ISBN 978-0-260-52190-3
PIBN 10953707

THE CONGRESSIONAL GLOBE:

CONTAINING

SKETCHES OF THE DEBATES AND PROCEEDINGS

OF THE

TWENTY-THIRD CONGRESS.

BLAIR & RIVES, EDITORS.

TWO VOLUMES IN ONE.....FIRST SESSION, VOL. I.

CITY OF WASHINGTON:
PRINTED AT THE GLOBE OFFICE FOR THE EDITORS.
1834.

INDEX

TO THE FIRST VOLUME OF THE CONGRESSIONAL GLOBE.

SENATE.

HOUSE OF REPRESENTATIVES.

THE CONGRESSIONAL GLOBE.

PRINTED AND PUBLISHED AT THE CITY OF WASHINGTON, BY BLAIR & RIVES.

23d Congress, 1st Session.   SATURDAY, DECEMBER 7, 1833.   Vol. I........No. 1.

TWENTY-THIRD CONGRESS.
FIRST SESSION.

IN SENATE,
Monday, December 2, 1833.

This being the day named in the Constitution of the United States, the two Houses assembled in their respective chambers in the Capitol.

Mr. WHITE, of Tennessee, took the Chair at twelve o'clock, in the absence of the Vice President, the Hon. Martin Van Buren.

The credentials of Messrs. Morris of Ohio, Grundy of Tennessee, Swift of Vermont, Ether Shepley of Maine, Nathan Smith of Connecticut, and Kent of Maryland, were severally presented; after which they respectively qualified and were permitted to take their seats.

The PRESIDENT pro tem. informed the Senate, that he found on his table a document which went to show, that Mr. E. R. Potter had been duly elected a Senator from the State of Rhode Island, in the room of Mr. Robbins, and which he proposed should be read; which being read accordingly by the Clerk—

The PRESIDENT pro tem. said, that during the last session of Congress, a document had been presented from the State of Rhode Island, also authenticating the election of Mr. Robbins. Under this state of things, it was for the Senate to determine what course they would adopt.

Mr. POINDEXTER observed, that he would not offer any opinion upon the merits of the case in controversy; but would state that it appeared to him a matter of course, that the member first chosen [Mr. Robbins] should be permitted to qualify and take his seat, that Mr. Potter should then present his credentials, which might be referred either to a Committee on the Judiciary, or to the Committee on Elections, the question being yet to be decided whether he was duly elected or not. In the meantime, he would move that Mr. Robbins be admitted to take the usual oath, and to refer the subject to the Judiciary Committee.

The credentials of Mr. Robbins, at the suggestion of Mr. CLAY, having been read,

Mr. KING, of Alabama, objected to this course being taken, deeming it proper that both the parties should be placed in a precisely similar situation, until the merits of the case were decided upon. He was aware it was the practice of the House of Representatives, in all cases of contested elections, to permit one of the parties contesting to take his seat; but in this case, there was this peculiar novelty attached to it: that each came before the Senate, having certificates of their being respectively elected. He therefore thought it better that neither should be permitted to qualify

until the rights of each party, to the seat, was fully investigated. He considered that if Mr. Robbins was now admitted to qualify, and take his seat, that a positive injury might be done to the State of Rhode Island, as he might vote on, and possibly decide, important questions, although his election should afterwards be set aside.

Mr. CLAY considered that it would be rather an injustice to the State of Rhode Island to restrict her from the exercise of the power given her by the Constitution, namely, to have herself represented in the Senate by one Senator instead of two, upon every question that should arise. The verification of the credentials of each Senator was the preliminary act, and it was their province, in case of any controversy, to say who was the Senator. This, it was not only their right, but it was their imperative duty, to do. Under all the circumstances, as they were bound to decide upon one of the parties, the question would be, simply, which of them? After adverting, at some length, to the circumstances attending the election of Mr. Robbins, by one Legislature, and that of Mr. Potter by a subsequent one, he argued that, as there was prima facie evidence that Mr. R. had been duly elected, that the certificate thereof was duly presented, and filed in the Senate, he had a priority of right, and ought to be admitted to qualify and take his seat.

Mr. KING observed, that he had not been prepared, nor intended, to enter into the legal points that were involved in this question. His only desire was, to act in a way that would be perfectly fair to both, and to give to the State an opportunity, if represented at all, to be fairly so. If the consequence of his suggestion was to deprive the State of the number of Senators she was entitled to under the Constitution, it was a state of things which arose solely from her own acts; and it often happens, that from various causes, other States had not more than one vote; yet no such very great injury was supposed to arise thereby. He asked for some delay, from a sense of justice, and not from any desire to prejudice the case of either, considering that the Senate owed it to themselves to wait for a report on the subject from a select committee, before they would make any selection.

Mr. CHAMBERS denied that the Senate had, constitutionally, the right to prevent Mr. Robbins from qualifying and taking his seat, inasmuch as the effect would be to deprive Rhode Island of one of her Senators, after having performed all that was required by the Constitution for her to do to entitle her Senator to his seat. In the absence of all precedent to guide them in this novel case, he thought they were to be governed by the rules followed in all other contested elections. It appeared that

one of these parties was duly elected; he occupies the post; his right to do so becomes rather the subject of subsequent examination than anything else, and as to any objection made as to the validity of any act so done by him, although his election might be vacated, it was expressly provided for, that, as the House of Representatives were the sole judges of the validity of their members, so were the Senate also of theirs. Under all the circumstances, the clear and proper course was, to give permission to Mr. R. to take his seat, until an investigation could be had in such a form as those better experienced than he was would decide was best, to do perfect justice.

Mr. KING rose to bring the attention of the Senate to a case, which he thought would establish the views he had taken on this subject. The case of the Hon. Mr. Lanman, of Connecticut, and which would operate as a precedent in this.

It appeared that Mr. L. was elected as Senator in 1825, from that State, his credentials were presented. On the motion of Mr. Holmes, that he should qualify, and take his seat, a debate arose, the subject was postponed, and a motion was made, that the subject should be referred to a select committee, which motion having been carried, a committee was appointed, and Major Eaton, who was chairman of the committee, presented a report on the facts, by which Mr. L. was prevented from qualifying. His election had taken place under circumstances which were not warranted by the law of Connecticut; and the Senate did not hesitate to pronounce his election invalid, inasmuch as he was not constitutionally elected.

Mr. CHAMBERS said in this case it clearly appeared that the election was invalid.

Mr. KANE argued that it would be an injustice to Rhode Island, by admitting the Senator to qualify, whom her Legislature had pronounced disqualified, and moved that the question should be postponed till to-morrow.

The question thereon being put, was negatived : ayes 16, noes 17.

After an animated and lengthened discussion, in which Messrs. CLAY, FRELINGHUYSEN, WRIGHT, EWING, BIBB, POINDEXTER, MANGUM, and BENTON participated,' Mr. BENTON moved, in substance, that the whole subject should be referred to a select committee ; which was decided by yeas and nays, as follows :

YEAS—Benton, Brown, Grundy, Hill, Kane, King, Morris, Rives, Robinson, Shepley, Tallmadge, Tipton, White, Watkins, Wright—15.

NAYS—Bell, Bibb, Chambers, Clay, Ewing, Frelinghuysen, Hendricks, Kent, Knight, Mangum, Moore, Naudain, Poindexter, Prentiss, Smith, Swift, Silsbee, Tomlinson, Tyler—19.

So the question was lost, and the motion of Mr. Poindexter being put, prevailed ;

1

upon which Mr. Robbins qualified and took his seat.

The Senate resolved to pay their usual tribute of respect by wearing mourning, &c., for the Hon. Mr. Buckner and Hon. Mr. Johnson, lately deceased.

The customary resolutions were then passed, that a message should be sent to inform the House of Representatives that the Senate were ready to proceed to the despatch of business, for the usual number of newspapers to be furnished to each Senator: and that a committee should be appointed to wait on the President to inform him they were ready to receive any communication he might make.

Adjourned.

HOUSE OF REPRESENTATIVES.
Monday, December 2, 1833.

At twelve o'clock, the House was called to order by the Clerk.

The Clerk proceeded to call the names of the several members by States. The names of the Kentucky delegation being called—

Mr. ALLAN, of Ky., rose and said: Gentlemen of the House of Representatives, by the law apportioning the Representatives in Congress among the States, the State of Kentucky is entitled to thirteen members; and the Legislature of Kentucky, by a law passed at their last session, accordingly divided the State into thirteen congressional districts, from each of which one member was required to be elected. But he perceived that fourteen gentlemen· had presented themselves as representatives from that State. From the district composed of the counties of Mercer, Garrard, Jessamine, Lincoln, &c., two persons presented themselves in this Hall, both claiming to be members. It was obvious that this controversy must be settled at this stage of the proceeding. The question was deeply interesting to the district where the election was made and to ⁀the State of Kentucky. The delegation from that State had examined the vouchers which had been presented, and come to an opinion on the subject, which he, as the organ of the delegation, was deputed to express. He rose to perform this duty under circumstances of peculiar embarrassment. This was a new Congress and was composed of a majority of new members. If left to his own feelings, he would have been content to keep his seat and give a silent vote. It was a painful duty to him to be obliged to express an opinion affecting the rights of gentlemen with both of whom he had been long acquainted, and with whom his associations had been of the most agreeable character, but he should do it in a manner most respectful to their feelings. To enable the House to decide the question, he would call for the reading of the credentials which were in the possession of the Clerk, of the individuals claiming to be elected,

The Clerk, after explaining the manner in which the papers were received, commenced to read a letter from the Executive

of Kentucky, inclosing the certificates of the election from the different districts.

Mr. WAYNE here rose, reluctantly, he said, to interrupt the proceedings. He took no part in the controversy, but he wished to know, whether any and whose name was entered upon the roll of members, from the fifth congressional district of Kentucky.

The Clerk stated the name of "THO-MAS P. MOORE" appeared on the roll.

Mr. WAYNE. Then I ask permission to call upon that gentleman to exhibit his credentials, to those who were about to qualify as members, for none of us were members until we were duly qualified. This had been the former usage of Congress. Each member formerly presented his credentials prior to qualification. No one could be sworn in without some credentials. He felt it his solemn duty, springing from his oath, to stop the proceeding, so irregular in its character, by which the right of any member to his seat might be contested. He knew no gentlemen here as members of Congress, for they were not members until they were sworn in as representatives from different States; and those who were furnished with the usual credentials were alone entitled to be qualified. With these remarks, he called for the reading of the evidence of the election of the gentleman whose named was upon the roll.

Mr. ALLAN. Does the gentleman object to the further reading of the certificates?

Mr. WAYNE. No. But I object to anything conflicting with the right of any person to take his seat and qualify as a member, he being able to exhibit the usual evidence of his election. If the credentials are found sufficient, the gentleman has a right to be qualified and to take his seat.

The Clerk proceeded to read the certificate of the election of THOMAS P. MOORE, from the Fifth Congressional District' of Kentucky.

Mr. WAYNE. Is that paper presented by the member?

The Clerk, in reply, stated that no paper had been read from Mr. Moore.

Mr. ALLAN wished, he said, to ask the gentleman from Georgia, whether he contended that any person presenting himself, as a member, and whose name appears upon the roll, is entitled to be qualified?

Mr. WAYNE. If the member will show the credentials in virtue of which he claims his seat the House can judge of their sufficiency. I, for one, am ready to pass judgment upon them.

Mr. MOORE, of Kentucky, rose and said: Gentlemen of the House of Representatives: Had I not been informed, from various quarters, that this movement would be made, it would have greatly surprised me. Unprecedented as it is, I am prepared to meet it calmly, and to submit it to the decision of the House, although unformed and not having the power to give a legal decision, as is now the case. It is upon *prima facie* evidence only that any member of this House is entitled to be qualified, and it cannot be known to us, as a constitutional body, whose election is to be contested and whose not, until the House is organized. Until then, there is, in fact, no one entitled to qualify; no one entitled to decide; and no one entitled to decide

it. I come here with the *prima facie* evidence of my election, like the honorable gentlemen around me. I have in my possession the certificate of a majority of the sheriffs, convened according to law to compare the polls, and the Clerk of this House has received the same evidence from the Governor of the State of Kentucky, that I am the Representative of the fifth district, that he has transmitted to establish the claims of the other members from Kentucky. If these documents are informal or defective, a committee of this House, after it is duly organized, will so decide; and until they do so, and it is sanctioned by the House, I am as much entitled to my seat here as any member on this floor. I not only have the *prima facie* evidence of my right to the seat, but if any one, at a proper period, shall come forward to contest it, I shall I hope be prepared to show that I am duly elected, or, that the election was marked by such gross irregularities as ought to refer it again to the decision of the people. Nothing but a deep conviction of the truth of what I have stated, would have brought me here, and if my wishes could have controlled all doubts, as to who is legally entitled to the seat, it would have been decided by the people themselves, without troubling this House. But as that appeal to decide ultimate as well as *prima facie* rights was declined, I have no alternative but to assert my rights and those whom I claim to represent.

Ever inclined to pursue that course which may preserve order and decorum in this Hall, and not being disposed to retard the organization of the House, I shall cheerfully submit to any decision the gentlemen present shall make; but it is my duty to do it with a proper assertion of my rights, and the rights of those whom I claim to represent. I therefore, respectfully, deny the right of any one to vote on the subject in its present stage, and if I am prohibited from qualifying, I protest against it as an arbitrary exertion of power, which will form a most dangerous precedent, and not only deprive me of my just rights, but the people of the fifth Congressional district of their representative.

The Clerk then read the fifth Congressional election return.

After a few words of explanation between Mr. MOORE and Mr. ALLAN, which we could not hear,

Mr. ALLAN said, I now understand the gentleman to say that he rests his right to a seat upon the paper which has just been read. I now contend that, according to the law and usage of Kentucky, the certificate just read is a mere nullity. The case presented is the extraordinary and novel case of an individual claiming a seat without a certificate of his election. A majority of the delegation from Kentucky having examined the paper, pronounce it a nullity.

He would proceed briefly to sustain this conclusion. By the law passed at the last session of the Legislature of Kentucky to regulate this subject, it was made the duty of the county sheriffs to meet at a particular place, to count the votes, give a certificate of election, &c. What was the object of this law? It was to ascertain who has the majority, and to furnish the person having it with the legal evidence of the fact. Mr. ALLAN here read the law.

Mr. WAYNE here made a remark, in an under tone, addressing himself to the gentleman from Kentucky.

Mr. ALLAN continued: So far as I understand my duty, I take it that I have a right to present this question. This is a House as soon as a quorum has assembled, and is competent to do anything as a House. It is its first and imperative

duty, before its organization, to ascertain who are its members.

Mr. FOSTER wished the gentleman from Kentucky to give way for a moment, while he moved that we appoint some member to the chair. All bodies, parliamentary or otherwise, on getting together, can appoint a chairman. The House, he perceived, was becoming confused, and it would be difficult to proceed without a chairman, to whom gentlemen would address themselves.

Mr. SPEIGHT suggested that the Clerk had better proceed to call the names of the members, that those as to whom there was no contest might be qualified. He hoped the question would not be moved till a Speaker was chosen and the members qualified.

Mr. ALLAN would have no objection, he said, to this course, were it the usage of the House to qualify the members before the election of Speaker. The election of Speaker is one of the most important functions of the House, the character of the House much depending upon its organization. In the exercise of this important function, was not his State entitled to be fully represented on this floor? He repeated that he was unwilling to take any course which would lead to any embarrassment. This was a case of difficulty, he would admit; but it was a case of high importance. We had time enough to act upon it now. There was no occasion for hurry in the organization of the House. Believing that he had a right to the floor, he would now proceed respectfully to examine this certificate, confining his remarks to the face of the paper.

Mr. BOON. Will the gentleman give way for one moment?

Mr. ALLAN. No; I will now finish what I have to say, and the gentleman will have an opportunity to be heard afterwards. This certificate shows that the sheriffs met—

Mr. LETCHER here interposed and stated that he would cease to press this question until the House was organized.

The call was continued, and 229 members answered to their names.

ELECTION OF SPEAKER.

The House proceeded to ballot for a Speaker, Mr. CLAY, of Alabama, and Mr. JARVIS, of Maine, acting as tellers. Upon the first ballot, it appeared that the whole number of votes given was 218, of which 110 were necessary to a choice, and that there were for

Andrew Stevenson	142	C. F. Mercer	1
Lewis Williams	39	John Davis	1
Edward Everett	15	Samuel A. Foot	1
John Bell	4	Joseph Vance	1
Richard Coulter	2	James K. Polk	1
R. H. Wilde	2	Blanks	8

The Hon. ANDREW STEVENSON, of Va., having 142 votes, was declared to be duly elected, and having been conducted to the chair by Mr. WILLIAMS, of N. Carolina, addressed the House as follows:

GENTLEMEN: This is the fourth time that you have been pleased to call me to this high office. For this new and distinguished mark of your confidence and favor, I pray you to accept my warm and grateful acknowledgments; and whilst it will be deeply valued and cherished by me as the best reward for any past service that I may have rendered, it shall inspire me with a zeal so to conduct myself as to justify, in some measure, the choice of my friends, and merit the continued approbation of my country. Would to God that I was better qualified to fulfil the arduous duties of this chair, in a manner suitable to its dignity and importance, my own wishes and honor, and the just expectations of the House. There are few stations, gentlemen, under our Government, either in relation to their elevation, or the nature and extent of their duties, more laborious or responsible, than that of Speaker of this House; and there probably has been no period in the past history of our country, when the duties of the Chair were more important, or calculated to impose higher responsibilities, than at the present moment; enhanced, as they necessarily must be, by the enlarged number of the House; by the increased mass of its ordinary business; and by those interesting and important subjects, which will, no doubt, be presented for consideration, and probably give rise to deep political excitement.

For the last six years, my experience in this Chair has taught me, not only to know and feel its responsibilities and trials, but to know likewise how difficult and indeed impossible it is, in an office like this, whose duties must often be discharged amidst the warmth of party feeling, for any man, whoever he may be, to free himself from censure or give unqualified satisfaction; and especially in times like these, when the acts of public men are not passed lightly over, nor any very charitable judgment pronounced upon their motives.

Under these circumstances, gentlemen, sincerely distrustful of my abilities, both in their character and extent, I come again, at your bidding, to this high office. All that I dare hope or promise, will be to proceed in the path marked out, and in the spirit of the principles which I laid down for my government when I first came to this Chair. It shall be my constant and ardent desire to discharge my duty with all the ability and address in my power, with the temper and moderation due to the station and the House, and at least with a zeal and fidelity of intention which shall bear me up under every embarrassment and difficulty, and entitle me to the approbation of the just and liberal portion of my country. But all my efforts must prove unavailing without that liberal and cordial co-operation which the House have heretofore so kindly extended to the Chair. How much will depend upon yourselves, gentlemen, individually and collectively, in preserving the permanent laws and rules of the House, and giving dignity and character to its proceedings, it is not necessary that I should attempt to impress on you; nor is it needful, I am sure, that I should admonish you of the magnitude of your trust, or the manner in which it ought to be discharged. But this I will take occasion to say, that if it be true that this House is justly to be regarded as the great bulwark of liberty and order, if here—here in this exalted refuge, the people are to look for the security and safety of their free institutions, and to repose with unlimited confidence and affection, how important, how deeply important is it, that we prove ourselves worthy of the trust, and act as becomes the representatives of a free and enlightened nation.

Yes, gentlemen, animated by a virtuous and patriotic zeal, let all our proceedings, I pray you, be marked with forbearance, moderation, and dignity; let us diligently and steadfastly pursue those measures, and those only, which are best calculated to advance the happiness and glory of our beloved country, and render that Union, which our fathers established for the protection of our liberties, imperishable and immortal.

ELECTION OF CLERK.

On motion of Mr. MANN, the House then proceeded to the election of a Clerk.

Mr. MANN nominated Walter S. Franklin, of Pennsylvania.

Mr. KING nominated Matthew St. Clair Clarke, of Pennsylvania.

The House proceeded to the election, and upon the first ballot, it appeared that the whole number of votes given was 231, of which 116 was necessary to a choice, and that there were for—

Matthew St. Clair Clarke	113
Walter S. Franklin	107
Eleazar Early	2
Walter F. Clarke	3
Thos. C. Love	1
Blanks	3

There being no choice, the House proceeded to a second ballot, and it appeared that 228 votes were given—necessary to a choice 115, and that there were for—

Matthew St. Clair Clarke	107
Walter S. Franklin	114
Blanks	2

A message was received from the Senate that that House was organized and ready to proceed to business.

The House then proceeded to a third ballot for Clerk, when it appeared that 229 votes were given, of which Mr. Walter S. Franklin received 117 votes, and Matthew St. Clair Clarke 110; whereupon, Walter S. Franklin was declared duly elected, having received a majority of the whole number.

Adjourned till to-morrow at 12 o'clock.

IN SENATE.

TUESDAY, December 3, 1833.

A message was received from the House of Representatives, that they had elected ANDREW STEVENSON, Esq., of Virginia, Speaker of their House; also, that they were then ready to proceed to business; and that a resolution had been agreed to, to appoint a committee, to join such committee as should be appointed by the Senate, to wait on the President of the United States, and receive from him such communication as he might be pleased to make.

THE PRESIDENT'S MESSAGE.

Messrs. WILKINS and GRUNDY, who had been appointed on the joint committee to wait on the President, reported, that they had performed the duty to which they had been appointed, and that he had informed them he would make his communication at one o'clock, this day.

The following Message was delivered by the Private Secretary of the President, and read:

Fellow-citizens of the Senate and
House of Representatives:

On your assembling to perform the high trusts which the people of the United States have confided to you, of legislating for their common welfare, it gives me pleasure to congratulate you upon the happy condition of our beloved country. By the favor of Divine Providence, health is again restored to us; peace reigns within our borders; abundance crowns the labors of our fields; commerce and domestic industry flourish and increase; and individual happiness rewards the private virtue and enterprise of our citizens.

Our condition abroad is no less honorable than it is prosperous at home. Seeking nothing that is not right, and determined to submit to nothing that is wrong, but desiring honest friendships and liberal intercourse with all nations, the United States have gained throughout the world the confidence and respect which are due to the character of the American people, and to a policy so just, and so congenial to the spirit of their institutions.

In bringing to your notice the particular state of our foreign affairs, it affords me high gratification to inform you, that they are in a condition which promises the continuance of friendship with all nations.

With Great Britain, the interesting question of our northeastern boundary remains still undecided. A negotiation, however, upon that subject has been renewed since the close of the last Congress; and a proposition has been submitted to the British Government, with the view of establishing, in conformity with the resolution of the Senate, the line designated by the treaty of 1783. Though no definitive answer has been received, it may be daily looked for, and I entertain a hope that the overture may ultimately lead to a satisfactory adjustment of this important matter.

I have the satisfaction to inform you that a negotiation which by desire of the House of Representatives was opened some years ago with the British Government for the erection of light-houses on the Bahamas, has been successful. Those works, when completed, together with those which the United States have constructed on the western side of the Gulf of Florida, will contribute essentially to the safety of navigation in that sea. This joint participation in establishments interesting to humanity and beneficial to commerce is worthy of two enlightened nations, and indicates feelings which cannot fail to have a happy influence upon their political relations. It is gratifying to the friends of both to perceive that the intercourse between the two people is becoming daily more extensive, and that sentiments of mutual good will have grown up befitting their common origin, justifying the hope that, by wise counsels on each side, not only unsettled questions may be satisfactorily terminated, but new causes of misunderstanding prevented.

Notwithstanding that I continue to receive the most amicable assurances from the Government of France, and that in all other respects the most friendly relations exist between the United States and that Government, it is to be regretted that the stipulations of the convention concluded on the 4th July, 1831, remain, in some important parts, unfulfilled.

By the second article of that convention it was stipulated that the sum payable to the United States should be paid at Paris, in six annual instalments, into the hands of such person or persons as should be authorized by the Government of the United States to receive it; and by the same article the first instalment was payable on the second day of February, 1833. By the act of Congress of the 13th July, 1832, it was made the duty of the Secretary of the Treasury to cause the several instalments, with the interest thereon, to be received from the French Government and transferred to the United States in such manner as he may deem best; and by the same act of Congress the stipulations on the part of the United States in the convention were in all respects fulfilled. Not doubting that a treaty thus made and ratified by the two Governments and faithfully executed by the United States would be promptly complied with by the other party, and desiring to avoid the risk and expense of intermediate agencies, the Secretary of the Treasury deemed it advisable to receive and transfer the first instalment by means of a draft upon the French Minister of Finance. A draft for this purpose was accordingly drawn in favor of the cashier of the Bank of the United States for the amount accruing to the United States out of the first instalment and the interest payable with it. This bill was not drawn at Washington until five days after the instalment was payable at Paris, and was accompanied by a special authority from the President, authorizing the cashier or his assigns to receive the amount. The mode thus adopted of receiving the instalment was officially made known to the French Government by the American chargé d'affaires at Paris, pursuant to instructions from the Department of State. The bill, however, though not presented for payment until the twenty-third day of March, was not paid, and for the reason assigned by the French Minister of Finance, that no appropriation had been made by the French Chambers. It is not known to me that up to that period any appropriation had been required of the Chambers; and although a communication was subsequently made to the Chambers, by direction of the King, recommending that the necessary provision should be made for carrying the convention into effect, it was at an advanced period of the session, and the subject was finally postponed until the next meeting of the Chambers.

Notwithstanding it has been supposed by the French Ministry, that the financial stipulations of the treaty cannot be carried into effect without an appropriation by the Chambers, it appears to me to be not only consistent with the charter of France, but due to the character of both Governments, as well as to the rights of our citizens, to treat the convention made and ratified, in proper form, as pledging the good faith of the French Government for its execution, and as imposing upon each department an obligation to fulfil it; and I have received assurances through our chargé d'affaires at Paris, and the French minister plenipotentiary at Washington, and more recently through the Minister of the United States at Paris, that the delay has not proceeded from any indisposition on the part of the King and his Ministers, to fulfil the treaty, and that measures will be presented at the next meeting of the Chambers, and with a reasonable hope of success, to obtain the necessary appropriation.

It is necessary to state, however, that the documents, except certain lists of vessels captured, condemned, or burnt at sea, proper to facilitate the examination and liquidation of the reclamations comprised in the stipulations of the convention, and which, by the sixth article, France engaged to communicate to the United States by the intermediary of the Legation, though repeatedly applied for by the American chargé d' affaires, under instructions from this Government, have not yet been communicated; and this delay, it is apprehended, will necessarily prevent the completion of the duties assigned to the commissioners within the time at present prescribed by law.

The reasons for delaying to communicate these documents have not been explicitly stated, and this is the more to be regretted, as it is not understood that the interposition of the Chambers is in any manner required for the delivery of those papers.

Under these circumstances, in a case so important to the interests of our citizens and to the character of our country, and under disappointments so unexpected, I deemed it my duty, however I might respect the general assurances to which I have adverted, no longer to delay the appointment of a minister plenipotentiary to Paris, but to despatch him in season to communicate the result of his application to the French Government at an early period of your session. I accordingly appointed a distinguished citizen for this purpose, who proceeded on his mission in August last, and was presented to the King early in the month of October. He is particularly instructed as to all matters connected with the present posture of affairs, and I indulge the hope that, with the representations he is instructed to make, and from the dispositions manifested by the King and his Ministers, in their recent assurances to our Minister at Paris, the subject will be early considered and satisfactorily disposed of at the next meeting of the Chambers.

As this subject involves important interests and has attracted a considerable share of the public attention, I have deemed it proper to make this explicit statement of its actual condition; and should I be disappointed in the hope now entertained, the subject will be again brought to the notice of Congress in such manner as the occasion may require.

The friendly relations which have always been maintained between the United States and Russia have been further extended and strengthened by the treaty of navigation and commerce, concluded on the 6th of December last, and sanctioned by the Senate before the close of its last session. The ratifications having been since exchanged, the liberal provisions of the treaty are now in full force; and, under the encouragement which they have received, a flourishing and increasing commerce, yielding its benefits to the enterprise of both nations, affords to each the just recompense of wise measures, and adds new motives for that mutual friendship which the two countries have hitherto cherished towards each other.

It affords me peculiar satisfaction to state that the Government of Spain has at length yielded to the justice of the claims which have been so long urged in behalf of our citizens, and has expressed a willingness to provide an indemnification, as soon as the proper amount can be agreed upon. Upon this latter point, it is probable an understanding had taken place between the Minister of the United States and the Spanish Government before the decease of the late King of Spain; and, unless that event may have delayed its completion, there is reason to hope that it may be in my power to announce to you, early in your present session, the conclusion of a convention upon terms not less favorable than those entered into for similar objects with other nations. That act of justice would well accord with the character of Spain, and is due to the United States from their ancient friend. It could not fail to strengthen the sentiments of amity and good will between the two nations which it is so much the wish of the United States to cherish, and so truly the interest of both to maintain.

By the first section of an act of Congress passed on the 13th of July, 1832, the tonnage duty on Spanish ships arriving from the ports of Spain, was limited to the duty payable on American vessels in the ports of Spain, previous to the 20th of October, 1817, being five cents per ton. The act was intended to give effect, on our side, to an arrangement made with the Spanish Government, by which discriminating duties of tonnage were to be abolished in the ports of the United States and Spain, on the vessels of the two nations. Pursuant to that arrangement, which was carried into effect, on the part of Spain, on the 20th of May, 1832, by a royal order dated the 29th of April, 1832, American vessels in the ports of Spain have paid five cents per ton, which rate of duty is also paid in those ports by Spanish ships; but as American vessels pay no tonnage duty in the ports of the United States, the duty of five cents payable in our ports by Spanish vessels, under the act above mentioned, is really a discriminating duty, operating to the disadvantage of Spain. Though no complaint has yet been made on the part of Spain, we are not the less bound by the obligations of good faith, to remove the discrimination; and I recommend that the act be amended accordingly. As the royal order, above alluded to, includes the ports of the Balearic and Canary Islands, as well as those of Spain, it would seem that the provision of the act of Congress should be equally extensive; and that for the repayment of such duties as may have been improperly received, an addition should be made to the sum appropriated at the last session of Congress for refunding discriminating duties.

As the arrangement referred to, however, did not embrace the islands of Cuba and Porto Rico, discriminating duties, to the prejudice of American shipping, continue to be levied there. From

the extent of the commerce carried on between the United States and those islands, particularly the former, this discrimination causes serious injury to one of those great national interests which it has been considered an essential part of our policy to cherish, and has given rise to complaints on the part of our merchants. Under instructions given to our Minister at Madrid, earnest representations have been made by him to the Spanish Government upon this subject, and there is reason to expect, from the friendly disposition which is entertained towards this country, that a beneficial change will be produced. The disadvantage, however, to which our shipping is subjected by the operation of these discriminating duties, requires that they be met by suitable countervailing duties during your present session—power being at the same time vested in the President to modify or discontinue them as the discriminating duties on American vessels or their cargoes may be modified or discontinued at those islands. Intimations have been given to the Spanish Government that the United States may be obliged to resort to such measures as are of necessary self-defence; and there is no reason to apprehend that it would be unfavorably received. The proposed proceeding, if adopted, would not be permitted, however, in any degree to induce a relaxation in the efforts of our Minister to effect a repeal of this irregularity by friendly negotiation; and it might serve to give force to his representations, by showing the dangers to which that valuable trade is exposed by the obstructions and burdens which a system of discriminating and countervailing duties necessarily produces.

The selection and preparation of the Florida archives, for the purpose of being delivered over to the United States, in conformity with the royal order, as mentioned in my last Annual Message, though in progress, has not yet been completed. This delay has been produced, partly by causes which were unavoidable, particularly the prevalence of cholera at Havana; but measures have been taken, which it is believed will expedite the delivery of those important records.

Congress were informed, at the opening of the last session, that "owing, as was alleged, to embarrassments in the finances of Portugal, consequent upon the civil war in which that nation was engaged," payment had been made of only one instalment of the amount which the Portuguese Government had stipulated to pay for indemnifying our citizens for property illegally captured in the blockade of Terceira. Since that time, a postponement for two years, with interest, of the two remaining instalments, was requested by the Portuguese Government; and as a consideration, it offered to stipulate, that rice of the United States should be admitted into Portugal, at the same duties as Brazilian rice. Being satisfied that no better arrangement could be made, my consent was given; and a royal order of the King of Portugal was accordingly issued on the 4th of February last for the reduction of the duty on rice of the United States. It would give me great pleasure if, in speaking of that country, in whose prosperity the United States are so much interested, and with whom a long subsisting, extensive, and mutually advantageous commercial intercourse has strengthened the relations of friendship, I could announce to you the restoration of its internal tranquillity.

Subsequently to the commencement of the last session of Congress the final instalment payable by Denmark, under the convention of the 28th day of March, 1830, was received. The commissioners for examining the claims have since terminated their labors, and their awards have been paid at the treasury as they have been called for. The justice rendered to our citizens by that Government is thus completed, and a pledge is thereby afforded for the maintenance of that friendly intercourse becoming the relations that the two nations mutually bear to each other.

It is satisfactory to inform you that the Danish Government has recently issued an ordinance by which the commerce with the island of St. Croix is placed on a more liberal footing than heretofore. This change cannot fail to prove beneficial to the trade between the United States and that colony; and the advantages likely to flow from it may lead to greater relaxations in the colonial systems of other nations.

The ratifications of the convention with the King of the Two Sicilies have been duly exchanged, and the commissioners appointed for examining the claims under it, have entered upon the duties assigned to them by law. The friendship that the interests of the two nations require of them being now established, it may be hoped that each will enjoy the benefits which a liberal commerce should yield to both.

A treaty of amity and commerce between the United States and Belgium was concluded during the last winter, and received the sanction of the Senate; but the exchange of the ratifications has been hitherto delayed, in consequence, in the first instance, of some delay in the reception of the treaty at Brussels, and subsequently, of the absence of the Belgian Minister of Foreign Affairs at the important conferences in which his Government is engaged at London.

That treaty does but embody those enlarged principles of friendly policy which, it is sincerely hoped, will always regulate the conduct of the two nations, having such strong motives to maintain amicable relations towards each other, and so sincerely desirous to cherish them.

With all the other European Powers with whom the United States have formed diplomatic relations, and with the Sublime Porte, the best understanding prevails. From all, I continue to receive assurances of good will towards the United States—assurances which it gives me no less pleasure to reciprocate than to receive. With all, the engagements which have been entered into, are fulfilled with good faith on both sides. Measures have also been taken to enlarge our friendly relations and extend our commercial intercourse with other States. The system we have pursued of aiming at no exclusive advantages, of dealing with all on terms of fair and equal reciprocity, and of adhering scrupulously to all our engagements, is well calculated to give success to efforts intended to be mutually beneficial.

The wars of which the southern part of this continent was so long the theatre, and which were carried on, either by the mother country against the States which had formerly been her colonies, or by the States against each other, having terminated, and their civil dissensions having so far subsided, as, with few exceptions, no longer to disturb the public tranquillity, it is earnestly hoped those States will be able to employ themselves without interruption in perfecting their institutions, cultivating the arts of peace, and promoting, by wise counsels and able exertions, the public and private prosperity which their patriotic struggles so well entitle them to enjoy.

With those States our relations have undergone but little change during the present year. No reunion having yet taken place between the States which composed the Republic of Colombia, our chargé d'affaires at Bogota has been accredited to the Government of New Grenada; and we have therefore no diplomatic relations with Venezuela and Equador, except as they may be included in those heretofore formed with the Colombian Republic. It is understood that representatives from threee States were about to assemble at Bogota to confer on the subject of their mutual interests, particularly that of their union; and if the result should render it necessary, measures will be taken on our part to preserve with each that friendship and those liberal commercial connexions which it has been the constant desire of the United States to cultivate with their sister republics of this hemisphere. Until the important question of reunion shall be settled, however, the different matters which have been under discussion between the United States and the Republic of Colombia, or either of the States which composed it, are not likely to be brought to a satisfactory issue.

In consequence of the illness of the chargé d'affairs appointed to Central America at the last session of Congress, he was prevented from proceeding on his mission until the month of October. It is hoped, however, that he is by this time at his post, and that the official intercourse, unfortunately so long interrupted, has been thus renewed on the part of the two nations so amicably and advantageously connected by engagements founded on the most enlarged principles of commercial reciprocity.

It is gratifying to state that since my last annual message, some of the most important claims of our fellow-citizens upon the Government of Brazil have been satisfactorily adjusted, and a reliance is placed on the friendly dispositions manifested by it that justice will also be done in others. No new causes of complaint have arisen; and the trade between the two countries flourishes under the encouragement secured to it by the liberal provisions of the treaty.

It is cause of regret, that, owing probably to the civil dissensions which have occupied the attention of the Mexican Government, the time fixed by the treaty of limits with the United States for the meeting of the commissioners to define the boundaries between the two nations, has been suffered to expire without the appointment of any commissioners on the part of that Government. While the true boundary remains in doubt by either party, it is difficult to give effect to those measures which are necessary to the protection and quiet of our numerous citizens residing near that frontier. The subject is one of great solicitude to the United States, and will not fail to receive my earnest attention.

The treaty concluded with Chili, and approved by the Senate at its last session, was also ratified by the Chilian Government, but with certain additional and explanatory articles of a nature to have required it to be again submitted to the Senate. The time limited for the exchange of the ratifications, however, having since expired, the action of both Governments on the treaty will again become necessary.

The negotiations commenced with the Argentine Republic, relative to the outrages committed on our vessels engaged in the fisheries at the Falkland Islands, by persons acting under the color of its authority, as well as the other matters in controversy between the two Governments, have been suspended by the departure of the chargé d'affaires of the United States from Buenos Ayres. It is understood, however, that a minister was subsequently appointed by that Government to renew the negotiation in the United States, but though daily expected, he has not yet arrived in this country.

With Peru no treaty has yet been formed, and with Bolivia no diplomatic intercourse has yet been established. It will be my endeavor to encourage those sentiments of amity and that liberal commerce which belong to the relations in which all the independent States of this continent stand towards each other.

I deem it proper to recommend to your notice the revision of our consular system. This has become an important branch of the public service, inasmuch as it is intimately connected with the preservation of our national character abroad, with the interest of our citizens in foreign countries, with the regulation and care of our commerce, and with the protection of our seamen. At the close of the last session of Congress I communicated a report from the Secretary of State upon the subject, to which I now refer, as containing information which may be useful in any inquiries that Congress may see fit to institute with a view to a salutary reform of the system.

It gives me great pleasure to congratulate you upon the prosperous condition of the finances of the country, as will appear from the report which the Secretary of the Treasury will, in due time, lay before you. The receipts into the Treasury during the present year, will amount to more than thirty-two millions of dollars. The revenue derived from customs will, it is believed, be more than twenty-eight millions, and the public lands will yield about three millions. The expenditures within the year for all objects, including $2,572,240 99 on account of the public debt, will not amount to twenty-five millions; and a large balance will remain in the treasury after satisfying all the appropriations chargeable on the revenue for the present year.

The measures taken by the Secretary of the Treasury will probably enable him to pay off, in the course of the present year, the residue of the exchanged four-and-a-half per cent. stock, redeemable on the first of January next. It has, therefore, been included in the estimated expenditure of this year, and forms a part of the sum above stated to have been paid on account of the public debt. The payment of this stock will reduce the whole

debt of the United States, funded and unfunded, to the sum of $4,760,082 08. And as provision has already been made for the four-and-a-half per cent. above mentioned, and charged in the expenses of the present year, the sum last stated is all that now remains of the national debt; and the revenue of the coming year, together with the balance now in the treasury, will be sufficient to discharge it, after meeting the current expenses of the Government. Under the power given to the commissioners of the sinking fund, it will, I have no doubt, be purchased on favorable terms within the year.

From this view of the state of the finances, and the public engagements yet to be fulfilled, you will perceive that, if Providence permits me to meet you at another session, I shall have the high gratification of announcing to you that the national debt is extinguished. I cannot refrain from expressing the pleasure I feel at the near approach of that desirable event. The short period of time within which the public debt will have been discharged, is strong evidence of the abundant resources of the country, and of the prudence and economy with which the Government has heretofore been administered. We have waged two wars since we became a nation, with one of the most powerful kingdoms in the world—both of them undertaken in defence of our dearest rights, both successfully prosecuted and honorably terminated; and many of those who partook in the first struggle, as well as the second, will have lived to see the last item of the debt incurred in these necessary, but expensive conflicts, faithfully and honestly discharged; and we shall have the proud satisfaction of bequeathing to the public servants who follow us in the administration of the Government the rare blessing of a revenue sufficiently abundant—raised without injustice or oppression to our citizens, and unencumbered with any burdens but what they themselves shall think proper to impose upon it.

The flourishing state of the finances ought not, however, to encourage us to indulge in a lavish expenditure of the public treasure. The receipts of the present year do not furnish the test by which we are to estimate the income of the next. The changes made in our revenue system by the acts of Congress of 1832 and 1833, and more especially by the former, have swelled the receipts of the present year far beyond the amount to be expected in future years upon the reduced tariff of duties. The shortened credits on revenue bonds, and the cash duties on woollens, which were introduced by the act of 1832, and took effect on the 4th of March last, have brought large sums into the treasury in 1833, which, according to the credits formerly given, would not have been payable until 1834, and would have formed a part of the income of that year. These causes would of themselves produce a great diminution of the receipts in the year 1834, as compared with the present one; and they will be still more diminished by the reduced rates of duties which take place on the first of January next, on some of the most important and productive articles. Upon the best estimates that can be made, the receipts of the next year, with the aid of the unappropriated amount now in the treasury, will not be much more than sufficient to meet the expenses of the year and pay the small remnant of the national debt which yet remains unsatisfied. I cannot, therefore, recommend to you any alteration in the present tariff of duties. The rate, as now taxed by law on the various articles, was adopted at the last session of Congress as a matter of compromise, with unusual unanimity; and unless it is found to produce more than the necessities of the Government call for, there would seem to be no reason at this time to justify a change.

But while I forbear to recommend any further reduction of the duties, beyond that already provided for by the existing laws, I must earnestly and respectfully press upon Congress the importance of abstaining from all appropriations which are not absolutely required for the public interests, and authorized by the powers clearly delegated to the United States. We are beginning a new era in our Government. The national debt, which has so long been a burden on the treasury, will be finally discharged in the course of the ensuing year. No more money will afterwards be needed than what may be necessary to meet the ordinary expenses of the Government. Now, then, is the proper moment to fix our system of expenditure on firm and durable principles: and I cannot too strongly urge the necessity of a rigid economy, and an inflexible determination not to enlarge the income beyond the real necessities of the Government, and not to increase the wants of the Government by unnecessary and profuse expenditures. If a contrary course should be pursued, it may happen that the revenue of 1834 will fall short of the demands upon it: and after reducing the tariff in order to lighten the burdens of the people, and providing for a still further reduction to take effect hereafter, it would be much to be deplored if, at the end of another year, we should find ourselves obliged to retrace our steps and impose additional taxes to meet unnecessary expenditures.

It is my duty, on this occasion, to call your attention to the destruction of the public building occupied by the Treasury Department, which happened since the last adjournment of Congress. A thorough inquiry into the causes of this loss was directed and made at the time, the result of which will be duly communicated to you. I take pleasure, however, in stating here, that by the laudable exertions of the officers of the department, and many of the citizens of the District, but few papers were lost, and none that will materially affect the public interest.

The public convenience requires that another building should be erected as soon as practicable; and in providing for it, it will be advisable to enlarge, in some manner, the accommodations for the public officers of the several departments, and to authorize the erection of suitable depositories for the safe-keeping of the public documents and records.

Since the last adjournment of Congress, the Secretary of the Treasury has directed the money of the United States to be deposited in certain State banks, designated by him, and he will immediately lay before you his reasons for this direction. I concur with him entirely in the view he has taken of the subject; and some months before the removal, I urged upon the department the propriety of taking that step. The near approach of the day on which the charter will expire, as well as the conduct of the bank, appeared to me to call for this measure, upon the high considerations of public interest and public duty. The extent of its misconduct, however, although known to be great, was not at that time fully developed by proof. It was not until late in the month of August that I received from the Government directors an official report, establishing beyond question, that this great and powerful institution had been actively engaged in attempting to influence the elections of the public officers, by means of its money; and that, in violation of the express provisions of its charter, it had, by a formal resolution, placed its funds at the disposition of its President, to be employed in sustaining the political power of the bank. A copy of this resolution is contained in the report of the Government directors, before referred to; and however the object may be disguised by cautious language, no one can doubt that this money was in truth intended for electioneering purposes, and the particular uses to which it was proved to have been applied, abundantly show that it was so understood. Not only was the evidence complete as to the past application of the money and the power of the bank to electioneering purposes, but that the resolution of the Board of Directors authorized the same course to be pursued in future.

It being thus established by unquestionable proof that the Bank of the United States was converted into a permanent electioneering engine, it appeared to me that the path of duty which the Executive Department of the Government ought to pursue, was not doubtful. As by the terms of the bank charter, no officer but the Secretary of the Treasury could remove the deposites, it seemed to me that this authority ought to be at once exerted to deprive that great corporation of the support and countenance of the Government in such an use of its funds and such an exertion of its power. In this point of the case, the question is distinctly presented, whether the people of the United States are to govern through representatives chosen by their unbiased suffrages, or whether the power and money of a great corporation are to be secretly exerted to influence their judgment and control their decisions. It must now be determined whether the bank is to have its candidates for all offices in the country, from the highest to the lowest, or whether candidates on both sides of political questions shall be brought forward as heretofore and supported by the usual means.

At this time the efforts of the bank to control public opinion through the distresses of some and the fears of others, are equally apparent, and, if possible, more objectionable. By a curtailment of its accommodations, more rapid than any emergency requires, and even while it retains specie to an almost unprecedented amount in its vaults, it is attempting to produce great embarrassment in one portion of the community, while through presses known to have been sustained by its money, it attempts, by unfounded alarms, to create a panic in all.

These are the means by which it seems to expect that it can force a restoration of the deposites, and, as a necessary consequence, extort from Congress a renewal of its charter. I am happy to know that, through the good sense of our people, the effort to get up a panic has hitherto failed, and that, through the increased accommodations which the State banks have been enabled to afford, no public distress has followed the exertions of the bank; and it cannot be doubted that the exercise of its power and the expenditure of its money as well as its efforts to spread groundless alarm, will be met and rebuked as they deserve. In my own sphere of duty, I should feel myself called on by the facts disclosed, to order a *scire facias* against the bank, with a view to put an end to the chartered rights it has so palpably violated, were it not that the charter itself will expire as soon as a decision would probably be obtained from the court of last resort.

I called the attention of Congress to this subject in my last annual message, and informed them that such measures as were within the reach of the Secretary of the Treasury, had been taken to enable him to judge whether the public deposites in the Bank of the United States were entirely safe; but that as his single powers might be inadequate to the object, I recommended the subject to Congress, as worthy of their serious investigation: declaring it as my opinion that an inquiry into the transactions of that institution, embracing the branches as well as the principal bank, was called for by the credit which was given throughout the country to many serious charges impeaching their character, and which, if true, might justly excite the apprehension that they were no longer a safe depository for the public money. The extent to which the examination, thus recommended, was gone into, is spread upon your journals, and is too well known to require to be stated. Such as was made, resulted in a report from a majority of the Committee of Ways and Means touching certain specified points only, concluding with a resolution that the Government deposites might safely be continued in the Bank of the United States. This resolution was adopted at the close of the session, by the vote of a majority of the House of Representatives.

Although I may not always be able to concur in the views of the public interest, or the duties of its agents, which may be taken by the other departments of the Government, or either of its branches, I am, notwithstanding, wholly incapable of receiving otherwise than with the most sincere respect, all opinions or suggestions proceeding from such a source; and in respect to none am I more inclined to do so than the House of Representatives. But it will be seen from the brief views at this time taken of the subject by myself, as well as the more ample ones presented by the Secretary of the Treasury, that the change in the deposites which has been ordered, has been deemed to be called for by considerations which are not affected by the proceedings referred to, and which, if correctly viewed by that department, rendered its act a matter of imperious duty.

Coming as you do for the most part, immediately from the people and the States, by election, and possessing the fullest opportunity to know their sentiments, the present Congress will be sincerely solicitous to carry into full and fair effect the will of their constituents in regard to this institution. It will be for those in whose behalf we all act, to decide whether the Executive Department of the

Government, in the steps which it has taken on this subject, has been found in the line of its duty.

The accompanying report of the Secretary of War, with the documents annexed to it, exhibit the operations of the War Department for the past year, and condition of the various subjects intrusted to its administration.

It will be seen from them that the army maintains the character it has heretofore acquired for efficiency and military knowledge. Nothing has occurred since your last session to require its services beyond the ordinary routine of duties, which upon the seaboard and the inland frontier devolve upon it in a time of peace. The system, so wisely adopted and so long pursued, of constructing fortifications at exposed points, and of preparing and collecting the supplies necessary for the military defence of the country, and thus providently furnishing in peace the means of defence in war, has been continued with the usual results. I recommend to your consideration the various subjects suggested in the report of the Secretary of War. Their adoption would promote the public service and meliorate the condition of the army.

Our relations with the various Indian tribes have been undisturbed since the termination of the difficulties growing out of the hostile aggressions of the Sacs and Fox Indians. Several treaties have been formed for the relinquishment of territory to the United States, and for the migration of the occupants to the region assigned for their residence, west of the Mississippi. Should these treaties be ratified by the Senate, provision will have been made for the removal of almost all the tribes now remaining east of that river, and for the termination of many difficult and embarrassing questions arising out of their anomalous political condition. It is to be hoped those portions of two of the southern tribes which in that event will present the only remaining difficulties, will realize the necessity of emigration, and will speedily resort to it. My original convictions upon this subject have been confirmed by the course of events for several years, and experience is every day adding to their strength. That those tribes cannot exist, surrounded by our settlements and in continual contact with our citizens, is certain. They have neither the intelligence, the industry, the moral habits, nor the desire of improvement, which are essential to any favorable change in their condition. Established in the midst of another and a superior race, and without appreciating the causes of their inferiority, or seeking to control them, they must necessarily yield to the force of circumstances, and ere long disappear. Such has been their fate heretofore, and if it is to be averted, and it is, it can only be done by a general removal beyond our boundary and by the reorganization of their political system upon principles adapted to the new relations in which they will be placed. The experiment which has been recently made has so far proved successful. The emigrants generally are represented to be prosperous and contented, the country suitable to their wants and habits, and the essential articles of subsistence easily procured. When the report of the commissioners now engaged in investigating the condition and prospects of these Indians, and in devising a plan for their intercourse and government is received, I trust ample means of information will be in possession of the Government for adjusting all the unsettled questions connected with this interesting subject.

The operations of the navy during the year, and its present condition, are fully exhibited in the annual report from the Navy Department.

Suggestions are made by the Secretary, of various improvements, which deserve careful consideration, and most of which, if adopted, bid fair to promote the efficiency of this important branch of the public service. Among these, are the new organization of the Navy Board, the revision of the pay to officers, and a change in the period of time, or in the manner of making the annual appropriations, to which I beg leave to call your particular attention.

The views which are presented on almost every portion of our naval concerns, and, especially, on the amount of force and the number of officers, and the general course of policy appropriate in the present state of our country, for securing the great and useful purposes of naval protection in peace, and due preparation for the contingencies of war, meet with my entire approbation.

It will be perceived from the report referred to, that the fiscal concerns of the establishment are in an excellent condition; and it is hoped that Congress may feel disposed to make promptly every suitable provision desired either for preserving or improving the system.

The General Post Office Department has continued, upon the strength of its own resources, to facilitate the means of communication between the various portions of the Union with increased activity. The method, however, in which the accounts of the transportation of the mail has always been kept, appears to have presented an imperfect view of its expenses. It has recently been discovered that, from the earliest records of the department, the annual statements have been calculated to exhibit an amount considerably short of the actual expense incurred for that service. These illusory statements, together with the expense of carrying into effect the law of the last session of Congress, establishing new mail routes, and a disposition on the part of the head of the department to gratify the wishes of the public in the extension of the mail facilities, have induced him to incur responsibilities for their improvement beyond what the current resources of the department would sustain. As soon as he had discovered the imperfection of the method, he caused an investigation to be made of its results, and applied the proper remedy to correct the evil. It became necessary for him to withdraw some of the improvements which he had made, to bring the expenses of the department within its own resources. These expenses were incurred for the public good, and the public have enjoyed their benefit. They are now but partially suspended, and that where they may be discontinued with the least inconvenience to the country.

The progressive increase in the income from postages has equalled the highest expectations, and it affords demonstrative evidence of the growing importance and great utility of this department. The details are exhibited in the accompanying report from the Postmaster General.

The many distressing accidents which have of late occurred in that portion of our navigation carried on by the use of steam power, deserve the immediate and unremitting attention of the constituted authorities of the country. The fact that the number of those fatal disasters is constantly increasing, notwithstanding the great improvements which are everywhere made in the machinery employed, and in the rapid advances which have been made in that branch of science, show very clearly that they are in a great degree the result of criminal negligence on the part of those by whom the vessels are navigated, and to whose care and attention the lives and property of our citizens are so extensively intrusted.

That these evils may be greatly lessened, if not substantially removed, by means of precautionary and penal legislation, seems to be highly probable: so far, therefore, as the subject can be regarded as within the constitutional purview of Congress, I earnestly recommend it to your prompt and serious consideration.

I would also call your attention to the views I have heretofore expressed of the propriety of amending the Constitution in relation to the mode of electing the President and the Vice President of the United States. Regarding it as all-important to the future quiet and harmony of the people that every intermediate agency in the election of these officers should be removed, and that their eligibility should be limited to one term of either four or six years, I cannot too earnestly invite your consideration of the subject.

Trusting that your deliberations on all the topics of general interest to which I have adverted, and such others as your more extensive knowledge of the wants of our beloved country may suggest, may be crowned with success, I tender you, in conclusion, the coöperation which it may be in my power to afford them.

ANDREW JACKSON.

WASHINGTON, *December* 3, 1833.

On motion of Mr. KING, of Alabama, 5,000 copies of the Message, and 1,500 of the accompanying documents, were ordered to be printed.

Adjourned.

HOUSE OF REPRESENTATIVES.

TUESDAY, *December* 3, 1833.

The resolution from the Senate, appointing a committee to wait upon the President and inform him that the two bodies are organized, and ready to receive his communications, was concurred in; and Messrs. WARD and SPEIGHT were appointed on the part of the House.

The oaths of office were then administered to the Clerk, WALTER S. FRANKLIN.

The House, on motion of Mr. MASON, proceeded to the election of Sergeant-at-Arms.

Mr. MASON nominated Thomas B. Randolph; and Mr. SPEIGHT nominated William Robinson. 220 ballots were given, of which number—

Thomas B. Randolph received	158	votes.
William Robinson	54	"
O. Crosby	3	"
Jackson	1	"
Blank	4	"

Mr. CLAY submitted the following resolution, which was agreed to:

Resolved, That Overton Carr be appointed Doorkeeper, and John W. Hunter, Assistant Doorkeeper of the House of Representatives.

The oath of office was then administered to the Sergeant-at-Arms and Doorkeepers elect.

The usual resolutions for the appointment of chaplains and for furnishing the members with newspapers were adopted.

Mr. HUBBARD moved that all the former rules for the government of the House be adopted, with the exception of the 56th and 76th.

Mr. WILLIAMS was unwilling to decide upon a matter involving a change in the rules of the House without some time for consideration. He did not exactly understand what would be the effect of the proposed alteration, and he moved that the motion lie on the table.

Mr. HUBBARD explained that one of his propositions would be to increase the number of the members of the standing committees from seven to nine, and of the other committees from three to five. He also intended to propose that the members should sit uncovered until the Speaker should otherwise direct.

After a few words from Mr. BURGES in favor of a postponement of the subject,

Mr. WILLIAMS said that the proposition to sit without hats had often been submitted, and had always been rejected. It had been rejected on the ground that there was no convenient place for putting our hats; but he supposed that those who proposed the change would provide a place. He doubted, also, whether we should increase the efficiency of the committees by increasing their number. It was difficult to get the attendance of four members, which was the majority of seven, and it would be still more difficult to get five, the majority of nine. He wished time for reflection on the subject, and renewed his motion to lay the matter on the table.

Mr. SUTHERLAND suggested that nothing would be gained by letting the subject lie on the table. The House would be embarrassed unless rules were adopted.

Mr. PATTON moved that the 9th rule be also excepted, stating that it was his intention to move a modification of the 9th rule, to the effect that the Speaker should vote in the first instance in all cases, and that if the House be equally divided the question should be lost.

The motion, as modified at the suggestion of Mr. PATTON, was agreed to.

On motion of Mr. DAVIS, of Massachusetts, the House then adjourned.

IN SENATE.

WEDNESDAY, *December* 4, 1833.

Mr. CALHOUN, of South Carolina, and Mr. SPRAGUE, of Maine, appeared and took their seats.

The PRESIDENT laid before the Senate a communication from the Treasurer of the United States, transmitting the annual statement of his accounts, &c.

The PRESIDENT also presented a report from the Secretary of the Treasury, giving his reasons for the removal of the public deposites from the Bank of the United States.

Mr. GRUNDY moved that the reading of the

report should be dispensed with, and that 5,000 copies of the report and 1,500 copies of the documents accompanying it be printed for the use of the Senate. Agreed to.

Mr. WRIGHT submitted the following resolution:

Resolved, That the proceeding of the Legislature of the State of Rhode Island, now upon the table of the Senate, showing the appointment of ELISHA R. POTTER as a Senator to represent that State in the Senate of the United States, be referred to a select committee of five Senators, to inquire and report upon the claim of the said Elisha R. Potter to the seat in the Senate now occupied by the Hon. ASHER ROBBINS.

After some discussion as to the point of order whether the resolution should be then acted on, and the mode of appointing the committee, Mr. CLAY moved to postpone the further consideration of the subject until to-morrow, which was agreed to without a division.

A resolution from the House of Representatives, for the appointment of two chaplains, was considered and agreed to.

Mr. BENTON submitted the following resolution; which was considered and agreed to:

Resolved, That the Secretary of the Treasury be instructed to report to the Senate upon the sufficiency of the provisions made by the act of March 2d, 1833, for the satisfaction of revolutionary bounty land warrants, and whether a further appropriation of land and issue of scrip is necessary to satisfy outstanding warrants.

Mr. BENTON gave notice that he would, on Monday next, ask leave to introduce a joint resolution, proposing an amendment to the Constitution of the United States in relation to the mode of electing a President and Vice President.

On motion of Mr. KANE,

The Senate then adjourned.

HOUSE OF REPRESENTATIVES.

WEDNESDAY, *December* 4, 1833.

After the Journal was read, Mr. ALLAN, of Kentucky, rose and said, that prior to the organization of the House, the question connected with the contested Kentucky election was depending; but it was withdrawn in order to permit the organization of the House, and he now proposed to proceed in it. We had before made some progress in the question, and had arrived at the merits of it. It would take but a few minutes to complete the view which he proposed to take in reference to the subject. [Here Mr. A. was interrupted by the question, whether there was any subject before the House.]

The SPEAKER replied that he considered the question to be, whether Mr. Moore was to be qualified as a member or not. Mr. Moore was supposed to present himself now to the Chair for qualification.

Mr. ALLAN continued. It is likely in the skirmish we had the other day, that there was some mistake as to the character of Mr. Moore's certificate. He saw, by the reports, that it was considered that Mr. Moore's election was certified by the Governor in the same manner as the election of the other members from Kentucky. But the fact was, the Governor had no right to perform such duty, nor had he undertaken to perform it. The Governor had simply transmitted the returns from the sheriffs, without expressing any opinion as to the election in either of the districts. If any one imagines that the Governor transmitted the same certificate in the case of Mr. Moore, as in that of the other members, he is mistaken. The certificates of every member, except Mr. Moore, were signed by the sheriffs of every county in the respective districts. But Mr. Moore's certificate was signed only by three of the five sheriffs of the fifth district. The question is, whether that certificate, which is thus defective, is *prima facie* evidence of Mr. Moore's election? What do they certify? That they met and counted the votes? No, but that they did not meet and count the votes. The result of the election in the fifth district was known. Everybody knew it. The newspapers had published it. Mr. Letcher was well ascertained to be elected. Under those circumstances, the sheriffs met, on the fifteenth day after the election, to count and compare the votes. Did they count and compare the votes of the several counties, and certify the election of the candidate who had the greatest number of votes? No. The sheriff of Lincoln, one of the oldest and most improved counties in the State, as to the vote in which there was no dispute, puts the poll-book of that county in his pocket, and marches off. How stood the vote in Lincoln? The majority for Mr. Letcher there was one hundred and fifty, which, added to the whole, gave him a majority over Mr. Moore. The sheriff, seeing this result, suppressed his return. In good old times, in Kentucky, (said Mr. ALLAN,) a certain candidate who had been defeated, was asked, what was the reason of his defeat? "Nothing but the want of a sufficient number of votes," was the reply. The want of votes was, at that time, in Kentucky, considered quite sufficient to account for the failure of a candidate, and no one ever dreamed of getting here in any other way than by a majority of votes. But if this paper is received as a sufficient evidence of election, then a new way to get to Congress has been discovered.

Mr. HAWES, of Kentucky, said he presented himself with unfeigned embarrassment to the House, on this question. He considered the question, which of the two gentlemen, Mr. Moore or Mr. Letcher, should take his seat, was to be decided by this House, and decided in favor of the member who should be found to have the greatest number of votes. Mr Moore's certificate was, he contended, as valid as that of any other member from Kentucky. The return had the sanction of the Governor, which showed that he was considered by the Governor to have been duly elected. He admitted that the certificate was, in some respects, informal, but that informality did not affect the right of Mr. Moore to take his seat and qualify in the first instance. If we pursue the mode which has ever been pursued since the foundation of the Government, there will be no difficulty in the case. Let the subject be submitted to a committee, to take its usual course; and, at a proper time, let the House, with all the facts before them, say which party has the majority of votes, and is therefore elected. Any other course would be highly improper and unusual. The law of Kentucky had not provided for the case; but he contended that the failure of the sheriff of Lincoln to make his return did not make the election void, nor affect the validity of the certificate furnished by the other sheriffs of Mr. Moore's election. He did not pretend to say whether Mr. Moore or Mr. Letcher had the majority, but that the House should proceed to ascertain this fact in the usual form. He then referred to the course pursued in the contested election of a delegate from Michigan, as a precedent. He knew that the sheriffs were obliged by law to count the votes; but he saw no reason why this House should depart from the precedents established in such cases. Every member of the House was prepared to act on this question without the slightest prejudice in favor of either party. He did not know which candidate was elected, but he should vote, in the first instance, in favor of qualifying Mr. Moore.

Mr. CHILTON, after expressing a reluctance to enter upon this question, suggested that his colleague [Mr. HAWES] had fallen into some inconsistency in proposing to refer the subject to a committee. If the position taken by his colleague [Mr. ALLAN] in reference to the character of the certificate was correct, it could not be supposed that the House would permit Mr. Moore to take his seat. The question for our consideration was, whether this certificate complies with the laws of the State of Kentucky. He thought it was plain that it did not comply with the law. It was admitted that the district was composed of five counties; that the sheriff of each must, at a certain time, attend at a certain place, for the purpose of counting and comparing the votes. There was no dispute as to this. After a faithful comparison and count, each of these sheriffs must put his name to a certificate, showing that one person has a majority of votes and is elected. This was perfectly plain. But the fact is not disputed, that there appear at the bottom of the certificate the names of but three sheriffs. Now, he denied that an informal certificate amounted to *prima facie* evidence. Can interested evidence be admitted in a court of justice, merely because no other evidence can be furnished? Can partial testimony be in any case received, merely because it is the best evidence the case admits of? The principle was, in his opinion, erroneous and dangerous. We were all interested in preserving the purity of elections, and should be cautious in introducing any principles which will open a door to fraud. While he said this, he fully and entirely acquitted the member [Mr. Moore] from the slightest participation in the proceedings to which he referred as so incorrect. But he believed that the acceptance of his certificate would strike a fatal blow at the freedom and purity of elections. It was due to the whole nation to discountenance the attempt to force into the House, as a member, an individual whose credentials are thus imperfect. He disclaimed, as his colleagues had done, all feeling of an unfavorable character to the interests of either party to this question.

Mr. LANE rose and called for the reading of the certificate testified by the Governor of Kentucky, and in the possession of the Clerk, which was as follows:

STATE OF KENTUCKY,
Fifth Congressional District: }

We, the undersigned, sheriffs for the counties of Mercer, Garrard, Anderson, Lincoln, and Jessamine, composing said Congressional district, do certify, that on the fifteenth day after the commencement of the late Congressional election for said district, to wit: on the 20th day of August, 1833, we met at the court-house in Harrodsburg, Mercer county, and, adjourning from day to day, made a faithful comparison and addition of the votes and polls for said Congressional election, for said district, and found, and accordingly certify, that Thomas P. Moore is duly elected a Representative to Congress from said fifth Congressional district, by a majority of the qualified votes of said district. Given under our hands, this 21st day of August, 1833. The vote of Lincoln county not taken into calculation.

JACOB KELLER, *Deputy*,
For G. W. THOMPSON, *S. M. C.*,
JOHN WALSH, *Sheriff Anderson co.*,
By R. WALKER, *D. M.*,
JAMES H. GAIRG, *Deputy*,
For JOHN DOWNING, *Sheriff J. C.*

Mr. L. then inquired if the specific question presented to the House was, Shall Mr. Moore be sworn and take his seat? To which the Speaker replied, it was. Then, sir, it being admitted that the inquiry is not, who shall or shall not in the final decision of this House be entitled to the seat; not who received the greater number of legal votes, but whether the certificate read furnishes *prima facie* evidence of that fact,—the question to my mind is a simple one. It is a principle, that all persons intrusted with authority do their duty until the contrary appears. It is easy to suppose why the return of Lincoln was rejected. It may have been so imperfect upon its face, as to forbid its being received. It is said by the gentleman at my left, that he would not suffer any one to take his seat unless he produced a certificate perfect in all its parts. How, then, will the other gentleman take his seat, having no certificate? Mr. L. said both the gentlemen were strangers to him; but that he could assure them and the House that when he should be called upon to vote upon the first decision, his vote should be cast for him who should satisfy his mind he had received the majority of legal votes.

Mr. MARSHALL said the question was now narrowed down to a small point. It was not easy to say what was sufficient *prima facie* evidence of election; but when a member's credentials were questioned, he must produce such credentials as other members bring of their election. Any one may present himself in the Hall for qualification, and upon this *prima facie* evidence might be sworn in, if no one disputed his right. He utterly denied that the certificate produced by Mr. Moore amounted to sufficient evidence of his election, and we would not undertake to guess at reasons which might account for its informality. Any court of justice would decide that this certificate did not prove the main fact which it was offered to prove, viz: the election of Mr. Moore by a majority of the votes in the five counties composing the fifth district. The poll books themselves were the very

best evidence of an election, and the certificate was simply a substitute for the record of the fact itself. Now it ceased to be a substitute, if it was not made according to the laws of the State. There was no pretence for saying that an informal certificate was a substitute for the legal evidence of an election. If it was informal, in any one point, it ceased to carry any authority with it. If all the sheriffs did not sign it, it might as well be signed only by one sheriff, or not signed at all. In the law of Kentucky there was no provision for this case. It was a *casus omissus*, which we had no right to provide for. We must be bound by the law of Kentucky regulating the elections, as that law now stands. The Michigan case was totally different from this. This certificate did not state a fact upon which the election of Mr. Moore could be inferred. In the first instance, he contended, that the person who received the largest number of votes was entitled to his seat, and, in the next place, that no individual had produced the evidence of his having received that majority.

Mr. ELLSWORTH said, that the difficulty presented to his mind was this: Does the gentleman, Mr. Moore, present us a paper which is an evidence of his election? It appeared to him that a majority of the sheriffs could not give a certificate, for the law of Kentucky expressly provided that all the sheriffs of the several counties should assemble and perform certain duties, one of which was, to sign this certificate. Suppose the certificate had asserted this: "We certify that, according to the votes in four counties in the 5th district, Thomas P. Moore is elected." Would that be sufficient? Certainly not. But, in fact, they have certified to nothing more, if to so much. The question now is, who shall sit as a member from the 5th district until the subject is investigated? And in his opinion the Hon. Mr. Moore did not present such testimony as entitled him to a seat.

Mr. BEARDSLEY said it was conceded that the preliminary question was to be decided upon the sufficiency of the certificate. It is said that it appears on the face of this certificate that the votes of the county of Lincoln are not counted. But does it appear on the face of the certificate that any votes from Lincoln county were presented to the sheriffs? The paper shows, upon the declaration of three sheriffs, that Thomas P. Moore is duly elected by a majority of the qualified votes of the district. The only question is, therefore, whether the certificate of three sheriffs is sufficient, for it is admitted that this paper would be deemed sufficient had it been signed by the five sheriffs. Where several persons are appointed to do a particular act, the law recognises as valid the act of a majority of those persons. This was a clear principle, and if this be so, it ends the question.

Mr. POLK rose to offer some precedents bearing on this case. He held in his hand the original manuscript report on a contested election in the 20th Congressional District of New York, which was in point. By the law of New York, certain officers called the State canvassers, must certify the election of each member. The canvassers returned the name of Daniel Huggenin, without the word *junior*, in consequence of which, Mr. Ten Eyck was returned as a member. Two hundred and seventy-four votes were lost to Mr. Huggenin by the omission of "Junior" in the return, and the certificate was given to Mr. Ten Eyck. The certificate stated the facts of the case, and Mr. Huggenin appeared at the bar of the House and alleged that he had been duly elected, for that he was the Daniel Huggenin, Jun., who had been voted for, as he offered to prove. But the House gave the seat to Mr. Ten Eyck for the time; and after investigating the facts, in the usual manner, gave the seat to Mr. Huggenin. He referred to another case of the same sort, in which Mr. Fisher was returned from New York, instead of Silas Wright, Jr., because some of the votes given for Mr. Wright were not counted by the canvassers. Mr. Fisher was qualified, and subsequently the seat was given to Mr. Wright. The House never pretended, at first, to go beyond the certificate; our course was a clear one, according to the precedents laid down.

Mr. WARDWELL went into some explanations of the New York cases referred to by the member from Tennessee. In the case of Mr. Wright, all the votes were not counted; but Mr. Fisher, contrary to the wishes of his own friends, and notwithstanding that the fact of Mr. Wright's election was undisputed, came here and presented himself for qualification. The evidence that Mr. Wright had been elected was so plain, that not a member of the House contradicted it. But still the House, following its usual course, suffered Mr. Fisher to take his seat; and subsequently, after the report of a committee, the seat was given to Mr. Wright.

Mr. ALLAN called for the reading of certain papers which he named, from which he would show that the votes given in the different counties were as follows:

	Letcher.	*Moore.*
Jessamine	581	489
Garrard	175	248
Anderson	99	436
Mercer	686	1469
Lincoln	650	501
	3191	3143

Majority for Letcher, 48.

The Clerk proceeded, at the request of Mr. ALLAN, to read certificates of the number of votes given in each county.

Mr. POLK interposed, and objected to the course pursued. If we went into the subject at all, we must hear the whole evidence in the shape of depositions and affidavits, which the two parties are prepared to offer. This would convert this House, at this stage of the business, into an examining committee. In his own opinion, we had no right to go beyond the certificate.

Mr. McKINLEY rose to point out a difference between this case and the New York cases; for in those cases, the certificates themselves showed that there were other candidates who were voted for. The evidence called for would not apply to this case.

Mr. BURGES said we must first ascertain whether there is any case to examine before a committee. If the law intended that each sheriff should certify the return from his own county, then a return of a portion of the sheriffs can give no one a certificate which will entitle him to a seat. Therefore, we have no knowledge that any one was elected in the 5th district. We must, to ascertain who is elected, go behind the certificate, and approximate to the people. We must go up to the poll books, if we wish to reach the truth. We have no paper which gives us any amount of the votes in the several counties, unless it be the papers, the reading of which was called for. The certificate did not assume to give the votes of every county.

Mr. POLK said he now understood that the gentleman who contested this seat had been engaged for two months in obtaining testimony, some of which was ready, and some of which was expected. The House, therefore, if it goes into the evidence at all, must continue to examine it, and proceed in it as it comes in from day to day, and no decision could be made until the whole of it had been received. Advertising the House of this fact, he would withdraw the objection to the reading of the paper.

Mr. EVANS moved an adjournment.

The SPEAKER communicated to the House the report of the Secretary of the Treasury on the removal of the deposites.

On motion, the reading of the report was dispensed with, and ten thousand copies ordered to be printed.

The SPEAKER communicated to the House a report of the Secretary of the Treasury on the cultivation of the sugar cane; a report from the Board of Engineers; the annual Treasury report; the annual report of the Treasurer; and the report of the late Clerk of the House, on the contingent expenses of the House; all of which were laid on the table, and ordered to be printed.

The House then adjourned.

IN SENATE.

THURSDAY, *December* 5, 1833.

On motion of Mr. GRUNDY, it was

Ordered, That when the Senate adjourns to-day, it will adjourn to meet again on Monday next.

The following message was received from the President of the United States, (through Mr. Donelson, his private secretary,) returning, with his objections, the bill which originated in the Senate at its last session, "appropriating for a limited time the proceeds of the sales of the public lands, and for other purposes."

To the Senate of the United States:

At the close of the last session of Congress, I received from that body a bill entitled "An act to appropriate for a limited time the proceeds of the sales of the public lands of the United States, and for granting lands to certain States." The brief period then remaining before the rising of Congress, and the extreme pressure of official duties, unavoidable on such occasions, did not leave me sufficient time for that full consideration of the subject which was due to its great importance. Subsequent consideration and reflection have, however, confirmed the objections to the bill which presented themselves to my mind upon its first perusal, and have satisfied me that it ought not to become a law. I felt myself, therefore, constrained to withhold from it my approval, and now return it to the Senate, in which it originated, with the reasons on which my dissent is founded.

I am fully sensible of the importance, as it respects both the harmony and union of the States, of making, as soon as circumstances will allow of it, a proper and final disposition of the whole subject of the public lands; and any measure for that object, providing for the reimbursement to the United States of those expenses with which they are justly chargeable, that may be consistent with my views of the Constitution, sound policy, and the rights of the respective States, will readily receive my coöperation. This bill, however, is not of that character. The arrangement it contemplates is not permanent, but limited to five years only, and in its terms appears to anticipate alterations within that time, at the discretion of Congress; and it furnishes no adequate security against those continued agitations of the subject which it should be the principal object of any measure for the disposition of the public lands to avert.

Neither the merits of the bill under consideration, nor the validity of the objections which I have felt it to be my duty to make to its passage, can be correctly appreciated without a full understanding of the manner in which the public lands, upon which it is intended to operate, were acquired, and the conditions upon which they are now held by the United States. I will, therefore, precede the statement of those objections by a brief but distinct exposition of these points.

The waste lands within the United States constituted one of the early obstacles to the organization of any Government for the protection of their common interests. In October, 1777, while Congress were framing the Articles of Confederation, a proposition was made to amend them to the following effect, viz:

"That the United States in Congress assembled, 'shall have the sole and exclusive right and power 'to ascertain and fix the western boundary of such 'States as claim to the Mississippi or South sea, 'and lay out the land beyond the boundary so ascertained, into separate and independent States, 'from time to time, as the numbers and circum'stances of the people thereof may require."

It was, however, rejected, Maryland only voting for it; and so difficult did the subject appear, that the patriots of that body agreed to waive it in the Articles of Confederation, and leave it for future settlement.

On the submission of the articles to the several State Legislatures for ratification, the most formidable objection was found to be in this subject of waste lands. Maryland, Rhode Island, and New-Jersey, instructed their Delegates in Congress to move amendments to them, providing that the waste or Crown lands should be considered the common property of the United States; but they were rejected. All the States, except Maryland, acceded to the articles, notwithstanding some of them did so with the reservation that their claim to those lands, as common property, was not thereby abandoned.

On the sole ground that no declaration to that effect was contained in the articles, Maryland withheld her assent, and in May, 1779, embodied her objections in the form of instructions to her Dele-

gates, which were entered upon the journals of Congress. The following extracts are from that document, viz:

"Is it possible that those States who are ambitiously grasping at territories, to which in our 'judgment they have not the least shadow of exclusive right, will use with greater moderation 'the increase of wealth and power derived from 'those territories, when acquired, than what they 'have displayed in their endeavors to acquire 'them?" &c., &c.

"We are convinced, policy and justice require 'that a country unsettled at the commencement of 'this war, claimed by the British Crown, and 'ceded to it by the treaty of Paris, if wrested from 'the common enemy by the blood and treasure of 'the Thirteen States, should be considered as a 'common property, subject to be parcelled out by 'Congress into free, convenient, and independent 'Governments, in such manner and at such times 'as the wisdom of that assemby shall hereafter 'direct," &c., &c.

Virginia proceeded to open a land office for the sale of her western lands, which produced such excitement as to induce Congress in October, 1779, to interpose and earnestly recommend to "the said State and all States similarly circumstanced to forbear settling or issuing warrants for such unappropriated lands, or granting the same during the continuance of the present war."

In March, 1780, the Legislature of New York passed an act tendering a cession to the United States of the claims of that State to the western territory, preceded by a preamble to the following effect, viz:

"Whereas nothing under Divine Providence can more effectually contribute to the tranquillity and safety of the United States of America than a federal alliance on such liberal principles as will give satisfaction to its respective members; and whereas the Articles of Confederation and perpetual Union recommended by the honorable Congress of the United States of America have not proved acceptable to all the States, it having been conceived that a portion of the waste and uncultivated territory within the limits or claims of certain States ought to be appropriated as a common fund for the expenses of the war; and the people of. the State of New York being on all occasions disposed to manifest their regard for their sister States and their earnest desire to promote the general interest and security, and more especially to accelerate the federal alliance, by removing, as far as it depends upon them, the before-mentioned impediment to its final accomplishment," &c.

This act of New York, the instructions of Maryland, and a remonstrance of Virginia, were referred to a committee in Congress, who reported a preamble and resolutions thereon, which were adopted on the 6th September, 1780; so much of which as is necessary to elucidate the subject is to the following effect, viz:

"That it appears advisable to press upon those States which can remove the embarrassments respecting the western country a liberal surrender of a portion of their territorial claims, since they cannot be preserved entire without endangering the stability of the general confederacy; to remind them how indispensably necessary it is to establish the Federal Union on a fixed and permanent basis and on principles acceptable to all its respective members; how essential to public credit and confidence, to the support of our army, to the vigor of our councils and success of our measures, to our tranquillity at home, our reputation abroad, to our very existence as a free, sovereign, and independent people; that they are fully persuaded the wisdom of the several Legislatures will lead them to a full and impartial consideration of a subject so interesting to the United States and so necessary to the happy establishment of the Federal Union; that they are confirmed in these expectations by a review of the before-mentioned act of the Legislature of New York, submitted to their consideration," &c.

"*Resolved*, That copies of the several papers, referred to the committee, be transmitted with a copy of the report to the Legislatures of the several States, and that it be earnestly recommended to those States who have claims to the western country, to pass such laws and give their delegates in Congress such powers as may effectually remove the only obstacle to a final ratification of the Articles of Confederation; and that the Legislature of Maryland be earnestly requested to authorize their delegates in Congress to subscribe the said articles."

Following up this policy, Congress proceeded, on the 10th of October, 1780, to pass a resolution pledging the United States to the several States as to the manner in which any lands that might be ceded by them should be disposed of, the material parts of which are as follows, viz:

"*Resolved*, That the unappropriated lands which may be ceded or relinquished to the United States by any particular State pursuant to the recommendation of Congress of the 6th day of September last, shall be disposed of for the common benefit of the United States, and be settled and formed into distinct republican States, which shall become members of the Federal Union, and have the same rights of sovereignty, freedom and independence as the other States," &c. "That the said lands shall be granted or settled at such times and under such regulations as shall hereafter be agreed on by the United States in Congress assembled, or nine or more of them."

In February, 1781, the Legislature of Maryland passed an act authorizing their delegates in Congress to sign the Articles of Confederation. The following are extracts from the preamble and body of the act, viz:

"Whereas it hath been said that the common ene y is encouraged by this State not acceding to the Confederation to hope that the union of the sister States may be dissolved, and therefore prosecutes the war in expectation of an event so disgraceful to America; and our friends and illustrious ally are impressed with an idea that the common cause would be promoted by our formally acceding to the Confederation," &c.

The act of which this is the preamble, authorizes the delegates of that State to sign the articles, and proceeds to declare, "that, by acceding to the said Confederation, this State doth not relinquish, nor intend to relinquish any right or interest she hath, with the other United or Confederated States, to the back country," &c., &c.

On the 1st of March, 1781, the delegates of Maryland signed the articles of Confederation, and the Federal Union under that compact was complete. The conflicting claims to the western lands, however, were not disposed of, and continued to give great trouble to Congress. Repeated and urgent calls were made by Congress upon the States claiming them, to make liberal cessions to the United States, and it was not until long after the present Constitution was formed, that the grants were completed.

The deed of cession from New York was executed on the 1st of March, 1781, the day the Articles of Confederation were ratified, and it was accepted by Congress on the 29th October, 1782. One of the conditions of this cession, thus tendered and accepted, was, that the lands ceded to the United States "*shall be and enure for the use and benefit of such of the United States as shall become members of the Federal alliance of the said States, and for no other use or purpose whatsoever.*"

The Virginia deed of cession was executed and accepted on the 1st day of March, 1784. One of the conditions of this cession is as follows, viz:

"That all the lands within the territory so ceded to the United States, and not reserved for or appropriated to any of the before-mentioned purposes, or disposed of in bounties to the officers and soldiers of the American army, *shall be considered as a common fund for the use and benefit of such of the United States as have become or shall become members of the Confederation or Federal alliance of the said States, Virginia inclusive, according to their usual respective proportions in the general charge and expenditure, and shall be faithfully and bona fide disposed of for that purpose, and for no other use or purpose whatsoever.*"

Within the years 1785, 1786, and 1787, Massachusetts, Connecticut, and South Carolina, ceded their claims upon similar conditions. The Federal Government went into operation under the existing Constitution on the 4th of March, 1789. The following is the only provision of that Constitution which has a direct bearing on the subject of the public lands, viz:

"The Congress shall have power to dispose of, and make all needful rules and regulations respecting the territory or other property belonging to the United States, and nothing in this Constitution shall be so construed as to prejudice any claims of the United States, or of any particular State."

Thus the Constitution left all the compacts before made in full force, and the rights of all parties remained the same under the new Government as they were under the Confederation.

The deed of cession of North Carolina was executed in December, 1789, and accepted by an act of Congress approved April 2, 1790. The third condition of this cession was in the following words, viz:

"That all the lands intended to be ceded by virtue of this act to the United States of America, and not appropriated as before mentioned, *shall be considered as a common fund for the use and benefit of the United States of America, North Carolina inclusive, according to their respective and usual proportions of the general charge and expenditure, and shall be faithfully disposed of for that purpose, and for no other use or purpose whatever.*"

The cession of Georgia was completed on the 16th of June, 1802, and, in its leading condition, is precisely like that of Virginia and North Carolina. This grant completed the title of the United States to all those lands, generally called *public lands*, lying within the original limits of the Confederacy. Those which have been acquired by the purchase of Louisiana and Florida, having been paid for out of the common treasure of the United States, are as much the property of the General Government, to be disposed of for the common benefit, as those ceded by the several States.

By the facts here collected from the early history of our Republic, it appears that the subject of the public lands entered into the elements of its institutions. It was only upon the condition that those lands should be considered as common property, to be disposed of for the benefit of the United States, that some of the States agreed to come into a "perpetual union." The States claiming those lands acceded to those views, and transferred their claims to the United States upon certain specific conditions, and on those conditions the grants were accepted. These solemn compacts, invited by Congress, in a resolution declaring the purposes to which the proceeds of these lands should be applied, originating before the Constitution, and forming the basis on which it was made, bound the United States to a particular course of policy in relation to them, by ties as strong as can be invented to secure the faith of nations.

As early as May, 1785, Congress, in execution of these compacts, passed an ordinance, providing for the sales of lands in the Western Territory, and directing the proceeds to be paid into the treasury of the United States. With the same object, other ordinances were adopted prior to the organization of the present Government.

In further execution of these compacts, the Congress of the United States, under the present Constitution, as early as the 4th August, 1790, in "an act making provision for the debt of the United States," enacted as follows, viz:

"That the proceeds of sales which shall be made of lands in the Western Territory, now belonging, or that may hereafter belong, to the United States, shall be, and are hereby, appropriated towards sinking or discharging the debts for the payment whereof the United States now are, or by virtue of this act may be holden, and shall be applied solely to that use, until the said debt shall be fully satisfied."

To secure to the Government of the United States forever the power to execute these compacts in good faith, the Congress of the Confederation, as early as July 13, 1787, in an ordinance for the government of the Territory of the United States northwest of the river Ohio, prescribed to the people inhabiting the Western Territory certain conditions which were declared to be "articles of compact between the original States and the people and States in the said Territory," which should "forever remain unalterable, unless by common consent." In one of these articles, it is declared, that—

"The Legislatures of those districts or new States shall never interfere with the primary disposal of the soil by the United States in Congress assembled, nor with any regulation Congress may find

necessary for securing the title in such soil to the *bona fide* purchasers."

This condition has been exacted from the people of all the new territories; and, to put its obligation beyond dispute, each new State, carved out of the public domain, has been required explicitly to recognise it as one of the conditions of admission into the Union. Some of them have declared through their conventions, in separate acts, that their people "forever disclaim all right and title to the waste and unappropriated lands lying within this State, and that the same shall be and remain at the sole and entire disposition of the United States."

With such care have the United States reserved to themselves, in all their acts down to this day—in legislating for the territories and admitting States into the Union—the unshackled power to execute in good faith the compacts of cession made with the original States. From these facts and proceedings, it plainly and certainly results—

1. That one of the fundamental principles on which the confederation of the United States was originally based was, that the waste land of the West within their limits should be the common property of the United States.

2. That those lands were ceded to the United States by the States which claimed them, and the cessions were accepted, on the express condition that they should be disposed of for the common benefit of the States according to their respective proportions in the general charge and expenditure, and for no other purpose whatsoever.

3. That in execution of these solemn compacts, the Congress of the United States did, under the Confederation, proceed to sell these lands and put the avails into the common treasury, and, under the new Constitution, did repeatedly pledge them for the payment of the public debt of the United States, by which each State was expected to profit in proportion to the general charge to be made upon it for that object.

These are the first principles of this whole subject, which, I think, cannot be contested by any one who examines the proceedings of the Revolutionary Congress, the cessions of the several States, and the acts of Congress under the new Constitution. Keeping them deeply impressed upon the mind, let us proceed to examine how far the objects of the cessions have been completed, and see whether those compacts are not still obligatory upon the United States.

The debt for which these lands were pledged by Congress may be considered as paid, and they are consequently released from that lien. But that pledge formed no part of the compacts with the States, or of the conditions upon which the cessions were made. It was a contract between new parties—between the United States and their creditors. Upon payment of the debts the compacts remain in full force, and the obligation of the United States to dispose of the lands for the common benefit, is neither destroyed nor impaired. As they cannot now be executed in that mode, the only legitimate question which can arise is, in what other way are these lands to be hereafter disposed of for the common benefit of the several States "*according to their respective and usual proportion in the general charge and expenditure?*" The cessions of Virginia, North Carolina, and Georgia, in express terms, and all the rest impliedly, not only provide thus specifically the proportion according to which each State shall profit by the proceeds of the land sales, but they proceed to declare that they shall be "*faithfully and bona fide disposed of for that purpose, and for no other use or purpose whatsoever.*" This is the fundamental law of the land at this moment, growing out of compacts which are older than the Constitution, and formed the corner-stone on which the Union itself was erected.

In the practice of the Government, the proceeds of the public lands have not been set apart *as a separate fund* for the payment of public debt; but have been and are now paid into the treasury, where they constitute a part of the aggregate of revenue upon which the Government draws as well for its current expenditures as for payment of the public debt. In this manner, they have heretofore and do now lessen the general charge upon the people of the several States in the exact proportions stipulated in the compacts.

These general charges have been composed not only of the public debt and the usual expenditures attending the civil and military administrations of the Government; but of the amounts paid to the States with which these compacts were formed, the amounts paid the Indians for their right of possession, the amounts paid for the purchase of Louisiana and Florida, and the amounts paid surveyors, registers, receivers, clerks, &c., employed in preparing for market and selling the western domain. From the origin of the land system down to September 30, 1832, the amount expended for all these purposes has been about $49,701,280; and the amount received from the sales, deducting payments on account of roads, &c., about $38,386,624. The revenue arising from the public lands, therefore, has not been sufficient to meet the general charges on the treasury which have grown out of them, by about $11,314,656. Yet, in having been applied to lessen those charges, the conditions of the compacts have been thus far fulfilled, and each State has profited according to its usual proportion in the general charge and expenditure. The annual proceeds of land sales have increased and the charges have diminished, so that at a reduced price those lands would now defray all current charges growing out of them, and save the treasury from further advances on their account. Their original intent and object, therefore, would be accomplished as fully as it has hitherto been, by reducing the price, and hereafter, as heretofore, bringing the proceeds into the treasury. Indeed, as this is the only mode in which the objects of the original compacts can be attained, it may be considered, for all practical purposes, that it is one of their requirements.

The bill before me begins with an entire subversion of every one of the compacts by which the United States became possessed of their western domain, and treats the subject as if they never had existence, and as if the United States were the original and unconditional owners of all the public lands. The first section directs—

"That from and after the 31st day of December, 1832, there shall be allowed and paid to each of the States of Ohio, Indiana, Illinois, Alabama, Missouri, Mississippi, and Louisiana, over and above what each of the said States is entitled to by the terms of the compacts entered into between them respectively upon their admission into the Union and the United States, the sum of twelve and a half per centum upon the net amount of the sales of the public lands which subsequent to the day aforesaid shall be made within the several limits of the said States; which said sum of twelve and a half per centum shall be applied to some object or objects of internal improvement or education in the said States, under the direction of their several legislatures."

This twelve and a half per centum is to be taken out of the net proceeds of the land sales before any appointment is made; and the same seven States which are first to receive this proportion, are also to receive their due proportion of the residue, according to the ratio of general distribution.

Now, waiving all considerations of equity or policy in regard to this provision, what more need be said to demonstrate its objectionable character, than that it is in direct and undisguised violation of the pledge given by Congress to the States before a single cession was made; that it abrogates the condition upon which some of the States came into the Union; and that it sets at naught the terms of cession spread upon the face of every grant under which the title to that portion of the public lands is held by the Federal Government?

In the apportionment of the remaining seven-eighths of the proceeds, this bill, in a manner equally undisguised, violates the condition upon which the United States acquired title to the ceded lands. Abandoning altogether the ratio of distribution according to the general charge and expenditure, provided by the compacts, it adopts that of the federal representative population. Virginia, and other States, which ceded their lands upon the express condition that they should receive a benefit from their sales, in proportion to their part of the general charge, are by the bill allowed only a portion—seven-eighths of their proceeds—and that not in the proportion of general charge and expenditure, but in the ratio of their federal representative population.

The Constitution of the United States did not delegate to Congress the power to abrogate these compacts. On the contrary, by declaring that nothing in it "*shall be so construed as to prejudice any claims of the United States, or of any particular State,*" it virtually provides that these compacts and the rights they secure, shall remain untouched by the legislative power, which shall only make all "*needful rules and regulations*" for carrying them into effect. All beyond this would seem to be an assumption of undelegated power.

These ancient compacts are invaluable monuments of an age of virtue, patriotism, and disinterestedness. They exhibit the price that great States, which had won liberty, were willing to pay for that union, without which they plainly saw it could not be preserved. It was not for territory or State power, that our revolutionary fathers took up arms; it was for individual liberty and the right of self government. The expulsion from the continent of British armies and British power was to them a barren conquest, if, through the collisions of the redeemed States, the individual rights for which they fought, should become the prey of petty military tyrannies, established at home. To avert such consequences, and throw around liberty the shield of union, States, whose relative strength at the time, gave them a preponderating power, magnanimously sacrificed domains, which would have made them the rivals of empires, only stipulating that they should be disposed of for the common benefit of themselves and the other confederated States. This enlightened policy produced union, and has secured liberty. It has made our waste lands to swarm with a busy people, and added many powerful States to our Confederation. As well for the fruits which these noble works of our ancestors have produced, as for the devotedness in which they originated, we should hesitate before we demolish them.

But there are other principles asserted in the bill which would have impelled me to withhold my signature, had I not seen in it a violation of the compacts by which the United States acquired title to a large portion of the public lands. It re-asserts the principle contained in the bill authorizing a subscription to the stock of the Maysville, Washington, Paris, and Lexington Turnpike Road Company, from which I was compelled to withhold my consent for reasons contained in my message of the 27th May, 1830, to the House of Representatives. The leading principle then asserted was, that Congress possesses no constitutional power to appropriate any part of the moneys of the United States for objects of a local character, within the States. That principle, I cannot be mistaken in supposing, has received the unequivocal sanction of the American people, and all subsequent reflection has but satisfied me more thoroughly, that the interests of our people, and the purity of our Government, if not its existence, depend on its observance. The public lands are the common property of the United States, and the moneys arising from their sales, are a part of the public revenue. This bill proposes to raise from and appropriate a portion of this public revenue to certain States, providing expressly, that it shall "*be applied to objects of internal improvement or education within those States,*" and then proceeds to appropriate the balance to all the States, with the declaration, that it shall be applied "*to such purposes as the Legislatures of the said respective States shall deem proper.*" The former appropriation is expressly for internal improvements or education, without qualification as to the kind of improvements, and therefore in express violation of the principle maintained in my objections to the turnpike road bill, above referred to. The latter appropriation is more broad, and gives the money to be applied to any local purpose whatsoever. It will not be denied that, under the provisions of the bill, a portion of the money might have been applied to making the very road to which the bill of 1830 had reference, and must of course come within the scope of the same principle. If the money of the United States cannot be applied to local purposes *through its own agents*, as little can it be permitted to be thus expended *through the agency of the State Governments.*

It has been supposed that with all the reductions in our revenue which could be speedily effected

by Congress without injury to the substantial interests of the country, there might be for some years to come a surplus of moneys in the treasury, and that there was, in principle, no objection to returning them to the people by whom they were paid. As the literal accomplishment of such an object is obviously impracticable, it was thought admissible, as the nearest approximation to it, to hand them over to the State Governments, the more immediate representatives of the people, to be by them applied to the benefit of those to whom they properly belonged. The principle and the object was, to return to the people an unavoidable surplus of revenue which might have been paid by them under a system which could not at once be abandoned; but even this resource, which at one time seemed to be almost the only alternative to save the General Government from grasping unlimited power over internal improvements, was suggested with doubts of its constitutionality.

But this bill assumes a new principle. Its object is not to return to the people an unavoidable surplus of revenue paid in by them, but to create a surplus for distribution among the States. It seizes the entire proceeds of one source of revenue and sets them apart as a surplus, making it necessary to raise the moneys for supporting the Government and meeting the general charges, from other sources. It even throws the entire land system upon the customs for its support, and makes the public lands a perpetual charge upon the treasury. It does not return to the people moneys accidentally or unavoidably paid by them to the Government, by which they are not wanted; but compels the people to pay moneys into the treasury for the mere purpose of creating a surplus for distribution to their State Governments. If this principle be once admitted, it is not difficult to perceive to what consequences it may lead. Already this bill, by throwing the land system on the revenues from imports for support, virtually distributes among the States a part of those revenues. The proportion may be increased, from time to time, without any departure from the principle now asserted, until the State governments shall derive all the funds necessary for their support from the treasury of the United States, or, if a sufficient supply should be obtained by some States and not by others, the deficient States might complain, and to put an end to all further difficulty, Congress, without assuming any new principle, need go but one step further, and put the salaries of all the State governors, judges, and other officers, with a sufficient sum for other expenses, in their general appropriation bill.

It appears to me that a more direct road to consolidation cannot be devised. Money is power, and in that government which pays all the public officers of the States, will all political power be substantially concentrated. The State governments, if governments they might be called, would lose all their independence and dignity. The economy which now distinguishes them, would be converted into a profusion, limited only by the extent of the supply. Being the dependants of the General Government, and looking to its treasury as the source of all their emoluments, the State officers, under whatever names they might pass, and by whatever forms their duties might be prescribed, would in effect be the mere stipendiaries and instruments of the central power.

I am quite sure that the intelligent people of our several States, will be satisfied, on a little reflection, that it is neither wise nor safe to release the members of their local Legislatures from the responsibility of levying the taxes necessary to support their State governments, and vest it in Congress, over most of whose members they have no control. They will not think it expedient that Congress shall be the tax gatherer and paymaster of all their State governments, thus amalgamating all their officers into one mass of common interest and common feeling. It is too obvious that such a course would subvert our well-balanced system of government, and ultimately deprive us of all the blessings now derived from our happy Union.

However willing I might be that any unavoidable surplus in the treasury should be returned to the people through their State Governments, I cannot assent to the principle that a surplus may be created for the purpose of distribution. Viewing this bill as in effect assuming the right, not only to create a surplus for that purpose, but to divide the contents of the treasury among the States without limitation, from whatever source they may be derived, and asserting the power to raise and appropriate money for the support of every State Government and institution, as well as for making every local improvement, however trivial, I cannot give it my assent.

It is difficult to perceive what advantages would accrue to the old States or the new, from the system of distribution which this bill proposes, if it were otherwise unobjectionable. It requires no argument to prove that if three millions of dollars a year, or any other sum, shall be taken out of the treasury by this bill for distribution, it must be replaced by the same sum collected from the people through some other means. The old States will receive annually a sum of money from the treasury, but they will pay in a larger sum, together with the expenses of collection and distribution. It is only their proportion of *seven-eighths* of the proceeds of land sales which they are to *receive;* but they must *pay* their due proportion of the *whole*. Disguise it as we may, the bill proposes to them a dead loss, in the ratio of *eight* to *seven*, in addition to expenses and other incidental losses. This assertion is not the less true because it may not at first be palpable. Their receipts will be in large sums, but their payments in small ones. The *Governments* of the States will receive *seven* dollars for which the *people* of the States will pay *eight*. The large sums received will be palpable to the senses; the small sums paid, it requires thought to identify. But a little consideration will satisfy the people that the effect is the same as if *seven hundred dollars* were given them from the public treasury, for which they were at the same time required to pay in taxes, direct or indirect, *eight hundred*.

I deceive myself greatly if the new States would find their interests promoted by such a system as this bill proposes. Their true policy consists in the rapid settling and improvement of the waste lands within their limits. As a means of hastening those events, they have long been looking to a reduction in the price of public lands upon the final payment of the national debt. The effect of the proposed system would be to prevent that reduction. It is true, the bill reserves to Congress the power to reduce the price, but the effect of its details, as now arranged, would probably be forever to prevent its exercise.

With the just men who inhabit the new States, it is a sufficient reason to reject this system, that it is in violation of the fundamental laws of the Republic and its Constitution. But if it were a mere question of interest or expediency, they would still reject it. They would not sell their bright prospect of increasing wealth and growing power at such a price. They would not place a sum of money to be paid into their treasuries, in competition with the settlement of their waste lands and the increase of their population. They would not consider a small or a large annual sum to be paid to their Governments and immediately expended, as an equivalent for that enduring wealth which is composed of flocks and herds, and cultivated farms. No temptation will allure them from that object of abiding interest, the settlement of their waste lands, and the increase of a hardy race of free citizens, their glory in peace and their defence in war.

On the whole, I adhere to the opinion expressed by me in my Annual Message of 1832, that it is our true policy that the public lands shall cease, as soon as practicable, to be a source of revenue, except for the payment of those general charges which grow out of the acquisition of the lands, their survey and sale. Although these expenses have not been met by the proceeds of sales heretofore, it is quite certain they will be hereafter, even after a considerable reduction in the price. By meeting in the treasury so much of the general charge as arises from that source, they will hereafter, as they have been heretofore, be disposed of for the common benefit of the United States, according to the compacts of cession. I do not doubt that it is the real interest of each and all the States in the Union, and particularly of the new States, that the price of these lands shall be reduced and graduated; and that after they have been offered for a certain number of years, the refuse remaining unsold shall be abandoned to the States, and the machinery of our land system entirely withdrawn. It cannot be supposed the compacts intended that the United States should retain forever a title to lands within the States which are of no value, and no doubt is entertained that the general interest would be best promoted by surrendering such lands to the States.

This plan for disposing of the public lands impairs no principle, violates no compact, and deranges no system. Already has the price of those lands been reduced from two dollars per acre to one dollar and a quarter, and upon the will of Congress it depends whether there shall be a further reduction. While the burdens of the East are diminishing by the reduction of the duties upon imports, it seems but equal justice that the chief burden of the West should be lightened in an equal degree at least. It would be just to the old States and the new, conciliate every interest, disarm the subject of all its dangers, and add another guarantee to the perpetuity of our happy Union.

Sensible, however, of the difficulties which surround this important subject, I can only add to my regrets, at finding myself again compelled to disagree with the legislative power, the sincere declaration, that any plan which shall promise a final and satisfactory disposition of the question, and be compatible with the Constitution and public faith, shall have my hearty concurrence.

ANDREW JACKSON.

December 4th, 1833.

The Message being read,

Mr. CLAY rose and animadverted with severity upon the course pursued by the President, in relation to the bill in question, and concluded by moving to lay the Message on the table.

Mr. KANE inquired whether the gentleman intended by his motion to preclude any future action on the subject?

Mr. CLAY replied that he supposed the bill must be considered as defunct, and no further action could be had upon it.

Mr. BENTON desired to make a few remarks before the subject should be finally disposed of, and if the motion to lay it on the table prevailed, he would move to resume the consideration of the subject, in order to attain his object.

The motion to lay the Message on the table was then agreed to.

Mr. BENTON moved to take up the Message and make it the order of the day for to-morrow.

Mr. POINDEXTER objected to the motion, on the ground that no further action whatever could be constitutionally had on the subject. The Message, like some others from the same quarter, was a departure from the usual practice of the Government, under similar circumstances, and was addressed to the public ear through this body, &c.

Mr. BENTON then rose and replied to the remarks made by Mr. CLAY, and in vindication of the course pursued by the Chief Magistrate.

Mr. CLAY rejoined.

Mr. BENTON then withdrew the motion to resume the consideration of the Message.

On motion of Mr. MOORE, 5,000 extra copies of the Message were ordered to be printed.

[The incidental debate above alluded to will be given in full hereafter.]

Mr. CLAY gave notice that he would on Tuesday next ask leave to introduce a bill "to appropriate for a limited time, the proceeds of the sales of the public lands."

Mr. CALHOUN gave notice that he would on Monday next move for leave to introduce a bill to repeal the act of last session entitled "An act to amend the several acts providing for the collection of duties on imports."

Mr. BENTON submitted the following resolution:

Resolved, That the Secretary of the Treasury be directed to report to the Senate—1st. A statement of the amount of public moneys in the Bank of the United States at the end of each month for each year from the establishment of the Bank to the present time. 2d. The average amount of the same for each year. 3d. The average of the same for the whole time.

Mr. SPRAGUE submitted the following resolution:

Resolved, That the 34th rule of the Senate shall be so amended as to read and stand as it did prior to the 24th day of December, 1828.

A message was received from the President of the United States, covering reports from the Secretaries of War and the Navy, made in pursuance of a resolution of the Senate, in relation to the regulation of the pay of the officers of the army and navy, &c.; which was laid on the table.

The PRESIDENT laid before the Senate a letter from the Secretary of the Senate, communicating his annual report of the disbursement of the the contingent fund of the Senate. Laid on the table.

On motion of Mr. WRIGHT, the following resolution, submitted by him yesterday, was taken up:

Resolved, That the proceedings of the Legislature of the State of Rhode Island, now upon the table of the Senate, showing the appointment of Elisha R. Potter as Senator to represent that State in the Senate of the United States, be referred to a select committee of five Senators, to inquire and report upon the claim of the said Elisha R. Potter to a seat in the Senate, now occupied by the Hon. Asher Robbins.

Mr. CLAY moved to amend the resolution, so as that the committee should be appointed by the Senate.

Some debate ensued, in which Messrs. CLAY, WRIGHT, and KING, participated. The amendment was then agreed to.

After a few remarks by Messrs. POINDEXTER and KNIGHT, the resolution was agreed to, as amended.

The Senate proceeded to ballot for a committee, which resulted in the choice of Messrs. POINDEXTER, RIVES, WRIGHT, SPRAGUE, and FRELINGHUYSEN.

The Senate adjourned over to Monday.

HOUSE OF REPRESENTATIVES.

THURSDAY, *December* 5, 1833.

Mr. GRENNELL submitted a resolution that the House should on Monday next, at one o'clock, proceed to the election of Chaplain; which was agreed to.

KENTUCKY ELECTION.

Mr. HARDIN said he was induced, in order to save the time of the House, and with a view to place the subject in controversy in a more tangible shape than it was likely from present appearances it would assume, to submit the following:

Resolved, That the Committee of Elections, when appointed, inquire and report to this House who is the member elected from the 5th Congressional district, in the State of Kentucky, and until the committee shall report as herein required,

Resolved, That neither Thomas P. Moore nor Robert P. Letcher shall be qualified as the member from said district.

Resolved, further, That the Committee of Elections be required to receive as evidence all the affidavits and depositions which may have been heretofore or which may hereafter be taken by either of the parties, on due notice having been given to the adverse party, or his agent, and report the same to the House.

Mr. H. said, he rose more for the purpose of referring to the laws of Kentucky, by which he would contend this case must be governed, than with any intention to enter at large into the discussion. He thought that nothing that had been previously said in the course of this debate, in relation to the cases of contested election, in either of the Territories, or to those which occurred in New York, had any bearing on the present question, as it should be recollected that, by the laws of the several United States, they respectively made provisions as to the way in which their elections should be conducted, both as to time, place, and manner. Here the honorable member recited at large the provisions of the act regulating elections in the State of Kentucky, and contended that, as it appeared by the certificate presented by Mr. Moore, that all the sheriffs did attend in pursuance of the mode prescribed by law on the fifteenth day after the election, for the purpose of comparing the votes in their respective districts, and yet only three of them had signed the certificate; their act was not in strict conformity to the laws of the State. He was sure that things would be received here as they are, on broad and liberal principles. The question was, whether a certificate of three sheriffs, representing only part of the district, should entitle a member to qualify here—the county of Lincoln, which polled 1,500 votes, not having been taken into the computation. There was one preliminary question to be settled first, and that was, who had the certificate substantially in conformity with the laws of Kentucky? He thought there was none such. He would suppose a case. Suppose all the sheriffs had attended with their poll-books in hand, and it was previously known who was elected. One of the sheriffs is the friend of the defeated man; he keeps his poll-book under his arm, and says, "You shall not count my votes, or learn the result on my book;" and the other sheriffs make out the certificate in conformity with the result on their books. Would that be such a certificate as will be accepted here? He contended that this was not a paper certifying that Mr. Moore was elected, but elected, if you don't count the votes in one county. It was not a certificate that a man was elected upon counting all the votes. It only certified that in *four* counties that Mr. Moore is elected, and even these four counties certified for by only three sheriffs. He hoped, therefore, that neither gentleman would be permitted to qualify until the subject had undergone the investigation of a committee, who, having the poll-books before them, could only decide this case, and do substantial justice by reference to them. By adopting this course, both the claimants to the seat should wait the decision of the committee; they would both be placed alike, and the subject would be thus dispassionately discussed and decided fairly upon its merits.

Mr. ARCHER expressed his surprise at the doctrine which was broached on this question, that in order to decide it, it should be decided solely upon the face of the paper which was presented by one of the parties. Did it not arise to the mind of those gentlemen who maintained such a doctrine, that it was expressly provided for by the Constitution, that this House was to be the sole judge of the qualifications of its members? In his opinion, the case now before them was very simple. It was merely to decide upon the sufficiency of the paper; in order to do which, they were to consider what made it a sufficient paper. He apprehended only two things were necessary to establish this, as making a good return; one was, that there was in itself sufficient matter; the other, that it was done by competent authority. As to the first, it was clear, on the face of it, that Mr. Moore was elected under certain circumstances, that made it apparent it was not a fair return. How, then, could they excuse themselves to their constituents for making it a matter of debate for three days, to the prejudice of other business. The paper states that Mr. Moore was elected by a majority of the qualified votes of the fifth Congressional district, the vote of Lincoln county not taken into calculation. This made it not only insufficient as to matter, but self-contradictory, and what would be styled, in legal phrase, an insensible return. Now, as to the act being done by competent authority, it appeared to have been a certificate signed by three sheriffs only, who certify for the majority in favor of Mr. Moore, and evidently for four counties; he would remark, in answer to the argument on this point, put forth by an honorable member from New York, [Mr. BEARDSLEY,] and whose high eminence in his profession he would not dispute, that honorable members, in maintaining that the question was to be settled solely on the face of the certificate, had argued that although the number of sheriffs certifying was less than the whole, yet, the principle of law applied, that in public bodies the act of a majority was the act of the whole number required by law; and he had asked, in support of this principle, if one of the sheriffs had died after the election, and had not previously certified, would the election have been therefore destroyed? He, (Mr. A.) however, would ask that honorable member to say, what would be the effect in the case of trustees, appointed to perform a certain trust? Would any one trustee be empowered to do the acts required to be done by two? Would there be, on the decease of one of them, any right devolving on the remaining trustee, in consequence? And would it not rather be necessary in order to execute such trust, to go to a court of justice and have the power conferred in case of either death, or refusal on the part of the trustee? He contended that the certificate wanted all that was necessary to make it an essential return; that as the House were then exercising their judicial functions, and it was, as he thought, fairly stated before in the debate, if a motion was made in any court of justice, to exclude it, as evidence of a fact, it would be excluded from its contradictory character. He maintained that the House were bound to consider its imperfectness, and asked, if it was stated that upon any return made by which a member claimed his seat, that such a return was a forgery, would there be any doubt that they would determine at once that it was, in consequence, imperfect, and should not be acted upon? He would not impute improper conduct in this instance, but would suppose the case of a deputy sheriff, who, in order to defeat an election, would withhold his poll book altogether. He appealed to the feelings which he knew pervaded honorable minds as to what would be their decision.

Mr. HUBBARD argued, at some length, to show that Mr. Moore's certificate proved that he had been elected a Representative from the fifth Congressional district of Kentucky. The statute of Kentucky required no more than the statutes of every State required. The votes, in every State, were returnable to some tribunal which had the power to pass judgment on them. The returns read here show conclusively that the claimant did receive the majority of the votes of his district. The provision of the statute of Kentucky was fully complied with. The certificate states that the sheriffs of the five counties composing the district did assemble and did proceed to discharge and execute the duty imposed upon them by the provision of the act. The sheriffs certify—what? That Thomas P. Moore is duly elected a Representative by a majority of the qualified votes of the district. We had no knowledge of the fact stated that the sheriff of Lincoln pocketed his poll-book. It does not appear on the face of the return. There might have been reasons for the omission to return the votes of the county of Lincoln.

If the sheriffs formed a judicial tribunal for the purpose of canvassing the votes, a less number than the whole body could act. He should propose an amendment to the resolution, in order that the subject should go to the Committee on Elections, in the usual course of proceeding. Not a single case had ever occurred in which the House refused to qualify the member actually returned. If we went into this subject, without the intervention of a committee, we should have as much as would employ us for some weeks; for both parties would institute a close scrutiny into the votes in every county. He was very happy that so much good feeling had been manifested in this discussion. He had entered into it, not in reference to the controversy between the two individuals, but because he felt bound to oppose the innovation attempted upon the usages of this House. He moved to strike out the whole of the resolution offered by the gentleman from Kentucky, and to insert the following:

"*Resolved*, That the certificate presented by Thomas P. Moore, of his election as a Representative from the fifth Congressional district in Kentucky, furnishes *prima facie* evidence of his having been duly elected, and that he is now entitled to be sworn accordingly."

Mr. HUNTINGTON said he should vote against the amendment, simply because it did not contain the truth. He meant that the assertion which it contained, that the certificate in question was evidence of the election of the claimant, was not supported by the facts of the case. Is the certificate duly authenticated according to the statutes of Kentucky? And, if it is, is there no other defect in it? The law of Kentucky requires that the sheriff of each county in the district should attach his signature to the certificate. Language could not be more precise nor full than that of the law on this point. It was not necessary to go into the examination of what, under other circumstances, would constitute the act of a body; but the gentleman from New York, who spoke yesterday, would not surely hazard his professional reputation by maintaining that when the statute, in express terms, requires each member of a body to act, the majority could act for the whole. Suppose Congress

should refer a fact for examination to a committee, and require, by a rule, that the evidence of this fact should be the assent of each individual member of the committee, would it be pretended that, in this case, the act of a majority of the committee would be taken in the room of the evidence required? The certificate required by the law of Kentucky is to be the result of the examination by the sheriffs. Those who suppose that this certificate complies with the statute of Kentucky, must consider that the Legislature, in requiring the signature of all the sheriffs, in fact only meant to require the signature of a majority of them. He presented the following view as a test question: Is the law of Kentucky requiring the signature of all the sheriffs complied with by a certificate which is signed by only three out of five of the sheriffs? But suppose that a majority of the House determines that five means the same thing as three, is there no other deficiency in it? He did not rely on technicalities. The gentleman from New Hampshire excluded the last clause of the certificate as surplusage. In fact, the legal effect and common sense of the certificate is, that Thomas P. Moore has the majority of all the votes which they, the sheriffs, thought proper to count—or, what is the same thing, that Thomas P. Moore had all the votes which were not given to other candidates. Was this a certificate that Thomas P. Moore was elected by a majority of the votes of the district? Is this legal evidence that Thomas P. Moore is elected? The sheriffs superadd to the declaration that Thomas P. Moore is duly elected, that they did not count all the votes. That instrument has neither authenticity nor substance. It is not legally authenticated, and if it was, it does not show that Thomas P. Moore was duly elected. In regard to what had been said on the subject of precedents, he contended that a case like this had never before occurred. Suppose a member from the District of Columbia should present himself for qualification, would it be necessary to refer it to a committee? Would not the credentials be called for? Suppose the claimant had brought a certificate signed by a constable, or by half a dozen of his neighbors, would it be received as *prima facie* evidence of election? In the cases which had been referred to committees, and which the gentleman from Tennessee [Mr. Polk] relied on, the claimants presented duly authenticated certificates, If Mr. Moore had brought a formal certificate, there would have been no difficulty in the case. Bu the has brought a paper which is a mere nullity. The question to be settled on this occasion vitally affected the dearest interests of this country. You place the election of members to this House on a loose, indefinite, and unsafe foundation, if you depart from the express words of the laws which are made to guard the purity of elections.

Mr. JONES said, it appeared to him that the honorable gentleman from New York [Mr. Beardsley] had not taken the distinction between judicial and ministerial offices. The sheriffs were bound not to return an opinion, but a fact. He contended that the law required the signatures of all the sheriffs. Some gentlemen had suggested that we had no evidence that any poll was held in Lincoln county. This was an error. At the close of the certificate the sheriffs say, almost in terms, that a poll was taken in Lincoln county, and, it was not taken into the computation. The certificate was insufficient, for the reason that it was not properly authenticated, and for the further reason that on its face it does not declare that the claimant has a majority of all the votes.

Mr. BEARDSLEY said, he could not look behind the certificate, as the usage had been, in all such cases as the present, not to go behind them. Mr. Moore had presented his certificate here, and so had every gentleman his, or it had been sent here by the competent authorities. No objection had been taken to any, except that presented by Mr. Moore, although it was possible to make such, and then the same question would have been presented as in the case before them. He contended, then, that the whole matter came to the simple question, whether the certificate was a substantial compliance with the laws of Kentucky? The material fact in the case is, does the certificate say that all the votes were returned on its face? It does not appear that any votes, if any were taken in Lincoln county, were returned; and saying that the votes in that county were not taken into the calculation, is saying they were not returned.

Mr. HARDIN said, that he had just conversed with both the gentlemen, and they had agreed that the whole subject should be referred to the Committee on Elections, and proposed to modify his first resolution.

Mr. HUBBARD observed, if that was the understanding, he would withdraw his amendment.

After some conversation between Mr. POLK and Mr. HARDIN, the resolutions were read, when—

Mr. STEWART suggested that further action on the subject ought to be suspended, until the appointment of the committees was announced.

Mr. CHILTON thought the resolution ought to be amended, so that the papers produced before the committee should be subject to all legal exceptions.

Mr. ARCHER called for a division on the question.

Mr. POLK said, if any difficulty was to arise from the arrangement, he hoped the House would proceed upon it as it was originally presented. Notices had been given by the gentlemen of the taking of depositions on both sides, and, in order to prevent difficulty, and protract a decision of the question, it was now agreed, between the parties interested, to read all the papers.

Mr. HARDIN assented to this understanding.

Mr. ARCHER said that, although he had no objection to any arrangement which the gentlemen might make, yet he could not consent that the House should ratify anything between them which might compromit the rights of the people of Kentucky. The rights of every elector in the district would be infringed upon; and if he stood alone, he would protest against the House buying terms from Mr. Moore, or any other gentleman, for settling this question.

After some further debate, between Messrs. ARCHER, POLK, HUBBARD, J. DAVIS, and BURGES—

Mr. WATMOUGH moved an adjournment; which, being negatived,

The question was taken on the resolution of Mr. Hardin, as modified, and agreed to, without a division.

Mr. STEWART moved the consideration of the 9th, 56th, and 76th rules, excepted in the adoption of the rules of the House.

Mr. WHITTLESEY expressed a hope that the subject would not be acted upon until after mature consideration. It is extremely difficult to obtain the presence of a majority of a committee even of seven. It often happened that the chairman of a committee could not report, because a majority of the committee could not be brought together. The difficulty would be greatly increased by increasing the number of members of each committee. The responsibility would be so much divided that the committee would not attend to their duties.

Mr. HUBBARD was persuaded, he said, that some of our important committees should consist of a greater number than seven. In some committees every section of the country ought to be represented, and what was the argument urged against the measure? Why, that members of this House would not do their duty.

Mr. WHITTLESEY moved to amend the resolution by adding, "and the absence of a majority of each committee shall be reported to the House;" which was agreed to.

The 56th rule, as amended, was then adopted.

On motion of Mr. WILDE, it was ordered that when this House adjourns, it adjourn to meet on Monday.

On motion of Mr. POLK, it was ordered that the standing committees be appointed.

On motion of Mr. POLK, the House then adjourned.

REPORT OF THE SECRETARY OF WAR.

Department of War,
November 29th, 1833.

Sir: In submitting to you, agreeably to your instructions, a report of the operations and administration of this Department for the past year, it affords me pleasure to bear my testimony to the zeal and ability of the respective officers at the head of the various bureaus, and of those employed to aid them in the performance of the important functions committed to this branch of the Executive Government.

A reference to the accompanying reports and documents will show the state of the army; as well with relation to its numbers, and their position and condition, as to the progress of the various works intrusted to them, and the collection and preservation of the necessary *materiel* for offensive and defensive operations, which is indispensable to the safety of the country. The principle, which governed the reduction of the army, from a war to a peace establishment, has been found by subsequent experience to be salutary; and its practical operation has been to form a body of officers equal in all the requisites of military knowledge and efficiency to those of any other service which is known to us. The army is organized, that, should an increase become necessary, in consequence of those conflicts of interest and opinion, to which all nations in their intercourse with one another have been exposed, and from which we have no right to expect perpetual exemption, any reasonable addition may be made to it, without disturbing its arrangement; and the professional knowledge and experience, embodied in it, will be immediately felt in the new corps, and will identify them with those previously in service. The military experience of other countries, as well as of our own, has shown that the system of extension, by which new and old troops are incorporated together, is much better calculated to produce discipline and subordination, and thus to meet the exigencies of a service, which does not allow large bodies of troops to be kept up in time of peace, than the organization of separate corps, composed of inexperienced officers and men, with all their military knowledge to acquire, and all their military habits to form. And this is more particularly true of the staff department of an army, upon which its movement, its subsistence, and the economy of its administration, must principally depend. The system, established in our service, is equally creditable to the army and satisfactory to the Government, and may be applied to any necessary extent, without any diminution of that economy and efficiency, which have heretofore marked its operation.

Much advantage is anticipated from the operation of the act, passed at the last session of Congress, for improving the condition of the army. Already its effects have been felt, as the subjoined documents will show, in the decrease of desertion, and in the increase of the business of recruiting. The addition to the pay of the rank and file, the reduction of the term of service, and the improved condition of the non-commissioned officers, promise important meliorations in the character of the army. This prospect cannot but be interesting to the Government and the country. Although the numerical strength of the army is comparatively small, it is yet sufficient to excite public solicitude; and this must be increased by the consideration, that the character of our military establishment may hereafter essentially depend upon the measures now taken for its moral and intellectual advancement. Although it were idle, in the present state of the country, to apprehend any danger from the force which is employed, still the lessons of experience taught by the progress of events in other nations, ought not to be neglected, nor the possibility overlooked, that other circumstances may lead to the increase of our military strength, and to the diminution of that wise jealousy, which is now one of our national characteristics. Moral habits in the soldiery constitute one of the best safeguards against the abuse of military power, and their inculcation has engaged the attention of this department during successive periods of its administration. Amongst other measures, which have been adopted, with this view, you have recently directed the discontinuance of all parades on Sunday, in order that that day may be exclusively devoted to the purposes of instruction and improvement. Certainly in time of peace, no just reason can exist, for converting a day of rest and devotion into a day of military parade.

The act for the better defence of the frontiers, by raising a regiment of dragoons, is in the process of execution. About six hundred men have been enlisted, and most of the officers appointed, and five

of the companies have been ordered to proceed to Fort Gibson, upon the Arkansas, where they will be stationed during the winter. The remainder of the regiment will be concentrated at Jefferson Barracks this season, and it is intended in the spring to order the whole to proceed through the extensive Indian regions between the western boundaries of Missouri and Arkansas and the Rocky Mountains. It is deemed indispensable to the peace and security of the frontier, that a respectable force should be displayed in that quarter, and that the wandering and restless tribes, who roam through it, should be impressed with the power of the United States, by the exhibition of a corps so well qualified to excite their respect. These Indians are beyond the reach of a mere infantry force. Without stationary residences, and possessing an abundant supply of horses, and with habits admirably adapted to their use, they can be held in check only by a similar force, and by its occasional display among them. Almost every year has witnessed some outrage committed by them upon our citizens; and, as many of the Indian tribes from the country this side of the Mississippi, have removed, and are removing to that region, we may anticipate their exposures to these predatory incursions, unless vigorous measures are adopted to repel them. We owe protection to the emigrants, and it has been solemnly promised to them. And this duty can only be fulfilled by repressing and punishing every attempt to disturb the general tranquillity. Policy and humanity equally dictate this course, and there is reason to hope that the display of this force will itself render unnecessary its hostile employment. The more barbarous tribes will perceive that their own safety is closely connected with the permanent establishment of pacific relations, both with the United States and with the other Indians.

It is due to the regiment of dragoons to remark, that its composition is believed to be good, and I anticipate it will do honor to the army, and render effectual service to the country.

I feel it a duty once more to ask your favorable interposition in behalf of the medical corps. There is no portion of the army whose compensation is so utterly inadequate to their services. The pay of the highest grade but little exceeds that of a captain, and the pay of the lowest that of a first lieutenant; and these two grades constitute the whole range of service within the reach of medical officers. In the line of the army and most of the staff departments, there are successive gradations of rank, each with increased emolument, to stimulate the exertions and to reward the services of the officers. The importance of professional skill and talent in the medical corps will not be doubted. And the dispersed condition of our army in time of peace, and its exposure to the effects of various climates, render the conservation of its health an object of much solicitude. And in time of war this solicitude will be increased by the perils of active service.

In order to place in proper condition this branch of our military establishment, a system of examination has been recently instituted, by which the pretensions of medical gentlemen, seeking appointments in the army, will be subjected to rigid scrutiny. A board, composed of able and experienced surgeons, has been organized, and the various members of the department have been examined by them. The result has already been highly useful, and cannot fail to be so for the future. But while the standard of professional acquirements is thus increased, justice demands that the rate of compensation should be examined, and that it should be rendered commensurate with the duties and responsibility of this most useful class of officers. It is not to be expected that the medical corps can retain the able men who now compose it, or see others join it, unless their services are adequately rewarded.

The act organizing the Subsistence Department expires by its own limitation on the second day of March next. It was originally passed in 1818, and has been continued by successive temporary acts till the present time. The reason of this course of legislation is undoubtedly to be found in the fact, that the introduction of the system was an experiment, and it was deemed prudent to test its operation before a permanent character was given to it. This has been fully done, and the result is, in every point of view, satisfactory. All who were acquainted with the mode of supplying the army previously to, and during, the late war, and for a few years after its termination, must be sensible of the superiority of the present plan. In the quality of the provisions, in the certainty of the supply, and in the economy of administration, its operation is decidedly superior to the old system, where contractors furnished and issued all the subsistence required. The continued failures that took place, and frequently in the most critical state of affairs, the controversies arising out of perpetual attempts to issue unsound provisions, and the serious obstacles which these and the other operations of the system interposed to the public service, must be fresh in the recollection of every military man who participated in the events of those periods. The army is now well and promptly supplied, and the faithful officer at the head of the Subsistence Department has established a system of purchasing, of issuing, and of responsibility, which, while it insures this result, guards the public interest against loss and imposition, as far as a business, necessarily so extended, permits. During the fifteen years in which this department has been in operation, more than five million and a half of dollars have been expended under its direction, and the whole loss which has been incurred by the defalcations of its officers, does not amount to sixteen thousand dollars.

I consider that the time has arrived when the present arrangement should be rendered permanent, and I therefore present the subject with that view to your notice. And I also beg leave to suggest that the compensation of the clerks in the office should be increased. It is now lower than the average amount allowed in the other public offices, and less than is due to their labor and responsibility.

The report of the Visiters, appointed to examine the Military Academy, shows that the institution is in a prosperous condition, and is fulfilling the duties committed to it, in the education of the young men destined for the military service of the country. The suggestions, made by the visiters, for the improvement of this national school, are the result of a careful examination, and coming, as they do, from a body of able and impartial citizens, are entitled to much consideration. They appear to me just in themselves, and promising, in the event of their adoption, salutary consequences to the institution.

There is one subject which I feel particularly desirous of placing before you. The situation of teacher of drawing corresponds, neither with the nature and importance of the duties required of that officer, nor with the professional merit of the distinguished artist, who has relinquished the fair prospects held out to him in a foreign country, to accept it. The art itself is highly important to military men, and its acquisition is essential to a respectable standing at the Academy. It is very desirable that the instructor should unite in his person those high qualifications, natural and acquired, which have in all ages been the lot of those who have attained eminence in the art, and which have placed it among those pursuits, that are at once the cause and the effect of advanced improvement in society. I respectfully recommend, that this officer be placed in the same situation as the Professors at the Academy, and I cannot but believe, that such a measure would not only be just in itself, but would be a proper tribute of respect to the liberal arts, and a proper notice of one, whose professional talents and success have been honorable to his country.

I have had the honor heretofore to submit to your consideration my views in relation to brevet commissions in the army, and I am induced, as an act of justice to those entitled to them, again to present the subject. If no new legislation is contemplated nor any action of the Senate, which shall change the principle or practice heretofore prevalent, no objections occur to me to delay, any longer, these promotions. The officers have earned them by length of service, agreeably to the established usage, and to make a discrimination, without any previous declaration, so as to exclude from this advantage those who are at this time entitled to it, does not seem called for by the exigency of any circumstance, connected with this subject. And in fact, there are no very obvious reasons, occurring to me, why these professional honors, which in common cases make no demand upon the treasury, but serve to foster those professional feelings, which give elevation to the military character, should not be granted, as they have heretofore been. Under ordinary circumstances, they would produce no practical operation, either with relation to emolument or command. When they should do either, it would be precisely when their value would be enhanced by the very state of things, producing this change in their operation; when the greater experience of the brevet officer would entitle him to an enlarged command, and to a corresponding rank over those, whether in the regular army or the militia, whose qualifications, so far as these depend upon service, are less than his.

The attention of the army has been frequently drawn to a project for the establishment of a fund for the support of invalid officers, and of the widows and children of such as may die in the service. The object is a commendable one, and as the only aid expected of the Government is such legislative provision as may be necessary to give effect to the measure, in conformity with the general views of the officers of the army, it is certainly entitled to the favorable regard of the Government. A moderate and stated deduction from the pay of each officer would create a fund which would afford essential relief to many who otherwise would be exposed to want and penury, and might soothe the declining years of meritorious officers, who may have necessarily expended in the maintenance of their families the whole allowance made to them by law, and who, without such an arrangement, would look forward with anxiety for the future. Whatever plan may be ultimately adopted, a legal organization is essential to its operation and success. And as the funds will be provided by the officers themselves, and for their own advantage, the administration will no doubt be committed to them, to be exercised by such persons, and in such manner, as they may direct. The considerations connected with this measure are so obviously just, and in accordance with the dictates of prudence and humanity, that I trust they will be favorably considered. And I also feel it my duty to bring before you a kindred subject, connected with the rank and file of the army, and having for its object a provision for the support of superannuated soldiers. In our service, as at present organized, a soldier can only be retained as long as his physical powers are sufficient to enable him to perform the duties required of him. When his constitution fails, unless it is the result "of disability incurred in the line of his duty," he is discharged without any provision for his support, and generally, from the *habits of his life*, without the disposition, and too often the power to labor, and without the means of support. He is then thrown upon the charity of the community, after devoting the best of his life to the service of his country.

This result may be easily obviated, without expense to the Government, and an ample provision made for those discharged soldiers who are unable to procure the means of support. The principle, which has been long and wisely applied to the navy, may be safely applied to the army. An inconsiderable deduction from the pay of each soldier would go far towards the creation of a fund for this purpose. And if this deduction were to commence with those who might enlist after the passage of the law, there could be no objections on account of the previous engagements formed with the soldiers. And there are three auxiliary sources of revenue which may be applied towards the former object. These are—

Fines assessed by courts martial;

The pay due to soldiers who may die without leaving any heirs to claim it;

A proportion of the post fund, which is principally derived from a tax upon sutlers.

It is believed that the means which may be realized agreeably to this suggestion would be found sufficient to provide for the maintenance of this class of persons, whose condition is now so hopeless, and so unsuited to the character of the Government and the feelings of the community.

The experience of every year adds to the conviction, that the sooner the Indians, remaining east of the Mississippi, migrate to the region west

of that river, the sooner will they be relieved from the embarrassments of their present position, and placed in a situation where they may physically and morally improve, and look forward to a prosperous and permanent destiny. All the reports which reach the department upon this subject, concur in the representation that the emigrants already there are comfortable and contented. That the region assigned to them is fertile, salubrious, and as extensive, as they and their descendants for many generations can require. They are making improvements and erecting dwellings, and evidently laying the foundations of a social system, which it is to be hoped will afford them security and prosperity. As a striking proof of their improvement, and of the quantity of provisions raised among them, it may be stated that one of the contracts for furnishing provisions has been taken by a Choctaw, who is said to have a supply of his own amply sufficient to enable him to meet his engagement. It is fortunate for the Indians themselves and for the great cause of humanity, that the efforts of the Government to persuade them peaceably and voluntarily to remove, are every year crowned with more and more success. Since the last annual report from this department, the conditional arrangement made by the Seminoles for their emigration has been rendered absolute by a personal inspection of the country proposed for their residence. They have examined and are satisfied with it, and if the treaty should be ratified by the Senate, they will soon leave the Territory of Florida. An arrangement has also been made with the separate bands in that Territory, by which they have agreed to emigrate, and thus provision has been made for the removal of the whole Indian population from Florida.

The treaty with the Chickasaws has terminated all difficulties with that tribe. It is understood that the exploring party, provided for in that instrument, are about to commence their journey with a view to select a residence west of the Mississippi. If they succeed, they will remove within the period limited. If they do not, and choose to remain, they will become, with their own consent, citizens of Mississippi, and will occupy, as absolute owners, the several tracts of land assigned to them.

The obligations assumed by the United States in the treaty with the Choctaws, for the removal of those Indians, have been fulfilled. From the reports which have been made to the department, it appears that about fifteen thousand individuals of this tribe have been removed. A party, estimated to contain from fifteen hundred to three thousand persons, have changed their usual place of residence in Alabama, and have declined accompanying the other Indians in their emigration. It is believed that this party is composed principally of the worst portion of the tribe, and that they intend to hang upon the white settlements, in order to indulge the vicious habits they have acquired. As the Government has scrupulously fulfilled its engagements with these people, which terminate with this year, and as every exertion has been made by the proper agents to induce them to remove, nothing remains but to leave them to the results of their own experience. It cannot be long, before they will see the necessity of rejoining the great body of the tribe.

Satisfied as you have been, that the very existence of the Creeks in Alabama, required their establishment in the country west of the Mississippi, where so many of their tribe already reside, you have not hesitated to embrace every opportunity which offered of accomplishing this object. Instructions have been three times given to ascertain their views, and to endeavor to persuade them to acquiesce in this course. The two first attempts proved unsuccessful. The results of the last is unknown. Independent of the general reasons, arising out of our Indian relations, which operated to induce these efforts, the peculiar state of things among these Indians, and a strong desire to remove the difficulties connected with them, had much influence in directing the negotiations.

The Sacs and Foxes have quietly removed to the region assigned to them, and the Winnebagoes have left the country upon Rock river, agreeably to the stipulations of the treaty with them, and retired across the Mississippi, to their lands north of the Ouisconsin.

Treaties have been formed with the Pottawatamies, Chippewas, and Ottawas, claiming the district on the west side of Lake Michigan, south of Green Bay and north of Chicago, for its cession to the United States, and with the Pottawatamies of the peninsula of Michigan for the relinquishment of their reservation south of Grand river.

With the exception, therefore, of the Miamies in the State of Indiana, of a band of Wyandots at Upper Sandusky in Ohio, and of scattered portions of the Ottawas and Chippewas in the peninsula of Michigan, north of Grand river, and of Saginaw Bay, probably not exceeding altogether five thousand individuals, the whole country north of the Ohio and east of the Mississippi, including the States of Ohio, Indiana, and Illinois, and the Territory of Michigan, as far as the Fox and Ouisconsin rivers, has been cleared of the embarrassments of Indian relations, and the Indians themselves have either already emigrated or have stipulated to do so within limited periods, and upon such terms as will ensure them adequate subsistence, and the means of establishing themselves comfortably in their new residence, unless, indeed, the aid and efforts of the Government are rendered useless by their habitual indolence and improvidence. The Cherokees occupying portions of land in Georgia, Alabama, North Carolina, and Tennessee, and probably not exceeding eleven thousand persons, are the only Indians south of the Ohio and east of the Mississippi with whom an arrangement has not been made, either for emigration or for a change of political relations. It is to be regretted that the same causes which have heretofore prevented an adjustment of the difficulties of that tribe and their removal west yet continue to defeat the efforts of the Government. These causes are no doubt principally to be traced to the ascendency of particular individuals, and to their desire to retain political influence and power. It is expected that about five hundred of these Indians will remove, west this season, and the residue of the Cherokees then remaining east of the Mississippi will be, agreeably to previous computations, about ten thousand five hundred.

The commissioners west of the Mississippi are engaged in the execution of the duties connected with our Indian relations in that quarter. They have succeeded in arranging satisfactorily the disputed question of boundaries between the Creeks and Cherokees, which has for some time occasioned much embarrassment. They have also formed treaties with the Creeks, the Cherokees, the Senecas, and Shawnees, the Quapaws, and the Seminoles of Florida, by which all matters connected with these tribes have been satisfactorily adjusted. Their labors will be now directed to the other subjects, indicated in their instructions, and which are important to a permanent arrangement of the various questions arising out of the new state of things which will be created in that region. Among these, one of the most interesting is a practical plan for regulating the intercourse of the various tribes, indigenous and emigrant, with one another, and with the United States, and for the establishment of some general principles, by which their own internal government can be safely administered by themselves, and a general superintending authority exercised by the United States, so far as may be necessary to restrain hostilities among them, and incursions into our borders. Until such a system is adopted, it is evident that the condition of those Indians cannot be secure, nor will the obligation imposed upon the Government be fulfilled. The task requires an intimate knowledge of the local circumstances of the tribes of that region and of the country they inhabit, and a practical acquaintance with Indian habits, feelings, and mode of life. I trust the commissioners will be able to report a plan which will fulfil the expectation of those who have observed with solicitude the course of this matter, and which will eventually secure the prosperity of the Indians. As it is probable, however, that this cannot be effected within the time limited for the duties of the commissioners, I would respectfully suggest the propriety of their term of service being prolonged until the close of the next year.

There have been presented for allowance under the pension act of June 6, 1832, thirty thousand six hundred claims. Of these of these have been examined, and either admitted, rejected, or

returned to the parties for supplementary action. Twenty-three thousand four hundred and thirty-eight certificates have been issued; eleven hundred and eleven claims have been rejected; three hundred returned cases are in the office awaiting or undergoing re-examination; thirteen hundred and fifty-one, which are incomplete in their proofs, are suspended until these are furnished; and four thousand four hundred and twenty-five are in the hands of the parties for additional evidence, or authentication, or in transitu between them and the office.

It is creditable to the industry and efficiency of the Pension Office, that such a mass of business should have been performed within the period which has elapsed since the passage of the above law. I have the honor to be, very respectfully, sir, your obedient servant,

LEW: CASS.

To the President of the U. States.

Notwithstanding it is positively asserted in the Prospectus for this paper, *that no subscription will be received unless payment is made in advance*, many persons have requested it to be sent to them without making the advance. We cannot comply with such requests. The price is fixed so low, that we would lose money on the publication if we were to open accounts for it, *even should every one be finally settled.*

Postmasters' who have received such sums as cannot be remitted by mail, will please refund it to the subscribers.

We will print a sufficient number of copies to supply all who have subscribed, whenever they comply with the terms.

From the Pennsylvania Reporter.

CLERK TO CONGRESS.

Our readers will perceive, by the Congressional news copied from the Washington Globe of yesterday, that Col. Walter S. Franklin, of this place, has been elected Clerk of the House of Representatives, by the friends of the Administration in that body. This intelligence will be truly gratifying to the numerous friends of Col. Franklin in Pennsylvania, and will meet the hearty approval of the democratic party at large, who, in this instance, see an honorable and patriotic member placed in an enlarged sphere of usefulness, both as regards the public interests and his own private welfare. We have long been acquainted with Col. Franklin, and feel a most perfect assurance in the belief that he will hold the esteem of the august body in which he now occupies so responsible a station, while official fitness, sound principles, and liberal manners, are held in deserved veneration by its members.

WALTER S. FRANKLIN, ESQ.

This gentleman has for a number of years officiated as Clerk to the State Senate, and is now announced by the Washington Globe as a candidate for the Clerkship in the House of Representatives.

As an individual, qualified by long experience, talent, a high sense of moral and political integrity, we doubt whether his superior can be found. Col. Franklin has always been a staunch and thorough-going Democrat, and zealously devoted to the National Administration. We hope he may be elected.—*Upland (Penn.) Union.*

THE CONGRESSIONAL GLOBE.

PRINTED AND PUBLISHED AT THE CITY OF WASHINGTON, BY BLAIR & RIVES.

23d Congress, 1st Session.   SATURDAY, DECEMBER 14, 1833.   Vol. 1....No. 2.

IN SENATE.

Monday, *December 9*, 1833.

The PRESIDENT *pro tem.* presented the credentials of the Hon. WILLIAM C. PRESTON, elected a Senator from the State of South Carolina, to supply the vacancy occasioned by the resignation of the Hon. Stephen D. Miller.

Also, the credentials of the Hon. SAMUEL McKEAN, elected a Senator from the State of Pennsylvania, in the place of the Hon. George M. Dallas, whose term of service had expired.

He also informed the Senate of the receipt of the credentials of the Hon. DANIEL WEBSTER, reelected a Senator from the State of Massachusetts.

Mr. FRELINGHUYSEN presented the credentials of the Hon. SAMUEL L. SOUTHARD, elected a Senator from New Jersey, in the place of the Hon. Mahlon Dickarson, whose term of service had expired.

Whereupon, Messrs. WEBSTER, SOUTHARD, and PRESTON, appeared, were qualified, and took their seats.

On motion of Mr. POINDEXTER, the credentials of the election of the Hon. Mr. ROBBINS were referred to the special committee appointed on that subject.

On motion of Mr. GRUNDY, the Senate proceeded to the election of a Secretary, when it appeared that WALTER LOWRIE was unanimously elected, he having received 39 votes.

The Senate then proceeded to the election of a Sergeant-at-Arms; when it appeared that

William Robinson had..............5 votes.
Mountjoy Bailey 2   "
John Shackford...................25   "
O. S. Hall.........................1   "
Edward Wyer......................1   "
W. Henry.........................1   "
Major Randolph...................3   "

So it appeared that John Shackford, having received a majority of votes, was duly elected Sergeant-at-Arms and Doorkeeper.

The Senate then proceeded to the election of an Assistant Doorkeeper; when it appeared that Stephen Haight was elected on the 6th ballot.

The ballotings were as follow:

	1st.	2d.	3d.	4th.	5th.	6th.
Stephen Haight 6	12	15	19	20	20
William Robinson....8	2	14	16	16	17
O. S. Hall...........5	6	5	3	1	1
Watkins 6	-3	0	0	0	0
James Young 2	1	0	0	0	0
W. H. Campbell.....2	0	0	0	0	0
Edward Wyer........1	2	2	0	1	0
Thomas Fillebrown, jr...1	0	0	0	0	0
Charles Curtis.......1	1	0	0	0	0
Nerins...............2	0	0	0	0	0
John Taliaferro......2	3	3	0	0	0
J. Coxe.............0	0	0	1	2	0
T. Brown, jr........0	0	0	0	1	1

Mr. CLAY moved the postponement of the choice of Chaplain, which, on motion of Mr. CHAMBERS, of Maryland, was appointed to take place to-morrow.

Mr. BENTON proposed a resolution calling for information from the Secretary of the Treasury relative to the amount of public moneys deposited in the United States Bank.

Mr. CLAY moved that the resolution be laid on the table; not that he had any objection to the resolution itself, but he wished that the country should have an opportunity of ascertaining the condition of other banks as well as that of the United States.

The resolution was laid on the table.

Mr. CALHOUN, on leave given, presented a bill to repeal the act of last session, providing for the collection of duties on imports; which passed to a second reading.

Mr. BENTON, pursuant to notice and on leave given, presented a bill granting to the State of Missouri a certain quantity of land for purposes

2

of internal improvement, &c.; which was read a first time and passed to a second reading.

Also, a joint resolution relative to an alteration of the Constitution of the United States, in relation to the election of President and Vice President of the United States; which, on motion of Mr. BIBB, was laid on the table and ordered to be printed.

Also, a bill to graduate the prices of the public lands longest in the market; which was passed to a second reading.

Mr. MOORE, on leave given, presented a bill to establish a pension agency in North Alabama, which passed to a second reading.

Mr. WEBSTER gave notice that he would, on to-morrow, introduce a bill to provide for compensation certain citizens of the United States for French spoliations upon their commerce.

The Assistant Doorkeeper, Stephen Haight, here presented himself and was sworn into office.

The resolution altering the 34th rule of the Senate, in relation to the appointment of standing committees, was taken up for consideration.

Mr. SPRAGUE was in favor of the proposed amendment of the rule. His object was to restore to the Senate the business of choosing its own committees. Power should never be unnecessarily delegated. He thought the appointment of committees was of the utmost importance; and should always be exercised by the Senate itself, unless great inconvenience should be found to result from it. Committees might be denominated the eye of the body. Their information is sent forth to the world, and that had a material effect in the formation of public opinion. He was not presenting to the Senate, to adopt, anything of a novel nature, but to return to the usages of the body long since adopted. From the first Congress until the year 1823, the standing committees were elected by the Senate. In 1826 or '29, the change was made, giving to the Vice President the power of appointment, and he thought it ought now to be resumed.

Mr. GRUNDY was opposed to any alteration of the rule, and was not prepared to vote for any, unless there was strong probability that some benefit was to result from it. He admitted that there had been a great diversity of practice in that body on that subject. Originally the Senate had elected its own committees, but were induced to change the practice from the embarrassments which arose out of it. And he saw a great difficulty that would arise again. A plurality would elect a committee. Five votes might, and ten in many instances would, place particular members on important committees. He had seen but little inconvenience result from the rule as it at present stands: too little, indeed, to authorize a change now to be made. Some gentlemen had ability to discharge duties which others had not; and giving the power of appointment to one individual would enable him to equalize and distribute the duties and labors of gentlemen than would result by leaving it to chance. He was glad to hear that this motion was not predicated upon any objection to the present presiding officer, and until some better objections could be produced against the present rule, he should vote to support it.

Mr. BIBB wished to understand what would be the rule of the Senate if this resolution was adopted. A majority would elect a chairman and a plurality choose the other members of the committees. He would move an amendment to the proposition, that a majority should be necessary to a choice of each of the members of the committee. He had seen four or five elect a committee. This was no election by the eye, but was entirely the result of chance. He would therefore move the amendment which he had suggested, which was adopted.

Mr. KING, of Alabama, was in favor of the whole proposition. He thought it must be apparent, that if it was adopted three-fourths of the time would be consumed in the election of standing

committees. The inconvenience of the balloting system had caused the Senate to run into the other extreme, and give the whole power of appointment to one individual, the Vice President. This seemed like something indelicate to the presiding officer. The proposed system would place many of the same members on so many committees, as to make it objectionable in that respect. The existing rule ensures a parcelling out and equalizing of the duties and burdens of business, and members would be selected with reference to their various qualifications.

Mr. CHAMBERS made a few remarks in support of the proposed alteration, which were inaudible in the gallery, except that he was understood as maintaining the position that the political complexion of the committees ought to accord with that of the Senate.

Mr. WRIGHT was unfavorable to an alteration of the rule for the present. He had not the advantage of experience, but he had reflected on the subject; the committees require a duplicate of all the members of the Senate, and, therefore, choice and not chance ought to prevail in selecting them. The former objection was, that the Vice President not being selected by the Senate, nor accountable to them, should not appoint the committees, and it was transferred to the presiding officer, who was one of the body. The adoption of the rule in 1826 was considered as an intimation to the Vice President that he should relieve the Senate from the inconvenience of electing committees, and give them an opportunity of acquiring one of their own body to perform that duty.

The honorable gentleman here referred to the journals to show that the Vice President was not in the habit of taking his seat in the Senate until a much later period in the session than the present.

The honorable gentleman did not know why the Vice President had absented himself, but he [Mr. W.] believed he had done so from respect to the Senate, and in compliance with the practice of the Senate and existing rules.

Mr. CLAY made some remarks in support of the amended rule, which we are compelled to omit.

Mr. BIBB then moved to reconsider the vote adopting his amendment; which was agreed to, and the amendment was then negatived.

The question of adopting the resolution (in its original shape) being about to be put, the Presiding Officer, [Mr. WHITE,] asked to be excused from voting; which

Mr. POINDEXTER briefly objected to.

Mr. FRELINGHUYSEN said he felt seriously embarrassed by the present proposition, and as he wished time to consider of it, he moved that the Senate adjourn, which was agreed to.

Adjourned.

HOUSE OF REPRESENTATIVES.

Monday, *December 9*, 1833.

Messrs. WISE and PLUMMER appeared, were qualified, and took their seats.

The several Standing Committees were announced from the Chair, as follows:

Elections.—Messrs. Claiborne, Griffin, Hawkins of North Carolina, Banks, Vanderpoel, Jones of Georgia, Peyton, Hamer, and Hannegan.

Ways and Means.—Messrs. Polk, Wilde, Cambreleng, Gorham, McKim, Binney, Loyall, McKinley, and Hubbard.

Claims.—Messrs. Whittlesey of Ohio, Barber, McIntire, Grennell, H. King, Gholson, Cramer, Forester, and Bynum.

Commerce.—Messrs. Sutherland, Davis of Massachusetts, Harper, Foot, McKay, Lawrence, Pinckney, Heath, and Selden.

Public Lands.—Messrs. Clay, Duncan, Boon, Mason, Clayton, Slade of Vermont, Leavitt, Ashley, and Inge.

Post Offices and Post Roads.—Messrs. Conner, Kavanagh, Pearce of Rhode Island, Thomas of

Louisiana, Briggs, Murphy, Lane, Lytle, and Laporte.

District of Columbia.—Messrs. Chinn, W. B. Shepard, McKennon, Stoddert, Allen of Virginia, Dennis, Hiester, Fillmore, and Taylor.

Judiciary.—Messrs. Bell of Tennessee, Ellsworth, Foster, Gordon, Beardsley, Thomas of Maryland, Hardin, Parks, and Pierce of New Hampshire.

Revolutionary Claims.—Messrs. Muhlenberg, Crane, Bates of Massachusetts, Standifer, Bouldin, Marshall, Young, Bayliss, and Turrill.

Public Expenditures.—Messrs. Davenport, Lyon, Paige, Clarke of Pennsylvania, Tweedy, Gillet, Hall of Vermont, McLene, and Kinnard.

Private Land Claims.—Messrs. Johnson of Tennessee, Mardis, Carr, Galbraith, Mann of New York, Cage, Felder, Casey, and Bull.

Manufactures.—Messrs. Adams of Massachusetts, Huntington of Connecticut, Deany, Davis of South Carolina, Corwin, Dickerson, Martindale, McComas, and Osgood.

Agriculture.—Messrs. Bockee, Taylor of Virginia, Hathaway, Barnitz, Bean, Dunlop, Clowney, Turner, and Davis of Kentucky.

Indian Affairs.—Messrs. Lewis, Gilmer, McCarty, Everett of Vermont, Graham, Allen of Ohio, Dickinson of Tennessee, Howell, and Love.

Military Affairs.—Messrs. Johnson of Kentucky, Vance, Speight, Ward, Blair of South Carolina, Thompson of Ohio, Burd, Coffee, and Bunch.

Naval Affairs.—Messrs. White of New York, Williams, Watmough, Patton, Lansing, Reed, Grayson, Parker, and Smith.

Foreign Affairs.—Messrs. Archer, Everett of Massachusetts, Wayne, McDuffie, Hall of North Carolina, Coulter, Jarvie, Pierson, and Carmichael.

Territories.—Messrs. Williams, Allan of Kentucky, Potts, Johnson of New York, Anthony, Wilson of Virginia, Jones of Ohio, Ewing, and Gamble.

Revolutionary Pensions.—Messrs. Wardwell, Barringer, Tompkins, Moore of Virginia, Lea, Deming, W. K. Fuller, Fowler, and Bell of Ohio.

Invalid Pensions.—Messrs. Burges, Evans, Beale, Schley, Adams of New York, Schenck, Chilton, Chaney, and Mitchell of Ohio.

Roads and Canals.—Messrs. Mercer, Blair of Tennessee, Vinton, Stewart, Rencher, Johnson of Maryland, Lucas, Pope, and Slade of Illinois.

Revised and unfinished business.—Messrs. Dickson, Harrison of Pennsylvania, McVean, Shinn, and Beatty.

Accounts.—Messrs. Mann of Pennsylvania, Lee of New Jersey, Mitchell of New York, Crockett, and Miller.

Expenditures in the Department of State.—A. H. Shepperd, Day, Beaumont, Bodle, and Patterson.

Expenditures in the Department of the Treasury.—Messrs. Allen of Vermont, P. C. Fuller, Harper of Penn., Spangler, and Clark of N. Y.

Expenditures in the Department of the Navy.—Messrs. Hall of Maine, Huntington of New York, Ramsey, Sloane, and Van Houten.

Expenditures in the Department of the Post Office.—Messrs. Hawes, Fulton, Wagner, and Lee of New Jersey.

Expenditures in the Department of War.—Messrs. Whittlesey of New York, Deberry, Chambers, Webster of Ohio, and Halsey.

Expenditures on the Public Buildings.—Messrs. Whallon, Darlington, Brown, Henderson, and Hard.

The SPEAKER announced that on Wednesday next the several States would be called in their order for the presentation of petitions.

Mr. PATTON submitted the following:

Resolved, That the following shall be established as the 9th rule of this House:

"In all cases the Speaker shall vote, and if the House be equally divided, the question shall be lost."

Mr. PATTON said that the object which he had in view was not in the slightest degree to change the effect of the vote that might be given by the Speaker for the time being, nor to increase any of his powers; but it was to restore to his constituents, and to himself, those high and valuable privileges, of which, by the present rule, he considered he was unjustly deprived, and which pertained to every Representative sent to the House. The

honorable member argued at some length in support of his resolution, from the rules, practices, and usage of the House of Commons in England, some of which he cited, and contended at some length that they were not applicable to the institutions of this country. Where the Speaker, having to be aproved of by the King, is not chosen simply by the Representatives of the people, there might exist a reason for the present rule, which did not exist here. The practice of the Senate was in strict accordance with the rule he proposed for their adoption; as in all cases the President *pro tem.* chosen by that body in the absence of the President provided by the Constitution, exercised the power of voting. Such was also the practice in the great majority of the Houses of Assembly, in the various States of the Union, although differing in some slight degree as to the time when the right should be exercised. He hoped, therefore, that his motion would be sustained by the House, and thus they would restore to the personage himself those rights, in the exercise of which he would then be in the same respect as other Representatives, subject to the control of that which now constituted the great moral lever which governs the world—public opinion.

Mr. SUTHERLAND said that the rule proposed to be modified had been in operation ever since the year 1789. Coming from a State where every member of the legislative body votes *viva voce,* he thought the present rule ought to be abolished. There was nothing in favor of the present rule but ancient usage. The Speaker's vote should, in his opinion, be recorded, with that of other members, in order that his constituents may see it, and the nation at large be able to judge, by his vote, whether he is worthy of the chair or not. Here, in the great national council, every vote ought to be given, *viva voce,* and at a proper time, he should make a motion for the change of the rules to that end. We should then have no dispute about the counting of ballots.

Mr. WAYNE was unable, by indisposition, he said, to enter fully into the subject at this time. The gentleman from Virginia talks of giving the Speaker the right to vote, as if he had not that right at present. But the fact is, that the present rule gives him additional power and privileges, as a member. In his own opinion, the rule ought to continue to stand as it now stood; but as he was unable to go fully into the question at present, he would move the postponement of the further consideration of the motion till Monday next.

Agreed to.

The SPEAKER laid before the House the following messages, which were appropriately referred.

WASHINGTON, December 6, 1833.

To the House of Representatives:

I transmit herewith to the House of Representatives, a communication from the War Department, showing the circumstances under which the sum of $5,000, appropriated for subsistence of the army, was transferred to the service of the Medical and Hospital Departments; and, which, by the law authorizing the transfer, are required to be laid before Congress during the first of their session.

ANDREW JACKSON.

WASHINGTON, December 6, 1833.

To the House of Representatives:

I transmit herewith, for the information of the House, the report of the survey made in pursuance of the fourth section of the act of Congress of the 4th July, 1832, authorizing "the survey of canal routes in the Territory of Florida."

ANDREW JACKSON.

ELECTION OF CHAPLAIN.

On motion of Mr. GRENNELL, the House proceeded to the election of a Chaplain.

Mr. WARD nominated the Rev. Thomas H. Stockton.

Mr. CLAY nominated the Rev. J. A. Copp.

Mr. WHITE nominated the Rev. Wm. Hammet.

Mr. ELLSWORTH nominated the Rev. R. R. Gurley.

Mr. EVANS nominated the Rev. Mr. Palfrey.

The several members proposing the respective candidates were appointed tellers.

On the first ballot, 210 members voted—106 being necessary to a choice. There were for the—

Rev. Mr. Stockton	104
Rev. J. A. Copp	33
Rev. Wm. Hammet	50
Rev. R. R. Gurley	6
Rev. Mr. Palfrey	9
Rev. Mr. Smith	1
Blank	6
Scattering	1

None of the candidates having the requisite number, a second ballot took place; when 194 members voted—98 required a choice. For the—

Rev. Mr. Stockton	143
Rev. Mr. Copp	10
Rev. Mr. Hammet	34
Rev. Mr. Gurley	2
Rev. Mr. Palfrey	2
Rev. Mr. Smith	1
Blanks	6

Whereupon the Rev. Mr. Stockton was declared duly elected.

After which, on motion of Mr. STEWART, The House adjourned.

IN SENATE.

TUESDAY, *December* 10, 1833.

Mr. WEBSTER presented a petition from citizens of the city of Cincinnati, praying Congress to purchase all private interests in the Louisville and Portland canal; which was laid on the table, and ordered to be printed.

Mr. CLAY, on leave given, introduced a bill to appropriate, for a limited time, the proceeds of the sales of the public lands.

Mr. CLAY said that the bill contained no material alteration from that of last session; and, on his motion, the bill was read the first time by its title.

Mr. CLAY moved to take up for consideration the resolution submitted by Mr. BENTON, in relation to the amount of moneys deposited in the Bank of the United States; which was agreed to. When

Mr. CLAY offered the following amendment, as an additional resolution; which was read and agreed to:

And resolved, also, That the Secretary of the Treasury be directed to report to the Senate the names of all banks, and where they are respectively situated, which have been selected by him, in place of the Bank of the United States, as depositories of the public money; the amount of the capital of the said banks respectively, distinguishing between what has been actually paid in by the stockholders and what has not been paid; the amount of public money in each of the said banks on the first of October, the first of November, and the first of December, 1833, distinguishing between the sums standing to the individual credit of the United States, and those standing to the credit of any public officer, or other distinguished agent of the Government; the amount of debts due from each of the said banks on each of the days aforesaid; the amount of notes in circulation, and the amount of specie in their vaults respectively; the names of the stockholders in each of the said banks on the first day of September and the first day of October last, distinguishing between foreigners and citizens of the United States; the mode in which transfers of the public money were made from the Bank of the United States to the said banks respectively, whether by warrants or otherwise; if by warrants, whether they were issued in pursuance of appropriations previously made by law; and whether any such transfers were requested by the said banks, or either of them, or made by the treasury, to sustain the credit of the said bank, or any of them; and a copy of all the correspondence between the Department of the Treasury and the said banks, or either of them, relating to the said transfers, or any of them; at what periods the several charters of the banks so designated as depositories of the public money expire; copies of the said charters; and whether the Secretary of the Treasury has been able to obtain at all the ports of the United States at which banks are established, the consent of banks to receive and deposite the public money upon such conditions as he approved, and if not, at what ports has he been unable to obtain such consent.

Mr. FORSYTH, on leave given, presented a bill to provide for the fulfilment of the compact of 1802, between the United States and Georgia.

Mr. CLAY moved that the report of the Secre-

tary in relation to the removal of the public deposites be taken up and considered.

Mr. C. said, that the charter of the Bank of the United States provided for the deposite of the public moneys in that bank and its branches. It also vests in the Secretary of the Treasury the power of removing them to other places of deposite when he may think proper, but it also requires him to give his reasons for so doing to the next Congress. The removal of the deposites had taken place, and the Secretary had told us it was by his order, and he submitted his reasons for doing so. When the charter of the bank authorized a removal of the public moneys from its vaults, it intended and expected, that when the act was done, some sufficient reasons should be given for it, and that Congress should look at them, and examine into their sufficiency. Those reasons are now before us, and we are to decide whether the measure was a proper one, according to the Constitution and laws of the country; and if there was one question of public consideration of more importance than another, it was that which related to the custody of the public treasure. Now was the time to inquire into the condition of the Treasury. The present Vice President had once said that we ought to inquire where the lost rights of the States were. Now he (Mr. C.) wanted to inquire where the Treasury of the United States was. He conceived it to be his duty, as a Senator here, to bring this question up. And as we were to judge whether the Secretary of the Treasury had acted wisely in this matter, we ought to judge of his reasons before the whole Senate, and not refer it to a committee. In order to do this, he hoped a day not far distant would be appointed for its consideration. He would therefore propose that the report of the Secretary be made the order for Monday next.

Mr. BENTON said that the Secretary of the Treasury had announced distinctly his reasons for the removal, to be on account of the misconduct of the Bank of the United States. He has charged the Bank distinctly with interfering with the purity of elections, with corrupting and subsidizing the press, with dishonoring its own paper, and that of its branches. Here were charges of great criminality on the part of the Bank, and the question was, whether we ought to go into a trial of the case here, or refer it to some committee in the Senate. The House of Representatives, he contended, was the proper body before which the subject ought to be investigated, although he confessed the Senate could entertain it. He wanted to examine these charges against the Bank, and therefore he thought the report ought to be referred to a committee.

The postponement was agreed to.

Mr. CLAY submitted the following resolution; which was read and laid on the table:

Resolved, That the President of the United States be requested to inform the Senate whether a paper under date the ———— day of September, 1833, purporting to have been read by him to the Heads of the several Departments, relating to the deposites of the public money in the treasury of the United States, and alleged to have been published by his authority, be genuine or not; and if it be genuine, that he be also requested to lay a copy of said paper before the Senate.

Mr. WEBSTER, on leave given, presented a bill to provide satisfaction for the claims of citizens of the United States for French spoliations; which passed to a second reading.

Mr. WILKINS, on leave given, presented a bill for the relief of A. G. Ralston and Girard Ralston; which passed to a second reading.

Mr. KING submitted the following resolution; which was read and laid on the table:

Resolved, That the Committee on Indian Affairs be instructed to inquire into the expediency of authorizing the President of the United States to appoint an agent to receive evidence of losses sustained by the inhabitants of the now State of Alabama, by a hostile eruption of a party of Creek Indians, in the year 1814, by which Fort Mims was taken, and those who had fled there for protection, massacred.

The Senate then proceeded to the election of a Chaplain, which resulted in the choice of the Rev.

Mr. HATCH, on the 6th ballot. The ballotings were as follows:

	1st.	2d.	3d.	4th.	5th.	6th.
Mr. Post,	13	14	16	15	14	11
Mr. Pise,	10	6	1	1	1	1
Mr. Smith,	8	11	11	11	8	6
Mr. Hatch,	6	10	12	12	17	23
Mr. Orr,	1	0	0	0	0	0

Mr. BENTON submitted the following resolution:

Resolved, That the Secretary of the Treasury be directed to communicate to the Senate any information in his power or possession to show that the Bank of the United States or its branches, at any time heretofore, have refused, or delayed to receive the notes, of any of the branches in payment or deposite.

The Senate then proceeded to the order of the day, and resumed the consideration of Mr. SPRAGUE's resolution to alter the mode of electing their standing committees by the Senate, instead of being, as formerly, appointed by the President *pro tem.*

Mr. WHITE (President *pro tem.*) renewed the request which he had previously made to be excused from voting.

Mr. CLAY, believing that the President was impelled to make this request from a sense of delicacy, and disposed to feel the highest respect for him and his motives, he presumed the Senate would not hesitate to agree to it, and he submitted a motion to that effect.

Mr. GRUNDY could not, from a sense of duty, consent to this motion, and trusted that on further reflection the President himself would withdraw it. He (Mr. G.) was opposed to it, because he thought the right of voting belonged to the office, and ought to be exercised by the occupant of the chair until the rule itself was altered. The request, he knew, had proceeded from a nice sense of honor on the subject at issue, and he would have been happy if he could, consistent with his sense of duty, comply with it. If he had asked to be excused, he saw little if any difference in the respective situations of himself and the President if he was excused. In that case, if he (Mr. G.) voted for the motion, he voted to give himself that increase of power which he voted to take away from the President, the only difference being that the President might have it in his power to vote to retain a greater portion than he could have. There was another consideration which to him appeared of some force; the chair was occupied only temporarily; circumstances might arise by the following day by which the Vice President appointed by the Constitution to occupy the chair might arrive; and in the meantime, by now declining to vote, or the Senate by agreeing to excuse, a radical change in the rule of their proceeding, and having an important influence, might thereby be produced, which he thought it desirable to avoid. For these reasons he regretted that he could not comply with the wishes of the President.

Mr. CLAY, in explanation, said that he was influenced in acceding to the wishes of the President to be excused simply from the consideration that it appeared that he continued to feel, after due reflection upon the subject—after the intervention of a night since the request was first made—the same delicacy as to voting on this question. He could not see any force in the grounds upon which the motion was to be opposed. He denied that the honorable Senator and the President were in the same situation as to the relative power to be acquired by them under the circumstances, the relative power of the honorable Senator being only in the proportion of forty-one to one, whilst on the other side it was a question whether the power would devolve altogether upon one man. He was always disposed to applaud the motives by which it appeared the honorable President was actuated. He, it appeared, was not disposed to retain power in the present instance. With respect to the suggestion that the Vice President should arrive on the morrow, he would say he regretted his absence; for if he had been here, as he ought to have been, at the post assigned him by the Constitution, the Senate would have been saved the necessity of the present motion, as it would then follow, as matter of course, that the former practice of electing committees by ballot would of right devolve

upon them. He repeated, that he was only influenced by motives of delicacy and respect towards the high-minded gentleman who occupied the chair in submitting the motion in accordance with his wishes, and he would willingly withdraw it, but could not do so until he had an intimation to that effect from him.

Mr. GRUNDY said, when the Vice President would arrive here, he was not informed. He would say, however, what he knew on the subject, and that was, that for the last three or four sessions, the Vice President never had arrived in the Senate until the presiding officer had appointed the committees. He did not argue upon the propriety or impropriety of his absence, but he would say that his predecessors had acted in the same way. It might be wrong, but if that gentleman had acted in conformity to practice and usages of his predecessors, which had not been objected to, why ought it now to be complained of? As to avoiding or assuming responsibility, he viewed that matter in this way—when it was the duty of an officer to act, let him act. He objected to the presiding officer being excused from voting on this question, because he could not consent that the State of Tennessee should have but one voice in determining it.

Mr. CALHOUN said that as allusions had been made to himself, he felt compelled to make a remark, although he had intended not to have taken part in the discussion. He never knew that there was an understanding that the Vice President should absent himself to enable the presiding officer to appoint the committees. He trusted that no gentleman would charge him with having absented himself at the commencement of the session to avoid the responsibility of appointing the committees. His absence had been solely caused by domestic affliction or some other unavoidable cause. He never had absented himself on that account. He concurred with the gentleman from Mississippi [Mr. POINDEXTER] that appointments should be made by the Senate itself.

Mr. WHITE, the presiding officer, begged leave of the Senate to make a few remarks. (Leave was granted.) Mr. W. then said that he felt very delicately situated on this subject. If he voted against the proposition, it might be supposed he acted on the principle that power is never so well exercised as when it is in our own hands. If he voted to take the power away from the presiding officer, he might be charged with having been governed by the principle that he dreaded the responsibility. There was no duty more unpleasant than the appointment of the standing committees, and he thought no one had so performed that duty as to give entire satisfaction to every member of the Senate, and it was difficult, if not impossible, for any gentleman to perform it with satisfaction to himself. If it was the pleasure of the Senate to excuse him, it would give him pleasure, but if he were compelled to vote, he should do so to the best of his judgment, and according to the dictates of his own conscience.

On the question of excusing Mr. WHITE from voting, Mr. GRUNDY called for a division, when there were, yeas 21, nays 19.

Mr. FORSYTH said that the manner in which the committees were constituted, was a matter of perfect indifference to him. But from the manner in which the conduct of a distinguished gentleman, (the Vice President,) then absent, had been treated, he felt bound to make a few remarks in his defence. He had always understood that the rule was an invitation to the Vice President to absent himself so as to give the Senate an opportunity of appointing its committees by one of its own members. As to the absence of the Vice President he knew that that gentleman remained away from respect to the rule, from respect to himself, and from respect to the members of the Senate. He knew well, from the known character of the gentleman whose conduct is here impeached, as well as from his past history, that he never shrunk from any duty, which the station to which he had been called, imposed upon him. Committees were appointed to collect facts and to state them fairly; they were not to be understood as expressing the voice of the Senate. We speak by our laws and resolutions. God forbid that we should speak by our committees, which very frequently report and say very strange things. The object of commit-

Louisiana, Briggs, Murphy, Lane, Lytle, and Laporte.

District of Columbia.—Messrs. Chinn, W. B. Shepard, McKennon, Stoddert, Allen of Virginia, Dennis, Hiester, Fillmore, and Taylor.

Judiciary.—Messrs. Bell of Tennessee, Elleworth, Foster, Gordon, Beardsley, Thomas of Maryland, Hardin, Parks, and Pierce of New Hampshire.

Revolutionary Claims.—Messrs. Muhlenberg, Crane, Bates of Massachusetts, Standifer, Bouldin, Marshall, Young, Baylies, and Turrill.

Public Expenditures.—Messrs. Davenport, Lyon, Paige, Clarke of Pennsylvania, Tweedy, Gillet, Hall of Vermont, McLene, and Kinnard.

Private Land Claims.—Messrs. Johnson of Tennessee, Mardis, Carr, Galbraith, Mann of New York, Cage, Felder, Casey, and Bull.

Manufactures.—Messrs. Adams of Massachusetts, Huntington of Connecticut, Denoy, Davis of South Carolina, Corwin, Dickerson, Martindale, McComas, and Osgood.

Agriculture.—Messrs. Bockee, Taylor of Virginia, Hathaway, Barnitz, Bean, Dunlop, Clowney, Turner, and Davis of Kentucky.

Indian Affairs.—Messrs. Lewis, Gilmer, McCarty, Everett of Vermont, Graham, Allen of Ohio, Dickinson of Tennessee, Howell, and Love.

Military Affairs.—Messrs. Johnson of Kentucky, Vance, Speight, Ward, Blair of South Carolina, Thompson of Ohio, Burd, Coffee, and Bunch.

Naval Affairs.—Messrs. White of New York, Williams, Watmough, Patton, Lansing, Reed, Grayson, Parker, and Smith.

Foreign Affairs.—Messrs. Archer, Everett of Massachusetts, Wayne, McDuffie, Hall of North Carolina, Coulter, Jarvis, Pierson, and Carmichael.

Territories.—Messrs. Williams, Allan of Kentucky, Potts, Johnson of New York, Anthony, Wilson of Virginia, Jones of Ohio, Ewing, and Gamble.

Revolutionary Pensions.—Messrs. Wardwell, Barringer, Tompkins, Moore of Virginia, Lea, Deming, W. K. Fuller, Fowler, and Bell of Ohio.

Invalid Pensions.—Messrs. Burges, Evans, Beale, Schley, Adams of New York, Schenck, Chilton, Chaney, and Mitchell of Ohio.

Roads and Canals.—Messrs. Mercer, Blair of Tennessee, Vinton, Stewart, Rencher, Johnson of Maryland, Lucas, Pope, and Slade of Illinois.

Revisal and unfinished business.—Messrs. Dickson, Harrison of Pennsylvania, McVean, Shinn, and Beaty.

Accounts.—Messrs. Mann of Pennsylvania, Lee of New Jersey, Mitchell of New York, Crockett, and Miller.

Expenditures in the Department of State.—A. H. Shepperd, Day, Beaumont, Bodle, and Patterson.

Expenditures in the Department of the Treasury.—Messrs. Allen of Vermont, P. C. Fuller, Harper of Penn., Spangler, and Clark of N. Y.

Expenditures in the Department of the Navy.—Messrs. Hall of Maine, Huntington of New York, Ramsey, Sloane, and Van Houten.

Expenditures in the Department of the Post Office.—Messrs. Hawes, Fulton, Wagner, and Lee of New Jersey.

Expenditures in the Department of War.—Messrs. Whittlesey of New York, Deberry, Chambers, Webster of Ohio, and Halsey.

Expenditures on the Public Buildings.—Messrs. Whallon, Darlington, Brown, Henderson, and Hard.

The SPEAKER announced that on Wednesday next the several States would be called in their order for the presentation of petitions.

Mr. PATTON submitted the following:

Resolved, That the following shall be established as the 9th rule of this House:

"In all cases the Speaker shall vote, and if the House be equally divided, the question shall be lost."

Mr. PATTON said that the object which he had in view was not in the slightest degree to change the effect of the vote that might be given by the Speaker for the time being, nor to increase any of his powers; but it was to restore to his constituents, and to himself, those high and valuable privileges, of which, by the present rule, he considered he was unjustly deprived, and which pertained to every Representative sent to the House. The

honorable member argued at some length in support of his resolution, from the rules, practices, and usage of the House of Commons in England, some of which he cited, and contended at some length that they were not applicable to the institutions of this country. Where the Speaker, having to be approved of by the King, is not chosen simply by the Representatives of the people, there might exist a reason for the present rule, which did not exist here. The practice of the Senate was in strict accordance with the rule he proposed for their adoption; as in all cases the President *pro tem.* chosen by that body in the absence of the President provided by the Constitution, exercised the power of voting. Such was also the practice in the great majority of the Houses of Assembly, in the various States of the Union, although differing in some slight degree as to the time when the right should be exercised. He hoped, therefore, that his motion would be sustained by the House, and thus they would restore to the personage himself those rights, in the exercise of which he would than be in the same respect as other Representatives, subject to the control of that which now constituted the great moral lever which governs the world—public opinion.

Mr. SUTHERLAND said that the rule proposed to be modified had been in operation ever since the year 1789. Coming from a State where every member of the legislative body votes *viva voce,* he thought the present rule ought to be abolished. There was nothing in favor of the present rule but ancient usage. The Speaker's vote should, in his opinion, be recorded, with that of other members, in order that his constituents may see it, and the nation at large be able to judge, by his vote, whether he is worthy of the chair or not. Here, in the great national council, every vote ought to be given, else *voce,* and at a proper time, he should make a motion for the change of the rules to that end. We should then have no dispute about the counting of ballots.

Mr. WAYNE was unable, by indisposition, he said, to enter fully into the subject at this time. The gentleman from Virginia talks of giving the Speaker the right to vote, as if he had not that right at present. But the fact is, that the present rule gives him additional power and privileges, as a member. In his own opinion, the rule ought to continue to stand as is now stood: but as he was unable to go fully into the question at present, he would move the postponement of the further consideration of the motion till Monday next.

Agreed to.

The SPEAKER laid before the House the following messages, which were appropriately referred.

WASHINGTON, December 6, 1833.

To the House of Representatives:

I transmit herewith to the House of Representatives, a communication from the War Department, showing the circumstances under which the sum of $5,000, appropriated for subsistence of the army, was transferred to the service of the Medical and Hospital Departments, and which, by the law authorizing the transfer, are required to be laid before Congress during the first of their session.

ANDREW JACKSON.

WASHINGTON, December 6, 1833.

To the House of Representatives:

I transmit herewith, for the information of the House, the report of the survey made in pursuance of the fourth section of the act of Congress of the 4th July, 1832, authorizing "the survey of canal routes in the Territory of Florida."

ANDREW JACKSON.

ELECTION OF CHAPLAIN.

On motion of Mr. GRENNELL, the House proceeded to the election of a Chaplain.

Mr. WARD nominated the Rev. Thomas H. Stockton.

Mr. CLAY nominated the Rev. J. A. Copp.

Mr. WHITE nominated the Rev. Wm. Hammett.

Mr. ELLSWORTH nominated the Rev. R. R. Gurley.

Mr. EVANS nominated the Rev. Mr. Palfrey.

The several members proposing the respective candidates were appointed tellers.

On the first ballot, 210 members voted—106 being necessary to a choice. There were for the—

Rev. Mr. Stockton	104
Rev. J. A. Copp	33
Rev. Wm. Hammett	50
Rev. R. R. Gurley	6
Rev. Mr. Palfrey	9
Rev. Mr. Smith	1
Blank	6
Scattering	1

None of the candidates having the requisite number, a second ballot took place; when 194 members voted—98 necessary to a choice. For the—

Rev. Mr. Stockton	143
Rev. Mr. Copp	10
Rev. Mr. Hammett	34
Rev. Mr. Gurley	2
Rev. Mr. Palfrey	2
Rev. Mr. Smith	1
Blanks	6

Whereupon the Rev. Mr. Stockton was declared duly elected.

After which, on motion of Mr. STEWART, The House adjourned.

IN SENATE.

TUESDAY, *December* 10, 1833.

Mr. WEBSTER presented a petition from citizens of the city of Cincinnati, praying Congress to purchase all private interests in the Louisville and Portland canal; which was laid on the table, and ordered to be printed.

Mr. CLAY, on leave given, introduced a bill to appropriate, for a limited time, the proceeds of the sales of the public lands.

Mr. CLAY said that the bill contained no material alteration from that of last session; and, on his motion, the bill was read the first time by its title.

Mr. CLAY moved to take up for consideration the resolution submitted by Mr. BENTON, in relation to the amount of moneys deposited in the Bank of the United States; which was agreed to.

When

Mr. CLAY offered the following amendment, as an additional resolution; which was read and agreed to:

And resolved, also, That the Secretary of the Treasury be directed to report to the Senate the names of all banks, and where they are respectively situated, which have been selected by him, in place of the Bank of the United States, as depositories of the public money; the amount of the capital of the said banks respectively, distinguishing between what has been actually paid in by the stockholders and what has not been paid; the amount of public money in each of the said banks on the first of October, the first of November, and the first of December, 1833, distinguishing between the sums standing to the individual credit of the United States and those standing to the credit of any public officer, or other distinguished agent of the Government; the amount of debts due from each of the said banks on each of the days aforesaid; the amount of notes in circulation, and the amount of specie in their vaults respectively; the names of the stockholders in each of the said banks on the first day of September and the first day of October last, distinguishing between foreigners and citizens of the United States; the mode in which transfers of the public money were made from the Bank of the United States to the said banks respectively, whether by warrants or otherwise; if by warrants, whether they were issued in pursuance of appropriations previously made by law; and whether any such transfers were requested by the said banks, or either of them, or made by the treasury, to sustain the credit of the said bank, or any of them; and a copy of all the correspondence between the Department of the Treasury and the said banks, or either of them, relating to the said transfers, or any of them; at what periods the several charters of the banks so designated as depositories of the public money expire; copies of the said charters; and whether the Secretary of the Treasury has been able to obtain at all the ports of the United States at which banks are established, the consent of banks to receive in deposite the public money upon such conditions as he approved, and if not, at what ports has he been unable to obtain such consent.

Mr. FORSYTH, on leave given, presented a bill to provide for the fulfilment of the compact of 1802, between the United States and Georgia.

Mr. CLAY moved that the report of the Secre-

tary in relation to the removal of the public deposites be taken up and considered.

Mr. C. said, that the charter of the Bank of the United States provided for the deposite of the public moneys in that bank and its branches. It also vests in the Secretary of the Treasury the power of removing them to other places of deposite when he may think proper, but it also requires him to give his reasons for so doing to the next Congress. The removal of the deposites had taken place, and the Secretary had told us it was by his order, and he submitted his reasons for doing so. When the charter of the bank authorized a removal of the public moneys from its vaults, it intended and expected, that when the act was done, some sufficient reasons should be given for it, and that Congress should look at them, and examine into their sufficiency. Those reasons are now before us, and we are to decide whether the measure was a proper one, according to the Constitution and laws of the country; and if there was one question of public consideration of more importance than another, it was that which related to the custody of the public treasure. Now was the time to inquire into the condition of the Treasury. The present Vice President had once said that we ought to inquire where the lost rights of the States were. Now he (Mr. C.) wanted to inquire where the Treasury of the United States was. He conceived it to be his duty, as a Senator here, to bring this question up. And as we were to judge whether the Secretary of the Treasury had acted wisely in this matter, we ought to judge of his reasons before the whole Senate, and not refer it to a committee. In order to do this, he hoped a day not far distant would be appointed for its consideration. He would therefore propose that the report of the Secretary be made the order for Monday next.

Mr. BENTON said that the Secretary of the Treasury had announced distinctly his reasons for the removal, to be on account of the misconduct of the Bank of the United States. He has charged the Bank distinctly with interfering with the purity of elections, with corrupting and subsidizing the press, with dishonoring its own paper, and that of its branches. Here were charges of great criminality on the part of the Bank, and the question was, whether we ought to go into a trial of the case here, or refer it to some committee in the Senate. The House of Representatives, he contended, was the proper body before which the subject ought to be investigated, although he confessed the Senate could entertain it. He wanted to examine these charges against the Bank, and therefore he thought the report ought to be referred to a committee.

The postponement was agreed to.

Mr. CLAY submitted the following resolution; which was read and laid on the table:

Resolved, That the President of the United States be requested to inform the Senate whether a paper under date the ——— day of September, 1833, purporting to have been read by him to the Heads of the several Departments, relating to the deposites of the public money in the treasury of the United States, and alleged to have been published by his authority, be genuine or not; and if it be genuine, that he be also requested to lay a copy of said paper before the Senate.

Mr. WEBSTER, on leave given, presented a bill to provide satisfaction for the claims of citizens of the United States for French spoliations; which passed to a second reading.

Mr. WILKINS, on leave given, presented a bill for the relief of A. G. Ralston and Girard Ralston; which passed to a second reading.

Mr. KING submitted the following resolution; which was read and laid on the table:

Resolved, That the Committee on Indian Affairs be instructed to inquire into the expediency of authorizing the President of the United States to appoint an agent to receive evidence of losses sustained by the inhabitants of the now State of Alabama, by a hostile eruption of a party of Creek Indians, in the year 1814, by which Fort Mims was taken, and those who had fled there for protection, massacred.

The Senate then proceeded to the election of a Chaplain, which resulted in the choice of the Rev. Mr. HATCH, on the 6th ballot. The ballotings were as follows:

	1st.	*2d.*	*3d.*	*4th.*	*5th.*	*6th.*
Mr. Post,	13	14	16	15	14	11
Mr. Pise,	10	6	1	1	1	1
Mr. Smith,	8	11	11	11	8	6
Mr. Hatch,	6	10	12	12	17	23
Mr. Orr,	1	0	0	0	0	0

Mr. BENTON submitted the following resolution:

Resolved, That the Secretary of the Treasury be directed to communicate to the Senate any information in his power or possession to show that the Bank of the United States or its branches, at any time heretofore, have refused, or delayed to receive the notes, of any of the branches in payment or deposite.

The Senate then proceeded to the order of the day, and resumed the consideration of Mr. SPRAGUE's resolution to alter the mode of electing their standing committees by the Senate, instead of being, as formerly, appointed by the President *pro tem.*

Mr. WHITE (President *pro tem.*) renewed the request which he had previously made to be excused from voting.

Mr. CLAY, believing that the President was impelled to make this request from a sense of delicacy, and disposed to feel the highest respect for him and his motives, he presumed the Senate would not hesitate to agree to it, and he submitted a motion to that effect.

Mr. GRUNDY could not, from a sense of duty, consent to this motion, and trusted that on further reflection the President himself would withdraw it. He (Mr. G.) was opposed to it, because he thought the right of voting belonged to the office, and ought to be exercised by the occupant of the chair until the rule itself was altered. The request, he knew, had proceeded from a nice sense of honor on the subject at issue, and he would have been happy if he could, consistent with his sense of duty, comply with it. If he had asked to be excused, he saw little if any difference in the respective situations of himself and the President if he was excused. In that case, if he (Mr. G.) voted for the motion, he voted to give himself that increase of power which he voted to take away from the President, the only difference being that the President might have it in his power to vote to retain a greater portion than he could have. There was another consideration which to him appeared of some force: the chair was occupied only temporarily; circumstances might arise by the following day by which the Vice President appointed by the Constitution to occupy the chair might arrive; and in the meantime, by now declining to vote, or the Senate by agreeing to excuse, a radical change in the rule of their proceeding, and having an important influence, might thereby be produced, which he thought it desirable to avoid. For these reasons he regretted that he could not comply with the wishes of the President.

Mr. CLAY, in explanation, said that he was influenced in acceding to the wishes of the President to be excused simply from the consideration that it appeared that he continued to feel, after due reflection upon the subject—after the intervention of a night since the request was first made—the same delicacy as to voting on this question. He could not see any force in the grounds upon which the motion was to be opposed. He denied that the honorable Senator and the President were in the same situation as to the relative power to be acquired by them under the circumstances, the relative power of the honorable Senator being only in the proportion of forty-one to one, whilst on the other side it was a question whether the power would devolve altogether upon one man. He was always disposed to applaud the motives by which it appeared the honorable President was actuated. He, it appeared, was not disposed to retain power in the present instance. With respect to the suggestion that the Vice President should arrive on the morrow, he would say he regretted his absence; for if he had been here, as he ought to have been, at the post assigned him by the Constitution, the Senate would have been saved the necessity of the present motion, as it would then follow, as matter of course, that the former practice of electing committees by ballot would of right devolve upon them. He repeated, that he was only influenced by motives of delicacy and respect towards the high-minded gentleman who occupied the chair in submitting the motion in accordance with his wishes, and he would willingly withdraw it, but could not do so until he had an intimation to that effect from him.

Mr. GRUNDY said, when the Vice President would arrive here, he was not informed. He would say, however, what he knew on the subject, and that was, that for the last three or four sessions, the Vice President never had arrived in the Senate until the presiding officer had appointed the committees. He did not argue upon the propriety or impropriety of his absence, but he would say that his predecessors had acted in the same way. It might be wrong, but if that gentleman had acted in conformity to practice and usages of his predecessors, which had not been objected to, why ought it now to be complained of? As to avoiding or assuming responsibility, he viewed that matter in this way—when it was the duty of an officer to act, let him act. He objected to the presiding officer being excused from voting on this question, because he could not consent that the State of Tennessee should have but one voice in determining it.

Mr. CALHOUN said that as allusions had been made to himself, he felt compelled to make a remark, although he had intended not to have taken part in the discussion. He never knew that there was an understanding that the Vice President should absent himself to enable the presiding officer to appoint the committees. He trusted that no gentleman would charge him with having absented himself at the commencement of the session to avoid the responsibility of appointing the committees. His absence had been solely caused by domestic affliction or some other unavoidable cause. He never had absented himself on that account. He concurred with the gentleman from Mississippi [Mr. POINDEXTER] that appointments should be made by the Senate itself.

Mr. WHITE, the presiding officer, begged leave of the Senate to make a few remarks. (Leave was granted.) Mr. W. then said that he felt very delicately situated on this subject. If he voted against the proposition, it might be supposed he acted on the principle that power is never so well exercised as when it is in our own hands. If he voted to take the power away from the presiding officer, he might be charged with having been governed by the principle that he dreaded the responsibility. There was no duty more unpleasant than the appointment of the standing committees, and he thought no one had so performed that duty as to give entire satisfaction to every member of the Senate, and it was difficult, if not impossible, for any gentleman to perform it with satisfaction to himself. If it was the pleasure of the Senate to excuse him, it would give him pleasure, but if he were compelled to vote, he should do so to the best of his judgment, and according to the dictates of his own conscience.

On the question of excusing Mr. WHITE from voting, Mr. GRUNDY called for a division, when there were, yeas 21, nays 19.

Mr. FORSYTH said that the manner in which the committees were constituted, was a matter of perfect indifference to him. But from the manner in which the conduct of a distinguished gentleman, (the Vice President,) then absent, had been treated, he felt bound to make a few remarks in his defence. He had always understood that the rule was an invitation to the Vice President to absent himself so as to give the Senate an opportunity of appointing its committees by one of its own members. As to the absence of the Vice President he knew that that gentleman remained away from respect to the rule, from respect to himself, and from respect to the members of the Senate. He knew well, from the known character of the gentleman whose conduct is here impeached, as well as from his past history, that he never shrunk from any duty, which the station to which he had been called, imposed upon him. Committees were appointed to collect facts and to state them fairly; they were not to be understood as expressing the voice of the Senate. We speak by our laws and resolutions. God forbid that we should speak by our committees, which very frequently report and say very strange things. The object of commit-

tees is to facilitate and mature business for the action of the Senate. The ordinary business did not require that committees should be appointed by ballot; he admitted there might be extraordinary matters for consideration, when the committees ought to be chosen in that way, but in such exigencies the choice of committees was completely within the power of the Senate. He thought the present rule was better calculated to attain the desired end than any other. Were committees, he would ask, to be chosen with reference to parties? How many parties are there here? One, two, three, four, or five? Certainly three, and there was not a majority of that body of either party. Were they to be chosen by arrangements made out of doors, and with reference to partisan feelings? He hoped not; and as the present mode of choosing prevented such an interference, he thought that it was the best.

Mr. SPRAGUE made a few additional remarks in support of the proposed amendment of the rule, after which the question being taken on his resolution, was decided in the affirmative:

YEAS—Messrs. Bell, Calhoun, Chambers, Clay, Ewing, Frelinghuysen, Kent, Knight, Mangum, Naudain, Poindexter, Prentice, Preston, Robbins, Silsbee, Smith, Southard, Sprague, Swift, Tomlinson, Tyler, and Webster—22.

NAYS—Messrs. Benton, Bibb, Brown, Forsyth, Grundy, Hendricks, Hill, Kane, King, Moore, Morris, Rives, Robinson, Shepley, Talmadge, Tipton, Wilkins, and Wright—18.

HOUSE OF REPRESENTATIVES.

TUESDAY, *December* 10, 1833.

On motion of Mr. McDUFFIE, the report of the Secretary of the Treasury on the removal of the deposites, was taken up and referred to the Committee of the Whole on the state of the Union.

DEATH OF THE HON. T. D. SINGLETON.

Mr. PINCKNEY, of South Carolina, rose and stated that he held in his hand certain resolutions which he would respectfully ask leave to offer for adoption by the House. He believed that it had always been customary for the House to adopt suitable tributes of respect to its deceased members. The South Carolina delegation had heard, with deep regret, of the death of their colleague, the Hon. THOMAS D. SINGLETON, and it was his painful duty to communicate that mournful information to the House. He died at Raleigh whilst on his journey to the capital, whither he was hastening to assume his seat, and to discharge his duties as a member of this body. It was a source of grateful consolation to his colleagues to learn, as they had done, that he received every possible attention, during his illness, from the kindness and humanity of the citizens of Raleigh, and that the Legislature of North Carolina, in a manner equally honorable to him and to themselves, had evinced their respect for his public character and private virtues, by attending his remains to the tomb. It was true that the deceased had not had it in his power to appear and qualify as a member of the House; but as it was well known that he was a Representative elect, and that he died whilst in the very act of endeavoring to reach this city, he certainly deserved every testimonial of respect to which he would have been entitled if he had actually qualified, and might justly be considered as having literally fallen in the discharge of his duties and in the service of his country. It was the fortune of Mr. P. to have had but a slight personal acquaintance with the deceased, but that acquaintance, slight as it was, was sufficient to impress him with a high respect for his intelligence and virtues as a man, and with a deep conviction of his exalted purity and devotion as a patriot. He would not detain the House, however, with anything like a regular eulogy of his departed colleague. To those who knew him, it would be entirely unnecessary—to those who did not, it might prove uninteresting. It would be sufficient, therefore, to say, that he was eminently honored and beloved by his constituents, amongst whom he possessed, as he deserved, almost unequalled popularity and influence; and that whilst his death inflicts a deep wound and an irreparable loss upon his immediate relations and friends, it may well be regarded also as a public calamity to his particular district, and will assuredly be a subject of regret to the people of his State in general. Under these circumstances, he proposed that the House should pay a becoming tribute to his memory—well knowing that it was not only in conformity with the usages of the House upon similar occasions, but that it could not be bestowed on a more worthy man, on a purer patriot; a man of whom all who knew him concurred in saying that his private life was a beautiful exemplification of every Christian virtue, and that as a politician and patriot, he uniformly exhibited an ardent attachment to the rights of the people, and to the great cause of constitutional liberty. With these few remarks, which he had felt it his duty to submit in justice to the character of one whose memory deserved a far better tribute than any he could offer, he now proposed the following resolutions for the consideration of the House:

Resolved, That this House has received with deep regret the melancholy intelligence of the death of the Hon. THOMAS D. SINGLETON, a Representative elect from the State of South Carolina.

Resolved, That this House tender the expression of their sympathy to the relatives of the deceased, upon this mournful event, and that, in testimony of their regret for his loss, and respect for his memory, the members will wear crape upon the left arm for thirty days.

On motion of Mr. PINCKNEY,
The House then adjourned.

IN SENATE.

WEDNESDAY, *December* 11, 1833.

Mr. BIBB, pursuant to notice given, presented certain joint resolutions providing for an alteration in the Constitution of the United States in relation to the mode of electing the President and Vice President, and then moved to lay the same on the table and print them. Mr. B. said he felt no disposition to press the consideration of the resolutions now, and therefore moved that the second Monday in January next be assigned for taking them up, and also the resolutions offered by Mr. BENTON some days since, on the same subject, at the same time; which was agreed to.

Mr. BENTON, on leave given, presented a bill to increase the pay of the medical staff of the army of the United States.

Mr. KING, on leave given, presented a bill for the relief of Thomas Rhoads and Jeremiah Austen.

Mr. KING also, on leave given, presented a bill for the relief of John Chalender and William Johnson.

The abovementioned bills passed to a second reading.

Mr. CLAY moved the consideration of Mr. BENTON's resolution relative to the amount of moneys in deposite at particular periods in the Bank of the United States.

The question being upon the adoption of Mr. CLAY's amendment, Mr. C. suggested a modification of it, and a further amendment, inquiring to know the "current market value of the stock of each of the said State banks on the first of September and first of November, 1833;" which was agreed to, and the amendment adopted.

The following resolution, submitted yesterday by Mr. CLAY, was taken up for consideration:

Resolved, That the President of the United States be requested to inform the Senate whether a paper under date the 18th day of September, 1833, purporting to have been read by him to the heads of the several departments, relating to the deposites of the public money in the treasury of the United States, and alleged to have been published by his authority, be genuine or not; and if it be genuine, that he be also requested to lay a copy of said paper before the Senate.

The blank was then filled with the 18th.

Mr. FORSYTH remarked that this was a very unusual call. He should like to know its purpose, and what use was to be made of the paper when obtained. Everybody supposes the paper to be genuine. He had always taken it for granted that it was so.

Mr. CLAY said that the reasons for the call were so apparent, that he had thought it entirely unnecessary to offer any. The President, on the 18th of September, is said to have read to his Cabinet a certain paper. That paper has been promulgated to the people of the United States as his paper. But we have had no official communication of the document, nor anything affirming it to be an authentic document. If the President had merely read the paper to his Cabinet, without promulgating it, it might be a doubtful matter whether we had the right to call for its communication to us. But we have certainly the right to know from the highest source whether the paper is genuine or not, and, if it is, we had the right to be put in possession of it. At present, we we had no proof of its genuineness, except the assertion of a newspaper; and it was not every assertion of a newspaper that could be relied upon. The only proof we had was the statement of the editor of a newspaper, and upon such evidence we ought not to presume that the paper is genuine. The proceeding of the President in promulgating the document—supposing the paper to be what it purports to be—is without a precedent in the annals of the country. It introduces a new feature into the executive government of the country. The President has the constitutional authority to call upon the heads of departments for their opinions in writing, to assist him in the formation of an opinion. But here is a reversal of the case. A paper from the President is read to the heads of department, to assist them in the formation of an opinion. He would not go into the question why the deposites were removed from the place which the law authorizes to a place which the law does not authorize. That was a subject which, at a proper time, would come up for consideration. He had now risen merely to say, in reply to the gentleman from Georgia, that he had not assumed the document to be genuine, and that if it was genuine, we had a right to call for it. But, if the gentleman from Georgia objects to the question whether the paper be genuine—why, I want the paper. I wish to treat the Executive Department with all possible respect. I do not assume the paper to be genuine, because I do not know the fact.

Mr. FORSYTH. If I understand the gentleman from Kentucky, he admits that with the intercourse between the President and his Cabinet, we have nothing to do.

Mr. CLAY. I made no admission, either one way or another. I consider it would have been a difficult question, had not the document been promulgated.

Mr. FORSYTH. I consider the question precisely the same, for the paper was addressed by the President to his confidential advisers. But he could not see that the gentleman had given any reason for desiring to have the paper. Why should we depart from the rules which have heretofore governed us in relation to such papers, in order to obtain a paper which we do not want? There was another branch of Congress which might have occasion for this document. If a criminal charge was to be made against the President, this paper would be adduced as the evidence of his criminality. When the President should be brought to our bar, and put on a trial for his violation of the Constitution, that paper would be produced in support of the charge. He could see no reason why we should call for the document in question. We have access to it, and for any purpose, whether of judgment or argument, on the subject to which it relates, it is already before us. He demanded the yeas and nays on the question, and they were ordered.

Mr. BENTON said the President had already communicated the paper to America, and to Europe. For every purpose, it was in our possession. But it was probably supposed that the President, being called upon to communicate it to this body, would refuse to send it; and by such refusal, he would, in his (Mr. B.'s) opinion, exhibit a proper respect for himself and his office. Shall we follow out the question, and call upon the President to say whether any newspaper article attributed to him be genuine or not? I wish some person capable of analysis would tell me the difference between calling upon the President for this paper and calling upon him for his speeches to his Cabinet, the

substance of which may have got into a newspaper. We may then go one step further, and call upon him for what he says in his Cabinet, while sitting in his chair, or for what he says to a single member of the Cabinet in his walks, the substance of which remarks may have been overheard and reported. Where shall we stop? We might just as well call for what the President said that day, on the subject of the deposites, as for what he wrote that day. There would be no distinction in law. It was all parole. He could see no reason why any Senator might not take up the Globe, which contains the article, and read it and rely upon it, with as much certainty as if he had received it from the President himself. He objected not to the use of the paper, but to the proposed call for it. He did not seek to protect the President, but to protect ourselves from the reproach of making a demand upon a coördinate branch of the Government which we had no right to make.

Mr. POINDEXTER said that the paper in question was one of great importance, and intimately connected with the affairs of the Government. If it was not so, he would be the last man to vote for a resolution requiring it. The paper was in the nature of instructions to Heads of Departments, and being so, he claimed the right on the part of the Senate, to call on the President for a copy of it. He viewed it in the same light as instructions given by the President to a foreign minister, under his own sign manual. He would inquire, what was the question ultimately to be submitted? It was, whether the President should have the unlimited control of the purse of the country. Under the construction contended for of the power of the President, what would prevent him drawing from the treasury ten millions of dollars? Suppose he should ask ten millions of dollars from the Secretary of the Treasury, and the Secretary should say, "I cannot sign a warrant for the money without an appropriation made by law." What then? Why, the President turns round and says, "Mr. Taney, I appoint you Secretary of the Treasury;" and thus he appoints an officer who will accede to his wishes, and so obtains the complete control of the treasury. Now, he (Mr. P.) insisted on his right to call for a copy of this official act, and therefore he would vote for the resolution.

Mr. FORSYTH said, that the propriety of this course of proceeding depended on the use which was to be made of the desired information when obtained. He could see none. Certainly no official use could be made of it. He believed there could be no doubt of the genuineness of the paper; he thought that was known. Such a paper could only be officially used when the President was called to the bar of the Senate, on a charge of criminal conduct. He thought this call was to be understood as a desire to prompt the other House to a proceeding by impeachment, and to condemn the President in advance. He thought that the similarity of this proposition to the Executive correspondence with a foreign minister, as alluded to by the gentleman from Mississippi, [Mr. POINDEXTER,] was not analagous. He, Mr. F., viewed the paper more as a private letter, read to the head of a department. Suppose the President should write to such an officer, "You are to give certain instructions to a foreign minister." Could you call for that? He presumed not, no matter what was in it. And if it contained the *directest treason*, it was a subject within the proper sphere of action of the other House, and it only.

Mr. WEBSTER said, that if the resolution presented itself in a modified form, he thought there could be no objection to it. He viewed the question in a different light from the gentleman from Georgia [Mr. FORSYTH.] The only doubt could be whether the paper was an official act of the President, and he thought it was so. It was possible that the motion of the gentleman from Kentucky [Mr. CLAY] might be premature, but as he had no doubt that something would be before the Senate during the present session, which would make it necessary to know the genuineness of the paper, he thought the Senate ought to be in possession of it. He would express no opinion of it. He did not regard it in the nature of a private letter, but rather as a public document, and designed for the public eye, and containing opinions of great importance. It stands before the public like the proclamation. He knew of no law authorizing copies of proclamations to be sent to Congress, and yet he believed the President had sent copies of his proclamation last session both to the Senate and House of Representatives. He (Mr. W.) would suggest that that part of the resolution inquiring into the genuineness of the paper be struck out, and that it simply call on the President for a copy of the paper.

Mr. CLAY said he might say with accuracy that no paper ever was attempted to be used by the Senate without a call for it from the authority from which it emanated. It was the parliamentary usage, and had always been the practice. As to the uses to which the paper was to be applied, the gentleman from Georgia [Mr FORSYTH] seemed to think it could be used for no other than one purpose, that of impeachment. He (Mr. C.) had no such design. It was a document affecting the whole treasure of the United States. The gentleman from Massachusetts [Mr. WEBSTER] thought it premature. Why so? It was the duty of Congress to look into the source of the removal of the deposites; where they were removed; the cause and the authority of their removal. He did not know whether the paper was genuine; he could not know it except from the highest authority, and it was out of respect to the Chief Magistrate that he wished to inquire whether it was genuine, and to obtain a copy of it. As that was his object, he would accept of the proposed modification.

Mr. BIBB said he had no disposition to interfere in this matter, except upon a sense of imperious duty. He would not have risen on the subject except for the grounds on which the gentleman from Georgia [Mr. FORSYTH] had placed the question, that the paper was to be taken as genuine because it had appeared in the newspapers. God forbid that he should tax upon the President everything which appeared in the papers. He could not act on this document from a newspaper publication of it—he wanted an authentic copy of it. The President in his message, had referred to the removal of the deposites; and the Secretary of the Treasury too, had given his reasons for so doing. This paper emanated from the President, as the President, to the heads of the departments, and was read to them, relative to a removal of the deposites. In his (Mr. B.'s) sense of it, it was an official act of the President, and a public document which the Senate is entitled to, without assuming the copy in the newspapers as genuine. The modification of the gentleman from Massachusetts [Mr. WEBSTER] was more congenial with his taste, and he hoped it would be agreed to.

Mr. CALHOUN said he should vote for the resolution, with no feeling of disrespect towards the President, but because it was due to him, and due to the Senate itself, that it should have the paper in its most authentic form.

Mr. FORSYTH observed he had not said that the paper was to be taken officially as genuine by the Senate from the newspapers. He knew the newspapers too well. The gentleman from Massachusetts [Mr. WEBSTER] viewed it as an Executive act. He (Mr. F.) viewed it in a very different light. He thought you might, with just the same propriety, call on the President for his correspondence with Mr. Duane, as for this paper. The deposites are removed, and if it was the wish of gentlemen to go behind that act and see where the criminality was, he would say it was not a proper subject for the Senate. He had not said that the only purpose for which the paper could be used was an impeachment. He had only used that as an argument; and as he did not consider it as an official paper, but merely a letter addressed to the members of the Cabinet, he should vote against the resolution.

Mr. KING, of Alabama, said that the paper was one which it was supposed the President had read to his Cabinet for the purpose of influencing his Cabinet. If so, he would ask, could either branch of Congress call on that officer to produce the deliberations of his Cabinet—confidential communications—that they might be spread before the public? Its being in the newspapers did not alter the case. He (Mr. K.) could not, with a proper respect for the President or ourselves, vote for the resolution. It was a call for what we had no right to ask—a confidential communication to the Cabinet. It had been said that the President shrinks from no responsibility. He (Mr. K.) believed he shrunk from no proper responsibility, and he trusted he never would.

Mr. CLAY observed that we had no right to call for a confidential communication to the Cabinet so long as it remained confidential. But this paper had been promulgated by the official organ of the Government, and its promulgation had given us the right to call for it. It had been said, that the paper was published and its genuineness not contradicted, and therefore we ought to act upon it as if it were so. But when we can obtain evidence of the fact, we ought to call for it. It had been said that the President might refuse to give it, and if he should do so, accompanied with a denial of the paper, then we would have a right to use the public version of it. Suppose the correspondence of a foreign minister were *published*, would we not have a right to call for it? Suppose the President should give an order upon the Secretary of the Treasury for payment of a sum of money, and he should pay it, and place the order on file, would we not have a right to call for it? It was in consonance with precedence and all usage, to appeal to the highest authority for evidence of a paper.

Mr. KANE said that the reason which would influence him in his vote, had not been touched on by any of the gentlemen who had spoken on the question. [Here the honorable gentleman read that part of the President's Message which referred to the removal of the deposites.] Now, the gentleman from Kentucky [Mr. CLAY] wished to know who had removed the deposites. This seemed to him (Mr. K.) a very unnecessary inquiry, because the President had informed them that they had been removed by the Secretary of the Treasury. Now, is the object of this proceeding to show that the Secretary has been guilty of a criminal act? If so, it is a matter entirely for the other House, and the paper cannot be used here with any such view. Has the President acted falsely in giving this information? If so, he (Mr. K.) could hardly conceive of a more criminal act. He laid this out of the question, then, and took the object of the inquiry to be, to learn the President's reasons for directing the Secretary to remove them. But the reasons have been given by the officer appointed by the law to do so, and if they are not good, what is the remedy? How are the deposites to be restored, but by a new compact between the parties? If the Secretary, the officer appointed by law to the act, has removed them, what right have we to call on the President for reasons?

The question on the resolution, as modified, was then taken, and decided in the affirmative, as follows:

YEAS—Messrs. Bell, Bibb, Calhoun, Chambers, Clay, Ewing, Frelinghuysen, Hendricks, Kent, Knight, Mangum, Naudain, Poindexter, Prentiss, Preston, Robbins, Silsbee, Smith, Southard, Sprague, Swift, Tomlinson, Webster—23.

NAYS—Messrs. Brown, Forsyth, Grundy, Hill, Kane, King of Alabama, Moore, Morris, Rives, Robinson, Shepley, Tallmadge, Tipton, Tyler, White, Wilkins, Wright—17.

Mr. MOORE, on leave given, presented a bill for the relief of Eli Robinson; also, a bill for the relief of John McCarty; which were both read a first time, and passed to a second reading.

Mr. BENTON's resolution, calling on the Secretary of the Treasury for information relative to the United States Bank refusing to receive in payment the notes of its branches, was taken up and agreed to.

Mr. CHAMBERS presented a memorial from the directors of the Baltimore and Ohio Railroad, praying for an extension of the time allowed by law for completing that work.

The CHAIR announced the receipt of a communication from the Secretary of the Navy; which was laid on the table.

After which, the Senate were engaged in Executive business until the hour of adjournment.

HOUSE OF REPRESENTATIVES.

WEDNESDAY, *December* 11, 1833.

After the presentation of sundry petitions—

The SPEAKER laid before the House the following message:

WASHINGTON, *December* 11, 1833.

To the House of Representatives:

I transmit herewith a report from the Secretary of the Treasury, exhibiting certain transfers of appropriations that have been made in that Department in pursuance of the power vested in the President by the first section of the act of Congress of the 3d of March, 1809, entitled "an act further to amend the several acts for the establishment and regulation of the Treasury, War, and Navy Departments."

ANDREW JACKSON.

Which message, on motion of Mr. POLK, was referred to the Committee of Ways and Means, and ordered to be printed.

The SPEAKER also laid before the House the annual report from the Comptroller of the Treasury; a statement of the unsettled balances and accounts for the last three years; and a report in relation to ——— Moore; which were severally laid on the table, and ordered to be printed.

The House then, on motion of Mr. CLAY, suspended the rule, and went into Committee of the Whole on the state of the Union.

Mr. J. Q. ADAMS was nominated to the Chair.

Mr. CLAY said, as the subject of the President's message was undoubtedly familiar to the members, he, in moving that the committee should proceed to the consideration of the message, would also move that the reading of it should be dispensed with.

The motion to consider having been agreed to,

Mr. C. submitted the following resolutions:

1. *Resolved*, That so much of the President's message as relates to the political relations of the United States with foreign nations, and as recommends a "revision of our consular system," be referred to the Committee on Foreign Affairs.

2. *Resolved*, That so much of said message as relates to the state of the finances, the public debt, revenue, and the Bank of the United States, be referred to the Committee of Ways and Means.

3. *Resolved*, That so much of said message as relates to the commerce of the United States with foreign nations, and their dependencies, be referred to the Committee on Commerce.

4. *Resolved*, That so much of said message as relates to the report of the Secretary of War, and the public interest intrusted to the War Department, be referred to the Committee on Military Affairs.

5. *Resolved*, That so much of said message as relates to the report of the Secretary of the Navy, and the naval service, be referred to the Committee on Naval Affairs.

6. *Resolved*, That so much of said message as relates to the Post Office Department, and the report of the Postmaster General, be referred to the Committee on Post Offices and Post Roads.

7. *Resolved*, That so much of said message as relates to the Indian tribes and to their removal beyond the limits of the States, be referred to the Committee on Indian Affairs.

8. *Resolved*, That so much of said message as relates to "amending the Constitution in relation to the mode of electing the President and Vice President of the United States," the removal of "every intermediate agency in the election of these officers," and to limiting their eligibility to "one term, of either four or six years," be referred to a select committee.

9. *Resolved*, That so much of said message as relates to "accidents which have occurred in that portion of our navigation carried on by the use of steam power," and lessening or removing those evils "by means of precautionary and penal legislation," be referred to a select committee.

10. *Resolved*, That so much of said message as relates to "the destruction of the public building occupied by the Treasury Department," and the erection of another building for that purpose, be referred to the Committee on the Public Accounts and Expenditures, which relate to the public buildings.

Mr. WILDE expressed his desire that any action on one of the resolutions—that in reference to the proposition to amend the Constitution of the United States—should, for the present, be deferred. He would briefly state his reasons for desiring this postponement. It was well known that various propositions and amendments had been suggested, both in the several States and on the floor of that House, none of which had as yet found favor, so as to satisfy the scruples of those who deemed the propositions unconstitutional, or otherwise; yet in the course he was about to suggest, although he did not expect himself to be able to satisfy all parties, he entertained the conviction that there was not at present any other means left to dispose of a question which, more than any other, would tend to promote the harmony and to increase the prosperity of the Union. It was his intention, if the honorable mover of the resolutions would defer for the present the part to which he had reference—after a conference which might be had with members in the House of the various political parties, and from various sections of the country who would possess the advantage of longer experience, and of more influence than he could possibly pretend to—to move that a committee should be raised for the special purpose of inquiring what amendments to the Constitution should be recommended to the several States. If, in taking this course, he should not get encouragement that would justify him in going on with it, he would not press it further, and he wished the delay, to enable him to have the matter tested.

Mr. CLAY said he would readily comply with the request of the gentleman, if it was consistent with his own notions of propriety to do so. But it should be recollected that the proposition announced by the honorable member was one involving a most important topic. In submitting his (Mr. C.'s) resolutions embracing all the points comprised in the President's message, he had followed the course that was usually taken; and as regarded any amendment which the honorable member from Georgia might wish to make, he did not think that the course which he had taken could, in the slightest degree, interfere with his views: the usual course was to refer the matter in the message to the usual committees, and he could not consent to depart from it, and it would as well suit the honorable member's purpose to move his amendment hereafter as a distinct proposition.

Mr. ARCHER begged to remind the honorable member from Georgia of what must have escaped his recollection, that a committee had been raised for the same purpose during the last session, and of which he had the honor to be a member. He could do that committee the justice to state, that no persons could evince more anxious desire than they did to fulfil the public expectation; but they found it impossible to come to anything like unanimity upon it, and, with the knowledge of this result, he would say, the only effect of the honorable member's now going into such a committee would be to embarrass other proceedings. He therefore prayed the honorable member to take the course suggested.

Mr. WILDE replied, (but in so low a tone as to be almost inaudible. The reporter understood him to say,) that it was with regret he learned that there was no hope of settling this all-important subject, and that it was, at all events, his desire that his constituents should know the fact, that there was no such thing as even a prospect of having any amendments made to the Constitution—a matter upon which, as connected with other subjects, he could take upon himself to say that they felt the most intense anxiety.

Mr. WAYNE hoped to get credit, as a representative from Georgia, of also knowing something of the sentiments of his constituents. He thought it was rather premature, not having any expression from the State Legislature or from the people on the subject, to suppose there was so much anxiety felt by them; and it would be certainly, in his opinion, more becoming to them that such an expression of their will should come from themselves, than it should be presumed to exist by any of her representatives. He thought that if the honorable member from Alabama should consent to defer his resolution, and that the course suggested by his colleague should be agreed to, the certain effect would be to burden the committee with so much business that there could not be any action on the message, in conformity to the public desire. He thought, therefore, that it would be better to go on with the usual reference, and for his colleague to make a distinct proposition on such points as he deemed expedient; however anxious he was to hear them hereafter, he would disclaim on the part of their common constituents that they now had any desire they should be acted on, or have the important objects contained in the message retarded.

The CHAIRMAN inquired if the honorable member from Georgia required that the question on the resolution should be taken on the part in discussion separate from the other part?

Mr. WILDE responded in the affirmative, and expressed his regret that his colleague should have thought it necessary to make a disclaimer that the people of Georgia did not feel anxiety on this subject—claiming, with all due respect for him, to have some knowledge of their sentiments. Did he not recollect that the Legislature had made more than one proposition to amend the Constitution? His intention was to consider what amendments might be made to it; and in doing so, he meant to include all the propositions that the people, or the States, had at various times proposed. He had no wish to embarrass the other business, and thought no embarrassment could arise from his proposition to defer, for a short time, a resolution on a subject which had no immediate urgency—which had slept for four years, and which, if it had taken even a longer *nap*, there would not have been any very serious injury incurred. He asserted that there was throughout the Union—in the North as well as the South—much anxiety felt, that some amendments should be made to the Constitution; that this anxiety not only embraced the subject of the Presidential election, but it extended to other important questions, affecting the bank and the currency of the country, the public lands, the tariff, and other topics which he would not enlarge upon; not desiring to prolong what appeared an unprofitable discussion. He would now move that the question on the resolution as to the election of President, be taken separately.

Mr. WAYNE did not intend to intimate that his colleague has not as good a right to speak for the people of Georgia as himself, but he insisted that the people of Georgia, so far as he knew their opinion, were opposed to the agitation of any question which would disturb the harmony which prevailed.

Mr. WILDE said, with respect to everything being harmonious and tranquil, he would remind his colleague that at a large meeting in Georgia the present tariff was denounced and its further modification called for. That meeting was so composed that his colleague would not doubt that it represented the sentiments of the people of Georgia. We cried peace, peace, when there was no peace. It was not all harmony and peace. Of the condition of this "rising empire, but falling republic," as it had once been called, he had taken a wide view, and he had come to the opinion that it was possible to adopt some amendments to the Constitution, if the great parties in the nation would lend themselves to the work, in the spirit of peace and patriotism. The great question of restrictive construction, or liberal construction, might still be left open, and it necessarily must be; but the dangerous questions of the bank, the tariff, internal improvement, and other disputed powers, might be settled at once and forever. It was urged against his proposition, that by blending so many topics in the same proposition, the whole would be lost. But he thought that, by presenting at once what concerned different parts of the country, a compromise of prejudices and interests might be effected. He would compromise anything but principle.

Mr. GILMER reminded his colleague to the right [Mr. WAYNE] that the amendment to the Constitution proposed by the President, had been expressly rejected by the Legislature of Georgia. He also contended that the people of Georgia were deeply interested in the settlement, by some compromise, of the questions which had so long agitated the country. As to the tariff, was it not exceedingly important, was it not necessary to the safety of the Union, that the Constitution should be definite on that subject? It is necessary, in order to save the country from continual agitation and excitement, to settle the great questions relative to the bank, the tariff, and internal improvements. The subject to which his colleague refer-

red was of secondary importance in the estimation of the people of Georgia to these.

Mr. WAYNE had no doubt that his colleague would sacrifice his prejudices and interests—principle he knew he would never sacrifice—to the attainment of national harmony and the preservation of the Union. But he insisted that the manner in which his colleague had introduced his proposition was, though unintentionally, calculated to disturb the harmony of the country, and produce infinite confusion and agitation. The people of Georgia would, he believed, be content to stand still, at least until her grievance should become too oppressive for freemen to bear.

The question being stated,

Mr. McDUFFIE moved that so much of the message as relates to the Bank of the United States, &c., be also excepted.

The CHAIR read the second resolution, and asked if the member from South Carolina wished to except the whole, or that part alone which relates to the bank.

Mr. McDUFFIE. The whole.

Mr. JARVIS moved to except the 10th resolution, relating to the destruction of the building of the treasury.

The resolutions submitted by Mr. CLAY were then agreed to, and reported to the House, with the exception of the 2d, 8th, and 10th.

The question being on the 2d resolution—

Mr. McDUFFIE rose and suggested to the honorable mover, Mr. CLAY, the propriety of omitting from the resolution the words "Bank of the United States," in order to avoid, for the present, the discussion which must otherwise inevitably ensue at this stage of the business.

Mr. CLAY said it had been usual to refer the subjects of finance, revenue, and the bank, to the same committee, and he could not consent to any unusual course on this occasion.

Mr. McDUFFIE said that the gentleman from Alabama wholly misapprehended his object. His purpose was to avoid a discussion on a preliminary question; and the motion to refer the clause in the message, implies an admission of the authority of the President to remove the deposites, whereas it was well known that he had no such power.

Mr. CLAY did not see, he said, why the discussion alluded to should necessarily arise upon the usual motion for the reference of the several parts of the message to the usual committees. He could not be persuaded of the propriety of the course suggested by the gentleman from South Carolina.

Mr. McDUFFIE said that it was evident that the discussion of this topic must now take place. But as the House, at this hour, was not prepared for it, he would move that the committee rise.

The committee then rose and reported progress.

Mr. POLK rose to move a re-consideration of the vote by which the report on the removal of the deposites was yesterday referred to the Committee of the Whole on the state of the Union. He voted for the motion with the understanding that the object of the mover was to move the report and message together, when the question of reference should come up. He regarded it as important that there should be a full and deliberate investigation of this subject by a committee. But he presumed that it was intended to involve the House, suddenly and without investigation or deliberation, in a full discussion of the merits of this important subject, on a preliminary question. He would not make the motion to reconsider at this late hour, if the rules of the House would permit him to make it at a subsequent time.

Mr. CHILTON moved that the House do now adjourn.

The House then adjourned.

IN SENATE.

THURSDAY, *December* 12, 1833.

A message from the President was received by the hands of Mr. Donelson, his Private Secretary, which was read as follows:

WASHINGTON, *December* 12, 1833.

To the Senate of the United States:

I have attentively considered the resolution of the Senate of the 11th instant, requesting the *President* of the United States to communicate to the Senate "a copy of the paper which has been published, and which purports to have been read by him to the heads of the Executive Departments, dated the 18th day of September last, relating to the removal of the deposites of the public money from the Bank of the United States and its offices."

The Executive is a coördinate and independent branch of the Government, equally with the Senate; and I have yet to learn under what constitutional authority that branch of the legislature has a right to require of me an account of any communication, either verbally or in writing, made to the heads of departments, acting as a cabinet council. As well might I be required to detail to the Senate the free and private conversations I have held with those officers on any subjects relating to their duties and my own.

Feeling my responsibility to the American people, I am willing upon all occasions to explain to them the grounds of my conduct; and I am willing upon all proper occasions to give to either branch of the Legislature any information in my possession that can be useful in the execution of the appropriate duties confided to them.

Knowing the constitutional rights of the Senate, I shall be the last man, under any circumstances, to interfere with them. Knowing those of the Executive, I shall at all times endeavor to maintain them agreeably to the provisions of the Constitution, and the solemn oath I have taken to support and defend it.

I am constrained, therefore, by a proper sense of my own self-respect, and of the rights secured by the Constitution to the Executive branch of the Government, to decline a compliance with your request. ANDREW JACKSON.

After the message had been read,

Mr. CLAY said that a call had been made on the President for a copy of a document which had been published and extensively circulated by the papers in this city—a document intimately connected with the safety of the treasure of the country. The call for it was made under the full conviction that the Senate ought to have that document. It had been refused under the pretext that the rights of the Chief Magistrate were invaded by it. He always would be disposed to respect the rights of every public officer, but the President could have no more confidence in his rights than I feel in the rights of the Senate. The right of the Senate to call for this paper was founded on the ground that the whole world was already in possession of it. It was made because the document was sent forth to the American people upon an all-important subject, and because it was the right of the Senate to have it. Nor was it made because the call was in violation of precedent or an established usage. But the President has refused to give us this document, and it was not necessary to proceed further in the pursuit. One result happens from it: the President don't deny the genuineness of the paper. It is before the world, and as we have endeavored to get it, and it has been refused, I have a right to take the next best evidence of the document, and that is, as it has been published in the official paper. In every instance, therefore, where I have occasion to use it, I shall avail myself of that publication of it as genuine.

Mr. GRUNDY said he thought when the proposition was made it was a very unnecessary procedure.

Here the Presiding Officer interposed, that the debate was out of order, unless some motion was intended to be made.

Mr. GRUNDY said he intended to move before he concluded that the message be laid on the table; and then resumed that he thought it unnecessary, because we only wanted evidence when the facts had not come to our knowledge, or when they were denied. Now, he believed that both friends and enemies admitted this document to be genuine—to be what it purported to be. He therefore had thought that nothing beneficial could result from this proposition, and this was what induced him to vote against it. The President has given his objection to complying with the call, and what is it? Why that the Senate has asked for a private communication from the Chief Magistrate to his Cabinet. He (Mr. G.) would never question the propriety of the motives of the Senator who wanted this information. But the President has said that it is a matter which you have no right to interrogate him about; and his opinion is, too, that to comply with the request would be setting a dangerous precedent. He (Mr. G.) was not inclined to say anything on the subject of the removal of the deposites when that matter should come up for consideration. But if he did, he could not, even if he were so disposed, speak of that paper as any other than a genuine one, or deny its authenticity. He therefore moved to lay the message on the table; which was agreed to.

On motion of Mr. BENTON, the memorials and resolutions of the several States upon the subject of the public lands were ordered to be printed, and a tabular statement prepared by the Secretary.

STANDING COMMITTEES.

The PRESIDENT *pro tem.* announced that this was the day assigned for the appointment of standing committees.

Mr. GRUNDY said, before the election was gone into, he wished to preface it by a few observations. The Senate had determined to deprive the presiding officer of the power of appointing the committees, and he was not disposed to question the propriety of the decision. But the reason assigned for this course, and that which seemed to him of most weight, was, that the committees should be the legitimate and true organs of this body. What, then, he would ask, was the present condition of the Senate? There were seven vacant seats here. Five of these have been filled by appointments or by elections by the Legislatures of the different States, but none of the gentlemen chosen were here. Two of these vacancies have not yet been supplied. The five, however, are expected here every day. The Senator from Pennsylvania was expected to-night; indeed, he had been told he was already in town. The Senator from Georgia was elected, and would be here shortly. The Senator from Louisiana, and another from Delaware, were neither of them here. Most of the gentlemen would be here, he thought, on Monday; and, under the circumstances, there would be danger of not securing a correct expression of opinion by proceeding to the election to-day. Another matter occurred to him as being of importance. Three of the five gentlemen have been appointed by the Governors of their respective States, and have *not yet been qualified* as Senators. If his idea on the subject was correct, to be a Senator, the person chosen ought to be here, and take the oath prescribed. He would ask, can we appoint those gentlemen on committees at all, until they are sworn? He could not hear what had been the practice in such case, of appointing Senators on committees, who had never been here or taken their seats. Mr. CLAYTON, of Delaware, and Mr. WAGGAMAN, of Louisiana, (he believed he might mention their names,) might be so appointed, but can the others? He did not think they could yet be recognised as members, and therefore to give them an opportunity of coming in, he moved to postpone the election till Monday next.

Mr. CLAY hoped the postponement would not take place. The Senate was as full as it would be, on the average, during the session. We were now at the close of the second week of the session, and we were urged to put off the appointment of committees, a matter about which, he supposed, the minds of all gentlemen were made up. This day had been assigned for the appointment, some days ago, and it was as well known then that there were absentees as it is now. No such objection was urged then. There were important bills now lying on the table that ought to be referred to the committees. The time for the meeting of the committees was approaching, and it was of importance that they should be appointed now. If gentlemen were absent, he regretted it; but we were not in fault, and he thought if we were to look at the political character of the absentees, that things would be as they now are, if they were here. As to the objection of the gentleman from Tennessee, as regards the practice of the Senate of appointing absent gentlemen on committees who had not been sworn, his impression was, that they had always been appointed, whether they were here or not. Qualification will precede the commencement of service, and, therefore, he could see no reason for the delay, but that we ought rather to proceed to

the appointment, and he would therefore call the yeas and nays upon the question.

Mr. WEBSTER said he had voted for the change of the rule, in regard to the appointment of committees, with a good deal of reluctance. It appeared to him likely there would be some difficulty in making so good a selection in respect to where pluralities were to prevail. It appeared to him an early period to proceed to the consideration of important business. He thought there was reason in giving time to the absent gentlemen to be here, and it is said they will be here. We had changed the rule—they could not know it, and if gentlemen request postponement, he thought it was reasonable, and that the motion should prevail.

Mr. CLAY. I understand the gentleman to say it is early time to proceed to the appointment of committees.

Mr. WEBSTER. I said it was an early period to take up important business.

Mr. CLAY. At no time, he believed, had the appointment of committees been delayed beyond the second week of the session.

Mr. GRUNDY said that the present was a new case in the Government. It was new in this, that the Senate, at the commencement of the session, had changed an important practice. Formerly, the presiding officer appointed the standing committees, and it was well known that he exercised that power. The gentlemen absent, therefore, had no right to expect that they would be called on at this early period of the session, to perform the duty of choosing the committees.

The question of postponement was determined in the affirmative.

YEAS—Messrs. Benton, Bibb, Brown, Frelinghuysen, Forsyth, Grundy, Hendricks, Hill, Kane, King, Knight, Moore, Morris, Prentiss, Rives, Robinson, Robbins, Shepley, Silsbee, Smith, Swift, Tallmadge, Tipton, Tomlinson, Webster, White, Wilkins, and Wright—28.

NAYS—Messrs. Bell, Calhoun, Chambers, Clay, Ewing, Kent, Mangum, Naudain, Poindexter, Preston, Southard, Sprague, and Tyler—13.

The Senate then, on motion of Mr. MANGUM, adjourned over to Monday next.

HOUSE OF REPRESENTATIVES.

THURSDAY, *December* 12, 1833.

After the presentation of sundry petitions,

Mr. EVANS, of Maine, reported from the Committee on Invalid Pensions, a bill granting pensions to certain persons therein named; which was read a first time, and ordered to a second reading.

REMOVAL OF THE BANK DEPOSITES.

The motion submitted yesterday, by Mr. POLK, for the reconsideration of the vote by which the report of the Secretary of the Treasury on the removal of the deposites was, on Tuesday, referred to the Committee of the Whole House on the state of the Union, was taken up.

Mr. CHILTON had no desire to address the House on this question, when he moved the adjournment yesterday. But he wished that, on so important a subject, some time should be afforded for reflection; and, after reflection, he had come to the conclusion that the motion ought to be resisted. It was not to be presumed that the gentleman from South Carolina, [Mr. McDUFFIE,] entertaining, as he did, the opinion that the removal of the deposites was an act of usurpation, intended to suffer a reference of the subject in the usual manner. He had not understood that gentleman as assenting to any such course, when he made the motion, and he could not see how the gentleman from Tennessee [Mr. POLK] could have misunderstood his intention. He was also surprised at the remark of the gentleman from Tennessee, that the subject ought to be deliberately approached and illuminated by rays of light to be shed upon it by some committee; he was too modest to say the Committee of Ways and Means. There are some subjects as to which new lights are indispensable and as to which it would not be safe to legislate without investigation. But was this a subject of that kind? And was there any light, which the Committee of Ways and Means could shed on this subject which did not already shine upon the Committee of the Whole House? The gentleman must excuse him if he said, in the words of a distinguished individual of no very remote antiquity, "some things can be done as well as others,"—and "some things could be done by some people as well as by others," nor indeed could he sit by, patiently and see the whole weight of this massive Government imposed on the shoulders of his friend from Tennessee. He wished, moreover, that the laurels as well as the responsibilities and labors of legislation should be divided among the members. He had no doubt, in fine, that this subject could be as well examined by a committee of the whole House as by any standing committee. The gentleman from Tennessee had sought to smother the question. There was something peculiar in the character of his motion. It was made in consequence of the intimation from the member from South Carolina to go into the question before the Committee of the Whole. Is not the member from Tennessee satisfied with the reasoning of the Secretary of the Treasury? Can he improve upon it? The Secretary has made up an issue,—will not the gentleman abide by it? Every new light on this subject which had been presented to us on this question, consisted in newspaper scrapings of the most miserable character. He knew what he said. It was now time to have fair play, and to disabuse the public of its delusions on this subject. We ought to put a stop to the artificial excitement which has been kept up with a view to disturb the currency of the country, and to destroy an institution of great national utility. He pleaded, as an apology for presenting himself before the House on this question, that it had been trumpeted in the official organ of the Government, that all the members who should raise their voices in favor of the bank, were bribed. He was sensible of the hazard, personally and politically, to which he exposed himself, by declaring his sentiments. But no man should desire to outlive the honor and glory of his country. He entertained the highest respect for the gentleman from Tennessee. His talents were known to the Union. He was on excellent terms with himself, and his amicable relations he had no disposition to disturb.

The SPEAKER. The gentleman is discussing the question of whether the report should be sent to the committee, which is not in order. The question now before the House is, whether it shall be brought back into the House, and he will confine himself to this.

Mr. CHILTON continued. He was opposed to the reference which the gentleman from Tennessee seemed to desire, for he knew the result of it would be to prevent any action on the subject. It was wholly unnecessary to refer the subject at all.

The SPEAKER interposed, and said, it was not in order to speak to the point of reference. The question was on reconsideration.

Mr. CHILTON. One of the arguments in favor of the removal of the deposites was that the charter would expire. Could it take us five minutes to find out whether the charters of the State banks selected are not also soon to expire. But he proceeded no further, as he might wander, in the estimation of the Speaker, from the precise question before the House.

Mr. POLK rose only to say, that this was the first time that any great subject of national policy was ever referred, in the first instance, to the Committee of the Whole on the State of the Union. If we should plunge into the discussion of this question, in the Committee of the Whole, there would be no end to it. If it was necessary to act speedily on this subject, it need not be delayed. The action of the House would be facilitated by taking the usual course. The Bank of the United States itself ought not to shrink from the investigation which he proposed. But in the Committee of the Whole, this could not be done. The discussion would be limited to the face of the papers themselves, and we could bring into it nothing else. The discussion, too, would occupy days, weeks, and even months. He insisted that the House ought to pursue the usual and parliamentary course. He had nothing more to say.

Mr. McKIM called for the yeas and nays on the question; which were ordered.

Mr. McDUFFIE said, the gentleman's object, I understand to be, to bring the subject before a standing committee. [Mr. POLK. That, or any other committee the House will direct.] The object could not in that way be attained. A discussion must take place on every presentation of the question. The only fact involved in the case, which can be referred, is that fact relating to printing documents. But he was willing to admit the fact that the bank defended itself. State the sum, if you please, at fifty, sixty, or a hundred thousand dollars. The facts are immaterial. They have nothing to do with the question. Congress provided a certain depository for the public money, providing for its removal in a certain contingency. But the Secretary of the Treasury takes a view of the transactions of the bank for five years, and directs a removal of the deposites, in the face of an almost unanimous resolve of this House, and for reasons which must have existed then, if they ever existed. The Secretary, unauthorized, nay, in opposition to the will of Congress, transferred the public treasure from the safest institution on the face of the earth to banks upon whose solvency no member in the House could pronounce. The gentleman speaks of a scrutiny into the affairs of the bank. The bank, he says, was reluctant to stand scrutiny. But this had nothing to do with the matter. We were to look at it upon fundamental principles, and had nothing to do with facts. It is said that the State banks had relieved the pressure by issuing bills on the credit of the deposites. Why, children would not act so imprudently. To flood the country with currency, based on no foundation but the temporary and unauthorized deposite of public money in their vaults, was the veriest piece of folly ever heard of. Great embarrassments must ensue, if we remove the deposites from the State banks; but we must do it, if we are not bound, hand and foot, to the Executive.

Mr. CAMBRELENG said he believed this question depended on great principles connected with the expiration of the charter of the United States Bank. He heard with alarm the intimation that the deposites should be restored to the Bank of the United States—the only object of which procedure must be, to force the renewal of the charter, to avoid the embarrassments it would create. He was surprised, too, to hear doubts expressed as to the solvency of some twenty banks, whose capitals were infinitely larger than the whole revenue of the country. Let the gentleman, if he chooses, introduce his resolution for the restoration of the deposites. He would pledge himself not to shrink from the question. But the subject of the bank and the letter of the Secretary of the Treasury ought, in conformity with ancient usage, to go to a standing committee.

Mr. BINNEY understood, he said, that the sole object of the motion to reconsider, was to delay the discussion on this subject until it had been investigated by a committee. The interest with which his constituents viewed this question was his apology for appearing himself so early after his introduction into the House, in a discussion. A large view of this subject, which could not be too soon met, was presented by the gentleman from South Carolina, and there was a narrower, but large view, involving the public faith, the obligations of a contract, and the honor of this House, as the guardians of the public faith. The contract was between the people and the stockholders of the bank, the latter giving their services, and the former certain immunities, and the privilege of the public deposites. The question was submitted to us by the contracting parties, whether the compact has been fulfilled. The Secretary of the Treasury had made an award against the bank, and in virtue of his power he had removed the deposites. He now calls upon us to confirm his judgment. The reasons of the officer are placed together with his power—and his act and his reasons for it, come before us. If any inquiry in respect to the bank was wished, let it be made. But let it be prosecuted independently of the question of the Secretary's reasons. We are here upon a question of contract. What is the object of the inquiry asked for? Is it to suggest reasons for the Secretary's act which had not occurred to the Secretary himself, and had not influenced his judgment? If you bring in other facts, other judgment, other reasons, you annul the judgment of the Secretary, agree that it was wrong, and assume to exercise an ori-

ginal instead of a derivative power. Does the Secretary ask for further inquiry? He gives facts and inferences, upon which he rests the case. He does not ask Congress for new facts and reasons; and if Congress goes in quest of them, it is an acknowledgement that the Secretary's facts and reasons are insufficient; that he acted, in a word, in the dark on this important subject. The charter says, that the reasons shall be immediately communicated to Congress. Why? That Congress may immediately judge whether those reasons are sufficient; his judgment being in the nature of an award between the people and the bank, the parties who are interested. The Secretary had not asked for further inquiry. If, then, he acted on sufficient reasons, it was for the House, on behalf of the people, to pronounce their judgment, and if they were sufficient, then there was an end of the question. New reasons cannot justify the measure. This view of the matter, he felt bound to submit to the House. He must be permitted to say, that it was not only important that we act on the lights before us, but that there was never a question before this House which so much required an instantaneous decision. The control of the treasury was in a new and unsafe position. The safeguards of the public money adopted by law, were inapplicable to the present control of the deposites. What knowledge had we of the condition of the banks selected by the Government? The people would not long be content with the present state of things. Embarrassments were gathering in the commercial community. The best paper was at a discount of 12 or 15 per cent. Still the crops were abundant, and trade was thriving. The scarcity of money was owing to the state of uncertainty which now existed. If the public money was to be restored, it must be done immediately, for in a few weeks it would be beyond our reach. It would become blended with the interests and business of the local banks so far that we would not withdraw it.

Mr. McKINLEY said the Secretary of the Treasury had the power of removing these deposites whenever he thought proper, and was to report his reasons for their removal. The inquiry was, therefore, whether the reasons were sufficient and the facts stated true. The Committee of the Whole was not the usual and proper place for such an inquiry. When all the facts were examined and reported upon, we could proceed to the discussion. He asked whether the House, in the Committee of the Whole, had the power to order the deposites to be replaced? That was to be done by resolution. The question could not be determined in the Committee of the Whole.

Mr. CLAYTON said he should not vote against the motion to reconsider, and might, therefore, expose himself to the charge of inconsistency. At the last session he voted that the public deposites were unsafe in the Bank of the United States, and he still thought so. But it did not follow that he did not also consider them to be unsafe at the bottom of the Potomac. The Bank of the United States was unsafe as a depository, and they had been removed to another which was still less safe. He was opposed to the Bank of the United States, and always should be. But he thought that the removal of the deposites to the State banks made them, *pro tanto*, the Bank of the United States.

The SPEAKER called the member to order, as he was going into the merits of the case, which had not been touched in the argument.

Mr. CLAYTON professed his desire, at all times, to bow to the decision of the Chair, yet he did not think he had gone more into the merits than had been done by the members from Pennsylvania and South Carolina, who had preceded him.

The SPEAKER again reminded the gentleman from Georgia that he did not confine his remarks to the question.

Mr. CLAYTON said, then, that he would endeavor to keep within order, and try to get in only occasionally what he wanted. It was, he thought, highly important to settle this matter at once. If it were proposed to authorize the Secretary of the Treasury to establish as many banks as he pleases, would it be entertained for a moment? But the Secretary has undertaken to exercise such a power. The reasons reported to the House are not of new discovery. They have been acted on formerly by the House, and we need no time to act on them again. Has it not been stated that the bank had influenced elections—that it had expended money for printing? All this he admitted, and it proved that the bank ought not to exist. But the Secretary has multiplied the institution upon us. He should vote, when the question should come up, for the removal of the deposites back to the Bank of the United States.

Mr. POLK would not, he said, fatigue the House with speaking. He rose only to reply to a few of the suggestions which had been thrown out. The report contains the various facts which governed the Secretary of the Treasury in his action, and some of those facts may involve the charter of the bank; and, for both reasons, ought now to be inquired into by a committee. In reply to the gentleman from Pennsylvania, [Mr. BINNEY,] he said, that it was not material to the question of reference whether the action of the House would be original or in review. It was also suggested that the State banks were unsafe. This constitutes one of the chief objects of the examination proposed. Again, it was said that this was a question of public faith. Well, be it so. Is it not proper, then, for a committee of the House to inquire by which party the contract was violated? It seems to me that it is. It had also been said that the treasury was going out of the bank daily. Well, I consider that the treasury is the public money, wherever it may happen to be, in one bank or twenty. He would only add one additional reason why the motion should prevail, and it was this: the subject is intimately connected with the finances of the country. It was formerly contended in this House, by a gentleman now a member of it, that the connexion between the bank and the finances was as intimate as that which exists between the soul and the body. He would repeat that the debate in the Committee of the Whole would be protracted for days and weeks. He hoped there would be ample opportunity for full discussion, but not, he trusted, in this general and unsatisfactory manner.

Mr. WAYNE replied briefly to the arguments adduced against the motion to reconsider; and, having deprecated any discussion upon the merits of the bank question, at the present moment, as unnecessary and out of order, with a view to terminate it, he announced his determination to act in the same manner in which he had been himself treated at the last session, by the honorable member from South Carolina, [Mr. McDUFFIE,] when about to explain his views on the resolution of the bank being a safe depository of the public funds, by calling for the previous question.

The question thereon being put, the House refused to sustain the call—

Ayes 104, noes 107.

Mr. WATMOUGH moved an adjournment, which he subsequently withdrew in favor of

Mr. BURGES, who moved that when the House should adjourn, it would adjourn until Monday.

Mr. POLK objected to this motion, as out of order.

After a remark to the point of order from the SPEAKER,

Mr. BURGES said, as the motion was objected to by that gentleman, [Mr. POLK,] he would withdraw it.

Upon which,

Mr. WATMOUGH again moved an adjournment, which was carried.

The House then adjourned.

HOUSE OF REPRESENTATIVES.

FRIDAY, *December* 13, 1833.

Mr. BULLARD, of Louisiana, appeared, was qualified, and took his seat.

The SPEAKER presented to the House a memorial from Messrs. Gilpin, McElderry, and Wager, the three Government directors of the Bank of the United States, in relation to the conduct of the directors, and especially of the president of that institution.

Mr. POLK moved that it should be referred to the Committee of Ways and Means.

Mr. WATMOUGH moved to amend that motion, by moving that it should be referred to the Committee of the Whole on the state of the Union.

The SPEAKER said it was not necessary to amend—a motion to refer to the Committee of the Whole having precedence.

Mr. POLK demanded that the question should be taken by yeas and nays.

Ordered.

Mr. VANCE called for the reading of the memorial.

Mr. ARCHER objected to the reading, and suggested that it might, for the present, be better not to give any direction to it; that it might lie on the table, and follow such course as should be given to the report of the Secretary of the Treasury on the removal of the deposites. He moved that it should be laid on the table.

Mr. POLK called for the yeas and nays on this motion.

Ordered.

Mr. ARCHER said, if requested by the member from Tennessee, and to save the time of the House now, he would withdraw his motion, but gave notice that he should renew it.

The motion was then withdrawn, upon which,

Mr. POLK said, that the present was altogether a question whether they were to follow the usual course heretofore adopted in referring matters connected with the bank to the Committee of Ways and Means. This was a memorial made by the Government directors, on a subject of deep interest to the Government; it involved the conduct of those entrusted with the management of its affairs, bringing various facts and allegations against them for misconduct. It was their duty to communicate to the House the knowledge of all such facts as they should discover in the management of that institution, which they should deem prejudicial to the public interest. Having been presented by them, the usual course was, surely, to refer it to the committee which, heretofore, had cognizance of all the matters connected with the finances of the country. They all knew the intimate connexion which existed between the Government and the bank. It had an interest in it arising from the large share of the stock which they held. They (the bank) were, in part, keepers of its funds; they had, in consequence, been called on to make weekly statements of their transactions, and the Government had wisely secured to itself the power of appointing five directors, for the special purpose of seeing that the public interests were not jeoparded. The memorial now presented was made by them in pursuance of that duty, and he saw no reason why it should not be sent to the usual committee. If the motion of the honorable member from Virginia to lay it on the table should be made, he trusted that it would not be sustained. He was not desirous to shrink from the general subject involved, but he would oppose and avoid any general skirmishing upon it.

Mr. FOSTER said, that it seemed almost impossible to avoid entering into the merits of the question, and he would urge the propriety of this report being laid on the table for the present, and that the honorable member from Virginia would move, in addition, that it should be printed.

Mr. ARCHER assured the honorable member from Tennessee, that he could not have any desire to give the subject any other direction than the one he wished, but there was a difficulty attendant upon now doing it. He would ask him what he would desire to be done with it, if the question recently under discussion, as to the reference of the report of the Secretary, should be decided by a reference to the Committee of the Whole on the state of the Union? Would he not in that case desire that this memorial should be associated with it? His only desire was for the present to suspend any final action upon it until the fate of the other was ascertained. He would conclude by a motion to have it laid on the table also, and in accordance to the suggestion of the honorable member from Georgia, that it should be printed.

Mr. POLK demanded the yeas and nays. Ordered.

Mr. SPEIGHT then called for the division of the question.

The question on the motion to lay the memorial on the table was then taken, and decided in the negative, as follows:—Yeas 107, Nays 119.

YEAS—Messrs. J. Q. Adams, Allan, Archer, Ashley, Banks, Barber, Barnitz, Barringer, Bates,

Beale, Beatty, James M. Bell, Binney, Bouldin, Briggs, Bullard, Bull, Burd, Burges, Cage, Carmichael, Chambers, Chilton, Choate, Claiborne, Clark, Clayton, Clowney, Corwin, Coulter, Crane, Crockett, Darlington, John Davis, Warren R. Davis, Amos Davis, Davenport, Deberry, Deming, Denny, Dennis, Dickson, Duncan, Ellsworth, Evans, Edward Everett, Horace Everett, Ewing, Felder, Fillmore, Foot, Foster, Fowler, Philo C. Fuller, Fulton, Gamble, Gholson, Gilmer, Gordon, Gorham, Grayson, Grennell, Griffin, Hiland Hall, Hard, Hardin, James Harper, Hazeltine, Heath, Hiester, Jabez W. Huntington, Wm. Cost Johnson, Seaborn Jones, Lay, Lee, Lewis, Love, Martindale, Marshall, Mason, McKennan, Mercer, Milligan, Patton, Pinckney, Potts, Reed, Selden, Shepard, Shepperd, William Slade, Sloane, Spangler, Stewart, Taylor, Philemon Thomas, Tompkins, Tweedy, Vance, Vinton, Watmough, Frederick Whittlesey, Elisha Whittlesey, Wilde, Williams, Young—107.

NAYS—John Adams, Heman Allen, John J. Allen, William Allen, Anthony, Bayliss, Bean, Beardsley, Beaumont, John Bell, James Blair, John Blair, Bockee, Bodle, Boon, Brown, Bunch, Burns, Bynum, Cambreleng, Carr, Casey, Chaney, Chinn, Samuel Clark, Clay, Conner, Cramer, Day, Dickerson, Dickinson, Dunlap, Forrester, Wm. K. Fuller, Galbraith, Gillet, Joseph Hall, Thomas H. Hall, Halsey, Hamer, Hannegan, Joseph M. Harper, Harrison, Hathaway, Hawkins, Hawes, Henderson, Howell, Hubbard, Abel Huntington, Inge, Jarvis, Noadiah Johnson, Cave Johnson, Benjamin Jones, Edward Kavanagh, King, Kinnard, Lane, Lansing, Laporte, Lawrence, Lea, Leavitt, Loyall, Lucas, Lyon, Lytle, Abijah Mann, Joel K. Mann, Mardis, McComas, McIntire, McKay, McKim, McKinley, McLene, McVean, Miller, Robert Mitchell, Moore, Muhlenberg, Murphy, Osgood, Page, Parks, Parker, Patterson, Pearce, Peyton, Pierce, Pierson, Polk, Pope, Ramsay, Rencher, Schenck, Schley, Shinn, Charles Slade, Smith, Speight, Standifer, Stoddert, Sutherland, William Taylor, Francis Thomas, Thomson, Turner, Turrill, Vanderpoel, Van Houten, Wagener, Ward, Wardwell, Webster, Whallon, Campbell P. White, and Wise—119.

Mr. POLK withdrew his call for the yeas and nays on that part of the motion—that the memorial be printed; but the call was renewed by Mr. DAVENPORT, and the question having been ordered to be taken by yea and nays, was decided in the affirmative, as follows:

YEAS—Messrs. John Q. Adams, John Adams, Heman Allen, John J. Allen, Chilton Allan, Wm. Allen, Anthony, Archer, Ashley, Banks, Barber, Barnitz, Barringer, Bates, Bayliss, Beale, Bean, Beardsley, Beatty, John Bell, James M. Bell, Binney, James Blair, John Blair, Bockee, Bodle, Boon, Bouldin, Briggs, Brown, Bullard, Bull, Bunch, Burd, Burges, Burns, Bynum, Cage, Cambreleng, Carmichael, Carr, Casey, Chambers, Chaney, Chilton, Chinn, Choate, Claiborne, Samuel Clark, William Clark, C. C. Clay, Clayton, Clowney, Coffee, Connor, Coulter, Cramer, Crane, Crockett, Darlington, John Davis, Amos Davis, Davenport, Day, Deberry, Deming, Dennis, Dickson, Dickerson, Dickinson, Duncan, Ellsworth, Evans, Edward Everett, Horace Everett, Ewing, Felder, Fillmore, Philo C. Fuller, Fulton, Galbraith, Graham, Grayson, Grennell, Griffin, Hiland Hall, Thomas H. Hall, Halsey, Hamer, Hannegan, Joseph M. Harper, Harrison, Hathaway, Hawes, Heath, Henderson, Howell, Hubbard, Jabez W. Huntington, Abel Huntington, Inge, Jarvis, William C. Johnson, Richard M. Johnson, Noadiah Johnson, Cave Johnson, Seaborn Jones, Benjamin Jones, Kavanagh, King, Kinnard, Lane, Lansing, Laporte, Lawrence, Lay, Lea, Leavitt, Lee, Lewis, Love, Loyall, Lucas, Lyon, Lytle, Abijah Mann, Joel K. Mann, Martindale, Marshall, Mardis, Mason, McCarty, McComas, McDuffie, McIntire, McKay, McKennan, McKim, McKinley, McLene, McVean, Mercer, Miller, Milligan, E. Mitchell, Moore, Muhlenberg, Murphy, Osgood, Page, Parks, Parker, Patton, Patterson, Pearce, Peyton, Pierson, Pinckney, Polk, Pope,

Potts, Ramsay, Reed, Rencher, Schenck, Schley, Selden, Shepard, Shepperd, Shinn, William Slade, Charles Slade, Sloane, Smith, Spangler, Speight, Standifer, Stewart, Stoddert, Sutherland, William Taylor, William P. Taylor, Francis Thomas, Philemon Thomas, Thomson, Tompkins, Turner, Turrill, Tweedy, Vanderpoel, Van Houten, Vinton, Wagener, Ward, Wardwell, Watmough, Wayne, Webster, Whallon, Campbell P. White, Elisha Whittlesey, Wilde, Williams, Wilson, Wise, and Young—294.

NAYS—Messrs. Dunlap, Joseph Hall, Hawkins, and Vance—4.

The question, that the memorial should be referred to the Committee of the Whole on the state of the Union, was then decided in the negative, as follows:

YEAS—Messrs. J. Q. Adams, Heman Allen, Chilton Allan, Ashley, Banks, Barber, Barnitz, Barringer, Bates, Beatty, James M. Bell, Binney, Bouldin, Briggs, Bullard, Bull, Burd, Burges, Cage, Chambers, Chilton, Choate, William Clark, Clayton, Clowney, Corwin, Coulter, Crane, Crockett, Darlington, John Davis, Amos Davis, Davenport, Deberry, Deming, Denny, Dennis, Dickson, Duncan, Ellsworth, Evans, Edward Everett, Horace Everett, Felder, Fillmore, Foot, Foster, Philo C. Fuller, Gamble, Gilmer, Gordon, Gorham, Grayson, Grennell, Griffin, Hiland Hall, Hard, Hardin, James Harper, Hazeltine, Hiester, Jabez W. Huntington, William C. Johnson, Seaborn Jones, Lay, Lewis, Love, Martindale, Marshall, McDuffie, McKennan, Mercer, Milligan, Moore, Pinckney, Potts, Reed, Rencher, Selden, William B. Shepard, William Slade, Sloane, Spangler, Stewart, Philemon Thomas, Tompkins, Tweedy, Vance, Vinton, Watmough, Frederick Whittlesey, Elisha Whittlesey, Wilde, Williams, Wilson, and Young—96.

NAYS—Messrs. John Adams, John J. Allen, William Allen, Anthony, Archer, Bayliss, Beale, Bean, Beardsley, Beaumont, John Bell, James Blair, John Blair, Bockee, Bodle, Boon, Brown, Bunch, Burns, Bynum, Cambreleng, Carmichael, Carr, Casey, Chaney, Chinn, Claiborne, Samuel Clark, Clay, Coffee, Connor, Cramer, Day, Dickerson, Dickinson, Dunlap, Ewing, Forrester, Fowler, William K. Fuller, Fulton, Galbraith, Gholson, Gillet, Joseph Hall, Thomas H. Hall, Nicoll Halsey, Hamer, Hannegan, Joseph M. Harper, Harrison, Hathaway, Hawkins, Hawes, Heath, Henderson, Howell, Hubbard, Abel Huntington, Inge, Jarvis, Richard M. Johnson, Noadiah Johnson, Cave Johnson, Benjamin Jones, Kavanagh, King, Kinnard, Lane, Lansing, Laporte, Lawrence, Luke Lea, Leavitt, Thomas Lee, Loyall, Lucas, Lyon, Lytle, Abijah Mann, Joel K. Mann, Mardis, Mason, McCarty, McComas, McIntire, McKay, McKim, McKinley, McLene, McVean, Miller, Robert Mitchell, Muhlenberg, Murphy, Osgood, Page, Parks, Parker, Patton, Patterson, Dutee J. Pearce, Peyton, Franklin Pierce, Pierson, Polk, Pope, Ramsay, Schenck, Schley, Augustus H. Shepperd, Shinn, Charles Slade, Smith, Speight, Standifer, Stoddert, Sutherland, William Taylor, William P. Taylor, Thomson, Turner, Turrill, Vanderpoel, Van Houten, Wagener, Ward, Wardwell, Wayne, Webster, Whallon, Campbell P. White, and Wise—133.

The memorial was then referred to the Committee of Ways and Means, without a division.

On motion of Mr. WARD, the House agreed, when they would adjourn, to adjourn until Monday.

Mr. C. P. WHITE, with consent of the House, submitted the following resolution, which was read and agreed to:

Resolved, That the Committee on Naval Affairs be instructed to inquire into the expediency of making an appropriation to construct and equip two small vessels of war, to be rigged either as brigs or schooners, under the direction of the Navy Department, to supply the places of the Porpoise and Dolphin, and that said Committee be authorized to report by bill or otherwise.

Mr. WHITTLESEY, of Ohio, from the Committee of Claims, reported a bill in favor of certain persons therein named, which was read twice and referred to the Committee of the Whole.

Mr. McINTIRE, from the same committee, re-

ported a bill for the relief of Joseph M. Harper and others.

Mr. CAVE JOHNSON, from the Committee on Private Land Claims, reported a bill for the relief of Abraham Forbes.

Mr. CARR, from the same committee, reported a bill for the relief of John Bills.

All which bills were read and committed.

And on motion of Mr. GRENNELL, the House adjourned.

REPORT OF THE SECRETARY OF THE NAVY.

NAVY DEPARTMENT,
November 30th, 1833.

To the President of the United States:

Sir: In submitting to your consideration a review of the operations of the naval branch of the public service during the past year, I would beg leave to invite attention to its administration in this plan.

The separate organization of the Navy Department, and the manner originally established by Congress, and the change since made by the addition of a Navy Board, have, with the several clerks now allowed, furnished a sufficient number of persons for the suitable discharge of all ordinary duties immediately connected with this office. So far as my knowledge extends, those duties have generally been performed with promptitude and accuracy. But some changes in the present laws respecting them, would probably prove beneficial. Though the number of clerks, and the aggregate amount of salary paid to them, are deemed sufficient, yet more substantial justice could be effected, if that amount was so appropriated as to permit the department to divide it in conformity to the usefulness of their respective services. It has happened that some of them, receiving large salaries, perform no greater or more difficult duties than those receiving less pay; and no power exists here to equalize their compensation, except by an occasional transfer of duties, not always convenient, appropriate, or useful.

A different arrangement of the Navy Board has for a few years, been a subject of consideration by Congress. The Board itself, and the head of this department, once united in recommending such a change as to apportion its ordinary business among the several members with a view to greater convenience, despatch, and responsibility. This could be accomplished without any material increase of expense; and it seems on many accounts very desirable. The reasons for the change have been already detailed in former reports, as not to need, at this time, further explanation.

There might be some useful alterations connected with the administration of the naval branch of the service in the office of the Fourth Auditor, whose duties, though nominally belonging to the Treasury Department, are intimately allied with, and very essential in most of, the operations of the navy. The great amount of property which is in charge of that department, and which is yearly increasing, seems to require that a regular account of it should be opened in that office, and kept in such manner as to insure safety and responsibility. In another particular, improvement could be made. The old balances on his books, due from default ers who were once in the naval service, are large and though few such balances have occurred lately yet the collection of all of them would doubtless be promoted, if it were devolved upon him, as the person who, from his official station, is best acquainted with the situation of the claims, and the means of payment possessed by the debtors, as who could act with the most promptitude in securing the public.

Auxiliary to the central administration of the naval service, the inspection of our ordnance was a few years since, assigned to an officer of rank residing in this neighborhood, and authorized to receive the usual extra allowances while engaged in actual duty. His employment during the past season has been much extended, having embraced the inspection of all our ordnance and ordnance stores in depot of all the naval stations. This result, it is hoped, may prove highly beneficial to our future operations. Under a similar arrangement, the custody and correction, as well as cost

tionally the purchase of charts, chronometers, compasses, and nautical instruments generally, were devolved on two intelligent officers stationed at this place. The system has worked favorably, and the small increase of expense attending it has been amply repaid in the better preservation and quality of those articles, and in the probable increase of safety to our vessels afloat, and to the lives of their gallant officers and crews. A specific estimate for the purchase and maintenance of a lithographic press, is submitted as a means of saving, under charge of these officers, still more to the public in the procurement of charts, circulars, and blank forms, of such kinds as are employed, not only in this office, but at the several yards, and on board vessels in commission. (A.) Its various conveniences and usefulness in other respects, and especially in the drawings and plans connected with the survey of our coast now in progress, are more particularly detailed in the reports annexed. (B, 1 and 2.) To prevent any nominal or real increase of appropriations in consequence of the purchase of this press, it will be seen in the general estimates that a corresponding, or, indeed, a larger reduction has been made in what is asked for the general contingent appropriations for this office and for the service, and out of which appropriations most of the above articles are now provided.

It was formerly recommended to organize at this place a Naval Medical Bureau, and a bill is now on the files of Congress reported for that purpose. As that bill was not finally disposed of, I did not deem it proper to adopt any different system for attaining in a different manner, most of the benefits expected to be accomplished by that measure. But if nothing be done during the ensuing session of Congress, regulating this subject, it is intended, under our present laws, that one of the older surgeons, in connexion with other services either at the barracks or navy-yard in this city, shall be detailed and employed in performing many of the duties contemplated for a surgeon general.

The whole expenses the past year, for all persons situated here, and belonging to the administration of this department, as well as the expenses for the care and repair of our furniture, buildings, and the grounds appurtenant, were about $48,000. This amount, I trust, will be thought to bear a favorable comparison with the same class of expenses at former periods, or in similar establishments, when the large increase and extent of duties at this place are duly considered.

Passing from the central administration of this department to that of the persons connected with its operations elsewhere, I would next submit to your consideration a few remarks on the situation of such of those persons as fill official stations, but are not technically denominated naval officers. They are a large and useful class, belonging to what may be considered our civil list; and consist of agents, storekeepers, constructors, builders, schoolmasters, secretaries to commanders, clerks of yards, engineers, live-oak superintendents, and some others attached to stations and hospitals.

In an establishment growing, like the navy, in a few years from so small a beginning to its comparatively great size at the close of the late war, and at the present moment, it was perhaps unavoidable that many measures and appointments, considered as incidental to other important objects expressly authorized, should be left to the discretion of the department. In this way, most of the above persons have been employed and paid, usually by virtue of estimates and general appropriations, without any specific provision in any act of Congress regulating the manner of their appointment, or the amount of their compensation. Indeed, a system similar in some respects has been extended to others; as the only limit which now exists to the number of every class of naval officers is the same discretion, restrained solely by estimates and appropriations, and by the confirmation required from the Senate in the case of commissioned officers. These practices have not, in my opinion, been the safest; though the custom of this department to submit to Congress, through the Executive and otherwise, full communications of its doings in relation to most of these subjects, enables the Government to exercise any control deemed necessary over any supposed abuse. My own desire has been, whenever convenient and practicable, to impose still further limits on that discretion. With this view, on a former occasion, the estimates for the contingent appropriations were made by me more specific, and settled rules of allowances and compensation, in most cases, were established or collected, and then digested and published. The revision of our whole naval regulations by the board heretofore appointed for that purpose, will, when finished and adopted, probably introduce greater system and certainty in relation to some of these matters. But it still deserves consideration, whether additional legal provision might not judiciously be made concerning the appointment and wages of some of the classes before named. All the persons on the civil list now under consideration, are believed to have conducted, during the past year, with fidelity to their duties. The only essential changes in relation to them have been the following. There has been a discontinuance of two naval constructors, whose services were no longer needed; and new and more economical arrangements have been made as to the duties of some of our agents and storekeepers abroad. The few live-oak agents, appointed for certain districts, who remained in office last December, have been dispensed with; and no salary is now paying on that account, except to one person, in temporary employ, for a few months, in the examination of an unfinished district. In some cases in which we have had warrant officers competent to perform the labors assigned to persons belonging to civil life, and hired at some of the yards, it has been deemed sound economy to order the former upon such duty, and to discontinue the services of the latter.

It has not been found necessary to select a permanent engineer, as the superintendents of the dry-docks and of the erection of the hospitals have been able for the present to peform such duties as would have been required of him. But the additional schoolmasters authorized at the last session have been employed, and, it is hoped, with increased benefit to the class of the younger officers. A general order has recently been issued with a view to improve the education of these officers, by requiring all midshipmen, whether passed or not, after suitable relaxation under leave of absence, to attend on one of the naval schools for further instruction in the studies and proficiency in the duties belonging to their profession. It is intended to employ them not only in appropriate reading, nautical observations, and recitations, but in forming a more practical acquaintance with the several materials used in the construction and equipment of vessels, and with the manner of preserving them, and of applying them in building and repairs. A due portion of their leisure will also be devoted to the peformance of such services connected with our most important naval stations where the schools are established as will be useful to the public, and at the same time advance them in a more thorough knowledge of the active duties which may soon devolve on them in higher and more responsible stations.

Excepting these variations, the civil establishments at the yards and abroad have not been materially altered during the year. It will be seen that the whole expenses of the persons connected with them have been considerably reduced, and are now annually about $130,000. This does not include the wages of ordinary laborers, as these are more properly charged, according to their employment, under other heads, which will hereafter be considered—such, for example, as repairs of vessels, improvements at yards, or buildings of hospitals.

The only material change proposed in the civil list for the ensuing year is a small addition to the very low compensation of some of the clerks at a few of the yards.

The remaining persons belonging to the naval establishment are the various officers and seamen of the navy. The general conduct of these the past year has been highly commendable. The very small number of courts-martial, it is believed, has arisen from an improving spirit of harmony in the service, and from a mild but firm and uniform system of discipline. Seldom has the health enjoyed on every station been better; and the superior condition of the medical corps, as well as of the hospitals, exercises on this subject a very salutary influence.

The number of officers in the different classes has generally been kept within the estimates. It is proposed to continue the number much as it now exists. There are now quite as many captains and surgeons as can be usefully employed, the former having been increased about one-third and the latter one-fourth during the last ten years. There are somewhat more lieutenants and midshipmen than might be deemed indispensable, the former within that time having been increased about one-half and the latter one-fourth, though in making this comparison it is proper to state, that previous to 1824 all these classes had occasionally been more numerous than they were at that period. But in relation to the two classes no reduction from the estimates of last year is contemplated. It is considered that on a peace establishment they ought to possess ample and valuable materials for any sudden or large increase of the higher classes which any rational emergency may at any time require, whilst nothing is found to prove more injurious to older officers than to be placed in a condition where no further incentives to improvement by anticipated promotion exist, and where the classes they already fill contain so large a number as to permit many years to elapse without the possibility of putting them all on active duty, unless at the expense, inconvenience, and injury of more frequent changes of the superior officers in stations and squadrons than the public interests appear to justify.

The whole number of naval officers at this time, including those under warrants as well as commissions, is about one thousand; and our whole annual expenses, of every kind, for their maintenance is about $850,000, or on an average about eight hundred and fifty dollars for each officer. These expenses have not been increased during the last ten years, except what has been caused by the addition before mentioned to the numbers of some classes of officers, and the augmentation in pay in 1827 to passed midshipmen, in 1828 to surgeons and their assistants, and in 1830 to lieutenants. In the mean time, of late years, more useless officers have been placed on half pay, and some large allowances reduced. But no further essential reduction in these particulars can, in my opinion, be effected, without injury either to individual officers, or to the naval service. Whatever has been accomplished by myself on this subject, and on the requirement of a more equal portion of laborious duty from all officers of similar rank and date, who were not invalids, has often caused me much pain; but it has been prompted by a strong sense of the equal justice due to the officers themselves, and of the manifest propriety in this department of seeing that all those under its administration perform services for the public, when practicable, in some degree proportionate to the compensation they receive.

It is hoped that I may not be deemed importunate, if I once more urge on your attention a topic far more grateful to my feelings. I have long entertained a decided opinion that the compensation to some classes of officers ought to be increased. It is certain that more equal justice would be awarded to all; that services at sea could more easily be obtained; that greater cheerfulness and alacrity in the performance of duty would be evinced, and a higher grade of qualifications in some subordinate stations could be commanded, if the whole subject of pay was revised, and the compensation graduated in a fairer proportion among different ranks in the navy, and to similar ranks in the army; and if there was provision made for a larger and marked discrimination between duty afloat and leave of absence, or waiting orders, on shore. Such a discrimination formed a prominent feature in the act of Congress passed April 21st, 1806, and which regulates pay as now established. But that discrimination, amounting to one-half of the whole pay, was virtually abolished by a rule of this department in 1819. During the continuance of the small compensation to some classes of officers, and after so long a practice under that rule, with the yearly sanction of Congress by means of the estimates and corresponding appropriations in conformity to the rule, I have not felt at liberty to alter it. Further details on this subject at this time are not deemed necessary, as they have fully and recently been laid before you in a special report from this

department on a resolution of the Senate passed at the last session of Congress.

The whole number of seamen in the navy, including all the different grades, does not vary much from five thousand; and the annual expenses of their pay, rations, and enlistment, are not far from $1,130,000, or, on an average, about $226 for each seaman. These expenses are small, and indicate great popularity in the service, when we advert not only to our facility in obtaining good seamen, but to the high rate of wages the past year in merchant vessels, and to the great cost of this class of persons in the navies of some countries, where labor is generally much lower than in the United States. These expenses have not been increased the last ten years, except by an augmentation of about one-third in the whole number of seamen, arising chiefly from an increase of our force in commission. The complement of men to each vessel might advantageously, in some respects, be lessened, and the whole expenses on account of them be thus reduced, were it not considered of vital importance in so small a navy to have all our ships afloat as perfect as possible in every particular conducive to their efficiency, and to the reputation of the Government. It is expected that a laudable pride will then be felt and encouraged by all connected with the service, on a comparison of the condition of our own ships with those of other nations, and that the moral force of our navy—as a model for a larger one when wanted—as likely to vindicate its country's rights and honor in war, and protect its commerce in peace—will always be much greater with a small number of vessels afloat, built of the best materials and in the best manner, supplied with the most approved equipments, commanded by well-educated and well-disciplined officers, and navigated by full crews of hardy and contented seamen, with the whole ready on any emergency for immediate and efficient action—than with double the number of vessels half manned, and in other respects defectively provided. Every improvement in our materials, whether timber, cordage, or cannon—in our yards, docks, or harbors—in our hospitals or asylums—will add strength to this moral force, and better prepare us for any future conflict in which the violence or injustice of other nations may involve us.

In connexion with this part of the service, it is deemed proper to present some remarks concerning the condition of the Marine Corps. The subject of its allowances, in addition to pay, was not specially noticed by Congress the last year, though, in that way, it has of late been customary to regulate them. But, under a belief that the omission probably arose from accident, I have not interfered to revise the difficulties which have so long existed under that head. It will, however, be considered my duty, the ensuing year, to investigate, and attempt to adjust them, if not otherwise provided for. The commutation of the whisky part of the ration, while the marines are at sea, has been extended to this corps; and the army regulation, entirely abolishing that part, has been applied to their rations while on shore.

The whole expenses of the corps, independent of the erection of barracks and officers' quarters, are yearly about $190,000. The expenditures for such erections, on an average for the last ten years, have been about $5,000 annually. The quarters authorized at Philadelphia have been completed; but the comfort and proper accommodation of the men require new barracks at New York. The estimates for this purpose, and for the support of this corps, are herewith submitted. (C, 1 and 2.)

The examination of the state of the pensioners upon the Navy Pension Fund, as those enjoying its privileges, have been, or are now, in the service, or were connected with those once in it, may also be deemed to come properly under the head of persons attached to the navy. Though the annual expenditures from that fund are about $33,000, yet the fund itself did not spring from the public treasury, except as derived from prizes captured by our public vessels. It was not till lately that its disbursements were classed with the navy expenditures; and now the only yearly expense this fund and its administration here impose upon the treasury, is the portion of time they occupy of the head of this department, and of one clerk. Its annual income now exceeds the annual expenses about $20,000; and, during the past year, rules have been prepared, and the benefits of this surplus extended, as originally contemplated by the act of Congress creating the fund, so as to embrace those officers and seamen who, without being wounded, have, during long and faithful services, been visited by infirmities entitling them to relief. Five persons, coming under this description, have been added to the pension list, and are allowed suitable clothing, food, and medical attendance. The number of pensioners under this and the other provisions is 298.

The condition of the privateer pensioners, placed under the exclusive administration of this department, has not essentially changed during the year. The fund for their relief, like that for navy pensioners, does not come from the public treasury, and its management is no charge upon that treasury, except in the particulars before mentioned. As the whole of this fund was derived from captures by privateers, it has been deemed expedient to exhaust it in the support of those disabled, and of proper persons connected with those, whose bravery and enterprise made the captures. It has therefore become gradually reduced to $44,667. The annual charge on it at this time is about $3,000, exceeding considerably the annual income, and thus, in due time, carrying into effect the original policy of the system. For further particulars about these two funds, reference can be had to the annexed statement. (D, 1 to 5.)

On a review of the entire personal branch of our naval establishment, it will be seen that its annual cost, not including the marine corps, is about $2,000,000; and, of that sum, about $1,964,000 is an annual charge on the public treasury. Considering the size and usefulness of the whole naval establishment, it is believed that this part of it, at the present time, bears a judicious and economical proportion to the whole, except in the particulars heretofore enumerated. Should improvements be made in those particulars, I am satisfied that the number and condensation of the persons employed, both on the civil list and in the navy, will be found to be such as to ensure the due care and preservation of the public property, to furnish officers and men sufficient for the present protection of our commerce and rights abroad, and to maintain among all classes a state of discipline and activity indispensable to efficiency in the discharge of ordinary duties, and to a supply of suitable candidates for promotion in the extraordinary exigencies of the future.

The deaths, dismissions, and resignations, in the service since my last report, may be seen in the tables annexed. (E. F. G.)

When we advert to the other subjects connected with the navy, and more especially to what may be considered as belonging to its materials, it is deemed proper to notice, first, the employment and condition of our public vessels. Those in commission have consisted of one ship of the line, four frigates, eleven sloops, and seven schooners. They have been distributed, as usual, on four foreign stations, keeping up a greater intercourse than formerly with the western coasts of Portugal and Africa, and with the adjacent islands, extending our cruises into various parts of the Indian ocean, and making the West India squadron act somewhat more as a home squadron, by requiring a portion of it to visit twice annually some of our Atlantic ports. By properly regulating these visits, much exposure in the two most dangerous months in a tropical climate is avoided, and great facilities are obtained to furnish necessary supplies, to relieve parts of their crews and exchange officers, as well as to have nearer at hand, during those visits, vessels in commission, which, if any emergency should occur, may be despatched at once on any distant or important service. Efforts have been made to relieve seasonably all our vessels which have been more than two years abroad. The Fairfield and Vincennes have been sent to the Pacific to succeed the Potomac and Falmouth; the Natchez and Ontario, to the Brazilian station in place of the Lexington and Warren; the Experiment to the West Indies in the place of the Shark; and the Shark and Delaware to the Mediterranean in the place of the Concord, Boston, John Adams, and Brandywine. In making these changes so early as to prevent the expiration abroad of the service of our seamen, much discontent has been avoided, though this system has necessarily subjected the Department to some additional expense, by having occasionally, for short periods, double sets of vessels afloat attached to the same station. But it has enabled us to perform our engagements faithfully with their crews, and to keep up a more regular and constant force on each station for protection. At the same time, caution has been taken to guard against an increase of our whole expenditures for the current year beyond the appropriations connected with this subject.

All those squadrons have been actively and efficiently employed; and it gives me great satisfaction to state, that our commerce in all quarters of the globe was probably never known to be more free from menaces, danger, or actual violence.

The estimates for the ensuing year are for the same amount of force as was authorized the past year, consisting of about 530 guns, and distributed in such a proportion among vessels of every class belonging to our service, as to combine the greatest efficiency for naval purposes during peace, with the soundest economy. Few will deem that force either too large or extravagant, when it is considered that our foreign commerce exposed on the ocean, exceeds one hundred millions of dollars in imports, and almost an equal amount of exports, with vessels exposed in their transportation of over half a million of tonnage, and probably twenty millions in value; and when it is remembered how much the security, not only of those vessels and their cargoes, but of their numerous crews, and of other classes of our citizens resident in some countries abroad, depends upon our navy being actively and widely distributed. On this point it may be well to reflect further, how safely that navy enables us, not only to send to new and the most distant markets, and thus to give increased value to the surplus proceeds of our agriculture, manufactories and fisheries, and to obtain in return whatever may conduce to comfort, improvement, or wealth, but what protection and enhanced worth it confers on most of our immense coasting trade; how much our national reputation abroad is everywhere known and appreciated by it; the respect it inspires, the security it yields, and the weight it affords in all our claims of justice, and negotiations with semi-barbarous nations; and how justly it may be apprehended that new perils will, ere long, await a portion of our trade, and the tranquillity of a part of our maritime frontier, from the operations of a new course of legislation by some foreign powers concerning an unfortunate portion of their population; and against which perils, as well as against the ordinary aggressions and piracies in peace, and much of the depredations which may threaten us in war, the navy, from the insular situation of the country, as to the most of the world, must always be regarded as our great safeguard.

The facilities for the examination and repair of our vessels have been much increased the past year by the completion, in most respects, of the two dry-docks; and the expenses in refitting the classes of larger vessels will thereby become sensibly reduced.

The present policy of this department is [illegible] launch no more vessels of the same size with those in ordinary, until the latter are worn out. But [illegible] is proposed to build, from time to time, and pr[illegible] tect on the stocks till wanted, such new vessels [illegible] Congress may authorize to be constructed; be[illegible] cause, in that condition, their timber will improve rather than decay, and the expense of taking care of them will be trifling compared with that of vessels in ordinary. This course has been adopted the past year with the Macedonian, now building. It is recommended, as sound policy, that autho[illegible] should be given to procure the frame for ano[illegible] sloop, to be called the Levant, after the conso[illegible] gallantly captured with the Cyane; and the fr[illegible] for another frigate, to be called the Paul Jones, [illegible] grateful memory of one of the earliest, brav[illegible] and most distinguished commanders in our [illegible] service during the Revolution. The estimates [illegible] the purchase of these are submitted. Fr[illegible] could not be bought for vessels of these [illegible] under any existing laws; and the timber, if p[illegible] cured and seasoned, whether soon set up or [illegible]

would become more valuable, being sheltered under either our present excellent sheds or ship-houses, and live oak probably becoming scarcer and dearer as our southern frontier is cleared for cultivation.

The vessels in ordinary and on the stocks, as well as the frames for others in depôt, have all been examined, and found to be in a good state of preservation, except a few of those in ordinary. Some of them are defective by their long continuance afloat before being covered, some by their great age, and some by the original imperfection of their timber. Those unworthy of being refitted are used at times for receiving-ships; and the rest, as wanted, are placed in a proper state to go into commission for the relief of other vessels returning from long cruises, and needing extensive repairs. As vessels afloat grow older, their repairs must of necessity become more expensive. The cost of all repairs of all our vessels the past year has been about $580,000. During the last ten years, the repairs have been, on an average, about $500,000 annually.

A table, showing the vessels in commission, with their commanders and stations, is submitted. (I.) The names and condition of those in ordinary and on the stocks, may be seen in the documents annexed, (K, 1 and 2.) Proceeding from the vessels to the materials used in their construction and equipment, not much has occurred the past year deserving notice. Some additions of valuable and durable articles have been made to our various stores on hand at the time of my last annual report. All these stores, and especially the timber in the docks and under sheds, are in good condition; and means have been taken to ascertain and supply any deficiency, in any article not perishable, which may be wanted for the building and perfect equipment of every vessel on the stocks, and every frame in depôt. As more timber may be needed, or thought proper to be purchased in advance, our means for the supply of live oak, it being the most important species, have been fully investigated and discussed in a special report to Congress from this department during the last session. Referring to that for detailed information on this point, I would only add, that subsequent examinations in some of the then unfinished districts, have fully confirmed the impressions entertained concerning the great quantity of live oak timber on portions of the public lands in those districts. In respect to the other kinds of timber needed in ship-building, the Government has made little public provision; and doubts exist whether it will be necessary to make any further public provision for its growth or preservation while the prices continue so moderate, and the resources of the country in such timber are likely, for many years, to remain so very abundant.

The erection of two new magazines, where none before existed, is proposed the next season; and an estimate for that purpose is submitted. (L.) Connected with this, a thorough inspection has been made not only of our present ordnance stores, but, as previously mentioned, of all our arms on hand, with a view to the sale of such as are defective or unsuitable, and to the procurement of what may be found necessary to produce uniformity, and the greatest power in our future armaments. The usual sum of about $10,000 has been expended for the purchase of such ordnance and ordnance stores as the current wants of the service required. The buying and manufacture of iron tanks for all our vessels in commission are in rapid progress under the late appropriation for that purpose; and, should Congress sanction the making of our own cordage, as heretofore asked, and as now again proposed in the general estimates, the equipment of our vessels would soon become, throughout, all which the friends of the service could desire, for health, safety, efficiency, and national reputation.

After much deliberation, the department has become convinced that the building or purchase of two store-ships for the Pacific station, to be used in the transportation and the preservation there of supplies of all kinds, would promote sound economy, and increase the comforts of our seamen. An estimate for the procurement of one the ensuing year, is submitted. (M.) We are obliged to pay freight for these supplies, heavy duties either on their being landed or re-shipped, and large rent for store-houses. The duties are a burden from which we are almost entirely exonerated under similar circumstances in other quarters of the world. The proposed measure would relieve us from them, as well as the other charges; and the store-ships, by going out and returning separately and alternately, would afford great facilities to exchange or bring home invalid officers and seamen, without incurring the expense of their passages in merchant vessels from so distant a station.

The construction of two or three small steam-batteries, for reasons heretofore recommended, is still deemed highly important to our future interests; and too long delay in making further experiments, and in acquiring further science on this subject, in our naval service, may, on the sudden occurrence of hostilities, place us in a position not a little mortifying to our pride, and hazardous to our welfare.

The different navy yards are essential portions of our naval establishment, connected with its materials. The condition of most of them has been improved the past year either by new buildings for officers' quarters, or new store-houses and timber-sheds, or new wharves and other conveniences.

The two dry-docks at the yards near Norfolk and Boston having been successfully completed in all essential particulars, the details on that subject will be found in the report annexed, (N, 1, 2, and 3.) This report shows the whole expenditures the last year, not only on that subject, but on all others, under the head of gradual improvement. From the great advantages already realized in the ease and rapidity of repairs in vessels at the yards where these dry-docks are situated, I am satisfied that others would be found very beneficial. Surveys were formerly had for two more—one at New York and one at Portsmouth; and a report in favor of these two was once made and approved in the House of Representatives. Much can be urged in favor of the former place, on account of its central position, and great resources for repairs, stores, seamen, and workmen; and of the latter place, on account of the low price of labor, small cost of constructing a dock, and the easy access to it by vessels of all classes at all seasons of the year. But whether one or both, or neither, shall be selected at this time, is submitted to the proper authorities, on a review of the whole subject. It must be obvious that the relative importance of different stations must undergo changes, as the capacities of different quarters of the country become more fully developed; and that some places, now employed as naval depots, can be of very little use on the occurrence of war; while the positions of others, when that event may happen, will greatly increase their usefulness.

Among the new places which, on such an occasion, if not earlier, the interest of the country may require the Government to occupy for naval purposes, will undoubtedly be, Newport harbor on the north; and one or more positions on the long range of coast to the south, between Norfolk and Pensacola. Whether the last selection should be made near Charleston or Savannah, at Key West or the Dry Tortugas—each of which possesses advantages for such purposes—can be better decided when the time and circumstances occur rendering immediate action necessary.

The continuance of Pensacola as a naval station seems to me judicious. This opinion arises not only from its convenient position as to the whole Gulf of Mexico, but its proximity to the mouths of the Mississippi and Mobile rivers, whose great and growing commerce is so amply entitled to the best protection. In the depth and size of its bay, in the excellent defences of its mouth, in its healthy situation, in its easy access to all our vessels, except the two highest classes, Pensacola has no prominent rival in that neighborhood. The correspondence and documents annexed (O, 1 and 2) are submitted to aid yourself and Congress to judge of the practicability and propriety of deepening the entrance to the bay, so as to admit vessels of the largest class. This, it is supposed, can be effected at a small expense, compared with the importance of such a measure to the full operations of our navy on that coast, and to the greater security and strength of our southern maritime defences.

The exchange of lands at the yard near New York, authorized at the last session of Congress, has been carried into effect. The controverted claim of the heirs of Mr. Harris to a part of the navy-yard near Boston, has once been laid before Congress; and a new action having been instituted by them against the commander of that station, as will be seen by the letter annexed, such course will be pursued in its defence as Congress may be pleased to direct. (P.)

Some new pretensions have been set up to different parcels of land included in our possession and purchases at Norfolk; but their justice cannot be recognised on the facts known to the department, and those making them have been informed that no steps can be taken for their adjustment, unless the parties previously obtain the sanction of Congress, or a judgment in their favor by the courts of law.

The expenditures on all the yards the last year, exclusive of the dry docks, but including houses, sheds, stores, wharves, enclosures, workshops, marine barracks, and incidental labor, have been about $360,000. The expenditures on the dry docks are chargeable to a distinct appropriation for gradual improvement, and were about $180,000. The other expenditures under the last head were about $150,000. (N, 1) The estimates for the usual objects at the yards the ensuing year are about the average amount for the last two years. Besides those objects, they include an extra sum towards the erection of ropewalks, in conformity with the plan adopted by Congress in 1827; and yet the whole amount requested towards these and all other improvements, at all the yards, is only $354,000.

Immediately connected with the subject of our yards, is that of our naval hospitals and the naval asylum. Under the appropriations lately made by Congress, new hospitals have been commenced near Pensacola, New York, and Boston, on retired and healthy sites, combining great convenience and beauty. The plans of these have been formed on a scale suited only to the present wants of the service, but capable of easy and appropriate enlargement hereafter, whenever our necessities may require it. An additional sum will be needed to finish them in the manner proposed, and to make further progress in the hospital before built at Norfolk. (Q.)

Such expenditures have been made the past year on the latter, from the general hospital fund, as could well be spared, and as the comforts of its inmates seemed most urgently to demand. This is much larger than our present necessities require, and therefore it is not proposed to finish the whole interior of it. But the exterior of this hospital is now chiefly completed, and it has become one of the most beautiful and useful public buildings belonging to the Government. The naval asylum at Philadelphia has been finished, and partly furnished; but it is much regretted that the department has not been able to obtain a cession of jurisdiction over it, without reservations that render the cession wholly nugatory. Besides retaining the usual power in the State to execute criminal and civil process, the reservations subject it to, and it is actually burdened by, the assessment of large taxes which are paid from the hard earnings of our seamen, and an unlimited right is retained to cut up the property by new streets. Further efforts are now making by the department to obtain relief from these onerous taxes and liabilities, so disadvantageous, if not fatal, to the success of this public and charitable institution. Should these efforts fail, all the correspondence and documents in the case will be submitted, in order that such legislation may be had as the whole circumstances connected with the subject shall be thought to require. The general condition of the hospital fund may be seen in the statement before referred to. (D, 6.)

The ordinary purchases of medicines and surgical instruments for use in hospitals and yards, and in vessels afloat, are included under a specific appropriation, and are about $35,000 yearly. The pay and subsistence of the surgeons and assistant surgeons attached to the hospitals are provided for under the general appropriation for navy officers. The other annual expenses of our hospital establishment, independent of buildings, furniture, and repairs, are about $1000. These are defrayed wholly from assessments on the seamen and officers. From the same quarter come all other re-

sources for the establishment, with the exception of such appropriations as Congress have made from time to time, to aid in erecting and furnishing buildings. These last appropriations have been made but seldom, and have, within ten years, amounted to a sum which would be on an average, about $22,150 annually; and for the same purposes, during that period, the fund has furnished, from its annual increase and former accumulations, about $45,000 annually. Should Congress grant what is now asked, more will probably not be wanted for many years. In immediate connexion with the yards, hospitals, and other real estate belonging to our naval establishment, is the live oak plantation. Being situated only seven miles from our most southern yard, it has the past year been placed under the same general superintendence. The purchase of the land, and the cutting and removal of the underwood and common timber from about 200 acres of the plantation, had been accomplished before the charge of this department was placed in my hands. It seemed to me judicious in that state of things to attempt to preserve any benefits already attained, or fairly anticipated, by continuing to destroy a few years longer the annual growth of other wood injurious to the young live oak trees, to trim and train the thriftiest new ones appearing, and to employ merely the leisure of the hands so engaged in extending this process to more of the land. From 200 acres of land, and 22,000 live oak trees to which, in 1829, the above system had been applied, it has, since 1831, been so continued and extended, that the nursery has become enlarged to 225 acres, and includes over 60,000 trees. The expense attending this has been about $1,200 a year; but should any considerable portion of the trees ever reach maturity, and attain a size suitable for ship building, the Government will be amply repaid. As the trees grow larger, the annual expense concerning the same number will rapidly diminish. Doubts exist whether some of them, from the poverty of the soil, and their apparently dwarfish character, will ever attain a valuable size. But it is now too early for forming a decisive opinion on the extent to which the operation of these causes may affect the whole plantation, and, under existing circumstances, sound policy appears to require that the experiment, having gone so far, should be allowed a further and full trial. The nearness of the plantation to the Pensacola yard, and to water transportation, enhances much the value of any timber it may produce. Lately, I have not only placed this land under the superintendence of the commander of that yard, but required his particular and constant vigilance over the live oak reservations in all that region of country. The whole agencies heretofore connected with our live oak have, as before suggested, been discontinued; all the districts, except small portions of two, having been explored as fully as is deemed useful till the surveys of the land into townships and sections shall be completed. Fast as they may be completed, arrangements have been made for additional reservations of public land on which live oak has been ascertained to abound, and the prospect of a sufficient supply of that kind of timber in future is flattering, if that on private lands, as these are wanted to be cleared for cultivation, be from time to time purchased at moderate prices, and placed in depot for the frames of vessels specially authorized or collected under the head of gradual improvement. On this whole subject I have so recently, at such length, submitted to Congress the views of this department, that further observations here are not deemed necessary. [See report on live oak to the House of Representatives December 14, 1832.]

Some miscellaneous matters connected with the navy, deserve a brief notice. The usual attention has been bestowed on the suppression of the slave trade. The colony of Liberia has been visited by the schooner Porpoise while in pursuit of a piratical vessel, and which vessel, it is gratifying to add, is supposed to have been since captured by a British brig, and her criminal career terminated near the Island of St. Thomas, on the coast of Africa. One-half of the usual appropriation on the subject of the slave trade will probably be sufficient for the ensuing year, as may be seen by the state of the account herewith submitted.

The renewal of an appropriation for the relief of Alexander Claxton, made in May, 1830, has become necessary, in consequence of its having been transferred to the surplus fund before all the persons entitled to it were able to procure the necessary vouchers.

The proceedings of the board appointed, under a resolution of Congress, to revise the naval regulations, will be soon submitted in a separate report.

The survey of our seacoast having been placed in charge of the Treasury Department, it is not in my power, officially, to state its progress; but officers have been detailed, and all available facilities provided, whenever the wishes of those superintending the subject have been communicated.

Some expenses, under the contingent appropriation for enumerated objects, have not been included under any of the amounts already mentioned, but they belong to courts martial, to pilotage of vessels, to transportation of materials, to the purchase of charts and books, and various other small items, forming an aggregate of about $80,000.

On a review of the whole affairs of this department, it appears that its expenditures on all naval subjects, the past year, have been somewhat less than four millions of dollars. It will be seen how this result compares with former periods, by adverting to the fact that, during the last twenty years, these expenditures, except during five years of that time, have never fallen so low as three millions; and, except during six years of that time, have never exceeded four millions.

The whole estimates made the past year, for the general wants of what is technically considered the navy, were only $3.176,766. Those for the year previous were $3,227,383. Those for the present year are $3,292,224. (S, 1 to 8.) But it is to be remembered, that under the head of naval expenditures, besides what is paid from the amount voted on the annual naval estimates, it is customary to class what is paid from half a million appropriated for a term of years to gradual improvement, almost $200,000 for the marine corps; the payments from the navy pension, hospital, and privateer pension funds, and several miscellaneous sums voted by Congress on motions, resolutions and petitions; and part of which sums, though charged under this head, have little or no concern with our naval establishment. On the contrary, some of the expenses connected with the administration of the department, at this place, are included in the general appropriation bills for the support of Government, and are not usually classed under the head of naval expenditures.

It is a high gratification to be able to state that, since 1827, nearly half a million a year has been disbursed for gradual improvement; that within ten years a larger number than formerly of seamen and officers, with increased pay for four classes of the latter, have been maintained; very great and valuable improvements, besides the dry-docks, have been begun and accomplished at many of the yards, and our force in commission considerably augmented; and yet that all our ordinary naval expenditures are, and probably can be, kept within four millions of dollars annually.

The smaller appropriations originally made for the navy served to maintain the few officers and seamen then employed, and supplied us with several fine vessels, four of which are still in existance. The subsequent appropriations on a more extended scale, besides supporting the current expenses of our force in its infancy, furnished the purchase money for most of our present yards, and defrayed the expenses of our brilliant hostilities with France, and afterwards with Tripoli; till a few years of comparative inactivity having ensued, the commencement and progress of the last war with England led to a great addition to the naval establishment, and to expenditures much larger than at present. The liberal appropriations that were continued for some years after that war aided in laying a good foundation for the gradual increase of the navy, and helped to build, not only many of the vessels now in commission and ordinary, but most of those upon the stocks. The appropriations for some years past have been similar in amount, and have enabled the department to enlarge its policy and widen the sphere of its operations. Besides building some additional vessels, and defraying all the current expenses of an increased force, both personal and material, it has been able to erect hospitals, to construct dry-docks, to improve greatly the old yards, to add and maintain a new one on our southern frontier, and to collect in depôt a large amount of valuable stores as a part of the due preparation in peace for the various contingencies of war. With a careful regard to system and economy, and with strict accountability in agents and officers, this policy can long be pursued and extended without making the ordinary annual demands for this branch of the service often exceed four millions; and if, without essential changes by Congress, increasing our present expenses, and without any unforeseen and extraordinary wants, our fiscal operations can usually be confined within that amount yearly, it is confidently hoped the naval establishment will not be considered wasteful or burdensome beyond its benefits to the country.

In disbursing between three and four millions the past year, it is not known that a single instance of any loss has occurred.

The balances on hand, unexpended, are about $1,400,000; but most of them will probably be wanted to close the different accounts, on all the different subjects, when finally adjusted.

Connected with our financial concerns, is one other circumstance of urgent importance. The period of time at which the annual appropriations for this branch of the service are usually made, is a source of great inconvenience and injury.

The estimates and appropriations are known generally not to extend beyond the current year. Consequently, it happens that after the 1st of January, there is nothing on hand under some heads to meet the daily demands of the service, amounting, on an average, to $10,000 per day, unless a new appropriation has been made, or there happen to be some balances of the former year not called for. Under some heads, such balances always exist, because some disbursements, by means of absence, distance, and other causes, are not completed within the year. But they seldom exist under other important heads; and ought not to, if the accounts are seasonably settled, and the estimates were accurate, and the appropriations, as is usual, conform to the estimates. The power now vested in the President to transfer a balance from one appropriation to another, is confined to certain classes of claims small in amount; and hence, as to all others, no transfer can legally be made, and if no balance remain at the end of the year, and the new naval appropriation bills have not passed, payment is entirely stopped, or the whole operations of this department dependant on them are suspended. Considering how large a part of these operations, and of our expenditures, necessarily takes place in distant quarters of the world, it will be seen that the embarrassment in this branch of the service must often be peculiar and aggravated. In the case of bills of exchange drawn abroad chargeable to appropriations already exhausted, the public faith, under the above circumstances, is sometimes in danger of being violated; our credit in foreign countries becomes injured; and the treasury, as actually happened during the last winter, is exposed to large losses if the holders choose to resort to protests and claims for the mercantile rate of damages.

Under the present system of passing so late the naval appropriation bills, it happens that, unless money voted under one head is, without authority, as was once the practice, applied under other heads, this unfortunate condition continues every short session of Congress about two months, and every long session about four months. It can easily be remedied in two methods: One of them is to make, previous to the 1st of January, new appropriations for a quarter or half of the year towards all permanent objects. By limiting them to such a time, and to such objects, and by taking the estimates of the former year as a guide, no inconvenience will interpose, and no error can occur which may not be readily corrected when the residue of the appropriations for the whole year is voted at a later period in the session. Another mode is, to authorize the President to make necessary transfers from one head to another, in all cases where the new naval appropriation bills do not pass by the commencement of the year, and to require from him a report to Congress of the amount and causes of such transfers. If the authority be thus restricted, it is difficult to discover any danger likely to result from

its exercise; and it is believed that the surplus of balances on hand under some of the appropriations would usually prove sufficient to supply the wants under others. The detail and earnestness with which legislation on this subject is now urged, must find their excuse in my strong convictions that no measure whatever, requiring like this no increased expenditures, could be more conducive to the reputation and efficient operations of our naval establishment.

Thus, sir, under an examination of its central administration, of its personal, or civil and navy list, of its materials, with the appurtenants thereto, and of its miscellaneous concerns, I have submitted a review of all its transactions and expenditures, during the past year, that possess any great degree of importance. This has been accompanied by suggestions for such improvements as observation and reflection have convinced me might be useful; and should they meet with the approbation of yourself and Congress, I look forward with confidence to a long continuance of prosperity in the affairs connected with this department.

With great respect,
Yours, &c.,
LEVI WOODBURY.

REPORT OF THE POSTMASTER GENERAL.

General Post Office Department,
November 30, 1833.

To the President of the United States:

Sir: When, in 1829, the functions of this department devolved upon me, the annual transportation of the mail amounted to 13,700,000 miles. The contracts then in existence, with the other expenses of the department, had, within the year ending the 30th of June, 1829, diminished its surplus revenue $101,256 03, and those contracts were still in force from one to four years in prospect.

The surplus available revenue had been reduced to the nominal amount of........	$230,849 07
But it has subsequently been ascertained that there had been expenses incurred for transportation performed prior to the 1st of July, 1829, which were not embraced in that account, to the amount of......................	64,248 76
which reduced the real surplus to....	$166,600 31

The annual transportation of the mail was, on the 1st of July, 1833, 26,854,485 miles.

The annual amount of the transportation of the mail in stages and steamboats, on the 1st of July, 1829, was 6,507,818 miles.

The annual amount of the transportation of the mail in stages and steamboats, on the 1st of July, 1833, was 18,322,576 miles.

The expense of transporting the mail for the year ending the 30th of June, in 1829, was $1,153,646 21.

The expense of transporting the mail for the year ending 30th of June, 1833, was $1,894,688 08.

The gross amount of postages, constituting the revenues of the department, was, for the year ending 30th of June, 1829, $1,707,418 42.

The gross amount of postages for the year ending 30th of June, 1833, was $2,616,538 27.

The incidental expenses of the department for the year ending 30th of June, 1829, amounted to $69,249 08.

The incidental expenses of the department for the year ending 30th of June, 1833, amounted to $87,701 61.

The number of post offices in the United States on the 1st of July, 1829, was 8,004.

On the 1st of July, 1832, the number of post offices in the United States was 10,127.

The increase of the annual transportation of the mail within the four years ending the 30th June, 1833, is 13,154,485 miles, nearly equal to the whole amount of transportation in 1829.

The increase of the annual amount of postages within the same period is $909,119 85, and the whole amount is more than the double of what it was in 1825.

The average expense of transporting the mail in 1829 was eight cents and four-tenths of a cent per mile.

The average expense of transporting the mail in 1833 is seven cents and fifty-seven hundredths of a cent per mile; making a difference in the rate per mile of eighty-three hundredths of a cent, equal, for the whole service, to $222,692 22 per year less, in proportion to the service performed, than the expense of transportation in 1829, besides a great increase in expedition between the principal commercial cities, and a much greater proportion of the whole performed in stages.

After carrying into effect the law of the last Congress establishing new mail routes, the present length of railroads in the United States amounts to 119,916 miles, viz:

	Miles.
In Maine	3,824
New Hampshire	2,460
Vermont	2,531
Massachusetts	4,845
Rhode Island	491
Connecticut	2,701
New York	13,256
New Jersey	1,961
Pennsylvania	11,010
Delaware	494
Maryland	2,102
Virginia	10,588
North Carolina	6,850
South Carolina	4,516
Georgia	5,274
Florida	1,131
Alabama	4,433
Mississippi	2,462
Louisiana	1,462
Arkansas	2,309
Tennessee	6,761
Kentucky	5,993
Ohio	8,977
Michigan	1,495
Indiana	5,361
Illinois	4,459
Missouri	2,170
Total	119,916

Over these roads, the annual transportation of the mail on the first of July last, was,

	In stages.	In steamboats.	On horseback and in sulkeys.	Total.
	Miles.	Miles.	Miles.	Miles.
In Maine	708,184	3,398	267,010	978,592
N. Hampshire	622,238	-	111,854	734,092
Vermont	634,666	-	106,260	740,926
Massachusetts	1,563,640	23,712	150,037	1,737,389
Rhode Island	117,988	-	16,692	134,680
Connecticut	598,987	17,376	175,608	791,971
New York	3,053,558	155,339	854,937	4,063,834
New Jersey	548,330	-	100,840	649,170
Pennsylvania	2,414,801	-	762,873	3,177,674
Delaware	92,674	-	17,264	109,938
Maryland	585,792	58,380	161,588	805,760
Virginia	1,277,848	88,500	778,906	2,145,232
North Carolina	829,415	15,288	427,076	1,271,779
South Carolina	658,524	-	275,548	934,072
Georgia	368,012	-	498,626	866,638
Florida	47,112	41,860	86,612	175,384
Alabama	429,978	96,360	353,652	879,990
Mississippi	78,002	-	282,756	360,758
Louisiana	48,516	15,704	156,676	220,896
Arkansas	-	-	231,556	231,556
Tennessee	513,453	-	502,320	1,015,773
Kentucky	628,072	45,000	540,240	1,213,312
Ohio	1,216,801	47,150	618,190	1,882,141
Michigan	144,932	-	89,512	234,464
Indiana	196,268	21,000	487,814	705,082
Illinois	236,522	-	293,278	529,800
Missouri	79,508	-	184,184	263,692
Total	17,693,839	628,737	8,531,909	26,854,485

The increase of transportation from the 1st July, 1832, to the 1st July, 1823, has been,

In Stages	1,471,096	miles.
In steamboats	129,436	"
On horseback and in sulkeys	1,628,932	"
Making together	3,229,464	"

The method in which the accounts of the expenses of transporting the mail haye always been kept in this department, has led to a misapprehension of the means of extending improvements in mail facilities. It appears, from the earliest records of the department, to have been a rule not to enter to the credit of a contractor, nor to charge to the account of transportation, the expense of carrying the mail on his route, till after he had signed his contract and bond, and returned them to the department with proper security, though the service may have been regularly performed, and, in many instances, the moneys actually paid. It has sometimes happened that contracts of the greatest magnitude have, from various causes, remained for more than a year unreturned. In such cases, though the expenses have been incurred, they do not appear in the transportation account; and though the moneys may have been paid to the contractors, they stand on the books as balances to that amount due from them to the department, constituting a part of its surplus fund; when, in fact, they constitute a part of the actual expense incurred for the transportation of the mail. The consequence has been, that the expenses for transporting the mail within any given period of time, as shown in the accounts, and reported annually through the Executive, have been always calculated to exhibit an amount considerably less than what has actually been incurred. This is an imperfection not of recent origin, but one which appears to have been co-existent with the department. When the number of contracts was few, and the surplus revenue bore a large ratio to its whole annual amount, the effect was unimportant; but in the increased number of mail routes, and the diminution of its surplus revenue, it was calculated to produce serious inconvenience. From the statements growing out of this system, thus illusory in their results, together with the great expense of carrying into effect the law of the last Congress establishing new mail routes, and a disposition to gratify the wishes of the public in the improvement of mail facilities, I was led to carry those improvements to an extent which it was found the resources of the department would not well sustain. When the inconvenience was felt, the cause was carefully investigated, and the following result was disclosed. Prompt directions were given for the correction of the error in future. It is not possible to determine, to an exact certainty, the whole expense incurred for transportation within any recent period; because it will often happen that improvements will become necessary, even for the fulfilment of existing laws, the expenses of which, for want of proper evidence, must be reserved for subsequent adjustment, and so come into the account for a later period than that in which the services were performed. But these variations are of an inconsiderable amount compared with the differences resulting from the system heretofore observed.

On the 30th of June 1829, which was the close of the first quarter in which I had assumed the functions of the department, the expenses which had been incurred for transporting the mail were $64,248 76 more than the amount stated in my report to that day.

On the 1st day of July, 1832, the day to which my last report reaches, there was stated to be a surplus of available funds, after defraying all the expenses of the department up to that day, of $202,811 40

It is, however, now ascertained, that the expenses incurred for transportation which had actually been performed prior to the 1st July, 1832, beyond the amount stated in that report, were..............	205,656 07
So that, instead of a surplus on that day, the department was actually indebted on the 1st day of July, 1832, beyond the whole amount of its available funds, admitting that no losses of postages should be sustained......................	2,844 67
The gross amount of postages for the year ending the 30th June, 1832, was......................	2,258,570 17
The gross amount of postages for the year ending the 30th of June, 1833, was......................	2,616,538 27
Making an increase for the year over the former year of..............	$357,968 10

The net proceeds of postages, after deducting commissions to postmasters and the contingent ex-

penses of their offices, for the year ending 30th
June, 1832, was.............$1,543,098 49
For the year ending June 30, 1833,
it was.........................1,790,254 65

Making an increase of net proceeds
for the year, of.................$247,156 16

The expenses of the department, incurred for
the year ending June 30, 1833, were as follows,
viz:
Compensation to postmasters, including the contingent expenses of
their offices—
3d quarter, 1832.... $202,431 26
4th quarter, 1832.... 200,151 51
1st quarter, 1833.... 214,935 50
2d quarter, 1833.... 208,765 35
                         $826,283 62
Transportation of the mail—
3d quarter, 1832.... $435,892 95
4th quarter, 1832.... 441,183 01
1st quarter, 1833.... 499,185 96
2d quarter, 1833.... 518,496 16
                         1,894,688 08
Incidental expenses for the year.... 87,701 61

Making together.............2,808,673 31
The gross amount of postages for the
same period was—
3d quarter, 1832... $642,689 22
4th quarter, 1832.... 630,464 47
1st quarter, 1833.... 673,957 67
2d quarter, 1833.... 669,426 91
                          2,616,538 27

Leaving a deficit of........... 192,135 04
Add to this sum paid into the Treasury by irregular deposites, having
been placed by the receiving officer
to the credit of that department instead of this.................... 228 69
The balance due by the department
on the 1st July, 1832, as above
stated........................ 2,844 67
And the department was indebted on
the 1st July, 1833, beyond the
amount of available balances due
to it, in the sum of.............. 195,908 40

The annual expense of transporting
the mail under existing contracts,
with all their improvements, is.... 2,033,289 42
The incidental expenses of the department, estimated at......... 90,000 00

Making the aggregate expense for a
year........................2,123,289 42
The net proceeds of postages for the
year ending the 30th June, 1833,
amounted to......$1,790,254 65
The net increase for that
year over the prece-
ding year, and which
may be safely estima-
ted as continuing, was 247,156 16

Making the net revenue for the current year...............2,037,410 81

Leaving a deficit of........... 85,878 61

The former method of keeping the accounts of
the expenses of transportation would have left out
of this report expenses for transportation, as if
they had not been incurred, because not entered
under their proper dates, the sum of $91,658 82,
viz:
For services performed prior to July 1,
1832.......................$29,294 44
For services performed during 3d quarter, 1832.................... 9,480 50
  "   4th quarter, 1832...... 9,932 91
  "   1st quarter, 1833...... 23,872 70
  "   2d quarter, 1833...... 27,138 27

Making, together...............$91,658 82

This, had the imperfection of that system remained unobserved, would have made the department appear to be less indebted, by that amount,
than what it is in reality.

This discovery of the excess of expenditures
beyond its revenues at once showed the necessity
of retrenchment. The only practicable means of
doing this was the withdrawal of some of the improvements which had been made, and on such
routes as would be least injurious to the public, and
least prejudicial to the revenues of the department.
This has been done with great care and attention
to these two points.
The reductions have been directed on the transportation to take effect from the 1st of January
next, to the annual amount of........$202,370
The contracts have been renewed for the
southwestern section, comprising the
States of Louisiana, Mississippi, Alabama, Tennessee, Missouri, Illinois,
and Indiana, and the Territory of Arkansas, with a greater amount of improvements than curtails, at an annual
saving of........................... 71,893

Making, together, an annual retrenchment in the expenses of the department
of.................................$274,263

In making these retrenchments many of the
principal contractors who were to be affected by
them, seeing the necessity which induced the measure, have readily declared their cordial acquiescence in it, and, with a patriotic spirit becoming
their character, have shown a determination to sustain the department, as a paramount object, at any
sacrifices which it may require on their part.
After the reduction shall take effect, the annual
transportation of the mail will still be 25,527,957
miles, viz:

	In stages.	In steam-boats.	Horseback & sulkeys.	Total.
In Maine....	826,400	3,386	971,374	910,004
N. Hampshire.	623,408	–	111,554	734,962
Vermont......	636,192	–	104,076	740,198
Massachusetts	1,553,348	33,712	145,230	1,732,189
Rhode Island..	117,968	–	16,692	134,660
Connecticut..	567,720	17,276	175,596	760,792
New York....	3,989,520	125,339	864,649	4,892,908
New Jersey...	517,654	–	100,540	618,208
Pennsylvania.	3,080,089	–	764,323	3,845,350
Delaware....	104,910	–	17,064	191,374
Maryland....	570,726	58,386	161,585	790,694
Virginia.....	1,544,246	46,360	776,026	1,870,032
North Carolina	733,483	15,268	413,660	1,189,271
South Carolina	609,364	–	973,548	577,804
Georgia.....	978,994	–	496,898	776,850
Florida.....	47,118	41,600	86,619	175,384
Alabama.....	493,378	26,380	253,632	879,360
Mississippi..	78,000	–	990,756	350,756
Louisiana....	45,516	15,704	156,676	998,196
Arkansas....	–	–	231,556	231,556
Tennessee....	513,459	–	506,320	1,813,773
Kentucky....	595,869	45,800	598,804	1,158,816
Ohio.......	1,003,369	37,150	617,358	1,669,877
Michigan....	119,086	–	97,414	309,504
Indiana.....	190,260	21,600	467,814	705,089
Illinois......	536,569	–	963,978	595,900
Missouri.....	79,506	–	184,184	983,689
Total.....	16,400,851	587,137	8,540,189	25,527,957

Thus, it will appear that but a part of the
improvements will be withdrawn, to enable the
department still to rely exclusively on its own resources, as the annual transportation will still be,
after the 1st January next, 1,902,936 miles more
than it was on the 1st July, 1832.
I have the honor to be, very respectfully, your
obedient servant,   W. T. BARRY.

From the American Sentinel.
THE LAND BILL.
The President's veto on this bill (which
we published in the Sentinel of yesterday)
will satisfy every disinterested mind in the
community. The sketch given of the
manner whereby the United States were
first put in possession of these lands is interesting and judicious, and demonstrates
that they had originally been ceded specifically to pay the debt created by the revolutionary war, and as a source of revenue—evidently therefore intended to constitute an integral part of the national
income. Can the income thus devoted to
a special purpose be alienated in good

faith? Is not it intended as a part of the
revenue of the United States in general,
and not for the advantage of any State in
particular? If the revenue were thus
despoiled or defalcated by applying the
resources arising from these public lands
to any other purpose than that of supporting the General Government of the Union,
would not the deficit thence arising compel an impost of another kind for a supply
or succedaneum? How, then, could it be
for the advantage of any State or States—
not desiring a fraudulent preference—to
seek to despoil the general revenue in one
branch, which must be compensated by
some other means? And is not the revenue arising from public lands less oppressive in its being levied, than almost
any other accessible source of revenue?
But what right has any State to expect of
demand a bonus or dividend of the net
proceeds of the public lands revenue,
which is joint, not individual property?
Even if a dividend were effected for a
short period for specific purposes of improvement in some States, would that
alienation or dividend be constitutional, or
would it be expedient, since unfortunately expediency, not integrity or justice, has
become the order of the day?
No: let the revenue of the public lands
form an unalienable portion of the revenue
of the General Government; and let us
not degenerate into the absurd practice of
robbing Peter to pay Paul : for though our
revenue in this year is in happily flourishing condition, we cannot hope for the same
surplus funds in any subsequent year,
when the income arising from the reduced
scale of tariff duties will inevitably decrease those funds. So that it is much
better, being thus forewarned and forearm-
ed, to maintain the fidelity of the general
revenue ; to apportion the surplus funds
to meet the likely demands hereafter of
the General Government; and thus to obviate the necessity of again resorting to an
excessive and oppressive increase in the
tariff duties—which has already alienated
the affections of many portions of the
Union, exposed the integrity of Congress
to plausible suspicion, and the integrity of
the Union to a contemplated rupture.

There have been two or three fires in the
city lately, but the firemen put them out
so quick that we could learn nothing about
them. In no city in the world, we will
venture to say, does there exist a fire department so well drilled or so active as
that of Cincinnati. There is no chance
for a fire when they take it in hands. We
shrewdly suspect that they could have extinguished the late meteoric phenomenon,
if they had tried it.—*Cincinnati Rep.*

Governor Hayne, in his message to the
Legislature of South Carolina, complains,
in the same sentence, of the removal of
the ruffian Randolph and of the late Secretary of the Treasury. Mr. Duane will
feel himself highly complimented by the
association.—*Albany Argus.*

THE CONGRESSIONAL GLOBE.

PRINTED AND PUBLISHED AT THE CITY OF WASHINGTON, BY BLAIR & RIVES.

23d Congress, 1st Session.   SATURDAY, DECEMBER 21, 1833.   Vol. I.........No. 3.

IN SENATE.

Monday, December 16, 1833.

The VICE PRESIDENT of the United States appeared, was conducted to the Chair by the PRESIDENT *pro tem.*, and upon calling the Senate to order, delivered the following address:

Senators: In entering upon the duties of the station to which I have been called by the people, deference to you and justice to myself, require that I should forestall expectations which might otherwise be disappointed. Although for many years heretofore a member of the Senate, I regret that I should not have acquired that knowledge of the particular order of its proceedings which might securely be expected. Unfortunately for me, in respect to my present condition, I ever found those at hand who had more correctly appreciated this important branch of their duties, and on whose opinions as to points of order I could at all times safely rely. This remissness will doubtless, for a season, cause me no small degree of embarrassment. So far, however, as unremitted exertions on my part, and a proper respect for the advice of those who are better informed than myself can avail, this deficiency will be remedied as speedily as possible; and I feel persuaded that the Senate, in the mean time, will extend to me a considerate indulgence.

But however wanting I may be for the time, in a thorough knowledge of the technical duties of the Chair, I entertain, I humbly hope, a deep and solemn conviction of its high moral obligations. I am well aware that he who occupies it, is bound to cherish towards the members of the body over which he presides, no other feelings than those of justice and courtesy—to regard them all as standing upon an honorable equality—to apply the rules established by themselves for their own government with that impartiality, and to use whatever authority he possesses, in the manner best calculated to protect the rights, to respect the feelings, and to guard the reputations of all who may be affected by its exercise.

It is no disparagement to any other branch of the Government to say, that there is none in which the Constitution devolves such extensive powers as it does upon the Senate. There is scarcely an exercise of constitutional authority in which it forms an important, and, in some respects, an indispensable part of each of the three great departments—Executive, Legislative, and Judicial; and is, moreover, the body in which is made effectual that share of power in the Federal organization so wisely allowed to the respective State sovereignties.

Invested with such august powers, so judiciously restricted, and so safely adapted to the purposes of good government, it is no wonder that the Senate is regarded by the people of the United States as one of the best features, in what they at least consider to be, the wisest, the freest, and happiest political system in the world. In fervent wishes that it may long continue to be so regarded, and in a conviction of the importance of order, propriety, and regularity in its proceedings, we must all concur. It shall be an object of my highest ambition, Senators, to join with you, as far as in me lies, in effecting those desirable objects, and in endeavoring to realize the expectation formed of this body, at the adoption of the Constitution, and ever since confidently cherished, that it would exercise the most efficient influence in upholding the Federal system, and in perpetuating what is at once the foundation and the safeguard of our country's welfare—the union of the States.

Mr. BENTON presented the credentials of the Hon. Lewis F. Linn, appointed by the Governor a Senator from the State of Missouri to supply the vacancy occasioned by the death of the Hon. A. Buckner.

Mr. Linn attended, was qualified, and took his seat.

The Hon. Samuel McKean, Senator elect from

Pennsylvania, appeared, was qualified, and took his seat.

The VICE PRESIDENT laid before the Senate the memorial from the Government directors of the Bank of the United States; which, on motion of Mr. WEBSTER, was laid on the table and ordered to be printed.

The VICE PRESIDENT also laid before the Senate a letter from the Secretary of the Navy, enclosing a report of the disbursement of the contingent fund for the Navy Department for the last year; which was laid on the table.

STANDING COMMITTEES.

The VICE PRESIDENT having announced the standing order to be the election of the Standing Committees, the Senate proceeded to that duty.

For chairman of the Committee of Foreign Relations—

Mr. WILKINS received, on the 2d ballot, 26 votes; Mr. FORSYTH, 18 votes.

Whereupon Mr. WILKINS was pronounced duly elected.

Mr. CLAY then observed that it was now necessary to decide whether the Senate should proceed to the election of the chairman of the several committees first, or continue to ballot for the other course the best, and therefore made a motion to that effect.

Mr. KING, of Alabama, said it made but little difference what course was pursued. He would only say that the practice had always been different. He believed the rule had uniformly been to choose all the members of each committee in their order.

Mr. CHAMBERS said he believed the practice had been as the gentleman from Alabama-[Mr. King] has stated. He hoped, therefore, the gentleman from Kentucky would accede to the usual course.

Mr. CLAY said it was a matter of perfect indifference to him, and therefore he would withdraw his motion.

Mr. POINDEXTER renewed the motion. He thought it would save some trouble to choose the several chairmen first, and then there would be no difficulty in filling up the bodies of the committees afterwards.

Mr. BENTON asked the Secretary to read the rule, which was done.

Mr. CLAY. From the rule as read, it would appear that the practice has been to choose the chairmen severally, and then the other members of the committees, as I at first supposed.

The motion was then agreed to.

The result of the ballotings for the chairmen of the other committees is as follows:

Committee on Finance—Mr. Webster, 22; Mr. Wright, 18. Mr. Webster chosen.

Committee on Commerce—Mr. Silsbee, 23; Mr. King of Albama, 19. Mr. Silsbee chosen.

Committee on Manufactures—Mr. Frelinghuysen, 23; Mr. Clay, 16. Mr. Frelinghuysen chosen.

Committee on Agriculture—Mr. Brown had 49 votes, and was chosen.

Committee on Military Affairs—Mr. Benton had 36 votes, and was elected.

Committee on the Militia—Mr. Robinson had 43 votes, and was chosen.

Committee on Naval Affairs—Mr. Southard had 25 votes, and Mr. Rives, 18. Mr. Southard chosen.

Committee on Public Lands—Mr. Poindexter had 28 votes, and Mr. Kane 18. Mr. Poindexter chosen.

Committee on Private Land Claims—Mr. Kane had 41 votes, and was chosen.

Committee on Indian Affairs—Mr. White had 44 votes, and was chosen.

Committee on Claims—Mr. Bell had 29 votes, and Mr. Brown 11. Mr. Bell chosen.

Committee on the Judiciary—Mr. Clayton had, on the second ballot, 21 votes, and Mr. Forsyth 15. Mr. Clayton chosen.

Committee on the Post Office and Post Roads—Mr. Grundy had 43 votes, and was chosen.

Committee on Roads and Canals—Mr. Hendricks was chosen.

Committee on Pensions—Mr. Tomlinson had 34 votes, and Mr. Clay 11. Mr. Tomlinson chosen.

Committee on Revolutionary Claims—Mr. Moore had 38 votes, and was chosen.

Committee on the District of Columbia—Mr. Chambers had 28 votes, and Mr. Tyler 9. Mr. Chambers chosen.

Committee on the Contingent Expenses of the Senate—Mr. Knight had 37 votes, and was chosen.

Committee on Engrossed Bills—Mr. Shepley had 23, Mr. Robbins 11. Mr. Shepley chosen.

The Senate then proceeded to ballot for the remaining members of the several committees, a plurality only being necessary to a choice. The result was as follows:

Committee on Foreign Relations—Messrs. Forsyth, Rives, Mangum, and Sprague.

Committee on Finance—Messrs. Tyler, Ewing, Mangum, and Wilkins.

Committee on Commerce—Messrs. King, Wright, Waggaman, and Sprague.

Committee on Manufactures—Messrs. Knight, Prentiss, Morris, and Linn.

Mr. HENDRICKS here moved an adjournment, which was negatived, and the Senate then proceeded with the balloting, which resulted as follows:

Committee on Agriculture—Messrs. Robinson, Kent, Swift, and Wright.

Committee on Military Affairs—Messrs. King, Clayton, Benton, and Preston.

Mr. WILKINS here moved an adjournment on a division. Yeas 19, nays 24.

The Senate then resumed the ballotings, which resulted as follows:

Committee on the Militia—Messrs. Hendricks, Waggaman, McKean, and Clayton.

Committee on Naval Affairs—Messrs. Robbins, Bibb, Chambers, and Tallmadge.

Committee on Public Lands—Messrs. Moore, Prentiss, McKean, and Clay.

Committee on Private Land Claims—Messrs. Linn, Naudain, Poindexter, and Silsbee.

Mr. CLAY here moved an adjournment, which was carried. Adjourned.

HOUSE OF REPRESENTATIVES.

Monday December 16, 1833.

Mr. WHITE of Louisiana, appeared, qualified, and took his seat.

Mr. CARR, from the Committee on Private Land Claims, reported a bill for the relief of Alexander Boyd.

Mr. SUTHERLAND, from the Committee on Commerce, reported a bill for the relief of Ezekiel Foster & Co.; also, a bill for the relief of the owners of the schooner Three Sisters, of Saybrook.

All which bills were read twice, and committed.

On motion of Mr. STEWART, a resolution of the Legislature of Pennsylvania, instructing the Senators and requesting the Representatives of that State in the Congress of the United States to endeavor to procure the passage of a law authorizing a subscription of a million of dollars, on the part of the General Government, to the stock of the Chesapeake and Ohio Canal Company, to be expended on the western section, was referred to the Committee on Roads and Canals.

Mr. PATTON submitted the following resolution; which was read and agreed to:

"*Resolved*, That the Committee on the Post Office and Post Roads, be instructed to inquire into the expediency of establishing a mail route from Orange Court-house, in Virginia, to the town of Stanardsville, in the county of Orange."

Mr. PATTON'S motion to change the 9th rule

of the House so as to require the Speaker to vote in the first instance, on every question, and providing that when the House is equally divided, the motion shall be lost, was taken up for consideration, as the special order of the day. The yeas and nays having been ordered, some conversation took place on a question of order; the 9th rule was read as follows:

"In all cases of ballot by the House, the Speaker shall vote: in other cases he shall not vote, unless the House be equally divided, or unless his vote, if given to the minority, will make the division equal; and in case of such equal division, the question shall be lost."

And the question stated to be to strike out the rule, and insert the rule moved by Mr. PATTON.

Mr. WAYNE was convinced, by reflection, that the rule, as it stands, is founded in experience, and cannot be changed without producing much disorder. He had suggested the other day, and now repeated, that the motion proceeded on the supposition, that we were about to restore to the Speaker certain rights of which he has heretofore been deprived. If we give the Speaker the right to vote on every question, we must also give him the right of speaking on every question. The reason for depriving him of the right of speaking was, to prevent him from exerting the influence o his official station upon the questions before the House, and no member could ever be raised to that station without some party influence. It was our duty to render the Speaker independent of party relations, and put him out of the reach of temptation. He also suggested, that in questions of order, upon which the Speaker was to decide in the first instance, it was improper to allow him to vote, when an appeal was made to the House. If we do allow the Speaker to vote, from the connexion which he must have with a powerful Administration, we make him the victim or instrument, against his will, of that Administration. The more deeply we interest the Speaker in the proceedings of the House, the more reason we have to apprehend that, in all his decisions, votes, and appointments of committees, he will be made the instrument of a party. Here Mr. W. went into the history of parliamentary law, in England, to show that there had there always existed a jealousy of the power of the Speaker of the House of Commons. The present rule had existed from the foundation of the Government, and had been found practically convenient and useful, and the example of some few State Legislatures, to the contrary, was wholly inapplicable to the proceedings of this body.

Mr. PATTON replied to the gentleman from Georgia, and supported his motion. He denied the fact that the rule proposed would make the Speaker interested between the parties of the day, any more than he has ever been interested. It was not to be supposed that any member would become suddenly divested of all party feelings upon his elevation to the chair. Every member, in the chair and out of the chair, was influenced by party feelings;—he was sorry it was so—he could wish that we were all free from party feelings and motives. He would not insult the good sense and feelings of the House by proposing any rule to guard against the wilful, malicious, and corrupt miscounting of votes, by a Speaker. He had no political object to obtain, and no personal feeling to gratify in his course on this question. Whatever he had said had no reference whatever to any individual Speaker, past, present, or to come.

The question was here taken by yeas and nays, and decided in the negative, as follows:

YEAS—Messrs. Heman Allen, John J. Allen, William Allen, Anthony, Archer, Banks, Barber, Barringer, Bates, Beale, Beatty, Beaumont, Bouldin, Burd, Burges, Carmichael, Carr, Chaney, Chilton, Chinn, Claiborne, Clayton, Clowney, Corwin, Coulter, Crockett, Darlington, Warren R. Davis, Amos Davis, Davenport, Deming, Denny, Dunlap, Evans, Horace Everett, Ewing, Foster, Fowler, Fulton, Galbraith, Gamble, Gholson, Gordon, Grayson, Grennell, Griffin, Joseph Hall, Hannegan, Hardin, James Harper, Harrison, Hazeltine, Heath, Hiester, Henderson, Howell, Jabez W. Huntington, William Cost Johnson, Kinnard, Laporte, George W. Lay, Lee, Lewis, Loyall, Lucas, Lyon, Marshall, Mardis, Mason, McCarty, McKennan, Miller, S. McD. Moore, Patton, Pinckney, Pope, Potts, Ramsay, Reed, Rencher, William B. Shepard, Shinn, Standifer, Stewart, Stoddert, Sutherland, William P. Taylor, Philemon Thomas, Tompkins, Vance, Vinton, Wagener, Webster, Frederick Whittlesey, Wilde, Williams, Wise—96.

NAYS—Messrs. John Q. Adams, J. Adams, C. Allan, Ashley, Barnitz, Baylies, Bean, Beardsley, John Bell, James M. Bell, Binney, James Blair, Bockee, Bodle, Boon, Briggs, Bull, Bunch, Burns, Bynum, Cambreleng, Casey, Chambers, Choate, Samuel Clark, William Clark, Clay, Connor, Cramer, Crane, John Davis, Day, Deberry, Dennis, Dickson, P. Dickerson, D. W. Dickinson, Duncan, Ellsworth, Edward Everett, Fillmore, Foot, Forester, P. C. Fuller, W. K. Fuller, Gillett, Gilmer, Gorham, Hiland Hall, Thomas H. Hall, Halsey, Hamer, Joseph M. Harper, Hathaway, Hawkins, Hawes, Hubbard, Inge, Jarvis, Richard M. Johnson, Noadiah Johnson, Cave Johnson, Seaborn Jones, Benjamin Jones, Kavanagh, King, Lane, Lansing, Lawrence, Lea, Leavitt, Mann, Martindale, McComas, McIntire, McKay, McKim, McKinley, McLene, McVean, Mercer, Milligan, R. Mitchell, Muhlenberg, Murphy, Osgood, Page, Parks, Parker, Patterson, D. J. Pearce, Peyton, Franklin Pierce, Pierson, Polk, Schenck, Schley, A. H. Shepperd, Singleton, William Slade, Charles Slade, Sloane, Spangler, Speight, William Taylor, Thomson, Turner, Turrill, Tweedy, Vanderpôel, Van Houten, Ward, Wardwell, Watmough, Wayne, Whallon, C. P. White, E. D. White, E. Whittlesey, Young—121.

The ninth rule of the House was then adopted without amendment.

The SPEAKER presented to the House a communication from the Secretary of the Navy, with the petition of Judge Tucker; which had been referred to that department, and which was now referred to the Committee on Naval Affairs.

Also, a communication from the Comptroller of the Treasury, in relation to the unsettled balances and accounts, and one from the Secretary of the Navy, with an account of the expenditures in that department; which, on motion of Mr. WHITTLESEY, of Ohio, were ordered to be laid on the table and printed.

REMOVAL OF BANK DEPOSITES.

The motion of Mr. POLK, to reconsider the vote by which, on motion of Mr. McDUFFIE, the report of the Secretary of the Treasury on the removal of the deposites, was referred to the Committee of the Whole on the state of the Union, was taken up as the unfinished business of Thursday.

Mr. ALLAN, of Kentucky, opposed the motion. The consequence of sending the document in question to the Committee on Ways and Means would be a long delay of the discussion and decision of the bank question. The subject would be buried, for weeks or months, in the committee, and weeks and months would elapse—yes, we would see hot weather—before we should hear of the matter again. It was due to the public interest and to public expectation, that an early decision should be made on the solvency and condition of the State banks which were selected as the depositories of the public money. The evil and calamity of the removal of the deposites would fall heaviest upon his State. The great commercial cities of the east had their currency and the use of the public money, but such advantages his constituents had no share in.

The SPEAKER interposed, and said, that the merits of the case could not be discussed. The question was where it should be discussed.

Mr. ALLAN went on to say that the State of Kentucky was interested in this question, having an extensive commerce with every part of the Union, and this he used as an argument in favor of an early disposition of the question. Every mail brought him letters showing that the people of the West were about to establish local banks to supply a currency in the room of that of which they were to be deprived, and he anticipated the recurrence of the pecuniary distresses and embarrassments of 1818, and another consideration was, that all the public treasure had not yet been withdrawn from its legal depository. From what had passed he inferred what was to come. Out of forty millions heretofore deposited in the local banks, a million and a half had been lost. To prove this, he referred to the statement of the Secretary of the Treasury of what he called the unavailable funds. The local banks had not the public confidence, individually or collectively. He regretted that he was unable, from the narrow point in which the question was now presented, to show the general effect of the measure upon his constituents, and he would now conclude, reserving to himself the right to take some other opportunity for the purpose.

Mr. SELDEN spoke in opposition to the motion. He viewed it as a question of time, and to the point of time he should confine his remarks. A very speedy disposition of the question ought to be made, and for that reason he was opposed to the delay which would be occasioned by the reference of the subject to a standing or special committee. The ordinary length of commercial paper was 60 or 90 days. Was every contract now in existence to be exposed, by the delay of this subject, to all the effects of doubt and uncertainty? Was it prudent to suffer doubts on such a subject long to hang over the commercial community? If he understood the chairman of the Committee of Ways and Means, he advocated the reference of the letter to the standing committee, first because it was the usual course, and, second, because there was more important business which would be interrupted by its discussion now. But if the chairman agreed with him as to the character of this question, he would deem it of sufficient importance to devote to it the whole time of the House until it was disposed of. As to the usage urged by the chairman, he would ask him to refer to a case where the whole amount of the public funds had been subjected to a removal, and then point out what had been the usage in such cases. The ordinary length of commercial paper was not equal to the time during which this subject would rest in the hands of the standing committee. Was it necessary to show to this House the extent of the fever now felt along the whole Atlantic coast? If it was so, he would point out the sales of stock recently made in the city of New York, from which it would appear that the commercial pressure was never so extensive and severe as now. Was it prudent, under such circumstances, to keep up this alarm and uncertainty, till every note and bill of exchange had become payable, and until every merchant had stood and passed the day of trial. In the city of New York, which he in part represented, there were eight millions of country bank paper afloat, to redeem which there were only half a million in specie. Here Mr. S. made several statements of the amount of paper in circulation compared with the quantity of metallic currency, from which he inferred that, in the whole State of New York, there was only one dollar in specie for every fifteen dollars in paper. In other States there was a similar scarcity of metallic currency. In Massachusetts, by a late return, it appeared that there were twenty-four millions of paper in circulation, and only nine hundred thousand dollars with which to redeem it. The country was prosperous, and every section of it was pouring fourth its products, but still there was not in the country a sufficient amount of metallic currency to meet a sudden run among the banks. Will the House, under such circumstances, suspend their action for ninety days? He pointed them to the history of the currency in this country. In the year 1814 the banks in New York passed a resolution, that it was unnecessary for them to suspend specie payments. But in five days from that time, such was the panic and pressure, that they did stop specie payments; and from that time forth, for many months, there was not a single paper dollar redeemed in specie from this metropolis to the New England line. This shows the effect of alarm upon the currency. Ninety days, sir—ninety days may carry ruin through every part of the country, so far as ruin can take place from pecuniary embarrassments. In 1814, the banks were, in five days, compelled to rescind their resolve to pay in specie. The disposition of six millions of public funds was, in itself, a matter of no moment. If the whole sum were at once sunk in the sea, the people would forget it in a day. But if the disposition of that sum be such as to create alarm, you cannot meas-

are its mischievous effects upon the community. Every man, in the general panic, husbands what he has. Every banker keeps what he has got, and asks for more. The panic spreads and pervades the whole community, and finally results in the ruin of thousands, who, under ordinary circumstances, would be able to meet their engagements. From what part of the world, he would ask, did gentlemen expect new supplies of specie in ninety days, to meet the pressure and panic? He who attended to the peculiar sensitiveness of those who engaged in commercial transactions; to the diligence and enterprise of the stock speculators—they would have their spies in every public house in this city, watching the progress of the secret discussion of the subject in the standing committee, and avail themselves of the information thus obtained, to the disadvantage of the public interests. Why should we not proceed without delay, to an open discussion? Let those who wish to impeach the act of the Secretary of the Treasury do it upon the reasons which he has furnished in his report. Let the act be judged of according to the reasoning and facts of the report.

Mr. FOOT concurred in the views taken by the honorable member from New York, who had preceded him, and observed, that although, from the novelty of the present case, no precedent had been adduced by those who justified that the proper course to be taken in acting upon this question, was to retain it in the Committee of the Whole, yet, in an authority always looked up to, Jefferson's Manual, the principle was fully laid down, that it was necessary for all important questions to be referred to that committee, that they might be there digested and put into a shape to meet the views of the majority, and which afterwards being reported upon, could then be referred to one or other of their standing committees. He concluded by observing, that as the act of removal of the Secretary of the Treasury was consummated; that he had given his reason for that removal, the question was now before the House in a form for them to act upon, and that as they did not want the intervention of any committee, to direct them how they should act upon it, he hoped further time would not be spent in discussing what was only a preliminary question.

Mr. BEARDSLEY asked the indulgence of the House while he should submit a few remarks, and in which he would promise to avoid all allusion to the merits of the report of the Secretary of the Treasury, and confine himself, as the rules of propriety and order required he should do, to such points as were properly at issue in the present limited discussion. The act incorporating the Bank of the United States declared that the moneys of the United States should be deposited in the bank and its branches, unless otherwise directed by the Secretary of the Treasury, in which event he is required to report his reasons for such direction to Congress. That officer had, in the performance of the duty thus assigned to him, removed these deposites from the Bank of the United States, and placed them in certain State institutions; and as the act of Congress directed, he has reported at large his reasons for that measure. This report, without any apparent consideration, and certainly without discussion, was referred to the Committee of the Whole on the state of the Union. A motion is now made to reconsider that vote of reference, in order to bring the subject under the control of the House, when the House will be enabled to dispose of it as in its deliberate judgment shall be deemed fit and proper.

The honorable mover of the present question stated to the House, that the vote of reference was obtained, or rather assented to, by himself, under a misapprehension of what had been said by the honorable gentleman who moved that reference, [Mr. McDuffie,] as to his object. Under such circumstances, Mr. B. submitted that it was not unusual, and indeed that it was rather a matter of course, to reconsider a vote so given, and thus subject the question to the considerate determination of the House. But this course, it appeared, was not to be taken on the present occasion. And it was manifest that if anything had been gained by the former vote of reference, that advantage was not to be given up without a struggle. The House, therefore, must necessarily pass upon the proposition submitted.

The report of the Secretary, he would observe, was upon two important and distinct subjects—one, the propriety of the removal of the public funds *from* the Bank of the United States, the other, the propriety of placing those funds in the particular State banks which had been selected by the Secretary. And the report presents a mass of facts and of reasons in support of both these measures. These different acts of the Secretary stand on distinct and independent grounds. The reasons given for the removal may be abundant and satisfactory, and yet those presented in the report in favor of the particular banks which have been selected as depositories of the public funds may be altogether insufficient. These banks may be badly located for the convenience of the public, or may be unsound in credit or capital, either of which would render that act of the Secretary objectionable. The report, however, covers the whole ground, and asserts and maintains, not only the propriety of the removal, but the perfect convenience and solidity of the substituted institutions. But it is now urged as a reason for immediate discussion and decision by this House, that the public treasure is in danger; that these State banks are unsound; "that their charters, their capitals, their condition, are alike unknown;" that this, in truth, is not so much a question about the United States Bank as about the rights of this House, and the security of the treasure of the people themselves, endangered, as is asserted, by this unwarrantable act of the Secretary. In fact, sir, it is said that the public money might as well be at the bottom of the Potomac, as where it has been placed by the Secretary.

Mr. CLAYTON here rose and said that he had been misapprehended: he did not insinuate anything to the prejudice of the State banks; that if he voted against the United States Bank as being an unsound depository of the public money, it did not follow that he was bound to think it would be safe at the bottom of the Potomac.

Mr. B. continued, and said, that he might have mistaken the precise import of the language of the honorable member, but certain it was, that the immediate decision of the question had been pressed upon the House on the alleged ground of the insecurity of the State institutions, and the consequent extreme danger of the public treasure. Upon these grounds of alarm the House had been urged to act and decide at once, without waiting the slow movement of a committee.

Sir, said Mr. B., these very reasons, so pathetically urged in favor of retaining this document in the Committee of the Whole on the state of the Union, are, with me, controlling for an opposite course. The reasons given by the Secretary for what he has done, consist as well of matters of fact, as of his deductions from these facts. But the facts stated and relied upon by him, not only in justification of the removal of the deposites, but also to show the perfect security of the State institutions, are called in question and disputed by honorable gentlemen who have addressed the House. Indeed, with the exception of his colleague, [Mr. Selden;] the stress of the argument had been directed to that object. The argument of that gentleman, he admitted, had been different. It was consistent and fair. It admitted, unqualifiedly, that if the report of the Secretary should remain in Committee of the Whole, and be there discussed and acted upon, its statements must all be taken as true, and the result would of course depend, not upon their accuracy in point of fact, but upon their sufficiency in sound reason and propriety. If the House would act upon this view of the case, Mr. B. said he, for one, would be satisfied to see this motion fail, and the discussion on the merits proceed without delay. But how and where shall we ascertain the truth of these adverse and contradictory allegations? Not in Committee of the Whole. There, gentlemen may argue and debate; and there every one will feel himself at liberty to assume and abide by his own version of the facts. But in a standing or select committee, proof, if necessary, may be taken, the truth elicited and reported to the House. If truth, upon controverted allegations, is desirable, this is the only way in which it can be arrived at by the House. This consideration, Mr. B. said, was decisive of the vote he should give. He chose to learn whether the information which the Secretary had received, upon which he had relied, and which he had given to the House, was correct or not, before he passed upon the soundness and accuracy of his views.

It was admitted by the honorable member from Pennsylvania, [Mr. Binney,] that documents from the Secretary of the Treasury, of this description, were usually referred to a standing or select committee, and not to a committee of the Whole House. What adequate reason had been given, or existed, for departing, in this instance, from the usual course? He maintained there was none whatever. Why was immediate discussion necessary? One honorable gentleman had said that this House, in vindication of its authority, should at once order a restoration of the deposites. This, to him, was extraordinary language—a most extraordinary proposition. He would ask, what authority of this House had been violated by this act of the Secretary? Had he done more than he was authorized to do by the public law of the land? This House had, singly, as he contended, no power to act upon this subject; although, as a component part of the Legislature of the Union, it might with propriety act and decide. It was only, however, as he supposed, in the passage of a law, that it could contribute towards a restoration of the deposites, or vindicate its own authority. It had no other authority in this matter than the ordinary law-making power of the House.

Mr. B. said he had understood the honorable member from Pennsylvania, [Mr. Binney,] to maintain that Congress could only exercise in this case an appellate power over the decision of the Secretary of the Treasury; that this House could not look beyond the report for reasons to influence its decision. This seemed to him altogether too technical and limited a view of the matter, and he thought could not receive the sanction of the House. It was urged that the bank, by accepting its charter, had assented that the Secretary might first decide upon the removal or retention of the public deposites, subject, however, to the controlling power of Congress by way of appeal from that decision, but upon those grounds, and those alone, which had been acted upon and advanced by the Secretary. But he could not find this limitation to the power of Congress in the charter or elsewhere. The charter gave to the Secretary the unqualified power of removal. True, it made it his duty to report his reasons; but it did not profess, in any respect, to limit the supervising power of Congress. That power was left upon the broad basis of the Constitution, and if the reasons assigned in the present instance by the Secretary, should turn out to be unsatisfactory and insufficient, which he was very far from conceding or supposing would be the case, yet if others existed of a more cogent nature, and of themselves confessedly sufficient, he asked if it could be supposed that Congress, under such circumstances, would direct a restoration of the public deposites to be made? He supposed not, although the argument of the honorable gentleman led to a different conclusion.

His colleague [Mr. Selden] had urged the importance of *time* in making a final disposition of this question; that a reference to a standing or select committee would extend the period of final determination beyond sixty or ninety days, the ordinary time for commercial paper to run in the banks. The honorable gentleman insisted, that in this aspect, the action of this House ought to be instantaneous. Mr. B. said, that his colleague seemed to have overlooked the fact, that the deposites were removed about ninety days since, during which time, the whole community had acted upon the assumption, that they would remain in the State institutions. The State banks had regulated their discounts accordingly, and every one, he believed, had conducted his own affairs upon that supposition, and they would no doubt continue to manage their concerns in the same way, unless alarmed by the agitation here. He would ask, in all seriousness, if gentlemen could hope, in any way, to procure a passage of a law, of any description, in time to meet this critical period of ninety days, from the time when the decisive step was taken by the Secretary of the Treasury? As to the pretence that immediate discussion and decision were required or expected by the country

at large, he could concede nothing of that nature. A restoration of the deposites to the Bank of the United States, was, as he believed, the very last thing looked for, if not the last thing desired, by our constituents. As far as public opinion was to be regarded, he looked upon the deposites as forever gone from the bank: the die had been cast: they would never be restored to that institution. And the agitation now said to prevail, if it existed in the large cities, and to some extent here, did not extend to the country. That was prosperous, decided, and tranquil.

Mr. B. said he had thus given to the House the views which would induce him to vote for the motion. He could not, with the honorable member from Georgia, [Mr. CLAYTON,] with whom, upon most questions relating to the bank, it had been his good fortune hitherto to act—he could not, he said, with that honorable gentleman, now say that although he believed the bank to be unconstitutional—although he believed and had voted that the public deposites were unsafe in its vaults—and although he knew nothing about the State banks which had been selected by the Secretary of the Treasury, yet, that he would vote to restore these deposites to this unconstitutional and unsafe institution. These reasons might satisfy the mind of the honorable gentleman himself, but he believed would tend very little to the satisfaction of others.

Mr. GORHAM advocated the necessity of a speedy decision, and remarked, in answer to the argument of the honorable member from New York, [Mr. BEARDSLEY,] who wanted to know by what authority the House could possibly act on the Secretary's report, that he thought there was sufficient authority vested in the House, deeming it to be the concentration of public opinion, which if once expressed, and that if there was any refusal on the part of the Secretary to obey such expression, a remedy could be found by passing a law on the subject.

Mr. POLK replied briefly to the arguments adduced against his motion, and maintained that the principles now claimed by the present Secretary of the Treasury were the same upon which Mr. Secretary Crawford had acted and justified his former removal of public moneys from the bank; that, so far from the State institutions being insolvent, or weak in public estimation, he found that their respective stock bore at market higher prices than the stock of the United States Bank did in all the eastern cities, which he would take as the best possible thermometer of the public confidence in those institutions. He desired to bring this preliminary debate to a close, feeling perfectly satisfied that an earlier decision would be had by referring it to a standing committee, than even if it was to remain in Committee of the Whole; the effect of which would be, by the flood of speeches that would be there made on one side and upon the other, rather to darken than enlighten the public mind on the merits of the great question itself.

Mr. BURGES having obtained the floor, moved an adjournment; which was carried.

IN SENATE.
TUESDAY, December 17, 1833.

A message was received from the President of the United States by the hands of Mr. Donelson, his Private Secretary.

Mr. TYLER, on leave, introduced a bill for the relief of the legal representatives of Captain Robert White, and a bill for the relief of the legal representatives of Major William Mosby; which were read, and ordered to be read a second time.

Mr. ROBINSON, on leave, introduced a bill to provide payment for horses lost in the late expeditions against the hostile Indians; which was read, and ordered to be read a second time.

Mr. TIPTON, on leave, introduced a bill further to extend the provisions of the act granting preemption rights to the settlers on the public lands, &c.; which was read, and ordered to be read a second time.

STANDING COMMITTEES.

The Senate then proceeded to elect the remaining members of the several standing committees, which resulted as follows:

Committee on Indian Affairs.—Messrs. Frelinghuysen, Tipton, Smith, and Swift.

Committee on Claims.—Messrs. Brown, Naudain, Tipton, and Wright.

Committee on the Judiciary.—Messrs. Bibb, Preston, Smith, and Bell.

Committee on Post Offices and Post Roads.—Messrs. Clayton, Ewing, Knight, and Rives.

Committee on Roads and Canals.—Messrs. Hill, Southard, Shepley, and Kent.

Committee on Pensions.—Messrs. Prentiss, McKean, Tallmadge, and Kane.

Committee on the District of Columbia.—Messrs. Tyler, Southard, Bibb, and Tomlinson.

Committee on Revolutionary Claims.—Messrs. Swift, Hill, Smith, and Shepley.

Committee on the Contingent Expenses of the Senate.—Messrs. Tomlinson and Tallmadge.

Committee on Engrossed Bills.—Messrs. Morris and Robinson.

The VICE PRESIDENT laid before the Senate the annual report of the Secretary of the Treasury; which, on motion of

Mr. WEBSTER, was referred to the Committee on Finance, and 1,500 copies thereof ordered to be printed.

The Senate then proceeded to the consideration of Executive business; when the doors were opened the Senate adjourned.

Note.—We omitted to state yesterday that Mr. CLAYTON, of Delaware, and Mr. WAGGAMAN, of Louisiana, appeared, and took their seats.

HOUSE OF REPRESENTATIVES.
TUESDAY, December 17, 1833.

Mr. POLK, from the Committee of Ways and Means, reported a bill making appropriations for the support of Government for the next year; which was read twice and committed.

Mr. E. EVERETT, from the Committee on Foreign Affairs, reported a bill for the relief of Philip Beason.

Mr. WATMOUGH, from the Committee on Naval Affairs, reported a bill for the relief of the legal representative of —— Rowe; also, bills for the relief of Horatio N. Crabb and John G. Reynolds.

Mr. REED, from the same committee, reported a bill for the relief of John Percival.

Mr. MARSHALL, from the Committee on Revolutionary Claims, reported a bill for the relief of Francis and Judith Taylor.

Mr. CAVE JOHNSON, from the Committee on Public Land Claims, reported a bill for the relief of John L. Lobdell.

Mr. MUHLENBERG, from the Committee on Revolutionary Claims, presented a bill for the relief of Pressly Thornton, deceased; also, for the relief of Thomas Minor.

Which bills were severally read and committed.

Mr. ARCHER and Mr. MUHLENBERG, from their respective committees, made unfavorable reports on the petitions of Jane Baker and Stephen Kingston.

On motion of Mr. ALLEN, of Virginia,

Resolved, That the Judiciary Committee be instructed to inquire into the expediency of changing the time of holding the United States Court for the Western District of Virginia, at Clarksburg, and that they have leave to report by bill or otherwise.

On motion of Mr. HANNEGAN,

Resolved, That the Committee on Roads and Canals be instructed to inquire into the expediency of making an appropriation for the purpose of removing the obstructions to the navigation of the Wabash river.

On motion of Mr. CAGE,

Resolved, That the Committee on the Judiciary inquire into the expediency of establishing a new circuit or circuits, extending the Circuit Court system to the new States, which are now without a full participation in the benefits growing out of the establishment of the Federal Judiciary.

On motion of Mr. SEVIER,

Resolved, That the Committee on the Territories be instructed to inquire into the expediency of permitting the people of the Territory of Arkansas to form a constitution and State Government, and for the admission of such State into the Union, on an equal footing with the original States.

On motion of Mr. HAWES,

Resolved, That the Committee on Roads and Canals be instructed to inquire into the expediency of making an appropriation for the improvement of the navigation of Green river, in the State of Kentucky.

On motion of Mr. LANE,

Resolved, That the Committee on Public Lands be instructed to inquire into the expediency of permitting the public lands which have been fifteen years in market, to be purchased by actual settlers or resident cultivators, at a reduced price, under the same regulations and restrictions as are prescribed by the act of April 5th, 1832, for the purchase of forty-acre tracts; and of granting to every settler (being a housekeeper) on such lands, the right of preëmption to enter the quarter quarter sections which he has improved; with leave to report by bill or otherwise.

On motion of Mr. STANDIFER,

Resolved, That the Committee on Roads and Canals be instructed to inquire into the expediency of making an appropriation to improve the Tennessee and Coosa rivers, and connect their waters by canal or railroad.

On motion of Mr. CARR,

Resolved, That the Committee on Roads and Canals be instructed to inquire into the expediency of making an appropriation, either in money or in Government lands, for the purpose of improving the great western thoroughfare and mail-route between Louisville, Kentucky, and St. Louis, in the State of Missouri.

Be it further resolved, That the Committee on Roads and Canals be instructed to inquire into the expediency of making an appropriation for the purpose of improving the navigation in the Indian Chute, through the falls of the Ohio river, opposite Louisville, Kentucky—a sum sufficient to accomplish which, and make the Indian Chute navigable for keel and flat boats, in a low stage of water, would not, it is presumed, equal the sum liable to be collected as tolls from keel and flat boats for a passage through the canal, within the term of one year.

And be it further resolved, That the Committee on Roads and Canals be instructed to inquire into the expediency of making an appropriation for the purpose of surveying a route for the construction of a railroad, commencing at the falls of the Ohio river, or at some other convenient commercial point, thence to Indianapolis, the seat of government of the State of Indiana, and from thence to Michigan city, on Lake Michigan, in the State of Indiana.

On motion of Mr. LYON, of Michigan,

Resolved, That the Committee on Roads and Canals be instructed to inquire into the expediency of making appropriations for the following objects, viz: 1st. An appropriation for constructing a ship canal, to connect the navigable waters of the River Raisin with Lake Erie or La Plaisance bay, in the Territory of Michigan, agreeably to the survey and estimate of the War Department. 2d. An appropriation for surveying the Flats, so called, in Lake St. Clair, at the mouth of St. Clair river; and also for removing the bar and building a pier, if necessary, at the mouth of Clinton river, in Lake St. Clair, in Michigan Territory. 3d. An appropriation for constructing a harbor at the mouth of the St. Joseph's river, on Lake Michigan, in Michigan Territory. 4th. An appropriation to defray the expenses of surveying the obstructions to the navigation of the St. Joseph's and Kalamazoo rivers, as far up as the said streams may be considered navigable.

Resolved, That the Committee on the Post Office and Post Roads be instructed to inquire into the expediency of establishing a post route from Sussex Court-House, by Comanns's Mill and Williamson's Store, in Virginia, to Pleasant Hill, in Northampton county, in North Carolina.

On motion of Mr. E. EVERETT,

Resolved, That a Committee of three be appointed, who, together with a like number to be appointed by the Senate, shall direct the expenditure of the money appropriated for the Library of Congress.

On motion of Mr. EVANS,

Resolved, That the Committee of Ways and Means be directed to inquire into the expediency

of paying to Morgan S. Gordon, from the Treasury of the United States, the amount received from the Brazilian Government as indemnity to him for injuries sustained and expenses incurred in consequence of the illegal capture of the schooner Sarah George, of which said Gordon was master.

On motion of Mr. SLADE, of Vermont,

Resolved, That the Committee on Invalid Pensions be instructed to inquire into the expediency of extending the invalid pension of Russell Jefferson, of the State of Vermont, back to the commencement of his disability.

On motion of Mr. McVEAN,

Resolved, That the Committee on Revolutionary Pensions be instructed to inquire into the expediency of allowing to Andrew Michael, of Montgomery county, New York, a pension for services rendered the United States during the Revolutionary war.

On motion of Mr. McVEAN,

Resolved, That the Committee on Revolutionary Pensions be instructed to inquire into the expediency of allowing to Reynhart Tougot, of Montgomery county, New York, a pension for services rendered the United States during the Revolutionary war.

On motion of Mr. CHILTON,

Resolved, That the Committee on Claims be instructed to inquire into the expediency of allowing to the heirs of Thomas Clemmons, deceased, an artificer of the late war, compensation for services rendered by the said Thomas Clemmons, as artificer to Colonel Nicholas Miller's regiment, Kentucky militia.

On motion of Mr. SLADE, of Vermont,

Resolved, That the Committee on Invalid Pensions be instructed to inquire into the expediency of placing the name of Harvey Reynolds, of the State of Vermont, on the roll of invalid pensioners.

On motion of Mr. McKINLEY,

Resolved, That the Committee on Public Lands be instructed to inquire into the propriety of disposing of the public lands by settlement rights of 160 acres to each actual settler thereon, upon the payment of all expenses incurred by the United States for surveying, &c., with the right of preemption of 160 acres adjoining, at the minimum price.

Resolved, That said committee also inquire into the propriety of granting to the States in which they lie, all public lands which have been offered for sale and remained unsold ten years, on which there are no actual settlers.

On motion of Mr. DUNCAN,

Resolved, That the Committee on the Public Lands be instructed to inquire into the expediency of reducing and graduating the price of the public lands, so that the future proceeds of sales shall not exceed the general charges for surveying and selling them.

Resolved, That the same committee be instructed to inquire into the expediency of granting the right of preëmption to all settlers on the public lands.

Resolved, That the same committee be instructed to inquire into the expediency of selling 160 acres of land to each actual settler, who shall cultivate the same for five years, at a less rate than the minimum price of the public lands.

Resolved, That the same committee inquire into the expediency of abolishing all auction sales of the public lands, and of permitting them, in future, to be purchased at private sale as soon as they are surveyed.

On motion of Mr. PAGE,

Resolved, That the Committee on Invalid Pensions be instructed to inquire into the expediency of allowing to the widow and children of the late Lieutenant Benjamin Fitch, late of the United States army, the arrearages of pension to which, by his rank, he was entitled from the time he was placed on the pension roll, up to the time of his death, and that the petition and other documents in relation to the same, on the files of this House, heretofore presented, be referred to said committee.

Mr. MERCER submitted the following resolution; which has one day for consideration:

Resolved, That the President of the United States be requested to lay before this House a copy of any contract which may have been made for the construction of a bridge across the Potomac river, opposite the city of Washington, together with the authority under which such contract may have been made; the names of the contractors, and of their securities, if any; and the plan and estimate of the cost of such bridge.

On motion of Mr. JARVIS,

Resolved, That the Committee on the Post Office and Post Roads be instructed to inquire what amount of postage has been paid into the treasury of the United States; and also to inquire into the expediency of restoring to the Post Office Department such portion of the amount so paid into the treasury as will enable the Postmaster General to carry into effect an act of Congress, approved June 15, 1832, entitled "An act to establish certain post roads, and to alter and discontinue others, and for other purposes."

On motion of Mr. LEAVITT,

Resolved, That the Committee on Private Land Claims be instructed to inquire into the expediency of confirming the right of the heirs and representatives of the late Henry Dohrman to sections Nos. 8, 11, 26, and 29, in township 13, range 7, of the Steubenville land district, in the State of Ohio, which said township was intended to be granted entire to the said Dohrman, by a resolution of Congress, adopted October 1, 1787.

On motion of Mr. STEWART,

Resolved, That the report of the Secretary of War on the subject of a national road from Uniontown, by way of Pittsburg, to the lakes, be referred to the Committee on Roads and Canals.

On motion of Mr. CROCKETT,

Resolved, That a select committee be appointed by this House, consisting of seven members, whose duty it shall be to inquire into and report the most equitable and advantageous mode of disposing of that portion of the lands belonging to the United States south and west of the Congressional reservation line.

Resolved further, That all papers heretofore on the files of this House, relative to said subject, be referred to said committee, and that they have leave to report by bill or otherwise.

On motion of Mr. EWING, "the several memorials and joint resolutions of the Legislatures of Indiana and Illinois, praying of Congress to grant and to defray the expense of removing all obstructions to the navigation of the Wabash river and White river, (reserved national highways,) which have been presented to the House heretofore, at different periods," were referred to the Committee on Roads and Canals; and "the several memorials and joint resolutions of the Legislature of Indiana, praying of Congress to appropriate and to improve the great western thoroughfare and mail route leading through said State of Indiana and the State of Illinois, from Louisville, Kentucky, to St. Louis, in Missouri," heretofore presented to the House, at different periods, were also referred to the Committee on Roads and Canals.

REMOVAL OF THE DEPOSITES.

The resolution of Mr. POLK, to reconsider the vote by which the report of the Secretary of the Treasury upon the removal of the deposites was referred to the Committee of the Whole, coming up—

Mr. BURGES, who was in possession of the floor from the previous day, after apologizing to the honorable member from Georgia [Mr. CLAYTON] for having interrupted him, said that, from various reasons, he was induced to decline addressing the House, and would now yield the floor to him.

Mr. CLAYTON said he had only risen from a desire to protest against the manner in which it had been sought to involve him in a charge of inconsistency, in a speech which was unfinished. From that charge he could, however, justify himself, and he would still maintain that he was perfectly consistent in his former opposition to the bank—an opposition which he still avowed—and his now voting, as he meant to do, against this motion to reconsider. He maintained that as his opposition to the Bank of the United States was grounded solely upon principle—from its unconstitutionality, in having a connexion with the Government—he could not see any difference could arise when it appeared that the Government was connecting itself with the State banks. It was upon this ground, if no other, he was justified. But, apart from this, he was opposed to any action on this subject, by a committee out of doors; knowing the encouragement that such a direction to it would, no doubt, give to speculators in stocks, who would, in some shape or other, get insight into their proceedings, by reports to the House, or otherwise. He desired to have the reasons of the Secretary of the Treasury examined in the House, to ensure a speedier action than could be had elsewhere. He argued, that if the reasons of the Secretary were not sufficient for the removal of the deposites, then he ought not to have removed them. But he begged to be understood distinctly, that he did not war against the directors of the bank; he warred against the institution on principle alone. He would not lend his aid to have it crushed suddenly. No! He knew, too well, the ruin and suffering that must ensue from the sudden winding up of an institution in which the public had so deep a stake—sufferings in which the Government itself must participate. He rather wished the institution to be let easily down, and that no attempt would be made to press on measures which must terminate in the destruction of thousands.

Mr. SPEIGHT declared, that as he thought the debate was carried on long enough, upon what was only a preliminary question, he would move the previous question.

Messrs. BRIGGS and WARD having been appointed tellers: the House refused to sustain the motion—Ayes 102, noes 113.

Mr. DENNY thanked the House for having rejected the motion, and said it would go well to the country as a good augury for this question, and show also that there were in the House those who would not suffer any attempt to force upon them the operation of what was aptly termed the gag-law, made only with a view to prevent the expression of their sentiments. He contended that if the report was sent to a select committee it would have the effect of preventing any discussion, or letting the public have any lights upon it. He asked, to use the language of the gentleman from Tennessee, why the friends of the Administration retreat from the discussion? He was not one of those who wished to do so, and that gentleman and those who acted with him ought to stand, to use the trite motto *semper paratis*. They ought to have been prepared for the result when they presented to the Congress the reasons of the Secretary, and have a prompt and immediate discussion upon it, affecting, as it confessedly did, the public credit and all the other important interests of the country. If it was sent to the Committee of Ways and Means it might lie there, as was said by the member from New York, full ninety days, and it would then have to come here and meet a similar delay. Adverting to what was argued by the honorable member from New York, [Mr. BEARDSLEY,] that it was unnecessary to have the report acted upon here, as public opinion had settled that the public deposites would not be restored, he, (Mr. D.,) however, differed from him as to this being a proper view of the public opinion; but if it was so, he asked, was that a reason why there should not be any discussion here? That honorable member also observed that the private or standing committees were best, as they could investigate the facts; but he maintained it was perfectly competent for the House itself to have any examination they thought proper to have as fully as any committee. He thought that much injustice would be done to the people if full discussion upon the reasons of the Secretary was not now had, and contended, at length, that as the Secretary was bound by law to furnish his reasons, they (the House of Representatives) were bound to examine—to pronounce upon them, and thus restore the nation to that state in which it was before the removal took place; to do which, they should not defer investigation until after the evils had been increased tenfold.

Mr. VANDERPOEL said that he could not boast the honor claimed by one of his colleagues, [Mr. SELDEN,] of representing the largest commercial city in the Union, but he might claim the honor of representing a people as deeply interested in the action of this Government as are the worthy constituents of the gentleman from New York—a

district agricultural, commercial, and deeply interested in manufactures—and (said Mr. V.) I only echo the sentiments of my constituents in the avowal that the removal of the public deposites from the Bank of the United States was loudly called for by the best interests of the country.

It must (said Mr. V.) be conceded that the disposition which the adversaries of the motion to reconsider propose to make of the document in question would be a departure from the ordinary usage of the House; that it ever has been customary, and must, from the nature and fitness of things, be customary, to refer papers of this description to the Committee of Ways and Means.

And on what ground is this departure from precedent and principle attempted to be justified? Oh, say gentlemen, expedition, immediate action is everything in this matter. They tell us that the subjection of this report to the ordinary routine of legislation would scatter bankruptcy and distress, if not desolation, through your commercial cities. Indeed! Whence do gentlemen derive this argument? Is it from the report of the Secretary, which is said to be so all-sufficient for immediate action, and beyond which they object to go? No, sir; I have not read it there, and the enemies to a reconsideration feel themselves, therefore, compelled to go beyond the report, in quest of an apology for the unprecedented course for which they are contending.

But (said Mr. V.) is it indeed true that the commercial distress resulting from the removal of the deposites is so great as to justify the precipitancy in proceeding which is now asked for? Is it true that Pandora's box was opened upon this devoted country, when the fiat of the Secretary of the Treasury to remove the public deposites went forth? Not so, sir, according to the statements of a document, the truth of which gentlemen propose to admit, by going immediately into Committee of the Whole—I mean the report of the Secretary of the Treasury.

This very able and triumphant document assigns other reasons for the commercial distress which has been depicted to us in such frightful colors. It tells us that in two short months immediately before the removal of the deposites, the Bank of the United States reduced its loans upwards of SIX MILLIONS OF DOLLARS; that this enormous amount was in so short a time withdrawn from the business of the country; that it had shortly before the Presidential election increased its loans to an unprecedented amount, for purposes which none can misunderstand; that the Government deposites were accumulating in the bank, and instead of loaning them, or discounting on the strength of them, as it had been accustomed to do, it was, after having thus stretched itself to its utmost tension, withholding its usual accommodations from the public, and thus producing great embarrassment and distress in your commercial cities; and the Secretary of the Treasury in this same document tells us, that the alleviation of this distress, thus occasioned by the sudden contraction of the bank, was one great object in ordering a removal of the deposites.

Sir, (said Mr. V.,) I may be permitted to go a step further on this point. I have the same right that other gentlemen exercise, to speculate and conjecture as to the causes which have produced the great dearth of money which has here been so much deplored. I might suppose, that the demand for money was much increased by reason of the new adjustment of your tariff, that all your woollens now pay cash duties; that the old bonds to Government are now falling due; and that nearly two years of imposts are now paid in one! This, no doubt, has contributed much to the scarcity in the money market which is now said to prevail.

Whence, sir, comes this astounding cry about the public distress? Does it not proceed from the friends of the bank, and do they not sound the tocsin of alarm louder than the actual state of things warrants? The great mass of the people, sir, are prosperous and happy, beyond all example; the fruit of the husbandman is abundant, and commands most liberal prices; lands are rapidly appreciating, and your people are everywhere making the most rapid strides in enterprise and prosperity. There may, indeed, be a pressure in the money market in your cities; but, sir, have there not always been fluctuations there? Yes, sir, they are the inevitable results of improvident over-trading and mad speculation—the tide of the ocean ebbs and flows not more certainly, than does the active capital of your commercial cities. An unprecedented inundation has lately taken place, as the Secretary of the Treasury tells you, and if a little sickness and distress are occasioned by the too sudden evaporation of the unnatural waters, we should take consolation from the prospect, that the deleterious fountain from which they flowed, is soon to be dried up, rather than dole out our lamentations about a little partial and temporary distress.

But it is said, that the suspense which now occupies the public mind, contributes largely to that distress; that the depository banks dare not discount upon the Government deposites, because they are fearful that the deposites will again be taken from them.

Of the actual existence of such suspense (said Mr. V.) I know nothing; but what has transpired to justify it? What has occurred to induce the belief, that the public deposites will be removed by this Congress? What cause is there to alarm the depository banks? Is it to be found in the vote of last Thursday in relation to the memorial of the Government directors? Is it to be found in the inconstancy and irresolution of the Secretary of the Treasury, or of that distinguished patriot, who presides over the Executive Department of this Government? No, no, sir. The history of the past is enough to admonish the world, not to found any hopes upon the fickleness or instability of those public functionaries who have ordered the removal of the deposites: with the sagacity to see plainly the path of duty, they unite the energy to follow it.

The necessity of committing the report in question to the Committee of Ways and Means is demonstrated by the strange incongruities, in which gentlemen who oppose the motion to reconsider, involve themselves. We were told by an eminent gentleman from Pennsylvania a few days ago, [Mr. BINNEY,] whose very ingenious remarks I listened to with great interest, that a reference of this report to a Committee of the Whole on the state of the Union would, in effect, and for the purpose of discussion in Committee of the Whole, be an admission of the truth of the facts set forth in the report, and the gentleman resorted to certain legal analogies to illustrate the view he took of the question. He told us that we were a court of review, called upon to revise the act of the Secretary of the Treasury; that his report was his award, and that as an appellate tribunal, we could not look *beyond the report:* that it embodied all the facts and reasons of the Secretary, and that the report must stand or fall by itself; and that nothing extrinsic could be received; and yet, strange as it may seem, he tells us almost in the same breath that the public deposites are unsafe in the State banks! Whence does he derive this fact? From the report of the Secretary? No, sir. He travels out of the record to support his case. This proves the necessity of referring the subject to the Committee of Ways and Means, who have power to inquire into this all-important question, whether the public deposites are safe. The Committee of the Whole on the state of the Union have no means of shedding any new light upon this all-important point. The question of the security or insecurity of your public treasure, is one of vital interest to this nation, and should be referred to a committee that can make the necessary inquiry.

Gentlemen tell us that they are willing, for the purpose of bringing the matter immediately before the Committee of the Whole on the state of the Union, to admit the facts set forth in the report, or in other words, they seem to demur to the report of the Secretary. I deny, sir, that any gentleman has a right to put in a demurrer that shall conclude the House. We may not be disposed to be very sceptical in relation to the facts and deductions of the Secretary of the Treasury, and yet we may and should be disposed, from a spirit of justice to the bank, to refer this matter to a committee, to examine and report whether the Secretary had not misconceived or given undue weight to facts; and I deny that gentlemen have a right to make any admission that shall supersede this further investigation. While, on the one hand, I would not sanction the relaxation of those over-indulgent prosecutors, who have heretofore filed their bills of indictment against the bank—so, on the other, I would not be too ready to try and condemn it upon the admissions of those who have undertaken its defence. I shall vote for a reconsideration, to the end that the subject may be referred to the appropriate committee.

Mr. McDUFFIE said, the invariable rule of all legislative bodies was, to settle great principles in the Committee of the Whole, and then to settle questions of detail in the standing committees. This was the parliamentary rule. Our course should be, first, to ascertain whether we have the right to violate the stipulations of the charter, and second, whether the President, on speculative conjectures as to the interference of the bank in elections, can direct the Secretary of the Treasury to remove the deposites. When these questions are settled, the House can direct any committee to report a bill in conformity with its decisions. The public mind would thus be quieted. He besought the House not to permit the great interests of the community to be sacrificed, while we carried on these petty disputes. It might be sport to us, but to the community it was death. Any man who, to serve any party purpose, shall keep back this question from a decision—but there is no such member here—deserves the execration of the community. There was no reason to go before a standing committee, unless for the purpose of obtaining another report in favor of the President's course. Had not the President given reasons, sufficiently ample and at length, for his course? Had not the Secretary of the Treasury taken time and pains enough to report his reasons for an act which he did two months before the commencement of the session? If the House went into the Committee of the Whole on the subject, he would introduce resolutions for the action of the House upon it.

Mr. SUTHERLAND said he had voted twice for the previous question, and again he should vote for it when he had an opportunity. He belonged to that class of representatives who were more anxious for the settlement of this question than of any other question. His constituents were deeply interested in an immediate decision of the question. But he thought the most speedy way of obtaining a decision was, to refer the subject to the Committee of Ways and Means. If we went into the discussion in the Committee of the Whole, we should never reach a decision. The Committee of Ways and Means would immediately give us a resolution, upon which our action would be definite and speedy. There must be an issue made up, and upon what issue would the House sooner act than upon one presented in a regular form from a standing committee? In the Committee of the Whole, we should have a dozen projects—one from the gentleman from South Carolina, others from many members. He hoped the question of reference would be settled this day. If the Committee of Ways and Means did not present a speedy report, he pledged himself to call upon them for the report. Action, action, was what he demanded.

Mr. FOOT said that the House could act upon the resolutions proposed to be submitted by the gentleman from South Carolina, as well as upon the issue which may be presented by the Committee of Ways and Means. To avoid a discussion on the subject was impossible, and the sooner we went into it the sooner we should arrive at a result. He referred to the rules of the House to show that the usage was to refer certain subjects to the Committee of the Whole, and contended that this was a subject which should take that direction.

Mr. JONES, of Georgia, did not agree with the gentleman from South Carolina, that the reasons given by the Secretary of the Treasury for the removal of the deposites were insufficient, but he had made up his mind that the proper place for the discussion of the subject was in the Committee of the Whole. He had twice voted against the previous question, and again he should vote against it. He was in favor of free and full discussion of every question of public importance. The discussion of this question was due to all those who were parties to it; it was due to the bank—to the State banks—to the public. As the matter must be finally settled in Committee of the Whole, he saw

no reason why we should delay to bring it before that committee.

Mr. PEYTON said, the people had pronounced a judgment upon this subject, which we were now called upon hastily to reverse. The American people dread no power—that of a corporation, or of any other power. The alarm attempted to be excited was without foundation. His own opinion was, that the subject ought to be referred first to a committee, and upon the report of that committee the House should act. The movement of the Secretary of the Treasury, two months in advance of the meeting of Congress, was necessary, he contended, in order to prevent the bank from withdrawing from the general circulation of the country nine millions of dollars more. He referred to many charges against the bank, which, unless gentlemen on the other side admitted them, ought to be subjects of investigation in a standing committee. Facts, as to which any dispute should arise, could not be settled in the Committee of the Whole.

Mr. DAVIS, of Massachusetts, wished the House to understand the nature of the question: it was a motion to reconsider a vote sending the report of the Secretary to the Committee of the Whole. Why is the motion made? It is to send the paper to the Committee of Ways and Means. What purpose is to be served by that course? First, it is said to be the usage of the House to refer such papers to that committee. But we referred, at the commencement of every session, the President's message to the Committee of the Whole. Why? Because it relates to great and general subjects—the great matters of the Union. There it was dissected and disposed of. The principle was, that all great subjects should be referred to the Committee of the Whole. The usage on smaller questions was exactly opposite. The argument of usage, therefore, falls to the ground. What is the next reason? The Committee of Ways and Means is to furnish facts. What right has that committee to give us facts? We are to look to the Secretary for the facts upon which the Secretary has acted. When we have his reasons, what more do we want? Why, it is said that there must be a report, echoing some public documents already before us. Well, if it is to go there for political purposes, let it be so understood. Let a political report, for political effect, be made. But one thing he desired: that these two matters—the report of the Secretary and the President's message, should not be separated.

Mr. LANE said, that so far as he had been able to gather the intentions of gentlemen, all were agreed in desiring as speedy a conclusion as could be arrived at; and, so far as his own vote was concerned, it should be on that side which he considered best calculated to reach that end. He was willing to put the question as to the proper disposition of the report of the Secretary, on a single proposition advanced by the gentleman from South Carolina, [Mr. McDuffie.] That gentleman said the paper must go to the Committee of the Whole, in order that the great and obvious principles involved might there be settled. Now, he had supposed that the great and obvious principles of truth were always known and always settled; that they were firm and settled as the course of time; and that great principles were only useful in their practical application to things. He had now, for the first time, learned what was the real object of that gentleman: it was to discuss the report of the Secretary of the Treasury, together with the weekly reports of the bank; and the gentleman had had the candor to tell the House that those weekly reports do contradict the averments of the Secretary; so that it appeared an issue was to be made up between the statements of the Secretary and the statements of the bank reports. Now, how was this issue to be settled? By first discussing great and obvious principles in Committee of the Whole? No. By sending both, together with the reports of the directors of the bank, to the Committee of Ways and Means. Let the committee settle the issue; and let them bring back, as speedily as possible, their report into the House. When once the facts were settled, what was the object of discussion? To ascertain the truth. Was the Secretary right, or were the directors right? When this was the question brought before the Committee of the Whole on the state of the Union, how simple and how obvious would be the inquiry which would occupy its attention! It was easy to apply great principles—they were as simple as light. Inasmuch as the saving of time was the great object on all hands, let the paper go to the Committee of Ways and Means; let it be accompanied, if gentlemen pleased, with instructions; and let the investigation, the decision, and the report follow each other in quick succession.

The House had been told that a great state of alarm existed in the country, and that a further continuance of the present state of uncertainty was much more to be apprehended than any result of the question. Since this had been stated, and facts had been referred to in support of it, he would inquire of gentlemen (he did it with great reluctance—and should not, had not the statements made compelled him to such a course) who had spread this alarm? Who had proclaimed it abroad? The Secretary had declared in his report that all was well; here was the voice of peace. Did the gentleman learn it from the venerable man who filled the Executive chair? No. Did he hear it from gentlemen on that floor who were the avowed friends of the Administration? No. The alarm came from a different quarter entirely. The cry of "fire!" came from the opposite side of the House. No doubt the cry was raised in all sincerity, but it came not from those who acted with him. Mr. L. concluded by expressing his hope that the paper would go to the committee of Ways and Means; that they would report without delay, and that all would act upon the subject without reference to local or to party feelings, and like members of one common family, would all conspire to allay the alarm which was said to prevail.

The question was then taken by yeas and nays, and decided in the affirmative, as follows:

YEAS—Messrs. John Adams, John J. Allen, William Allen, Anthony, Baylies, Beale, Bean, Beardsley, Beaumont, John Bell, James Blair, John Blair, Bockee, Bodle, Boon, Brown, Bunch, Burns, Bynum, Cambreleng, Carmichael, Carr, Casey, Chaney, Chinn, Claiborne, Samuel Clark, Clay, Coffee, Connor, Cramer, Day, P. Dickerson, D. W. Dickinson, Dunlap, Forester, Fowler, William K. Fuller, Fulton, Galbraith, Gholson, Gillet, Joseph Hall, Thos. H. Hall, Halsey, Hamer, Hannegan, Joseph M. Harper, Harrison, Hathaway, Hawkins, Hawes, Henderson, Howell, Hubbard, A. Huntington, Inge, Jarvis, R. M. Johnson, N. Johnson, C. Johnson, B. Jones, Kavanagh, Kinnard, Lane, Lansing, Laporte, Lawrence, Lea, Leavitt, Lee, Loyall, Lucas, Lyon, Abijah Mann, J. K. Mann, Mardis, Mason, McCarty, McComas, McKay, McKim, McKinley, McLene, McVean, Miller, R. Mitchell, Muhlenberg, Murphy, Osgood, Page, Parks, Parker, Patton, Patterson, D. J. Pearce, Peyton, F. Pierce, Pierson, Polk, Pope, Ramsey, Schenck, Schley, A. H. Shepperd, Shinn, Charles Slade, Smith, Speight, Standifer, Stoddert, Sutherland, William Taylor, John Thomson, Turner, Turrill, Vanderpoel, Van Houten, Wagener, Ward, Wardwell, Wayne, Webster, Whallon, C. P. White, and Wise—124.

NAYS—Messrs. John Q. Adams, H. Allen, C. Allan, Archer, Ashley, Banks, Barber, Barnitz, Barringer, Bates, Beatty, J. M. Bell, Binney, Bouldin, Briggs, Bullard, Bull, Burd, Burges, Cage, Chambers, Chilton, Choate, W. Clark, Clayton, Clowney, Corwin, Coulter, Crane, Crockett, Darlington, John Davis, W. R. Davis, A. Davis, Davenport, Deberry, Deming, Denny, Dennis, Dickson, Duncan, Ellsworth, Evans, Edward Everett, Horace Everett, Ewing, Felder, Fillmore, Foot, Foster, Philo C. Fuller, Gamble, Gilmer, Gordon, Gorham, Grayson, Grennell, Griffin, Hiland Hall, Hard, Hardin, James Harper, Hazeltine, Heath, Hiester, Jabez W. Huntington, W. Cost Johnson, Seaborn Jones, King, Lewis, Love, Martindale, Marshall, McDuffie, McKennan, Mercer, Milligan, Moore, Pinckney, Potts, Reed, Rencher, Selden, W. B. Shepard, Wm. Slade, Sloane, Spangler, Stewart, Wm. P. Taylor, Philemon Thomas, Tompkins, Tweedy, Vance, Vinton, Watmough, E. D. White, Frederick Whittlesey, Elisha Whittlesey, Wilde, Williams, Wilson, and Young—102.

So the House agreed to reconsider the vote referring the report of the Secretary of the Treasury to the Committee of the Whole.

Mr. POLK then moved that the report of the Secretary of the Treasury be referred to the Committee of Ways and Means.

Mr. McDUFFIE moved the following instructions to the Committee on Ways and Means:

"To report a joint resolution providing that the public revenue hereafter collected be deposited in the Bank of the United States, in conformity with the public faith pledged in the charter of the said bank."

Mr. McDUFFIE then moved [at half past three o'clock] that the House do now adjourn.

Messrs. PATTON and WARDWELL, being appointed tellers, the question was taken on the adjournment, and decided in the affirmative—ayes 110, noes 102.

The House then adjourned.

IN SENATE.

WEDNESDAY, *December* 18, 1833.

A message was received from the President of the United States by Mr. Donelson, his Private Secretary.

Various memorials and petitions were presented by Messrs. WILKINS, SILSBEE, CHAMBERS, WRIGHT, KENT, FRELINGHUYSEN, HENDRICKS, TYLER, PRENTISS, McKEAN, SPRAGUE, SHEPLEY, TIPTON.

Mr. EWING, on leave, introduced a bill for the relief of the legal representatives of Hugh McGinnis, deceased; which was read twice, and referred to the Committee on Claims.

Mr. HENDRICKS, on leave given, introduced a bill for the relief of the heirs and legal representatives of Captain Robert Beal, deceased; which was read twice, and referred to the Committee on Revolutionary Claims.

Mr. TYLER, on leave given, introduced a bill for the relief of the legal representatives of William McKinley; which was read twice, and referred to the Committee on Finance.

Mr. BIBB, on leave given, introduced a bill for the relief of the sureties of John H. Morton; which was read twice, and referred to the Committee on the Judiciary, together with additional documents in relation thereto.

Mr. SILSBEE, on leave given, introduced a bill for the relief of Phineas Sprague and others; which was read twice, and referred to the Committee on Commerce.

On motion of Mr. POINDEXTER, so much of the President's Message as relates to the public lands, was referred to the Committee on the Public Lands.

On motion of Mr. GRUNDY, so much of the President's Message as relates to the post office, was referred to the Committee on Post Offices and Post Roads.

On motion of Mr. SILSBEE, so much of the President's Message as relates to commerce, was referred to the committee on that subject.

On motion of Mr. WEBSTER, so much of the President's Message as relates to finance, was referred to the committee on that subject.

On motion of Mr. WHITE, so much of the President's Message as relates to Indian affairs, was referred to the committee on that subject.

On motion of Mr. BENTON, so much of the Message as relates to military affairs, was referred to the Committee on Military Affairs.

On motion of Mr. SOUTHARD, so much of the said Message as relates to naval affairs, was referred to the committee on that subject.

The VICE PRESIDENT laid before the Senate communications from the Secretary of War and Commissioner of Pensions; which, on motion of Mr. TOMLINSON, were referred to the Committee on Pensions, and ordered to be printed.

On motion of Mr. KING, the following resolution, offered by him on Tuesday the 11th instant, was considered and agreed to:

Resolved, That the Committee on Indian Affairs be instructed to inquire into the expediency of authorizing the President of the United States to appoint an agent to receive evidence of losses sustained by the inhabitants of the now State of Alabama, by a hostile eruption of a party of Creek Indians, in the year 1814, by which Fort Mims was taken, and those who had fled there for protection massacred.

On motion of Mr. BENTON, the bill granting to the State of Missouri a certain quantity of public land for purposes of internal improvement, and the bill graduating the price of the public lands, were referred to the Committee on Public Lands.

On motion of Mr. MOORE, the bill to establish a pension agency in North Alabama, was referred to the Committee on Pensions.

On motion of Mr. MOORE, the bill authorizing a relinquishment of the sixteenth section of the public lands, granted for the use of schools, and granting other lands in lieu thereof, was referred to the Committee on Public Lands.

On motion of Mr. CLAY, the bill to distribute the proceeds of the public lands to and among the several States, for a limited period, was referred to the Committee on the Public Lands.

On motion of Mr. FORSYTH, the bill providing for the fulfilment of the compact of 1802, between the United States and Georgia, was referred to the Committee on Indian Affairs.

On motion of Mr. WEBSTER, the bill to provide indemnity for French spoliations, was referred to a select committee consisting of Messrs. WEBSTER, CHAMBERS, GRUNDY, and BENTON. And,

The special order of the day being announced by the Chair to be the consideration of the resolution relative to the removal of the deposites—

Mr. CLAY said he was aware that the subject was one which ought to be disposed of at as early a period as was practicable. Some information had been called for, in relation to this matter, which has not been had, and which it was necessary to obtain before he could go into the discussion of the question, and therefore he moved a postponement of it until Monday next; which was agreed to.

On motion of Mr. WILKINS, the bill for the relief of A. G. Ralston and G. Ralston was referred to the Committee on Finance.

On motion of Mr. BENTON, the bill to regulate and fix the pay of the Medical Staff of the Army was referred to the Committee on Military Affairs.

On motion of Mr. KING, of Alabama, the bill for the relief of Thomas Rhoads and others, and the bill for the relief of John Hanmer and William Johnson, were referred to the Committee on the Post Office and Post Roads; and

The bill for the relief of Theodore Brightwell was referred to the Committee on the Judiciary.

On motion of Mr. MOORE, the bill for the relief of Eli Robbins, and the bill for the relief of John McCarty, were referred to the Committee on Claims.

On motion of Mr. TYLER, the bill for the relief of Robert White was referred to the Committee on Revolutionary Claims.

On motion of Mr. TYLER, the bill for the relief of William Mosby was referred to the Committee on Claims.

On motion of Mr. ROBINSON, the bill granting compensation to certain persons for horses lost in the late war, was referred to the Committee on Claims.

On motion of Mr. TIPTON, the bill granting preëmption rights to settlers on the public lands, was referred to the Committee on Public Lands.

Mr. POINDEXTER submitted the following resolution:

Resolved, That the Commissioner of the General Land Office be directed to communicate to the Senate—

1st. The whole amount of public lands belonging to the United States, exhibiting the net proceeds, and distinguishing between those which have been sold within the limits of Louisiana, Florida, and other parts of the United States, respectively, and including the latest returns.

2d. The whole amount of public lands which have been surveyed and exposed to sale in the several States and Territories; and showing the amount sold and the amount remaining to be sold, according to the last returns.

3d. The amount which has been actually patented in bounties to the army, during the late war.

4th. The amount granted to each of the several States and Territories, and for what purposes.

5th. The amount set apart or reserved for schools in the several States and Territories.

6th. The amount granted in donations for the cultivation of the vine and olive, to Lafayette, and for all other purposes.

Mr. HENDRICKS submitted the following resolution:

Resolved, That the Committee on Commerce be instructed to inquire into the expediency of making an appropriation to remove obstructions to the navigation of the Wabash river, and that the documents on that subject now on file in the office of the Secretary of the Senate, be also referred to the same committee.

Mr. ROBBINS submitted the following resolutions:

Resolved, That the Committee on Naval Affairs be instructed to inquire into the expediency of establishing a naval depôt, and post of expedition and rendezvous, within the waters of Narraganset Bay.

Resolved, That so much of the report of the Board of Navy Commissioners, made December 19, 1829, and of the report of the Secretary of the Navy, made December 6, 1830, as relates to the establishment of a depôt within said waters, together with the report of the survey of said bay, communicated to the Senate December 19, 1832, with the several charts relating to the same, be referred to said committee.

Mr. HENDRICKS submitted the following resolution:

Resolved, That the Committee on the Post Office and Post Roads be instructed to inquire into the expediency of establishing a post route from Greensburg by Fugitaville, Hartville, Goshen, and Newburg, to Columbus.

Resolved, Also, a post route from Indianapolis, by Danville, Bainbridge, and Chiltonville, to Rockville.

Mr. TIPTON submitted the following resolution:

Resolved, That the Committee on Commerce be instructed to inquire into the expediency of making appropriations for the following objects, viz:

1st. An appropriation for constructing a ship channel to connect the waters of the River Raisin with La Plaisance Bay, in the Territory of Michigan, under the direction of the War Department.

2d. An appropriation for constructing a harbor at the mouth of St. Joseph's river, on Lake Michigan, in Michigan Territory.

3d. An appropriation to defray the expense of surveying the obstructions to the navigation of St. Joseph's river, and its tributaries, as far up as the said streams may be considered navigable.

4th. An appropriation for constructing a harbor at the mouth of Trail Creek, on Lake Michigan, in the State of Indiana.

Mr. MOORE submitted the following resolution:

Resolved, That the Secretary of War communicate to the Senate the correspondence between that department and the several agents, and other persons who have been employed in the removal, or in the arrangement for removal of the Indian tribes. Also, all correspondence between the department and other individuals on the subject of Indian affairs, including the names of agents or other persons who have been employed in making Indian treaties, in the removal of Indians, taking the census of Indians, or in locating the reservations allowed by treaties to Indians, with a statement of the several sums disbursed by each, showing the amount expended, the persons to whom it has been paid, and the specific services or consideration for which they have been paid.

Mr. CLAY submitted the following resolutions:

Resolved, That the Secretary of the Treasury be directed to communicate to the Senate a copy of the entire letter, addressed by Mr. Crawford, when Secretary of the Treasury, under date the 13th February, 1817, to the President of the Mechanics' Bank of New York, an extract from which is recited in his report to Congress of the 3d December, 1833; and copies of the other correspondence of Mr. Crawford with the banks, about that period, to passages in which the Secretary alludes in the same report.

Resolved, also, That the Secretary be directed to communicate to the Senate a copy of the correspondence between the agent appointed during the

last summer, to inquire upon what terms the State banks would undertake to perform the services to the Government which had been performed by the Bank of the United States, and the said bank; a copy of the report made, if one was made, by the said agent to the Secretary or the Executive; the name of the agent, his compensation, and in virtue of what law he was appointed.

The Senate then adjourned.

HOUSE OF REPRESENTATIVES.

BANK OF THE UNITED STATES.

Mr. BINNEY presented a memorial from the President and Directors of the Bank of the United States, asking redress for the violation of their charter by the removal of the public deposites. He did not desire any action upon it now, but would move that it should be laid on the table and printed.

Mr. POLK moved that the memorial should be referred to the Committee of Ways and Means, and demanded that the question should be taken by yeas and nays, which were ordered: yeas 95—nays not counted.

Mr. WATMOUGH rose to address the House, but the SPEAKER informed him it was not in order to debate a motion to lay on the table.

Mr. POLK called for a division of the question.

Mr. BINNEY asked for the reading of the memorial, which was as follows:

To the Senate and House of Representatives of the United States:

The Board of Directors of the Bank of the United States, respectfully represent—

That by the charter of the Bank, it was stipulated between the Congress of the United States, and the stockholders of the Bank of the United States, that in consideration of a full equivalent rendered by them, in money and services, they were entitled to the custody of the public moneys, which were not to be withdrawn from it, unless for the reasons, of the sufficiency of which Congress, and Congress alone, was the final judge.

That the Bank has in all things faithfully performed the stipulations of the charter.

Nevertheless, since the adjournment of Congress, the Secretary of the Treasury has issued an order on the 26th of September last, withdrawing from the possession of the bank the custom-house bonds deposited therein, and has subsequently transferred to certain State banks a large portion of the public moneys then in the safe-keeping of the bank, with the purpose of making them hereafter the permanent depositories of the public revenue.

The Board of Directors therefore deem it their duty forthwith to apprise your honorable bodies of the violation of the chartered rights of the stockholders, and to ask such redress therefor as to your sense of justice may seem proper.

By order of the board:

N. BIDDLE,

President of the Bank of the U. States.

PHILADELPHIA, *December* 9, 1833.

The question on that part of the motion—to lay it on the table—was put, and decided in the negative, as follows:

YEAS—Messrs. John Q. Adams, H. Allen, C. Allan, Archer, Ashley, Banks, Barber, Barnitz, Barringer, Beaty, James M. Bell, Binney, Bouldin, Briggs, Bullard, Bull, Burd, Burges, Cage, Chambers, Chilton, Choate, Wm. Clark, Clowney, Corwin, Coulter, Crane, Crockett, Darlington, Amos Davis, Davenport, Deberry, Deming, Dickson, Ellsworth, Evans, Edward Everett, Horace Everett, Felder, Gordon, Gorham, Grayson, Grennell, Griffin, Hiland Hall, Hard, Hardin, J. Harper, Hazeltine, Heath, Hiester, J. W. Huntington, Wm. C. Johnson, Seaborn Jones, King, Love, Martindale, Marshall, McComas, McKennan, Mercer, Milligan, Patton, Pinckney, Potts, Rencher, Shepard, Shepperd, Wm. Slade, Sloane, Spangler, Philemon Thomas, Tompkins, Turner, Tweedy, Vance, Vinton, Watmough, Edward D. White, Frederick Whittlesey, Elisha Whittlesey, Wilde, Williams, Young—84.

NAYS—Messrs. John Adams, John J. Allen, William Allen, Bates, Baylies, Beale, Bean, Beardsley, Beaumont, John Bell, James Blair,

John Blair, Bockee, Bodle, Boon, Brown, Bunch, Burns, Bynum, Cambreleng, Carmichael, Carr, Casey, Chaney, Chinn, Claiborne, Samuel Clark, Clay, Clayton, Connor, Cramer, Day, Dickerson, Dickinson, Duncan, Dunlap, Ewing, Fillmore, Forester, Fowler, Philo C. Fuller, William K. Fuller, Fulton, Galbraith, Gholson, Gillet, Gilmer, Joseph H. Hall, Thomas H. Hall, Halsey, Hamer, Hannegan, Joseph M. Harper, Harrison, Hathaway, Hawkins, Henderson, Howell, Hubbard, Abel Huntington, Inge, Jarvis, Richard M. Johnson, Noadiah Johnson, Cave Johnson, Benjamin Jones, Kavanagh, Kinnard, Lane, Lansing, Laporte, Lawrence, Lee, Leavitt, Lee, Loyall, Lucas, Abijah Mann, Joel K. Mann, Mardis, Mason, McCarty, McIntire, McKay, McKim, McKinley, McLene, McVean, Miller, R. Mitchell, Samuel McD. Moore, Muhlenberg, Murphy, Osgood, Page, Parks, Parker, Patterson, Pearce, Pierce, Pierson, Polk, Pope, Ramsey, Schenck, Schley, Shinn, Charles Slade, Smith, Speight, Standifer, Stoddert, Sutherland, William Taylor, William P. Taylor, John Thomson, Turrill, Vanderpoel, Van Houten, Wagener, Ward, Wardwell, Webster, Whallon, Campbell P. White, Wilson, Wise—126.

The memorial was then ordered to be printed.

Mr. CHILTON moved to amend Mr. POLK's motion, by instructing the Committee of Ways and Means, in substance, to report a joint resolution, directing the Secretary of the Treasury to restore the public deposites to the Bank of the United States.

[Mr. C. addressed the House at length in support of his amendment, and went into the general subject of the bank; but having concluded with a request to the reporters, that, although they might, if they thought proper, present their own views, they should abstain from giving his remarks, until further directions from him; and, as will be seen in the subsequent proceedings that the amendment was withdrawn by Mr. C., the reporter feels pleasure in acceding to his wishes.]

The yeas and nays having been ordered on the call of Mr. CHILTON, and the question on his amendment stated,

Mr. McDUFFIE requested the gentleman from Kentucky to withdraw his proposition, as it seemed to forestall the other proceedings, which were then undisposed of, and about to come up for discussion.

Mr. CHILTON consented to withdraw his amendment; and the memorial was then referred to the Committee of Ways and Means.

On motion of Mr. SLADE, of Vermont,
Resolved, That the Committee on Invalid Pensions be instructed to inquire into the expediency of restoring to the roll of invalid pensioners the names of those who have relinquished their claim to such pensions, for the purpose of obtaining the benefit of the pension laws of the 18th March, 1818, and 1st of May, 1820.

On motion of Mr. JARVIS,
Resolved, That a committee be appointed, whose duty it shall be to consider all matters referred to them touching the public buildings and public grounds within the city of Washington, with leave to report by bill or otherwise.

On motion of Mr. McINTIRE,
Resolved, That the Committee on Revolutionary Claims be instructed to inquire into the expediency of making appropriation by law for paying Nicholas Scammon, the bearer of a prize certificate, the amount due thereon, which certificate issued from the War Office of the United States, under date of the 29th of April, 1780, for $500, with interest annually, payable to Thomas Cutts, or bearer, numbered 228.

On motion of Mr. DEMING,
Resolved, That the Committee on Revolutionary Pensions be instructed to inquire into the expediency of granting a pension to Jonathan Elkins, of Caledonia county, in the State of Vermont, on account of his services and sufferings during the war of the Revolution.

On motion of Mr. WARDWELL,
Resolved, That the Committee on Revolutionary Pensions inquire into the expediency of granting a pension to Abel Potter, of the State of New York, for his services in the revolutionary war.

Mr. STEWART submitted the following resolution; which lies one day for consideration:
Resolved, That the Secretary of War be directed to communicate to this House the report of the engineer employed to make a survey, plan, and estimate, with a view to the improvement of the steamboat navigation of the Monongahela river.

On motion of Mr. BEAUMONT,
Resolved, That the Committee on Revolutionary Claims be instructed to inquire into the propriety of making compensation to the heirs of Benjamin Harvey, deceased, for bounty lands, and services rendered the United States during the Revolutionary war.

On motion of Mr. FULTON,
Resolved, That the Committee on the Post Office and Post Roads be instructed to inquire into the expediency of establishing a post route from Abingdon, Va., to Grayson Court-house, in the same State.

On motion of Mr. R. M. JOHNSON,
Resolved, That the Committee on the Public Lands be instructed to inquire into the expediency of making an additional appropriation of land to satisfy the warrants in scrip which have issued, or which may hereafter issue, according to the resolutions and laws of the United States and Virginia, for revolutionary services.

Resolved, That the Committee on the Judiciary be instructed to inquire into the expediency of amending and continuing the act of Congress, entitled "An act in addition to an act entitled an act for the relief of certain insolvent debtors of the United States," which expires the 4th of March next.

On motion of Mr. C. JOHNSON,
Resolved, That all the papers and documents now on the files of the House in relation to the establishment of an armory on the western waters, be referred to the Committee on Military Affairs, and that they have leave to report by bill or otherwise.

Mr. E. WHITTLESEY submitted the following resolution, which lies one day:
Resolved, That so much of the 13th rule of the House as follows, to wit: "and other persons introduced by the Speaker or by a member of the House, shall be admitted within the Hall of the House of Representatives," be and the same is hereby rescinded.

On motion of Mr. HANNEGAN,
Resolved, That the Committee on Roads and Canals be instructed to inquire into the expediency of making an appropriation for the necessary survey and construction of a harbor at the mouth of Trail creek, on Lake Michigan.

On motion of Mr. KINNARD,
Resolved, That the Committee on Public Lands be instructed to inquire into the expediency of embracing the State of Indiana and the Territories of Michigan and Huron, in one surveyor general's district; and of locating the office of surveyor general, for said district, at Indianapolis, in the State of Indiana.

On motion of Mr. SLADE, of Illinois,
Resolved, That the Committee on Roads and Canals be instructed to inquire into the expediency of causing a survey and estimate of the expense of improving the navigation of the Kaskaskia river, in the State of Illinois, from the town of Shelbyville to its junction with the Mississippi river.

Resolved, That the same Committee be instructed to inquire into the expediency of causing a re-survey of the national road from Vandalia, the seat of government, in the State of Illinois, to the Mississippi river.

On motion of Mr. DUNCAN,
Resolved, That the Committee on Roads and Canals be instructed to inquire into the expediency of affording some efficient aid to the State of Illinois, in the construction of a steamboat canal from lake Michigan to the Illinois river.

Mr. ASHLEY submitted the following preamble and resolution, which was agreed to:
Whereas the President of the United States entertains doubts of the action of Congress on the claims of six companies of Missouri militia, for services rendered during the late war with the Indians, on the northern frontier, consequently payment to those companies has been withheld; therefore,

Resolved, That the Committee on Ways and Means be instructed to inquire whether an appropriation for the purpose aforesaid was made at the last session of Congress, and if not, to inquire into the expediency of appropriating a sufficient sum for that purpose.

Mr. EWING submitted the following resolution:
Resolved, That the Committee of Ways and Means be instructed to inquire into the expediency of authorizing a national currency of $35,000,000, to be founded upon the faith of the United States, and to be unconnected with, and independent of, all direct Executive control, except as may be required for the nomination of directors; said currency to be struck, perfected, and issued in a department of the mint of the United States, under regulations to secure an impartial distribution thereof among the several States respectively, according to representative population, if the same be required in virtue of the plighted faith and resources of each State so requiring, to the United States for its redemption, according to the legal stipulations on its face, and the payment of such bonus to the treasury of the United States to defray expense, and to guaranty ulterior responsibility, as may be prescribed; and said currency so authorised and loaned according to the prescribed ratio to States requiring its use, when loaned to the people through State instrumentality, shall be received in payment of public lands, and in payment of all other revenue accruing to the General Government, and shall be obligatory upon the State issuing the same to redeem on demand at her office of discount and deposite, which said State office, when established, under State guarantee, to loan and to redeem said currency, shall be the place of deposite of all public money collected or belonging to the General Government, within the limits of the State where it existed; also, to inquire into the comparative expediency of establishing a national bank, based upon a specie capital, to be furnished by the several States, as sole stockholders thereof, on a scale proportionate to the representative population of each, with a branch in each State, the institution to be regulated in strict accordance with uniform general rules, adopted by Congress under a directory of State appointment, and each State to enjoy the benefit of a capital, and exercise a power in accordance with her vested interest therein; said committee to report by bill or otherwise.

Mr. EWING said this was a momentous question. This Union was dependent on no corporations. This House had the power of creating a sound currency for the country, if the local currency should become disordered. He could show that the institution which he proposed would produce a safer and more uniform currency than we now had. It would also enrich the States, and promote those improvements on which the prosperity of the country depends.

The resolution was agreed to.

On motion of Mr. STEWART,
The House then adjourned.

IN SENATE.

THURSDAY, *December* 19, 1833.

Petitions and memorials were presented by Messrs. PRENTISS, LINN, BIBB RIVES, HILL, PRESTON, CHAMBERS, WRIGHT, FRELINGHUYSEN, BELL, TOMLINSON, SPRAGUE, TYLER, CLAY, WILKINS, SILSBEE, and KING of Alabama.

Mr. POINDEXTER, on leave given, presented a bill for the relief of Elihu Hall Bay, which was read twice and referred to the Committee on Private Land Claims.

Mr. CHAMBERS, on leave given, introduced a bill providing for payment of interest on the claims of the several States for moneys advanced during the last war; which was read twice and referred to the Committee on the Judiciary.

Mr. POINDEXTER submitted the following resolution:
Resolved, That the Sergeant-at-Arms be authorised to subscribe for three daily papers published in the District of Columbia, for the use of the Senate.

On motion of Mr. TYLER, the bill for the relief of Moses Sheppard, was referred to the Committee on Claims.

Mr. TYLER, on leave given, presented a bill to repeal the act for the better organization of the Treasury Department, passed in May, 1820.

On motion of Mr. TYLER, the bill was read twice and referred to the Committee on Finance.

Mr. CLAY presented a petition from citizens of Schenectady, New York, requesting the attention of Congress to the frequent fires on board steamboats. Mr. C. hoped that the committee to whom it might be referred would also direct its attention to another subject of immense importance, and intimately connected with this, which was the frequent lamentable accidents and loss of life resulting from the bursting of steamboat boilers. He suggested the reference of the petition to the Committee on Naval Affairs.

Mr. BIBB thought the most proper reference would be the Committee on Commerce. He thought that so far as Congress was authorized to interfere on such a subject, it must be with a view to regulate the commercial intercourse of the community; therefore he thought the Committee on Commerce was the most appropriate one.

Mr. CLAY said, it was indifferent to him.

The petition was referred to the Committee on Naval Affairs.

Mr. GRUNDY submitted the following resolution, calling for information which, he said, every member of the Senate would desire to be laid before the House, and he hoped no objection would be made to its being immediately considered:

Resolved, That the Postmaster General be directed to communicate to the Senate a statement of all the allowances made by him beyond the sums stipulated in the original contract, since the 6th of April, 1829, specifying, in every case, the service to be performed by the original contract, and the sums to be paid thereon; the nature and extent of each facility or improvement, and the extra allowance made therefor, and the names of the persons to whom the allowance has been made, and at what time.

2d. A statement of the curtailments of facilities lately made by the department, specifying each route and the names of the respective contractors, and the amount of the diminutions of service, and of compensation in each case; also, what routes, if any, have been discontinued.

3d. The expense incurred in putting into operation the post routes established by the act of the 15th of June, 1832, and the cost of transporting the mail on said routes in each year.

Mr. CLAY said he was glad that the gentleman from Tennessee had offered this resolution. There was no branch of the General Government, the correct administration of which was of more importance than that of the Post Office Department. If there were abuses in it—he did not say there were any—they ought to be corrected. He would, however, suggest to the gentleman, that if the resolution was not limited as to time, much delay would ensue. If there was any truth in what rumor said on the subject, great abuses existed in that branch of the Government. The Postmaster General, if the inquiry were not limited, might go back to the time of Mr. Habersham's administration in search of information supposed to be wanted, and thus we would never have a report.

Mr. GRUNDY thought the gentleman from Kentucky had not attended to the phraseology of the resolution; if he had, he would have perceived that it only went back to the commencement of Mr. Barry's administration. The gentleman had observed that if what rumor said was true, there were great abuses in the department. He (Mr. G.) hoped gentlemen would not trust to rumor. We want the truth; we want facts. His object was this: He wanted the facts to come out, and if there be anything wrong there, let it come out, and let the people know it. But if nothing censurable shall appear, let all rumors be put down. Let us see what the present head of that department has done, and then let opinion be formed. He could not believe it possible that any delay could occur. In a very few weeks we could have all the information required, and more, if the Senate desired it. The resolution embraced the whole administration of that department from the commencement of Mr. Barry's administration of it, and he hoped all would suspend their opinions—would wait until the information to be obtained should justify either censure or approbation.

The resolution was then agreed to.

Mr. SOUTHARD, from the Committee on Naval Affairs, reported a bill for the relief of John A. Webster.

Mr. WEBSTER submitted the following resolution:

Resolved, That the Committee on Naval Affairs be instructed to inquire into the expediency of passing a law for preventing, as far as may be, accidents to vessels employed in the foreign or coastwise commerce of the United States, from the explosion of steam.

Mr. MANGUM said it was with profound regret that he rose to call the attention of the Senate to a subject involving important principles. He alluded to the message of the President of the United States to the Senate of the 12th instant. He regretted that the duty devolved upon him. He had hoped some other gentleman than himself would have directed the attention of the Senate to it. The subject was one involving matters of grave moment, as it touched the great constitutional rights of the Senate, and as it touched that high courtesy and mutual respect which ought to subsist between the various branches of the Government. That the Senate should prove deficient in these respects, would to him be matter of great regret. That the Senate had transcended its constitutional rights, in the request which it had made on the Executive in the matter alluded to, must not be admitted. It was, therefore, due to the dignity of the Senate, and due to the institutions of the country, to review its whole course in this matter, and if the Senate had done wrong—if it had transcended its rights—to retrace their steps. But if it had not transcended its just rights, it was our duty to maintain the constitutional rights of the Senate. He (Mr. M.) was one who, in the simplicity of his heart, had voted for the resolution calling for information of the President—never dreaming of its being an invasion of Executive power. And he would suppose it impossible that the Senate should lose sight of that respect which was due to the highest functionary of the Government. His object was to take up the message for consideration, and to move its reference to a select committee.

Which was agreed to.

The Senate then balloted, when the following gentlemen were announced as the committee: Messrs. MANGUM, WHITE, FORSYTH, EWING, SOUTHARD, RIVES, and BIBB.

Mr. FORSYTH asked to be excused from serving upon the committee.

Mr. GRUNDY hoped the gentleman would not be excused, or all might be excused.

Mr. FORSYTH said, gentlemen did not seem to perceive the awkward situation in which he was placed. He would be compelled to sit in judgment between the President of the United States and the majority of the Senate upon a matter in which his opinion was unchanged and he might say unchangeable.

Mr. BIBB opposed Mr. FORSYTH's request, which was not agreed to.

On motion of Mr. ROBBINS, the Senate concurred in the joint resolution from the House of Representatives for the appointment of a Library Committee, and Messrs. ROBBINS, POINDEXTER, and BIBB, were chosen on the part of the Senate.

Mr. KING submitted the following resolution:

Resolved, That the Committee on Public Lands be instructed to inquire into the expediency of authorizing the Secretary of the Treasury to pay over to the State of Alabama, to be applied to the construction of a railroad from the Tennessee to the Alabama river, two per cent. of the proceeds of the sales of the public lands, which has been set apart for making roads to and from said State, under the direction of Congress.

The following resolutions, submitted yesterday, were taken up and agreed to—

By Mr. ROBBINS:

Resolved, That the Committee on Naval Affairs be instructed to inquire into the expediency of establishing a naval depôt and post of expedition and rendezvous within the waters of Narraganset bay.

Resolved, That so much of the report of the Board of Navy Commissioners, made October 19, 1829, and of the report of the Secretary of the Navy, made December 6, 1830, as relates to the establishment of a depôt within said waters, together with the report of the survey of said bay, communicated to the Senate, December 19, 1832, with the several charts relating to the same, be referred to said committee.

By Mr. HENDRICKS:

Resolved, That the Committee on the Post Office and Post Roads be instructed to inquire into the expediency of establishing a post route from Greensburg by Fugitsville, Hartville, Goshen, and Newburg, to Columbus.

Also, a post route from Indianapolis, by Danville, Bainbridge, and Chiltonville, to Rockville.

Mr. HILL presented a memorial from the Legislature of New Hampshire, requesting the Senators and Representatives in Congress from that State to use their exertions to procure a more perfect organization of the militia of the United States; which was referred to the Committee on the Militia.

Mr. TIPTON submitted the following resolutions:

Resolved, That the Committee on Commerce be instructed to inquire into the expediency of making an appropriation for building a light-house at the mouth of the Kalamazoo and Grand rivers, on Lake Michigan, Michigan Territory, and for surveying the bars at the mouths of both these rivers.

Resolved, That the Committee on Commerce be instructed to inquire into the expediency of an appropriation for surveying the flats in Lake St. Clair, at the mouth of St. Clair river; and also for removing the bar, and building a pier, if necessary, at the mouth of the river Clinton, in Lake St. Clair, in the Territory of Michigan.

The following resolution, offered yesterday by Mr. TIPTON, was taken up, considered, and adopted. We are compelled, for want of time, to omit Mr. TIPTON's remarks upon the resolution.

Resolved, That the Committee on Commerce be instructed to inquire into the expediency of making appropriations for the following objects, viz:

1st. An appropriation for commencing a ship channel to connect the waters of the River Raisin with La Plaisance bay, in the Territory of Michigan, under the direction of the War Department.

2d. An appropriation for constructing a harbor at the mouth of St. Joseph's river, on Lake Michigan, in Michigan Territory.

3d. An appropriation to defray the expense of surveying the obstructions to the navigation of St. Joseph's river and its tributaries, as far up as the said streams may be considered navigable.

4th. An appropriation for constructing a harbor at the mouth of Trail creek, on Lake Michigan, in the State of Indiana.

The following resolution, submitted yesterday by Mr. POINDEXTER, was taken up and agreed to:

Resolved, That the Commissioner of the General Land Office be directed to communicate to the Senate—

1st. The whole amount of public lands belonging to the United States; exhibiting the net proceeds, and distinguishing between those which have been sold within the limits of Louisiana, Florida, and other parts of the United States, respectively, and including the latest returns.

2d. The whole amount of public lands which have been surveyed and exposed to sale in the several States and Territories, and showing the amount sold and the amount remaining to be sold, according to the last returns.

3d. The amount which has been actually patented in bounties to the army during the late war.

4th. The amount granted to each of the several States and Territories, and for what purposes.

5th. The amount set apart or reserved for schools in the several States and Territories.

6th. The amount granted in donations for the cultivation of the vine and olive, to Lafayette, and for all other purposes.

The following resolutions, submitted yestesday by Mr. CLAY, were taken up, when Mr. C. spoke at length in their support, and was replied to by

Mr. Forsyth. Their remarks we are compelled to omit, for want of time.

Resolved, That the Secretary of the Treasury be directed to communicate to the Senate a copy of the entire letter addressed by Mr. Crawford, when Secretary of the Treasury, under date the 13th February, 1817, to the President of the Mechanics' Bank of New York, an extract from which is recited in his report to Congress of the 3d December, 1833; and copies of the other correspondence of Mr. Crawford with the banks about that period, to passages in which the Secretary alludes in the same report.

Resolved, also, That the Secretary be directed to communicate to the Senate a copy of the correspondence between the agent appointed during the last summer to inquire upon what terms the State banks would undertake to perform the services to the Government which had been performed by the Bank of the United States, and the said banks; a copy of the report, if one was made, by the said agent to the Secretary, or the Executive; the name of the agent, his compensation, and in virtue of what law he was appointed.

The VICE PRESIDENT laid before the Senate the annual statement of the Commissioner of the Public Buildings.

The Senate then adjourned over to Monday next.

HOUSE OF REPRESENTATIVES.

Thursday, *December* 19, 1833.

On motion of Mr. C. P. WHITE,

Resolved, That the report of the Director of the Mint, presented to this House on the 11th instant, and also the consideration of the state of the coins, and the relative value thereof, and the valuation of the foreign gold and silver coins in circulation in the United States, be referred to a select committee, and that said committee have leave to report by bill or otherwise.

On motion of Mr. WILSON,

Resolved, That the Committee on Revolutionary Pensions be instructed to inquire into the expediency of placing the name of Robert Reynolds on the roll as a revolutionary pensioner.

On motion of Mr. POPE,

Resolved, That the Committee on Public Lands inquire into the expediency of appropriating two sections of the public domain in aid of the support of the Marine Hospital, at Louisville, Kentucky.

On motion of Mr. CONNOR,

Resolved, That the papers in relation to the establishment of assay offices in the gold regions of North Carolina, Virginia, and Georgia, be again referred to a select committee.

On motion of Mr. CHILTON,

Resolved, That the Committee on Claims be instructed to inquire into the expediency of making compensation to James McCarty, for a horse belonging to him, which was wounded in an engagement with the Indians during the last war, while in the possession of Duff Green.

On motion of Mr. PATTON,

Resolved, That the Committee on Revolutionary Claims be instructed to inquire into the expediency of paying to George Stephens, executor of James Buren, deceased, the five years' commutation of full pay in lieu of half pay for life due to said Buren, under the resolves of Congress.

On motion of Mr. BOON,

Resolved, That the Committee on Roads and Canals be instructed to inquire into the expediency of making an appropriation to authorize a survey of the two White rivers in the State of Indiana, with a view to ascertain the practicability and expediency of removing certain obstructions to the navigation of these rivers.

Mr. SEVIER submitted the following resolution, which lies one day for consideration:

Resolved, That the Secretary of War be instructed to inform this House whether a survey of White and St. Francis rivers in Arkansas has been made, in obedience to an act of Congress of the last session, and if so, to report the same to this House; and if not, to state the reasons why they have not been surveyed.

The resolution offered yesterday by Mr. WHIT-

TLESEY, of Ohio, that so much of the 13th rule, " and other persons introduced by the Speaker, or by a member of the House, shall be admitted with in the Hall of the House of Representatives, be rescinded," coming up,

Mr. W. remarked that he was induced to submit this alteration in the rule only with a view to the despatch of business.

Mr. WILDE moved as an amendment to omit also from the rule the words, "Treasurer, Comptroller, Register, and Auditor."

[So that these personages should be deprived of the *entrée* into the privileged places outside the bar.]

Mr. WHITTLESEY accepted this amendment as a modification.

The SPEAKER here said, that there was so much noise beyond the bar of the House that he could not hear what was addressed to the Chair.

Mr. C. C. CLAY. That convinces me of the necessity that exists of adopting the original motion, but the amendment offered by the gentleman from Georgia he did not understand.

Mr. J. Q. ADAMS objected to any alteration of the rule as it stood.

Mr. WILDE consented to make his amendment a distinct question.

Mr. HARDIN complained that there was generally so much noise outside the bar that he and those who sat near it could not hear what was passing at the Speaker's table, and expressed a hope that, if the noise was not discontinued, from a sense of politeness, some of the members in the pit or gallery of the Hall would exchange places with those who were unfortunately on the mountain.

Mr. THOMAS, of Louisiana, said that as he was the father of the rule which it was desired to abolish, and consequently had been the cause of the present discussion, he might be permitted to say, that when he had introduced this part of the rule for their adoption, it was because he felt it was the duty of every representative to accommodate and satisfy the ladies in every particular; but things were now altered, as they had a large erection for their satisfaction, an extensive gallery for them, where they could see and be seen, and hear every thing that passed in the Hall; he therefore could now concur in the propriety of the proposed amendment of the honorable member from Ohio.

After some desultory conversation, the question on the motion made by Mr. WHITTLESEY was taken and carried in the affirmative.

Mr. WARD desired to know from the honorable member from Georgia for what reason it was sought to exclude the persons named in his amendment—persons who had so long been in the enjoyment of that privilege, as it seemed to be rather an invidious uncalled-for exclusion.

Mr. JARVIS inquired if it was in order to act on the amendment without being laid on the table for one day?

The SPEAKER replied it was.

Mr. WILDE said he did not wish to prolong the discussion, recollecting the adage, *de minibus lex non curat.* But in answer to the member from New York, he would say, that the only reason that he wished to strike out of the rule the words giving the privilege of *entrée* to the Hall to the treasurer, &c., was, that he did not see any reason why they should ever have had it.

Mr. WARD called for the yeas and nays on the question. The House refused to sustain the call; and the question on the amendment of Mr. WILDE being put, Messrs. BRIGGS and SLADE, of Illinois, were appointed tellers, and it was rejected. Ayes 94—N0es 107.

Mr. WATMOUGH reported a bill from the Committee on Naval Affairs, granting certain allowances to captains of marine corps.

Mr. PARKER, from the same committee, reported a bill to extend the time for persons on the pension fund.

Mr. PATTON, from the same committee, reported a bill to compensate Susan Decatur and others.

Mr. MUHLENBERG, from the Committee on Revolutionary Claims, reported a bill for the relief of the legal representatives of Fuller Claiborne.

Mr. WARD, from the Committee on Military Affairs, reported a bill for the relief of —— Bloodgood.

Mr. CAVE JOHNSON, from the Committee on Private Land Claims, reported bills for the relief of —— Fisher and —— Prossck.

Mr. POLK, from the Committee of Ways and Means, a bill for the relief of —— Beaucompiere.

Mr. R. M. JOHNSON, from the Committee on Military Affairs, reported a bill to satisfy the claims of the State of Connecticut against the United States, for the military services of the militia, with some private bills.

Mr. CARR, from the Committee on Private Land Claims, reported a bill for the relief of Archibald Small.

All which bills were severally read twice, and committed.

THE BANK DEPOSITES.

The House proceeded to consider the motion of Mr. POLK, to recommit to the Committee of Ways and Means the report of the Secretary of the Treasury on the removal of the deposites, together with the following instructions to the Committee, moved by Mr. McDuffie:

"To report a joint resolution providing that the public revenue hereafter collected, be deposited in the Bank of the United States, in conformity with the public faith pledged in the charter of the said bank."

Mr. McDUFFIE said, although he agreed with the gentleman from Kentucky [Mr. Chilton] that in point of strict justice, the bank was entitled to indemnity for the past removal of the deposites, yet he would not add to the embarrassment of the community by restoring the money already transferred to the State banks. He thought, however, that, to direct the future deposite of all public money in the Bank of the United States, was a measure demanded by justice and expediency. The deposites had been removed, and he should proceed to prove that their removal was illegal. The President, in his Message, formally and solemnly informs us that the Secretary of the Treasury had removed the deposites. There was reason to believe that this was not the fact. Technically and strictly, the deposites were not removed by the Secretary. We had the word of the President, in a public document, [from which he read some passages,] that he had himself directed the removal of the deposites. After giving the reasons why he thinks the deposites should be removed, he adds, "the President thinks," &c., and concludes, "the President wishes this measure to be considered as his own," &c.; and he therefore names a particular day for the revenue bonds to be placed in the State banks. Now, he would put it to every man acquainted with the ordinary import of language to say, whether the President had not usurped the power of removing the deposites, which, in the same document, he admits to belong exclusively to the Secretary of the Treasury. From some passages in the paper one would think that the President would rather cut off his right hand than interfere with a subject belonging, as he acknowledges this to belong, to the office of the Secretary of the Treasury. He admits that the power of the Secretary over the subject is unqualified, and that he must exercise the power under his responsibility to Congress. But three days before the Secretary of the Treasury went out of office, the removal of the deposites is officially announced in the Government gazette. The Treasury Department is an Executive Department: it has distinct duties from those devolved upon the President; but yet the President assumes the exercise of those duties, and renders the office of the Secretary of the Treasury a merely ministerial office. The object of Congress in giving this separate power to the Secretary, was evidently to keep asunder the purse and the sword. He doubted whether any monarch now in existence would dare to usurp the power of the purse. One French king had lost his throne by a usurpation of a smaller extent than this. It was curious to read what the President says on this subject. [Here Mr. McDUFFIE read long extracts from the paper submitted by the President to his Cabinet on the subject of Congress.] It seemed, he said, the President had exercised this authority with extreme pain and reluctance, and merely from the necessity of the case. Usurped power was always accepted with reluctance. Cæsar thrice refused the kingly crown.

Richard the Third accepted the honors forced upon him, although "they were against his conscience and his soul." The President's explanations were, however, more difficult to be understood than these. They had but one precedent, and that was the manner in which Henry the Fourth set forth his title to power, which he read from Hume. He distrusted pretensions which were set forth with such glosses. The President says to the Secretary, The law has vested this power in you: I would be as unwilling to dictate to you as to have you dictate to me; but, in the face of this, he turns out the Secretary because he will not sign the paper, and puts in another man who will. He never had met anything like this, except a story of the decision of a magistrate in some little town in New York—Kinderhook, perhaps—on the subject of liberty of conscience: "Oh, yes," said the judge, "every man has a right to tink for himself, provided he tinks with the court." The President gives the Secretary the right to think for himself, provided he thinks just as he directs him to think. The Secretary did not remove the deposites. It was a false statement. The President removed them, who had no more right than I have.

The history of usurpation contained nothing equal in impudence to the pretensions by which all power was now attempted to be concentrated in the President. The law showed that the deposites were to be removed only for reasons connected with the convenience and safety of the treasury, and at the order of the Treasury Department alone could they be removed. Had the Secretary shown that the bank was corrupt, that it violated its faith, or even that he could make a better arrangement with the State banks, his reasons would have been sufficient. But so far from giving these reasons, no person, not the Secretary, not a member of the House, will pretend that the bank is unsafe. On the other hand, it is charged against the bank, that it embarrasses the country by hoarding up specie. What one of the stipulations of the charter has the bank violated? No government in the world, be its sphere of operations large or small, has had its money concerns so well and cheaply transacted as ours have been by this bank. The government creditors have never waited one moment for their money from the disbursing officers, so far as the bank was concerned, and when they got their money, it was money. God grant they may say the same thing two years hence. Not a dollar has been lost for sixteen years, of all the money collected for the Government, and deposited in this bank. But still the safest bank in the world was to be put down, the public money was to be hazarded, the interests of widows and orphans were to be destroyed, to gratify, the malice of a tyrant, madly seeking his personal revenge in the destruction of the institution. Mr. McD. here took up the charge made against the bank of having interferred with elections. In the first place, he contended that the bank directors had not interfered in elections—they had, he said, studiously avoided them, and endeavored to conciliate all parties. In fact, they attended to their business. But what right had the President to disfranchise bank officers? They had as good a right as any men to vote at elections, and take a part in public affairs. The truth was, that the charge meant nothing more than that the bank would not interfere in elections, according to the directions sent to it from Washington. It refused to turn out Jonathan and put in John at the order of the President. The President says, "it is his desire that the control of the bank and the currency be entirely separated from the political power of the country." A wiser sentiment never was uttered. Here is the precept, what was the example? He punishes the Bank of the United States, because it could not be made a political instrument. He had done more. He had distributed the whole funds of the country among the local banks according to their political character. So help me God, he would rather trust Andrew Jackson with fifty thousand soldiers, than with the privilege of disposing, through his pliant instrument—for the Secretary of the Treasury would never be anything more than a pliant instrument—the revenue of the country among banks, judiciously chosen by him. The deposite banks had been selected expressly with a view to their party character, and the officers of those banks had already begun to figure in the political arena. He did not charge General Jackson with duplicity, in stating his principles. He believed that he assumed them in sincerity, but that in the language of the late Secretary of the Treasury, he had no fixed principles—impulse and passion ruled him.

Mr. McDuffie here adverted to the support which he gave General Jackson, as a candidate for the Presidency. One of the principles on which he was brought into power was, the necessity of keeping out of public office all those who interfered with elections. But now the officers of the Government were transformed into an army of electioneering agents. The reform had ended in turning out independent men, and putting political partisans in their places. What (Mr. McD. asked) will be the result, if we suffer the public deposites to be removed at the will of the President? Would not every election be controlled by money influence? Even now, the whole power and means of the Government are exerted to secure the succession to the Presidency, which had been resolved upon. Almost every reason given by the President for removing the deposites was conclusively answered by the fact, that the charter of the Bank of the United States expires in 1836. The bank, before that time, could do nothing to undermine the liberties of the country. The real object was, therefore, as he believed, to concentrate the moneyed power where the political power was concentrated, and to exert both in the control of the Presidential election. The State banks would be actuated with one common spirit; they would be Government banks, and political agents of the Government. Every man acquainted with the practical operations of the bank, must know that the removal of the deposites would not in the least degree relieve the commercial embarrassments which must take place upon the expiration of the charter. This was, therefore, no good reason. But the Secretary says it is necessary to provide a new currency to take the place of the bills of the Bank of the United States. Bills of better credit? No, that was not pretended. They are, then, to carry on the exchanges. But they had not stipulated to do it. Would the deposite bank at Richmond take the bills of the Bank of the Metropolis? They will for the Government, but not from individuals. It was idle to attempt to give the notes of the State banks any general credit. So far from having their credit improved by the destruction of the United States Bank, the State banks will be the first to suffer by it, and would soon find themselves, if they did not already, in a very critical situation. There was a rumor that the deposite banks had actually petitioned the Government to restore the deposites to the Bank of the United States. Here we have a bank too strong, too solvent, with too much specie in its vaults; but the next reason for removing the deposites is, that the notes of the bank will depreciate when the bank winds up. This was like telling a countryman, who holds the note of a rich farmer, that, when the day comes for its payment, it will be depreciated in value. No one who knew anything of banking, believed that the paper of the bank would be depreciated one-fourth of one per cent. It was idle to say so.

Here Mr. McDUFFIE gave way, at the instance of Mr. Davis, of Massachusetts, to a motion for adjournment; and the House then adjourned.

HOUSE OF REPRESENTATIVES.

Friday, *December* 20, 1833.

Mr. WHITTLESEY, of Ohio, submitted the following resolution, which lies one day for consideration:

Resolved, That the Secretary of War report to this House the survey of a canal route from Pittsburg to Akron, made by Colonel James Kearney, with the estimates of the expenses of construction, accompanied with the maps and profiles.

Mr. KINNARD submitted the following resolutions, which also lie one day on the table:

Resolved, That the Secretary of the Treasury be requested to communicate to this House, a statement of the quantity of lands included in the grant made to the State of Indiana, to enable her to construct the Wabash and Erie canal, which have been sold under the proclamation of the President, dated 3d September, 1833, or any previous proclamation, ordering sales of land, at Bucyrus and Wapawkonetta, in the State of Ohio.

2. That the Secretary aforesaid be requested to accompany said report with a statement of the amount of money arising from the sale of said canal lands, together with a map of the same, distinctly marking their contiguity to the canal line, and communicating such other information of said lands in his possession, as will enable the House to form an estimate of their intrinsic value.

3. That a select committee be appointed to inquire into the expediency of making provision by law, to reimburse the State of Indiana for the loss which she may sustain in consequence of the sale of the lands aforesaid: to report by bill or otherwise.

On motion of Mr. EWING,

Resolved, That the Committee on the Territories be instructed to inquire into the expediency of extending the northern boundary of the State of Indiana, so as to embrace a slight tract of land (now attached to the territory of Michigan) south of St. Joseph's river, so as to render said river the boundary line, from its junction with Lake Michigan, and allow concurrent jurisdiction to Indiana, at its mouth.

On motion of Mr. DUNCAN,

Resolved, That the Committee on Commerce be instructed to inquire into the expediency of making Chicago a port of entry.

Mr. STEWART submitted a motion, that when the House adjourned, it should adjourn over until Monday. Agreed to.

Mr. BEARDSLEY, from the Committee on the Judiciary, reported bills for the relief of W. Sanders, W. R. Porter, Joel Wright, and for the legal representatives of Nathaniel Patton, deceased.

Mr. MUHLENBERG, from the Committee on Revolutionary Claims, a bill for the relief of —— Mortimer.

Mr. McKENNAN from the Committee on the District of Columbia, a bill, granting donation of lots to the Alexandria Free School, and Orphan Asylum.

Mr. CAVE JOHNSON from the Committee on Private Land Claims, bills for the relief of the heirs of —— Ermendorf, and of Eliza Dickenson.

Mr. TURRILL, from the Committee on Revolutionary Claims, bills for the relief of the legal representatives of Walter Livingston, deceased, and of Thomas Wallace, deceased.

Mr. BULL reported a bill for the relief of Isadore Moore.

All of which bills were read twice, and committed.

The resolutions heretofore submitted, and given in our paper, by Mr. MERCER, in relation to the bridge over the Potomac: by Mr. STEWART, of Pennsylvania, in relation to the improvement of the Monongahela river: and by Mr. SEVIER, calling on the Secretary of War for information in relation to a survey of St. Francis and White rivers, were severally adopted.

Mr. STEWART submitted the following resolution, which lies one day on the table:

Resolved, That the Secretary of War be directed to communicate to this House the reports of Colonels Abert and Kearney, and also the recent report of Captain William Gibbs McNeil, of the corps of Topographical Engineers, on the plan, construction, costs, and actual condition of the Chesapeake and Ohio canal.

On motion of Mr. CHILTON,

Resolved, That the Committee on Roads and Canals be instructed to inquire into the expediency of making an appropriation to aid in the turnpiking and improvement of the road leading from Louisville, in the State of Kentucky, to Nashville, in the State of Tennessee, in the manner proposed in an act of the late Legislature of said State of Kentucky; and that said committee have leave to report by bill or otherwise.

Mr. WHALLON submitted the following resolution, which lies one day:

Resolved, That the Secretary of War be instructed to lay before this House the survey and estimates for the erection of a pier or breakwater in the harbors of Burlington, Port Kent, and Plattsburg, on Lake Champlain.

On motion of Mr. H. EVERETT,

Resolved, That the Committee on Revolutionary Pensions be instructed to inquire into the expedi-

ency of placing the name of Elisha Lucas on the roll of revolutionary pensioners.

On motion of Mr. VINTON,

Resolved, That the Committee on Public Lands be instructed to inquire into the expediency of confirming by law all selections of school lands granted by the act of May 20th, 1826, entitled "An act to appropriate lands for the support of schools in certain townships and fractional townships not before provided for," which may have been made and returned to the General Land Office, or to the Register and Receiver's Office of any land district in any State or Territory.

Mr. STEWART submitted the following resolution, which lies one day:

Resolved, That the Secretary of War be directed to communicate to this House an estimate of appropriations required by the public service for the first quarter of the year 1834, so far as relates to his department.

Mr. MERCER submitted the following resolution, which lies one day:

Resolved, That the Secretary of the Treasury be directed to lay before this House a statement of the amount of duties received in the year 1833, the payment of which would have been deferred till the year 1834, had not the system of cash payments been adopted.

On motion of Mr. WARDWELL,

Resolved, That the Committee on Revolutionary Pensions inquire into the expediency of placing the names of Ebenezer Horne and Solomon Tracy, of the State of New York, on the list of revolutionary pensioners, for their services in the revolutionary war.

Mr. SELDEN, submitted the following resolution, which lies one day:

Resolved, That the Committee on Ways and Means be instructed to report a bill requiring the commissioners of the sinking fund, forthwith to purchase or otherwise redeem the five per cent. stocks of the United States, and directing the Secretary of the Treasury from time to time to place under the control of said commissioners, such funds, not otherwise required for the purposes of the Government, as shall be necessary for that object, and in case of deficiency, to sell so much of the stock of the Bank of the United States belonging to the Government as will enable them to complete the purchase.

On motion of Mr. HUBBARD,

Resolved, That the Committee on the Post Office and Post Roads be instructed to inquire into the expediency of establishing a mail route from Stoddard, through Sullivan, in the county of Cheshire, and State of New Hampshire, to Keene in said county.

On motion of Mr. F. WHITTLESEY,

Resolved, That the Committee of Claims be instructed to inquire whether any additional relief should be extended to Joel Byington.

On motion of Mr. GILLET,

Resolved, That the Committee on the Post Office and Post Roads be instructed to inquire into the expediency of establishing a post road from Hopkinsburg, in the county of Franklin, through Rusher and Stockholm, to the town of Parishville, in the county of St. Lawrence, in the State of New York.

Resolved, That the Committee on Invalid Pensions be instructed to inquire into the expediency of allowing Russell Atwater, of Norfolk, in the county of St. Lawrence, and State of New York, his pay as an invalid pensioner, from the time of the passing the law allowing invalid pensions to soldiers of the Revolution, to January 1st, 1832.

Mr. JARVIS submitted the following resolution, which lies one day on the table:

Resolved, That the Postmaster General be instructed to report to this House the net amount of postage received during the year ending the 30th of September, 1833, in each of the States and Territories, and the amount which would have been paid for the transportation of the mail in each of the States and Territories, under the new contracts, provided no reductions had been made.

On motion of Mr. PEARCE, of Rhode Island,

Resolved, That the Committee on Revolutionary Pensions be instructed to inquire into the expediency of extending the provisions of the act of June 7th, 1832, entitled "An act supplementary to the act for the relief of certain surviving offi-

cers and soldiers of the Revolution," to the officers, non-commissioned officers, marine or marines, who served on board private armed vessels, during the war of the Revolution.

The SPEAKER presented to the House a report from the Superintendent of Public Buildings in relation to the expenditure; which was laid on the table, and ordered to be printed.

The SPEAKER announced that this day was set apart for private business.

The House then went into Committee of the Whole, (Mr. STEDGRT in the chair,) on several private bills, which were severally reported to the House.

A message was received from the Senate, informing the House that they had agreed to the joint resolution for the appointment of a library committee, and that they had appointed a committee on their part.

The House again went into committee, and were occupied with private business until they adjourned.

REPORT ON THE FINANCES.

In obedience to the directions of the "Act supplementary to the act to establish the Treasury Department," the Secretary of the Treasury respectfully submits the following report:

1. *Of the Public Revenue and Expenditures.*
The receipts into the treasury, from all sources, during the year 1831, were..... $28,526,820 82

The expenditures for the same
year, including payments on account of the public debt, were.. $30,038,446 12

The balance in the treasury on 1st
of January, 1832, was.......... $4,502,914 45
The receipts from all sources, during the year 1832, were...... $31,865,561 16
Viz:
Customs......... $28,465,237 21
Lands, (statement
D.)............. 2,623,381 03
Dividends on bank
stock, (E.)..... 490,000 00
Sales of stock in
the Bank of the
United States,
(E.)............ 169,000 00
Incidental receipts, (E.)..... 117,942 89

Making, with the balance, an aggregate of.................... $36,368,475 61
The expenditures of the same year were (F.)..................... $34,356,698 16
Viz:
Civil list, foreign
intercourse, and
miscellaneous .. $4,577,141 45
Military service,
including fortifications, ordnance, Indian affairs, pensions,
arming the militia, and internal
improvements.. 7,982,877 03
Naval service, including the gradual improvement
of the navy.... 3,956,370 29
Public debt..... 17,840,309 29

Leaving a balance in the Treasury
on the 1st of January, 1833, of.. $2,011,777 55
The receipts into the treasury, during the first three quarters of the present year, are estimated
at $24,355,317 95
Viz:
Customs.. $21,256,089 77
Lands, (G.) 2,919,957 35
Dividends on
bank stock,
(H.)........ 474,985 00
Sales of stock
in the bank
of United
States, (H.)..91,000 00

Third instalment under
the convention with
Denmark,
(H.) 221,315 17
Incidental receipts, (H.) 91,970 66

The receipts for the
fourth quarter,
are estimated at .. $7,675,000 00
Making the total estimated receipts
of the year.................. $32,030,317, 95
And with the balance of the first of
January, 1833, forming an aggregate of................ $34,042,095 50
The expenditures for the first three quarters of the present year, are estimated at (I.) $18,248,389 15
Viz:
Civil list, foreign
intercourse, and
miscellaneous,
including $667,-
160 87 duties refunded under the
3d section of the
act of the 2d
of March, 1833,
and $661,160 95
awards under the
convention with
Denmark...... 4,951,462 84
Military service including fortifications, ordnance,
Indian affairs,
pensions, arming
the militia, and
internal improvement.........9,950,349 29
Naval service, including the gradual improvement
of the navy.... 3,076,051 39
Public debt........270,524 63

The expenditures for the
fourth quarter, including $2,301,716 36 on
account of the public
debt, are estimated,
on data furnished by
the respective departments, at........$6,409,915 45
Making the total estimated expenditures of the year.......$24,658,304 60

And leaving in the treasury on the
1st of January, 1834, an estimated balance of................ $9,383,790 90

This balance, however, includes the funds, estimated at $1,400,000, heretofore reported by this Department as not effective.
The appropriations remaining unsatisfied at the close of the year are estimated at $5,964,571 23, but of this amount, it is estimated by the proper departments—
1. That the sum of $5,190,297 62 only will be required for the objects for which they were appropriated.
2. That the sum of $449,434 04 will not be required, and may therefore be considered as an excess of appropriation, and is proposed to be applied without being re-appropriated, in aid of the service of the year 1834, as will more fully appear, when the estimates of the appropriations for that year are presented.
3. That the sum of $324,859 57 will be carried to the surplus fund, either because these moneys will not be required for, or can no longer be applied to them.

2. *Of the Public Debt.*

Notice has been given of the intended reimbursement of the residue of the exchanged 4½ per cent. stock, on the 1st of May, 1834. This stock was subject to redemption, at the pleasure of the United States, at any time after the 31st of December, 1833, upon six months' public notice of such intended reimbursement. The time at which the

notice was given does not enable the United States to insist on reimbursing it, so as to stop the interest, before the 1st of May, 1834. A small portion of it was however purchased for the United States, in the months of September and October, by an agent employed for that purpose—and on the same day that notice was given of the intended reimbursement, on the 1st of May next, an offer was made to the holders, by public advertisement, to pay them the whole amount of the principal, with interest to the day of payment, upon their making the proper transfers of the certificates. Many of the holders have already accepted this offer, and portions of it continue almost daily to be presented for payment. It is believed that the greater part, if not the whole of this stock, will be redeemed by the end of the present year. Under these circumstances it seems proper to charge the whole amount to the expenditures of the present year, rather than to the next; the account is accordingly stated on this principle, and the interest calculated to the first of January; and if a part of it should not come in by that time, it will make no material difference in the result, because the interest saved upon the stock, paid before the end of the year, will, it is expected, be equal, or nearly so, to the amount of interest which may afterwards accrue on the portion remaining unpaid. And if the whole of it should be reimbursed within the present year, the interest saved will increase the estimated balance in the treasury, in but a very small degree. In the following account, therefore, the whole of this stock is charged to the expenditure of 1833, and the interest on it calculated, as if it would be reimbursed on the 1st of January, 1834. The disbursements on account of the public debt, during the year 1833, will amount, as has already been shown, to $2,572,240 99
Of which there will have been applied to the payment of the principal.................. $2,240,950 80
And to interest........ 331,290 19

The stocks which will have been redeemed by the application of this sum, during the year, are as follows:
The residue of the exchanged 4½ per cent. stock, issued under the act of the 26th May, 1824............ $2,227,363 98
A part of the five per cent. stock issued under the act of 3d March, 1821........................... 13,036 01
Also, certain portions of the old registered debt, which have been presented for payment; being part of the unfunded debt of the Revolution 50 81
And treasury notes 500 00

On the 1st of January next, it is estimated, the public debt will be reduced to (K.)................. $4,760,082 08
Viz:
1. The funded debt, consisting of the residue of the five per cent. stock, under the act of the 3d of March, 1821, and redeemable after the 1st Jan. 1835...$4,722,260 29
2. The unfunded debt, amounting to.......... 37,821 79
Consisting of the registered debt, being claims registered prior to the year 1798, for services and supplies during the revolutionary war......$27,476 70
Treasury notes issued during the late war.. 6,025 00
And Mississippi stock........ 4,320 09

These last sums, composing the unfunded debt, are payable on the presentation of the certificates.

3. *Of the Estimates of the Public Revenue and Expenditures for the year 1834.*

According to the best judgment the department is able to form on the subject, the receipts into the treasury from all sources, during the year 1834, may be estimated at................................... $18,500,000 00
Viz:
Customs.............$15,000,000
Public Lands 3,000,000
Bank dividends, and miscellaneous rec'ts of all kinds........ 500,000
To which add the balance estimated to be in the treasury on the 1st of January, 1834, after deducting the unavailable funds... 7,983,790 90
Making, together, the sum of .. $26,483,790 90
The expenditures for the year 1834, including the reimbursement of the whole of the public debt, are estimated at............... 23,501,994 85
Viz:
Civil, foreign intercourse, and miscellaneous $2,800,897 33
Military service, including fortifications, ordnance, Indian affairs, pensions, arming the militia, and internal improvements. 8,654,942 25
Revolutionary pensions, under the act of the 7th of June, 1832, including arrearages from the 4th of March, 1831, in cases in which payment has not been made 3,000,000 00
Naval service, including the gradual improvement of the navy 4,051,073 19
Public debt:
Prin'l,$4,760,082 08
Interest.. ,235,000 00
$4,995,082 08

Which will leave in the treasury, on the 31st of December, 1834, a balance estimated at........... $2,981,796 05
The value of the exports of the year ending on the 30th of September last, is estimated at $90,663,403, of which $70,642,030 were of domestic and $20,021,373 of foreign articles, showing an increase in the exports of domestic produce of $7,504,560 over the exports of the same character for the year ending 30th September, 1832, and a diminution in foreign articles of $4,018,100. The value of the imports for the year ending on the 30th of September last is estimated at $109,000,000 being greater by the sum of $8,000,000 than the imports for the year ending 30th September, 1832. Of the imports for the year ending 30th September last, it is estimated that $34,000,000 were in articles free from duty.
It will be seen, from the foregoing statement of the receipts of the present year, that they very much exceed the amount at which they were estimated in the last annual report.
The excess has been derived chiefly from customs, which are estimated to produce more than $28,000,000.
The large receipts of this year, have been principally occasioned by the act of July 14, 1832, which abolished the system of long credits on revenue bonds, and required the duties on woollen goods to be paid in cash, and on other articles in three and six months. The new regulation took effect on the 4th of March last, and the cash duties and shortened credits have brought into the treasury, during the present year, a large amount of revenue, which, under the former system of credits would not have been payable until 1834, and would have formed a part of the receipts of that year. The income of 1833 has therefore had the advantage of the new system, as well as of the former one; and the receipts are much greater than they would have been under either of them, according to the established rate of duties.

The expenditures for the present year have also been unusually large, and are estimated at $22,086,063 61, exclusive of the expenditure on account of the public debt.
The appropriations for the year were heavy, and exceeded by three millions the appropriations for 1832, and the balances of unexpended appropriations, at the close of that year have been for the most part applied during the present one to the various objects authorized by law, and therefore enter into the account of its expenditures. Several items of appropriation, however, for the present year cannot be considered as forming a part of the ordinary expenditures of the Government. Without enumerating all objects of this description, it may be sufficient to mention some, which have contributed materially to enhance the amount actually expended. The duties refunded at the treasury, under the law of the last session, and the awards under the convention with Denmark, are included in this account; and the expenses occasioned by the Indian aggressions in 1832 have been for the most part paid in this year. These three items amount to nearly two millions of dollars. But when this sum is deducted from the whole annual expenditure it shows that more than twenty millions of dollars have been expended during the present year, for the various other objects authorized by law, exclusive of the amount set apart for the reimbursement of the 4½ per cent. stock. The pensions for life, granted under the acts of 1818 and 1832 to the officers and soldiers of the Revolution have increased considerably the annual expenditure. More than four millions of dollars have been already paid on that account during the present year. There is, indeed, no item in the list of appropriation which our citizens generally more cheerfully contribute to pay than the one last mentioned; but in the order of nature it must be annually decreasing; and in the estimates of the coming year, those payable under the acts of June, 1832, are set down at three millions of dollars. The different sums above mentioned, therefore, show six millions of dollars, paid for purposes which cannot be considered as entering into the ordinary and regular expenses of the Government, and form no rule by which its future annual expenditure ought to be estimated.
The receipts of 1834 must be very much below those of the present year. A large portion of the receipts from customs, as already stated, has been derived from the importations of previous years. But from the change in the system of credits, only a small part of the duties accruing in this year will go into the receipts of the next. And the diminished rate of duties, which takes effect on the first of January next, on some of the most productive articles, and the entire exemption of others, will contribute still more to reduce the receipts of the coming year, as compared with the present.
In estimating the receipts from customs, for the year 1834 at fifteen millions of dollars, I have assumed that the imports of that year will nearly equal those of 1832. This estimate is higher than the average of the last five or six years; but it is believed to be a safe one. For although the importations of each of the two last years were unusually large, yet the imports of the present one have gone still higher. And the general state of our commerce, and the situation of the country, justify the belief that there will be no serious diminution in the coming year. The condition of the mercantile classes does not indicate any excess of importation. Indeed, the short credits, and cash duties, will be found to contribute greatly to prevent overtrading in that respect. Moreover, many articles, in common use, are admitted free from duty. This will produce an increased ability in the community to buy those which pay duty, and consequently a greater consumption. There appears, therefore, to be no reason to apprehend any serious diminution in the importations of 1834, and it will be safe to estimate its receipts by the standard above mentioned. Yet any material excess beyond that amount cannot, I think, be counted on. The produce of the public lands can hardly fall short of the sum at which it has been stated, and will perhaps exceed it.
In this view of the receipts of 1834, the income of the year will about equal the estimated expenditure. And with the aid of the balance in the

treasury on the first of January next, it will be sufficient for all the wants of the Government, including the amouut necessary to pay off the residue of the national debt. It must, however, be observed, that, in addition to the appropriations now asked for, there will be an unexpended balance of former appropriations, amounting to the sum of $5,190,287 62, which will probably be required in the course of the ensuing year for the objects for which it has been appropriated. And if the entire amount of appropriations proposed in the estimates for 1834 were also to be required within the year, there would not be money enough in the treasury to meet them, after satisfying the balances above stated, and paying off the public debt. But the experience of former years shows that a portion of the appropriations may always be expected to remain unexpended at the end of the year. And the average of these unexpended balances for the last four years is about $5,300,000. In estimating the balance in the treasury at the close of 1834, I have therefore assumed that a portion of the estimates of expenditure, herewith submitted, will not be used during the year; and that balances of appropriations, equal to the amount at the close of the present year, will in like manner remain in the treasury at the end of the year 1834, and go into the expenses of the succeeding year. And it is not necessary to raise money for the public use sooner than it will probably be needed.

But the balance stated at the end of 1834 is not to be considered as a clear surplus. It will still be chargeable with the amount of appropriations estimated to remain unexpended at that time.

From this state of the finances, and of the proposed appropriations, it is evident that a reduction of the revenue cannot at this time be made, without injury to the public service. Under the act of the last session, the receipts of 1835 will be less than those of 1834, as a further reduction in the rate of duties will take effect on the 1st of January, 1835. And if the appropriations should be kept up, to the amount authorized for the present year, the charge upon the treasury in 1835 would be more than it could probably meet. But the debt will then have been entirely paid, and if a guarded rule of appropriation is at once commenced, there will be no difficulty in bringing down the expenditure, without injury to the public service.

If the revenue is not to be reduced more than the existing law provides for, there seems to be no sufficient reason to open at this time the vexed question of the tariff. The manner in which duties are now apportioned on different articles would be liable to insuperable objections, if it were to be considered as a settled and permanent system. But the law is temporary on the face of it, and was intended as a compromise between conflicting interests; and, unless the revenue to arise under it should hereafter be more productive than is anticipated, it will be necessary in two years from this time, to impose duties on articles that are now free, in order to meet the current expenses of the Government. There would seem, therefore, to be no advantage in agitating the question at the present moment; yet some modifications of the existing laws will be necessary, in order to carry into effect the intentions of the Legislature, and to guard against attempts to evade its provisions, without in any degree affecting its principles.

It is however respectfully recommended that the appropriations for 1834 should be regulated by a proper regard to economy. Heretofore the receipts to be expected could be ascertained with some degree of certainty, because they were principally derived from the imports of previous years; and the bonds taken for the duties on such imports showed the amount of receipts which might safely be counted on: but under the new system of cash duties, and short credits, each year must mainly depend for its income on its own imports. And as commerce is always more or less liable to fluctuations, the public interest requires that there should be at all times in the treasury a sufficient sum to provide for unforeseen contingencies, and to guard against disappointment in the estimated receipts. The calculations on the income of a succeeding year is necessarily more uncertain under the present system than under the former one of long credits; and if the anticipations of the receipts of 1834 and 1835 should be fully realized, there will not be more than ought to be provided on the estimated scale of expenditures. At the last session of Congress, the appropriations exceeded twenty-one millions five hundred thousand dollars, being nearly three millions five hundred thousand above the estimates presented at the beginning of the session. A similar amount of expenditure, authorized at the present session, might render it necessary to provide additional revenue earlier than is now contemplated.

It is understood to be conceded on all hands, that a tariff for protection merely, is to be finally abandoned, and that the revenue is to be reduced to the necessary wants of the Government. Various causes have contributed to enlarge the proposed expenditures for 1834, as will be seen by the particular estimates from the different departments. But it is believed that all the objects for which this Government was established can be effectually attained at much less annual expense hereafter; and the harmony and mutual good feeling of this extensive country will be best secured and perpetuated by rigidly confining the operations of the General Government to its appropriate sphere. If this is done, and its expenditures are regulated by a strict economy, the burdens it imposes will scarcely be felt by our citizens, while its blessings are inestimable.

As the public debt will soon be extinguished, it is proper that the books and papers which belong to the various loan offices should be transmitted to the seat of Government, and placed among the archives of the nation. It is believed that the outstanding debt can be purchased on favorable terms in the course of the ensuing year, and that it can be most conveniently purchased at the treasury. It appears therefore desirable that provision should be made by law for immediately transmitting to this department all the books and papers relating to the national debt. The money can be readily transmitted to the public creditor without charge to him or to the Government, and he can be paid at any place where he may wish to receive it.

The act of March 3, 1807, abolished the office of Commissioner of Loans, and transferred the duties to the Bank of the United States. The money necessary to pay the public creditors has, from time to time, been advanced to the bank by the treasury; and it appears that large sums have remained for a considerable time in the bank without being applied to the purposes for which they were intended. The amount has been reduced within a few months past. But the statement from the Register's Office, herewith presented, marked L, will show that $773,111 98 still remained in their hands on the first of October last. A portion of this sum, as appears by the paper referred to, was advanced some years ago. And there is no reason why this money should continue in the hands of the bank, where it is useless to the Government as well as to the creditor. The delay in the payment has probably in some instances been caused by the death of the party entitled, and the ignorance of his representatives as to his claims on the United States. The situation of these outstanding claims renders it still more necessary that the books and papers relating to the public debt should be forthwith transmitted to this department, where the proper inquiries could be made as to the cause of the delay, and measures taken to ascertain who is entitled to receive the money. As the amount is justly due from the United States to some one, and may belong to persons who are ignorant of their rights, justice seems to require that the Government should take measures to apprise them of their claims, and of the readiness of the United States to discharge them.

The destruction of the building occupied by the Treasury Department, has occasioned the loss of some valuable papers. But it is believed that none have deen destroyed that can materially affect the public interest. It will become necessary to provide another building, and the loss already sustained in the documents and records of this office, shows the propriety of erecting it upon a different plan from the former one, and of placing the archives of the Government in a situation less exposed to danger. The inconveniences which are felt from the present situation of the offices connected with this department, as well as the more exposed condition of the papers, induce me to invite the early attention of Congress to this subject.

The report from the Commissioner of the General Land Office is herewith presented, showing the condition of that branch of the public service, and containing suggestions for its improvement.

All which is respectfully submitted.

R. B. TANEY,
Secretary of the Treasury.

TREASURY DEPARTMENT,
December 17, 1833.

Continuation of Thursday's proceedings.

IN SENATE.

THURSDAY, *December* 19, 1833.

The following resolutions, submitted yesterday by Mr. CLAY, were taken up:

Resolved, That the Secretary of the Treasury be directed to communicate to the Senate a copy of the entire letter addressed by Mr. Crawford when Secretary of the Treasury, under date the 13th February, 1817, to the President of the Mechanics' Bank of New York, an extract from which is recited in his report to Congress of the 3d December, 1833; and copies of the other correspondence of Mr. Crawford with the banks, about that period, to passages in which the Secretary alludes in the same report.

Resolved, also, That the Secretary be directed to communicate to the Senate a copy of the correspondence between the agent, appointed during the last summer to inquire upon what terms the State banks would undertake to perform the services to the Government which had been performed by the Bank of the United States, and the said banks; a copy of the report made, if one was made, by the said agent to the Secretary, or the Executive; the name of the agent, his compensation, and in virtue of what law he was appointed.

When Mr. BENTON moved to amend the resolution, by adding the following:

"Also, That the Secretary communicate to the Senate the monthly statements of the affairs of the Bank of the United States for the current year, which have not been heretofore communicated.

"Also, the entire correspondence between the Secretary of the Treasury and the President of the Bank of the United States for the first half of the year 1819."

The amendment was agreed to.

Mr. CLAY said that he felt it his duty to submit to the Senate some explanation of the motives which had induced him to ask it to adopt these resolutions. The Secretary in his report concerning the public deposites, had labored very hard, through two or three of the first pages of it, to prove that he possessed the *exclusive* power to decide when they should be removed. This power, he contended, was not restricted to any particular contingencies, but "was absolute and unconditional, as far as the interests of the bank were involved." "It is not necessary," says that officer, "that the deposites should be unsafe, in order to justify the romoval. The authority to remove is not limited to such a contingency. The bank may be *perfectly solvent*, and prepared to meet *promptly* all demands upon it: it may have been *faithful* in the performance of *all* its duties, and yet the public interest may require the deposites to be withdrawn; and, as that cannot be done *without* the action of this department, the Secretary of the Treasury would betray the trust confided to him, if he did not cause the deposites to be made elsewhere, whenever the change would advance the public interests *or* the public convenience. The *safety* of the deposites—the *ability* of the bank to meet its engagements—its *fidelity* in the performance of its obligations, are *only* a part of the considerations by which his judgment must be guided. The *general* interest and convenience of the people must regulate his conduct."

Here is the assumption of a power analagous to the old exploded doctrine of the general welfare, in a most odious form. According to that doctrine, it was claimed by certain Federalists of 1798-9, that the Constitution vested in Congress power to legislate on all subjects for the general welfare. But, according to the new version of the heresy, a Secretary of the Treasury—a subordinate officer of the Government, the creature of

Congress, arrogates to himself a power to administer the duties of his office, and to regulate the currency of the country, in conformity with his sense of the general interest and convenience of the people! And at the very moment of setting up this enormous pretension, he denies any such power to Congress!

But this is not all. This modern doctrine assumes for the Secretary not only a power equivalent to its ancient prototype, but it demands that it be respected as absolute and unconditional, and exclusive even of Congress. "For," to quote the language of the Secretary, "although Congress should be satisfied that the public money was not safe in the care of the bank, or should be convinced that the interests of the people of the United States imperiously demanded the removal, yet its passage of a law directing it to be done, would be a breach of the agreement into which they have entered."

Is this possible? Can it be true that an official being, brought into existence by the will of Congress, having no authority, and charged with no duties but such as that will has conferred, has more power than its creator? Can it be true that the agent may do what the principal cannot do? Can it be true that the Secretary, representing one of the parties to a contract, without a violation of a single stipulation of that contract by the other party, may, upon a general notion of public interest or convenience, violate, at his pleasure, the most essential stipulation of the whole contract for that other party? May he do that, whilst Congress is restrained from ordering a removal of the deposites, under any circumstances; even if the bank had failed to fulfil all the provisions of the charter, and the deposites were unsafe, and the interests of the people of the United States imperiously demanded the removal? May the Secretary remove them, without any breach of the charter on the part of the bank, whilst the hands of Congress are fast tied, although the bank had broken every stipulation of the charter?

The Secretary appears to have been conscious that this most extraordinary doctrine required all the bolstering which he could give it; and he has accordingly retreated behind a precedent which he alleges to have been furnished by Mr. Crawford, one of his predecessors. He says: "This principle" [that is, the absolute, unconditional, and exclusive power of the Secretary over the deposites] "was distinctly asserted by Mr. Crawford." "In a postscript to his letter to the President of the Mechanics' Bank of New York, dated February 13, 1817, he says: The Secretary of the Treasury will always be disposed to support the credit of the State banks, and will invariably direct transfers from the deposites of the public money in aid of their legitimate exertions to maintain their credit." The Secretary alludes to other passages in the correspondence of Mr. Crawford with the banks about the period of the 13th February, 1817. But he contents himself with a single citation from the postscript; perhaps supposing that Congress, like the fairer portion of our species, would deem that the most important part of the letter.

Now, Mr. President, what must be your surprise, when he (Mr. C.) stated that Mr. Crawford never, in the correspondence referred to, distinctly asserted any such principle as his successor attributes to him?—never did claim for himself, on that occasion, any such extraordinary and exclusive power over the deposites; and that his correspondence was conducted under an authority totally different from that contained in the bank charter?

It will be recollected that when the Bank of the United States was incorporated, a general suspension of specie payments prevailed throughout the United States, with the exception of New England. The taxes and duties were paid in depreciated paper, of which the million and a half (a sum equal to the bonus paid by the Bank of the United States) of unavailable funds, now annually reported by the treasury, is a part. To produce a restoration of a sound currency was the main object in establishing that bank. About that period a convention of representatives from the State banks was held, and some were, and others were not, willing to resume specie payments. It was feared by Congress that the bank alone might not prove competent to produce the desired effect.

An auxiliary measure was deemed necessary; and that was adopted in the following resolution which passed on the 30th April, 1816:

"Resolved, &c., That the Secretary of the Treasury be, and he hereby is, required and directed to adopt such measures as he may deem necessary to cause, as soon as may be, all duties, taxes, debts, or sums of money, accruing or becoming payable to the United States, to be collected and paid in the legal currency of the United States, or treasury notes, or notes of the Bank of the United States, as by law provided and declared, or in notes of banks which are payable and paid on demand in legal currency of the United States; and that, from and after the twentieth day of February next, no such duties, taxes, debts, or sums of money accruing or becoming payable to the United States, as aforesaid, ought to be collected or received otherwise than in the legal currency of the United States, or treasury notes, or notes of the Bank of the United States, or in notes of banks which are payable and paid on demand, in the said legal currency of the United States."

The letter of Mr. Crawford, the postscript of which the Secretary has communicated to Congress, bears date the 13th of February, 1817, only one week before the day fixed for the resumption of specie payments by the resolution to which he had called the attention of the Senate. That letter, beyond all doubt, was written under the authority contained in that resolution. What, then, must be thought of the official candor and honor of the Secretary of the Treasury, who has endeavored to palm upon Congress and the country, the authority of Mr. Crawford for the enormous power which the Secretary assumes under the charter, when Mr. Crawford was acting under a resolution which, having produced its object, has long since expired.

The object of the first resolution submitted by him (Mr. C.) yesterday, is to obtain an entire copy of the correspondence of Mr. Crawford. The second resolution carries its own explanation.

Mr. CLAY begged permission to trespass a few moments longer on the Senate, to make a statement concerning himself personally. He had heard that one high in office had allowed himself to assert that a dishonorable connexion had subsisted between him (Mr. C.) and the Bank of the United States. When the present charter was granted he voted for it; and having done so, he did not feel himself at liberty to subscribe, and he did not subscribe for a single share in the stock of the bank, although he confidently anticipated a great rise in the value of the stock. A few years afterwards, during the presidency of Mr. Jones, it was thought by some of his friends in Philadelphia expedient to make him (Mr. C.) a director of the Bank of the United States; and he was made a director without any consultation with him. For that purpose, five shares were purchased for him by a friend, for which he (Mr. C.) afterwards paid. When he ceased to be a director, a short time subsequently, he disposed of those shares. He does not now own, and has not for many years been the proprietor of a single share.

When Mr. Cheves was appointed president of the bank, its affairs in the States of Kentucky and Ohio were in great disorder; and his (Mr. Clay's) professional services were engaged during several years for the bank in those States. He wrought a vast number of suits, and transacted a great amount of professional business for the bank. Among other suits was that for the recovery of the 100,000 dollars, seized under the authority of a law of Ohio, which he carried through the inferior and Supreme Court. He was paid by the bank the usual compensation for these services, and no more. And he ventured to assert, that no professional fees were ever more honestly and fairly earned. He had not, however, been the counsel for the bank for upwards of eight years past. He does not owe the bank, or any of its branches, a solitary cent. About twelve or fifteen years ago, owing to the failure of a highly estimable, now deceased friend, a large amount of debt had been, as his endorser, thrown upon him, (Mr. C.,) and it was principally due to the Bank of the United States. He (Mr. C.) established for himself a rigid economy, a sinking fund, and worked hard, and paid off the debt long since, without receiving from the bank the slightest favor. Whilst others around him were discharging their debts in property, at

high valuations, he periodically renewed his note, paying the discount, until it was wholly extinguished. It has been said of professional men of the greatest eminence, that their fate is to work hard, live well, and die poor.

Such was a true account of his connexion with that institution; and he defied its disproof in any particular.

He hoped the resolution would be adopted.

Mr. FORSYTH said, that perhaps the gentleman from Kentucky was not aware that the letter which he wanted was upon record. [Mr. F. referred to page 47 Senate documents of that year.] Here is the letter and the postscript alluded to; there can be no mistake about it, for it refers to the renewal of specie payments. He thought it rather unkind in the gentleman to charge the Secretary with taking a false position, when the record of it was before the world. He ought to have been certain of it first. He thought the Secretary could fully sustain the position he had taken. He thought if there were an error, it was rather a matter of inference than of fact.

Mr. CLAY wanted the whole correspondence at one view.

The resolution was adopted.

HOUSE OF REPRESENTATIVES.

WEDNESDAY, December 18, 1833.

Wednesday, December 18, 1833.

Mr. CARR, of the Committee on Private Land Claims, reported a bill for the relief of Luther L. Smith, which was read a first and second time, and committed to a Committee of the Whole House, and made the order of the day for to-morrow.

Thursday, December 19, 1833.

Mr. CARR, of the Committee on Private Land Claims, reported a bill for the relief of Archibald Small, of Indiana; which was read a first and second time, and engrossed for its third reading on Monday next.

Friday, December 20, 1833.

Mr. CARR, of the Committee on Private Land Claims, reported a bill for the relief of Elijah Lincoln, which was read a first and second time, and committed to a Committee of the Whole House, and made the order of the day for to-morrow.

A vast amount of damage was done by the gale of yesterday, which blowing directly down the sound, and the East River, accumulated the water at high tide in the bay, and caused it to encroach upon the streets in the lower part of the city. Cellars and kitchens were filled, the fires put out in the stores in the lower part of the buildings, hogsheads of sugar were spoiled, barrels of flour, piles of mahogany, and vast quantities of lumber were floated away. The damage was not confined to this city: Brooklyn came in for its share, and at Hoboken the wharf erected for the ferry lies almost in ruins, the meadows are covered with a sheet of water, and Hoboken Point is an island. The Hudson is probably opened by the storm to Albany. It was raining at that place on Monday morning.

New York Evening Post.

King Leopold has appointed a commission for the encouragement of steam-carriages into Belgium. The country being almost a perfect plane, is peculiarly well adapted to this mode of conveyance. Two have already been started from Brussels; one of enormous size, capable of exercising 120 horse-power.

THE CONGRESSIONAL GLOBE.

PRINTED AND PUBLISHED AT THE CITY OF WASHINGTON, BY BLAIR & RIVES.

23D CONGRESS, 1ST SESSION.   SATURDAY, DECEMBER 28, 1833.   VOL. I........No. 4.

IN SENATE.

MONDAY, December 23, 1833.

A message from the President of the United States was received by the hands of A. J. DONELSON, Esq., his Private Secretary.

Mr. POINDEXTER presented the credentials of the Hon. JOHN BLACK, a Senator elect from the State of Mississippi.

Mr. BLACK appeared, was qualified, and took his seat.

Petitions and memorials were presented by Messrs. FORSYTH, SILSBEE, SHEPLEY, EWING, BELL, WRIGHT, TYLER, GRUNDY, SMITH, KING of Alabama, ROBINSON, TIPTON, MOORE, PRESTON, LINN, RIVES, WILKINS, SOUTHARD, ROBBINS, and CLAY.

Mr. KING, of Alabama, submitted the following resolution:

Resolved, That the Committee on Military Affairs be directed to inquire into the expediency of repealing so much of the law relative to brevet rank as authorizes the President to confer that rank on officers who shall have served ten years in any one grade.

Mr. TIPTON, on leave given, introduced a bill to aid in the construction of roads in the territory of Michigan, which was read twice and referred to the Committee on Roads and Canals.

Mr. PRENTISS submitted the following resolution:

Resolved, That the Committee on the Post Office and Post Roads be instructed to inquire into the expediency of establishing a post route from Bethel, through Stockbridge, Pittsfield, and Windsor, to Rutland, in Vermont.

Mr. WHITE submitted the following resolutions:

Resolved, That the Committee on Naval Affairs be instructed to inquire into the expediency of restoring to the pension list Mrs. Ellen Dix, widow and relict of the late Dr. Dix, was surgeon in the navy of the United States.

On motion of Mr. WHITE, the resolution was considered and agreed to.

Mr. KING, of Alabama, reported a bill for the relief of Mountjoy Bailey.

On motion of Mr. WILKINS, the following resolution, offered on Wednesday, by Mr. MOORE, was taken up, considered, and agreed to:

Resolved, That the Secretary of War communicate to the Senate the correspondence between that department and the several agents, and other persons who have been employed in the removal, or in the arrangements for removal of the Indian tribes. Also, all correspondence between the department and other individuals on the subject of Indian affairs, including the names of agents or other persons who have been employed in making Indian treaties, in the removal of Indians, taking the census of Indians, or in locating the reservations allowed by treaties to Indians, with a statement of the several sums disbursed by each, showing the amount expended, the persons to whom it has been paid, and the specific services or consideration which they have been paid.

ORDERS OF THE DAY.

The following resolution submitted by Mr. WEBSTER on Thursday last, came up for consideration:

Resolved, That the Committee on Naval Affairs be instructed to inquire into the expediency of passing a law for preventing, as far as may be, accidents to vessels employed in the foreign or coastwise commerce of the United States, from the explosion of steam.

Mr. WEBSTER said that the great importance of this subject in its relation to the public welfare had induced him to offer this resolution. It seemed to be the general expectation with the public, that the subject would be taken up by Congress and efficiently acted on. The history of the country for the last three years presented a most startling list of accidents from explosions by steam, and the general opinion seemed to be that they arose, in many instances, from very culpable negligence, but in some from a more positive criminal offence than negligence, to wit: steamboat racing. This was a most unpardonable offence, as tending immediately to the destruction of life, by an agent so salutary and useful when under proper restraint, but awfully destructive and calamitous when in inexperienced hands. He had no doubt that it was within the power of Congress to interpose in this matter. They were licensed commercial vessels, and it seemed within the general scope of the powers of Congress to regulate commerce and preserve the lives and property of our citizens, and unless the power can be exercised by Congress he thought it could not be by the States. He desired to express an opinion, but it had occurred to him that a law might be framed having a two-fold character, to prescribe and regulate the manner in which steam-boilers should be tried, and then to prohibit the application of more than one-half or one-third of the pressure to the boiler, which it might be pronounced capable of sustaining; the regulation of the safety-valve connected to something without, by which every one might examine into the degree of pressure for himself, was also important. As it was the opinion that culpable negligence was the chief cause of so many disasters, it seemed necessary that there should be some provision for an immediate examination of all the circumstances whenever they occur; that the collector of the district ought to take measures to bring the subject to a judicial investigation, and that no excuse should avail unless it should turn out that the accident was such as could not have been prevented even by the greatest degree of skill. He was satisfied that there could be no efficient security until the owner of the boat was brought to feel his responsibility to the public by a legal provision for punishment and forfeiture. It was within the principle to look to that as the great remedy; that when explosions do take place, the owners should be held responsible, and he was persuaded that such a provision would put an end to three-fourths of such occurrences. As to the punishment imposed, that is another consideration. As negligence was highly culpable, how much more so was the system of racing, whether of a boat against a boat or against time, and in such cases the owner ought to be punished in a most exemplary manner, together with forfeiture of the boat. There was another thing: collisions had been of frequent occurrence, or boats running foul of each other. Something like a law or rule ought to be adopted to regulate the course which boats meeting each other at night ought to take, and to require them to be well lighted. Complaints, too, had been frequent of gunpowder being carried on board of steamboats. Perhaps that ought to be entirely prohibited, owing to the terror which prevented people from going in boats on that account, and that for that reason gunpowder had been frequently shipped on board in disguise. He had brought forward the resolution because so much terror existed in the public mind as greatly to impede that most comfortable and useful mode of travelling.

Mr. BENTON said he did not rise to oppose the resolution—he would give it his hearty support, as he agreed to everything which he had heard on the subject. He believed that from four to five thousand lives had been lost in the United States from such accidents. He was in New Orleans when the steamboat was blown up on the Red river—and was informed there that fifty kegs of gunpowder was on board that boat at the time. He had also been told by the captain of a steamboat, that two hogsheads had been shipped on board his boat without his knowing the contents of them; he had placed them immediately under the boilers of the boat, and it was not until they arrived safely at their place of destination, that the captain discovered that they contained gunpowder. There was another class of accidents peculiar to this species of travelling in the West which ought to be provided against—that of assaults and batteries, and homicides. He did not oppose the resolution, but rose merely to say that in his view of the subject, the Committee on the Judiciary, having the judicial affairs of the country in charge, was the most appropriate committee to consider this subject. He thought so, because the resolution embraced the jurisdiction of the private waters of the States, and it seemed to contemplate an interference with their sovereignty. In the West, during high waters, steamboats passed over plantations, and up to the heads of springs on private property. He had reflected much on this subject, with a view to devise some means of preventing the great evils complained of, but had always met with difficulties at a time when he thought he had accomplished his object. He would say, however, notwithstanding so many calamitous accidents had occurred, that his acquaintance with the captains and owners of boats enabled him to speak of them as men generally of great skill and high character, although, to be sure, there were exceptions. In twelve years' experience, in this mode of travelling, he (Mr. B.) had never met with any accident, and he attributed his good fortune solely to the minute inquiries he had always been in the habit of making when he went on board as to the perfection of the machinery, and the care and skill of the persons having it in charge. He moved to amend the resolution so as to refer it to the Judiciary Committee.

Mr. WEBSTER did not know that there was any standing committee which could appropriately take charge of it; but he was governed by precedent. A resolution offered a few days since, in relation to fires on board steamboats, had been referred to the Committee on Naval Affairs, and he thought this had better take the same course. It was his purpose to carry the regulations to boats registered and licensed plying upon the public waters only.

The motion to amend was disagreed to, and the resolution was then adopted.

The bill to repeal the act, commonly called the "Force Bill," came up in order.

Mr. FORSYTH thought, if it was the intention to discuss the bill now, that we ought to have the South Carolina ordinance.

Mr. CALHOUN said he wished to move a postponement of the bill to this day two weeks; by which time that document should be had; he accordingly made a motion to that effect, which was agreed to.

Mr. POINDEXTER'S resolution for purchasing three daily papers for the use of the Senate, came up in order.

Mr. FORSYTH did not understand the object of the resolution.

Mr. POINDEXTER. I wish the papers to be filed for the purpose of reference by the members of the Senate.

The resolution was adopted on a division—18 to 17.

The following resolution, submitted by Mr. KING on Thursday last, was taken up, considered, and agreed to:

Resolved, That the Committee on Public Lands be instructed to inquire into the expediency of authorizing the Secretary of the Treasury to pay over to the State of Alabama, to be applied to the construction of a railroad from the Tennessee to the Alabama river, two per cent. of the proceeds of the sales of the public lands, which has been set apart for making roads to and from said State, under the direction of Congress.

The following resolutions, submitted by Mr. TIPTON on Thursday last, were taken up, considered, and agreed to:

Resolved, That the Committee on Commerce be instructed to inquire into the expediency of making an appropriation for building a light-house at the mouth of the Kalamazoo and Grand rivers, on

Lake Michigan, Michigan Territory, and for surveying the bars at the mouths of both these rivers.

Resolved, That the Committee on Commerce be instructed to inquire into the expediency of an appropriation for surveying the Flats in Lake St. Clair, at the mouth of St. Clair river, and also for removing the bar, and building a pier, if necessary, at the mouth of the river Clinton, in Lake St. Clair, in the Territory of Michigan.

REMOVAL OF THE DEPOSITES.

The consideration of the report of the Secretary of the Treasury on the removal of the deposites, came up in order.

Mr. CLAY said, he regretted he was compelled to ask for a further postponement of this subject. The unexampled pressure in the money market, he was aware, required some expression on the part of the Senate, with as little delay as possible. It would be well recollected, that a call had been made upon the Secretary of the Treasury for certain papers alluded to in his report; these have not yet been received; he had supposed that they would have been ready by to-day, and that he should not have been compelled to ask for any further delay. But as the correspondence alluded to has not been received, he asked a further postponement until Thursday next.

Mr. FORSYTH said he had no kind of objection to the postponement. But he would suggest to the gentleman from Kentucky, that if he would turn over the printed public documents, he would find all the correspondence he wanted. He (Mr. F.) understood that all the gentleman wanted, was to ascertain whether the Secretary had put the proper construction upon Mr. Crawford's letters. The call of the gentleman seemed to Mr. F. very extensive, and he thought it would require more time to copy it all than was allowed by the proposed postponement.

Mr. CLAY hoped there would be no objection to the day suggested. The documents alluded to by the gentleman were in four volumes, and it was impossible to select out of them the correspondence referred to. But he would say, that he had read a great portion of it, and he was unable to find in it a single passage justifying the construction put on it by the Secretary; but, on the contrary, doctrines the very reverse of it. He asked, what was no more than fair, that the Secretary should state his own case.

The postponement till Thursday was agreed to.

On motion of Mr. FORSYTH, the bill for the relief of John A. Webster was laid on the table.

On motion of Mr. BENTON, the Senate then went into the consideration of Executive business, which occupied their attention to the hour of adjournment.

HOUSE OF REPRESENTATIVES.

MONDAY, December 23, 1833.

On motion of Mr. FULTON,

Resolved, That the Committee on Revolutionary Pensions be instructed to inquire into the expediency of granting a pension to John Carmack, of the county of Washington, Virginia, for services rendered the United States in and prior to the war of the Revolution.

On motion of Mr. STEWART,

Resolved, That the Committee of Ways and Means be instructed to inquire into the expediency of authorizing the application of a part of the annual appropriation under the act of 1824, for surveys, &c., to geological investigations, and to the formation of a geological map of the United States.

On motion of Mr. FILLMORE,

Resolved, That the Committee on Military Affairs be instructed to inquire into the expediency of so modifying the existing law in relation to the militia of the several States, as to permit each State, in time of peace, in the discretion of its legislature, to require no person to bear arms under 21 or over 40 years of age; and to permit the inspection of arms to be taken by companies, instead of by regiments or battalions; and, also, into the propriety of providing arms and accoutrements at the public expense for those liable to bear arms; and that they be required to report to this House by bill or otherwise. [Mr. F. subsequently, by unanimous consent, changed the reference of the foregoing resolution to a select committee, previously raised on subjects of a similar character.]

On motion of Mr. McKIM,

Resolved, That the Committee on the Post Office and Post Roads be instructed to inquire into the expediency of authorizing the clerk of the United States Supreme Court to receive and transmit all records, documents, and letters, concerning the duties of his office, free of postage.

On motion of Mr. DAVENPORT,

Resolved, That the Committee on the Post Office and Post Roads, be requested to inquire into the expediency of establishing a post route from Weldon, in North Carolina, by Charlotte Court-house and Brook Neal, to Green Hill, in the county of Campbell, Virginia; also, one other route from Green Hill, in the county of Campbell, by Rice Meeting-house and Spring Garden, to Danville, in Pittsylvania county, Virginia.

On motion of Mr. BOCKEE,

Resolved, That the Committee on Revolutionary Pensions be instructed to inquire into the expediency of granting a pension to Robert Brush, a soldier of the Revolution.

On motion of Mr. VANCE,

Resolved, That the deposition of Josiah Smith and others, relative to the loss of a horse while he was in the service of the United States, and for which he claims compensation from the Government, be referred to the Committee of Claims.

On motion of Mr. McKAY,

Resolved, That the Committee on Commerce be instructed to inquire into the expediency of making an appropriation for the building of a marine hospital in or near Wilmington, North Carolina.

On motion of Mr. PINCKNEY,

Resolved, That the Committee on Naval Affairs be instructed to inquire into the expediency of making remuneration to Lieutenant E. R. Shubrick, of the United States Navy, for certain expenses incurred by him during the period he commanded the United States ship Vincennes in the West Indies, and that the memorial of Lieutenant Shubrick, with the accompanying papers, presented at the last session of Congress, and now on file in the office of the Clerk of the House, be committed to said committee.

On motion of Mr. TOMPKINS,

Resolved, That the Committee on Roads and Canals be instructed to inquire into the expediency of making an appropriation for the improvement of the navigation of Big Barren river, in the State of Kentucky, and that said committee report by bill or otherwise.

On motion of Mr. DUNLAP,

Resolved, That the Committee on Post Offices and Post Roads be instructed to inquire into the expediency of establishing a post route from the town of Perryville, in the county of Perry, State of Tennessee, to the town of Reynoldsburg, in the same State.

Resolved, That the Committee on Post Offices and Post Roads be instructed to inquire into the expediency of establishing a post route from Antrim, of Van Buren, in the county of Hardiman, State of Tennessee, by Nubbin Ridge, Simpson's Bridge, on the Hatchee river, Cypress, Chambers' Store, Wolf's Ferry, on the Tennessee river, to Lilley's, on the stage road from Florence, Alabama, to Savannah, Tennessee.

On motion of Mr. EWING,

Resolved, That the Committee on Invalid Pensions be instructed to inquire into the expediency of providing by law for the payment of half-pay pensions to the widows and orphans of those officers and soldiers of the late six companies of mounted rangers who died while in the line of their duty on the northwestern frontier.

Mr. EVERETT submitted the following resolution, which, by a rule of the House, lies on the table one day:

Resolved, (if the Senate concur therein,) That when the two Houses of Congress adjourn to-morrow, they adjourn to meet on Monday next.

Mr. POLK said it was unusual to adopt a course of this kind. The usage had been for each House, during Christmas week, to adjourn to the third day from the day preceding Christmas. He did not expect that the House would do much business during this week, but he hoped it would do some business.

Mr. EVERETT said, it had been usual, when Christmas occurred on Wednesday, to adjourn over to the following Monday. At this stage of the session, it was not usual for the House to sit on Saturdays.

Mr. WILLIAMS, of North Carolina, moved that the resolution lie on the table indefinitely.

Mr. FOOT suggested that the resolution must, according to the rule, lie one day, and claimed the enforcement of the rule; but subsequently withdrew it, at the request of several members, who wished the sense of the House to be taken at once upon the adjournment.

Mr. POLK renewed the call for the application of the rule, and the joint resolution lies accordingly on the table for one day.

On motion of Mr. WHITE, of Louisiana,

Resolved, That the Committee on Public Lands be instructed to inquire into the expediency and justice of granting to the State of Louisiana, in aid of internal improvements, the same extent of land which has heretofore been granted by Congress to other western States, and particularly to the State of Alabama.

On motion of Mr. LEAVITT,

Resolved, That the Committee of Ways and Means be instructed to inquire into the expediency of refunding to James Maley a sum erroneously paid by him to the marshal of the district of Ohio, in the purchase of certain real estate, sold by said marshal, upon an execution issued at the suit of the United States.

On motion of Mr. BELL, of Ohio,

Resolved, That the Committee on the Post Office and Post Roads be instructed to inquire into the expediency of establishing a mail route from Cambridge, in Guernsey county, Ohio, through Liberty, in said county, to Plainfield, in Coshocton county.

On motion of Mr. STANDIFER,

Resolved, That the Committee on the Post Office and Post Roads be instructed to inquire into the expediency of establishing a mail route from Dallas, in Hamilton county, Tennessee, to Ashville, in the State of Alabama, passing through Wills's Valley.

On motion of Mr. CLAY,

Resolved, That the Committee on Revolutionary Claims be instructed to inquire into the expediency of establishing an agency for the payment of pensions at the branch of the Bank of the State of Alabama in Decatur.

On motion of Mr. LYON, of Kentucky,

Resolved, That the Committee on the Post Office and Post Roads be instructed to inquire into the expediency of establishing a post road from Wadesboro', Kentucky, by Humility, to the mouth of Sandy, Tennessee.

On motion of Mr. SLADE, of Illinois,

Resolved, That the Committee on Public Lands be instructed to inquire into the expediency of authorizing the relinquishment of the sixteenth sections reserved for the use of schools in the State of Illinois, in all cases where the same is barren and unproductive, and the selection and entry of others in lieu thereof.

On motion of Mr. ASHLEY,

Resolved, That the Committee on Claims be instructed to inquire into the expediency of allowing to Morris James, or his legal representatives, compensation for wood cut and taken away from his land by the troops of the United States.

On motion of Mr. HANNEGAN,

Resolved, That the Committee on Roads and Canals be instructed to inquire into the expediency of donating to the State of Indiana each alternate section heretofore reserved to the United States by the act of March 2, 1827, for the purpose of insuring a speedy completion of the said canal, under a provision, that if the same be accepted by the State of Indiana, the work shall, after its completion, become forever a free and public highway for all the citizens of the United States, and the transportation of their property, subject to the collection of no higher amount of toll or other charge than will be sufficient to keep said canal in proper repair.

On motion of Mr. EVERETT, of Vermont,

Resolved, That the Committee of Ways and Means be instructed to inquire into the expediency of refunding to Jesse Gove a sum of money paid in 1814, by mistake, to the district attorney for the Vermont district, for the use of the United States.

On motion of Mr. LYON of Michigan,

Resolved, That the Committee on Roads and Canals be instructed to inquire into the expediency of making an appropriation to construct certain roads in the Territory of Michigan, described in a bill (No. 85) which passed the Senate at the last session of Congress; and also that said committee be instructed to inquire into the expediency of making an appropriation to survey and mark a road, and to cut away the timber and bridge the streams on the same, from Taginaw to Mackinac, and thence to the Sault Sainte Marie, in Michigan Territory.

Mr. WHITTLESEY, of Ohio, from the Committee of Claims, reported a bill for the relief of Joseph Byington.

Mr. BOULDIN, from the Committee on Revolutionary Claims, reported bills for the relief of the legal representatives of George Herbert, and of the heirs at law of Richard Wilson.

Mr. MUHLENBERG, from the same, reported bills for the relief of Dr. Robert Wilmot and Ephraim Whitaker.

Mr. CRANE, from the same, reported a bill for the relief of Mary Anne Brooks, and other heirs at law of Daniel Reeves.

Mr. GRENNELL of Massachusetts, reported a bill for the relief of Asa Wilkinson.

Mr. WARDWELL, from the Committee on Revolutionary Pensions, reported a bill for the relief of Daniel Payne.

Mr. McINTIRE reported a bill for the relief of Laurentius M. Hyler.

Mr. MARSHALL, from the Committee on Revolutionary Claims, reported bills for the relief of the legal representatives of Captain Thomas Blackwell, and for the administrators of Michael Pratts.

Mr. EVANS of Maine, from the Committee on Pensions, reported a bill granting pensions to certain persons therein named.

Mr. CAVE JOHNSON reported a bill for the relief of J. Dutee and others.

All which bills were read twice and committed.

The SPEAKER presented the following message from the President of the United States:

WASHINGTON, *December* 23, 1833.

To the House of Representatives:

The rules and regulations herewith submitted have been prepared by a board of officers, in conformity with an act passed May 19, 1832. They are approved by me; and, in pursuance of the provisions of said act, are now communicated to the House of Representatives for the purpose of obtaining to them the sanction of Congress.

ANDREW JACKSON.

The said message, on motion of Mr. WATMOUGH, with the accompanying documents, was referred to the Committee on Naval Affairs, and ordered to be printed.

The SPEAKER also presented a report from Robert Mills, in relation to the recent alteration made in the House of Representatives; which, on motion of Mr. WHITTLESEY, was referred to the Committee on Public Buildings.

REMOVAL OF THE DEPOSITES.

The House resumed the consideration of the motion to re-commit the report of the Secretary of the Treasury to the Committee of Ways and Means—the question being on the following instructions, moved by Mr. McDUFFIE:

"To report a joint resolution providing that the public revenue hereafter collected be deposited in the Bank of the United States, in conformity with the public faith pledged in the charter of the said bank."

Mr. McDUFFIE said, the only substantial ground alleged by the Secretary of the Treasury for the removal of the deposites, he would now proceed to consider. It was a ground which, if founded in fact, was entitled to the serious consideration of this House. The Secretary alleged, that the curtailments of the bank made this step so necessary that he could not wait two months for the meeting of Congress. Mr. McD. insisted that the ground taken was not founded in fact. The whole amount of the reduction in the circulation of the bank, from the first of August to the first of October, was, in fact, only one million and sixteen thousand dollars. But the Secretary has informed us that the amount of the reductions, or, as the Secretary called them, "of collections from the community," during that time, was upwards of six millions of dollars. The document, therefore, speaking technically, or in the language of common sense, was a gross imposition on the public. The Secretary had arrived at this result by alleging that the amount of deposites received by the bank was equivalent to a withdrawal of so much money from the circulation of the bank. The actual amount of discounts on the first of August was $43,237,000, and on the first of October, $42,221,000; so that this extraordinary reduction, which produced so much distress, was only $1,016,000. The actual amount of capital taken from the vaults of the bank, within the same time, was $8,000,000; for the threat to take it away rendered it necessary for the bank to be prepared to pay it. The domestic bills discounted by the bank were not actually loans. They were bought by the bank, and paid at maturity, for the accommodation of the community, and to save the time of transporting specie. On no commercial principle, therefore, could the diminution in the amount of these bills be considered as a diminution of the circulation. He had seen it stated in the Government press of this morning that the bank, from the first of August to the present time, had diminished its circulation twelve millions of dollars. But the fact was, that, to this time from the first of August, the diminution of its circulation had been only four millions and a half of dollars; and adding to this amount the diminution in bills of exchange, it was less than ten millions, a sum but little exceeding the amount drawn by the Government from the bank.

The Secretary next accuses the bank of hoarding up specie—of accumulating a large amount of specie, which the Secretary infers was drawn from the State banks. But if the fact were true, which the Secretary alleges, and if all the suffering had ensued from the curtailments of the bank, still the Executive was entirely answerable for it. He had never read, in his life, a more unfair, uncandid, and jesuitical statement than that, by which it was attempted to throw the responsibility of the present pressure upon the bank. After reading the passage referred to, he adverted to the declaration of the President, made by public manifesto, in September, that the deposites ought to be removed as soon as practicable, and fixes for that purpose the first day of October. Yet, the Secretary says the bank should not have taken the removal for granted. They should have come to him—to the Secretary of the Treasury, for information as to this fact. But who was the Secretary of the Treasury? Mr. Duane held the office, and would he, if applied to, have given any information counter to that communicated in the manifesto? The bank, he insisted, ought, in common prudence, to consider the deposites as removed as soon as the manifesto of the Executive was published. Mr. McD. then referred to the charge that the bank had violated its charter in not requiring the concurrence of seven directors in every act. Why was not the *scire facias* issued on this charge? Why, he believed that not one respectable lawyer in the United States would be found to bring the suit. The board of directors constituted the legislature of the bank, but the president and certain committees were the executive authority of the bank. It was not necessary that any act authorized by the board should be performed in the presence of and with the assent of the board. The President of the United States, he imagined, would not consent to decline the exercise of all Executive authority which had not the concurrence of Congress. But it was said that the Government directors were excluded from all participation in the proceedings of the bank. He went into a statement of the ordinary management of the bank, to show that the proceedings of the exchange committee were duly reported to the board, and that no act of that committee could be consummated without the knowledge of every member of the board. The Government directors could see the whole proceedings of that committee on the books before their consummation. The old matter of the three per cents. had been again looked up, as a charge against the bank. In that case the bank stepped in to avert a pressure which the Government was about to produce. By the arrangement of the bank, they were enabled to continue their discounts to the amount of six millions; the Government was released from responsibility, and the certificates came into the hands of the bank. In fact, the bank, by this arrangement, expedited instead of retarded the payment of the debt. The bank paid the interest of the stock to the Government; the Government lost nothing, and the bank had now paid the whole amount of the certificates to the holders, and had at the same time averted from the community a pressure as severe and as extensive as the present. For what purpose this charge was brought up again he could not tell, but it served to shew the spirit in which the bank was persecuted.

On the subject of the charge against the bank, founded on the demand made by the bank upon the Government, for damages on a bill of exchange drawn by the Government on France, purchased by the bank and protested, he stated that the bank, in this transaction, stood to the Government precisely as an individual purchaser of a bill, and were exposed to the same loss and inconvenience by its protest, as an individual purchaser would have been. The Government itself had always most rigidly exacted damages, to the full legal amount, whether inconvenience had been suffered or not. Yet the Government had the audacity to charge the bank with stabbing the public credit, whereas the Government itself had stabbed the public credit by refusing to pay its just debts. The Government alleges that the money was deposited in the bank, to the whole amount paid for the draft, and that the bank had therefore the use of it. But this was an assertion not founded in fact. Congress provided by law, that the money should be deposited in the bank, and appropriated to loans for the use of the distributees of the fund

He came next to the charge that the bank had conferred upon its president the power of printing certain documents. He was astonished that the President, of all others, should have made this charge. By a law of last session, an unlimited power—the disposition of the whole wealth and revenue of the country—was placed in the hands of the President, at his own special instance. He could not match this inconsistency with anything but with another Dutch story; he had got in the habit of relating Dutch stories; they were so very apposite, at the present time, as affording illustrations of Dutch wisdom. But he would not locate this story, like the other, at Kinderhook, lest some question might arise upon it. In a certain Dutch village, there was once upon a time, as all old stories begin, a certain lottery to be drawn, having many blanks and few prizes. In the revolving of the wheel, before the assembled crowds interested in such event, dame fortune, who presided, showered her favors upon but few. There were more blanks than prizes. This was felt a great grievance, until at length, the public excitement getting to the highest pitch, a large bully mounted the platform upon which the wheel was placed, with the intention of breaking it all to smashes, because, as he said, "de whole bushness war a piece of willainous cheatrery"—when up starts one of the managers, before he had time to put his threats into execution, and exclaimed to him, "softly, softly, my good friend; do you know what this is in my hand for you?" The honest Dutchman said, "no, he did not." "Why, then," said the other, "'tis a large prize for you." "Oh, then," on second thought, responded the Dutchman, "this cannot be a willainous piece of cheatrery; it is as fair a thing as ever was." The President complains of the power vested in the president of the bank as subversive of the liberty of the country, but when he himself takes the exercise of a power ten thousand times greater, he says "it is as fair a thing as ever was." The charge was, that the bank had expended so much for printing—but, in fact, only 46,000 dollars of the sum stated was for printing—the remainder being for blank books, bank notes, &c. He mentioned this merely to show that the statement of the Secretary could not be relied upon. He wished to God that the President, as the representative of the government interest in the bank, had discharged his duties as well as the president of the bank. His daily and nightly effort had been to destroy the institution; and it was greatly to the credit of the bank that it had withstood the whole combination of the government—stockjobbers and all. Any

other institution would have fallen under the assault. The Bank of the United States is the only institution which stands safe amidst the general shock produced by the course of the Government; and yet the President had denounced it, last year, as an unsafe depository for the public money. The bank, too, had made a generous use of its power; for he was told that it had assisted to preserve the banks in its vicinity from entire destruction. The bank, too, was charged with interfering with elections. The charge was, that the bank, from the first of January, 1831, to May, 1832, had increased its loans from forty-two to seventy millions of dollars—making an increase of twenty-eight millions in sixteen months. But this statement was, he contended, a gross, and he was sorry to say, an intentional misrepresentation. On the first of January the amount of discounts was thirty-three millions. On the first of May, they had increased to forty-seven millions—being an increase of fourteen millions. This was put forth as a crime against the bank. But the Secretary of the Treasury had, in suppressing some facts, which must have been known to him, left himself open to the charge of wilfully attempting to impose upon the Congress and the country: for he had known, that by various means, the collecting of its debts, and repayments from England, the bank had increased the cash in its vaults, during that same period, to nearly eleven millions—and yet he urges as a complaint, "that the bank had increased its discounts from forty-two to seventy millions." So the extraordinary increase of discounts turns out to be nothing more than the exchange of one debtor for another; and, besides, the bank was able to discount more than the actual amount of the money thus repaid to it. Another consideration was, that the year 1831 was one of most excessive importation, and although there was an unprecedented amount of commercial debt created, there was, through the wise administration of the bank, no ruinous re-action or depression. The bank eased every thing down quietly and safely. The merchants got through the crisis with ease, and in spite of all predictions, refused to fail or become embarrassed. The main proof brought by the President and his Secretary in support of the charge of interfering with elections, was this inerease of discounts. They could imagine no other reason for the increase than an attempt to defeat his election. Most horribly must that intellect be perverted which could see, in such a measure, nothing but a desire to interfere in a presidential election.

He had now gone through with all the charges against the bank, and he called upon Congress to interfere and save the country from the distresses impending over it. Shall we not interfere to stop the extending ruin? We are called upon by every consideration connected with the liberties of the people, to arrest the arbitrary arm of the Executive. Where is the public treasure? No man can tell where it is. By what authority has it been taken out of the treasury? No man can answer. Then let us tell the Secretary of the Treasury, if he attempts to forestall our proceedings, he shall not accomplish his object. Why had the President removed the deposites before the meeting of Congress? Because he knew that he could not persuade Congress to do it, though he might induce them to confirm the act after it was done. The President, as a military man, knows the effect of throwing himself into a breach and crying to his followers, "Save your general." The Executive government had thrust itself into this matter in such a manner as almost to preclude any action upon our part. We could not now, without producing great embarrassments, interfere by ordering the deposites, already withdrawn from the United States Bank, to be restored to it; and he had, therefore, confined his object to the future deposite of all public money in that bank. The instructions to the committee, for the restoration of the deposites, he desired now to have only a prospective effect, in order to avert the ruin which would ensue from their being suddenly withdrawn from the State banks. He knew that the pictures drawn of the calamities all over the country would be said to have been too highly colored. It was in fact said the other day, by an honorable member from New York, [Mr. VANDERPOEL,] that the removal had nothing to do with these calamities—that all that was said about commercial distress, was a humbug. Ay, sir, these were the words; but to him it was a most melancholy humbug. Was there any man now, in his senses, to join in that opinion? Who now would say that the removal of the deposites had not something to do with the distress overspreading the land? He presumed no man would have the audacity now to say so, for any picture of that distress must fall short of its sad reality. Even he himself, until he had various letters from different sections of the country, could not have formed any idea of its extent. And this, he contended, would not be confined, as was alleged, to the cities only; it must finally increase, and find its way into the country at large—as one class of the country could not be affected by commercial distress, without all the others feeling it, and most sensibly too. That the effect of the commercial distress on the South had already been felt, he could testify. The crop of cotton, when brought to market, had borne in Charleston, as compared with the prices in Liverpool, a loss of five cents per pound. What produced this difference? Nothing else assuredly than the scarcity of money; in consequence of which the usual purchasers of this article were disabled from entering into the market; and within the last four weeks a further difference had been made of at least two cents. With the knowledge of this, as to one important interest, he might predict that the same result would be produced in others. Did they not know that great losses had arisen to the dealers interested in stocks of the State banks, even in some of the favored ones? Was there not in the Girard bank stock a decline from 70 to 54? And yet they were to be told there was no commercial distress in consequence of the scarcity of money. But if there was such a depreciation in the value of this bank stock, must it not be apparent that the stock of others would also become depreciated? From what cause could such depreciation arise, if it was not from the panic created in consequence of the absurd and wicked interference with the monetary institutions?

He would conclude by saying, what would be the end of this? He would not say. The object of all these measures, if not retraced, must be to make a sacrifice of the interests of all the industrious classes in the country, for the sole benefit of speculators and stockjobbers. For them, there was a full harvest to be reaped. The speculating broker, and rapacious money-vender, would have every opportunity afforded them to prey upon the necessities of those who were the main dependence of the country. These meritorious classes must be depressed, whilst others would rise, upon their necessities, to princely fortunes. To those persons, however, who, if connected with the recent measures of the Government, and speculating on their effect, had hoped to gain by depreciating the United States Bank stock, it was some consolation that they would be disappointed: for whilst the State bank stock had, in many instances, fallen, the other had advanced; the bank was too strong for them. Mr. McD., after deprecating, at some length, the ruinous consequences that would follow, as a consequence of the late measures, in connecting the executive with the finance power of the country, concluded by calling upon the House to interpose its power, before it became too late to do so, to wrest impending ruin from the country.

Mr. POLK then rose and moved an adjournment, which was carried.

And the House adjourned.

IN SENATE.

TUESDAY, *December* 24, 1833.

A message was received from the President of the United States, by the hands of A. J. DONELSON, Esq., his Private Secretary.

Petitions and memorials were presented by Messrs. HENDRICKS, TOMLINSON, KING of Alabama, TALLMADGE, LINN, and SHEPLEY.

Mr. ROBINSON, on leave given, introduced bills for the relief of Noah Stehley and George Stehley, which were read twice and referred to the Committee on Public Lands.

Mr. POINDEXTER, from the Committee to whom was referred the bill for the relief of Elihu Hall Bay, reported the same without amendment.

Mr. BELL, on leave given, introduced a bill for the relief of Caleb Stark; which was twice read, and referred to the Committee on Claims.

Mr. POINDEXTER, from the Committee on Public Lands, to which was referred the memorial of the Legislature of Missouri, praying for a grant of lands, reported adverse to the prayer of the petitioners.

Mr. SPRAGUE, on leave given, presented a bill for the relief of Ebenezer Roberts, which was twice read, and referred to the Committee on Claims.

Mr. GRUNDY, from the Committee on Post Offices, reported two bills for the relief of John Chalender and William Johnson, and Thomas Rhoads and Jeremiah Austen.

Mr. POINDEXTER, on leave given, introduced a bill for the relief of Calvin Smith; which was twice read, and referred to the Committee on Private Land Claims.

Mr. KENT submitted the following joint resolution:

Resolved by the Senate and House of Representatives of the United States of America in Congress assembled, (two-thirds of both Houses concurring,) That the following article be proposed to the Legislatures of the several States as an amendment to the Constitution of the United States, which, when ratified by three-fourths of said Legislatures, shall be valid as part of the Constitution.

When a bill which, having passed the Senate and House of Representatives, shall be returned by the President of the United States, with his objections, upon the reconsideration thereof, a majority of all the members elected to each House shall again pass such bill, notwithstanding the objections of the President, it shall become a law, and the requisition of two-thirds in such case, according to the existing Constitution is revoked.

ORDERS OF THE DAY.

The following resolution, offered yesterday by Mr. KING, came up for consideration, and was adopted:

Resolved, That the Committee on Military Affairs be directed to inquire into the expediency of repealing so much of the law relative to brevet rank, as authorizes the President to confer that rank on officers who shall have served ten years in any one grade.

The following resolution, offered yesterday by Mr. PRENTISS, was considered and adopted:

Resolved, That the Committee on the Post Office and Post Roads, be instructed to inquire into the expediency of establishing a post route from Bethel, through Stockbridge, Pittsfield, and Windsor, to Rutland, in Vermont.

The resolution of Mr. ROBBINS, directing the Library Committee to procure a bust of the late Chief Justice Ellsworth, to be executed by an American artist, was considered and agreed to.

The bill for the relief of Mountjoy Bailey, was read a second time and ordered to be engrossed for a third reading.

A joint resolution was received from the House of Representatives, for an adjournment of Congress till Monday next.

Mr. KANE moved to concur in the resolution.

Mr. CLAY opposed it on account of the unusual pressure of business.

The motion was lost on a division, 18 to 17.

Mr. FRELINGHUYSEN then moved, that when the Senate adjourns, it will adjourn to meet again on Thursday next, which was agreed to.

Mr. LINN submitted the following resolution:

Resolved, That the Committee on Public Lands be instructed to inquire into the expediency of making a grant of land to the widow and heirs of the late Felix St. Vrain, who was killed by the Indians in the late disturbance in the Northwest.

On motion of Mr. SHEPLEY, the Senate then proceeded to the consideration of Executive business, in which they were engaged till the hour of adjournment.

HOUSE OF REPRESENTATIVES.

TUESDAY, *December* 24, 1833.

The House suspended the rule for the purpose of taking up the joint resolution submitted yesterday by Mr. EVERETT, that when the House adjourned, it should adjourn over to Monday next.

After some opposition from Mr. CLAY, who moved to postpone the third reading until Saturday, the motion was rejected, and the resolution was read twice, and ordered to be engrossed for a third reading, was engrossed, finally passed, and sent to the Senate for concurrence.

Subsequently, a message was received from the Senate, informing the House that the Senate had not concurred in the resolution for a temporary adjournment.

Mr. EVERETT moved that when the House adjourned this day, it should adjourn until Friday next, which motion did not, he said, require the concurrence of the Senate: agreed to.

On motion of Mr. HATHAWAY,
Resolved, That the Committee of Claims be instructed to inquire into the expediency of paying Daniel Brown the amount certified to be due to him by a jury, in a suit instituted against him by the United States.

Mr. ANTHONY submitted the following resolution, which, by the rule of the House, lies one day on the table:
Resolved, That the Secretary of War be directed to communicate to this House the report of Major Bache, of the corps of Topographical Engineers, of his survey and estimate of the Williamsport and Elmira railroad, in the States of Pennsylvania and New York.

On motion of Mr. GALBRAITH,
Resolved, That the Committee on Roads and Canals be instructed to inquire into the expediency of making an appropriation for the harbor at Wightua's Point, near the mouth of the Twenty-mile Creek, Erie county, Pennsylvania, and that the Secretary of War be directed to furnish to this House a copy of the report of a survey made by the United States engineer at said point.

Mr. PINCKNEY submitted the following resolutions, which lie one day on the table:
Resolved, That the President of the United States be requested to communicate to this House, if not incompatible, in his opinion, with the public interest, a copy of the instructions given to our Minister at Madrid, relative to the trade between the United States and the islands of Cuba and Puerto Rico, and such information as may be in his possession, touching the prospect of an abolition by the Spanish Government of the discriminating duties referred to in his message.

Resolved, That the President be requested to cause to be laid before this House a statement of the discriminating duties levied upon American vessels in the islands of Cuba and Puerto Rico, and also of the duties now imposed by the Government of the United States upon articles imported from those islands.

On motion of Mr. DUNLAP,
Resolved, That the Committee on the Post Office and Post Roads be instructed to inquire into the expediency of establishing a post route from Durhamsville, in Tipton county, Tennessee, to Ashport, in said county of Tipton.

On motion of Mr. KINNARD,
Resolved, That the Committee on the Post Office and Post Roads be instructed to inquire into the expediency of establishing a mail route as follows, viz: continuing the present route from Richmond, via Newcastle, Pendleton, and Strawtown, from the latter place to Kirk's Cross Roads, in the State of Indiana.

On motion of Mr. CASEY,
Resolved, That the Committee on the Post Office and Post Roads be instructed to inquire into the expediency of establishing a mail route from Alton, by Fairfield, Malding's Mills, and Mount Vernon, to Nashville, in the State of Illinois.

Mr. DUNCAN submitted the following resolution, which, according to a rule, lies one day on the table:
Resolved, That the Secretary of the Treasury be requested to communicate to this House whether any attempts have been made to evade the revenue laws of the United States, by the introduction of lead in 56 pound weights, in statues, or any other form, and whether any further legislation be necessary to protect the revenue and the manufacture of lead.

On motion of Mr. MARDIS,
Resolved, That the Committee on the Post Of-

fice and Post Roads be instructed to inquire into the expediency of establishing a mail route from Selma, via Valley Creek Settlement, Weaver's Store, to Marion, Perry county, Alabama.

On motion of Mr. SEVIER,
Resolved, That the Committee on Indian Affairs be instructed to inquire into the expediency of increasing the salary of the sub-agent to the Choctaw Indians west of the Mississippi river.

On motion of Mr. McCARTY,
Resolved, That the Committee on the Post Office and Post Roads be instructed to inquire into the expediency of establishing the following post routes in Indiana, to wit: From Connersville, in Fayette county, to Louisville, in Henry county; from New Castle to Munceytown; from Brownsville, by Philomith, to Centreville; from Richmond, by Winchester and Missisiniwa, to Fort Wayne; and from Oxford, in Ohio, by Fairfield and West Union, to Rushville, in Indiana.

Mr. H. EVERETT submitted the following resolution; to lie one day:
Resolved, That the Secretary of War be directed to communicate to this House the names, and places where employed, of the superintendent of Indian Affairs, Indian agents, and sub-agents, interpreters, and clerks, and all other persons now in the employ of the United States in the Indian Department; the salary and emoluments of each; by whom appointed; the dates of their appointments, with a reference to the treaty, law, or authority under which they were appointed; and his opinion whether a part of said agencies may not be discontinued without prejudice to the public service.

On motion of Mr. GILLET,
Resolved, That the Committee on Private Land Claims be instructed to inquire into the expediency of granting to Amos W. Brown, of St. Lawrence county, in the State of New York, a warrant for bounty land, to which he was entitled as a Canadian volunteer, during the late war, and that the petition presented by him at the last session of Congress, together with the report of the Committee of Claims, be referred to said committee.

On motion of Mr. DAVIS, of Massachusetts,
Resolved, That a select committee be appointed, to be called the Committee on Patents granted for Useful Inventions.

On motion of Mr. HARD,
Resolved, That the Committee on Commerce be instructed to inquire into the expediency of making an appropriation for constructing a breakwater at the Niagara river, near Youngstown, in the State of New York.

Mr. PAGE submitted the following resolution; which lies one day on the table:
Resolved, That the Secretary of War be requested to transmit to this House the report and drawings of the survey of the New York and Erie Railroad, made under the direction of De Witt Clinton, Esq., United States civil engineer, in 1832.

Mr. CAVE JOHNSON reported bills for the relief of Wyatt Singleton, and James Andrews, and others.

Mr. NICHOLSON reported a bill for the relief of John McClenahan.

Mr. CASEY, for the relief of Richard Max.

Mr. MUHLENBERG, for the relief of John Polhemus.

Mr. EVANS, for the relief of James B. Folsom and others.

All which bills were read twice, and committed.

Mr. CARR, of Indiana, from the Committee on Private Land Claims, reported a bill for the relief of Baptiste Jean Sonne; which bill was read a first and second time, referred to a Committee of the Whole House, and made the order of the day for to-morrow.

Mr. CLAY, from the Committee on Private Land Claims, reported a bill granting lands in the Western Reserve to the State of Ohio, for the support of certain schools; which was read twice, and ordered to be engrossed for a third reading on Monday next.

The SPEAKER presented to the House a communication and some accounts from the Secretary of the Treasury.　Also a communication from the War Department, with a survey of the White and St. Francis rivers, Arkansas, as ordered by the

House; which were appropriately referred, and ordered to be printed.

The resolutions for inquiry, heretofore offered, were severally considered and adopted.

The resolution heretofore offered by Mr. SELDEN, relative to the sinking fund, was taken up for consideration.

Mr. POLK suggested a modification of the resolution, so as to give it the form of an inquiry.

Mr. CAMBRELENG stated that the existing laws on the subject of the sinking fund, made all the provisions required by his colleague, except one.　Mr. C. stated what were the existing laws on that subject.

On motion of Mr. WHITTLESEY, the resolution was laid on the table, on account of the absence of the mover.

The following engrossed bills were, severally, read a third time and passed:
A bill for the relief of Archibald Small.
A bill granting pensions to certain persons therein named.
A bill for the relief of Samuel Thomson.
A bill for the relief of Sarah Thomson.
A bill for the relief of George Chinn.
A bill for the relief of Benjamin Sherfey.
A bill for the relief of the heirs of widow Robert Avart.
A bill for the relief of Thomas Richardson.
A bill for the relief of William S. Anderson.
A bill for the relief of George H. Jennings.
A bill for the relief of James H. Brewer.
A bill for the relief of the legal representatives of James Morrison, deceased.
A bill for the relief of John Thomson.
A bill for the relief of Richard Bagnall, executor of J. B. Vaughan.
A bill for the relief of Whitford Gill.
A bill for the relief of Peregrine Gardner.
A bill for the relief of Edward Willett.
A bill for the relief of Jonathan Lincoln, administrator of Samuel Lincoln, deceased.
A bill for the relief of John H. Maguire.
A bill for the relief of Russell Hunt, David Hunt, and Amos Hunt.
A bill for the relief of Philip Hickey.
A bill for the relief of John Bills.
A bill for the relief of Daniel Hazleton and William Palmer.
A bill for the relief of Francis Barnes.
A bill for the relief of Joseph M. Harper.
A bill for the relief of Martha Bailey, and others.

On motion of Mr. WARD, the House then adjourned.

The select committee on the Militia, consists of Messrs. Hubbard, Lyon, Beale, Griffin, Plummer, McCarty, Bull, Graham, and Anthony.

[The following preamble and resolution was submitted in the House of Representatives on Monday last, by Mr. HANNEGAN, of Indiana, but on the suggestion of Mr. MERCER, the preamble was withdrawn, (it being unusual upon subjects of inquiry.)　The resolution was adopted.　It is now republished, together with the preamble, in order to a more full understanding of the objects of the mover.]

Whereas by an act of Congress, approved May 26, 1824, the State of Indiana was "authorized to survey and mark through the public lands of the United States, the route of a canal by which to connect the navigable waters of the river Wabash with those of Lake Erie;" and under certain provisions in said act stipulated, 90 feet of land on each side of said canal were reserved from sale and the use thereof vested in the State aforesaid for a canal, and for no other purpose whatever; and whereas, by a subsequent act of Congress, approved the 2d of March, 1827, there was granted to the said State of Indiana, for the purpose of aiding her "in opening a canal to unite at navigable points the waters of the Wabash river with those of Lake Erie," a quantity of land equal to one half of five sections in width, on each side of said canal, and at the same time reserving each alternate section to the United States, to be selected by the Commissioner of the Land Office, under the direction of the President, from one end thereof to the other, with a proviso, that said canal, when

completed, "should be, and forever remain, a public highway for the use of the Government of the United States, free from any toll or other charge for any property of the United States or persons in their service, passing through the same," and a further proviso, "that the canal should be commenced by said State within five, and completed within twenty five years:" Now, therefore, as the State of Indiana has accepted the grant, and in good faith commenced the execution of the work under all the provisions of the several acts referred to, and the same is a work entirely national in its character, and its completion an object of general interest—

Resolved, That the Committee on Roads and Canals be instructed to inquire into the expediency of donating to the State of Indiana each alternate section heretofore reserved to the United States by the act of March 2, 1827, for the purpose of ensuring a speedy completion of the said canal, under a proviso that if the same be accepted by the State of Indiana, the work shall, after its completion, become forever a free and public highway for all the citizens of the United States, and the transportation of their property, subject to the collection of no higher amount of toll or charge than will be sufficient to keep the said canal in proper repair.

IN SENATE.

THURSDAY, *December* 26, 1833.

A bill for the relief of Mountjoy Bailey was read a third time, and, on motion of Mr. WRIGHT, laid on the table.

The following resolution, submitted by Mr. LINN on Tuesday, was agreed to:

Resolved, That the Committee on Public Lands be instructed to inquire into the expediency of making a grant of land to the widow and heirs of the late Felix St. Vrain, who was killed by the Indians in the late disturbance in the Northwest.

PUBLIC DEPOSITES.

The VICE PRESIDENT having announced the orders of the day to be the consideration of the report of the Secretary of the Treasury upon the removal of the deposites—

Mr. CLAY said as he was desirous of avoiding any interruption upon the question of order, he would submit the following resolutions:

1. *Resolved*, That, by dismissing the late Secretary of the Treasury because he would not, contrary to his sense of his own duty, remove the money of the United States in deposite with the Bank of the United States and its branches, in conformity with the President's opinion; and by appointing his successor to effect such removal, which has been done, the President has assumed the exercise of a power over the treasury of the United States not granted to him by the Constitution and laws, and dangerous to the liberties of the people.

2. *Resolved*, That the reasons assigned by the Secretary of the Treasury for the removal of the money of the United States deposited in the Bank of the United States and its branches, communicated to Congress on the third day of December, 1833, are unsatisfactory and insufficient.

The resolutions being before the Senate—

Mr. CLAY said, we are in the midst of a revolution, which, although bloodless, yet we are rapidly advancing to a concentration of all the powers of government in the hands of one man. By the exercise of the powers assumed by the President of the United States, in his letter to his Cabinet, the powers of Congress are paralyzed, except where they are in compliance with his own will. These powers he had exercised in repeated instances, by withholding his signature from bills involving no constitutional questions, which had been passed by both Houses, and even where that had been done by the most unusual unanimity. The power of the Senate, which was intended by the Constitution as a most salutary control over the President, had become an idle ceremony. How often (said Mr. C.) have we felt the injustice of the power of removal. How often have we said among ourselves that the office could not remain vacant, but must be filled by some one. The powers of the judiciary, too, had not escaped the prevailing rage for innovation—the sanctity of treaties had been disregarded. In our relations with the Indians their rights had been violated, and the privileges of the aborigines of our soil had been trampled in the dust. Our public domain, the richest that ever fell to the lot of any nation on earth, had been threatened with sacrifice. Our currency had been menaced with disorder and confusion. The American system, at the last session of Congress, had only been snatched from destruction, and now we have been coolly told, by the Secretary of the Treasury, that a tariff, only for the protection of our industry, was to be abandoned. If the progress of innovation should continue unarrested to the year 1837, we shall, in a little term of years, less than that employed in the achievement of our independence, have changed our Government. He did not desire to give an undue coloring to the melancholy picture, for melancholy it was, but he would implore the people of the country and the Senate calmly to view it and to apply the remedy which the emergency seemed to require. It was not the least unpleasant symptom prevailing abroad that good men of all parties were giving themselves up to despondency. Feelings of distrust and want of confidence were prevailing; he hoped, however, that spirits and confidence would revive. There was room for patriotic vigor, none for despair. If our ancestors had yielded to despair we would never have attained that liberty which we are now enjoying. It was in the memorable years 1776-'77, that our country was covered with darkness; it was a most remarkable epoch, and remarkably similar to the present time. He would observe that this day fifty-seven years ago, a man who was most truly called the father of his country, had achieved a most glorious victory—a striking coincidence; but he had gone; and let us hope that the superintending Power which contributed to that result, will interpose some happy deliverance from the dangers with which our country seems threatened. When (said Mr. C.) we assembled here this time last year, the most dreadful forebodings had entered the public mind. On one side civil war appeared to be impending, and on the other we seemed threatened with the immediate destruction of our most cherished policy. Congress proved able to avert these calamities, and he would be wofully disappointed, if those who then differed from us and were mistaken in their views, shall not now be found among the foremost in arresting the progress of Executive encroachment. Up to the period of the termination of the last session of Congress, the power of Congress over the treasury of the country had never been contested.

Among the earliest acts of Congress, in September, 1780, was one passed to guard the public treasury. He begged leave to call the attention of the Senate for a moment to some of its provisions. It was "An act to establish the Treasury Department," and was altogether unlike any of the acts placing the other departments under the Executive direction. [Here Mr. C. read extracts at length from the law.] Prior to the establishment of the present Bank of the United States, there was no treasury designated by law for keeping the money of the United States, for the clause in the present bank charter was not in the charter of the old bank. The Treasury of the United States, he took to be that place where the moneys of the people were kept—the buildings erected for that purpose was the Treasury. By designating the Bank of the United States and its branches, as the depository of the public moneys, Congress had made the bank and its branches for the time being, the Treasury of the United States. Sir, said he, the safety of this treasure or the public deposites in that institution, was drawn in question for the first time by the President of the United States. Prior to the last session, the President appointed an agent to scrutinize and examine into the affairs of the Bank of the United States. That agent diligently and faithfully performed his duty, and reported that the treasure of the country was perfectly safe in its guardianship. But the President was not yet satisfied, and threw out opinions in his next message, which induced the appointment of a committee, who made a most diligent and laborious investigation, and reported, as the result, that the moneys were safe, and the report was followed by a resolution of Congress to that effect. After all this, who could have supposed that a change would have been ordered? Who could have supposed that sixty days before the meeting of Congress, the President of the United States would have ordered a removal of the deposites from the Bank of the United States? Who would have dreamed that the Treasurer of the United States should have thrown away the key, over which Congress and he alone had the control, and selected some dozens of keys of treasuries, over which Congress had no control? Yet all this had been done! If we could suppose that the Chief Magistrate desired to possess unlimited control over the treasury of the country, (he suspected no such thing of the President; but, supposing such a thing,) what would he do? He would first throw out suspicions that the moneys of the country were not safe, and finally seize hold of them, and say, they were not safe there, but they are perfectly safe in my hands. And now all this having been done, it became the solemn duty of the Senate to inquire, 1st, by whose authority it had been done; and 2d, if the act was done in accordance with the Constitution and laws of the United States. There was one thing, however, in which Mr. C. could agree with the President of the United States, and that was in regard to the importance of this question. [Here Mr. C. read extracts from the paper read by the President to the Cabinet.] In his view, Mr. C. said, the bank was as nothing, compared with the principles involved. However faithful it had been in the performance of its duties, (and he believed it had been perfectly so,) however successful it had been in regulating and establishing a sound currency, and in promptly meeting all its engagements, and intimately as the best interests of the country were blended with its prosperity, yet all these were of minor importance in comparison with the executive power assumed by the President in that paper. This assumption affects the very existence and control of the Government in its grasping at the public purse of the country.

Entertaining these views, he should not, to-day, examine into the reasons of the President or Secretary for the removal of the deposites. For, if the Secretary was clothed with no power to do the act, no matter how urgent the necessity for it might seem, no reasons could justify the commission of an unconstitutional and an illegal act. The first question, then, which presented itself was, by whose decision the removal had been made? And was there any man here, within reach of his voice, who required proof of that? It was a matter of universal notoriety. Did any man doubt that it was done by the President of the United States? The President himself had furnished conclusive evidence of the fact. Although he had refused the Senate a copy of the paper, yet it had been given to the world, and Mr. C. hoped that Senators would avail themselves of all it contained, and he believed it would be conclusive. That was a paper of a most extraordinary character. The Constitution of the United States admits that calls may be made upon the heads of departments in writing; but the President, not satisfied with the power given to him in the Constitution, reads a paper to his Cabinet, with a view to indoctrinate them into his views and principles. It was the first time a paper had been read to the Cabinet and published to the world; it was a most unprecedented proceeding. Those in power seemed inclined to hold their opponents in contempt; but although disregarding them, yet they seemed disposed to retreat behind the influence of precedent when it was sufficient to avail them. But he would inquire again, who had transferred the public deposites of the country from the place where Congress declared they should be kept, to places where Congress as especially declared they should not be kept? And here he would tell gentlemen that he was not to be amused with a reply that it was by an order signed R. B. Taney. He did not look to the hangman as accountable for the infliction of death, but to the tribunal sanctioning it—not to who removed the deposites, but by whose order, by whose command, it had been done.

After reading the following extract from the paper read by the President to his Cabinet:

"In the remarks he has made on this all-important question, he *trusts* the Secretary of the Treasury will see only the frank and respectful declarations of the opinions which the President

'has formed on a measure of great national interest, deeply affecting the character and usefulness of his Administration; and *not a spirit of dictation*, which the President would be as *careful to avoid*, as ready to resist. Happy will he be, if 'the *facts* now disclosed produce uniformity of 'opinion and unity of action among the members 'of the Administration"—

Mr. C. said: Sir, how kind, how genial, how gracious, must these expressions have sounded in the ears of the Secretary of the Treasury. It reminded him of a historical anecdote of Oliver Cromwell. While that remarkable man was contending for the mastery of Great Britain, he besieged a Catholic town. The place made a stout resistance, but in the end being likely to be taken, the Catholics proposed terms of capitulation, stipulating for the toleration of their religion. The paper containing the terms was brought to Oliver, who exclaimed, "Granted, certainly; but if any of the Catholics shall be found attending mass, they shall be hanged." Thus the Secretary is told very mildly by the President that he has not the slightest wish to dictate—nothing is farther from his wishes; but what does he say in the sequel? "If you don't obey my orders, why, you go out of office." And what then follows? This document, which Mr. C. considered imperative upon the Secretary, is dated 18th September. He read from the official paper of the Government of the 20th September:

"We are authorized to state that the deposites 'of the public money will be changed from the 'Bank of the United States to the State banks, as 'soon as necessary arrangements can be made for 'that purpose, and that it is believed they can be 'completed in Baltimore, Philadelphia, New York, 'and Boston in time to make the change *by the first of October, and perhaps sooner*, if circumstances should render an earlier action necessary on 'the part of the Government."

We find, then, said Mr. C., that the measure was determined on on the 18th September, to take place on the first of October. Mr. Duane is dismissed on the 23d, and between the 23d and 26th Mr. Taney signs the order which goes forth for the removal of the deposites. On this point, the evidence is conclusive in the President's letter to that gentleman, dated 23d, which concludes by saying, that "your further services as Secretary of the Treasury are no longer required." Now, such is the testimony on one side of this question, to prove that the removal of the deposites was determined on by the President against the will of the Secretary, and while he was still in office; and although Mr. Taney signed the order on the 26th, it was issued in conformity with the previous determination of the President. Mr. C. said he would now call the attention of the Senate to the testimony of the other party. He would not read the whole of Mr. Duane's address, but it concluded as follows:

"Thus I was thrust into office—thus was I 'thrust from office; not because I had neglected 'any duty—not because I had differed with the 'President on any other point of public policy—'not because I had differed with him about the 'Bank of the United States—but because I refused, without further inquiry or action by Congress, to remove the deposites."

Can testimony be more complete to establish the proposition that these deposites were removed by the authority of the President, and that it is his act alone? Is it possible, from a review of the testimony on both sides, that any man can doubt it was done in accordance with his commands? And now, having seen that the removal was by command of the President, let us inquire next whether the authority assumed is in conformity with the Constitution of the United States. He would not inquire into the reasons given for this act, except so far as they set up an authority for the exercise of this power. If he possesses no power, it is useless to look for the exercise of a power which he does not possess. What power, then, has the President over the treasury? Is it in the bank charter? Let us advert to it. That part of it relating to the deposites declares—

"That the deposites of the money of the United 'States, in places which the said bank and branches thereof may be established, shall be made in 'said bank or branches thereof, unless the Secretary of the Treasury shall at any time otherwise 'order and direct; in which case the Secretary of 'the Treasury shall immediately lay before Congress, if in session, and, if not, immediately after 'the commencement of the next session, the reasons of such order or direction."

This clause is in strict consonance with the character of the Treasury Department, as organized in the year '89. The Secretary is by that act required to make annual reports on the state of the finances, as the agent of Congress. And if he undertakes to remove the Government deposites from the place designated by law as the depository, he is to report his reasons. To whom? Why to Congress. By the charter of the bank, the President is clothed with two powers in relation to it, the appointment of the Government directors, and the issuing of a *scire facias*, when he shall believe the charter has been violated. These are the only powers given him; all others are denied him, and are delegated to others. The weekly statements of the bank are to be made to the Secretary of the Treasury, and when anything further shall be necessary, the appointment of a committee of investigation by Congress, is authorized. The powers of the President are restricted to the appointment of the Government directors, and the issuing of the *scire facias*. Has the President, then, any powers over the treasury given him by the Constitution of the United States? None. The Constitution is express, that no money shall be drawn from the treasury, except by authority of appropriations made by law. But the President says, "upon him has been devolved, by the Constitution and the suffrages of the American people, 'the duty of superintending the operation of the 'Executive departments of the Government, and 'seeing that the laws are faithfully executed."

In another part of this same paper the President refers to the suffrages of the American people in approbation of his opinions. Mr. C. thought differently from him, on that point. When the American people reëlected him, they thereby expressed no approbation of all his opinions. It could not be that the State of Pennsylvania, so appropriately termed the key-stone of the Federal arch, intended to reverse their own opinions so repeatedly expressed through their representatives in favor of the bank and domestic industry. But the President says "the duty has devolved upon him to remove the deposites, by the suffrages of the American people." Why does he say that the suffrages of the American people devolved upon him the duty of superintending the interests of the American people? There is no color in the Constitution for that idea. The laws have established the several Executive departments, and the heads of them are required to execute duties given them from time to time, under the direction of the President. But there are many duties to be performed by these officers over which the President has no control and no right to interfere with. This was no new case. Thirty-two years ago the Supreme Court of the United States, in deciding a case—"Barbary and Madison"—delivered these sentiments:

"By the Constitution of the United States, the 'President is invested with certain important political powers, in the exercise of which he is to use 'his own discretion, and is accountable only to his 'country in his political character, and to his own 'conscience. To aid him in the performance of 'these duties, he is authorized to appoint certain 'officers, who act by his authority, and in conformity with his orders. In such cases their acts 'are his acts; and, whatever opinion may be entertained of the manner in which Executive discretion may be used, still there exists, and can exist, 'no power to control that discretion. The subjects 'are political. They respect the nation, not individual rights, and being intrusted to the Executive, the decision of the Executive is conclusive. 'The application of this remark would be perceived by adverting to the act of Congress for 'establishing the Department of Foreign Affairs. 'This officer, as his duties were prescribed by that 'act, is to conform precisely to the will of the President. He is the mere organ by whom that will 'is communicated. The acts of such an officer, 'as an officer, can never be examinable by the 'courts.

"But when the Legislature proceeds to impose 'on that officer other duties; when he is directed 'peremptorily to perform certain acts; (that is, 'when he is not placed under the direction of the 'President;) when the rights of individuals are dependent on the performance of those acts, he is so 'far *the officer of the law;* is amenable *to the laws* for 'his conduct, and cannot, at his discretion sport 'away the vested rights of others.

"The conclusion from this reasoning is, that 'where the heads of departments are the political 'or confidential agents of the Executive, merely to 'execute the will of the President, or rather, to act 'in cases in which the Executive possesses a constitutional or legal discretion, nothing can be 'more perfectly clear than that their acts are only 'politically examinable. But where a specific duty 'is assigned by law, and individual rights depend 'upon the performance of that duty, it seems 'equally clear that the individual who considers 'himself injured, has a right to resort to the laws 'of his country for a remedy."

Although the President is mistaken in saying that the Constitution devolves upon the President the duty of superintending the departments, yet he has recited one clause in that instrument in which he is right. It is that, making it his duty to see that the laws are faithfully executed, and under this provision, the most enormous pretensions are set up for the President.

It has been contended, that if a law shall pass, which the President does not conceive to be in conformity with the Constitution, he is not bound to execute it; and if a treaty shall have been made, which, in his opinion, has been unconstitutional in its stipulations, he is not bound to enforce them. And it necessarily follows, that, if the courts of justice shall give a decision, which he shall in like manner deem repugnant to the Constitution, he is not expected or bound to execute that law. Sir, let us look a little into this principle, and trace it out into some of its consequences.

One of the most important acts performed at the departments, is to settle those very large accounts which individuals have with the Government; accounts amounting to millions of dollars; to settle them, an auditor and a comptroller have been appointed by law, whose official acts may affect, to the extent of hundreds of thousands of dollars, the property of individual contractors. If the pretensions of the President are well founded, his power goes further than he has exerted it. He may go into the office of the Auditor, or the office of the Comptroller, and may say to him, Sir, Mr. A. B. has an account under settlement in this office, one item of which, objected to by you, I consider to be in accordance with the Constitution: pass that account and send it to the Auditor; and he may then go to the Auditor and hold similar language. If the clause of the Constitution is to be expounded, as is contended for, it amounts to a complete absorption of all the powers of Government in the person of the Executive. Sir, when a doctrine like this shall be admitted as orthodox, when it shall be acquiesced in by the people of this country, our Government will have become a SIMPLE machine enough. The will of the President will be the whole of it. There will be but one bed, and that will be the bed of Procrustes: but one will, the will of the President. All the departments, and all subordinate functionaries of Government, great or small, must submit to that will; and if they do not, then the President will have failed to "see that the laws are faithfully executed."

Sir, such an extravagant and enormous pretension as this must be set alongside of its exploded compeer, the pretension that Congress has the power of passing any and all laws which it may suppose conducive to "the general welfare."

Let me, in a few words, present to the Senate what are my own views as to the structure of this Government. I hold that no powers can legitimately be exercised under it but such as are expressly delegated, and those which are necessary to carry these into effect. Sir, the Executive power, as existing in this Government, is not to be traced to the notions of Montesquieu or of any other writer of that class, in the abstract nature of the Executive power. Neither is the legislative nor the judicial power to be decided by any such reference. These several powers with us, whatever they may be elsewhere, are just what the Constitution has made them, and nothing more.

And as to the general clauses in which reference is made to either, they are to be controlled and interpreted by those where these several powers are specially delegated, otherwise the Executive will become a great vortex that must end in swallowing all the rest. Nor will the judicial power be any longer restrained by the restraining clauses in the Constitution, which relate to its exercise. What, then, it will be asked, does this clause, that the President shall see that the laws are faithfully executed, mean? Sir, it means nothing more nor less than this, that, if resistance is made to the laws, he shall take care that resistance shall cease. Congress, by the 1st article of the 8th section of the Constitution, is required to provide for calling out the militia to execute the laws, in case of a resistance. Sir, it might as well be contended, under that clause, that Congress have the power of determining what are, and what are not, the laws of the land. Congress has the power of calling out the militia; well, sir, what is the President, by the Constitution? He is commander of the army and navy of the United States, and of the militia when called out into actual service. When, then, we are here told that he is clothed with the whole physical power of the nation, and when we are afterwards told, that he must take care that the laws are faithfully executed, is it possible that any man can be so lost to the love of liberty, as not to admit that this goes no further than to remove any resistance which may be made to the execution of the laws? We have established a system in which power has been carefully divided among different departments of the Government. And we have been told a thousand times, that this division is indispensable as a safeguard to civil liberty. We have designated the departments, and have established in each, officers to exercise the power belonging to each. The President, it is true, presides over the whole; his eye surveys the whole extent of the system in all its movements. But has he the power to enter into the courts, for example, and tell them what is to be done? Or may he come here and tell us the same? Or when we have made a law, can he withhold the power necessary to its practical effect? He moves, it is true, in a high, a glorious sphere. It is his to watch over the whole with a paternal eye; and, when any one wheel of the vast machine is for a time interrupted by the occurrence of invasion or rebellion, it is his care to propel its movements, and to furnish it with the requisite means of performing its appropriate duty in its own place.

That this is the true interpretation of the constitutional clause to which I have alluded, is inferred from the total silence of all contemporaneous expositions of that instrument on the subject. I have myself, (and when it was not in my power personally, have caused others to aid me,) made researches into the numbers of the Federalist; the debates in the Virginia Convention, and in the Conventions in other States, as well as all other sources of information to which I could obtain access, and I have not, in a solitary instance, found the slightest color for the claims set up in these most extraordinary times for the President, that he has authority to afford or withhold at pleasure the means of enforcing the laws, and to superintend and control an officer charged with a specific duty, made by the law exclusively his. But, sir, I have found some authorities which strongly militate against any such claim. If the doctrine be indeed true, then it is most evident that there is no longer any control over our affairs than that exerted by the President. If it be true that when a duty is by law specifically assigned to a particular officer, the President may go into his office and control him in the manner of performing it, then is it most manifest that all barriers for the safety of the treasury are gone. Sir, it is that union of the purse and the sword, in the hand of one man, which constitutes the best definition of tyranny which our language can give.

The charter of the Bank of the United States requires that the public deposites be made in its vaults. It also gives the Secretary of the Treasury power to remove them. And why? The Secretary is at the head of the finances of the Government. Weekly reports are made by the bank to him. He is to report to Congress annually; and to either House whenever he shall be called upon. He is the sentinel of Congress—the agent of Congress—the representative of Congress. He has been created by Congress. Congress has prescribed and has defined his duties. He is required to report to them, not to the President. He is put there by us as our representative: he is required to remove the deposites when they shall be in danger, and we not in session; but when he does this, he is required to report to Congress the fact, with his reasons for it. Now, sir, if, when an officer of Government is thus specifically assigned his duty, if he is to report his official acts on his responsibility to Congress, if in a case where no power whatever is given to the President, the President may go and say to that officer, "Go and do as I bid you, or you shall be removed from office"—let me ask you whether the danger apprehended by that eloquent man has not already been realized?

But, sir, let me suppose that I am mistaken in my construction of the Constitution; and let me suppose that the President has, as is contended, power to see every particular law carried into effect: what, then, was it his duty to do in the present case, under the clause thus interpreted? The law authorized the Secretary of the Treasury to remove the deposites on his responsibility to Congress. Now, if the President has power to see this, like other laws, faithfully executed, then surely the law exacted of him that he should see that the Secretary was allowed to exercise his free, unbiased, uncontrolled judgment in removing or not removing them. That was the execution of the law. Congress had not said that the Secretary of War, or the Secretary of State, might remove the public deposites from the treasury.

The President had no right to go to the Secretary of War and ask him what the Secretary of the Treasury ought to do. He might as well have consulted the Secretary of the Treasury about a contemplated movement of the army, as to ask the Secretary of War about the disposition of the public moneys. It was not to the President and all his Secretaries combined, that the power was given to alter the disposition of the deposites in the bank. It was to the Secretary alone, exclusive of the President and all the other officers of Government. And according to gentlemen's own showing, by their construction of the clause, the Secretary ought to have been left to his own unbiased determination, uncontrolled by the President or anybody else.

[I would thank the Secretary of the Senate to get me the Sedition Law. It is not very certain how soon we may be called to act upon it.]

Now, sir, said Mr. C., let us trace some of the other sources of the exercise of this power, or motives for it, or by whatever other name they are to be called. He says to Mr. Duane, "the President repeats that he begs the Cabinet to consider 'the proposed measure as his own, in the support 'of which he shall require no one of them to make 'a sacrifice of opinion or principle. Its responsibility has been assumed, after the most mature deliberation and reflection, as necessary to preserve the 'morals of the people, the freedom of the press, and 'the purity of the elective franchise." The morals of the people! What part of the Constitution has given to the President any power over "the morals of the people?" None. It does not give such power even over religion, the presiding and genial influence over every true system of morals. No, sir; it gives him no such power.

And what is the next step? To-day he claims a power as necessary to the morals of the people; to-morrow he will claim another, as still more indispensable to our religion. And the President might in this case as well have said that he went into the office of the Secretary of the Treasury and controlled his free exercise of his authority as Secretary, because it was necessary to preserve "the *religion* of the people!" I ask for the authority. Will any one of those gentlemen here, who consider themselves the vindicators of the Executive, point me to any clause of the Constitution which gives to the *present* President of the United States any power to preserve "the morals of the people?"

But the "freedom of the press," it seems, was another motive. Sir, I am not surprised that the present Secretary of the Treasury should feel a desire to revive this power over the press. He, I think, was a member of that party which passed the Sedition law, under precisely the same pretext. I recollect it was said, that this bank, this monster of tyranny, was taking into its pay a countless number of papers, and by this means was destroying the fair fame of the President and his Secretary, and all that sort of thing. Sir, it is sometimes useful to refer back to these old things—to the notions and the motives which induced men in former times to do certain acts which may not be altogether unlike some others in our own time.

The famous Sedition Act was passed, sir, in 1798; and it contained, among others, the following provision:

Sec. 2. "That if any person shall write, print, utter, or publish, or shall cause or procure to be written, printed, uttered, or published, or shall, knowingly and willingly, assist or aid in writing, printing, uttering, or publishing, any false, scandalous, and malicious, writing or writings, against the Government of the United States, or either House of the Congress of the United States, or the President of the United States, with intent to defame the said Government, or either House of the said Congress, or the said President, or to bring them, or either of them, into contempt or disrepute; or to excite against them, or either or any of them, the hatred of the good people of the United States, or to stir up sedition within the United States; or to excite any unlawful combinations therein, for opposing or resisting any law of the United States, or any act of the President of the United States, done in pursuance of any such law, or of the powers in him vested by the Constitution of the United States; or to resist, oppose, or defeat any such law or act; or to aid, encourage, or abet, any hostile designs of any foreign nation against the United States, their people, or Government, then such person, being thereof convicted before any court of the United States having jurisdiction thereof, shall be punished by a fine not exceeding two thousand dollars, and by imprisonment not exceeding two years."

We have now, sir, in the reasons for the removal of the Government deposites, the same motives avowed and acted upon. The abuse of the Government, bringing it into disrepute, using contemptuous language to persons high in authority, constituted the motives for passing the sedition law; and what have we now but a repetition of the same complaints of abuses, disrespect, &c. As it is now, so it was then: for, says the next section of the same sedition act, "That if any person shall be prosecuted under this act for the writing or publishing any libel aforesaid, it shall be lawful for the defendant, upon the trial of the cause, to give in evidence in his defence, the truth of the matter contained in the publication charged as a libel. And the jury who shall try the cause, shall have a right to determine the law and the fact, under the direction of the court, as in other cases."

It is only for the sake *of the truth* said they who favored the passage of the law—for the sake of justice, as it is now said, that it was necessary to remove the deposites in order to preserve the purity of the press. That's all, sir. But there is one part of this assumption of power by the President much more tyrannical than that act. Under that law the offending party was to have a trial by jury, the benefit of witnesses and of counsel, and the right to have the truth of his alleged libels examined. But what is the case now under consideration? Why, sir, the President takes the whole matter into his own hands; he is at once the judge, the jury, and the executioner of the sentence, and utterly deprives the accused party of the opportunity of showing that the imputed libel is no libel at all, but founded in the clearest truth.

But "the purity of the elective franchise," also, the President has very much at heart. And here again I ask, what part of the Constitution gives him any power over that "franchise?" Look, sir, at the nature of the exercise of this power. If it was really necessary that steps should be taken to preserve the purity of the press or the freedom of elections, what ought the President to have done? Taken the matter into his own hands? No, sir; it was his duty to recommend to Congress the passage of laws for the purpose, under suitable sanctions—laws which the courts of the United States could execute. We could not have been

worse off under such laws (however exceptionable they might be) than we are now. We could then, sir, have reviewed the laws, and seen whether Congress or the President had properly any power over this matter, or whether the article of the Constitution which forbids that the press shall be touched, and declares that religion shall be sacred from all the powers of legislation, applied in the case or not. This the President has undertaken to do of himself, without the shadow of authority, either in the Constitution or the laws.

Suppose, sir, that this contumacious institution, which committed the great sin in 1829 of not appointing a new president to a certain one of its branches—suppose that the bank should go on and vindicate itself against the calumnies poured out upon it—that it should continue to stand upon its defence, how inefficient will have been the exercise of power by the President! How inadequate to the end he had in view of preserving the press from being made use of to defend the bank! Why, sir, if we had had the power, and the President had come to us, we could have laid Mr. Nicholas Biddle by the heels if he should have undertaken to publish another report of General Smith or Mr. McDuffie, or another speech of the eloquent gentleman near me, [Mr. Webster,] or any other such *libels* tending to bring the President or his Administration into disrepute. But the President of the United States, who thought he had the bank in his power, who thought he could stop it, who was induced to believe, by that "influence behind the throne greater than itself," that he could break down the bank at a word, has only shown his want of power over the press by his attempt to exercise it in the manner he has done. The bank has avowed and openly declared its purpose to defend itself on all suitable occasions. And, what is still more provoking, instead of being a bankrupt, as was expected, with its doors closed, and its vaults inaccessible, it has now, it seems, got more money than it knows what to do with; and this greatest of misers and hoarders cruelly refuses to let out a dollar of its ten millions of specie to relieve the sufferings of the banks to which the Government deposites have been transferred.

Sir, the President of the United States had nothing to do with the morals of the community. No, sir; for the preservation of our morals we are responsible to God, and I trust that that responsibility will ever remain to Him and his mercy alone. Neither had the President anything to do with the freedom of the press. The power over it is denied even to Congress by the people. It was said, by one of those few able men and bright luminaries whom Providence has yet spared to us, in answer to complaints by a foreign minister, against the freedom with which the American press treated certain French functionaries, that the press was one of those concerns which admitted of no regulation by the Government; that its abuses must be tolerated, lest its freedom should be abridged. Such, sir, is the freedom of the press, as recognised by our Constitution, and so it has been respected ever since the repeal of the obnoxious act which I have already quoted, until the detestable principles of that law have been reasserted by the President in his assumption of a power in nowise belonging to his office, of preserving the purity of the press.

Such, sir, are the powers on which the President relies to justify his seizure of the treasury of the United States. I have examined them one by one, and they all fail, utterly fail to bear out the act. We are irresistibly brought to the conclusion, that the removal of the public money from the Bank of the United States has been effected by the displacement from the head of the Treasury Department of one who would not remove them, and putting in his stead another person who would; and, secondly, that the President has no color of authority in the Constitution or the laws for the act which he has undertaken to perform.

Let us now, said Mr. C., for a few moments examine the consequences which may ensue from the exercise of this enormous power. If the President has authority, in a case in which the law has assigned a specific duty exclusively to a designated officer to control the exercise of his discretion by that officer, he has a right to interfere in every other case, and remove every one from office who hesitates to do his bidding, against his judgment of his own duty. This, surely, is a logical deduction not to be resisted. Well, then, how stands the matter? Recapitulating the provisions of the law prescribing how money should be drawn from the Treasury, and the deduction above stated, what, asked Mr. Clay, is to prevent the President from going to the Comptroller, and, if he will not countersign a warrant which he has found an accommodating secretary to sign, turning him out for another; then going to the Register, and doing the same; and then to the Treasurer, and commanding him to pay over the money expressed in the warrant, or subject himself to expulsion?

Where is the security against such conduct on the part of the President? Where the boundary to this tremendous authority which he has undertaken to exercise? Sir, every barrier around the treasury is broken down. From the moment that the President said, "I make this measure my own—I take upon myself the responsibility," from that moment the public treasury might as well have been at the Hermitage as at this place. Sir, the measure adopted by the President is without precedent—in our day at least. There is, indeed, a precedent on record, but you must go down to the Christian era for it. It will be recollected, by those who are conversant with ancient history, that after Pompey was compelled to retire to Brundusium, Cæsar, who had been anxious to give him battle, returned to Rome, "having reduced Italy (says the historian) in sixty days—[the exact period, sir, between the removal of the deposites and the meeting of Congress, without the usual allowance of three days' grace]—in sixty days, without bloodshed." The historian goes on: "Finding the city in a more settled condition than he expected, and many Senators there, he addressed them in a mild and gracious manner, [as the President did his late Secretary of the Treasury,] and desired them to send deputies to Pompey, with an offer of honorable terms of peace, &c. As Metellus, the tribune, *opposed his* taking money out of the public treasury, and cited some laws against it—[such, sir, I suppose, as I have endeavored to cite on this occasion,]—Cæsar said, 'Arms and laws do not flourish together. If you are not pleased at what I am about, you have only to withdraw. [Leave the office, Mr. Duane!] War, indeed, will not tolerate much liberty of speech. When I say this, I am renouncing my own right, for you and all those whom I have found exciting a spirit of faction against me, are at my disposal.' Having said this, he approached the doors of the treasury, and as the keys were not produced, he sent for workmen to break them open. Metellus again opposed him, and gained credit with some for his firmness; but Cæsar, with an elevated voice, threatened to put him to death, if he gave him any farther trouble. 'And you know very well, young man,' said he, 'that this is harder for me to say than to do.' Metellus, terrified by the menace, retired; and Cæsar was, afterward, easily and readily supplied with everything necessary for the war."

And where now, sir, is the public treasury? Who can tell? It is certainly without a local habitation, if it be not without a name. And where is the money of the people of the United States? Floating about in treasury drafts on checks to the amount of millions, placed in the hands of tottering banks, to enable them to pay their own debts, instead of being appropriated to the service of the people. These checks are scattered to the winds by the Treasurer of the United States, who is required by law to let out money from the treasury, on warrants signed by the Secretary of the Treasury, countersigned, registered, &c., *and not otherwise.*

Mr. C. here referred to a correspondence, which he quoted, between the Treasurer and the officers of the bank, complaining of these checks drawn without proper notice, &c., in which the Treasurer says, they were only issued to be used in certain contingencies, &c. Thus, sir, said Mr. C., the people's money is put into a bank here, and a bank there, in regard to the solvency of which we know nothing, and it is placed there to be used in the event of certain contingencies—contingencies of which neither the Treasurer nor the Secretary have yet deigned to furnish us any account.

Where was the oath of office of the Treasurer, when he ventured thus to sport with the people's money? Where was the Constitution, which forbids money to be drawn from the treasury without appropriation by law? Where was the Treasurer's bond when he thus cast about the people's money? Sir, said Mr C., his bond is forfeited. I do not pretend to any great knowledge of the law, but, give me an intelligent and unpacked jury, and I will undertake to prove to them that he has forfeited the penalty of his bond.

Mr. President, said Mr. C., the people of the United States are indebted to the President for the boldness of this movement; and as one, among the humblest of them, I profess my obligations to him. He has told the Senate, in his message refusing an official copy of his Cabinet paper, that it has been published for the information of the people; as a part of the people, the Senate, if not in their official character, have a right to its use. In that extraordinary paper he has proclaimed that the measure is *his* own; and that *he* has *taken* upon himself the responsibility of it. In plain English, he has proclaimed an open, palpable, and daring usurpation!

For more than fifteen years, Mr. President, I have been struggling to avoid the present state of things. I thought I perceived, in some proceedings, during the conduct of the Seminole war, a spirit of defiance to the Constitution and to all law. With what sincerity and truth—with what earnestness and devotion to civil liberty, I have struggled, the Searcher of all human hearts best knows. With what fortune, the bleeding Constitution of my country now fatally attests.

I have, nevertheless, persevered; and, under every discouragement, during the short time that I expect to remain in the public councils, I will persevere. And if a bountiful Providence would allow an unworthy sinner to approach the throne of grace, I would beseech him as the greatest favor he could grant to me here below, to spare me until I live to behold the people, rising in their majesty, with a peaceful and constitutional exercise of their power, to expel the Goths from Rome; to rescue the public treasury from pillage; to preserve the Constitution of the United States; to uphold the Union against the danger of the concentration and consolidation of *all* power in the hands of the Executive; and to sustain the liberties of the people of this country against the imminent perils to which they now stand exposed.

At half past 2 o'clock, Mr. CLAY gave way to a motion, by Mr. EWING, that when the Senate adjourns, it will adjourn until Monday next.

The VICE PRESIDENT observed, that the motion would require the unanimous consent of the Senate, as the subject was not concluded.

Mr. BENTON said he objected to the motion.

Mr. EWING then moved to postpone the further consideration of the question till Monday next; which was carried, ayes 26, noes not counted.

On motion of Mr. EWING, the Senate then adjourned to that day.

HOUSE OF REPRESENTATIVES.

Friday, *December* 27, 1833.

Mr. MASON, of Maine, appeared, was qualified, and took his seat.

After the presentation of petitions,

On motion of Mr. WATMOUGH,

Resolved, That a committee be appointed to inquire into the expediency of equalizing the compensation of the officers of the army and navy and fixing the amount of compensation by law, instead of allowances now made by the department. [The committee was ordered, to consist of five.]

On motion of Mr. PINCKNEY,

Resolved, That the Committee on Revolutionary Claims be instructed to inquire into the expediency of granting relief to the legal heirs and representatives of Major Alexander Garden, deceased, and that their petition, with the accompanying documents, now on file in the office of the Clerk, be committed to that committee.

On motion of Mr. STEWART,

Resolved, That the Committee of Ways and Means be instructed to inquire into the expediency of making an appropriation to pay the salary and disbursements of Valentine Geisey, as late superintendent of the Cumberland road.

On motion of Mr. FOSTER,

Resolved, That the Committee on Invalid Pensions be instructed to inquire into the expediency of placing the name of Stephen Gatlin, of Green county, State of Georgia, on the invalid pension roll, and that the papers herewith submitted be referred to said committee.

On motion of Mr. GAMBLE,

Resolved, That the Committee on the Post Office and Post Roads be instructed to inquire into the expediency of establishing a post route from Waynesborough, in Burke county, through Louisville and Sandersville, to Milledgeville.

On motion of Mr. GILLET,

Resolved, That the report made to the Legislature of the State of New York by the Committee on the Militia and the Public Defence, together with the resolutions passed by the said Legislature at its last session on that subject, which have been officially transmitted to the representatives from the said State, be referred to the Select Committee on the Militia.

Mr. CHILTON submitted the following resolution:

Resolved, That the Committee on Revolutionary Pensions be instructed to inquire into the expediency of so extending the provisions of the act of Congress, passed 7th June, 1832, granting pensions to certain classes of troops therein named, as to embrace in its provisions those who were engaged in the wars against the Indians subsequent to the close of the revolutionary war, and down to the treaty of Grenville, with leave to report by bill or otherwise.

Mr. WARDWELL suggested that the Committee on Revolutionary Pensions had no concern with services rendered subsequent to the Revolution.

Mr. HARDIN would be glad, he said, if his colleague would bring the time down to 1794. He had intended, before he left home, to bring this subject before Congress. The western lands were brought into market, and were settled in 1780, and from that period till the treaty of 1783, the settlers were exposed to the hostilities both of the northern and southern Indians. After 1783, Great Britain retained the western military posts, and the hostilities continued without cessation till 1794. Innumerable battles, of a kind and character much more desperate and bloody than those fought on the seaboard from 1780 till 1794, were fought by these settlers with the Indians. Conflicts frequently took place of thirty on each side, in which not five men escaped with their lives. They fought, literally, for victory or death. These men received no compensation for their services at the time, nor had they received any pay, pension, or bounty since, and no men ever shed their blood more freely. If ever men deserved to be pensioned, it was these. Many of them had asked him why they were not put on the pension list, and he had been able to give no reason for their exclusion. He hoped the proposition would be adopted—and if he had presented it, he would have given it the form of an instruction instead of an inquiry.

Mr. WARDWELL did not, he said, rise to oppose the resolution, but again to suggest that it referred the inquiry to the wrong committee. It ought to go to the Committee on Military Pensions, or Military Affairs. The Committee on Revolutionary Pensions had nothing to do with the services rendered in the late war.

Mr. EVERETT, of Vermont, thought the subject ought to be referred to a select committee.

Mr. CHILTON modified the resolution so as to require its reference to a select committee, to be appointed, whose duty it shall be, &c.

Mr. WHITTLESEY moved an amendment, bringing the time down to 1794. The subject, he said, was before Congress when the last pension law was passed, and was very favorably received, and he had no doubt the same Congress would have included these men in that law, if the subject had been thorougly examined and the facts presented in a report. It was true that the war in the west did not close till after Wayne's victory, and, for that reason, those who thus continued the war were as much worthy of the bounty of the Government as those who fought before 1783.

Mr. CHILTON accepted the motion as a modification of the resolution.

Mr. LANE, of Indiana, said, that a body of more meritorious men than these had never been provided for by Congress; any one who reads their history would find that the perils which they encountered, and the sufferings which they endured, were unparalleled in our history. He had intended himself to bring this subject before Congress, and he was gratified that it had come from another quarter.

Mr. BURD of Pennsylvania, proposed so to amend the resolution as to embrace all persons who, at any time during the Revolution, had been engaged in conflicts with the Indians.

Mr. WILLIAMS of North Carolina, said, that so far as this proposition went to pension the revolutionary soldiers, he was in favor of it; but so far as it continued the pension system, after the period of the Revolution, he was opposed to it. Something like this was offered in 1832, and rejected, after full consideration. The principle assumed by that Congress was, that revolutionary service was distinct from all other service in character. To pension all those who have been at any time engaged in military service was beyond the means and resources of the country. We had not yet fully extended the pension system to the soldiers of the Revolution—the militia were not placed on the same footing with those of the continental troops. Believing that the tendency of the resolution was not fully apprehended by the House, he moved to lay it on the table.

Mr. CHILTON (the motion being withdrawn) objected to the amendment moved by Mr. BURD, as out of order, and altering the phraseology of the whole resolution.

Mr. BURD withdrew his amendment.

Mr. CHILTON remarked that he was not usually very tenacious of his own phraseology. He remembered that in the retrenchment discussion his resolution on that subject underwent so total a change that the word "Resolved" was the only word left in it.

At the suggestion of a member he further modified the resolution so as to require the committee to report by bill or otherwise.

Mr. HARDIN would remark, he said, in reply to the member from North Carolina, that the pension list would be too large for the revenue, that he was perfectly satisfied that the whole number of persons added to the pension list by this proposition would not exceed two thousand. He had good reason to believe that not one man in ten was alive of those who were embraced in the provisions proposed, and their number was every day diminishing. He did not propose, in any case, to extend the provision to the heirs. Very little of the public money was expended beyond the mountains. Nearly the whole revenue was diffused east of the Alleghany. The receipts from the public lands amounted to three millions and a half, while not half a million was expended in the West. Any system by which the distribution of public money could be equalized deserved the consideration of the House. He hoped his honorable friend from North Carolina would withdraw his opposition to the measure until the committee should report and the merits of the claims be laid before the House.

Mr. ALLAN of Kentucky, said it was true that the claims of those who fought the Indians after the revolutionary war were brought before the last Congress, and were very favorably received. But they were not passed or fully considered. The war continued beyond the mountains after the peace of 1783. The signature of that treaty did not put a stop to hostilities in the West, and he was at a loss to know why the gentleman from North Carolina should consider those who continued to fight after the treaty were less entitled to a pension than those who fought before the treaty was concluded.

Mr. BLAIR, of South Carolina, was opposed to this proposition for the same reason that he opposed the law of 1832. By that law we taxed the descendants of the soldiers of the Revolution, and he believed that the best of them had died before pensions were granted—for the benefit of their wealthy survivors. The gentleman from Kentucky says there will be but two thousand added to the pension list by this bill. He believed the number would exceed ten thousand. If we adopted this proposition, we should not be troubled with surplus revenue. He moved that the resolution be laid on the table, and upon that motion he required the yeas and nays.

The yeas and nays being ordered, the question was taken and decided in the negative.

YEAS—Messrs. Archer, Bean, James Blair, Cambreleng, Chinn, Claiborne, Clowney, Connor, Warren R. Davis, Day, Felder, Foster, William K. Fuller, Gillet, Gilmer, Gordon, Grayson, Griffin, Thomas H. Hall, Joseph M. Harper, Hubbard, Jarvis, Noadiah Johnson, Seaborn Jones, Kavanagh, King, Lewis, Loyall, Lucas, Abijah Mann, Mardis, McDuffie, McIntire, McKay, Muhlenberg, Page, Pierce, Pinckney, Ramsay, Rencher, William B. Shepard, Smith, Speight, Francis Thomas, Turrill, Vance, Vanderpoel, Van Houten, Vinton, Williams—50.

NAYS—Messrs. John Q. Adams, John Adams, Heman Allen, John J. Allen, Chilton Allan, Wm. Allen, Ashley, Banks, Barber, Barringer, Baylies, Beale, Beardsley, Beatty, Beaumont, John Bell, James M. Bell, John Blair, Bockee, Bodle, Boon, Bouldin, Briggs, Brown, Bull, Bunch, Burd, Burns, Bynum, Carr, Casey, Chaney, Chilton, Choate, William Clark, Clay, Coulter, Cramer, Crane, Crockett, J. Davis, A. Davis, Deberry, Deming, Denny, Dennis, Dickson, Dickinson, Duncan, Dunlap, Evans, Edward Everett, Horace Everett, Ewing, Filmore, Foot, Forester, Fowler, P. C. Fuller, Fulton, Gamble, Grennell, H. Hall, Halsey, Hamer, Hannegan, Hard, Hardin, Harrison, Hathaway, Hazeltine, Henderson, Huntington, Inge, William C. Johnson, Richard M. Johnson, Cave Johnson, Benjamin Jones, Kinnard, Lane, Lansing, Laporte, Lawrence, Lay, Luke Lea, Leavitt, Love, Lyon, Joel K. Mann, Martindale, Marshall, McCarty, McComas, McKim, McLene, McVean, Mercer, Miller, Henry Mitchell, Robert Mitchell, Moore, Murphy, Osgood, Parker, Patterson, Pearce, Peyton, Pierson, Polk, Pope, Potts, Reed, Selden, Augustine H. Shepperd, W. Slade, C. Slade, Sloane, Spangler, Standifer, Stewart, W. Taylor, Philemon Thomas, J. Thompson, Tompkins, Tweedy, Wagener, Ward, Wardwell, Watmough, Wayne, Webster, Whallon, Edward D. White, Elisha Whittlesey, Wilde, Wise, Young—137.

The question then recurring on the resolution—

Mr. BOULDIN rose and said that, as he had voted with the majority, refusing to lay the resolution on the table, whilst he fully accorded in the sentiments expressed by the honorable member from North Carolina, [Mr. WILLIAMS,] he felt it necessary to state that he was influenced in thus voting, by his coinciding in opinion with the member from Kentucky—that his constituents, whatever might be the ultimate decision of the House on the subject, had a right to have their petition heard. But he would now propose the following amendment:

Strike out all after "inquire," and insert "into the moral and political effects of the pension laws of the United States, and how far the same ought to be modified or repealed."

Mr. B. said he was induced to offer the foregoing amendment, feeling satisfied that there could not be imagined a more corrupt and corrupting system to the morals of any country than had been created by the present pension system in this. He sought revision of it because it had no other than the most painful effect upon the industrious classes of the community, by inducing them—instead of following the true course by which wealth was to be acquired and the treasury of the country to be filled—to rather look up to that treasury as a never-failing spring, from whence their draughts were to be always supplied. In support of this view, he asked members to consider the number of applicants who were daily seeking information as to the best manner in which they could prosecute their claims to be put on the list, and to further consider the species of evidence by which these claims were supported; in too many instances from recollection of facts occurring nearly half a century back. But if the House agreed with him to raise the committee proposed, he thought they would be convinced, as he was, of its ruinous and demoralizing effect. If they were not, then, after full investigation, and a report presented to them, they would be better able to act on the subject, and decide as to the persons or

periods at which time, if at all, they would have the present system extended.

Mr. CHILTON considered that the proposed amendment had at least novelty to recommend it, and if adopted, its effect would be to do what was sought to be done elsewhere, to involve the House by introducing into it a new principle of legislation—an inquiry into principles of morality, &c. He denied that there was in the present pension system, as asserted by the honorable member, anything to warrant him in describing it in the terms he did, and after an eloquent and energetic eulogy upon the people of the West for their bravery in repeated battles with the Indians, and for the untiring fortitude with which they endured their privations in the early settlement of that once desert, but now flourishing country, he insisted that, even if there were, as alleged, some Tories, to get upon the list, or other persons by fraud, that was no reason why they were not entitled as well as the other patriots who enjoyed, in his opinion, so deservedly the munificence bestowed upon them by their country. He, upon this subject, felt warmly and deeply the debt due to the remnant of those by whom arms our liberties and present happiness were achieved, and instead of rewarding them niggardly, he was rather disposed, as he trusted the House would be, to apply to them the beautiful words of the poet Burns, who says:

"——Were I as rich as day,
I would be as generous as the sun."

Mr. C. concluded by an animated and lengthened appeal to the magnanimity of the House, in support of his resolution.

Mr. BOON called for the previous question, but the House refused to sustain the call, after which

Mr. HORACE EVERETT remarked that it was a bad practice for them to adopt, namely—on leave given, to have any subject introduced by resolution that was likely to create debate: to avoid which, on such a case occurring again, he would suggest the propriety of its being withdrawn; and with a view to the despatch of the ordinary business of the House, he would now move that the farther consideration of the resolution should be postponed until Tuesday next. The motion was agreed to.

Mr. THOMAS moved that when the House adjourned, it should adjourn over until Monday. Agreed to.

Mr. CARR, from the Committee on Private Land Claims, reported a bill for the relief of Amos W. Brown, which was read a first and second time by its title, and, on motion, was committed to a Committee of the Whole House, and made the order of the day for Monday next, and the bill and report ordered to be printed.

Mr. CLAY, from the Committee on Public Lands, reported a bill to reduce and graduate the price of public lands; which was read twice, and with the report ordered to be printed, and referred to the Committee of the Whole on the state of the Union.

The House refused to suspend the rule to enable Mr. ASHLEY to submit a motion that 5,000 extra copies of the report and bill should be printed.

The resolution heretofore submitted by Mr. HORACE EVERETT, and given in our paper, calling on the Secretary of War for information as to the appointment of Indian agents, was taken up and agreed to.

Mr. WHITTLESEY reported a bill for the relief of John Morot.

Mr. LEWIS reported a bill for the relief of George Elliott.

Mr. MERCER reported a bill to authorize a further subscription to the Chesapeake and Ohio Canal Company; with, with the report and resolutions of the Legislature of Pennsylvania, accompanying the same, were ordered to be printed.

M. ASHLEY reported a bill to establish an additional land office in Missouri.

Mr. LEAVITT, a bill granting an additional quantity of land for the satisfaction of revolutionary land warrants.

Mr. CAVE JOHNSON, a bill for the relief of James L. Stokes.

Mr. MUHLENBERG, a bill for the relief of

the legal representatives and heirs at law of John Taylor, deceased; and

Mr. McCARTY, a bill for the relief of John Wilstead.

All which bills were severally read twice, and committed.

Mr. EVANS, of Maine, moved an adjournment, but withdrew his motion at the request of Mr. POLK.

After which, the House went into Committee of the Whole on the state of the Union, Mr. FOOT in the chair, for the purpose of considering the bill making appropriation for the service of the Government for 1834, commonly called the House appropriation bill.

On motion of Mr. POLK, the bill was considered, and the blanks therein filled up, and agreed to, as follows:

For pay and mileage to members of Congress, $555,400.

For pay and mileage to members of Congress, $32,900.

For printing and contingent expenses, $150,000.

The committee then rose, and reported the bill to the House; which was read twice, and ordered to be engrossed for its third reading on Monday next.

And the House adjourned.

PAPER
READ TO THE CABINET ON THE 18TH OF SEPTEMBER, 1833.

Having carefully and anxiously considered all the facts and arguments which have been submitted to him, relative to a removal of the public deposites from the Bank of the United States, the President deems it his duty to communicate in this manner to his Cabinet the final conclusions of his own mind, and the reasons on which they are founded, in order to put them in durable form, and to prevent misconceptions.

The President's convictions of the dangerous tendencies of the Bank of the United States, since signally illustrated by its own acts, were so overpowering when he entered on the duties of Chief Magistrate, that he felt it his duty, notwithstanding the objections of the friends by whom he was surrounded, to avail himself of the first occasion to call the attention of Congress and the people to the question of its re-charter. The opinions expressed in his Annual Message, of December, 1829, were reiterated in those of December, 1830 and 1831, and in that of 1832, he threw out for consideration some suggestions in relation to a substitute. At the session of 1831-'2, an act was passed, by a majority of both Houses of Congress, re-chartering the present bank, upon which the President felt it his duty to put his constitutional veto. In his message returning that act, he repeated and enlarged upon the principles and views briefly asserted in his Annual Messages, declaring the bank to be, in his opinion, both inexpedient and unconstitutional, and announcing to his countrymen, very unequivocally, his firm determination never to sanction, by his approval, the continuance of that institution, or the establishment of any other upon similar principles.

There are strong reasons for believing that the motive of the bank in asking for a recharter at that session of Congress, was to make it a leading question in the election of a President of the United States the ensuing November, and all steps deemed necessary were taken to procure from the people a reversal of the President's decision.

Although the charter was approaching its termination, and the bank was aware that it was the intention of the Government to use the public deposite as fast as it has accrued, in the payment of the public debt, yet did it extend its loans from January, 1831, to May, 1832, from $42,402,304 94

to $70,428,070 72, being an increase of $28,025,766 68 in sixteen months. It is confidently believed that the leading object of this immense extension of its loans, was to bring as large a portion of the people as possible under its power and influence; and it has been disclosed that some of the largest sums were granted on very unusual terms to the conductors of the public press. In some of these cases, the motive was made manifest by the nominal or insufficient security taken for the loans, by the large amounts discounted, by the extraordinary time allowed for payment, and especially by the subsequent conduct of those receiving the accommodations.

Having taken these preliminary steps to obtain control over public opinion, the bank came into Congress and asked a new charter. The object avowed by many of the advocates of the bank, was to put the President to the test, that the country might know his final determination relative to the bank prior to the ensuing election. Many documents and articles were printed and circulated at the expense of the bank, to bring the people to a favorable decision upon its pretensions. Those whom the bank appears to have made its debtors for the special occasion, were warned of the ruin which awaited them, should the President be sustained, and appeals were made to alarm the whole people by painting the depression in the price of property and produce, and the general loss, inconvenience, and distress, which it was represented would immediately follow the re-election of the President in opposition to the bank.

Can it now be said that the question of a re-charter of the bank was not decided at the election which ensued? Had the veto been equivocal, or had it not covered the whole ground—if it had merely taken exceptions to the details of the bill, or to the time of its passage—if it had not met the whole ground of constitutionality and expediency, then there might have been some plausibility for the allegation that the question was not decided by the people. It was to compel the President to take his stand, that the question was brought forward at that particular time. He met the challenge, willingly took the position into which his adversaries sought to force him, and frankly declared his unalterable opposition to the bank as being both unconstitutional and inexpedient. On that ground the case was argued to the people, and now that the people have sustained the President, notwithstanding the array of influence and power which was brought to bear upon him, it is too late, he confidently thinks, to say that the question has not been decided. Whatever may be the opinions of others, the President considers his re-election as a decision of the people against the bank. In the concluding paragraph of his veto message, he said:

"I have now done my duty to my country. If sustained by my fellow-citizens, I shall be grateful and happy; if not, I shall find in the motives which impel me, ample grounds for contentment and peace."

He was sustained by a just people, and he desires to evince his gratitude by carrying into effect their decision, so far as it depends upon him.

Of all the substitutes for the present bank which have been suggested, none seems to have united any considerable portion of the public in its favor. Most of them are liable to the same constitutional objections for which the present bank has been condemned, and perhaps to all there are strong objections on the score of expediency. In ridding the country of an irresponsible power, which has attempted to control the Government, care must be taken not to unite the same power with the Executive branch. To give a President the control over the currency and the power over individuals now possessed by the Bank of the United States, even with the material difference that he is responsible to the people, would be as objectionable and as dangerous as to leave it as it is. Neither one nor the other is necessary, and therefore ought not to be resorted to.

On the whole, the President considers it as conclusively settled, that the charter of the Bank of the United States will not be renewed, and he has no reasonable ground to believe that any substitute will be established. Being bound to regulate his course by the laws as they exist, and not to antici-

pate the interference of the legislative power, for the purpose of framing new systems, it is proper for him seasonably to consider the means by which the services rendered by the Bank of the United States are to be performed after its charter shall expire.

The existing laws declare, that "the deposites of the money of the United States, in places in which the said bank and branches thereof may be established, shall be made in said bank or branches thereof, unless the Secretary of the Treasury shall at any time otherwise order and direct, in which case the Secretary of the Treasury shall immediately lay before Congress, if in session, and if not, immediately after the commencement of the next session, the reasons of such order or direction."

The power of the Secretary of the Treasury over the deposites, is *unqualified*. The provision that he shall report his reasons to Congress, is no limitation. Had it not been inserted, he would have been responsible to Congress, had he made a removal for any other than good reasons, and his responsibility now ceases, upon the rendition of sufficient ones to Congress. The only object of the provision, is to make his reasons accessible to Congress, and enable that body the more readily to judge of their soundness and purity, and thereupon to make such further provision by law as the legislative power may think proper in relation to the deposite of the public money. Those reasons may be very diversified. It was asserted by the Secretary of the Treasury without contradiction, as early as 1817, that he had power "to control the proceedings" of the Bank of the United States at any moment, "by changing the deposites to the State banks," should it pursue an illiberal course towards those institutions; that "the Secretary of the Treasury will always be disposed to support the credit of the State banks, and will invariably direct transfers from the deposites of the public money in aid of their legitimate exertions to maintain their credit;" and he asserted a right to employ the State banks when the Bank of the United States should refuse to receive on deposite the notes of such State banks as the public interest required should be received in payment of the public dues. In several instances he did transfer the public deposites to State banks, in the immediate vicinity of branches, for reasons connected only with the safety of those banks, the public convenience, and the interests of the treasury.

If it was lawful for Mr. Crawford, the Secretary of the Treasury, at that time, to act on these principles, it will be difficult to discover any sound reason against the application of similar principles in still stronger cases. And it is a matter of surprise that a power which, in the infancy of the bank, was freely asserted as one of the ordinary and familiar duties of the Secretary of the Treasury, should now be gravely questioned and attempts made to excite and alarm the public mind, as if some new and unheard-of power was about to be usurped by the Executive branch of the Government.

It is but a little more than two and a half years to the termination of the charter of the present bank. It is considered as the decision of the country that it shall then cease to exist, and no man, the President believes, has reasonable ground for expectation that any other Bank of the United States will be created by Congress. To the Treasury Department is intrusted the safekeeping and faithful application of the public moneys. A plan of collection different from the present, must therefore be introduced and put in complete operation, before the dissolution of the present bank. When shall it be commenced? Shall no step be taken in this essential concern until the charter expires, and the treasury finds itself without an agent, its accounts in confusion, with no depository for its funds, and the whole business of the Government deranged? or shall it be delayed until six months, or a year, or two years before the expiration of the charter? It is obvious that any new system which may be substituted in the place of the Bank of the United States, could not be suddenly carried into effect on the termination of its existence without serious inconvenience to the Government and the people. Its vast amount of notes are then to be redeemed and withdrawn from circulation, and its immense debt collected. These operations must be gradual, otherwise much suffering and distress will be brought upon the community. It ought to be not a work of months only, but of years, and the President thinks it cannot, with due attention to the interests of the people, be longer postponed. It is safer to begin it too soon than to delay it too long.

It is for the wisdom of Congress to decide upon the best substitute to be adopted in the place of the Bank of the United States, and the President would have felt himself relieved from a heavy and painful responsibility if, in the charter to the bank, Congress had reserved to itself the power of directing, at its pleasure, the public money to be elsewhere deposited, and had not devolved that power exclusively on one of the Executive departments. It is useless now to inquire why this high and important power was surrendered by those who are peculiarly and appropriately the guardians of the public money. Perhaps it was an oversight. But as the President presumes that the charter to the bank is to be considered as a contract on the part of the Government, it is not now in the power of Congress to disregard its stipulations; and by the terms of that contract the public money is to be deposited in the bank, during the continuance of its charter, unless the Secretary of the Treasury shall otherwise direct. Unless, therefore, the Secretary of the Treasury first acts, Congress have no power over the subject, for they cannot add a new clause to the charter, or strike one out of it, without the consent of the bank, and consequently the public money must remain in that institution to the last hour of its existence, unless the Secretary of the Treasury shall remove it at an earlier day. The responsibility is thus thrown upon the Executive branch of the Government of deciding how long before the expiration of the charter the public interest will require the deposites to be placed elsewhere. And although, according to the frame and principle of our Government, this decision would seem more properly to belong to the legislative power; yet as the law has imposed it upon the Executive department, the duty ought to be faithfully and firmly met, and the decision made and executed upon the best lights that can be obtained, and the best judgment that can be formed. It would ill become the Executive branch of the Government to shrink from any duty which the law imposes on it, to fix upon others the responsibility which justly belongs to itself. And while the President anxiously wishes to abstain from the exercise of doubtful powers, and to avoid all interference with the rights and duties of others, he must yet, with unshaken constancy, discharge his own obligations, and cannot allow himself to turn aside, in order to avoid any responsibility which the high trust with which he has been honored requires him to encounter; and it being the duty of one of the Executive departments to decide in the first instance, subject to the future action of the legislative power, whether the public deposites shall remain in the Bank of the United States until the end of its existence, or be withdrawn some time before, the President has felt himself bound to examine the question carefully and deliberately, in order to make up his judgment on the subject: and in his opinion the near approach of the termination of the charter, and the public considerations heretofore mentioned, are of themselves amply sufficient to justify the removal of the deposites without reference to the conduct of the bank, or their safety in its keeping.

But in the conduct of the bank may be found other reasons very imperative in their character, and which require prompt action. Developments have been made from time to time of its faithlessness as a public agent, its misapplication of public funds, its interference in elections; its efforts, by the machinery of committees, to deprive the Government directors of a full knowledge of its concerns; and above all, its flagrant misconduct, as recently and unexpectedly disclosed, in placing all the funds of the bank, including the money of the Government, at the disposition of the president of the bank, as means of operating upon public opinion and procuring a new charter, without requiring him to render a voucher for their disbursement. A brief recapitulation of the facts which justify these charges, and which have come to the knowledge of the public and the President, will, he thinks, remove every reasonable doubt as to the course which it is now the duty of the President to pursue.

We have seen that in sixteen months, ending in May, 1832, the bank had extended its loans more than $28,000,000, although it knew the Government intended to appropriate most of its large deposite during that year in payment of the public debt. It was in May, 1832, that its loans arrived at the maximum; and in the preceding March, so sensible was the bank that it would not be able to pay over the public deposite when it would be required by the Government, that it commenced a secret negotiation, without the approbation or knowledge of the Government, with the agents, for about $2,700,000 of the three per cent. stocks held in Holland, with a view of inducing them not to come forward for payment for one or more years after notice should be given by the Treasury Department. This arrangement would have enabled the bank to keep and use during that time the public money set apart for the payment of these stocks.

After this negotiation had commenced, the Secretary of the Treasury informed the bank that it was his intention to pay off one-half of the three per cents. on the first of the succeeding July, which amounted to about $6,500,000. The president of the bank, although the Committee of Investigation was then looking into its affairs at Philadelphia, came immediately to Washington, and upon representing that the bank was desirous of accommodating the importing merchants at New York, (which it failed to do,) and undertaking to pay the interest itself, procured the consent of the Secretary, after consultation with the President, to postpone the payment until the succeeding first of October.

Conscious that at the end of that quarter the bank would not be able to pay over the deposites, and that further indulgence was not to be expected of the Government, an agent was despatched to England secretly to negotiate with the holders of the public debt in Europe, and induce them by the offer of an equal or higher interest than that paid by the Government, to hold back their claims for one year, during which, the bank expected thus to retain the use of $5,000,000 of the public money which the Government should set apart for the payment of that debt. The agent made an arrangement on terms, in part, which were in direct violation of the charter of the bank, and when some incidents connected with this secret negotiation accidentally came to the knowledge of the public and the Government, then, and not before, so much of it as was palpably in violation of the charter was disavowed! A modification of the rest was attempted with the view of getting the certificates without payment of the money, and thus absolving the Government from its liability to the holders. In this scheme the bank was partially successful, but to this day the certificates of a portion of these stocks have not been paid, and the bank retains the use of the money.

This effort to thwart the Government in the payment of the public debt, that it might retain the public money to be used for their private interests, palliated by pretences notoriously unfounded and insincere, would have justified the instant withdrawal of the public deposites. The negotiation itself rendered doubtful the ability of the bank to meet the demands of the treasury, and the misrepresentations by which it was attempted to be justified, proved that no reliance could be placed upon its allegations.

If the question of a removal of the deposites presented itself to the Executive in the same attitude that it appeared before the House of Representatives at their last session, their resolution in relation to the safety of the deposites would be entitled to more weight, although the decision of the question of removal has been confided by law to another department of the Government. But the question now occurs, attended by other circumstances and new disclosures of the most serious import. It is true, that in the message of the President, which produced this inquiry and resolution on the part of the House of Representatives, it was his object to obtain the aid of that body in making a thorough examination into the conduct and condition of the bank and its branches, in order to enable the Executive Department to decide whether the public money was longer safe in its

hands. The limited power of the Secretary of the Treasury over the subject, disabled him from making the investigation as fully and satisfactorily as it could be done by a committee of the House of Representatives, and hence the President desired the assistance of Congress to obtain for the Treasury Department a full knowledge of all the facts which were necessary to guide his judgment. But it was not his purpose, as the language of his message will show, to ask the representatives of the people to assume a responsibility which did not belong to them, and relieve the Executive branch of the Government from the duty which the law had imposed upon it. It is due to the President that his object in that proceeding should be distinctly understood, and that he should acquit himself of all suspicion of seeking to escape from the performance of his own duties, or of desiring to interpose another body between himself and the people in order to avoid a measure which he is called upon to meet. But although, as an act of justice to himself, he disclaims any design of soliciting the opinion of the House of Representatives in relation to his own duties, in order to shelter himself from responsibility under the sanction of their counsel, yet he is at all times ready to listen to the suggestions of the representatives of the people, whether given voluntarily or upon solicitation, and to consider them with the profound respect to which all will admit that they are justly entitled. Whatever may be the consequences, however, to himself, he must finally form his own judgment where the Constitution and the law makes it his duty to decide, and must act accordingly; and he is bound to suppose that such a course on his part will never be regarded by that elevated body as a mark of disrespect to itself: but that they will, on the contrary, esteem it the strongest evidence he can give of his fixed resolution conscientiously to discharge his duty to them and the country.

A new state of things has, however, arisen since the close of the last session of Congress, and evidence has since been laid before the President which he is persuaded would have led the House of Representatives to a different conclusion if it had come to their knowledge. The fact that the bank controls, and in some cases substantially *owns*, and by its money *supports* some of the leading presses of the country, is now more clearly established. Editors to whom it loaned extravagant sums in 1831 and 1832, on unusual time and nominal security, have since turned out to be insolvent, and to others apparently in no better condition, accommodations still more extravagant, on terms more unusual, and some without any security, have also been heedlessly granted.

The allegation which has so often circulated through these channels, that the treasury was bankrupt and the bank was sustaining it, when for many years there has not been less on an average than six millions of public money in that institution, might be passed over as a harmless misrepresentation, but when it is attempted, by substantial acts, to impair the credit of the Government and tarnish the honor of the country, such charges require more serious attention. With six millions of public money in its vaults, after having had the use of from five to twelve millions for nine years, without interest, it became the purchaser of a bill drawn by our Government on that of France for about $900,000, being the first instalment of the French indemnity. The purchase money was left in the use of the bank, being simply added to the treasury deposite. The bank sold the bill in England, and the holder sent it to France for collection, and arrangements not having been made by the French Government for its payment, it was taken up by the agents of the bank in Paris with the funds of the bank in their hands. Under these circumstances, it has, through its organs, openly assailed the credit of the Government, and has actually made, and persists in a demand, of fifteen per cent. or $158,842 77 as damages, when no damage, or none beyond some trifling expense, has in fact been sustained, and when the bank had in its own possession on deposite several millions of the public money which it was then using for its own profit. Is a fiscal agent of the Government which thus seeks to enrich itself at the expense of the public worthy of further trust?

There are other important facts not in the contemplation of the House of Representatives, or not known to the members at the time they voted for the resolution.

Although the charter and the rules of the bank both declare that "not less than seven directors" shall be necessary to the transaction of business, yet the most important business, even that of granting discounts to any extent, is intrusted to a committee of five members, who do not report to the board.

To cut off all means of communication with the Government in relation to its most important acts, at the commencement of the present year, not one of the Government directors was placed on any one committee. And although, since, by an unusual remodelling of those bodies, some of those directors have been placed on some of the committees, they are yet entirely excluded from the committee of exchange, through which the greatest and most objectionable loans have been made.

When the Government directors made an effort to bring back the business of the bank to the board, in obedience to the charter and the existing regulations, the board not only overruled their attempt, but altered the rule so as to make it conform to the practice, in direct violation of one of the most important provisions of the charter which gave them existence.

It has long been known that the president of the bank, by his single will, originates and executes many of the most important measures connected with the management and credit of the bank, and that the committee, as well as the board of directors, are left in entire ignorance of many acts done, and correspondence carried on in their names, and apparently under their authority. The fact has been recently disclosed, that an unlimited discretion has been, and is now, vested in the president of the bank to expend its funds in payment for preparing and circulating articles, and purchasing pamphlets and newspapers, calculated, by their contents, to operate on elections, and secure a renewal of its charter. It appears, from the official report of the public directors, that on the 30th November, 1830, the president submitted to the board an article published in the American Quarterly Review, containing favorable notices of the bank, and suggested the expediency of giving it a wider circulation at the expense of the bank; whereupon the board passed to following resolution, viz:

"*Resolved*, That the president be authorized to take such measures in regard to the circulation of the contents of the said article, either in whole or in part, as he may deem most for the interest of the bank."

By an entry in the minutes of the bank, dated March 11th, 1831, it appears that the president had not only caused a large edition of that article to be issued, but had also, before the resolution of 30th November was adopted, procured to be printed and widely circulated, numerous copies of the reports of General Smith and Mr. McDuffie in favor of the bank, and on that day he suggested the expediency of extending his power to the printing of other articles which might subserve the purposes of the institution. Whereupon the following resolution was adopted, viz:

"*Resolved*, That the president is hereby authorized to cause to be prepared and circulated such documents and papers as may communicate to the people information in regard to the nature and operations of the bank."

The expenditures purporting to have been made under authority of these resolutions, during the years 1831 and 1832, were about $80,000. For a portion of these expenditures, vouchers were rendered, from which it appears that they were incurred in the purchase of some hundred thousand copies of newspapers, reports, and speeches, made in Congress, reviews of the Veto Message, and reviews of speeches against the bank, &c., &c. For another large portion, no vouchers whatever were rendered, but the various sums were paid on orders of the president of the bank, making reference to the resolution of the 11th March, 1831.

On ascertaining these facts, and perceiving that expenditures of a similar character were still continued, the Government directors, a few weeks ago, offered a resolution in the board, calling for a specific account of these expenditures, showing the objects to which they had been applied, and the persons to whom the money had been paid. This reasonable proposition was voted down.

They also offered a resolution rescinding the resolutions of November, 1830, and March, 1831. This also was rejected.

Not content with thus refusing to recall the obnoxious power, or even to require such an account of the expenditure as would show whether the money of the bank had in fact been applied to the objects contemplated by these resolutions, as obnoxious as they were, the board renewed the power already conferred, and even enjoined renewed attention to its exercise, by adopting the following, in lieu of the propositions submitted by the Government directors, viz:

"*Resolved*, That the board have confidence in the wisdom and integrity of the president, and in the propriety of the resolutions of 30th November, 1830, and 11th March, 1831, and entertain a full conviction of the necessity of a renewed attention to the object of those resolutions, and that the president be authorized and requested to continue his exertions for the promotion of said object."

Taken in connexion with the nature of the expenditures heretofore made, as recently disclosed, which the board not only tolerate, but approve, this resolution puts the funds of the bank at the disposition of the president, for the purpose of employing the whole press of the country in the service of the bank, to hire writers and newspapers, and to pay out such sums as he pleases, to what person and for what services he pleases, without the responsibility of rendering any specific account. The bank is thus converted into a vast electioneering engine, with means to embroil the country in deadly feuds, and, under cover of expenditures, in themselves improper, extend its corruption through all the ramifications of society.

Some of the items for which accounts have been rendered show the construction which has been given to the resolutions, and the way in which the power it confers has been exerted. The money has not been expended merely in the publication and distribution of speeches, reports of committees, or articles written for the purpose of showing the constitutionality or usefulness of the bank. But publications have been prepared and extensively circulated, containing the grossest invectives against the officers of the Government; and the money which belongs to the stockholders and to the public has been freely applied in efforts to degrade, in public estimation, those who were supposed to be instrumental in resisting the wishes of this grasping and dangerous institution. As the president of the bank has not been required to settle his accounts, no one but himself knows how much more than the sum already mentioned may have been squandered, and for which a credit may hereafter be claimed in his account under this most extraordinary resolution. With these facts before us, can we be surprised at the torrent of abuse incessantly poured out against all who are supposed to stand in the way of the cupidity or ambition of the Bank of the United States? Can we be surprised at sudden and unexpected changes of opinion in favor of an institution which has millions to lavish, and avows its determination not to spare its means when they are necessary to accomplish its purposes? The refusal to render an account of the manner in which a part of the money expended has been applied, gives just cause for the suspicion that it has been used for purposes which it is not deemed prudent to expose to the eyes of an intelligent and virtuous people. Those who act justly do not shun the light, nor do they refuse explanations when the propriety of their conduct is brought into question.

With these facts before him, in an official report from the Government directors, the President would feel that he was not only responsible for all the abuses and corruptions the bank has committed, or may commit, but almost an accomplice in a conspiracy against that Government which he has sworn honestly to administer, if he did not take every step within his constitutional and legal power likely to be efficient in putting an end to these enormities. If it be possible, within the scope of human affairs, to find a reason for removing the Government deposites, and leaving

the bank to its own resource for the means of effecting its criminal designs, we have it here. Was it expected when the moneys of the United States were directed to be placed in that bank, that they would be put under the control of one man, empowered to spend millions without rendering a voucher or specifying the object? Can they be considered safe, with the evidence before us that tens of thousands have been spent for highly improper, if not corrupt purposes, and that the same motive may lead to the expenditure of hundreds of thousands, and even millions more? And can we justify ourselves to the people by longer lending to it the money and power of the Government, to be employed for such purposes?

It has been alleged by some as an objection to the removal of the deposites, that the bank has the power, and in that event will have the disposition, to destroy the State banks employed by the Government, and bring distress upon the country. It has been the fortune of the President to encounter dangers which were represented as equally alarming, and he has seen them vanish before resolution and energy. Pictures equally appalling were paraded before him when this bank came to demand a new charter. But what was the result? Has the country been ruined, or even distressed? Was it ever more prosperous than since that act? The President verily believes the bank has not the power to produce the calamities its friends threaten. The funds of the Government will not be annihilated by being transferred. They will immediately be issued for the benefit of trade, and if the Bank of the United States curtails its loans, the State banks, strengthened by the public deposites, will extend theirs. What comes in through one bank will go out through others, and the equilibrium will be preserved. Should the bank, for the mere purpose of producing distress, press its debtors more heavily than some of them can bear, the consequences will recoil upon itself, and in the attempts to embarrass the country, it will only bring loss and ruin upon the holders of its own stock. But if the President believed the bank possessed all the power which has been attributed to it, his determination would only be rendered the more inflexible. If, indeed, this corporation now holds in its hands the happiness and prosperity of the American people, it is high time to take the alarm. If the despotism be already upon us, and our only safety is in the mercy of the despot, recent developments in relation to his designs and the means he employs, show how necessary it is to shake it off. The struggle can never come with less distress to the people, or under more favorable auspices than at the present moment.

All doubt as to the willingness of the State banks to undertake the service of the Government, to the same extent, and on the same terms, as it is now performed by the Bank of the United States, is put to rest by the report of the agent recently employed to collect information; and from that willingness, their own safety in the operation may be confidently inferred. Knowing their own resources better than they can be known by others, it is not to be supposed that they would be willing to place themselves in a situation which they cannot occupy without danger of annihilation or embarrassment. The only consideration applies to the safety of the public funds, if deposited in those institutions. And when it is seen that the directors of many of them are not only willing to pledge the character and capital of the corporations in giving success to this measure, but also their own property and reputation, we cannot doubt that they, at least, believe the public deposites would be safe in their management. The President thinks that these facts and circumstances afford as strong a guarantee as can be had in human affairs for the safety of the public funds, and the practicability of a new system of collection and disbursement through the agency of the State banks.

From all these considerations the President thinks that the State banks ought immediately to be employed in the collection and disbursement of the public revenue, and the funds now in the Bank of the United States drawn out with all convenient despatch. The safety of the public moneys, if deposited in the State banks, must be secured beyond all reasonable doubts; but the extent and nature of the security, in addition to their capital, if any be deemed necessary, is a subject of detail to which the Treasury Department will undoubtedly give its anxious attention. The banks to be employed must remit the moneys of the Government without charge, as the Bank of the United States now does; must render all the services which that bank now performs; must keep the Government advised of their situation by periodical returns; in fine, in any arrangement with the State banks, the Government must not, in any respect, be placed on a worse footing than it now is. The President is happy to perceive by the report of the agent, that the banks which he has consulted have, in general, consented to perform the service on these terms, and that those in New York have further agreed to make payments in London without other charge than the mere cost of the bills of exchange.

It should also be enjoined upon any banks which may be employed, that it will be expected of them to facilitate domestic exchanges for the benefit of internal commerce; to grant all reasonable facilities to the payers of the revenue; to exercise the utmost liberality towards the other State banks; and do nothing uselessly to embarrass the Bank of the United States.

As one of the most serious objections to the Bank of the United States is the power which it concentrates, care must be taken in finding other agents for the service of the treasury not to raise up another power equally formidable. Although it would probably be impossible to produce such a result by any organization of the State banks which could be devised, yet it is desirable to avoid even the appearance. To this end it would be expedient to assume no more power over them, and interfere no more in their affairs than might be absolutely necessary to the security of the public deposite, and the faithful performance of their duties as agents of the treasury. Any interference by them in the political contests of the country, with a view to influence elections, ought, in the opinion of the President, to be followed by an immediate discharge from the public service.

It is the desire of the President that the control of the banks and the currency shall, as far as possible, be entirely separated from the political power of the country, as well as wrested from an institution which has already attempted to subject the Government to its will. In his opinion the action of the General Government on this subject ought not to extend beyond the grant in the Constitution, which only authorizes Congress "to coin money and regulate the value thereof;" all else belongs to the States and the people, and must be regulated by public opinion and the interests of trade.

In conclusion, the President must be permitted to remark that he looks upon the pending question as of higher consideration than the mere transfer of a sum of money from one bank to another. Its decision may affect the character of our Government for ages to come. Should the bank be suffered longer to use the public moneys in the accomplishment of its purposes, with the proofs of its faithlessness and corruption before our eyes, the patriotic among our citizens will despair of success in struggling against its power; and we shall be responsible for entailing it upon our country forever. Viewing it as a question of transcendent importance, both in the principles and consequences it involves, the President could not, in justice to the responsibility which he owes to the country, refrain from pressing upon the Secretary of the Treasury his view of the considerations which impel to immediate action. Upon him has been devolved by the Constitution and the suffrages of the American people, the duty of superintending the operation of the Executive Departments of the Government, and seeing that the laws are faithfully executed. In the performance of this high trust, it is his undoubted right to express to those whom the laws and his own choice have made his associates in the administration of the Government, his opinion of their duties under circumstances as they arise. It is this right which he now exercises. Far be it from him to expect or require that any member of the Cabinet should, at his request, order, or dictation, do any act which he believes unlawful, or in his conscience condemns. From them, and from his fellow-citizens in general, he desires only that aid and support which their reason approves and their conscience sanctions.

In the remarks he has made on this all-important question, he trusts the Secretary of the Treasury will see only the frank and respectful declarations of the opinions which the President has formed on a measure of great national interest, deeply affecting the character and usefulness of his Administration; and not a spirit of dictation, which the President would be as careful to avoid as ready to resist. Happy will he be if the facts now disclosed produce uniformity of opinion and unity of action among the members of the Administration.

The President again repeats that he begs his Cabinet to consider the proposed measure as his own, in the support of which he shall require no one of them to make a sacrifice of opinion or principle. Its responsibility has been assumed, after the most mature deliberation and reflection, as necessary to preserve the morals of the people, the freedom of the press and the purity of the elective franchise, without which all will unite in saying that the blood and treasure expended by our forefathers in the establishment of our happy system of Government will have been vain and fruitless. Under these convictions, he feels that a measure so important to the American people cannot be commenced too soon, and he therefore names the first day of October next as a period proper for the change of the deposites, or sooner, provided the necessary arrangements with the State banks can be made.

ANDREW JACKSON.

REPORT OF THE COMMISSIONER OF THE GENERAL LAND OFFICE,

To the Secretary of the Treasury, on the annual operations of the office, dated Nov. 30, 1833.

General Land Office,
November 30, 1833.

Sir: I have the honor of submitting to your examination, and for the consideration of the Government, a report of the operations of this office during the past year; and the present condition of the same, with its arrears of business, and the necessary action of Congress, to enable it to discharge its various duties with more promptness, and with that justice which is due to the parties interested, and to the public service.

The annexed document, marked A, shows the periods to which the quarterly accounts of the receivers have been rendered to this office, as also the monthly abstracts of sales and receipts, and the admitted balances remaining in the hands of the receivers at the respective dates of their last returns. With few exceptions, the land officers have been very prompt in transmitting to this office their monthly and quarterly statements, as required by law, and the regulations of the department.

The accompanying statement, marked B, exhibits for the year 1832, and the first three quarters of 1833, the amount of public lands sold in the respective States and Territories; the several amounts received in cash, in forfeited land stock, in military bounty land scrip, and the total amount of purchase money, with the amount paid into the treasury. From which statement, it will appear that the sales of the first three quarters of 1833 have exceeded those of the corresponding quarters of 1832, 532,838 acres, $655,060 of purchase money; and of amount paid into the treasury, the sum of $609,838. This excess can be accounted for, in the increasing disposition for emigration which pervades the Atlantic States and many portions of Europe, and in the persevering industry and enterprise of our western and southwestern population. It is not improbable that the sales for the present year will amount to three millions of acres, and the money paid into the public treasury exceed three millions of dollars. In many of the districts, the largest sales frequently occur in the last quarter of the year.

I have caused to be prepared the tabular statement marked C, which presents, at one view, the sales of the public lands, under the cash system, from its commencement, on the 1st of July, 1820, to the end of the year 1832. It exhibits the quantity sold at the several land offices in each year, with the aggregate amount at each office during the whole of that period, as also the amount sold in each year in the several States and Territories, together with the total amount in each State and Territory, with the grand total. This statement also

shows the progressive increase of the ordinary sales, with the exception of the year 1832, which did not equal those of 1831 by 315,514 acres; in consequence, principally, of the general prevalence of the Asiatic cholera in many of those districts to which emigration tended, and from which it usually emanates, and the Indian war which pervaded the northern frontier of Illinois and the western part of Michigan.

A schedule of forfeited land stock, issued and received at the several land offices, under the provisions of the acts of Congress of May 23, 1828, March 31, 1830, and July 9, 1832, is herewith appended, marked D. It shows the amount issued and received at each office in each of the years 1828, 1829, 1830, 1831, 1832, and the first three quarters of 1833; the total amount issued and received in each year; the whole amount at each office during that period; with their respective grand totals. The small balance of less than 16,460 dollars of the whole amount issued, remained to be received and accounted for at this office on the 30th of September last.

By the act of May 30, 1830, there were appropriated 260,000 acres of land, subject to private entry, in Ohio, Indiana, and Illinois, to satisfy the unlocated military bounty land warrants of the Virginia State line and navy; 50,000 acres of the Virginia Continental line, and an unlimited quantity for the United States military warrants, for services rendered in the revolutionary war; and scrip was authorized to be issued in eighty-acre tracts, in lieu of said warrants. The act of July 13, 1832, made an additional appropriation of 300,000 acres for the Virginia Continental line, and the State line and navy; and, by the act of March 2, 1833, the further quantity of 200,000 acres was appropriated for the Virginia warrants, to be located on *any* of the public lands liable to sale at private entry; making a total for Virginia warrants of 810,000 acres. Of this quantity, scrip had been issued, or prepared to be issued, by the Secretary of the Treasury, on the 15th of November instant, for 772,424 acres, leaving a balance of 37,576 acres, the warrants for which have been filed, and the scrip will be issued thereon so soon as the title papers thereof shall be completed. The schedule hereunto annexed, marked E, exhibits a summary statement of the number of warrants which have been satisfied, of each class or description; the quantity of land for which scrip has been issued; its amount in money, at one dollar and twenty-five cents per acre; together with the total number of certificates of scrip issued. Virginia warrants have already been filed for about 10,000 acres, exceeding the amount which can be satisfied with scrip out of the appropriations which have been made. I have no means of ascertaining the amount of outstanding Virginia warrants not yet filed in this office, and it will be for the decision of Congress whether further provisions shall be made to satisfy the same.

The annexed statement, marked F, shows the amount, in money, of the military land scrip received in payment for public lands, at the several land offices, in the years 1830, 1831, 1832, and the first three quarters of 1833, with the total amount in each year in each State and at each office, with the grand total. It will appear from this statement, that, of the whole amount of scrip issued, ($1,063,592,) there had been received at the land offices and accounted for at this office, on the 30th of September last, the sum of $754,827; and that, of this sum, more than one-half has been taken at the Zanesville office, in Ohio, and at the office of Indianapolis, in Indiana. It is altogether, in my opinion, irreconcilable with the ordinary course of such business, and the usual current of public sales, that so large a portion should have been received at these two offices, without the connivance or direct agency of the land officers and their clerks, or one or more of them, at each office, by which scrip has been taken in cases where otherwise cash would have been received. Other offices have also received and transmitted an unexpected amount; in consequence of which, measures have been taken to ascertain the facts and circumstances connected with these transactions, and explanations have been required of the officers. Before the close of the present session of Congress, the department will be able to show the causes and agencies which have contributed to throw this species of property so rapidly upon the Government.

The appropriation of seven thousand dollars, made at the last session of Congress, for extra clerk hire for this office, has enabled me to progress with its current business to a very considerable extent, and to great advantage to those most interested, and to the Government. Out of that appropriation there have been opened twenty-two tract books, containing the entries of the tracts of 504 townships; the posting of about 17,000 entries of lands sold, besides the writing and recording of more than 13,000 patents, and the performance of a large amount of miscellaneous business, equally pressing and important. Yet, notwithstanding the benefits which have resulted from that appropriation, the force of the office, provided by law, has been inadequate to the discharge of its current duties, and leaving, at the close of the present year, a greater aggregate amount of arrears than existed on the 1st of January last.

On the passage of the act of March 2, 1833, providing for the appointment of a secretary to sign patents in the name of the President, there were written and recorded, and prepared for signature, more than twenty thousand patents for lands sold. In consequence of the provisions of that act, it became necessary to alter the date of execution of each patent and the record thereof, and the endorsement of the certificate on which the same was founded. This service was an expense to the office of more than six hundred dollars, requiring, on all the documents, more than sixty thousand alterations or additions, and, in effect, abstracted that sum from the appropriation for the salaries of the permanent clerks. I would, therefore, for the purpose of reimbursing that amount to the office, respectfully recommend a special appropriation of six hundred dollars, to be expended in writing and recording four thousand patents, which would diminish that branch of arrears, without interfering with current duties.

The unfortunate destruction of the treasury building by fire admonished me of the propriety and absolute necessity of adopting every precautionary measure to secure the safety of the title papers, records, and other important documents which constitute the archives of this office. On a particular examination, with a view to that object, it was found that about two tons of the papers, embracing a large portion which belong to the credit system of the land sales, were deposited in the attic story of the building, immediately under the roof, in the utmost confusion, in bundles arranged neither in chronological order nor in the order of consecutive numbers. On a representation of these facts to the then Secretary of the Treasury, and by his advice, I have adopted those means which would secure to the Government and to the extensive regions of the Ohio and Mississippi the safety and security of those documents, which are connected with the land titles of more than three millions of white population. Portable cases for all papers and documents not of daily use, and fire-bags for each room of the office, have been contracted for, and will be delivered in the course of two or three weeks, while the assortment and the arrangement of the title papers are in rapid progress by persons especially employed in that service. The plan adopted, and which, when completed, as it will be in two or three months, will enable twenty able-bodied men, in case of fire, to remove from the office every paper, document, book, and record of the same to a place of security in *fifteen minutes*, without the derangement of either, so that in case the roof and second story of the building should be in flames, everything belonging to the Land Office, except its furniture, could be saved and removed by the ordinary assistance which is found in the case of fires. The whole expense of these necessary and precautionary measures will amount to about twenty-six hundred dollars, for which a special appropriation is respectfully requested.

One of the most serious causes which have produced the delays and embarrassments to the performance of the ordinary business of this office is the want of the statutes and the reports of the adjudicated decisions of the highest courts of justice in the several States. The daily necessity of a recurrence to such documents, and the difficulty of obtaining access to the same, has been the occasion of vexatious delays, in numerous instances, to the parties immediately interested, and to the prompt discharge of official duty. This can be remedied by a special appropriation, for that purpose, of about twenty-five hundred dollars, which is respectfully and urgently recommended. It is frequently the case that a resort to these statutes, and the reported decisions thereon, is absolutely necessary to a correct action on questions arising under the law of descent, the jurisdiction of probate matters, the settlement and distribution of intestate estates, the law of judgments and executions, and the lien created thereby, with the law of assurances, or conveyances in relation to real estate. Access to these sources of information is often indispensable to the security of individual rights, and important to the pecuniary interests of the Government. In many of the States, some of the principles of the common law have been declared inapplicable to the peculiar circumstances of the people and the country, and inconsistent with the genius and provisions of our political institutions, and others have been substituted by legislative adoption, compatible with constitutional rights and the immunities of the citizen. Hundreds of questions are presented every year, in the administration of the powers and duties of this office, involving the examination and application of legal principles, connected with the subjects above enumerated; and it is a matter of surprise to me that more complaints have not been made against the decisions of the Commissioner in cases where he has been called upon to decide, without the requisite legal information to do so understandingly. In many instances, I have no doubt they have been submitted to rather than incur the expense of an appeal to the administrative justice in the United States courts. These evils should no longer prevail, and the excuse for them should cease to exist, by the appropriate action of Congress. The small sum necessary to be appropriated cannot come in competition with the resulting benefits to individuals and to the Government. There is, probably, no bureau under the Executive departments which requires so frequent recurrence to the statutes and judicial decisions of the several States, as that of the General Land Office, and in which they are so necessary to the administration of right and justice. In truth, it has become in practice, from necessity, a court of exchequer, where its decisions are tacitly assented to, from ignorance of the law, or acquiesced in from pecuniary considerations. My duty to the Government and to individual rights requires this statement from me, as an act of justice to the parties interested, and as highly proper and important for the legislative action of Congress.

Although the above statements and exhibits show that the duties of this office are annually increasing and rapidly accumulating, it is proper for me to say, that they present but a small portion of the items of such increase. Exclusive of the correspondence with the Secretary of the Treasury, in relation to the issue of military bounty land scrip since the first of January last, which is equal to the writing and recording of 342 letters, and the letters written to the several land officers, acknowledging the receipt of their monthly and quarterly returns, amounting to 1,150 to the 15th of the present month, there have been written in the office, on other subjects, from the first of January last to the 15th instant, including copies of a portion of the same, 4,529 letters, occupying on the record thereof 3,047 large folio pages. During the present year, there will have been issued and transmitted from the office more than *forty thousand* patents, leaving an arrear of patents for land sold, at the close of the year, in amount exceeding SEVENTY THOUSAND. To this should be added, besides other increasing demands upon the office, the requirements of individuals for copies of the papers, records, correspondence, and other documents, to be used in the administration of justice, the settlement of intestate estates, to supply the loss or destruction of the originals, and for other lawful purposes, which will amount for the present year, at twelve and a half cents per one hundred words, to a sum exceeding three thousand dollars. This class of requisitions upon the time and duties of the office must annually increase with the progress

of the sales of the national domain, the opening and clearing the forests, and the extension of the western settlements. Another source of expense to the office, and which is constantly increasing with the accumulation of its arrears, is the issuing, in ignorance of the fact, of patents to purchasers, or to their assigns, after the death of the patentees. To remedy this defect in the system of legal grants for lands sold, which has now become serious and embarrassing, it is necessary for Congress to provide by law that patents issued to persons deceased, the legal title shall inure to the heirs or devisees, to every lawful effect and extent, as if they had been executed and delivered in the lifetime of the same.

The surveys of the public lands have progressed to a very considerable extent, a large portion of which, however, are rendered immediately unavailing, in consequence of the deficiency of aid provided by law in the offices of the surveyors general. At the present time I am not able to make a particular report thereof; but it is expected that statements in detail of the progress of this work, and the condition and necessities of each office on the first of January next, will be returned, as soon as practicable after that date, by the several surveying departments. When these statements are received, they will be communicated in extenso, or in a condensed form, as may be required. It is known, however, that the surveys of about eight hundred townships have been made and paid for, the plats and descriptive notes of which should be returned to this office, and to the proper land offices, in the course of six or eight months. A large amount of surveys have been made and are in progress, which will be completed and paid for, and the returns thereof made, during the year 1834, if the necessary means should be provided by Congress. I consider it my duty to state, in connexion with this subject, that is is impossible for the public surveys to progress, and the sales and disposition of the national domain to be facilitated and extended with advantage to the Government, and without injury to individuals, unless more discretionary power is vested in the Treasury Department, to meet unforeseen evils and the defects of legislation, to bring up and prevent the accumulation of arrears, and to secure a prompt and efficient discharge of public duty. I would, therefore, respectfully propose that the Secretary of the Treasury, on a reported statement of the facts by the Commissioner of the General Land Office, be authorized and directed by law to cause all the arrears of the surveying departments to be brought up as soon as practicable; to require an authenticated transcript of the records of the field notes to be transmitted to the General Land Office; to cause renewed township plats to be furnished to the land offices, where the originals have become so defaced and injured, and the entries thereon obliterated by constant use, as to be no longer available, in every particular, as public documents; and to make reasonable allowance for the surveys of the principal and guide meridians and base lines, and particular sections of the public lands, in cases where they cannot be executed for the prices allowed by law; and that this expense thereof be paid out of the general appropriation for the surveys of the public lands.

In making this annual report, I am again required, by a sense of public duty, to present a brief view of the arrears of business in this office, and the means necessary to bring up those arrears, in connexion with a proper discharge of current duty. Under the head of,

1st. *Private land claims.*—The printing and publication of State papers, by Gales & Seaton, and Duff Green, supersede much of the duty previously required by this bureau. The arrears of this branch of business can now be brought up by one competent clerk in one year.

2d. *Military bounty lands.*—The duties now required to be performed under this head would require the time of three clerks for one year.

3d. *Posting the entries and sales of public lands, and adjusting the quarterly accounts thereof,* would occupy the time, for one year, of six intelligent and industrious clerks.

4th. *Indexes to the records of patents,* a work of the most pressing necessity, and which is almost entirely in arrears from the commencement of the public land sales, cannot be accomplished in less than one year, by fifteen active and competent clerks.

5th. *The opening of tract books for surveys already returned to the office,* as rendered necessary by the quarter-quarter section subdivision, would require the service of two clerks for one year.

6th. *Writing, recording, and examining patents for land sold.*—The amount of arrears under this head, for lands sold to the first of January next, will exceed seventy-two thousand patents. To write, record, and examine the same, would require the services of eighteen diligent clerks for a year.

7th. *Suspended cases under the credit system,* from a difficulty of completing the title papers, and the great labor of examination, will demand the service of two clerks one year, who are acquainted with this duty.

8th. *The draughtsmen's bureau.*—There are now in the office 926 township plats to be protracted on the maps of the proper land districts, besides about 800 other plats, which are expected to be returned in the course of six or eight months; information having been received that the surveys thereof have been made and returned to the respective surveyors general. To make the protractions and connexions, which should be done in the course of the ensuing year, will require the labor of one competent and industrious draughtsman at least twelve months. The lands selected by the States of Ohio, Indiana, Illinois, and Alabama, under grants for canal purposes, and those selected under grants for other purposes, with the school lands selected in lieu of section sixteen, have all to be entered and marked on the township plats and maps of the proper districts. To perform this service, as also that of making similar entries, under the act of April, 1832, authorizing a subdivision of the fractional sections into forty-acre tracts, would occupy the time of a draughtsman more than one year. If it is contemplated by the Government to complete the service as far as practicable, required by a resolution of the Senate of February 26, 1823, the labor of one draughtsman acquainted with the duty would be required for six years. The daily interruption to the proper discharge of public duty, and the expense resulting to the office, in consequence of the continuance of these arrears, have become evils of the most serious character, and should be done away immediately.

9th. *Miscellaneous arrears,* other than those enumerated, would occupy the time of four clerks one year. These arrears, now amounting to the services of fifty-nine clerks for one year, have been accumulating for a long period of time, a large portion of which existed before the administration of the office was committed to my hands. They have arisen from the physical impossibility of the office to discharge all the duties required of it by law, with the force provided for that purpose; from the injudicious and unfortunate reduction of six of its clerks in 1827; from the great increase of business arising under the relief laws since 1826; from the establishment of additional land and surveying districts; from the numerous reservations made in Indian treaties; from the many grants of public lands for canal, road, literary, and other purposes; and from the great increase of miscellaneous business, within the last four or five years, not previously demanded of the office.

To bring up these arrears, I would respectfully recommend that the Secretary of the Treasury be authorized to cause the same to be done, and the expenses thereof paid out of any moneys in the treasury not otherwise appropriated, to such an extent as, in his judgment, the necessities of the Government and justice to individuals may require. And to enable the office to discharge its current duties, I propose the employment therein of one chief clerk at a salary of $1,700 per annum; one clerk at $1,500; five at $1,400; ten at $1,150; thirteen at $1,000; making, in all, thirty clerks; and also one draughtsman at $1,150; one assistant draughtsman at $1,150; one messenger at $700, and two assistant messengers at $350. For the reasons of this additional aid, and the increase of pay to a portion of the same, I refer you to my report made to the Secretary of the Treasury on the 21st of January last, and which has been printed as number 50 of the Senate documents of last session. If, however, it should not be deemed

expedient by Congress to adopt this proposition, an appropriation of $6,000 per year, for the writing and recording of patents for lands sold, and a like appropriation for six extra clerks in the office, would greatly facilitate its business, and very much lessen the embarrassments under which it now labors.

All which is respectfully submitted.

ELIJAH HAYWARD.

Hon. R. B. TANEY,
Secretary of the Treasury.

DELAWARE BREAKWATER.

In the Quartermaster General's report, accompanying the President's annual message, is a statement of the condition of the Delaware breakwater. General Jesup pronounces the experiment fairly made, and successful. The work already affords a good harbor for vessels engaged in transporting the materials for its construction, as well as for such vessels engaged in commerce as have found occasion to take shelter in time of storm.

The whole length of the breakwater, according to the plan, is *thirty-six hundred* feet, and the deposites of stone already extend two thousand seven hundred feet, in the following proportions: about one thousand feet are elevated five feet above the plane of high-water: nine hundred and fifty feet are nearly level with high-water, and nearly seven hundred and fifty feet are elevated fifteen feet above the sea-bottom.

The whole length of the ice-breaker is to be one hundred and fifty feet, and the deposite of stone extends one thousand four hundred feet; of which, nearly one thousand are above high-water mark, three hundred feet nearly up to that level, and the remainder about fourteen feet above the bottom.

The quantity of stone deposited during the last season was one hundred and fifty-four thousand four hundred and fifty-nine tons, and as much more could have been deposited, with but little increase of contingent expenses, if the means had been provided to pay for it.

If adequate appropriations are made, the work can be completed in 1835.

The estimate, by General Bernard, of the cost to complete the whole work, was $2,216,950. Of this sum, $1,160,000 has been appropriated, leaving a balance of $1,056,950.

Among the estimates is $20,000 for a light-house at the western extremity of the breakwater, which can be constructed at less expense while the main work is going on, than after it is completed.

Balt. Amer.

It may be safely estimated that the average number of letters received, delivered, distributed, and mailed, in our city post office, is not less than *fifteen thousand* each day.—*N. Y. Eve. Post.*

'THE CONGRESSIONAL GLOBE.'

PRINTED AND PUBLISHED AT THE CITY OF WASHINGTON, BY BLAIR & RIVES.

23d Congress, 1st Session.   SATURDAY, JANUARY 4, 1834.   Vol. 1........No. 5.

IN SENATE.

Monday, December 30, 1833.

The VICE PRESIDENT communicated to the Senate a letter from the Secretary of the Treasury, responding to the following resolution of Mr. CLAY, submitted on the 19th instant, with the accompanying documents.

"*Resolved,* That the Secretary of the Treasury be directed to communicate to the Senate a copy of the entire letter addressed to Mr. Crawford, when Secretary of the Treasury, under date the 13th of February, 1817, to the President of the Mechanics' Bank of New York, an extract from which is recited in his report to Congress of the 3d December, 1833; and copies of the other correspondence of Mr. Crawford with the banks about that period, to passages in which the Secretary alludes in the same report."

"*Resolved, also,* That the Secretary be directed to communicate to the Senate a copy of the correspondence between the agent appointed during the last summer to inquire upon what terms the State banks would undertake to perform the services to the Government which had been performed by the Bank of the United States and the said banks; a copy of the report made, if one were made, by the said agent to the Secretary, or the Executive; the name of the agent, his compensation, and in virtue of what law he was appointed."

The communication was read in part by the Secretary, when

Mr. CLAY moved that the further reading be dispensed with, unless some other Senator desired it should be read.

Mr. FORSYTH hoped the paper might be read.

The reading was then proceeded in, followed by the reading of the documents accompanying it.

Mr. CLAY. I rise to make an observation. Sir, this response is a most extraordinary and unprecedented document. We have called for information, and the Secretary gives us argument. Let him have the benefit of it. I undertake to prove, sir, that the financial officer of the Government has grossly perverted and misstated Mr. Crawford. He has entirely misinterpreted him. He has suppressed documents. A most important passage has been withheld. At another time, I undertake to prove my premises. Sir, we have called for certain things which we have not got, and obtained others not called for. We have asked for bread, and the Secretary has given us a stone. We have asked for the name of the agent and his compensation, but it has been withheld. We asked for the law in virtue of which the agent was appointed, and he recognizes not our authority. Sir, I have seen all the letters of Mr. Crawford, with the exception of the circular, and I undertake to prove, at another period, that that gentleman has been misquoted and misinterpreted.

Mr. FORSYTH thought the Senator from Kentucky was unkind and unjust to the Secretary of the Treasury. He accuses him of suppressing what was not asked for. What, sir, is it that has been asked for? The opinions of Mr. Crawford; and has he not given them? He refers to documents in possession of the Senate. Are they not in the Senate? He (Mr. F.) would recall to the gentleman what, the other day, he said he wanted, that the Secretary should state his own case. The gentleman says that he can disprove what the Secretary has stated. Well, there is in, with reference to chapter and verse. Mr. Crawford was charged with having violated the sixteenth section of the charter of the bank, by the suppression of the fact of the transfer of the deposites having been made. But the gentleman says the answer don't correspond with the call—don't state the name of the agent, and his compensation, &c. But all this is plaid in the papers accompanying this report, as he will perceive, if he will refer to them.

Mr. CLAY. No man can have feelings for the

5

Secretary more different than those attributed to him by the honorable member from Georgia. He had a slight personal acquaintance with the Secretary, and no other feelings towards him than in his official character. The Senate called for those documents that he might make out his case. The Senate asked for documents, and he has given us arguments. If the name of his agent is in the appendix, well: it certainly did not appear in the report. In reference to Mr. Crawford's opinions, he would repeat, that although there was a plausibility for the construction which the Secretary had given to them, yet he (Mr. Clay) would undertake to show that the opinions ascribed to Mr. Crawford in reference to the bank charter were never asserted by him.

On motion of Mr. CLAY, the report was laid upon the table and ordered to be printed.

The report of the Committee on Public Lands, adverse to the memorial of the Legislature of Missouri, was taken up and agreed to.

Mr. POINDEXTER, from the Committee on Public Lands, reported a bill for the relief of Andrew Knox, which was read the first time.

Mr. POINDEXTER, from the Committee on Public Lands, reported a bill for the relief of Noah Stehley and John Stehley, without amendment.

Petitions were presented by Messrs. CHAMBERS and WILKINS.

On motion of Mr. WILKINS,

Resolved, That the Secretary be directed to procure, for the use of the members of the Senate not heretofore supplied, one copy each of the Debates on the adoption of the Federal Constitution.

The order, being the consideration of the report of the Secretary of the Treasury upon the removal of the deposites,

Mr. CLAY said, before I proceed, sir, I wish to anticipate an objection to the resolutions. They say that the President, by dismissing the Secretary of the Treasury, for refusing to remove the deposites, has exercised a power which is unconstitutional and dangerous to the liberties of the people.

It may be said, sir, that the Senate ought not to say this. But I will say, sir, that the Senate, in its organization, is possessed of three characters—its legislative, its executive, and finally, its judicial character. Of these three, the most important I conceive to be its legislative character. And this will appear upon considering how strange would be the condition of this body in case its powers were abridged by the Executive, if it could not protect those powers, because we might be called on to perform certain judicial duties in case of impeachment. The Senate is rarely called on to act in its judicial character; I believe, sir, in forty years, it has thus acted only in three instances.

The President may perform an unconstitutional act with very good intentions, and, therefore, if the objection has any weight in it whatever, it would go to prevent the exercise of certain duties, because certain contingencies might arise—a position which ought not to prevail. It is not intended to controvert the fact of the removal of the deposites by the Secretary, but if it be contended that it was done by his own authority, and of his own mind, I say he is flatly contradicted—contradicted by the President himself.

Let us look at the case, sir. This measure, the removal of these deposites, was decided on, on the 18th September, and the order for that purpose was formally given on the 26th. I contend, sir, that the Secretary ought to have stated the whole truth, and not a part only, as he has done. He ought to have stated that his predecessor, Mr. Duane, the particular friend of the President, selected for his peculiar fitness for the office, had refused to remove these deposites, and that he, the Secretary, as his colleague, was by at the time. He ought to have stated, too, that Mr. Duane was dismissed for his contumacy, and he, Mr. Taney,

put in to do that which Mr. Duane would not do. Mr. Duane is a son of one of the fathers of the democracy of the country; he was dismissed from the Cabinet councils, and a man introduced who was an enemy to that democracy—a man who gave his vote against the admission of Missouri into the Union, without the slavery restriction, and who has been introduced for the purpose of practising a system of proscription unexampled in the country. It is this system of proscription which is making its way into the halls of legislation, displacing honest, faithful, and tried public servants, expelling fathers from their places, and depriving wives and children of support from their services. And I caution our Secretary to beware of a like fate. But, sir, I will tell him that if he dares to interfere with a hair of the head of a single individual under him in regard to his opinions, I myself will be the first man to move for his expulsion. The Secretary of the Treasury, sir, ought further to have stated that in the Cabinet deliberations upon the contemplated removal, the Secretaries were divided two and two. What, sir, I ask, would the ministers of a foreign government have done under similar circumstances? Why, sir, they would have resigned their seats and retired, and more especially would they have done so, if there had been a cabal behind the throne, countenacting and subverting their best efforts for the good of their country. There are no men in the country, sir, of honorable feelings, who would not have given up their places with dignified pride on seeing the sullions enter the palace. The Secretary ought to have told us, also, that this measure was ordered by the President and not by him. I will then inquire, in the first place, into the power of the Secretary to remove these deposites; and, secondly, into the sufficiency of his reasons for that act. The Secretary says in his report, the power reserved "to the Secretary over the deposites is not 'restricted to any particular contingencies, but is 'absolute and unconditional, as far as the stockholders' interests are involved." And again, the 'power of the Secretary is unrestrained and that 'of Congress is totally excluded." This, sir, is the Secretary's own statement of his own power. He comes before us expanding his own authority to its utmost dimensions, with what modesty will readily be seen. And who would have supposed that after excluding Congress from any participation in it, and that he alone has the power, that he would yet admit the Executive into a share of the authority. Yet we find him when commenting upon the Executive authority, corseted up and squeezing himself into the most lady-like proportions; yet when commenting upon those of Congress, he distends himself like a balloon and flirts as if conscious of total irresponsibility." He says:

"And as the Secretary of the Treasury presides 'over one of the Executive departments of the 'Government, and as his power over this subject 'forms a part of the executive duties of his office, 'the manner in which it is exercised must be sub-'ject to the supervision of the officer to whom the 'Constitution has confided the whole executive 'power, and has required to take care that the laws 'be faithfully executed."

Now, sir, the Secretary is in one of the departments, and yet he mistakes its true character. Where, I ask, and in what law does he find it established as an Executive department? Congress has totally excluded the President from all control over the Treasury Department. The Secretary is the financial agent of Congress; makes his reports to Congress, and it is within their exclusive control. In some instances, I admit, sir, Congress has placed him under the supervision of the President—in some things which he is directed to do, in regard to the negotiation of loans, for instance; but he is never placed in that situation except expressly and by some positive law. I read from the law on Thursday that the moneys of the United States were confided by law to the Treasurer of the United States. It is not true that the public moneys are put under the care of the Secretary; they are

always placed under the care of the Treasurer of the United States alone. Now, if the Secretary is vested with a power by which Congress is prohibited from acting with him, upon what ground can he call on the President to do it? But the Secretary says, "The power over the place of deposite 'for the public money would seem properly to belong to the legislative department of the Government." If this power then belongs exclusively to the legislative, how does the Executive derive any authority? Sir, I deny the correct interpretation of this power as claimed by the Secretary. Congress has not given up its powers over the treasury of the country. How stands the matter, then? The charter of the Bank of the United States says, that the moneys of the United States shall be deposited in that bank, unless the Secretary shall otherwise order and direct; and in case of removal he is to report his reasons. To whom? Why, to Congress. Why was not the power and absolute control given to the Secretary himself? Why, because the Secretary is the agent and financial sentinel of Congress, appointed to watch over the treasury, and in case prompt action might be necessary, where the treasure of the nation was in danger, to remove it to a place of safety; but to report to Congress his reasons for so doing. Sir, does not all this prove that Congress intended that the Secretary should act in obedience to the injunctions contained in the charter of the bank, and upon the obligation of giving the reasons which led him to the act? It is important to discriminate between the parties to this contract, the Government and the stockholders of the bank. The power given for the removal of the public deposites is a reservation for the benefit of the people, not the stockholders. I assume this principle then: that there being two parties to this charter, which is for the benefit of the people, those which are for the benefit of the people Congress may control and modify as they please. But the Secretary contends that he alone should exercise this power. Congress has said to the bank, we put the money of the nation in your keeping, but place it under the care of our agent. And was it material to the bank who that agent should be? or whether any Secretary should be the agent? It is no matter to the bank who the agent is. Suppose the office of the Secretary of the Treasury should be abolished, and the duties of his office were assigned by law to either of the other Secretaries, could the bank complain? The Secretary is the mere agent. The substance, the essence is reserved to Congress. Suppose a corrupt understanding should be had with the Secretary in relation to the appropriation of the public money, has Congress no control over it? Suppose the bank refuses to fulfil its engagements and is faithless to its trust, has Congress no power to interpose?

I contend that it is an universal principle in all contracts, that your obligation to fulfil your part of the covenant rests on mine, and when you fail to perform on your part, I am discharged. And in either private or public contracts, when either party fails, the judicial tribunals of the country must decide fairly and impartially between them.

The doctrine of the Secretary, denying the powers of Congress in this case, to be exercised in any contingency, I oppose in every view, and assert that Congress possesses the right now to withhold the public moneys from the impending danger. As to the absolute power contended for, to himself alone, sir, it is contrary to the genius of all our laws. I must be allowed to repeat that the Secretary is the mere agent of Congress; the mere substitute of Congress; bound to report to Congress; responsible only to Congress; and by all the laws of principal and agent, his powers are no more extensive than are those whom he is chosen to represent. The Secretary, then, being the mere agent, there comes in another principle applicable to the case; and that is, that all agency is liable to revocation, unless expressly declared to be irrevocable. In this case there is no such clause, no such provision superadded to the authority, but the Secretary is called the agent in the ordinary terms. And when, therefore, you have ascertained the measure of power of the principal, you have discovered the utmost stretch of it which the agent can exercise.

This brings me to the clause on this subject, contained in the charter. And here I will remark, that the whole instrument must be expounded together. The whole contract must be interpreted according to known rules. Then, Congress has the power to remove the deposites in times of danger, and when the provisions of the charter have been violated; but Congress would only have the right upon the known rules of principal and agent, and upon one contingency, and that is, a breach of the contract upon the part of the bank. If we will look at the whole contract, we shall see that the bank pays a heavy bonus, engages to transmit the moneys of the Government from place to place free of charge. There are but two stipulations in the contract to be performed on the part of the Government. The first is, that the bank shall have the use of the public deposites for twenty years, and its notes shall be receivable in payment of debts due the United States. If, then, the bank has performed its stipulations, both parties are bound by their mutual engagements. But suppose at the time of chartering the bank, it had been proclaimed, we have reserved the power of removing the deposites, and we give notice that the Secretary can remove them when he pleases, and if he refuses to do it, the President may remove him: if this had been offered to the people, I ask, sir, would they have subscribed to the stock? Would they have risked their property upon the whim of any man, upon such an arbitrary responsibility? I come, then, to this conclusion, that Congress has not parted with its power, but may modify it for the benefit of the people, and to prevent corrupt collusions. If all this be true, the Secretary being restrained in the exercise of the power, could only interfere in cases where the principal could interfere.

I proceed to the second point in the argument: the reasons which the Secretary has given for the removal of the deposites. And here it is necessary to enter into this discussion with correct views of these reasons. And first, whatever the reasons are, they ought to be of a financial nature. Whenever Congress gives power to an agent, the extent of that power must be interpreted by the act giving him existence. If we view the Secretary, then, as a financial agent, we shall pretty quickly dispose of his reasons. But there is another principle which we must take along with us in the discussion. The Treasury Department is not one of the Executive Departments of the Government. Its duties are to Congress; its reports and its responsibilities are to Congress, and all this without acknowledging any assumption of authority by the Executive. Whenever the Secretary of the Treasury is placed under the direction of the President, it is by the requirements of positive laws, such as relate to loans, &c. With these guides before us, then, let us examine his reasons. The first reason given is the expiration of the charter. The Secretary says, that as the charter has only about two years and a half to run, it became necessary for him to interfere. A gentleman just appointed, and but three days after coming into office, perceives it necessary to do an act which ought to require great experience and observation to enable him to act rightly. And was not this a subject upon which it was proper for Congress to exercise its discretion? Upon what principle did the Secretary interfere with a case which was for the action of Congress alone? Would it not have been better to have waited sixty days? Why anticipate the approach of the session, which was only sixty days off, and when he had been only three days in office, remove these deposites, because the charter would soon expire? Sir, he admits the safety of the deposites, that there is no danger to be apprehended, and therefore he makes out no case.

Sir, is there a man here within the hearing of my voice who doubts, that when the President issued his proclamation last September, instead of ordering a removal of the deposites, he had proclaimed there was no doubt of their safety in the bank, the stability of the bank, and its capacity to meet all its engagements—if this had been done, I say, there is no doubt that all the trouble and distress under which the country is suffering would have been averted. The despatching of an agent last summer upon a secret mission made it necessary for the bank to guard against Executive interference. Was there no motive for waiting till Congress should convene? Did not a decent respect for Congress require that the Secretary should wait? Before turning the treasure of the nation out of doors, he ought to have procured an adequate place for their security. I am sorry to say there is no doubt of the motive of this precipitate action. There is no doubt that the object was to place the public moneys where Congress could not restore them or displace them. If the 2d resolution pass, or if it pass both branches of Congress, we shall see what the Secretary will do. The next reason given is, that the reëlection of the President has decided this question, and that the people, by that act, intimated an expression against the bank. Admitting all this for a moment, and what will it amount to? Nothing more than that there should be no bank, or that the bank should not be renewed. But, I would ask, was the question of the removal of the deposites submitted to the people of the United States by that act? Why, sir, is this perpetual reference to the reëlection of the President? It seems to be a favorite topic either with him or the Secretary. What right has the Secretary to look into it and be constantly recurring to it? Surely the immense majority he received ought to have satisfied them. It is only those who lost, who have reason to be dissatisfied. The winners surely ought to be content. For myself, sir, I have adopted this rule: when the election is over and it is lost, I give it up, and think no more about it. I recognise in every freeman of this nation the right to vote for whom he pleases, and do as a freeman ought.

But, Mr. President, if I show you that the question of rechartering the bank or that of the removal of the deposites were neither of them submitted to the people of the United States, what becomes of the argument of the Secretary on that subject? I refer, in the first place, to the Annual Message of the President in 1829. He says:

"The charter of the Bank of the United States 'expires in 1836, and its stockholders will most 'probably apply for a renewal of their privileges. 'In order to avoid the evils resulting from precipi'tancy in a measure involving such important prin'ciples and such deep pecuniary interests, I feel 'that I cannot, in justice to the parties interested, 'too soon present it to the deliberate consideration 'of the Legislature and the people."

His attention is next drawn to the subject in 1830. He says:

"Nothing has occurred to lessen in any degree 'the dangers which many of our citizens appre'hend from that institution, as at present orga'nized. In the spirit of improvement and compro'mise which distinguishes our country and its 'institutions, it becomes us to inquire whether it 'be not possible to secure the advantages afforded 'by the present bank, through the agency of a 'Bank of the United States, so modified in its prin'ciples and structure as to obviate constitutional 'and other objections."

So far from being opposed to any United States Bank, he admits the practicability of establishing a national bank based upon the public deposites, which shall be as useful as the present bank. All this, sir, you will perceive is non-committal. It does not embody his own opinions, but only those of a large part of the community. He thinks that a bank may be so organized as to obviate all constitutional objections. Here, sir, are three messages alluding to this all-important subject, and if any man can ascertain from them what the opinions of the President were upon it, he must see through different spectacles from those I am in the habit of using. Sir, I affirm, that up to the last moment when the act for rechartering the bank was passed by Congress it was unknown what the President would do. I do not speak of those having his confidential ear, but of gentlemen in Congress. In the message of 1831 he says:

"Entertaining the opinions heretofore expressed 'in relation to the Bank of the United States as at 'present organized, I felt it my duty in my former 'messages frankly to disclose them, in order that 'the attention of the legislature and the people 'should be seasonably directed to that important 'subject, and that it might be considered and 'finally disposed of in a manner best calculated to 'promote the ends of the Constitution and sub'serve the public interests. Having thus con-

'scientiously discharged a constitutional duty, I 'deem it proper on this occasion, without a more 'particular reference to the views of the subject 'then expressed, to leave it for the present to the 'investigation of an enlightened people and their 'representatives."

These are all the messages until we have the veto.

[Here Mr. C. read various extracts from the veto message.]

The Secretary says that the extensive credit possessed by the Bank of the United States results from its being the Government depository, and its notes being made a legal tender in payment of debts due the United States. Now, sir, could you, by making your little Bank of the Metropolis the public depository, and by enacting that its notes should be receivable for debts due the United States, could you make its notes five per cent. above par in foreign countries? Sir, don't we know the real causes of the extensive credit of the United States Bank notes? Is it not its large capital, its connexion with the Government, and the ability with which it has been administered, but, above all, like the Bank of England and the Bank of Amsterdam, that, if there is anything wrong in its management, the Government will expose it? These are the causes; and not that its notes are made receivable for debts due the United States. Another argument used is, the expansion of its powers and the contraction of its loans, and that all this is done for political effect. Sir, how does the Secretary know this? What is there to authorize this inference? Why does he see in every effort of the bank to protect itself that it is me you attack? What does he see in the people of this nation so corrupt as to justify the belief that they can be bought up by the money of the bank? Sir, every consideration required that the Secretary should give a correct motive—never a wrong one. Cannot every man account for the contraction of the loans of the bank, when the Government had despatched an agent to pry into its concerns—and such an agent! Sir, the power to remove the moneys, it is true, is with the Secretary; but to keep them is with the Treasurer. By the act of '89, he is put under an oath, and bound to take care of the moneys. Suppose the Secretary usurps the power of the Treasurer, and the moneys are lost, is the Secretary liable? No, sir.

The next objection is, that the bank has devolved some of its duties upon the executive committee, which ought to be done by the whole board of directors. Now, sir, every bank doing an exchange business in the United States has an exchange committee. The directors meet and do the ordinary business, and leave the presiding officer to execute their directions. This is the invariable practice. But the Government directors are excluded! Well, sir, if the Government choose incompetent, inexperienced men, they cannot expect anything else.

The next objection is, the affair of the French bill. And this is a mere ordinary mercantile operation; and the bank did no more than it was justified by its charter in doing to preserve its credit. But the bank is aiming at political power! Now, sir, let us advert to what this reckless Secretary says. [Here Mr. C. read from the Secretary's report.] Where, sir, is the proof—where the positive evidence of this exercise of political power? Has it come to this, that, in a country where there is a free press, a public banking institution shall not be permitted to publish articles in its own defence, and upon the finances of the country? Is it come to this, that a Secretary of the Treasury has a right to animadvert upon publications made in the press? Under what new sedition law has he done this? Has he forgotten his party who passed that old law? and that the country is yet free?

Here Mr. C.'s remarks were arrested by a motion of Mr. POINDEXTER to adjourn; which was agreed to.

And the Senate adjourned.

HOUSE OF REPRESENTATIVES.

MONDAY, *December* 30, 1833.

Mr. WHITE, of Florida, appeared, qualified, and took his seat.

Mr. PLUMMER presented the petition of Joseph W. Hegeman, praying for a preëmption right to land on Pawpaw alias Mynifes' Island, situate in the Mississippi river, near the town of Vicksburg; which was referred to the Committee on Private Land Claims.

On motion of Mr. PLUMMER,

Ordered, That the petition of John K. Groff, praying for a preëmption right to a certain tract of land presented to the House, at the last session, be referred to the Committee on Private Land Claims.

On motion of Mr. PLUMMER,

Ordered, That the petition of the heirs of John Ellis, deceased, praying for the passage of a law authorizing them to locate three thousand and six hundred arpens on any of the unappropriated lands of Mississippi, Louisiana, or Arkansas, in lieu of a Spanish claim, reported by the Board of Commissioners, and confirmed by an act of Congress, which has been subsequently sold by the United States, presented at the last Congress, be referred to the Committee on Private Land Claims.

On motion of Mr. PLUMMER,

Ordered, That the petition of Wm. L. S. Dearing, praying to be indemnified for the loss of his surveying instruments, field notes, &c., in Red river, presented to the last Congress, be referred to the Committee on Claims.

On motion of Mr. PLUMMER,

Ordered, That the petition of James S. Douglass, Stephen Douglass, William House, Alford Douglass, Samuel House, and James Tant, praying for the passage of a law giving them the right of preëmption to one quarter section of land each, in lieu of that quantity sold by the Government, to which they were entitled to a preëmption right, under the act of May 29th, 1830, be referred to the Committee on Private Land Claims.

Mr. PLUMMER presented some additional testimony in support of said claims, which was referrid to the same Committee.

On motion of Mr. PLUMMER,

Ordered, That the petition of Hartwell Vick, of Mississippi, presented to the last Congress, praying to be indemnified for the loss of certain lands purchased by him from the General Government in 1818, which, on a resurvey in 1828, were found to be covered by a private land claim previously located, be referred to the Committee on Private Land Claims.

On motion of Mr. PLUMMER,

Ordered, That the petition of Woodson Wren, presented to the last Congress, praying for a preemption right to locate a quantity of land on any of the unappropriated lands of Louisiana, Arkansas, or Mississippi, in lieu of a claim confirmed to him by an act of the 2d session of the 21st Congress, on the Bayou Biloxi, be referred to the Committee on Private Land Claims.

On motion of Mr. PLUMMER,

Ordered, That the account and accompanying documents of John C. Naylor, for services rendered as Clerk in the Surveyor General's office, South Tennessee, presented to the last Congress, be referred to the Committee on Public Lands.

On motion of Mr. PLUMMER,

Ordered, That the papers and documents presented to the last Congress, in support of the claim of Right Fore, a citizen of Rankin county, Mississippi, and soldier of the last war, to a pension, be referred to the Committee on Invalid Pensions.

On motion of Mr. PLUMMER,

Ordered, That the documents in support of the claim of George Turnbull, for building a bridge over Labusha creek, in the Choctaw nation, on the great mail route leading from New Orleans to Nashville, presented to the last Congress, be referred to the Committee on Claims.

On motion of Mr. PLUMMER,

Ordered, That the petition of the Board of Trustees of Oakland college, praying for a grant of land to that institution, presented to the last Congress, be referred to the Committee on Public Lands.

Mr. PLUMMER presented the petition of the President and Trustees of Mississippi college, praying for a donation of land to said institution. Referred to the Committee on Public Lands.

On motion of Mr. PLUMMER,

Ordered, That the Committee on Private Land Claims be instructed to inquire into the expediency of granting to John A. Bares, of Claiborne county, Mississippi, a preëmption right to purchase, at one dollar and twenty-five cents per acre, so much of a certain tract of land confirmed to John Anderton by the Board of Commissioners, under and by virtue of the provisions of an act of Congress, passed March 3, 1803, as exceeds the quantity of six hundred and fifty acres.

BANK OF THE UNITED STATES.

Mr. BINNEY presented the following memorial from several of the banks in Philadelphia.

To the Senate and House of Representatives of the United States in Congress assembled:

The memorial of the undersigned the Presidents of the State Banks located in the city and county of Philadelphia, acting under the authority of the Boards of Directors of the several Banks, respectfully represents:

That they address themselves to your honorable bodies as the guardians of the general interests of the country, and as possessing alone the power of remedying the existing distress, and of averting the greater calamities which are obviously impending.

That one of the first blessings a nation can possess is a sound and well-regulated currency—the solid and sure reward of industry, and the uniform measure of property; and it was not the least among the many advantages anticipated from the Constitution that the whole Union would, by the legislative power, be relieved and preserved from the dangers and disgrace of a depraved and irresponsible circulating medium. Such a sound currency this nation has enjoyed, by means of the Bank of the United States, established by the wisdom of Congress; and the peculiar occupation of the undersigned justifies them in stating their conviction, that it is owing in a great degree to the judicious operations of that institution, that for ten years past our moneyed system has been so perfect—and that whether its solidity, its adaptation to the wants of all classes of the community, its facilities for internal commerce, and its protection against the vibrations of foreign trade be regarded, it has no superior in any country. It is therefore with deep regret that the undersigned are now constrained to inform Congress that, in their belief, this system, with the signal prosperity it has produced, has undergone a sudden and painful change. The moneyed operations of our commercial cities are almost at a stand; the commerce between the States is again laboring under a tax, which must continue increasing, of a loss on all its exchanges; the circulating medium already begins to arrange itself on the scale of depreciation; while in the train of these evils, and not far behind them, may be apprehended a general abandonment of specie payments.

In looking for the cause of this state of things, the undersigned feel no difficulty in naming that which is at once obvious and adequate. On the 1st of October last, the whole moneyed system of this country commenced a total change. To the eye of a common observer, it seemed to be the mere transfer of the public revenue from one bank to many banks. But it was in fact the disorganization of the whole moneyed system, and the whole revenue system of the country. Until the 1st of October, the revenue paid by the whole country was diffused by the bank and its branches throughout the whole community, to be used for the support of the industry of the whole, and gently recalled when needful for the service of the whole; while the bank, as the common friend of all sound State banks, uniting with and sustaining them, was enabled to supply an adequate circulating medium from its own resources, and to preserve in a uniform and sound condition the issues of the State institutions. Now, the public revenue is no longer diffused throughout the whole Union; it cannot even be advantageously used where it is collected; and the Bank of the United States, whose expansive power and credit have been so frequently employed to relieve the community, must look necessarily and primarily to its own security.

Happily for the country, the remedy for this distressing state of things is as evident as the cause of it. The undersigned do not hesitate to express their belief, that as the removal of the deposites of the United States from the Bank of the United

States is the real cause of this distress, so the restoration of them to that institution is the real, and will be the effectual, remedy for them. With a view to remove from that measure all reasonable apprehension, the undersigned venture to request that the deposites of the public revenue now in the State banks should remain with those institutions until withdrawn in the course of the public service, or as the wisdom of Congress may please to direct; but that hereafter, the accruing revenue of the United States should be collected and deposited in the Bank of the United States. And your memorialists will ever pray.

H. NIXON,
President of the Bank of North America.
JAMES DUNDAS,
President of the Commercial Bank of Penn.
S. LAMB,
President of the Mechanics' Bank.
ELIJAH DALLET,
President of the Bank of Penn Township.
THOMAS H. GRAIGE,
President of Manufacturing and Mechanics' Bank.
J. HOLMES,
President of Moyamensing Bank.
W. MEREDITH,
President of Schuylkill Bank.
S. HARVEY,
President of Bank of Germantown.
J. TAGERT,
President, by order of the Directors of the Farmers and Mechanics' Bank.

Mr. B. remarked, that as the main question was under discussion, and no person could yet say what disposition would be made of it, and as he had no wish to embarrass the other proceedings of the House by any premature discussion, he would, for the present, move to have the resolution laid on the table and printed.

Mr. POLK reminded the member from Pennsylvania that the memorials on the same subject, from the president and directors of the bank, and from the Government directors, had already been referred to the Committee of Ways and Means; he would suggest that this should take the same course. Deprecating discussion on the subject now, he moved that the memorial should have the same reference.

The question on laying the memorial on the table was put, and negatived: Ayes 79, noes not counted.

The memorial was then referred to the Committee of Ways and Means, and ordered to be printed.

Mr. BOULDIN reported a bill for the relief of John Syme.

Mr. MUHLENBERG, for the relief of Christian Ish, and

Mr. WARDWELL, for the relief of Robert Reynolds; all which bills were severally read twice and committed.

The SPEAKER laid before the House a communication from the Secretary of the Treasury, with a report of evidence taken in the case of Charles Gibbs; which, on motion of

Mr. WHITTLESEY, was referred to the Committee on Claims.

The SPEAKER also presented a report from the person appointed to superintend the works on Pennsylvania Avenue; which was referred to the Committee on the District of Columbia.

REMOVAL OF THE DEPOSITES.

The House proceeded to consider the motion of Mr. POLK, to re-commit to the Committee of Ways and Means the report of the Secretary of the Treasury on the removal of the deposites, together with the following instructions to the committee, moved by Mr. McDUFFIE:

"To report a joint resolution providing that the 'public revenue hereafter collected, be deposited 'in the Bank of the United States, in conformity 'with the public faith pledged in the charter of the 'said bank."

Mr. POLK rose and said, in entering upon the discussion of this great question, he would beg leave to remind the House of the true state of the question, and of the manner in which this discussion was forced so prematurely upon us. The Secretary of the Treasury removed the public deposites from the Bank of the United States. The bank sent to us a memorial complaining that the removal was a violation of its chartered rights, and praying the restoration of the deposites. The House, on full consideration, referred the memorial to the Committee of Ways and Means, for further investigation. The Government directors of the bank also sent us a memorial, respecting the management of the institution—making grave and heavy charges against it—charges which, if true, not only forfeit public confidence in the bank, but also its charter. After full consideration, this memorial was, by a large majority, referred to the Committee of Ways and Means for investigation. The letter of the Secretary of the Treasury, giving us his reasons for the removal of the deposites, was, in the first place, through a misunderstanding, referred to the Committee of the Whole on the state of the Union. But the House reconsidered this reference, and withdrew the paper from the Committee of the Whole, in order to refer it to the standing committee. The House had thus solemnly pronounced that it would not go into a discussion of the subject, until a full investigation had been made by the standing committee; and, at this stage of the proceeding, the gentleman from South Carolina offered his instructions to the standing committee, prejudging the question which was by that committee to be investigated.

This course Mr. P. viewed as a departure, by the bank, from the light of truth. It shunned the investigation which was preferred and invited, and the discussion was pressed now without any investigation. Why was this course pursued? He was unwilling to attribute motives to others, but he would suggest that it might be deemed important to bring on an early discussion in order to flood the country with inflammatory speeches, and with statements of facts made up for the occasion. May it not, too, be deemed advisable, by a discussion here, to fan the flame of the excitement, and to increase the panic of which we have heard so much. All understood the operation of this thing: on the same principle, the bank hoped, by turning its screws, to induce the people to do what they would not do, except in the moment of excitement. Sir, are we children, not to understand what is going on out of this House? This day was presented to us, a memorial praying the restoration of the deposites, from the same banks in Philadelphia which asked the renewal of the bank charter. What other object, he asked, can be attained by the course pursued—a speedy decision? This was the worst possible mode of reaching an early decision. If the standing committee presented something definite and tangible for us to act upon, it would greatly facilitate and expedite the action of the House. One more preliminary remark he would make. The previous question had been called for, and gentlemen exclaimed, "do you wish to gag us?" But the very same gentlemen had, when the bill for rechartering the bank was before us, applied the previous question in order to cut off the debate. That, too, was a final question, and we were not allowed to offer any reasons against the passage of the bill. When the bank had the majority here, no member was permitted to answer the argument of an honorable member in favor of the bill rechartering the bank. So, too, when the question of the safety of the public deposites, in the United States Bank, was before us, the previous question was moved, carried, and all argument cut off. Although this was the course of the friends of the bank, we are charged with endeavoring to avoid a discussion. But we do not seek to avoid it—we are desirous of a full and searching examination, and of an early decision. But we are called upon to do now what we ought to do after an examination—to pronounce a judgment in the case. Without examination the gentleman from South Carolina now comes forward and accuses the Secretary of the Treasury of falsehood in his statements, relative to the concerns of the bank.

Forced, then, into the discussion, thus prematurely, he was obliged to occupy some time in noticing the arguments of the gentleman from South Carolina. If delay should be the consequence, and the universal ruin which he predicts as the sure effect of delay, should befall us, he and his friends are alone answerable for it. If, said Mr. P., I was sure that the House would now vote upon the question, I would resume my seat without a reply to the member from South Carolina. What was the end proposed by that gentleman's motion he did not pretend to say. But its prototype, the proposition of the gentleman from Kentucky [Mr. CHILTON] answered as a hook to hang a speech upon, and was then withdrawn. Whether this will take the same direction, I, of course, have no means of knowing.

The gentleman from South Carolina assumes that the President, in reference to the removal of the Secretary of the Treasury, has acted as a usurper and a tyrant; he did not, however, furnish us the facts on which he grounds the accusation, but argued upon them as granted. In unmeasured terms, he accused the President of tyranny, usurpation and injustice, and seemed to be as much in a rage with him as the Dutch bully was with the lottery wheel. Like the Dutchman, he seemed ready to break everything into smashes, and with about as much reason; for if, in some capricious turn of fortune's wheel, the gentleman and his friends had obtained a prize, he would have pronounced it "as fair a thing as ever was." It was easy to call hard names, but the President had too long and too faithfully served his country to be within the reach of such assaults. But the President is an usurper and a tyrant, and the Secretary of the Treasury, we are assured, is not responsible to the President, and is independent of him. Now, I affirm, said Mr. P., that the Secretary of the Treasury is not independent of the President; and, furthermore, that if Congress should undertake to render him so, by express law, they would exceed their power, and their act would be void. Yes, sir, I affirm that the Secretary of the Treasury is not independent. The Secretary is appointed by the Executive authority of the country. I beg pardon of the House for entering into an argument to prove what has been acquiesced in for forty years—that the Secretary of the Treasury is dependent upon the President. Do gentlemen mean to say that the President has not the power to remove the Secretary of the Treasury from office? The Constitution, on this point, says: "The President shall nominate, and, 'by and with the advice and consent of the Senate, 'shall appoint ambassadors or other public minis'ters, &c., and all other officers of the Unite 'States, whose appointments are not herein other'wise provided for, and which shall be established 'by law. But the Congress may, by law, vest 'the appointment of such inferior officers as they 'think proper in the President alone, in the courts 'of law, or in the heads of department." The heads of department were not inferior officers, and Congress had no right to appoint them; Congress had no power to appoint any officer, and further, they had no right to invest themselves with the power of appointing any officer. By what tenure does the Secretary of the Treasury hold his office? Although there was no express power given in the Constitution for the removal of that officer, yet it was evident that he held the office "*durante bene placito*"—during the pleasure of the President. The Judges of the Supreme Court hold their office by a different tenure—during good behavior; and from that express provision he derived an argument that the Secretary of the Treasury did not hold by that tenure, but at the pleasure of the President. The tenure of the President and Vice President was expressly settled by the Constitution—they hold for a term of years. But other officers hold during pleasure: so it was understood by the framers of the Constitution, and so it has been understood ever since. The appointing power is the Executive power, and the appointing power must necessarily be the removing power. If the one branch had the power of appointment, and another of removal, endless confusion would be produced in the Government. The President "shall take care that the laws be faithfully executed;" can he do this by authorizing each officer to execute the law according to his own understanding? In that case there would be no uniformity or consistency in the action of the Government. One Secretary would execute the embargo law, but another would say that in his conscience he believed the law to be unconstitutional, and, therefore, he was not bound to enforce it. Was it contemplated that each of the inferior officers should construe the law for himself? Did

the Constitution mean, as had been elsewhere suggested, merely to empower the President to put down resistance to the laws. Unquestionably this was one of his duties. But the President, I affirm, cannot see that the laws are faithfully executed, except as he understood them, and it was necessary for him to remove those assistants whose construction of the law differed from his own, and to put in others in their places. Else how had it happened, upon the accession of each new President, that a new Cabinet was appointed? Else how, in the great political revolution of 1801, could the new President have brought into office a cabinet of his own; and how, without a new Cabinet, would he have provided for the faithful execution of the laws? Sir, said Mr. POLK, these are questions so long settled, that I fear I weary the House by referring to them. How happens it that the President is authorized to require the opinions of his Cabinet in writing, if he has not a supervising power over them? The power of removal is left with the President, because he is the Chief Executive, and is responsible to the country for the faithful execution of the laws.

But it was said that the Treasury Department is differently organized from any other. What power, then, has Congress over this officer? Congress, though they saw the public treasure wasting, and the officer unfaithful to his duty, have no power to reach him but by an impeachment. Must there be no method of removing the officer but by the tedious process of impeachment? I apprehend not, sir. The whole duties of the Secretary are executive; in their execution he is responsible to the Chief Executive, who is himself responsible to the country for the acts of his assistants. But let us reverse the question: suppose the President entertained a different opinion on this subject, and that the Secretary of the Treasury had given notice that, on a certain day, he would remove the deposites, and to the President says, I am independent of you, sir; and the bank charter gives me express power to remove the deposites. Suppose the President to fold his arms and say, I have no power to intefere. What would be the indignation of the people at such conduct in the President, on the supposition that the proposed measure was deemed by them unnecessary and mischievous? What, on the other hand, would be the hosannas of the bank, if the President should say, I dismiss you, Mr. Secretary. But independently of these views, the power of removal is expressly recognised. It is an unqualified power, and if it can be exerted without reasons, surely it may be used with reasons. Gentlemen may differ as to the sufficiency of reasons, but there can be no dispute as to the power. The President is not empowered to remove the Secretary at will by the charter of the bank, for such a provision would have looked to Congress as the source of the appointing and removing power; but the charter recognises the power on the part of the President to remove the Secretary. It provides that, in case the office of Secretary becomes vacant by death, resignation, or removal, the deposites should be removed by another officer. The only question raised here, said Mr. Polk, by the gentleman from South Carolina, is the power of the President to remove the Secretary from office. The President is a usurper, a tyrant, yet he has done nothing more than the Constitution authorized him to do. Sir, I have taken some pains to collect the views which were entertained on this subject by those who framed the laws regulating the Executive Departments. It was contended, in Congress, by some member, that the advice and consent of the Senate was as necessary to the removal as to the appointment of an officer. [Mr. P. here read from Lloyd's Debates, extracts from the speeches of Messrs. Madison, Sedgwick, Fisher Ames, Jackson, Gerry, and others, showing the opinions of those gentlemen on the very points now under discussion.]

[The passages in the authorities referred to by Mr. Polk were not furnished to the reporters for the Globe; and they have to regret, as a consequence, that it is not in their power to give as perfect a report of Mr. P.'s excellent speech as they could have wished.]

The opinion was strongly expressed by these gentlemen, that the President was responsible to the people for the conduct of the persons appointed to aid him in the Executive departments. If any power of the President is settled beyond dispute, it was the power of overseeing and controlling those who execute the laws. I take it, then, sir, continued Mr. P., that the power which the President has, in this case, exerted, is clearly given by the Constitution; is clearly conferred by the legislative acts creating the Treasury Department, and has been acquiesced in from the commencement of the Government. Has the power been exerted without adequate reason? If the President uses his power capriciously, he is responsible to the people; if he uses it corruptly, he can be reached by impeachment. But it is said that the Secretary is bound by law to make his annual report to Congress, and that, by the bank charter, he must present his reasons for removing the deposites to Congress, and that, therefore, he is independent of the President. But why does he make his report on the finances to Congress? Because this House is the money-raising House, and it was proper, therefore, that he should lay before them the means of raising revenue, and the sums required for the public service. But does that supersede his responsibility to the Executive? No, sir. But his reasons for removing the deposites must be presented to Congress. In the charter of the old bank, there was no provision requiring the Secretary to deposite the public money in the United States Bank. But he chose to do it in part. In the present bank, the public money is to be deposited, until the Secretary sees fit to withdraw it; and when he does, he is to assign us a reason, that we may know where he has put them, and for what purpose they were removed. We are guardians of the public money, and we say to the Secretary, you must assign to us your reasons, that we may see if you have acted properly. Does this make him independent of the President? Gentlemen had affected to regard the power of removing the public deposites as one never before exercised in this country. He would now undertake to show that, from the days of Alexander Hamilton to this time, all the Secretaries, prior and subsequent to the bank charters, had exercised power over the public deposites, and that it was never esteemed an arbitrary assumption of power, but a power, the exercise of which, was necessary to preserve the currency from confusion. He would show what were the views of those cotemporary with the establishment of the present bank, in relation to the power of the Secretary of the Treasury over the deposites. Mr. Crawford, in a letter dated February 13, 1817, asserts the power to control the bank by removing the public money to the State banks.

In another letter, to the Mechanics' Bank of New York, he claims the right to withdraw the deposites and place them so as to equalize the benefits derived from them, and to support the credit of the State banks. In a report to Congress, of December 10, 1817, Mr. Crawford gives what he deemed satisfactory reasons for detaining the deposites from the United States Bank. He deemed it expedient to suffer the balances remaining in certain banks in Philadelphia, New York, and the District of Columbia, to continue there for some time, in order to enable those banks to renew specie payments. On the 16th of May, in the same year, the Secretary deposited five thousand dollars in the Mechanics' Bank of Georgetown, which had not previously been a depository of the public money.

His reasons were communicated to Congress, in which the right was expressly asserted as a justification for the act he had done. They were acquiesced in by Congress. But the bank did not then complain that there was any violation of their chartered rights being interfered with. No, the bank had not then set themselves up as an antagonist power to that of the Government. No, the bank had not then dared to attempt the control of all the monetary institutions of the country: when these reasons were so presented, they were then deemed all satisfactory and all sufficient, and they established the full and complete power of the Secretary of the Treasury over the deposites. Mr, P. here referred, in illustration of this position, to the letter of Mr. Secretary Crawford, communicated in obedience to a call to that effect by Congress, on the 25th February, 1823, in which various instances were cited to show that this power was used by his predecessors, and he particularly referred to the report presented in 1817, by Mr. Secretary Hamilton, who had claimed the right to remove the deposites as a peculiar province of the Government, even to sustain the credit of State institutions, instancing several loans made by that eminent statesman to the Georgetown Bank and others, and yet, said Mr. P., at that time no dissatisfaction was ever expressed at the propriety of the measures, or were they ever called in question. There were again other instances of loans to the Bank of Columbia, the Bank of the Metropolis, and other lodgments made, and still no complaint. There was even a stronger instance in the case of the Bank of Alexandria, which had applied for a loan of 130,000 dollars to save them from then impending ruin. This relief was only afforded upon consultation with the then President, for it appeared in the correspondence between that bank and the treasury, he had written that the bank must wait for a day for an answer to the application, as he felt it his duty to communicate with the President, and to obtain his order or sanction for complying with the application. Accordingly consultation was had with the President, he gave his sanction to it, and the loan was afforded. But this assumption of power on the part of Mr. Crawford had not altogether passed unobserved, or had not passed without notice of the Congress. It would be in the recollection of many, that a memorial had been presented by the celebrated N. Edwards, making grave charges against the Secretary. Amongst them was one that he had deposited in the local banks the public moneys, and in places where there were branches existing of the Bank of the United States. The Secretary was then highly distinguished for his financial ability; he stood at this very time prominently before the country for the highest office in the gift of the people. Did he then shrink from meeting this, and defending the exercise of the power? No. What was the conduct pursued, when the charges were presented to the House? A committee was immediately raised, of which Governor Floyd, of Virginia, then a member of this House, was the chairman. Evidence was brought forth from various quarters from Missouri, to establish what the Secretary had not attempted to conceal; for he had sought to maintain this right, and the result was, after full investigation, a long report on the subject, which fully justified him.

It was useful and necessary to refer back to reminiscences of similar occurrences to those of the present day, to see what was then thought and said upon them at that time, and contrast them with the present time. The power now exercised was then openly claimed, asserted, and exercised, without question and without complaint. But now for the same exercise, the same sanction, the President is stigmatized as a tyrant, as an usurper, and the Secretary his most miserable instrument, in an act which is styled nothing less than one of despotism—yes, of absolute despotism; and yet these acts, so stigmatized now, received the sanction of Congress and of the nation, for no man then gainsaid the views taken either by Secretary Crawford or by Governor Floyd, though they were then engaged in all the heat engendered by party conflicts. No man then descended so low as to make the points now so gravely discussed. Mr. P. read various extracts from the report, and commented at some length upon it, after which he referred to the correspondence between Secretary Ingham and the Bank, in which the same power to remove the deposites as exercised by his predecessors was claimed by him, and when he stated "that he would exercise it," the bank was altogether silent upon that subject. Mr. Secretary Ingham in that correspondence expressly endorsed and ratified the former opinion of Secretary Crawford; and at the conclusion of his letter of 5th October, 1829, deprecates the idea of the bank being made the engine of a political party—yes, an engine of a political party! But before he (Mr. P.) would have done he would have something to say upon the subject—something upon the political character of this purest of all institutions! If he had succeeded in making himself understood, he had shown that the exercise of the power by the

Secretary of the Treasury was only the exercise of an ordinary and usual power. The President had also exercised the usual and ordinary power; he had removed the Secretary of the Treasury for refusing to act. But he begged pardon; if the argument of the member from South Carolina was good, Mr. Duane was still Secretary; Mr. Taney had no authority at all. He, however, would contend that Mr. Duane was removed by the exercise of power that the President possessed, that this removal was a matter of right, devolving upon the President, he having refused to act in conformity to his directions. Upon his removal Mr. Taney is appointed; the removal is made by him or by his order, and yet it was asked by the member from South Carolina, [Mr. McDuffie,] "Was it the Secretary who done this act? No; it was the act of a tyrant, forsooth, and the Secretary had no more agency in it than the iron pen with which the order was writen." But he (Mr. P.) would state, that it was fortunate for the country, most fortunate for the individual himself, that his character stood too high to require anything to be added by him, or which would render it necessary to say more than that the present Secretary was not the person to be rendered the blind instrument of any man, be he whom he might. He was not such a blind instrument as was charged in this transaction. He could state, as he was authorized to do, that the opinions given by him, and upon which he had acted in the removal, were similar to those given by him, in writing, in the month of March previous, when he was Attorney General, when consulted upon the subject as Cabinet minister. Well, then, was he to be blamed and thus stigmatized for having honestly entertained the opinion that the deposites ought to be removed, for removing them, when, upon the refusal of Mr. Duane and his dismissal that he, appointed his successor, should do so? Yet for this removal, a question upon which his mind had been long made up, he was the "miserable instrument of tyranny!"—he was to be stigmatized as "one of those miserable sycophants who literally crawled in their own slime to the footstool of Executive favor."

[Mr. McDUFFIE here rose and said, that this designation was not intended to be applied to the Secretary.]

Mr. POLK continued, and said he was happy to hear such a disclaimer of an expression, but which must therefore apply to somebody else, he did not know whom; and proceeded to justify the course taken by Mr. Taney, as one which he was induced to take, from having his opinion on the necessity of removal long made up, and which being in full accordance with the opinion of the Chief Magistrate, he had carried into effect when appointed to office. Adverting to the argument and complaint, that the contract made by the Government with the bank had been violated, he denied that the contract was violated, and maintained at length that it was a part of the agreement, by which the very power of removal was reserved expressly to the Secretary of the Treasury, as the agent of Government, and that was a part of the contract, that the Government could remove them at pleasure. To this the bank had agreed, and it was no part of the contract that the deposites were to remain there; but, on the contrary, they might be removed. He referred to the fourteenth section of the charter to the bank, and argued to show, that, under the provision of that section, by which their notes were to be received in payment of Government duties, yet, if Congress passed a law that the notes of the bank should not be received, they might do so, under cases of emergency, without being liable to a charge of violating that contract; he apprehended it would not be any violation to pass such a law; and yet one was as much a contract as the other. After some further arguments in support of this view, Mr. P. said, before he would go into the consideration of the real question at issue, he was desirous to dispel from the minds of the House an insinuation that was as unfounded as any that had been made by the bank, and which, if he was not mistaken, was an insinuation that had been also made by the honorable member from South Carolina, [Mr. McDuffie.] Mr. P. here read an extract from the correspondence with the bank, which he pronounced to be false, and challenged the proof; he maintained the proof could not be produced. The charges against the President were founded upon this; and shortly after he came into power, the war of persecution was commenced. The President had committed the heinous crime of informing Congress, and through them the country, "that the constitutionality and expediency of the bank were questioned by himself, and, so far as he understood, by the people." But was this a new opinion on this subject, and for the first time entertained by the President? No! Was it only an opinion formed between the March at which he was elected and his first inauguration speech in the December following? No! The President's opinion was a fact well known to many. It was known that he had formed opinions adverse to the bank, because he thought it an institution which had too much power, and was as unconstitutional as it might be dangerous to the country. The President's opinion had been known long previous to this, and expressed in the case of McColloh, in Maryland. It was matter of notoriety, that he had so expressed himself to his friends at the Hermitage, and elsewhere; and, when he came into power, and made his first inauguration speech, he felt it his duty, on that, his first public opportunity, to call the attention of the country to the subject. In this he was only consistent throughout. What, then, became of the insinuation thus made in the bank manifesto, that the Government, failing to get possession of the funds of the bank, their next attempt was to break it? Mr. P. here referred to the correspondence with the Portsmouth branch, from which he made various quotations, and upon which he commented at length, to show the views with which Secretary Ingham replied to the parent bank, asserting the right of the Government, under certain emergencies, as a right which pertained to the department; which, when disclaimed by the bank, was re-asserted by Mr. Ingham, and the bank had, in consequence, by their letter to him of October, 1829, backed out of the ground which they had assumed, on the plea, "that the circumstances were no longer applicable." But he would again revert to this subject; and, as he could not then conclude his remarks, and as it was suggested to him that the usual hour for the adjournment of the House had arrived, before he would yield the floor for the purpose of having a motion for an adjournment made, he pledged himself to the House and to the country, that every charge made by the Secretary of the Treasury against the bank would be established to the word—even to the letter; and that, so far from that personage—as was pronounced by the honorable member from South Carolina, but he trusted, on reflection, he would retract—having given to the world unfair, uncandid, or jesuitical arguments in his report, or from his having been guilty of falsehood or wilful suppression of any fact, he (Mr. P.) would undertake to show the truth of every one of them, from documents presented by the bank itself, so that, if there should have been any erroneous statement in the report, the bank alone was the cause of it.

On motion of Mr. CLAY,

The House then adjourned.

IN SENATE.

TUESDAY, *December* 31, 1833.

Mr. WHITE, from the Committee on Indian Affairs, asked to be discharged from the further consideration of the petition of Asher P. Dedrick, and that the petitioner have leave to withdraw his papers; which was agreed to.

Mr. WHITE, from the same committee, reported unfavorable to the petition of Thomas Talbert and others, for the loss of property by Indians, on the return of the petitioners from Mexico. The petitioners alleged that they considered the United States as underwriters for property lost in that manner by trading associations—a principle the Committee did not recognise. The committee asked to be discharged from the further consideration of the subject, and that the petitioners have leave to withdraw their papers; which was agreed to.

Petitions and memorials were presented by Messrs. EWING, HENDRICKS, ROBBINS, McKEAN, WAGGAMAN, LINN, KING of Alabama, and ROBINSON.

Among the memorials was one from citizens of Philadelphia, praying indemnity for French spoliations prior to 1800, which was referred to the Committee on Finance; and another from the State banks of said city, in reference to the moneyed depression now experienced by the mercantile community, which was also referred to the same committee.

The following resolution was submitted by Mr. EWING:

Resolved, That the Postmaster General lay before the Senate a statement of the amount of money, if any, which has been borrowed within the current year, for the use of the department, and that he designate the persons, or corporations, of whom such loans (if any) may have been made, and the date, amount, and terms of each loan.

Mr. HENDRICKS submitted the following resolution:

Resolved, That the Committee on Post Offices and Post Roads be instructed to inquire into the expediency of extending the post route from Terre Haute to Crawfordsville, through Pleasant Hill, Newtown, Rob Roy, Attica, Williamsport, Gregory's Settlement, and Parish's Grove, to Buskum, on the Iroquois, where it intersects the road from Vanville to Chicago.

Mr. WRIGHT, from the Committee on Claims, asked to be discharged from the further consideration of the petition of Moses Shepherd, and that it be referred to the Committee on Roads and Canals; which was agreed to.

Mr. WRIGHT, from the same committee, reported unfavorable to the petition of Daniel Bradley, which was partially read, and ordered to be printed.

Mr. WRIGHT, from the same committee, reported a bill from the House of Representatives for the relief of Hugh McGennis, with an amendment.

Mr. FORSYTH presented the credentials of JOHN P. KING, recently elected a Senator from Georgia, which were read, when Mr. KING was qualified and took his seat.

Mr. WEBSTER, from the committee on Finance, reported a bill for the relief of Benjamin G. Winter.

Mr. POINDEXTER, from the Committee on Public Lands, asked to be discharged from the further consideration of the petition of Green Derrington, and that the petitioner have leave to withdraw his papers; which was agreed to.

Mr. POINDEXTER, from the same committee, reported unfavorable to the memorial of the Legislature of Missouri, with regard to the registers of land offices; when, upon his motion, the committee were discharged from the further consideration of the same.

Mr. POINDEXTER, from the same committee, made a similar report with regard to the memorial of the trustees of Union College in Illinois, and St. Charles College, and asked to be discharged from the further consideration of the same; which was agreed to.

Mr. TIPTON, from the Committee of Claims, reported a bill for the relief of John Timberlane of Indiana; which was read and ordered to be printed.

Mr. TIPTON offered the following resolution:

Resolved, That the Committee on Military Affairs be instructed to inquire into the expediency of an appropriation for paying two companies of volunteers, commanded by Captains McGeorge and Siegler, of the State of Indiana, for service rendered against the hostile Indians in the year 1832.

The following resolution was submitted by Mr. KING of Alabama:

Resolved, That the Committee on Indian Affairs be instructed to inquire into the expediency of indemnifying the heirs of J. Phillips and W. Walker, for losses by them sustained by the depredations of the Creek Indians.

The VICE PRESIDENT presented a communication from the Commissioner of the Public Buildings; which was laid on the table.

The Senate then took up the resolution offered yesterday by Mr. WILKINS, viz:

Resolved, That the Secretary be directed to procure, for the use of the members of the Senate not heretofore supplied, one copy each of the Debates on the adoption of the Federal Constitution.

Which was considered and adopted.

Mr. EWING submitted the following resolution:

Resolved, That the Secretary of State lay before the Senate a copy of the commission under which William J. Duane lately acted as Secretary of the Treasury, and a copy of the commission under which Roger B. Taney now acts as Secretary.

Mr. EWING asked for the unanimous consent of the Senate for its immediate consideration, which being objected to by Mr. KING of Alabama, the resolution lies one day of course.

On motion of Mr. GRUNDY, it was

Resolved, That when the Senate adjourns it adjourn until Thursday.

The following bills from the House of Representatives were read the first and second time, and referred to the appropriate committees, viz:

A bill granting pensions to certain persons.
A bill for the relief of Samuel Thomson.
A bill for the relief of George Chinn.
A bill for the relief of Benjamin Shepley.
A bill for the relief of the widow and heirs of Robert Le Baine.
A bill for the relief of Thomas Richardson.
A bill for the relief of William S. Anderson.
A bill for the relief of George H. Jennings.
A bill for the relief of James H. Brewer.
A bill for the relief of the legal representatives of James Morrison, deceased.
A bill for the relief of John Thomson.
A bill for the relief of Richard Bagner, executor of N. P. Vaughan.
A bill for the relief of Peregrine Garner.
A bill for the relief of Edward Willett.
A bill for the relief of the administrator of Samuel Burr, deceased.
A bill for the relief of John H. Maguire.
A bill for the relief of Russell Hunt, David Hunt, and Amos Hunt.
A bill for the relief of Philip Hickey.
A bill for the relief of John Bills.
A bill for the relief of Daniel Hazleton and William Palmer.
A bill for the relief of Branset Barnes.
A bill for the relief of Joseph M. Harper.
A bill for the relief of Martin Bailey and others.
A bill for the relief of Archibald Smalf.

REMOVAL OF THE DEPOSITES.

Mr. CLAY concluded, as follows:

I have but a few words more, Mr. President, to say upon this subject, and it cannot afford yourself and the Senate more pleasure than it does me, from the fatigue of the two last days, from which I have not yet recovered. I attempted to show, yesterday, that the Secretary of the Treasury had no right to remove the public deposites, and then that the reasons he had given for exercising that power were insufficient. It remains for me now to examine the manner in which he has exercised the power. While the money of the United States was in the Bank of the United States, it was so much added to the effective capital of the bank, and it was enabled, by means of its branches, to distribute its capital, and also the benefits of its capital, into all parts of the country, for the benefit of the people. This use of the capital of the United States is of the utmost importance to the people, and especially in the section from which I come, where the moneyed wants of the people are great. While the bank exists, with its ample means and resources, this western want is supplied by means of its branches, and it has hitherto been of the greatest benefit to them, by increasing their industry and stimulating their enterprise. When the process of abridging these facilities and these means shall have been completed, there will be a degree of distress and embarrassment in the country which no language can describe. By this exercise of power by the Secretary, this use of the capital of the bank and of the nation is withdrawn from the bank and its branches, and placed in local banks in the large cities and on the seaboard, and the people are prevented from having the use of it. The city of New York, particularly, will derive almost the whole benefit from it; or, rather, a few local banks in one single port will have the exclusive use of one moiety of the whole revenue of the United States. Upwards of three months have elapsed since the removal of the deposites, and yet we are told by the Secretary, in his report, that arrangements have not yet been made in all the ports of the United States for receiving the public moneys, and that in one port, that of Charleston, there have been no such arrangements made. Where, sir, are the collector's bonds put in Charleston? Where is the money placed which has been removed from the Bank of the United States, and who has the care of it in Charleston? Although three months have elapsed since this act was done, the Secretary has not yet obtained copies of the charters of the banks selected by him as the depositories of the public money. Can there be anything more dangerous or improvident than to order the public moneys into the vaults of particular banks without knowing the extent of their powers, their liabilities, their obligations, or when their charters expire? Yet he says that, when their charters are received, he will communicate them. But, sir, he ought to have seen *first* what were their powers, their duties, the extent to which they could lawfully contract, their debts, and the amount of specie in their vaults. But he says he has found some banks with whom he has contracted; and the very first step he has taken is in open violation of an express statute of the United States.

[I will thank the Secretary to get the act of 1st May, 1820.]

By this law, sir, the Secretary of the Treasury, as well as the other Secretaries, are prohibited from making any contracts whatever. The provision I allude to is as follows:

"SEC. 6. *And be it further enacted*, That no contract shall hereafter be made by the Secretary of State, or of the Treasury, or of the Department of War, or the Navy, except under a law authorizing the same, or under an appropriation adequate to its fulfilment, and excepting, also, contracts for the subsistence and clothing of the army and navy, and contracts by the quartermaster's department, which may be made by the Secretaries of these departments."

Thus, by this act, the Secretaries are expressly forbid to contract unless by express authority of law.

Where then is the law, and under what authority has this Secretary undertaken to make these contracts? Is it that because the power is given to the Secretary to remove the deposites, it carries with it an implication to repeal this law?

Sir, if it be possible that the provisions of a prior statute can be construed to repeal a subsequent one, it would apply equally to the Treasurer of the United States. It is the Treasurer who has the care and custody of the treasury. What, sir, let me inquire, is the theory of the treasury? It is this. It is the legislative department. The Secretary has authority to draw warrants. It is the duty of the Comptroller to countersign them. The Register records the warrants, and finally the Treasurer is required to pay the warrants thus registered, and not otherwise. Why all this caution? Because the Constitution requires that no money shall be drawn from the treasury, except in pursuance of appropriations made by law. This provision of the Constitution would be nugatory without these four checks, each upon the other. When the Treasurer is thus made the officer to pay the moneys, he is the man to take care of them? If I am right then, the contract of the Secretary with the banks is void: 1st. Because he had no power to remove the deposites, and next because the act is in violation of the law of 1820. The Secretary has no more power than the law gives him, and if he makes a contract when he has no power, it is void. But let us look at the implied powers claimed by the Secretary for this usurpation. It implies the repeal of the act of 1820—and here again the necessity for a little patience by the Secretary in exercising this power, is manifest. Congress had the powers assumed by him, and could have passed a law and specified the terms upon which the deposites should be made in the other banks, the bonus which should be given by them, the interest which should be paid, and the security which they should give, as well as any other terms which might be thought necessary. But acting in direct violation of the charter and assuming powers not granted to him, he anticipates the meeting of Congress, and now it has become necessary for Congress to look into the terms of these contracts. But suppose I am wrong in the position I have taken, and the Secretary had the power assumed: I will show, sir, that a more injudicious contract could not have been entered into by a man possessing the least soundness of judgment or discretion.

[Here Mr. C. read the terms on which the deposite banks would receive each other's notes.]

Instead of the Bank of the United States, whose credit is uniform, and whose notes circulate everywhere; instead of stipulating to do for the Government what the Bank of the United States does, they only stipulate to receive, for the time being, the notes of banks in their immediate vicinity. Now, they may receive these notes to-day and refuse to do so to-morrow. But the Secretary says, it is important to have in due [illegible] a paper circulation, to be substituted for that of the Bank of the United States, and intimates that it may be a better paper.

[Here Mr. C. read, "that the banks were to submit their books and papers to the inspection of the Government agents," &c.]

In lieu of the ample means furnished in the charter of the Bank of the United States, the Secretary has contracted with banks, without seeing their charters, or knowing anything about it.

[Here Mr. C. read, "that if the deposites shall at any time exceed half the capital of said bank, it shall give security," &c.]

Here the officer charged with the care of the public moneys is found placing them in the hands of banks instead of procuring prior security, but says the security is to be given afterwards, when the deposites shall exceed half their capital. The public funds have no security but the stock and bonds, and when they are gone, the money is lost. Sir, a schoolboy would not dispose of his father's money in so loose and unguarded a manner; a freshman would not be so unmindful of paternal regards.

[Here Mr. C. read "that the banks were to transfer the funds to other banks, as may be wished, reasonable notice being first given," &c.]

Now, according to the charter of the United States Bank, no such notice as this is required. In its origin, I believe, Mr. Crawford did give this notice, but it is not done now. What is a reasonable notice? Cannot any one of these banks shelter itself behind what it may deem reasonable notice, when unable to comply with its contract?

[Here Mr. C. quoted the remarks relative to the compensation to be paid to the agents appointed to investigate, &c.]

Here, then, is the whole scheme developed. It is to introduce the safety-fund scheme of New York that these banks are to be leagued together. They are to submit their books to the examination of the Government agent or agents, and this league of banks is to pay these agents such amount of salary, not as Congress shall determine, but as the Secretary shall say. Sir, can you conceive of a more dangerous power distributed through the country, acting under one common direction, than exists here? And what State, sir, choosing to exercise its own authority over the banks of its own creation, will authorize the Secretary of the Treasury to exert such a power over their own creations? Sir, one of these very banks (the Union Bank of Baltimore) has already done what the old Bank of the United States never dared to do. It has stepped forward by its president, in defence of the Secretary, in opposition to an article in the National Intelligencer. And what has been said? Nothing. Sir, if the Secretary wants to purify the press, let him first apply the remedy to the official organ, to the press nearest him; let him first cleanse the Augean stable in his own vicinity, and when he has done that, if his powers are not then exhausted, he can attend to the correction of others. Allow me, sir, to call your attention to one of the banks selected by the Secretary as one of the depositories of the public money. I will take, for convenience, the one nearest me, the Bank of the Metropolis. By its charter this bank is required to communicate its condition annually to Congress. Its last communication was made two year ago. The capital of this bank, paid in, is $500,000—how, it is not said. Whether in stock-notes, or money, this deponent saith not.

Now, sir, what do you suppose the amount of specie in its vaults to be? The bank is at the seat of government—made the depository of all the disbursing officers of the Government here—and what do you suppose, sir, is the amount of specie in its vaults? Why, *just ten thousand nine hundred and seventy-four dollars and seventy-six cents!!!* Here the Secretary of the Treasury, a modern *Tergot*, withdraws the deposites from the United States Bank, with its capital thirty-five millions, and its specie of ten millions, and selects a bank with a capital of $500,000, and only $10,000 of specie; and this, too, is a bank with which a contract is made that when the deposites in it shall *not exceed* $250,000, it shall give security. Sir, we have got a most wonderful man for our financier; a man, sir, who sits by and sees an officer anxious to discharge his duties, refusing to obey the command of the Chief Magistrate where his conscience dictated he was wrong; a man in trouble and distress, between his attachment to the President and his duty to his country. He sees a case, too, (a most rare one, sir,) of a man preferring retirement to all the honors, emoluments, and patronage of office. He sees him driven from his office, and coolly slips into it himself, without remorse or sympathy. Sir, this Secretary discovers, after he has been but three days in office, that Mr. Madison, the Supreme Court, the people, and all who have pronounced upon the expediency and constitutionality of the bank, have been wrong, and that he alone is right. He tells us that it is his solemn conviction that the bank is not in conformity to the Constitution, and upon three days' consideration, he dismisses the bank, scatters the treasure of the country, and undertakes to regulate the press, the morals of the people, and the elective franchise. An amount of labor which no one man ever before performed—a quantum of labor which no man ever before attempted. But, sir, let us look at the financial reasons of the Secretary.

He withdraws the public money from the United States Bank. He requires no bonus from the present depositories, and depreciates the stock of a bank in which the Government holds seven millions. Sir, I undertake to say, that if it be settled that these deposites are to remain in these banks permanently, their stocks will rise from ten to fifteen per cent., and in the same proportion our seven millions in the Bank of the United States will depreciate. These, sir, are the certain results. To what extent the item of unavailable funds which is annually reported will be run up, we shall see when the day of reckoning arrives. Now, sir, as I am anxious to dispose of this subject, let me ask what is it the duty of Congress to do? I ask if the proposition in the first resolution is not established? If the President has not assumed powers not granted to him by the Constitution and laws, and dangerous to the liberties of the people? And if I have not shown that the reasons of the Secretary are insufficient and unsatisfactory? Sir, the eyes and the hopes of the people are directed to us. Let us fulfil those hopes—let us meet their expectations. Sir, the people feel themselves deceived, betrayed, and their liberties in danger. They behold the rapid concentration of all the powers of government in the hands of one man. By the positive authority of the Executive, he controls the legislative action, and is engrossing the entire power of the Government. The question is now not what laws Congress shall pass, but what laws the Executive will not veto. What have we beheld here, sir? A faithful officer, fully competent to do his duties—a man who had received, from the very company over whom he presided, a vote of thanks and a gratuity of $5,000 for his services—has been discharged from his presidency, and a man appointed in his stead, totally unacquainted with the duties of his office, and appointed to propitiate the Executive authority. Sir, we behold around us the usual symptoms of approaching despotism—spies and informers are lurking among us. The incumbents in this place speak in the cautious whispers of trembling slaves, instead of the open frankness and independence of manly freedom. Sir, the premonitory symptoms of despotism are upon us—the collapsed state is rapidly approaching, and if we are not soon relieved we shall die, ignobly die, the contempt of mankind, unpitied, unwept, and unmourned.

Mr. BENTON moved an adjournment, which was lost—ayes 15, noes 22.

The Senate then proceeded to the consideration of Executive business; after which, it adjourned until Thursday.

HOUSE OF REPRESENTATIVES,

TUESDAY, *December* 31, 1833.

Mr. DAVIS, of Massachusetts, rose and said: I hold in my hand, sir, the memorial of Noah Fletcher, formerly of Massachusetts, a citizen of this District, and recently employed as a clerk in the office of the Clerk of the House of Representatives. He represents that, from his youth upward, nearly the whole of his time has been employed in the public service—not in any post of honor or emolument, but of humble and laborious occupation as a clerk; that he has contracted, in this place, the relations of a husband and a father, and is surrounded by those who look to him for protection and support, and that whatever he has been able to save from his earnings has become connected with the concerns of this community. The memorialist, said Mr. D., is highly esteemed among the citizens of this place for probity and courtesy, and holds among the members of this body an honorable and respectable standing. He comes here demanding redress from this body, representing that he has been removed from his employment here, without premonition, and, so far as he knows, without cause. He considers this House as the sanctuary of liberty, and that here every free citizen may come and lay hold of the horns of the altar. Allow me to say, sir, that the eyes of this nation are always fixed with intense interest on this body, as the last refuge and the strong hold of their constitutional liberties. To us they look for the dispensation of justice, confidently trusting that here there will be no wrong, no violence, no arbitrary use of power. Under all circumstances, they rely upon us for protection, and think it enough to say to any one who lifts the scourge over them, I am an American citizen. Sir, it is one of the great privileges of American citizens to think and act according to their own judgment. This high prerogative we all claim, and whenever it is impugned, I hold it the peculiar duty of this House to defend it from the assaults of any power which may rise up in any quarter. No abuse of power should be tolerated by us.

Mr. CLAY, of Alabama, rose to a question of order. The gentleman was debating a proposition which was not before the House, whereas, by the 45th rule, a member, in presenting a petition, must confine himself to a statement of its contents.

The SPEAKER said the gentleman from Massachusetts must content himself with a brief statement of the contents of the memorial.

Mr. DAVIS resumed. He was unwilling to excite any unpleasant feelings on the part of any body, particularly of the learned member from Alabama. It was his intention to confine his remarks to the contents of the paper. The memorialist alleges that the course pursued towards him has been arbitrary and unjust, and it seems proper to me that the House should entertain the memorial, and ask who has exercised this power. He says he was removed by an officer of this body, an individual who, within a few days, was elevated to a responsible office in this House.

The SPEAKER here interposed. The gentleman must limit his remarks to the contents of the memorial.

Mr. DAVIS. That, sir, is my design. I am stating the reasons for which the memorial ought to be entertained. The memorialist goes on to represent that he has been removed without cause. It has not been alleged that he is incompetent to his duties, or unfaithful in their discharge, or that he has been uncourteous or disrespectful to the members of this House. On the other hand, it is universally admitted that he is a man of respectful and courteous deportment, and is seldom seen within this Hall. Well, sir, he has been removed by the exercise of an arbitrary power alone, and it becomes us to inquire whether the spirit of proscription has entered these walls, and whether that despot has at length come here to crush its victims or mould them to its purpose. The memorialist is a man of sensibility and of honor. But, sir, I find myself so much restricted in my remarks by the rules of proceeding, that I cannot present to the House the considerations suggested by this topic. It is a topic of fearful moment. It concerns this House, as the last refuge of liberty, and therefore it ought not to be embarrassed by any mere questions of order. He sent the memorial to the Chair, and requested its reading.

The memorial was then read, as follows:

To the Honorable the House of Representatives of the United States:

The memorial and representation of Noah Fletcher, late an assistant clerk in the Clerk's office of said House, respectfully sheweth—

That in the year 1819, your memorialist was appointed by Thomas Dougherty, then Clerk of the House, as an assistant, *pro tempore*, and that afterwards he was recognised by a resolution of said House, and directed to be continued in service; since which time, until Friday last, your memorialist has continued to discharge his duty with assiduity, and according to the best of his abilities, to the satisfaction of the late Clerk, and, so far as known, to the satisfaction of the members of the House: That on Friday last your memorialist was dismissed from the service of the House, by the present Clerk, without any reason assigned, and, as he alleges, without any good cause, and another person appointed in his place: That your memorialist considers this proceeding as oppressive, contrary to the good feelings of the House of Representatives, and against the true spirit of the Government under which we live.

Your memorialist, therefore, feels it his duty to make this communication to the House, and claims its interposition.

NOAH FLETCHER.

Mr. DAVIS then offered the following resolution:

Resolved, That Noah Fletcher was removed from his office of assistant clerk in this House, without any sufficient cause, and ought to be immediately reinstated.

The SPEAKER said, a resolution was not in order.

Mr. DAVIS. It is in order to make some motion to dispose of the subject of the memorial.

Mr. CLAY rose to submit a remark. No motion can be made accompanying a petition, except one immediately relating to its reference. While up, sir——

The SPEAKER interposed. The motion is, I consider, in order, as it is connected with the subject of the memorial presented. But it must lie on the table one day, without unanimous assent to its consideration.

Mr. PATTON, of Virginia, asked whether it was now in order for him to move the reference of the memorial and motion to a select committee.

The SPEAKER stated that the motion could be received to-morrow, as an amendment to the motion of the gentleman from Massachusetts.

Mr. BAYLIES presented a memorial praying for an appropriation to be made for the removal of obstructions and placing buoys in Great Taunton river, which he moved to have referred to the Committee on Commerce.

Mr. MERCER objected to this reference, and moved that so much only of the memorial as related to placing buoys, should be referred to that committee, and that the residue, in relation to the obstructions in the river, should be referred to the Committee on Roads and Canals.

A desultory discussion arose as to the appropriate duties of these respective committees—in which Messrs. SUTHERLAND, WHITTLESEY of Ohio, REED of Massachusetts, FOOT, HALL of North Carolina, SELDEN, and EWING, participated.

And the question on the motion to refer to the Committee on Commerce, was put and negatived; yeas 65, nays 76.

And the motion submitted by Mr. Mercer prevailed.

Mr. WARD, of New York, presented the memorial of James D. Woodside, of Washington city, on the subject of steam navigation, and steam engines. Referred to the Committee on Naval Affairs.

On motion of Mr. THOMAS, of Louisiana, the House agreed that when they should adjourn this day, they should adjourn over till Thursday next.

A memorial was presented by Mr. WARD-WELL, from sundry inhabitants of New York, praying an appropriation for the erection of a harbor and light-house at Sandy creek and at Salmon river, on Lake Ontario.

Upon this memorial, a second lengthened discussion, of no public interest, arose, as to the most appropriate committee to which it should be referred, in which Messrs. SUTHERLAND, MERCER, GORHAM, VINTON, STEWART, and BOULDIN, participated.

Mr. WARDWELL having moved that the memorial should be referred to the Committee on Commerce, the question was ordered to be taken by yeas and nays, the motion prevailed—yeas 105, nays 97.

Mr. CLAY, of Alabama, moved to refer to the Committee on Indian Affairs the petition and accompanying documents of John McCartney, of Madison county, in that State, asking indemnity for certain property taken by a military officer of the United States on Cherokee lands; which was referred accordingly.

Mr. CARR, from the Committee on Private Land Claims, reported a bill for the relief of Paul Pointis, which was read twice by its title, and referred to a Committee of the Whole House, and made the order of the day for to-morrow, and the bill and report ordered to be printed.

Mr. CARR, from the Committee on Private Land Claims, made an unfavorable report on the claim of Benjamin Oden, representative of William Williams; and, on motion, the report was ordered to be printed.

Mr. DUNCAN reported a bill, granting preemption rights to certain settlers.

Mr. MARSHALL, a bill for the relief of the heirs or legal representatives of Doctor Berrien, deceased.

Mr. FOOT, a bill for the relief of Atwater Daggett and others, owners of the brig Hero.

Mr. HUBBARD, a bill to refund tonnage duties in certain cases.

Mr. LEWIS, a bill for the relief of sundry citizens who have lost property by depredations committed on their property by Indian tribes.

Mr. POLK, a bill making appropriations for the Indian department for 1834, and for the Naval service.

Mr. BINNEY, a bill returning duties paid on certain pieces of sculpture.

Mr. MUHLENBERG, a bill for the relief of Frederick Rayner.

Mr. CAVE JOHNSON, a bill for the relief of Antoine Crozet and Abraham Kinkle.

Mr. McKAY, of N. C., a bill making appropriation for a marine hospital near Wilmington, North Carolina; and

Mr. SUTHERLAND, bills regulating compensation of certain officers of revenue cutters; for the relief of the owners and crew of the schooner Adamant; and for the relief of Henry Gardner. All which bills were severally read twice and committed.

The bill making appropriations in part for the service of Government for 1834, commonly called the House appropriation bill, and the bill granting certain lands in Ohio to that State for the support of schools, were severally read a third time and passed. After which,

The House adjourned.

IN SENATE.

Thursday, January 2, 1834.

A message was received from the House of Representatives, by their Clerk, with sundry bills which had passed that House; which were referred to appropriate committees.

Mr. SILSBEE, from the Committee on Commerce, reported a bill for the relief of John Hagerty and David Austin.

Mr. SILSBEE, from the same committee, reported a bill for the relief of John Hone & Sons.

Mr. HENDRICKS, from the Committee on Roads and Canals, reported a bill for appropriating certain money for the improvement of roads in Arkansas Territory.

Mr. NAUDAIN, from the Committee on Claims, reported a bill for the relief of Andrew Rappalye.

Mr. POINDEXTER, from the Committee on Public Lands, made an unfavorable report upon the petition of Daniel Rhode; which was concurred in.

Mr. POINDEXTER, from the Committee on Public Lands, made an unfavorable report upon the petition of sundry citizens of Mobile, in Alabama; which, on motion of

Mr. KING, of Alabama, was laid upon the table.

Mr. TOMLINSON submitted the following resolution:

Resolved, That the Committee on Revolutionary Claims be instructed to inquire into the expediency of compensating Phineas Taylor, of Danbury, in the State of Connecticut, for a horse and other property taken from him for public use during the revolutionary war.

Mr. WEBSTER, from the Committee on Finance, reported a bill from the House of Representatives in favor of George Chinn, without amendment.

Petitions and memorials were presented by Messrs. KNIGHT, TOMLINSON, MOORE, ROBBINS, LINN, KENT, TIPTON, FORSYTH, and WILKINS.

Mr. GRUNDY gave notice that he should to-morrow ask for leave to introduce a bill for the amendment of the laws regulating the Post Office Department.

On motion of Mr. CHAMBERS, the memorial of James H. McCulloh, which had been laid upon the table, was referred to the Committee of Commerce.

Mr. CHAMBERS, after some explanatory remarks, moved that the subject of a penal code for the District of Columbia, which had been referred to a joint committee of both Houses, be referred to the Committee of the District of Columbia; which was ordered accordingly.

The VICE PRESIDENT presented a memorial from the Legislature of Missouri, relative to the navigation of the Mississippi; which was read, and ordered to lie upon the table.

Mr. SOUTHARD, from the Committee on Naval Affairs, asked to be discharged from the further consideration of the petition of —— Anderson, and that it be referred to the Committee on Claims.

Mr. TIPTON, from the Committee on Claims, reported a bill for the relief of Felix Spencer; which was read twice, and committed.

Mr. TIPTON offered the following resolution:

Resolved, That the Committee on Claims be instructed to inquire into the expediency of granting indemnity to Samuel and James Smith, of Indiana, for improvements made by them on property of the United States, under a lease given claimants by the United States' trustees on certain property of the United States.

Mr. TIPTON offered the following resolution:

Resolved, That the Committee on Claims be instructed to inquire into the expediency of paying Hiram A. Hunter (now of Indiana) for a horse lost by him while in the service of the United States as orderly serjeant in Captain Robert F. Crittenden's company of volunteers, in the Seminole campaign.

Mr. SPRAGUE submitted the following resolution:

Resolved, That the Secretary of the Treasury be directed to communicate to the Senate, so far as the documents and returns received will permit, the amount of trade between the United States and the British North American colonies, the British West Indies, the Danish West Indies, and the Swedish West Indies, since the 30th day of September, 1832—distinguishing the amount of American, British, and other foreign tonnage, which has entered and departed to and from those places respectively; or the West Indies generally. Also, the amount of imports and exports of American and foreign produce, distinguishing between the same.

Mr. LINN submitted the following resolution:

Resolved, That the Committee on Claims be instructed to inquire into the expediency of making compensation to Joseph T. Cirtick, for a boat taken from him by the officers of the General Government, during the last war with Great Britain.

A bill from the House of Representatives making appropriations for the use of Congress, was read twice, and referred to the Committee on Finance.

Mr. CHAMBERS moved that the bill for the relief of Mountjoy Bailey be taken up; but upon the suggestion of Mr. KING, of Alabama, it was again laid on the table.

A bill from the House of Representatives, granting certain lands in the Connecticut Reserve, in Ohio, for the use of schools, was read twice, and referred.

Mr. BLACK introduced the following resolution:

Resolved, That the Committee on the Judiciary be instructed to inquire into the expediency of directing by law the terms of the District Court of the United States for the District of Mississippi, to be hereafter held at Jackson, the seat government of that State.

ORDERS OF THE DAY.

The Senate then proceeded to the consideration of the resolution offered on Tuesday by Mr. HENDRICKS, in the following words:

Resolved, That the Committee on the Post Office and Post Roads, be instructed to inquire into the expediency of extending the post route from Terre Haute to Crawfordsville, through Pleasant Hill, Newtown, Rob Roy, Attica, Williamsport, Gregory's Settlement, and Parish's Grove, to Bunkum, on the Iroquois, where it intersects the road from Vanville to Chicago.

Which resolution was adopted.

The following resolution, submitted by Mr. TIPTON on Tuesday, was taken up and adopted:

Resolved, That the Committee on Military Affairs be instructed to inquire into the expediency of an appropriation for paying two companies of volunteers, commanded by Captains McGeorge and Siegler, of the State of Indiana, for service rendered against the hostile Indians in the year 1832.

The following resolution of Mr. EWING was then taken up, and adopted:

Resolved, That the Secretary of State lay before the Senate a copy of the commission under which William J. Duane lately acted as Secretary of the Treasury, and a copy of the commission under which Roger B. Taney now acts as Secretary.

The following resolution offered by Mr. KING, of Alabama, was taken up and referred to the Committee on Indian Affairs, viz:

Resolved, That the Committee on Indian Affairs be instructed to inquire into the expediency of indemnifying the heirs of J. Phillips and W. Walker, for losses by them sustained by the depredations of the Creek Indians.

The following resolution offered by Mr. EWING, was taken up and adopted:

Resolved, That the Postmaster General lay before the Senate a statement of the amount of money, if any, which has been borrowed within the current year, for the use of the department, and that he designate the persons, or corporations, of whom such loans (if any) may have been made, and the date, amount, and terms of each loan.

A bill for the relief of Daniel Bradley, reported by the Committee of Claims, was ordered to lie upon the table.

Mr. KENT'S resolution, with regard to altering the Constitution of the United States, relative to the election of President and Vice President, was taken up, when the mover suggested the fact that a very important subject was now before the Senate, and as his resolution involved a principle of great moment, he moved that, for the present, the resolution be laid upon the table.

A bill for the relief of Thomas Rhoades and Jeremiah Austin, being under consideration, Mr. GRUNDY made a few observations explanatory, when the bill was ordered to be engrossed and read a third time.

A bill for the relief of John Chandler and William Johnston, having been called up, gave rise to a desultory conversation, in which Messrs. GRUNDY, POINDEXTER, KING, of Alabama,

CHAMBERS, and EWING, participated, when it was laid upon the table: Yeas 22, nays 16.

The VICE PRESIDENT presented a communication from the Secretary of the Navy; which was read and laid on the table.

REMOVAL OF PUBLIC DEPOSITES.

The Senate resumed the consideration of the resolutions submitted by Mr. Clay, on the 26th ultimo.

The VICE PRESIDENT observed, that before the discussion was commenced, the Chair would take occasion to state, that any expressions of their opinions or feelings by spectators in the Senate Chamber, in regard to anything said in debate, were inconsistent with the order of the Senate, and could, on no account, be tolerated. Under the hope that the officers of the House might have it in their power, by the use of ordinary means, to suppress any such acts, and being indisposed to confound the many respectable citizens who are obviously desirous of preserving the decorum demanded by their situation, with the few who are forgetful or unmindful of their duty in this regard, the Chair had hitherto forborne to direct the galleries to be cleared upon the exhibition of such improprieties. The experience of the last few days, however, clearly indicated that such feelings could not be indulged with safety to the order of the Senate, and has induced the Chair to state that there must be perfect silence and order observed on the part of the spectators; and that if this admonition was in the least degree disregarded, the Chair would feel it to be a duty to take effectual measures to put a stop to the irregularity by directing the galleries to be immediately cleared.

Mr. BENTON said he would take leave, before he took up the subject under debate, to vindicate an officer of the Senate who had been unjustly assailed, and who had not the right of speaking for himself. He alluded to the Secretary of the Senate, [Mr. Lowrie,] and to the threat publicly expressed in open debate by a Senator from Kentucky, [Mr. Clay,] to move to expel him from his office if he should remove any of his clerks for their political opinions. The threat implied a knowledge or belief that the Secretary intended to make such removals, when in point of fact no such intention existed. The Secretary now had every clerk in his office which was in it when he came in many years ago. He was living in the utmost harmony with these clerks, and could not but feel himself deeply wounded by a threat which raised an implication which had no manner of existence. Mr. B. said that an acquaintance of fourteen years with the Secretary enabled him to say that he was incapable of the dishonorable conduct attributed, by implication, to him; that he was a high exemplification of the character of a Christian and a gentleman, and would conscientiously discharge his duties to the Senate and his clerks without the slightest regard to unmerited threats. Mr. B. also spoke of the animadversion which had been made at the same time, and for the same cause, upon an officer of another body, [the Clerk of the House of Representatives.] Mr. B. was a stranger to him, knew nothing of what he had done, had no opinions to give as to his conduct; but he would say, in vindication of the privileges of the House of Representatives, that the conduct of their Clerk belonged to them, not to the Senate, and that it was unparliamentary for the Senate to take notice of it.

Mr. B. then proceeded to the order of the day, the resolutions submitted by a Senator from Kentucky, [Mr. Clay,] on the removal of the public deposites from the Bank of the United States, and asked for the reading of the resolutions.

The Secretary reads—

1. "*Resolved*, That, by dismissing the late Secretary of the Treasury, because he would not, contrary to his sense of his own duty, remove the money of the United States in deposite with the Bank of the United States and its branches, in conformity with the President's opinion; and by appointing his successor to effect such removal, which has been done, the President has assumed the *exercise* of a power over the Treasury of the United States, *not* granted to him by the Constitution and laws, and *dangerous* to the liberties of the people.

2. "*Resolved*, That the reasons assigned by the Secretary of the Treasury, for the removal of the money of the United States, deposited in the Bank of the United States and its branches, communicated to Congress on the third day of December, 1833, are unsatisfactory and insufficient."

Mr. B. said that the first of these resolutions contained impeachable matter, and was in fact, though not in form, a direct impeachment of the President of the United States. He recited the constitutional provision, that the President might be impeached, 1. for treason; 2. for bribery; 3. for high crimes; 4. for misdemeanors, and said that the first resolution charged both a high crime a a misdemeanor upon the President: a high crime in violating the laws and constitution to obtain a power over the public treasure to the danger of the liberties of the people; and a misdemeanor in dismissing the late Secretary of the Treasury from office. Mr. B. said that the terms of the resolution were sufficiently explicit to define a high crime, within the meaning of the Constitution, without having recourse to the arguments and declarations used by the mover in illustration of his meaning. But if any doubt remained on that head it would be removed by the whole tenor of the argument, and especially that part of it which compared the President's conduct to that of Cæsar in seizing the public treasure to aid him in putting an end to the liberties of his country; and every Senator in voting upon it would vote as directly upon the guilt or innocence of the President as if he was responding to the question of guilty or not guilty, in the concluding scene of a formal impeachment.

We are then, said Mr. B., trying an impeachment. But how? The Constitution gives to the House of Representatives the sole power to originate impeachments; yet we originate this impeachment ourselves. The Constitution gives the accused a right to be present; but he is not here. It requires the Senate to be sworn as judges; but we are not so sworn. It requires the Chief Justice of the United States to preside when the President is tried; but the Chief Justice is not presiding. It gives the House of Representatives a right to be present, and to manage the prosecution; but neither the House nor its managers are here. It requires the forms of criminal justice to be strictly observed; yet all these forms are neglected and violated. It is a proceeding in which the First Magistrate of the Republic is to be tried without being heard, and in which his accusers are to act as his judges.

Mr. B. called upon the Senate to consider well what they did before they proceeded further in the consideration of this resolution. He called upon them to consider what was due to the House of Representatives, whose privilege was invaded, and who had a right to send a message to the Senate, complaining of the proceeding, and demanding its abandonment. He conjured them to consider what was due to the President, who was thus to be tried in his absence for a most enormous crime: what was due to the Senate itself in thus combining the incompatible characters of accusers and judges, and which would itself be judged by Europe and America. He dwelt particularly on the figure which the Senate would make in going on with the consideration of this resolution. It accused the President of violating the Constitution, and itself committed twenty violations of the same Constitution in making the accusation! It accused him of violating a single law, and itself violated all the laws of criminal justice in prosecuting him for it. It charged him with designs dangerous to the liberties of the citizens, and immediately trampled upon the rights of all citizens in the person of their Chief Magistrate.

Mr. B. descanted upon the extraordinary organization of the Senate, and drew an argument from it in favor of the reserve and decorum of their proceedings. The Senate were lawgivers, and ought to respect the laws already made; they were the constitutional advisers of the President, and should observe as nearly as possible the civil relations which the office of adviser presumes. They might be his judges, and should be the last in the world to stir up an accusation against him to prejudge his guilt, or to attack his character with defamatory language. Decorum, the becoming ornament of every functionary, should be the distinguishing trait of an American Senator, who combines in his own office the united dignities of the Executive, the legislative, and the judicial character. In his judicial character especially he should sacrifice to decorum and propriety, and shun as he would the contagious touch of sin and pestilence the slightest approach to the character of prosecutor. He referred to British parliamentary law to show that the Lords could not join in an accusation, because they were to try it; but here the Senate was sole accuser, and had nothing from the House of Representatives to join, but made the accusation out and out, and tried it themselves.

He said the accusation was a double one, for a high crime and a misdemeanor, and the latter a more flagrant proceeding than the former, for it assumed to know for what cause the President had dismissed his late Secretary, and undertook to try the President for a thing which was not triable or impeachable. From the foundation of the Government it had been settled that the President's right to dismiss his Secretaries resulted from his constitutional obligation to see that the laws were faithfully executed. Many Presidents had dismissed Secretaries, and this was the first time the Senate had ever undertaken to found an impeachment upon it, or had assumed to know the reasons for which it was done.

Mr. B. said that two other impeachments seemed to be going on at the same time against two other officers—the Secretary of the Treasury and the Treasurer, so that the Senate was brim full of criminal business. The Treasurer and the Secretary of the Treasury were both civil officers, and were both liable to impeachment for misdemeanors in office, and great misdemeanors were charged upon them. They were, in fact, upon trial without the formality of a resolution; and if hereafter impeached by the House of Representatives, the Senate, if they believed what they heard, would be ready to pronounce judgment, and remove them from office without delay or further examination.

Mr. B. then addressed himself to the Vice President [Mr. Van Buren] upon the novelty of the scene which was going on before him, and the great change which had taken place since he served in the Senate. He commended the peculiar delicacy and decorum of the Vice President himself, who, in six years' service, in high party times, and in a decided opposition, never uttered a word, either in open or secret session, which could have wounded the feeling of a political adversary if he had been present and heard it. He extolled the decorum of the opposition to President Adams's Administration. If there was one brilliant exception, the error was redeemed by classic wit, and the heroic readiness with which a noble heart bared its bosom to the bullets of those who felt aggrieved. Still addressing himself to the Vice President, Mr. B. said that if he should receive some hits in the place where he sat, without the right to reply, he must find consolation in the case of his most illustrious predecessor, the great apostle of American liberty, (Mr. Jefferson,) who often told his friends of the manner in which he had been cut at, when presiding over the Senate, and personally annoyed by the inferior—no, young and inconsiderate—members of the old Federal party.

Mr. B. returned to the point in debate. The President, he repeated, was on trial for a high crime, in seizing the public treasure in violation of the laws and the Constitution. Was the charge true? Does the act which he has done, deserve the definition which has been put upon it? He had made up his own mind that the public deposites ought to be removed from the Bank of the United States. He communicated that opinion to the Secretary of the Treasury; the Secretary refused to remove them; the President removed him, and appointed a Secretary who gave the order which he thought the occasion required. All this he did in virtue of his constitutional obligation to see the laws faithfully executed; and in obedience to the same sense of duty which would lead him to dismiss a Secretary at War, or of the Navy, who would refuse to give an order for troops to march or a fleet to sail. True, it is made the duty of the Secretary of the Treasury to direct the removal of the deposites; but the Constitution makes it the duty of the President to see that the Secretary performs his duty; and the Constitution is as much above law as the President is above the Secretary.

The President is on trial for a misdemeanor—*for*

dismissing his Secretary without sufficient cause. To this accusation there are ready answers: *first*, that the President may dismiss his Secretaries without cause; *secondly*, that the Senate has no cognizance of the case; *thirdly*, that the Senate cannot assume to know for what cause the Secretary in question was dismissed.

The Secretary of the Treasury is on trial. In order to get at the President, it was found necessary to get at a gentleman who had no voice on this floor. It had been found necessary to assail the Secretary of the Treasury in a manner heretofore unexampled in the history of the Senate. His religion, his politics, his veracity, his understanding, his Missouri restriction vote, had all been arraigned. Mr. B. said he would leave his religion to the Constitution of the United States, Catholic as he was, and although "*the Presbyterian might cut off his head the first time he went to mass*." His understanding he would leave to himself. The head which could throw the paper which was taken for a stone on this floor, but which was in fact a double-headed chain-shot fired from a 48-pounder, carrying sails, masts, rigging, all before it, was a head that could take care of itself. His veracity would be adjourned to the trial which was to take place for misquoting a letter of Secretary Crawford, and he had no doubt would end as the charge did for suppressing a letter which was printed *in extenso* among our documents, and withholding the name and compensation of an agent, when that name and the fact of no compensation was lying on the table. The Secretary of the Treasury was arraigned for some incidental vote on the Missouri restriction, when he was a member of the Maryland Legislature. Mr. Benton did not know what that vote was; but he did know that a certain gentleman, who lately stood in the relation of *sergeant* to another gentleman in a certain high election was the leader of the forces which deforced Missouri of her place in the Union for the entire session which he first attended, not served, in the Senate of the United States. His politics could not be severely tried in the time of the alien and sedition laws, when he was scarce of age; but were well tried during the late war, when he sided with his country and received the constant denunciations of that great organ of federalism—the Federal Republican newspaper. For the rest, Mr. B. admitted that the Secretary had voted for the elder Adams to be President of the United States; but denied the right of certain persons to make that an objection to him. Mr. B. dismissed these personal charges for the present, and would adjourn their consideration until his trial came on, for which the Senator from Kentucky [Mr. Clay] stood pledged; and after the trial was over, he had no doubt but that the Secretary of the Treasury, although a Catholic and a Federalist, would be found to maintain his station in the first rank of American gentlemen and American patriots.

Mr. B. took up the serious charges against the Secretary, that of being the mere instrument of the President in removing the deposites and violating the Constitution and laws of the land. How far he was this mere instrument, making up his mind in three days to do what others would not do at all, might be judged by every person who would refer to the opposition papers for the division in the Cabinet about the removal of the deposites, and which constantly classed Mr. Taney, then Attorney General, on the side of removal. This classification was correct and notorious, and ought to exempt an honorable man, if anything could exempt him, from the imputation of being a mere instrument in a great transaction of which he was a prime counsellor. The fact is, he had long since, in his character of legal adviser to the President, advised the removal of these deposites; and, when suddenly and unexpectedly called upon to take the office which would make it his duty to act upon his own advice, he accepted it from the single sense of honor and duty, and that he might not seem to desert the President, in flinching from the performance of what he had recommended. His personal honor was clean; his personal conduct magnanimous; his official deeds would abide the test of law and truth.

Mr. B. said he would make short work of long accusations, and demolish in three minutes what has been concocting for three months, and delivering for three days in the Senate. He would call the attention of the Senate to certain clauses of law, and certain treasury instructions, which had been left out of view, but which were decisive of the accusation against the Secretary. The first was the clause in the bank charter which invested the Secretary with the power of transferring the public funds from place to place. It was the 15th section of the charter; he would read it. It enacted that whenever required by the Secretary of the Treasury the bank should give the necessary facilities for transferring the public funds from place to place within the United States or Territories thereof; and for distributing the same in payment of the public creditors, &c.

Here is authority to the Secretary to *transfer* the public moneys from place to place, limited only by the bounds of the United States and its Territories; and this clause, of three lines of law, puts to flight all the nonsense about the United States Bank being the *treasury*, and the Treasurer being the *keeper* of the public moneys, with which some politicians and newspaper writers had been worrying their brains for the last three months. In virtue of this clause the Secretary of the Treasury gave certain transfer drafts to the amount of two millions and a quarter; and his legal right to give the draft was just as clear under this clause of the bank charter as his right to remove the deposites was under another clause of it. The *transfer* is made by *draft; a payment* out of the treasury is made upon a *warrant;* and the difference between a transfer draft, and a treasury warrant, was a thing necessary to be known by every man who aspired to the illuminating of a nation, or even to the understanding of himself. To make this clear, Mr. B. read extracts from the treasury instructions to banks of deposite in 1829, and from certain letters from the Treasurer of the United States to the cashier of the Bank of the United States in the month of November last, which would justify the issue of the transfer drafts, and quiet the alarms of all those who thought the Treasurer had forfeited the penalty of his bond, and the Secretary had violated the clause of the Constitution which forbids money to be drawn from the treasury except upon warrants and under appropriation laws. They would show that the transfer drafts were not warrants; that they drew nothing from the treasury, but made a treasury in every place into which they carried money within the limits of the United States or its Territories, whether there was a branch of the United States Bank there or not.

Extract of circular instruction to the banks employed as depositories of the public moneys, dated

"Treasury Department, *May* 28, 1829.

"All public moneys received on or subsequently to the 1st of June, will be placed to the credit 'of Mr. Campbell, as Treasurer. They will be 'drawn for by him in the following manner, *and 'no other:*

"1st. The *Secretary* of the Treasury will issue his '*warrant* upon the *Treasurer*, directing the payment, which warrant will be *countersigned* by the '*Comptroller* of the *Treasury*, and recorded by the '*Register*, who will authenticate the record by his 'signature, and upon a suitable part of the warrant 'the *Treasurer* will give his order directed to the 'proper bank for the payment of the money.

"2d. When transfers are to be made of the 'public funds from one *bank* to *another*, the *Treasurer* will issue a *transfer draft* upon the bank in 'which the funds may be at his credit, in favor of 'the bank to which they are transferred, for the 'amount required, stating that it is to be placed to 'his *credit* in such bank. This draft will be *recorded* by the *Register*, who will authenticate the record by his *signature* upon the draft; and it will 'finally receive the written sanction of the *Secretary* of the Treasury.

"☞ *No deduction whatever is to be made from 'the moneys placed to the credit of the Treasurer, except in these two modes.*"

Extract of a letter from the Treasurer of the United States to the cashier of the Bank of the United States, dated 25th November, 1833.

"The charter of the Bank of the United States 'has given to the Secretary of the Treasury the 'sole power of ordering *transfers* of the public 'funds from *place* to *place* for the convenience of 'the public service, and he of course must judge 'of their necessity and legality. It would, therefore, be out of place in me to offer any observations as to the character of the drafts to which 'some allusion has been made. He is responsible 'to the nation for the proper exercise of this power, and of course cannot be controlled in it by any 'officer in the treasury or of the bank, as I conceive. The charter of the bank provides, 'that, '*whenever required by the Secretary of the Treasury*, 'the said corporation shall give the necessary facilities for transferring the public funds from *place* 'to *place*, within the United States or the Territories thereof, and for distributing the same in payment of the public creditors.' The form in which 'this power, thus confided to the Secretary, is to 'be carried into effect, he has prescribed in his instructions to the bank, of May 28, 1829, which 'were accordingly communicated to all the banks 'in which there were public funds. These instructions are as follows:

"'When *transfers* are to be made of public funds 'from one bank to another, the Treasurer will issue 'a *transfer draft* upon the bank in which the funds 'may be at his credit in favor of the bank to which 'they are to be transferred, for the amount required, 'stating that it is to be placed to his credit in such 'bank. This draft will be recorded by the Register, who will authenticate the record by his signature upon the draft, and it will finally receive 'the written sanction of the Secretary of the Treasury.'

"The transfer draft, signed by the Treasurer, 'Register, and Secretary, in pursuance of these 'instructions, is the form prescribed by the Secretary for carrying into effect the power confided 'to his discretion, of ordering transfers of the 'public funds from place to place. It was adopted 'to give authenticity to the order, and to enable 'the Treasurer to give an accurate account of the 'state of the public funds in the bank and its 'branches, and not in consequence of *his having 'any discretion or control over the subject*. He has 'therefore rigidly and strictly conformed to all the 'instructions given by the Secretary of the Treasury on this subject, and whenever he shall direct 'that notices of *transfer drafts*, as well as of *warrants*, shall be transmitted to the banks by this 'office, those instructions shall, with great pleasure, 'be complied with on my part; but until such instructions are given, the practice of this office will 'be continued as heretofore.

"*When disbursements of money are to be made out 'of the treasury, the law has pointed out the* duties of 'the Treasurer. Such disbursements are to be 'made *alone upon the warrant* of the *Secretary of 'the Treasury, countersigned* by the *Comptroller*, 'and recorded and authenticated by the signature 'of the Register. And by the regulations of the 'treasury, of the 28th of May, 1829, which were also '*communicated to all the banks in which there were 'public deposites*, the Treasurer is required to write 'his order for the payment of the money upon the 'warrant; and by another regulation, the Treasurer is required to transmit to the bank a *daily 'list* of the *warrants* thus directed during the day 'to the bank for payment. These regulations 'have been, and will continue to be, uniformly 'complied with."

After reading these extracts, Mr. B. took a position, and defied all attacks to dislodge him from it. It was this: that a warrant for the payment of money out of the treasury must, in addition to other requisites, be countersigned by the Comptroller of the Treasury; and the bank is forbid to pay, and pays at its peril, any warrant not so countersigned; the transfer draft is not so countersigned; the Comptroller does not so countersign it; yet the Bank of the United States paid these drafts, to the amount of two millions and a quarter, without the countersigning of the Comptroller, and in so doing, admitted that the money was not drawn out of the treasury. This was conclusive, and put the Bank of the United States in the position of contradicting itself, and contradicting all its advocates, in the assumption that the bank is the treasury

Mr. B. took a further view of the newfangled conception that the Bank of the United States was the Treasury of the United States. It followed from that doctrine, that where there was no branch of the United States Bank there could be no treasury, and no public moneys. Now, six or

eight States of this Union had no branch; the three territories had none; by consequence no public moneys could be sent to those States and Territories. Again: the Bank of the United States was not obliged to establish a branch in a single State, only in the District of Columbia, so that if she withdraw her branches, no public money could be kept except in Philadelphia and Washington. He traced the origin of this assumption that the bank was the treasury, to the great measure introduced by President Jackson in the first year of his Administration for the protection of the treasury, which was, that the treasury warrant should be filed in the bank which paid the money. Before that time the Treasurer issued his check on the bank for the money, and it was paid on his single check; since then three other names must go to the bank with his, to wit, that of the Comptroller, that of the Register, and that of the Secretary of the Treasury, and this formed the true defence and security of the treasury. The Treasurer's bond for $150,000 was nothing to a man who would check for thirty millions in a year. President Jackson, in the first months of his Administration, supplying the deficiencies of all 'his predecessors, applied the true remedy. Secretary Ingham wrote the circular: he (Mr. B.) had read extracts from it; it did high honor to the new Administration. It put the treasury beyond the reach of being injured by any Treasurer. The Treasurer's check could not now draw one dollar without three other names upon it, and the filing of the warrant under the seal of the treasury. The bank is now to see the warrant, and to hold it, and because this warrant was formerly retained by the Treasurer, the bank thinks itself the treasury because for six years it has had the treasury warrants, instead of the Treasurer's check. Mr. B. here commented upon the strangeness of fortune, that President Jackson, who was the only President who had devised a true and impregnable safeguard for the treasury, should be charged with seizing it, and his conduct compared to that of Cæsar in pillaging the gold which Pompey, the Consuls, and the Senate were silly enough to leave behind in the temple of Jupiter when they fled from Rome.

Mr. B. held that the Secretary of the Treasury was now acquitted; that the Treasurer himself was freed from the penalties of the act of 1789; that both were found to be borne out by law; and he regretted that these officers had not had an opportunity of showing to their accusers and judges the difference between a treasury warrant and a transfer draft, before sentence of condemnation had been passed upon them for mere defect of that knowledge.

Mr. B. proceeded to the second of the resolutions submitted by the Senator from Kentucky, [Mr. CLAY;] and to avoid all questions about order, he took leave to give notice that he should, at the proper time, move an amendment to that resolution, namely, to strike it all out, and to substitute another of a different import.

He considered this second resolution to be illegal, futile, and nugatory.

Illegal, because it assumed an appellate jurisdiction over the act of the Secretary of the Treasury in a case in which no right of appeal had been reserved to the two Houses of Congress in their joint legislative capacity, much less to the Senate alone. The act of the Secretary is definitive. His report to Congress is for their information, not for their revision. The condemnation of his reasons by either, or both Houses of Congress, cannot restore the deposites, or alter their destination. It will require a law, or a joint resolution to do that. The resolution was illegal in assuming a jurisdiction over a subject of which the Senate had no cognizance. It was a single resolution, and could not legally be communicated to the House of Representatives.

It was futile and nugatory in leading to no action, or practical result. It declared a naked proposition, but indicated no consequence resulting from it. It declared the Secretary's reasons to be insufficient and unsatisfactory; but did not say what was to be done with the Secretary, or with the deposites, if the Senate found them to be so. He would still remain Secretary, and the public moneys would still remain removed, whether the resolution was passed or rejected by the Senate. The mover seemed to foresee this objection and to understand the unparliamentary character of his resolution when he alluded to the effect which its adoption might have upon the public mind. He (Mr. B.) denied that the Senate was the place to adopt barren resolutions for popular effect. He doubted the propriety of the trial, and the success of the experiment. He remembered a case in which the Senate's condemnation had been the highest passport to public favor; and it might be that a vote on this resolution in favor of the bank might be equally unprofitable to the Senate which gave it, and to the bank which received it.

On motion of Mr. KANE, the Senate then adjourned.

HOUSE OF REPRESENTATIVES.

Thursday, January 2, 1834.

Several private bills were reported, which will be noticed hereafter. After which,

Mr. DAVIS inquired if it was then in order to take up the resolution submitted by him on the petition presented from Noah Fletcher, one of the Clerks of the House, recently dismissed.

The SPEAKER explained the practice of the House at length, and in accordance to it, decided that after the expiration of the first thirty days sitting of the House, it was not in order to discuss any petition except on Mondays.

After a protracted discussion on the point of order between Messrs. CLAY, MERCER, WILLIAMS of North Carolina, and WAYNE, the latter took an appeal from the decision of the Speaker to the House, but subsequently withdrew it.

REMOVAL OF PUBLIC DEPOSITES.

The House proceeded to consider the motion of Mr. POLK, to recommit to the Committee of Ways and Means the report of the Secretary of the Treasury on the removal of the deposites, together with the following instructions to the committee, moved by Mr. McDUFFIE:

"To report a joint resolution providing that 'the public revenue hereafter collected be deposited 'in the Bank of the United States, in conformity 'with the public faith pledged in the charter of 'the said bank.'"

Mr. POLK resumed and concluded his remarks, which, from the early hour we are obliged to go to press, we are precluded from giving, but shall hereafter.

Mr. BINNEY having obtained the floor; moved an adjournment, which prevailed.

IN SENATE.

Friday, January 3, 1834.

A message was received from the President of the United States, by the hands of his private secretary.

Mr. HENDRICKS submitted the following resolutions, which lie one day on the table:

Resolved, That the Committee on Roads and Canals be instructed to inquire into the expediency of making a further appropriation for the construction of the Cumberland road, in the States of Ohio, Indiana, and Illinois.

Resolved, That the Committee on Pensions be instructed to inquire into the expediency of placing upon the pension list, applicants who shall be able to prove three months' service in the revolutionary war, agreeably to the requisitions of the law of 1832.

Mr. ROBINSON, from the Committee on Engrossed Bills, made a report of the examination of certain bills referred to that committee.

Mr. ROBINSON also presented a memorial from the Legislature of Illinois, on the subject of canals; which, on his motion, was referred to the Committee on Roads and Canals.

Mr. GRUNDY, in pursuance of notice given yesterday, introduced a bill to amend the several acts relative to the Post Office Department; which was read a first and second time, and referred to the Committee on Post Offices and Post Roads.

Mr. BELL, from the Committee on Claims, made a report unfavorable to the petition of Guy Bradford; which was ordered to lie on the table.

Mr. BELL, from the same committee, reported

a bill in favor of Caleb Starke, without amendment.

Mr. SILSBEE, from the Committee on Commerce, reported a bill in favor of Phineas Sprague, without amendment.

A communication, responsive to the following resolution of Mr. EWING—

"That the Secretary of State lay before the Senate a copy of the commission under which William 'J. Duane lately acted as Secretary of the Treasury, and a copy of the commission under which 'Roger B. Taney now acts as Secretary,"

Was made by the Secretary of State; which was ordered to lie on the table, and, with the accompanying documents, be printed.

Mr. BROWN, from the Committee on Claims, made an unfavorable report upon the petition of James Starke, and moved that the petitioner have leave to withdraw his papers, and that the committee be discharged from the further consideration of the same; which was agreed to.

Mr. BROWN, from the same committee, made a similar report in the case of the heirs of John Mercer, deceased; upon which a like order was made.

Mr. CHAMBERS moved that the report of the Commissioner of Public Buildings, now lying upon the table, be referred to the Committee of the District of Columbia, and be printed; which was agreed to.

Mr. POINDEXTER, from the Committee on Public Lands, made an unfavorable report upon the petition of John Martindale; which was concurred in.

Mr. POINDEXTER, from the same committee, reported unfavorably upon the petition of Andrew Henshaw, and moved that the petitioner have leave to withdraw his papers.

Mr. KING, of Alabama, suggested the peculiar hardships under which the petitioner labored, and moved to lay the report upon the table; which, after a few observations in reply by Mr. POINDEXTER, admitting the hardship of the case, was so directed to be done.

Mr. SWIFT submitted the following resolution:

Resolved, That the Committee on the Post Office and Post Roads be instructed to inquire into the expediency of establishing a post route from St. Alban's in Vermont, to Plattsburg, in New York.

Mr. KING, of Alabama, moved that the Senate take up, for consideration, the bill for the relief of Mountjoy Bailey.

Mr. WRIGHT stated that his object in moving to lay this bill on the table, some days ago, was to take this opportunity to settle the question whether interest should be allowed in all cases upon commutation or not. There were precedents, he remarked, on both sides.

The motion to take up the bill was rejected: Ayes 12, noes not counted.

Mr. KING, of Alabama, gave notice that he should, on Monday, ask leave to introduce a bill granting lands for the endowment of female schools in certain Western and Southwestern States.

Petitions and memorials were presented by Messrs. HENDRICKS, ROBINSON, WAGGAMAN, LINN, TOMLINSON, TIPTON, McKEAN, ROBBINS, WILKINS, and PRESTON, all of which were referred to appropriate committees. Among the petitions was one presented by Mr. McKEAN, praying the aid of the Government in rendering navigable the Susquehanna river.

ORDERS OF THE DAY.

The Senate then proceeded to the consideration of the several orders of the day, viz:

The resolution of Mr. BLACK,

That the Committee on the Judiciary be instructed to inquire into the expediency of directing by law the terms of the district court of the United States for the district of Mississippi, to be hereafter held at Jackson, the seat of government of that State.

The resolution of Mr. TOMLINSON,

That the Committee on Revolutionary Claims be instructed to inquire into the expediency of compensating Phineas Taylor, of Danbury, in the State of Connecticut, for a horse and other prop-

erty taken from him for public use during the revolutionary war.

The resolution of Mr. LINN,

That the Committee on Claims be instructed to inquire into the expediency of making compensation to Joseph T. Cirtick, for a boat taken from him by the officers of the General Government, during the last war with Great Britain.

The resolution of Mr. TIPTON,

That the Comittee on Claims be instructed to inquire into the expediency of paying Hiram A. Hunter, (now of Indiana,) for a horse lost by him while in the service of the United States, as orderly sergeant, in Captain Robert F. Crittenden's company of volunteers, in the Seminole campaign.

The resolution of Mr. TIPTON,

That the Committee on Claims be instructed to inquire into the expediency of granting indemnity to Samuel and James Smith, of Indiana, for improvements made by them on property of the United States, under a lease given claimants by the United States' trustees, on certain property of the United States.

The resolution of Mr. SPRAGUE,

That the Secretary of the Treasury be directed to communicate to the Senate, so far as the documents and returns received will permit, the amount of trade between the United States and the British North American Colonies, the British West Indies, the Danish West Indies, and the Swedish West Indies, since the 30th day of September, 1832—distinguishing the amount of American, British, and other foreign tonnage, which has entered and departed to and from these places respectively, or the West Indies generally. Also, the amount of imports and exports of American and foreign produce, distinguishing between the same.

All of which were adopted.

Upon the consideration of Mr. SPRAGUE'S resolution, Mr. SPRAGUE said, his object was to ascertain the present state of the trade and navigation between this country and the British Colonial possessions. It was a subject which had heretofore attracted much attention, and had now lost none of its intrinsic interest. It had been the subject of controversy between the United States and Great Britain from the origin of our Government to the year 1830, when the celebrated "Arrangement," as it was called, was made between the United States and Great Britain. The whole matter of the controversy was, whether the United States should have an equal and fair proportion of the carrying trade from our own ports to the British Colonies.

Sir, up to the year 1830, from the superior advantages of the United States, at least nine-tenths of the whole carrying trade was in our hands. The amount of British tonnage employed in the trade was only one-tenth of the amount of our tonnage. How is it since the arrangement? The very first year the British tonnage came up to forty-six per cent. of the whole amount. For 1832, the British tonnage employed in the trade was more than double that of the United States. In that year the British tonnage employed in navigation between the ports of the United States and the British Colonial ports was 146,292 tons, and the American tonnage was only 66,056. Since the arrangement of 1830, and he believed in consequence of it, our tonnage had dwindled from nine-tenths of the whole to less than half that of the British. He wished to have the means of ascertaining what was the present state of the trade.

On motion of Mr. SHEPLEY, it was

Resolved, That when the Senate adjourned, it adjourn until Monday.

A bill for the relief of Thomas Rhodes and Jeremiah Austin, was read a third time and passed.

A bill for the relief of Elihu Hall Bay being under consideration, on motion of Mr. CLAY, it was laid upon the table, and the Senate took up the subject of the

REMOVAL OF PUBLIC DEPOSITES.

The Senate resumed the consideration of the resolution submitted by Mr. CLAY, on the 26th ultimo.

Mr. BENTON resumed his remarks—

Having now got rid of the outworks which impeded his progress, Mr. B. said that he would arrive at the main point, and take up the subject which was more immediately before the Senate. For the sake of avoiding questions about order, he would give notice that he should submit at the proper time a motion in amendment of the second resolution under discussion, which amendment should be strictly appropriate and naturally flowing from the course of the argument he should follow. And first, he would take leave to read a paper replete with facts and sentiments applicable to the present attitude of the Bank of the United States and the Government of the United States, though written thirty years ago, and a reference to which he should have frequent occasion to make. It was part of a letter from the great apostle of American liberty (Mr. Jefferson) to Albert Gallatin.

Mr. KANE, at the request of Mr. B., read the paper.

"This institution is one of the most deadly hostility existing against the *principle* and the '*form* of our *Constitution*. The nation is, at this 'time, so strong and united in its sentiments, that 'it cannot be shaken at this moment; but suppose 'a series of untoward events to occur, sufficient to 'bring into doubt the competency of a *Republican* 'Government to meet a crisis of great danger, or '*to unhinge the confidence of the people in the public* '*functionaries;* an institution like this, *penetrating* 'by its branches every *part* of the Union, acting 'by *command* and in *phalanx*, may, in a critical 'moment, *upset the Government*. I deem no Government safe which is under the vassalage of any 'self-constituted authorities, or any other authority than that of the nation, or its regular functionaries. What an obstruction could not this Bank 'of the United States, with all its branches, be in 'time of war? It might dictate to us the peace we 'should accept, or withdraw its aids. *Ought we,* '*then, to give further growth to an institution so powerful, so hostile?* That it is so hostile, we know, '*first*, from a knowledge of the principles of the '*persons* composing the body of *directors* in every 'bank, principal or branch, and those of most of 'the stockholders; *secondly*, from their opposition 'to the *measures* and *principles* of the Government, 'and to the *election* of those friendly to them; and, '*thirdly*, from the sentiments of the *newspapers* 'they support. Now, while we are *strong*, it is the 'greatest duty we owe to the *safety* of our *Constitution*, to bring this *powerful enemy* to a perfect 'subordination under its authorities. The first 'measure would be to *reduce* them to an equal footing only with *other banks* as to the favors of the 'Government." (*That is, as to public deposites.*)—*Jefferson's letter to Gallatin*, 1803.

This brief extract, Mr. B. said, soared above party politics, and averred the Bank of the United States to be hostile to the *pinciples* and to the *form* of our Constitution; an assertion which would be proved to be true in the course of this debate. It recommended the people of the United States, while they were strong, to provide for the safety of their Constitution, and to bring the great enemy of their liberty under subordination to the laws, and to do it by depriving him of the public deposites, and thus reducing him to a level with State banks.

He would now take up one of the reasons for removing the deposites, and become infinitely stronger since for not restoring them. It was the expansion and contraction of currency. This was the vice of all banks, especially powerful ones, such as the Bank of England and that of the United States. To make fortunes for individuals connected with the bank—to favor gamblers in the stocks—was generally the object of these expansions and contractions; but political ends were sometimes the main object, and the acquisition of fortunes a secondary and subordinate one. Once in a certain number of years the cycle for these operations came on in England, and always attended with the making and breaking of many fortunes.

The last operation of the kind in England was performed in 1824–'5, and Mr. Baring, who gave an account of it in the British House of Commons, described the effect to be such that many millions changed hands, and men who in a regular train of business could have wound up with a clear estate of two hundred thousand pounds sterling, were left paupers on the hands of the parish. It was done by pouring out a flood of paper, lending money to everybody, then calling all in, and lending money to nobody but the favorites of the bank. This operation (Mr. B. said) had been three times performed in the United States by the present bank, first in 1818–'19 from mercenary motives, to gamble in the stocks and riot on the distresses of the country, and to make fortunes for the directors and their friends; once in 1831–'2 to effect a political object, when near thirty millions of loans were made in a few months, and suddenly called for at the appearance of the bank veto message; but the happy termination of the presidential election stopped the progress of the contraction, and gave the community time to breathe. The removal of the deposites was the next great occasion, and for the contraction and pressure at that time the bank began to prepare as soon as it was ascertained that the removal would be made. This was early in the last summer. Many circumstances, growing out of the state of the country and the legislation of Congress, favored the operation. The shortened credits on the revenue bonds was about to take effect; the cash payments on a part of the imports came into play at the same time; a great accumulation of revenue on hand, which made large balances against other banks in whose notes much of it was paid. All this made of themselves an unusually large demand for money in the commercial cities towards the close of the year. The bank took advantage of these circumstances to make her contraction the more violent upon the community; they prepared for it in secret for several months beforehand. The first great measure was to accumulate bills of exchange in the Atlantic cities, payable at a brief date, and all falling due about the same time. For this purpose a resolution was passed applicable to the "*five western branches*," as they were called, of the most insulting, degrading, and injurious nature. They were forbid to purchase bills of exchange except payable in one of the Atlantic cities, and with not more than ninety days to run. This extraordinary fact and extraordinary resolution was communicated to Congress in the report of the Government directors, which had been printed, and was now a part of our documents. It would be found at page 21 of the original report. Mr. B. called upon any member who stood in a relation to know the secrets of the bank to account for this extraordinary resolution, which prevented the western banks from dealing in exchange with one another, or giving any citizen a bill in one branch for his money at the place where another was, or taking from an exporter of western produce or a drover a bill payable in New Orleans or Charleston. He wished to hear a reason. To him the object stood revealed. It was to make a great accumulation of these bills in New York, Philadelphia, and Baltimore, towards the close of the year, and thus to increase the demand among the merchants for money in those places at the very moment that the bank intended to deny them all aid, and was to press them for former debts. The next great act of preparation on the part of the bank was incredible and diabolical: it was to dishonor its distant branch bank notes at that time, and thus render as unavailable as possible the masses of those notes which might be on hand.

Mr. B. regretted that he had to allude to this act without the proofs in hand. They had been called for, and furnished, and were now in the hands of the printer, and would be used by him on a future occasion, and he trusted that a proceeding would be had which would put the bank before a tribunal where the history of this incredible transaction would be brought to light. He alluded to a *scire facias* for the violation of the charter. He said that the notes of the branches had been dishonored at New York, at Baltimore, and at Mobile, about the same time, and at that time, in the crisis of this contraction, and with such similarity of circumstances as to announce that all was done with the connivance, if not with the orders of the Bank of the United States. He denied that there was any possible assignable reason for dishonoring the distant branch notes at this time. The bank was full of specie, five millions more than it had in 1832, at which time it considered about six millions to be enough, and the president of the bank treated as a mere surplus about five millions which had been parted with in a few months; the greater part being sold to France and England. Yet they

were refused for near a week in New York, till the cashier of the branch could first write, and then fly in person to the mother bank to get leave to receive them, perhaps about $50,000; refused the same way in Baltimore, until a like communication could be had with the mother bank; and refused absolutely and without explanation at the bank in Mobile, which was too distant to communicate with the mother bank. Mr. B. said that he stated these facts from a mere sight of the letters which proved them; the proof would be before the Senate soon, and he should endeavor to fix public attention upon a transaction which he might qualify as diabolical and infernal. The result of the whole was, that when all these circumstances growing out of the state of the country had made an unusual demand for money—when the bank had increased that demand by an extraordinary accumulation of bills of exchange—the contraction was commenced at the rate of several millions a month, including the bills at ninety days; and at the moment their own distant bank notes would have become unavailable in the hands of the holders if it had not been for the energy of the Secretary of the Treasury, who coerced the payments of the branch notes by those celebrated transfer drafts for about two millions and a quarter, the view of which, and the fear of more to follow, compelled the Bank of the United States to relax her policy, permit her branch notes to be received as usual, and thus saved the country from the shock of an unconvertible currency.

Mr. BENTON had, he said, already demonstrated that the present pressure in the money market was not only unnecessary, but wanton. He would now proceed to prove that the curtailment, so reprehensible in itself, was conducted in a manner which was illegal and violated the charter of the bank; and in the next place, he would prove that the curtailment was unequal and partial in its character and operation. He hoped that he fully felt the responsibility which he undertook in making charges against any individuals or bodies corporate out of this House, and it was from the thorough conviction that what he asserted could be proved, that he was induced to bring forward these charges; and, moreover, it was his intention to give the United States Bank a fair and full opportunity to vindicate itself from the charges, if they were unfounded.

First, the mode of curtailment was illegal. He repeated the words of the charter, stating that the business of the bank could not be transacted by less than seven directors, one of whom should be the president. These being the words, he held that the curtailment of twelve millions in five months, was a portion of that business which could be legally transacted only by a board of directors. Now, sir, here is a paper that has come before us as a public document, and may be taken as evidence of the truth of what it contains till it is contradicted. Mr. B. than read from the memorial of the Government directors, the following paragraph: which he read, and then said—

This, sir, shows that the curtailment was not made by the board of directors, nor even by a committee appointed by the board, but by the president. Yes, sir, this enormous pressure which was to bear upon the whole community, was the work of one single individual. It appears that the removal of the deposites being supposed to be probable, the bank began to take steps to meet it, as early as May or June, by curtailing its business.

The Government directors give us an account, in a narrative of several pages, of the steps taken to get at the reduction to be made. He read first an order of the board in May, directing a committee to report a plan of curtailment; and remarked, so far, so good. That resolution he held to be a wise one—but that was by the board and was legal. He read the resolution of the 13th of August, and the whole history of the curtailment, from the report of the Government directors.

"Resolved, That for the present, and until the 'further order of the board, the amount of bills 'discounted shall not be increased at the bank and 'the several offices. That the bills of exchange 'purchased at the bank, and all the offices, except 'the five western offices, shall not have more than '90 days to run. That the five western offices be 'instructed to purchase no bills of exchange, ex-

cept those payable in the Atlantic cities, not having more than ninety days to run, or those which may be received in payment of existing debts to the bank and the offices, and then not having more than four months to run."

"We perceived at once, in this measure, the commencement of a system of reduction, in conducting which, wisely and impartially, the welfare of the whole community was involved. No notice of these resolutions had been given, and therefore, while we concurred, as we stated, in the propriety and expediency of reducing the business of the institution, we required that the plan should be carefully weighed, so as to bear equally on all parts of the country, and on all debtors to the bank. We desired also to have the result of the views and inquiries of the committee already appointed. With these objects, we asked that the resolutions might be postponed for one week, or even until the next meeting, it being understood that the subject should be then definitely acted upon. Our request was refused. The resolutions were passed at once, and, as usual, by the vote of all present except one other director and ourselves. Believing that this measure was not only precipitate, but partial, and that it would lead to curtailments unequal and oppressive, and entertaining the opinion that a system might easily be formed, on a just basis, we offered the following resolution:

"Whereas a resolution was adopted on the 7th of May last, instructing the Committee on the state of the bank to report to the board a scale of reduction in the business of the institution, and no report has been made in pursuance thereof—And whereas, a resolution, passed at the last meeting, which places certain restrictions on the business of the institution, confines the same to five of the western offices:

"Resolved, That the Committee on the state of the bank be instructed to report to the board, at as early a day as possible, a system for the gradual reduction of the business of the institution throughout all sections of the country, having regard to the interest of the stockholders, the debtors of the bank, and the community in general."

"This plan, which would have prevented an oppressive and partial system of curtailment, confined to particular portions of the country, and exerted at particular times, which would have given to the subject full and fair consideration, and which, above all, would have enabled every member of the board to exercise his deliberate judgment, was as usual rejected. Nor was this all; when we offered the resolution, temperately expressed as it is, the president himself asked the question of consideration upon it, though no motion to that effect had been made—a course never before adopted in the board nor sanctioned by the by-laws, and evidently introduced to curtail more effectually, if possible, the very limited interference in the affairs of the institution which was still allowed to the public directors. On this suggestion of the president, the majority refused even to consider our resolution, by the vote of all present except one director and ourselves. This plan was persisted in, and subsequently carried still further. A series of resolutions were adopted for reducing the business of the institution, and authority was given to the committee on the offices, which is appointed by the president alone, to modify them in such manner as they should deem expedient; and eventually that committee was authorized to direct such measures for the general reduction of the business of the bank as they should think best. We offered, as an amendment to the resolution giving to a committee this extraordinary power, a request that 'they should report to the 'board such measures as they directed.' This request was rejected by the usual vote. It is of course impossible for us to know by what principles of policy the committee have been governed. The proceedings are secret, and we can only ascertain at intervals some of the results to which they had led. We attribute to them the excessive curtailment in the business of the institution, which has lately been so sudden and oppressive; and which was not necessary either to the extent to which it has been carried, or in the manner in which it has been made to bear on the community. With these sentiments, and in the hope

that the board itself might be induced, at a time like this, to interpose and to exercise for the welfare of the community some portion at least of that unlimited power it had intrusted to the committee, we lately offered the following resolutions:

"Whereas the pressure on the commercial community at this time may be removed by a liberal spirit of accommodation on the part of the banks generally; and whereas the State banks complain that in consequence of the balances being largely in favor of the Bank of the United States, they are unable to afford the necessary facilities to their customers without subjecting themselves to increased demands from this bank; and whereas it is believed, that were the banks in this district to extend their loans twenty per cent. beyond the income, for a period of thirty days, it would relieve the money market, restore confidence, and have a salutary effect on the industry and enterprise of our citizens: Therefore,

"Resolved, That a committee of three be appointed, to confer with similar committees that may be appointed by the other banks, for the purpose of uniting in some arrangement to carry into effect the object of the foregoing preamble; and that the cashier be requested to send copies of the above resolutions to the presidents and directors of the other banks, with a request that their determination on the subject may be communicated as early as practicable.'

"These resolutions, the effect of which would have been to produce a concert of action among the banks, for the relief of the mercantile community, at a period of difficulty, and to display on the part of the Bank of the United States a determination to afford it, which could not have been unsuccessful, the board refused even to consider; they were rejected in the usual summary manner, and the whole subject remains as before, in the power of the committee on the offices.

"It will thus be seen, that while the unlimited authority of the president to expend the funds of the bank had been deliberately confirmed, and while the committee on exchange, selected and appointed by him, had been officially permitted to discount notes and carry on the proper business of the board; now, in addition to all this, the measures of the institution in the regulation of its vast business, at this most important crisis, were intrusted to the committee on the offices, also selected and appointed by the president, accompanied by an explicit refusal to require them to report any of their acts to the board."

Mr. B. continued—

It was not to a breach of the by-laws that he alluded as a breach of the charter.

This high function of the board was delegated to a committee. This was equivalent to a delegation by Congress to one of its committees of that legislative power which the Constitution vests in the two Houses of Congress.

Here an authority is given to a committee 'to make an enormous reduction; an authority, too, unlimited by the terms of the resolution which bestows it. The whole power of the board is surrendered to a subaltern board. Sir, said Mr. BENTON, I denounce it as an atrocious violation of the charter of the bank. He hoped the question would be brought, for decision, before some tribunal competent to try the law and the facts, whether this was a violation of the charter and a forfeiture of it.

Does the Senate hear me?'exclaimed? Mr. B. This paper was a single individual whose ears had not caught the words, he would read them again. He reads, and exclaims:

The five Government directors appointed by the President and Senate of the United States, to represent seven millions of public stock, and to act as guardians over a greater amount of public deposites, were left in the dark as to the immense business which might be transacted by a committee, left to find out what was done, like mere strangers to the board!

One of these resolutions was, that the Bank of the United States should act in concert with the city banks in the adoption of measures for the relief of the money market. In what manner was it received by this imperious board? They would not even consider it! They did not consider and

then reject it, but they *refused to consider it*. They left their course to its results, be the effect on the community whatever it might.

I have not, Mr. President, said Mr. Benton, in the charge which I have made—no, sir, I cannot be considered as having made it, but the charge which I have brought out of the document which both Houses have ordered to be printed as a public document—against the bank for having violated and forfeited its charter in the mode of curtailment which it has carried on, one branch of the charges was, that the mode of curtailment was illegal, the other was that it was unequal and partial; and it was now for him to prove the assertion. He would have recourse to the same report of the Government directors, (page 14.) Two facts only, out of a number, he would bring before the Senate, which would show the favoritism and inequality of this curtailment. On the 16th of August, we find the extent of the authority assumed, one hundred thousand dollars was loaned to one individual.

"On the 16th of August, we perceived a striking 'instance of the extent of authority they assumed. 'We observed that, a week before, a single loan 'of no less than one hundred thousand dollars was 'made by the committee to one person, without 'any authority from the board, although it had 'been in session that very day; although the proposition for the loan must have been made before 'the meeting of the board, for it was submitted to 'the committee, by its chairman, immediately on 'the adjournment, and although the board had, 'on the same day, refused good mercantile paper. 'When we made inquiry, we ascertained that the 'loan was not in fact done for the person whose 'name was entered on the books, but for a bank 'of which he was a director, and on account of a 'large debt then due from it to the Bank of the 'United States, the regular payment of which was 'thus postponed. We cannot doubt that the board 'would have refused this proposal, had it been 'submitted to them; but however that might have 'been, the assumption of such a power, exercised 'in such a manner by the committee, is not to be 'sanctioned, unless the other members of the 'board have become utterly useless."

Although the board had the same day refused the paper of good men, merchants in the city, on the 16th day of August, when the curtailment was in full operation, the exchange committee, without the authority of the board, discounted one hundred thousand dollars to an individual, and refused the business paper of mercantile men, though well endorsed. He held that it was an improper partiality, at the very moment when the screws were turning on the merchants of Philadelphia, to make such a loan to an individual. Who was that individual? He figures at the head of a memorial praying for the restoration of the deposites! He was one of those who were busy in getting up public meetings and *fac simile* memorials in favor of the restoration of the deposites, which were to be repeated in showers from every part of the country, like the memorials which two years ago we had in favor of the renewal of the charter. Could anything be a more remarkable evidence of favoritism and partiality, than this screwing of one part of the community with one hand, and, with the other, pouring out favors upon those who were to aid the bank in getting up excitements and sending memorials to Congress.

Mr. B. read again:

"Another instance was lately exhibited of the 'injustice arising from this unlimited and irresponsible power of the committee on exchange. The 'policy adopted by the board has caused curtailments in the loans to the community to a great 'extent. These ought at least to be *general* in their 'operation. Yet, on a loan for a very large sum, 'secured on stock, being offered for renewal on the '8th of November, all reduction was refused, on 'the ground that it had been originally made by 'the committee on exchange, some years before, 'for an indefinite period, and that the faith of the 'bank was therefore pledged for its continuance. 'These resolutions, passed three years since, at a 'time when there was great abundance of money, ''authorized the committee on exchange to loan 'large sums on approved collateral securities.' Assuming, by virtue of these, a power which we believe the board never intended to confer, they have 'thus entered, it seems, into contracts which will 'extend to the *termination of the charter, if not beyond it*. These contracts, too, so far as we can 'learn, were not reduced to writing—in fact, the 'notes themselves were drawn at the usual short 'periods. It is now, at least, apparent that these 'proceedings were at variance with the true policy 'of the institution, and that they operate unequally 'on the community, whose interests ought to be 'impartially consulted."

The name of this individual was not given, but there were circumstances which would enable him (Mr. B.) to identify him. The committee appointed two years ago to investigate the affairs of the bank, reported that a loan of eleven hundred thousand dollars was made, at one time, to a broker, who was a relative of the president of the bank—a loan, too, for an indefinite term of years, and at five per cent. interest. This, sir, was the loan on which no reduction was to be made—a loan standing at five per cent., when the merchants were driven to the brokers for money, at exorbitant premiums, to maintain their credit. There was an entire class of debtors to the bank, who were not subjected at all to the curtailment; but they were politicians and friends, and men who were busy in getting up meetings, for the purpose of producing that instantaneous action which was to restore the deposites to the bank, without any examination into the truth of the charges made against it.

I trust, Mr. President, continued Mr. B., that I have now made out the case of illegality, partiality, favoritism, and violation of the charter, upon the testimony of a document which would stand before us, and before the American people, as true, until it should be disproved. He would not go further into instances of favoritism; they were abundant, but time forbade the detail.

He wished now to say a word of the meetings everywhere getting up to influence Congress on the subject of the deposites—to coerce their "*instantaneous restoration*." He had observed that merchants were often engaged in these meetings. Allow me to say, sir, that my historical reading, and my professional studies, have led me to entertain an exalted opinion, and high respect, for merchants as a body. He need not go back to the middle ages, when merchants were the founders of States, and raised the free cities of Italy to a level with kingdoms and empires. He would refer to the merchants of England and America, who had a potential voice with statesmen in all matters of finance and commerce. The opinions of such men, whenever expressed, would command from him respect and deference; but to maintain their right to that respect and deference, they must express the opinions of *merchants*, and not of *political partisans*. Their meetings must be those of merchants, in which they speak and act for themselves, and not the meetings of lawyers and politicians, in which the merchants made no figure. In such meetings, the voice coming from merchants was lost; it was their own fault for merging their own high character in that of faction. The heat and passion of a political meeting was not their theatre when they wished to enlighten the councils of the nation in matters of finance and commerce, and they must not think it amiss if they shared the fate of their company, and saw their opinions no better treated than those of lawyers and partisan politicians.

Mr. B. then descanted, with some keenness, upon the *fac simile* meetings which were getting up all over the United States, and adopting resolutions bearing the impress of the same mint, to coerce Congress into "*immediate action*." He treated the motives of such meetings with considerable levity, made some cuts at lawyers and politicians who could decide all the points connected with the immense question of removing and restoring the public deposites, without evidence, without facts, without hearing but a small piece of one side of the question, and then put forth their resolves to govern the opinions of the country. He said he should not pay much regard to such sudden verdicts, although they might be communicated by a procession of *grown men*, who should make a circuit round the city, like the soldiers of Joshua round the walls of Jericho, and deliver their resolves in a blast of rams' horns, loud enough to blow down the walls of the Capitol.

[The hour for making up our paper having arrived, we are obliged to close the report. It will be continued on Monday.]

Mr. BENTON, without concluding, gave way to a motion to adjourn, and,

On motion of Mr. GRUNDY, the Senate adjourned.

HOUSE OF REPRESENTATIVES.

FRIDAY, *January* 3, 1834.

The following bills were reported from standing committees, read twice, and committed, viz:

By Mr. WATMOUGH, a bill relative to naval schools.

By Mr. EVANS, a bill granting pensions to certain persons therein named.

By Mr. CAMBRELENG, a bill to exempt merchandise imported under certain circumstances, from the operation of the provisions of the act of 19th May, 1828, in alteration of the several acts imposing duties on imports.

By Mr. MUHLENBERG, a bill for the relief of the legal representatives of John M. Gregory.

By Mr. CHINN, a bill for the relief of the widow and heirs of Lewis P. Davidson.

Also, a bill for the relief of Edmund Brooke.

By Mr. WHITTLESEY, of Ohio, a bill for the relief of James Kilgore.

By Mr. YOUNG, a bill for the relief of the legal representatives of Benjamin Bird and ——— Pomeroy.

By Mr. BOULDIN, a bill for the relief of the legal representatives of Amasa Soper, deceased.

Mr. WARDWELL, from the Committee on Revolutionary Pensions, reported a bill authorizing the Secretary of War to establish a pension agency in the town of Decatur, Alabama, and to provide for the payment of certain pensioners in said town; which was read twice, and ordered to be engrossed and read a third time.

Mr. MERCER, from the Committee on Roads and Canals, reported the following resolution, which, under a rule of the House, lies one day on the table:

Resolved, That the Secretary of the Treasury be directed to lay before this House a copy of any contract which may have been made by that department for the construction of a bridge over the Potomac river opposite to the city of Washington, and to transmit with the same the names of the contractors and their sureties, if any, and copies of such reports or estimates, if any, as have been made of the plan and probable cost of such bridge, and a statement of any sums of money that may have been paid, or have become due, under such contract.

The following resolution, heretofore offered by Mr. SELDEN, was taken up:

Resolved, That the Committee of Ways and Means be instructed to report a bill requiring the commissioners of the sinking fund forthwith to purchase or otherwise redeem the five per cent. stocks of the United States, and directing the Secretary of the Treasury from time to time to place under the control of said commissioners such funds, not otherwise required for the purpose of the Government, as shall be necessary for that object, and in case of deficiency to sell so much of the stock of the Bank of the United States belonging to the Government as will enable them to complete the purchase.

The resolution was briefly debated by Messrs. SELDEN and CAMBRELENG, when

Mr. POLK moved to amend it by striking out the instructions to the committee to "report a bill," and directing them merely to "inquire into the expediency" of the proposed measure.

And the resolution, as amended, was agreed to.

Mr. LANE then rose to address the House on the subject, but the hour allotted to morning business having expired, he was precluded from proceeding.

The SPEAKER communicated a letter from the Secretary of the Navy, transmitting copies of the Annual Navy Register.

ORDERS OF THE DAY.

The House then went into Committee of the Whole, Mr. POLK in the chair, on the following private bills:

A bill for the relief of John Webber.
A bill for the relief of Abraham Forbes.
A bill for the relief of Alexander Boyd.
A bill for the relief of Ezekiel Foster.
A bill for the relief of the owners of the schooner Three Sisters.
A bill for the relief of Philip Beasom.
A bill for the relief of the representatives of Joseph Rowe, deceased.
A bill for the relief of Horatio N. Crabb.
A bill for the relief of John G. Reynolds.
A bill for the relief of John Percival and others.
A bill for the relief of Francis and Judith Taylor,
A bill for the relief of the representatives of George Hurl, deceased.
A bill for the relief of the heirs of Presley Thornton, deceased.
A bill for the relief of Thomas Minor.
A bill for the relief of the representatives of Enos Grennis.
A bill for the relief of John Lobdell; and
A bill for the relief of Thomas Ap Catesby Jones.
The committee rose, reported the bills to the House, and they were ordered to be engrossed and read a third time.
On motion of Mr. P. THOMAS, it was ordered that when the House adjourn it will adjourn to meet on Monday.
The House then again resolved itself into Committee of the Whole (Mr. ELLSWORTH in the chair) on the following bills:
A bill granting pensions to several persons therein named.
A bill for the relief of Francis Barham, and others;
A bill for the relief of Aaron Bellamy.
A bill for the relief of Luther L. Smith.
A bill for the relief of Pearson Freeman.
A bill for the relief of the representative of Buller Claiborne, deceased.
A bill for the relief of the heirs and legal representatives of Doctor John Berrien.
A bill to extend the term of certain pensions charged on the privateer pension fund.
A bill to compensate Susan Decatur.
A bill making certain allowances, as to the captains, &c., of the marine corps.
A bill for the relief of the widow, &c., of George Ludlum, deceased.
A bill for the relief of Coleman Fisher.
A bill supplementary to the act for the relief of Guarringer Flaujac, of Louisiana.
A bill for the relief of Chasterlain and Pouvert.
A bill for the relief of Lucy Loomis.
A bill for the relief of Archibald Small.
A bill for the relief of Joel Wright.
A bill for the relief of Nathaniel Patten.
A bill for the relief of Ann Mortimer Barron.
And a bill for the relief of the representatives of Everard Meale.
The committee rose and reported the bills to the House, with the exception of the bill to compensate Susan Decatur, which, on motion of Mr. PATTON, was passed over, and the committee asked leave to sit again on the same, which was granted. The bills for the relief of the widow, &c., of George Ludlum, deceased, and for the relief of Nathaniel Patten, were postponed till Friday next, and the residue of the bills reported from the Committee of the Whole, were ordered to be engrossed and read a third time.
On motion of Mr. CLAY, a Committee on Enrolled Bills, to consist of five members, was ordered to be appointed.
The House then adjourned until Monday.

TURNER'S FALLS.—These exist in Connecticut river, near the point where the towns of Montague, Gill, and Greenfield meet. They are by far the most interesting waterfalls in the State, and I think I may safely say in New England. At least, to my taste, the much broader sheet of water, the higher perpendicular descent, and the equally romantic scenery of the surrounding country give to this cataract a much higher interest than is excited by a view of the more celebrated Bellows' Falls, on the same river, in Walpole, New Hampshire, and probably the latter are generally regarded as the most striking object of this kind in New England.

Above Turner's Falls the Connecticut, for about three miles, pursues a course nearly northwest, through a region scarcely yet disturbed by cultivation; and all this distance it is as placid as a mountain lake, even to the verge of the cataract. Here an artificial dam has been erected, more than a thousand feet long, resting near the centre upon two small islands. Over this dam the water leaps more than thirty feet perpendicularly, and for half a mile continues descending rapidly, and foaming along its course. One hundred rods below the falls, the stream strikes directly against a lofty greenstone ridge, by which it is compelled to change its course towards the south at least a quarter of a circle.

The proper point for viewing Turner's Falls is from the road leading to Greenfield, on the north shore, perhaps fifty rods below the cataract. Here, from elevated ground, you have directly before you the principal fall, intersected near the centre by two small rocky islands, which are crowned with trees and brushwood. The observer perceives at once that Niagara is before him in miniature. These islands may be reached by a canoe from above the falls in perfect safety. Fifty rods below the cataract, a third most romantic little island lifts its evergreen head, an image of peace and security, in the midst of the agitated and foaming waters, swiftly gliding by. The placid aspect of the waters above the fall, calmly emerging from the moderately elevated and wooded hills at a distance, is finely contrasted with its foam and tumult above the cataract.

The country around the falls is but little cultivated. On the opposite side of the river the observer will, indeed, perceive a few dwellings and the head of a canal; but a little beyond, wooded elevations, chiefly covered with evergreens, terminate the landscape; while in every other direction, the scenery is still more wild and unreclaimed from a state of nature.

A sailing excursion from the falls, three miles up the stream, has all the attractions of a passage over a mountain lake. And probably the coves along the shore furnish as good sports for fishing as now exist in the river. The geologist too, will find the vicinity of these falls full of interest.

During high water, the roar of Turner's Falls may be heard from six to ten miles. The magnificence of the cataract is greatly heightened at such a season.

In order to visit Turner's Falls, one must turn aside from every great public road; and although but four miles from the village of Greenfield, this circumstance shows why they are so seldom resorted to by travellers.—*Hitchcock's Geological Report.*

. OLD BRANDY.—We are informed by the collector from Great Egg Harbor, that during the late gale, four pipes of brandy and some pieces of silk were found on Peck's Beach, which no doubt came from the brig Perseverance, wrecked on that beach eighteen years ago. The liquor possesses all the good properties of age, but tasted strongly of bilge water. It was sold on the 25th by the commissioner of wrecks, in Cape May county, for 63 a 76 cents a gallon. The silk was as bright and nearly as strong as new. The Perseverance was from Bordeaux, bound to Philadelphia, bilged and sunk in the year 1815.—*Philadelphia Coffee House Books.*

It is said the police duties in London, are much more active during the sitting of Parliament, as the thieves, when that body is prorogued, follow the aristocracy into the country. Every class of animals, like those of the vegetable kingdom, are infested with a particular class of parasites and vermin that feed upon them.

It is not, perhaps, generally known in this country, that one of the most gifted and powerful writers and poets of the age, Allan Cunningham, was a mason by trade, and is at present, and has been for years, occupying the humble birth of foreman in the workshop of the celebrated sculptor Chantrey, at London. Allan is about publishing a new edition of his Life of Burns, and other works.

The herring, salmon, and other fisheries of G. Britain alone, amount to £700,000 per annum, and employ over eighty thousand persons.

Some robbers at London were lately discovered upon the roof of a house, from which, contrary to their usual custom, they were about making a descent into the apartments below. The night being dark, the people set fire to the chimney, by the help of which, the culprits were pursued and taken.

A member of Parliament presenting a petition of the weavers, complaining of the pressure of the times and want of employ, said they had worked so hard and spun so much yarn, that they had not a shirt to cover their backs.

From the recent numerous murders committed in England, by administering arsenic, and the pretext set up by the accused that the poison was purchased to destroy rats, and from the narrow escape from death of three children while asleep, who were attacked by a ferocious rat, we should imagine that the country was overrun with the vermin.

The new police lately created in London being under the direction of the Government, has awakened the jealousy of the people, who apprehend that it may become an engine of despotic power and tyrannical espionage, as in France and some other countries.

The back numbers of the Congressional Globe are exhausted, or will be before this sheet reaches subscribers. Therefore, those who may subscribe hereafter, cannot be furnished with a complete file.

THE CONGRESSIONAL GLOBE.

PRINTED AND PUBLISHED AT THE CITY OF WASHINGTON, BY BLAIR & RIVES.

23d Congress, 1st Session.   SATURDAY, JANUARY 11, 1834.   Vol. I........No. 6.

[The conclusion of Mr. Polk's speech on Thursday, January 2d, commenced in the last number of the Congressional Globe, cannot be continued in this, for want of room.]

IN SENATE.

MONDAY, January 6, 1834.

A message was received by the hands of Mr. Donelson, his Private Secretary, from the President of the United States, stating that he had received a communication from the consul of the United States at Tangier, advising him that he had obtained a present, in his official character, of a lion and two horses; but conceiving that he had no right, under the Constitution, which he felt himself bound to support, to accept these presents, he thought it to be his duty to submit the animals to the control of the national authorities.

Mr. CLAY remarked that he had an idea of moving that the message be referred to the Committee on Agriculture; but, upon reflection, he moved that it be referred to the Committee on Foreign Relations; which was agreed to.

Mr. WAGGAMAN presented the credentials of the Hon. ALEXANDER PORTER, a Senator from the State of Louisiana, in the place of the Hon. Josiah S. Johnston, deceased; which were read; and took his seat.

Mr. WEBSTER, from the Committee on Finance, reported a bill from the House of Representatives, making appropriations for the service of the Government, with amendments; which were considered; and, after some explanatory remarks by Mr. WEBSTER, was ordered to be read a third time.

Mr. POINDEXTER, from the Committee on Public Lands, reported a bill for the relief of John Pusbell.

Mr. POINDEXTER, from the same committee, also reported a bill in favor of the widow and heirs of Felix Adrain.

Mr. POINDEXTER, from the same committee, reported unfavorably to the petition of the Common Council of ———.

Also, unfavorably to the petition of Stephen P. Payne, for a township of land for missionary services rendered by him.

The VICE PRESIDENT presented a communication from the Secretary of State, responsive to the following resolution of Mr. EWING, which was inadvertently stated by our reporter to have been presented to the Senate on Friday:

Resolved, That the Secretary of State lay before the Senate a copy of the commission under which William J. Duane lately acted as Secretary of the Treasury, and a copy of the commission under which Roger B. Taney now acts as Secretary.

Which was read, and ordered to be printed.

Mr. WHITE submitted the following resolution:

Resolved, That the Secretary of War be, and he hereby is, requested to transmit to the Senate, a copy of the evidence furnished him by Mountjoy Bailey, to prove that he was entitled to his commission of five years full pay, as a captain in the Maryland Line in the war of the Revolution, and that he never received the same from the United States, agreeably to the proviso in the act of Congress of the 26th May, 1830, entitled "An act for the relief of Mountjoy Bailey."

Which was adopted, the standing order being dispensed with by unanimous consent.

Mr. McKEAN presented memorials from certain State Banks in Pennsylvania, asking that the public deposites might be restored to the Bank of the United States; which, on his motion, were ordered to be upon the table, and be printed.

Mr. TIPTON submitted the following resolution:

Resolved, That the Committee of Commerce be instructed to inquire into the expediency of an appropriation for erecting a light-house at Michigan City, on Lake Michigan, in the State of Indiana, and of establishing a port of delivery at that place.

Mr. SHEPLEY offered the following resolution:

Resolved, That the Committee on Military Affairs be instructed to inquire into the expediency of making an appropriation for the repair of the military road constructed by the United States in the State of Maine, leading from the river Mattanawcook to Houlton.

Mr. SHEPLEY submitted the following resolution:

Resolved, That the Secretary of War be directed to communicate to the Senate any information within the department showing the injury done by storms during the month of December last to the pier on the western side of the entrance to Kennebunk river in the State of Maine, and the necessity of an immediate repair; and to furnish an estimate of the sum required to make the necessary repairs.

Mr. KING, of Alabama, in pursuance of notice the other day, introduced a bill granting a certain amount of public lands for the benefit of female schools in particular States, which was read twice, and referred to the Committee on Public Lands.

ORDERS OF THE DAY.

The resolution of Mr. HENDRICKS—

Resolved, That the Committee on Roads and Canals be instructed to inquire into the expediency of making a further appropriation for the construction of the Cumberland road in the States of Ohio, Indiana, and Illinois.

The resolution of Mr. HENDRICKS—

Resolved, That the Committee on Pensions be instructed to inquire into the expediency of placing upon the pension list applicants who shall be able to prove three months' service in the revolutionary war, agreeably to the requisitions of the law of 1832.

The resolution of Mr. SWIFT—

Resolved, That the Committee on the Post Office and Post Roads be instructed to inquire into the expediency of establishing a post route from St. Alban's, in Vermont, to Plattsburg, in New York.

Were severally taken up and adopted.

A bill for the relief of Noah Stayley;
A bill for the relief of John Kimberlin;
Were severally ordered to a third reading.
A bill for the relief of Andrew Knox being under consideration, Mr. BLACK moved an amendment, and suggested that it lie upon the table, but at a subsequent hour it was taken up on motion of Mr. POINDEXTER, and the amendment, ordered to be engrossed.

The bill for the relief of Eli Robinson being called up, Mr. MOORE moved that it be made the special order for Monday next, but at the suggestion of Mr. NAUDAIN it was laid upon the table upon the motion of Mr. MOORE.

Petitions and memorials were presented during the morning, by Senators SILSBEE, SPRAGUE, McKEAN, and LINN; among them the memorial of certain citizens asking the construction of a breakwater at Sandy Bay in Massachusetts.

The Senate then proceeded to the special order of the day.

REMOVAL OF PUBLIC DEPOSITES.

The Senate resumed the consideration of the resolutions submitted by Mr. CLAY on the 26th ultimo.

Mr. BENTON continued—[We are compelled to omit his remarks in the Congressional Globe for want of room.]

HOUSE OF REPRESENTATIVES.

MONDAY, January 6, 1834.

Mr. SELDEN presented the memorial of the Board of Trade of the city of New York, on the subject of the currency. Mr. S. remarked, that a memorial had been published in the newspapers, without the knowledge or approbation of the Board of Trade. This board, he would add, represented the great body of New York merchants who were engaged in the internal trade of the country. The memorial was referred to the Committee of Ways and Means.

Mr. BINNEY presented a similar memorial from the Board of Trade, in Philadelphia, and remarked that, as the memorialists had gone more at length into the causes of the existing distress, consequent upon the present derangement of the currency, and suggested remedies to alleviate it, he desired to have it read. It was read accordingly, referred to the Committee of Ways and Means, and ordered to be printed.

The SPEAKER presented a memorial from a meeting of merchants, held in Philadelphia, of which Mr. Robert Patterson was chairman, on the same subject; which was also referred to the Committee of Ways and Means.

The SPEAKER presented a memorial from Commodore Barron, stating that he had invented a steam plough-ship, calculated for the destruction of ships of war; which was referred to the Committee on Naval Affairs.

On motion of Mr. PINCKNEY,

Resolved, That the Committee on Revolutionary Claims be instructed to inquire into the expediency of making compensation to the heirs and legal representatives of John Gordon, deceased, who served as an officer during the revolutionary war, in the Legion commanded by Colonel Henry Lee, and that the papers accompanying this resolution be committed to said committee.

On motion of Mr. FOSTER,

Resolved, That the Committee on Revolutionary Pensions be instructed to inquire into the expediency of placing the names of Thomas Leverett, William Brooks, and Benjamin Joiner, of the State of Georgia, on the roll of revolutionary pensioners: and that the papers and documents herewith presented be referred to said committee.

On motion of Mr. LYTLE,

Resolved, That the Committee on Commerce be instructed to inquire into the expediency of making an appropriation in aid of the marine hospital of Cincinnati.

On motion of Mr. LYTLE,

Resolved, That the Committee on the Post Office and Post Roads be instructed to inquire into the expediency of authorizing the Postmaster General to contract for the transportation of the mail by steamboat navigation from Louisville to New Orleans.

The CHAIR presented a message from the President of the United States, which was read as follows:

WASHINGTON, *January* 6, 1834.

To the House of Representatives:

I communicate to Congress an extract of a letter recently received from James R. Leib, consul of the United States at Tangier, by which it appears that that officer has been induced to receive from the Emperor of Morocco a present of a lion and two horses, which he holds as belonging to the United States. There being no funds at the disposal of the Executive applicable to the objects stated by Mr. Leib, I submit the whole subject to the consideration of Congress, for such direction as in their wisdom may seem proper.

I have directed instructions to be given to all our ministers and agents abroad, requiring, that, in future, unless previously authorized by Congress, they will not, under any circumstances, accept presents of any description from any foreign State.

I deem it proper, on this occasion, to invite the attention of Congress to the presents which have heretofore been made to our public officers, and which have been deposited, under the orders of the Government, in the Department of State. Those articles are altogether useless to the Gov-

ernment; and the care and preservation of them in the Department of State are attended with considerable inconvenience.

That provision of the Constitution which prohibits any officer, without the consent of Congress, to accept any present, from any foreign power, may be considered as having been satisfied by the surrender of the articles to the Government, and they might now be disposed of by Congress to those for whom they were originally intended, or to their heirs, with obvious propriety in both cases—and in the latter would be received as grateful memorials of the character of the present.

As, under the positive order now given, similar presents cannot hereafter be received, even for the purpose of being placed at the disposal of the Government, I recommend to Congress to authorize by law, that the articles already in the Department of State, shall be delivered to the persons to whom they were originally presented, if living, and to the heirs of such as may have died.

ANDREW JACKSON.

The House suspended the rule, for the purpose of enabling Mr. LEWIS, of Alabama, to offer the following resolution:

Resolved, That the Committee on Indian Affairs be instructed to inquire whether the provisions of the treaty of March, 1832, with the Creek tribe of Indians, in the State of Alabama, be inconsistent with the sovereign right of jurisdiction of said State, within its limits; and whether the execution of said treaty has so far conflicted, or is likely to conflict, with the operation of the laws of said State over the country ceded by such treaty, and if so, to inquire whether some act of legislation, consistent with the rights of said Indians, may not be necessary to prevent such conflict; and that said committee have leave to report by bill, or otherwise.

Mr. L. said, he felt it his duty to submit to the House the reasons that induced him to bring this subject before the House. It was for the purpose of preventing any conflict between the Executive and the authorities of the State of Alabama. It might be sufficient for him in the outset to state, that long before the execution of the treaty made with the Indians in Alabama, the lands in question had been under the jurisdiction of the State, and the laws of Alabama were in full force over the country, when the Government of the United States claimed the right, under the act of 1807, to send there the deputy marshal to impede such improvements as were made by resident inhabitants of the State, and to remove them as intruders. This power in the treaty was objected to at the time the treaty was made by the people of Alabama, but it was supposed that all matters connected with it would be subjected to the decision of the judicial tribunals of Alabama. The recent act of the Government, however, amounted to a total abolition of the State jurisdiction. It was hoped, that as the execution of the orders for the removal had been delayed, there would not be any further action on those orders, and the people of the State had a right to believe so. The subject had not been alluded to in the annual message, as he contended it was the duty of the President to have done, that Congress might have its attention called to such a state of things, and have taken such measures as would have prevented the possibility of any conflicts. But he supposed this was not done in this instance, because the Executive thought proper to do what was now become an every day practice, to exert the military power of the Government at his will against the constituted State authorities, without deigning to inform Congress. Upon consultation with his colleagues, they agreed with him in opinion, that it was hardly possible that the Government would proceed in the steps they have taken to remove the persons from the lands, as it was impossible that the contemplated locations could be made before the 15th of this month, the time named in the order for removal. He had, however, applied to the Secretary of War to delay the execution of the order, that the locations might be made, and the removal rendered unnecessary, and he had received his answer, that the time could not be lengthened, and that the order was not revoked. He, under these circumstances, felt it his duty to offer this resolution. He had a further object in submitting it, that it might immediately arrest the action of the Executive, who would, he hoped, not feel it his duty to enforce the orders, whilst the subject itself was before the House, and when he, as a representative from the State of Alabama, had applied for a repeal of the law, under which the right of removal was claimed.

He could not anticipate that any objections would be made to the resolution, as it was one simply of inquiry, and was presented with a view to prevent any collision by force, and did not compromise the rights or merits of either side of the question. It might be objected that Congress had no jurisdiction in this case; that it had no power to violate a treaty which had been duly ratified; but if, on inquiry, the treaty itself was found to be unconstitutional, he maintained that it was not only the right, but it was the duty of Congress to repeal the act, and they could, if necessary, indemnify any party who might have claims for indemnity upon the country in consequence of it. Gentlemen might speak of the obligations of treaties, and of the necessity that existed for fulfilling their stipulations; but he thought a stronger and higher duty was imposed on them, namely, to preserve the Constitution of the country—to preserve the rights of the States, which, resting on the Constitution as their basis, could not in any respect be impaired without a gross violation of that Constitution. He hoped the House, considering the collision which had already taken place, and what was still likely to take place, if the orders of the Executive were not delayed, would be induced to reconsider the basis upon which the treaty was founded, and thus prevent a resort to military force, the *ultima ratio regum*. He would remark, in anticipation of objections as to the powers of Congress, in cases where treaties were made, as it was a mooted point, whether Congress had the power to withhold an appropriation for a treaty that had been ratified, that treaties could not be made except between sovereigns, and that he maintained the Creek Indians could not be considered a sovereign State or people, at the time the treaty was made, as they and their lands were then subject to, and under the acknowledged laws of Alabama. He believed that a timely survey of the lands would have prevented all this difficulty. He did not impute blame to any person for this delay; but felt that it was unfortunate, and that a greater delay had taken place than was expected. The people of Alabama had no right to suppose that the present conflict could have arisen between them and the present Executive, knowing that the President had on so many occasions notoriously asserted the complete right of the States to extend their laws over the Indian tribes within their limits. But if the act of 1807 had been, or is to be now enforced, he would show not only that the President did not on other occasions believe it his duty, but if he did, that he knowingly and willingly violated his duty in not acting upon it. The President had, in the conflict between the State authorities in Georgia, and the Cherokee and Choctaw tribes, expressly recognised the right of that State; he did not enforce the law against the State authorities in that case, because he believed it to be incompatible with their rights. Georgia took the Indian lands—had them surveyed, and since disposed of by lottery, and yet their acts were not called in question, nor any military force displayed, as was recently done at Fort Mitchell. The Indians had not originally made any other stipulation in the treaty, than that "they were to remain on the lands until their crops were gathered." The State had reason to suppose that they would have removed immediately upon that being done, and were justified in extending their laws and taking the country under their jurisdiction.

So far from deserving punishment, these settlers were considered as pioneers and were encouraged as such both by the Government and the State of Alabama. No government land had been so profitably sold as that which was settled by those pioneers. It was not true that they injured the lands in any respect or incommoded the Indians. They had also the express pledge of the Government that they should not be removed till the selections were made. Yet military force has been employed to remove persons as intruders who settled by express permission from the Secretary of War. Their numbers had now increased to thirty thousand, and he submitted to the House, with what propriety their instantaneous removal had been ordered, after repeated declarations from the Government that they should remain till the selections were made." Mr. Speaker, it is a matter of curiosity to look at the cause of that change of policy. Why has the President so suddenly changed his views? It is not pretended that the public lands have sustained any injury from the settlers, or that they have set up an adverse title to that of the United States, or that they have interfered with the rights of the Indians. On the contrary, the interests of the Indians have been promoted by the settlement; many of the Indians had reservations to sell, the value of which was increased by the competition of the settlers. But still those settlers were to be driven away—for what purpose? To enable a few government pet agents and surveyors to purchase these very reservations for a trifle. It was under the influence of those individuals that the order for the removal of the Indians had been given. The character of the settlers, for this purpose, had been slandered by these men, and the feelings of the Indians towards the settlers had been grossly misrepresented. The great body of the Indians never did oppose the settlement of these people among them. No two people, he would undertake to say, distinct in language, color, and habits, ever lived together more harmoniously. The rights of the Indians were respected and protected. The laws were equitably enforced against all persons who infringed, in any way, upon their rights. Public opinion there would not tolerate the least injustice to an Indian. He knew the character of the settlers of that country—they were his constituents, and he knew that they were unjustly represented as intruders on the public lands. Their character was as respectable—he called his colleagues to witness—as that of any portion of the people of Alabama. They had been slandered by those who were interested in procuring their removal. These people were not intruders, within the meaning of the laws. They had settled under the protection of the Government of the State of Alabama and of the United States, with a view to become purchasers of Indian reservations. The deputy marshal now undertook, upon *ex parte* testimony, to decide who were intruders. The jurisdiction of the courts of Alabama, in all cases of trespass, was wholly set aside. If a white man intruded upon the Indians, relief was given by our laws; but it was now to be given summarily by the United States' marshal. The Executive was impatient of the law's delay, and he orders the marshal to decide, and to enforce his decision by the bayonet of the United States as soon as it is made. One individual had already lost his life in consequence of this usurpation of authority—a more atrocious act than the murder of Owens was never perpetrated in any country calling itself free. Here Mr. L. read an account of the transaction, as given by the deputy marshal. Thus a citizen of Alabama was shot down by order of a deputy marshal under the instructions of the President. With the deputy, he had nothing to do. His case was before the proper tribunal. My business, is with the President, by whose order the act was done. I hold the Government responsible for the deed, until it disavows it. The Secretary of War justified the act. Is the army and navy to be prostituted to such purposes of oppression? If so, I will vote for their abolition. We want no such aid to the Executive power. They ought to be disbanded to-morrow, if they are kept up, not for foreign foes, but to enforce Executive decrees. If the army was the bulldog of the President, ready to make an attack and draw blood at his bidding, he submitted whether the military power did not govern in Alabama, and whether the republican form of government guarantied to each State by the Constitution, now existed there. Where is the law? In the mouth of a deputy marshal. Who executes it? A hireling soldiery.

The act of 1807 was incompatible with State sovereignty. It was passed at a time when the condition of lands and Indians was very different from what it now is. He had not gone so fully as he could have wished into this subject. He came forward to demand for his constituents a restoration of the right of trial by jury, and of a republican form of Government.

Mr. STEWART, of Pennsylvania, thought, he said, we had subjects of excitement enough before us without the addition of this. Its introduction into the House, at this time, would hasten the collision which the gentleman deprecates, by agitating the citizens of Alabama. He saw no cause for the intervention of Congress in the case, and there was certainly no occasion for any action on the subject before the 15th.

Mr. LEWIS said if anything was to be done, it most be done quickly. The order for removal was unrevoked, and would be executed by military force on the 15th of this month. It was a question of peace or war.

Mr. JONES, of Georgia, said, of what use would be the action of this House after the 15th? That is the time when the mischief is to be done; when the orders of the Executive are to be enforced. The gentleman from Pennsylvania says there is no cause for the interposition of Congress. If the threatened removal of people from lands to which they have been invited, and if the subjection of the country to military law be not cause for intervention, in a free Government, he knew not what could be. Last year, instructions were sent to the marshal of Alabama to remove all persons against whom any Indian had made a complaint. There were always some individuals who, from interested motives, would induce the Indians to complain of him. He knew the fact, that immediately after the murder of Owens, the land which he had occupied was taken possession of by another white man. Owens was killed that another white man might possess his improvements. The State of Alabama extended its laws over the Indians and Indian lands within its limits. Now the archives of the Government would show that any law in contravention of the jurisdiction of the States over Indians and Indian lands, was held by the President and Secretary of War as null and void. The laws of Alabama were in full operation over the district of country occupied by the Indians. This was also a sufficient cause for the intervention of Congress in this case. Mr. J. read a number of documents showing that the President disclaimed the right of arresting the laws of any State within the limits of that State, and that this House had sanctioned the President's views on the subject by appropriating large sums for the removal of the Indians, according to the recommendation of the Executive. The opinion of the Attorney General, that the law of 1802 authorized the removal, was, in his opinion, incorrect. It might apply to public property in a territory, but not in a State. But, in this case, the action of the Government was upon the reservations of Indians, which were individual property. Where was the difference between property owned by a white citizen and an Indian, and why should the summary Government process apply to one and not to another? The gentleman from Alabama had remarked that the President was impatient of the law's delay; would to God he were, equally so of the insolence of office. If he were, he would not subject free citizens to the arbitrary decisions of a deputy marshal. It was in the knowledge of every one here that one man had been killed in Alabama. It was also true that the marshal, and his assistants, had been indicted for murder, and true bills had been found against them. Suppose they are condemned, and suppose a citation is issued to carry up the case, by appeal, to the Federal courts. Suppose the citation is not attended to by the State courts, and that the murderers are hung, as Tassels was in Georgia—will not such a conflict of jurisdiction present a case for the intervention of Congress?

Mr. McKINLEY was not prepared (he said) to vote for this resolution. It appeared extraordinary to him that the action of the House should be asked on a state of things on the 7th of January which would not occur till the 15th of January. The subject was important, and deserved some further inquiry. As it was near the usual hour of adjourning, he now moved that the House adjourn.

The motion to adjourn was lost.

Mr. McKINLEY moved to lay the resolution on the table till to-morrow, but withdrew it, and moved to postpone its further consideration till to-morrow.

Mr. FOSTER remarked that this motion would

have the effect to defer the consideration of the resolution for two months, until the debate on the deposite question was over.

At the request of Mr. MARDIS, the ayes and noes were ordered on the motion.

The question being taken, the motion was decided in the affirmative—yeas 110, nays 107.

On motion of Mr. GRENNELL,
The House then adjourned.

IN SENATE.

TUESDAY, January 7, 1834.

Mr. TIPTON, from the Committee on Claims, reported a bill for the relief of Edward Whillet.

Mr. NAUDAIN, from the same committee, reported bills for the relief of George H. Jennings and others.

Mr. BELL, from the same committee, reported without amendment a bill from the House of Representatives for the relief of Russel, David, and Amos Hunt; which was read twice.

Mr. BELL, from the same committee, reported a bill for the relief of Thomas Fillabrown; which was read, and ordered to be printed.

Mr. WRIGHT presented the memorial of the Board of Trade of the city of New York, relative to the removal of the deposites; the reading of which was dispensed with, and the memorial referred to the Committee on Finance.

Mr. WEBSTER said he thought it his duty to avail himself of the present occasion to make an observation or two. Several papers and memorials of a character similar to the one just presented had been referred to the Committee on Finance. Among others, he alluded to those presented yesterday by an honorable gentleman from Pennsylvania, not now in his seat, [Mr. McKean.] They were memorials from several banks in the city of Philadelphia, and some from banks in the interior of the State of Pennsylvania, ascribing the present distress (for there could be no doubt there was great distress existing in the community) to the change which had taken place respecting the removal of the Government deposites. Undoubtedly this agitating subject could not have escaped the attention of the Committee on Finance—a subject so atrocious could not be supposed to have been overlooked by that committee. He would state that it was the intention of the committee to submit their sentiments to the Senate on this question, but they could not with propriety do so until the committee were put in possession of the paper which was now the subject of discussion before the Senate—he alluded to the report of the Secretary of the Treasury on the removal of the deposites. At an earlier day he had intended to have moved its reference to that committee, but that the subject was before the Senate, and he did not wish to deprive gentlemen of an opportunity of expressing their views upon it who were desirous of doing so. He rose now to state, that at as early a day as he could, consistently with a disposition to afford to every gentleman an opportunity of expressing his sentiments, he should move the Senate that the whole subject be referred to the Committee on Finance.

Mr. BROWN, from the Committee on Claims, reported bills for the relief of Wm. Anderson and Robert Claiborne; which were read twice.

Mr. CHAMBERS, from the Committee on the District of Columbia, reported a bill in favor of the Baltimore and Ohio Railroad Company; which was read twice.

Mr. MOORE presented additional papers of Harrison Thomas and others; which were referred to the same committee who had charge of their petition.

Mr. WEBSTER called up the bill for the relief of Benjamin G. Lincoln, and asked the reading of a letter from the Solicitor of the Treasury, explanatory of the claims of the petitioner; after which the bill, on motion of Mr. W., was ordered to be engrossed and read a third time.

The VICE PRESIDENT communicated a letter from the Secretary of State, accompanied by a statement of the names and compensation of the clerks employed in that department.

The VICE PRESIDENT also communicated a letter from the Postmaster General, detailing the amount of moneys ($350,000) borrowed for the

use of that department, and the names of the banks; which was read and ordered to be printed.

The VICE PRESIDENT also presented a communication from the Secretary of the Navy, detailing the names and compensations of the clerks in that department, and in the office of the Navy Commissioners.

On motion of Mr. GRUNDY, the bill for the relief of John Chandler and William Johnston was taken up, and recommitted to the Committee on Post Offices and Post Roads.

Mr. WILKINS presented the memorial of the Board of Trade of Philadelphia, in reference to the removal of the public deposites from the Bank of the United States; which was referred to the Committee on Finance, and on motion of Mr. CLAY, was ordered to be printed.

A message was received from the House of Representatives by the Clerk, stating that they had appointed on their part a Committee on Enrolled Bills, and asked the concurrence of the Senate to complete the joint resolution on that subject.

Mr. KING, of Alabama, suggested that the appointment should be made by the Chair, but a Senator objecting to that course, the Senate proceeded to ballot, when Messrs. KING of Georgia, and LINN, were chosen.

A bill for the relief of John Timberlane;
A bill for the relief of Andrew Knox;
A bill for the relief of George Sinyley;
A bill for the relief of Noah Stayley;
A bill for the relief of the representatives of William McGinnis, deceased; and
A bill for the relief of John Haggerty and David Austin;
Were severally read a third time and passed.

The following resolution was submitted by Mr. LINN:

Resolved, That the Committee on Post Offices and Post Roads be instructed to inquire into the expediency of transporting the mail from Louisville, Kentucky, to St. Louis, Missouri, in steamboats.

The following resolution was submitted by Mr. KING, of Alabama:

Resolved, That the Committee on Post Offices and Post Roads be instructed to inquire into the expediency of making an appropriation for the completion of the post road from Lime creek to the Chattahoochee.

Petitions and memorials were presented by Messrs. NAUDAIN, PORTER, WRIGHT, SOUTHARD, WILKINS, WAGGAMAN, and EWING; which were severally referred to the usual committees.

The Senate then proceeded to the

ORDERS OF THE DAY.

The resolution of Mr. TIPTON,
That the Committee of Commerce be instructed to inquire into the expediency of an appropriation for erecting a light-house at Michigan City, on Lake Michigan, in the State of Indiana, and of establishing a port of delivery at that place.

The resolution of Mr. SHEPLEY,
That the Committee on Military Affairs be instructed to inquire into the expediency of making an appropriation for the repair of the military road constructed by the United States in the State of Maine, leading from the river Mattanawcook to Houlton.

The resolution of Mr. SHEPLEY,
That the Secretary of War be directed to communicate to the Senate any information within the department, showing the injury done by storms, during the month of December last, to the pier on the western side of the entrance to Kennebunk river, in the State of Maine, and the necessity of an immediate repair, and to furnish an estimate of the sum required to make the necessary repairs.

Were severally adopted; when the Senate proceeded to the special order of the day.

REMOVAL OF PUBLIC DEPOSITES.

The Senate resumed the consideration of the resolution submitted by Mr. CLAY, on the 26th ultimo.

[Mr. BENTON concluded his remarks to-day. We reluctantly, from their great length, are compelled to omit them in the Congressional Globe.]

The Senate then, on motion of Mr. SOUTHARD, adjourned.

HOUSE OF REPRESENTATIVES.

TUESDAY, *January* 7, 1834.

Mr. CLAY reported bills for the relief of William Weeden; of Jeremiah Wasson; and a bill to grant preëmption to land to settlers in township ten, in the St. Stephen's land district, Alabama; which were severally read twice, and committed.

Also, a bill for the relief of Joseph Clift; which was read twice, and ordered to be engrossed for a third reading.

Mr. WHITTLESEY, of Ohio, bills for the relief of the legal representatives of John Thompson, junior; and for the relief of Samuel A. Edmondson.

Mr. MUHLENBERG, a bill for the relief of John Emerson.

Mr. DUNCAN, a bill to create additional land districts in Illinois, and two additional land districts in Michigan.

Mr. YOUNG, bills for the relief of the legal representatives of Lucy Vaughan, and others; of Margaret Riter; and for the relief of the legal representatives of Joseph Torrey.

Mr. CHINN, bills to incorporate the Washington City Insurance Company; and the Clerks' Savings Company.

Mr. GILMER, a bill to carry into full effect the fourth article of the treaty made with the Creek Nation of Indians on the 8th January, 1821.

Mr. ADAMS, of New York, a bill for the relief of Joseph H. Osgood, and others; and

Mr. PIERCE, of New Hampshire, a bill for the relief of Henry Okes.

All which bills were severally read twice, and committed.

The SPEAKER presented a communication from the President of the United States, with a report from the Secretary of the Treasury, in compliance with a request from the House, relative to the Potomac bridge; which, with the accompanying documents, on motion of Mr. MERCER, were referred to the Committee on Roads and Canals, and ordered to be printed.

Also, communications from the Secretaries of State and of the Navy, with lists of the clerks employed in their respective departments; which were laid on the table, and ordered to be printed.

The bill making an appropriation for the service of Government, in part, for 1834, having been returned with amendments, made thereto by the Senate, was, on motion of Mr. HUBBARD, committed to the Committee of the Whole.

The bills for the relief of Thomas Rhodes and James Austin were, on motion of Mr. CONNOR, committed to the Committee on the Post Office and Post Roads.

Mr. CARR, from the Committee on Private Land Claims, reported a bill for the relief of Marguerite Baron, widow of Jean Pierre Ledoux; which bill was twice read, and committed to a Committee of the Whole House, and made the order of the day for to-morrow; and, on motion, the bill, with the report, was ordered to be printed.

Mr. CARR, from the Committee on Private Land Claims, reported a bill for the relief of George Douglass, James Douglass, Stephen Douglass, William House, the heirs of Joseph Douglass, deceased, Samuel House, and James Tant; which bill was read twice, and committed to a Committee of the Whole House, and made the order of the day for to-morrow, and the bill and report ordered to be printed.

Mr. CARR, from the Committee on Private Land Claims, reported a bill for the relief of George K. Jackson, of Indiana; which was read twice, and engrossed for its third reading on to-morrow.

The House refused to suspend the rule, to enable Mr. FOSTER, of Georgia, to submit a resolution to extend the time allowed to morning business.

REMOVAL OF THE DEPOSITES.

The House having resumed the consideration of the motion to refer the Secretary of the Treasury's report on the deposites to the Committee of Ways and Means; and the question being upon the motion of Mr. MCDUFFIE, to add to the motion for reference the following instructions to the said committee:

"With instructions to report a joint resolution, 'providing that the public revenue hereafter collect- 'ed shall be deposited in the Bank of the United 'States, in compliance with the public faith, pledged 'by the charter of the said bank."

Mr. BINNEY rose and said, the gentleman from South Carolina proposes a joint resolution providing that the public money shall hereafter be deposited in the Bank of the United States, in conformity with the stipulations of the charter of the bank. It, therefore, presents directly the question of the sufficiency of the reasons given by the Secretary of the Treasury for the removal of the deposites, and brings up the topic of public faith as connected with the transaction. He meant to discuss this question as it became him to discuss it, on his first entrance into this House, and as it became one who was but a short time to be connected with the House—he meant to say nothing which hereafter could be a source of regret. As the Secretary's report had come into the House wearing the form, and bearing the name of reasons, he would receive it as such, and try it by the standard of reason. He meant to take the Secretary's motives as he alleged them to be, and to take his facts as he stated them, unless those facts should be contradictory to each other on their face, in which case he must arrive at the truth in the best manner he could. He should add no facts to those adduced by the Secretary, which were not notorious and undisputed. Sir, the effort is almost unnecessary. The great practical answer to the Secretary's reasons is given by the condition of the country—an answer which nothing can refute, and which it requires no argument to sustain. It comes to us in the language of truth, and soberness, and bitterness, from every part of the country. He who can see in the complaints, remonstrances, and prayers of the whole business community nothing but a theatrical trick, got up for effect by the friends of the bank, will remain blind till the catastrophe of the drama shall render them sensible of their delusion. Sir, the change produced in this country in the short space of three months, is without example in the history of any nation. In the course of the preceding summer, the people were delighted and contented with the adjustment of several of the most fearful questions which ever agitated the country. The President, upon his re-election, was receiving, in the Middle and Eastern States, more than the honors of a Roman triumph from the people of every party, rank, and age. Nature poured out abundant harvests; trade rewarded the enterprise of our merchants; the spindle and the shuttle, and every other instrument of the mechanic art, was laboriously and successfully plied; and internal improvement was bringing contributions to the general prosperity from the remote West. Universal content appeared on the broad and happy face of the land. What causes have dashed to the earth this full cup of national happiness and prosperity? Sir, we have in this country one peculiar subject of derangement, and it is an interest which is inseparably involved and connected with every other—he meant our currency. We had twenty scores of banks from which our currency was derived. They issued from eighty to a hundred millions of bank paper, and to this amount our usual metallic currency bore the proportion of not more than one to seven. Every one can see that the safety of these banks depends entirely upon the confidence of the public; that confidence depends upon the regularity of the machine; and that regularity must depend upon the proper control of the whole. Every one can see that this system is liable at any time to derangement; that it has worked well since the incorporation of the United States Bank; and that it has worked well only in consequence of the establishment of that bank. That regularity which was imparted to the system by the United States Bank is at an end—so far as it can be put at an end by the orders of the Secretary of the Treasury. The balance-wheel of this system—the principle of control, regularity, and confidence—we have thrown away as contemptuously and wantonly as a boy throws away a whistle. The Government, without warning to the public, had, in one moment, deranged and dislocated the most important and critical of all the interests of the country. The State banks are paralyzed. The bank of the United States stands still, and it can do nothing with safety, till the extent of the mischief is ascertained and limited. Bank notes were falling—prices of everything were falling—stocks were falling—and some had fallen dead. The whole gravitation of the system was stopped. No one here can predict the extent of the derangement, or from what new contrivance we shall obtain relief. What, then, has caused this general stagnation? It was contrary to true philosophy to assume more causes than would be sufficient to account for a particular effect. We have one cause—the removal of the public deposites, and the consequent withdrawal of all regularity or control from the bank paper currency of the country.

This, and no other cause, he should attempt to show, had produced this general embarrassment. The Secretary of the Treasury, in his poor judgment, had fallen into one error, for which he could not be easily excused. The honorable member from Tennessee had committed the same mistake. They held up two great objects for our sole consideration—the Bank and the Administration. The principles and views of the Administration, according to them, are to be carried out, and the bank must yield and give way to them. But the country, upon which the whole consequences of the measure are to fall, is not considered as having any interest in the question. Those consequences we have in full view before us—the bank stands undismayed, undisturbed—the Government struggles and shifts—the country is paralyzed, stupified, sacrificed. The question for this House to determine is, whether we, too, shall forget and neglect the country, or whether we shall use our endeavors to put it again on its feet, and aid it in recovering from the effects of an envenomed shaft which was aimed at the bank, but which glanced off and struck deep into the vitals of the country.

In the year 1832, the amount of bills of exchange purchased by the bank, was $67,516,600; in the next half year upwards of forty-one millions. The amount of bills collected in the same time was thirty-one millions. The bank drafts and the notes received out of the place where the bank was obliged to pay them, amounted to a still larger sum. The notes of State banks received where they were not payable was over twenty millions. Mr. B. went into statements to show that the whole amount of the sums exchanged by the bank in 1832, was $241,717,910. The foreign exchange, in addition to this, was over nine millions. The whole expenses of this agency to the country was less than one-eleventh of one per cent. upon the amount exchanged. This showed the inseparable manner in which this bank was connected with the business and interests of the country. The average amount of loans and discounts of the bank, in 1832, was sixty-six millions. In 1833, sixty-one millions. Now, it appeared to him that he did no injustice to the Secretary of the Treasury to say, that it was the design of the act of removal to break up the whole machine—that it was not a casual act, the results of which were unforeseen, but intended to force the circulation from the people back into the bank—to cut off the connexion of the bank with the people, and confine her within her own marble walls. Whether this was the design or not, this was the effect—to take her away from the people and compel her to wind up. Can any one wish a better reason than this for the stagnation, the syncope, the embarrassment of the country? Sir, the only and the true reason lies in that act—the removal of the deposites. It is not the consequence of the removal of ten millions of dollars from one bank into another, but it was the consequence of the removal, taken together with the object of removal. The removal of the deposites, as an insulated circumstance, could be productive of no important results. The consequences arose from the state of the country, in connexion with the doctrine he had advanced. The bank in six months previous to January, 1834, had reduced her currency about nine millions of dollars. The Bank of the United States, on the 11th of August, 1833, held nine or ten millions of dollars of public money. How was she to pay it? The answer was, whenever and wherever the Secretary of the Treasury orders. The opponents of the bank say she should have paid it in specie. Suppose she had—if it had any

effect, except to take the money across the streets and bring it back again, it would have been a most pernicious effect. She had her eighteen millions of currency to sustain. She could not keep all her sails set, and throw all her ballast overboard. She was obliged to meet the payment by curtailing her discounts, by calling upon her own debtors. This was the only safe or prudent course for her to take. When a bank calls upon her debtors to return a part of the amount due to her, every individual debtor who has a deposite in the bank, will necessarily draw upon it. Two and two do not always make four in a bank curtailment. The curtailments of the bank made in August, were in part met by the withdrawal of a portion of the private deposites from the bank. Mr. B. then showed that the curtailment made by the bank in August, of four millions of discounts, drew from the community less than one million. The reduction might be very large and the effect very small; and the bank, in his opinion, ought to strengthen herself; yet the curtailments which had been made tended very little to that object. The whole amount of reduction from August to January increased the means of the bank only to the amount of the sum which the Government took away.

They are right, who say that the removal of the deposites from the bank did not produce the distress; but it was the universal want of confidence and stagnation produced by the measures necessarily taken by the bank to pay the public deposites. The object might have been accomplished with less embarrassment to the community, if the Treasury Department had rendered it certain at what time, and when the money should be paid. But the bank found that it had to deal with an enemy, who sought to come upon it by surprise, and in the dark. The daily and weekly lists of sums deposited by the Government, were discontinued, and large drafts were sent without notice. Some of these were drafts to be paid on certain contingencies, beyond the knowledge or control of the bank. Every reflecting man must say that the course of the Secretary of the Treasury, in keeping these drafts hovering between Baltimore and Boston, to the amount of three millions, was alone sufficient to account for the alarm of the bank, and to render advisable a much larger amount of curtailment than was resorted to. When the removal of the public deposites to a State bank in Philadelphia was made, it was found not to be so valuable a present as was at first supposed. The private deposites lessened in the proportion that the Government deposites increased; for private individuals found that the Government was a preferred depositor, and, in case of any difficulty, would sweep the whole. Several other views he presented, to show that the State banks could not, so well as the United States Bank, discount upon the public deposites. The days of one and one and a half per cent. were days of disaster to both borrower and lender. There was (he spoke from personal knowledge) a vast amount of private capital in Boston, New York, and Philadelphia, ready to be loaned at five per cent., upon security of stocks; but the universal want of confidence kept it out of the market. The great amount of money in the country was employed in bringing the crops to market, and in transporting merchandise in exchange for the crops.

I ask, what was the structure of the bank, that it could provide at every point for the wants of the Government, and, at the same time, promote the interests of the country, by carrying on their exchanges? But the bank having no share in the deposites removed, but being obliged to distribute them at any point, she must diminish her assistance to the community. The State banks, he contended, could not pay the public deposites, and at the same time assist the community. Let them try it, and in three months' time they will give it up, or, in violation of their charters, consolidate their relics into a United States Bank. The remedy that was to be applied for this state of things was apparent to every one—the restoration of the deposites. But the gentleman from Tennessee wants a sifting inquiry, before he acts upon the question; a sifting inquiry must be had into the miserable driblets of printing accounts, and into the fact whether the National Intelligencer belongs to the bank or not; while, in the meantime, the great interests of the country are set aside and neglected.

The question for the consideration of the House, was, whether the reasons adduced by the Secretary of the Treasury were such as ought to be satisfactory to Congress? If not, then whether they were not bound to consider if there was any, and what remedy should be applied to avert the dangers that were now more than apprehended to fall on the country in consequence of his removal of the deposites? It was necessary for him, then, to take them as given; and here he would observe, and it could not have escaped observation, that the Secretary of the Treasury had submitted various propositions as the basis of his action, with a statement of some particular facts, by which he justified that action. The arguments in the statement of facts, made for his justification were large and numerous enough; whilst for the groundwork, the basis, there was no argument at all, neither had they been enlightened on this point, by the honorable member [Mr. Polk] who had preceded him (Mr. B.) in the debate. The Secretary broadly asserted, that whether he was right, or whether he was wrong, he alone was authorized to remove the deposites. The bank, by the removal, were, in legal parlance, put out of court—in fact, they were not entitled to a hearing as a party in the cause. For this, however, no reason was given. He next asserts, as another of his propositions, that Congress tied themselves up by the act incorporating the bank, and in which they had given him alone the absolute and unconditional power of removal. So that if this assertion was founded correctly, it must follow, as a matter of course, that Congress could not interfere, with even the best reasons in the world for doing so—the very safety of the deposites themselves—they could not take this money from the bank. Another proposition submitted by him was, that the removal having even a tendency towards public convenience, was sufficient for him in making the removal; and he went further to say, that the power to remove, conferred the power to place the public money elsewhere. But to sustain these various propositions, no argument was given; they rested on mere dogmas, and he could only, therefore, in the absence of any argument to sustain them, proceed to discuss them negatively, and to show that if they were examined into attentively and admitted, it would be conceding that which he believed the House never would sanction. Mr. B. here proceeded to review at length the reasons of the Secretary, and read from his letter to Congress the passages in which it was stated that, by repeated adjudications, the charter granted to the bank was in the nature of a contract, and by which it was alleged by the Secretary that the power reserved to the Secretary over the deposites should not be restricted to any particular contingency, but was absolute and unconditional; and thus, as he (Mr. B.) contended, he must be supposed as assuming the ground that, be his reasons for the removal right or wrong, it could be no breach of the contract to remove the deposites.

The Secretary admits that the bank obtained their privileges for a consideration, paid by them in money and services; he must admit also that the bank is still performing services in various ways. He says that the power is absolute, although it is stated that the charter was in the nature of a contract, one part of which was, that he was obliged to report to Congress his reasons for any use of the power given to him; but he (Mr. B.) asked what fair construction could be put on that obligation, if it was not that Congress had a right to consider those reasons? Why else was it required that they should be given at all? This was the common-sense doctrine, and which is the legal doctrine, because the law says expressly, that the reasons shall concern the party whom they affect; and if this be so, how could the Secretary be correct in asserting that the bank had no concern in the reasons, which he was bound to furnish, by the terms of what he admits is a contract—a pecuniary contract, between the stockholders on the one part, and the sovereignty (the United States) granting it? He contended that the bank, being thus the admitted party to a contract made, by which the Secretary was bound to furnish his reasons, he in compliance with that obligation, done no more than his duty; the bank then were the party who were only concerned in the sufficiency of these reasons, and ought to have their justice examined into by the House. He found that this very right of the House was conceded, in the communication read in the debate, from Secretary Crawford to the House—one of the charges made against him was, that he had removed the deposites from the United States Bank to the Bank at Chilicothe, without communicating his reasons for such removal to Congress. Well, then, did the Secretary of that day assume the ground now taken? Did he not say, rather in terms, that the omission was owing to inadvertence? And what further? That this very provision—the submitting the reasons to Congress—"was intended for the benefit of the bank." Mr. Secretary Crawford again admits that the reasons were to be communicated to Congress. Why? Because it was necessary that Congress should know where the public money should be deposited. He concluded, therefore, and maintained, that the assertion that the power of the Secretary was absolute and unconditional was not made out; was in the face of this former precedent of Secretary Crawford; and had only arisen from the very poverty of the case. He trusted that Congress would not sanction such a principle, as that, in a case of actual contract, after a bonus had been paid by the bank, and services rendered by them, estimated at nearly 200,000 dollars per annum, the Secretary could, for insufficient reasons, thus commit what was a breach of the contract for which this bonus and services were paid; and Congress supposing his reasons to be insufficient, had not power to bring the subject back, and reverse a decision which might be proved to be contrary to a sense of common justice. The House had the right to inquire into these reasons and into their justice. They were bound to do this, lest they might have been dictated by caprice, and thus the public faith had been violated, and the bank turned away from the enjoyment of what was their purchased rights.

The next proposition assumed by the Secretary, which he meant to discuss, was, that the power reserved to the Secretary did not depend for its exercise on the safety of the money, or the fidelity with which the bank had conducted itself, but that he (the Secretary) had the right whenever the public interest required it. Mr. B. would, however, defer this until the next day, if favored by the House with an adjournment.

Mr. MERCER rose and submitted a motion to that effect; which prevailed.

IN SENATE.

WEDNESDAY, *January* 8, 1834.

Mr. ROBINSON, from the Committee on Engrossed Bills, made a report.

Mr. TOMLINSON gave notice that he should ask leave to-morrow to introduce a bill, the nature of which could not be understood.

Mr. WEBSTER, from the Select Committee, reported a bill, with an amendment, on the subject of French spoliations prior to 1800; which was read, and on motion of Mr. W., was made the special order of the day for Wednesday, the 5th of February.

Mr. MORRIS made a report from the Committee on Engrossed Bills.

Mr. WAGGAMAN introduced a letter from the Governor of Louisiana, enclosing the following resolutions, which were read:

Resolved by the Senate and House of Representatives of the State of Louisiana, in General Assembly convened, That our Senators in Congress be instructed, and our Representatives requested, to support such measures as they may deem expedient to terminate equitably the disputes existing between occupants of land in the county of Feliciana, who claim under titles derived from the Government of the United States, and those claiming the same land under grants from the Spanish or other authorities.

And be it further resolved, &c., That the Governor be requested to transmit copies of these resolutions to our Senators and Representatives in Congress.

ALCEE LABRANCHE,
Speaker of the House of Representatives.
C. DERBIGNY,
President of the Senate.

Approved December 19, 1833.

A. B. ROMAN,
Governor of the State of Louisiana.

Mr. WAGGAMAN proposed that the resolutions be referred to the Committee on Foreign Relations.

Mr. POINDEXTER conceived that the proper reference would be to the Committee on Public Lands.

After some conversation between these gentlemen, the vote was taken upon the reference to the Committee on Foreign Relations, and carried—ayes 24, noes not counted.

The following resolutions were submitted, and lie one day upon the table:

By Mr. SPRAGUE,

Resolved, That the Committee on the Library be instructed to inquire into the expediency of subscribing, for the use of Congress, to a new statistical work proposed to be published by George Watterston.

By Mr. MANGUM,

Resolved, That the resolution adopted on the 14th of May, 1830, directing the Secretary of the Senate to contract with the printer of the House of Representatives for copies of the documents printed by order of the House, be, and the same is hereby rescinded.

By Mr. KENT.

Resolved, That the Committee on the Post Office and Post Roads be instructed to inquire into the propriety of so modifying the law regulating the Post Office Department, as to authorize the transmission by mail of such books and public records, whether bound or in boards, as the Executives of the respective States are in the habit of interchanging with each other, upon such terms as will best comport with the importance of the object.

By Mr. PORTER:

Resolved, That the Postmaster General be directed to report to the Senate the number of failures which have occurred during the last twelve months in carrying the mail between the city of Washington and New Orleans, by the southern route, and the number and amount of forfeitures enforced by him in consequence of those failures, during the same period.

ORDERS OF THE DAY.

The resolution of Mr. LINN—

That the Committee on the Post Office and Post Roads be instructed to inquire into the expediency of transporting the mail from Louisville, Kentucky, to St. Louis, Missouri, in steamboats;

And the resolution of Mr. KING, of Alabama, That the Committee on Post Offices and Post Roads be instructed to inquire into the expediency of making an appropriation for the completion of the post road from Line Creek to the Chattahoochee—

Were taken up and adopted.

Petitions and memorials were presented by Messrs. TOMLINSON, FRELINGHUYSEN, BIBB, WAGGAMAN, LINN, and PORTER, which were referred to appropriate committees.

Mr. WILKINS presented a petition from the Board of Trustees of Alleghany College, in Pennsylvania, stating that they proposed incorporating manual labor with collegiate studies, and asking Congress to grant them lands to carry into effect their object; which, on motion of Mr. WILKINS, was referred to the Committee on Public Lands.

The following bills from the House of Representatives were ordered to be engrossed and read a third time:

A bill for the relief of John Haggerty and David Austin. [This bill was improperly stated yesterday as having passed.]

A bill for the relief of Benjamin G. Minturn.

A bill for the relief of John Hone and Sons, of New York.

A bill for the relief of Enoch Spencer.

A bill for the relief of Phineas Sprague and others.

A bill for the relief of John Harter.

A bill for the relief of the widow and heirs of Felix Adrain.

A bill for the relief of Ebenezer Lobdell.

A bill for the relief of the Baltimore and Ohio Railroad Company.

A bill for the relief of the heirs of Robert Labarr.

Mr. RIVES presented a memorial of the representatives of General Thomas Nelson, deceased, praying compensation for services in the revolutionary war; which was referred to the Committee on Revolutionary Claims.

Mr. RIVES also presented the memorial of certain citizens of Virginia, asking relief for damages sustained by French spoliations prior to 1800, which he declined sending for the present to the select committee on that subject, they having made a report this morning, and moved that the memorial be laid upon the table.

Mr. HENDRICKS reported a bill for the relief of George Kinn; which was read and committed.

The Senate then proceeded to the consideration of the special order of the day.

THE REMOVAL OF THE DEPOSITES.

The question being on the motion of Mr. BENTON to strike out Mr. CLAY's second resolution and insert the amendment—

Mr. SOUTHARD said that he desired to express his views on this question, but a resolution had been interposed as an amendment, on which he had no wish to say anything. Any remarks which he might be disposed to make now, ought, agreeably to parliamentary usage, to be upon the amendment, and therefore it was his desire that the question should be put on the amendment, and he would therefore reserve what he had to say on the general question until that should be disposed of: he therefore asked the yeas and nays on the amendment.

Mr. FORSYTH said that this question had come up very unexpectedly. The gentleman who offered the amendment [Mr. BENTON] was not in his seat, and as he could not possibly have expected this state of things, he would move to lay the subject on the table.

Mr. CLAY hoped not.

Mr. GRUNDY did not feel willing to lay the matter on the table. He would rather the gentleman from Missouri [Mr. BENTON] should be present, but yet he thought the motion of the gentleman from New Jersey [Mr. SOUTHARD] a very proper one. He (Mr. G.) had no desire to say a word on the main question, but he wished that the Senate might be full. The gentleman [Mr. B.] lived very near the Capitol, and if the Senate would delay a few minutes, he thought he would be in.

The motion to lay on the table was lost.

Mr. KING, of Alabama, said he thought the gentleman from New Jersey [Mr. SOUTHARD] was not right in his view. The whole subject was open for discussion on the motion to strike out, and he hoped the gentleman would take up the subject as he proposed to do.

Mr. POINDEXTER said he had a single remark to make. The great subject under consideration grew out of the reasons of the Secretary of the Treasury for his removal of the Government deposites. The amendment of the gentleman from Missouri [Mr. BENTON] has no relevancy to this question whatever. It was a distinct substantive proposition, and one in which he would certainly succeed if it were made agreeably to parliamentary usage. The gentleman could have Mr.

Biddle's testimony, as well as that of any other person. He could have it by the appointment of a committee of investigation. But while the Senator from Missouri was considering the reasons of the Secretary, he concludes his speech of four day's continuance, by moving a question which was in no way connected with the subject. He thought the Senator [Mr. SOUTHARD] was right in desiring to disentangle this from the great subject, and therefore he hoped an immediate question would be taken upon the amendment, which he considered frivolous. Placed where it was, it might, indeed, be said to be ridiculous, because it placed the Senate in the attitude of a grand jury, impanelled to try certain charges against the officers of the United States Bank. He hoped the Senate would either get rid of or adopt the proposition, so that an inquiry might be had into the sufficiency of the reasons of the Secretary of the Treasury for the removal of the deposites.

Mr. FORSYTH said, that the Senator not now in his seat, could not have anticipated that such would be the fate of his resolution. He hoped to hear the remarks of the Senator from New Jersey; he desired no delay, but he trusted that this proposition would be not be hurried on when it had been thus violently assailed by the gentleman, [Mr. POINDEXTER.] But he, Mr. F., would say that the proposition has relation to the question before the Senate. He begged leave to call attention to it. Mr. F. read the amendment.

Now, sir, said Mr. F., what is the subject before the Senate? It is a condemnation of the reasons of the Secretary of the Treasury for an official act. And among those reasons, there was a charge against the Bank of the United States for the improper curtailment of its discounts, and the improper manner of doing it, and that it had interfered in elections, and prostituted its means for political purposes. Now, has it not relation to the subject? As respects the propriety of the proposed course of calling witnesses to the bar of the Senate, that was a very different question. He was not quite satisfied that it was correct. But the proposition was certainly in order, and it ought not to excite the surprise of the gentleman from Mississippi [Mr. P.] He, Mr. F., concurred in some respects with the views of the gentleman, [Mr. BENTON,] but he was not satisfied to take the statements of the Secretary of the Treasury.

Mr. F. was here told that Mr. BENTON was in the Chamber, and he then resumed his seat.

The VICE PRESIDENT having stated the question,

Mr. KANE asked for a division of it, to end with striking out.

The VICE PRESIDENT read the rule, to show that the motion was not in order.

Mr. BENTON said, he did not wish to embarrass gentlemen by pressing his amendment, but suggested his readiness to modify it by a motion to strike out and afterwards to insert, but he did not consider it material.

The question being on the adoption of the amendment, in lieu of the second resolution,

Mr. CHAMBERS demanded the yeas and nays, which were ordered, and are as follows, to wit:

YEAS—Messrs. Benton, Brown, Grundy, Hill, Kane, Linn, Morris, Shepley, Tallmadge, Tipton, White, and Wright—12.

NAYS—Messrs. Bell, Bibb, Black, Calhoun, Chambers, Clay, Ewing, Forsyth, Frelinghuysen, Hendricks, Kent, King of Alabama, King of Georgia, Knight, McKean, Mangum, Moore, Naudain, Poindexter, Porter, Prentiss, Preston, Rives, Robbins, Robinson, Silsbee, Smith, Southard, Sprague, Swift, Tomlinson, Waggaman, Webster, Wilkins—34.

The question recurring on the adoption of Mr. CLAY's resolutions,

Mr. SOUTHARD said, that as the question recurred upon the reasons of the Secretary of the Treasury for the removal of the deposites, and the resolutions of the gentleman from Kentucky founded upon them, he would endeavor to meet it. It presented a serious and very important question. For sixteen years past, the money of the people had been deposited in the place selected by Congress and the laws for its reception, and it has now been removed and deposited in places where Congress has not directed it to be placed, to wit: in some twenty or thirty of the State banks. It was, before the removal, in the place which Congress had created, and it is now where Congress has no control over it. It therefore presents a question most intimately connected with the safety, welfare, and best interests of the country. It was not a question of office or of place, or whether the Bank of the United States should be rechartered or not. It is a question placed far above it; it rises higher, and fixes and determines forever after, the powers delegated to a high functionary of the Government; and when political aspirants shall be forgotten, and the scramble for office shall be at an end, it will stand in bold relief before posterity as the assumption and exercise of an enormous power. It becomes us, therefore, to consider the subject with calmness and deliberation, and he proposed to consider, first, what the Secretary has done; second, the principles by which he has been governed; and third, the reasons he has given for doing the act.

1st. What has the Secretary done? He has ordered the inferior officers and debtors of the Government to place the money of the Government in places which he has selected, so that hereafter, the money shall be placed there according to his orders, and on terms which he has prescribed, and these terms are to be found in the agreement made with the banks where the moneys are to be deposited. In page 40 of the pamphlet copy of the report, we find the terms, or the agreement, which has been made with the banks to receive the money. To know what is done, and how it has been done, it is necessary to refer to that agreement. The first item is, that "the said bank 'agrees to receive and enter to the credit of the 'Treasurer of the United States all sums of money 'offered to be deposited on account of the United 'States, &c., whether in gold or silver, or notes of 'the Bank of the United States or branches, in notes 'of any bank which are convertible into coin in 'its immediate vicinity, or in notes of any bank 'which it is, for the time being, in the habit of 'receiving." Which it is in the habit of receiving! Let it be remarked that these receiving banks confine themselves to a particular specified kind of money, which they receive in their immediate vicinity. The second item is, "that, if the deposites in said bank shall exceed one half of its capital 'stock actually paid in, it is agreed that collateral 'security shall be given," &c. Then let it be observed, too, that here is no present security for the people's money. It has been placed in certain banks, without first taking the necessary security, even if the Secretary possessed the power to do so. And if hereafter it should be taken, it must be done by the Secretary, not by Congress. The Secretary has not obtained the security, and he could not possibly know the necessity for it, for he says expressly he has not seen the charters of the selected banks. And he was in such a hurry to effect the removal, that one of the banks was actually incapable of receiving them. Another item is, that the banks are to make transfers of the public moneys from place to place on reasonable notice given. And what is to be understood by reasonable notice? Suppose an order should be issued to transfer $200,000 to a particular place in five days: is that reasonable notice? and would the bank notified agree that it was reasonable notice? Another item is, that all the services required of these banks are to be performed in their immediate vicinity. And here there is a perfect surrender of the rights which Congress should possess of transferring the money to any point in the country. Another item is, that an agent or agents are to be appointed by the Secretary of the Treasury, and the compensation and expenses of this agency are to be fixed by him, placed under the control of the Secretary, and as to the banks, why they are to pay for it. And, sir, the consequences are apparent. The seventh item authorizes the Secretary to dismiss the receiving banks at his will and pleasure. But the Secretary has omitted to tell us *when* contracts were made with most of the banks. The dates of some he has given, but as to the others the time at which they were entered into he has altogether omitted to state. Sir, when the Secretary was about to give his reasons for the act in question, was it ingenuous, was it honest, to conceal from Congress when these contracts were made as going to operate on those very reasons? There was another thing, the solvency or insolvency of the selected banks, which the Secretary had not inquired into, and therefore he could know nothing about it. He had not seen the charters, but was so imprudent as to act without the necessary information; and now Congress was called on to justify him in an act which affects the treasury of the nation. The time selected by him, the period at which the action took place, manifests too truly that he did not desire this information. On the 18th September he determined to remove the deposites. The action upon this determination took place on the 26th; and was there time to make the necessary inquiry, which in justice to the country the importance of the act rendered it necessary should be made? But, perhaps, it may be suggested that everything necessary to be known was known, because a negotiating agent had been appointed on this subject the August preceding. But his report could have been made only a few days preceding the action of the Secretary, and, by the well-known course of time and distance, it could only have been known as to two or three banks in the cities in this vicinity. But as to the banks from Maine to Louisiana it could not have been known. It is true the Secretary assures us that the banks are of undoubted credit. He (Mr. S.) was not disposed to impeach the word of the Secretary; but when we were called on to act on this important question, he could not take the dictum of the Secretary. He wished to know the fact, and without obtaining it the Secretary has been guilty of a most gross and palpable violation of his duty. He tells us he was obliged to draw money out of the Bank of the United States and give it to the State banks for the purpose of sustaining them, and yet he says they are of undoubted solvency. It may be so. But when they are given duties to perform not authorized by their charters, their very act becomes an act of insolvency. In regard to what the Secretary did in making the contract, he was not satisfied; but there was another greater and paramount cause of dissatisfaction: it was the power to make these contracts. If the Secretary is invested with no power to make the contract, the contracts are void. But this was a question which it was unnecessary to argue, because, unless authority can be shown for it, it is void, except so far only as it depends upon the honor of those with whom he has made the contract. He would like to know and be informed of the power and authority given to the Secretary for making these contracts, which affect the whole treasure of the United States. He could find none, and he had searched carefully. But, on the contrary, he had found something the very opposite of it—something directly against it. He referred to the act read by the gentleman from Kentucky, passed in May, 1820. He would ask, does that act mean what that gentleman contended for, or not? He had heard the construction given to it by that gentleman, and perfectly coincided with him in it. But there was another remark which he had to make on the Secretary's argument on this subject. The Secretary says that the power to remove necessarily draws after it the power to fix the place of deposite. Sir, it is a *non sequitur*. It does not follow of course. The Secretary is the agent of the law, and can act only by the law. The Secretary of the Treasury is to decide as to the general management of the treasure of the Union. But the Treasurer himself is the officer designated by Congress to perform express acts to be done in the disbursement of the public moneys. He hoped to be able to show that it was the Treasurer, in the absence of all laws to the contrary, who was to select the places for the safekeeping of the public moneys. There was another thing to be considered—the influence which this act was calculated to exert upon public sentiment in relation to the extent of delegated powers. Looking into it as the act of the Secretary, and he would ask if it was not a power enormous in itself, and dangerous to the institutions of the country? This agreement places the receiving banks at the will and mercy of the Secretary. He can destroy them all at a single blow; he may require payments to be made agreeably to his own direction; he may determine when, how, and in what time, they shall transmit money from place to place. He may retain, dismiss, or discharge them, whenever he sees fit, and this from other motives than should govern a public officer in the discharge of his duties. He may show favor and partiality to whom he pleases, for by this act he has created an army of sycophants and supporters. Sir, have we not seen the answer of one of these banks to the notification of its selection? The president says: "I take the occasion to express the high sense of honor conferred upon the 'bank by so distinguished a mark of your confi'dence;" thus stooping and cringing to the dispenser of favors. All this is not according to the laws of the land, but the authority of the Secretary, and he says, "I am under the President of the United States." He has no official will of his own, and all this power is to be in the hands of the President. If Senators are willing to have it there, let them do so; but if not, he hoped they would say so. Congress had *regulated* the intercourse between the Government and the Bank of the United States; but as to the banks selected in its stead as the public depository, at the whim of the Secretary, they were taken out of those regulations, and placed under his sole control; and would Senators countenance such acts? But the Secretary has done another act. He has recommended that the holders of public money, disbursing officers, who are under bond for the safekeeping of that money, and its faithful disbursement, to deposite those moneys in certain banks, (and this act is approved by the President in page 41-'2 of the pamphlet.) Sir, by this act the President has violated his duty. He has directed the Secretary to do an act by which he has placed all the disbursing officers of the Government at his own will and discretion. What, he would inquire, would be the consequence of that act on every such officer of the Government? Suppose three or four large disbursing officers here had been in the habit of placing their money in the Patriotic Bank, and the order of the Secretary should be received to remove them from the Patriotic Bank and place them in the Bank of the Metropolis, and afterwards supposing they should be lost: what would the consequences be? If the Bank of the Metropolis should not safely keep it, the officers would be released from their bonds, or if not released, they would be placed at the mercy and under the power of one man, and an officer of the law not empowered to interfere with them. The Secretary has ordered the deposites to be made to the credit of the United States, but he has made no contract that the money placed in the receiving banks shall be secured to the United States. He has drawn the public money from the Bank of the United States and the Treasury of the United States, in direct violation of law. He has given drafts in favor of the Union Bank of Maryland, the Girard Bank, the Mechanics' and Manhattan Banks of New York, for sums amounting to nearly three millions of dollars. How much more to other banks we do not know; and these drafts are not countersigned by the Comptroller in the usual way. And as to the time when they were drawn, that is not known; but after they had been issued some time, it was discovered that they had been out and in the hands of the cashiers of these banks a month before they were presented for payment.

Where had the Secretary told us that he had placed these sums at the disposal of the banks for their relief? Nowhere. He has concealed it, and it was a most disingenuous concealment. We know it now from the correspondence of the banks with the Treasurer. But the drafts are said to be contingents, and that the banks should use the money if pressed by the United States Bank. He has drawn this money, or made it subject to be drawn, and placed it on a contingency to be judged of by the banks to whom they were given. What, then, is this but a loan to these banks to support their credit? What else could it be? Was it for the purpose of doing what the laws required? Are Senators prepared to say that the Secretary could loan the people's money to the banks for their own use, and this done, too, without security? Where is the security? Is it in the bond of the cashier? Would the bank itself have been bound to answer to the Government for this money? Certainly not, until it was placed within its vaults? The cashier might have drawn it and gone off with it, and not a single dollar of it could ever have been recovered —it would have been thrown on the waves without the means of ever reaching it again. And while these drafts were in the cashier's hands, what was the situation of the books of the treasury? They would have shown the transfer, and if it had been lost, the loss would have been on the Treasurer himself. This act of the Secretary is a most extraordinary transaction, and he would only say, that if the Secretary can do this, and Congress has been so negligent of its duty, and has provided no guards to the public treasury, it becomes us now to repair the defect, and if anything had been omitted, he hoped it would be so no longer. But Congress has not neglected its duty. It has secured guards enough around the treasury. But we are told that new guards have been placed round it to save it from plunder. And what are these new guards? The mode of sending notices to the banks of drafts, to prevent frauds. Sir, the mode of drawing money out of the Treasury has always been a uniform one. Four years ago, we heard much about these treasury guards. And this is only another instance to the many preceding it, of trifles lighter than air, being used for political effect, and to promote political objects. The drafts were in violation of the charter of the bank and of the laws. They were secret. The officers had not the courage, or if they had they had not the honesty, to announce the possession of them. And the danger impending from that cause over the public treasure, and the imprudence of the act, were not creditable to the sagacity of the Secretary. Two millions of drafts were in the hands of cashiers totally irresponsible, which might have been presented at a moment's warning, and yet we are told that the Bank of the United States acted dishonestly and oppressively in guarding against them. That in these very guards it had violated its charter and been guilty of gross misconduct, because it had placed a shield around itself to avoid the assaults of those who ought to protect and sustain it. Sir, said Mr. S., if the Senate will sustain the reasons of the Secretary, there are no longer any guards upon the public treasury. The President of the United States and Secretary of the Treasury may take it when and to where they please, and he would ask, was the Senate prepared to justify the act? But an apology had been offered for this act of the Secretary, that they were transfer drafts. And what, he would ask, is a transfer draft? It is simply this: the money of the Government is in a particular place where it is not wanted, and they wish it transferred to a place where they do want it for disbursement. For instance, the money is in the bank at Philadelphia, and it is wanted in Norfolk. A draft is drawn on the bank in Philadelphia to place it in Norfolk, to meet the demands of the Government there. It is a mere letter of advice to place it where the Government wants it. It is not properly a draft to take money away from the bank on which it is drawn, but merely to change its place of disbursement. When was this transfer draft ever used to place the people's money in the hands of other banks for their own use? Never. Was it ever to be used to take money from one part of a town to another part? The object of the Government is to pay its debts, and nothing else. And what is the effect of this transfer, according to the doctrine of the Secretary? Why, if in taking

it from one man and giving it to another it should be lost, the Government loses it and not the bank. It is an entire change of the responsibilities of the agents, and the moment the bank loses possession of the money, it loses its liabilities. The transfer must always be made where the legal responsibility is the same in the agent to which it is transferred, as in that from which it is taken. While he viewed the subject in this light, he must believe, and he must vote too, that there has been here a most shameful abuse of power and violation of official duty by the Secretary. There is no relief for the act to be found, in saying that Congress has placed no guard around the treasury, and therefore it can be done. Congress has provided ample guards. He viewed it as a direct violation of law. The law has directed the manner in which the money should be taken out of the treasury, and its directions have not been pursued. The proofs offered by the gentleman from Kentucky were, to his mind, conclusive. And he felt impelled to say, that the *time* when this act was done drew none of his respect towards it. It was done when the Secretary knew he could not accomplish the act and the purposes designed, unless done before the meeting of Congress. He knew it was a question of momentous interest and importance; that if deferred, it must agitate Congress in their deliberations, while they were making arrangements for depositing the public money elsewhere. He knew that he would be insulting Congress, and that Congress would not approve of the act. Recollect, almost the last act of the representatives of the people, when called on by the highest authority to act, was to express their opinion, as the representatives of the people, that the public money was safe in the United States Bank; and yet, in six months, and within sixty days of the next meeting of Congress, a Secretary of the Treasury is found disregarding the opinion of Congress, and it may be said, acting in direct violation of their instructions. The Secretary knew all this—ay, more; he knew that if the money was once removed, it would require a law, or a joint resolution of Congress, to restore it. He knew, and he believed, too, if he could get the money out, that unless two-thirds of both Houses could be obtained in favor of the restoration, a single word from the President would veto it. Sir, it was to prevent the legislative action that this act was done. And is there a parallel to it in history? Is there in all history an instance of greater scorn towards the legislature? No, sir! A Secretary does an act within sixty days of the meeting of Congress, and by this act bereaves Congress of their whole power over the treasury of the Union. He (Mr. S.) stood here to maintain the authority of Congress, and he would maintain its power over the treasury of the country.

Here Mr. SOUTHARD yielded the floor to Mr. FRELINGHUYSEN, upon whose motion the Senate adjourned.

HOUSE OF REPRESENTATIVES.

WEDNESDAY, January 8, 1834.

The SPEAKER laid before the House the following letter from Mr. BULLARD:

HOUSE OF REPRESENTATIVES,
January 8, 1834.

SIR: I have the honor to inform you that my seat in the House of Representatives of the United States, over which you preside, has become vacant, by my resignation addressed to the Executive of the State of Louisiana.

I have the honor to be, very respectfully, your obedient servant,   H. A. BULLARD.

Hon. ANDREW STEVENSON,
Speaker of the House of Representatives.

Which was laid on the table.

Mr. WHITTLESEY reported a bill for the relief of François Suzor;

Mr. GHOLSON, a bill for the relief of Henry and Robert Sewell;

Mr. McKIM, a bill for the relief of the crew of the brig Sarah George;

Mr. SELDEN, a bill making an appropriation for the improvement of the Hudson river;

Mr. R. M. JOHNSON, a bill to provide for the support of the widows and orphans of such officers of the army as die whilst in the service of the United States;

Mr. HARPER, a bill making an appropriation for the erection of a marine hospital at Portland, Maine;

Mr. MANN, a bill for the relief of W. L. Cock. erill; and

Mr. SUTHERLAND, a bill for the relief of James Marsh;

All which bills were severally read twice and committed.

Mr. POLK, from the Committee of Ways and Means, reported that that committee had agreed to the amendments made by the Senate to the bill making an appropriation in part for the service of Government for 1834; and the bill was then committed to the Committee of the Whole on the state of the Union.

REMOVAL OF THE DEPOSITES.

The House having resumed the consideration of the motion to refer the Secretary of the Treasury's report on the deposites to the Committee of Ways and Means, and the question being upon the motion of Mr. McDuffie to add to the motion for reference the following instructions to the said committee:

" With instructions to report a joint resolution, 'providing that the public revenue hereafter col'lected shall be deposited in the Bank of the Uni'ted States, in compliance with the public faith, 'pledged by the charter of the said bank;".

Mr. BINNEY rose and said, that in the remarks which he had the honor to address to the House yesterday, he had concluded what he had to say upon the first of the general propositions to be found in the letter of the Secretary of the Treasury, but which was not sustained by any argument from him. He would now proceed to discuss the second proposition, which was one affecting, as he viewed it, the House as a component part of the legislature, and affecting also their whole legislative power in the most critical and vital parts, as would appear from the statement of the Secretary, itself. It was in terms that the power reserved to the Secretary of the Treasury does not depend for its exercise, merely on the safety of the public money in the hands of the bank, nor upon the fidelity with which it has conducted itself; but that he has the right to remove the deposites, and it is his duty to remove them, whenever the public interest or convenience will be promoted by the change; that even although Congress should be convinced that the depository was unsafe, or that the interests of the people imperiously demanded the removal, he alone, not they, had any control in the matter. These were the terms of the Secretary himself, and the House must perceive, that this must be their plain meaning; and for thus stating it so plainly, he acknowledged that much benefit was thereby procured for those gentlemen who were disposed to controvert him; for if his propositions had not been put so plainly, or had been given in an ambiguous manner, when they discussed the subject, it might be alleged, that, what they urged, was not an answer to the proposition at all. Now, he called on the House to recollect, that this proposition denied the power of the House, and was put forward by the Secretary as a justification of his own acts. This was a question as to the interpretation to be given to the terms of a statute; it was a question of the extension of authority or restraint to be ascertained from the reasons and within the

scope presented. What, then, must be the surprise of the House at finding in the letter this remarkable expression, " that ' the power over the place of deposite ' would seem properly to belong to the ' legislative department of the Govern- ' ment;" further adding, " that it was diffi- ' cult to imagine why the authority to ' withdraw it from this bank was confined ' to the Executive." Difficult to imagine! thinks the Secretary, why Congress should deprive themselves of this power? But, to any person accustomed to the inter- pretation of statutes, their surprise must be, that he had not come to a contrary conclusion—that the House did not de- prive themselves of it, regarding him as their officer, and their power over the money, supreme ; it is to remain where placed, until drawn from, by appropria- tions, made in conformity to law.

The Secretary says, that the charter de- volves upon the Executive the exclusive power of removing the deposites. Mr. B. submitted that the power was given not to the Executive, nor to an agent of the Ex- ecutive, but to the agent of Congress. He then passed to the consideration of arguments drawn from the acts organizing and regulating the departments. The first act was passed in 1788. This regards the department of Foreign Affairs. It provides that the head of this department shall per- form and execute such duties as shall be devolved upon him, from time to time, by the President, and shall conduct the busi- ness in such manner as the President shall, from time to time, prescribe. The next act established the War Department, and pro- vides that the Secretary of War should ex- ecute such duties as the President, in pur- suance of the Constitution, should devolve upon him. When they came to establish the Department of the Navy, they did it in the same words. But when they came to establish the Department of the Treasury, we see that they changed the title of the act and its whole language. It was, as first reported by the committee, entitled an act to establish an Executive Depart- ment, &c., but the title was subsequently changed. This act makes it the duty of the Secretary of the Treasury to propose plans to be submitted to Congress for rais- ing and collecting the revenue, to prescribe the form of keeping accounts, and to exe- cute such duties as by law might be re- quired of him. All the three other de- partments are presidential departments, belonging to the office of President. Now the Treasury Department was not a depart- ment of the executive branch of the Gov- ernment in name or design. To have placed the public money in an executive department, under the control of the Pres- ident, would have been a solecism in the Constitution. The money was to be drawn from the treasury by warrant alone. Such a thing as making the treasury an execu- tive department, and at the same time giving Congress the sole power of appro- priations, would have been a solecism and constitutional absurdity. His position,

therefore, was, that nothing is placed in the hands of the Executive but what the Constitution has put there.

The gentleman from Tennessee assumes that the President may exercise entire power over the Treasury Department in virtue of his power of removal. This suggested a theme so vast that he could but barely touch some few of its points. Mr. B. then argued at considerable length, against the position of the member from Tennessee, that the power of removal was incidental to the appoint- ment. In illustration of his views, he put a case. Who directs the marshal in the discharge of his duties? The court. Who appoints and removes the marshal? The court? Certainly not. But does it follow that the courts are therefore unable to give directions to the marshal? The doctrine contended for was a political absurdity. He ad- mitted that the President had the right of direction, but it did not result from his power of appointment and removal, but from official connexion and sub- ordination. Again, it is said, that all power must be judicial, ministerial, or executive; that this power is not ministerial nor judicial, and is, there- fore, executive. But there were certain acts per- taining to one department, which were oftentimes committed to another department. Again, it was said, that the President has power to demand the opinion, in writing, of each head of department, and that this must be for the purpose of giving directions in regard to the subject of the opinion called for. He had nothing to do with the Pres- ident's organization of his cabinet; but if he was not misinformed, the Attorney General and the Postmaster General were members of it. The cabinet was not made by the Constitution. The President had no power from the Constitution to ask the opinion of the Secretary of the Treasury which at all interfered with his argument. The Attorney General and Postmaster General were cabinet officers, but they were not recognised as executive officers by the Constitution.

The Constitution says that the President may require the opinion of the principal executive offi- cers in each department, &c. If the Treasury De- partment was not an executive department, then the President has no power to ask the opinion of the Secretary of the Treasury. So we may leave this revision out of the question. Finally, it was said by the gentleman from Tennessee, that it was the duty of the President to take care that the laws be faithfully executed; and from this he derived the power of the President over the Treasury De- partment. It was a good rule in logic, that what proves too much proves too little. This argument goes beyond the concerns of the departments, and gives the President the power of directing the Su- preme Court in the discharge of their duty. It turned the whole structure of the Government up- side down—fused all departments into one. He admitted the power of the President to remove an officer who wilfully disobeyed the law. The clause in question was given, not to enlarge the powers of the President, but to remove all obstructions to the discharge of the duties devolved upon him by other clauses of the Constitution. He assumed, therefore, as to the right of removal, that it gave the power or direction over such officers as prefer- red office to duty; but that it left the question at issue where it found it.

If his view was generally true, how much clearer was the truth in regard to the matter in hand—the removal of the deposites. The Secretary was to give reasons for their removal. Whose reasons— his own, or the President's? Doubtless his own. How does that square with his responsibility to the President? If he is responsible to the Presi- dent, must he not give his reasons to the President? To his own master he must answer, and not to another. The right of removal was, moreover, a charter regulation—a regulation by compact. Look at the language of the charter. There were author- ities given to the President, and authorities given to the Secretary of the Treasury. If all these du- ties were to be performed by the President, they would all have been assigned to him by the char- ter. But a portion was given to the President by name, and a portion to the Secretary by name. The powers of the President are, to appoint direct- ors on the part of the Government, with the advice and consent of the Senate, and to direct the issue of a scire facias, to ascertain whether the Bank had

violated its charter. The powers of the Secretary were, to direct transfers of the public funds, and to withhold from the bank the public deposites.

I repeat, said Mr. B., that the entire and exclu- sive control of the public deposites is inherent in Congress, except so far as it is given to the bank. Here he did not confound power with right. Con- gress, he contended, had absolute right over the deposites to the whole extent to which they had not parted with it to the bank. Congress is the treasurer of the people. It represents the people in raising revenue, in guarding it, and in appro- priating it to the public service. It gives certain rights to the bank, subject to a covenant. If the bank violated the covenant, there was an equiva- lent discharge from obligation on the other side. If the bank violated the agreement, the right re- verts to Congress to dispose of the deposites as it pleases. Now, gentlemen might make the rights of the bank as broad or as narrow as they please; as soon as one part of the agreement was violated, Congress could resume the whole power. The object of Congress was to provide for the safety of the deposites. The instant the bank ceases to perform her duty, that instant Congress might act. Here, in the charter, the power is given to the Secretary of the Treasury to act when it was im- possible that Congress could act—that is, when Congress was not in session. The dangerous consequences of the doctrine contended for, must strike every one. It stripped Congress of all power over the public money. Shall we stain the memory of the Congress of 1816 by supposing that they intended to give away this money to the bank and the Secretary of the Treasury, to enable them to hold it and control it as long as they mu- tually connived at each other's conduct, while Congress stood by with their hands tied?—for the doctrine comes to this. Did the Congress of 1816 intend to act in this manner? No, sir. They made a plain, obvious, and useful provision, giving the Secretary the power to withhold the deposites from the bank in a certain case, because, from his situation, he would necessarily be apprised of any approaching danger to the public money. This act was implicitly and almost expressly subjected by the terms of the charter to the revision of Con- gress.

So much for the proposition that Congress can- not interfere.

[The remainder of Mr. Binney's remarks for this day are unavoidably omitted.]

IN SENATE.

Mr. KANE, from the Committee on Private Land Claims, reported a bill for the relief of the heirs and legal representatives of Thomas H. Boyle; which was read a first and second time.

Mr. KANE also, from the same committee, re- ported a bill for the relief of the legal representa- tives of Lawrence Whitaker, deceased; upon which a similar order was had.

Mr. POINDEXTER, from the Committee on Public Lands, reported a bill for the relief of Cal- vin Smith, with an amendment.

Mr. POINDEXTER, from the same committee, made a location of land; which bills were read and committed.

Mr. ROBINSON made a report from the Com- mittee on Enrolled Bills.

Mr. ROBBINS, from the Library Committee, reported a resolution for the purchase of a bust on the part of Congress, of the late Chief Justice Ellsworth.

Mr. TOMLINSON, in conformity with notice given yesterday, asked and obtained leave to in- troduce a bill for the relief of Ithiel Town; which was read ; and

On motion of Mr. TOMLINSON, referred to the Committee on the Judiciary.

Mr. WHITE, from the Committee on Indian Affairs, made a report unfavorable to the petition of Mathew Irwin, which was concurred in.

Mr. MANGUM, from the Committee on For- eign Relations, moved that Enos Leavy have leave to withdraw his memorial and accompanying pa- pers; which was agreed to.

Mr. SHEPLEY presented a petition of David

Pearce and others, for the abolition of slavery in the District of Columbia, which was referred to the Committee on the District of Columbia.

After a short time, Mr. PRESTON moved to reconsider the vote of reference, with a view to lay the same on the table for a few days. Mr. PRESTON said, as the petition related to a question which was of a very interesting character in the Senate, he desired an opportunity of examining into it.

Mr. SPRAGUE made a few remarks against the motion.

After some further conversation between Messrs. CHAMBERS, PRESTON, and SHEPLEY,

Mr. PRESTON withdrew his motion to reconsider.

Mr. HENDRICKS, from the Committee on Roads and Canals, reported a bill with amendments, concerning certain public roads; which was read and committed.

The VICE PRESIDENT presented communications from the Secretary of the Navy and the Secretary of War, in reference to expenditures made in those departments; which were read and laid upon the table.

The VICE PRESIDENT also laid before the Senate a letter from the Secretary of War, responsive to the resolution offered by Mr. SHEPLEY, on the 7th inst:

"That the Secretary of War be directed to communicate to the Senate, any information within the department showing the injury done by storms, during the month of December last, to the pier on the western side of the entrance to Kennebunk river, in the State of Maine, and the necessity of an immediate repair; and to furnish an estimate of the sum required to make the necessary repairs."

The following bills were read a third time and passed:

A bill for the relief of George Chinn;

A bill for the relief of the widow and heirs of Robert Lahary;

A bill for the relief of Phineas Sprague and others;

A bill for the relief of Ebenezer Lobdell;

A bill for the relief of John Hone and Sons;

A bill making appropriations for constructing certain roads in the Territory of Arkansas;

A bill for the relief of Felix Spencer;

A bill for the relief of John Hartal;

A bill for the relief of the widow and heirs of Felix Adrain;

A bill granting certain privileges to the Baltimore and Ohio railroad.

A bill granting privileges in constructing a lateral branch of the same company.

Mr. POINDEXTER, after reading the message of the President of the United States of the 6th inst., relating to the presents made to the American consul at Tangier by the Emperor of Morocco, made a few explanatory observations previous to introducing the following resolution:

Resolved, That the President of the United States be requested to cause to be laid before the Senate a schedule of the several articles received by the ministers, consuls, or other agents of the Government of the United States at foreign courts, as presents from the Governments at which they were respectively accredited, and by them deposited in the Department of State; specifying each article, and its estimated value, and the name of the minister, consul, or agent to whom the present was made.

Mr. POINDEXTER asked its consideration at this time; when, no objection having been made, it was considered and adopted.

Mr. WILKINS adverted to an order made the other day by the Senate, requiring to be printed, for the use of its members, 5,000 copies of the Reasons of the Secretary of the Treasury for the removal of the public deposites. Another paper, in conformity with a call from the Senate, had subsequently been furnished by the Secretary. As both reports were upon the same subject, Mr. WILKINS moved that a similar number (5,000) be printed for the purposes of distribution.

Mr. CLAY objected to the motion, and hoped the Senate would not make the order, at least at this time. We (said Mr. C.) asked of the Secretary documents, sir, and he chose to respond to our demands by an argument. I repeat, sir, we called, for documents, for documents, and he has given us an uncalled-for argument. I object to the printing, because it would be an implied approbation of the unwarrantable attempt of the Secretary; a precedent which I, for one, sir, am not disposed to sanction.

Mr. CLAY concluded by moving that the resolution lie upon the table; which being assented to by Mr. WILKINS, such order was taken upon it.

Petitions and memorials were presented by Messrs. TYLER, SHEPLEY, and SWIFT, which obtained the usual reference.

The following resolutions were proposed, and lie one day of course:

By Mr. ROBBINS,

Resolved, That the Joint Library Committee be instructed to inquire into the expediency of a proposition to be made by Congress to the Parliament of Great Britain, to interchange and exchange copies of the acts and proceedings of their respective bodies, from year to year, and also the expediency of doing the same thing with regard to the legislative Chambers of France.

By Mr. HENDRICKS,

Resolved, That the Secretary of War be directed to communicate to the Senate, a report of the agent recently employed on a survey of the Cumberland road, west of the Ohio river.

The Senate then proceeded to consider the

ORDERS OF THE DAY.

The resolution of Mr. SPRAGUE—

That the Committee on the Library be instructed to inquire into the expediency of a proposition to be made by Congress, to a new statistical work proposed to be published by George Watterston—

Was adopted.

The resolution of Mr. MANGUM—

That the resolution adopted on the 14th of May, 1830, directing the Secretary of the Senate to contract with the printer of the House of Representatives for copies of the documents printed by order of the House, be, and the same is hereby rescinded—

Was, on motion of Mr. FORSYTH, laid upon the table: Ayes 25, noes not counted.

The resolution of Mr. KENT—

That the Committee on the Post Office and Post Roads be instructed to inquire into the propriety of so modifying the law regulating the Post Office Department, as to authorize the transmission by mail, of such books and public records, whether bound or in boards, as the Executive of the respective States are in the habit of interchanging with each other, upon such terms as will best comport with the importance of the subject.

The resolution of Mr. PORTER—

That the Postmaster General be directed to report to the Senate the number of failures which have occurred during the last twelve months in carrying the mail between the city of Washington and New Orleans, by the southern route, and the number and amount of forfeitures enforced by him in consequence of these failures during the same period—

Being under consideration, Mr. GRUNDY proposed the following amendment, viz:

After the word "route" insert "the names of the contractors who may have failed to fulfil their contracts, together with," and before the words "the number," &c.

Which being accepted by Mr. PORTER, the resolution, as modified, was adopted.

The Senate then proceeded to the special order of the day.

THE REMOVAL OF THE DEPOSITES.

The Senate resumed the consideration of the resolutions submitted by Mr. CLAY, on the 26th ultimo.

Mr. SOUTHARD said, that the adjournment took place yesterday just before he had closed the consideration of the last act performed by the Secretary in his withdrawal of the deposites from the United States Bank. He was then showing that the Secretary could not perform what he had undertaken to do. He now proceeded to show that the Secretary had, since the meeting of Congress, forbidden the Bank of the United States from performing its accustomed duty to the Government, as commissioner of loans. A most marked insult to Congress. Mr. S. then went into a minute statement to show that the Postmaster General had been authorized to borrow, and had borrowed from certain State banks, about $400,000, to meet the deficiency in the revenue of that department, besides over drafts, the extent of which he did not know, and (he continued) all this scheme was going on while the Secretary was placing the money of the Government in irresponsible places. Mr. S. contended, that if the charter of the bank was to expire in fifty hours, he would compel the agents of the Government to restore the deposites to the place from whence they were taken. But the Senate were to investigate the reasons of the Secretary, and in doing so he should not undertake to examine the issue formed between the President and the Secretary in relation to it—he would let them try that themselves. We are to look to its consequences, not upon the Government itself, and the people of the United States. The President of the United States and the bank were but as a feather compared to the interests of this Union and the violated laws of the land. He was willing, for the sake of the argument, to regard the reasons of the Secretary as true, and that he was acting by his own impulse, and upon his own judgment, but it required great faith to believe it, when it was considered that we had the positive assertion of Mr. Duane, that he was to act by the orders of the President, and upon his responsibility alone. Let the feeling be what it may, the issue he meant to try was between the violated laws of the country, and the punishment, he might call it, due to the violators of them. It was necessary to look first in the Secretary's principles for his reasons, for if they be untrue or unsound, his conclusions must be false also. The Secretary speaks of the treasury and the Treasury Department as one and the same thing. Now, there is a great distinction between the Secretary of the Treasury, who is required to perform certain general and known duties, and the Treasurer, a ministerial officer, from whom certain specific duties are required. We shall see what he says by adverting to pages one and two of his report. Mr. S. then read an extract, showing the duties of the Secretary in the absence of any legislative provision applicable to the act he felt called on to perform.

Mr. S. continued. He admits that the deposites are safe in the Bank of the United States, but the bank having violated its charter, he has a right to remove them as he thinks proper. The power thus claimed is an original power, emanating out of that belonging to his office, and the President's power emanating from his general power to see the laws faithfully executed. Mr. S. took leave to say that the reasons are unsound and unjustified by the law or the duty of the Secretary of the Treasury. Mr. S. here read at length extracts from the several laws establishing and regulating the Treasury Department, for the purpose of showing that the general powers and duties of the Secretary were defined and prescribed, and that they gave no color to the power assumed by him for the removal of the deposites, and then contended that the power to take the money of the nation and appoint the agents of the Government belonged to the Congress of the United States alone, and that the Secretary has assumed duties which did not belong to him. What, he would ask, is the character of the power? Is it not as purely legislative power as any other known to the Constitution? Does not the Constitution place in the hands of Congress to deal with and manage and control the purse of the nation? It is a legislative power, and of the very highest legislative character under our Government. But if the Secretary were to argue that it was an executive power, what then? Must it not be conferred? as if it is not conferred, how can he act? The Secretary will find no relief from those who claim it as an executive power. But his claim is for unlimited and an unrestricted power, and he presses his wonder that Congress should be conferred such a power upon him. In this, Mr. S. said, he would most cordially join him; really wondered at the assumption of a power which was not granted by the laws. But suppose the Secretary had said in his report that the President ordered him to remove the deposites, and had done it in pursuance of such order, would the

be any relief to him, or would it remove the Secretary's responsibility? The President was not authorized, under our Constitution and laws, to take off the responsibility of any officer of the Government on whom Congress has imposed such responsibility. He would suppose a case. Suppose an officer of the Government to violate a law, by order of the President, will his responsibility be removed? Certainly not. There were only two modes by which the responsibility could be taken off. One was by the power of an armed force. The other, where a man says a thing and it is believed where he does it, and is applauded, be the act what it may. Popularity may justify assuming the responsibility, but it is a most dangerous experiment. Mr. S. said that the whole result in his mind was, that if there was a single power which could relieve any officer of his whole responsibility, it was an unmitigated despotism. What, he would inquire, is a despotism, but that one man should say to another, you are to act on my responsibility? Could the Autocrat of the Russias, could the Sultan of Turkey do more? If one man can take upon himself the whole responsibility of every agent of Government, it is a revolution already, which, although bloodless, yet, in the emphatic language of the gentleman from Kentucky, may not continue so when the people, in their throes, shall begin to feel the chains riveted upon them. He had always thought the Constitution of the United States expressly designed to keep the Executive apart from the treasury of the nation. At the time of the formation of that instrument the subject engaged the attention of some of the most enlightened men of our country, and the cry of every patriot was, to keep them far asunder; and, accordingly, the Treasury Department was established for the purpose of preventing the Executive from having the control of the money of the nation.

Mr. S. here read at length from the laws of the United States the manner in which money was to be drawn from the treasury: that the Treasurer was to give bond; and asked, why was the Treasurer to give bond, if the Secretary was authorized to draw the money, put it where he pleased, and select his own agents? Why was not the Secretary himself required to give bond? There is not a man in the Government a disbursing officer, who is not obliged to give bond; and why is it that the Treasurer is to give it, and not the Secretary himself? There is but one solution to the question—that he alone is the officer appointed to receive and keep the moneys of the United States. Before Congress had provided the place for keeping the public money, the Treasurer was obliged to keep it safely. But when a place was provided by Congress for its reception, the Treasurer was not held responsible, but the guardians of that place; it was only when no place was provided for it, that the Treasurer was bound to keep it. It was the object of Congress to remove the treasury as far as possible from the Executive, or otherwise Congress would not have required the Secretary to make his communications to Congress only. If it had been otherwise, why was he not required to make his reports to the President, like the Secretary of War and Navy? But it is said that all this reasoning is of no validity, because the President retains the power of dismission; and therefore the inference is, that this power of dismission is to give to the President the entire control over our whole political system. Is this, can this be true? He did not deny the power of dismission. That was a question which had been agitated and settled at a very early day; but then it was not designed to be exercised as it has now been. The celebrated Elbridge Gerry, a prophet, and more than a prophet, foresaw the result of an abuse of this power, for he fixed the period at the year 1829. At his day, there was not a man in the Congress of the United States that ever dreamed that that power could or would be exercised for party purposes, or for enabling the Executive to obtain the control over the treasury of the Union. They went no further than to admit that it might be done. It was a power that was to be exercised under the control of the laws, and it has always been so exercised, until very lately. Where there is a power and a duty to be exercised agreeably to law, and there is a mental or other physical incapacity to exercise the duty, Mr. S. admitted that there was a power reposed in the Executive to see that the act enjoined should be either done or forbidden, as required by law; but then only until the legislative action could be brought to control both the act and the cause of the act. Could the President undertake to say how a man should perform his duty under the laws? The legislative power has directed its agent to perform a certain act according to his discretion. How, then, can he do so, if the President can interpose? and if he can, how is there anything, either of judicial or legislative power, left? There is none; the President possesses the whole judicial power of the country. If it be so, he can direct the marshal to bring before your courts all and any person, at his pleasure or his enmity; and where, then, is your trial by jury, that sacred guarantied right, which is the life and soul of this country? He would ask, then, if Senators were prepared to sanction such powers? If they were, they were prepared to be slaves. He was not prepared to say the President would abuse his power. But if he did not, who could know who his successor, or the successors of his successor, might be? He (Mr. S.) would not trust any man on earth with such a power. The conclusion of his mind, then, was, and he had come to it on anxious reflection, that it was a high abuse of power in the Executive to displace an officer because he would not execute his duties by the Executive standard. He regarded the dismissal of Mr. Duane, not as a triumph over the Secretary or the bank, but over the people and over the law of the land. But to return to the preëxisting power. If the Treasurer is to receive and keep the money, does it not follow that he shall select the place where it shall, on his own responsibility, be safely kept? But suppose we should admit the power claimed by the Secretary. What is his reasoning upon it? He says it was reserved in the sixteenth section of the bank charter; but if it is to be found nowhere else, it is a useless provision, for it will not bear him out in his position.

Mr. S. having again argued at length upon the contract entered into between the Government and the bank by the charter, and also upon the general nature and proper and legal construction of contracts, said this contract was a voluntary act or offer on the part of the Government; the formation of it was not called for by the bank or the individuals who were to be concerned in it. It was not, however, uncalled for by the Government, for the Government was forced by the necessities of the nation to offer the charter, and it prescribed the terms of its own accord—it made a voluntary offer to the people, which, having been embraced, the contract is sealed, and the nation would disregard its own honor if it should now stand by and see it violated by the officers of the Government. At the time the Government made this offer the evils of the country were great, and it was wished to create a fiscal agent for its own use. It therefore prescribed the terms on which it should act. True it might have left this to the State banks, but it had passed an act on the 15th of January, 1815, which created such an agent; the President, however, vetoed the bill, but let it be remembered, not on constitutional grounds. But at the next session Congress saw the immense difficulties upon the country which they were compelled to cut through, and being on the eve of chartering the present bank, they required of it the performance of certain terms, the payment of specie, the restoration of the currency, to act as the fiscal agent of the Government to keep safely the public money, and transfer it to any place where it might be required, without any expense to the Government. On the other hand, Congress had given it an act of incorporation—had subscribed seven millions to its stock—had made it its fiscal agent, and held out invitations to the people to subscribe the remainder of the stock. All this was the act of Congress, and it was dishonorable now to violate a contract which was the result of its own proposition. It was not a question of this man or that man at that day. The bank was required to perform certain duties, and if it failed to do them the charter prescribed a remedy. But when it had performed all the duties required of it, it had a right to profit for themselves—to heap up as much as it could for the stockholders. What was the subscription of Congress to the stock? Was it more than a subscription of the people, whose interest in the bank the Government directors were appointed to superintend and watch over? Sir, these directors were not sent to act as spies and informers upon the bank, but to represent one of the parties in the concern. By the acceptance of the terms by the people which were dictated by the Government, it had no right to travel out of its terms and require others. Mr. S. was no friend to the bank; was not a stockholder, and never had been; he did not know ten of its directors, and had enjoyed as little of its benefits as any other man, but it had performed the terms required of it. The Secretary admits that the deposites are safe; the bank did restore the currency of the country, and in doing so passed millions into the treasury which would otherwise have been lost. From a depreciation of twelve or fifteen per cent. it had raised the paper money then in the hands of the Government to par, by which it was enabled to pay nine millions of the national debt years sooner than it would have been paid. Everything which had been obtained by the Government through the Bank of Columbia (and it had not lost a single cent) had been saved by the branch here, at a loss to the branch of at least $150,000. And yet the Secretary says that although the bank may have performed all the terms of its stipulation, he may violate the terms offered by the Government, and remove the deposites. No matter what are his reasons or motives—no matter how vile they may be, he contends that he is the agent of the Government, and can remove them whenever he thinks fit. If this could be, Mr. S. thought it proved a deep and degraded state of both public and private morality. But he says further that he may do it whenever in his judgment the public interest and convenience in any degree require it—the slightest notions of convenience are to justify him in trampling down a contract which the pledged honor of the Government required him to uphold. Convenience was a stale apology, which usurpers could readily grasp hold of for the assumption of power. Did Congress, when it adopted that section in the bank charter on which this assumed power is founded, believe that it was conferring such a power? Did the honorable Senator from Massachusetts now here, but then a member of the House of Representatives, who penned that section, understand at the time that it was conferring such a power?

Mr. WEBSTER. No, no, no.

Mr. S. then continued, by reading at length an extract from an opinion given by Mr. Taney when Attorney General of the United States, for the purpose of showing that he held opinions on the doctrine of powers and delegated trusts different from those on which he acted in the removal of the deposites. Mr. S. then went into an examination of the opinions imputed to Mr. Crawford by the Secretary of the Treasury, in relation to the removal of the Government deposites. He read the resolution of Congress from Story, third volume, page 1616, upon which he contended that Mr. Crawford's correspondence was founded; and that it proceeded from the anxiety of Congress to restore specie payments before the Bank of the United States went into operation, and to withhold the large amount of Government funds in State bank paper from the United States Bank, to protect them from that bank. Mr. S. had just concluded his argument on that point, when he yielded the floor to Mr. SPRAGUE, on whose motion the Senate adjourned.

HOUSE OF REPRESENTATIVES.

THURSDAY, *January* 9, 1834.

The following bills were reported from the standing committees, read twice, and committed to the Committee of the Whole.

By Mr. WHITE, of New York, a bill authorizing the purchase of live oak frames for a frigate and sloop of war, and for other purposes.

Also, a bill to authorize the President of the United States to direct transfers of appropriations in the naval service, under certain circumstances.

By Mr. INGE, a bill for the relief of John C. Nailor.

By Mr. CASEY, a bill to continue the Cumberland road from Mississippi to the city of Jefferson, in the State of Missouri.

By Mr. CAVE JOHNSON, a bill approving sundry preëmption claims in the southeastern dis-

trict of Louisiana. [The consideration of this bill was postponed to Tuesday next.]

By Mr. ASHLEY, a bill authorizing the relinquishment of the sixteenth section of public lands granted to the use of schools, and the entry of other lands in lieu thereof.

Also, a bill granting the right of preëmption to John Yantis. Read twice, and ordered to be engrossed.

By Mr. MUHLENBERG, a bill for the relief of the legal representatives of William Rogers, deceased.

By Mr. CRANE, a bill for the relief of Benjamin Jacobs, surviving executor of John Baird, deceased.

By Mr. CLAY, a bill for the relief of William Innis, of Arkansas.

By Mr. CASEY, a bill for the location and survey of the Cumberland road from Vandalia to the Mississippi river.

Mr. JONES, from the Committee on Elections, made the following report:

The Committee of Elections, to which was referred the letter of Matthew St. Clair Clarke relative to "the compilation of all the cases of contested elections before Congress since 1789," have had the same under consideration, and have directed me to report—

That, upon an examination of the work, they are of opinion the same would be useful and conduce to lighten the labor of the said committee and of the House in future contests, and calculated to produce uniformity and consistency of decision, which is highly desirable on all such occasions; and have directed me to offer the following resolution:

Resolved, That 600 copies of said work be printed, as other public documents, and that the Committee on Accounts do ascertain and allow to said Clarke a reasonable compensation for his time and labor in compiling the same.

The resolution was agreed to.

REMOVAL OF THE DEPOSITES.

The House having resumed the consideration of the motion to refer the Secretary of the Treasury's report on the deposites to the Committee of Ways and Means; and the question being upon the motion of Mr. McDuffie to add to the motion for reference the following instructions to the said committee:

"With instructions to report a joint resolution 'providing that the public revenue hereafter collect-'ed shall be deposited in the Bank of the United 'States, in compliance with the public faith, pledged 'by the charter of the said bank"—

Mr. BINNEY continued his remarks. The Secretary assumes that the bank has violated its charter, and that the violation consists mainly and principally in the mode in which the committees of the bank were appointed and its operations conducted by the committees. The mode of appointing committees, he understood the Secretary to charge, as a plain violation of the charter. This was a small matter, but he wished to be right in small things. But the Secretary was in this, as in other things, wholly wrong. He then read the clause in the charter which requires that business should be transacted by a board of directors, consis ing of not less than seven members, of whom the president should always be one, unless prevented by sickness, &c. The Secretary alleges that it was not competent to the bank to do anything unless seven directors contributed to the act. This phrase, "transaction of business," was explained by another phrase in another section. In the 10th section, the directors for the time being are empowered to appoint such officers and clerks under them, as they might deem necessary for the execution of business. A distinction was made between the transaction and execution of business. To hold that every act of the bank was to be executed by seven directors and the president, was absurd. If that construction was correct, not a note could be paid nor a deposite received except by this quorum of directors. In the sickness of the president, his place is to be filled by any one else. What is the necessary business of the president, as prescribed by the charter, he was at a loss to find. Any other special duty than the signature of notes he had not found prescribed in the charter. The meaning of the section was plain; a quorum of seven must authorize the business to be done. The charter requires a quorum to give effect to what was proposed to be done. Sir, the Secretary of the Treasury seems not to be aware what the constitution of the charter was and is, as to by-laws. The power of making by-laws is necessary to every corporation. There are gentlemen here who know that it has been settled for a hundred years, that a power given to a whole body may be delegated to a portion of that body. The first act done by the corporation of the bank was to make its by-laws. The 10th section of the charter gives the directors the express authority of appointing committees to transact business, and they have exercised it. The expediency of its exercise is not a question for this body: it was enough that it was expedient in the opinion of the directors. They had the right, and they deemed it necessary to exercise it. As to the extent of the business transacted by the exchange committee, that was not a subject of inquiry here. There was not a bank in the country which has not its exchange committee, and does not discount notes without the presence of a quorum of directors. Whether this exchange committee made reports or not of their proceedings to the board, is not a matter for inquiry here; but, in fact, they did report.

Then comes the charge of concealment of the operations of the bank. Now, there were some points which he would leave to the discussion of those who think they can make anything of them. The old affair of the three per cents. had been so fully and so often discussed here that he would pass that by. To one matter he would in passing give a slight notice—the statement of the gentleman from Tennessee that there was a contradiction between the bank report of 1832 and the statement since made at the call of the Senate, in relation to the printing accounts. The fact is that there is no contradiction. The call was specific, for the sums paid to editors—the report embracing three different items: 1st. Money paid for printing; 2d. To editors for publishing and circulating documents; and 3d. For the purchase and distribution of printed documents. There was nothing at all, in these statements, involving any contradiction. This, however, was a small matter, and he would pass that also. The point of concealment referred to he would examine. It is charged that the committee of offices did not report to the board of directors what measures they had ordered in reference to the reduction of discounts. It was difficult to conceive what this charge was grounded upon. Another charge is, that the Government directors were kept in ignorance of the proceedings of the exchange committee, and that neither of them was a member of that committee. This was a matter which greatly concerned the bank and all banks, the right of particular directors to be placed on committees. The Government directors claimed the right to be placed on the committees appointed by the board. They had no more right to be put on a particular committee than any member of this House has to be placed on a particular committee. Any member here has as good a right to complain that he is not a member of this or that committee, as the Government directors have to complain that they were not put upon the exchange committee. It was not the right of a director to require his appointment to a particular committee; if the board refused it, the director must submit. The operations of this House were subject to the will of the House, but the appointment of committees is subjected by the House to the absolute control of the Speaker. Now he would take up the question of expediency of refusing to appoint the Government directors upon committees. In times past, the Government directors had been in the fullest confidence of the board of directors, and acted with them in the utmost harmony. Mr. Biddle was himself a Government director for some years, and at that time there was no distinction between the Government directors and the private directors, either in policy or design. But in 1833, it began to be vehemently suspected by the majority of the board that the Government directors entertained very peculiar notions of their duty. It was, he repeated, vehemently suspected that these gentlemen considered it to be their duty to use their post for the purpose of making partial and unfair representations of the business transacted, and of impeaching to the President the conduct of the directors of the bank, with whom they were associated. He said it was, at that time, vehemently suspected —for the gentlemen did not care to avow their object—that the Government directors considered themselves as clothed with political power to represent and comment upon the transactions of the bank in a manner which would be acceptable to their superiors. If this suspicion was well founded, it did not become the bank to assist the gentlemen in their objects. If the Government directors thought it their duty to use their information for political purposes, for the purpose of misrepresenting the transactions of the bank, and for the purpose of abusing the confidence and wounding the feelings of honorable men with whom they were associated, what inducement, he would ask, had the private directors to sit on a committee by the side of the Government directors? But one answer would be given to the question by any honorable man. This, which was suspected at the time referred to, was now known to be true by the public confession of the Government directors. He would put himself to the proof of what he asserted. As early as April, 1833, it appears they had an object which they did not dare to avow. He did not envy them the feelings which dictated their letter to the President on the 22d April, 1833. The letter was signed by Messrs. Gilpin, Sullivan, and Wager, from which he read the following passage:—

"Without considering any portion of our re-'marks as falling within the limits of those pri-'vate accounts, which, as you state, the charter 'has so carefully guarded, since the whole relate 'to the action of the board on matters fully open 'and discussed before them, and extend in no in-'stance to the private debtor and creditor account 'of individuals; yet we may be excused for ex-'pressing much gratification at your assurance that 'the information requested is for your own satis-'faction, and that you do not wish it extended 'beyond our personal knowledge. We may be 'permitted also to add, that the wishes and opin-'ions which we took the liberty of expressing in 'our former letter, have since been more strongly 'confirmed, and that we should not only feel more 'satisfaction ourselves, but be enabled to convey 'to you more full and correct information, were 'we to proceed in an investigation whose object 'was avowed, and if we were strengthened by that 'official sanction which we suggested."

No wonder they did not feel comfortable, and wished to have the written authority of the President for making their investigations openly and avowedly, while they were daily sitting by the side of honorable men. It did not appear, however, that the authority sought was ever granted. But this was not all. We have, in their memorial to Congress, their confession of faith. These gentlemen here undertake to state what they are:

"Nothing can be plainer, than that the public di-'rectors were devised as instruments for the attain-'ment of public objects; that their being insisted 'upon in the charter itself, was in obedience to the 'will of those who elected the legislative body by 'which it was passed; and that their appointment 'was given to the President, with the advice and 'consent of the Senate of the United States, (not 'to the mere fiscal representative,) in order to 'clothe them with all the character of official rep-'resentation, and to exact from them a discharge 'of all the duties, public, political, and patriotic, 'incident to a trust so conferred."

Yes, sir, they say they are "devised as instruments, and given to the President," &c. Mr. B. commented on this phrase at some length.

Now, if their theory of their offices is correct, my answer to it is this: If these were the political directors, the others were the anti-political directors, and the private directors did well to go on and discharge their duties. But, sir, the heads of these gentlemen were made dizzy with their political elevation. But they were not "devised as instruments," though they choose to make themselves so. There was no distinction made by the charter between the private and Government directors. The private directors owed a duty to the public, and they performed it; the Government directors owed a duty to the bank, and they did not perform it.

The public directors were not placed there to

make inquiries for the President. The President had no authority to make such inquiries. The charter had not given the authority to him, but to the Secretary, to a limited extent, and to Congress, through the means of a committee, to an unlimited extent. Both of these modes were open and public modes of investigation, and might be carried to any extent, while, at the same time, the bank would have an opportunity to vindicate itself from false representations. But these gentlemen were bound, by their oath of homage and fealty, to give representations without the knowledge of the bank. The charter never meant to deal thus with the character and feelings of the honorable men who, it must have presumed, would be placed there. The Secretary of the Treasury received weekly returns of the condition of the bank, its notes, specie, debts, &c.

The authority given to the Secretary of the Treasury to investigate the concerns of the bank, was for the purpose of enabling him to ascertain whether the deposites were safe, and every power necessary for this purpose he possessed. I say, said Mr. B., that the board did right to resist the claims of these Government directors. They should be praised, instead of censured, for excluding them from an association in the business of the committees. In what a state of things did this doctrine place the United States Bank. The deposites were removed. The Government was in an attitude of hostility to it. The bank made a statement weekly of the position of the bank, and it went into the hands of a gentleman who was disposed to put the worst possible construction on everything done by the bank, and would counteract every measure attempted to enable the bank to wind up. But the Secretary of the Treasury only knows the results of the measures taken by the bank for its security. He now wants the *quo modo*—where is the money to be placed, and whence is it to be taken? The Government directors must inform him what course the bank is to take, in order that he may take such steps as will embarrass it in winding up. He had remarked that the power of the Secretary was subject to some limitations; this question would doubtless receive an investigation before Congress. He asked gentlemen to look at it in one aspect. The contract made by the Secretary with the Girard Bank enlarges his authority to the extent which the Government claimed in regard to the United States Bank, on account of a similar clause in the contract with the Bank of Virginia. The stockholders of that bank had refused to sanction the contract. What is this new authority? An inquiry into accounts of A and B, not to see whether the deposites were safe, but to see who has bank dealings, and, in reference to their political character, to exercise the authority of transferring deposites.

Another objection made against the bank, is, that it neglected to furnish the necessary means to the Government directors to furnish an accusation against its existence. If there were no means to be furnished, no authentic allegation to be supported by any means within the cognizance of the bank directors, are they to be condemned for not providing what did not exist? And if they did exist, are they to be condemned for not furnishing evidence against themselves, and endeavoring to ruin the stockholders, who had intrusted property to their custody and care? But no just grounds for accusation did exist: no feasible objection can therefore be made for not furnishing unjust grounds.

Another charge made by the Secretary of the Treasury, or another of his reasons assigned in his report, for his removing the deposites, is the allegation for concealment or faithlessness relative to the French bill for $1,000,000; a bill that had been protested by the French Government, and the responsibility of which had been immediately assumed by the bank. For this service the bank had made a charge, as it would have done in any and every other instance. But the gentleman from Tennessee assumes the law and the fact in this matter. The only law applicable to the case is an old statute of Maryland made in 1785—valid, perhaps, within the jurisdiction of Maryland—but obscure or obsolete elsewhere. The bank was undoubtedly entitled to make a claim for damages on assuming the responsibility of a protested bill of this nature; yet, because it had taken no step to enforce its claim; because it had not peremptorily demanded immediate payment; because it had merely entered the amount in the usual account with Government; because it had relied on the integrity of the Government to pay a reasonable demand, and felt conscious, not only of the propriety of its own claim of damages, but of the ability of Government to meet the claim—the bank is therefore accused, by the Secretary of the Treasury, with want of faithfulness, or with concealment. Is it not the privilege of the lowest in society to make the lowest charge, on any reasonable demand, upon the highest and most powerful in the nation? Well do they know this, who make such a charge, and make it but to swell the catalogue of allegations; to make that appear something, which in itself is nothing; to make that appear popularly base, which is radically correct. The bank bought the bill, and paid the money due on it. It consequently made a claim of damages, precisely similar to the customary claims for damages insisted on by the United States during the last forty years. Is it not, then, a strange perversion of mind to look on the fact of a claim being instituted by the bank, analogous to claims justified by a forty years' procedure of the Government of the country, as a sufficient warrant for the breach of faith implied in the contract given by the charter to the Bank of the United States? How can such a charge be sustained—how justified?

The last reason assigned by the Secretary of the Treasury for removing the deposites is contained in the accusation that the bank had exhibited a determination to obtain political power. Had I (said Mr. B.) been a director of the bank, and sitting by the side of men who are an ornament to their city and an honor to their country; who from their youth to their more matured age have been beloved, respected, and honored; men whose characters are not only without reproach, but whose reputation is held in the highest estimation; and if I had been called on for my opinion relative to the transactions of the directors, and if I had differed from them, I would have considered it tantamount to treason to superior intelligence, and an assumption of arrogance which should have justly exposed me to merited contempt. During the years 1829, '30, and '31, I had no concern as a director in the affairs of the bank. In January, 1832, I was chosen a director; but being appointed on a committee to examine the affairs of the bank, I have since kept apart from all immediate interference in its control, and have been informed of its course only as the public and the House have been informed—by published statements. And, as to his professional relations to the bank, he would not condescend to notice the idle rumors that had been interestedly circulated; nor would he attempt to vindicate the integrity and honor of that profession to which he and many members of both Houses of Congress belonged; neither would he wait to inquire what compensation would induce one of an honorable mind to sell his conscience and his principles of rectitude to the purposes of his client.

But the bank has been charged with having exercised political power. Granted, granted—the charge is granted; but the bank has not succeeded in its exercise of this alleged power. The letter of the Secretary of the Treasury proves that the bank did not succeed. The last election, he asserts, proves that it did not succeed. The force of array, legislative and executive, was against the bank; and it did not succeed. The act of removal was, therefore, not an imperative or retributive act; but one of a malignant dye—an act vindictive. It was an act for which there was no necessity; an act which not only has disturbed the affairs of the bank, but has cursed the country; an act not to punish for what had been done or supposed to have been done, but ostensibly and interestedly alleged, to prevent what is not improbable or impossible to be hereafter done or supposed. 'Tis true that the bank has printed and published papers and documents giving information of opinions and testimonies in its own defence; but never in any instance is he aware that it has given currency to scurrility in any pamphlet. If it has, he does not know. He is aware of nothing which has in any instance emanated from the bank—not even the review of the veto message—which is not within the verge of constitutional law. It has but claimed the common privilege asserted in the Constitution, of the natural and political right of all to defend themselves. It has but claimed the free expression of opinion, the liberty of the press in its own defence. What is the Constitution worth, if such a right is to be submerged in the case of a bank publicly and politically accused? if the liberty of the press is to be arbitrarily abridged in any devoted instance? What would the nation assert if Congress were to pass an enactment abridging the liberty of the press—if it enacted a law that such and such persons, parties or companies, should not be permitted to print anything in their own defence? Would not all instantly exclaim against such an act as an arbitrary violation of the Constitution? To what less, therefore, does the charge of the Secretary of the Treasury amount, because the bank had used the liberty of the press to disseminate accurate information of its conduct by authentic statements and views counter to other views and opinions interestedly promulgated? Is the bank to be denied the right claimed by all and every citizen of the Union, agreeably to the charter of the Constitution? Certainly not. If not, then has no gentleman the right to make an exception against the use of any constitutional privilege. The bank is like all—responsible for the abuse not the use of the privilege. It is responsible to the judicial tribunals of the land. It is to be arraigned before a jury, to be heard, tried, and then sentenced. But to condemn without being heard; to sentence on club conviction, without being tried by the legal and prescribed tribunals of the land, is not to be tolerated in a land of freedom.

But the treasury has evinced no slight assumption of political power, in unconstitutionally endeavoring to destroy one bank, and substitute fifty banks; in subverting one bank where it had legislative control without direction, and where the accounts of stockholders were perfectly secure, and establishing others whose accounts (by contract) are to be opened to investigation, and therefore as a necessary consequence, to direction.

Even had the bank assumed the power imputed, it was exerted for the safety of the nation against power in office. Now any capability of assuming power in any bank receiving the deposites, must be exerted not in opposition to Executive power or interference, but fearfully in its support or augmentation—a support which may prove ruinous to the interests and freedom of the country.

If the bank had been guilty of any error or crime, the law was open, and specified. Why did not the Executive resort to the *scire facias* prescribed by the law, and give the bank the constitutional right to be heard by a jury of the country—give its directors that which has been secured to them as their birthright as citizens, and that which has been ensured to them in their official capacity by the terms of their charter? Why not grant them the common privilege to have their case tried; and then that they should abide by the result!

In his historical researches, he has not been enabled to ascertain more than one parallel case, in which a charter had been destroyed on the alleged ground of assumption of political power. That was in the reign of Charles 2d of England. He had obtained possession of the charter of the city of London, from the same alleged reason; yet had obtained it then with all his power, solely by his tampering and packing court and jury. The indictment charged the corporation of London with having practised sedition, and interfered with political power. By means of the then Attorney General, who was very well disposed to serve the Crown—he held in obeisance the tribunal before which the trial took place; yet not till he had turned out one judge, and another had been afflicted with apoplexy. Then obtained he possession of the charter of London—which he held during the balance of his reign; and which was held during the short reign of his successor, James the 2d. But it was restored when constitutioual liberty dawned over the political horizon of that period, at the Revolution—at the accession of the house of Orange to the throne which had been disgraced so by the Stuarts. Then was the decision reversed unanimously by the House of Peers; and then and since was the tribunal which pronounced that decision subjected to the odium of all—as the op-

probium of the bench and the scorn of the people. Mr. BINNEY then read the account as detailed by Bishop Burnett, in his "History of his own Times."

The state of the country requires that the deposites should be restored, without any immediate or ultimate reference to the renewal of the charter. If the charter will be renewed, then should the deposites be restored, in order to preserve the equilibrium of the currency; and if not, still should they be restored, agreeably to the terms of the charter, till Congress should consider it proper to order otherwise. But if he were careless of the consequences resulting to the country from a deranged currency, and a pecuniary pressure, he would by all means advise that they should not be restored, but scattered about as at present, till ruin would inevitably stare them in the face, and disorder brood over the ruins of the commerce of the country.

At the expiration of its charter, the bank and its customers, those at least to whom the bank is indebted, and those who are indebted to it, must exercise a mutual forbearance. The bank will be as much compelled to conciliate to its debtors as its debtors must do to it. Punctuality cannot be expected on both sides; for it will be no trifling matter for the bank to withdraw its circulation of fifty millions of discounts and bills. But if the pressure is to be continued in reversion at the expiration of the charter, it is perhaps better that it should now be encountered, while there is some hope of being enabled to arrest some of the evils necessarily consequent upon a state of derangement and constitutional violation. The country will not then be better enabled to bear the evils than now. The nation will gain nothing by delay. The people will be but little benefited, except that they will, to their cost, perceive the indispensable utility of the present bank, or one established on a similar basis. There is no true wisdom, no true courage in postponing the evil day; a shipwreck of the State will occur, and few will perhaps prove fortunate to save even a plank from the wreck, except by means of their own devisal. All are as well braced now as they will be hereafter, except they acquire additional means of support. And unless some remedy be speedily and surely provided, those evils will be found true, oppressive, disastrous.

Mr. B. concluded his address by an eloquent peroration; but which was unfortunately not distinctly heard in the reporter's seat, partly from the hurried enunciation of the speaker and the smothered accents of his cadences in their die-away falls. Yet sufficient was heard to learn that he pronounced a warm eulogy on Mr. McDuffie; to learn that he besought the House not to treat the question as one of party pretensions, but rather as one affecting the general interests of the community; as one involving the purity of the Constitution, the stability of contracts, and the permanence of a free Government; as a question involving public faith, national existence, and the honor and integrity of the country at home and abroad. All friends of freedom throughout the earth are interested in the decision of the question. Justice and patriotism—impartial justice and enlightened patriotism, will view the decision as one of common importance and feeling; and if defeated, they will surrender their hopes of liberty prostrated at the altar of the spirit of party.

Mr. B. spoke to-day for one hour and a half.

Mr. CAMBRELENG said, that he was sensible of the responsibility he had assumed in attempting to follow the able and eloquent gentleman from Pennsylvania, [Mr. BINNEY.] He did not now rise for the purpose of proceeding with the debate, although he was prepared to do so should such be the decision of the House. Before doing so, he felt bound to waive all personal considerations, and to submit a motion to arrest, if possible, the further progress of the debate. He knew that the previous question was obnoxious to a portion of the most decided opponents of the bank—he respected the motives of the gentlemen, and if the House should decide against it, he should submit with great deference to its judgment and go on with the question. He begged the House to understand that he submitted the motion with reluctance. He had never, to his recollection, made such a motion before. He felt himself compelled, from his peculiar position, to take the earliest opportunity to arrest the further agitation of a question which was so distressing, not only to the district which he had the honor to represent in part, but to the whole country. Whether this debate should be continued weeks or months—if the question should be kept in suspense for two years—the country must continue to be disturbed. It was nothing but a struggle of the Bank of the United States for a new charter, and it would ultimately turn its batteries on the North, South, East, or West. He did not mean to impute to the president and directors any other motives than those common to all such institutions; any other bank would struggle in the same manner. Believing as they do that the institution is absolutely necessary to the country, they conduct their measures regardless of all other considerations but the main one of obtaining a renewal of its charter. The more the country is distressed, as they think, the more certain they are of obtaining their object. By arresting the progress of the debate at this stage, after the able defence of the gentleman from Pennsylvania, the friends of the bank could have no right to complain. They had a month ago evinced great anxiety to have this question promptly decided. He was satisfied if it continued another month, it would terminate at last only with the previous question. The motion now pending had been effectually decided three different times by the House. The last question upon the memorial of the Philadelphia banks—which memorial concluded with the very words of the motion of the gentleman from South Carolina—was referred to the Committee on Ways and Means. He begged the House to understand that he submittde the motion from a sense of public duty; if they decided against it, he should proceed with the debate.

The motion of Mr. CAMBRELENG was lost by a majority of 108 to 89.

He then made a motion to adjourn the debate till to-day.

The House then, by consent, proceeded to transact ordinary business.

The SPEAKER presented a communication from the Secretary of War, with an account of the expenditure of the contingent fund; also from the Secretary of the Navy, with a statement of various contracts for the last year; which were severally laid on the table and ordered to be printed.

Several private bills from the Senate were read by their titles, and having been passed through their first and second stages, were referred to the standing committees.

The House then, on motion of Mr. POLK, resolved itself into Committee of the Whole on the state of the Union, (Mr. MCINTIRE in the chair,) and proceeded to consider the bills making appropriation for the service of the navy for 1834, and for the Indian department; which were severally agreed to.

The bill making appropriation in part for the service of Government, commonly called the House appropriation bill, having been returned by the Senate with an amendment thereto, striking out a proviso, originally in the bill when sent from the House, to prohibit either House from directing the purchase of books or the printing of them, not warranted by law;

Mr. POLK moved that the committee disagree to the amendment; which motion was briefly debated by Messrs. McDUFFIE, WHITTLESEY, ADAMS, EDWARD EVERETT, GORHAM, and CLAY.

An amendment to the amendment of the Senate, moved by Mr. EVERETT, granting $1,000 to the Joint Library Committee, was agreed to. And the question on Mr. POLK'S motion being put, it was negatived.

Thereupon the committee rose, and reported the several bills to the House.

The bills granting appropriations for the Indian department, and for the naval service, were then ordered to be engrossed for their third reading to-morrow.

The amendment granting $1,000 to the Library Committee was not concurred in by the House, and the question then being on concurring with the amendment of the Senate to the bill making appropriations for the service of Government for 1834, before any final action was had thereon,

The House adjourned.

IN SENATE.

FRIDAY, *January* 10, 1834.

A message was received from the President of the United States by the hands of Mr. Donelson, his Private Secretary.

Mr. FRELINGHUYSEN submitted the following resolution, the immediate consideration of which he asked of the Senate:

Resolved, That that Secretary of the Treasury be directed to inform the Senate of the construction which has been given by that department to the act passed at the last session of Congress, entitled "An act to modify the act of the 14th of July, 1832, and all other acts imposing duties on imports," and also to furnish copies of such instructions as may have been given to collectors regulating their duty under the said act.

Mr. CLAY said he was glad the gentleman had presented this resolution. If the information which he had received, relative to the construction given to the act of last session by the Secretary of the Treasury, was correct, it was necessary that there should be prompt legislation on the subject. He had heard that the Secretary had put a construction on that act by which the minimum duties on cotton fabrics were entirely swept away, and the duties brought down from 80 to 20 per cent. It was a construction which, if persevered in, would expose to inevitable destruction the whole cotton manufacture of the country, and especially that of printing. He wished that a fair experiment should be made under the act of last session, and that that might be done, the construction ought to be in accordance with the plain meaning and intent of Congress, and not by treasury interpretation.

Mr. WEBSTER said that this subject had never attracted his attention, or come under his notice, until this morning. He had received the same information which the gentleman from Kentucky had, in relation to this matter, and he did not hesitate to say that if the construction given by the Secretary of the Treasury be correct, it would be an entire prostration of the whole cotton manufacture of this country. While the bill was pending, during the last session, he gave an opinion as to the fair and just construction of the act, and some of the gentlemen near him would remember that he then asked from them the expression of their opinions on the subject in writing, which were given, adverse to that supposed to be held by the Secretary. He, therefore, concurred in the opinion of the necessity of obtaining the imputed construction, whatever it might be. If that were true, millions upon millions would not compensate for the injury which would be inflicted upon that branch of the national industry, the manufacture of cotton fabrics. The information came upon him at a blow—he was not prepared for it. Opposed, as he was, to the passage of the law at the last session, he then saw no such consequences to be apprehended from it, and he was sure the gentleman from Kentucky himself, who introduced the bill, did not and could not have anticipated such a thing. It was true he saw that such a construction might be given to it, and he did hope that it might turn out that the Secretary did not give it such a construction as had been imputed to him. He was, therefore, in favor of the immediate adoption of the resolution.

Mr. FORSYTH said, he was not opposed to the resolution. But he thought that when the Secretary's construction was asserted, we could understand better whether it was in violation of the law, or only a mistake. He thought the terms of the resolution were too broad—it asked for the construction given to all the laws on the subject.

Mr. FRELINGHUYSEN explained his object.

Mr. FORSYTH thought that the construction given to the act of last session would, perhaps show everything that was wanted.

The resolution was then agreed to.

Mr. ROBBINS, from the Library Committee reported a joint resolution for the purchase of copies of the Laws of the United States; which was read a first and second time.

Mr. TIPTON, from the Committee on Indian Affairs, reported a bill for the relief of Francis I

Fontaine and Sons; which was read a first time, and the report accompanying it ordered to be printed.

Mr. TIPTON, from the Committee of Claims, reported a bill for the relief of Thomas Richardson.

Mr. TIPTON, from the same committee, to whom was referred the petition of Samuel and James ———, of Indiana, believing the subject involved a legal question, moved its reference to the Committee on the Judiciary; which was ordered.

Mr. WRIGHT, from the Committee on Claims, reported a bill for the relief of Philip Hickley.

Mr. WRIGHT, from the same committee, moved that the petition of Thomas Cutts, jr., be referred to the committee on the Judiciary.

Mr. POINDEXTER, from the Committee on Public Lands, reported a bill favorable to the settlers on public lands, with an amendment.

Mr. POINDEXTER, from the same committee, reported unfavorably to the petition of William Churchill; which was agreed to, and the petitioner had leave to withdraw his papers.

Mr. WEBSTER, from the Committee on Finance, to whom was referred the petition of ——— Langlorn, moved that it be referred to the Committee on Private Land Claims; which was agreed to.

Mr. POINDEXTER, from the Committee on Public Lands, reported a bill in favor of John Kirkpatrick; which was read a first and second time.

Mr. POINDEXTER, from the same committee, reported a bill for the relief of Anna Howard Penrose; which was read twice and committed.

ORDERS OF THE DAY.

The resolution of Mr. ROBBINS,

That the Joint Library Committee be instructed to inquire into the expediency of a proposition to be made by Congress to the Parliament of Great Britain, to interchange and exchange copies of the acts and proceedings of their respective bodies, from year to year, and also the expediency of doing the same thing with regard to the legislative Chambers of France;

The resolution of Mr. HENDRICKS,

That the Secretary of War be directed to communicate to the Senate a report of the agent recently employed in examining the Cumberland road, west of the Ohio river—

Were taken up and adopted.

Mr. POINDEXTER moved that when the Senate adjourn it will adjourn to meet on Monday next.

Mr. WEBSTER hoped the gentleman would not press his motion, but that the Senate would meet tomorrow, so as to proceed in the discussion of the important question now under consideration. It was important to have as early an expression of the Senate upon it as could be obtained consistently with a desire to accord to gentlemen an opportunity of debating it.

Mr. POINDEXTER said he was as anxious as the gentleman could be to dispose of the question alluded to, but it was the usage to adjourn over to Monday, and besides, there was a mass of business of importance in the Senate, which should be acted on by the committees. He thought, however, that an early expression of opinion upon that important question was very desirable, and he would be the last man to interpose any difficulty to delay or prevent it.

Mr. WEBSTER thought the reason sufficient.

Mr. FORSYTH wished to learn what was to be gained by the delate upon the question in its present attitude before the Senate. He had understood the gentleman from Massachusetts, the other day, to express a desire to afford Senators an opportunity of expressing their opinions upon it; if he understood him correctly now, he expressed a wish to have the opinion or action of the Senate upon it.

Mr. WEBSTER designed the expressions as equivalent, and to be understood in either sense. He said the other day, that it was proper to refer the report to the Committee on Finance, and that the committee should report thereon before the ultimate decision of the Senate should be had on it. It was a matter of indifference to him, whether the decision of the Senate should precede or succeed

the report of the committee. As to its reference, that, too, was entirely at the pleasure of the Senate.

Mr. FORSYTH said it was his impression that the report ought, in the first instance, to have been referred to the Committee on Finance as the appropriate committee. He wished to be informed in what shape the question was to be finally presented to the Senate for its decision.

Mr. WEBSTER said, if he had the volition of the Senate in his hand, he could reply to the gentleman. He could not give an opinion what the Senate might choose to do; he could only say, for one, that before the appointment of the Committee on Finance, the discussion of the resolutions had begun and been progressed in. He wished to interpose for the purpose of bringing it before the committee as early as possible; but when was he to do it, and what gentleman was he to cut off by the motion? He said the other day that as soon as he could, with propriety and courtesy to Senators, he would move the reference of the report. Whether he voted for the resolutions or against them, he desired the action of the committee on the report.

Mr. POINDEXTER'S motion was adopted.

At ten minutes before one, Mr. CHAMBERS moved that the Senate proceed to the special order of the day—

THE REMOVAL OF THE DEPOSITES.

Mr. SOUTHARD then resumed, and concluded his speech, when—

Mr. CALHOUN rose, and after expressing a wish to be heard, moved that the Senate adjourn; but, at the suggestion of Mr. POINDEXTER, he withdrew it, for the present, and on Mr. P.'s motion, the Senate went into the consideration of Executive business until adjournment.

HOUSE OF REPRESENTATIVES.

Friday, January 10, 1834.

Mr. EVANS, from the Committee on Invalid Pensions, reported a bill for the relief of Judith Thomas and Daniel Palmer.

Mr. CONNOR reported a bill for the relief of George Brown.

Mr. MARSHALL, a bill for the relief of the legal representatives of Samuel Gibbs.

Mr. CLAY, of Alabama, a bill for the relief of William K. Paulding; and another for the relief of William Hazlett.

Mr. LAWRENCE, a bill for the relief of Joseph W. Walstead, of Marblehead, master and owner of the schooner Sally, and for the crew of said vessel.

Mr. POLK, from the Committee of Ways and Means, reported a bill making appropriations for different fortifications throughout the United States, for the year 1834; and a second bill making appropriations for Indian annuities, and other similar objects for the year 1834. Both were read twice and committed to the Committee of the Whole on the state of the Union.

The order of the day was then stated to be the consideration of Mr. SELDEN'S bill as amended, that the Committee of Ways and Means be instructed to inquire into the expediency of requiring the commissioners of the sinking fund forthwith to purchase or otherwise redeem the five per cent. stocks of the United States, and directing the Secretary of the Treasury, from time to time, to place under the control of said commissioners such funds not otherwise required for the purpose of the Government, as shall be necessary for that object, and in case of deficiency, to sell so much of the stock of the Bank of the United States belonging to the Government as will enable them to complete the purchase.

Mr. STEWART, of Pennsylvania, strenuously objected to the resolution as proposed by the gentleman from New York; because, by rendering it imperative to redeem the public debt, it will have the effect of increasing the price of the debt, and there are not funds adequate to extinguish the debt, without doing injustice to others. The commissioners of the sinking fund have already the power, if they had the means, to redeem the debt. He would, therefore, move that the motion of Mr. SELDEN be laid on the table.

Mr. SELDEN, of New York, being permitted to enforce his resolution, asserted that, from the report of the Secretary of the Treasury, there were now in the treasury funds sufficient to extinguish the debt; and that if there are funds to pay the outstanding debt of the nation, it is imperative on the Government to redeem, rather than maintain it by a system of oppressive taxation. The Secretary reports that his balance is 9,389,000 dollars, deducting appropriations made. Is it not, therefore, proper, that with this accumulation of unavailable funds in the hands of the Government, that the debt should be extinguished? The argument that an order for a compulsory redemption of the debt would advance the article in the market, is not valid, because compulsory no more than voluntary payments, will not and cannot tend to increase the demand; and, therefore, not enhance the price. It is merely fanciful to assert that the debt will thus be liable to increase; for as there is but a certain amount of principal bearing a determinate interest, no increase can be effected of either principal or interest. They can produce but a particular amount. They are not subject to fluctuation, and never can advance in price. Demand or supply does not affect the five per cent. stocks. They are as bank notes, bearing a specific value, but not like bank stocks subjected to all the fluctuations of demand and supply. He therefore considers it essential that they should be paid off in a certain time. Is the Secretary of the Treasury to be permitted to keep in the treasury finances for no available or appropriated purpose, while the outstanding debt of the nation is unredeemed, and the country taxed to maintain it; taxed at an amount of five per cent. yearly, while the unvaluable funds bear no income whatever? The Government derives nothing from the surplus revenue; the banks receiving the deposites derive all that can be expected. He hoped that the Committee of Ways and Means will prepare a law, instructing the Secretary of the Treasury to pay off all stocks before the first of May next; then a greater premium than 1 per cent., and all short of 1 per cent. after the 1st of September. He is willing to submit his motion to that committee, because the chairman concurs with him in opinion that it is necessary the debt should be extinguished now while there are funds which may be safely appropriated for that purpose. He will, from time to time, give notice of the funds and finances of the nation, and ask that committee why they do not act.

Mr. LANE, of Indiana. I rise, not for the purpose of taking any part in the debate before us, but to congratulate the House on the recovery of the lost treasury of the United States. Where is the treasury? has long been asked by all. Where is the treasury? ay, where is the treasury? The treasury is at length found. The President has seized it from the grasp of those with whom it was lost, and borne it off in triumph. The Government can now preserve the treasury; the people can know where it is to be found; and the nation can have the advantage of it. Nine millions of the people's money has been at last recovered. Old Hickory can rejoice every day he sees it, and the people can look to their beloved and determined President, to guaranty its safety from the speculations of bank jobbers. What complaint can there be about the trifle of a debt, while there are nine millions in the treasury? I will not longer detain the House, but to congratulate them on the recovery of the lost treasury of the United States. Let there be great joy, from Georgia to Maine, that the treasury is rich, and bountifully replenished.

Mr. STEWART, of Pennsylvania, said the resolution intended to compel the Commissioners of the Sinking Fund to extinguish the debt, whether they had or had not funds. If they had funds, they have already the power; if they have not funds to pay the four and three-quarter millions, they cannot obtain them within the time proposed by the gentleman from New York. The Secretary of the Treasury states expressly, that the surplus revenue will not be sufficient to meet next year the appropriations already made, and the public service will be materially injured.

His motion to lay it on the table was lost—yeas 80, nays 85.

Mr. SELDEN said his motion was, that if there was a surplus in the treasury adequate to redeem the debt, it would be better to apply it to that purpose, than have it fluctuating in unavailable funds; and if there was not sufficient in the surplus revenue, that the deficiency would be supplied by the sale of the bank stock.

Mr. STEWART said this would be a singular remedy—to sell bank stock, bearing an interest of seven per cent., in order to redeem stock bearing an interest of only five per cent.; making the country a considerable loser by the difference received and paid.

Mr. MERCER, of Virginia, took the same view of the question; and said it would go to make the country a loser of two per cent. yearly on a much larger principal than the debt amounted to.

Mr. POLK said, as the resolution was a mere matter of inquiry, he could not oppose its being referred to the Committee of Ways and Means. That committee will judge whether it is expedient to use the surplus revenue (if any) to extinguish the debt; or whether it would be well to dispose of the bank stock that the national debt might be redeemed.

The resolution was agreed to. Yeas 126, nays 81.

The House, on motion, resolved that when they should adjourn this day, to adjourn over until Monday next; and having refused to suspend the rule by which this day is set apart for the consideration of private business, the following engrossed bills were read a third time and passed:

A bill for the relief of William Walker, and the heirs of Samuel Brown;
A bill for the relief of Abraham Forbes;
A bill for the relief of Alexander Boyd;
A bill for the relief of Ezekiel Foster;
A bill for the relief of the owners of the schooner Three Sisters;
A bill for the relief of Philip Bessom;
A bill for the relief of the representatives of Joseph Rowe, deceased;
A bill for the relief of Horatio N. Crabb;
A bill for the relief of John G. Reynolds;
A bill for the relief of John Percival and others;
A bill for the relief of Frances and Judith Taylor;
A bill for the relief of the representatives of George Hurlbut, deceased;
A bill for the relief of the heirs of Presley Thornton, deceased;
A bill for the relief of Thomas Minor;
A bill for the relief of the representatives of Enos Grannis;
A bill for the relief of John Lobdell; and
A bill for the relief of Thomas Ap Catesby Jones.

The bill granting pensions to several persons therein named, was taken up for consideration. After some discussion,

Mr. GILMER moved to re-commit the bill, with instructions so to amend it as to cause the pension to Leslie Combs, of Lexington, Kentucky, to take effect from the year 1822, instead of the year 1813, (the time of the alleged disability.)

Some further debate ensued. The question was then taken, and the motion to re-commit agreed to—yeas 169, nays 30.

On motion, the House then adjourned.

[In our report of Thursday's proceedings, it is stated, by mistake, that Mr. CASEY reported a "bill for the continuation of the Cumberland road, &c.," and a bill "for the location and survey of the Cumberland road, &c." These bills were both reported by Mr. SLADE, from the Committee on Roads and Canals.]

[We omitted, in its proper place, to say, that Mr. BENTON concluded his remarks by submitting the following resolution, which he moved to insert in lieu of the 2d resolution offered by Mr. CLAY. On the following day the resolution was considered and rejected.]

"Resolved, That Nicholas Biddle, President of the Bank of the United States, and ———, be summoned to appear at the bar of the Senate, on the —— day of ——, then and there to be examined on oath, touching the causes of the late large curtailment of debts due to the Bank of the United States, and the manner of conducting the said curtailment; also to be then and there examined touching the application of the moneys of the bank to electioneering and political objects."

We have received files of Buenos Ayres and Rio Janeiro papers, the former to the 19th October, and the latter to the 15th November, inclusive.

Buenos Ayres was in a state of great confusion and excitement. The Governor, on the 15th instant, issued a Proclamation addressed to the inhabitants of the Province, to the effect that if in time of tranquillity it be necessary for the Executive to act so as to give confidence to the people, and security for the preservation of constitutional liberty, it was more than ever so at the present moment, from the scandalous insurrection promoted by some deluded men, and every measure would be taken to restore order and tranquillity. Troops had, in consequence, been ordered to the capital. Riots and tumult were frequent in the city.

The Congress of Buenos Ayres, on the 15th October, passed a law suspending, for fifteen days, the liberty of the press, and forbidding, under the heaviest penalties, the publication of any article of a political nature in the journals; the editors are compelled, therefore, to withhold any comment on passing events.

Another conspiracy against the Government of Chili had been discovered and suppressed in the capital of that Republic in September last. Some discharged military officers were at the head of it.

In an article on Rio Janeiro, in the English journal published at Buenos Ayres, a complaint is made that the Americans have lately completely driven the British out of the coffee market of Rio, by their superior enterprise and skill in speculation.—Balt. Daily Adv.

Another invention.—An article, called the Patent India Rubber Floating Mattress, invented by J. D. Elliott. It is cased with india rubber water-proof cloth, and filled in part with cork shavings. It is said to be soft, elastic, and comfortable to sleep on, and will not imbibe or retain infection or dampness. It will be a grand article at sea or on rivers, as it is sufficiently buoyant to support two persons, and will keep six from sinking in the water, by laying hold upon it. Commodore Elliott, of the navy-yard, Boston, recommends them highly as beds and as life preservers.—N. H. Spect.

Louisiana.—The message of the Governor of Louisiana alludes to the dreadful ravages of the cholera throughout that State during the year, and of the yellow fever, immediately after, in the capital of the State, and adds that the expiring year is the most sickly since Louisiana has ever experienced since her first establishment. It then proceeds to congratulate the Legislature on the universal restoration of health, and the agricultural and commercial prosperity of the State.

"The products of our agriculture," says the message, "will equal those of the last crop; our commerce has never been more flourishing; and New Orleans, where edi-

fices of the value of more than two millions are now rising up, is every day acquiring a development worthy of the city which must be considered not only the capital of Louisiana, but of the whole valley of the Mississippi.

"The exports of New Orleans, for the year 1831, will probably be as follows:

Cotton—45,900 bales, at $55.....	$24,730,000
Tobacco—30,000 hhds., at $40.....	1,200,000
Sugar—70,000 hhds., at $65.....	4,550,000
Molasses—4,500,000 galls., at 20 cts.	700,000
Western produce.....................	5,400,000
	$36,700,000
Deduct for home consumption.....	2,000,000
Total of exports for 1831.....	$34,700,000

"Of these exports, the produce of Louisiana and the charges of transit will amount as follows:

Cotton—180,000 bales, at $55......	$9,900,000
Sugar—70,000 hhds., at $65......	4,550,000
Molasses—3,500,000 galls., at 20 cts.	700,000
Charges on produce in transit, and on the produce of Louisiana, exported at.................	5,000,000
Total value of the produce and profits of Louisiana......................	$20,150,000

"To which may be added near $2,000,000 profits made this year by our merchants on the last crop of cotton. Whence it results that the produce of Louisiana and profits of her commerce amount in value to more than one-half of that of her whole exports, and that New Orleans alone realizes profits equivalent to one-third of the total proceeds of the industry of the State.

"The policy which England has just adopted in relation to her colonies, however disastrous it may be to those intended to be benefited by it, can produce no other than a favorable effect on that branch of our agriculture, which, in consequence of the early frosts which we have experienced, is the least flourishing at the present time. The English colonies will, for the future, produce less sugar, and the increase which must necessarily take place in price may compensate us henceforward for the injury produced by the diminution of the duty on that article."—Courier.

"When all other means fail in arresting hæmorrhage, a little oil of tobacco has immediately succeeded. That which collects in the stems of pipes which have been long smoked will answer perfectly. The discovery was made by Humel, a chemist at Berlin, and his mixture is eight ounces of distilled water, two drachms of oil of tobacco, and a few drops of ethereal animal oil. This has been found so effectual, that by a recent decree of the Minister of the Interior at Munich, all apothecaries are ordered to keep it prepared."

The back numbers of the Congressional Globe are exhausted. Those persons, therefore, who may subscribe for it hereafter, will receive only the number containing the proceedings of the week in which their subscriptions are received at this office, and all the future numbers as they are published.

THE CONGRESSIONAL GLOBE.

PRINTED AND PUBLISHED AT THE CITY OF WASHINGTON, BY BLAIR & RIVES.

| 23D CONGRESS, 1ST SESSION. | SATURDAY, JANUARY 18, 1834. | VOL. I........No. 7. |

IN SENATE.

MONDAY, January 13, 1834.

The VICE PRESIDENT laid before the Senate the following communication from the Secretary of the Treasury, in compliance with the resolution of Mr. FRELINGHUYSEN, adopted on Friday, which was read as follows:

TREASURY DEPARTMENT,
January 13, 1834.

SIR: In obedience to the resolution of the Senate of the 10th instant, directing " the Secretary of the 'Treasury to inform the Senate of the construc- 'tion which has been given by that Department to 'the act passed at the last session of Congress, 'entitled 'An act to modify the act of the 14th of 'July, 1832, and all other acts imposing duties on 'imports,' and also to furnish copies of such in- 'structions as may have been given to collectors 'regulating their duty under said act,'" I have the honor herewith to transmit a printed copy of the letter of instructions from this Department to the officers of customs, dated April 20, 1833, stating the principles on which the duties were to be cal- culated under the act of the 14th of July, 1832, and that of the 2d of March, 1833, modifying said act; and also a printed copy of the instructions given by the Comptroller on the 26th ultimo.

No other instructions have been issued from this de- partment in relation to the subject mentioned in the resolution.

Under the construction of the law as given by the department in the circular letter of April last, the duties on manufactures of cotton, or of which cotton shall be a component part, are to be calculated according to the act of the 14th of July, 1832, and the act of the 2d of March, 1833, reducing the duty, will operate upon the rate of duty calculated in the minimum principle; and instructions will forthwith be given to the collectors accordingly.

No decision has been made by the department since that of the 20th of April, 1833, before refer- red to.

I understand from the Comptroller that his in- structions were intended by him to carry into effect that decision according to what he supposed to be his intention.

I have the honor to be, very respectfully, your obedient servant, R. B. TANEY,
Secretary of the Treasury.
Hon. MARTIN VAN BUREN,
Vice President of the United States, and
President of the Senate.

Mr. CLAY said he was glad to see that the error in the interpretation of the act of last session was now corrected, and that new instructions, conformable to the meaning of the act would issue. That the Secretary of the Treasury and the Comptroller had given to the act the interpre- tation imputed to them, he had received, he might say, a half peck of letters and communications to prove, and not only that, but also a communica- tion from one of the officers of the customs in the city of New York, informing him that such were the instructions which had been issued to him from the department. He was glad to see that the error was corrected, and that the construction given would be repealed, and others conformable to the spirit and plain meaning of the act would be is- sued. He moved the reference of the report to the Committee on Manufactures.

Mr. CALHOUN added thereto the motion to print.

Mr. FORSYTH thought the Committee on Fi- nance the most appropriate committee. The question involved had reference to the revenue alone. He therefore moved to amend the mo- tion so as to send the report to that committee. It was very obvious that no decision of the head of the Treasury Department had been made in the subject, except that which was made in April last by Mr. McLane—and it seemed that in carrying out the decision of the Secretary, the Comptroller was mistaken. He thought the gen- tleman [Mr. CLAY] was in error in supposing that 7

the Comptroller and Secretary were both equally mistaken.

Mr. CLAY thought that, as it regarded the re- ference of the report to the proper committee, if the Treasury Department meant to do what they said they would do, it was of no consequence what committee it were sent to. But it related, in a much greater degree, to the manufacturing interests of the country than to the revenue. He thought, therefore, that the Committee on Manu- factures was the most proper committee. As re- spected the adjustment of the mistake, between the Secretary and the Comptroller, the gentleman [Mr. F.] might settle that as he thought proper. But had the present Secretary been so devoted to the removal of the deposites, and the regulation of the present depositories of the public money, that he could not attend to it? There had been at least as culpable an omission in his not super- intending the carrying out the instructions of his predecessor, as there was in the Comptroller.

Mr. FORSYTH replied, that he had no doubt but that Secretary had been properly employed in his official duties—what the nature of them might be, he [Mr. F.] would not pretend to say. But the gentleman from Kentucky himself had fur- nished him with a good deal to do. The Secre- tary certainly had not attended to the details of this matter. They were properly left to the sub- ordinates in the office. It would be impossible for him to attend to the details in his office—that would require ten men. But he [Mr. F.] was anxious the error, whatever it were, should be fixed on the proper person, because it would do him no harm. As regarded the reference of it to the Committee on Finance, it was obviously the most proper one, as immediately affecting the rev- enue, for the minimum duties by this construction were got rid of entirely, and great difficulty was likely to be given in carrying it into effect, and it would require some general rule to be made by that committee on the subject.

Mr. CLAY said, there could not be the slight- est difficulty in carrying the act into effect. The act of 1832 subjects cotton fabrics to a duty of 25 per cent. ad valorem, and a further duty, in the form of minimums, of 30 cents and 35 cents. The compromise act of last session provides for a bien- nial reduction of 10 per cent. upon all duties im- posed by previous acts. He held in his hand a calculation in figures, which was as clear as the sun at noon-day, made by a collection officer him- self, going to show conclusively that there was no new legislation necessary, if the act was carried out according to its plain import. As to the de- tails which it was said the Secretary could not at- tend to, he [Mr. C.] would say, that when im- mensely important duties, affecting the collection of imposts on manufactures, were committed to him, he would have thought he could find time to attend to them. But if he could not find time to attend to his duties as Secretary of the Treasury, how was he able to attend to those duties which were exclusively assigned to the Treasurer of the United States?

Mr. FORSYTH would not attempt to defend the Secretary from the gentleman; he was deter- mined to find fault with him. Mr. F. thought the circular of the Comptroller was the mere practical application of the rule as it was established, and he was mistaken in it. It was not the Secretary's duty to superintend the carrying out the provisions of the act. The act declares that if the duties shall exceed 20 per cent. on the value, a reduction of one-tenth shall be made. Now, what is the value spoken of? Upon what is the calculation to be made? The minimum value is supposed by the treasury to be totally destroyed, but the actual value of the article is to be taken into view in fix- ing the duty.

Mr. CLAY said, there was not the slightest change made in the ad valorem. The act of last session assumes that the collection shall continue the existence of duties imposed by law prior to the act of last session.

Mr. PRESTON observed, that as far as the South were concerned, they were disposed to carry into effect the law of last session, in its plain and obvious terms, whatever might be the consequen- ces, with the most perfect good faith. As regarded the reference of this report, it was a question ex- clusively of revenue, and instructions to revenue officers, and therefore most peculiarly appropriate to the Committee on Finance. It might be that the law was for the purpose of fostering manufac- tures; but as it now was, it was solely a revenue law.

Mr. CLAY remarked, that as he was perfectly indifferent what committee the communication of the Secretary was referred to, he would move to lay it on the table, for the purpose of asking the last instructions which had issued from the depart- ment on this subject.

Mr. FORSYTH thought it would be more con- venient for the committee to write for the instruc- tions.

Mr. CLAY said he wanted to see the instruc- tions.

The motion to lay on the table was agreed to.

And afterwards, on motion of Mr. WEBSTER, it was ordered to be printed.

Mr. BIBB, from the Committee on the Judici- ary, reported sundry bills, which were ordered to be printed.

The VICE PRESIDENT laid before the Sen- ate a communication from the Secretary of the Treasury, containing a report from the several banks of the District of Columbia.

Mr. POINDEXTER, from the Committee on Public Lands, asked to be discharged from the further consideration of the petition of Andrew Knox; which was agreed to.

Mr. HENDRICKS, from the Committee on Public Lands, reported a bill for the relief of the heirs and legal representatives of Moses Shepherd; which was read and committed.

A message was received from the House of Representatives by their Clerk, stating that they had passed certain bills, and asking the concur- rence of the Senate.

Mr. KANE, from the Committee on Private Land Claims, reported certain bills, which were ordered to be printed.

Mr. TIPTON, from the Committee on Public Lands, reported a bill for the relief of Hiram A. Hunter; which was read and committed.

Mr. WILKINS presented a memorial from the Chamber of Commerce of Philadelphia, ascribing the present pecuniary distress of the country to the removal of the deposites from the Bank of the Uni- ted States; which, on motion of Mr. POINDEX- TER, was referred to the Committee on Finance, and ordered to be printed.

The following bills from the House of Repre- sentatives were read, and severally referred to ap- propriate committees:

A bill for the relief of William Walker and the heirs of Samuel Brown, deceased.

A bill for the relief of the heirs of Dr. John Berrien, deceased.

A bill for the relief of George Hurlbut.

A bill for the relief of Captain Thomas ap Cates- by Jones.

A bill for the relief of John L. Lobdell.

A bill for the relief of Thomas Minor.

A bill for the relief of the heirs and legal repre- sentatives of Presbry Thornton.

A bill for the relief of Frances and Judith Tay- lor.

Petitions and memorials were presented by Messrs. SHEPLEY, WRIGHT, WILKINS, TYLER, and SILSBEE, which, without reading, were severally referred.

The following resolutions were offered pending the morning session, and lie one day:

By Mr. CLAY—
Resolved, That the Committee on Finance be directed to inquire into the expediency of affording

temporary relief to the community from the present pecuniary embarrassments, by prolonging the payment of revenue bonds, as they fall due, the obligors paying interest, and giving satisfactory security.

By Mr. MOORE—

Resolved, That the Committee on Military Affairs be instructed to inquire into the accounts of Colonel Samuel Dale, as settled under the act of 1832, and whether said Dale is not justly entitled to the money received by ——— Weir, for provisions furnished the troops in the Territory of Alabama, in 1818; and whether the said sum of money ought not to be paid to the said Dale.

By Mr. ROBBINS—

Resolved, That the Committee on the Library be instructed to inquire whether any, and if any, what amendments are necessary to the existing laws providing for the distribution of the laws and the reports of the Supreme Court of the United States.

The VICE PRESIDENT then announced the special order to be

THE REMOVAL OF THE DEPOSITES.

The Senate resumed the consideration of the resolutions submitted by Mr. CLAY, on the 28th ultimo.

Mr. CALHOUN then addressed the Chair for an hour and a half in opposition to the report of the Secretary. On concluding,

Mr. SHEPLEY rose, and after expressing a wish to be heard, moved that the Senate adjourn. Whereupon

The Senate adjourned.

HOUSE OF REPRESENTATIVES.

MONDAY, *January* 13, 1834.

The petition of Noah Fletcher coming up in its order—

Mr. DAVIS, of Massachusetts, rose, and after referring to the postponement of any action on the petition when first presented by him, said, that, although he did not agree that the rules of the House, under which it was postponed had been always uniform, yet, that he had acceded to it, because he had every desire to accommodate the House, and not entangle it with a contention about the rules of their proceedings. He would not now go into an elaborate view of the subject, and had nearly closed what he had to say upon it, when, on the former occasion, the member from Alabama [Mr. CLAY] had interposed by his objections, that, under the rule of the House, the subject could not then be discussed; but he would merely remark now, as he did then, that the petitioner was a person in an humble situation of life: he had been a laborer in the service of the Government for nearly the whole of his life, and of which fourteen or fifteen years had been passed as a subordinate officer of the House; that he had discharged his duty so far, as he had reason to believe, in a satisfactory manner, for no complaint had been preferred against him. Under such circumstances, it, however, appeared that he had been removed from the office which he so filled by the fiat of power; he had been removed by virtue of an instrument with which they had become latterly somewhat familiar—an instrument in writing, a little paper, unceremoniously addressed to the object, beginning "I," not the House, "have no further occasion for your services." This, then, being the mode in which one of their agents for the transaction of their business had been dismissed, and without previous admonition, he thought it was a duty incumbent upon the human character, wherever an exercise of power had been made, in either an offensive manner, or in a way to prove injurious to our fellow creatures, that the party was called upon to lay before the world some justification for such injurious or offensive exercise, some plausible apology for the conduct pursued. But was such the case here? No; it was not pretended that there was any charge against the petitioner, and nothing but this brief notice of dismissal was sent to him; being thus dismissed, his plans in life altogether broken up; this act, too, being done by an officer who holds and exercises that power from the House, it became their duty to see, by what authority the act had been done. Whether the power was legally or illegally exercised was not so material; it was enough for them, if the power was exercised unjustly or improperly to entitle them to call upon the individual thus exercising it. The House, he contended, had this power in their hands, and they could not go forth to their constituents and say they witnessed such an exercise of power as was displayed in this instance without affording redress. No apology having been made for it, the natural inference was, that the power had been exercised in a proscriptive manner. And here he was induced to consider what was proscription? It was the power of a tyrant; it was the power which said, "Think as I think," "Do as I bid you do." Does the Autocrat of all the Russias demand from his humblest serf more than this? What could the Sublime Porte itself require of the humblest slave within his realms, than, Think as I think, act as I wish? This was the very essence of tyranny. This spirit it was, which, with powerful arm, grapples and regulates and guides everything as it pleased; which made the man for the place, and not the place for the man. This was proscription; this was the spirit which addressed itself to the ambitious man, and says, Give up your independence or your place shall be forfeit; to the avaricious it says, You must barter your conscience for gold; and this it was which addressed itself to the hungry and to the naked, saying, Be ye warm, be ye fed, be ye clothed, *but*, be ye also of my faith. This was the true character of proscription; to avoid which, it would seem, that every man upon entering into office, must crawl to the footstool of its known disposer, and first undersign and seal, give bond by which he will engage to become the slave of that power. This was one effect of proscription, but not the worst. If they wanted to see its effect upon the proscribed, they need not travel out of the present case; the case of an humble individual, who would not be permitted to sit in a private chamber of the capitol, there to enjoy even the privilege of neutrality, but he must be bound to bark and to hunt for the power which employed him. There was another view of all this, which seemed to him to be still more offensive and more obnoxious to public justice. He was led to consider who was this "I," who said "I have no occasion for your services." The gentleman in the office of chief clerk need not suppose that these remarks were intended to be personal, for they were not so. Mr. D. would not apply them so, as he now believed that this officer had acted inconsiderately rather than from any other motive in the matter. But, in considering the effects of the system, and who the personage was, who thus claimed this power, they would find that it was one whom they had elevated into an office, connected with which was the power to use all the money of the House, and all the vast patronage which that money could give as a capital to trade upon; and if this was so, in truth and in fact, was it not time that such a power was taken out of the hands of their chief officer? The salaries at his disposal amounted to some twelve or fifteen thousand dollars, and being so large it was in the power of any band of men to conspire together to elevate whom they pleased to the office, and then have the patronage to trade upon; but he trusted that the House would not tolerate such a system. He knew the character of the petitioner to have been without spot or blemish; and as he claimed it as a right to have his petition presented, he (Mr. D.) had presented it as a duty due, not only to him, but, under the circumstances, to the whole country, and in a manner as little offensive as possible.

Mr. CLAY, of Alabama, said he must claim the attention of the House for a few moments on this all-important question, (as the gentleman from Massachusetts seemed to consider it,) particularly as he had been referred to in the course of the remarks which had just been made. He ought to do so, (Mr. C. said,) if it were only for the mere purpose of rendering some suitable apology for having called the gentleman from Massachusetts to order, when he presented the memorial the other day. Mr. C. said the gentleman had not been satisfied to accompany the presentment of the memorial with "a brief statement of the contents thereof," as the rule of the House required; but was going on to declaim at large upon the freedom of the people, and the safety of the citizen. He (Mr. C.) had thought this course a departure from the rule of practice in such cases, and an unnecessary consumption of time, and had therefore called upon the Chair to interpose. To require a member to conform to rules, adopted for our government and the orderly transaction of business, certainly demanded an apology!

I had supposed, Mr. Speaker, the House had sufficient business to occupy its time and attention, and sufficient matter for excitement, too, at least for the present, without the introduction of this most unnecessary, if not unprecedented question. It seems to me, sir, that any one will be satisfied, on the least examination, or the slightest reflection, that the memorialist has no claim to the interposition of the House, founded either upon its practice or the law of the country. It may serve to occupy the time of the House, which all must agree to be so precious, and so much demanded by legitimate subjects for its consideration; and it may serve to produce some excitement, which may be desirable in *these calm and quiet times.*

But the gentleman from Massachusetts, [Mr. DAVIS,] who introduced the memorial with so much pure benevolence and deep pathos, disclaimed any intention to excite the feelings of gentlemen, by any remarks he had made. Far from him! He only wished to do justice to an injured individual, an oppressed American citizen! No, sir, it was not *his* purpose

"To stir men's blood."

He only showed the supposed *wrongs* of Mr. Fletcher—

——————"poor, poor dumb mouths,
And bid *them* speak *for him.*"

But, notwithstanding the gentleman's disclaimer, if it had so happened that the eloquence of those "dumb mouths" had roused a general feeling of indignation, likely to overwhelm the object of his assault, he would doubtless have been ready to exclaim with his great prototype,

——————"Mischief, thou art afoot;
Take thou what course thou wilt."

But, sir, what is the ground assumed and set forth by the memorialist, upon which he claims the interposition of this House? It consists in his having been appointed about fourteen or fifteen years ago, and having ever since quietly held the office, and enjoyed its emoluments: ergo, he is entitled to it the remainder of his life. This, sir, is the sum and substance of Mr. Fletcher's claim: he has held the office so long, that he now believes his title indefeasible. The claimant, in this instance, however, is not the only one who has arrived at the conclusion, that once getting into office in this District gives a *freehold title.* That notion, Mr. C. believed, prevailed extensively, not only in reference to clerkships and other offices in the House of Representatives, but to all the officers in the several departments. It remains to be seen whether the House will give sanction to the claims of such *tenants.*

The gentleman from Massachusetts, [Mr. DAVIS,] however, was not satisfied to rest the claim of Mr. Fletcher upon the ground set forth in his petition. He urges the additional consideration of the petitioner's long residence here, during which he has made investments in property in this District; and that he has here contracted the private relations of husband and father. For all this good fortune, the gentleman would seem to conclude that the petitioner should hold his office for life. If a man has held an office many years, it is a good claim, according to this new doctrine; but if he shall have had the good fortune, in the mean time, to get married, and to get rich, *forsooth*, it is much better—it is an indefeasible freehold, at least. Why, sir, acquiesce in this doctrine for a few years more, and we shall have office claimed here by inheritance. The son of Noah Fletcher, or some one else, who has settled here, obtained a good office, got married, been blessed with children, and has realized a fortune, will come forward and claim the place which was held by his father. And could he not sustain his claim? Yes, sir, with as much plausibility as the gentleman from Massachusetts sustains that of the father. He would only have to add to the family history, with which we have already been favored, by saying he had been born here, raised and educated here, perhaps brought up in his father's office, and accustomed to its duties, unaccustomed to any other business, and unacquainted with the manners and

habits of any other place. He might add to all this, by urging the *conclusive* objection to his emigration, which is said to have been made by a starving washerwoman, of this or some other city—that he could not go to a remote part of the country, (the West, perhaps,) because there is no society there.

To enhance the importance of this grave matter, the gentleman from Massachusetts told you, upon introducing it, that it was "intimately connected with the *freedom and safety* of the people." The removal, or rather *the failure to reappoint a clerk—a subordinate clerk—endangers the safety of the people!* This is truly touching. What a lively sensibility the gentleman from Massachusetts has, to the "freedom and SAFETY of the people!" It certainly ought to enrol him, not only with the patriots, but the philanthropists of the age. But, sir, has he satisfied you of the truth of the fact he assumes? The time was, (and yet is, in some parts of the country,) when *rotation in office* was supposed to be intimately connected with the freedom and safety of the people; when the power and emoluments of office were supposed to be corrupting in their tendency; and when frequent changes were deemed indispensable to the purity of our institutions. It is true that the party to which the gentleman belongs—once called Federal, now ycleped National Republican—did, in the early history of the country, insist that some of the higher officers of the Government should be appointed for life; but *they* did not then insist, so far as I am informed, that clerks, or any class of subordinate officers, should be so appointed. That, I suppose, has been left for one of the improvements of this more enlightened age. We must now sanction the doctrine, that when a man once gets into office, he is to hold it for life, or during *his own* will and pleasure.

But, sir, how long has this been a favorite principle with the gentleman from Massachusetts, or his political friends? Did they entertain it during the late Administration? Did they raise the cry then, that "the freedom and safety of the people" was in danger? The Secretary of State of that Administration thought proper to change the publishers of the laws throughout most parts of the Union, as well as I recollect. Did the gentleman, or his friends, then consider the "freedom and safety of the people" in danger? Did they then tell you that the liberty of the press had been assailed, that the freedom of the people was identified with that great palladium of their liberties, and that, if one were cloven down, the other must fall likewise? No, sir. Not one of those watchful sentinels of liberty then sounded the tocsin. "It was all the fairest thing in the world." Why, sir, the principle of rotation in office has been carried to the utmost extremity by the party to which the gentleman belongs. When did they ever have power, and not exercise it? When did they ever have patronage, and bestow it on those who were guilty of differing with them in opinion? If newspaper authority can be relied on, it was but the other day that no less than *fifty-eight watchmen* of Philadelphia were dismissed because they were not of the true political faith. If I am correctly informed, the city administration has lately changed hands. A new mayor, friendly to the bank, and a believer in its claims to perpetuity, has been elected—and this is among the first fruits of his administration. Where was the sympathy of the gentleman's friends when this was done?

The late printer to this House had been in office four years, and, so far as regarded the discharge of his *mechanical duty*, I am not aware that there was any well-grounded complaint. Other considerations than the mere business of printing for the House, operated upon his reflection; and, I believe, justly operated. Did the gentleman, or his then political friends, vote for him? I presume he will answer no. But, sir, it is useless to waste time in enumerating instances in which similar acts have been done, even by those who belong to the orthodox school of National Republicanism. The omissions to exercise power, when they have it, will be found to be mere exceptions from their general rule of action. Their whole history proves that they act upon the assumption that no man is qualified for office, no man is worthy of trust or confidence, unless he is of the true faith according to their creed: it is immaterial what may be the grade or character of the station, from the *Chief Magistracy* down to a *watchman*.

But, sir, looking to the real object of the resolution, rather than to the question properly involved, I had nearly omitted it. The 2d section of the first article of the Constitution, declares that each House of Representatives shall have the power to "choose their Speaker and other officers." That the Clerk of the late House was not clerk of this, has been demonstrated by the election of our present clerk as his successor. Can it be maintained that a subordinate clerk, who derives his appointment and his powers from his principal, has a better tenure? Who directs his labors? Who superintends the performance of his duty? Who is responsible to the House for the performance of them? All must agree that the principal clerk is the source of his power and authority, the superintendent of his performance, and responsible to the House. It will be found by an examination of all the laws and resolutions of the House, in relation to the subordinate clerks, that every one of them, by the authority of the House, has been employed by the principal clerk. The House has never appointed one of them. I had intended to have gone into a more minute examination of the subject; but, as the gentleman has not thought proper to say anything upon what would seem to be, properly, the main ground of his motion, I deem it unnecessary.

Mr. C. concluded by saying that he hoped the House was satisfied that the removal, or, more properly, the failure to re-appoint, Mr. Fletcher, was not fraught with such awful consequences to the freedom of the people, and the safety of the country, as the gentleman from Massachusetts had supposed, and, consequently, they would not adopt the resolution he had proposed.

Mr. MANN moved to lay the resolution on the table, but subsequently withdrew the motion.

Mr. CHILTON then advocated the necessity of inquiry, as a means of justifying the Clerk; for, if there could be any cause shown that the petitioner had neglected his duty, no person, whatever was his political creed, would pronounce that he had done wrong in removing him. It would appear that the whole sympathy of the member from Alabama had been swallowed up for the Philadelphia watchmen, and in apprehension that their removal had been caused by that ten-headed monster, the Bank of the United States. But no matter where proscription might be found to exist, or to originate, it was important to the House and to the nation that it should be put down, and he expected to have the coöperation of that gentleman to put it down. Had they forgotten the scenes that occurred in 1827 and 1828, before the last presidential election, upon this very subject? Did they not all recollect the hue and cry that was then raised, when Mrs. Bailey was removed from an office, connected with the public printing? His (Mr. C.'s) sentiments were the same now as then. Although charged with deviation, he was determined to maintain the principles for which he had at that period contended.

Mr. C. went on to say that this was the first occasion on which the principles of proscription had been introduced and practised upon in this House, and he considered it as a proof that the reign of terror was restored. Beginning in high places, the stream branched off into every place, however small. He saw distinctly in the course of this Administration, in its large and small operations, a strong tendency to despotism, &c. If it should be found, after giving the Clerk of the House a fair opportunity to explain, that he has turned out able and faithful officers to put in political friends I, (said Mr. C.) will be in favor of teaching him a lesson which shall operate upon public officers beneficially hereafter. He would have a committee to inquire into the facts of the case, and he submitted the following motion as an amendment:

Mr. C. then moved to refer the resolution of Mr. DAVIS, on the memorial of Noah Fletcher, to a select committee, with instructions to inquire into, and report to this House, the causes which have led to the removal of the memorialist; and whether it was from neglect of duty, or from political considerations, that he has been removed; and that said committee have leave to send for persons and papers, and to report by resolution or otherwise.

Mr. MILLER, of Pennsylvania, remarked that very little remained to be said in reply to the gentleman from Massachusetts, without travelling over the same ground taken by the gentleman from Alabama. He had himself, for a long series of years, enjoyed an intimate acquaintance with the gentleman who now fills the station of Clerk of this House, and he knew that there was not anywhere to be found a more high-minded and honorable man. He possessed the confidence of his fellow-citizens in Pennsylvania to a very high degree, and he enjoyed the confidence of his political opponents to as great an extent as any man in that State. I can therefore vouch, said Mr. M., that he is incapable of a dishonorable act. But what is the question which we are now discussing? Has it not been usual for the Clerk of the House to appoint his assistants? Has the right ever been denied to him? How can we make a question of his right to employ such assistants in the discharge of his duties as he himself sees fit to select? As well might the late Clerk, Mr. Clarke, come before us with a memorial for redress, as any one of the assistant clerks. He had never heard Mr. Clarke had been neglectful of his duties; on the contrary, he had always heard him spoken of as a very competent and efficient officer, and an amiable and agreeable man. But still we chose to elect another Clerk. We did not recognise his right to remain in office because he had held it ten or eleven years. If this was the democracy of the gentleman from Kentucky, he could not accede to it, when predicated on the principle of right. It was not the democracy of the people of Pennsylvania, nor did he believe it was of Kentucky. Rotation in office had always been a favorite doctrine with the Democratic party, and very properly. It was the nature of man to misuse powers and privileges long remaining in his hands. He did not apply this to the case of the memorialist, who was, as he had been informed, a respectable man, and had discharged his duties well. Maintaining, as he did, that the Clerk of the House being responsible to the House for the discharge of his trust, had the right of choosing his assistants, he saw no reason for an inquiry into the motives of the removal of the memorialist. He knew very well that all this talk about proscription was meant to operate upon the people. But gentlemen wholly misapprehended the sentiments of the people, if they supposed that the people were in favor of rendering every civil office permanent, during the good behavior of the incumbent. The cry of the minority about proscription he had always regarded as a dishonorable mode of party warfare. Were he in the minority, he would be the last man to ask political favor from adversaries whose election he had opposed. He appealed to the candor and good sense of the gentleman from Massachusetts for the acknowledgment that it is usual for every majority to appoint its own friends to office in preference to its opponents. Was not this the case in the gentleman's own State? Were the offices of trust and profit in the gift of the majority there conferred upon individuals belonging to the minority? Would the gentleman himself, as Governor of Massachusetts, appoint an opponent to office, or would he permit one to remain in office to the exclusion of a political friend? Let him answer this, and then say what becomes of his doctrine of proscription. He was of opinion that this subject ought not to have been introduced into the House, and he was willing to believe that the gentleman from Massachusetts had acted under a momentary excitement, and without mature reflection; and that, upon reflection, he will come to the conclusion that his proposition is unwise and inexpedient.

Mr. SPEIGHT moved to lay the whole subject on the table.

Mr. PINCKNEY rose and asked permission to address the House, but the SPEAKER remarked, that no discussion was in order, the motion being to lay the subject on the table.

Mr. WHITTLESEY, of Ohio, requested the member from North Carolina [Mr. SPEIGHT] to withdraw his motion. There were, he said, in his possession, some important facts, bearing on this subject, which the House should be acquainted with, before the subject was disposed of.

The motion not being withdrawn, Mr. W. called for the yeas and nays upon it, and they were ordered.

Mr. WILLIAMS, of North Carolina, moved that the member from Ohio have leave to submit his information to the House.

The CHAIR said the motion was not in order, Mr. WILLIAMS then moved a call of the House. Agreed to, 83 to 76.

The Clerk called the roll, and 210 members having answered to their names, on motion of Mr. WILLIAMS, the continuance of the call was dispensed with.

Mr. MERCER desired that the first article of the amendment of the Constitution of the United States be read before the question was taken.

The Clerk read it, as follows:

"Congress shall make no law respecting an establishment of religion, or prohibiting the free 'exercise thereof; or abridging the freedom of 'speech or of the press; or the right of the people 'peaceably to assemble and to petition the Government for a redress of grievances."

Mr. WHITTLESEY called for the reading of the resolution under which the memorialist (Noah Fletcher) was appointed to office, and it was read by the Clerk.

The question then being taken on the motion to lay the whole subject on the table, it was decided in the affirmative, as follows: 120 to 83.

YEAS—Messrs. John Adams, William Allen, Anthony, Bernitz, Baylies, Bean, Beardsley, Beaumont, John Bell, James Blair, John Blair, Bockee, Bodle, Boon, Brown, Bunch, Burd, Burns, Bynum, Cage, Cambreleng, Carmichael, Carr, Casey, Chaney, Chinn, Claiborne, Samuel Clark, Clay, Coffee, Connor, Coulter, Cramer, Day, Dickerson, Dickinson, Dunlap, Fowler, William K. Fuller, Gillet, Joseph Hall, Thomas H. Hall, Halsey, Hamer, Hannegan, Joseph M. Harper, Harrison, Hathaway, Hawkins, Hawes, Heath, Henderson, Hubbard, Abel Huntington, Inge, Jarvis, Richard M. Johnson, Noadiah Johnson, Cave Johnson, Benjamin Jones, Kavanagh, King, Kinnard, Lane, Lansing, Laporte, Lawrence, Lay, Luke Lea, Thomas Lee, Leavitt, Loyall, Lyon, Lytle, Abijah Mann, Joel K. Mann, Mardis, M. Mason, McIntire, McKay, McKim, McKinley, McLene, McVean, Miller, Robert Mitchell, Muhlenberg, Osgood, Page, Parks, Parker, Patterson, Dutee J. Pearce, Peyton, Franklin Pierce, Pierson, Plummer, Polk, Pope, Ramsay, Schenck, Schley, Selden, Shinn, Speight, Standifer, Sutherland, William Taylor, Francis Thomas, Thomson, Turner, Turrill, Vanderpoel, Van Houten, Wagener, Ward, Wardwell, Webster, Whallon, C. P. White—120.

NAYS—Messrs. John Quincy Adams, Heman Allen, Chilton Allan, Ashley, Banks, Barber, Barringer, Bates, Beatty, Bouldin, Briggs, Burges, Chambers, Chilton, Choate, William Clark, Clowney, Crane, Crockett, Darlington, Amos Davis, Davenport, Deberry, Denning, Denny, Dennis, Dickson, Duncan, Evans, Edward Everett, Horace Everett, Ewing, Fillmore, Foot, Foster, Philo C. Fuller, Fulton, Gamble, Gordon, Gorham, Grayson, Grennell, Hiland Hall, Hard, Hardin, James Harper, Hazeltine, Hiester, Jabez W. Huntington, Seaborn Jones, Lewis, Love, Martindale, Marshall, McCarty, McKennan, Mercer, Milligan, Moore, Murphy, Patton, Pinckney, Potts, Reed, Rencher, William B. Shepard, Augustine H. Shepperd, Slade, Sloane, Spangler, William P. Taylor, Philemon Thomas, Tompkins, Tweedy, Vinton, Watmough, Edward D. White, Frederick Whittlesey, Elisha Whittlesey, Wilde, Williams, Wise, and Young—83.

On motion of Mr. SLADE, of Vermont, Resolved, That the Committee on Revolutionary Pensions be instructed to inquire into the expediency of placing the name of Joseph Plumb, of Bangor, in the State of New York, on the roll of revolutionary pensioners.

On motion of Mr. DEMING, Resolved, That the Committee on the Post Office and Post Roads be instructed to inquire into the expediency of establishing a post road from Danville, through Waldin and Lamoile village, in Hardwick, to Wolcott, in the State of Vermont.

On motion of Mr. McINTIRE, Resolved, That the Committee on the Post Office

and Post Roads be instructed to inquire into the expediency of establishing a post road from Great Falls, in the State of New Hampshire, to Wells, in State of Maine.

Mr. TURRILL submitted the following: Resolved, That the Committee on Commerce be requested to inquire into the expediency of causing a survey to be taken of the coast of Lake Ontario and of Lake Erie, in which shall be designated the islands and shoals, with the places of anchorage; and also the courses and distances between the harbors, capes, or headlands, together with such other matters as may be deemed proper for completing an accurate chart of every part of said coast.

Mr. GILLET moved to amend the resolution by including "the river St. Lawrence, to the 45th degree of north latitude," which was accepted as a modification by the original mover.

Mr. MERCER then moved to refer the subject to the Committee on Naval Affairs, instead of the Committee on Commerce, which was agreed to, and the resolution, as amended, was adopted.

Mr. McKENNAN, of Pennsylvania, with consent of the House, moved that it be

Resolved, That the Clerk of the House be directed to procure 300 copies of Elliot's Debates on the adoption of the Federal Constitution, for the use of the new members, and the residue for the future disposition of the House.

Mr. PINCKNEY, of South Carolina, warmly opposed the adoption of such a resolution, as being contrary to law, for the House alone, without the sanction of the other two branches of the Government, to make any appropriations for any purpose. He could see no reason why gentlemen who wish to furnish their libraries with any particular book, should do so at the expense of the nation. If for their own particular use, then why not themselves purchase desired works? He was so determined against all appropriations made for books, in the manner proposed by the resolution, that he would move it should be laid on the table. He, however, waived pressing his motion, to permit

Mr. CLAY, of Alabama, to speak on the subject. This gentleman said, that such a resolution was directly against an act of last session, allotting provisional funds for contingent expenses. That act appropriated a sum for either House; that for the House of Representatives was 100,000 dollars for contingent expenses, including printing, &c., among the contingencies. He said, therefore, that the House had no power to act upon the resolution proposed.

Mr. HAWES, of Kentucky, considered that the new members of the House had equal right to obtain copies of the work, as had the old. He would ask one question—Did Mr. CLAY receive, or return, the copy presented to him, which had been ordered by act of Congress?

Mr. WAYNE, of Georgia, moved that the resolution be referred to the Library Committee.

Mr. ELLSWORTH, of Connecticut, did not wish to renew the agitation of a topic so often debated before; and which always produced the same results. He wished that the resolution should be so modified as to call for only as many copies as would be necessary to furnish each new member with a copy.

Mr. PINCKNEY again pressed his motion to have the resolution laid on the table; which was lost by a large majority.

The debate was then resumed by Messrs. COULTER, SUTHERLAND, J. Q. ADAMS, &c., after which the resolution was amended so as to embrace sufficient copies not only of Elliot's Debates, but also of the volume on the Land Laws, and of the Journals till the end of the 13th Congress, formerly published by order of Congress.

Mr. HARPER presented the memorial of the Philadelphia Board of Trade relative to the deposites, which was in part read; but owing-to the lateness of the hour and the pressure of business, it was referred to the Committee of Ways and Means.

After the presentation of other petitions concerning different individuals, or for purposes merely local, from the members representing the various States, in their customary order, The House adjourned, about 4 o'clock.

IN SENATE.

TUESDAY, January 14, 1834.

A message was received from the President of the United States, by the hands of Mr. Donelson, his Private Secretary.

Mr. NAUDAIN reported a bill for the relief of John Thompson, without amendment.

Mr. GRUNDY, from the Committee on Post Offices and Post Roads, made a report upon the resolution offered the other day by Mr. LINN, instructing that committee to make an inquiry into the expediency of carrying the mail between Louisville, Kentucky, to St. Louis, Missouri, by steamboats. Mr. G. stated that he was instructed to move that the committee be discharged from its further consideration. He thought it dangerous for Congress to legislate upon the subject. It appeared an intrusion upon the privileges and rights of the department, and would lead to the derangement of public business and establish a bad precedent.

The report was adopted.

Mr. WHITE, from the Committee on Revolutionary Claims, reported a bill for the relief of Elizabeth Scott, which was, on his motion, ordered to be printed.

Mr. BROWN, from the Committee of Claims, reported a bill for the relief of Samuel Thompson, which was read.

Petitions and memorials were presented by Messrs. PRENTISS and LINN.

Mr. MORRIS presented the following resolutions from the Legislature of the State of Ohio, relative to the Bank of the United States; which were read and ordered to be printed.

Whereas, there is reason to apprehend that the Bank of the United States will attempt to obtain a renewal of its charter at the present session of Congress; and whereas, it is abundantly evident that said bank has exercised powers derogatory to the spirit of our free institutions, and dangerous to the liberties of these United States; and whereas, there is just reason to doubt the constitutional power of Congress to grant acts of incorporation for banking purposes, out of the District of Columbia; and whereas we believe the proper disposal of the public lands to be of the utmost importance to the people of these United States, and that honor and good faith require their equitable distribution; therefore

Resolved by the General Assembly of the State of Ohio, That we consider the removal of the public deposites from the Bank of the United States, as required by the best interests of our country, and for a proper sense of public duty imperiously demanded that that institution should be no longer used as a depository of the public funds.

Resolved, also, That we view, with decided disapprobation, the renewed attempt in Congress, to secure the passage of the bill providing for the disposal of the public domain upon the principles proposed by Mr. Clay, inasmuch as we believe that such a law would be unequal in its operations and unjust in its results.

Resolved, also, That we heartily approve of the principles set forth in the late Veto Message, upon that subject; and

Resolved, That our Senators in Congress be instructed, and our Representatives requested, to use their influence to prevent the re-chartering of the Bank of the United States to sustain the Administration in its removal of the public deposites; and to oppose the passage of a land bill containing the principles adopted in the act upon that subject, passed at the last session of Congress.

Resolved, That the Governor be requested to transmit copies of the foregoing preamble and resolutions to each of our Senators and Representatives in Congress.

JOHN H. KEITH,
Speaker of the House of Representatives.
DAVID T. DISNEY,
Speaker of the Senate.

January 9, 1834.

The following resolutions were offered, and lie one day on the table, viz:

Resolved, That the Committee on Commerce be instructed to inquire into the expediency of establishing at some suitable point on the Ohio river, within the State of Indiana, a marine hospital for

the accommodation of sick and disabled seamen, and river-faring men.

By Mr. POINDEXTER,

Resolved, That the Secretary of the Senate procure from Gales and Seaton, as many copies of their Register of Debates as will supply one copy thereof to each member of the Senate, not already supplied therewith, and ten copies to the office of the Secretary of the Senate.

By Mr. ROBBINS,

Resolved, That the Secretary of the Senate purchase fifty sets of the American Annual Register, and deliver one set to each member of the Senate.

ORDERS OF THE DAY.

The resolution of Mr. ROBBINS, reciprocating on the part of Congress an exchange of copies of proceedings, &c., with the British Parliament and the French Chambers, was taken up and adopted.

The resolution of Mr. CLAY, of yesterday—

"That the Committee on Finance be directed to inquire into the expediency of affording temporary relief to the community from the present pecuniary embarrassments, by prolonging the payment of revenue bonds, as they fall due, the obligors paying interest, and giving satisfactory security," being under consideration—

Mr. CLAY observed, that the resolution just read sufficiently explained its object—it proposed to instruct the Committee on Finance to inquire what relief can be afforded to the community by delaying the collection of revenue bonds. He was not sure that the object desired to be accomplished could be attained; he was not sure that the state of the treasury was not such as to require, for the unavoidable calls of the Government upon it, the immediate possession of all its means. If we were to judge of that department of the Government by the situation of one of the other departments—he meant the Post Office—it was certain we could not do what the resolution contemplated, because the Government will want all its available means. But the subject was worthy of inquiry, and he hoped it might appear that the treasury could do something—could grant some relief, by delaying the collection of the revenue bonds. As regarded the distress existing in the community, that was what no one could deny. What was the situation of the country four months ago? Then, every interest, every branch of trade was flourishing. In the section of country from which he came, every production of agriculture and manufactures was in demand, the most unexampled prosperity prevailed, and what was true of that section was equally true as respected other parts of the Union; the same unexampled prosperity prevailed. What was the condition of the country *now*? What branch of industry was there that had not received a most serious fall? In one week, as he had been credibly informed, the great staple commodity of the State of Pennsylvania had been reduced from 115 cents to 90 cents per bushel; an extraordinary depression in the Southern staple had also taken place. Everything was falling and going down, and it would continue, unless something was done. The immediate cause of all this distress was now under discussion in the Senate; he did not mean to take it up; but if the deposites should be restored, relief could not be produced by it immediately. When the public credit is destroyed, and confidence shaken, it requires a long time to restore it. But if it should take place, and if it should be found practicable to do what is proposed, something would have been done to restore our former prosperity, and at some future day he hoped to see a permanent restoration of it. By adopting the resolution and the purpose it contemplated, relief would be afforded to some classes of the community. The pressure was occasioned by the want of money for the purchase of the produce in market. The resolution proposed an inquiry, and he hoped the Committee on Finance would find that the Government were able to give some relief.

Mr. BROWN was opposed to the resolution, because it was entirely inexpedient for Congress to hold out to the community the idea of relief, unless they intend that relief to be permanent. But he was opposed to it on another ground. It was the practice, when the Government granted relief to those who were indebted to them, for their debtors to look for further relief. It was true there might be distress in the community, but he did not believe that it existed to the extent which had been represented; he believed it had been greatly exaggerated. A great depression in the Southern staple, cotton, had been spoken of; but he would ask, could this measure have reduced the price of cotton in England and in Europe? The general price of cotton and of tobacco was higher here now than it was this time last year. But the cause to which it has been referred is intimately connected with the true cause; and he would remark, that if an institution is capable of exerting a power such as is given to the Bank of the United States for such purposes, it is time for the people to pause. If a remedy for the distress be necessary, it should be the removal of that power which is capable of exercising such deleterious influence. He had been told that the markets and produce of the country, and the diminution in the price of cotton, were to be attributed to the removal of the deposites; and if any other great phenomenon should happen, no doubt that too would be ascribed to the same cause. This excitement got up on this floor might have its political effects: he did not attribute political effect as the design of gentlemen—far, very far from it; but he was opposed to the resolution of inquiry, because it was entirely inexpedient.

Mr. FORSYTH had no objection to the resolution, or to an inquiry, or to legislative aid, if any were necessary, but he proposed to amend the resolution—to strike out all after the word "resolved," and insert the following:

"That the Committee on Finance inquire into 'the extent and causes of the alleged distress of 'the community, and into the propriety of legis'lative interference to relieve them."

Mr. CLAY observed, that as compromises had become fashionable, he would be willing to accept it, not as a substitute, but as an addition to his resolution. He did not know of any other mode of giving constitutional relief, except that contemplated.

Mr. SHEPLEY intended to vote against both the amendment and the resolution. We live in an intelligent community, and among a people who know what their distresses are, and what relief is necessary. They have asked no interference on the part of Congress, nor petitioned for relief; and they were as competent to say what relief they required as merchants were. He should wait till we were asked to legislate on the petitions of the people. Much had been said of the distress of the people, but he thought there was more in imagination than in reality—a distress which did not make itself known, except in chambers of commerce and in banking institutions. But so far as his own State was concerned, he could say that the most prominent newspaper there opposed to the Administration of the Government, admitted that wild lands had risen in Maine at least one-fifth in price; and if that were true, why should not other classes of the community be benefited by it? He should wait till those classes should interpose for relief.

Mr. SILSBEE said the gentleman had spoken of the rise of wild lands in Maine. Now, he (Mr. S.) knew the cause of that rise to be the large speculations which had recently been made in them—six thousand emigrants had but lately gone into them—that was the cause. The gentleman seems to think there has been no depression in anything. But Mr. S. would say that he knew and *felt* that some articles had fallen, and fallen much. He hoped the original resolution would pass and the object of it be accomplished. He had received letters from various parts of the country, informing him that such distress as existed now never was felt before. The banks and the individual lenders of money have granted indulgence to their debtors, and this has prevented more general insolvency. But if they had been indebted to the Government, a most merciless creditor, the debt must have been paid. There was a loud call for what was contemplated by the resolution.

Mr. PRESTON would state a single fact. He had just received a letter from a gentleman in South Carolina, a large planter, and for many years a director in the Bank of Columbia. He states that the effect of the recent public measures is, to have brought down the price of cotton so low, as to be within three to five cents of what the prices at Liverpool would authorize, and in fact, that such is the pressure that it is impossible to furnish such facilities to the planter as are necessary to carry on the business, and no money can be got from any quarter to pay for the cotton which is brought there. The gentleman from Maine says, that the cries of distress are only from chambers of commerce and banking houses. And what are chambers of commerce? Do they not represent the vast commercial interests of the country? And what are banking houses? Do they not regulate and represent the whole fiscal affairs of the nation? And are they under the influence of this institution, which it is so desirable to look into? But, if so, we ought to look farther—we ought to look to that power which has seized on the bank and disorganized the country. He spoke with some knowledge of his own part of the country. He knew that the staple there had fallen greatly and suddenly. A great many people had embarked in the business, and they did not believe it possible that the Executive could so interfere as to reduce their property from twenty-five to thirty per cent. There was another matter. South Carolina held more of the stock of the United States Bank, in proportion to her means, than any other State—it amounted to about five millions, and by one fell swoop of the Executive, one million of this sum was lost—the people of the South were losing daily from three to five cents per pound upon their great staple article, not positively, but relatively, to the price in the Liverpool market. The exchange was struck down and money was not to be had to purchase anything. He heartily desired that if it was in the power of Congress, as general a relief might be granted as was practicable.

Mr. FORSYTH had no objection to the amendment, either as a substitute or an addition. There was nothing unfair in the resolution, but it was not necessary. His general inquiry included the gentleman's [Mr. CLAY's] particular inquiry. All he seemed to desire was, that the specific mode of relief might be under the inquiry of the committee. He (Mr. F.) had no objection that the Committee on Finance should take the general welfare into consideration, and he had no wish but that a constitutional remedy should be applied. He believed that distress did exist in the community. It had been alleged that the distress was very great. This he believed was incorrect; he thought it greatly exaggerated. For we had been just told by a distinguished gentleman, lately one of the directors of the United States Bank, that the *mere* removal of the deposites did not and could not have produced the distress. Whence, then, does it arise? From the conflict, the war which the institution is waging to get back the deposites. The deposites having been removed, it stands still to see what may follow, and it stands still, too, that its power may be felt in every nerve and fibre of the community—that every man shall feel the *necessity* of the institution. As to the wisdom or policy of this course of conduct, he would leave that to the gentleman to settle. The relief contemplated, he thought, could at best only benefit the importers.

Mr. CLAY asked if the gentleman did not see that if the inquiry proposed by himself were adopted, Mr. F.'s would not be excluded? Had the gentleman suggested any other mode of relief than that? In regard to relieving the importers only, what is it, he would ask, that the Executive has done? What has the Secretary of the Treasury in his late edict said? Give relief to the importers. And what did his resolution ask but an inquiry with a view to relieving the same class? He should vote against the amendment.

Mr. SPRAGUE said, as it had been argued that the distress produced was not the effect of the removal of the deposites, it was not of much moment what resolution was adopted.

[Mr. FORSYTH observed that the gentleman alluded to in his speech had said that the *mere* removal of the deposites *could* not have produced the present distress.]

If so, then the answer does not meet the question. It was the manner of the removal, and the gentleman in his speech attributed the distress to the execution of the act. That the way in which it was done impelled the bank to a course of self-defence. The issuing of contingent checks, to be

presented only upon the will of the enemy, and upon the will of the local banks, armed by the Executive to be made as and how they chose. It was this which compelled the bank to guard against the attacks of the Executive.

Mr. BENTON inquired whether any petitions or memorials had been presented by the importing merchants, praying for relief from the payment of their bonds?

The VICE PRESIDENT replied there were none.

Mr. B. then said, as none had been presented, he should wait till the request was made. This proceeding was a work of supererogation, and it was making a direct reflection upon that most respectable class of our citizens, the importing merchants, which they did *not* deserve. He was always disposed to listen to their applications with patience and respect, but he was unwilling to act until they solicited it.

Mr. CHAMBERS thought the proposition of the gentleman from Georgia a most proper and expedient one. But when the gentleman rose and said there was no pressure in the community, there was nothing more important than that the *fact* should be put at rest. His section of country was a grain-growing country, and he would be happy if the gentleman from North Carolina, [Mr. BROWN,] could make his assertion in relation to that interest with the least appearance of reality. There was not a man in his vicinity who sells his bushel of grain, who did not pay his tax for this attack upon, and derangement of the pecuniary affairs of the country. It was the agricultural interests which always suffered most from such a state of things: and was the absence of all political power in them a cause for neglecting them? A neglect, too, aggravated by saying that it was ideal.

Mr. BROWN said, that was another string, fortunately got up to play on. A few days since, we had the manufacturing interests, depicted as being in a shocking state; a little while ago, the cotton business; and now, the agricultural interests were destroyed. In regard to the distress in the South, which the gentleman [Mr. PRESTON] had depicted, it was a fixed rule in commerce, that where capital was most wanted, it would seek investment, and he assured the gentleman that when it should be known that he wanted money, there was capital enough to come to his relief. We had been told by the gentleman from Maryland, [Mr. CHAMBERS,] that the distress was real. But there was no prophecy so true, as that which the prophet himself wishes to have realized. Why was there distress? what caused the distress? These walls rung with the alarm—the newspapers resounded with exaggerations of it, while themselves produced dismay, apprehension, and distress; but there were no more failures in our commercial cities than was common in the ordinary course of trade.

Mr. KING, of Alabama, said, it was not his habit to oppose any resolution which the public interests might require. But he felt compelled to observe, that no subject had been recently introduced into the Senate, in which the question of the removal of the deposites had not been introduced also. The gentleman from Kentucky was peculiarly fortunate in this respect—he would not, however, discuss that question now. Whether the prevailing distress, so vividly depicted by honorable gentlemen, were so or not, he did not know; he was willing that an inquiry might be made into it. He rose merely to reply to the gentleman from South Carolina—he could not agree with him in relation to the depression in the price of cotton. He would go to the fountain head for the truth, and if the gentleman would look to the price of cotton in Liverpool, he would find that the price here corresponded with it there. The price there was from seven to nine pence, equivalent to 13 and 16 cents. The expense of sending the article from here to Liverpool is four cents per pound—deduct that from the price in Liverpool and add it to the price here, and he would find that it was uniform. In 1825-6, cotton ran up to 25 and 26 cents per pound, and in a few months it fell to 10 and 12 cents. The deposites were then not removed—the country was in the utmost prosperity, so far as the Bank of the United States was concerned. But the depreciation arose from the fact that it was ascertained in England that the crops were abundant, and failures then took place in consequence of inordinate speculation in the article, and the same state of things existed now to a certain degree. Before he left home, and before the removal of the deposites could have had any effect upon the trade, gentlemen were selling out their cotton at considerable loss from the same causes. But as he was anxious to hear the gentleman from Maine [Mr. SHEPLEY] on the main question, he moved to lay the subject on the table for the present.

Mr. K., however, withdrew his motion, to allow Mr. PRESTON to reply.

Mr. WILKINS said, that having just taken his seat, he had not heard all which had been said upon this subject. But he would give the reasons why he should vote both against the resolution and the amendment. The relief contemplated was but a temporary expedient, and in the present situation of the country, it was our duty to avoid anything like temporizing, for he could call it nothing more. We should carry out and sustain the Administration in the removal of the deposites, or adopt an order for their immediate restoration. He was therefore unwilling to adopt any temporizing relief. There was no expression in any of the memorials which had been presented on this subject suggesting or requesting any temporary mode of relief. True, the memorialists ascribe the prevailing distress to the action of the Secretary of the Treasury, in the removal of the deposites, and that *nothing* can give relief but their restoration.

Another reason why he would oppose the resolution was, that the present complaints were greatly exaggerated. There was nothing whatever to justify the fears and apprehensions which had been entertained. He believed the settlement of the resolutions, now the subject of the main discussion, would relieve the pressure. If the resolutions pass, the deposites will be restored; and if we bear out the Administration in their removal, the same happy results will be produced by it, and trade and business would accommodate itself to the existing state of things. He was exceedingly anxious to terminate this discussion. The gentleman who had been alluded to [Mr. BINNEY] thought that the present distress did not arise from the mere removal of the deposites. And it could not be denied that the mere change, the mere transfer from one side of the street to the other, did not, and could not, have produced it. But the gentleman from Maine [Mr. SPRAGUE] contended that it was the secrecy, the stealth, with which it was done, and the forbearance to disclose the existence of the transfer drafts that had issued, which caused all this calamity. Well, what was that? What did it amount to? The transfer drafts only amounted to one million of dollars; and could the abstraction of this sum have produced all this wide-spread national calamity? There was no secrecy in the transaction—nothing disingenuous in it. It was all known to the bank a month before the demand of the money. The drafts had issued in the regular uniform prescribed mode; they were signed, countersigned, recorded, and passed through all the required forms, without the least concealment or secrecy; and any man who could read, might have seen their amount. The cashier of the bank, too, says their existence was known. But if there had been any secrecy in the warrants, so much the better for the bank. The holders were instructed not to present them unless it should be found that the vindictive spirit of the bank made it necessary. There was no part of the country which did a more extensive and important business than the city and vicinity of his residence, and he had not heard a word, complaining of distress, from that quarter. It was confined to the vicinity of the bank, and it was a part of the system adopted by the bank to coerce the restoration of the deposites. And upon whom had it brought down this calamity? Upon the heads of their own innocent neighbors. Nothing but the final adjustment of this question would give relief—this temporizing would not avail.

Mr. POINDEXTER suggested as an amendment to the amendment, that the committee inquire into the "extent and causes" of the pressure; which

Mr. FORSYTH accepted.

Mr. POINDEXTER observed that the subject was particularly interesting to him, coming as he did from a cotton-growing country, and he felt desirous of being heard briefly upon it. But as the hour had arrived for resuming the general debate, he thought we ought to proceed with it—he would therefore move to postpone the question till another day, when he would show that the present financial arrangements have had a most deleterious effect upon the cotton trade. He then moved to lay the resolution on the table; which was agreed to.

The VICE PRESIDENT having announced the special order to be the

REMOVAL OF THE DEPOSITES,

The Senate resumed the consideration of Mr. CLAY's resolutions.

Mr. SHEPLEY addressed the Senate at length against the resolutions of Mr. CLAY, and in support of the reasons of the Secretary, and at three o'clock gave way to a motion of Mr. BENTON to adjourn.

Mr. BENTON, however, withdrew his motion, to allow the introduction of the following resolutions submitted by Mr. WEBSTER:

Resolved, That the Secretary of the Treasury lay before the Senate a copy of the official order or direction for changing the place of the deposite of the public money.

Resolved, That the Secretary of the Treasury cause to be laid before the Senate a copy of the official bond of the Treasurer of the United States.

Resolved, That the Secretary of the Treasury cause to be laid before the Senate copies of all drafts, checks, or orders issued by the Treasurer of the United States, in order to transfer the public moneys from the Bank of the United States and its branches, to the several State banks, selected as banks of deposite.

And the Senate adjourned.

HOUSE OF REPRESENTATIVES.

TUESDAY, *January* 14, 1834.

Mr. ARCHER, from the Committee on Foreign Relations, reported a bill for the relief of the legal representatives of Richard W. Meade, deceased. Also, a bill to provide for the settlement of the claims of Mary O'Sullivan; which were severally read twice, and committed to the Committee of the Whole.

Mr. ADAMS, of Massachusetts, submitted the following resolution:

Resolved, That the Secretary of the Treasury be directed to communicate to this House copies of such instructions as have been given to the collectors of the customs since the 26th of December last, regulating their duty under the act passed at the last session of Congress, entitled "An act to modify the act of the 14th of July, 1832, and all other acts imposing duties on imports."

Mr. ADAMS said his object was merely to obtain the treasury instructions given since the 26th of December, that being the day on which the erroneous instructions were issued by the Comptroller, and had greatly agitated the public mind. The information which would be elicited by the call would satisfy the public mind on the subject.

The resolution was agreed to.

The following resolution, heretofore offered by Mr. ANTHONY, was, on his motion, taken up and agreed to:

Resolved, That the Secretary of War be directed to communicate to this House the report of Major Bache, of the corps of Topographical Engineers, of his survey and estimate of the Williamsport and Elmira railroad, in the States of Pennsylvania and New York.

On motion of Mr. BOCKEE,

Resolved, That the Committee on Revolutionary Pensions be instructed to inquire into the expediency of granting a pension to John Wardin, a soldier of the Revolution,

On motion of Mr. EWING,

Resolved, That the Committee on the Post Office and Post Roads be instructed to inquire into the expediency of establishing a post road from Bedford, in the county of Lawrence, through Mount Pleasant, in the county of Martin, to the town of Portersville, in the county of Dubois, and of ex-

tending post route No. 3014, (Post Office Register,) from Green Castle, through Manhattan and Pleasant Garden, towns in the county of Putnam, Bowling Green and New Brunswick, (Rowley's Mill,) towns in the county of Clay, to Caledonia, and thence to Carlisle, towns in the county of Sullivan, in the State of Indiana.

Mr. GILMER submitted the following resolution, which, by the rules, lies one day on the table:

Resolved, That the Secretary of War be directed to communicate to this House all correspondence which he may have had, or other information in his possession, in relation to the death of Hardiman Owens, a citizen of Alabama, who was lately put to death by a party of regular soldiers; whether said Owens was put to death in pursuance of orders from the War Department, or any officer of the United States; and that he also communicate to this House any correspondence which he may have had, or other information in his possession in relation to any obstruction thrown in the way of the execution of the process of the courts of Alabama, issued for the purpose of bringing to trial those by whom said Owens was killed, and any correspondence in relation to the removal of said prosecutions to the District Court of the United States.

On motion of Mr. BEATTY,

Resolved, That the Committee on Roads and Canals be instructed to inquire into the expediency of appropriating a sum in ——— dollars, to complete the improvement of the navigation of the Cumberland river, from Nashville up to the falls on said river.

On motion of Mr. WARD,

Resolved, That the Committee on Naval Affairs be instructed to inquire into the expediency of constructing a dry-dock at or near the city of New York, and of causing a survey to be made of the present navy yard at Brooklyn, and also of other sites in the vicinity of New York, which may be selected for the construction of such dry dock.

On motion of Mr. STEWART,

Resolved, That the Committee on Roads and Canals be instructed to inquire into the expediency of making provision for the improvement of the steamboat navigation of the Monongahela river, as far as the survey, plan, and estimates have been completed, and for the extension of the surveys to the highest practicable point of such improvement.

On motion of Mr. WILDE,

Resolved, That the report of the Secretary of the Treasury, of the 24th February, 1830, on the currency, made in obedience to the resolution of the House of Representatives, be printed for the use of Congress.

On motion of Mr. McKIM,

Resolved, That the Committee on Commerce be instructed to inquire into the expediency of requiring all American vessels, of 200 tons burden and upwards, bound to any ports in Europe, or south of the equator, to have, as a part of the crew of said vessels, one or more apprentices, in proportion to their tonnage.

Mr. MARDIS submitted the following resolution, the consideration of which, on his motion, was postponed until Monday next:

Resolved, That the Committee of Ways and Means be instructed to inquire into the expediency of designating, by law, the future depository of the public moneys of the United States, and also as to the expediency of defining by law all contracts hereafter to be made with the Secretary of the Treasury in relation to the safe-keeping, management, and disbursement, of the same.

Mr. ADAMS, of Massachusetts, submitted the following resolution, which lies one day on the table:

Resolved, That the President of the United States be requested to cause to be laid before this House a list of the presents now deposited in the Department of State, and referred to in his message of the 5th instant, received by persons holding offices of profit or trust under the United States, from any king, prince, or foreign State, from whom, the name and office of the person by whom, the time when, and the authority, if any, by which such present was received, and the estimated value of the same.

On motion of Mr. POTTS,

Resolved, That the Committee on the Post Office and Post Roads be instructed to inquire into the expediency of establishing a mail route from Nottingham, in Chester county, Pennsylvania, to the Brick Meeting-house, in Cecil county, Maryland.

On motion of Mr. McCOMAS,

Resolved, That the Committee on the Post Office and Post Roads be instructed to inquire into the expediency of establishing a post road from Poplar Hill, in the county of Giles, the residence of Thomas Shannon, up Walker's Creek, to the town of Mechanicsburg, in the county of Giles, and from thence to the head of Walker's Creek, and down the Holston river to the Salt Works in the county of Smythe; and that they have leave to report by bill or otherwise.

On motion of Mr. DAVENPORT,

Resolved, That the Committee on the Post Office and Post Roads inquire into the expediency of establishing a post route from Danville, by the way of Rocky Mount, in the county of Franklin, to Salem, in Botetourt county, Virginia.

Mr. SEVIER submitted the following resolution, which, by a rule of the House, lies one day on the table:

Resolved, That the Secretary of the Treasury be directed to inform this House how many patents for land, sold at either public or private sale, in the Territory of Arkansas, *have been suspended*; together with the name or names of each purchaser, and the quantity of each purchase or entry, and the reasons which have induced such suspensions.

Mr. FOOT submitted the following resolution, which lies one day on the table:

Resolved, That the Secretary of the Treasury be directed to prepare, and lay before this House, a plan for the reorganization of the Treasury Department; with a view to simplify the forms of keeping and settling accounts, and rendering them more intelligible; of making a more equal distribution of the labor and duties; of abolishing some of the subordinate branches, and reducing the number of clerks in the Executive departments.

On motion of Mr. FOSTER,

Resolved, That the report of the Secretary of the Treasury, with regard to the removal of the public deposites, shall be the standing order of the day, at one o'clock daily, Fridays and Saturdays excepted; and that, until that hour, the business of the House shall proceed in the order prescribed by the rules of the House.

On motion of Mr. HARRISON,

Resolved, That the Committee on Revolutionary Pensions be instructed to inquire into the propriety of placing John Myers, of Butler county, Pennsylvania, a revolutionary soldier, on the pension roll.

On motion of Mr. McKENNAN,

Resolved, That the Committee on the Post Office and Post Roads be instructed to inquire into the expediency of establishing a mail route from Washington, Washington county, Pennsylvania, by Dock's Mill, Buckingham, and Jefferson, to Wayneaburg, in Greene county; and of altering so much of the present route between those points as will be rendered unnecessary thereby; and that the accompanying papers be referred to said committee.

On motion of Mr. CLAY, of Alabama,

Resolved, That the Committee on the Post Office and Post Roads be instructed to inquire into the expediency of establishing a post route from Carrollton, Georgia, by way of Drayton, in Burton county, Nail's Island, in Cocea river, to Ashville, Alabama. Also, a post route from Montgomery, Alabama, by way of the Court-houses of Cocoa, Taladega, and Burton counties, to the head of Cocea river, in Georgia.

On motion of Mr. LYON, of Michigan,

Resolved, That the Committee of Ways and Means be instructed to inquire into the expediency of making an appropriation for constructing a ship canal between the navigable waters of the river Raisin and Lake Erie, or La Plaisance Bay, being a part of the improvements at that place already authorized by law.

Mr. POLK, from the Committee of Ways and Means, reported a bill from the Senate for the relief of John Haggerty and David Austin, with an amendment. Also, a bill from the Senate, authorizing the Secretary of the Treasury to compromise a claim against the firm of Minturn and Champlin. Also, a bill from the Senate, for the relief of John Hone & Sons, of New York; read twice, and committed.

Mr. DUNCAN, from the Committee on Public Lands, reported a bill to establish the office of surveyor general in certain States and Territories; read twice, and committed.

The following bills were also reported, read twice, and committed to the Committee of the Whole:

By Mr. CASEY: Senate bill for the relief of Noyes Daily.

Also, a bill for the relief of George Terry.

By Mr. HUBBARD: A bill for the relief of the owners of the schooner Joseph and Mary.

By Mr. McKIM: A bill for the relief of Samuel P. Walker.

By Mr. LEWIS: A bill for the relief of Alexander J. Robertson.

On motion of Mr. MUHLENBERG, the Committee on Revolutionary Claims was discharged from the further consideration of the petition of General Thomas Nelson, of Virginia; and,

On motion of Mr. WISE, the same petition was ordered to be referred to a Select Committee of seven.

Mr. CLAY, from the Committee on Public Lands, reported a bill further to provide for locations of certain land claims in the Territory of Arkansas; and on his motion the further consideration of the same was postponed to and made the order of the day for this day week.

Mr. CARR, from the Committee on Private Land Claims, reported a bill for the relief of the heirs at law of William G. Christopher, deceased. Read twice and committed.

Mr. THOMPSON, from the Committee on Military Affairs, reported a bill for the relief of David Kilburn. Read twice and committed.

Mr. JOHNSON, of Kentucky, from the same Committee, reported a bill to authorize the establishment of an army asylum. Read twice and committed.

A resolution was proposed that, in future, the time of the House, after the hour of one, pending the discussion relative to the public deposites, should be devoted to the discussion solely of that topic, till it shall have been definitely decided—on every day except Fridays and Saturdays.

Motion lost.

REMOVAL OF THE DEPOSITES.

The House having resumed the consideration of the motion to refer the Secretary of the Treasury's report on the deposites to the Committee of Ways and Means, and the question being upon the motion of Mr. McDUFFIE to add to the motion for reference the following instructions to the said committee:

"With instructions to report a joint resolution, 'providing that the public revenue hereafter collected shall be deposited in the Bank of the United 'States, in compliance with the public faith, 'pledged by the charter of the said bank'"—

Mr. CAMBRELENG rose and addressed the House in a speech of much point and pungency, levelled against all classes of bank monopolies.

After Mr. CAMBRELENG had concluded, Mr. MOORE moved an adjournment of the House, but withdrew his motion to enable Mr. SEABORN JONES to submit the following, in lieu of the amendment submitted by Mr. McDUFFIE: viz. to strike out of his amendment all after "with instructions to," and insert—

"Inquire into the expediency of depositing the 'revenue hereafter collected in the State banks in 'the different States where the same is collected, 'in proportion to their respective capitals paid in, 'and to prescribe the terms on which the same 'shall be deposited; and to report by bill or 'otherwise."

The engrossed bill making appropriations for the naval service for 1834, was read a third time and passed.

The SPEAKER presented a communication from the Secretary of the Treasury, with a report on the state of the incorporated banks in the Dis-

trict of Columbia; which was laid on the table and ordered to be printed.

Also, a communication from the War Department, with a report and some surveys by Captain McNeil and others, which was ordered by the House on the 24th ultimo; which was referred to the Committee on Roads and Canals; and, on motion of Mr. EVERETT,

The House adjourned.

IN SENATE.

WEDNESDAY, January 15, 1834.

Mr. GRUNDY, from the Committee on the Post Office and Post Roads, reported a bill authorizing and regulating the transportation of acts and laws of the several State Legislatures in the mails; which was read.

Mr. HENDRICKS gave notice that he should to-morrow ask leave to introduce a bill for the benefit of South Hanover College.

The VICE PRESIDENT communicated a letter from the Secretary of War, stating the impracticability of furnishing the documents called for in the case of Mounjoy Bailey; which was read.

The VICE PRESIDENT also communicated a letter from the Secretary of the Treasury, relative to imports; which, on motion of Mr. WEBSTER, was ordered to be printed.

Mr. EWING presented the petition of certain citizens of the State of Ohio, praying that slavery may be abolished in the District of Columbia; which was referred, without reading, to the Committee on the District of Columbia.

Mr. SPRAGUE presented the memorial of sundry citizens of Maine, on the same subject; which had the same reference.

Mr. KING, of Georgia, presented the memorial of several citizens of Savannah and Macon, in Georgia, relative to the construction of an iron steamboat; which was referred to the Committee on Finance.

Petitions, generally of a private nature, were also presented by Messrs. EWING, WAGGAMAN, RIVES, SMITH, BELL, and WEBSTER, which were severally referred, without reading, to the usual committees.

Mr. KANE gave notice that he should to-morrow ask leave to bring in a bill for the construction of a canal from St. Andrew's Bay to Apalachicola river.

Mr. BELL, from the Committee on Claims, reported a bill for the relief of Daniel Halsey and William Palmer; which was read.

Mr. POINDEXTER introduced a bill for the relief of Elizabeth Magruder; which was read, and on his motion referred to the Committee on Private Land Claims.

Mr. CLAY moved that certain papers which had recently been discovered, belonging to Paschal Hickman, be referred in the same committee which had charge of his petition.

Mr. MOORE, from the Committee on Revolutionary Claims, reported a bill for the relief of the heirs of Richard Wilde, deceased; which was read, and, with the accompanying report, ordered to be printed.

The following bills from the House of Representatives were read a first and second time, and referred to appropriate committees:

A bill for the relief of John Webber;

A bill for the relief of Abraham Forbes;

A bill for the relief of the heirs of Alexander Boyd;

A bill for the relief of Ezekiel Foster & Co.;

A bill for the relief of the owners of the schooner Three Sisters;

A bill for the relief of Philip Bessom;

A bill for the relief of the heirs of Joseph Rowe, deceased;

A bill for the benefit of the Baltimore and Ohio Railroad Company, [authorizes the construction of a lateral road in the District of Columbia, and appropriates $350,000 to that object.]

A bill for the relief of Horatio N. Crabb;

A bill for the relief of John G. Reynolds;

A bill for the relief of Master Commandant John Percival.

The VICE PRESIDENT communicated a letter from the Secretary of the Treasury, in compliance with a resolution of Mr. SPRAGUE, ask-

ing information relative to tonnage employed in the trade between the United States and the various West India Islands, &c.; which, on motion of Mr. WEBSTER, was ordered to be printed; but afterwards, at the suggestion of Mr. SHEPLEY,

Mr. FORSYTH moved the reconsideration of the order to print, which gave rise to some conversation between Messrs. SHEPLEY, WEBSTER, and SPRAGUE; when the question to reconsider was lost.

A message was received from the House of Representatives, by Mr. Franklin, their Clerk, stating that they had passed certain bills, in which they desired the concurrence of the Senate.

ORDERS OF THE DAY.

The resolutions offered yesterday and the day before, by Messrs. HENDRICKS, POINDEXTER, MOORE, ROBBINS, and WEBSTER, were severally read and adopted.

The resolution of Mr. ROBBINS, that the Secretary of the Senate purchase fifty sets of the American Annual Register, and deliver one set to each member of the Senate, being under consideration, Mr. ROBBINS made a few explanatory remarks, which were inaudible in the gallery.

Mr. SPRAGUE objected to the adoption of the resolution in its present form, and offered an amendment, that the "copies be deposited in the Library of Congress."

Mr. HILL objected to the resolution. He said there was enough of such books in the library to answer the purposes of Congress. There was no particular merit in the work in question. It was tinged with party feeling, and we might as well purchase, said Mr. H., old files of newspapers. Besides, the work could be had at the bookstores for a great deal less cost, ($1,750.)

On motion of Mr. FORSYTH, the resolution was referred to the Committee on the Library.

The joint resolution for the purchase of ten copies of the Laws of the United States, in seven volumes complete, being the same laws which were originally contained in the first six volumes thereof, to be deposited in the Library of Congress, was ordered to be engrossed.

The following resolution, offered by Mr. McKEAN, was adopted, the rule having been dispensed with, which would have required it to lie one day on the table:

Resolved, That the Committee on the Post Offices and Post Roads be instructed to inquire into the expediency of establishing a post route from the next office at Franklindale, in the county of Bradford, through Granville or Sperryfield, to the post office at Ridgeberry, in the State of Pennsylvania.

The following resolution was submitted by Mr. ROBINSON, which lies one day:

Resolved, That the Committee on the Judiciary be instructed to inquire into the expediency of more explicitly fixing the amount of the fees of the attorneys of the respective districts of the United States, and of equalizing said fees according to the services rendered.

Mr. POINDEXTER stated that he had yesterday moved, and it was so ordered, that the resolution of the Senator from Kentucky, inquiring into the expediency by the Committee on Finance, of "affording temporary relief to the community from the present pecuniary embarrassments" should lie upon the table. He stated that if it was the pleasure of the Senate, or the wish of the gentleman from Kentucky, he would now move to take the resolution up; he preferred himself, that the main debate upon the resolutions of the same Senator (disapproving of the course of the Secretary of the Treasury in removing the public deposites) be allowed to proceed.

Mr. CLAY assented to the wishes of the Senator from Mississippi.

The VICE PRESIDENT having announced the special order to be

THE REMOVAL OF THE DEPOSITES.

The Senate resumed the consideration of the resolutions submitted by Mr. CLAY, on the 26th ultimo.

Mr. SHEPLEY then resumed his speech, and continued until 3 o'clock, when he gave way to a motion by Mr. KANE, for an adjournment.

The Senate then adjourned.

HOUSE OF REPRESENTATIVES.

WEDNESDAY, January 15, 1834.

The SPEAKER presented a letter from Mr. DAVIS, stating he had informed the Legislature of Massachusetts, that he had resigned his seat in Congress.

He also presented a communication from the Secretary of the Treasury, in accordance with the resolution passed yesterday, relative to the rules and regulations adopted by the Treasury Department, in pursuance of the 9th section of the act of July, 1832, on the tariff. The following is a copy of the circular sent to the collectors from the Comptroller's Office:

TREASURY DEPARTMENT,
Comptroller's Office, January 15, 1834.

SIR: In giving the instructions in the circular of the 28th ultimo, in relation to the item of forty bales of blue cotton cloths, I was under the impression that, according to the views expressed by the Secretary of the Treasury, in his circular of the 20th April, 1833, the reduction of duties provided for by the act of 2d March, 1833, was to be ascertained by calculating the duty of 35 per cent. imposed by the act of 14th July, 1832, on the actual or real value of this description of goods, instead of the minimum, or assumed, or artificial value of 35 cents per square yard, when costing less than that sum.

The Secretary of the Treasury has, however, decided that such was not the intention of the circular of the 20th April, 1833, and has directed that the duty of 25 per cent., imposed by the act of 14th July, 1833, is to be calculated on the minimum principle, or assumed value of such goods; and that the duty of 20 per cent., under the act of 2d March, 1833, is to be estimated on the real or actual foreign cost or value of such goods—the difference between the two amounts thus produced, constituting the excess upon which the one-tenth is to be deducted.

You will, accordingly, be pleased to make alterations and additions in relation to the item of forty bales of blue cotton cloths, in the form of the importer's entry subjoined to the circular from this office of the 26th ultimo, in the manner specified in the accompanying statement.

Respectfully, _____, Comptroller.

Mr. MUHLENBERG, of Pennsylvania, presented a letter from the relief of the heirs and legal representatives of Philip Turner; read twice and committed.

Mr. WARDWELL, of New York, a bill for the relief of Benedict Galvert and Robert Rush; read twice, and committed.

Mr. BAYLIES, a bill for the relief of the heirs of F. Sampson; read twice, and committed.

Mr. GRAYSON, a bill for the relief of Nathaniel Therens; also, a bill for the relief of Henry Whitney; committed.

Mr. POLK presented a bill from the Committee of Ways and Means for the relief of Jonathan Walker and John Clay De Kraft.

THE PENSION LAWS.

The order of the day was then declared to be the resolution of Mr. CHILTON, to appoint a select committee to inquire into the expediency of extending the general pension law as to embrace within its provisions those persons who were engaged in the Indian wars, down to the year 1794; and the amendment on it by Mr. BOULDIN, to appoint a committee to inquire into the moral effects of the pension system upon the community, and how far it ought to be abolished or repealed.

Mr. McCOMAS admitted that the effect of the present pension laws is calculated to corrupt many, but not a majority, or rather to corrupt some, but not many. But who will reject a law because in its effects it may produce a few evils; although in its general operation it is capable of producing beneficial results, which greatly overbalance any concomitant evils? Such a principle, if adopted in practice, would upturn the very foundations of society itself. He sees no satisfactory reason why the heroes of the frontier war should not be entitled to the relief provisions of the pension laws; and thinks the distinction between them and those who fought in the Revolution to be invidious. The soldiers of one period and campaign are as well re-

paid, while those of another do not receive a solitary cent. Nor can he see either the propriety or justice of abolishing or repealing the pension laws, as suggested in the amendment of his colleague from Virginia. The law will, in the lapse of time, repeal itself, by the deaths of the soldiers pensioned, many of whom are now on the verge of eternity, and many having already passed the bounds of time. There is, therefore, a reduction of at least twenty per cent. on the original grants, and a further reduction may still be expected; few, if any of the pensioners being under seventy years of age. Why then gravely deliberate on the repeal of laws which have their own period of existence assigned them in the lives of veterans?

It is true that many soldiers are patriots, and from their love of country and opinions of civil and religious liberty, would enter into the military service in case of absolute necessity. Yet, where is the soldier devoid of the hope of remuneration, who will continue in the forces of his country to fight her battles, if his objects of reward are thus frustrated by prohibiting all ideas of this hope? Take it away, and the musket will fall nerveless from his grasp, the bayonet will fall pointless, and few will ardently oppose the enemy. If troubles originate again, the soldier will find that he can obtain nothing but empty honors; and who will covet honors that will but beggar him? He will point to the resolution of the House, that the Government will take no care of him; that his father had fought at periods of our revolutionary history, and had his petition for assistance, in his old age, slighted, rejected; and this at a time when the funds of the treasury were locked up—when (like the river Nile) it overflowed its banks, and was hoarded as a sinking fund to make Presidents out of.

He sees no difference between the soldiers who fought at a time when their fight was equivalent to treason, and their punishment death by hanging; and those who fought with the Indians, when their deaths would be by the scalping knife or tomahawk. He thinks none have such an aversion to being hung, as voluntarily to enrank themselves among the opponents of the Indians, by whom they will have their heads skinned, their brains knocked out, and then subjected to enduring excruciation till death becomes a relief. Those who fought against the Indians in the West were subjected to equal privations and difficulties, as the pensioners who fought in the Revolution. They had volunteered their services in defence of their country, had spent for her the energies of their youth,—and are their claims to be rejected, now that the frosts of seventy years have rendered them wretched and helpless?

Mr. SPEIGHT thought that some term of service should be ascertained, whereby a soldier should be entitled to the provision of the pension system. This should be regulated by a committee, rather than have abrogated the whole laws. It would prevent the corruption insinuated in the amendment.

Mr. DICKINSON, of Tennessee, said, I hope the House will not think me intrusive in offering a few remarks upon this question. A small remnant of a race of men now nearly extinct, yet lingers in the section of country from which I come, and if others who have never seen them, and who have never heard from their own lips the story of the privations and perils through which their early life was past, may be permitted to speak doubtingly or slightly of their claims upon the gratitude of their country, I, who have both seen them, and heard them, cannot be silent.

A militiaman of the revolutionary war, who was in camp or upon a march for the period of six months, receives a pension from the bounty of the Government. Sir, the first settlers of the West may be said to have past fifteen or twenty years in a camp, or upon the scout, or in battle. Every private dwelling, every piece of enclosed ground, was an encampment, and so continued for nearly a third of the ordinary period of the life of man. Sir, the fields were cultivated at periods of time snatched from the pursuit of an enemy, and then under sentinel guards. But how often did it happen in the history of the settlement of the western country, that the cultivator was shot down in the furrow his plough had made? Sir, in many of our fields, may the spot be pointed out, which drank the blood thus shed, of the primest stock that ever trod its surface. Ay, the primest, in the true and natural sense of the word. For who shall stand in a higher rank, even among the benefactors of mankind, than that hardy, brave, and devoted class of men, who plunged into the wilderness, a handful in numbers only—drove out the savages after a twenty years war, and gave to the people of the eastern States—to the people of the world, I may say, at the end of that time, a safe and peaceful entry into such a region as the valley of the Mississippi? Whether we look at the perils encountered and overcome, the value and magnificence of the object achieved, or the actual sufferings endured, it has no parallel in history, that I know of, save only the first planting of this continent itself by the adventurers from Europe. But even this great enterprise was not attended with more real suffering.

It has been said during the debate upon this resolution, that the practice of pensioning has not gone beyond the Revolution, and that it would be a dangerous precedent to extend the system this side of that period. I suppose, sir, for I have not heard it stated in debate, that it was thought by our predecessors, that the precedent of granting pensions to persons who rendered services to the country during the Revolution, could not be drawn into precedent, and very plausibly too, for I agree that the war of the Revolution and of Independence can never occur again any more than it can happen to man to be twice born. But I will go further, and agree that no military service ever has done, or ever can do so much for liberty—for human rights and human happiness, as the military service of the Revolution. I agree that none can be more glorious, both to those who achieved it, and to those, their descendants, who enjoy the prize. But, sir, what argument is there in all this against the proposition now before the House? To go back to the foundation of this claim of some of the surviving pioneers of the West to receive a pension, they were in reason and truth soldiers of the Revolution, though never so long as six months upon any one tour of service which was recognised by the public authorities of the country as belonging to any regular national force. But, sir, from the very commencement of the revolutionary war, and from that period onwards to its close, some of the early settlers stood firmly upon the western frontier, or deep in the forest far beyond the general line of frontier settlements, breasted the savage charge, and often broke its fury before it reached the regular frontier settlements. They furnished employment, and furnished victims too, to the savage knife and tomahawk, nearer to their haunts than the more dense settlements of the interior. Such men as these constituted a wall of defence throughout the whole period of the Revolution, which was of immense service, though it was not always sufficient, for want of the common munitions of war, to resist or drive back the numerous hordes of savages who pressed heavily upon the western frontier during the war.

I call upon gentlemen to say what principle, or reason, or sound policy, forbids that these men should share the bounty and the honors of the Republic with the regular soldier of the Revolution. Sir, they who shared the perils and dangers of the Republic should share its bounty too. I plead the cause of a class of men who, with the most scanty means, almost without powder and lead, resisted the Indians for a period more than twice as long as the Revolution lasted. What men of the Revolution risked more or suffered more severely than these? There is no regular history of the exploits and sufferings of these brave men; their story is only to be found in their own recollection, or in that of their children and countrymen, with whom it is traditionary. But many memorials of their actions and their fate are scattered over the State that I have the honor, in part, to represent upon this floor. A mountain has given immortality to the name of the brave Spencer of the Yadkin. The Black Fox's Camp is associated with the name of John Peyton and others, who signalized themselves against an Indian chief of that name, and his party—a valor and enterprise surpassed by few warriors of any age. This class of worthies are represented by but few survivors; they are rapidly passing away. Very soon, and not one of them will remain; and if there was but one survivor only, I would vote to cheer his declining life and rouse his drooping spirits by the generous notice and bounty of the Government. The largest class of those men who perilled everything in the early settlement of the western country (and they are now but a feeble band) are those who emigrated about the close of the revolutionary war. Many of them had been soldiers in that war, and after having established with their swords the liberty and independence of the country, sought in the wilderness and in the midst of savage hostility the means of personal independence for themselves and their posterity. Those of this class that remain are already provided for; and I have nothing further to say of them, than to express my gratitude for their noble daring, and a fervent desire that they may enjoy a protracted and happy old age. But, sir, with the soldiers of the Revolution there went to the West many more—their friends and kindred, just grown up, and who gave all the vigor of their manhood, and too many of them their lives, to the defence of the early settlements in the West. The Indian hostilities, commencing with the revolutionary war, never ceased upon the western frontier for ten or twelve years after the Revolution ceased. It was not until 1795 that the Indian wars growing out of the revolutionary struggle closed. It lasted more than twice as long as the revolutionary war, and was waged throughout that time, on the part of the Indians, upon women and infants in the cradle; on the part of the settlers, by a courage, hardihood, and persevering fortitude, beyond any example to be found in the Revolution proper. Sir, so long, so fierce, and indiscriminate was the war, that the very brute creation sympathized with man in his fears and sufferings, and learned to snuff the approach of the Indian, and give the alarm. Such is a well-attested fact in that country. Sir, who here does not sympathize with the survivors of such a war-bred race? Who would not cheer them with the bounty of the Government, equally with the soldier of the Revolution himself?

I know that we ought to act here upon other principles than those of mere sympathy and feeling. Policy and State expediency must be consulted. Well, sir, let us examine for a moment the objection that it is a most dangerous precedent. Bring the case of these men to the same test that was applied to the men of the Revolution. When again will it happen in the history of this country that such a valley as that of the Mississippi will be thrown open to the safe and comfortable dwelling of man by an enterprise so daring? There is no such country remaining upon the globe to be rescued from the dominion of savages, that we know of; and as for the race of men who achieved that great object, I do not know that it will ever be renewed. It is just as possible that the revolutionary war can occur again, and bring with it its public debt, as that the conquest of the valley of the Mississippi can ever be re-acted. The pensioning of the survivors of the first settlers and warriors of the West in danger of being drawn into precedent! Who can seriously indulge in such a fear? Sir, this country may have many wars; the late war may often be renewed in type and effect in the future history of this country. But the fifteen or twenty years' war waged by the early settlers of the West against its savage inhabitants can never be acted over again.

An argument was suggested by the gentleman from Kentucky [Mr. HARDIN] when this subject was before the House which I thought had great force in it. This protracted Indian war was but a continuation of the revolutionary war, and the claims of these men to receive a pension should be placed upon the same ground with the soldiers who rendered services to the country during the first six or seven years of the Revolution. If I have read the history of that period aright, Great Britain did not relinquish the idea of limiting the boundary of the United States in the West and Northwest by the Ohio river until the treaty of 1795, when she finally agreed to deliver up the posts within the limits of the territory ceded to the United States by the treaty of 1783. The Spaniards, soon after the treaty of 1783, adopted the policy of limiting the new Republic in the Southwest. And by these two Powers the Indians in the North and the South were encouraged and supplied with arms to carry on the war. Under this state of the facts, are we not warranted in saying that the con-

quest of the valley of the Mississippi was not achieved in 1783?

How could the western country be said to have been wrested from Great Britain as long as her military posts were occupied by her arms, and the numerous Indian tribes, her open allies during the first six or seven years of the revolutionary war, continued to be excited to hostilities, and furnished by her with munitions of war? The country had not been delivered up. The peaceable and actual possession of it was not enjoyed, but was in a state of war. Yes, sir, a British war was carried on by British mercenaries for ten or twelve years after the treaty of 1783. Then the revolutionary war was not ended. It raged upon the western frontier until the final pacification in 1795. It was then, and not till then, that Great Britain acquiesced in the extension of our boundary to the westward, and refused any longer to afford the means of hostile incursions to the Indians.

Mr. Speaker, another objection is started to the proposition, which, when duly considered, I think is entitled to but little weight. It is proposed to add a few hundred, perhaps a thousand, names more to the pension list, and not one of them who may not be said to have passed many years in the service of the country. It is objected that the whole system of pensioning is demoralizing, and ought, there are, to be extended no further. Such an objection—I speak it with deference—seems to me to come with a bad grace just now, and against such men as are proposed to be added to the pension list. Sir, I am not disposed to go into an argument of the policy of the pension system. Much, no doubt, may be said on both sides, to show the fitness or unfitness of such a system, in such a Government as ours. Perjuries and corruptions of various kinds, doubtless, attend the granting pensions in every country. The unworthy and perjured applicant often steps in and enjoys the reward due to valor and actual service only. The community is taxed to pay the cowardly and undeserving soldier, as well as the one that is patriotic and deserving. Many who receive this bounty from the Government do not need it, and many misapply it when they receive it, and find no permanent relief from their poverty. It may be true that the granting pensions for military services may tend to create a mercenary spirit in our citizens, and cause them to regard the sordid pay which they may or may not receive, according to circumstances, when called upon to defend the country when threatened or invaded by a foreign foe, instead of cultivating that patriotic chivalry and devotion to country which is always the surest, safest, and strongest defence any people can have. All these views may be true, and yet, sir, there are some views on the other side of the question worth considering. The young and discreet soldier who engages to exhaust the energies of his youth and the prime of his life in the service of his country, may often find his courage fortified and his patriotism receive a new impulse from the reflection, that his old age would be rescued from the miseries attendant on destitution, by a generous and grateful country. A country acquires a higher moral elevation, and gives a finer tone to all its public actions, and furnishes a new incentive to honorable and hazardous enterprises, by the practice of that sort of justice which is voluntary, and not yielded in obedience to law. The spectacle of a Republic (a form of Government that has been denounced by monarchists in all ages of the world, for being ungrateful) yielding that kind of voluntary but substantial homage to its greatest benefactors, which is implied in the pensions which have been granted, and which are now proposed to be granted, may not be without a salutary effect upon the feelings and judgment of the world, in deciding upon that form of government which is best suited for the protection of human rights and human happiness.

Mr. BURGES, of Rhode Island, could not see the propriety of confounding the Indian with the revolutionary war; nor was he before aware of the existence of an Indian war carried on for the space of twenty years. The principle on which the pensions were granted to the soldiers of the revolutionary war was, that those soldiers had been unpaid for their services at the time, and were therefore justly entitled to a public compensation. But this is not applicable to the case of those who

fought against the Indians. The claim for arduous or difficult service has not been recognised by Congress; nor has a claim for any term of service. As to the twenty years' war, if any has ever been, it must have been private, not public; and have merely exhibited reciprocal energy on the part of the invaders and the invaded—on the part of the Indians to obtain forcible possession of the territories of the frontier settlers; and on the part of the frontier settlers to repel those attacks, and defend their own possessions. So has it ever been in this country, since first colonized. Those occupying the frontier settlements have always voluntarily or compulsorily repelled the Indian attack, and have pushed their frontiers further westward. But which of them have ever demanded, or thought of demanding, public remuneration for services so performed? Where is the frontier which had formerly existed? There will always be frontier settlements. There will always be settlers on these frontiers. There will always be wars after wars on these frontiers, so long as Indians exist beyond them. Must those settlers be perpetually making demands on the public purse for defending their own possessions? be continually affecting claims, or asking alms? Is it consistent to tax itself that they may be secured in their possessions? and are we to subsidize or maintain every race of settlers who may find it necessary to band together for mutual defence? He thinks it better to retain the principle on which the pension system was founded, than to have it enlarged so as to embrace every variety of individual claim, continued from age to age. It should extend no further than the revolutionary war.

The House proceeded, at 1 o'clock, in accordance to the resolution adopted yesterday, to the order of the day, being the

REMOVAL OF THE DEPOSITES.

The House resumed the consideration of the motion to refer the Secretary of the Treasury's report on the deposites to the Committee of Ways and Means, and the question being on the amendment submitted by Mr. JONES, as an amendment to that previously submitted by Mr. McDUFFIE, viz: to add to the motion for reference the following instructions to that committee:

" Inquire into the expediency of depositing the 'revenue hereafter collected in the State banks in ' the different States, where the same is collected, ' in proportion to their respective capitals paid in, ' and to prescribe the terms on which the same shall ' be deposited; and to report by bill or otherwise."

Mr. MOORE, having had the floor from the previous day, rose, and claimed the right to vote on this question, untrammelled by party, and with the single view of promoting what should appear to be for the best interests of the country, considering himself not so much the organ of the sentiments of any particular party as a representative of the whole people. Acting upon this principle, he would vote, not upon the responsibility of any party, but upon his own, and for such measures as would be most conducive to the interests of those whom he had the honor to represent. Before he would address the House upon the general subject involved, he wished to explain some circumstances as to the vote given by him on a former occasion; and which explanation he had hitherto been desirous, but was unable, to make. He had voted against the motion submitted by the honorable member from Tennessee, [Mr. Polk,] for reconsidering the vote by which the subject had been referred to the Committee of the Whole on the state of the Union, because he thought, from the reasons given in the report, the House could judge whether the Secretary had done right or not in making the removal, and he desired to have discussion on the subject in the whole House, that hereafter they could act understandingly and knowingly on the subject; for this reason, he wished the debate to go forth to the nation, that they could come to a right conclusion, in this way, rather than through the corrupt medium of the press, which, from all that appeared, was charged as being influenced, on the one side, by the Bank of the United States, and upon the other, by those State banks who were interested in pulling down that institution. He denied that he was one of those whom the member from Tennessee had hinted "was desirous to stifle all debate," and would

maintain that if the subject had been left in the committee where it was first placed, the House could have decided the question; whilst, if they had desired further investigation as necessary for that purpose, he would have supported it. He would desire investigation, in order to act impartially between the bank and the Administration; and after quoting the various passages from Mr. Polk's speech, in which " he pledged himself to ' prove that every word contained in the Secretary's report could be established, if a committee ' of investigation was appointed," and that he viewed the conduct of the friends of the bank in declining investigation " as a departure from its light of truth," &c., he commented upon this, and said he could not see what light could have been shed on the subject that would not be the same if presented to the House, as to any of the individuals on the Committee of Ways and Means. He contended that, so far from light being desired, there was a party made to sustain the views of the Secretary, and that the investigation which the honorable member from Tennessee, and those with whom he acted, sought, should not have been for the purpose of sustaining this or that officer of the Government. It was true that gentleman had said he had no right to impute motives, but he was induced to consider, if he had, what sort of motives would he have imputed. That gentleman had again said that the object of those opposed to him was, in debating the question, to pour out upon the country, through speeches made in that House, a torrent of misrepresentation and falsehood as to the Secretary's report. But it was easy to see that his object in stifling debate, by referring it to the Committee of Ways and Means, was, to let the Secretary's report go to the people, and which afterwards being backed by a report from that committee, which would be in opposition to the bank, the people would have been thus prejudiced against the institution. This was his object, and the method taken to effect it seemed to be the same which was taken by the pastors of a certain religious sect, who, professing to inspect their flock in the doctrines of Christianity, would not permit them to look into the Scriptures—into that inspired book which established it.

He disclaimed any intention of using disrespectful terms towards any officer of the Government, and would not enter into the question of Mr. Duane's dismissal, as not properly belonging to the present discussion, but would merely remark, that from the tenor of Mr. D.'s correspondence with the President, the friends of the Administration would have some difficulty in showing why he was originally selected for the office from which he had been dismissed; however, being put there, he ought not to have remained in office, under these circumstances, so long; neither ought the President to have dismissed him, solely for having entertained a different, but honest opinion; for he should have known, that in that matter he was the officer of Congress, not of the Executive. Mr. M. proceeded to quote various other passages from the Secretary's report, and contended at length that the Secretary was not justified in removing any money from the bank, which, once placed in it, ought not to have been withdrawn, except by virtue of that article of the Constitution which provides that no money should be drawn from the treasury under by appropriations made in conformity to law. There was no power that he knew of conferring this right. The act of 1789 did not give it; that act only authorized warrants to be issued to draw money from the treasury, and had prohibited expressly any other interference with the public money. He could not accord in the precedent referred to by the Secretary as to Mr. Crawford; for that officer had rather appeared to have acted as trustee, and by consent, between the bank and the United States Government. Mr. M. next referred to the opinion of the Secretary, as to the power originally in Congress, but of which the Secretary alleged Congress had divested themselves by granting their charter to the bank, and given it to him. The whole history of the English people showed that they would not subscribe to such views and doctrines; and he trusted that the people of the United States would not be backward in following their example. The origin of parliaments, or representative bodies in England was closely connected with this very money power. They

first parliament had been called in the reign of Henry Third, by the government of Leicester, solely to obtain grants of money. Their most absolute sovereigns had been compelled to economize, because they knew that when they wanted money they must ask the Commons for it. The very civil war which, in part, drove so many of their ancestors to seek an asylum on this continent, commenced with a struggle who should have the disposal of the public treasure; and when that war, towards its close, had brought one monarch (Charles the First) to the block, the country maintained their money powers, which they did not part with until the restoration of Charles the Second. Then, indeed, they parted with it, and felt, in consequence, all the evils of uniting the purse and the sword; for to the act conferring the disposal of the public revenue in the king for life much of the subsequent atrocities of Jeffries and others were to be mainly attributed. If such a doctrine was suffered to prevail in this country, he saw nothing to prevent any young or ambitious President from becoming the absolute monarch of these United States, as he did not think any difficulty could be interposed to prevent such a design being accomplished. There was little difference in the President's having the power, through his Secretary, to put the money in his pocket at his own will and pleasure, and the power to hire a band of armed mercenaries for such an object. Would he be told, in answer to this, that the President could not take out the money of himself? True, he could not; but he had a power tantamount to it, namely, to turn out of office him who should refuse to comply with his wishes. The Secretary denies the power of Congress to interfere; says that "it is a breach of the agreement made with the bank." So that it would follow, in any case, Congress could not interfere.

He had not, in the foregoing remarks, the remotest idea to charge the President with any improper design, believing that, however he misapprehended the powers of the Executive in the present case, if he had any such views, he also had sufficient moral courage, under any circumstances, to assert them openly. He contended that the power conferred by the bank charter had been given to the Secretary, as the officer of Congress, as Congress was not always in session, and therefore could not act upon any emergency arising, which would require instantaneous action; but the Congress had never divested themselves of their constitutional rights. They had not the power to do so. The Secretary was in fact a mere trustee; the House had, in consequence of the powers he now claimed, the novel circumstance of a trustee claiming a right to act contrary to the wishes of the very parties by whom he had been appointed and chosen to act as trustee. And if his construction was carried out, there could not be any interference with him by any of the other branches of the Government. He thought the deposites ought of right to be lodged in the Bank of the United States, as a part of the contract for which they paid a large bonus originally. Yet, if the Secretary's construction was correct, he could remove them at will; but this was such a palpable breach of contract as he hoped never could be tolerated between individual and individual. Neither should it be countenanced between the bank and the nation. The Secretary had also undertaken to instruct them on the law by which the bank was incorporated—"that it was a law not warranted by the Constitution." But what authority had he to decide such a question?

Mr. M. here referred to that passage in the Secretary's report, which alluded to the public convenience as a proper motive for the removal of the deposites. This, he contended, was an assumption of legislative power by the Secretary. When Congress established the bank, they took into view, first, their constitutional authority, second, the commercial interests of the country, and third, the convenience of the Government. These several considerations resulted in a legislative act. So, if Congress should undertake to remove the public deposites from the bank to the State banks, they would consider the commercial advantages to be derived from the removal, and the ability of the State banks to promote the convenience of the Government. The Secretary, from the same considerations, arrived at the result that the deposites ought to be removed to the State banks, and proceeds to effect the removal. In what particular, then, does his decision fall short of a legislative act? It was an assumption by the Secretary of a power to legislate. He claims to act on every consideration which could have been brought before Congress. Where did the Secretary get the power to place the deposites in the State banks? He would be thankful to any gentleman to inform him. He did not get it from the bank charter. But he gets it, he says, from the necessity of the case. Mr. M. denied the existence of the authority, from whatever source it might be pretended to be derived. We have a Treasurer, whose duty it was to keep the public money. The Secretary might have left it in the hands of the Treasurer or of the collectors—men who had given adequate security for the performance of their trust. The plea of necessity was always suspicious. It was the tyrant's plea. Mr. M. might, he said, undertake to show that the State banks were calculated to do as much mischief in the manner in which they were employed by the Secretary as a national bank. The national bank was a check upon the State banks. One moneyed institution was opposed to another moneyed institution. But it was now in the hands of a single individual to control the operations of the bank. The whole report of the Secretary appeared to be drawn with a view to sustain an act already done, instead of being a simple statement of the Secretary's reasons for doing an act. Mr. M. then read from the report the following passage:

"The manifestations of public opinion, instead 'of being favorable to a renewal, have been decidedly to the contrary. And I have always regarded the result of the last election of President 'of the United States as the declaration of a majority of the people that the charter ought not 'to be renewed. It is not necessary to state 'here what is now a matter of history. The 'question of the renewal of the charter was introduced into the election by the corporation itself. 'Its voluntary application to Congress for the renewal of its charter, four years before it expired, 'and upon the eve of the election of President, 'was understood on all sides as bringing forward 'that question for incidental decision at the then 'approaching election. It was accordingly argued 'on both sides, before the tribunal of the people, 'and their verdict pronounced against the bank 'by the election of the candidate who was known 'to have been always inflexibly opposed to it."

He could not see exactly with what propriety the Secretary brought forward such considerations. Everybody knew that General Jackson would have been elected if he had chartered forty banks, and his election was not decisive of the opinions and wishes of the people on the subject. The Secretary objected to the bank that it had increased its discounts. The proper way to remedy this, would, he supposed, be to call the money back again into the bank. The bank did so, and the Secretary condemns the curtailment. He complains of the curtailment as oppressive to the community. The Secretary also undertakes to show that the bank acts as the fiscal agent of the Government, and he goes into an argument to show that the bank had been guilty of such misconduct as justified the Government in withdrawing from it all confidence. Well, why did he not then take away the money at once from the bank. But he leaves it there for some time afterwards. Either, therefore, his argument was unsound, or he had improperly left money in the bank.

We hear, said Mr. M., of pressure for money. The distress was great, even if it was but one-tenth as great as it was represented to be. It was, in his opinion, destined to become greater. We were getting back to the period of 1814, when the country was inundated with depreciated bank paper. The State of Ohio was about to establish a bank with a capital of four or five millions; Indiana another, with eleven or twelve branches; and North Carolina had established three new banks and was about to charter a fourth. In other States the same experiment was making. The day was not distant when we should have as much depreciated paper as we formerly had. He was not disposed to discuss this question on party grounds. It ought not, he thought, to be looked at as a party question. He was aware that some editors had assumed the office of dictators, and had instructed the friends of the Administration to support the course of the Administration in regard to the removal of the deposites. But he denied their right to instruct him in his duty. Although he believed that a national bank was necessary, and that the State banks were unconstitutional, yet he was not a friend to the present Bank of the United States. He was not satisfied with its conduct in lending large sums of money to editors upon insufficient security, and there were facts alleged by the Government directors which must be explained before he would vote for the renewal of its charter; nor was he inimical to the present Administration, though he set up no claim to its friendship. He had come here in the hope that he might be able to sustain the measures of the Administration; but he would not degrade the body to which he belonged by doing an act which his conscience would not justify. He had heard it suggested that though the act of the removal might have been improper, yet that it ought now to be sustained by the friends of the Administration. Now, he had always understood that justice ought to be done, even should the Heavens fall. But the people of the United States were not disposed to condemn a man or a set of men on account of any single error—nor would he utterly condemn the Administration on account of what he considered its errors on this subject. It might be true that the restoration of the deposites would defeat some of the arrangements of the State banks. Mr. M. then alluded to the doctrine of nullification, which he strongly condemned, though for many of the Nullifiers he had a strong personal regard. But he would not support an act which he believed to be wrong, merely because it was supported by those who have on some questions been wrong.

Mr. M. here referred to some remarks which had fallen from the member from New York [Mr. CAMBRELENG] on the subject of State rights. Mr. M. was not, he said, exactly a State-rights man, though he admitted the States had rights, and he would go far to sustain them. He was under obligations to the President for the defence of State rights in his proclamation. That document met with his entire approbation. The gentleman had complimented Virginia on her principles, and on having been always right. He believed that she was as apt to think right as any State; but still she sometimes thought one way, and sometimes another. She was, in his opinion, right now, in condemning the removal of the deposites. He had now more reason to be proud of her than ever. She still acts on her high and honorable principles, and refuses to sustain an act which she deems improper, though it is directed against an institution, to the establishment of which she was always opposed.

Mr. BEARDSLEY, of New York, took the floor, and on his motion,

The House adjourned.

IN SENATE.

THURSDAY, *January* 16, 1834.

A message was received from the President of the United States by the hands of Mr. Donelson, enclosing a report from the Director of the Mint; which was read.

Mr. SMITH presented a memorial from John Watts; which was referred to the Committee on Naval Affairs.

The VICE PRESIDENT laid before the Senate a communication from the Secretary of War, relative to licenses of traders with Indian tribes; which, on motion of Mr. TIPTON, was ordered to be printed.

Mr. SILSBEE gave notice that he should, to-morrow, ask leave to introduce a bill for the relief of Christian Coffin.

Mr. KANE, in pursuance of notice given yesterday, introduced a bill for the construction of a canal from St. Andrew's to Apalachicola river; which was read, and referred to the Committee on Roads and Canals.

Mr. KING, of Alabama, presented a memorial from the Legislature of Alabama, relating to the preëmption rights of settlers upon the public lands, and also praying that the price of refuse lands be

reduced so as to come within the means of purchase of the poorer classes of the community. The memorial was ordered to be printed on motion of Mr. KING, of Alabama, and referred to the Committee on Public Lands.

Mr. HENDRICKS presented the memorial of the Legislature of Indiana, relative to the Louisville and Portland Canal; which was referred to the Committee on Roads and Canals.

Mr. HENDRICKS, agreeably to notice given yesterday, introduced a bill for the benefit of South Hanover College; which was read, and referred to the Committee on Public Lands.

Mr. TYLER, from the Committee on Finance, reported a bill, without amendment, for the repeal of certain sections of the act establishing the Treasury Department.

Mr. NAUDAIN gave notice that he should, tomorrow, ask leave to introduce a bill for the relief of Henry Warren.

Mr. RIVES presented the petition of Henry Drummond; which was referred to the Committee of Ways and Means.

Mr. TIPTON gave notice that he should, tomorrow, ask leave to introduce a bill granting compensation to Captain John Hamilton.

Mr. PORTER gave notice that to-morrow he should ask leave to introduce a bill for the relief of certain persons in Louisiana.

Mr. WRIGHT gave notice that he should, tomorrow, ask leave to introduce a bill for the relief of Baron de Stocks.

Mr. CLAY presented the petition of Lieutenant Green, a revolutionary officer; which was referred to the Committee on Revolutionary Claims.

ORDERS OF THE DAY.

The resolutions offered yesterday, were taken up and adopted.

The resolution, which was ordered to be engrossed yesterday, for the purchase of ten copies of the Laws of the United States, was passed.

A bill from the House of Representatives, making appropriations for the naval service for the year 1834, was read, and referred, on motion of Mr. WEBSTER, to the Committee on Finance.

A bill for the relief of the heirs of Dr. John Berrien, deceased, was read a second time, and referred to the Committee on Revolutionary Claims.

The following bills, from the House of Representatives, were read, and ordered to be engrossed:

A bill for the relief of George H. Jennings;
A bill for the relief of James H. Brewer;
A bill for the relief of Richard Baker, executor of James B. Ball;
A bill for the relief of Peregrine Gardner, (amended on motion of Mr. TIPTON;)
A bill for the relief of Edward Willett;
A bill for the relief of Russel Hunt, David Hunt, and Amos Hunt.

RESOLUTIONS.

The following resolutions were submitted during the morning:

By Mr. KNIGHT,
Resolved, That the Secretary of the Senate cause to be engraved, upon a reduced scale, the map of Narraganset Bay, now on the files of the Senate, and that two thousand copies of the same be printed.

By Mr. SHEPLEY,
Resolved, That the Secretary of the Treasury be directed to communicate to the Senate, so far as the returns received will permit, the tonnage departing from the United States in each collection district thereof, to the British North American colonies, and to the British West Indies, since the 30th September, 1832, distinguishing the domestic and foreign tonnage; and also, the value of the exports to those places respectively, from each collection district, during the same period.

By Mr. WAGGAMAN,
Resolved, That the Committee on Commerce be instructed to inquire into the expediency of erecting a light-house at the mouth of Tchifuncta, on Lake Pontchartrain.

By Mr. TIPTON,
Resolved, That the Committee on Pensions be instructed to inquire into the expediency of placing on the roll of revolutionary pensioners, all persons who served as wagoners, or were engaged in the

transportation of provisions or munitions of war to the army of the Revolution, on their producing such proof of their services as is required to establish a claim to a pension under the pension act of 7th June, 1832.

By Mr. LINN,
Resolved, That the Committee on Manufactures be instructed to inquire whether the duty on lead has not been eluded, or attempted to be eluded, by the importation of lead, in the form of busts, clock and sash weights, bullets, large bowls, &c., &c., &c.

The VICE PRESIDENT having announced the special order to be

THE REMOVAL OF THE DEPOSITES.

The Senate resumed the consideration of the resolutions submitted by Mr. CLAY, on the 26th ultimo.

Mr. SHEPLEY resumed, and concluded his speech in support of the removal of the deposites; when Mr. RIVES took the floor, and moved an adjournment. He withdrew the motion, however, at the suggestion of Mr. WEBSTER, and the Senate then, on his motion, went into the consideration of Executive business. After some time spent therein,

The Senate adjourned.

HOUSE OF REPRESENTATIVES.

THURSDAY, January 16, 1834.

The SPEAKER presented a communication from the Secretary of the Treasury, with a copy of the instructions given to the custom-house officers by the Comptroller of the Treasury; also, a communication, ordered by the House on the 24th ultimo, in relation to lands in Indiana, and from the Secretary of War, with an abstract of accounts;

Which were severally laid on the table.

Mr. CLAY, of Alabama, presented a memorial from the Legislature of that State, asking the enactment of a law to grant preëmption rights to settlers on the public lands; and also, a reduction of the price of land heretofore offered for sale, and remaining unsold; which was, on his motion, laid upon the table, and ordered to be printed.

Mr. CLAY reported a bill from the Senate of the relief of John Hurtell.

Mr. JARVIS, a bill making appropriations for the public buildings and public grounds, and for other purposes.

Mr. DUNCAN, a bill granting certain lands in Michigan, for the construction of a rail or Macadamized road, to connect Detroit river with Lake Michigan, and for other purposes: also, to authorize the President of the United States to cause the lead mines in Michigan to be sold; and for other purposes.

Mr. YOUNG, a bill for the relief of James Bell.

Mr. HARPER, bills for the relief of Samuel Case, Charles Burden, and others; all which bills were read twice and committed.

The SPEAKER presented the following message from the President of the United States, with the following report from the Director of the Mint:

WASHINGTON, January 15, 1834.

SIR: I transmit to Congress a report from the Director of the Mint, exhibiting the operations of that institution during the year 1833.

ANDREW JACKSON.

To the Hon. the Speaker
of the House of Representatives.

MINT OF THE UNITED STATES,
Philadelphia, January 1, 1834.

SIR: I have the honor to submit a report on the general transactions of the mint during the last year.

The coinage effected within that period amounts to $3,765,710, comprising $978,550 in gold coins, $2,759,000 in silver, $28,160 in copper, and consisting of 10,307,790 pieces of coin, viz:

Half eagles, 193,630 pieces, making $968,150
Quarter eagles, 4,160 " " 10,400
Half dollars, 5,206,000 " " 2,603,000
Quarter do. 156,000 " " 39,000
Dimes, 485,000 " " 48,500

Half dimes,	1,370,000	"	"	68,500
Cents,	2,739,000	"	"	27,390
Half cents,	154,000	"	"	770
	10,307,790			$3,765,710

Of the amount of gold coined within the past year, about $85,000 were derived from Mexico, South America, and the West Indies; $13,000 from Africa; $868,000 from the gold region of the United States; and about $13,000 from sources not ascertained.

Of the amount of gold of the United States, above mentioned, about $104,000 may be stated to have been received from Virginia, $475,000 from North Carolina, $660,000 from South Carolina, $216,000 from Georgia, and about $700 from Tennessee.

The annexed statement exhibits the quantity of gold received from the several districts of the United States which have thus far produced it in sufficient quantities to be an object of regard, commencing with the year 1824. Previously to that period, gold had been received at the Mint only from North Carolina, from which coinage it was first transmitted for coinage in 1804. During the interval, however, from that date to 1823, inclusive, the average amount had not exceeded $2,500.

In the report of last January, 1833, it was remarked that the quantity of gold of the United States brought to the Mint in the year 1832, was regarded, according to estimates entitled to great respect, as not much exceeding one-half the quantity produced from the mines within that year; nearly an equal amount being supposed to have been exported uncoined, or consumed in the arts. Nothing has since occurred to create a doubt of the correctness of that conjecture. It is altogether probable that the remark is equally true in regard to the last year, and that the amount of gold derived from the United States, within that period, has exceeded one million and a half of dollars. The sum, it is believed, is not less than about one-half of the amount of gold produced within the same period from all other sources, in Europe and America, estimated according to the best authorities.

I have the honor to be, with great respect, your obedient servant, SAMUEL MOORE,
Director of the Mint of the U. States.

To the PRESIDENT OF THE UNITED STATES.

	Virginia.	N. Carolina.	S. Carolina.	Georgia.	Tennessee.	Alabama.	Total.	Statement of this amount of gold produced annually from the gold region of the United States, from the year 1824 to 1833, inclusive.
1824		$5,000					$5,000	
1825		17,000					17,000	
1826		20,000					20,000	
1827		21,000					21,000	
1828		46,000					46,000	
1829	$2,500	134,000	$3,500				140,000	
1830	24,000	204,000	26,000	$212,000	$1,000		466,000	
1831	26,000	294,000	22,000	176,000	1,000		520,000	
1832	34,000	458,000	45,000	140,000	7,000		678,000	
1833	104,000	475,000	66,000	216,000	700	$9,000	870,000	
	190,500	1,674,000	162,500	744,000	9,000	3,000	2,781,000	

THE PENSION LAWS.

The resolution submitted by Mr. CHILTON, to appoint a select committee to inquire into the expediency of so extending the general pension law as to embrace within its provisions those persons who were engaged in the Indian wars down to 1794, with the amendments thereto submitted by Mr. BOULDIN, to appoint a committee to inquire into the moral effects of the pension system, coming up as the unfinished business—

Mr. ALLEN, of Virginia, rose and advocated the original resolution submitted by Mr. CHILTON. The pension system having been established, he thought equal justice required that those persons embraced under the resolution of Mr. C. were as fully entitled to participate in its benefits as many others who had been placed upon the roll. The resolution, at all events, being only for inquiry, whether a class of citizens who had encountered many dangers in the service of their country, should have any claims to it, it was with much regret he observed that his colleague [Mr. B.] had embarrassed the resolution with the amendment proposed by him. Had that gentleman proposed his amendment as a distinct proposition, as it was the right of every representative to have the policy of the laws discussed, he would not have objected to it, although he could not concur with him in the propriety of abandoning the pension system, which he took for granted, the nation having after due consideration established, they would not now retrace their steps. The inquiry proposed by his colleague went to establish a new principle of legislation, which, if once sanctioned, it would become as necessary to have the same inquiry made into the moral effects of all the laws heretofore passed, or to be passed, or they may as well be dispensed with.

It was doubtless true there were abuses on the pension system, as there would be on any other; but the Congress which adopted it must have been aware of the abuses to which this, in common with any other law, was liable, and they preferred risking that, rather than leave what they considered just claims on the country undischarged. He did not agree with the opinion of the member from Rhode Island, [Mr. BURGES,] who objected to the inquiry on the ground "that pensions had been 'granted on account of the justness of the claims 'which the applicants had upon the nation, as 'arising from the circumstance that they had been 'paid for their services in a depreciated currency, 'and therefore had not received that which the 'Government ought to have paid." For if this was so, he asked, how it happened that there was as much paid to those who served only twelve months as to those who served a longer period? If that gentleman's principle was correct, it would follow that the pensions ought to be in proportion to the time of service; and if it was a payment actually due as a debt, it would be deciding that there was still a larger proportion who were entitled to it, if we regarded the national faith or common honesty, viz: those, or rather the heirs of those who had since departed this life; equal justice required, if this construction was to be put on the question, that the principle should be so carried out. He, however, thought that the principle upon which the pension system was founded had been more correctly laid down by the gentleman from Kentucky, [Mr. C.,] that it was not strictly so much an act of justice, as it was an appeal to the nation, and who chose in this way to testify their gratitude, and thus evince to the world the nation's deep sense of the services of those coming under its provisions.

The member from Rhode Island was not justified in terming the conflicts had with the Indians on the frontiers "as a mere predatory warfare from time to time," for it was a continual war, kept up with them down to 1794, and under circumstances which conferred upon the people engaged in it the strongest possible claims to the relief now sought for. It would be recollected by those conversant with the history of those times, that the Indian frontiers were in a state of comparative quiet, after the treaty made in 1765, with the Indians, by Sir W. Johnson, and that quiet remained until 1774, when the tea was destroyed in Boston. But after the occurrences of that day, the regal Government instigated these frontier Indians to commit hostilities, doubtless to divert and distract the attention with which the Commonwealth of Virginia viewed the encroachments of the Government, and prevent the measures which they had undertaken, in concert with the Confederacy. This, according to the traditionary history of the country, was the motive in which the Dunmore campaign originated; and notwithstanding the treaty with Great Britain, by which our independence was acknowledged, these hostilities continued on the frontiers down to the treaty of Grenville, in 1795, the period to which the proposed inquiry is limited. This inquiry was sought, as by the present law it was necessary that the applicants, under its provisions, should have been enrolled for six months, but it happened that scarcely any of these were enrolled at all; the State of Virginia, then, as well known, had an extensive frontier to the west, and she wisely determined not to call upon the inhabitants, scattered over that part, for their services to be enrolled along with the others whom she sent to join the confederate force, preferring to leave the care of the frontier settlements to them; and well did they take care of them; every field was tilled by them with the rifle by their side. Every block-house was a fortress to impede the incursions of the savages. Under such circumstances, he contended, they were entitled equally with others, as coming within the spirit, if not the letter of the law, which gave the rewards of the nation to others, for services during the revolutionary war. Mr. A. went at length into the history of the war, and contended that it was by the exertions of the frontier men, with a detachment under the command of Rogers Clark, a great and valuable domain in the West, which was now possessed by the several States, had been acquired, and for which they never had received any proportion of the bounty which had been given to others. He therefore trusted that Congress, considering they had not been heretofore importunate beggars, knocking at their doors, would consider them, under all the circumstances detailed, as entitled to participate in it, even at this late hour. Mr. A. then concluded by expressing his hopes that the amendment of his colleague [Mr. BOULDIN] would not prevail.

Mr. PEYTON rose and indignantly repelled (as he was understood by the reporter) some expressions used on the previous day by the honorable member from Rhode Island. He denied that the persons engaged in these Indian wars, as termed, were "merely bands of armed plunderers," and insisted that it was owing to their intrepidity and daring in penetrating into the western forests in pursuit of the Indians that the quiet subsequently enjoyed, and the public lands, now the object of so much desire, had been secured. He eulogized the leaders of various detachments in these conflicts, and particularly the exertions of Boon, Wickliffe, and Lewis. The history of Robinson and his warlike deeds would fill a volume. He had been to Virginia what Boon had been to Kentucky, the pioneer of the West, Spencer, too, was a name which would have imperishable renown. He had been the pilot of all these daring bands for years, until at length he fell, gallantly fell, covered with wounds, and his flesh, with that of many of his gallant companions, devoured by the wolves. No monument had yet been raised by the nation for such services, but nature had raised a prouder monument to his fame than man could raise. It stood in the far West; he gave a name to a hill which would last to all time. Even the women in those times aided their husbands, casting bullets and supplying them for their conflicts with means to obtain victory over the savages, whilst the tomahawk was uplifted over their heads. And thus, as they had all contributed their share of services to secure the benefits of civilization to the country, he hoped they would be permitted to enjoy some share of the common bounty.

The debate was cut off at 1 o'clock, in accordance with the resolution adopted on the 14th instant, and the House proceeded to the orders of the day, being the

REMOVAL OF THE DEPOSITES.

The House resumed the consideration of the motion to refer the report of the Secretary of the Treasury on the deposites to the Committee of Ways and Means, the question being on the amendment submitted by Mr. JONES, as an amendment to that previously submitted by Mr. McDUFFIE, viz: to add to the motion for reference the following instructions to that committee: "Inquire 'into the expediency of depositing the revenue 'hereafter collected in the State banks in the different States where the same is collected, in proportion to their respective capitals paid in, and to 'prescribe the terms on which the same shall be 'deposited, and to report by bill or otherwise."

Mr. BEARDSLEY, of New York, commenced his remarks by adverting to the posture in which the United States Bank now stood before us. The bank had gathered a golden harvest from the exclusive use which, for many years, it had enjoyed of the public money, and it was never to have been expected that it would use on any occasion, all its efforts to prostrate the interests of the country. The transfer of the deposites to other banks increased the ability of those banks to the same extent that it diminished the resources of the United States Bank. It was to be expected some temporary and inconsiderable derangement of the usual train of bank business would have been the consequence of the removal; but, if all had acted with a view to the general good, no serious disaster would have occurred. The removal of the deposites was an act unquestionably legal and valid. The expediency of the measure was a distinct question, and one which the bank had no right to judge upon under any circumstances. But the measure had been met by the bank with a general and oppressive system of retaliation. He believed that the effect of those measures had fallen short of their object. The whole fury of the institution had been poured out upon the devoted heads of citizens of the seaboard. Where men congregate in cities, they are easily brought to move in masses, and any derangement of the currency is immediately and generally felt. The bank, with cool deliberation and design, set about the production of the greatest possible amount of distress and embarrassment, and its whole coercive energies had been applied to the object, with a considerable degree of success. A different course would have gained to the bank many friends from among those who had been enemies. But the course adopted by the bank bore equally upon friends and enemies; it was prosecuted with a view to coerce all to the support of its own views. The pressure having now somewhat subsided, and the cities which were lately writhing under its effects, being now restored to a comfortable condition, it remains for us to do our duty. We have seen that the credit of our local institutions is based on a safe foundation, and that public confidence in them cannot be easily shaken. Let us go forward and do our duty, remembering that "the blood of the martyrs is the seed of the church;" and complete by our success the entire overthrow of this dangerous institution.

For two months previous to the meeting of Congress, it was notorious that the deposites were removed from the bank to the State institutions. The Secretary, not sheltering himself under the authority of the President, had officially announced the act as his own; but the truth of his annunciation is disputed. It has been charged here in debate that the President did the act through the Secretary, who was the passive instrument of his tyranny, and to enable him to gratify his revenge against the bank he had hurled the former Secretary of the Treasury from office. To these charges he should look somewhat in detail. In fairness to the officer, so far as he was personally concerned, we ought to consider the act as done by him. This was required in justice to the Secretary; but, in reference to the act itself, was wholly unessential. It was proper also to advert to the fact, that before the present Secretary came into the department, his views on this subject were known to correspond with those of the President. If he understood the character of the Secretary, he was not a man to be driven from his purpose. This report was a monument of the vigor of his understanding. His disinterestedness was shown in the acceptance of an office which he knew he must hold at the pleasure of his political foes, while he gave up an office which he held upon a tenure as permanent as the personal regard and confidence of a friend. As to the removal of the former Secretary, he would take leave to deny that he had been dismissed because he refused to transfer the deposites.

But this refusal, in his estimation, would have been a sufficient reason for his dismissal, and he would, for that reason alone, have been dismissed. He was an agent, and not an independent branch of the Government, and he was bound in all respects, to give effect to the judgment of the President. But clinching office with a death-gripe, he at the same time opposed the will of the President. As a subordinate officer, it was his duty to aid the President, instead of opposing him in the execution of the laws; and if his views did not permit him to afford that aid, it became him to stand out of the way.

It has been assumed that the Secretary of the Treasury is the fiscal agent of Congress, and not of the President. The gentlemen from South Carolina and Pennsylvania both concurred in this position, and all those who had spoke on their side of the question had expressed the same opinion. He thanked gentlemen for being so intelligible on this subject. They make their whole argument dependent on the position that the Secretary of the Treasury is independent of Executive control—that the President has no right to control him in the performance of his duties. The order, prejudgment, and consideration with which the act was done, has been said to characterize it as a legislative act. But these were not characteristics exclusively belonging to any one department of the Government, and it was not to be inferred from the character of the act itself to what department it pertained. Let us look a little further, and see to what branch of the Government the Secretary of the Treasury belongs. The allegation is not that the act of removing the deposites is judicial, but legislative in character. It appeared to him that it could not be legislative, for the reason that, by the Constitution, all legislative power was vested in Congress. Congress was the law-making power, and it was a power inalienable in its character, not to be exercised through agents, but by the legislative body itself. The execution of these laws depended on other branches. The legislative power terminated in the framing and passing of laws—their execution was confided to another branch. But three departments of power were known to our Constitution—legislative, judicial, and executive. If the act of the Secretary was neither judicial nor legislative, it must have been executive. Where was the executive power lodged? The Constitution of the United States vested it in the President of the United States of America. Not a part of the executive power, but the whole mass, was lodged in the President alone, and it could not exist elsewhere. There it was vested, and there it must remain, until the Constitution was altered by an amendment. A law of Congress could not transfer the power from the President, in whom the Constitution has vested it. Legislative and judicial power could not be exerted by a substitute; but it was not so with executive power. The powers in the executive head may be exercised by executive agents. On the President devolves the high duty of seeing that the laws be faithfully executed. He, and not Congress, nor the judiciary, nor subordinate officers, were to discharge that high trust. That all the executive power should be exercised by one individual in person was impossible, and the President had substitutes, to give effect to his orders in every part of the country. No one man can take into view all the cases to which the laws must extend, and hence aids and assistants must be provided for their execution. War demanded its armed legions, and the officers of the civil departments were spread into every part of the country. It was perfectly clear that all the officers of the Departments of State, War, Navy, and Treasury, were aids of the President in giving effect to the laws of the country. Hence, what was said by the Executive a few years ago, was well applied to them all. It was necessary that they should form an unit, that they might oppose no obstacle to his execution of the laws according to his own views. The Secretary of the Treasury could not, in the nature of things, under the Constitution, be any other than an executive officer. As such officer, all his official acts must necessarily be of that character, and of course subject to the final direction of the President, in whom is lodged the whole executive authority. Not that the Secretary was bound to obey illegal orders; but that the exercise of judgment and discretion, in the execution of the laws, was conferred upon the President, and upon him alone, and that the President in the first instance is to determine what is a faithful execution of the law.

But it is said, by the gentleman from South Carolina, [Mr. McDuffie,] that if this act of the President be not arrested, it will certainly destroy the liberties of the country. Why, sir, we have heard acts of legislation denounced before from the same quarter, and in the same terms. We hold our liberties too cheap if they stand, in our estimation, upon such a basis as the gentleman from South Carolina has indicated. The tariff was denounced in the same phrase. The bloody bill, so called to frighten children, and render it odious among the people, was also to put an end to our liberties. But we yet live, move, and have our being, and are in the enjoyment of as much liberty as any other people in the world—the bloody bill, the tariff, and political prophecy, to the contrary notwithstanding. It was strange that this single act should be considered as destructive to our liberties. If the President is corrupt, let us impeach him: but while he is the President, let him have fair play, and fair treatment. We might canvass his acts and pass judgment on them, without imputing to him corrupt and unworthy motives. Other branches of the Government may impute sinister motives to our acts, and any such imputation of one branch upon another, was reprehensible.

The doctrine for which he contended was as old as the Constitution, and was as well settled as anything which pertained to the history of the Government. The bank had kindly lent to us the light of its instructions, and had informed us that the act of the Secretary was a legislative act, and the Secretary was independent of the President.

The opinion seemed to have been adopted here, and was argued upon as one which was settled. We were enlightened on this subject by the Richmond resolutions, which tell us that the treasury is a legislative branch of the Government. We must now go back and show how the Treasury Department was organized, however uninteresting might be the detail. In May, 1789, the House of Representatives came to a resolution to establish three executive departments, the heads of whom should be removable by the President. Bills were brought in by the committee in pursuance of the resolution, on the 4th of June, for the establishment of the three departments—of War, of Foreign Affairs, and of the Treasury. The House acted on these as executive departments, and intended all as executive in their nature, and dependent upon the Chief Executive. They were all run in the same mould. The bill establishing the office of Foreign Affairs was the one first acted upon. That bill contained a clause providing that the Secretary should be removable at the pleasure of the President. A motion was made to strike out that provision, and upon this motion arose the debate reported by Lloyd. It was contended that the power of removal ought to be exercised by the President and Senate. The motion was negatived, 23 to 34. In this shape the bill was reported to the House, where two motions were made, to strike out the provision of removal, and to insert in another clause, the words "when the principal officer is removed," &c. The mover [Mr. Benton] contended that these words were a sufficient recognition of the power of removal, and the motions were carried, by the same vote which had been given in the Committee of the Whole.

Thus the amendments proposed by Mr. Benton substantiated the principle that all executive power is vested, constitutionally, in the President, as the head of the executive; and its being inserted in the acts creating the departments merely proves its recognition more plainly. Hence it is, therefore, that, since that period, in the judgment of the country, and Government, this department has beeen recognised as an executive department. No new power was conferred by the bill; the old power, conceded by the Constitution to the Executive, was but recognised or confirmed. But it was reserved for this day and this debate, to question the principles or deny the propriety of its application.

Returning, however, to the bills constituting (according to the resolution) the departments of Foreign Affairs, of War, and of the Treasury, he thought that the enacting clauses of each bill elucidates the meaning of the others, or the objects contemplated by the Legislature of that period, in instituting those departments. These bills were passed by the same Congress, and at the same period, and were founded on the same resolution. Therefore the clauses of the bills creating the War and Treasury Departments are to be interpreted in precisely the same manner. The act appointing the department of Foreign Affairs passed on June 24th, that for the War Department on June 27th, and that for the Treasury on July 2d—making but an interval of eight days: so that Congress certainly did not forget the clauses or meaning of the clauses of the first act when it had passed the last. Nor is it to be presumed that they meant differently on the same resolution, when the acts were expressed in terms precisely the same. There is no change of opinions indicated in the recorded proceedings of the day. Passing over the bill appointing the War Department, we come to that regulating the Treasury Department. Now, as it has never been questioned that the War or the Foreign Affairs Departments belong strictly to the executive, not the legislative branch of the Government, it cannot with good reasons be contended that the Treasury Department belongs to the legislative, not the executive branch. In all these departments a head is appointed, with powers to nominate his subordinate; and over all is the control of the President, expressed in his being empowered, as the Constitution had asserted, to appoint and remove these heads of departments, as he judged best for the public interests. There is equally a recognition of the heads of the departments; there is equally a power of removal.

Again, during the same session of Congress, an act was passed regulating the salaries of the executive departments; and in this act are specified the salaries of the different Secretaries, with their subordinates; among whom are classed the Secretary of the Treasury, with his subordinates—evidently, therefore, recognising the Treasury Department as a department of the executive government. Indeed, all the acts of the first Congress are thus in accordance. They exhibit an indication of the same principle, of one fact, one truth, that the Treasury Department is a branch of the executive government; and that the head of that department is amenable to the power of the head of the executive. Nor can we form this conclusion from the acts only of that Congress; but we find the same indication of principle interspersed in the discussions on those bills as reported in Lloyd's Debates, much of which has been before referred to, as clearly proving the agreement between the sayings and doings of that Congress. Ames says, that the Constitution has placed all executive power in the hands of the President; and that if it were possible for him to perform all the executive duties, then would he alone engross all executive power. But as this is impossible to be done by any one man, he is obliged to employ auxiliaries for the various operations and minutiæ of Government, subject to his control, but removable whenever he loses confidence in them. To the same effect speaks Stone, when he says, that the President appoints agents or subordinates for the convenient despatch of business. And so says Mr. Madison, when asserting that, by the Constitution, the President is bound to see that the laws are faithfully executed; and if so, that it is therefore indispensable he should be invested with sufficient power to accomplish this end. But if the officers of the executive departments are independent of the President, and these departments are armed with separate or distinct powers, he could not see how the President could effect the object designed in the Constitution. Now, the gentleman from Pennsylvania thinks differently from those gentlemen. He says, in answer to the argument, that if the President is empowered to see the laws properly executed, and that therefore he extends his control over the departments, he may extend it also over the Judiciary—reasoning that, by a known rule in logic, what proves too much, proves too little. But the gentleman forgets that the President is empowered to judge of the means whereby the laws are executed in the executive branch of the Government, as he is responsible for their faithful performance; but he is not bound to adjudge concerning the means employed by the judicial. True, he has the

power of appointing the judges of the supreme and inferior courts, but he has no control over them when appointed—no power of removal, no right of dictation. The judicial branch is perfectly distinct from the executive; each has its own rights and own duties. The argument is therefore nugatory. The judges being once appointed, hold their offices independent of the President; they depend not on him for their term of office.

Not so with the departments of the executive governments. The President is bound to see that their operations are in accordance with the laws. They hold their offices by his choice, and they are appointable and removable at his will, being in the eye of the law considered but as his auxiliaries, and performing for him the functions of his department of the Government. The executive power is not vested in them, but in him.

In the first debate on passing the bill in Congress, Sedgwick is reported to have said, that a great majority of the House had acknowledged that all the officers of the Treasury Department were dependant on the President for their continuance in office, and rightfully so, as he was responsible for their conduct. Thus, therefore, have we the acts and speeches of the House of that Congress agreeing together, and agreeing with the practice of the present Executive; and the acts of the Senate at that period, although we have not their sayings, for then they sat with closed doors, but we may reasonably infer that they came to the same result, on the same grounds, with the House, and therefore infer that their doings and sayings were alike in concert.

There is, therefore, no doubt of the true purpose of the first Congress in instituting the Treasury Department, at the same time with the departments for Foreign Affairs and for War; and there can be no justifiable doubt that these several departments were intended as branches of the executive government, not as dependencies of Congress—not all, nor one.

But this is also strikingly exemplified in the clauses specifying the duties of the Secretary of the Treasury, in the bill creating that department. These duties are of two kinds. The first are strictly official; as requiring him to superintend the collection of the public revenues; to regulate the sales of public land; and to control the finances. These duties are evidently executive in their character; not, certainly, of a legislative nature. The second duties, not official, require no use of public power, and have no immediate effect on public right; no official authority whatever is exerted; such are the digesting of plans to regulate commerce, to be laid before Congress; his forming estimates of finances, &c.

These acts are nullities in the eye of the Constitution and law, conveying no authority or power; having no responsibility nor effect. They require skill, intelligence, and fidelity; and nothing more. But in the former duties he acts as an executive agent, invested with authority as such.

Mr. B., in continuation, (which we are compelled merely to glance at or omit, from the lateness of the hour at which he ceased speaking,) said that the same arguments which would deny the Treasury Department to be a branch of the executive government, are equally applicable to nullifying the Executive control of the Post Office; for here, also is a head, with subordinates, to be appointed, in turn, by the Postmaster General; and he also is required to make an annual report to the Congress, not the President. The gentleman proved, therefore, that if the Treasury Department is not under the control of the head of the executive government, neither is the Postmaster General; which is against all experience in the Government. He continued, in conclusion, to answer the objections of Mr. Binney, to the validity of the reasons assigned by the Secretary for removing the deposites. We regret we are compelled to break off abruptly.

Mr. SEABORN JONES obtained the floor, and moved an adjournment.

And the House adjourned.

HOUSE OF REPRESENTATIVES.

Friday, *January* 17, 1834.

Mr. C. P. WHITE reported a bill for the relief of the legal representatives of John Coleman, deceased.

Mr. WATMOUGH reported a bill for the relief of William P. Zantzinger, late a purser in the United States navy.

Mr. ALLEN, of Ohio, reported a bill for the relief of —— Fisher; all which bills were read twice and committed.

Mr. WATMOUGH reported a bill concerning navy pensions and the navy pension fund; and

Mr. POLK, a bill making appropriations for revolutionary and other pensioners of the United States for the year 1834; both of which bills were severally referred to the Committee of the Whole on the state of the Union, and ordered to be printed.

THE PENSION LAWS.

The resolution submitted by Mr. CHILTON, to appoint a select committee to inquire into the expediency of so extending the general pension law, as to embrace within its provisions those persons who were engaged in the Indian wars down to 1794, with the amendments thereto, submitted by Mr. Bouldin, to appoint a committee to inquire into the moral effects of the pension system, coming up as the unfinished business—

Mr. PEYTON resumed his remarks. He said that any vote of the House, by which the services of the persons engaged in the conflicts with the Indians might be recognised, would be to them the proudest day of their existence, and its effect would be to relieve many who had long experienced undeserved want and misery. Adverting to the statement, made by the honorable member from Rhode Island, [Mr. Burges,] "that this was a petty warfare," he asked, could that be considered a petty warfare, which raged from Georgia to Canada, and in which thousands and tens of thousands of savages had been engaged for years? But to show that those wars were neither petty nor inglorious, he referred the gentleman to an instance in which a small party of only nineteen whites had resisted and proved victorious, over a band of Indians, who outnumbered them in the proportion of one hundred to one, and he described these conflicts, and said that, although after the savages obtained victories, they had used their powers barbarously; that in every Indian camp, the remnants of human skeletons, the remnants of those whose bodies were consumed at the stake, were to be met with; even the skeletons of women and children; yet he must repel the insinuation that the whites had committed similar atrocities, and asked the gentleman if he ever heard of a white man injuring women and children, begging him, when he should hear such a charge made, to set it down as false. That gentleman was unsparing of his censure upon these hardy bands for defending themselves, or for pursuing the savages. But was he equally so upon the privateering of those from his own State, during the last war? No. Yet his patriotic blood seemed to curdle in his veins when he reflected upon the conduct of the white man, who was forced to peril his life against the most fearful odds. He talked, too, "of atrocious acts of retaliation having been committed by the frontier men," but Mr. P. denied the justice of this charge, and referred the gentleman to the history of Kentucky and of the times, by which he would learn such was not the conduct of Boon, when he penetrated into the deep forest in pursuit of the two Miss Calloways, whom he regained from the Indians, and restored to their homes. Boon was not alone in such achievments. There was a long list, in which the name of Weeks and others were to be enrolled. There were 1500 women and children who were taken captive, wounded, or slain; at least 2000 horses, and not less than 5000 dollars worth of property taken from the harassed and bleeding hunters. Yet this was all "petty" in the gentleman's opinion. Mr. P. contended at length, that it was owing to their gallant exertions the standard raised by Cornwallis in the South, at the instigation of the tories, had been pulled down; and after detailing the events of the Battle at King's Mountain, as having contributed as much as any other to establish the independence of the United States, he expressed his hope, that the glory of that and their other actions would be permitted to stand as a proud monument of their fame; that the surviving remnant of such an heroic band would be considered as not the least deserving of those who now enjoyed the bounty of the nation.

Mr. PINCKNEY said that he valued as highly as any person the rich inheritance of independence that was left them by their fathers, and duly appreciated the price at which it was purchased. But he would prefer showing his veneration for those engaged in the Revolution in some other way than by increasing taxation, or the burdens of the nation. The mover of the resolution had certainly taken such captivating ground, that even he, deprecating, as he must ever do, the consequences of its adoption by the House, was almost tempted to give freely the pittance which was claimed so eloquently for the warworn veterans of the West. But he had a higher duty to perform than to give way to his feelings; as he must contend that the House had no constitutional right to adopt the resolution. The whole pension system was established without constitutional authority, and he defied the utmost ingenuity to point out any one article in the Constitution from which the power to establish it could be inferred. If, then, it was not constitutional to establish the system for the soldier of the Revolution, how much more unjust was it to include within the provisions of that law those who, whatever were their services elsewhere, had no agency in that war? Their services having been subsequent to that event, they had not contributed to lay the glorious foundation on which the Federal Constitution was raised. He could not assent to the pension system being established, much less being extended; for, by the Annual Message of the President, as well as the report from the Secretary of the Treasury, they were plainly told that economy was necessary; that there were some doubt that the revenue of the country would keep pace with the expenditure; and they were warned of this in order to prevent them indulging their feelings by making appropriations of this character. But notwithstanding this warning, scarcely a day passed without some schemes being presented which had for their object an extension of the public expenditure. There were propositions to distribute the public lands; to make appropriations for subscriptions to various roads and canals; and lastly, the pension system, as now sought, was to be increased. He called on the House to consider that the certain effect of proceeding in this way must be to oblige them again to have recourse to most onerous taxation; and that for this purpose, notwithstanding all the agitation which prevailed on the subject of the tariff had been sealed by the compromise bill, that subject must be again opened. But were Congress prepared to convulse the country as it had been on that question? Would they have the country so torn and distracted as it was, and this, too, not for the benefit of any great manufacturing interest, but for such a measure as this, which was only based on an appeal to their feelings of generosity? He trusted not, for his motto was justice, rather than generosity; and it was not justice to tax the public for the benefit of a class of persons who had no claims whatever. He would rejoice to see the pension system abolished altogether, considering that it was notoriously a branch which had its origin in the protective system; it had been devised under color of showing gratitude to those who achieved the independence of the country; but, in reality, to keep up the system of high duties; and this being the understanding of the people of the South as to its origin, it was most odious to them, for they knew that so long as the expenditure of the Government was increased, or kept up unnecessarily, taxation must be resorted to. They were now about to commence a new era; the public debts were to be paid off. There was no longer a pretext for the continuance of taxation. Economy was one principle on which the present Administration came into office; to correct abuses and reform institutions was another. But how had these promises been fulfilled? Where was the retrenchment, where was the expenditure reduced? Instead of retrenchment, they found such extravagance to prevail, that some of the departments were insolvent; and, in such a state of things, ought Congress to increase the expenditure, or to reduce the revenue to the legitimate wants of the people? As long as there was the pretext of the public debt, the people bore taxation; but now that they know that pretext is removed, they demand as a right that no more taxation, no more appropriations, shall be made than

was absolutely necessary. If there was one objection stronger than another to taxation, it would be to taxation for their pension system, because it was not only burdensome in itself, but because, as it operated unequally, it therefore operated unjustly. Who, he asked, enjoyed its benefits? Not one in twenty in the South participated in the benefits of it, although the South, more than any other portion of the United States, contributed to the revenue of the country.

After some further remarks, Mr. P. concluded, by a motion to postpone the resolution indefinitely.

Mr. BURGES rose to say, that he had been greatly misrepresented in his observations formerly made on this resolution concerning military pensions. It has been asserted he had termed the Indian war, to which honorable gentlemen had referred, a "petty" war. Now he had not said that it was a petty war, although he certainly had said that it was a private, not a public war. And to this remark he was stimulated by an observation of one who advocated the passage of the resolution—that the war had continued for twenty years: therefore, giving the gentleman credit for his assertion, he could not but consider it a private war: for with no Indian war of a public nature of twenty years' continuance, has he been made acquainted in his historical researches. It must have been a private war; because those who were engaged in it had not been enlisted in the public service; had not been even employed in the service of the country, nor had they been equipped or designed as militia. Where then is the nature of a public war? Where the test of evidence to prove that those engaged were engaged in the service of the public? And if not engaged in the service of the nation, why should the nation be publicly taxed to remunerate private services so performed? He does not deny the men—Boon, Spencer, and their associates—were brave men; nor that any of those who may have contended in the alleged wars with the Indians may have been actuated by a chivalrous spirit—the bravery they possessed, they possessed for themselves. They were pioneers for themselves, not from a love for the nation. They were stimulated by a desire to better their own condition—not to defend their country's rights: and their condition they did better. Have they not taken forcible possession of the most fertile lands in the most fertile districts, and entailed their property on their sons and grandsons, while they have been enabled to settle all their cousins around them? What more would they desire? They have monopolized territories, and now they want to become pensioners on the public bounty. Gentlemen are very loud in applauding the chivalry of these men, but they disdain to give more than their praise. They exclaim that those whom they eulogize are in straits and misery; but so far from being ready to contribute to these alleged wants of applauded chevaliers, they are anxious to exonerate themselves from their craving demands, and to burden the public with those from whose claims they appear not otherwise willing or able to obtain redemption. They give praise when they should give alms; and think that this applause and the aid of public pensions should relieve themselves from the necessity of maintaining them. [The speaker then instanced several examples from ancient and modern history wherein there had been pioneers on the frontiers of extending countries, and discoverers of previously unknown regions.] He alluded to extending the frontiers from Rhode Island to Connecticut, and thence westward still; but which of all the adventurers so employed, ever asked the support of the public funds for private services so performed?

He alluded to the wanderings of Hercules in Italy, and the barbarity of the tyrant Cacus, filching his neighbor's cattle, and drawing them backward into his den; but that Hercules discovered the cattle by their lowing—so says the poetical version of the tale, but whether true or not, he can't say. Yet this Hercules is now deemed a hero, from such exploits of his pioneering bravery, and Cacus condemned as an aboriginal savage. So with the pioneers of the West. They are deemed heroic cavaliers; and the aborigines of the soil, whom they conquered and expatriated, are denominated savages, whom it was a glory to extirpate, in whom it was a crime to endeavor to regain their own lands, and over whom it was bravery to triumph, and deserving of public pensions. But we are told that the civilization disseminated by the conquest, improves the condition of these reputed savages; and for this, those instrumental in extending the boon of civilization, deserve public approbation and reward. For himself, he has no desire to reward any for killing the Indians in party or pioneering conflicts. The Indians were the original possessors of the soil, and cannot be condemned for struggling to retain their own. The Indian names and fame are interwoven in the annals and statistics of the country; and when that mountain, to which Spencer had given his name, may dwindle into obscurity or change its epithet, the mighty rivers of the land—the Ohio, Mississippi, &c.—will roll on, a reminiscent record of their fame to posterior ages: their waters, in rolling onward to the ocean, will resound their fame; and the literature of the country will redeem them from infamy. The Indians were attacked, routed, expatriated. They were driven from the lands of their fathers; and well might they exclaim that they had scarcely left land enough to die on. At that period the frontier settlers thought but of their own condition—how they might improve it, by acquiring fertile possessions: and now that the dangers of those adventurous days have passed away—now that the days of their enjoying the war-whoop of their much wronged opposers have gone—they turn round and demand the right of having bestowed on them pensions for so acting for themselves against a self-raised foe. If pensions are granted for the display of chivalry, such as this is commended to have been, then will pensions swell the expenses of the nation, and engross the revenues of the country; for the frontiers of the West will still be extending westward, and opportunities be still given for the display of chivalrous spirit at every such extension. We shall therefore keep alive the spirit of chivalry, and eternally awaken the spirit of war. There will always be Sansoons and Herculeses among those cavaliers; and a demand will always be made to pension them or their sons, as the heroes of the twenty years' war have been rewarded before them. The evils will thus be extended. It is therefore much better to narrow the pension system while we may; and before we afford injurious precedents for expenditures of the public bounty, and rewards for monopolizing skirmishes with the Indians. He is not disposed to reward such chivalry, nor to participate in such exploits. If, in such a contest, the gentleman to whom he is now more immediately opposed, should take a fancy to tomahawk him, and to carry about his venerable scalp as a trophy of victory, he might consider himself as deserving a pension of the Government; but if he was fortunate enough to master his enemy, and had taken his scalp, he would not think it worth his trouble to take it away.

A motion was then made to suspend the rules of the House, relative to the duties of Friday, in order that the preceding debate might be continued; but it was lost.

On the motion of Mr. POLK, several bills for the relief of individuals, as reported by the Committee of Ways and Means, were then read a third time and passed.

A few petitions were then proposed, with the consent of the House, and some private bills.

The SPEAKER presented a public document containing the list of clerks belonging to the public departments.

A resolution passed by a small majority, conceding to the Colonization Society the use of the Hall of Representatives for a meeting to be held on Monday evening next.

Mr. POLK moved to suspend the standing orders of the House, in order to propose the bill of appropriations (returned with amendments from the Senate) concerning the contingent expenses of Congress, in the articles of stationery, &c. The gentleman said it was absolutely necessary that the appropriation should be made as soon as possible. The House concurred.

Mr. POLK then said that the Committee of Ways and Means had agreed to the amendments proposed by the Senate, except that one which proposed to strike out altogether a clause which had first been passed in 1830, and continued every year since, which restricted this appropriation for contingencies to mere stationery, &c., and the printing of such public documents as may be ordered by both houses in the routine of business, unless it were otherwise ordered by a joint resolution of both Houses. Although he did not wish to originate discussion on this clause, he thought it prudently restrictive, as it tends to prevent the ordering of books, &c., without making any appropriation for them; and prevents the action of either House without the concurrence of both. But this restriction cannot extend to the vote lately passed for Elliot's Debates—its effects being solely prospective. Nor can it prevent the ordering in future any books—its object being solely to prevent such orders without the joint resolution of both Houses, which is required to make any appropriation. Appropriations may be specially made for any particular purpose; so that the clause proposed is to prevent the appropriation made for the contingent expenses of both Houses, amenable to the orders of either only, in any resolution not jointly passed.

Mr. FOOT objected to the clause, and thought it should be admitted, as the Senate had proposed. It is rather singular that either House should be denied the privilege of printing what it adjudges proper to order, when that privilege is extended to all the departments, which are allowed to print ad libitum, what is considered necessary; nor is it consistent that the Senate should be denied the privilege which is appropriated by the House. This will bring both Houses into an improper collision. He sees, therefore no sufficient reason why they should endeavor to tie up their own and other persons' hands.

The discussion was continued by Messrs. C. C. CLAY and POLK, who supported the motion, and by Messrs. EVERETT of Massachusetts, ADAMS of Massachusetts, WHITTLESEY, and BATES of Massachusetts, who opposed the motion to disagree to the Senate's amendment.

On motion of Mr. McKIM, the yeas and nays were ordered on the question.

The question being taken, it was decided in the affirmative, by a vote of 70 to 119.

So the House disagreed to the amendment of the Senate.

On motion of Mr. VANCE, it was
Ordered, That when the House adjourn, it adjourn to meet on Monday.
The House then adjourned.

Jamaica papers to the 5th ult. have been received at New York. The House of Assembly was closely engaged in the discussion of the slavery bill.—Balt. Amer.

Two or three letters from Buenos Ayres to the 13th November, have been received in this city, by the brig Heroine, arrived at Lewistown, Delaware, bound to Philadelphia. They state that the revolutionary disturbances at Buenos Ayres has ceased, and that peace was proclaimed on the 10th of November.—Balt. Amer.

The Legislature of Massachusetts have elected John Davis, Esq., Governor, for the year ensuing, on the first ballot.—Baltimore Gazette.

THE CONGRESSIONAL GLOBE.

PRINTED AND PUBLISHED AT THE CITY OF WASHINGTON, BY BLAIR & RIVES.

23d Congress, 1st Session.　　　　SATURDAY, JANUARY 25, 1834.　　　　Vol. I........No. 8.

In the House of Representatives, January 16, 1834, on Mr. Chilton's resolution to appoint a Select Committee to inquire into the expediency of so extending the general pension law as to embrace within its provisions those persons who were engaged in the Indian wars, down to the year 1794; and the amendment on it by Mr. Bouldin, to appoint a committee to inquire into the moral effects of the pension system upon the community, and how far it ought to be abolished or repealed.

Mr. PEYTON, of Tennessee, rose and said—

Mr. SPEAKER: I arose on yesterday from the impulse of the moment, not to make a speech, but rather to repel what I considered an imputation cast upon men whom I was early taught to look upon as patriots, most of whom are gone, than to ask for them an act of justice and charity from their country.

The venerable gentleman from Rhode Island, [Mr. Burges,] spoke lightly of the early settlers of the West—talked of their scalps—classed them with "plunderers and savage murderers." I, sir, am proud to trace my origin to that race of men. But, sir, no pension law can benefit my ancestors now. It would come too late for them. They never asked a pension while they lived. I value the reputation of that band of patriots as dearer than gold. You have a right to deny the survivors bread, but no right to cast obloquy upon their names.

They were no "plunderers." No, sir, they were soldiers, true and pure; and a soldier never stains his hand with "plunder." The brave are always tender and humane. They "plunderers !" What temptation was there in the frowning forest of the West to invite to "plunder?" None, sir, none.

The wild beast and the naked savage, armed with all his instruments of death, the gun, the knife, the axe, and fagot, were the allurements held out. It was not every one whose train would have led him to partake in such "plunder." I question if the gentleman, in the unrestrained ardor of his could have been induced to throw a sickle and reap for "plunder" there. The harvest, was often smoking cabins, murdered wives and children, scalped and mangled sires. They "murderers !" They left their firesides and patriarchal farms in Carolina and Virginia to protect our mothers from murder—from savage torture; and, sir, the social and domestic virtues found an asylum in the forest. The strongest rampart was thrown around them—the chivalry of these men. And this reflection soothed and quieted the pang which wrung their bosoms when they stood upon the last hill which overlooked their homes, where youthful feelings clung and hovered.

What! cast an imputation upon the names of Boon, Robinson, and Spencer, and their brave compeers!! Class these men with the savage in point of honor and humanity! They were patriots, benefactors of the West, who deserved to live in marble, and not to be remembered with reproach and scorn.

The history of Boon and Robinson is known. Robinson was to Tennessee what Boon was to Kentucky. Spencer, who has been referred to by my friend and colleague, [Mr. Dickinson,] was the first white man who spent a winter in my native county, (Sumner county.) He lived in the hollow of a tree at Bledsoe's Lick, alone, surrounded by the savages, and no other of his race on that side of the mighty mountains which lay between him and his native Carolina. When the spring opened, and the desert bloomed around him, he returned, described the country, its game, its fertility, its rich inviting loveliness. His neighbors came; he was their pilot; he killed their meat; he dressed while they slept. Thus he spent his time for years. At last, upon the hill which bears his name he fell, valiantly fell, fighting between the women and the ambushed savage. His flesh was devoured, and his bones bleached and mouldered in the woods, until an old man, the companion of his youth, collected them together, and placed them in a cave, where they are yet. No marble pillar marks the spot, but nature, in that proud hill which rears its head above the clouds, has raised for him a grander monument than man can raise. It is Spencer's Hill, and will remain so forever. But, sir, he was no "plunderer," but a generous, kind, and hospitable man. He would divide his meat, to the last morsel, with a hungry dog. He was no "murderer," but a soldier, who would defend himself and friend—fit to have stood beside Bruce, Leonidas, or Kosciusko.

Boon and Spencer thought that nature did not intend that mighty West—all that valley which is watered by the "King of Floods" and its tributary streams, to be kept forever for the savage war dance—a wild hunting ground. I know that some few gentlemen have always differed with them, and have opposed emigration to the West, and looked with jealousy upon its rising prospects—have saved their sympathy for the red man, and their spears and darts for the white man. I never could understand such enlarged patriotic sympathy, much less did I expect to find one ready to pierce the dead. I agree with Boon and Spencer, that the West should have been settled, and how was that to be accomplished? My answer is, by just such men as did effect it, and such a race as will never see again—so resolutely brave, so pure and warm in patriotism, so kind to one another, (I wish their spirit filled these legislative halls,) so patient under all the pangs of war, and wants, and wretchedness. Women then were more than soldiers.

I question, sir, if old Mrs. Buchanan did not distinguish herself in these "petty feuds," of which the gentlemen seems never to have heard, as much as that worthy and venerable man has done in all the mighty struggles through which his country has passed. Women then, sir, would come around with bullets in their aprons, encouraging their husbands, sons, and brothers. They would hold an aching head, or bind a bleeding wound, and all this was in the service of the country, in the war of the Revolution.

The gentleman seems to be uninformed of the early occurrences in the West, and looks down with scorn upon the struggles there. I could refer him to a man who would be able to supply his want of local knowledge—a venerable man, about his own age—his name is Gennings—Edmund Gennings. He was in Dunmore's war; fought all day long in the battle of the Point, at Big Kenhawa. The gentleman no doubt remembers that battle; it was fought in 1774, just 20 years before Wayne's victory in 1794. But, sir, this old soldier, bent by war and time, who is now a wanderer, without a home, I left him in my district when I came away—he performed an exploit in the Nickajack expedition worthy of a monument. Now, sir, perhaps that gentleman who never heard of Nickajack; if so, he should talk no more of Indian wars in the West, but keep close upon the borders of Rhode Island. Whitley was at Nickajack—brought down his soldiers from Kentucky, and joined Robinson at the French Lick Station, (now Nashville.) There are men alive, and now upon this floor, who can attest that Whitley deserves not to be degraded to the level of a savage; he was the patriot of two wars. But, sir, Edmund Gennings, he swam a river in the dark, a mile in width, (the Tennessee below the Muscle Shoals,) and went into an Indian town, which lined its banks, with one companion only—ascertained its strength, and brought the canoes over to Robinson and Whitley. His companion was Joshua Thomas. He went the way which the gentleman seems to think was right, for he was scalped—a truer soldier never lived or died. That gentleman may think such men "murderers" and "plunderers," and that it is a bad example to reward or even admire them. But, sir, I rank them with the bravest of the brave, the most deserving of the revolutionary soldiers.

Mr. Speaker, if I were to ask you to point me to the most cruel, bloody, and vindictive of all the mother country's acts which marked her war upon the colonies, what would be the answer? That she excited the savages, unkennelled the bloodhounds of the forest, who knew no mercy, who spared neither age nor sex, to war upon the American people. "In the issue which was made before high Heaven," "whether England should rule or America be free," were not the savages used as instruments and allies of Great Britain to subjugate the colonies? Was it not a part of our revolutionary struggle to resist those savages? Were did this vindictive and unrelenting policy fall most heavily? Upon the West; and, sir, the West met it, as she has since met perils from the same quarter, and as I trust she will ever meet them, come from where they may.

It was patriotic in Washington to resist the civilised nature of Great Britain, but not so in Boon to resist her gentle and permissive instruments of savage warfare in the West. What kept back the depredations of these allies from the interior? The bust of ramparts for a nation's safety—the chivalry of its frontier citizens. And, sir, shall such a race of men, who achieved so much, be branded with epithets?—have their scalps put, in their country's estimation, against an Indian scalp, their humanity against the humanity of an Indian, their honor against the honor of a savage, while other soldiers of the Revolution have won for themselves immortal honor and freedom for their country? No, sir, it is not just to treat them so. If any soldier of the Revolution should stand in patriotic merit above another, it is he who fought the solitary fight, in far and distant parts. No flag like that [pointing to the flag in the House]—no spirit-stirring fife and drum to cheer him on—so Washington to lead him up in confidence to battle—no pay, no arms, nor ammunition furnished—no clothes, nor meat; his name no roll—he fights from high impulse and love of country—not for pay nor "plunder;" and if he falls, no stone to tell the spot—no book is written about him; but if a monument at all, it is left by the hand of a hunter, carved in the bark of the tree that shades his grave. And if he lives, and is old and poor, a wanderer from house to house, there is no pension for him. No, sir, no pension. Why? His name is not enrolled in a book.

And was not he who found his own arms, and grappled with the foe in the deep forest, in that sacred cause which won so much for men, without the aid of anything but valor—was not he a soldier of the Revolution, standing on prouder ground than if he had been drafted, and forced to follow his commander and that glorious banner? [pointing again to the flag in the House.]

FRIDAY, January 17, 1834.

Mr. PEYTON continued his remarks in reply to Mr. Burges as follows: I have but a few observations to offer in addition to those I made on yesterday. My intention has never been to make an argument upon the question now under consideration. Nothing was farther from my thoughts or wishes than to have found it necessary for me to say a word upon the subject. I expected to have given a silent vote. And I assure the House I feel less anxious to obtain a pension for the early emigrants to the West (richly as I think they deserve it) than to save their memory from censure and reproach—and show that it would not be wrong in itself, nor the example demoralizing, for them to receive their country's notice and its gratitude. And now, sir, after all that has been said, a vote of this House recognising them to be, what I contend they are, soldiers of the Revolution, would be to those who live, the proudest day of their existence, and a grateful tribute of regard to those who are no more. It would carry joy and gladness to their bosoms, and afford the means of independence to those who scorn to live on private charity. But, sir, the gentleman from Rhode Island speaks with contempt and censure of those petty feuds and private wars which raged on the western frontiers. What does the gentleman mean by petty feuds and

private wars? Does he call that a petty private war which raged unceasingly for more than twenty years; which called forth all the savage tribes from Georgia to Canada? Yes, sir; bands united into armies of painted warriors, counting thousands. If that gentleman had been in Buchanan's station when it was surrounded by more than seven hundred Creeks and Shawnees, with only nineteen men and a few resolute women to defend the fort, I question whether it would have struck him as a petty feud, or inglorious defence. Sir, Tecumseh, since the most celebrated warrior of the Red Men, then but a boy, was there. This fact I learned from the granddaughter of General Robinson, a lady who unites the spirit of her ancestor with taste and learning. Why is it that the gentleman's sympathies are all with the red men? Sir, at that time, they were as a hundred to one when compared with the whites. They used their superior strength most barbarously; at all their camps were to be seen stakes with human skeletons hanging around them—some small and short—infants which had perished with their mothers. The gentleman spoke of retaliation; did he ever hear of a white man's torturing a female or infant Indian? If he has, I beg the gentleman to set it down as false; cowards and barbarians only are capable of misusing those whom it is the duty of man to protect. Sir, no coward ever showed his face there. He spoke of retaliation, and seems to think it the duty of the Government to discourage it as practised in the West. Was not the gentleman in favor of privateering during the late war? Did he not think it right in his own State to fit out privateers of war to capture merchant vessels; not that those vessels had done them any wrong, but because their nation was at war with ours? Yet the gentleman's patriotic blood curdles in his veins at the thought that a rude backwoodsman, with a cabin just sufficient to shelter his family, and a poney to pack in meat for their support, when robbed of all by the harassing allies of a powerful nation at war with his country, should retake his horse or take another, not by attacking a defenceless neutral, but at the hazard of his life. Retaliation, indeed! How could Boon retaliate in 1776, when his daughter and the Miss Calloways were carried prisoners, by the savages, far, far into the deep cane-tangled wilderness? What, catch and kill an Indian girl! Could Boon do that? No; no more than he could give up his Gertrude—not of Wyoming, but of Boonsborough. They must be saved from the stake and flame! He raised his friends and resolutely followed on; he fought and won a battle, and brought the trembling captives home to their mothers. He talked of private wars and petty piracy. The lives of a few soldiers were prized at that day in the West, and when they fell were greatly missed. The West was weak, and faint, and bleeding, and scarce of soldiers. Let us examine and see if those wars were so private as the gentleman seems to think. From 1783 to 1790 the loss of property was immense. There were killed and wounded and taken prisoners 1500 men, women, and children. This is the estimate made of the loss in seven years of that war, which raged with unceasing fury for more than twenty years upon that harassed people, which the gentleman may learn, if he ever reads a book published on the other side of the Alleghanies.

But, sir, as to the services performed by these hunters: At the most gloomy period of the Revolution, when despair clouded the brow of the patriot, and hundreds were flocking to the British standard, giving up their liberty and their country's independence as gone forever—when Cornwallis was in the centre, and Ferguson had taken his position near the mountains in Carolina, encouraging the Tories and dispiriting the Whigs—who drove that British general from his post? 'Twas the hunters of Watага. They pursued him with the impetuosity of a mountain torrent for thirty-six hours, stopping only one hour for refreshment at the Cowpens. At King's Mountain they overtook the royal army, drawn up upon its summit: who climbed that steep, and dragged down the tyrant power, and by the bold exploit not only cheered the drooping spirits of the Whigs and carried terror to the Tories, but made Cornwallis quail and retreat? Sir, when that conflict began, the mountain appeared volcanic; there flashed along its summit, and around its base, and up its sides, one light sulphureous blaze. That [pointing to the eagle and flag of the House] eagle's eye shone bright in victory—that banner floated proudly out. Historians give this as the most patriotic and illustrious achievement of the Revolution. And, sir, need I tell that gentleman, who has at least noticed Marshall's history, that it was achieved by the hunters of the West, without the aid, or even the knowledge, of Government. And upon that proud mount still let them stand! Who would drag them down to the low estate of savages? Who would tear one laurel from their brow? If you can't spare for those who live the means of living, be it so—the West will feed her patriarchal soldiers; they are old and few; when they are gone, may their mantles fall, to warm the patriot's bosom and nerve the soldier's arm. But you *dare* not reproach them; their honor and patriotic worth are our richest inheritance, and, sir, we will hug and defend it as our country's honor. Let the warworn soldier, when pressed to live, and disappointed in his expectations here, look to the West—it is what his country has done in the hour of her peril and day of her distress.

IN SENATE.

FRIDAY, *January* 17, 1834.

Mr. BELL, from the Committee of Claims, reported unfavorably to the petition of John Donley; which was agreed to.

Mr. BELL, from the same committee, reported a bill for the relief of John McCartner; which was read, and, together with the report, ordered to be printed.

Mr. ROBINSON, from the Committee on Engrossed Bills, made a report.

Mr. TIPTON, in pursuance of notice given yesterday, introduced a bill for the relief of Captain John Hamilton; which was read, and referred to the Committee on Pensions.

Mr. HENDRICKS, in pursuance of notice, introduced a bill for the relief of Henry Warren, which was read and referred to the Committee on Claims.

Mr. SILSBEE, in pursuance of notice, introduced a bill for the relief of the heirs of Christopher Coffin; which was read, and referred to the Committee on Revolutionary Claims.

Mr. KANE, from the Committee on Private Land Claims, made several reports, upon which the usual orders were made.

The VICE PRESIDENT communicated a letter from the Secretary of War, including a report from the agent of the national road in Indiana; which, on motion of Mr. HENDRICKS, was referred to the Committee on Roads and Canals.

The VICE PRESIDENT also communicated a letter from the Secretary of War, enclosing a statement of the number, names, and compensation of the clerks employed in his department during the year 1833.

Mr. POINDEXTER, from the Committee on Public Lands, reported several bills of a private nature.

Mr. POINDEXTER, from the same committee, asked to be discharged from the further consideration of the resolution of the State of Missouri, respecting land districts.

Mr. PORTER, in pursuance of notice, introduced a bill for the relief of certain persons in Louisiana;

Which was read, and referred to the Committee on Public Lands.

Petitions were presented by Messrs. TOMLINSON and PORTER.

Mr. POINDEXTER, who moved to lay the resolution of Mr. CLAY (submitted on Tuesday last) upon the table, called it up.

Mr. CLAY moved the following as an amendment to the amendment of Mr. FORSYTH:

"By extending the period of payment of revenue bonds, under suitable precautions or otherwise, within the constitutional powers of Congress."

Mr. POINDEXTER then addressed the Senate for some considerable time, and was followed by Mr. BENTON, for a few moments; when Mr. WEBSTER, expressing a wish to be heard upon the subject, moved that the resolution lie upon the table; which, after an intimation from Mr. CLAY, that he should expect it to be taken up on Monday, was so ordered.

[A sketch of the debate upon this resolution will be furnished in continuation.]

On motion of Mr. EWING, it was

Resolved, That when the Senate adjourn, it will adjourn until Monday.

The VICE PRESIDENT then announced the special order of the day to be Mr. CLAY's resolution upon

THE REMOVAL OF THE DEPOSITES.

Mr. RIVES expressed the reluctance with which he obtruded himself upon the attention of the Senate, as it better became him to be a listener than a speaker. But the importance of the question, and the occasion, left him no other alternative. The subject was admitted to be of the highest moment on account of the distress which prevailed in the community, but which was much exaggerated by panic, and which, such as it was, he hoped would be of transient existence. And in providing the remedy care should be taken not to mistake the symptom for the disease. He believed the disease more deeply seated than the gentleman from Kentucky supposed; a disease which would require the cautery and the knife to eradicate. But the distress came to him with the alleviating reflection that it would pass over with the destruction of its great cause. In vain did the patriots of '91 warn us that the Bank of the United States was most dangerous to the institutions and government of the country—in vain did the voice of the gentleman from Kentucky, on a former occasion, warn us that the institution was dangerous to our liberties, if we were now to close our eyes against its conduct; but he trusted gentlemen would open their eyes to its character. It was in vain to say the panic was caused by the removal of the deposites—it could not be. That was no novelty—it had been done before; we had been told by the bank that when the protested bill came back from France, there was less than $2000 of public money in the bank; and was not this in effect a removal of the deposites? Yet there was no pressure at that time. Some other cause, then, must be found for it, and that had been assigned by a gentleman in the other House, [Mr. Binney.] He ascribed it to the doctrine on which the act was done, by which the people were to be separated from the bank; and it was said that the people were so connected with the bank that the separation could not be effected without inextricably involving one and the other.

Mr. RIVES then briefly recapitulated statements showing the annual operations of the bank; the domestic exchanges amounting to two hundred and forty-one millions; the foreign to thirteen millions; which, added to the discounts and deposites, make an aggregate of three hundred and forty-one millions, the annual operations of the bank. Could any one look at that exhibit, without having a sense of the danger of the institution to the country from the manner in which it had mixed itself up with the affairs of the country? It was impossible but that it must exert an influence hostile to the best interests of the country. He conceived the true danger and the real cause of its distress to be in the existence of this institution with its overpowering monopoly. What, then, was the remedy? Was it by increasing its means? Could any man fail to see that this would be the effect of restoring the deposites? And how then could its effects on the country be resisted, when it wound up its concerns? It must cease to exist; and how was the nation to get rid of this immense power without producing a pressure upon the country? Did gentlemen forget the non-renewal of the charter of the old United States Bank, and the report of the Secretary of the Treasury to Congress, that such would be the consequence? It would be singular if any one could suppose we could get rid of this institution without some distress and panic in the community.

But the gentleman from South Carolina said, the question was not, bank or no bank, but whether there should be a league of State banks, subject to the absolute control of the Executive. Could he suppose that the State banks, under the direction of the Governments of the States, totally unconnected with each other, could possibly be made the instruments of an influence

formidable as an institution like the United States Bank? Could he suppose that a portion of the public moneys, amounting to no more than four millions, distributed among the State banks, could seduce them to be the tools of the Executive? What was lately seen in Virginia in regard to this matter? The deposites were not considered there so great and desirable a boon as was supposed. But he would say to that gentleman, that this was not the true issue presented—it was not the alternative. He admitted that when the plan of a metallic currency, which would do away with the necessity of a United States Bank, should be presented, that then the question of constitutionality of the bank would come up. Mr. R. thought nothing was more practicable than this. There were inherent vices in a paper currency which it was the duty of every patriot to provide against; it was a vice, too, which was not obviated by the operations of the United States Bank—a vice which the Constitution, as a hard money Constitution, intended to provide against. Mr. R. thought the means by which the metallic currency might be established would be easy; but first the Bank of the United States should be put down, and then by correcting the inequality in the relative value of gold and silver, gold would take the place of small notes for travelling and other ordinary purposes; the small notes might then be discouraged, and the revenue of the country prohibited from being paid in notes under the denomination of $10 or $20. Believing that this grand reform was called for, and that Congress ought to prepare the way for it, he would pledge himself to introduce a plan for that end. The issue was now presented between the Constitution, having in view a metallic currency, and the Bank of the United States; he was anxious that the preliminary measures should have their effect. Yet, notwithstanding all this, if he could be persuaded that the faith of the Government had been violated by the removal of the deposites, he would vote, at all hazards, to sustain that faith. The act of the Government, of necessity, involved the whole conduct of the bank, and brought it up for consideration. His idea of the power given to the Secretary of the Treasury was, that it was to be exercised by him in case of any misconduct whatever on the part of the bank.

In answer to the argument that the bonus paid by the bank was the consideration given for the deposites, Mr. R. contended that it was given as the *quid pro quo* for the chartered privileges, the banking monopoly; the Government having restrained itself from establishing any other bank; that the deposites were not considered as a source for enlarging its discounts indefinitely, nor as a privilege or advantage altogether, but a charge for safekeeping, and, further, that it was the intention of the Government to reserve to itself, by the 16th section of the bank charter, the absolute control over the public moneys; that the Secretary had the general authority to deposite or withdraw them whenever he should think proper; that it was most extraordinary that Congress was not more explicit in their language, if their meaning had been otherwise than to give the broadest and most extensive power to the Secretary. The language was as general as it could be to empower the Secretary to remove, for any reasons growing out of the conduct of the bank. Mr. R. then went into a detailed account of the conduct of the bank in relation to the payment of the three per cent. Government stocks, amounting to six millions. That although it had due and timely notice from the Secretary of the wishes of the Government in this particular, and although it had nine millions of public money in its vaults, it was unable or unwilling to pay six; that at the bank's request the Secretary postponed the time of payment, and then, when the ultimate day of payment was approaching, it sought to attain its object in another manner to thwart the wishes of the Government by secret arrangements with her creditors. That by these acts it proved itself incapable of paying, and interposed to defeat the great object of the Government. Mr. R. contended, that if, in making this arrangement, the bank had become insolvent, the Government would have lost their funds, and therefore this conduct itself, was sufficient to justify the removal of the deposites. Mr. R. argued at length upon the palpable violation of the charter by the bank, in excluding the Government directors from a participation in its affairs; that the Government stock was entitled to a representation; that those directors were provided by Congress for that purpose; that the charter required the business of the bank to be transacted by *not less* than seven members, and yet that the whole business of discounting was confided to the committee on exchange, composed of directors elected by the president himself; that the whole of its operations were covered by a veil of impenetrable mystery, and that the manifest object of Congress in seeking to guard against such an event, by providing the transaction of business should be by seven directors, was frustrated and lost. He further contended that the institution was designed for the good of the people and the nation at large, and *nothing else*, and above all things it ought to abstain from the politics of the country. Yet in a period of sixteen months its private accounts rose from forty to seventy millions of dollars, all of which was justly considered by the President and Secretary as having been done for political effect, since it was this enormous extension of its loans which prevented the bank from paying her honest debts. And in answer to the argument that these loans were made necessary by the extraordinary amount of imports at that time, he contended that excess was stimulated by the excessive liberality of the bank. Then the authority given to the president of the bank to expend its funds for the purchase and circulation of political pamphlets was unexampled in banking operations. It was a public institution, and had no right to make any such defence, except as regarded the public interests. The press and the various other public channels by which public opinion could be operated upon, were amply sufficient for defending it. Some of the publications which had issued at its expense, particularly that alluded to by the gentleman from Missouri, was filled with party politics throughout, and with the most abusive epithets and coarsest ribaldry. The interests of the bank were involved in the elections—its profits depended upon its re-charter. It was the first instance in banking where a political fund had been placed under the direction of the president for any purpose. He was glad the attention of the people had been called to the subject by the Executive, and he should regret if Congress would countenance such an appropriation of its funds. He thought enough had been said to show that the bank had forfeited all claim to the advantages of the deposites, that the Secretary was justified in removing them; and having shown a legal authority in him for doing the act, he might terminate the discussion, but that it was necessary to consider certain grave and important constitutional questions which had been urged.

Mr. R. then proceeded to reply at length to the charge of the executive invasion of the legislative power over the purse—the alarming cry of the union of the purse and sword. What, he asked, was the power of the purse? It was the power of raising a fund by means of taxes, and appropriating it. In England, the sword was in the hand of the King. He had the power of declaring war, although the Parliament withheld or furnished the supplies as they pleased. It was not so here. All this was withheld from the President, and placed within the power and control of the Congress of the United States: both the purse and the sword were in Congress. Before the United States Bank was established, the Secretary of the Treasury could deposite the money *where he pleased;* and was this an encroachment on the public purse? In reply to the argument that the bank itself was the treasury, Mr. R. contended that if it were so, it was only so *sub modo*—while the Secretary choose the money should remain there. But this was a mistake. The treasury had no fixed locality—it was not a given place, but the charge and condition of keeping the moneys. The treasury was where the moneys were, in the legal custody of the Treasurer. By the act establishing the Treasury Department, the Secretary was required to furnish a true account of the moneys in the treasury, not in any one bank or particular place, but wherever they might be. What, then, he inquired, was the true effect of the removal of the deposites? Were they not in the treasury, subject to the control of the Treasurer? Were they any more out of the treasury in the State banks than in the United States Bank? And yet we were told they were in the uncontrolled power of the President of the United States, and general denunciations were uttered against the Executive for the exercise of this power, which were not justified by a sober view of the case.

Mr. R. read more at length from the opinions of Patrick Henry, part of which had been cited by Mr. Clay, to show that those opinions were not in any manner applicable to the removal of the deposites. He also adverted to the argument that the President had not only usurped the power of the purse, but had interfered with the appropriate duties of one of the departments. He said he was as much opposed to the executive power as any man, but he would always maintain the proper distribution of power made by the Constitution. Mr. R. then went into an elaborate exposition of the theory of executive power. He reverted to the debates in the convention of 1789, which formed the Constitution, to show that the members of that enlightened body were in favor of a single executive head, to whom was committed a sole and undivided responsibility; that throughout the debates it would be seen that the Constitution, and not the laws, gave the President the power of superintending and controlling the officers of Government in the performance of their duties. He read from the opinions of Mr. Jefferson, Mr. Madison, Fisher Ames, and others, expressed in various letters and public documents, proving that they considered the Chief Magistrate as responsible for the acts of all the executive departments; that this responsibility was looked to as the great security of the people; and that of consequence he possessed the unqualified power of superintending and controlling the executive departments; and that his general duty was, to see that the laws were faithfully executed, not by force, but by the intervention of the subordinate officers of Government.

Mr. EWING then took the floor, and moved an adjournment; which was carried.

IN SENATE.

Monday, *January* 20, 1834.

A message was received from the House of Representatives, by Mr. Franklin, its Clerk, stating that that House had passed several bills, the titles of which were read, and the concurrence of the Senate asked.

Mr. BIBB, from the Committee on the Judiciary, reported a bill for the relief of the executor of Stephen Morris, deceased.

Mr. FRELINGHUYSEN presented the following resolutions, passed by the Legislature of New Jersey, which were read and laid upon the table, and, on motion of Mr. HILL, were ordered to be printed:

STATE OF NEW JERSEY.

JOINT RESOLUTIONS.

Whereas the present crisis in our public affairs calls for a decided expression of the voice of the people of this State; and whereas we consider it the undoubted right of the Legislatures of the several States to instruct those who represent their interests in the councils of the nation, in all matters which intimately concern the public weal, and may affect the happiness or well being of the people: Therefore,

1. *Be it resolved by the Council and General Assembly of this State*, That while we acknowledge with feelings of devout gratitude, our obligations to the great Ruler of nations, for his mercies to us as a people, that we have been preserved alike from foreign war, from the evils of internal commotions, and the machinations of designing and ambitious men, who would prostrate the fair fabric of our Union, that we ought, nevertheless, to humble ourselves in His presence, and implore His aid for the perpetuation of our republican institutions, and for a continuance of that unexampled prosperity which our country has hitherto enjoyed

2. *Resolved*, That we have undiminished confidence in the integrity and firmness of the venerable patriot who now holds the distinguished post of Chief Magistrate of this nation, and whose purity of purpose and elevated motives have so often received the unqualified approbation of a large majority of his fellow citizens.

3. *Resolved*, That we view with agitation and alarm the existence and gigantic power of a great moneyed incorporation, which threatens to embarrass the operations of the Government, and by means of its unbounded influence upon the currency of the country, to scatter distress and ruin throughout the community, and that we therefore solemnly believe the present Bank of the United States ought not to be rechartered.

4. *Resolved*, That our Senators in Congress be instructed, and our members of the House of Representatives be requested to sustain, by their votes and influence, the course adopted by the Secretary of the Treasury, Mr. Taney, in relation to the Bank of the United States, and the deposites of the Government moneys, believing, as we do, the course of the Secretary to have been constitutional, and that the public good required its adoption.

5. *Resolved*, That the Governor be requested to forward a copy of the above resolutions to each of our Senators and Representatives from this State in the Congress of the United States.

HOUSE OF ASSEMBLY, *January* 11, 1834.

These joint resolutions having been three times read and compared in the House,

Resolved, That the same do pass.

By order of the House:

DANIEL B. RYALL,
Speaker of the House of Assembly.

IN COUNCIL, *January* 11, 1834.

These joint resolutions having been three times read in the Council,

Resolved, That the same do pass.

By order of the Council:

MAHLON DICKERSON,
Vice President of the Council.

Petitions and memorials were presented by Mr. EWING, Mr. MANGUM, Mr. CHAMBERS, Mr. GRUNDY, and Mr. WEBSTER, which were severally referred. Among them was a petition from sundry citizens of Maryland and the District of Columbia, praying that the bridge across the Eastern Branch may be made free.

The following resolution was submitted by Mr. CHAMBERS:

Resolved, That the Committee on the District of Columbia be instructed to inquire into the expediency of continuing the improvements of Pennsylvania Avenue, from the Executive offices to Georgetown.

Mr. BENTON submitted the following resolution:

Resolved, That the Secretary of the Treasury be directed to inform the Senate, provided any information in his power or possession will enable him to give the information, whether the Government directors of the Bank of the United States for the year 1833 have continued to act as directors in the year 1834.

The following resolution was submitted by Mr. WHITE:

Resolved, That the Secretary of War be, and he hereby is, requested to furnish to the Senate an estimate of the number of Indians that will probably emigrate during the *present year*, from the country now occupied by the Creeks, to the country assigned them west of the river Mississippi; and also, a detailed estimate of the sums of money which may be necessary during the present year, to comply with the various stipulations of the treaty made with the Creek Indians.

The VICE PRESIDENT laid before the Senate a communication from the Secretary of State relative to patents.

Mr. KING, of Alabama, from the Committee on Military Affairs, reported a bill for the relief of Eliza F. Hickman.

Mr. WEBSTER rose to state that he was prevented by circumstances from moving, this morning, that the Senate proceed to the consideration of Executive business, but be desired to give notice that he would do so to-morrow.

He took the present occasion to say, that a paragraph which had just appeared in a morning paper in relation to the Government directors of the United States Bank was unfounded both in law and in fact. The directors appointed last year hold over and are still in office.

Mr. WEBSTER then submitted some resolu-

tions, adopted at a meeting of citizens of Boston; which were read and referred to the Committee of Finance.

Mr. EWING having the floor upon the main question, in relation to the removal of the deposites, gave way for a short time, at the request of Mr. CALHOUN, who rose to correct Mr. RIVES, in relation to part of his speech, delivered on Friday last.

Mr. RIVES made some remarks in reply, after which,

Mr. EWING proceeded in the general debate, and after some time gave way to a motion by Mr. SMITH, to adjourn.

The Senate then adjourned.

HOUSE OF REPRESENTATIVES.

MONDAY, *January* 20, 1834.

The early part of the day was occupied with the presentation of petitions and memorials. They were chiefly of a private or local nature—embracing claims on the revolutionary pension fund, requests to have roads, &c., constructed, &c.

Among the memorials presented may be noticed one by Mr. DICKERSON, of New Jersey, complaining of the manner in which the Legislature of that State have resolved relative to the United States Bank; asserting that they had been elected pending the meeting of the topic affecting that bank by the Governor of that State, and inferring that therefore they but spoke the sentiments of a party.

Mr. CHAMBERS, of Pennsylvania, presented a memorial from the bank at Chambersburg, Pennsylvania, complaining that the pecuniary pressure had arrived at the interior of that State, and requesting relief.

Three petitions were presented, praying that Congress would adopt some means for the effectual and exemplary abolition of slavery within the District of Columbia.

The SPEAKER presented a memorial from Robert Mayo, stating that he had issued proposals to print an analytical digest of the laws of the Union; and requesting that the House would subscribe to the work.

Mr. CARR presented a memorial from the Legislature of the State of Indiana, relative to the great western mail route between Louisville, Kentucky, and St. Louis, in Missouri; which, upon his motion, was referred to the Committee on Roads and Canals.

The petition of Benjamin Roach, of Mississippi, praying permission to relinquish certain lands purchased by him at Mount Salus Land Office, and locate other lands in lieu thereof, for reasons therein stated, was referred to the Committee on Public Lands.

Mr. PLUMMER presented the petition of Silvia C. Vick, on behalf of the heirs and legal representatives of Hartwell Vick, late of the county of Warren, Mississippi, deceased, praying for the grant of two sections of land, in lieu of a tract of land purchased by said Hartwell Vick during his lifetime. Referred to the Committee on Private Land Claims, to whom was referred the petition of Hartwell Vick on the same subject.

Ordered, That the petition of the heirs of Henry King, deceased, heretofore presented to Congress, praying an allowance for money expended and services rendered as Assistant Commissioner of Issues during the revolutionary war, be referred to the Committee on Revolutionary Claims.

On motion of Mr. PLUMMER,

Resolved, That the petition and accompanying documents in support of the claim of the heirs of Elisha Winter and Sons to a tract of land granted to them by the Baron de Carondelet, Governor General of the Provinces of Louisiana and West Florida in 1797, heretofore presented to Congress, be referred to the Committee on Private Land Claims.

On motion of Mr. E. WHITE,

Resolved, That the Committee of Ways and Means be instructed to inquire into the expediency of making an appropriation for enclosing the lot of the custom-house and Federal court in New Orleans, and providing the indispensable accommodations.

On motion of Mr. McCARTY,

Resolved, That the Committee on Roads and Canals be instructed to inquire into the expediency of an appropriation in money, or a grant of lands, to be applied to the opening of a road through the public lands, from the rapids of Grand river, in Michigan Territory, by Fort Wayne, Winchester, Centreville, and Connersville, to Lawrenceburg, in Indiana; and of a like appropriation for making a road through the public lands, from Oxford, in Ohio, by Liberty, Milles, New Castle, Munceytown, and Goshen, in Indiana, to Edwardsburg, in Michigan Territory, upon the principles of a bill reported to this House, No. 241, upon this subject, at the first session of the last Congress, and that the memorials of the Legislature of Indiana, in reference to this subject, heretofore presented, and upon the files of this House, be referred to said committee.

On motion of Mr. HANNEGAN,

Resolved, That the Committee on Commerce be instructed to inquire into the expediency of making the town of Lafayette, on the Wabash river, a port of entry.

On motion of Mr. McKIM,

Resolved, That the Committee on Military Affairs be instructed to inquire into the expediency of making an appropriation for the commencement of the works of the first and second class, projected by the Board of Engineers, for the defence of the river Patapsco and the city of Baltimore.

On motion of Mr. LANE,

Resolved, That the Committee on the Post Office and Post Roads be instructed to inquire into the expediency of establishing a post route from Lawrenceburg, in the county of Dearborn, to the town of Versailles, in the county of Ripley, in the same State.

On motion of Mr. PINCKNEY,

Resolved, That the Committee on Private Land Claims be instructed to inquire into the expediency of renewing a warrant for 400 acres of land, which has been lost, and still remains unsatisfied.

On motion of Mr. WHITE, of Florida,

Resolved, That the Committee on the Judiciary be instructed to inquire into the expediency of providing, by law, for running and marking the boundary line between the State of Georgia and the Territory of Florida.

Mr. HAWES moved a call of the House. Negatived.

Mr. C. C. CLAY remarked that a call was necessary, as there did not appear to be a quorum present.

On motion of Mr. WHITE, of Florida, the message of the President respecting the disputed boundary between Florida and Georgia was referred to the Committee on the Judiciary.

Mr. PLUMMER moved to suspend the rule, in order to permit the States to be called for resolutions. Lost.

REMOVAL OF THE DEPOSITES.

The House resumed the consideration of the motion to refer the report of the Secretary of the Treasury on the deposites to the Committee of Ways and Means, the question being on the amendment submitted by Mr. JONES, as an amendment to that previously submitted by Mr. McDUFFIE, viz: to add to the motion of reference the following instructions to that committee: "Inquire 'into the expediency of depositing the revenue 'hereafter collected in the State banks in the dif'ferent States where the same is collected, in pro'portion to their respective capitals paid in, and 'to prescribe the terms on which the same shall 'be deposited, and to report by bill or other- 'wise."

Mr. SEABORN JONES, of Georgia, rose and addressed the House in support of his motion. If he had consulted his own feelings only, he would not (he said) have troubled the House at all with his views on this question, but he felt it to be a duty which he owed his constituents. He had not the vanity to believe that anything which he could offer would induce any gentlemen to change their opinion, but he hoped that the facts and principles which he should bring before them would persuade those whose minds were not finally made up to

conform their opinions to those facts and principles. He could not say with the gentleman from Virginia who preceded him, [Mr. Moore,] that he belonged to no party. He did belong to a party which the President is supposed to have prostrated in the dust. He had belonged also to the Jefferson party, which produced the glorious political revolution in this country. He belonged to that State Rights party which was said to be prostrated in the dust, but which, like Antæus, had arisen from the earth with fresh strength for the struggle. The Proclamation he considered as akin in principle to the alien and sedition laws, and fraught with the most high-toned federal sentiments. But what the gentleman disapproved in the President he (Mr. Jones) entirely approved—the veto of the bill renewing the bank charter. This act was the brightest plume in the crown of the President's glory. He had magnanimously thrown himself into the breach, and won the approbation of posterity. It was not his belief that the Government was intended to act upon the States. He referred to the fable of the wind and sun striving which would strip the traveller of his cloak. The wind blew, but served only to induce the traveller to wrap his cloak the closer around him. The sun's mild rays soon overcame him, and induced him voluntarily to lay aside what could not be forced from him. The moral he drew from this was, that the Government of the United States should only be felt in kindness by the States. Thus much he was compelled to say to show wherein he agreed and disagreed with the gentleman from Virginia. Before he proceeded to discuss the question in the manner he had proposed to himself, he would ask leave to attend to a few of the preliminary remarks of the gentleman from Pennsylvania, [Mr. Binney.] The gentleman informed us that but a short time ago, from the influence of the United States Bank, the country was in a state of unparalleled prosperity; commerce, agriculture, and manufactures, were all flourishing. But suddenly, as if touched by the magic wand of a wizard, all this prosperity disappeared; and fortunate for the country was it, in Mr. Jones's opinion, that the country was so touched.

Under the Circean enchantments of the bank, the country enjoyed a fleeting and delusive prosperity. But suddenly the spell was dissolved, and we had awakened to the sober realities of our situation. We found ourselves slaves; and those to whom the bank belongs we found to be our lords and masters. He would read a few remarks made by a man who was now gone, but who would long live in the veneration of his country, (Mr. John Randolph,) in his speech on granting the original charter of this bank. He then read from that speech a passage in which Mr. Randolph remarks, that if he must have a master, he would have something that he could respect. He would prefer a master with epaulettes to one with a quill behind his ear. We were told by the gentleman from Pennsylvania, that if the bank was engaged in political schemes, if it aided in putting forth scurrilous publications against the President, he would be ready to join in the denunciation of the institution. Without stopping to inquire whether those charges were true or not, he would ask the gentleman how far, in that case, he would join in the denunciation. Would he simply say to the bank, this is your only offence, and we will therefore overlook it for the sake of the good you have done? or would he join us in punishing the bank for malversation? Another observation of the gentleman from Pennsylvania did credit to his understanding and his heart; he referred to the remark that, if the bank was not to be rechartered, nor one like it, the deposites might as well be removed now as some time hence; that the bank and the country were as well prepared for the removal now as they ever would be. Mr. J. hoped that no consideration of the convenience of the bank to the country in carrying on exchange, nor any reasons whatever would induce us to recharter the bank. If the bank was not to be rechartered, this was the best time that could be taken, he believed, for removing the deposites; and he would admit that if the bank was to be rechartered, this was a proper time to restore the deposites. The restoration and the recharter was one and the same question; for if we restored the deposites, it would be vain to resist the recharter. He therefore attacked the measure at the threshold. He would defend the outposts, and then he would know that the citadel was safe. He here called the attention of the House to the figures and calculations of the gentleman, which were produced by that gentleman for the purpose of showing the magnitude of the operations of the bank; and showed, at some length, that the sum of the operations was greatly exaggerated by the enumeration of the same operation several times. He then passed to the argument urged by the gentleman from Pennsylvania in favor of the course taken by the bank to meet the payment of the deposites. He tells us that the bank was obliged to keep its specie to sustain its circulation. What was that circulation? Only eighteen millions; less than double the amount of the specie retained in the vaults of the bank. Now, he recollected that the president of the bank said, on oath, when the paper circulation was twenty-two millions, that five millions of specie was sufficient to sustain it, and hence the bank had sent a part of its specie to Europe. He believed, with Mr. Biddle, five or six millions in specie was sufficient to support a currency of twenty-two millions: and he could not believe that it now required ten millions to sustain a currency of eighteen. He thought, therefore, that the bank had not acted solely with a view to self-defence. We are told that the industry of the country must stop unless the deposites be restored. But there were other causes which had, in his opinion, contributed more to the general distress than the removal of the deposites. The cash payment of duties, added to the reduction of the currency by the bank, was sufficient to account for the pressure upon the money market. We are told, from high authority, that another cause was, the want of confidence in the stability of the present state of things. Who created this uncertainty, but the advocates of the restoration of the deposites? The capital exists, whether in one bank or another, and every one knows that the State banks are willing to lend money on their deposites. Could any bank do more?

Mr. J. perfectly agreed in the opinion that want of confidence in the permanence of the present state of things, was the main cause of the continuance of the pressure. Let this House act, then, and confidence will be restored. Let this House declare that the deposites shall remain where they are.

Mr. J. said he would call the attention of the House to the nature of the contract made with the bank; and, in answer to an argument put by Mr. Moore, of Virginia, contended, from the conduct of Mr. Secretary Dallas, that it was no part of the bargain between the Government and the bank, that the bonus of $1,500,000 was paid as a consideration for the bank having any right to the public deposites. It appeared, that in 1815, a communication had been made by the President to Congress, on the subject of the currency; in consequence of which a committee was raised, having at its head Mr. J. C. Calhoun. After some deliberation, as to what remedy should be applied to restore the currency to a sound state, the committee came to the conclusion that it was necessary for that purpose to establish a Bank of the United States, and the chairman was directed by the committee to ascertain the opinions of Mr. Dallas, whose financial abilities were duly estimated. Mr. Calhoun accordingly addressed him a letter, requesting information; to which his reply was given immediately, with that opinion upon the six following points, viz: On the amount of capital necessary for the bank; its government, privileges, and duties; organization; the bonus to be paid for granting the charter; and, lastly, such measures as should be taken by Government to aid in the establishment of the institution. For the present, it was not necessary for him to refer to more than what was stated in the opinion in reference to the bonus. Upon this, Mr. D. expressly stated "that 'it was to be paid for the exclusive privileges to 'be granted to the stockholders for the space of 'twenty years;" and there was nothing in it to warrant a supposition that the right to the deposites was one of the considerations for which the bonus was paid. They were rather considered as an incidental benefit; for further on, with a prophetic eye as to futurity, it would be seen that he had expressly stated that the deposites were absolutely, and almost in terms, excluded from being so considered, for he includes, amongst others, as advantages to be derived from the bank, the collection and transfer of the public revenue, and that of the keeping of the deposites; and there was no claim of right, therefore, as to them, inserted in the charter, although there was a clause by which the bank was bound to transfer the public money as the exigencies of the Government should make it necessary. It might be asked, in reference to this obligation to transfer, how could the money be transferred, if there was not thereby an implied obligation that the deposites had been previously secured? But he thought that this could be effected by the Secretary of the Treasury—in whom the control lay, and wanting such a transfer much—presenting a check on the State banks for that purpose, and that the Bank of the United States were bound, under their stipulations, to make the transfer. He, and everybody who knew Mr. Calhoun, would acknowledge the keenness and accuracy with which he understood these matters, and it was clear that he had not thought that the deposites were a part of the bargain for which the bonus was paid, or it would have been inserted in the charter. From this omission, he argued at length, that the bank had not, by the contract, any right to them, and contended that they would not have been named in the charter at all, if Congress had not, in their discretion, by a subsequent clause, determined that they should put some limit to the power given by them to the Secretary of the Treasury. It was admitted by the advocates for the bank, that the Secretary had the right to remove the deposites upon the failure of the bank, in complying with their stipulation to transfer, or to pay over the public money when demanded. But if the objection to the Secretary's acting was closely canvassed, it would appear from this that he could not act, until after the commission of an act by which the charter itself was violated: for how was he to ascertain that the depository was unsafe until he had established it by proof? Mr. Webster, who drew the clause in the charter, never understood that the bank had the right to hold the deposites until proof had been made that they were in an unsafe institution, or he would have used other language than he did. He could not assent to the doctrine that the Secretary was bound to satisfy the bank for the exercise of the power of removal vested in him by the charter, for the Secretary was only bound to satisfy the representatives of the people; and if they were satisfied, that was sufficient for him, as it would be altogether useless for him to endeavor to satisfy the bank that the deposites ought to be removed from it. He trusted that they would come to the conclusion that he did, that the Secretary had the right to exercise this power, in pursuance of the discretion vested in him, and that the reasons rendered by him for so doing were sufficient. He contended that there were other reasons than those admitted by the friends of the bank, which would justify the action of the Secretary, and these were, whenever the bank should do any act having a tendency to injure the Government; to destroy the purity of election; prevent the Government of its due influence, or sought to make unconscionable gains at its expense; and above all, when the interest of the people should require it. To sustain his views as to the construction of the charter, he called the attention of the House to the recorded opinions of Mr. Secretary Crawford, in 1817, 1818, and 1823, on this subject, as he was, if not the ablest, certainly inferior to none of his predecessors or successors in office, and he felt it a high gratification, as he had been the friend of his boyhood, as well as of his maturer years, to find that he was quoted on all sides, as one of their ablest financiers. These opinions, as to the power of the Secretary and upon the constitutional law, had been so recently given, it was not necessary for him to do more than remind the House of them. Mr. Crawford was not alone in his opinions, for they found Mr. Secretary Ingham had reiterated the same opinions, and that he told the bank, if they should interfere with the Government, or with the elections, that he would exercise the power now claimed. He told Mr. Biddle in terms, if the bank entered the political arena, he would exercise the power placed in his hands. Did Mr. Biddle then deny that right? Not at all. It had been urged that this power vested in the Secretary was too great; that a *scire*

facias ought to have been issued, &c. But on referring to the report of 1819, presented by the committee, of which Mr. Spencer of New York was chairman, to inquire into the malversation of the bank at that time, they would find, that after the various matters had been enumerated, the conclusion was substantially "that the bank had violated its charter, that it was unnecessary to issue a *scire facias*, as the powers vested in the Secretary of the Treasury were fully sufficient, if the stockholders of the bank, or the directors thereof, should not correct the evils then charged against it." Thus Congress had then thought, and they had the other precedents of Secretary Crawford and of Secretary Ingham to sustain the same opinion.

Mr. J. next called the attention of the House to the statement made, that one reason why the old Bank of the United States was not rechartered was, that it was interfering in politics, and thus had been denied; but his friend, the member from Tennessee, [Mr. Polk,] had only urged that it had been suspected of this. He would now remark, that if it were innocent, they had the highest possible authority to satisfy them that these suspicions were correct; for Mr. Clay, upon his going home, after voting for the chartering of the present bank, had expressly stated to his constituents, that one of the considerations which induced him not to sustain it was, that it had abused its powers, and had sought to subserve the views of a political party; which charges, though denied by its friends, were yet, in his judgment, fully borne out; and the member from Pennsylvania [Mr. Binney] would have, therefore, the opportunity afforded him, either of denying the charge, or joining, as he asserted he would do, in its denunciation. Mr. J. was proceeding, when he gave way, at the suggestion of

Mr. POLK, who submitted a motion to adjourn; which prevailed.

IN SENATE.

Tuesday, January 21, 1834.

A message was received from the President of the United States, by Mr. Donelson, his Private Secretary.

The VICE PRESIDENT communicated a report from the Secretary of State, responsive to the resolution of Mr. Poindexter, calling for a statement of the articles deposited in that department, which had been received as presents by our foreign functionaries. The report was read, referred to the Committee on Foreign Relations, on motion of Mr. Wilkins, and ordered to be printed. A few minutes afterwards,

Mr. POINDEXTER rose, and hoped that no notice of the report would be taken upon the journals. He asked that the report and accompanying documents would be returned to the department; it was not made in compliance with the resolution. The resolution asked this information of the Executive, and there was a discrepancy in the proceedings, by reason of the response coming from another quarter. He hoped no notice would be taken of the report.

Mr. KING, of Alabama, and Mr. FORSYTH, made a few remarks in reply to Mr. POINDEXTER; when the latter gentlemen intimated that his object had been achieved by the information asked for being furnished; and that if any Senator objected, he would not press the matter.

Mr. FORSYTH: I object.

Mr. POINDEXTER: Then, sir, I withdraw the motion.

The VICE PRESIDENT laid before the Senate a communication from the Commissioner of the Land Office, relative to private land claims.

Mr. TIPTON, from the Committee on Military Affairs; Mr. BELL, from the Committee of Claims, Mr. HENDRICKS, from the same committee; Mr. BROWN, from the same committee; Mr. POINDEXTER, from the Committee of Private Land Claims; Mr. WRIGHT, from the Committee of Claims; and Mr. BENTON, from the Committee on Military Affairs;—made reports upon various private bills and petitions.

Memorials and petitions, generally of a private nature, were presented by Messrs. McKEAN, TIPTON, BENTON, and BIBB; which were generally, without reading, referred to the usual committees.

The resolution submitted by Mr. Knight, on Thursday, relative to the engraving and printing a chart of Narraganset Bay, being under consideration,

Mr. KNIGHT stated, that since he had offered the resolution, he had understood that the chart had been engraved, and he asked to modify it so as to call for the printing of 1000 copies.

Mr. FORSYTH remarked that this was certainly a small affair, but he would at least like to know for what purpose this multiplication of copies was desired.

Mr. KNIGHT replied, that Narraganset Bay was in the public eye as a naval station. A survey had been made with that intention. It was a place of very great interest, and the object of the resolution was to give everybody an opportunity of examining the subject, and estimating the advantages of Narraganset Bay. He wished to convince the public of the strong claims which this bay had upon the notice of the Government and the people.

Mr. FORSYTH objected to the proposition, as involving an expense without a commensurate advantage.

Mr. ROBBINS remarked, that Narraganset Bay possessed preeminent advantages as a naval station. It was superior to any other site on the whole Atlantic frontier. It was better calculated as a depot and station from whence to wage a maritime offensive or defensive warfare, than any other part of the coast. As a station, it was not only calculated to repel invasion, but to furnish facilities to carry the war into the enemy's waters —to drive him back to his own channels. It was a station calculated to reduce the expense of a naval war at least one-half. The cost of printing was trifling: a knowledge of the bay of great importance.

Mr. FORSYTH said that he was really ashamed to rise again, but he could not conceive that any good would arise by an expenditure of three or four hundred dollars for printing additional copies of a chart, when all who had occasion to examine it could be furnished at any time. These repeated calls for printing involved in the aggregate heavy expenditures. He could not conceive that any public benefit would be derived from the adoption of this resolution, and consequently he should vote against it.

The resolution was adopted—ayes 23, noes not counted.

Mr. WEBSTER moved to take up the bill making appropriations, in part, for the support of Government for the year 1834.

Mr. W. remarked, that the bill, when it passed the House, contained a provision restricting the Senate in the expenditure of the contingent fund, to its ordinary expenses, and not to the purchase or publication of any books, maps, charts, &c.; and that not a dollar could be expended, under that provision, for any thing but their ordinary printing business. He thought the Senate ought to be allowed the privilege of using their contingent fund at their pleasure, and he therefore moved to adhere to the amendment.

Mr. FORSYTH thought the restriction imposed by the House a very necessary one. Very great abuses had certainly taken place in the expenditure of the contingent fund. It had been frequently appropriated to the purchase and publication of books of any kind, whether good or bad, if the owners of them could induce a friend to make the motion, believing they were good and useful. He recollected, and mentioned several instances of such expenditure, and even now there was an annual appropriation of $2,500 for purchasing Gales & Seaton's Register of Debates, as long as they might choose to publish them. He thought there was no other way to prevent these abuses but by agreeing to the restriction imposed by the House.

Mr. KANE thought the question was not whether the Senate acted unwisely in the expenditure of the contingent fund, but whether this body, having ordered certain printing, should pay for it. He agreed with the gentleman from Massachusetts that the Senate ought to insist on their amendment.

Mr. KING, of Alabama, was of a different opinion. It was certain there had hitherto been a disposition to squander the contingent fund. The same provision had been introduced into similar

bills some years ago, and was a very proper one. We had the law before us for our government, and why had we ordered this printing? He was in favor of the course pursued by the House.

Mr. WEBSTER viewed the question as affecting the relative rights of the two Houses; it was not in true taste to be in controversy on this act, object. To restrict the Senate thus, was to impugn the very idea of a contingent fund. Such a fund was, by its terms, to be used as the Senate might think fit.

Mr. POINDEXTER moved that the question be taken by yeas and nays, which were ordered, and are as follow:

YEAS—Messrs. Bell, Bibb, Black, Calhoun, Chambers, Clay, Ewing, Frelinghuysen, Hendricks, Kane, Kent, Knight, Linn, McKean, Mangum, Moore, Naudain, Poindexter, Porter, Prentiss, Preston, Robbins, Robinson, Silsbee, Smith, Southard, Sprague, Swift, Tipton, Tomlinson, Tyler, Waggaman, Webster, and Wilkins—34.

NAYS—Messrs. Benton, Brown, Forsyth, Grundy, Hill, King of Alabama, King of Georgia, Morris, Rives, Shepley, Tallmadge, White, and Wright—13.

The special order of the day (Mr. Clay's resolution) was then called up, when

Mr. CLAY continued his remarks until about half past two o'clock, when he gave way to Mr. WEBSTER, for a motion to proceed to Executive business. After the consideration of which,

The Senate adjourned.

HOUSE OF REPRESENTATIVES.

Tuesday, January 21, 1834.

Mr. WHITTLESEY, of Ohio, reported a bill for the relief of John Bruce.

Mr. BLAIR, of Massachusetts, a bill for the relief of Colonel George Gibson.

Mr. WARDWELL, a bill for extending the provisions of an act, supplemental to an act for the benefit of the surviving officers and soldiers of the Revolution.

Mr. CHINN, a bill to organize the several Fire Companies in the District of Columbia.

Mr. HAMER, a bill for the relief of Mr. P. Mix.

Mr. LEAVITT, a bill authorizing the surrender of certain bounty lands by soldiers of the Revolution, that they might locate on others in lieu thereof, and for other purposes.

Mr. McKIM, a bill authorizing the continuance of the Cumberland road to Indiana and Illinois, and for its repairs, &c. Also, a bill for the relief of Tuffs & Clark.

Mr. SELDEN, a bill for the relief of Stephen Kingston.

Mr. BINNEY, a bill supplemental to the act passed for the relief of certain insolvent debtors of the United States.

Mr. REED, of Massachusetts, a bill for the relief of Commodore Isaac Hull.

Mr. LOYALL, a bill for the relief of Humphry B. Gwathmey.

All which bills were severally read twice and committed.

Mr. CLAY reported a bill for the relief of Asa Hartfield; which was read twice, and ordered to be engrossed for its third reading to-morrow.

The SPEAKER presented the annual report from the State Department of the patents for inventions taken out, and of those which had expired in 1832; which was laid on the table.

Mr. BEARDSLEY obtained leave of the House to submit the following resolution, which lies on the table one day for consideration:

Resolved, That the Secretary of the Treasury be directed to inform this House what amount of money had been received into the treasury on the before the 30th of September, 1833, as proceeds of lands embraced in the Louisiana purchase, of which had been sold by the United States, exhibiting also a statement of payments from the treasury for roads or other improvements within the limits of said purchase; also, exhibiting the amount of payments by the United States for or upon any debts or claims to lands within said purchase; also, payments and expenditures to extinguish any Indian rights to such lands; also, payments to commissioners, officers, &c., who have been employed in the management and sale of lands within said purchase, &c., so as to exhibit

clearly the receipts and expenditures (except the original purchase money) for said lands so purchased by the United States to the day aforesaid; also, similar information concerning the lands embraced in the Florida purchase.

Mr. JOHN Q. ADAMS submitted the following resolution; which lies one day on the table:

Resolved, That the President of the United States be requested to cause to be laid before this House, if not inconsistent with the public interest, a copy of the instructions of Richard Rush, Envoy Extraordinary and Minister Plenipotentiary to the Court of Great Britain, of the 6th of November, 1817; and also a copy of the instructions referred to in his message of the 6th instant, forbidding all the ministers and agents of the United States abroad to accept in future, unless previously authorized by Congress, presents of any description, from any foreign State, under any circumstances.

THE PENSION LAWS.

The order of the day was then declared to be the resolution of Mr. CHILTON, to appoint a select committee to inquire into the expediency of so extending the general pension law, as to embrace within its provisions those persons who were engaged in the Indian wars down to the year 1794, and the amendment of it, by Mr. BOULDIN, to appoint a committee to inquire into the moral effects of the pension system upon the community, and how far it ought to be abolished or repealed.

Mr. PEYTON rose and said: Mr. Speaker, I intended to have made my acknowledgments to the honorable gentleman from Rhode Island, [Mr. BRIGGS,] for a kindness which others have so often received at his hands before. But, sir, that gentleman is not in his seat—he was not there yesterday morning—and I have no remarks to make. The *absent* and the *dead—nature's bourne* and *ocean's waves*, alike with *me*, afford a sacred shield.

Mr. HARDIN said he did not understand the history of the Indian wars in the manner in which it was understood by the gentleman from Rhode Island. Those wars were the most desperate and bloody which history recorded, and continued, without intermission, from 1778 to 1794. He went into a recital of some of the principal events of those wars, and allowed that they were connected with the war of the Revolution, and grew out of the hostility of the Indian allies of Great Britain.

These were not the petty conflicts which the gentleman from Rhode Island supposed them to be. Mr. H. passed a high eulogium on the character of the Kentucky militia, as exhibited in the Indian wars and during the late war with Great Britain. When the Governor of Rhode Island, with an army of fifteen men, was hesitating whether he could constitutionally take the field or not, the venerable Governor of Kentucky was facing the enemy with two thousand of the bravest and best of the sons of Kentucky: no constitutional scruples were felt there. The gentleman from Rhode Island deemed it a reproach to take the spoils of his vanquished foe. He had taken the idea from the story of Ajax and Ulysses, but had forgotten the part which best applied to the case. The Grecian generals awarded the arms to Ulysses, and left the old vaunting chief in mortification and despair. Mr. H. greatly regretted that this subject should be attempted to be turned into ridicule. The people of the West have as strong claims to pensions as any in America. He repeated, that they bore a part in the revolutionary war, and were entitled to the same consideration with those who fought on the east side of the mountains. The gentleman from South Carolina [Mr. PINCKNEY] contended that the whole pension system was unconstitutional. Was it unconstitutional to pay men who are engaged in the land and naval service of the United States? If they are wounded in service, is it unconstitutional to pension them? If they die in service, is it unconstitutional to give half-pay for five or ten years to their widows? Certainly not; and for the same reasons it is not unconstitutional to pension those who have rendered military services. The military pension system was dictated by sound national policy. He would never pension officers who were engaged in civil service. When a man is ordered to storm a battery or scale a fort, if he knows that it is unconstitutional for the Government to provide for his wife and family, if he falls, or for himself, if he is wounded, his courage and ardor are damped. But if the Government says to him, Go on, we will be a father to your family, and take care of you, he has no longer any hesitation, and braves death without dismay. He hoped never to see the time when we should be such sticklers for the Constitution that we could do nothing of a useful or practical kind. Some remarks had been made as to the probable number of the persons who would be entitled to pensions under the proposed measure. The number of those engaged at different times in the wars with the Indians did not exceed twenty thousand, and of these not more than three or five thousand could now be alive; but this was a subject proper for the inquiry of a committee.

A message was received from the Senate, informing the House that the Senate *adhered* to their amendment to the bill making appropriations, in part, for the support of the Government.

REMOVAL OF THE DEPOSITES.

The House resumed the consideration of the motion to refer the report of the Secretary of the Treasury on the deposites to the Committee of Ways and Means—the question being on the amendment submitted by Mr. JONES, as an amendment to that previously submitted by Mr. MCDUFFIE, viz: to add to the motion for reference the following instructions to that committee: "Inquire into the expediency of depositing the revenue hereafter collected in the State banks in the different States, where the same is collected, in proportion to their respective capitals paid in, and to prescribe the terms on which the same shall be deposited; and to report by bill or otherwise."

Mr. JONES, of Georgia, resumed his remarks.

He read some extracts from the speech of Mr. Clay against the recharter of the old bank, showing that Mr. Clay was satisfied that the charges made against the old bank of abuse of power, and oppressive conduct, had been fairly made out. Whether the bank was obnoxious to these charges was not now the question; but there was sufficient proof of their truth to satisfy the honorable member, whose remarks he had read. Mr. J. then passed to the manner in which the transfer drafts were made, and expressed the opinion that the Secretary of the Treasury ought to have apprised the bank of the existence of the drafts, in the weekly lists, and to have stated the contingency upon which they would be presented.

From the circumstances of the times—the payment of duties in cash, the transfers, and the curtailments of discounts made by the bank—great distress had befallen the community. It was his opinion that the removal of the deposites ought to have been made at an earlier period. The time chosen was unfortunate, and he believed they could have been removed at an earlier period, without embarrassment to the public, had the President acted with less forbearance towards the predecessor of the present Secretary of the Treasury. Mr. Jones here read a passage from the Secretary's report, showing the reasons which governed him in fixing upon the time of removal. He says—

"It was impossible that the commercial community could have sustained itself much longer under such a policy. In the two succeeding months, the collections of the bank would probably have exceeded five millions more, and the State banks would have been obliged to curtail in an equal sum. The reduction of bank accommodations to the amount of nineteen millions of dollars in four months, must have almost put an end to trade; and before the 1st of October this pressure in the principal commercial cities had become so intense, that it could not have been endured much longer without the most serious embarrassments. It was then daily increasing; and from the best information that I have been able to obtain, I am persuaded that if the public moneys received for revenue had continued to be deposited in the Bank of the United States for two months longer, and it had adhered to the oppressive system of policy which it pursued during the two preceding months, a widespread scene of bankruptcy and ruin must have followed. There was no alternative, therefore, for the Treasury Department, but to act at once, or abandon the object altogether. Duties of the highest character would not permit the latter course, and I did not hesitate promptly to resort to the former.

"I have stated the condition of the mercantile classes at the time of the removal, to explain why it was impossible to postpone it even for a short period. Under other circumstances, I should have been disposed to direct the removal to take effect at a distant day, so as to give Congress an opportunity of prescribing, in the meantime, the places of deposite, and of regulating the security proper to be taken."

In reply to these views, the gentleman from Pennsylvania has furnished us with the reasons which rendered necessary the curtailments made by the bank. He would inquire how far these reasons were sufficient for the curtailments. He had before him a statement of the specie possessed by the bank for a course of several years, and of the circulation and discounts of the bank for the same periods. From this it appeared that, in 1824, the bank had six millions in specie, of bills in circulation eleven millions, and of discounts thirty-three millions; in 1825, the bank had in specie six millions, bills eleven millions, and discounts thirty-three millions; in 1826, specie three millions, bills sixteen millions, and discounts thirty-three millions; in 1827, specie six millions, bills seventeen millions, and discounts thirty-one millions; in 1828, specie five millions, bills twenty-two millions, and discounts thirty-five millions; in 1829, specie six millions, bills thirteen millions, discounts thirty-nine millions; in 1830, bills fifteen millions, discounts forty-four millions; in 1831, bills eighteen millions, discounts forty-four millions; in 1832, specie six millions, bills twenty-four millions, discounts sixty-seven millions; and in 1833, specie ten millions, bills eighteen millions, discounts seventy millions. He called the attention to the continual increase of discounts shown by this statement. He would also direct the attention of the House to the fact, that six millions in specie were, in 1832, deemed sufficient to sustain a paper circulation of twenty-four millions; and that in 1833, with ten millions in specie, and bills amounting only to eighteen millions, the bank deems it necessary to curtail her discounts in order to sustain the credit of her circulation. The directors probably know well what to do in this matter, but they ought to give us better reasons for their acts.

Mr. J. now proceeded to consider the reasons offered by the Secretary of the Treasury for his act, and he did not entertain a doubt that he could fully demonstrate the efficiency of those reasons. But here he met the objection that these were not the reasons of the Secretary of the Treasury, but of the President, and that the Secretary had no more to do with them than the iron pen with which he wrote the order. This, he thought, did injustice to the Secretary, and it was a matter of surprise to him that the gentleman from South Carolina, who was so well acquainted with the subject, should have assumed such a position in regard to the act of the Secretary. He was no apologist for the Secretary, but he was free to award censure where it was due, and praise where it was deserved. Mr. Duane tells us that the President, when on his eastern trip, transmitted to him four written opinions on the subject of the removal of the deposites, which opinions he had demanded from his Cabinet.

Mr. McDUFFIE rose to explain. He knew that the Secretary honestly entertained the opinions on which he acted. If the gentleman would look at his speech, he would find what his views were on this subject. His idea was, that when the President turns out one officer who will not obey his will, and puts in another who is willing to obey his will, the President is the author of the act which he has in view, no matter whether the officer deems the act legal and expedient or not.

Mr. JONES was happy, he continued, that he had afforded the gentleman from South Carolina an opportunity to make this explanation. Lest any one should misunderstand the subject, he would read Mr. Duane's published statement of the opinions expressed by the members of the Cabinet. The character of Mr. Taney placed him above the suspicion that he would prefer office to duty. The President had no right to exercise such control as to force his Ministers to agree with him; but where they disagreed on vital principles,

it was the President's duty and right to remove them. The Secretaries were not responsible to us, but to the President, and the President was responsible to the people and to the representatives of the people. In support of this position, Mr. J. read several passages from the debates in Congress on the organization of the departments.

If the President is responsible for the due execution of the laws, it is necessary that those under him should be responsible to him for the manner in which those laws are executed, as he may direct or judge best. The principles in which the laws are executed, should be alike maintained by all in subordination to the executive government; and these principles are based on opinions. The President is therefore in a sensible degree affected by the opinions of those under him concerning the mode of executing the laws; and more so, concerning whether the law should or not have its proper efficacy. Having nominated his subordinates, he is responsible for their conduct in office. He has therefore properly a control over their opinions, relative to the duties of their station; and has the power of removal for a contradiction of opinion; for it would beget a contrariety of action. And if he has thus constitutionally the power of removing whole gangs of those in office under him, who can deny him the power of removing one?

He will merely put the case instanced by Mr. Calhoun. Suppose, that instead of the Secretary of the Treasury being opposed to the removal of the deposites, and the President determined in favor of them, that the Secretary of the Treasury was as determinedly in favor of their being removed, while the President was decided against such a measure: are there any of the opposite party declaiming now in favor of the bank, who would not exult at the proper exercise of the constitutional power vested in the President, of removing one so opposed in opinion and practice, because such a measure would be coincident with their own interests or views? There are, therefore, more spectacles to be found than those of Major Jack Downing; which, when turned on the patent screws, will enable their user to see things adversely from reality; to view in bold relief objects discernible only in perspective; to observe black things as white; and all as they would be desired, not as they in reality exist. We need not go to England for these patent spectacles; for they are to be found on the floor of the House.

But it had been alleged as dangerous that the Government should hold purse and sword, and asserted, that having already the sword, the Executive, by this removal of the deposites, would obtain such a control over the treasury as to possess also the purse. The former part of this assertion has been amply disproved by the gentleman [Mr. Beardsley] from New York, who has shown that not the executive but the legislative branch of the Government possesses virtually and actually the sword; for it possesses the command of the army and navy and their equipment, the power to declare war and make peace, the right to raise taxes and make appropriations; all which are properly the duties of that part of any government which can properly be said to possess the sword of the nation. And as to that part of the assertion which insinuates that the Executive becomes possessed of the purse of the nation, by ordering the transfer of the deposites from one place to another, it is equally nugatory or invalid; because the transfer from the United States Bank to a State bank is no greater in its effects than the transfer from the United States Bank to one of its branches, or from one branch bank to another—indeed, no more than changing the deposites from one side of the vaults of the banks to another. And why? The Executive can make no demand for expenditure on the deposites, wherever situated, without a definite appropriation by Congress. Thus Congress possesses in reality both the purse and the sword of the nation. So that the argument concerning the power of the White House of the Executive, more properly belongs to the White House of Congress. There is no evil to be apprehended from the power of the former, till the power of the latter be invoked into exertion. The loaded ass of Philip was never able to enter the walls of a Grecian city, till those within were prepared to receive him. The heads of any department will not be capable of succeeding in any contemplated plan of violating the Constitution, till the people themselves become corrupted. So was it in every Republic of any age. The Republics of Greece and Rome maintained their pristine vigor till the people became corrupted, and deadened to a sense of their own degradation. Cæsar was not able to seize the treasury of Rome, till the people cried "All hail!"

The Executive will be unfaithful in the discharge of the trust conferred on him by the public, if he does not see practised what he judges best. If any Secretary, whether of the treasury or of any department, disagrees with the President, it is then a duty which he owes no less to the country than to himself, to turn that Secretary out of office. Let the case be thus illustrated: Suppose this country was again involved in war with England, and that the British troops were landed in this country; suppose that the bank had agreed to loan largely to the commissary of that army, and that this fact became known to the Executive, would it not be the duty of the President to order that no public funds should continue deposited in the vaults of the bank, in order to be so applied to aid and abet, comfort and convenience, the arms of the common enemy? If then the Secretary of the Treasury should depend on the power with which it is alleged the charter arms him, of judging of and for himself, concerning the expediency of removing these deposites, and should in consequence persist in refusing to order any transfer, would he not be guilty of misprision of treason, by free consent, and subject to impeachment?

The honorable gentleman next adverted to the sufficiency of the various reasons adduced by the Secretary of the Treasury as having induced him to order the removal of the deposites, in answer to the arguments by Mr. Binney and others. He dwelt first on the transaction of the bank relative to the purchase and deferring of the three per cents, although it was expected the Government would redeem that debt. He asserted that the bank was responsible for what its agent had done, particularly when that agent was General Cadwalader, who was intimate with the relations and designs of the bank—was himself a director; and had even been a president *pro tem.* of the bank. Not till the public indignation was roused by the publication of the circular of the Barings of London, did the bank think proper to disavow the proceedings. To disavow afterwards the proceedings of an agent is no uncommon occurrence in commercial as well as political transactions. He instanced that of passing over the Florida line, and seizing the towns of St. Marks and Pensacola; and when the Spanish Ambassador complained of the trespass, it was found convenient to disavow it, and to throw the weight of the responsibility on the agent. So was the disavowal in the case of the three per cents; and a similar instance occurred during the existence of the old bank, in a substitution of two millions of debt for another two millions of a different kind, which the Secretary claimed the right of redeeming. This latter was a feasible objection against the former bank; the present charge is therefore tenable against the present bank.

He instanced next the interference in elections, and referred to cases before quoted by Mr. Polk, of Tennessee.

The loans of the bank to different individuals connected with the public press, formed his next topic of animadversion. These loans, he said, were given without any specification as to time or security, to responsibility or manner, and given evidently to sustain the interests of the bank, and to an undefined amount, larger than was required. [The honorable gentleman here quoted the items specified in the report of the Secretary of the Treasury of the amount of discounts of the bank on the 31st December, 1830, ($42,403,404) and that in 1831, ($63,026,452) and compared it with that in the May following, ($70,000,000,) to prove that the bank had extravagantly enlarged its discounts at the time the President delivered his message counter to its being re-chartered; and this was only four years before its charter was expected to expire. He compared the account of the Secretary with that given by the bank itself, in the report of its directors, and showed that the actual increase in the amount of the loans at that period was at an average of seven millions for four months. He also demonstrated that as in February and March, '32, the amount of specie was six millions, and of currency twenty-four millions, and the present amount of specie ten millions, and of currency only eighteen, that the withdrawing of the discounts of the difference between the present circulation and the sixty-three or seventy millions, was the real cause of the distress—not removing of the deposites.

He touched cursorily on the topic of the bank having published some documents, &c., which had been ordered to be printed and circulated by Congress, because they contained reports favorable to that institution. This he considered a gratuitous and uncalled-for act, and that it was evidently an exertion of electioneering policy in favor of having granted a new charter. Whoever does not perceive in the transaction testimony sufficient to warrant such a conclusion, requires more evidence than would satisfy him.

Mr. J. then discussed the topic of concealing the affairs of the bank from the Government directors. This was faintly denied by the other bank directors, but fully admitted and justified by the gentleman from Pennsylvania, [Mr. Binney.] Here Mr. J. quoted the discussion in Congress at the time of appointing Government directors of the bank, to prove it was deemed then essential that a national bank should be for national interests, and be controlled by the Government of the nation; and to prove it could not properly subserve public interests if its affairs or administrations were kept close. Yet have the Government directors been excluded not only from all participation in the management of the bank, but have had its proceedings studiously concealed from them. The whole executive power of the directors has devolved upon the committee of exchange, who have intrusted to them an irresponsible power. For even Mr. Biddle himself, when examined, confessed that that committee need not necessarily report its proceedings to the board of directors. They had power to order loans without regard to length of time or security, when and to whom they pleased; and hence they were enabled to discount notes of hand for Webb and for Burrows, for Noah and for others; to grant facilities as they judged advantageous to secure the advocacy of those connected with the public press; and to do so in a manner not tolerated in any other instance by any banks. Yet all these notes were duly recognised by the executive committee; and even Mordecai Noah's authorized, though unendorsed by Burrows, as it should have been. But this was in contemplation of a renewal of the charter, done precisely at the period necessary to influence the public mind when the President delivered his message disapproving of the re-charter.

He disproved the allegation of Mr. Binney relative to the power of any corporation to delegate its authority to others. This delegation is partial, not entire. If the board of directors institute general rules for the administration of the bank, the committee cannot run counter to these rules. If the board decree that all transactions shall be submitted to a quorum of seven, and that the committee infringes this general rule, then is the committee wrong, and the administration of the bank improper.

The honorable member from Georgia continued to declaim in detail against the proceedings of the bank on the French bill; to show the greater responsibility, safety, and stability of depositing the public funds in State banks to one bank with many heads; of their being more independent of the Executive, and therefore of separating moneyed influence from governmental patronage; and advocated the superior nature and efficacy of the amendment he had proposed in lieu of that by the gentleman from South Carolina, viz: that the Committee of Ways and Means should be instructed to inquire on what terms the different State banks, &c.

Mr. HUNTINGTON having obtained the floor moved an adjournment.

The House adjourned at half past three o'clock.

IN SENATE.

WEDNESDAY, *January* 22, 1834.

ORDERS OF THE DAY.

The resolution of Mr. SHEPLEY, offered on Thursday, relative to the amount of tonnage on

ployed in the West India trade, came up for consideration; when

Mr. SHEPLEY gave his reasons at length for asking the information called for by the resolution, accompanied with tabular statements of the value of trade and the amount of tonnage between the United States and the British West Indies.

Messrs. POINDEXTER and KNIGHT also made a few remarks, when the resolution was adopted.

The resolutions offered on Thursday by Messrs. WAGGAMAN, TIPTON, and LINN, the resolutions of Monday, submitted by Messrs. CHAMBERS, BENTON, and WHITE, those offered yesterday by Messrs. WAGGAMAN, PORTER, SWIFT, and SHEPLEY, were severally taken up and adopted.

Mr. WEBSTER, from the Committee on Finance, reported favorably on the petition of sundry citizens of Georgia praying that the duty upon iron which was about to be imported to construct a steamboat may be remitted, in order that the experiment about being made might be attended with as little expense as possible.

The bill was read and committed.

Mr. HENDRICKS gave notice that he should to-morrow ask leave to introduce a bill for the relief of Charles G. Hand.

Mr. MOORE, from the Committee on Revolutionary Claims, made an unfavorable report upon the petition of Benjamin Holmes; which, on his motion, was laid upon the table, and ordered to be printed.

Mr. WILKINS presented the petitions of sundry officers of the late war; which was referred to the Committee on Military Affairs.

Mr. WILKINS submitted a memorial from a number of citizens of Philadelphia, complaining of the improper conduct of the board of directors of the Bank of the United States, approving of the course of the Secretary of the Treasury in removing the public deposites, and praying that Congress would not interfere in restoring them to the Bank of the United States.

The memorial was referred to the Committee on Finance.

Petitions of a private nature were presented by Messrs. SHEPLEY, TOMLINSON, WILKINS, SPRAGUE, and PORTER; which were referred to appropriate committees.

The following resolution, submitted by Mr. WAGGAMAN, was considered and adopted:

Resolved, That the Committee on Public Lands be instructed to inquire into the propriety of granting —— acres of land to Major General Philemon Thomas, in consideration of the military services rendered by him in taking possession of that portion of West Florida included in the district of Baton Rouge.

The following resolution was submitted by Mr. LINN:

Resolved, That the Committee on Indian Affairs be instructed to inquire into the expediency of extending the northern boundary line of the State of Missouri westward to the Missouri river, and eastwards from the rapids of the Des Moines to the Mississippi river, and inquire whether the northern boundary line has been ascertained of the State of Missouri according to compact.

At one o'clock Mr. CLAY moved that the Senate proceed to the consideration of the special order of the day, being his resolutions upon the removal of the deposites.

Mr. EWING then resumed and concluded his remarks; when

Mr. PRESTON moved an adjournment, but gave way to

Mr. WEBSTER, upon whose motion the Senate, at five minutes past two o'clock, proceeded to Executive business.

Previous to the galleries being cleared a communication was laid before the Senate from the President of the United States, in compliance with the resolution of Mr. POINDEXTER, relative to presents made to public functionaries resident in foreign countries, now deposited in the Department of State; which, on motion of Mr. FORSYTH, was referred to the Committee on Foreign Relations; and, on motion of Mr. POINDEXTER, was ordered to be printed.

When the doors were opened the Senate had adjourned.

HOUSE OF REPRESENTATIVES.

WEDNESDAY, *January* 22, 1834.

As soon as the Journal was read,

Mr. POLK moved to take up the bill making appropriations, in part, for the service of the Government during the year 1834. His object was to propose a conference with the Senate in relation to the amendment to which the Senate had adhered, and he had no doubt that, through means of a conference, the difficulty might be settled.

The bill having been taken up,

Mr. POLK moved that the House insist upon the disagreement to the amendment of the Senate, striking out the clause relative to the appropriation of the contingent fund of the two Houses to the purpose of printing, and purchase of books, maps, &c.

Mr. HARDIN said that his impression was, in regard to the point of order, that a conference between the two Houses could not be asked after one of them had *adhered*. The Senate having adhered, the House must recede, or lose the bill. For his part, he would rather recede than lose the bill.

Mr. POLK. I am not prepared to say that I would. As to the point of order, he was satisfied that the motion which he had made was strictly in order. The position in which the House was placed might be undesirable, but being so placed, he was prepared to act. He should abstain from any debate, unless it was forced upon him. He believed that the committee of conference would settle the question in the manner in which it ought to be settled, and that it was due to the Senate and to ourselves to ask a conference.

The CHAIR stated that the motion was in order.

Mr. J. Q. ADAMS said, that according to the practice of Congress for the last thirty years, when either House announced to the other its adherence, there could be no conference. We must either recede or adhere and lose the bill; and this practice, he contended, had its advantages. The chairman of the Committee of Ways and Means has intimated, that, if we now *insist*, and ask a conference, the question will be finally settled. I ask, sir, where the honorable chairman got his information, and I pause for a reply.

Mr. POLK replied, that he had proposed the conference, under the impression that the two Houses would ultimately agree; because, when the conferees came together, they would find the proposition of the House so reasonable, that they would agree to it. He had not received any information as to the probable course of the Senate from any member of that body.

Mr. ADAMS thanked the gentleman for the information that his impressions were not derived from that source. Now, sir, said he, if the gentleman rests upon the reasonableness of his proposition, it is my impression that the Senate will not agree to it, and he was sure that they ought not. What would be the consequence? When we send a message to the Senate asking a conference, they will reject it. It will then go before the world as a quarrel between the two Houses, provoked by the Senate. He did not expect that the gentleman had this design in view, but that the effect would be to put the two before the country in that attitude. The consequences of making such an impression on the public mind would, in his opinion, be more injurious than the loss of the bill. He hoped that we should give up our provision, or adhere and let the bill go. It would be better to lose this bill, however urgent it may be, and to get up another in its place, after much inconvenience from the delay, than to put the two Houses before the nation in a quarrelling attitude. I say it is my impression that the Senate will reject the conference; but that impression has not been derived from conversation with any Senator. The provision introduced into the bill by the House, he regarded as useless and insulting to the Senate; and the House, in his opinion, ought not to adhere to it. The honor of the House, and the peace and quiet of the nation, required that the House should recede. If the gentleman was so tenacious of the provision, let him bring forward a separate bill, and enact it as a general law.

Mr. FOOT said the decision of the Chair was correct as to the parliamentary rule; but the practice had not prevailed in this country. The Senate had adhered in the first instance, without insisting, and the door to conference was therefore closed. The Senate, by *adhering*, had signified that there was something in the bill which was insulting to the dignity of their body, and that it was a subject for further consideration. The gentleman from Tennessee supposes that the Senate will recede, but the record of their proceedings in regard to the matter does not encourage the supposition. Look at the vote on the question—

The CHAIR interposed, and stated that it was not in order to refer to the vote of the Senate.

Mr. FOOT said the whole object of a conference, at this stage of the proceedings, was to put on record the reasons of the two Houses for adhering now; he had no reason to give for the course of this House; and he was not willing to put upon record that this House had denied to the Senate the exercise of a privilege which we claim for ourselves.

Mr. EVERETT, of Massachusetts, asked whether the Chair was of opinion that the motion of the gentleman from Tennessee was in order.

The CHAIR replied, certainly. In the British Parliament it was once the usage not to confer after adherence, but that rule had been changed, and it was the practice to ask a conference after an adherence by both Houses. The practice here had been different. After an adherence by both Houses it had never been the usage to ask a conference. But when one House mounted up at once to an adherence, and the other did not, the other could ask a conference. This last course was taken in two prominent instances—in regard to the Missouri restriction bill and the judiciary bill, as he showed by reference to the Journals. It was for the House now to *adhere*, in which case there could be no conference—or to *recede*—or to *insist*, and ask a conference.

Mr. EVERETT, after some remarks upon the decision of the Chair, remarked that he had understood the gentleman from Tennessee to say that he had no doubt the Senate would give way.

Mr. POLK explained. He had no doubt that, in a conference, the two Houses would agree, and he would give a reason for that opinion. The provision would be so modified as to impose no further restriction upon the Senate than upon this House. This was the only mode of ascertaining whether the two Houses could agree without bringing forward a new bill. He asked the conference in order to avoid the adherence, and the consequent loss of the bill.

Mr. EVERETT understood, he said, that it was now admitted that the clause in question was copied by inadvertence from the bill of last session, and that the provision was of one year's standing alone. He had repeatedly stated to the House, during the progress of this bill, that the provision had not been inserted in any former bill except that of the last year. But it was insisted upon that it had been a standing provision for four years. But he objected to any limitation of the contingent fund in this way. Let this bill fall, and some other way can be provided by which the members may receive their pay and mileage. If the two Houses must quarrel, let it be on some more important point than this.

Mr. SUTHERLAND made some remarks on the point of order.

Mr. McKENNAN said, the contingent fund of the House was about one hundred and fifty thousand dollars, and to restrict the House in its application, implied a want of confidence in the integrity of a majority of the House. Suppose that the House, by unanimous vote, declares that the purchase of some book, map, or chart, is necessary for the instruction of the House, must we then apply to the Senate for leave to use a portion of our contingent fund for the purchase? He was not willing to tie the hands of the House in this way, for it implied a want of confidence in the integrity of the House. The contingent fund of the Senate was only $34,000; but we undertake to say, that having no confidence in the Senate, they shall not use a dollar of that fund for the purchase of books, &c., without our leave. The restriction was a direct and palpable insult to the Senate.

Mr. EVERETT, of Vermont, considered it almost a loss of time to continue debating on a trifling amount concerning the contingent expenses of the House, rather than attend to the

more important amounts embraced in the general appropriations.

In answer to a question—

Mr. POLK said, that the proposed Committee of Conference would be empowered either to agree in whole or in part with the Senate, or to reject if they pleased. Or they would be empowered to substitute another clause or amendment, as might be agreed on by the conferees of both Houses, and then ask the concurrence of their respective bodies. He considered it better thus to submit the views of either House, to avoid the collision of both. He again explained the tendency of the obnoxious clause—that it was to confine the compensation for any books which may be ordered to appropriations for the objects specified, not to have them paid for from the contingent funds—and to prevent either House from making appropriations without the concurrence of the other, as by the Constitution established. The same principle contained in the restrictive clause has been consecutively adopted by both Houses during the last four years; and maintained, with but one exception, in the case of a book ordered by the House. He had not the slightest intention, by his motion, to offer an insult to the Senate; nor was it in the contemplation of the House to distrust themselves. The motion was in the parliamentary course of proceedings, and was meant to adjust difference, rather than agitate dissension. A conference being granted can do no harm, and it may effect much good.

Mr. BARRINGER asked the Speaker what would be the result, if the conference were granted by both Houses, and then no agreement resulted. Would there be an alternative on the part of the House to recede, or would the bill lie on the table of the Senate and be lost?

The SPEAKER said that the clause of adhering, not insisting, being connected with that for the conference, would have the effect of placing the bill on the table of the Senate, in case of refusal to compromise.

Mr. BARRINGER considered it better to insist and retain the bill, rather than adhere, and have it lost in case of refusal.

Mr. BOULDIN said he had voted for the proviso in debate, when it was originally proposed in the bill of appropriation for contingent expenses, because he expected it would limit the range of expenditure under the head of general appropriation. But finding that, instead of so limiting, it had the effect of actually enlarging those expenses and appropriations—because all not specifically prohibited, are supposed to be countenanced—and the prohibition being only on the purchase of books, everything analogous to books is supposed to be included in the general appropriation for contingent expenses; he would therefore now reverse his vote; acting on the same principle as that which induced him originally to support the proviso. Every expense not embraced in the particular interdiction is countenanced; and therefore may adroitly be foisted into the contingent expenses. The bill was originally made on the spur of the moment, and therefore more obnoxious to error; for he remembers that Lord Coke has distinctly asserted that few good laws are ever made on the spur or excitement of the occasion. The proviso of the present bill is a proof of his assertion.

Mr. BROWN addressed a few words to the House, which were inaudible in the reporter's seat.

Mr. POLK was willing to modify his resolution so as to obtain only the committee of conference, without the clause insisting on the disagreement.

Mr. FOSTER considered that the House should have a respect for itself as well as for the Senate; and that they should have a laudable jealousy for the expenditure of the public money. The members of that House are, the representatives of the people, and from them should all appropriations emanate. It was therefore the duty of the Senate to request the conference after the House had so unequivocally disagreed to the amendment on an appropriation bill; to receive it as proposed by the House or to reject it in toto—not certainly to send it back with a message that they had adhered to their own amendment. He would prefer that the bill should be lost, rather than the dignity of the House should be lost. The Senate is not to respon-

sible to the country for the appropriations made; courtesy might therefore have prevented them from making an amendment; at least from adhering to an amendment which met the disapprobation of that House, whose duty and right it more immediately is, to control the expenses of the nation. He is reluctant to surrender the principle contained in the proviso; and rather than have it lost, he desires to have the whole bill lost; and that the responsibility should then rest on the other House. In a similar discussion in that House, he had asserted that the contingent fund ought to be more properly designated the convenient fund; and this he now repeated: for it was too well known that it was generally used as a matter of convenience; and that a dash of the pen often could draw on it for $30,000. He hoped the House would be mindful of its own privileges and rights, as well as regardful of the liberties and taxes of the people, not to concede the proviso; and he trusted that the gentleman from Tennessee would not withdraw his motion insisting on the disagreement, if he did not withdraw that demanding a conference.

The debate was continued for some time, when The question on the motion being divided it was put on the first part, viz: that the House insist on the disagreement, &c., and lost.

And the second part, viz: that the House request a conference, and it was carried in the affirmative, upon which a committee of five were named to act as conferees.

The SPEAKER laid before the House a communication from the department for Indian Affairs, with a list of persons employed, and their stations, &c., which was referred to the Committee on Indian Affairs.

The House then, by consent, waived the consideration of the removal of the deposites, and proceeded to take up several engrossed bills, which were on the Speaker's table.

The bill to authorize the construction of the branch railroad from Baltimore to Washington, coming up for its third reading,

Mr. CHINN moved to recommit the bill to the Committee on the District of Columbia, as the people of the District were deeply interested in the subject, and claimed to be heard upon it before that committee. They considered that this would lay an annual tax upon all passengers travelling upon the road, which ought not to be made; but if it was made, that some part of this emolument should belong to them, as well as to the State of Maryland.

Mr. McKIM said that the present bill was only a renewal of a former one, which had expired by its own limitation. This law having been passed by the State of Maryland, her Legislature had subscribed to it $500,000, in consideration of which a tax of 50 cents was given to them. He could not assent to this justice of the claims of the people of the District to any portion of this tax, they not having subscribed to it, and the road being through a very small portion of the District.

Mr. CHINN would not then discuss the right of the matter; but he would insist that they had a right to be heard upon the bill, before their own committee.

Mr. VINTON rose, not to object to the recommitment of the bill, but to its being sent to the District committee; and he contended that it should be sent to the Committee on Roads and Canals.

Mr. STODDERT said, there were many considerations, of a purely local nature, connected with the bill, which made the Committee on the District the most appropriate one to send it to.

Mr. VINTON moved to re-commit it to the Committee on Roads and Canals.

Mr. STODDERT remarked, that the bill had originally been reported from the Senate's Committee on the District.

Mr. HEATH opposed both the motions to recommit, and advocated its immediate passage.

After a few remarks from Mr. McKIM, the bill was recommitted to the Committee on the District of Columbia.

A bill for the relief of John Hurtell;

A bill granting certain allowance to officers of the marine corps, and,

A bill to establish a pension agency at Decatur, in Alabama, and for other purposes, &c.,

Were severally read the third time, and passed.

The bill making appropriations for the Indian Department of 1834, coming up for its final passage—

Mr. HORACE EVERETT said, that the Committee for Indian Affairs had instructed him to move that the bill should be recommitted to that committee, in order that they might examine it, and ascertain if there were any appropriations made for persons whose offices were not recognised by law.

Mr. CLAY said, that from the accidental absence of Mr. POLK, the chairman of the Committee of Ways and Means, who reported the bill, he was induced to move that its further consideration should be postponed; which was agreed to.

A bill for the relief of Colonel Coombs, after a few remarks from Messrs. CLAY, HARDIN, ELLSWORTH, EVANS, and McKENNAN, was also postponed.

And the House adjourned.

IN SENATE.

THURSDAY, January 23, 1834.

A message was received from the House of Representatives, by Mr. FRANKLIN, their Clerk, asking a conference with the Senate on the disagreement of the two Houses, relative to amendments in the appropriation bill.

Mr. WEBSTER asked for the immediate consideration of the message. He intimated that there was no settled practice on the subject of conferences, and moved that the message be referred to the Committee on Finance; which was agreed to.

Mr. WEBSTER asked permission, which was granted, to take up the bill making appropriations for the naval service for the year 1834; which was read a third time and passed.

The VICE PRESIDENT communicated the proceedings of a public meeting in Cincinnati, Ohio, disapproving of the course of the Secretary of the Treasury in removing the public deposites, and asking their restoration to the Bank of the United States.

The communication, on motion of Mr. EWING, was read, and referred to the Committee on Finance, and ordered to be printed.

Mr. BENTON read a letter from Benjamin Phillips, of New Albany, in Indiana, stating that he had made an improvement in the machinery of steamboats, so as to prevent accidents by the explosion of boilers, and intimating his wish to be summoned before the Committee on Naval Affairs, in order to be examined upon the subject. The letter, on motion of Mr. BENTON, was referred to the Committee on Naval Affairs.

Mr. HENDRICKS, agreeably to notice, introduced a bill for the relief of Charles R. Hand, of Indiana.

Mr. HENDRICKS, from the Committee on Roads and Canals, introduced a bill for the construction of certain roads in Arkansas.

Mr. MANGUM presented the memorial of sundry citizens of North Carolina, disapproving of the removal of the deposites, and asking their restoration to the Bank of the United States. Mr. M. took occasion to say, that he knew many of the signers of the memorial. His personal knowledge enabled him to testify to their respectability and intelligence; that they resided in the centre of a dense population, and that at least one-half of them were fast friends of the Administration, and had supported it through good and through evil report. On motion of Mr. M. the memorial was referred to the Committee on Finance, and ordered to be printed.

Mr. TIPTON gave notice that he should ask leave to introduce a bill to authorize the people of Michigan Territory to frame a constitution preparatory to being admitted into the Union.

Mr. KANE introduced a bill to establish an additional land office in Illinois.

Mr. TALLMADGE reported a bill for the relief of John H. Maguire.

The resolution of Mr. LINN, submitted yesterday, was taken up and adopted.

A number of bills of a private nature, from the House of Representatives, were read a first and second time, and referred to the appropriate committees.

Petitions were presented by Messrs. EWING, ROBBINS, and TYLER.

The following resolutions were submitted, and lie over one day:

By Mr. TIPTON:

Resolved, That the Commissioner of the General Land Office be directed to inform the Senate what progress has been made in connecting the surveys of the public lands with the line of demarcation between the States of Indiana and Illinois, agreeably to the provisions of an act of Congress entitled "An act authorizing the President of the United States to cause the public surveys to be connected with the line of demarcation between the States of Indiana and Illinois," approved the 2d March, 1833.

By Mr. SHEPLEY:

Resolved, That the Secretary of War be directed to inform the Senate whether any and what evidence has been received by the department, showing that the beacon on Steele's Ledge, in Penobscot Bay, has been destroyed, and to furnish an estimate for its reconstruction or repair in such a manner that it may be secure.

By Mr. TIPTON:

Resolved, That the Commissioner of the General Land Office be directed to report to the Senate what progress, if any, has been made in surveying and preparing for sale the lands acquired by purchase from the Potawattamie Indians, in the State of Indiana, and that he report the number of surveyors and deputy surveyors that have been engaged in that work, with their names and residence.

By Mr. TIPTON:

Resolved, That the Committee on Public Lands be requested to inquire into the expediency of removing the office of the Surveyor General of the land district, composed of the States of Ohio and Indiana, and the Michigan Territory, to a point more convenient to the country now remaining to be surveyed than that at which said office is now kept, and that said committee also inquire into the expediency of allowing office rent to the Surveyor General, and of an appropriation to purchase an iron chest for the safekeeping of the public moneys received at the land office of La Porte, Indiana.

The Senate, on motion of Mr. WEBSTER, proceeded to the

SPECIAL ORDER OF THE DAY,

Being Mr. CLAY'S resolutions in reference to the removal of the deposites.

Mr. PRESTON rose and said that the interest excited by this debate, and the feeling which had been produced in the country, was entirely disproportioned to what the mere abstraction of so much money from the Bank of the United States would produce. The cause of the deep interest excited was to be found elsewhere. When the manner of removal and the principles which led to it were reflected on, surprise would vanish, and it would be found that the effects were not disproportioned. The Bank of the United States was the great incorporated credit of the United States, the great censorium of the United States, and consequently any blow which should be made on it must cause such a derangement of public affairs, especially if done in the temper in which this was done. Such a shock upon the incorporated wealth of the nation must drive the bank to seek its own protection. We were in the midst of most extraordinary circumstances, more extraordinary than any which have occurred in modern times. It was only the other day, since the last adjournment of Congress, that the country was in a most unparalleled state of prosperity, everything abundant, party heats subsiding, everything joyous, large crops and high prices for them; when at one moment there came a blow which instantly reversed the scene, depriving the husbandman and the manufacturer of the avails of their labor; and rousing up all the vindictive passions of our nature. And all this referable to the act of the Executive of a republican government. Gentlemen had said that another agent had been called in to produce this result, and that it was continuing it by the most nefarious means; that the Bank of the United States were making efforts to spread abroad calamity and wo, that the cries of the people may have an effect on Congress to compel its re-charter. That the bank could not fail to act thus, followed as a necessary consequence—a blow aimed at it must cause it to contract its muscles. But the true cause laid deeper. It was the dread and dismay produced by this blow, struck at high and sacred chartered rights. If anything, it was the reverence for chartered rights, such as shook the Whigs of England, which produced this state of things, and he hoped to show that, from the very inception of this object, it was a violation of high chartered rights. What was the first step and foundation-stone of this proceeding? Why, the President of the United States, upon certain rumors, without knowing whether true or false, addresses a letter to the Government directors of the Bank of the United States, requiring them to investigate and look into the proceedings of the bank and expose them to him: a request which the President had no right to make, and when made, the directors had no right to communicate to him, even if he had the power. The mode of investigation is pointed out in the bank charter, and any other mode pursued is a violation of that charter. The President supposes the Government directors are the agents of the Government—not of the Government, but of the President. But is this their office? Are they placed there to act differently from the other directors? The charter provides for the appointment of twenty-five directors; that establishes their character; and yet gentlemen assume that they are not directors in this sense, but that they have a higher power, to wit: to represent the people of the United States, and not only that, but the President of the United States. Sir, when the President addressed these directors, he mistook his power and their duty, and violated the charter of the United States Bank. But the President enjoined it upon those gentlemen to act secretly; yes, gentlemen who were homogeneous with the other directors, were invested with secret powers to be exercised by secret means. Could this strike the public mind favorably? The gentlemen were wrong thus to proceed. But having got into the bank, and having insinuated themselves by means of executive power, behind the counter, what did they do? By their own showing they prosecuted their investigations as far as they were able, and the private accounts of individuals have been exposed to the public gaze of the world by the agency of these directors. When the charter should be thus violated under the sanction of the President, and by the officers of the Government, was it surprising that public feeling should revolt against the act? And when such was their conduct and such their motives, was it surprising that the other directors did not treat them as they expected? The directors know, and we know, that the President regarded the institution as an anomaly, denounced it, and was determined to put it down; and when they found these feelings were to be indulged, they would have been worse than idiots to have given their confidence to them. Their highest duty was to the interests of the bank and the country, and then the stockholders; and if they found an antagonist interest seated at the board with them, were they to say, Gentlemen, although you are enemies, give us your assistance; we trust the whole management of the bank to you? Sir, they were right to exclude them, and they did exclude them. The gentleman from Virginia [Mr. RIVES] had argued that the chief executive duty of the President was to look into the manner of executing its affairs, and that by the necessity of the case, the President could only look through them. But there were other modes prescribed by the charter, which ought to have been pursued; the charter had pointed out the power and duty of the Secretary, and the power of the Executive in the inspection of the accounts of the bank was given with the utmost caution. Secrecy is esteemed, to a great extent, a necessary part of the existence of such a corporation, and in the power given there is a special reservation of the rights of individuals. But there was another circumstance fully adequate to produce this shock. *When* was this investigation instituted, and when did these rumors reach the ears of the President? He says in one of his early messages, that the only mode of investigation was by Congress, through the medium of a committee; that committee was appointed and sent to investigate, and what then was the action of the Government? There was nothing then like authorizing the issuing of a *scire facias*. But the purpose of the Government was not accomplished. Congress had not done what the Executive wanted, and when the report of the committee was adopted, then this new proceeding was instituted. But there were other circumstances of a still higher character, which would have produced this shock upon the public mind. Mr. P. hoped to establish the fact, that not only had the charter been violated, but all the rights of the Government had been violated. The Executive had usurped both the judicial and legislative power, and was concentrating all the power of the Government in his own hands. Mr. P. put himself upon general positions. Had the bank failed to discharge its duty? Had a single cent been lost? Nothing of the kind had been alleged. Both as a public and private agent, it had been perfectly honest and faithful. In the performance of its public functions, all would bear witness to its capacity, fitness, and solvency as such; and what do the stockholders say? Sir, said Mr. P., at the commencement of these proceedings, when all these attacks and the disclosures consequent upon them had been made, the stock was at 128; his constituents, with an interest in the institution amounting to five millions, after all these attacks, held their stock at 28 per cent. advance. As the instrument of private gain, all were satisfied with the bank. But all this was not necessary as regarded the assumption of power in the Executive. The radical error was that the Executive had assumed penal powers over the bank, as though there was no provision in the charter for this case. Is not this a penal power which has been exercised? Look at the action of the Executive; was it not to punish the bank for its delinquencies, and delinquencies too, which, if proved, are otherwise specially to be proceeded against as provided for in the charter? There was not a charge adduced against the bank by any of the gentlemen, a mode of punishment for which was not pointed out in the charter; and the last clause in the charter guaranties a trial by jury in the courts of law; this trial by jury was guarantied to the bank in all questions involving the chartered privileges. Why, then, did the Executive shrink from the trial by jury, when, in but a little time, the truth might be winnowed from falsehood. Why not now issue a *scire facias*? Why concentrate all these sacred powers in the marble palace of the Executive?

Mr. P. then contended that the connexions of the United States with the bank were exclusively fiscal in their character, to be superintended by the fiscal agent of the Government, and yet, notwithstanding this, he is taken up and endowed with all the powers which are divided among all the branches of Government. The charter shows that the whole is purely fiscal, and ought to be so considered, but gentlemen contend for a penal power in the Secretary to punish at his pleasure. If this had been the design of Congress, the Attorney General, and not the Secretary, would have been selected for that purpose. But the Secretary deserts his own department, and takes the position of the Attorney General and the courts of the United States, to pronounce sentence against the bank. Regarding this as the proceeding of the Executive, no man is as safe in the country as before the assumption of this power. The courts and the laws are superseded, and next will be the jury, and next would be the habeas corpus act, that glorious palladium of both English and American freedom, which had recently been so signally exercised to the rescue of a free citizen from another executive assumption of power.

Mr. P. being here interrupted by a noise in the gallery, the Vice President ordered them to be immediately cleared.

Mr. POINDEXTER rose and observed, that as the trespass was very slight, he hoped there might be a relaxation of the rule for the present, and made a motion to that effect.

Mr. WEBSTER thought no motion necessary; that the Senate would always be disposed to sustain the President in preserving order; but as the violation was very slight, he respectfully suggested a relaxation of the rule in this instance.

The VICE PRESIDENT then countermanded the order, but remarked that, on the slightest violation hereafter, the rule would be strictly enforced.

Mr. PRESTON then resumed, and proceeded for a few minutes, when he gave way; and

Mr. POINDEXTER, at three o'clock, made a motion for adjournment, but gave way to Mr. WEBSTER, who offered the following resolution:

Resolved, That the Secretary of the Treasury lay before the Senate the statements, so far as received at the present time, of the condition of the several State banks in which the public money is deposited.

Mr. WEBSTER, from the Committee of Finance, to whom was referred the message of the House of Representatives, received this morning, made the following report:

The Committee on Finance, to whom was referred the resolution "that the House of Representatives do ask a conference with the Senate on the subject-matter of the second amendment to the disagreeing votes of the two Houses, on the bill (No. 36) entitled 'An act making appropriations in part for the support of Government for the year 1834,'" have had the same under consideration, and now report:

The House requests a conference after the Senate had *adhered* to its amendments, to which the House had previously disagreed. It cannot be denied that the Senate has a right to refuse such conference, a case exactly similar having been so disposed of by the Senate in 1826, as will be seen by the extracts from its journals, which are appended to this report; but the committee think it equally clear that such is not the usual and ordinary mode of proceeding in cases of this kind. It is usually esteemed more respectful, and more conducive to that good understanding and harmony of intercourse between the two Houses, which the public interest so strongly requires, to accede to requests for conferences, even after an adhering vote. Such conferences have long been regarded as the established and approved mode of seeking to bring about a final concurrence of judgment, in cases where the two Houses have differed; and the committee think it unwise either to depart from the practice altogether, or to abridge it, or decline to conform to it in cases such as these, in which it has usually prevailed. It should only be, therefore, as the committee think, in instances of a very peculiar character, that a free conference invited by the House, should be declined by the Senate.

The committee recommend the adoption of the following resolution:

Resolved, That the Senate agree to the conference proposed by the House of Representatives, upon the subject matter of the disagreeing votes of the two Houses, on the said amendment, and that four managers be chosen to manage the said conference on the part of the Senate.

The Senate then adjourned.

HOUSE OF REPRESENTATIVES.

THURSDAY, *January* 23, 1834.

Various private bills were reported for the relief of individuals, from some of the standing committees.

Mr. HUBBARD, from a select committee, reported the following resolution, which was agreed to:

Resolved, That the report of the board of officers relative to the militia, a document from the War Department, accompanying the President's message to Congress at the commencement of the second session of the 19th Congress, be printed for the use of the House.

THE PENSION LAWS.

The order of the day was then declared to be the resolution of Mr. CHILTON, to appoint a select committee to inquire into the expediency of so extending the general pension law, as to embrace within its provisions those persons who were engaged in the Indian wars, down to the year 1794, and the amendment of it by Mr. BOULDIN, to appoint a committee to inquire into the moral effects of the pension system upon the community, and how far it ought to be abolished or repealed.

Mr. LANE said, that should any apology be considered necessary for trespassing upon the time of the House and the patience of its members, in considering the principles involved in the resolution, that apology would be found in the importance given to the subject by the people whom he had the honor in part to represent.

For the few patriots, affected by this resolution, who yet linger among us, there is but one feeling and but one opinion. We entertain a lively and respectful recollection of their services, and a strong desire to relieve their wants by a nation's gratitude.

This being the object of the resolution, it was expected that it would be permitted to take the usual course, unobstructed by amendments, and unopposed by objections. This we had a right to anticipate, from respect to the wishes of the western people, and to the persons sought to be relieved, if not as a matter of courtesy to the western delegation.

Such has not been the good fortune of the resolution. On the contrary, it has been resisted at the threshold. An attempt is made, not only to alter its character entirely, and prevent all *inquiry*, but to dash from the statute book the pension laws—from the pension list, the names of all the wounded and warworn soldiers of the Revolution, and to stamp the National Legislature with folly, and the Republic with ingratitude.

All this is sought to be done upon the extraordinary discovery made by the honorable gentleman from Virginia, [Mr. BOULDIN,] that the practice of nations to reward individuals for perilous and important services to the public, is founded in a principle *immoral*, *corrupt*, and *corrupting*.

The honorable gentleman from North Carolina, [Mr. WILLIAMS,] has urged an objection of a very different complexion: that the resolution sought to place the soldiers of the West, for services performed since the Revolution, on an equality with those of the Revolution, whom he had supposed a distinct class, more elevated and meritorious than any others.

The gentleman from Rhode Island has urged other objections, equally extraordinary and infinitely more novel. That pensions have been granted to officers and soldiers of the Revolution, not as a mark of national gratitude, not as a reward for eminent services, but in the character of arrearages of pay, upon a close calculation of dollars and cents, showing the exact difference between the payments received in a *depreciated* and a *sound* currency. That if any such war as spoken of by western gentlemen, ever existed, it was a *private*, not a *public* war. That if any claim existed it was upon individual, not national gratitude. That they had been paid in the acquisition of land for themselves and children. That it was uncertain whether the white man or the Indian was the aggressor. That it could not be known whether they fought for defence or private revenge. That they were not *enlisted*, *drafted*, nor *regularly* entered into the public service.

The honorable gentleman from South Carolina, to whom he had heretofore listened with pleasure, has still graver objections; objection, which, if correct, would render the resolution fearfully dangerous. He declares *all* pension laws unequal, and therefore unjust; that they are calculated to substitute indolence for industry and enterprise; that they swell the patronage of the Government, and tend to demoralize the people; and this at the expense of the South.

These, Mr. Speaker, (continued Mr. LANE,) are substantially, if not literally, the objections urged against the original resolution, and in favor of the amendment. That they proceed from opinions honestly entertained, I have no doubt, I will go farther, and concede the point, that if any portion of these objections be *well taken*, the resolution ought not to pass. On the contrary, if met and answered, a large majority may be expected to support it.

For that purpose, (said Mr. LANE,) I throw myself upon the indulgence of this House, and respectfully request the kind attention of its members, while I briefly examine the several objections. Those which asserted the corrupting tendency of the pension system upon the individual pensioners he first considered. That such was the effect, will not be admitted by those who consider that these pensioners are from seventy to ninety years of age before the aid of the Government is extended to them. Are such men to be corrupted by a comfortable provision in their declining years? Are their habits to be demoralized by receiving a merited reward for their services? Such men are too old to learn new vices, even if they were as morally degraded as the gentleman's objection seems to imply. But this implication is inapplicable and unjust. The high character of the great body of those proposed to be relieved renders it unnecessary to answer the objection. The eminent services of their earlier years, and the old age, given only to good habits, are certain safeguards against corruption, even if such an effect was seriously apprehended.

The same answer (continued Mr. L.) may be given to the charge, that the pension system tends to substitute indolence for industry and enterprise, and to make pensioners a burden on society. What energy or enterprise can be expected from men of eighty? What indolence fostered?

Is energy checked and indolence nourished by rewarding services which required the highest degree of active exertions? Will the provision for their declining years render them a burden to society? *Without* it many might, indeed, be thrown upon the charity of the community, and be forced to the wretched necessity of begging alms from door to door. It is the usage of all nations to reward those who peril their lives in the service of their country, either by civil honors or pecuniary compensations. Yet he would not rest wholly on precedent and practice, which are often at variance with correct principles of action. The wars of other nations are generally caused by the passions or interests of those who have the direction of the Government. The caprice of a single ruler has been too often the cause of national ruin. The people might well object to pensioning the hirelings who had been the willing tools of such a ruler. But our wars have been of a very different character. They have been deemed necessary by the people either to acquire their independence or to secure its enjoyment. The people themselves dictate the war, and come forward to cary it on. The services were performed for the *public*, and have a far higher value, because they secure far more important rights than the military services in any other country. Petty rivalry, ambition of conquest, the desire to set up or pull down a particular dynasty, or motives still more paltry, are the usual causes of ordinary wars. But, with us, our liberties, our republican existence, or sheer self-defence, are the only sufficient causes of war. To the public the service has been rendered, and by the public it should be rewarded. The same good faith of moral obligation binds the Government and the individual: if service is done to repay; if a benefit is secured or obtained, to be grateful to him whose exertions have effected it. The same principle is binding on all. The only proper difference of opinion is as to the manner in which it shall be applied.

Fortunately the laws already made furnish a plain and excellent rule to direct us in the applica- tion. The invalid pensioners are provided for in the first instance, and the compensation given proportioned to the amount of disability. To others who served during the same period, until old age had disabled them from supplying their own wants, and then it is that the debt owed by the public may be paid with benefit to the veteran survivors and with honor to the Government.

This, Mr. L. said, he believed to be the tru principle of our pension system. By accident o design the several laws made and proposed to b made, fixed forty years as the time which shoul elapse after the service was performed before th pension was granted.

This principle was applicable alike to the soldie of the West and the soldiers of the Revolution. I a few months it will be *forty* years since the la services were performed for which compensation claimed by this resolution. And I hope it will b as cheerfully granted. As to the objection th revolutionary pensions are granted as arrearages pay—as difference between payments made in depreciated and a sound currency, a moment's co sideration proves its utter inapplicability.

By the law, those who served two years are a par with those who served seven, and recei equal amounts. The man who dies before t pension law passes, receives nothing. He w

dies in one year, receives one-tenth as much as he who lives ten years.

The nice calculations of the gentlemen from Rhode Island would show that the compensation should be equal to all; for surely, the dying a few days earlier or later cannot alter the so-much-talked-of difference between a depreciated and a sound currency. It is obvious that the fancied rule of the gentleman has no application. The true principle unquestionably is that which has been stated. The same principle runs throughout all our pension laws, and applies to invalid pensioners, and to those whom age has disabled from exertion. The provision is proportioned, in every class of pensioners, to his inability to supply his wants. When forty years have elapsed, Government kindly steps in to supply the place of those energies which were exerted and exhausted in its service. The time has now come to apply this principle to those who fought in the Indian wars, previous to the treaty of Grenville, in 1794.

But gentlemen say, that we exhaust the treasury, that we tax the South to sustain the pensioners. The number of revolutionary pensioners is at the highest 35,000. One-half of these in ten years will be no more; three-fourths in fifteen years; and in twenty years, all will probably have died.

Those now claiming will not amount to more than fifteen hundred, and their number will rapidly diminish. The whole amount of expenditure for pensions will be increased, during the first year after the proposed law passes; but will thenceforward rapidly decline, and before the period shall arrive for applying the same principle to the soldiers of the last war, the pension list will contain the names of no revolutionary pensioners.

It has been said, [by Mr. Burges,] continued Mr. L., that these Indian wars were *private*, not public. I must confess my inability to comprehend this distinction. If regular lines, constant hostilities, alternate defeats and successes, large numbers killed and great advantages secured by a definitive treaty of peace, be distinctive marks of public war, these were public. Will the gentleman say that the campaigns of Harmar, St. Clair, and Wayne, were the incursions of a private war?

Mr. L. said, he had listened with great regret to the remarks made by the honorable gentleman from Kentucky, [Mr. Hardin,] as to the conduct of General St. Clair, at Ticonderoga, and in his western campaign. The misapprehension of his character and conduct, was so general, that he begged to place it before the public.

On no man has the ingratitude of his country fallen so heavily and so unjustly. The Revolution found him wealthy, and with every prospect of advancement that his aristocratic connexions and individual abilities could present.

He embraced the cause of his country, cast off the ties which bound him to his mother country, and placed his property and himself at the disposal of the new Government. Throughout the Revolution, distinguished for his abilities, but still more for the chivalric purity of his character, he was the intimate friend of Washington, and his house was the home of Lafayette. As President of Congress, as Governor of the Western Territory, with powers and responsibilities almost unlimited, he was still the same chivalric and capable officer. Well may it be said of him, that his misfortunes were his only faults—them alone it is necessary to explain, and heavy is the debt that public opinion owes to his memory.

The evacuation of Ticonderoga was wakened into a fault by the subsequent defeat at the West. In the long interval he had received the strongest proofs of public confidence. It is true that the evacuation of the work was condemned in the general opinion. The public are too ready to impute calamities to the malconduct of individuals, when in truth, the cause is found in their failure to furnish the proper means.

The defence of Ticonderoga was impossible with the force under General St. Clair. The evacuation saved the garrison, and enabled them to join the main army, and thereby secured the surrender of Burgoyne. Mr. Lane then read the following extracts: (Wilkinson's Memoirs, p. 199.)

Extract from a letter dated Mape's Creek, July 28, 1777:

"Believe me, sir, if virtue or justice have existence, the man (General St. Clair) who stands 'condemned for retreating from Ticonderoga, will 'ere long *be thanked* for the salvation of 3,000 men, 'who, *instead of being in captivity are now opposing 'the enemy*."

Again, page 216, General Wilkinson says:

"I shall ever believe that General St. Clair, *by 'the abandonment of Ticonderoga, laid the foundation of our good fortune* in the convention at Saratoga."

The court martial which inquired into the conduct of General St. Clair, and of which Major General Lincoln was president, found as follows:

"That having duly considered the charges preferred against Major General St. Clair, (in reference to the evacuation of Ticonderoga,) and the 'evidence, are UNANIMOUSLY of opinion, that he is '*not guilty* of either or any of them, and do *unanimously* acquit him of all and every of them with 'the HIGHEST HONOR.

"B. LINCOLN, *President, and Major General.*"

Mr. Lane read extracts from Marshall's *Life of Washington*, corroborating the correctness of General St. Clair's conduct, and giving the reasons for the act, showing that it was *unavoidable*, was done with the approbation of a council of war, and was productive of the happiest consequences.

Mr. Lane quoted extracts to the same effect, from Ramsay's History: "Subsequent events '*clearly* proved the *wisdom* and *propriety* of the retreat from Ticonderoga."—Vol. 2, p. 35.

Mr. L. remarked, that all concurrent testimony clearly showed that this was an act characterized by General St. Clair's usual sagacity, and one which entitled him to gratitude, not *censure*.

The other misfortune which has blighted a long life of useful and eminent service, and withered in the public estimation a reputation more nearly allied in purity, ability, and common achievements with those of Washington and Lafayette, than that of any other man, has been equally misrepresented, equally misunderstood. Mr. L. said he would not detain the House by an examination of the circumstances connected with St. Clair's defeat. It need only be remembered that he was stricken in years; that public opinion inconsiderately and most unjustly decided against him; that the then Secretary of War, to whose misconduct the defeat was mainly owing, endeavored to cast the whole blame on General St. Clair. The examination was made by a committee of this House, and at its head was *Giles*, one of Virginia's most distinguished sons. After a full and careful investigation, that committee made the report which I hold in my hand. The Secretary of War, on whom the blame was by this report justly thrown, obtained a reëxamination, the result of which was alike complimentary to General St. Clair, and condemnatory of himself.

Mr. L. then read the following extract from the report of a committee made on the 8th of May, 1792, on the causes of failure of the expedition under Major General St. Clair:

"From the foregoing state of facts, the committee suggest the following, as the principal causes, 'in their opinion, of the failure of the late expedition under Major General St. Clair:

"The delay in furnishing the materials and estimates for, and in passing the act for the protection of the frontiers; the time after the passing of 'which was hardly sufficient to complete and discipline an army for such an expedition, during 'the summer months of the same year.

"The delays consequent upon the gross and various mismanagements and neglects in the Quartermaster's and Contractor's Departments; the 'lateness of the season at which the expedition 'was undertaken, the green forage having been 'previously destroyed by the frost, so that a sufficiency of subsistence for the horses necessary for 'the army, could not be procured.

"The want of discipline and experience in the 'troops.

"The committee conceive it but justice to the 'Commander-in-Chief to say, that in their opinion, 'the failure of the late expedition can, in no respect, be imputed to his conduct, either at any 'time before or during the action; but that as his 'conduct in all the preparatory arrangements was 'marked with peculiar ability and zeal, so his conduct during the action furnished strong testimonies of his coolness and intrepidity.

"The committee suggest as reasons for leaving 'the numbers of troops, at particular periods, and 'the dates of some facts blank, the want of sufficient time to complete the report with minuteness, 'and in some instances the want of the necessary 'evidence."

"7th November, 1792.—Committed to a committee of the whole House on Wednesday next. '14th November, 1792.—Committee of the whole 'House discharged, and report recommitted to a 'select committee. 15th February, 1793.—Amendatory report made, stronger in its character and 'more highly complimentary to General St. Clair."

The history of General St. Clair is a humiliating lesson of injustice and ingratitude. One of the ablest and best of all our public men—his services important and long-continued, his character above suspicion, his fortune and his life spent in the public service, and all this could only procure him contemptuous disregard of just claims while he lived, and the mockery of scorn, after a death in indigence and sorrow had relieved him from the weight of a nation's ingratitude.

Mr. L. said he was sure that the honorable gentleman from Kentucky [Mr. Hardin] was not aware of these facts. He felt sure that had that gentleman known, as he knew, the descendants of that distinguished man, respect for them would have prevented him from wounding his memory. General St. Clair, unfortunate in all things else, has the rare merit of being truly represented in integrity and ability by his posterity. To them this country owes a heavy debt of reparation. But there is in my eye an honorable gentleman [Mr. Denny, of Pennsylvania] who can, far better than myself, tell the tale of injustice and ingratitude.

Mr. L. then proceeded to answer the objection that the law proposed, and pension laws generally, conferred benefits on the worthless. This, he said, was an abuse in the administration of the public bounty, and required to be vigilantly guarded against. But the perjury of a few impostors should not be allowed to militate against the legitimacy of the provision. It should not be allowed to deprive the really deserving of the recompense to which they were fairly entitled. Such an argument will apply to every possible law. Yet surely the fear of abuse is not a sufficient argument against an equitable law.

[Mr. L. was obliged here to break off abruptly, to observe the order of the day.]

REMOVAL OF THE DEPOSITES.

The House resumed the consideration of the motion to refer the report of the Secretary of the Treasury on the deposites to the Committee of Ways and Means, the question being on the amendment submitted by Mr. Jones, as an amendment to that previously submitted by Mr. McDuffie, viz: to add to the motion for reference the following instructions to that committee: "Inquire into 'the expediency of depositing the revenue hereafter 'collected in the State banks, in the different 'States where the same is collected, in proportion 'to their respective capitals paid in, and to prescribe the terms on which the same shall be deposited; and to report by bill or otherwise."

Mr. HUNTINGTON having the floor from the previous day, rose and called for the reading of the two resolutions submitted to the House. After which, he said, that no question of more thrilling interest had been brought before them since the adoption of the Constitution. It was not so much a matter of local importance, or of some thousand dollars, but one in which the interests of the whole country were embraced; which affected the value and security of all property, of all labor, and the currency of the country so much, that that person who supposed that the recent measures could pass off without injury, must, in his opinion, prove himself the smallest of all politicians. He, therefore, was glad that the resolution submitted by the member from South Carolina [Mr. McDuffie] had been presented in a form by which the subject in all its bearings could have a full discussion; a

discussion, too, which was due to the House, the character and private faith of the nation, and, above all, due to the citizens of this entire community, who would thus have an opportunity of seeing for themselves the existing state of things, know the causes thereof, and what was the remedy to be applied. He would ask the House to look to the nature of the two propositions before them. One was, that the public money was hereafter to be lodged in the Bank of the United States; and what sort of a bank was that? Why, it was a bank, the control over which, by the people, through guardians appointed by themselves, was greater than was permitted to any monarch in Europe over such institutions; it was a bank whose resources were ample to meet all the demands that could be made upon it, and which was so constituted as to be under every proper and necessary check by the executive, the legislative, and the judiciary, who could, in their respective capacities, if they saw fit, bring it before the tribunals of the country, take away its corporate rights, or examine into its condition. This was the institution which was proposed by the resolution of the gentleman from South Carolina, whilst they should also ask themselves what was the condition, in all respects, of the State banks, which was proposed by the honorable gentleman from Georgia as a safe depository for the public money. Were not these State banks altogether independent of the same control? And what dependence had they to enforce the performance of the duties which must necessarily be required from them? What had they, but a simple contract, the very enforcement of which depended on the will of the party making it, upon the will of a Secretary who will not allow that the House has any control in removing the public money?

The subject now therefore at issue was, whether that public money would be placed, where it was safe, and where it was subject to their control; or have it in those places where the House could not have any control, but that which he had already described. He disclaimed altogether her being actuated by private or political motives in this discussion, for it was a subject he felt to be far above such considerations, and he trusted that the House, in coming to a decision upon it, would not decide it as a mere party question, but as one affecting all the great interests of the country, which by their oaths, they had bound themselves to maintain. The honorable gentleman from Tennessee [Mr. Polk] had stated, that this question was presented in the shape of an issue between the Government and the bank; he, however, would take leave to differ from him in this opinion, as to who were the parties in the contest. If that gentleman meant by the term Government, the treasury, he might be correct, but if he meant the Government, as it was understood by freemen, to be composed of other tribunals, the executive along with the legislative and judicial departments, they could not be considered as the parties; for so far as they could act, they had decided by their vote that the public money had been placed where it ought to be. The gentleman was equally in error, when he supposed the bank was the other party. No. Their interest in the question dwindled into insignificance, when compared with the interest of the people, and the contest was rather one between the Treasury Department and the people of the country. The bank was but a mere cipher in the controversy; and the result must fall upon the people. He considered that our condition for three years past, and up to the removal of the deposites, was a period of unparalleled quiet, ease, and prosperity to the country, in which every class had full employment given them, the laborer, mechanic, farmer, as well as the professional man; whilst the Bank of the United States had regulated the machinery by which these various interests were upheld, and kept in order. And this they were enabled to do, by preventing the State banks from over-issues; by keeping down the rates of foreign exchange, and thus, in preventing an exportation of specie, they had equalized the currency, giving health and soundness to it to such a degree, as never before existed in any country, and which called forth thanksgiving to the beneficent Author of all mercies for such a state of things. What was it now, however, and how sad the contrast! What was the condition of every large city? And this was a question which came home to the humblest individual. So far as regarded the state of the cities, was it not well known—for the sufferings of these communities could not be concealed—that the whole course of mercantile operations was wholly suspended; that every channel of industry was choked up; that there appeared to be a perfect paralysis upon all business. No new contracts were now making, for the currency was in so disordered a state, money could not be obtained. It had been said by the member from New York that all this had proceeded from a spirit of hostility displayed by the bank to the Government; but this was not the true cause; and he argued at length to show that there had been a depression in foreign exchange from 4 per cent. premium, to a discount of a half or one per cent. for cash; that there was a complete stoppage to the sale of all produce, and that money had become so scarce as to produce offers for it in New York, on good security, as high as 18 per cent. Stocks of all kinds had fallen. Foreign commerce was annihilated, and the domestic exchanges of the country, in which the Bank of the United States done formerly so large a portion of the business, was at so low an ebb that State bank notes west of Albany were at a discount of a half to two per cent.; whilst bills of exchange on the southern and western cities were wholly unsaleable. If this, then, was the true picture of their condition, did it not follow that these evils must increase, unless there was a timely remedy applied, and that the local banks must be driven to one of two alternatives, either to hazard their stock, by further curtailments of loans, or to a suspension of specie payments. He contended that, from the pressure, the local banks would not be enabled to collect in their debts much longer, the result of which must be to create a panic as to their own stability, which, once raised, they might as well attempt to resist, as to stem the torrent of Niagara. The cord had been tightened so long, and the pressure so felt by the State banks at its ultimate point of tension, that it must snap at last, and in the end, the Bank of the United States, whose resources had been so underrated, would be found to ride out the storm. He disclaimed the idea of representing the State banks as unsound, but he could not be blind to what he honestly believed must be the result to those institutions, if there was not some strong efforts made to replace the currency as it was, and this could now be only effected by the success of the motion submitted by the gentleman from South Carolina.

Mr. H. then adverted to the statement in the Secretary's report that the curtailments of the Bank of the United States had been, in the months of September and October, upwards of four millions, whilst, in the same months, there had been an increase of the public deposites of more than two, which the Secretary had made a charge against the institution as having withdrawn six millions from the business of the country. But he would show that the bank had not made any unusual curtailment. And, further, that the Secretary must have known that they did not, nor had they evinced any intention of contracting their loans. This was to be proved by referring to the bank's corresponding statement in 1832, where it would appear that the reduction of that time was $249,000 more than that of 1833. So he inferred the reduction was made in the natural course of banking operation, and not from a design, as charged upon the bank, of creating a pressure for ulterior purposes; and he asked, could such a reduction, at this period, be fairly considered as made with the intention of distressing the community, when it appeared that in these months the bank had been previously accustomed to make them? The bank, he said, regularly furnished their accounts to the treasury, and although he would not impute motives, or act upon them, except so far as they had been disclosed, yet he could not help feeling some surprise that, with the knowledge that this reduction was not unusual on the part of the bank during these months, the Secretary could have come to the conclusion that he was warranted in taking the steps he did, with a view, as he alleged, to remedy the pressure complained of on the part of the community.

Mr. H. went into some statements to show that the bank had not made any great reduction of its discounts in 1833, and that the amount of bills discounted and facilities afforded in 1832 did not much exceed the amount in 1833. The statement, that the commercial facilities afforded by the branch bank at New Orleans had been diminished, was untrue. The purchase of bills on the northern cities in preference to those on the western cities by that branch had the effect, and was intended to have the effect, of benefiting the agricultural interests of the Southwest. From official documents he attempted to show that the course of the bank had not occasioned the distress, and he would go on to show what was the cause. It was the unwise and unwarrantable hostility waged against the Bank of the United States by the Government. A systematic attempt, as we all knew, had (he said) been made to villify and slander the directors of the bank, and impair the credit and character of the institution. This course of proceeding had brought the country to its present state of embarrassment and distress. The country, he believed, would have sustained the bank so long as its administration was conducted faithfully in regard to the interests of the stockholders and the public. But the bank had to contend with the hostility of the Government and the slanders of the press. The time chosen for the removal of the deposites was such as to render it necessary for the bank to curtail its accommodations to the community to a greater extent than would have been necessary at any other period. It had been often said that the mere withdrawal of eight millions could not produce the effect which had been experienced. If the bank had been required to pay that sum of money for the use of the United States Bank, no such injurious consequences would have been realized. He would tell us in what way the removal of the deposites produced these results. It was by breaking up the relations of amity and confidence between the Government and the Bank of the United States. We feel great distress, and we apprehend greater. Can we apply a remedy? He thought we could. A proper and adequate remedy was, in his opinion, to restore the deposites, to restore confidence, and to restore amity between the bank and the Government. Could the local banks provide a safe, sound circulating medium? Could they facilitate exchanges between different parts of this widely-extended country? Could they restore the country to its former healthy and prosperous condition? If they could, it must be by their notes. But we know that their notes are not current beyond their own immediate vicinity. He appealed to former experience to show that the local bank paper could not afford a general and uniform circulating medium. You can't get the intelligent bank directors in New York to take the paper of distant local banks. The Government deposites instead of strengthening weakened the local banks, because their notes were not equivalent to coin. He doubted whether even the sound banks in the city of New York would afford any facilities to exchange. Suppose those banks authorize drafts upon them from the western towns, who is to buy them? Not the local western banks. But the branches of the United States Bank purchased drafts to an immense amount in those places upon New York. Fifty millions in specie would not give to the western States the facilities to exchange with the North which were afforded to them by the United States Bank. He had thus given a general view of the nature, cause, and remedy of the present distress. It remained to inquire whether this remedy should be applied by Congress.

Mr. HUNTINGTON here yielded the floor without concluding, to

Mr. GORHAM, on whose motion the House adjourned.

IN SENATE.

Friday, *January* 24, 1834.

On motion of Mr. WEBSTER, the Senate proceeded to the consideration of the report of the Committee on Finance, on the subject of a conference of the two Houses of Congress, on their disagreement upon the amendment to the appropriation bill.

Mr. WEBSTER moved to strike out the number four, and insert three managers on the part of the Senate; which amendment was agreed to, and the resolution was adopted.

The Senate then proceeded to ballot for managers, when Mr. WEBSTER, Mr. POINDEXTER, and Mr. PORTER, were chosen.

Mr. KANE, in pursuance of notice given yesterday, introduced a bill for the establishment of an additional land office in the State of Illinois; which was read a first and second time, and referred to the Committee on Public Lands.

Mr. POINDEXTER, from the Committee on Public Lands, asked to be discharged from the further consideration of the memorial of the trustees of Allegheny College, in Pennsylvania; which was so ordered.

Mr. POINDEXTER, from the same committee, also requested to be discharged from the further consideration of the memorial of the Legislature of Missouri, relative to land districts. The report of the committee, on motion of Mr. P., was laid upon the table.

Mr. POINDEXTER, from the same committee, moved the indefinite postponement of the bill for the relief of Joseph Tiff, of Arkansas; which was agreed to.

Mr. POINDEXTER gave notice that he should, on Monday next, ask leave to introduce a bill for the relief of the town of Washington, in Arkansas.

Mr. ROBINSON presented the petition of James Adams; which was referred to the Committee of Claims.

Mr. TIPTON, from the Committee of Claims, reported a bill for the relief of John Webber.

ORDERS OF THE DAY.

The resolutions submitted yesterday by Messrs. TIPTON and SHEPLEY were adopted; that of Mr. WEBSTER, upon his own motion, was laid upon the table.

The following bills, from the House of Representatives, were read a first and second time, and committed:

A bill for the relief of the officers of the navy and the marine corps;

A bill for the relief of the widows of persons slain in public or private armed vessels;

A bill providing for the appointment of a pension agent, to reside at Decatur, in Alabama;

A bill for the relief of George K. Jackson;

A bill for the relief of John Yancey;

A bill for the relief of Asa Hartsfield.

Mr. WILKINS said, that he held in his hand a petition of a man who had devoted a long life in doing good, in pouring the healing balm upon the wounded soul, but who had also turned his attention to relieving the bodily complaints of his fellow men, by inventing a valuable medicine. He had secured a patent for his physic, and the period prescribed by law which secured to him the advantages of his invention was about to expire, without the profits having been anything like adequate to his just expectations. To use the language of the petitioner, the patentee had not made money enough to enable "one hand to wash the other." The petition is signed by Lorenzo Dow.

Mr. WILKINS moved that it be referred to the Committee on the Judiciary; which was ordered.

Mr. POINDEXTER submitted a motion that when the Senate adjourn, it will adjourn over to Monday next.

Mr. WEBSTER hoped the gentleman would not persist in his motion. The business of the Senate was of engrossing interest, and he would suggest to postpone the special order of to-day till Monday, and meet to-morrow for the purpose of considering and deciding on the other resolution, submitted by the gentleman from Kentucky, (relative to extending the time of payment upon revenue bonds.)

Mr. POINDEXTER replied, that the reasons for this motion were, that an important subject, the inquiry into the right of the sitting member from Rhode Island to his seat here, was before a committee of investigation. The papers to be examined by the committee were very voluminous, and the gentleman opposed to the sitting member desired that a long written argument might be read before the committee, and the sitting member also desired to be heard. The committee could not sit during the sessions of the Senate without permission: and during the discussion of the important

question now before the Senate, no gentleman desired to be absent from his seat. But as it seemed to be the wish of gentlemen that the discussion upon the resolution of the gentleman from Kentucky should proceed, he would withdraw his motion, and leave the investigation for another day.

Mr. P. observed, that on the 19th of December last, he had submitted a resolution which had been adopted, calling for information from the Secretary of the Treasury relative to the public lands; no communication had been made by the department, and the information called for was important. He knew not why this delay had occurred.

Mr. P. then submitted the following resolution:

Resolved, That the Secretary of the Treasury be directed to communicate to the Senate, the causes, if any, which have prevented an answer to a resolution of the Senate of the 19th day of December last, calling for certain information in relation to the public lands.

Mr. P. asked its consideration at this time, but it being objected to in a few explanatory remarks by Mr. FORSYTH, the resolution lies on the table one day, according to rule.

The following bills were read a third time and passed:

A bill for the relief of George H. Jenning;

A bill for the relief of James H. Brewer;

A bill for the relief of the executor of James Dehall;

A bill for the relief of Peregrine Gardner;

A bill for the relief of Edward Willet;

A bill for the relief of Russel Hunt, David Hunt, and Amos Hunt.

The following bills were considered in Committee of the Whole, and read a first and second time:

A bill for the relief of Joseph M. Harper;

A bill for the relief of Benjamin Shupp.

The following resolution was submitted by Mr. SPRAGUE:

Resolved, That the Committee on Military Affairs be instructed to inquire into the expediency of erecting fortifications for the defence of Penobscot bay and river in Maine, or of causing surveys with a view to that object.

The Senate, on motion of Mr. WEBSTER, proceeded to

THE SPECIAL ORDERS OF THE DAY.

The VICE PRESIDENT having announced the special order to be the consideration of the Secretary's report on the removal of the deposites, and Mr. CLAY's resolutions thereon,

Mr. PRESTON resumed and concluded his speech.

Mr. FORSYTH then rose, and observed, that there was not time to proceed to the discussion of the other resolution offered by the Senator from Kentucky, but he begged to call the attention of the Senate to one remark which had just fallen from the Senator from South Carolina in relation to his (Mr. F.'s) course on the compromise bill of last session. The gentleman adverted to his opposition to it as an evidence of the hostility of the President of the United States to a peaceful settlement of that question. He called it to the recollection of the Senate, that his opposition to that bill was founded on a single point. In his opinion, the constitutional rights of the Senate were violated by its introduction here, as it belonged exclusively to the other House. But when it had been acted on by the other House, and came back here, he overlooked the objection, and gave his assent to its passage, but with the hope of making it better. He hoped the gentleman from South Carolina, and all who knew him during his political life, as well in the Senate as in the other House, would do him the justice to know that none of his acts emanated from any branch of this Government, or that his support of any measure was given to it because it was an Administration measure. He had always done justice to every Administration, approving or condemning according to the dictates of his own judgment. And he felt that he ought to do the President the justice to say, that it was his ardent wish to do justice to the South as regarded the tariff. Further, he would also say that he believed that the unfortunate situation of our sister State might have been more favorably

settled for her than under the auspices of the gentleman from Kentucky, by whose assistance it was settled.

Mr. PRESTON replied, that when the compromise bill was pending, it was not thought as good as the South could have wished or expected. But until it was expected to pass, he never heard that the Administration intended to give them a better bill than the tariff of '32. Then he did. But he never heard any proposition of a modified tariff till the compromise bill was introduced.

Mr. FORSYTH made the remarks just offered in justification of the President. As to his (Mr. F.'s) course upon the compromise bill, he observed that the final question on the bill was suspended till the action of the other House was had; and then it was admitted that the ground he had taken was correct. In reference to the President, he would only say, that his opening message to Congress, at the period alluded to, was hailed by the whole South as the harbinger of peace and justice to that section. And the gentleman from Kentucky appealed to that circumstance to show that the President had determined the bill should go down, and that his popularity was sufficient to carry it through.

Mr. WEBSTER then moved that the Senate proceed to the consideration of Executive business; which was agreed to; and, after some time spent therein,

The Senate adjourned.

HOUSE OF REPRESENTATIVES,
FRIDAY, January 24, 1834.

Mr. ADAMS, of New York, reported a bill for the relief of John Hunt.

Mr. GALBRAITH, a bill confirming the title of Samuel Tait to a certain tract of land in Baton Rouge, Louisiana; and

Mr. SUTHERLAND, a bill for the relief of Marcus Quincy and William Gorham.

All of which bills were read twice, and committed.

Mr. CARR, from the Committee on Private Land Claims, made an unfavorable report on the petition of Elory Sequrd, and others; which, upon his motion, was ordered to be laid on the table.

Mr. CARR, from the same committee, asked to be discharged from the further consideration of the petition of sundry citizens of Florida, on the subject of certain land claims therein named; and, on motion, it was ordered to lie on the table.

On motion of Mr. R. MITCHELL,

Resolved, That the Committee of Claims be instructed to inquire into the expediency of making compensation to certain contractors for work done on the Cumberland road, west of Zanesville, in the State of Ohio.

On motion of Mr. THOMPSON, of Ohio,

1st. Resolved, That the Committee on the Post Office and Post Roads be instructed to inquire into the expediency of establishing a mail route from Carrollton, in the county of Carroll, by Minerva, to Uniontown, in Stark county, Ohio.

2d. That the same committee inquire into the expediency of establishing a mail route from Copp's Mill, by Strain's Mill, to Gorton, in Carroll county.

3d. That the same committee inquire into the expediency of establishing a mail route from New Lisbon, Columbiana county, in the State of Ohio, by Clarkson, Mail's Cross-roads, to Beavertown, in the State of Pennsylvania.

4th. That the same committee inquire into the expediency of establishing a mail route from Canton, Stark county, by Sandy and Georgetown, to Salem, in Columbiana county, Ohio.

5th. That the same committee inquire into the expediency of establishing a mail route from Petersburg, through Beaver Township, Green Village, and New Albany, to Salem, Columbiana county, in the State of Ohio.

On motion of Mr. H. EVERETT,

Resolved, That the Committee on Revolutionary Pensions be instructed to inquire into the expediency of placing the name of Joseph Porter, a soldier of the Revolution, on the pension roll.

On motion of Mr. PLUMMER,

Resolved, That the Committee on Public Lands

be instructed to inquire into the expediency of extending to the heirs and legal representatives of Edmund Jones, late of the county of Amite, in the State of Mississippi, deceased, the provisions of the act of Congress passed March 21st, 1828, entitled "An act to revive and continue in force the several acts making provision for the extinguishment of the debt due to the United States, by the purchasers of public lands," and of making the relinquishment of the west half of the northwest quarter of section No. 13, of township No. 3, in range 3 east, in the land district west of Pearl river, made by Samuel B. Marsh, administrator of said Jones, of the same effect and validity as if the said relinquishment had been executed prior to the 4th of July, 1829.

On motion of Mr. SEVIER,

Resolved, That the Committee on Indian Affairs be instructed to inquire into the expediency of changing the location of the office of Superintendent of Indian Affairs, from St. Louis, in Missouri, to Arkansas; and that said committee be instructed to inquire of the Secretary of War into the expediency of making the change in the location of said office.

On motion of Mr. McCARTY,

Resolved, That the Committee on Revolutionary Pensions be instructed to inquire into the expediency of placing the name of Philip C. Hayle, of Indiana, a soldier of the Revolution, upon the pension list.

THE PENSION LAWS.

The order of the day was then declared to be the resolution of Mr. CHILTON, to appoint a select committee to inquire into the expediency of so extending the general pension law, as to embrace within its provisions those persons who were engaged in the Indian wars, down to the year 1794, and the amendment of it by Mr. BOULDIN, to appoint a committee to inquire into the moral effects of the pension system upon the community, and how far it ought to be abolished or repealed.

Mr. LANE resumed his remarks, and having said that he was not surprised at the quarter from whence the objections to conferring the benefits of the pension system to the frontier men of the West had come, he proceeded to combat these objections, and contended that the constituents of those gentlemen were those who had principally derived benefits from the exertions of the persons whom it was the object of the bill to relieve—their claims were strong, because by them millions had been brought into the treasury by the sale of the public lands, and millions had been otherwise acquired to the country. It was not necessary for him to go into a comparison of the justice of their claims and those of the soldiers of the Revolution. It was sufficient that it was shown that they had those claims. Their wars were not, as was said, waged from petty or private motives, and although not enlisted, enrolled, or drafted as volunteers, as it was said they ought to be to entitle them to be put on the pension list, many of these men wasted their whole lives in this dangerous service. They were the pioneers of the West, and in their conflicts were always fighting at a greater disadvantage than others, who in the hour of danger could either retreat or be relieved.

It had been said that if these men were placed on the pension list it would be thereby swelled to an extent beyond the resources of the country; but in addition to what he had urged against this objection on the previous day, he would remark that the entire number which appeared to be on the list, under the acts passed for the soldiers of the Revolution, did not at present exceed 25,000, and that the whole number that was supposed to be entitled to be put on the list, did not exceed thirty-five thousand; and he contended, from a calculation made of their respective ages and services, that the persons now sought to be put on the list would only supply the vacancies created by the death of those previously on it. He advocated their claims because their services were not of a common or ordinary nature; for, whilst the soldiers of other countries were acting from mercenary motives, to gratify the passions of some powerful ruler, these were, under numerous privations, fighting for themselves to defend the Republic, and in preserving to those who were left at home all the enjoyments of society. Was it not, then, only just that, having devoted their lives for such purposes, they should be entitled, at a certain period, to some aid? Their right to such aid was not a question which rested upon the practice of any legislature, or upon the quantum of services rendered, but it was founded on a truer principle, that when given by the gratitude of the people, it operated to aftertimes as an incentive to noble deeds. The gentleman from South Carolina [Mr. PINCKNEY] had, however, said that the whole system of pensions had a demoralizing effect; that it was unconstitutional. We had truly fallen upon extraordinary days. Nothing could be done now, or attempted, but the cry was raised, that the Constitution was violated, and that usurpation was the order of the day. Was this, however, consistent with good policy? Was it right that every measure should be denounced, and that nothing should be done that was contrary to the letter of the Constitution? However opposed, as he acknowledged he was, to the doctrine of implication, yet he could not agree that it was any violation of the Constitution to extend their gratitude to those who performed extraordinary services; and such, he contended, must be deemed the services of those engaged in the conflicts with the Indians on the frontiers; for where once the savage Indian roamed were now the seats of commercial cities, farm houses, and all the enjoyments of society.

These were some of the benefits derived from their exertions. Immense territories had been acquired, now peopled by emigrants from all the other States; and all these had been obtained, not by warfare carried on in the usual manner, but by warfare by night as well as by day. Too often they had to meet in the dark hour of night, the savage lurking to surprise and pounce upon his prey. There was not a breeze of wind upon which the war-whoop did not float; not a step that was not a step of danger, if not of death; not a tree of the forest, or a valley in the West, which did not witness the scenes of the barbarians, revelling, with hands reeking and knives drenched in the blood of the whites. The very snows were stained with their blood. Yet all this was but petty in the estimation of some honorable members. He acknowledged he was astonished that imputations should have been cast upon the valor of men who had, under such chivalrous circumstances, acquired and retained the possessions of which others had now the enjoyment. But their valor had descended unto their children, as the history of the last war told too well. They had nobly defended their country, and if some of them had been where they could have aided the gallant efforts of a Barney, the Capitol would not have been in flames, and the Speaker's chair would not have been polluted by the audacity of a British Admiral. He was inclined to give to the Constitution a liberal construction; to the Executive department a liberal, but yet a watchful confidence, deeming it a fearful practice, at all times, and for all things, to be constantly sounding the tocsin of alarm, that whatever was done was unconstitutional; for it would follow from such an unceasing cry, that when danger really did come, the cry was so often unnecessarily raised, the people could not give credit to it. The Capitol was not the spot from whence such alarms should proceed; for if safety could be found anywhere, it ought to be at the hands of those whom the people had honored with their confidence, and not at the hands of those who could deny to the warworn veteran of the West the miserable pittance now sought for him, or who say they had all for revenge, but nothing for gratitude. He would not say as others did, that he belonged to no party, for he did belong to one, but that party was his country, her honor, and her glory; and he called on those who really loved their country to cease such useless alarm; to unite rather in rewarding the claims of the meritorious, and do justice to those who performed eminent services. By taking this course with their venerable Chief Magistrate, in whom they could safely trust, they could hear his voice from the watchtower, and then could exclaim with him, all's well.

The hour allotted for morning business having expired, the House proceeded to the orders of the day.

The SPEAKER laid before the House the following letter received from the Postmaster General;

POST OFFICE DEPARTMENT,
January 23, 1834.

SIR: In obedience to a resolution of the House of Representatives, passed March 1st, 1825, I have the honor to transmit you herewith a statement of the net amount of postage accruing at each post office, in each State and Territory of the United States, for one year, ending March 31st, 1833, and showing the net amount accruing in each State and Territory.

With great respect, I have the honor to be, your obedient servant,

W. T. BARRY.

Hon. ANDREW STEVENSON,
Speaker of the House of Representatives.

Mr. WISE, of Virginia, on leave, submitted the following resolution:

Resolved, That the Committee on Public Buildings be instructed to inquire into the propriety and expediency of employing American artists to execute four national paintings, appropriate to fill the vacant niches in the rotundo of the Capitol, corresponding to those executed by Trumbull.

The question being taken, the resolution was agreed to—83 to 49.

The joint resolution from the Senate, providing for the purchase of ten copies of the laws of the United States for the library, was read twice and referred to the Committee on the Library.

The bill granting pensions to certain persons therein named, was taken up and read a third time.

Mr. CONNOR moved to amend the bill by reducing the pension of Leslie Combs from twenty dollars to five dollars per month.

The SPEAKER decided that the motion to amend was not in order.

Mr. CONNOR then moved to recommit the bill with instructions to the committee to strike out the clause granting a pension to Leslie Combs.

Mr. BURGES opposed the motion, and advocated the claim of the individual to a pension.

The discussion was continued by Mr. WARDWELL and Mr. PARKS, who opposed the claim.

Mr. WHITTLESEY, of Ohio, being very anxious, he said, that the House should dispose of some business to-day, felt constrained to move the previous question—but he yielded the floor to

Mr. LOVE, who wished to make some explanation.

The motion for the previous question was then made and lost.

The discussion was further continued by Mr. HAWES, Mr. MANN, and Mr. CHILTON ALLAN, of Kentucky, who spoke in panegyrical terms of Combs. The House was also briefly addressed on the subject by Messrs. BURGES and EVANS in favor of retaining the name of Comb[s] on the list; and by Messrs. PARKS, BROWN, BOULDIN, and DICKERSON, against it. Th[e] discussion was of a desultory and unimportant na[-] ture, affecting chiefly the character and claims o[f] Combs himself—with the exception that the Hous[e] should hesitate concerning the pretensions of ind[i-] viduals, for whose claims, a commissioner and distinct office were specially appointed. If th[e] pretensions had been of a valid nature, they wou[ld] have been properly appreciated and rewarde[d] without having had recourse to Congress.

The question was then put, that the name [of] Leslie Combs be struck off the bill. But a d[e-] mand being made to have the yeas and nays [on] the question, a considerable lapse of time was o[c-] cupied; when about 3 o'clock, the result was d[e-] clared to be 124 yeas for striking off the name, a[nd] 66 nays.

Mr. EVANS, of Maine, then moved that wh[en] the House adjourn, it adjourn over to Mond[ay.] Adopted.

A couple of private bills were read a seco[nd] time and committed.

The House then adjourned over till Mond[ay] next.

We have disposed of all the back numbers [of] the Congressional Globe. Those who subsc[ribe] for it hereafter, *will receive the number for the w[eek] in which their subscription is received, and all the [fu-] ture numbers.*

THE CONGRESSIONAL GLOBE.

PRINTED AND PUBLISHED AT THE CITY OF WASHINGTON, BY BLAIR & RIVES.

23d Congress, 1st Session.　　SATURDAY, FEBRUARY 1, 1834.　　Vol. I........No. 9.

IN SENATE.

Monday, January 27, 1834.

A message was received from the President of the United States, by the hands of Mr. Donelson, his Private Secretary.

Mr. FRELINGHUYSEN rose to present a memorial of the citizens of Newark, New Jersey, on the subject of the agitations in the business and currency of the country.

Mr. F. said the memorial was signed by 1341 citizens of that place, comprising the great mass of the business population of that place, without distinction of party, or political feeling, deploring the late direction of the Secretary of the Treasury, to which they ascribe the shock which the public credit and confidence has sustained. It proclaimed the voice of the hardy sons of honest industry in that place, who feel that a severe blow has been struck at their interests and prosperity. Mr. F. thought there was no political economist on earth who would not agree with them, that when this blow was struck, it was such a blow as would produce the effects complained of. And why was it not so? At that period we had arrived at a crisis, as has been most appropriately and truly said by other gentlemen, of the most unexampled prosperity, when public business and pursuits were restored to the utmost stretch of public confidence, and a stroke at this must affect the whole credit of the community. He said the memorial was signed without distinction of party, that it was far above party; and it was so. The paper contained the names of some of the President's best friends, who had adhered to him through good and through evil report. What motive could they have for making such representation? What motive could any Senator have to pluck a feather from his crown? They would rather (he spoke with confidence for himself) add another laurel to his well-earned wreath, not as a victory, but rather that he should retrace a step which had proved no calamitous to the country. Mr. F. would wish to persuade him that such a course would place his fame far above the lures of calumny. It was strange it did not occur to him, when he was fulminating his anathemas against the bank, that their effects never would reach it. There sits Mr. Biddle, in the presidency of the bank, as calm as a summer's morning, with his directors around him, receiving his salary, with everything moving on harmoniously; and has this stroke reached him? No, sir. The blow has fallen on the friends of the President and the country. But, he thought the sympathies of every Senator would be excited, when he called it to the recollection of the Senate, that himself and his colleague had received instructions from the respective Legislature of New Jersey, relative to the course they should pursue upon this question. Instructions, in terms unequivocal and not to be mistaken, requiring them to approve the course of the Secretary in the removal of the deposites. The subject was one of great interest, and he paused to ascertain the claims and character of those who had given the instructions. Was the Legislature invested with a power to instruct their Senators here what to do? No: if so, we had better change places. He felt that he trod on delicate ground, but he was not afraid of it. Where the Legislature pronounced the full expression of public sentiment, he would feel himself bound to give that expression his support, or to afford them an opportunity of choosing some one who would comply with their wishes. But while he held on one hand the instructions of the State representatives, he held in the other a much deeper and louder voice, that of the people. They were perfect antipodes to each other. Where, then, shall we go? And he would say, he would go for the people, where their will could be ascertained. By this he was willing to rise or fall, and he felt that he should be sustained in it by his constituents. But he would not leave this subject without admitting one exception. It was no part of his belief that a Representative must follow the voice of

his constituents, or resign his trust. But he thought there were occasions when the public exigencies required that such a charge must be thrown upon him, and, in such a case, he had nothing to consider him but the vindication of his own conscience. In this instance he would follow the dictates of his own judgment, and he believed he should be sustained by his constituents, in which, he thought, his colleague joined him. The reasons for the difference of opinion between the resolutions of the Legislature of his own State and himself, he would not now give, but he designed, at some suitable time, to ask leave of the Senate to state them.

He requested that the memorial should be read; which being done, he moved its reference to the Committee on Finance; which was agreed to.

The VICE PRESIDENT laid before the Senate a communication from the Secretary of the Treasury, in conformity with the resolution of Mr. Benton, inquiring whether the Secretary had received recently reports from the directors of the Bank of the United States. The department was not in possession of the information sought for by the resolution.

Mr. WEBSTER, from the Committee of Conference of the two Houses on the appropriation bill, made a report, which on his motion was laid upon the table, and ordered to be printed. Mr. W. remarked that the committee had agreed, and when the report was called up, he should explain the reasons which led to that result.

Mr. SILSBEE presented the memorial of sundry citizens of Boston, praying the establishment by Government of marine seminaries; which was referred to the Committee on Naval Affairs.

Mr. POINDEXTER, agreeably to notice, introduced a bill for the benefit of the inhabitants of Fayetteville, in the county of Washington, and Territory of Arkansas; which was read and referred to the Committee on Public Lands.

Mr. POINDEXTER presented a memorial from the Legislature of Mississippi, asking Congress for a grant of land for the construction of a canal; which was referred to the Committee on Roads and Canals.

Mr. POINDEXTER also presented a memorial from the same Legislature, praying that public lands which might remain undisposed of for two years after they were thrown into market, might be surrendered to the counties in which they were situated, for the purposes of education.

Mr. POINDEXTER also presented a memorial from the same Legislature, praying that certain modifications may be made in the act constituting the city of Natchez a port of entry; which was referred to the Committee on Finance.

Mr. POINDEXTER also presented a memorial from the same Legislature, praying aid in the construction of a road through the interior of the State; also suggesting some regulation in the transportation of the mails, and to make Vicksburg, on the Mississippi, a port of entry; which was referred to the Committee on Roads and Canals.

Mr. POINDEXTER also presented a memorial from the same Legislature, asking that provision may be made changing the location in certain cases of school lands; which was referred to the Committee on Public Lands.

Mr. TIPTON, agreeably to notice, introduced a bill to enable the inhabitants of Michigan Territory to frame a constitution preparatory to admission into the Union; which was read and referred to a select committee of five.

Mr. TIPTON, Mr. GRUNDY, Mr. PORTER, Mr. NAUDAIN, and Mr. EWING, compose the committee.

Mr. LINN made a report from the Committee on Enrolled Bills.

Petitions were presented by Messrs. ROBBINS, WEBSTER, KANE, and SOUTHARD, of a private nature; which were referred to the usual committees.

Mr. TOMLINSON presented the petition of inhabitants of several of the wards in the city of Washington, asking Congress to make an appro-

priation to MacAdamize certain streets and avenues in said city; which was referred to the Committee on the District of Columbia.

Mr. HENDRICKS, from the Committee on Roads and Canals, reported a bill making appropriations for the Cumberland road passing through the States of Ohio, Indiana, and Illinois; which was read a first and second time.

The VICE PRESIDENT here announced the special order to be the motion of Mr. CALHOUN for the repeal of the Force Bill.

Mr. CALHOUN not feeling disposed to interrupt the debate now in progress on the removal of the deposites, declined calling it up, but intimated that he should do so this day two weeks.

The resolutions offered on Friday were adopted, with the exception of that of Mr. POINDEXTER, calling for information from the Secretary of the Treasury relative to the public lands, Mr. FORSYTH having made a statement of the causes which prevented the Commissioner of the Land Office from complying with the call of the 19th of December.

Mr. POINDEXTER was under the impression that the Commissioner had misunderstood the character of the information sought for; and from the statement of the gentleman from Georgia, [Mr. FORSYTH,] had gone into unnecessary labor. The resolution merely called for abstracts. He hoped in a few days the Senate would get the information, and he therefore should not press the subject, and moved that it be laid upon the table; which was agreed to.

The VICE PRESIDENT then announced the special order of the day to be the

REMOVAL OF THE DEPOSITES.

Mr. FORSYTH rose and addressed the Senate until the usual hour of adjournment; when, without concluding, he gave way to a motion for adjournment.

On motion of Mr. MANGUM,
The Senate adjourned.

HOUSE OF REPRESENTATIVES.

Monday, January 27, 1834.

Mr. LYTLE, of Ohio, presented a memorial containing resolutions from a meeting of citizens in Cincinnati. The memorial stated that the resolutions had been passed at a meeting convened by a call from upwards of six hundred citizens. The resolutions urged the restoration of the deposites to the United States Bank; and concluded by a resolution that their representative in Congress be instructed to support the prayer of the petition.

On presenting the memorial, the following remarks were made by Mr. LYTLE:

The House will discover that, by this memorial, I am specially instructed to sustain the views of those who have presented that paper. As a public servant, acknowledging as I do the right of the people to instruct their representative, and pledged as I am, and ever wish to be, to sustain that doctrine to its fullest legitimate extent, I claim the indulgence of this House, while I assign a few reasons why I am constrained to question the right of my instructors, in this particular instance, to induce me as they have done, and distinctly to declare, that I cannot, and will not, obey them. When the voice of a majority of my constituents is heard to direct me in the path of my legislative duties, it shall most implicitly obeyed; I will promptly yield to that authority; and if I cannot conscientiously pursue its mandate, I will be the last man on earth to obstruct a full expression of the popular will. But knowing, as I do, that these resolutions only emanate from a minority, a meager minority, of those chiefly who opposed my election, I would be most faithless to the principles which I have here declared should ever govern an honest representative, if I did obey them. No, sir, I have those proofs with me now, which declare, in a language not to be misunderstood, that upon this subject my constituents are still with me in feeling

and in sentiment, as they were at the time when, at *the polls*, they instructed me. Shall I, then, when possessed of the unchanged evidence of my district upon this subject, turn traitor to the trust confided to me? Shall I disappoint the wishes of a majority of some eight or ten thousand voters, to gratify a meeting called by some seven hundred? And that meeting composed, too, mainly of my opponents? for in the whole catalogue of names which appear upon the paper calling this meeting, I only recognise the names of some half a dozen who supported me. Sir, I would be recreant to that trust, apostate to those principles which I avowed should ever govern me, and a craven culprit at the forum of my own conscience, if I were now to act in obedience to their instructions. I never can, then, and never will, give a vote by which I shall aid directly or indirectly the power or perpetuity of this most odious institution. Why, sir, you have, in the language of this memorial, nothing more than a reiteration of the same fallacies which were employed by the signers to defeat my election. The issue, sir, between the bank and the country was fairly and fully tried a year ago. A jury of the *whole district* sat in judgment upon them, and by a large majority of more than six hundred of the panel, I had a verdict against the bank. Sir, the judgment was a righteous one, and no aid of mine shall ever be given to reverse it.

I have said, sir, that the memorialists were of the most elevated and respectable character—individuals towards whom I entertain a high personal regard, but who lost no opportunity that their wealth, their talents, their high standing, their long residence among the people, or their untiring industry could effect, to defeat my election, in virtue of all these auxiliaries, and upon the very principle which gave birth to this memorial. As I could not compromise then, I will scarcely accommodate them now.

But is it not strange, and worthy of some notice, Mr. Speaker, that several of the most efficient managers of *this* meeting were men who have, through a long life, been attached to a party which has ever denied the whole doctrine of instruction—staunch Federalists, who have made the representative independent of his constituents, and who now, for the first time, come forward as converts to the old republican doctrine of representative amenability, and purport, or attempt to apply, to me their newly-adopted principles, and on an occasion when they are most singularly inapplicable? Why, sir, if I had never heard of my constituents since my election, the very names on that paper would be enough to satisfy me, (I mean the great body of them,) that those who supported me then were opposed at this time to the views of the memorialists.

It is only by elections, Mr. Speaker, that a perfect expression of the popular will can ever be obtained. The worthy gentlemen who here claim to instruct me in their views of the policy and expediency of sustaining the United States Bank, at the expense of what I humbly conceive to be every principle of constitutional liberty, had an opportunity (to do so at the last congressional election. Heaven and earth will bear witness that they did make this effort, and if they failed, God knows it was not by neglecting the *side* which their high standing in the community afforded them to carry these points, in their exertions to prostrate me. But those exertions were met, boldly and fairly met, and triumphantly resisted, by the opposing suffrages of an honest, unbiased, and unbought yeomanry.

Sir, do I hazard anything in this declaration, with the evidences of public opinion that I have before me? I will call the attention of the House to some indication of popular feeling on this subject, in the form of resolutions adopted by the people of Ohio, since the removal of the public deposites.

[Mr. L. here read the resolutions adopted by his constituents, advocating the removal of the public deposites, and expressing a confidence that he would sustain the Administration in that measure.]

Sir, I have not presented these resolutions to the House; nor do I mean to do it. It was neither expected nor required of me. But it was the voice of a convention of delegates, assembled, sir, not upon a *six hours'* notice, but by public advertisements for days and weeks previous to its as-

sembling, and composed of delegates from the various wards of the city, and townships of the county, comprising the district: and what is their mandate?—what their instructions? Why, sir, so far from instructions, they do not even *request* anything from me. But thank God they express an unshaken confidence in my firmness in sustaining, so far as my abilities permitted, the views and principles on which we all agreed at the period of my election, and which, I am proud to tell them, I never will desert. These teach me, sir, that the people of my district are unchanged in their hostility to the United States Bank; that they are strengthened in their conviction of its hourly inroads upon the Constitution, and upon our constituted authorities, and that the very safety of the country requires the destruction of this lawless aggressor.

But, sir, this is not all: the feeling is general, out of Cincinnati. These sentiments are entertained, as I will undertake to show by resolutions passed on the 8th of January last, at the seat of Government in Ohio. [In submitting these, Mr. L. was interrupted by Mr. WATMOUGH, who called Mr. LYTLE to order, but after some conversation, withdrew his call, when Mr. L. proceeded to read the resolution of the convention, and also of the General Assembly of the State of Ohio—which he said had been adopted in the one case by an unanimous vote, and in the other by large majorities of both branches.]

Mr. LYTLE continued. I have here, then, to sustain me, not only the opinions of my friends, those who elected me, in my own immediate district, but also the voice of a whole convention of more than two hundred delegates, from every section of the State, the largest that ever met in Ohio, a public act of the General Assembly of that State, supported by the Senators and Representatives from my immediate district. Are all these to be disregarded and set at nought, as the dictation of a few, who were ever opposed to me on this subject? Shall the mass of the people govern, or shall the country be controlled by the selfish and contracted views of an interested fraction of the people? Sir, this may be the republican reading which your memorialists derive from the Constitution of their country. But I take leave to say, that I, for one, read no such version of it from other *instructors*. And while I avow my determination to take the testimonials of public opinion as my guide in reference to the bank, I indulge the hope that they will be regarded by this House as entitled to at least an equal respect with the swarm of memorials which have lately crowded our tables from boards of trade, chambers of commerce, counting-house establishments, stock-jobbing associations, who seem to have taken Congress under their especial patronage, for the purpose of teaching them the vital necessity of sustaining this invaluable institution.

In conclusion, then, sir, I have the consolation of knowing that both from my district and State, I am sustained by the will of that majority, which I freely admit should in all cases control the representative: and I have only to add, that if the worthy gentlemen (to whom I feel indebted for their support at my election, and whose signatures to this paper would indicate a change of opinion) will, in addition to their own, procure the names of those five or six thousand others, who, in October, 1832, thought with them, that the power and influence of the bank was, instead of a blessing, a growing *curse* upon the people, I here publicly declare that, although my vote shall never be given to uphold the bank, I will no longer oppose myself as a barrier to their will, however pernicious I may regard its consequence. Sir, under such circumstances, I pledge myself to cease my zeal, and again try the question before the same tribunal, by whose judgment I now occupy a place upon this floor.

But, sir, I will beg leave to say to my Cincinnati friends, that before they took it upon them, as a minority, to instruct me in the form and manner which they have done, it would have been well to have thought of the operation that their course would produce on the minds of another representative in another place, possessed of their confidence, and adopting their views, and who stands instructed by the public voice of that body which created him a Senator.

[Here Mr. L. was called to order by the CHAIR, and informed that any reference to a member of the Senate was out of order, and unparliamentary.]

Mr. L. explained, and said, I may at least be allowed to state the case hypothetically. If a representative is bound by the instructions of his immediate constituents, in whatever form they may come to him, (where the difficulty is so great of procuring the actual sense of the majority of electors,) how much more imperative should be the clearly expressed will of a State Legislature upon a Senator of their own appointment, and under the most direct and absolute amenability to the creating power.

In the one case, there must always be uncertainty; in the other, no room left for doubt or cavil. In this sentiment I am borne out and sustained by the opinions of another, occupying also a high and responsible situation before the people, who told the Legislature, as their Chief Magistrate, in as official manner, only one short year ago, that "the people of New Jersey, by themselves, through their *representatives here*, and to *their representatives there*, have the right, and are bound by duty to themselves, to convey their commands on this, as on any other interesting topic; and it is *their* business *both to watch and control* the doings of their general agents, and, as they appointed them, so correct their wanderings and errors."

And yet, sir, this very functionary is now placed in the most awkward and embarrassing of all positions by the operation of his own principles, front and new-born as they are. He is constrained either to vote against his speech, or to speak against his vote!

Instructed, sir, as I feel myself to be, by the expression of the people, given so decidedly against the bank at my election, I feel safe in a strict reference to the poll-book record. From this course I shall not depart, until the same people shall instruct me otherwise; and in this act of obedience I shall indeed feel that I have been faithful and consistent as a representative, in w'thholding all aid from this most subtle, dangerous, and lawless invader of the Constitution and the country's peace.

Mr. SUTHERLAND presented some memorials, signed by a number of the inhabitants of the first Congressional district, approving of the removal of the deposites.

Mr. McCARTY presented the petition of sundry citizens of Fayette county, Indiana, praying for the abolition of slavery in the District of Columbia; which, on motion of Mr. McCARTY, was referred to the Committee for the District of Columbia.

Mr. EWING submitted the following resolution:

Resolved, That the schedule of lands within five miles of the surveyed line of the Wabash and Erie canal, (and bordering on the Maumee river, from the State line of Indiana eastwardly as far as the towns of Maumee and Perrysburg, in the State of Ohio,) sold by authority of a proclamation of the President of the United States, regardless of the act of Congress previously sanctioned, deemed the same to the State of Indiana, upon certain accepted conditions, (which schedule is herewith presented,) be referred to the Select Committee on the Wabash and Erie Canal Lands.

Mr. EWING asserted that the sale of the public lands on the Wabash river was in opposition to the act of Congress in 1827, and involved the conduct of the Commissioner of the Land Office.

Mr. CLAY, of Alabama, considered it unfair to pledge the House by such a resolution, stating as a fact that of which they had no knowledge, nor previous information whereon to come to the conclusion adopted in the resolution. If the resolution required merely an inquiry concerning the sale, it would not be obnoxious to his objection, and it might ultimately obtain the end sought by the gentleman from Indiana.

A desultory debate followed between Messrs. EWING and CLAY, which terminated in a motion by Mr. CLAY, that the consideration of the resolution should be postponed till next day.

This motion was adopted; and an attempt subsequently made by Mr. VINTON, of Ohio, to consider the motion of postponement, was negatived without a division.

Mr. WHITTLESEY reported bills for the relief of Samuel Butler, and of Francis Lasselle and others.

Mr. BINNEY, a bill making appropriations for the support of West Point Academy for 1834; also, a bill to extend the provisions of the act to release from duty iron intended, and actually used, for the purpose of railroads, &c.

Mr. SUTHERLAND, bills making appropriations for light-boats, light-houses, beacons, monuments, and buoys, for 1834.

Mr. BELL, of Ohio, a bill for the relief of Elizabeth Swain.

Mr. CAMBRELENG, a bill to repeal certain duties on goods imported, &c.

Mr. HUBBARD, a bill authorizing the Secretary of the Treasury to refund certain duties paid on goods imported by D. Watson & Co.

Mr. WARDWELL, a bill authorizing the Secretary of War to establish a pension agency at Milledgeville, Georgia; and

Mr. POLK, a bill making appropriations for the support of the army for 1834. All which bills were read twice and committed.

Mr. POLK, from the committee appointed by the House to meet the committee appointed by the Senate, to confer on the disagreement of the House to the amendment proposed by the Senate to the bill commonly called the House appropriation bill, reported that the committee had unanimously agreed to strike out that part after the 183 section of the bill, and proposing for adoption, in lieu thereof, in substance, viz: that neither House shall subscribe or purchase any books, &c., in future, unless an appropriation shall be specially made for that purpose; that 5,000 dollars additional, shall be appropriated to the joint library of Congress, and that all books and printing, heretofore ordered by either House, shall be paid for out of any moneys not otherwise appropriated. Mr. P. having moved to refer the report to the Committee of the Whole on the state of the Union—

Mr. J. Q. ADAMS rose, not to offer any objection to the report itself, but to inquire as to a question of order, whether the conferees had the right to submit the proposition just read? It seemed to him that they had entered upon an entirely new subject. An appropriation to subscribe to the library, which had not any relation to the question upon which the disagreement took place—the power of either House to make appropriations for the purchase of books; for if it was in order for them to do this, he thought they might as well have reported a complete and general appropriation bill.

The SPEAKER said that there was nothing in the report to prevent its being sent to the committee; the subject matter of it was a question upon which the House were to decide. He thought that the proposition might have been entertained by the committee of conference, as being connected with the subject upon which the House had disagreed, namely, the printing and purchasing of books; but it was for the House to say whether the committee of conference had transcended the powers vested in them by the House.

Mr. POLK remarked that the propositions were substantially connected with the subject matter in dispute between the two Houses. The committee being unanimously agreed that in future neither House should use their contingent funds for the purchase of books, &c., it had been suggested to them that there might arise a necessity to purchase various important works for the Library, for which there would not be adequate funds; and as this occasion did not arise from the giving up of any principle, but was necessary to promote that harmony which should ever exist between the two Houses, they had agreed to recommend that an additional subscription of 5,000 dollars should be made to the Congress Library for that purpose for this year; some of the Library Committee supposed to be on the committee of conference, and the appropriation had been considered coming within the duties assigned them, and connected with the same subject.

Mr. WILDE inquired if he was to understand that a decision had been made as to the point of order.

The SPEAKER repeated, that it was for any member of the House, when the report was in committee, to urge objections if he thought proper.

The report was then referred to the Committee of the Whole on the state of the Union, and the House suspended the rule, and went into that committee, Mr. CLAY in the chair, for the purpose of taking it up.

Mr. FILLMORE asked for the reading of the clause.

Mr. FOOT called for the reading of the entire bill. It was read accordingly.

Mr. WILDE said, although he would not object to any subscription to be made for the Library, yet he apprehended that the committee of conference having been appointed for a certain purpose only; it was not competent for them, under such limited authority, to recommend to the House to strike out any part of a bill which had previously received its sanction. There was in fact no difference between the present recommendation for the subscription to the Library, than if it had been submitted as a distinct proposition: however good, therefore, was their intention, it was manifest that they had exceeded their authority, in consequence of which excess, their acts, like the acts of other agents, became void.

Mr. EVERETT contended that the lines recommended to be stricken out formed an integral part of that which was the subject of disagreement, and that the committee had not gone beyond the point assigned them.

A desultory conversation then arose, in which the power of the committee of conference to make the recommendation, &c., was combated by Messrs. WILLIAMS, ARCHER, FOOT, and J. Q. ADAMS, and sustained by Speaker STEVENSON and Mr. POLK.

A motion was made by Mr. WILLIAMS, for the committee to rise, and was negatived—ayes 55, nays not counted.

The question was then taken on the committee concurring in the report, and decided in the affirmative—ayes 86, nays 79.

The committee, thereupon, rose and reported the same to the House, and,

On motion of Mr. WILLIAMS,

The House adjourned.

IN SENATE.

TUESDAY, January 28, 1834.

A message was received from the President of the United States by Mr. DONELSON, his Private Secretary.

The VICE PRESIDENT communicated a letter from the Secretary of the Treasury, transmitting certain documents relative to the removal of the deposites from the Bank of the United States; which,

On motion of Mr. WEBSTER, was laid on the table.

Mr. McKEAN presented a memorial from certain citizens of Pennsylvania, approving the course of the Secretary of the Treasury in removing the deposites, and praying that they may not be restored to the Bank of the United States; which was referred to the Committee on Finance, and ordered to be printed.

Mr. FRELINGHUYSEN, from the Committee on Manufactures, reported a bill relative to duties upon hardware; which was read.

Mr. KING, of Alabama, temporarily occupying the chair, presented a communication from the Secretary of the Treasury, in compliance with the resolution of Mr. SHEPLEY, calling for information relative to the amount of tonnage employed in the West India trade.

After the letter had been read a discussion ensued, in which Messrs. SPRAGUE, SHEPLEY, KNIGHT, and SILSBEE participated; when the communication and documents were referred to the Committee on Commerce, and ordered to be printed.

A message was received from the House of Representatives, by Mr. FRANKLIN, its Clerk, accompanied with sundry enrolled bills which had received the Speaker's signature.

Mr. TIPTON presented a joint resolution of the Legislature of Indiana, praying for the establishment of a harbor within the limits of that State; which was referred to the Committee on Commerce.

Mr. TIPTON, from the Committee on Claims, reported a bill for the relief of the administrator of

Bolitha Laws, deceased; which was read a first and second time, and, with the report, ordered to be printed.

Mr. TIPTON gave notice that he should to-morrow ask leave to introduce a bill to enable the inhabitants of Arkansas to form a constitution previous to the admission of that Territory into the Union.

A communication was presented by the CHAIR from the War Department, in relation to the destruction of the beacon on Steele's Ledge; which,

On motion of Mr. SHEPLEY, was referred to the Committee on Commerce.

Also, a communication from the same department relative to the number of Indian emigrants; which,

On motion of Mr. WHITE, was laid upon the table, and ordered to be printed.

The bill establishing land districts in the State of Illinois was read a second time, and,

On motion of Mr. KANE, was referred to the Committee on Public Lands.

Mr. WRIGHT, from the Committee on Claims, reported a bill for the relief of Martha Bailey and others, with an amendment.

Mr. BROWN, from the same committee, reported a bill for the relief of Henry Warrow.

Petitions and memorials were presented by Messrs. MOORE, McKEAN, TIPTON, and SWIFT.

The following bills were read a third time and passed:

A bill for the relief of Joseph M. Harper;

A bill for the relief of Benjamin Shirbley.

The following resolution was submitted by Mr. TALLMADGE:

Resolved, That the Committee on the Judiciary be instructed to inquire into the expediency of declaring by law the effect of liens of judgments obtained in the courts of the United States, and of limiting such liens to the same extent as judgments in the supreme or superior courts of the several States.

The Senate then proceeded to the special order of the day, being the

REMOVAL OF THE DEPOSITES.

Mr. FORSYTH resumed and concluded his speech.

Mr. SPRAGUE and Mr. GRUNDY simultaneously rose to move an adjournment. The Chair decided in favor of Mr. SPRAGUE, upon whose motion

The Senate adjourned.

HOUSE OF REPRESENTATIVES.

TUESDAY, January 28, 1834.

The standing committees reported bills—

For the relief of the heirs of William Pollard;

For the relief of Sutton Stephens;

For the relief of Thomas Dixon & Co.;

For the relief of John Barton;

For the relief of Noah Chittenden;

All of which were referred to the Committee of the Whole House, and made the order of the day for Wednesday.

On motion of Mr. HALL, of North Carolina,

Resolved, That the Committee on Ways and Means be instructed to inquire into the expediency of taking, immediately, such measures as may restore a metallic currency of gold and silver coins to the country, and, at as early a day as practicable, report on the subject by bill.

On motion of Mr. McKIM,

Resolved, That the Committee on Commerce be instructed to inquire into the expediency of making an appropriation for the purchase of a site, and the erection of a marine hospital, in or near the city of Baltimore.

On motion of Mr. MANN, of Pennsylvania,

Resolved, That the Committee on the Post Office and Post Roads be instructed to inquire into the expediency of establishing a mail route, commencing at the Spring House, in Montgomery county, thence by Acuff's to Heister's Tavern, on the Allentown road, thence by Thomas White's, Franconia Post Office, Gerhart's Tavern, Trumbowersville, Everhart's, Hertzel's, to Fryesbury, on the old Bethlehem and Allentown road, in Lehigh county.

Mr. H. EVERETT, from the Committee on

Indian Affairs, reported the following resolution, which, under a rule, lies one day on the table:

Resolved, That the Secretary of War be directed to-day before this House a statement of the present and future liabilities of the United States to Indians and Indian tribes under existing Indian treaties, exhibiting, in a tabular form, the dates of the treaties; the names of the tribes parties thereto; the several sums and annuities, designating whether in money or goods, stipulated to be paid or delivered; the term of payment or delivery; the place where to be paid or delivered; and the specific services and specific articles stipulated to be performed for and delivered to them; the terms thereof; the place where to be performed or delivered, with an estimate of the expense of the performance of such stipulations; and the stipulations for removing Indians from the States, with an estimate of the number of Indians to be removed, and of the expenses of their removal.

A message was received from the President of the United States by the hands of Mr. Donelson, his Private Secretary, giving a detailed account of the penitentiary in the District, from the warden; which was referred to the Committee on the District of Columbia.

THE PENSION LAWS.

The order of the day was then declared to be the resolution of Mr. Chilton, to appoint a select committee to inquire into the expediency of so extending the general pension law, as to embrace within its provisions those persons who were engaged in the Indian wars, down to the year 1794, and the amendment to it by Mr. Bouldin, to appoint a committee to inquire into the moral effect of the pension system upon the community, and how far it ought to be abolished or repealed.

Mr. Denny, of Pennsylvania, ably supported the original resolution, and encountered the objections urged both against the pension system in general, and against its extension to the soldiers of the frontier in particular. It had been said that by the Constitution, Congress had no power to pension even the soldiers of the revolutionary war, and much less had they power to pension those of the frontier. The gentleman from South Carolina, [Mr. Pinckney,] who had used this argument, asserted that the pension system originated with the much abused protective system. This, Mr. D. denied. He said the pension system was not only coeval with the Constitution, but existed before it, as it does now. What existed before, with, and after the adoption of the Constitution, is not, therefore, unconstitutional; nor did it appear unconstitutional to General Washington, who patriotically recommended it to the special attention of Congress. Indeed, the power of Congress to establish a pension fund is granted in that part of the Constitution which empowers it to raise and support an army.

The gentleman from South Carolina asserts also that the pension laws are unequal in operation, and therefore unjust, for a great majority of those on the pension list reside north and west of the Potomac. This is certainly the case. But why? Because most of the soldiers of the revolutionary war were from places situated north and west of the Potomac. Within their territories originated the war with the British, and with them were the enemy first encountered. Nay, when the war was changed towards the southern States, there were the northern and western soldiers to be found incorporated with the army of the Confederation. At the defeat of General Burgoyne, no less than thirty thousand soldiers were from the northern States; and these marched wherever the enemy was to be found.

With regard to the argument of the gentleman from Rhode Island, that the war was private, not public, it is only necessary to refer to the complaint made by the western Indians, that they were not included in the treaty of peace made with the British in '83; and that in consequence, the belligerency was continued separately with them as having been first the allies of Britain, and next the principals—the war being evidently continuous and the same. So speak all historians of the Indian war, classing it invariably as a concomitant and a consequence of the revolutionary war.

But an equally strong argument is, that the result of that war was for the national benefit in the cession of the public lands. These were for the benefit of the national treasury, not for the benefit of any particular State; from these funds of the national Government with the soldiers (whose exertions secured them) be entitled to look for compensation. The national Government were bound to remunerate them by a public bounty either of lands or moneys.

Mr. D. defended Generals Harmar and St. Clair from the attacks made on them, and concluded his address by hoping Congress would administer oil to the glimmering lamp of life of those soldiers engaged in the Indian wars, before it became extinguished.

The discussion was postponed to consider the prevalent order of the day at one o'clock, viz:

REMOVAL OF THE DEPOSITES.

The House resumed the consideration of the motion to refer the report of the Secretary of the Treasury on the deposites to the Committee of Ways and Means—the question being on the amendment submitted by Mr. Jones, as an amendment to that previously submitted by Mr. McDuffie, viz: to add to the motion for reference the following instructions to that committee: "Inquire into the expediency of depositing the revenue hereafter collected in the State banks in the different States, where the same is collected, in proportion to their respective capitals paid in, and to prescribe the terms on which the same shall be deposited; and to report by bill or otherwise."

Mr. Huntington, (of Connecticut,) resumed, directing his arguments chiefly to that part of the discussion whether Congress had the power to apply a remedy for the existing public distress, and whether they could, and how they should, exert that power, if it existed. This question of the power of Congress is involved in the sufficiency of the reasons assigned by the Secretary of the Treasury for withdrawing the deposites from the bank; for if they are insufficient, the right of Congress to restore them is a necessary consequence. Now, as the Secretary of the Treasury has made specified principles the basis of facts adduced to justify his order for the removal, it will be essential to consider the truth or propriety of those principles themselves, before treating of the facts superinduced on them.

The first of these arguments is, that the Treasury Department, being an executive department, is subject to the supervision of the President, who being bound by the Constitution to see that the laws shall be faithfully executed, is bound to control as he pleases the manner or means of their being executed; and therefore that he is not only justified in specifying to the Secretary of the Treasury the manner in which that officer should conduct the affairs of his department, but should see they are conducted as he shall so dictate, and shall remove any who prove refractory. But without waiting to notice the assertion that the Treasury Department is an executive department, which thinks it not a little remarkable, as well as contradictory, that the President denies in theory (in his last annual message) the power of the head of the executive which he maintains in practice. To deny the freedom of action is a slander on any who claim to be a citizen.

Again: The very language with which the orders of the Secretaries of State and of the War and Navy Departments, are introduced to public notice, is of itself conclusive as to the authority of the President over the Treasury Department. Every document issued from the offices of the former three departments is asserted to be by *the authority of the President;* but no such language is found in a treasury order.

But the argument to prove the power of the President to control the heads of the departments by the clause of the Constitution cited by the advocates of the Administration, will prove that there is but one executive department, dependent on the will of one person. So the argument to prove the power of control, by deducing it from the right to appoint and remove from office, will prove singular consequences, at variance with the freedom granted to every citizen of these United States. Take, as an example, the judiciary branch of the Government in that part which has not been made heretofore the subject of debate. The marshal of the United States is to have published the decrees of the Supreme Court. The President has the power to appoint and remove the marshal. But should the President think proper to require the marshal not to publish the decrees, would he be entitled to the asserted right of removal if the marshal did publish contrary to his order? Thus we would have to rest on the thorns of a Republican Government, whence every vestige of liberty had fled, if the doctrine of control, broached by the opposition, became general in its application.

Suppose another instance in that of Territorial judges, whose term of office is four years. If a Territorial judge of Florida thought proper to issue a decree from the district court of that Territory relative to a sale of land; and that the President thought proper to send his interdiction that no such decree should pass, under the penalty of removing the judge from his office, where could there be freedom of the exercise of will and wisdom of constitutional right and official privilege?

Suppose, again, the situation of the Librarian to the Library of Congress: the President appoints him, and has the power of removal. But suppose that the Joint Library Committee thought proper to order an invoice of books for the use of the Library, and that the President, in his wisdom, thought proper to order the Librarian not to make out the order, under pain of removal, would not the Librarian be justified in obeying his order?

Indeed, the unlimited power advocated for the President over those whom he may appoint to office, and can remove, would prevent the discretionary exercise of the very power with which any officer of Government may be invested as officer. No treaty or contract could be performed without the dictum of the President.

But if the control over the deposites had not been given by the bank charter to the Secretary of the Treasury, but to the Speaker of the House, or the Chief Justice of the Supreme Court, would the President have the power to control those officers in the exercise of the discretionary power vested in them by law? Or would he have the right to remove them, because they insisted on their right to decide for themselves? And suppose further, that the control was not given to the Speaker by virtue of his office, but to Andrew Stevenson of Virginia: would the authority of the President to see the laws executed empower him to control the exercise of the discretionary authority given by Congress to Andrew Stevenson?

And if not in such an instance, neither can the controlling authority in any other to whom Congress has specially delegated the power of removal. If Congress saw fit to entrust the discretionary power to the President, in conformity with his general authority, they would have no specified; but they have particularly exonerated him from all responsibility and all execution of the law, by throwing the responsibility and execution on another. So that whether by name or office, the person on whom the responsibility and power are devolved, it is taken off the President, who is consequently supposed to have no control nor interference whatever.

The main inquiry therefore resolves itself into the question, can that law which invests a discretionary power in one person, be faithfully executed by another? If so, then is the President clear; if not, then is the law given him none. His power after the removal of the deposites would control where the law gave him none.

If the law contemplated that the reasons of the President should be the authority of the Secretary of the Treasury for removing the deposites, the sum of his task would be merely to give a report stating that he had received such and such reasons (like those mentioned in the message or the Cabinet) from the President, and that he was guided and bound by them. Would this report be satisfactory to Congress? Would the reasons be another be sufficient where he was demanded to furnish his own?

Mr. H. next combated the assertion by which served power not only to remove the deposites but to remove them where he judged best. The only power over the deposites with which the Secretary was invested lay in the charter of the bank; if he had no power granted, he had none reserved. His power after the removal of the deposites was precisely that which he possessed over them before

the charter. By this charter he had no power granted. Before this charter, he had none reserved over the custody or control of the deposites. To the Treasurer, not to the Secretary of the Treasury, was the custody committed, guarantied by a bond. The custody taken from the Treasurer to be confided to the bank, reverted to the Treasurer when taken from the bank. Now, the Secretary pretends to derive his custody power from a previous authority, with which he was invested before the deposites had been confided to the bank; if such reserved power is proved not to have so existed, then the necessary consequence is, that the Secretary has exceeded his authority in removing the deposites to other banks. The Secretary has, indeed, depended for his reserved power on the authority given him to collect the public revenues; but the collection gives him no power as to the custody—which is invested by law in another.

Mr. H. said, that as no member had been found willing to justify the reason put forth by the Secretary of the Treasury—that he, not the House, had the sole right of removing the deposites, by the terms of the charter—he thought it hardly required argument or illustration to refute such a pernicious doctrine. However beneath the subject almost to discuss such a dogma, he might be permitted to refer to an article that lately appeared in one of the public prints, which occurred in the reign of Charles the 2d, as not inappropriate to the present times, and in reference to the Secretary's opinion. In that scrap of history, the Secretary would find something like a precedent. [Mr. H. here quoted an occurrence, in which the advisers of Charles the 2d had interfered, to prevent the House of Commons of his time from appointing supervisors, by whom the public money could be secured.] After which he said he could not concur with other reasons, that this power to remove was absolute and unconditional; for the people and the bank, being both equally interested in his acts, he thought that the true reason for which it was given was, to enable the House, if that power was not rightfully or satisfactorily exercised, to restore the deposites, and thereby the faith of the nation, which was plighted by the charter, that the deposites should be given to the bank; and he argued to show, that if the Secretary's power was thus as claimed by him, to be unconstitutional, that it must follow, that, although the House might come to the conclusion that he, in withdrawing the public funds from the bank, had done wrong, and from which they would direct them to be restored, yet, that this direction—that they should be restored—would be rendered of no effect, as he might subsequently act independent of Congress, and again and again withdraw them, as often as they should be restored. But was it denied that Congress had the power of ordering them to be restored? If the doctrine was sound, it must follow that the Congress was powerless. He could further show that the Secretary himself had, in a subsequent part of his report, stood self-contradicted on this very assumption, for he admits that the power given him by the act incorporating the bank is the same; neither more nor less than that which was previously conferred on the Treasury Department, and which he might have rightfully exercised under the laws existing before the charter was granted; which authority, to use his own words, "gave him the power to 'take care of the public money, and deposite it 'for safe keeping, and in convenient places.'" But where was it that the power was given, unlimited, to him, previously to that given by the charter? Nowhere; and he therefore contended that if the bank was safe as respected the care of the public money; if it had acted as a faithful fiscal agent, and had disbursed their money according to the wants of the Government, then the Secretary had not, on his own admission, the authority given him to remove the public funds, and he had overstepped his authority.

Neither could he assent to his doctrine that he could remove the deposites whenever the public interest would, in his opinion, require such removal. This was both unsound and dangerous; for as it would be difficult to ascertain exactly the precise point of convenience by which he would be really justified, he thought Congress never intended to vest such a power, to be acted upon by any single individual, at his sole will and pleasure. He would not go at length over the other grounds assumed by the Secretary in relation to this, but he would submit to the House, and maintain, that from the true construction to be given to the act, the bank had not only a legal, but they had an equitable, right to the use and benefit arising from the care of the public moneys, until the expiration of the charter granted them, if it discharged all those duties which had been enjoined by the charter.

The Secretary seemed to suppose that there were no other powers given, and the money could only remain there, until he might otherwise order and direct. But were there not many other provisions in the act, granting important privileges, and imposing on the institution many onerous duties, and were there not ample provisions to compel the faithful discharge by the bank of those duties? Was there not amongst them, that one imposing a bonus, to be paid for their privileges? Although the gentleman from Georgia [Mr. Jones] denied that this was to be deemed an equivalent for depositing the public money, yet the only reason he had given for that denial was, that in the act, introduced in 1814, such a right to the custody of the public money was not inserted; but as it was inserted in the present charter, it seemed to him a more correct inference to suppose that the right was inserted to show that it was to be secured to the bank; and looking then to all the circumstances connected with the granting of the charter, its provisions, and the remedy that was to be applied in case any of the provisions were not complied with, or looking to what ought to be done for any misconduct committed in the management of the institution, he thought that the Secretary had mistaken his rights, and proceeded to exert a penal power over the institution which did not rightfully belong to him, in virtue of his office, as the fiscal officer of the Government.

If it was objected that the bank has violated the charter, then it was in the power of the President to cause the charter to be broken, and this was in the power of the judicial tribunals of the country to do, by the usual process of issuing a *scire facias*.

Mr. H. proceeded to examine the other reasons given by the Secretary of the Treasury, "that the bank was a monopoly," &c. Whilst he agreed that the bank had no actual right to the renewal, he called to the recollection of the House, that when the bank was incorporated, it was not considered a monopoly; at the commencement much difficulty had occurred in procuring subscriptions. But now, there was, owing to this very institution, such stability given to all other banking institutions, that their stock lists were filled up with avidity. The speculations of the Secretary however on this head goes on—he tells you that the institution is dangerous to the liberties of the people. But this was not a new idea, the same had been broached by the travelling agent, appointed by Government to inquire into these bank matters. Who gave the Secretary power to declare all this, or to regulate his action upon speculations as to our liberties? The Secretary states also, that public opinion had been declared against the institution. On this, he would only remark, that in the last presidential election, the question of rechartering the bank was not made at all. The Secretary also feared that there would be a large surplus revenue in 1836, but this was disproved by the statement made in his annual report on the finances, in which he expresses a doubt, that the revenue would be adequate to the expenditure. In this doubt, he fully concurred, as he had reason to know by information from mercantile men that importations, upon which of course duties were raised, owing to the depressed state of credit, and the want of funds, must decrease enormously. The bank had hitherto been enabled to sustain the merchants, from the superior confidence placed in it; owing, he presumed, to its ubiquity, as well as its ample resources. This institution now, however, dared not to increase their issues, and he would deny that, in the event of this bank being suffered to expire, without renewing it, the State banks could supply the chasm that must arise upon such an event in 1836.

He wished to know, did the inducements held out for the last three months warrant them in supposing that there could be any alteration in the system of the bank, so as to justify an opinion as to its being unsound? During this period, under all adverse circumstances, it not only paid all demands upon it promptly, but it was seen coming forward to sustain public credit, even the credit of banks in the first commercial city in the country. He desired they would appeal to the experience they had of the value of the institution, in giving to the country a sound and uniform currency. He, knowing this, could not assent to the doctrine of the Secretary, that his act would confer similar benefits, or give uniformity to the circulating medium furnished, or to be furnished, by the several State banks which he selected as depositories for the public money. He thought it right that the public mind should be disabused of the impression that the bank had, by improper curtailments, produced the depreciation of the day. No orders had been given for such curtailment; but, on the contrary, when such a resolution had been submitted to the board by the Government directors, for a gradual curtailment, this resolution, he could state, was opposed by every stockholder-director, save one. The bank had gone on in assisting the commercial interests of the country, and had performed all the duties assigned it as the fiscal agent of the Government.

But it was said (continued Mr. H.) that, in excluding the Government directors from its committees, the bank had violated its charter. If this were so, he thought the proper remedy was to apply to the judicial tribunals. He could not agree to the doctrine, that all the bank duties required seven directors to execute them. The board of directors, he would presume, had a right to regard, in the selection of the committees, the qualifications of each person to be placed on them. This was the usual course taken here in their own committees in the House; and it would appear rather strange, if umbrage upon this point should be taken by those who might not be selected by the Speaker, upon their own opinion of their fitness for such appointments, whilst the House vested that discretion in the Speaker which the directors of the bank claimed for themselves. He would not discuss the objection raised as to the three per cents, for it had already been so often dissected; for him, it never required any other refutation than that a committee of this House had investigated the subject, and reported that it neither called for nor needed any action on this subject. He would have passed by the charge as to the printing concerns of Gales & Seaton, and to the ownership of the National Intelligencer, but that they flamed in the report. But he would take leave to bear testimony to their high character—that no persons were less likely to be employed in works of corruption. The bank had been assailed by the Government, and by the press in its influence, and was justified in repelling the calumnies by which it was assailed. It was rather hard that this should be made a matter of reproach. In conclusion, Mr. H. remarked, that as the country was on the eve of a precipice, from which alone it could be saved by a rightful decision in this question, he trusted that their decision would be such as to establish the industrious of all classes on the sound and healthy position from which they had been so recently driven.

Mr. ARCHER having obtained the floor, moved an adjournment; which prevailed.

The House then adjourned.

IN SENATE.

WEDNESDAY, *January* 29, 1834.

A message was received from the President of the United States, by Mr. DONELSON, his Private Secretary.

Mr. TIPTON, agreeably to notice, introduced a bill to enable the people of Arkansas Territory to form a constitution preparatory to their admission into the Union.

The bill was read twice, and referred to the select committee upon a similar bill for the admission of Michigan into the Union.

Mr. BELL, from the Committee of Claims, reported a bill for the relief of John Watson.

Mr. BELL, from the same committee, asked to be discharged from the further consideration of the petition of George M. Grouard; which was agreed to.

Mr. BROWN presented the memorial of the Legislature of North Carolina, praying that the title to Indian lands lying within the boundaries of that State may be extinguished; referred to the Committee on Indian Affairs.

Mr. FRELINGHUYSEN presented another memorial, signed by about one hundred citizens of Newark, New Jersey, being similar in its character to that submitted by him yesterday; which, without being read, was referred to the Committee on Finance.

Mr. WILKINS presented two petitions from citizens of Pennsylvania, praying the abolition of slavery within the District of Columbia; which were referred to the Committee on the District of Columbia.

Mr. WILKINS rose to present a petition which had been transmitted to him on the great subject which was now agitating Congress and the country. The petition was most respectably and numerously signed, by citizens of the city and vicinity of his residence, his neighbors and friends—though not his political friends—and was produced in consequence of what he had said the other day on this subject. At the meeting which was held in Pittsburg, and which was very respectably, and he would say numerously attended, a resolution was passed which bore on him for an expression which he used on the occasion referred to, and out of that meeting grew the petition he held in his hand. It represented that he was mistaken in his remarks, and that they were received at Pittsburg with the utmost regret and astonishment. They represent that distress exists in the western country to a very great extent, and they ascribe it to the late removal of the Government deposites from the United States Bank. He did not know that they spoke of the actual distress existing, so much as of the alarm and consternation which prevails, and the distress which will arise from the removal of the deposites.

The petition attributes the breaking up of the internal and domestic exchanges and the business of the western country to the removal of the deposites. But, notwithstanding the respectability of the meeting, and the facts stated in the petition, he did not acquiesce with them in the belief that the distress did prevail in the western country, to which he referred. He admitted that the commerce and business of that country had been interrupted by the measures which had been adopted by the Bank of the United States in consequence of the removal of the deposites. But his constituents were mistaken in ascribing this derangement of the western exchanges to the removal itself; and for this reason, because the resolution of the Bank of the United States, which broke up the western exchanges, passed the direction of the Bank of the United States two months before the removal, and the distress complained of is founded on rumor. This resolution passed on the 13th August. A voluntary and unnecessary act on the part of the bank produced these effects, and broke up the western business.

The bank had the whole internal exchange of the country in its own hands, and by one stroke of the pen it was all broken up, and dissolved on the 13th of August before the deposites were removed at New Orleans. Why, sir, these mistakes were very natural, and likely to occur when gentlemen assembled in a tavern to decide on great constitutional questions. At this meeting, gentlemen were appointed to give their opinions on these important questions, on which the greatest diversity of opinion exists here. The resolutions of the gentleman from Kentucky are of a most grave, intricate, and difficult character to decide; and yet, at this meeting, a committee of five gentlemen are appointed, who retire to a bar room, perhaps, and thence report resolutions deciding these most important national questions. They allege that there was no authority in the Secretary of the Treasury for removing the deposites; and that, on this point, it was a most unwarrantable assumption of power. If these remarks had been applied to the President there would have been some plausibility in them. But when declared of the Secretary, that no law or authority existed for this assumption of power, they were so much mistaken as when they say that the internal exchanges were broken up by the removal of the deposites. There is no distress in the western country. He would tell his constit-

uents to look at their bank note exchange list; to their prices current, their profits, their flour, their coal, their glass, and to the whole circle of their manufactures; to their sales of real estate, since the removal of the deposites, and it will be seen that they are mistaken. From the day when the French and Indians first settled there to the present time, the highest prices have been since the removal. He was mortified that the intelligent enterprising citizens where he lived should believe their prosperity depended on the United States Bank or the State banks. Their means and resources are infinitely beyond what the bank can control. Let them look at their machinery, their fuel, their raw material, their enterprise, their industry, their steam power, their capital, which the bank cannot deprive them of. He would ask them to depend on their own skill, industry, and enterprise, which were sufficient to place them far beyond anything the bank could do against them. There was another fact, which, as Pennsylvania was deeply interested in it, he would allude to. He observed in the published list of the prices of stocks that those of the State of Ohio were at 119, while those of Pennsylvania were only at 101. Why was there this difference? This quotation was from the Philadelphia prices, regulated by the Philadelphia brokers, who have an interest in the depreciation of the stock of Pennsylvania. But why is she placed by her own city, and her own metropolis, in this mortifying situation? Either of the stocks are reimbursable at the same period. But with all respect for the enterprise of our sister State, Ohio, he asked why was this difference? May it be not effected by a combination between the brokers of Philadelphia? Pennsylvania is looked on as debateable ground at this time. It is designed to operate on the Legislature of the State to induce them to act for the purpose of compelling a restoration of the deposites. But it will not do. He thanked the gentleman from Massachusetts [Mr. WEBSTER] for the complimentary allusion to Pennsylvania, made in his remarks the other day. And he would assure him Pennsylvania would go on with her great system of internal improvements. No combination of any kind or character could stop her, till she shall deprive her neighbor, the empire State, of the great western trade which she now enjoyed. Under the superintendence of a wise, vigorous, and economical State administration she would proceed. We were now engaged in an honorable emulation for the rich dowry which Ohio now holds in her lap; and they would proceed till they had secured it.

He moved that the petition be read, and then referred to the Committee on Finance.

Mr. WEBSTER said he was not in his seat when the gentleman [Mr. WILKINS] began his remarks. But he understood that the memorial which had been presented was respectably and numerously signed by citizens of Pittsburg, complaining of the late treasury measures. These persons, thus respectable and numerous, declare that they experience severe evils and great distress. Complaining in reply to the gentleman, he would move to lay the memorial on the table till to-morrow, when he would ask the indulgence of the Senate for a few minutes.

The motion was agreed to.

Mr. WEBSTER asked permission, which was granted, to take up the bill reported by the Committee on Finance to enable an enterprising individual in Georgia to import a quantity of iron free of duty, for the purpose of making an experiment in the construction of an iron steamboat. The bill was considered and ordered to be engrossed for a third reading.

ORDERS OF THE DAY.

The resolution of Mr. TALLMADGE, sub-

mitted to the Senate yesterday, was taken up and adopted.

Petitions were presented by Messrs. TIPTON, HILL, and LINN, which were severally referred to the usual committees.

The following bills were ordered to be engrossed and read a third time:

A bill for the relief of John Bills, with an amendment.

A bill for the relief of Archibald Small.

[After this bill had been ordered to be engrossed for a third reading, Mr. POINDEXTER, after making several remarks, and expressing a wish that a principle involved in it might be settled, as several other bills were in a similar situation, moved the reconsideration of the order which had just been taken.

Some remarks were made by Mr. KANE, chairman of the Committee on Private Land Claims, in reply; when

Mr. FORSYTH suggested that there was no need of a reconsideration, as the argument which the gentleman from Mississippi, [Mr. P.,] wished to make, might be offered to the Senate upon the passage of the bill; upon which

Mr. POINDEXTER withdrew his motion with the understanding that the bill would not be taken up during his absence.]

A bill making appropriations for certain roads in Michigan Territory, with an amendment;

A bill for the relief of Calvin Smith;

A bill for the relief of the heirs of Thomas H. Boyle;

A bill for the relief of the heirs of Lawrence Milligan.

The Senate then proceeded to the special order of the day, being Mr. CLAY'S resolutions upon the

REMOVAL OF THE DEPOSITES.

Mr. SPRAGUE addressed the Senate until half past three o'clock, when he concluded his speech.

On motion of Mr. GRUNDY,
The Senate adjourned.

HOUSE OF REPRESENTATIVES.

WEDNESDAY, January 29, 1834.

Mr. CASEY reported a bill for the relief of Joseph Bates; and

Mr. CLAY, a bill for the relief of Samuel H. Dobson; which were severally read twice and committed.

Mr. BOCKEE reported a bill to incorporate the Columbian Horticultural Society in the District of Columbia; which was read twice and ordered to be engrossed for a third reading.

Mr. C. P. WHITE reported a bill to regulate the value of certain foreign silver coin in the United States.

Mr. J. Q. ADAMS inquired if there was any report accompanying the bill from the committee.

Mr. C. P. WHITE replied that there was not, as the subject had been reported upon by the committee two sessions ago.

The bill was then read twice and committed.

Mr. J. Q. ADAMS said, that as many new members complained that they were not enabled to procure a work, the publication of which was ordered by the last Congress, and which was essentially necessary for them to have, he was induced to submit a resolution on the subject now, lest any difficulty might arise hereafter as to its being procured, by the new understanding, as to the provision inserted in the House appropriation bill in respect to the purchase of books, &c.

Resolved, That the Clerk of this House be directed to purchase a sufficient number of copies of the Legislative and Documentary History of the Bank of the United States to furnish one copy to each member and delegate who was not a member of the last Congress.

The resolution was agreed to.

On motion of Mr. GORHAM,

Resolved, That the Committee on the Post Office and Post Roads be instructed to inquire into the number of failures of the mail between the city of Washington and the city of Boston, in Massachusetts, which may have occurred within the last

eight weeks; and whether any fines have been exacted for such failures, from the mail contractors, and to report to this House.

On motion of Mr. BURD,

Resolved, That the Committee on Invalid Pensions be instructed to inquire into the expediency of increasing the pension of William Keller, of Bedford county, in the State of Pennsylvania, a soldier in the United States dragoons, and an officer in the army of the United States in the late war with Great Britain.

On motion of Mr. VANCE,

Resolved, That the act of last session of Congress for the relief of Riddle, Becktel, & Co., together with the decision of the 3d Auditor of the Treasury, be again referred to the Committee of Claims, for their decision and explanation.

Mr. WHITE, of Florida, submitted the following resolution; which lies on the table one day:

Resolved, That the President of the United States be requested to communicate to this House, the correspondence and remonstrance of the Spanish Governors and Ministers, in relation to the invasion of East Florida, in the years 1812 and '13, and the invasion of West Florida in 1814, and the demands upon the American Government for indemnity up to the conclusion of the Florida treaty, together with the instructions of the Government to our Minister in Spain to tender to the Government of Spain satisfaction for the invasion of the Spanish territory at Foxardo, by Commodore Porter.

Mr. HAWES submitted the following resolutions:

Resolved, That the Committee on Military Affairs be directed to inquire into the expediency of erecting a public armory on the waters of Green river, in the State of Kentucky.

Resolved, That the Committee on Military Affairs be directed to inquire into the expediency of abolishing the military institution at West Point, in the State of New York.

The question being taken on their adoption, the numbers voting were—ayes 41, noes 54. (No quorum.)

The reading of the resolutions was then called for. They were read accordingly.

Mr. WARD called for a division of the question. The first resolution was then agreed to.

Mr. BROWN, of New York, then moved to lay the resolution in relation to the academy at West Point on the table.

Mr. BOULDIN called for the yeas and nays on that motion; which were ordered, and the question to lay the resolution on the table was put and negatived.

YEAS—Messrs. John Adams, Heman Allen, Anthony, Archer, Ashley, Banks, Barnitz, Barringer, Bates, Bayliss, Bean, Binney, Bockee, Bodle, Briggs, Brown, Bull, Burns, Cage, Cambreleng, Chambers, Clark, Corwin, Cramer, Crane, Deberry, Denny, Dennis, Dickson, Evans, Edward Everett, Horace Everett, Foot, Fowler, Fuller, Fulton, Gillet, Gorham, Graham, Grennell, Halsey, Hannegan, Hard, Hardin, Harper, Hathaway, Hazeltine, Howell, Huntington, Jarvis, King, Lansing, Lay, Loves, Loyall, A. Mann, Martindale, McIntire, McKennan, McKim, McKinley, McVean, Muhlenberg, Page, Pearce, Ramsey, Reed, Schley, Selden, Slade, F. Thomas, Turrill, Tweedy, Vance, Vanderpoel, Van Houten, Vinton, Wagener, Ward, Wardwell, Watmough, Wayne, Campbell P. White, Edward D. White, E. Whittlesey, Wise, Young—85.

NAYS—Messrs. J. Q. Adams, John F. Allen, Chilton Allan, William Allen, Barber, Beale, Beatty, Beaumont, John Bell, James M. Bell, James Blair, John Blair, Bouldin, Bunch, Burd, Burges, Bynum, Carr, Casey, Chaney, Chilton, Chinn, Claiborne, Wm. Clark, Clay, Clayton, Clowney, Connor, Coulter, Crockett, Darlington, Davis, Davenport, Deming, Philemon Dickerson, David W. Dickinson, Duncan, Dunlap, Felder, Fillmore, Forester, Foster, Gamble, Gholson, Gilmer, Gordon, Grayson, Griffin, Joseph Hall, Hiland Hall, Thomas H. Hall, Hamer, Hawes, Hubbard, Inge, William Cost Johnson, Cave Johnson, Jones, Kavanagh, Kinnard, Lane, Laporte, Luke Lea, Thomas Lee, Leavitt, Lyon, Lytle, Joel K. Mann, Marshall, Mardis, John Y. Mason, Moses Mason, McDuffie,

McKay, Miller, Milligan, Mitchell, Osgood, Parks, Parker, Patton, Patterson, Franklin Pierce, Pinckney, Polk, Pope, Potts, Schenck, Shepard, Shinn, Smith, Speight, Standifer, Stoddert, Sutherland, Taylor, Philemon Thomas, Thomson, Turner, Webster, Williams, Wilson—102.

The question then recurring on the adoption of the resolution,

Mr. J. Q. ADAMS called for the yeas and nays; which were ordered.

Mr. LYTLE offered an amendment, but it was not considered in order.

Mr. HUBBARD proposed to amend the resolution, by striking out the words " *Committee on Military Affairs,*" and inserting " *a select committee, to consist of one member from each State.*"

Mr. H. remarked that he had voted against the motion to lay the resolution offered by the gentleman from Kentucky upon the table, and he had done so from a settled conviction that the time had arrived when some inquiry into the affairs of this institution ought to be made. It was perfectly manifest, from what had transpired heretofore, and from passing events, that there was an opposition, and an increasing opposition, to the academy at West Point; the reasons why, he could not distinctly tell, but such he believed to be the fact; whether it arises from the manner of administering the affairs of the institution, or whether from the creation of the institution itself, he was unable to say.

From what had come to his knowledge, he believed that the Legislatures of two at least of the States of this Union have expressly instructed their respective delegations in Congress to oppose all appropriation and every other measure for the benefit of this academy; and in other parts of the Confederacy there were objections to this institution. He therefore was of the opinion, that an inquiry should be composed of one member from each State; and he would be it understood, in preparing this amendment, he had not done it as of any disrespect to the Committee on Military Affairs; nor had he done it with a view of being placed upon the select committee, as it was his particular wish to be excused from that service.

Mr. SPEIGHT expressed his regret that the original resolution had been opposed; as it was adopted, the committee would have it in their power to investigate whether there were any abuses connected with the institution; however, the select committee proposed by the member from New Hampshire would no doubt do ample justice to the subject.

Mr. HUBBARD said, he was induced to offer his amendment in con sequence of the various opinions which were held as to the expediency and utility of the academy. These opinions had been carried so far as to have produced resolutions from some of the State Legislatures; he therefore thought that the subject should be investigated by a select committee, consisting of one person from the several States in the Union; that it was the only way to arrive to a proper decision, whether it was to be abolished, or have appropriations made for its support. In taking this course, he begged to be understood as declining being on the committee, if his proposition should be adopted.

Mr. BROWN, of New York, offered another amendment, but it was withdrawn.

Mr. MILLER moved to postpone the further consideration of the subject until Tuesday.

Mr. WILLIAMS called for the yeas and nays on this motion, but subsequently withdrew his call.

Mr. HAWES accepted the amendment offered by Mr. HUBBARD as a modification.

Mr. MANN, of New York, was about to address the House, but was prevented by the expiration of the hour allotted to morning business. (So the subject stands over.)

The House refused, on motion of Mr. POLK, to suspend the rule, and proceeded to the consideration of the House appropriation bill: ayes 109, noes 66—(not two-thirds.)

REMOVAL OF THE DEPOSITES.

The House resumed the consideration of the motion to refer the report of the Secretary of the Treasury on the deposites to the Committee of Ways and Means—the question being on the amendment submitted by Mr. Jones, as an amendment to that previously submitted by Mr. McDervie, viz. to add to the motion for reference the following instructions to that committee: " Inquire into the expediency of depositing the revenue hereafter collected in the State banks in the ' different States, where the same is collected, in ' proportion to their respective capitals paid in, ' and to prescribe the terms on which the same ' shall be deposited; and to report by bill or otherwise."

Mr. ARCHER, of Virginia, addressed the Chair. The question, he said, had been so long debated that it was almost impossible to present it in any new light. He should endeavor to compress the remarks which he had to offer in relation to it, for many reasons admonished him to be brief. He owed it to the peculiar position in which the State, which he in part represented, stood to this question, and he owed it to himself to express his views in regard to it. The gentleman from Georgia, [Mr. Jones,] the other day made an allusion to himself, by remarking that he [Mr. Jones] had, during his whole political life, been an advocate of the doctrine of strict construction of the Constitution. My principles (said Mr. A.) require that I should advocate the strict construction of the constitutional powers of the executive as well as of the legislative branch of the Government. Sir, what was this question of the deposites when we first took it up? It was a question of construction of a statute by a judicial officer. What is the question now? Not only in conversation, and in the public press, but in our own debates, it has become a question whether the Bank of the United States should be rechartered. Are gentlemen, who have made this new issue, aware of what admissions they make by it? They told us that the question of the recharter of the bank had been decided by the people. How, then, can it be made a question now? They say now that we cannot restore the deposites without securing the removal of the bank charter. Who brought us into this predicament? If this was the result, it was the President who had produced it—that person who had already taken so much responsibility in the affairs of this country had brought us into this predicament. A talismanic wand of responsibility rules over the destinies of this country. It was not the wand of a magician. He exercises his spells covertly and in secret, a higher power than his overrules the spirits of men by openly assumed responsibility. He would inquire whether this was the real question, and whether we were prevented from correcting the proceedings of the Executive, by the fear of perpetuating the use of the Executive. What is this new issue? At the beginning of this trial, the question was whether the Executive exceeded the bounds of his constitutional powers. How was this got over? It was by instituting a hunt of the bank—a hunt, too, in which the bank had no chance for escape, for it was a predetermined that the object of the chase should be run down. The accused being hopeless of defence, makes a new issue to save himself, and he did not at all object to it. The Executive first submitted to this House the question whether the deposites in the Bank of the United States were safe. The House, after due deliberation, determined that they were safe, and expressed this determination, by an overwhelming majority only a day or two before the close of the session. But the Executive will remained unchanged, and it was determined that the deposites should be removed without the assent of Congress; arrangements were accordingly made, by transferring the Secretary of the Treasury [Mr. McLane] to another department; and next, by appointing an agent to make provision for the future deposite of the public money in the State banks, and for the removal of the deposites from the Bank of the United States. An inquiry was instituted, not for the purpose of ascertaining

whether the decision of Congress was correct, but of finding means to carry out the predetermined will of the Executive. Was this all? No, sir. Such was the hurry to complete the removal, lest, perchance the representatives of the people should again oppose it, that it was ordered before the arrangements which were deemed necessary with the State banks had been completed. It was admitted by the Executive that certain arrangements were necessary to the removal of the deposites; but he would not await their progress, lest Congress should interpose and prevent the execution of his will. The Executive had hoped to obtain the aid of Congress in the execution of his scheme. He was disappointed. Has he then stopped and laid aside his plan? No. It was his character to defy all obstacles which were opposed to his will. The President assumed the responsibility, and said to his executive officer, Do this thing, or I will remove you. Suppose the President had signed the order with his own hand for the removal? There was no man in the country who would not have regarded it as a gross outrage. Suppose the Secretary of the Treasury had said that he had acted in obedience to the President, and that that was his reason for the act. Suppose he had said, that he knew the act to be wrong, and hostile to the interests of the country, but he had done it because the President ordered him to do it, or quit his office. How would that report have sounded in this Hall? It would have been received as an insult and an outrage by every person who holds a seat here. What is the case now? This case has not occurred, but something that is not very far short of it. He knew well it was supposed that there were in this House men who wear the harness of party. He did not say it was so; but if it were true, he was sure that those manacles would be rent asunder and hurled at any Executive or any Secretary of the Treasury who should come here with such a report as he had supposed. After a few words more, Mr. A. yielded the floor to

Mr. GRENNELL, who expressed a hope that the House would indulge the member from Virginia with an adjournment, as he was laboring under evident indisposition.

The House then adjourned.

IN SENATE.

THURSDAY, *January* 30, 1834.

The VICE PRESIDENT laid before the Senate a communication from the Secretary of the Treasury, transmitting a report from the Commissioner of the General Land Office, in compliance with the resolution of Mr. POINDEXTER of the 19th December last.

Mr. KANE, from the Committee on Private Land Claims, reported a bill for the relief of an individual whose name was not distinctly heard by the reporter.

Mr. WRIGHT submitted to the Senate resolutions of the State of New York, approving of the course of the Secretary of the Treasury with regard to the removal of the deposites. Mr. W., in presenting the resolutions, addressed the Senate as follows:

I hold in my hand, Mr. President, and am about to ask leave to present to the Senate, certain proceedings of the Legislature of my State, in which that body expresses its sentiments in regard to the removal (as it is called) of the public moneys from their deposite in the Bank of the United States, made by order of the Secretary of the Treasury; in regard to the re-charter of the Bank of the United States, and in regard to the existing pressure upon the money market in some portions of the country, with its views of the character and causes of that pressure; and in which, also, the Legislature expresses its pleasure as to the course which the representatives of the State, upon this floor, shall pursue when called to act upon these questions.

In presenting, a few days since, the proceedings of limited portions of the people of their respective States upon the same subjects, honorable Senators took occasion, no doubt properly, to inform the Senate of the number, character, and standing, political as well as personal, of those whose sentiments they laid before us; to tell us as well who they were, as who they were not. I beg the indulgence of the Senate, while, following the example set me, I detail some facts in relation to the body whose proceedings it has become my duty to present, tending to show the extent to which the proceedings themselves claim the respectful attention of Congress.

The whole number of members allowed by the Constitution of the State of New York to its Legislature, is one hundred and twenty-eight members of Assembly and thirty-two Senators. The members of Assembly are apportioned to the fifty-five counties of the State according to their respective population, and the whole territory is divided into eight districts for the election of Senators, each district having four, and electing one of the four every year. The proceedings which I am about to present, were passed in the House of Assembly by a vote of one hundred and eighteen for, to nine against, and in the Senate by a vote of twenty-three for, to five against them; thus showing the very unusual occurrence, that of the one hundred and sixty members elected by the people to that Legislature, one hundred and fifty-five were present and acting upon these interesting and important questions.

But, sir, if this unexampled strength and unanimity of expression be entitled to weight, and it surely must be, while authentic evidence of public opinion is allowed an influence in our deliberations, that weight is greatly enhanced by the peculiar circumstances attending the expression. All these members of the popular branch of that Legislature, and eight of the thirty-two Senators, were elected during the first week in November last, one full month after the removal of the deposites, while the vote shows that more than thirteen to one of the members of Assembly voted for, while but one of the eight Senators, thus elected, voted against the resolutions. Still the strength of this vote, taken as an expression of public opinion, will be much increased by an examination of its territorial distribution.

It is well known here, and throughout the country, that the extreme western district of the State of New York has been unhappily, but most severely, agitated, in consequence of an outrage several years since committed against the liberty, and probably upon the life, of a citizen. The effects of this outrage have been, not only the engendering of the most bitter domestic feuds, but the partial establishment of a geographical line of separation in feeling between that and the other sections of the State. It is, however, a source of high gratification to myself to be able to state, as I trust it will be of pleasure to liberal-minded men to learn, that this unnatural warfare of feeling is most rapidly subsiding; that the deep wounds which have been created by it, in the social relations of that otherwise highly-favored section of the State, are healing fast, and that the time is not distant when the evidence of its existence and effects will entirely disappear. In this section of the State, however, not an expression of complaint, as to the pecuniary pressure, has been heard, and from the best advices, I believe that, at this moment, its business relations of every description are in a more prosperous and easy condition than they have ever before been. Yet to the west and northwest must we look for every vote against the resolutions, and to this section alone for eleven out of the fourteen of these votes. The remaining three are, with one exception, senators not elected at the election of November last, but in previous years, and all are located beyond the reach of the present pressure—in the agricultural, not in the commercial sections. In those portions of the State embracing our great commercial emporium, (and which I think I may, without arrogance or presumption, style the commercial emporium of the United States,) and the extensive cities of Hudson, Albany, Troy, Schenectady, and Utica, and an almost endless number of incorporated trading towns and villages, all surrounded by a dense, intelligent, and watchful population, amounting together to at least one million eight hundred thousand souls, there was not found a single member of the popular branch of that Legislature absent from his seat, or not with cheerfulness and alacrity recording his name in favor of the resolutions. Of the hundred and twenty-eight members composing this branch of the Legislature, it is worthy of remark that the city of New York alone elects eleven, and that every representative from that city, in either branch of the State Legislature, responds to the resolutions which I now lay before the Senate.

Of the members of this Legislature, personally, it is not my intention to speak. The situations they hold, and their public acts, are the legitimate evidence of the capacity and respectability of the individuals. It is as the organ, upon this occasion, of this deliberative body, representing as they do two millions of freemen, nearly the one-sixth part of the entire population of the Union; a population, too, as commercial—nay, sir, I may say more commercial—and employing more capital, than any other portion of the country, and collecting and paying into the national treasury full one-third of its whole revenue; a people having as deep a stake, pecuniary and otherwise, in the prosperity of this country, and as firmly and ardently devoted to its welfare as any other equal portion of its citizens; it is as the organ of such a body, representing such a people, that I submit to the Senate this part of their public proceedings—that I ask to place their almost unanimous opinions as to the conduct of the President, of the Secretary of the Treasury, and of the United States Bank, upon your files, by the side of similar expressions from the States of Ohio and New Jersey; also by the side of different expressions from portions of the people from Boston and New Bedford, in Massachusetts; of Salisbury, in North Carolina, and Newark, in New Jersey, and such other expressions of opinion as are, or as may come, before the Senate upon the subjects; and at this interesting crisis in the affairs of our common country, I respectfully solicit from the Senate that consideration for these proceedings of the Legislature of my State which a liberal, just, and unprejudiced estimate of the views and feelings of any respectable portion of the citizens of the country may demand, and no more.

Here, sir, I might resume my seat, and I should do so with pleasure, were it not that a part of what I have felt to be an imperative duty upon this occasion remains to be performed.

In presenting the proceedings of a meeting of a portion of the town of Boston, the honorable Senator from Massachusetts availed himself of the occasion to express his own views as to the existence of a public pressure, of its cause, and of the appropriate mode of relief. He went further, sir, and called upon all, and especially upon those who sustain the Administration upon this floor in relation to the change of the deposites, to give their views as to the future as well as the present posture of the pecuniary affairs of the country. As an individual, and as one considering it one of my highest duties to sustain the Administration in this measure, I am ready to respond to the Senator with entire frankness; but in thus accepting his call, I must not be understood as for one moment entertaining the vain impression that opinions and views pronounced by me, here or elsewhere, will acquire any importance because they are my opinions and my views. I know well, sir, that my name carries not with it authority anywhere, but I also know, that so far as I may entertain and shall express opinions which are, or which shall be found, in accordance with the enlightened public opinion of this country, so far they will be sustained, and no farther.

Following, then, Mr. President, the example which has been set for me, I shall abstain from a discussion of controverted points, so far as that can be done, and enable me to state unreservedly my opinions, and to make my views intelligible.

First, then, as to the fact of an existing pressure upon the money market: I believe that the recent extensive and sudden curtailment, by the Bank of the United States, in the facilities for credit, which had before been lavished upon the community, has caused very considerable embarrassment to those in our commercial cities, who had extended widely their moneyed operations, and who had made themselves dependent upon these facilities; but, at the same time, I believe that these inconveniences have been in an unimportant degree, either directly or consequentially, extended to other classes of citizens. I therefore believe, further, that the extent of the pressure has been greatly exaggerated, and that the motives for the exaggeration are to be found, primarily, in the belief that the present Administration may b

brought into disfavor with the people, and may be overthrown through the agency of the panic which is attempted to be gotten up, and, secondarily, in the hope that the same panic, if successfully produced, may subserve the interests of the institution by which it has been and is to be raised.

Secondly, as to the immediate cause of the pressure, I concur fully with the Senator from Massachusetts that it is an error to attribute it to the mere fact of the change of the deposites. The reasons he has assigned for that opinion are sufficient. They might be amplified and enforced, but it is unnecessary upon the present occasion. Past experience, concurring facts, and the nature of the transaction, all combine to demonstrate that such a change would not, necessarily, draw after it such a result. I concur also with the honorable Senator [Mr. WEBSTER] in the position that the evil complained of is to be attributed to the change which has taken place in the positions which the Government, the Bank of the United States, and the State banks have heretofore occupied relatively towards each other, and to the acts which have followed that change. These positions, as at present existing, are pronounced by the honorable Senator to be false. That the attitude which the Bank of the United States has chosen to assume towards the Government and the State banks is a false position I most cheerfully admit; but that there has been anything in the conduct of either the Government or the State banks to justify or even excuse that attitude, I deny, and hope to have an opportunity to attempt to disprove. From the Government directly no loans could be obtained or were expected, and it was well known that the State banks which have been selected as the fiscal agents of the Government, had extended their loans many millions, and to the utmost limit authorized by the public deposites in their vaults. It is neither shown nor pretended that the other State banks have curtailed their loans in consequence of the change of the deposites, except when the curtailments by the Bank of the United States and its branches have compelled them to do so. We have, however, record evidence from itself that the Bank of the United States has curtailed its loans, since the first day of August last, and up to the first day of December last, to the enormous amount of $9,697,000, and all this curtailment has taken place in the entire absence of any revulsion in trade, of any scarcity in the country, or any other peculiar cause of embarrassment existing or anticipated. We need not then grope in the field of speculation for the cause of the present pressure. It stands before us recorded in letters and figures which cannot lie, and which leave us without excuse for misunderstanding or for affecting to misunderstand it.

Thirdly. As to the motives for this conduct on the part of the bank, I have already said, I deny that a justifiable one is to be found either in the conduct of the Government or of the State banks towards it; and I repeat the assertion. Whether or not this curtailment of its business has been rendered necessary on the part of the bank, in consequence of former mismanagement, I need not inquire, inasmuch as the bank itself, and all its friends and supporters, here and elsewhere, most strenuously deny that its present condition furnishes any necessity for increased means. I have looked carefully into the instructions originally given by the Secretary of the Treasury to the State banks in relation to the course to be pursued by them towards the Bank of the United States, and I find there nothing to warrant an apprehension that any disposition existed on the part of the Government to injure the bank, or to embarrass it in the prosecution of its lawful business. I have examined, with equal care, the instructions given in regard to the transfer drafts, and the circumstances under which they were to be, and were in fact, used. And these acts of the Government, taken in connexion with the large amount of money still left in the bank, and which, upon a different supposition, would assuredly have been also withdrawn, I hold to furnish undeniable evidence that no disposition was entertained or manifested on the part of the Government to wrong this institution. The only design evinced was, to exercise a legal right, reserved by the charter, to change the deposites, and to continue an uncompromising, to be sure, but constitutional opposition to the renewal of the charter of the bank. That, for these constitutional and legal acts, it has pleased the bank to wreak its vengeance upon the community, I neither allege nor believe: that the State banks have made the slightest hostile movement against it, neither is nor can be pretended. What, then, is the motive for this rapid curtailment? I have not the slightest doubt, Mr. President, that, in the language of the resolutions I hold in my hand, it is to be found, and found only, in an attempt of the bank, "at a time 'of general prosperity, to produce pecuniary dis'tress and alarm, and in exercising its power with 'a view to extort a renewal of its charter from the 'fears of the people." So much for the pressure, and the causes of it.

I will now consider the remedy for the evil which the Senator proposes. Leaving the discussion of everything constitutional, political, and expedient, the Senator, with his usual tact, goes directly to the matter in hand; and with the utmost confidence he tells us that the remedy is not to be found in the restoration of the deposites, but in the re-charter of the present bank. Whatever else may be said of this avowal, it must, at least, be admitted that it does credit to the candor of the Senator. For myself, I thank him, and the country will thank him also. It is time, Mr. President, high time, that things should be called by their right names in relation to the depending controversy; that the veil with which it has hitherto been attempted to disguise the subject should be torn off, and that the people should know what is the question which is, in fact, occupying the attention of Congress. This being done by the declaration of the Senate, there is reason to hope that we may hereafter be, if we have not heretofore been, aided by contributions of public sentiment, so far as the Senate may think proper to allow influences of that sort to enter into its deliberations. And, sir, I venture the prediction, that if the expressions now upon our files, or those which shall hereafter be placed there, as evidences of public sentiment, shall be examined, it will appear that the good sense and ingenuity of the Senator, in devising this remedy, has only placed him upon a level with the common opinion of the whole community, as to the real question in dispute: that every paper favoring the views of the opponents of the Administration, has and will, expressly or impliedly, recognise the fact, that the question before the public is, "Bank, or no bank," and that the real issue has that direction—not the disposition of the Government deposites. A petition for re-charter is a mere matter of form which can at any time be brought forward. A few days, or even a few hours, are sufficient for that object, and we ought not to permit ourselves to doubt that such a petition will be forthcoming or not, according to the decision of this merely incidental question, now made to assume the place and importance of the real issue.

But, Mr. President, while I highly approve of the open and manly ground taken by the Senator from Massachusetts, I differ with him *toto cœlo* as to the remedy he proposes. There is no inducements which can prevail upon me to vote for the recharter of the Bank of the United States. I would oppose this bank upon the ground of its flagrant violations of the high trusts confided to it; but my objections are of a deeper and graver character. I go against this bank, and against any and every bank to be incorporated by Congress, whether to be located at Philadelphia, or New York, or anywhere else within the twenty-four independent States which compose this confederacy, upon the broad ground which admits not of compromise, that Congress has not the power, by the Constitution, to incorporate such a bank.

I may be over-sanguine, Mr. President, but I do most firmly believe that, in addition to the invaluable services already rendered to his country by the President of the United States, he is, under Providence, destined still to render her a greater than all, by being mainly instrumental in restoring the Constitution of the country to what it was intended to be by those who formed it, and to what it was understood to be by the people who adopted it. In relieving that sacred instrument from those constructive and implied additions under which Congress have claimed the right to place beyond the reach of the people, and without responsibility, a moneyed power, not merely dangerous to public liberty, but of a character so formidable as to set itself in open array against, and to attempt to overrule, the Government of the country. I believe the high destiny is yet in store for that venerable man, of disproving the exalted compliment long since paid him by the great Apostle of Republicanism, "that he had already filled the measure of his country's glory," and that he is yet to accomplish, what neither Thomas Jefferson nor his illustrious successor could accomplish, by adding to the proof which he has so largely contributed to afford, that his country is invincible by arms, the consolatory fact that there is, at least, one spot upon earth where written constitutions are rigidly regarded. I know, sir, that this work which the President has undertaken, and upon the success of which he has, with his usual moral courage, staked the hard-earned fruits of a glorious life, is full of difficulty. I know well that it will put the fortitude and patriotism of his countrymen to the severest test; but I am happy also to know that he has, in this instance, as heretofore, put himself upon the fortitude and patriotism of a people who have never yet failed him, or any man who was himself faithful to his country in the hour of peril.

Of the course which the State which I have the honor in part to represent here, will take in this great contest, it becomes me, forming so humble a part of its voice in the councils of the nation, and known only by the favors I have received at its hands, to speak with great diffidence. In the resolutions I now lay before the Senate, it has spoken for itself upon most of the points involved. As to the others, I feel that my knowledge of the character of its people, and of the known sentiments of whole masses of its public men, will justify me in the confident expression of an opinion that the State will sustain the Executive to the utmost in this controversy; and that I may say to those who are, and long have been, desirous to restore the Constitution, in this regard, to its true reading, "now's the day and now's the hour" for its accomplishment. At all events, I have the right to say, that I will place myself by the side of the President, to the full extent of the views I have given, and that I desire to stand or fall with my constituents, as they shall determine the result.

I have thus responded, and I hope the Senator from Massachusetts will allow fully, to so much of his appeal. I will go on, sir, and cover the whole ground. He has asked, if you will neither recharter the present bank, nor establish a new one, what will you do? As an individual, sir, and speaking for myself only, I say I will sustain the executive branch of the Government by all the legal means in my power, in the effort now making to substitute the State banks instead of the Bank of the United States, as the fiscal agent of the Government. I believe they are fully competent to the object. I am wholly unmoved by the alarms which have been sounded, either as to their insecurity, or influence, or any other danger to be apprehended from their employment. I hold the steps so far taken in furtherance of this object well warranted by the Constitution and laws of the land, and I believe that the honor and best interests of the country imperiously require that they should be fully sustained by the people, and by their representatives here.

That these views are correct, it is not, of course, my intention, at this time, to attempt to show. In some stage of the debate upon this great subject, I hope to be able, without trespassing upon the superior claims of others, to have that opportunity.

We have been told, and told emphatically, that things cannot remain as they are; that the powers now vested in, and exercised by, the Secretary of the Treasury, are too broad, and that legislative aid is required. If I have not misunderstood the import of remarks, it has also been told to us that such aid will be withheld. To this, I for the present only answer, that things are now, in this respect, precisely as they were before the incorporation of the present bank; that the same powers which the Secretary of the Treasury then had, he has still; that by the change of the deposites from the Bank of the United States, the executive department of the Government has been restored to the control over the places for the safe-keeping of the public moneys, which it had by law before these moneys were deposited with that institution; and that all the law formerly existing

unaltered, the only effect of the provision in the charter of the bank, being to suspend their operation until the Secretary of the Treasury should order and direct that the deposites be made elsewhere than in the vaults of that bank. I further state, as my opinion of the law, that by the act of the Secretary of the Treasury ordering a change of the deposites, and by that act only, the full power of Congress over the whole subject, has been restored.

If, then, the powers of the Secretary are too broad, as the law now stands, it is the duty of Congress to restrict them; while, if the powers of the executive branch of the Government are not now fully adequate to the making and executing of all needful orders, rules, and regulations, for the safe-keeping and convenient management of the public moneys, it is equally the duty of Congress to legislate further upon the subject. And whether Congress do or do not legislate in either case, is a matter wholly between its members and their constituents, for which the Secretary of the Treasury is in no way responsible.

But, Mr. President, while I am prepared to give to this effort of the Government, to make the State banks our fiscal agent for the safe-keeping and convenient disbursement of the public moneys, a full support and a fair experiment, any effort, come from what quarter it may, to return to a hard money currency, so far as that can be done, by the operations of the Federal Government, and consistently with the substantial interests of the country, shall receive from me a cordial and sincere support; and no one would more heartily rejoice than myself, to meet with propositions which would render such an effort in any degree practicable.

Still are we told by the Senator from Massachusetts, that things cannot remain as they are; that unless something, which, according to his views of the subject, would afford relief, be done, the pressure, the distress, and the agitation, will continue. I have already stated the source from which, and from which alone, in my judgment, the present pressure proceeds. I have stated, also, without reserve, the object which is, in my opinion, intended to be accomplished by it. Of the correctness of my conclusions, the Senate and the country must judge. If they are, as I believe them to be, well founded, it is undoubtedly in the power of the bank to continue the pressure, and consequently the agitation of the public mind, to some extent, so long as it shall think it to be for its interest, and not incompatible with its safety to do so. It is not for me to speak as with a knowledge of its intentions in this respect, and the Senator from Massachusetts disclaims all information upon the point. I can, therefore, only state my opinion; and it is, that the bank has not entered upon this bold measure without the deepest consideration, and that it will not abandon it, the design not being accomplished, but upon the most stern necessity.

Yet, Mr. President, I trust in God that that necessity will soon, very soon, be made manifest, by the attitude which the nation will assume towards this daring and dangerous institution. The glorious American Revolution was but resistance to moneyed power—yes, sir, to the exercise of a moneyed power, without the consent, and beyond the reach, of the people of this country. To this our fathers opposed a stern and uncompromising resistance. Appeals were made to their fears. Distress in their pecuniary affairs were pictured to them in colors to have deterred any but the pure spirit of patriotism and love of liberty which led them forward. Then the pictures were not imaginary but real; the distresses were not fancy but fact. The country was not then strong and rich and prosperous, but weak and poor and disheartened; and still their march was onward. They armed themselves upon the side of their country, and stood by their Government; and when their hard and perilous services were paid in paper, worth a fortieth or sixtieth part of its nominal value, the representative of the dollar was the dollar to them, for it gave liberty to the people, and freed them from the rule of avarice. And have we, their immediate descendants, so soon lost their noble spirit? Are we to fold our arms and obey the dictates of a moneyed power, not removed from our soil, and wielded by stronger hands, but taking root among us; a power spoken into existence by our breath and dependant upon that breath for life and being? Are our fears, our avarice, our selfish and base passions to be appealed to, and to compel us to re-create this power, when we are told that the circulation of the country is in its hands—that the institutions established by all the independent States of the Confederacy are subject to its control, and exist only by its clemency—when we see it setting itself up against the Government and vaunting its power, throwing from its doors our representatives placed at its board, and pronouncing them unskilful, ungenteel, or incorrigible—nay, Mr. President, when it lays upon our tables in this chamber, its annunciation to the public, classing the President of the United States with counterfeiters and felons, and declaring, that as kindred subjects, both should receive like treatment at its hands,—I say, sir, are we to be driven by our fears to recharter such an institution, with such evidences of its power, and of its disposition to use that power, lying before us authenticated by the bank itself? Are we to do this after the question has been referred to the people of the country, fully argued before them, and their decision pronounced against the bank, and in favor of the President, by a majority such as never before in this Government marked the result of a contest at the ballot boxes?

Gentlemen talk of revolutions in progress. When this action shall take place in the American Congress, then, indeed, will a revolution have been accomplished—then will your Constitution have been yielded up to fear and favor, and your legislation to be the *sic volo, sic jubeo*, of a bank. But, Mr. President, I do not distress myself with any such forebodings. I know the crisis will be trying, and I know, too, that the spirit and patriotism of the people will be equal to the trial. As I read the indications of public opinion, I see clearly that the true question is understood by the country, and that it is assuming an attitude towards the bank which the occasion calls for. Be assured, sir, whatever nice distinctions may be drawn here as to the share of influence which expressions of the popular will upon such a subject are entitled to from us, it is possible for that will to assume a constitutional shape which the Senate cannot misunderstand, and understanding, will not unwisely resist. The country, Mr. President, has approved of the course of the Executive in his attempts to relieve us from the corrupt and corrupting power and influence of a national bank, and it will sustain him in the experiment now making to substitute the State institutions for such a fiscal agent. I have the fullest confidence in the ultimate and complete success of the trial; but should it not prove satisfactory to the country, it will then be time enough to resort to the conceded powers of Congress, or to ask from the people what, until every other experiment be fairly and fully tried, they will never grant, the power to establish a national bank.

Mr. WEBSTER replied to Mr. WRIGHT at considerable length.

Mr. CHAMBERS followed also in reply to the Senator from New York.

Mr. TALLMADGE continued the debate for some time in support of the position and arguments of his colleague.

Mr. GRUNDY, in order that the Senate might proceed to the special order of the day, moved that the resolutions be laid upon the table, which was upon the subject is now in full force, and wholly carried—

Ayes 23, noes 22.

Mr. WEBSTER gave notice that he should call up the subject to-morrow morning.

The Senate then proceeded to the special order of the day, being the resolutions offered by Mr. CLAY, upon the

REMOVAL OF THE DEPOSITES.

Mr. GRUNDY rose and said that it was a part of the history of every free country for persons who were out of power to charge those who were in power with oppression. Sometimes the charge was true, and sometimes only imaginary, and sometimes neither, but made to operate on the people, when the accusers themselves did not believe it. Frequently great injustice ensued from such charges, and often much good. Such occurrences were frequently wholesome and useful, as they enabled the people to apply the proper corrective if true, and if not, those who were assailed would receive the approbation of the community for their acts. Believing that there was no unwarrantable assumption of power in this instance, he would proceed as briefly as possible to give his reasons for the belief. And first, he considered the removal of the deposites as emphatically the act of the President; he had caused it to be done, and whatever of praise or censure the act merited was due to him alone. He would not deprive him of an act which was his, and it was well suited to the occasion when he said, "I take the responsibility." Although he did not feel so much alarmed as honorable gentlemen did at the act complained of, yet he felt astonished when they censured the Secretary. What has the Secretary done? He had previously filled a high station, and when his opinion was asked he gave it distinctly, and when he was afterwards called to be Secretary of the Treasury, he freely and fearlessly stepped forward and carried that opinion into execution; and would he not have been entitled to the execration of every honest man if he had given an opinion when in one office, and in another capacity refused to carry it into effect? It would not have accorded with the high character he sustained in the State from which he was taken. In that State, where there were high party feelings, he was called to the high office of Attorney General, and should we declaim thus against a man having so high a store of character laid up? Should we censure a man with a character spread over the whole country. He doubted the good effect of the Senate's denouncing him.

He thought gentlemen did not look with their ordinary care to the true structure of the Government in which we live. What is the great preservative principle in its theory? In order to prevent the concentration of all the necessary powers in one head, those powers were divided and distributed among three branches, the executive, legislative, and judicial. These are the great preservatives of American liberty, calculated to give safety to the people. The Constitution speaks of but one will to be obeyed, when that will is expressed. Take, for instance, the judiciary department. When the Supreme Court have pronounced a judgment, is it not the duty of every judge and subordinate officer to surrender to the supreme tribunal of the country? And if you should say to the subordinate, the judge is a mere tool, a driveller, you must disregard him, would not every man condemn you? Suppose Congress should pass an act with the sanction of the President, what is the duty of every officer of the Government and citizen of the United States? Conformity to the legislative will. It is the universal law of the land, made by the constitutional authority, and if it be unwise, the people can cause it to be repealed; but, until then, it must be rigidly observed. Now for the application of these principles to the executive departments. To the Executive is conferred the execution of the laws, and if any one department ought to act with more despatch than another, it is that. In order to have one uniform will and action in the executive department, the Convention which framed the Constitution, decided that it should be confided to a single individual. Now, if the Senate and House of Representatives determine that anything but the executive will shall prevail, they entirely obstruct that department. If they should say that any one of the Secretaries of any of the Departments should not be responsible to the President, you remove and destroy all his responsibility. But if you require him to conform to his will, you hold him to his responsibility. This has been the whole practice of the country. The people elect the President, and hold him responsible to them, but do they elect the Secretary? No. The Congress of 1789, declared that the operations of Government could not proceed, and all their hopes would be frustrated, if the power of displacing the executive officers could not be given to the President, so that he might see that they discharged their duties. It was for this reason, that this power was given to a single individual. This was the true construction of the Constitution, and acted on by every President down to the present time, and it was hardly necessary to prove its existence. But, it would appear, by reference to the recorded opinion of Mr. Madison, that the

power of the President to remove each executive officer under his control, was unqualified and unrestricted.

[Mr. G. here read an extract from Mr. Madison's opinion.]

The Constitution says that the executive power shall be vested in one individual, and if Mr. Madison's opinion was to be regarded, what inference was to be drawn from it? Whenever there is a difference of opinion in the President and the subordinate, the latter should yield his opinions or quit his station. He considered it settled by the Constitution, the first Congress, and by the practice of forty years, that the power exists in the President, and he is the only person responsible to public opinion. But the gentleman from Maine, [Mr. Sprague,] said, suppose it should turn out that the President ordered a thing to be done and the officer was of opinion that he could not perform it, what then was to be done? He (Mr. G.) would say, let him resign and go home, if he could not conform to the opinions of those who had authority to command him. He had another remark to make. It was true Congress created offices, and the President and Senate appoint the officers. But did it therefore follow that the officer belonged to Congress? No. The Constitution ranges him into his appropriate department. If it be the Judiciary, no one has a right to interfere with its duties or rights. But it is not so with the Comptrollers or Auditors; theirs are ministerial, not executive duties. But let us see to what branch of Government the Secretary of the Treasury belongs. What are his duties? To superintend the collection of the revenue, together with several other duties. And are they not ministerial? Sir, they are every one ministerial. And if they are of this description, they belong to the executive department, and you cannot change them. We prescribe the duties of all officers, and when that is done our powers are at an end. We cannot carry a single law into effect, because that duty is assigned to another. When the law is made, we have done all we can do. We can repeal, alter, change, or modify it; but the execution of the law belongs to the Chief Magistrate, and we have no power over it. The great argument is drawn from the sixteenth section of the bank charter, that although the Secretary may remove the deposites, he must give his reasons to Congress for so doing. Now the argument from this is, that the responsibility is not upon the President, but upon the Secretary, who is under our control. The great error lies in this view of the case. You may require of every officer in every department to give statements, and their reasons for an act. Suppose you should require of the District Judge of the District of Columbia, the number of causes decided in his court in a given time, would that make him executive? You get your information and act upon it, and still you cannot touch that independent branch of the Government, except to require information. And so when you require of the Secretary to report, it is to give you the foundation on which to make legal provisions, but this does not show that the Secretary was acting under your control in this department.

Having shown that the collection of the moneys of the United States is confided to the department which is bound to see that the laws are faithfully executed, Mr. G. proceeded to show, from historical documentary evidence, the practice of the Government from the origin to the present day. Gentlemen need feel no alarm about these things. Their ancestors saw the same things performed before, and never then thought them violations of the Constitution. The first impost law was passed in 1789, and the Treasury Department was then formed, and he begged gentlemen to observe, that by it the Secretary could not touch a single dollar of the public money. It was not so in 1789, when it was contended that the collection of the revenue devolved on the Executive Department. He referred to the first letter ever written on the subject by General Hamilton to the collectors in Georgia and Savannah, requiring the money collected to be sent to Mr. Habersham.

Mr. GRUNDY here observed that he could not conclude to-day; and,

On motion of Mr. BROWN,

The Senate adjourned.

HOUSE OF REPRESENTATIVES.

THURSDAY, *January* 30, 1834.

Mr. MARSHALL, from the Committee on Revolutionary Claims, reported a bill providing for the settlement of certain revolutionary claims; which was twice read.

Mr. MARSHALL stated that the object of this bill was to refer all claims for commutation and other similar claims to the Secretary of the Treasury for settlement, and the committee had suspended its action upon these claims until this bill should be decided upon. The committee hoped the House would give it an early consideration, and he moved its reference to the Committee of the Whole on the state of the Union.

Agreed to.

Mr. EVERETT, of Vermont, was directed, he said, by the Committee on Indian Affairs, to call up for consideration the following resolution, reported from the Committee on Indian Affairs on the 28th instant.

Resolved, That the Secretary of War be directed to lay before this House a statement of the present and future liabilities of the United States to Indians and Indian tribes, under existing Indian treaties; exhibiting, in a tabular form, the dates of the treaties; the names of the tribes parties thereto; the several sums and annuities, designating whether in money or goods, stipulated to be paid or delivered; the term of payment or delivery; the place where to be paid or delivered, and the specific services and specific articles stipulated to be performed for and delivered to them; the terms thereof; the place where to be performed or delivered; with an estimate of the expense of the performance of such stipulations, and the stipulations for removing Indians from the States; with an estimate of the number of Indians to be removed, and of the expenses of their removal.

The motion being objected to, Mr. EVERETT moved a suspension of the rule, to enable him to call up the resolution.

The question having been put, it was found that a quorum had not voted.

Mr. EVERETT asked the yeas and nays on the question, and they were ordered.

The question being then taken, on the motion to suspend the rule, it was decided in the affirmative:

Ayes 144, noes 29.

The resolution was then taken up for consideration and adopted.

THE PENSION LAWS.

The order of the day was then declared to be the resolution of Mr. CHILTON, to appoint a select committee to inquire into the expediency of so extending the general pension law as to embrace within its provisions those persons who were engaged in the Indian wars, down to the year 1794, and the amendment of it, by Mr. BOULDIN, to appoint a committee to inquire into the moral effects of the pension system upon the community, and how far it ought to be abolished or repealed.

Mr. HANNEGAN addressed the House in favor of the motion of Mr. CHILTON, and in opposition to the amendment of Mr. BOULDIN, until the expiration of the hour.

[Some of the dates in Mr. HANNEGAN's remarks, as reported, are incorrect, and they cannot be corrected in time for this paper. His remarks are, therefore, wholly excluded.]

REMOVAL OF THE DEPOSITES.

The order of the day was declared to be the discussion of the question concerning the removal of the deposites; but it being understood that Mr. ARCHER, who had the floor, was too indisposed to proceed, a motion of adjourning that debate was almost unanimously adopted.

Mr. POLK then moved that the House concur in the appropriation bill, as reported by the Committee of Conference of both Houses, and agreed to by a Committee of the Whole on the state of the Union which (after a short debate on a question of order) was made the order of the day.

Mr. HUBBARD said that some objections having been taken against the bill, as compromised by the conference of both Houses, on account of a variation having been made from the original bill, he had made special researches on the subject, that he might ascertain how far the House could act on a bill thus altered; and he had found two cases in point, both of which occurred in 1816. The first was on an action for a bill authorizing a convention to regulate the commerce between the United States and his Britannic Majesty. An objection had been made to the insertion of the word *declare* in the bill as originally drafted; and this produced a collision between the two Houses, which resulted in a conference. At this conference amendments were introduced, not to be found in the original bill. Again, in the same year, a bill was drafted, appropriating a compensation to the Secretary of the Senate and the Clerk of the House. The objections to this also produced a conference, which resulted in amendments altering the original appearance of the bill. As he therefore saw no point of disagreement between the practice of Congress in the two instances adduced, and that now before the House, the report of the Committee of Conference should have his support.

Mr. WAYNE, of Georgia, spoke chiefly as to a question of order. The bill had been sent from the Senate with amendments; it was returned with a motion of disagreement; it went back to the House with a message of adherence by the Senate in their amendment; and then the House refused a motion to recede, and granted one to confer. Now, Mr. WAYNE considers that the papers (bills) should invariably accompany each motion made, and that when not so, the action was not according to parliamentary usage. When the Clerk of the House carried the resolution to the Senate asking the conference, he should have carried also the bill on which the motion had been made to the Senate; and with the Senate should it have remained till a definite action was had on it. Instead of this course, the papers had not been sent to the Senate; but had been brought by the committee from the House to the conference and brought back again. This he considered irrelevant to parliamentary order, for which he is a decided stickler; and he considered that the bill was not strictly in the possession of the House—therefore that no action could now be had on the compromised bill as reported by the committee. To prove this view of the matter, he quoted the rules of order, as given in Jefferson's *Legislative Manual*. A conference he considered to be two-fold in its object, as a simple and a free conference. When simple, the attention of a conference was limited to objections stated in writing; but when free, the objections were not submitted in writing; and the conference was entitled to act as far as parliamentary usage permitted. This, Mr. W. considers, has not been done, and that the conferees have exceeded their authority in making amendments to the original bill. Such an alteration is particularly objectionable; because the power of the House is limited with regard to agreement or disagreement on it, as they must either reject or adopt the bill *in toto*. But if the House had been restrained in making any amendment to the bill as first returned from the Senate, or at any future procedure, surely the committee appointed by the House will be equally restrained, unless, indeed, the committee has greater power than the House itself. With regard to such amendments, the two instances quoted by the gentleman from New Hampshire do not form a practice calculated to supersede all the rules and precedents previously established.

But, again, the alteration contains an appropriation which is at variance with the powers entrusted to the conferees—to which he thought they had no right to assent in any compromise. The addition of five thousand dollars to the library of Congress, is different from the general appropriations made by the bill. To this he could not assent, and he regretted that he must therefore vote for the rejection of the bill as a whole, because he cannot alter it in part—the House having no power to modify a bill so reported by a committee of conference, and adopted by a committee of the whole House. He then referred to a transaction of the Senate of the 24th of May, 1796, and to the 188th page of the Manual, to prove that a report of a committee of conference cannot be modified as a report of any other committee.

Mr. CLAYTON was opposed to concur in the agreement; 1st, on account of the bad mode of legislation, which would be sanctioned by a concur-

rence; and, 2d, on account of the appropriation which formed the subject-matter of the obnoxious alteration. Legislation should be simple: straight forward, and according to rule. There were laws laid down for the proceedings of legislation—rules which were founded on reason; and any mode of legislation which violates those rules, must violate the reasons on which they are founded.

Both Houses had legislated so badly on this subject, that they had now reduced themselves to the predicament of being compelled to choose between two evils. The basis of liberty and efficiency in legislation is, that the members of the Legislature should have the right of freedom of debate, and the right auxiliary of rejecting or adopting any amendment which might in any manner or by any person be proposed. Yet by the proceedings of the conference, the House was completely precluded from the power of noticing the amendment, without rejecting the whole bill, and were debarred the freedom of debate on the subject.

Again: with regard to the appropriation made of 5,000 dollars by the compromise, he does not so much consider the amount of that sum as the principle on which it had been foisted into the bill. An appropriation for any, the most extraneous purpose, might have similarly been introduced—one (for instance) for clearing all the rivers of the country; or increasing all the salaries, which he informs us is contemplated, of the executive officers of the Government. He would object equally to one dollar as appropriated as to one million. A small sum should not thus be stolen no more than a large. Important consequences often result from small beginnings. No one (as Mr. CLAYTON illustrated his position) can succeed in his attempts at reduction, if there have not been compliances granted to him.

In conclusion, he said that it would be better to reject the bill than to pass it with such an objectionable amendment as that reported by the committee, even at the risk of having the appropriations deferred. He expected the House would ultimately be obliged to act as had been done in the case reported by Martinus Scriblerus—begin all its proceedings de novo.

Mr. SUTHERLAND considered it ridiculous to advocate a rigid adherence to parliamentary usage, else would this country sanction a painted chamber, &c. It is good to depend on rules founded on reason. But the reasons which may sanction rules for one Legislature may not be calculated to found rules for a Legislature of a different country. He is more solicitous to frame rules regulating the legislative proceedings of this country, from reasons more immediately affecting the interests and customs of the country, rather than from any foreign reasons, however appropriate they might have been to institute the rules for other proceedings.

Mr. S. cited some cases from the English Parliament, in the reign of Elizabeth, and from the Legislature of Pennsylvania, to show, according to the practice there, that the power to add new sections to bills was given to their committees of conference. These committees, if he might be allowed the term, possessed the majesty of both Houses, and they were often resorted to as measures of expediency, to prevent, as was the case in this instance, the loss of a bill upon which the two Houses might have differed. He fully concurred in the opinion expressed by the Speaker, that the present question was not strictly one so much of order as it was of discretion, and which it was for the House to sanction or not, as it thought proper.

Mr. HARDIN contended that it was not consistent with the dictates of common sense to suppose that a committee of conference could rightfully originate any new clause to a bill.

Mr. POLK expressed his regret that this question had been—instead of being discussed on its merits—embarrassed with so many points of order. However, as an opinion on these points had been given by the Speaker, it was unnecessary for him now to entertain them. He justified the committee for having recommended the proposition, as it was made by them, with a sincere desire on their part, to settle the differences which existed between the two Houses, and which might have caused the loss of the entire bill. This was done in

good feeling; but, as their acts were not binding, it was for the House to decide whether their recommendation was to be carried into effect. They had considered all the circumstances connected with the question, and he entreated the House would now decide it fairly upon its merits, as if any defect should be found to exist hereafter, it could be provided for by another bill; which was better than to have the present bill lost.

Mr. J. Q. ADAMS requested the title of the bill should be read.

The title was read accordingly.

Mr. A. then called for the reading of the entire bill, which being also read, he insisted that the insertion of the clause recommended by the committee was in total variance with the title of the bill, which was an act making appropriation for the service of Government, in part, for 1834; and he asked what possible connexion was there to warrant such a proposition as a library subscription in a bill of this character?

Mr. POLK remarked, that if the honorable member examined the bill, he would find that the proposition was fairly connected with the clause, making a limitation to the purchase of books, &c.

Mr. ADAMS would also contend, that even that clause ought not to have been in the bill, as it was inconsistent with its title. The present question was not only of order, but one that involved the principle of legislation, consistency, and the very honor of Congress, which was bound to maintain, when it passed any bill, that there should be some connexion between the title of the bill and its provisions. If the worst came to the worst, that the House adhered to their original intention, by which the present bill would be lost, another could be reported in the general appropriation bill; and this, he believed, would hasten, not retard, their measures.

After a few brief remarks from Messrs. E. EVERETT, HORACE EVERETT, HUBBARD, WAYNE, BATES, LANE, and FOOT, and after two ineffectual motions for adjournment, the question on concurring with the vote of the Committee of the Whole, on their agreement to the proposition made by the committee of conference, was put, and decided in the negative.

YEAS—Messrs. John Adams, Beale, Bean, Beardsley, Jr'n r Bell, Barber, John Blair, Bockee, Boule, Brown, Bunch, Burns, Chambers, Chinn, Sam'l Clark, Clay, Darlington, Davenport, Deberry, Dennis, P. Dickerson, Dunlap, Edward Everett, Horace Everett, Foster, Wm. K. Fuller, Fulton, Galbraith, Gillet, Gorham, Joseph Hall, Thomas H. Hall, Halsey, Joseph M. Harper, James Harper, Harrison, Hathaway, Hawkins, Hinsler, Howell, Hubbard, A. Huntington, Inge, Jarvis, R. M. Johnson, N. Johnson, Kavanagh, King, Lane, Lansing, Laporte, Lawrence, Lea, Leavitt, Joel K. Mann, Mardis, John Y. Mason, M. Mason, McKim, Robert Mitchell, Moore, Muhlenberg, Murphy, Osgood, Page, Parks, Patterson, Pierson, Polk, Pope, Schenck, W. B. Shepard, Shinn, Spangler, Speight, Standifer, Sutherland, William Taylor, Philemon Thomas, Turner, Turrill, Vanderpool, Van Houten, Ward, Wardwell, Campbell P. White, E. D. White, and Wilson—88.

NAYS—Messrs. John Q. Adams, H. Allen, C. Allan, William Allen, Barber, Barringer, Bean, Baylies, Beaty, Beaumont, Jas. M. Bell, Binney, Bouldin, Briggs, Bull, Bynum, Cage, Carmichael, Casey, Chaney, Chilton, Choate, Claiborne, W. Clark, Clayton, Coffee, Connor, Corwin, Coulter, Crane, Amos Davis, Day, Deming, Denny, Dickerson, Duncan, Evans, Felder, Fillmore, Foot, Philo C. Fuller, Gamble, Gholson, Gilmer, Gordon, Graham, Grayson, Griffin, Hiland Hall, Hamer, Hardin, Hawes, Hazeltine, Henderson, J. W. Huntington, Cave Johnson, Seaborn Jones, Benjamin Jones, Kinnard, Lay, Lewis, Love, Lucas, Lyon, Lytle, Martindale, Marshall, McComas, McDuffie, McIntire, McKay, McKennan, Miller, Milligan, Parker, D. J. Pearce, Franklin Pierce, Pinckney, Potts, Ramsay, Rencher, Schley, Selden, A. H. Shepperd, William Slade, Charles Slade, Sloane, Smith, Stoddert, Wm. P. Taylor, Francis Thomas, Thomson, Tompkins, Tweedy, Vance, Vinton, Wagener, Watmough, Wayne, Webster, Whallon, Frederick Whittle-

sey, Elisha Whittlesey, Wilde, Williams, and Wise—108.

Mr. WILDE then moved that the House re. cede.

The SPEAKER decided that; as the House had heretofore refused to recede, it was not in order to renew it.

Mr. BEARDSLEY rose, and moved an adjournment, which prevailed.

And the House adjourned.

IN SENATE.

FRIDAY, January 31, 1834.

The VICE PRESIDENT laid before the Senate a communication from the Secretary of the Navy, relative to the disbursements of appropriations made for the benefit of that department.

The VICE PRESIDENT also presented a communication relative to a railroad through Michigan Territory; which, on motion of Mr. HENDRICKS, was referred to the Committee on Roads and Canals.

A message was received from the President of the United States, by Mr. DONELSON, his Private Secretary.

Mr. POINDEXTER, after some prefatory remarks, submitted the following resolutions:

Resolved, That the resolutions of the Legislature of New York, presented to the Senate, be referred to the Committee on Finance, to which has been referred sundry other petitions, memorials, and resolutions, on the subject of the removal of the public deposites from the Bank of the United States, and placing them in certain State banks, by the orders of the President of the United States.

Resolved, That said committee be instructed to inquire into the present condition of the currency of the United States, and the effects of said removal of the deposites on the same.

Resolved, That said committee be instructed to inquire into the facts and circumstances under which an alleged to have rendered said removal of the deposites necessary and proper, at the time the order was given for that purpose; and also into the legal and constitutional power of the President of the United States to direct and control the Secretary of the Treasury, in the performance of special duties confided to the discretion of that officer by law, as connected with the power of appointment and removal of the heads of the several departments of the Government.

Resolved, That the said committee be further instructed to inquire into the present distress and embarrassments of the mercantile community, and the pressure experienced throughout the country, by the sudden depression in the prices of agricultural products, and every branch of industry; and also into the causes which have produced these results, and the means, if any, by which they may be averted.

Resolved, That the said committee be authorised, in the inquiries aforesaid, to send for such persons and papers as they may deem necessary to the investigation of the matters referred to them by the preceding resolutions.

On motion of Mr. POINDEXTER, the resolutions were ordered to be printed.

Mr. WEBSTER, according to notice given yesterday, called up the resolutions of the Legislature of New York approving the course of the Secretary of the Treasury, relative to the removal of the deposites.

Mr. WEBSTER occupied the floor a considerable time, with unusual animation.

He was followed by Mr. WRIGHT in a few remarks, who declined replying to the Senator from Massachusetts at large, as he did not wish to supersede the gentleman from Tennessee, [Mr. GRUNDY,] who had the floor upon another subject.

The special order of the day was then announced, being Mr. CLAY's resolutions upon the

REMOVAL OF THE DEPOSITES.

Mr. GRUNDY continued his remarks upon the authority exercised by General Hamilton, to order the deposites in the South to be placed in the hands of Mr. Haberaham. He inquired, where did Gen.

eral H. derive this right? Congress had not spoken on the subject. It was part of the Executive duties, and now we hear it proclaimed, that because the President has selected some of the State banks as depositories of the public money, he has broken into the treasury and seized and plundered its contents. In General Hamilton's time, Mr. Habersham, as had been significantly said, made his breeches pockets the depository of the public money, and yet at that day, when there were as pure patriots as now—Jefferson, Madison, Ames, Sherman, and the Adamses—intently watching and looking to the administration of public affairs, they saw nothing dangerous in this. It may be said, however, that there was no party spirit then. But when party spirit raged, as it did, at the latter part of Hamilton's administration, there were no complaints then. The department had always been managed as it now is, and the Government could not operate in any other way. In 1791, when Congress established the first Bank of the United States, were not the executive powers of the Government then ascertained? Mr. Hamilton was then controlling and regulating the transmission of the public money from place to place, and Congress did not then provide that the deposites should be made in the bank. If this had not been an improper use of the executive power, would not Congress have discovered it then, and required them to be deposited in the bank? When they made the bank, they did not require it, and why not? Because the executive department of the Government was charged with the collection and disbursement of the money, and held responsible for it.

Having shown that prior to 1816, Congress made no provision for the deposite of the public moneys, he proposed to inquire whether anything had been done since on the subject. It was right and proper for Congress to decide whether the bank was or was not the proper place of deposite, and when that was done, when they said the experiment should be made, they also made a proviso, lest the bank should act unwisely, or improperly, that it should be so unless the Secretary should order and direct otherwise. A set of expressions more powerful to clothe the Secretary with full power, could not have been devised. If it had been intended that nothing should be authority for him to remove the deposites, but the danger of the public money, and that that should be the only reason for it, it was the easiest thing in the world so to have declared. Who, then, can construe powers so general, as to level them down to a particular case? He was surprised that the gentleman from South Carolina, [Mr. CALHOUN,] possessing such powers and compass of language, and so eminently possessing the *multum in parvo*, in his writing and speaking, could draw such an argument from such a clause. And is it likely that that gentleman and others of that day, who participated in the passage of the bank charter, would have given the power to any men to be used for such dangerous purposes? He could give no credit to it. He believed the power was given to the fullest extent, and it had been used by every President of the United States; and if the present Chief Magistrate was an usurper, so was every President from the organization of the Government down to the present time. Talking of Executive usurpation, he asked, was it never seen when the charter was to expire, that Congress never devised a place for keeping the public money? It was a strange disregard and neglect of public duty. But the explanation of it is, that the charge of the money was an executive duty. How were your loans made last war? Did Congress make them? No. The Executive raised the money, and took it, and disbursed it to your soldiers and sailors. How do you erect fortifications, but by the Executive? Every expenditure is made by the Chief Magistrate, under a law. Now, to show these measures of the President and Secretary were nothing new, but had been done by Mr. Gallatin, long before, and by these same transfer drafts too, which were so objectionable, he referred to the 14th volume of the State Papers, document 40. [Here Mr. G. read an extract to show that the public money had been drawn and deposited in the State banks.] And how was it done, he asked? Why, by the Executive authority. This was the case now. The draft was drawn in the usual form; for instance, on the Bank of the United States in favor of the Manhattan Bank, and the money placed to the credit of the Treasurer of the United States there; it is put there for legal disbursement, and is only a change from place to place. He was surprised, therefore, to hear that the Treasurer had violated his bond for this act, when he was bound to draw his draft at the requisition of the Secretary. If the Government has a million of dollars in a State bank in Tennessee, where there is no branch, what can the Treasurer do with it? The Secretary has ample authority to say when and where it shall be placed. But the Bank of the United States has delivered up the money on these transfer drafts, and why have they done it? Shall it be said that it was done out of respect to the treasury? But it has refused to deliver up the pension fund in its possession when required. He only mentioned this to show that where the bank thought it had a right to retain the public money, it did so. Had the cashier of the bank said, you have no right to take this money? No. But it has merely objected that certain rules were not observed in removing it. So that the bank has given up the controversy. Did not Mr. Crawford loan money to a considerable amount to banks in Georgetown and Alexandria? He did; and it was for the purpose of enabling them to protect themselves from the purposes of the Bank of the United States, and that act was approved of, although a loss of some forty thousand dollars accrued to the Government from the failure of one of them, and yet his fame did not suffer by it. But further authority is at hand; that of Mr. Rush, the Secretary of the Treasury under the late Administration; he has said that the President did possess the power of removal, and that it was safely vested in him. Mr. G. thought he might say, then, that prior to 1816, the President possessed and exercised the power of removal, and that there was nothing in the act of 1816 to repeal or gainsay it.

Then as to the second branch of the subject, whether the time for the removal was well selected. And here he would say distinctly, that if he was in favor of the recharter, he would vote for the restoration of the deposites, for he could see no difference in the questions. But suppose today the deposites were to be restored: would you not cramp and embarrass the State banks, and afterwards, in March, 1836, we should have to go through the same operation? And if it be true that distress were produced by one removal, another removal then would bring utter ruin upon the community. Now, as he intended to vote against the recharter, it was useless to attempt to disguise that this was a question of recharter. What claim, then, he would ask, has this corporation upon Congress for a recharter? Moneyed monopolies were contrary to the genius of our Government. But if we could not do without a bank, destroy this monopoly; let it come to an end, and give others an opportunity to embark their funds in a new one. He was against the renewal, because the bank had flagrantly abused its charter—among other things, under the false pretence of defending itself against attacks of power. What is self-defence? Why, to repel attacks or invasion. And what has the Chief Magistrate done? In 1829 he said that the question of recharter was an important one, and that he desired to bring the subject before the Representatives of the people. Here was no attack. And yet for this the bank has put forth all its means to accomplish a victory over the Chief Magistrate of the Republic; and yet it calls this a defence of its rights. The bank—a mere creature of our hands—sets itself up in opposition to the Chief Magistrate of the country. Mr. G. differed with his friend from Georgia, [Mr. FORSYTH,] who thought that the bank did not possess political power. Men were not freemen who depend on a moneyed power or were controlled by it; and if for this reason alone that it had exerted this power and influence, he would vote against it, that others might not be guilty of a repetition of its offences. We allege that the Government directors were excluded from any participation in the administration of the bank. Why were these agents of the Government appointed, but that the Government might know how its funds were applied and administered? But another thing: if the Government sell its stock, it still maintains the power to vote at the Board of Directors. This subject was fully debated when the bank charter was before Congress; and although it was objected to by Mr. GOLDSBOROUGH, the provision was still retained for governmental inspection and control.

Among other things, Mr. G. remarked, that the Senator from Maine, [Mr. SPRAGUE,] to prove that the people were prone to idolatry, that the people of every nation were prone to idolatry, had made a reference to the history of the Jews, when travelling to the land of promise. If the honorable Senator had been more minute, he would not only have reminded us of the history, but have enabled us to make the application to our own times. The history tells us, that when Moses had remained in the Mount longer than was expected, the people became clamorous and demanded of Aaron to make them gods to worship and go before them; he required them to bring their gold, and their ear-rings, and their bracelets, and those of their wives and their daughters. They did so, and poured them down before him, and made a great pile, or BANK of them. Of these, Aaron made a molten calf and they worshipped it, and they sat down to eat, and to drink, and rose up to play, as many a thoughtless man now does who has obtained a discount in bank and has the money in his pocket. But when Moses came down from the Mount he was exceedingly offended, and he put HIS VETO upon the whole proceedings. He burned the calf, and ground it into dust, and scattered it upon the waters. Now, sir, who are worshipping the golden image which they themselves have made—let the people judge. Not the Levites: they followed, and now follow the counsels of Moses.

[Mr. G.'s remarks will be concluded on Monday.]

When Mr. GRUNDY concluded—

Mr. WILKINS and Mr. FRELINGHUYSEN rose almost simultaneously.

The CHAIR decided in favor of Mr. WILKINS, who remarked,

That as he had power now in his hands, he wished to use it discreetly. He rather desired that there should be alternate speaking, and he would give way to the gentleman [Mr. FRELINGHUYSEN] if it were understood that he could be allowed to take the floor next. He inquired whether such a bargain could be made.

Mr. WEBSTER observed that coalitions were dangerous.

Upon an intimation that the course suggested by Mr. WILKINS might be pursued, he yielded the floor to Mr. FRELINGHUYSEN, upon whose motion,

The Senate adjourned till Monday next.

HOUSE OF REPRESENTATIVES.

FRIDAY, *January* 31, 1834.

The Standing Committees of the House presented bills for the relief of individuals, and reported unfavorably to the claims of others.

On motion of Mr. ALLEN, of Ohio,

Resolved, That the Committee on Military Affairs be instructed to inquire into the expediency of establishing a national armory on the western waters, to include those in the State of Ohio.

Mr. SPEIGHT submitted the following joint resolution:

Resolved by the Senate and House of Representatives, That the members of the present Congress, who have not heretofore received them, be supplied with the same books that have been ordered to be furnished to the members of the 22d Congress; the cost thereof to be paid out of any money in the treasury not otherwise appropriated.

Mr. SPEIGHT'S resolution having been read a second time—

Mr. WHITTLESEY, of Ohio, thought it should be modified in one of its clauses, which assigned to all members of this Congress who were not members of the 22d Congress those books. Many who had been members of the Senate last Congress, were members of the House this Congress; and had not received the books mentioned. They would therefore be excluded from the benefit contemplated.

Mr. SPEIGHT is not tenacious of forms; if he

can accomplish his object, he cares not in what manner.

After a few words from Messrs. POLK and WAYNE, to learn what books and what number of books, with their cost, were to be embraced in the resolution; and Mr. WAYNE having said he expected the Documentary History of Gales and Seaton were embraced, and that he was informed additional volumes of that history were not now extant, so that to supply it would require a heavy tax, upwards of 20,000 dollars;

Mr. SPEIGHT said the works more immediately required, were a Register of Debates, and the Documentary History mentioned.

The SPEAKER said he was then informed by the Clerk that unsold copies were extant of Gales and Seaton's history, or were in press.

The resolution was engrossed and read a third time.

Mr. KINNARD submitted the following resolution, which lies on the table one day.

Resolved, That the Secretary of the Treasury be directed to communicate to this House the correspondence between his department and the Executive authority of the State of Indiana, on the subject of locating and selecting Wabash and Erie Canal lands, together with the correspondence relative thereto between the Commissioner of the Land Office and the Canal Commissioners of said State or their authorized agent.

2. That he communicate, if any, the correspondence of any Engineer or Engineers appointed by the Secretary of War to survey a line of the Wabash and Erie Canal.

3. That he communicate, also, a map within five miles of either side of the Maumee river, between the line of Indiana and the termination of the canal line at the foot of the Rapids of said river, together with information of the period or periods when said lands were brought into market, and copies of instructions to land officers under which they have been sold. Also, a statement of the amount of the purchase money, the names and residence of the purchasers, designating the portion of such lands which have been located for public use, as well as those which have been taken at private and public sale.

Private bills were then presented for the relief of Asa Armington; David Kincaid; Stephen Smith and others; the heirs of Robert Abbott; Matthew C. Perry and E. R. Shubrick, masters commandant of the U. S. Navy; the heirs of Leonard Holley; John J. Avery, &c., &c.

Mr. CARR, from the Committee on Private Land Claims, reported a bill for the relief of Robert Abbott, in behalf of himself and the other heirs of James Abbott, deceased; which was read twice, and committed to the Committee of the whole House, and made the order of the day for to-morrow; and the bill and report were ordered to be printed.

An act was read a first and second time making an appropriation to clear harbors and rivers for the year 1834.

PENSION LAWS.

The order of the day was then declared to be the resolution of Mr. CHILTON, to appoint a select committee to inquire into the expediency of so extending the general pension law as to embrace within its provisions those persons who were engaged in the Indian wars, down to year 1794, and the amendment to it by Mr. BOULDIN, to appoint a committee to inquire into the moral effects of the pension system upon the community, and how far it ought to be abolished or repealed.

Mr. HUBBARD, having referred to the part which he had taken in the pension act of June 1832, as chairman of the committee which reported the bill, he said he would use his utmost endeavors to prevent its repeal, or to lessen its benefits, from a decided conviction of the justice on which that act had been founded, from its necessity, and the advantages attending its existence. He never will consent that those to whom the public bounty has been honorably and justly extended; who have had the evening of their days gladdened by even this pittance, should be deprived of it at their time of utmost need.

The gentleman from South Carolina had objected, not only to the pension system at large, but to the pension act of 1832 in particular, from its origin and injustice. His objection to its origin was because it had been passed by that Congress which adopted the modification of the tariff or American System; and that therefore the pension system was but a ramification of the tariff, and equally obnoxious. This is an unjustifiable conclusion. The gentleman from South Carolina forgets that the same Congress thus repudiated passed a bill for the relief of the claimants of South Carolina, which drew very largely upon the National Treasury. Does he consider this act also a branch of the tariff measure, because adopted by the same Congress? Is this act also an attack (as that gentleman said of the pension act) upon the policy of the southern States, and upon the broached idea of sovereignty?

But the same gentleman [Mr. PINCKNEY] said that though the bill was ostensibly for the relief of the soldiers of the Revolution, it was really to swell the power of the Federal Government. Now under the act of June 1832, only a limited number of soldiers were pensioned—those chiefly who were objects of private and should justly be objects of public charity, those who could demonstrate a continuous service of nine months at least. These are not supposed likely to increase executive patronage. This their age virtually negatives; and this the circumstances in which they had been placed, for which they are thus remunerated, gives a strong denial. It is generally known that acquisitions are most esteemed by those who have been instrumental in acquiring them. Hence it is that those who had been instrumental in acquiring or establishing the freedom of the country, are not likely to esteem lightly their subsequent liberty: and having formerly spent their whole fortunes in that acquisition, are not now likely to have their feelings of independence deadened by a small pittance which they and others consider as justly their due and not a corruptive boon. Their remembrance of their exploits is as dear to them as the pittance is necessary and just.

But as to the bill promoting sectional jealousies by sectional preferences, or as to its interfering in any manner with the tariff system, or being any way incidental to it, or in the contemplation of the committee who reported the bill, he peremptorily denied. Among the members of that committee were some from South Carolina; and never did he (Mr. H.) hear any suggestion whatever, urged in committee upon the tariff or any sectional questions.

He considers that there being more pensioners relieved who are residents north than there are south of the Potomac, should be no feasible objection against the bill—when it was understood that the war in which those veterans had fought was general, calculated to establish independence north and south, and therefore the remuneration should be general as the benefits conferred; when it was considered that thus was a proof that more Whigs and less Tories resided north of the Potomac—that there were more persons who performed public service during the revolutionary war, resident north of the Potomac, or that mortality had been greater among those south.

He spoke also concerning the numbers of persons now on the pension roll, which was indeed greater than had been contemplated by the committee who reported the bill, from the paucity of documents relative to the subject—thus debarring them of authentic information; but the number was not greater than justice required.

He then spoke concerning the amendment of Mr. BOULDIN, which he considered unjust in principle, and unlikely to be countenanced by the House.

Lastly, he directed his arguments against the original resolution of Mr. CHILTON. He would not consent to repeal the pension act of '32, but neither would he consent to have it extended to more than the specifications of that act warranted. The pensions were granted as just debts due from the national Government to those who had been unpaid, or been but paid at a per centage of twenty-five, perhaps not more than twelve, of what they should have received. Those so pensioned had embarked their whole fortunes in the war, and had won the liberty of their country, while they lost their own means of living. The pensions were therefore a just demand of compensation. But the same arguments cannot exist in any other circumstances. These men had acted before the establishment of a General Government; all that have served since, have been appointed and paid by the General Government, and have not therefore the same claims to urge as the survivors of the Revolution.

He admits that the Indian war between '83 and '95 was a public war; and is so treated in the public statutes and history of the country. But the soldiers so serving were adequately paid. If pensions are granted to them, where shall they not be extended? To the veterans of the last war, and to those who may survive any future war. Thus will the country be burdened perpetually with a pension roll, incompatible with the Constitution. If they overstep the soldiers of the revolutionary war, where will they stop? No man should be pensioned for mere service alone.

Mr. POPE, of Kentucky, had the floor when this debate was adjourned according to the rules of the House.

Mr. SPEIGHT moved that his resolution should be made the order of the day; and that it should be considered by a Committee of the Whole House.

This being agreed to, the SPEAKER called Mr. CONNOR to fill the chair.

Mr. SPEIGHT then amended his resolution by adding, that the whole of the Register of Debates from the first to the ninth volume inclusive, and the whole of the Documentary History published, should be purchased for those members of Congress who had not yet received copies of those works.

Mr. FOSTER asked the probable cost of those books; and whether it was intended to furnish members with vacant copies of these works.

Mr. SPEIGHT did not know the cost of the books.

Mr. FOSTER thought it rather extraordinary that the House should be called on to pass a resolution granting away a large portion of the public treasure, without knowing the amount. He thought this secret appropriation highly unconstitutional; and he was not persuaded the constituents of members would be content to find their representatives enriching themselves by their own votes of unknown appropriations—adding as they pleased to their private libraries; as they had added salaries to their duties. This was indeed improving on the system of appropriation; and shortly a civil list and other contingent expenses will be granted wholesale, without compunction or apparent responsibility. Members seem determined to take care of themselves during their continuance in office. Appropriations will soon be made for their establishments of other descriptions than libraries. Private enrichments and emoluments are for the public good, because obtained by the public bounties.

Mr. SPEIGHT said, that the object of his amendment seemed to be mistaken by the honorable member from Georgia. It was simply to supply the new members with such books as had been supplied to former members, by order of the last Congress.

Mr. FOSTER considered that the resolution would, if adopted, have the effect of leading to a greater expenditure than was contemplated; for it would entitle former members, for years past, to call upon the officer of the House to have their sets completed. He asked when and where was all this to stop? He now moved that the committee should rise and report, and gave notice that he would move to refer the subject hereafter to the Library Committee.

The question on his motion, that the committee rise, was put; but it appeared that there was not a quorum voting.

Mr. WHITTLESEY thereupon moved that the committee should rise, and the chairman to report the fact to the House.

Mr. POLK suggested that the House should be counted, as he apprehended there was a quorum present.

The CHAIRMAN ascertained there was not a quorum; upon which, Mr. WHITTLESEY renewed his motion.

Mr. FOSTER then withdrew his motion, that the committee rise, and the amendment, submitted by Mr. SPEIGHT, was agreed to: thereupon the committee rose, and reported their concurrence to the House.

HOUSE APPROPRIATION BILL.

Mr. McINTIRE moved the reconsideration of the vote of yesterday on the report of the Committee of Conference, and to postpone the subject till Monday next; which was agreed to.

The SPEAKER presented the report of the Register and Receiver of the Land Office of New Orleans; which, on motion of Mr. WHITE, was referred to the Committee on Private Land Claims.

The SPEAKER communicated to the House a report from the Secretary of the Navy, showing the expenditures of that department during the year 1833; which, on motion of Mr. WATMOUGH, was referred to the Committee on Naval Affairs.

The House then proceeded to the orders of the day, being the consideration of sundry private bills lying on the Speaker's table.

The bill to compensate Susan Decatur and others was postponed until Friday next.

On motion of Mr. BATES, of Massachusetts, the rule was suspended in order to permit him to move that when the House adjourns, it adjourn to meet on Monday next.

On motion of Mr. BATES, it was ordered that when the House adjourns, it adjourn to Monday; 110 to 46.

The House went into Committee of the Whole on the bill making appropriations for the payment of revolutionary and other pensions for the year 1834, and reported the same without amendment. The bill was then ordered to be engrossed, was read a third time, and passed.

The House then adjourned.

[In the House of Representatives on Monday, the 27th instant, the following resolutions and petitions were presented, which we omitted to insert in the proceedings of that day.]

On motion of Mr. BATES,
Resolved, That the Committee on Military Affairs be instructed to examine and report upon the claim of the legal representatives of the late Colonel Roswell Lee, deceased, for services performed by him as an inspector, and otherwise, as set forth in his account on file in the Department of War.

On motion of Mr. E. D. WHITE,
Resolved, That the Secretary of War be directed to communicate to this House a copy of the correspondence of the department with the superintendent of the work of clearing away the raft in Red river.

On motion of Mr. LANE,
Resolved, That the Committee on Revolutionary Pensions be instructed to inquire into the expediency of placing the name of Joseph Seal, a soldier of the Revolution, upon the pension roll, with leave to report by bill or otherwise.

On motion of Mr. BYNUM,
Resolved, That the Committee on the Post Office and Post Roads be instructed to inquire into the expediency of establishing a semi-weekly post route, commencing at Winton, in the county of Hertford, running through Pitch Landing, in the county of Hertford, Coleman and Windsor, in the county of Bertie, through Williamson, in the county of Martin, to Tarborough, in the county of Edgecomb, in the State of North Carolina.

On motion of Mr. HANNEGAN,
Resolved, That the Committee on Commerce be instructed to inquire into the expediency of making an appropriation for the erection of a light-house at or near Michigan City, on Lake Michigan.

On motion of Mr. CARR,
Resolved, That the Committee of Claims be instructed to inquire into the expediency of providing by law for the payment of the horses which belonged to individuals of Captain Bigger's and other companies of United States mounted rangers, which were stolen by the Indians, died, or otherwise lost by unavoidable accidents, whilst in the service, in the late war with Great Britain; also, into the expediency of providing by law for the payment of the horses which belonged to individuals of the late six companies of United States mounted rangers, organized for the protection of the northwestern frontier, which were stolen by the Indians, died, or otherwise lost by unavoidable accidents, whilst in the service of the United States.

On motion of Mr. DUNCAN,
Resolved, That the Committee of Ways and Means be instructed to inquire into the expediency of appropriating a sufficient sum to complete the harbor at Chicago within the year 1834.

Resolved, That the same committee be instructed to inquire into the expediency of increasing the appropriation heretofore made for removing the obstructions in the channel of the Mississippi river at the rapids of the Des Moines and Rock rivers, with a view to the speedy completion of that object.

Resolved, That the Committee on the Public Lands be instructed to inquire into the justice and expediency of granting 320 acres of land to the widow and heirs of each person killed by the Indians on the frontiers of Illinois and Michigan, in 1832.

Mr. WHITE, of Florida, submitted the following resolution:
Resolved, That the Secretary of the Treasury be directed to report to this House the causes which have suspended the issuing of patents upon pre-emption claims in Florida, in whose favor the courts of the Territory have decided, under the laws of the United States.

On motion of Mr. CASEY,
Resolved, That the Committee on the Public Lands be instructed to inquire into the expediency of establishing a land office at Charleston, in Illinois.

On motion of Mr. CAGE,
Resolved, That the Committee on Commerce be instructed to inquire into the expediency of increasing the compensation of the collector of the port of Pearlington, in the district of Pearl river, in the State of Mississippi.

On motion of Mr. ASHLEY,
Resolved, That the Committee on Private Land Claims be instructed to inquire into the expediency of granting a patent to Daniel Kincaid for a tract of land confirmed, but not embraced in the report of the commissioners appointed to examine and adjust private land claims in Missouri.

On motion of Mr. BULL,
Resolved, That the Committee on Roads and Canals be instructed to inquire into the expediency of making an appropriation for improving the navigation of Missouri river, and that of the Mississippi river, above the mouth of the Ohio river.

On motion of Mr. McCARTY,
Resolved, That the Committee on Commerce be instructed to inquire into the expediency of making Michigan City, in Indiana, a port of entry.

On motion of Mr. SEVIER,
Resolved, That the Committee on Public Lands be instructed to inquire into the expediency of providing by law for coercing those entitled to military land in Arkansas to draw their patents for the same.

Mr. MASON, of Virginia, submitted the following resolution, which lies one day on the table:
Resolved, That the Secretary of the Treasury be directed to communicate to this House the names of the officers of the revolutionary army to whom or whose heirs commutation pay has been made by the United States for their services in the war of the Revolution, and the names of the persons to whom the payments have been made, and the sums respectively paid.

On motion of Mr. WHITE, of Florida,
Resolved, That the Committee on Naval Affairs be instructed to inquire into the expediency of deepening the bar of Pensacola Bay, according to the report of the engineers of the United States and that of the Secretary of the Navy.

On motion of Mr. LYON, of Michigan,
Resolved, That the Committee on Territories be instructed to inquire into the expediency of authorising the Legislative Council of the Territory of Michigan to extend their present session to sixty days; and that the accompanying letter on this subject from the President of the Council be referred to said committee.

On motion of Mr. DUNLAP,
Resolved, That the Committee on the Post Office and Post Roads be instructed to inquire into the expediency of establishing a post route from Huntington, in the county of Carroll, State of Tennessee, by Pleasant Exchange and Lexington, in Henderson county, to Purdy, in McNairy county, in the same State; and also, of establishing a post route from Jackson, Madison county, Tennessee, to Purdy, in said State.

On motion of Mr. DICKINSON, of Tennessee,
Resolved, That the Committee on Invalid Pensions inquire into the expediency of granting a pension to Heartwell Mills, a soldier of the Revolution.

On motion of Mr. DICKINSON, of Tennessee,
Resolved, That the Committee on Revolutionary Claims inquire into the expediency of making compensation to the heirs of Guilford Dudley, for loss of property sustained and services rendered by him in the revolutionary war.

On motion of Mr. DAVIS, of Kentucky,
Resolved, That the Committee on Revolutionary Pensions be instructed to inquire into the expediency of placing on the pension roll the name of John Young.

On motion of Mr. MARSHALL,
Resolved, That the Committee on Revolutionary Claims be instructed to inquire into the propriety of authorizing by law the payment to the representatives of William Boyce of such sum as may appear to be justly due and payable on account of his services as a lieutenant in the revolutionary army.

Mr. BEATTY submitted the following resolution, which lies one day on the table:
Resolved, That the Postmaster General be instructed to furnish the Committee on Post Offices and Post Roads with the entire correspondence and proof furnished the department by Elisha Smith, of Mount Vernon, Rock Castle county, Kentucky, in relation to post-route No. 1757, in the aforesaid State.

Mr. PATTERSON submitted the following resolution, which lies one day on the table:
Resolved, That the Secretary of War be requested to inform this House whether there has been a survey and location of a road running southwardly from Lower Sandusky, in the State of Ohio, to the boundary line established by the treaty of Greenville, pursuant to the act of Congress of the 12th December, 1811, and if such location has been made, that he communicate the plats, drafts, reports, and other documents concerning the same, together with such other information respecting the survey and location of said road as the files and records of the department will furnish. Also, that he report to this House whether the sum of $6,000, appropriated by the act aforesaid for the survey and location of said road and the road from the foot of the rapids of the Miami of Lake Erie to the western line of the Connecticut Reserve, has been expended for said objects, and what is the amount expended, if any, on the first-mentioned road.

On motion of Mr. PLUMMER,
Resolved, That the Committee on Public Lands be instructed to inquire into the expediency of providing by law for the payment of office rent to the registers and receivers of land offices, and to provide for the better preservation of the records, books, papers, &c.

Resolved, That the Committee on Public Lands be instructed to inquire into the expediency of repealing so much of the act entitled "An act supplemental to the several laws for the sale of public lands," passed April 5, 1832, as provides that "no person shall be permitted to enter more than one-half quarter section of land, in quarter-quarter sections or tracts of forty acres, and in no case unless he intends it for cultivation, or for the use of his improvement;" also, into the expediency of repealing so much of said act as requires the person applying to make an entry under its provisions to file an affidavit before making the purchase; and also, into the expediency of extending the right of pre-emption to a small quantity of land to all actual settlers and housekeepers for the term of six or twelve months.

Resolved, That the Committee on the Public Lands be instructed to inquire what States have received donations of land from the General Government for the purpose of making roads, bridges,

canals, and improving water courses; the quantity of land received by each State, and into the expediency of granting to such of the new States as have no portion of the public domain for such purposes, a quantity of land equal to that granted to the other States, to be applied under the direction of the Legislatures thereof, to objects of internal improvement within their respective limits.

Resolved, That the Committee on Indian Affairs be instructed to inquire into the expediency of making an appropriation for the purpose of aiding the Choctaw nation of Indians in establishing a printing press in the country to which they have recently emigrated, west of the Mississippi river.

Resolved, That the Committee on the Post Office and Post Roads be instructed to inquire into the expediency of establishing a post route from Columbus, by way of Plymouth, Mayhem, and Oakacheckina, to Troy, Mississippi.

Mr. LYON, of Michigan, presented the petition of numerous citizens of Calhoun county, praying that that county might be set off to, and form a part of the western land district in said Territory: referred to the Committee on Public Lands.

Also, the petition of Benjamin Franklin Stickney, Esq., praying compensation for services rendered the United States during, prior, and for some time subsequent to, the last war: referred to the Committee of Claims.

Also, the petition of Joseph Rolettee, praying for the balance of a private land claim at Prairie du Chien, to which he, as the assignee of the heirs of John Campbell, was entitled under the act of Congress by which the other claims were confirmed at that place: referred to the Committee on Private Land Claims.

Also, the petition of Robert Abbott, for himself and in behalf of the other heirs of James Abbott, deceased, for 640 acres of land in lieu of a like quantity to which they were entitled under the act of Congress of 11th May, 1820, and former acts for regulating grants of land in the Territory of Michigan: referred to the Committee on Private Land Claims.

Also, the petition of sundry citizens of Michigan, praying for the establishment of a post route from Pontiac to the Rapids of Grand river, in said Territory: referred to the Committee on the Post Office and Post Roads.

Also, the petition of Charles Jackson, for compensation for loss sustained in building a light-house at Chicago, Illinois: referred to the Committee on Commerce.

Also, the petition of Jeremiah Moore, for loss and damage sustained in building a light-house on Outer Thunder Bay Island, in Lake Huron: referred to the Committee on Commerce.

Also, the petition of the inhabitants of Chippewa county, in the Territory of Michigan, praying to be set off to the new territory, west of Lake Michigan, whenever said territory may be organized: referred to the Committee on Territories.

Also, a memorial of the citizens of Brown county, at Green Bay, praying for the organization of a separate territorial government west of Lake Michigan, &c., &c.: referred to the Committee on Territories.

Also, a petition from the inhabitants of Branch county, Michigan Territory, praying to be set off to the western land district in said territory; referred to the Committee on Public Lands.

Also, a petition from numerous citizens of Michigan Territory, praying for an appropriation of money, to aid in the construction of a territorial road from Sheldon's, on the Chicago road, to the mouth of the St. Joseph's river: referred to the Committee on Roads and Canals.

Also, the petition of Shubael Conant, Esq., for compensation for money advanced for forage for mounted rangers at Detroit during the last war, at the request, and under the direction of the United States quartermaster at that place: referred to the Committee of Claims.

Also, a petition of numerous citizens of Washtenaw, Oakland, Kent, and Ionia counties, in the Michigan Territory, praying for a change in the location of the Grand River road, in said Territory: referred to the Committee on Roads and Canals.

Mr. ALLEN, of Vermont, presented the petition of many citizens of Detroit, remonstrating against the change of the Grand River road, in Michigan Territory.

From the New York Mirror.

DESCRIPTION OF A BALL ON BOARD THE FRIGATE UNITED STATES: By N. P. WILLIS.

TRIESTE.—The guns were run out of the ports; the main and mizen masts were wound with red and white bunting; the capstan was railed with arms and wreathed with flowers; the wheel was tied with nosegays; the American eagle stood against the mainmast, with a star of midshipmen's swords glittering above it; festoons of evergreens were laced through the rigging; the companion-way was arched with hoops of green leaves and roses; the decks were tastefully chalked; the commodore's skylight was piled with cushions, and covered with red damask, for an ottoman; seats were laid along from one carronade to the other; and the whole was enclosed with a temporary tent, lined throughout with showy flags, and studded all over with bouquets of all the flowers of Illyria. Chandeliers made of bayonets, battle-lanterns, and candles in any quantity, were disposed all over the hall. A splendid supper was set out on the gun-deck below, draped in with flags. Our own and the Constellation's boats were to be at the pier at nine o'clock, to bring off the ladies; and at noon everything promised of the brightest.

First, about four in the afternoon, came up a saucy-looking cloud from the westernmost peak of the Friuli. Then followed, from every point towards the north, an extending edge of a broad, solid, black sheet, which rose with the regularity of a curtain, and began to send down a wind upon us, which made us look anxiously to our ball-room bowlines. The midshipmen were all forward, watching it from the forecastle. The lieutenants were in the gangway, watching it from the ladder. The commodore looked seriously out of the larboard cabin port. It was as grave a ship's company as ever looked out for a shipwreck.

The country about Trieste is shaped like a bellows, and the city and harbor lie in the nose. They have a wind that comes down through the valley called the "bora," which several times in the year is strong enough to lift people from their feet. We could see by the clouds of dust on the mountain roads that it was coming. At six o'clock the shrouds began to creak; the white-tops flew from the waves in showers of spray, and the roof of our sea-palace began to shiver in the wind. There was no more hope. We had waited even too long. All hands were called to take down chandeliers, sword-stars, and ottomans; and before it was half done the storm was upon us, the bunting was flying and flapping, the nicely-chalked decks were washed with rain, and strewn with leaves of flowers, and the whole structure, the taste and labor of the ship's company for two days, was a watery wreck.

Lieutenant C——, who had the direction of the whole, was the officer of the deck. He sent for his peajacket, and leaving him to pace out his watch among the ruins of his imagination, we went below to get early to bed and forget our disappointment in sleep.

The next morning the sun rose without a veil. The "blue Friuli" looked clear and fresh; the southwest wind came over softly from the shore of Italy, and we commenced retrieving our disaster with elastic spirit. Nothing had suffered seriously except the flowers, and boats were despatched ashore for fresh supplies, while the awnings were lifted higher and wider than before, the bright-colored flags replaced, the arms polished and arranged in an improved order, and the decks re-chalked with new devices. At six in the evening everything was swept up, and the ball-room astonished even ourselves. It was the prettiest place for a dance in the world.

The ship has an admirable band of twenty Italians, collected from Naples and other ports, and a fanciful orchestra was raised for them on the larboard side of the mainmast. They struck up a march as the first boat-full of ladies stepped on the deck, and in the course of half an hour the waltzing commenced with at least two hundred couples, while the ottoman and the seats under the hammer cloths were filled with spectators. The frigate has a lofty poop, and there was room enough on it for two quadrilles after it had served as a reception room. It was edged with a temporary ballustrade, wreathed with flowers and studded with lights, and the cabin beneath (on a level with the main ball-room) was set out with card tables. From the gangway entrance the scene was like a brilliant theatrical *ballet*.

An amusing part of it was the sailors' imitation on the forward decks. They had taken the waste shrubbery and evergreens, of which there was a great quantity, and had formed a sort of grove, extending all around. It was arched with festoons of leaves, with quantities of fruit tied among them; and over the entrance was suspended a rough picture of a frigate with the inscription, "*Free trade and sailors' rights.*" The forecastle was ornamented with cutlasses, and one or two nautical transparencies, with pistols and miniature ships interspersed, and the whole lit up handsomely. The men dressed in their white duck trousers and blue jackets, sat round on the guns playing at draughts, or listening to the music, or gazing at the ladies constantly promenading fore and aft; and to me this was one of the most interesting parts of the spectacle. Five hundred weatherbeaten and manly faces are a fine sight anywhere.

The dance went gaily on. The reigning belle was an American, but we had lovely women of all nations among our guests. There are several wealthy Jewish families in Trieste, and their dark-eyed daughters, we may say at this distance, are full of the thoughtful loveliness peculiar to the race. Then we had Illyrians and Germans, and Terpischore be our witness—how they danced! My travelling companion, the Count of Friuli, was there; and his little Viennese wife, though she spoke no Christian language, danced as featly as a fairy. Of strangers passing through Trieste we had several of distinction. Among them was a fascinating Milanese Marchioness, a relative of Manzoni's, the novelist, (and as enthusiastic and eloquent a lover of her country as I ever listened to on the subject of oppressed Italy,) and two handsome young men, the Counts Niepperg, sons-in-law to Maria Louisa, who amused themselves as if they had seen nothing better in the little Duchy of Parma.

We went below at midnight to supper, and the ladies came up with renewed spirit to the dance. It was a brilliant scene indeed. The officers of both ships, in full uniform, the gentlemen from shore, mostly military, in full dress, the gayety of the bright red bunting, laced with white and blue, and studded, wherever they would stand, with flowers, and the really uncommon number of beautiful women, with the foreign features and complexions, so rich and captivating to our eyes, produced altogether an effect unsurpassed by anything I have ever seen even at the Court *fêtes* of Europe. The daylight gun fired at the close of a *gallopade*, and the crowded boats pulled ashore with their lovely freight by the broad light of morning.

Mr. Editor: The following mournful intelligence, I have just received from a gentleman from the neighborhood where the scene occurred. A Mr. Shrader, of Henry county, who has long been addicted to habits of intoxication, on the night of the 9th instant, after a fit of debauch, killed three of his children, and abused his wife in such a way that her life is despaired of. What will the opponents of temperance societies in Kentucky and elsewhere say to this? A like catastrophe occurred in the same neighborhood about five or six years ago. In this case the man shot his wife dead, and immediately afterwards despatched himself in the same way.—*Frankfort Argus.*

Yankee Speculation.—It will be recollected that the ship Tuscany sailed from Boston last spring with a cargo of ice for Calcutta. Accounts have been received of her safe arrival out, and that very little of her ice had melted. The Hindoos will soon use it up, however, and, it is to be hoped, to a good advantage to the shipper.

THE CONGRESSIONAL GLOBE.

PRINTED AND PUBLISHED AT THE CITY OF WASHINGTON, BY BLAIR & RIVES.

23D CONGRESS, 1ST SESSION.   SATURDAY, FEBRUARY 8, 1834.   VOL. I........No. 10.

SPEECH OF MR. HANNEGAN,

OF INDIANA,

In the House of Representatives, January 30, 1834.

On the resolution of Mr. CHILTON, to appoint a Select Committee to inquire into the expediency of so extending the general pension law as to embrace within its provisions those persons who were engaged in the Indian wars, down to the year 1794, and the amendment of it by Mr. BOULDIN, to appoint a committee to inquire into the moral effects of the pension system upon the community, and how far it ought to be abolished or repealed.—

Mr. HANNEGAN said, he did not wish to intrude upon the time of the House; but the present question was one in which he felt a more than ordinary anxiety, arising not alone from the fact that some few of those who would be benefited by the resolution under consideration were his immediate constituents; but he had a higher interest, an interest springing from another and a broader source—a wish to see some slight public recognition, some token of national gratitude to those who in youth and vigorous manhood had devoted themselves exclusively to the service of their country.

In the fulfilment of this obligation, he was not, like the gentleman from South Carolina, [Mr. PICKENS,] deterred by constitutional scruples. Those who framed the Constitution, it would seem, had not such scruples, for the pension system was established at least as far back as 1789, and he (Mr. H.) was willing to take for his text on all constitutional questions, the acts and the opinions of those who framed the instrument. It would seem, too, that South Carolina herself did not formerly regard it as unconstitutional, for by a reference to the journals it will be found that in the year 1804 her pensioners were placed upon the roll of the United States, without any apparent objection on her part.

It was not, however, to argue the constitutionality of the matter that he had risen. His main object was, by a brief review of the history of the times, to show that the honorable gentleman from Rhode Island [Mr. BURGES] had, he would not say wilfully, misrepresented, but that he must have forgotten the real facts, when he spoke of these wars as "mere petty feuds, predatory excursions, waged by way of retaliation for purposes of robbery and plunder." He (Mr. H.) estimated the wars, the character, and the standing of that gentleman too highly to suppose for a moment that he would wilfully and unjustly defame the acts, and the reputation of any, far less those of the time-worn soldier and patriot, who in defence of his country had stained her soil with his blood. Unwilling to believe such things of that honorable gentleman, he was bound to presume that he had forgotten. The version given to the House by the honorable member would be found to be widely different from what he (Mr. H.) had learned alike from history and tradition.

Of tradition, however, he would not speak, but refer alone to history to sustain his remarks.

The honorable gentleman from Pennsylvania, [Mr. DENNY,] both the honorable members from Tennessee, [Messrs. DICKINSON and PAYTON,] had stated to the House the atrocious character of this war on the part of the savages throughout the revolutionary struggle. At that period it had raged in the most horrid manner, and if the honorable gentleman from Rhode Island was still not satisfied of the fact, he would refer him for confirmation of the fact, and also for the character of the war, to Marshall's Life of Washington, representing in the year 1778, that whilst various "diplomatic concerns employed the American Cabinet, and whilst the war seemed to languish on the Atlantic, it raged to the West in its most savage form." Would this appear to speak simply of some petty feud? He thought not.

But, said Mr. H., as the honorable gentleman from Rhode Island has disavowed all knowledge

of the existence of such a war as had been spoken of by the honorable gentleman from Tennessee, [Mr. DICKINSON,] he would ask the honorable gentleman from Rhode Island if there could be found any general treaty of peace, or suspension of the struggle with hostile Indians at the conclusion of the struggle with Great Britain? That gentleman could not. Upon the contrary, although various treaties had been occasionally formed with separate tribes at Fort Stanwix, Fort McIntosh, at Hopewell on the Keowee, and at the mouth of the Great Miami of the Ohio, they had proved entirely ineffectual. In pursuance of all these, however, a new treaty had been made at Fort Harmar in the year 1789, with numerous tribes, and almost the same stipulations adopted that had been agreed upon at the four places just named.

At this last treaty, (said Mr. H.,) the Wabash and Miami Indians, though specially urged, had refused to attend. They were bent upon war alone.

But, sir, to show how far this last treaty accomplished its object, it is only necessary to refer to a communication made to Congress by General Washington, in the year 1790; in which he informed that body that he had been compelled to call out the militia in the western country in aid of the regular troops against the increasing depredations of the savage enemy. This force was composed of one thousand men from Virginia and Kentucky, and five hundred from four counties in Western Pennsylvania.

Sir, (said Mr. H.,) the pay could not have been the object with these men. What was it? Contrast it with the pay that has been given in later times. It was $22 per month to a lieutenant, $5 per month to a sergeant, $3 per month to a private. And they were to receive this only in time of actual service, when required by imminent peril. Mr. H. said he believed he used the very words of the instructions given to the commanding general. The documents were within the reach of the House, showing that up to the period just mentioned, savage outrages had increased with even greater violence, and the whole frontier was stained with a repetition of the most shocking barbarities.

Shortly after these men were raised, the melancholy campaign of Harmar and St. Clair followed in quick succession. They surely did not head mere predatory bands, they were each followed by a strong and organized force, at the direction and under the auspices of the Government. The bare recollection of the names of those who fell on these fields, would certainly destroy any impression as to the character of the war, that might have been produced on a portion of the House by the remarks of the honorable gentleman from Rhode Island. For years after, their loss had been deplored as a public calamity all over the Union. The Father of his Country, on receiving the news of St. Clair's defeat, was represented to have shed tears: bitter and scalding they must have been, for numbered with the dead was many a revolutionary comrade.

Sir, (said Mr. H.,) I concur with the honorable gentleman from Pennsylvania [Mr. DENNY] in his remarks upon the conduct of General Arthur St. Clair. Injustice has been done his memory, notwithstanding a complete vindication at the hands of those who best knew, and whose province it was to judge of the facts. He was sorry that the honorable gentleman from Kentucky [Mr. HARDIN] had, in review of his remarks on a former day, joined in the censure of that man whom he considered amongst the most meritorious this country had ever produced. His disasters in that campaign were caused entirely by circumstances beyond control. Their introduction, however, at this time, he (Mr. H.) considered as unnecessary, perhaps unbecoming the present discussion. He hoped, however, that history would finally do justice to the memory of this gallant soldier and accomplished gentleman, whose name stood so intimately blended with some of our proudest national recollections.

But, said Mr. H., to return to the subject. In

September, 1791, a report from the Secretary of War, to which he had before alluded, would be found to contain, amongst many other statements, a representation that "a strong coercive force" would be required to carry into effect the object then contemplated by the campaign. And the same report clearly explained the principles of justice and of policy which dictated a most vigorous prosecution of this war.

It was not for success against the Indians alone that we were contending. Would the honorable gentleman from Rhode Island, [Mr. BURGES,] or any other gentleman on that floor, hazard an assertion to the contrary? They could not; for an object which all must admit to have been of the highest importance, was still further to be attained. It was the possession and subjugation of the British posts on Lake Michigan, and of Niagara and Detroit, withheld from us contrary to the treaty with Great Britain. From these posts, the hostile Indians were constantly furnished with arms and munitions, and excited to continue their career of indiscriminate butchery and massacre to such an extent that the frontiers were made desolate from Georgia to Canada.

From this state of things, the country had been redeemed by the successful engagement of General Anthony Wayne, with the combined Indian force and a large auxiliary body of Canadian volunteers, on the 20th of August, 1794. Yes, a body of Canadian volunteers, drawn from around the British post of Detroit, and encouraged by Colonel McKee, the British agent at that place, together with Captain Elliott, and others of the British army, who were actually in view amongst the Indians at, the commencement of the engagement, which was fought within sight of a British post and garrison.

But, said Mr. H., still further to show how little this war deserves the unkind description given of it by the honorable gentleman from Rhode Island, [Mr. BURGES,] let any gentleman look at the report of General Wayne, shortly after taking command of the army, then composed of 2600 regular officers and soldiers, and 360 mounted volunteers from Kentucky, under the command of General Charles Scott. This force he reported at the time as utterly inadequate to the difficulties of the enterprise, and the formidable enemy against whom he was to act. To supply the requisite force, a draft of the militia was deemed indispensable. This officer had, as was known to all, succeeded in the end, and the treaty of Grenville, made on the 3d day of August, in the year 1795, had constituted the basis of all subsequent treaties held with the Indians northwest of the Ohio river, and it was the first and only sincere peace made by them with this Republic, having, he (Mr. H.) believed, remained unbroken until within a short period anterior to the late war with Great Britain.

Throughout the whole of this war, it would be found, upon examination, that instructions had been uniformly given by the department to the commanding general to procure, by all means, the services of some influential and intelligent gentlemen resident in the West. A Logan, a Shelby, a Hardin, or a Spencer, were uniformly found with their little bands around them, opening the way, and directing the march of the advancing army. To the temporizing policy of the Government, the valuable life of Colonel John Hardin had been finally sacrificed; he having, at the request of the Government, undertaken a mission to the Wabash and Miami Indians, accompanied only by an interpreter, for the purpose, if possible, of effecting a reconciliation. Shortly after entering their country, he was seized as a prisoner, and, regardless of the character in which he came, he was barred at the stake with every circumstance of savage cruelty.

Are the survivors of these men now asking for some little pecuniary aid to cheer their declining existence, to be treated only with contumely? After having served for years, armed at

their own expense, carrying their provisions in their wallets, without tents, with no shelter from the piercing night save a single blanket, their humble request is to be rejected without even an inquiry, whilst those who fought on this side the mountains have been so freely provided for.

It could not be that greater devotion to their country had characterized the soldiers of the East and the North, than those of the West; a more striking instance of genuine patriotism could not be found either in the history of this country or any other, than that displayed by some early settlers (intruders as they were termed) upon the vacant lands in East Tennessee. They were removed in a large body by a military force despatched for the purpose, under Major Bradly, some short time previous to the defeat of General St. Clair. Sir, these very men, although they had just beheld their families in the most distressing possible situation, naked, houseless, and starving, were among the first to volunteer in the expedition then contemplating, and met their fate in the ensuing campaign gallantly fighting for the very Government that had just driven them from their cabins.

Sir, from the brief history of facts I have given, it will be seen that down to the year 1795, no general cessation of hostilities had occurred, and that the savages were continually urged by British emissaries, to the commission of the most brutal outrages. I have given this sketch to satisfy the honorable member from Rhode Island, and the House, that in no point of view can this long and protracted war be deserving of the character he has seen proper to bestow upon it.

If at any period it had assumed a predatory character, the fault was in the Government, and not in the inhabitants of the frontier. They were left alone to defend themselves against the public enemy, and at the same time by their own labor and exertions to procure the necessaries of life for the subsistence of their families. It is well known that after the treaty of peace with Great Britain in 1783, the Government could control neither men nor means, and consequently these people were compelled for some years to defend the lives and property of all around them, as they best could, from their own resources.

I have aimed in my remarks, sir, at nothing more than the performance of an act of simple justice to the surviving representatives of former days, so unjustly and unfeelingly denounced as robbers and plunderers.

Whether the resolution shall utimately prevail or not, I hope their services at least may be regarded in a proper light. By their valor, their constancy, their unshrinking fortitude, a title to the whole wide-spread country of the West was secured. In giving protection to an extensive frontier, of which they constituted the only means of succor and defence, every danger, every privation, every toil was encountered without murmur or complaint. Year after year they freely suffered; their only reward the warm and heartfelt prayer of the lonely woman and her offspring acknowledging their preservation from captivity, violation, and death.

I have (said Mr. H.) in my possession the petition of John Ritchie, one of these men, now upwards of 64 years old, who, from the age of 16, was constantly engaged in the service of his country; he went throughout his whole campaign with Colonel Logan; he fought in and was one of the few who fortunately escaped from the disastrous action at the junction of the St. Mary's and St. Joseph's, generally known as the defeat of General Harmar; he was with the five hundred picked men who performed one of the boldest tours on record against the Indians under the command of General Charles Scott, that chivalric hero of almost a hundred fields, with whose name history at least associates no ideas of robbery and plunder. This same individual was afterwards with the first force that ever penetrated to the Upper Wabash under General Wilkinson, and was present at the destruction of the Wea towns; and, sir, he finally followed the steps of Anthony Wayne throughout the whole of his memorable and glorious campaign, concluded by the treaty of Grenville in 1795. Years afterwards, when the Government again required the services of her citizens in the field, this man, although advanced in life, was amongst the first of the gallant and patriotic Kentuckians who so freely flocked to her standard; he was at the siege of Fort Meigs, and, if my recollection of the events of his life serves me right, although it is not stated in his petition, an honorable and highly distinguished gentleman on this floor, from Kentucky, [Colonel Richard M. Johnson,] one distinguished alike by his preëminent civil and military services on every occasion, so cheerfully and efficiently rendered his country, can bear individual testimony to the gallant conduct of my old friend in that field, where, by the defeat and death of the most justly celebrated man of all their warriors, the Indian power in the West was finally and forever broken: I allude to the battle of the Thames.

In declining age he now finds himself a prey to poverty; a constitution broken, and health enfeebled by early hardships, disable him from ordinary agricultural labor. Sir, should such a man, as life wanes lower and lower in the socket, be left alone to the "cold charity of the world?" His youth and manhood—that vigorous portion of existence which in these times men devote to hoarding up for age—were by him passed in the constant and arduous service of his country.

It may be said that this is but a single instance, and that the provisions of the resolution are general. Sir, this brief sketch would represent the claims of a majority of those benefited by the ultimate success of the principle contained in the resolution. The instance I have given is far from being solitary. It is in reality the history of a peculiar body of men, whose services cannot be obliterated by time, who, regardless of personal peril, seeking no individual advantage, dared everything in a most hazardous cause. Mr. Speaker, did they effect nothing? They fought amid a wilderness, boundless in extent; they fought for a wilderness, they succeeded; the result is known to all. That wilderness is now peopled by more than five millions of rational and intelligent beings, as happy, as free, as generous, and as brave as the sun ever shone down upon. The eye is everywhere greeted with smiling and beautiful farms, with flourishing villages; in the midst, cities have risen; and, over all, law and order, the lights of revealed religion and the blessings of civil liberty prevail.

Sir, it is for the surviving patriarch whose toils have brought so rich a harvest to others, that some little memento of national gratitude is now asked. It is not sought for robbers and plunderers. The gentleman from Rhode Island knows them not; from nothing on earth could they be more remote. Wanton aggression and unlicensed pillage stain not the history of their lives. Their devotional love of liberty was united to a singleness of heart and a simplicity of manner that might vie with the shepherd of old "watching his flocks on Chaldea's hills."

Mr. H. said that before concluding he wished to bestow a few observations on the amendment offered by the honorable gentleman from Virginia, [Mr. Bouldin,] proposing to abolish all pension laws. Throughout the entire discussion of the question, this amendment, in reality the legitimate subject of debate, had been totally overlooked, until the gentleman from South Carolina [Mr. Pinckney] had raised it from the condition of deep apathy, to which common consent had apparently consigned it. To that honorable gentleman, [Mr. Pinckney,] it was indebted for at least the active portion of its existence. For at the moment of its first appearance "in this breathing world," it had seemingly fallen stillborn into the hands of the Clerk, without, so far as he (Mr. H.) recollected, even a show of fatherly fondness from the honorable mover for his unfortunate and ill-conceived bantling. Notwithstanding this neglect of the natural protector, however, the imp has been so far resuscitated, as to chirp in the fostering arms of its late fond nurse.

The policy or the justice of that amendment are alike beyond my comprehension. Even a well-founded reason for its adoption, is more than I can imagine; no suggestions of necessary economy can be brought in aid of the proposition. No national debt hangs over us, no national pecuniary embarrassment of any nature or character whatsoever. Is the Government, then, so poor that she cannot pay this slight acknowledgment of gratitude for services rendered in a cause that has been sanctified beyond all others, by its result upon the happiness and the liberties of mankind? We have thousands to give annually for the improvement and repairs of Pennsylvania avenue; we have thousands to give for trimming the bushes, and turning the walks around this building; thousands to make "Goose Creek once, the Tiber now," flow in a direction something different from what nature intended it; thousands to give for innumerable other purposes of about equal importance to the country, but not one cent to those who fought to make that country free.

What, sir, strike out the pension act? When you do so, when you efface it from the statute book, blot out at the same time from the history of your country the name of every consecrated field on which these veterans fought, whether of victory or disaster. Do it, sir! erase the one, but leave no vestige of the other. Let not posterity be left to blush, that we sedulously preserved the record of those glorious fields, but consigned to poverty and misery the individuals who had rendered them immortal. Shall we tell the gallant mariner who has borne our flag in triumph over every sea, that hereafter, when worn down and unfit for service, he will be cast aside unnoticed—unregarded; the country he has so fondly loved, so proudly defended, with millions in her treasury, will leave him, the neglected victim of age, disease, and poverty combined?

For myself, I cannot concur in such sentiments; patriotism alone forbids the thought, and it is to be hoped that the justice and the generosity of this House will forever preclude it. My vote shall never deny to him who aided either in establishing or defending the Union and the liberties of this Republic, a just reward, sufficient to render easy his declining years.

He had no fear, however, that the amendment of the gentleman from Virginia would prevail, and sincerely hoped that a law would be passed pursuant to the principle proposed by the resolution.

IN SENATE.

Monday, *February* 3, 1834.

The VICE PRESIDENT communicated a letter from the Governor of Michigan relative to the improvement of the navigation of certain rivers in that Territory.

Mr. SHEPLEY presented the resolutions of a large number of the citizens of Portland adverse to a change of the mode of collecting the revenue from credit to cash, and also disapproving of the course of the Secretary of the Treasury in removing the deposites; which was read, referred to the Committee on Finance, and ordered to be printed.

On presenting these resolutions, Mr. SHEPLEY observed, that the signers were known to him to be gentlemen of great respectability, although differing from him in opinion in relation to many matters contained in those resolutions. It may not be improper to remark, that they do not assume to represent the opinion of the city of Portland, but only of a large number of its citizens.

The resolutions were read and referred to the Committee on Finance, and ordered to be printed.

Mr. SHEPLEY rose and said—

Mr. President, I ask leave to present certain resolutions of the Legislature of the State of Maine, expressing the opinion of that Legislature in relation to the Bank of the United States; to the cause of the distress upon the commercial community; and to the removal of the public deposites; and instructing her Senators to oppose a restoration of the deposites and a renewal of the charter of the bank.

On presenting these resolutions, I ask the indulgence of the Senate for a few moments, to state that the State of Maine, presenting a seacoast of more than three hundred miles in extent, and rivers of no inconsiderable magnitude extending from the sea shore far into the interior of the State, and there connecting themselves with large inland bodies of water; and a very large tract of land, covered with forest timber trees, portions of which are annually felled, floated on these waters, and manufactured into building materials, and trans-

ported to market; and having also extensive quarries of limestone and marble, which are worked, and the lime and marble shipped to a market; she is deeply interested in trade, commerce, exchange, and a sound currency. So great are the quantities of these materials and of domestic manufactures, and so extensive her intercourse with the British provinces, and with the other States, that her coasting trade is very valuable. Her tonnage employed in that trade, and other commerce, is to such an amount that there are now, it is believed, but two States whose tonnage is greater. Much of the success of her industrious and very enterprising people depends upon the successful prosecution of this trade and commerce; and her people must therefore be supposed to understand their own interests.

Little more than five years ago, and but one out of nine of her electoral votes was given to the present Chief Magistrate. At the last election, the whole vote of the State was given to him.

The resolutions now offered were passed in her House of Representatives by a vote of 119 to 53; and in her Senate, by a vote of 22 to 2. The election of these members, it is true, took place before the removal of the deposites, but the persons elected remained among the people electing them until after the discussion of the question commenced here; and they carried with them the opinions of the people whom they represented; and those opinions are embodied in their resolutions. These facts show that a large majority of the people of Maine do not regard the conduct of the President in the manner that my colleague does.

What he understands to be an accumulation of power in the Executive by the exercise of the veto power, as it is called, they understand to be a prostration of power attempted to be accumulated. They have seen the President exercise a power given to him by the Constitution, to break down that assumption of power which would control and manage the internal improvements of the States. They have seen him exercise the same power to prostrate a bank charter, calculated to control their own moneyed concerns, and to bring them and all their great and growing interests within its influence, and to enable it to brighten or blacken their prospects at its will. They desire to be delivered from such a power; and hence the vote on these resolutions. The other topics alluded to by my colleague, have all been discussed, and an opinion formed upon them in Maine, and that opinion is so distinctly made known in these resolutions, that it is not necessary that I should say anything respecting them. I concur in all the opinions expressed in these resolutions.

Mr. SPRAGUE said he was always disposed to be governed by the voice of the people when expressed. That while the resolutions of the Legislature of Maine emanated from that body in a party character almost exclusively, the resolutions from the city of Portland spoke the voice of the people of that city, that they were suffering serious distress and embarrassment. While he differed in opinion from the Legislature of Maine, a body for which he entertained great respect, and also from his honorable colleague, yet he was always ready and willing to render an account to the people for his public acts.

Mr. SHEPLEY, in reply, said he would only state a fact or two: all the representatives of the city of Portland were among the 119 voting for the resolutions; that all the Senators from the county of Cumberland, in which that city is situated, were also among the number of Senators who voted for them; that one of the Senators from Kennebec county, and an opponent to the Administration, asked to be excused from voting, on the ground that he was of opinion that the President had assumed a power that did not belong to him, and yet he could not vote to restore the deposites, thinking it would be inexpedient.

The resolutions were then read, and referred to the Committee on Finance, and ordered to be printed.

Mr. McKEAN presented the petition of sundry citizens of Pittsburg, disapproving of the course of the Secretary of the Treasury in removing the deposites; which was referred to the Committee on Finance.

Mr. McK. observed that this memorial had been committed to his care for presentation by the Representative in the House of Representatives from Pittsburg, Pennsylvania, [Mr. DENNY,] who desired him to say that the memorial was numerously and respectably signed by citizens of that place, without distinction of party. He had also in his possession a letter, left with him by Mr. DENNY, which any gentleman might see who desired it.

Mr. WILKINS presented two or three memorials from Pittsburg, sustaining the Secretary of the Treasury upon the removal of the deposites; which were referred to the Committee on Finance, and ordered to be printed.

Mr. WEBSTER suggested the propriety of having the names of the memorialists to all the petitions on this subject printed.

Mr. WILKINS presented the petition of the heirs of Andrew Gardner; which was referred to the Committee on Revolutionary Claims.

Mr. TYLER presented two petitions of a private nature.

Mr. TIPTON communicated the memorial of the Legislative Council of Michigan relative to the improvement of certain rivers in that Territory; which was referred to the Committee on Commerce.

Mr. POINDEXTER, from the Committee on Public Lands, reported a bill for the removal of the office of the surveyor general from Ohio to Indiana.

Which was read twice and committed.

Mr. POINDEXTER, from the same committee, reported a bill from the House of Representatives for the relief of George K. Jackson, and gave notice that he was instructed by the committee that, when the bill was called up, he should move its indefinite postponement.

Mr. KING, of Alabama, gave notice that he should to-morrow ask leave to introduce a bill for the relief of John Donelson and Stephen Heard.

The following resolution was submitted by Mr. POINDEXTER:

Resolved, That the President be requested to cause to be laid before the Senate a copy of any correspondence, if any shall have taken place, between the War Department or any officer attached to it, and the Bank of the United States, in respect to the agency of the said bank, under the act of 7th June, 1832, or any other act of Congress, in the payment of pensioners.

The resolutions of Mr. POINDEXTER submitted on Friday, were then taken up.

Mr. WEBSTER suggested to the gentleman from Mississippi, and the gentleman from Kentucky, the propriety of referring these resolutions, and the letter of the Secretary of the Treasury on the removal of the deposites, to the Committee on Finance, and allow the resolutions thereon to remain before the Senate, so that the debate might proceed without interruption.

Mr. POINDEXTER suggested a question of order, whether that could be done without taking the whole subject from the possession of the Senate.

Mr. CLAY said he had no objection to the proposition, if it was understood that the debate on the resolutions could go on. He hoped nothing would be allowed to interrupt that.

Mr. WRIGHT said it seemed to him, as the second resolution related exclusively to the reasons of the Secretary, that if it were referred to the committee, the debate upon it could not proceed. He objected to withdrawing it from the Senate, as he desired, when a convenient opportunity presented, to give his views to the Senate upon it.

The VICE PRESIDENT was understood to say, that the reference to the committee would withdraw the subject from the Senate.

Mr. CLAY observed that the President's message was before the committee, and there was nothing to prevent them from proceeding upon it.

Mr. WEBSTER said the message was not the Secretary's reasons. The message was before the committee, and they were not to be supposed to be inattentive to it, or the memorials on the subject of the deposites, and if the Secretary's reasons were before the committee, they would not require to have possession of them more than a day. He thought if the paper was to go to the committee it was time it was there.

Mr. POINDEXTER asked that Mr. CLAY's second resolution might then be read; which was done.

Mr. POINDEXTER said it did not follow that the reference of the report carried the resolution with it. Every Senator had the original report printed and on his file. The reasons of the Secretary were in possession of every Senator. It was competent for the Senate to go on with the discussion and put the committee in possession of the paper at the same time. If he was right, he preferred that the report should go to the committee now; no inconvenience would result from it, and the report would be had in a day or two.

Mr. WEBSTER would relieve the apprehension of gentlemen by saying, that at the close of the debate to-day he would move to refer the Secretary's letter to the Committee on Finance, and the report should be made to-morrow at the meeting of the Senate.

Mr. KING, of Alabama, said that this difficulty, which was apparent, arose from the eagerness with which these various resolutions had been pressed upon the Senate. If the resolutions were separated from the subject on which they were founded, the whole matter would be taken out of the possession of the Senate, and would go to the Committee on Finance, where it ought to have gone in the first instance. Now, he asked the gentleman from Mississippi what object he had in his resolutions? Did they vary the powers of the committee upon the memorials, or was it necessary to coerce the committee upon the subject? Was it necessary to instruct the committee upon the condition of the currency? That was a part of their duty. They had it before them in the message and the various memorials which had been referred to them. All the gentleman's resolutions were to the same point except the one relating to the distress existing in the community. He was opposed to the adoption of the resolutions, because it was not customary to authorize the committee to send for persons and papers without an intimation from the committee that they wished it. It was usual to ask for the power, and when it was necessary we gave it to them.

Mr. POINDEXTER remarked, the gentleman [Mr. KING] had opened the discussion, which from the first he wished to avoid. He would not follow his example.

Mr. WILKINS said there was something to him quite objectionable in the mode suggested. He thought the proposition, as he understood the gentleman from Massachusetts, would carry the whole subject from the Senate, and he understood that the Chair had so intimated. He had no objection to the reference to the Committee on Finance, but he hoped an arrangement could be made, that the debate might continue. That was all he asked. He had yielded the floor to the gentleman from New Jersey [Mr. FRELINGHUYSEN] with that expectation. If it was the subject of any arrangement, he hoped his claim to the floor in the line of succession justified him in expressing the hope that it would be made.

Mr. WEBSTER remarked, that he was surprised he had been misunderstood. He said he would propose at the conclusion of the discussion to-day to refer the subject to the Committee on Finance, and that the report of the committee should be made to-morrow. He did not recognise any line of succession in the debate; but if the gentleman objected to that course, or thought he would be affected by it, he would postpone his motion until the gentleman had spoken.

Mr. WILKINS replied, that if the report of the committee could be made to-morrow, he would not interrupt the debate. He heartily concurred in the proposition.

Mr. FORSYTH thought the Senate were likely to be greatly embarrassed by these resolutions. If he was not mistaken, they would entirely stop the discussion. The resolutions instructed the committee to inquire into the whole subject embraced by the resolutions of the gentleman from Kentucky. They swept away the whole of the Secretary's reasons. It was impossible, without the Secretary's reasons, for the committee to enter into it. He thought it better to let the subject lie on the table for the present, and not to press it till the report of the Secretary was disposed of.

Mr. CHAMBERS suggested that it was desirable to bring before the committee the lately-dismissed Secretary, who had intimated that he would disclose nothing unless legally required.

Mr. POINDEXTER said a general investigation was desirable, with a view to bring all the members of the Cabinet before the committee, as well those who had, as those who had not given their opinions in writing.

Mr. BIBB said he had no objection to an inquiry. But he hoped the gentleman [Mr. POINDEXTER] would not press the question. He felt that we were touching on delicate ground, in proposing to call before a committee the President's cabinet counsellors. He had no objection to a call on the President; there could be no doubt of the right of the Senate to make such a call. But he wished time to think of the propriety and dignity of the Senate calling for what took place before the President's Cabinet, out of respect for the constitutional authorities of the country.

Mr. CLAY then moved that the subject be laid on the table; which was agreed to.

SPECIAL ORDER OF THE DAY.

The special order having been taken up,

Mr. FRELINGHUYSEN took the floor, and addressed the Chair in opposition to the reasons of the Secretary of the Treasury for removing the deposites, until three o'clock, when he gave way to a motion by Mr. WILKINS, that the Senate adjourn; which prevailed.

And the Senate adjourned.

HOUSE OF REPRESENTATIVES.

MONDAY, *February* 3, 1834.

After the reading of the journal, the several States being called for the presentation of memorials, &c.,

Mr. PARKS rose and said, that, by the courtesy of his colleague, he had to present to the House certain resolutions from the Legislature of the State of Maine, in relation to the recent removal of the deposites, and the question of rechartering the Bank of the United States. These resolutions went to justify the course pursued by the Administration in that removal, and showed that they were opposed to any recharter of that bank. He took leave to say, that the Legislature of that State was composed of one hundred and eighty-six members in the House of Representatives, and of twenty-five in the Senate. These resolutions had been passed in the House of Representatives by the large vote of 119 to 53, and through the Senate by a vote of 22 to 2; and he believed they were passed by a body of men as able, as intelligent, and patriotic, and as truly respectable, as any body of men in the Union. This respectable body, then, came forward to state, that in their opinion, the bank was unconstitutional, and they believed this, because they thought that Congress had no power given to them by the Constitution to grant such a charter; holding that all powers not expressly granted by the Constitution are reserved to the several States. They further believe, that upon this question of removal of the deposites now depends, and is identical with, the recharter of the bank; and that, if the bank is not to be rechartered, their restoration would be improper. Thus believing, they had instructed their Senators and requested their Representatives in Congress to oppose the restoration of the deposites and the renewal of the charter of the United States Bank.

They also believe that the distress which has been brought upon our commercial communities, has been produced by the improper action of the bank upon the public, with a view to cause discontent at the recent measures of Government, and thus force from Congress a restoration of the deposites. It was evident, then, that if the bank, by producing this distress, was successful in their object—when she would think the proper moment had arrived for her to do so, to ask for a renewal of the charter—she would only have to put her machinery in motion, rack her victims, and through the agonizing throes thus produced, compel Congress to yield to her application. Thus yielding once to her, it would only be a prelude to their yielding again. He therefore felt with them, that the present was the time to meet the question, and resist it.

The Legislature of his State were the advocates of State rights. They fully adopted the doctrines put forth by the State of Virginia, and they believed if the bank should prove successful in throwing her golden chains around them, the words State rights, nullification, and secession, would be mere terms, more fit to be bandied by the lips of children than to be used by freemen.

Mr. P. having called for the reading of the resolutions, they were read as follows, and subsequently referred to the Committee of Ways and Means.

STATE OF MAINE.

Whereas, at an early period after the election of Andrew Jackson to the Presidency, in accordance with the sentiments which he had uniformly expressed, the attention of Congress was called to the constitutionality and expediency of the renewal of the charter of the United States Bank; and whereas the bank has transcended its chartered limits in the management of its business transactions, and has abandoned the object of its creation, by engaging in political controversies, by wielding its power and influence to embarrass the administration of the General Government, and by bringing insolvency and distress upon the commercial community; and whereas the public security from such an institution consists less in its present pecuniary capacity to discharge its liabilities, than in the fidelity with which the trusts reposed in it have been executed; and whereas the abuse and misapplication of the powers conferred have destroyed the confidence of the public in the officers of the bank, and demonstrated that such powers endanger the stability of republican institutions; therefore

Resolved, That in the removal of the public deposites from the Bank of the United States as well as in the manner of their removal, we recognise in the Administration an adherence to constitutional rights, and the performance of a public duty.

Resolved, That this Legislature entertain the same opinion as heretofore expressed by preceding Legislatures of this State, that the Bank of the United States ought not to be rechartered.

Resolved, That the Senators of this State in the Congress of the United States be instructed, and the Representatives be requested, to oppose the restoration of the deposites and the renewal of the charter of the United States Bank.

Resolved, That the Governor be requested to transmit a copy of this preamble and these resolves to the President of the Senate of the United States, and to each of our Senators and Representatives in Congress.

IN THE HOUSE OF REPRESENTATIVES,
January 25, 1834.

Read and passed.

NATHAN CLIFFORD, *Speaker*.

IN SENATE, *January* 25, 1834.

Read and passed.

JOSIAH PIERCE, *President pro tem.*

January 25, 1834. Approved.

ROBERT P. DUNLAP.

Mr. SMITH, of Maine, said: I hold in my hand a communication in the shape of resolutions passed at a public meeting holden in the city of Portland, in the district which I have the honor to represent on this floor. They relate to the existing state of the currency in this country, and to the removal of the public deposites from the Bank of the United States. They also embody a request, that the Representatives from Maine would cause them to be laid before the House, and give their support to them.

In compliance with that part of the request which asks to have them laid before this House, I beg leave to lay them upon your table. In relation to the other part, which asks my support of them, I feel constrained to decline. With the permission of the House, I will briefly advert to some of the reasons why I do so decline.

It will be observed that in one of the resolutions the alleged distress in the money market is attributed to the measures of the National Government in the removal of the public deposites from the Bank of the United States. This resolution proceeds to say, "that the removal of the public 'money from the Bank of the United States has 'had a *tendency* to derange the currency of the 'country, and to produce the embarrassments 'which now exist in the money market, *for the* 'bank *having* curtailed its accommodations to the 'public over $9,000,000, *in the five months prece-* '*ding the first of January*, has not only withdrawn 'that large amount from circulation, but has pro- 'duced a corresponding curtailment in the accom- 'modations of the State banks, and thus increased 'the evil and created alarm throughout the whole 'commercial community."

Sir, (said Mr. S.,) that there exists a pressure in the money market of that region whence these resolutions have emanated, is not for me to deny. That it is attributable, properly, to the removal of the deposites from the United States Bank, is a proposition to which I cannot assent: and I think that in the resolution itself, to which I have adverted, an argument is embodied, which illustrates to every candid mind the fallacy of such a conclusion. In order to show the *tendency* of the measure complained of, reference is had to the operations of the bank for *five months* preceding the first of January last. This reference, sir, embraces a period of *two* months anterior to the existence of the measure complained of. The fact that the authors of these resolutions felt compelled thus to go back of the period when that measure first existed, in order to prove *the tendency of it after* it existed, and in order to trace the existing state of things home to it, is to my mind a satisfactory exposure of the fallacy of the reasoning upon which these resolutions rest.

In another of these resolutions it is said, that the pressure in the finances of the country is so great, that an union of all parties existed to give utterance to them. In yet another of them, however, we are told, that they express only the opinions of "a portion" of the citizens of Portland. Sir, this was prudent. If they had undertaken more—if they had assumed to attribute these opinions to the generality of the citizens of Portland, or to the generality of the citizens of Cumberland district, I am sure that the rush of the multitude would have been down upon them, and their feeble utterance would have been drowned by popular acclamation of an opposite import, ere they could have reached this hall of legislation.

Sir, I have had an opportunity of becoming acquainted with the political history and opinions of *all* the gentlemen whose names are associated with these resolutions. And, sir, I am pleased to say—I am pleased in being able to say, that with a single exception, there is not an individual among them who has not been, from the beginning, either opposed to all the leading measures of the present national administration, or a friend of the Bank of the United States. A majority of them, sir, have had their names associated no less distinctly with every measure of opposition to the present Administration, which has been at any time concerted in the city of Portland. If they had now presented themselves in any other attitude than that of hostility to the measure complained of, it would have excited my surprise. I must admit, sir, still, that I feel surprise at the association of two or three of these names with these resolutions. Not, sir, that the gentlemen to whom I allude exhibit *now* evidences of their opposition to the Administration; but I am surprised at it from other considerations. I am surprised, because I know them to be directors of a bank in the city of Portland, which was among the *first* and *swiftest* of the banks to make application to the Treasury Department for the keeping of these same public deposites and before their removal from the United States Bank. I hold in my hand, sir, a copy of the official application of the bank of which the gentlemen alluded to are directors, tendering the services of their bank to the Government, and thus encouraging and inducing the very removal now complained of! Sir, it cannot be doubted that these gentlemen *then* regarded this measure as necessary, just, and patriotic. Then, sir, they regarded this measure, to use the language of the gentleman from South Carolina, [Mr. McDUFFIE,] "as fair a thing as ever was." But *now*, sir, the deposites having been removed, and these gentlemen having found that another bank in Portland has been preferred by the Government to their own, for keeping those deposites, the measure of removal is censured by them, and condemned, and they gravely resolve in public meeting that it i

destructive of the commerce and business of the country, or, to use the language of the gentleman from South Carolina once more, they declare it to be "*all a piece of villanous cheatery!*"

Sir, with the views which I entertain of these resolutions, I cannot do more than to move that they be laid upon your table and be printed, with the application of the Exchange Bank in Portland for the deposites. [These resolutions were in favor of the restoration of the deposites, and have been heretofore published.]

Mr. EVANS, of Maine, wished his colleague to withdraw his motion, as he desired to submit a few remarks in relation to the resolutions; which request having been acceded to—

Mr. E. believed that the first of the propositions just submitted from the Legislature of Maine, had a similar origin with others presented to them. But, although he had as much respect as any one could have for the body from whence it emanated, he might be permitted to say, without being considered disrespectful to them, that they were not exactly competent to pronounce, as they did, that the whole policy pursued by Madison, Jefferson, and others, for nearly forty years, was unconstitutional. The assertions set forth in the preamble to the resolution not being supported by any evidence, he would take leave to be excused from coming to the conclusion that they did, to govern his conduct upon these measures.

With respect to the memorial presented from inhabitants of Portland, which was of a different character from the other, he could testify that it emanated from a body of men who were influenced in presenting them by a knowledge of the actual state of things in their neighborhood, and not with any reference to party, many of them having been always, and for aught he knew still were, friendly to the existing administration from its first accession to power; and this he would assert, notwithstanding it had been said that the resolutions came from those who were always friendly to the bank. But did it follow that although they might be friendly to that institution, that they were not friendly to the Administration?

Mr. E. then briefly adverted to the position in which the bank was placed by the conduct pursued towards it by the Secretary of the Treasury. He denied that the curtailments made by the bank arose from any intention on their part to create distress, as he considered it was a duty incumbent upon them, when they were called upon to pay up the public deposites, to make such a curtailment as would best comport with the safety of the institution under such circumstances and their own interests, in which the safety of the whole community was also involved. He thought they were justified throughout, and would conclude by commending the resolutions from Portland to the calm consideration of Congress.

Mr. POLK rose to warn the House not to be drawn into these wide discussions, on the general subject, upon every memorial which should be presented to them. It had already occupied their attention to the exclusion of almost all other important business for nearly two months; and he rose also to express his hope that the House, after these two months thus spent in a discussion which otherwise appeared to be endless, would at length see how important it was that the subject should be brought to a close. He could affirm that this was demanded from them by a due regard for the public interest, now suffering heavily in consequence of this discussion. If the memorials were referred at once to the Committee of Ways and Means, that committee would not be long in presenting to the House a report with their views; then the whole subject would be open for full consideration, and they would have something tangible—some distinct proposition upon which they could deliberate and act.

Sir, the whole business community is agitated by the continued discussion of this question, and their interest requires that it should be settled. He hoped that the House would sit late and hear the discussion until it should be brought to a close. To-morrow or next day, he trusted, we should meet with the determination of disposing of the motions before the House. There was not a member of this House who did not, every day, receive letters from a distance, urging the speedy action of Congress on this subject. He would appeal to the friends of the bank, and ask whether they did not, at the commencement of this discussion, press the importance of the early action of Congress on the subject?

Mr. GORHAM rose to a question of order, and asked whether it was in order for the gentleman to go into the general character of the debate?

The CHAIR said the general discussion, on the presentation of a petition, could only be gone into with the assent of the House.

Mr. POLK said he had only claimed the indulgence which had already been extended to those gentlemen who preceded him. He would repeat, that he hoped the House would to-morrow meet with a determination to dispose of the question now pending.

The resolutions were then referred to the Committee of Ways and Means, and ordered to be printed.

Mr. MANN, of New York, presented the joint resolutions of the Legislature of New York, approving the removal of the deposites, and instructing her Senators and requesting her Representatives to oppose the recharter of the Bank of the United States.

Mr. M. said that he had intended to submit a few remarks on this occasion, explanatory of the views and opinions of a very large majority of the people of the State which he had the honor in part to represent, on the subject to which the resolutions refer; but the explanation of those views and opinions, which had already been given to the public in the other branch of the Legislature, [by Mr. WRIGHT,] rendered it unnecessary for him to trouble the House at this time.

In the exposition of those views and opinions to which he alluded, Mr. M. said he was authorized to believe that a large majority of his colleagues on this floor fully concur.

The resolutions were then read, ordered to be printed, and laid on the table.

Mr. SELDEN rose and said, that he held in his hand a memorial from the merchants of New York, representing the present deranged state of trade and currency, and the causes of their derangement.

In presenting the memorial, he would take occasion to say, that it was signed by three-fourths of the commercial interest of the city, and by three-fourths, in number, of the merchants of the city. He would further suggest that these merchants, more than any other traders in the Union, were connected with the commerce of this country. In the last six years they had paid to the Government more than fifty millions of dollars. The signers of this memorial had paid more than three-fourths of the sum collected in the city of New York, and more than half of what had been paid by the whole country. He would go further, and say, that the memorialists had fulfilled their contracts to the Government from month to month and year to year, with unexampled punctuality; that they were not connected with either of the belligerent parties of the day; that they were men of no party, but were deeply interested in every measure connected with the trade and commerce of the country. They were men upon whose operations depended the successful prosecution of the trade of this country. They speak from practical knowledge of the effect of the destruction of the national currency upon trade. Whenever occasions have called for the exertions of these men for the preservation of public interests, both in peace and war, they have not withheld their aid. In carrying on a conflict against their interests, you strike at the very vitals of trade; for when the centre of commerce was afflicted, those sections of country which least expect it will also be reached by the distress. Let me ask, sir, whether petitioners like these are not entitled to the favorable consideration of this House; whether men whose relations to the Government are as intimate as our own, when they represent that they cannot carry on trade without the agency of a national bank, are not entitled to be attentively heard, and their opinions carefully considered? He had said that the memorialists belonged to no party, but a large portion of them were friendly to the present Administration. He had looked over the paper, and was able to say that as large a number of friends as of opponents of the Administration had signed it. They say that the currency is in a state of derangement and does not answer the purposes of business. Mr. S. went on to point out some prominent facts in relation to the effect of the disturbance upon business. At the commencement of the month of September, exchange on Europe was 10 per cent. above par, thus affording to the producer an advance of 10 per cent. on his nominal prices. But, within the last month, drafts upon London were offered, in New York, at 5 per cent. discount. The relations between the towns on the Ohio and Mississippi and the city of New York were such, until recently, that exchanges could be carried on at the small expense to the producer of one-half of one per cent; but now it costs the producers from two to five per cent. to effect those exchanges. This was an actual draft upon the industry of the country, for the benefit of brokers and shavers. As to the extent of commercial distress, does any one doubt it? I tell gentlemen that some of the oldest and first-established houses in this country have failed, and that this is but the forerunner of greater difficulties. The memorialists were intimately connected with the local banks of New York, and knew their capacity for the transaction of business, and yet represent them as unable to afford any relief. What class of citizens are to be benefited by the present condition of things? He had heard the poor spoken of, and it had been said that the bank was to be destroyed for the benefit of the poor, at the expense of the rich. But was it a fact that the poor were to be benefited? The rich men, with money in their pockets, will not suffer. The bank was for the benefit of enterprise, and poverty, struggling, with the aid of credit, against the competition of wealth.

Mr. JARVIS here interposed, and asked if the gentleman from New York was in order.

The CHAIR replied, the gentleman is perfectly in order, if the House is willing to hear him, but not if any objection is made.

Mr. JARVIS then objected, and Mr. SELDEN asked the permission of the House to go on.

The House granted leave, and

Mr. SELDEN proceeded: He was sorry to see those gentlemen who had been so fully heard on this subject, now endeavoring to suppress the discussion. [The Chair stated that it was not in order to allude to the course taken by members.] Mr. S. adverted to the abolition of credit on duties. Formerly, the duties were paid after a credit of ten or twelve months, now they were paid in cash. At the very moment when this change was made, it was prepared to put an end to the currency of the country. Who would be the first to suffer? It might be that the Government itself would be the first to suffer. Instead of prompt and punctual payment of the duties, we may find nothing but protested bonds in the custom-house. It had been rumored in the Capitol for some days that we were to return to a specie currency. How were we to get the specie for the purpose? Send our local bank paper to Europe for it? Will our paper be more current there than here? But the evils of the paper system bore no proportion to its profits. The labor and enterprise of this country had been maintained by credit. The vast improvements which had of late years been made in this country had been accomplished by bank paper. The roads, canals, factories, storehouses, &c., which had sprung up everywhere, were the results of paper credit. It was true that this required regulation, and the memorialists say that it can only be regulated by a national bank. Mr. S. went on to argue that the paper system could only exist in a free Government. It was the offspring of free institutions. Mr. S. argued at some length, to show the inefficiency of local banks in equalizing the exchanges of the country. But the derangement of the paper system was not so great as to render it necessary to abandon it. The petitions sent to us from every part of the country do not exhibit any intention on the part of the people to abandon the paper system. There was nothing in the resolutions of the Legislature of the State of New York or of Ohio which favored the scheme of abandoning the paper system; and both of these States were carrying their paper system to a still greater extent, by the establishment of new local banks. But the bank was said to be a political machine. What was the evidence of this charge? The largest operations of the bank were in New York and Pennsylvania, but in those States the

Administration had very large majorities, and show me a vote which has been bought up, or a vote which has been controlled by the bank. Mr. S. also took up the constitutional question, but was prevented, by the restriction of the Chair, from going into it.

Mr. S. proceeded to read a tabular statement of the depreciation of the stock of the different banks in New York—the Manhattan Bank had suffered a depreciation of 11 per cent. on its capital, or $220,000; the Merchant's Bank 10, or $140,000; the Mechanics' 6, or $200,000; the Bank of America 9, or $180,000 on its property—making a depreciation of the bank stock in New York, amounting to upwards of three millions. Will not such a loss of stock, in one particular, reach other stocks, and eventually affect the whole system of internal improvements now in progress throughout the country? Already has the stock of some of the companies engaged in internal improvements, suffered in depreciation. The Delaware and Hudson has suffered a loss of $720,000; and the Ohio Canal Company, a loss of 10 per cent., or of $100,000 on every million of their property. So will all engagements for internal improvements suffer; for what affects the commercial interests of the community must necessarily affect all others, as commercial men and interests are more or less intimately connected with all others. And so of other interests. The stock of many insurance companies has sunk to one-half per cent. of its value. Indeed, as banking capital consists chiefly of a combination of debts, all capitals—and they are many—in the country must suffer in proportionate ratio as the banking capital becomes depreciated. The evil will be, that all property will lose one-half its real value; and what had been deposited will be repaid only with one-half; and what was paid in money, will average twice as much as when contract was made.

Mr. S. then made an exposé relative to the investment in our funds of foreign capital—which will become useless under the present derangement of the currency. Foreign capital has been invested from the confidence with which the faith of the country appeared to be pledged for its security; how much longer will that confidence continue, when that faith is lost? Will not then that capital be reclaimed, and required from us of its investers? Are we prepared to meet such a demand on the monetary concerns of the country? What means has Louisiana to discharge her debt of foreign capital amounting to ten millions? How can Ohio immediately answer the call on her for five millions owed in Europe? Or is Pennsylvania now able to reimburse her loan of twelve millions, owed by her in Europe? Thus has the Government sunk the credit of the country; and in consequence, will militate against the commercial interests of the country, by creating an alarm among the European creditors of the nation, who may require that their American stocks shall be redeemed or returned by a recall of their capital; and this would produce the actual absorption of all the substantial capital of the country.

There are fifty millions of British capital now afloat, or in use, in this country. Besides being of material advantage to the internal improvements and commercial interests of this nation, is not this large sum the best security for peace with the British nation? Are not these funds equivalent to hostages against British attack and aggression? Would to God that every other nation had capital so invested in this country; then should we have the best hostages for a continuance of friendly feeling with them, and be entitled to all the advantages of an amicable understanding—not only a protection against aggression and insult, but a guarantee for respect and friendship.

In conclusion, Mr. S. moved that the memorial be printed, and referred to a select committee of five; and he asserted that it contained the names of about 3500 firms in New York, and over 6000 signatures.

Mr. WILDE, of Georgia, moved an amendment, that the select committee so appointed should be instructed to inquire into the extent and nature of the pecuniary distress, and to what causes it was to be attributed; to inquire into the derangement of the currency of the country, and how produced; and to ascertain what remedies are best calculated to remove the distress, and restore the currency. In order to effect this judiciously and accurately, impartially and extensively, he added that they be empowered to examine documents and persons as they adjudged necessary.

Mr. W. supported his amendment by arguments drawn from the urgency of some action to be had efficiently and radically on the subject. The excitement in the House has tended to increase the excitement in the nation. If the distress did not exist, then would the conduct of the Chief Magistrate be made the subject of approval; but if distress existed—and this no man can doubt who has heard of the cries which have been made extensively, who has known that various memorials have been presented to Congress proclaiming the distress by men of every party and by men of no party—then will an inquiry be the best mode of coming to a candid result, where opinions are so various that asseverations are made on one side of the House that the distress is imaginary, and when on the other side the asseverations are equally strong and strenuous that the distress is too real.

In his opinion, we stand on the brink of a dangerous precipice, down which the measures now pursued by Government are likely to hurl us with a fearful, if not a fatal rapidity. Universal bankruptcy and suspension of specie payments stare us in the face. The present state of things cannot last. We shall go on from bad to worse, unless a remedy be adopted, and adopted speedily. The inquiry should therefore be on the broadest basis possible.

He next combated the scheme of the Secretary of the Treasury for adopting the agency of State banks, instead of the United States Bank, and in commenting upon the proposition of a metallic currency, he said that a restoration to specie payments would be more injurious to the interests of the country than restoring the deposites to the custody of the treasury.

Mr. POLK had been anxious to arrest the debate on the presentation of the resolutions from Maine, as being premature; he was equally anxious to arrest the debate on the present memorial, as being also uncalled for, and out of place. He saw no reason why the memorial, presented by the gentleman from New York, should not take the direction of all similar petitions, memorials, and documents on the same subject. He moved, therefore, that it be referred to the Committee of Ways and Means.

Mr. GORHAM said that the discussion and distress will not end till Government retrace its steps.

He entered into an elaborate statement on the question of a deranged currency, on specie payments, or a metallic currency; which our limited time, by the prolongation of the debate, prevents us now from giving.

Mr. HUBBARD observed that he had the honor of being a member of the Committee of Ways and Means, and he heard with utter astonishment the remarks which fell from the gentleman from Massachusetts, that this memorial, with the instructions, ought to be referred to a select committee, and not to the Committee of Ways and Means, because, forsooth, the committee had prejudged the matter—had formed their opinion—that the sentiments of some portion of that committee, had already been given to the public, and that the subject-matter of this memorial would not receive an impartial examination by that committee. Upon what authority, sir, has that gentleman presumed to declare, in the presence of this House, such sentiments? Does he know the opinion of one individual member of that committee upon the question involved in that memorial? Most assuredly not, for during all the meetings of that committee, since the commencement of the present session of Congress, (and he was confident that he had not been absent at a single meeting,) the subject of the Bank of the United States had not in any way or manner been presented to their consideration. The question in relation to the deposites—the renewal of the charter—the cause of the distress (whether real or pretended, he would not say) have in nowise engaged the attention of the committee at their sittings. How, sir, can the gentleman say that the Committee of Ways and Means have prejudged the case, or expressed opinions upon the subject. The gentleman from Tennessee, I admit, sir, has given his opinion at large upon the report of the Secretary of the Treasury, touching the removal of the deposites. He was followed by the gentleman from Pennsylvania, upon the same subject, and the gentleman from Pennsylvania was followed by the gentleman from New York, all members of the Committee of Ways and Means; and this morning we have been favored with the views of the gentleman from Massachusetts, in relation to the Bank of the United States. And how stands the account? Has the gentleman from Kentucky stated the case fairly, that, inasmuch as the opinions of the gentleman from Tennessee had gone forth to the American people in his printed speech, he was not a fit person to take charge of this memorial? Sir, does not the gentleman from Kentucky well know that the opinions of the gentleman from Pennsylvania had also gone forth to the American people, in his printed speech. The one, sir, followed close in the track of the other. It follows, then, that two members of that committee have expressed their opinions one way, and that two other members of the same committee had expressed their opinions the other way, on the absorbing question now before Congress, in relation to the bank; and the opinion of no other individual member could be known, unless it be that of the gentleman from Georgia, (who is also a member of the Committee of Ways and Means,) who has been pleased to make to the House, this morning, some general remarks in reference to the bank.

Although he (Mr. HUBBARD) had intended, for some time past, to have spoken upon the subject of the deposites, he had not been successful in his attempts to get the floor, yet he could not doubt that, if this memorial should be referred to the Committee of Ways and Means, it would receive its impartial, deliberate, and candid examination—that it would receive, from that committee, all the attention which its importance demanded.

It has been said that it ought not to be referred to the Committee of Ways and Means, because it speaks not of the deposites or of the Bank of the United States, and the gentleman from New York has said that it is a totally different question. Now, sir, what is the memorial? He could not be mistaken as to its importance. It speaks of the distresses which pervade the land; of the Pressure which bears heavily upon the various classes of the community, and tells us that the moving cause of this great calamity is to be found in the new relation produced between the Bank of the United States and the local banks. In other words, it has been produced by the removal of the deposites from the Bank of the United States and placing them in the State banks. Disguise it as you may, this is the plain English of the memorial. And it further says that the sovereign remedy for all these evils is the rechartering of the United States Bank, or the creating of some bank with similar powers. And yet, sir, it has been reiterated that the question involved in the memorial is wholly distinct and different from the question of removing the public deposites, or of rechartering the Bank of the United States, and therefore it should not be sent to the Committee of Ways and Means.

And what are the instructions proposed by the gentleman from Georgia to accompany this memorial? Why, sir, the committee are to inquire into the "truth of the recent complaints of general pecuniary distress and loss of credit, and into the truth of the alleged derangements of the currency and commercial exchanges." And that, if the complaints be well founded in the opinion of the committee, they are to report the causes of the said evils.

And what is the pretended cause of the alleged derangement of the currency and commercial exchanges? Nothing more nor nothing less than the removal of the deposites. There is then no difference in fact or in principle between this memorial and the hundred others which have heretofore been presented, and by order of the House referred—memorials and resolutions from Legislatures, from chambers of commerce, from boards of trade, and highly respectable individuals in different parts of the country. And what has been the order of the House in relation to all these? They have been referred, one and all, to the Committee of Ways and Means. And why give to this memorial a different direction? Why send it to a select committee?

The gentleman from Massachusetts has been pleased to state the reasons which would influence him; they had been repeated by the gentleman from Kentucky. He verily believes that the committee did not merit the reflection thus, in his view, cast upon them.

The subject properly and legitimately comes within the jurisdiction of the Committee of Ways and Means. It belonged to them, and properly to no other committee. It was most intimately connected with, and had relation to, the public finances, and thus should follow the disposition of all similar memorials which had come in before it. Before resuming his seat, he would make a single remark in reply to what fell from the gentleman from Kentucky, in relation to some observations which were made this morning by his friend from Tennessee. That gentleman did not say that he purposed to move the previous question, and thereby to cut short the debate.

He said no such thing. He said what he ought to have said, the force of which every member must feel, and must acknowledge. He said that this House had been in session nine weeks; that the question of the bank, in one way or other, had engaged most of the time and attention of this House during that whole period; that the complaints were floating on every breeze, coming from every quarter; that they were long and loud, and that he would most earnestly appeal to the House to unite with him in producing speedy and prompt action upon the subject.

The country demanded it; the time had come when there should be action—prompt and speedy action; and to bring this about, he most earnestly entreated the members of the House to hear all that was to be heard, and then deliberate and decide upon the great matters in controversy. This was in substance, what his friend said, and it was all that he said; and is there a man who does not most heartily respond to these sentiments? If the distress be real, the cause should be known and divulged at once; if it is fictitious or exaggerated, the imposition should be exposed—if the panic is got up for political effect, its aiders and abettors should receive public execration.

The sentiment of every man should be, it ought to be, whatever is to be done, let that be done quickly.

Mr. S. JONES moved an adjournment, which he withdrew, as there were loud calls for the question to be taken.

Mr. BARRINGER renewed his motion to adjourn, which was negatived.

After a few brief remarks from Messrs. WILDE, ARCHER, and SELDEN,—

The question on referring the memorial to the Committee of Ways and Means was put, and decided in the affirmative:

YEAS—Messrs. John Adams, William Allen, Baylies, Beale, Bean, Beardsley, Beaumont, John Bell, James Blair, John Blair, Bockee, Bodle, Boon, Brown, Bunch, Burns, Cambreleng, Carr, Casey, Chaney, Chinn, S. Clark, Clay, Coffee, Connor, Cramer, Day, Dickerson, Dunlap, Ewing, Forester, Fowler, William K. Fuller, Galbraith, Gillet, Joseph Hall, Thomas H. Hall, Halsey, Hamer, Joseph M. Harper, Harrison, Hathaway, Hawkins, Henderson, Howell, Hubbard, Abel Huntington, Inge, Jarvis, Richard M. Johnson, Noadiah Johnson, Cave Johnson, Seaborn Jones, Benjamin Jones, Kavanagh, Kinnard, Lane, Lansing, Laporte, Lawrence, Lea, Lee, Leavitt, Lucas, Lytle, A. Mann, Joel K. Mann, Mardis, McIntire, McKay, McKim, McKinley, McVean, Miller, Mitchell, Muhlenberg, Murphy, Osgood, Page, Parks, Parker, Patterson, Pearce, Peyton, Pierce, Pierson, Plummer, Polk, Pope, Ramsay, Schenck, Schley, Shinn, Charles Slade, Smith, Speight, Standifer, Sutherland, William Taylor, Francis Thomas, Thomson, Turner, Turrill, Vanderpoel, Van Houten, Wagener, Ward, Wardwell, Wayne, Webster, Whallon, C. P. White—113.

NAYS—Messrs. J. Q. Adams, Heman Allen, John J. Allen, Chilton Allan, Archer, Ashley, Barber, Barnitz, Barringer, Bates, Beatty, James M. Bell, Binney, Bouldin, Briggs, Bull, Burd, Cage, Carmichael, Chambers, Chilton, Choate, Claiborne, William Clark, Clayton, Clowney, Corwin, Coulter, Crane, Crockett, Darlington, Warren R. Davis, Amos Davis, Davenport, Deberry, Deming, Denny, Dennis, Dickson, Duncan, Evans, Edward Everett, Horace Everett, Felder, Fillmore, Foot, Foster, Fulton, Gamble, Gholson, Gilmer, Gordon, Gorham, Graham, Grennell, Griffin, Hiland Hall, Hard, Hardin, James Harper, Hazeltine, Heath, Hiester, Jabez W. Huntington, William C. Johnson, King, Lewis, Martindale, Marshall, J. Y. Mason, McComas, McKennan, Milligan, Moore, Patton, Potts, Reed, Rencher, Selden, Augustus H. Shepperd, William Slade, Sloane, Spangler, Stoddert, Wm. P. Taylor, Tompkins, Tweedy, Vance, Vinton, Watmough, Edward D. White, Frederick Whittlesey, Elisha Whittlesey, Wilde, Wilson, Wise, and Young—97.

So the memorial was referred to the Committee of Ways and Means.

And the House, on motion, at six o'clock, adjourned.

IN SENATE.

TUESDAY, *February* 4, 1834.

The following message from the President of the United States was received by Mr. DONELSON, his Private Secretary:

To the Senate and House of Representatives:

I deem it my duty to communicate to Congress the recent conduct of the Bank of the United States, in refusing to deliver the books, papers, and funds in its possession, relating to the execution of the act of Congress of June 7, 1832, entitled "An act supplementary to the act for the relief of certain surviving officers and soldiers of the Revolution." The correspondence reported by the Secretary of War, and herewith transmitted, will show the grounds assumed by the bank to justify its refusal to make the transfer directed by the War Department. It does not profess to claim the privilege of this agency as a right secured to it by contract, nor as a benefit conferred by the Government, but as a burden from which it is willing to be relieved. It places its refusal upon the extraordinary ground that the corporation has a right to sit in judgment upon the legality of the acts of the constituted authorities, in a matter in which the stockholders are admitted to have no interest; and it impedes and defeats, as far as its power will permit, the execution of a measure of the Administration, because the opinion of the corporation, upon the construction of an act of Congress differs from that of the proper officers of the United States.

The claim of this corporation thus to usurp the functions of the judicial power, and to prescribe to the Executive Department the manner in which it shall execute the trust confided to it by law, is without example in the history of our country. If the acts of the public servants, who are responsible to the people for the manner in which they execute their duty, may thus be checked and controlled by an irresponsible money corporation, then, indeed, the whole frame of our Government is changed, and we have established a power in the Bank of the United States above what we derive from the people.

It will be seen, from the accompanying statement, (marked A,) that according to the latest accounts received at the War Department, the Bank of the United States and its branches have in their possession near half a million of the public money, received by them under the law of 1832, which they have not yet accounted for, and which they refuse to pay over to the proper agents, for the use of those persons for whose benefit it was withdrawn from the treasury. It is to be regretted that this attempt on the part of the bank to guide and direct the Executive upon the construction and execution of an act of Congress should have been put forward and insisted on in a case where the immediate sufferers from their conduct will be the surviving veterans of the revolutionary war; for this evil falls exclusively upon the gallant defenders of their country, and delays and embarrasses the payment of the debt which the gratitude of the nation has awarded to them, and which, in many instances, is necessary for their subsistence and comfort in their declining years.

The character of the claim set up by the bank, and the interest of the parties to be immediately affected by it, make it my duty to submit the whole subject to the consideration of Congress; and I leave it to their wisdom to adopt such measures as the honor of the Government and the just claims of the individuals injured by the proceedings may be deemed to require.

Having called for the opinion of the Attorney General upon this occasion, with a view to a thorough investigation of the question which has thus been presented for my consideration, I enclose a copy of the report of that officer, and add my entire concurrence in the views he has taken.

ANDREW JACKSON.

February 4, 1834.

Mr. CLAY said that we had heard early in this month, whilst the conduct of the Executive in seizing the public money was under discussion, and before the decision of Congress was had upon it, the Executive, not choosing to wait for the decision of Congress, that he was proceeding to carry into effect the measures of September last. We have heard that an attempt was made to take from the Bank of the United States the agency committed to it by law, for payment of the Government pensioners. He had not heard it with surprise; he was surprised at nothing which was done by the executive branch of the Government. But he had looked into the nature of this agency, and he had found that it was confided to the Bank of the United States by law, and the Executive could not touch it but by a palpable usurpation of power. He was glad the bank had resisted this further violation of executive usurpation. Nothing was heard on this subject, until the call for the correspondence with the bank in relation to it, made by the resolution of the gentleman from Mississippi, was taken up yesterday; and he had not a doubt that information of it had previously reached the President's mansion. There could not be a doubt of it. The powers of the bank were heretofore adverted to in the Albany case. The law confided the agency to the bank, and it was so acknowledged by the Department of War. Yes, sir, it was acknowledged by that department, by his retracing his steps. And now we have a message, that because the bank would not yield to the executive mandate, Congress is asked to interfere. He hoped the message would be referred to a committee, that it may be subjected to a thorough examination, and a proper corrective applied where the real violation of law existed. He thought the Judiciary Committee was the most proper one to commit the subject to, and he moved its reference accordingly.

Mr. GRUNDY said that he had not made a thorough examination of the subject, but he was of opinion the gentleman from Kentucky was mistaken when he supposed the money referred to in the Bank of the United States was under the pension law of 1832, and that the bank was the agent for its disbursement. He thought the law made no such provision, but that the Secretary of the Treasury was to make payment of the money as he thought best. And by a resolution these powers were now transferred to the Secretary of War. But if this was a legal question, as he thought it was, there was no propriety in pronouncing an opinion now. The President was of opinion that the law authorized the transfer, and he applied to the bank and was refused. And what has the President done? He has laid the whole subject before Congress, and it seemed to him he could not have adopted a better, more correct, or more decorous course. He concurred in opinion that the subject ought to be examined by the Judiciary Committee. The opinion of the highest law officer had been taken by the Chief Magistrate, who agreed with him in opinion that the bank had no right to hold this money. He thought we ought to postpone the expression of any opinion on the subject, until the investigation could be had.

Mr. CLAY replied that the investigation must not be confined merely to the act of 1832, but should be extended to all the pension laws. He would have been glad if the gentleman [Mr. GRUNDY] had given his counsel to the President. What was the character of the message? Denunciation. Denunciation of the bank for withholding the papers given to it in charge, and attributes to it purposes of usurpation. And we are told that the opinion of the Attorney General had been given on this subject. But he had ceased to respect the opinions of the executive officers of the Govern-

ment the moment that they were bound to submit to one controlling voice. Those officers are mere automata. And when we know that dismission is inevitably the consequence of disobedience, how can we respect their opinions as free and independent? He had great respect for the Attorney General as a man; he knew his high character, and if he had remained at Albany, and had not come into this pestilential atmosphere, he would have continued to respect his opinion; but did the gentleman suppose that when he came here, where he was in constant danger of losing his place, I could respect his opinion? No, sir; no, sir.

Mr. WRIGHT observed that probably he was not so fortunate as the gentleman from Kentucky in being able to pronounce opinions upon questions so important as those embraced in the message. The question arose out of the pension laws, among which he thought the gentleman would find a marked difference. The payment of one class of pensioners was to be made by the bank—of another class, by the Secretary of the Treasury. He would only make a single remark further upon the manner in which the gentleman had spoken of the opinion of the Attorney General. That gentleman was his esteemed friend. He was a gentleman who could not be affected by the Senator's remarks to his prejudice. The country knew the character of the Attorney General too well to approve of such reflections upon his integrity. If there was any man within his acquaintance whose character Mr. W. respected, it was the Attorney General. He knew him well; so well that he might safely assert that neither authority nor interest could coerce him into an opinion which his conscience dictated to him was not right.

The message was referred to the Committee on the Judiciary.

Mr. WRIGHT rose, and said he held in his hand a memorial signed by citizens of the city of New York, in which they express their opinions in relation to the embarrassments in the money market, and representing that they believe a Bank of the United States to be useful and necessary. He was bound to say that he received the paper from a most respectable committee of gentlemen from New York, who were now in attendance here. He felt bound to say, also, that the signatures to the memorial, amounting to about six thousand, embraced some of the most respectable merchants, traders, and active business men in that city, and that their expression was entitled to as much weight here as that of any equal number in New York. He knew many of the gentlemen, and their representations ought to have great weight. He moved that the memorial be read, referred to the Committee on Finance, and printed, with the signatures appended.

After the paper had been read—

Mr. WEBSTER said, that the great number of signatures to the memorial was a just testimonial to the character and respectability of the signers. He thought it equivalent to actual proof of the existence of great distress in the commercial community. He doubted whether, in the whole history of the Government, memorials had ever come before Congress, where so much pains had been taken forcibly to express the deep, wide-spread conviction of embarrassment, distress, and impending ruin, as was exhibited in this. It reminded him more of some instances of occurrences in an European Government, in some respects a popular one, but not so much so as our own House of Representatives, not springing so directly from the people. He meant the British House of Commons, where in times past the House was invoked by petitions with vast amounts of names to them. We well remember how the tables of the House of Commons were loaded by petitions and memorials at the commencement of our Revolutionary War. He remembered an instance of a Whig member from one of the northern counties of England having presented a petition against the war, and while the messenger was carrying it along to the clerk's table, the end dragging on the floor and not being visible, a member observed, there was the head of the petition, but where was the tail? He was answered, that the tail had not yet left Yorkshire. The memorial proved this fact, too, that the distress and embarrassment was too serious to be scoffed at; it was too plain to be mistaken. They feel a pressure which they do not know how adequately to describe, and a fear of consequences which they cannot trust their lips to express to their most intimate friends. This was the state of things, and the country was now to pass on this great question. By some it has been contended that it is the consequence of the removal of the deposites, and the breaking up of the bank; by others, that it is owing to the conduct of the bank itself, and that it is in the power of the bank to triumph over the danger and relieve the community. He thought it the duty of the bank to do all it could to relieve the distress; to exert its whole power, even to the verge of its own safety, to avert this distress, which every man of business in the community feels. It was the duty of the bank to do this; but it was the duty of the bank, too, to look at its own situation—its debts were spread over the whole surface of the country, and any sudden expansion of its capacity for relief, must be followed by a sudden contraction on every emergency; it required the greatest deliberation in winding up its concerns, or the greatest distress must inevitably ensue. The Government had taken its stand, and declared its purpose to be, to collect and distribute its revenue through the State banks alone. Still, he trusted the bank would discharge its duties, and show that no fault remained on it; that it would relieve distress to its utmost capacity, and show that it could go no farther. He knew not to what extent these shocks of public credit and of property would go; but he thought he could perceive the end of those public men who closed their ears against the cries of distress which were coming in from all parts of the country. We have now the fact before us of great distress and pressure existing, and he besought gentlemen to believe it; he implored them to believe it, and to be assured that through all ranks and ranges of the commercial community, there had not been such distress for the last twenty years—he thought no man could refuse to believe it; although it extended now chiefly along the Atlantic coast, yet the wave would roll inward over the mountains, and across the Mississippi valley until it pervaded all parts of the Union.

Mr. WRIGHT observed, he did not rise to comment upon the memorial, but it was his duty to say, that too great an extension had been given to the scenes of distress, and that the memorial was not to be considered as conclusive evidence of the facts stated. He was aware that a controversy existed on the subject, and he was unwilling to discuss it in this incidental manner. He differed from the petitioners as to the cause of the distress, and the proper remedy to be applied.

The petition was referred to the Committee on Finance.

SPECIAL ORDER—PUBLIC DEPOSITES.

The VICE PRESIDENT having announced the special order to be the report of the Secretary of the Treasury on the removal of the deposites, and the resolutions of Mr. CLAY thereon—

Mr. FRELINGHUYSEN resumed and concluded his remarks against the report.

Mr. WILKINS then took the floor, and moved an adjournment; but withdrew the motion at the request of

Mr. WEBSTER, who remarked that he was perfectly willing the gentleman should proceed, as he had intimated the other day; but he wished to move the reference of the report and the second resolution thereon [Mr. CLAY's] to the Committee on Finance; and he would venture to say, if the gentleman would consent to the reference, that the report should be made by to-morrow morning. He wished the committee might have an opportunity of expressing the opinions they had formed on the financial part of the report. The resolutions were twofold. The first was of a high political character, and not for the Committee on Finance; but if the Senate wished it, they would not shrink from expressing their opinions upon it.

Mr. WRIGHT thought that if the whole subject went to the committee, it would form the basis of a report, and could not be considered as the direct subject of debate before the Senate when it was returned.

Some further remarks were then made by Messrs. WEBSTER, SPRAGUE, POINDEXTER, and CLAY, on a point of order, who contended that, when the subject came back from the committee, it would be substantially before the Senate as it left it.

Mr. KING took the opposite ground; when

The VICE PRESIDENT decided that the subject would be open for discussion when it came back, just as it was now.

The reference was then agreed to.

Mr. POINDEXTER then moved to take up his resolutions, submitted on Friday; and he withdrew his call for the ayes and noes.

The VICE PRESIDENT decided that the first resolution and a part of the third could not be entertained, because they were identical with other resolutions before the Senate, [Mr. CLAY's.]

Mr. POINDEXTER then consented to modify them, so as to destroy their identity.

Mr. GRUNDY then moved that the Senate adjourn; which was not agreed to.

The first resolution was then agreed to.

Mr. CALHOUN then moved that the third resolution be laid on the table; which was agreed to—23 to 14.

Mr. MORRIS then moved that the remaining resolutions be laid on the table; which was agreed to—yeas 21, nays 18.

The bill to allow —— Lamar, a citizen of Georgia, to import iron for a steamboat, free of duty, was read a third time, and passed; and then

The Senate adjourned.

HOUSE OF REPRESENTATIVES.

TUESDAY, *February* 4, 1834.

THE PENSION LAWS.

The order of the day was declared to be the resolution offered by Mr. CHILTON, to appoint a select committee to inquire into the expediency of so extending the general pension law, as to embrace within its provisions those persons who were engaged in the Indian wars, down to the year 1794, and the amendment of it by Mr. BOULDIN, to appoint a committee to inquire into the moral effects of the pension system upon the community, and how far it ought to be abolished or repealed.

Mr. POPE, of Kentucky, observed that he had but a few remarks to make, and that they should be hastily submitted. In fact, he should have contented himself with giving a silent vote on the resolution under consideration, had not the discussion which it provoked, assumed an objectionable aspect. But he felt constrained to say something, from the fact that the debate had unnecessarily wandered from its legitimate sphere, and partaken of a spirit foreign from that good feeling and mutual harmony which should prevail in the House. He felt impelled to speak, for the double purpose of presenting a few reasons why he thought the resolution should be adopted, and of redeeming from unmerited, but perhaps unintended imputation, the conduct of those who participated in the struggles to which the resolution refers. And although, during the discussion, unwarrantable imputations have been cast upon the pioneers and early warriors of the West, yet this circumstance should not provoke him to perpetrate injustice upon his unoffending fellow-citizens of the North. He should not retaliate by fulminating charges against the people of that quarter—nor should he seek to place their conduct in our warlike struggles, in disadvantageous contrast with that of their more western brethren. His purpose was to vindicate the conduct and the cause of his neighbors, of his friends, and of their fathers, not to cast reproach, perhaps unmerited, upon others. He was willing to admit that the people of the North had been ever animated by a disinterested attachment to country. He was willing to admit that the late war found their gallant tars upon the deep, asserting, with the cannon's voice, their country's rights—that it found them boldly careering through every sea, and giving our stars and stripes to the breezes of every clime; but he asserted that it also found the western warrior bleeding at every pore, and expiring upon every battle-field.

Mr. POPE inquired why the usual courtesy was not extended to the resolution under discussion? Why was it so bitterly opposed in its very incip-

ency? Why a committee were not permitted to examine and report its merits? Were not the objects whom it seeks to benefit worthy of the kindness and consideration of the House? Had they not shed their blood, periled their lives, and fought the battles of their country?

But it is objected by the gentleman from Rhode Island [Mr. Burges] that the wars in which they were engaged were *private* wars; that they were waged for the defence of individual rights and property. Can this be so? inquired Mr. P. Look (said he) to western history, and see if the fallacy of the assertion is not stamped upon every page. Look to general history, and it will be found that at the close of the revolutionary war, when the Atlantic States were enjoying the blessings of "profound peace and undisturbed repose"—when the last cannon's roar had died away upon the breeze—when the shrill notes of the fife had been succeeded by the busy hum of revived and awakened occupation—when the instruments of death were laid aside for those of more peaceful vocation—did the people of the West enjoy the same happy state of things? Did they bask in the same sunshine? Or were their midnight forests still lighted with the flames of continued war, and the very air loaded with the screams of murdered and mangled victims?

But *how* (said Mr. P.) were these private wars? Of what character were the campaigns under Hardin and Harmar and Clark, the great Clark, who has been justly styled the Hannibal of the West? Of what character was the campaign under the unfortunate St. Clair? Were these conducted to carry on private wars or predatory wars to protect *individual* rights and property? Certainly not. The rich blood that flowed in torrents at St. Clair's defeat, flowed not in a *private* but in a *public* war. St. Clair did not head a self-constituted band, congregated for the purposes of plunder, or the prosecution of a private feud, but he commanded an army under the direction and control of the Government of the United States, from which authority he derived his commission of command, and to which he was amenable for his conduct. Mr. P. repeated that it was a public war, and, in support of that view, referred to the resolution of Congress of the 21st July, 1787, directing "the 'Secretary of War to place the troops of the United States in such positions as should afford the 'most effectual protection to the frontier inhabitants of Pennsylvania and Virginia from the incursions and depredations of the Indians; for 'preventing intrusions on the Federal lands, and 'promoting a favorable issue to the intended treaty." He also referred to another resolution of the same body, requesting the Executive of Virginia "to give orders to the militia in the district 'of Kentucky to hold themselves in readiness to 'unite with the Federal troops in such operations 'as the officer commanding them might judge necessary for the protection of the frontiers; and 'that on the application of the commanding officer 'of the Federal troops, the said Executive be requested to give orders that a part of said militia, 'not exceeding one thousand, be embodied and 'take such positions as the said commanding officer should direct for acting in conjunction with 'the Federal troops in protecting and defending 'the frontier inhabitants, *and in making such expeditions against the Indians, in case they continued hostile*, as Congress should thereafter order and 'direct."

These resolutions, continued Mr. P., incontestably establish the fact that the Federal Government looked upon these wars as national in their character, and betray an anxiety on the part of the public functionaries of that day to bring them to a speedy termination. Yet, in despite of this testimony to the contrary, it is now gravely contended that they were private wars. Certainly this assertion cannot be predicated on the fact that the western country happened to be the exclusive theatre of the shocking butcheries that occurred. Because in that view of the case, Kentucky and Tennessee and other States might with equal propriety contend that the late war was a private war, it not having been waged within their territorial limits. But, sir, they did not assume that ground. The people of those States were animated with the same hopes and fears that were felt by the patriots of other States. They mourned over the reverses and rejoiced at the successes of their country; and their swords were ready then, as they ever will be, "to leap from their scabbards" at the call of duty.

It has been well remarked (said Mr. P.) by one of my colleagues [Mr. Hardin] that the wars spoken of were a *continuation* of the revolutionary war. If this be so, said he, the question is at an end. He proposed briefly to examine that point, and desired it to be borne in mind that when the revolutionary war commenced we were at *peace* with *every tribe of Indians*; that the British Government adopted the cruel policy of stimulating the savages to confederate with her troops in the war, and to imbrue their hands in our blood; that that Government literally bargained in American blood, and trafficed in American scalps. To such a murderous extent was this horrible policy pursued that it roused the matchless Chatham to one of the noblest efforts of his life, and induced him to pour out his indignant feelings in strains of fervid eloquence unparalleled in the efforts of the times. When peace ensued what was the course (inquired Mr. P.) pursued by the British Government? Did that Government surrender the posts on the lakes, or did it retain them in open violation of the treaty concluded between the two nations? It not only retained them, said he, but its agents actually supplied the savages from thence with all munitions necessary to continue the war and harass us with their butcheries and depradations. The savages did continue the war; and it was from these very posts that the victors of the unfortunate St. Clair and his army derived their implements of destruction. In the face, then, of all these facts, asserted by history and corroborated by the concurring testimony of the survivors of the scenes that occurred, how can it be asserted that those were private wars or predatory wars? How can it be doubted that they were a continuation of the revolutionary war? It is true (said Mr. P.) there was a *written* treaty of peace; but it is equally true there was no peace. It is true there was an avowed and stipulated suspension of hostilities, but it is equally true that the British Government prolonged the war through the means and agency of the savages. The glad tidings of peace had officially gone forth; but still murder and rapine reigned with unmitigated fury. Mr. P. considered there was no peace until the actual suspension of all hostilities; until the allies and confederates of the British Government had ceased to brandish the infernal tomahawk, and until the military posts alluded to were actually surrended by the British Government into the hands of that of the United States. He dismissed this part of the subject by the avowal of an opinion that every drop of patriot blood that was spilt in those wars, every soldier that was slain, every scalp that was taken, and every victim that was butchered, was all done in a common cause, for the common defence, and during the continuance of the war of the Revolution.

Mr. P. next proceeded to notice the objection taken to the pension system by the gentleman from Virginia, [Mr. Bouldin.] He was opposed to the amendment offered by that honorable gentleman. He could not agree that the tendency of pensions was demoralizing. In this particular case, it could not generate the spirit of idleness which the gentleman from Virginia so earnestly deprecated, because the objects to be pensioned had already reached an age when their habits, good or bad, were fixed. They were now in the "sere and yellow leaf," and their habits were immutable. It had been also stated in debate that the pension system was of demoralizing tendency, inasmuch at it held out inducements to perjury. Mr. P. did not think this a sound objection. It was an objection that would apply with equal force to the laws and judicial proceedings of every State in the Union. In many, or all the States, a man seeking the collection of a debt, or the enforcement of a claim, is allowed to swear to the statements of his bill or affidavit. Assuredly there is as great temptation to perjury held out in this practice as in the pension laws. The system (said Mr. P.) is like everything else of human contrivance, liable to be abused. But surely, said he, the possibility of such an occurrence can constitute no legitimate objection to the system itself. Let us discharge our duty. Let us discharge a long-existing debt of gratitude. And if any unworthy citizen in seeking to obtain that to which he is not entitled, shall forswear himself, let us leave him to abide the judgment of his own conscience and that of his Maker. So far from objecting to the system, Mr. P. was its advocate. He was so, because he believed all its tendencies were good; he believed it calculated to nerve the warrior's arm in the hour of battle, to stimulate him to deeds of nobler daring; to induce him to leap, with a lion's bound, into the storm of the conflict, convinced of the justice and beneficence of his Government, and of its protection and support of those whom his possible death in the struggle would leave unsheltered and forlorn.

Mr. P. said he had deemed it his duty thus feebly to raise his humble voice in support of the resolution offered by his worthy friend and colleague, [Mr. Chilton;] a resolution which embraces within its provisions a remnant of a race of men, many of whom still linger in the district he had the honor to represent in Congress—a race of men whose hands, he thanked Heaven, were unstained with plunder; who were revered where they were best known for their virtues and their valor; who were ardently attached to the honor and glory of their country, and whose last breath, he doubted not, would be expended in invoking for it the blessings and protection of their God.

Mr. BOULDIN rose to address the Chair, and, at the same moment, rose Mr. CROCKETT.

The CHAIR decided that the member from Tennessee [Mr. Crockett] was entitled to the floor, inasmuch as the member from Virginia had spoken already on this question.

Mr. CROCKETT said he had risen not to make a miscellaneous speech. There had been too many speeches of that sort already. He rose to move the previous question.

The CHAIR decided that the previous question was not in order at present, as the gentleman from Virginia would be entitled to the floor after the gentleman from Tennessee had yielded it.

Mr. CROCKETT. Well, sir, I will make a little short speech. It is well known to this House and to the nation (he said) that he had always supported the pension system. He had always contended that the volunteers and militiamen were even better entitled to pensions than the regular troops. The regulars sell themselves to the Government for a fixed price, but the volunteer goes into the war for the love of his country. He had no doubt that the Indian fighters were as much entitled to the bounty of the Government as any of the soldiers of the Revolution. There was no question that they suffered as much as any men who engaged in any other service. They suffered as much by the scalping-knife and from the want of provisions. He had been accustomed to that sort of thing, and had taken a hand in it himself. His object was to move the previous question, and if it was not in order now, he hoped it would be when the gentleman from Virginia had spoken. He had now finished his speech.

Mr. BOULDIN rose to speak, but

The CHAIR reminded Mr. B. that but a few minutes remained before the expiration of the hour.

Mr. ADAMS, of Massachusetts, had but a few words to say, which, with the leave of the gentleman in possession of the floor, he would say now. If the pension system was inconsistent with good policy it ought to be abandoned, and something else substituted. But as the system was in existence, he had nothing to say on that point. The inquiry proposed by the resolution as to the propriety of pensioning the persons who were engaged in the Indian wars prior to 1794 was not, in his opinion, liable to a single objection.

Against the object of the inquiry he had met with but one objection, and that was, that the Indian wars which took place within the period mentioned were private wars. Sir, I believe this opinion is not well founded. He believed they were not private wars, and that they were as much public as the war with Great Britain during the Revolution, or the late war with Great Britain. The conclusion of peace in 1783 left us still at war with the Indian tribes. He held in his hand the journals of the Congress of the old Confederation, from which it appeared that in 1784 it was proposed to disband the United States army. A report was made in relation to Indian affairs, showing that the

United States were at war with the Indians, and that the Indians were the aggressors. He read several passages, to show that the Indian wars were considered by Congress as public wars.

Mr. CHAMBERS, of Pennsylvania, rose to address the House, but

The SPEAKER stated that the hour had expired.

BANK—PENSION AGENCY.

The SPEAKER presented a message from the President of the United States, relative to the refusal of the United States Bank to deliver up the books, papers, or funds, belonging to the pension agency, together with the correspondence between the Secretary of War and the President of the bank, with the opinion of the Attorney General.

[The message will be found in the Senate proceedings.]

Mr. HUBBARD moved that the message and accompanying documents be printed, and referred to the Committee of Ways and Means.

Mr. WILLIAMS made a motion, which he afterwards withdrew, to read the opinion of the Attorney General.

Mr. WATMOUGH trusted that no such course as the reference to the Committee of Ways and Means would be taken on the documents then presented. They were of importance equivalent to any which had come before the House during the session. They mark a new set of principles on which the conduct of the executive government is made to depend. They assail an institution whose officers have been appointed by law, without regard to the existing laws of the land. The Committee of Ways and Means have got a voracious appetite, and seem desirous to devour all that comes before the House. This is a question of law, and should be decided by a committee on law. He therefore moved that the message, with the documents, be referred to the Judiciary Committee.

Mr. ALLAN moved the postponement of the subject till to-morrow.

The SPEAKER having put this question, there appeared

Ayes 95, and noes 113, on it.

Mr. HUBBARD considered the subject belonged properly to the Committee of Ways and Means, as it is but auxiliary to the main question, already referred, in conjunction with various petitions, memorials, and documents, on the bank topic, to that committee. It is not a question of law, but of fact. It is a question to decide concerning the moneys appropriated for a particular purpose—whether the Secretary of War has seen that the pension agency is properly discharged, and the appropriations properly disbursed. It is a topic of facts relative to the funds—the jurisdiction of which belongs expressly to the Committee of Ways and Means.

Mr. BARRINGER thinks that the collision has arisen concerning the construction of the law, and therefore that the topic belongs to the Judiciary Committee, as the expounders of a law in contestation. He desired that the communication of the President of the United States Bank be read.

[This was accordingly done; and on the request of the members, the letter of the Secretary of War and the opinion of the Attorney General were also read.]

Mr. B. said that the question was not one relating to the finances of the country, to which the jurisdiction of the Committee of Ways and Means was limited.

An appropriation for the pension fund had been made by Congress, and placed in the custody of the bank, beyond the control of the Executive, further than to specify the drafts in each instance for those purposes for which the appropriation had been given. The bank was appointed the agent to pay the pensions to the men entitled by law to receive it; and it was permitted to pay it in its own local currency. The agency had been intrusted to the bank by law; and that agency it cannot surrender but by law. It is necessary, therefore, to examine the legal bearings of the subject. This belongs to that committee which had assigned to it a peculiar fitness for peculiar purposes. This committee was that on the Judiciary. There did not appear to be any other difficulty than what arose out of the construction to be given to a particular statute, and he could not hold that any difference of this kind should constitute an offence of such a grave character, that it was necessary to punish the bank by sending the subject to the Committee of Ways and Means, instead of to the appropriate committee, the Committee of the Judiciary. He complained that the Executive had denounced the bank for having only done that which they had a right to do, believing that they were the agents appointed by law for the payment of these pensioners, and he felt warranted, from the tone throughout the message, in believing that if the President had the power, he would have used it, to coerce the bank for so doing. He requested honorable members to consider for what object was the message sent to Congress; was it not that legislation might be had on the subject?—that they might take such steps as were necessary to be taken by them as would bring the controversy to an end, without causing any further trouble? This being, in his opinion, the President's object, the subject for their determination then was, to what committee should it be sent? He asked honorable members to say, if in all cases where a difference arose on points of law, it was not the practice of the House to refer such matters to the Committee of the Judiciary, which, as the judicial organ of the House, was considered the appropriate one? But it would seem that it was necessary to send this to the Committee of Ways and Means. Why was it necessary that that committee should be disposed to grasp at and to have all the subjects to be presented to the House of importance, under its control? He could not assent to such a disposition of this message, and was proceeding to discuss some topics connected with the general bank subject, upon which

The SPEAKER called him to order.

Mr. B. then advocated the propriety of sending the subject to the Committee on the Judiciary, as he believed, that he might safely predict, that the House, in order to settle the controversy, would be compelled to enact a law on the subject, and upon which the Judiciary Committee would ultimately have the subject before it.

Mr. CLAY rose to ask the gentleman from North Carolina, in reply to the interrogatory put by him, by what authority was it that he could predicate the assumption that the Committee of Ways and Means had endeavored to grasp at subjects which had not been, and usually were not, referred to it? He had no recollection of any such case, and he desired to know why it should be deemed so extraordinary now to refer this matter to that committee, when every other, connected with the bank and the revenue of the country had always been sent there? That this was the case, was as well known to the gentleman who made the interrogatory, as it was to every other member in the House. Were not all the other memorials in relation to the bank committed to that committee? Had not the gentleman himself repeatedly, by former votes given by him, contributed as much as any one could, to cause such a direction to be given to such subjects? Why then were they to be called on by him, whom he challenged to give a single instance in which this practice was departed from, to renounce it? He was unwilling to go into motives, but if he were inclined to do so, as he might be justified from the imputation that was endeavored to be cast upon the Committee of Ways and Means, was he not entitled to put this interrogatory with more justice, and with certainly more difficulty to answer: Will the bank have the impudence, as has been said elsewhere, to make the attempt to dictate to Congress at the expense of pensioners who may be starving?

The SPEAKER here reminded the gentleman of the necessity of confining his remarks to the question to which of the committees the message should be sent.

Mr. CLAY continued and said, that although he had as much confidence in the integrity, intelligence, and capacity of the members composing the Committee of the Judiciary, and thought that they could do as full justice to the subject as any other committee, yet it was not advisable to send this question there; the effect of which must be to make this a separate question from others in relation to the bank which had been sent to the Committee of Ways and Means. He could not conceive any possible necessity existed to justify this being divided from the others sent to that committee. He considered that this was unquestionably nothing less than tantamount to the question embraced in the question of the removal of the deposites. What did the pension law of 1832 enact? Was it not attempted to be violated by the bank?

The SPEAKER here reminded the gentleman of the necessity of confining his remarks to the question to which of the committees the message should be sent.

Mr. CLAY hoped it was not necessary to admonish him, as he knew not when he could be rightfully charged with departing from the rules of debate.

The SPEAKER reminded him, that he had prevented the member who preceded him from going into the general discussion, and that he must do so to every other member.

Mr. C. expressed his willingness to submit to the decision of the Chair, and proceeded to argue, that inasmuch as all bills making appropriations of the public money emanated from the Committee of Ways and Means, the money to pay these pensions was appropriated, and the bill doing this had originated in that committee. It should therefore be now deemed the most appropriate committee to dispose of the matter at issue between the bank and the Government. He referred to and quoted the 57th rule of the House, which showed that upon that committee was enjoined the duty of taking into consideration all the reports from the Treasury Department, into which they were to examine, report thereon, examine into the state of the public departments, and particularly into the laws themselves making such appropriations. After a few remarks in explanation, between Mr. Barringer and himself, Mr. C. expressed his hope that the subject would be sent to the Committee of Ways and Means.

Mr. CHILTON humorously remarked, that the anxiety of his friend, the member from Alabama, [Mr. Clay,] to discuss the general subject connected with the bank, as was evinced by his several attempts to do so during the present debate, and which, in his mind, had nothing to do with it, reminded him of the story told of a truant schoolboy, who, when questioned by his master, "how it happened that he was generally late or absent from school," gave for excuse, "that the ground was so slippery with ice, that for every step he went forward, he went two backwards." "Well, then," rejoined the master, "how do you account for coming here at all?" The boy logically accounted for it by stating "that he was only enabled to do so, by starting off in an opposite direction;" and the boy's practice was followed out by the member from Alabama, to effect his purpose in the present discussion. Mr. C. advocated the propriety of sending the message to the Committee on the Judiciary, in preference to the Committee of Ways and Means It appeared that the Executive, before sending it to the House, had laid it before his judicial officer, the Attorney General, as he felt there was a difficulty in the way. He considered that a judicial tribunal was the first to be resorted to, and was competent solely to pronounce upon it. Why, then, he would ask, should they hesitate to follow this example, and for what object?

A reason had been given the other day by the honorable mover of the reference to the Committee of Ways and Means, upon some matter before the House, "that it was an imputation to withhold." If this was a good reason for that honorable member to urge, might he not retort now, and say, that as it was usual to refer such a subject as this message to the Judiciary Committee, it would be an imputation upon that committee not to do so, as it was their usual practice in such cases? He entreated, if there was anything like order or consistency in their rules to be observed, that this would be done, and that the House would not be induced, by any political or other considerations, to give the subject any other than the direction they ought to give it. If it was in order for him to go into inuendoes, he might say, we have seen a rising storm——

The SPEAKER here called to order.

Mr. C. assured the Chair he was only going to allay the storm, and remarked, that although he presumed that he himself ought to know where he should stop, but as the Chair was of a different opinion, he would yield to that opinion, and then conclude.

Mr. BINNEY said, he understood the rule of order as the honorable Speaker had already more than once stated it. The opinion of the Attorney General had not been submitted to the bank or to this House, and it was proper that, before it was discussed, it should be examined by the Judiciary Committee. As to the old soldiers, he had the utmost possible kindness for them, and his personal regard for the bank would not, in any way, conflict with his feelings towards them. But the bank had not refused to pay the pensions to the old soldiers, but would continue to pay them, as heretofore, in the manner authorized by law. He went into a view of the duties of the Committee of Ways and Means, to show that they related entirely to the means of raising revenue, and the sums necessary for public uses. But it was said that the memorials, relative to the bank, had all gone to the Committee of Ways and Means, and, therefore, that was the proper committee for the consideration of this subject. To this he had two answers: first, that the memorials were improperly referred to that committee, but, as it had been decided that it was proper, he would waive that objection. The other answer was, that the question of restitution was connected with the subjects belonging to the Committee of Ways and Means. The bank had asserted no right over this public money, but they say that, though this was an onerous duty imposed upon them, yet they had undertaken it, and were, therefore, bound to discharge it in the manner authorized by the committee of Congress. It was, therefore, a question of the interpretation of a judicial statute. It referred, in no possible form, to the subject of revenue. But he was averse to its going to the Committee of Ways and Means, even if it had any relation to the questions properly belonging to that committee. Man was man, and the excitement already produced among the members of that committee, would necessarily be extended to this subject, and influence their decision upon it. Another reason was, that it was due to the old soldiers to have a separate discussion and decision of this question. If it was referred to the Committee of Ways and Means, it would become mixed up with the whole question of the deposites, and its decision would be postponed until a final decision of that question should be had, which would not be until the close of the session. The bank, upon a decision of the House that she shall be relieved from the duty of disbursing this money, will be very willing to give up the money. What does she want with this half a million of dollars? He hoped the question would be decided very speedily, and he was sure that an early decision would not be obtained if the subject was referred to the Committee on Ways and Means.

Mr. BELL, of Tennessee, said, if it was the object to have the legal question inquired into and reported upon, then, according to parliamentary practice and the rules of the House, the subject ought to be referred to the Judiciary Committee; not, however, because that committee was more competent to the duty, but because it related to duties assigned to them. If he was compelled to say which committee embraced the best legal ability, he would say that it was the Committee of Ways and Means, but that was not the question. If, again, the object of the inquiry was to find where the blame of the transaction lies, or to institute a legal proceeding against the bank, the Judiciary Committee was the proper one. If we are to go to a legislative act, and express a declaratory law of the meaning of the act of 1832, the subject belongs to the Judiciary Committee. But if the House thinks that a regard for the public interests require that the agents should be changed—that by a new law new agents should be constituted for the disbursement of pensions, then the subject belongs properly to the Committee of Ways and Means.

Mr. FOSTER said that though a member of the Judiciary Committee, he was averse to engaging in this contest between committees. But the importance of the question involved here induced him to express his opinion. We could make no question, it seemed, which was not involved with the deposite question. We placed the pension fund under the control of the Secretary of War. The Secretary placed it in the Bank of the United States, not as a place of deposite, but as the agent for disbursing the fund. The Secretary had no control over the money. Why has the question been given to the Attorney General? Because it was a question of the construction of a law. The Committee of Ways and Means had nothing to do with the question, because the money had long since been appropriated.

Mr. WAYNE expressed the opinion that the duties assigned to the Committee of Ways and Means related to the appropriation of money, and to the proper and legal disbursement of the money appropriated. Now the question arose, under the law of 1832, who should make the disbursement; and it fell upon the Committee of Ways and Means to consider how the money was to be disbursed in conformity with the law. The disbursement of a fund was necessarily connected with the subject of the revenue, and therefore belonged to the Committee of Ways and Means.

Mr. LANE said that, upon examination, he had found that the question presented by the message was intimately connected with the subjects heretofore referred to the Committee of Ways and Means. He understood the 57th rule of the House to devolve this subject expressly upon that committee. By the 57th rule it was made the duty of the Committee of Ways and Means "to examine particularly into the laws making appropriations of moneys, and to report whether the 'moneys have been disbursed conformably with 'such laws." If this was a controversy whether one or another should disburse the pension fund, it belonged, by the very letter of the rule, to the Committee of Ways and Means. The 63d rule assigns duties to the Committee on the Judiciary touching all judicial proceedings. Would any one say that this was a judicial question—whether money was to be disbursed by A or B? It was said that the President had sent the papers here without motive. He was very happy to hear it acknowledged for once that the President had sent us documents without any unworthy motives. The gentleman from Pennsylvania says that the communication from the president of the bank is full, clear, and candid. Yes, sir, all that comes from the bank is pure and unsullied as snow.

Mr. JONES, of Georgia, considers the subject a judicial question, arising from the construction of an act of Congress—whether the bank is the proper disbursing agent, and is legally empowered to pay the pensions ordered. It is neither more nor less than this. There is no question concerning a sum to be raised, nor any concerning an appropriation to be raised; but whether some other officers shall be elected to pay the pensions.

The President's call on the Attorney General for a legal opinion, shows that in his judgment at least it is a legal question, requiring a legal investigation. Had it been a question of finance, the Secretary of the Treasury, not the Attorney General, would have been called on to express an opinion. This is therefore a presumptive proof that the question is within the peculiar jurisdiction of the Committee on the Judiciary, not the Committee of Ways and Means.

He regrets that his friends, or those with whom he votes and concurs in opinion on the deposite question, should intermingle this subject with that. He considers it better not to have them entangled. By the bank charter, the Secretary of the Treasury has full power to remove the deposites from the United States Bank, if he assigns sufficient reasons for his so doing. But the present subject is, whether one officer or agent shall be preferred to another.

The Committee of Ways and Means have such an accumulation of business before them, that they will not have time, even if they have inclination, to devote that attention requisite to the pension agency of the bank. With that committee it must necessarily be but auxiliary to the main question; which would be reported on perhaps previously to considering this question; and the pension agency must be suspended in the interval. But when it is exhibited as an isolated question, consigned to the Judiciary Committee, who have less business on hand, it will receive proper and prompt attention.

Mr. BEARDSLEY thinks that a due consideration of the rules of the House which explain the proper functions of the several standing committees, would point to the committee under whose jurisdiction this subject more immediately comes. The object of the Judiciary Committee is stated in the 63d rule to be limited to judicial proceedings. Now there is no topic of that kind before the House, no judicial proceedings in any court, nor any action of that nature, to obtain the moneys and papers withheld by the bank from the Secretary of War; and as there are not now any judicial proceedings, the House cannot contemplate any. If the Executive desired to institute an action on the subject, there is already sufficient power invested in the Government for the recovery of all moneys, &c., due to it. Its authority being now ample, no additional will be required; and as it has not been thought proper to appeal to judicial proceedings under this authority, no such proceedings can be contemplated by an appeal to Congress to arm the Government with further powers.

The bank has received an appropriation of $500,000 for the pension agency fund. The control over this fund has been given to the Secretary of War, who has the appointment of what agents he pleases in the management of the concerns of his department. If the bank will not pay the pensions, which will be payable in March, and refuses to submit to a transfer of the pension fund, then must Congress be required to order another appropriation for that purpose. This is surely not the business of the Committee on the Judiciary, nor of the Committee on Pensions, nor of any other committee but that of Ways and Means. By the 57th rule, the functions of this last committee extend to the control of everything relating to collecting, keeping, and appropriating the revenues or moneys of the nation. This committee is to decide concerning the means of raising revenue, and the mode whereby it is expended. The subject is therefore strictly referable to the Committee of Ways and Means.

Mr. McKINLEY asserted that the question really is, the jurisdiction of the respective committees. Now every executive department is accountable to the Committee of Ways and Means for the due discharge of its duties, and this committee is to investigate every transaction relative to the receipts and expenditures of the National Treasury. Were the question one on an action to recover money, it might belong to the Judiciary Committee; but where it involves the accountability of an agent in the disbursement of the public funds, it is a question properly within the cognizance of the Committee of Ways and Means.

Mr. BELL, of Tennessee, explained. He stated that the alternative of reference should be decided only according to the object contemplated by the reference. If the House merely sought to have an investigation of a legal question, and to have an opinion expressed in a report of a committee on that subject, then should the reference be made to the Judiciary Committee; but if something farther, if legislative action consequent on a legal investigation, be required, then should the reference be to the Committee of Ways and Means. So if it is only to try who is wrong in the construction of the act relative to the agency of the pension fund, still it is the province of the Judiciary Committee; but if it is to try whether the bank shall continue its agency, or if it is thought necessary to change the paying agents and officers of the pension fund in accordance with the new fiscal arrangements contemplated by the executive government, then the subject devolves on the Committee of Ways and Means; for to this committee, not to any other, belongs the question of agency in all matters affecting the national revenue. To continue former agents, or appoint new ones, belongs more properly to the Committee of Ways and Means than to the Judiciary Committee.

Mr. BRIGGS moved that the first two pages of the President's message be read, which was done accordingly.

Mr. DENNY submitted an amendment to instruct the Committee of Ways and Means to report a bill requiring the Secretary of War to re-

scind the order given to the Bank of the United States, &c., for the payment of pensioners.

Mr. MANN, of New York, called for the previous question, and the House having seconded the call—ayes 108, noes not counted—

Mr. DENNY demanded the yeas and nays on the previous question, which were ordered, and the House decided that the main question should be put—yeas 119, noes 96.

The main question then being to refer the message, &c., to the Committee of Ways and Means, it was decided in the affirmative, as follows:

YEAS—Messrs. John Adams, William Allen, Beale, Bean, Beardsley, Beaumont, John Bell, James Blair, John Blair, Bodle, Boon, Brown, Bunch, Burns, Cambreleng, Carmichael, Casey, S. Clark, Clay, Coffee, Connor, Cramer, Day, Dickerson, Dickinson, Dunlap, Forester, Fowler, W. K. Fuller, Gillet, Joseph Hall, T. H. Hall, Halsey, Hamer, Hannegan, Joseph M. Harper, Harrison, Hathaway, Hawkins, Hawes, Heath, Henderson, Howell, Hubbard, Abel Huntington, Inge, Jarvis, Richard M. Johnson, Noadiah Johnson, Cave Johnson, Benjamin Jones, Kavanagh, Kinnard, Lane, Lansing, Lawrence, Lake Lea, Thomas Lee, Leavitt, Lyon, Lytle, Abijah Mann, Joel K. Mann, Moses Mason, McIntire, McKim, McKinley, McLene, McVean, Miller, Henry Mitchell, Robert Mitchell, Murphy, Osgood, Page, Parks, Patterson, Peyton, D. J. Pearce, Franklin Pierce, Pierson, Polk, Pope, Schenck, Shinn, Charles Slade, Smith, Speight, Standifer, Stoddert, Sutherland, W. Taylor, Francis Thomas, John Thomson, Turner, Turrill, Vanderpoel, Van Houten, Wagener, Ward, Wardwell, Wayne, Webster, Whallon, C. P. White—107.

NAYS—Messrs. J. Q. Adams, Heman Allen, C. Allan, Archer, Ashley, Barber, Barnitz, Barringer, Bates, Bayliss, Beatty, James M. Bell, Binney, Bockee, Bouldin, Briggs, Bull, Burd, Cage, Carr, Chambers, Chilton, Choate, Claiborne, W. Clark, Clayton, Clowney, Corwin, Coulter, Crane, Crockett, Darlington, W. R. Davis, Amos Davis, Davenport, Deberry, Deming, Denny, Dennis, Duncan, Evans, Edward Everett, Horace Everett, Ewing, Felder, Fillmore, Foot, Foster, Philo C. Fuller, Fulton, Gamble, Gilmer, Gordon, Gorham, Graham, Grayson, Grennell, Griffin, Hiland Hall, Hard, Hardin, James Harper, Hazeltine, Hiester, Jabez W. Huntington, W. C. Johnson, Seaborn Jones, Laporte, Lay, Lewis, Love, Martindale, Marshall, Mardis, McComas, McKay, McKennan, Milligan, Muhlenberg, Parker, Patton, Pinckney, Potts, Ramsey, Reed, Rencher, Schley, Selden, William B. Shepard, Augustus H. Shepperd, Wm. Slade, Sloane, Spangler, Stewart, P. Thomas, Tompkins, Tweedy, Vance, Vinton, Watmough, E. D. White, Elisha Whittlesey, Wilde, Williams, Wise, Young—106.

The result having been announced that the motion for reference to the Committee of Ways and Means prevailed, there was some marks of applause, by clapping of hands, &c., heard.

The SPEAKER directed the galleries to be cleared by the Sergeant-at-Arms.

A motion made for adjournment was suspended until that was done.

The Sergeant-at-Arms proceeded to execute his duty; during which

Mr. WHITTLESEY remarked that he believed the noise that had been heard did not proceed from the gallery, but came from the Hall.

The motion of adjournment was then carried, and at half past six o'clock,

The House adjourned.

IN SENATE.

WEDNESDAY, February 5, 1834.

On motion of Mr. POINDEXTER, the vote of yesterday on one of his resolutions, referring it to the Committee on Finance, was reconsidered, and the resolution was laid on the table.

Mr. WEBSTER, from the Committee on Finance, made a long report on the subject of the Secretary of the Treasury's reasons for the removal of the deposites, which was read.

[One hour and a half was occupied in its reading.]

The report concluded by recommending the adoption of Mr. CLAY's second resolution.

Mr. WEBSTER moved that the report be printed.

Mr. CHAMBERS moved that 6,000 additional copies of the report be printed for the purpose of distribution.

The remainder of the day was occupied in discussing this motion, which resulted in its adoption.

The Senate then, on motion of Mr. WILKINS, adjourned.

HOUSE OF REPRESENTATIVES.

WEDNESDAY, February 5, 1834.

The standing committees reported various private bills for the relief of individuals.

A report was presented relative to marine apprenticeships.

A bill was reported making appropriations for the surveys, &c., of various enumerated harbors, for 1834.

Mr. POLK, from the Committee of Ways and Means, reported a bill making appropriations for the civil and diplomatic expenditure of Government, for 1834.

The SPEAKER presented various communications from minor branches of the executive departments, in obedience to resolutions passed recently by the House.

Mr. WHITTLESEY, of Ohio, asked the unanimous consent of the House that so many of the engrossed bills as practicable should be read a third time, before the hour of resuming the discussion of the deposites. Granted.

The House proceeded to the orders of the day, being

THE REMOVAL OF THE DEPOSITES.

The House having resumed the consideration of the motion to refer the report of the Secretary of the Treasury on the deposites to the Committee of Ways and Means—the question being on the amendment submitted by Mr. Jones as an amendment to that previously submitted by Mr. McDuffie, viz: to add to the motion for reference the following instructions to that committee: "Inquire into the expediency of depositing the 'revenue hereafter collected in the State banks in 'the different States where the same is collected, in 'proportion to their respective capitals paid in, 'and to prescribe the terms on which the same 'shall be deposited, and to report by bill or otherwise"—

Mr. ARCHER had the floor from the previous adjournment of the debate, but gave way at the instance of

Mr. McKINLEY, who desired to express the hope that some disposition would be come to by the House, as had been come to by the Senate on this question, and that after the gentleman from Virginia should conclude, that the House would be prepared to take the question. Although he had not spoken himself, as he was desirous to do, he would forego his purpose of doing so for the present, that if the subject was referred, they might have a report presented, upon which they could have full discussion. This, in his opinion, was in every point of view the most desirable course to take; but in giving this notice to the House, he did not wish to coerce them.

Mr. ADAMS wished to know what was the notice submitted by the gentleman. Did he mean by his notice that the House were to stop the debate?

Mr. McKINLEY regretted that his language should have been construed into anything more than what he intended to express, which was his wish that there would be some termination to the debate on this preliminary part of the subject.

The SPEAKER here interposed, upon which

Mr. ARCHER resumed his remarks. He said, on the former day when interrupted, he was about to examine the arguments used to sustain the exercise of the power upon which the removal of the deposites was made. The first question related to the relative power exercised on either the President or the Secretary. In the outset of his remarks, he felt it due to himself, and he owed it to them to state, that he did not believe they had knowingly transcended their powers. Yet,

---

in thus acquitting them of intentionally acting in this matter, they were not to be altogether excused, when they respectively commited what he considered gross dereliction of their duties. He viewed the act of the removal, as had not been denied, to have been the act of the President; the Secretary of the Treasury was only his agent. The language used in his paper, read to the Cabinet, wherein the time was announced that the removal should take place, fully proved that the measure was, beyond doubt, his own. He considered that if the doctrines advanced, to maintain that the Executive possessed rightfully any control, went to sap the foundations of all that was essential to free governments, and that were contradicted by the whole course taken by the framers of the Constitution, whose endeavor had been to place such guards upon the treasury, as would prevent what was termed the union of the purse and sword, and thus place guards to the designs of an ambitious Chief Magistrate. He could not assent to what was urged by the members from New York and Georgia, who had justified the Executive measure, that because Congress had the power to declare war, raise money, &c., that there was no danger to be apprehended. But the dangers to be apprehended, consisted not in his raising troops, but in commanding them. The argument advanced seemed to prove that we ought to give the whole money-power to the Executive.

He next contended that when the department of the Government were fixed and established in 1789, the Secretary of the Treasury was not made strictly an executive officer, as other heads of departments in the Government; for there was associated with him in that department an officer—the Treasurer of the United States—in whom was lodged at least some of the power to act in relation to all the transfers to be made of the public money. If this were not so, he asked why was it that the Treasurer, not the Secretary, was required to give bonds, &c., for the faithful discharge of the high trust reposed in him? Reviewing, then, all the circumstances connected with the first formation of that department, and its connexion with the fiscal affairs of the nation, he thought there could not be any doubt now that the Secretary was merely a legislative agent, and not an executive one, to carry into effect the directions so be given by Congress. He argued thus from the fact that Congress had appointed other official persons in that department, who might just as well claim to be executive officers as that officer. The Chief Justice was appointed to transact important business along with the Secretaries and others, as commissioners to pay off the public debt; and yet, could he turn about and say that he was other than a legislative agent, created by Congress to do a certain act? Surely not.

Mr. A. next proceeded to review the argument used, "that because the power was given to the President by the Constitution to dismiss the Secretary, therefore that the power to direct that officer was thereby implied." But reasoning on the by analogy with other powers given and used by the President, he came to the conclusion that it was not the intention of the framers of the Constitution to give to the President any such power. He argued at length against the reasons adduced by the Secretary to support the position that he not Congress, had any control over the funds lodged in the Bank of the United States. He considered that the Secretary had, in assuming this, contradicted the doctrine held by Mr. Dallas upon the duties of the treasury officers. Mr. D. had, when the bank was incorporated, showed that he placed the Secretary and the Treasurer to act, in their respective capacities, as checks, upon one another, the Secretary being to direct the payments, whilst the Treasurer was to perform. He alone was to do the act, and in accordance with this the various transfers were literally made, resting the revenue of the public, wherever placed to be lodged, not to the Secretary's credit, but to that of the Treasurer; and from this he argued against the right of exclusive control assumed by the Secretary as either it must have been injustice that he claimed in requiring him to give bonds and security for the faithful performance of a duty, the control of which he was deprived.

Mr. A. proceeded to comment at great length upon the several reasons given by the Secretary of the Treasury for the removal of the deposites. He denied the power of the Secretary to interfere with the currency, upon reasons founded on public convenience. Such a power submitted to the discretion of the Secretary the control of the property, the credit, and the honor of every individual. The course taken by the bank in its defence, by curtailing its operations, he defended as proper and necessary. The course of the Administration he thought would not be tolerated by the people. Indications from every quarter, especially from the South and from the State of Virginia, showed that the spirit of the people was roused against the usurpations of the Executive.

When Mr. ARCHER concluded his remarks, several members simultaneously addressed the Chair, but the floor was obtained by Mr. PEYTON, of Tennessee.

Mr. PEYTON commenced his remarks by alluding to the combination arrayed against the Executive on this question. Gentlemen who had formerly stood like tigers, ready to spring at each other's throats, now embrace each other in their patriotic arms. Are not the leaders of this coalition those who recently brought the country to the brink of ruin? What had united them? Was it love, or deadly hate, or patriotic zeal? It was patriotic in gentlemen to guard the people's liberty; for man should love his country more than self and next to God. Should to-morrow's sun behold this Administration swept away—if every member of it should meet his Brutus while he sleeps, would the new attachment which has thus sprung up between these individuals continue? As soon would winter combine with summer, as those factions with each other. Their fixed and settled determination was to rule or ruin. They talk of Cæsar and all other tyrants whom poets or historians have handed down to us. Now, he would ask any man to reflect on all the examples of the subversion of popular liberty, and then say whether it has not always been effected through the means of disappointed factions. They induce the people to consider themselves as slaves; shed their patriotic tears over the Constitution, and on either side of the same question; and then they are prepared for the struggle. Mr. P. went back to see how Cæsar obtained his power, and showed that it was by uniting two contending factions and through them breaking down the influence of Cato with the Senate and the people. In this way would the liberties of this country be destroyed. Some gentlemen of transcendent talent, and mortified ambition, would unite to wield the press and the money-power of the country. But the gentleman from South Carolina gives us his plan for preventing the union of the purse and the sword, the apprehension of which so much alarms him. He says that the Bank of the United States ought, by constitutional provision, to be compelled to take the political field on every election, for he wishes the bank to throw its weight against the Administration. Thirty-five millions must be thrown into the scale of him who is the opponent of the incumbent. As the bank has elected one candidate, it must turn round and oppose him. In this way, the bank would elect all the Presidents, and the sword and the purse would be effectually united.

It seems that the present incumbent is governed by impulse and passion, and has no fixed principles. The gentleman from South Carolina had never discovered this from his own acquaintance with the President, but he had told us that he derived the information from the ex-Secretary of the Treasury, who himself had not discovered it till he went home and consulted his *daddy*.

He should like to see one question settled. It had been said that seventy-five men elected the incumbent. They must deserve great credit for their talents. But he was inclined to believe that those who claimed the least credit for the service, had most to do with it; to wit—the people.

Mr. P. then adverted to the power and influence of the bank, its control of the State banks, and its power to fix the value of property in any part of the United States, by expanding and contracting its currency, as furnishing a strong reason for inhibiting it from interfering in any manner with elections. The power of the institution was now felt in every part of the country. High charges were made against it, and it tortured the people, to wring from them their reluctant support. If the bank could, at this day, move the people by torture, at another and later period, it might say of an opponent, "Off with his head."

The President, with all his power, cannot print a single document of any kind. If the bank can do this, with the public money, they can find daggers for public servants. The bank asserts, in fact, the right to spend every dollar in its vaults in carrying on a war with its adversaries.

Here Mr. PEYTON, without concluding, yielded the floor to Mr. BELL, of Tennessee, on whose motion the House adjourned.

IN SENATE.

THURSDAY, *February* 6, 1834.

After the presentation of petitions and reports of committes,

The Senate then proceeded to the special order of the day, being Mr. CLAY'S resolution on the

REMOVAL OF THE DEPOSITES.

Mr. WILKINS rose and said that, more than forty years ago, on an occasion like the present, the venerable Mr. Madison observed, that "the 'present question should be conducted with moderation and candor; and tragic representations, 'warmth, and passion, ought not to assume the 'preponderance, instead of reason." He would endeavor to profit by the recommendation of that sage and patriot, although he had but little hope of shedding new light on a subject which had been so exhausted by those who had preceded him. Wide, and unnecessarily wide, as the field had been enlarged, those skilful gleaners had passed over it without leaving scarcely a grain behind. He declared that he entered upon this debate reluctantly, not to shun responsibility, but from an indisposition to tax the patience of the Senate farther. For the truth of this remark, he might appeal to the fact, that since he had had the honor of a seat here, he had been rather a listener than a debater. During the last Congress, by an almost unanimous vote of the Legislature of his State, he was instructed to vote for the Bank of the United States, and he did not scruple to vote for its recharter, in obedience to those instructions. He voted for the bill which was reported by the committee. It was fortunate that on all sides of the House the question of recharter of the bank was laid on the shelf. The present was an abstract, insulated question, having no reference to the objects which arise out of it. And without any danger, therefore, of coming into collision with his own State, he was left to pursue his own course upon the resolutions of the gentleman from Kentucky. Tragic representations, and frightful pictures of distress in the country, the Constitution lying bleeding under foot, and approaching civil war and bloodshed, were presented to our view. The gloom of '76 was said to be overhanging us. The President is called a despot, grasping at all the powers of the Government, seizing upon the purse and sword of the nation, a public robber of the rights and treasure of the people—these are placed in the foreground of the picture, while the real merits of the question are cast entirely in the background. If we were to judge of politics by the same rules which govern in physical phenomena, it might be said that all these evils were to overtake us. Until this debate began, and long after the removal of the deposites, we enjoyed an entire calm; the people confided in an almost unparalleled degree in the Administration; and if there was any change known, it was only in the increase of its popularity. This wide-spread evil existed in this second resolution alone. It admitted the power of removing the deposites—there was no infraction of the charter—the money was all safe—the treasure was there—not a dollar was drawn out or appropriated but in accordance with law. If to touch this money corporation was to involve us in the gloom of '76, gentlemen ought to deliberate before they vote to revive such a corporation, which can revisit us with such disasters.

[An explanation here ensued between Mr. WEBSTER, Mr. SOUTHARD, and Mr. WILKINS, relative to some imputed expressions, which the two former gentlemen disclaimed.]

Mr. WILKINS continued, protesting that the pictures drawn by the two gentlemen were too highly colored, calculated to keep up the panic in the country, and were uncalled for by any act of the Government; because, if the late report of the Committee on Finance were analyzed, although it was written with great ability, yet it amounted to no more than that the great emergency for the removal of the deposites had not arrived when the act was done; the Secretary had the power, but the time and occasion was not justified by expediency. It did not state that an emergency might not happen, but that it had not happened. On the first of December, 1833, when he left home for this place, there was not a cry or whimper among the people. He travelled through Pennsylvania, the elections were over, the removal of the deposites had taken place, and the whole political character of the State was changed in favor of the man who caused the removal. The distress, then, was caused by the bank: he wished it had taken a different course, and negotiated with the Administration and with Congress, and had suspended its oppressive course, until Congress had acted. But they have concluded to pursue a different course; although the agent of the Government, they have warred with its principles, and adopted a system of cruel restriction with the people, when it was as much in their power to have adopted a different system. He had no objection to this course, but he only asked of them to yield to Congress the right of resisting them. If the bank had exercised kind feelings and charity, it would have been far better and more creditable to them.

But, it is said, the President has united the purse and the sword. Sir, there can be no such thing. So long as the people are enlightened and uncorrupt, the thing is impossible. If his object had been corrupt; if he had designed to unite the purse with the sword, he would have seized on the bank. But what has been his course? He has thrown away power; he has disclaimed it. The union of the purse and the sword, in the Chief Magistrate, supposes that when he had, after an eventful life, reached the Presidency, he had abandoned his patriotism and all those high honors which have been heaped upon him, and was now governed by a low, grovelling ambition, and a sordid passion. Yet, what has he done? Instead of uniting with the most powerful institution on earth, he has removed the deposites to the local banks. Has he gone to that bank where all power is concentrated—to that bank capable of producing all this distress and pressure? No. If his object had been power, he would have gone to that bank seeking to obtain a recharter, and there have made his bargain. He would have gone to an institution having so much influence over the people, not to the State banks, which cannot have any uniformity of action, but to the Bank of the United States, rich in coin, influence, and power, which it thinks neither the Government or people can control—to the bank which says it can annihilate the State banks. If all this proves anything, it proves his high-mindedness. He says to the bank, begone; although you have a majority in the House of Representatives, I have vetoed you. This would not have been his course, if he had contemplated a union of the purse and sword. He came now to speak of the Government directors—officers holding their commissions under the Government; and he contended the President was right in the course he pursued, in obtaining information from those directors, and they were right in communicating it to him. He had turned his attention to this subject, and he had found it was the friends of the bank who insisted, at the time it was chartered, that the Government ought to have sentinels at the board. But take up the charter for a moment, and on its face the President is justified in the course he has pursued, as well as the directors, and it will also be found that the President took the only course that was within his reach.

Mr. W. then adverted to each article of the charter in succession, to show that the President could arrive at no knowledge of the conduct of the bank, except through the Government directors.

He continued. Take up the charter itself, and it will be seen he had no other source of information, but through the public directors. And what was the attitude of the bank in reference to those directors? That of rank hostility. It would have

been in vain to apply for information to the body of the directors.

The President, therefore, addressed a letter to the Government directors. There was no secrecy enjoined in it, as had been contended. It enjoined on them not to take rumor or newspaper publications for their guide; but to let their information come from their own actual knowledge. The simple injunction upon them was, to give him what they knew to be true, because he had a public duty to perform, which made it necessary for him to know the conduct of the bank. Mr. W. here read a letter of Mr. Crawford's, dated 3d July, 1817, addressed to the directors of the Bank of the United States, in reply to the complaints which had been made against the bank, on the subject of the internal exchanges of the country. The letter was written with the knowledge of the President, and claimed the right to apply to the Government directors alone for information. The President had the right then, and it was the duty of the directors, to answer as they did. They were public officers, and by the words of the charter, the President could remove them. And how had they performed their duty? Not as spies; but as trusty sentinels, they had given the truth in a manner which would justify the Senate in confirming their nominations. Since this discussion commenced, he had adverted to another fact. He alluded to the recent refusal of the Bank of the United States to transfer the books and papers relating to the Government pensioners. The bank directors say the Government had no authority to make this requisition. This, Mr. W. considered another link in the chain of hostility which had long actuated the directors towards the Government. The bank says the business is of no consequence to them. They only withhold the books and papers *to see that the laws are faithfully executed*—on them devolved the duty of the President. The requisition of the Secretary of War to make these transfers, did not relate to pensions under the act of 1818—it referred to the *pay* law of 1832.

The requisition to transfer is by a *pay* law, not a *pension* law. It only sought to transfer the funds to the banks selected as the public depositories, and it was done by the Secretary of War to avoid the embarrassment of transferring funds from the local banks to the United States Bank to meet the applications there. If the bank wished to promote the good of the country why did they not give up the books and papers? or why not pay the pensioners? But they would do neither—they showed a disposition which every man ought to resist. In inflicting distress they did not spare the holy remnant of revolutionary officers; so sweeping were their exertions that even the surviving soldiers of the war of Independence were not spared. In vain did those patriots achieve the prize which we are now enjoying; in vain did they shed their blood if we are are to submit to an oligarchy which stands in the hall of our independence, if we are to submit to rulers who are attempting to oppress us.

He proposed now to take up and examine the resolutions of the gentleman from Kentucky. The first relates to the assumption of political power by the President. It charges him with no corruption, but rather that he has particular views and opinions as to the powers of removal of Executive officers. He (Mr. W.) thought that the Senate would acquiesce in the *power* of removal, when they were confirming or rejecting nominations every day. This resolution admits the right of removal, but simply charges the President with a usurpation of power. It seemed divisible into two parts: the first referring to Mr. Duane, the second to the appointment of Mr. Taney. With regard to the former gentleman, there was something so peculiar in his situation, in reference to the opinions of the President, that it was impossible the President could retain him, if upon personal considerations only. What was Mr. Duane's situation? He came into office holding opinions adverse to the President's. According to his own views, when he entered the Cabinet the Chief Magistrate was arbitrary in his acts, surrounded by a cabal—had no fixed principles, or if he had any, he carried out none of them. Under these circumstances he was called to a seat in the Cabinet among the President's confidential advisers and counsellors, to aid him in administering the affairs of Government; and having these secret opinions, that everything was proceeding from corruption, how could they pull together? But this was not all. He tells the President, you are governed by no consideration for the public good—your acts are vile, vindictive, and arbitrary. Vindictive and arbitrary are his very epithets. How, then, was it possible that a Secretary of the Treasury, with these sentiments, could coöperate with the President?

Yet this was not all. When serious difficulties were likely to arise in the councils of the nation, he promised to resign, and afterwards refused; the promise, when made, he did not expect to be called on to fulfil, and he determined to remain, to fix on the President the charge of interfering with the duties of his office. The President was right, therefore, in removing him—he had the power to do so by the Constitution and laws; its exercise was not dangerous to the liberties of the people; it was no assumption of power. The Executive was impressed with the conviction that the removal of the deposites was necessary, and it was his duty to take the step he did. The right of removal of the officer was admitted, on the principle that the President was responsible for the faithful execution of the laws. But it was argued that the treasury was not an executive department, and not under the supervision of the President; that the Secretary was not responsible to the executive, but to the legislative branch of the Government. Now, all the laws which speak of that department, speak of it in no other character than as an executive department. The officer, subject to removal by the President, is a member of the Cabinet surrounding the Executive. To be sure, the purse and the finances of the nation are under the control of Congress; but when Congress has passed laws and imposed duties, then the executive power attaches. Congress had passed a law imposing a duty on the Secretary. But the performance of that duty was placed under the care of the President. The omission of the word executive in the law of '89 was entirely accidental. By turning to the laws passed at the same Congress, it will be found that it was only an omission. Mr. W. read from a law of that year, for paying the salary of the Secretary of the Treasury, "as one of the executive officers of Government." In all the laws on the subject, the Secretary was recognised and called an executive officer. Mr. W. here read various passages from the Constitution, and Kent's Commentaries on American Law, to show that the Executive may require the opinions of either of the heads of departments in writing, and that General Hamilton was called on by General Washington, as an executive officer, to give him his opinions. It being an executive department, then, the President, under his general power and duty to see that the laws are faithfully executed, was bound to watch and see the proper time when the removal of the deposites should take place. This constitutional injunction never was to be suspended, either in time of peace or in rebellion—a general power of supervision was indispensable in every well-regulated Government, and the injunction to see that the laws were faithfully executed, was connected with his oath of office. In exercising this power, he interfered with no duty of another officer. The law had given the Secretary the power to remove, but was silent as to the time and manner of removal. Suppose Congress should adopt the second resolution, and order the restoration of the deposites, and the Secretary should refuse to execute the order, you might impeach him; but would it be a wise course? When a national calamity was prevailing in the nation, would it be right to wait for a tedious investigation? Every man would call for his removal; and if the President should refuse to remove him, universal condemnation would follow the conduct of the President. Suppose it had been absolutely and undeniably necessary to remove the deposites, and the Secretary had refused: would the President have been justified in not removing him? The President, then, was justifiable in the removal of Mr. Duane. Mr. Taney succeeded him; not because he moulded his opinions to the will of the President, but because he had given an opinion in favor of the removal, when in another high office under the Government. It was no sudden opinion of his. As early as March last, Mr. Taney was of opinion the deposites ought to be removed, and the bank ought to prepare to wind up its concerns. Mr. Taney came into office to execute an act upon which his opinion coincided with that of the President. It was right, if the President entertained the opinion he did, to select an officer holding his opinions. It was no assumption whatever. When did a President ever select the head of a department not holding his opinions? It was always the right of the President to select a person agreeing with him; and Mr. Taney came in with honor, to execute what he had advised to be done.

Mr. WILKINS, at three o'clock, gave way, without concluding, to a motion, by Mr. CLAY, to adjourn; but, on

Mr. WEBSTER'S suggestion, he withdrew the motion. Mr. W. then gave notice that when Mr. WILKINS concluded, to-morrow, he would move to go into the consideration of Executive business.

The Senate then adjourned.

HOUSE OF REPRESENTATIVES.

THURSDAY, *February* 6, 1834.

On motion of Mr. J. Q. ADAMS,

Resolved, That the Committee on Commerce be instructed to inquire into the expediency of making Dorchester, in the State of Massachusetts, a port of delivery.

On motion of Mr. C. JOHNSON,

Resolved, That a select committee be appointed, whose duty it shall be to inquire whether any and what steps should be taken on the part of the United States, for ascertaining the true northern boundary of the Chickasaw Indians, between the Tennessee and Mississippi rivers; and, also, the true line between the State of Tennessee and Mississippi; and, also, into the propriety of delaying the sales of the public lands in the northern part of Mississippi, until the true boundary line between the States be ascertained.

On motion of Mr. S. JONES,

Resolved, That the Committee on Naval Affairs be instructed to inquire into the expediency of substituting lead for iron as the material for balls for the use of cannon on board our vessels of war and batteries on land.

Mr. BOON reported a bill to remove the United States land office from Clinton to Jackson, Indiana; and

Mr. SUTHERLAND, a bill to annex part of Bridgeton, New Jersey, to the western district of Philadelphia; which were both read twice and committed.

PENSION LAWS.

The order of the day was then declared to be the resolution of Mr. CHILTON, to appoint a select committee to inquire into the expediency of so extending the general pension law as to embrace within its provisions those persons who were engaged in the Indian wars, down to the year 1794; and the amendment of it by Mr. BOULDIN, to appoint a committee to inquire into the moral effects of the pension system upon the community, and how far it ought to be abolished or repealed.

Mr. CHAMBERS, who had the floor from the previous day, said that he believed both public principle and policy was involved in the present question; he therefore desired to assign the reasons which should govern his vote. Many arguments had certainly been adduced in support of the extension of the pension system generally, which were of more than ordinary interest, and were entitled to the grave consideration of the House. They had heard, during the discussion, eloquent eulogiums upon the merits, and expressions of sympathy for the sufferings, of those engaged in those Indian wars, calculated to awaken a strong feeling in their behalf. These were of such a character as not to be heard with indifference, for they were calculated to raise the American character, as they brought forth to public notice men previously but little known to fame. He had listened with delight to the panegyrics bestowed by the member from Kentucky; yet he felt some regret at the censure which he seemed to cast upon Generals Harmar and St. Clair; in their defence, however, he thought it only necessary to say that they, notwithstanding all their misfortunes and distress continued to retain the confidence of the Father of his country's independence. However he rejoiced at the praises thus bestowed, he felt constrained, by

a sense of duty, to oppose their claims to be put on the pension list; for how much or how justly their sympathies might be raised in their favor, he must maintain that such feelings should not be permitted to prevail or be exercised in legislation, unless in cases that were clearly on the side of right. This House were guardians of the public treasure, and if they did not strictly regard the right of all claims to it, they must be deemed faithless to their trust: if they did not, what security had the country against that extravagance and prodigality which would inevitably prevail, and which at once disgraced and corrupted their citizens? He considered that all claims of this nature ought to be viewed in the nature of a contract made by the soldier with the Government, who, when he got what the Government undertook to give him for his services, he could not reasonably complain, unless in peculiar cases of disability, by wounds received whilst employed in the service. So far he would go, but could not go beyond that. If they did, they would increase the present list, and thus waste the public treasure. Having these views, he could not even vote for the resolution of inquiry, lest from so voting it might be deemed an evidence of his intention to vote for the extension of the system itself, and thus he might be charged with raising expectations which in all probability would not be realized. He could not see how it was possible for them to ascertain the numbers who could—taking for granted the justice of their claims to be placed on the roll—be considered entitled to this. He could not understand the principle upon which it could be maintained that Congress had the right in the case of those persons engaged in the Indian warfare, although it was alleged that Congress, having the right to declare war and raise armies, the right to grant pensions was to be implied. But this power extended only to those soldiers so engaged, in consequence of the terms upon which they might be engaged in the service. The instance, then, of the pensions formerly granted to the soldiers of the Revolution ought not to be referred to as a precedent to govern their decision upon this question, but should rather operate as a beacon to warn them of its dangerous consequences. The persons engaged in those wars were not engaged as the soldiers of the Revolution were, fighting on the side of principle; they fought not for themselves alone, but to give liberty and independence to every American citizen. They fought against a foreign Government which aspired to govern this exclusively. They fought, too, not under leaders and banners of their own, but under the orders of an organized Government, under privations of no common character, and received for their services a depreciated currency.

The officers and soldiers of the Revolution have claims for services which they had rendered without pay; they claimed the justice, not the bounty of Congress. Gentlemen of legal ability, in both Houses of Congress, advocated the bill granting pensions to those men, as a compensation for services, which compensation had been promised and withheld. The claim was both advocated and allowed as a matter of right. Not such was the character of the claims now presented. Much as he respected the men who fought after the treaty of peace, he must say that they did not present a case which called for the bounty of the Government. They were paid in good money, dollar for dollar, the whole sum which the Government promised them. They fought, too, not for the independence of the country, for that was secured. It was certainly never apprehended that the Indians would reconquer America. Where would the system stop, if we went to the extent proposed? Would not the officers and soldiers who were engaged in the late war with Great Britain be equally well entitled to military rewards? They rendered meritorious services on the land and on the sea. Why not go back to the Indian wars preceding the Revolution, and pension those who were engaged in them, or their surviving representatives? Some of those wars were of an extensive range, along the whole northern and western frontiers. He referred particularly to the wars growing out of the war between France and England in 1755. The pioneer settlers and the militia who engaged in them, received no compensation for their services, though they suffered the greatest privations in protecting the frontier settlements. But they participated in the benefits resulting from the contests, and were thus rewarded for their services. He could not see any reason why the system should be confined to military services. If we went on, we should find strong arguments in favor of pensioning those who had rendered important civil services. But he was not in favor of extending the system; on the contrary, he thought that this was the proper time for fixing its limits to those engaged in the revolutionary contest. Past experience had shown that the estimates of the expenditures under this system had always fallen short of the real amount. We were told, when the present pension act was before the House, that the number of applicants would not exceed seven or eight thousand. But it appears that the number was 30,625. He went into some statements of the sums which the pension system had cost us—amounting, altogether, to twenty-six millions of dollars.

The state of the treasury would not warrant an extension of the system. The present Administration came into power upon the principle of retrenchment, but it had gone on increasing the expenses instead of reducing them. The Secretary of the Treasury now cautions us to be economical, lest we should exceed the means of the Government. The revenue expected for the next year would not exceed the necessary expenses of the Government.

Here Mr. C. was obliged to suspend his remarks on account of the expiration of the hour.

REMOVAL OF THE DEPOSITES.

The House resumed the consideration of the motion to refer the report of the Secretary of the Treasury on the deposites to the Committee of Ways and Means—the question being on the amendment submitted by Mr. Jones, as an amendment to that previously submitted by Mr. McDuffie, viz: to add to the motion for reference the following instructions to that committee: "Inquire 'into the expediency of depositing the revenue 'hereafter collected in the State banks in the different States where the same is collected, in proportion to their respective capitals paid in, and to 'prescribe the terms on which the same shall be 'deposited, and to report by bill or otherwise."

Mr. PEYTON resumed his remarks. Every one (he said) must be aware that the present excitement against the President did not grow out of the removal of the deposites. That act was seized upon by the party leaders, to inflame the minds of the people, and to promote their chances of success in the deep game they were playing. The party was led by some of the highest order of talent, who were united by the common tie of disappointed ambition. One obstacle stood in their way—a man of stern integrity and inflexible patriotism stood as a pillar of the State. That pillar was to be overthrown, not by the removal of the deposites, but by a continued and organized system of slander and abuse and agitation. All efforts were directed to one object—to hold up the President as a tyrant, to resist whom will be patriotism.

We are taunted as a drilled majority. When gentlemen talk of the exercise of majority powers they certainly forget examples which they left behind them at home. Where has the majority-power fallen, in this country, with the heaviest hand? Where have patriots of the Revolution, and thousands of worthy and estimable citizens, been disfranchised and debarred from all the privileges of citizenship, for opinion's sake? It was in that State where the majority imposed upon every citizen the test oath. A dark cloud lowers over our horizon, and we hear the muttering of distant thunder. Where was the bolt to fall? He would like to know one thing. If, in the coming storm, the Administration and its friends should be overwhelmed and destroyed, into whose hands would the Government fall? We would be left without one, he supposed. Upon which of the opposing factions would the power fall? Which would say to the other, Be yours the profit, and mine the revenge?

The gentleman from South Carolina is disturbed by frightful images of treachery and murder. The idea of the President brings to his imagination everything frightful which he has read of in history. He pictures the President as a Richard, murdering his helpless and infant competitors while they are asleep in the tower. He says, too, that the acts of the President would have caused rebellion in the subjects of a king. What was there of torturing jealousy or mad ambition in the bosom of the President which would make the allusion to Richard applicable to him? What more had the President to hope, wish, or expect, from his country than he had already obtained? What personal feeling or advantage was to accrue to him from the removal of the deposites? By that act Andrew Jackson had won for himself immortal honor. His open and manly features would live in monumental marble long after the gentlemen who now assailed him should moulder in common earth.

The wit of the gentleman from South Carolina all runs along the Hudson, and hovers about the vicinity of Kinderhook. It was useless to be so much disturbed about the Dutchmen, for they were too phlegmatic to be at all disturbed themselves. But the gentleman's fancy has found a new thing under the sun. He has found a Dutch nullifier—a Being that was never before heard of in the world. Had the gentleman made the tickets for the wheel scene in 1824, the Dutchman would not have got his prize. Mr. P. went on to turn the anecdote against its author, but his remarks were indistinctly heard by the reporter.

Those who had been opposed to the bank on constitutional grounds, had now got rid of their constitutional objections. The President, they said, had done wrong, and this was a sufficient reason for them to abandon their constitutional objections to a bank. But there was at least one member from Georgia whose conscience could not be quieted by this panacea. How could those gentlemen drop so suddenly all their constitutional principles, because one man in the nation had, in their opinion, done wrong?

Mr. P. here adverted to the conduct of the bank in withholding the pension fund. Was it a legislative, judicial, or executive duty, he asked, to collect money according to law, and to disburse it according to law? But the bank says it will lock in the iron jaws of its vaults the little pittance granted by the Government for the warworn veterans of the Revolution; and if either House of Congress sustains the bank, the money must remain forever in the vaults of the bank. He denounced this act of the bank as the greatest outrage upon law and public opinion that was ever heard of.

But it was said that the Secretary of the Treasury ought not to act upon his own reasons, but upon those of his opponents, who think differently from him. This point Mr. P. remarked upon at some length. He eulogized the firmness and disinterestedness manifested in the course of Mr. Taney on this subject; yet it was said that the Secretary had nothing more to do with the act than the iron pen with which he signed the order, or than the hangman has with an execution. Why, then, was Mr. Taney abused for the act? What was the Secretary to do? There were some grounds necessary for the measure. The directors were appointed by the President and Senate. But that guard had been broken down. The Government directors were spurned as spies and informers. The gentleman from South Carolina says that the duty of the Government directors was to assist in increasing the profits of the bank, and that there their duty was to stop. They tell about the deposites and the safety of the institution. He would rather that the whole public treasure were deposited in the ocean, than that the use made of it by the bank should be tolerated. Write me, says the bank, one hundred thousand libels against the President, and we will pay you one hundred thousand dollars. Was the Secretary to acquiesce in such abuses?

He next referred to the singular restriction of the administration of the bank affairs by its exchange committee. Mr. Sergeant had only to say, "Let 50,000 copies of such a work be printed," and Mr. Biddle, "Let all (as many as are required to forward our interest) be published." And this is the very responsible way by which the people's money goes.

In concluding, Mr. P. referred to the threadbare charge against the President, of his being a military man. Yes, he is a military man; and thank Heaven we have such a military man to stand at

this time in the breach; one who has always been found ready and able to stand in the breach, between the nation and the nation's foe, whenever stern necessity demanded. He stood in the breach when he fought the battles of his country; when he overpowered the Indian amid his scalping warfare, and firmly grasped his sword when assailed by a foreign foe. He it was who then stood in the breach, and amid the wild torrent of the country's confusion, said "Peace!" and to the raging tumult "be still!" Who could now revert to the period, when our cities were in flames, when the foe had penetrated into the heart of the land, and plunged the reeking dagger in the bleeding bosoms of the country—who could look on that period when the enemy "cried havoc, and let slip the dogs of war," and not recognise and recollect the arm that then interposed in the breach to save the nation from plunder and the land from being enslaved? Shall he be thus subjected to abuse, for whom every heart panted with grateful remembrances; for whom bonfires blazed from north to south; for whom feasts in various cities were generously spread; for whom the chivalrous, grateful, and patriotic feelings of every individual breathing the spirit of American freedom—for whom even the Legislatures of the States and the Legislature of the Union, expressed their heartfelt generosity of ardent valor; shall he who thus stood in the breach to redeem the nation's glory, and thus gained the nation's gratitude, shall he be stigmatized as being a military man!

He has stood in the breach to save the country once in the field; he has again stood in the breach to save her in the cabinet.

Mr. WISE then rose and addressed the House on the subject.

Mr. BOULDIN took the floor, and expressed a desire to be heard on this question, and asked the House the indulgence of an adjournment, the hour then being twenty minutes past three.

Mr. BEARDSLEY demanded the yeas and nays on the motion, and they were ordered.

The question being taken by yeas and nays, it was decided in the affirmative by a vote of 113 to 103.

The House then adjourned.

IN SENATE.

FRIDAY, *February* 7, 1834.

Mr. POINDEXTER, from the Committee on Public Lands, reported a bill compensating to aid General Philemon Thomas, for services rendered by him in West Florida.

Mr. POINDEXTER, from the same committee, reported a bill, with an amendment, granting lands for the benefit of South Hanover college, to enable the trustees to establish a school for the education of deaf and dumb persons.

Mr. POINDEXTER, from the same committee, reported a bill relative to school lands for the benefit of the State of Ohio, without amendment.

Mr. WRIGHT presented the petition of the clerks in the navy-yard at Brooklyn, New York, praying additional compensation for their services; referred to the Committee on Naval Affairs.

On motion of Mr. WRIGHT, the resolutions of the Legislature of New York, relative to the removal of the deposites, was taken up, and Mr. W. then moved that the resolutions be referred to the Committee on Finance and printed, which was so ordered.

The VICE PRESIDENT communicated a report from the Commissioners of the Sinking Fund; which was read.

Mr. TALLMADGE presented a memorial and a series of resolutions from the manufacturers, mechanics, and laborers of the Second Ward in the city of New York, condemning the course of the Administration in removing the deposites from the Bank of the United States, and ascribing to that fact the present pecuniary distress of the country.

On Mr. CLAY'S motion, the memorial and resolutions were read, and afterwards, on his motion, ordered to be printed.

On motion of Mr. TALLMADGE, they were referred to the Committee on Finance.

Mr. GRUNDY, from the Committee on the Post

Office and Post Roads, reported a bill, with an amendment, for the relief of John Campbell and William Johnson.

On motion of Mr. CLAY, the resolution offered by him some time ago, extending the time for paying revenue bonds, in order to afford the commercial community relief, was taken up.

The resolution was discussed at length, until four o'clock, when it was laid on the table.

The following resolutions were submitted:

By Mr. POINDEXTER:

Resolved, That the Secretary of War be directed to communicate to the Senate the settlement of the accounts of William Thorp, late sutler in the army of the United States, made in pursuance of "An act for the relief of William Thorp," passed on the 23d day of May, 1826, specifying the items in said accounts, which have been disallowed, and the grounds on which they were rejected by the accounting officers, and also whether, in his opinion, any further legislation is necessary to the final settlement of said accounts on principles of equity and justice.

By Mr. WEBSTER:

Resolved, That the Committee on Finance be instructed to inquire into the probable effect of the present state of commercial affairs on the revenue of the United States.

A message was received from the House of Representatives by Mr. FRANKLIN, its Clerk, stating that that House had receded from its amendment to the appropriation bill.

Mr. CHAMBERS moved that when the Senate adjourn, it will adjourn until Monday next, which was agreed to.

Mr. WEBSTER suggested the propriety, after the morning business of Monday was over, that the Senate should go into Executive business, if the gentleman from Pennsylvania, [Mr. WILKINS,] who had the floor upon the deposite question, had no objection.

Mr. WILKINS not objecting, Mr. WEBSTER gave notice that he should, on Monday, at an early hour, move the Senate proceed to the consideration of Executive business.

The Senate, on motion of Mr. MANGUM, adjourned.

HOUSE OF REPRESENTATIVES.

FRIDAY, *February* 7, 1834.

Mr. C. P. WHITE submitted the following resolution, which lies one day on the table:

Resolved, That the Clerk cause to be printed, for the use of this House, one thousand additional copies of the Rules and Regulations for the government of the navy, as communicated to Congress by the President on the 23d of December, 1833.

On motion of Mr. BLAIR, of South Carolina, *Resolved,* That the Committee on the Judiciary be instructed to inquire into the expediency of providing a suitable building in the city of Charleston, in which to hold the Federal Court for the district of South Carolina, and of allowing a salary to the district attorney.

On motion of Mr. BRIGGS, *Resolved,* That the Committee on the Judiciary be directed to inquire into the expediency of extending to parties in suits commenced in the circuit court of the United States, where rights claimed under patents issued under the laws of the United States shall come in question, the right to a writ of error, or an appeal when the amount in controversy, or the judgment recorded in said court, shall exceed $500.

The SPEAKER communicated to the House the annual report of the Commissioners of the Sinking Fund; which was referred to the Committee of Ways and Means, and ordered to be printed.

Mr. MITCHELL, from the Committee on Indian Affairs, reported a bill for the relief of Thomas Bull; which was read twice, and committed.

Mr. POLK, from the same committee, reported a bill exempting from duty a quantity of iron imported by Mr. Lamar, of Georgia, for the purpose of making the experiment of an iron steamboat.

The bill was twice read, and, On motion of Mr. POLK, ordered to be engrossed and read a third time to-morrow.

Mr. HUBBARD, from the select committee on the militia, reported a resolution referring to that committee the militia returns for the last year, transmitted to the House from the President of the United States.

THE PENSION LAWS.

The order of the day was then declared to be the resolution of Mr. CHILTON, to appoint a select committee to inquire into the expediency of so extending the general pension law as to embrace within its provisions those persons who were engaged in the Indian wars, down to the year 1794; and the amendment to it by Mr. BOULDIN, to appoint a committee to inquire into the moral effects of the pension system upon the community, and how far it ought to be abolished or repealed.

Mr. CHAMBERS, of Pennsylvania, continued his remarks on the subject—arguing the impracticability of appropriating any fund, or any part of the revenues of the United States, to the purpose specified in the resolution of the gentleman from Kentucky. To prove this, he entered into a statistical survey of the revenue, as stated by the Secretary of the Treasury in his message this session—remarking on that part of it which deprecates any unnecessary appropriation of the surplus funds of the past year, as it was apprehended that the receipts would be less for the year 1834 than for 1833. He also remarked on the phrase of the Secretary, that "no serious diminution is, however, apprehended." Mr. C. thinks that if the present pecuniary pressure prevails longer, it will have the effect of leaving merchants in such an embarrassed condition that they would have no facilities to make purchases, nor to send to Europe for merchandise, whereon revenue may be raised. What money they may possess, they will in all probability lay out in internal management, considering the adventitious value which money must have, from the pressure on monetary concerns. This will therefore produce a sensible diminution in the revenue, which will fall short of the receipts contemplated by the Secretary of the Treasury, fifteen millions receipts of duties, and three millions from public lands. Indeed, if the distress is continued, if some safety or stability is not given to the currency of the country, it will be immaterial where the public deposites shall be placed.

With regard to the amendment of the gentleman from Virginia, concerning an inquiry into the moral effect of the pension system; frauds, imposition, and false swearing, undoubtedly exist in the enlargement of the pension rolls, owing to the cupidity or the love of money of many who may be indigent or indolent. That the pension laws should have produced fraud and falsehood was to be expected or apprehended; not merely in the persons who may be more immediately benefited by the fraud, but even by others who may be instrumental in the imposition, by giving their testimony; for such is the infirmity of human nature that the fading memory of the veterans may unwillingly or unknowingly falsify the circumstances which they testify. The number of names at present on the pension roll proves that fraud of an extensive kind must necessarily exist. According to censuses taken, [which the gentleman quoted,] the whole number of persons in the United States, between the ages of 70 and 80, was in one instance 50,000; and in another (the last census) 57,000. Now making the proper draw backs on this number for persons who could not possibly have been in the war—such as emigrants &c.—the reasonable number remaining of persons over the age of 70, who might be supposed to have been engaged as soldiers in the revolutionary war, would be only about 12,000. There are there now 47,000 pensioners on the public bounty. An inquiry into such a state of things evidently required. He thinks that the Secretary of War ought to be required to make some investigation into these impositions on the pension roll and have them rectified.

Mr. WILDE rose to make a suggestion to bring this discussion to a definite termination as soon as possible. The business of the House is impeded

THE CONGRESSIONAL GLOBE.

PRINTED AND PUBLISHED AT THE CITY OF WASHINGTON, BY BLAIR & RIVES.

23d Congress, 1st Session.   SATURDAY, FEBRUARY 15, 1834.   Vol. 1........No. 11.

by these preliminary discussions on presenting petitions or resolutions, which will receive all the consideration due to them from the committees to which they may be referred, particularly all regarding an inquiry.

The hour allotted for morning business had expired.

THE HOUSE APPROPRIATION BILL.

The House, on motion of Mr. POLK, suspended the rule by which this day is set apart for the consideration of private bills, in order to take up the bill making appropriation, in part, for the service of Government for 1834—

Ayes 104, noes 44.

Mr. WILDE inquired the state of the question?

The SPEAKER informed him, as he believed he was not in the House at the time, that he took the first opportunity to correct the decision given by him, to say that this motion, submitted by the honorable member from Georgia—for the House to recede from its disagreement to the amendment that was made to the bill by the Senate—was in order.

Mr. WILDE then inquired whether, under these circumstances, the motion to recede would be reinstated in the position it was when proposed by the Chair in error to be out of order?

The SPEAKER informed him that if the motion to reconsider the vote, by which the House had refused to concur with the vote of the Committee of the Whole prevailed, the motion to recede would be in the same situation for him to effect his object.

A desultory discussion upon a point of order, of no interest out of the House, arose, in which Messrs. J. Q. ADAMS, WAYNE, HARDIN, MILLER, and EVERETT of Vermont, participated.

After which,

The SPEAKER decided that the motion to reconsider took precedence of any other motion, and after which, the motion to recede was in order.

Mr. WILDE demanded the yeas and nays on the motion to reconsider; which were ordered.

The question being taken by yeas and nays, it was decided in the negative—yeas 103, nays 116.

Mr. WILDE then moved that the House do now recede from their disagreement to the amendment of the Senate.

Mr. POLK regretted the difficulty, he said, in which the House was placed in regard to this bill. An attempt had been made to effect a compromise by the Committee of Conference, but the House had rejected their proposition. But as another conference was in order, and as it was now understood what was the objectionable matter in the compromise which had been rejected, he had risen to move a new conference with the Senate.

The SPEAKER explained the state of the question. The rejection of the proposition of the Committee of Conference left the question precisely as it was before the conference was ordered. The House had the choice of three alternatives: first, they could recede, in which case, the amendment of the Senate would be agreed to, and the bill passed. The motion to recede had the preference of the two other motions. If the House refuse to recede, they may ask a conference with a view to a compromise; or the House may adhere to their disagreement, which will be tantamount to a rejection of the bill.

Mr. POLK regarded the principle on which the House had, in the first place, refused to recede, as one which he could not yield. He should vote against receding, and, in giving that vote, he should insist only upon the precedents established by Congress. If the motion to recede were lost, he should propose a new conference, which he hoped would result in a compromise. The committee of the Senate, in the concession which they made, manifested a disposition to settle the matter, with a

11

similar disposition by the committee on the part of the House.

Mr. HARPER, of Pennsylvania, stated the considerations which would influence his vote. He believed that it was never the intention that any but incidental expenses should be paid without an appropriation by law, and, in this belief, he found that he was supported by the earliest acts of Congress.

Mr. WILDE spoke in favor of his motion to recede. Appropriation bills were, he said, intended for objects previously authorized by law, and it was highly important that every item in an appropriation bill should be, as nearly as possible, indisputable. By putting into this bill matter which, if proper in a distinct bill, was improper here, we had got into this difficulty. He was in favor of the proposition of the conference, to increase the library appropriation; but the easiest way of getting out of the difficulty was to recede, and to leave the matter of restricting the two Houses in the use of their contingent fund, if it was deemed so very important, to be provided for in an express bill.

He deprecated the want of confidence insinuated in the objectionable clause against the Senate, and considered it improper that greater restrictions should be placed on Congress, in the matter of expense, than had been done in the other departments of Government.

Mr. BROWN would vote against the motion to recede, because it was still open to conference.

Mr. HARDIN thinks it a mark of courtesy to submit to partial amendments made in a bill by the Senate, particularly such an amendment, of that trifling nature, which has been made the subject of so much minute discussion. The privilege of printing, conceded to the Senate, is to disseminate authentic information on every topic of political importance. It is immaterial whether books composed of documents of former years be ordered, or whether an order be given for printing documents relative to the present year. To order printing, merely incurs a debt, not makes an appropriation. The spirit of concession, and the advantages of free orders for printing useful documents, ought to have prevented the introduction of the restrictive clause, or to have erased it, when discovered to be obnoxious.

Mr. FOOT thought nothing very material was embodied in the appropriation bill, as to render it of such importance as it appears to be in the eyes of the chairman of the Committee of Ways and Means. The bill cannot reach the evil it is intended to obviate, nor can the remedy reach the disease. Let a law, founded on the principle of restricting Congress from purchasing books, be reported, but let it not be appended to an appropriation bill, which is ineffectual.

Mr. TURRILL thinks the restriction useful. If orders are made for books, a demand will be made on the contingent appropriation to such an extent, that the regular printing, nor the appointed clerks, &c., of Congress, will receive their salaries: another appropriation must therefore be made. Every appropriation should have a specific object, and no demand should be tolerated on it, but for the purposes distinctly specified.

Mr. HAWES thinks the House the proper guardian of the treasury of the people; and responsible for its proper expenditure. He would not consent to any compromise of its dignity, nor admit that the Senate should make demands at pleasure on the treasury.

Mr. LYTLE referred to the provisions of the bill, and contended that, as the House had at all times the power to review any appropriations made by it, it was absurd, unworthy, and undignified for them not to recede.

Mr. BYNUM contended that the quantum of money was of comparatively small importance in competition with the principle that was involved, which was, in effect, whether the House would yield to the Senate the control vested in them by the Constitution over the purse of the nation. He

had voted for the original proposition, that one House might be, as was contemplated by the framers of the Constitution, a check upon the other. If it was not adopted, the result might produce a contest for power between the two Houses at the expense of the nation, and he trusted that the majority, who supported the bill as it went from the House, would continue to support a principle which was sacred to the welfare of the nation.

Mr. BAYLIES said he was as well disposed to contend, upon every proper occasion, for the dignity of the House as any other member, but he believed there was some misapprehension about the bill itself. He had examined it, and believed that the Senate could not appropriate any of the money voted by the bill to improper purposes; it was said that they might do so, but the bill restricted them.

Mr. MILLER would not have obtruded himself, but that he wished to free himself from a charge of inconsistency, in now voting to recede, which he had previously opposed. He had, since that, examined the bill, and discovered that the principle for which he was contending was retained as fully in the bill as before; for the restriction as to the printing clause secured that object, and it would be in the power of the House, if the Senate expended their money improperly, and should ask for more, to withhold it. He confessed, if he had been a Senator, he would have stood out for their amendment, and he especially supported it, because it gave to the House the same privilege which it gave them.

Mr. WHITTLESEY expressed his wish that the question might be taken, that the House might proceed to the consideration of private bills.

Mr. MANN, of New York, called for the yeas and nays; which were ordered.

The House then receded from their disagreement by the following vote—

Yeas 111, nays 104.

So the bill was finally passed, with the amendment made by the Senate.

Several engrossed bills were read a third time, and passed.

The following bills were ordered to be engrossed:

A bill for the location of lands in the Territory of Arkansas; and

A bill in reference to preemption rights.

Mr. SPEIGHT moved that when the House adjourn it adjourn to meet on Monday next. An objection being made, Mr. WAYNE moved to suspend the rule, in order that the motion to adjourn over to Monday might be made. The motion was lost, two-thirds not voting in the affirmative.

A bill for the relief of Arnold Henry Dorman, after some discussion, was postponed. On motion of adjournment,

The House adjourned.

IN SENATE.

FRIDAY, February 7, 1834.

On motion of Mr. CLAY, the resolution offered by him some time ago, extending the time for paying revenue bonds, in order to afford the commercial community relief, was taken up.

Mr. C. proposed an inquiry into this subject only; and when the accents of distress were reaching us from every quarter, it was due to the people that every practicable effort should be made to give relief, and he was particularly desirous that it should come from the Senate, and that the Senate should apply all its constitutional powers to that end. When the resolution was first offered, the fact of the distress was not admitted. Its universality and severity was not now denied. While he was up, he would offer a few remarks in reference to an observation made by the gentleman from Pennsylvania [Mr. Wilkins] a few days since. He then stated a fact, which, if he were now pre-

sent, Mr. C. was sure he would correct. It was, that he was surprised to find the State stock of Ohio selling at 115, while that of Pennsylvania was at 100 or 102. Mr. C. was himself surprised at the fact, as he supposed it was, when it was stated, but he thought it was correct. Upon the assumption of its truth, the gentleman insinuated that it was owing to a combination between the Bank of the United States and the brokers, with a view of producing effect upon the Pennsylvania Legislature, and thus reach Washington. Now, what must be the surprise of the Senate, when he told them the truth of the fact. The truth is, the stock of Pennsylvania selling at 102, was bearing an interest of five per cent., while that of Ohio bore an interest of six per cent. Any one might make a calculation showing that the five per cents. being less in the market, the stock of Pennsylvania was really the highest. Yet the member threw out the insinuation against the bank on these grounds. He thought the gentleman owed it to himself, to his constituents, to justice and to truth, to rectify the mistake, and to retract the injustice he had done. Scarcely a day passed that he did not hear of distress prevailing in Pennsylvania. It was only this morning he had received a letter from Pittsburg on this subject, which he begged leave to read. [Mr. C. here read the letter.] This letter was from a man in Pittsburg, than whom there was no one more respectable, and few more opulent.

He proposed the resolution with a view to a specific inquiry, and he hoped that it would be adopted.

Mr. KANE. The historian of Charles the Fifth of Spain, among the achievements of that eventful reign, has recorded the fact that that monarch made the Pope of Rome his prisoner, and whilst Charles held down upon him the screws of a rigid captivity, and at a moment when a wink of his eye or a shake of his finger would have given freedom to his captive, he coolly turned around, and directed all the priests of his extensive dominions to offer up their prayers to Heaven for the speedy restoration of the Holy Father to freedom. Such, said Mr. K., is the course of the Bank of the United States. The doctrines recently promulged here, show us that the control of the currency is in the hands of that institution, that she may flood the country with her notes to any extent not forbidden by the charter, and that there is no power in the State to prevent her from withdrawing it as suddenly and as entirely as she pleases. The Government deposites may be restrained by the bank, for the purpose either of enabling it to enlarge its accommodations, or for the object of withdrawing so much of the currency from circulation, neither to be issued by itself nor any other bank. This is undoubtedly true, if the Secretary of the Treasury has no other power over the deposites than that allowed to it by the report of the Committee on Finance. If the deposites can be withdrawn by the Secretary, only in cases where he deems them unsafe, or when the bank refuses to the Government the necessary facilities for transferring the public funds, how is the bank to be compelled to relieve the wants of the country to the extent which the deposites may authorize? Not by *scire facias*, nor by any judicial process, because such refusal presents no violation of the terms of the charter. The Government cannot reach the conduct of that institution in any other mode than through the agency of courts and juries, and if the Secretary does not hold in his hands the corrective, the great and sovereign right to regulate the currency, so indispensable to the freedom of the country, and to the security of all private property, belongs to the bank, and the Government itself is made to contribute to the distresses of its own citizens, whenever the bank may choose to withhold from circulation the public deposites.

That some parts of the country are now in a condition of great embarrassment, I have no right to deny, because the evidences of it upon the table are numerous and conclusive. The withdrawal of the deposites cannot be the cause, unless by that operation the amount of the means of banking accommodation, both State and Federal, has been diminished. It may have been the means of exciting the bad passions of boards of directors, and thus of dissocializing the Federal and State banks. The correction for this evil is not within the jurisdiction of Congress, and the applications of our fellow-citizens for relief should be addressed to the directors and stockholders of the bank, to convince them that they consult their own interests by making peace.

Now, the course the Administration felt themselves authorized to take, might be gleaned from what had been said by the gentleman from New York, [Mr. Wright,] and that appeared to be to do nothing on this subject. There was no relief to be expected from that quarter, because it was said that the question of restoring the deposites was connected with the question of the recharter of the present bank, or the establishment of another in its place. Here, then, was the course, as far as one side had laid it down—and what had been done by those Senators who had talked the most, the longest, and the loudest? The Senate had been six weeks in discussing a question which cannot, let it be decided one way or the other, effect anything. It would settle nothing. The subject had been referred to the Committee on Finance, who had made a report on it; and what did it propose? Precisely what we have been talking about for the last six weeks; it stated that the reasons of the Secretary of the Treasury for the removal of the deposites were not sufficient. The report did not go into any reasons to show why the deposites should be restored, nor did it look into the effect of a restoration of the deposites. The committee had abstained from expressing an opinion as to whether a restoration would or would not effect relief. The Senate, then, had been discussing a subject which would eventuate in nothing—had been debating a mere abstract proposition.

Gentlemen did not propose any relief, but took occasion to find fault with the Administration. They said there is distress, but said nothing else. Mr. K. attributed a want of confidence on the part of the community, in a great degree, to the language that had been used by Senators in speaking of distress. To show that what was said in this body had made an impression on the public mind, he needed only to refer to the memorial which had been just presented by the gentleman from New York; it was almost a copy of the language that had been used here. If the people were to be told that the powers of the Government had been usurped—that the President was a tyrant—that the sword and the purse were united in the same hand, and that dreadful consequences were likely to grow out of this single act of the Secretary of the Treasury—why, it would be most extraordinary indeed, if these assertions did not make some impression on the public mind.

Members of Congress must have had less weight in the community than they deserved, if somebody could not be found who would believe what they said. Here, said Mr. K., in this chamber, where the vestal lamp should be always lighted, where the oil should be pressed from the leaf of the olive and poured upon the troubled waters, is the volcano from whence is thrown, all over the country, the material which alarms our fellow citizens. The remedy which had been proposed for the present distress, by the resolution of the Senator from Kentucky, was to extend credit to the merchants upon their duty bonds. This he considered as a partial relief, and it did not reach the whole object. It was a partial measure for the relief of one class of men, not only to the disregard of all others, but to the positive injury of all others. It was a question whether there should be any deposites at all in any bank. The importers having credits extended, will be relieved, and all other classes of men will be deprived of the advantages of the deposites in any bank, State or Federal. Would it be said that because relief was thus afforded, it would be extended in consequence to all others—tradesmen, farmers, and manufacturers? The answer to that suggestion is, that you relieve the importers *by law*, and leave the rest of the community to be dealt with by them according to *their* tender mercies. Why should gentlemen select importers in preference to any other class? Because Senators say we do not know how it is in our power to relieve others. And has the Constitution drawn this distinction? Have these men superior claims upon the public indulgence? Why, sir, were we not told over and over again, during the tariff discussions, that to a very great extent the importers were foreign agents, who could undersell the regular trader, and that auction sales, so much encouraged by them, were destructive to manufactures?

He was perfectly willing, for one, when any measure should be proposed which in his judgment would relieve all classes from the present state of embarrassment, to give it his support—but not by restoring the deposites, by rechartering the bank, or by establishing a new bank.

It seemed, according to the views of some gentlemen, that there was no plan in the world that could be adopted to rid us of our difficulties, but by establishing a bank—there was no living without a Bank of the United States. It had been said by one gentleman, that the people, after trying the State banks, which he called bark canoes, would call for old *Ironsides* again. *Old Ironsides, indeed!* That was the *nom de guerre* of the "Constitution." Was it intended to be intimated that the Bank of the United States was to be regarded as the Constitution, to which everything was to be confided? And who, he asked, is *old Ironsides* to be commanded by? The gallant commodore who had spread her name and fame everywhere all over the world? or by the patriotic chief now at the head of our affairs? No, sir! She was to be commanded by Nicholas Biddle, president of the Bank of the United States. Let the bank hold on to the motto, *Ne sutor ultra crepidam*, and let president-making alone. Let it loan all the money it can with safety, and make all the profit it can for the stockholders. That is its duty.

Mr. K. concluded by repeating his intention to vote for any measure that would have the effect of *general* relief.

Mr. WILKINS having resumed his seat during the previous discussion, said that he had been informed by the gentleman from Kentucky, that in the remarks he had just made, and while he (Mr. W.) was not in his seat, he had referred to a statement made by him, in relation to the prices of Pennsylvania and Ohio State stocks in Philadelphia, and presumed he (Mr. W.) would make the correction on the authority of letters, &c., received by the gentleman. He was glad the call had been made on him—he had been waiting for it. It was not his duty to introduce the subject, because it might be thought it was an acknowledgment of his error. It was no error. He said he took it from a newspaper publication—he had no correspondence in Philadelphia on the subject. The prices of stocks were always published in the newspapers; and he stated upon such an authority that Pennsylvania State stock, bearing an interest of five per cent., and redeemable in 1850, was at 101 or 102, while that of Ohio, redeemable at the same period, and bearing the same interest, stood at 110 and 112. He referred to the quotation in a newspaper, the American Sentinel, dated January 24, 1834. [Mr. W. read the statement.] He was not responsible for the correctness of the editor of the paper. Did he need anything further, then, to bear him out? If it was an error, he was at a loss to know how it occurred. He would lay the statement on the table, for gentlemen to refer to if they pleased. So much for this. The other day, and also this morning, the gentleman from Mississippi [Mr. Poindexter] referred to him as speaking by *authority*. That was a significant phrase, and bore a well-known meaning here. He did speak by authority; but it was an authority within his own bosom. It was an authority proceeding from his conviction of the rights and interests of his fellow-citizens, and upon his own best judgment. He took his cue from no man, however deeply he might be implanted in the affections of the people. In all his life, he never had one word of private or confidential communication on any bill or subject, public or private, with the President. He had never in his life seen General Jackson alone. He was independent of him and of every other consideration except what bore upon the best interests of his fellow-citizens. When he held conferences, he would go to the fountain head—the people. He did not allude to any executive measure, but only as to his own impression that the people would adapt themselves to any condition which might result from this state of things. The gentleman had a very favorite word here: it was the word *pet*. Now he presumed he used it in its family signification—he had his pet, but that was only one—

Mr. W. had many. One pet in a family was more dangerous than many, and if the gentleman did not take care, he feared his pet would shortly rule the family.

But the distress of his constituents had been brought into view. He stated his belief, the other day, in the absence of distress in his neighborhood. He left home the latter end of November; all was then calm and tranquil at Pittsburg, and yet the bank commenced its curtailments on the first of August preceding, and broke up the domestic exchanges on 13th August. The high prices of property in Pittsburg were not affected; there were no complaints before. Since then he had received many letters breathing complaints, and this morning two others, uttering threats which were a disgrace to the writers. He had been told by gentlemen, now within the range of his voice, that there would be serious distress in Pittsburg. He told them that it was strange it never had been communicated to him, till his declarations here on the subject went home. The question rested between his constituents and himself; he admitted they were in difficulties, but the difference between them was as to the source of the real cause of the evil. He told them they saw the removal of the deposites, and they feel the pressure, and they ascribed it to the action of the Government. He told them there might be other and secret causes for it. Now, they were not aware that between the month of November last, and the 13th of January, the bank curtailed its accommodations half a million; they were not aware of the amount abstracted from circulation in that time. He had a word to say respecting the relation in which the bank stood at this moment to the State of Pennsylvania. It was well known that the Messrs. Allen, brokers in Philadelphia, took the late State loans to the amount of three millions, an operation which involved them deeply and compelled them to throw up a portion of the stock, and in consequence of this the Governor proposed to borrow $300,000—the stock was taken by four Pennsylvania banks; two in Philadelphia, and two in the county. Now when it was necessary for Pennsylvania to borrow large sums of money on her own vast resources, what was the conduct of the United States Bank? The ability of the State to borrow depended upon the banks located in Philadelphia. The State banks are required by their charters to loan the State five per cent. on their capital when required, and to pay into the State treasury a certain commission on their dividends. Standing as they now do, their capacity to loan depends entirely on the course of the United States Bank, because it is able to control the State banks—they live, as the directors say, only at the mercy of the United States Bank—it can annihilate them at a blow. Whether the State can obtain loans, therefore, depends upon a bank which is capable of holding such language as, "we will cripple you the moment you allow the Legislature to pass resolutions against us." As much had been said of domestic exchanges, Mr. W. referred to the letter of Mr. Crawford, dated 3d July, 1817, showing that even the attempt, on the part of the bank, to deal in domestic exchanges, with a view to profit, and not for the benefit of the commercial community, was reprobated by him, and that in such an event, the President and Secretary would have no other alternative left but to exercise the conservative power, reserved in the charter, of removing the deposites.

Mr. SILSBEE earnestly hoped the resolution would pass. The distress was not now to be doubted. We had heard it from gentlemen who were most likely to know. He thought when creditors of all classes were granting indulgence to their debtors, the Government ought to be equally lenient to theirs.

Mr. BLACK said he had no objection to the resolution; but he had no idea that any benefit could grow out of it. He thought that specific relief could not be extended, but that the distress could only be alleviated by the bank itself. The bank was a fiscal agent, having two duties to perform; the one to the Government, the other to the country. As respected its duty to the Government, the bank was absolved from that by the removal of the deposites; but its other duties to the community were still binding. It was a corporation designed to facilitate the business of the commercial community. And what was the condition of the bank? It was fully demonstrated that it was entirely solvent. Its duties, then, were still existing, and the performance of those duties were consistent with the desire of gain by the bank, because distress in the community must diminish the profits of the bank. The contingent drafts, amounting to a million and a half, had all been met and paid. The amount which the bank held, due to the Government, had also been paid. It was incumbent on the institution, then, to exhibit a good will, a friendly disposition towards the community, to grant relief as far as was in their power. He would not say to what extent they could go. They ought, however, to go as far as they could; and if the bank should proceed in a way which indicated a wish to force a recharter, there were those who would recollect it. As to his opinions of a Bank of the United States, he thought he ought now to express them. There were but two courses that could be pursued to attain a sound currency. One was by means of a national bank, and the other by State banks. As to a metallic currency, he had thrown that out of the question; there was no principle upon which it could be founded, and there was no power in Congress to secure it. Suppose we should throw out of circulation the paper of the National Bank, it must be followed by issues from the State banks, and this must throw specie almost entirely out of circulation. Look to the Corporation of this city—they issue small notes, and the metallic currency in Washington is driven out of circulation—it has almost disappeared. And it must necessarily be so. There was no power in Congress to restrain the issues of State banks or control the currency, except by a national bank. The instance given by the gentleman from Virginia, [Mr. RIVES,] of the success of the metallic currency in France, is in no way analagous. France is a consolidated empire, having a chartered national bank; there the Government has the same power in one part of the kingdom as in another, and therefore it has the whole control of the currency. This General Government does not possess these means, through any laws already made or which it is in their power to make. We have, then, only two choices: the one is the currency of a national bank, the other the currency of bills issuing from State banks. The great extent to which the bills of State banks may be, and are counterfeited, is a great evil. How was a man in Mississippi to know the genuineness of bills of banks in Maine? He would not know there was such a bank as the note in his hand purported to issue from, much less its genuineness. Another evil consequence resulting from such a currency, is the over issues of the State paper, producing an alternate rise and depreciation in the price of property: this must inevitably bring distress on the community. Another destructive effect on his State, alluded to by his colleague, [Mr. POINDEXTER,] was, that it must render the valley of the Mississippi tributary to New York. How can facilities be furnished through the medium of State banks for conveying funds to the eastern cities? Every State in the West must have funds to the amount of at least half a million dollars in the eastern cities to carry on their business. If a merchant in the West takes bills on to the East from his own banks, the brokers may fix their own rates of exchange, and the holders could force no other terms than they chose to dictate; and there was not much favor to be found in their lenity. He, therefore, preferred the present system.

Mr. POINDEXTER then rose and addressed the Senate at length in support of the resolution.

Mr. KING, of Georgia, rose and said that the sudden arrival of the debate on these resolutions reminded him that, shortly after the resolutions were introduced, he had made an effort to say a few words upon one branch of the question raised by them, and to which the honorable Senator from Mississippi had professed mainly in his first speech to direct his attention. He then failed to get the floor, and had abandoned all idea of addressing the Senate upon the subject. He said, however, as the subject had been revived, he would like still to make a few remarks, but in doing so, that he might not interfere with the privileges of the gentleman who had the floor upon the special order of the day, he would move to lay the resolutions upon the table until to-morrow. However, (said Mr. K., turning to Mr. WILKINS,) on this point I would consult the wishes of the honorable gentleman himself.

Mr. WILKINS having expressed his willingness that Mr. K. should proceed, Mr. K. continued—

I do not sufficiently disagree, Mr. President, with several gentlemen who have addressed the Senate upon these resolutions, (either directly or incidentally,) to feel myself called on to pay any particular attention to their remarks. He should (he said) himself vote for the resolution, but he dissented from some of the reasons given by gentlemen for their support of it; and he deemed it of the first importance in the present condition of the country that we should not only act advisedly, but endeavor to give reasons for our acts that would be respected by the community to which they were addressed.

Mr. K. said he would mainly direct the few remarks he intended to make to the observations of the honorable Senator from Mississippi on the low prices of our articles of export and the causes of their depression. This was a subject in which the South was particularly interested, and for that reason the honorable Senator from Mississippi had given it particular notice.

I do not profess, Mr. President, (said Mr. K.,) to be very intimately acquainted with the nature of commercial operations. I have bestowed but few thoughts in the course of my life on this subject, and am, perhaps, still less familiar with the usual influence of a deranged and fluctuating currency upon the commercial interests of the country. But, sir, (said he,) with my unlearned notions upon these subjects, the views of some gentlemen have been so exceedingly wild, or, at least to me so unsatisfactory, that I hope I may not be charged with presumption, or even with affording evidence of a degree of confidence in my own opinions which I do not feel, if I should attempt very briefly to explain why it is that I differ so widely in my views with other gentlemen who have preceded me in the discussion.

The honorable Senator from Mississippi had contended, if he understood him, that the present low price of cotton was to be attributed to the derangement of the currency, and the inequality and depression of exchanges, which produced a want of fair relation between the home and foreign market, all of which was to be attributed to the removal of the deposites. Here Mr. K. turned to Mr. P. and said that he had taken no notes, and being suddenly called up in the debate, he might, possibly, not recollect accurately some of the positions of the honorable Senator, and he hoped if he should misstate his arguments, that he (Mr. P.) would take the liberty of correcting him. Mr. P. bowing assent, Mr. K. proceeded.

Sir, (said Mr. K.,) that the home price of an article of export, in which the speculator usually deals for cash, and ships to a foreign market, which being the market of its greatest consumption, confessedly regulates its price in all parts of the world where it is produced; or, (to take the other branch of the proposition,) that the relation between the home price of an article of export and the price of the same article in such foreign market, should be materially influenced by the derangement of the currency, the fluctuations of the currency, the inequality in domestic exchanges, or (what seems most relied on) the want of confidence and the want of credit *in this country*—seemed to him to be doing violence to all just reasoning upon the subject, and to be marked with a total disregard of the most obvious laws of trade, and the plainest principles of commerce.

Sir, (said Mr. K.,) what renders this assumption the more extraordinary, is the admission on all hands that the country has never been so full of capital as it is at this time. Yes, said Mr. K., all accounts I have seen recently from the Atlantic cities concur in proving that there has rarely been such an accumulation of *private deposites* in the banks of the Atlantic cities, and especially in New York, as there was at the date of the last accounts. Of money and currency in the country, then, there was a plethoric abundance, and that, too, not alone belonging to the banking institutions, and subject

to their control, *but belonging to individuals*, and which, by a law common to speculating men, they would always invest whenever they could honorably expect a profitable return. But, notwithstanding this admitted abundance of capital in the country, it is said "there is a want of confidence and a want of credit," and "hence the low prices of our articles of export." Sir, said Mr. K., you might as well say, "hence the low condition of the western waters," during the fall of 1833. What, said Mr. K., has a want of confidence or a want of credit *in this country* to do with the matter? The capital is now idle in the hands of individuals, and the capitalist who has money *unemployed* wants neither confidence nor credit. He has money, and always wishes to employ it profitably, when invited by a market that offers a large profit. Why, said Mr. K., so far from the position of gentlemen being true, it may be safely assumed that if every dollar of currency were, "by one fell swoop," stricken from the face of the earth, within the limits of the planting States; yes, from the Potomac to the Sabine, unless it were driven beyond the confines of the commercial world, and its circulation *forcibly* prevented—the influence of such a local disaster to the currency on the price of cotton in the planting States, would be merely temporary. What, said Mr. K., plenty of capital in the country at the command of individuals *unemployed*, and a tempting foreign market before them, offering, it is said, large profits, and yet the capital will not circulate in the purchase of it! Why, said Mr. K., you might as well expect to stop the flow and circulation of the blood to the heart of the animal during the continuance of respiration, as to stop the flow and circulation of currency to those points where it can be most profitably employed.

But an attempt has been made (said Mr. K.) to account for the fall of cotton by the loss on exchanges. To attempt anything like a lucid exposition of the nature and operation of exchanges, (said Mr. K.,) would require both detail and time; and he was disposed to save himself the trouble of the one, and the Senate the consumption of the other. But a few remarks would dispose of this part of the subject. The gentleman from Mississippi had said, (if he understood him,) that, as one of the effects of the removal of the deposites, foreign exchanges had fallen, and domestic exchanges had risen; or rather, that the *premium* on foreign bills had fallen, and the *discounts* on inland bills had risen, which, thus explained, seemed to assert a depression in both species of exchange, as the effect in both cases was to reduce the proceeds of the bill in the hands of the seller.

If (continued Mr. K.) the honorable Senator intended to assert that domestic exchange has been unusually high or unequal during the fall of 1833, he must insist that the honorable Senator was—unintentionally, of course—mistaken in point of fact. Mr. K. stated that he lived in a central city, about equi-distant between this and New Orleans; and mentioned some facts, and referred generally to the exchange tables, as found in the southern papers, to prove that, from the city of his residence, exchange north and south, had rarely, if ever, been lower than since the removal of the deposites. What it was at New York or New Orleans, he knew not. But if it were as stated by the Senator from Mississippi, when last up, greatly against New Orleans, he could only say, what the Senator and all others must readily perceive, that the effect was in direct hostility to the proposition which this fact was brought forward to sustain. If Louisiana bank bills were ten or twelve per cent. discount in New York, as had been stated, and exchange were so heavily against New Orleans, the inevitable effect must be to transfer capital from New York to New Orleans, for the purchase of cotton. When speculators with $1000 in New York, could place $1100 in New Orleans, for the purchase of cotton, *they would purchase cotton nowhere else*, and such a state of its currency would shortly make New Orleans the greatest exporting and importing city in the Union.

But (said Mr. K.) a practical answer to all this theory is readily found in the relation between the prices of cotton in the different ports of the Union. The quotations in the different seaports would show no unusual inequality in price. And he would ask gentlemen why it was, that if cotton were low in New Orleans, from the difficulty of supplying funds from New York to purchase, why did it not bear a better price in New York, *the place from which the money is said to be supplied?* These are both exporting and importing cities, and there seems no unusual want of relation of prices between the city supplying and the city supplied, with capital to purchase this article of export. And this alone would prove that nothing could be lost to the producer by the inequality of domestic exchanges. But (said Mr. K.) I will make a more unanswerable inquiry still—why is it, said he, that cotton does not bear a better price in Texas, Mexico, and South America? He hoped there had been no removal of the deposites there.

But (Mr. K. said) the shortest way to dispose of this whole charge of loss on account of the depression of exchanges, would be (for the sake of argument) to admit the facts as charged, and we would instantly see such a want of agreement between the alleged cause and the alleged effects, as clearly to show that there was no proper connexion between them. He had seen in the public prints, that some who had agreed with the views of the gentleman from Mississippi, insisted on a loss to the producer of 2½ or 3 per cent. *on this account*. For no one, he believed, contended for a loss to the producer *of the whole amount* of the depression of exchange, or attempted to impute the *entire* decline in *foreign* exchange to the measures of the Administration. But to be liberal in our admissions, for the sake of argument, (said Mr. K.) let us say 5 per cent. He presumed the Senator from Mississippi would not contend for more. What would this amount to? In estimating cotton at 10 cents per pound, it would amount to a half cent per pound. How shall we account for the balance of the loss? It is alleged that the loss is from 3 to 5 cents per pound.

But (said Mr. K.) I must say a word on foreign exchange; though the loss on that is included in the admission just made for the sake of argument. It is said, I think, that the planter loses the premium on foreign exchange, which formerly added to the price of his productions. [Here Mr. POINDEXTER begged leave to explain. He said, that by the depression of foreign exchanges, cotton would not now be used as a remittance to the same extent as formerly, as the depression destroyed the competition among that class of purchasers who purchased cotton for remittance instead of exchange.] Mr. K. resumed. He said, with the explanation he perfectly understood the argument of the honorable Senator, and thought it easily answered. No one had shown how the condition of our own money market had exerted any agency in depressing foreign exchange. It is never dealt in as an article of speculation; it is only needed for the payment of our foreign debt; and the price and competition depend upon the demand, and the demand is regulated by the state of trade between the two countries. It is admitted, then, (said Mr. K.,) on all hands, even in the complaining memorials upon your table, that the balance of trade is largely in our favor. This was a state of things long desired by us, and the Senator might as well expect the laws of gravity to be disturbed, and the waters of the Mississippi to turn up stream, and continue in that direction, as for exchange to be against us when the balance of trade is in our favor. The premium of exchange (he said) should not be expected to resist the balance of trade.

So much, then, for the home prices of our articles of export in connexion with the measures of the Administration. We are, however, confounded by another proposition, brought in aid of the first; and though no attempt is made to explain it, for an obvious reason, yet it asserts a most disastrous state of things; and, unless it can be explained by others—like all other inexplicable phenomena, charged with mischief—it will be put down of course to the account of the Administration: I allude to the alleged want of proper relation between the home and foreign markets.

Now, (said Mr. K.,) the relation between the home price of an article of export, and the foreign price of the same article, (which, being the market of its greatest consumption, confessedly regulates its price in all parts of the world, wherever produced,) depends upon a variety of commercial incidents, but mainly and principally *upon the confidence of the dealer in the stability of the foreign market*. And it is a law of trade, that a rising foreign market will usually be anticipated by the dealer, *provided he have a reasonable confidence in the continuance of the causes of the advance*. And, for a like reason, a falling foreign market will be anticipated by the dealer, provided he have a continued confidence in his belief of the causes of the decline. Practical men reason in these matters just as they reason in the every-day transactions of life. They use the plain logical proposition, that what has happened once, will most likely, under the same circumstances, and during the continuance of the same causes, happen again. Hence they say, that "if cotton fluctuated in price, either on the rise or decline, a given amount, during the lapse of thirty days *previous* to the dates of the last European quotations, and we know, and feel confident in the continuance of the causes of the fluctuation, it is safe to conclude that the fluctuation has been in an equal ratio for the thirty days which it has required to receive the accounts."

Let us illustrate by a few practical references; we should never resort to theory when we have the lights of experience to guide us. What, then, was the relation between the home and foreign markets for cotton in the year 1825? Ask the speculator of that year, or get information from more infallible sources, and it would (if he mistook not) be found, that, during a portion of that year, the home price was nearly equal to, quite equal to, and perhaps, for a short period, even beyond the last European quotations. What was the cause of this? Why, in that year, the dealers, both in Europe and America, had become fully convinced that the crop then in market was an unusually short one; that the supply would fall far short of the usual demand. *The whole commercial world was fully satisfied of this fact.* And, without recollecting that the high price of an article of consumption will greatly diminish the consumption itself, the belief was general, and much encouraged by speculators, that the price would continue to advance *indefinitely*, until it should be checked by the distribution of the new crop! But consumption was checked, the speculating bubble burst, and the sequel was known. Cotton went down at a few leaps from 32 or 3 cents to 7 or 8! Oh! said Mr. K., what a glorious year this would have been for the removal of the deposites! The President, with all his alleged usurped power, and unrighteous popularity, aided by all his "collar men," and his "collar presses," could not have stood up a moment against the torrent of discontent which the disappointments and distresses of that year produced! *It would all have been attributed to the removal of the deposites.*

This relation, then, (said Mr. K.,) between the home and foreign market, in 1825, was owing to *the universal belief* in the causes on which the maintenance of prices was based. But what is the fact in 1833–4? Why, said Mr. K., such has been the want of confidence among American speculators, in the maintenance of prices at which cotton opened in the fall of 1833, that thousands of experienced dealers have not touched a lock of the article. And those who ventured, at the higher prices of the opening market, had so little confidence in the maintenance of prices, that there has been a precipitate rush by holders to the European markets, which has swelled the exportations, for the last quarter of 1833, far beyond those of the corresponding quarter of the previous year. This hasty glut of the market would, of itself, have produced some decline.

But, (said Mr. K.,) what has been the reason of this want of confidence with the American dealers in 1833, which has made them cautious of approaching the European quotations at the opening of the market, and which has made them anticipate the decline, and endeavor to keep ahead of it, after the decline commenced? The reasons are well known. In the first place, they had the experience of 1825 before them. They knew that cotton was at a price very far beyond its natural price, that is, the price at which the article can reasonably and profitably be made by the planter,

and that the high price itself would greatly diminish the consumption. And, secondly, they believed that the assumption upon which the market opened, and upon which these high prices were maintained, was, *in point of fact, untrue*. These high prices, at the opening of the market, were based on the supposition that the crop was unusually short. This was doubted by most dealers in this country, *and the event has shown that their doubts were well-founded. The crop has turned out to be fully equal to the last year's crop, and probably larger*. And no speculating dreamer has ever supposed, at any part of the season, that, if the crop should turn out to be as abundant *as it is now ascertained to be*, that prices could be maintained beyond the present quotations.

American dealers, then, *have not had confidence in the stability of the foreign market* during the present season; and when the decline commenced, *they knew the causes, had confidence in their continuance*, and endeavored, prudently, to anticipate the decline. And this brings us to a practical answer to the whole complaint. Ask the unfortunate speculator of the present season, who, *somehow or other*, in despite of the measures of the Administration, and of the removal of the deposites, unluckily for himself, has obtained the requisite cash or credit, and, tempted by these high Liverpool prices, with a hope of making an easy fortune, has embarked in large exporting speculations; ask him, I say, if he has realized "from three to five cents per pound" *more than the usual profit*. He will answer you, with a sigh, sir, "I am ruined by my speculations." Why, sir, (said Mr. K.,) it may be safely assumed, that if all the treasure that ever was extracted from the mines of Golconda and Potosi, were heaped up in one common mass before the merchants of this country, with privilege to borrow *ad libitum* on good security, the effect of such a privilege would have no sensible effect on the cotton market of this country.

Do you expect men, sir, to give prices for exports beyond those prices at which they are daily ruined? Sir, dealers have no other inducement to make investments on speculation than the hope of realizing a profitable return. This practical view of the operations of the present season, it is hoped, is a full and conclusive answer to all complaints of an unfair and losing relation between the home and foreign market, unless indeed you expect exporters to speculate against all the maxims of human prudence.

But, (said Mr. K.,) I have said more than I intended when I arose, and will only say a few words on the relief proposed by the resolution, and the question of reference. Mr. K. said he would vote for the specific inquiry proposed in the resolution, because it proposed to relieve a want *created by the action of Congress*, and he thought it therefore peculiarly fit that Congress should relieve it. This, he said, was a large item in the wants of the merchants, and contributed largely to the public distress.

The wants of the merchants, said he, are ordinary and extraordinary. Their *ordinary* wants, as borrowers, in this country, are *always* heavy, which arises out of our abominable paper banking system. Merchants do not trade upon solid capital, but trade upon their credit, that is, upon the chances of borrowing; always expecting to make up any deficiencies between their investments and returns, by further loans from the banks. The directors of banks are generally ready to mistake the wants of sinking merchants for the wants of currency, and by pouring out floods of their paper trash, *when not needed for circulation*, ease only the merchants for a time, but occasion reactions that carry in their sweep, wide-spread ruin to all other portions of the community.

But, said Mr. K., I find myself likely to digress. I do not intend to discuss the banking system; only to state it as an incident to account for the great extent of the ordinary wants of our merchants.

The extraordinary wants of the merchants during the present season consist, 1st. In deficiencies occasioned by a falling market. *The returns of the speculator do not repay his investments.* He is, therefore, in debt, and wishes to borrow the deficiency, and this deficiency constitutes one of his extraordinary wants. 2dly. The want which this resolution proposes to relieve, and which constitutes the heaviest item in the class of extraordinary wants. This want has been occasioned, not by the acts of the Executive, but by the action of Congress. The importing merchants have given the usual credit to their customers, and Government does not extend the usual credits to them. To these extraordinary wants, perhaps, a few others might be added, but it is unnecessary to notice them.

The above positions, if true, will prove that the *wants* of the merchants are precisely what they would have been, independent of the measures of the Administration. But what I intend to admit is, that these measures have, for the present, cut off, or choked up, many of the sources from which these wants have been too liberally supplied. There is a panic in the community, which, for the present, destroys all confidence in our domestic trade and exchanges. The fixed property, and all property for domestic use and consumption, have depreciated, partly as an incident to a falling market upon exports, but largely owing to the shock upon our monetary system. Again, a large curtailment in the usual means of supply, may be found in the withdrawal from circulation of the amount of the Government deposites. These may be considered as taken from circulation, and withdrawn from the uses to which they have heretofore been appropriated. The Bank of the United States cannot discount upon them, because it has them not to discount upon. The State banks cannot, or will not, discount upon them, because, whilst the debate on the removal continues, the deposites do not constitute a fund upon which they can safely rely.

This state of things, sir, must continue to a certain extent, at least, until this uncertainty ceases, and some measure decided on, to give stability to our monetary system, and restore confidence in the domestic trade of the country.

For the reasons before given, I shall vote for the specific inquiry proposed in the resolution.

The debate was further continued by Mr. WEBSTER, Mr. SILSBEE, Mr. WRIGHT, Mr. MANGUM, and Mr. CHAMBERS, when, on motion,

The Senate adjourned till Monday.

HOUSE OF REPRESENTATIVES.

SATURDAY, *February* 8, 1834.

The journal of the preceding day having been read,

The standing committees were called to present any report ready.

A bill was reported for the relief of Elijah King.

Mr. MARDIS, of Alabama, presented a memorial from the Legislature of that State; which was referred to the Committee on Private Land Claims.

On motion of Mr. PEYTON, it was

1. *Resolved*, That the Committee on the Post Office and Post Roads be instructed to inquire into the expediency of establishing a post route from Gainsboro', Tennessee, by Major Thomas Butler's and Celina, to Burksville, Kentucky.

2. *Resolved*, That the same committee be instructed to inquire into the expediency of establishing a post route from Monroe, *via* Locust Shade, in Overton county, Tennessee, by Celina, Jackson county, Tennessee, by Garret Moore's, to Tompkinsville, Kentucky.

On motion of Mr. LAY, of New York, it was

Resolved, That the Committee on Invalid Pensions be instructed to inquire into the expediency of placing the name of Salathiel Harris on the pension roll.

On motion of Mr. LYON, it was

Resolved, That the Committee on Military Affairs be directed to inquire into the expediency of making an appropriation to pay any unsatisfied claims for military services in the Territory of Michigan, growing out of the Indian disturbances in that Territory in the year 1832.

On motion of Mr. GILMER, it was

Resolved, That the President be requested to communicate to this House all papers which he may have received from, or correspondence which he may have had with, the Executive department of Georgia upon the subject of the boundary line between the State of Georgia and the Territory of Florida, which has not already been communicated to this House.

On motion of Mr. WATMOUGH,

Resolved, That the Committee on Commerce be instructed to inquire into the expediency of extending the limits of the port of entry and delivery of the port of Philadelphia northwardly to the foot of Hanover street, in the district of Kensington.

Mr. EWING, of Indiana, submitted the following:

Resolved, That the Committee on Military Affairs—in considering the resolutions already referred, upon the subject of a national armory on the western waters—be instructed to embrace the Wabash and White rivers, in the State of Indiana.

Mr. SEVIER moved, as an amendment, to append the words, "and the waters of the Arkansas river, in the Territory of Arkansas."

To this Mr. EWING objected, as he did not perceive the necessity so urgent of extending the benefits contemplated to the Territory of Arkansas, as there existed to extend them to the waters on the northwestern frontiers in Indiana.

Mr. SEVIER briefly supported the claims of the Territory which he had the honor to represent, to be included in the benefits to be derived from the adoption of the resolution. The gentleman from Indiana talked of cornstalk militia; but he believed if they were to be found at all, they would be rather found in his own State. Arkansas was entitled to some attention from the House; for whilst other States got several hundred thousand acres of land, to enable them to make roads and canals, this Territory got nothing but that which she procured for herself.

Mr. ASHLEY wished to submit an amendment to the amendment.

Mr. SPEIGHT rose, not to prolong the discussion, but to apprize the House that this matter was already before the committee for consideration, and that it was unnecessary for further resolutions to be offered, as before the committee would come to any conclusion, they would necessarily take this subject into their consideration.

Mr. MASON remarked, that after what had been stated by the preceding member, he would, to save the time of the House, move to lay the resolution on the table.

Which motion prevailed.

PENSION LAWS.

The order of the day was then declared to be the resolution of Mr. CHILTON, to appoint a select committee to inquire into the expediency of so extending the general pension law as to embrace within its provisions those persons who were engaged in the Indian wars, down to the year 1794; and the amendment of it by Mr. BOULDIN, to appoint a committee to inquire into the moral effects of the pension system upon the community, and how far it ought to be abolished or repealed.

Mr. LAY, of New York, who had the floor from the previous day, rose and said, that it was not his intention to detain them long; neither did he intend to go over the whole ground covered by the debate which had so long occupied the House; as he should confine himself to an examination of the principles involved in the propositio is submitted, and by which their respective merits should be tested. It had been pressed upon the consideration of the House, and urged by the honorable members from Kentucky [Messrs. HARDIN and POPE] with much force and plausibility, that the contest with the savages in what had been termed "the Indian wars on our frontiers," was "but a 'continuation of the revolutionary struggle; and 'that, on this account, the individuals engaged 'were entitled to the same pecuniary recompense 'awarded to the soldiers of the Revolution." From an examination of the facts in the case, it will readily be seen that there is no analogy whatever between a claim for remuneration for services rendered by the persons contemplated in this resolution, and the cases provided for by the bill to compensate the officers and soldiers of the revolutionary war. The character and nature of the two cases are entirely distinct and dissimilar. The claims of the revolutionary soldier were not merely equitable, but legal in the strict sense of the word, and were peculiarly addressed to the justice and honor of the nation; whilst, on the contrary, the

claims of those sought to be embraced by the original resolution of the honorable member from Kentucky, [Mr. Chilton,] appeal solely to our sympathies and generosity, and do not possess any of those strong and peculiar features which justified Congress in passing the bill to compensate the surviving officers and soldiers of the Revolution. One was a debt, acknowledged to be due for services rendered under a contract made with the Government under the old Confederation, and which every sense of national faith, justice, and honor, required us to cancel; the other, a claim where the services performed were for the protection of the person and property of individuals who have already received a full and adequate compensation, yet who now demand of Government a permanent pension for having protected them.

Had the claims of the revolutionary soldier no other basis than that growing out of the perils, the sufferings, and the privations of those who successfully fought the battles of our country, and by a perseverance and courage unparalleled in the annals of history, steadily adhered to the principles of the Declaration of Independence,—he had no hesitation in saying that the present pension system would never have been adopted. No, sir; had this been the principle, it would have been in vain at this time for the friends of this proposition to have sought for a precedent which could, by any analogy of reasoning, or any perversion of language, have justified the adoption of this resolution. The obligation of the Government to remunerate the patriotic soldier, who had sealed his devotion to the liberties of his country with his blood, and by years of the most toilsome and dangerous service, was never denied. It was always conceded by the constituted authorities of the Government, whenever the subject was discussed, that the old Congress had failed to comply with the spirit and morality of the contract made with our revolutionary soldiers, and that payment was only delayed in consequence of the embarrassments and poverty of our country. When, therefore, peace returned, and with it the agricultural and commercial interest of the United States had revived and infused new life and vigor into the exhausted and wasted energies of the country, she set the bright and glorious example of declaring to the world that the national character was of as much importance as independence, and that wealth and prosperity were but as dust in the balance compared with the dictates of humanity and justice.

The honorable member from South Carolina, [Mr. Pinckney,] to whose purity of feeling and correct purpose every member of this House will most cheerfully bear testimony, has been pleased to say in regard to this act, that it is not only unconstitutional, but partial in its benefits, oppressive in its operation and tendency. The indebtedness of the United States having always been admitted, it is now too late to discuss the constitutionality of the act. The sixth article of the Constitution expressly recognises the obligation of the Government to pay "all debts contracted, and 'engagements entered into, before the adoption 'of the Constitution; and that they should be as 'valid against the United States, under the Con'stitution, as under the Confederation." The principles of this act have been sanctioned by our most enlightened statesmen, and the gratitude of millions has hallowed its adoption. It is most unquestionably true, sir, that far the greater portion of that remnant of patriots, who were engaged in the service of their country in the revolutionary struggle, and who are now receiving a compensation under this act, reside in the northern States; but are they, on this account, the less entitled to a remuneration for services so meritorious as these are acknowledged to be by every member on this floor, and to which even the member from South Carolina has paid so handsome a tribute? Was not the war of the Revolution waged and carried on in defence of principles common and dear to every American citizen? Did not its successful termination bring liberty and independence to the South as well as the North? Is the justice and liberality of this Government, then, to be restricted by geographical lines or boundaries? Ought the legislation of Congress to be influenced by any prejudices growing out of sectional considerations? Do we stand here to represent the district or State only in which we reside? Surely not. The great body of the American people, by their representatives in Congress, are to be governed by more extended and liberal views—by far higher considerations. They are to legislate for the whole nation, not a part, and provide for and consult the general interest and welfare. The cause is obvious, and the answer easy, why so great a number of the revolutionary pensioners are to be found in the northern States. It was these States, sir, that furnished by far the greater proportion of troops for the contest, and the bones of our northern soldiers, who fell in this glorious struggle for life and liberty, now lie scattered through the land, in every portion of this Union, wherever danger assailed, or the interest of their country called them. The surviving few, whose claims have at length been recognised by a grateful country, are now, in a great degree, dependent upon the trifling pittance allotted to them; and which serves to comfort their declining years for the few days they may linger among us, before they shall be called away to join their co-patriots in arms, who have already gone before them; and for whom the acknowledgment of their services, by their country, came too late. Let not, then, the agitation of this question disturb the peace and quiet of this remnant of our revolutionary fathers now alive, nor let it embitter the evening of their days with the appalling apprehension of penury and want.

But whilst he differed from honorable members as to the policy and legality of the pension system, he agreed with them, and with the honorable member from New Hampshire, [Mr. Hubbard,] upon the propriety of rejecting the claims of those embraced in the resolution,—not but that the acts performed, and which have been so feelingly and eloquently portrayed, are highly meritorious and worthy of praise—not but that the individuals are entitled to all our sympathies and admiration; but simply because, in their case, they can have no possible claim upon the Government for services rendered, however beneficial and useful, beyond the express and implied terms of their contract.

It may be said, that it is the duty of every Government to protect its own citizens in their lawful pursuits and avocations. This, as a general proposition, is undoubtedly true, in time of peace as well as war; yet, who ever heard of an instance, even in our late war, when our whole western frontier was laid waste by the invading enemy, our villages laid in ashes, and our citizens, without regard to age, sex, or condition, shot down, butchered, and scalped by their Indian allies—where a pension has been given, even to one out of the thousands who daily, and without pay or remuneration, went forth as volunteers to meet and repel the enemy? The farthest that our Government have ever gone to sustain any principle which can be assimilated to this, has been to compensate sufferers for property taken and destroyed in war, under peculiar circumstances; but in no instance had the principle been extended so far as to remunerate our officers and soldiers beyond the terms of their contract or enlistment. To adopt such a principle at this time would be subversive of all the best interests and the true political economy of this Government. The evil would not stop with establishing a system which, by its terms, would embrace every individual in the service of the Government, either in the revolutionary or recent war; but, when once adopted as a precedent, its force and effect will be felt to be forever obligatory upon the country, and we shall have a pensioned army fastened upon and living upon the substance of the people; the consequence of which will be more dangerous, more oppressive, and more to be dreaded, than the odious pension system of Great Britain. In matters of such great and vital interest to this nation, the utmost care and caution should be used, lest by an indiscreet zeal for doing some particular act in which we have suffered our feelings to become too much enlisted, we inflict an irreparable injury on our country. We are placed here as the guardians of the public treasure; and as the trustees of the American people, it is our solemn duty to watch carefully, and deliberately examine every principle submitted, which has for its object the disbursement of that treasure, or the establishment of a precedent which is to be co-extensive with the Government.

Mr. L. argued at length to show the dangerous tendency of precedents, when a due regard to the interests of the country was lost sight of, and referred to several instances of the pernicious effect of such incautious legislation; after which, he continued and said, it was not necessary for him to go into a particular examination of the daring exploits and "hair-breadth escapes" of the several individuals who had immortalized themselves in border warfare and personal contests with the savages, the detail of which had excited such lively and thrilling interest; nor into the motives which induced the brave pioneers of the West, to leave their cultivated farms, their homes, and firesides, and penetrate into the recesses of the forest, whether influenced by the love of gain, the hunt and the chase, or that peculiar eccentricity characteristic of the old trapper, so beautifully described by our talented novelist, or that instinctive love of solitude, and of the charms of the forest, which induced the celebrated Boon, so often alluded to in this debate, to leave his habitation, and again plunge into the wilderness many hundred miles beyond the abode of civilized man, merely because, to use his own language, "a yankee had the audacity to come and plant himself directly under his nose, within one hundred and fifty miles of his cabin." All this it was not necessary for him to inquire into. Suffice it to say, that no precedent exists which will justify such an appropriation, nor can human ingenuity bring these cases within the principles established by the revolutionary pension bill, and no cause can be shown why a pension should be granted to those persons when thousands, even of our revolutionary veterans, are excluded from enjoying the liberal intentions of Congress, by the rigid construction of the pension laws. Mr. L. here argued to show that the same principle which would give pensions to those persons engaged in the conflicts with the Indians, would necessarily lead to the extension of the pension system to every person engaged in military service; and he contended that the soldier who fought at Queenstown, Chippewa, Lundy's Lane, and New Orleans, was more deserving, and better entitled to a pension, than they could possibly be; and he concluded by asserting that it was the principle of the resolution, and the inevitable consequences that would flow from it, that he condemned, and which, if once sanctioned, would bring ruin and beggary upon the country. These principles once adopted as a precedent, there would not be an instance of meritorious conduct, or of a conscientious discharge of duty, in any department of the Government, or even in private life, in which an individual may not, with the same propriety, demand a pension. He hoped, therefore, that the time of the House would not be longer occupied with the discussion of the resolution, for every incident, which could give strength to the claims, had been fairly presented, and its advocates had furnished every detail necessary for the House to form a deliberate opinion upon its merits. He must deprecate the idea of its being sent to a committee to be examined and reported upon, as this, in all probability, would only lead to a further protracted debate, and which was wholly unnecessary. Every member now fully understood the principles upon which the resolution was based, and was prepared to act upon it. He desired to have the question taken, and the resolution and the amendment both rejected.

Mr. BOULDIN rose to reply, but the hour allotted for morning business having expired,

The House proceeded to the consideration of private bills.

The resolution offered yesterday, for printing one thousand copies of the Navy Regulations, was adopted.

The House resumed the consideration of the bill for the relief of Arnold Henry Dohrman; which, after a long discussion, was ordered to a third reading.

The bill for the relief of John Moret was taken up, and, after some discussion, recommitted.

On motion of Mr. MARSHALL, of Kentucky,

The House took up, in the Committee of the Whole, the bill to provide for the settlement of certain commutation and other revolutionary claims.

The bill and the report accompanying it having been read, the committee rose and reported the bill to the House, without amendment; and the bill was then ordered to be engrossed and read a third time.

The House then adjourned.

IN SENATE.

MONDAY, February 10, 1834.

A message was received from the President of the United States, by Mr. DONELSON, his Private Secretary.

Mr. MOORE presented a memorial from the Legislature of Alabama, praying the establishment of a pension agency within that State; which was referred to the Committee on Finance.

Mr. MOORE presented a memorial from sundry citizens of Alabama, praying the establishment of pension agencies at Tuscaloosa and Montgomery; which was referred to the same committee.

Mr. MOORE presented a memorial from the Legislature of Alabama, stating that the 16th section of the public lands, reserved for the use of schools, in many instances was utterly valueless, and praying Congress for the privilege of changing such entries, when occasion called for it. The memorial was laid upon the table.

Mr. CHAMBERS presented the memorial of a large number of the inhabitants of the city of Washington, praying aid from Congress relative to the debt incurred by the Corporation in subscribing for stock in the Chesapeake and Ohio Canal Company. Referred to the Committee on the District of Columbia.

Mr. CHAMBERS, in pursuance of notice, introduced a bill for the benefit of the Baltimore and Susquehanna Railroad Company.

Which was read twice, and referred to the Committee on Finance.

Mr. HENDRICKS, from the Committee on Roads and Canals, to whom was referred the memorial of the President and Directors of the Pontchartrain Railroad Company, asked to be discharged from the further consideration of the same, and that it be referred to the Committee on Commerce; which was agreed to.

Mr. TOMLINSON, from the Committee on Pensions, made an unfavorable report on the petition of John Smith, which was read and ordered to be printed.

Mr. KING, of Alabama, presented a memorial of the Legislature of that State. The memorial states that Congress had granted 400,000 acres of land for the improvement of the navigation at the Muscle Shoals; all the good lands had been disposed of, and the object of the Legislature was to ask Congress to permit the refuse lands to be sold for what they would bring. The memorial was referred to the Committee on Public Lands, and, on motion of Mr. MOORE, was ordered to be printed.

Mr. KING, of Alabama, presented the petition of the trustees of the Female Academy at Franklin, praying a grant of four sections of land. Referred to the Committee on Public Lands.

Mr. WEBSTER, from the Committee on Finance, reported a bill from the House of Representatives making appropriations for the payment of revolutionary pensioners, without amendment.

Mr. TYLER, from the Committee on Finance, reported a bill for the benefit of the crew of the privateer Rodgers.

Mr. CLAYTON presented two memorials from inhabitants of Delaware, asking aid of Congress in improving the navigation of the Christiana; which was referred to the Committee on Commerce.

Mr. TIPTON, from the Committee on Claims, reported a bill from the House of Representatives, without amendment, for the benefit of certain inhabitants of the frontiers of the States of Illinois and Indiana.

Mr. CHAMBERS presented the memorial of the President and Directors of the Baltimore and Susquehanna Railroad Company. Referred to the Committee on Finance.

Mr. TALLMADGE presented the petition of the heirs of Major General Lord Stirling, of the revolutionary army; which was referred to the Committee on Military Affairs.

Mr. WILKINS presented the proceedings and resolutions of a large meeting recently held at Pittsburg, disapproving of the course of the Secretary of the Treasury in removing the deposites. The proceedings were read, referred to the Committee on Finance, and ordered to be printed.

Mr. WILKINS also presented the proceedings and resolutions of a numerously-attended meeting of citizens of Philadelphia, approving of the course pursued by the Secretary of the Treasury in removing the deposites, and advocating the public measures of the Executive of the United States. Read and referred to the Committee on Finance, and ordered to be printed.

Mr. WILKINS presented the memorial of the Chamber of Commerce of Philadelphia and others, praying the reconstruction of a light-house in Delaware bay, near the Brandywine Shoals. Referred to the Committee on Commerce.

Mr. KENT presented the memorials of sundry citizens of Baltimore, praying aid for the improvement of that harbor; which was referred to the Committee on Commerce.

Mr. KENT also presented the petition of many of the inhabitants residing in the eastern section of Washington city, praying Congress would purchase the bridges over the Eastern Branch, in order to make them free. Referred to the Committee on the District of Columbia.

Mr. SOUTHARD presented the proceedings and resolutions of meetings held in New Jersey, the one in the county of Morris, in the eastern part of the State, the other in the county of Burlington, in the western part, disapproving of the course of the Secretary of the Treasury in removing the deposites. Read and referred to the Committee on Finance.

Petitions of a private nature were submitted by Messrs. PORTER, BIBB, WAGGAMAN, and WILKINS; which were referred to the usual committees.

RESOLUTIONS.

The following resolutions were submitted during the morning:

By Mr. TOMLINSON:

Resolved, That the Committee on Commerce be instructed to inquire into the expediency of making an appropriation to complete and secure the works at Cedar Point, in the State of Connecticut.

By Mr. CHAMBERS:

Resolved, That the Committee on Military Affairs be instructed to inquire into the expediency of making an appropriation for the expediency of the first and second class, as projected by the Board of Engineers, for the defence of the city of Baltimore.

By Mr. HENDRICKS:

Resolved, That the Committee on Naval Affairs be instructed to inquire into the expediency of authorizing the accounting officers of the Treasury Department to adjust and settle the claims of Lieutenant James Noble, of the United States Navy, for services as lieutenant on board the Dolphin, and until his return to the United States, from the 10th March, 1830, to the 1st December, 1832.

Resolved, That the Committee on Pensions be instructed to inquire into the expediency of granting a pension to Henry L. Montain, of Indiana, and that his papers be referred to said committee.

By Mr. HENDRICKS:

Resolved, That the Committee on the Post Office and Post Roads be instructed to inquire into the expediency of establishing a post route from Jeffersonville, by way of Charlestown, Indigan Collins's, Vienna, Slateford, Stanfield's Mills, and Rockford, to Indianapolis, or so much thereof as may not heretofore have been established by law.

At one o'clock, on motion of Mr. WEBSTER, the Senate proceeded to Executive business, and, after spending some time therein,

Adjourned.

HOUSE OF REPRESENTATIVES.

MONDAY, February 10, 1834.

BANK OF THE UNITED STATES.

Mr. CAMBRELENG presented four memorials, all relating to the present condition of the country, and proposing modes of relief. The first memorial was from the merchants of New York engaged in the foreign trade of the country, praying for the establishment of a warehousing system. The act of 1833 would effectually destroy the carrying trade in dutiable articles, unless some such remedy should be promptly applied. The operation of that act since the 4th of March last, had almost prostrated that branch of trade; it had withdrawn a capital equal to more than twenty millions of dollars. The amount existing on the 1st January, 1833, was twenty-one millions and a half. We have not only (said Mr. C.) withdrawn that vast capital from one branch of trade since the 4th of March last, but we have compelled our importers to advance the revenue to the Government. It is impracticable, under that act, to realize the amount of duty from the sales before they are obliged to advance. Under this double operation, this single branch of trade had been called upon for thirty millions, one-half of which at least had been called upon from the city of New York. I am not, sir, for constituting Government a borrower or a lender to any branch of trade. The terms of credit should not be so long as to encourage age injudicious speculations, nor so short as to embarrass and restrict the foreign trade. They should be so graduated as to enable the importer to realize the duty by sale of the merchandise before he is called upon to pay the duty.

Gentlemen may save themselves the trouble of devising means to employ our surplus revenue at the end of the year—the operation of the act of July, 1832, would cause a large reduction in importations of dutiable articles, and he was much mistaken if there would not be a very considerable falling off in the revenue of the present year; unless foreign trade could not recover or flourish, unless some remedy is speedily applied. If gentlemen are sincerely desirous of extending relief to this branch of trade, let them come forward, establish a warehousing system, permit importers to deposite their merchandise for three years, and to pay the duty in three and six months from the date of the entry for consumption. We hear much, sir, about measures of relief. There is none that can be proposed which would afford more substantial and permanent relief of the foreign trade of the country, a branch of trade which has been fatally embarrassed by our own measures.

The second memorial which I shall present, is from the "workingmen of New York, against paper money, and in favor of the constitutional currency." The currency proposed by the memorialists is that which was contemplated by the framers of the Constitution; and well would it have been for the country, had we never, since 1789, introduced by law, another of a fluctuating character. I am surprised to hear the language lately reiterated upon the subject of a metallic currency. However we may differ about the remedy, I had heretofore supposed that gentlemen all agreed that the bank note circulations of the country were sustained by too small a metallic basis, to secure stability to commercial credit and steady employment to the laboring classes. It is unnecessary for gentlemen to be alarmed or to attempt to spread unfounded apprehensions. No one proposed to rush headlong from one extreme to the other. Whatever reform might be attempted should be effected by slow degrees, and with a just regard to the existing condition of the trade of the country. No interest should be disturbed or deranged by any abrupt measures. Sir, I am of those who believe it practicable to reclaim our gold coin from foreign countries, and that it is to such very difficult matter for the trade of this commercial country to abstract from the four thousand millions of the current coin of the world, one hundredth part, to be added to the existing metallic circulations of our country. But whatever reformation of the currency shall be attempted, it must be made gradually; and I hope, sir, that gentlemen who profess sound regard for the soundness of our currency, will, at least, throw no impediment in the way of those anxious as we are to improve its character, without interrupting the prosperity of the country, and to secure permanent and great stability to the operations of trade and industry.

Sir, I have two other memorials to present, signed by more than ten thousand of my fellow-citizens, and other memorials to the same effect are yet to come; praying that the deposites may not be restored, and that the Bank of the United States

may not be rechartered. Under the peculiar circumstances which produced these memorials, I feel a proud satisfaction in presenting them to this House. They speak the language of independent men, of a community suffering under oppression, but determined never to submit to their oppressors, or to surrender their rights. The Bank of the United States has made a bold experiment upon the country. Since the commencement of this session, its presses and its friends abroad—ay, sir, even the capitalists of this country—have been instrumental in an attempt to destroy commercial confidence, by circulating the most alarming predictions of approaching ruin and calamity. These rumors of distress, of frightful disasters, of panic, have been echoed here by distinguished gentlemen of both Houses. Sir, no other country upon earth could have stood firm under such a general attack upon commercial confidence as has been made by the bank and its friends abroad during the last seventy days. If the distinguished men of both Houses of Parliament had indulged in the same gloomy anticipations, had they for more than two months predicted universal wreck and ruin, and general panic, it would have broken half the country banks in England, and half their merchants and manufacturers. It is, sir, a bold experiment of the Bank of the United States, and has fallen with dreadful severity upon my constituents; produced many bankruptcies, and ruined many families. But, sir, were their losses and sufferings ten times as great, so long as they are animated with the spirit of freemen, they will never subject a Government of their own to the dominion of the Bank of the United States. These memorials, sir, are the result of the policy pursued by the bank, and such will be the sentiment of the country. This experiment upon the fears of the country has totally changed the question; it is no longer a contest between the bank and the treasury, or the Executive; it is a question between the bank and the people; a question between the moneyed power of a corporation and popular sovereignty. Gentlemen had understood the intelligence and patriotism of the people, and this last experiment would fail. But, sir, whatever may be the political result, I hope those who have been instrumental in destroying commercial confidence, by predicting ruin, will unite with us in endeavoring to restore it. I trust, sir, that the ninety days referred to by a gentleman [Mr. SELDEN] at the commencement of the session, are now drawing to a close, and that we are approaching those days of grace when the Bank of the United States will, in its mercy, relieve the country. I hope, sir, the bank will do now what it ought to have done two months ago—announce to the local banks that they have nothing to fear from its measures—and restore confidence. The president and directors have now no apology for persisting in its mysterious course towards the State banks. Nay, sir, they have been called upon by their own friends—they have been admonished to change their course—the mandate has been issued from the other wing of the Capitol. It cannot be misunderstood, and I have no doubt it will be obeyed, and that commercial confidence will be once more restored. Sir, if gentlemen really intend to do something for the relief and permanent benefit of the country, let them reëstablish our foreign trade on a secure foundation, either by a warehousing system or by extending the credit on duties. And if they wish to secure a durable prosperity to trade, and a steady employment to labor, let them unite with us in our measures to enlarge the metallic basis of our circulation, and improve the condition of our currency. Mr. C. concluded by moving the reference of these memorials to the Committee of Ways and Means.

The memorials were then referred accordingly.

Mr. SELDEN presented a memorial of working men, mechanics, and others, in the city of New York, detailing their present embarrassments, which they attribute to the derangement of the currency; and praying Congress to restore the deposites to the Bank of the United States, or to adopt other measures for their relief.

Mr. S., to give some idea of the present distress in that city, said that there were upwards of ten thousand workingmen generally employed in the building of houses, but who, owing to the present pressure for money, were now out of employment, no contracts being made for the putting up of buildings. He was happy to hear from his colleague, [Mr. CAMBRELENG,] that there was something contemplated to alleviate their distress; that it was at length intimated that the intention of resorting at once to a metallic currency was abandoned, and that that project would be only gradually proceeded with. With respect to what had fallen from his colleague as to the prophecy he had made in the beginning of the debate on the restoration of the deposites, "that unless Government retrace their steps within ninety days, there must be produced a scene of wide-spread and unexampled ruin," he would ask, was not his colleague satisfied that the prophecy had been unfortunately verified? Had there not been seen, and within the time specified, at their doors, the merchants and mechanics of almost all their principal towns and cities, stating their distress, and praying Congress to adopt some measures for their relief? He had then been justified in the view which he had presented so early to the House. He now regretted that the memorial presented by his colleague had not been read, that it might be seen whether a very important part, and which, if the journals were to be believed, was subsequently appended to it, went to confirm the memorial presented by him, and equally called on the House for relief. He desired that the memorial he presented should be read, and would state to the House that it was signed by three thousand persons.

The memorial was then read, and referred to the Committee of Ways and Means.

Mr. MUHLENBERG presented the proceedings of a meeting held in the town of Lancaster, Pennsylvania, on the subject of the currency. The meeting was large and respectable, and they adopted resolutions highly approving of the removal of the deposites; referred, and ordered to be printed.

Mr. CHAMBERS presented the memorial of a public meeting held in Franklin county, Pennsylvania, on the subject of the public distress. The memorialists were not stockjobbers, but farmers and millers. They attribute the distress to the removal of the deposites, and request their restoration. Read, and ordered to be printed.

Mr. DENNY presented the memorial of a meeting of citizens held in Pittsburg, representing the embarrassed condition of their business, and praying the adoption of measures for their relief. Mr. D. spoke at considerable length in support of the views of the memorialists; and, on his motion, the proceedings of the meeting were referred to the Committee of Ways and Means, and ordered to be printed.

Mr. BINNEY rose to present a memorial of the Chamber of Commerce of Philadelphia, requesting an appropriation to be made for rebuilding a light-house on the Brandywine shoal of the Delaware.

Mr. BINNEY also presented a memorial from the merchants, mechanics, manufacturers, traders, &c., of the city and county of Philadelphia, praying that the Government deposites should be restored to the United States Bank. In doing this, he embraced the opportunity of animadverting upon the impropriety of violating the rules of the House by those (presenting petitions) who made the occasion a means of commenting upon the topics agitating the House in other discussions, which are irrelevant to the subject before the House. One violation begets others in replies. He would therefore content himself with making a simple statement of the memorial; and nothing more is necessary than to notice the simple facts announced in the paper; the connexions, characters, and occupations, the present and apprehended amount of sufferings, and the numbers of those who have signed the appeal to the representatives of the nation. These facts ought to surpass any arguments which could be presented by the most commanding and persuasive eloquence. If, by famine, pestilence, or any plague, and not by the conduct of the Administration, the memorialists had been reduced to the state of suffering which they have described, it would excite a throb in the hearts of all, and plead for sympathy and relief. He trusts that still there will be those who have ears to hear, and hearts to feel, who will not have their understandings misled, and who will not deny the existence of the calamity, nor refuse the proper remedy.

The memorial was signed by 10,259 residents of the city and county of Philadelphia, each name having attached to it the trade or profession of the subscriber, so that the authenticity of the whole proceeding might be better ascertained. The gentleman under whose immediate protection the memorial was got up, took care to exclude the name of every minor, and of every person not a resident in Philadelphia. Nearly every profession or calling in that city, and every species of property, are represented by those who subscribed the memorial. The subscribers, he said, are intelligent men, and of practical experience, competent to estimate the causes of the calamity and suffering they assert. Nor is the memorial the production of a party: for all feel the pressure; and bankruptcy, want, and beggary is likely to know no distinction of parties. If no relief is afforded in time, all party distinctions will be broken into *one* which bankruptcy, want, and beggary have made—a party ruined and undone.

The memorial breathes the language of men who feel their suffering, and are competent to ascertain the cause and point out the remedy. They are in the midst of distress; yet they have the foresight to apprehend that their distress will be made greater if means are not taken to remove it. They represent that one part of the citizens will suffer insolvency and bankruptcy; and that the other will be destitute of food and raiment. They believe—and he also believes—that their suffering arises from the total destruction of confidence in every branch of business; and this destruction they attribute to the removal of the deposites.

Mr. B. continued, saying that the present state of things is quietly, secretly, and imperceptibly undermining all the State banks; that their notes are at a discount and still going down; and that shortly they will be compelled to stop specie payments. He asserted that the deposites did not so much go into the State banks as *into* the private coffers of individuals, who were thus resolved to sustain themselves in the day of anticipated calamity. He added, that nothing but the restoration of public confidence could remedy the evils complained of; and this could be produced only by a restoration of the confidence between the General Government and the Bank of the United States.

He moved that the memorial be read, and printed entire, with the signatures and occupation of the subscribers. Unwilling to provoke any discussion on its reference, he moved that it be referred to the Committee of Ways and Means.

Mr. SUTHERLAND presented a memorial from inhabitants of the 8th Congressional district, also, one from a number of Democrats who lately assembled at the court-house of the city of Philadelphia, against the restoration of the deposites. The signers of the memorial say, that this is the general voice of their party, and he would remark, that it spoke the voice of what he apprehended would be the larger portion of the inhabitants of that city.

The SPEAKER presented memorials on the same subject, from Moyamensing and Harrisburg, Pennsylvania.

Mr. WATMOUGH presented one from the 3d Congressional district, Philadelphia, in favor of the restoration of the deposites; all which memorials were referred to the Committee of Ways and Means.

Mr. W. presented another from the same district, *against* the restoration of the deposites.

Mr. SPEIGHT called for the reading of the memorial.

Mr. WATMOUGH did not object to its being read; but he desired to have the other one also read.

The SPEAKER said that the first memorial having been referred, it was not in order now to call for the reading.

The memorial *against* the restoration of the deposites having been read—

Mr. WATMOUGH insisted that this memorial having been read, it was only an act of justice to his constituents to have the first one also read; he had not moved this, originally, being unwilling to consume the time of the House, and he did not suppose any gentleman would withhold such an act of courtesy.

The SPEAKER called Mr. W. to order. It was not in order to reflect upon any member;

Mr. SPEIGHT disclaimed having been actuated by any motives to treat the gentleman with disrespect. He called for the reading of the last memorial, as he had in presenting the other, favored the House, if not with elaborate, certainly with a very strong statement.

Mr. WATMOUGH was happy to hear the disclaimer, and moved the suspension of the rule, in order that the memorial might be read; and upon this motion, he asked the yeas and nays.

The House refused to order the yeas and nays, and the motion to suspend the rule was rejected.

Mr. WATMOUGH moved to re-consider the vote referring the memorial to the committee, in order that he might call for its reading. Rejected, 88 to 102.

Mr. LANE presented the petition of the citizens of Ripley and Switzerland counties, in the State of Indiana, and of the county of Gallatin, in the State of Kentucky, praying the establishment of a mail route from Georgetown, in the State of Kentucky, by the way of Owington, Ghent, Verry, Mount Sterling, Cross Plains, and Versailles, to Napoleon, in the State of Indiana; to be conveyed in stages.

Mr. WHITE, of Florida, submitted the following resolution, which lies one day on the table:

Resolved, That the Secretary of War be directed to communicate to this House the correspondence and reports of the agents charged with superintending the repairs of the fort and sea-wall at St. Augustine, Florida, or such parts as will show its condition, with an estimate of the sum required to complete the improvements, and also the report and estimate for the completion of the improvements of certain rivers and roads in Florida.

Mr. J. Q. ADAMS submitted the following resolution, which lies one day for consideration:

Resolved, That the following be adopted as one of the standing rules for conducting business in this House, to follow immediately after the fifty-seventh rule:

At every session of Congress, commencing on the first Monday of December, it shall be the duty of the Committee of Ways and Means, within thirty days after their appointment, to report the general annual appropriation bills for the support of Government, of the army and navy, and for the Indian department, and Indian annuities; or, on failure thereof, the reasons of such failure.

Mr. HAWES submitted the following resolution, which lies one day on the table:

Resolved, That the Secretary of War be instructed to communicate to this House the names and numbers of all the cadets who have been received into the United States Military Academy, in each year, from the 31st of December, 1829, till the present time; the States and Territories, including the District of Columbia, from whence they came, respectively, distinguishing between those who have been graduated and have received commissions and those who have withdrawn or have been dismissed from the institution; stating, also, the names and number of those graduates now in the army of the United States, and designating (as far as practicable) those whose fathers or guardians were, or now are, members of Congress, or Governors of States or Territories, or holding offices in the District of Columbia.

On motion of Mr. MARDIS, the House suspended the rule, to permit him to offer the following resolution:

Resolved, That the Committee on the Post Office and Post Roads be instructed to inquire into the expediency of establishing the following post routes in Alabama: from Erie, Green county, to Livingston, Sumpter county; from Marion, Perry county, to Cahawba, Dallas county; from Pickensville, Pickens county, to Jackson, Mississippi; from Benton Court-house, Benton county, via Kelly's Spring, to the Court-house in Talladega county; and from thence to Wetumpka, Alabama.

Mr. CAVE JOHNSON reported a bill supplemental to an act passed for the final adjustment of land claims in Louisiana.

Mr. HARPER, a bill for the relief of William Harrison and others.

Mr. R. M. JOHNSON, a bill to provide more effectually for the defence of the Arkansas frontier.

Mr. McKINLEY, a bill for the relief of Ebenezer Reed.

Mr. JARVIS, from the Committee on Public Buildings, reported a resolution that Robert Mills be paid 1,000 dollars out of the contingent fund of the House, for his services as architect in making alterations, &c., in the Hall.

Mr. J. remarked, that Mr. Mills had been employed by the last House of Representatives to make the alterations, which conduced so much to their comfort; and he thought the present House were only performing an act of justice in paying him.

Mr. WHITTLESEY objected to the resolution, as he contended that the subject should be referred to the Committee of Claims, that they might report upon it.

Mr. HAWES moved an amendment to strike out 1,000 dollars and insert 250 dollars.

After a few brief remarks by Mr. JARVIS in support of the resolution—

Mr. EWING moved to recommit the resolution to the Committee on Public Buildings, with a view that further experiments might be made to improve the Hall, which at present was so constructed that scarcely a word of the ordinary business could be heard whilst in progress.

Mr. PARKER objected to the payment being made out of the contingent fund:

After a few brief remarks from Messrs. BURGES and EVANS, the resolution was recommitted to the Committee of Claims.

The House went into Committee of the Whole on the state of the Union, Mr. THOMSON in the chair, and considered the bill making appropriation for the commissariat for 1834.

The bill was considered, and having been reported to the House, was ordered to be engrossed for a third reading to-morrow.

The House then adjourned.

IN SENATE.

TUESDAY, February 11, 1834.

Mr. McKEAN presented a memorial signed by 10,250 citizens of Philadelphia, relative to the pecuniary distress, assigning the cause to be the removal of the Government deposites from the Bank of the United States.

Mr. McKEAN rose and said, he had been honored with the charge of a memorial, signed, as he had been informed, by about ten thousand citizens of the city and county of Philadelphia, complaining of the existence of great distress and pressure in that community, which they attributed to the removal of the Government deposites. Mr. McK. said he had been waited on by a very respectable committee of gentlemen from that city, now here, who expressed their views to him at length on the subject. And although he differed from them in opinion as to the causes of the distress and pressure, yet he could no longer disbelieve the fact that such a state of things did exist there. He moved that the memorial be read, referred to the Committee on Finance, and printed. He also presented a letter from that committee to himself, which he desired might be read.

After the memorial had been read,

Mr. CLAY suggested that the motion of the gentleman from Pennsylvania might comprehend the printing of the signatures, and the accompanying letter; which

Mr. McKEAN assented to.

After some remarks by Mr. WEBSTER, the memorial was referred.

Mr. GRUNDY, from the Committee on the Post Office and Post Roads, reported a bill for the regulation of the Post Office Department, with amendments; which was ordered to be printed.

Mr. MANGUM presented the preamble and resolutions of a meeting held in Burke county, N. C., of a similar character with those presented a few minutes before by Mr. McKEAN.

Mr. BROWN asked for the reading of the paper; and the paper was accordingly read.

Mr. MANGUM then sent a letter to the table, which he desired might be read.

The letter having been read—

Mr. BROWN rose and said, that although he had not been apprized, but a few moments before, that this preamble and resolutions were to be presented to the Senate, he felt it to be his imperative duty, as one of the representatives of the State of North Carolina, on this floor, in consequence of the tone of this preamble and resolutions, and of the remarks of his colleague, to take the present occasion to explain some of his views in reference to this subject.

He was one of those who, in his representative capacity, felt every disposition to respect public opinion, whenever that opinion could be properly ascertained. Whenever he should be brought to feel a settled conviction that the opinion of the people of North Carolina was in opposition to the course which he had felt it to be his duty to take on great political measures, and whenever that opinion should be fairly presented to him, he would be either prepared to obey it, or to relinquish the seat which he had the honor to hold on this floor. If he did not adopt one of these alternatives, he should consider that he was acting in opposition to the most principles of our republican institutions, and following the practice of those who, while they were issuing denunciations of Executive usurpations of power, were themselves acting in opposition to the expression of opinion of their own constituents, and were thus violating the great principles of republican government. But he could not consent to take the opinions of these petitioners, respectable as he admitted them to be, as the sense of the people of North Carolina. It was true that some of the signers of this paper had been supporters of the present Executive, but it was equally true that others of them were his decided opponents. From the tone of the resolutions, and the character of the newspapers selected for their publication, he inferred, indeed, that the greater number had been always in opposition to General Jackson. What were those papers? The National Intelligencer—the U. S. Telegraph—the Richmond Whig. He admitted that some of the signers of the paper were once among the friends of the Executive, but this document came to the Senate in a very questionable shape.

In regard to the great question which was agitating the country from one end of it to the other, his own opinion had been firmly and deliberately made up. From a view of all the circumstances, he was satisfied that the agitation and embarrassment which prevailed, resulted from the conduct of the bank itself, and the conduct of that political party, the existence of which seemed to depend on that of the bank. He should deem himself recreant to all republican principles, and to his own feelings, did he not place himself in zealous and determined opposition to such a course. What had been the course of the bank? When about eight millions were drawn from the bank—a sum small in comparison to its capital—every effort was immediately put in operation to produce distress and embarrassment in the country. While the bank thus put the screws down hard upon the people, politicians, men in high places, newspapers, the whole squadron of paid agents and corps, spread an alarm that the country was to be plunged into ruin by the removal of the deposites. Was not that conduct alone calculated to produce the distress which was foretold? Would it not alarm the capitalists of the country, the man who had any superfluous money, and prevent them from loaning to others? Unquestionably.

Believing, as he himself did, that the freedom and independence of the people and the maintenance of the Constitution depended on the issue of this contest, he would not consent for himself, and the State he represented, that they should be influenced by the cry of alarm which had been sent abroad. The public distress was a fertile theme for declamation; but could it be doubted that politicians feed on this distress; that it is the fund from which they draw their arguments, and they speculate on it to the greatest advantage? Let the condition of the bank be as unjustifiable as it could be, these gentlemen were uniformly skeptical; and be the action of the Executive as unexceptionable as it might, they could find nothing to justify.

There was another view which he was desirous

to present. He should be opposed now to the restoration of the deposites, because the inevitable result of such a measure would be the rechartering of the United States Bank. It was true, that it had been denied by many gentlemen that there was any connexion between the two questions. But what did they hear? Were they not told that it was impossible for the Government to carry on its financial operations without a fiscal agent; and that, without such agency, the whole of our revenue system would be involved in ruin? There were many who contended that the questions were distinct, and, while they were insisting on the restoration of the deposites, declared that they had no desire to touch the question of chartering the bank; but it was evident that, while affecting to hate the traitor, they cherished the treason. If the bank possessed all this power to cripple the commerce of the country, to shackle industry, and injure our markets, it was an establishment repugnant to the Constitution, and one which might ultimately seize the reins of Government. If it possessed all this tremendous power, in time of peace, what if, in the moment of war, it should take upon itself the power to control all the State banks? It was his settled opinion, that if, in a great war of national rights, the stockholders of the United States Bank should choose to array themselves against the Government, as was the case with some of the owners of capital in the late war, they could arrest all the operations of the country, stop the progress of resistance, and compel the Government to conclude a treaty—a disgraceful treaty. Could he sanction the institution when it was admitted to possess such power? Although he placed a high value on the honor of a seat on this floor, if he were constrained to hold it only as the advocate of such an institution, the seat would lose all its value in his estimation, and he would surrender it without regret.

What did the Senate already begin to see? In Pennsylvania, where the bank was situated, public opinion was rising up against it. The honest and indignant voice of the people were denouncing it. It had been tried by a jury of the vicinage—tried by its own State—and there was no doubt that the public judgment would be recorded against it. Entertaining these views, and without desiring to throw any imputation on other gentlemen, he had found himself impelled to offer them to the Senate. He could not doubt that his colleague, in presenting his remarks on offering the resolutions, had honestly obeyed the convictions of his mind; and, while he accorded this tribute of justice to him, he hoped to receive for himself an equal charity.

One word further. He protested against the influence of this bank being exerted in his State. He denied that the State was in any way dependent on the institution. There was never a greater degree of prosperity among the people than at this time. Its population consisted of industrious farmers, mechanics, and planters, and over these he denied that the bank had any control. They had their own resources, drawn from their industry, by means of which they carried on their own operations. No national bank could reach them. They were entirely beyond its influence and control.

It had been stated, in a letter presented by his colleague to the Senate, and which had been read, that some of the notes of the State banks had been at eight per cent. discount in the western part of North Carolina. That bank was in as good credit as any bank in the Union. It was a specie-paying bank, and all that he should say was, that if its notes were at a discount of eight per cent. in the State, it was a greater discount than was asked in New York, or anywhere else. In New York, he believed, the discount was only two per cent.; and it was strange indeed if it was two per cent. in New York, and eight per cent. at home. He had noticed in a recent paper, that commissioners had been appointed to receive subscriptions of stock for a new bank, and they were receiving the notes of the State Bank for stock, because it was a specie-paying bank. There was a difficulty in selecting a bank in the State for the public deposites, until there had been an action of the Legislature on the subject. His colleague had said, that the flame was extending in the mountain region; that this was one of the strongholds of the Ad-

ministration, but that the flame was spreading and threatening a general conflagration. Now, he himself had no doubt that North Carolina would sustain the Administration; that the opinions of the people, republican as they were, were decidedly against domestic foes as well as foreign enemies, and would support the Government against both. He had no doubt that these mountain men—mostly the descendants of that gallant band which so valiantly maintained the honor of their country at King's Mountain—would, on this occasion, exhibit a firmness and courage which would not dishonor the achievement of that day.

Mr. BENTON asked, what could be the object in printing so many names as were appended to this memorial, twice over? They had been ordered to be printed in the other House already.

Mr. WEBSTER said that the gentleman from North Carolina [Mr. Brown] had adverted to the rates of exchange of certain bank notes. He said that the bills of North Carolina were at a discount of two per cent. The prices current of January 24th last, rate the notes of North Carolina at a discount of five per cent. Those of Kentucky at from five to eight. Alabama eight to twelve. The notes of Louisiana and Mississippi at eight to twelve. In these States, in August last, North Carolina notes were at one and a half to two. South Carolina one and a half to two. Kentucky four to six; and he supposed these indications of the currency and rate of exchange were as correct as any. He had but one word more to say. The gentleman had repeated what had often been repeated, and what was a subject only fit for a further inquiry, that the bank was making every effort to produce the pressure and distress which now exists. Would the gentleman tell us what the bank has done, and what it should not do? He surely did not mean to take up the common cry, founded upon no data. If the bank has not discounted to the utmost of its ability, show us the grounds for the objection. What is his grounds? So far as we know, it has not curtailed a dollar of its accommodations beyond the amount of deposites removed from it. We see from its condition in New York, where it had three millions of deposites, and has now but $75,000, it has discounted to the amount of half a million. This did not seem like screwing down the community. Mr. W. wished what the bank had done to be known, and so far as there was any known fact in relation to its conduct, he should interrupt no gentleman in exposing it. But he thought the charge ought to be made so that the people may judge whether the bank was in fault or not.

Mr. BIBB was one of those who desired to repel the idea of wishing to recharter the United States Bank. He was no bank man, and never had been. He was hostile to that bank, and to all the State banks; but if we were compelled to submit to one of many evils, he would choose the least: he would rather oppose the whole system; but if he must submit to a tyrant, he would rather yield to one than to four hundred. The man who should invent a different sort of system than the present, which shall press so lightly upon the business, the debts and credits of the country, as that they cannot be materially affected by it, should have his hearty support. This, however, was not the question presented in these memorials, but it was convenient to seize on them as reasons for evading the true causes of the distress. There was nothing in the natural elements calculated to account for the distress; the multiplication of these memorials attested the fact of the stoppage of the money concerns of the country. There is a deep distress, a cold mildew which has benumbed the commercial and business transactions of the country. It is so, or gentlemen are inattentive to the sources of information; they are the representations of merchants, dealers, and traders, speaking the language of soberness and truth. The charter of the bank is a contract made by the authorities of the Government, and sanctioned by the Supreme Court of the United States; and now to refuse to abide by the terms of the contract and carry it into effect, would be to stultify the Congress which made the bank: for President Jackson to stultify President Madison. It is a contract for which a consideration has been given; and he, for one, would not be willing to tarnish the faith of the Government in the eyes of Europe and the civ-

ilized world by proclaiming that the former Congress did not know their duty. By the eighth article of the bank charter it was required and compelled to confine its debts within its capital, and by its charter it was bound to curtail its debts and its discounts in proportion to the reduction of its public and private deposites; and he would presume that it had done all this, until some actual case to the contrary was brought to his mind. He was a Republican; but he was equally opposed to the tumult of democracy as he was to the calm of despotism. He was in favor of the will of the people to be expressed in its most effective form.

Mr. BROWN wished to say a word or two in reply to the gentleman from Massachusetts. He had referred to the rate of exchange, to show the value of North Carolina and other notes at Philadelphia. I [said Mr. B.] had remarked that North Carolina notes of the State Bank were at two or three per cent. in the northern cities, and had inferred that they could not have depreciated down to eight per cent. in their own State, when they were at two per cent. at so remote a distance. It seemed that North Carolina notes were reported at only five per cent. discount in Philadelphia, which was not so much as the alleged discount in the western part of North Carolina.* But he considered the Philadelphia market to be an unsafe guide, as it was under the control of brokers who might be connected with the bank, and nothing could be more easy than for a combination of brokers, who wished to depreciate the price of notes for a few weeks, to do so. But they were not so omnipotent as to be able to do this for any length of time. There were no notes in better credit than those of the North Carolina State Bank, which was a specie-paying bank. The banks in the State were in the possession of public confidence; their charters were on the point of expiring, except one, which had been lately rechartered by the Legislature, and they were in the daily fulfilment of their obligations. The gentleman from Massachusetts had stated that he [Mr. B.] had made grave charges against the bank, and asked him for the proof. He thought that there was strong proof before the world. What was its conduct when the public deposites were at first removed? Did it not immediately curtail its discounts to an amount far beyond that which had been withdrawn? The gentleman from Pennsylvania [Mr. Wilkins] had, some days since, read a paper, to show that bills of exchange were sold on better terms by some of the State banks of Pennsylvania, than by the United States Bank, showing the disposition on the part of the United States Bank to embarrass domestic exchange. That was some proof. What other proof was there? Is rapid and great curtailment of its accommodations everywhere, except, perhaps, in New York, where it might have pursued a different policy. There was yet an amount of ten millions of specie in its vaults, yet it continued to reduce its discounts. The great danger was in the secret operations of the bank. If all its schemes could be developed, and the public could have a knowledge of all its secret machinery, which was employed in spreading distress through the community, they would discover that, like the electric stroke, it was not seen until it had fulfilled its fatal mission.

Mr. MANGUM said he reciprocated the kind feelings towards his colleague. The Philadelphia stock market had been objected to by him. Perhaps he would have none to the New York market, where the same prices prevailed. The question was not one of bank or no bank, but to restore the faith of the Government, and to repair the injury inflicted on it.

Mr. PRESTON entered the Senate Chamber with much agitation, just as Mr. Mangum had finished his remarks; when,

Mr. FORSYTH having obtained the floor, gave way to—

Mr. PRESTON, who said he did not rise with

a wish to interrupt the debate, but to announce the fact that he had just witnessed an awful occurrence. A distinguished member of the House of Representatives, [Mr. BOULDIN, of Virginia,] while in the discharge of his official duties, and actually upon the floor, addressing the Chair, had fallen from his position, and then lay a corpse in the Hall!

The Senate then, on motion of Mr. PRESTON, immediately adjourned.

HOUSE OF REPRESENTATIVES.

TUESDAY, *February* 11, 1834.

Mr. CLAY, from the Committee on Public Lands, reported a bill for the relief of George Davenport: read twice and committed.

Mr. CLAY gave notice that he would, on Tuesday next, move that the House go into Committee of the Whole on the state of the Union, on the "bill to reduce and graduate the price of the public lands," pursuant to instructions from the committee by whom the bill was reported.

Mr. WILLIAMS, from the Committee on Territories, reported a bill repealing certain acts of the Legislative Council of Florida: read twice and committed.

PAYMENT OF PENSIONS.

Mr. POLK, from the Committee of Ways and Means, reported "a bill to describe the mode of paying pensions heretofore granted by the United States," accompanied by a detailed report, as follows:

The Committee of Ways and Means, to whom was referred the message of the President of the United States, of the 4th of February, 1834, with the accompanying documents communicating to Congress the refusal of the Bank of the United States to deliver over to the order of the Secretary of War, the books, papers, and funds, connected with the disbursements to be made under the act of June, 1832, entitled "An act supplementary to the act for the relief of certain surviving officers and soldiers of the Revolution"—

REPORT

That they have given to the subject all the consideration which its importance demands, as well from its intrinsic character as from the class of most meritorious persons whose interests may be affected by the delay which may take place, in the payment of the sums respectively due to them, in consequence of the refusal of the Bank of the United States to deliver over the funds heretofore provided by law for their payment, together with the books and papers connected with its disbursement.

The bank, by the appointment of the Secretary of War, has heretofore been the disbursing agent of the Government, under the act of June 7, 1832, "for the relief of certain surviving officers and soldiers of the Revolution." In ordinary circumstances, all disbursing officers are responsible for the faithful performance of the duty assigned them, and are removable by, the Executive. This control over them has been deemed essential to the correct performance of their duty, as well as to the just security of the public interests. The bank, however, under the act of June 7, 1832, claims to be the disbursing officer of the Government independent of the appointment of the Executive, to hold the office by law, and to be beyond the power of removal by the executive authority. Such a claim, to be supported, should be clearly established, as it is at variance with the general principles of the Constitution and laws.

The committee, on an examination of the documents accompanying the President's message, find that an order was given by the Commissioner of Pensions, which order was authorized by the Secretary of War, for removing from the Bank of the United States and its branches, to the local banks of deposite, at places where such local banks had been selected, the books, papers, and funds, relating to the execution of the act of June 7, 1832. With this requisition the bank has declined a compliance, on the ground that the bank is constituted by law the agent for making payments under the act of 1832, and that the Secretary of War has consequently no right to transfer these duties to any other agent.

The question is, therefore, one of authority between one of the departments of the Government and the Bank of the United States, in which the bank has undertaken to retain the money and other property of the Government, until some measure, legislative or judicial, can be adopted, whereby the authority of the Executive over the public money and property, and the right claimed by the bank to retain them, can be determined, and provision made for their ultimate disposition.

The committee are of opinion that the bank has taken a position, and set up a claim to the possession of the funds, books, and papers in question, which cannot be supported. The opinion of the Attorney General, communicated by the President, contains a history of the agency of the bank in the payment of pensions, and of claims under the act of 1832, and also a full, and as the committee think, a correct view of the law of the case. To this opinion they refer, as greatly diminishing their labors on this part of the subject. It is conceded that, by various legislative enactments, direct and indirect, the bank was constituted the disbursing agent for paying invalid and revolutionary pensioners prior to and under the act of March 18, 1818. The Secretary of War has given no directions for the change of this agency, and the bank remains as it was, the disbursing officer for the payment of pensions under these laws. But the case is otherwise under the act of June 7, 1832. Under that act, the bank was not, by the terms, or any fair construction of the law, constituted the disbursing agent for paying the annuities which it granted. That act is supplementary to the act "for the relief of certain officers and soldiers of the army of the Revolution," passed May 15, 1828. These two acts form parts of the same system. The act of 1832 has reference to that of 1828, and the phraseology of both is nearly identical. They provide for making payments to the surviving officers and soldiers of the revolutionary army, in consideration of services, and the sums to be paid are denominated pay; and before any payment can be made under either of these laws, if the persons claiming their benefit are already receiving *pensions* under former laws, such pensions are required to be relinquished. No wounds are required to entitle a man to this "*monthly pay*," as they are agreeably to the system of the invalid pension laws; nor is poverty essential to this aid, as it is under the acts of March 18, 1818, and the act of May 1, 1820, supplementary thereto. But the whole claim seems to be placed on the ground of services, and, in consideration of them the "annuity" is given and received. The execution of both these acts was confided to the Secretary of the Treasury, and that officer was authorized to cause the payments to be made *at such times and places* as he thought proper. The act of 1828 provides "that the pay allowed by this act shall, under the direction of the Secretary of the Treasury, be paid to the officer or soldier entitled thereto, or to their authorized attorney, *at such places and days as the said Secretary may direct*." The act of 1832 provides "that *the pay allowed by this act* shall, under the direction of the Secretary of the Treasury, be paid to the officer, non-commissioned officer, musician, or private, entitled thereto, or his or their authorized attorney, at *such places and times as the Secretary of the Treasury may direct*." And both acts contain a permanent appropriation of the sums necessary to carry them into effect. The Secretary of the Treasury, under the authority given by the act of 1828, has caused the payment to be made at the Treasury directly to the individuals entitled. The bank never had any agency whatever under this law, nor is it known to the committee that they ever interposed any claim to make these payments. It is very clear that if the payments under the act of 1828 could be made at the Treasury, or at such other *place* as the Secretary of the Treasury might direct, without the intervention of the bank as the disbursing agent, so could the payments under the act of 1832 be made in like manner, had the execution of the act of 1832 remained with the Secretary of the Treasury. The execution of this act was, however, by a joint resolution of June 28th, 1832, devolved upon the Secretary of War, and the duties which the act required to be performed by the Secretary of the Treasury were "transferred to the Secretary of War." The Secretary of War was, by this resolution, clothed with the same authority to make payments to those entitled under the act of 1832, at such times and places as he might direct, as was previously possessed by the Secretary of the Treasury. In whatever mode the payments could have been made by the Treasury Department previous to the adoption of the resolution of June 28th, 1832, in the same mode they can be made at the War Department after the adoption of that resolution. The whole business, then, was to be done under the "direction" of the Secretary of War, and the payments made at such "*times and places*" as he may direct. It will not be disputed that the words of the law confer upon the Secretary of War a general supervisory authority over the payments to be made under it. They authorize the payments to be made whensoever, wheresoever, and by whomsoever the Secretary may direct. If the Secretary were to direct the payments to be made at the Treasury, (as by the law he has a clear right to do,) it surely cannot be maintained that an agent of the bank must stand by to receive the money and pass it over to those entitled. It surely cannot be contended that the money is not properly disbursed, unless it first pass through the hands of the bank. If the Secretary of War thinks the convenience of those entitled to pay under this act, or the public interest requires that places of payment should be designated where there are no branches of the United States Bank, may the bank, by refusing to establish an agency at such places, (and there is no law requiring them to do so,) defeat the contemplated arrangement? It appears to the committee, that the power confided to the Secretary of War, to designate *times* and *places* of payment, necessarily includes the authority to select the persons who are to act as agents in making the payments, as without such authority, the power to direct the *times* and *places* of payment would be wholly nugatory.

The committee are of opinion that upon no correct principles can the bank claim the legal right to make these payments—either in their character of commissioners of loans, or as disbursing agent of the Government. The charter does not confer on the bank the right of being in all cases the agent for the payment of pensions. It reserves to Congress the power to impose on the bank the duty which was before performed by the commissioners of loans; and as those commisioners, at the date of the bank charter, performed the duties of agent for paying the invalid pensions, the reservation in the charter authorized Congress to impose that duty on the bank. But Congress may or may not, at its own pleasure, exercise the power it has thus reserved. The bank can have no right to demand its exercise. The charter, therefore, in this respect, confers no right on the bank. It merely reserves to Congress the power to impose a duty, and the duty of the bank in this particular cannot be more extensive than the laws passed subsequently to the charter shall be found to require of it. The act of the 3d of March, 1817, made it the duty of the bank to pay, as agent, the pensions which, before that time, were paid by the commissioners of loans; but it does not require that all pensions afterwards created shall be paid in like manner by the bank. Its provisions are expressly confined to the duties which were then performed by the commissioners of loans, and no allusion is made in the law to pensions which may afterwards be created. The act of 1818 directs the pensions which it gave to be paid in the same manner as pensions to invalids had before that time been paid, and it is by virtue of this provision that the bank pays the pensioners under this law. But this act, like that of 1817, makes no general provision on the subject of paying pensions. It directs the manner in which the particular pensions it created should be paid; but it does nothing more.

From this statement it appears that the duty of pension agent has been imposed on the bank by law, in those cases where the pensions were given by the act of 1818, or by some previous act of Congress. But it is not the duty of the bank to act as pension agent in relation to pensions created since the law of 1818, unless some subsequent act of Congress has imposed that duty on it.

If, then, it be assumed that the payments under the act of 1832 are to be regarded as pensions,

yet the bank would not be bound to take upon itself that duty, unless it was required of it by act of Congress. For it is not enough that new pensions are created—there must also be some law directing the bank to act as agent in paying them; otherwise the bank can be nothing more than a voluntary agent, and at liberty, therefore, to surrender their trust whenever they think proper.

But there is no pretence that the law or resolution of 1832 contains any direction that the bank should act as agent in paying these claims. There is no reference in the law to any former act of Congress from which such an intention can be inferred, even by the most strained and forced construction; and, therefore, if these *payments* be considered *pensions*, in the legal sense in which the word is used in the acts of Congress, yet the duty of paying them has not been imposed on the bank, and they were not bound to perform the duty, unless they supposed it to be their interest to do so.

There is another point of view in which the subject presents itself, and which it is believed is still more important; and that is the attitude assumed by the bank. They do not claim the books, papers, and funds, as belonging to them. These are confessedly the property of the Government. But they claim the right to retain the possession of them, not from any interest which they have in them, for this is disavowed, but merely that they may take care that the laws be faithfully executed. This is certainly a novel pretension, and it is believed is now for the first time asserted by a corporation, at least in the United States. By the Constitution, the execution of the laws is confided to the Executive.

The allegation of the bank, as contained in the letter of the president of the bank of January 23, 1834, that "it is no justification to the bank to obey any other authority," (than Congress,) "for 'if it pays money or transfers money, without the 'authority of Congress, its accounts may be dis- 'allowed by the accounting officers," does not, in the opinion of the committee, deserve to be seriously considered or refuted. It is impossible to conceive upon what grounds such an apprehension as is here pretended could be seriously entertained; for whatever authority the bank had to disburse the annuities under the act of June 7th, 1832, was derived, not from Congress, for the act directs the payments to be made "*under the direction of the Secretary*," but from their appointment as paying agent, by the Secretary of War; and if he gave the authority, it would be strange, indeed, if he could not revoke it. The public money had been placed in the hands of the bank, by order of the Secretary of War, and if he revokes that order, and directs the money to be returned to the treasury, or transferred to other agents, it is absurd to suppose that the bank, by obeying, should be in any way embarrassed in the settlement of their accounts. There was not the slightest ground for such a belief; and it cannot, therefore, be urged as any extenuation or apology for the course of the bank.

In no view of the subject can the bank, in the opinion of the committee, rightfully retain possession of the money and property of the Government. If the law of 1832 had constituted the bank (which the committee do not concede, but, on the contrary, maintain it did not) the paying agent of the Government, it would not necessarily follow that they must keep possession of these books, papers, and funds. Many cases might be conceived in which it would be not only proper, but the duty, of the Government to resume the possession of them. The books and papers might be wanted for copying, examination, or correction, or other conceivable purposes. The money appropriated for these payments might be accumulated in an unnecessary degree at a given point, and might be wanted elsewhere, in consequence of a diminished supply at other "*places*" designated by the Secretary for the payments. But the ground taken by the bank excludes all possibility of the exercise of this supervisory regulation of the head of the department, whose duty the law makes it to see that the "*pay*" allowed by the act shall be made under his "*direction*," and at such "*times*" and "*places*" as he may designate. The bank, in effect, says, we have decided that we are the proper agents to make the payments, and therefore the Government shall in no case have any power to withdraw the property which it has heretofore placed in our possession. Such a principle, if applied to all other cases of disbursing officers who may assume the ground that they have been illegally dealt with, would lead to consequences which do not require to be stated, and could not, for a moment, be tolerated.

If the bank when the demand was made for the books, papers, and money of the Government in its possession had "protested," if they thought the demand illegal, and had then delivered them up, and had afterwards appealed to Congress or the judicial tribunals for such redress or decision as the nature of the case might call for, their position would have been far different from what it is now. Assuming to decide the law for themselves, and arrogating the power to see that the laws be faithfully executed, they assume a power heretofore unknown to our laws and institutions. Claiming to define their own legal rights, they have so far forgotten the rights of the public as to withhold vouchers and funds to which they can have no title.

It further appears to the committee that the change directed to be made by the Secretary of War was called for by the circumstances. It is understood that the change has been confined to a substitution of the local banks of deposite for the Bank of the United States and its branches at those places where local banks of deposite have been selected. Where the public funds are yet deposited in the branches of the United States Bank, these branches are yet the agents for making the payments, by appointment of the Secretary of War, under the act of June 7, 1832. Where the change has been made, the business is to be done by the new agency without any charge whatever to the Government.

The reason and propriety, therefore, of the measure, are obvious. The object is to direct the banks holding the public money to pay out this money to persons claiming it under the act of June 7, 1832, instead of having the funds drawn from these banks and placed in the United States Bank and its branches, for the mere purpose of doing what the former may do as well. To have continued the agency of the Bank of the United States in making these payments, when the public moneys were in other banks, would have been unnecessarily to put it in the power of the Bank of the United States, by means of the public funds, to draw large amounts of specie from time to time from the selected banks, to hoard in its own vaults, thereby to increase for its own purposes, a needless and unjustifiable pressure on the people.

It remains to be considered what effect this unwarrantable act of the bank may have upon the future payments to be made to the officers and soldiers entitled to the benefits of the provisions of the act of 1832. The committee called upon the Secretary of War for information on this point, and herewith submit the answer which has been received. It appears that on the 1st of January last, the bank, as disbursing agent for the payment of claims under the act of June 7th, 1832, held of public moneys drawn from the treasury for this object, the sum of $470,546 98. Since then, other payments, to a comparatively small amount, may have been made, and it is possible that subsequent settlements may further reduce this balance. This sum had been regularly drawn from the treasury by warrants in the usual way, and placed in the possession of the bank to be disbursed. The act of 1832 makes a standing appropriation of the amount necessary to carry its provisions into effect. The bank, by withholding the sum which it has in possession, stands in the situation of any other defaulting disbursing agent, and a sum equal to that which it thus wrongfully retains, must be drawn from the treasury and applied to the payments until the amount withheld by it shall be recovered. The detention of the books and papers by the bank, will not necessarily postpone the payments until the possession of such books and papers may be recovered from the bank; but it will render it necessary for the Department of War to make out new lists of those entitled to pay, and there is no probability that this can be done sufficiently early to enable the payments under the act of June 7, 1832, to be made on the 4th of March next, especially at the distant agencies, agreeably to the established usage. The labor of preparing new lists and papers is understood to be great, and with all the care that can be taken, there will be a liability to error, in many cases, until the present agents settle their accounts, resulting from the uncertainty of the periods to which the payments may have been made. But as no surviving claimants have been paid to a period later than the 4th of September last, all who are now living may be paid on the 4th of March for the half year ending at that time.

If any inconvenience should be felt by any of those veterans of the Revolution, as the committee believe it will be by all, by the delay which will take place in the payment of the next annuity due to them, it is to be attributed to the unjustifiable conduct of the bank in interposing to thwart the views of the Government, in withholding from the officers of Government the public money and public property, to which they do not pretend to have any claim. The committee cannot condemn, in terms too strong, the conduct of the bank in this transaction. The bank withholds from the public service the large sum of four hundred and seventy thousand five hundred and forty-six dollars and ninty-eight cents, and thus puts the Government to the inconvenience of applying other funds to the objects for which the sum they retain was appropriated and drawn from the treasury.

So far as respects the delivery of the public property in their possession, they refuse to obey the instructions issued; but so far as respects the termination of the duty of making payments, they yield a ready acquiescence, and yet there is the same authority for the one order as for the other. But in the former case, they have a direct pecuniary interest in the course they pursue. In the latter, their interest is not at stake, and no one suffers but the Government, which must advance other funds to supply the place of those illegally retained by the bank, and the veterans of the Revolution, who must wait for the amount due them until the necessary documents can be prepared to justify the payment.

The existing laws are, in the opinion of the committee, adequate to enable the Government to effect a recovery from the bank of its money and property, and therefore they propose no measure of legislation in this respect. Neither is any further appropriation required to supply the place of the sum thus retained by the bank; for, as has been already remarked, the act of June 7, 1832, makes a standing appropriation of the sums necessary to carry its provisions into effect. If the bank, or any other disbursing agent for the payment of these claims, become defaulters, and refuse to pay over the public moneys placed in their hands to make such payments, the meritorious class of citizens provided for by the act, cannot, on that account, be deprived of their rights, though some of them may experience delay in receiving the sums due to them, as in this case they probably will, in consequence of the conduct of the bank, in withholding the public books and papers, by which the exact amount of their claims is to be ascertained.

The committee deem the course of the bank such in this case, as to justify the repeal of the several provisions constituting them pension agents, under the invalid acts and the acts of 1818 and 1820. There seems to be no propriety in the separation of these duties; but as one may be conveniently performed by the agents selected by the Secretary of War, so may the other. There seems to be a propriety, too, in confiding to a responsible officer of the Government the duty of making these payments, rather than leave it in the hands of an irresponsible corporation. They therefore recommend this course, and report a bill accordingly.

On motion of Mr. POLK, the bill and report were ordered to be printed.

Mr. BLAIR, of South Carolina, said, that the subject was one of high interest to the public, and he moved a suspension of the rule, to allow him to move the printing of an extra number of copies.

The motion was agreed to, and Mr. BLAIR moved that 10,000 copies of the report and accompanying documents be printed.

The SPEAKER stated the motion must lie one day before it could be considered.

NATIONAL PAINTINGS.

Mr. JARVIS, from the Committee on the Public Buildings, reported a joint resolution for the procurement of four national paintings to fill the vacant panels in the Rotundo of the Capitol; which was read the first time.

The following bills were reported, read twice; and committed to the Committee of the Whole, viz:

By Mr. BARRINGER, a bill for the relief of John Carruck;

By Mr. JOHNSON, of Kentucky, a bill for the relief of Paschal Hickman;

By Mr. DEMING, a bill for the relief of Elijah Loose;

By Mr. DUNCAN, a bill to establish an additional land office in the Territory of Arkansas;

By Mr. YOUNG, a bill for the relief of Peter Jacquett;

By Mr. YOUNG, a bill for the relief of H. Winett.

Mr. ADAMS, of Massachusetts, remarked that yesterday the member from New York, [Mr. CAMBRELENG,] presented a memorial from sundry merchants of New York in relation to the establishment of a warehousing system, and it was referred, with three other papers relating to the Bank of the United States, to the Committee of Ways and Means. He had no disposition nor desire that the three other papers should be otherwise referred than they have been; but the memorial on the warehousing system involved principles other than those relating to finance. It related to the subject of commerce, and also to an interest which he was bound to advocate in this house, and with the care of which he was charged as the chairman of the Committee on Manufactures. He had not read the memorial, nor was it now in his power to read it; but he apprehended that it was most deeply interesting to the manufacturing interest. He wished it to be referred to the Committee on Manufactures, and asked a suspension of the rule to allow him to submit the motion.

The motion to suspend the rule was put and lost.

PENSION LAWS.

The order of the day was then declared to be the resolution of Mr. CHILTON, to appoint a select committee to inquire into the expediency of so extending the general pension law as to embrace within its provisions those persons who were engaged in the Indian wars, down to the year 1794; and the amendment to it by Mr. BOULDIN, to appoint a committee to inquire into the moral effects of the pension system upon the community, and how far it ought to be abolished or repealed.

Mr. CHILTON ALLAN said he was unwilling to be the cause of further consumption of time upon this subject. He understood that the House was anxious to have it disposed of, as many resolutions had been and would be offered for the consideration of the House. He would, therefore, waive his right to speak on the subject, with the understanding that no gentleman should continue the debate.

Mr. GILMER said he was extremely anxious that the amendment offered by the gentleman from Virginia should be discussed.

Mr. ALLAN then moved the previous question, with a view to ascertain the sense of the House as to the continuance of the discussion.

Mr. MASON, of Virginia, expressed a wish that the motion would be suspended till his colleague, the mover of the amendment, should appear in his seat.

The motion for the previous question was seconded by the House.

Mr. MASON demanded the yeas and nays on the previous question, and they were ordered.

The question being taken whether the main question should be put, it was decided in the affirmative—yeas 136, nays 66.

The question was then taken on the resolution as submitted by the member from Kentucky, and determined in the affirmative—yeas 119.

So the resolution was adopted.

POTOMAC BRIDGE.

Mr. MERCER obtained leave to report a bill from the Committee on Roads and Canals, authorizing the construction of a bridge over the Potomac, and repealing all former acts passed on this subject; which was read twice.

Mr. M. then moved that it should be referred to the Committee of the Whole on the state of the Union, as he considered that committee the most appropriate in which a measure was to be discussed by which a great saving was to be effected; he also moved that the report, with the accompanying documents, should be printed.

Mr. McKENNAN remarked, that, as he did not see in his seat the chairman of the Committee on the District, he would state that the improvement contemplated had originated with that committee, and he would move that the subject should be referred to it.

Mr. MERCER disclaimed having any intention of trenching upon the rights of any committee, and he explained that he felt it his duty—as the Committee on Internal Improvements were about to adjust their improvements to meet the revenue of the country, that as the expenditure about to be undertaken, involved, he was credibly informed, the large amount of full three millions, if not five millions—to recommend the present proposition, which would only require $130,000, as sufficient for every reasonable purpose.

Mr. McKENNAN said he had every respect for the chairman of the Committee of Roads and Canals, but nevertheless he could not see why any views which had been submitted to that committee, to create such a change in the construction of the bridge, could not be considered by the committee in which it originated; and after detailing the proceedings taken by the Committee on the District, to effect the construction of the bridge, he desired that their claim to have the subject before them should be recognised.

Mr. MERCER remarked, that the proceedings had originated in consequence of a report to the House by Mr. WICKLIFFE, which had, thereupon, made an appropriation of sixty thousand dollars for the repairs of the bridge, and of twenty thousand dollars for purchasing the rights of the company. Nothing was, however, done, and the President of the United States had reported various plans to Congress. He was assured that the plan subsequently adopted would cost fully five millions to complete it, as proposed. It was, therefore, a serious consideration whether they should determine to go on with it, or proceed with what was now recommended, the expense of which would not amount to a year's interest of the cost required for the other.

Mr. CHINN said, it never was the understanding of the House that the Committee on Roads and Canals should have proceeded to annul the contracts that had been made for the construction of the bridge; and as there could not be a doubt that the Committee of the District had, under all the circumstances, the most appropriate jurisdiction over the subject, he advocated the reference to it accordingly.

Mr. MANN, of New York, knowing the anxiety of the House to proceed with the other important business before it, and seeing that there was such a variety of opinion on this subject, which was likely to occupy their time, he would move to postpone its further consideration until to-morrow; which motion prevailed—ayes 86, nays 72.

REMOVAL OF THE DEPOSITES.

The House resumed the consideration of the motion to refer the report of the Secretary of the Treasury on the deposites to the Committee of Ways and Means—the question being on the amendment submitted by Mr. JONES, as an amendment to that previously submitted by Mr. McDUFFIE, viz: to add to the motion for reference the following instructions to that committee:

"Inquire into the expediency of depositing the 'revenue hereafter collected in the State banks in 'the different States, where the same is collected, 'in proportion to their respective capitals paid in, 'and to prescribe the terms on which the same shall 'be deposited; and to report by bill or otherwise.'"

Mr. BOULDIN, of Virginia, having the floor from the previous day, rose and said:

Sir, before I proceed to submit a few remarks—and they shall be but few—on the merits of the serious question which is now before the House, I must revert to the rebuke which I, in all due humility, received the other day from my colleague, [Mr. WISE.] Sir, he stated, and he stated truly, that, although Mr. RANDOLPH was a member elect of this House, that fact had not been formally announced to the House. Sir, I am not in the habit of taking any general remark whatever to myself; but when a general remark is made, and under such circumstances as will apply to no one else so appropriately as to myself, I am compelled to do so. Sir, my colleague did not as kindly suggest that the thing ought to be done, which another colleague [Mr. ARCHER] most kindly, and in the most delicate manner, through another colleague, did suggest—that this ought to be done; and now, as it has become my bounden duty, I must tell my colleague, and this House, and, through them, my constituents, the reason why Mr. RANDOLPH's death was not here announced. But, sir, I cannot tell the reason why the thing so kindly suggested was not done, without telling what I have already told my friends, and more than one, what I should say if I done that thing—

Here it becomes our painful duty to state, that Mr. BOULDIN, after some moments pause, was observed to totter and lean forward upon the desk from which he had been addressing the House; he was seized with an apoplectic fit, and although medical assistance was promptly rendered, having been carried into the esplanade and bled, the vital spark had fled.

The House adjourned on the instant.

IN SENATE.

Mr. CHAMBERS presented the memorial of between two and three thousand inhabitants of the city of Baltimore, disapproving the course of the Secretary of the Treasury in removing the deposites, and asking their restoration to the Bank of the United States.

Mr. C. addressed the Senate for a few minutes, but declined extending his remarks, on account of the state of the feelings of members at this moment. He however requested that the memorial might be read, and referred to the Committee on Finance, and printed.

The reading was proceeded in for some time, when a message was announced from the House of Representatives, when it was suspended—

Mr. FRANKLIN, the Clerk of the House of Representatives, then announced to the Senate the death of the Hon. THOMAS T. BOULDIN, a Representative from Virginia, and that his funeral would take place from the hall of the House to-morrow morning, at eleven o'clock.

Mr. RIVES rose, and said:

Mr. PRESIDENT: The Senate were yesterday apprised by the honorable Senator from South Carolina, [Mr. PRESTON,] in the momentary absence of my colleague and myself, of the melancholy event which has just been communicated to us by the House of Representatives, and which has deprived the State of Virginia of one of her most distinguished Representatives in the Legislature of the Union. The event, sir, was, in all its circumstances and associations, of the most solemn and affecting character, well calculated to remind us, in the midst of our busy cares here, "what shadows we are, and what shadows we pursue!" I now rise, Mr. President, to ask, at the hands of the Senate, the accustomed marks of respect to the memory of our deceased associate, and which are so eminently due to the high character he maintained in all the relations both of public and of private life. I therefore beg leave to offer, for the adoption of the Senate, the following resolution:

Resolved, That the Senate will attend the funeral of the Hon. THOMAS TYLER BOULDIN, late a member of the House of Representatives, from the State of Virginia, at the hour of 11 o'clock A. M., to-morrow, and as a testimony of respect for the memory of the deceased, will go into mourning, by wearing crape round the left arm for thirty days.

On motion of Mr. RIVES, it was

Resolved, That when the Senate adjourn, it adjourn to meet to-morrow morning, at half past ten o'clock, to take order in attending the funeral of the late Hon. THOMAS T. BOULDIN.

On motion of Mr. RIVES,

The Senate adjourned.

HOUSE OF REPRESENTATIVES.

WEDNESDAY, February 12, 1834.

After the Journal of the preceding day had been read—

Mr. ARCHER rose and said: I rise, Mr. Speaker, not to announce to the House—that were superfluous—but to submit the resolutions rendered proper by the dreadful catastrophe of which we were all appalled, and, I am sure I may add, afflicted spectators, yesterday, by which I have been deprived of an esteemed friend, and the State to which we both belonged, at a moment of the extremest public excitement, of one of the most valued and valuable of her Representatives on this floor.

I know, sir, that I should outrage the feelings of the House, as I should violate my own, were I to avail myself of this occasion to pay at large the tribute of esteem to my departed colleague and friend, which would, under other circumstances, be due to the annunciation of his loss. He was of a character which might well be fruitful of panegyric, if it were now allowed me to dwell upon it. It was his fortune to have raised himself, from the humblest condition in life, to rank in his profession—to a high judicial station at home—and to a seat, and that no undistinguished one, on this floor, by the aid of merit alone. At an age approaching to majority he was following the plough; and, so far from regarding this circumstance with shame, or desiring to conceal it, he had the superior mind to regard and to speak of it with exultation, as, what it truly was, an honor. Without fortune or influential friends, or the aid even of education, he had lifted himself to general esteem, to independence, and to a place which he regarded, as I do, inferior to none in point of honor—a seat in this House.

Sir, if I felt at liberty to pursue the theme, no man would be better authorized, from knowledge, to bear the high testimony which it merited, to his character, as a private and a public man; nor, let me add, would there be any one who would be more glad and proud to render this just tribute to his memory and virtues. But I dare not pursue the theme, just and grateful as it would be. The awful catastrophe we have been called to witness and deplore, speaks to our hearts; and, let me add, to our horror, in a language which forbids it. I feel that I ought not, may I say that I cannot, add more; and I content myself, therefore, after this brief and impartial notice, with sending to the Chair the resolutions I hold in my hand, such as are ordinarily adopted on occasions of this description:

Resolved, That the members of this House will attend the funeral of the late THOMAS TYLER BOULDIN, at eleven o'clock to-morrow.

Resolved, That a committee be appointed to take order for superintending the funeral of THOMAS T. BOULDIN, deceased, late a member of this House from the State of Virginia.

Resolved, That the members of this House will testify their respect to the memory of THOMAS T. BOULDIN, by wearing crape on the left arm for thirty days.

Ordered, That a message be sent to the Senate, to notify that body of the death of THOMAS T. BOULDIN, late one of the Representatives from the State of Virginia; and that his funeral will take place to-morrow, at eleven o'clock in the forenoon, from the Hall of the House of Representatives.

Mr. ARCHER, Mr. CLAYTON, Mr. WILLIAMS, Mr. MUHLENBERG, Mr. C. P. WHITE, Mr. HARPER, and Mr. MARSHALL, were appointed the committee to superintend the funeral ceremonies.

On motion of Mr. ARCHER, it was ordered, that when the House adjourn, it adjourn until to-morrow morning at eleven o'clock.

On motion of Mr. DAVENPORT, of Virginia, the House then adjourned.

HOUSE OF REPRESENTATIVES.

MONDAY, February 10, 1834.

On motion of Mr. LYON, of Michigan, Ordered, That the memorial of the Legislative Council of Michigan Territory, praying for an appropriation to improve the navigation over the flats, in Lake St. Clair, and also an appropriation

for removing the bar at the mouth of Clinton river, in said Territory, be referred to the Committee on Roads and Canals.

On motion of Mr. LYON, of Michigan,
Ordered, That a petition from numerous citizens of Cass and Berrien counties, in Michigan Territory, praying that the location of the Chicago road may be so changed as to run from Edwardsburg to Niles, and thence to the mouth of St. Joseph's river, in said Territory, be referred to the Committee on Roads and Canals.

On motion of Mr. LYON, of Michigan,
Ordered, That the petition of sundry citizens of Cass county, Michigan Territory, praying that the location of the Chicago road may be so changed as to run directly from Edwardsburg, through Berrien, to the mouth of the St. Joseph's river, be referred to the Committee on Roads and Canals.

On motion of Mr. LYON, of Michigan,
Ordered, That the memorial of a Territorial Convention, assembled at Jonesville, in Michigan Territory, on the 8th of January, 1834, praying for an appropriation to survey and locate the route for a railroad across the peninsula of Michigan, and also for an appropriation of lands or money to construct said road, be referred to the Committee of the Whole House on the state of the Union, to whom was referred the bill reported by Mr. DUNCAN on the 16th ult., for making an appropriation of a certain quantity of the public land, to aid the Territory of Michigan in constructing such a work as is here prayed for.

On motion of Mr. LYON, of Michigan,
Ordered, That the petition of Ensign J. G. Odall, and also the petition of Henry Myers, for arrears of pension, be referred to the Committee of Claims.

On motion of Mr. LYON, of Michigan,
Ordered, That the petition of sundry citizens of Michigan, praying for the erection of a light-house at the mouth of the Kalamazoo river, and another light-house at the mouth of Grand river, on Lake Michigan, in Michigan Territory, be referred to the Committee on Commerce.

IN SENATE.

THURSDAY, February 13, 1834.

The Senate was called to order at half past ten o'clock.

Immediately after the reading of the Journal of yesterday, Mr. WHITE suggested that the hour had arrived when the Senate had agreed to meet the House of Representatives to attend the funeral obsequies of the Hon. THOMAS TYLER BOULDIN; and, on his motion,

The Senate adjourned.

The Senators, preceded by the Sergeant-at-Arms, and headed by the Vice President and Secretary of the Senate, proceeded to the Hall of the House of Representatives.

HOUSE OF REPRESENTATIVES.

THURSDAY, February 13, 1834.

The House met at eleven o'clock, pursuant to adjournment.

After prayers and the reading of the Journal, on motion,
The House adjourned, to meet to-morrow morning at twelve o'clock.

FUNERAL OF HON. THOMAS T. BOULDIN.

The members of the Senate, preceded by their officers, entered the Hall at twelve o'clock.

The President of the United States, Heads of Departments, and Judges of the Supreme Court, also attended, and took seats in front of the Chair.

The remains of the deceased were brought into the Hall, preceded by the Committee of Arrangements, the Pall Bearers, and the Virginia delegation as mourners.

The Episcopal Church service was read by the Rev. Mr. HATCH, Chaplain to the Senate; after which an appropriate discourse was pronounced by the Rev. Mr. STOCKTON, Chaplain to the House of Representatives.

The Funeral Procession was then formed, and proceeded to the eastern portico, whence it moved to the Congressional Cemetery in the following order:

The Chaplains of both Houses.
Physicians and Clergymen who attended the deceased.
Committee of Arrangements:
Mr. Archer, Mr. Clayton, Mr. Williams, Mr. Muhlenberg, Mr. White, of New York,
Mr. Harper, of N. Hampshire,
and Mr. Marshall.
Pall Bearers:
Mr. Pinckney, Mr. Kencher, Mr. McIntire, Mr. Bell, of Tenn., Mr. Crane, and Mr. Murphy.
The Family of the deceased.
The members of the House of Representatives and Senators from Virginia, as mourners.
The Sergeant-at-Arms of the House of Representatives.
The House of Representatives, preceded by their Speaker and Clerk.
The Sergeant-at-Arms of the Senate.
The Senate of the United States, preceded by the Vice President and their Secretary.
The President of the United States.
The Heads of Departments.
Judges of the Supreme Court and their Officers.
Foreign Ministers.
Citizens and Strangers.

IN SENATE.

FRIDAY, February 14, 1834.

A message was received from the President of the United States by Mr. Donelson, his Private Secretary.

Mr. HENDRICKS presented the memorial of the Legislature of Indiana, praying that measures may be taken by Congress for the improvement of the navigation of the Ohio river. The memorial was referred to Committee on Roads and Canals.

Mr. HENDRICKS gave notice that he should ask leave to-morrow to introduce a bill for the improvement of the navigation of the river Wabash, in the State of Indiana.

Mr. SOUTHARD, from the Committee on Naval Affairs, reported several bills of a private nature from the House of Representatives; which were read and committed.

Mr. SOUTHARD, from the same committee, reported a bill for the relief of Anna Stone, widow of John Stone.

Mr. SOUTHARD, from the same committee, asked to be discharged from the further consideration of the resolution inquiring into the expediency of placing Mrs. Allen Dix upon the pension roll; which was agreed to.

Mr. SOUTHARD, from the same committee, asked to be discharged from the further consideration of the petition of the clerks in the navy-yard at Brooklyn, New York, praying additional compensation; which was agreed to.

Mr. SOUTHARD, from the Committee on Roads and Canals, reported a bill incorporating a company, and extending certain benefits, for the purpose of cutting a canal in the Territory of Florida, with an amendment.

Mr. POINDEXTER gave notice that he should, on Monday next, ask leave to introduce a bill prescribing the time when the sales of public lands shall take place.

The VICE PRESIDENT communicated a letter from the War Department, transmitting statements of contracts made by that department in the year 1833.

The VICE PRESIDENT also communicated a letter from the Secretary of the Treasury, transmitting weekly statements of the State banks, in which the public deposites are now made; which, on motion of Mr. WEBSTER, was ordered to be printed.

Mr. LINN, from the Committee on Private Land Claims, reported a bill for the relief of Sebastian Butcher and others; which was read twice and committed.

Mr. BIBB, from the Committee on the Judiciary, reported a bill for changing the time of holding the term of the United States Court of the western district of Louisiana; which bill was read, and considered in Committee of the Whole, and, on its being reported to the Senate, was, on motion of Mr. BIBB, ordered to be engrossed for a third reading.

Mr. CLAY presented the memorial of sundry

citizens of Illinois, relative to a preëmption law; which was laid on the table.

Mr. NAUDAIN, from the Committee on Claims, asked to be discharged from the further consideration of the petition of E. Y. Dyer, and that it be referred to the Committee on the Judiciary; which was so ordered.

Mr. NAUDAIN, from the same committee, asked to be discharged from the further consideration of the memorial of William Waller, and that it be referred to the Committee on Military Affairs; which was agreed to.

Mr. WRIGHT presented the memorial of about 3,000 mechanics and artisans of the city of New York, ascribing the deranged state of the currency to the removal of the deposites; which was read, referred to the Committee on Finance, and ordered to be printed.

Mr. McKEAN presented the proceedings of a numerous meeting of the Democratic citizens of the third congressional district of Pennsylvania, in opposition to the recharter of the Bank of the United States, and the restoration of the public deposites.

Mr. McKEAN also presented the proceedings of Democratic citizens of Philadelphia, of the same tenor.

Mr. McKEAN also presented the proceedings of citizens of Spring Garden, Philadelphia, in favor of restoring the deposites.

Mr. McKEAN also presented similar proceedings of inhabitants of the Northern Liberties, Philadelphia.

Mr. McKEAN also presented a memorial signed by 500 citizens of Philadelphia, of the like tenor, with the memorial presented by him on Tuesday, in favor of a restoration of the deposites.

Mr. McKEAN also presented the memorial of 1100 citizens of Moyamensing, county of Philadelphia, opposed to the removal of the deposites.

Mr. McKEAN also presented the memorial of a number of the inhabitants of the county of Schuylkill, Pennsylvania, opposed to the Bank of the United States, and against the restoration of the deposites.

Mr. McKEAN also presented a memorial of the inhabitants of Tamaqua, Pennsylvania, in favor of the restoration of the deposites.

These several proceedings and memorials were read and referred to the Committee on Finance, and ordered to be printed.

Mr. FORSYTH asked and obtained leave to withdraw the papers of Isaac B. Roberts.

Mr. TIPTON, from the select committee to whom was referred the propriety of admitting Michigan and Arkansas into the Union, reported a bill forming a Territorial Government for Wisconsin; which was read twice and committed.

Petitions and memorials were presented by Messrs. LINN, EWING, KNIGHT, SHEPLEY, and TIPTON.

The following resolutions were submitted:

By Mr. HENDRICKS:

Resolved, That the Committee on Revolutionary Claims be instructed to inquire into the expediency of paying John Peck the balance of interest due on three final settlement certificates, and which is withheld at the treasury in consequence of an error in the act of the last session of Congress (No. 445) "for the relief of John Peck."

By Mr. LINN:

Resolved, That the Committee on Claims be instructed to inquire into the expediency of making an appropriation to pay the claim of the heirs and legal representatives of the late Mr. Spencer Pettis for services rendered the United States by said Pettis.

The Senate then, on motion of Mr. MANGUM, took up for consideration the memorial and resolutions submitted by him on Tuesday last, from a meeting of citizens in the western part of North Carolina, in relation to the removal of the deposites.

The motion was agreed to, and thereupon a protracted debate ensued, which continued till half past four o'clock, in which Messrs. FORSYTH, WEBSTER, CLAY, BROWN, WRIGHT, PRESTON, and WILKINS, participated.

The Senate then adjourned till Monday next.

HOUSE OF REPRESENTATIVES.

FRIDAY, *February* 14, 1834.

Mr. WISE, of Virginia, asked leave of the House to occupy the floor for a few moments, on a subject personally relating to himself. Leave being granted, Mr. WISE said—

Mr. SPEAKER: I ask the indulgence of this House, at its first meeting since the melancholy occasion of the funeral of my lamented colleague, [Judge BOULDIN,] whilst I discharge a delicate and solemn duty to his memory and myself. His death, so sudden, and so shocking to all, was peculiarly distressing to me. It happened at a moment when he was about to reply to what he termed my "*rebuke*" to him. I hope it is not improper for me now to state to members, his family and friends, and my own, that there was not the slightest emotion of unkind feeling between us at the time he expired. Sir, when I had the honor of addressing this House, but the other day, on the momentous question which so excited his ardent mind, and which still agitates this nation, as a father to a young colleague, he sat by my side, and gave me the cheering encouragement of his countenance and his smile. When I alluded to the fact that the death of his illustrious predecessor had not been announced to this House, I bowed to his venerable person, and disavowed the intention to "*rebuke him*" who filled the seat of Mr. Randolph with honor to himself and usefulness to the country. But the day before he was cut down in the midst of his usefulness, we met in this Hall, and had a free and friendly conversation, which left nothing, on either side, unexplained. And I am confident that, if he had been spared but few words more, he would have left no room for misunderstanding the relations in which we stood to each other. My object in making the allusion which I did to the death of Mr. Randolph, was solely what I professed at the time, sincerely disclaiming any personal reflection upon my colleague, who, I never doubted, had good and sufficient reasons for failing to perform what seemed to be his appropriate duty. These reasons have since been made public. He said he would announce them fully when he came to speak on the deposite question. Alas! little did he anticipate that death would seal his lips and bury him, too, in silence, before he should finish what he meant to have said on the death of his predecessor! I have the consolation to know, that he died with a full knowledge that I intended no wound to his feelings, and no reproach to his conduct. And it becomes me to pay my humble tribute to his memory when dead, as I paid him the homage of my respect, and confidence, and admiration, when living. I became acquainted with him late in the session, and from that time until the moment he expired in the public service on this floor—a glorious death it was!—I have the proud satisfaction of believing that I daily increased in his good will, whilst I know he grew in my affections and in my estimation as a noble, generous, and warm-hearted friend, an able and honest and useful man, and a bold and true patriot, who "had done the State some service." He is gone!—lamented by none here more than by one who is, comparatively, a stranger to all his merits, his high worth, and exalted virtues; and whose fervent prayer to Heaven now is, that his departed spirit is reposing in peace in the bosom of his GOD!

Mr. CONNOR, from the Committee on the Post Office and Post Roads, made a report upon the resolution referred to that committee relative to the failure of the mails between the cities of Washington and Boston. Laid on the table, and ordered to be printed, together with the accompanying communication of the Postmaster General.

Mr. CHILTON, from the Committee on Invalid Pensions, reported a bill for the relief of John Collins. Read twice, and committed.

Mr. CARR, from the Committee on Private Land Claims, reported a bill for the relief of George Gordon, assignee and representative of Matthew Rennie, deceased. Read twice, and ordered to be engrossed.

Mr. LANSING reported a bill for the relief of the heirs and sureties of Melancthon W. Bostick, deceased. Read twice, and committed.

The resolution from the Committee on Roads and Canals for information relative to the Potomac bridge, was taken up, and, on motion of Mr. MERCER, laid on the table.

The resolution from the committee relative to the Rules of the House was taken up, on motion of Mr. MERCER, and postponed to and made the order of the day for Monday next.

Several resolutions for inquiry, heretofore offered, were considered and agreed to.

The following resolution, submitted on the 6th instant by Mr. LEWIS, of Alabama, was taken up:

Resolved, That the Committee on Indian Affairs be instructed to inquire whether the provisions of the treaty of March, 1832, with the Creek tribe of Indians, in the State of Alabama, be inconsistent with the sovereign right of jurisdiction of said State within its limits, and whether the execution of said treaty has so far conflicted, or is likely to conflict, with the operation of the laws of said State over the country ceded by such treaty, and if so, to inquire whether some act of legislation consistent with the rights of said Indians may not be necessary to prevent such conflict, and that said committee have leave to report by bill or otherwise.

On the reading of the resolution,

Mr. McKINLEY said, that as the subject was amicably adjusted which was contained in the resolutions, he thought it better that it should be noticed no further He therefore moved that the resolutions be laid on the table; but he withdrew it immediately at the request of Mr. LEWIS.

Mr. LEWIS did not believe that the subject was yet amicably adjusted, as he had received a letter from the Secretary of War that the removal of the Indians had been postponed from the 15th of January till the 16th of March, and that by that time the lands would be disposed of, so that it would not be necessary to execute the orders of Government by military force. He hoped so; but still, as the resolution was one of inquiry, he trusted it would be permitted to go to the Committee on Indian Affairs. It might still be a question of peace or war, and he did not wish it to be subject to the control of the President or his subordinate officers. The act of 1827 he considers unconstitutional.

Mr. McKINLEY considers the question is not now of importance to the State of Alabama. He does not agree with many of the expressed opinions of the President; and was with many of those who thought with his colleague, [Mr. LEWIS.] Yet he considered it extremely injudicious to go into the question, while the causes of complaint—the invasion of the sovereign rights of Alabama within her own State—were likely to be obviated by the removal of the Indians. When an amicable settlement of the question was thus likely to be effected, it was not necessary to refer to any committee—particularly considering the temper displayed by his colleague in moving its reference, making it uncertain what action might be had by a committee. He considered that the act of 1827 had nothing to do with the question.

Mr. LEWIS said that the removal of the Indians is not the only difficulty apprehended.

Mr. McKINLEY having renewed his motion to have the resolution laid on the table,

Mr. LEWIS demanded the ayes and noes on the question, which being agreed to by the House, the division resulted in 107 ayes and 88 noes, to lay it on the table.

The SPEAKER laid before the House communications from the President, in conformity to resolutions for information, adopted on the 8th instant and the 16th ultimo; which, on the motion of Mr. ADAMS, of Massachusetts, were referred to the Committee on Foreign Affairs, and ordered to be printed.

The SPEAKER presented also the annual account from the Secretary of War relative to the service of public contracts; and from the Department of War a communication in answer to the resolution adopted on the 27th ultimo.

A bill from the Senate was read a third time and passed, authorizing G. B. Lamar, of Georgia, to import iron for steamboats and machinery, to be used in the inland navigation, free of duty.

A bill for the relief of Arnold Henry Dohrman, was, after some amendments were made thereto, read a third time and passed.

The bill for the relief of the representatives of Walter Livingston, deceased, was read a third time and passed.

The bill to provide for the settlement of commutation and other revolutionary claims, was read a third time. The question being on its passage—

Mr. PIERCE, of New Hampshire, said that this bill had been passed to a third reading without due consideration. It transferred to the Treasury Department important duties which had heretofore been examined by Congress. He had not given that attention to it himself which the subject deserved; and he moved the postponement of the bill till Monday. Agreed to.

The bill for the relief of Nathaniel Potter, formerly postmaster in the town of Franklin, Missouri, which had been debated for several years since 1826, in both Houses of Congress, and as often rejected; but which had, in January of this year, been reported by the Committee on the Judiciary, and had passed the Committee of the Whole House—became again the subject of a protracted debate, in which Messrs. CONNOR, BEARDSLEY, ASHLEY, CAGE, and WHITTLESEY, BULL, and McDUFFIE, participated, and was rejected without a division

The House, on motion of Mr. POLK, suspended the rule by which this day was set apart for private business—ayes 90, noes 34.

The House then resolved itself into Committee of the Whole on the state of the Union, Mr. BRIGGS in the Chair, and proceeded to consider the bill making appropriations for fortifications for 1834; which, having been considered, the committee thereupon rose and reported it to the House; and it was ordered to be engrossed for a third reading.

The House then went into committee on sundry bills; Mr. HUBBARD in the chair.

The bill to compensate Susan Decatur and others, was postponed.

The following bills were considered, and reported to the House:

A bill for the relief of citizens, sufferers by Indian depredations;

A bill to return the duties on certain pieces of sculpture, (intended for the Philadelphia Exchange;)

A bill for the relief of Frederick Raymer;

A bill for the relief of Antoine Crusat;

A bill for the relief of Abraham Wrinkle;

A bill for the relief of the owners of the schooner Admiral;

A bill for the relief of Henry Darling;

A bill for the relief of Paul Poissot;

A bill for the relief of Terence Le Blanc;

A bill for the relief of the heirs and legal representatives of William Teas, deceased.

A bill granting pensions to certain persons therein named.

Mr. CARR, from the Committee on Private Land Claims, reported a bill for the relief of George Gordon, assignee and representative of the heirs of Matthew Ramey; which was read twice, and ordered to be engrossed for a third reading.

A bill was reported from the Committee on the District of Columbia, to authorize Edmund Brooke to introduce some slaves for his use from the State of Virginia into the District of Columbia, as an exception to the law in existence. Having been debated by several gentlemen, it was eventually postponed.

A bill for the relief of James Tilford;

A bill for the relief of William Weedon;

A bill for the relief of Jeremiah Worsham;

A bill for the relief of John Thompson, jun.;

A bill for the relief of Samuel A. Edmondson;

A bill for the relief of John Emerson;

A bill for the relief of Marguerite Baron;

A bill for the relief of George Douglass;

The above bills were ordered to be engrossed, and read a third time.

The House then adjourned till to-morrow, at twelve o'clock.

From Allan Cunningham's Biographical and Critical account of English Literature.

BYRON.

The cynical, sneering, and sarcastic spirit of our times—the doubting of everything, and believing in nothing—found a poet in George Gordon Lord Byron. He was born with the noblest faculties; his imagination was boundless, his intellect lofty and vigorous, and his application unceasing: nor did he want a passionate energy, and a sensibility keen and acute—in short, a union of those fine qualities which fit a man for the highest flights of poetry. How and when much of this was blighted and seared, will never perhaps be discovered: of the sterner and darker parts of his character, there is no intimation in the 'Hours of Idleness,' and the change which came over him, as a cloud comes over the sun, has been imputed to the contemptuous and unjust criticism in the *Edinburgh Review*, which nearly drove him distracted—turned his blood to gall, and dipped his pen in nitric acid, and influenced all his subsequent compositions. This is not easily reconciled with the circumstance mentioned by Moore, that a good deal of his satire on the reviewers was written before the critique alluded to appeared. I know not how it came to pass, but it is certain, from this period Byron became cynical and moody, and recalled too often for his own peace of mind, the language of the article, which he continued long to resent.

His high birth and singular story united in helping him on to fame. He was born in London in 1788: his father was a spendthrift and a libertine, and his mother an heiress, who paid as a penalty for her ill-placed love, her whole fortune, save some two hundred a year, on which this descendant of princes educated her only child, and maintained her household. Between the poet and a lordship many life-like people stood; but by the time he had half completed his education, relations were removed one by one, till at last the title descended to him, and he found himself Lord of Newstead and of himself—"that heritage of wo." Like Burns, whom in many things he resembled, with him began love and poetry; when some twenty years old he gathered his poems into a volume—the source of all his fame and much of his sorrow. In reply to its reception from the critics of the North, he wrote that sharp satire, "English Bards and Scotch Reviewers," and, having done so, sailed away, to give his wrath a cooling on Mount Parnassus and in the Hellespont. He was beginning to be forgotten, when he returned suddenly to England, surprised the country by the publication of "Childe Harold," and his Whig reviewers, by siding with them in the Lords, and uttering bitter speeches against the tories. This noble poem raised him at once above criticism, and gave him rank with the highest spirits of English poesie.

From this time forward he continued to pour his verse before the public, with a rapidity only equalled by the originality of his compositions, and the brighiness of his handling. A succession of poems, all impressed with an Eastern character, and wearing the hue and lineament of the people with whom he had sojourned among the Mediterranean isles, confounded the critics, and awakened such rapturous applause as had only been heard when the Ariosto of Scotland sent forth his "Marmion," and "Lady of the Lake." Of these, "The Giaour," "The Corsair," "The Siege of Corinth," "The Bride of Abydos," and "Lara," appeared within a wonderous short space of time: which proves that the poet's passions, like those of another bard, raged like so many devils, till they got vent in verse. Having wearied himself rather than the public with rhyme, he took a sudden stride into the realms of blank verse, and gave us his mysterious "Manfred," his splendid prodigal "Sardanapalus," with other dramatic compositions scarcely less regal and surprising. Having on many occasions displayed an irritability of nature, and a quick susceptibility in all things personal, together with a love of showing that he was inflammable and voluptuous, his friends, in the joy with which mariners welcome a storm-tossed ship to a secure and calm anchorage, hailed his marriage with a lady reckoned every way worthy of her envied fortune. The result was unfortunate; from the moment of his marriage his muse was silent; his creditors were not so: three executions in this proud man's house invaded his studies and hurt his temper; his lady, under pretence of a journey to the country, forsook him; the world, always ready to strike the proud, and trample on the famous, assailed him with its thousand weapons, and drove him, in a moment of despair, from the land which gave him birth, and now inherits his glory. His course from this moment was wayward, and more like a will-o'-the-wisp than an inspired being: yet, between this and the grave, he wrote some of his boldest compositions; he concluded "Childe Harold," wrote "Mazeppa," and alarmed the sedate and the scrupulous with his wild "Don Juan." The poet seems to have been sitting between angels of light and darkness when he wrote it, and to have been influenced by the former at the rate of ten stanzas to the canto. It exhibits some of his brightest and some of his blackest moods. How he tried to restore the extinguished fire of liberty in Italy, and, with a helmet of a Spartan pattern on his head, sailed to revive heroism among the hordes of Greece—how he failed, and how he fell, have been made known to the world. He died at Missolonghi, and was buried at Newstead, after being refused admission into Westminster Abbey.

The poetry of Byron is singularly bold in conception: the thoughts are generally new and striking, and the language audaciously powerful and fluent. He looks at nature through his own eyes; he refuses to feel with others; and this is visible in the characters he employs, as well as in thoughts on the present and the future, which he scatters always with a daring, and sometimes with a profane prodigality. He has no desire to claim the virtues of mercy and generosity for his bandit heroes; he dips them in the hues of darkness, and then seeks to bring them back towards humanity, by shedding on them one ray or so of virtue, which, like a light in a charnel-house, renders all more ghastly around. His heroines are neither feminine nor natural; they seem formed on the Nut Brown Maid pattern, whom neither robbery, bloodshed, nor love elsewhere bestowed, could appal. This is an offence against the feeling and pride of woman's heart, which all the other charms in which he arrays, or the grandeur of soul with which he sometimes endows them, cannot atone for. Yet, with all the repulsiveness of his men, and the melodramatic sort of characters of his women, he invests them with such life—paints their thoughts so truly, and their actions with such wondrous force of light and shade, as render them welcome, with all their sins against virtue and decorum. His chief excellence is in the calm dissection of the human heart, and in expressing sentiments dark and terrible. We follow him, not through the charm of love, but the spell of fear; and while we cannot find an echo in our own hearts for the third of the fearful things he utters, we follow him still. His radical defect is the want of sympathy with universal nature; in this the peasant Burns far surpasses the lordly Byron; the humble tiller of the ground, who had but the sweat of his brow and seven pounds a year for his inheritance, loved the earth and all that was in it ten times more than did the Lord of Newstead, with his high rental, and pedigree reaching to the Conquest. The noble poet did not see and feel great Nature's plan, as the rustic felt it; he wrote of everything as if in scorn; he treated virtue as an accident, and error as a certainty; and his fame must pay the penalty of his pride or his presumption. We read his noblest strains with an uneasy heart and a troubled brow: those who desire to draw the honey of happiness from divine verse, will not readily obtain it in the works of the gifted Byron.

The Zion's Herald (Methodist) says a pamphlet will shortly be issued in vindication of the result of the trial of E. K. Avery. The pamphlet maintains his entire innocence, and a mass of evidence will be introduced which was excluded at the trial. A relation by Mr. Avery of his acquaintance with S. M. Cornell will occupy a part of the pamphlet.

Worthy of imitation.—It is stated in the Journal of Commerce that "*all* the members of the Union College have signed a pledge of entire abstinence from ardent spirits, to be binding during the whole of their college course, and we trust to be acted upon during life. They have addressed circular letters to other colleges and academies, soliciting the *coöperation* of the students in the same glorious cause."

THE CONGRESSIONAL GLOBE.

PRINTED AND PUBLISHED AT THE CITY OF WASHINGTON, BY BLAIR & RIVES.

23d Congress, 1st Session. SATURDAY, FEBRUARY 22, 1834. Vol. I........No. 12.

HOUSE OF REPRESENTATIVES.

Saturday, *February* 15, 1834.

On motion of Mr. A. H. SHEPPERD,

Resolved, That the Committee on Indian Affairs be instructed to inquire into the expediency of compensating the Society of Moravians, or United Brethren, for their missionary improvements and expenditures in the Cherokee country, within the State of Georgia.

ALABAMA CONTROVERSY.

The following resolution, submitted on the 14th ult. by Mr. Gilmer, of Georgia, was taken up:

Resolved, That the Secretary of War be directed to communicate to this House all correspondence which he may have had, or information in his possession, in relation to the death of Hardeman Owens, a citizen of Alabama, who was lately put to death by a party of regular soldiers; whether said Owens was put to death in *pursuance* of orders from the War Department, or any officer of the United States; and that he also communicate to this House any correspondence which he may have had, or other information in his possession, in relation to any obstructions thrown in the way of the execution of the process of the courts of Alabama, issued for the purpose of bringing to trial those by whom said Owens was killed, and any correspondence in relation to the removal of said prosecutions to the District Court of the United States.

Mr. G. said, that knowing many of the friends and relatives of the deceased, he was induced to bring this subject to the attention of the House, and he could testify that, as they were mostly all his neighbors and constituents, they were of respectable standing in society. The father of Mr. Owens had commanded a company in the service against the Creeks, and died nearly in that place where his son was subsequently put to death. Owens himself had been, in 1830, chosen to survey the public lands, and he had means of knowing that whilst in that employment he had given full satisfaction. With this knowledge, then, of his and their general good conduct, he had seen, with surprise, those who had brought odium on themselves, endeavoring to free themselves from it by making aspersions on the character of the deceased. He had seen him, during the last summer, at his residence, which was situate on the great road to New Orleans; many white settlers were around him. At that time, he understood from him that he had raised and possessed extensive crops, which had been cultivated for him by his Indian neighbors, peaceably, and with perfect good feeling; that he had purchased many valuable Indian reserves from them whilst living there, for the time he had been amongst them, being about twelve months. He knew that, at this period, there was much excitement on the subject of Indian purchases, and Government were trying to collect the Indians together with a view to purchase their lands. He saw Owens on the most amicable terms with the Indians, and there was not any allegation then made by them against him that he was an intruder. But shortly after this, he was informed that he had been put to death, and he had received a letter from his bereaved widow, detailing the circumstances, and entreating him to obtain for her redress. To do this, he wrote to the President of the United States, and soon afterwards received a communication from the Secretary of War, couched in such terms as precluded any hope of obtaining redress from that quarter.

Mrs. Owens, he was sorry to state, was not only left with a numerous and young family, but she was afflicted with a chronic disease; all these circumstances made it difficult to conceive what situation could more justly claim their sympathy. It was in consequence of this feeling, that he desired inquiry to be made into the circumstances which attended the death of her husband. He understood that it was occasioned by some soldiers acting under orders given by the Secretary of War. But was this to be the employment given to their army? He thought such duties were incompatible with the duty that ought to be assigned them, and nothing but the strongest case of necessity could justify their being so employed. The House, then, as the grand inquest of the nation, were bound to inquire into the circumstances attending this act; and if a sufficient justification for it was not found, they should see that the outrage upon their laws should be amply vindicated. The fourth article of the Constitution expressly provided, that it was the right of the people to be secure in their persons, houses, &c., against unreasonable searches and seizures; and that no warrant should issue but upon probable cause, supported by oath or affirmation, and particularly describing the place to be searched, and the person or things to be seized; and such was the feeling of the framers of the Constitution, that but for this amendment, it never would have been adopted. This would be proved on reference to the various conventions held in Massachusetts, New York, and other places. He desired, therefore, in pursuance of this article, to know by what authority, by what warrant it was, that process had been issued and given to the soldiers of the United States, in consequence of which, one of the citizens of this country, entitled to the benefits of this article of the Constitution, had been deprived of his life? It was not his purpose to charge the persons implicated in this transaction; his object was to have the transaction itself investigated. The second clause in the resolution submitted by him, was for the purpose of ascertaining whether, after the act was perpetrated, and process thereupon had been issued for the purpose of having justice done in the premises of the State courts of Alabama, any obstruction had been given to that process by the officers of the army, acting under the orders of the Secretary of War? He understood that this was the case. That the death having been caused by some soldiers of the regular army stationed at Fort Mitchell, proceedings had been instituted; writs of *subpœna ad testificandum* had been issued, directed to those who were most cognizant of the circumstances, and that when the officer in command of the fort was requested to aid the civil authority, that aid was not given by him; but the parties implicated refused obedience to it, did not give the required assistance, and finally, that they were permitted to leave the country for the purpose of avoiding the process which had been issued against them. The proofs of all these facts, he believed, were in the possession of the Secretary of War, and could be communicated by him to the House. He required proof of this fact, because it was made the bounden duty of all officers in the service, by the twenty-third article of regulations, commonly called the articles of war, to aid the civil authority, and if this was refused or wilfully neglected, then, in such cases, the officer so refusing was to be cashiered. The House would from this see the importance there was, if the facts as alleged were true, of having that truth ascertained. The third clause in the resolution went to require a copy of any correspondence on the subject of removing the prosecutions commenced against the parties from the State courts of Alabama, in which they had commenced, to the circuit courts of the United States. He had reason to believe there was such a correspondence, as he held in his hand a printed copy of letters that passed on this subject from the Secretary of War to the Governor of Alabama, to Major McIntosh, Mr. Key, and to Mr. Austin, the deputy marshal of the southern district of that State, and from which it would appear that the United States Government had so far interfered with the State laws as to have endeavored to effect this removal of a cause which was then in progress, and pending before these courts, and that the right to do this was claimed by Government to have been conferred on it by the authority of what was called the Force Bill. If this was to be one of the first fruits of that bill, he hoped it would be the last. Mr. Secretary Cass, in his letter to Major McIntosh, says, that the seventh section of that bill makes ample provision for taking from the State tribunals, and carrying before those of the United States, all persons prosecuted for proceedings under that act. But if the law was fully examined, he contended that it would appear there was no such power to be found in it, nor was there any appointment of a special agent authorized by it. That act gave only the right of issuing a habeas corpus, to release from prison such persons as might be confined under the State laws. He referred to a decision given by the supreme court, in New York, where it was determined, in the case of a soldier killed at Fort Niagara, that the Supreme Court of the United States had not authority to act in similar cases, but that the power was possessed exclusively by the State courts.

He concluded by saying that, although he did not intend to make any charge against the Secretary of War, for whom he acknowledged he had the highest respect, in this matter, yet he was induced to submit the resolution, believing that the Government owed it to itself to have a matter investigated in which there were grave violations of their laws; the House were also bound to see that those laws were not wilfully violated.

Mr. CLAY rose, and said, before he would proceed to submit a few brief remarks on this subject, he wished that a message sent by the Governor of Alabama to the General Assembly of that State, should be read by the Clerk, that the House might know how this matter stood, and was viewed by the Governor of that State.

The message having been read accordingly—

Mr. SEABORN JONES expressed his desire that the documents which were sent with the message should be also read.

Mr. CLAY said, he had no objection to this being done.

[The following letters were then read by the Clerk, viz: one from Secretary Cass to Governor Gayle, an extract from same to F. S. Key, Esq.; letters to Major J. S. McIntosh and J. S. Austill, Esq.; all of which, with Governor Gayle's message, have been heretofore published in our paper.]

Mr. CLAY observed that, as it appeared from the documents that were just read, the matter in controversy had been adjusted, to the perfect satisfaction of Governor Gayle; and as there was no practical purpose suggested, he could not see the propriety or the necessity, now, of instituting the proposed inquiry. He could moreover state, that the Legislature of Alabama had exercised their opinion, and, in conformity to the recommendation of the Governor, passed a law which would regulate hereafter the intercourse with the Indians, and prevent any collision with them or their lands by intruders, which law, he was happy to be able to say, was considered satisfactory by the Executive of the United States

It would be recollected, that in this case a prosecution had been commenced against the deputy marshal of the district, and others implicated with him, for the death of Owens, in one of the circuit courts of Alabama, and although it was true, that, in the first instance, Major McIntosh had declined paying obedience to the process issued by the court, yet when this circumstance was made known to the Secretary at War, he promptly directed Major McIntosh not only to submit himself to the process, but he was instructed to facilitate by all the means in his power, any investigation which the civil authority should consider it necessary to make into the transaction, among those under his command. He considered that, as the whole matter was more properly a subject for judicial cognizance and investigation, the House was not the proper place to have it entertained. For it would be conceding, what he did not suppose the courts in Alabama ought, or would do, a surrender of their right to have exclusive jurisdiction in the matter. The resolution was objectionable, also, in its phraseology; for it called on the Secretary at

War to say whether Owens had not been put to death by his orders. This language, to say the least of it, was not very respectful to that personage. Under all the circumstances, viewing the transaction as one that had been adjusted, and as no ultimate practical benefit was suggested to arise from the proposed inquiry, he would abstain from further discussing it, and for the present move that the resolution be laid on the table.

Mr. LEWIS hoped the gentleman from Alabama would withdraw his motion to enable him to submit a few remarks.

Mr. CLAY having withdrawn the motion, in compliance with this request—

Mr. LEWIS said, he witnessed with much surprise the present opposition to the proposed inquiry. He would not discuss the merits involved in the present question, but as it was the usual course to adopt such resolutions, when presented to the House, he could not see any reason why that course should be departed from, although, as was alleged, the matter was satisfactorily adjusted. There was much importance attached by the gentleman to the law that was passed, having given satisfaction in that importance, or as having any weight on the present question. The resolution submitted, applied solely to the facts connected with Owens's death. These facts it was only right the country should be in full possession of. The resolution called for information whether there had been any improper interference with the jurisdiction claimed by, and, as he contended, rightfully belonging to, the State courts of Alabama, and it was proper that these facts should be substantiated. The gentleman [Mr. CLAY] could not perceive any object as likely to grow out of the resolution; but he thought there might be various objects anticipated from its adoption. Restitution to Mrs. Owens, of property of which she was despoiled, might be one object. To restore the jurisdiction of the State tribunals, another; and many others might be named. He owed it to his constituents and to himself to state, that the investigation sought for was necessary and proper, and that the gentleman from Georgia had his thanks for having proposed it.

Mr. BEARDSLEY having obtained the floor, he gave way to

Mr. GILMER, who disclaimed the intention of using any language that could be deemed disrespectful to the Secretary of War; he had not the slightest intention of casting any reflections upon him. He had meant to convey, that the deputy marshal was acting under the general orders of the Secretary, and he was willing to attend to any suggestion which the honorable member from Alabama might conceive to be necessary to free the Secretary from what he apprehended was an improper imputation. He had not charged him with the crime of killing Owens, but that the orders issued were of a character to justify the act. He would, however, modify the resolution, by substituting the words "the proper execution," for "in pursuance" of orders, &c., and add the words "or order," after any correspondence.

The resolution being modified accordingly—

Mr. BEARDSLEY rose, but was prevented by the expiration of the hour for morning business, from renewing the motion to lay the resolution on the table.

Mr. JONES moved to suspend the rules of the House, in order to proceed in the discussion of the resolution. Lost.

The House then proceeded to the order of the day.

The following bills were read a third time, and passed:

A bill for the relief of George Jones, assignee of Matthew Ramsey, deceased;

A bill for the relief of Frederick Raymer;

A bill for the relief of Antoine Cruzat;

A bill for the relief of the heirs of Lewis Grant Davidson;

A bill for the relief of H. A. De Saussure, executor of Alexander Garden, deceased;

A bill for the relief of the heirs and legal representatives of Philip Turner;

A bill granting pensions to certain persons therein named;

A bill for the relief of the representative of John M. Gregory;

A bill for the relief of William Weedon;

A bill for the relief of James Tilford;

A bill for the relief of Jeremiah Worsham;

A bill for the relief of the representatives of John Thompson, jr.;

A bill for the relief of Samuel A. Edmondson;

A bill for the relief of John Emerson;

A bill for the relief of Marguerite Baron.

Mr. WARD moved that the House do now adjourn.

Mr. STEWART asked for the yeas and nays on the motion, but the House refused to order them.

On division, the motion was carried, 132 rising in the affirmative—negatives not counted.

The House then adjourned.

IN SENATE.

MONDAY, *February* 17, 1834.

A message was received from the President of the United States, by Mr. DONELSON, his Private Secretary.

The VICE PRESIDENT laid before the Senate a communication from the Secretary of the Treasury, relative to surveys of public lands, with a report of the Commissioner of the General Land Office; which, on motion of Mr. TIPTON, was ordered to be printed.

The VICE PRESIDENT communicated a letter from the Secretary of the Treasury, on the subject of revolutionary bounty and warrants; which was read and referred, and ordered to be printed.

The VICE PRESIDENT communicated a letter from the Commissioner of the General Land Office, transmitting the number and names of surveyors and deputy surveyors employed in that branch of the Treasury Department; which, on motion of Mr. TIPTON, was ordered to be printed.

The VICE PRESIDENT communicated a memorial of the Legislative Council of Arkansas, and also of the Legislative Council of Michigan, praying the establishment of post routes; which were referred to the Committee on the Post Office and Post Roads.

Mr. BELL, from the Committee on Claims, reported a bill from the House of Representatives, for the relief of Aaron Bellamy, without amendment.

Mr. BELL, from the same committee, asked to be discharged from the further consideration of the motion of James Addis; which was agreed to.

Mr. BELL presented a memorial from the city of Portsmouth, New Hampshire, complaining, as Mr. B. said, of great embarrassment and pecuniary distress in that city, and ascribing the same to the removal of the deposites from the Bank of the United States. The memorial, Mr. B. said, was numerously signed by merchants, ship-owners, traders, and laboring men, all men of integrity and respectability, and entitled to as much weight as an equal number of men in any part of the country. He moved that the memorial be read, referred to the Committee on Finance, and printed, with names attached.

Mr. HILL said he had not had the privilege of a sight of the original memorial from Portsmouth; but a member of the House, who had a copy of it, had kindly shown that to him. Of the two hundred and fifty petitioners, so far as can be ascertained by gentlemen personally acquainted, there is not a solitary friend of the Administration upon it.

In relation to this memorial, he would ask leave to read extracts from a letter he had recently received from that town:

"On Saturday I perceived, by a notice stuck up at one end of the brick market, that the Federalists of this town were about to memorialize Congress upon the subject of the public deposites. Although this invitation was given to all, 'without distinction of party,' yet I feel persuaded that you will not find the name of a single friend of the Administration. If they have told you that there is any unusual pressure in this town, it is not true. There is no man here that feels embarrassed for the want of money, save those who have unaccountably extended their business upon a borrowed capital. Everything here commands a high price. The agriculturists feel no pressure. They are reaping richly of the blessings of a wise and judicious Administration, and of the bounties of a kind Providence. The merchants here might do the same, if it were not for the corrupt and corrupting, and shameful management of the banks—I say banks, because the most of the local banks in this town sympathize strongly in politics with Mr. Biddle's bank and its branches.

"I will venture to assert, and pledge my veracity upon the assertion, that the branch bank in this place has in her vaults at least fifty thousand dollars in specie, and at least thirty thousand dollars in local bills. If the fact be so, it would enable that bank alone to discount over a hundred thousand dollars. How much has been discounted at that bank I have not the means of knowing.

"This bank also refuses to send home the bills of the Commercial Bank, although the cashier has been repeatedly requested to do so, and receive the specie for them."

Mr. H. continued: Sir, the number of petitioners attached to the Portsmouth memorial is less than one-half the number of votes that have sometimes been cast by the opposition party in that town.

For some time past, it will be seen that the discount of the Portsmouth branch has averaged about $400,000. On the first of January it was $395,033—it was reduced in that month, when it was necessary to prepare for a petition, to $392,375—making a contraction of more than a thousand dollars in a day.

The Portsmouth petitioners probably owe the bank at least three-fourths of the whole debt. There are but few debts due out of that town; and of the bank's debtors the names of some of these few are on the petition.

Sir, very few persons at Portsmouth, or elsewhere in New Hampshire, would think of moving in favor of the bank, except those who act in this matter from party motives; for the bank has been a blighting curse to the men of business of that place.

There are, sir, on this petition several names of persons who failed in business four and five years ago, and whose names are on bad paper at the branch bank, five, ten, twenty, and up to sixty thousand dollars each.

There are also other names on the paper of respectable gentlemen, men of reputed wealth, who are reported to have permanent accommodation at the bank of from five thousand to twenty thousand dollars, which is employed in navigation or manufacturing establishments.

The branch at Portsmouth, Mr. President, ever since 1826, has been managed for the purpose of political favoritism; since that time very few, except political friends, have had loans on personal security; and of the whole loss incurred, it is believed not a dollar has been lost directly by any defalcation of any friend of the Administration.

We have a right to presume, as well from the character of the petitioners and their small number, as from the efforts that the friends of the bank have there made, that less than one-fourth of the people of Portsmouth is in favor of the bank. Independent of political bias, which a few men entertain, the friendship to the bank is forced, from the fears of those who are dependent on it. These men are generally under whose capital is or has been furnished by the bank.

There is on the petition scarcely the name of a mechanic or artisan who labors with his own hands. The workingmen, mechanics, and mariners, and farmers of that town, are made of too stern stuff to be compelled to petition for an object like this; and the party favored by the bank has too often been defeated in its attempts to coerce those resolute, highminded men, at this time to embark on such an undertaking. These men have long followed in the train with such men as Langdon, and Manning, and Hall, and Gardner; and it is too late in the day for the Havens, and the Ladds, and the Pierces, to lead them up to any encounter against popular rights.

The public voice in the State of New Hampshire sustains the President's opposition to rechartering of the bank by nearly three to one.

No meetings in that State have been called to

express opinions on this subject; but the friends of the State and National Administrations have recently had meetings in nearly every town, to elect delegates for their Council and Senatorial District Conventions for the present year. No organized opposition has yet appeared to the prevailing party, nor is there a probability that there will be any opposition. Yet never have the primary meetings been as full, or the conventions been so generally attended. More than two hundred of the two-hundred and thirty-eight towns, in each convention, have been represented. The delegates, in some instances, travelled a distance of seventy miles to attend them. And it is the interesting position of the country in relation to the Bank of the United States that thus called out these full conventions. Without any previous concert, the five council district conventions and eleven of the twelve senatorial conventions, have passed strong resolutions against rechartering the bank, and entirely approving the removal of the deposites. The conventions have not sent their resolutions here, but they have published them to the world.

At least three to one of the people of New Hampshire are opposed to this bank; and was it not that the question is identified with the two parties—the old Federal and Democratic parties—there would be none but the debtors and immediate dependants of the bank favorable to a renewal of its charter.

The retaining the bills of the Commercial Bank, which is the deposite bank, by the bank at Portsmouth, is proof conclusive of the predetermined hostility of the branch bank to the State banks that will not obey its commands. The manner of redeeming the notes of the interior banks in New England, has become a system, bringing all to a par value. Boston being the emporium to which all these notes flow, soon after they are issued, each bank has its specie fund at Boston to redeem them. If a bank should stop payment, the fact would be known at Boston before it was known at its own place of location. The funds are in Boston for the redemption of the bills. The Commercial Bank of Portsmouth keeps its funds there. The branch at Portsmouth, instead of either sending the notes of the Commercial to the counter of that bank at its own doors or sending them to Boston for redemption, chooses to hold on to them. Why? Because the managers of that bank know that by so doing they can pounce upon the Commercial Bank either at one place or the other; and thus compel the bank to provide a specie fund at both places at the same time for this single amount of money.

In 1832 I was surprised to find petitions coming in here from banks in New Hampshire, favorable to renewing the charter of the Bank of the United States. Those banks, generally, had had very little to do with the United States Bank; they never had been in a position to ask favors from it, or to be much affected in business by it. The banks in New Hampshire are generally in the hands of our political opponents.

After my return home, I was made acquainted with the process of procuring these petitions. The bank attorney at the head of the branch at Portsmouth was the agent to write to some political friend connected with each bank, urging that petitions might be forwarded. In some instances the directors of these banks having before their eyes the declaration of Mr. Biddle in 1830, that it was in the power of his bank, at almost any time, to annihilate the State banks, obeyed the command. In other cases, after a warm controversy, a majority of the directors voted the proposition down. And, in some few cases, no attention was paid to the call.

I have information from various parts of New England that calls from the South have been there made to get up agitation meetings on the subject of the deposites. But little impression as yet has been made out of the commercial towns; for there is an innate hostility to the United States Bank and its management throughout the whole interior of New England. The Massachusetts Legislature, opposed as it is to General Jackson and the Administration, has disobeyed the instructions which have been sent to Boston, and manifested the wise determination of not molesting the deposite banks in that State in the exercise of their rights. The effort on the State of New Hampshire thus far, has resulted in obtaining in a single town about one-half of the party in opposition to the Administration to put their names to a somewhat equivocal request that the deposites may be restored.

Mr. BELL said it would be inexcusable in him to answer all the remarks of the gentleman. But little of what he had said was applicable to the subject. But his observations in relation to the character of the signers of the memorial, required a few words in reply from him. He knew many of the memorialists, and he would undertake to affirm that they composed a very considerable portion of the merchants and business men of the city of Portsmouth. It was signed by the presidents, cashiers, and principal clerks in the five banks in that place. True, the memorial was not large, and probably contained no more names than had been mentioned. As to the misconduct of the branch bank at Portsmouth, he knew nothing. It might be that it had acted improperly. But the opinion there was, that in its general operations it had acted with great propriety, and had extended its accommodations to gentlemen of all political parties; and some of the directors were friends of the present Administration.

Mr KNIGHT presented the memorial of sundry citizens of Providence, Rhode Island, ascribing the distress of the mercantile community to the removal of the deposites, and asking their restoration to the Bank of the United States.

On presenting the memorial, Mr. K. addressed the Senate for a few minutes, and was followed by Mr. ROBBINS at some length.

The memorial was then referred to the Committee on Finance, and ordered to be printed.

Mr. WILKINS moved the special order of the day, but gave way to

Mr. CLAYTON, who made a report from the Committee on the Judiciary, relative to the message of the President of the United States of the 3d instant, in reference to the Bank of the United States refusing to pay over to the order of the Government the pension fund.

Mr. CLAYTON moved that the report, without being read, be laid upon the table and printed.

Mr. CLAY moved that six thousand copies be printed.

Mr. FORSYTH moved to lay the motion to print on the table, which was lost.

Mr. KING, of Alabama, renewed the motion to lay upon the table, when the yeas and nays were called, and are as follows:

YEAS—Messrs. Benton, Black, Calhoun, Forsyth, Grundy, Hendricks, Hill, Kane, King of Alabama, King of Georgia, Linn, McKean, Mangum, Moore, Morris, Robinson, Shepley, Sprague, Tallmadge, Tipton, Tyler, Waggaman, White, Wilkins, and Wright—25.

NAYS—Messrs. Bell, Bibb, Clay, Ewing, Knight, Naudain, Poindexter, Porter, Prentiss, Robbins, Silsbee, Smith, Southard, Swift, Tomlinson, and Webster—16.

The Senate then proceeded to the

SPECIAL ORDER OF THE DAY,

Being the memorial of inhabitants of Burke county, North Carolina, which, on motion of Mr. MANGUM, was laid upon the table.

Mr. CLAY'S resolution, extending the time for the payment of the revenue bonds, was then announced to be in order, but which, on motion of Mr. FORSYTH was laid upon the table.

The Senate then proceeded to the remaining order, being Mr. CLAY's resolution upon

THE REMOVAL OF THE DEPOSITES.

The special order of the day, being Mr. CLAY's resolutions relative to the removal of the deposites, coming up for consideration—

Mr. WILKINS rose and said, he hoped he would not be accused of affectation when he declared that he felt great apprehension and embarrassment in proceeding in a debate which had already occupied two months. As he intimated before, however, he felt it to be his duty, and he hoped the Senate would bear with him. He could neither promise brevity or expect to have influence—the dictates of his own conscience and the rectitude of his intentions were his own justification.

The resolution of the gentleman from Kentucky, and the report of the Committee of Finance upon that resolution, and the memorial of the Bank of the United States, all admit that the removal of the deposites was effected by the Secretary of the Treasury himself. The resolution tacitly admits the unqualified power of the Secretary over the deposites, and the report of the Committee on Finance admits his power and control, but assumes that it should only be exercised on important occasions, and that no emergency had happened which justified it; and they both admit the power of the Secretary to be contained in the 16th section of the charter. After these admissions, he could not but be surprised that in the memorials presented, and in the arguments of gentlemen here, the power was still denied. The second resolution charges no assumption of unconstitutional power on the Secretary, but fairly tenders the true issue. Was the removal of the deposites justified as a measure of public expediency? or, in the language of the charter, are the reasons sufficient and satisfactory? Believing that this was the proper issue, he was unwilling to listen to any change of it, and hence he voted against the amendment of his friend from Missouri, [Mr. BENTON.] Take up the 16th section of the charter as connected with the removal of the deposites, and there are three positions presented: the power unrestricted and absolute in the Secretary, the manner of executing it, and the propriety and sufficiency of the reasons for the act. To show the unrestricted power of the Secretary, he observed that the 16th section was divided into two parts. The first gives the absolute power in any emergency to place the public money in the Bank of the United States, or anywhere else he may deem proper. Now, this section gives the power and limits it, if it can be called limiting it, to placing the money there, unless otherwise ordered. The second paragraph requires him to give his reasons. There is here no qualification of authority or diminution of it in any way; but it says you may exercise it as you please, only let Congress know how you have exercised it, so that they may know whether any further legislation is necessary on the subject. It seemed difficult to ascertain how the 16th section found its way into the bill. He had traced it up, and discovered that it was offered as an amendment by the distinguished Senator from Massachusetts, [Mr. WEBSTER,] then a distinguished member of the House of Representatives. If he (Mr. WILKINS) might be allowed to conjecture, he had no doubt it was intended as a benefit to the bank; but it was a contingent one, to be enjoyed at the volition of the Secretary. And he thought there was some ground for the conjecture, that the friends of the bank had rather the deposites should be made there, and there continued, at the will of the Secretary, than that they should be subject to the will of Congress. They may have been afraid of the operations of the local banks upon Congress, when at any time the bank should become unpopular.

But whether the conjecture be correct or not, on recurring to the history of the Treasury Department ample authority for the exercise of the power as the Secretary has exercised it, would be found. Tracing it up from the first Continental Congress, it would be found that the Board of Treasury, as it was called by the ordinance of July 3, 1779, were to deposite the moneys in the most proper and safest places, and the Treasurer was to receive and keep them; and in the act of 1789 the phrase "the Treasurer is to receive and keep" is preserved, so that from the time of Robert Morris down through all the laws on the subject, we find the control of the Secretary over the deposites absolute. In the act of 1791 chartering the first bank, there is nothing said of the public deposites, but they are left to the Secretary. During the existence of the charter of the old bank it and the local banks shared in the public deposites, and they were managed by the Secretary as the public interests required; and when we come down to the bill submitted to Congress by Mr. Dallas in 1814, there was no provision in it, leaving them under the control of the Secretary. Nothing was intimated on this subject until the 16th section of the bank charter, the amendment offered by the gentleman alluded to, was introduced. It attracted no attention, or debate, but passed with other amendments.

And why? Because no change was made in the power of the Secretary over the public moneys. If it had made a change it would have attracted attention; but it was so unimportant that it passed without, because Congress left the power as they found it. Mr. Crawford, too, contended for the power, and whenever he spoke of the expediency of exercising it, referred to this same 16th section; and it was after that that he exercised it. But it had been said that the deposites were a part of the charter, and could not be removed without a violation of the contract. He acknowledged it was a contract, but he denied that the deposites were any consideration for the contract. The 14th section of the charter imposed the obligation on the Government to receive the notes of the bank and its branches as coin, and as a legal tender in all debts due the Government, and for this the bank contracted to transfer the Governmant funds wherever required. The deposites could not have been considered then, because they were contingent and could not have been viewed as part of the contract on the part of the bank. By the 14th section the notes of the bank were to be received, unless otherwise ordered by act of Congress. Mark the difference. The 16th section, alluding to a lighter matter, leaves the power with the Secretary, because Congress did not wish to impair the usage. If the deposites had entered into the consideration of the contract, why was it not said they should remain there until changed by act of Congress? The conclusion was irresistible that they were to be left to the exclusive control of the Secretary, and therefore they never could have entered into the consideration of the contract. The committee of investigation into the affairs of the bank, in 1829, of which Mr. McDuffie was one, unanimously agree in saying that whatever errors and abuses the bank may have been guilty of, they offer no remedy, but say that the Secretary has the power to apply a prompt remedy—the removal of the deposites. And in the debate upon the bank, on a motion to strike out the provision for the five Government directors, it was resisted, on the ground that all depended on the power of the Secretary to remove the deposites. This was the argument of Mr. Wells, of Delaware, who was opposed to the bank and to the Government; and none of those gentlemen applied the language of the section, or restricted it to the misconduct of the bank. He referred also to the report of Mr. McDuffie in 1830, where the power is admitted in general terms, and is in its nature a salutary corrective. Now there were two things admitted in the report—the removal of the deposites for any political interference of the bank, and that the power may be used upon any light occasion, for their withdrawal. But the Secretary would take care not to exercise it on any light occasion, because he was to give his reasons to Congress. A regard for his character would restrain him from its exercise on any light occasion. Mr. Crawford, in his correspondence, admits that they should not be removed from capriciousness, but for good reasons. The bank then had no reason to complain, because it was a contingent benefit, and the Secretary was amenable to Congress for the exercise of the power. The argument was not correct that the removal dissolved the connexion between the principal and the fiscal agent. These relations still remain, and the agency was retained by the bank, knowing that the deposites were contingent, and that universal usage and precedent united, gave the Secretary the absolute control over them.

The next objection was as to the manner and mode of removal. This, he did exactly as all his predecessors had done—in the form of transfer, which was always adopted. The objection of the gentleman from Kentucky, that the Treasurer ought to have selected the place of deposite, was quite novel. From the ordinance of '79, the Secretary was to choose the place, and he has done so from that day to this. The Treasurer to dictate to the Secretary! Is the Treasurer to say to the Secretary, I am determined to remove the deposites? If so, the Secretary certainly might, if he pleased, put them back again. The Treasurer puts no money into the treasury—but it is his duty to take care that none goes out of it without warrants lawfully issuing. "The treasury," means nothing local; it means a fund, on which Congress may draw—a credit established by the Secretary, and when established, then arises the jurisdiction of the Treasurer. He has nothing to do with the custom-house officers or revenue bonds. If he had, he would have authority to say, deposite the moneys here or there, where I choose to designate the place. The Treasurer's bond has been referred to—that instrument is in the penalty of $150,000. But could a bond in that paltry sum have been designed to secure the whole treasure of the United States? It was simply to control his own credit, not to sign warrants improperly. If, when the public moneys are taken from the Bank of the United States, the Treasurer can say, go there, or there, could not the Secretary order them back? Who would incur the responsibility of removal, if he had not also the power of fixing upon the place of deposite?

The next objection was the contingent transfer drafts; and when gentlemen spoke on this subject, it was with considerable asperity, which the conduct of the Secretary did not justify. If we examine his whole conduct, we will find that he was governed by vast liberality towards the bank, and with an ardent desire to promote the commercial facilities of the country. The forms of transfer were precisely the same as were uniformly used by the Government, and the same kind of draft which carried the public deposites into the Bank of the United States originally. He was determined to draw the money out gradually; but he was driven, by the conduct of the bank, from his amicable disposition towards it, and then the public money was spread over the various cities of the Union for the commercial good. But it has been said that the Secretary's conduct was disingenuous in reference to the transfer drafts. Now, if the Senate would look over his conduct, they will find that there was in it no concealment or disingenuousness whatever. If the bank had condescended to inquire, it would have known of the existence of the drafts. Why did the bank, on the 1st August, 1833, begin a rapid and ruinous curtailment, merely to meet these drafts? Some of them were contingent drafts, not to be presented till the second week in November. The paper read to the Cabinet was published in September, and all knew the removal would ensue on the 1st October. It was in consequence of the uncertain state of things produced by the fear of the deposite banks that a run would be made upon them by the Bank of the United States, that these drafts were given them, only to be used in case of the contemplated rush. [Mr. W. here read the letter of instructions of the Secretary to the Girard Bank; also, his letter enclosing the contingent drafts; also, the letter dated 7th October, 1833, to the deposite bank in Baltimore.] These letters show the liberal disposition of Mr. Taney towards the Bank of the United States, and show that the transfer drafts were only to be used in case of a run. Where, then, was the want of candor on the part of Mr. Taney, or an illiberal or disingenuous feature in his conduct? His instructions were, use the drafts in your own defence—wait till you are attacked; if there is no rush, no demand for coin, founded on the public deposites, don't use them, but return them to me. How different the conduct of the Bank of the United States, when, the other day, a rush was made by it on the Bank of the Metropolis here. It had accumulated $150,000 of their bills, and refused to take their branch drafts, but took from the deposite bank $50,000 in coin, when the branch had a larger amount in its vaults and the parent bank had its millions. This was the return for Mr. Taney's liberality. If he could advise Mr. Taney, and he would be governed by a spirit of retaliation, he would tell the Secretary to stand by the public deposites and reject these branch drafts. But he designed no such thing, although it had been intimated that such was his intention. It was a mistake, although it had been decided that they were not bank notes, yet he would not take advantage of the decision. He was governed by the wishes of the country, and an anxious regard to facilitate its commercial facilities, and therefore he went on receiving these false and spurious branch drafts. If he had been governed by the vindictiveness of the bank, he would say, reject them, who cares for the country? We will curtail them; who cares for the good of the country?

Another objection, urged by the gentleman from New Jersey, [Mr. Southard,] as to the situation in which the disbursing officers of the Government would be placed in case the public money should be lost—that it would be the loss of the officer, and not the Government. But this is a fallacy. The fourth section of the act of 4th March, 1809, provides that the "public agents shall keep the public money in the incorporated banks designated." Now, when it is placed there by the disbursing officer, agreeably to law and the directions of the President, the officer would, in no case of loss, be liable. And yet this law was passed during the existence of the old bank, authorizing the public moneys to be placed in any incorporated bank, which showed that they never looked to the Bank of the United States as the *only* depository at that time.

Well, the public moneys have been transferred to local incorporated State banks, and the Secretary had made contracts for their disbursement, which have been scrutinized, and their whole validity denied. The gentleman from Kentucky, alluding to the law prohibiting the heads of departments from making any contracts, says the Secretary had no power to make contracts with the State banks. To this Mr. W. had a short but conclusive answer. The power to make these arrangements was an incident to, and followed the right to remove the deposites. It therefore follows that the power to make the contract, and to carry it into execution, arises out of the high political power of the United States.

Mr. W. here gave way to a motion for adjournment.

And the Senate adjourned.

HOUSE OF REPRESENTATIVES.

Monday, *February* 17, 1834.

Mr. ADAMS, of Massachusetts, reminded the House that he had given notice that he would this day renew his attempt to have the memorial from the city of New York, in favor of a warehousing system, referred to the Committee on Manufactures. Mr. A. had since received a copy of the memorial, and he proceeded to review its contents. The general object of the memorial was, to change the law of 1832,—a law which had been sometimes termed a compromise. It had not been expected that the subject of the tariff would be touched at the present session, nor was he disposed to bring it before the House. Mr. A. then moved a reconsideration of the vote by which the memorial had been referred to the Committee of Ways and Means.

Mr. CAMBRELENG expressed his surprise that any gentleman should oppose this measure, especially a gentleman who was so intimately connected with gentlemen who were now so clamorous for relief, and constantly, in both Houses, demanding it from their opponents. He was surprised that the very first measure of relief should meet with hostility from that quarter. The petitioners ask nothing more than an extension of the warehousing system, which was already adopted in regard to wine and spirits, to teas also, as long as the duties existed. Under the present law, if the duties on certain merchandise were not paid within three months after their importation, they were to be sold at auction. For this law he voted, for no other reason but to prevent the effusion of blood in the country. It was certainly proper at this time, to remove some of the objectionable features of that law. What would be the result, if the prayer of the memorial was not granted? The dry goods which are imported must, in many cases, come to auction, and be sacrificed by forced sales for cash, daily and weekly, at all seasons, whereby not only the merchant, but the domestic, as well as the foreign manufacturer, would be greatly injured. The merchants ask permission to deposite their goods in the custody of the customs until they can find an opportunity to dispose of them advantageously, and to be allowed a credit of three, six, and nine months upon the duties. They do not ask you to lend them the money of the Government, as proposed in the Senate. Nine tenths of those interested in the trade would infinitely prefer the measure asked for in the memorial. He regretted to see the gentleman from Massachusetts, [Mr. Adams,] throwing this impediment in the way of the petitioners. There were, on the

6th of February last, sixteen hundred and thirty packages of merchandise, which would soon be sent to auction under the 6th section of the act of July, 1832. They belonged chiefly to those who were unable to raise money to pay the duties at such a crisis. If relief was not promptly granted, the merchandise would be sacrificed and it would add to the ruin now existing. He hoped that the House would not reverse its decision, and send the memorial to the Committee on Manufactures, where we should never hear from it again, which was too manifestly the object of the motion. It was indispensably necessary to extend relief promptly to this branch of trade. The memorialists asked for nothing but an act of sheer justice, and a measure founded in the soundest policy. It related to the collection of the revenue, and belonged to the Committee of Ways and Means, and he hoped the House would not sustain the motion to reconsider its decision.

Mr. HUNTINGTON thought, he said, that the resistance of the motion to reconsider came with an ill grace from the gentleman from New York. He, Mr. H., voted against the bill of 1822, and the bill of 1833; but the gentleman from New York voted for both of those acts. Then he said nothing about a warehouse system, nothing of the danger of losing our carrying trade. The effect of the proposition of the memorial, which the gentleman advocated, would be to open the whole subject of the tariff for discussion. Does any man suppose that the compromise bill would have passed, without the provision for the cash payment of duties? Those who wished to agitate the country again with this subject, would press the proposition of the memorialists. A word on this subject of relief.

The CHAIR interposed, and restricted the range of Mr. H.'s remarks.

Mr. CAMBRELENG agreed with the gentleman from Connecticut, as to the impropriety of opening the tariff question again for discussion. He was not disposed to draw any contrast between his votes and those of the gentleman from Connecticut. It was true that he (Mr. C.) voted for the compromise bill, and he would tell the gentleman he knew of no interest in this country, commercial, agricultural, or manufacturing, which he was not ready to sacrifice in order to avert from the country the calamities of a civil war.

Mr. SELDEN said that he apprehended that the reading of the memorial would at once put an end to this quarrel between the two committees, and induce the House to send it to a third committee. At his request, the memorial was read. Mr. S. then proceeded to comment upon the objects of the memorial. The whole was peculiarly a commercial subject, and, in his opinion, ought to go to the Committee on Commerce. Should the motion to reconsider prevail, he would move the reference of the memorial to that committee.

Mr. ADAMS made some remarks in reply to the gentleman from New York, [Mr. CAMBRELENG,] and said that the gentleman was incorrect in supposing that he made the motion from hostility to the object of the memorial. He made it with a view to prevent the opening of a question which had so long and seriously agitated the country. What he contended for was, that this memorial goes to destroy the compromise of the last year. Some other remarks he made which we could not distinctly hear.

Mr. CAMBRELENG spoke in reply to the gentleman from Massachusetts, and contended that it had been the uniform practice of the House to refer subjects of this sort to the Committee on Ways and Means.

Mr. DICKSON called for the yeas and nays, and they were ordered.

The question was then taken on the motion to reconsider the vote by which the memorial had been referred to the Committee of Ways and Means, and was decided in the negative, 84 to 123.

Mr. HARPER, of New Hampshire, presented the memorial of certain inhabitants of Portsmouth, New Hampshire, which he moved be referred to the Committee of Ways and Means.

Mr. H. said, that the petition complained of the distress of the times, which it attributed to the removal of the public deposites from the Bank of the United States. The memorial stated, that, previously to the establishment of the present bank, the same state of things existed that now exists; the same general want of confidence, the same scarcity of money, and the same inequality in the exchanges of the country. That the establishment of the bank restored mutual confidence, established a sound currency, and equalized exchanges, and was followed by general prosperity. The memorial concluded by praying Congress that the deposites may be restored, or that some other measure be devised to bring back confidence to the public mind. The petition, he said, was signed by two hundred and fifty citizens of Portsmouth, of highly respectable character, men of wealth and of influence, and who were entitled to his respect.

The memorialists, he observed, set forth in their petition, that it was the duty of the people to make known to their representatives the wants and grievances of those whom he represented, and the duty of the representative to lay those before the legislature. In this doctrine Mr. H. said that he fully concurred. But it was due to the House and to himself, to state the means he possessed of becoming acquainted with the sentiments and wishes of his constituents.

The town of Portsmouth contained between eight and nine thousand inhabitants, of whom more than one thousand were voters. This memorial was signed by two hundred and fifty persons only. Such a number constituted a minority even of the voters alone, and did not include more, or but little more, than half of the minority who has opposed his election.

There were different opinions as to the cause of the difficulty experienced by the commercial community. That difficulty did exist he was not prepared or disposed to deny; but there might be other causes for it besides the removal of the deposites from the Bank of the United States. One cause might have been over-trading, an abuse of the credit system, the dependence on fictitious capital, the habit of living beyond men's income, and not the least was undoubtedly the conduct of the bank itself. The president and cashier of one of the banks in Portsmouth had petitioned that the deposites, when removed, might be placed there; but the Government had seen fit to place them elsewhere, and now the names of these same gentlemen were found appended to a memorial praying that the deposites might be restored to the United States Bank.

These memorialists declared their belief that the directors of that bank had conducted its affairs rather with a view to the public good than to mere private emolument; but he saw attached to this memorial the names of some who had petitioned those directors, that the president of the Portsmouth Bank might be removed from office for favoritism. New Hampshire contained (he said) five councillor districts, eight counties, and twelve senatorial districts. In all of these, meetings had been held, and candidates had been nominated, in view of the election to take place three weeks from to-morrow. These were all primary meetings of the people; delegates, consisting of twice the number they were entitled to in the State Legislature, had been present; and in nearly all of these meetings, resolutions had been passed, approving of the removal of the deposites, and against the recharter of the bank; some of these he would read.

[Mr. H. here read a number of resolutions passed at district meetings in the State of New Hampshire, of which the following was the first, and the rest of a similar character:

Resolved, That each successive year of the Administration of our venerable Chief Magistrate increases our confidence in the wisdom of his measures, and our admiration of his firmness and decision in carrying those measures into effect.

Resolved, That the removal of the public deposites from the Bank of the United States, by the Secretary of the Treasury, has our unqualified approbation.]

These (Mr. H. said) were, in his judgment, much more conclusive evidence of public opinion, than the two hundred and fifty signatures got up to a petition in the manner well known to most who heard him. It was to be presumed that the opponents of the Administration had got all the signatures to such a memorial that they conveniently could.

Senatorial convention, in District No. 4, passed, among others, the following resolutions:

Resolved, That we recognise in the Secretaries of the different departments of our national Government men of patriotism, talents, and integrity; and that in all their official acts, (especially that of Mr. Secretary Taney in removing the deposites,) they merit the confidence and gratitude of the American people.

Resolved, That in the systematic opposition that has been so perseveringly urged to General Jackson and his Administration, we recognise the principles of old-fashioned Federalism, as exhibited in the days of John Adams, the embargo, and the late war—which principles we will fearlessly and unceasingly oppose.

Resolved, That our Representatives in Congress be requested to use all constitutional means to resist a return of the public deposites to the United States Bank, and a recharter of that aristocratic and dangerous *monopoly*.

Grafton and Coos counseller District passed, among others, the following:

Resolved, That we regard the Bank of the United States as an institution unconstitutional in its origin, and dangerous in its operations to the liberties of the country; that its history for the last five years unfolds a degree of crime and corruption in the conduct of its affairs without a parallel in our annals, and richly entitling its managers to the scorn and indignation of the American people.

Resolved, That the removal of the public deposites from an institution so dangerous and corrupt, was but an act of justice to the outraged moral sentiments of an abused and insulted people, and that, instead of making the removal a subject of complaint, the bank should have borne the deprivation with the meekness of a contrite, convicted culprit.

Senatorial District No. 1, among others, passed the following:

Resolved, That the withdrawal of the public deposites at the present juncture is wise, just, and necessary, and the only means of parrying the blow which the bank meditated, and has partially inflicted, on the business community.

Resolved, That the President of the United States has, in withstanding the gigantic advances of this common enemy, merited the lasting gratitude of his country, and is entitled to the support of all good citizens.

District No. 10, I find the following:

Resolved, That the firm and patriotic course which General Jackson has pursued in relation to the United States Bank, particularly as evinced by the removal of the deposites from that institution, increases and strengthens his claims upon the gratitude and admiration of his countrymen.

Resolved, That we approve of the conduct of the Secretary of the Treasury in relation to the removal of the deposites from the United States Bank, deeming the measure both expedient and necessary, in order to prepare the country for the closing up of the concerns of that institution, and to prevent, in a measure, any act of mischief, which it may be disposed to commit in order to compel a renewal of its charter.

The memorial was then referred to the Committee of Ways and Means, and ordered to be printed.

Mr. BURGES presented a similar petition from Providence, in Rhode Island, in which he stated that they allege, that the prosperity heretofore enjoyed, could not be secured, unless the former relations of amity that existed between the Government and the bank were restored. The memorial was signed by 1065 persons, who were nearly all the voters of that city. And after enlarging upon the stability and industry which was found to pervade the State of Rhode Island generally, he remarked that those persons were actuated by one mind, and not from sinister motives, in giving their present sentiments. He called for the reading of the memorial, and would then move that it be referred to the eternal Committee of Ways and Means.

The memorial having been read—

Mr. PEARCE remarked that the signatures to it seemed to be, many of them, in one hand writing.

Mr. BURGES explained, that the original memorial, of which this was a counterpart, was presented to the Senate.

Mr. PEARCE denied that the memorial spoke the voice of the city of Providence; for as there were 19,000 inhabitants in the city, 1050 could not be considered such a number as to be called the voice of that city. He had no doubt that there was some pressure, but it must evidently be exaggerated, and he thought that they wanted light and information as to the cause of it. It was not more than three weeks since large sums, amounting to nearly $300,000, had been loaned by inhabitants of Providence to merchants of New Bedford and of New York. This evinced that there was not so great a scarcity of money as was represented, and he argued that if there was, that the Legislature of the State of Rhode Island would have given some expression of their opinion, as well as other States. He could affirm that the views contained in this memorial were not generally felt, for at a meeting last week held at Newport, called to discuss the measures of the Administration, the meeting separated without adopting any resolutions whatever. The statements made of the existing distress must be received with some grains of allowance. He thought that what was most wanting at the present crisis was decision, decision to restore the country to its former state, and thus prevent the country from having its property made one general wreck.

Mr. BURGES said he was much embarrassed at the flat contradiction which had been given to him by his colleague, and expressed his surprise that the correctness of those whom he and his colleague knew so well, should be questioned by him. He proceeded to support the views taken by the memorialists, and did not consider that his colleague could, with any propriety, call in question the statements he had made in regard to a memorial expressly committed to his care from the citizens of Providence. His colleague had made this attack upon him without giving him any notice of his intention to speak on the subject, and he expressed his regret that his colleague should take this occasion to sunder the ties of amity which had heretofore subsisted between them.

Mr. PEARCE, in reply, insisted that he had made no attack upon his colleague. His colleague had gone out of his course in his remarks, to make some statements which, as a representative in part of the State of Rhode Island, he felt bound to correct. The facts which he (Mr. P.) had stated, were not denied. In what, then, had he made any misrepresentation on the subject of the memorial? His object was to exhibit the views of the people of Rhode Island on this subject in a true light. He believed that if the question of bank or no bank were presented to the people of that State, there would be found a majority in opposition to the bank. Three years ago there would not have been five hundred votes in opposition to the bank. But a great change had taken place in public opinion on this subject in Rhode Island. His colleague had given to the House part of a speech which had been concocted for another occasion. This was, perhaps, as good an occasion as any for delivering it; and it was not his intention to make any reply to his argument. He wished his colleague to learn that he was not to consult him in regard to his course in this House. In relation to his colleague's course, he should never express any regret, and he hoped that his colleague would cease to express his regrets at his (Mr. P.'s) course. Personally, he entertained a regard for his colleague, and, before this session, they had commonly acted together. That he now differed from his colleague, was only a proof that his colleague differed from him.

Mr. BURGES rejoined, in a few words, which were not heard by the reporter.

Mr. HARPER, of Pennsylvania, presented the memorial of sundry citizens of Philadelphia, engaged in the manufacture of boots and shoes, representing that their business is embarrassed by the deranged state of the currency, and praying the restoration of the deposites and the recharter of the Bank of the United States. Mr. H. accompanied the presentation with some remarks in support of the views of the memorial, and, on his motion, the memorial was read, and ordered to be printed.

Mr. GALBRAITH presented two memorials from citizens of the county of Erie, in Pennsylvania, one in support of the removal of the deposites, and the other praying their restoration. Ordered to be printed.

Mr. SUTHERLAND presented a memorial from citizens of Southwark and Moyamensing, praying the restoration of the public deposites; which was read, and Mr. S. moved to have it printed.

Mr. MANN, of New York, objected to the memorial being printed. After some remarks from Mr. WATMOUGH and Mr. SUTHERLAND, he withdrew his objection, and the memorial was referred to the Committee of Ways and Means and ordered to be printed.

The SPEAKER presented similar resolutions from the chairman who presided at the meeting.

Mr. SUTHERLAND presented resolutions on the same subject from Germantown and Bristol, Pennsylvania, for the restoration of the deposites; and from a meeting of cordwainers, held at Independence Hall, Philadelphia, the reverse of that presented by his colleague, [Mr. HARPER,] and which went to contradict the statement put forth "that the shoemakers were out of employment." Mr. S. took that occasion to say, that there was more mischief brought upon the country by the waste of time in debating the question of the removal than by any other cause; he would therefore entreat the House to come up to the question at once, and have a decision upon it, one way or the other.

Mr. HARPER disclaimed having said that the shoemakers were out of employment; he said that the master-shoemakers were afraid that their resources would soon be cut off, and thus, that those they employed must soon be thrown out of employment if there was not some change made in the present state of the pecuniary relations of the country.

Mr. LYON, of Michigan, presented a memorial of the Legislative Council of Michigan Territory, praying the establishment of certain post routes in said Territory. Referred to the Committee on Post Offices and Post Roads.

Mr. HEATH presented the memorial of a meeting of citizens of Baltimore, praying the restoration of the deposites to the Bank of the United States.

Mr. HEATH spoke in support of the views of the memorialists. He said he came to this House not as a party man, but as an independent citizen; and he declared that no man in this nation had been a more pure, sincere, and disinterested friend of General Jackson than himself, and that he had uniformly supported his measures. He appealed to the friends of the President on this floor to say whether, if the President should to-morrow send us a message informing us that he had directed the deposites to be restored to the United States Bank, they would not give their hearty approbation and support to the measure.

The memorial was read, and ordered to be printed.

The SPEAKER presented the resolutions of eight hundred citizens of Richmond, Virginia, in favor of the restoration of the public deposites to the Bank of the United States.

Mr. PATTON called for the reading of the resolutions; and after they were read, Mr. P. said he felt it his duty to state, after having, in courtesy to the memorialists, asked for the reading of the resolutions, that he dissented almost wholly from the views expressed in the memorial. At another time he hoped to have an opportunity to lay his views fully before the House on this subject. He only wished now to say that he dissented from the opinion that the President had exercised an unconstitutional authority. He concurred in the opinion that the measure of the President was unwise and ill-timed, but at the same time he believed that he had acted honestly, and that he had done that which he had a right to do, and which it was, moreover, his constitutional duty to do. In regard to the policy of restoring the deposites to the Bank of the United States, he also dissented wholly from the memorialists. The question whether the bank should be rechartered, was, in his opinion, inseparably connected with the question whether the deposites should be restored. What good were we to do by restoring the deposites, without accompanying it with an assurance that the bank should be rechartered? The dismay and distress would, in a few months, return upon us with aggravated severity, unless the bank felt assured that its charter would be renewed. He saw no reason, for his own part, to believe that the bank would be rechartered. He believed that if the question, whether the bank should be rechartered, or a bank should be chartered, were now put to this House, there would be a majority of this body against it. If the bank was certainly to be rechartered, he would, without hesitation, vote for the restoration of the deposites.

On Mr. PATTON's motion, the resolutions were ordered to be printed.

Mr. GRAHAM presented the resolutions adopted by a meeting of citizens of Bertie county, North Carolina, praying the restoration of the public deposites, and representing that the resolutions "were sustained with considerable ability by the Hon. Samuel P. Carson, and adopted without a dissenting voice." Read, and ordered to be printed.

Mr. TOMPKINS presented the resolutions of the lower branch of the Legislature of Kentucky, condemning the removal of the deposites, and the exercise of the veto power by the President. Read, and ordered to be printed.

Mr. LYON, of Kentucky, presented the memorial of thirty-three citizens of Kentucky, disapproving of the removal of the deposites: ordered to be printed.

Mr. LYON also presented the memorial of the Endless Life Society, praying a grant of land, with a view to the promotion of their scheme of rendering perpetual human life on this earth: referred to the Committee on Public Lands, and ordered to be printed.

Mr. CARR presented a preamble and joint resolution of the members of the Senate and of the House of Representatives of the Legislature of the State of Indiana, on the subject of improving the navigation of the Ohio river at the falls, particularly through the Indian Chute, instructing their Senators and requesting their Representatives in Congress to use their best endeavors to procure the passage of a law appropriating a liberal sum of money, to be expended in improving the navigation at the place aforesaid, under the superintendence of some qualified person or persons; which, after a brief explanation made by Mr. C., was, upon his motion, referred to the Committee on Roads and Canals.

Mr. CARR presented a petition, asking for the establishment of a mail route from Charleston, Clarke county, to Rockford, Jackson county, Indiana; also, for the establishment of a mail route from Charleston to New Providence, in Clarke county, Indiana; which, on his motion, was referred to the Committee on the Post Office and Post Roads.

Mr. PINCKNEY presented the resolutions of a public meeting of the citizens of Charleston, South Carolina, praying the restoration of the deposites: read, and ordered to be printed.

On motion, the House then adjourned.

IN SENATE.

TUESDAY, *February* 18, 1834.

A message was received from the President of the United States, by Mr. DONELSON, his Private Secretary.

Mr. HENDRICKS, agreeably to notice, introduced a bill appropriating $20,000 for the purpose of improving the navigation of the Wabash river; which was read twice, and referred to the Committee on Roads and Canals.

Mr. TYLER presented the memorial of a number of the inhabitants of Richmond, Virginia, asking Congress to adopt measures to relieve the distresses, of the community; and asserting the cause of that distress to be the removal of the public deposites from the Bank of the United States.

Mr. TYLER also presented a similar memorial from inhabitants of Franklin, in Virginia; which,

after some remarks made by Mr. T., were read, referred to the Committee on Finance, and ordered to be printed.

Mr. BIBB presented resolutions of the House of Representatives of Kentucky, protesting against the dangerous power exercised by the President of the United States, in causing the public moneys to be removed from the Bank of the United States, and complaining of the use of the veto power by the Executive. The resolutions were read, referred to the Committee on Finance, and ordered to be printed.

On motion of Mr. MANGUM, the order to print 6,000 copies of the report of the Judiciary Committee on the message of the President, relative to the pension fund, was taken up.

Mr. CALHOUN called for the reading of the report.

After the reading; which occupied an hour and five minutes—

Mr. MORRIS moved as an amendment, that 6000 copies of the President's message, the opinion of the Attorney General, and the accompanying documents, also be printed; which amendment was adopted, and the resolution, as modified, was agreed to.

At two o'clock the special order of the day was taken up, being the report of the Committee on Finance, and Mr. CLAY's resolution relative to

THE REMOVAL OF THE DEPOSITES.

Mr. WILKINS having resumed his remarks, said that he endeavored yesterday, in an humble manner, not only to show that the removal of the deposites was a rightful exercise of authority on the part of the Secretary of the Treasury, but the mode sanctioned by the usage of the department, by all the statesmen who have heretofore acted in the department, and by the laws of the country. The expediency of the measure bore the Secretary out in his reasons for the removal. And in justifying him, Mr. W. would assume the following positions. The attitude of the bank in respect to the near termination of its charter; the rapid curtailment of its accommodations adopted on the 1st of August; that the State banks are the only proper depositories, in the absence of all law providing for any other; that the present distresses of the country were not owing to the removal of the deposites, but to the harsh, vindictive spirit of the bank; and lastly, that they ought not to be restored to the Bank of the United States, because the crisis must be met, and the restoration would only produce the same, and greater disorder, when they should ultimately be removed. When a head of a department is about to discharge a duty devolved upon him by an act of Congress, which would seriously affect the finances of the country, he must find his justification in the laws imposing the duty on him. That he is confined to acting, not on rumor, but to the provisions on the statute book, and the Secretary was bound to look no farther than the charter, by which the bank was to close its concerns on the 4th of March, 1836, two years and five months from the order of removal. The term being thus fixed, the Secretary could not suppose it would be extended one hour longer. He knew the bank was created on the termination of the war to correct the disorder of the currency, and assist the financial operations of the country; that the crisis and emergency had passed, and that no consideration of the same kind existed for the continuance of the charter now. And he had stronger reason for believing that the two years given it after the expiration of its charter contemplated its determination, and that the farther provision in the 16th section, gave the power preparatory to the final closing of the bank. But if we were disposed to tell the Secretary that he ought to have looked to public sentiment for his course of action, what is the conclusion? Everything justified him in the conclusion he came to. The bill for rechartering the bank had been lost, and the very Chief Magistrate who vetoed it was reëlected by the people. Mr. W. did not think, with some gentlemen, that his reëlection was a decision against the bank. He thought the people looked beyond the bank question, and that thousands voted for General Jackson, who, to-morrow, would vote to recharter the bank. His reëlection proved that during his second term the question of rechartering was settled and at an end. Gentlemen on this floor declared, after the veto message was received, that the President had assumed the responsibility of putting an end to the bank, and that the country ought to prepare for the termination of its charter. This was the condensed argument of the gentleman from Massachusetts, and the whole country, the Government, and every individual, were bound to prepare for its downfall; and was the Government to be the last to prepare? Mr. W. contended that the question presented was the renewal of the charter of the bank, and the bank ought to come forward and have it settled; for if it is not to be renewed, the deposites ought not to be restored. The question, then, was merely one of time *when* the removal should take place. It was an experiment that was to be done, and there was little time for doing it in.

It was an experiment to ascertain whether the country could get along without the Bank of the United States, and whether the State banks were sufficient for the purposes of Government? If it were doubtful, the earlier it was made the better; and if it failed before the 4th of March, 1836, it would be testing the necessity of the bank to the Government. [Mr. W. then read from the memorial of the bank to Congress in 1831–'2, to show that it admitted that the earlier the question was decided that the country could prepare for the change arising from the non-renewal of the charter, the better for the nation and the bank.] The allegation that the Secretary ought to have waited the sixty days till the meeting of Congress, had no weight; for if the bank had the right to the public money, nothing could give Congress jurisdiction over it but the previous action of the Secretary. Neither the President nor the Secretary could bring it before Congress, nor could Congress say the Secretary must act. But it was the original intention of the Secretary to have waited for the meeting of Congress, and his determination was only changed by the improper and resentful conduct of the bank itself. The declaration of the Secretary, at page nineteen of his report, Mr. W. referred to as fully showing this. In August, while Mr. Duane was Secretary, and supposed to be protecting the interests of the bank, they commenced an immediate and ruinous system of curtailment, which clearly justifies the wisdom of the act, and shows that the immediate action of the Secretary was necessary. And now the bank seeks to press the country by the same means which it used to prevent the removal. The most proper places, then, for depositing the public money—there being no national bank, no private depository, and no provision for the approaching termination of the charter—was the local banks. This selection was in accordance with all usage and precedent. All the Secretaries, and Mr. Duane himself, pointed to the State banks as the proper depositories for the public money. And it was argued by some of the most distinguished men opposed to the old bank, that the State banks were the most appropriate depositories. And this, too, was argued by the gentleman from Virginia, opposite, [Mr. TYLER,] in the House of Representatives, when contending for the greater safety of the public money. And if the State banks were safe then, (during the war,) why was not the argument as good now, when banking is better understood, when capitals are larger, and they have had ample experience since the war? They are now on a more solid foundation, they are all specie-paying banks, and are infinitely more substantial than the branch banks. In regard to the contracts of the Secretary, they are discreet and cautious, and were made with prudence and liberality, and with a true regard to the interests of the commercial community. Look at his arrangements, and it will be seen that they secure the same control which was provided by Mr. Crawford, and followed up by Mr. Rush in 1826; and it is not correct now to say that the people have confidence only in the Bank of the United States: because, wherever there are branch banks, it will be found that the individual deposites are greater in the State banks than they are in the branches, and this remark equally applies to the private and public deposites in all the large cities.

[Mr. W. here read the late statements of the Bank of the United States to this point of his argument.]

As to the Secretary's arrangements with the State banks, it was attended with no expense whatever to the Government, but was borne by the banks themselves. His next point was, that the conduct of the bank was resentful and coercive, and although distress and pressure did exist, that it was much magnified by the newspapers and the discussions here, which, if terminated, the distress would subside, and the strength and elasticity of the country would enable the community to accommodate itself to the new condition of things. There was abundance of resources in the country, and the report of the New York committee, who have just returned home from a visit to this place, distinctly declares that they believe there is no project here for any national bank—that there is no struggle between Chesnut street and Wall street; and they exonerate both the first and second officers of the Government from any such view or intention. There is no such object, and if he (Mr. W.) believed it was to terminate in a contest between Chesnut street and Wall street, he would abandon the course he had now taken, and cease to sustain the act of the Secretary. There was no such project; he could not be mistaken, and the moment that question was presented, he should instantly determine in favor of Chesnut street, in the good city of William Penn. No. The rivalry between Philadelphia and New York was of a higher and more honorable character—it was a struggle in the great internal improvements which they were both prosecuting, for the trade of the Great West, from which Pennsylvania would not depart till she had succeeded in obtaining it. These distresses were local, not national, or extending over the whole land. He could not believe that they had fallen on that class of citizens so valuable to the country, and which he greatly respected—he meant the American merchant—for which he would make any sacrifice except the rights of the Government to the ambition of the bank. Where is the real evidence of distress? There are no more bankruptcies now than there were when the bank was in the full enjoyment of its power; they were confined to brokers, stockjobbers, and those who live on every morning's discount obtained at the bank. The great mass of the people were undisturbed—the bone and sinew of the country were unembarrassed—all the elements of prosperity are among us, and our resources abundant; and therefore the time was peculiarly appropriate for the removal of the deposites. But the bank effected its ruinous curtailment, when the late instalments of the public debt which were paid, had not time to seek investment, and now we have the same alarm resounded as when the old bank went down in 1811. What has produced the present calamities of the country, is an important question, and he (Mr. W.) believed it was the bank, which, in the spirit of resentment which it had exhibited, in the language of the gentleman from Massachusetts, broke up the amity existing between it and the local banks. If the bank thought proper to quarrel with the Administration, was that a reason for breaking up the amity between it and the State banks?

Mr. W. then proceeded at some length to explain the effect which the system of cash duties had in producing the prevailing distress, when he gave way, at half past three o'clock, to

Mr. MANGUM, who observed that a meeting was about assembling in the Supreme Court room, in consequence of the melancholy death of Mr. Wirt, which had just taken place, and, with the permission of the gentleman from Pennsylvania, he would move that the Senate adjourn.

Mr. WILKINS having yielded the floor,

The Senate adjourned.

HOUSE OF REPRESENTATIVES.

TUESDAY, *February* 18, 1834.

Mr. GORHAM presented a report from the minority of the Committee of Ways and Means on the subject of the pension agency by the Bank of the United States; which was referred to the Committee of Ways and Means, and ordered to be printed.

Mr. J. Q. ADAMS submitted the following resolution, which lies on the table one day for consideration:

Resolved, That the Secretary of the Treasury be directed to report to this House a statement of the facts relating to the disallowance by the accounting

officers of the treasury, of a payment made by the Bank of the United States, under instructions from the Commissioner of Pensions, referred to in the letter of the President of the Bank of the United States to the Secretary of War, of the 23d of January last; and copies of all the correspondence between the War and Treasury Department and the Bank of the United States relating thereto.

Mr. PAGE reported a bill for the relief of the administrators of Charles Williams.

Mr. CAVE JOHNSON reported a bill for the final adjustment of land claims in Louisiana and the Territories of Florida and Arkansas. Also, for the heirs of Eugene Jenet; which were read twice, and committed.

Mr. CARR, from the Committee on Private Land Claims, to whom was referred the petition of the citizens of the reserved townships in Monroe county, Indiana, reported a bill for their relief, granting them a quantity of land for the use of schools in said township, in lieu of the 16th section in said township, which was granted by Congress to the State for the use and benefit of a State college; which bill was read twice, and committed to a Committee of the Whole House, and made the order of the day for to-morrow, and ordered to be printed.

Mr. CARR, from the same committee, asked to be discharged from the further consideration of the application of the representatives of Louis Tesson, alias Horoni; which, upon motion, was ordered to lie on the table.

The House then took up the resolution submitted by Mr. GILMER, of Georgia:

Resolved, That the Secretary of War be directed to communicate to this House all correspondence which he may have had, or information in his possession, in relation to the death of Hardeman Owens, a citizen of Alabama, who was lately put to death by a party of regular soldiers; whether said Owens was put to death in *pursuance* of orders from the War Department, or any officer of the United States; and that he also communicate to this House any correspondence which he may have had, or other information in his possession, in relation to any obstructions thrown in the way of the execution of the process of the courts of Alabama, issued for the purpose of bringing to trial those by whom said Owens was killed; and any correspondence in relation to the removal of said prosecutions to the district court of the United States.

Mr. BEARDSLEY having the floor from the previous day, gave way to Mr. CLAY.

Mr. CLAY said, when he submitted some brief remarks on this subject the other day, owing to the *general* terms of the resolution, and his inability to hear the remarks of the gentleman from Georgia, at the distance he was from him, he objected to the resolution, because he did not perceive that its adoption would lead to the attainment of any practical purpose. But Mr. C. said, that, as he understood from remarks subsequently made by his colleague, [Mr. LEWIS,] that the widow and children of the deceased had suffered injury, in the loss of property, and that facts might be elicited by the resolution which might lead to restitution; and as he had moreover understood that the officers in command of Fort Mitchell were charged with having sent off beyond the jurisdiction of the courts of Alabama, or facilitated the escape of the soldier or soldiers charged with the homicide, he should withdraw all opposition to the inquiry sought. A practical purpose is now said to be within the scope of the resolution, and he hoped it would be adopted by general consent.

Mr. C. also said, he would take this occasion to correct an error into which he was now informed he had fallen, when he submitted the remarks alluded to the other day. Mr. C. said he had then admitted what he believed to be true, *that Major McIntosh had, in the first instance, resisted or obstructed the execution of process within the fort*; but that he had been promptly instructed by the Secretary of War not only to submit to process himself, but to afford all the facility in his power for its execution upon others under his command. Mr. C. said he had since been informed, by a gentleman entitled to implicit confidence, that he had done injustice to Major McIntosh, who, (as Mr. C.'s informant said) never had resisted or obstructed the execution of process in the case alluded to. This explanation (Mr. C. said,) was due to Major McIntosh, and he made it with pleasure. We should, however, be correctly informed when the resolution came to be answered.

Mr. BEARDSLEY said, that as it seemed to be the general wish that the resolution should be adopted, he would not oppose it, although he did not approve of the adoption of resolutions of this character. It was, however, clear that the time of the House ought not to be wasted in debating it, and he was therefore induced to move the previous question.

The House refused to second the call—ayes 98, nays 104.

Mr. HARDIN then said that he understood that Mr. Owens had been living quietly and peaceably on the lands, when he was shot down by a party of the military, acting under the order of a higher authority; and, under these circumstances, the House were surely bound to ascertain by what authority he was thus put to death. He contended that the rights of the United States over the lands ceded by the Indians to them, gave them no other rights than those which should devolve upon individuals purchasing; if Owens, then, was killed for merely living on the Indian lands, upon what principle could his death be justified? Whoever did the act, although in obedience to orders, was guilty—the soldiers, as well as the deputy marshal, or the person who directed the deputy marshal. Yet, under the circumstances, the gentleman from Alabama [Mr. CLAY] could not see any practical object to result from the adoption of the resolution.

Mr. CLAY remarked, that he had not been heard by the member, when this day he withdrew his objections to it.

Mr. HARDIN resumed and said, that he wanted to know who issued the orders; that whatever was his situation, who had directed such measures, or who dared to issue orders to shoot a man down merely because he was living on the public lands of the Government, should be held accountable for it. It behooved every man to condemn such conduct. He did not know whether the act had originated with the marshal or with the officer commanding; but whoever was the cause, him only the resolution would affect.

Another part of this transaction to which he wished to advert, and which required investigation, was the attempt to transplant the proceedings in this case from the judicial tribunals of Alabama to the Federal courts. He denied this right, and contended that the parties should be tried for the offence by the State courts of Alabama. There appeared to be a disposition to extend the judiciary system of the Federal Government into the States; but the General Government had no right to extend it. If this was permitted, he thought they might as well take away the State Governments at once. He would vote for the resolution, as an outrage had been committed, by which the life of a citizen was violated, and which it was the duty of the House to have investigated.

Mr. MARDIS did not rise to discuss the merits of the resolution, as this did not appear to be necessary. The honorable member [Mr. HARDIN] was discussing a subject which there did not appear to be any objection made to have inquired into. Did not that member recollect, that by going into it now, he was prejudging the case of some individuals? He hoped that there would not be any further discussion upon it, and that the resolution would be adopted unanimously.

Mr. WILDE deprecated unnecessary discussion as much as any member, but he must rise to protest against the ground upon which the resolution was advocated by some gentlemen. The argument was, that the resolution was to grant restitution of property. It was not, it seemed, to be to make inquiry why a citizen's life was taken away. The time was passed, that it was enough to say, I am a Roman citizen, or that the death of an American citizen did not furnish ground for inquiry.

The resolution was then agreed to.

The resolution submitted by Mr. MERCER, relative to the duties of the committees, was postponed until Tuesday next.

The resolution submitted by Mr. SEVIER, to suspend patents of lands, and that submitted by Mr. FOOT, to organize the Treasury Department, were agreed to.

The resolution submitted by Mr. MARDIS, to instruct the Committee of Ways and Means to report a bill regulating the deposites of the public money, coming up in its order,

Mr. MARDIS was prevented from addressing the House by the expiration of the hour for morning business, and the House proceeded to the order of the day, being the

REMOVAL OF THE DEPOSITES.

The House resumed the consideration of the motion to refer the report of the Secretary of the Treasury on the deposites to the Committee of Ways and Means, the question being on the amendment submitted by Mr. JONES, as an amendment to that previously submitted by Mr. McDUFFIE, viz: to add to the motion for reference the following instructions to that committee: "Inquire into 'the expediency of depositing the revenue hereafter 'collected in the State banks, in the different 'States where the same is collected, in proportion 'to their respective capitals paid in, and to prescribe the terms on which the same shall be deposited; and to report by bill or otherwise."

Mr. MUHLENBERG rose and said, that this was merely a preliminary question, the decision of which would not affect the decision of the main question. It was merely a question whether the subject should go to the committee, with or without instructions. The question had been under consideration the greater part of seventy days, and he thought it quite time to decide it. The country was calling for it in every direction. He felt compelled, therefore, from an imperious sense of duty, to call for the previous question.

Mr. CHILTON asked a call of the House.

The SPEAKER stated that the call of the House was not in order, as there was a motion for the previous question, which was not yet decided. The question was now whether the House would second the motion for the previous question.

Mr. WILDE said, there was a principle of courtesy which was above any consideration upon which the gentleman from Pennsylvania, [Mr. MUHLENBERG,] had made his motion for the previous question. He considered that after what had been said in the debate, in relation to his connexion with the Committee of Ways and Means, that he had a right to expect from the House an opportunity of being heard. By the courtesy of the House he was entitled to make a reply to some of those who had participated in the debate. He, therefore, appealed to the gentleman for the withdrawal of his motion.

Mr. CHILTON appealed from the decision of the Chair on the question of order, and he argued at some length to prove that a call of the House could be required at any time.

The SPEAKER went fully into the grounds of the decision, stated that the practice of the House had not been uniform, and expressed a wish that the House would now solemnly settle the question.

Mr. BURGES said there was no good reason for not calling the House before the seconding of the previous question. If there was a necessity for the call, it existed before the motion for the previous question was put.

After some remarks from Mr. HARDIN, Mr. CHILTON withdrew his appeal.

Mr. J. Q. ADAMS renewed the appeal. He thought, he said, that the decision of the Chair was incorrect. It appeared to him that if there was ever an occasion for the presence of all the members, it was precisely when the previous question was demanded. The decision of the Speaker rested on the technical construction of the rule, and he thought it ought to be reversed.

The SPEAKER said, that he was never more satisfied with the correctness of a decision than that which he had now given. He was perfectly satisfied that it was correct, according to the rules and usages of the House. But he only felt solicitous for the distinct settlement of the question, as it was one of much importance in reference to the future despatch of business.

Mr. FOSTER, Mr. VINTON, Mr. GHOLSON, and Mr. CLAYTON, also made some remarks in

opposition to the decision of the Chair, and Mr. BROWN, of New York, in support of it.

Mr. WILDE asked whether, before the decision of the House on the appeal, it would be in order to move a call of the House.

The SPEAKER replied that it would not be in order.

Mr. WILDE then demanded the yeas and nays on the appeal, and they were ordered.

Mr. CHILTON remarked that there was nothing in the rule of the House that forbade a call of the House, and hoped that upon a great question like this, the fundamental rights of their constituents to give, through their representatives, a vote, would be respected.

Mr. BYNUM said he did not rise so much to enter the discussion of the parliamentary usages of the House, in relation to the subject under debate, as to reply to the remarks of his honorable friend from Virginia, [Mr. GHOLSON,] and the gentleman from Georgia, who had just taken his seat. Mr. B. said he had heretofore invariably voted against the call of the previous question. His object had been, to allow the fullest latitude to a free discussion of the suject then before them, which had been carried on upwards of two months, without interruption, and which he thought, in all conscience, a reasonable length of time for the discussion of one subject. But the honorable gentleman from Virginia had said, or insinuated, that the House was about to use the brutal force of numbers to put a stop to the debate. This he denied, and contended that he had every disposition to extend to every gentleman on the floor an opportunity to address the House, but that he thought such was the nature of this protracted debate, and the circumstances growing out of it, that the interest of the country at large required that it should be terminated in some form or other; that hundreds and hundreds of thousands of dollars of the people's money had been spent in this protracted discussion, without the least benefit, in his judgment, being afforded to the nation; he could not, therefore, upon grounds of policy, feel himself justified in voting in favor of a continuation of so fruitless a discussion. Mr. B. said, that the gentleman from Georgia, [Mr. CLAYTON,] had stated, that he thought it a very hard case that a call of the House should not be made, in order to allow gentlemen who were absent an opportunity of voting. Mr. B. said, he could not recognize the principle of having a call of the House on every occasion to get members in to vote. He thought it rather their duty to be in their seats, and that they should be excused only for sickness or unavoidable absence, for which he had no doubt they always would be excused both by the House and their constituents, to whom they were more immediately responsible. He, therefore, thought there was little weight in the argument of the gentleman from Georgia in relation to the hardness of the cases of those who were absent. Gentlemen had complained, said Mr. B., of the majority's determination to bring this debate to a close—he thought this complaint wholly unfounded. Who (he asked) was most responsible for this protracted discussion? Who would be censured for the evil consequences which had, and would continue to grow out of it? The friends of the Administration, no doubt. Yes, sir, the very party that now is opposed to the termination of this already too protracted and perplexing question, will be the first to cry out, in voices of bitterest censure, against the majority in favor of the Administration having suffered so much time of the House to be consumed at such enormous expense to the country in idle and profitless debate; that they had the power to put a stop to it whenever they might have thought proper. He thought courtesy at this time required immediate action on the subject. Indeed, gentlemen of the opposition had so declared themselves, again and again.

Mr. B. was proceeding to show that the present excitement in the country was owing more to the incertitude of the action of the House on the subject than to the simple act of the removal of the deposites, when the debate was arrested by the Speaker's informing Mr. B. that the merits of the question could not be gone into on the motion for a call of the House.

Mr. WILLIAMS believed that a call of the House was at all times in order, as it was preliminary to, and necessary to, all other questions. He would move a call of the House before the question on the appeal was taken.

The SPEAKER decided that this motion was not in order.

Mr. WAYNE considered, as the House was not in possession of the motion for the previous question, the call of the House was then in order.

Mr. REED said that the very seconding of the question was the decision of the House, and which must ultimately affect the question. He hoped that the decision made by the Speaker would be reversed.

Mr. BURGES deemed the continuance of the present question in debate as one of the most important questions that ever had been presented.

The SPEAKER called to order.

Mr. B. continued and said, he desired therefore to have a full expression of the representative voice, that the fetters of tyranny should not be riveted so as that on this great question hereafter, no man could say, in excuse, that he was not here to vote upon it.

Mr. BEARDSLEY said he would not debate the merits of the question, but he meant to call the attention of the House to what had been its practice on former occasions; and in doing so, he could not help adverting to the former vote given by the honorable member from Rhode Island, two years ago, upon an occasion which that honorable member must well remember. Notwithstanding the horror which he now expresses against the call for the previous question, he had twice concurred in such a call on one and the same day, to carry through the question of rechartering the Bank of the United States. Then there was not a word from him as to tyranny. If the present call was tyranny, what, he asked, was the conduct of those acting then with him?

The SPEAKER rose to order.

After a few remarks from Mr. BURGES and Mr. BEARDSLEY,

Mr. ADAMS said it was his intention to have asked the member from Pennsylvania [Mr. MUHLENBERG] to withdraw his motion for the previous question, that he might have addressed a few remarks, not on the merits of this question, but to show that the report of the Secretary ought not to be sent to the Committee of Ways and Means without the instructions moved by the member from South Carolina, [Mr. McDUFFIE;] but as a similar favor had been refused to another member, he could not, with propriety, now make the request. He hoped, however, hereafter to have an opportunity of addressing the House on the abstract question; and feeling, then, unwilling to waste the time of the House, and at the same time desirous to avoid a decision upon what he feared would be a most pernicious precedent, he would withdraw his appeal from the decision of the Chair.

Mr. FOSTER, however, renewed the appeal, and the question thereon being stated—

Mr. HARDIN remarked, he regretted to differ with his friends, but he must say, that the call of the House was not in order after the previous question was moved.

The House sustained the decision of the Chair, by the following vote: 115 to 112.

The question was then taken on the call for the previous question, and the call was seconded by the House, by a vote of 115 to 109.

Mr. CHILTON then moved a call of the House. Lost.

The question being, "Shall the main question be now put?" the yeas and nays were ordered.

Mr. BURGES moved that the House do now adjourn, and thereupon asked the yeas and nays, which were ordered.

The question being then taken on the motion for adjournment, it was decided in the negative—yeas 84, nays 142, as follows:

YEAS—Messrs. John Quincy Adams, Heman Allen, Chilton Allan, Banks, Barber, Barnitz, Barringer, Bates, Beatty, James M. Bell, Binney, Briggs, Bull, Burd, Burges, Chambers, Chilton, Choate, Claiborne, William Clark, Clayton, Clowney, Coulter, Crane, Crockett, Darlington, Warren R. Davis, Amos Davis, Davenport, Deberry, Deming, Denny, Dennis, Dickson, Evans, Edward Everett, Horace Everett, Felder, Foot, Foster, Fulton, Gamble, Gholson, Gordon, Gorham, Grayson, Grennell, Griffin, Hiland Hall, Hard, Hardin, James Harper, Hazeltine, Heath, Jabez W. Huntington, William Cost Johnson, Lewis, Martindale, Marshall, McComas, McKennan, Mercer, Milligan, Moore, Pinckney, Potts, Reed, Selden, W. B. Shepard, W. Slade, Sloane, Spangler, Wm. P. Taylor, Philemon Thomas, Tompkins, Tweedy, Vance, Vinton, Watmough, Edward D. White, Frederick Whittlesey, Williams, Wilson, and Young—84.

NAYS—Messrs. John Adams, John J. Allen, William Allen, Archer, Baylies, Beale, Bean, Beardsley, Beaumont, John Bell, James Blair, John Blair, Bockee, Bodle, Boon, Brown, Bunch, Burns, Bynum, Cage, Cambreleng, Carmichael, Carr, Casey, Chaney, Chinn, Samuel Clark, Clay, Coffee, Connor, Cramer, Day, Philemon Dickerson, David W. Dickinson, Duncan, Dunlap, Ewing, Fillmore, Forester, Fowler, Philo C. Fuller, William K. Fuller, Galbraith, Gillet, Gilmer, Graham, Joseph Hall, Thomas H. Hall, Halsey, Hamer, Hannegan, Joseph M. Harper, Harrison, Hathaway, Hawkins, Hawes, Henderson, Hiester, Howell, Hubbard, Abel Huntington, Inge, Jarvis, Richard M. Johnson, Noadiah Johnson, Cave Johnson, Seaborn Jones, Benjamin Jones, Kavanagh, King, Kinnard, Lane, Lansing, Laporte, Lawrence, G. W. Lay, Luke Lea, Leavitt, Love, Loyall, Lucas, Lyon, Lytle, Abijah Mann, Joel K. Mann, Mardis, Moses Mason, John Y. Mason, McCarty, McIntire, McKay, McKim, McKinley, McLene, McVean, Miller, H. Mitchell, Robert Mitchell, Muhlenberg, Murphy, Osgood, Page, Parks, Parker, Patton, Patterson, Dutee J. Pearce, Peyton, Franklin Pierce, Pierson, Plummer, Polk, Pope, Ramsay, Rencher, Schenck, Schley, Augustine H. Shepperd, Shinn, Charles Slade, Smith, Speight, Standifer, Stoddert, Sutherland, William Taylor, F. Thomas, Thomson, Turner, Turrill, Vanderpoel, Van Houten, Wagener, Ward, Wardwell, Wayne, Webster, Whallon, C. P. White, Elisha Whittlesey, Wilde, and Wise—142.

Mr. CHILTON again moved a call of the House.

The CHAIR decided that the motion was not in order, as the House had just decided against the motion.

The yeas and nays were then taken on the question, whether the main question should be now put, and it was decided in the affirmative, yeas 116, nays 112, as follows:

YEAS—Messrs. John Adams, William Allen, Beale, Bean, Beardsley, Beaumont, John Bell, James Blair, John Blair, Bockee, Bodle, Boon, Brown, Bunch, Burns, Bynum, Cambreleng, Carmichael, Carr, Casey, Chaney, Samuel Clark, Clay, Coffee, Connor, Cramer, Day, Dickerson, Dickinson, Dunlap, Forester, Fowler, William K. Fuller, Galbraith, Gillet, Joseph Hall, Thomas H. Hall, Halsey, Hamer, Hannegan, Joseph M. Harper, Harrison, Hathaway, Hawkins, Hawes, Henderson, Howell, Hubbard, Abel Huntington, Inge, Jarvis, Richard M. Johnson, Noadiah Johnson, Cave Johnson, Benjamin Jones, Kavanagh, Kinnard, Lane, Lansing, Laporte, Lawrence, L. Lea, Leavitt, Lucas, Lyon, Lytle, Abijah Mann, Joel K. Mann, Mardis, Moses Mason, McCarty, McIntire, McKay, McKim, McKinley, McLene, McVean, Miller, Henry Mitchell, Robert Mitchell, Muhlenberg, Murphy, Osgood, Page, Parks, Parker, Patterson, Dutee J. Pearce, Peyton, Franklin Pierce, Pierson, Polk, Pope, Schenck, Schley, Shinn, Charles Slade, Smith, Speight, Standifer, Stoddert, Sutherland, William Taylor, Francis Thomas, Thompson, Turner, Turrill, Vanderpoel, Van Houten, Wagener, Ward, Wardwell, Wayne, Webster, Whallon, Campbell P. White—116.

NAYS—Messrs. J. Q. Adams, Heman Allen, John J. Allen, Chilton Allan, Archer, Ashley, Banks, Barber, Barnitz, Barringer, Baylies, Beatty, James M. Bell, Binney, Briggs, Bull, Burd, Burges, Cage, Chambers, Chilton, Chinn, Choate, Claiborne, William Clark, Clayton, Clowney, Corwin, Coulter, Crane, Crockett, Darlington, Warren R. Davis, Amos Davis, Davenport, Deberry, Deming, Denny, Dennis, Dickson, Duncan, Evans, Edward Everett, Horace Everett, Ewing, Felder, Fillmore, Foot, Foster, Philo C. Fuller, Fulton, Gamble, Gholson, Gilmer, Gordon, Gorham, Graham, Grayson, Grennell, Griffin, Hiland Hall, Hard, Hardin, James Harper, Hazeltine, Heath, Hiester,

Jabez W. Huntington, William Cost Johnson, Seaborn Jones, King, Lay, Lewis, Love, Loyall, Martindale, Marshall, John Y. Mason, McComas, McDuffie, McKennan, Mercer, Milligan, Moore, Patton, Pinckney, Plummer, Potts, Ramsay, Reed, Rencher, Selden, William B. Shepard, Augustine H. Shepperd, William Slade, Sloane, Spangler, William P. Taylor, Philemon Thomas, Tompkins, Tweedy, Vance, Vinton, Watmough, Edward D. White, F. Whittlesey, Elisha Whittlesey, Wilde, Williams Wilson, Wise, Young—112.

Mr. CLAY asked the yeas and nays on the main question, and they were ordered.

The main question, on the motion of Mr. POLK to refer the letter of the Secretary of the Treasury to the Committee of Ways and Means, was then taken, and decided in the affirmative, as follows:

YEAS—Messrs. John Adams, William Allen, Baylies, Beale, Bean, Beardsley, Beaumont, John Bell, James Blair, John Blair, Bockee, Bodle, Boon, Brown, Bunch, Burns, Bynum, Cambreleng, Carmichael, Carr, Casey, Chaney, Chinn, Samuel Clark, Clay, Coffee, Connor, Coulter, Cramer, Davenport, Day, Philemon Dickerson, David W. Dickinson, Dunlap, Ewing, Forester, Fowler, William K. Fuller, Galbraith, Gholson, Gillet, Gilmer, Joseph Hall, Thomas H. Hall, Halsey, Hamer, Hannegan, Joseph. M. Harper, Harrison, Hathaway, Hawkins, Hawes, Henderson, Howell, Hubbard, Abel Huntington, Inge, Jarvis, Richard M. Johnson, Noadiah Johnson, Cave Johnson, Seaborn Jones, Benjamin Jones, Kavanagh, King, Kinnard, Lane, Lansing, Laporte, Lawrence, Lea, Leavitt, Loyall, Lucas, Lyon, Lytle, Abijah Mann, Joel K. Mann, Mardis, John Y. Mason, Moses Mason, McCarty, McIntire, McKay, McKim, McKinley, McLene, McVean, Miller, Henry Mitchell, Robert Mitchell, Muhlenberg, Murphy, Osgood, Page, Parks, Parker, Patton, Patterson, Dutee J. Pearce, Peyton, Franklin Pierce, Pierson, Plummer, Polk, Pope, Schenck, Schley, Selden, Shinn, Charles Slade, Smith, Speight, Standifer, Stoddert, Sutherland, William Taylor, William P. Taylor, Francis Thomas, Thomson, Turner, Turrill, Vanderpoel, Van Houten, Wagener, Ward, Wardwell, Wayne, Webster, Whallon, Campbell P. White—130.

NAYS—Messrs. J. Q. Adams, Heman Allen, John J. Allen, Chilton Allan, Archer, Ashley, Banks, Barber, Barnitz, Barringer, Bates, Beaty, Jas. M. Bell, Binney, Briggs, Bull, Burd, Burges, Cage, Chambers, Chilton, Choate, Claiborne, William Clark, Clayton, Clowney, Corwin, Crane, Crockett, Darlington, Warren R. Davis, Amos Davis, Deberry, Deming, Denny, Dennis, John Dickson, Duncan, Evans, Edward Everett, Horace Everett, Felder, Fillmore, Foot, Foster, Philo C. Fuller, Fulton, Gamble, Gordon, Gorham, Graham, Grayson, Grennell, Griffin, Hiland Hall, Hard, Hardin, James Harper, Hazeltine, Heath, Heister, J. W. Huntington, William Cost Johnson, Lay, Lewis, Love, Martindale, Marshall, McComas, McDuffie, Potts, Ramsay, Reed, Rencher, William B. Shepard, A. H. Shepperd, W. Slade, Sloane, Spangler, Philemon Thomas, Tompkins, Tweedy, Vance, Vinton, Watmough, Edward D. White, F. Whittlesey, Elisha Whittlesey, Wilde, Williams, Wilson, Wise, Young—98.

Mr. JONES, of Georgia, asked the unanimous consent of the House to offer a resolution for the instruction of the Committee of Ways and Means. Refused.

On motion, the House adjourned.

IN SENATE.

WEDNESDAY, February 19, 1834.

A message was received from the President of the United States, by Mr. DONELSON, his Private Secretary.

Mr. KANE presented the petition of sundry inhabitants of Illinois, praying the passage of a pre-emption law; which was referred to the Committee on Public Lands.

Mr. TIPTON, from the Committee on Military Affairs, reported a bill for the relief of Lucy Loomis.

Mr. TIPTON presented resolutions of the Legislature of Indiana, asking an appropriation by Congress for the improvement of the Wabash river; which was referred to the Committee on Roads and Canals.

Mr. POINDEXTER, from the Committee on Public Lands, reported a bill for the relief of Thomas S. Martin.

Mr. POINDEXTER, from the same committee, asked to be discharged from the further consideration of the memorial of the Legislature of Alabama, relative to a grant of lands for the endowment of male and female academies. Mr. P. stated that committee had the subject at large before them, and they thought it unnecessary to report specifically upon this memorial. He moved that it be laid upon the table until other bills of a similar character were taken up.

Mr. POINDEXTER, agreeably to notice, introduced a bill limiting the time of advertising public lands for sale at not less than four, nor more than six months; which was read twice and committed.

Mr. LINN asked that the report of the Committee on Private Land Claims on the petition of Colonel White, together with the petition and accompanying documents, be printed; which was so ordered.

Mr. TOMLINSON presented the memorial of the Selectmen of Norwalk, Connecticut, asking an appropriation for the improvement of that harbor; which was referred to the Committee on Commerce.

Mr. TOMLINSON, from the Committee on Pensions, reported a bill, from the House of Representatives, making appropriations for the payment of certain pensioners, with various amendments.

Mr. MOORE, from the Committee on Revolutionary Claims, reported a bill from the House of Representatives, without amendment, for the relief of the heirs of the late Dr. John Berrien.

Mr. TALLMADGE presented the petition of the officers and crew of the privateer General Armstrong, asking remuneration for services performed during the late war; which was referred to the Committee on Naval Affairs.

Mr. TALLMADGE presented the proceedings of a meeting of citizens of New York, disapproving of the course of the Secretary of the Treasury in removing the deposites, and asking their restoration to the Bank of the United States.

Also, the proceedings of a great Democratic Republican meeting, held in the Park, city of New York, sustaining the Administration in its measures in removing the deposites from the Bank of the United States.

Also, the proceedings of a numerous meeting of Democratic citizens at Tammany Hall, in New York, (which was brought to this city by a highly respectable committee,) of similar import with those at the Park.

These several proceedings were read, referred to the Committee on Finance, and ordered to be printed.

Petitions of a private nature were presented by Messrs. TIPTON and TALLMADGE; which were referred to the usual committees.

The following resolutions were submitted:

By Mr. TIPTON:

Resolved, That the Committee on Public Lands be directed to inquire into the expediency of authorizing the Secretary of the Treasury to correct an erroneous entry of the numbers of three sections of the lands granted to aid the State of Indiana in constructing a road from the Ohio river to Lake Michigan.

By Mr. EWING:

Resolved, That the Committee on Indian Affairs be instructed to inquire into the justice and expediency of paying to George C. Johnston, out of the annuities accruing to the Shawnee nation of Indians, the amount of ten several bonds for $2000 each, which he holds against the chiefs and warriors of said nation.

Mr. McKEAN presented a memorial from a meeting of citizens of the county of Erie, in the extreme west of the State of Pennsylvania; and also another from a meeting of citizens in Germantown, in the extreme east of the State; both expressing directly opposite views on the topic which

now agitates the country. He regretted to say that both the memorial contained expressions which did not meet his approbation.

He moved that they be separately read, and referred to the Committee on Finance, and be printed.

After the memorials were read,

Mr. KING, of Alabama, said it was with great reluctance that he rose at any time to say anything upon petitions or memorials presented to the Senate. But the characters of both these memorials are so exceptionable, that the Senate owed it to its own dignity and the preservation of its own character, to refuse to print them, but should lay them on the table, where they ought to lie, under the indignant frown of the Senate. If we allow denunciations of the Senate, and its presiding officer, in such unqualified terms, where shall we stop? It is right that gentlemen should state the substance of petitions on presenting them, and if they are found calculated to mislead the public mind, we should refuse to countenance them. He regretted that the gentleman from Pennsylvania [Mr. McKEAN] thought it his duty to present these memorials. For himself, he would not have done so. He made no exception to a decent expression of opinion. The doors of the Senate and the ears of Senators were open, and they would always be heard. But where denunciation, abuse, and calumny characterized their petitions, we should suffer ourselves to be merely the channel through which denunciatory pamphlets, not calculated to promote the interest of the country, were sent abroad, if they were to be received, printed, and referred. He was certain no Senator here thought they ought to be received, and with permission of the gentleman who presented them, he would make a motion to that effect.

Mr. McKEAN said he felt no anxiety that his motion should prevail. He had consulted his colleague on the subject, who thought it was better to present them. He stated, on presenting them, that they contained expressions which he deprecated, and he did so still. But he had brought the memorials before the Senate; he disapproved of their language, and he hoped he should receive no more of them. The gentleman [Mr. KING] might make the motion if he chose.

Mr. KING then moved that the Senate refuse to receive the memorials.

Mr. FORSYTH observed that there were expressions in these memorials which were certainly very offensive, and in very bad taste. But he did not know how the Senate could prescribe the manner in which the people should express themselves either to this or any other body. He had no objection to laying these memorials on the table; but he objected to refusing to receive them: for there was scarcely one presented here which did not contain some exceptionable expression. He did not defend these; they were very obnoxious, and in bad taste; but he held that the people had a right to express themselves, and they had also a right to choose the language in which to convey their expressions. He hoped the gentleman [Mr. KING] would not press his motion, but allow them to lie on the table.

Mr. SPRAGUE entirely concurred with the gentleman who had just sat down, that the expressions were highly offensive. But in times like the present, when the people were laboring under so severe pressure and distress, and the most gloomy apprehensions of the future occurrence, he for one, would not refuse to hear them, in any language, and the Senate were bound to listen to them. The expressions in the first memorial which was read referred to the Senate—they were certainly very disrespectful in calling this an aristocratic body; but we could not close our ears to them; and if people were taught to view this body as dangerous to the liberties of the people, let us hear their voice. This was not the first time the Senate had been attempted to be prostrated—had been struck at, and we could not ward off the blow by refusing to receive them. He would not consent to print them, but he held that the people had a right to send their memorials here, and we were bound to receive them, and bound to give them such consideration as they merited. But the reflections upon the presiding officer of the Senate were peculiarly offensive and objectionable, and he would be among the foremost to condemn it, because that officer had

not an opportunity to answer them, by reason of his having no voice here.

Mr. MANGUM coincided with the sentiments expressed by the gentlemen in regard to the terms of these memorials. As regarded the reflections upon the Senate, he would observe, that in every nation in Christendom the Court language was considered the standard of purity, and he thought the memorialists had not departed widely from the Court language here.

Mr. KING, of Alabama, consented to vary his motion to lay the memorials on the table. But if we were to sit here and receive violent abuse, and individual Senators calumniated, we would have but little to do. He did not exactly understand the gentleman's [Mr. MANGUM] Court language! Did the gentleman assimilate the abusive epithets in these papers to the Court language?

Mr. SMITH said, it was the undoubted right of every American citizen to address themselves to Congress, to make known their wants; but this right should be enjoyed by addressing Congress in respectful language. He was disposed to observe the same rule here which prevailed in the courts of law. The right of petitioning the courts for a redress of grievances was guarantied to the citizen; but if he should address the chancellor in scurrilous language, would he receive the petition or complaint? Certainly not. He recollected an instance of an application to the chancellor, and it was referred to the master to expunge the offensive passages, and the chancellor observed, that if another similar instance occurred, he would inquire who drafted the application. Mr. S. would receive these memorials, but would lay them on the table.

Mr. BIBB said, the right of petition and remonstrance was not the right to abuse and degrade the body to whom the petitions were addressed; and it was the duty of the body thus reflected on to protect itself, and it would be wanting in its duty if it failed to do it. The morals of the people and a respect for truth flowed, in a very considerable degree, from the examples of those in power. Example was more effectual than precept. He would not like the preacher, who should say, do as I preach, regardless of my own conduct. He was disposed to adopt a medium course in reference to these memorials; he would rather refer them to a committee, or an officer to be appointed, to strike out the objectionable parts; he was unwilling to let them lie on the table, with those obnoxious words in them. And if he was at liberty, he would move to refer them to a committee, to expunge the objectionable matters.

Mr. POINDEXTER said, that the right to petition Congress was guarantied by the Constitution, but petitions should be couched in temperate, respectful language; and he was as ready as any Senator to treat with disrespect any petition couched in vituperative language, addressed to this body. But in reference to the memorial from Erie, there was some apology for the harshness of its language. They resided in a remote part of the country, and referred to a particular event, and connected with that, the character of the Senate as an aristocratic body. And he would ask, were we not to blame for this in a great measure? We had been told by a gentleman here, in reference to this event, that the censure of the Senate was no reproach; and shall we, then, censure the citizens of Erie for reëchoing this language? Let us begin at home; let us begin here, and compel our own body to treat us with proper respect, and then we would command the respect of the people. What are the people to believe, when they hear from a Senator on this floor, that a rejection by the Senate is the high road to popular favor? But we were not without a higher precedent. A late message from the President of the United States charges the Senate with being guilty of a corrupt violation of the Constitution of the United States. Under this high sanction, then, the citizens of Erie are excusable for their warmth. He was willing to consider these petitions, and he was unwilling to treat them with rudeness, when he considered the sanction which they had received from the President. There were petitions here containing worse expressions than these. We could not expect to have them just as we would wish. He was willing therefore to refer them; they could not injure him; and he was willing to send them to the Committee on Finance, and let them go for what they were worth.

Mr. KING then renewed his motion to lay on the table; which was agreed to.

The Senate then proceeded to the special order of the day, being Mr. CLAY's resolutions, and the report of the Committee on Finance on the

REMOVAL OF THE DEPOSITES.

Mr. WILKINS said, on the adjournment yesterday, he was proceeding to ascribe the existing distress in the community to the resentful deportment of the Bank of the United States itself—it was to be ascribed to measures of the bank intervening between the removal of the deposites and the pressure. There were one or two facts more which he would offer as evidence of this disposition. And a prominent one was, the refusal of the bank to join the local banks in any arrangement for the relief of the commercial community, when the bank well knew the Government and the Secretary would have gone hand in hand with them in the attainment of that object. Hence the State banks all over the country were memorializing Congress for the restoration of the deposites, because the bank was only to be thus appeased. Another fact of which there was undeniable evidence, was, its disposition to oppress the country by a resort, in August last, to breaking up the domestic exchanges between the Atlantic cities and the interior. The vast West, and particularly his city, at the head of the Ohio river, connected with the Mississippi, have felt this more sensibly than any other part of the country. This was two months anterior to the removal of the deposites, and therefore that could not have produced it. The bank, by means of its great capital and extensive circulation of its notes, had complete control over the debts of the United States and the domestic exchanges, and by referring to the letter of Mr. Crawford in 1817, it would be found that the conduct of the bank, when considered according to his views, fully justified the Secretary in the removal of the deposites, if he had had nothing else. The bank at that time was about to adopt a system of exchanges injurious to the country, and Mr. Crawford informed them that if they did so, the Government had no other alternative but to take away the public deposites. Why, then, was there distress, unless it was caused by the bank itself? The late bank of Mr. Girard went down without creating any distress, although his loans amounted to four millions. He admitted that the bank ought to reduce its discounts, because of the removal of the deposites; but the reduction should be proportioned to the demand likely to be made on them. But they were disproportioned, and holding, as it did, the entire control over the currency, and holding the discounts of the country in its hands, there was no necessity for its pursuing such a course, and entailing calamity on the country. He referred to the newspapers of the day, as proving that the removal was not thought of any consequence to the bank.

It was asked, what could the bank do to relieve the country? He answered, everything. It was rich and powerful, and by a single breath could restore confidence in the community—let it cease any further curtailment—stand still—restore amity between itself and the local banks, and the Secretary would go hand in hand, and do all in the power of the department to restore confidence in the commercial community, and dispel embarrassment. If the termination of the charter was not near enough to justify the removal, it has not approached near enough to justify such excessive curtailments. It ought to go to the verge of the precipice, and even peril its own safety to give relief—its hostile attitude to the Governmen ought to be no impediment. Its notes cannot be affected. They are secured as a legal tender in payment of debts, and they are admitted to be perfectly sound and solvent. Indeed, the bank is said to be the soundest and safest in the world, and if so, why not grant relief? In March, 1831, it parted with a portion of its coin as surplus specie, leaving afterwards six millions of hard dollars in its vaults, which, added to its other available funds, amounted to fifteen millions and upwards; and it had a circulation to meet this of only nineteen millions. In the last month it has decreased its business more than one million, and added half a million of specie to its vaults. In Pittsburg, the reduction from the maximum of its loans, in one year, was (he spoke in round numbers) $557,000, and in the two last months, $72,000, extorted from the citizens of Pittsburg, when the bank was perfectly safe from all accident, and beyond the reach of the world. And in Boston, in the same period, a curtailment of $600,000 had taken place. Mr. W. proceeded to show the views of Mr. Biddle as to the readiest means of averting a panic, and contended that he could dispel the embarrassment, and, by the magic of his pen, afford relief in a moment. Mr. W. adverted to the House of Representatives' report of the spring of 1832, page 460, to the answer of Mr. Biddle to a question put by Mr. McDuffie, one of the committee of investigation.

[Here Mr. W. read Mr. Biddle's answer, detailing the account of the panic in 1825 in England, when the Bank of England was about suspending specie payments, from which national calamity the country was only saved by the timely arrival of 200,000 sovereigns, and the discovery, accidentally, of a large quantity of one pound notes in the vaults of the bank.]

This Mr. W. considered strong evidence of what the Bank of the United States could do to give relief, and was conclusive of its ability, in that respect, when taken in connexion with the fact that by an extension of discounts in New York of $50,000, the country was saved from a crisis of great danger and difficulty.

[Mr. W. here read Mr. Biddle's letter of instructions to the branch in New York at that time.]

Why could not the bank (said Mr. W.) adopt the same course on the present occasion, when it was not pressed for coin; when it owed nothing? When coin was flowing into her vaults, why not let it out? When $50,000 before averted an apprehended calamity, why not adopt the same course now? He denied that there was any disorder in the currency; there was not a single note of any Bank of the United States in circulation, which was not as good now as when the deposites were removed. Although at a small discount, apart from the vicinity of the bank issuing them, they are all promptly paid in coin on presentation at the counter, according to the promise on their face. The only real difference in them, arises from the expense of carrying them to the bank, and procuring the coin. But when the period arrives when some pay specie and others do not, then he would be willing to admit that the currency was disordered. And when it is known that the circulation of the United States Bank notes could not be impaired, and could not be checked, where is the disorder? But the Secretary charges the bank with having exercised political power; and, if he has sustained the position, no one will deny that it is of itself sufficient ground to justify the removal of the deposites; for on the purity of our elections depends the integrity of the administration of the Government. In answer to this objection, the directors explain away the facts, but substantially admit them. And what should we think of the bank which would use the public funds for vilifying the public men of the country? The evidence of the charge was the best evidence of which the case was susceptible; for although the bank labors to conceal it, it admits the fact charged, but excuses itself, by saying it was for self-defence; thus yielding the point, and going to the full extent of the principle. Could the same evidence be expected as was admissible in a court of justice? He was willing to yield to them the right of a proper expenditure in the publication of essays upon the currency and banking, and, indeed, he would say speeches and reports; but he would like to hear an explanation of the twenty or thirty thousand dollars expended for "miscellaneous" publications. Why conceal this, if it was only for self-defence? Let them explain these expenditures for "miscellaneous" publications, and he would give up the charge of meddling in the politics of the country. For if they only defend the bank, they should be disclosed to the people. He was opposed to the restoration of the deposites, because he was unwilling to yield to the bank; which, if it could force a restoration, would rule now and forever. Restore the deposites and the bank will continue its excessive curtailments; and how miserable must be our

country—now represented as the best and most prosperous on earth—which relies for its prosperity on the restoration of the deposites. The report of the late New York committee, who were on a visit here, says the country is blessed with abundance, and they spoke like men honorably relying on the resources of the country. Frankly believing the original question to be changed, he would yield for a moment, that it might not have been expedient to remove the deposites; but as the act had been fairly and honorably done, and the experiment made, which must be made, the question presented a new aspect, and it would now only add to the disorders of the country to restore them. If the bank is not to be rechartered, and he presumed it was conclusive that it would not be—why restore the deposites? If he could be satisfied that there was a reasonable likelihood of a recharter, he would rise at midnight to vote for the restoration of the deposites.

There was one point more which he would advert to. It was said that the bank ought to have been proceeded against by *scire facias*, thus giving to the bank the advantage of a judge, and a trial by jury. If this course was calculated to meet all the errors and abuses charged against it, he would admit the justice of the argument. The charter says, either the President or Congress may direct a *scire facias* to be issued, in case of a violation of the charter. But for other vast abuses, infinitely above a mere violation of the charter, the proceeding by *scire facias* is not to be used, but the removal of the deposites resorted to. For interfering in the politics of the country, for proceeding in various ways to cripple the commerce of the country, the *scire facias* affords no remedy. But suppose Congress had ordered a *scire facias:* would not the removal of the deposites also follow of course? Would you pursue the judicial proceeding, and yet leave the deposites? To prevent a greater disorder of the currency, the Administration pursued the most discreet course? For if the removal of the deposites could affect the country so seriously, what would have been the consequence of a total overthrow of the bank? Mr. W. said he gave way to no despondency—he feared no revolution, present or prospective. The bank might control the currency of the country, and produce distress for a time, but it would emerge from it with still greater strength; and while it was attempting to arrogate to itself power over the Government, he would appeal to his own State to resist its unwarrantable assumption, and call on Congress to drive back so usurping an institution.

Mr. TYLER obtained the floor, and moved an adjournment. He gave way, however, at the instance of

Mr. CLAY, who suggested that considerable business had accumulated, and the usual hour of adjournment not having arrived, he hoped that the Senate would continue its session, and dispose of a portion of it.

Mr. TYLER withdrew his motion for adjournment.

Mr. WAGGAMAN submitted a resolution, which lies one day, restricting the issuing of any notes within the District of Columbia, of a less denomination than five dollars.

ORDERS OF THE DAY.

The resolutions of Messrs. CHAMBERS, TIPTON, and HENDRICKS, previously submitted, were taken up and adopted.

The bill to repeal the force bill was then taken up, and, on motion of Mr. CALHOUN, made the order of the day for Monday fortnight.

Mr. CLAY presented the memorial of sundry citizens of New York, praying an extension of time for the payment of revenne bonds; which was referred to the Committee of Finance.

The special order, being Mr. CLAY's resolution and the report of the Committee of Finance, was postponed till Monday next.

On motion of Mr. TYLER,

The Senate adjourned.

HOUSE OF REPRESENTATIVES.

WEDNESDAY, *February* 19, 1834.

Mr. CHANEY, from the Committee on Pensions, reported a bill for the relief of Manasseh U. Stith; which was read twice and committed.

Mr. WHITE, of New York, from the select committee on coins, reported a bill regulating the value of certain foreign gold coins in the United States; read twice, and committed.

Mr. WHITE, of New York, from the same committee, reported a bill concerning the gold and silver coins of the United States, and for other purposes. Read twice, committed, and, together with the accompanying report, ordered to be printed.

Mr. JARVIS, from the Committee on the Public Buildings, made a report on the subject of the public buildings; which, on his motion, was laid on the table, and ordered to be printed.

PUBLIC DEPOSITES.

The following resolution, submitted on the 14th ultimo by Mr. MARDIS, of Alabama, was taken up:

Resolved, That the Committee of Ways and Means be instructed to inquire into the expediency of designating by law the future depository of the public moneys of the United States; and, also, as to the expediency of defining by law all contracts hereafter to be made with the Secretary of the Treasury in relation to the safe-keeping, management, and disbursement of the same.

Mr. MARDIS then modified his resolution, so as to make it read as follows:

Resolved, That the Committee of Ways and Means be instructed to inquire into the expediency of reporting a bill requiring the Secretary of the Treasury to deposite the public moneys of the United States in the State banks; and, also, as to the expediency of defining by law all contracts hereafter to be made with the Secretary, for the safe-keeping, management, and disbursement of the same.

Mr. MARDIS said, that in submitting his views on the subject of the resolution, he did not feel called upon to prove that the Treasury Department was an Executive department, or to consider whether the President of the United States has or has not been guilty of improper acts in relation to the treasury. He knew that grave charges had been brought against the President in reference to the transaction, but he did not think it incumbent on him to undertake the vindication of the President from these charges. A long life, spent in the faithful service of his country, was the best and a sufficient answer to them. Neither should he institute an inquiry into the reasons of the Secretary for the removal of the public deposites from the United States Bank, nor into the several charges made against the Bank of the United States. His views on these topics were sufficiently indicated by his recorded votes on the proposition sent to the Committee of Ways and Means. He had introduced this resolution, on the thorough conviction that the public deposites would not be restored to the Bank of the United States, and that the Bank of the United States would not be rechartered. If he was right in this supposition, then it follows, as a necessary consequence, that some other depository of the public money must be sought for and regulated by law. Sir, (said Mr. M.) am I right in these conclusions? I ask the House to refer to the state of public opinion on the subject of the bank in 1832. The subject, at that time, was not much agitated. We could learn the sense of the community through their representatives on this floor. Was not the general feeling of Congress and of the community then in favor of the bank? Is it not recollected that there was a decided majority in favor of renewing the charter of the bank? It was then thought an idle matter by some gentlemen to investigate the concerns of the bank. The feelings of the House then corresponded with those of the community. The people were then in favor of rechartering the bank. Has any individual forgotten the state of feeling then exhibited in Congress? Has any one forgotten the indictment against the bank then filed by the gentleman from Georgia, [Mr. CLAYTON?] Has any one forgotten his predictions at the time? I have the charges before me, seven in number, and all of grave import. It now becomes a matter of great importance to see what they are. Mr. M. proceeded to read them, as follows:

"1. The illegal issue of seven millions of branch 'bank orders as currency.

"2. Usurious contracts relative to depreciated 'bank notes at the West. [Mr. CLAYTON read a part of the reported case in the United States Supreme Court, Bank of the United States *vs.* Owings *et al.*, which proved, he said, a distinct case of usury, and there were many other instances in Ohio and Kentucky, involving nearly a million dollars in each of those States.]

"3. The practice of compelling borrowers to 'draw domestic bills at an usurious discount, in 'cases where simple loans of money were re-'quested.

"4. The non user of charter from 1819 to 1829, 'in not issuing notes from the branches of the 'South and West.

"5. Building houses for rent. [Mr. C. contended that purchases of plantations, or any speculations in real estate, were contrary to the charter.]

"6. Of the capital stock, there was not a due 'proportion of coin. [He said the Government deposites were $16,000,000; those of individuals $8,000,000; the circulation above $20,000,000. To meet all these, they had not more than $7,000,000.]

"7. Foreigners voting for directors through 'trustees."

These charges were submitted to the House by the gentleman from Georgia, at the time when the proposition to send a committee of investigation to Philadelphia was under consideration. Were these charges, sir, sustained? The gentleman was a member of the committee, and he had pledged himself to examine into the matter. What was his report? Why, that he had found all these allegations to be true. This report, in connexion with another important document, was sent abroad to the people in every part of the country. It had everywhere aroused the public mind to a sense of the dangerous character of the institution. Does any one say that these charges are not sustained? The gentleman assured the country that they were all made out. Last year, the gentleman added another item to the list of charges. When the question was raised, whether the Bank of the United States was a safe depository of the public money, the gentleman said that it was not a safe depository. What was the result, sir, of all these investigations? The people of the United States sustained the bill of indictment which the gentleman had filed. They had rendered their verdict upon it, both by the reëlection of the President and by the return of Representatives to this Hall. He would ask gentlemen to look for a confirmation of the fact to the representation of New York, of Ohio, and of Pennsylvania. The charges of the gentleman from Georgia had been sustained by the people, and there was now a general feeling of hostility against the bank. The people had pronounced their verdict by sending to this House a decided majority against the bank. Now, he understood it to be the wish of the gentleman from Georgia to enter a *nolle prosequi* in the case. This may be considered as proper practice in the State of Georgia, but he doubted whether it was a practice which would be found to prevail in any other State, even if it was the practice there.

But, sir, am I not right in the conclusion that there has been a great change of sentiment in relation to the bank since 1832; that the bank will not be rechartered, and that the deposites will not be restored, unless there should occur some great and unexpected change in public sentiment? But we are told by gentlemen that there is to be a great change of public sentiment. A great revolution is expected. The people are modestly told that they are laboring under a gross delusion on the subject, and that they are to be enlightened and freed from a tyrant's grasp. By whom are they thus told? Is it true that the President of the United States alone has produced an entire revolution in public sentiment? Would it not deprive the gentleman from Georgia, and the gentleman from Virginia, [Mr. ARCHER,] of much of the credit due to them, by attributing the change of popular sentiment wholly to the President? Did not the gentleman from Virginia, last year, tell the people that the Bank of the United States was an unsafe depository of the public money? Will he now tell the people who confided in him that he formed an opinion last session without proper information? No. The nature of the evidence which he sent

out to the world would contradict any declaration of this kind. No, sir; he said that the public money was unsafe in the Bank of the United States, because he honestly believed that it was unsafe. He acted, last year, on the fullest information, on the highest authority, and on his responsibility to his constituents. Now, sir, people do not usually apply twice to the same physician, first for a prescription, and then for relief from the operation of the prescription. The same doctors who brought the disease on the country now tell the people that they were deceived, and that their case was maltreated. Will the people trust to them again? Will they not, at least, inquire something as to the individuals who offer to give them this new light? If, sir, (said Mr. M.,) I have misrepresented the past or present opinions of any of these gentlemen, I have done it unintentionally. If the people inquire who are the men that now propose the restoration of the deposites, they will find that some of them are the very men who, last year, recommended the removal of the deposites. Certainly these gentlemen must then have intended to give a different destination to the deposites, when they wished to remove them from the Bank of the United States.

But are these gentlemen now in favor of rechartering the bank? He believed not. He had heard from them no declaration to that effect. They are in favor of restoring the deposites to a bank which they deem unconstitutional.

Gentlemen say that they are in favor of restoring the deposites, because they wish to relieve the public distress. He would examine whether the measure would effect what it was designed to effect. If the removal of the deposites did all the injury, he would ask whether it would afford any relief to put them back? Would we not be obliged to pass through the same scene of suffering, in 1836, when the bank winds up? Taking their own assumptions, he would ask gentlemen what would be the condition of the country at the expiration of the charter, and whether the restoration of the deposites, at this time, would afford any permanent relief. But it was not the trifling amount withdrawn from the bank which had shaken public confidence. The bank derived its credit mainly from the fact that it was the depository of the public money, coupled with the fact that the notes of the bank were made receivable in the payment of dues to the Government. If the restoration of the deposites afforded any present relief, it would bring upon the country fourfold distress at the expiration of the charter.

Sir, the fact that the enemies of the bank are now uniting with its friends on the question of the deposites is not calculated to produce a reaction in favor of the bank. In my opinion, (said Mr. M.,) it must have a directly contrary tendency. On one side, it was said by the friends of the bank, that we cannot get along without a Bank of the United States; that the institution is essential to the existence of the Republic. What was the view of the gentlemen who had now joined them? Why, they say the bank is unconstitutional and inexpedient, and that the happiness of the people and the stability of our institutions depend upon the abolition of the bank. Is not this a singular contradiction of opinion? Doubtless they were honest in their opinions. But does it not fill the mind with astonishment to see men entertaining such opposite opinions voting together? The truth must be told here as well as elsewhere, and the people have a right to know these facts.

But it was said that the rights of the bank were to be restored by a restitution of the deposites, and that the President and the Secretary had been guilty of a gross violation of vested rights. Does, then, an unconstitutional law give such sanctity to vested rights that they cannot be disturbed? Do not gentlemen see that their theory is utterly put to flight when they assume that rights once vested can never be divested by any political power?

These gentlemen had heretofore insisted that unconstitutional law was no law, and that a State could so declare it. In opposing the present course of the Executive they have entirely changed their sentiments on this point. We heard a great deal said in the debates about magicians. Now, he apprehended that if one party in the House had its magicians, the other had also. He apprehended that both parties had their leaders and wire-workers. Gentlemen on the other side, therefore, did not so much object to the use of magic as to the superior skill of the magicians opposed to them. They found that their own magicians were not of the order of Aaron, and they fear that the rods of our magicians will swallow up all their rods. He did not know whether his views on this subject corresponded with the views of any other gentlemen. He certainly did not impeach the motives of any gentleman. He did not suppose that any one in the House was disposed to legislate in reference to men. He knew that the object of the people was not merely to put down one and put up another individual. Principle alone should and does govern a great majority of the people of this country in all their sentiments on public topics. There could be no community of feeling between the people and men who suffer merely personal considerations to control their acts. The intelligence of the people had, he thought, been underrated, and those politicians who predicated their course upon the ignorance of the people would find themselves deceived in the results which they anticipated. In the other end of the Capitol there were individuals who might profit by this suggestion. The people understand their rights, and would never suffer them to be sported with by politicians for party purposes. If gentlemen should learn to put more confidence in the people and less in their own management, they would better represent the interests of the people.

Taking it for granted, then, (said Mr. M.,) that the public deposites will not be restored to the Bank of the United States, and that the bank will not be rechartered, I now come to the main object of the resolution. The President is charged with having seized upon the purse-strings of the nation. Is there any one so ignorant as to believe this to be true?

These gentlemen wished to convey the idea that the President has attempted to corrupt the people by his use of the public moneys. There was not an individual on this floor who believed it. The people would never believe it; for it was not true. Does the simple removal of deposites produce the effect of giving the President any new powers over the public treasure? Had the President attempted the exercise of any new power?

[Here the remarks of Mr. MARDIS were broken off by the expiration of the hour assigned to the consideration of resolutions; and the House proceeded to the order of the day.]

The SPEAKER laid before the House a communication, as ordered by the House, from the Secretary of War, with the report and survey made of a railroad route from the Hudson river to the Portage Summit Level of the Ohio canal; which was referred to the Committee on Roads and Canals.

A bill to provide for the payment of certain revolutionary claims, coming up for its third reading and final passage,

Mr. SMITH moved that it should be postponed until Tuesday next, in consequence of the absence, from indisposition, of Mr. FRANKLIN PIERCE, who wished to submit his views upon it.

Mr. MARSHALL said it was important that the bill should be acted upon.

Mr. VANDERPOEL inquired if it was in order to move to postpone the bill indefinitely?

The SPEAKER said the motion was not in order.

Mr. WISE remarked that a number of his constituents were interested in the passage of the bill, and he hoped it would not be delayed on account of the absence of one member.

Mr. MASON thought that the friends of the bill would not suffer any injury in acceding to the delay that was asked. This was due as an act of courtesy, and would not prevent the discussion of the principles involved in the bill.

Mr. HARPER, of New Hampshire, advocated the postponement under the circumstances; which finally was carried.

The bill to render more permanent the mode for supplying the army of the United States, having been taken up for its third reading,

Mr. WILDE objected to the increased number of clerks employed in the commissariat service under the bill.

Mr. THOMSON said, that on inquiry from the Secretary of War, he had ascertained that these clerks had not been taken from the line, but were placed on the same footing as other clerks, and that the service required the proposed number.

Mr. VANCE eulogized the present mode of supplying the army as more economical than the mode heretofore adopted; and he contended that, as the commissariat department had thrown upon it, in addition to the duties formerly required from it, the labor and trouble of supplying the Indians, there was nothing improper in asking for an increased force. He could testify, from his own knowledge, that the clerks were most laboriously employed, and that more competent persons were not employed in any other department. The House should bear in mind the numerous and heavy defalcations that formerly took place, whilst now there was not an instance of a single cent being lost.

After a few remarks in opposition from Mr. McKAY, which were not heard by the reporter—

Mr. R. M. JOHNSON insisted upon the advantages, in a pecuniary point of view, to be gained by employing competent persons to discharge the various duties of the Government. He could perceive no force in the objections to the increased number of clerks in the commissariat service. Was not the head of that department (Colonel Gibson) a man whose integrity was not questioned, and who accounted, as he was obliged to account, for every single cent that passed through his hands? From what he knew of the service, he was only surprised that the business could be so well done, and at so moderate an expense.

Mr. BLAIR, of South Carolina, moved to recommit the bill to the Committee on Military Affairs.

Mr. WILDE submitted an amendment—

With instructions to divide the two distinct subjects contained in this bill, and to report a bill for each, inserting in both a clause limiting the continuance thereof to three years, and until the end of the next session of Congress thereafter.

Mr. H. EVERETT proposed to recommit the bill to the Committee of the Whole House.

Mr. MILLER and Mr. WARD objected to the recommitment.

The question to recommit, with the amendment proposed by Mr. WILDE, was then put, and decided in the negative: Ayes 60, noes 82.

And the motion to recommit the bill to the Committee on Military Affairs prevailed.

The bill making appropriations for certain fortifications for the year 1835, was then taken up; and the question being, Shall this bill pass?

Mr. McDUFFIE said that he regretted he had been prevented by indisposition from hitherto attending to the progress of this bill through the House, for if he had been well, he would have objected to many of the items contained in it, as it made appropriations for four or five new fortifications. Two years ago he had announced his intention to oppose, in future, all such appropriations. He would now, in the spirit of perfect frankness, and in order to have a free discussion upon this subject, move to recommit the bill to the Committee of the Whole on the state of the Union. There were appropriations for four new fortifications in the present bill, which had not been appropriated for until last year, but it was not too late to correct the error, in having made them.

Mr. BARRINGER was decidedly opposed to any new fortifications being made. He had examined the bills making appropriations for the last year, and none had been made except for what might be considered preliminary measures to their being erected. He deprecated the inconsistency of making appropriations for fortifications, whilst the House had uniformly declined making appropriations large enough to man them, or have them sufficiently armed. The report on this subject, formerly presented by Mr. Graydon, demonstrated clearly that the sums usually appropriated for that purpose would not accomplish it in forty years. Why, then, add to their number?

Mr. POLK insisted that there were no appropriations in the present bill for any place for which there had not been previous appropriations made by the House. He looked to the three bills passed during the last session, and he there found that the

places now designated as new, were appropriated for. He could state that the committee who reported the bill had duly considered the subject, and in answer to their application for information, they had received a special communication from the Secretary of War, which he would beg to have read by the Clerk, and satisfied the committee of the propriety of the course they pursued. He found that there was an appropriation made of $25,000 for the fort on George's Island, Boston harbor. There were also appropriations made for a fort on Throg's Neck, New York. If the general argument was to be brought up on the policy of our system of fortifications, that is a different question. It might be that the system was too much extended. But, taking the appropriations now proposed, in the aggregate, he believed that they did not exceed those of former years. He desired the reading of some of the communications from the Secretary of War in relation to several of the forts and fortifications in progress. He could see no reason for discontinuing the present policy in regard to this system, and if it was to be continued, the appropriations were proper and necessary.

Mr. McDUFFIE said it had been the determination of Congress not to make appropriations for new fortifications. The items appropriated last year must have passed *sub silentio*. They did not meet his eye. He was not in favor of abolishing the fortification system. The fortifications of the first order were already finished, and there was no use in continuing to build fortifications which we could neither man nor equip. He adverted also to the necessity of economy and retrenchment as another reason for discontinuing the appropriations. The next year we should hardly be able to meet our necessary expenses. He made the proposition to recommit the bill with a view to attempt to amend it, and not from any unkind or unfair spirit towards the Committee of Ways and Means, or to the Administration; but it seemed that he could do nothing without exposing himself to the charge of acting from hostility to the Administration.

Mr. POLK explained that he had not intimated or supposed that the gentleman's motion had arisen from hostility to the Committee of Ways and Means, or the Administration. He added that the fortifications embraced in the bill, belonged to the regular system which we had adopted, and by discontinuing the appropriations now, we should lose what we had already expended on them.

Mr. SELDEN spoke in reference to the importance of continuing the appropriations for the defence of the harbor of New York.

Mr. WAYNE replied to the views of the gentleman from South Carolina, and showed that he was in error in the supposition that the appropriations now called for exceeded those of former years.

Mr. GORHAM opposed the motion to recommit the bill, and contended that the appropriations proposed for Boston harbor were essential to its defence. The inner harbor was well protected; but the outer harbor was wholly defenceless. To this day, though the United States have made Boston the grand naval depôt of the Eastern States, the Government has done nothing towards the defence of the outer harbor. The last place which the Government should abandon was this important depôt of their naval strength, and he was only surprised that it had not been fortified before. The estimates were not, in his opinion, too high.

Mr. HALL, of North Carolina, said he should vote for the recommitment, not, perhaps, precisely for the same reasons that some others did, but because he was really and thoroughly a retrenchment man; and in saying this, he meant not the slightest reflection on any one. But gentlemen had spoken of retrenchment. He was willing to go with them, not only upon this bill—this particular case—but all others where it was proper. He would go with the gentleman from New York [Mr. SELDEN] to the *Blue Book*, as he had alluded to that as a proper object. Mr. H. said this was a very good ground to stand upon. It might not be critically correct to say a good ground on which to raise a *superstructure* of retrenchment, but it was a good ground to stand upon to carry into effect very large retrenchments. But he would tell the gentleman that it was very inadequate. It was entirely useless to expect any great or beneficial results from attempting to cut off a little here and a little there. He had learned from long experience and observation, through a term of between fifteen and twenty years that he had been a member of the House, the utter futility of attempting to lop off the branches piecemeal; the only remedy was to go at once to the main body of the evil. Reduce the revenue; this was the only remedy. Sir, (said he,) I am willing to lop off the branches as I go along, but I am for going to the source of the evil, to the body and soul of the mischief. And, I repeat, that I am convinced, from what I have seen and experienced, that, so long as we have a surplus revenue, we shall continue to scramble for and apply it to purposes many of them entirely valueless or mischievous. As to the bill now under consideration, he had said he should vote for the recommitment, because he believed that many (he would by no means say all) of the objects were entirely unnecessary.

Mr. HARPER, of Pennsylvania, contended that the appropriation proposed in the bill for the forts on the Delaware were necessary. There was at this time no point of defence on the approach to Philadelphia. The whole range of the Delaware was unprotected. The old fort had fallen into ruins. Last year its rebuilding was commenced, and to stop the appropriation now would be to expose the city of Philadelphia to be laid in ashes at any moment by an enterprising enemy.

Mr. BROWN said, he was willing to give his vote for the bill under consideration, if the state of the revenue would admit such an expenditure of the public money, without serious embarrassment to the treasury. He would vote for the bill, not because a portion of the money was to be expended in the State of New York, which he had the honor, in part, to represent upon this floor; nor would he vote for it because it contained an appropriation for the harbor of Boston, or the mouth of the Delaware: but he would do so because it was a part of our great system of public defence, provided and projected for the security and defence of the whole country. Before he did vote for the bill, however, he should be glad to have some information from honorable gentlemen upon the Committee of Ways and Means, as to the probable state of the revenue. We had been admonished by the President, in his annual message, to be cautious of making unnecessary appropriations of the public money. Our revenue laws had undergone a very recent, and a very important change, and the effect of such change upon the treasury was the subject of uncertainty if not anxiety.

He (Mr. B.) therefore thought that the suggestions which had fallen from the honorable gentleman from South Carolina, [Mr. McDUFFIE,] entitled to the serious consideration of the House. If there was to be any considerable falling off in the receipts of the revenue for the coming year, he thought this very bill, above all others, making appropriations, should be drawn with reference to that deficiency; and before he was called upon to vote for its final passage, he hoped that the House would be put in possession of the views of the Committee of Ways and Means upon the subject of the revenue for the coming year.

Mr. EVERETT, of Massachusetts, admitted that there had been an understanding that works of the second class should be discontinued, but there had been no understanding, express or implied, that works of the first class should be abandoned. The representatives of Massachusetts would never have assented to any understanding that the outer harbor of Boston should be left defenceless. The great points on our coast were the mouth of the Mississippi, Philadelphia, New York, and Boston. These were the four great points, and the last point had not been defended. Fort Independence, in the inner harbor, was not built by the United States. It was built one hundred and fifty years ago, under the Colonial Government. He was in favor of retrenchment, and would always aid his friend from South Carolina in effecting it. But he did not think that the work of retrenchment ought to be commenced by abandoning the defences of one of the most important and exposed points on our coast.

On motion,

The House then adjourned.

IN SENATE.

THURSDAY, *February* 20, 1834.

A message was received from the President of the United States, by Mr. DONELSON, his Private Secretary.

Mr. CHAMBERS rose to say, that many members of the Senate had a duty of a painful character to perform to-day, which would necessarily take them from their seats. He alluded to the funeral of the Hon. WILLIAM WIRT. He was not authorized, by any usage or precedent, to offer anything to the Senate on the occasion, but, in consideration of the many distinguished public and private virtues of the deceased, and in order to give the members of the Senate an opportunity of paying the last token of respect to his memory, he moved that the Senate adjourn; whereupon

The Senate adjourned.

HOUSE OF REPRESENTATIVES.

THURSDAY, *February* 20, 1834.

After the reading of the Journal, Mr. MASON, of Virginia, rose and said:

Mr. SPEAKER—Sir: It has become my melancholy duty to advert to a recent dispensation which has deprived the bar and the country of one of the greatest ornaments of both: I allude to the death of WILLIAM WIRT! The funeral ceremony takes place this day; and it is the wish of many members of this House to pay that tribute of respect to his memory which all feel to be due—the accompanying of his mortal remains to the tomb. It is not my intention to pronounce an eulogium, an unnecessary eulogium on the deceased, but I may be permitted to speak of his urbanity of manners, his fidelity to his friendship, his gentleness of disposition, his benevolence of heart, and of those eminent literary attainments, which have shed so bright a lustre on his country.

It is due to the exalted merits, to the virtues, and to the purity of mind and heart of the lamented and illustrious dead, that some signal mark of public respect should be awarded to his name. To us, in Virginia, where the prime of his life was passed, and where his example can have, as it *has* had, the most beneficent effects, the honor rendered to him will be the more peculiarly gratifying.

Mr. Speaker, I move, sir, that the House do now adjourn.

And the House adjourned.

IN SENATE.

FRIDAY, *February* 21, 1834.

A message upon executive business was received from the President of the United States, by Mr. DONELSON, his Private Secretary.

Mr. SOUTHARD presented a memorial from the town of Trenton and its vicinity, signed by four hundred and twenty-three individuals; another from the township of Howell, signed by upwards of three hundred citizens; and a third from Burlington county, signed by two thousand seven hundred and eighty-five voters, against the removal of the deposites from the Bank of the United States, which, after some remarks from Mr. SOUTHARD, were read, referred to the Committee on Finance, and ordered to be printed.

Mr. WILKINS presented the proceedings of upwards of 1000 citizens of Pittsburg and its vicinity opposed to the domination of the Bank of the United States, and friendly to the measures of the Administration in relation to that institution. The resolutions as passed declared that the Bank of the United States is an institution exercising powers and extending an influence which, if not arrested, must eventually greatly endanger, if not totally overthrow our free system of Government. The proceedings were read, referred to the Committee on Finance, and ordered to be printed.

Mr. WILKINS presented the memorial of the two local banks in Pittsburg, asking the interference of Congress to restore the public deposites to the Bank of the United States; upon which a similar order was made.

Mr. SPRAGUE presented a similar memorial signed by six hundred and forty-six citizens o

Portland, Maine, and moved the usual reference, and that it be printed.

Also, the proceedings of a town meeting of Bangor, Maine, and a memorial signed by three hundred citizens of that town, of the same tenor as the above.

After the memorials were read, a protracted discussion ensued, which continund till four o'clock; in which Messrs. SPRAGUE, SHEPLEY, FORSYTH, and CHAMBERS, participated—when Mr. WEBSTER rose, and after expressing a wish to make some remarks, moved an adjournment; but, on the suggestion of Mr. POINDEXTER, withdrew it; and after a short time spent in executive business,

The Senate adjourned.

HOUSE OF REPRESENTATIVES.

FRIDAY, *February* 21, 1834.

Before the Journal of yesterday's proceedings had been read,

Mr. ADAMS, of Massachusetts, addressed the Speaker as follows:

Mr. SPEAKER: A rule of this House directs that the Speaker shall examine and correct the Journal *before it is read*. I therefore now rise, not to make a motion, nor to offer a resolution, but to ask the unanimous consent of this House to address to you a few words, with a view to an addition which I wish to be made to the Journal, of the adjournment of the House yesterday.

The Speaker, I presume, would not feel himself authorized to make the addition in the Journal which I propose, without the unanimous consent of the House; and I therefore now propose it before the reading of the Journal.

I ask that, after the statement of the adjournment of the House, there be added to the Journal words, importing that it was to give the Speaker and members of the House the opportunity of attending the funeral obsequies of William Wirt.

At the adjournment of the House on Wednesday, I did not know what the arrangements were, or would be, for that mournful ceremony. Had I known them, I should have moved a postponed adjournment, which would have enabled us to join in the duty of paying the last tribute of respect to the remains of a man who was an ornament of his country and of human nature.

The customs of this and of the other House of Congress warrant the suspension of their daily labors in the public service, for attendance upon funeral rites, only in cases of the decease of their own members. To extend the usage farther might be attended with inconvenience as a precedent, nor should I have felt myself warranted in asking it upon any common occasion.

Mr. Wirt had never been a member of either House of Congress. But if his form in marble, or his portrait upon canvass, were placed within these walls, a suitable inscription for it would be that of the statue of Moliere, in the Hall of the French Academy—"Nothing was wanting to *his* glory. *He* was wanting to ours."

Mr. Wirt had never been a member of Congress; but for a period of twelve years, during two successive Administrations of the National Government, he had been the official and confidential adviser, upon all questions of law, of the Presidents of the United States; and he had discharged the duties of that station entirely to the satisfaction of those officers and of the country. No member of this House needs to be reminded how important are the duties of the Attorney General of the United States, nor risk I contradiction in affirming, that they were never more ably or more faithfully discharged than by Mr. Wirt.

If a mind stored with all the learning appropriate to the profession of the law, and decorated with all the elegance of classical literature; if a spirit imbued with the sensibilities of a lofty patriotism, and chastened by the meditations of a profound philosophy; if a brilliant imagination, a discerning intellect, a sound judgment, an indefatigable capacity, and vigorous energy of application, vivified with an ease and rapidity of elocution, copious without redundance, and select without affectation; if all these, united with a sportive vein of humor, an inoffensive temper, and an angelic purity of heart—if all these, in their combination, are the qualities suitable for an Attorney General of the United States, in him they were all eminently combined.

But it is not my purpose to pronounce his eulogy. That pleasing task has been assigned to abler hands, and to a more suitable occasion. He will there be presented in other, though not less interesting lights. As the penetrating delineator of manners and character in the British Spy; as the biographer of Patrick Henry, dedicated to the young men of your native Commonwealth; as the friend and delight of the social circle; as the husband and father in the bosom of a happy, but now most afflicted family; in all these characters I have known, admired, and loved him; and now, witnessing, from the very windows of this Hall, the last act of piety and affection over his remains, I have felt as if this House could scarcely fulfil its high and honorable duties to the country which he had served, without some slight, be it but a transient, notice of his decease. The addition which I propose to the journal of yesterday's adjournment, would be such a notice. It would give his name an honorable place on the recorded annals of his country, in a manner equally simple and expressive. I will only add, that, while I feel it peculiarly incumbent upon me to make this proposal, I am sensible that it is not a fit subject for debate; and, if objected to, I desire you to consider it as withdrawn.

The SPEAKER said, that according to the sixth rule of the House, it was the duty of the Chair to examine and correct the Journal before it was read. It had been examined, and according to the rule, was now to be read. But it was competent for the House to revise and correct it, in the manner proposed by the gentleman from Massachusetts. The Journal now reads:

"THURSDAY, *February* 20, 1834.

"The House met according to adjournment; and after reading the Journal of the preceding day,

"On motion of Mr. MASON, of Virginia,

"*Ordered*, That the House adjourn until to-morrow, twelve o'clock, meridian."

The CHAIR was not authorized to make any correction of it. If there was no objection, and if it was the pleasure of the House, the Chair would amend the Journal according to the suggestion of the gentleman from Massachusetts.

An objection having been made by a member,

Mr. BLAIR, of South Carolina, asked if there were no means by which the objection could be obviated.

The SPEAKER said it was competent for the gentleman from Massachusetts to submit his motion, but he had understood him to say that he should withdraw the motion, if an objection should be made to it.

Mr. PARKER said that it was a matter of fact that the House did adjourn to enable the members to attend the funeral of Mr. Wirt.

Mr. J. Q. ADAMS had hoped, he said, that no objection would be offered to the proposition. But as the objection seemed not to be sustained by the sense of the House, he would move that the Journal be altered so as to read as follows:

"The House met pursuant to adjournment; and after the reading of the Journal of the proceedings of yesterday,

"On motion of Mr. MASON, of Virginia, and for the purpose of affording the Speaker and the members of this House an opportunity of attending the funeral obsequies of WILLIAM WIRT, deceased, it was

"*Ordered*, That the House do adjourn."

The motion was agreed to.

Mr. WHITTLESEY, of Ohio, from the Committee on Claims, reported a bill for the relief of M. Gelston, executor of William Gelston, deceased; which was read twice, and committed.

Mr. WHITTLESEY, from the same committee, reported a bill for the relief of George Taylor and Betsy Taylor. Read twice, and committed.

Mr. HARPER, of New Hampshire, from the Committee on Commerce, reported a bill making appropriations for the erection of two custom-houses in Massachusetts. Read twice, and committed.

Mr. CARR, from the Committee on Private Land Claims, made an unfavorable report upon the petition of William G. Davis and Mary Ann his wife; which was ordered to lie on the table.

On motion of Mr. CARR,

The petition of Benjamin Ogden, the representative of William Williams, deceased, was recommitted to the Committee on Private Land Claims.

PUBLIC DEPOSITES.

The House resumed the consideration of the following resolution, offered by Mr. MARDIS, of Alabama:

Resolved, That the Committee of Ways and Means be instructed to inquire into the expediency of reporting a bill, requiring the Secretary of the Treasury to deposite the public moneys of the United States in the State banks; and, also, as to the expediency of defining by law all contracts hereafter to be made with the Secretary for the safe-keeping, management, and disbursement, of the same.

Mr. MARDIS resumed his remarks, which had been suspended by the expiration of the hour on Tuesday. He was defending (he said) the President of the United States from the charge of having seized upon the purse of the nation, and had adverted to the fact that he could not take one cent from the treasury, without an appropriation by law. But we were told that, although he would not take it for his own purposes, yet he might seize upon it with a view to corrupt the people, to manage elections, and to control public sentiment. The act, it was said, was unauthorized on the part of the Secretary, and was prompted to him by the President of the United States. Now, sir, (said Mr. M.,) I had promised, at the commencement of my remarks, not to institute any inquiry into the reasons given by the Secretary of the Treasury; but I trust it will not be considered as a breach of that promise, if I look at the main objection offered to the act of the Secretary. It was said, that his power of removing the deposites was limited in its operation to a removal, solely in case the deposites should be considered as unsafe in the Bank of the United States. The Secretary, it was contended, had only to look to the safety of the deposites, and beyond that he could not go; and it was said that this was a just inference from the words of the charter, taking one clause with another. But he would refer to another provision of the charter, which would completely overthrow this position. It was conceded also by the friends of the bank, that there were ample inducements and reasons for the removal of the deposites, else why would they intrench themselves behind this argument? The provision of the charter under which the Secretary exercised the power, authorized him to remove the deposites from the bank, "until otherwise ordered." This power was conferred for some purpose. Any power, it was argued, which was given to the Secretary, must have been given for the purpose of securing the public revenue. Now, if he proved that the power given would be no such security, the argument must fall to the ground.

The SPEAKER here stated, that it was not in order to refer to any arguments used by members in a debate gone by.

Mr. MARDIS said he should confine himself to objections generally made to the act of the Secretary. At what time would the deposites in the bank be most endangered? Assuredly not in time of universal prosperity—not when the bank was entirely sound. When would the deposites be endangered? When, he answered, public confidence was lost in the institution, when it refused specie for its notes, then they would be unsafe. If this was true in point of fact, for what purpose was the 16th section inserted in the charter? Would it not be a strange proceeding to withdraw the deposites, when, at the same time, we continued to receive the notes of the bank in payment of dues to the Government? Would the withdrawal of the deposites be any security, when the very paper, the depreciation of which led to the removal, was still received at the treasury? Would any additional security be given the Government by depositing the notes in the State banks? Would not the removal of the deposites, under such circumstances, be altogether nugatory, and fail to effect the purpose of securing their safety? But has the Secretary the discretionary power of refusing to receive the notes of the Bank of the United States in payment of dues to the Government? He has not; and yet it was said that the provision in the charter was intended to be

operative only when the Secretary considered the deposites as unsafe in the bank. Then, sir, if the Secretary has the right to remove the deposites for other reasons than the belief that they are unsafe, does not the main argument which is urged against the act of the Secretary, fall entirely of effect?

Has there been no cause for the act of the Secretary? There had been abundant cause, and he contended that the existence of adequate causes had been conceded by the argument used on the other side. The President had fulfilled the expectations of the country, and we have strong evidence on our tables that the voice of the people, from Maine to Louisiana, concurs in the act. Then the President had been guilty of no usurpation of authority, and of no wanton abuse of power. But is it true that he is desirous to retain the discretion imposed upon him in the honest discharge of his duty? Is any individual desirous of enabling the Secretary of the Treasury to retain any control of the subject? Not one. From his humble station in the Government, he had but little intercourse with those to whose hands the administration of our affairs was confided; but he had never heard any intimation from any one that the discretion assumed by the Secretary should remain to him. He would ask gentlemen on the other side to go with us in putting this question at rest. But, sir, it is said, that though it is desirable to change the destination of the public deposites, and though the country may desire to get rid of the Bank of the United States, yet such is the present condition of things, that it is impracticable. We are told that, owing to the peculiar organization of the banking system, and the influence which the Bank of the United States is capable of exercising, and does exercise, it is impossible that the country can do without the agency of the Bank of the United States. We are told that this bank is necessary to enable the people of the country to receive the reward of their labor. We are told, in a word, that the enterprise and industry of the country are in the hands of this institution. How is this made manifest? They say that the bank understands the interests of the country so well, knows so well the places where, at particular seasons, capital is required, and has such facilities through her branches, that it is able to shift its capital from one place to another, to meet the emergencies of the business community. Now, sir, carry out this argument. If the bank controls the enterprise and industry of the country, it can also control the elections of the country. If it can force a recharter now, he would ask, whether, if at some future day, when its friends and enemies came into conflict, it would not put down its foes and uphold its friends? It could control an election by the same means by which it could control the wishes of the people and the sentiments of this House at the present time.

Is not the assumption on the part of the friends of the bank at war with the liberties of the people? If the existence of the bank is necessary to the industry and enterprise of the country, then all is lost. Its power is without compass, and is already extended beyond the control of the people. But, though doubtless the bank was anxious to acquire the power attributed to it, it had not yet succeeded in the attempt. He thought its friends were mistaken in the belief that the enterprise and industry of the country were dependent upon it. He would ask the sugar planter of Louisiana in what manner he was paid for his produce. Nine-tenths of the sugar of Louisiana was paid for in money, of the local banks. The cotton growers of Mississippi will tell you that for nine-tenths of their cotton they were paid in notes of the local banks. He would appeal to any one who was conversant with the course of business in Alabama, to say whether the sale of the cotton crops in that State depended upon the branch of the United States Bank at Mobile. Nine-tenths of the money paid for cotton in Alabama was paid in local bank paper.

One thing, he thought, was plain, that at whatever point there was a demand for capital, there it would be brought; and he thought it would be much better to leave the transfer of capital to individual sagacity and enterprise than to create such a tremendous engine as the United States Bank to do it.

But, desirable as it is to get rid of this institu-

tion, we are told that we cannot get rid of it. We are told that the country can establish no institution which will supply the place of the bank. Do we contemplate, say they, a league of local banks No. We cannot, then, it is said, make the local banks perform all the operations required from a national bank. It was said, too, that the power which, to be efficient, must be confided to the confederated banks, would be as dangerous to the liberties of the people as a national bank. No such thing as a confederation of banks was contended for. It was required from each bank to perform the duties now performed by the United States Bank, and if each bank does its duty, the duties will be as efficiently performed by them as they can be by the United States Bank. What was to prevent them from transferring their funds from one part of the country to another? Had they not the same facilities? What had given the United States Bank the universal credit and currency of its notes? Was it not these two circumstances, that it was backed by the Government deposites, and that its notes were receivable in payments to the Government? Suppose the same advantages to be extended to the local deposite banks, in what would their facilities fall short of those enjoyed by the United States Bank? If the notes of the branch bank at Mobile were good in New York, is it because the bank is more solvent, or better managed, than the State bank of Alabama? If all the news he had heard were true, the preponderance was in favor of the State institution. Each pays specie; why then is the paper of the Bank of Alabama less current than that of the branch bank of Mobile? Simply because the paper of the branch bank is receivable in payment of the public revenue. So the branch bank at Charleston and Savannah had a circulation throughout the country. But if the same facilities were extended by law to local banks in those cities, in what respect would the credit of their notes differ from those of the branch banks?

[Here Mr. M. was compelled to suspend his remarks, without concluding, in consequence of the expiration of the hour—the House having refused to suspend the rule.]

The SPEAKER presented to the House a communication from the Secretary of the Treasury, with an account of contracts made in 1833 for light-houses, &c.; which was laid on the table, and ordered to be printed.

The House went into Committee of the Whole, (Mr. CONNOR in the chair,) on sundry private bills.

A bill to compensate Susan Decatur and others, whose claims have been so long before the House, was taken up and considered.

Mr. PATTON detailed the circumstances under which Commodore Decatur performed the gallant exploit—first projected by himself, and carried into effect with a party of volunteers, from the squadron of Commodore Preble, in the Mediterranean—to enter the harbor of Tripoli, in 1804, where he succeeded in destroying the United States frigate Philadelphia, which had been previously captured by that Power, and was lying at anchor, protected by the batteries of the harbor. Having eulogized the exploit as one that more than any other had raised the character of the American flag, he advocated the claims of the persons engaged in it and their representatives to the bounty of the nation.

[The bill grants $100,000, to be paid in the following proportions:
To the widow of Commodore Preble..$5,000 00
To Mrs. Decatur, and the widows of
  the officers in the first class.........31,412 42
To the officers in the second class, their
  equal proportions of...............12,564 96
To the officers of the third class.......14,958 26
To the persons in the fourth class......12,215 93
To the persons in the fifth class........11,074 88
To the sixth class, consisting of forty-
  two seamen and marines.........12,773 59]

Mr. GRAYSON concurred in the views submitted by Mr. P., and described in strong colors the advantages that resulted to the United States, the Barbary Powers having been inspired with such dread, by the gallantry of the exploit, that they immediately sued for peace, and thus the commerce of the country was protected from depredations to which it had long been subjected.

Mr. CRANE thought the claims just, under the circumstances upon which the various projects acts had been usually passed, to reward the gallantry of our seamen; but he objected to the mode of distribution, and contended that it should be made in conformity to that adopted in former acts.

Mr. PARKER thought that this claim was not one of law, so much as it was of equity, and which, being founded solely on an appeal to their honor and generosity, the House had therefore the right to apportion the amount to be given, in such a manner as they should conceive the respective parties had deserved it.

Mr. CHILTON said, he had for years opposed these claims, and he felt still compelled to do so, by a sense of what he felt due to his constituents; and he knew that the late Commander Decatur, if now alive, would not have presented any claim, but would have been satisfied with what he valued above all other things—the fame and distinction he had acquired.

On motion of Mr. HAWES, the committee rose, reported progress, and obtained leave to sit again.

The House suspended the rules to permit Mr. WHITTLESEY to submit a motion, granting the use of the Hall to the Temperance Society, on Tuesday evening next: Ayes 95, noes 19.

Which motion having prevailed—

Mr. THOMAS, of Louisiana, remarked, that as the natal day of WASHINGTON ought to be kept by every patriot, he would ask a similar favor, for the House to suspend its rules, to enable him to submit a motion, that when the House should adjourn, it should adjourn over until Monday.

The House suspended the rules for that purpose: Ayes 114, noes 7; and the motion being agreed to,

The House adjourned.

The excitement in Upper Canada against the Provincial Assembly, for their arbitrary course towards Mr. McKenzie, continues to increase, and the Assembly remain obstinate. Since his last expulsion, on the same ground of objection as the four preceding, every motion favorable to his right to a seat has been voted down. Some of the people of his district—the county of York—indignant at this persevering exclusion of their representative, have copied some of the temper of the English on the Reform Question, and determined to pay no taxes. This they effect peaceably, by refusing to appoint a collector or assessor of taxes. In the township of King, at the regular meeting of the 6th ult., the determination to refuse to appoint the taxing officers was universal. One man dissented, but he subsequently joined in an address to Mr. McKenzie. The matter, if followed up in this spirit, must produce serious consequences.—*Balt. American.*

SPECIE.—The packet ship Erie, d expected from Havre, has on board a l amount of specie,—how large, we ca ascertain, but the shipments were suspended by the refusal of the un writers in Havre, to insure any fu amount. The balance was then sent board the Albany, which ship was expected to have on board all that ca be insured.—*N. Y. Jour. Com.*

Famine prevails to such an exten the Crimea, that two villages in the ne borhood of Odessa, have been enti deserted by their inhabitants.

THE CONGRESSIONAL GLOBE.

PRINTED AND PUBLISHED AT THE CITY OF WASHINGTON, BY BLAIR & RIVES.

23D CONGRESS, 1ST SESSION. SATURDAY, MARCH 1, 1834. VOL. 1........No. 13.

IN SENATE.

SATURDAY, *February* 22, 1834.

Mr. TYLER presented resolutions of the Legislature of the State of Virginia, instructing the Senators and requesting the Representatives in Congress to exert themselves to effect the restoration of the public deposites to the Bank of the United States.

After a few remarks by Mr. TYLER, the resolutions were read.

Mr. RIVES rose and said:

Mr. PRESIDENT: The Senate will indulge me, I hope, standing in the position I do, with a few remarks on the subject of the resolutions just read. It is very far from my intention to attempt to impugn, in any manner, the force of those resolutions, or to derogate, in the slightest degree, from the high respect to which they are entitled here and elsewhere. On the contrary, I recognise them as the legitimate expression of the opinion of my State, conveyed through the only authentic organ known to her constitution and laws.

The Senate will have perceived, from the reading of the resolutions, that it is my misfortune to entertain, and to have expressed, on the grave questions now occupying the public mind, opinions very different from those asserted by the resolutions. Notwithstanding this difference of opinion, I should feel it my duty, as one of the representatives of Virginia on this floor, to conform to the views expressed by her Legislature, if, in the circumstances in which I am placed, I could do so without dishonor. I hold it, sir, to be a vital principle of our political sytem, one indispensable to the preservation of our institutions, that the representative, whether a member of this or the other House, is bound to conform to the opinions and wishes of his constituents, authentically expressed; or if he be unable to do so, from overruling and imperious considerations operating upon his conscience or honor, to surrender his trust into the hands of those from whom he derived it, that they may select an agent who can better carry their views into effect.

On all occasions involving questions of expediency only, it is, I conceive, the bounden duty of the representative to conform implicitly to the instructions of the constituent body, where those instructions are to be carried into execution by a legislative act, which, as a mandate of the public will, prescribes and directs what *shall* be done for the public good. But where the instructions contemplate a *declaration of principles or opinions*, which are contrary to the sincere and honest convictions of the representative, as there is no means of forcing the assent of the understanding to abstract propositions, the only course left to him is, by the surrender of his commission, to put it in the power of his constituents to confer it on another, whose opinions correspond with their own.

To apply these principles to my own case, I do not hesitate to say, that if the instructions of the Legislature of my State had required me specifically to vote for a law or other legislative act, providing for the restoration of the public deposites to the Bank of the United States, however highly inexpedient I deem such a measure to be, I should nevertheless have felt it my duty to give the vote required. Such, it will be recollected, was the precise demand of the memorial of the citizens of Richmond presented a few days ago by my honorable colleague, and which concluded by asking, that Congress "would provide *by law* for the immediate restoration of the public moneys to the Bank of the United States."

But, sir, this is not the shape in which the question is presented to me, by the resolutions of the General Assembly of my State, or by the proceedings pending in this body. Those resolutions instruct the Senators of Virginia, in general terms, "to use their *best exertions* to procure the adoption by Congress of *proper measures* for restoring the public moneys to the Bank of the United States." Now, sir, I am bound to inquire what are those proper measures, in the contemplation of the Legislature of Virginia.

We all know that the only measures proposed, or contemplated in this body, are the two declaratory resolutions offered by the Senator of Kentuky: the first, affirming that the conduct of the President with reference to the removal of the public deposites, was a dangerous and unconstitutional assumption of power; the second, declaring the reasons assigned by the Secretary of the Treasury for that removal, to be unsatisfactory and insufficient. When the latter of these resolutions, together with the report of the Secretary of the Treasury, was referred some days ago to the Committee of Finance, that committee did not report a bill, or joint resolution, for the restoration of the deposites, but simply a recommendation, that the Senate adopt the declaratory resolution of the Senator from Kentucky. In short, it is now avowed and understood on all hands, that all that is deemed necessary, or will be proposed here, to effect a restoration of the public moneys to the Bank of the United States, is a *mere declaration* by Congress, of the insufficiency of the reasons assigned for their removal.

The only measures, then, on which I shall be called to carry into effect the instructions of the Legislature of my State are, the *declaratory* resolutions moved by the Senator from Kentucky, and now depending before the Senate. That these resolutions are, in the estimation of the General Assembly of Virginia, *proper measures*—that the opinions and principles declared by them, are believed by the General Assembly to be correct and well founded—it would be unpardonable blindness to the language and tenor of their instructions not to see. At the same time, it is well known to the Senate, that on each of the propositions declared in these resolutions, I had (and I will take leave to add, after the most careful and anxious investigation,) come to opposite conclusions, which I had earnestly asserted and maintained on this floor. I am, therefore, placed, by the instructions of the Legislature of my State, in this dilemma—either to vote for the declaratory resolutions of the Senator from Kentucky, and thereby express opinions which I not only do not entertain, but the reverse of which I have sincerely and earnestly maintained on this floor; or, by voting against them, to oppose the *only measures* which are likely to come before this body, having in view the restoration of the public deposites to the Bank of the United States, and thus appear in the attitude of disregarding and thwarting the declared wishes of the General Assembly of Virginia. I am sure I but respond to the honorable feelings of all who hear me, in saying, that the first branch of the alternative is *impossible*, while the latter is no less forbidden by my principles, and a proper sense of duty to the constituted authorities of my State. The only course left to me, then, is one which the Senate can be at no loss to anticipate.

Before I close the few remarks with which I have felt myself called on to trouble the Senate, I beg leave to say, that, while I recognise implicitly the resolutions just read as the legitimate and constitutional expression of the opinion of my State, I wish not to be understood as saying that they express the *real* public opinion of the State—that of the PEOPLE. On the contrary, my firm and clear conviction is, that the sentiments of the people in the present instance are not in unison with the proceedings of the legislative authority. The manifestations of popular sentiment already commencing in various quarters of the State—the principles and opinions heretofore steadily cherished by Virginia—multiplied communications received from the most respectable sources—and my own knowledge, I may be permitted to add, of a people with whom I have been connected, in the relations of public service, for now near twenty years, assure me that they are not; and the revolution of a few months will, I confidently believe, render the fact manifest to all the world. But in the regulation of my *official* conduct here, I am not permitted to look beyond the constitutional expression of the opinion of the State, by its regular and proper organ. If a Senator were allowed to set up against the public opinion of his State as officially and solemnly declared by her Legislature, a *hypothetical* public opinion, which may or may not be that of the people of the State, it is obvious that a door would be opened for the total evasion of all effective responsibility of this body to public opinion. It is on the Legislatures of the States that the Constitution has devolved the choice of members of this body, and the same Legislatures must be the interpreters of the public opinion of their respective States to the Senators chosen by them, whenever an occasion shall arise which may call for a solemn manifestation of that opinion.

This is indeed the only *practicable* mode of bringing the opinion of the sovereign communities represented in this body to act, with authoritative influence, on its proceedings; and when it is considered that the Senate is, by the greater permanency of its official tenure, farther removed from the salutary controls of the representative system than any other branch of the Government, all will see the necessity of keeping open a clear and designated channel by which public opinion may promptly reach it, in an authoritative form, and be made effectual on its deliberations. It is thus essential to the practical supremacy of the popular will itself, that the State Legislatures should be recognised as the authentic and constitutional exponents of the popular opinion of the respective States, in all relations with this body. If, in any instance, the Legislatures of the States shall mistake the opinions of the people, it is, as I conceive, for the people themselves, and not for us, to correct the mistake.

These, Mr. President, are very briefly the opinions I entertain on the delicate questions presented for my consideration by the instructions of the Legislature of my State just read; and the only alternative they leave me, in the circumstances in which I am placed, is to surrender the trust with which I have been honored as a member of this body into the hands of those from whom I received it. I know well, Mr. President, and I feel how much of honor and of satisfaction I give up in abandoning my seat on this floor. I abandon what I have ever regarded the highest honor of my public life—an honor than which none higher, in my opinion, can be presented to the ambition of an American citizen. I sacrifice social and kindly relations with many members of this body—I would fain hope with *all*—which have been the source of the highest satisfaction to me here, and the remembrance of which I shall cherish with sincere pleasure in the retirement whither I go. I know and feel the weight of these sacrifices, but great as they are, I make them without a sigh, as the most emphatic homage I can render to a principle I believe vital to the Republican system, and indispensable to the safe and salutary action of our political institutions.

The resolutions were read, referred to the Committee on Finance, and ordered to be printed.

Mr. McKEAN presented the following:

The memorial of six hundred and seventy-nine citizens of Pottsville;

The memorial of sundry citizens of Schuylkill county;

The proceedings of a meeting of boot and shoe dealers of Philadelphia;

The memorial of the President and Directors of the Western Bank of Philadelphia;

The proceedings of a meeting of citizens of Southwark and Moyamensing.

All of which were in favor of restoring the public deposites to the Bank of the United States; which, on motion of Mr. McKEAN, were read, referred to the Committee on Finance, and ordered to be printed.

The VICE PRESIDENT presented a communication from the Secretary of the Treasury, transmitting an account of the expenditures of that department.

Mr. POINDEXTER, from the Committee on Public Lands, reported a bill for the relief of Oliver M. Spencer; which was read twice, and committed.

Mr. POINDEXTER, from the same committee, asked to be discharged from the further consideration of the memorial of sundry inhabitants of Illinois, praying the passage of a preëmption law, and that the same be laid upon the table, as a general bill on that subject would probably be reported. Agreed to.

Mr. TIPTON, from the Committee of Claims, reported a bill for the relief of James Taylor; which was read, and, on motion of Mr. TIPTON, the report was ordered to be printed.

Mr. KANE, from the Committee on Private Land Claims, reported, without amendment, a bill for the relief of Alexander Boyd, and a bill for the relief of the heirs of George Penrose.

Mr. TYLER presented the memorial of citizens of Richmond, Virginia, praying aid from Congress to improve the navigation of the lower part of James River; which was referred to the Committee on Commerce.

Petitions of a private nature were presented by Mr. ROBBINS and Mr. KING of Alabama.

The following resolution was offered by Mr. ROBBINS:

Resolved, That the Library Committee be instructed to inquire into the expediency of procuring to be executed an equestrian statue of Washington, in bronze, to be placed in the square east of the Capitol.

The Senate then proceeded to the consideration of the motion to refer the petition from Portland and Bangor, in Maine, upon the subject of the deposites, when Messrs. WEBSTER, FORSYTH, KANE, and CHAMBERS, severally addressed the Senate.

The orders of the day having been announced a few minutes before three o'clock, Mr. FORSYTH moved the Senate do now adjourn, but gave way to

Mr. PORTER, who suggested that a large amount of private business had accumulated upon the table, and he therefore gave notice that he should on Friday and Saturday move, to the exclusion of all other matters, that the Senate should proceed to such business.

Mr. WEBSTER, adverting to the fact of some members having been sick, which lead to the suspension of executive business, gave notice that he should, on Wednesday, immediately after the reading of the Journal, move the Senate to proceed to executive business.

On motion of Mr. FORSYTH, the Senate adjourned.

IN SENATE.

MONDAY, February 24, 1834.

A message upon executive business was received from the President of the United States, by Mr. DONELSON, his Private Secretary.

Mr. SMITH presented the following petitions: From 700 inhabitants of New Haven, Connecticut;
From 300 citizens of Hartford;
From 900 citizens of the same place;
From the Phœnix Bank of Hartford;
From the Connecticut River Bank;
From the Insurance Company of Hartford; All in opposition to the course pursued by the Secretary of the Treasury, in removing the deposites; which, after some remarks by Mr. SMITH, were laid upon the table, with an understanding that they would be called up for consideration and reference at some other day.

The following resolution was submitted by Mr. SILSBEE:

Resolved, That the Committee on Commerce be instructed to inquire whether any, and if any, what alterations ought to be made of the amount and manner of compensation to the collectors and other officers of the revenue; and, also, whether the fees and charges, on some of them, which are now paid at the custom-houses, may not be discontinued.

On motion of Mr. CLAY, the Senate proceeded to the special order of the day, being Mr. CLAY's

resolution, and the report of the Committee on Finance, upon

THE REMOVAL OF THE DEPOSITES.

Mr. TYLER, after a brief exordium, said that, borne into office as the President of the United States was, upon the shoulders of party, and by a popularity entirely unprecedented in the nation, it would have been remarkable if he had not had advocates and supporters, let his conduct have been what it might. Hence, in all that is past in our history, the President, no matter what was his course, found a support from the men of his party, and it was to be expected that no expedient would be left unresorted to to support him. The Bank of the United States was a corporate existence, and therefore whatever could affect it affected individual rights; and if the President of the United States could control those rights, your armed him with all power, even that of life and death: and even the courts of justice afforded no security for the liberty of our citizens. This was his (Mr. T.'s) aspect of this question, and it was also that of the State of Virginia, a State which was at all times opposed to the exertion of arbitrary power. And in illustrate that assertion, he referred to the case of Philips, a celebrated bandit before the Revolution, whom the Legislature of Virginia outlawed, and whose decision was overruled by the people, and he who had gloated upon crime in all its deformities was allowed the benefit of a trial by jury.

The formidable array of precedents which had been urged for justifying the President for the removal of the deposites were, in their best form, but poor reasons for the reliance of gentlemen. For what justification would it be to a criminal in a court of law to say that he next door neighbor had committed the same offence for which he was arraigned? The judge would certainly teach him otherwise. And Mr. T. thought if precedent was to govern in one case, it was applicable in the other. But look at the precedents; and in this aspect of the case, what then becomes of the veto power, for the exercise of which the President has obtained the greatest credit, and which it is said has reflected the highest honor upon him. If we look at precedent, what is to become of the glory which he is said to have won by it? Mr. T. dissented from precedent as an authority, for if it came to anything, it was only that the agent might override his principal. On the accession of the President of the United States to office, "Reform, Reform," was inscribed on his banner, and yet now we hear the cry of "Precedent, Precedent," resounded on all sides —cries which operate only as false lights to decoy us.

But the Chief Magistrate has thought proper to throw before the world certain anonymous letters containing threats against himself, through his own journal, and the pretended assassins even fix upon the very day when the deeds of blood are to take place. He did not say anything as to the motives of these letters, but if assassins had thus proclaimed their intentions, they would have proclaimed their own madness and folly. But the only question in this investigation with which we have any concern, is that the Secretary proceeded unjustifiably. It was admitted that the public moneys were safe in the bank; that it had fulfilled all its engagements; that it had established a sound currency, and that the Government was deeply interested in the stock; and with these admissions, how much surprised would a foreigner have been at the removal of the deposites? Would he not naturally have inquired into the necessity of a change? But if he had referred to the act of 1789, establishing the Treasury Department, how would he have been amazed? That act requires of the Secretary of the Treasury to make plans for the improvement of the revenue, and to furnish stability to public credit. And has he prepared his plans and submitted them to Congress; and has he improved the revenue or added anything to it? All this was his duty; but, so far from doing it, the revenue has diminished, and the Government stock depreciated from which the revenue is to be derived. So that, when all is taken together, there has been an aggregate loss to the Government of at least two millions. So much for the improvement of the revenue and the management of the revenue now, when contrasted with the operation as performed by the bank. By it

this was all done without difficulty; the public money was distributed over the whole country through the various conduits of the bank, unseen, and therefore there could be no improvement in its management, and the attack upon the public faith was well calculated to weaken the public confidence. But has he improved the currency? It is hardly necessary to answer. We had a currency, than which there was none better on earth, which approached nearer to an equality with the precious metals than any other. But what was our condition now? The voice of distress from all parts of the country was a sufficient answer to this inquiry. We perceive an instance of a war waged against the public treasury by the person at the head of the Treasury, and he (Mr. T.) thought the case of a financier making war upon his own treasury was really a new one. And under what pretence was it done? The Secretary converts his office into that of a judge, takes the bank into his own hands, relies on the newspapers for the support of the charge, and the accuser is the President of the United States. The judge is on the bench, and not have been the design of Congress. In the event of the public deposites being unsafe, these words were to be his authority for acting, and the whole authority was contained in those seven words alone. The charter looks to this as giving him his whole power; the weekly statements so he made—everything is for the purpose of enabling the Secretary to decide on the solvency of the bank and the safety of the funds committed to its charge; and the Congress would not even trust itself with more than this. The power of issuing a *scire facias* was guaranteed to the bank on a charge of forfeiture of charter. If this position was true, the Secretary could look no further than to the safety of the public deposites; and nothing else, therefore, could avail him in his defence. But in looking to the reasons, he complains of the discretion given to the president of the bank in the expenditure of limited sums of money; and notwithstanding its limitation he had forgotten the vast powers he had himself assumed, and yet complained of this mere penny-post affair.

His next charge was the attempt at corrupting the press: the press which Mr. T. recognised as the great palladium of liberty; and never would he countenance the attempt to corrupt it by rewards. But had the Secretary forgotten the rewards which had been given by the Administration to editors? Had he failed to see the streets filled with them? And did he not know when their nominations were rejected here, the newspapers of the next morning announced their appointment to offices, the rewards of which were as great as those from which they had been rejected. He had voted against such nominations, and would continue to do so, that editors might rely upon public sentiment for support. He held the subsequent conduct of the Secretary equally as censurable as what preceded it. The Treasurer of the United States is the officer appointed to keep the public money, and he is responsible for the fidelity of his agents, but he cannot be responsible for agents which are not appointed by himself. But it is said the Treasurer's bond is no security for him. The argument is a mockery of the law and an insult to the common sense of the community. But, it is said, this act was done by the command of the President, and that there could be no danger, as the money was placed beyond his reach for his own purposes. But was it not used for enlarging his powers when the stockholders of these various banks were installed in his cause? Money works by corruption —it works in secret. Look to its influence in parliament.

was life, exercised through the brokers and money lenders.

Mr. T. came to the conclusion that the deposites ought to be restored, and that the Constitution ought to be amended so as to allow a Bank of the United States to be established—that was his only objection to it. Let this be done, and it would enable Congress to confer the greatest possible benefit on posterity, and put to rest a question which would never be settled in any other way. The considerations for the amendment were great and powerful—and it could be effected before the expiration of the bank charter; so that the present bank might be rechartered, or a bill for another passed.

Mr. T. concluded by contrasting the republicanism of Mr. Jefferson with that of the present Administration, and condemning the principles of the Proclamation.

HOUSE OF REPRESENTATIVES.

Monday, February 24, 1834.

Mr. PARKS rose and said:

Mr. Speaker: I am requested to present a memorial, report, and resolutions, adopted at a meeting convened, as it is said, without distinction of party, in the town of Bangor, in Maine, and which memorial is signed by two hundred and eighty-eight inhabitants of said town, praying for a recharter of the present Bank of the United States, or that another, on similar principles, may be chartered.

Before, sir, passing this memorial to the Chair, there are a few observations which I feel myself called upon to make, not only on the subject-matter of the papers themselves, but as regards the relation in which I stand to the petitioners.

The town, sir, from which this memorial comes, has, for a number of years past, been progressing in a state of flourishing prosperity, such as has seldom been equalled, never surpassed, in New England. It now contains, sir, six thousand people, all actively engaged in commercial pursuits, and the various avocations incident thereto. It is from a town so circumstanced, that this memorial, signed by two hundred and eighty-eight only of its citizens, comes.

It is professed, Mr. Speaker, that the meeting when this memorial was got up was called without distinction of party. It is no doubt true, sir, that it was so called, but it is not true that it was so attended. It was a political meeting, got up for political purposes, and attended by one political party only. I will not undertake to say, sir, that no man was there who ever gave a vote in favor of the Administration. There is, sir, in every community where political parties run high, some few persons without any fixed opinions, who are always vacillating from one party to the other, as the one or other may to them seem to preponderate in power and strength. That some such persons, who may have occasionally given a vote to the Administration, were present, and acting on that occasion, I do not deny. But, sir, I do deny that any one firm friend of the Administration was present acting there. Sir, the attempt was made to give this meeting the appearance of being what it purports to be, "without distinction of party," by putting on to a committee three gentlemen, friends of the Administration, whom I am glad to call such, and with whom I am always proud to act. I have before me, sir, one of the daily papers of that town, in which those gentlemen state that their names were made use of without their knowledge or consent; and they add, further, that "we regret that any of their citizens are disposed to countenance or approve the course pursued by the United States Bank, in its unhallowed attempts to perpetuate its power by its oppression; and that they can never lend their aid, however feeble, to aggravate the public distress which that institution is attempting everywhere to produce." So much, sir, with regard to its being without distinction of party.

I show me now, sir, to call the attention of the House to some of the statements and admissions in the report and resolutions. In the first place, the petitioners say, and very truly so, that there has been no unusual pressure in Bangor—that there has been no failures, but such as might have occurred in ordinary times. Sir, from the very nature of the business of Bangor, it is impossible there could have been any pressure of a very serious nature there. The principal of the business of that place in the lumber trade; the lumber is cut in the winter, brought down the river in the spring, manufactured, and sent to market during the summer. During the winter season, nature lays a very effectual embargo on the foreign commerce of that port, by closing the river for miles below with ice. The goods, therefore, which are wanted for the winter consumption are brought there in the fall, and no payments, to any amount are either expected or promised to be made until the produce of their winter's work is ready to be shipped for market in the spring and summer.

But these memorialists state further, that although there has been no pressure as yet, they fear there may be. I am not, sir, entirely without apprehension of that event myself; but, sir, there are other causes to which, if such an event happens, I can ascribe it, as well as to the removal of the deposites, or to the deranged state of the currency. Until within a very few years, the immense resources for trade and enterprise of every description which are to be found in the Penobscot section of Maine, appear to have been passed by unheeded and unknown. It appeared that, as if by magic, the veil which had hitherto concealed them from the eyes of men had suddenly been lifted, and as if all the advantages and opportunities for enterprise, which were so abundant, were for the first time made known. Wealth, population, enterprise of every character flowed in upon us. Everything seemed as if touched by Midas to be turned to gold. This state of things has continued to the present hour, so that instead of suffering, a state of actual prosperity has existed, such as I never saw before, and had never supposed to be capable of existing. In such a state of affairs, a population composed principally of active, enterprising young men, would naturally, with new inducements daily opening before them, extend their operations to the full extent of their means and credit. No evil has yet resulted from this state of things; it has been supported by the ample resources which have been hourly developed; and, sir, the probability is, that these will still support it. But there is always danger lest some in such a state of affairs, should overtrade. Therefore it is not impossible, although improbable, that some of the fears entertained by these memorialists may be well grounded.

In the next place, sir, these memorialists go on to say, that even if there had been any pressure among them, they should not have known what cause to have assigned for it: whether it was the conduct of the bank, or the course of the President. The committee even say that that was a question upon which they differed so much that they concluded to leave it as they found it. So, sir, with regard to the question whether the bank has forfeited its charter, whether it has fulfilled its duty to the country or not—all these questions, and others of a similar character, they come to leave undecided; and yet, Mr. Speaker, they ask this Congress to recharter a bank whose conduct, according to their own account of it, may well be considered a matter of doubt and suspicion.

There is one other matter here, Mr. Speaker, to which I wish to allude. In the papers, sir, which I am about to present, immediate action is asked for. The memorialists, sir, and the persons who attended that meeting, are most faithful and thorough-going party men; they live, sir, in a remote quarter of the Union, and we are now receiving from them the echo of the petition of the advocates of the bank, on the floor of this House, at the commencement of this session, asking for action, action, no matter what it might be. Sir, had the petition who got up that meeting and this memorial known the facts of the bank on this floor had changed their course of policy, and that they had, from the beginning of the session, voted against action, and for some time past ceased to ask for it, these same persons, sir, who have here asked for action, would have begged for delay, investigation, debate, till doomsday, and it so doing, would have acted with no more inconsistency than their friends upon this floor.

One subject more, Mr. Speaker, and I have done; and that, sir, is of so extraordinary a character, coming from the source it does, that I must ask leave of the House to read the resolution to which I refer. It is as follows:

"Resolved, That the custody and control of the public money was never intended by the Constitution to be intrusted exclusively to the President of the United States; and when they considered this power in connexion with the extraordinary military power granted to that officer by Congress last session, slight memorials, indeed, seemed to remain either in the people or in the States, of 'freedom, sovereignty, and independence.'"

And this resolution, Mr. Speaker, has been adopted by men who are consolidationists, who last year claimed the President as their President. The very men, sir, who defended and insisted upon exclusively justifying and supporting that very grant of power, as an act based upon the principles of the party to which they belong. Sir, my feeble voice was drowned among the shouts of triumph which they uttered. "Redress! redress! regnat" was their cry then. But there has been, sir, a wonderful change of opinion in these people on this subject within a very few months. I know not, sir, to what this remarkable alteration can be attributed, but to the equally remarkable union that has evidently taken place in this House, between the ultras of the North and those of the South, heretofore antipodes in principle, and that these very worthy constituents are willing to consummate the alliance by a total abandonment of all their own principles and the adoption of those of nullification, as remarkable a countermarch of opinion, within three short months, as can be found in all the annals of history. What advantage is to be gained by all this, beyond a more united opposition to the present Administration, is beyond my power to perceive. Their creed to this moment has always been, that the General Government cannot have too much power, nor the States too little. This resolution, sir, is from the very men who opposed my election to a seat in this House, upon the alleged ground of my being a nullifier, and an opponent of the bank. Sir, there was no subject upon which the opinions of the people of the district I have the honor to represent upon this floor, are more decidedly formed than upon that of the Bank of the United States. As to nullification, they knew there was none of it in Maine. The result, sir, was my return to this House by a majority of nearly seventeen hundred votes. I allude to this, sir, simply as showing the opinions of the people of my district upon the subject of the bank. I am not vain enough, nor foolish enough, to suppose that that result was owing to any personal popularity. Let my opinions on the subject of the bank have been but favorable to it, and I should have been defeated by a large majority, and very possibly larger than that by which I was elected. Sir, there are from fifteen to eighteen hundred voters in the town of Bangor; a majority of them were opposed to the Administration; an active committee was appointed to obtain signatures to this memorial; they have presented here the names of only two hundred and eighty-eight persons. What must be the inference? I, sir, need not state it.

Sir, when I had the honor the other day to present the resolutions of the Legislature of the State of Maine, I avowed myself an advocate for State rights, and of the Virginia construction of the Constitution. My colleague [Mr. Evans] in replying to my observations, asked, in a very significant manner, what are the doctrines of Virginia now? Sir, it is not for me to answer for Virginia: but if, as he intimated, Virginia has forgotten or repudiated the doctrines of her Jefferson and her Madison, I thank God, sir, there are some States who have not forgotten them, but who still remember them, and believe them the only construction of the Constitution which can preserve the rights and liberties of a free and happy people. In conclusion, Mr. Speaker, I shall merely move to refer these papers to the Committee of Ways and Means. I shall not move for their printing; they are, in my opinion, inconsistent and contradictory, and do no honor to the hand that penned them, the committee that reported them, the meeting that adopted them, nor to the citizens who signed the memorial. If, however, my colleague, or any other, shall choose to move the printing, I shall make no objection; but in that case, request that the names to the memorial be likewise printed.

Mr. REED would enter his protest against the manner in which memorials were this session presented by some honorable members, who took the occasion of presenting them to cast discredit upon those who sent them. He would deny that these memorials had been got up for any political purpose whatever; for he knew that there was, in many cases that he had presented petitions, the existence of very great distress and suffering, solely caused by the derangement given to the pecuniary relations throughout the country. In answer to the charge made, that those who now called for action, action on this subject by Congress, to restore the country to its former state of prosperity, continued to debate the subject, it was enough for him, perhaps, to say, that the debate was not protracted to prevent relief being given, but that it was done in total despair of effecting it in any other way—that, by such debating, there would be a change of opinion of those in power, if not in Congress, as would ultimately lead to a change of measures on their part. It was hoped that in this way, when the true condition of the country should be made known, Congress would afford the relief that was sought for so urgently. He insisted that those who alleged that there was no distress in the country, were utterly mistaken in supposing so. The distress, first felt on the seaboard, was fast spreading into the country, and if the honorable member could now congratulate his constituents, who were, as he said, engaged in the lumber trade, from being at present exempt from it, he could venture to predict such would not be their case sixty days hence. He objected strongly to the memorials being slighted, because they had been signed by those who had not supported General Jackson.

Mr. EVANS defended the character of the persons who signed the memorial, and moved that it should be printed.

After a few remarks in reply by Mr. PARKS, the memorial was ordered to be printed, and referred to the Committee of Ways and Means.

Mr. HUNTINGTON presented memorials from the Phœnix and Hartford Banks, Hartford, and from four banks in the city of Norwich, praying the restoration of the deposites, and the rechartering of the Bank of the United States; which were referred.

Mr. FOOT presented resolutions of the citizens of New Haven, in favor of the restoration of the deposites, and the recharter of the bank. Referred to the Committee of Ways and Means, and ordered to be printed.

Mr. SELDEN presented a memorial from the city of Troy, in relation to the state of the currency. Referred to the Committee of Ways and Means, and ordered to be printed.

Mr. SHINN rose and said:

I have been requested to present to this House a memorial from a part of the citizens of the county of Burlington, in the State of New Jersey. The memorialists, after stating the derangement of the currency of the country, pray that the public deposites be restored to the Bank of the United States. This, sir, is a large and respectable memorial, signed, as is said, by twenty-seven hundred and eighty-five persons, many of whom are my personal acquaintance and friends. I move its reference to the Committee of Ways and Means. This memorial has been printed in the Senate, therefore I do not move that course.

Mr. POTTS presented two memorials from his constituents, representing that there exists a general and severe embarrassment, in currency and business, attributing the same to the removal of the deposites, and praying their restoration. Mr. P. said that he fully concurred with his constituents as to the cause, remedy, and extent of the evils which they represented to exist; and on his motion the memorials were referred, and ordered to be printed.

Mr. MUHLENBERG presented the memorial of 1850 citizens of Berks county, Pennsylvania, disapproving the removal of the deposites and demanding their restoration as a measure of public justice and expediency.

In presenting this paper, Mr. M. wished to be indulged with some remarks, and he promised those who had petitions to present that they should be very brief. He represented a district composed of the single county of Berks, with a population of 60,000 souls. The 1850 signers to the memorial were a part of that population and but a small part of his constituents. He deemed it proper for a representative to present any petition from any part of his constituents, whether he concurred with their views or not. In the present instance, he differed *toto cœlo* from the memorialists, and he believed that a large part of the citizens of the county coincided with him in his views. He believed that the restitution of the deposites would lead to the recharter of the Bank of the United States, to which result he would undertake to say that two-thirds of his constituents was opposed. What change of opinion would be produced by the continuance of the present pressure and derangement of currency, he was not prepared to say, for he was neither a prophet nor the son of a prophet. Time and experience would show. These men were a minority of his constituents, but they were a respectable minority. He observed among the names, many of the highest respectability, whose opinions were entitled to great respect. But the great mass of the signers had always been opposed to the present Administration; with how much effect, the result of the election had shown. Another portion of the signers were friendly to the President and his Administration until the President signed the bank veto message. Another portion were still warmly attached to the President, but differed with him in relation to the policy of a bank. His duty compelled him to add, that by some persons he had been requested to say, that many were induced to add their names to this memorial by statements and coloring which were unfounded in truth. Without expressing an opinion as to the expediency of removing the deposites, he must say, that he was opposed to their restoration at the present time, because it must have the effect to produce the recharter of the present bank. The one measure would necessarily lead to the other. If he thought that the opinions of his constituents differed from his own, he would not say that he would conform his views to their opinions. No. An opinion deliberately formed, with reference to the interests of the whole people, he would not compromise. But, sir, said Mr. M., I would instantly resign my seat, and give my constituents an opportunity to elect an individual who would represent their sentiments. But he believed that a large majority of his constituents coincided with him in opinion on this subject. He was sustained in this belief by two large meetings held in the same county, one of them consisting of eight hundred citizens, with the proceedings of which he had not thought proper to trouble the House. As a mark of respect to the memorialists, and to show for what purpose the memorial was circulated, and what object it was covertly and insidiously made to subserve, he would ask that the memorial be read.

After the memorial had been read,

Mr. McKENNAN said, he wished to ask whether he had correctly understood his colleague to say that the memorialists had approached their object in a covert and insidious manner.

Mr. MUHLENBERG denied that he had made any such charge upon the memorialists.

Mr. McKENNAN said his object was merely to resist an attack which he supposed to be made upon men with many of whom he was personally acquainted.

Mr. BINNEY asked whether a copy of the memorial in the German language was annexed to it. Most of the subscribers were acquainted with no other language than the German.

Mr. MUHLENBERG replied, that there were two copies of the memorial: one in English, and the other in German; which last, for convenience, had been detached.

Mr. BINNEY would further ask whether it was so detached by the gentleman who presented it.

Mr. MUHLENBERG. Certainly.

Mr. WATMOUGH desired to ask whether his colleague, in the concluding remarks of his speech——

The SPEAKER interposed, and said it was not in order to propose interrogatories to members.

Mr. WATMOUGH wished to know, he said, whether his colleague did mean to say that subscriptions were obtained to the memorial through improper means, and that the doctrines contained in it emanated from a quarter upon which the people were not accustomed to rely. The gentleman seemed to convey this idea; if so, knowing the opinions of the people of Pennsylvania, he would say that when the questions now agitated were clearly presented to their strong and discriminating minds, they would not be prevented from coming to a decision, by the intimation that their opinions came from the Philadelphia school or any other quarter. He had propounded the question, and he had no doubt that his colleague would answer it with his usual promptness.

Mr. MUHLENBERG. If my honorable friend will take care of his own district, I will take care of mine. I am responsible to my own constituents for my course here, and forbid any interference of this kind. I have spoken respectfully of my constituents. I intended to convey the idea that signers to the memorial were obtained with a view to the recharter of the bank, whereas there is not one word in the memorial about the recharter of the bank. If the question was put to his constituents, whether they were in favor of General Jackson, two-thirds of them would say yes; and if they were asked whether they were in favor of the recharter of the bank, two-thirds of them would say no.

Mr. McKENNAN asked how his colleague could say that an attempt was made to mislead the people by producing the effect of rechartering the bank, when there was nothing of the kind on the face of the paper. He would undertake to say that many of the signers to this paper were men who would spurn the suggestion that any deception had been attempted.

Mr. MUHLENBERG had no doubt, he said, that many men whose names were on this paper would spurn the suggestion that they had attempted to make a false impression, but among the large number of signers there were many other men. He would like to know how many of the names subscribed to the memorial were known to his colleague.

Mr. McKENNAN, instead of answering the question, would, he said, ask his colleague to state to the House the names of the underlings to whom he had attributed deception. His constituents might then judge as to the correctness of the imputation. It was not for him to intefere with his colleague and his constituents, but he wished to vindicate respectable individuals from unjust imputations.

The SPEAKER asked whether the gentleman from Pennsylvania intended to embrace the names in the motion to print.

Mr. MUHLENBERG said he did not.

The memorial was then ordered to be printed.

Mr. WATMOUGH moved the printing of the names appended to the memorial.

Mr. BINNEY said this motion was connected with the inquiry as to the original memorial. Most of the names would be found in the German character, and many of the signers understood that language better than the English. He wished to have the German original before the House, as an answer to the suggestion, whenever and wherever it might be made, that the memorial had been submitted to the Germans in a language they did not understand. He could see no reason for printing the names, unless the German copy was annexed to the memorial.

Mr. MUHLENBERG rose only to explain the circumstances in connexion with the separa[illegible] from the memorial of the German translat[illegible] The original memorial, as brought to him, written in English and German. It was so mutilated, that he handed it to the person whom he received it, to make a new copy fo[illegible] sentation to the House. It was not pro[illegible] him, nor did he think it necessary to prese[illegible] the German copy. He had no objection presentation of the German copy. If gen[illegible] wished it they could have it.

Mr. MERCER said that the memorial d[illegible] to be presented was written in two language[illegible] therefore the House was not put in posses[illegible] the real memorial.

Mr. BINNEY would simply request the man to hand the German copy to the Clerk.

Mr. WAYNE said if it would be supposed a single individual who had signed the mem[illegible] would not have signed it, if the German copy

not been appended, it was a sufficient reason for presenting the German copy with the other.

Mr. MUHLENBERG had no objection to it, and should comply with the request. He also stated that he had no objection to the printing of the names.

Mr. WATMOUGH demanded the yeas and nays on his motion, and they were ordered.

Mr. TURRILL objected to printing names to this or any similar memorial. It was time to put a stop to this kind of operation. We had already printed half the names in Philadelphia at the public expense. What was the object? Not to enlighten the members of this House in regard to this question: Any one who wished to see what weight was attached to the names, could go and read them in the Clerk's office, without drawing any money from the treasury. In the first place, the bank gets up its panic meetings, and then they come and ask us to pay the expenses of printing and circulating their proceedings, memorials, and even the signatures. He could see no possible benefit to result from printing the names. If gentlemen who advocate the printing would give a reason for it, he would then withdraw his objection.

Mr. MILLER was indifferent whether the names were printed or not. But he was at a loss to imagine why this system of catechising members was introduced. His colleague had stated expressly that the memorialists were many of them highly respectable men. The effect that the memorial was intended to have could be seen by any one. He believed himself that it was impossible to draw a distinction between the question of a restoration of the deposites and a recharter of the bank. Who could doubt that the restoration would produce a recharter? And he had understood his colleague, [Mr. Binney,] with his accustomed frankness, to avow the opinion that unless the bank was rechartered the restoration of the deposites would be of no avail. In regard to the duplicate memorials we were contending about, they were both the same, and it was of no consequence which was presented to the House.

Mr. McKENNAN contended that the restoration of the deposites was not necessarily connected with the question of the recharter of the bank. But gentlemen (he said) had connected the questions with a view to excuse their course to their constituents.

Mr. BINNEY made a few remarks in reply to Mr. Miller.

Mr. SUTHERLAND said it was rather strange so much should have been made upon so small a matter. His colleague did throw out an idea that there was something insidious—owing to some misapprehension in the signers—in the manner by which some names were withdrawn from this petition. Generally speaking, he wished gentlemen to consider the propriety of having names printed to the memorial as calculated to do little good except to benefit the public printer. Although there are many persons who signed this and other memorials from Pennsylvania, they were the steady friends of the Administration, but who thought that in this matter a mistake or error had been committed by General Jackson, for whom they did not claim absolute infallibility, or that he was more than man. He wished that the names would be printed, that it could be hereafter seen they would be found again, as they always had been, ardently supporting the principles of the Republican party.

Mr. McKENNAN congratulated his colleague for the motive he had avowed that he was actuated in desiring the names of the memorialists to be printed. He thought that they were men of whom any country should be proud, inasmuch as they showed that they could dare to act up to their opinion in opposition to the Administration, even if it were only on one solitary point.

Mr. MUHLENBERG said there was some misapprehension as to what had fallen from him. He had not objected to the printing of the names of the memorialists. He, however, would state, that he held a letter in his hand, signed by nineteen persons, whose signatures were affixed to this memorial, in which they expressly state that they had been induced to sign it from some misconception of its purport, and they had authorized him to state so to the House.

Mr. WATMOUGH withdrew his call for the yeas and nays.

Mr. MANN, of New York, wished to know whether the printing was to be in Dutch, that there might be no cheatery.

The SPEAKER said he had announced his intention of having the memorial printed in the Dutch.

The question being stated on the printing of the names to the memorial—

Mr. WATMOUGH a second time called for the yeas and nays, and they were ordered.

Mr. FELDER remarked, that as the signatures were in both languages, there would be some injustice in printing them twice over.

Mr. MERCER said that the value of the time engaged in the discussion would suffice to pay the expense of printing.

Mr. TURRILL would oppose, if he stood alone, the printing of all such petitions. It was surprising to him to hear such an unnecessary expense advocated. There was, among others, a petition already printed on this subject, with sixty-two pages of names, at a considerable expense. These petitions, he believed, were got up originally by the bank, and those who procured the signatures were paid for their trouble out of Mr. Biddle's breeches pocket. He felt that it was time for the House to take a stand, and save the treasury from this expense which was sought to be thrown upon it. It was possible that many of those who signed the petitions from the large cities, were stimulated by the *assurances that their names would appear in a printed book.*

Mr. H. EVERETT did not think the member from New York [Mr. Turrill] warranted in taking for granted that all the memorials presented on account of distress were got up by the bank, and he desired to know if it was the design of gentlemen, by making such statements, to forestall public opinion, and thus prevent them coming forward to testify their deep sense of that distress. If such denunciations were made, it must have the effect of deterring, in future, any petitions being sent. He hoped that the representatives would not consider themselves so much the representatives of any particular district, as of the whole people; and that when petitions should be presented, that they would be treated by members in a respectful manner. They should look to considerations affecting the general good, and ought to be above those of party.

Mr. BURGES was astonished at the opposition given to the printing of the names to memorials on the ground of expense, and he advocated it as necessary to establish, beyond question, whether the distress which now agitated the country was real or pretended—was got up by the people themselves, or by the influence, as charged, of the bank.

Mr. LANE believed that the statements they had heard that these memorials about distress were got up by the bank, were justly founded. They had been known to originate almost at the doors of the bank, and only from those places directly under its influence. There was no voice of distress from Indiana or Illinois.

Mr. EWING corroborated the statement that there was no distress felt in Indiana; and he maintained that there was a general feeling that the people should have some benefit from the profits derived by the bank; that they thought these profits should not be monopolized by any institution which properly belonged to themselves. As other memorials had been printed, he would vote for the printing of this, in both German and English.

Mr. CROCKETT rose and said: Sir, as I am the only person from Tennessee in this House who am opposed to the Administration, I hope I may get a few words in: that I may say what are my own notions on these matters. Sir, I think the member from New York, [Mr. Turrill,] who has just spoke, has been a little testy in his objections. He talks much about this, as if it was a great matter. Sir, are we to stick at such trifles as a few dollars in the printing a matter so important? It seems, sir, to me to be something like loading a twenty-four-pounder to shoot a flea. Sir, is it not so? We are spending three or four thousand dollars in discussing the printing of a matter that, perhaps, after all, will not be twenty cost. But, sir, this is retrenchment; but it is the old rule for retrenching. I love, sir, to see the petitioners come here, and my life on it, sir, they will come; ay, and from Indiana, for all that we here to the contrary; and yet from my own State, every day my letters tell me they wish this question settled. They know very well, in my district, the character of the man, who, when he takes anything into his head, will carry it into effect. They know how I should act in this bank business, for I told them, before I was elected, how I should vote—that I would recharter the bank, and restore the deposites. Sir, I get letters every day, from all parts, which tell me these acts are disapprobated. The question is now, whether we shall be under the old and happy state of things, or have a despot. Sir, the people have a right to tell their grievances, and, sir, I tell you, they must not be refused—I can't stand it any longer—I won't.

Mr. ASHLEY, of Missouri, said that he could not undertake to state, with any degree of precision, how the people of Missouri were divided on the important question of the removal of the deposites, nor could he account for not having received memorials from his constituents on that subject. Perhaps the people of Missouri have come to the conclusion that memorials, petitions, or prayers of any kind touching this subject would avail nothing; that should they be favorably disposed of by Congress, they might be disregarded in another quarter. Mr. A. thought the people of Missouri as deeply interested in this measure as those of any other portion of the Union. The State had been a few years ago literally inundated with local bank paper, when everything in relation to the currency of the country was confusion and distrust. On the introduction of the paper of the Bank of the United States, this unsound and fraudulent currency (local bank paper) gradually diminished, and at length entirely disappeared. Since that time, up to the present, everything in relation to the currency of the country has moved on smoothly; but he feared, from present appearances, this state of things would not long exist.

Mr. LANE made some explanations in reply to his colleague, [Mr. Ewing.]

The question was then taken on the motion to print the names signed to the memorial, and decided in the affirmative—yeas 112, noes 90.

On motion of Mr. THOMAS,

The House then adjourned.

IN SENATE.

TUESDAY, *February* 25, 1834.

Mr. SMITH moved that the petitions and memorials presented by him yesterday, from sundry citizens and institutions of Connecticut, disapproving of the removal of the deposites, be taken up, read, referred to the Committee on Finance, and ordered to be printed.

Mr. CLAYTON presented a memorial, praying a grant of lands for soldiers of the late war; which was referred to the Committee on Military Affairs.

Mr. CLAYTON, from the Committee on the Judiciary, reported a bill, without amendment, relative to interest on advances made to the United States.

Mr. FRELINGHUYSEN presented the petition of eight hundred citizens of the county of Cumberland, praying the restoration of the deposites and the recharter of the Bank of the United States; which, after some remarks by Mr. F. and Mr. CLAYTON, was read, referred to the Committee on Finance, and ordered to be printed.

Mr. WRIGHT, from the Committee on Commerce, asked that the memorial which was referred to that committee, on the warehousing system, might be printed; which was so ordered.

Mr. WRIGHT, from the Committee of Claims, asked to be discharged from the further consideration of the memorial of Lyman Foote, surgeon in the army of the United States, praying additional compensation for services rendered by him at Prairie du Chien, and the memorial might be referred to the Committee on Military Affairs; which was agreed to.

Mr. WRIGHT presented the memorial from one thousand seven hundred and thirty citizens of Troy, New York, praying legislative relief from the pecuniary distress of the community; which,

Mr. CHILTON thought, under all the circumstances, that it was only an act of courtesy to accede to the motion.

Mr. POLK explained the grounds upon which the Committee of Ways and Means had acted in reporting the bill, in conformity to estimates furnished from the War Department, and said, although he did not think it necessary himself to recommit the bill, yet as there was a general desire to have a discussion upon it, and as he could not have anything to fear from that discussion, he would at once withdraw his opposition to the motion.

Mr. McDUFFIE thereupon, by unanimous consent of the House, withdrew his call for the yeas and nays.

So the bill was committed to the Committee of the Whole on the state of the Union.

The bill making appropriations for Indian annuities for 1834, having been taken up—

Mr. HORACE EVERETT withdrew a motion made by him for its recommitment.

The question then being, Shall the bill pass?

Mr. McKAY desired to know if there was any intention, on the part of the Committee on Indian Affairs to report a bill for the regulation of intercourse with the Indian tribes.

Mr. H. EVERETT replied, that it was his intention to do so.

After some conversation, in which Messrs. McKAY, POLK, FILLMORE, ASHLEY, and H. EVERETT, took part—

Mr. McKAY moved to recommit the bill to the Committee on Indian Affairs—negatived, 70 to 102.

On motion of Mr. BROWN, the House then adjourned.

IN SENATE.

WEDNESDAY, February 26, 1834.

A message upon executive business was received from the President of the United States, by Mr. DONELSON, his Private Secretary.

Mr. CHAMBERS presented the memorial of 3558 citizens of Baltimore, composed of merchants, mechanics, manufacturers, &c., attributing the depression in the money market exclusively to the conduct of the Bank of the United States, and expressing the greatest confidence in the Executive. It was the wish of the memorialists that the deposites might not be restored, and that the Bank of the United States might not be rechartered. Mr. C. remarked that the committee, now in this city, was composed of gentlemen of respectability and worth. On his motion, the memorial was read, referred to the Committee on Finance, and ordered to be printed.

Mr. WHITE, from the Committee on Indian Affairs, made a report on the petition of James Vernon; which was read, and ordered to lie on the table.

Mr. WEBSTER moved, in pursuance of notice, that the Senate proceed to executive business.

Mr. CHAMBERS, in consequence of the indisposition of his colleague, [Mr. KENT,] hoped this motion would not be pressed.

Mr. WEBSTER then waived the motion, but signified his determination to renew it at an early hour to-morrow.

On motion of Mr. GRUNDY, the Senate proceeded to the election of a member of the Committee on the Post Office and Post Roads, vacated by the resignation of the Hon. Mr. RIVES, of Virginia, when Mr. ROBINSON was appointed.

Mr. McKEAN presented a memorial signed by 1878 citizens of Berks county, Pennsylvania, in favor of a restoration of the deposites.

Also, the proceedings of a meeting of inhabitants of the Northern Liberties of Philadelphia, of the same tenor.

Also, one from citizens of Schuylkill county, opposed to the restoration of the deposites.

The memorials and proceedings were read; when Mr. McKEAN moved that they be referred to the Committee on Finance, and be printed.

After some remarks by Mr. McKEAN, Mr. CLAY, and Mr. CLAYTON, the motion was agreed to.

Mr. WHITE submitted the following resolution:

Resolved, That the Committee on Military Affairs be instructed to inquire into the propriety of providing by law for the appointment of a chaplain to ...... attached to the battalion of mounted rangers ...... ed for the defence of the frontiers.

Mr. CLAY presented a copy of a memorial from a large number of citizens of the city of Louisville, Kentucky, which had been presented in the House of Representatives, complaining of great pecuniary distress in that city, and attributing it to the removal of the deposites. Mr. C. took the occasion to speak at length of the prosperous state of affairs in Kentucky, when he left home in September, as compared with the representations he had received of its situation now. That such was the panic existing there, that all who had bank notes were getting specie for them and hoarding it up as fast as they could, and that the only remedy was a restoration of the deposites and the recharter of the bank. Mr. C. said that the existence of distress was now admitted by all. That although the gentleman from Georgia spoke a short time ago of the exemption of the city of his residence from the prevailing pressure, yet that he (Mr. C.) had this morning seen an account of a town meeting held there on this very subject. He admitted that the cause of the distress was a subject of much dispute; but that whatever the cause might be, it was the duty of all to consider whether it was practicable to afford relief, and if it was, to apply it without regard to party. The President and Secretary had both said that a leading motive with them for removing the deposites, was to compel the bank to wind up its concerns and close its doors. But now it was said that the bank was the cause of the distress, because it had begun to wind up, and that it could grant relief by not doing so. He had no doubt but it could give relief, but it must be under different circumstances from what gentlemen thought. If it could be rechartered, and receive an assurance that it would meet with no attack from the Executive, he believed it could give relief in thirty days. He complained of gentlemen calling on the bank for relief, if it were guilty of all the charges which were brought against it.

Mr. C. then adverted to the safety fund banking system of New York, and the attempt by the President, and Secretary of the Treasury, to introduce the same system among the deposite banks, and took up and examined the list of banks in that State, and spoke of the insecurity and danger of the whole system. That of the sixty-nine banks, thirty had less than ten thousand dollars in specie, six of them less than five thousand dollars, and one—the Bank of Ithaca, with nearly three hundred thousand dollars of bills in circulation—had four thousand dollars in specie. He thought such a state of things in relation to those banks might exist in times of public confidence and security, but in case of overtrading, or a panic, such as now prevailed, they must blow up. Although he was in favor of a recharter of the bank, yet he trusted no opposition for that purpose would be submitted till the violated laws and Constitution of the country should be vindicated. The struggle we were engaged in, was an arduous one; but it was one between a single man with a standing army of forty thousand officers on the one side, and the people on the other. Still he doubted not that the people would ultimately prevail. Mr. C. then commented on the report of the Philadelphia committee who visited the President a short time since for the purpose of explaining to him their views of the prevailing distress in the community, and condemned in unmeasured terms the reply of the President as reported by those gentlemen.

Mr. TALLMADGE said he was unwilling to occupy the time of the Senate on a mere incidental question, and more especially was he reluctant to interfere with the Senator, [Mr. HILL,] who was entitled to the floor on the main question of debate. But he could not forbear to say a word or two in relation to the Safety Fund System of New York, which had been the subject of animadversion by the Senator from Kentucky, [Mr. CLAY.] It was a topic which the Senator seemed to cherish with much care. It had afforded him occasion for remark from the very commencement of the session to the present time. In the main debate on the deposites, he had dwelt upon it in a manner calculated to excite the public mind against

those banks in the State of New York, which were denominated Safety Fund Banks. Mr. T. said he had intended, at a proper time, to reply to the Senator on that subject, and the opportunity might yet offer to enable him to do it. At present, he would confine himself to a few remarks, as the time had already arrived to proceed with the special order of the day.

It would, no doubt, afford gratification to some gentlemen, if the safety fund banks were in a worse condition even than they themselves have represented them; or if disaster should befall any of them. The Senator from New Jersey, [Mr. SOUTHARD,] as well as the Senator from Ohio, [Mr. EWING,] had, on a former day, alluded to them; and the latter gentleman, whilst he considered all State banks unsafe and unfit to sustain the currency of the country, was pleased to say, he deemed the safety fund banks of New York more unsafe than any others; that they were far behind the banks of Ohio and the western States; and we are now told, on his authority, that the want of confidence in the banks of his own State, is such, at this time, that the people of the country are rushing for specie, and carrying it away by bushels. This alarm, Mr. T. said, might be true; still he had confidence in the banks of Ohio; but did it show the condition of those banks to be preferable to the safety fund banks? Mr. T. said, when he heard gentlemen talk so much about this system, and decry its safety, he could not persuade himself that they possessed any very accurate information in relation to it. He had hoped that some one of those who had taken this subject into their special charge, would, whilst they were arraigning it before the Senate, condescend to explain it. Mr. T. said he would yield the floor to the honorable Senator from Kentucky, if he would vouchsafe an explanation.

Mr. CLAY said, he understood by the safety fund system, the sixty-nine banks were connected together and responsible to each other. That they each contributed a certain per centage to protect the people against a blow up of any one, or all of them. He had understood that they had raised a fund of some $290,000 for that purpose, and that the responsibility was only to the cases of the fund so raised. The gentleman thought it hard that others should notice this system, and if it was confined only to New York, and no other State was to be affected by it, perhaps it would not be proper to notice it. But as every State was more or less affected by the banking operations of the others, it was right to look to the condition of those banks, and especially, too, when the Secretary of the Treasury announced his purpose of trying the same system in other parts of the United States. The gentleman did him great injustice by saying that he would see with satisfaction the fall of the New York banks. He would be happy if the gentleman could make out that they were safe. Mr. C. had seen the report of the commissioners of the safety fund, and there was one item in it, of which he had not heard a satisfactory solution by any New York gentleman to whom he had spoken on the subject—it was the item of the five millions. He was not cognizant of the trade of New York as the gentleman seemed to suppose. He was aware that the banks in the interior drew on the city banks, and while public confidence was not impaired, it might go on safely. But now, if the farmer would say he did not want their paper, but must have specie, what would become of them? The gentleman thought he knew nothing of the safety fund system, and he hoped he would have no occasion to know any more of it.

Mr. TALLMADGE resumed—

From the Senator's explanation, he perceived his knowledge of the system was as imperfect and as limited as he had anticipated. The very application of it which he has made to the State banks employed by the Secretary of the Treasury for deposite of the public funds shows that he has a very inadequate idea of the system. He objects to the system being extended through the Union by the Secretary of the Treasury under Executive management. He has told us that a fund is provided by the contribution of the banks of a certain per cent., and that that fund is responsible for the deficiency of an insolvent bank. Wherein (asks Mr. T.) does the Senator find any resemblance of

the branches to take each other's notes, why should a branch demand a premium on a check? This view proved conclusively, that the universal circulation of the paper of the United States Bank was not owing to its accommodating disposition, but to the causes which he had mentioned. If the bank did not charge the same rate of premium on exchange which the brokers in New York and Philadelphia charged, how could the brokers exist in those places? Why did any person resort to the bank? From the flourishing condition of the brokers in the neighborhood of the bank, he was led to the conclusion that exchange was afforded as cheap by the brokers as by the bank. Why, he would ask, should not the notes of a local deposite bank, paying specie for its notes, giving weekly statements of its condition, its notes being also receivable in payment of dues to the Government, be quite as current as the notes of the United States Bank? Would the people have no security, if his plan were adopted? They would have the same security for the safety of the deposites which the charter of the United States Bank gave them. The condition of the deposite banks would be made known in the same manner. But it may be said that these reports are not alone sufficient, and that the charter of the United States Bank offered other security by the appointment of Government directors. But these were merely nominal directors. The Government has directors, but they can know nothing of the concerns of the bank, because all information is denied to them. Of this fact we had the most conclusive evidence. It came to us in such a manner that we should do violence to our judgment in supposing that the Government directors had any direct participation in the management of the institution. But were not the State banks, under the management of individuals, quite as respectable and trustworthy as the United States Bank? Were they not also accountable to the Legislatures in their respective States? Were they not under the direct supervision of the people, through their Legislatures? They were directly amenable to the people, who were affected by the management of the institution. The United States Bank was amenable to the people of the Union. But an act done at that board might be justified by nine-tenths of the Union, and the tenth portion, to whom the act was injurious, would have no redress. An act which was injurious to the interests of Alabama, might be approved of in New York, or in other northern cities. The people, therefore, could be better secured in their rights through the immediate responsibility of the State banks, than through the general responsibility of a national bank. This liability, connected with the safeguards which he had referred to, would afford perfect security to the people of the nation.

It was said that the whole commercial interests of the country would be prostrated by the measure which he had advocated. But if the commercial prosperity of the country depended upon the amount of capital in employment, no such effect would take place. Not a cent of capital would be annihilated by the measure. The mere withdrawal of capital from one bank, and its transfer to others, did not diminish the capital of the country to the amount of a single cent. The amount of revenue would be the same whether it was received by the State bank or a national bank, and it was likely that the local banks would make as much use of it as the United States Bank would make. What inducement would the local banks have to withhold discounts? The people would have the same use of their own money, and it would be distributed more generally than it would if deposited in the United States Bank. He might be told that the rate of exchange would be so injuriously affected by the measure, that internal exchanges could not be carried on. Mr. M. went on to show that though the equalization of exchange was one of the objects for which the United States Bank was brought into existence, yet the bank had not effected this object. In 1832 and 1833, the bank received from premiums on exchange $917,244. The bank, by this course, had violated the great principle on which it was founded. In support of this view, he read a passage from a letter of Mr. Crawford. The universality of the currency of the United States Bank enabled it to carry on exchanges at a low rate of premium; but the local deposite banks, when they have, from similar Government facilities, the same general currency for their notes, will be able to effect the internal exchanges at the same low rates.

Mr. M. would now proceed to the last view of the case. Gentlemen seem to think that the whole business of the country rested in the hands of the United States Bank. They forget that there is any private capital in the country. They forget even what the organ of the bank had announced, that the distress of the community was not so much owing to the withdrawal of capital from the bank, as from the want of confidence which it produced. He would ask gentlemen not to come to the support of General Jackson's measures, but to come forward, at this crisis, and arrest the further progress of bank tyranny—to come forward and assist in restoring the lost rights of the people. We are told that we are in the midst of a revolution; and he concurred in the opinion. A mighty struggle was going on between the people and the bank, between money-power and the rights and liberties of the people. The people had made up the issue, and they would abide by it. They know that it was in the power of the bank to bring much suffering and calamity upon them, but they would meet it all as they would the privations and toils of a war declared for their independence.

Mr. CLOWNEY rose and obtained the floor.

The hour allotted for the consideration of resolutions having expired, the order of the day was taken up.

The House proceeded to the orders of the day, and took up the bill making

APPROPRIATIONS FOR FORTIFICATIONS.

The question thereon before the House being a motion submitted by Mr. McDufeie to commit the bill to the Committee of the Whole on the state of the Union—

Mr. McD. remarked, that he had been induced to submit his motion in consequence of the bill having passed through the House without objection. The bill being in its final stage, he wished to have it committed, that it might be in the power of the House to reject such of the appropriations for places which, upon full discussion, would be found expedient. With a view to ascertain whether there was any spirit of economy existing in the House, he would call for the yeas and nays; which were ordered.

Mr. POLK would not then enter into any discussion upon the policy of the system of fortifications, but he wished to remind the House of the state of the present bill. It has been regularly reported with the usual appropriations, and there had been appropriations made in it for four new works, for which some small appropriations had been made the last session. A portion of the money had been expended preparatory to their completion. One was intended for the protection of Boston harbor, another at New Orleans, and one at Foster's Bank, Florida, which was part of the system of defence for Pensacola. It was for the House, then, to consider whether they would go on with these works or have them prostrated. It was deemed important that these should be completed; and although the appropriation for all these places in the aggregate exceeded that of last year by $64,000, yet it was less than the appropriations made in other years for these purposes. The defence of the country must mainly be aided by such fortifications, and he had been given to understand that the contemplated works were most important.

Mr. WILDE objected to the whole system which had been adopted for erecting and supporting fortifications for years past; and said he feared that the gentleman from South Carolina had fallen upon a wrong subject to expect that coöperation from the House which it merited on the ground of economy. He maintained that as the fortifications were now extended, they could not be sufficiently manned or armed in less than twenty years, and that as they were useless in a time of peace, they must, when unarmed be more pernicious than any thing else in the event of any sudden war.

Mr. CAMBRELENG, although he differed in opinion on this subject with the honorable member from South Carolina, expressed his hope that, in order to accelerate the passage of the bill, the motion to commit would be acceded to. He desired that every opportunity should be given for inquiry into the expenditures of the country; and he did not think that when these inquiries were made that the excess complained of would be found in the appropriations made for the support of the army or navy, but in the appropriations made by the House on other subjects.

Mr. PINCKNEY said, unless the bill was committed, he would be compelled to vote against it; but whilst he fully agreed in the policy of supporting fortifications, as it appeared there had been large increased appropriations, it was necessary that some economy should be practised. That it should be looked into whether any of the places might be abandoned with propriety; whether there was any immediate necessity, from the state of the country, for the appropriations now made.

Mr. P. was proceeding on the general subject, when—

The SPEAKER interposed, and said it was not in order to discuss it.

Mr. PINCKNEY resumed, and said he wished to state he desired the commitment of the bill that he might move an amendment to strike out the clause in relation to the appropriation for a fortification in Charleston, $50,000, which was utterly useless unless it was intended that they should be used, as they had been, not outward to the ocean, but against the citizens themselves. He could not vote for any fortifications in Charleston, whilst the force bill was in existence. They had enough of tyranny from the Federal Government, and he would stand upon the Constitution, and put the question at once, whether there could be any fortifications erected without the consent of the States themselves. He would submit whether it was intended to erect these forts without the consent of the State, asked or obtained. If so, he maintained it would be a gross infraction of the agreement entered into between the several States.

Mr. WAYNE could not recognise the propriety of recommitting the bill unless it could be speedily pointed out that there was extravagance in any of the appropriations made, and that the recommitment might be thus found necessary. He did not believe that the observations that were made by the honorable member from South Carolina [Mr. Pinckney] would find any corresponding voice in the House. It seemed to that gentleman, that the contemplated works were for the protection of Charleston alone. This was not so. The importance of that harbor in a time of war, as convenient to the West Indies, was of the highest order. The Government was acting on a general system for the benefit of those to come after them, as well as with a view to their present safety.

Mr. McKAY went into some statements to show that the appropriations for fortifications were increasing in amount. He advocated the recommitment, that there might be a more regular and economical appropriation made than we had been in the habit of having. The increase appeared to be since 1831, at the rate of twenty-five per cent. upon the first item in the bill, for the preservation of Castle Island. He trusted that the bill would be recommitted, that the estimates submitted by the engineers for these various fortifications should be inquired into. He was going into the general subject, when—

The SPEAKER reminded him he was not in order.

Mr. PARKER said, as there appeared to be instances in which the appropriations made last year for the peparatory measures, were not applied, it might induce the Committee of the Whole to see that there was no necessity for appropriations being made for the completion of the works themselves.

Mr. VANDERPOEL said, although he believed he should vote for the bill, yet, under the circumstances in which the House had been placed latterly, he did not think that the request of the honorable member from South Carolina, in asking for a delay, unreasonable, and particularly when it was stated that it had passed *sub silentio*. He could not see that there should be any objection to a scrutiny by the Committee of the Whole into a bill which appropriated so large a sum as $800,000. There might be some members who might object to appropriations for particular places, for, although willing to swallow a single pill, it did not therefore follow that they should swallow an apothecary's shop.

Mr. CHILTON thought, under all the circumstances, that it was only an act of courtesy to accede to the motion.

Mr. POLK explained the grounds upon which the Committee of Ways and Means had acted in reporting the bill, in conformity to estimates furnished from the War Department, and said, although he did not think it necessary himself to recommit the bill, yet as there was a general desire to have a discussion upon it, and as he could not have anything to fear from that discussion, he would at once withdraw his opposition to the motion.

Mr. McDUFFIE thereupon, by unanimous consent of the House, withdrew his call for the yeas and nays.

So the bill was committed to the Committee of the Whole on the state of the Union.

The bill making appropriations for Indian annuities for 1834, having been taken up—

Mr. HORACE EVERETT withdrew a motion made by him for its recommitment.

The question then being, Shall the bill pass?

Mr. McKAY desired to know if there was any intention, on the part of the Committee on Indian Affairs to report a bill for the regulation of intercourse with the Indian tribes.

Mr. H. EVERETT replied, that it was his intention to do so.

After some conversation, in which Messrs. McKAY, POLK, FILLMORE, ASHLEY, and H. EVERETT, took part—

Mr. McKAY moved to recommit the bill to the Committee on Indian Affairs—negatived, 70 to 102.

On motion of Mr. BROWN, the House then adjourned.

IN SENATE.

Wednesday, *February* 26, 1834.

A message upon executive business was received from the President of the United States, by Mr. Donelson, his Private Secretary.

Mr. CHAMBERS presented the memorial of 3558 citizens of Baltimore, composed of merchants, mechanics, manufacturers, &c., attributing the depression in the money market exclusively to the conduct of the Bank of the United States, and expressing the greatest confidence in the Executive. It was the wish of the memorialists that the deposites might not be restored, and that the Bank of the United States might not be rechartered. Mr. C. remarked that the committee, now in this city, was composed of gentlemen of respectability and worth. On his motion, the memorial was read, referred to the Committee on Finance, and ordered to be printed.

Mr. WHITE, from the Committee on Indian Affairs, made a report on the petition of James Vernon; which was read, and ordered to lie on the table.

Mr. WEBSTER moved, in pursuance of notice, that the Senate proceed to executive business.

Mr. CHAMBERS, in consequence of the indisposition of his colleague, [Mr. Kent,] hoped this motion would not be pressed.

Mr. WEBSTER then waived the motion, but signified his determination to renew it at an early hour to-morrow.

On motion of Mr. GRUNDY, the Senate proceeded to the election of a member of the Committee on the Post Office and Post Roads, vacated by the resignation of the Hon. Mr. Rives, of Virginia, when Mr. Robinson was appointed.

Mr. McKEAN presented a memorial signed by 1878 citizens of Berks county, Pennsylvania, in favor of a restoration of the deposites.

Also, the proceedings of a meeting of inhabitants of the Northern Liberties of Philadelphia, of the same tenor.

Also, one from citizens of Schuylkill county, opposed to the restoration of the deposites.

The memorials and proceedings were read; when Mr. McKEAN moved that they be referred to the Committee on Finance, and be printed.

After some remarks by Mr. McKEAN, Mr. CLAY, and Mr. CLAYTON, the motion was agreed to.

Mr. WHITE submitted the following resolution:

Resolved, That the Committee on Military Affairs be instructed to inquire into the propriety of providing by law for the appointment of a chaplain to be attached to the battalion of mounted rangers [illegible]ed for the defence of the frontiers.

Mr. CLAY presented a copy of a memorial from a large number of citizens of the city of Louisville, Kentucky, which had been presented in the House of Representatives, complaining of great pecuniary distress in that city, and attributing it to the removal of the deposites. Mr. C. took the occasion to speak at length of the prosperous state of affairs in Kentucky, when he left home in September, as compared with the representations he had received of its situation now. That such was the panic existing there, that all who had bank notes were getting specie for them and hoarding it up as fast as they could, and that the only remedy was a restoration of the deposites and the recharter of the bank. Mr. C. said that the existence of distress was now admitted by all. That although the gentleman from Georgia spoke a short time ago of the exemption of the city of his residence from the prevailing pressure, yet that he (Mr. C.) had this morning seen an account of a town meeting held there on this very subject. He admitted that the cause of the distress was a subject of much dispute; but that whatever the cause might be, it was the duty of all to consider whether it was practicable to afford relief, and if it was, to apply it without regard to party. The President and Secretary had both said that a leading motive with them for removing the deposites, was to compel the bank to wind up its concerns and close its doors. But now it was said that the bank was the cause of the distress, because it had begun to wind up, and that it could grant relief by not doing so. He had no doubt but it could give relief, but it must be under different circumstances from what gentlemen thought. If it could be rechartered, and receive an assurance that it would meet with no attack from the Executive, he believed it could give relief in thirty days. He complained of gentlemen calling on the bank for relief, if it were guilty of all the charges which were brought against it.

Mr. C. then adverted to the safety fund banking system of New York, and the attempt by the President, and Secretary of the Treasury, to introduce the same system among the deposite banks, and took up and examined the list of banks in that State, and spoke of the insecurity and danger of the whole system. That of the sixty-nine banks, thirty had less than ten thousand dollars in specie, six of them less than five thousand dollars, and one—the Bank of Ithaca, with nearly three hundred thousand dollars of bills in circulation—had four thousand dollars in specie. He thought such a state of things in relation to those banks might exist in times of public confidence and security, but in case of overtrading, or a panic, such as now prevailed, they must blow up. Although he was in favor of a recharter of the bank, yet he trusted no proposition for that purpose would be submitted till the violated laws and Constitution of the country should be vindicated. The struggle we were engaged in, was an arduous one; but it was one between a single man with a standing army of forty thousand officers on the one side, and the people on the other. Still he doubted not that the people would ultimately prevail. Mr. C. then commented on the report of the Philadelphia committee who visited the President a short time since for the purpose of explaining to him their views of the prevailing distress in the community, and condemned in unmeasured terms the reply of the President as reported by those gentlemen.

Mr. TALLMADGE said he was unwilling to occupy the time of the Senate on a mere incidental question, and more especially was he reluctant to interfere with the Senator, [Mr. Hill,] who was entitled to the floor on the main question of debate. But he could not forbear to say a word or two in relation to the *Safety Fund System* of New York, which had been the subject of animadversion by the Senator from Kentucky, [Mr. Clay.] It was a topic which the Senator seemed to cherish with much care. It had afforded him occasion for remark from the very commencement of the session to the present time. In the main debate on the deposites, he had dwelt upon it in a manner calculated to excite the public mind against those banks in the State of New York, which were denominated Safety Fund Banks. Mr. T. said he had intended, at a proper time, to reply to the Senator on that subject, and the opportunity might yet offer to enable him to do it. At present, he would confine himself to a few remarks, as the time had already arrived to proceed with the special order of the day.

It would, no doubt, afford gratification to some gentlemen, if the safety fund banks were in a worse condition even than they themselves have represented them; or if disaster should befall any of them. The Senator from New Jersey, [Mr. Southard,] as well as the Senator from Ohio, [Mr. Ewing,] had, on a former day, alluded to them; and the latter gentleman, whilst he considered all State banks unsafe and unfit to sustain the currency of the country, was pleased to say, he deemed the safety fund banks of New York more unsafe than any others; that they were far behind the banks of Ohio and the western States; and we are now told, on his authority, that the want of confidence in the banks of his own State, is such, at this time, that the people of the country are calling for specie, and carrying it away by bagfulls. This alarm, Mr. T. said, might be true; still he had confidence in the banks of Ohio; but did it show the condition of those banks to be preferable to the safety fund banks? Mr. T. said, when he heard gentlemen talk so much about this system, and decry its safety, he could not persuade himself that they possessed any very accurate information in relation to it. He had hoped that some one of those who had taken this subject into their special charge, would, whilst they were arraigning it before the Senate, condescend to explain it. Mr. T. said he would yield the floor to the honorable Senator from Kentucky, if he would vouchsafe an explanation.

Mr. CLAY said, he understood by the safety fund system, the sixty-nine banks were connected together and responsible to each other. That they each contributed a certain per centage to protect the people against a blow up of any one, or all of them. He had understood that they had raised a fund of some $280,000 for that purpose, and that the responsibility was only to the extent of the fund so raised. The gentleman thought it hard that others should notice this system, and if it was confined only to New York, and no other State was to be affected by it, perhaps it would not be proper to notice it. But as every State was more or less affected by the banking operations of the others, it was right to look to the condition of those banks, and especially, too, when the Secretary of the Treasury announced his purpose of trying the same system in other parts of the United States. The gentleman did him great injustice by saying that he would see with satisfaction the fall of the New York banks. He would be happy if the gentleman could make out that they were safe. Mr. C. had seen the report of the commissioners of the safety fund, and there was one item in it, of which he had not heard a satisfactory solution by any New York gentleman to whom he had spoken on the subject—it was the item of the five millions. He was not quite so ignorant of the trade of New York as the gentleman seemed to suppose. He was aware that the banks in the interior draw on the city banks, and while public confidence was not impaired, it might go on safely. But now, if the farmer would say he did not want their paper, but must have specie, what would become of them? The gentleman thought he knew nothing of the safety fund system, and he hoped he would have no occasion to know any more of it.

Mr. TALLMADGE resumed—

From the Senator's explanation, he perceived his knowledge of the system was as imperfect and as limited as he had anticipated. The very application of it which he has made to the State banks employed by the Secretary of the Treasury for the deposite of the public funds shows that he has a very inadequate idea of the system. He objects to the system being extended through the Union by the Secretary of the Treasury under Executive management. He has told us that a fund is provided by the contribution of the banks of a certain *per cent.*, and that that fund is responsible for any deficiency of an insolvent bank. Wherein (said Mr. T.) does the Senator find any resemblance of

relation between this system and those banks employed by the Secretary of the Treasury? There is no responsibility; the one for the other—no contribution—no common fund. How, then, can it be said that the Secretary is endeavoring to extend this system through the Union? There is nothing in the Secretary's plan that assimilates it to the safety fund system. What bearing, then, has this system on the Secretary's plan for depositing and disbursing the public money through the State banks? None. And its introduction to the Senate so frequently can only serve to gratify those who wish to create distrust in its security. He knew that no one on this floor would desire to produce a panic in relation to any of our banks; but there were those out of this Chamber who had contributed all in their power to do it. But he trusted, in regard to the banks in New York, that their efforts would be unsuccessful. The people of that State had entire security. The bill-holders and depositors under that system were altogether safe, and from their safety arises their confidence in the system itself. They are protected against the possibility of loss. The Senator, however, tells us that the safety fund consists of about $300,000, and that that sum would be but little more than sufficient to cover the circulation of a single bank. That fund is to be increased, it should be observed, till it equals three per cent. on the whole banking capital of the State. If in case of insolvency of any bank the fund should not be sufficient after applying its effects, then the banks again contribute to the fund as before, and the creditor receives the amount due him, with interest from the time his claim was presented. A case can scarcely be imagined where the effects of the bank itself, on winding up, would not be sufficient to meet all its engagements without a resort to the safety fund. Its stockholders might sustain loss, but its creditors would not. Thus it will be seen that unless gentlemen can suppose an entire insolvency of all the banks of the State under this system, there is not the possibility of loss to the creditors of any of them. The community, therefore, is safe. But there is another feature that adds still more to that safety, and which guards the banks themselves—it is the power of the bank commissioners to supervise all their concerns. Their frequent and periodical examinations keep them in perfect order, and within the limits prescribed by their charters. This power of examination and supervision is of the most salutary tendency. Its silent operation is useful. It is a preventive to fraud or improper conduct of any kind. No board of directors, if under other circumstances they might be induced to exceed their bounds, would presume to undertake it whilst this power could reach them and expose them at any moment.

The Senator also alluded to the capital paid in stock notes in many of the State banks. Whatever application this remark may have elsewhere, it has none to the safety fund banks. Their capital is all actually paid in. There is no nominal capital known to the system. This, too, must be done, and the most positive and indubitable proof furnished that it is done, before the bank can go into operation. The same proof, in addition to the personal examination of the commissioners, may be required, at any time, that none of the capital has been withdrawn. It will be perceived, then, that the operations of these banks are on substantial capital, and the supervision of the commissioners is a guarantee to the public, and to the stockholders, of the fidelity of those who manage and direct their affairs.

So far, then, from this system having anything in it objectionable, it presents the strongest safeguards and security to the community. The great evil heretofore, in our banking system, has been the insecurity of the people. By this system perfect safety and security are obtained. These are the main objects. We do not incorporate such institutions for the sole benefit of stockholders—they are at best monopolies—and the people should always require and receive sufficient guarantees for their own safety. Whatever panic, therefore, may be created, the people, the creditors of the safety fund banks of New York, cannot suffer; and (said Mr. T.) I trust there is intelligence enough amongst the people of that State not to permit themselves to be deluded by these panic cries that are so industriously sent through the country.

Sir, (said Mr. T.,) the Senator from Kentucky has exhibited to us what he calls a statement of the small amount of specie in the vaults of our country banks. Why, sir, to those who know the course of trade and business in New York, this would excite no surprise. The country banks have never been in the habit of keeping large amounts of idle funds in their vaults. They know their own interest better—they know the interest of the community better. Their surplus funds are deposited in Albany and New York, on which they can draw, at any time. Those funds are convertible into specie at any moment. A western merchant, for instance, wishes to remit to the city of New York, where, from the course of trade, his payments are to be made; he would much prefer a draft on one of the banks in that city, than the bills of the bank in his neighborhood, or even the specie—the draft is better to him than the specie. Where, then, is the necessity of hoarding up a large amount of specie in their own vaults, when they can deposite their surplus funds in New York and Albany, and, under certain stipulations, receive interest on them? This mode is for their own interest, and for the benefit of the community. These funds, which are convertible into specie at any moment, together with the specie in the vaults of the banks out of Albany and New York, amounted, according to the report of the bank commissioners, on the 1st of January last, to *forty-four per cent.* on their whole circulation. Allowing, then, that this panic operation should succeed so far as to throw upon them, *in one instant*, nearly one-half of the whole amount of the bills of those banks now in circulation, they have the means at command to meet them; and this, too, without looking to their large and substantial note account, which is daily becoming due and receivable.

There are no banks, (said Mr. T.,) which have more ready or substantial means to meet all their engagements of every description. There are no banks, in the aggregate, more sound. The United States Bank itself is not more so. It cannot present more, if it can as much, substantial means. He did not doubt its safety; but he should be glad to believe that it had as much substantial means to meet all engagements as the safety fund banks of New York. If, (said Mr. T.,) this panic, about which so much is said, can be made to extend amongst the people, as some seem to desire it should, he would rather be a creditor of those banks than of the Bank of the United States. If any serious disasters follow from this panic, from the loss of confidence, and the consequent loss of credit, rely upon it, the Bank of the United States will come in for its full share of the calamity. But, says the Senator from Kentucky, if public confidence should be impaired, and these banks should be run for specie, they could not redeem their bills. This is true of any bank—of the United States Bank—of all banks—none of them ever have an amount of specie equal to the redemption of all their bills in circulation—of course if public confidence, as to their solvency, should be so far impaired as to bring in upon them all their bills, they could not redeem them in *specie*. But still, if they have been managed properly, they will have abundance of *means* to answer all the demands that can be made upon them. Mr. T. said, so far as his acquaintance extended, the safety fund banks were in the most discreet and substantial hands. He knew instances where some individual stockholders and directors were worth double and treble the whole amount of the capital of the bank to which they belong. Can the community lack confidence in such banks? Can the people doubt their solvency? Can they doubt their own security from loss, even if any one should fail, as long as an ample fund is provided for their safety? No, sir; there are individuals, (said Mr. T.,) such as he had described, who would give ample security, by bond and mortgage, for any amount of bills that could be presented.

Sir, the Senator from Kentucky, on some newspaper authority, has stated, that the bank commissioners have taken a large amount of money belonging to the canal fund, and loaned it in New York, to meet the redemption of the bills of country banks. Mr. T. said he had seen no such statement; but come from what source it might, he did not hesitate to pronounce it untrue—and for the best of reasons, that the bank commissioners have no power, by law, over the canal fund, and can, in no event, nor under any circumstances, use it.

One word (said Mr. T.) for the Senator from Ohio, [Mr. Ewing.] He condemns the safety-fund system, from its tendency to destroy that watchfulness of the banks over each other, which would otherwise exist. That, inasmuch as they are responsible for each other, in case of failure, they would not return the paper of each, with that vigilance, which they would do, acting independently—that they are perfectly safe, says he, in issuing paper to any amount they please—that there is no limit to their issues. Perhaps (said Mr. T.) the gentleman will allow something to experience and observation. He (Mr. T.) had witnessed all these operations; and he had found, under this system, a far greater watchfulness of the banks over each other than formerly existed. A healthy watchfulness—not a disposition to harass and vex, as was sometimes the case under the old system, but to see that each kept within its proper limits as prescribed by the charter. There is competition between them, but it is a healthy competition—it is salutary in its operation. As to their issues, the gentleman need give himself no alarm on that subject. They are limited by law, and he would venture to say, there were no banks in the Union which were so much restrained in their issues. They were far less than the banks under the old system were allowed to issue—and he had no doubt that in proportion to capital and the increased business of the State, the circulation was, at this time, in a less ratio than before this system was adopted.

Whatever efforts, then, may be made, and from whatever quarter they may be made, to increase the panic, Mr. T. said he trusted that the confidence of the country could not easily be shaken. He hoped the honorable Senator from Kentucky would soon get round Point Judith, to which he had alluded, and speedily arrive in that calm haven which he so much desired. And if he (Mr. T.) could judge from the symptoms of distress which usually attend those who perform that voyage, he should suppose the honorable Senator was now doubling that point.

Mr. CLAY replied, if the gentleman from New York would refer to the report of the Secretary of the Treasury, and the agent of the Government, he would see the outline of the system very clearly defined. Mr. C. regretted that the gentleman could not explain the item of the five millions in the report of the commissioners.

Some further brief remarks were made by Mr. CHAMBERS, Mr. EWING, and Mr. TALLMADGE.

Mr. WRIGHT said he regretted to enter into this debate at all, but he felt it due to himself and the subject, to give the answer which he had promised to the honorable Senator from Kentucky, [Mr. Clay,] and before he did that, he would say that he rejoiced that there was no intention in this body to produce an excitement in the country; that the Senator did not intend to produce that effect by the remarks he had made, but that he was able to add the gentleman's distinct denial that such was his intention.

He must be permitted further to say, before he replied to the interrogatory of the Senator, in justice to the bank of Ithica, in his State, the bank which the gentleman had named, that the remarks he had made in relation to it are most eminently calculated to produce the very effect upon that institution which the Senator did not mean to produce. He must not be misunderstood. He imputed no intention; but he must say that the statement of the honorable gentleman [Mr. Clay] as to the bank of Ithaca, the large amount of bills he had stated to be in circulation from that bank, and the very small amount of means to redeem them, unexplained, was directly and most happily calculated to produce a panic in the public mind in the vicinity of that bank, and to cause the run upon it which he was happy to find it was the desire of all to avoid.

He must further say, that while he would not

make the imputation against any individual in or out of this body, he deeply feared that certain presses in the country were daily and constantly publishing articles, and giving, very erroneously, what purported to be facts, most strongly calculated to excite the panic which the honorable Senator [Mr. CLAY] had so often and so emphatically mentioned with disgust in the course of his remarks. In answer to these attempts to influence the public mind, he would say to the customers and bill-holders of, and to the depositors in, the Bank of Ithica; what the honorable Senator had said, and so confidently repeated to the people of the whole country, "Be calm, be serene and confident." This ship of State is not to be run upon the rocks, nor are the disasters predicted, to be experienced, unless the panic produces the result. We shall ride out the present storm in safety, and peace and plenty will return to the land, if the public mind remains unshaken.

I will now answer the honorable Senator in reference to the $5,000,000 of bank notes possessed by the safety fund banks of the State of New York, and which are set down by the bank commissioners as a part of their available means. I know not from what statement or authority the gentleman reads, but presume it is from the summary of the bank commissioners of that State. I think they, in their annual report, after giving the detailed statement of the condition and means of each bank, gave a summary statement of the aggregate condition of all the banks under their charge and supervision; and I presume that this item is drawn from that summary statement. If I am right in this, it shows that all these banks, which the gentleman says are sixty-nine in number, have this five millions of the notes of other banks. The only error in the statement of which I have a right to complain, (and that is a very material one at this period, and in the present agitated state of the public mind,) is, that the gentleman says he assumes that all these are notes of the safety fund banks themselves. Now, sir, this is a violent presumption. The item is undoubtedly composed of all the notes of other solvent banks, held by the safety fund banks at the moment the statement was prepared. The amount, and the description of notes of which it would be composed, would be as fluctuating as the circulation of bank paper, but at any period the notes on hand would be those which the banks should think it desirable to receive, or safe to keep, and therefore it may be confidently assumed that they were the notes of the best banks of the country. The proportion of safety fund bank notes would depend upon the proportion of these and other bank notes in circulation at the points where the collections are made and security felt in the institutions whose notes should be thus kept in deposite. I speak from some acquaintance with those banks and their business, when I say that I fearlessly venture the prediction, that if an account of these notes were given, there would be found to be an amount of the notes of the Bank of the United States and its branches, greater, by five or ten times, than the amount of the notes of any one safety fund bank. Sir, we were told the other day by the honorable Senator from Massachusetts, [Mr. WEBSTER,] that the notes of the Bank of the United States were received and used by the State banks as capital, and that they made discounts and did business upon them as such; and this was given to us as one of the merits of such an institution. This was and is true as to the notes of that bank, but is equally true as to the notes of any solvent State bank. The banks all consider the notes of their solvent neighboring institutions in their vaults as specie, and they do business upon them as such; nor does it make any difference as to what bank issued them, provided they be notes current at their counter.

Why, Mr. President, should it not be so? Such notes are convertible into specie at will, and therefore are safe capital.

But, sir, suppose all this $5,000,000 of bank notes held by the safety fund banks of New York, were the notes of the safety fund banks themselves: would it injuriously affect the standing of this aggregate account of all these banks? No, sir, it would show that the account was well made up. Take an instance: the Bank of Ithaca, in its statement, debits itself with the whole amount of its bills out, without reference to the place where they are, and credits itself with its means to meet those bills when they are called for. Ten thousand dollars of those bills are in one of its neighboring banks, and in making its account, it credits itself with these ten thousand dollars of Ithaca notes as a part of its means. Now the charge in the one case, and the credit in the other, counterbalance each other, and, so far as the general summary statement of all the banks is concerned, the ten thousand dollars of bills are redeemed. This is the nature of the item to which the Senator [Mr. CLAY] refers, and this must be the only explanation of which that item, in this general summary, is in any way susceptible. How far it is satisfactory, is left to the Senate. To me it seems to be perfectly satisfactory, because the explanation shows that where the item consists of bills of the safety fund banks, the credit as means by one, must be countervailed by a charge as debit by another. So much for the explanation I have promised.

I must correct the Senator in another and much more important error into which he has fallen in relation to the manner in which the country banks in the State of New York do their business. The Senator [Mr. CLAY] says, when they have a call which they have not the power to meet by the means in their vaults, they are in the habit of answering it by a draft drawn upon the commercial cities of Albany or New York, on time. Such I understood to be the declaration of the Senator.

[Here Mr. CLAY signified that such was not the purport of his statement.]

Mr. W. continued: I will then state, Mr. President, distinctly what I did understand the Senator to say, and he will surely correct me if I am wrong. I did understand him to allege that the banks in the interior were in the habit of making drafts upon the commercial cities before named, to answer calls which they had not the means to answer at their counters, without having, at the time, funds in those cities to meet such drafts. Whether or not he said the drafts were made upon time, is immaterial to my purpose. Am I right in this understanding?

[Mr. CLAY said the Senator had better go on.]

Mr. W. continued: Sir, I speak from personal knowledge, when I say no such drafts are made. It is the practice of those banks in the interior to keep nearly the whole of their surplus funds in the cities. There these banks meet the great portion of their liabilities, and there they most need those funds; there also, they obtain an interest upon those funds, and therefore, as a matter of profit, as well as security, they are kept there.

Their usual and almost universal course is, to make an arrangement with some solvent city bank; and these arrangements are made either in Troy, Albany, or New York, and they receive an interest, I believe, as a general rule, varying from four to five per cent., the stipulation being always accompanied with the condition, either that notice of the drafts shall be given, the drafts be made upon time, or that the amount in deposite shall exceed a certain stipulated sum, before interest is chargeable. I have recently understood that a very few of the western banks have made their arrangements with stockbrokers, and keep their accounts with them, but these cases only form an exception to the general rule. The solvent city banks are the general depositories of these funds.

Sir, these country banks would not, if they had it, keep large amounts of specie on hand, in ordinary times, and when business was regular and undisturbed by any unusual excitement; they would transfer it to the cities, where they would be most likely to need it, and where it would earn an interest, until they should require its use. What, then, can be inferred from the exhibit made by the Senator of the condition of these banks, so far as their specie funds in their vaults is concerned? I say, confidently, nothing. Their funds are not kept idle in their vaults, but are placed where they are more needed, and where they can be usefully employed when not needed. I am asked, what are those funds? I will answer. The bank accommodates the merchant; he wants to use the accommodation in the city, and does so, and the bank meets the payment there. When the time of payment comes, the merchant sends to the market some commodity, out of which he makes the money, and deposites it the credit of the bank at the place in the city where the account of the bank is kept. This replaces the amount substracted for his accommodation, and thus the fund in the city is kept good. No country bank draws upon the city bank, but upon funds previously placed there to meet the draft; I say, none. There may be cases where such drafts are made, but never without previous arrangement for their acceptance; and I hazard nothing in saying that there is not a country bank in the whole State whose draft would be accepted, but upon funds placed in the city to meet it, or upon an arrangement for its acceptance. There is no drawing upon time, or upon the contingency of a general credit.

The honorable Senator tells us that certain brokers in New York have sent a quantity of country bank notes to Albany to be redeemed, and that their redemption was refused. Sir, I know not from what authority the gentleman speaks, but this I do know, that if the bills of any country banks were sent to Albany for redemption, and the banks which issued the bills had not funds in Albany for the purpose of their redemption, they would, of course, not be redeemed by the Albany banks. Why should they be? Upon what principle could the banks at Albany be expected to redeem notes not their own, and without funds from the banks which issued them? Surely upon none which belongs to the principles of safe and correct banking.

Again, Mr. President, we are told that large sums of money belonging to the canal fund of the State of New York have been, by the bank commissioners of the State, withdrawn from the banks in New York, where these moneys were drawing an interest, to be applied to redeem the notes of the safety fund banks. I have no doubt, the honorable Senator [Mr. CLAY] has been informed and believes this statement; but from what source he derives his information I knew not. I will tell him, however, what I do know, derived from personal and official knowledge, and it is, that his assertion cannot be true; that the bank commissioners of the State of New York have no more power over the moneys belonging to the canal fund of the State of New York, than the honorable Senator himself has. Those moneys are in the care of entirely different officers—officers holding the most high and responsible offices in the State. They have always been loaned where they were considered perfectly secure, and would command the highest rate of interest, and they never have been changed or withdrawn when so invested to consult the wants or interests of any bank. The law would not allow the officers having the charge of them to dispose of them from such motives, and those officers have not done so. They have, during the last year, and as I think very wisely, used every effort to sink these moneys in the redemption of the stocks which they are destined to redeem; and they have, to a great extent, succeeded. Those efforts are still making, and notwithstanding the great cry we hear in this body of distress and ruin, and scarcity of money, and almost starvation, overspreading the whole land, such is the state of things that the guardians of this fund cannot purchase these stocks (five per cent. stocks redeemable in 1845) at a lower rate than about 16 per cent. above their par value.

Mr. President, I regret exceedingly to have been compelled to enter into an incidental debate of this character; and I would not have done so, had I not considered myself called upon to explain allegations made in reference to the business affairs of my own State, and to transactions which no members of this body but my honorable colleague and myself could be supposed to understand. I have done this, and will merely reply to a remark or two made by the honorable Senator from Ohio, [Mr. EWING,] when I will resume my seat. The gentleman has denounced, in no measured terms, the safety fund system of my State, as applied to our banks. He thinks, as others have thought, that the safety of the banks is endangered by it; but he seems wholly to overlook the security afforded to the community, to the bill holders and depositors. He seems to suppose that because the fund is not large enough to redeem all the bills in circulation, of all the banks at once, he

proves that the security is fallacious. Sir, he is mistaken. The bill holder, the depositor, and the whole community, with the exception of the stockholder, is ultimately perfectly safe, unless every bank subject to the system be broken and destroyed. The fund may not be large enough *in presenti*, but the contributions must continue until the claims of the bill holders and depositors are fully paid. What, then, is the difference between this system and the ordinary system, where there is no such security? I hold the notes of an insolvent bank which has stopped payment. I cannot, in either case, get coin for my notes; but if they be safety fund notes, I will eventually get dollar for dollar, and if they be not, I will get nothing. This is the simple difference, and this is the system which the gentleman thinks so mischievous and dangerous. I am not disposed to discuss with him the question whether these banks, by being made thus measurably reponsible for each other, are more or less safe. I will only say that, if it be proper for legislation to consult any other object than that of filling the pocket of the stockholders, any portion of safety transferred from a bank to the bill holders, the depositors and the community in general, is not objectionable to me. Such is the object of the safety fund system of New York, and I verily believe that, in consulting the safety of the public, it has, in the best manner, consulted the greatest safety of the banks.

[Mr. EWING having made some reply to what had been said by Mr. W.]

Mr. WRIGHT said he would relieve the gentleman; he did not answer his main argument because he could not believe that it required an answer. The argument was, that making these safety fund banks mutually responsible for each other, prevented them from keeping that salutary guard over each other's transactions, and especially over each other's issues, which banks in no way connected with, but acting as rivals to each other, would keep. The statement of the proposition seemed to him to be a sufficient answer to the argument drawn from it. What, sir, will a bank at this capital watch with less care the operations of a bank at the other end of this avenue, when it is fully responsible for all the notes of that bank, than when it has no connexion with, or responsibility on account of it? If that be the effect of such a responsibility, Mr. W. said he had mistaken the influence which the interests of men had over their actions. The motive to increased watchfulness was direct and palpable, and that such a motive would have the effect to destroy that watchfulness, he could not see or believe.

While up, he would say one word in answer to a suggestion which had fallen from the honorable Senator when he first addressed the Senate, and to which he had intended to reply. The Senator [Mr. Ewing] seems to suppose that the circulation of the notes of the Banks of New York has been less extensive and less broadly diffused since the establishment of the safety fund system, than before that time. He mistakes the fact. Mr. W. said he spoke from knowledge when he asserted that from about one year after the establishment of that system, the public confidence had increased greatly as to the security of the notes of the safety fund banks, and that the circulation of those notes out of, and beyond, the limits of the State had been two or three times as great as at any former period. Yes, sir, they flew over into the territory of the Senator's own State, and even beyond it. He (Mr. W.) had himself known instances where remittances had been directed to be made to Kentucky, in the notes of the safety fund banks, when the notes of the other banks of the State, entirely solvent, but not subject to the safety fund law, would not be received.

At first, (said Mr. W.,) fears were entertained. The banks were fearful, and the bankers and politicians wrote and spoke against the plan, but time soon convinced all that the system was most valuable. The most experienced bankers of the State yielded their assent to it, and the old banks came in and took new charters subject to the law. He did not feel disposed to institute a comparison between the science and skill and prudence and success of the bankers of his State, and those of other States, but he was willing that their history, from the institution of banks in the State to the present time, should be examined, and he believed they would not be found to have been the least successful of all the bankers of the country. These men are now the warmest and strongest friends of the safety fund system. Indeed, (Mr. W. said,) he verily believed, if the honorable Senators themselves, [Mr. Ewing and Mr. Clay,] would examine the legislation of New York upon this subject, not as politicians, but as intelligent lawyers, as they are, they would yield their full assent to its wisdom and safety.

Mr. WEBSTER said he would draw the attention of the gentleman from New York, [Mr. Wright,] and others, to a consideration which seemed to have been overlooked. The question of the insolvency of the bank was not the true question when speaking of the currency of the country. The question was the ability of each individual bank to meet the demands which might be made on it, in specie. He was not acquainted with the banking system of New York, but there seemed to him one insuperable objection to it: it was, that there was too much confidence it; so that all individual responsibility was removed. The true question in all our institutions was, not the ultimate means of meeting all its liabilities, but the present means for present calls. He had not heard it stated what was the actual proportion of specie to the whole circulation in New York; but in England, from long experience, it was found that less than one-third was not safe, and the Bank of the United States had adopted that as its proportion. He thought the case was not helped by saying that the banks in the interior of New York draw on those in the city, for it was but an exchange of paper; John Doe drawing on Richard Roe, and Richard Roe drawing on John Doe again. There could be no security longer than the circulating paper was redeemable at the banks from which it issued. And it was not bettered by the bond of mortgage security, spoken of; that system had been tried for a hundred years, over and over again, and had uniformly failed, and never could succeed. No matter how many men of wealth you had, heap Ossa upon Pelion, and it would not do.

Mr. FORSYTH said, that the gentlemen from New York, [Mr. Wright and Mr. Tallmadge,] if they had taken his advice, might have saved themselves a great deal of trouble. They could not recommend the safety fund system, be it good or bad. It came from New York. He rose, not for the purpose of discussing that system, or the Secretary's system, as proposed to be introduced into the United States, according to the views of gentlemen, but to reply to the remarks of the gentleman from Kentucky in relation to the distress which he said existed in Georgia, in the cities of Savannah and Augusta. Mr. F. thought that by reference to the documents, the gentleman would perceive that he was mistaken. How long they might remain exempted, he could not say; he trusted it would be long, but at present they were exempt; their withers were unwrung. The call for the meetings in Savannah and Augusta, was for the pupose of deliberating upon the distress of the country, and to express their opinions that the bank ought to be rechartered. In Savannah there were some cries of pressure, because certain citizens wanted to swell the voice of distress; but they were voted down by an immense majority, and there was no cry from Savannah now. As regarded the meeting in Augusta, a memorial and resolutions were prepared, but there was not a syllable in them about distress there. They knew better. The journals published there, the one containing these proceedings, show the prices of produce and of public stocks to be unaffected. They desire that the bank may be rechartered—they ask not that the deposites may be restored; but restore the deposites and recharter the bank. [Mr. F. here read a passage from the Augusta memorial.] He knew the individuals; they were highly respectable men—merchants and members of the bar. They were friends of the Bank of the United States; they thought it a necessary and useful institution, and wished to promote its recharter.

The gentleman from Kentucky had referred to a certain document lately prepared and signed by several respectable citizens of Philadelphia, who came here as the representatives of some ten thousand citizens of that city, for the purpose of obtaining relief for their distresses, and to report the result of their labors. And Mr. F. thought he would be very much wanting in respect to those gentlemen if he did not say that they got what they wanted, and they went away when they obtained it. Did they expect that any representation from citizens of Philadelphia would make any impression upon the firm convictions of the President? They did not come from the proper quarter, nor from the proper persons, because they were not without bias and interest. Would any one say that there was a man in Philadelphia who was a safe judge of the true policy on this subject? Every expenditure made in Philadelphia was for its benefit; all her citizens were deeply interested in it, and it was as much as his patriotism was worth for any man to resist an application for a recharter of the bank. The gentleman from Kentucky places great reliance upon the remarks of the President of the United States, made to the Philadelphia committee; but he (Mr. F.) thought they ought to be taken with many grains of allowance. They did not state the words of the President, but the substance of what he said in a long conversation. But it was said the gentlemen were not political partisans. Now, he (Mr. F.) knew the gentleman who was chairman of the meeting, and he was a most bitter, "rantancorous" politician. He came here to get friends, and went back to make enemies against the President of the United States. He was, perhaps, successful in the first, but whether he would succeed in the second operation remained yet to be seen. He hoped he would not. Mr. F. said he had desired to make some further remarks, but as this debate had sprung up on a memorial from Louisville, he was really ashamed to do it.

Some further brief remarks were made by Mr. CLAYTON, Mr. WEBSTER, and Mr. FORSYTH.

A message was received from the House of Representatives, by Mr. Franklin, their Clerk, stating that the Speaker had signed the bill which had passed both Houses making appropriation for the payment of pensioners.

On motion of Mr. EWING, the Senate adjourned.

HOUSE OF REPRESENTATIVES.

Thursday, *February* 27, 1834.

Mr. WHITTLESEY reported a bill for the relief of the heirs of Thomas F. Townsley.

Mr. McKINLEY, a bill for the relief of L. H. Bates and W. Lacon; which were severally read twice and committed.

Mr. FOOT, a bill to authorize the Secretary of the Treasury to issue a register for the brig American, of Savannah; which was ordered to be engrossed for a third reading to-morrow.

The House then resumed the consideration of the following resolution, submitted by Mr. Mardis, viz:

Resolved, That the Committee of Ways and Means be instructed to inquire into the expediency of reporting a bill requiring the Secretary of the Treasury to deposite the public moneys of the United States in the State banks; and, also, as to the expediency of defining by law the contracts hereafter to be made with the Secretary for the safe-keeping, management, and disbursement of the same.

Mr. CLOWNEY, who had the floor from the previous day, rose and said, that the resolution offered by the member from Alabama, and the arguments adduced by him in support of it, appeared to be predicated on the assumption that the public deposites would not be restored to the Bank of the United States. If he was satisfied that the honorable member was correct in that assumption, he must agree with him in considering that some such resolution would be expedient. He, however, could not concur in this, and he did not think that the recent votes of the House, referring the subject to the Committee of Ways and Means, afforded a just criterion to entitle him to pronounce that the question of restoration was thereby finally decided. He regarded, therefore, the present resolution as altogether premature; but he was glad it was brought forward, because it gave to him, as well as to others so disposed, an opportunity to explain their views before the question itself would come up for general discussion,

on the report to be presented by the committee. He considered the present resolution, in substance, the same as that submitted by his colleague, [Mr McDuffie,] the future disposition of the deposites being the object of both—one being to restore them to the bank, the other to place them in the State banks.

After the display of learning, talents, and research, that had already been displayed on the subject, he had not the vanity to suppose that he could offer anything new to the House in the shape of argument, or by which he could hope to influence any member. But it was due to his constituents that he should exercise his privilege of addressing them; and in the peculiar situation in which he was placed, as arguments had been given, by which the question of restoring the deposites and that of rechartering the bank were identified, he, being opposed to the recharter of the bank, yet, strange as it might seem, opposed to the removal of the deposites, there was a necessity imposed upon him to explain his reasons for what appeared to be inconsistency. He was at a loss to conceive why questions so different in themselves should be thus associated together; for the principle objections that had been urged against the bank were on account of its unconstitutionality, and its capacity, by the great pecuniary powers which it possessed, to destroy the institutions of the country. Those who were honest in opposing the bank on these grounds could not abandon their opinion. He found that these objections were principally what was urged in the several memorials, and in the reasons presented by the Secretary of the Treasury in his justification for the removal of the deposites. They were also urged by the President of the United States as the great grounds upon which he predicated the exercise of the veto power by him upon the bill passed to recharter the bank, and they were the great objections on the part of the people. They could not be removed by any argument of expediency. He could not coincide in the opinion that the two questions were the same, and he asked if it was not for the purpose of alarming the fears of those who were opposed to the bank, on grounds of unconstitutionality, and who might be induced to dread that if they lent their aid to effect the restoration of the deposites, it might be the means of rechartering the bank. He avowed that he was opposed to the establishment of all banks by the power of Congress, unles there should be such an amendment made to the Constitution as would obviate his objections on this score. He had no fears as to the great danger to be incurred by the present bank enslaving the Government. The manner in which it had been hitherto conducted, and the services it had rendered in correcting a spurious paper currency, and acting as the public fiscal agent faithfully, forbade him to entertain such an opinion; and in his opinion, entitled the bank to have strong claims on the gratitude of the country. The fears of what the bank might do, had been urged in argument from what it had done; but this could have no effect upon him now; and although he would have been unwilling to commit such powers originally, yet he saw nothing to dread in making a restoration for the remainder of the time that was given by the charter, of which the bank had been so unjustly deprived. He regarded the act of removal so much an act of executive usurpation, that, although if the question of bank or no bank was brought up, he would say no bank, yet he, at the same time, would vote for the restoration of the deposites. He could not assent to any action being justified by the doctrine of expediency, at the expense of principle. He could not do evil that good may come from it, and felt that such a doctrine was mischievous in its effects, and more properly belonged to tyrants and persecutors. By them it was ever used,—by all who found courtly morality convenient to practice. It was resorted to by the Inquisitions, to justify the cruelties they inflicted; and, according to Paley, it was a doctrine, the adoption of which must involve the world in confusion, and put an end to all society—who, being therefore bound to avoid the evils it must produce, ought to adhere rigidly to principle, leaving consequences to God. He would act so; for in voting upon this question, he was not actuated by any feelings of personal hostility, nor was he so drilled in the schemes of any party as to oppose the measure that would be submitted, or do fealty to any individual, right or wrong. And although he would acknowledge he saw in the acts of the President much to admire; that he considered the veto power had been judiciously exercised by him to check legislative usurpation,—he would vote for the restoration of the deposites, because, in this instance, he believed that the authority claimed to do the act was not confided to him by law, and the exercise of it was dangerous to the Constitution. Before he would proceed to consider the arguments, he felt bound to remark, as to what was said on the opposition to this measure having its origin in a coalition between two distinguished individuals—that it arose from a conspiracy between them to rise to power on the ruins of the present Administration. But he desired to know upon what evidence this charge was made.

What evidence was there to justify the opinion that all resistance to usurpation was only to gratify disappointed ambition? Was there not in this conspiracy to be found included all who were in favor of the restoration, one-half the members, and the majority of the Senate, amongst them many who had grown gray in the service of the public, and whose patriotism had not ever been suspected? It was not, however, his purpose to retort, or to defend those with whom he intended to act. The public services of these persons had already secured those to whom he alluded a glorious immortality in the affectionate remembrance of the country. He would not speak on one side and vote upon another. He could not exhaust his strength combating the arguments of those who were enlisted with him on the same side. He would not, he trusted, be reduced to come forward with an apology for the strangeness of such conduct, or have the modesty to state in the face of the House that of all those who acted with him I am alone honest, pure, and disinterested—I alone consult the public good, whilst others only consult their selfish aggrandizement, and above all, I hope (said Mr. C.) that I may not be reduced in the course of my argument to attest my attachment to the President by offering prayers for the success of his Administration; that my speech, when it goes home to my constituents, will not leave open to any question of doubt whether the glory of that Administration ranks higher in my estimation than the great principle of Executive usurpation which is involved in the question of the deposites. Mr. C. did not feel it necessary to go into the arguments upon the reasons submitted by the Secretary of the Treasury, for on examining the proceedings of the Committee of the House, he could not find there was any new fact of which the House was not in possession, when, by a large majority, they resolved that the deposites were perfectly safe. He held that the Secretary of the Treasury had no powers vested in him but such as related to the safety, the disbursement of the public money, and generally whether the bank had peformed the duties which were assigned to it. His reasons, therefore, sunk into insignificance when compared with the principle involved in the act of removal and the arguments urged in its support. The removal, although conceded to have been the act of the Secretary, was not denied to have originated with the President. In justification of this act some alarming doctrines were advanced. It was contended that the Executive department was not only Executive as organized, but it was not in the power of Congress to interfere; that any law rendering the Secretary independent of the Executive would be a violation of the Constitution; so that it would follow, from many of the arguments, that many officers appointed by the President hereafter may execute their office independent of him. But were not such opinions adverse to the doctrines entertained, or that should be entertained of a republican Government? They were sufficient to induce him to vote against any measure that they were brought forward to support. The extraordinary power claimed for the Executive was attempted to be deduced from that part of the Constitution which enjoined on the President the duty of seeing the laws faithfully executed; but in opposition to this, he would contend that the President had no prerogative except what was expressly granted by the law or the Constitution. He would also contend that Congress had the power to create offices over which the President had no power by law or the Constitution. He contended further, that Congress had the right to define the duties of the Secretary of the Treasury as to the public money, of which they alone had the control, and that the President had no right to interfere with his performance of such duties; that the President had no constitutional power except to nominate and appoint, by and with the consent of the Senate, for the sole power of removal was was not given by the Constitution; it was a mere veto power, used under the provisions of a law passed by the first Congress, and which, at the pleasure of Congress, might be again abolished or repealed.

If they wanted to know what were the Executive departments, the Constitution, not Johnson's dictionary, must be referred to. In that instrument, the three departments were particularly defined, with the power that pertained to each. They would, also, there find the definition of the term "Executive." Mr. C. read the clause conferring powers on the President, from which he argued that although he might claim full control over the Army, the Navy, and State Departments—they being, from the nature of their duties, as well as from their title, Executive—and over which he might safely rest his claim to control them by his mere anthority, yet, when he claimed to exercise the same power over officers whose duties were not connected with him, he must look elsewhere than to that which gave to Congress, and Congress alone, full power over the public purse, and in support of his views he would state, that Congress had the power to have declared, if they had deemed it necessary—the Treasury Department as independent of the President as they had made the judiciary, or any other. He contended that it was established originally by the Congress, with that object; which was evidenced by the circumstance, that there was no power granted the President, as was given expressly over the other departments, except where the lines occurred, which gave the power "to remove from office." Mr. C. gave way before he had concluded, to

Mr. CLAY, who moved that the House should proceed to the orders of the day.

The SPEAKER presented a communication from the Secretary of War, transmitting a report from the Topographical Bureau. Referred to the Committee on Commerce, and ordered to be printed.

The SPEAKER also presented a communication from the Secretary of the Treasury, transmitting an answer to a resolution of the House on the subject of the violation of the revenue laws by the evasion of the duties on imported lead: referred to the Committee on Manufactures.

The House resumed the consideration of the bill making appropriations for the Indian Department for the year 1834.

Mr. McKAY moved the recommitment of the bill to the Committee of the Whole on the state of the Union.

After some remarks from Messrs. POLK, COULTER, HAWES, SEVIER, McKINLEY, HORACE EVERETT, McKAY, FILLMORE, MERCER, WILLIAMS, VINTON, CAMBRELENG, BEARDSLEY, and WILDE—

The question was taken on the motion to recommit the bill, and decided in the affirmative, yeas 106, nays 101.

On motion, the House then adjourned.

IN SENATE.

Thursday, *February* 27, 1834.

Mr. SILSBEE, from the Committee on Commerce, reported a bill for the relief of Peter C. Phillips; and, on his motion, the report accompanying it was ordered to be printed.

Mr. WEBSTER presented the petition of Isaac Folier, of Boston; which was referred to the Committee on Commerce; and the petition of Marion Baldwin, which was referred to the Committee on Naval Affairs.

Mr. WEBSTER presented the memorial of all the banks of New Bedford, Massachusetts;

Of three hundred and three inhabitants of Warren county, New York;

Of eight hundred and sixty-six citizens of Northampton county, Pennsylvania;

All in favor of the restoration of the public deposites, and the rechartering of the Bank of the United States, with modifications; which were read, referred to the Committee on Finance, and ordered to be printed.

Mr. CLAYTON presented the memorial of a number of citizens of Schuylkill county, Pennsylvania, in favor of the restoration of the deposites; which was read, referred to the Committee on Finance, and ordered to be printed.

Mr. HENDRICKS presented the joint resolutions of the Legislature of Indiana, praying that Congress would pass a law compensating persons who lost horses in the recent campaigns with the Indians; which were referred to the Committee on the Judiciary.

Also, the joint resolutions of the same Legislature, stating the sparseness of the population of the Wabash country in the neighborhood of Lawrenceburg; attributing it to the difficulties of intercourse, and praying aid in constructing a railroad; which resolutions were referred to the Committee on Roads and Canals.

Also, another resolution of the same Legislature, of a similar character of that first presented, on the subject of compensation for loss of horses; which had the same reference as the former.

Mr. McKEAN presented the petition of Stephen G. Rollins, which was referred to the Committee on Finance; and the petition of Elizabeth Josiah, which was referred to the Committee on Revolutionary Claims.

Mr. SPRAGUE presented the petition of James Thomas; which was referred to the Committee on Claims.

Mr. BLACK presented the petition of the heirs of John George, deceased; which was referred to the Committee on Public Lands.

Mr. BLACK asked that the petition of William Borax, which was not acted on at the last session, might be again referred to the Committee on Public Lands; which was agreed to.

Mr. NAUDAIN, from the Committee on Private Land Claims, asked to be discharged from the further consideration of the petition of Asher Homer, and that it be referred to the Committee on Public Lands; which was agreed to.

Mr. NAUDAIN, from the Committee on Claims, asked to be discharged from the further consideration of the petition of James Rinker, surviving partner of Bailey & Rinker; which was agreed to.

Mr. TOMLINSON, from the Committee on Pensions, reported a bill for the relief of Aaron Fitzgerald.

Mr. TYLER presented a memorial of a number of the inhabitants of Wheeling, Virginia, praying for the restoration of the deposites, and the recharter of the Bank of the United States.

Also, a memorial from a number of the citizens of Norfolk, Virginia, praying the restoration of the deposites to the Bank of the United States; which memorials were read, referred to the Committee on Finance, and ordered to be printed.

The following resolutions were submitted, and lie on the table one day; the consideration of them at this time being objected to, that of Mr. WEBSTER by Mr. POINDEXTER, and that of Mr. POINDEXTER by Mr. HILL.

By Mr. WEBSTER:

Resolved, That the Secretary of the Treasury lay before the Senate the monthly returns of the Bank of the United States, from August, 1833, to February, 1834, inclusive.

By Mr. POINDEXTER:

Resolved, That the Secretary of the Treasury be directed to communicate to the Senate copies of any order or treasury draft, which may have been given by that department for the removal of the deposites of the public money from the Planters' Bank at Natchez, specifying the amount of the deposite; the bank or banks to which said money is removed, or intended to be removed; whether the same is required for the public service at the place to which it is so transferred, or intended to be transferred; and, if not, for what other purpose the said deposites are directed to be withdrawn from said bank. And, also, that he transmit copies of any letters which may have passed between any officer of the Treasury Department and the President of said bank on this subject.

On motion of Mr. WEBSTER,

The Senate, shortly after one o'clock, proceeded to Executive business.

The Senate continued in secret session to a very late hour. When the doors were opened, it had adjourned.

HOUSE OF REPRESENTATIVES.

THURSDAY, *February* 27, 1834.

Mr. ASHLEY reported a bill for the relief of John Jordan and the legal representatives of Vincent Fisher.

Mr. R. M. JOHNSON, a bill for the relief of William Piatt.

Mr. HORACE EVERETT, a bill to provide for the appointment of agents and sub-agents of Indian affairs and interpreters.

PUBLIC DEPOSITES.

The House resumed the consideration of the following resolution offered by Mr. MARDIS:

Resolved, That the Committee of Ways and Means be instructed to inquire into the expediency of reporting a bill requiring the Secretary of the Treasury to deposite the public moneys of the United States in the State banks; and, also, as to the expediency of defining by law all contracts hereafter to be made with the Secretary for the safe-keeping, management, and disbursement of the same.

Mr. CLOWNEY resumed his remarks. He contended that the powers of the Secretary of the Treasury related exclusively to the legislative department of the Government, over which the President had no control. On the other side, the power to remove was considered as incidental to the power to appoint. Such an idea had never entered the head of a single member of the illustrious body which framed our Constitution. The question as to the power of removal was not agitated in the convention. Why not? Because it was so clearly incidental to the powers granted in the Constitution, and so reasonable and just in itself, that it was deemed unworthy of notice? No, sir, it was either not considered at all, or it was, at that time, thought that the term of office was sufficiently restricted by the power of impeachment. Mr. C. read some passages from the 77th number of the Federalist, in which the doctrine of removal was laid down. In the first Congress which assembled under the Constitution, the question was, for the first time, seriously agitated. The sole power of removal was not then considered as vested in the President, and we find that, on this question, many members of Congress who had been members of the convention, were arrayed against each other. Messrs. Madison and Matthews maintained the existence of the power, and Messrs. Gerry and Sherman denied it. The existence of the power was, after debate, finally affirmed by the House of Representatives. The Senate was equally divided upon the question, and the question was decided in favor of the present construction, by the casting vote of the Vice President. Thus it appears that the advocates of consolidation, in the first Congress, by a majority of twelve votes in the House, and a casting vote in the Senate, gave to the Constitution, then fresh from the hands of the people, a different form from that which those who framed, and those who adopted it, had contemplated and designed, and clothed the President with powers which Alexander Hamilton, with all his prejudices in favor of a strong government, acknowledges that the States would never have assented to. To give this first act of legislation the authority of the Constitution, Congress inserted in the acts organizing the departments, the words "and when removed from office, &c., another officer shall, for the time being, discharge the duties of the office." Against the power, it was contended that it would be liable to great abuse, and would render the officers of the Government dependant on the whim and caprice of a single individual. This objection was met by the advocates of the construction, that the abuse of power by the President of the United States would render him liable to impeachment and removal from office. Here Mr. C. read and commented upon the arguments used in the debate referred to.

If the doctrine contended for on the other side was correct, it followed that the Clerk of this House and all other officers whose duties were not executive, were subject to the control of the President. He defied gentlemen to draw a distinction between the duties of the Clerk of this House and those of the Secretary of the Treasury. One was charged with the disposition of the contingent fund of this House, the other with the funds of the nation. One was subject to the control of this House; the other to the control of Congress. None of the duties of the Secretary of the Treasury relate to any power vested in the President, and, therefore, the President would have no power over that officer. He was aware that the judges of the Supreme Court, and some other officers, were considered as constitutional exceptions to the general power of the President to control all officers. But he asked gentlemen to point out the general grant of power to which there were exceptions. It was not to be found. If, then, the power could not, as he contended, be derived from the power to appoint, and was not granted expressly by the Constitution, whence do gentlemen derive the power? The last ground on which they rest the construction for which they contend, is the clause of the Constitution which provides that the President shall "take care that the laws be faithfully executed." To the misconstruction of this clause was to be traced every act of executive usurpation of which we had cause to complain. It was construed and acted upon as a distinct grant of power, clothing the President with authority above the laws, instead of requiring him to adhere to, and direct the execution of the laws. In virtue of this construction, we had seen a President send an armed force into the heart of a sovereign State, to compel her to relinquish her rights over a large part of her soil. It was honorable to the then Executive that he either abandoned his construction or waived his claim—and peace and the sovereign rights of a State were preserved. But scarcely had the apprehensions of the people become quieted, than they were alarmed again, by a thundering proclamation emanating from the President, and directed against the laws which a sovereign State, in its legislative character, had passed. Under the same specious pretexts, we have seen the ministers of the law and public justice rudely thrust aside, and the army of the United States substituted as the ministers of an executive measure. In a time of profound peace, we had seen the arms of a paid soldiery turned against peaceful citizens, who were acting under the laws of a sovereign State. All this had been done upon no other authority than this construction. It was true that one of the acts was, at the modest request of the President, legalized by the force bill; an act which Mr. C. said was already recorded in blood, and threatened the entire subversion of the liberties of the country. For power to call out the militia to execute the laws, suppress insurrection, &c., the President was indebted, as Mr. C. contended, not to the Constitution, but to law. His power over the Secretary of the Treasury, he went on to argue, stood on the same footing with his power over the militia.

[Here the hour having expired, Mr. CLOWNEY yielded the floor, without concluding, and the House proceeded to the order of the day.]

Mr. CAMPBELL, a Representative from South Carolina, elected in the place of Mr. SINGLETON, deceased, appeared, was qualified, and took his seat.

POTOMAC BRIDGE.

On motion of Mr. MERCER, the House took up the bill reported from the Committee on Roads and Canals, authorizing the construction of a bridge over the Potomac, and repealing all previous acts on the subject.

The SPEAKER stated that there were two propositions pending in reference to the bill: one to refer it to the Committee of the Whole on the state of the Union; and another to refer it to the Committee for the District of Columbia.

Mr. MERCER explained the views of the committee. He said that the cost price of the bridge, according to the plan proposed by the committee, would not exceed $130,000, whilst the estimates presented to the Secretary of the Treasury of the cost of the bridge proposed by the President would exceed $3,000,000. This was so important a difference, that the House ought to take up the question at once and dispose of it.

Mr. CHINN did not desire to express any views as to the construction of the bridge; but he would merely say, that he had been formerly against it, knowing that the House was deceived when they supposed that it could have been constructed for the sum at which it was estimated when the appropriation was made. The question was of reference as to this bill. As a member of the Committee for the District, he had no desire to have it sent there, if it ought not in strict right to be sent there. The principal reason that induced him to desire it to be sent there was, that there were various other subjects before that committee which were connected with the construction of the bridge, and upon which all action by the committee was necessarily suspended. That committee had jurisdiction over all matters in relation to the District, and it was due to them, as all other bills making appropriations had originated there, as well as due to the people of the District, to have the subject sent where they could be heard.

Mr. RENCHER considered, as the Committee on Roads and Canals had, after much laborious exertion, and in the faithful discharge of their duties, examined into this subject, made their report, and presented a bill in conformity to it, that the objections raised to their jurisdiction over this subject came too late. He considered that the claims of the Committee for the District to exclusive jurisdiction ought only to have reference to such matters as were merely of a local nature.

Mr. CHAMBERS remarked, that the subject was in such a shape before them, that it was manifest there ought to be immediate action upon it. As the House were in possession of information necessary for them to have that action, it was surely immaterial to them from what committee the information came to them. There was a greater question involved than a contest between two committees for jurisdiction: whether the Secretary of the Treasury had the right to make contracts involving the expenditure of large sums; and this ought to induce the House not to refer the subject a second time, but act upon it.

Mr. FILLMORE advocated the claims of the Committee of the District to have this subject referred to them, and he considered that it was unreasonable to suppose that this committee would not be as much disposed to check extravagance as any other committee. Without, therefore, wishing to detract from the intelligence, patriotism, and purity of conduct, which the chairman of the Committee on Roads and Canals, and the other members of that committee acted, it was only fair to suppose, that if the subject was sent to the Committee on the District, they would act up to their economical views, and having an opportunity to examine witnesses, from their testimony, have new light thrown upon the subject.

Mr. FOOT expressed some surprise at a discussion which seemed to him to be so unnecessary. He asked, what was the object of rules for the regulation of their proceedings, if, when a subject of this kind came up, was regularly referred to a standing committee, and by them reported upon, the bill they reported was not to be acted upon?

Mr. STODDERT said, that the Committee on the District intended to have called upon the Secretary of the Treasury for information to enable them to act upon this subject, when they were anticipated by the chairman of the Committee on Roads and Canals. They had various matters before them connected with this, which prevented the committee from coming to a definite conclusion what should be done with them. He contended that this subject should now be referred to that committee, as, amongst others, there was a memorial referred to them from Alexandria, praying Congress for additional aid to construct an aqueduct over the Potomac; and the committee, in considering the two subjects, might combine them, and thus effect a saving of $20,000 and upwards. This could not be done if the present bill was put into effect, as the bridge was directed to be constructed on the old site.

Mr. WILLIAMS advocated the reference to the Committee of the Whole on the state of the Union, as he considered it would be a most unprecedented course, at a time when the very object of a reference was attained, to change it by sending the subject back to another committee. It was not a respectful course towards the Committee on Roads and Canals, and if there was any objectionable matter found in the bill, when it was in Committee of the Whole, that was the time and place to consider the necessity of a reference to the Committee on the District.

Mr. McKENNAN disclaimed having any intention of showing any disrespect, or of throwing any reflection on the Committee on Roads and Canals in advocating a reference to another committee; but, as he considered this altogether a question of jurisdiction, it was clear that the Committee on the District ought to have the subject referred to it. The practice had been, he contended, uniformly, to send all bills making appropriations for the District to it; even one making appropriations for clearing obstructions in the Potomac was so referred; and he therefore apprehended the question of jurisdiction was thereby settled. Although a member of the committee, he was not prepared to say what conclusion he would come to in regard to this appropriation, for there might be a further reduction found necessary in the sum appropriated by the present bill.

Mr. WARDWELL adverted to the proceedings by which, on the motion of Mr. MERCER, the chairman of the Committee on Roads and Canals, the Secretary of the Treasury communicated to the House all the facts in relation to the contracts that were proposed for the erection of the bridge, and said that the matter was referred to that committee almost without consideration, or without objection on the part of the Committee on the District.

Mr. CHINN rose to correct this statement; he had consented to the reference, having understood from the chairman that his object was to ascertain the cost of the bridge.

Mr. WARDWELL resumed, and contended that there was nothing in the reference then, which should be deemed giving that committee an authority to do more than that. They had, nevertheless, taken upon themselves to report a bill for the construction of the bridge. He considered this was a subject which ought to be peculiarly under the cognizance of the Committee on the District.

Mr. STEWART remarked, that it was not so material to what committee the question properly belonged, for as the bill had been reported to the House on the subject, it was competent for any member of the Committee on the District to move any amendment or alteration he wished, when the bill should be in Committee of the Whole on the state of the Union. There was one subject, however, which he wished to state, that the House might see the necessity that existed of acting promptly upon the bill. The House were doubtless aware that the President had various propositions submitted to him for the construction of the bridge; that a contract was entered into, which was given up, and finally that a proposition was made by Mr. Dibble, and accepted of; although the contract with him was not formally executed, yet he was told to go on, collect his materials, &c., for it. The previous evening, Mr. D. called upon him and stated, that in consequence of this intimation, he had gone on making purchases to the extent of $120,000, and that he would go on further. Was it not therefore important that the House should come to some decision; either to rescind this contract, or pass some law upon the subject? While we were going on discussing the propriety of a reference to one committee or another, Mr. Dibble would be going on with his purchases, and the House would be hereafter called upon to indemnify him.

Mr. McDUFFIE said, from what had occurred, it was evident there was more than met the eye in the zeal displayed to get this subject from one committee to another. That the President of the United States had, on the faith of a bill making an appropriation of $200,000 for the construction of this bridge, pledged the faith of the nation for a much larger amount. If there was any design to have this act ratified, he would say the House were called upon, by regard for their own legislative rights, not to give it countenance, by referring it a second time.

Mr. WAYNE said, if the facts were as supposed by the honorable member from South Carolina, the House would be indebted to him for the observations he had made; but although they were, when made, supposed to be founded in truth, they were, nevertheless, not so. Mr. W. here referred to the report from the Secretary of the Treasury on the subject, by which it appeared that he stated there was nothing contemplated to be done by the President, unless with the consent of the House; and although Mr. Dibble might have gone on purchasing, yet he did so at his own risk.

After a few further remarks from Mr. STEWART, Mr. MERCER, and Mr. CHINN, in explanation—

The question on referring the bill to the Committee of the Whole on the state of the Union was put, and it prevailed—ayes 103, noes not counted.

REVOLUTIONARY CLAIMS.

The House proceeded to the consideration of the bill reported from the Committee on Revolutionary Claims, "to provide for the settlement of certain revolutionary claims."

Mr. PIERCE, of New Hampshire, thanked the House for having kindly deferred, on the suggestion of his indisposition, the consideration of the bill which has just been read, and he felt under particular obligations for the generous courtesy manifested on that occasion by the gentleman from Virginia, a friend of the bill, upon his right, [Mr. MASON.] He had expressed, the other day, when moving the postponement of the bill, his conviction, that it had been passed to a third reading without having received all the consideration due to its importance. That conviction had been strengthened by further examination and subsequent reflection. Nothing, however, but a sense of what he conceived to be his duty, as an humble member of that body, could have induced him to arrest its progress then, or now to ask for a few moments the indulgence of the House. He should be brief in his remarks, having nothing to say for political effect or for home consumption; but, with the opinions he entertained of the bill, he should do injustice to himself did he permit it to pass, *sub silentio*, feeble and unavailing as his voice might prove. He had hoped that its importance, and the new order of things to be had under it, would have called up some gentleman whose experience and whose reputation might have insured general attention. He had waited to the last moment, and waited in vain; and now, upon its passage, he called upon gentlemen to pause before they proceed to provide, *by presumption*, for satisfying claims of any character, from any quarter.

Mr. T. said, he was not insensible of the advantages with which the bill now under consideration came before the House. It came, as he understood, with the unanimous approbation of a committee entitled to the most entire respect, and it related to services, the very mention of which moved our pride and our gratitude. They were services beyond all praise, and above all price. He spoke of the revolutionary services generally. But while warm and glowing with the glorious recollections which a recurrence to that period never fails to awaken; while we cherish with affection and reverence the memory of the brave men of that day, now no more; while we would grant, most cheerfully grant, to their heirs all that is justly due; and while we do extend to those who still survive our grateful thanks, and our treasure also, he trusted we should not, in the full impulse of generous feeling, disregard what was due from the gentlemen composing this House as the descendants of such men.

What then, sir, (said Mr. P.,) are the objects to be answered by the bill, and what are its provisions? The general object is plainly and briefly stated in the introduction of the committee's report. They say:

"Finding many petitions before them asking 'the commutation of five years' full pay, promised 'by the resolution of Congress of the 22d of March, '1783, to certain officers of the revolutionary army, 'they have been induced, by several considera-'tions, to present to the House a bill, the object of 'which is to remove these and some other similar 'claims from the action of the committee and of 'Congress, and have them settled at the Treasury 'Department."

Mr. P. would not be disposed, at any time, much

less was he disposed now, when so much was said as to the tendency of power and patronage, and of responsibility to the Executive, to cast from us any duties which have been performed, or any responsibilities which have hitherto rested here, unless the reason for such transfer shall appear obvious and conclusive.

It was more than fifty years since the passage of the resolution referred to by the committee as the foundation of commutation claims. The subject of making suitable provision for the officers of the army of the Revolution was one of the deepest and most intense interest, not only to the officers themselves, but to the country generally, from 1778, down to the passage of the commutation resolve of 1783. Mr. P. apprehended that individuals having substantial claims against the Government did not often remain long in ignorance of the fact, and he was curious to know how it happened that these claims had slumbered during the whole of this period. Considering the frequency and earnestness with which the subject was urged upon Congress by the Father of his country, and the anxiety with which it was regarded by the officers themselves, it was not *to be presumed* that any were so listless as to remain in the dark with regard to their own rights. In his judgment, it was reasonable to suppose that the number of legal and just claims would by this time have been so far diminished as to leave little for the action of Congress or of any department.

Since, however, that which might naturally have been expected to occur, seemed not to have obtained in this particular instance, he knew not that he should have raised any serious objections to sending the claims to the Treasury Department, provided they were to go there relying upon their merits, and depending for their allowance upon evidence, ordinarily required, of revolutionary services, and not upon *presumptions*. If the bill did not embrace the rules that are to be regarded as fixed principles, and to which he trusted he should be able to satisfy the House there were strong, if not insurmountable objections, it would still be exceptionable. He understood that it was not formerly the practice of Congress to allow interest upon these claims, even where they were brought by satisfactory evidence within the provisions of the resolution of 1783; and it struck him that a different practice never should have obtained, except in cases where the claimant furnished sufficient reasons for his delay, showing that it was attributable to no fault or negligence on his part. If correct in this view, it would be clearly wrong to sanction the principle generally, as is provided by the third section of the bill.

In speaking of what he considered to be the most objectionable features of the bill, Mr. P. said he should confine himself chiefly to its operation upon those who were entitled to half pay for life under the resolve of 1780, at the second important change in the arrangement of the army after its establishment. And to some portion of the history of the subsequent action of Congress upon the subject, it might be proper for him to call the attention of the House. By the resolution just referred to, those who were reduced by the arrangement which then took place, as well as those who served to the close of the war, were entitled to half pay for life. That this provision was made under very peculiar circumstances, was matter of history, and it was well known to all within the reach of his voice, that it was regarded with jealousy and dissatisfaction, both by the soldiers, who had behaved with equal valor and endured equal hardships, and by the citizens generally. They regarded it as anti-republican—they thought it setting up, in the then young republic, invidious distinctions, and establishing for that generation, at least, a privileged and pensioned class, inconsistent with the equal rights for which they had been contending, and at variance with the genius and spirit of such a government as they hoped to see established and maintained.

In March, 1783, a change was made; and what was the moving cause of that change? A memorial from the officers themselves. The preamble of the resolution recites, that, "Whereas, the officers of the several lines, under the immediate 'command of his Excellency General Washington, 'did, by their late memorial transmitted by their 'committee, represent to Congress, that the half 'pay, granted by sundry resolutions, was regarded in an unfavorable light by the citizens of some 'of these States, who would prefer a compensation 'for a limited term of years or by a sum in gross, 'to an establishment for life," &c. To satisfy the memorialists and the country, five years' full pay was granted, in lieu of half pay for life; and it is for this commutation that petitions are now pouring in upon you, and claims, arising under the resolution just referred to, and those, the adjustment of which the bill proposes to transfer to the Treasury Department, with rules of evidence, which might possibly facilitate, as the committee suppose, the allowance of some just claims, but which will at the same time open a wide door for imposition and for the assertion of rights which have no legal or equitable foundation, and which may still be honestly urged by the heirs of deceased officers. Sir, said Mr. P., is it not admitted, by the report, that this will be the operation to some extent? Speaking of these rules, the committee say:

"It is possible that their universal application 'may lead to the allowance of some claims which 'do not come strictly within the original terms; but 'this will be no new evil; and it is certain that if 'they are not applied many just claims must be 'rejected for the want of techinical proof."

To the correctness of this last clause he must be excused for withholding his assent.

If evil has heretofore arisen, or is liable to arise, from application of the said rules of evidence, is that now to be used as an argument in favor of transferring duties from the House to one of the departments, and transferring them with instructions binding the Secretary, and making certain the continuance of the evil? He trusted not. If *presumption* and not evidence was to be the ground on which claims are to be allowed, in any instance, would it not be more wise to retain them here, where a spirit of liberality, and yet a sound discretion, may be exercised in each particular case, according to its circumstances, than to give them a direction anywhere else, accompanied by instructions which it was admitted might lead, and which, in his humble judgment, would inevitably lead, to the acknowledgment of many unjust claims?

Again the committee say—

"If there is any apprehension that the principles 'here declared are too liberal, it must be recollected 'that the tendency of legislation for individual 'claims is constantly to enlarge the basis of right, 'while the effect of transferring them to another 'tribunal more judicial in its character, will probably be to retain that basis essentially within the 'limits fixed at the moment of transfer. If, therefore, it should be supposed, or even admitted, 'that the principles asserted in the bill are more 'liberal than the present practice of Congress, it 'may be considered certain that, in its continued 'action, they would soon be surpassed in liberality."

That is, if we are acting upon too liberal principles—too much upon presumption—we had better at once send out these presumptions to be the guide of others than longer to trust ourselves. Why? Because "the tendency of legislation for individual claims is constantly to enlarge the basis of right;" and we are in danger of being further from those principles which should govern prudent legislators, watchful of the interest of those whom they represent as they would be of their own, than we now are. Mr. P. said, however just this might be in point of fact, he was not yet prepared to admit it as a principle of action, and while no one would lend his support more readily to any claim that might come here sustained by proper evidence, he trusted the correctness of such a proposition might never find support in any vote of his.

Speaking of the operation of the limitation acts, the committee say further:

"Driven from the ordinary means of redress, individual claimants, from time to time, resorted to 'Congress for relief. At first it may have been matter of consideration and of serious question whether 'relief should be afforded after the limitation had 'expired, and the party was at least held *to account* '*for his delay;* but in the process of time it became, 'as it is now, a matter of course to grant relief in 'every case in which the claimant brings himself, 'by proof, within the terms of the resolutions on 'which the claim is founded, and has not been 'already paid."

Mr. P. trusted that wrong practice and precedent, founded in error, were not to be regarded as a guide here. He solemnly believed that if precedent and practice were to be relied upon, gentlemen might readily find justification for going almost any length in any direction.

In the case before the House, it was so exceedingly probable, that all claims founded in right were adjusted, and so fallible and uncertain was human testimony, after a lapse of fifty years, that he had no hesitation in declaring it as his firm conviction that the former course was the proper one; and that applicants, who came in after the extension act of 1792, should always have been held to account for their delay. It was not, of course, intended to give commutation to those, or the heirs of those, who received certificates in 1784, or who have, at any time since, under any circumstances, received commutation.

Before, then, examining more particularly the presumptions which this bill directs the Secretary to assume, let us consider, for a moment, what are the natural presumptions in the case. The commutation, provided for by the resolution of 1783, was originally directed to be adjusted by commissioners or other accounting officers, appointed by Congress, and it was supposed that certificates were almost universally granted in 1784. Why should it not have been so? They were ready upon application, and the production of the proper evidence; and he put it to the House whether the provisions of that resolution, and the rights accruing under it, considering the circumstances under which it was passed, upon the application of the officers themselves, must not have been known to every officer living within the limits of the United States. Mr. P. thought it utterly incredible that it should have been otherwise. Whenever there had been any action upon the subject of pensions, in latter times, what period had elapsed before that action, whether favorable or unfavorable, and almost every particular attending it, had, through one channel or another, reached the humble dwelling of every survivor of that noble band. But upon the supposition of their remote situation from the accounting officers, some might, by possibility, have been precluded from obtaining their rights, an act was passed on the 27th of March, 1792, suspending the operation of the limitation acts for two years, and, under this extension, remaining claims, or such as were presented, were adjusted at the Treasury Department, by what were then termed certificates of registered debt. Again, he inquired whether it was within the bounds of reasonable probability that any claims were held up after this period, if they were ever intended to be enforced? Sir, (said Mr. P.,) it is to be remembered that during all this time, it was not as it unfortunately now is. There were hosts of living witnesses among the officers with whom the claimants served, and the soldiers whom they commanded. Nor is the advantage which the officer had, from his position over the private soldier, of proving every particular connected with his service, and its duration, to be overlooked. Men engaged in the same great cause, and serving in the same camp, were no strangers to each other; never, perhaps, was there a band bound together by such ties of affection, intimacy, and confidence. Genius and honor and unshaken valor then went hand in hand, and were in exercise, not from low considerations of personal aggrandizement, but to vindicate a nation's rights. The links that bound men together at that day, exist not now. Their intimacies and their friendships were those which, perhaps from our very natures, can only spring up and flourish amidst the mutual dangers and privations of a camp. At the period of which he spoke, every incident of the exciting and eventful struggle through which they had just passed, must have been fresh and vivid in the recollection of all; nothing need then have been left to doubt, nothing *to presumption*. But this is not all. From 1794 down to this hour, there had been the same opportunity to obtain equitable rights, by application to Congress, that exists at present.

With these facts before us, (said Mr. P.,) if the natural presumption be not that all just claims have been satisfied, according to the provisions of the resolution of 1783, he confessed that the conclusions at which he had arrived were singularly erroneous.

The House had nothing to do with the question of the value of the certificates; they were, without doubt, nearly valueless in the hands of a large portion of the original holders. This subject was most satisfactorily discussed in the able and elaborate reports made to both Houses, at the first session of the twenty-first Congress, when the act was passed providing for the officers who were entitled to half pay by the resolve of 1780, and for the non-commissioned officers and soldiers who enlisted for, and served to the close of the war. The views taken in these reports were interesting and instructive upon this subject; but he was considering what was the natural presumption as to commutation rights, still existing; and if his views were in any tolerable degree correct, it was diametrically opposed to the legal presumption to be established by the passage of this bill.

Sir, (said Mr. P.,) we are told that the evidence of records is exceedingly imperfect, and he assured the House that such was the fact to a much greater extent than he had supposed before applying to the department for information. The muster-rolls had been almost entirely destroyed by fire, and all the records, from various casualties, were broken; but this deficiency of record evidence was, in his estimation, much more the misfortune of the Government than of the claimants who came here after the lapse of fifty years; but pass your presumptions, sir, said he, and you will have little occasion for evidence.

It is said that the rules which are to be regarded as fixed principles by the department, provided this bill pass, are the same which the committee have adopted in the investigation of claims coming before them. If so, and they accorded with the sentiments of the House, he confessed it was a matter of very little consequence whether they were applied here or elsewhere; and he was happy that the bill had been reported, that the opinion of the House might be deliberately and understandingly expressed upon the propriety of their adoption.

Sir, (said Mr. P.,) will not their operation be that of a new law upon the subject of commutation? Look at the first presumption of the bill; it has the advantage of being plain, there is no ambiguity about it—

" It being established that an officer of the continental line was in service as such on the twenty-first of October, seventeen hundred and eighty, and until the new arrangement of the army 'provided for by the resolution of that date was 'effected, he shall be presumed, unless it appear 'that he was then retained in service, to have been ' reduced by that arrangement, and therefore enti- 'tled to half pay for life, or the commutation in ' lieu of it.''

The onus probandi was shifted; the burden of proof was not left where it was intended it should rest, with the claimant, but it was thrown upon Government. He presumed it was not expected that the Government would send agents abroad to obtain negative evidence from living witnesses. How, then, was it to be shown, in the present imperfect state of the records, that an officer was not reduced, and did voluntarily leave the service?

The effect of such instructions would virtually be to give commutation to all who were in service on the 21st of October, 1780, and until the new arrangement was effected, instead of to those only who were actually reduced, as was originally contemplated. He called the attention of the House to the second presumption:

" 2d. A continental officer proved to have re- 'mained in service after the arrangement of the ' army under said resolution of October, seventeen ' hundred and eighty, shall be presumed to have ' served to the end of the war, or to have retired ' entitled to half pay for life, unless it appear that ' he died in the service, or resigned, or was dis- 'missed, or voluntarily abandoned an actual com- 'mand in the service of the United States.''

This, also, manifestly made new provision, granting commutation to those who were in service after the new arrangement, in 1780, instead of to those who actually served to the close of the war. For in the state of record evidence, as the claimed by the committee, how was it possible for the Government to prove, in very many instances, that the claimant, or the ancestor of the present

claimants, "died in the service, or resigned, or was dismissed, or voluntarily abandoned a command in the service of the United States?" There was no possible means of doing it.

Mr. P. would pursue the subject no further. If there was no fallacy in these premises, and the conclusions were legitimate, they were sufficient for his purpose. The House would not think of passing the bill in its present shape. He ought not longer to ask the attention of gentlemen, for which he was already under great obligation.

Such were some of the objections to the bill that had occurred to Mr. P., and thus much he thought it his duty to say. For the committee making the report he entertained the highest respect, and he believed that he was no less disposed than they were to grant to the uttermost farthing all that was due to revolutionary officers or their heirs.

But (said Mr. P.) pass this bill, and you will do great injustice to the country; you will make a most exhausting draft upon your treasury, to answer, it may be, some equitable claims that may as well be liquidated without it, and you will, it is morally certain, be compelled, under it, to acknowledge a vast number which have no foundation in justice—no foundation anywhere, except in lost records and violent presumptions.

Mr. VANDERPOEL followed in opposition to the bill; and, without concluding, gave way to a motion to adjourn.

On motion of Mr. CLAY,
The House then adjourned.

IN SENATE.

FRIDAY, February 28, 1834.

A message was received from the President of the United States, by Mr. DONELSON, his Private Secretary.

ORDERS OF THE DAY.

The resolutions previously submitted by Messrs. HENDRICKS, TOMLINSON, CHAMBERS, TIPTON, LINN, EWING, WAGGAMAN, ROBBINS, SILSBEE, CLAYTON, WHITE, and WEBSTER, were severally taken up, and adopted without discussion.

The resolution submitted yesterday by Mr. POINDEXTER, in relation to the Planters' Bank at Natchez, was read.

Upon this resolution a long and spirited debate ensued, much of which was of a personal nature, between Mr. POINDEXTER and Mr. FOR-SYTH. Mr. KING of Alabama, Mr. CLAY, Mr. MOORE, Mr. GRUNDY, Mr. BLACK, and Mr. WHITE, also participated in the discussion; when the resolution was adopted.

On motion of Mr. CLAY, it was ordered that when the Senate adjourn it will adjourn until Monday.

The Senate then went into the consideration of a large number of bills from the House of Representatives; which were read by their titles, and referred.

On motion of Mr. SILSBEE, at half past three o'clock, the Senate went into executive business, and, after some time spent therein, the Senate adjourned.

HOUSE OF REPRESENTATIVES.

FRIDAY, February 28, 1834.

Mr. HALL, of North Carolina, submitted the following resolution:

Resolved, That the Committee of Ways and Means be instructed to inquire into the expediency of reporting a plan, accompanied by a bill, to reduce the revenue to the necessary expenses of the Government.

Mr. STEWART moved that the question should be taken whether the House should consider the resolution.

Mr. McDUFFIE desired that the resolution should be referred to the Committee of Ways and Means.

Mr. CONNOR called for the yeas and nays on the motion to consider; which were ordered.

The House refused to consider; which is a rejection of the resolution:

Yeas 70, nays 115.

The House resumed the consideration of the following resolution, offered by Mr. MARDIS:

Resolved, That the Committee of Ways and Means be instructed to inquire into the expediency of reporting a bill requiring the Secretary of the Treasury to deposite the public moneys of the United States in the State banks; and, also, as to the expediency of defining by law all contracts hereafter to be made with the Secretary for the safe-keeping, management, and disbursement of the same.

Mr. CLOWNEY resumed, and said, when he last addressed the House, he was endeavoring to show that the President derived his power to remove from office, from the law, not the Constitution. He maintained that as the Secretary of the Treasury was an officer created by Congress, he was bound to obey their orders; and he desired to know, upon a review of all the circumstances attendant upon the removal of the deposites, if the Secretary could be considered to have faithfully complied with the duties enjoined upon him by law?

Referring to the paper read by the President to his Cabinet, it would be found that he had not pretended to deny that it was the right of the Secretary to exercise his own judgment, from which he (Mr. C.) argued that if the Secretary had retained the control, that he would have kept it where it was placed by the Constitution. It was said in the arguments, that although the President had no right to compel the Secretary to deviate from what he conceived to be an honest discharge of his duties, yet that he had a right to dismiss an error? He thought not, and that in such case the Legislature could only blame themselves for trusting any matter of importance to the discretion of their own agent. He was forced to conclude that the President, in this matter, had assumed powers which belonged to the Legislative body, and to regard which, as a mere abuse of power, was too mild a term. The President assumed the power, which rested in the representative body alone, over the public purse; for he considered that the means taken by the President to effect his object by the removal of an officer who would not carry out his views, for the purpose of appointing another who would, is tantamount to his doing the act in person, and that it must be deemed on his part an unlawful assumption of power, not properly belonging to him.

Mr. C. had not concluded at the expiration of the hour; after which, this day is set apart for the consideration of private bills.

The House went into committee thereon, Mr. CONNOR in the chair.

Several private bills were considered in the Committee of the Whole, reported to the House, and ordered to a third reading.

The bill to compensate Susan Decatur and others, was taken up for consideration in the Committee of the Whole.

Messrs. HAWES and HARDIN spoke in opposition to the bill, and Mr. PINCKNEY in its support.

On motion of Mr. HUBBARD, the committee rose, reported progress, and had leave to sit again.

On motion of Mr. WAYNE, the rule was suspended to enable him to submit a motion.

Mr. WAYNE then moved, that when the House adjourns, it adjourn to meet on Monday.

Mr. CARR demanded the yeas and nays, but the House refused to order them.

The motion was agreed to:
Yeas 115; nays 39.

On motion,
The House then adjourned.

THE CONGRESSIONAL GLOBE.

PRINTED AND PUBLISHED AT THE CITY OF WASHINGTON, BY BLAIR & RIVES.

| 23d CONGRESS, 1st SESSION. | SATURDAY, MARCH 8, 1834. | VOL. I.......No. 14. |

IN SENATE.

FRIDAY, February 26, 1834.

Debate on Mr. POINDEXTER's resolution, calling on the Secretary of the Treasury for information relative to transfer of the public money from the bank in Natchez to banks in the Atlantic cities.

Mr. POINDEXTER said he had intended to have made some remarks upon the resolution, but if there was no objection to its passage, he would suspend what he had to say until the answer to the call came in.

Mr. FORSYTH had he had certainly no objection to a call for any information which any gentleman thought proper to make—he had no disposition to keep back facts, but he thought it an act of justice to state to the gentleman from Mississippi, that he was entirely misinformed. In the remarks which the gentleman made yesterday in submitting the resolution, he was mistaken in every fact which he had stated. Mr. F. made this statement in justice to the Secretary of the Treasury, and for the satisfaction of the gentleman from Mississippi, for he was sure it would give him satisfaction to know, that there was no foundation whatever in the charge he had made. The facts were these: On the 19th of the present month, in answer to a letter of inquiry from the bank at Natchez, upon the subject of the removal of the deposites from that institution, the Secretary said he had no intention to withdraw or transfer any of the deposites to the Atlantic cities. That it had become necessary for payment of services in the removal of the Indians, to transfer $250,000 to the Commercial Bank of Louisiana on the 1st of May next. And for other like expenses, $250,000 more on the 1st of June, to the Union Bank of Louisiana, at New Orleans, or to the Union Bank at Nashville, at the option of the bank at Natchez. The gentleman from Mississippi, therefore, would perceive that the whole of his information was founded in mistake. He has said that a million has been drawn out of the bank. Why, the fact is, there is not as much in it. He says the bank is prevented from discounting, but no drafts are made to prevent them, and the letter to the bank says expressly that no transfers are contemplated to the Atlantic cities.

Mr. POINDEXTER said he might have been misinformed, but he believed himself to be correct. The fact was, the President of the United States had brought into the market an immense body of very valuable lands, which the people could not purchase without accommodation at the banks—that the sale was on very short notice, and before the crops were sold, so as to enable the people to purchase—and that the removal of the deposites to the Planters' Bank, prevented the United States Bank from discounting. That the Planters' Bank had ceased to discount, because it was compelled to hold the deposites ready to pay over at a moment's warning at the requisition of the Secretary of the Treasury.

Mr. FORSYTH said he hoped the Senate would take nothing from him in lieu of the Secretary's report. But when he stated anything here, he stated what he believed. His information was obtained from his own examination of the documents. There was not a single fact in the statement of the gentleman from Mississippi that would not be contradicted by the public documents.

Mr. POINDEXTER. Does the gentleman mean to impute to me the wilful misstatement of a fact?

Mr. FORSYTH. I call the gentleman to order. The gentleman will please take his seat. I mean just what I say.

The VICE PRESIDENT here interposed, and called Mr. POINDEXTER to order, and took his seat.

Mr. FORSYTH resumed. It was very probably true that the Planters' Bank was not in as good condition to benefit the community as the Bank of

the United States was. But no money was drawn from the bank, and the bank was expressly informed that no money was intended to be drawn from it for banks in the Atlantic cities.

Mr. POINDEXTER read the report of his remarks of yesterday from the National Intelligencer, which he said were substantially correct. He had not stated the facts on his own knowledge. If the gentleman from Georgia [Mr. FORSYTH] meant to impute to him here the assertion of a fact on his own authority which he knew to be untrue, he departed from the character of an honorable man, and he would hold him accountable for it. No man should speak in such a way of him but at the hazard of his life, and no honorable man would make such an imputation. As to the subject under consideration, he desired to make the inquiry. He had heard that great speculations had been made in the West and also in the Creek country by a Tennessee company, nephews and other relatives of the President of the United States.

Mr. FORSYTH said, when he made a statement here which he believed to be correct, he would say so, in utter disregard and contempt of the gentleman's displeasure. He would not enter into an argument with the gentleman. The Government has not drawn a dollar out of the bank, nor does it intend to draw a dollar to send to the Atlantic cities. The inference of the gentleman is false and without any foundation. And he (Mr. F.) was sorry that the gentleman was not glad to find he was mistaken.

Mr. POINDEXTER replied that two-thirds of his remarks yesterday was matter of inference that the money was to be sent to support the failing banks in the East by transferring it to the Atlantic cities. He now distinctly asked the gentleman from Georgia if he meant to charge him with wilful misrepresentation?

Mr. FORSYTH. Then I shall not answer the gentleman.

Mr. POINDEXTER. Very well.

Mr. KING, of Alabama, said the gentleman from Mississippi had done great injustice to the President of the United States, not only on this but on many other occasions. The President had no more agency in the sale of the lands in Mississippi than the gentleman himself. Nor had the President's nephews, and the gentleman's colleague knew that it was not the fact. He had derived his information from those who either knew nothing of the facts or wilfully misrepresented them. True there were speculators there. There always had been, and there ever would be, so long as there should be sales of lands in the United States. In Alabama, in consequence of an unfortunate difference between the government of that State and the Government of the United States, the President, with a paternal solicitude characteristic of him, and worthy the highest praise, determined to do everything which could be done to effect justice between the Creeks and the unfortunate settlers. He knew that if they were driven off at a moment's warning, downright ruin would overtake them. And when the position assumed by the Executive of Alabama was made known to the President, he ordered the location of numerous reservations, and when they were made, in order to contribute to the removal of the Indians and furnish a home to those who had removed, the lands were brought to market. He mentioned this to show that it was to save the ruin and expense of a removal that the sales took place. Had the gentleman information that a single Tennessean was there? Mr. K. had information that there was not one there. The lands were sold, but settlers obtained them at the reduced prices of the Government.

Mr. POINDEXTER said there were persons here ready to give evidence of the facts. He did not say the President was concerned in the speculations, but his relatives. He intended bringing the whole subject up for investigation before the Senate.

Mr. GRUNDY said he did not rise for any other purpose, but to allude to the imputation upon the

character of Mr. McLamore, the locating agent. Mr. McLamore was his neighbor; he knew him well, and there was not a more honest or honorable man in any country. He had had a great deal more to do in locating public lands in Tennessee than any other man, and he had never heard a single word to his prejudice in any of his land transactions. And he was the only dealer in public lands that he had ever heard complained of. He was looked up to by his fellow-citizens as the guardian and securer of their rights and business. But this Tennessee Company—he would like to know their names; this whole of it was a secret to us at home. He had never heard of it, although he had heard as much of the business of Tennessee as most gentlemen; but he thought the gentleman would find that he was mistaken in his information. Mr. G. knew that some individual Tennesseeans had gone to the South for the purpose of speculating in land, but there were no combinations of men so far as he had learned. The gentleman from Mississippi had been so informed, but the only exception he (Mr. G.) made to that gentleman was, his greater facility of belief. Now, he ought not lightly to make such imputations against respectable men, or give credit to them.

Mr. CLAY said, perhaps the gentleman who had just sat down, was as liable to the objection he himself had urged, as the gentleman from Mississippi. As to the sale, the notice was unprecedentedly short, and well calculated to produce these speculations. He knew nothing of it himself, but he believed other Senators had also some information of the sort. But he hoped an end would be put to these disputes, by passing the bill which he had the honor of submitting on a former occasion.

He rose, however, at this time, to express his deep regret at an incident which had just occurred between two honorable Senators. He would submit to the gentleman from Georgia, whether the two gentlemen were on terms of perfect equality? How was it? The gentleman from Mississippi rose in his place yesterday, and submitted a resolution. From information he had received, he made certain inferences, and drew certain conclusions, and argued upon those inferences. Now, how was the gentleman from Georgia situated? He, standing in different relations with the Government from the gentleman from Mississippi, resorts to the Secretary of the Treasury. The Secretary gives him information, and submits the documents on the subject to his perusal. And the gentleman from Georgia was thus prepared with the whole official matter, and the gentleman from Mississippi, deprived of it; in this state of inequality, the gentleman from Georgia rises in his place, and pronounces language which he (Mr. C.) thought was rather strong. The gentleman's course here had always been courtly, manly, and open. But, on this occasion, he applied language which Mr. C. hoped he would reconsider: he hoped both the gentlemen would reconsider what had fallen from them, and let the matter go no farther. He hoped all would wait for the information, which would be here in a few days, and, in the meantime, all would take pleasure in seeing a reconciliation and an adjustment of those circumstances which had given great pain.

Mr. FORSYTH said, that the gentleman from Kentucky was mistaken in point of fact. He had not gone to see the Secretary. The Secretary came to him, and requested him to communicate to the Senate what he had stated. As respected the inequality of situation which the gentleman had spoken of, he did not reprehend the gentleman from Mississippi. He gave the information he had obtained, and it was not until that gentleman cast a doubt upon him, that he used the strong language spoken of. His simple purpose was to give to that gentleman and to the people, a knowledge of the fact, so that the statement of the gentleman from Mississippi might not injure the Secretary of the Treasury. He never used language which he did not think befitted the occasion

Mr. POINDEXTER. Unless the gentleman meant to say that he (Mr. P.) intended to convey here, what he knew was not true, common courtesy required of him to say so. But when the gentleman made an imputation, and on being asked for an explanation, refused to disavow it, he (Mr. P.) felt bound to consider the matter ended, and he did consider it at an end.

Mr. BLACK said, he was in favor of calling for the information which the resolution contemplated. But there was one or two matters in which his colleague [Mr. POINDEXTER] had done great injustice to the President of the United States. The sales of the Choctaw lands were advertised sixty days, and he thought no inconvenience resulted from that notice instead of a longer period. He thought all purchasers were as well prepared as they would have been with longer notice, and that no injury resulted to the citizens of the State from it. In regard to the company formed for speculating there, he believed his colleague did the persons implicated great injustice. He (Mr. B.) was there, and was a close observer of the sales, although he bought no land. After the first day, a company was formed, but it was not from Tennessee. The proportion of persons concerned was not greater than one in six, from Tennessee. And there was no agreement among the company not to bid against each other. He knew many of the persons engaged in it, and he would say, confidently, there were no men more honest or honorable. He knew, also, Mr. McLamore, and he knew that his pecuniary abilities at that time were extremely limited, and he believed him to be an honest and honorable gentleman, and there was nothing whatever improper in his conduct.

Mr. MOORE said, he felt no interest in the subject of the resolution; being local in its character, he should not have arisen to say a word, except for some of the topics accidentally lugged into the debate.

The first fact stated by his colleague, and repeated by the Senator from Mississippi, [Mr. BLACK,] he had heard for the first time, that gentlemen from Alabama had participated in the recent speculations in the purchase of the public lands referred to, and he was bound to presume if any purchases were made by those, they were with the view to establish cotton farms, and not for the purpose of speculation—indeed, one gentleman of the first respectability he knew had purchased with this view only.

But whilst his colleague is willing to exonerate the Tennesseeans (no doubt properly enough) from the censure, he has transferred it to Alabamians; and the gentleman from Mississippi, whilst he says Alabamians were concerned, justifies, and says, the transaction was altogether innocent. Now, this might be so; he did not know the character of the land speculation to which reference had been made. But there was a species of land speculation known to have existed in the country in which he resided, which he considered censurable, and ought to be deprecated by all; and that he might not be misunderstood, he would endeavor to explain this system, which is as follows: The moneyed men and capitalists throughout the country meet at the land office, form a common stock with their funds for the mutual benefit of all. The effect of which is to put down all other competition; for the poor settler, although he may be prepared to purchase his improvement at the Government price—although he may have prepared himself with a sufficiency at one dollar and twenty-five cents per acre—yet, by this immense common stock, he is driven out of the market, and compelled to make the best terms he can. This company then ascertain the highest price he can, or is willing to give for his improvement, and if he can be screwed up to any point over the minimum, then they promise him if he will not bid, they will purchase the tract, including his improvement, and transfer it to him at the stipulated price. Having thus removed him from the competition in bidding, they obtain it at the minimum, and put in their own pockets all they get from him over the said minimum. Now, said he, this is the system of which his constituents complain, and of which he did not approve. The other fact was as to the sufficiency of the notice. The Senator from Mississippi [Mr. BLACK] had said the notice, as regarded the sale in that State, had been sixty days, and he viewed it as sufficient, and this he said might be so, he would not pretend to dispute it. But, as regarded the notice in Alabama, it was not more than half that time. It had been made the subject of complaint, and he thought that, considering the distance and the locality of the country to be sold, such notice made more in favor of the capitalist than the actual settler, who might find it necessary to make an application to the State bank for the one thing needful.

And here he would beg leave to say to the honorable Senator from North Carolina, [Mr. MANGUM,] that although he would be highly pleased to see him settle a cotton plantation in Alabama, yet the fact that foreigners were not accommodated had not excited his sympathies at all. Again, it had been said, that an expeditious sale was necessary as a means of preventing the difficulty that was threatened between the authorities of the State and the General Government. The life of a citizen had been sacrificed by order of a deputy marshal, which had given rise to an apprehension of the most serious results.

It is true it had been said that this unfortunate individual was a turbulent man, and had attempted to blow up his own house in order to injure others, &c.; but he believed this was mere rumor, and not sanctioned by evidence. The sales of the lands, however, it had been said, removed all difficulty, and therefore justified the very short notice that had been given, and he was not disposed to controvert this point. What he wished mainly to say was, that he had not been consulted as to the time of sale, nor had he given any advice relative to it. He was glad, however, that the sales had been suspended, because if the bill which has been reported by the Committee on the Public Lands, and is now progressing in the Senate, shall become a law, (and he hoped it would,) the settlers would be protected from the iron grasp of the *speculator*, by means of the preëmption right which this bill gives them. And experience had proved that the Government could lose nothing by this mode of disposing of the public lands; for if any of the lands were worth more than the minimum, the surplus was pocketed by speculators.

Mr. KING replied that he never said or intended to say that any one was consulted. He said he knew nothing of the intended sale till he heard that gentlemen were consulted. He presumed that the letters of gentlemen in the other House stated things correctly. In carrying the treaty into effect, an individual intruded, and thereby lost his life, while he was himself attempting the lives of others. The President used every possible exertion to locate the reservation as soon as possible, but the great source of controversy remained, and the lands were brought to market to narrow down the controversy. A portion of the population might have been dissatisfied with the sales; he did not know how that was. As to a settlement of the difficulties, he did not know how that could be effected by the plan of the gentleman from Kentucky, which provided for a distribution of the proceeds of sales among the several States.

Mr. WHITE said, from the terms in which gentlemen had spoken of the Tennessee company, he felt bound to make a few remarks, lest his silence might be misinterpreted into an acquiescence in the correctness of the statements. The gentleman from Mississippi [Mr. POINDEXTER] had spoken of a Tennessee speculating company. For himself he could not say whether such a company existed or not. But about twelve months ago a story of the same kind was in circulation. He was shortly afterwards in Nashville, and made inquiry of several gentlemen there into its truth, who assured him that there was no such company there. Last fall, shortly before he left home for Washington, he was in Nashville again, and while there, several gentlemen went to Mississippi to make purchases of land, and he was satisfied from what he learned, that no one of them was a member of any company whatever. The people of Tennessee, like those of other States, were an enterprising, money making people, but their characters were as fair and respectable as any others. It might seem invidious to say they were more so, he therefore made no claim to go higher. There was a great variety of character and population there, and some might no doubt be found who had gone to purchase land in Mississippi, believing they could better their condition in life. And there may also have been a company formed in Tennessee; but so far as he knew, he believed that the gentleman's information that there was such a company, was founded in mistake. If it were so, he had no information whatever about it. The place of his residence was two hundred miles from the place where the company was said to be formed. Being from Tennessee, it might have been inferred if he had been silent, that he possessed knowledge of a fact which he would not avow. Mr. McLamore's name had been mentioned. That gentleman was a nephew of the President, and it had been said was a member of the company. He had had a long and intimate acquaintance with Mr. McLamore, and he willingly added his testimony to his character. His land transactions were as numerous as those of any other man in Tennessee—he was an active, business-doing and faithful man, and was the only man within his acquaintance who dealt largely in lands, who never was subjected to any imputation which would take from his character as a man of honor and integrity. It had been said that the notice of sale was short, and that the Tennessee company was formed of nephews and relations of the President of the United States. And in the absence of any disclaimer on his part, it might be thought that he admitted the charge. But he was persuaded, if inquiry were made into the motive for the short notice, it would be found that there was none other than what the public ought to approve, because the object was to promote the public interest. He was perfectly satisfied if any Tennesseean, either a relative or not of the President, had, either directly or indirectly, intimated to him a wish that he should give him an advantage in the purchase of land over any other citizens of the United States, he would have received such an answer from the President as would forever after have placed him beyond the pale of his friendship. And in regard to the short notice, if it should be found that the motive was the public interest, he hoped the President would be acquitted on that point. He was desirous that the Committee on Public Lands should inquire into the whole subject, and if it should be discovered that there had been violations of the public interests, that the names of the guilty should be held up to the scorn and indignation of the community. And while he confidently indulged the hope that no countryman of his would be found guilty, God forbid that he should screen him from exposure, if his guilt should be made to appear. It had been said that the agent for locating the lands in the Choctaw country was concerned in the purchase of lands. But he thought it would appear that in this, too, the gentleman was mistaken. But if it be known, and if it can be authentically made known to the President, from that time forth he would be instantly dismissed, and a person appointed who would promptly and faithfully perform his duty. Mr. W. said he felt it his duty to say thus much, and perhaps he ought to apologize to the Senate for this consumption of their time. And he would further say, that if it was in the power of the committee to devise a plan which should effectually guard against frauds, hereafter, in the sale of the public lands, it would meet his hearty concurrence and support.

Some further remarks were made by Messrs. POINDEXTER, BLACK, MANGUM, and MOORE, when the resolution was adopted.

IN SENATE.

MONDAY, *March* 3, 1834.

Mr. CLAYTON presented the memorial of one thousand six hundred and forty citizens, and the proceedings of a public meeting in Newcastle, Delaware, praying that measures may be devised for restoring the deposites to the Bank of the United States. After some remarks, made by Mr. C., the memorial and proceedings were read, referred to the Committee on Finance, and ordered to be printed.

Mr. POINDEXTER rose, not to revive the discussion upon the public lands. He would not argue it now, but contented himself with saying that the subject would undergo a most rigid inves-

tigation before the Committee on Public Lands, when the subject came before them.

Two of the leading journals of this city, from motives highly proper in themselves, refrained from publishing any report of the unpleasant debate which took place in the Senate on Friday last. For one, he rejoiced at the discretion which had been exhibited by the gentlemen at the head of those journals; but the third, the official journal, had published a report of that description which contained scarcely a semblance of the truth. As to his remarks, that report did not give one-tenth of what fell from him, and so changed as to give a very different view from that which he had really given. Other gentlemen had been as much misrepresented. He had made this statement in order that no undue impression might be made on the public mind from this publication. It would have been better that the report had been suppressed altogether. As far as related to himself, he had deemed it his duty to make these remarks. If other gentlemen were satisfied, be it so. He took occasion to say thus much, and concluded by submitting the following resolutions, and asked their immediate consideration:

1. *Resolved*, That the Secretary of the War Department be directed to communicate to the Senate the name or names of the agent or agents appointed by the President of the United States to locate the reservations granted to individuals of the Choctaw tribe of Indians, by the treaty of Dancing Rabbit Creek; and, also, copies of such instructions as may have been given to the agent or agents so appointed; and of any correspondence which may have taken place between any officer in the Department of War and said agent or agents, or any other person or persons whose correspondence may be in the department, touching the locations of said reservations, and the manner in which the duties of said agent or agents may have been performed.

2. *Resolved*, That the said Secretary be directed to transmit to the Senate a copy of the register of the names of such Choctaw Indians as claim reservations of lands under the 14th and 19th articles of said treaty.

Mr. POINDEXTER moved the consideration of the resolutions now, with a view to give the Secretary of War time to make out the papers.

Mr. GRUNDY said he was much pleased with the movement which was now made, because if there was anything wrong in the matter to which the resolutions alluded, he was as desirous to expose it to public reprobation as any other man. His object in rising now, was to move that the resolutions be printed. He wished to have an opportunity of considering the resolutions with a view of ascertaining if some further direction on the subject could not be given to the committee.

The consideration of the resolutions was agreed to, and they were adopted.

On motion of Mr. GRUNDY, the resolutions were then ordered to be printed.

Mr. POINDEXTER also submitted the following resolutions:

1. *Resolved*, That the Committee on the Public Lands be instructed to inquire into the circumstances attending the recent sales of the public lands in the States of Mississippi and Alabama, and whether the proclamation of the President of the United States, causing the public lands in the district of country acquired from the Choctaw tribe of Indians, in Alabama, to be offered at public sale, were issued and promulgated a reasonable length of time prior to the day on which said sales were directed to be commenced in said districts, to give proper notice to the people of the United States of the days appointed for said sales.

2. *Resolved*, That the same committee inquire whether any fraudulent practices to the injury of the public interest took place at said sales, by reason of combination of companies or individuals interdicting, or unfavorable to a fair competition between bidders for the public lands, offered for sale in the said districts; and if so, whether the officers superintending said sales had knowledge of, or participated in such fraudulent practices or combinations.

3. *Resolved*, That the said committee be instructed to inquire whether the registers of the lands offices and the receivers of the public moneys at

---

any of the land offices, of the United States or either of them, have, in violation of law and of their official duties, demanded, or accepted a bonus or premium from any purchaser or purchasers of the public lands at public or private sale, for the benefit of such officer or officers, as a condition on which such purchaser or purchasers should be allowed to enter or purchase any tract or tracts of land offered for sale by the United States; and, also, whether any register or receiver as aforesaid, has been guilty of fraud or partiality in the sales of the public lands, by adopting rules and regulations in their respective offices, inconsistent with the laws of the United States.

4. *Resolved*, That the said committee inquire whether the public lands at any land office in the State of Mississippi have been sold otherwise than for cash; and whether any register or receiver in said State has, at any time, taken in payment the promissory note of any purchaser or purchasers, bearing an interest to accrue to the benefit of such register or receiver.

5. *Resolved*, That, in prosecution of said inquiries, the said committee have power to send for persons and papers, and to examine witnesses before them on oath, touching the matters aforesaid.

Mr. ROBINSON presented the petition of inhabitants of Barkland, Illinois, praying the establishment of a land office; which was referred to the Committee on Public Lands.

Mr. ROBINSON presented the memorial of inhabitants of Adams county, Illinois, praying the construction of a railroad from Buffalo to the river Mississippi; which was referred to the Committee on Roads and Canals.

Mr. ROBINSON presented the petition of inhabitants of Crawford county, Illinois, praying the establishment of a post route from Chicago to Vincennes, which was referred to the Committee on the Post Office and Post Roads.

Mr. ROBINSON, in pursuance of notice, obtained leave to introduce a bill to authorize the State of Illinois to dispose of the lands reserved for the use of public schools; the bill was read and referred to the Committee on Public Lands.

Mr. POINDEXTER asked that the bill regulating the manner of advertising the public lands, when offered for sale, be read a second time, in order that it might be referred; which was agreed to, and the bill referred to the Committee on Public Lands.

Mr. KING, of Alabama, gave notice that he should, to-morrow, ask leave to introduce a bill compensating the register and receiver of the land office in West Florida.

Mr. KING, of Alabama, submitted the following resolution, the immediate consideration of which he asked; which was agreed to:

Resolved, That the Committee on Public Lands be instructed to inquire into the expediency of authorizing by law the sale of four sections of land, being part of the grant made to the French emigrants for the cultivation of the vine and olive, and parcelled out to each grantee in small allotments.

Petitions of a private nature were presented by Messrs. ROBINSON, POINDEXTER, MANGUM, and McKEAN, and severally referred to appropriate committees.

Mr. McKEAN presented a memorial, signed by inhabitants of Oxford, Lower Dublin, and the unincorporated parts of the Northern Liberties, in favor of the restoration of the deposites to the Bank of the United States;

Also, a memorial from inhabitants of Roxborough and Manayunk, of the same character;

And also, one of a similar nature, from the city and county of Lancaster;

All of which were read, referred to the Committee on Finance, and ordered to be printed.

SPECIAL ORDERS.

Mr. CHAMBERS moved to postpone all the special orders, for the purpose of taking up the bill providing compensation for French spoliations. Mr. C. said, he made this motion in pursuance of notice that he would do so on to-day. The importance of the bill, the pecuniary interests involved in it, required at the hands of the Senate as early a consideration of it as was practicable. He did not urge the bill in violation of the wishes

---

of the Senate. Whatever the decision might be, he would of course acquiesce in it.

After some conversation between Messrs. CLAY, CHAMBERS, and GRUNDY, all the special orders were postponed till to-morrow, except that in relation to the

REMOVAL OF THE DEPOSITES.

Which, having been announced by the VICE PRESIDENT,

Mr. HILL rose, and spoke at some length in support of the reasons of the Secretary; when, at four o'clock, without concluding, he gave way to Mr. WRIGHT; upon whose motion,

The Senate adjourned.

HOUSE OF REPRESENTATIVES.

MONDAY, *March* 3, 1834.

Petitions and memorials were presented by Messrs. HIESTER, WAGENER, ANTHONY, GALBRAITH, HARRISON, BINNEY, HARPER, DENNY, McKENNAN, POTTS, KING, RAMSEY, STEWART, SUTHERLAND, LAPORTE, BEAUMONT, HENDERSON, and WATMOUGH, of Pennsylvania;

Mr. MILLIGAN, of Delaware;

Messrs. McKIM, STODDERT, and HEATH, of Maryland; and by

Messrs. ARCHER and GORDON, of Virginia.

Mr. HIESTER presented the proceedings of a meeting held by the citizens of Lancaster county, Pennsylvania, in favor of the restoration of the deposites to the United States Bank. Read, referred, and ordered to be printed.

Mr. HIESTER also presented fourteen petitions, signed by 2800 citizens of Lancaster county, also praying the restoration of the deposites. Referred, and ordered to be printed.

Mr. WAGENER presented the petition of 350 citizens of Northampton county, Pennsylvania, praying the recharter of the Bank of the United States, and the restoration of the deposites. Referred, and ordered to be printed.

Mr. BINNEY presented the memorial of 1700 citizens of Northampton county, Pennsylvania, representing the existence of great distress in the country, and praying the recharter of the United States Bank. Read, referred, and ordered to be printed.

Mr. HARPER presented the memorial of a bank in Pennsylvania, praying the restoration of the deposites. The memorial was referred, and ordered to be printed.

Mr. DENNY presented the petition of the Bank of Pittsburg, praying the recharter of the Bank of the United States.

Mr. DENNY also presented the resolutions adopted by a meeting of citizens of Alleghany county, Pennsylvania, declaring that great pecuniary embarrassment pervaded the western country, and that the only and the proper remedy for the evil was the restoration of the deposites to the United States Bank. Read, referred, and ordered to be printed, with the names.

The SPEAKER presented the proceedings of a large meeting of citizens of Chester county, ascribing the public distress to the removal of the deposites, representing the necessity of a recharter of the Bank of the United States, and also proposing a general convention of the citizens of Pennsylvania, to be held at Harrisburg, with a view to express their sentiments on this subject.

Mr. POTTS said he could bear testimony to the fact that this meeting was emphatically a meeting of the people. It was composed of persons of all parties, and it was the largest meeting ever held in the large and flourishing county of Chester. The individuals who took part in the proceedings of the meeting, were among the most intelligent, and honorable men in the county, and were attached to different political parties. On motion of Mr. P. the proceedings were referred, and ordered to be printed.

The SPEAKER presented the proceedings of a meeting of citizens, held in Philadelphia, on the subject of the removal of the deposites and the recharter of the bank, declaring the opinion that the deposites were removed and the bank charter restored, with a view to the establishment of a national bank in the city of New York, and recommending such an alteration of the Constitution as will re-

move all constitutional objections to a national bank.

On motion of Mr. SUTHERLAND, the proceedings were read.

Mr. SUTHERLAND presented a memorial from the citizens of Roxborough, Philadelphia county, Pennsylvania, in favor of the restoration of the deposites, and for rechartering the Bank of the United States. He called for the reading of the memorial, and knowing the persons who signed it, he wished to bear testimony to their high respectability. They were men friendly to the present Administration; they were men who felt that it was their right as freemen to give their sentiments on the present state of things. But he would take occasion to remark, that although they had signed and sent this memorial, not one of them would be found abandoning the Administration in the day of trial.

Mr. HARPER, of Pennsylvania, said he was happy to have it in his power to concur with his colleague in bearing testimony to the respectability, intelligence, and patriotism, of the memorialists. The memorial was agreed to at a meeting composed of six or eight thousand persons, and with only one dissenting voice. This would be, he hoped, sufficient evidence, if any was wanting, that the present was no longer viewed as a question of party, but that it originated in motives that were entitled to the consideration of the House.

The memorial was then read, referred, and ordered to be printed.

Mr. KING presented a memorial from inhabitants of Pottsville, Schuylkill county, Pennsylvania, against the restoration of the deposites and recharter of the bank.

Mr. STEWART presented forty-one memorials from divers places, praying aid for the Chesapeake and Ohio canal.

Mr. SUTHERLAND presented a memorial said to be signed by nearly four thousand workingmen, in the Third Congressional District, asking that the deposites might not be restored, and protesting against the recharter of the bank.

Mr. WATMOUGH remarked that he had heard some floating rumor that such a memorial was to be presented. He claimed to know something of the sentiments, and of the inhabitants of the district, and he desired that his colleague would state what he knew of the persons who had signed the memorial. The people of the district felt that the presentation of the memorial was such an imputation upon their character, that they called a meeting, which was to be held on Wednesday next; that when this should have been presented, the character of the persons signing it should be placed in their proper light.

Mr. SUTHERLAND said, if the men who signed the memorial were not to be found, as was apprehended by his colleague, when the great question came up hereafter, it would be, perhaps, so much the better for him, as to the contest that was approaching. He did not himself know the memorialists, but he might be allowed to say, that the memorial was presented to him by as gallant a soldier as was in the country, and that it was sent on by a committee of the workingmen from the district. He could state further, as he was instructed to do, that they were men who were determined to hold on to their opinion in support of the President still more than they had done. He had intended presenting it last petition day, when the gentleman who gave it was here, and who brought with it a letter to him from the gentleman who was now editor of the Workingman's Advocate. He would move for the printing of the names, to gratify the gentleman, that he may hereafter see the memorialists have not such a character as he would represent them; that they are not mere men of of straw.

Mr. WATMOUGH rose to order. The gentleman misrepresented what he had said; he had not said they were men of straw.

The SPEAKER remarked that Mr. S. had not attributed this expression to him.

Mr. SUTHERLAND made the remark in answer to what was said by the gentlnman when he wished he might know where these persons were to be found. He moved the printing of the names for that purpose.

Mr. WATMOUGH desired this equally with his colleague, and he hoped that he would be as well prepared as he was at the approaching contest, to account for every word and every act which he had done or said in the House or elsewhere, in reference to the interests of their constituents. He wanted to be convinced of the fact whether those 4000 persons came from the Northern Liberties.

Mr. SUTHERLAND could not, from his own knoweledge, say they did; but he supposed they lived there, or round about it.

Mr. WATMOUGH: Round about, indeed! Why, the whole number of voters in the district is not 3000. He knew that the whole of the Third Congressional District had an almost unanimous voice upon this subject. They had, hitherto, come forward in mass, and they were about doing so in detail. He was not going to impute anything derogatory to the character of any man, or detract from that of a gallant soldier, but the circumstances of this memorial were so remarkable, it was only right that the matter should be fairly stated. It did not appear that there was any public meeting called to give it sanction.

Mr. SUTHERLAND had always tried to keep from intermeddling in the affairs of other districts. He knew, therefore, but little of the memorialists, or about the manner in which it was got up; and when doubts were attempted to be cast upon them and it, he felt he owed it to himself, and to the House, to state that he presented it because he was requested to do so. He alluded to the gallant soldier, because, from the knowledge he had of his character, he was convinced he would not do a thing so derogatory to his character as bringing a petition with false names. Although he did not himself know the persons, he had no hesitation in saying that he believed the sentiments contained in the memorial were felt by a large body of the working men in the district.

The memorial, with the names, was then ordered to be printed, and referred.

Mr. WATMOUGH presented two memorials from the mechanics and workingmen of the Northern Liberties, and from the farmers, mechanics, &c., in the smaller districts, in favor of the restoration of the deposites, and rechartering of the bank; which were read, referred, and, with the names, ordered to be printed.

Mr. MILLIGAN presented the memorial of sundry inhabitants of Newcastle county, Delaware, praying the restoration of the deposites to the United States Bank.

Mr. MILLIGAN said, that when the subject to which the petition referred should be brought before the House by the Committee of Ways and Means, he should feel it his duty to throw aside the character of listener, which he had hitherto sustained, and advocate the views of his constituents before this house. At present, it was his purpose to say that the petition was signed by one thousand six hundred persons, embracing a majority of the voters of the county, and to bear testimony to their respectability, intelligence, industry, and enterprise. They were influenced in their views by no party considerations, and they were men of different occupations, and of every grade of wealth. Mr. M. proceeded, at some length, to explain and support the views of the memorialists, after which, on his motion, the memorial was read, referred, and ordered to be printed.

Mr. MILLIGAN also presented the proceedings of the meeting at which the above memorial was adopted, which was also read, and ordered to be printed.

Mr. McKIM rose and said:

I am requested to present two memorials signed by 3624 citizens of Baltimore, stating that they approve of the course of the Administration in relation to the Bank of the United States, and praying that the charter of said bank may not be renewed.

I shall not, Mr. Speaker, trespass on the time of the House, by detailing the various trades and professions of the signers to this memorial; it is sufficient for my purpose to say, that they are *American freemen*, and as such, entitled to be heard, and to have equal weight and consideration in proportion to their numbers, as to any memorial yet presented to this House.

On motion of Mr. McKIM, the memorial was read and ordered to be printed, and referred to the Committee of Ways and Means.

Mr. GORDON presented the resolutions of the Legislature of Virginia, requesting the Representatives and instructing the Senators from that State to exert their efforts to procure the restoration of the deposites, &c. The Legislature considered this as a great question, and regarded the action of the President on the subject as violative of the Constitution. The people of Virginia heretofore yielded to no portion of the people of this nation in admiration and respect for our Chief Magistrate. But the Legislature of Virginia, standing on constitutional grounds, now opposed his assumptions of power, and the voice of the Legislature was, he believed, reëchoed by almost all the people of the State. They characterize the measures of the President, as a dangerous and alarming assumption of power, and they say that they have seen an intention or a tendency to concentrate all power in the hands of the Executive. They witness the exercise of legislative functions by the Executive, and they see the rights of this House trampled under foot.

The Executive Magistrate was authorized by the charter of the bank, in case of a violation of the charter, to issue a *scire facias* and try the question; but, prejudging the question, he has himself decided it, instead of the judge. The laws direct that the Secretary of the Treasury, if he have good cause, shall remove the deposites. The President abused his power of appointment, to thrust from office a Secretary who had decided that he had no sufficient reason for removing the deposites, and put in one whose opinions were known to coincide with his own. The President had done that indirectly which he had no power to do directly. The President had no right to go into the treasury except under the orders of Congress—he had no right to interfere directly in any way with the treasury. The Legislature admitted, and he himself admitted, the right of removal from office; but to make use of the power of removal to effect an illegal act was, in their and his opinion, a dangerous assumption of power. A power to put in and out forty thousand officers, would become, if wielded for political effect by the President, utterly inconsistent with the political freedom of the country. This golden ladder of preferment, with forty thousand rounds, held out to every climber-up the prospect of reaching to the top. Human virtue could not withstand the temptations which power and patronage presented to their followers. He should feel himself degraded to stand here as a representative of the people, if such a construction of the Constitution should prevail as would give the President the power to put out and in, without just cause, almost every functionary of the Government. He did not believe that it was the intention of the President to grasp the liberties of the country; he believed he viewed the Bank of the United States as a monster standing in the way of public liberty. But the State of Virginia, though likewise opposed to a national bank, viewed the question as one concerning the powers of the different branches of the Government. All legislative power was vested in Congress. The veto power of the President was not a legislative power, but merely a negative power. The Constitution directs that no money shall be drawn from the treasury without an appropriation by law.

It had been assumed that, in the interval between the collection and the disbursement of the revenue the President might do what he pleased with it. But Mr. G. contended that the President had nothing to do with the public money excepting as appropriated by law. The assumption violated the groundworks of free government, and he expressed his surprise and regret that the representatives of the people did not condemn the course of the Executive *instanter*. He had no doubt, however, that the members of this body acted from honest convictions of their duty.

Mr. G. then alluded to the President's proclamation, the principles and objects of which he condemned. That was the first measure as to which the people of Virginia differed from the President. Sixty days before the meeting of Congress, after various transmutations in the Cabinet, a blow was struck which carried alarm through the whole community. The deposites were removed. The measure he deemed unnecessary, as the bank had been

killed by the veto; and as the time of the President's term of office was longer than the remaining term of the charter, there was no possibility that the bank would obtain a renewal of its charter. It did not require memorials from Philadelphia, or elsewhere, to tell us that the measure was productive of distress and embarrassment. Its necessary result was general distrust and despondency.

Mr. G. considered the power of removal as a legal, not a constitutional power; and while he was a Representative of the people, he meant to watch over its exercise. The only way to preserve liberty was to diffuse power. Where it was concentrated, it became corrupt.

Virginia stood in opposition to the power assumed by Congress to charter any bank; her doctrines, as to the rights of the States, were well known, and by them he was determined to stand or fall.

The resolutions were then read, after which,

Mr. PATTON rose and called for the reading of the following letter, which was sent by the Governor of Virginia, with the resolutions, to the Representatives in Congress from Virginia:

VIRGINIA.

Executive Department,
February 13, 1834.

Sir: In compliance with the request of the General Assembly of the Commonwealth, it gives me great pleasure to transmit to you the accompanying resolutions, adopted by that body, disapproving of the recent act of the President, in withdrawing and withholding the public deposites from the bank where they had been placed by law.

This dangerous and alarming assumption of power has already inflicted deep and lasting injury upon the citizens of this Commonwealth, which your efforts and exertions in the Congress of the United States, it is hoped, will aid in alleviating as far as practicable, and restraining the disposition which the President has manifested to extend his official authority beyond its just and proper limits, which he has so clearly manifested in his recent interference with the Treasury Department of the Federal Government.

I am, sir, with respectful consideration, your obedient servant,
JOHN FLOYD.

Mr. P. rose to perform the unpleasant and ungracious task of showing that the Governor of Virginia, in thus sending his missive to the representatives of that State in Congress, had manifested a disposition to extend his authority beyond its proper and defined limits. And he desired to know by what right the Executive was authorized to do more than to transmit the resolutions. But when he did thus denounce the acts of the President in withdrawing the deposites, as a dangerous and alarming assumption of power, which he felt pleasure in doing, he ought to have given a better and more accurate description than he had chosen to do, of the state of public opinion, and have added, that Virginia had not deserted the opinions which she had always entertained in opposition to the bank—that Virginia still held to the opinions which she promulgated in 1798, and which she reiterated in 1811, that the power to establish such an institution by Congress, was a dangerous violation of the Constitution, and a dangerous encroachment upon the sovereignty of each of the United States. The Governor had been pleased, also, to express his hopes that the efforts of the representatives of Virginia here would be used in restraining the disposition manifested by the President, in extending his judicial authority. But, whilst he would acknowledge with gratitude any opinions with which he might be favored, to instruct him, as to the path he should pursue, and give such instruction the consideration it would merit, he could not recognise the Governor's right to do so, under the official garb of his authority, addressed by letters missive, more in the style of a great potentate, to an ambassador selected by him to do his bidding, than in anything else. No person had more loudly joined in the universal burst of indignation with which the President's proclamation had been received in Virginia, than the present Governor of Virginia. And he had upon all occasions joined in denouncing the President for having assumed what he considered to be an authority which did not belong to him; and should, or ought, the representatives, the free representatives of Virginia, submit with complacency to him, in what was as great an assumption, and look on, or listen with complacency to the anathemas he dealt forth at his pleasure against the President? He felt that it became them to treat the executive authority, at all times, with becoming respect, and when the Governor proceeded in this style, he was reminded of the anecdote told of the honest Dutchman, Henry Snyder, who, passing judgment upon himself, was forced to acknowledge, that in taking too much toll—but which he gave to the poor—"he might go along vid the sheep, but it was a *tammed tight squerze.*" There was but little difference between this assumption by the Governor, and that by the President. He would regret his missive, the President's proclamation, and the manifesto read by the President to his Cabinet, as of one and the same class, *par nobile fratrum*, and all as being efflorescence from the soil of Executive pruriency.

In noticing the resolutions of the Legislature, he would do so with all the respect to which they were entitled. His own opinions on the subject-matter were well known to be at variance with them; he had given the subject every consideration, and he saw no reason to change the opinion he had entertained. Although he might best consult his own interest by doing so, and joining in the cry that was endeavored to be raised of tyranny and despotism, he would not until he was directed so to do by that authority which only he could recognise—that of the people whom he represented. He would not float into the stream, which must finally lead to the gulf of despotic consolidation, into which the country was rapidly falling. He remembered well, and the time was not long gone by, when Virginia stood alone in resisting the encroachments of the Federal Government. The doctrine, however, spread. The Bank of the United States was one of the first-born that sprung from these encroachments. He therefore rejoiced that, as it was the most powerful, it was then reeling and tottering under the same blow which had nearly destroyed the two others, which had a similar origin—internal improvement and the tariff. He could not wish to mitigate its fate, and hoped that those who contended so successfully in arresting the progress of consolidation, would not be led away under the influence of excitement, and thus abandon their principles. Mr. P. referred to the opinions expressed by Mr. Madison, in his various letters under the signature of Publius, showing the dangers of concentrating power, and argued at length to prove, that if the preamble to the resolutions was adopted, as there was in it what he contended was an unfounded assumption of power, the natural conclusion must be that it must result in erecting a principle which is alike unsound. In commenting upon the resolutions adopted by the Legislature of his State, he was compelled to deny that the framers of the Constitution deemed the act of the President in removing from office to be a dangerous or alarming usurpation. He maintained that the power of removal was more properly an executive than a legislative power.

Mr. P. said that no one contended that the President had the right to use capriciously the power of removal and appointment. Such a right would set up all the offices of the country to be scrambled for, and establish the detestable principle that the spoils of the vanquished belong to the victors. He would oppose this principle by whomsoever it might be advanced. Mr. P. here read a passage from the speech of Mr. Calhoun, stating that the power of removal could be constitutionally exercised, and viewing its exercise, in the present case, as an abuse, and not as an assumption of power. This gentleman rested his opposition to the measure on the supposed impropriety of the motives of the President in exercising the power. If he could believe that the President's motives were corrupt, he would go as far as any one in condemning them, and he would be willing that any inquiry should be instituted into the facts.

But the question did not rest upon reason or argument. There was the highest authority for the right of the President to exercise the power. It rested on a legislative act, passed in 1789, nine days after the organization of the department, establishing the salaries of the Executive Departments. But the question was put forever at rest by the fact that the act creating the Treasury Department imposed upon the Secretary of the Treasury to report to Congress plans for the improvement of the revenue, &c., and that Congress is not bound to act upon those plans, but may lay them aside. He censured Mr. Duane, not for refusing to resign, but for giving a pledge to resign. He maintained that the President had acted honestly and faithfully in this matter, and that he had the constitutional right to remove Mr. Duane, and that he would have been recreant to his trust, if he had not removed him.

If the correctness of the President's motives were questioned, let them be inquired into and ascertained.

But it was said that the House of Representatives had declared that the deposites were safe in the Bank of the United States. To this he answered that the opinion was forced from Congress by the application of the gag, without consideration or the examination of evidence. There was nothing in the vote of Congress, or that resolution, which ought, in the least degree, to have influenced the action of the President on this subject. But it was said that the House of Representatives had the exclusive control of the treasury. There was not a clause in the Constitution which gave countenance to this assertion. The bills were to originate in the House of Representatives. This had no reference to the present question. All laws respecting the keeping of the deposites belong to the legislative department, in the constitutional use of the term, and are not the peculiar province of the House of Representatives. But General Jackson had not seized the purse; he could not touch even a dollar of his own salary without the forms of law. It was said that he could turn out the officers, and put in those creatures who would sign such warrants as were presented to them. But it was as vain to talk about that as to say that the legislative department might take the whole surplus revenue and distribute it among ourselves, as extra compensation. We had the power to do it; but should that prevent us from exercising our just and proper powers? It was idle to argue against the existence of powers from their possibility of being abused. It was the part of wisdom to restrain the powers of Government within just limits, and, by proper checks, to prevent those limits from being transcended. If gentlemen think that this is an arbitrary assumption of power by the President, he submitted that they ought to proceed to inquire into the facts. Let us not act as accusers and judges. If the charges were true, the President ought to be impeached; and if they were true, he ought to be convicted. According to his present impression, he could not see the distinction between this question and that of rechartering the bank. Unless he could be convinced that the restoration of the deposites would relieve the community, he should vote against their restoration.

He could not agree with the Legislature that the safety of the public treasure was the only reason for which the deposites could be removed—on the contrary, he did not think it a leading consideration. If that were intended by the charter it would have been so stated. Why should the charter require the Secretary of the Treasury to give "*reasons*," when they contemplated but one reason? The charter also required that the notes of the bank should be received in payment of the revenue; and if, in giving this power to remove the deposites, their safety was alone considered, would not some provision have been made for discrediting their notes at the treasury, at the same time that the deposites were removed? It was not his design to advert at present to many other points which had been brought into discussion, but which were not presented by the resolutions of the Legislature. He, however, resisted the idea that the United States Bank was the treasury, and contended that the treasury was the public money, wherever it was kept. If the bank had violated its charter, and engaged in party contests, the Secretary had the right to remove the deposites. One of the charges against the bank had been attempted to be met by ridicule. But the charge was too serious to be got over in that way. He then went into a detail of the printing expenses of the bank, during the late contest, for the presidency, at the very moment when the main ques-

tion between the two parties was bank or no bank. He read an extract from a report made to this House, two years ago, which was thought to be so excellent an argument in favor of the recharter of the bank, that a large number of copies were distributed by the bank. In this passage, the writer laid down, in broad terms, the very principles on which the Secretary of the Treasury claimed the right to remove the deposites. He also referred to the opinions of Mr. Sergeant and Mr. Mc Lane, as authority for the measure. The argument then was, that the Legislature had no right to investigate the concerns of the bank, or in any way to interfere with it. In relation to the selection of the places of depositing the public money, he had only to say that, before the establishment of the bank, the Secretary of the Treasury exercised the exclusive control of this subject. The Secretaries of the Treasury had exercised the power, without dispute, of transferring the public money from one bank to another, and choosing what banks they pleased as its depository.

In conclusion of the remarks, of which the above is a very slight sketch, Mr. P. strongly expressed the opinion that this was a contest between the Constitution and the laws on one hand, and a moneyed obligarchy on the other.

Mr. GHOLSON obtained the floor, and signified a wish to speak on the subject, but as the hour was very late, he would defer his remarks for the present. On his motion,

The House then adjourned.

IN SENATE.

TUESDAY, *March* 4, 1834.

Two messages upon executive business were received from the President of the United States, by Mr. DONELSON, his Private Secretary.

The VICE PRESIDENT presented the proceedings of a large meeting of the citizens of Philadelphia in favor of the restoration of the deposites to the Bank of the United States.

Mr. McKEAN moved that the proceedings be printed, and referred to the Committee on Finance.

Mr. CLAY and Mr. McKEAN made a few remarks in support of the respectability of the character of the individuals composing the meeting; when the motion for reference and printing was agreed to.

The VICE PRESIDENT presented the proceedings of a meeting of the inhabitants of West Chester, Pennsylvania, of a similar character to those of Philadelphia; upon which the same order was taken.

The VICE PRESIDENT presented a communication from the Treasury Department, in compliance with a resolution of Mr. POINDEXTER, concerning the removal of public deposites from the Planters' Bank of Natchez.

Mr. GRUNDY moved that the reading be dispensed with, and the communication and documents be printed; which was agreed to.

The VICE PRESIDENT presented a lengthy communication from the Post Office Department, the reading of which was dispensed with, on motion of Mr. GRUNDY, at whose instance an index was ordered to be prepared of the various subjects contained in the communication, and that it be printed.

The VICE PRESIDENT presented a communication from the Treasury Department, in compliance with the resolution of Mr. WEBSTER, transmitting a statement of the monthly returns of the Bank of the United States since August, 1833.

Mr. POINDEXTER, from the select committee to whom was referred the credentials of the Hon. ASHER ROBBINS and ELISHA R. POTTER, on the subject of the contest between those two gentlemen for a seat in the Senate, made a report, which Mr. P. read at the Secretary's table, adverse to the claims of Mr. POTTER, and favorable to the right of Mr. ROBBINS, the sitting member, to his seat.

After the report had been read,

Mr. POINDEXTER said he declined making any observations upon the subject now. He merely wished to move the printing of the report and the documents. He understood that the minority of the committee wanted to submit a counter report, and he wished to give them time for that purpose, and when the report came up for consideration he would submit his views.

Mr. WRIGHT said he was bound, in justice to himself and to the honorable Senator from Virginia, [Mr. RIVES,] who, it would be recollected by the Senate, was a member of this select committee, but who had, upon a late day, resigned his seat in this body, to state a few facts in relation to the proceedings of the committee. According to his recollection, the meeting of the committee to decide the important matters referred to it was held three weeks ago on Saturday last. At that meeting the views of each member of the committee were fully expressed, and it was found that himself and his honorable friend from Virginia, entertained the same opinions, and that their opinions differed with those entertained by the other three members of the committee. He (Mr. W.) then understood that the report of the majority of the committee would be drawn up and submitted to the minority at a much earlier period; but he found no fault with the treatment which the minority of the committee had received from the majority. He knew from his own experience how little time any member of the Senate could get, from his other duties, to think and write upon subjects important as those submitted to this select committee. The honorable chairman of the committee, as much pressed with other official duties as any other member of the body, had found it necessary to retain the papers upon which the report was to be, predicated until the present time, to enable him to draw up the report of the majority of the committee; and his (Mr. W.'s) knowledge of the case enabled him to say, that no person could write a report upon this subject without the possession of the papers before the committee. Such had been the course permitted to the parties by the committee, that those papers were indispensable in drawing a report taking either side of the great question.

He, (Mr. W.,) by the resignation of the gentleman from Virginia, was now left alone as the minority of the committee, and unexpectedly the labor of drawing up a report, expressing the opinion of the minority of the committee, was devolved upon him; as before the resignation of the honorable Senator, it was understood between them, that that able and much more competent individual, should perform that labor. He (Mr. W.) should have asked the Senate to elect a member of the committee to fill the vacancy occasioned by the resignation of his honorable friend, had it not been for the fact that the case had been finally decided by the committee before that event happened; but, with his best reflection upon the subject, he had come to the conclusion that placing at this late period of their action, a new member upon the committee, would give little aid to their deliberations, while it would impose an arduous labor upon some member of the Senate.

A question had bben suggested in the committee as to the right, under the rules and practice of the Senate, of the minority of its committees to submit a report. His present object was to say, that himself and his colleague before named upon the committee, had discussed this subject, and in view of the importance of the questions involved, they had considered it to be their duty to present their views to the Senate, in case it should be considered admissible for them to do so. He was aware that he ought to have been prepared, at this time, to submit those views, but want of possession of the papers had prevented him from having made that preparation, and his expectation, entertained until one week ago on Saturday last, that the Senator from Virginia would perform the labor, furnished another reason for his want of preparation.

He would now submit to the Senate the disposition of the whole matter, declaring his disposition, according to his best ability, to discharge his duty as a member of the committee, but entertaining no feeling as to the course which the Senate should indicate. The honorable chairman had moved the printing of the report of the majority, and if the Senate should so order, and no other expression should be made, he should feel it to be his duty, as soon as he could obtain the possession of the papers from the committee, to draw up a report containing the views of the minority of the committee, so far as they came in conflict with those which had been given to the Senate by the majority. Still, if such a report would not be received by the Senate, he desired to be saved the labor of making it, and, therefore, he hoped such expression would be now made as might direct him as to his duty. For himself, he felt no anxiety whatever, but rather regretted that this responsible duty had devolved upon him; but under the circumstances, and standing alone in the minority, he felt so strongly the importance of the questions, that he should not shrink from the attempt to present his views of them, in case they would be received by the Senate, and in that event those views should be presented at the earliest day at which his other duties, and the possession of the papers, would enable him to give them.

Mr. CLAY said, that the time had arrived for proceeding to the orders of the day; but he would say, that the parliamentary propriety of allowing a counter report of a committee, no doubt, was not warranted by usage, as it had been applied in this country, until within a few years past. As regarded the practice of the Senate on this subject, he did not know what it was, but he thought it a bad one to introduce. He had no objection to receiving the report of the minority, but he wished now to move the postponemet of the subject till to-morrow, and proceed to the consideration of the special order.

Mr. KING, of Alabama, said, he was aware that, until a late period, it was not the practice to present counter reports; it grew up in the House of Representatives, and this morning there were two reports made in that body on the same subject. A few years since, the question was raised in this body. A Senator from South Carolina presented a majority report on the subject of reducing the duty on imported iron; a Senator from New Jersey presented the minority report on the permission of the Senate. The report was received for the purpose of enabling the minority fairly and fully to express their views and opinions. He hoped the view of the gentleman from Kentucky would not be carried into effect. If the report could be sent back to the committee, so that the opinions of both the majority and minority could be presented in one view, he thought it would be the preferable course.

Mr. CLAY said the gentleman from Alabama misunderstood him. He was not opposed to a minority report. He only said the practice was unparliamentary. The gentleman relied upon a single precedent, and Mr. C. would submit, whether a single precedent ought to control the Senate now and hereafter. As he understood that case, a paper was reported by a majority, and another by the minority. In this instance, he would prefer allowing a minority report, but at the same time with an expression of opinion that it should not be considered as a general rule, because he thought it a bad one. But he hoped the subject would be postponed till to-morrow, and the gentleman from New Hampshire, who had the floor, be allowed to proceed in the speech which he had begun upon the special order.

Mr. POINDEXTER thanked the gentleman from Alabama for referring to the precedent. He was quite willing that the minority should have an opportunity to make their report.

Mr. SPRAGUE was very unwilling the minority should be deprived of the opportunity of making a counter report. But he thought it could not be yielded to them as a matter of right. He would rather lay down a prospective rule, than appeal to the present. He hoped such a course would be adopted as would enable the gentleman from New York [Mr. WRIGHT] to make his report; as he believed, from his statement, that he would have had much difficulty before in doing so.

Mr. CLAYTON understood the proposition of the gentleman from Alabama was, to recommit the whole subject, which he was opposed to. He hoped every facility would be given the gentleman from New York to make his report, but he thought the rule, as a matter of practice, objectionable, as it would in every case of difference of opinion in a committee, enable a minority to obstruct and delay the action of a majority. He thought it better to print the report, and give an opportunity to the gentleman to examine it and the documents, and then submit his report.

Mr. CHAMBERS said he recollected the case alluded to by the gentleman from Alabama, and if his object was to recommit this report, he thought if the gentleman examined it more closely, he would find himself mistaken in the extent to which he supposed the precedent went, as a justification of a minority report. [Mr. C. here read an extract from the Senate Journal.] Here there was no recommitment. In the progress of the proceeding, the minority presented a paper expressive of their views, which was received; and he was willing to extend the same indulgence to the gentleman from New York.

Mr. CALHOUN said he was in the Chair on the occasion alluded to, and had a distinct recollection of it. It was submitted as a paper, and printed as a paper, not as a report.

Mr. KING replied that the minority made a report, and it purported to be the report of a minority of the committee, call it by what name you please, and it was also ordered to be printed. What distinction was there in calling it a paper, when it was a report, and was called a report? Now, he was anxious to know the grounds, not only on which the majority, but also the minority, founded their opinions; and when a subject of so much importance was presented, as one involving the right of an individual to a seat in the Senate of the United States, it was highly desirable to have the whole subject before us, so that Senators might be enabled to examine it thoroughly. He would withdraw his motion to recommit the report, and he hoped the gentleman from New York, on the part of the minority, would present his views on the subject.

Mr. WRIGHT said it was immaterial to him what disposition was made of the question. His object was to discharge his duty as a member of the committee to the best of his ability, and if it was not a part of his duty to draw up a counter report, he had no desire to do it; but if it was, he would cheerfully undertake it. But from the general expression of the gentleman from Alabama and others on the subject, he would endeavor to do his duty as early as he could get possession of the papers, and prepare the report.

Mr. GRUNDY moved that the correspondence between the Committee on the Post Office and Post Roads and the Postmaster General, be printed; which was agreed to.

Mr. GRUNDY submitted the following resolution; which was considered and adopted:

Resolved, That the Postmaster General be directed to report to the Senate the amount of money paid by the Post Office Department since the 1st of July, 1829, for services rendered and expenses incurred prior to that date; also the amount of money paid since the 1st of April, 1829, for services rendered and expenses incurred prior to that date; and also, whether any balance remains due from that department, and if any, what amounts for services rendered and expenses incurred prior to the above periods.

The Senate then proceeded to the special order of the day, being Mr. CLAY's resolution, and the report of the Committee on Finance on the

REMOVAL OF THE DEPOSITES.

When Mr. HILL resumed and concluded his speech in favor of the course pursued by the Secretary of the Treasury; when,

On motion of Mr. CHAMBERS,

The Senate proceeded, at a quarter before four, to executive business, and after spending a few minutes therein,

Adjourned.

HOUSE OF REPRESENTATIVES.
TUESDAY, *March* 4, 1834.

Mr. CAVE JOHNSON reported a bill for the relief of Nicholas C. Coleman; which was ordered to be engrossed for a third reading.

Mr. WATMOUGH, a bill to authorize the payment of a certain balance of prize money due to Henry Bell.

Mr. CAVE JOHNSON, bills to authorize the sale of certain land reservations in Ohio, and in Arkansas.

Also, bills for the relief of Pierre Lafitte and Jean Baptiste Granger.

Mr. ADAMS, of New York, a bill for the relief of Josiah H. Brown and John Conkin.

Mr. SCHLEY, a bill for the relief of Isaac Janvier.

Mr. BLAIR, a bill to appropriate certain lands within the State of Alabama for the purpose of improving the Tennessee and Coosa rivers, and connecting their waters by canal or railroad.

Mr. POPE, a bill in relation to the Louisville and Portland canal; all which were read twice and committed.

Mr. R. M. JOHNSON reported the bill making amendments to the bill in relation to the commissariat; which was referred to the Committee of the Whole on the state of the Union.

Mr. CARR, from the Committee on Private Land Claims, asked to be discharged from the further consideration of the petition of L. H. Lorriens, attorney in fact for P. Lorriens, widow of Peter Juzon, deceased; which was ordered to be laid on the table.

BANK OF THE UNITED STATES.

Mr. POLK presented, from the Committee of Ways and Means, a report and resolutions founded upon the letter of the Secretary of the Treasury in relation to the deposites, and the sundry memorials referred to them. He said he was instructed by the committee to move that the further consideration of the report should be postponed until Wednesday in next week; and, in the mean time, that the report and accompanying documents be printed.

Mr. CLAY called for the reading of the report, &c.

Mr. McDUFFIE suggested that the reading of the resolutions might be sufficient.

Mr. CLAY desired to have the whole read.

The SPEAKER remarked that it was the right of every member to call for the reading. It was so settled repeatedly.

Mr. McDUFFIE moved to dispense with the reading.

The SPEAKER decided that such a motion was not in order. According to the *lex parliamentaria,* it was settled that every member had the right to have papers read on their first presentation, that he might not be forced to vote upon what he did not understand.

Mr. BINNEY stated he had a report to present from the minority of the committee, and he wished to know the proper time for presenting their views.

The SPEAKER informed him, after this question was disposed of.

Mr. HARDIN inquired if it was not competent for the majority of the House to dispense with the reading. He suggested to the member from Alabama, that it was unnecessary to have their time occupied, as the report, &c., were to be printed.

The SPEAKER replied in the negative, for the reason he had previously given.

Mr. CLAY said he wished the report to be read, as it was his intention to move for the printing of an extra number of copies.

Mr. PATTON remarked, that there would not be any objection to having an extra number printed.

The report having been partly read—

Mr. CLAY said he would yield to the wish of the House, not to proceed with it, upon the understanding that there would not be any objections to the printing of 10,000 copies of the report and documents.

The resolutions appended to the report were then read next.

The question then being on postponing the further consideration of the report until Wednesday week.

Mr. McDUFFIE requested that the motion would be withdrawn by the honorable member from Tennessee, to enable him to submit an amendment.

Mr. POLK said, that he moved the postponement of the question to the day mentioned, in order that the House, having the report printed, could then take it up, and dispose of it as they thought proper. He could not now withdraw his motion, without incurring the hazard of a premature and unnecessary discussion.

The motion of Mr. P., to postpone the further consideration, was then agreed to.

Mr. BINNEY presented a report on behalf of the minority of the Committee of Ways and Means, and he moved that the reading of the report should be dispensed with, and that it should take the same direction as the other report: agreed to.

Mr. CLAY then moved, that 10,000 copies of the two reports should be printed.

Mr. HAWES moved 50,000; which was rejected.

Mr. REED moved 20,000: rejected.

Fifteen thousand copies was then suggested, and was finally agreed to, after a few remarks from Mr. EWING, in opposition.

Mr. WILDE moved to suspend the rule, to enable him to submit an amendment, which he intended to move when the subject should come up.

The House refused: ayes 108, noes 91.

Mr. BINNEY obtained leave to submit the following resolution:

Resolved, That the Committee on the Judiciary be instructed to inquire into the expediency of providing by law for the registry of assignments or transfer of copy-rights:

Mr. GAMBLE submitted the following:

Resolved, That the Committee on the Judiciary be instructed to inquire into the expediency of building a court-house in the town of Milledgeville, in the State of Georgia.

Mr. VINTON, from the Committee on the Patent Laws, reported a bill for the relief of Francis P. Oyder: read twice, and committed.

The SPEAKER presented a report from the War Department, in answer to a resolution of the 18th ultimo, on the subject of Indian Affairs: laid on the table, and ordered to be printed.

The SPEAKER presented a communication from the Commissioner of the Land Office, in answer to a resolution of the House of the 18th ult.: laid on the table, and ordered to be printed.

REVOLUTIONARY CLAIMS.

The House resumed the consideration of the bill reported from the Committee on Revolutionary Claims, providing for the settlement of certain revolutionary claims by the Secretary of the Treasury.

Mr. VANDERPOEL resumed and concluded his remarks, in opposition to the bill.

Mr. MUHLENBERG supported the bill at some length, vindicating it from the objections urged by Messrs. PIERCE, of New Hampshire, and VANDERPOEL.

Mr. BROWN rose, and intimated an intention to speak upon the subject, but as the usual hour of adjournment had arrived, he moved that the House adjourn. The motion prevailed, and

The House adjourned.

IN SENATE.
WEDNESDAY, *March* 5, 1834.

Mr. PRESTON presented the credentials of the Hon. BENJAMIN WATKINS LEIGH, elected a Senator from Virginia, to supply the vacancy occasioned by the resignation of the Hon. WILLIAM C. RIVES; which being read,

Mr. LEIGH appeared, was qualified, and took his seat.

Mr. TIPTON, from the select committee with regard to the admission of the Territories of Michigan and Arkansas into the Union, asked that certain documents of the Legislative Council of Michigan might be printed; which was agreed to.

Mr. TOMLINSON presented the memorial of the directors of all the banks in Norwich, Connecticut, in favor of restoring the deposites to the Bank of the United States, together with the proceedings of a town meeting in the same place; which, after some remarks by Mr. TOMLINSON, were read, referred to the Committee on Finance, and ordered to be printed.

Mr. HILL presented a memorial signed by three hundred and fifty-seven citizens of Portsmouth, New Hampshire, praying that a sea wall may be erected in that harbor. Referred to the Committee on Commerce.

Mr. FRELINGHUYSEN presented the memorial of inhabitants of Bloomfield, New Jersey, together with one from Orange township, Essex county, New Jersey, in favor of the restoration of

the deposites to the Bank of the United States; which, after some remarks by Mr. F., were read, referred to the Committee on Finance, and ordered to be printed.

Mr. McKEAN presented the memorial of inhabitants of the county of Chester, Pennsylvania, asking the restoration of the deposites to the Bank of the United States; which was read, referred to the Committee on Finance, and ordered to be printed.

Mr. MOORE, from the Committee on Revolutionary Claims, reported a bill for the relief of the heirs and legal representatives of General Lord Stirling; which was read, and, on his motion, the report and accompanying documents were ordered to be printed.

Mr. MANGUM presented the memorial of inhabitants of Fayetteville, North Carolina, praying a restoration of the deposites to the Bank of the United States; which was read, referred to the Committee on Finance, and ordered to be printed.

Mr. HENDRICKS presented the memorial of the General Assembly of Indiana, relative to appropriations for the Cumberland Road; which was referred to the Committee on the Post Office and Post Roads.

Mr. POINDEXTER, from the Committee on Public Lands, reported the following bills:

A bill for the relief of James P. Hainesworth;

A bill for the relief of E. Homer;

A bill for the relief of William Burrows;

A bill for the relief of Hishe Homa, otherwise called Captain Red Pepper;

Which bills were severally read, and committed.

Mr. POINDEXTER, from the same committee, asked to be discharged from the further consideration of the memorial of the Legislature of Alabama, and the petition of inhabitants of Mobile, in that State, relative to the prices of public lands and preëmption rights, and that the memorials be laid upon the table; which was agreed to.

In pursuance of notice, Mr. KING, of Alabama, asked and obtained leave to introduce a bill, authorizing the Secretary of the Treasury to make additional compensation to the register and receiver of the land office established at Tallahassee, Florida; which was read, and referred to the Committee on Public Lands.

Petitions of a private nature were presented by Messrs. TIPTON, HILL, MANGUM, and HENDRICKS, which were severally referred to the appropriate committees.

On motion of Mr. GRUNDY, the report of the Postmaster General made yesterday, was referred to the Committee on the Post Office and Post Roads.

Mr. EWING moved to take up the resolution offered by Mr. MANGUM, in relation to the printing of the Senate; which being agreed to—

Mr. MANGUM offered the following as a substitute for the original resolution, observing that its object was merely to place the printer of the Senate upon a footing with the printers of the House.

Resolved, That the resolution adopted on the 14th of May, eighteen hundred and thirty, directing the Secretary of the Senate to contract with the printer of the House of Representatives for copies of the documents printed by the order of the House, be, and the same is hereby, repealed, and that the orders of the Senate for printing be executed without regard to the printing of the House.

Mr. FORSYTH asked that the letter written by the Secretary of the Senate to the printers of the House in relation to the printing authorized under that rule, might be read, together with their answers; which being done, Mr. F. said, that under the rule proposed to be repealed, the printers of the House have refused to contract to furnish extra documents. Of course the printer of the Senate must furnish them. He did not know why the change was sought for. It was to him rather a singular refusal, and on a strange ground of a breach of contract between the Senate and the printer of the Senate. He rose now, however, to inquire of the Secretary of the Senate what the difference would be, in the expense of the printing, by changing the rule. It was not of much importance, but the printing of the Senate was already sufficiently heavy, and he was not disposed to increase it.

Mr. CHAMBERS said that he had made inquiry on the subject, and he thought the amendment was proper. He understood that, according to the rules of each House, the positions of the two printers were not parallel, or their duties the same. If the rules were the same, the amendment would not be necessary.

Some further remarks were made by Mr. FORSYTH and Mr. PRESTON, when Mr. FORSYTH moved to lay the whole subject on the table till to-morrow, and asked the yeas and nays on the motion; which, being ordered, are as follows, to wit:

YEAS—Messrs. Benton, Black, Brown, Forsyth, Grundy, Hendricks, Hill, King of Alabama, King of Georgia, Knight, Linn, McKean, Morris, Prentiss, Robinson, Shepley, Tallmadge, Tipton, Tomlinson, Waggaman, White, Wilkins, and Wright—23.

NAYS—Messrs. Bell, Bibb, Calhoun, Chambers, Clay, Clayton, Ewing, Frelinghuysen, Leigh, Mangum, Moore, Naudain, Poindexter, Porter, Preston, Robbins, Silsbee, Smith, Sprague, and Swift—20.

On motion of Mr. POINDEXTER, all the special orders were postponed, in order to relieve the table of the mass of business which had accumulated upon it, and the Senate proceeded to the consideration of the

ORDERS OF THE DAY.

The communication from the War Department, transmitting the report of the Third Auditor upon the accounts of William Tharp was taken up, and, on motion of Mr. POINDEXTER, was laid upon the table, and ordered to be printed.

PUBLIC LANDS.

The resolutions offered by Mr. POINDEXTER on Monday last, requiring the Committee on Public Lands to make certain inquiries with regard to the land offices, were taken up for consideration:

1. *Resolved*, That the Committee on the Public Lands be instructed to inquire into the circumstances attending the recent sales of the public lands in the States of Mississippi and Alabama, and whether the proclamations of the President of the United States, causing the public lands in the districts of country acquired from the Choctaw tribe of Indians, in Alabama, to be offered at public sale, were issued and promulgated a reasonable length of time prior to the day on which said sales were directed to be commenced in each of said districts, to give proper notice to the people of the United States of the days appointed for said sales.

2. *Resolved*, That the same committee inquire whether any fraudulent practices, to the injury of the public interest, took place at said sales, by reason of combination of companies or individuals interdicting, or unfavorable to a fair competition between bidders for the public lands, offered for sale in the said district; and, if so, whether the officers superintending said sales had knowledge of, or participated in such fraudulent practices or combinations.

3. *Resolved*, That the said committee be instructed to inquire whether the registers of the land offices and the receivers of the public moneys at any of the land offices of the United States, or either of them, have, in violation of law, and of their official duties, demanded or accepted a bonus or premium from any purchaser or purchasers of the public lands at public or private sale, for the benefit of such officer or officers, as a condition on which such purchaser or purchasers should be allowed to enter or purchase any tract or tracts of land offered for sale by the United States; and, also, whether any register or receiver as aforesaid, has been guilty of fraud or partiality in the sales of the public lands by adopting rules and regulations in their respective offices inconsistent with the laws of the United States.

4. *Resolved*, That the said committee inquire whether the public lands at any land office in the State of Mississippi have been sold otherwise than for cash; and whether any register or receiver in said State has, at any time, taken in payment the promissory note of any purchaser or purchasers, bearing an interest to accrue to the benefit of such register or receiver.

5. *Resolved*, That in prosecution of said inquiries the committee have power to send for persons and papers, and to examine witnesses before them on oath, touching the matters aforesaid.

Mr. MORRIS said that these resolutions embraced very extensive grounds, and invested the committee with very extensive powers, and it was necessary to know and understand the grounds on which they intended to proceed. He thought that in order properly to proceed in the way which was indicated by the resolutions, some gentleman ought to have presented a memorial, or some specific subject of complaint. The power was given to send for persons and papers to all parts of the United States. He was not opposed to the investigation, but he wished to place it on the true grounds, so as to preserve individual rights and the public good. We had been told that abuses existed. It might be so; and if it were, and the guilty persons could be discovered, he would be in favor of dismissing them instantly. He rose now to offer the following additional resolution as an amendment to those under consideration:

Resolved, That the committee before they proceed to inquire into the conduct of any register or receiver of the public moneys at any land office in the United States, make out a specification of charges and facts which the committee believe to be true, and into which they shall be of opinion an inquiry ought to be made; that they transmit a copy of the same to such register or receiver, who shall have the privilege to produce before the committee such testimony in his favor as he shall think proper.

Mr. POINDEXTER said the resolution was entirely unnecessary, as the committee would pursue the course they would think right. The committee knew nothing, and were presumed to know nothing, of the facts, but they would take proper steps to make the investigation; and if it became necessary to give notice, that course would be pursued. He thought the resolution improper and unnecessary.

Mr. CLAYTON thought it a bad precedent for future cases. It was calling on the committee to make out the specifications of charges without having any facts before them.

Mr. MORRIS said the resolutions of the gentleman from Mississippi were altogether accusatory in their character. What, then, was the real character of them? Were they to correct abuses? Not at all. What was to be the result of the inquiry? He rose for the purpose of protecting, to the extent of his ability, the rights of the free citizens of the country. Implications were contained in the resolution against the character of the public officers in their private reputations, and as long as he had the honor of a seat here, he would raise his voice to protect them against such an inquisitorial power. Did the committee ask this power without any evidence of the offence existing? Were they to draw before them just such persons as should be accused, and shut out from them all knowledge of their accusers, upon charges which, if explained, would perhaps vanish as air? He could not believe it. He asked the gentleman from Mississippi for a precedent for such a power being conferred without some previous call for it. He knew of none. He wished to impose no burden on the committee, but he felt it a duty to himself and the people he represented that when called on to perform a trust he would do it. It was the right of every man accused to be heard. This proceeding might be right, but it was not according to his ideas of what was due to every American freeman.

Mr. SHEPLEY desired, if it was in order, that the question might be taken on each resolution separately. He was disposed to afford a full and fair examination into the conduct of all the officers of Government, and the sale and disposition of the public lands. He was not desirous of excluding any information relating to the subject. He was disposed to vote for the first and second resolutions, but not for the third and fifth. They were imperative, *instructing*, not *authorizing*, the committee to inquire into the conduct of a whole class of public officers in any branch of that service, which he did not think was fair. There might be abuses, but they should be designated, that we may know on whom the imputation is to rest. But in the present shape of the resolutions, it is on all, without exception. The authority to send

for persons and papers was very proper, but it should not be given without the Senate knowing what was necessary. It was great oppression to send for, and compel the attendance of, individuals here, without first becoming acquainted with the necessity for it.

Mr. POINDEXTER said, the other day this investigation was invited by the gentleman from Tennessee, [Mr. GRUNDY,] and other gentlemen, and now the shoe pinched, they objected. A general investigation was proposed to protect purchasers of public lands from being swindled by the officers. There was no power given the committee, except what was indispensably necessary.

Mr. GRUNDY said he made no objection to the inquiry whatever, but he desired to do justice. And that every individual officer, be he whom he may, if he had not consulted the public interest, should be known and published. But he was desirous, at the same time, of securing justice to all. Without pretending to know, he thought it was right, according to the spirit and genius of our institutions, that the men who were implicated should have an opportunity of cross-examining the witnesses who should be brought to testify against them. He would go further: he would give them an opportunity to give exculpatory evidence. He moved to add, as an amendment to the end of the first resolution, "and the causes why the usual public notice was not given."

After some remarks between Mr. POINDEXTER, Mr. CLAYTON, and Mr. GRUNDY, Mr. POINDEXTER accepted the amendment as a modification.

After which, some further remarks were made by Mr. FRELINGHUYSEN, Mr. KING, of Alabama, Mr. PORTER, Mr. PRESTON, and Mr. CLAY.

The first resolution was then agreed to unanimously.

The second resolution was agreed to, 39 to 1—Mr. SHEPLEY dissenting.

The fourth resolution was then agreed to unanimously.

Mr. MORRIS then withdrew his amendment.

Mr. SHEPLEY offered the following amendment to the fifth resolution.

Strike out all after the first line, and insert "have power to cause testimony to be taken on 'oath, where any misconduct is supposed to have 'taken place, touching the matters aforesaid; and 'in case any person is implicated, such person be 'notified and be entitled to introduce testimony in 'exculpation of himself, and to cross-examine all 'witnesses introduced against him."

Mr. POINDEXTER then modified the fifth resolution, by inserting after the word "papers," the words, "and also to take depositions."

Some further remarks were then made by Messrs. SMITH, BELL, SPRAGUE, WRIGHT, and SHEPLEY.

The question on Mr. SHEPLEY'S amendment was determined as follows:

YEAS—Messrs. Brown, Forsyth, Grundy, Hill, King of Alabama, King of Georgia, Linn, Morris, Shepley, Tallmadge, Tipton, White, Wright—13.

NAYS—Messrs. Bell, Bibb, Black, Calhoun, Chambers, Clay, Clayton, Ewing, Frelinghuysen, Hendricks, Knight, Leigh, Moore, Naudain, Poindexter, Porter, Prentiss, Preston, Robbins, Smith, Sprague, Swift, Silsbee, Tomlinson, Waggaman, Webster—27.

So the amendment was lost.

The question was then taken on adopting the resolution, and it was adopted.

On motion of Mr. BELL,

The Senate adjourned.

HOUSE OF REPRESENTATIVES.

WEDNESDAY, March 5, 1834.

The Hon. LEVI LINCOLN, elected a Representative in Congress from Massachusetts, in the place of the Hon. JOHN DAVIS, resigned, appeared, was qualified, and took his seat.

Mr. EWING moved to suspend the rule, in order to proceed in the call of the States for petitions; but withdrew it.

Mr. VANCE renewed the motion, and called for the yeas and nays upon it; which were ordered.

Mr. GORHAM asked whether the Virginia res-

olutions would not have the preference in case the motion prevailed?

The CHAIR replied, Yes, unless those resolutions were postponed.

Mr. J. Q. ADAMS moved to amend the motion to suspend, by adding the words "for the purpose of receiving petitions and memorials, with the exception of the Virginia resolutions."

After some conversation on the question of order, the CHAIR suggested that the member from Virginia, who was entitled to the floor, might obviate the difficulty by yielding the floor till Monday.

Mr. GHOLSON said he was not disposed to speak to an unwilling audience, and if the House wished to pass over the Virginia resolutions for the present, he would yield the floor for that purpose, with the understanding that he should proceed in his remarks when the call of the States was concluded.

Mr. WAYNE made some remarks in reference to the impropriety of allowing so wide a range of discussion upon the presentation of petitions, memorials, &c.

The SPEAKER replied, that the Chair had endeavored to restrict the discussions within the rule, but that he had been repeatedly overruled by the House. He did not consider that the Chair was responsible for the course which the House had determined to take.

The question being taken upon the motion to suspend the rule, it was determined in the affirmative: yeas 155, noes 54.

Mr. GHOLSON then waived his right to the floor till Monday next.

Petitions and memorials were accordingly presented by Messrs. MASON, CHINN, WILSON, MERCER, and LOYALL, of Virginia;

Messrs. CONNOR, W. B. SHEPARD, and DEBERRY, of North Carolina;

Messrs. WAYNE, FOSTER, CLAYTON, and WILDE, of Georgia;

Messrs. CHILTON, BEATTY, LYON, HARDIN, JOHNSON, POPE, DAVIS, and TOMPKINS, of Kentucky;

Messrs. STANDIFER and LEA, of Tennessee;

Messrs. LYTLE, BELL, VANCE, LEAVITT, SLOANE, MITCHELL, McLENE, VINTON, CRANE, CORWIN, WHITTLESEY, and ALLEN, of Ohio;

Mr. WHITE, of Louisiana;

Messrs. LANE, McCARTY, EWING, CARR, HANNEGAN, and KINNARD, of Indiana;

Mr. CAGE, of Mississippi;

Messrs. DUNCAN, CASEY, and SLADE, of Illinois.

[Mr. CASEY presented the petition of sundry citizens of the State of Illinois, praying an appropriation of land to improve the road from Chicago to Vincennes; which, on his motion, was referred to the Committee on the Public Lands.]

Messrs. CLAY, MURPHY, McKINLEY, and MARDIS, of Alabama.

[Mr. CLAY, of Alabama, presented the memorial of sundry citizens of Blount county, in that State, praying for the establishment of a post route from Village Springs to Frontier Post Office, on the route from Huntsville to Selma, via Ashville; which was referred to the Committee on the Post Office and Post Roads.

Mr. CLAY also presented the memorial of sundry citizens of Jackson county, asking relief for William Gunn, in relation to a certain tract of land therein described; which was referred to the Committee on the Public Lands.]

Messrs. ASHLEY and BULL, of Missouri;

Mr. LYON, of Michigan;

Mr. SEVIER, of Arkansas;

Mr. WHITE, of Florida;

Messrs. ADAMS and REED, of Massachusetts;

Messrs. BURGES and PEARCE, of Rhode Island;

Mr. ELLSWORTH, of Connecticut;

Messrs. MARTINDALE, DAY, WARDWELL, McEVAN, BEARDSLEY, SELDEN, GILLET, HAZELTINE, CAMBRELENG, CRAMER, and HALSEY, of New York.

Mr. FOSTER, of Georgia, presented certain resolutions of that State, on the subject of the public lands.

Mr. LYON presented a memorial from inhabitants of Salem, Kentucky;

Mr. R. M. JOHNSON, from Boon County, Kentucky; and

Mr. MITCHELL, from Zanesville, Ohio, in favor of, and one from Norwich, against the restoration of the deposites.

Mr. REED, from 1990 citizens of New Bedford, whom he stated to be deeply engaged in the whale fishery, and who were now suffering much embarrassment in consequence of the difficulty they experience in procuring capital to carry on their business. They attribute their embarrassment to the recent measures of the Government, which have affected the operations of the State banks generally. He called for the reading of the memorial.

It was then read, and, with the others, laid on the table, and ordered to be printed.

Mr. CARR rose to present certain proceedings, &c., and remarked that he held in his hand the proceedings of a meeting holden in the town of Madison, in the State of Indiana, on the 7th of February, 1834, in pursuance to previous notice given, for the purpose, as is alleged, of taking into consideration the embarrassed state of the country and derangement of its currency; and remarked that he had not been furnished with a copy of the proceedings adopted by the meeting, in the usual manner in which proceedings of the like kind are generally received; that the proceedings were sent to him by the gentlemen who acted as secretaries to said meeting, in a paper printed in the town of Madison, together with a letter addressed to him by the same gentlemen. Mr. C. remarked that he had not been requested, by any individual who attended the meeting, to present the proceedings to the House, nor did he know that it was the wish of those who did attend it, that he should do so; that he had not been informed as to the extent of the meeting, but that he was acquainted with the gentlemen who acted as officers to said meeting, and also with those who composed the committee whose duty it was made to draft the proceedings, and he knew them all to be highly respectable individuals. Under all the circumstances, he felt it to be his duty, with the leave of the House, to present the proceedings. Upon his motion, the memorial was read, and ordered to be printed, and the same directions given to them, as to the other memorials on this subject.

Mr. WILSON presented a memorial signed by 500 inhabitants of Green county, Virginia, praying the restoration of the deposites.

Mr. LOVALL, from sundry merchants and others, of Norfolk, for the same.

Mr. CONNOR, from inhabitants of Cabarras county, North Carolina, for the same.

Mr. DEBERRY, from inhabitants of Fayetteville, North Carolina, for the same; which were ordered to be printed, and laid on the table.

Mr. WAYNE, a memorial from inhabitants of Savannah, praying an appropriation to be made for the erection of a custom-house there; which was referred to the Committee on Commerce.

Mr. WILDE, a memorial from Augusta, signed by four hundred inhabitants of that town, praying the restoration of the deposites.

Mr. W. briefly stated, that although one of the inland towns, yet it was one of the most extensive commercial towns in the Union—its prominent and exports being 180,000 bales of cotton annually, which formed one-twelfth part of the whole of the value of the exports of the United States. The memorial was signed by the Mayor of the town, and was generally from that party styled Union men, who had been opposed to the doctrine of nullification, and many of whom were supporters of the Administration. He believed a more independent or enlightened body of men of this same number, never brought their complaints to the House; for they were men of that character, that they seldom interfered in the management of public affairs, except to discharge the ordinary duties of good citizens. He called for the reading of the memorial. It was read accordingly, and Mr. W moved to postpone its further consideration until Wednesday next.

Mr. WAYNE rose and remarked, that in all that had been said by his colleague of the respectability of the memorialists, he was altogether correct. But standing, as he did, a representative of the whole people of Georgia, and not as a representative of a particular district only; and as he viewed this memorial as only the commencement

of the presentation of others from other parts of the State, he felt it right to assume that responsibility which belonged to a representative of the whole people, and to state that he differed, in *toto*, from the sentiments expressed in the memorial; and as he learned, through the medium of the newspapers, that some of the memorials were to be sent to fill the representatives of Georgia, he must frankly state, that he could not give any aid to procure the result which they desired. He would also state, that his impression of the sentiments of the inhabitants of the State generally, from all that he was able to learn, and more particularly by letters from the community in which he resided, was, that they were decidedly in opposition to the sentiments expressed in this memorial, and that, unless he had been grossly deceived, another memorial would be sent on from that same city, which will confirm his opinion, and prove that the sentiments ought only to be regarded as the sentiments of the individuals who signed it.

The consideration of the memorial was then postponed.

Mr. POPE presented two memorials signed by upwards of a thousand inhabitants of Louisville, Kentucky, complaining of great pecuniary distress and commercial embarrassment, ascribing it to the removal of the deposites, and praying Congress to adopt such measures of relief as its wisdom might suggest. And also, to pass an act rechartering the Bank of the United States, with modifications.

Mr. P. observed that he recognised among the signatures to the memorial, the names of many active, industrious, enterprising, and intelligent merchants, mechanics, manufacturers and professional gentlemen of that city—gentlemen whose opinions were entitled to great respect and consideration, either in Congress or elsewhere, and to whose judgments he would willingly defer on any occasion, if the act did not, in his own opinion, involve the sacrifice of vital interests. He moved that the memorials be read, laid upon the table, and printed.

Mr. ALLEN, of Vermont, presented a memorial from the inhabitants of Burlington, Vermont, in favor of, and

Mr. BEARDSLEY, a memorial signed by 570 persons, residents of Jamestown, and its vicinity, Chautauque county, New York, against the restoration of the deposites, and against the recharter of the bank.

The memorial were read, referred, and laid on the table.

And the several States having been gone through, The House adjourned.

IN SENATE.

THURSDAY, *March* 6, 1834.

A message upon executive business was received from the President of the United States, by Mr. DONELSON, his Private Secretary.

Mr. SILSBEE, from the Committee on Commerce, reported a bill without amendment, from the House of Representatives, for the relief of Philip Bessom; and a bill for the relief of ―――― Deberry.

Mr. SILSBEE presented the memorial of Major George Bender, late of the army of the United States; which was referred to the Committee of Claims. Also, the petition of Benjamin G. Adams; which was referred to the Committee on Finance.

Mr. CHAMBERS presented the memorial of the Washington Canal Company, asking an appropriation to complete said canal; which was referred to the Committee on the District of Columbia.

Mr. WAGGAMAN presented the resolutions of the Legislature of Louisiana, recommending that James H. Caldwell may be permitted to import certain articles free of duty, necessary to be used in lighting the city of New Orleans with gas. The resolutions were referred to the Committee on Finance.

Mr. TOMLINSON, from the Committee on Pensions, reported a bill from the House of Representatives, without amendment, authorizing the Secretary of War to establish a pension agency at the town of Decatur, in the State of Alabama; which was read and committed.

Mr. TOMLINSON, from the Committee on Pensions, asked to be discharged from the further

consideration of the resolutions of the Legislature of Alabama, relative to the establishment of a pension agency at Tuscaloosa, Montgomery, or Decatur, in that State; which was agreed to.

Mr. TOMLINSON, from the same committee, reported, without amendment, a bill from the House of Representatives for the relief of Pierson Freeman; which was read and committed.

Mr. WRIGHT presented the memorial of 316 inhabitants of Buffalo, New York, praying the restoration of the deposites to the Bank of the United States, and asking a recharter of said bank. The memorial was read, referred to the Committee on Finance, and ordered to be printed.

Mr. KING, of Georgia, presented the petition of certain officers of the United States Army, stationed in Alabama, praying a grant of land for services rendered during the late war; which was referred to the Committee on Military Affairs.

Mr. BIBB presented the resolutions of the Legislature of Kentucky, requesting their Senators and Representatives to endeavor to procure an act of Congress granting franking privileges to the adjutant general of that State, and major and brigadier generals, when engaged in correspondence relative to the militia. The resolutions were referred to the Committee on the Post Office and Post Roads.

Mr. ROBINSON presented the memorial of inhabitants of Illinois, praying the removal of the land office from Quincy, in that State.

Mr. MOORE suggested that the petition of Benjamin S. Cope had been referred, at the last session, to the Committee on Public Lands, which committee had not acted upon it; when, on his motion, it had the same reference.

Mr. BLACK presented the petition of the chiefs and captains of the Choctaw Nation of Indians, asking Congress for the grant of a section of land, for certain purposes therein mentioned; which was referred to the Committee on Public Lands.

Mr. SHEPLEY, in pursuance of notice, asked and obtained leave to introduce a bill in relation to drawbacks on goods, wares, and merchandise; which was read, and referred to the Committee on Commerce.

The Senate then proceeded to the consideration of the

ORDERS OF THE DAY.

The following bills were read a third time, and passed;

A bill for the relief of John Bills;

A bill changing the terms of holding the terms of the Court of the Western District of Louisiana.

The bill for the relief of Archibald Small being upon its third reading, was, on motion of Mr. POINDEXTER, laid upon the table.

The memorial of citizens of Louisville, Kentucky, relative to the removal of the deposites, presented some days ago, by Mr. CLAY, was then taken up, and referred to the Committee on Finance, and ordered to be printed.

The report of the Committee on Pensions, unfavorable to the petition of John Smith, was taken up, read, and concurred in.

The report of the Committee on the Judiciary, relative to the pension fund and the Bank of the United States, was taken up; when some conversation occurred between Messrs. WRIGHT and CLAYTON, which resulted in a motion by Mr. C. that the report be laid upon the table, and made the special order of the day for Friday week.

On motion of Mr. PRENTISS, the Committee on Pensions were discharged from the further consideration of the petition of Ichabod Nye;

The report from the Committee on Indian Affairs, unfavorable to the petition of James Vernon, was read and concurred in.

Petitions of a private nature were presented by Messrs. SILSBEE, PRELINGHUYSEN, HILL, PRENTISS, SPRAGUE, BLACK, LINN, and KING, of Alabama; which were referred to the usual committees.

The Senate took up, for consideration, the bill to revive the act granting preëmption rights to settlers upon the public lands, dated 29th of May, 1830.

Mr. TIPTON offered an amendment to authorize any person inhabiting one quarter section, and cultivating another, to enter either at his discretion.

Mr. TIPTON'S amendment being under considera-

tion, Mr. EWING suggested a further amendment, by adding, "provided that he shall designate to the receiver, within six months after the passage of this act, which he elects."

Mr. TIPTON accepted this as a modification, and the amendment was then agreed to; when the bill was reported to the Senate.

Mr. KING, of Alabama, then offered an amendment, giving preëmption rights to all persons located on the public lands previous to 1829. Mr. K. observed that he thought the amendment necessary, as the consideration given to the law by the Secretary of the Treasury was, that only few of the actual settlers could receive preëmptions.

The amendment was agreed to, and the bill was then ordered to be engrossed and read a third time.

The bill to procure a marble bust of the late Chief Justice Ellsworth, to be placed in the Capitol, was taken up, and the blank filled with $600, on motion of Mr. ROBBINS, when it was ordered to be engrossed for a third reading.

The following resolutions were submitted during the morning:

By Mr. CHAMBERS:

Resolved, That the Committee on Commerce be instructed to inquire into the expediency of making an appropriation to erect a light-house on Lost Point, at the mouth of Chester river.

By Mr. WRIGHT:

Resolved, That the Committee on Pensions be instructed to inquire into the expediency of placing the name of William Pattie upon the pension roll, under the act of the 7th of June, 1832.

By Mr. WAGGAMAN:

Resolved, That the Committee on Commerce be instructed to inquire into the expediency of erecting a light-house at the mouth of the bayou St. John, on Lake Pontchartrain, in Louisiana.

By Mr. PRENTISS:

Resolved, That the Committee on Manufactures be instructed to inquire into the expediency of increasing the duty on foreign marble imported into the United States.

By Mr. PRENTISS:

Resolved, That the President of the United States be requested to communicate to the Senate a copy of the memorial addressed to him by the heir at law of the late General Ira Allen, relative to the capture, detention, and condemnation of the ship Olive Branch, and her cargo, by the British Government; and also a copy of the instructions given to the Minister of the United States at the Court of Great Britain, and of the correspondence between him and the British Government on the subject; or so much of the said instructions and correspondence as may be communicated, in the opinion of the President, consistently with the public interest.

By Mr. SPRAGUE:

Resolved, That the Committee on Finance be directed to inquire into the expediency of making certain foreign coins, particularly Spanish milled dollars, and five-franc pieces, a legal tender, and current by law.

The Senate, at twenty minutes after one o'clock, proceeded to Executive business, and continued until a little before three. When the doors were opened,

Mr. CHAMBERS presented the memorial of the Female Orphan Asylum of Georgetown, District of Columbia, which had been presented at the last session, and which, on his motion, was referred to the Committee on the District of Columbia.

On motion of Mr. CLAYTON, all the orders of the day were suspended, and the Senate proceeded to the consideration of the bill changing the time of holding the district court of Delaware; which was ordered to be engrossed for a third reading.

A bill reported by the Committee on Indian Affairs, for the relief of Francis Lafontaine & Son, was considered, and ordered to be engrossed for a third reading.

Mr. KNIGHT moved an adjournment, but withdrew it at the instance of Mr. POINDEXTER.

The Senate then, in Committee of the Whole, proceeded to the consideration of the following bills; which were reported without amendment, and ordered to be engrossed for a third reading;

A bill for the relief of John Kirkpatrick;

A bill for the relief of the widow of Clement B. Penrose;

A bill for the relief of Philip Hickey.

On motion of Mr. BELL, the Senate adjourned.

HOUSE OF REPRESENTATIVES.

THURSDAY, *March* 6, 1834.

Mr. EVANS reported a bill to restore to certain individuals pensions by them relinquished; which was read twice and committed.

The House suspended the rule, to enable Mr. J. Q. ADAMS to submit the following resolution, which lies one day for consideration:

Resolved, That the Secretary of the Treasury be directed to report to this House, a statement of all the sums denominated in the treasury accounts *unavailable funds;* specifically designating the several banks or individuals indebted to the treasury therefor; the time when each debt first became due; the time when failure of payment thereof first occurred; the security, if any, which the public have for payment thereof, at any time, and the prospect of such eventual payment.

On motion of Mr. DUNLAP,

Resolved, That the Committee on the Judiciary be instructed to inquire into the expediency of establishing a third judicial district in the State of Tennessee, and of requiring the judge of the district of East and West Tennessee to hold one or more terms of said court annually, at the town of Jackson, in said State.

On motion of Mr. McCARTY,

Resolved, That the Committee on Private Land Claims be instructed to inquire into the expediency of authorizing the officers of the land office at Fort Wayne, and the Commissioner of the General Land Office, to correct an error in the entry of an eighty acre lot of land, in the name of William O'Neal, of Delaware county, Indiana, made at the Fort Wayne land office, on the 29th of September, 1831.

Mr. CLAY reported a bill for the relief of James Kitchens; which was read twice, and ordered to be engrossed for a third reading to-morrow.

Mr. SLADE, of Illinois, a bill for the survey of certain roads and canals, and improvement of harbors in Michigan.

Also, a bill granting a certain quantity of land to Ohio and Indiana to open a navigable communication between the Wabash river and Lake Erie; which were read twice, and committed.

PUBLIC DEPOSITES.

The House resumed the consideration of the following resolution offered by Mr. MARDIS:

Resolved, That the Committee of Ways and Means be instructed to inquire into the expediency of reporting a bill requiring the Secretary of the Treasury to deposite the public moneys of the United States in the State banks; and, also, as to the expediency of defining by law all contracts hereafter to be made with the Secretary for the safe-keeping, management, and disbursement of the same.

Mr. CLOWNEY resumed. He considered that Mr. Duane had been improperly removed from the office of Secretary of the Treasury, to make way for one whose first act was to deny the power of the House, from whom he alone constitutionally derived it. But the House were to judge of the importance of the doctrines he advanced, and if they sanctioned them, they might tell the people to be undeceived as to their notions of independence; for they would, in effect, decide that the President of the United States having thus, through the medium of this officer, the control of the purse as well as the sword, he possessed more power than any king of Great Britain. He would, in conclusion, avow, that it was his determination to vote against this resolution, and every resolution with a similar object, until the deposites were restored; after which, he was prepared to vote for any measure which should be deemed necessary for their ultimate security.

Mr. CLAYTON said he would have been glad, on a former occasion, if the rules of the House had permitted him to go into some explanation which seemed to be called for from him, from the peculiar situation in which he stood with regard to this bank subject. He would, in the outset, consider the question of the power of removal that was involved, leaving the question of the influence which the restoration of the deposites would have in rechartering the bank, to those who deemed it of more importance than he did. Before, however, he would proceed in the discussion, he must advert to what had fallen from the honorable member from Alabama, [Mr. MARDIS,] when he had done him the honor of making him the subject of his speech. If that honorable member professed his wonder as to what he thought of his conduct, what was to be thought of his own, in submitting his present resolution for legislative interference? Did he not, by his own proposition, condemn the measures of the President? For if he had the right to take the deposites from the bank, by virtue of a lawful power vested in him, he asked where was the necessity for legislation on the subject? It would, in this point of view, be impertinent. But thus it was with those persons who spoke in one place, what they wished only to be heard in another; and they pointed out inconsistency in another, which they overlooked in themselves. He avowed that he wanted no other proof of the illegality of the act of the removal, when the bad consequences that followed it were evinced by this attempt to bolster it up by future legislation.

The honorable member from Alabama professed not to understand his (Mr. C.'s) conduct, but this was, he thought, because he did not want to do so. The honorable gentleman seemed to think that the two questions of restoration and recharter were the same; but he must be permitted to suspect the motives of those who pretended to think so; and he hoped to be able to satisfy that gentleman himself, that his conduct was not so inconsistent as he would have it appear, notwitstanding the astonishment which he feels, or affects to feel. He, however, would rather appear inconsistent at any time than unjust; and he would give two answers, by way of illustration, which, he trusted, would be sufficient. It was the practice in Georgia, where actions were brought to obtain by one means what could not be obtained by another, to put in plea, that the purpose of the action was for selfish purposes; and the courts, holding this sufficient, would dismiss the action, on the ground of being vindictive, arbitrary, and unjust. This, however, might not be the practice in the State of Alabama. There, their practice might be, to hold on to the case, the worse it would appear. His second answer to the charge might be found in an anecdote told, and which happened in Alabama; where, a man having been charged with the crime of murder, the jury found him guilty of—shop-lifting! The court pronounced that it was impossible such a verdict could be received. The jury retired, and, after a long absence, they came to the logical conclusion, that, if the man was not guilty of shop-lifting, he most certainly was of—sheep-stealing. And to this most righteous conclusion they availed themselves of their constitutional privilege as jurors to cling. And he argued to show, that as he had preferred his indictment for murder against the bank, on various charges, of which it had been acquitted, he was not bound to think as others did, and bring in a verdict that the bank was guilty of shop-lifting or of sheep-stealing. He arraigned the conduct of the President of the United States as inconsistent, in removing the deposites, after the action of Congress upon his messages, in pronouncing the deposites safe, and which he could not support. His purpose, originally, was honestly to prevent a continuance of the bank, because he believed that it was unconstitutional. But he referred to the proceedings of the bank committee, to justify him that their motives were different from what was attributed to him. Congress had considered these reports, and in acting upon them, did not say the deposites should be removed, or the charter revoked. On the contrary, he asked, was there not a bill passed by them to recharter the institution—a vote of the House that the deposites were safe? And yet, upon weaker testimony than that by which these verdicts of acquittal had been pronounced, gentlemen who voted for these measures were to be found now arrayed on the opposite side. He thus contended, whatever was his private opinion of the justice of the verdict, that, as the bank had two verdicts against him, instead of his having a verdict against it, he was not inconsistent in yielding. He remained, however, still unconvinced as to the opinion he had entertained against its constitutionality. But upon the question of the expediency of having such an institution, he must candidly confess he had changed his opinion, and this change was brought upon him from seeing the consequences which followed the rash and vacillating acts of the Executive, in substituting other institutions for the bank. He considered the act of removing the deposites to be much more unconstitutional than the bank, because it was a plainer case, and it had perpetrated more mischief. The country and the Administration had been divided upon the question of constitutionality. And he went on to argue, from the letters of Mr. Duane, (which he read extracts from,) that the removal was improper, and had been prompted by two motives, by which, he alleged, from public rumor, the present Administration were malignly influenced. These motives were, avarice and ambition; which were to be gratified by obtaining riches, by speculation in stocks, &c., to be used as a stepping-stone to office. For these purposes, as the bank stood in the way, and as it would not do to wait for the expiration of its charter, it was deemed necessary to have it cut down, and to organize such a moneyed regency here, as had been successfully practised elsewhere. He was therefore compelled, if opposed to the bank on the grounds of unconstitutionality, to be much more so to these measures of the Administration. Having argued against the power claimed by the Executive, he said that the effect of the withdrawal of the public moneys must be to make the bank what it never was intended by the charter to be—a private institution, the control over which was, by the act, given up to the directors.

Mr. C. here gave way, without having concluded, to a motion to proceed to the order of the day.

Mr. LYON, of Michigan, presented a resolution of the Council of Michigan, requesting the establishment of a separate territorial government west of Lake Michigan, and a recognition of the line running west from the southern extreme of Lake Michigan, established by the 5th article of the ordinance of 1787 as the southern boundary of that Territory. Referred to the Committee on the Territories, and ordered to be printed.

Mr. LYON, of Michigan, presented a memorial of the citizens of Oakland county, in the Territory of Michigan, praying the grant of a township of land to aid the establishment of a seminary of learning in said county. Referred to the Committee on Public Lands.

Mr. LYON, of Michigan presented a petition from numerous citizens of the counties of Monroe and Lenawee, in the Territory of Michigan, praying the establishment of a post route from Port Lawrence, through Adrian and other places, to intersect the Chicago road, in the county of Hillsdale, in said Territory. Referred to the Committee on the Post Office and Post Roads.

Mr. LYON, of Michigan, presented a petition of numerous citizens of Michigan Territory, praying that a road may be laid out and established from Fort Gratiot, at the foot of Lake Huron, through the county seat of Lasseur county, to the Grand river, and thence to intersect the road leading from Detroit to Chicago. Referred to the Committee on Roads and Canals.

The House resumed the consideration of the bill reported from the Committee on Revolutionary Claims, to provide for the settlement of certain revolutionary claims.

Mr. BROWN, who was entitled to the floor, spoke at considerable length in favor of the bill.

Mr. WISE followed on the same side.

Mr. GILMER spoke in favor of passing a general bill on this subject, but to the bill reported by the committee he was decidedly opposed. He suggested many considerations, which he thought ought to induce the House to recommit the bill for amendment. He accordingly moved the recommitment of the bill, but withdrew it for the present.

Mr. MARSHALL spoke in support of the bill, and in reply to the gentleman from Georgia, [Mr. GILMER.] At half past three o'clock, without concluding, he gave way to a motion to adjourn.

On motion of Mr. BURGES,

The House then adjourned.

IN SENATE.

FRIDAY, *March* 7, 1834.

Mr. BELL, from the Committee of Claims, reported a bill without amendment, from the House of Representatives, for the relief of Christian Lynch and others; which was read, and committed.

Mr. BELL, from the same committee, reported a bill for the relief of William D. Aikin; which was read, and committed.

Mr. CHAMBERS presented the memorial of Tench Ringgold, formerly Marshal of the District of Columbia, praying certain allowances may be made to him; referred to the Committee on the Judiciary.

Mr. McKEAN presented a memorial signed by 2530 inhabitants of the county of Lancaster, Pennsylvania, in favor of the restoration of the public deposites and the recharter of the Bank of the United States, with modifications.

Mr. McK. moved that the memorial be read, referred to the Committee on Finance, and be printed.

After some remarks by Mr. WEBSTER, the motion was agreed to.

Mr. McKEAN also presented the memorial of three hundred and thirteen inhabitants of Marietta, in the same county, in favor of the restoration of the deposites; upon which the same order was taken.

Mr. WEBSTER presented the memorial of persons engaged in house building in the city of Philadelphia, praying the restoration of the deposites to the Bank of the United States.

Mr. WEBSTER addressed the Senate at some length, on presenting the memorial.

Mr. CLAY also made some remarks; when the memorial was read, ordered to be printed, and referred to the Committee on Finance.

The following memorials were submitted, and lie on the table one day:

By Mr. EWING:

Resolved, That the Secretary of the Treasury cause to be transmitted to the Senate a statement of all contracts for the transportation of the mail, entered into since the 30th day of June, 1829, and of the proposals respecting such contracts, as the same may appear in the books and files of the Comptroller of the Treasury.

By Mr. EWING:

Resolved, That the Postmaster General be directed to transmit to the Senate a statement of the items which make up the sum of $64,248 76, which, in his annual report of November 30, 1833, he charges as the excess of expenses incurred for transporting the mail prior to the 30th of June, 1829, over and above the amount stated in his report to the last named day. And also, that he set forth the amount which the expenses actually incurred for transportation of the mails exceeded the amount stated in his annual reports of those expenses for the years ending the 30th of June, 1830, and the 30th of June, 1831; and that he give the items which make up the excess in each year. Also, that he set forth, or state particularly the items which make up the sum of $205,656 07, stated in his annual report of the 30th of November, 1833, as the expenses incurred for transportation which had actually been performed prior to the 1st day of July, 1832, and which were not included in his report for that year.

Also, that he report to the Senate the items making up the sum of $91,658 82; which in his report of November 30th, 1833, he says, would, according to the former method of keeping the accounts of the expenses of transportation, have been left out of his said report, because not entered under their proper dates.

Resolved, That the Postmaster General be directed to report to the Senate the amount of compensation and extra allowance for transporting the mail, omitted in the Blue Book of 1833, if any be omitted, and that he communicate the names of the individuals entitled to such compensation or extra allowance.

Resolved, That the Postmaster General be directed to report to the Senate the items which make up the incidental expenses of the Post Office Department from the 1st day of October, 1831, to the 1st day of January, 1834, and that he communicate the names of the individuals to whom, and

designate the services or objects for which, the money may have been paid, or such expenses incurred.

Resolved, That the Postmaster General be directed to report to the Senate the amount, if any, due to mail contractors on the 1st day of January, 1834, which has not yet been paid; and also, that he state the amount, if any, which the department has overdrawn, the sums due at that date from any postmaster or postmasters; also, the amount which the department has, or shall have, overdrawn its deposites in any bank or banks prior to the time of sending in the report called for by this resolution; also, that he set forth the amount which has been borrowed for the use of the department, or which shall have been borrowed prior to the time of sending in said report, and then unpaid, and that he designate the contractors to whom the department is so indebted, and the postmasters and banks on whom such overdrafts have or shall have been made, and the banks or individuals of whom such moneys shall have been borrowed, with the respective sums due to, overdrawn on, or borrowed from each.

Mr. CLAY rose, and said he held in his hand four resolutions, which he wished to present, and which he was desirous should be considered at no very distant day. They presented subjects of grave inquiry, and of deep importance, involving the purity of the Administration, if not the very durability of the Government. The three first resolutions assumed that the Constitution gave so power of removal from office by the President of the United States at his pleasure. He was fully aware that this power was conceded to the President by the first Congress which sat under the Constitution. But since that period, except in an incidental discussion here four or five years ago, it has never been discussed in Congress. He had carefully looked into the Constitution, as it related to the power of removal in the President, and the result was that the power was not reposed in the President in the instance indicated in the resolutions. He believed the assertion of the power by the first Congress was improvident, and not the least reason for this opinion was the confidence which that Congress reposed in the wisdom, the prudence, and the patriotism of the first President, the father of his country. And, as to the precedent, the fact was worthy of consideration; and, while he conceded that it was made, he contended that it was made with qualifications which have been utterly disregarded by this Administration. The doctrines of this Administration and the principles of its supporters, as avowed in the discussion upon the deposite question, are, that all persons are bound to conform to the will of the President, no matter how opposite that will may be to their own opinion and judgment. The total number of employees under the Government is estimated to be at least forty thousand; and, if we look at the Blue Book, where only a portion of them are registered, the estimate will be found to be much below the true mark. If we suppose that this mass of forty thousand officers are actuated by one spirit, governed by one impulse, and by one mind, it would act with certainty decide the succession to the Presidential chair as the Praetorian band of ancient Rome decided on the disposition of the imperial throne. He hoped gentlemen would soon turn their attention to the subject seriously; examine the Constitution carefully, and not intrench themselves behind one solitary precedent. He admitted the force of precedent, it was entitled to respect; but yet it was only evidence. He therefore invoked gentlemen to point out the part or parts of

the Constitution which gave to the Chief Magistrate the power contended for. He had looked for it in vain. The effect of the plan indicated by the resolutions was to secure the independence of the officer, to place him less under the control of one man, to restore that equilibrium in the Government which was wanting, and which, if permitted to go on, would lead to the total absorption of the power of Government by one head, to the exclusion of all other departments. He was guided in this movement by considerations of public good, and he looked to the operations of Government and its effects upon the institutions of the country. He submitted the resolutions, moved that they be printed, and made the order of the day for the first Monday in April.

1. *Resolved*, That the Constitution of the United States does not vest in the President power to remove, at his pleasure, officers under the Government of the United States, where offices have been established by law.

2. *Resolved*, That in all cases of offices created by law, the tenure of holding which is not prescribed by the Constitution, Congress is authorized by the Constitution to prescribe the tenure, terms, and conditions, on which they are to be holden.

3. *Resolved*, That the Committee on the Judiciary be instructed to inquire into the expediency of providing by law, that in all instances of appointment to office by the President, by and with the advice and consent of the Senate, other than diplomatic appointments, the power of removal shall be exercised only in concurrence with the Senate; and, when the Senate is not in session, that the President may suspend any such officer, communicating his reasons for the suspension to the Senate at its first succeeding session; and if the Senate concur with him, the officer shall be removed; but if it do not concur with him, the officer shall be restored to office.

4. *Resolved*, That the Committee on the Post Office and Post Roads be instructed to inquire into the expediency of making provision by law for the appointment, by and with the advice and consent of the Senate, of all deputy postmasters whose annual emoluments exceed a prescribed limit.

The resolutions having been read,

Mr. BIBB said, that in connexion with the motion of his colleague, he would move that the debate which took place in the first Congress on the subject of the power of removal by the President, be collated by the Secretary, and printed for the use of the Senate.

The VICE PRESIDENT said, that according to the rules, it was a resolution which required notice; that it was appropriating money out of the contingent fund.

Mr. BIBB then gave notice that he would introduce a resolution to that effect on Monday next.

Mr. POINDEXTER submitted the following resolution:

Resolved, That the Committee on Public Lands be instructed to inquire into the expediency of employing a draughtsman (by resolution or otherwise) to make a manuscript map, from official documents, of each State and Territory wherein the public lands are situated; to comprise the survey of the public lands, the topographical surveys, the surveys of coasts, the post roads, the boundaries of counties, and the precise location of towns, and such other matter as is useful, and usually found on State maps, or that may be ordered by any of the committees of this body.

Mr. FORSYTH moved to take up for consideration the resolution submitted by Mr. MANGUM, relative to the public printing of the Senate.

Mr. WRIGHT made some remarks in opposition to the resolution, and concluded by moving to refer it to the Committee on the Contingent Expenses of the Senate, with a view to an inquiry into the subject; but, on the suggestion of

Mr. KNIGHT, the motion was withdrawn, and Mr. K. then offered the following substitute as an amendment to the resolution:

Resolved, When any message, report, or other document, communicated to both Houses of Congress, shall be ordered to be printed by the Senate, the Secretary shall ascertain whether the same has been ordered to be printed by the House of Rep

resentatives; if so, the copies will be furnished by the printer to the House for the use of the Senate, under the law and usage now in force.

And when the same person shall be printer to both Houses of Congress, and any message, report, or other document, communicated to both Houses, and printed by the House, and an additional number of copies thereof shall be ordered to be printed by the Senate, the printer shall charge for the same after the rate allowed by law for press-work, including paper, folding, stitching, and excluding composition; and that the resolution of the 14th May, 1830, be and the same is hereby repealed.

Mr. CLAY expressed his desire to become acquainted with the subject, and hoped it might have the action of a committee.

Mr. FORSYTH said he concurred in the opinion, and renewed the motion to refer; which was agreed to.

Mr. POINDEXTER, from the Committee on Public Lands, made a report of several private bills; which were read by their titles, and committed.

ORDERS OF THE DAY.

The resolutions submitted by Messrs. CHAMBERS, WAGGAMAN, WRIGHT, SPRAGUE, and PRENTISS, were severally taken up, and adopted.

On motion of Mr. CLAY, it was ordered, that when the Senate adjourns, it stand adjourned until Monday.

The following bills were read a third time and passed:

A bill for the relief of Peter Mills, assignee of Joshua Sprague;

A bill for the relief of Philip Hickey;

A bill reviving the act of May 29, 1830, granting preëmption rights;

A bill appropriating $800 for the purchase of a marble bust, to be placed in the Supreme Court room, of the late Chief Justice Ellsworth;

A bill for the relief of Francis La Fontaine and Son;

A bill for the relief of John Kirkpatrick;

A bill for the relief of the Widow Penrose;

A bill for the relief of the Collector of Franklin, New York;

A bill changing the time of holding the terms of the United States Courts in Delaware.

The following bills were considered in Committee of the Whole, reported to the Senate, and ordered to be engrossed for a third reading:

A bill for the relief of Thomas Richardson;

A bill for the relief of the sureties of John H. Morton;

A bill for the relief of the legal representatives of Moses Shepherd, deceased;

A bill for the relief of Hiram A. Hunter;

A bill for the relief of Samuel Thompson;

A bill for the relief of John Thompson;

A bill for the relief of Daniel Hazleton and William Palmer;

A bill authorizing the Governors of the several States to transmit, by mail, copies, bound or unbound, of all laws and reports, which may pass the several Legislatures;

A bill authorizing the construction of a lateral road to the District of Columbia, by the Baltimore and Ohio Rail Road Company.

The bill for the relief of Elizabeth Robinson being under consideration, Mr. MOORE moved that it be recommitted to the Committee on Revolutionary Claims. This gave rise to a discussion, in which Messrs. MOORE, NAUDAIN, HENDRICKS, KING of Alabama, and CHAMBERS, participated; when the motion to recommit was lost. The bill was then laid upon the table.

The following resolution was submitted by Mr. CLAYTON:

Resolved, That the Postmaster General be directed to inform the Senate how many, and what postmasters, clerks, and other agents in his department have been by him removed from office since the 3d day of March, 1829. Also, to state the names of those who have been appointed in lieu of the postmasters so removed, their places of residence, and to furnish the originals (or copies thereof) addressed to him as Postmaster General, communicating the political character of those re-

moved, or those who have been appointed to supply their places.

Resolved, That the Postmaster General be directed to communicate to the Senate a copy of any and every circular or order to his deputies, directing them, or any of them, to transmit to his department the names of the newspapers taken at their respective offices, or the names of the subscribers to such newspapers, and generally to state whether his department receives quarterly returns of newspapers taken in the United States, and the names and places of residence of their subscribers.

The bill for the relief of Elizabeth Robinson was again taken up, when, at a quarter past four, on motion of Mr. SHEPLEY,

The Senate adjourned.

HOUSE OF REPRESENTATIVES.

FRIDAY, March 7, 1834.

Mr. CAMBRELENG, from the Committee on Ways and Means, reported a bill to authorize merchandise to be deposited in the public stores, and for other purposes. Read twice, and committed to the Committee of the Whole on the state of the Union.

Mr. McKENNAN, from the Committee on the District of Columbia, reported a bill to amend an act incorporating the Fire Insurance Company of Georgetown. Read twice and committed.

Mr. ELLSWORTH, from the Committee on the Judiciary, reported a bill for the relief of the heirs of Thomas ——— and others. Read twice and committed.

On motion of Mr. WATMOUGH, five thousand extra copies of the report on the bill to equalize the pay of the army and navy were ordered to be printed.

Mr. ADAMS, of New York, from the Committee on Invalid Pensions, reported a bill for the relief of Enoch Blaisdell. Read twice, and committed.

Mr. GILMER asked, and obtained leave, to lay on the table an amendment which he proposes to move to the revolutionary claims bill; and the amendment was, on his motion, ordered to be printed.

Mr. THOMPSON, with the leave of the House, submitted the following resolution:

Resolved, That the Committee on Roads and Canals be instructed to inquire into the expediency of granting to the State of Ohio a quantity of unsettled lands, within the same, for the purpose of aiding said State in the construction of a canal to connect the Ohio canal with the Pennsylvania canal, by way of what is called the Sandy and Beaver route.

Mr. CLAY would have no objection to the inquiry, if the gentleman would modify it so as to refer it to the Committee on Public Lands.

Mr. THOMSON refused to modify the resolution, and

Mr. CLAY moved to lay it on the table. Lost.

After some opposition to the resolution from Mr. WHITTLESEY, of Ohio,

Mr. STEWART moved to amend the resolution, by striking out that part which gives any land to the State of Ohio, and the latter clause, which indicates the route. The subject, he considered, properly belonged to the Committee on Roads and Canals, as the proposition was to make a canal.

Mr. THOMSON said that if the amendment should be adopted, he should be compelled to vote against his own resolution. His object was to connect the Ohio and the Pennsylvania canal, and he presumed that his colleague, [Mr. WHITTLESEY,] whose opposition to the resolution had surprised him, was in favor of the same object, though he had in view a different route from that proposed in the resolution. He went on to make some remarks in favor of the route which he had proposed.

Mr. WHITTLESEY said he objected to the designation of any route in the resolution, and especially of one which had been condemned by every person who had examined it.

Mr. STEWART made some remarks in support of his motion to amend. The proposition was to give the land to the State of Ohio, that the

State of Ohio might sell it and subscribe the proceeds to the stock of the company. He did not see why the Government should not make the subscription to stock, whether it was in land or money, and have the benefit of it.

Mr. THOMSON made some statement in support of his views of the eligibility of the route designated in the resolution. He had, however, determined, rather than continue the debate, to accept the amendment as a modification of the resolution.

Mr. FULLER, of New York, said if there was to be an inquiry, he would like to have it extended a little further. We in New York (said he) would like to have a canal from Rochester to Olean, and we happen not to have any public land. The canal would terminate on the Alleghany river, and would be highly important to all the interests below. The work contemplated by the resolution was highly important, but not more so than this.

Mr. STEWART said that, without objecting to the proposition of the gentleman from New York, he thought he had better offer it in a distinct resolution.

Mr. FULLER. I think not. I would a great deal rather be in good company than alone. Both canals were important, and are connected with the same interests. He accordingly offered his amendment, instructing the committee also to inquire into the expediency of making a grant of land for the purpose of constructing a canal from Rochester to Olean.

[Here the discussion was interrupted by the expiration of the hour assigned to the consideration of resolutions, and the House proceeded to the orders of the day, which were private bills.]

The following bills were read a third time, and passed:

A bill granting pensions to certain persons therein named;

A bill for the relief of Henry Oakes;

A bill for the relief of Henry Sewall and Robert Sewall;

A bill for the relief of W. L. Cockerille;

A bill for the relief of James Marsh;

A bill for the relief of Stephen Kingston;

A bill for the relief of John C. Naylor;

A bill for the relief of William Enos;

A bill for the relief of Judith Thomas and Daniel Palmer;

A bill to authorize the Secretary of the Treasury to issue a register to brig American, of Savannah;

A bill for the relief of Nicholas C. Coleman and James Kitchens;

A bill for the relief, in part, of the crew of the brig Sarah George, having been reported with an amendment, by the Committee of the Whole,

Mr. McKIM supported it, and called for the reading of the report accompanying the bill; after which, the further consideration was postponed until to-morrow.

Mr. POLK asked the unanimous consent of the House to suspend the rules by which this day is set apart for private bills, in order to take up appropriation bills.

Mr. WHITTLESEY objected.

Mr. POLK moved the suspension of the rule for that purpose.

The members voting were—ayes 67, noes 40—(not two-thirds, nor a quorum.)

The SPEAKER said he must enforce the rule of the House—that all members shall vote upon one side or the other; and having ascertained there was a quorum in the House—the members voting being ayes 74, noes 49, (not two-thirds,)—the House proceeded with private bills.

Sundry bills (heretofore stated in our paper to have been passed in the Senate) were read twice, and referred to the standing committees.

The House resolved itself into committee, Mr. CONNOR in the Chair.

The bill to compensate Susan Decatur and others; the bills for the relief of John S. Fleming and of Richard W. Meade, were severally laid aside.

The following bills were then considered, reported to the House, and ordered to be engrossed:

A bill for the relief of George Bowen;

A bill for the relief of W. K. Pauling;

A bill for the relief of W. Haslett;

A bill for the relief of Joseph W. Wormstead;

A bill for the settlement of the claim of Mary O'Sullivan;

A bill for the relief of John Kimberlin;

A bill for the relief of Peleg Spencer;

A bill for the relief of Haggerty and Austin;

An act to authorize the Secretary of the Treasury to compromise the claims of Minturn & Champlin;

A bill to refund to certain owners of the schooner Joseph and Mary the sum paid into the Treasury by reason of the condemnation of said vessel;

A bill for the relief of Samuel P. Walker;

A bill for the relief of Alexander J. Robinson;

A bill for the benefit of the heirs at law of the representatives of William G. Christopher, deceased;

A bill for the relief of John Hone & Sons;

A bill for the relief of William B. Doliber and others, owners, and the heirs of the crew, of the schooner Mary & Hannah;

A bill for the relief of the legal representatives of James Brown;

An act for the relief of Noah Staley;

A bill for the relief of Benedict Alford;

A bill for the relief of the heirs of Crocker Sampson, deceased;

A bill for the relief of Henry Whitney;

A bill for the relief of Jonathan Walton, and John J. De Graff;

An act for the relief of the widow and heirs of Felix St. Vrain.

The bill for the relief of David Kilbourn was also reported, and taken up for consideration.

Mr. GRENNELL and Mr. CHILTON opposed the bill, and it was supported by Mr. THOMSON and Mr. WARDWELL; after which, its further consideration was postponed to Friday next.

Mr. THOMAS moved that the rule be postponed, in order to permit him to make a motion that when the House adjourns, it adjourn to meet on Monday next.

Mr. WHITTLESEY, of Ohio, called for the yeas and nays, but the House refused to order them.

The motion to suspend the rule prevailed.

Mr. WHITTLESEY, of Ohio, moved that the House do now adjourn. Negatived.

Mr. THOMAS then submitted his motion.

Mr. CLAYTON asked the yeas and nays upon it, but they were not ordered.

The motion to adjourn to Monday was agreed to by a vote of 129 to 49.

Mr. POLK gave notice that he should, on Monday next, or as soon as possible, call up for consideration some of the appropriation bills.

Several bills from the Senate were taken up, read the first time, ordered to a second reading, and referred.

On motion, the House then adjourned.

REMARKS OF MR. WRIGHT,

OF NEW YORK,

In Senate, *Thursday, March* 6, 1834.

[The question being upon the fifth resolution offered by Mr. Poindexter, and he having modified the resolution so as to authorize the committee to have depositions taken at a distance, as well as to examine witnesses before themselves, and Mr. Shepley having moved an amendment to direct the committee, when the testimony to be taken was of a character to implicate the official conduct of any officer, to give that officer notice, and an opportunity to attend at the taking of the testimony, and to cross-examine the witnesses]—

Mr. WRIGHT said, he should have considered the modification made by the honorable chairman of the committee full and sufficient, but for declarations which had fallen from other members of the Senate. He did not rise to express any want of confidence in the committee. Under the modification of the resolution, he should have assumed that the committee would have given notice to any officer of the Government whose official acts were impugned by any evidence appearing before them, and that they would have given such officer an opportunity for exculpation by testimony, before they would report matters of accusation or impeachment. He would have entertained this opinion, because the course would be so palpably required in justice to accused public officers; and, but for the declarations to which he referred, he would have cheerfully concurred in the remark made by the honorable Senator from Alabama, [Mr. King,] and would have presumed that the course of the committee, in making their investigations, would be such as he had indicated.

He was, however, not now at liberty to make this presumption, because it had been distinctly declared by the honorable Senator from Connecticut, [Mr. Smith,] and intimated by several other members, in the course of their remarks, that it would not be the duty of the committee to give any notice to any accused officer; that the committee were a mere inquest; that they were to act as grand jurors, and in no other character; that they were not to hear exculpatory evidence, if offered; but that they were to act exclusively in an *ex parte* and accusatory character. This was presenting the duties of the standing committees of this body in a new light to him. Were they mere bodies of inquest, mere *ex parte* examiners of the subjects referred to them? He had not so understood the matter. He had understood that the duty of a standing committee of the Senate was to examine the merits of the questions referred to them, and to advise the Senate as to its final action. Now, it seemed that they were mere bodies of *ex parte* inquiry; and what, he would ask, was to be done with such a report when it came in? What was this ulterior and final action of which gentlemen spoke? Was it to refer the report back to the same committee, with instructions to examine the other side of the subject? What else could it be? If the Senate was not to obtain full information through its committees, how was that information to be obtained? What was the course of the committees upon ordinary subjects? Was it merely to make *ex parte* inquiry? If so, where was the testimony upon the other side to come from? Mr. W. said, the position was a mistaken one. The committees of this body are not placed in the situation of grand jurors. It is not their duty to make *ex parte* examinations, but to inquire into the merits of all subjects referred to them, and to make a report advising the Senate as to its final action. Until, therefore, he could receive some intimation that this committee would so consider its duties, that it would feel bound to notify such officers as might be accused before it, and to give them an opportunity to be heard in their defence, he could not vote for the resolution, as modified by the honorable mover, but must vote for the amendment which made that an express duty. He could not believe it was the intention of the Senate to make the duties of this committee under the resolutions accusatory only; to put whole classes of officers within their power for the purpose of having them report to the Senate, and spread before the public, *ex parte* examinations and accusations which the persons accused had had no opportunity to answer or explain. Still such had been the practical effect of the opinions and views expressed by the honorable Senator from Connecticut, [Mr. Smith,] and, as he understood, assented to by others, and until counter indications should be given by the committee, he must be in favor of the amendment.

[Mr. CLAY replied, referring to companies which had been formed to speculate in the purchase of lands, and inquired who were to be notified? That if the committee were to be compelled to give notice, it would defeat the whole object of the inquiry; that gentlemen seemed to be mistaken, and constantly to suppose that officers were to be accused; that such was not the object of the inquiry; that the inquiry was to be made for the purposes of general legislation and to correct abuses alleged to exist in the system of selling the public lands, &c., &c.]

Mr. WRIGHT said, the second resolution refers to the combinations and companies to which the honorable Senator from Kentucky [Mr. Clay] alludes. To those persons he did not ask that notice should be given. He cared not what the result of an investigation might be to them. They were not public officers, and had acted upon their private responsibility only. But if the honorable Senator had cast his eye over the third resolution, he would have seen that he was widely mistaken in supposing that the express direction to the committee was not to inquire into the official conduct of every land office in the whole United States. He would read the resolution. It was as follows:

"3. *Resolved*, That the said committee be instructed to inquire whether the registers of the land offices, and the receivers of public moneys, at any of the land offices of the United States, or either of them, have, *in violation of law*, and of their official duties, demanded or accepted a bonus or premium from any purchaser or purchasers of the public lands at public or private sale, *for the benefit of such officer or officers*, as a condition on which such purchaser or purchasers should be allowed to enter or purchase any tract or tracts of land offered for sale by the United States; and, also, whether any register or receiver, as aforesaid, has been guilty of fraud or partiality in the sales of the public lands by adopting rules and regulations, in their respective offices, inconsistent with the laws of the United States."

Here was a positive direction to inquire into the conduct of these officers, and *into their violations of the laws of the United States*, and to make those inquiries only. It was to such officers that he thought notice should be given. He did not believe that they should be condemned unheard. If the honorable Senator would look further, he would find that the fourth resolution contained the same direction, confined to the land offices in the State of Mississippi, and to a particular description of illegal acts. [Here some Senator remarked that this resolution had been so modified as to extend to all the land offices of the United States.] Mr. W. proceeded. He said he stood corrected: that he was told this resolution also had been made as broad as the third, and it only strengthened the ground for which he contended.

The Senate would see that he could feel no interest in these inquiries. The land offices were so far removed from his State that neither himself nor his constituents knew much about them or the officers which occupied them. That abuses might exist was more than likely, and he hoped to be believed when he said that no member of the Senate was more willing or anxious than he was that where they existed they should be ferreted out and the guilty punished. Still he was unprepared to say that *ex parte* accusations should be spread before the public against any officer of the Government. All ought to be heard and to have an opportunity for explanation and defence, and his present object was to cause the question before the Senate to be clearly understood, that every member might vote as his judgment should dictate. For his own part, after the distinct declaration of the honorable member of the committee, [Mr. Clay,] that notice ought not to be given, that he, as a member of the committee, should not feel bound to give such notice, but should consider it improper to give it, he (Mr. W.) had no alternative but to vote for the amendment, which required that notice should be given to any accused officer, and that he should be allowed to cross-examine the witnesses against him, and to make his defence.

Conclusion of the Report of the Committee of Ways and Means, on the removal of the deposites.

It will be seen by the views already taken by the committee, that in their opinion, the deposites have been lawfully removed from the Bank of the United States, and the money now in the treasury has been legally deposited in the State banks.

In these circumstances, it remains to be considered, whether any, and if any, what legislation is necessary, in consequence of the change of the deposites.

It is the opinion of the committee that the Bank of the United States ought not to be rechartered. The constitutional objections to it are, in their judgment, insuperable; and if its charter could be justified by the Constitution, recent events have demonstrated that the continued existence of such a vast concentrated money power, must prove dangerous to the freedom and purity of our institutions.

And after the great abuses of which it has been guilty, a recharter, under any modifications, would be offering the high legislative sanction and approbation of Congress, to the various acts of misconduct detailed in this and former reports to Congress. It is impossible that a corporation, which is prove

to have used its money to corrupt the press, to influence elections, and control the Government, can ever be selected as the peculiar object of the favor and bounty of the Government. The bank ought not, therefore, to be rechartered on any terms. And as the charter ought not to be renewed, it is manifest that the deposites ought pot to be restored to it. For, setting aside the various acts of misconduct, by which the present corporation has justly forfeited the public confidence, it is obvious that the restoration of the deposites to the present bank, to be removed again in two years, would produce nothing but the most serious evil and distress to the country, without any possible advantage. The restoration of the deposites and the recharter of the bank, are, in the judgment of the committee, inseparably connected together, and neither can, with any propriety, be adopted without the other.

The question then arises, whether the State banks should be continued as the fiscal agents of the Government.

The committee are satisfied that the State banks are fully competent to perform all the services which the General Government ought to require, in the collection and disbursement of the revenue; and to afford also all the facilities to the internal commerce and exchanges of the country, which have been derived from the Bank of the United States.

The collection and disbursement of the public revenue may be safely placed where the sages who framed the Constitution left it. They did not deem a national bank essential, either to the Government they were forming, or to the successful administration of its finances. The opinion has already been expressed, that the State banks are competent to perform all the duties which the Government or the public convenience may require. And there are many circumstances which strongly recommend them to a preference over the Bank of the United States. No one of them can exercise a general control over all the others, and expand and contract the whole currency of the country at its pleasure, to favor the private speculations of individuals, or to increase its own profits. And they can never combine together for political objects, nor hope to gain possession of the Government, and control its operations. The State banks are now firmly interwoven with the institutions of the country. They are generally under the management of citizens as respectable, as trustworthy, as any directors of the Bank of the United States. And it would be unjust, and contrary to the spirit of our institutions, for Congress to sustain a great moneyed power to overawe and oppress them, and bring ruin upon multitudes of our citizens, whenever cupidity or ambition shall tempt them to exercise their power. The stock of the Bank of the United States has fallen for the most part into the hands of the great capitalists of this, and foreign countries, who have but little sympathy for the suffering of our people, when their own sordid or ambitious views make it their interest to inflict it.

If it should be urged as an objection to the State banks, that they cannot afford a general currency, the answer is obvious. If it were necessary to create a paper currency, possessing equal credit with that of the present Bank of the United States, the object can be as well accomplished with the State banks, as with the Bank of the United States. The provision which has made the latter current everywhere, is the clause in the charter which compels the Government to receive their notes in payment of all debts due to the public; and a similar provision in favor of the State banks, which might be selected as the depositories of the money of the United States, would immediately make their notes equally current, and ensure for them equal confidence in any part of the United States.

But the committee are not prepared to recommend the adoption of such a measure. They are convinced that all which public convenience requires, in this respect, will soon be accomplished by arrangements among the banks themselves; and that there ought to be no legislation of Congress for the purpose of establishing a currency of paper.

The main object of legislation should be, to enlarge the basis of specie, on which the paper circulation of the State banks is to depend for support. And the committee are persuaded, that by the adoption of the State banks as the fiscal agents of the General Government, and a judicious course of legislation founded upon it, that a sounder state of the currency than now exists would soon be attained, and the country rescued permanently from the danger of those sudden expansions and contractions of the paper currency which have been constantly succeeding each other, since the Bank of the United States was established, which have brought such severe and extensive evils upon the country. The aid and coöperation of the several States may be relied on, to banish gradually the smaller notes, and introduce in their place silver and gold, for ordinary domestic purposes, and the convenience of travel between distant places. Such a reform is strongly called for by sound policy, and the best interests of the country, and the accomplishment of an object so desirable, may be mainly accelerated by laws passed by Congress, adjusting the standard of value of our coins, and regulating the deposites and collection of the revenue. If gold and silver were brought into common use, and the small notes banished from circulation, payments of small sums would probably be made in specie. The great object is, not to diminish the amount of the ordinary circulating medium, but to give it a broader and firmer foundation on the precious metals.

With these views, the committee are of opinion that the State banks ought to be continued as the depositories of the money of the United States, and that measures ought forthwith to be taken, to regulate by law the manner in which they shall be selected, and to ensure the safety of the public money.

According to the law, as it now stands, the duty of selecting the banks, and of prescribing the securities to be taken, is devolved upon the Secretary of the Treasury, under the supervision of the President. This power has been heretofore exercised by the head of the Treasury Department, and in a manner advantageous to the public, and it is not doubted, if the law should continue unchanged, that it may and will continue to be so exercised by the head of that department; yet it is the opinion of the committee, that discretionary power should never be given, in any case, to any officer of the Government, where it can be regulated and defined by law. They think that it would be more consistent with the principles of our Government, for Congress to regulate by law, the mode of selecting the fiscal agents, the securities proper to be taken, the duties they shall be required to perform, and the terms on which they shall be employed.

In accordance with these views, they accordingly report for the consideration of the House, resolutions declaring that the Bank of the United States ought not to be rechartered, and that the State banks ought to continue to be employed as the fiscal agents of the Government, under such regulations as Congress shall prescribe.

Before they close this report, the committee consider it to be their duty to state, that in their judgment a necessity exists for an immediate examination into the conduct of the bank, and they proceed to state the grounds which make it absolutely necessary that a strict and rigorous scrutiny should be instituted. They think such an examination necessary in reference to the security of the interests which the United States, as a stockholder, have in the bank, as well as to correct, as far as practicable, the abuses of which it has been guilty, and to prevent it from using its corporate power and money for purposes of corruption and oppression.

Numerous memorials have been referred to the committee, complaining of embarrassment in mercantile transactions, some attributing them to the removal of the deposites, and others chiefly to the subsequent conduct of the Bank of the United States. That serious embarrassments exist in many of the commercial cities, cannot be doubted; and it seems necessary clearly to ascertain the cause, before an attempt be made to prescribe the remedy. The powers possessed by the committee are inadequate to that object, and they are unable to do more at present than to submit the facts which have come to their knowledge, with the course they seem to suggest. That the simple transfer of a sum of money from one bank of deposite to another, could have produced the commercial embarrassments complained of, is impossible. The public deposites have not been annihilated, nor have they been transported from the country; they are still in the country, and in the use of the community.

It is in vain that they look for the cause of embarrassment in the state of our markets, or the operations of trade. Our agricultural productions, and manufactures generally, bear a good price; foreign exchange is at its lowest rate; the balance of trade is decidedly in our favor, and the precious metals are flowing in upon us from South America, Mexico, and Europe. None can doubt the power of the bank to create embarrassment whenever its managers deem it expedient. In four months, commencing with August last, and ending with November, it called in $9,707,245 of its loans. As the State banks could not commence extending until they began to receive the public deposites in October, and from that till December could not, in their extension, keep pace with the curtailment of the Bank of the United States, it is evident that such rapid curtailment by the bank of the United States must have created some sensation in the commerce of the country. But it is easy for the Bank of the United States to produce universal embarrassment, without any aggregate curtailment of its accommodations, by calling in rapidly one month, letting out the next, and calling again during the third; while it loans out in one place what it curtails in another, and, in this manner, falls upon all the commercial cities in rotation, it may more effectually embarrass trade than by a steady curtailment. When the policy of the bank is unsteady and capricious, producing a scarcity of money to-day, and an abundance to-morrow, to be succeeded by a greater dearth the next day, it is impossible for merchants to conduct business with safety, and prudent men will restrict or discontinue their operations. The bank has long enjoyed a large portion of the business of domestic exchange, and whenever it chooses to cut off the supply in any or all directions, embarrassment and difficulty naturally ensue.

There is much reason to suspect that the bank has been managed, for the last six months, with a view to embarrass the community, as a means of operating on public opinion, and controlling the action of Government.

In the proceedings of the bank, in relation to domestic exchange, as far as known, are perceived indications of a disposition to use the power it possesses through that branch of its business, for the purpose of producing excitement and distress.

The Government directors inform us, in their memorial, that on the 13th of August last, two weeks before the treasury agent returned from his mission to confer with the State banks, and five weeks before the determination of the Executive was announced, the Board of Directors adopted a resolution, declaring—

"That the bills of exchange purchased at the 'bank, and all the offices, except the five western 'offices, shall not have more than ninety days to 'run. That the five western offices be instruted 'to purchase no bills of exchange, except those 'payable in the Atlantic cities, not having more 'than ninety days to run, or those which may be 'received, in payment of existing debts to the 'bank and the offices, and then not have more 'than four months to run."

The Government directors inform us, that on a subsequent day, a series of resolutions were adopted for reducing the business of the institution, and *authority given to the committee on the offices to modify them at pleasure*, and although a strenuous effort was made to require them to report such measures as might be directed by them to the board, the *proposition was voted down.*

Thus, in direct violation of the charter, and in defiance of all prudence and propriety, was the whole power of this vast and powerful corporation to relieve or to oppress vested in a committee, who are not subject to the responsibility of even making reports to the Board of Directors. A few irresponsible men, issuing secret orders from their private chamber, possess more power to distress the American people, than any department of their Government, or all departments, by an act short of a declaration of war. What the resolves and orders of this potent body have been, we have no means of knowing. The President of the bank,

who is ex officio a member of this committee, and undoubtedly directs its operations, is also clothed with unlimited power to set the press in motion for the purpose of promoting the views of the bank. For months, those presses which are known to have been sustained by enormous loans, and those which have received the most liberal allowances for printing, have been incessantly engaged in an effort to spread alarm and dismay throughout the land. It is impossible not to suspect that the secret management of the bank, and the use of its funds by its President, are in perfect concert with their dependent and devoted presses, all aiming to create a general panic, and produce the same result. That result is the restoration of the deposites, and, its certain consequence, the recharter of the bank.

If anything was wanting to confirm these suspicions, the alleged refusal of this bank to co-operate with the State banks in their laudable efforts to relieve the existing pressure upon the community, in the larger commercial cities, is sufficient to remove all doubts from the minds of the most incredulous.

It is due to the country that the source of the embarrassments which oppress a portion of its commerce shall be laid bare. Should they appear to spring solely from the management of the bank, wantonly and wickedly directed to produce them, it may become the duty of Congress to resort to all the means within their constitutional authority to check its career.

If it shall appear that the bank, by means of its money and the papers under its control, has wilfully and intentionally produced these embarrassments; and if its power has thus been abused, it cannot be endured that, for two years longer, it shall be suffered wantonly to excite alarm in the country, and then on another, enlarge at one place, and contract in another, for the purpose of continuing to the end of its existence the evils which there is too much reason to believe it has already inflicted on the community. If, upon examination, it shall be found that it has been guilty of such offences, its charter cannot be too soon terminated, and a scire facias would be imperatively demanded to put an end to its machinations against the peace and interests of the people. The Government owns seven millions of its stock, equal to one-fifth of the whole amount. It is the duty of Congress to see that it be not used to oppress the people and subvert the principles of our Government. Of every hundred thousand dollars spent by the President of the bank, or distributed to advocates under the name of loans, and forever lost, $20,000 belong to the people of the United States. That their property may not be wasted, that the cause of their distress may be ascertained and a remedy applied, and above all, that their own funds, and the money and power of this corporation may not be employed to subvert the principles of their Government by controlling their elections—the committee deem it necessary that there should be a thorough investigation into the alleged abuses and corruptions of that institution, and particularly into the details of its management for the last six months. To this end, they propose a resolution to invest a committee of the House with power to make such investigations.

1. Resolved, That the Bank of the United States ought not to be rechartered.

2. Resolved, That the public deposites ought not to be restored to the Bank of the United States.

3. Resolved, That the State banks ought to be continued as the places of deposite of the public money, and that it is expedient for Congress to make further provision by law, prescribing the mode of selection, the securities to be taken, and the manner and terms on which they are to be employed.

4. Resolved, That for the purpose of ascertaining, as far as practicable, the cause of the commercial embarrassment and distress complained of by numerous citizens of the United States, in sundry memorials which have been presented to Congress at the present session; and of inquiring whether the charter of the Bank of the United States has been violated, and also what corruptions and abuses have existed in its management; whether it has used its corporate power, or money to control the press, to interfere in politics, or influence elections; and whether it has had any

agency, through its management, or money, in producing the existing pressure—a select committee be appointed to inspect the books, and examine into the proceedings of the said bank, who shall report whether the provisions of the charter have been violated or not; and also what abuses or malpractices have existed in the management of said bank; and that the said committee be authorized to send for persons and papers, and to summon and examine witnesses on oath, and to examine into the affairs of the said bank and branches; and that they are further authorized to visit the principal bank, or any of its branches, for the purpose of inspecting the books, correspondence, accounts, and other papers connected with its management or business; and that the said committee be required to report the result of such investigation, together with the evidence they may take, at as early a day as practicable.

Mr. EWING, of Indiana, has written us a note, correcting some mistakes which occurred in reporting his remarks of the 24th ult. The remarks he made, we understand, were mistaken as well by the reporters of the other prints, as by the reporter for the Globe. Mr. EWING's voice is not distinctly audible at some times throughout the Hall. This we have felt it our duty to say in justice to the reporters. In justice to Mr. EWING, we give the following extract from a note which he has written, correcting the misapprehension in regard to his expressions:

"I do not think it necessary now to write out all that I uttered on the occasion alluded to, but every member within hearing upon this floor, will, I think, verify my declaration, that, I did not 'corroborate,' but, on the contrary, felt myself called upon to correct and refute some of the inferences my colleague, particularly his idea that 'there is no distress felt in Indiana,' and that 'memorials about distress are got up by the United States Bank.' I disclaimed any such belief, and dissented from the grounds assumed. At the same time I distinctly declared that I was no advocate of the existing United States Bank, nor did I believe any few corporate individuals should have the authority or the name of the existing institution. That a free people, entitled to equal rights and equal privileges, were not satisfied to continue dependent for a safe circulating currency upon either State or United States individual corporate bodies. That it is known I am the advocate of an institution that would strengthen the Union, and advance the interest of every section. That the institution I proposed, (now referred, and not yet reported upon,) would enlarge the resources, and increase the capital of local banks, at the same time by certain facilities perform all the functions of exchange and transfer, without the agency of brokers; and that paper speculators only should oppose the establishment of such an institution. That if such an institution be refused, I should in that case disapprove of allowing public money to be deposited in State banks under the influence of any executive officer. That the people had experience enough of such places of deposite, and lost enough by a depreciated and corrupting currency during and after the last war, &c.

"I do not consider it necessary to say more to show that I did not, and could not corroborate the statements made by my colleague on behalf of Indiana; but it is proper here to add, that I have various letters from my constituents, which manifest their apprehensions at the existing state of things, and express great fear of loss when the spring trade opens, and they reach market with the last year's crop. I only hope their fears may not be realized; and wishing the truth to reach them, I now ask of you to give this note a circulation equal to the matter which rendered its publication necessary. I am, &c.,
       "JNO. EWING."

NAVY DEPARTMENT.

Extract of a letter from Commodore J. D. Henley to the Secretary of the Navy, dated

"Pensacola Bay, February 18, 1834.

"Enclosed is the copy of a communication from Lieutenant Commanding Paine, of the Experiment, relative to the report of a piratical brig having been cruising off St. Thomas's, which appeared in the Kingston paper of the 21st December last.

"Lieutenant Commandant Paine and the officers of the Experiment disavow having made any such report to the editor of the Kingston paper, if there were any truth in the report, it is indeed remarkable that I, being in the Vandalia, in the port of St. Thomas, and in that neighborhood for twelve or fifteen days, at the same time that the Experiment was, heard nothing of said piratical vessel.

"I must, therefore, believe the report entirely unfounded.

"Lieutenant Commandant Paine states, that on the day he left Havana, (which was a few days before the occurrence off Cape Antonio, reported by the schooner Davenport, Norton, from Kingston,) a small British cruiser also sailed, with the view of cruising off Cape Antonio for slave vessels, and I think it is highly probable that the firing and other movements, deemed suspicious by the Davenport, was nothing more than an attempt on the part of the cruiser to bring that vessel to in order to ascertain her character.

"The Vandalia and St. Louis, as I have heretofore informed you, have both orders to touch at Havana and St. Thomas, and the Grampus, on her return, to cruise on the northern coast of Cuba, as far down as Cape Antonio. In the meantime, I propose visiting said coast myself in the Experiment, so that if there be pirates in either quarter, they will be carefully looked after."

Extract from a letter to a gentleman in this city, dated

PHILADELPHIA, March 4, 1834.

"This afternoon the whole city has been thrown into confusion. Just as the Baltimore boat, William Penn, came to the Point, she took fire; the State-House bell rung, and in a few minutes the wharves were crowded.

"The sight was beautifully grand, but the anxiety of all was great, for the safety of the passengers. It was past seven o'clock; and the hour which went from the city, have just returned, and the report is, that four or five of the passengers are drowned. How it caught, or how many were on board, no one can tell. All is confusion and anxiety. The boat is now floating up past the city, all on fire; and ten to twenty thousand persons looking at it."

"We understand that seven of the Ohio banks have been forced to stop payment, and that others are tottering."

LAND AND COMMERCIAL AGENCY
AT NATCHEZ.

THE subscriber offers his services to the public as agent to purchase or sell lots and houses, plantations and uncultivated lands; and particularly to purchase Government lands at the public land sales, or to make entries at the different land offices of Louisiana, Mississippi, and Arkansas Territory, of Mississippi, Red River, and Tombigbee bottom or uplands, from Baton Rouge to Memphis. To purchase or sell all kinds of stocks and other interests, liquidate claims on accounts, otherwise make collections of debts, and remit as may be required. Also, to purchase cotton for the western and northern manufactories, and receive and sell cotton bagging and rope.

His residence has been at Natchez nearly nineteen years, during which time he has become extensively acquainted with the lands alluded to and its inhabitants, having been the greater part of that time actively employed in commerce, and for the last three or four years collecting information relative to the above lands.

Letters (post paid) on any of the above subjects, will be attended to promptly.
       WOODSON WREN.
Sept. 16, '33—swlyr.

THE CONGRESSIONAL GLOBE.

PRINTED AND PUBLISHED AT THE CITY OF WASHINGTON, BY BLAIR & RIVES.

23d Congress, 1st Session.   SATURDAY, MARCH 15, 1834.   Vol. I........No. 15.

IN SENATE.
Monday, March 10, 1834.

Mr. SILSBEE, after a few remarks, presented a series of resolutions passed by the Legislature of Massachusetts, complaining of the State of the currency of the country, recommending the restoration of the public deposites to the Bank of the United States, and praying the recharter of the said bank. Mr. S. asked that the resolutions might be read, referred to the Committee on Finance, and printed.

After they were read—

Mr. WEBSTER said he fully concurred in the sentiments expressed by his colleague. These resolutions were undoubtedly the opinions of the people of Massachusetts. In every town and parish, the removal of the deposites was disapproved of, if not severely reprobated; and himself and colleague would not be the true representative of Massachusetts, if they did not hold language clear and strong, that the cause of the distress was to be found in the removal of the deposites, and if they did not declare, in her name, that her interests were greatly injured, and the distress on all parts of her population was deep and severe. She expected them to say this, and also to say, that they look to Congress alone for prompt relief. In one of the resolutions, an opinion that a national bank, and the restoration of the deposites, are the appropriate remedy, is intimated. It was now several weeks since he had given a pledge here that he would submit to the Senate some measure of relief. It was now three months since the existence of a pressure was asserted. It was then denied, but now no one seriously denied or doubted the alarming state of the country. He could not but suppose that the Executive saw and lamented the distress; but yet no new remedial measure was proposed from that quarter, except the experiment which was going on; and it was fair to receive the late report, made by the Committee of Ways and Means in the other House, as a manifestation of the views of the Executive, made in authentic language, and having the merit of being unequivocal, that the deposites were not to be restored, and the bank was not to be rechartered. This being the case, it seemed to him time to redeem his pledge; the subject had been before the Committee on Finance, and he was authorized to say it met the approbation of a majority of the committee. He therefore gave notice, that on Monday next he would introduce a bill for rechartering the Bank of the United States for some limited time. He saw the difficulty attending such a proposition, but his sense of duty would not allow him to shrink from the effort. He had two objects in view, in submitting this measure. The first was, to give to the community prompt relief, and this it was the duty of Congress to do. He knew of no remedy but the restoration of the deposites and the recharter of the bank for a limited time. And when he spoke of prompt measures, he laid out of the question a new bank, because that could not be done before the 4th of March, 1836. The remedy proposed would be a prompt and efficient one. Secondly, a great object to be regarded was, to propose measures in such a light as to conciliate anything, and to give up everything, so that the object could be attained, and relief given—such measures as the whole country would say ought to be adopted. When he considered the present state of opinion in the capital, and entertained by the Executive, he was convinced that any measures proposed would be attended with difficulty in their accomplishment, and should be submitted to the people, and receive the destiny of the people; and under the impulse of intelligence in the community, which would be sure to be attracted to any such measure, full attention would be given it; and his only hope and wish was, that their decision would decide this question. His opinion, also, was, that while the present state of things continued in the country, the adjournment of Congress ought not to be thought of. Our constituents would not, and ought not, to

welcome us to our homes, till relief shall have been given. We have the power of giving relief, and they look to us for it. The State Governments are not competent to it. The evil arises from political action, and the remedy must be by political action. No vote of his, therefore, should be given to vacate our seats here, or to consent to their being vacated, till something efficient and satisfactory be done.

Mr. FORSYTH said, he congratulated those who were constantly pouring in their memorials here, that their prayers were at last likely to be heard and to be attended to by the appropriate organ of the Senate. Not one petition had been presented which had not urged that prompt attention to the subject was necessary. The honorable gentleman from Massachusetts had said that we were not permitted to speculate; but such had been the progress and condition of things here for three months, there has been nothing but speculation. We are told legislative action is necessary, and yet we are to speculate another week, and then we are to have the proposition. Why not submit it now? After a delay of three months, we are at last come to the object of the petitioners and of gentlemen here: it is the recharter of the bank. And that no difficulty might arise as to himself, he would distinctly announce the terms on which his aid would be given towards that object. First, the rate of interest must be reduced to five per cent.; next, the power of the State Governments to tax the funds of the bank in each of the States, where attested, should be distinctly recognised, and the vexed question of the power of the Government directors must be distinctly understood, and must be admitted to be what the President understands it to be. It could not receive his approbation, without a greater control over it were given to the Government than was contemplated in 1816. It was with surprise and regret that he heard the annunciation of the honorable gentleman, that we ought to sit here till the existing distress should be relieved. Were we to sit here till August or September, to compel the House of Representatives or the Executive to action? Were the coordinate branches of the Government to submit their judgments to our behests? He thought it passing strange; and more especially so, when we were told that the State Governments possessed no power of relief, but that it was in us alone, who hold all the power we possess from the State Government. But are we to be told that the State Governments don't desire relief? Can any man shut his eyes to the fact, that the majority of the State Governments and of the people have said that this bank charter shall cease to exist? If the fact were otherwise, and the people say it shall exist, it will exist, and provision could be made for it two years hence. And it appeared to him that the object of the honorable gentleman was to raise a question which was to be settled two years hence. Mr. F. believed the question was already settled, and he believed every effort which was made to raise it, only the more strongly confirmed it. He trusted we should not sit here till August or September, when this question could be as well settled at home.

The debate was further continued by Messrs. WEBSTER, KING of Georgia, CHAMBERS, and FORSYTH; when the resolutions were referred, agreeably to Mr. SILSBEE'S motion.

The Senate then proceeded to the first special order, being the consideration of the bill for the relief of Elizabeth Robinson, daughter of Lieutenant Wilde, a revolutionary officer.

Mr. MOORE moved the recommitment of the bill to the Committee on Revolutionary Claims.

A considerable debate ensued, upon the propriety of allowing interest on the claim, in which Messrs. SHEPLEY, MOORE, NAUDAIN, FORSYTH, LEIGH, BIBB, CHAMBERS, CLAYTON, WHITE, TALLMADGE, TOMLINSON, and SPRAGUE, participated.

Mr. MOORE withdrew his motion to recommit

it to the Committee on Revolutionary Claims, and moved that it be referred to the Committee on Pensions. Lost.

Mr. FORSYTH revived the motion to recommit to the Committee on Revolutionary Claims; which was agreed to.

Mr. CLAYTON, from the Committee on the Judiciary, reported a bill for the relief of George Read, and, on his motion, the report accompanying it was ordered to be printed.

Mr. C., from the same committee, reported a bill for the relief of Stephen Pleasonton, upon which a similar order was made.

Mr. SHEPLEY, from the Committee on Engrossed Bills, made a report.

On motion of Mr. ROBBINS, leave of absence for three weeks was granted to Mr. Bell.

On motion of Mr. FORSYTH, a few minutes after four o'clock,

The Senate adjourned.

HOUSE OF REPRESENTATIVES.
Monday, March 10, 1834.

Mr. J. Q. ADAMS rose, and intimated a wish that the call of the States for the presentation of memorials, might be commenced as usual, with the understanding that the memorials presented, in reference to the bank, should be accompanied only with very brief remarks, explanatory of the circumstances under which they were adopted. He wished himself to have an opportunity of presenting certain resolutions adopted by the Legislature of Massachusetts. If the gentleman from Virginia, [Mr. Gholson,] who was entitled to the floor to-day, would yield it for the purpose of calling the States, there would, he presumed, be ample time left for the gentleman to address the House on the subject of the Virginia resolutions.

Mr. GHOLSON replied, that the honorable member from Massachusetts must be aware that Virginia had already once yielded the right of proceeding with this discussion for the convenience of the House. Being disposed, however, to extend every courtesy to the venerable member, he would, with the consent of the House, waive his right to the floor till one o'clock.

Mr. MOORE, of Virginia, objected, he said, to the further postponement of the Virginia resolutions.

Mr. J. Q. ADAMS said, he was now more anxious than he was before, to obtain an opportunity to present his resolutions; for, if not only the gentleman in possession of the floor, but every other member from Virginia was to express his sentiments to the House on the subject of the Virginia resolutions, it was evident that it would be a long time before the States could again be called.

VIRGINIA RESOLUTIONS.

Mr. GHOLSON having the floor from the previous day, rose and said, he, too, had received from Governor Floyd a letter similar to that which his colleague [Mr. Patton] had animadverted upon, but it had not occurred to him that the letter contained anything so objectionable as his [Mr. P.'s] remarks would seem to convey. And it never could have induced him to arraign—as his honorable colleague had felt it his duty to do—the conduct of the Governor of his native State, before Congress, or to charge upon him that he had manifested a disposition to extend beyond its due limits his official authority.

Mr. PATTON remarked that he had been misunderstood: he had expressly disclaimed imputing improper dispositions to Governor Floyd.

Mr. GHOLSON resumed. The Governor of Virginia was blamed for designating the resolutions as he had done; for expressing his pleasure on having to communicate that the resolutions disapproved of the recent act of the President in removing the deposites. But whilst he [Mr. G.] hailed this concurrence in the opinion of the Gov-

ernor with the Legislature of Virginia as a most auspicious omen, which would have a salutary influence elsewhere, after investigating the principles upon which the Government was founded, he could not conceive in what way he had transcended his official limits. For this inoffensive matter, however, this act is to be classed along with the manifesto of the President, and with other dangerous assumptions of power on the part of the Executive, and the Governor, when about to retire into his wilderness, is sought to be made as a scape-goat to cover other Executive assumptions. He would not pretend to say that the sacrifice would be so accepted by the people, but he might be permitted to say, that so long as there was on the watch-tower a person so cautious as his colleague, little danger could arise from the Governor's assumptions. He must deny, as alleged by his colleague, that the State Legislature, in adopting these resolutions, had abandoned the ancient principles which the State had so long acted upon; and he referred to the various numbers voting on the several resolutions adopted by the Legislature, to show that public opinion was not misrepresented by the votes by which they were severally passed, and which, as they varied in number, proved that the members of the Legislature had been actuated by a deep sense of the responsibility which devolved upon them. They had judged each resolution upon its own proper merits, and, as he was happy to inform the House, they had not in that Legislature any party machinery, caucusses, or conventions, which were ultimately destined, instead of representing, to bury the voice of the people. His colleague had objected to the preamble to the resolutions; but while Virginia had enough of abuse heaped upon her; while she had been denounced by the press, abused as being second only to South Carolina, he little expected to find one of her sons, and one of whom she was justly proud, joining with those who wished to expose her; and he might be permitted to wish that, after the excitement which prevailed in debate had subsided, his honorable colleague, in his cooler moments, had not reiterated his objections in the terms he did, but that he would have dropped a tear of regret upon them, and have blotted them out forever.

Mr. G., after adverting to the arguments adduced to maintain the power of the President over the treasury, contended that their great error was in supposing that the Treasury Department was an executive one, and he referred to the proceedings of the conventions held in New York, Virginia, Massachusetts, and Pennsylvania, to show that it was not considered so, either prior to, or by the articles of, the Constitution itself. The position that had been assumed was, that the President, in his executive character, being responsible to the people, had the right of supervision or control, and could remove from office such officers only as were given to aid him in the discharge of his executive duties. He did not conceive that the President had any right to remove from office those who were not responsible to him, for a mere difference of opinion; and he argued to prove that if the doctrines maintained, that the President had this unrestricted right of removal, were correct, that ultimately he must ingulf all the powers vested by the Constitution in all the other branches of the Government.

Mr. G. proceeded to argue that the power of removing the deposites was not an executive power. The very fact that the Secretary was obliged to come here with his reasons was sufficient proof of the fact that Congress intended to render the Secretary independent of the President in the exercise of the power of removing the deposites. The President had powers in reference to the bank, but of a different nature from this. He could issue a *scire facias* against the bank, and try the question of its alleged violations of the charter. But the President says he had not time to issue a *scire facias*, and that he must, therefore, in order to see the laws faithfully executed, remove the deposites, and remove the Secretary of the Treasury in order to remove the deposites. This construction of Executive duties, Mr. G. pronounced to be dangerous as well as absurd.

Mr. G. then passed to the consideration of the principles contended for by the Secretary in his reasons, and asked, who had made the Secretary the political and moral monitor of the nation? Who had authorized him to travel beyond the laws and his leger to pick up newspaper charges against the bank, and exert his financial powers for the preservation of the public morals, &c.? He averred that the Secretary had not offered one single financial reason for his act.

Mr. G. submitted to the House whether a single evil alleged as a reason for the removal of the deposites, had been avoided or cured by the act. The Secretary knew that the bank was a hard master, reaping where it had not sown, and it was his duty to foresee the results of his rash measure. It was his duty to know that the act would not only embarrass the business of the country, but would, by diminishing the revenue one-third in amount, render necessary a resort to an increased tariff of duties. Mr. G. could not help coming to the conclusion that there were other reasons for the act than those which met the eye. He could hardly believe that the Secretary himself was satisfied with the reasons which he had presented. His impressions were strengthened by the fact that Mr. Duane, in his third letter, states that the President had said of the last Congress, that if it had sat one week longer it would have been bribed by the bank to renew its charter; and that the same would be the case with this Congress if he did not interfere by removing the deposites before the commencement of the session. He asked whether the House was prepared to sustain the President in acts which were founded on such suspicions. He himself felt assured, and upon his representative responsibility he would express his belief, that the President asked and used the influence of persons who were unworthy of his confidence. He compared his administration to the reign of Elizabeth, beginning in brightness and glory, and ending, through the influence of bad counsels, in disgrace and gloom. The cry of "Recharter, recharter," which was raised whenever this subject was touched, was wholly unfounded. The whole of the southern States, in a body, were opposed to the recharter of the bank. The President, the Vice President, and a majority of this House were opposed to a recharter; and the object, whoever might have it in view, was altogether unattainable. For himself he thanked the chairman of the Committee of Ways and Means for his second resolution, that "the bank ought not to be rechartered," and would support it. But he wished to see the injury done to the Constitution and to public faith, by the removal of the deposites, repaired by their restoration.

Mr. MOORE, of Virginia, spoke in earnest vindication of Governor Floyd, from the charge of having addressed an offensive and improper letter to the representatives of Virginia. If the Governor had committed an offence, he was entitled to a fair trial and to be confronted with his accusers. But to drag the Governor to the bar of this House, to answer to the House, as judges and accusers, for an offence against the dignity of its measures, was a measure which the sense of the House would revolt at. For his part, he would rather that the waves of the ocean should roll over the State and blot it out forever, than it should undergo such a degradation. His colleague had asked where Governor Floyd had got his notions. I can tell the gentleman. He got them in the mountains of Virginia, where men are as free as the air which they breathe. He would suggest, too, that if Governor Floyd had no right to comment upon the course of the Virginia delegation, his colleague had no right to comment upon the Richmond resolutions. It is settled by the practice of the House, that a man might abuse his own constituents, but not that he may call in question the views of those who are not his constituents. It seemed that his colleague had heard a voice from Virginia, differing from the sentiments of the Legislature. It was true, that the question of removing the deposites had sunk into insignificance. It was now a question between liberty and slavery; and it was much to be feared that the removal of the deposites was but the first in a series of measures by which it was designed to transform our institutions into a corrupt monarchy, based on the influence of office-holders and State banks. He spoke much of the danger to be apprehended from the forty thousand office-holders, and stated that the danger from this course of a consolidation of powers in the Government had early attracted the attention of the Legislature of Virginia. The talk about the political influence of the bank was absurd. In the great State of Pennsylvania, where last year the Legislature voted unanimously in favor of the bank, the national Administration was stronger than in any other State. If the bank could not control the politics of the State where it is located, how idle it was to apprehend its influence over the politics of other States. The people could not much longer be deceived. The southern merchants when they go to New York to buy goods, and find that they have to pay four or five per cent. discount on their money, will come home and tell their neighbors what is the effect, and what is the object of the experiment of the Administration. He would suggest to the advisers of a specie medium, the expediency of first trying the experiment of depriving the people of the facilities and comforts which they have derived from the paper system. The services of General Jackson would not much longer blind the people to the fact that he is under improper influence. The day of reckoning was at hand. The people would require an account of the twenty-two millions which had been squandered during the last year. He knew the operations by which the public sentiment of Virginia was to be revolutionized; but he was also certain that they would fail of effect. The people of Virginia would not be reduced to political prostitution by the offer of the Vice Presidency to Virginia. He did not know that it had been offered, but he expected soon to see, in some distant newspaper, the nomination of a son of Virginia as the next Vice President. Mr. M., in conclusion, alluded to the party divisions of Virginia which now weakened her strength, and declared his belief that those dissensions would soon vanish, and that the whole State would present an undivided front against executive abuses and usurpations.

Mr. PINCKNEY rose and said, he must deny the right that was assumed by the member from Virginia, [Mr. PATTON,] on a former day, to censure the convention and other proceedings which were held in South Carolina; but as the State had been thus assailed, he hoped he might be permitted to defend it. Upon this occasion, he felt he must lament the want of that member from Virginia whom they had so lately followed to the grave, [Mr. BOULDIN,] for *he* would not have thus charged South Carolina, but would have thrown himself into the breach, and have gallantly maintained the rights of South Carolina, as he would have his own beloved Virginia. He was the steadfast advocate of State rights. It was a remarkable fact, that this worthy successor of Randolph, and dying with that name upon his lips, shortly previous to his death, stated to him (Mr. P.) that he had defended his State from charges similar to those which had been preferred against her.

The gentleman said South Carolina had acted "rashly." He should like, if so, to know what constituted prudence. Was it not notorious, that she petitioned, and by her Legislature sent remonstrances to Congress, for ten long years? And with what result?—that her petitions and remonstrances were treated with neglect, until at length that act (the tariff) was passed, which went to make her slaves to the North, and filled up the measure of her degradation. Would the honorable member from Virginia have had her fold her arms and make no effort in her own defence? But the men who were thus charged with acting "rashly" well understood the perils of their situation. They looked, however, to the consequences; they looked to the cost; they found there was nothing so intolerable to bear as the chains of slavery that were *forged* for them.

The gentleman said if they were not so rash, Carolina would have got better terms; but he contended that what they desired they had generally obtained. Although there were some objectionable provisions in the Compromise bill, yet she obtained by her own exertions, much that was substantial and valuable, for which she had contended. He would ask, what better terms could she have made. The Compromise bill, bad as it might be in some respects, found no favor from the Administration, and if it were not for the exertions of the distinguished statesmen, whom Carolina honored, little indeed would the South have obtained at their hands. He would here remark, that hereafter, as the people of Carolina now knew their situation,

and their eyes were opened, they would no longer kneel to the foot of the throne for relief; he desired that they would hold on to that determination, for no persons could be enslaved, except those who were willing to be so. He wished to hear testimony as to the state of public feeling in relation to the deposites, and he had the gratification to know, that on this question, Nullifiers and Unionists joined in reprobating the act of removal as one of executive usurpation; they had abstained, however, from giving any opinion, and he thought wisely, on the question of the constitutionality of the bank; as when that question came up it would be the proper time to express their opinion upon it. Whilst he could not assent to the power of Congress to charter the bank, without an amendment of the Constitution for that purpose, he was bound to confess that the institution had done much good; and he would say, when this amendment should be made, the State-rights party generally would feel themselves bound to give their suffrages in favor of the present bank.

After reviewing the charges brought against the bank, he could not agree that there was anything to blame in its conduct. The outcry was however made, that it was curtailing its discounts to produce a recharter. He denied this, and attributed all the evils the country was suffering, to a desire on the part of the Executive to crush the institution. The question now, however, at issue, would decide whether the House would rise in the majesty of the people, and assert their right to have the constitutional control over the public purse, or lay at the feet of the President the Constitution and the laws.

Mr. P. dwelt, at some length, on the various measures of the President and the heads of departments, all of which he denounced as usurpations of authority, founded upon the assumption that each officer may execute the law according to his own construction of it, and according to his own notions of its general expediency. Who made the Secretary of the Treasury the conservator of our liberties, and the censor of our morals? It was bad enough to listen to such language from the President; and if the House would hear it from the President, they deserved to hear it from the Secretary.

Here Mr. P., without concluding, yielded the floor to a motion to adjourn; and,

On motion of Mr. MERCER,

The House adjourned.

IN SENATE.

Tuesday, March 11, 1834.

Several messages, upon executive business, were received from the President of the United States, by Mr. Donelson, his Private Secretary.

Mr. PRENTISS presented the memorial of 130 inhabitants of Burlington, Vermont, praying for a restoration of the public deposites to the Bank of the United States. Mr. P. accompanied the presentation of the memorial with some explanatory remarks, and concluded with a motion that it be read, referred to the Committee on Finance, and ordered to be printed. The memorial was read; when

Mr. SWIFT made some remarks in favor of the petition of the memorialists.

Mr. CLAY said he wished to take this occasion to correct a mistake in a matter of fact, made by one of the honorable gentlemen from New York, the other day, in presenting a memorial from the citizens of the city of Troy, on which occasion it was said that the names of but one hundred friends of the Administration were upon the memorial. The remark was made on the authority of the Representative from that district in the House of Representatives. He held in his hand a letter, signed by several respectable citizens of Troy, stating, among other things, that not less than four hundred of the friends of this Administration had signed that memorial, which he would read. [Here Mr. C. read the letter.]

Mr. WRIGHT said that the remarks in the Troy papers on this subject, were made through mistake. He was reported as having said, on presenting the Troy memorial, that the memorialists imputed their distress to the removal of the deposites. He did not so state, because the memorial had not said so. From this error arose the charge of an alteration having been made in the memorial after its circulation, which was respectful and temperate in its language. In justice to the representative in the other House from Rensselaer county, he would say that gentleman needed no man's endorsement for the truth of his remarks. Whether there was a mistake of one per cent. in the number of signers, friends of the Administration, he did not know. But that gentleman was daily calling on him for a printed copy of that memorial—he had heard of his having made a misrepresentation in this respect, and he wanted to see it.

Mr. CLAY replied that the Troy representative might be fully as respectable as he was said to be, but he believed he resided some fifteen miles from Troy, and it was hazarding a good deal in him to say there were but one hundred friends of the Administration on the memorial.

The memorial from Burlington, Vermont, was then referred, according to Mr. PRENTISS'S motion.

Mr. WHITE presented the petition of Robert Butler, of Florida, praying compensation for services rendered; which was referred to the Committee on Military Affairs.

Mr. WHITE, from the Committee on Indian Affairs, asked to be discharged from the further consideration of the petition of David Brearley; which was agreed to.

Mr. FRELINGHUYSEN presented the memorial of 454 voters of Patterson, New Jersey, asking the interference of Congress for the restoration of the public deposites to the Bank of the United States, alleging their removal as the cause of the pecuniary distress of the country.

Also, a petition signed by 670 citizens of the same town, of a counter character, ascribing the distress to the course of the Bank of the United States, and praying that the deposites may not be restored.

Also, the proceedings of a public meeting, held in pursuance of notice, of the inhabitants of the four upper townships of the county of Morris, New Jersey, expressive of the confidence of the meeting in the patriotism and wisdom of the Executive, recognising the right of the Legislature to instruct Senators, and approbatory of the measures of the Secretary of the Treasury in the removal of the deposites.

Mr. FRELINGHUYSEN said, that in regard to the great subject of complaint in the country, even the friends of the Administration did not justify the measure of the Secretary of the Treasury. The elder Senator from Georgia [Mr. Forsyth] had said but yesterday, that if he had been consulted upon it, he would never have advised the measure; and the other Senator, his colleague, said, that if it were not a party question, two-thirds of each House of Congress would have voted for the restoration of the deposites, and yet the Legislature of New Jersey have instructed their Senators here to vote to sustain the Administration in a measure which its own friends do not approve. But gentlemen say the bank is a monster, and must go down; and we are advised to sit still, and submit to the acts of the Administration in relation to it, and listen calmly, and cease our cries. He would not cease; he would go on until their cries of distress should reach every hill and valley, and he would be willing to sit here till the end of the year, and if the ballot-boxes decided for power, he would submit, but not till then.

Mr. BROWN said there was not a man who regarded the right of petition on the part of the people, and the obligation of their representatives to hear it, as more sacred than himself. The gentleman from New Jersey [Mr. Frelinghuysen] need not have informed us that he intended to sound the notes of alarm. Mr. B. admitted that the notes of alarm were not *to be* sounded, but that they *had been* sounded, for the last three or four months, in language used to overawe the Congress of the Union. This not availing, the language of supplication had since been resorted to, and the gentleman from Kentucky had recommended you, sir, to go to the Executive and supplicate him to retrace his steps. The gentleman from New Jersey seemed to think that public opinion was against the Administration; but so far as that had been experienced in its proper form—so far as the legislative expressions were an index to public opinion, it was strongly in favor of the Administration. And the Legislature of New Jersey, too, had passed approbatory resolutions; and so far as they were an exponent of the public will there, it was also in favor of the Administration. But he had just heard language used here—Senators rising in their places and threatening revolution—which struck him with some surprise. The gentleman from Delaware, [Mr. Clayton,] a few days since, stated that there were two remedies for the alleged evils—one by the ballot-box, and the other the right of revolution; that his constituents had strong arms and stout hearts, for taking the means of redress in their own hands. And who did this extraordinary language proceed from? Why, from gentlemen who were constantly ringing in our ears a reverence for the laws and the Constitution. While in one breath the Executive was charged with trampling the laws and the Constitution in the dust, they were in the next inviting freemen to rally under the flag of rebellion; and yet they are the exclusive guardians of the law and the Constitution. If he had no other objection than this to the bank, the daily events which are passing before our eyes, would make him its opponent. The bank was shaking this free Government to its centre, and its partisans and friends were threatening revolution. The power to create a bank was of the most doubtful character, and to say that the Constitution granted a power which was capable of producing this state of things, was a libel on the wisdom and patriotism of its framers.

The bank was operating on the liberties of this country to a greater extent than all the delegated powers in the Constitution put together were capable of doing. He needed no other arguments to establish its unconstitutionality than this. It had been said by honorable gentlemen that the question of constitutionality had been settled. But he did not regard it as settled. In 1810 or '11, the Congress of the United States decided against it. He admitted the decision in its favor by the Supreme Court of the United States; and while as a citizen he would yield every respect and obedience to that decision, yet, as a Senator here, he would yield to no judicial decision. He would recognise its doctrines only to the extent of his own reason, and no further. Suppose the legislative branches of the Government were to submit to the Supreme Court, that court would absorb all the powers of Congress. He was opposed to the existence of the bank, or the prolongation of its existence in any shape. He viewed it as a question of liberty. It had undertaken to harass the people, to overawe Congress; and should we present the spectacle of yielding to its menaces? He held, that to give it a single day of life beyond the time specified in its charter, was to compromise the Constitution and the independence of the people. The people owed it to themselves to vindicate themselves from the gross libel which had been promulgated against them, that they could not get along without the bank, and to show to the world that the sources of their prosperity were in their industry and the fertility of the soil and the genial climate of the country. But he had heard another expression from the honorable gentleman from Massachusetts equally alarming, that Congress should be kept here without rising, unless some relief should be devised. What, sir, have we arrived at such a period, that Congress should be compelled to sit longer than ever it had done before, only on account of the bank? This was not the least alarming of the expressions we had heard. Mr. B. contended that it was high time to take a decided stand against the bank. We were told that the distress was accumulating, and that we must listen to the will of the people. But gentlemen were greatly mistaken if they supposed that the people were to be driven to submit. In proportion to their distresses, the people would feel an elasticity of spirit which would enable them to surmount them. They would manifest the same feeling which they did when this Capitol was in flames, during the last war—they would only be roused to greater exertions to overcome the evil.

Mr. CLAYTON said the gentleman from North Carolina [Mr. Brown] misunderstood him in the remarks he made the other day. If that gentleman

had not postponed his reply so long, but had honored him with his notice at the time, he would have taken pleasure in correcting him.

What he said was, that the people of the whole country were suffering distress, and that they would not be content till they had produced a change through the ballot boxes. Mr. C. said he did go for a revolution, but it was for that kind of revolution which should bring back the Government to the true principles of the Constitution, and until that was done, he cared not whether we were driven to power to accomplish it. But he preferred the ballot box, and when, as men, we complained of the Constitution being trampled under foot, he held to the right of exercising that power, which our fathers exerted in the war of the Revolution. The gentleman from North Carolina had said that the distress had not reached his constituents; probably the fact would be otherwise by and by. He (Mr. C.) was convinced that two months would not elapse till the tone of many of those who have sustained this Administration will be completely changed. We had been told, too, by another honorable gentleman, that our cries were like those made in obedience to the mandate of the preacher who cried, Groan, sinner, groan. But he thought there was a certain class of politicians who would not be less loud in their groans by and by. The gentleman [Mr. Brown] complained of the power of the bank, but could see no danger from the assumption of executive power; none coming from the White House. He proudly acknowledged himself to be one of those who sustained the Jeffersonian principles, and yet the very men whom he sustained, rose into power on the contest between the Executive and the people.

Mr. BROWN said he should not have noticed the gentleman's observations, if he had not been led to it by the remarks of other gentlemen. The gentleman from Delaware [Mr. Clayton] yet tells us that he approves of the people releasing themselves from their alleged embarrassments at the polls; but if they cannot effect it in that way, they must do it at any rate. He has stated that they must be released at all events; and we are to understand him as having adopted the maxim "Peaceably if we can, forcibly if we must." Sir, the great mass of the people will scowl at and contemn the invitation to repair to the standard of revolt. They never can be induced to rally in support of a great moneyed aristocracy. He admitted the right of the people, to the fullest extent, to resist the unlawful measures of the Government, but he never would believe that the people would submit to the rule of a moneyed aristocracy. The gentleman said that he (Mr. Brown) perceived great dangers in the bank, but could apprehend none from the White House. Mr. B. said he had thoroughly and carefully examined the subject alluded to, and his vision was too obtuse to see the dangers in it which some other gentlemen saw. But if it were otherwise, he would not place the custody of the public money in the power of the bank, which was irresponsible to the people. The President of the United States was responsible to the people every four years—it was not so with the bank, which was chartered for twenty years, and thus removed from the people during that whole period; its influence was invisible—its operations removed from the public eye—it insinuated itself into a thousand places where the public eye could not trace it out. The conduct of the Executive was visible, while that of a great moneyed institution, and an irresponsible power, was secret, and therefore dangerous to the liberties of the people.

Mr. FORSYTH said we had now presented to us a fair advertisement of the avowed purpose of petitioning Congress and adding to the groans already sounded in our ears, and here we have the result. He thought there was sufficient now before us to teach gentlemen not to be misapprehending the conduct of the country. The gentleman from New Jersey had made a long speech on the subject, and yet from the State of New Jersey we had three cheers for one groan. The gentleman from Delaware thought there was a certain class of politicians who would groan for their political sins, instead of by commands from the pulpit. Mr. F. congratulated the gentleman on the discovery he had made. But the gentleman from New Jersey was mistaken in regard to his (Mr. F.'s) situation. He had not said that he condemned the removal of the deposites, or that he did not defend it. He had defended it, and his defence was before the world. He had said that he would have delayed it. As a party man, he said he regretted there had not been more delay; but for the good of the country, perhaps the decision of the President was best. But he had another cause of complaint against the honorable gentleman from New Jersey. The gentleman said that he (Mr. F.) complained of the complaints made here.

Mr. FRELINGHUYSEN disclaimed any allusion to him.

Mr. FORSYTH resumed. It was but the other day that he complained of talking too much—of throwing too much light on the subject. One thing was certain, if the people were suffering or had any cause of complaint, so far as the Senate were in fault, the sin laid at the door of gentlemen on the other side of the house. In vain could they expect relief from the President or the Administration—they know the sentiments of the Administration not to be theirs. Why, then, did they not act upon their own views? Why not act? Do they decline acting here because they want the action of the people on the other end of the house, with a view to make their action correspond with the majority here? If gentlemen imagine that by delay they may expect the people to act on the other end of the Capitol, why they will have the benefit of the experiment. It was impossible to shut our eyes to the fact that the recharter of the bank was what was sought for. If we could be blind now, our eyes would be opened shortly. But there surely was enough in a neighborhg State within a few days past to determine what the views of the people were on this subject. Here was a State almost the largest in the Union—a State whose Legislature was but a short time since unanimous in favor of the institution. And what was the state of the case now? A thorough change had taken place, and the cry rung from one end of the State to the other, "Down with the bank!" Mr. F. said he thought this would have been sufficient to startle gentlemen, and to satisfy them that their anticipations were without foundation. When gentlemen look to the light which they perceive to be breaking through for the purpose of prostrating those in power, he would suppose they would not be very sorry for it, or that the experiment, as they termed it, had been made. Supposing there should be distress, and the widow and the orphan should be made to feel it, what a glorious reason it would afford for exclaiming against the tyrant, and for hurling the despot from his throne. But he thought gentlemen would find themselves mistaken in their expectations of the effect to be produced by it. We shall soon see.

Mr. FRELINGHUYSEN observed, that if he had fallen into complaints, if he had been making long speeches, he had only been doing what the gentleman from Georgia did, not what he said. His situation surely was sufficiently embarrassing, but his wheel, was turning, might yet place himself and the gentleman in a similar situation; and when he should receive instructions, if he be determined to disobey them, he should have his hearty support and countenance.

Mr. FORSYTH disclaimed anything personal in his observations. He thanked the gentleman from New Jersey, for his good wishes. As to the situation of the honorable gentleman from New Jersey, he sincerely sympathized with him, and hoped that, before long, the Lord would send him deliverance.

Mr. SPRAGUE rose to protest against the gentleman from Georgia imputing sentiments here to Senators, which he, for one, entirely repudiated, that we were not party this experiment had been tried. The gentleman was not authorized to say so. All deeply lamented the Executive experiment on the business and finances of the people of the United States. The gentleman hoped the experiment would not be so fatal as those trying it would make it. He (Mr. S.) protested against its being made a mere party question, for he believed he, and those with whom he acted, would almost agree to perpetuate the Administration of the present Chief Magistrate, if he would grant relief. When he looked at the effect of this measure on his constituents, and that this effect would go on, he saw that it was a measure which must prostrate their happiness, their business, and their prosperity.

Mr. FORSYTH replied that the gentleman from Maine [Mr. Sprague] protested against the injustice of having ascribed to him gratification at the "experiment," as he calls it. Well, nobody knew his motives better than he did himself. But when his course here, for the last four years, had been marked with a constant succession of charges against this Administration, he must have a strangely constituted mind, if he did not desire the Administration to be thrown out of power. Now, where was the injustice of supposing this, when the gentleman thought he had his foot upon the neck of the tyrant? He might shut his eye on the operations of his own mind, but others could see it. And when declarations are daily made here against the whole party, are we not justified by the gentleman's example? Did he not every day impute unworthy motives to his opponents here? Let the gentleman's conduct go to his constituents; he tells us we don't understand public opinion. Does the noise he hears come from his constituents, or does he know more of other parts of the United States than he does of his own? If not, he is in error; if in other parts of the United States, he can't be at his own home. He was accused by the gentleman of groaning, and yet groaned himself; yet he would not change his condition for that of the honorable gentleman, under any circumstances. I maintain a situation far above party, which, so help me God, I will stand in. I hope the gentleman will give and take; and when he makes imputations broadcast upon others, he will be willing to receive them in return again.

Mr. SPRAGUE said it was easy to make broad general declarations, impugning the motives of others. He would be obliged to the gentleman from Georgia, if he would specify particular instances. He had always endeavored to treat gentlemen here with respect, and would have been obliged to the gentleman to have mentioned an instance when he had not done so. The gentleman had referred to the opinions of his constituents. But the time might arrive when the people of Georgia would express opinions against the gentleman's course. He (Mr. S.) knew the people of Maine—he was bound to consult their interests, although he knew his political life would be sacrificed by it. He believed that if they knew all could perceive the truths which were poured in here, in relation to this Administration, they would sustain him in the stand he had taken against it. If personal objects had been in his view, could he not have seen the means of obtaining Executive patronage, and have yielded his support to the Administration?

Mr. FORSYTH thought the issue had been made between us. The question was about devotion to power; to those possessing patronage within a few years past. If the gentleman cast his eyes back some twelve years, he would find that his devotion to the powers that be, had been much greater than his. It was his (Mr. F.'s) misfortune to have differed with most of the Administrations since he had had the honor of a seat in the Congress of the United States, and with one, also, on some points. The cries of patronage against the powers that be, were nothing more than that those who were out of power might displace those who were in power. It was not policy to get power from the people, as place from those in power. Let gentlemen, then, get their places if they had no higher ambition than to get a place under the Government. For himself, his ambition laid higher.

Some further remarks were made by Messrs. SHEPLEY and SPRAGUE, when the memorials were referred to the Committee on Finance.

Mr. GRUNDY presented the memorial of trustees of Nashville University, asking the relief in position of Congress in effecting a change of certain lands formerly granted for the use of that institution; which was referred to the Committee on Public Lands.

Mr. WRIGHT, from the Committee on Claims, reported a bill for the relief of Peter H. Green.

Which was read a first time, and the report and accompanying documents were then ordered to be printed.

Mr. WRIGHT, from the same committee, reported a bill for the relief of the heirs of Samuel Gibbs, with an amendment. The report and amendment were ordered to be printed.

Mr. WRIGHT, from the same committee, reported a bill from the House of Representatives for the relief of the executors of Samuel Peers, and the executors of Joseph Falconer, with an amendment; which was ordered to be printed.

Mr. SMITH, from the Committee on the Judiciary, reported a bill for the relief of Ithiel Town; which was read.

Mr. SMITH, from the same committee, reported a bill for the relief of the heirs of Thomas Worthington, deceased; which, at his instance, without being read, was laid on the table.

Mr. NAUDAIN, from the Committee on Claims, reported a bill from the House of Representatives, without amendment, for the relief of James Tilford; which was read.

Mr. NAUDAIN, from the same committee, reported a bill for the relief of Joseph Tilghman and Benjamin Bird, without amendment, and of Job Pomeroy with an amendment.

Mr. ROBINSON presented a petition from sundry inhabitants of Vermillion county, Illinois, praying the establishment of a post route.

Mr. KING, of Alabama, pursuant to notice, introduced a bill relative to certain land claims in Alabama; which was read twice, and referred to the Committee on Public Lands.

The following resolution was submitted by Mr. GRUNDY:

Resolved, That the President of the United States be requested to communicate to the Senate the dates of the proclamations, and the times of sales specified in each, for the sales of the public lands in the district of country acquired from the Choctaw tribe of Indians by the treaty of Dancing Rabbit Creek, and from the Creek tribe of Indians in Alabama; and also the causes, if any existed, of a shorter notice being given for the sale of these lands, than is usual in the sale of the other public lands.

Mr. KING, of Alabama, presented the memorial of Samuel Smith and others, setting forth their claims to a reservation of lands; which was referred to the Committee on Public Lands.

Also, a petition from an officer in the late war, who was disbanded at its close, praying a grant of land for himself and other officers in similar circumstances, in consideration of the embarrassments proving out of a change thus effected in their situation. The memorial was referred to the Committee on Military Affairs.

Mr. EWING called up the resolution submitted by him the other day, when, after some modifications and amendments, made by Mr. GRUNDY and the mover, they were severally adopted.

Mr. TIPTON, from the Committee on Claims, reported a bill for the relief of John McClanahan; which was read.

Mr. TIPTON presented the petition of Robert Harris, which was referred to the Committee on the Post Office and Post Roads.

Mr. CLAYTON called up, for consideration, his resolutions, submitted a few days since; which were considered, modified, and amended by Mr. GRUNDY and the mover, and adopted.

Mr. HENDRICKS presented the petition of Oliver Cromwell; which was referred to the Committee of Claims.

On motion of Mr. POINDEXTER, the Senate, a little before four o'clock, proceeded to executive business, and continued therein until half past five o'clock, when

The Senate adjourned.

HOUSE OF REPRESENTATIVES.

TUESDAY, *March* 11, 1834.

Mr. J. Q. ADAMS said, that not having had an opportunity yesterday, to present the resolutions of the Legislature of the Commonwealth of Massachusetts, he now asked the unanimous consent of the House to present them.

An objection being made,

Mr. ADAMS moved the suspension of the rule of the House, for the purpose of enabling him to present the resolutions.

The motion was rejected.

Mr. THOMSON, from the Committee on Military Affairs, reported a bill for the relief of the heirs of Colonel Rosewell Lee: read twice.

Mr. JOHNSON, of Kentucky, reported an act for the benefit of Pamela Adams: read twice, and committed.

Mr. CARR, from the Committee on Private Land Claims, reported a bill for the relief of Henry Stoddard, representative of Francis Duchoquet; which was read twice, committed to a Committee of the Whole House, and made the order of the day for to-morrow.

Mr. CARR, from the same committee, reported a bill from the Senate, for the relief of Lafontaine and Son, without an amendment; which was referred to a Committee of the Whole House, and made the order of the day for to-morrow.

Mr. CARR, from the same committee, reported a bill for the relief of William O'Neale, of Indiana; which was read twice, and ordered to be engrossed for its third reading to-morrow.

Mr. CARR, from the same committee, reported a bill for the relief of John Bills, with an amendment from the Senate; which was committed.

On motion of Mr. CARR, the papers in the case of Louis Honore Tesson are ordered to be recommitted to the Committee on Private Land Claims.

Mr. DUNCAN, from the Committee on Public Lands, reported a bill from the Senate; which was committed.

Mr. ARCHER, from the Committee on Foreign Affairs, reported the following resolution; which was agreed to:

Resolved, That the Committee on Foreign Affairs be instructed to inquire into the expediency of purchasing the library and the official and private manuscript papers of General Washington, to be deposited in the Department of State.

Mr. BELL, of Tennessee, from the Committee on the Judiciary, reported a bill from the Senate, for changing the time of holding the courts of the United States in the district of Delaware; which was twice read, and ordered to be engrossed.

Mr. CAVE JOHNSON, from the Committee on Private Land Claims, reported a Senate bill with amendments, for the adjustment of land claims in Louisiana.

Mr. CAVE JOHNSON moved that the Committee of the Whole be discharged from the further consideration of the bill to provide for the final settlement of land claims in Louisiana, Arkansas, and Florida; so as to bring the bill into the House.

Mr. ELLSWORTH opposed the motion, as it gave preference to the bill over other business.

Mr. MANN, of New York, urged the necessity of speedy action on the bill, in order to relieve the Committee on Private Land Claims from the necessity of acting, without sufficient evidence, upon a large mass of claims.

Messrs. JOHNSON and SEVIER supported the motion; and the question being taken, the motion was agreed to:

Ayes 85; noes 60.

Mr. CLAIBORNE stated that he was requested by the Committee of Elections to ask leave for the committee to sit during the sittings of the House; and leave was accordingly granted.

Mr. PARKS, from the Committee on the Judiciary, reported a bill for the relief of Joseph V. Garnier; which was read twice and committed.

Mr. WILLIAMS, from the Committee on Territories, reported a bill providing for taking a census of the inhabitants of the eastern division of the Territory of Michigan, and of the Territory of Arkansas; which bill was read twice and committed.

Mr. WHITTLESEY, from the Committee on Claims, reported a bill for the relief of the legal representatives of William Finley; which was read twice and committed.

It wanting two minutes of one o'clock, Mr. CLAYTON, of Georgia, rose and said, he must throw himself on the indulgence of the House for permission to proceed with his remarks on the resolution submitted by the gentleman from Alabama. He had had the misfortune, he said, to be knocked from one week into another.

Mr. POLK hoped the gentleman would be willing to suspend his remarks, in order that he might be enabled to call up the appropriation bills.

Mr. CLAYTON said he would willingly assist in that object after he had finished his speech, and he would promise not to say all now that he knew.

A motion was then made to proceed to the orders of the day, and agreed to.

THE PUBLIC DEPOSITES.

The House resumed the consideration of the following resolution, submitted by Mr. MARDIS, of Alabama:

Resolved, That the Committee of Ways and Means be instructed to inquire into the expediency of reporting a bill requiring the Secretary of the Treasury to deposite the public moneys of the United States in the State banks; and, also, as to the expediency of defining by law all contracts hereafter to be made with the Secretary for the safe-keeping, management, and disbursement of the same.

Mr. CLAYTON resumed, and proceeded to controvert the positions assumed by the Secretary of the Treasury, in relation to his powers over the public money, and to the duties enjoined upon the bank when incorporated; arguing to show that the bank was established by the Government from the necessity that then existed to have their funds transferred from one part of the Union to the other, to revive commerce, preserve the currency from the ruinous state to which it was reduced by the bad paper currency, and for other purposes. The act of incorporation being in the nature of a contract, he could not agree, however desirous the Government might be to succeed with their present experiment, that they had the same right which a sovereign State might have, to nullify their own contract. But reviewing all the circumstances of the act of removing the deposites, it was evident to him that the President had taken the responsibility of the act upon himself, he had made up an issue which was to be decided upon, whether he or Congress was to have the future control over the purse of the nation. The arrangements made with the State banks by him, proved that he had transferred to them the rights to regulate commerce, coin money, and all other powers given by the Constitution to the Government over the currency. It never had been contended, that when the charter was granted, Congress had usurped any power which rightfully belonged to the Executive. And he maintained, that as the power over the public money belonged to Congress of right, they alone, standing, as contracting parties with the bank by the act incorporating it, had the control over it. The Secretary was directed to give his reasons, but if the power was contended to be vested in the Executive, it would follow that Congress might have also required the President to give his reasons. Was not this an absurdity that naturally followed the doctrine? But where was there any precedent for a law requiring the President to give his reasons to Congress for any official act? Suppose Congress had provided in the charter that the President should give his reasons for the removal of the deposites, if he did remove them: would he, as a coördinate branch of the Government, have submitted to the degradation? Was it not idle, then, to suppose that Congress had required reasons of an officer who had no will of his own, and was the mere organ of the will of the President?

It was further attempted to support the power of the President by arguments: That the Treasury was only a branch of the Executive department, and that the appointing power, as well as the power of removal, gave the President the power of controlling the officer executing the duties of the office. But he argued to show, that if such doctrines were true, then they must apply to all the other civil officers of the Government, and the President would be thus enabled to put at defiance every law which regulated the performance of duties specified by Congress. For example, he might interfere with the obligation of the Secretary to report his reasons to Congress, and desire him to report to himself, although this obligation to report to Congress was introduced by them in order to retain within their own hands the full control over the deposites, which the Secretary in his reasons had assumed they had parted with,

to him. When the charter was framed, it was in the power of Congress to appoint any individual officer to remove the deposites and give his reasons for the same. Suppose they had appointed the Reporter to the Supreme Court; does any one suppose that he would have attempted to deprive Congress of its rights over the public deposites, or that any such attempt could be for a moment sustained? Was it not, then, an abuse of power to attempt to deprive Congress of its rights by controlling the action of its agents, and for a purpose which was bringing ruin and dismay throughout the land?

Mr. C. said, that to give the bank a blow and make it reel, and then say go on, was mockery. To require the bank to do what it had always done, after taking away ten millions of dollars from it, was unjust and ungenerous. But the consequences did not stop with the United States Bank—they reached the State banks, and compelled them to redeem their discounts. Mr. C. referred to the paper read by the President to show, he said, that the President did not believe that the Bank of the United States would be able to go on and continue its accommodations to the community after the removal of the deposites; yet now he told the merchants and mechanics of New York and Philadelphia to go to Nicholas Biddle for relief. Suppose the President had laid a powder magazine under the vaults of the bank, laid a train, and asked the vote of Congress to apply the match: would it not send a tremor to the heart of every member? But the cause was the same in principle, but not in effect. Wrong in both cases was attempted to be done to the bank, and no man could reconcile one act to his conscience more than the other. Right-conusses, it ought ever to be remembered, exalteth a nation; and injustice is a reproach to it. He characterized the act of the President as an abuse and perversion of power, and appealed to his friends of the State-rights party for aid in resisting the principles on which the act was founded. After the glorious triumph which they had achieved, he implored them not to submit to this new abuse of executive authority. Mr. C. passed to some statements respecting the Post Office Department, and said that it was reported that contracts were given, and new routes made where they were not needed, for political purposes, and for the advantage of political friends; and that to pay the expenses of these revenues, large loans were required from the deposite banks, &c.

Mr. CONNOR here interrupted Mr. CLAYTON, and stated that the loans referred to by the gentleman had been, for the most part repaid. He would take this occasion to say, in reply to a member who remarked that the Post Office Department had involved the Government to the amount of 500,000 dollars, that the department had not involved the Government to the amount of one cent.

Mr. CLAYTON proceeded. His object was, he said, to defend the bank from the charge of interfering with elections. What he had mentioned he gave only as common report, and he put it against the reports of the corruptions of the bank. He went on to state that it was also reported that the mails were irregular, and that many necessary routes were discontinued in consequence of the favoritism which he had referred to. It was also said, and he would pledge himself to prove that report, that postmasters are removed from office upon secret information, without a hearing, on account of their political opinions. He should believe all those reports, unless the Post Office Department should require and submit to a rigid investigation of all these subjects; which investigation should proceed at the same time with that which the President was claiming into the affairs of the Bank of the United States. Mr. C., after a few further remarks in relation to his former opposition to the bank, concluded his speech.

Several members addressed the Chair simultaneously, and the floor was obtained by Mr. BURGES.

The House then proceeded to the orders of the day.

On motion of Mr. POLK, the House went into Committee of the Whole on the state of the Union, Mr. WAYNE in the chair, on the bill making appropriations for the army of the United States, for the year 1834.

The bill having been read by sections, Mr. McKAY remarked, that as the expenditure for the support of the army was progressively increasing, he wished to show distinctly what was the expenditure in each year; for this purpose, he moved to strike out 1,381,772 dollars for the support of the army and support of officers, and to make a separate provision for the pay of arrearages for 1833, (which were included in this sum;) he would move to insert for support, &c., for 1834, $1,286,986, and for the arrearages of 1833, $94,786.

Mr. POLK assented to the amendment being made in such a shape as would effect the purpose; and defended the present appropriation as necessary under various increases which had been made to the service.

The amendment was then agreed to.

The next section being an appropriation of $50,179 for forage,

Mr. McKAY objected to it as too large, and moved to reduce it to $54,331.

Mr. POLK contended that the establishment required the sum appropriated; after which,

Mr. KAY having withdrawn his motion, the appropriation was agreed to.

The appropriation for the medical staff having been read—

Mr. E. EVERETT moved to amend the bill by inserting, for extra allowance to Surgeon Beaumount, $1,825.

Mr. E. remarked, that he was instructed by the Joint Library Committee to propose this as a remuneration for expenses incurred by him in making experiments on a soldier of the army to illustrate the digestive system of human economy.

Mr. POLK, not knowing anything of the circumstances further than was stated, wished the subject to be reported on by some of the committees.

Mr. JONES objected to the allowance, and desired to know upon what principle it was sought to be granted.

Mr. E. EVERETT felt it unnecessary to go into a constitutional argument. He thought the claim perfectly just and proper to make an appropriation for.

Mr. McDUFFIE said he had looked into the work giving an account of these experiments, and he considered that they were of an extremely valuable character, he would not therefore too nicely scrutinize such an appropriation, and which appeared to have been done by an officer in the line of his duty.

Mr. CHILTON bore testimony to the merits of the work, and supported the amendment, as the experiments made would be the means of saving thousands to the public.

Mr. CROCKETT said: Sir, I ask; as there is an experiment trying upon the currency, what possible objection ought there to be to one on science? Sir, I begin to think it is time to object to all appropriations as unnecessary. What is the use of them until we know where the money is? If the money can be taken at will, may it not be distributed by the same hand? It is all a mockery. What is the use of law at all? I am sorry the gentleman from Georgia opposes this claim; for, although I will vote for one experiment, I will vote against the other.

The amendment was agreed to; ayes 80, noes 50.

After several other sections were gone through, Mr. McKAY proposed to reduce the miscellaneous appropriation $50,000; but before any action could be had on this,

Mr. WILDE moved that the committee do rise; which motion prevailed, ayes 66, noes 64.

The committee thereupon rose, and reported progress.

The bill, as amended, was ordered to be printed, and

The House adjourned.

IN SENATE.

WEDNESDAY, March 12, 1834.

Mr. ROBINSON presented the memorial of Marcus Ball; which was referred to the Committee on Private Land Claims.

Mr. HENDRICKS, from the Committee on Roads and Canals, reported a bill for the improvement of the navigation of the Wabash river; and, on his motion, the report and documents, together with the memorial of the Legislature of Indiana, were ordered to be printed.

Mr. McKEAN presented the memorial of the tin-plate workers, workers in sheet iron, &c., of Philadelphia, praying the restoration of the public deposites to the Bank of the United States. Also, the memorial of a similar class of mechanics in Southwark, Philadelphia, of a like tenor. And, also, the proceedings and memorial of a public meeting in Carlisle, Cumberland county, Pennsylvania, of like import. Which memorials and proceedings were severally read, referred to the Committee on Finance, and ordered to be printed.

Mr. LEIGH presented the memorial of sundry inhabitants of Petersburg, Virginia, praying the restoration of the public deposites to the Bank of the United States.

Mr. LEIGH said, he desired to present a memorial from citizens of the city of Petersburg, Virginia, on the subject which had so long agitated this great country. It was signed by merchants, manufacturers, artisans, and some members of the learned professions, of that city; a place as much distinguished for its devotion to Republican principles as any other in the Union. He could not say which of the signers were, and which was not, friends of the present Administration; but he could not refrain from expressing his surprise and dismay that the friends of those who were complaining found it necessary to say that the signers of these various memorials were friends of the Administration. Was it come to this, that the friends of the Administration were entitled to more respect here than its opponents? These signers were often actuated by impulses? And yet their representations are the least to represent the real will of the people. He hoped when memorials were presented hereafter, there would be no detraction from them when their temper and tone, and remarks, accorded with the business in which their signers were engaged. These memorials say their distresses arise from the curtailments of the Bank of the United States, and that this is the necessary consequence of the removal of the deposites. No system of public credit can consist with any one man's absolute and unlimited power in government. Frederick of Prussia, in an essay on political subjects, entertained the idea that it was impossible to establish a bank in a government of civil monarchy. But he was determined to try it. He established a bank, and by his fostering care it did linger out his reign, but how long afterwards it continued to breathe, Mr. L. could

not tell. Bank credit was one of the most sensitive of all plants. At the touch of arbitrary power it shrinks its leaves; but remove it and it expands again and revives. But let power remain inexorably pressed on it, and the plant must perish. He had seen the evidences of efforts which were made to reverse the sentiments of Virginia on this subject, and if it succeeded he must yield, not with any concern for himself, but rather for his children. The effort was made, to get a majority by claiming to have a majority here; and a gentleman had thought proper to say, that he knew better the sentiments of Virginia than he did. He mentioned this, for the purpose of making this remark—that for a State-rights man to say a single word to detract from the dignity of a State Legislature, was to do more harm to State rights than all the powers of this Government united could do. For himself, he believed Virginia was not changed from the complexion presented by her Legislature, and would not be found chained again.

He would not fatigue the Senate by an argument on the constitutional point of this subject, but follow the President to the sequel of this transaction. As soon as the order for removing the deposites was given, transfer checks were issued to the State banks on the United States Bank, to use as might suit their purposes. And this was done with the avowed purpose of enabling the State banks to meet the demands of the branches of the United States Bank upon them, and so by lending money relieve their distress. When the Manhattan Bank (for illustration) presented its check on the branch in New York, it was debtor to the Government some $200,000. It then received credit for that sum and balances due from other State banks transferred to it, to meet the balance. So that this draft was put in the hands of the Manhattan Bank to trade on till called for by the Government, and thus as complete a loan was effected for its use, as if the President had loaned directly out of the treasury. Could gentlemen point out in the Constitution any authority for thus lending the people's money, or any implication of authority? Is the lending out of this money to be upheld as a proper exercise of Executive power in such a limited Government as ours. In any days of the British Government, such an exercise of power would cost the minister, not his head, (for sanguinary punishments are much curtailed there,) but certainly his rights as a freeborn citizen of the country. He would have been impeached and declared incapable of further serving the crown in any capacity whatever. It was immaterial whether these evils were designed or not. He did not suspect the President of design, and not suspecting him, he acquitted him of it. But he stated the *fact* that here was an assumption of power, and it was the duty of freemen to oppose it, by whoever and wherever asserted. He desired to be informed whether there was any statute of the United States giving the Postmaster General power to borrow money on the credit of the United States. He thought not. And yet we had seen it avowed that the Postmaster General had borrowed some four or five hundred thousand dollars; a power which is only given to Congress. Here, then, is the Executive Government lending the people's money to the State banks to pay their debts to the United States—the money lent out by one hand and borrowed by the other: the Secretary of the Treasury lending money without interest, and the Postmaster General borrowing money at six per cent.

But we had been told that if the removal of the deposites had been put upon an error in judgment, instead of an usurpation of power, there would have been two-thirds of both Houses of Congress in favor of the restoration. Why then not retrace his steps? If the President of the United States would retract this error of his own accord, and restore the deposites, and thereby confidence to the country, not all the fame he received from the victory of New Orleans would equal that peal of thanks which would resound from all quarters of this Union for the act. But alas, there is no hope of it. If the newspaper reports are to be relied on, nothing will cause him to relent, and it therefore behooves Congress to take such steps as the best interests of the country require and demand.

Mr. FORSYTH replied. [The notes of our reporter were given to Mr. Forsyth, who has not returned them; and it is now impossible to prepare his speech in time for this paper.]

Mr. KING, of Georgia, said he cared not to interfere in the controversy between his honorable colleague and the honorable Senator from Virginia, touching the respect due to memorials, or to examine the motives of those by whom they were usually got up and sent here. He would only say that he not only acknowledged the right of the citizens of all parties to be heard in this form, but approved the practice on all subjects of importance to the interests of the country. But he must say, (what few would deny,) that when looked to as a test of public sentiment on questions purely political in their character, these memorials should be most carefully watched and diligently guarded, to prevent imposition. And perhaps (said Mr. K.) a better illustration of this truth will not be required than a reference to the very memorial now before the Senate, which, notwithstanding heaven and earth had been moved for many weeks to stir up the people to sign it, contained (as he understood and believed) the names of a mere fraction of the voters in the district from which it came. We must not too readily suppose that memorials represent the feelings of the whole district from which they come. We only hear from those who are dissatisfied with the Government. Oppositions are always better organized, and more active, than those who are satisfied with the established order of things—who rarely move so long as they continue satisfied with their condition.

But (said Mr. K.) enough of this. I will leave the discussion on this branch of the subject to the two honorable Senators who commenced it, and return to the subject of the memorial now before the Senate, on a question of reference. The object of this memorial, I believe, (said Mr. K.,) is the recharter of the Bank of the United States, and the restoration of the deposites.

[Here Mr. Leigh interrupted Mr. K., and said the memorial only prayed the restoration of the deposites.]

Mr. K. said he was glad to be thus corrected. The correction would shorten what he had to say upon the memorial; and he had, in fact, a few days since, on another memorial, from Massachusetts, expressed briefly his opinion upon a recharter, and professed a friendship—rather a cool one, to be sure, for a national bank under existing circumstances. I am glad this single question is presented, as it gives me at once a proper occasion to refer to some remarks which I made a few days since, and which seem to have been, by some gentlemen, imperfectly understood, or entirely perverted and misapplied.

Sir, (said Mr. K.,) what I said, I said, and have no disposition to retract or modify it. But why (said Mr. K.) are the remarks referred to constantly called "*admissions?*" I call them *statements*, for which I am alone responsible. By what authority (said Mr. K.) do gentlemen so connect a party with me as to embarrass it either by my statements or admissions? What I did state, Mr. President, and am willing to repeat, is, that I had travelled in several States in the South and Southwest, and that the measure adopted by the Administration in the removal of the deposites, at the time the act was done, was very generally disapproved as *inexpedient*. But was I not sufficiently explicit as to the nature and reasons of this disapprobation? It was not because the people in the South generally believed that the President acted from bad motives; not because they believed he had violated and trampled the Constitution under foot; not because in so doing he had usurped dangerous powers, and united the purse and the sword; not because they are in favor of the Bank of the United States; not because they believe that the institution has not abused its functions, by corrupting presses, and purchasing up politicians, and in many other ways; not because they disagree with the President in the *great end* of destroying this institution, which they think dangerous to liberty. No, sir. Whatever my own opinion may be, I think the great majority of the people to whom I referred are with the President on all these points. But they disapproved the act, because, whatever may have been the conduct of the bank, they knew it possessed immense power, and was fixed on the country till the 4th of March, 1836. They also, perhaps, had not full confidence in the patriotism of the combination of parties opposed to the Administration, who they feared would avail themselves of this pretext to use this most powerful engine in the cause of party, and thereby inflict cruel calamity upon an unoffending community. They, therefore, said, let the lion sleep, and quietly expire for want of congressional breath—peaceably die for want of a charter.

I stated further, sir, (said Mr. K.,) (but with the added caution that I only stated my conjectures,) that I thought these were the sentiments of a majority even of the friends of the Administration when Congress assembled, and if the question of restoration had been viewed only as one of expediency—had not been made a party question, and forced upon the friends of the Administration in a form to make it one upon which the existence of an Administration, which was preferred for higher reasons, was to depend, and a vote taken on the subject before these apprehended mischiefs had occurred, and by which they might have been prevented; in that case, a majority of two-thirds of both Houses might have voted a restoration of the deposites. I say so still, without professing, either before or now, to make anything more than a conjecture of my own. It is said all around me, that I am mistaken on this point. I think it very likely, sir, and so stated before. But what I am most anxious in this place to notice and correct is, the misconstruction of my admission, as it is called by the honorable Senator from Maryland. *I did not say, or even intimate—I did not then, nor do I now, believe*, that there is a majority of two-thirds, or any other majority, *in either House*, who believe it would be expedient, or beneficial to the country, *now* to restore the deposites, unless the Bank of the United States is to be rechartered. Nay, sir, I will go further. As it seems I have bound one party, I will now bind the other. I stated when last up, that, if I liked the project for a renewal of the charter, for a short time, I would vote for it. My favor to this and all paper-issuing banks is, to be sure, a cool one; but, if the gentleman gets my vote, I presume he will not care much with what feeling it is given. I am, then, sir, the gentleman must admit, at least in a modified sense, a bank man; and, therefore, for a much stronger reason than any he showed, have a right to bind him and the whole bank party. I say, then, distinctly, that there are, in my opinion, few, in or out of this House, even of that party, who care a snap of the finger for a restoration of the deposites, unless the recharter of the bank is to accompany or follow that measure. All must know, or at least believe, that restoration, without recharter, must only add an additional shock to the currency, and prolong the distresses of the people. I cannot permit honorable gentlemen to escape from the obligations of my "admission." I certainly have better authority for making this "admission" than that which they have attempted to use against the friends of the Administration.

Sir, (said Mr. K.,) having endeavored to relieve the friends of the Administration from the embarrassment of what is called my "admission," I will proceed to notice the remarks of the honorable Senator from Virginia, who thinks it strange I should not have heard of the constitutional objections until they were raised in this Hall. I state so again, and I presume the honorable gentleman does not intend to call in question *the truth* of this statement.

Mr. LEIGH. Certainly not.

I did not (said Mr. K.) state that the objections had not been before made, only that I had no recollection of having seen or heard them; by which alone I intended to prove that among plain people the objections were not obvious, and for that reason alone should not be readily trusted, as, in fact, no reasoning was to be trusted but that which was natural and easy. This very power had been before exercised, was a power which seemed literally given by the bank charter, and had even been exercised, without a whisper of complaint, he believed, for purposes the most obnoxious, (according to the views of the honorable Senator,) that is, *for the assistance of the State banks*. What discourses may have been early made, or views expressed by the learned circles of Richmond, Kentucky, or elsewhere, and which had escaped his observation, he knew not. He only meant to say, that a con-

struction which required the penetration of practised politicians, or even the aid of a learned professor, whose very professional duties led to the habitual use of subtleties, should not readily be countenanced by those who have a real regard for the Constitution.

Why, Mr President, (said Mr. K.,) I can truly say, even now, that although I have listened attentively here for two months, and paid strict attention to the subject, I do not now distinctly understand any definite and well-understood ground upon which the power of the Secretary to remove the deposites is denied. There is such a confusion of ideas on the subject—so much difference of opinion, and such a mixture of objections to the power itself, and the insufficiency of the reasons for its exercise in this particular instance, that I find it impossible to understand gentlemen upon this point. This may be, and probably is, owing to my own obtuseness of intellect, but may be taken as some evidence of the danger of this novel construction of the charter. He had, however, no disposition to enter into an argument on a point so much discussed already, and if he had, he could not be expected to refute arguments which he could not clearly understand. Suffice it to say, then, Mr. President, that the power exercised by the Secretary is plainly given in the bank charter.

But it seems we are very unexpectedly surrounded by strict constructionists, who, to prove their principles, instead of reading a charter, make a charter. New friends to the Constitution. Yes, sir, gentlemen who for years have been mutually charging each other with a habitual contempt of the Constitution, all at once claim to be the only exclusive guardians of that instrument; and to show their new-born affection, instead of expounding the Constitution, they go into elaborate arguments to prove what the Constitution ought to be. The continual cry is, the "Constitution, the Constitution! the bleeding Constitution!" There are no constitutional measures but their measures. There is no people but their people. All is tyranny that keeps their party out of power. All is oppression that forces the equal and regular operation of the laws. "Liberty! Liberty!" is the cry of these exclusive patriots. An oppressed, enslaved, and degraded people are called on to rescue the Constitution, and recover the liberty they have lost; and in the very next breath we hear the complaint that the Senate alone can save the country, as the majority of the people are against them. In the name of reason, sir, what kind of liberty is this? It can be no other, by their own confessions, than the liberty of governing—the liberty of a few to govern the great body of the people, and not the liberty of the great body of the people to govern themselves.

Those who prefer the present Administration are continually taunted with the question, "And will you submit?" I answer, ay, sir; I will submit to the laws of my country, and the Government of my choice. But, sir, I will tell you what I am not disposed to submit to: I never can, willingly, submit to the dictates of an ambitious and disappointed faction.

But, sir, we have just heard again the oft repeated alarm that we are living under a despotism. Paper currency, it is stated, cannot be sustained under despotic government. And why, sir, these continual insults offered to the majority of the American people for sustaining the government of their choice? Sir, gentlemen may cease their lamentations, and the band of leagued tyrants on the other side of the water, to whom they afford so much joy, may hush their triumphs. The people of this country will protect their own liberties, and march on to the highest destiny of nations. Yes, sir; they may meet with impediments—the extremes of political doctrine may hang heavily on each skirt; they may be loaded down with bank paper—tripped up or jostled by bank monopolies—and meet with the various obstacles thrown in their way by party dissensions, but still, sir, the great body of this nation will move on with the gathering strength of a growing giant—not to "despotism," sir—not to tyranny; but until they shake tyranny from the earth, and crumble the despotism of the world to atoms.

Sir, (said Mr. K.,) the people of the United States are free, and under God, I think they are determined to remain so.

The memorial was referred to the Committee on Finance, and ordered to be printed.

The following resolution was submitted by Mr. McKEAN:

Resolved, That the Committee on Pensions be instructed to inquire into the expediency of granting relief to Ann Holland, widow of Thomas Holland, deceased, a revolutionary soldier.

At half past two o'clock the special order of the day was announced, being the

REMOVAL OF THE DEPOSITES.

Mr. TALLMADGE rose and addressed the Senate until half past three o'clock, sustaining the Secretary of the Treasury in removing the deposites from the Bank of the United States; when he gave way to

Mr. CLAY, upon whose motion

The Senate adjourned.

HOUSE OF REPRESENTATIVES.

Wednesday, March 12, 1834.

BANK OF THE UNITED STATES.

Mr. POLK rose and said, that as the documents appended to the report presented by the Committee of Ways and Means, which was ordered to be printed, had not been yet laid on the table by the public printer; and as the object of postponing the consideration of the report was to have them printed for the information of the House, before there was any discussion on the subject, he felt it necessary to move that the further consideration of the report be postponed until Tuesday next.

Mr. WILDE 'hoped the motion to postpone would not prevail. Every member already had the principal documents, and was therefore prepared to proceed with the discussion. He desired to submit his views, and he would suggest, that as he was prepared now to go into it, which would take up some time, and as Friday and Saturday were set apart for private business, the subject would at all events have to stand over till Tuesday.

Mr. ELLSWORTH said that it could not be doubted, when the state of the public feeling was considered, that this subject ought to be proceeded with, as it was the duty of the House at once to decide, if it was to be so decided, that the deposites were to remain where they were now placed.

Mr. DICKSON, of New York, viewing it as all-important that the House should have full information preparatory to full discussion, was in favor of the postponement, for the reason given by the chairman of the Committee of Ways and Means.

Mr. CHILTON would not stop now to remark upon the charge of attitude which those who formerly so strenuously opposed delay on this subject now presented, in seeking for it. He felt compelled, however, to agree with them, because he wished the present question should be settled coolly and dispassionately, and because, if it was in order to refer to what was done elsewhere, he might say there was a proposition made (in the Senate) which might restore the lost and murdered tranquillity of the country. He did not desire that his acquiescence to postpone should be considered any acquiescence with the views by which the Executive was influenced, but as a means to have the present question satisfactorily settled.

Mr. WAYNE rose only to remark that the chairman of the Committee of Ways and Means had no disposition to delay this discussion; but he felt that if he pressed it, under the circumstances he stated, that he would have left himself subject to a very heavy imputation, and deservedly so, if he pressed discussion without having documents declared to be important, but which were ordered to be printed. There were some of the documents which had never been in print, and although anxious, himself, that the discussion should go on, yet he must say, that he was not prepared to go on with it, without these documents. He desired that the postponement should be fairly understood, as desired, because that information, to which the members were entitled, had not been printed. For if the discussion were on without this information, they might be called on to vote on a sub-

ject upon which they had not had information which they had a right to call for. From these views, and believing that the discussion could go on next week; and as he hoped it would uninterruptedly until its close, he hoped the postponement would be acceded to.

Mr. BURGES deprecated any further delay, for nothing was so oppressive to the heart as that feeling which ariseth from hope deferred. They could not justify themselves to their constituents for delaying a discussion upon a subject in which delay was ruin to their hopes and prospects, and he thought so certain as delay would be now made, so certainly would the people scrutinize with severity their conduct. He could not agree that it was necessary to wait for the documents. It was not necessary to wait for precedents or dicta to ascertain whether the Secretary had violated the law and brought ruin and destruction on the country, when it was openly maintained that it was not the Executive, living or dead, if God, he would arraign his memory for the perpetration of acts of such gross usurpation, that he ought to have been hurled from office. The delay sought for would be followed by calls for the perusal question, by committees of investigation # set during the summer; and thus there would be so relief given to the community.

Mr. MASON, of Virginia, said, it appeared from what had fallen from the member from Rhode Island, that his opinion was made up on this subject, and that nothing that could be adduced would justify what he pleased to term acts of gross usurpation. But he trusted that the House were not prejudiced on the same extent which that honorable member had avowed. He thought it was a most novel proposition, that, upon a question of such a grave character, there should be a desire to precipitate discussion, when information, ordered to be printed, was within their reach. He would make an additional remark; he had been hitherto a silent, but not inattentive observer of the past discussion; and he must say, that for one, he entertained the opinion that the distress which they had heard, was attributable, in a great degree, to the delay that had taken place in deciding this question. He hoped, therefore, that when the question should come up in a tangible shape, that the honorable member from Rhode Island would show the same disposition to act speedily upon it, that he now did. In voting to postpone now, [Mr. Mason] was not for continuing the evils which were brought upon the country, and which were brought upon it by a variety of causes, but he desired to have all the means presented to the House, that voting upon the question, they should be enabled to come to a right conclusion.

Mr. CHILTON ALLAN expressed his alarm at the indications thrown out, and that there was some intention to prevent ample discussion upon a subject which, upon all hands, was agreed to be so necessary. He desired that the discussion should proceed, and that it should be sent to the Committee of the Whole on the state of the Union for this purpose. He might however be mistaken in what he was afraid was the meaning of what had fallen from honorable members, and he called on the chairman of the Committee of Ways and Means to say at once whether it is his intention to send this into the Committee of the Whole.

Mr. POLK replied, that although he did not know that the honorable member was authorized to propound such an interrogatory, yet he would answer it. He would avow, that he was unwilling that the subject should be sent to any place whence a decision could not be had upon it; although he

the same time, would not desire to take any course which should preclude full discussion by those who were desirous to give their views upon it. Under the circumstances stated by the honorable member from Georgia, [Mr. Wayne,] he was perfectly correct in stating that the only motive which he had in moving the postponement, was to avoid the charge that might have been urged against him, for precipitating the House into a discussion upon a report, the evidence upon which the report was founded not having been, under circumstances which he could not control, furnished to them. He had no design to procrastinate the subject unnecessarily, or to give it the go-by. On the contrary, he desired to have the fullest expression that could be given upon each and every one of the resolutions which the committee, of which he was chairman, had felt it their duty to present to the House for adoption.

In respect to the remarks made by the honorable member from Rhode Island, he would only say, that he hoped he would be prepared, when the question should come up, to assist, then, in preventing unnecessary delay to a decision upon the question. He, and those with whom he acted, were not to blame for the seventy or eighty days discussion that had already taken place. And when the subject had taken the course they had always desired, there was not much delay by the committee in presenting their views. He considered that the documents that were appended were of the most important character; and although he could not say what weight would be attached to them by the House, he could say that they had much weight in inducing the committee to come to the conclusion they had on the various matters referred to them. He repeated, that he had no wish whatever to procrastinate the subject, and if such an impression was thrown out to the country, for himself, he felt compelled to say, that there was no foundation for it. To evince his determination to bring this subject to a close, he would state that it was his intention, when strictly in order to do so, to submit a motion, for the purpose of insuring discussion and speedy action upon it, that it shall be made the special order of the day, to sit daily until a final decision should be had upon it. When that motion would be made, it would be seen whether the honorable member from Rhode Island would coöperate with him to avoid delay.

Mr. MILLER advocated the postponement, not for the purpose of putting off the debate on the subject, which, from all appearances, was likely to be of the same length as the session; but he was desirous that the intervening days between this and Tuesday would be passed in despatching other business, which was necessary, for the public good, to be acted upon. He felt it his duty to repel, with indignation, the remarks in which the honorable member from Rhode Island had, by indulgence, attempted to cast censure upon the venerable Chief Magistrate, for whose life of service the country was so much indebted.

Mr. WAYNE remarked, that as he had been misunderstood by some honorable members, he wished to remind the House that, by its rules, there was a positive obstacle to going on at present with the discussion. It was the right of every member to know what it was he was to be called upon to vote for; and if the right of calling for the reading of matters connected with it was exercised, if the documents were not printed, it must at once put a stop to their proceedings. He would give notice, that if the postponement was not acceded to, he, in justice to himself, would call for the reading of the documents.

Mr. BAYLIES did not wish to be subject to the imputation which the honorable member from Rhode Island cast upon those who favored the postponement. Whilst this honorable member felt so much for the distress over the country, others, however, were just as anxious as he was to avoid delay; but he thought it was not just to go into such a subject as the present, without having the fullest means to come to a right conclusion upon it. He appealed, confidently, to his own conduct, in not having occupied the time of the House, or causing any delay; but he had not desired to prevent others from being heard. The postponement now, will not prevent those who are desirous of giving their views, to do so hereafter.

Mr. ASHLEY thought, as the debate on this subject was likely to be protracted, that the House ought to postpone the discussion now, for the purpose of taking up and acting upon the several appropriation bills which were necessary for the public service.

Mr. HUBBARD rose and said that it would seem that no discussion can be had in this House upon any subject connected with the public deposites, without the manifestation of an extraordinary excitement. This is certainly to be regretted.

In order to ascertain the propriety of adopting the motion presented by the chairman of the Committee of Ways and Means, we should inquire in the first place what were the subjects referred to that committee.

It will be found that not only the report of the Secretary of the Treasury was committed to that committee, but also various memorials touching the bank and the deposites were also referred. Many of the memorials called for a recharter of the Bank of the United States, others petitioned for a restoration of the public deposites to that institution.

What has been the report of the committee in relation to those subjects? The committee has recommended the adoption of a resolution that it is inexpedient to recharter the Bank of the United States. They have assigned their reasons for this. The committee have also recommended the adoption of a resolution, that it is inexpedient to restore the deposites to the Bank of the United States. They have stated in the body of their report the considerations which induced them to present this last resolution. And it must occur to every member of this House that the power of the Secretary of the Treasury over the public deposites has been questioned and denied; and in relation to that power the committee have, at great labor, collected, prepared, and arranged a body of documents fully sustaining the power of the Secretary. They have considered this as of the utmost importance, and they think that the documentary history appended to the report will clearly show that this same power has been exercised by the head of the Treasury Department from the foundation of the Government to the present time.

And now, sir, what is the motion of the gentleman from Tennessee? It is, that the further consideration of this subject be postponed until Tuesday next. And why? Because, sir, the report, thus prepared, with the documents, have not been published and placed upon the tables of the members,—that no opportunity has yet been given to examine that report.

His honorable friend has not asked for the postponement for his own accommodation, or for the accommodation of the other members of the Committee of Ways and Means; but with reference to the report, the motion has been made in justice to himself, and in justice to the other members of the committee. It is due to them, and it is due to the House. The grounds taken by the committee have been distinctly presented in their report. They think that the members of this House should have an opportunity fully to examine and well to consider those grounds, even before the debate should commence. It is no more than an act of justice to them. No fault can be imputed to the committee; they cannot be answerable for the delay which has taken place in the printing of their report with the accompanying documents. On every consideration, therefore, it did seem to him that the motion should be adopted, and the consideration of the subject postponed.

Mr. EVERETT, of Vermont, advocated the motion, as a courtesy due to the committee; and if (he said) the committee had not made the motion, he should have made it himself. He was opposed to going into the discussion before the documents were furnished.

Mr. HARDIN felt no disposition (he said) to urge the debate until the documents were submitted. Kentucky had not yet been heard on the question, and he was anxious that the discussion should be renewed; and when it was renewed, he hoped it would be prosecuted daily, till a decision was obtained.

Mr. McKENNAN was in favor of the postponement, for the reason that he thought the House ought to become acquainted with the opinions and wishes of the people on the question. He wished to postpone the decision of the question till the voice of the people had been heard in this House from every part of the country. If there was to be any relief from public distress, the people must look for it to this House. They could expect nothing from the Executive. He was also in favor of the motion, because we ought to act upon some important business which was now before us. He therefore moved that the consideration of the motion be postponed to next Tuesday.

Mr. BURGES said, he wished to move an amendment to the resolutions reported from the Committee of Ways and Means, recommitting the report and resolutions, with instructions to report a resolution declaring that the reasons of the Secretary of the Treasury for the removal of the deposites were insufficient. His object in opposing the motion to postpone was, not to press the discussion, but to put the subject in a proper condition for discussion. Now, the discussion is to come up in the House, when the previous question can at any time cut off the debate. He wished to put the simple question to the House, whether they would keep the control of the subject in the Committee of the Whole or not? He claimed to be permitted to call the President a tyrant without asking leave, for he was called so by thousands who once admired him, and he was felt to be so throughout the suffering country. The President said, in reply to the complaints of the people, Go home—I can govern: I have been accustomed to govern all my life.

Mr. BYNUM spoke in favor of the motion to postpone. He wanted the facts, to examine for himself. He could not take them upon trust from the gentleman from Georgia, nor from any gentleman. Gentlemen seized on every opportunity to set up a cry of distress, desolation, ruin, and tyranny. The people understood this, and could not be misled by it. They would take no man's word for it. They understand that these denunciations are for political effect, and these gentlemen who are crying wolf, wolf, when they can show no wolf, would be dealt with by the people accordingly. If the postponement for a month would enable us to receive any additional light, let us have it. Hoping that the question would receive a full discussion, and be decided in reference to the best interest of the country, he should vote for the postponement.

Mr. McDUFFIE said that the report of the Committee of Ways and Means was better calculated than any other measure to increase the alarm and distress of the country, and he was, therefore, in favor of pressing it to any early decision. He understood that the chairman did not intend to speak, and that the gentleman from Georgia was ready to speak; but if the chairman had any special reasons for the postponement, he would, in courtesy, consent to it.

Mr. LANE said, if the gentleman from Georgia was ready to go on with his argument, he was not ready to hear him. He had neither read or even seen the report of the Committee of Ways and Means, and therefore would not be able to judge of the applicability of the argument for or against it, and for that reason should vote against the motion to postpone until Tuesday week, and for the one till Tuesday next. He had remained a silent and patient listener to the arguments upon the subject of the deposites for the last three months; that he would not have broken that silence on the present occasion, but for the imputation attempted to be thrown upon the chairman of the Committee of Ways and Means, and those with whom he acts, by the gentleman from Rhode Island; that he trusts he will never be capable of calling in question the motives or intentions of any gentleman in this House; nor was he willing quietly to sit and hear the motives of others arraigned. The gentleman says the object is delay. This is a voice that falls upon the ear with an ill grace from gentlemen on that side of the House. To review the past, is always attended with advantage. On the 12th of December last, the gentleman from Pennsylvania said, action was called for, immediate action; that in a few weeks, unless the deposites should be returned, it would be too late. The gentleman from South Carolina on the same day said, discussion might be sport to the members, but was death to the people. Mr. L. said, that

on that occasion he had also said, his vote should be given on that side which should be most likely to bring the subject to a satisfactory and speedy conclusion. So much for the past. Now to whom is delay to be justly attributed? After seven weeks' delay, each of these gentlemen voted against bringing that preliminary discussion to a close. The report is now before the House for action, ordered to be printed; but not printed, not read, or yet seen. The motion is to put off the debate, for that purpose, is now resisted, on the ground of delay.

Mr. L. desired not only to see and read the report and appendix, but also to hear the gentleman from Rhode Island, whose illuminated mind would no doubt throw much light around it. That he should avail himself of all the means in his power, all the *lights* of the gentleman, to arrive at a just conclusion, always excepting *a blue light*.

Mr. BURD made a few remarks in favor of the postponement. On another occasion, he might go into details in relation to the distress pervading the country. He thought the question ought to be decided within a reasonable or proper time, after due consideration of every fact connected with the condition of the country, and the laws and the Constitution of the country.

Mr. WILDE said that so far as he was concerned, he hoped the House would acquit him of any extraordinary urgency. At one time his speech was cut off by the previous question, and though he did not suppose that the object of the motion to postpone was again to cut off his speech, yet he was somewhat surprised that when he was ready to proceed, and the chairman of the committee did not wish himself to speak, the House should not be willing to hear him. He assured the gentleman, as the determination was to keep the tourniquet on the debate, so as to amputate it at any time, he could not tell how long the debate would last. But if he could be allowed to consume these two days, there would certainly be left two days for others who were to follow him. He stated that documents, to procure which the postponement was asked, would be of no aid to the gentleman from Indiana, in understanding his speech, as he should not refer to them, and as they had no relation to the points he should discuss. He also said, that the main positions of the majority of the committee, that the deposites ought not to be restored, and that the bank ought not to be rechartered, &c., would not be at all affected by the documents referred to. He had no disposition to facilitate or hasten the passing of the appropriation bills. He did not certainly know what would follow the passage of those bills. But he was enabled to guess that, when they were passed, an attempt would be made to precipitate the decision of other questions, in a manner which to him appeared inexplicable. As, however, the question whether he should speak to-day or not, was likely to occupy the whole day, he would withdaw his objection to the motion.

The question was then taken on the motion of Mr. McKENNAN, to postpone the subject till Tuesday week, and rejected.

The motion to postpone till Tuesday next was agreed to without division.

Mr. J. Q. ADAMS asked the unanimous consent of the House to present certain resolutions of the Legislature of Massachusetts; which was objected to.

Mr. ADAMS moved the suspension of the rule; which was negatived.

Mr. POLK moved the suspension of the rule, so as to permit him to offer the following resolution:

Resolved, That the report of the Committee of Ways and Means on the removal of the deposites from the Bank of the United States, be the standing order of the day for Tuesday next, at one o'clock, and on each succeeding day in every week, Saturdays excepted, at the same hour, until disposed of; and that until the hour of one o'clock, P. M., on each day, the business of the House shall proceed in the order prescribed by the rules of the House.

The motion to suspend was agreed to.

The SPEAKER stated that the resolution must lie on the table one day.

Mr. POLK moved to suspend the rules of the House in order to proceed to the consideration of the resolution.

Mr. McDUFFIE asked whether the resolution, if it was acted upon now, would not fall behind all other resolutions.

The CHAIR replied in the affirmative.

Mr. McDUFFIE said he was therefore in favor of its consideration now.

The motion to suspend was agreed to.

Mr. HANNEGAN moved also to except Mondays as well as Saturdays.

Mr. POLK said it would be understood, that for the purpose of receiving memorials, the House might suspend the rule on Mondays; but he would consent to modify his resolution so as to except Saturdays and Mondays, after the presentation of petitions.

Mr. McDUFFIE moved a proviso, that petitions and memorials shall be received on Monday.

Mr. POLK accepted the proviso, and Mr. HANNEGAN withdrew his motion.

Mr. ELLSWORTH asked whether the report, if this resolution was carried, would be discussed in the House or in committee.

The CHAIR replied, that when the report was taken up, it would be in order to move the commitment of the report.

Mr. MERCER opposed the resolution, for the reason that it would embarrass and delay the business of the House.

Mr. ADAMS, of Massachusetts, opposed the resolution. If it passed it was extremely probable that no other subjects could be considered at this session. He alluded to the presentation of the Virginia resolutions, which were not expected to produce any debate. But one gentleman from Virginia rose and made a speech of three hours upon it, with the force and eloquence of which he was much delighted. The debate had been continued ever since, and was likely to continue, whenever it should be in order to take up resolutions. He referred also to the fact that the debate had gone far beyond the subject of the Virginia resolutions, and might continue till the first Monday of next December, should the House sit so long. The speech of the eloquent gentleman from South Carolina did not at all relate to the subject of the resolutions.

Mr. A. wished to say, that he did not care one straw whether the question in relation to the deposites should be taken now, or three months hence. He did not believe that a decision here would decide the question. Those who laid that flattering unction to their souls would find themselves mistaken. It had been said to-day by a member, that it would be vain for the people to go to the Executive for relief. He would add, that it were vain for the people to come to us for relief. They must look to themselves, and to themselves alone. He believed that the decision of this House three months hence would be the same that it would be now. Where was the necessity of pressing this subject? He cared very little when or how the House acted upon the propositions of the committee. He could see no reason why the House should clog itself with this resolution; for no member of the House could lay his hand upon his heart, and say that the decision of the House would be different three months hence from the decision which it would make now. If we go on with the debate, we cannot take up the appropriation bills, about which the gentleman from Tennessee was so justly anxious.

Well, sir, it is circulated in whispers in the House, and around about the House, that as we have not had sufficient specimens of the exercise of royal prerogative, after due time, when the chairman thinks that the subject has been sufficiently debated, the discussion will be closed by the previous question, preparatory to such a disagreement of the two Houses as will render this House the instrument of the exercise of another royal prerogative. He was not disposed to credit everything which he heard, but from what he had seen this morning, he was led to believe that the minority of this House would be deprived of its just rights, and the people would be deprived of their constitutional right to present their grievances to this House.

The SPEAKER said that he would take this occasion to inform the House that these discussions had not the approbation of the Chair, and that the Chair was not responsible for them.

Mr. POLK said that he could not consider that much that had fallen from the gentleman from Massachusetts was very relevant to the question before the House: it was not necessary for him to reply at large to it. He would, however, say, that his object in presenting the resolution that he had submitted, was for the purpose of insuring to the great subject full discussion, yet, at the same time, have some regard for other interests to come up before the House.

With respect to what the gentleman had remarked about the previous question, he begged to inquire if his actions formerly were consistent with his present opinion? Was not that gentleman found voting for the previous question, when the motion to recharter the bank was only carried by the very turning of the screws which he now deprecates so much? He could not help feeling that such repeated reference to the call for the previous question was intended to reflect upon him for the use of it. But in the discharge of the duty assigned him, he would not be deterred; he would always take such a course as a sense of duty only would dictate. It was well understood that, from the nature of all numerous legislative bodies, Congress ought to have a proper control over all subjects to be debated in it; and when the subject should come up on Tuesday, they would then have to decide whether they would send the subject into Committee of the Whole on the state of the Union—where there could be no previous question—or not. The country, however, expected action from them upon it, and whether their decision might or not, as was said, be obligatory or not upon the people, yet they were bound to give that decision—the decision of Congress. The course taken by him in attaining it, by making the subject the special order of the day, to the exclusion of other subjects, was following that of last session, upon the tariff, and this session upon the question of the deposites. But notwithstanding this, he trusted that full opportunity would be afforded to the honorable member to present the Massachusetts resolves, and that the debate on those from Virginia, which he so much dreaded, would ere long be brought to a close.

Mr. McDUFFIE remarked that it did not appear to him that any actual change was made by the resolution, to prevent the reception of petitions and memorials. The previous question was always in the power of the majority for them to use over the minority; it was not therefore for the minority to provoke them into the use of it by unprofitable discussion. As a certain time would in all probability be granted by the majority, if any more time was wasted, the minority would only be burning out their own candle. He was most anxious to meet the question fairly, and then have a decision upon it.

Mr. VINTON submitted an amendment "that so much only of the report of the Committee of Ways and Means as related to the removal of the deposites" should be the order of the day.

Mr. COULTER considered that, under all the circumstances, the postponement sought by the chairman of the Committee of Ways and Means ought to have been acceded to, and that it was for the advantage of those in favor of the bank, to agree to the resolution making the subject the special order of the day.

After a few remarks from Mr. HARDIN,

Mr. McDUFFIE inquired the state of the question?

The SPEAKER explained, and said the question would be subject to all the rules of other privileged questions when it came up on Tuesday next.

Mr. DICKSON asked if it would be in order for a majority of the House on Tuesday next to order the subject to be referred to the Committee of the Whole on the state of the Union?

The SPEAKER replied in the affirmative.

The resolution, as modified, was then read, and agreed to; after which,

The House adjourned.

IN SENATE.

THURSDAY, *March* 13, 1834.

Mr. HENDRICKS, from the Committee on Roads and Canals, reported a bill appropriating

lands for cutting a canal from the Wabash river to Lake Erie, and for other purposes; which was read, and ordered to a second reading, and the documents accompanying it directed to be printed.

Mr. WEBSTER presented the proceedings of a public meeting, and the memorial of persons composing the same, of Brooklyn, New York, in favor of a restoration of the deposites, and the recharter of the Bank of the United States; which were read, referred to the Committee on Finance, and ordered to be printed.

Mr. WRIGHT presented the memorial of inhabitants of Suffolk, New York, praying an appropriation for the improvement of certain inlets of Long Island; which was referred to the Committee on Commerce.

Mr. TOMLINSON, from the Committee on Pensions, reported a bill from the House of Representatives relative to pensions; which was read, and ordered to a second reading.

Mr. TOMLINSON, from the same committee, asked to be discharged from the further consideration of the petition of Christopher Casey, and that it be referred to the Secretary of War; which was agreed to.

Mr. SPRAGUE presented two memorials, one from Eastport, and the other from Lubec, Maine, praying the restoration of the deposites, and the recharter of the Bank of the United States; which were read, referred to the Committee on Finance, and ordered to be printed.

Mr. KENT presented the petitions of James Williams and Benedict I. Heard; the first of which was referred to the Committee on Foreign Relations, and the latter to the Committee of Claims.

Mr. SPRAGUE, from the Committee of Claims, reported a bill for the relief of David and Ebenezer Robinson; which was read, and ordered to a second reading.

Mr. KANE presented the petition of Susannah Pratt; which was referred to the Committee of Claims.

Mr. KANE, from the Committee on Private Land Claims, reported a large number of private bills, (the titles of which could not be heard distinctly by the reporter,) from the House of Representatives; which were laid upon the table.

The following resolution was submitted by Mr. SPRAGUE:

Resolved, That the Committee on the Judiciary be instructed to inquire into the expediency of continuing, for a limited time, the act entitled "An act for the relief of certain insolvent debtors of the United States," passed on the 2d of March, A. D. 1831.

Mr. TYLER presented the memorial of inhabitants of the towns of Fredericksburg and Falmouth, in Virginia, praying the restoration of the deposites to the Bank of the United States.

Also, the proceedings of a public meeting of inhabitants of Accomac county, Virginia, of similar import.

Mr. TYLER observed, on presenting these memorials, that the memorialists prayed a restoration of the deposites as the proper remedy for their sufferings; and why should we not restore them? It is not the Bank of the United States that they look to, but the country, the wants of the country, and the requirements of the Constitution and the laws of the country. He cared not for the bank, nor had he inquired whether the bank required the restoration of the deposites. He rather desired to see it put to death tranquilly, and that public confidence may be restored by producing harmony between the President and his Secretary and the bank. He condemned the remark of the gentleman from Georgia, [Mr. FORSYTH,] that the President could not in honor retrace his steps. The country was in deep distress, and the honor of the President required him to consult the best interests of the country. The honor of consistency in continuing in error was to bring contempt upon the country. Virginia, too, was the constant theme of the gentleman's attacks. The State of his birth, which had given as many evidences of her attachment to the Union as any other, had been condemned because a former Administration, under a Virginia President, had done the same thing which she now complains of in this, without receiving condemnation from her. Mr. T. then proceeded at length to prove there was no analogy between the act of Mr. Crawford, in 1817, and that of the present Secretary, and that the precedent was nothing, as all those acts passed without notice at that time, because no one called the proceedings in question.

Mr. BROWN thought he might throw some light on the subject of the distress complained of. It would be recollected that the great staple of the State of Virginia was tobacco. That State had been long engaged in its cultivation, from her earliest history. He held in his hand a paper containing the prices current in Richmond, and it would be found by it (the Richmond Enquirer of the 8th instant) that good tobacco was now selling at from $8 to $9 per hundred, and fine at from $9 to $10, which was better than the average price of the article had been for five years past, and it was considered not only a handsome, but a rich compensation, to receive $6. The price of bank stocks was also given, and exhibited the stocks of the State and Farmers' Banks of Virginia at 108½, being 8½ per cent. above par. This threw some more light on this picture of distress; and yet if we listen to representations abroad, that ancient Commonwealth is prostrated by this removal of the deposites. The gentleman from Virginia [Mr. TYLER] wished the bank to expire in tranquillity. And who disturbed it? Surely not the President of the United States. Did he seize on its rights, or any member of the Government obstruct its operations? No. It still carried on all its operations. The deposites, to be sure, were taken away; but they were not the property of the bank. By the gentleman's argument, the bank had an unlimited, unqualified property in the deposites. If prayers were to be sent forth against the President, it struck him the Executive was not to be responsible, but the president and directors of the bank. They were responsible for the distress of this operation. The gentleman from Virginia [Mr. LEIGH] had mistaken the individual for the object upon which the responsibility rested. As respected the matter of honor upon the President in retracing his steps, he supposed the mere question of honor would be but a small consideration with him. He looked to a higher, a nobler duty—a duty to the Constitution of the country and the people of the country. He protested against any gentleman taking into custody the President's honor. He had no doubt the President would bear and would wear his own honors with honor to himself.

Mr. LEIGH said the memorial lately presented from Richmond was signed by every tobacco merchant there, and they asserted that the price of the article was reduced from 15 to 20 per cent. But the true test of the value was the price of the article in foreign markets. In Richmond the price varied at from $3 to $25 and $30. And as regarded the price of bank stocks in Virginia, they were affected lately by the determination not to recharter the bank. Before that question was settled, the prices were low. But afterwards, when it was settled the bank was not to be rechartered, capitalists sought investment, and stock rose to 112 and 113½. But since the treasury measure, they have fallen to 108½.

Mr. FORSYTH said the first memorial presented came to him under circumstances of great force. It was couched in very respectful language, and came from most respectable persons in Virginia, and a portion of its signers resided upon the spot where he first saw the light. Of course he could not say anything which was not respectful or kind of them. No doubt they expressed their own wants and their distress, and they asked a restoration of the deposites; upon which subject he differed with them in opinion.

The gentleman from Virginia charged the friends of the Administration with having changed their language upon the subject of the deposites. As to himself, (Mr. F. said,) this was a great mistake. From the first, he said the removal of the deposites could not produce the distress. This was the very language he held now. The gentleman from Massachusetts had told us, in express terms, that the deposites was a matter of no material consideration. That the only mode of restoring public confidence, and relieving the public distress, was to reconcile, to harmonize the Administration and the bank, and that the only way of satisfying the people was to continue the bank for a limited time. This was the uniform language. Restore the deposites to-morrow, and let there be no well-founded hope of a recharter of the bank, and things will remain precisely as they are. The bank could do nothing more with than without the deposites. If it was to wind up, it must wind up, and that could not be done without continuing the pressure. These were the universal sentiments entertained, and the gentleman from Virginia, [Mr. TYLER,] in view of his former convictions, must be blind to the true question. The questions could not be separated; it was not a triumph to be achieved over the Administration in the restoration of the deposites, but a triumph over it in the recharter of the bank.

The gentleman from Virginia [Mr. TYLER] said, in reference to him, (Mr. F.,) that he had said Virginia never condemned a change of the Government deposites when the act was done under the administration of a Virginia President. Now what was the fact? The present Executive was not a Virginian, and his course was denied to be legal and constitutional by the Legislature of Virginia. The question, then, was the removal of the deposites from one place of safety to another place of safety. And did not Mr. Gallatin, under the administration of Mr. Jefferson, do the same thing? He was a Virginian. And the deposites were removed, not only with the approbation of Congress, but without a murmur of complaint from any quarter. And was this union of the purse and the sword, this usurpation of power, this trampling the Constitution in the dust, condemned by Virginia? Never, never. And for what purpose were the deposites removed by Mr. Crawford? Why, for the sole purpose of sustaining the tottering State banks. And who thought at that day of abusing the President of the United States for a usurpation of power? No man. Mr. Crawford's conduct, too, was the subject of accusation before Congress. He was charged with transferring the public funds without giving his reasons to Congress for the act, and what was the report of the committee of investigation? They unanimously acquitted him, and accepted of his reasons. But what was then said as to the usurpation of power, the plundering of the public money, the violation of vested rights, the trampling of the Constitution under foot? It never entered into the imagination of man that it was an act violating either the letter or spirit of the Constitution and laws. Here was an example sustaining him in point of fact. It might have been condemned, but if it had been, he had yet to learn it. But the gentleman had told us he heard with some surprise an accusation against Virginia by a native son of Virginia. He (Mr. F.) had made no accusation—he intended to make none. He referred only to the fact to establish the course the State had taken, and that which she now desired, and would hereafter pursue; and which, if she did pursue, she would act inconsistently with her course when one of her own distinguished sons [Mr. Jefferson] was at the head of the Government.

The gentleman had also said it was dishonorable in the President not to retrace his steps when in error. It was true, an honest and courageous man would retrace his steps when he was convinced he was in error. But what must be the character of that man who retracts when he is not convinced? Could the gentleman doubt, could any man doubt, that the President of the United States thought this step was necessary, not only to the public good but to the public liberty? And entertaining this opinion, he would be covered with everlasting infamy if he recoiled from the act or its resposibility.

The debate was further continued by Messrs. WEBSTER, EWING, PRESTON, TYLER, and FORSYTH.

When, at half past three o'clock, on motion of Mr. PORTER,

The Senate adjourned.

HOUSE OF REPRESENTATIVES.

THURSDAY, *March* 13, 1834.

Mr. CLAY, from the Committee on the Public Lands, reported a bill to change the boundaries of certain land districts in Michigan, and for other

purposes. Read twice, and ordered to be engrossed for a third reading.

Mr. HARDIN, from the Committee on the Judiciary, reported a bill for the relief of Nathaniel Tyler. Read twice, and committed.

Mr. DUNCAN, from the Committee on the Public Lands, moved that the Committee of the Whole be discharged from the bill providing for the establishment of two additional land offices in the State of Illinois, &c., for the purpose of having the bill immediately considered.

Mr. DUNCAN informed the House that a large district of country had been surveyed, and the plats filed in the General Land Office, and only wanted the passage of this bill to be brought into market. He said that sales of public land usually took place in the spring and fall; that if this bill could not be passed out of its present order on the files of the House, the sale would be postponed until fall, which would be equally injurious to the interests of the Government, and the citizens residing in the country, who wished to purchase their homes, and make permanent improvements. The motion was lost.

PUBLIC DEPOSITES.

The House resumed the consideration of the following resolution, offered by Mr. MARDIS, of Alabama:

Resolved, That the Committee of Ways and Means be instructed to inquire into the expediency of reporting a bill requiring the Secretary of the Treasury to deposite the public moneys of the United States in the State banks; and, also, as to the expediency of defining by law all contracts hereafter to be made with the Secretary for the safekeeping, management, and disbursement of the same.

Mr. BURGES took the floor, and asked if it was in order to move an amendment to the resolution, so as to move a different instruction on the same subject.

The CHAIR said the motion would be in order under certain restrictions, which he indicated.

Mr. BURGES proceeded to reply to the argument of the gentleman from Alabama, (Mr. MARDIS,) and after speaking about half an hour, gave way to a motion to proceed to the orders of the day.

The SPEAKER *pro tem.* (Mr. FOOT) announced that the pension bill was the special order.

Mr. POLK moved that the House resolve itself into Committee of the Whole on the state of the Union, for the purpose of taking up the bill making

APPROPRIATIONS FOR THE ARMY.

Mr. MARSHALL contended for his right to the floor.

The SPEAKER decided that the order of the day not having been announced, the motion of Mr. POLK was in order.

Mr. POLK then called for the yeas and nays; which were ordered.

The House decided to go into Committee, Mr. WAYNE in the chair—yeas 134, nays 37.

The bill having been taken up, the motion pending being one made by Mr. McKAY, to reduce the miscellaneous appropriation from $356,000 to $306,000.

Mr. McKAY said that, having had an interview on this subject with the chairman of the Committee of Ways and Means, who had, on examination of some of the items, consented to reduce them considerably, he would withdraw his motion.

Mr. POLK admitted that there might be a reduction made in the item of fuel, which was comprised in this; and he moved to strike out $356,000, and insert $344,000. Agreed to.

The next item being for transportation of clothing, subsistence, ordnance, &c., $150,000;

Mr. POLK moved to reduce it to $145,000; which was agreed to.

The allowance to officers for the transportation of their baggage, when on duty, and for *per diem* allowance to officers in topographical duty, was reduced from $70,000 to $55,000.

The item for the rewards, and other expenses incident to the apprehension of deserters, $8,000, was stricken out.

For contingencies of the army, $10,000, was agreed to.

For carrying on the works in the city of Savannah, Georgia, $25,000.

Mr. VANCE inquired what sort of works this appropriation was for?

Mr. POLK said this was to complete the erection of barracks, for which there was an appropriation made the last year.

Mr. VANCE was opposed to the whole barrack system, as unnecessary and burdensome. He thought it ought to be curtailed. Barracks were often erected at great expense, after which they would be abandoned. He instanced the case of Fort Gibson, for which there was an item in this bill making an appropriation of $25,000 to erect barracks there, whilst there was on the table a bill reported, which went to change the military station from that place into the Territory of Arkansas.

Mr. POLK said, that when the bill alluded to by the member from Ohio came up, he hoped to be able to show him that it ought not to pass. The present appropriation was absolutely necessary, to afford protection to the army. The appropriation of last year had been applied to the purchase of the site on which the erections were to be made. With respect to the erection of barracks at Fort Gibson, it would be recollected, that in consequence of the removal of the Indians, it became one of the most important posts in the West. The present building was in a state of decay, and as it was deemed more economical to erect a permanent building of brick and stone, the Secretary of War had directed an estimate to be submitted for that purpose, upon which the committee felt it their duty to report an appropriation for it.

Mr. R. M. JOHNSON pledged himself to show to the House, that it would not be politic to change the military station from Fort Gibson into the Indian territories; for the troops of the United States ought to be placed on our own borders, as much to protect our own citizens as to keep peace among the Indian tribes.

Mr. JONES, of Georgia, and Mr. WILLIAMS, objected to the appropriations for barracks.

Mr. GAMBLE bore testimony to the necessity there was of them in Savannah.

Mr. POLK said, that where there were no barracks, the health of the officers and soldiers must be hazarded, by being turned into the open air. It would not require more that twenty dollars a man to furnish them with comfortable barracks.

Mr. WARD enlarged upon their importance in a military point of view, and advocated the appropriations.

The appropriation was agreed to.

The items for continuing repairs and alterations, &c., at Baton Rouge, Louisiana, $10,000;

For erecting officers' quarters at Fort Severn, Annapolis, $5,000;

For carrying on the works at Green Bay, Michigan, $10,000; were severally agreed to.

For extending the works and erecting additional barracks at Fort Gibson, Arkansas, $25,000.

Mr. SEVIER moved to strike out this appropriation and insert $10,000 for erection of a fort on the Arkansas river. He stated that the garrison was in an unsuitable place, where it was of no use, and as long as it was there, he was not in favor of appropriating a cent for its accommodation.

Mr. POLK went into some explanations to show that, in the opinion of the War Department, Fort Gibson was one of the most important posts in the western country. If there had been a force there formerly, it would have saved the Government the expense of a million of dollars. All the information which he had received on this point went to assure him that this appropriation was necessary.

Mr. ASHLEY was surprised at the opinion of the Secretary of War, that so large a sum as $10,000 should be expended for the erection of barracks at Fort Gibson, because so many Indians were located there. The great mass of Indians were farther north on the Missouri river, and the commissioners appointed to look out for proper locations for Indians had brought them five hundred miles up the Missouri for proper situations. A post at Fort Gibson was not so important, therefore, as had been represented.

Mr. EVERETT, of Vermont, said he was willing to make such an appropriation for the repairs

of the barracks at Fort Gibson as might be necessary to render them comfortable. He did not think it would be good policy to retain a post within the settlements of the Indians, and he should object to appropriations which contemplated any permanent posts in their vicinity.

Mr. VANCE thought, he said, that the soldiers ought to erect their own barracks generally. He was not in favor of this bill when it was reported, but he thought that those who had charge of the defence of the country were better judges of the eligibility of different posts than the people of Arkansas. Believing, however, that the general appropriation for the repairs of barracks was sufficient, without this specific appropriation, he should vote for striking out the clause.

Mr. SEVIER made some further remarks in support of his motion, dissenting from the opinion of the Secretary of War, and contending that the garrison might as well be in Cuba as the place where it was. It was true that in that portion of Arkansas a post was highly necessary, but the Indians and the people of Arkansas were both opposed to the present position of the garrison, and no one was in favor of it, except the Secretary of War.

Mr. CAGE opposed the motion to strike out, and contended that the Secretary of War, obtaining, as he did, the best information from the officers of the army, was better qualified than any one else to form an opinion as to the advantages of different positions for the establishment of military posts. The gentleman says that the people of Arkansas do not wish to have the post in its present position, does not afford them so good a market for their eggs, chickens, and ducks, as it might in another situation; but that consideration might not have guided the Secretary of War in forming his opinion. Mr. C. spoke earnestly in support of the policy and justice of making ample provision for the defence of the frontiers from the hostilities of the Indians.

Mr. CLAYTON supported the motion. The Cherokee Indians, against whom the people of Arkansas wished to be protected, were between them and the fort; and the fort was, therefore, as beneficial to the Cherokees as to the people of Arkansas. If the fort was to protect Arkansas, it ought to come back to the Arkansas line.

Mr. R. M. JOHNSON regretted that a matter so easily understood had consumed so much time, and proceeded to make some explanations respecting it. The question was whether we should keep a post forty miles within the Indian country or bring it back to the Arkansas line. He contended that the intercourse between the garrison and the Indians was highly disadvantageous to the morals of the latter.

Mr. HUBBARD opposed the motion. Permanent barracks were not wanted, but the Secretary merely proposed to repair the barracks for the accommodation of the troops now at the post. As to the position of the fort, he contended that every fort ought to be in advance of civilization, and that it was absurd to erect a line of posts on the frontier for its defence against the Indians. The gentleman from Kentucky was mistaken in supposing that the fort was built on lands belonging to the Indians, the land having been reserved to the United States. Had the gentleman informed us of any acts of depredation committed by Indians east of Fort Gibson? He had not. He hoped the House would decide upon the motion, in order that we might get the bill through the committee.

Mr. SPEIGHT remarked, that the reservation referred to by the gentleman from New Hampshire was so limited, that it could not be used for the purpose of this fort. The Committee on Military Affairs wish to check the disturbances which grew out of the vicinity of the posts to the Indian settlements.

Mr. EVERETT, of Vermont, proposed an amendment to the bill, which the Chair pronounced to be out of order.

Mr. H. EVERETT said that in case the amendment of the gentleman from Arkansas should be rejected, he would move to strike out the words "creating additional barracks at Fort Gibson," and the word "twenty," so as to reduce the appropriation to five thousand dollars.

Mr. SEVIER protested against the use of the opinion of the Secretary of War as an oracle in this House, though he had (he said) as much respect for the Secretary as any other gentleman. He went on to speak at some length in support of his motion.

Mr. WATMOUGH supported the motion, and contended that no precise information had been given by the Committee of Ways and Means for dissenting from the Committee on Military Affairs, whose opinion he thought was entitled to as much weght as that of the Secretary of War. The opinion of the people of Arkansas, as expressed through their representative, was also entitled to respect.

Mr. GILMER said it was highly important to the success of the plans for meliorating the condition of the Indians, that they should cease to entertain any jealousies of us. The Choctaws and Cherokees were, essentially, peaceful in their habits and feelings; their warlike spirit had been broken down. It was now necessary to remove from them the apprehension which they entertain of our control, by withdrawing our troops. A small force only is necessary to be retained in the Indian country to prevent collisions between the different tribes themselves. He did not think it advisable now to withdraw the post, but he was in favor of reducing the appropriation to $5,000.

Mr. POLK said that it was plain that if the post was to be continued at Fort Gibson, some arrangement ought to be made for the accommodation of the troops there stationed. The Secretary of War stated that the post could not be safely removed from Fort Gibson, and he certainly understood the locality of the post, the situation of the Indians, and the proper means of defending the frontier, as well as any gentleman here.

After some further remarks from Messrs. WATMOUGH, HUBBARD, ASHLEY, and DUNCAN,

Mr. GAMBLE moved that the appropriation be rise.

The motion was rejected: Yeas 65, nays 81.

Mr. CLAYTON then contended that the best location for a fort, would be on the western line, between the lands occupied by the Choctaws and the Territory of Arkansas.

Mr. GORHAM said that the communication made on this subject by the Secretary of War to the Committee of Ways and Means, was predicated on the assumption that Fort Gibson was to be hereafter a permanent military station. He did not think, unless the House was prepared to assent to this, that so large an appropriation as twenty-five thousand dollars was necessary; twelve or fifteen thousand would be sufficient to keep the present buildings in repairs for two or three years; after which, if it should be found necessary to keep it up as a permanent military station, then would be the time to make the large erections that were contemplated.

The question on the amendment proposed by Mr. SEVIER was put, and rejected.

Mr. HORACE EVERETT thereupon moved to strike out the appropriation for erecting additional works, &c., at Fort Gibson, $25,000, and to insert "for making temporary repairs there, $5,000;" which was agreed to.

Mr. POLK said, as the appropriation of ten thousand dollars for the erection of new barracks at Fort Armstrong, also of the same amount for the repairs of the barracks, and for defences at Fort Brady, might be postponed until next year, he would move to have these items stricken out. Agreed to.

Mr. ASHLEY moved an amendment, for erecting an arsenal at St. Louis, Missouri, $8,500. Agreed to.

The following items were then read, and severally agreed to:

For the purchase of land adjoining Fort Sullivan, Eastport, Maine, $3,500.

For national armories, $360,000.

For the armament of fortifications, $100,000.

For the current expenses of the ordnance service, $96,400.

For arsenals, $150,000.

For the purchase of five thousand sets accoutrements for the artillery and infantry regiments, $14,250.

For the recruiting service, in addition to $29,388 unexpended of a former appropriation, $6,000.

For contingent expenses of the recruiting service, in addition to $6,043 unexpended of a former appropriation, $14,000.

For arrearages prior to the first of July, eighteen hundred and fifteen, payable through the office of the Third Auditor, in addition to an unexpended balance in the treasury, $3,000.

To enable the Second Auditor to close the accounts under the act of third March, eighteen hundred and twenty-one, allowing three months' gratuitous pay to disbanded officers and soldiers, $1,000.

For the payment of the general and staff officers and six companies of Missouri militia, ordered into service by the Governor of that State, in the year eighteen hundred and thirty-two, $35,000.

For finishing gun-racks and building window shutters to the new arsenal; rebuilding middle water shop, one hundred and ten by fifty feet; and for building a house for steam engine, including a store-room for iron, fifty-two by forty-six feet, at the national armory, Springfield, Massachusetts, $12,900.

For additional machinery and fixtures at the same armory, viz: three water wheels for grinding musket barrels, six water wheels and twenty-two forges required in the middle water shop, blast machinery for eleven double forges, and for the purchase of new and improved labor-saving machinery, $17,800.

For slating roof and rebuilding water wheel of upper workshop, renewing and repairing fences on the public ground, and for painting public buildings at the same armory, $3,500.

For repairing dam, (and removing obstructions in way of,) supplying the water to the rifle factory on the Shenandoah river, at the national armory, Harper's Ferry, Virginia, $2,000.

For the completion of the machinery in the three shops, for turning, boring, and stocking muskets; the completion of the canal, furnishing the water power; erecting an annealing shop and proof-house; erecting two shops for tempering springs and polishing barrels; erecting two engine houses, and making addition to stocking shops; and for erecting a carpenter's and machine shop, at the same armory, $36,114 86.

For erecting store-houses for iron and pit coal, repairing paymaster's and clerk's quarters, constructing a river wall, sinking three wells on Camp Hill, grading and paving the open spaces between the public shops, and for painting some of the public buildings at the same armory, $8,588 87.

For the payment of the taxes assessed by the State of Pennsylvania on the United States arsenal on the Schuylkill river, $568 89.

For the purchase of three acres of land on the Alabama river, and building a warehouse and dock at the Mount Vernon arsenal, in the State of Alabama, $1,800 50.

Mr. CONNOR proposed an additional clause, giving the franking privilege to the Chief Engineer.

Mr. ADAMS warned the House not the sanction such a doctrine as the insertion of such matters into their bills making appropriations. He thought that the franking privilege ought to be curtailed rather than enlarged.

Mr. CONNOR said, that the proposition which he had made was under the sanction of the Secretary of War, and he believed that such a privilege was inserted with the assenting vote of the honorable member from Massachusetts in a former bill.

The clause was rejected; and,

On motion of Mr. POLK, the committee rose and reported the bill as amended to the House; after which, the House adjourned.

IN SENATE.

FRIDAY, March 14, 1834.

Mr. WRIGHT presented the proceedings of a large meeting of the citizens of Brooklyn, New York, together with a memorial of the same, approving of the course of the President of the United States, and regarding the reasons of the Secretary of the Treasury for the removal of the deposites as sound and conclusive, and praying that the bank may not be rechartered. The proceedings and memorial were read, referred to the Committee on Finance, and ordered to be printed.

The VICE PRESIDENT communicated a memorial from the Legislative Council of Michigan, praying remuneration for losses sustained by the citizens of that Territory during the late war; which,

On motion of Mr. NAUDAIN, was referred to the Committee of Claims, and ordered to be printed.

Mr. PRENTISS presented the proceedings of a convention of delegates from the several towns in the county of Windsor, Vermont, held at Woodstock, disapproving of the removal of the deposites, and asking their restoration to the Bank of the United States; which were read, referred to the Committee on Finance, and ordered to be printed.

Mr. McKEAN presented the proceedings of the largest meeting which had ever assembled in Philadelphia, held on the 4th of March, 1834, sustaining the Executive in the acts of his Administration; attributing the present distress of the community to the course of the bank; approving of the veto of the bank bill; of Governor Wolf's late message relative to the bank, and approving of the call of a national convention for the nomination of high Executive officers, as the only practicable mode of preserving the union of the Democratic party.

Mr. McK. said he fully agreed in the opinions and views expressed in the proceedings of this meeting, with the exception of that part approving of a national convention for the nomination of candidates for the Presidency and Vice Presidency of the Union. Mr. McK. moved that the proceedings be read, referred to the Committee on Finance, and printed. Agreed to.

Mr. McKEAN also presented the proceedings of three public meetings in different townships of Perry county, Pennsylvania, disapproving of the action of the Government in relation to the United States Bank, and the removal of the deposites, and opposed to a national convention. Mr. McK. said he was not in favor of all the sentiments expressed in these proceedings, but he did concur in the political sentiments therein avowed.

On his motion, the proceedings took the same order as those preceding.

Mr. WILKINS, from the Committee on Finance, reported a bill from the House of Representatives, without amendment, to exempt merchandise imported under certain circumstances from the operation of the act of the 19th of May, 1828, entitled "An act in alteration of the several acts imposing duties on imports;" which was read, and ordered to a second reading.

Mr. POINDEXTER, from the Committee on Public Lands, reported a bill, without amendment, prescribing the mode of advertising the public lands.

The Senate then proceeded to the special order of the day, being the report of the Committee on Finance, and Mr. CLAY's resolution on

THE REMOVAL OF THE DEPOSITES.

Mr. TALLMADGE rose and concluded his speech, sustaining the reasons of the Secretary; when

Mr. WRIGHT moved an adjournment, but gave way to

Mr. WAGGAMAN, upon whose motion it was agreed, that when the Senate adjourn, it adjourn until Monday.

On motion of Mr. WRIGHT,
The Senate adjourned.

HOUSE OF REPRESENTATIVES.

FRIDAY, March 14, 1834.

Mr. WHITTLESEY, of Ohio, from the Committee of Claims, reported a bill for the relief of Marinus W. Gilbert; which was read twice, and committed.

Mr. CARR, from the Committee on Private Land Claims, asked to be discharged from the further consideration of the petition of William C. Hazzard; which was ordered to be laid on the table.

The House then resumed the consideration of the following resolution, submitted by Mr. MARDIS, viz:

Resolved, That the Committee of Ways and Means be instructed to inquire into the expediency of reporting a bill requiring the Secretary of the

Treasury to deposite the public moneys of the United States in the State banks; and, also, as to the expediency of defining by law all contracts hereafter to be made with the Secretary, for the safe-keeping, management, and disbursement of the same.

Mr. BURGES resumed, and after addressing the House a few moments on the general bank subject, he gave way, from indisposition; and the further consideration of the resolution having been, on motion of Mr. WHITTLESEY, postponed,

Mr. POLK asked the unanimous consent of the House to take up the army appropriation bill.

Mr. WHITTLESEY objecting,

Mr. POLK moved the suspension of the rule setting this day apart for private bills, for that purpose. The House refused: ayes 93, noes 50.

The following engrossed bills were read a third time, and passed, viz:

A bill for the relief of Haggerty & Austin;

A bill for the relief of Peleg Spencer;

A bill for the relief of Noah Staley;

A bill for the relief of John Hone & Sons;

A bill to compromise the claims of the United States against Minturn & Champlin;

A bill for the relief of John Kimberly;

A bill for the relief of the widow and heirs of Felix St. Vrain;

A bill for the relief of Andrew McCollum;

A bill for the relief of George Bowen;

A bill for the relief of William K. Paulding;

A bill for the relief of W. Hazlett;

A bill for the relief of Joseph W. Wormstead;

A bill for the relief of Richard W. Meade;

A bill for the relief of Mary O'Sullivan;

A bill for the relief of the owners of the schooner Joseph and Mary;

A bill for the relief of Samuel D. Walker;

A bill for the relief of Alexander J. Robinson;

A bill for the relief of the heirs at law and representatives of William G. Christopher;

A bill for the relief of William B. Doliber and others;

A bill for the relief of the legal representatives of James Brown;

A bill for the relief of Benedict Alford and Robert Brush;

A bill for the relief of the heirs of Crocker Sampson, deceased; and

A bill for the relief of Henry Whitney.

The bill for the relief of Jonathan Walton and John De. Graff being on its final passage,

Mr. WHITTLESEY remarked, that this bill had passed through, unnoticed by him. He considered the principle upon which it was sought to grant compensation to those parties, for having received payments from the Government in treasury notes, to be dangerous, and as tending to involve the Government in other similar claims. He was induced to move that it should be recommitted.

Mr. POLK suggested a postponement of the bill till to-morrow.

Mr. WHITTLESEY assented, and withdrew his motion to recommit.

Mr. CAMBRELENG wished to explain.

Mr. HUBBARD moved to postpone the bill until Saturday in the next week.

Mr. EWING moved to recommit the bill.

The SPEAKER decided this motion was not in order, as there was a motion to postpone to a day certain, and which it was not in order to debate.

The motion of Mr. HUBBARD prevailed.

Mr. POLK moved to suspend the rule of the House in order to take up the army bill; but in relation to the Cumberland road; and several other appropriation bills. Lost.

Mr. POLK then varied his motion so as to suspend the rule for the purpose of taking up the army bill alone.

Mr. McKENNAN moved to amend the motion, so as to include the bill for continuing and repairing the Cumberland road.

Mr. POLK accepted the amendment as a modification of his motion, and called for the yeas and nays on the question, and they were ordered.

Mr. EWING requested a division of the question.

Mr. LANE requested his colleague to withdraw the motion, as it would embarrass the House.

Mr. EWING persisted, and accordingly the question was first taken on the motion to suspend the rule for the purpose of taking up the army bill, and was decided in the affirmative. Yeas 125, nays 82.

The question was then taken on the second branch of the motion—to suspend the rule for the purpose of taking up the Cumberland road bill, and decided in the negative—yeas 94, nays 91—[not two-thirds.]

The House then took up the bill making appropriations for the support of the army for the year 1834.

ARMY APPROPRIATION BILL.

The amendment adopted in the Committee of the Whole, granting $1,825 to Doctor Beaumont of the army, by way of extra allowance, in consideration of extra services in making professional experiments, being under consideration,

Mr. HALL, of North Carolina, opposed the amendment, and asked the yeas and nays upon the question of concurrence, and they were ordered.

Mr. CAMBRELENG opposed the amendment, for the reason, he said, that he was unwilling to make the appropriation bills a pack-horse for every private claim.

Mr. HARDIN opposed the provision for the same reasons.

Mr. E. EVERETT, in reply to a question from Mr. CAGE, stated that Dr. Beaumont was a surgeon in the United States army, and that the person upon whom the experiments were made was a soldier in the service. In reply to the remark of the gentleman from New York, he said that the reason for making the provision in the appropriation bill was, that in the present state of business in the House, there was no hope of obtaining its passage in any other way.

Mr. BROWN said that this reason would admit the attachment of a provision of any subject to the appropriation bill. If the subject was brought up in a separate bill, he would support it.

Messrs. FILLMORE and WAYNE spoke in favor of the amendment, and contended that the provision properly belonged to the army appropriation bill.

The debate was continued by Messrs. HARDIN, EVERETT, and CHILTON.

Mr. POPE expressed his hope, as the subject was well understood by the House, that a vote would be taken at once upon the amendment, that they might go on to the consideration of the other parts of the bill.

Mr. WAYNE presented various letters from Doctor Douglass and others, descriptive and approbatory of the experiments, which were submitted to the Joint Library Committee, and which had influenced them in recommending this extra allowance. He called for the reading of them.

The letters were read accordingly.

Mr. CAMBRELENG said, although he did not desire to undervalue the justice of the claim, yet he could not conceive that an appropriation bill was the proper place to have it attended to. If the claim was to reward merit, there was an appropriate committee for that purpose to take it up, if it was connected with the military affairs of the country.

Mr. SUTHERLAND would vote for this amendment, and thought nothing could be more important to the country than anything which could tend to illustrate the diet system for the army, which the experiments of Surgeon Beaumont unquestionably did in an eminent degree. Surgeon B. had advanced the cost of making these experiments out of his own funds. He contended that he was, upon every view that could be taken of the subject, fully entitled to the amount, in justice to science, to the army, and to the country.

Mr. MANN, of New York, said, if all other objections to this were waived, there was something due to the considerations of the danger that would ensue from creating a precedent for remunerating services of this kind in this way.

Mr. TURRILL opposed the allowance.

Mr. P. C. FULLER supported it.

Mr. BEARDSLEY desired, if it was in order, to call for the previous question, that a decision might be procured without debate.

The SPEAKER explained that the previous question must cut off this, and all other amendments.

Mr. JONES went into a constitutional argument against the allowance, and proposed that each member should purchase one or more copies of the book, which, in his opinion, would be the most constitutional way that the House could reward the meritorious services for which it was made.

Mr. SCHLEY adverted to the refusal on the part of the old Confederation to grant to Congress the power of rewarding discoveries in science. He was therefore compelled to oppose it on constitutional grounds.

Mr. HARD justified the allowance, on the ground of expense incurred by Surgeon Beaumont, which was to produce results beneficial to the public generally.

Mr. J. Q. ADAMS objected to the mode and form by which the allowance was proposed. It appeared to have come up upon a memorial presented to the other branch, the Senate, and which had by that body been referred to the Joint Library Committee. He reminded gentlemen, although he was not opposed to the claim, if presented in another shape, that it was the peculiar province of the House to originate all bills making appropriations for money. He had no constitutional objections to the power of Congress granting rewards for discoveries in science; but he thought they ought to be only granted upon memorials presented to the House, and which being referred by them to a committee to report, the House would be in a situation fairly to decide upon their merits.

The question on concurrence with the Committee of the Whole in the amendment, was taken by yeas and nays, and decided in the negative—yeas 56, nays 126.

The question being on concurrence with the amendment reducing the appropriation for works and barracks at Fort Gibson, Arkansas, from $25,000 to $5,000,

Mr. SEVIER opposed the amendment, objecting strongly to the maintenance of the post within the limits of the Indian territory.

Mr. H. EVERETT said that the amendment only went to prevent the extension of the works at Fort Gibson. All that it decided was, that we should not erect permanent works at Fort Gibson; not saying where a permanent post shall be established. So far the amendment aided the object of the gentleman from Arkansas, and he was surprised at his objecting to it.

The House concurred in the amendment.

Mr. SEVIER moved to strike out the section, as amended, from the bill, and insert in lieu thereof an appropriation of $10,000, to establish a military post at Fort Smith, on the Arkansas line.

The motion was rejected.

The other amendments reported from the Committee of the Whole were severally concurred in, without debate.

The question being on the engrossment of the bill,

Mr. JONES, of Georgia, moved to add a provision to the bill, restricting the application of the sums granted for the erection and repairs of barracks, to the purchase of materials necessary to be used.

Mr. JONES said his object was to reduce the expense of these buildings by making it necessary for the soldiers to do the work themselves.

The motion was rejected.

The bill was ordered to be engrossed for a third reading.

On motion of Mr. J. Q. ADAMS, the use of the Hall, on Tuesday evening, was granted to the members of the bar of the Supreme Court, for the purpose of hearing an eulogium on the late WILLIAM WIRT.

The House then adjourned.

In our report of the proceedings of Mr. POLK's motion, we mistook the remark which fell from the Chair as to the debate which had taken place on the presentation of memorials. The Speaker said the Chair was not responsible for the course of the debate. He had attempted to prevent debate; but the House had permitted it when appealed to, and it was for the House, and not the Chair, to arrest it.

REMARKS OF MR. MUHLENBERG,
OF PENNSYLVANIA,
IN THE HOUSE OF REPRESENTATIVES,
TUESDAY, *March* 4, 1834.
On the Bill to provide for the settlement of certain
Revolutionary Claims.

I am pleased, Mr. Speaker, that some of our young friends have found an opportunity of exhibiting their talents at speechmaking, and delivering animated addresses upon a new subject. It is, however, to be regretted, that both the subject and the time appear to be ill-chosen. Indeed, I cannot but express my surprise and regret that there should be opposition to a bill of the description of that now before you—a bill providing for the settlement of the most just and best founded of all revolutionary claims; and particularly that the opposition should only show itself in the last stage of the bill, when amendment can no longer be admitted.

The report which accompanied the bill when it was brought into the House, and which was read at the Clerk's desk when it was under consideration in the Committee of the Whole on the state of the Union, amply explains the nature of the claims to be provided for, and the principles upon which they are to be settled. That report has, also, no doubt, been read, examined, and considered by the great mass of the honorable gentlemen around me in their own chambers. It would, therefore, appear unnecessary to take up much of the time of the House in discussing the provisions and merits of the bill. Its nature and objects must be understood; the utility and even necessity of its passage be generally felt. Under such circumstances its fate might readily be left to the good sense, to the justice and experience of the House, without another word in its defence.

As, however, there has been an opposition unlooked for, a sounding of trumpets to the right and left, to collect forces for a further onset, I must be permitted to say a word in regard to the objects of the committee, and a word in reply to a few of the objections raised against the bill, leaving a reply to the remainder to other gentlemen of the committee, who will, no doubt, triumphantly vindicate its provisions.

The committee under whose orders the bill was reported, had several objects in view, which seemed to them laudable, and which it was thought might be accomplished by its passage.

One of these objects was, to save the time of the House; a point considered as of some importance. A large number of cases, about two hundred, all of a similar character, and embraced in the provisions of the bill, were referred to the Committee on Revolutionary Claims during the present session of Congress. The mass of these have remained unacted upon; they have been held back in the hope of a prompt action and speedy passage of the present general bill which provides for the settlement of this whole class of claims at the Treasury Department. Should the bill not pass, a majority of these cases must

necessarily be placed on the calendar in as short a period as possible. This will, of course, greatly increase the business of the House, and in the same degree prevent its action upon other private claims, a large number of which have been pending for years without receiving any further notice than being placed from time to time, from year to year, upon the calendar, some proof, at least, that they are just, that the claimants are entitled to relief as they have the favorable testimony of the investigating committees. Sir, this delay in the settlement of private claims is a growing evil. Anything which may decrease their number, and thus enable the House to give more time to the remainder, should, I think, be calculated to find favor in this Hall.

Another object of the committee was, to accelerate the settlement of such of these claims as are just and sustained by sufficient evidence. Probably—and I judge from some experience, Mr. Speaker—probably it would take Congress five or more years to pass definitively upon those cases which are now before the Committee on Revolutionary Claims, if, as is at present the practice, a special act is to be passed in each individual case. But, sir, it is not to be presumed that the cases at present before the committee are the only existing cases. More will no doubt be referred during the present, and more at the next session of Congress. There may be from fifty to one hundred more cases scattered through the Middle, Eastern, and Western States, the present cases being principally from the South. Should the bill fail, I grieve for the delay of cases which must inevitably be the consequence. In many highly meritorious cases it will be equal to an entire denial of justice, and he who fought your battles gallantly and shed his blood freely, and sacrificed his all without hesitation, to secure your independence, will go down to his grave with sorrow, and bequeath no blessing to an ungrateful country. Whereas, should the bill become a law, this whole class of cases may be disposed of in a twelvemonth, and thereby speedy justice be ensured to the still surviving meritorious officer of the Revolution; or, if he has gone to rest with his brave associates, at least to his descendants, who have become impoverished by the sacrifices of their ancestor.

Another object of the committee was, to render the rejection of all unjust, unfounded claims of this class nearly certain; at least more so than can now be expected. Whatever evidence may exist in favor of these claims, it is of course sought out and invariably presented to Congress, or rather its committees; whereas that of a contrary description—that adverse to the claimants, if there be any—is either not known to them, or held back. This evidence, adverse to the claims, is scattered throughout the public offices. The members of the committee are obliged to go in search of it, and yet, after their utmost care and assiduity, it may escape their search; they may fail to apply at the proper source. This difficulty would at once be obviated,

if, as provided for in the bill on your table, a decision on these cases and a settlement were left to the Treasury Department. All the evidence in the possession of the Government would then at once be collected to one point, and made to bear upon every individual case. Few unjust claims would, in this mode of procedure, escape a rejection, whereas now they may at times escape the vigilance of any committee upon whom the House may choose to throw the burden of investigating them.

The bill before you, Mr. Speaker, would then, should it become a law, save the time of the House and the money of the Government. It would go far to ensure the rejection of unjust claims, and accelerate the settlement of such as are just, not only of this class, but of all others left for the decision of Congress. It would ensure the same measure of justice to one citizen which is granted to another, and could not fail, by equal, exact, and speedy justice, of giving satisfaction to all parties.

But the gentleman from New Hampshire, [Mr. PIERCE,] complains that all proofs for the validity of these claims are made to rest upon presumption, and mere presumption. Far from it, Mr. Speaker. The gentleman has misapprehended the intentions of the committee. Under the bill, absolute, positive proof of service is required to the year 1781, when the army of the Revolution was reorganized under the resolution of October, 1780; it is in fact required to the virtual close of the war, when the equity of the case would require the admission of the claim. If presumptions are admitted after that period, who will venture to assert that they are unreasonable? It is unreasonable to suppose that an officer who had served until the war was considered as at an end, would voluntarily resign his commission, and that he would not hold to the advantages promised him if he should continue in the service a short time longer, when there was in fact little fatigue and less danger connected with the service! Surely there is nothing unreasonable in such a presumption. Would not self-interest, honor, the known attachment formed to military life by a long continuance in it, lead to the presumption that the great mass of officers would hold to their commissions until a disbandment of the army took place?

If there be presumptions as to any part of the evidence, they are such, Mr. Speaker, as have been admitted by wiser heads than mine, or perhaps, than that of my young, estimable, and talented friend from New Hampshire. The fathers of the nation—the Senate, have acted upon them for many years past, and the House has followed the example set by the Senate. Nay, sir, both Houses have for years past, not only acted upon some presumptive proof, they have acted upon the admitted fact, that service was not continued longer than the capture of York in 1781. Thus in the case of General Hamilton's heirs, when the General was known to have retired after that event, considered as the close of the war, commutation pay

was granted by both Houses, with little or no difficulty.

The argument of the gentleman from New Hampshire goes, however, in fact, not so much against the admission of presumptive evidence, as against the admission of any claim on the part of the retiring officers under the resolves of 1780. If I understood him correctly, his arguments, if they are to have any weight, must lead to that result—an injustice he certainly could never have intended—an injustice, at all events, so crying, that this House never will never can think of sanctioning it.

As to the objections raised by the gentleman from New York, [Mr. VANDERPOEL,] they are so evidently founded upon a misapprehension of the whole subject, that it is scarcely necessary to give them a reply. Leaving the mass of the gentleman's strange assertions to other gentlemen of the Committee on Revolutionary Claims, I will make a few remarks upon his principal objection. He says the act of May 15, 1828, made provision for these claims, and was intended for that purpose. Now, sir, if I understand it, the object of that act was and must have been an entirely different one. It provides for officers and *soldiers*; whereas officers alone are entitled to commutation. It provides for living officers only, while commutation is a right descending to heirs. It grants no higher pay than that of a captain, no matter what rank may have been held; whereas five years' full pay, according to the rank of the officers, is the commutation of half pay for life, granted by the resolve of March, 1783.

Sir, the object of the act of 1828 was to show the gratitude of the nation for the services rendered by the officers and soldiers who continued in the service to the close of the war, and to compensate in some measure for the endured losses and privations of every description. The claims provided for by the present bill, on the other hand, are founded upon express contract between the then existing Government and the officers of the army. The original contract was, that those who had served until the spring of 1781, when the reorganization of the army under the resolutions of October, 1780, took place, should have half pay for life, and that those also who continued in the service to the end of the war, in addition to their full pay during such continuance, should be entitled to half pay during life, to commence from the time of their reduction. In 1783, owing to the unpopularity of this mode of payment, it appearing to create something like a privileged class, the contract was changed with the consent of parties. The half pay for life was commuted by a grant of five years full pay. This was accepted, not by officers individually, but by lines and corps not belonging to particular States, by the officers of the hospital department, and by the retired officers in each State *collectively*. Can it be doubted for a moment that the officers of the army who fulfilled their part of the con-

tract, have a right to look to the Government for a fulfilment of its promise? Can it be doubted whether the Government is bound to make its contract good? There is no escaping, Mr. Speaker. Pay them you must—those I mean who retired under the resolves of 1787, and the consequent new arrangement of the army, and those who served to the end of the war, unless you choose condescending to plead the limitation act, and to commit the most gross and outrageous injustice.

The great mass of these claims, it is admitted, have already been paid, perhaps nineteen out of every twenty. If, comparatively speaking, some few remain unpaid, it was in most cases not owing to an ignorance of their rights in the claimants, as the gentleman from New York would seem to say the committee had insinuated, but to the particular mode (collectively by a majority) in which the commutation had been accepted; to patriotism, which held many back from asking what they well knew an impoverished Government could not easily pay; to a knowledge that the certificate granted in lieu of pay was, at that time, scarcely worth asking for; and to other causes detailed by the committee in their report.

Sir, instead of the act of May, 1828, being considered as making compensation for commutation pay, the very reverse is the case. Having received commutation, entitles to the benefits of the act of 1828, and receiving the benefits of that act, entitles to commutation, if not before received, although half pay under the Virginia laws, notwithstanding the assertion of the gentleman from New York, will exclude, and necessarily exclude from commutation. A right to commutation, and a title to the benefits of the act of 1828, are necessarily connected one with the other, both requiring the same services, although they are entirely different rewards. Thus, when the Treasury Department, under whose direction the act of '28 is executed, asks for the proofs which are to entitle the claimants to the benefit of that act, it requires them to declare—this being the strongest possible proof the claim being a valid one—it requires them to declare that they have received their commutation certificates. Here, sir, is the form of a declaration, prepared at the Treasury Department, which applicants for the benefits of the act of 1828 are required to sign. It runs thus:

"For the purpose of obtaining the benefits of an 'act entitled ' An act for the relief of certain surviving officers and soldiers of the army of the Revolution,' approved May 15, 1828, I, &c., do hereby declare, that I was an officer of the Continental line of the army of the Revolution, and served as such (note: here insert, ' to the end of the war,' or as the case may be) to the time when the arrangement of the army, provided by the resolves of Congress of the 3d and 21st of October, 1780, was carried into effect, and that I was reduced under that arrangement; and I also declare, that I afterwards received certificates (commonly called commutation certificates) for a sum equal to the amount of five years' full pay, which sum was offered by the resolves of Congress of the 22d of March, 1783, instead of the half-pay for life, to which I was entitled under the resolve ' of the 21st of October, 1780.''

Can anything, Mr. Speaker, be more clear, positive, and decisive? Thus the Treasury Department has acted, and continued to act. And what has been the course of Congress? Does the action show in what light the case has been received? Most distinctly. At one session, it passes an act to give to Job I. Jacobs the benefits of the act of 1828, and at another session it passes an act giving him his commutation. At one session it gives to Ephraim Whitaker the benefits of the act of '28, and at another it gives him commutation. Do

gentlemen, can gentlemen, desire anything more? If the gentleman from New York will be candid, he will admit that he was under wrong impressions. Upon the last case—the case of Whitaker—he has himself acted but a few weeks since; he approved of it, because, though he may not have voted, silence here gives consent. In cases of this kind, there is, in fact, no excuse. Let no man complain that a bill passes *sub silentio*, as the gentleman has said. When bills of this description are reported to the House, they are invariably accompanied by a report, detailing the facts of the case, and the evidence by which it is supported. This report is laid upon the desk of members—if they do not choose to read it—if they do not choose to be in their places when the bill is considered in the Committee of the Whole—if they do not sit in the proper time make objections—are they entitled afterwards to complain of a bill passing *sub silentio*, or is it expected that committees shall themselves raise objections to their own bills and reports, and thus call upon gentlemen to deliver speeches where they are deemed unnecessary by the committees?

But, Mr. Speaker, I will not myself take up the time of the House unnecessarily. If ever justice and expediency required the passage of any law, I will venture to assert that it is the passage of this. Sir, I have waded in these claims for three years, and I make the assertion, after a full examination. The passage of the law on your table, I repeat it, will save the time of the House and the money of the treasury; it will render the rejection of unjust claims nearly certain, and accelerate the settlement of just claims of this description, and of all others left for the decision of Congress. It will ensure the same measure of justice to one citizen which another has received, and will, by speedy, exact, and equal justice, go far to satisfy all parties.

With these few observations, I cheerfully leave the fate of the bill to the good sense, the justice, and experience of the House. Its decision, after hearing some of my colleagues of the Committee on Revolutionary Claims, will no doubt be correct.

CORRECTION.—We are requested by Mr. BROWN, of the Senate, to say that he was incorrectly reported in his remarks on Thursday, on the memorials presented by Mr. TYLER. Our reporter made him say—

"He held in his hand a paper containing the prices current in Richmond, and it would be found by it, (the Richmond Enquirer of the 8th inst.,) that good tobacco was now selling at from $8 to $9 per hundred, and fine from $10 to $10, which was better than the average price of the article had been for five years past, and it was considered not only a handsome, but a ample compensation, to receive $6."

It should have been as follows:

"He held in his hand a paper containing the prices current in Richmond, and it would be found by it, (the Richmond Enquirer of the 8th instant,) that good tobacco was now selling at from $8 to $9 per hundred, fine from $9 to $10, fine manufacturing 10 dollars and 11 dollars; and although there had been a slight decline in the price of that article lately, in consequence of the state of the market in Europe, yet, according to the prices quoted, if he did not much err in his recollection, it was now commanding a better price than it had on an average generally, for the last five years. It had sometimes been higher during that period, but generally, it had been much lower. So far as he was acquainted with the opinions of intelligent tobacco planters, an average price of six dollars per hundred was considered a fair remuneration for those engaged in its culture."

The 13th number of the CONGRESSIONAL GLOBE dated the 1st March, 1834, for Pennsylvania, an the States north and east of it, was on board of the steamboat William Penn, which was burnt on the 4th, and the greater part of them destroyed.

We give this notice, for the purpose of informing those subscribers who have failed to receive that number, of the reason of its failure, as that we have not that number on hand to supply the loss.

THE CONGRESSIONAL GLOBE.

PRINTED AND PUBLISHED AT THE CITY OF WASHINGTON, BY BLAIR & RIVES.

23d Congress, 1st Session.   SATURDAY, MARCH 22, 1834.   Vol. 1......No. 16.

The Senate did not sit on Saturday.

HOUSE OF REPRESENTATIVES.

Saturday, March 15, 1834.

Mr. R. M. JOHNSON asked the unanimous consent of the House to submit a motion to grant the use of the Hall, on Monday evening, to Mr. Whitlow, for the purpose of lecturing upon Asiatic cholera and dyspeptics. An objection being made, Mr. JOHNSON moved the suspension of the rule. It appearing by the vote, 80 to 21, that there was no quorum, Mr. THOMSON moved that the House do now adjourn.

Mr. CARR called for the yeas and nays, and they were ordered.

Mr. PARKER asked if a call of the House was in order, and was informed by the Chair that it was not.

The question being taken by yeas and nays on the motion to adjourn, it was decided in the negative—ayes 7, noes 121.

The question being taken on the motion to suspend the rule, to permit Mr. Johnson to make his motion,

Mr. WATMOUGH asked for the yeas and nays, which were refused.

The motion was rejected.

Mr. SHINN, from the Committee on the District of Columbia, reported an amendment to the bill respecting the Potomac Bridge; which was ordered to be printed.

Mr. BEALE, from the Committee on Revolutionary Pensions, reported a bill granting pensions to certain persons therein named. Read twice, and committed.

Mr. WARDWELL, from the same committee, reported a bill for the relief of Peter Triplett. Read twice, and committed.

The resolution of Mr. MARDIS, respecting the public depositories, was taken up.

The SPEAKER informed the House that he had received a letter from Mr. Burges, a member of the House, stating that he was prevented by indisposition from attending the House to-day, and requesting that the consideration of the resolution be postponed till Monday.

On motion of Mr. WHITTLESEY, of Ohio, the further consideration of the resolution was postponed till Monday.

Mr. POLK asked the unanimous consent of the House to permit the army appropriation bill to be read a third time; and no objection being made, the bill was read a third time, and passed.

Mr. SPEIGHT moved the suspension of the rule, in order to take up a joint resolution relative to the purchase of certain books. Agreed to.

The House proceeded to consider a joint resolution for the purchase of certain books, the question being on an amendment reported from the Committee of the Whole, for the purchase of additional copies of Gales & Seaton's Debates.

Mr. SPEIGHT submitted an amendment to the amendment, which the Chair stated was not now in order.

Mr. FOSTER said that when the subject was formerly, he stated that he would endeavor to get our constituents to be informed of the amount of money which we appropriated to ourselves. He wished to have a law providing what books should purchase, and should appropriate for them. He was willing to get Gales & Seaton's nine volumes, and Elliot's book, and Gibbon's Decline and Fall of the Roman Empire, and Hume's England, and Kent's Commentaries, &c., pay for them out of a certain and fixed contingent fund, as far as it goes, and pay the balance out of our own pay. Some one asked whether members who opposed these appropriations received the books. He replied to the question that he did receive them. But if the would leave the money in the treasury, instead of appropriating it to the contingent fund, would suffer the books to remain on the printer's shelves. He then moved that the resolution

be recommitted to the Committee on the Library, with instructions to inquire and report what books ought to be purchased, and the amount which they will cost.

Mr. J. Q. ADAMS asked if it was in order to move an amendment to the instructions requiring the committee to report a bill.

The SPEAKER said the motion was not now in order.

Mr. ADAMS had no objection to the object of the inquiry, but he wished to have a bill, instead of a joint resolution, reported. He conceived that the resolution, as it stood, was unconstitutional. His objection was not to the object, but to the form of the proceeding. Mr. A. proceeded to sustain his objections, when

Mr. SPEIGHT rose to a question of order. The merits of the question were not now open for discussion. If the gentleman would defer his remarks to a proper time, he would meet him on the constitutional question.

The SPEAKER said it was not in order to discuss the merits of the resolution.

Mr. ADAMS. Is it not in order at any time and under any circumstances, to oppose the passage of a bill or resolution here on constitutional grounds?

The SPEAKER decided that it was not now in order to discuss the merits of the resolution.

Mr. ADAMS. I submit, sir, but am not convinced.

Mr. FOSTER said that as the members would not, he hoped, be unwilling to record their names upon a question whether the people should be informed of the amount of money which we appropriate to ourselves, he asked the yeas and nays on the question.

The House refused to order the yeas and nays, twenty-four only rising in the affirmative.

Mr. FOSTER'S motion to recommit was rejected, thirty-seven members had not voted for the call of the yeas and nays.

The amendment of the Committee of the Whole was concurred in.

Mr. SPEIGHT then offered his amendment.

Mr. J. Q. ADAMS opposed the amendment and resolution. The Constitution (he said) declared that no money should be drawn from the treasury but in consequence of an appropriation by law. Nothing could become a law but that which was introduced in the form of a bill. Every bill, before it shall become a law, must be presented to the President of the United States for his approval and signature. This, (said Mr. A.,) is the first instance of an attempt to appropriate money by joint resolution. There was not a single instance of the kind on the statute books. If the resolution passed, he hoped the appropriation would be stricken out.

Mr. SPEIGHT would say but a few words on the question. He would ask if the gentleman means to say that no appropriations have ever been made by resolutions? He would refer the gentleman to a resolution, which he himself introduced, at the commencement of the session, for the purchase of the bank book.

Mr. ADAMS. There was no appropriation in that.

Mr. SPEIGHT subscribed, he said, to the doctrine of the gentleman, that no money can be appropriated except by law. What is law? The expression of the will of the legislature, in joint resolution, was an expression of that will, and had all the sanction of law. He was surprised to hear the gentleman assert that no appropriations have ever been made by joint resolution. Appropriations had been, either directly, by resolution and he could point out to the gentleman a joint resolution of this kind, which he himself sanctioned during his administration.

Mr. ADAMS. I would be glad if the gentleman would show it.

Mr. SPEIGHT had, he said, but one motive in offering his amendment; it was to put the new members on the footing with the old members, in respect to being furnished with books. He proposed to furnish the new members with the nine volumes of the Register of Debates, and the old members with the last volume. He also stated, upon the authority of a letter from Messrs. Gales & Seaton, that this work must be discontinued, for want of patronage, unless the patronage of Congress should be continued to it. In conclusion, Mr. S. said, that unless we got books for the new members, he should propose that the old members should bring all the books which they have heretofore received, put them down in a pile, and divide them among all the members.

Mr. FOSTER. I will join you in that, sir.

Mr. McDUFFIE suggested that if "appropriated" was stricken out of the joint resolution, it might obviate the objection of the honorable member from Massachusetts.

Mr. Speight's amendment was read as follows: strike out after Resolved, and insert "That the members of the present Congress who have not heretofore received them be supplied by the Clerk with the same books that have been ordered to be furnished to the members of the last Congress; together with complete sets of the Register of Debates, to the ninth volume inclusive, and that such members of the last Congress as have received parts of the debates be also furnished with volumes necessary to complete their sets to the ninth volume inclusive, and the expense be paid out of the contingent fund."

Mr. FOSTER expressed regret that the honorable member, [Mr. Speight,] with whom he had so long felt pleasure in acting, should have taken the lead in making this proposition; but he begged to remind the House that upon a former occasion they had by a large majority declared that these books should not be paid for out of their contingent fund.

Mr. POLK said he, for one, could not vote for the amendment, because if he did he would thereby be abandoning the great principle for which he had always contended, viz: that the House had no right to use their contingent fund for such purposes, or cause any books to be ordered or paid for except by a law or by joint resolution. He would state that he was not opposed, but on the contrary, was willing to vote that the new members should receive such books as had been voted to the members of the last Congress; but he could not give the former members any in addition to what they had already obtained.

Mr. GALBRAITH called for the reading of the resolution and amendment.

They were read accordingly; after which Mr. SPEIGHT said that he coincided in the opinion avowed by the honorable member from Tennessee as to the principle about the contingent fund; but under the circumstances, he considered that it was only an act of justice that the new members should be placed on a similar footing with the old, and as the Senate did not choose to come to the House for a joint resolution for the purchase of such books as they desired, he would not go to them.

Mr. PARKER was opposed to the amendment. He thought at the time that the House had receded from their disagreement to the Senate's amendment to the House appropriation bill that there was an understanding that thenceforth all future purchases of books should be provided for by bills for that purpose, or by a joint resolution of both Houses.

Mr. BARRINGER rose to set the member from New Jersey right upon this. He had certainly not supposed there was any such understanding. The Senate, so far from having it, had by their acts soon after, completely negatived the idea that there was any understanding of the kind, for they had supplied themselves with books without regarding the disposition of the House on the subject. The resolution, as amended, therefore, only

authorized that to be done by the House which the Senate had already done for themselves.

Mr. JARVIS called for the reading of the clause in the House appropriation bill, specifying the items for which the contingent fund was to be applied.

The clause was read, viz: "granting $150,000, for printing, stationary, &c., to be applied for no other purpose;" after which,

Mr. JARVIS called for the yeas and nays on the question.

Mr. PINCKNEY inquired if a motion for indefinite postponement was then in order?

The SPEAKER replied in the negative.

The House refused to order the yeas and nays, ayes 27, noes 137.

Mr. PINCKNEY said, although he differed in opinion with the member from North Carolina, [Mr. Speight,] that a law and joint resolutions were similar; yet it was perfectly immaterial to him, by which mode the House should make the appropriation, for his objection was to the principle—that they could appropriate for the purchase of books, at all. He considered this an appropriation of the people's money for the private use of the members; as such it was unconstitutional, and for which, if they were justified in appropriating, they might just as well appropriate for their private uses all the funds in the treasury. He had another objection to this. The House were called on to vote in the dark; without knowing the amount of the people's money which they were thus going to dispose of. They did not know—they refused even to inquire, whether the cost of these books would be eight thousand, or eighty thousand dollars, and if he was correctly informed, the amount would be the latter. He desired to call the attention of the people to the question, whether the House had the right to do this, and he might at the same time inquire if he had not the right to avail himself of that order, although he would not make the objection—that members should not vote in cases in which they were interested? He moved to postpone the resolution indefinitely; and called for the yeas and nays on his motion; which having been ordered,

Mr. McDUFFIE said he felt bound by some feeling of paternity, to say something in vindication of the resolution. He could not agree with his colleague, [Mr. P.,] that this resoultion made an appropriation for the private uses of the members, or that it was unconstitutional for the House to vote upon questions that they were interested in. He would like to know, if the principle held good, by what right they voted their pay? Voting for the appropriation of $150,000 for their contingent fund to pay for stationary, pens, knives, &c., might be termed voting for their private uses on the same principle. He maintained that these books were all important to the members on public grounds to give them information that would the better enable them to discharge their public duties. He believed that the work could not be proceeded with without the aid of Congress, and in voting for the works, it was on public grounds he had done so; having so received them, he never should take them home, intending to leave them here, where they could be of equal advantage to his successors, as they had been to himself, and he could have desired that there was such an obligation inserted when the resolution was originally introduced, or even now, that all books should be left in the library for the benefit and use of their successors in Congress. In order to obviate the objection of the member from Tennessee, [Mr. Polk,] he must request the mover of the amendment [Mr. Speight] to modify his resolution so as to have it by joint resolution, and to strike out the part terming it "appropriate," which would also obviate the objections of the member from Massachusetts [Mr. Adams.]

Mr. SPEIGHT declined making any alteration, in consequence of the conduct pursued on this subject by the other branch of the Legislature. It was for the House, if they thought proper, to reject his amendment, and they might then pass a joint resolution, which would be equally satisfactory to him.

Mr. WAYNE inquired if it was not intended to confine the action of the resolution to the House only?

Mr. SPEIGHT replied such was his intention.

The resolution having been read, it was so modified, by inserting "House of Representatives."

Mr. J. Q. ADAMS considered the proposition of Mr. McDuffie the most advisable course to be taken.

The question on the amendment, as modified by Mr. Speight, was then put, and agreed to.

The question then being on the motion of Mr. Pinckney, to postpone indefinitely—

Mr. POLK expressed his deep regret that the House were about to abandon a principle for which they had contended, and to decide that they had a right to use their contingent fund as they thought proper. He had no objection to the purchase of any books that should be deemed necessary. All that he desired was, that the purchase should be made in pursuance of a specific and direct law; not by applying indirectly to attain the object by means of the contingent fund, which he maintained it was unconstitutional to use for such purposes. The consequence of all this must be, that the contingent fund would be exhausted, and would not be sufficient to defray their ordinary expenses. He considered the whole difficulty would have been obviated, if the member from North Carolina [Mr. Speight] had consented to the proposition to make it a joint resolution.

Mr. WAYNE said he should have preferred having the books procured by a joint resolution of both Houses, for that purpose; but if they were not to be procured in that way, he would vote for the amendment to obtain them. He considered that this was not a proposition to purchase books for the private uses of the members, or for the purchase of books of an ordinary character. No; it was the purchase of what had been done under the permission, if not under the authority of Congress, and which was more illustrative of their past proceedings, more necessary to assist members in the discharge of their public duties, than any other work that could be obtained. He considered that, as all reports of their proceedings; that reporters were permitted into the House for that purpose, by their authority, the registers of debates on subjects that came up, although not in the form of a record, were substantially a part of their proceedings, and which were highly valuable as well for the present use of the members, as for reference hereafter, to explain to posterity, what could not otherwise be explained, the grounds upon which, on all important subjects, they were induced to act. The question had come to this, that if they did not supply themselves with the works in their separate capacity, it appeared they could not have them at all, for the Senate had declared that the House had no right to interfere with them in the use of their contingent fund to make such purchases as they thought proper; the constitutional principle of touching it, for the purchase of books, was rejected.

Mr. CHILTON remarked that he was originally inclined to vote for the resolution, but upon more mature reflection, he was compelled, by a sense of what he owed to his constituents, to vote for the motion for indefinite postponement. He could not consider it anything else than as a practical increase by the members of their own pay; and if necessary to be done at all, he would submit the question, whether this ought not to be done by a direct law, and therefore in such a shape as the whole country could understand. As a new member, who was to be benefited if the resolution should be passed, he would rather give up any claims he could have than sanction what he must consider to be a dangerous principle for the House to act upon, and which must, if not timely arrested, make the printing of books for the use of members the most expensive department of the Government. He would vote against the purchase of even a solitary book.

Mr. BROWN said, it was with some reluctance he rose to address the House; but as he should feel himself compelled to vote against the resolution, in its present form, he desired to state his reasons, that he might not be misunderstood.

It must be manifest to all who had listened to this discussion, or looked into the previous action of Congress upon this subject, that a limit must, sooner or later, be put upon the practice heretofore pursued of furnishing members with books at the public expense. When this resolution was first introduced, he did not suppose it was intended to do more than place the new members, as to books, upon a footing of equality with the old; and if he was not mistaken, it not only did this, but also proposed to grant to all the members, indiscriminately, books not embraced within the resolutions of the last Congress. He was willing that as much should be done for the new members in this respect as had been done for the old; and he could, at the same time, unite his regrets with honorable gentlemen, that the practice had not, from its commencement, been confined exclusively to providing books for the use of members only during the time they remained in office. He begged the House to look at the practice as applied to individuals—himself, for instance. Long before the works contemplated in the resolution could be published, his time of office would expire, and the chances were as ten to one at least that he would never come back again; indeed, he was not yet prepared to say he wished to come back. The books would then become his own property, and his successor, whoever he might be, could not derive the slightest benefit from any information they contained.

He was opposed to the resolution in its present shape upon another ground. Upon a previous occasion, when one of the appropriation bills was under consideration, the House disagreed with the Senate, and he twice voted (and he believed rightly) to set a limit upon the power of both Houses over the contingent fund, to prevent its application to the purposes mentioned in this resolution. He would not now reverse those votes, nor would he, under the name of the contingent expenses of Congress, make appropriations for the purchase of books, but would prefer that they should be made the subjects of a specific appropriation.

Mr. McDUFFIE rose for the purpose of obviating what he considered the only objection that could be urged to the resolution, and which it was in their power to do, to make the books public instead of private property; for which purpose he moved the following as an amendment, viz., "the sixth, 'seventh, eighth, and ninth volumes of the Regis-'ter of Debates to be deposited in the Library when 'the present members retire, for the use of their 'successors."

Mr. VANDERPOEL inquired if such an amendment was in order when there was a motion to postpone?

The SPEAKER replied in the affirmative, and that the amendment had precedence of the motion to postpone.

Mr. VINTON objected to the new principle proposed by the amendment submitted by Mr. McDuffie, which he said would go to establish that each representative had no occasion for the information contained in these or other books that Congress had usually voted, except at the seat of Government. He considered that every member paid fully to his constituents a remuneration for the value of the books, by answering the calls made upon them in their representative capacity for information.

Mr. WISE spoke in favor of the resolution, and urged the claims of the new members to be put on the same footing with the old members. But even if it were an original question, he would vote for the purchase of such books as would tend to enlighten him in regard to the history of the legislation of this House. We, sir, (said he) are at home the oracles of our respective neighborhoods. To us the people look for information in regard to the business of this House. As a new member, he expected to acquire more knowledge preparatory to the discharge of his duties here, during the recess than he could acquire during the session, and he wished to carry with him such documents as were necessary to his instruction.

The question was taken on the amendment proposed by Mr. McDUFFIE, and rejected.

Mr. MANN, of New York, believed that the measure proposed was wrong in principle and in practice. Congress could not properly become the great patron of publishers. Is it true that this is the work on which the Clerk of this House gave his acceptances, and must we now redeem those acceptances? He trusted not. If the work could not be supported by the patronage of the public there was no way to prevent it from going down. He acknowledged that it was an important work and he should be very sorry to see it discontinued

But he would not consent, though one of the members for whose benefit the resolution was introduced, to pay the public money for our own private benefit. The member from Virginia, might be assured that, however it was in Virginia, there were no oracles in New York.

Mr. POLK said he would show the House what extent this system of pensioning publishers on our contingent fund, had been carried in another branch of Congress. He held in his hand a statement from the Secretary of the Senate, showing, that during the last year that body voted for the purchase of Gales & Seaton's Debates, $1,940, and for Duff Green's compilation of the Land Laws, &c., (1,600 copies,) over $46,000, and other sums for other works. He questioned whether any member of the Senate looked at the amount of this expenditure at the time when it was made. The same was the case with this House. He wished the House to understand what they were doing, and what they were likely to do. We had before us the example of the Senate for purchasing 1,600 copies of a work, at the expense of $46,000, to be paid out of a contingent fund of $36,000.

Mr. WISE asked whether the House had not uniformly been furnished with books by resolution. He hoped that the abuses of the Senate—he did not use the term in disrespect to that body—would not be followed by the House. We were told by the gentleman from New York, that in New York there are no oracles. He had not used the word "oracles" in the Delphic sense. The oracles to which he referred, were the stump orators of the country. If there were no such oracles in New York, there were a plenty of them in Virginia; and he hoped in God, that as long as there was a green court-yard and a stump to be found in Virginia, there would be no lack of such oracles. During the spring elections in Virginia, it was the custom for the competitors for office in the several counties, to address the people. During the last spring, he had himself, he believed, made as many as twenty-seven stump speeches, besides having one hundred and fifty cross-road skirmishes. But it seems that the constituents of the gentleman are so wise, that they listen to no such sources of instruction. No doubt they are the salt of the earth, and that wisdom will perish with them. But still, if he had not been much misinformed, there was an oracle in Albany, which does give law to the gentleman himself, and to his constituents.

Mr. MANN, of New York, had not intended, he said, to disturb the gentleman's equanimity, nor to draw from him any reflections upon New York. Sitting here as a listener, he had often heard the gentleman speak about New York, its parties, its discipline, and what not; but he had not regarded it. He knew that it was quite common, of late, to talk in the debates of New York politics, of New York magicians, and of the machinery by which the politics of the State were supposed to be managed. Sir, the gentleman is totally ignorant of New York. I referred, sir, to the gentleman's remark, that the members from Virginia were oracles in their own districts. I did not know whether he used the term in the Delphic sense, or the stump sense; but, as the gentleman is a classical scholar, I thought he had allusion to the classics, and I supposed—though, to be sure, it was rather an extravagant supposition—that the member from Virginia, a State distinguished in old times for its eminent men, called himself an oracle among his constituents. Let me tell the gentleman, and others who think with him, to come into New York, and go among the people. He will find them free, intelligent, virtuous, instructed, and as independent in their opinions as any on the face of the globe. Under the management at Albany, of which the gentleman speaks, we had a free and enlightened Government, a system of public instruction which was unrivalled in the world; a noble system of internal improvements; vast, increasing, and rapidly developing resources and individual wealth, virtue, and happiness. Let the gentleman look at all this, and then say, if he chooses, that such a people are governed by an oracle at Albany, or elsewhere. That population, he assured the gentleman, was not to be influenced either by stump speeches or by *oracles*. Mr. M. continued his remarks, contrasting the former public men of Virginia—upon whose political sentiments he was proud to say he had formed his own—with those of the present day. Can it be, that the State of Virginia has come to a premature old age? He trusted not. But the course of the gentleman almost induced him to believe—stranger as he was to this body—that the day of public men in Virginia had gone by.

Mr. McDUFFIE rose. Though he stood between the two gentlemen, yet he had no intention to interfere in their strife. He would say, since they had got upon classical ground,

"Non nostri tantas componere lites;"

but he wished to bring down the gentlemen from the high political and classical topics upon which they had been discoursing, to the small matter of figures which was before the House, &c.

After some conversation between Mr. J. Q. ADAMS and Mr. POLK, in reference to the document which the latter had read to the House, relative to the expenditures of the Senate—

Mr. LANE said, if the object of gentlemen who had occupied the floor for the last hour in opposition to the resolution, had been to convince members of the inexpediency of its adoption, he could only say, so far as it regarded himself, they had been truly unfortunate. So far from having heard anything to change, his first impressions had been confirmed. That no one had contributed more largely in producing that result than his honorable friend from Tennessee, [Mr. POLK.]

We are told by that gentleman that the Senate have, by a similar resolution, appropriated upwards of $40,000 in purchasing books for that body.

This fact, so far from proving the dangerous tendency of the resolution for which it has been thrown into the debate, was conclusive to his mind of not only the propriety of its adoption, but of its necessity.

If the Senate, of whose integrity and intelligence he entertained the most exalted opinion, composed of forty-eight members, had found it necessary for a full and faithful discharge of their duties to expend that sum, how much greater the necessity, and with how much more propriety, may this House, composed of two hundred and forty members, appropriate from the same fund, for a similar purpose, the sum of $4,000 contemplated by the resolution.

The gentleman from Kentucky [Mr. CHILTON] has told us gravely, he will vote against the resolution in any shape, though he had received the same books now contemplated to be furnished new members, in order to place them in that respect on an equality with the old, by virtue of a similar resolution.

The gentleman from South Carolina [Mr. PINCKNEY] informs the House that he has arrived at the same conclusions, and therefore had made the motion for indefinite postponement, with the exception that he had paid for the books out of his own funds. A most excellent reason for voting against the resolution, and especially for the gentleman from Kentucky.

The gentleman from New York, [Mr. MANN,] in reply to the gentleman from Virginia, [Mr. WISE,] informs the House, they have no *oracles* in New York; that his constituents will not consult him as to what had been done in this House. If that be true, so much greater the necessity of these books, that his constituents may read and judge for themselves.

Mr. L. said he was differently situated; his constituents would no doubt make many inquiries in relation to the action of this House and the part he had taken, and to answer, and satisfactorily to answer, any inquiry, he desired to have the books in the way they have been furnished to the old members. He considered the books for the new members not only as an act of justice, but to enable them to a discharge of their respective duties here and at home. He therefore should vote against the motion to postpone.

After a few remarks in explanation from Mr. WISE and Mr. MANN,

Mr. FOSTER repeated his objections to the purchase of books by the contingent fund of the House, instead of by a bill for that purpose.

The question on postponing the resolutions indefinitely was decided in the negative—yeas 80, nays 115.

Mr. CHILTON called for the yeas and nays on the question of agreeing to the resolution, as amended by Mr. SPEIGHT.

The House refused to order them; and the resolution as amended, &c., was agreed to, and

The House adjourned.

IN SENATE.

MONDAY, *March* 17, 1834.

Mr. POINDEXTER, agreeably to notice, asked and obtained leave to introduce a resolution to enable the Committee on Public Lands to employ a clerk to record the testimony about being taken before that committee, relative to alleged frauds in the land offices; which was read a first and second time, and ordered to be engrossed for a third reading.

The VICE PRESIDENT communicated the proceedings of a numerous meeting of freeholders and voters of the county of Shenandoah, Virginia, approving of the course of the Administration, objecting to the restoration of the public deposites, and against the recharter of the Bank of the United States. The proceedings having been read—

Mr. TYLER said he rose for the purpose of moving the printing of these proceedings, and their reference to the Committee on Finance. He further said, that as one of the representatives of Virginia here, he would have taken great pleasure in making known the sentiments of any portion of her citizens, if they had made known their sentiments to him, without any regard to their political principles; and he would have been pleased on this occasion, to have been the medium of presenting their views. But although they had not intrusted him with this duty, he was not unadvised of these proceedings. The people of the county of Shenandoah were Whigs from a period long anterior to the Revolution. In that struggle which terminated in the achievement of our independence, the people of that country stood by the side of those who fought for the country. And such was their zeal, at that eventful period, that after the consummation of the struggle, they even objected to the name which the county then held. It was then named Dunmore, after the last of the royal Governors of Virginia, and they thought that the name which it now bears, after the noble river which flows through its soil, was more compatible with their ideas of liberty. In subsequent contests in which the country was engaged they had been uniformly found with the Republican party, headed by Mr. Jefferson. What they were at a period anterior to our history, no one has a right to question, nor would he now question it. It was his misfortune to see some things in the present posture of our affairs, with different eyes from theirs, and if they had the same opportunities of observation which he had here, he believed they would not be found differing. But be this as it might, in relation to some of the principles contained in these resolutions, he cordially agreed with them. He was opposed to the Bank of the United States on broad constitutional grounds. And while he differed with them in the assumption of executive power, he would equally oppose the assumption of legislative power.

The motion to refer and print was agreed to.

The VICE PRESIDENT presented the proceedings of a meeting of the inhabitants of York county, Pennsylvania, opposed to the recharter of the Bank of the United States, and against the restoration of the public deposites.

Mr. WILKINS moved that it be read, referred to the Committee on Finance, and ordered to be printed.

After the memorial had been read,

Mr. WEBSTER said, indeed he agreed in opinion with these people of York, that "truth was mighty and would prevail;" and he thought this salutary maxim was likely to be verified in their own case. His attention had been requested to these proceedings by persons of York, who desired him to say that this paper grossly misrepresented them. He was requested to say this by persons who were present at the meeting, who were not willing that those puerilities contained in the paper should be charged upon one of the greatest counties in Pennsylvania. He had a paper in his hand, signed by a number of highly respect-

able people of York, protesting against these proceedings. [Here Mr. W. read some of the names, inquiring if the Senators from Pennsylvania were acquainted with them; upon which Mr. McKean replied, he knew some of them to be respectable.] Mr. Webster continued. These resolutions say that they were passed unanimously, with the exception of some half dozen yells of persons who came there to disturb the harmony of the meeting. The men signing this protest say that these resolutions were rejected by a vote of three to one, and that they neither express the sentiments of the people of York, nor of the people who attended the meeting. He submitted the letter, requesting that it might be read. And as it respected these memorials, if this was a specimen of those which were to be presented for the purpose of supporting the treasury measure, he thought they would require the particular attention of the Senate. He agreed with them that truth was mighty, and *would* prevail.

Mr. McKEAN said he had not been honored with the confidence of either of these parties; he believed, however, that many of the names he had heard were very respectable.

Mr. POINDEXTER did not object to the presentation of petitions or memorials, but he objected to this one. He did not know if it evidenced more of ignorance than of insolence; it was very remarkable for both. But on its face, in the resolution relative to the Bank of the United States, it made allusions of direct and palpable corruption, in charging an attempt by that institution to purchase members of this body. It was also objectionable, as being a printed paper cut out of some newspaper, and that, too, defaced, and a part struck out of it, making a direct personal reflection upon an honorable member of the Senate. For himself, he would not have presented such a paper. If it had been sent to him, he would have sent it back to the person from whom it came. [Here Mr. P. read one of the resolutions couched in offensive language, in reference to Mr. Webster's being bribed by the Bank of the United States, and his vote upon the bill chartering the bank in 1816.] Mr. P. said, it was time for the Senate to take care of its own dignity. It was assailed by friends of the present Chief Magistrate, in terms which looked like having been got up in the purlieus of the palace, and sent to York county, to be sent back here again. When a direct libel was contained in the paper upon an honorable member of this body, it was not fit to be recognised by the Senate. It bore no signature, no marks of authenticity, and contained the grossest libels against the two Houses of Congress. There were not two sentiments in the paper, which set forth the truth. He was against even the reception of the paper.

Mr. WILKINS asked Mr. Poindexter to mark the exceptionable passages, which he did.

Mr. PRESTON desired to be informed how the paper got before the Senate.

The VICE PRESIDENT replied, that the proceedings were transmitted to him under cover of a letter, which requested him to lay them before the Senate. He directed the letter to be read, which was done accordingly.

Mr. WEBSTER said, he had been told, a short time ago, that such proceedings would be presented here, and that one of the resolutions would be of a scandalous character. He then said, that he felt some reluctance about laying any of the papers before the Senate, because his duty to the Senate and his sense of self-respect dictated to him to take no notice of such idle scandals. It was due to the Chair, however, to say, that the presiding officer of the Senate informed him that one of these resolutions contained matter that he deemed was offensive to himself. He told that officer that he was aware of it; and the Vice President replied, that he would not lay the proceedings before the Senate, unless some one representing the petitioners would take upon himself the responsibility of striking out the offensive part. He (Mr. W.) had not seen the paper at all; but since he had heard it read, he thought it obnoxous to all the censure which the gentleman from Mississippi had made against it. He thought, therefore, it ought to lie on the table.

Mr. PRESTON desired to make but a single remark. He was astonished at the presentation of this petition. He considered the right of petition a sacred right, and therefore he protested against any changing or remodelling of petitions or memorials sent to the Senate for presentation. When the presiding officer, or any officer of the Senate, was in possession of documents to be submitted to the Senate, he should not be permitted, with his consent, to erase or mutilate them.

Mr. WILKINS said he owed it to the Senate to make an explanation on this subject. On coming into the Senate chamber this morning, just before they were called to order, and before he had time to look over these proceedings, they were put into his hands by the presiding officer of the Senate, who made some suggestions in relation to the application of a part of them to the honorable Senator from Massachusetts, and he had also suggested a consultation with his colleague upon the propriety of striking out the offensive paragraph. Upon this suggestion, the very difficulty urged by the gentleman from South Carolina [Mr. Preston] occurred to him—how far himself and colleague were right, as the representatives of Pennsylvania, in altering a petition or memorial presented from their constituents. If this had been the first case which had been presented, he would have said that they had no authority to interfere. But this was the course he adopted, and this paragraph had been stricken out. It was done upon consultation with his colleague, who consented to share the responsibility of it with him, and for himself he would have gone still further, and have stricken out the other part objected to by the gentleman from Mississippi. Whether there was error in this procedure or not, he did not know. It was done from feelings of delicacy towards an honorable member of this body, and not thinking it of any consequence to strike out what did not affect the substance of the petition. This was the extent of his interference, and this was the motive for it.

He was willing to say a word upon another part of the subject. There could be no doubt of the respectability of the meeting at which the proceedings were adopted. The person whose name stood at the head of it, Adam King, was a member of the House of Representatives in the last Congress. This was some apology for the people of York. We were all aware of the excitement which prevailed in reference to the bank. There was no question which came so directly home to the feelings of the people, and hence the numerous meetings which were assembling in the country. All were struggling to obtain a correct expression of public sentiment on the all-absorbing question before the Senate, and hence arose the question which party had the majority in York. All were aiming at public sentiment, because it was that, which, when obtained, would settle the question. He was quite willing the gentleman from Massachusetts should take public sentiment in Pennsylvania as his guide, and he was equally willing to adopt it as a rule for their decision here.

One word as to the meeting, and as to which party had the majority. He had received a letter from Mr. King informing him that the meeting was a very large one; that the room in which it met was full to overflowing. We had, then, *prima facie* evidence that the resolutions were carried by a large majority of the meeting, because the proceedings were signed by the officers of the meeting, who attested the correctness of the proceedings. So much for the *prima facie* evidence. Now, as to the protest of the gentleman from Massachusetts, that was signed by fifty-three persons of a meeting, and wherein you have the curious assertion that the resolutions were lost by a vote of three to one. Now, when fifty-three persons of a meeting composed the majority in the proportion of three to one, he asked how many must have composed the whole meeting? And how is it possible that so very small a minority, consisting of but sixteen or eighteen persons, of course, could have been sufficiently strong to retain the control of the meeting, and bold enough to authenticate and transmit the proceedings? The protest itself shows the improbability of its own story, and defeats the object which the signers have in view. As he had already said, very strictly speaking, the marking of this insulated paragraph, merely indicating to the Secretary that it should not be read, may not have been justifiable, but it was a question between him and a portion of his highly respected fellow-citizens of York, and he was not apprehensive that he should incur their censure. They would appreciate his motives. If not rigidly justifiable, it was certainly excusable, because the act was one of delicacy towards a Senator, and did not in any way change the sense of the proceedings. The great object of the gentlemen of the meeting was to express their sentiments on the all-absorbing question of the deposites, and that expression of sentiment you yet have entire.

Mr. PRESTON said the memorial which was the subject of discussion was not the memorial which purported to be adopted in York county. He would not interfere between the gentlemen from Pennsylvania and their constituents, but he wished to declare the fact, that after the remodelling of the petition, it was not the petition of the York district. Why had this been done? Why had that been obliterated from it which stamped it all over with its peculiar character, and which made it unworthy of reception, in order to make it palatable to us? It was now a thing of a totally different character. Members, perhaps, might assume the responsibility of standing between the Senate and their constituents, but the Senators from Pennsylvania had nothing to do with this. If a memorial may be changed by erasures, may it not also be changed by additions? These were very extraordinary times, and it was the duty of the Senate to be on its guard, and take care that there be no interception between the people and this body. This paper was addressed to us, and in its progress from the people here, it had been essentially changed, and afterwards it had been presented to this House. If the officers of this House had a right thus to change petitions, we had nothing certain. His constituents might send memorials here, and if they were altered here, they were not the representations of his constituents, but of the officers of this House. He was anxious that the Senate should look to its rights, and therefore he moved to lay the papers on the table, for the purpose of affording an opportunity to take further measures, in case they should be necessary.

Mr. CLAY thought that, under all the circumstances, it was the duty of the Senate to give a decision which might operate as a precedent in similar cases. He agreed with the gentleman from South Carolina, [Mr. Preston,] that the paper had lost its identity—that it was not the memorial of York county. And it could not be received without admitting that while it was *in transitu*, or while it was in possession of the officers of this House, it might be altered. And it was true that if a right to alter or erase existed, it might also be done by addition, and if so, what became of the right to petition? The gentleman from Pennsylvania [Mr. Wilkins] said in his place that he had received no communication from the petitioners themselves, or from any persons at the meeting. He believed if a private petition were sent to a member, he might alter it as might be necessary. But in this instance it was necessary for the Senate to sanction or disapprove of it, and it appeared to him necessary to make a decision once for all in such cases.

He (Mr. C.) was opposed to laying the paper on the table, which presupposed that it had been received. He thought it ought not to be received at all. By parliamentary usage the first question was, should the paper be received; and although it was not put, yet it was a question which was presupposed and comprehended in the presentation, and therefore he would make the motion that the petition be not received, because it was not genuine, but altered, and because it was couched in language which ought not to be received by the Senate.

Mr. CALHOUN suggested that the preliminary question always was, shall the paper be received?

Mr. KANE said the subject seemed likely to receive serious consideration. Petitions in grossest language against the presiding officer [of] the Senate had heretofore been received. [The] gentleman from South Carolina [Mr. Preston] said that the paper was in the hands of the offic[er] of the Senate, and could not, and should not [be] altered, and then said that it was to be presen[ted] on the responsibility of the presiding officer. [He] concurred with him in that responsibility, so

as that no member should violate the rules of this body, and the same in relation to the presiding officer. If the paper was consistent with the rules of the Senate, he would present it. If it contained charges against this body, it was his duty to withhold it. What, then, was to be done? The right of petition was sacred, and one which could not be infringed, and what was to be done in this instance? The presiding officer had a duty to perform. A Senator is attacked in a way which the presiding officer would not allow from one of his compeers on the floor, and the Senators interested had a right to strike out the offensive matter, so far as it could be done consistently with preserving and securing to the people the great right of petition. Was not the Senate right to correct and regulate its proceedings so as to secure their own dignity? Has it not a right to protect itself against abuses? Without infringing the rights of the people, it may receive the paper, and direct it to a committee, to expunge the objectionable matter.

Mr. KING, of Alabama, said, that a few days ago a very offensive memorial, containing highly derogatory expressions, was presented by some gentleman and objected to. We were then met by the gentleman from Mississippi, [Mr. Poindexter,] and told that the language there used was the court language, and, therefore, proper to be used in a memorial. Now, that gentleman objects to this memorial because the matter is offensive, charging corruption to gentlemen of this body. He (Mr. K.) had looked into the paper, and except the part which had been struck out, he perceived no direct or positive charges. The statements were altogether general, and not near so exceptionable as some resolutions which had been offered by the gentlemen here on their own responsibility. [Mr. K. here read the resolution alluded to from the meeting of tin-plate workers in Philadelphia.] Now, what could the gentlemen say upon this paper, when we had received memorials and resolutions here, calculated to throw discredit on the chief magistrate of the nation and the presiding officer of this body? What was the character of this memorial, or rather preamble, for it was no part of the proceedings, the resolutions only having passed which embody what the memorialists have in view? It was customary, in presenting memorials, when there were offensive remarks in them against any member of Congress, to strike a pen across them, because it was not violating or affecting the objects sought to be attained.

He did not agree with the gentleman from South Carolina, [Mr. Calhoun,] that it was a question as to the reception of the paper. The rules of the Senate require the contents of a memorial to be briefly stated, but when it is read, it is in possession of the Senate. By the Manual, the silence of the House, or dispensing with the formality of reading, was a reception of it. He was surprised at the honorable gentleman from South Carolina, [Mr. Preston,] protesting against the course which had been pursued by the honorable Senators from Pennsylvania. Nothing had been done, but what was proper to be done. It was nothing but expunging the offensive matter. And he would enter his protest against any attempt to influence the public mind that any officer of the Senate had any disposition to change a memorial presented here.

Mr. WRIGHT said he rose to state a fact, as he thought bearing directly upon what had been harshly termed the mutilation of the paper now under consideration, and he did it under a conviction that he was bound to do it as an act of justice to the presiding officer. A few days ago a memorial from the State of New York, from the county of Warren, in that State, was transmitted to an honorable Senator not from that State, with a request that he would present it to the Senate; that honorable Senator, upon examining the memorial, found in it a clause which he considered as containing offensive matter (said Mr. W.) towards himself. The honorable Senator, as he (Mr. W.) subsequently learned from him, handed the memorial to a member of Congress from that State, being in the vicinity of the petitioners, and told that member of Congress, if he considered himself authorized to strike out of the memorial the offensive clause, he should be willing to comply with the request of the petitioners, and present the paper to the Senate; but unless that was done, he must decline to present the memorial. The member took his pen and struck out the exceptionable clause, and in that shape the paper was presented by the Senator, received by the Senate, read, referred, and printed; and in that shape it is now upon our files. It was not the memorial which was sent here, but it was that memorial, altered as he had related. He (Mr. W.) met the presiding officer this morning, and in a casual conversation, he mentioned to Mr. W. his embarrassment in relation to the paper now before the Senate, in consequence of the offensive remarks contained in it towards a member of this body, and he (Mr. W.) related to him the circumstances which he had just detailed to the Senate. He did not doubt that this conversation might have induced the presiding officer's suggestion to the honorable Senators from the State from which this paper comes, and might have influenced them in striking out the paragraph from this paper.

Now, without having entertained a thought that the Senator, in the case he had related, had done an improper act, or made an improper suggestion, in speaking to the member of the other House as to striking out the offensive matter from the memorial, the transaction furnished conclusive evidence to his mind that the Senator's motives were highly honorable, and personally he felt under the strongest obligations to him for the course he had pursued.

He would add one word more in reference to what had fallen from the Senator from South Carolina, [Mr. Preston.] He (Mr. W.) always understood heretofore, and still did, that every member of this body was responsible for any paper he presented to this body, and that the presiding officer was equally responsible for papers he presented to the Senate; but Mr. W. did not understand that papers directed to the presiding officer, with a request that he will lay them before the Senate, were any more in the possession of this body than papers thus sent to any other member of the body; and he therefore supposed that the instance of the alteration of a paper, which he had related, was in all respects parallel to the case now before the Senate. Any attempt to distinguish the cases does not seem to him possible.

Mr. WEBSTER having suggested that if the Vice President now believed that the paper was one which ought not to have been presented to the Senate, the Senate ought to grant him leave to withdraw it. He merely made the suggestion upon the supposition that the presiding officer was satisfied the paper was exceptionable, and such a one as ought not to have been presented.

When the debate closed, and before putting the question on the motion made by Mr. Clay that the memorial should not be received, the VICE PRESIDENT rose and observed in substance—

That it was with much regret that the Chair felt itself compelled to detain the Senate at so late an hour by any observations of its own, upon a subject which had been already so fully discussed. But as the question to be decided was in its nature one of order, in respect to which it was not only proper in itself, but conformable also to parliamentary usage for the Chair to take a part, he felt it due as well to the Senate as to the Chair, to state briefly, not only the considerations by which its course had been influenced in the particular case now before the Senate, but also the general principles which the Chair had adopted for its government in regard to the subject matter out of which it had arisen. He believed such a course on his part, necessary to a correct understanding of the immediate question under discussion, and that it could not fail to be useful in future. By the express provision of the Constitution, the Senate is authorized to "determine the rules of its proceedings." By this provision of the Constitution, the rules of order in its proceedings are subjected to the legislation of the Senate without restriction, other than such as may be found to result from other and express provisions of the Constitution. This right has been exercised by the Senate by means of the rules which it has from time to time established.

These rules provide that every question of order shall be decided by the President, subject, nevertheless, to an appeal to the Senate. They provide further, that the President may call for the sense of the Senate on any question of order. This latter provision is peculiar to this body, and its rules are, in that respect, unlike those of the other branch of the legislature. But little conversant with questions of order, and anxious to regulate its course by the best lights that could be obtained, the Chair thought it proper, at an early day, to look into the practical interpretation which had been given to the authority thus conferred on it by those who had preceded the present incumbent in the occupation of the Chair. Upon that examination it was found that it had generally been the practice of the Chair, and especially upon important points of order, to take the sense of the Senate in respect to them in the first instance, whenever there was, in its judgment, sufficient question as to the proper course of proceeding to render such a step advisable. Having regard to the character and construction of the body, this mode of proceeding appeared to the presiding officer to be not only discreet in itself, but he thought it would give to this peculiar provision an effect more conformable to the respect which was justly due to the Senate from a presiding officer not chosen by itself. The Chair, therefore, felt no difficulty in adopting it as a rule for its own conduct. Why that course could not be pursued upon the first presentation of the papers in question, consistently with other and paramount considerations, and why it is not only most proper, but highly desirable, that the sense of the Senate should now be taken upon the immediate question before it, he trusted would be made quite obvious in the succeeding observations, which he felt it his duty to submit.

The subject-matter out of which the present question has arisen, presents two points for decision; that is to say, *first*, Does a communication intended to be laid before the Senate through the medium of the presiding officer, from the moment of its reception by the Chair, become, *ipso facto*, as is contended, the property and part of the archives of the Senate, so as to deprive the Chair of all discretion, as to the disposition to be made of it, without the approbation of the body? And, if that be not the case, then, *secondly*, Under what responsibility does the Chair rest to the Senate, in regard to the character of the communications which it suffers to reach the body through its agency.

These are certainly questions of a very grave character, well deserving the deliberate consideration of the Senate. They are questions in respect to which there would seem to be a diversity of opinion among the members; and it is certainly far from being the intention of the Chair to pass, in this form, upon the correctness of the conflicting deductions which have, in this respect, been drawn from the premises before us, by honorable Senators. Its only purpose is, to state its own views, and in doing so, it feels that it may safely assume, that if it be correct to say that the Chair has no rightful authority over communications addressed to it for the use of the Senate; no right to return them to those from whom they came; to deliver them over to their representative on this floor, and withhold them from the Senate, then most clearly the Chair cannot be held responsible for the contents of any paper thus presented. It can only be necessary to state this proposition, to render the incongruity and injustice of the opposing pretensions obvious to the meanest capacity, and to secure its rejection by every unprejudiced mind. What, then, is the true rule as to the power and duties of the Chair, in regard to the disposition of papers addressed to it, with a view to their submission to the Senate? Could the Chair allow itself to consult its convenience only, and to relieve itself from responsibility, there is no rule that could be suggested by which those objects would be more effectually accomplished, than that which has been contended for, by which its office, in this respect, is converted into one of a purely ministerial character, and by which every paper received by it for the use of the Senate is at once converted into a portion of the Senatorial archives. But the Chair has not been able to satisfy itself that it could thus be relieved from a duty which it owed to the Senate. It has, on the contrary, considered it to be a portion of that duty to withhold such communications, as, in the exercise of its best discretion, it considered to be so framed, as to render their presentation inconsistent with the respect due

to the Senate, as well as such as were, from other considerations, justly subject to the operation of the same rule. Scarcely a week passes in which communications are not received by the Chair, with a request to have them laid before the Senate, in respect to which it is apparent that their authors are suffering under mental aberrations. Communications of this sort, of which many are constantly in the possession of the Chair, would, on the supposition referred to, be entitled to the disposition which is claimed for the paper under consideration.

But the exercise of the discretion referred to, has not been confined by the Chair to papers of this description, which might justly be regarded as extreme cases. It has, on the contrary, felt it to be within the line of its duty to withhold from the Senate communications which, however high and sound the source from which they emanated, contained reflections upon the Senate plainly derogatory to its honor. It is but a few weeks since that the Chair received, with a request to lay them before the Senate, the proceedings of a public meeting held in the city of Philadelphia, which, it was obvious, had been a very large one, and which the Chair does not doubt to have been also very respectable, in which the severest censure was denounced against this body, for an act in which the present incumbent of the Chair happened to have had a particular interest. Under the influence of the sense of duty which has been expressed, the Chair did not hesitate to deliver the paper to one of the Senators from that State, with a request that it should be respectfully returned to the source from which it had come, with the information that the Chair felt it to be inconsistent with its duty to lay a paper containing such matter before the Senate. The Chair would have preferred in this, as it would in every similar case, to have pursued the course authorized by the rules of the Senate, and which has heretofore, in other respects, been so extensively adopted, of taking the sense of the Senate, in the first instance, upon the propriety of receiving the paper in question. But it has hitherto appeared to the Chair that that could not well be done without exposing the Senate to the indignity against which the discretion exercised by the Chair was calculated to protect it, viz: the indignity of having a paper read to it which reflected upon its character and motives.

The Chair has thought it proper to be thus particular in the statement of its views and practice, to the end, that if the opinion which has been so confidently advanced, that every paper received by the Chair becomes the property of the Senate, subject to its exclusive disposition, be that of the body, the fact may be authoritatively announced, either in the form of a rule or decision of the Senate, and thus made the rule of conduct for the future. If such a rule were adopted, the respect which the Chair entertains for the body over which it has the honor to preside, as well as a sense of duty, will induce it to carry the same into execution. But the Chair has felt itself constrained to regard this as an erroneous view of the subject, and it has already stated its own impressions as to the nature and extent of the responsibility under which it rested, to the Senate, in the discharge of this portion of its official duties.

In taking upon itself the exercise of the discretion before stated, the Chair was by no means unapprized of the extent and delicacy of the responsibility, which, without previous reference to the wishes of the Senate, it assumed, but which it cheerfully encountered with the view of upholding the true dignity of a body, to the advancement of whose highest interests it had determined to devote itself.

The difficulties of a successful discharge of this trust in the particular case under consideration, had, moreover, been in no small degree increased by the course which was taken by the Senate, and by the character of the debate, on the part of some of its members, in two cases similar in principle, which have recently been acted upon. It was well known that the Senate, although its attention was directly called to their exceptionable character, decided in those cases, to receive papers, which, on account of the reflections they respectively contained upon the body and its presiding officer, they refused to refer or to print; and that in the discussion which arose upon their presentation, the principle was distinctly and solemnly avowed, that in a period like the present, it did not belong to the Senate to prescribe to a suffering people the language in which they should call upon their representatives for a redress of grievances. In these proceedings the Chair was not inclined, on account of its relation to the subject, to take part; nor could it, perhaps, have done so with propriety, if its inclinations had been otherwise.

Although, as has been observed, the difficulties of the Chair in the performance of this part of its duties, at all times delicate, were thereby unavoidably increased, its opinion was not changed in respect to the principles which it had adopted. Acting upon that principle, the Chair declined to submit the proceedings in question to the Senate, although well satisfied of the respectability of the source from whence they emanated, because they contained improper reflections upon one of its members by name. Although the Chair participated so far, at least, in the sentiments alluded to, as to be willing to extend the most liberal indulgence to the right of petition, it could not regard it as consistent with the peculiar relations in which it stood towards this body, to permit others to say to it, in a petition presented through the agency of the Chair, that, for which it would be the duty of the Chair to call a Senator to order, when uttered orally in respect to one of his compeers on this floor. The Chair, therefore, delivered the paper to one of the Senators from Pennsylvania, and accompanied it by a declaration, that unless he and his colleague felt themselves authorized to suppress the exceptionable matter, the Chair could not reconcile it to its sense of duty to present it to the Senate. Upon that question, the Chair did not, of course, express its opinion; but it regards it as due, as well to the honorable Senators from that State, as to itself, to say, that if it had regarded such an act on their part to be liable to any just exception, it would never have submitted the paper to them with any such suggestion. It did not so regard it; and, least of all, could it have anticipated that an act done under the circumstances, and from the motives by which it was characterized, would have elicited the exceptions which have been made to it. The facts and circumstances of the case were now before the Senate, and whatever difference of opinion may exist as to their effect upon the question of the validity of the paper in its present state, the Chair is quite confident there can be none as to the correctness of the motives by which the transaction has been characterized.

This, however, is not the only objection that has been raised against the presentation of the paper. It was objected by an honorable Senator, that these proceedings, the erasure of a part of which is deemed so objectionable, are but a part of a common newspaper, without even the autograph signature of any of the presiding officers, or other mark of authenticity; and, therefore, not admissible according to parliamentary usage. That objection has, however, been fully answered by the reading of the original letter from the committee appointed by the meeting to communicate its proceedings to the Chair, and which is before the Senate in the state in which it was received, but which had been overlooked by the acting Secretary of the Senate.

But it is further objected that the paper in question does still contain exceptionable matter, inasmuch as it charges the corruption of Congress by the bank. The Chair has no hesitation to say, that if the paper had appeared to it to be susceptible of that construction, it would not have deemed it proper, upon its own mere motion, to lay it before the Senate. Upon the brief and cursory examination which it was alone in the power of the Chair to give to its contents, extended as they are, they did not strike the Chair as charging more than a disposition upon the part of the bank to corrupt Congress and the press. Nor is the Chair now satisfied that the proceedings in question, although upon the examination to which they have been subjected by the Senate, they are certainly found to contain many injurious insinuations, do contain the charge of practised corruption of the legislature. The Chair, perhaps, owes it to itself to state, that before presenting the proceedings, it suggested to the Senator more directly referred to by them, its willingness to hold them up for further advisement and examination, and that it was in consequence of hearing from that Senator that he had a response to the proceedings in his possession, that he would probably make some observations upon them, and that he would prefer to have them presented forthwith, that the Chair was induced to present them this morning. But, whatever may be the just construction of their contents, it is in the power of the Senate to make such a disposition of them, upon the motion made by the Senator from Kentucky, as may be deemed most consistent with justice and the respect that is due to the body.

In regard to the suggestion that the Chair should ask permission to withdraw the paper, it has only to say, that it thinks it in every respect desirable that the Senate should itself now express an opinion upon the point presented to its consideration by the pending motion. Such a decision is particularly important in the present agitated state of the country, and in view of the great probability that cases of the same kind may again arise, if not prevented by the formal decision of the Senate. To have taken its opinion upon the subject in the first instance under the rule of the Senate, would have been the choice, of course, of the Chair, had it not been for the difficulty which has been referred to. The subject is now before the Senate. Whatever room there may be for a difference of opinion as to the strict propriety of the course which had been taken, there cannot be any, it is hoped, in respect to the motives and intentions which prompted to that course. Upon this point, the Chair does not feel itself to be under the slightest necessity to indulge in protestations or assurances of any kind. It is fully persuaded that no unprejudiced mind will, for a moment, hesitate in believing, that its conduct in the whole matter has, so far at least as intention is involved, been controlled by the principles which were avowed by the Chair at the threshold of its duty, and which, it is well assured, have been most faithfully adhered to. Why, then, should the decision of the Senate be superseded through its agency? It can perceive no good reason for such a course, whilst many are opposed to its adoption. Independently of the intrinsic importance of such a decision, there are other considerations of a still more imperative character.

As has already been stated, the Senate has heretofore decided to receive communications from the people upon this subject, which, on account of the injurious reflections they contained, as well on the Senate as on its presiding officer, it refused to commit or print. The subject having, then, entered into the deliberation and decision of the Senate, it is desirable that all further action upon it should be under its control, when that can, as in the present case, be done without impropriety. Again, a grave question has been made, and fully discussed, as to the control of Senators over the communications of their constituents, under circumstances like the present. It is proper, also, that that point should be settled by the Senate. To render the proposed course admissible on the part of the Chair, there should at least be unanimity on the part of the Senate in desiring it. Such appears not to be the case. It is not only expressly objected to by Senators, but there obviously appears to be a diversity of opinion amongst the members upon the abstract question, whether the paper should be received or not. Under such circumstances, and without noticing an objection of order, which would render the step improper without unanimous consent—a consent which has already been refused—the Chair cannot but think that it will best discharge its duties to all parties, by allowing the question before the Senate, and upon which the ayes and noes have been already ordered, to be taken.

The discussion was further continued by Messrs. PRESTON, BIBB, FORSYTH, and others, when the question, "Will the Senate receive the paper?" was negatived, as follows:

YEAS—Messrs. Benton, Brown, Forsyth, Grundy, Hendricks, Hill, Kane, King of Alabama, King of Georgia, Linn, McKean, Mangum, Morris, Robinson, Shepley, Tallmadge, Tipton, White, Wilkins, and Wright—20.

NAYS—Messrs. Bibb, Black, Calhoun, Clay, Clayton, Ewing, Frelinghuysen, Kent, Leigh, Moore, Naudain, Poindexter, Porter, Preston,

Robbins, Silsbee, Smith, Southard, Sprague, Swift, Tomlinson, Waggaman, and Webster—24.

So the Senate refused to receive the proceedings of the York county meeting.

Mr. WEBSTER gave notice that he should to-morrow ask leave to introduce a bill to recharter the Bank of the United States.

On motion of Mr. WEBSTER, at a quarter before six o'clock,

The Senate adjourned.

HOUSE OF REPRESENTATIVES.

MONDAY, *March* 17, 1834.

Mr. WILLIAM JACKSON, elected a Representative from Massachusetts, appeared, was qualified, and took his seat.

The SPEAKER announced the Virginia resolutions as the unfinished business of Monday last; Mr. PINCKNEY, of South Carolina, being entitled to the floor.

Mr. J. Q. ADAMS asked leave of the House to submit a motion to call the States for the reception of petitions and memorials.

Mr. PINCKNEY would yield the floor, he said, to the gentleman from Massachusetts, for the purpose of enabling him to present the resolutions of his State, with the understanding that, after he had presented them, he (Mr. P.) should have an opportunity to proceed with his remarks.

After some further conversation, Mr. PINCKNEY yielded the floor, for the purpose of calling all the States in order, in compliance with the wishes of the House.

Mr. JARVIS, of Maine, presented a memorial from sundry citizens of Eastport, Maine, praying the restoration of the deposites. Read, and ordered to be printed.

Mr. EVANS presented a memorial of similar import, from citizens of some place in Maine, the name of which we could not hear.

The memorial, without reading, was ordered to be printed.

The SPEAKER presented to the House a communication signed by John C. Churchill and others, of Portland, in Maine, submitting to the House explanations in regard to some statements made on the floor of the House by a Representative from Maine, in relation to a memorial some weeks ago presented to the House, from a portion of the citizens of Portland. The letter having been read—

Mr. SMITH, of Maine, said, the communication which has just been read, quotes a portion of the remarks which he had the honor to submit to the House on the occasion of his presenting certain resolutions emanating from the city of Portland, relating to the public deposites. I ask the indulgence of the House in making a few observations respecting it.

Leave being granted, Mr. S. proceeded—

Although the communication has been written in a spirit of complaint, it will be found, upon examination, not to controvert any of the statements which he had previously made to the House. The gentlemen, said he, who have sent it here, know full well, and the community surrounding them know full well, that the truth would not bear out such a contradiction of me.

What, sir, says this communication? Why, that these eight gentlemen are not, and have not been, opponents of the National Administration. Sir, did I so represent them, be the fact how it may? Not at all. The language which they quote from me does not so represent them; and these gentlemen, therefore, only exhibit themselves in the suspicious attitude of pleading *not* guilty to a charge which had not been made against them. And what does the fact argue to an intelligent mind? Sir, a conscience void of offence fears no accuser. A conscience that is guilty of offence, needs no accuser.

But, sir, these gentlemen have not been pleased to quote the definite language which I used. I said, sir, that *a majority* of the signers of the resolutions had their names no less distinctly associated with every measure of opposition to the Administration which had been at any time concerted in the city of Portland. And do a majority of them deny it? Not at all. Do even these eight gentlemen deny it? Not at all. The gentlemen to whom I thus alluded, have been too open, too decided, and, as I have no doubt, *too honest* in their hostility to the Administration, to deny it here or elsewhere. They are, sir, as I willingly bear testimony, not of that class of politicians in Maine, who are capable of professing a friendship for the Administration which they do not feel. Besides, sir, I have before me documents* which bear their signatures to most decided, unequivocal, and unmeasured denunciations of the Administration. Thus was I fortified by truth in my representation.

I did not mean to include, and I did not include—for I said only what I meant, and what I am now ready to reassert—I did not include the writers of this communication among the open opponents of the Administration, nor with the majority of whom I spoke. But, sir, I might have said of at least six in the eight gentlemen, that which will account to the House for the extreme sensitiveness which they now manifest at a charge which I did *not* make against them. I might have said, sir, that they were, and still are, members of *a faction* in Portland, who supported a bought-up press in that city that was opposed to the election of both the *Administration* candidate for Governor in Maine, and the *Administration* candidate for Congress in Cumberland district,—of a faction, sir, so weak and impotent as to obtain no more than 407 votes of about 7,500 given in that district; and this, too, notwithstanding they were marshalled, and *led* on, and *urged* on, by an ex-minister plenipotentiary to the Netherlands—by a judge and clerk of the district court of the United States, who opened the court-room of the Government, night after night, to caucus and discipline their little squadron of political disorganizers in, and by the city postmaster, and the collector of the port of Portland, who had in his train some three or four subordinate officers, appointed but a short time before for the special purpose—yes, for no other reason under heaven than that of wielding an additional influence against the Administration party.

Sir, called upon, as I have been by this letter, to be thus particular in explaining the political relationships of the gentlemen who have sent it, I feel also bound to say, that such as the facts stated imply, is also the character of their friendship for the Administration. They do indeed profess friendship for the Administration, but they have recourse to measures, in conjunction with its most relentless opponents, calculated to defeat it, and overwhelm it in disgrace. They do, indeed, profess friendship for the President, and their arms are nerved amid proffered assurances of ready support of him. But, sir, their arms are in fact nerved only for an opportunity of thrusting home more successfully to the vitals of his exalted fame, the daggers which are concealed beneath their robes.

Sir, it has been the signal fortune of President Jackson, since presiding over the affairs of this nation, to have many such sunshine friends in different sections of the Union—men who are capable of betraying, under cover of a friendship not felt, but lacking moral courage to meet him and his measures in open combat, under the unfurled banner of that hostility which rankles at their hearts. But in despite of them, sir, he has triumphed as man never before triumphed. In despite of them, the gratitude and admiration of the American people—of a free, intelligent, independent people—have borne him on from one point of honor to another, and from one position of glory to another, until language itself fails in capacity to express the full measure of exaltation, which the hearts of the great mass of his countrymen most cheerfully accord to him.

But, sir, what more do these eight of the twenty-four gentlemen say? Why, that they are not friendly to a *recharter* of the United States Bank. Sir, I did not so represent them. The language which they quote from me does not so represent them. And again are they seen pleading *not* guilty to a charge that was not made against them. I said, they are friends to the bank: and do not their measures make good the declaration? It does not require a magician to see that the bank has many friends who are not yet committed in favor of its recharter. It requires not a prophet to foretell that the bank will rely, as it does now rely, upon many who are opposed to its recharter on high constitutional grounds, for support of measures which are of vital importance to it. And are not such persons to be regarded as friends of the bank?

Sir, there are but two sides to the great question now agitating the country.

[The SPEAKER said it was not in order to discuss the merits of the bank question.]

I was intending only to say, sir, (said Mr. S.,) that those who acted at all at this crisis, and who act not in support of the Administration, *act on the side of the bank*, and in a spirit of friendship for the bank. What, sir, do the resolutions of these gentlemen ask? A restoration—an immediate restoration of the public deposites. And is not this in a spirit of friendship for the bank? Is it not in opposition to the Administration?—to the great distinguishing feature of the Administration? a feature which, if not sustained, will overwhelm the Administration with defeat? Sir, it is among this class of friends to the bank that I represent these gentlemen. It is among this class that the community in which they reside will assign them a place.

In conclusion, sir, permit me to add, that if there be any issue between these gentlemen and myself upon this subject, most gladly will I go with it, at a proper time, to the people surrounding them. That people know them even as I know them. I respect, them, sir, as that people respect

*The following extracts from the documents to which Mr. Smith alluded, issued at Portland, *just preceding the last presidential election*, sanctioned by the names of a majority of those who signed the above-named "*no-party*" resolutions as committee-men, and with whom the above letter-writers are now in communion on the bank question. The first document commences in the following *no party* strain:

"The subscribers, merchants and ship-holders 'of Portland, *who have never before acted together* 'but for *commercial* purposes, nor even attempted, '*as a body*, to influence the *political* opinions of their 'fellow-men, although it will not be denied, perhaps, by any ship-holder here, that they have *had* '*the power* to a much greater degree than has ever 'been believed by their townsmen, who are not 'engaged in commerce, have come to the conclusion, after much and careful inquiry, that it is 'now their *duty* to manifest their political opinions, 'without reserve; and to call upon their *fellow-* '*sufferers*, who are engaged in navigation, or otherwise dependent upon trade or the mechanic arts 'for the support of their families, &c. * * * 'Hitherto, it has been comparatively of *no* consequence to the merchants of the United States 'who was President of the United States. Now, 'it has become a matter of *life and death*, as they 'believe."

Then follows a long appeal against the reëlection of President Jackson.

The second document, emanating from the same source, says: "We address ourselves to *no party*," &c. "Most of us are no politicians. Many have 'never before meddled with politics, &c. Many 'are about leaving the stage,' &c. However we 'may differ in all other things, we unite in a desire that this may be regarded as *no party* question," &c. The document then proceeds to say of the President, "after four years of trial, under 'every advantage of popularity and predetermined favor, multitudes of his warmest friends 'have been obliged to abandon him; while others 'declare that he has not only done all that was 'foretold of him by his ungenerous adversaries, 'but *more* and *worse;* and that had anything like 'the truth been apprehended, he would never 'have reached the place he now occupies." "Before his elevation, he professed to love his country, and to revere the Constitution; and even his 'adversaries believed him, and attributed his errors 'to a mistaken but honest zeal. Notwithstanding 'which, by a series of DIRECT USURPATIONS, &c., 'he has set himself *above* his associated co-executive, the Senate of the United States—*above* the 'supreme judiciary—*above* the supreme legislative 'power—thereby constituting himself the common 'superior of the Senate, the judiciary, and the 'Congress of these United States of America."

them. I hold them as they hold them, "enemies in war, in peace friends."

Mr. SMITH concluded with a motion to print the letter.

Mr. J. Q. ADAMS presented certain resolutions adopted by the Legislature of the Commonwealth of Massachusetts, in relation to the currency and the removal of the deposites from the Bank of the United States. Mr. A. proceeded to read and comment upon the preamble and the several resolutions. In conclusion, he said he was not, on this occasion, authorized to speak for any of his colleagues. Each one of them was able to speak for himself. Speaking for himself, he would say, he entirely concurred in the views expressed in the resolutions. He moved that the resolutions be read, printed, and laid upon the table. He, at the same time, laid upon the table a resolution in connexion with the subject, which he should call up, when the subject was taken up, in its order. The resolution is as follows:

Resolved, That the resolutions of the Legislature of the Commonwealth of Massachusetts, in relation to the currency, &c., be referred to a select committee, with instructions to report a plan for continuing to the people the advantages resulting to them from a national bank.

Mr. POLK rose and requested the gentleman from Massachusetts to withdraw his motion, for a moment, to permit him to make a few remarks.

The motion was withdrawn, and Mr. POLK having obtained the leave of the House, made some remarks in vindication of the President from the unjust and injurious imputations cast upon him by the gentleman from Massachusetts.

Mr. PINCKNEY rose to speak on the subject, but his remarks were arrested by the Chair.

Mr. PINCKNEY asked leave of the House to continue his remarks, and the House refused leave.

Mr. ADAMS renewed his motion to lay on the table and print; and it was agreed to.

MEMORIAL FROM BOSTON.

Mr. GORHAM presented a memorial from six or seven thousand inhabitants of the city of Boston, which (he said) they were induced to send a second time, asking for relief from Congress, under the present state of things, which appeared to him (Mr. G.) to be growing from bad to worse. He moved to have the memorial laid on the table, and printed, with the names; giving notice, that when the other petition from the Legislature of Massachusetts on this subject should be taken up and referred, he would then move that this should have a similar direction given to it.

Mr. CLAY called for a division of the question, as he considered it was perfectly useless to print the names.

The memorial having been laid on the table and ordered to be printed, the question then being on the printing of the names—

Mr. GORHAM remarked, that hitherto, from various motives, it had been the practice of the House to have the names appended to the memorials presented on this subject printed. It might be necessary to ascertain names, that it might be shown that the signers of the memorials consisted of the greater number of the qualified voters, with others in Boston. He would ask, what ground of objection there could be to the printing of this memorial more than any other?

Mr. CLAY objected to the printing of the names on the ground of the utter inutility of the practice, and as producing an expense which ought to be avoided. It was a practice that had grown up this session, so far as his observation had gone, and it was time that it should be discontinued. He could assure the gentleman from Massachusetts that he would have made the same objection if the petition had come from the other side of the question.

Mr. E. EVERETT advocated the printing, as he said that the expense would be inconsiderable, and as a counter petition would hereafter be presented, the names to which he himself would move to have printed. It would give an opportunity to scrutinize the character of the signers to each, and determine the weight that should be attached to each of the representations made by them.

Mr. PARKER contended that as the gentleman from Massachusetts, who presented the memorial, could state the character of the signers, this would be sufficient for the House; he had described that

it was signed by all the qualified voters, and more too in Boston; his word was therefore sufficient. The practice was novel, and ought not to be encouraged, as leading to unnecessary expense, and could do no good.

Mr. WHITTLESEY rose for the purpose of correcting some errors into which the two honorable members from Alabama, [Mr. CLAY,] and from New Jersey, [Mr. PARKER,] had fallen. It was not a novel practice to print the names to petitions. On the contrary, it was the early practice to have the names invariably printed, and it was a new practice not to do so. Many frauds had been committed in getting up petitions; he therefore thought it was necessary that the names should be printed, that means of detecting them, on whatever side they were presented, should be afforded.

Mr. BAYLIES said, that he must consider it would be a very invidious distinction now to refuse to this petition that which had been done to all the others that had been presented on this subject this session. He was in favor of the printing, and would consider it a mark of disrespect, which ought not to be evinced, to withhold it.

Mr. BEARDSLEY was opposed to the printing.

Mr. BARRINGER was in favor of it.

Mr. J. Q. ADAMS and Mr. GRENNELL spoke at some length, in favor of the motion to print the names.

Mr. JONES, of Georgia, in order to arrest the debate, moved to lay the motion to print the names on the table.

The SPEAKER decided that the motion was in order, and Mr. MERCER appealed from the decision, but subsequently withdrew the appeal.

Mr. JONES withdrew the motion to lay on the table, under the supposition that the question on the motion to print would be taken without further debate.

Mr. WAYNE spoke briefly in favor of the motion to print the names.

Mr. JONES, of Georgia, renewed his motion to lay the motion to print on the table, and thereupon demanded the yeas and nays; which were ordered.

The question was then taken, and decided in the negative:

Yeas 79, nays 107.

The question recurring on the motion to print the names,

Mr. REED demanded the yeas and nays, and they were ordered.

The question being taken, it was determined in the affirmative:

Yeas 108, nays 78.

Mr. LINCOLN presented, with some remarks, a memorial from two hundred and seven citizens of Worcester county, in Massachusetts, representing the prevalence in that county of great public distress, praying relief by the restoration of the public deposites to the United States Bank, and condemning the project of a specie currency. He called for the reading of the memorial, and moved that it be printed and laid on the table, to take such direction as should be hereafter given to the resolutions presented from the Legislature of Massachusetts.

Mr. H. EVERETT presented a memorial from a number of delegates assembled in Wyndham county, Vermont, in which, he remarked, although they prayed for the restoration of the deposites to the Bank of the United States, yet they had not connected with it any request for the recharter of any bank influence, and that in giving their views, as they were not influenced in favor of the bank by anything but an opinion of its general utility to the country, he hoped it would be received with the consideration to which it was entitled.

The memorial was laid on the table and ordered to be printed.

Mr. FILLMORE presented a memorial, with certain resolutions, from seven hundred citizens of Buffalo and its vicinity, called without reference to party, adopted on the 19th February last.

Mr. F. was proceeding to address the House at large, when

The SPEAKER reminded him it was necessary to confine his remarks to a brief discussion of the contents of the memorial.

Mr. FILLMORE asked the indulgence of the House, to give some explanation of the former box. tility which had prevailed in that district against the Bank of the United States.

The House having refused—

Mr. FILLMORE said he would only call for the reading of the memorial and resolutions.

The resolutions were then read, remonstrating against the removal of the deposites, and praying Congress to avert from them the ruin which they alleged was impending over them in consequence of that, and praying for the recharter of the bank. He moved to have the memorial laid on the table, and ordered to be printed, with the names.

Mr. MANN, of New York, wished to remark, that there was a branch of the Bank of the United States in the place from whence this memorial proceeded.

The SPEAKER here interfered, as it was not in order to debate a motion to lay on the table.

The memorial was laid on the table, &c.; and, On motion of Mr. VINTON,

The House then adjourned.

IN SENATE.

Two messages were received from the President of the United States, by Mr. DONELSON, his Private Secretary, one upon executive business, the other communicating a letter from the Secretary of State, relative to the adjustment of claims under the Neapolitan treaty. The message and documents, on motion of Mr. WILKINS, were referred to the Committee on Foreign Relations, and ordered to be printed.

Mr. WILKINS gave notice that he should tomorrow move the Senate to proceed to an election to fill the vacancy in the Committee on Foreign Relations, occasioned by the resignation of the Hon. WILLIAM C. RIVES.

Mr. EWING, on leave asked and obtained, withdrew the papers relating to the claims of the heirs of the late Thomas Worthington, deceased.

Mr. WEBSTER presented the protest and memorial of a meeting composed of 6,841 citizens of Boston, held at Faneuil Hall, protesting against the removal of the public deposites from the Bank of the United States, and praying their restoration.

After some remarks by Messrs. WEBSTER, SILSBEE, and SPRAGUE, the memorial, &c. were referred to the Committee on Finance, and ordered to be printed.

Mr. WEBSTER rose and said he desired, in pursuance of notice previously given, to ask leave to introduce a bill to continue in force for six years the act incorporating the subscribers to the Bank of the United States. Presuming on the indulgence which the Senate always extends in such cases, he would accompany the motion by a few preliminary observations, and then propose the reference of the bill to the Committee on Finance, and when reported, to be disposed of as the state of public opinion might seem to require. The condition of the country was most extraordinary. In a state of ordinary prosperity, it was suffering severe distress. Commerce, which was hitherto active, was stopped; the manufacturing industry of the country was suspended; the labors of agriculture were losing sight of their ordinary reward; and yet the resources of the country were abundant and active, and the health of the country was favorable, not only for retaining its hitherto prosperous condition, but for its rapid advancement to still greater heights of prosperity. Our condition was singular. It was like a strong man chained, who felt full of health and unabated strength, but who had lost all sense of performing his customary action—every limb bound down by manacles, with inherent vigor rendering him competent to do anything if he was but at liberty. We had nothing to do now but to unmanacle the country—to set the country free. It was truly a singular situation. A sudden spell had smitten the body politic; its numerous active powerless, and the blood had ceased to circulate through its veins. Six months ago the aspect of the country was more gratifying than

had been exhibited for many years before. Commerce, manufactures, agriculture, everything, and everywhere throughout the whole land, was in the highest state of prosperity. A more healthy state of general business never existed in the country from the fall of 1832 to the fall of 1833. It was possible there had been some overtrading, but the general condition of the country was one of unprecedented prosperity and activity. The commerce of the country was never surpassed. In 1833 the exports were ninety millions, and the imports were one hundred and nine millions, and the active coastwise trade, up to October 1833, never was surpassed. The circulating medium, too, was full, and supposed to be safe, and now the change was such as to strike the minds of all. He had inquired into the probable receipts into the treasury for the current year, and he was much deceived if the effects of this treasury measure would not so affect the receipts of the revenue as to make it a little startling. The Secretary had estimated the amount to accrue from the customs at fifteen millions, and the whole receipts into the treasury at eighteen millions, which, added to the balance in the treasury, would make a total of upwards of twenty-one millions. The estimated expenditures were twenty-three millions five hundred thousand dollars, by which there would be a deficiency of about two millions; but no doubt this deficiency would be made up by uncalled for approppriations made for the year 1834. The subject, therefore, was worthy the consideration of Congress. The Secretary makes no deduction for the reduction of the revenue from the late measurers, but he says, that in two years it will be necessary to reinstate the duty on articles made free by recent laws.

He (Mr. W.) had made a sort of estimate of the receipts at the custom-house for the last half of the year 1834, and the result of it was, that the deficiency would be near fifty per cent. He did not say that this would produce distress, but it might delay the payment of the public debt. The manufacturing interests, it was said, were last year menaced by the bill called Mr. Verplanck's bill; but what was that to this interposition of the hand of the Secretary of the Treasury into the public treasure of the country? Several cotton mills had already broken in some of the manufacturing States, besides several woollen factories. These changes were going on everywhere. Go where you would, you would not find men enjoying the same cheerfulness and happiness as formerly. But then it had been said, how was it possible such great effects could result from such trifling causes? And he thought every ordinary observer, every thinking man, would perceive how it was. The State banks were actually less able to extend relief to the country, with the deposites, than they were without them. The Government had ten millions in the United States Bank, and in two months it called out six millions, and the bank curtailed its discounts to that amount. Now, the deposites of a bank were one of its liabilities, and the State banks felt the enhancement of their liabilities, without a corresponding enhancement of their means. This, then, was an attack on the commercial credit of the country, which was composed of bank notes, bills of exchange, &c., and unless we were to repudiate all the lights of experience, we ought to maintain the beneficial exercise of this public credit; and public credit, too, depended on the security of good government, and of sound laws. Ours was a new country, and would continue to be a new country for a century to come. Land would be plenty in proportion to personal capital; and it was a country where a high state of commercial credit would be the most useful, and this showed why it was that the recent action of the Secretary had this effect.

But we were told that there was a war waging of the poor against the rich, against all monsters, and against the men of small capital. And how is it? We don't leave the poor man where he was, paying six per cent. for his loans; but we put him where he can be screwed down to twenty-five per cent., and thus enable the rich man to put his foot upon his neck, and keep him down. He had no doubt that not less than twenty millions of dollars had been abstracted from the pockets of the poor, in the shape of extra interest, by this measure of the Secretary. We ought to disabuse our country of this ribaldry—a country which the world sees needs credit and banks. But the bank is a lion or a sucking dove, according to circumstances. We had heard much from the Senator from New York, [Mr. Wright,] of the danger which the bank was to the liberty of the country. A bank with thirty-five millions dangerous to the liberty of this people! But how was it in the State of New York? Was it a death grasp there? New York has her safety-fund system—a league of fifty-nine affiliated banks, the whole of which was moved by the touch of a single finger. They might be under the supervision of one single intellect, and yet there was no danger from this system to New York. But the whole twenty-four States of this Union cannot resist the Bank of the United States with a capital but little more than that employed in New York. It was time to put an end to this notion of banks being the instruments of political power. There were three classes of persons who were friendly to the bank: those who believed it to be constitutional, and indispensably necessary—others who believed it necessary, but that Congress possessed no power to establish a bank—and those who admitted the power, but who were opposed to the renewal of this bank. Then there was a class of miscellaneous opinions—some in favor of a hard money system; some in favor of more, and some of less Government influence; and the question was, whether there was any common ground on which so many could unite as to secure an adequate remedy by law for the necessities of the country. Can we agree on anything, and if so, what is it? Probably a majority of those who were opposed to the measures of the Secretary were in favor of a national bank, perhaps of the present one. He preferred a permanent measure, that is, for fifteen or twenty years; but he hoped all who agreed with him, that if present relief could be obtained by means of the greatest concessions to opposite opinions, they would join him. To those who had constitutional scruples he would say, that never was a subject of reproach or fault-finding with him; but he put it to gentlemen, whether a more unconstitutional state of things could exist than now exists, if Congress were to make forty banks? There were also friends to a new bank, and he would say he was not an enemy to a new bank; if this bill should pass, he would next Congress join for a new bank. But gentlemen must know that project could afford no effectual relief—the object was to adopt some measure capable of affording relief in the present emergency. The country expected Congress to do something—and he thought, if this could not be accomplished, we could do nothing to effect relief.

The following is the bill which Mr. Webster proposed to introduce:

A BILL to continue for the term of six years the act entitled "An act to incorporate the subscribers to the Bank of the United States."

Be it enacted by the Senate and House of Representatives of the United States of America in Congress assembled, That the act entitled "An act to incorporate the subscribers of the Bank of the United States," approved on the 10th day of April, in the year 1816, shall continue in full force and effect for the term of six years, from and after the period therein limited for its expiration, to wit, the 3d day of March, 1836, and that all the rights, interests, properties, powers, and privileges, secured by the same act, with all the rules, conditions, restrictions, and duties therein prescribed and imposed, be and remain, after the said 3d day of March, 1836, during the said six years, as if the said limitation in the said act had not been made: *Provided nevertheless*, That so much of the said act as declares that no other bank shall be established by any future law of the United States, during the continuance of the corporation thereby created, shall not be continued by this act, but that it shall be lawful for Congress, whenever it shall see fit, to establish any other bank to come into existence and operation at any time on or after the 4th day of March, 1836.

And be it further enacted, That all public moneys accruing to the United States, and becoming payable from and after the passage of this act, in places where the said bank, or any of its offices, is established, shall be deposited in the Bank of the United States, and its offices, as heretofore; provided, that at any time after this act shall have been accepted, Congress may, by law or joint resolution, cause such moneys to be withdrawn and removed to any other custody or place of deposite.

And be it further enacted, That, in consideration of the benefits and privileges conferred by this act, the said bank shall pay to the United States the annuity or yearly sum of two hundred thousand dollars, which said sum shall be paid by the said bank on the 4th day of March, in each and every year, during the said term of six years.

And be it further enacted, That Congress may provide by law that the said bank shall be restrained, at any time after the 3d day of March 1836, from making, issuing, or keeping in circulation, any notes or bills of said bank, or any of its offices, of a less sum or denomination than twenty dollars.

And be it further enacted, That at any time or times, within the last three years of the existence of said corporation, as continued by this act, it shall be lawful for the president and directors to divide among the several stockholders thereof, such portions of the capital stock of the said corporation, as they may have withdrawn from active use, and may judge proper so to divide.

And be it further enacted, That so much of any act or acts of Congress, heretofore passed and now in force, supplementary to, or in anywise connected with the said original act of incorporation, approved on the 10th day of April, in the year 1816, as is not inconsistent with this act, shall be continued in full force and effect during the said six years after the 3d day of March, 1836.

And be it further enacted, That it shall be the duty of the president and directors of the said bank, on or before the first day of the next session of Congress, to signify to the President of the United States, their acceptance, on behalf of the Bank of the United States, of the terms and conditions in this act contained, and if they shall fail to do so, on or before the day above mentioned, then this act shall cease to be in force.

Mr. LEIGH thought he ought to embrace the present occasion to indicate the course which he should feel himself bound to pursue on this great and interesting subject. The remarks of the gentleman from Massachusetts seemed to require that he should state the position in which he stood. He would therefore state frankly the course he should pursue, and the reasons on which he should maintain it. The Legislature of Virginia had solemnly declared its opinion that the United States Government possessed no constitutional authority to establish a national bank; and the Senate must be aware that he accepted the trust which a seat here imposed upon him, knowing that these were the sentiments of the people of Virginia, and that he should not so far misrepresent them, as to vote for this or any other national bank. He concurred in those resolutions of the Virginia Legislature fully.

He (Mr. L.) thought there was no power in Congress to establish a United States Bank. In the expression of this opinion, he did not wish to be understood to say that it was a palpable assumption of power by the Government. It would be presumption in him to say, after the expression of opinion of so many distinguished men, and a majority of the sovereign States of this Union in favor of its constitutionality, that it was plainly wrong. He believed he understood the argument under which its constitutionality was urged, but it had not convinced his understanding. It was not claimed as an express delegation of power, but only as an incidental power. It was claimed as incidental to the fiscal operations of the Government; and he admitted it might be *convenient* for that purpose. He knew very well that the events of this year might show that the putting down of this bank was only the prelude to raising up another in New York, to be controlled by the President of the United States.

Mr. L. then spoke somewhat at length upon the danger of placing a national bank and the revenues of the country at the power and within the disposal of the President: and condemned the removal of the deposites, as an act which placed the deposite banks under the President's control.

When Mr. L. concluded, Mr. WRIGHT took

the floor, and after expressing a wish to reply to Mr. Leigh, on his motion,

Before the question of leave was taken,

The Senate adjourned.

HOUSE OF REPRESENTATIVES.

Tuesday, *March* 18, 1834.

Mr. WHITTLESEY, of Ohio, reported a bill for the relief of Jesse Smith and others.

Mr. BINNEY, an act to remit the duty on locomotive engines heretofore imported, and to allow their future importation duty free. Also, a bill for the relief of John F. Ohl; and an act to remit certain duties on goods imported by Alexander De Launay; and

Mr. CONNOR, a bill for the relief of Patrick Green; which was read twice, and committed.

Mr. CARR, from the Committee on Private Land Claims, reported a bill for the relief of James Keytes; which was read twice, committed to a Committee of the Whole House, and made the order of the day for to-morrow.

Mr. CARR, from the Committee on Private Land Claims, reported a bill for the relief of John A. Barnes, assignee of John Anderton; which was read twice, and committed to a Committee of the Whole House, and made the order of the day for to-morrow, and the report and bill ordered to be printed.

Mr. LEAVITT, a bill granting an additional quantity of land (150,000 acres in addition to the quantity heretofore appropriated) for the satisfaction of bounty land warrants.

Mr. R. M. JOHNSON, a bill for the erection of a national armory on the western waters.

Mr. CASEY, a bill for the relief of John Dement.

Mr. CAMBRELENG, a bill for the relief of Robert Dickey, of New York.

Mr. WHITTLESEY, a bill for the relief of Marinus W. Gilbert.

Mr. HUBBARD, a bill to authorize the Secretary of the Treasury to refund to Richard Butman certain duties imposed on the schooner Brandywine.

A message was received from the President of the United States, with a copy of a letter from the commissioners appointed to adjust the claims of our citizens under the late treaty with Naples, and suggesting the expediency of extending the term allowed for the performance of the duties assigned them. Referred, on motion of Mr. WHITTLESEY, to the Committee on Foreign Affairs.

Mr. PINCKNEY obtained leave to submit the following resolution, in relation to the trade between the United States and Cuba, which, he said, was deemed highly interesting to his constituents:

Resolved, That the documents communicated by the President of the United States, in relation to the trade between the United States and the Islands of Cuba and Porto Rico, be referred to the Committee on Commerce, and that said committee be instructed to inquire into the discriminating duties referred to by the President in his message, and into the expediency of adopting countervailing measures, for the protection of the American merchants and ship-owners.

Agreed to.

Mr. SLADE, a bill for the improvement of the mail road between Louisville and St. Louis; and

Mr. INGE, a bill for the relief of the representatives of Lawrence Milligan.

All which bills were read twice, and committed.

The House proceeded to the consideration of the following resolution, submitted by Mr. Mardis, of Alabama:

Resolved, That the Committee of Ways and Means be instructed to inquire into the expediency of reporting a bill requiring the Secretary of the Treasury to deposite the public moneys of the United States in the State banks; and, also, as to the expediency of defining by law all contracts hereafter to be made with the Secretary for the safe-keeping, management, and disbursement of the same.

Mr. BURGES took the floor, and continued his speech in opposition to the resolution.

At one o'clock, Mr. BURGES suspended his remarks; and

The SPEAKER announced the special order of the day, viz: the resolutions reported from the Committee of Ways and Means.

THE DEPOSITES AND UNITED STATES BANK.

The House proceeded to the consideration of the following resolutions, reported from the Committee of Ways and Means:

1. *Resolved*, That the Bank of the United States ought not to be rechartered.

2. *Resolved*, That the public deposites ought not to be restored to the Bank of the United States.

3. *Resolved*, That the State banks ought to be continued as the places of deposite of the public money, and that it is expedient for Congress to make further provision by law, prescribing the mode of selection, the securities to be taken, and the manner and terms on which they are to be employed.

4. *Resolved*, That for the purpose of ascertaining, as far as practicable, the cause of the commercial embarrassment and distress complained of by numerous citizens of the United States, in sundry memorials which have been presented to Congress at the present session; and of inquiring whether the charter of the Bank of the United States has been violated, and also what corruptions and abuses have existed in its management; whether it has used its corporate power or money to control the press, to interfere in politics, or influence elections; and whether it has had any agency, through its management, or money, in producing the existing pressure—a select committee be appointed to inspect the books, and examine into the proceedings of the said bank, who shall report whether the provisions of the charter have been violated or not; and also what abuses or malpractices have existed in the management of said bank; and that the said committee be authorized to send for persons and papers, and to summon and examine witnesses on oath, and to examine into the affairs of the said bank and branches; and that they are further authorized to visit the principal bank, or any of its branches, for the purpose of inspecting the books, correspondence, accounts, and other papers connected with its management or business; and that the said committee be required to report the result of such investigation, together with the evidence they may take, at as early a day as practicable.

Mr. WILDE said he would now proceed to offer some observations to the House, unless the gentleman from Tennessee desired to speak.

Mr. POLK having signified that he did not wish to speak,

Mr. WILDE took the floor, and offered the following resolution as a substitute for the first resolution reported from the Committee of Ways and Means:

Resolved, That the reasons submitted by the Secretary of the Treasury for removing the public deposites are insufficient and unsatisfactory.

The lips (said Mr. W.) which were open to discuss this question when it was last before us, are now closed forever in silence. The patriot fell, as he had ever stood, in the front rank, warring for the Constitution. Here, as in battle, if our companions fall, we close our ranks and hurry on. When our gallant and noble comrade fell in defence of constitutional liberty, who could have thought, as soon as the grave was closed over him, we should have witnessed in this Hall an attempt to restrict the freedom of debate? Silence was imposed upon us on pain of imprisonment. The honorable chairman of the Committee of Ways and Means assured him that if he would sit with him and vote against all the motions for adjournment, he would not have recourse to the previous question. He (Mr. W.) did sit, and did vote against the motions to adjourn. Mr. W. went on to remark upon the circumstances under which the discussion was cut off by the previous question, and upon the injustice and discourtesy of the measure towards himself personally.

Mr. W. then referred to the situation of this country. Our national debt was paid off; our exports and imports were of vast amount; we had an industrious population, and a cheap Government; and still, we have—what? Numerous bankruptcies, a deranged currency, imminent danger of a total suspension of specie payments, and an apprehension that the duty bonds will not be collected. The means by which this state of things was brought about was extraordinary. Our Constitution doubtless designed this for a hard-money Government, yet we had nothing but paper. Mr. W. went on, at great length, to exhibit a view of the general character and history of our currency. His object was to show that the State banks effectually subvert the intentions of the Constitution, if that intention was to establish a hard-money currency; and that the revenue could not be collected and disbursed, without great loss, by the State banks. If we wished to return to a specie currency, we must (he contended) begin by destroying, not the United States Bank, but the State banks. During the ten years preceding 1830, (Mr. W. said,) the amount of revenue collected was two hundred and thirty millions. The aggregate number of persons employed in the collection of this amount was over nine thousand. The collection and disbursements were made at all points in the country, and yet they were made without the loss of a single cent. In the ten years preceding the year 1816, when the United States Bank was established, the Government lost a million of dollars by broken banks alone. No part of the loss was in the receipts at the customs. It was in the collection of thirty-six millions from lands and internal taxes. Thus, one thirty-sixth part of our revenue from these sources was lost by State banks. This, however, was but a small part of the loss sustained by the Government. The expense of transportation, and the loss on loans, which were taken at a very reduced rate, amounted to a much larger sum. But still the loss of the Government sinks into insignificance in comparison with the loss to individuals. During the same term of ten years, on a domestic exchange of two hundred millions, the loss, at the low estimate of five per cent., was ten millions a year. The people were thus taxed ten millions a year for the benefit of banks and brokers. These were among the blessings of numerous State banks. But it might be said that the condition of the State banks now was not the same as it was in 1816. True, it was not the same; it was more than in 1816. The banks had not yet suspended specie payments, but in respect to the relative proportions of specie to circulation, the condition of the State banks was worse now than it was in 1816. He made statements, from which (he said) it appeared that the paper in circulation was, as to specie in the banks, as seven to one. The State banks must restrict their currency, at the risk of breaking their customers, or they must suffer themselves to be run upon and broken. The only question is, which shall break first—the banks or their customers?

Mr. W. entered, at some length, into the consideration of the project for substituting a hard-money currency for paper. He would not, at present, he said, go fully into the constitutional question; but he stated that a very minute examination of early documents, relative to our history, had convinced him that the term "Bills of Credit," as used in the Constitution, was intended to apply to all species of paper money. At the same time, he did not think it an open question whether the United States shall have a paper currency. Nature and habit had decided that point. He had heard it said, "Perish the banks, live the Constitution." So it was said during the embargo, "Perish commerce, let the Constitution live." But Mr. Jefferson himself, devoted as he was to restrictive measures, became convinced that such was the inveteracy of habit, that it was impossible to pursue his experiment, and he therefore abandoned it. Paper money became, at an early day, a financial expedient of the colonies. It carried them through the French war, and through the war of the Revolution. Paper money was born with the colonies and he had almost said would exist as long as the States existed. Whatever was the intention of the framers of the Constitution, it was certain that, at a very early day after its adoption, they found it extremely convenient and necessary to resort to a paper currency.

Mr. W. thought it might be useful to inquire why it was, that the precious metals were so much used in general circulation over the world. This was to be found in their value as arising from the

labor necessary to procure them; their ductility; non-susceptibility of great increase; as well as their various utility. When it was necessary to have payments made by weight, commerce had not advanced to that state to which it subsequently became; and when larger payments were required to be made, those marks and seals were made upon the metals, which gave to them a circulation beyond their intrinsic value, and from this system of convenience originally might be dated the practice of banks giving to paper a value and currency based on their (not intrinsic) being a representative of other securities—gold, silver, or that which was estimated as property. When it was gravely proposed to dispense with these improvements upon the ancient usages, and to dispense giving facilities to commerce, it might be as well attempted to return from the algebraic method of attaining certainty in calculations, to the rules of common arithmetic. It was scarcely necessary for him to advert to the cheaper medium of paper to assist in performing the necessary circulation for property exchanged from hand to hand. A mixed circulation of paper and gold has forced its way and would sustain itself. Paper convertible into gold for the larger payments—the precious metals for the smaller—neither of which could be destroyed until commerce itself was destroyed. This he argued would be the effect of the experiments now making, for as credit was the offspring of commerce, tyranny and usurpation was death to it.

He would now discuss another subject connected with these measures. Where, he must ask, was the difference between employing State banks as fiscal agents of Government, in a constitutional point of view, and employing the Bank of the United States? Which was the most dangerous? The answer to these questions must be obvious. Who, he also asked, had the greatest interest in having a sound circulation? Was it not the poor man, who required it as remuneration for his daily labor? Was it not wages that would be the first to feel it? And as the aggregate paid for labor was more than was paid to all the rest of the world, the poor man was surely the most interested in its preservation. Of the various modes of collecting the public revenue suggested, he considered that the least plausible was a Government bank; the least feasible was the State banks. The history of all times had showh in Europe, and in several of the States, that changes were sure to result from any paper circulation issued by a Government. He referred for evidences of this to the disastrous results in France, where the assignats, though on their face the national domains were pledged for their redemption, yet there was a failure of two hundred millions of dollars, which the public had to bear. In Russia the same experiment had been tried, and the result was, that four rubles in paper was reduced to one in silver. These were among the most prominent examples, and so well was this understood among commercial men, that even the celebrated Law, when he first projected his scheme, owned his ruin, and brought ruin upon the fortunes of others, in consequence of his objections to issue paper, not convertible into specie, being not only not attended to, but because he was compelled to give up the superintendence, and his was made a Royal Bank by an arret of State; after which the bank commenced making large paper issues. He considered that the great error of this day in depreciating paper currency, to be similar to what was formerly deemed the greatest of all crimes, defacing or reducing the value of the coin in olden times.

Mr. W. dwelt at some length on the utility of banks to commerce, and, proceeding to argue against the reasons adduced by the Secretary of the Treasury, he maintained that Congress had the legislative power, by the Constitution, to regulate and control the public money; and if they had divested themselves of it, as was maintained by the Secretary, he thought Congress might at once vote away their independence, and place themselves under a Lord Protector. The power of the Secretary of the Treasury over the deposites was restricted, as he contended, to the withholding of the deposites from the bank, and did not extend to their withdrawal. The justification of the act of the Secretary, so far as it was founded upon the measures of Mr. Crawford, failed altogether, as he contended, for the reasons that Mr. Crawford acted under a resolution of Congress, the object of which was to facilitate the resumption of specie payments by the State banks. He stated and commented upon the several reasons given by the Secretary in justification of the removal of the deposites. The object of sending the subject of the Secretary's reasons to the Committee of Ways and Means had not been obtained. The committee had reported an argument, but had not affirmed the sufficiency of the reasons offered by the Secretary. The only point which was referred to them for consideration, they had omitted to express any opinion upon in a shape for the decision of the House.

Mr. W., after speaking nearly three hours, yielded the floor, without concluding, to a motion to adjourn.

On motion of Mr. WILLIAMS,
The House adjourned.

IN SENATE.

WEDNESDAY, *March* 19, 1834.

REMOVAL OF THE DEPOSITES.

Mr. TOMLINSON presented the memorial of 380 citizens of Bridgeport, Connecticut, praying the restoration of the deposites to the Bank of the United States.

Mr. McKEAN presented the memorial of about 700 cabinet-makers, chair-makers, upholsterers, &c., of the city and county of Philadelphia, of the same tenor. And, also, the proceedings of a meeting of the same trades, of similar import.

Mr. MANGUM presented a memorial signed by 250 of the citizens of Plymouth, North Carolina, of like character.

Mr. BIBB presented the proceedings of a meeting of inhabitants of Madison county, Kentucky, of the same tenor.

Upon presenting these several memorials and proceedings, the gentlemen having them in charge, severally addressed the Senate. They were read, referred to the Committee on Finance, and ordered to be printed.

Mr. WAGGAMAN presented the proceedings of a meeting of citizens of New Orleans, praying a restoration of the deposites to the Bank of the United States. Also, a memorial from citizens of the same city of the same tenor.

Mr. PORTER presented the memorial of a number of merchants and others, of the same city, and of similar import.

These several proceedings and memorials were read, and followed by some remarks by both those gentlemen, upon the existing distress in New Orleans.

Mr. FORSYTH said, the reference made to him by his friend from Louisiana at his side gave him a fair occasion, for which he had been anxiously looking for several days, to correct an error he had committed about a fortnight since.

Speaking of the condition of the money-market of Augusta, Georgia, he had spoken of the prices of stock and produce as at their usual rate; and had mentioned that the Bank of Augusta, with a capital of six hundred thousand dollars, having authority to double it, had sold the extra stock at a profit of twenty per cent. Mr. F. had no information contradictory of this statement except as to the last particular. The bank had authority to double its capital, but had made no effort to do so. He had been misled by an account of the sales at auction of a portion of the stock of that bank at that rate of advance, and supposed it to be the whole additional stock of the bank, which was sold at twenty per cent. premium—it still bore that premium according to the last prices current of the city; but no such sale of double the capital stock had occurred.

In speaking of the condition of the Southern States, he had not intended to embrace New Orleans—that State is so identified with the West, that we speak of it as western or southwestern. From the character of the business of that city, no doubt the pressure there was great. It was done extensively on credit, and by exchanges. These being deranged, necessarily affected the business of the city. Mr. F. wished to God he had the power to relieve the distress; it would not be of long continuance if he had; yet he could not but hope it was exaggerated. One statement in the memorial gave grounds for this hope. In estimating the loss sustained by the pressure, the memorial, after establishing, no doubt fairly, as the signers of it believed, that it amounted to eight dollars per bale of cotton, they calculate the loss is $4,000-000—five hundred thousand bales being the estimate of the whole crop of cotton of the States of Louisiana, Mississippi, Alabama, and Tennessee; and here it must be obvious that this calculation is inaccurate. The loss can fall only on the cotton yet in the market on this side the Atlantic. That which was shipped before January last, certainly cannot be properly taken into the calculation. What portion of the crop of the States mentioned had been shipped before January, he could not tell, but this he knew, from the ports of Charleston, Savannah, and New Orleans, between sixty and seventy thousand bales of cotton had been shipped on the last quarter of the past year, *more* than there had been during the same period of the preceding year. How it was elsewhere, Mr. F. could not say. In Georgia, the planters, stimulated by the good prices with which the market opened, had hurried their produce into market, an operation in which they had been favored by an unusually fine season. The larger part of their crops being sold early, at good prices, comparatively, they were now easy in their money matters, and were holding the residue of their crops, with a reasonable hope of better prices in a short time.

Having corrected his own errors, he might be pardoned for adverting to those of others. In the course of discussion, some time since, the Senator from Maryland, [Mr. CHAMBERS,] not now in his seat, and the Senator from Maine, over the way, [Mr. SPRAGUE,] had spoken of the draw for specie made on the Branch Bank of the United States at Savannah, and had supposed it to be connected with a plan in connexion with the Government to injure the credit of the Bank of the United States, or else as a scheme to reduce the price of the stocks in order to enable the house in New York, who was supposed to have made large contracts for delivery at a coming day, to comply with those contracts at a profitable rate. What occurred in this Chamber, being, as usual, very roughly reported, had attracted the attention of the house in Augusta by whom the specie had been drawn at Savannah, and he begged permission, in justice to them, to read a letter just received, addressed to his colleague [Mr. KING] and himself:

"At this time of general excitement in the community on money affairs, it is a matter of no small 'regret to us to see our names thrust before the 'public, coupled with a transaction, in itself a '*'fair business transaction*,' but misrepresented and 'distorted into every and any shape, to suit the 'views of partisan politicians. We allude to the 'draw of specie made by us on the United States 'Branch Bank in Savannah, in November last. 'The simple and incontrovertible facts are these. 'The act of our Legislature, prohibiting the circulation of all notes under the denomination of 'fives, went into operation early in the fall. The 'sudden withdrawal of over $600,000 of small 'notes created a vacuum in our circulation, which 'had to be supplied in a great measure by specie, '*instanter*. You are well aware that we have large 'operations in specie, and perhaps know, that we 'have for years past been in the habit of contracting with banks to supply them. In this instance, 'we were applied to for specie by no less than nine 'different banks, in the space of eight or ten days. 'We made such contracts to deliver to these banks 'the amount they wanted, as we deemed to our 'interest. We then contracted with Mr. G. B. 'Lamar for the freight of the specie from Savannah to Augusta. All this was done before a dollar of specie was drawn.

"When we drew the specie, we did not 'offer 'the bank to take a check on the North in lieu of 'the silver.' Neither did we ask the bank or 'cashier 'to permit us to make a special deposite 'of the specie.' The bank had not silver enough 'to pay the whole amount, ($334,000,) and begged 'our clerk to wait until they could send and get '$10,000 from one of the local banks; and he did 'wait. The specie was delivered by us to nine 'different banks in this State, except twenty-seven 'thousand seven hundred *Spanish* dollars, which, 'being worth three or four per cent. premium at that 'time in New York, were shipped to our house at 'that place. Every dollar employed in the draw

'was our own. The operation was entirely and exclusively *our own*. Our New York house *knew nothing of the transaction*, until it was all over. 'Not one dollar of the notes with which the draw 'was made was sent to us from New York, or any 'other place out of the State. We have never had 'the first word of correspondence with the Executive, the Government, or any person in the employ of Government, relative to the United States 'Bank, the draw in question, or anything connected with it. The only correspondence we *ever* had 'with any person connected with the Government 'was with the Assistant Postmaster General, and 'that on business relating to that department exclusively. Such a thing as political effect was '*never intended or thought of by us.*"

The Senate had now information about that strangely represented transaction from the fountain-head. Mr. F. hoped Senators who had made representations or received impressions at variance with the statement now made, would be satisfied that they had been misled.

PETITIONS.

Petitions of a private nature were presented by Messrs. McKEAN, GRUNDY, BIBB, POINDEXTER, and TIPTON; which were severally referred to appropriate committees.

REPORTS OF COMMITTEES.

Mr. POINDEXTER, from the Committee on Public Lands, reported a bill authorizing in certain cases an exchange of land warrants for scrip.

Mr. POINDEXTER, from the same committee, asked to be discharged from the further consideration of the bill confirming certain land claims in the district of St. Stephens, in Alabama, and that it be referred to the Committee on Private Land Claims.

Mr. BROWN, from the Committee of Claims, reported a bill for the relief of Carlos D. Hall.

Mr. BROWN, from the same committee, reported a bill for the relief of John Winslett.

Mr. PRESTON, from the Committee on the Judiciary, reported a bill to regulate and increase the compensation of surgeons and assistant surgeons of the army.

Mr. TIPTON, from the Select Committee on the admission of Michigan and Arkansas into the Union, reported a bill granting additional compensation to the Governor and United States Judges of Michigan.

Mr. MOORE, from the Committee on Revolutionary Claims, reported two bills for the relief of certain persons therein named.

Mr. MOORE, from the same committee, to whom had been recommitted the bill for the relief of Elizabeth Robinson, daughter of Lieutenant Richard Wilde, of the revolutionary army, reported the same, with an amendment.

Mr. KING, of Alabama, from the Committee on Military Affairs, reported a bill making an appropriation for the construction of a military road in the State of Maine.

The engrossed resolution authorizing the Committee on Public Lands to employ a clerk, was read a third time, and passed.

The first special order of the day being the unfinished business of yesterday, (leave to introduce a bill continuing the charter of the Bank of the United States,) being announced,

Mr. WEBSTER moved its postponement until to-morrow, (intimating that he should then call it up at an early hour,) in order to afford Mr. TALLMADGE an opportunity of concluding his remarks upon the other special order, being the report of the Committee on Finance, and Mr. CLAY's resolutions relative to

THE PUBLIC DEPOSITES.

Mr. TALLMADGE resumed, and concluded his remarks, sustaining the reasons of the Secretary of the Treasury; when, at a quarter before five o'clock, on motion of Mr. CLAY,

The Senate adjourned.

HOUSE OF REPRESENTATIVES.

WEDNESDAY, *March* 19, 1834.

Mr. WHITTLESEY, of Ohio, from the Committee of Claims, reported, without amendment, several Senate bills, which were committed and made the order of the day for to-morrow.

Mr. WHITTLESEY, from the same committee, reported the following resolution:

Resolved, That the Committee of Claims be instructed to inquire into the expediency of providing by law for referring all claims for buildings burnt and destroyed by the enemy during the late war, because they were in the military occupation of the United States, by the order of an officer or agent of the United States, as places of deposite or as barracks, to the Third Auditor of the Treasury Department, on principles that have been heretofore prescribed in the settlement of such claims; and that they further inquire into the expediency of providing by law for the settlement of all claims arising from the loss of property in the military service of the United States by contract or impressment, and for horses lost during the late war; also, during the war with the Seminole Indians, and the late war with the Indians commenced by Black Hawk, on such principles as have heretofore been prescribed in such cases.

Mr. WHITTLESEY said that this resolution would relieve the committee and the House from much labor, and would subserve the purposes of justice.

The resolution was agreed to.

Mr. E. EVERETT obtained the consent of the House to submit the following resolution; which was considered and agreed to:

Resolved, That the Secretary of War be directed to submit to this House any information concerning the fortifications proposed to be built on Castle Island, in the harbor of Boston, and on Throg's Point, East river, New York, which may have been recently received at the War Department.

The House resumed the consideration of the resolution offered by Mr. MARDIS, of Alabama:

Resolved, That the Committee of Ways and Means be instructed to inquire into the expediency of reporting a bill requiring the Secretary of the Treasury to deposite the public moneys of the United States in the State banks; and, also, as to the expediency of defining by law all contracts hereafter to be made with the Secretary for the safe-keeping, management, and disbursement of the same.

Mr. BURGES resumed his remarks, and spoke till the expiration of the hour.

The CHAIR presented a communication from the Navy Department, transmitting a report on the case of Henry Eckford, referred to that department. Referred to the Committee on Naval Affairs.

THE DEPOSITES AND THE U. S. BANK.

The House resumed the consideration of the resolutions reported from the Committee of Ways and Means, together with the amendment moved by Mr. WILDE, declaring the reasons given by the Secretary of the Treasury for the removal of the deposites to be unsatisfactory and insufficient.

Mr. WILDE resumed his speech. The committee, he went on to contend, had not discharged the duty which was required of them. On the distinct question presented by the Secretary's reasons, the committee had reported an argument, but no resolutions in affirmation or denial of the sufficiency of those reasons. If the committee would not suffer the vote to be taken on that distinct proposition, the inference will be irresistible. He was somewhat an observer of days and times. The report came in on the 4th of March. Was this to be interpreted as an augury? Does it mean that on the 4th of March next the doctrines of the report will be exploded, and that, by the following 4th of March, nothing but a fragment will remain of the party which now supports them? If so, he accepted the omen. Mr. W. glanced at the topics and reasoning of the report. The great display of historical research—the merit of which he did not intend to controvert—would serve to prove the qualifications of the author for the high post of Secretary of the Treasury, if the incumbent should not, as is possible, be confirmed in the office. He would not travel over the threadbare topics of the three per cents, the protested bill of exchange, and the sums paid for printing. He first adverted to the nature of the contract with the bank. According to the theory of the chairman, the performance of its engagements by the bank established no claim upon the Government for the fulfilment of its promises. The committee, he said, had gone far beyond the President and the Secretary, in claiming power for the Executive. The committee contend that the power over the public deposites was originally an Executive power, always has been an Executive power, and still is an Executive power. If he were not aware of the alarming rapidity with which despotic power makes its progress, he should be surprised at the fact that a power which, six months ago, was acknowledged to be a legislative power, had become converted into executive power, to be exercised under the responsibility of the President to the people.

In considering the accusation against the bank, that by its curtailments it had produced the distress, the calculations evinced that this accusation was something like the statement that the distress was produced by the speeches in Congress. Both were unfounded. But it was not enough for the opponents of the bank to decry the speeches, or to decline, which they could have done, to add to the distress, by not speaking. It was the policy of the day to contemn the persons sending their petitions; in effect, telling the people, Be silent, wretches, even your groans shall not be heard. He referred to the printed report of the conversation of the President with the Philadelphia committee, when they waited upon him with their representations. Having read some extracts, as the accuracy of them was impugned, he said that their report was at least corroborated by that from the Baltimore committee, from which he read extracts; and as there was a member in the House who was capable of bearing testimony to the character of those who made it, he felt at liberty to assume that the statements were correct, if not contradicted by that honorable member.

[Mr. HEATH rose to say that if he was the member alluded to, he was ready to state, that the persons who made the report were highly respectable merchants in Baltimore, well known to him to be incapable of giving any misrepresentation.]

Mr. W. continued. This, then, settled the question of the veracity of the statements, and entitled him to contrast the conduct of the President, as stated by these committees, with that pursued by the Father of his country—WASHINGTON—when he received his white children. Mr. W. proceeded to review and comment upon the term "Government" and others, which he thought were so ambiguous as to induce him to suppose that the report and the message from the President read to his Cabinet were prepared by the same persons. He contended that the charges brought against the bank were altogether unsustained by evidence, and argued against the reasons adduced by the Secretary, that Congress had divested themselves of their money power, and said when it was attempted to defend the acts of the President and the Secretary, by pleading for them purity of intention, the adage—

"Nemo malus qui non stultus"

was brought to his recollection. This he did not use in any offensive sense; but he would urge that such a defence ought not to be allowed to prevail amongst statesmen. It was the Portuguese proverb which said "That hell was paved with good intentions." He went on to controvert the arguments and assertions in the report of the Committee of Ways and Means, to sustain the preference which they had recommended to be given to the State banks as the fiscal agents of the Government, and he contended, that as nothing sufficient was given by them, he must refer it to the language of the President to the Philadelphia committee, in which, among others, the President was alleged to have stated that the article giving power over the coin to Congress had reference to hard money alone. This position of the President he could not assent to, nor could he see how it was possible the power of the States could be invoked to carry into operation the plans which he had detailed for reducing the circulation of the notes of the State banks under the amounts of ten or twenty dollars. Mr. W. disputed the power of the Secretary of the Treasury to make contracts with the State banks, and contended, at length, against the views of the committee as to the capacity of the State banks to act as fiscal agents of the Government. He was in favor of enlarging the specie basis, and had formerly exerted his efforts in the House to that end. But the scheme adopted by the Pres

dent for this purpose was, he thought, the very worst that could be devised.

He dwelt upon the injurious effects which would follow a reduction of the currency. The whole property of the State of Georgia he estimated at seventy millions of dollars, and its circulating medium four millions. If the circulation was reduced to two millions, the property, he said, would be reduced in price to thirty-five millions, and another reduction of the currency to one million, would reduce the value of the property to seventeen and a half millions. What would be the effect upon individuals? A man who has a thousand dollars in property and owes two hundred and fifty dollars becomes bankrupt. Those who happen to have the money, become possessed of all the property in the States. Thus it had always been, and thus the fortunes of the poor were to be promoted by the present experiment. Mr. W. adverted to Mr. Duane's statement that the President had remarked that two-thirds of Congress would have been bribed by the bank if they had remained in session one week longer, also to the reports that it was the intention of the President to adjourn Congress, in case of a disagreement between the two Houses as to the time of adjournment, and commented upon them with much severity. The committee, Mr. W. said, had decided questions which they had not argued, and had argued questions which they had not decided. They shun putting to the House the simple proposition, that the rescue of the Secretary has satisfactory, and put before it the proposition that the bank ought not to be rechartered. We understand this, sir, said Mr. W. It is to show the strong wing to the enemy, and to keep out of view the weak one.

But of what use is the declaration that the bank ought not to be rechartered? The bank don't ask a recharter of us, and we cannot bind our successors. The Administration desire to commit us, but why should we desire to commit ourselves? Let the Government go on with its scheme. If the State banks fail, let them try a specie currency, and every other project. But when all their projects have failed, let us be left untrammeled to try a scheme which never has failed. He had intended to conclude his speech by a motion to lay the proposition of the committee on the table. But as many wished to express their opinions upon it, he had determined, instead of making that motion, upon offering the resolution which he had sent to the table. After some further remarks, Mr. W. concluded.

On motion of Mr PINCKNEY,
The House adjourned.

IN SENATE.

Thursday, March 20, 1834.

A message was received from the President of the United States, upon executive business, by Mr. Donelson, his Private Secretary.

The VICE PRESIDENT presented a communication from the War Department, transmitting the Army Register for 1834.

Also, a communication from [the same department,] enclosing a report from the Commissioner of Pensions, in compliance with a resolution of the 28th of February last.

Petitions of a private nature were presented by Messrs. SILSBEE and SWIFT, and referred.

Mr. SMITH stated the Committee of Claims had some days since made a report upon the petition of John Watson, which was laid upon the table; he now moved for leave to withdraw the papers of said Watson; which was granted.

Mr. NAUDAIN, from the Committee of Claims, moved to be discharged from the further consideration of the petition of Samuel Gray; which was agreed to.

Mr. NAUDAIN, from the same committee, made an unfavorable report upon the petition of Joseph Clark; which was concurred in.

Mr. WEBSTER moved to take up the first special order, being the consideration of the question of granting him leave to bring in a bill to continue the charter of the Bank of the United States for six years; which was agreed to.

Mr. WRIGHT then took the floor, and spoke at length against the constitutionality of the present or any Bank of the United States.

The debate was further continued by Messrs.

WEBSTER and LEIGH, a report of which will be made hereafter.

Mr. CALHOUN intimated his wish to address the Senate, but as the day was advanced, he proposed an adjournment.

Mr. WEBSTER said he was entirely willing to gratify the Senator from South Carolina, but hoped many days would not be consumed in the preliminary question of granting leave.

Mr. CLAYTON moved that the report of the Secretary and accompanying documents, responsive to the call of the Senate of the 26th of February, relative to pensions, be printed; which was agreed to.

On motion of Mr. CALHOUN,
The Senate adjourned.

HOUSE OF REPRESENTATIVES.

Thursday, March 20, 1834.

Mr. SUTHERLAND, from the Committee on Commerce, reported an act supplementary to an act to fix the limit of the port of entry and delivery for the district of Philadelphia.

Also, an act making Dorchester, in Massachusetts, a port of entry; and

An act to establish the collection district of Newark, New Jersey; which bills were read twice, and committed.

Mr. CLAY, from the Committee on Public Lands, reported a bill to authorize the construction of railroads and canals through lands of the United States. The bill was read twice. Mr. C. said he did not desire to have the bill committed; he desired only to have it printed and laid on the table for the present. Agreed to.

Mr. C. also reported a bill making grants of land to disbanded officers and others, for services during the late war; which was read twice, and he then moved to have it committed to the Committee of the Whole on the state of the Union.

Mr. MASON, of Virginia, objected to its commitment to any but the usual committee for such subjects, the Committee of the Whole House.

Mr. WILLIAMS said that bills as interesting as this had been referred to the Committee of the Whole House.

Mr. CLAY said the bill had been reported at the instance of various Legislatures of the Union. He wished to have its consideration insured during this session; for which purpose he moved its reference to the Committee of the Whole on the state of the Union.

Mr. MASON considered that this was in its nature a private bill; he could not, therefore, see any reason why precedence should be given to it over all others. He moved its commitment to the Committee of the Whole.

Mr. CLAY remarked, that although the bill should be sent to the committee which he desired, yet it did not follow that it would have any preference given to it, unless it should be the pleasure of the House to take it up.

After a desultory conversation, in which Mr. WILLIAMS, Mr. MILLER, and Mr. CHILTON participated,

The bill was referred to the Committee of the Whole House.

On motion of Mr. HARPER, of New Hampshire,

Ordered, That the Committee on Commerce be discharged from the further consideration of the petition of inhabitants of Massachusetts, for the improvement, &c., of Taunton river; also, from the consideration of a petition of inhabitants of Wilmington, Delaware, for the improvement of the navigation of the Christiana river.

On motion of Mr. THOMAS, of Louisiana,

Ordered, That the Committee on the Post Office and Post Roads be discharged from the consideration of the case of A. M. Pennyman.

The several bills referred to the Committee on Commerce, making appropriations for building light-houses, light-buoys, boats, beacons, &c., for 1834, for the improvement and survey of certain harbors, &c., were reported from that committee with amendments, and committed to the Committee of the Whole House, and made the order of the day.

The House proceeded with the following resolution submitted by Mr. Mardis:

Resolved, That the Committee of Ways and Means be instructed to inquire in the expediency of reporting a bill requiring the Secretary of the Treasury to deposite the public moneys of the United States in the State banks; and, also, as to the expediency of defining by law all contracts hereafter to be made with the Secretary for the safe-keeping, management, and disbursement of the same.

Mr. BURGES resumed his remarks, and spoke in opposition to the resolution until the expiration of the hour allotted for morning business.

The CHAIR communicated to the House a report from the Secretary of War, transmitting the annual register of the army. Laid on the table, and ordered to be printed.

THE DEPOSITES AND UNITED STATES BANK.

The House resumed the consideration of the resolutions reported from the Committee of Ways and Means, together with the amendment moved by Mr. Wilde, of Georgia, declaring the reasons offered by the Secretary of the Treasury for removing the deposites to be unsatisfactory and insufficient.

Mr. PINCKNEY, of South Carolina, took the floor. His reasons for rising to occupy the attention of the House for comparatively a short time, after the able arguments from the gentlemen who had preceded him, was the interest which his constituents felt in the question. He represented a city which was deeply concerned in commerce, navigation, and agriculture, and which now felt all the embarrassments growing out of the measures of the Executive. Recent advices from Charleston informed him that rice, which ordinarily was worth $3.50, was now scarcely worth $2.75. Lands, negroes, and town property, had fallen to a most alarming extent. The losses sustained by South Carolina alone, if accurately ascertained, would be found to be large enough to excite the sympathy of every individual on this floor, and perhaps of the President himself. Under these circumstances, he would be recreant to his duties did he not express his sentiments on the subject before the House. Before he proceeded to discuss the main question, he must be allowed to touch upon a few incidental points, even at the risk of provoking the ridicule of his friend from Kentucky, who had remarked that he [Mr. Pinckney] could talk upon nothing without introducing nullification. The opinions which he entertained on that subject, were, he believed, the same which the gentleman, under similar circumstances, would entertain. He reminded the gentleman, too, that the doctrine originated in Kentucky. It was in that State that resolutions were adopted, in reference to the alien and sedition laws, declaring that nullification was the rightful remedy; a principle upon which South Carolina had stood, and struggled, and triumphed. He had already, on a former occasion, noticed the attempt to create the belief that all who were opposed to the removal of the deposites, were in favor of the recharter of the bank. The merchants had also been attacked. Their deputations were not only repelled with indignity, but now they were denounced as enemies to liberty. As far as his constituents were concerned, he repelled the attack, and as to the great body of the merchants, he pronounced it to be unjust and unfounded.

Mr. P. went on to speak of the charter of the President's motives, which, he said, could not, if good, justify his measures; and he referred to Mr. Duane's letters for an explanation of the principles on which the President acted. It might be that his language was disrespectful to the President, and he might be told, as the Governor of Virginia was, that he had no right to hold any opinion in respect to the President's course. The gentleman from Virginia, [Mr. Moore,] exulted in the idea that the proclamation had destroyed nullification. Does he not know that this doctrine brought Mr. Madison and the Republican party into power? And does he exult that the doctrines of Jefferson have been destroyed by Jackson; that the doctrine of Virginia has been swept away by the proclamation? But he need not lay that flattering unction to his soul. The doctrine is now more firmly established than ever. Thousands were now convinced who formerly doubted. The proclamation had not only confirmed the State-rights party in South Carolina in their opinions, but has gained thou-

sands of converts to those opinions. It had united the whole South against executive usurpation, created State-rights societies in Pennsylvania, encouraged Alabama to resistance, and aroused the friends of the Constitution everywhere to a sense of the impending danger of consolidation.

The President, Mr. P. declared, would never have ventured to remove the deposites, if the force bill had been rejected. The passage of that bill by a large majority, taught him that he might venture upon anything. That same body which had put at his disposition the whole army and navy, to enable him to crush a sovereign State, would, he thought, justify him in grasping the money power of the country. They who had made him a despot, ought not to be surprised at his exertion of despotic power. Mr. P. then referred to the remarks made by the member from Tennessee, [Mr. Polk,] in reply to the remarks of his colleague, [Mr. McDuffie,] in respect to drilled majorities. The member from Tennessee spoke of the test oaths of South Carolina as an odious and tyrannical exercise of majority power. But the act alluded to was not a test act. A test act required conformity to certain religious opinions. There was no act of this sort in any of the States except the State of Tennessee; according to the Constitution of which State, no person can hold an office who does not believe in the existence of a Deity. He would not say that this was not a proper provision, and no one would regret more than himself the appointment of any man to office who disbelieved in the existence of a Deity. But the test law of South Carolina was not of that description. All the citizens of that State were on a footing of perfect equality. All which the law enjoins, is, that the citizens shall take an oath of allegiance to the State, and to support the Constitution of the United States. This was no new provision. The States of Georgia, Virginia, and Massachusetts had similar laws.

Mr. P. here took up the resolutions of the committee, and contended that they did not meet the question before the House. He spoke of the public distress, the existence of which was not, he said, denied by any one, and of the clamors for relief to which, he said, the committee had turned a deaf ear. The deposites, he declared, must be restored, or a revolution would take place. This House and this nation would never approve of their removal. Yes, sir, I repeat, said he, that either these deposites must be restored, or a revolution is at hand. The spirit which threw the tea overboard at Boston is at work in the northern and in the southern States. He dwelt long upon the President's words—the measure is my own, I take the responsibility; and took up the President's reason for the measure, which he commented upon at great length. He argued at length in support of the positions that the removal of the deposites was a violation of the Constitution; that it was a violation of the charter of the bank; and that it was the perversion of the power of appointment—a power which, he said, was not given by the Constitution, but which had been unfortunately acquiesced in.

When Mr. P. concluded, at about three o'clock, several gentlemen simultaneously addressed the Chair.

The floor was obtained by Mr. GILMER, on whose motion,

The House adjourned.

IN SENATE.

FRIDAY, *March* 21, 1834.

Mr. POINDEXTER, from the Committee on Public Lands, reported a bill from the House of Representatives authorizing the sale of school lands in Illinois, without amendment; and gave notice that when the bill was called up, he was instructed by the committee to move its indifinite postponement.

Mr. POINDEXTER, from the same committee, made a report upon the petition of Robert Stephens; which, without reading, was laid upon the table.

Mr. CLAY presented a memorial signed by about 3,000 clerks in the city of New York, ascribing the derangement of the currency and pecuniary distress to the removal of the deposites, and praying their restoration to the Bank of the United States;

Also, a memorial of merchants and traders from nine or ten different States, signed in Philadelphia, of a similar character;

The memorials were read by Mr. CLAY, and, on his motion, were referred to the Committee on Finance, and ordered to be printed.

Mr. SOUTHARD presented a memorial of the township of Lawrence, New Jersey, praying the restoration of the deposites;

Also, a memorial from the county of Monmouth;

The proceedings of a meeting of inhabitants of Shrewsbury;

A memorial of the State Bank of Camden, the Farmers' Bank of Mount Holly, and the Cumberland Bank;

A memorial signed by 1695 inhabitants of Gloucester county;

All of the same import; which were severally read, referred to the Committee on Finance, and ordered to be printed.

Mr. SOUTHARD presented the memorial of Henry Eckford; which was referred to the Committee on Naval Affairs.

Mr. EWING submitted the following resolution:

Resolved, That the Committee on the Post Office and Post Roads be instructed to examine and report the present condition of the Post Office Department; and that they have power to send for persons and papers, and to take testimony for that purpose; and that the Secretary of the Senate shall, on application of the committee, employ a clerk to attend them.

The VICE PRESIDENT communicated a letter from the Secretary of State, transmitting a register of American seamen for the year 1833.

Mr. KENT presented a memorial from three banks in Frederick, and one in Washington county, Maryland, praying the restoration of the deposites to the Bank of the United States; which was referred to the Committee on Finance, and ordered to be printed.

The VICE PRESIDENT announced the first special order to be the granting leave to introduce a bill to recharter the Bank of the United States; when

Mr. CALHOUN took the floor, and spoke for one hour and a half against the principles of the bill, as being only a temporary expedient, but in favor of establishing a new bank upon the present one, and prohibiting the issuing of notes under $10, and the payment of Government dues in any notes of banks under the denomination of $5. When Mr. CALHOUN concluded—

Mr. BENTON rose and expressed his satisfaction that the Senator from South Carolina [Mr. CALHOUN] had restored the debate to the elevation that belonged to the Senate. He did not mean to descend from that elevation, not of sentiment, thought and style, to which he had no pretension, but in the mode of conducting the debate, descending to no personal, or partisan object, but keeping solely in view the great interests of the country, and the means of accomplishing those interests. Mr. B. said it was now six years since he had begun to oppose the renewal of the charter of this bank, but he had not, until the present moment, found a suitable occasion for showing the people the kind of currency which they were entitled to possess, and probably would possess, on the dissolution of the Bank of the United States. This was a view of the subject which many wished to see, and which he felt bound to give; and which he should proceed to present, with all the brevity and perspicuity of which he was master.

I. In the first place, he was one of those who believed that the Government of the United States was intended to be a hard money Government; that it was the intention and the declaration of the Constitution of the United States that the Federal currency should consist of gold and silver; and that there is no power in Congress to issue, or to authorize any company of individuals to issue, any species of Federal paper currency whatsoever.

Every clause in the Constitution (said Mr. B.) which bears upon the subject of money—every early statute of Congress which interprets the meaning of these clauses—and every historic recollection which refer to them, go hand in hand in giving to that instrument the meaning which this proposition ascribes to it. The power granted to Congress to coin money, is an authority to stamp metallic money, and is not an authority for emitting slips of paper containing promises to pay money. The authority granted to Congress to regulate the value of coin, is an authority to regulate the value of metallic money, not of paper. The prohibition upon the States against making anything but gold and silver a legal tender, is a moral prohibition, founded in virtue and honesty, and is just as binding upon the Federal Government as upon the State Governments, and that without a written prohibition; for the difference in the nature of the two Governments is such that the States *may* do all things which they are not forbid to do, and the Federal Government *can* do nothing which is not authorized in the Constitution to do. The power to punish the crime of counterfeiting is limited to the current coin of the United States and to the securities of the United States, and cannot be extended to the offence of forging paper money but by that unjustifiable power of construction which founds an implication upon an implication, and hangs one implied power upon another. The word currency is not in the Constitution; nor any word which can be made to cover a circulation of bank notes. Gold and silver is the only thing recognised for money. It is the money, and the only money of the Constitution; and every historic recollection, as well as every phrase in the Constitution, and every early statute on the subject of money, confirms that idea. People were sick of paper money about the time the Constitution was formed. The Congress of the Confederation, in the time of the Revolution, had issued a currency of paper money. It had run the full career of that currency. The wreck of two hundred millions of paper dollars lay upon the land. The framers of the Constitution worked in the midst of that wreck. They saw the havoc which paper money had made upon the fortunes of individuals, and the morals of the public. They determined to have no more Federal paper money. They created a hard money Government; they intended the new Goverment to recognise nothing for money but gold and silver; and every word admitted into the Constitution upon the subject of money defines and establishes that sacred intention.

Legislative enactment (continued Mr. B.) came quickly to the aid of constitutional intention, and historic recollection. The fifth statute passed at the first session of the first Congress that ever sat under the present Constitution, was full and explicit on this head. It defined the kind of money which the Federal treasury should receive. The enactments of the statute are remarkable for their brevity and comprehension, as well as for their clear interpretation of the Constitution, and deserve to be repeated and remembered. They are: That the fees and duties payable to the Federal Government shall be received in gold and silver coin *only;* the gold coins of France, Spain, Portugal, and England, and all *other* gold coins of equal fineness, at 89 cents for every pennyweight; the Mexican dollar at 100 cents; the crown of France at 111 cents; and all *other* silver coins of equal fineness, at 111 cents per ounce. This statute was passed the 30th day of July, 1789, just one month after Congress had commenced the work of legislation. It shows the sense of the Congress, composed of the men, in great part, who had framed the Constitution, and who, by using the word *only*, clearly expressed their intention that gold and silver alone was to constitute the currency of the new Government.

In support of this construction of the Constitution, Mr. B. referred to the phrase so often used by our most aged and eminent statesmen, that this was intended to be a hard-money Government. Yes, (said Mr. B.,) the framers of the Constitution were hard-money men; but the chief expounder and executor of that Constitution was not a hard-money man, but a paper-system man!—a man devoted to the paper-system of England with all the firmness of conviction, and all the fervor of enthusiasm. God forbid (said Mr. B.) that I should do injustice to General Hamilton—that I should say, or insinuate, aught to derogate from the just fame of that great man! He has many titles to the gratitude and admiration of his countrymen, and the heart could not be American which could dishonor or disparage his memory. But his ideas

of government did not receive the sanction of general approbation; and of all his political tenets, his attachment to the paper-system was most strongly opposed at the time, and has produced the most lasting and deplorable results upon the country. In the year 1791, this great man, then Secretary of the Treasury, brought forward his celebrated plan for the support of public credit—that plan which unfolded the entire scheme of the paper system, and immediately developed the great political line between the Federalists and the Republicans. The establishment of a national bank was the leading and predominant feature of that plan; and the original report of the Secretary, in favor of establishing the bank, contained this fatal and deplorable recommendation:

"*The bills and notes of the bank, originally made 'payable, or which shall have become payable, on demand, in gold and silver coin, shall be receivable in 'all payments to the United States.*"

This fatal recommendation became a clause in the charter of the bank. It was transferred from the report of the Secretary to the pages of the statute book; and from that moment the moneyed character of the Federal Government stood changed and reversed. Federal bank notes took the place of hard money; and the whole edifice of the new Government slided at once from the solid rock of gold and silver money, on which its framers had placed it, into the troubled and tempestuous ocean of a paper currency.

Mr. B. said it was no answer to this most serious charge of having changed the moneyed character of the Federal Government, and of the whole Union, to say that the notes of the Bank of the United States are not made a legal tender between man and man. There was no necessity (he said) for a statute law to that effect; it was sufficient that they were made a legal tender to the Federal Government; the law of necessity, far superior to that of the statute book, would do the rest. A law of tender was not necessary; a forced, incidental tender resulted as an inevitable consequence from the credit and circulation which the Federal Government gave them. Whatever was received at the custom houses, at the land offices, at the post offices, at the marshal's and district attorney's offices, and in all the various dues to the Federal Government, must be received, and will be received, by the people. It becomes the actual and practical currency of the land. People must take it, or get nothing; and thus the Federal Government, establishing a paper currency for itself, establishes it also for the States, and for the people, and everybody must use it from necessity, whether compelled by law or not.

Mr. B. said it was not to be supposed that the objection which he now took to the unconstitutionality of the clause which made the notes of the Federal bank a legal tender to the Federal Government, was an objection which could be overlooked or disregarded by the adversaries of the bank in 1791. It was not overlooked or disregarded: on the contrary, it was denounced and combated, as in itself a separate and distinct breach of the Constitution, going the whole length of emitting paper money, and the more odious and reprehensible because a privileged company was to have the monopoly of the emission. The genius of Hamilton was put in requisition to answer this objection; and the best answer which that great man could give it was a confession of the omnipotence of the objection, and the total impossibility of doing it away. His answer surrendered the whole question of a currency. It sunk the notes of the bank, which were then to be tendered to the Federal Government, to the condition of supplies furnished to the Government, and to be consumed by it. The answer took refuge under the natural power, independent of all constitutions, for the tax receiver to receive his taxes in what articles he pleased. To do justice to General Hamilton, and to detect and expose the true character of this bank paper, Mr. B. read a clause from General Hamilton's reply to the Cabinet opinions of Mr. Jefferson and Mr. Attorney General Randolph, when President Washington had the charter of the first bank under advisement with his Secretaries. It was the clause in which General Hamilton replied to the objection to the constitutionality of making the notes of the bank receivable in payment of public dues.

"To designate, or appoint, the *money*, or *thing*, 'in which taxes are to be paid, is not only a proper, 'but a necessary, exercise of the *power* of collecting them. Accordingly, Congress, in the law 'concerning the collection of the duties, imposts, 'and tonnage, have provided that they shall be 'payable in gold and silver. But, while it was an 'indispensable part of the work to say in *what* they 'should be paid, *the choice of the specific thing was 'a mere matter of discretion*. The payment might 'have been required in the *commodities* themselves. 'Taxes *in kind*, however ill-judged, are not without precedents, even in the United States; or it 'might have been in the *paper money* of the several 'States, or in the *bills* of the Bank of North America, New York, and Massachusetts, all, or either 'of them; it might have been in bills issued under 'the authority of the United States. No part of 'this, it is presumed, can be disputed. *The appointment of the MONEY or THING in which the 'taxes are to be paid, is an incident of the POWER 'of collection*. And among the *expedients* which 'may be adopted, is that of bills issued under the 'authority of the United States."

Mr. B. would read no further, although the argument of General Hamilton extended through several pages. The nature of the argument is fully disclosed in what is read. It surrenders the whole question of a currency. Neither the power to furnish a *currency*, nor to regulate *currency*, is pretended to be claimed. The notes of the new bank are put upon the footing, not of money, but of *commodities—things—articles in kind*—which the tax receiver may accept from the tax payer, and which are to be used and consumed by the tax receiver, and not to be returned to the people, much less to be diffused over the country in place of money. This is the original idea and conception of these notes. It is the idea under which they obtained the legal capacity of receivability in payment of public dues; and from this humble conception, this degraded assimilation to corn and grain, to clothes and provisions, they have, by virtue of that clause in the charter, crept up to the character of money—become the real, practical *currency* of the land—driven the *currency* of the Constitution from the land—and so depraved the public intellect as now to be called for as money, and proclaimed to be indispensable to the country, when the author of the bank could not rank them higher than an *expedient* for paying a tax.

II. In the next place, Mr. B. believed that the quantity of specie derivable from foreign commerce, added to the quantity of gold derivable from our own mines, were fully sufficient, if not expelled from the country by unwise laws, to furnish the people with an abundant circulation of gold and silver coin, for their common currency, without having recourse to a circulation of small bank notes.

The truth of these propositions, Mr. B. held to be susceptible of complete and ready proof. He spoke first of the domestic supply of native gold, and said that no mines had ever developed more rapidly than these had done, or promised more abundantly than they now do. In the year 1824 they were a spot, in the State of North Carolina; they are now a region spreading into six States. In the year 1824, the product was $5,000; in the last year the product, in coined gold, was $868,000; in uncoined, as much more; and the product of the present year computed at $2,000,000; with every prospect of continued and permanent increase. The probability was, that these mines alone, in the lapse of a few years, would furnish an abundant supply of gold to establish a plentiful circulation of that metal, if not expelled from the country by unwise laws. But the great source of supply, both for gold and silver, (Mr. B. said,) was in our foreign commerce. It was this foreign commerce which filled the States with hard money immediately after the close of the revolutionary war, when the domestic mines were unknown; and it is this same foreign commerce which, even now, when Federal laws discourage the importation of foreign coins, and compel their exportation, is bringing in an annual supply of seven or eight millions of dollars. With an amendment of the laws which now discourage the importation of foreign coins, and compel their exportation, there could be no delay in the rapid accumulation of a sufficient stock of the precious metals to supply the largest circulation which the common business of the country could require.

Mr. B. believed that the product of foreign mines, and the quantity of gold and silver now in existence, to be much greater than was commonly supposed; and as a statement of its amount would establish his proposition in favor of an adequate supply of these metals, for the common currency of the country, he would state that amount, as he found it calculated in approved works of political economy. He looked to the three great sources of supply: 1. Mexico and South America; 2. Europe and Northern Asia; 3. The coast of Africa. Taking the discovery of the New World as the starting point from which the calculation would commence, and the product was:

1. Mexico and South America....$6,458,000,000
2. Europe and Northern Asia........628,000,000
3. The coast of Africa..............150,000,000

making a total product of seven thousand two hundred and thirty-six millions in the short space of three centuries and a half. To this is to be added the quantity existing at the time the New World was discovered; and which was computed at $2,300,000,000. Upon all these *data* the political economists, (Mr. B. said,) after deducting $2,000,000,000 for waste and consumption, still computed the actual stock of gold and silver in Europe, Asia, and America, in 1832, at about seven thousand millions of dollars, and that quantity constantly and rapidly increasing.

Mr. B. had no doubt but that the quantity of gold and silver in Europe, Asia, and America was sufficient to carry on the whole business of the world. He said that States and empires far greater in wealth and population than any now existing—far superior in public and private magnificence—had carried on all the business of private life and all the affairs of national government upon gold and silver alone, and that before the mines of Mexico and Peru were known or dreamed of. He alluded to the great nations of antiquity, to the Assyrian and Persian empires, to Egypt, Carthage, Rome, to the Grecian republics, the Kingdoms of Asia Minor, and to the empire transcending all these put together, the Saracenic Empire of the Caliphs, which, taking for its centre the eastern limit of the Roman world, extended its dominion as far west as Rome had conquered, and farther east than Alexander had marched. These great nations, whose armies crushed empires at a blow, whose monumental edifices still attest their grandeur, had no idea of bank credits and paper money. They used gold and silver alone. Such degenerate phrases as sound currency, paper medium, circulating media, never once sounded in their heroic ears.

But why go back (exclaimed Mr. B.) to the nations of antiquity? Why quit our own day? Why look beyond the boundaries of Europe? We have seen an empire in our own day, of almost fabulous grandeur and magnificence, carrying on all its vast undertakings upon a currency of gold and silver, without deigning to recognise paper for money. I speak (said Mr. B.) of France—great and imperial France—and have my eye upon that first year of the Consulate, when a young and victorious general, just transferred from the camp to a council, announced to his astonished ministers that specie payments should commence in France by a given day!—in that France which for so many years had seen nothing but a miserable currency of depreciated *mandats* and *assignats!* The annunciation was heard with the inward contempt and open distrust which the whole tribe of hack politicians everywhere feel for the statesmanship of military men. It was followed by the success which it belongs to genius to inspire and to command. Specie payments commenced in France on the day named, and a hard money currency has been the sole currency of France from that day to this.

Mr. B. here cited a passage from a letter of Mr. Gallatin to Mr. Ingham, then Secretary of the Treasury, (December, 1829,) to confirm what he said of the French currency.

The passage.

"For the last twenty-five years the coinage of 'France has been far greater than that of any 'other country. I hardly need to observe that 'this is due to the almost total expulsion of paper 'as currency. The Bank of France alone issues

'paper, and none of a denomination less than five 'hundred francs; so that it is used almost exclusively for commercial transactions, and remittances, *and makes no part of the currency, properly so called, of the country.* Paper, as all know, necessarily drives away the precious metals, which 'will naturally flow to the places where paper is 'not used. They (the precious metals) are a 'dearer, but the only *safe*, circulating medium; 'and no country that will resort to other means, 'can expect to have a *sound* and *uniform* currency.'"

Such (said Mr. B.) is the currency of France; a country whose taxes exceed a thousand millions of francs—whose public and private expenditures require a circulation of three hundred and fifty millions of dollars—and which possess that circulation, every dollar of it, in gold and silver. After this example, can any one doubt the capacity of the United States to supply itself with specie? Reason and history forbid the doubt. Reason informs us that hard money flows into the vacuum the instant that small bank notes are driven out. France recovered a specie circulation within a year after the consular government refused to recognise paper for money. England recovered a gold circulation of about one hundred millions of dollars within four years after the one and two pound notes were suppressed. Our own country filled up with Spanish milled dollars, French crowns, doubloons, half joes, and guineas, as by magic, at the conclusion of the revolutionary war, and the suppression of the continental bills. The business of the United States would not require above sixty or seventy millions of gold and silver for the common currency of the people, and the basis of large bank notes, and bills of exchange. Of that sum more than one-third is now in the country, but not in circulation. The Bank of the United States hoards above ten millions. At the expiration of her charter, in 1836, that sum will be paid out, in redemption of its notes—will go into the hands of the people—and, of itself, will nearly double the quantity of silver now in circulation. Our native mines will be yielding, annually, some millions of gold; foreign commerce will be pouring in her accustomed, copious supply; the correction of the erroneous value of gold, the liberal admission of foreign coins, and the suppression of small notes, will invite, and retain an adequate metallic currency. The present moment is peculiarly favorable for these measures. Foreign exchanges are now in our favor; silver is coming here, although not current by our laws; both gold and silver would flow in, and that immediately, to an immense amount, if raised to their proper value, and put on a proper footing, by our laws. Three days legislation, on these subjects, would turn copious supplies of gold and silver into the country, diffuse them through every neighborhood, and astonish gentlemen when they got home at midsummer, at finding hard money, where they had left paper. Mr. B. was against a small paper currency; not against large bank notes, and expressed a concurrence in much that was said on paper money by the Senator from South Carolina, [Mr. CALHOUN,] though differing so much on the subject of the national bank.

III. In the third place, Mr. B. undertook to affirm, as a proposition free from dispute or contestation, that the value now set upon gold by the laws of the United States, was unjust and erroneous; that these laws had expelled gold from circulation; and that it was the bounden duty of Congress to restore that coin to circulation, by restoring it to its just value. In this he had the pleasure to concur heartily with the Senator from South Carolina, [Mr. CALHOUN.]

That gold was undervalued by the laws of the United States, and expelled from circulation, was a fact (Mr. B. said) which everybody knew; but there was something else which everybody did not know; which few, in reality, had an opportunity of knowing; but which was necessary to be known, to enable the friends of gold to go to work at the right place to effect the recovery of that precious metal which their fathers once possessed; which the subjects of European kings now possess—which the citizens of the young republics to the south, all possess—which even the free negroes of San Domingo possess—but which the yeomanry of this America have been deprived of for more than twenty years, and will be deprived of forever, unless they discover the cause of the evil, and apply the remedy to its root.

I have already shown (said Mr. B.) that the plan for the support of public credit, which General Hamilton brought forward in 1791, was a plan for the establishment of the paper system in our America. We had at that time a gold currency which was circulating freely and fully all over the country. Gold is the antagonist of paper, and, with fair play, will keep a paper currency within just and proper limits. It will keep down the small notes; for no man will carry a five, a ten, or a twenty dollar note in his pocket, when he can get guineas, eagles, half eagles, doubloons, and half joes, to carry in their place. The notes of the new Bank of the United States, which bank formed the leading feature in the plan for the support of public credit, had already derived one undue advantage over gold on being put on a level with it in point of legal tender to the Federal Government, and universal receivability in all payments to that Government: they were now to derive another, and a still greater undue advantage over gold, in the law for the establishment of the national mint; an institution which also formed a feature of the plan for the support of public credit. It is to that plan that we trace the origin of the erroneous valuation of gold, which has banished that metal from the country. Mr. Secretary Hamilton, in his proposition for the establishment of a mint, recommended that the relative value of gold, to silver, should be fixed at fifteen for one; and that recommendation became the law of the land, and has remained so ever since. At the same time, the relative value of these metals in Spain and Portugal, and throughout their vast dominions in the New World, whence our principal supplies of gold were derived, was at the rate of sixteen for one; thus making our standard six per cent. below the standard of the countries which chiefly produced gold. It was also below the English standard, and the French standard, and below the standard which prevailed in these States before the adoption of this Constitution, and which was actually prevailing in the States at the time that this new proportion of fifteen to one was established.

Mr. B. was ready to admit that there was some nicety requisite in adjusting the relative value of two different kinds of money—gold and silver, for example—so as to preserve an exact equipoise between them, and to prevent either from expelling the other. There was some nicety, but no insuperable, or even extraordinary difficulty, in making the adjustment. The nicety of the question was aggravated in the year '92, by the difficulty of obtaining exact knowledge of the relative value of these metals, at that time, in France and England; and Mr. Gallatin has since shown that the information which was then relied upon, was clearly erroneous. The consequence of any mistake in fixing our standard, was also well known in the year '92. Mr. Secretary Hamilton, in his proposition for the establishment of a mint, expressly declared that the consequence of a mistake in the relative value of the two metals, would be the expulsion of the one that was undervalued. Mr. Jefferson, then Secretary of State, in his contemporaneous report upon foreign coins, declared the same thing. Mr. Robert Morris, financier to the revolutionary Government, in his proposal to establish a mint in 1782, was equally explicit to the same effect. The delicacy of the question, and the consequence of a mistake, were, then, fully understood forty years ago, when the relative value of gold and silver was fixed at fifteen to one. But, at that time, it unfortunately happened that the PAPER SYSTEM, then omnipotent in England, was making its transit to our America; and everything that would go to establish that system—everything that would go to sustain the newborn Bank of the United States—that eldest daughter, and *spem gregis*, of the *paper system* in America—fell in with the prevailing current, and became incorporated in the Federal legislation of the day.

Gold, it was well known, was the antagonist of paper; that from its intrinsic value, the natural predilection of all mankind for it, its small bulk, and the facility of carrying it about, would be preferred to paper, either for travelling or keeping in the house, and this would limit and circumscribe the general circulation of bank notes, and prevent all plea of necessity for issuing smaller notes. Silver, on the contrary, from its inconvenience of transportation, would favor the circulation of bank notes. Hence the birth of the doctrine, that if a mistake was to be committed, it should be on the side of silver! Mr. Secretary Hamilton declares the existence of this feeling, when, in his report upon the establishment of a mint, he says: "*It is sometimes observed, that silver 'ought to be encouraged, rather than gold, as being 'more conducive to the extension of bank circulation, 'from the greater difficulty and inconvenience which 'its greater bulk, compared with its value, occasions in the transportation of it.*" This passage in the Secretary's report proves the existence of the feeling in favor of silver against gold, and the cause of that feeling. Quotations might be made from the speeches of others, to show that they acted upon that feeling; but it is due to General Hamilton to say that he disclaimed such a motive for himself, and expressed a desire to retain both metals in circulation, and even to have a gold dollar.

The proportion of 15 to 1 was established. The 11th section of the act of April, 1792, enacted that every fifteen pounds weight of pure silver should be equal in value in all payments, with one pound of pure gold; and so in proportion for less quantities of the respective metals.* This act was the death warrant to the gold currency. The diminished circulation of that coin soon began to be observable; but it was not immediately extinguished. Several circumstances delayed, but could not prevent that catastrophe. 1. The Bank of the United States then issued no note of less denomination than ten dollars, and but few of them. 2. There were but three other banks in the United States, and they issued but few small notes; so that a small note currency did not come directly into conflict with gold. 3. The trade to the lower Mississippi continued to bring up, from Natchez and New Orleans, for many years, a large supply of doubloons, and long supplied a gold currency to the new States in the West. Thus, the absence of a small note currency, and the constant arrivals of doubloons from the lower Mississippi, deferred the fate of the gold currency; and it was not until the lapse of near twenty years after the adoption of the erroneous standard of 1792, that the circulation of that metal, both foreign and domestic, became completely and totally extinguished in the United States. The extinction is now complete, and must remain so, until the laws are altered.

In making this annunciation, and in thus standing forward to expose the error, and to demand the reform of the gold currency, he (Mr. B.) was not setting up for the honors of a first discoverer, or first inventor. Far from it. He was treading in the steps of other, and abler men, who had gone before him. Four Secretaries of the Treasury—Gallatin, Dallas, Crawford, and Ingham—had, each in their day, pointed out the error in the gold standard, and recommended its correction. Repeated reports of committees, in both Houses of Congress had done the same thing. Of these reports, he would name those of the late Mr. Lowndes, of South Carolina; of Mr. Sanford, late a Senator from New York; of Mr. Campbell P. White, now a Representative from the city of New York. Mr. B. took pleasure in recalling, and presenting to public notice, the names of the eminent men who had gone before him in the exploration of this path. It was due to them, now that the good cause seemed to be in the road to success, to yield to them all the honors of first explorers; it was due to the cause also, in the hour of final trial, to give it the high sanction of their names and labors.

* "The present rate was the result of information clearly incorrect, respecting the then value of gold and silver in Europe, which was represented as being at the rate of less than 15 to 1, when it was, in fact, from 15.5 to 15.6:1. It would be better, at all events, to discontinue altogether the coining of gold than to continue the present system. The average premium on the American gold coins, for the last four-and-a-half years, has been about 5 1-6 on the nominal value."—*Mr. Gallatin's letter to Mr. Ingham, Dec. 31, 1829.*

THE CONGRESSIONAL GLOBE.

PRINTED AND PUBLISHED AT THE CITY OF WASHINGTON, BY BLAIR & RIVES.

23d Congress, 1st Session. | SATURDAY, MARCH 29, 1834. | Vol. I........No. 17.

Mr. B. would arrest for an instant the current of his remarks, to fix the attention of the Senate upon a reflection which must suggest itself to the minds of all considerate persons. He would ask how it could happen that so many men, and such men as he had named, laboring for so many years, in a cause so just, for an object so beneficial, upon a state of facts so undeniable, could so long and so uniformly fail of success? How could this happen? Sir, exclaimed, Mr. B., it happened because the policy of the Bank of the United States required it to happen! The same policy which required gold to be undervalued in 1792, when the first bank was chartered, has required it to be undervalued ever since, now that a second bank has been established; and the same strength which enabled these banks to keep themselves up, also enabled them to keep gold down. This is the answer to the question, and this the secret of the failure of all these eminent men in their laudable efforts to raise gold again to the dignity of money. This is the secret of their failure; and this secret being now known, the road which leads to the reformation of the gold currency, lies uncovered and revealed before us: it is the road which leads to the overthrow of the Bank of the United States—to the sepulchre of that institution; for while that bank lives, or has the hope of life, gold cannot be restored to life. Here, then, lies the question of the reformation of the gold currency. If the bank is defeated, that currency is reformed; if the bank is victorious, gold remains degraded, to continue an article of merchandise in the hands of the bank, and to be expelled from circulation to make room for its five, its ten, and its twenty dollar notes. Let the people, then, who are in favor of restoring gold to circulation, go to work in the right place, and put down the power that first put down gold, and which will never suffer that coin to rise while it has power to prevent it.

Mr. B. did not think it necessary to descant, and expatiate upon the merits and advantages of a gold currency. These advantages had been too well known, from the earliest ages of the world, to be a subject of discussion in the nineteenth century; but as it was the policy of the paper system to disparage that metal, and as that system in its forty years reign over the American people had nearly destroyed a knowledge of that currency, he would briefly enumerate its leading and prominent advantages. 1. *It has an intrinsic value;* which gave it currency all over the world, to the full amount of that value, without regard to laws or circumstances. 2. *It had a uniformity of value;* which made it the safest standard of the value of property which the wisdom of man had ever yet discovered. 3. *Its portability;* which made it easy for the traveller to carry it about with him. 4. *Its indestructibility;* which made it the safest money that people could keep in their houses. 5. *Its inherent purity;* which made it the hardest money to be counterfeited, and the easiest to be detected, and, therefore, the safest money for the people to handle. 6. *Its superiority over all other money;* which gave to its possessor the choice and command of all other money. 7. *Its power over exchanges;* gold being the currency which contributes most to the equalization of exchange, and keeping down the rate of exchange to the lowest, and most uniform, point. 8. *Its power over the paper money;* gold being the natural enemy of that money, and, with fair play, able to hold it in check. 9. *It is a constitutional currency;* and the people have a right to demand it, for their currency, as long as the present Constitution is permitted to exist.

Mr. B. said, that the false valuation put upon gold had rendered the mint of the United States, so far as the gold coinage is concerned, a most ridiculous and absurd institution. It has coined, and that at a large expense to the United States, [illegible],717 pieces of gold, worth $11,852,890; and where are these pieces now? Not one one of them to be seen! all sold, and exported! And so regular is this operation that the Director of the Mint, in his latest report to Congress, says, that the new coined gold frequently remains in the mint, uncalled for, though ready for delivery, until the day arrives for a packet to sail to Europe. He calculates that two millions of native gold will be coined annually hereafter; the whole of which, Mr. B. said, without a reform of the gold standard, will be conducted, like exiles, from the national mint to the sea shore, and transported to foreign regions, to be sold for the benefit of the Bank of the United States.

Mr. B. said this was not the time to discuss the relative value of gold and silver, nor to urge the particular proportion which ought to be established between them. That would be the proper work of a committee At present it might be sufficient, and not irrelevant, to say that this question was one of commerce—that it was purely and simply a mercantile problem—as much so as an acquisition of any ordinary merchandise from foreign counties could be. Gold goes where it finds its value, and that value is what the laws of great nations give it. In Mexico and South America—the countries which produce gold, and from which the United States must derive their chief supply—the value of gold is 16 to 1 over silver; in the Island of Cuba it is 17 to 1; in Spain and Portugal it is 16 to 1; in the West Indies, generally, it is the same. It is not to be supposed that gold will come from these countries to the United States if the importer is to lose one dollar in every sixteen that he brings; or that our own gold will remain with us, when an exporter can gain a dollar upon every fifteen that he carries out. Such results would be contrary to the laws of trade; and therefore we must place the same value upon gold that other nations do, if we wish to gain any part of theirs, or to retain any part of our own. Mr. B. said that the case of England and France was no exception to this rule. They rated gold at something less than 16 for 1, and still retained gold in circulation; but it was retained by force of peculiar laws and advantages which do not prevail in the United States. In England the circulation of gold was aided and protected by four subsidiary laws, neither of which exists here; one which prevented silver from being a tender for more than forty shillings; another which required the Bank of England to pay all its notes in gold; a third which suppressed the small note circulation; a fourth which alloyed their silver nine per cent. below the value of pure silver. In France the relative proportion of the two metals was also below what it was in Spain, Portugal, Mexico, and South America, and still a plentiful supply of gold remained in circulation; but this result was aided by two peculiar causes: *first*, the total absence of a paper currency; *secondly*, the proximity of Spain, and the inferiority of Spanish manufactures, which gave to France a ready and a near market for the sale of her fine fabrics, which were paid for in the gold of the New World. In the United States gold would have none of these subsidiary helps; on the contrary it would have to contend with a paper currency, and would have to be obtained—the product of our own mines excepted—from Mexico and South America, where it is rated as 16 to 1 for silver. All these circumstances, and many others, would have to be taken into consideration in fixing a standard for the United States. Mr. B. repeated that there was nicety, but no difficulty, in adjusting the relative value of gold and silver so as to retain both in circulation. Several nations of antiquity had done it; some modern nations also. The English have both in circulation at this time. The French have both, and have had for thirty years. The States of this Union also had both in the time of the Confederation, and retained them until this Federal Government was established, and the paper system adopted. Congress should not admit that it cannot do for the citizens of the United States, what so many monarchies have done for their subjects. Gentlemen, especially, who decry military chieftains, should not confess that they themselves cannot do for America, what a military chieftain did for France. Above all, those who are now engaged in decrying the State governments, and representing them as unfit to be trusted with their currency without a master, should not come out with a practical confession, that this boasted Federal Government cannot perform for the Union what the State governments, each for itself, performed for its citizens, for the whole period which elapsed from the close of the Revolution to the establishment of this Government.

Mr. B. made his acknowledgments to the great apostle of American liberty (Mr. Jefferson) for the wise practical idea, that the value of gold was a commercial question, to be settled by its value in other countries. He had seen that remark in the works of that great man, and treasured it up, as teaching the plain and ready way to accomplish an apparently difficult object; and he fully concurred with the Senator from South Carolina, [Mr. Calhoun,] that gold, in the United States, ought to be the preferred metal—not that silver should be expelled, but both retained; the mistake, if any, to be in favor of gold, instead of being against it.

IV. Mr. B. believed that it was the intention, and declared meaning, of the Constitution, that foreign coins should pass currently as money, and at their full value, within the United States; that it was the duty of Congress to promote the circulation of these coins, by giving them their full value; that this was the design of the States, in conferring upon Congress the exclusive power of regulating the value of these coins; that all the laws of Congress for preventing the circulation of foreign coins, and underrating their value, were so many breaches of the Constitution, and so many mischiefs inflicted upon the States; and that it was the bounden duty of Congress to repeal all such laws, and to restore foreign coins to the same free and favored circulation which they possessed when the Federal Constitution was adopted.

In support of the first branch of his *first* proposition, Mr. B. quoted the words of the Constitution which authorized Congress to regulate the value of foreign coins; *secondly*, the clause in the Constitution which authorized Congress to provide for punishing the counterfeiting of current coin, in which term foreign coin was included; *thirdly*, the clause which prohibited the States from making anything but gold and silver coin a tender in payment of debts—a clause which did not limit the prohibition to domestic coins, and therefore included foreign ones. These three clauses, he said, were concurrent, and put foreign coin and domestic coin upon the same precise footing of equality in every particular which concerned their current circulation, their value, and their protection from counterfeiters. Historical recollections were the next evidence to which Mr. B. referred to sustain his position. He said that foreign coins were the only coins known in the United States at the adoption of the Constitution. No mint had been established up to that time. The coins of other nations furnished the currency, and the exclusive metallic currency, which the States had used from the close of the revolutionary war up to the formation of this Federal Government. It was these foreign coins, then, which the framers of the Constitution had in view when they inserted all the clauses in the Constitution which bear upon the value and current circulation of coin; its protection from counterfeiters, and the prohibitory restriction upon the States with respect to the illegality of tenders of anything except of gold and silver. To make this point still plainer, if plainer it could be made, Mr. B. adverted to the early statutes of Congress which related to foreign coins. He had seen no less than nine statutes, passed in the first four years of the action of this Federal Government, all enacted for the purpose of regulating the value, protecting the purity, and promoting the circulation of these coins. Not only the well-known coins of the principal nations were provided for in these statutes, but the coins of all the nations with whom we traded, how rare or small

might be the coin, or how remote or inconsiderable might be the nation. By a general provision of the act of 1789, the gold coins of *all nations* which equalled those of England, France, Spain, and Portugal in fineness, were to be current at 89 cents the pennyweight; and the silver coins of *all nations* which equalled the Spanish dollar in fineness, were to be current at 111 cents the ounce. Under these general provisions, a great influx of the precious metals took place. Doubloons, guineas, half joes, were the common and familiar currency of farmers and laborers, as well as of merchants and traders. Every substantial citizen then kept in his house a pair of small scales to weigh gold, which are now used by his posterity to weigh physic. It is a great many years—a whole generation has grown up—since these scales were used for their original purpose; nor will they ever be needed again for that use until the just and wise laws of '89 and '90, for the general circulation of foreign coins shall again be put in force. These early statutes, added to historical recollections, could leave no doubt of the true meaning of the Constitution, and that foreign coins were intended to be forever current within the United States.

With this obvious meaning of the Constitution, and the undeniable advantage which redounded to the United States from the acquisition of the precious metals from all foreign nations, the inquiry naturally presents itself to know for what reasons these coins have been outlawed by the Congress of the United States, and driven from circulation. The inquiring mind wishes to know how Congress could be brought, in a few short years after the adoption of the Constitution, to contradict that instrument in a vital particular—to repeal the nine statutes which they had passed in favor of foreign coin—and to illegalize the circulation of that coin whose value they were to regulate, and whose purity to protect.

Sir, (said Mr. B.,) I am unwilling to appear always in the same train, tracing up all the evils of our currency to the same fountain of mischief—the introduction of the paper system, and the first establishment of a Federal bank among us; but justice must have its sway, historical truth must take its course, facts must be told, and authentic proof shall supply the place of narrative and assertion. We ascend, then, to the year '91—to the exhibition of the plan for the support of public credit—and see in that plan, as one of its features, a proposition for the establishment of a national mint, and in that establishment, a subsidiary engine for the support of the Federal bank. We have already seen, that in the proposition for the establishment of the mint, gold was largely undervalued, and that this undervaluation has driven gold from the country, and left a vacuum for the circulation of Federal bank notes; we are now to see that the same mint establishment was to give further aid to the circulation of these notes by excluding foreign coins, both gold and silver, from circulation, and thus enlarging the vacuum which was to be filled by bank paper. This is what we are now to see; and to see it, we will look at the plan for the support of public credit, and that feature of the plan which proposes the establishment of a national mint.

THE REPORT.—*Extract.*

"The last point to be discussed, respects the 'currency of foreign coins. The abolition of this, 'in proper season, is a necessary part of the system contemplated for the national coinage. But 'this it will be expedient to defer, till some considerable progress has been made in preparing '*substitutes* for them. A gradation may, therefore, 'be found most convenient. The foreign coins 'may be suffered to circulate, precisely upon their 'present footing, for one year after the mint shall 'have commenced its operations. The privilege 'may then be continued for another year, to the 'gold coins of Portugal, England, and France, and 'to the silver coins of Spain; and these may be 'permitted to be current for one year more, *at the rates allowed to be given for them at the mint;* after 'the expiration of which, the circulation of all foreign coins to cease. The moneys which will be 'paid into the treasury during the first year, being 'recoined before they are issued anew, will afford 'a partial substitute, before any interruption is 'given to the preëxisting supplies of circulation. 'The revenues of the succeeding year, and the 'coins which will be brought to the mint, *in consequence of the discontinuance of their currency,* will 'materially extend the *substitute* in the course of 'that year; and its extension will be so far increased during the third year, by the facility of 'procuring the remaining specie to be recoined, 'which will arise from the *diminution of their current values,* as probably to enable the dispensing 'wholly with the circulation of the foreign coins 'after that period. THE PROGRESS WHICH THE 'CURRENCY OF BANK BILLS WILL BE LIKELY TO 'HAVE MADE, DURING THE SAME TIME, WILL ALSO 'AFFORD A SUBSTITUTE OF ANOTHER KIND. It may, 'nevertheless, be advisable to repose a discretionary authority in the President of the United 'States, to continue the currency of the *Spanish* 'dollar, *at a value corresponding with the quantity of fine silver in it,* beyond the period above mentioned for the cessation of the circulation of 'foreign coins."

Mr. B. would remark that four points were presented in this extract: 1st, The eventual abolition of the currency of foreign coins; 2d, The reduction of their value while allowed to circulate; 3d, The substitution of domestic coins; and 4th, The substitution of bank notes, in place of the uncurrent and undervalued foreign coins. Such were the recommendations of Secretary Hamilton; and legislative enactments quickly followed to convert his recommendations into law. The only power the Constitution had given to Congress over foreign coins was, a power to regulate their value, and to protect them from debasement by counterfeiters. It was certainly a most strange construction of that authority first to underrate the value of these coins, and next, to prohibit their circulation! Yet both things were done. The mint went into operation in 1794; foreign coins were to cease to be a legal tender in 1797; but, at the end of that time, the contingencies on which the Secretary calculated to enable the country to do without foreign coins, had not occurred; the substitutes had not appeared; the mint had not supplied the adequate quantity of domestic coin, nor had the circulation of *bank notes* become sufficiently familiar to the people to supersede gold. The law for the exclusion of foreign coins was found to be impracticable, and a suspension of it for three years was enacted. At the end of this time, the evil was found to be as great as ever; and a further suspension of three years was made. This third term of three years also rolled over; the supply of domestic coins was still found to be inadequate, and the people continued to be as averse as ever to the *bank-note substitute.* A fourth suspension of the law became necessary, and in 1806 a further suspension for three years was made; after that a fifth, and finally a sixth, suspension, each for the period of three years; which brought the period for the actual and final cessation of the circulation of foreign coins, to the month of November, 1819. From that time, there was no further suspension of the prohibitory act. An exception was continued, and still remains, in favor of Spanish milled dollars, and parts of dollars; but all other foreign coins, even those of Mexico, and all the South American States, have ceased to be a legal tender, and have lost their character of current money within the United States. Their value is degraded to the mint price of bullion; and thus the constitutional currency becomes an article of merchandise and exportation. Even the Spanish milled dollar, though continued as a legal tender, is valued, not as money, but for the pure silver in it; and is therefore undervalued three or four per cent., and becomes an article of merchandise. The Bank of the United States has collected and sold $4,456,000 of them. Every money dealer is employed in buying, selling, and exporting them. The South and West, which receives them, is stripped of them. The letter read in the Senate two days ago from the brokers in Georgia, to exculpate themselves from erroneous representations on this floor, contained a striking proof of this fact. It stated that, in the sum of $334,000 of silver drawn by them out of the United States branch bank in Savannah, there were 27,700 *Spanish* dollars; that these *Spanish* dollars were not paid over to the State banks in Georgia, which had contracted for the silver, but remitted to New York, where they commanded a premium of three or four per cent. Mr. B. did not mention this circumstance as a thing objectionable in those who did it; if they had not drawn them from the branch bank, that branch would have remitted them to the mother bank, and she would have sold them; and the fact of being paid any part of their demand in *Spanish* dollars, was proof that their specie was out! His object was to fix public attention upon the fact of the undervaluation of silver, as well as of gold, and the consequent abstraction of that coin from the South and West, and the exportation of it from the country.

Having gone through this narrative of facts, and shown the exclusion of foreign coins from circulation to be a part of the paper system, and intended to facilitate the substitution of a bank note currency, Mr. B. went on to state the injuries resulting from the measure. At the head of these injuries he was bound to place the violation of the Constitution of the United States, which clearly intended that foreign coins should circulate among us, and which, in giving Congress authority to regulate their value, and to protect them from counterfeiters, could never have intended to stop their circulation, and to abandon them to debasement. 2. He denounced this exclusion of foreign coins as a fraud, and a fraud of the most injurious nature, upon the people of the States. The States had surrendered their power over the coinage to Congress; they made the surrender in language which clearly implied that their currency of foreign coins was to be continued to them; yet that currency is suppressed; a currency of intrinsic value, for which they paid interest to nobody, is suppressed; and a currency without intrinsic value, a currency of paper, subject to every fluctuation, and for the supply of which corporate bodies receive interest, is substituted in its place. 3. He objected to this suppression, as depriving the whole Union, and especially the western States, of their due and necessary supply of hard money. Since that law took effect, the United States had only been a thoroughfare for foreign coins to pass through. All that was brought into the country had to go out of the country. It was exported as fast as imported. The custom-house books proved this fact. They proved that from 1821 to 1833, the imports of specie were $89,428,463; the exports, for the same time, were $88,891,433; lacking but three-quarters of a million of being precisely equal to the imports! Some of this coin was recoined before it was exported; a foolish and expensive operation on the part of the United States; but the greater part was exported in the same form that it was received. Mr. B. had only been able to get the exports and imports from 1821; if he could have obtained those of 1820, and the concluding part of 1819, when the prohibitory law took effect, the amount would have been about ninety-six millions of dollars; the whole of which was lost to the country by the prohibitory law, while much of it would have been saved, and retained for home circulation, if it had not been for this law. The loss of this great sum in specie was an injury to the whole Union, but especially to the western States, whose sole resource for coin was from foreign countries; for the coinage of the mint could never flow into that region; there was nothing in the course of trade, and exchanges, to carry money from the Atlantic States to the West; and the mint, if it coined thousands of millions, could not supply them. The taking effect of the law in the year 1819, was an aggravation of the injury. It was the most unfortunate and ruinous of all times for driving specie from the country. The western banks, from their exertions to aid the country during the war, had stretched their issues to the utmost limit; their notes had gone into the land offices, the Federal Government turned them over to the Bank of the United States, and that bank demanded specie. Thus, their necessity for specie was increased at the very moment that the supply was diminished, and the general stoppage of the western banks was the inevitable, and natural, result of these combined circumstances.

Mr. B. then read an extract from the memorial of the General Assembly of Louisiana, dated March, 1820, remonstrating against the PERNICIOUS CONSEQUENCES of the law for the exclusion of foreign coins, and praying that it might be REPEALED.

THE MEMORIAL.—*Extract.*

"The General Assembly of the State of Louisiana respectfully represent:

"That the law passed at the last session of Congress, providing that from and after the 1st day of November, 1819, foreign gold coin should cease to be current in the United States, has produced in this State *the most pernicious consequences.* * * Those real advantages (importation of gold from Spanish America) have disappeared under the operation of the law above mentioned. Inasmuch as doubloons have ceased to be current in the United States, no reasonable hope can be entertained that traders will persist in *bringing them here*, when in all parts of the West Indies they can easily, and at an advantageous rate, exchange them for every kind of commodities and necessary supplies. * * * Was that law intended to place at the disposal of Government, for coinage, a sufficient quantity of gold? If such was its object, it appears improbable that it will be attained, inasmuch as gold being received at a very high rate at the Havana, and several other places, it will be purchased here for *exportation* at a low price by the moneyed men.' * * * 'It appears that Congress, when they fixed a term after which that money should cease to be current in the United States, had reason to believe, that before the time prescribed, a quantity of American eagles, nearly equal to the amount of the foreign specie withdrawn, would be thrown into circulation; *but the General Assembly do not perceive* that that object has been fulfilled; *and even had it been, they could not have viewed, without regret*, the adoption of a measure which tends sensibly to affect the commercial relations between LOUISIANA and MEXICO, and which would flourish as formerly, if a more immediate protection was extended to our navigation in those quarters, (against pirates,) *and the above-mentioned law repealed.*"

Having shown the great evils resulting to the country from the operation of this law, Mr. B. called upon its friends to tell what reason could now be given for not repealing it? He affirmed that, of the two causes to which the law owed its origin, one had failed *in toto*, and the other had succeeded to a degree to make it the curse and the nuisance of the country. One reason was to induce an adequate supply of foreign coins to be brought to the mint to be recoined, the other to facilitate the substitution of a bank note currency.

The foreign coins did not go to the mint, those excepted which were imported in its own neighborhood, and even these were exported nearly as fast as recoined. The authority of the directors of the mint had already been quoted to show that the new coined gold was transferred direct from the national mint to the packet ships bound to Europe. The custom-house returns showed the large exportation of domestic coins. They would be found under the head of *Domestic Manufactures exported*, and made a large figure in the list of these exports. In the year 1832 it amounted to $2,058,474, and in the year 1833 to $1,410,941, and every year it was more or less, so that the national mint had degenerated into a domestic manufactory of gold and silver for exportation to foreign countries. But the coins imported at New Orleans, at Charleston, and at other points remote from Philadelphia, did not go there to be recoined. They were, in part, exported direct from the place of import, and in part used by the people as current money, in disregard of the prohibitory law of 1819. But the greater part was exported, for no owner of foreign coin could incur the trouble, risk, and expense of sending it some hundred or a thousand miles to Philadelphia to have it recoined, and then incurring the same expense, risk, and trouble, laying out of the use of the money, and receiving no interest all the while, of bringing it back to be put in circulation, with the further risk of a deduction for want of standard fineness at the mint, when he could sell and export it upon the spot. Foreign coins could not be recoined so as to supply the Union by a solitary mint on the Atlantic coast. The great West could only be supplied from New Orleans. A branch of the mint placed there, could supply the West with domestic coins. Mexico, since she became a free country, has established seven mints in different places,* because it was troublesome and expensive to carry bullion from all parts of the country to be coined in the capital; and when coined there, there was nothing in the course of trade to carry them back into the country, and the owners of it would not be at the expense and trouble of carrying it back and get it into circulation, being the exact state of things at present in the gold-mines of the southern States. The United States, upon the same principle, and for the same reasons, should establish branches of the mint in the South, convenient to the gold mine region, and at New Orleans, for the benefit of that city and the West. Without a branch of the mint at New Orleans the admission of foreign coins is indispensable to the West, and thus the *interest* of that region joins itself to the voice of the Constitution in demanding the immediate repeal of all laws for illegalizing the circulation of these coins, and for sinking them from their current value as money to their mint value as bullion. The design of supplying the mint with foreign coins for recoinage had then failed, and in that respect the exclusion of foreign coins has failed in one of its objects; in the other, that of making room for a SUBSTITUTE of BANK NOTES, the success of the scheme has been complete, excessive, and deplorable.

Mr. B. said, that in demanding the restoration of foreign coins, he was not preferring a new or unheard-of demand before the Senate. It was evident, from the great number of times that the law for the exclusion of foreign coins had been suspended, so as to postpone its final taking effect from 1793 to 1819—a period of twenty-six years—that the opposition of the community to it was deep and abiding, and only overcome after a quarter of a century of perseverance on the part of the Federal Government, and in the complete triumph of the paper system, in the establishment, for the second time, of a Bank of the United States, and making the promissory notes of its corporators a legal tender to the Federal Government, and equal in law to the gold and silver of the Constitution. The people had struggled for twenty-six years for the preservation of their ancient foreign coins, but were vanquished at last. In the course of this struggle, many reports from committees of Congress, and many memorials from State Legislatures, were brought before Congress, to arrest the impending fate of hard money. To read all these reports and memorials, would be tedious; to omit all, would be unjust to the subject. He (Mr. B.) had selected two of these papers, both of them peculiarly applicable to the present state of things. One of these papers (the memorial from the General Assembly of Louisiana) he had read; the other, being a report from a committee of the House of Representatives, of which Mr. Quincy, then a member from Massachusetts, was chairman, would now be read, and would derive peculiar interest from being the offspring of similar circumstances to those in which the United States are now placed. The report was made in 1811, in view of the approaching termination of the charter of the first Bank of the United States, and all its reasonings and conclusions are applicable to the present moment.

MR. QUINCY'S REPORT.—*Extract.*

"That the general design of the bill (from the Senate) being to increase the current money of the United States, by authorizing foreign gold and silver coins again to become a legal tender, is important in its object, and may be beneficial in its consequences. It is very apparent, that the denial to foreign coins of the privileges of currency, and of being a legal tender, has at once the combined effect of *circumscribing* the just sphere of mercantile action, and of encouraging the *exportation* of that species of coin, to which these privileges are denied. In the present circumstances of the United States, it seems peculiarly unadvisable to permit any statute prohibitions to continue, which have a tendency to produce such an effect. The statute currency of the United States, which now consists only of the coinage of the United States and the Spanish milled dollars, and parts of dollars, is also probably insufficient for the ordinary necessities of domestic exchange, and is certainly wholly inadequate to support any peculiar embarrassment of our circulating medium, which, in the event of the dissolution of the Bank of the United States, cannot but be anticipated. Your committee were, therefore, of opinion, that foreign coin ought to be made current money, and a legal tender."

The report of the committee, Mr. B. said, was complied with. Foreign coins were again made a legal tender, their value regulated, and their importation encouraged. This continued to be the case until after the present Bank of the United States was chartered; as soon as that event happened, and bank policy again became predominant in the halls of Congress, the circulation of foreign coins was again struck at; and, in the second year of the existence of the bank, the old act of 1793, for rendering these coins uncurrent, was carried into final and complete effect. Since that time the bank has enjoyed all her advantages from this exclusion. The expulsion of these coins has created a vacuüm, to be filled up by her small note circulation; the traffic, and trade in them, has been as large a source of profit to her as of loss to the country. Gold coin she has sold at an advance of five or six per cent.; silver coin at about two or three per cent.; and, her hand being in, she made no difference between selling domestic coin and foreign coin. Although forbid by her charter to deal in coin, she has employed her branches to gather $40,000,000 of coin from the States, a large part of which she admits that she has sold and transported to Europe. For the sale of the foreign coin, she sets up the lawyer-like plea, that it is not coin, but bullion! resting the validity of the plea upon English statute law! while, by the Constitution of the United States, all foreign coins, are coins; while by her own charter the coins, both gold and silver, of Great Britain, France, Spain, Portugal, and their dominions, are declared to be coin, and as such, made receivable in payment of the specie proportion of the bank stock; and, worse yet, while Spanish dollars, by statute, remain the current coin of the United States, of which Spanish milled dollars the bank admits the sale of $4,450,-142.

Mr. B. then took a rapid view of the present condition of the statute currency of the United States—of that currency which was a legal tender—that currency which a debtor had a right by law to protect his property from execution, and his body from jail, by offering it, as a matter of right, to his creditor in payment of his debt. He stated this statute currency to be, *first*, coins from the mint of the United States; *secondly*, Spanish milled dollars and the parts of such dollars. This was the sum total of the statute currency of the United States; for happily no paper of any bank, State or Federal, could be made a legal tender. This is the sum total out of which any man in debt can legally pay his debts; and what is his chance for making payment out of this brief list? Let us see. Coinage from the mint: not a particle of gold, nor a single whole dollar, to be found! very few half dollars, except in the neighborhood of the mint, and in the hands of the Bank of the United States and its branches; the 25, 10, and 5 cent pieces scarcely seen, except as a curiosity in the interior parts of the country. So much for the domestic coinage. Now for the Spanish milled dollars. How do they stand in the United States? Nearly as scarce as our own dollars; for there has been none coined since Spain lost her dominion over her colonies in the New World; and the coinage of these colonies, now independent States, neither is in law, nor in fact, Spanish milled. That term belongs to the coinage of the Spanish crown, with a Spanish king's head upon the face of it; although the coin of the new States, the silver dollars of Mexico, Central America, Peru, and Chili, are superior to Spanish dollars in value, because they contain more pure silver; still they are not a tender; and all the francs from France,

* By the Federal Constitution of Mexico, dated October, 4, 1824, the Federal Congress has the exclusive power to fix the weight, standard, and value of money, but the coinage goes on in Guanajuato, Zacatecas, Guadalajara, Durango, Chihuahua, and Sombrerete. Before the constitution of 1824 each State fixed the weight, standard, and value of its own money, and all uniformity of value was destroyed; now the general Congress fixes it, the value is uniform.

in a word, all foreign coin, except Spanish milled dollars, the coinage of which has ceased, and the country stripped of all that were in it, by the Bank of the United States, are uncurrent, and illegal as tenders; so that the people of the United States are reduced to so small a list and so small a supply of statute currency out of which debts can legally be paid, that it may be fairly assumed that the whole debtor part of the community lie at the mercy of their creditors, to have their bodies sent to jail, or their property sold for nothing, at any time that their creditors please. To such a condition are the free and high-minded inhabitants of this country reduced—and reduced by the power and policy of the first and second Banks of the United States, and the controlling influence which they have exercised over the moneyed system of the Union from the year 1791 down to the present day.

Mr. B. would conclude what he had to say on this head with one remark; it was this: that while the gold and silver coin of all the monarchs of Europe were excluded from circulation in the United States, the paper notes of their subjects were received as current money. The Bank of the United States was, in a great degree, a foreign institution. Foreigners held a great part of its stock, and may hold it all. The paper notes issued by this institution, thus composed in great part of the subjects of European kings, are made legal tenders to the Federal Government, and thus forced into circulation among the people; while the gold and silver coin of the kings to which they belong is rejected and excluded, and expelled from the country! He demanded if anything could display the vice and deformity of the paper system in a more revolting and humiliating point of view than this single fact?

Without concluding, Mr. B., at a quarter before four o'clock, gave way to

Mr. WHITE, on whose motion,

The Senate adjourned.

HOUSE OF REPRESENTATIVES.

Friday, *March* 21, 1834.

Mr. EVANS, from the Committee of Claims, reported a bill for the relief of Richard Hardesty. Read twice, and committed.

Mr. GRENNELL, from the Committee of Claims, made an unfavorable report on the petition of Horatio Tilden; which was read, and laid on the table.

Mr. PARKER, from the Committee on Naval Affairs, made an unfavorable report on the petition of Lieutenant Jonathan D. Ferris; which was read, and laid on the table.

Mr. ASHLEY, from the Committee on Roads and Canals, moved that the Committee of the Whole House be discharged from the further consideration of the two following bills, and refer them to the Committee of the Whole on the state of the Union:

A bill for the continuation of the Cumberland road from the Mississippi river to the city of Jefferson, in the State of Missouri; and

A bill for the survey and location of the Cumberland road from Vandalia to the Mississippi river.

On taking the vote, it was found that a quorum was not present.

Mr. WHITTLESEY, of Ohio, moved a call of the House; which was ordered.

After proceeding for some time in the call, on motion of Mr. WARD, of New York, the call was suspended.

The question being again put, the motion was refused, 81 to 51.

Mr. EVANS, from the Committee on Invalid Pensions, reported a bill granting a pension to John F. Wiley, and increasing the pension of George Field. Read twice and committed.

Mr. HAWKINS obtained leave to offer a resolution, referring a private claim to the Committee on Revolutionary Pensions; which was agreed to.

The House then resumed the consideration of the following resolution, submitted by Mr. Mardis, viz:

Resolved, That the Committee of Ways and Means be instructed to inquire into the expediency of reporting a bill, requiring the Secretary of the Treasury to deposite the public moneys of the United States in the State banks; and, also, as to the expediency of defining by law all contracts hereafter to be made with the Secretary for the safe-keeping, management, and disbursement, of the same.

Mr. BURGES resumed, but had not concluded his remarks when the hour expired.

THE PUBLIC DEPOSITES.

The House resumed the consideration of the resolutions reported from the Committee of Ways and Means, together with the amendment offered by Mr. Wilde, declaring that the reasons of the Secretary of the Treasury for removing the deposites from the United States Bank are unsatisfactory and insufficient.

Mr. GILMER, of Georgia, addressed the House. The subject, he said, was one of more interest than any which had been discussed since the origin of the Government, and he therefore wished to express the views which would govern his vote. His own situation in relation to the subject was peculiar; for he should not vote on the question of the removal of the deposites on the same grounds which others had taken. He begged leave, in the outset, to protest against the manner in which the subject had been discussed. When the gentleman from South Carolina [Mr. McDuffie] proposed his resolution declaring that the deposites ought to be restored, what question did we discuss? Not the question of restoration; for most of the arguments which we heard related to the conduct of the President of the United States in removing the Secretary, and appointing another. The consequence was, that public feeling was misled and excited, and we were led to consider that the question was to be determined, not on its merits, but on our like or dislike of the President of the United States. The question of the power of appointment was connected, in fact, with the removal of the deposites; yet it had no possible connexion with the question whether the public interests required their restoration to the bank. The public interests alone should determine that question. When the power of removal from office was before the first Congress, it was solemnly argued and decided. Were we now better prepared than they were to come to a proper decision of the question? Without saying that their determination was right, he would say that there never was a time when the state of public feeling was so little favorable to a proper determination as the present time.

Another question had been made here, whether the public money, after having been deposited by law, can be removed without the authority of law. Here he entered his dissent to the doctrine advanced in favor of this proposition. From the manner in which the question had been discussed, the people were misled as to the real question before us. What was the true question? It was whether Congress can sell the right to control the public money. In order to ascertain whether the position which had been assumed both by the majority and the minority of the committee, was correct, it would be necessary for him to go into a somewhat extended argument. We created a body corporate and gave it certain rights and privileges, in order to carry into effect the purposes of the Government. To effect these purposes both public and private rights were granted to the bank by law. The public rights were conferred with a view to effect public objects, such as the safe-keeping and easy transportation of public funds. The Government, he contended, had no right to change and modify these rights for the purpose of effecting the objects which were intended by law.

One of the consequences which he must deduce from this position was, that the public money was deposited, not so much for the benefit of the bank as for that of the Government, and that Congress could not sell their control over it or transfer it. An inference had been drawn that one of the benefits which were conferred on the bank arose from the keeping of the public money. But this inference was had, without regarding, what he laid down as incontrovertible—that the money could not be deposited with that view. He who contended that this right was conferred upon the bank by virtue of a contract made between them and Congress, contended for that which Congress had no power vested in them by the Constitution to confer. He argued that this conclusion did not necessarily follow from the act of 1816 incorporating the bank. This inference, however, had not only been drawn from the clause in the charter which conferred exclusive privileges on the bank, but it was also inferred that the bank was entitled to be the depository of the public money, in consequence of the bonus of one million and a half which they had paid. He contended that this bonus was paid for that only which the bank had the right to purchase or the Government the right to confer; and looking to the fact that there were many large capitalists now to be found who were willing to pay six, seven, or ten times the amount paid by the bank for similar exclusive privileges, and without any clause confirming the right of the Government depositing the public money, it was evident the terms upon which they held these privileges were too cheap. There was another argument which he confessed he heard with much surprise, by which it was attempted to excite public feeling in their favor—that was, talking of the sacred right of chartered privileges, and the House had been warned how they should infringe upon these sacred rights. This made it necessary to inquire into the origin of chartered societies, and there was no part, perhaps, of the history of human society so interesting to trace. When originally granted, the people had no rights, they were considered in a state of slavery to the church and feudal nobility; charters were then devised by the crown to enlarge those powers which had been taken from the people by the feudal system so prevalent in Europe in the earlier ages. To them, in consequence, the most liberal encouragement had been given, and society had derived from them more benefit than from any other thing whatever. Upon the original settlement of this country, the colonies had obtained them, to secure to themselves the enjoyment of such privileges as they conferred. But at the Revolution, by which our independence was established, they ceased to be of value. Every man became free, and that which was before so valued became regarded as exclusive monopolies which it was for the interest of society to abolish, as they took from, instead of adding to, the rights vested naturally in every member of society.

Having disposed of the argument by which the right of the bank to the deposites was maintained as arising from contract, he wished to call the attention of the House to what was the principal argument advanced to justify the exercise of the right of removal by the Secretary of the Treasury. He would not apply himself to the sufficiency or insufficiency of the reasons given by him; for he cared not whether they were or not—his argument being to establish the power of the House over the public money. It had been said that the Secretary might interfere in cases where the safety of the public money was concerned, and that this was the only case that could justify him. But he could not consider this reason applicable; for if the safety of the public money only was to be thought of, that safety might be attained as well by keeping the public money where it was collected, in the shape of revenue, at the custom-houses. Such a reason, when assumed as the only one, reminded him of those sages who were looking into a deep well for truth, which was to be found on the surface of the earth. He contended that the public moneys were lodged by the Government for other purposes than that of safety: that they might be used through the bank, to fill up the vacuum which was created by their collection, and thus be used to advance the prosperity of the whole people. Looking, then, to the question whether the deposites should be restored to the Bank of the United States, it becomes necessary to ascertain what the conduct of the bank had been, to satisfy us what it would be. He considered, according to the adage, banks had no soul; their end was to make profit, and their conduct was actuated by this motive. But although he would not go into the charges against the Bank of the United States, it was sufficient to say, that upon the expiration of their charter, a renewal of it was of more immediate importance than any profits they could have by discounts. Such had been proved to be the motive and conduct of the directors of this institution. Was not the first application to Congress for renewal of the charter made shortly before the Presidential election? Why, he asked, did they

select that time for their application? Was it not evidently under the expectation that, as their renewal would be acceded to by Congress, they could deter the President from the exercise of his constitutional veto, or make him immediately responsible for that act to the people? This was evident, when such an application was not necessary at that time for their operations. It was done to control the Government. Instead of curtailing immediately after the veto, they commenced extending their issues from forty-five to seventy millions. What was this increase for? Evidently under the belief that they could influence public opinion in their favor. But the bank was mistaken in this, for public opinion was not to be so influenced. However favors might be conferred on the individual, the bank, as the event proved, had been mistaken in the supposition that public opinion was to be bought up. Their curtailments then commenced, from which so much distress was produced. If, then, Congress were satisfied that the bank had, in any way, contributed to produce it for the purpose of effecting a renewal of their charter, what ought to be their course? Ought they to restore the deposites, and thus grant them additional power to be used for that purpose? Surely not. Those only who considered that the interests of the country would be advanced by renewing the charter, might adopt such a course without blame; but others, who did not agree with them, were bound by every sense of duty to keep from it all further power to do evil.

Mr. G. referred to the clauses in the Constitution giving the money power to Congress; from which he contended that as they had no specific power given to incorporate a bank, they were not authorized to do so by any doctrine of construction or expediency, and that this was a right appertaining to the several States, which they had not yielded, and therefore should not be exercised by the General Government. He knew it was said that it was impossible for the Government to get along without the aid of a national bank. But for one, he must say, that those who believed that the State banks could not discharge the various duties required for the fiscal offices, or supply the community with a safe circulating medium, must be disposed to doubt the stability of the Government under which they lived. The argument was, that the State banks were incapable of doing this, that their notes must be considered equivalent to specie. This, he thought, it was perfectly in their power to do, by the same means which had raised into credit the notes circulated by the United States Bank. The great argument upon which the charter for the United States Bank was advocated was, that it would restore the currency; that it would have the effect of making the State banks pay their notes in specie. Whilst now, what did they see in practice by the bank? Why, that when they received the notes of the State banks, instead of demanding specie from them, they re-issued it, so as to make the currency of the country one of paper alone; and this being the practice of the old United States Bank, had upon the State banks precisely the same effect, which was to render them less solvent than they otherwise would have been. It was said, however, that "it was idle, perfectly ideal and visionary to expect that the notes of the State banks could maintain as safe and general circulation as those of the present Bank of the United States." He would assert, however, that this was possible, and that the effect of encouraging the State banks would be, to make them a safer currency than that of the United States Bank was at present. For they would more effectually compete with one another, and thus each circulating in its own State or neighborhood, they would be the more likely to be called on to pay in specie, and must therefore be always prepared with specie for this purpose.

It was asked how the exchange could be carried on without a bank, between one part of the country and another. How were exchanges now carried on between New York and Liverpool? It was through an interchange of products. No two countries carried on a trade in which one was constantly drawing from the other. If this Government would do its duty as well as the State governments do theirs, all would be right. This Government has the power to coin money, and to regulate the value thereof. Gold was produced and coined in abundance in this country. But this Government, instead of retaining it in the country, suffers it to be transported out of the country, by neglecting to fix and regulate its value in a proper manner. But Mr. G. looked to consequences of vastly more importance. The question was at the foundation of individual interests, and of free government. He believed that he who contributed to the recharter of the Bank of the United States, struck a deadly blow at the liberties of the country. The original question between the federal and anti-federal parties comes up. Is it proper to strengthen this Government by connecting with it a bank of thirty-five millions capital? The Bank of the United States had it in its power to come into the market in every part of the country, and controlling the issues of the State banks, to fix the price of the whole product of the country. By establishing this bank, we give to twenty-five men the power to control the whole property of the Union, and they must use their power for the benefit of the stockholders. But we not only make the value of all property dependent on the use of the authority which we grant the Bank of the United States, but we take from the State authorities the power to resist the usurpations of the Government. There were but two means by which the States could resist oppression: the first by revolution, and the second by the power of the States to exercise authority within their respective limits. How are the States to use either of these means in opposition to the Federal Government? How can they organize any resistance? All the moneyed power is through the National Bank, dependent on Government, and it was the interest of the bank to strengthen the hands of the Government. A national bank, therefore, took from the people both the honor and the inducement to resist oppression. He called on his State-rights friends to look well at this subject. It was idle to say that we were under an obligation, by restoring the deposites, to put it in the power of the bank to force a recharter. The position was erroneous. They had not the power to give or sell to the bank the exclusive control of the public money. He called on them as advocates of the constitutional rights of the States, now to speak out, or to hold their peace forever. This talk of Andrew Jackson as an usurper, had drawn off the attention of the people from the true question before them. The real question for the people to decide was, will you maintain the right of the bank to the people's money; will you agree that you have sold to the bank the control over the public money? It is said this is not a question of recharter. But that was the only question worth contending for, and upon the decision of the question of restoration depended the decision of the question whether the bank shall be rechartered or not.

When Mr. G. concluded,

Mr. CLAY, of Alabama, obtained the floor, and on his motion, the House adjourned.

IN SENATE.

SATURDAY, *March* 22, 1834.

Several messages upon executive business were received from the President of the United States, by Mr. DONELSON, his Private Secretary. Also, a message transmitting a report from the Secretary of State in compliance with a resolution of the Senate of the 7th instant.

Mr. LINN, from the Committee on Private Land Claims, reported a bill for the relief of John B. Folesong and William Russell.

Mr. TIPTON presented a memorial of the Legislative Council of Michigan, praying a modification of the laws of that territory. Referred to the select committee on the subject of the admission of Michigan and Arkansas into the Union.

Mr. TIPTON, from the Committee on Claims, reported a bill for the relief of William Pursell, and on his motion the report accompanying it was ordered to be printed.

Mr. WEBSTER presented the proceedings of a public meeting of the citizens of Franklin county, held at Chambersburg, Pennsylvania, disapproving of the course of the Secretary of the Treasury in removing the deposites; and also a memorial from the same place, signed by upwards of 1800 inhabitants, praying the restoration of the deposites to the Bank of the United States. The proceedings and memorial were read, referred to the Committee on Finance, and ordered to be printed.

Mr. EWING, in pursuance of previous notice, asked and obtained leave to bring in a bill settling the northern boundary line of the State of Ohio; which was read and referred to the Committee on the Judiciary.

Mr. ROBBINS presented memorials from the towns of Newport, Cumberland, and Smithfield, Rhode Island, praying the restoration of the deposites to the Bank of the United States; which were read, referred to the Committee on Finance, and ordered to be printed.

Petitions of a private nature were presented by Messrs. TYLER, ROBINSON, and POINDEXTER, which were appropriately referred.

Mr. LINN submitted the following resolution:

Resolved, That the Committee on the Post Office and Post Roads be instructed to inquire into the expediency of establishing a post road from the town of Jackson, Cape Girardeau county, Missouri, to Bailey's store, in Stoddard county.

The first special order of the day being announced,

Mr. POINDEXTER moved to postpone it until Monday, in order to proceed with private business. This being objected to by Mr. WEBSTER, Mr. P. withdrew his motion.

On motion of Mr. PRENTISS, the message of the President, and the accompanying documents, were ordered to be printed.

Mr. SMITH, from the Committee on the Judiciary, reported a bill for the relief of Thomas L. Winthrop and others, directors of the New England Mississippi Land Company. The report was ordered to be printed.

Mr. FORSYTH presented a memorial of upwards of three hundred voters of the town of Petersburg, Virginia, complaining of a memorial lately presented to the Senate from that place, and expressing their approbation of the act of the Secretary of the Treasury in removing the deposites, and averse to the recharter of the Bank of the United States. The memorial was read, referred to the Committee on Finance, and ordered to be printed.

Mr. LEIGH presented the memorial of citizens of Princess Ann county, Virginia, of an opposite character to the foregoing, which was read, and referred as above.

The first special order, being the consideration of leave to introduce a bill extending the charter of the Bank of the United States, was then taken up.

Mr. BENTON continued and concluded his speech. [It is too lengthy for the columns of the Congressional Globe.]

Mr. WHITE obtained the floor, and intimated his disposition to proceed then, or postpone his remarks until Monday, as might be the pleasure of the Senate.

Mr. BENTON suggested an adjournment.

Mr. WEBSTER was desirous of extending every facility to gentlemen who wished to address the Senate on this subject, but as this was but a preliminary question, he trusted much time would not be consumed upon it, and hoped that gentlemen would not regard it as wanting in courtesy, if, after this, he should press the matter to a conclusion.

Mr. CLAY said he, too, had a special order long locked up in the debates of the Senate, and expressed his wish that another week would bring it to a close.

Mr. FORSYTH said gentlemen might have had decisions long ago, if they had forborne making long speeches upon the presentation of memorials.

On motion of Mr. WRIGHT, the Senate proceeded to executive business; and, after spending some time therein, adjourned.

HOUSE OF REPRESENTATIVES.

SATURDAY, *March* 22, 1834.

Mr. BINNEY, from the Committee of Ways and Means, to whom was referred the memorial of the Commercial Bank of New Orleans, made an unfavorable report thereon, and it was laid on the table.

Mr. KING reported a bill for the relief of David Bartlett; which was read twice, and committed.

The House proceeded with the unfinished business, being an engrossed bill for the relief of Walton & De Graff, to which

Mr. E. WHITTLESEY proposed an amendment, altering the phraseology of the bill, to read as follows: "To allow to them such sum as they 'shall prove they actually lost on the sale of treasury notes on account of current moneys previously advanced and paid by them out of their own 'individual funds for the United States, during the 'last war with Great Britain, for expenditures as 'agents aforesaid, provided they received said 'treasury notes under a contract or agreement that 'they were to be reimbursed in par funds; and 'provided said contract or agreement was not 'rescinded or waived by the parties." Also, restricting the payment on the interest "until the principal was refunded."

The amendment having been agreed to, the bill was ordered to be reëngrossed, and it was subsequently read a third time and passed.

The House proceeded to the consideration of the following resolution, submitted by Mr. Mardis, of Alabama:

Resolved, That the Committee of Ways and Means be instructed to inquire into the expediency of reporting a bill requiring the Secretary of the Treasury to deposite the public moneys of the United States in the State banks; and, also, as to the expediency of defining by law all contracts hereafter to be made with the Secretary for safe-keeping, management, and disbursement of the same.

Mr. BURGES resumed and continued his remarks in opposition to the resolution, until the expiration of the hour allotted for morning business.

Mr. McKIM moved that the rule setting this day apart for the consideration of private bills be suspended, in order to take up the bill making appropriations for the Cumberland road, and repairs, &c., in Ohio, Indiana, and Illinois.

Mr. MERCER proposed as an amendment that the bill for the construction of the Potomac bridge be taken up; and

Mr. ASHLEY, another, to take up therewith the bill for the continuation of the Cumberland road from the Mississippi to Jefferson City, Missouri.

Mr. McKIM accepted these amendments as modifications to his motion.

Mr. PARKER objected to the suspension of the rule, and called for a division of the question, and for the yeas and nays; which having been ordered,

The House refused to suspend the rule for the purpose of taking up the Cumberland road bill—yeas 103, nays 85, (not two-thirds.)

Mr. ASHLEY withdrew his amendment.

The question was then taken upon the second branch of the motion, to suspend the rule for the purpose of taking up for consideration the bill in relation to the Potomac bridge, and decided in the negative.

The following bill was read a third time, and passed:

An act for the relief of John Bills.

The bill to remit the duties on certain pieces of sculpture, was read a third time, and discussed by Messrs. FILLMORE, BINNEY, WILLIAMS, PEARCE of Rhode Island, HUNTINGTON, PARKER, EVERETT of Massachusetts, McINTYRE, and HARDIN, when, the question being taken on its passage, it was rejected: Yeas 135, nays 41.

On motion of Mr. CONNOR,

The House then adjourned.

IN SENATE.

Monday, *March* 24, 1834.

Mr. WEBSTER presented a memorial signed by upwards of 900 inhabitants of the town of Lynn, Massachusetts, praying the restoration of the public deposites to the Bank of the United States, and a recharter of the said corporation. Read, referred to the Committee on Finance, and ordered to be printed.

The VICE PRESIDENT communicated a letter from Lieutenant U. P. Levy, of the United States navy, presenting to Congress a colossal statue of Thomas Jefferson, in bronze, (now in the Rotundo of the Capitol,) made at the private expense of Lieutenant Levy, and under his immediate superintendence. The letter was read, and, on motion of Mr. TYLER, referred to the Joint Library Committee.

The VICE PRESIDENT stated to the Senate that he had received a communication from James Lewis and Adam King, the committee appointed by a meeting of a portion of the people of York, held on the 4th of March last, to communicate the proceedings of that meeting to the Chair, to be laid before the Senate. That the committee in their communication express their regret that any inadvertence in the performance of the duties enjoined upon them by the meeting, had led to the transmission of a paper to the Senate which was not directed to be sent, and was not proper to be received; that they now enclosed, and asked the Chair to lay before the Senate, such portion of the proceedings as the meeting intended for it; that they would have preferred to vary the language of some of the resolutions, but have not the power; that they cannot, however, find in them any disrespect to either House of Congress, and that they are confident none was intended by the meeting; that it is with reluctance they again bring the subject to the notice of the Chair, but that without doing so, they would consider themselves as having unperformed their obligation to their fellow-citizens. The paper now communicated was stated by the Chair to be the resolutions only which had on a former occasion been read to the Senate, without any portion of the preamble then attached to it. The Chair further stated, that the Senate, having heretofore decided not to receive the proceedings of this meeting in the form in which they were then presented, the Chair thought it due to the Senate to leave to its decision the question how far the objections then raised to them have been obviated by the condition in which they are now presented, and by the explanations of the committee, which would be read.

Mr. CLAY inquired whether the presiding officer thought the paper was couched in respectful language?

The CHAIR replied, that it had on a former occasion given its views as to the character of the expressions used in the resolution, which was deemed most objectionable, and which the Chair briefly repeated; but that, under the circumstances of the case, and in view of what had already taken place, the Chair thought it consistent with its duty, and most just to the body, to take its own sense upon that question.

Mr. CLAY said, by the rules and practice of both Houses of Congress, whenever a paper like this was presented, the person presenting it vouched for the respectfulness of its language. If the person did not so vouch, the paper could not be received. He understood that the presiding officer declined doing so, and therefore it ought not to be received. The paper did not come to the Senate in the form in which it ought to come. He therefore moved that the paper be not received.

Mr. WEBSTER said he knew no difference in the application of the rule between the Chair and an individual member of the Senate. If the Chair could decline saying whether the paper was in such language as made it fit to be received or not, then any member of the Senate could also refuse.

Mr. WRIGHT said, if he understood the facts in relation to this paper, it had already been before the Senate, and they had refused to receive it. The paper had since been returned to the place from whence it came, and the objectionable part, he believed, had been struck out; that part was not now here. The objection raised was to the preamble, which is not connected with the proceedings, and to certain mutilations of the paper, not now connected with it. If so, by presenting it in this manner the Chair signified its duty to lay the paper before the Senate, the exceptionable parts being now out of the question.

Mr. CLAY replied, there was some perseverance in this matter beyond what met the eye. The objection was not solely to the mutilation. The paper was now brought back, with an expression on the part of those who sent it that they did not feel authorized to alter the proceedings. In other words, that what had been done by the gentleman from Pennsylvania, [Mr. Wilkins,] in altering the paper, they do not feel authorized to do; and therefore they send it back, with the exception of the preamble. The rule that the preamble is not part of an enactment, was not applicable to the proceedings of public meetings; and that being stricken out, the Chair deems it somewhat questionable as to propriety of language, and throws the responsibility of receiving it on the Senate. Now, he would vote against receiving it, because it was the duty of the Chair to state, whether it was in respectful language or not. The Chair declined doing this, and he was not willing that the responsibility should rest on the Senate, the Chair having declined the preliminary question.

Mr. KING, of Alabama, did not know how far the gentleman from Kentucky intended his remark to go, when he insisted upon every individual who presented papers to the Senate, to vouch for the respectful language in which they were couched. Were they to vouch for every expression contained in them? Had the gentleman read these resolutions? There was nothing disrespectful in them. The preamble was every way exceptionable, but that has been stricken out, and now the resolutions come back in an unexceptionable form. In what terms, he would ask, are petitioners to clothe their meaning or their views? To what parts of these resolutions does the gentleman except. There was but one resolution which could be tortured to apply to any individual in either House of Congress; and that only says that the bank has used its funds to corrupt members of Congress, without designating any one. And had they not a right to say so, if they believed it? He hoped the resolutions would be read, in order that we may see whether there be anything objectionable in them.

Mr. CLAYTON was opposed to receiving the resolutions, because the preamble which had been appended to them was a component part of the whole proceeding, and no one had a right to strike it out.

Mr. PRESTON said that a change of circumstances had made an essential difference in the case. The preamble was now off, and the paper sent back; the agents in this matter say they were not empowered to send the preamble, and therefore they have sent the resolutions; and they have decided that the preamble is not a part of the proceedings. He thought they were the proper persons to decide upon this question; whether they had done so improperly was not for us to decide; but a liberal discretion ought to be allowed them. When the paper was sent to the presiding officer, he was bound to exercise a certain degree of discretion about presenting it. If he had doubts about its propriety, it was proper for him to submit it to the Senate, so that it might be read, and if, in the course of reading, it were found exceptionable, any gentleman might move to dispense with any farther reading, or to refuse to receive the paper. He hoped this might be read for that purpose.

Mr. POINDEXTER said that these proceedings had already been refused by the Senate. There was no power to strike out the preamble—it was as much a part of the proceedings as the resolutions. The same objections he urged to the proceedings before, exist now, and he did not think the letter from the committee cured the defect. There was another objection. Those gentlemen express their regret that they could not strike out the offensive resolution, but say they meant no offence to either House of Congress in the resolution. The resolution did not speak the voice of York county, and if it had, they ought to have called another meeting, and if their proceedings had been respectful, we would have received them. One of these resolutions stated that the Bank of the United States had used its money to purchase support in this and the other House. It was precisely the same paper as the other, and he was decidedly opposed to receiving it, and he thought it ought to be condemned by a vote of the Senate.

Some further remarks were made by Messrs. CALHOUN, LEIGH, EWING, and KANE, when,

On motion of Mr. FRELINGHUYSEN, Mr. Clay's resolution, that the paper be not received, was laid on the table.

SPECIAL ORDER.

The Senate then resumed the consideration of the question granting Mr. WEBSTER leave to bring in a bill to recharter the Bank of the United States.

Mr. WHITE took the floor, and spoke at length against the principles of the bill, as being unconstitutional and inexpedient. At half past three o'clock, Mr. WHITE gave way, without concluding, to Mr. KANE, on whose motion,
The Senate adjourned.

HOUSE OF REPRESENTATIVES.

MONDAY, *March* 24, 1834.

THE VIRGINIA RESOLUTIONS,

Being called, as the unfinished business from the last petition day—

Mr. GAMBLE said, he wished to address the House in reply to remarks by some members who preceded him.

The SPEAKER said, as this debate had already been before the House three weeks, to the prejudice of the presentation of other petitions, he must enforce the rule, to cut off further debate, unless the House should decide against him.

Mr. GAMBLE remarked, that he did not wish to trespass on the House, and would defer what he had to say until an appropriate opportunity should come up.

Mr. MASON then moved that the resolutions should be laid on the table, and printed.

Mr. GORDON hoped that they would be permitted to take the usual course.

The SPEAKER said, that was the usual course.

Mr. PATTON said, he wished to submit a few brief observations in reply; but,

The SPEAKER reminded him of the necessity of conforming to the rule of the House.

The motion to lay on the table, &c., prevailed.

Memorials, petitions, and resolutions, in favor of a restoration of the public deposites to the Bank of the United States, were presented as follows, severally laid on the table, and ordered to be printed, viz:

By Mr. TAYLOR, of New York, from the inhabitants of the village of Syracuse.

By Mr. SELDEN, the proceedings of a meeting of the inhabitants of Brooklyn.

By Mr. HAZELTINE, of Jamestown, Chautauque county.

By Mr. FILLMORE, of Buffalo and its vicinity, in the State of New York.

Mr. MILLER presented the proceedings of a meeting of the citizens of Cumberland county, Pennsylvania, held at the Borough of Carlisle, on the 22d February last. He stated that he had received these proceedings several days ago, perhaps a week, but that this was the first opportunity that had been afforded to present them to the House. This related (he said) complain by their resolution of a deranged state of the currency and of pecuniary embarrassment, which they attribute to the removal of the deposites of the public money from the Bank of the United States, and recommended a restoration of them to the bank, and a recharter of that institution. It was not his purpose to call in question or to canvass the political character or motives of any portion of his constituents. He might be permitted to say, however, that so far as he knew the individuals who composed the meeting, that they were respectable. Of the number attending the meeting, he had not been informed, but had no doubt it was respectable in point of number as well as character, and that their proceedings were entitled to respectful consideration. The proceedings were ordered to be printed, and laid on the table.

He also presented the proceedings of a meeting of the citizens of Carlisle and vicinity, at which resolutions were adopted *approving* of the removal of the deposites, and *opposed* to the recharter of the Bank of the United States. This meeting, he was informed, was numerously attended, and was respectable in point of character as well as number. The proceedings were ordered to be printed, and laid on the table.

He also presented the proceedings of a meeting of citizens of Buffalo township, in the county of Perry, Pennsylvania, disapproving of the removal of the deposites, and in favor of rechartering the bank. The citizens composing it were also respectable. But they had introduced matters of a political character, not connected with legislation, which he thought had better been omitted. But as they were sent to him, he thought it his duty

to present them. The proceedings were laid on the table, and ordered to be printed.

By Mr. WAGENER, a memorial of inhabitants of Northampton county, Pennsylvania.

By Mr. HIESTER, a memorial of inhabitants of the county of Lancaster, and from Berks county, Pennsylvania.

By Mr. SHINN, from the president and directors of the State Bank at Camden, the Farmers' Bank of New Jersey, and the Cumberland Bank at Bridgeton. Also, a memorial from the county of Gloucester, N. J., with the proceedings of a meeting held at Woodbury, on the 15th February last.

Mr. BEARDSLEY presented a memorial from R. B. Miller, and others, praying for an appropriation for the erection of a court-house at Utica, for the use of the United States district court.

Mr. DICKERSON presented resolutions from inhabitants of Paterson, protesting against the recharter of the bank, in favor of the removal of the deposites, and sustaining the course taken by the Executive.

Mr. PARKER, of New Jersey, presented certain resolutions from the Legislature of New Jersey, affirming that their recent instructions to their Senators in Congress spoke the voice of the people of New Jersey in opposition to the recharter of the bank and restoration of deposites, and censuring the conduct of the Senators from that State for not acting in compliance with the instructions given by them.

Mr. McVEAN presented a memorial from inhabitants of Montgomery county, New York, held at Johnstown on the 12th instant, against the restoration of the deposites, and in favor of the course taken by the President.

Mr. LEE, of New Jersey, presented two petitions from Cumberland county, one for and the other against the removal of the deposites and recharter of the bank.

Mr. PAGE presented the petition of inhabitants of Otsego county, New York.

Mr. MILLER presented a petition of a meeting of the citizens of Carlisle and its vicinity, against the renewal of the charter and the restoration of the deposites.

Mr. KING presented the memorial of certain farmers, iron-masters, and other citizens of the lower part of Schuylkill county, Pennsylvania, representing the existence of great embarrassments throughout the county, and praying the interference of Congress for their relief. Read, ordered to be printed, and laid on the table.

Mr. BINNEY presented various resolutions and petitions, praying the restoration of the deposites, from the building mechanics, coach-makers, cabinet-makers, gilders, painters, boot-makers, &c., of the city of Philadelphia, and a memorial also on the same subject from the young men of Philadelphia. Mr. BINNEY made a brief statement of the facts mentioned by the memorialists in support of their views.

The memorials, &c., were read, ordered to be printed, and laid on the table.

Mr. WATMOUGH presented several memorials from citizens of his district, praying the restoration of the deposites and the recharter of the United States Bank; also, the resolutions of a meeting held in that district condemning the measures of the Present Administration.

Mr. WATMOUGH presented the proceedings of a meeting of the third congressional district, in favor of a restoration of the deposites.

A debate ensued between Messrs. SUTHERLAND, WATMOUGH, and BINNEY, which will be given hereafter.

The SPEAKER laid before the House the proceedings of a meeting held in the county of York, in the State of Pennsylvania, approving the removal of the deposites, and expressing the opinion that the United States Bank ought not to be rechartered.

On motion of Mr. BARNITZ, the paper was laid on the table, and ordered to be printed.

Mr. JONES, of Georgia, asked and obtained the leave of the House to make an explanation in regard to some unpleasant difference which lately occurred between two members of this House.

Mr. J. read a paper stating that the difference between two members from South Carolina (Messrs.

PICKENS and BLAIR) had been amicably, satisfactorily, and honorably settled.

Mr. BARNITZ presented a memorial from other inhabitants of York, protesting against the sentiments expressed in the preceding memorial, and in favor of the restoration of the deposites, &c.

Mr. ANTHONY presented two memorials from inhabitants of Lycoming county in favor of the restoration of the deposites.

Mr. CHAMBERS presented three memorials from 1800 inhabitants of Franklin county; from the township of Washington, and from other inhabitants of that county, detailing the pressure that prevailed in that part of the country, which they attribute to the removal of the deposites, and praying their restoration.

Mr. HARPER presented resolutions of watch-makers and silversmiths of the city and county of Philadelphia.

Mr. BURD presented a remonstrance from certain officers on the Niagara frontiers against the passage of a bill before the House for the regulation of half pay.

Mr. SUTHERLAND presented three memorials from Penn township and Lower Dublin, and from a number of inhabitants in Philadelphia, against the restoration of the deposites.

Mr. GALBRAITH presented memorials for and against the restoration of the deposites.

Mr. BANKS, from inhabitants of Cleaveland, in Beaver county, for the restoration of the deposites.

Mr. STEWART, a memorial of 400 inhabitants of Brownsville, praying Congress to take measures to restore the currency.

Sundry memorials were presented by Mr. S. Mr. LEAVITT of Ohio, Mr. BURD, Mr. W. COST JOHNSON, Mr. THOMAS of Maryland, and Mr. CHAMBERS, presented petitions, from various places, for an appropriation to the Chesapeake and Ohio Canal.

Mr. LANE presented the petition of sundry citizens of Dearborn county, in the State of Indiana, praying the establishment of a post route from Rising Sun, in said county, to the town of Versailles, in the county of Ripley, which was referred to the Committee on the Post Office and Post Roads.

Mr. DICKERSON, of New Jersey, remarked, that he had received a memorial, which he presented to the House, signed by more than 700 of the inhabitants of the town of Paterson and its vicinity, in the State of New Jersey. That the memorialists admit that considerable pecuniary pressure and embarrassment exist, and ascribe it, in a great measure, to the vindictive course of the United States Bank, and the panic created by the hireling presses of that institution. They express an opinion that the existence of the bank is dangerous to the rights of the people, and repugnant to the principles of a republican Government. They protest against the restoration of the deposites and the recharter of the bank, and approve the plan suggested by the President and his friends, of gradually introducing into our country a specie currency—and urge upon the House the necessity of speedy action.

He would not say, as was frequently said in the House on similar occasions, that this memorial is signed *without reference to party*. He believed that they were all of one party, and that an inspection of all the memorials upon the tables of members would furnish a very accurate index (so far as they extend) of the political parties of the country. He further remarked that he should do no justice to his constituents and to the House if he attempted to impress a belief that the memorial expressed the views and sentiments of a majority of the wealthy and business part of the town of Paterson.

That he should do violence to his own feelings if he did not state explicitly that he looked in vain over the list annexed to the memorial for the names of many of his own friends and neighbors, who differed with him in their political views generally, and particularly in their views upon the subject of the memorial. That their names would be found upon a memorial of a different character, to be presented to the House, and signed, as he was informed, by about four hundred and fifty of the inhabitants of the same town.

But (Mr. D. remarked) that this memorial was also signed by his friends and neighbors—by more than seven hundred of those very men who admit

that they suffer, and to whom the blessings of property and liberty are as dear as they can be to any others; by men who, at the same time that they suffer, have the sagacity to discover the cause of their sufferings, the boldness to declare that cause, and the firmness to bear up under those sufferings, and support the policy of the Administration of their choice, because they believe that policy best calculated to promote the great and permanent interests of the Republic. In other words, he stated that the memorial was signed by the Democrats and independent workingmen of the town of Paterson and its vicinity.

Read, and laid on the table.

Mr. MASON, of Virginia, presented a memorial from certain inhabitants of Petersburg, stating there was great pressure at present, and their apprehension of greater; praying Congress to take measures by restoring the deposites to the Bank of the United States, in order to mitigate their distress.

Also, a second memorial, from three hundred inhabitants of the same place, denying the facts set forth, and in favor of the course taken by the Executive.

Mr. WISE, of Virginia, presented two memorials from inhabitants of his district, one in favor of, and the other against the restoration of the deposites.

Mr. LOYALL, Mr. CRANE, and Mr. HALL of North Carolina, presented memorials from places whose names we could not hear, and Mr. PATTON one from Fredericksburg and Falmouth, for the restoration of the deposites.

The SPEAKER presented a memorial from the Board of Officers at Jefferson barracks, Missouri, remonstrating against the passage of a bill before the House, regulating half pay; also, from the Legislative Council of Michigan, for claims against the United States for losses, &c.; and one from Commodore James Barron.

All which memorials were appropriately referred.

Mr. PEYTON obtained leave to submit the following resolution, which lies on the table one day for consideration:

Resolved, That the Secretary of War communicate to this House all the correspondence which has taken place in the Department of War since the 4th March, 1829, in reference to a removal or change of the Pension Office operations from the Bank of the United States and its several branches to any of the local banks.

Resolutions were offered, instructing the Committee on the Post Office and Post Roads to inquire into the expediency of establishing post routes from the following places, viz:

By Mr. POLK: From Williamsport, in Maury county, by way of Three-Stone and Snow creek, to Franklin, in Williamson county, Tennessee.

By Mr. BEATTY: From Richmond, Kentucky, passing Slaughter's Salt Works, Mt. Vernon, to Somerset, Pulaski county, and from Monroe to Locust Shade, in Tennessee, to Burkville, Kentucky.

By Mr. FULTON: from Fincastle, Virginia, to Cumberland Gap, Tennessee.

By Mr. LEA: From Maryville, Tennessee, by way of Mount Vail Springs, to intersect the route from Madisonville, Tennessee, to North Carolina, at Hugh Gormley's, on Tennessee river.

By Mr. MOORE: From Pattonsburg, in the county of Botetourt, Virginia, to Clifton Forge, Allegheny county, and from Waynesboro' to Greensville, Augusta county.

By Mr. GRAHAM: From Morgantown, in Burke county, up John's river, to John Mastin's, on Watauga river, in Ashe county.

Mr. DUNLAP submitted the following:

Resolved, That the Committee on Commerce be instructed to inquire into the expediency of establishing a marine hospital at the town of Memphis, on the Mississippi river, for the reception of all sick and disabled persons in anywise engaged in the navigation of said river. Agreed to.

Mr WHITTLESEY, of Ohio, presented a preamble and resolutions from the Legislature of the State of Ohio, praying a grant of land for the Ohio and Pennsylvania canal; which were referred to the Committee on Roads and Canals.

Mr. LYTLE, a memorial of inhabitants of Hamilton county, Ohio, censuring the course taken by one of the Senators from that State, [Mr.

Ewing,] and in favor of the course of the Executive in relation to the currency and the Bank of the United States.

Mr. LEAVITT, a memorial signed by 1700 agricultural inhabitants of Harrison county, Ohio, protesting against the restoration of the deposites, and against the recharter of the Bank of the United States. Also, one of a similar tenor from inhabitants of Jefferson county.

Mr. McLANE, a memorial from the Legislature of Ohio, in relation to the Academy at West Point. Also, one respecting the northern boundary of the State; which were laid on the table, and ordered to be printed.

Mr. MITCHELL, six memorials from inhabitants of Ohio, for the restoration of the deposites and recharter of the bank.

Mr. PATTERSON presented a petition of Silas Pearce, of Richland county, Ohio, a soldier of the Revolution, asking a pension.

Also, the petition of Aaron Mortner, of Huron county, Ohio, asking to be indemnified for property lost in the revolutionary war.

Also, a petition of Ebenezer Smith, of Huron county, Ohio, praying to be placed on the pension list.

Also, a petition of sundry persons for a post route from Tiffin to Bucyrus, in the State of Ohio; all of which were referred to the appropriate committees.

Mr. PATTERSON also offered a resolution directing the Committee on Indian Affairs to inquire into the expediency of making an appropriation to purchase the Wyandot reservation, in the State of Ohio; which was not acted upon for want of a quorum.

Mr. CAGE, of Mississippi, a memorial from inhabitants of Natchez, for the same; which, he stated, met his decided approbation.

Mr. PLUMMER asked leave of the House to address a few remarks in reply to his colleague, as he dissented entirely from the views of the memorialists.

The House refused: ayes 6, noes 15.

Mr. PEARCE moved an adjournment; which he subsequently withdrew.

Mr. CAGE moved a call of the House.

The House refused to second the call: ayes 15, noes 19.

Mr. SELDEN moved an adjournment.

Mr. CARR called for the yeas and nays, which having been ordered,

The motion to adjourn prevailed: yeas 24, nays 21; and the House adjourned.

IN SENATE.

TUESDAY, *March* 25, 1834.

A message upon executive business was received from the President of the United States, by Mr. DONELSON, his Private Secretary.

Mr. MANGUM presented a memorial from sundry citizens of Wilkesborough, in the western part of North Carolina, praying a restoration of the deposites to the Bank of the United States; which was read, referred to the Committee on Finance, and ordered to be printed.

Mr. MANGUM also presented a memorial from inhabitants of Halifax county, in the same State, of like import; same order as the preceding.

Mr. CLAY said he had just heard through the public prints, that one of the incorporated banks of Maryland, situate in Baltimore, had failed. He had also heard that in consequence of a supposed connexion between that bank and the Union Bank of Maryland, one of the banks selected by the Secretary of the Treasury as a depository of the public money in that city, a great run was made upon that selected bank yesterday for specie. He had been informed that the Secretary of the Treasury was a stockholder to some extent, he did not know how much, in the Union Bank, and there might be great danger to the public moneys now on deposite there. He hoped it would turn out the Union Bank was safe, and that the Secretary was not a stockholder to such an amount that his interest could be supposed to have induced him to select that bank as a depository of the public money. He had also heard that in apprehension of a run on the Union Bank, a treasury draft had been issued in its favor for $150,000 to that bank, and it was the duty of the Senate to look into it.

He had therefore prepared the following resolution, which he hoped no gentleman would object to being adopted immediately:

Resolved, That the Secretary of the Treasury be directed to report to the Senate what amount of public money is now on deposite in the Union Bank of Maryland; on what account it was deposited, and whether any treasury drafts, contingent or other, have been, during the month of March, 1834, furnished to the said bank to enable it to meet any demands which might be made upon it.

Mr. FORSYTH said, if the gentleman had introduced the resolution without any remarks, he could have had no objection to it. But after what had been said by the gentleman, he thought we ought to have some time to see the resolution. It was said the Secretary of the Treasury was a stockholder in the Union Bank—he knew nothing to what extent; but he had no hesitation in saying that the interest of the Secretary, wherever it might be, had not the slightest effect on him in selecting the bank as one of the public deposites.

The resolution lies one day.

The VICE PRESIDENT presented a communication from the Treasury Department, transmitting a report relative to insolvent debtors.

Mr. CLAYTON presented a memorial from a number of watchmakers, jewellers, and others, in favor of a restoration of the deposites to the Bank of the United States; which was read, referred to the Committee on Finance, and ordered to be printed.

On motion of Mr. HENDRICKS, the order of the day were postponed, and the Senate took up for consideration the bill making appropriations for the repairing and continuing the Cumberland road, through the States of Ohio, Indiana, and Illinois.

Several amendments were proposed, upon the adoption of which a desultory debate ensued, in which Messrs. HENDRICKS, WILKINS, TIPTON, FRELINGHUYSEN, EWING, PRESTON, and KING of Alabama, participated.

The bill, on motion of Mr. FRELINGHUYSEN, was laid upon the table.

Mr. KING of Alabama, gave notice that he should to-morrow ask leave to introduce a bill organizing an additional District Court of the United States in the State of Alabama.

BANK OF THE UNITED STATES.

The VICE PRESIDENT having announced the special order to be Mr. WEBSTER's motion for leave to bring in a bill to recharter the Bank of the United States for six years—

Mr. WHITE resumed, and concluded his argument against the bill.

Mr. WEBSTER then took the floor, and said that he had not expected that on a motion for leave to bring in a bill, such a protracted debate would have ensued. If he had foreseen it, he would have been restrained from interfering with the discussion upon the resolutions of the gentleman from Kentucky. In his judgment, say relief for the present distresses of the country can be carried through Congress by the action of public opinion out of doors. Such was the diseased state of the community, that no relief could be expected till public sentiment gives a direction to some specific measures. And with this object in view he had moved for leave to introduce this bill, with a view to action upon it in due season hereafter. But it had become the subject of debate, and if it went on, on a motion for leave, other topics were likely to be introduced into it. It was with great reluctance he interrupted the debate, but he could not consent to a thing so extraordinary; he believed it was the first time such a thing had ever occurred. There had been nothing like it since he had been in the Senate. He was unwilling, therefore, to endeavor to make disposition of this object was to place the proposition for relief before the country. His therefore moved to lay the subject on the table, and intimated his intention to call it up again on the first Monday in March next.

On this motion,

Mr. FORSYTH asked the yeas and nays were ordered, and are as follows, to wit: [?]

YEAS—Messrs. Black, Calhoun, Clay, [?] ton, Ewing, Frelinghuysen, Hendricks, King [?]

Georgia, Mangum, Moore, Naudain, Poindexter, Porter, Prentiss, Preston, Robbins, Silsbee, Smith, Southard, Sprague, Swift, Tomlinson, Waggaman, Webster—34.

NAYS—Messrs. Benton, Brown, Forsyth, Grundy, Hill, Kane, King of Alabama, Morris, Robinson, Shepley, Tallmadge, Tipton, White, Wilkins, Wright—15.

Mr. CLAY then inquired whether the gentleman from New York [Mr. WRIGHT] designed to speak on the other special order, (Mr. C.'s resolution relative to the removal of the deposites.) If he did not, he (Mr. C.) wished to make some remarks himself, in reply to some gentlemen who had already spoken.

Mr. WRIGHT was understood to express a wish to make a few observations upon the first resolution of the gentleman from Kentucky.

The Senate then, on motion, adjourned.

HOUSE OF REPRESENTATIVES.

Tuesday, March 25, 1834.

Mr. THOMSON reported a bill for the relief of Caroline E. Clitherall.

Mr. WARDWELL, a bill for the relief of Peter Dextator and Jacob Weaver.

Mr. TOMPKINS, a bill for the relief of John Id, of Maine.

Mr. CHINN, a bill to complete the improvements on Pennsylvania Avenue.

Mr. MASON, a bill for the relief of Peter Mills.

Mr. BELL, from the Committee on the Judiciary, reported, without amendment, the bill from the Senate for changing the term of the district court for the western district of Louisiana.

Mr. STODDERT, an act for the benefit of the city of Washington; authorizing the Secretary of the Treasury to pay a sum not exceeding $60,000 dollars annually, in quarterly instalments, for three years, to the Mayor of the city, to be applied under the direction of the Board of Aldermen and Common Council, to extinguish so much of the interest annually accruing on its public debt.

Mr. ARCHER, a bill for the relief of certain inhabitants of East Florida.

All which bills were read twice and committed.

Mr. ASHLEY obtained leave to present a memorial from sundry western merchants, who met in Philadelphia, praying that the Bank of the United States may be rechartered, and such other measures taken by Congress as would relieve the country from its present pressure. It was needless for him to say, that the memorial had his most hearty wishes; he now called for the reading of it. It was read accordingly, ordered to be printed, and laid on the table.

The House, by unanimous consent, proceeded to call the several States for the presentation of petitions.

A memorial from Natchez, presented by Mr. CAGE, praying the restoration of the deposites, being the unfinished business from yesterday, on which there was a motion that it should be laid on the table.

Mr. PLUMMER claimed the floor.

Mr. CAGE withdrew his motion, for the present, to lay on the table.

Mr. PLUMMER said he wished to make a few brief remarks, dissenting from the views of the memorialists.

The SPEAKER said it was not in order to do so, except with leave of the House.

Mr. PLUMMER then said, that in order to attain his object, he would move to have the resolutions and memorial referred to the Committee of Ways and Means, with instructions to make a report adverse to the memorial, &c., if he was in order to do so.

The SPEAKER informed him this motion was in order; but as the resolutions were not before the House, having by mistake been sent to the printer, the subject must stand over until next petition day.

Mr. HANNEGAN obtained leave of the House to submit the following:

Resolved, That the Committee on Revolutionary Pensions be instructed to inquire into the expediency of placing Dempsey Hicks, a soldier of the Revolution, on the pension roll. Agreed to.

Mr. SEVIER obtained leave to submit the following, which lies one day on the table for consideration:

Resolved, That the Secretary of War be instructed to inform this House whether a survey of the Memphis and Little Rock road has been made; and if so, whether that survey has been returned to the War Department; and if not, the reasons why it has not been returned; and further, that he inform this House when it is intended to commence the work upon that road.

Resolutions that the Committee on the Post Office and Post Roads be instructed to inquire into the expediency of establishing post routes from the following places were agreed to:

By Mr. BROWN: From Milton, in Ulster county, by way of Modena and Youngs post office, to Tuthill, and from thence across by the mountain at the Traps, to Acord, in the county of Rochester.

By Mr. SHEPPERD: From Germantown, in Stokes county, North Carolina, by Bethania, Vienna, and Shore's Ferry, to Rockford, in Surry county.

By Mr. PLUMMER: From Jackson to Winchester, Mississippi.

On motion of Mr. WARD, of New York, the memorial and documents of Jonathan Ward were recommitted to the Committee on Revolutionary Claims.

Mr. WARD also presented the memorial of the owners and captains of vessels navigating Long Island Sound, in relation to the light-house on Sands Point, New York: which was referred to the Committee on Commerce.

Petitions were presented by Mr. CAGE, of Mississippi, Mr. BULL, of Missouri, and Mr. LYON, of Michigan.

The SPEAKER presented a communication from the State Department, transmitting an abstract, showing the number of American seamen at each port. Referred, and ordered to be printed.

The SPEAKER also presented a communication from the War Department, in compliance with a resolution of the House of the 19th instant, transmitting information relative to fortifications, &c. Referred to the Committee on Military Affairs, and ordered to be printed.

The SPEAKER also presented a letter from the Secretary of the Treasury, in pursuance of an act of Congress, supplementary to an act for the relief of insolvent debtors of the United States, transmitting an abstract and returns, in pursuance of the provisions of that act.

On motion of Mr. ELLSWORTH, the letter was ordered to be printed.

The SPEAKER also laid before the House a letter from Lieutenant Levy, of the United States navy, asking leave to present to Congress, and through them to his fellow-citizens of the United States, a bronze statue of Thomas Jefferson, &c.

Mr. PATTON said, that having the pleasure of an acquaintance with Lieutenant Levy, he rose to make the proper motion on the subject. After investigation, he had found that the uniform course, on such occasions, had been to refer the communication to the Committee on the Library. Accordingly, he made that motion, that the committee might inquire what disposition should be made of this munificent and patriotic donation.

The motion was agreed to.

THE PUBLIC DEPOSITES.

The House resumed the consideration of the resolutions reported from the Committee of Ways and Means, together with Mr. WILDE's motion to amend the same.

Mr. GILMER, of Georgia, obtained leave to lay the following resolutions on the table, stating that it was his intention to offer them, as an amendment, at a proper time hereafter:

Resolved, That the right to control the possession of the public money is a trust, and delegated to the Government, of which it cannot divest itself: and, therefore, that Congress has no power to sell to the Bank of the United States, or other corporation, or to any individual, the right to possess the money of the United States.

Resolved, That the Congress of the United States did not, by the sixteenth section of the act to incorporate the subscribers of the Bank of the United States, which directs that the deposites of the

money of the United States shall be placed in the Bank of the United States and its branches, unless the Secretary of the Treasury shall at any time otherwise order and direct, relinquish its right of controlling the deposites of the money of the United States, whenever the public interest should require its exercise.

Resolved, That the right of Congress to fix by law the place of deposites for the money of the United States, does not depend in any degree upon the sufficiency or insufficiency of the reasons assigned to Congress by the Secretary of the Treasury, at the commencement of its present session, for the removal of the money of the United States from the Bank of the United States.

Resolved, That the application to Congress for a recharter by the Bank of the United States, in the session immediately preceding the last presidential election; the rejection of that application by the deliberate action of the Government; the general embarrassment of all business which has been carried on by banking credit; the great interest which the Bank of the United States has to increase the embarrassment, and to occasion general distress throughout the country; the power which the United States Bank would possess of compelling most of the State banks to stop the payment of specie, and all accommodation to the people if the deposites of the money of the United States were restored to the Bank of the United States, conspire to render it the imperative duty of Congress to deposite the money of the United States, in some other place than the Bank of the United States.

Resolved, That the United States possess no powers of Government, except such as have been delegated to it by the States through the Constitution.

Resolved, That the power to grant charters of incorporation is an attribute of sovereignty, and belongs to the States or the people, it never having been delegated to the United States.

Resolved, That the authority granted to the United States by the last clause of the 8th section of the 1st article of the Constitution, to pass all laws necessary and proper for carrying into execution the powers conferred upon it, does not justify the assumption of any sovereign power by the United States which belongs to the States or the people.

Resolved, That the creation of a national bank, or the rechartering the present bank, by the United States, is not only an exercise of power not authorized by the Constitution, but dangerous to the individual independence of the people; to the power of the States to resist the usurpation of their rights, and to the continuance of our present free institutions.

Resolved, That the money collected from the people, for the use of the Government, ought to be placed in the State banks until it shall be drawn therefrom in consequence of appropriations made by law, instead of permitting it to remain in the possession of the public officers—because, through the banks, the money may be made to return immediately into circulation, thereby lessening the burdens of taxation, keeping the quantity of circulating medium equal, and adding to the activity and prosperity of the community.

Resolved, That the State banks, to be made the depositaries of the public money, ought to be designated by law, as soon as possible, and the conditions and restrictions prescribed upon which they shall receive the public money and transfer it to such places as the Government may require.

The resolutions were ordered to be printed.

Mr. CLAY, of Alabama, who was entitled to the floor, rose and spoke two hours in support of the resolutions reported from the Committee of Ways and Means. When he concluded, several gentlemen simultaneously addressed the Chair, and the floor was obtained by Mr. SCHLEY, of Georgia, on whose motion, the House adjourned.

IN SENATE.

Wednesday, March 26, 1834.

A message was received from the President of the United States, by Mr. DONELSON, his Private Secretary, transmitting a report of the Secretary of War upon the petition of William Tharp; which was referred to the Committee on Claims.

Mr. SOUTHARD presented the proceedings of

a meeting of young men of Philadelphia, opposed to the course of the Secretary of the Treasury in removing the deposites.

Mr. PRESTON said that he desired to take this opportunity to make a remark or two upon a memorial which he intended to present, from a meeting of citizens of the third congressional district in Pennsylvania. It came from the young gentlemen of Philadelphia; and he thought, coming from such a source, it presented an instructive lesson. It proceeded from a class of citizens who were uncorrupted by the world, and it therefore spoke the lessons of wisdom. The sentiments thus avowed were natural and proper, and necessary to the times in which we lived. These young gentlemen represent that the Constitution has been violated, and the laws trampled upon. We had now been discussing this subject three months— the whole continent had been shaken by its absorbing influence; and in the midst of all these things, occurrences have taken place, and are daily taking place, which would shake our reason under other circumstances. We see one of the departments of this Government bankrupt to the amount of $500,-000, and it passes unnoticed. But who was it that performed this act? The Secretary of the Treasury? No. But the Secretary of the President of the United States—a Secretary not confirmed, or offered to be confirmed, by the Senate. We were now here, almost at the first of April, and the extraordinary spectacle was presented of three high officers of the Government exercising their duties, without their offices being confirmed by the Senate. And what was the situation of our foreign relations? One court, high up the Baltic, was entirely without a representative, kept open for negotiation. Another more important one, the Court of England, has been for two years without a representative there—a Government where, according to the President's admission, negotiations of the most important nature were left pending. An army of soldiers were marching and countermarching through several of the States of this Union, and yet nothing affected the public mind, such was the interest and anxiety in the present state of things. At no period of the Government had there ever been such a congregation of remarkable facts collected together. It may well be said that we were in a revolution, hitherto bloodless, but it was not so now. Murder had been committed; blood had been spilt; the life of an individual had been sacrificed, in performing a duty secured to him by the Constitution. And what impression did this make? The name of the individual who has fallen he hardly knew. Petitions and memorials were showering in here from all quarters, complaining of this usurpation of power, and gentlemen say, Have patience, and all will be well. Yes, when the distress has attained its utmost limit, then we shall have relief. When the storm has prostrated the forest, a new growth will take place. They make a solitude, and call it peace.

Mr. BROWN desired to make but a remark or two in reply to the gentleman from South Carolina, [Mr. PRESTON,] he he would take the occasion to congratulate gentlemen upon their reinstatement in their former situation. He thought he perceived for some days past their phalanx wavering—that there was not the same unity of sentiment upon the violated laws of the country. They stated the issue to be one thing. We said it was another; that the Bank of the United States was the issue, and a bill was afterwards brought forward to recharter the bank, and the honorable gentleman from Massachusetts opened the discussion. This was continued for several days; gentlemen now saw that it was not the proper question to be presented, and the issue was withdrawn. We were then upon the same ground upon which we had been placed for some days past, and the tones of sympathy and distress were again repeated. The gentleman from South Carolina prefaced his observations by stating that he had a memorial to present from the young men of Philadelphia; a circumstance which peculiarly marked the present time. It did mark the present time, when young men were forced to fight the battles of the United States Bank. It was eminently characteristic of the present time. What did the bank do? It was flying to take refuge among the boys of the country. But honorable gentlemen thought the elections would decide the

question. They would decide it. Look at the elections since the removal of the deposites. Have they not triumphantly sustained the Administration? Witness the result of the elections in Virginia and New Hampshire. The gentleman also asked, what was the situation of our foreign relations at this time? And what was it, Mr. B. would also ask? The dignity, elevation, prosperity, and success of the Administration in this branch of the public service was read in the eyes of the nation. Never was there a period in our history when a patriot's heart had greater reason to be gratified by the success of our foreign relations. What old subjects of controversy were there that were unsettled under this Administration? Subjects which had baffled the exertions of the most able statesmen of the country heretofore had been honorably adjusted. There was no foreign court where the nation was not represented by some one. The Minister to Russia had but just left there. And why was there not a Minister to England? the gentleman asked. Why not? The history of this body gave the response—that history would show that the nominations of the President were not always confirmed. But it was said that the tendency of power was to concentrate in the hands of one man. But if it were so, was there none in that great corporation which was wielding a power wholly unparalleled in the country. The bank could draw down no denunciations upon it from the other side of the House. Repeated efforts were made to persuade the people that the President was arrogating to himself the supreme power, the imperial purple. But when we look to his advanced age, and reflect upon the long life which he had devoted to the service of his country, can it be believed that he would do anything to tarnish that fame which is, and ought to be, so dear to him? He thought it necessary to say thus much in answer to the gentleman from South Carolina.

Mr. PRESTON remarked that the gentleman from North Carolina [Mr. BROWN] said that the memorial from these young men indicated the power of the bank over the people. Mr. P. thought that it was not in the ranks of the young men that advocates for the bank would be found. If they obeyed impulses, it would be to cry out for the party. It was not the character of the country to be bought. He scorned the imputation. If every bank in the United States was crushed to atoms, greater distress than now existed could not be produced. He did not know whether the absence of the Minister from England was necessary. But the Chief Magistrate has said that important matters were under discussion there. And the gentleman had said that the nominations were not made, because nominations to the Senate were not always confirmed.

Mr. BROWN rose to explain. He did not say that that was the reason why a nomination had not been made, but that it was the reason why no Minister was not now there.

Mr. PRESTON resumed. The Senate then did not think proper to confirm the nomination. It was a dangerous non-exercise of power to refuse to nominate when it was said important negotiations were then to be attended to. The powers of the Senate were superseded—there were no nominations to foreign courts—no nominations to three high offices in the Government. There was one instance in relation to our foreign affairs, to which he would allude. A part of the national debt, the 4½ per cents., was about falling due, and the department had actually forgotten to give notice of it, and the interest was running on to this day. Such were the circumstances under which the country was placed.

Mr. FORSYTH said there was one remark of the honorable gentleman from South Carolina [Mr. PRESTON] to which he wished to call the attention of the Senate. He alluded to the complaint which the gentleman made that the high officers of the Government—the Secretary of State, of the Treasury, and the Attorney General—were the officers of the President, and not of the United States. He believed the Constitution of the United States authorized the President, during the

recess of the Senate, to grant commissions to fill vacancies, which should continue until the end of the next session of Congress. The persons alluded to have their commissions from the President, and whether they were here or not, for confirmation, they were officers of the United States. He did not understand the point of the gentleman's complaint against the President for not sending their appointments for confirmation. Was it his duty to do so? It was his duty to send them before the time of adjournment, and then it was our duty to pass upon them, and we had a right to pass upon them. How we should do so, the majority in this body would determine. Was then an anxiety existing, in these allusions, to embarrass the public affairs when the disastrous effects of proceedings here were already so agitating the country? The President had pursued a just discretion, and he [Mr. F.] could see no objection to his exercising it. The two gentlemen [Mr. SOUTHARD and Mr. PRESTON] had dwelt much on the strong evidence of public opinion manifested in the proceedings of the young men in Philadelphia—the young men, the junior classes of the country—that they had no self-interest, but were guided by generous gentle affections. But we have had frequent exhibitions of this sort before. We have had other meetings of young men and conventions of young men, and if he recollected rightly, the course of the last young men's convention here had been over-shadowed by the young men at the ballot boxes, as they will be again. It was a very remarkable fact, that the city of Philadelphia, so conspicuous for her wealth, her virtue, and her intelligence, always had the misfortune of being opposed to the people of the United States. But the gentleman and the people saw other and more dangerous encroachments upon their liberties—that a formidable army had marched through one State to attack another, and all this created no attention. And why? Because the people knew the purpose of it—they knew the object in view, and approved the act—they went to enforce the laws of the country, and the State of Alabama approved the act, and was satisfied that the President was right. But the gentleman also says that the revolution is no longer bloodless—that one murder had been committed on a citizen exercising the elective franchise. True, rumor said that an individual had been lately severely beaten in Philadelphia, and had since died. But without a knowledge of the circumstances, would the gentleman say that murder done was committed, or that the deceased did not merit the blow by which he fell? The cause existed no attention here was, that it did not belong to the United States Government, but was the government of Pennsylvania, and he had no judicial justice would there be done. And he would say to that gentleman, that the introduction of this topic here did not properly belong to persons holding the opinions which we hold here upon State rights. It belonged to the action of the State Governments. The petitions complained of an intolerable deal of public distress. The people were deluded into a belief that they suffered greater distress than war and famine could produce. But could it not be said that it was greatly exaggerated? He had passed through the cities of Philadelphia and New York, when he saw not a living thing in the streets—when the noise of his own feet was terrifying to him. But was there anything prevailing distress to be compared to this? There was distress existing it was true, but it was not of

and fomented to foster political hopes—hopes that a while ago were dead, are now alive, and the bank was used as the instrument of promoting those hopes. But the issue was before the people, and he hoped they would feel it, and decide it; and he thought they would be as before, against the bank. But the gentleman was mistaken in supposing that the presentation of such masses of memorials was unexampled here. In 1811, (which, to be sure, was before his time,) innumerable petitions were presented for renewing the charter of the old bank, and complaining, as now, of great distress and embarrassment, and bushel baskets full of them might now be found in the State Department. Even in our own time, in the Cherokee case, there were more than there are now. And so of the Missouri question, (though he was out of the country then,) and more lately the tariff. There was hardly an exciting topic could come before Congress that did not produce a flood of memorials and petitions.

The memorials were read, referred to the Committee on Finance, and ordered to be printed.

The special order of the day was then announced, being the report of the Committee on Finance, and Mr. CLAY's resolutions upon the

REMOVAL OF THE DEPOSITES.

Mr. FORSYTH said he would, with the permission of the gentleman who was entitled to the floor, [Mr. WRIGHT,] correct a misrepresentation of his remarks yesterday, so great, that he was led to apprehend that it was designed to do him or another person injury. The Senator from Kentucky, in introducing his resolution of inquiry into the amount of the public moneys on deposite in the Union Bank of Maryland, had said, "he hoped it would turn out that the Secretary of the Treasury was not a stockholder in this bank to any extent which could authorize an impression that he had suffered his own interests to enter into the considerations which led him to select this bank as one of the depositories of the public money." Without then knowing, as he now did, that the amount of stock owned by Mr. Taney was small, Mr. F. rose to protest against the statement expressed, and to appeal to the justice and generous feelings of the Senator from Kentucky, that no amount of stock owned by Mr. Taney could justify an inference to his prejudice; that his character was a sufficient guarantee that his official acts could not be influenced by his pecuniary interests.

Now, (Mr. F. said,) he was represented in the National Intelligencer as endorsing the Senator's remark. He was made to say, "He did not imagine, however, that it could be found, on examination, that the Secretary held sufficient stock to render it an object with him to select this bank for the custody of any part of the public money;" thus admitting what he had risen to deny, that there was an amount of stock which, if owned in the bank by Mr. Taney, could, by possibility, govern his official conduct.

Mr. WRIGHT then rose, and spoke at large, sustaining the Secretary.

When he concluded,

Mr. CLAY obtained the floor, and intimated that if it was the wish of any gentleman to address the Senate, he would yield his privilege. No Senator rising, Mr. CLAY moved an adjournment, but gave way to Mr. POINDEXTER, upon whose motion the Senate proceeded to executive business; and after some time spent therein,

Adjourned.

HOUSE OF REPRESENTATIVES.

WEDNESDAY, *March* 26, 1834.

Mr. HARPER, of New Hampshire, from the Committee on Commerce, reported an act for the relief of Phineas Sprague, and others, late owners of the schooner Two Sisters, with an amendment.

Mr. OSGOOD, with leave, presented two private petitions for relief of revolutionary soldiers; which was referred.

The resolution submitted by Mr. MARDIS, of Alabama, respecting the public deposites, was taken up.

Mr. BURGES resumed and concluded his remarks on the subject, and

Mr. CHILTON ALLAN obtained the floor.

THE DEPOSITES AND UNITED STATES BANK.

At one o'clock the House proceeded to the consideration of the resolutions reported from the Committee of Ways and Means, together with the amendment submitted by Mr. WILDE, declaring that the reasons of the Secretary of the Treasury for the removal of the deposites are unsatisfactory and insufficient.

Mr. SCHLEY took the floor. He did not (he said) engage in the discussion with the expectation of changing the opinion of any gentleman here who differed from him, nor of confirming the opinion of those who thought as he did. He would have been content to give a silent vote, had it not been that the country had been flooded with inflammatory speeches and letters sent from this city to produce an artificial excitement and alarm. Those clamors had been echoed back from certain individuals who were under the influence of a power more potent than reason. The evidence of the fact lies on the table. It was these reiterated clamors, all tending to induce the people to believe in the existence of a state of facts which had no reality, that had led him to present the views which he entertained on this subject. A sort of factitious importance had been given to this question, which had swelled it far beyond its natural dimensions. The real cause and object of all this excitement every individual could tell. It was expected by these means to procure what otherwise could not be procured—the recharter of the bank, and a change of administration. While a certain individual was at the head of the Government, there were persons who could not be satisfied with any state of things. With Haman, they exclaimed, What are all these things to me, while Mordecai, the Jew, sits in the King's gate? His honorable colleague, [Mr. WILDE,] in reference to the speeches, letters, &c., which have been sent abroad to mislead the public mind, asked why their effect was not counteracted by our speeches. In answer to the interrogatory, he would say, that although we have usurped the purse and sword of the nation, yet we have no money to pay for printing speeches. He had been credibly informed that 100,000 copies of a certain speech delivered in this House had been purchased for distribution; of another speech 50,000 copies; and of a certain other speech 50,000 copies more. If we send speeches abroad, we have to buy them, and we are not able to pay for so great a number. This was the reason why the Administration party were not able to counteract the efforts of the friends of the bank. A distinguished party leader and Senator had said that we were in the midst of a revolution, rapidly tending to the concentration of all power in the hands of one man; that the premonitory symptoms of despotism were upon us, &c. He (Mr. S.) believed that we were in the midst of a revolution; but that, instead of concentrating power in the hands of one man, it would wrest power from hands where it had been unconstitutionally lodged.

Mr. S. proceeded to argue upon the nature of the several powers granted to the President of the United States and the Secretary of the Treasury in their respective capacities; and he maintained that there was no express power granted to the President. It was rather an incidental power growing out of the taxing power, granted by the Constitution. Congress, then, (he argued,) had, as a matter of course, the power to protect the public treasure. But supposing that they had not expressly designated the place where it should be kept, it seemed to him that it devolved as a necessary consequence upon the Executive, to see that it should be taken care of. This also seemed to him to be the practice of the Government, and it had not been hitherto opposed; no law having been, that he was aware of, ever passed, interfering with the right exercised by the Secretary of the Treasury—whom, he contended, was a branch of the Executive power. But although, by the act incorporating the bank, specified powers were given to the Secretary, it was not to be supposed that Congress ever intended to vest in this officer, the power over the public purse without having some responsibility, some accountability over it. The people had elected the President, believing him to be a man of talents, of integrity, and of honor—who would not do anything to violate their Constitution or their laws—and he inferred that Congress, when incorporating the bank, with the clauses so often referred to in the debate, had not the Secretary so much as the President *pro tempore* in view. He took for granted, from the usual motives by which men were actuated, that Congress considered him alone as responsible for the safe-keeping, &c., of the public funds, and that the Secretary was bound to carry into effect the orders of the Executive, unless, as in the case of Mr. Duane, he could not conscientiously do so. Mr. Secretary Taney had done no more than carry out views, which he had entertained, and which he was bound to do. In reference to the arguments that the power of the Secretary in this matter was independent, he would suppose that the Secretary was about to remove the deposites, in opposition to the will of the President, and that he had prevented him in removing them, and he must ask, what would be the conduct of those now opposed to any Executive control? Would there have been such an outcry as now? No. "It would have been as fair a thing as ever was."

An issue had been made, that this was a question between the bank and the President, while, in fact, it ought to have been advocated upon what it really was, an issue between the bank and the people, and an issue, too, upon which they (the people) had decided by their votes at the last election. The bank, like all other corporations, was an institution without a soul, created by the Government for the performance of certain fiscal offices. Its charter being about to expire, the President very properly brought to the notice of Congress this fact, and called their attention to it, that they might supply the want of such an institution as agent for the public business. Such being his duty, it was scarcely possible to suppose that this should have caused the results which the country had ever since experienced. It was hardly possible to credit, that for this the bank should have commenced, and been justified by its friends for so doing, to corrupt the press, and flood the land with pamphlets, &c., "for the purpose of enlightening the people," or "for defence," as it was termed. It then came to this, that, as the recharter of the bank was advocated only on the ground that it was necessary for the fiscal offices of the Government, and not so much for the benefit of the stockholders, should Congress—were they in fact justified—in aiding them, by granting any further powers to a corporation which was rising up every day and doing acts pernicious to public liberty, and which must ultimately destroy them? Could men be found to justify this conduct by the bank? Could legislators be found, could men who were sworn to defend the Constitution, aid them after these improper acts were brought home to them? He thought, if Government had come to that pass, that they would be overawed by an institution of their own creation; it was a degradation, a miserable state of things, that he never expected to witness. He asked if there did not appear to be a high-handed attempt to overawe Congress on this question, in a manner hitherto unexampled, and which ought to be resisted. In reference to the safety of our free institutions, he viewed the bank as a most dangerous incorporation, which must ultimately destroy the ramparts which surrounded the Constitution. His hopes were, however, grounded upon the intelligence and patriotism of the people, and that they would not permit it to be sustained. If not, then we should be a people with the name of liberty, but not having the substance. If the bank should be rechartered, the whole property of the nation would be made subject to it, to rise and fall, as it would extend or curtail its issues of paper. Referring to the opinions given by the President of the United States, "that the constitutionality and expediency of the bank might be well questioned," and to the opinions entertained by Mr. Madison in 1791, and his change of opinion on this subject in 1816, he said he regretted that he ever could have changed the opinion he had expressed against its constitutionality; for he (Mr. S.) could not yield up his opinion on the grounds which Mr. Madison had justified his—"that he believed it to be necessary."

Mr. S., after adverting to the powers exercised by the States in issuing "bills of credit," and which he contended bank bills could not be so considered, he eulogized the Constitution as the

great chart to which the people looked, and which, as it doubtless would be adhered to by the President in his conduct to the bank, it would alone be their safest guide, and ultimately would produce safety and continuance to their free institutions.

Mr. S. proceeded to show why, according to his views, the bank was not constitutional. The States had reserved to themselves all powers which were not granted to the Federal Government. The question arose, whether this power was so granted? The grant was not to be found in the Constitution. So far from that, it was a matter of history that it was proposed in the convention to give this power, and that the proposition was rejected. Mr. S. referred to the history of the convention, to prove this fact. The specific power to incorporate a bank was not proposed, but a power to incorporate companies generally was proposed and rejected. To this argument it had been replied that the proposition was rejected because it would have endangered the adoption of the whole instrument by the people. His view of the subject was, that the power did not exist, unless it was specifically granted.

Mr. S. referred to the argument that the faith of the Government being pledged, it was proper to return the deposites, even admitting the institution to be unconstitutional. The Secretary, he argued, had an uncontrolled discretion in regard to the disposition of the deposites, and that this power was granted in the charter. What right had the bank to complain of the exercise of the power, when it was secured to the Secretary of the Treasury by the very terms of the contract with the bank? It had been said that the President had assumed an illegal power over the public money. But the fact was that Congress had the same power over the public treasure now which they had before the deposites were removed; and the power of the President was not greater now than it was before. The question now is, what shall be done with the public money? He contended that legislative power was inalienable. No one disputed this, and the 16th section of the charter, reserving to the Secretary of the Treasury the power of removal, showed conclusively that Congress did not intend to legislate away their legislative power. The question what shall be done with the deposites? now came up as an original question. We could do with them whatever we pleased.

Mr. S. proceeded to inquire into the expediency of a national bank as a fiscal agent, and into the causes of the existing public distress. In many points of view, he represented this concentration of money-power as dangerous to the liberties of the country. He referred to the recent efforts of the bank to misrepresent the acts of the President, through memorials elicited from the people, as a proof of the capacity and disposition of the bank to abuse its influence. The bank represented all the distress which pervaded the community as resulting from a measure of the President—from the removal of eight or nine millions from its vaults. Mr. S., in answer to the views presented by the friends of the bank on this point, read a letter written by the President of the bank, explaining the causes of public embarrassments which existed at a time when the bank could not complain of the conduct of the President of the United States, or his Secretary of the Treasury. Mr. Biddle represented the distress, at that time, as arising from over-trading, brought on by over-banking. The same means, he went on to show, had produced the present state of things. He referred to a statement, which he was willing to take as true, that the bank had withdrawn from circulation only four millions of dollars. This was a sufficient proof that the removal of the deposites to the State banks, which continued to use those deposites for the benefit of the people, could not have produced any embarrassment. But it was said that the removal, *per se*, had not produced the effect, but that the panic and loss of confidence consequent on the removal, had produced it. But who produced the panic? Not the State banks, for they would be the first to suffer by it. Not the people, certainly, for they are its victims. But it was the United States Bank which created all this alarm and agitation. Without greatly reducing the amount of their discounts, they could produce agitation by diminishing their facilities at one point and increasing them at another, subjecting every place, in succession, to their influence. Mr. S. vindicated the Secretary of the Treasury from the aspersions cast upon him, eulogizing his character in warm terms.

When Mr. S. concluded,

The floor was obtained by Mr. ELLSWORTH, who moved that the House adjourn.

The question being taken by yeas and nays, the motion was negatived:

Yeas 64, nays 66.

Mr. CLAYTON moved a call of the House; upon which motion, Mr. EVANS demanded the yeas and nays; which were ordered.

Mr. McCOMAS moved that this House do now adjourn.

On this motion, Mr. GILLET demanded the yeas and nays, which were ordered.

Mr. ELLSWORTH rose to explain that he had moved an adjournment, after obtaining the floor, because, not expecting to speak to-day, he was not prepared with the papers which he should have occasion to use in addressing the House.

Mr. HARDIN said he had voted against the adjournment, and he wished to give a reason why he should now change his vote.

The SPEAKER decided that no explanations were in order.

The question on the motion to adjourn, was taken by yeas and nays, and decided in the affirmative:

Yeas 70, nays 62.

The House adjourned.

IN SENATE.

TUESDAY, *March* 27, 1834.

On motion of Mr. SILSBEE, leave of absence for ten days after Monday next, was granted to Mr. WEBSTER.

Mr. KING, *of Georgia*, presented a memorial from about four hundred citizens of the city of Augusta, asking a restoration of the deposites, and a recharter of the Bank of the United States.

Mr. K. said that as, from the proceedings of yesterday, he found it was still usual, on the presentation of memorials, to speak of the character of the memorialists, and, at the same time, to say something upon the subject of their complaints—although he disapproved the practice of discussing these memorials, and thought the compliments of respectability, &c., as mere formal ceremonies—yet, as the practice was continued, he could *not* consent that his fellow-citizens of Augusta, and their memorial, should suffer too much in comparison with those from various other quarters and sections of the Union, by refusing to bestow upon them something like the accustomed attention.

He said, then, he could state that he was personally acquainted with a very large portion of the memorialists; and he thought that, to a limited extent, they embraced all classes, characters, trades, professions, and interests, in the community from which the memorial came. He said he also found that a very respectable portion of the merchants and business men of the city had signed the memorial, and from his acquaintance with some of them, he thought their experience and general intelligence as merchants, qualified them as well to judge of those measures of State policy which would likely improve or injure their respective interests, as a like number of merchants taken promiscuously from any other southern city in the Union.

Of the politics of the memorialists, however, he said he could not say so much. He was not extensively acquainted with the political opinions and feelings of his neighbors. He did not know whether they were generally friendly, or opposed to the present Administration. But from the best information he could gain, the memorial was not originated, circulated, signed, or sent here, with any very marked reference to party distinctions upon this point. He might, perhaps, he said, make this exception. There was, he said, a very small, but at the same time a very respectable party in the city of Augusta (known as the Nullifying party) who, with a consistency with their former opinions upon the subject of the United States Bank, (which so far from censuring, he was much disposed to admire,) had generally, he believed, declined to put their signatures to the paper.

There was one characteristic, however, he said, by which he thought the memorial might be distinctly marked. So far as he was acquainted with the sentiments of the memorialists, they had been generally friendly to a United States Bank. They thought such an institution an useful instrument in the commerce of the country, and an efficient aid to the Government in the administration of its finances. The character and objects of the memorial, he said, might in fact be gathered from the language employed in it, which had been appropriately selected, and showed an evident intention in the memorialists to state nothing but the truth; but at the same time to state that in such a way as to forward, as far as possible, the object they had in view. They spoke of "indications" of distress in the commercial community; of "evils which they witness," and of still greater evils which they apprehend, &c. They nowhere pointedly state, said Mr. K., that *they are themselves* suffering under any very unusual pecuniary embarrassment or pressure in their money market. They could not so state, he said, as he apprehended such statement would have been contrary to the fact. The very mail, he said, which brought the memorial, brought the prices current, by which it appeared that local stocks, (always the thermometer of the money market, as they were not influenced by any foreign competition,) and in fact all vendible articles usually stated in the price current, maintained their prices, and indicated that all those who had the worth of money could procure money on the usual and customary terms. He referred, also, to the proceedings of the meeting, by which it was admitted, he believed, by the speakers on both sides, that the pressure had not *then* reached the city. If further evidence were wanting, he said he could state that he had conversed with *two of the memorialists themselves*, both highly respectable merchants, who had stated to him that the present season had not been marked by any unusual distress among the merchants. And, (said Mr. K.) if Senators should still be incredulous, I hold in my hand a letter from one of the committee who drafted the memorial itself, a line from which, he supposed, would conclusively settle this point. Among other things the writer states: "As yet, our money market is about as we left it."

Mr. K. said, he was thus particular in dwelling on these facts, not only to show the true character of the memorial and its object, but to sustain his colleague in a declaration he had made a few weeks past, *that at that time* the city of Augusta was suffering no unusual distress. The truth of this statement had been questioned by some honorable Senators, and particularly the honorable Senator from Kentucky had laughed at his colleague for this supposed mistake. The statement of his colleague, he said, was *strictly* true at the time it was made, and in fact so continued up to the date of the last accounts.

But (said Mr. K.) it is true the memorialists *apprehend* distress, and he thought with some reason, if he understood well the present state of affairs in that city. This pressure (said Mr. K.) has been almost periodical in the southern cities for several years, and may always be expected, to a certain extent, when the article of cotton opens at a price much beyond that which is afterward maintained. It is known (said Mr. K.) that northern exchange is principally furnished to southern merchants by the purchase and shipment of cotton. These are the means by and through which the southern merchants pay their northern debts. And when the trade continues regular throughout the season, the supply is generally equal to, and sometimes beyond the demand, and the premium on northern exchange is often a trifle, and sometimes nothing. But (said he) the planters, after they have sold a portion of their crop at good prices, sell the remainder with extreme reluctance at prices very far below what they have previously obtained. Every man (he said) at all in the habit of attending to the operations of his own mind, would understand the policy by which the planter was governed in such a case.

In fact, the planter was not only inclined, but *enabled*, during the present season, by a timely disposition of a large portion of his crop, at good prices, to hold on to the remainder, in expectation

of an advance. Since the fall in the foreign market had produced a heavy decline in the home market, sales had almost ceased in Augusta, and for the last sixty or seventy days, the planters had generally stored. The warehouses (he said) in Augusta, though numerous and spacious, were crowded to overflowing, very few preferring to sell at the current prices, but holding on with an obstinate confidence, hoping better might be obtained.

This policy (said Mr. K.) has cut off the most usual supply of northern exchange, which had risen since about the first of January from par to 2 per cent. premium, and even this rate being beyond the usual exchange; a further advance would probably produce a run upon the banks for specie, in the remittance of which the merchants (when remittances must go on as usual) would find a better account than in the purchase of exchange at these high rates. If, for these reasons, (said Mr. K.,) the merchants should commence drawing specie from the banks, the banks must stop their discounts, and reduce their debts, by calling upon their customers, and thus would commence the pressure.

There was another cause (he said) which might add something to the demand for money in the southern cities; and which, if he mistook not, had added to the apprehensions of some practical men in the city of his residence.

There were (he said) many northern houses which had southern connexions and business friends; and it will be recollected (said Mr. K.) that, when making a few remarks before the Senate a few weeks since, I stated that there was rather an unusual demand for capital in the northern cities, without the usual facilities of supplying them. The money market has been easier at the South, and he believed he had understood (at least it was reasonable) that many southern houses had exhausted their credit, to raise remittances to aid their northern friends. This might, if the facts were so, add something to the usual demand for northern exchange, which together would make something more than an ordinary demand, which was met in consequence of the policy of the planters, by a very inadequate and insufficient supply. Mr. K. said he hoped, however, that this apprehended pressure might yet be averted, by a change of policy by the planters, or such rise in their produce as would induce them to part with their property.

I might be disposed, (said Mr. K.,) under other circumstances, to say something in reference to the object of the memorialists, in a more methodical manner than I have done heretofore; but the proposed measure of the recharter is more directly before the Senate by the introduction of a bill for that purpose; and I will therefore conclude, by moving that the memorial be read, printed, and referred to the Committee on Finance, hoping that the bill, when brought forward for discussion, will have that deliberate attention to which the importance of the measure proposed so justly entitles it.

The memorial was read, referred to the Committee on Finance, and ordered to be printed.

Mr. WEBSTER rose to make a correction in a notice given a few days since, that he would, on the first Monday in May, call up the bill extending the charter of the United States Bank. He now gave notice that he would call it up on Monday, the 21st of April.

Mr. W. also presented a memorial of six thousand two hundred and seven inhabitants of Worcester county, Massachusetts, praying the restoration of the deposites to the Bank of the United States; which was read, referred to the Committee on Finance, and ordered to be printed.

Mr. CLAY said that it had been his intention to call up the resolution submitted by him, asking for information from the Treasury Department, relative to the amount of public deposites in the Union Bank of Maryland; but, observing an honorable Senator from Georgia [Mr. FORSYTH] absent from his seat, he should decline doing so at this time.

Mr. CLAY presented a memorial, signed by upwards of 1200 inhabitants of the city of Lexington and county of Fayette, Kentucky, praying a restoration of the deposites to the Bank of the United States; which was read, referred to the Committee on Finance, and ordered to be printed.

Mr. WHITE presented the petition of Benjamin Murphy, of Arkansas; which was referred to the Committee on Indian Affairs.

Mr. WILKINS presented the proceedings and resolutions of inhabitants of Beaver county, Pennsylvania, censuring the acts of the Secretary of the Treasury in removing the deposites; which were read, referred to the Committee on Finance, and ordered to be printed.

Mr. WILKINS, from the Committee on Finance, reported a bill from the House of Representatives, making appropriations for the army for the year 1834.

The special order was then announced, being the report of the Committee on Finance, and Mr. CLAY's resolution upon the

REMOVAL OF THE DEPOSITES.

Mr. CLAY said it was just three months yesterday since he opened the debate in the Senate, which was now drawing to a close. The period which had elapsed was long enough for a vessel to have passed the Cape of Good Hope, or to have made a return voyage from Europe. It was the longest period which had been occupied in a single debate in either House of Congress since the organization of the Government. But when the magnitude of the interests involved were considered, there was no disproportion between the time and the subject. He seriously believed the liberties of the country were involved in the measure under consideration arising out of the acts of the Executive of the Government. The present situation of the country was truly alarming. Would nothing open the eyes of those in power? Would nothing soften their hearts? Between the commotions which followed the downfall of the first Bank of the United States and the present state of things, there was no comparison. Why was this whole people agitated from one extreme of this great nation to the other? Nature was still unchanged in her various operations. Why was it, then? It had flown from the act of one man alone, honest and patriotic if you please, but still it had proceeded from that act.

Gentlemen deceived themselves as to the evidence of public sentiment, as manifested by the late elections. Except the elections of the Senator on his right, [Mr. LEIGH,] and another of a doubtful character in Virginia, there had been no demonstrations of public sentiment. It had been intimated that we should not adjourn till relief was effected; he would be willing to stay here till new year's day if that would procure relief, but he saw no relief till public sentiment effected it. And he would be willing to say, when the authority of the Constitution and laws should be vindicated, let us adjourn, and go home, and consult our constituents what was to be done for their relief, and then return and do their will.

The gentleman from New York [Mr. WRIGHT] considered the first resolution as judicial in its character; that the President was under trial; and if it were so, he could not have had a more eloquent or able defender than the gentleman had been. Mr. C. denied having any personal feelings to gratify against the President—his feelings were exclusively public. He contended that the resolution was not judicial, either in its form or purposes; that it was next to impossible to bring the President to trial upon an impeachment, if that were designed. That upon the doctrine contended for by gentlemen, if the marshal, or any civil officer of the Government, was sent to summon him, he could dismiss him, and put in another—he had the military and naval power in his own hands, and all the officers of Government held their offices at his will. The resolution was no way hostile to the President. Supposing it was admitted that there was an assumption of power over the Constitution and laws: could the Senate do nothing? It was the right and the duty of the Senate to express an opinion, and the resolution was nothing more. But it was said that the Senate could not act without acting on the *quo animo*. But the resolution only affirmed that the act done, was not in accordance with the sentiments of the Senate. What, then, he asked, had the President done? In his first speech on this subject, he (Mr. CLAY) had said that it was not the act of the Secretary, but of the President; and since then an honorable member from Tennessee, [Mr. GRUNDY,] had said distinctly, that this was not the act of the Secretary, but emphatically the act of the President, and whatever of praise or blame was due for it, was due to the President alone. This, Mr. C. considered as high authority, and entitled to great weight, coming from a gentleman who came from the same city as the President did. What the resolution affirmed was, that by the proceeding of the President he had assumed a power not granted to him by the Constitution and laws; and he defied gentlemen to point out an instance in the history of the Government, where a head of a department was required to perform a duty, and a President had interposed his authority. Mr. Gallatin, in the late report of the Union Committee, affirmed that this was the first instance of such an occurrence. A gentleman from Virginia, not now here, [Mr. RIVES,] had said that this was an abstract proposition, but Mr. Clay contended it was not so. It was a distinct affirmance of an opinion on the part of the Senate. And if both Houses should say—he did not care if it was by a majority of but one vote—that the reasons assigned by the Secretary were unsatisfactory and insufficient, it was his duty to restore them; his act was vacated, and no form of joint resolution or bill was necessary to effect the restoration. The subject could not be brought within the power of the veto. It was his duty to restore them, and he ought to perform it. Whether he would perform it or not, Mr. C. could not say; but public sentiment would compel him to do it.

Mr. C. then took up the argument urged, that all the executive power was vested in a President of the United States, without limitation. He had heard no limit to it whatever; but, on the contrary, the assertion of a power which was greater than that possessed by any king in Europe. He contended that the provision in the Constitution, that the "executive power shall be vested in a President of the United States," was not an express grant of power, but a designation of the person in whom the executive power should be vested. He then referred to the constitutional provision for the judicial department: that "the judicial department shall be vested in a Supreme Court of the United States, and such other courts as the Congress shall from time to time appoint." This, he maintained, was the recipient of the power, not the grant of the power. The Constitution proceeded in another part of it, to wit, the second section of the second article, to designate the powers granted to the President, beyond which he could not go, and that the argument that the President was invested with all the powers he had assumed by the provision that he should see "that the laws were faithfully executed," was without foundation; that this provision never was designed to give him the power of requiring public officers to perform their duties according to his will and pleasure; that the executive power was in its very nature fundamental; that where the Constitution gave him power, Congress could not impair it or take it away; but where Congress gave, Congress could shape or alter it as they thought proper. He denied that the President was invested with the power of control, as incident to the power of appointment. That the chief object in the establishment of the Government under the present Constitution, was to pay the debts of the United States: hence the provision for that purpose in the sixth article. With this object in view, the commissioners of the Sinking Fund were appointed, of whom the Vice President was one, and the Chief Justice of the United States was another, neither of whom were removable by the President. That although the heads of the State, War, and Navy Departments were emphatically the mouth-pieces of the President, yet the Treasury was one over which the control of Congress was complete, and therefore the President had no right to interpose his authority over the head of that department.

Mr. C. then adverted to the position maintained by some gentlemen, that all the officers of Government held their places at the pleasure of the President. He had never until now heard it contended that the President had a right to superintend and direct the action of an officer under his own will. He had, to be sure, a general controlling power to see the officer at his post in the proper discharge

of his duty. But he was to leave him there, to act upon his own responsibility. He had never heard such an interpretation of the President's power till in these more modern times. A similar provision that the Governor shall "see that the laws are faithfully executed," was to be found in the constitutions of several of the States; but it never was pretended that the Governors possessed power under it to the extent contended for here. The last foundation relied on by the advocates of this power was the responsibility of the President. What was responsibility? What was the responsibility of a President whose ambition was not satisfied? Where was the responsibility of a President who assumed all power—who wished to ascend the throne? Suppose that case. In 1789 the argument was used, that a removal from office by the President, on account of political opinions, rendered him liable to impeachment. Impeachment! Such a thing as impeachment, Mr. C. considered as almost impracticable. "I take the responsibility," was, in his view, an unmeaning sound. Was there really any responsibility? No. Was the President responsible for the conduct of the receiver of public moneys in New Orleans? Or even of the collector, almost under his eye, at Alexandria? No, he was not responsible. Suppose Mr. Duane had, or had not, removed the deposites, could the President have been impeached for it? Not at all. He was only responsible for his own act. In truth, it removed, it destroyed responsibility. A Secretary of the Treasury was called on to remove the deposites against his judgment—did it not annihilate his responsibility? Could he be put in a position to be liable to removal, if he did not obey the command, and liable to impeachment if he did obey it? It was impossible. What became of the oath of the officer, if this doctrine were true? He was sworn to perform the duties of his office according to his best judgment; and yet this doctrine spread the power of the President over the whole country and gave him a control over every officer in it.

Mr. C. then proceeded at length to answer the argument that the President was bound only to execute the laws according to his understanding of them, and contended that if this were true the Executive was the supreme department of the Government, and no others could move without him. He also contended that the President was bound to execute the laws in force; and if he assented to a law by approving it, he was bound by it. If he refused to sanction it, and exercised the veto, and it was afterwards passed by two-thirds, he could not refuse, but was equally bound to execute it.

Mr. C. here gave way to a motion to adjourn, which prevailed.

HOUSE OF REPRESENTATIVES.

THURSDAY, *March* 27, 1834.

The House proceeded with the resolution submitted by Mr. MARDIS:

Resolved, That the Committee of Ways and Means be instructed to inquire into the expediency of reporting a bill requiring the Secretary of the Treasury to deposite the public moneys of the United States in the State banks; and, also, as to the expediency of defining by law all contracts hereafter to be made with the Secretary for the safe-keeping, management, and disbursement of the same.

Mr. CHILTON ALLAN, who had the floor from the previous day, rose and said, that the occurrences which had taken place, made it difficult to state precisely whether the power of legislation still rested in the Congress, as given by the Constitution, or not. Every day the scenes were shifting. But yesterday, the people were told that Congress were possessed of virtue and intelligence, whilst to-day they were in terms denounced as being so corrupt, that it was impossible for them to legislate as they ought to do for the welfare of the people. He called on the House to say, whether this was not the state in which the country was placed. But yesterday, the whole country, the workshops, and all the pursuits of business, teemed with the hum of industry. To-day, that hum was silent. Yesterday commerce and agricultural labor were sure of their reward. To-day it was withering, its hopes were blasted, and in this new and extraordinary condition of affairs, Congress was brought into a debate upon reasons—forty pages of what the Secretary of the Treasury calls reasons—which were sent to the Committee of Ways and Means, who reported one hundred and forty pages more to prove he reasoned well; and thus, upon all these pages presented to them, the debate had been opened, no issue defined, but every subject had been introduced at the pleasure of each speaker upon them. The first question presented was naturally one upon which they could have met—the sufficiency or insufficiency of the reasons. But as these reasons, when exposed to the light of truth and reason, all evaporated, what did the chairman of the Committee of Ways and Means inform them? That there was a new question presented—he said it was bank or no bank. This the South declaring against, was then surrendered, and then they were told by the member from Tennessee it became a question of national honor. But the member from Alabama, not satisfied with this, said it was a question of liberty; anon, it was distress caused by the tyrant in his marble palace. But when it was rendered apparent that the bank, so far from curtailing, had not done so, nor to the extent which they were justified in doing, for the amount of deposites withdrawn from them, then what did they hear? Why, it was, "Mischief, do thy worst:" "Break, you ought to break!" Here, then, was a true picture of the question, and the remedy for the state the country was in.

He did not propose discussing minutely the reasons of the Secretary of the Treasury for his conduct, because the competent power—the last Congress—had already decided upon the facts he adduced. The very charges now brought against the bank had been previously brought against it, with some unimportant additions; and the result of the inquiry into them by Congress, was the solemn decision of Congress that the charges were untrue, and, therefore, that the bank ought to be rechartered. In Kentucky—he did not know what was the practice in other places—one fair trial was sufficient; that, he contended, the bank had, and with a verdict of acquittal in its favor. The question of removing the deposites had also been discussed, which, with the consideration that the friends of the Administration had abandoned the reasons, or any reason, to sustain the removal, made it unnecessary for him to take them up. He had, however, yet to learn that any person was to be found who had advised, or would advise, the removal. The question had been virtually waived.

The report was sent to the Committee of Ways and Means, that they might present their views on the reasons justifying the act. But they did not make such a report a part of their proceedings. He supposed they did not choose to risk doing that. Why? To avoid having any vote of Congress upon that very question. In this controversy he felt there was some credit due to the President for not having considered this a party question, and he could have wished, as his measures were opposed by Mr. Livingston, Mr. McLane, Mr. Cass, and others, whom he was not displeased with for so doing, that he had extended the same forbearance to Mr. Duane, for his opposition. The opinions of these Jackson men, showed this was not a party question, but one that ought to be decided upon its merits, and he was rejoiced at this, representing, as it was his good fortune to do, a district where, although it was the rule of conduct they adopted, that their representative was bound to follow the wishes of the majority, which was against the measures of the Executive, yet he wished to do so always with some deference to the views of the minority of his constituents.

Adverting to the state of the information which the people had as to the cause of the present distress, he could not help thinking that there was much mystification about it; and whilst various causes were assigned for it, it was matter of astonishment to him, that to meet them all, one wonder-working argument was deemed equally applicable to all subjects, to all objections; this was to be deemed triumphant through all the stages of the question; and that answer was found—in the battle of New Orleans.

Having made these preliminary observations upon the manner in which the argument was conducted, and upon the causes which produced the unhappy condition of the country, he would take now a nearer view. The subject of the controversy involved four propositions, all important in their nature. The first was, shall the regulation of the currency be vested in the General or State Governments? Second, shall the fiscal affairs of the nation be administered through the agency of the national or through the State banks? The third, shall the deposites of the public money be used for the benefit of a chosen body, in preference to that of the whole nation? And fourth, is the control of the currency to belong to the Executive or to the Legislature?

The President having proposed to use the State banks, a question was involved, whether the power of the House over the public money was to be surrendered? It then became necessary, before the power was surrendered, to inquire into their condition, that it might be ascertained whether they were capable of performing all that was required of them, and to supply the country with a sound currency. He proceeded to do so, and referring to their number being four hundred and fifty throughout the United States, having a paper circulation of one hundred millions of dollars, based on a supply of only twelve millions of specie in their vaults, he inferred that they would not have it in their power to maintain, as the Bank of the United States had done, a sound and general circulation throughout the Union; and he desired to have the name of any one statesman who could be said to have advocated the State banks in preference to the United States Bank for such purposes? Such was not to be given. On the contrary, Mr. Jefferson, he proved, by referring to the fourth volume of his correspondence with Mr. Eppes, denounced such institutions and their paper as trash; and Mr. Madison acknowledged that at the formation of the Constitution the mischief of a State bank currency was not foreseen. But they were to have a metallic currency, while he would be bound to say, that the very party engaged in crying it up were actively getting up State banks in many places. He instanced Indiana and other States, and then he argued to prove that after an experience of forty years, such banks were proved to be inadequate to do that agency which had been beneficially done by the Bank of the United States. He reverted to and denied the statement that the question of chartering the United States Bank was made a question to the people at the last election; when he was obliged to conclude his remarks, the hour allotted for morning business having expired.

The SPEAKER presented a report from the directors of the Mint, in relation to the assay of gold and silver. Laid on the table, and ordered to be printed.

THE DEPOSITES AND UNITED STATES BANK.

At one o'clock, the House resumed the consideration of the resolutions reported from the Committee of Ways and Means, together with the amendment offered by Mr. WILDE, declaring that the reasons of the Secretary of the Treasury for removing the public deposites are unsatisfactory and insufficient.

Mr. ELLSWORTH said, that the nature of the power exercised by the Secretary of the Treasury and the reasons which he has given for its exercise, had already been fully discussed here. The letter of the Secretary was finally referred to the Committee of Ways and Means, and from that enlightened committee we had received a report going over the same grounds. He was surprised that the committee had not seen fit to imbody in the resolutions concluding their report, a resolution expressive of the sense of the House as to the conduct of the Secretary. All the resolutions reported were prospective in their character. The question which was urged upon the consideration of the House and the country, had led to the impeachment of the conduct of men high in power. But, instead of giving an opinion upon that subject, the committee propose, first, that the Bank of the United States ought not to be rechartered. This was an abstract proposition, upon which he did not feel called upon to decide. It was possible, that, in the course of two years, more light might be thrown upon that subject, which might influence our ultimate decision. The committee also propose the appointment of a special committee, to investigate the causes of the public distress, and the condi

of the bank. To this he had no objection. He was willing that the conduct of the bank should be thoroughly probed. Not to dwell on this subject, he would only mention a few considerations which should induce the House to vote for the proposition of the gentleman from Georgia, [Mr. WILDE.] Our relations to the Bank of the United States, a proper respect to the Executive, to the excitement prevalent in the country, and to ourselves, all required us to place on our records our opinion whether the President of the United States has or has not exercised a power over the bank and the currency which this House is called upon to sustain. We are constituted by the bank charter as the court of ultimate appeal and decision in this case. Will not the majority of the House say whether the Secretary of the Treasury had good reasons or not for removing the deposites? He would not suppose that the House was afraid to meet the issue.

The Executive, Mr. E. contended, had drawn to himself a portion of the legislative power of the Government. This was the main view which he should present, and, in sustaining that view, he did not think it necessary to call in question the motives of the President. The removal of eight or nine millions of dollars was a matter, in itself, of small consideration. But the President had destroyed the legal fiscal agent of the Government, and created twenty other fiscal agents. He had entered upon an experiment to put down the Bank of the United States, and substitute for it the State banks—to fill up the vacuum created by the withdrawal of the United States Bank paper, with the currency of the State banks. The manner in which this was done was bold and daring—and there was, he believed, some charm in a bold and daring deed, which silenced the dictates of the judgment, and even of conscience. The unnatural war waged upon the bank appeared to him to spring from love of conquest, victory, and spoil. Mr. E. went on to argue that the experiment was uncalled-for, hazardous to the public interests, and illegal. He referred to the act of May, 1820, prohibiting the Secretaries from making any contract but by law. This act, he thought, rendered the contracts made by the Secretary of the Treasury with the State banks illegal. The gentleman from Indiana [Mr. LANE] not long ago exclaimed, in the language of exultation, that the treasury was found. Would any gentleman tell him where the treasury was? Where, he repeated, is the treasury? Does not the president hold in his hands all the money of the Government? Does he not claim authority to move the whole public treasure from one bank to another? What guards, what laws, secure the treasury? The treasury was not kept in any known place, under the safeguard of any known laws. Mr. E. declared that he would not give much for all the deposites in the State banks, should this House adjourn, leaving things as they are. He referred to some documents which, he said, would show that some of the deposite banks had more public money than the whole amount of their capital. The Bank of Natchez had at one time a million of dollars. Would any one say that that money was safe? The Secretary of the Treasury trembled when he sat down to pen the order to the bank at Natchez to be prepared to pay the money on a certain day. My word for it, (said he,) it will be a long day before that money is paid. So with the Girard bank, which had lent out a million and a half of public money. In reply to the congratulations of the gentleman from Indiana, upon the recovery of the treasury, he would say boldly, that there was no treasury at our disposal. Mr. E. also referred to the special message of the Governor of New York to the Legislature of that State, recommending measures for the relief of the banks and the business community of that State. He could not doubt that the Governor believed all the banks in that State to be in jeopardy. The idea of introducing a metallic currency was, he insisted, wholly absurd. We could not collect the revenue, nor carry on any commercial operations if the experiment should be attempted. But the States were going to extend the paper system. They show no disposition to return to a hard-money currency. They are increasing their paper currency to meet the withdrawal of the United States paper, and we have no control over their operations. He called upon gentlemen to tell him

what great interest of the country had suffered from the currency of the United States Bank. Had commerce, agriculture, or manufactures suffered from it? On the contrary, those interests had been fostered by the bank. This was a young and enterprising country, and required credit as a substitute for capital. In England it was estimated that one dollar in specie afforded to the community a currency of three dollars. The same facilities were still more requisite for us.

Mr. E. went into a view of the extent and causes of the distress, and asked whether there was any hope of relief. He would declare that he saw none. He spoke from personal observation. During the consideration of this question, he had visited his constituents, and he knew that the distress was great and pervading. The storm was but now beginning which was to pour destruction upon the business interests of this country. His constituents had extensive connexions with the South and West, but their trade was almost entirely cut off. Nothing was made to send abroad, because the difference of exchange was sufficiently great to swallow up all the profits on business. Many large manufacturing establishments had dismissed half of their hands, and some had stopped entirely. No relief was expected from any source, except the abandonment of the experiment attempted by the Government.

After speaking two hours, Mr. ELLSWORTH concluded, and

The floor was obtained by Mr. CHOATE, who moved an adjournment.

Mr. McKIM demanded the yeas and nays on the motion, and they were ordered.

The question being taken by yeas and nays, it was decided in the affirmative—yeas 85, nays 69.

The Senate then adjourned.

IN SENATE.

FRIDAY, March 28, 1834.

A message upon executive business was received from the President of the United States, by Mr. Donelson, his Private Secretary.

Mr. WEBSTER presented a memorial from inhabitants of the city of Albany, New York, asking the restoration of the deposites to the bank of the United States, and praying the recharter of the bank.

Mr. WEBSTER accompanied the memorial by a speech at some length; and, on concluding,

Mr. WRIGHT rose and expressed a desire to make some observations in reply, but that he did not wish to interrupt the discussion which was going on, unless the gentleman from Kentucky would yield his right to the floor upon the special order.

Mr. CLAY said it was his wish to conclude the debate which had been so long continued, and in order to give the gentleman from New York an opportunity of making the remarks he proposed, he moved to lay the memorial on the table; which was agreed to.

REMOVAL OF THE DEPOSITES.

Mr. CLAY then resumed his speech begun yesterday; and on concluding he offered the following modification of his second resolution, and asked the yeas and nays on both:

Resolved, That the President, in the late executive proceeding in relation to the public revenue, has assumed upon himself authority and power not conferred by the Constitution and laws, but in derogation of both.

Mr. MOORE then rose, and briefly explained the reasons why he should vote 'against both the resolutions, and was followed by

Mr. McKEAN, who said he thought it his duty to give, in one word, his reasons for the same vote. He considered the resolutions as purely censorious in their character, and the adoption of them would be no remedy whatever for the prevailing distress of the country. But he thought it right to say, that the vote he would give was not to be considered decisive evidence of what his course might be when decisive measures of relief should be proposed.

The question being upon the adoption of the resolution reported by the Committee on Finance, that " the reasons assigned by the Secretary of the Treasury for the removal of the public deposites

' from the Bank of the United States are insuffi- ' cient and unsatisfactory," it was decided in the affirmative, as follows, to wit:

YEAS—Messrs. Bibb, Black, Calhoun, Clay, Clayton, Ewing, Frelinghuysen, Hendricks, Kent, King of Georgia, Knight, Leigh, Mangum, Naudain, Poindexter, Porter, Prentiss, Preston, Robbins, Silsbee, Smith, Southard, Sprague, Swift, Tomlinson, Tyler, Waggaman, and Webster—28.

NAYS—Messrs. Benton, Brown, Forsyth, Grundy, Hill, Kane, King of Alabama, Linn, McKean, Moore, Morris, Robinson, Shepley, Tallmadge, Tipton, White, Wilkins, and Wright —18.

The question being on Mr. CLAY's second resolution, as modified, was also decided in the affirmative, as follows, to wit:

YEAS—Messrs. Bibb, Black, Calhoun, Clay, Clayton, Ewing, Frelinghuysen, Kent, Knight, Leigh, Mangum, Naudain, Poindexter, Porter, Prentiss, Preston, Robbins, Silsbee, Smith, Southard, Sprague, Swift, Tomlinson, Tyler, Waggaman, and Webster—26.

NAYS—Messrs. Benton, Brown, Forsyth, Grundy, Hendricks, Hill, Kane, King of Alabama, King of Georgia, Linn, McKean, Moore, Morris, Robinson, Shepley, Tallmadge, Tipton, White, Wilkins, and Wright—20.

Mr. WAGGAMAN moved, that when the Senate adjourns, it adjourn until Monday.

On a division, the motion was lost—yeas 21, nays 22.

On motion of Mr. NAUDAIN,

The Senate adjourned.

HOUSE OF REPRESENTATIVES.

FRIDAY, March 28, 1834.

Mr. J. Q. ADAMS asked leave to offer the following:

Resolved, That the Secretary of the Treasury be directed to lay before this House, copies of the charters of all the banks selected by him, as depositories of the public moneys in the place of the Bank of the United States and its branches—together with the names of the presidents, directors, and stockholders, in the said selected banks, with the amount of stock in said banks, held by each stockholder, and the amount of debt due by each president, cashier, and director, of each of the banks, to the said banks, at the time when it was selected as a depository, and at this time.

Mr. POLK said, as the information was already before the House, he must object.

Mr. ADAMS insisted that it was not, and he moved the suspension of the rule of the House to enable him to offer it.

Mr. WILLIAMS called for the yeas and nays.

Mr. POLK then said, that he would withdraw his objection.

The resolution having been read,

Mr. EWING rose for the purpose of submitting an amendment, calling for further information, which he said he desired to have. As there was such a cry made about lawyers and the solicitors, employed on behalf of the bank, he desired to know if any were employed in behalf of the State institutions.

Mr. WAYNE remarked, that as by the rule, the resolution must stand over one day, an amendment was not in order. He desired, as the information called for was of a comprehensive character, that it should lie over and be printed, that the House could be prepared to judge of the propriety of acceding to it or not.

After a few remarks from Mr. SPEIGHT, The SPEAKER explained the rule; after which Mr. ADAMS assented to the consideration of the resolution being postponed, upon the understanding that it should be taken up to-morrow. The amendment of Mr. EWING to insert, " and the names of the lawyers and solicitors" he accepted as a modification.

The Hon. JAMES W. BOULDIN appeared, was qualified, and took his seat as a Representative from Virginia—elected in the place of the Hon. THOMAS TYLER BOULDIN, deceased.

On motion of Mr. McKINLEY, the House agreed to meet, henceforth, at 11 o'clock, A. M.

Mr. LYON, of Michigan, obtained leave to offer the following:

Resolved, That the Secretary of War be requested to transmit to this House a copy of the map and report furnished the department by Lieutenant Allen, who accompanied H. R. Schoolcraft, Esq., to and beyond the sources of the Mississippi river, on a visit to the Northwestern Indians in 1832.

Agreed to.

Mr. PATTERSON obtained leave to submit the following:

Resolved, That the Committee on Indian Affairs be instructed to inquire into the expediency of making an appropriation for the purpose of purchasing the Wyandot Indian reservations in the State of Ohio, and removing the Wyandot tribe of Indians west of the Mississippi.

Agreed to.

Mr. GRENNELL, from the Committee of Claims, reported a bill for the relief of Joseph Nourse.

Read twice and committed.

Mr. POLK, from the Committee of Ways and Means, asked to be discharged from the consideration of the petition of certain sugar refiners of Boston, praying a reduction of duties on sugar.

Agreed to.

Mr. BELL, from the Committee on the Judiciary, reported a bill supplementary to the acts in relation to insolvent debtors of the United States. Read twice and committed.

Mr. HARPER, of New Hampshire, from the Committee on Commerce, reported a bill for the relief of Joseph Harbaugh and others. Read twice and committed.

Mr. CAVE JOHNSON, from the Committee on Public Lands, reported a bill to direct the sale of certain lands in Illinois. Read twice and committed.

Mr. WHITTLESEY, of Ohio, proposed that the House should, hereafter, devote a part of the morning to the offering of resolutions. He gave notice that he should, to-morrow, ask leave to submit a motion to call the States for resolutions.

The House proceeded to the consideration of the following resolution, submitted by Mr. MARDIS:

Resolved, That the Committee of Ways and Means be instructed to inquire into the expediency of reporting a bill requiring the Secretary of the Treasury to deposite the public moneys of the United States in the State banks; and, also, as to the expediency of defining by law all contracts hereafter to be made with the Secretary for the safe-keeping, management, and disbursement of the same.

Mr. CHILTON ALLAN resumed his remarks. He contended that the people had not decided the question of the recharter of the bank by their vote in favor of the election of General Jackson. This question was not (he said) distinctly submitted to the people at the election in a single county or district of the country; and, on the contrary, it was generally supposed that General Jackson thought a national bank not only expedient, but constitutional. The people, he insisted, were in favor of a national bank. Even at the South, where the bank was opposed on constitutional grounds, its general expediency was not questioned. Scarcely a single southern member had spoken on the subject, since the discussion commenced here, who opposed the bank on grounds of expediency. Mr. A. here asked the reading of Mr. Madison's opinion on the constitutionality of the bank. Among his constituents, the authority of that statesman was greater than that of any man living, and he wished to lay his opinions on this question before them. The paper having been read, Mr. A. said this was the first country in the world which had tried the experiment of a written constitution; but a written constitution would avail us nothing, if each party which obtained the majority power should, in succession, overthrow and change the settled construction of the Constitution. He alluded to the rumor of new State banks, some of which were to have branches in other States. Any State (he said) which should consent to receive a branch bank from another State, ought to be blotted out from existence. His constituents cared nothing about the bank. They only wished a sound currency, such as the Bank of the United States had uniformly given them. They wanted good money for their produce. The question, he argued, was one between money and paper rags—between the industrious classes and the drones. Here Mr. A. was interrupted in his remarks by the expiration of the hour, and the House proceeded to the special order of the day.

THE DEPOSITES AND UNITED STATES BANK.

The House resumed the consideration of the resolutions reported from the Committee of Ways and Means, together with the amendment offered by Mr. WILDE.

Mr. CHOATE rose, he said, with great reluctance, to address the House on a question which had been so long discussed. The House would, no doubt, be glad to hear that he did not intend to occupy its attention for any length of time. He thought that there was a point of view in which the majority had not looked at this question. He should ask them whether, if he conceded to them some of the main positions on which they stood, they could not consistently with their own grounds, consent, by restoring the deposites, to give relief to an agitated, anxious, and suffering community? On one side it had been urged that the President had gone beyond the legal and constitutional powers, and on the other, it had been argued that the President and Secretary of the Treasury had not exceeded their authority. He made haste, in the outset, to say, that he should not touch upon these more exciting and elevated points. He had nothing to say about the limits and extent of Executive power over the subject of the deposites and the currency. As to the bank itself, he should go throughout on the supposition that it would not be rechartered. He called on gentlemen to look upon the proposition to restore the deposites merely as a temporary measure for relief. The business of the country stood in need of all the aids which the public purse could afford. He went on the plain ground that the public stood in need of the public money. However resolutely determined we might be not to recharter the bank, it so happened that the public could not have the use of the public purse, in any beneficial way at present, but through the Bank of the United States. There was no one here now who did not admit and lament the prevalence of great distress throughout the country. Was it not possible, then, without any material compromise of opinion, for the House to concur in the restoration of the deposites, as a measure of relief from the great, unforeseen, and unintended calamity which had followed their removal? We had, he thought, obscured, varied, and endangered the most important question before us, by heaping too much matter upon it.

The only question was this: In what way can we dispose of the public deposites so as to afford practical and immediate relief to the community? On that question he could not but hope that he would yet have the concurrence of the majority of the House in his opinion. The immediate cause of the public distress was, that the public deposites no longer did their usual and proper office in supplying active capital, in sustaining loans, and in upholding the vast system of credits which was the basis of all the business operations of the country. Heretofore, the public money in the interval between its collection and disbursement, had been lent to the public. It was placed in banks, not only for safety, but to aid the currency. In this way some compensation was made to the people for the expenses of the Government. Taxes, it had been justly remarked, never a blessing, had been in this way rendered less intolerable. The United States Bank thinks that it cannot safely afford the same facilities to the country, without, as with the deposites; and, for many reasons, the State banks and private capitalists are led to follow the example of the United States Bank in curtailing their business. He would not stop to explain the *modus operandi*, but he stood upon the broad, practical fact, that capital to a vast amount was rendered inactive. There is as much blood as ever in the system, but it is congealed at the heart. Not only the amount of the deposites was rendered unavailable, but the great mass of capital in the country was hoarded or put to usury. The removal of the deposites had unexpectedly produced this state of things. He knew that while we all agreed as to the existence of the embarrassments in business, we disagreed as to the causes which led to them. Some maintain that but for the conduct of the United States Bank, the public deposites would have continued to afford the same facilities as formerly. But what hinders Congress from giving back the funds which have been withdrawn? It was said, that the State banks would ultimately afford relief. The practical question was, in what way could be soonest and most safely afforded the necessary relief? The effect of the restoration of the deposites would be immediate and great. It would enable the bank to make its will; to appoint its executors; to distribute its assets; to indulge its debtors; and to die something like a Christian. The people, too, would be enabled to prepare for the change. The transition would be less sudden, violent, and agitating to the community. The consequences of the experiment so far cannot be remedied. But because we cannot do everything, we should not refuse to do anything. Now, he would ask, does anybody see any prospect of early relief in any other way?

Mr. C. argued at some length to prove that it was the duty of the Government to restore the deposites to the bank, for the purpose of enabling it to wind up, as it was admitted there was a necessity to do, gradually, and not by a sudden contraction of their affairs, cause or increase distress. He held that the establishment of friendly relations between the Government and the bank would be instantly productive of restoring friendly relations between the banks; and thus the bank would, if a recharter was decided against, wind up with the least possible injury to the community. In this way only did he think they could do so. The directors of the bank would find it their interest, not hoping a recharter as a consequence from the restoration, would, he was convinced, be influenced by the views common to all other directors of banking institutions similarly circumstanced. The whole capital of the country, now under a sort of embargo, would be at once let out, and the currency placed in a condition by which alone the country could expect to be prosperous. He knew the bank had been called at some public meetings an "evil spirit;" but if it was a spirit of evil, was it safe to torment it as it had been, with this illegal violation of their chartered rights? the whole policy of the Executive having been directed to put down the institution. Whilst he would not object to the exercise of the constitutional right of the veto, he could not but regret, that, not content with this, the President had, to make assurance doubly sure, gone on by this act of removal to forestall the action which it was the right only of Congress to make. From this, he contended, all the evils and all the distress and embarrassment the country at present labored under was to be attributed. He would contrast this high-handed policy with that pursued by Mr. Gallatin, whom he described to have effected the object of winding up the affairs of the old Bank of the United States almost without the loss of a single private fortune.

Having shown the necessity that existed for a restoration of the deposites, he desired to proceed to the consideration of the new project submitted to them—a return to a metallic currency; and he must contend that this was, in the present state of things, nearly impracticable. He held that a paper currency, based on a metallic currency, had been productive of more vivifying influence than any other that had been ever introduced.

Having gone through the charges brought against the bank, he could not agree that the reasons of the Secretary were sufficient to justify him in removing the deposites. The only charge which seemed to him to be necessary to dwell upon, was the charge that the bank was producing the distress for the purpose of forcing a recharter. But whilst he agreed that those who entertained such feelings were justified in using the strong language they did, he could not act upon this, without having certain and sure knowledge that they had created it for this purpose. Until he was convinced of this, he could not but entertain the opinion, that the attitude which the Government assumed made it necessary for the bank to act with some caution. The question, then, would be, had the bank curtailed to such a degree as was unnecessary? This alone would entitle gentlemen to oppose it on the grounds they

THE CONGRESSIONAL GLOBE.

PRINTED AND PUBLISHED AT THE CITY OF WASHINGTON, BY BLAIR & RIVES.

23d Congress, 1st Session. | SATURDAY, APRIL 5, 1834. | Vol. 1........No. 18.

had done. He adverted to the contrariety of opinions held as to the mode in which the operations of banks should be conducted, as affording some evidence to show that they were not justified in attributing that conduct to a spirit of evil, which for ought they knew, might be the wisest measures of caution, and which certainly, therefore, should not justify Congress in withholding their assent to a measure which would at once relieve the community. The conduct of all banks, he contended, should be left to themselves. Under all the circumstances, he came to the conclusion, that if he were a political adherent of the President, (which he was not,) that although it was evident he desired to take all the responsibility of these measures, yet, as he could not have foreseen their consequences, he should advise him not to keep on, inflexibly, to a course which was bringing destruction on the community, and by means which were inroads on the Constitution. He considered the removal of one officer for not complying with his wishes, the act of removal, and the placing of the public money, as it had been, in State banks, as of this character. The public money had been treated as if it was private, and he referred to the alteration made in the resolutions by Mr. Mardis, as confirming these views. He did not go so far as to say this was the union of the purse and the sword in the hands of the Executive, in the sense it was first used, but he would say, that it was a vast transfer of power to the Executive, and as such, it was in opposition to the spirit of the Constitution. The whole plan of State banks to transact their fiscal affairs, or legislating to place the deposites in them, must have the most pernicious effect, by increasing, in an undue degree, the power and prerogative of one branch, and which entitled him to say Congress would have much boldness for conniving at. In the long run, much disposed as the people were to honor the public magistracy, they would rally under the flag raised here in conflict to assumptions of power. They inherited this spirit from their ancestors. It was this that they practised at the Revolution. Everywhere the people were disposed to take from, not add to, the power of Government. The people would not be contented with the restoration of the deposites, they would call for the supremacy of their branch in the Government. He would then entreat all the friends of liberty, of law, to lend their aid in supporting the restoration, and putting an end to the evils which are at present afflicting the country.

Mr. DICKERSON rose and said:

Mr. Speaker: I have listened with much pleasure to the remarks of the gentleman from Massachusetts [Mr. Choate] who last addressed the House. His views were new and interesting, and delivered in a tone and spirit becoming the representative of a free people.

But, sir, I was not prepared to hear the positions taken by the honorable gentleman, nor can I yield to the correctness of his views, although so eloquently expressed. I had thought that the idea of restoring the deposites as a means of relief from present distress had not been seriously entertained, except with a view to the recharter of the bank. It appears to me that it is the worst of all expedients, and its necessary consequence must be to prolong the distress which now prevails, instead of relieving it. Nor can I perceive of what possible benefit the possession of the public deposites would be to the bank if it is to close its operations in 1836. With that view, it is certainly now time that they should in good faith commence curtailing their business. They now have on hand—and in the process of drawing in their capital they must necessarily have on hand at all times—surplus funds lying useless in their vaults, and of consequence the possession of the public deposites, with their attendant duties and liabilities, would be worse than useless to them.

I do not propose, sir, to attempt to answer the arguments of the gentleman in detail upon this point. But I would remark, that the foundation of his whole argument rests upon the idea, that if the deposites are restored, the bank at the termination of its present charter will calmly cease to exist, and (as he remarked) "die something like a Christian." If I believed this, sir, I should, indeed, think it worth while to inquire seriously into the expediency of restoring the deposites. But in this respect the gentleman begs the question. He asks more than will be conceded. I believe with him, that the bank will cease to exist at the termination of its present charter, but it will die hard. It will struggle as long as it can hope to perpetuate its existence, and I am not disposed to add to it any further power to protract its dying struggles.

I intended, sir, to give a silent vote upon the question now under discussion. But I consider it the privilege of the people to know the sentiments of their representatives upon all subjects involving their interests; and as I have been instructed by my constituents upon this subject, a silent vote might not be considered as expressive of my own sentiments, but only as a response to theirs. Under these circumstances, I must ask the indulgence of the House whilst I briefly state my views of the matter now under discussion.

By the report of the Committee of Ways and Means the following propositions are submitted for the consideration of Congress:

1st. That the Bank of the United States should not be rechartered.

2d. That the deposites should not be restored.

3d. That the State banks should be continued as the places of public deposite, and that they should be regulated by law; and

4th. That a committee should be appointed to investigate the concerns of the bank, &c.

In place of these resolutions the gentleman from Georgia [Mr. Wilde] has proposed an amendment, declaring that the reasons assigned by the Secretary of the Treasury are insufficient, and the present discussion turns upon that proposed amendment.

I do not intend to trespass upon the time of the House by recapitulating the many arguments and reasons which have been urged upon the different topics involved in this discussion, and which must be familiar to this House, but propose to state briefly my conclusions drawn from those arguments, and to show that the proposed amendment should not be adopted.

I understand that very little difference of opinion exists as to the propriety of adopting the proposition contained in the last resolution of the Committee of Ways and Means.

The second and third of those resolutions appear to me to depend very much upon the decision of the first; and the question involved in the first resolution, whether the Bank of the United States shall be rechartered, I consider as the real and important question now under discussion before Congress and the people. No matter how this question may be connected with other considerations—no matter how ingenuity may strive to conceal it from public view—no matter how political aspirants may use the occasion for their ambitious purposes—it must result in the important inquiry whether it be consistent with the great interest of this republic that the United States Bank shall be continued. Before I proceed to explain my views upon this point, permit me, sir, to dispose of some subjects which have been pressed into this discussion, as I consider, improperly, and for political effect.

The question of the power and authority of the President of the United States to remove his Secretary, in the manner he has done, I consider has no necessary connexion with, and ought to have no bearing upon, the decision of the question of the renewal of the charter of the Bank of the United States, nor of the present disposition of the public deposites. And as I am unwilling that the real point in issue should be involved in any extraneous matter, or obscured from view by any other subjects not necessarily connected with it, I shall not at present remark upon that point, except to observe, that if the President has been guilty of a corrupt, or arbitrary, or unconstitutional exercise of power, in removing his Secretary, or in appointing another, or in recommending the removal of the public deposites, in the manner he has done, he is responsible to his country for his conduct. Let him be called to account, and put upon his defence. And permit me to say, that if he does not answer promptly, and defend himself triumphantly, it will be a new era in his history.

But it has been said that he shields himself behind a majority in this House, and, therefore, that such an effort would be useless. The allegation proves too much for those who use it, unless they can show, as they sometimes appear to believe, that the minority should govern the majority. It is true, I have no doubt, that this House would shield him from oppression, but never from a fair and impartial investigation.

As to the claim of the bank to retain the public deposites until the termination of the charter, it appears to me to be without foundation. The right of the Secretary of the Treasury to withhold those deposites from the bank, is reserved in the charter by express and unequivocal words. The assignment of his reasons is an act necessarily subsequent to the act of removal, and consequently presupposes the existence of the right to remove.

The object of the provision contained in the 16th section of their charter, requiring the Secretary to assign his reasons, was to enable Congress to judge whether the Secretary had consulted the public interest in making the removal, and not to inquire how far the interests of the bank had been consulted. And if it had been the intention of Congress to limit the discretion of the Secretary in this respect to the single question of the *safety* of the deposites in the United States Bank, I cannot understand why they should require him to assign his *reasons*, when but one *reason* could exist, and that reason ascertained by law. For these, and many other reasons, which have been urged before this House, and which I do not intend to repeat, I conclude that the claim of the bank, by their charter, to retain the public deposites, is not well founded, and that it was the right and duty of the Secretary of the Treasury to remove those deposites, whenever the exigencies of the country required their removal.

But, sir, it has been seriously urged that the deposites should be restored to the United States Bank, for the purpose of rebuking the President of the United States for his arbitrary and corrupt exercise of power, in the removal of his Secretary. I am well aware, sir, that there may be many gentlemen, whose chief and favorite object it is to rebuke the President, rather than relieve the people. But I was not prepared to hear this reason for the restoration of the deposites publicly urged; and I cannot consider that its tendency has been well considered.

In this country, no man can be tried for the most trifling charge, without having an opportunity of being heard in his own defence. It is the great security of the people against oppression. And shall we, here, now undertake to try the Chief Magistrate of our country, upon a charge, which, if true, should hurl him from the high place which he now fills with so much honor to himself and his country, without giving him the privilege common to every American citizen—the privilege of being heard in his own defence? Sir, the very act would render us guilty in the highest degree, of the offence charged against him. If gentlemen wish to rebuke the President, let them meet him, as he has always met his opponents, in fair, open, and manly conflict, and not strive to rebuke him by indirect means, by the union of the influence of nullifiers, bank men, and aspiring politicians. Let them resort to impeachment, or to the ballot boxes, and not to a method heretofore unknown to our laws and Constitution.

It is true, sir, that the several questions growing out of this subject—which, for the reasons stated,

I have not undertaken to discuss—are of great moment, and deserving of most serious consideration, and will without doubt receive that consideration when properly presented to this House. And I certainly have no wish to screen the President of the United States from an investigation of any act of his political life, nor do I wish that the conduct of the Secretary of the Treasury, nor of any other officer of Government, should escape the strictest scrutiny. But I do protest against this indiscreet mode of trial. I contend that every measure should rest on its own merits; that the several questions are of sufficient importance to require separate discussion, and that the combination of those important questions only tends to obscure the truth, and mislead the public mind.

But, sir, it is said that the great and important question now to be discussed and settled is, whether the reasons assigned by the Secretary of the Treasury for the removal of the deposites are sufficient; and to ascertain the opinion of Congress upon this point, is the ostensible object of the proposed amendment of the gentleman from Georgia, [Mr. Wilde,] and also of the proposed amendment of the gentleman from Rhode Island, [Mr. Burges,] and early in this session it was the ostensible object of the gentleman from South Carolina, [Mr. McDuffie,] in an amendment then proposed by him.

With due deference for the opinions of other gentlemen on this floor, and notwithstanding the factitious importance which has been thrown about this view of the subject, I must be permitted to say that, in my opinion, the decision of that question would be unimportant, except for its political effect; and it would have no necessary influence upon the real question now under discussion.

The Secretary of the Treasury is not upon his trial; it is not a question between Congress and the Secretary; nor should it be a question between Congress and the bank.

It is in fact a question between Congress and the people. We find the country and the public treasure in a certain condition, and we are bound to make such disposition of them as shall appear to us most conducive to the public welfare, and best calculated to promote their present and future happiness and prosperity.

I have said that the decision of the question of the sufficiency of the reasons assigned by the Secretary of the Treasury for the removal of the deposites would be unimportant, and that it would have no necessary bearing or influence upon the real question under discussion.

In order to test the correctness of this assertion, let us suppose, for the sake of the argument, that we shall determine those reasons to be insufficient: what is the result? I beg gentlemen to recollect the real question—and I ask again, what would be the effect of the decision?

It might, indeed, show that we were of opinion that the Secretary had acted without sufficient reasons—or it might show that, in our opinion, he had acted corruptly or illegally. But it would not necessarily show either of those results. For it might show only that in our opinion he had offered insufficient reasons for an act which was right and proper in itself, and for which good and sufficient reasons existed; and I presume it will not be contended that the deposites should be restored to the United States Bank, merely because the Secretary of the Treasury may not have assigned sufficient reasons for their removal, when, in point of fact, sufficient reasons did exist.

But the decision of the question against the sufficiency of the reasons assigned by the Secretary of the Treasury, would furnish us with no guide to direct us in the true course now to be pursued. It would lay the basis of no legislative action. For surely it does not follow, as a necessary consequence, that because it may have been inexpedient then to remove the deposites, that it must now be expedient to restore them. The two propositions are distinct, and depend upon entirely different reasons.

But, Mr. Speaker, let us suppose, on the other hand, that by the vote of this House we shall decide that the reasons assigned by the Secretary are sufficient, and that he was wholly justified by them in making the removal: what then? Would that decision furnish a true guide for our conduct, or form the basis of any legislative action at this time? Certainly not, to my mind. For although his reasons may have been sufficient at that time; and although the situation of the country may then have demanded the immediate removal of the deposites from the United States Bank, yet circumstances may have rendered it expedient that those deposites should now be restored. By way of illustration, I would remark, that if I were now convinced that the United States Bank would be rechartered in 1836, or at any prior period, I would, without hesitation, now vote for the restoration of the deposites, although I am entirely satisfied with the reasons for their removal.

I make these remarks, Mr. Speaker, to show that, by expressing our opinion, and deciding upon the sufficiency of the reasons of the Secretary of the Treasury for the removal of the deposites, we really do not advance one step, and no important conclusion can fairly be drawn from the decision.

Although it may not be considered strictly in order, upon the discussion of the proposed amendment, to inquire into the causes of the distress which now prevails; yet as that subject has been made the topic of debate upon this occasion, I must ask the indulgence of the House for a few minutes to explain my views upon this point.

It is certainly true that the Bank of the United States, during the period between the month of May, 1830, and the month of May, 1832, increased their loans more than twenty-seven millions of dollars. I will not inquire into the motives of the bank, in thus extending their business. But one of two conclusions must evidently flow from the fact: either that the bank, before that time, had not issued as much paper as the country required for its healthful use, or, upon that occasion, that they issued more. The first of these conclusions cannot be adopted, without charging the directors of the bank with want of discernment to discover, or inclination to promote, the interests of their stockholders, which will not be pretended. And recent events have made most manifest the truth of the latter conclusion.

It is also true, that between the month of May, 1832, and the meeting of this Congress in December last, the bank had reduced their loans about sixteen millions of dollars, and since that time they have continued to reduce.

It is not important, according to my view of the case, here to inquire whether they have made that reduction of their loans, *bona fide*, to close their own concerns, or, *mala fide*, to close the concerns of other people. But it must be obvious to every mind, that the necessary consequence of such a rapid expansion and contraction must be to produce a scarcity of money, and consequent distress in all branches of business. And what in fact has been the situation of the country in the meantime? Why, sir, during the time of the expansion, of course money was plenty, and all kinds of business prosperous and flourishing. But as soon as the contraction commenced, a reaction also commenced, and a pressure was soon felt in the money market, which continued to increase regularly, but not rapidly, until the meeting of Congress; since which time, it has marched with most rapid strides, and from pressure it soon became high-pressure. A panic ensued, which brought distress and ruin in its train.

Such is a brief history of the rise and progress of this pressure. And now, sir, let us inquire more particularly into the cause of its extraordinary character.

It is not pretended, by any one, that the mere act of changing the place of deposite could have produced the result. But it is said, that it is the great breach of national faith, and of chartered rights, and violated laws and Constitution, occasioned by that act, which has destroyed all confidence between man and man, and brought panic and distress among the people.

If that has been the true cause, the effect (so far as that effect could have been produced by want of confidence or panic) would have been felt at once in its greatest force. The people would not have waited sixty days for the meeting of Congress to inform them that there had been a great breach of national faith, and of chartered rights, and that their Constitution and laws had been trampled upon, and that it was time for them to be alarmed. But so far from that, sir, we find that during the interval between the removing of the deposites and the meeting of Congress, business was going on as usual; no loss of confidence, no panic, and under no other pressure in the money market than would necessarily have resulted from the situation of the country if the deposites had not been removed. I say, therefore, that it is not true that the present distress in the community has been occasioned by the removal of the public deposites. The cause was not adequate to the effect.

But, sir, that distress is occasioned by the struggle of the United States Bank for a recharter, combined with the struggle of aspiring politicians for power, acting upon the people by means of the inflammatory and panic-making speeches of honorable members of Congress—speeches which are multiplied by means of the public presses, and scattered gratuitously by hundreds of thousands, amidst a people who were placed in a situation easily to be alarmed and distressed by the improvident designing conduct of the bank itself. Here, sir, are causes enough for the effect—causes which would have existed in full force if the deposites had never been removed. And the only difference is, that they now charge the distress to the removal of the deposites; and if they had not been removed, they would have charged it, with the same effect, to the veto.

Mr. Speaker, in reflecting upon the present situation of the country, I was forcibly struck with the remarks of the honorable gentleman from Rhode Island, [Mr. Burges,] some days ago, when addressing the House upon this subject. He represented the Government bank directors as becoming drunk by looking at the immense masses of gold and silver in the vaults of the bank. The idea serves as an apt illustration of my views, and I shall therefore take the liberty of using the gentleman's figure, and extending its application, by comparing the people of the United States to drunken men. Yes, sir, for six years past we have been too much excited, we have taken too much stimulus, too much wine for our substantial food. Some three years ago, the Bank of the United States (whom I shall consider upon this occasion as the wine dealer) administered most copious draughts of the intoxicating liquor. We were told that it was good wine, and would pass current everywhere. We seized it with avidity, and drank it with delight. It gave us additional strength, vigor, and animation. We became drunk with prosperity. But, sir, it is with bodies politic, in this respect, as with natural persons—an over excitement cannot continue for a long time. A corresponding depression must ensue, and we are now in that condition. The wine merchant has ceased to supply our appetites with their wonted quantity, and left us feeble, and tremulous, and distressed. And shall we, sir, again return to the dangerous practice, and for the sake of a few bright and joyous years of excess and intoxicating prosperity, condemn ourselves to a premature old age, and drag out a miserable, decrepid, and gouty existence, dependent upon the wine dealer for our lazy comforts, and leave to our posterity, instead of the bright inheritance which we received from our ancestors, an inheritance encumbered for more than it is worth? A moneyed aristocracy? No, sir, we have yet sufficient physical power to redeem ourselves. Let us rise in our strength, and shake off the drowsy and sickly feeling, which is the result of excess, and by one spirited and manly exertion, restore ourselves to health, and prosperity, and happiness.

I have said that the present question is a question of the recharter of the Bank of the United States. By this I mean, that it is not only the question now technically before the House, but that it is the real question before the people—the question which we are called upon most urgently to decide. And let me say, sir, it is a question, the decision of which will do more to restore confidence and relieve the present distress than the decision of any other question which can be proposed to Congress at this time. It is indeed a momentous question, upon which the greatest talents of the country have been exercised. I do not intend to discuss it. In making up my mind upon this subject, I have not found it necessary to resort to the much-vexed question of the constitutionality of the measure, nor to the arguments deduced from the abuse of power in conducting the

present institution. Nor am I disposed to detract from its merits by denying its utility. I do believe, and always have believed, that, in some respects, and for certain purposes, it has exercised a beneficial influence over this country. But, when it is admitted that it has the power at once to embarrass, if not crush, all the local banks in the country, and to bring distress and ruin upon a great part of the community; when I consider that this bank, either designedly or casually (and I care not which) has been the cause of the distress which now prevails; when I perceive, as I think I do here, the interest of that institution placed paramount to the interest of the people; when I reflect that the union of the influence of that institution with the patronage of the executive branch of this Government would create a power against which the people might strive and strive in vain; when I hear on this floor, and before the people, an issue made up, and now trying between that institution and this Government, the result of which trial is to determine the political character of the next Administration; and when I hear the harsh and discordant sounds of revolution echoing through these halls, and honorable gentlemen proclaiming that the deposites must be restored to the Bank of the United States, or that revolution will be the consequence,—when I see and hear these things, and reflect upon consequences, I have no difficulty nor hesitation in concluding that the existence of a bank, with such capital and such power, is dangerous to our liberties, and utterly inconsistent with the spirit of our free political institutions.

Mr. HARDIN expressed a wish to speak on the question, and moved that the House do now adjourn.

Mr. MERCER requested him to withdraw the motion, in order to take up the bridge bill for half an hour.

The motion not being withdrawn, the question was taken upon it, and it was rejected:

Ayes 40; noes 56.

The SPEAKER stated that there was not a quorum present. The Speaker, after some conversation, stated that no business could be transacted until a quorum should be present.

Mr. CHILTON moved that the House adjourn. The motion was negatived:

Ayes 52; noes 63.

The SPEAKER directed the Sergeant-at-Arms to invite the members to attend.

Mr. HARDIN rose to say that he had not, on this question, been troublesome to the House. He had patiently listened to the discussions without participating in them, and some of his constituents had inquired why he had not expressed his views. He could not tell within three months, when he should get the floor again, and he was unprepared with the necessary documents to proceed in the discussion now. If the House would indulge him on this occasion, he would pledge himself never to ask of them a similar favor again; for he would rather at any time starve than beg his bread. He renewed the motion to adjourn.

The motion was agreed to, without a count, and The House then adjourned.

IN SENATE.

Saturday, *March* 29, 1834.

On motion of Mr. KANE, leave was given to withdraw the papers of Thomas Harrison.

Mr. WEBSTER presented a memorial of sundry citizens of the State of New York, praying an alteration in the patent laws; which was referred to the Committee on the Judiciary.

Mr. WEBSTER presented memorials from the borough of Muncy, the township of Muncy Creek, Lycoming county, Pennsylvania; and also from the township of Watervleit, New York, praying the restoration of the deposites to the Bank of the United States. The memorials were read, referred to the Committee on Finance, and ordered to be printed.

Mr. PORTER presented the petition of George Whiteley; which was referred to the Committee on Military Affairs.

Mr. McKEAN presented a memorial signed by upwards of five hundred authors, printers, &c., of Philadelphia; and also the proceedings of a meeting of the inhabitants of the township of West Manchester, York county, Pennsylvania, asking the restoration of the deposites to the Bank of the United States; which were read, referred to the Committee on Finance, and ordered to be printed.

Mr. TYLER presented the memorial of 312 inhabitants of Culpepper, Virginia, praying a restoration of the deposites to the Bank of the United States, which he prefaced with a few remarks.

Mr. LEIGH said he would take this opportunity to make a remark. He had observed that when anything occurred particularly agitating to the public mind, an unusual commotion was produced in some of the counties of Virginia. He was a new comer here, and until he came here, he could not have formed an adequate conception of the movements and action of this Government. Many valuable tracts on its structure, and the nature of our institutions, had been published. But he held in his hand a book better calculated to inform the people than any other; he meant the Blue Book, in one page of which he saw a reference to Culpepper county, Virginia. At page 256, would be found the contract prices for carrying the mail, with an asterisk affixed to those where extra allowances had been granted. This began at New York, and after proceeding down to Virginia, the asterisms increased to a perfect galaxy; hence the excitement in Culpepper county, where so many of these extra allowances were granted. He felt curious to see what effect the passage of the resolutions here yesterday, would have upon the Executive of this Government. According to his notions of law, the 16th section of the bank charter was the law of the land, and that prescribed the Bank of the United States as the stong box of the Government. By that section the Secretary, in case of removal of the deposites, was required to report his reasons to Congress, in order that Congress might see and approve or disapprove them. If they approved the reasons, the 16th section was repealed *pro tanto*, and if the other House disapproved the reasons, as this had done, the law was in force, and the deposites must be restored. He did not wish to speak with asperity of the President. Mr. L. believed the President thought he was aiming a blow at the bank, but he believed the blow he was aiming was struck at the liberties of the people.

Mr. BENTON rose in reply to the Senator from Virginia, [Mr. Leigh.] He did not know what the President, or the Secretary of the Treasury, might think it necessary to do in consequence of the vote given by the Senate yesterday on the deposite resolutions; but he did know that the Senate was not the Congress; and that it was to Congress only that the Secretary was to make his report of reasons for removing the deposites from the Federal bank. When the voice of Congress was heard, it might be proper for the President and Secretary to consider what ought to be done; but a voice from a single branch of Congress would never be taken, he presumed, for that of the whole body, much less the solitary voice of the Senate in a case relating to the revenue, a subject placed by the Constitution under the peculiar guardianship of the House of Representatives as the immediate representatives of the people. The Secretary was to report his reasons to Congress—at once, if in session, if not in session, immediately after the commencement of the next session. Now, said Mr. B., the Senate may be in session, and Congress not. The President may convene the Senate without the House of Representatives. The Senate may have its separate session; and has had many. He, (Mr. B.,) in the course of his service, had attended three such sessions himself; and yet if the deposites had been removed during one of these Senatorial sessions, no report of his reasons would have been due from the Secretary to that body. If the President had convened the Senate last fall, a month, or two months before the meeting of Congress, no report of the Secretary's reasons would have been due to them; because they would not have been the Congress; that session of Congress would not have commenced, immediately after which the reasons should be reported. Mr. B. said Congress could have but one voice; the two Houses might have two voices; and, if the voice of the Senate was one way, and that of the House of Representatives the other way, which was to govern?—especially, was the smaller body to govern the greater?—the one most remote from the people to govern the one nearest to the people?—the one which could not originate a money bill, to govern the one, in a question of revenue, which has the peculiar charge of the revenue, and the sole power of orginating money bills?

Mr. B. did not know what the President an Secretary might think they ought to do in consequence of yesterday's vote; he knew what he thought they ought to do, and that was, *nothing*. So far from having the voice of Congress, there was no way for the Executive, or for the other half of Congress, to know what the Senate had done. Their resolutions were single, not joint. There was no way to communicate them to the President, or to the House. Joint resolutions went to both; single ones did not; and these resolutions might lie on the Senate journals till doomsday, and neither the President or the House of Representatives could legally, regularly, or in any parliamentary way, know of their existence. They could not regularly take notice of them. These resolutions are anomalies. They have no relation to the House, or the President; they lead to no action; they tend to disunite the two Houses, and to segregate their opinions. A joint resolution goes from one to another; it receives the action of both; it unites the sense of both; but this single resolution stays where it was born; it leads to no joint action, but to separate action—to no unanimity of opinion, but to diversity of opinion—to no harmony, but to discord between the Houses. For, what is the House to think of a pretension on the part of the Senate to assume to itself the powers of Congress?—to assume supreme jurisdiction over a subject, and that subject an affair of revenue, and set up its will as superseding the will of the House, and standing for the voice of the whole Congress? In every point of view, he (Mr. B.) considered the Senate's proceeding as an anomaly; and that the best thing that could happen for the Senate would be for the President, and the House of Representatives, to take no notice of it until a parliamentary communication of the proceeding could be made to them; and as that never could be done, so they would remain in ignorance of it forever. Certainly neither House can know what the other does, except from an authentic communication; certainly the President cannot know what is done in either House, except upon a regular communication, under the authority of the House. Newspaper reports, verbal intelligence, the statements of members, are no authority for coördinate branches of the Government to act upon; and, in parliamentary understanding, neither the House of Representatives, or the President knows anything of the resolutions which were adopted here yesterday.

Being on his feet, Mr. B. would take notice of another remark which fell from the Senator from Virginia, [Mr. Leigh.] He spoke of the Bank of the United States as being the Treasury of the United States. It was not the first time he had so spoken of that bank; but this was the first time that he (Mr. B.) had found it convenient to call the attention of that Senator to an argument against his assumption, which had been several times used without drawing an answer from those who held, as he [Mr. Leigh] did, that the Federal bank was the Federal treasury. Doubtless they did not answer, because they thought the argument too insignificant to merit an answer. There were some, however, who thought otherwise—who thought that this argument annihilated their whole assumption, and that the only way to get over it was to go round it—the only way to answer it, was to seem not to hear it. He (Mr. B.) wished to know if the Senator from Virginia was of the same mind, and therefore would state this argument to him. It was founded on the 14th fundamental article of what the charter called the constitution of the bank—the article which provided for the establishment of branches—and was in these words:

"The directors of said corporation *shall* establish a competent office of discount and deposite in the District of Columbia, whenever any *law* of the United States shall require such an establishment; also one such office of discount and deposite in any State in which 2,000 shares shall have been subscribed, or may be held, whenever,

'upon application of the Legislature of *such State*, 'Congress may, by law, require the same: *Provided*, The directors aforesaid shall not be bound 'to establish such office before the whole of the 'capital of the bank shall have been paid up. 'And it shall be lawful for the directors of the said 'corporation to establish offices of discount and 'deposite wheresoever *they shall think fit*, within 'the United States or the territories thereof, to 'such persons, and under such regulations, as they 'shall deem proper, not being contrary to law, or 'the constitution of the bank. *Or, instead of establishing of such offices, it shall be lawful for the directors of the said corporation, from time to time, to 'employ any other bank, or banks, to be first approved 'by the Secretary of the Treasury, at any place, or 'places, that they may deem safe and proper, to manage 'and transact the business proposed as aforesaid, other 'than for the purposes of discount, to be managed and 'transacted by such offices under such agreements, and 'subject to such regulations, as they shall deem just 'and proper.*"

Mr. B. went on to remark upon this article, that it placed the establishment of but one branch in the reach, or power, of Congress, and that one was in the District of Columbia—in a district of ten miles square—leaving the vast extent of twenty-four States, and three Territories, to obtain branches for themselves upon contingencies not dependent upon the will, or power, of Congress, or requiring her necessities, or even her convenience to be taken into the account. A *law* of Congress could obtain a branch in this District; but with respect to every State, the establishment of the branch depended, first, upon the mere will and pleasure of the bank; and, secondly, upon the double contingency of a subscription, and a legislative act, within the State. If, then, the mother bank does not think fit, for its own advantage, to establish a branch; or, if the people of a State do not acquire 2,000 shares of the stock of the bank, and the Legislature, therefore, demand it, no branch will be established in any State, or any Territory, of the Union. Congress can only require a branch, in any State, after two contingencies have happened in the State; neither of them having the slightest reference to the necessities, or even convenience, of the Federal Government.

Here, then, (said Mr. B.,) is the treasury established for the United States! A treasury which is to have no existence but at the will of the bank, or the will of a State Legis'ature, and a few of its citizens, enough to own two thousand shares of a stock worth one hundred dollars a share! A treasury which Congress has no hand in establishing, and cannot preserve after it is established; for the mother bank, after establishing her branches, may shut them up, or withdraw them. Such a thing has already happened. Branches in the West have been—some shut up, some withdrawn; and in these cases the treasury was broken up, according to this newfangled conception of a national treasury. No! (said Mr. B.,) the Federal bank is no more the treasury of the United States than the State banks are. One is just as much the treasury as the other, and made so by this very fourteenth fundamental article of the constitution of the bank. Look at it! Look at the alternative! Where branches are not established, the State banks are to be employed! The Bank of the United States is to select the State bank; the Secretary of the Treasury is to approve the selection; and if he does so, the State bank so selected, and so approved, becomes the keeper of the public moneys; it becomes the depository of the public moneys; it transfers them; it pays them out; it does everything except make discounts for the mother bank and issue notes; it does everything which the Federal Government wants done; and that is nothing but what a bank of deposite can do. The Government makes no choice between State banks and branch banks. They are all one to her. They stand equal in her eyes; they stand equal in the charter of the bank itself; and the horror that has now broken out against the State banks, is a thing of recent conception—a very modern impulsion; which is rebuked and condemned by the very authority to which it traces its source. Mr. B. said the State banks were just as much made the Federal treasury by the bank charter as the United States Bank itself was; and that was sufficient to annihilate the argument which now sets up the Federal bank for the Federal treasury. But the fact was, that neither was made the treasury; and it would be absurd to entertain such an idea for an instant; for the Federal bank may surrender her charter, and cease to exist—it can do so at any moment it pleases; the State banks may expire upon their limitation; they may surrender; they may be dissolved in many ways, and so cease to exist; and then there would be no treasury! What an idea, that the existence of the treasury of this great republic is to depend, not upon itself, but upon corporations, which may cease to exist, on any day, by their own will, or their own crimes. Mr. B. hoped that the Senator from Virginia, [Mr. LEIGH,] who had just referred to the Federal bank as the Federal treasury, would find an argument in this fourteenth fundamental article of the constitution of the bank sufficiently large to claim his attention, and to receive from him that answer which others had deemed it too insignificant to merit.

Mr. LEIGH rose, and pledged himself to answer the argument of the Senator from Missouri, as soon as the course of the debate would allow him to do so, without interfering with the rights of others who were now entitled to the floor.

Mr. GRUNDY said he was at a loss to perceive any connexion between the extra allowances in the post office department and the memorial from Culpepper county, Virginia. He was not in the habit of making *de bene esse* speeches here, but he was anxious to have these extra allowances fully investigated. We had the report of the Postmaster General made on this subject—it was ordered to be printed, and would be ready for our examination, he had been informed, in a few days. Was it not better, then, to wait until we should have the means of ascertaining for what purpose these extra allowances were made, what services were rendered for them, and whether or not the public had been materially benefited by them? And as soon as we saw for what purpose they were made, and that they were not for the public good, he would be as ready to condemn the act as any man. We might all perhaps join in saying he had extended his accommodations too far, but before we censured, we should see that the head of the department had heaped the money upon favorites. Extra allowances had been paid to contractors on the Piedmont route, a highly important one, and if it should be found that the allowance was not more than the services rendered were worth, he thought no one ought to complain. It was not treating the department fairly to take up the Blue Book, pick out a contract for $5,000, and then because 3, 4, or $5,000 more were allowed for extra services, to say it was worthy of censure. We should first see what were the original terms of the contract, and if additional services were rendered, compare them with the additional price, and then censure as might be necessary.

Mr. TYLER rose to propound an inquiry to the chairman of the Committee on Post Offices, &c. We had been now nearly four months in session. The public have had proceedings from the Postmaster General, from which it was manifest that the department was out of order. The public had, therefore, anticipated a report from the Post Office Committee, and he desired to know what progress the committee had made in the development of the true condition of the department, and what were the impediments in the way of a development of its true condition. He wished to know, if the inquiry was proper, why the committee were not more prompt in their action.

Mr. LEIGH inquired of the gentleman from Tennessee [Mr. GRUNDY] if he had discovered, and could explain, the cause of the starry corruscations in the firmament over Virginia.

Mr. GRUNDY replied, that he believed Virginia always had more stars than any other State in the Union, and therefore he was not a little surprised that any Virginian should be startled at it. In answer to the other gentleman from Virginia on his left, [Mr. TYLER,] he said that he did not question the right of any gentleman to inquire how far he had done his duty. But the Senate might be sure of one thing, that the greatest vigilance would be exercised, and a full, fair, and impartial exposition of the whole state of the deparment should be made to the Senate. To say at what stage the committee had now arrived was a very difficult thing. If the Senate had passed the resolution offered by the gentleman from Ohio [Mr. EWING]—and he hoped it would be adopted to-day—the committee might have progressed more rapidly. But he gave the gentleman his solemn assurance, that they would proceed till everything was known which it was desirable to know, and more than he could wish.

Mr. CLAYTON trusted we would learn something of the propriety of these extra allowances. But we never could ascertain their whole amount. He was waited on the other evening by an officer of the Treasury Department, who informed him that they could not give the original contracts in the Comptroller's office, owing to their destruction in the late Treasury building. The department was known to be bankrupt—it was not responsible to the public—it owed no responsibility to Congress. It was so constituted that it laid in the will of one man to dispose of the funds as he pleased. And this state of things would never be remedied till the department was placed on the same footing as the other departments. The post office law provided that extra allowances should be apportioned according to the original contract. But he could prove that in fifty cases the Postmaster General had violated that law. It was a department which had more power than all the other departments in the Government put together. It was able to secure the election of any man they pleased, or to put out any man who was in. The Postmaster General could create as many clerks as he pleased—he could make fifty to-morrow, at a salary of $1,000 each. The contingent expenses were voted for by law, but the incidental expenses were incurred and paid at the pleasure of the department, without knowing what the items were. From twenty to thirty thousand agents were subjected to the will of one man; and if they had all been in Tennessee before the late senatorial election, he did not know what effect they might have had on the honorable member's election. It was his conviction that this department exercised more power than all the others combined; it was also increasing, appointing political partisans everywhere, and was exercising more influence over the elecive franchise than any other.

Mr. GRUNDY said it was his principle to leave as little to the discretion of the department as was possible, only leaving it the means of performing its appropriate duties to the country; and when the gentleman from Delaware [Mr. CLAYTON] should introduce a measure to bring its discretion down to that point, it should have his hearty support. We could get all the information we desired, notwithstanding the recent burning of the Treasury building. The people ought not to be told that the original contracts were destroyed, and that, therefore, their contents could not be ascertained. For supposing all the originals were consumed, could we not ascertain what they were, as easily as if we had the originals? When a contract was laid off, a record was made of it, and therefore, although we could not have the originals, we could have abstracts from the record, giving the price, the name of the contractor, and the extra allowances, and therefore the public ought not to be induced to believe that we cannot obtain full and accurate information; the only error could be (which was not probable) in making the record. He would not go back to the investigations four years ago. But although the gentleman then said the department was bankrupt, yet the gentleman from Kentucky [Mr. BIBB] and others, at the very time, denied it. They said it was rich and productive, and advocated a reduction of the postage on newspapers upon that belief, which would have had the effect of breaking down the mails and coaches. And it was probable this state of prosperity would have continued, had it not been for the post office bill of that session, which passed the House of Representatives, creating from forty to fifty thousand additional miles of post road; but when the bill came here, we reduced it to from twenty to thirty thousand, yet it still increased the expenses of the department enormously. The gentleman thought it the most powerful department in the Government; and he (Mr. G.) agreed with him that it was so, and must necessarily be so, from its very nature, because it had more intercourse

with the people, and more business with a greater number of individuals than any other. The gentleman, too, complained of the power to appoint so many clerks, and that partisans were appointed to offices. In regard to the first objection, Mr. G. admitted the power to appoint was in the Postmaster General, and so long as we passed resolutions making so many calls upon him, which gave so much labor, the power to made clerks must exist somewhere, and the clerks must be paid. As to the next objection, he would remark, that Mr. Abraham Bradley, whom the gentleman would not suspect of partiality to this Administration, declared on oath, at the period alluded to, that a majority of the clerks in the Post Office were opposed to the Administration. And as to the deputy postmasters, some of the most important of them were certainly of that political character. He instanced the postmasters at Albany, at Richmond, and in the city of New York; and he thought if the fact could be ascertained, it would appear that all the postmasters in the United States were pretty equally divided in their political sentiments. The Postmaster General made no report of the contingent expenses, because there was no law requiring it, and because none of his predecessors had done so. Mr. G. repeated, that it was his intention, if his health continued to improve as it had done, to completely eviscerate the department, that its true situation might be fully made known.

Some further remarks were made by Mr. EWING and Mr. CLAYTON, when the memorial was referred to the Committee on Finance, and ordered to be printed.

Mr. GRUNDY moved that the Committee on Private Land Claims be discharged from the further consideration of the petition of William D. Ferguson, and that the petitioner have leave to withdraw his papers; which was so ordered.

Mr. KENT presented a resolution of the Legislature of Maryland, instructing their Senators and requesting their Representatives to exert themselves in obtaining aid from Congress for the benefit of the Chesapeake and Ohio Canal; which was referred to the Committee on Roads and Canals.

Mr. TOMLINSON, from the Committee on Pensions, reported a bill from the House of Representatives, relative to pensions, with an amendment.

Mr. TOMLINSON, from the same committee, asked to be discharged from the further consideration of the petition of Benjamin Sampson; which was agreed to.

On motion of Mr. TOMLINSON, the documents relative to the improvement of the harbor of Bridgeport were referred to the Committee on Commerce.

The resolution offered by Mr. EWING, empowering the Committee on the Post Office and Post Roads to send for persons and papers, and appointing a clerk to aid them, was taken up and adopted.

Mr. SOUTHARD, from the Committee on Naval Affairs reported a bill from the House of Representatives for the relief of John G. Reynolds, and gave notice that he was instructed by the committee when the bill came to be acted upon to object to its passage.

Mr. SOUTHARD, from the same committee, reported a bill regulating the compensation of certain officers in the marine corps.

Mr. SOUTHARD, from the same committee, reported a bill for the relief of Samuel C. Reid, and the officers and crew of the privateer General Armstrong.

Also, a bill for the relief of the heirs and legal representatives of Henry Eckford, deceased; which was ordered to be printed.

Also, a bill for the relief of James Noble, and a bill for the relief of Laomi Baldwin.

Mr. WILKINS, from the Committee on Foreign Relations, reported a bill extending for six months the time allowed the Commissioners of the Neapolitan treaty to settle claims of the citizens of the United States under that treaty.

Mr. BENTON submitted the following resolution, and on his motion, without being read, it was ordered to be printed:

Resolved, That a committee be appointed on the part of the Senate, jointly with such committee as may be appointed on the part of the House of Representatives, to consider and report to the Senate and to the House respectively, what alterations, if any, are necessary to be made—

1. In the value of the gold coined at the mint of the United States; so as to check the exportation of that coin, and to restore it to circulation in the United States.

2. In the laws relative to foreign coins, so as to restore the gold and silver coin of foreign nations to their former circulation within the United States.

3. In the joint resolution of 1816 (for the better collection of the revenue) so as to exclude all bank notes, under twenty dollars, from revenue payments after a given period, and to make the revenue system of the United States instrumental in the gradual suppression of the small note circulation, and the introduction of gold and silver for the *common currency* of the country.

Mr. PORTER gave notice that as numerous bills had accumulated, he should, on Monday, move that the Senate proceed to the consideration of private business.

Mr. GRUNDY moved to take up the resolution calling for information from the President of the United States, relative to the proclamations for the sale of public lands in the southwestern country; which was considered and adopted.

Mr. PRESTON presented the memorial of the city authorities of Charleston, South Carolina, praying the establishment of a naval hospital at that place, which was referred to the Committee on Naval Affairs.

Mr. PRESTON, from the Committee on the Judiciary, reported a bill for the relief of the heirs and legal representatives of Walter Livingston, deceased.

Mr. LINN presented the petition of George F. Bollinger; which was referred to the Committee on Military Affairs.

Mr. HENDRICKS presented a memorial from the officers of Fort Dearborn; which was referred to the Committee on Military Affairs.

On motion of Mr. WRIGHT, the Senate went into executive business, when, after spending some time therein,

The Senate adjourned.

HOUSE OF REPRESENTATIVES.

SATURDAY, *March* 29, 1834.

Mr. J. Q. ADAMS asked the unanimous consent of the House to take up the following resolution, submitted by him yesterday:

Resolved, That the Secretary of the Treasury be directed to lay before this House copies of the charters of all the banks selected by him, as depositories of the public moneys in the place of the Bank of the United States and its branches, together with the names of the presidents, directors, and stockholders, in the said selected banks, with the amount of stock in said banks, held by each stockholder, and the amount of debt due by each president, cashier, and director, of each of the banks, to the said banks, at the time when it was selected as a depository, and at this time.

Mr. FOSTER objecting—

Mr. ADAMS moved a suspension of the rule, for the purpose of taking it up.

Mr. WILLIAMS called for the yeas and nays; which having been ordered—

Mr. FOSTER said, that as he was anxious to save the time of the House, he would withdraw his objection.

The resolution was then taken up and read.

Mr. ADAMS desired to have the following inserted as a modification to the resolution:

"And that the Secretary of the Treasury be directed to report to this House a statement of all sums, denominated in the treasury accounts *unavailable funds*, specifically designating the several banks or individuals indebted to the treasury therefor; the time when each debt first became due; the time when failure of payment thereof first occurred; the security, if any, which the public have for payment thereof, at any time, and the prospect of such eventual payment."

Mr. HARPER, of Pennsylvania, considered that it was not right to call for information with respect to the private accounts "or debts of the president, cashier, and directors of each of the banks." It might be ruinous to them. He would, therefore, move to have that part stricken out of the resolution.

Mr. ADAMS said that it would have been a matter of much satisfaction to him, if a similar forbearance with the private accounts of individuals had been attended to on other occasions. He had himself urged this as an objection two years ago, when the committee was appointed to investigate into the affairs of the Bank of the United States. But he was overruled, and numerous private accounts of individuals were exposed to the committee in opposition to his remonstrance and protest on that occasion. A similar investigation was now proposed for the adoption of the House, in the report presented by the Committee of Ways and Means, and which, if adopted, not only the debts of the president, cashier, and directors of the Bank of the United States would be brought before the public gaze, but many others, which should not be. For this reason it was he introduced this resolution for inquiring into the State banks as a set-off to that proposed into the Bank of the United States; as it was only fair that the measure meted to one, should be meted to the others. If this kind of investigation was to be permitted into the affairs of those persons connected with the United States Bank, it was only in conformity to all equitable principles of action, to have it extended to those connected with what he would term "trap" banks, being a better term for them than "pet" banks. His object was to obtain information as to the precise condition of these selected depositories for the money of the people. He was not acquainted himself with their state, although he had been informed many of the State banks so selected, were, what was called, "family concerns." The inquiry, therefore, into the debts of those controlling them, was an inquiry into their condition, involving considerations of the solvency of the banks themselves, as well as their fitness for being depositories. He called for the yeas and nays on the resolution.

Mr. WAYNE desired to correct a misconception which appeared in the Intelligencer, "that he had promised to vote for this resolution" when submitted by the gentleman from Massachusetts, yesterday. He had not done so. He had expressed a wish that the consideration of it should be postponed, to give the members an opportunity of understanding the subject, and then deciding whether or not it should be adopted by them. The resolution appeared to him to be in some respects unnecessary, as there were two of the subjects upon which information was called before the House. They had copies of the charters of all the banks selected by the Secretary of the Treasury, already on their files in the documents furnished by him, in answer to a call for that purpose by the Senate in December last. They had also the names of the stockholders, as far as they could be ascertained, although they had not the amount of the stock held by them. For this he would perhaps be willing to vote, also for the names of the lawyers and solicitors employed.

There were some other objections to the resolution on its merits, for there was now a much wider inquiry demanded than when the resolution was first proposed. He would ask the honorable member from Massachusetts, if this inquiry was consistent with the position he had formerly maintained? at the same time, reminded him that he [Mr. W.] went with him on a former occasion, in objection to examination into the private accounts of any individuals. The inquiry now proposed was one which could not be effected. They had no control over the State banks; and it was one which could be of no benefit, whilst, at the same time, it might prove to be eventually injurious. If the resolution was adopted, the Secretary might fairly and truly say that he could not give the information, because he certainly had no authority to procure it, and if he had, he would contend that its effect would be to give to Government an influence over the State banks more direct than was desirable.

The resolution was, in another point of view, unnecessary for the objects stated by the honorable member from Massachusetts. The report presented by the Committee of Ways and Means recom-

mended the adoption of a law regulating the deposite of the public money with the State banks; "that they should be made as Congress would direct." The consequence of the adoption of the resolution, and of action upon it by the Secretary of the Treasury, would be this, although he did not say such was the object of the member proposing it: the State banks might tell the Secretary that he had no power to call for the information. They might be induced to refuse the call from a desire to preserve their perfect independence, and put themselves in an improper position as respected the Government. He contended, also, that one effect of the proposition might be to induce the public to suppose that these banks were unsafe as depositories. It was unnecessary, with a view to inquiry as to the safety of these institutions for that purpose, as they were obliged to furnish statements weekly, and when called upon, of their affairs. Why, then, as their condition was thus known, should they be called on for that information which there had been an objection made to demand from the Bank of the United States? The member from Massachusetts said his resolution was intended as a set-off to inquiries that were contemplated to be made for improper uses into the affairs of individuals having transactions with the Bank of the United States. If he (Mr. W.) thought such was to be the use to which the resolution proposed for adoption, in the report of the Committee of Ways and Means, was to be applied, he would feel bound to vote against it. He was willing to vote for inquiry, if it was limited to cases in which there had been violations of their charters by any of the State banks, but he considered it altogether unnecessary to inquire into the subjects of any loans made by the State banks to any individuals. Where such loans were secure the inquiry was unnecessary.

In every point of view, and as additional subjects for inquiry had been proposed, further time was necessary before they should act on the resolution. He would not now move to postpone its consideration to a day certain, being desirous to give a fair opportunity to any member who wished to reply. After that he would do so, that there might be full discussion upon it, and after which they could determine whether the inquiry was a proper one to make, or whether the information on their table was not sufficient.

Mr. McKINLEY would willingly assent to the inquiry into the condition of the State banks, if the resolution proposed to ascertain that of which the Secretary had official knowledge; or if he could be shown to have the power to procure the information sought for by the resolution, he would vote for it, without any regard to the object for which it was proposed. He considered that all the power which vested in the Secretary of the Treasury, over the State banks, was that which was given him by the contracts into which they entered with him. There was no such power in the contracts. How, then, could the House require the Secretary to procure this information?

Mr. SPEIGHT said, that although he had supported the Secretary of the Treasury, yet he, for one, was willing to vote for any inquiry that should be proposed to elucidate the affairs of those State banks that were selected by the Secretary for the safe-keeping of the public money; and so far from thinking with the gentleman from Georgia [Mr. WAYNE] that the Secretary had not the power to procure the information, he should think he had, and that if he had not, he had been guilty of a great neglect of his duty in not having it. With respect to what had been said by the gentleman from Alabama, [Mr. McKINLEY,] he would only reply, that if the power to procure such information as was now asked for by the resolution, was not inserted, or given to the Secretary by the various contracts entered into, it ought to have been in them. He was surprised at the motion offered by the member from Pennsylvania, [Mr. HARPER,] to strike out the parts respecting the debts of the individuals, for he was always at a loss to conceive what good reason there could be for having any concealment about debts to any banks. He agreed with the gentleman from Massachusetts, that it was necessary to have the inquiry proposed by his resolution. He desired to know everything about the condition of the State banks, and wished him to extend the same inquiry to the Bank of the United States. There should be no objection to give information on the subject that would be desired.

Mr. WILDE said he would support any and all amendments that should be proposed, unless they should be such as would change the character of the inquiry. He desired here to tender his thanks to the member from North Carolina [Mr. SPEIGHT] for the aid which he had given. The system—if system it could be called, which system it was none—into which the money affairs of the country had been brought by the conduct of the high officers of the Government, was rapidly developing. He, however, agreeing with the sentiments expressed by him, wished to put the vote he should give on grounds still more distinct than those of the member from North Carolina. The views which he had were, that the whole control over the public money—viz: to raise it, to pay it out, and to deposite it for safe-keeping—belonged to Congress. They were told now, that Congress had no right to inquire into the condition of those banks having it. If this was the fact; if the money had got into depositories into which they had no right to inquire, then came the natural inquiry, how came it to be placed there? If this was true, what (he asked) was the condition of the country? He desired to be understood as maintaining that Congress had no right to put the public money in places, into the safety of which they had not the right to inquire. He was at a loss to determine whether the resolution embraces a sufficient range of inquiry. He had no objection that the inquiry should be made as extensively in regard to the United States Bank as to the State banks; but he saw no propriety in connecting the two inquiries.

Mr. MANN, of New York, said there were but two points in the inquiry proposed which had not already been laid before the House, in answer to the former inquiries. The names of the lawyers and solicitors were desirable, in his opinion. The amount of debt due by each president, cashier, &c., was perhaps desirable and useful. He saw no objection to it, and he trusted that the gentleman from Pennsylvania [Mr. HARPER] would withdraw his motion to strike out this clause.

Mr. HARPER rose and said he would withdraw his motion to strike out the clause.

The hour here expired for the consideration of resolutions.

Mr. POLK moved the suspension of the rules of the House, for the purpose of proceeding to consider the general appropriation bill.

Mr. McDUFFIE suggested that the adoption of the motion would not promote the despatch of public business, as the Senate, it was well known, had not yet acted upon the bills already sent to them.

Mr. WILLIAMS objected to the motion, that no notice had been given of it, and he called for the yeas and nays upon it; which were ordered.

Mr. MERCER moved to amend the motion, by adding the Potomac bridge bill. Rejected.

The question being taken on the motion to suspend the rule, for the purpose of taking up the bill making appropriations for the support of Government for the year 1834, it was determined in the negative—ayes 107, noes 82, (not two-thirds.)

The House proceeded to the consideration of private bills.

The following bills were considered, and ordered to be engrossed for a third reading:

A bill for the relief of Edward Brooke;

A bill for the relief of the legal representatives of William Rogers, deceased;

A bill for the relief, in part, of the crew of the brig Sarah George;

A bill to authorize letters patent to be issued to Morris B. Ogden.

The bill for the relief of David Kilbourn was taken up. A discussion ensued, in which Messrs. WHITTLESEY of Ohio, BURD, CHILTON, THOMSON, BURGES, LANE, VANCE, BRIGGS, WARDWELL, GRENNELL, McKENNAN, EWING, GILLET, and FILLMORE participated.

The question being on ordering the bill to be engrossed for a third reading, it was taken by yeas and nays, and determined in the negative: Yeas 72, nays 86.

On motion, the House then adjourned.

IN SENATE.

MONDAY, *March* 31, 1834.

Mr. BIBB submitted the following resolution, and asked the unanimous consent of the Senate for its immediate consideration; which was granted, and the resolution adopted:

Resolved, That the Secretary of the Department of State be requested to lay before the Senate, as soon as practicable, all the information which has been obtained under a resolution of the Senate of the 26th February, 1833, touching the population of the United States, of all kinds, native and alien, the militia, and such other statistical information as the Secretary might deem useful and expedient; and particularly that he lay before the Senate all the information that has been obtained under the circulars issued by Mr. Livingston, propounding queries to obtain information, as well on the subjects particularly mentioned, as upon the subjects confided to his direction by that resolution.

Mr. MANGUM presented a memorial from inhabitants of the county of Wilkes, North Carolina.

Also, a preamble and resolutions adopted at a meeting of citizens of Mountsville, Rowan county, North Carolina.

Also, a memorial signed by 500 citizens of Beaufort county, North Carolina, in favor of the restoration of the deposites to the Bank of the United States.

All of which, after explanatory remarks by Mr. M., were read, referred to the Committee on Finance; and ordered to be printed.

Mr. KING, of Alabama, presented a memorial from citizens of the city of Mobile, in the State of Alabama.

Mr. K. said he had a personal acquaintance with a majority of the signers of the paper; they were persons of the greatest respectability, many of them merchants of the highest standing in society. They say they are not carried away by party considerations, and they express themselves in the most decorous and respectful language. They said that for five or six years past the city of Mobile, as well as the State of Alabama, had enjoyed a great and increasing degree of prosperity, but that for the last four or five months this prosperity had received a check, which had unsettled the exchanges of the country, and which they attributed in some degree to the removal of the deposites. They complained that the pressure in the money market had reduced the price of cotton; and they further stated that they had no interest in the United States Bank, not being the owners of any stock in the institution. They submit it to the wisdom of Congress to adopt such measures to relieve the pressure in the country as might be most expedient. The memorial was read, and, on motion of Mr. K., was referred to the Committee on Finance.

Mr. KING, of Alabama, in pursuance of notice, asked and obtained leave to bring in a bill for the better organization of the district court of the United States in Alabama; which was read, and referred to the Committee on the Judiciary.

Mr. CLAY called up for consideration his resolution calling for information from the Treasury Department of the amount of deposites made in the Union Bank of Maryland. Mr. C. modified his resolution as follows:

Resolved, That the Secretary of the Treasury be directed to report to the Senate what amount of public money is now on deposite in the Union Bank of Maryland; when, and on what account it was deposited; and, also, whether any treasury drafts, contingent or other, have been, during the month of March, 1834, furnished to the said bank, or at any time heretofore to the Bank of Maryland, for any and for what purpose. And that he likewise report what amount of stock in the capital of the said Union Bank was held by R. B. Taney, Esq., when the said bank was selected as one of the banks to receive on deposite the public money, and what amount of said stock he now holds.

The resolution, as modified, was adopted.

Mr. POINDEXTER presented the petition of Thomas Mullen; which was referred to the Committee of Claims.

Mr. POINDEXTER submitted the following resolution, and asked the immediate consideration

of the Senate; which being agreed to, the resolution was adopted:

Resolved, That the Commissioner of the General Land Office be directed to communicate to the Senate the number of patents in his office prepared for the signature of the President of the United States, which have not been signed, and the number of final certificates filed in his office, on which patents have not been prepared for signature.

Mr. POINDEXTER submitted the following resolution:

Resolved, That one thousand copies of the Journals of the old Congress, and of the Senate, including, in separate volumes, the confidential proceedings, with a compendious index to the whole, in each volume, be printed for the use of the Senate, and that the same be retained subject to the further order of the Senate.

On motion of Mr. WRIGHT, the Senate proceeded to the consideration of the reference of the memorial of the citizens of Albany, New York, to the Committee on Finance.

Mr. WRIGHT rose, and spoke at length. He was followed by Messrs. EWING and CLAY; when the memorial was referred to the Committee on Finance, and, with the names, ordered to be printed.

Mr. WRIGHT presented the memorial of 1,700 citizens of the city of Albany opposed to a restoration of the deposites to the Bank of the United States; which, on his motion, was ordered to be printed, with the names, and referred to the Committee on Finance.

Mr. TYLER presented the petition of Josiah Hopkins; which was referred to the Committee on Pensions.

Mr. LINN, from the Committee on Private Land Claims, reported a bill relative to land claimants in Missouri.

Mr. EWING gave notice that he should to-morrow call up for consideration the bill making appropriations for extending the Cumberland road through the States of Ohio, Indiana, and Illinois, and as the Senate was not full, and the hour was late, he moved an adjournment, but withdrew the motion at the instance of

Mr. POINDEXTER, upon whose motion the Senate proceeded to

THE ORDERS OF THE DAY.

The following bills from the House of Representatives were ordered to be engrossed and read a third time:

A bill for the relief of Peleg Sprague, with amendments; and,

A bill for the relief of John Haggerty and David Austin, with amendments.

The following bills were read a first and second time, and referred:

A bill for the relief of Joseph W. Armistead;
A bill for the relief of the owners of the schooner Joseph and Mary;
A bill for the relief of Samuel D. Walker;
A bill for the relief of William B. Dohber and others;
A bill for the relief of Stephen Kingston;
A bill for the relief of James Marsh;
A bill for the relief of William K. Paulding;
A bill for the relief of William Hasleti;
A bill for the relief of William O'Neal;
A bill for the relief of Nicholas D. Coleman;
A bill for the relief of James Kitchens;
A bill for the relief of William Enos;
A bill for the relief of John C. Naylor;
A bill for the relief of John Walton and John J. DeGraff;
A bill for the relief of Henry Sewall and Robert Sewall;
A bill for the relief of Francoise Suzone.
A bill for the relief of Henry Oakes;
A bill for the relief of the heirs of William G. Christopher;
A bill for the relief of William L. Cockerille;
A bill for the relief of Benedict Alford and Robert Brush;
A bill for the relief of Judith Thomas and Daniel Palmer;
A bill granting pensions to certain persons therein named;

A bill authorizing issue of the register of the brig American;
A bill for the relief of Mary O'Sullivan;
A bill for the relief of Alexander J. Ross;
A bill for the relief of the heirs of James Brown;
A bill for the relief of George Bowen;
A bill for the relief of the heirs of Thomas Sampson;
A bill for the relief of Henry Whitney.

The following bills were read a third time, and passed:

A bill for the relief of Samuel Thompson;
A bill for the relief of Thomas Richardson;
A bill for the relief of John Thompson;
A bill for the relief of Daniel Hasleton and William Palmer;
A bill for the relief of the sureties of John H. Morton.

Upon the bill for the relief of the heirs and legal representatives of Moses Shepherd, deceased, being called up upon its passage—

Mr. SPRAGUE rose and said, that considerable litigation had previously occurred upon the merits of that claim, and as the Senate was thin, and the usual hour for adjournment had long since passed, he should not urge any member to explain its provisions, but would move that the Senate adjourn.

The Senate then adjourned.

HOUSE OF REPRESENTATIVES.
MONDAY, *March* 31, 1834.

In pursuance of the rule of the House, the States were called for the presentation of petitions, memorials, &c., beginning with Mississippi, where the call was suspended on Monday last, after the presentation by Mr. CAGE, of the resolutions of sundry citizens of Natchez, condemning the removal of the deposites, and recommending their restoration, &c.

Mr. PLUMMER said that he had not inflicted on the House a speech during its present session. His silence during all this time had not been owing to a want of confidence in himself, so much as to ill health. The ague and fever with which he had been afflicted during the chilling blasts of winter, and on the opening of spring, left him suffering under a much more fashionable and prevalent disease in this climate. It was a disease common to most of the members of Congress, and seemed to be contagious. It was not his purpose to enter into a discussion of the various symptoms of the disease in its different stages, nor was he capable of throwing any light on the subject, although he had paid some attention to the effects which it had on both the body and mind. The general symptoms, he said, were an apparent restlessness of the whole body, palpitation of the heart and uneasiness of mind. It frequently caused the features of the patient to be distorted, muttering a jargon of high-sounding and unmeaning words; sometimes it affected him in a manner not unlike the hydrophobia, causing foaming at the mouth; at others, stamping of the feet, clenching of the fists, wise and *learned* looks and ludicrous motions of the arms and other parts of the body, and not unfrequently a perversion of the truth. Owing to the want of a classical education he did not understand the technicalities of the learned professions, but he had heard those who talked Greek and spoke Latin call the disease of which he had spoken the " *Cacoethes loquendi.*" It was, he said, considered incurable; temporary relief might, however, be obtained, by talking from one to three days. Although the members of the House might have cause to regret it, he most heartily congratulated himself on a change of diseases. He no longer felt inclined to yawn, pains in his bones, and cold flashes running up his back, intimations of the approaching ague, but he felt strong symptoms of the other disease. Unless, however, his case should become more aggravated than it was at present, he trusted that he should not occupy the time of the House long on the subject under consideration. If, in the few remarks he intended to submit, he should fail to command the attention of the House, he hoped that he should be so well satisfied with his own effort, as not to be under the necessity of procuring an anonymous puff of himself to be published in the newspapers; nor of falling into the fashionable practice of addressing a note to the editors, complaining of the reporters, because they do not make a good speech out of a bad one, or because they fail to report what he would have said, if he had not forgotten it.

Mr. P. said, when he rose to address the House the other day on the presentation by his colleague of the resolutions under consideration, he did not intend to occupy more time than would have been necessary to correct an erroneous impression made here and elsewhere in relation to public sentiment in Mississippi on the all-engrossing subject of the bank. Since that time circumstances had developed themselves which had caused him to consider it due to the House, to the country, to his constituents, and to himself, that he should rise in his place and speak forth the words of truth and soberness. He did not intend, however, to discuss at that time the merits of the bank question, nor inquire into the legality or expediency of the conduct of the Secretary of the Treasury in removing the public deposites from the Bank of the United States to the local institutions. He rose more particularly for the purpose of explaining some of the reasons why he could not consistently comply with the requests of his constituents who contemplated the meeting that adopted the resolutions under consideration. He agreed with them in the opinions therein expressed relative to the apparently prosperous condition of the State of Mississippi a few months ago and the present distress of which they complained, but differed with them altogether as to the origin of these difficulties and reverses, and was opposed to the remedy which they recommended. It was unnecessary, he presumed, for him to bear testimony to the high standing and respectability of those whose names were mentioned in the resolutions. The most of them were known to some of the gentlemen on that floor, and, to say the least of it, as favorably known as those who had the honor of representing them. There were (he said) several gentlemen in his eye besides his honorable colleague who would not hesitate to vouch for the names of Wilkins, Grayson, Quitman, Bingaman and Merrill. The right of the people to instruct the representatives of their own choice (he said) was one which he held more sacred than any other right claimed or exercised by the citizens of a free Government. He held that it was the imperious duty of the Representative, who was the public servant of the people, to obey the mandates of his constituents on all questions of expediency, when clearly expressed. He went farther, and admitted that it was the bounden duty of a Representative to obey the known will of his constituents on all questions which might come before him, either of a general or a local nature, or resort to the other alternative, and follow the praiseworthy example set them by a distinguished gentleman from Virginia a short time since in the other end of the building.

What is the will of the people, and whether there has or has not been a fair expression of that will, are questions of which every one must judge for himself, and upon his own responsibility. He professed to know the sentiments of the great mass of the people of Mississippi as well, but not better, than any other man. He had been among them from boyhood. He had grown with their growth, and strengthened with their strength, and undertook to assert that three-fourths of the whole number of voters in the State were opposed to a recharter of the United States Bank, and, consequently, to a restoration of the deposites. He might, he said, be mistaken in his opinion with regard to public sentiment in Mississippi, but as evidence of his sincerity, he was willing to stake his popularity, which he prized as high any man, and all of his political prospects on the question, to make up an issue on that subject, before the people of that State.

In 1828, the General Assembly of Mississippi passed a set of joint resolutions remonstrating against the introduction of a branch of the United States Bank within the limits of that State. Mr. P. said he was a member of the Legislature which adopted those resolutions, and gave them his support. In 1829 and '30, efforts were made to repeal the resolutions, and invite the location of a branch within the State, which he opposed. They were not repealed until the next session of the Legislature, after he became a member elect of

Congress. At the first session of the 22d Congress, he voted uniformly with the opponents of the bank, and recorded his vote against the bill to recharter that institution. After his vote on the bank, and after the Executive veto on that bill, in August, 1832, his name went before the people of Mississippi for a reëlection. He was opposed by the presses in support of the bank, on the ground of his vote, and his opposition to that institution. The whole power of the bank was brought to bear on him, and at a time, too, when absent, and unable to defend himself. With these things known to the people of the State, for they were not done in the corner, he was reëlected by a majority of the whole number of votes given at the election. Although he was under no positive pledge to oppose the bank, nor support the measures of the Administration, there was an implied pledge on his part to support the measures advocated by the laboring part of the community—by the working-men of Mississippi—to whom alone he was indebted for his seat on that floor.

He was (he said) opposed to rechartering that moneyed monster, and opposed to a restoration of the deposites, not because he wished to conciliate General Jackson, for he said he had never found favor in his sight, but because he was opposed to all licensed monopolies, to the conferring of exclusive privileges on any man, or corporation of men. The President advocated the principles of the working men of the country, therefore did he support him; whenever he abandoned those principles, he was in honor bound to his constituents to abandon him. Mr. P. said he should be recreant to those who had honored him with their suffrages, and unworthy of the station he occupied, if, under the circumstances, he should vote for a restoration of the deposites, or a recharter of the bank. He had a high respect for the opinions of those whose names were mentioned on the face of the resolutions, but for the purpose of showing that there had been no change in public sentiment, as had been inferred, in Mississippi, he must be permitted to state, that all of them excepting one, had always belonged to the National Republican (he would not say Federal Bank) party, and uniform opposers of the present Administration; and the one excepted, was an admitted Federalist, and President of the Branch Bank located at Natchez.

[Mr. CAGE here corrected Mr. PLUMMER, and said, if he had reference to Colonel Wilkins, that it was a mistake.]

Mr. P. said if he was mistaken, it was because he had recently resigned.

Mr. P. said that he would here take occasion to repel a charge that had been made from a quarter which he did not think proper to name, because it might be a violation of order, that his course on this question "was the effect of party trammels;" that he was "under the influence of decided party discipline;" that he had "become a mere automaton," and disposed to "surrender his judgment, and what he believed to be the best interests of the people of Mississippi, at the shrine of party." Mr. P. said he, too, with his honorable colleague, should "fearlessly do what he believed to be his duty;" that he, too, with his honorable colleague, could safely say, that "he had no interests" here, "unconnected" with the interests of the people he had the honor in part to represent. Charges such as he had named came with a bad grace from those who were under the necessity of placing themselves under "trammels" and "party discipline" to procure their election to a seat in that Hall. It was well known, he said, that he had never been a favorite of those who stood at the head of, and controlled the destinies of the Administration party in Mississippi. That he might not be misunderstood, he would particularize. He had never been supported by the Governor of the State, who was considered by the party as their champion. The patronage of the General Government had been arrayed against him, if that could be considered the patronage of the Government, which caused the United States officers within the State of Mississippi to oppose his election. There were, at the time he was elected to the station which he then held, five newspapers within his district in support of the Administration. Two of them, he said, assailed him with all of the violence of political partisans; two of them admitted communications against him, and refused, or neglected, to defend him; and the fifth one, a new paper, just then established, had since discarded him. He had, he said, received no favors at the hands of the Executive branch of the Government, nor had he any to ask. He mentioned these things, not in a spirit of complaint towards the President, or and of the Heads of Departments; not out of any feelings of disrespect to the Governor of the State, (who commanded from him that respect due to a generous heart, and the high and responsible station which he occupied,) or any one else; but in justification of his course there, and in reply to an attack made against him and others on that floor, with whom he acted, on the all-absorbing question of the bank, in one of the newspapers printed in the State he had the honor in part to represent.

Mr. P. said, he did not propose to occupy the time of the House in responding to the common newspaper slang of those who were under the influence of the bank, nor did he deem it necessary to notice the vulgar and abusive communications of the letter-writers, whether over the signature of "Major Downing," "The Spy," or any other poor, anonymous, irresponsible devil, who earned his daily bread by fabricating libels on the characters of those who would not bow down and worship at the footstool of their master and employer, the Bank of the United States. But (he said) when he saw a communication from a *responsible source*, over the signature of an *honorable gentleman*, published in a public journal, and evidently intended for the public eye, misrepresenting the opinions of high public functionaries, and containing slanderous charges against a portion of the members of that House with whom he was associated on a question of great national importance, he considered it not only his right, but his duty to notice it in his place on the floor of that Hall, even though it might possibly have been written by *one* entitled to a seat within its walls. If (said Mr. P.) the publication should have been first made in his own State, and intended to mislead those whom he had the honor, in part, to represent, and calculated to injure him (if believed) in their estimation, it would be due to his constituents as well as to himself, that the misrepresentation should be corrected, the slanderous charges contradicted; and things called by their right names.

For the purpose of bringing the Administration, and those who support its measures, into disrepute among the people of Mississippi, it had been asserted by that high authority to which he had already made allusion, that "there is no complaint that the bank did not discharge promptly and efficiently all the duties required of it by its charter." Now, sir, (said Mr. P.,) I undertake to say, that this statement is a wholesale perversion of truth, and misrepresentation of facts. Let us inquire what is meant by this statement. It cannot refer to the bank, nor those opposed to the Administration, for they have made no complaints against the bank. It must, then, be intended to convey the idea that no charges or complaints have been made from any source "that the bank did not discharge promptly and efficiently all of the duties required of it by its charter," but that the Secretary of the Treasury removed the deposites in violation of law, without any complaint being made, without any provocation whatever; and, if he might be allowed to use a legal phrase, with malice aforethought, and without the fear of God before his eyes; and that those who sustained his course on that floor were *particeps criminis* in the transaction.

To show the falsity of that statement, he would only mention such charges made against the bank as had been not only clearly proven, but admitted by its friends, and attempted to be justified. He begged leave to call the attention of that letter-writer to the fact of the transaction of the most important business by the bank, by the President, and one or two others, when the charter expressly provides that "not less than seven directors shall constitute a board for the transaction of business," to the exclusion of the Government directors altogether from the board; to the effort on the part of the bank to postpone secretly, without the consent of the Government, the payment of a portion of the public debt, called the three per cent. stocks; to the unconscientious demand on the part of the bank for damages to the amount of $158,842 77, on the protested bill drawn by the United States on the French Government; to the enormous sums of the people's money appropriated illegally to editors and printers for the purpose of abusing the President of the United States.

Again, (said Mr. P.,) this distinguished letter-writer says, "It certainly never was intended to 'give to the Secretary of the Treasury the regulation of the currency of the country, by an unlimited control over the moneyed institutions; and 'yet the Secretary, in his report to Congress, has 'claimed all this power." Now, I undertake (said Mr. P.) to say that he has neither claimed nor exercised any such power. He has not, on any occasion, attempted to regulate the currency of the country. He has never at any time exercised, or attempted to exercise, any control over the moneyed institutions. The 16th section of the bank charter enacts "that the deposites of the money 'of the United States in places in which the said 'bank or branches thereof may be established, 'shall be made in said bank or branches thereof, 'unless the Secretary of the Treasury shall at any 'time otherwise order and direct." In conformity with the provisions of that act, the public moneys were deposited in the United States Bank and branches until September last, when the Secretary of the Treasury ordered and directed that thereafter they should be made in the State banks, for reasons which he communicated to Congress at the commencement of the session, as he lawfully might do. Was this regulating the currency of the country? Was this claiming a control over the moneyed institutions? Or was it only designating the place where the money should be deposited for safe-keeping?

The honorable letter-writer, (said Mr. P.,) from whom he had made sundry quotations, had propounded to the people of Mississippi a series of interrogatories, which he read, and begged leave to answer in their order. Mr. P. said, if an apology was due for occupying the time of the House in responding to newspaper scribblers, it might be found in the fact that he stood by *himself* in support of the democracy of the State *here*, and unsupported by any of the presses at home. If he should respond by a written communication to that renowned letter-writer, there was no certainty of its being published in the State which he had the honor in part to represent. During the last session of Congress, he said that he wrote several letters, and delivered speeches on several important questions, that were published in the city papers, and republished in different parts of the Union, none of which found their way into the newspapers of Mississippi. He therefore hoped the House would allow him to do an act of justice to himself and the democracy of the State, which, from his peculiar situation, he could not otherwise well do. In answer to the following interrogatory—

"How do the people of Mississippi stand affected in relation to the removal of the public deposites?"

Mr. P. said that the Democracy of Mississippi stood unmoved and immovable—resolved to sacrifice "their lives, their fortune, and their sacred honor," in defence of those rights and privileges handed down to them by their fathers, rather than permit themselves to be made the slaves and vassals of an irresponsible corporation, wielding a moneyed power which already shook our institutions to the centre, and threatened to break down the Constitution, trample on the laws, and prostrate the liberties of the people. This, said Mr. P., is the way the great mass of the people, the working-men of the State, stand, and the way they will continue to stand, even if the pecuniary distress should be greater than at present. There is, however, said Mr. P., another party, differently situated, and differently affected. The Federalists of '98, of alien and sedition law memory—the anti-war party, of Hartford Convention memory—the old aristocracy of the State—the National Republican party—the bank party, and all of the discordant materials (not exceeding one fourth of the State) who have uniformly opposed the measures of the present Administration, (excepting the proclamation and enforcing bill,) "stand affected" in favor of rechartering the United States Bank, and, consequently, in favor of restoring the deposites. Not an original Jackson-man was there

among them, excepting a few of the followers of that ingenious politician who had recently invented a mode by which those opposed to the bank on constitutional grounds can consistently vote for a recharter of that institution, and a few disappointed old Federalists who crept into the Democratic ranks for the sake of office. These, said Mr. P., are the individuals who are following in the wake of their leaders, and responding to the inflammatory panic speeches of Congress by passing distress resolutions at public meetings, for the purpose of influencing the action of this House. The question before the people of the United States is the same now, said Mr. P., that it has been ever since the adoption of the Constitution, between the Federalists and Republicans—between the Aristocracy and Democracy—between those who are in favor of enlarging the powers of the General Government, by implication, and those who are for confining it within the limits prescribed by the Constitution. Gentlemen might disguise it as they would, that, he said, was the real state of the question. In answer to the second interrogatory, "Do they believe good or evil is to come of it?" Mr. P. said that if their representatives did not violate the trust reposed in them, and forfeit the confidence of the people who sent them there, by voting for a restoration of the deposites, and a recharter of the bank, they believed that the great cause of the "evil" would expire by limitation, and that "good" would eventually "come of it." Mr. P. read from the same paper the following interrogatories:

"Do they, or do they not feel that something is 'wrong, in relation to the money operations of the 'country? Do they, or do they not feel that a 'blow has, from some quarter or other, fallen upon 'and paralyzed their best interests? Do they trace 'the fall in price, and stagnation in the operations 'of the great staple of our country, to any parti- 'cular cause, and if so, what is it?"

The people of Mississippi, (said Mr. P.) do believe that something is legally and morally wrong in relation to the moneyed operations of the country; and that wrong, they believe, consists in destroying private credit, driving the gold and silver out of the country, and collecting the loanable capital at one point, and placing it under the control of the Bank of the United States—an institution exempt by law from liabilities to which individuals are subject—a corporation clothed with powers repugnant to the fundamental principles of a republican Government—a moneyed monopoly upon which exclusive privileges have been conferred by charter, and an aristocratic institution, under no moral obligations, which respects the laws and public opinion only so far as is necessary to promote its own interest. The democracy of that State (continued Mr. P.) do believe that a blow has fallen upon and paralyzed their best interests, and that there is a stagnation of business, and fall in the price of the staple of the country. He said, however, that they did not trace the cause to the Secretary of the Treasury, nor to the President of the United States, but to the evils of the banking system. They did not believe that the mere transfer of eight millions of dollars from one bank to another could cause such distress, and affect the price of cotton. The bright and cheering prospect a few months ago, described in the resolutions, was, he said, owing to the extensive accommodations of the bank during the past year. The effect of bank paper, every one would admit, was to drive the gold and silver out of the country. Experience had demonstrated that specie and paper money could not circulate together. As long as the bank continued to extend its discounts, money, or that which represented money, was plenty, and the country apparently in a prosperous condition. When the bank curtailed its discounts, the system contracted, and the pressure on the community was in proportion to the curtailment. This (said Mr. P.) is the effect of the whole system, and the necessary consequence of banking operations. What (inquired Mr. P.) were the facts? In the short period of sixteen months, prior to the first day of May, 1832, the bank extended its loans from forty-two to seventy millions of dollars, being an increase of twenty-eight millions, a much larger [illegible] of loans than was ever made by the bank within the same period, since the granting of its charter.

This expansion of the bank (said Mr. P.) made "money plenty," caused a sudden rise in the prices of cotton and the staple commodities, and the country was apparently in a prosperous condition. During the months of August and September last, the bank curtailed its loans four millions sixty-six thousand one hundred and forty-six dollars, while there was an increase of the public deposites, during that period, of two millions two hundred and sixty-eight thousand five hundred and four dollars. In the short period of two months, the enormous sum of six millions three hundred and thirty-four thousand six hundred and fifty dollars was withdrawn by the Bank of the United States from the business of the country. This curtailment of its loans and contraction of its issues, (said Mr. P.,) was what caused the price of cotton to fall, and brought pecuniary distress on the country. The contraction, he said, had been in fact greater than he had named. The policy adopted by the United States Bank, compelled the State banks to curtail in equal proportion. Such was the extraordinary power of that institution over, not only a portion of the community, but the State banks, and the whole currency of the country. Without, however, entering into an argument at that time on the subject, he begged leave to state one fact, which he considered conclusive on that point. Whether the bank was or was not compelled to pursue that course in self-defence, all the combined powers of the nationals, nullifiers, and bank party put together, could not, he said, induce the intelligent people of Mississippi to believe that there would have been any distress or pressure in the money market, at this time, if there had been no Bank of the United States. That position admitted, (and no man could deny it,) it followed as a necessary consequence that the evil must be traced to the bank, and not to the executive branch of the Government.

"Do they believe that the action of the execu- 'tive branch of Government in relation to the 'United States Bank, the removal of the public 'deposites from, and its declared hostility to, this 'institution, has or has not had an effect upon the 'present state of things?" To this, the last interrogatory, (said Mr. P.,) this writer had in the same communication (by mistake, he presumed) furnished a full and satisfactory answer. "If the 'amount of deposites (says the letter-writer) had 'been cast into the ocean, or disposed of in any way, 'leaving the bank the full enjoyment of its chartered 'rights and privileges, its action uninfluenced by 'hostility towards it on the part of the Executive, 'things would have gone on well: and if it had 'been the sense of the nation that it should have 'died a natural death, its existence would have 'terminated, with its constitution or charter, with- 'out a *struggle*, and without affecting the body 'politic in which it had figured as the great moder- 'ator of the currency of the country." Here (said Mr. P.) is an admission made by this bank advocate which overturns every argument adduced to show that the present distress in the country is produced by the action of "my old friend the Gineral," (as this letter-writer calls him,) and not by the voluntary and malicious conduct of the bank. Mark his words: "If the amount of the 'deposites had been cast into the ocean, *things* '*would have gone on well!*"—that is, the mere removal of the deposites would not have caused any distress in the country, if the bank had not sought to revenge itself on the people, for a supposed injury done to the institution, by the Secretary of the Treasury, by contracting its issues, and thereby causing universal distress in all classes of society throughout the land; that, but for this spirit of revenge, aroused into action by the pretended hostility of the Executive, "the existence 'of the bank would have terminated with its char- 'ter, without affecting the body politic, and that 'it would have died a natural death, without a 'struggle," notwithstanding the removal of the deposites. When it comes to the test, this (said Mr. P.) is what they all are bound to admit. But the public moneys were not cast into the ocean; they were not thrown away; they were not locked up in the strong box of the Government, for the purpose of oppressing the people; they were placed in the State banks, for the accommodation of the community.

Mr. P. said he did not claim the right of advising or lecturing his honorable colleague, for whom he entertained the kindest of feelings; but the character of the State was suffering under charges and imputations which he had been instrumental in bringing about. He therefore begged leave, most respectfully, to address to the House, for the benefit of his colleague, a few observations in relation to the sudden change of public sentiment in Mississippi, and the hostile attitude which that State had assumed towards the measures of the Administration, spoken of in that Hall and elsewhere.

[The SPEAKER reminded Mr. P. that it was not in order to speak personally of any member of the House.

Mr. CAGE requested that his colleague might be allowed to proceed, if the Chair could permit him, without too great a violation of order, as he was prepared to reply.]

Mr. P. thanked the Chair for the timely admonition, and his colleague for his polite request in his behalf, and begged leave, most respectfully, to inform them that he had no intention of violating the rules of the House, as they would have learned, if they had been a little more patient. That there should be no dispute or misunderstanding about his allusions, Mr. P. said that he would read from the newspaper the charge against the character of his State to which he referred

He then read from the "Richmond Whig" as follows:

"MISSISSIPPI.—This State has assumed an at- 'titude of decided hostility to the moon-struck 'measures of the Administration. The Natchez 'Courier publishes a letter from Mr. Cage, one of 'the Representatives of the State in Congress, an- 'nouncing his purpose of throwing off the tram- 'mels of party, and sustaining the interests of the 'people. Judge Black, of the Senate, elected a 'Jackson man, has taken the same decided stand, 'and in both Houses Mississippi is unanimous in 'the course, unless Mr. Plummer be an excep- 'tion, which the Telegraph regards as doubtful."

Mr. P. pronounced this statement false. The State of Mississippi has not assumed, he said, "an attitude of decided hostility to the measures of the Administration." If there was any hostility on the part of that State to the Administration on the bank question, it was not among the great mass of the people, for he had already remarked that they stood firmly by the Old Hero, who stood by them in the hour of peril and danger; but it was among those who were elected to sustain him in his efforts to put down a moneyed monopoly, about to enslave the people, and who had knowingly and wilfully violated the plighted faith of their constituents, and forfeited the confidence reposed in them by the much abused people of Mississippi.

Mr. P. referred to another article, stating that "Mr. Cage of Mississippi, a member of the House, elected as a friend to the Administration, is a friend no longer, but speaks loud and strong against it." In order to explain this strange state of things, he said, he deemed it necessary for the world to know a few facts that he hoped would not be considered entirely irrelevant to the subject under consideration, which he understood to involve, among other things, the question of what was public sentiment in Mississippi. His colleague and himself, he said, were elected to the stations which they occupied, in August, 1832, immediately after the adjournment of the first session of the 22d Congress. The presses in support of the Administration, charged a distinguished Senator from that State with being hostile to the leading measures of the Administration. One of the specifications was, that he had voted for the bill to recharter the United States Bank, which the President had just put his veto upon. The presses in opposition to the Administration, charged his colleague, another Senator, with having supported the leading measures of the Administration. One of the specifications was, that he had voted against the bill to recharter the United States Bank. They were toasted at dinners and barbacues got up for the purpose by their respective friends and partisans—the lines of party were distinctly drawn—every politician took sides—there was no equivocation allowed—the people advanced boldly up to the mark and took their stand—they took their motto from the good book, "those who are not for us,

are against us." The people were agitated on the question. The excitement was never greater in the State. Mr. P. said that the "whole animal" Jackson men kicked him out of company, notwithstanding he had been a uniform supporter of the Administration, because he had been so unfortunate as to be a native of Massachusetts, and was so inprudent as to use the following language in a speech on that floor: "I am no man-worshipper; I do not belong to the leaders of any of the numerous parties who figure upon the political theatre; I go for measures and not for men." A higher honor could not, in his opinion, have been conferred on a native of the "Ancient Commonwealth."

Mr. P. then asked his honorable colleague—(however, Mr. P. said, for the purpose of avoiding *personalities*, he would include *himself*)—he then asked the *delegation from Mississippi*, with which party *they* took sides—with those who sustained the bank and Clay's land bill, and opposed the Administration, or with those who sustained the Administration on those questions? By whom (said Mr. P., addressing himself to his colleague, in an emphatic tone) were *we* supported—by those who sustained the bank, or by those who sustained the Administration? When the Jackson presses urged *our* pretensions on the ground that *we* were more of Jackson men than *our* opponents, and made an appeal to the partialities and prejudices of the people, exhorting them to rally at the polls, and give their votes for *us*, who were the personal and political friends of the hero of New Orleans in preference to one whose motto was "measures and not men;" what, he asked, was the course of his honorable colleague (and himself?)

Did *we* mount the stump and tell the people that *we* would not wear "party trammels," that *we* would not be under the influence of "party discipline," that *we* would not bow "at the shrine of party," and that *we* would not pledge *himself* to support the measures of the Administration, right or wrong, like an independent *man* resolved not to be *trammelied?* or did *we*, under these circumstances, tell the people that *we* was a native of *Tennessee*, from the same neighborhood, and personally acquainted with the President; that General Jackson had known *us* intimately from his infancy; had often dandled *him* on his knee in childhood; and that *we*, while yet a boy, had followed him to the tented field, and fought by his side in his country's defence, when he achieved those victories, and won those laurels which placed him in the chair of state; and that *therefore* they could not question *his* Jacksonism? And for fear that additional evidence would be wanting, did *we* not shed tears in speaking of his "old friend the General." In short, did *we* not take advantage of the peculiar state of excitement existing at that time, and ride into Congress on the popularity of General Jackson? He said that he could readily answer these questions if certain that it would be in order to do so; but as he was an orderly man, he would leave that for the *rest* of the delegation. Admitting them to be answered in the affirmative, what do they prove, said Mr. P.? They prove (he continued) one of two things; either that *we* pledged *himself* to the people of the State to vote for the measures of the Administration *generally*, or that *we* would sustain such leading measures of the Administration in *particular*, as were then under discussion and consideration before the people of the State. He cared not, he said, which *we* meant; the people understand *us* as being, at least, tacitly pledged to oppose the bank.

Mr. P. said, if an apology was due to the House for having treated a letter-writer with so much respect, it must be found in the fact that he had no other way of disabusing the public mind. He hoped that the newspapers would do the people of Mississippi the justice to give his remarks a circulation as extensive as the letter-writers had the slanders to which he had referred. With regard to the merits of the main question, he had intended to embrace the opportunity then offered to express himself fully, but the feeble state of his health would not admit of it at that time; he should therefore defer it, and seek some other occasion, on the report of the Committee of Ways and Means.

Mr. P. protested against any intention of disrespect to any one; repeated that he had a high regard personally for the individuals who composed the meeting at Natchez. He made some further general remarks in relation to the distress in the country and the cause of it, not distinctly heard by the reporter, and earnestly contended that no man who was well versed in the banking operations could attribute it to any cause other than the pernicious and baneful operations of the banking system, which he feared would some day destroy the Government. He concluded by declaring that it was with wounded feelings of national pride that he heard it gravely asserted by intelligent, and he believed patriotic gentlemen, on that floor, that the Government could not exist, nor the various branches of industry prosper without the aid of the United States Bank, or some other similar moneyed corporation, to afford facilities and regulate the currency of the country. If the body politic, said he, was so debilitated; if the energies of the people were reduced so low that they could not continue to exist without a moneyed monopoly to lean upon for support, it was evidence to him that they were prepared for slavery; it was time that they had a master; they were, in his opinion, unworthy of that rich inheritance handed down to them by the patriots of the Revolution; they were incapable of self-government.

Mr. CAGE briefly replied, when the resolutions were laid on the table and ordered to be printed.

Mr KAVANAGH presented a memorial signed by inhabitants of Bath, in the State of Maine, complaining of the present stagnation of business, which they attribute to the removal of the public deposites. He remarked, that although he felt great regret in differing from so respectable a portion of his constituents in some of the views which they presented, yet it gave him great pleasure to assure the House that their memorial was couched in language becoming them as highly respectable citizens, and the body which they address—that it was altogether free from those harsh criminations which characterize many of the communications on the same subject which have been addressed to the House. The memorialists, with great candor, suggest the course which they believe necessary to relieve the country from the embarrassments of which they complain.

On motion of Mr. KAVANAGH, the memorial was read, ordered to be printed, and laid on the table.

Mr. EVANS presented a memorial, praying the restoration of the public deposites from sundry citizens of the town of Somersworth. Read, ordered to be printed, and laid on the table.

Mr. BRIGGS presented the memorial of 370 citizens of the town of Adams, in the county of Berkshire, Massachusetts, praying the restoration of the deposites, and representing the prevalence of great embarrassment in their business, &c. Read, laid on the table, and ordered to be printed.

Mr. BAYLIES presented a memorial from 2,429 inhabitants of Bristol county, Massachusetts, representing that all business in that county labors under unexampled embarrassments, and suggesting, as a remedy for the evil, the restoration of the deposites, and the extension of the bank charter for two years. Read, laid on the table, and ordered to be printed.

Mr. BAYLIES also presented resolutions of the Legislature of the Commonwealth of Massachusetts, in relation to the improvement of the navigation of Taunton river. Read, and referred.

Mr. CHOATE presented a memorial from citizens of the town of Lynn, praying the restoration of the deposites, and the recharter of the United States Bank. Read, laid on the table, and ordered to be printed.

Mr. OSGOOD said he had to present certain resolutions adopted by the citizens of Boston, at one of the largest meetings ever held, remonstrating against any restoration of the deposites, and against the rechartering of the bank, as well as professing their determination to support the Executive in their measures to employ the agency of the State banks, and to restore to the country a metallic currency. He called for the reading of the memorial and resolutions.

They were accordingly read, ordered to be printed, and laid on the table.

Mr. BURGES presented a memorial, which he said was signed by a majority of the voters in Paterson, New Jersey, praying the restoration of the deposites and recharter of the bank; also, one of a similar tenor from Smithfield and Cumberland, Providence county, Rhode Island.

Mr. PEARCE remarked that he had received some communications in relation to this latter memorial, which he desired should be read.

Mr. BURGES said he would not object.

The letters were read, and there were in them sundry charges that the memorial was not signed exclusively by the inhabitants of the place from whence it purported to come; that it was improperly get up for political objects, &c.

Mr. BURGES asked whose signature was to one of the letters read?

Mr. PEARCE informed him it was by Mr. Owney Ballou.

Mr. BURGES pronounced it a forgery.

Mr. PEARCE asked and obtained leave of the House to address a few remarks in defence of the statements contained in the letters, as well as their authenticity; upon which a debate of a very lengthened and recriminatory character arose between the two honorable members from Rhode Island, in which the local politics of the State were discussed, [but which we are obliged to defer for the present.] It was finally arrested by a successful motion of Mr. EVANS to have the memorial laid on the table; and it was ordered to be printed, with the others presented.

Mr. BURGES then presented another memorial of the same tenor from inhabitants of Newport; which was read, ordered to be printed, and laid on the table.

And the House adjourned.

IN SENATE.

Tuesday, *April* 1, 1834.

A message was received from the President of the United States, by Mr. Donelson, his Private Secretary, transmitting a report from the Secretary of State on the subject of preventing the counterfeiting of foreign coin.

Mr. WRIGHT asked leave to present to the Senate a report from the minority of the select committee to whom was referred the credentials of the Hon. Mr. Robbins and the Hon. Mr. Potter, each claiming a seat as a Senator from Rhode Island.

Mr. POINDEXTER inquired whether this was a substantive view taken of the subject, or a response to the report of the committee. He objected to anything but a substantive view of the question on the part of the minority. He had been told (he had not seen it) that the paper was a response, in the shape of a speech or argument, to the report of the committee.

Mr. WRIGHT did not wish the gentleman to be in doubt about the report. He answered, that the paper was both a substantive view of the questions involved, and also a response to the positions assumed by the majority of the committee in their report. He was entirely unacquainted with the practice of the Senate on such subjects, but the practice of the House of Representatives was, that a minority was authorized to make a report. When the majority made their report, he distinctly stated he desired to avoid the duty of making a minority report unless it was acceptable to the Senate. But under expressions from different sides of the House, he then said he would present his own views, and he had done so. He had not intruded upon the Senate.

Mr. FRELINGHUYSEN thought a presentation of the substantive views of the gentleman was as far as the Senator could go. He was willing that a minority of a committee should have an opportunity of making known their own views, but not to take up the majority report and tear it to pieces, because it would be putting them in the back ground. He hoped the gentleman from New York would give such a direction to the subject as to enable him to give his own views on general principles, and then subject them to the consideration of the Senate.

Mr. SPRAGUE was willing and desirous that the gentleman should present his views; but that it should be done in the same manner, and in the same character, as the report of the majority which was presented. It was going very far, when a select committee made their report, to

permit an individual member of the committee to make an answer to the report presented, by way of counter report.

Mr. EWING, in order to give an opportunity to examine the paper, moved to lay the motion on the table for the present; which was agreed to.

The VICE PRESIDENT presented a communication from the Governor of Michigan, relative to the southern boundary of said territory; which, on motion of Mr. NAUDAIN, was referred to the Committee on the Judiciary.

Mr. TIPTON presented a memorial from sundry citizens of Arkansas Territory; which was referred to the select committee on the admission of Michigan and Arkansas into the Union.

On motion of Mr. FRELINGHUYSEN, the Senate took up the bill making appropriation for repair and completion of the Cumberland Road through the States of Ohio, Indiana, and Illinois.

Mr. HENDRICKS moved an amendment, to apply a portion of the appropriation to building toll-gates and toll-houses on the road.

Mr. POINDEXTER opposed the application of the money to any purpose but the repair of the road.

Mr. HENDRICKS said he opposed the amendment, because the act of the Legislature of Pennsylvania contemplated the taking of the road, when the toll-gates and houses were put up.

Mr. CLAYTON opposed the whole bill on principle. The improvement system was designed as a national system; and this proposed cession to the States through which the road passed, would be destructive of this great principle, if the States were to exercise unlimited jurisdiction over it.

Mr. EWING replied, that it would not be giving the exclusive jurisdiction over the road to the State. Congress still retained its power over it. The States were the agents of the General Government. They were to take only enough tolls for repairing the road. It must go out of repair, or the States must take it under their control.

Mr. FRELINGHUYSEN thought this was one of the most substantial improvements of the General Government. It was a highly national object, and to stop it now, would be sounding the funeral knell of the system; and, therefore, he was not in favor of it. He had reason to believe, from the reports on the subject, that by a further expenditure of $400,000 or $700,000, it could be put in complete order, and then the States would take it under their control.

After some further remarks, Mr. HENDRICKS withdrew his amendment.

Mr. PRESTON then made some remarks in opposition to the bill, and then offered the following amendment to the appropriation:

" Provided, The States of Maryland and Pennsylvania consent to receive those portions of the road passing through their respective territories, upon the said sum of $300,000 putting the said road in repair."

Mr. WILKINS opposed the amendment, because it would tend to defeat the bill. He did not know how the consent of the States could be obtained. We must trust to their good faith to take the road, and he doubted not they would do so.

After some further remarks by Messrs. CLAY, EWING, and KANE, the amendment was disagreed to.

The question on ordering to be engrossed, and read a third time, recurring, it was decided as follows:

YEAS—Messrs. Benton, Bibb, Clay, Ewing, Frelinghuysen, Hendricks, Kane, Kent, Linn, Morris, Poindexter, Porter, Prentiss, Robbins, Robinson, Silsbee, Southard, Tipton, Waggaman, Wilkins—20.

NAYS—Messrs. Black, Brown, Calhoun, Clayton, Forsyth, Hill, King of Alabama, King of Georgia, Knight, Leigh, Mangum, Moore, Naudain, Preston, Shepley, Smith, Sprague, Swift, Tomlinson, Tyler, White, and Wright—22.

Mr. SOUTHARD moved that the Committee on Naval Affairs be discharged from the further consideration of the memorial of the city authorities of Charleston, South Carolina, for the establishment of a naval hospital, and that it be referred to the Committee on Commerce; which was agreed to.

Mr. SILSBEE presented the memorial of Benjamin Adams & Co. and others, praying the remission of excess on certain duties; which was referred to the Committee on Finance.

On motion of Mr. WAGGAMAN,
The Senate adjourned.

HOUSE OF REPRESENTATIVES.

TUESDAY, April 1, 1834.

The SPEAKER laid before the House a written communication from the President of the United States, transmitting a report from the Secretary of State, relative to measures for preventing the counterfeiting of coin, and for preventing the importation of foreign counterfeit coin.

On motion of Mr. CAMBRELENG, the report and message were referred to the Committee on the Judiciary.

Mr. J. Q. ADAMS asked the unanimous consent of the House to present a petition.

There not being a quorum in the House, a call was moved by Mr. LYTLE.

The House refused—ayes 21, noes 34.

A quorum having in the interim come into the House—

Mr. ADAMS renewed his application. Objected to.

Mr. WILLIAMS moved a suspension of the rule, for the purpose of receiving petitions generally. Negatived.

Mr. GRENNELL moved a call of the House; which prevailed—yeas 101, nays 18.

The call was proceeded with; and,

On motion of Mr. MERCER, it was suspended.

Mr. ADAMS then obtained leave to present the petition of sundry inhabitants of Scituate, Marshfield, Hanover, and Pembroke, Plymouth county, Massachusetts, praying that the navigation of the North River, in that State, be improved, by cutting a canal from the northeast bend, below Wille's Island, to the town of Scituate. Referred to the Committee on Roads and Canals.

Mr. WILLIAMS then renewed his motion to suspend the rule generally, for the presentation of petitions, and demanded the yeas and nays thereon; which having been ordered, the House refused to suspend the rule—yeas 82, nays 54.

Mr. CHANEY reported a bill for the relief of William Slocum.

Mr. SUTHERLAND, from the Committee on Commerce, reported a bill granting compensation to the surveyor of Town Creek, Maryland.

Mr. MERCER, from the Committee on Roads and Canals, to whom was referred the bill from the Senate to aid in the construction of certain roads in the Territory of Michigan, reported the same without amendment; and the bill was committed.

Mr. CARR, from the Committee on Private Land Claims, asked to be discharged from the further consideration of the petition of John Lawe; and leave was given the petitioner to withdraw his petition.

Mr. CARR, from the same committee, asked leave to be discharged from the further consideration of the petition of Augustin Grignon and others; and leave was granted said petitioners to withdraw their petition.

The consideration of the bill to provide for the settlement of certain revolutionary claims was resumed as the unfinished business.

Mr. MARSHALL resumed the speech in support of the bill which he commenced some weeks ago, when the subject was last up, and spoke till one o'clock, without concluding, when the special order of the day was announced.

THE DEPOSITES AND UNITED STATES BANK.

The House resumed the consideration of the resolutions reported from the Committee of Ways and Means, together with Mr. Wilde's amendment thereto, declaring the reasons offered by the Secretary of the Treasury, for the removal of the deposites to be unsatisfactory and insufficient.

Mr. HARDIN, who had the floor from Friday last, spoke in support of the amendment, and in opposition to the resolutions, as reported. Before calling the attention of the House to the report of the committee, Mr. H. made some preliminary remarks upon the relative position of different parties in regard to this question. He thought (he said) that there was nothing unnatural in the union of the National Republicans with the State-rights party on this question. He knew of nothing inconsistent or incompatible with the acts or doings of either party in their present union against the Executive. He was only surprised that their unanimity was not more perfect, and that there was a solitary instance of a State-rights man supporting the doctrines of the President. The two parties might differ again, as they have differed heretofore, in regard to the tariff, the question on discriminating duties, &c.; but, on the present occasion, when a vital principle of the Constitution was boldly invaded, they must necessarily unite. He viewed the charge of an unnatural coalition of parties against the Administration, as a manœuvre to divert the attention of the people from the real issue.

The Committee of Ways and Means had promised, when they should get possession of this subject, to eviscerate it, and lay it fully before the House. Some gentlemen remarked, at the time, that the report would thereby reëcho the letter of the Secretary, and so it had turned out. But one thing he gave the committee great credit for. He never saw a master-stroke of policy that he did not do it justice. He alluded to the subject introduced in the first resolution—the declaration that the Bank of the United States ought not to be rechartered. He asked, who had a right to present that proposition to the House? The corporation being composed, principally, of private stockholders, we had no right to renew their charter unless they applied to us for it. Why, then, was the question introduced? Because the committee knew that some States of this Union which were opposed to the course of the President in regard to the deposites, were also opposed to a national bank. Mr. H. took up the constitutionality of the bank, and pursued the topic at great length. He examined it as an original question by former Administrations and the decisions of the Supreme Court. It was the right and duty of Congress, he contended, to regulate the currency. Congress were required to maintain an army, a navy, and an extensive civil list. In ordinary times, these expenses may amount to twenty or thirty millions, and, in time of war, to sixty or a hundred millions, which sums must be annually raised and disbursed by Congress. Congress had power to use expedient and competent means to carry these powers into effect. They had the power to regulate the currency, to sustain armies, navies, and a civil list, and defray the national debt. What kind of means had Congress to effect these leading objects? What means had Congress the right to resort to for such purposes? Any means, he contended, could be used which were conducive to the end. Congress was not confined to express means, but could devise means from implication. They were not confined to indispensable means, but could select means which were convenient. In fine, he contended that any means were within the scope of the powers of Congress, which would conduce to carry into effect the powers of Congress.

Mr. H. argued that the means of raising and disbursing revenue by a national bank were fully within the constitutional power of Congress, because no other means would answer the purpose so well. The Bank of the United States had enabled the Government to manage its fiscal affairs without loss or inconvenience, and he entered into a long series of remarks to show that a metallic currency was impracticable and undesirable, and that the State banks could not be relied upon as safe depositories of the public money, or as faithful agents for its disbursement. He then viewed the question of the constitutionality of the bank in reference to authority and precedent. There ought to be some mode, he contended, to settle disputed constitutional questions, and he went into the history of the bank, to show that the question of its constitutionality had been solemnly affirmed and established, and was no longer to be questioned. He read extracts from the veto message, from which he argued that General Jackson was fully committed in favor of the constitutionality of a national bank. Mr. H. here remarked that the Globe-man, with whom he was well acquainted, and who he liked very well himself, (he said,) though many others did not, had notified him that

If he made a speech on this question, he would publish in the Globe the speech which he (Mr. H.) made in 1816 against the bank. Having due notice, he might as well explain that matter now, for if he was handled in the Globe, as the Senators sometimes were, he was fully aware it would not be with silk gloves. He did oppose the incorporation of the Bank of the United States, because he considered its capital as too large, and because he apprehended that it would have a baneful influence on the liberties of the country, and the purity of our institutions. His fearful forbodings had not been realized. The bank had refused to become a political tool to any party. It had been attempted (he said) to render the bank subservient to the views of the Administration in the same manner as the Post Office Department was. He spoke of the number of mail contractors, &c., under the influence of the department, forming a disciplined corps, every member of which wore a collar, with the inscription of "Andrew Jackson, his dog." The bank alone had stood out, and the vengeance of the party—not of the party, for nine-tenths of them were as respectable as any men in the world—but the vengeance of some of the party managers was poured out upon the bank, because it would not do—what? Because it would not contribute its aid to the plan of merging all the powers of the Government in the executive power. His fears had not been realized. Few men, when taken up to the top of a high mountain, and tempted with the offer of wealth and power, would say, "Get thee behind me, Satan." None but Biddle and Duane had withstood the tempter. He had voted against the bank in 1816, because he then thought it unconstitutional. Then, he was a young and inexperienced member. He had since reviewed that opinion, and reversed it. It afforded him pleasure to retract the opinion, and he wished to God that General Jackson could find the same pleasure in retracing his steps and restoring the deposites. He had no pride of opinion to sustain, and no interest to promote, in deciding the question. He had never had any connexion with the bank in any way. He had been employed in one or two causes against the bank, and in one for it. He retracted his opinion because he believed it was an erroneous opinion, and because he believed that his constituents and State wished the bank to be rechartered.

Mr. H. then proceeded to discuss, at length, the expediency of rechartering the bank, as a measure for regulating the currency.

About three o'clock, Mr. H. gave way to a motion to adjourn; and Mr. McCOMAS moved an adjournment.

Mr. CARR called for the yeas and nays on the motion.

Mr. McCOMAS withdrew his motion; and Mr. HARDIN proceeded.

At half-past three, Mr. H. yielded the floor to Mr. CHILTON, who moved an adjournment.

Mr. BROWN asked the yeas and nays; and they were ordered.

The question being taken, by yeas and nays, it was decided in the negative:

Yeas 68, nays 89.

Mr. HARDIN resumed, and spoke till ten minutes past four, upon the reasons of the Secretary for removing the deposites; when he yielded the floor to

Mr. CHILTON, who moved an adjournment. The question was taken by yeas and nays, and determined in the negative—yeas 76, nays 84.

Mr. HARDIN resumed, and felt flattered (he said) at the decision of the House, as it showed that the House was fascinated with his speech. He went on for a few minutes, and

Mr. CLARKE moved an adjournment.

Mr. GILLET called for the yeas and nays; which were ordered.

Mr. MERCER proposed to amend the motion, by inserting the hour.

Mr. FOOT (Speaker pro tem.) said this was in the pleasure of the House.

Mr. POLK rose to order. He wished to know if such a motion could be submitted, the member from Kentucky not having gave way.

Mr. FOOT understood the member to have given way.

The motion prevailed—yeas 82, nays 80, and The House adjourned.

IN SENATE.
WEDNESDAY, April 2, 1834.

Mr. WHITE moved a reconsideration of the vote of yesterday, upon the rejection of the Cumberland road bill.

Messrs. WHITE, CLAY, SPRAGUE, and KING of Alabama, briefly expressed the reasons which should actuate them in the vote they were about to give.

The question on reconsideration, on motion of Mr. PRESTON, was taken by yeas and nays.

YEAS—Messrs. Benton, Clay, Ewing, Grundy, Hendricks, Kane, King of Alabama, Knight, Linn, McKean, Morris, Poindexter, Porter, Prentiss, Robbins, Robinson, Shepley, Silsbee, Smith, Southard, Sprague, Swift, Tallmadge, Tipton, Tomlinson, White, Wilkins, Wright—28.

NAYS—Messrs. Brown, Calhoun, Hill, King of Georgia, Leigh, Moore, Preston, and Tyler—8.

On motion of Mr. EWING, the bill was recommitted to the Committee on Roads and Canals.

A message was received from the House of Representatives, by Mr. FRANKLIN, their Clerk, transmitting the following order:

Ordered, That a message be sent to the Senate, to notify that body of the death of JAMES BLAIR, late one of the Representatives from the State of South Carolina, and that his funeral will take place this day, at four o'clock in the afternoon, from the Hall of the House of Representatives.

Mr. PRESTON said, I am sure the Senate will sympathize with me in those emotions of profound sorrow, with which I rise to propose the customary resolutions upon such an event. The sudden death of General BLAIR, in the vigor of life, and in the midst of his most strenuous pursuits, cannot fail to impress all minds with the most solemn feelings, which to us are enhanced by his association with us in the same pursuits, and by the fact that this is the second instance this session of such an awful and sudden dispensation of Providence. We, his colleagues of the South Carolina delegation, lament his loss—not the less that he has differed with us in some points of public policy. Such differences have never extended to personal separation, for each has excused the zeal of the other by a mutual and equal acknowledgment of zeal, and God forbid that any such difference should impede for a moment the sad current of feeling which now passes through my heart. To whatever the deceased addressed himself, he brought uncommon force of character, firmness of purpose, and vigor of intellect. His country and his constituents will mourn the loss of these qualities at this important juncture of our affairs, and upon me devolves the melancholy duty of moving the following resolution:

Resolved, That the Senate will attend the funeral of the Honorable JAMES BLAIR, late a member of the House of Representatives from the State of South Carolina, at the hour of four o'clock this evening; and as a testimony of respect for the memory of the deceased, they will go into mourning, by wearing crape on the left arm for thirty days.

The resolution was adopted unanimously.

On motion of Mr. PRESTON, The Senate adjourned.

HOUSE OF REPRESENTATIVES.
WEDNESDAY, April 2, 1834.

After the Journal was read—

Mr. McDUFFIE said:

Mr. SPEAKER: I rise to discharge a painful and melancholy duty, by announcing the death of General JAMES BLAIR, a Representative from the State of South Carolina. The occurrences of the few last weeks, furnish to us all an impressive and awful admonition of the precarious tenure by which we hold this fleeting and feverish existence, while we are but too prone to act as if it would never have an end. Scarcely have our feelings recovered from the violence of the shock produced by the extraordinary and unexpected spectacle of one of our number falling dead before our eyes, while in the act of addressing the House on a great question of deep and absorbing interest, when we are summoned to pay the last melancholy offices of humanity to another, whose death was equally sudden.

Mr. Speaker, I never have been able to feel that on occasions of this kind, panegyric is an appropriate tribute to the memory of the dead. They are beyond the reach of praise, and it is not by this that they are judged, either in this world or the next. Biographical details, however brief, are, in my opinion, not more appropriate. When the deceased is unknown, they are seldom of any interest. His name should be his epitaph; and however blank it may appear to the vacant eye of the passing stranger, it will always have power to call up the recollection of his virtues in the bosom of friendship, and the tear of undissembled sorrow in the eye of affection—offerings more grateful and congenial to the disembodied spirit than the proudest monument which human art can erect, or the most pompous eulogium which human eloquence can pronounce. Without saying more, sir, I now ask the House to bestow upon the memory of the deceased the customary testimonials of respect, by adopting the resolutions I hold in my hand.

Resolved, That the members of this House will attend the funeral of the late JAMES BLAIR, at four o'clock, this afternoon.

Resolved, That a committee be appointed to take order for superintending the funeral of JAMES BLAIR deceased, late a member of this House from the State of South Carolina.

Resolved, That the members of this House will testify their respect for the memory of JAMES BLAIR, by wearing crape on the left arm for thirty days.

The resolutions were adopted.

The usual notification thereof having been ordered to be sent to the Senate.

On motion of Mr. McDUFFIE, The House then adjourned.

Messrs. McDUFFIE, WHITTLESEY of Ohio, SPEIGHT, THOMAS of Louisiana, GILMER, BOON, and BRIGGS, were appointed a committee to conduct the funeral ceremonies.

IN SENATE.
THURSDAY, April 3, 1834.

A message was received from the President of the United States, by Mr. DONELSON, his Private Secretary, transmitting communications from the Governors of the States of New York and New Jersey, relating to the settlement of the boundary lines of those States.

Mr. PRENTISS presented a memorial signed by about four hundred freemen of the county of Chittenden, Vermont, praying a restoration of the public deposites to the Bank of the United States; which was read, referred to the Committee on Finance, and ordered to be printed.

The VICE PRESIDENT presented the following communication from the Secretary of the Treasury, responsive to Mr. CLAY's resolution of the 31st March:

TREASURY DEPARTMENT, April 3, 1834.

SIR: In obedience to the resolution of the Senate of the 31st ultimo, requiring the Secretary of the Treasury "to report to the Senate what amount of public money is now on deposite in the Union Bank of Maryland, when and on what account it was deposited, and also, whether any treasury drafts, contingent, or other, have been, during the month of March, 1834, furnished to the said bank, or at any time heretofore to the Bank of Maryland, for any and what purpose; and that he likewise report what amount of stock in the capital of the said Union Bank was held by R. B. Taney, Esq., when the said bank was selected as one of the banks to receive on deposite the public money, and what amount of the said stock he now holds," I have the honor to transmit herewith a statement (marked A to U) of the public money deposited in the Union Bank of Maryland, showing when it was deposited and on what account. The difference between the balance on credit of the Treasurer, in his statement, and that furnished by the bank, arises from warrants which have been issued by the Treasurer on the bank, but which have not yet been presented for payment, and a deposite to his credit since the last weekly return.

No treasury drafts, contingent or other, were furnished to the Union Bank of Maryland during the month of March, 1834. And no transfer draft of any description, contingent or other, has ever been furnished to the Bank of Maryland since I came into office.

In answer to that part of the resolution which calls for information as to the amount of stock held by Roger B. Taney in the Union Bank of Maryland, "when the said bank was selected as one of 'the banks to receive in deposite the public money, 'and what amount of the said stock he now holds," I have the honor to state, that, inasmuch as the inquiry does not embrace the stockholders generally, but is confined to the stock of a particular individual, it must, by necessary implication, be understood as pointing the inquiry to the motives which influenced the individual named in the transactions he may have had in the stock of the said bank—and under such circumstances, it is due to his official relations to the Senate, and to the public, that his motives in any such transactions should be fully and clearly disclosed. I therefore transmit to the Senate a copy of a letter from this department to the President of the Union Bank of Maryland, dated the 31st day of March, 1834, apprizing him of the information required by the Senate, requesting him to forward to the department a statement of the amount of stock in the Union Bank of Maryland held by Roger B. Taney at the time the deposites were removed—time at which it was purchased—and the amount now held by him—and the original private letter of Roger B. Taney, authorizing him to sell certain shares of stock which were lately sold.

Also, the letter from the President of the Union Bank of Maryland, in reply, dated April 1, 1834, enclosing the statements and papers above-mentioned, which are herewith transmitted, and are as follows:

1. The statement of the cashier, showing that at the time of the selection of the said bank as one of the banks to receive in deposite the public money, Roger B. Taney held, in the stock of the said bank, seventy-one full shares and four half shares, the par value of which amounted to $5,475. That the last of these shares were purchased by him on the 12th of May, 1831, before he received any appointment under the Government of the United States; and that he now holds sixty-three full shares of stock in the said bank, showing that eight full shares and four half shares, which were held by him at the time the deposites were removed, were sold and transferred on the 20th February, 1834.

2. The original private letter of Roger B. Taney, of the 18th February, 1834, to the President of the Union Bank, directing so many shares to be sold, for the purpose of paying the debt therein mentioned, as might be necessary for that purpose, and the balance of the shares to be returned to him; and the affirmation of the President of the Union Bank that he sold, under the power of attorney mentioned in that letter, eight full shares, and four half shares, and returned to Roger B. Taney a certificate of the remaining one share. The letter states the certificate sent to the president of the bank at nine full shares; the affirmation of the president of the bank shows that it contained nine full shares and four half shares, the half shares being omitted in the letter, but included in the power of attorney to sell.

I also transmit herewith the *original* letter, dated 15th February, 1834, from Somerville Pinkney, Esq., of the city of Annapolis, the counsel for the creditor to whom the debt was due from Roger B. Taney, as trustee, requesting the payment of the said debt.

I have the honor to be, sir, very respectfully, your obedient servant, R. B. TANEY,

Secretary of the Treasury.

Hon. Martin Van Buren,
Vice President of the United States,
and President of the Senate.

On motion of Mr. CLAY, the communication and accompanying documents were ordered to be printed, and referred to the Committee on Finance.

The VICE PRESIDENT presented a communication from the Department of State, transmitting an account of the number of passengers who arrived in the United States from foreign countries during the year 1833; which,

On motion of Mr. SPRAGUE, was laid upon the table, and ordered to be printed.

Mr. SPRAGUE presented a memorial signed by upwards of 300 citizens of Bath, Maine, praying a restoration of the deposites to the Bank of the United States; which was read, referred to the Committee on Finance, and ordered to be printed.

On motion of Mr. FRELINGHUYSEN, the message of the President of the United States, and the accompanying documents, relating to the boundary lines between the States of New York and New Jersey, was ordered to be printed.

Mr. BENTON rose to present the resolutions adopted by the friends of the Administration, and opponents of the United States Bank, at their great meeting, in Fanueil Hall, on the 14th of March last. He said, that in the great multitude of petitions, memorials, and resolutions, which had been presented to the Senate, few, if any, ever came forward with more imposing claims to the respectful consideration of the Senate. They come from a city, great in itself, and greater still in the commerce which enriches it—the arts and literature which adorn it—and the historic recollections which illustrate it. They come from a large portion of the population of that eminent city—5,000 being computed to be within the walls, and 2,000 without—making a mass of 7,000 citizens, whose voices were united and embodied in these resolutions. They were adopted on a spot sacred to American history, and memorable for scenes of patriotic impulsion—in that Fanueil Hall, whose name alone imparts an interest to everything which emanates from it.

These resolutions (said Mr. B.) are twenty-eight in number. They embrace all the points which have grown out of the question which has occupied and engrossed the public attention, since the meeting of Congress; and are full and explicit in approving the conduct of the President and Secretary of the Treasury, and in condemning the conduct of the United States Bank. Concurring, as he heartily did, in the sentiments expressed by these resolutions, he felt a particular gratification in being the organ of their communication to the Senate. They would be read, and would speak for themselves; and would show that any attempt on his part to add to their point and power, would be vain and nugatory. He should not make the attempt—he should not pretend to go over ground so fully occupied, and so ably explored; but he would take leave to make a few remarks on some points mentioned in the resolutions, either of a more general application, or of a nature not to be sufficiently illustrated in the limited scope of a resolution.

Mr. B. remarked upon the identity of the scene which was now presented with the one which was witnessed at the approaching termination of the first bank charter in 1811, when there was no removal of deposites to be charged with the distresses of the country. All the machinery of alarm and distress was in as full activity at that time as at present, and with the same identical effects—town meetings, memorials, resolutions, deputations to Congress, alarming speeches in Congress. The price of all property was shown to be depressed. Hemp sunk in Philadelphia from $350 to $250 per ton; flour sunk from $11 a barrel to $7½; all real estate fell 30 per cent.; 500 houses were suspended in their erection; the rent of money rose to 1½ per cent. per month on the best paper; confidence destroyed, manufactories stopped, workmen dismissed, and the ruin of the country confidently predicted. This was the scene then; and for what object? Purely and simply to obtain a recharter of the bank! Purely and simply to force a recharter from the alarm and distress of the country; for there was no removal of deposites then to be complained of, and to be made the scape-goat of a studied and premeditated attempt to operate upon Congress through the alarms of the people and the destruction of their property. There was not even a curtailment of discounts then. The whole scene was fictitious; but it was a case in which fiction does the mischief of truth. A false alarm in the money market produces all the effects of real danger; and thus as much distress was proclaimed in Congress in 1811—as much distress was proved to exist, and really did exist, then as now—without a single cause to be alleged then, which is alleged now. But the power and organization of the bank made the alarm then; its power and organization make it now; and fictitious on both occasions; and men were ruined then, as now, by the power of imaginary danger, which, in the moneyed world, has all the ruinous effects of real danger. No deposites were removed then, and the reason was, as assigned by Mr. Gallatin to Congress, that the Government had borrowed more than the amount of the deposites from the bank; and this loan would enable her to protect her interest in every contingency. The open object of the bank then, was a recharter. The knights entered the list with their vizors off—no war in disguise then for the renewal of a charter under the tilting and jousting of a masquerade scuffle for recovery of deposites.

That the real object of all this alarm in the country—all this pressure upon some *parts* of the country—for the section south of the Potomac had enjoyed a remarkable exemption—he was permitted to believe, was to secure the recharter of the bank. Such must have been the design of the bank; and the manner in which the bill for the recharter was brought forward, and then laid over, certainly favored the idea. It was brought forward under an agonizing cry of distress, and a vehement appeal for immediate relief from actual, insufferable distress. It was then laid down that it might not interfere with another debate; that other debate came to a close in two days; then the bill, which was fixed for the first of May, was taken up to be fixed again for the 21st of April; and before the 21st of April came, a set of important elections will take place in the two great States of New York and Virginia. Thus, after working the machinery of alarm for three months, and filling the Union with cries for the restoration of the deposites, the bank suddenly presents a demand for a recharter; and then adjourns that demand, urgent as it might be, until certain important elections were over.

Mr. B. remarked upon the political character of this bank. He said it was born a political institution, and was the first measure of the Government to develop the line which so long and so distinctly marked the political parties of this country. The creation of this bank went to the origin of party. It went to the source where parties should be formed—to principles, to great and fundamental principles in the administration of the Government. It involved the question of constructive and of granted powers; and was the entering wedge to all the implied powers afterwards assumed by Congress. Prohibitory tariffs—local internal improvement—and the whole American system. He said the bank was the head of the American system; and if it was rechartered, it would reëstablish that system in greater power and glory than it ever possessed. That it would do so, was proved (he said) by what it was now doing, struggling for those deposites which were the fruit of the high tariff policy—struggling for money which many a gentleman held to have been unconstitutionally levied, and therefore not levied at all, but taken tortuously. He warned gentlemen who were opposed to the American system, not now to reëstablish this eldest and strongest member of that system; and which, if reëstablished, would certainly set up the whole family again, especially that high tariff which furnished her with those surplusses of revenue, for the keeping of which she now shows such an invincible inclination.

Mr. B. remarked upon the resolution which spoke of the exclusion of the Government directors from a knowledge and participation in the affairs of the bank, for the purpose of reminding the American people that there were no Government directors at this time in the bank. The institution, in its management, was now a mere private affair, governed by the directors of the individual stockholders, wielding and using the money, the name, the character, and the influence of the United States precisely as they pleased. The immense power which the Government had put into the hands of the bank was now used independently of the Government; and in the absence of directors, it became a matter of the highest moment to the people to have a thorough investigation into the affairs of the bank, to see how far its tremendous powers had been used for good or for evil, for favor or affection, for the relief or oppression of the American

people. Until that examination was made, and especially in the absence and exclusion of the Government directors, it was certainly an extraordinary case of presumption for the bank to come forward and demand a recharter.

The equality of the State banks with the branches of the Federal bank as places of deposite for the public moneys, as mentioned in one of the resolutions, was next adverted to by Mr. B. He did it for the purpose of remarking that the strong and conclusive argument against the assumption that the Federal bank was the Federal treasury, growing out of the 14th fundamental article of the constitution of the bank, could no longer escape public attention. The notice which was taken of it in such a meeting and such a place would ensure it a general and conspicuous regard in time to come.

Mr. B. referred to another of the resolutions, as claiming a particular notice, because it had a reference to a great practical measure now depending before the Senate, and which he hoped would end in legislative action. It was the one which related to the reform of the currency—the real currency of the Constitution—by enlarging the specie circulation and diminishing the paper circulation within the United States. This was the true way to reform the currency. Let Congress raise gold to its just value, and restore it to its ancient place of current money among the people; let it repeal all its unwise, if not unconstitutional laws against the circulation of foreign coins; let it get rid of its own unwise legislation, and permit the enterprise of the people and the commerce of the country to take their course, in bringing in coin, and the country will immediately fill up with the precious metals. Small bank notes will become odious to everybody; they will be suppressed by the power of the people through the action of the Federal and State Legislatures; and labor will receive its appropriate reward in a currency really sound, intrinsically valuable, dependent upon no contingency for its safety, and susceptible of being used with due regard to a beneficial economy.

Mr. B. had listened with great satisfaction to the various declarations which had come from the other side of the House, as to the prosperity of the country previous to the removal of the deposites in October last. A state of unparalleled felicity and prosperity was affirmed to exist in the country. The memorials which were introduced upon the same side of the question, were equally full, copious, and glowing, in describing the happiness of the people, and the prosperity of their affairs, up to that period. According to all their representations, a state of Arcadian felicity seemed to be prevailing up to that time in this country—in this same country, which, according to incessant predictions for nine years, was to be covered with ruin and desolation if General Jackson was elected President. Mr. B. said it was not for so small an object as raising contrasts, or exciting disagreeable recollections, that he referred to these prophecies, so profusely made, for so long a period, and now so publicly contradicted by the whole body of the prophets themselves. A higher and nobler object animated him—an object connected with the safety and the good of the country. He wished, by recalling the recollection of these unfortunate predictions, to inspire distrust, if possible, in those who make them; if not, in those who hear them. Those who have been so greatly mistaken, heretofore, ought to admit the possibility of their being mistaken once more, and should adhere with less confidence to their predictions of ruin, if the Federal bank is allowed to expire; those who have heard these predictions, and believed in them, and acted upon them, should now be careful how they believe and act again upon new prognostications from old sources which have led them into so much error heretofore. They should hesitate before they believe in a prediction of ruin to the country, from the dissolution of this bank, coming from the same prophets who so long prophesied ruin to the country from the election of General Jackson, and who have been employed for three months past in proclaiming the happiness of the country under his Administration. They will doubtless be as much mistaken in time to come, as they have been in time past; and should no longer put faith in predictions which have been so delusive and deceptious.

Mr. B. then moved that the resolution be read, printed, and take the usual reference to the Committee on Finance.

Mr. BIBB said he was not actuated in the course which he should pursue by any question of renewal or otherwise of the charter of the Bank of the United States; and since the gentleman from Missouri [Mr. Benton] had suggested that the proposition to recharter the bank had been permitted to sleep for three weeks to come, until certain important elections should have transpired, he would observe that if it had a tendency to produce political effect on these events, a fair statement of facts should go forth. From 1807 to 1811 the country was laboring under the stricture of an embargo. He was here when the nation was disengaged from that policy, and when a war was the result. In consequence of this, the money market was reduced, and upon the going down of the old bank in the limited state of the circulation, a severe pressure was felt. This the gentleman attributed to a fictitious alarm, which he [Mr. Bibb] knew to be a mistake, for great distress did in fact and verity exist, a distress which was felt by the property holders from one end of the country to the other. And what succeeded? We got rid of the old bank, but in its place we had a litter of State banks substituted, which, like the blood of the Hydra in fabulous history, when it was shed, many Hydras sprang up from it, and which have been increasing to this day. And the great question was, how were we to counteract it. The proposition alluded to, to lay the bill to recharter the bank on the table, was not made with a design to cover this or that election, but because the gentleman from Massachusetts found he could not get on with the bill; he discovered that the majority was against it, and, like a prudent general, he moved to lay it on the table himself. When the war of 1812 closed, the bank was chartered, and the gentleman from Missouri said that it was a political bank. And who made the war but the great body of politicians to whom he [Mr. Bibb] then belonged? On looking at the votes of those who made the bank, he discovered that without the concurrence of a majority of those who professed to be State-rights men, it could not have gone into operation. The bank was made by the Republican party, and by a Republican President; it was not sustained by any paper-money system, and those who sustained it held the stock of the Government. The patronage of the Government went hand in hand with the patronage of the bank. The stock of the bank, as of all other banks, would make its way, and be held by the rich and wealthy men who desire to live on the interest of their money; and the Board of Directors, of course, if chosen from among the stockholders, will be composed of such men.

Mr. B. disclaimed any friendship to the United States Bank, and also to the State institutions. He believed the whole system was vicious in its nature, liable to convulsions, storms, and tempests, putting it in the power of men, by alternate issues and contractions of bank paper, to bring ruin and destruction on the community; and therefore, instead of rechartering the United States Bank as a permanent system, he thought we ought to turn our attention to a much greater evil—the checking of the paper system; not rashly, because honest men were in possession of the paper for value given. Wo to the Government who should knock it down suddenly and without providing an adequate substitute. He had no design to defend the United States Bank, but he thought whenever gentlemen objected to the power of the bank, they ought to remember that if the same amount of capital were divided among sundry State banks, the same influence would be produced by them as was now produced by that bank, and to a greater extent. The effect was as inseparable as the shadow from the substance. And if the indications of the extraordinary increase of banks in all quarters were not soon checked, he thought it would be necessary for Congress to enforce the provision in the Constitution which prevents the States from issuing bills of credit, or a necessary consequence would be general bankruptcy. By being in favor of the restoration of the deposites, he was not in favor of the bank. He proceeded on the imperious obligation imposed on every individual citizen to be honest, to do justice, and to comply with his engagements; and when the Government had made an engagement with the bank, and received value for it to the amount of one million and a half of dollars, besides other important advantages, it now found the bank unconstitutional, and were waging a crusade against it which he did not and could not approve of, and which was in violation of justice and honesty.

Mr. BENTON rose in brief reply to the Senator from Kentucky, [Mr. Bibb.] He said that he hoped he had kept himself both within the bounds of truth and parliamentary practice in what he had said relative to the deferred recharter bill. That bill was certainly brought forward under a great press of urgent necessity—of immediate action—to relieve the distresses of the country. After some debate, it was laid on the table until the first of May, that its discussion might not interfere with a debate of prior origin. That debate, of prior origin, ceased in two days; and then the recharter bill was called up, not for action—that immediate action which the distresses of the country were supposed to require when it was first brought forward—but to be fixed for discussion for the 21st of April, a period of time which would certainly cover important elections in the two great States of Virginia and New York. It was not for him (Mr. B.) to assign motives for this delay; it was sufficient that he should state facts; but he might be permitted to suggest a doubt as to the correctness of the motive assigned for the mover of the bill, by the Senator from Kentucky, [Mr. Bibb.] That Senator supposed it was from a conviction of the impossibility of getting his bill through, that he had delayed it; he (Mr. B.) thought the contrary; for the natural consequence of such a conviction would have been to move the indefinite postponement of his bill; at all events to let it remain at the later period to which it was already fixed, namely, first of May; but he had shortened that period; he had fixed it for an earlier day; and that certainly indicated, not a conviction that he should lose the bill, but a hope that he should carry it.

In the allusion which he had made to the political character of the Bank of the United States, Mr. B. did not refer to the party designations of the day. They were too much qualified by ephemeral and subaltern distinctions, to stand for national denominations. He did not use the term federal or republican; for, in these times, those terms have lost their signification—they no longer indicate the true original grounds of the national parties—those grounds which were worthy to divide a nation—grounds on which patriots stood and patriots divided in 1791—grounds which went to the fundamental principles of the action of the Government, and which drew the great line between those who were for a government of *constructive* powers and *delegated* powers. The political grammar (Mr. B. said) was now strangely confused. Many men have got into wrong places. They wear the name of one party, and act on the principle of the other. Parties, as the Senator from South Carolina who sat farthest to his left [Mr. Preston] had well said—the description was meant for only one party—were now strangely chequered—they were ring-streaked, and speckled. This was their state now; but this bank question, carrying all back to the year 1791—ascending to the true fountain of party distinction—would set all right, and come back to the two plain colors, which would be a true index to every one's political principles. Bank or no bank will be the question for years to come. That question will involve the question of constructive and delegated powers; it would involve the question (Mr. B. believed) of Constitution or no Constitution; for the construction which could let in this bank, with all its various breaches of the Constitution, would make a breach in it wide enough to let in every other unconstitutional measure which the varying times, and the passions, or interests, of parties might seem to require. Mr. B. then read an extract from a speech of a son of Virginia, and a son-in-law of Mr. Jefferson, made at the attempted renewal of the first bank charter, to confirm and establish the political importance, and the political character which he had ascribed to the United States Bank. It was the speech of the late Mr. Eppes, and was a valuable piece of historical truth and political doctrine:

"The charter of the bank was granted in 1791. 'On this great measure, the two great parties 'were, for the first time, arrayed against each

'uther. It was at that time considered a PARTY
'QUESTION, inasmuch .as it involved the very
'PRINCIPLES on which the parties divided,
'to wit: DELEGATED powers and CONSTRUCTIVE
'powers. Unfortunately for his country, General
'WASHINGTON, on this occasion, took side with
'the FEDERALISTS. The creation of a MONEYED IN-
'TEREST, CONNECTED with the GOVERNMENT, was
'a favorite measure of those who were willing
'to ingraft energy on the Constitution, and was
'warmly opposed by the party unwilling to add,
'by CONSTRUCTION, the extraneous right of a
'MONEYED capital, to a Constitution, considered,
'on a fair' construction, sufficiently energetic.
'The defeat of General St. Clair took place in the
'November following the establishment of the
'bank; and the subsequent DISASTERS of the In-
'dian war, by INCREASING the wants of the Gov-
'ernment, drew more closely the ties of connexion
'between the FEDERAL PARTY and the BANK.
'Through all the periods of the Federal Admin-
'istration, this MONEYED POWER was their
'SHIELD and their SWORD."

Mr. SILSBEE moved to have the names to the
memorial printed.

Mr. BENTON observed that the proceedings
which he had introduced were the resolutions of
the meeting. They were duly signed by the President and Secretaries. A letter to himself, from
the same gentleman, stated the number at the
meeting to be estimated at seven thousand, namely, five thousand within the walls of the building,
and two thousand without.

The resolutions were then read, ordered to be
printed, and referred.

Mr. McKEAN presented a memorial from the
Commissioners of the Northern Liberties, praying
that the boundaries of the port of entry of Philadelphia may be extended, so as to comprehend
those Liberties; which was referred to the Committee on Commerce.

Mr. McKEAN offered the following resolution,
which was agreed to:

Resolved, That the Committee on Pensions be
instructed to inquire into the expediency of granting relief to Ann Holland, widow of Thomas
Holland, a revolutionary soldier, deceased.

Mr. WRIGHT gave notice that he should to-
morrow, as soon as he could obtain the floor, move
the Senate take up his motion for leave to introduce the report of the minority of the select
committee, to whom was referred the credentials
of the Hon. Messrs. ROBBINS and POTTER for a
seat upon the floor of the Senate.

Mr. WRIGHT moved that the Senate proceed
to executive business; which, upon a division,
was lost.

The Senate then proceeded to the

SPECIAL ORDERS OF THE DAY.

The bill for the relief of the heirs and legal representatives of Moses Shepherd, deceased, was, on
motion of Mr. CLAYTON, laid upon the table.

The resolution of Mr. POINDEXTER, authorizing the preparation of manuscript maps of the
country in which public lands lie, was taken up
and adopted.

The resolution of Mr. McKEAN relative to a
revolutionary claim, was adopted.

The report and resolution of the Committee on
the Judiciary upon pension agencies, was, on motion of Mr. CLAYTON laid upon the table, and
made the order of the day for Tuesday next.

Mr. WEBSTER'S bill relating to French spoliations prior to 1800, was, on motion of Mr.
WRIGHT, laid on the table.

The bill repealing the act commonly called the
force bill, was, on motion of Mr. CALHOUN,
laid upon the table, with an intimation that he
would call it up hereafter.

The bill for the relief of Elihu Hall Bay and
others, was taken up, when a long and desultory
debate occurred, in which Messrs. POINDEX-
TER, BLACK, CLAYTON, MOORE, PRES-
TON, CALHOUN, PORTER, KANE, LINN,
and KING of Alabama, participated.

Mr. BLACK moved to lay the bill upon the
table. Lost—

Ayes 14, nays 14; the chair (occupied by Mr.
SILSBEE,) deciding in the negative.

The debate was further continued, 'when the
question upon an amendment offered by Mr. KING
of Alabama, to confine the location of the claims
to the State of Louisiana, was taken by yeas and
nays, and lost.

YEAS—Messrs. Black, Forsyth, Hill, King of
Alabama, Moore, Morris, Robinson, Shepley,
White, Wright—10.

NAYS—Messrs. Brown, Calhoun, Clay, Fre-
linghuysen, Hendricks, Kane, King of Georgia,
Knight, Leigh, Linn, Mangum, Poindexter, Por-
ter, Prentiss, Preston, Robbins, Silsbee, Swift,
Smith, Southard, Tipton, Tomlinson, Tallmadge,
Waggaman—24.

Mr. MOORE offered an amendment modifying
the amendment of Mr. KING of Alabama, upon
which the yeas and nays were ordered.

YEAS—Messrs. Black, Forsyth, Hill, King of
Alabama, King of Georgia, Moore, Morris, Shepley, White, Wright—10.

NAYS—Messrs. Brown, Calhoun, Clay, Frelinghuysen, Hendricks, Kane, Kent, Leigh, Linn,
Mangum, Poindexter, Porter, Prentiss, Preston,
Robbins, Silsbee, Smith, Southard, Swift, Tipton, Tomlinson—21.

The question on ordering the bill to a third
reading was then taken, and agreed to.

The bill for the relief of Hiram A. Hunter was
read a third time, and passed.

The bill authorizing the Governors of the several States to transmit, by mail, legislative documents and reports, bound and unbound, was, on
motion of Mr. PORTER, laid upon the table.

On motion of Mr. CLAY,
The Senate adjourned.

HOUSE OF REPRESENTATIVES.
THURSDAY, April 3, 1834.

Mr. WHITTLESEY, of Ohio, reported a bill
granting compensation for losses incurred during
the late war; which was read twice, and made the
special order of the day for the 11th instant.

Mr. CHANEY, from the Committee on Pensions, reported a bill granting a pension to William Wilges. Read twice, and committed.

Mr. E. EVERETT, from the Committee on
Foreign Relations, reported a bill making compensation for certain diplomatic services, and for other
purposes. Read twice, and committed to the Committee of the Whole on the state of the Union.

Mr. H. EVERETT obtained leave to present
a petition; which was referred.

Mr. CLAY, by leave of the House, presented
the memorial of the Tennessee Canal Commissioners, asking further aid for the accomplishment of
that work, and some modifications of the grant;
which was referred to the Committee on Roads
and Canals.

The House resumed the consideration of the
resolution respecting the public deposites, submitted by Mr. MARDIS.

Mr. CHILTON ALLAN resumed his remarks
in opposition to the resolution. The question
which arose in '91 as to the constitutionality of
employing bank agency in the fiscal affairs of the
Government, was no longer a subject of dispute.
In 1791 there were three banks, now there were
four hundred and fifty. The President assumes
that bank agency is necessary. The Secretary of
the Treasury assumes the indispensable necessity
of bank agency. All parties proceed on the assumption that bank agency is necessary. It was
no longer a question whether such agency should
be employed. The question now was, which department of the Government should create and
employ such agencies. Another question was before us, as to the regulation of our funds through
our fiscal agent, in such manner as to give certainty and stability to our revenue. After treating
this point briefly, Mr. A. passed to another portion, that the public funds ought to furnish capital
to the people. Eight millions was the amount of
public funds generally on hand, and that far constituted banking capital. Through the agency of
the Bank of the United States that capital was
equally distributed, as it ought to be. Being paid
by all, it should be used for the benefit of all. The
valley of the Mississippi was entitled to one-fourth
of the sum, and it was essential to its prosperity,

in aiding in the transportation of produce to market. Now, this money was taken away and deposited only in those local banks where the money
was collected. We, in the West, are therefore
utterly deprived of the use of our own money as
banking capital. Mr. A. said he would now look
at the political aspect of this question. He understood the Secretary of the Treasury to maintain
that he was not the officer of Congress or the people, but of the President; that he was bound to
discharge the duties of the office according to the
directions of the President. He had always supposed it to be a vital principle that the people
should have the control of their own money, &c.
After some remarks on this point, Mr. A. concluded, and

Mr. CORWIN obtained the floor.

Mr. WHITE, of Louisiana, moved the suspension of the rules of the House, in order to move
that the House be called for the presentation of
petitions from twelve to one o'clock, beginning the
call at the extreme South.

The question was divided at the request of Mr.
PARKER, and the motion was put and lost.

The House resumed the consideration of the
bill ' to provide for the settlement of certain revolutionary claims."

Mr. MARSHALL continued and concluded his
remarks in support of the bill, and in reply to the
speeches of Messrs PIERCE, of New Hampshire,
VANDERPOEL, and GILMER.

Mr. BAYLIES obtained the floor.

THE DEPOSITES AND UNITED STATES BANK.

The House, at one o'clock, resumed the consideration of the resolutions reported from the
Committee of Ways and Means, together with the
amendment offered by Mr. WILDE, declaring the
reasons given by the Secretary of the Treasury for
removing the deposites to be insufficient and unsatisfactory.

Mr. HARDIN resumed, and expressed his
regret that he had been compelled to detain the
House with his remarks, but he would endeavor
to detain them as little as possible. It was not his
intention to have discussed at large the reasons of
the Secretary for removing the deposites; but he
would now do so. He concluded that the matters
stated in relation to the three per cent. stock had
been brought forward in a spirit rather to inno-
beat and insult Congress, than to illuminate the
revenue of the country. He treated the charge
that the bank had not complied with its charter, by
having its business done by the medium of sub-
agents, or exchange committees, as perfectly ridiculous, to be urged as an argument, when the bank
was empowered by its by-laws to delegate such
functions to these committees. The complaint that
these Government directors were not placed on the
exchange committee, was not deserving of consideration, when it must be recollected that this
appointment was by law vested in the bank. They
could not, or should not, he contended, appoint to
such places of trust those in whom they had not
confidence; and surely no person would stand up
and say, that these directors could be considered
anything but spies, obeying the orders of the
Kitchen cabinet. These directors had undertaken
to do the drudgery required from them; and he
could not therefore see that they had any right to
complain that they were not elevated into high
places from the low offices which he considered
they had voluntarily chosen to fulfil.

Mr. H. animadverted with much severity on the
act of removal, as having produced distress of
unparalleled magnitude, which was at present
raging in the cities amongst the commercial world,
but which would finally extend in a fourfold degree
into the interior of the country. He condemned
the assumption of this power of removal, when
unsustained by any strong grounds, as trenching
upon the high privileges conferred by the Constitution on the House of Representatives, who alone
had the right to place it where they pleased—in
custom houses, or banks, and from which, when
so placed, he argued, that it should not, by any
power placed in another place, ever be attempted ' to
be scooped out." The doctrines of the member
from Georgia [Mr. GILMER] on this point, he considered untenable in principle, and he maintained
that the people, having in the free Government of
England, always claimed the right of withholding

or granting supplies, it had been productive to them of much good, and he would ask the member from Georgia, if he was prepared to abandon it in this country?

He acknowledged that General Jackson had, in the display of talents, done great service to his country hitherto, for which he was deservedly popular; but he contended, that this very popularity, an attendant upon the military success which crowned him with glory, ought rather to make the people view his conduct in a spirit of jealousy, than of blind devotion to his wishes. The history of all countries showed the dangerous consequences arising from intrusting power, too much power, in the hands of those whom success in war generally left despots over the free institutions which they were bound to protect. The statement in defence of the President, that we were respected abroad, had no weight with him in any argument upon a subject connected with the regulation of our internal affairs. In the state of our internal affairs, there was but too much to awaken the jealous spirit which should ever actuate a people who desired to transmit to their posterity the rich inheritance they had received from their ancestors.

He alleged that the great principles upon which General Jackson was brought into office, had been altogether violated. Instead of retrenchment, there was lavish expenditure; offices had been increased instead of being abolished; and, more than all, for the charge alleged against Mr. Adams, that he had put into office improperly members of Congress, the present Chief Magistrate was more obnoxious to it than any other President who had preceded him. The liberty of the press never had been invaded until the present Administration came into power. This was not invaded by attacks upon it, but was undermined by the patronage given to those who directed it. A deadly attack had been made upon that which should have been left as free as the air they breathe—the right of free suffrage—which had been accomplished by proscribing those who voted against, and rewarding those who voted for, the favorites of the Government. Efforts had been made by the official organs of the Government to degrade the legislature itself in the eyes of the people. Cougress were charged by the President with being corrupt—this was read to the Cabinet.

They were told—what was a poor compliment to the House—that there was some danger in leaving the money power of the Government to its proper guardians, the next Congress; and this was given as a reason for instantaneous action. What were the usual steps taken to acquire and concentrate all power into the hands of one, if they were not measures such as these? What measures, he inquired, could better effect this object than the cry raised, "that one man, the President, is the man for the Democracy of New York, of Pennsylvania?" But who are the Democracy? Are they not the freemen, the republicans of the United States? All these things induced him to feel a foreboding of great evil. He, however, rejoiced that the States were at length taking the alarm; and, although he would disclaim all personal reflections upon General Jackson, he considered that all his faults might be attributed more to a too great devotion to his friends, and to their machinations, than to anything else. He considered that they were all members of one great family, and that they should consult the interests of the country rather than the wishes of any man.

In conclusion, Mr. H. would say, that in submitting these remarks, he was solely induced to do so by a sense of what he felt to be his duty, and from a desire to induce the House to reflect upon the present situation of the country. For, as had been heretofore said by a great and good man, if but one mind was brought to reflection upon it he would be satisfied.

Mr. McDUFFIE rose and said that the member from Tennessee [Mr. Polk] was pleased to complain, that on a former occasion, when he addressed them on this subject, he had brought a grave charge against the President, of having perpetrated an act of oppression, by which the President of the United States had trampled into dust the rights of orphans and of others—which charge (he said) was unsustained; and so seeming to regard it, he had declined making any answer to it. If, however, the charge then made was not sustained by sufficient evidence, this would doubtless redound the more to the honor of the person against whom it was preferred. He would, however, endeavor now to supply that evidence—the *desiderata* required. But before he would proceed to do so, he asked their indulgence for a few moments, that he might explain the course which he had pursued. Before he left South Carolina, he thought he could perceive some symptoms of a disposition on the part of the President, to a course of action which, if sanctioned, must ultimately prove subversive of the Constitution. It was from an apprehension of this, that his opening remarks were made; and rather as a skirmishing attack on the outposts of the enemy in his front, in order to compel them to come out from behind their intrenchments, expose their position, and take their line of battle in the open field. In this he had been, he felt, successful. The honorable member from Tennessee did come out boldly and manfully, took his position, and, whatever views he might entertain of his generalship, he was ready to bear testimony that the position which he had assumed was the only one he could assume, without leaving unprotected and undefended the very part which it was his duty to defend. But, having done so, with a tact and skill and zeal worthy of a better cause, he prudently retreated behind his intrenchments, under cover of the previous question, to see, according to signal, what reinforcements were to be expected from the Pennsylvania line. Then, having ascertained this, he again comes from behind his intrenchments, not, however, to assume the old position which he had abandoned, but to form an entirely new line of battle. In this new move, however, he was met with corresponding skill by the member from Georgia, [Mr. Wilde,] whose motion must compel him to assume that original position, unless he would a second time feel that the better part of valor was discretion, and would again return behind his intrenchment, for a similar protection. However, having thus given the condition of the question before the House, and the proceeding of the member from Tennessee, in military figures—for which he asked their pardon—he would proceed to supply those deficiencies which that honorable member was so kind as to point out.

He had, with much attention, listened to the debates; and after surveying the whole field, which appeared to be covered with monumental beacons, conveying at every step lessons of wisdom, he ventured to assert that there was, in no history of any nation, one in which the progress of the usurpation of the Executive upon the other branches of the Government was more rapid, more bold, or more successful, than had been witnessed in the United States for the last fifteen months. The last of the Tarquins had been expelled from the throne of his ancestors, and Charles 1st and Louis 16th were condemned and executed under charges made against them, with only a difference of modification, of having subverted the fundamental laws of their respective countries, and trying to subvert the supreme power, which vested in their Senates. Strange, then, as it may sound to loyal ears, he would assert that the proof of those charges, for which one monarch was banished, and two others executed, was not made more conclusive against them than similar charges were against the President of the United States, who was borne into his elevated office pledged to reform—pledged to recover the lost rights of the States, and pledged to bring back the spirit of their free institutions to their primitive state. God forbid, however, that in these allusions there should be any idea that he had a desire that the President should meet for conduct similar to that on their part a similar fate. No, he thanked his God we lived in an age and a country where its punishments were not conceived in a spirit of vengeance.

Mr. McD. alluded to a subject which (he said) had given him great pain—the publication of letters in the official journal threatening the President of the United States with assassination. It was barely possible that some misguided man might suppose that the President would be influenced by alarm to change his course; but the threat deserved reprobation only inferior to the reprobation due to the design of rendering such threats subservient to the designs of ambition. The infernal machine contributed to the establishment of the empire; and he would remark, if ever it should come to pass that the President was assassinated, he would be the last President constitutionally elected. Let the President of the United States have a fair, and, if possible, an impartial trial. He now stands arraigned before the people of the United States, who now sit in judgment upon him, and from whom he was sure he would not take an appeal, as it was his practice to appeal from other tribunals. It was charged that the President, being moved and seduced by wicked miscreants and evil counsellors, without proper regard for the Constitution and the laws, has assumed power belonging to another branch of the Government, had contemned the authority of the legislature, and had pursued a course having the certain and fatal tendency to subvert liberty, and exhibit, for the first time, to the world, the political paradox of a constitutional despotism.

Mr. McD. said he would exhibit evidence of the fact that the President had designed to assume a position which would tend to the complete subversion of the principles of the Constitution. In the first place, he would say, that it had never happened that the people had occasion to examine and limit the extent of executive power. In all ages the best precedents had been established in the worst reigns. Magna Charta was obtained in the reign of the basest and meanest of the Kings of England. He hoped that executive power in this country would find its limits during the presidency of the most self-willed, obstinate and encroaching of all our Presidents. The position to which he alluded as having been assumed by the President he would proceed to establish. In the official journal, soon after the removal of the deposites, appeared an article, which he read, expressing the opinion that the power over the deposites was not legislative nor judicial, but executive; and being executive in its character, Congress could not vest it in any branch but the executive. To show that this opinion was not accidental, he went on to say, that it had received the support of the chairman of the Committee of Ways and Means, and he read several extracts from his speech which (he said) supported this official exposition of the extent of executive power. But, that there might be no doubt on the subject, he would advert to the opinion expressed in the speech of the gentleman from New York, [Mr. Beardsley,] extracts from which he read. With a felicitous confusion of ideas, the gentleman went on, combining two questions as different from each other as light from darkness, and stated that Congress could neither delegate its power nor exercise it by agency. In the Senate the same doctrines were maintained by a Senator from Virginia, [Mr. Rives.] Such was the evidence, the proof which he adduced to them that the President had asserted political doctrines which blotted out from the Constitution all the powers in it except the executive power. The clause in the Constitution which was relied upon to maintain this odious and revolting heresy, so far from vesting all power in the President, in fact vested in him no power at all. In the President shall be vested executive power. What power? All power? This simple clause, intended as a sort of title page, had been construed to confer greater and more extensive executive powers than were ever exercised by any monarch under the sun, for there had been no monarch whose power had not limit. The gentleman from New York had given us reason to hope that if we were tricked out of our liberties, it would be according to the most approved and practised modes. The interest of the people was to be the President's excuse for every measure. The syllogism presented was this: take any power, and say it is not legislative nor judicial, and therefore it must be executive. The executive is made the residuary legatee of all other power. No tribunal is to be consulted in reference to the legality of the testament. The executive is judge of the extent of its own powers, and consequently of the extent of the powers of all the other branches of the Government. Every State constitution has the same words, from which it is attempted to invest the President with absolute power. In Virginia there is but a shadow of executive power; but the constitution provides that the executive power shall be vested in a Governor. In South Carolina the Governor has not the power to make or unmake

THE CONGRESSIONAL GLOBE.

PRINTED AND PUBLISHED AT THE CITY OF WASHINGTON, BY BLAIR & RIVES.

23d Congress, 1st Session.   SATURDAY, APRIL 12, 1834.   Vol. I........No. 19.

single officer; but the constitution of the State says, that is the Governor shall be vested the executive power; and, moreover, it says that the Governor "shall see that the laws are faithfully executed;" the other caballistic words from which the newly-claimed powers are to be derived. But where, he asked, did the gentleman learn that Congress could not create an agency for the execution of its powers? Were we schoolboys, on the first form, that we should entertain such notions? In what catastrophe would this doctrine end? He asked the House to look at its foundation. It revived the feudal doctrine. All the executive power, exercised by the infinite number of officers appointed to carry on the Government, was vested in the President, proceeded from, and returned to him. Everything odious in history, or personified in fable, was here exhibited to us—a hydra with a thousand heads, a Briareus with a hundred hands, was this executive power.

Mr. McD. went on to comment upon particular passages in the speech of the gentleman from New York. The gentleman lamented, what was truly unfortunate, that the President, in addition to constitutional omnipotence, should be possessed of ubiquity, that he could exercise all executive power himself. There was something alarming in the idolatry of these doctrines, and in the tone and manner of their propagation. He repeated that these were attributes which never belonged to any monarchical government, constitutional or unconstitutional. There was nothing like it even in the mythology of the Greeks and Romans; for there Neptune ruled the sea, and Pluto the realms below; to Mars was assigned the province of war; to Venus of love, and to Minerva of wisdom. But Jupiter, armed in the panoply of all the gods, claims from all obedience to his will. He

"Shakes his ambrosial curls, and gives the nod,
The stamp of fate, the sanction of a god."

Here Mr. McD. yielded the floor to Mr. ARCHER, who moved an adjournment.

Mr. LANE demanded the yeas and nays on the motion; and they were ordered.

The question being taken on the motion, it was determined in the affirmative, by a vote of 117 to 93.

The House then adjourned.

IN SENATE.

Friday, April 4, 1834.

A message from the President of the United States, upon executive business, was received by Mr. Donelson, his Private Secretary.

The VICE PRESIDENT presented a memorial from certain persons of Louisiana; which was referred, on motion of Mr. HENDRICKS, to the Committee on Private Land Claims.

The VICE PRESIDENT presented a communication from the Postmaster General, transmitting a list of the clerks employed in that department; which, on motion of Mr. GRUNDY, was referred to the Committee on the Post Office and Post Roads.

Mr. McKEAN said, he had been requested to lay before the Senate the proceedings of a public meeting, said to be the most numerous ever held in the county of Centre, in the State of Pennsylvania, composed of the friends of the national and State Administrations, to take into consideration the present situation of our public affairs. He said he had been requested to state, and he did so with pleasure, as a matter of his own knowledge, that the prominent actors at the meeting, are those whom we denominate decided and consistent democrats, and friends of the present Chief Magistrate of the Union. The venerable Andrew Gregg, who reported the resolutions, was once a member of this body, and must be known personally, or by character to many, if not all the members of the Senate. Mr. G. was also a member of the first Congress that assembled under the Constitution, and with little intermission had been in active public life ever since. Mr. McK. knew he had been

19

throughout a decided friend and supporter of the present national executive. This meeting, among other things, resolved, that they have continued confidence in the integrity and patriotism of our present venerable President, and that they see no reason to doubt the purity of his purpose, and honesty of intention, which guided him in his recent course against the United States Bank; but as Congress alone possesses the power under the Constitution to raise revenue, and direct its appropriation, so, in accordance with the same principle, the place of deposite and safe-keeping of the public money should be provided for by law; and they request their Senators and Representatives in Congress to use their best exertions to procure an early and satisfactory adjustment of the questions affecting the currency of the country.

The proceedings were read, referred to the Committee on Finance, and ordered to be printed.

Mr. McKEAN again rose, and said he had been charged with presenting the proceedings of another meeting of the citizens of the same county, on the same subject, and held at the same place; and it afforded him pleasure to bear testimony to the respectability of those concerned, so far as he had the honor of their acquaintance. However, respectable as they were, they could not, he believed, be counted among the friends of the present Administration. He stated this merely to show the distinct character of the two meetings, not because it ought or would have any weight with the Senate, and, indeed, under other circumstances, ought not to be mentioned here at all.

These proceedings, however, in moderate and dignified language, disapprove the conduct of the President in relation to the United States Bank and the public deposites, to which cause they attribute the present distresses of the country, and recommend, for a limited time, the extension of the charter of the present bank, and that the public revenues to be collected hereafter shall be deposited in it and its branches.

The proceedings were read, referred to the Committee on Finance, and ordered to be printed.

Mr. WRIGHT moved to take up for consideration the report of the committee upon the contested election of the Senator from Rhode Island; which was agreed to.

Mr. W. then said, that when he offered the paper on the table, he was called on to know whether it was responsive in its character to the report of the majority, and he been answered frankly that it was; that it contained the substantive views of the minority of the committee, as also a response to the views of the majority. A suggestion was then made as to the propriety of such a course. He did not now contend for the propriety of a minority making their report, but he supposed, that in preparing the paper he was acting under the express assent of the Senate to make a report; and the only question now was, whether he had forfeited that right by the manner of his making it. He had reflected on the subject, and he was unable so to alter the document substantially as to change its character. He could alter it so as to avoid saying that it was a response; but still it must continue to be so in substance; and it would not have been a respectful course to have affected that the report of the majority was not before the Senate, and, therefore, he had endeavored to submit a fair argument on the questions submitted to the committee.

Mr. CLAY thought the question could be determined without any influence in reference to the main question, by the gentleman from New York [Mr. Wright] deriving the paper into the form of a speech, and presenting it to the public. He thought this was the first case of a minority report being made in the Senate; which he thought wrong in principle. It was best to adhere to the settled practice of receiving the report from the majority only.

After some further desultory remarks between Messrs. KANE, KING of Alabama, CLAYTON, POINDEXTER, CLAY, BENTON, and

SPRAGUE, the paper was received, laid on the table, and ordered to be printed.

The Senate then proceeded to the consideration of the

ORDERS OF THE DAY

The bill authorizing the Governors of the several States to transmit by mail, free of postage, legislative documents, was taken up, read a third time, and passed. The question was taken by yeas and nays, as follows:

YEAS—Messrs. Benton, Bibb, Clayton, Frelinghuysen, Grundy, Hendricks, Hill, Kane, Kent, Knight, Linn, McKean, Morris, Poindexter, Porter, Prentiss, Robbins, Robinson, Shepley, Silsbee, Southard, Sprague, Swift, Tallmadge, Tipton, White, Wilkins—27.

NAY—Mr. King of Georgia—1.

Mr. BIBB moved a postponement of the orders of the day; which was agreed to.

Mr. BIBB, from the Committee on the Judiciary, reported a bill for the relief of Pierre Menard.

Also, from the same committee, a bill for the relief of Joseph Bogy, of Missouri.

Mr. SOUTHARD, from the Committee on Naval Affairs, reported a bill from the House of Representatives, without amendment, for the relief of Henry Whitney.

Mr. SOUTHARD, from the same committee, asked to be discharged from the further consideration of the petition of Henry Lavely; which was agreed to.

Mr. SOUTHARD presented the petition of Thomas Tenant and others, of Baltimore, on certain claims arising from the Danish treaty; which was referred to the Committee on the Judiciary.

On motion of Mr. SPRAGUE, the Senate took up the bill for the relief of Thomas Fillebrown, Jr.

After a considerable debate, in which Messrs. SPRAGUE, SHEPLEY, SOUTHARD, PORTER, BIBB, and BENTON participated, the latter moved to lay the bill upon the table; which was lost. The bill was then ordered to be engrossed and read a third time.

Mr. POINDEXTER moved to take up the bill from the House of Representatives, reported by the Committee on Public Lands, for the relief of Garrigues Flaujac; which was ordered to be engrossed and read a third time.

Mr. GRUNDY, from the Committee on the Post Office and Post Roads, reported a bill from the House of Representatives, without amendment, for the relief of George Bowen.

On motion of Mr. WAGGAMAN, it was ordered that when the Senate adjourned, it would adjourn to meet on Monday.

Mr. TALLMADGE presented the petition of Thomas Blanchard; which was referred to the Committee on the Judiciary.

Also, the petition of Archibald W. Hamilton; which was referred to the Committee on Military Affairs.

Mr. HENDRICKS, from the Committee on Roads and Canals, to whom was recommitted the bill for the repair and extension of the Cumberland road through the States of Ohio, Indiana, and Illinois, reported the same with an amendment.

On motion of Mr. SILSBEE, the bill reported by the Committee on Commerce, from the House of Representatives, authorizing the issue of a register for the brig American, was taken up, considered, and ordered to be engrossed for a third reading.

Mr. WRIGHT, from the Committee on Claims, reported a bill for the relief of Robert Sewall and others.

On motion of Mr. POINDEXTER, the bill authorizing corrections to be made in locations of land granted to the State of Indiana, for the purpose of enabling that State to construct the Michigan road, was taken up, and ordered to be engrossed for a third reading.

The following resolutions were submitted:

By Mr. LINN:

Resolved, That the Committee on Claims be instructed to inquire into the expediency of making a grant of land to Jean Baptiste Janis, appointed ensign of militia in 1778, by Col. George Rogers Clark, under authority derived from his Excellency Patrick Henry, Governor of Virginia, who served in the campaign at the siege and capture of Vincennes, and into the expediency of granting him a pension.

By Mr. CLAYTON:

Resolved, That the following be added to, and form a part of the rules of the Senate:

"As soon as the Journal is read, the President 'shall call for petitions from the members of each 'State, beginning with Maine, and if on any day, 'the whole of the States shall not be called, the 'President shall begin on the next day where he 'left off the previous day."

Mr. TOMLINSON, from the Committee on Pensions, reported a bill from the House of Representatives, without amendment, granting pensions to certain persons therein named.

Also, a bill from the House, without amendment, for the relief of Robert Reynolds.

Mr. NAUDAIN, from the Committee of Claims, asked to be discharged from the further consideration of the petition of the widow of James Leomaster; which was agreed to.

On motion of Mr. POINDEXTER,

The bill reported by the Committee on Public Lands, for the relief of Hishe Homa, otherwise called Captain Red Pepper, a Choctaw Indian, was taken up, considered, and ordered to be engrossed for a third reading.

Mr. WILKINS asked leave to withdraw the papers of Jonathan Kearsley. Granted.

Mr. TIPTON, from the Committee of Claims, reported a bill for the relief of James Ord.

Mr. TIPTON presented the petition of James Wallman; which was referred to the Committee on the Judiciary.

Mr. BIBB asked leave to withdraw from the files of the Senate of 1st session of the 23d Congress, the essay upon currency, by Thomas Law, Esq., of Washington city. Granted.

Mr. SOUTHARD moved to take up the bill rom the House of Representatives, for the relief of John A. Webster; which was agreed to, and the bill ordered to be engrossed for a third reading.

On motion of Mr. TIPTON, the bill from the House of Representatives for the relief of William S. Anderson, was taken up, considered, and ordered to be engrossed and read a third time.

Mr. WAGGAMAN stated, that he had several important documents relative to the claims of Spanish grantees in Louisiana, which had been obtained from the archives of the French Government, which he moved to refer to the Committee on Foreign Affairs, who had that subject under consideration.

After some conversation, the motion to refer was agreed to.

Mr. KENT presented the petition of James F. Southeron; which was referred to the Committee on Claims.

Also, a memorial from the corporate authorities of the city of Baltimore, stating that that city, owing to its commercial intercourse with foreign countries, was liable to afflictions from pestilence, and praying Congress to aid them in the establishment of an hospital for the reception of foreign patients. The memorial was referred to the Committee on Commerce.

On motion of Mr. SWIFT,

The Senate adjourned.

HOUSE OF REPRESENTATIVES.

FRIDAY, *April* 4, 1834.

Mr. WHITTLESEY, of Ohio, from the Committee of Claims, made unfavorable reports on the petitions of Gates Hoit, Vincent Taylor, Ahaz Hayes, and James D. Harding; which reports were severally ordered to lie on the table.

Mr. CHILTON reported a bill for the benefit of Samuel M. Asbury;

Mr. CARR, a bill for the relief of John M. Carroll, junior; and

Mr. CONNOR, from the select committee appointed for the purpose of making inquiry into the propriety of establishing assay offices in the gold regions in the southern States, made a report, accompanied by a bill to establish assay offices of the United States Mint in the gold districts of North Carolina, South Carolina, Georgia, and Virginia;

All which bills were severally read twice and committed.

The SPEAKER communicated a message, received from the President of the United States, with a communication from the Governor of New York, and the Governor of New Jersey, addressed to him with a view of obtaining the consent of Congress to an agreement which had been entered into by those States, to settle the boundary line between them.

On motion of Mr. MANN, the message, with the accompanying documents, were referred to the Committee on the Judiciary.

The SPEAKER laid before the House a letter from the Secretary of the Treasury, with a statement, prepared in obedience to the order of the House, of the duties received in 1833, the payment of which would have been deferred till 1834, had not the system of cash duties been adopted.

Also, a letter from the Postmaster General, transmitting a list of persons employed as clerks in the Post Office Department in 1833, with their salaries. Which were laid on the table.

The House took up the resolution submitted by Mr. MARDIS, in relation to the deposites.

Mr. CORWIN, of Ohio, having the floor, after professing that he felt much embarrassment in addressing the House on a subject which had been already discussed so ably, spoke until the expiration of the morning hour, in opposition to the views given by the Secretary of the Treasury in justification of the removal; contending that Congress had never intended to confer the exclusive power over the public funds in the President, as they had assigned, in one section of the act incorporating the bank, particular duties to him, whilst they had, in another section, assigned certain duties to the Secretary, which went to show, that the Secretary was to exercise them without any of the supervisory control, which it was claimed on the other side, that the President had, over all the acts of his subordinates; and he gave way, without concluding his remarks, to

Mr. MARSHALL, who moved that the House should proceed to the orders of the day, being the bill to provide for the settlement of certain revolutionary claims.

Mr. BAYLIES spoke till the expiration of the hour, generally in support of the bill.

Mr. CRAMER, of New York, followed, and replied to the arguments adduced in opposition to the bill.

THE DEPOSITES AND UNITED STATES BANK.

The House, at one o'clock, resumed the consideration of the resolutions reported from the Committee of Ways and Means, together with the amendment submitted by Mr. WILDE.

Mr. McDUFFIE resumed his remarks in opposition to the resolutions. The gentleman from New York, by his Executive syllogism, had discovered a power more efficient than any ever dreamed of by Archeinedes. The gentleman had found a place for a fulcrum, and by the application of his newly-discovered lever power, was able to tottle the fabric of this Government into ruins. The gentleman had argued that, though legislative power could not be exercised by agency, yet the executive power could be. If he had taxed his ingenuity to frame an absurd proposition, he could not have better succeeded. Where did the gentleman learn that the President, our dread sovereign, could appoint an agent for the exercise of his power, without authority of law? The President of the United States was clothed with two kinds of power, wholly separate from each other. Every power which the President could exercise was by the law and under the law. The executive power cannot create an agency! Why, sir, cannot we, before to-morrow's sun, strike from existence this whole machinery of Government—executive departments, army, navy, judiciary, and all—and the next moment rear up another fabric of equal magnificence? And yet (says the gentleman from New York) Congress cannot create an executive agency. But let all these agents be ministers to the executive will, and where is the legislative power? You might as well talk to me of the power of a sleeping man, as of a legislative power without practical means for its exercise. How was the President to execute the laws of the Union? By inherent power? By such agents as he chose to appoint? No; in such manner and by such means as the law directs. The President was nothing more than the grand marshal to execute the decrees of legislation.

He passed to the power of appointment. He could not (he said) conceive how the power of dismissal from office came to be considered as an inherent constitutional power in the President, independent of legislation. Nor was the question an immaterial one, whether this right of dismissal was derived from the Constitution or from law, as he should show. Was it not a legislative power, to create an office, to prescribe its duties, to fix upon the degree of malversation which should be cause for dismissal? Sir, I will tell you my opinion. Congress has a right to say for what causes officers of the Government should be dismissed, except the judges, whose tenure was settled by the Constitution. He believed, too, that it was time to interpose this legislative power, and let the officers of the Government know that they hold their places by a tenure less frail than that of the will of a single individual. He had a deep and solemn conviction, that unless Congress interposed on this subject, the day was not far distant when the Government would sink into absolute corruption and monarchy. Has it occurred to you, Mr. Speaker, (said Mr. McD.,) that upon the change of ministry and measures in England, the whole system of administration remains still in the hands of the same officers? Here, on the other hand, the doctrine is maintained and practised upon, that each President may turn out his opponents and put in his friends. It was boldly claimed for the President that he should have this power in order to secure his responsibility to the people for his measures. It was strange, he thought, to secure responsibility by putting at the disposal of a President a standing army of civil officers, scattered abroad through the Union; they were of more efficiency than ten times the number of soldiers. Look at the Blue Book, now rising in envious rivalry to the Red Book of England, and say what can resist such a powerful array of Executive influence. When Cromwell usurped power, he used to say he sought it not—he received it by the grace of God, through the army, &c., the usual channel through which, in these latter days, the mercies of God are dispensed to his faithful worshippers. What have we seen in Ohio? A convention to nominate a candidate for the Presidency, two-thirds of it consisting of office-holders. Look at Pennsylvania. Twelve months ago, the Legislature of Pennsylvania voted unanimously that the bank ought to be rechartered; now they reverse the opinion, and for what reason? For no other reason than that which the grenadier gave for dispersing the Council of Five Hundred: "The General has ordered it." God forbid that the people should confirm the order. He warned the gentleman from Tennessee that if this doctrine of executive omnipotence was established, in connexion with the aid of those who worship at the shrine of a saint whose name was unknown to the Christian calendar, the President would be armed with an incantation more potent to call spirits from the vasty deep to do his bidding. The President, in his old age, when his vigor had survived his intellect, delirious with the adulation of sycophants, invokes the vengeance of Heaven upon those who support an institution which he wishes to destroy, &c.

He then adverted to what he said was an i
nious contrivance to encroach upon the limi
constitutional power—it was to represent the
ple in the President. If this doctrine was
lished, there never would be a President who w
not be able to claim all power, as the represent
of the people. Every President could as we
sume that the people had approved his meas
and adopted all his principles, by electing
Suppose the doctrine to be true, it would p
nothing in this case; for the people of the U
States never had any reason to suppose that
eral Jackson was opposed to a national bank.
his messages, he expressed his hostility to
bank; but always introduced a saving clause

favor of some bank, differently framed. He had seen with surprise in the newspapers, the doctrine that the members of this House are elected to represent the President—to obey his will! The doctrine was acted upon in this Hall. Who, sir, are we, and what are we? If we have lost the substance, let us down with its forms. Why sit we here prating about the laws, and the public funds? Let us, in obedience to a New York organ, pass the appropriation, and go home. Let us grease the wheels of the idol, and go home and tell our wretched and distressed constituents to prostrate themselves before it, and be crushed to atoms.

It had been intimated that the President would order us to go home, and that we should shortly receive the royal mandate. If the President intends to prorogue his Parliament, he hoped he would do it with historic forms. Cromwell, after calling together a parliament which at first supported him, though the majority afterwards turned against him, determined to prorogue them. He called them to his presence in the painted Chamber; (we, he supposed, would be convened in the east room.) He told them that they had been in session five months and had passed no bill; (our time was not quite out yet.) They had done nothing, except to encourage the levellers to intrigue with the cavaliers; (the nullifiers with the national republicans.) By their dispersion they had aided to throw the nation into confusion. By their slowness of proceeding, the soldiers had been compelled to take free quarters. (It had not come to that here yet, though we had not yet got the army appropriation bill through.) You suppose, continued Cromwell, that I cannot raise money, except through you. But he reminded them that he was inured to difficulties, and that God, on whom he relied, had helped him through all. The people would be compelled, by necessity, to furnish him with supplies. The very same language, (Mr. McD. said,) had been officially used here in reference to Congress. Cromwell concluded his harangue by declaring that the good of the nation did not require the continuance of the session, and he, therefore, did then and there dissolve the Parliament. For one, (said Mr. McD.,) I am not disposed to take the hint. I will not, with my own consent, adjourn without doing something to relieve the people. We had now a practical illustration of the small degree of capacity necessary to enable a man to do an infinite deal of mischief. He would not trust those to redeem the country who had involved it in the present calamities. On all sides we heard the cry, uttered on this floor by the gentleman from New York, perish commerce, perish credit, perish banks, rather than force the President to retrace his steps.

[When Mr. McDuffie finished this part of his speech, Mr. Beardsley interrupted him to make an explanation in reference to his allusion to some words which he attributed to him (Mr. B.) If the gentleman from South Carolina had quoted the sentence correctly he would not have thought it necessary to interrupt him. But, as he had misquoted, undesignedly, no doubt, in justice to the gentleman and to himself, he would set him right. The gentleman represented him as having said that he would see commerce perish, &c., rather than that the President should be compelled to retrace his steps. What he did say was, that he would see all these calamities fall upon the country rather than see it prostrated beneath the power of the bank. He would see commerce, &c., perish, rather than the country should be compelled to submit to the dictation of that corporation, or any other. This was his position, and it was precisely the converse of that which the gentleman from South Carolina maintained.]

Mr. McD. continued. He did not profess to give the gentleman's words, but his interpretation of them. The explanation did not vary their meaning. He would suffer these evils because their removal involved submission to the power of the bank. It all came to the same thing.

Mr. McD. then proceeded at considerable length to speak of the present distress, and the remedies by which the country could be relieved from it. Mr. McD. having concluded—

Mr. MASON rose and said—

It will be remembered, sir, in the commencement of the brilliant and powerful effort, which has just received such fixed and merited attention, the honorable gentleman from South Carolina alluded, with somewhat of reproach, to the only parliamentary measure by which a legislative assembly can restrain discussion or compel a decision of a debated question, however essential to the public interests. He called it, sir, a "signal of retreat."

I am not a military man, as is that gentleman: but if I may be permitted to use his martial figure, I would call it the stern order of "charge bayonet," to which the most skilful general has sometimes to resort, to terminate a protracted conflict and bring a manœuvring adversary to decisive action. I feel assured that there can be no just ground of complaint, if, in the very presence of the blaze of his eloquence; if, having received the unanswered fire of that tremendous park of artillery which that gentleman supplies and commands, those who approve the resolutions of the committee are willing to abide this decisive charge.

It cannot be necessary, sir, that I should remind the House, how long the subject of this debate has been under consideration; how injuriously the uncertainty of its result affects the business of the whole community; how necessary it is, as far as may be, by our decision, to allay the agitation and excitement which distract the country. In my poor judgment, the time has come when our duty requires a definitive disposition of this great and absorbing question. Impelled by a sense of duty, I demand the previous question.

Mr. BRIGGS, and Mr. HALL of North Carolina, were appointed tellers, and the House seconded the call—

Ayes 114, nays 105.

Mr. SELDEN rose to a question of order. By the 36th rule of the House, no member should vote upon a question in which he was interested.

The SPEAKER decided that such a question could not then be raised; the House having seconded the call for the previous question.

Mr. SELDEN said he understood there were many members who, being stockholders in the State banks selected by the Secretary for the depository of the public money, were interested in the present question, and came within the rule.

The SPEAKER said, when any member who was interested was about to vote, then was the time to raise such an objection.

Mr. VANCE moved an adjournment.

Mr. POLK called for the yeas and nays on his motion; which were ordered.

The motion was decided in the negative—yeas 103, nays 119.

Mr. DICKSON, of New York, moved a call of the House, and called for the yeas and nays; which were ordered, and a motion for a call was rejected:

Yeas 100, nays 120.

Mr. CHILTON said, if it was in order, he would move that the first resolution, viz: "That the Bank of the United States ought not to be rechartered," should be laid on the table.

The SPEAKER decided, that inasmuch as a motion to lay on the table was of the second class of privileged questions, whilst a call for the previous question was in the third class, the motion of Mr. C. having precedence, was in order.

Mr. CHILTON then asked for the yeas and nays on his motion to lay the first resolution on the table, which were ordered; and the question thereon having been put, was decided in the negative:

Yeas 82, nays 136.

YEAS—Messrs. John Quincy Adams, Heman Allen, J. J. Allen, Chilton Allan, Ashley, Banks, Barber, Barringer, Baylies, Beatty, James M. Bell, Binney, Briggs, Bull, Burges, Cage, Chambers, Chilton, Choate, William Clark, Corwin, Coulter, Crane, Crockett, Darlington, A. Davis, Deberry, Deming, Denny, Dennis, Dickson, Duncan, Ellsworth, Evans, Edward Everett, Horace Everett, Fillmore, Foot, Philo C. Fuller, Graham, Grennell, Hiland Hall, Hard, Hardin, James Harper, Hazeltine, Heath, Jabez W. Huntington, Jackson, King, Lay, Lincoln, Martindale, Marshall, McCarty, McComas, McKennan, Mercer, Milligan, Moore, Pinckney, Potts, Ramsay, Reed, Selden, William B. Shepard, A. H. Shepperd, W. Slade, Sloane, Stewart, Philemon Thomas, Tompkins, Tweedy, Vance, Vinton, Watmough, Edward D. White, Frederick Whittlesey, Elisha Whittlesey, Williams, Wilson, and Young—82.

NAYS—Messrs. John Adams, William Allen, Anthony, Archer, Beale, Bean, Beardsley, Beaumont, John Bell, Blair, Bockee, Boon, Bouldin, Brown, Bunch, Burd, Bynum, Cambreleng, Campbell, Carmichael, Carr, Casey, Chaney, Chinn, Claiborne, Samuel Clark, Clay, Clayton, Clowney, Coffee, Connor, Cramer, W. R. Davis, Davenport, Day, Dickerson, Dickinson, Dunlap, Felder, Forester, Foster, William K. Fuller, Fulton, Galbraith, Gholson, Gillet, Gilmer, Gordon, Grayson, Griffin, Joseph Hall, Thomas H. Hall, Halsey, Hamer, Hannegan, Joseph M. Harper, Harrison, Hathaway, Hawkins, Hawes, Henderson, Howard, Hubbard, Abel Huntington, Inge, Jarvis, William Cost Johnson, Richard M. Johnson, Noadiah Johnson, Cave Johnson, Seaborn Jones, Benjamin Jones, Kavanagh, Kinnard, Lane, Lansing, Laporte, Lawrence, Luke Lea, Thomas Lee, Leavitt, Loyall, Lucas, Lyon, Lytle, Abijah Mann, Joel K. Mann, Mardis, John Y. Mason, Moses Mason, McIntire, McKay, McKinley, McLene, McVean, Miller, H. Mitchell, Robert Mitchell, Muhlenberg, Murphy, Osgood, Page, Parks, Parker, Patterson, D. J. Pearce, Peyton, Franklin Pierce, Pierson, Plummer, Polk, Pope, Rencher, Schenck, Schley, Charles Slade, Smith, Spangler, Speight, Standifer, Stoddert, Wm. Taylor, Wm. P. Taylor, F. Thomas, Thomson, Turner, Turrill, Vanderpoel, Wagener, Ward, Wardwell, Wayne, Webster, Whallon, and Wilde—136.

So the House refused to lay this resolution on the table.

Mr. WILDE appealed to the courtesy of the House, as it was obvious there could be no further debate, to permit a vote to be taken, that his friends might have an opportunity of recording their sentiments on the amendment submitted by him, "that the reasons of the Secretary of the Treasury for removing the deposites were insufficient."

The SPEAKER said this was not in order, except by unanimous consent of the House.

Mr. POLK objected.

Mr. BURD then moved to lay the other resolutions (being the 2d, 3d, and 4th) of the committee on the table.

Mr. BARRINGER called for a division on this question. Ordered.

Mr. DAVENPORT demanded the yeas and nays; which were ordered.

The question on the 2d and 3d resolutions, viz:

2. *Resolved*, That the public deposites ought not to be restored to the Bank of the United States.

3. *Resolved*, That the State banks ought to be continued as the places of deposite of the public money, and that it is expedient for Congress to make further provision by law, prescribing the mode of selection, the securities to be taken, and the manner and terms on which they are to be employed.

Was then put and decided in the negative—yeas 95, nays 125.

YEAS—Messrs. J. Q. Adams, Heman Allen, John J. Allen, Chilton Allan, Archer, Ashley, Banks, Barber, Barnitz, Barringer, Baylies, Beatty, James M. Bell, Binney, Briggs, Bull, Burd, Burges, Cage, Campbell, Chambers, Chilton, Choate, Claiborne, William Clark, Clayton, Clowney, Corwin, Coulter, Crane, Crockett, Darlington, A. Davis, Davenport, Deberry, Deming, Denny, Dennis, Dickson, Duncan, Ellsworth, Evans, E. Everett, H. Everett, Ewing, Felder, Foot, Foster, Fulton, Gholson, Gordon, Grayson, Grennell, Griffin, H. Hall, Hard, Hardin, J. Harper, Hazeltine, Heath, J. W. Huntington, William Cost Johnson, H. King, Lincoln, Martindale, Marshall, McComas, McKay, McKennan, Mercer, Milligan, Moore, Pinckney, Potts, Reed, Rencher, Selden, A. H. Shepperd, W. Slade, Sloane, Stewart, William B. Taylor, Philemon Thomas, Tompkins, Tweedy, Vance, Vinton, Watmough, Edward D. White, F. Whittlesey, Elisha Whittlesey, Wilde, Williams, Wilson, Young—95.

NAYS—Messrs. John Adams, William Allen, Anthony, Beale, Bean, Beardsley, Beaumont, J. Bell, Blair, Bockee, Bouldin, Brown, Bunch, Bynum, Cambreleng, Carmichael, Carr, Casey, Chaney, Chinn, Samuel Clark, Clay, Coffee, Connor, Cramer, Warren R. Davis, Day, Dickerson, Dick-

inson, Dunlap, Fillmore, Forester, Philo C. Fuller, William K. Fuller, Galbraith, Gillet, Gilmer, Graham, Joseph Hall, Thomas H. Hall, Halsey, Hamer, Hannegan, Joseph M. Harper, Harrison, Hathaway, Hawkins, Hawes, Henderson, Howell, Hubbard, Abel Huntington, Inge, Jackson, Jarvis, Richard M. Johnson, Noadiah Johnson, Cave Johnson, Seaborn Jones, Benjamin Jones, Kavanagh, Kinnard, Lane, Lansing, Laporte, Lawrence, Lay, L. Lea, T. Lee, Leavitt, Loyall, Lucas, Lyon, Lytle, Abijah Mann, Joel K. Mann, Mardis, John Y. Mason, Moses Mason, McCarty, McIntire, McKinley, McLene, McVean, Miller, Henry Mitchell, Robert Mitchell, Muhlenberg, Murphy, Osgood, Page, Parks, Parker, Patterson, Dutee J. Pearce, Peyton, Franklin Pierce, Pierson, Plummer, Polk, Pope, Ramsay, Schenck, Schley. W. B. Shepard, Shinn, Charles Slade, Smith, Speight, Standifer, Stoddert, Sutherland, William Taylor, Francis Thomas, Thompson, Turner, Turrill, Vanderpoel, Wagener, Ward, Wardwell, Wayne, Webster, Whallon—125.

So the House refused to lay these resolutions on the table.

Mr. WILDE renewed his appeal to have a vote taken on his amendment.

Mr. ARCHER suggested that the member from Georgia could have an opportunity hereafter of submitting his amendment as a distinct proposition.

The question then being—Shall the main question now be put? (which cuts off the amendments,) the House decided in the affirmative. Yeas 114, nays 106.

YEAS—Messrs. John Adams, William Allen, Anthony, Beale, Bean, Beardsley, Beaumont, John Bell, John Blair, Bockee, Boon, Bouldin, Brown, Bunch, Bynum, Cambreleng, Carmichael, Carr, Casey, Chaney, Chinn, S. Clark, Clay, Coffee, Connor, Cramer, Day, Dickerson, Dickinson, Dunlap, Forester, W. K. Fuller, Galbraith, Gillet, Joseph Hall, T. H. Hall, Halsey, Hamer, Hannegan, Joseph M. Harper, Harrison, Hathaway, Hawkins, Hawes, Henderson, Howell, Hubbard, Abel Huntington, Inge, Jarvis, Richard M. Johnson, Noadiah Johnson, Cave Johnson, Seaborn Jones, Benj. Jones, Kavanagh, Kinnard, Lane, Lansing, Laporte, Lawrence, Luke Lea, Thos. Lee, Leavitt, Loyall, Lucas, Lyon, Lytle, Abijah Mann, Joel K. Mann, Mardis, John Y. Mason, Moses Mason, McIntire, McKay, McKinley, McLene, McVean, Miller, Henry Mitchell, Robert Mitchell, Muhlenberg, Murphy, Osgood, Page, Parks, Parker, Patterson, Dutee J. Pearce, Peyton, Franklin Pierce, Pierson, Plummer, Polk, Pope, Schenck, Shinn, Charles Slade, Smith, Speight, Standifer, Stoddert, Sutherland, William Taylor, Francis Thomas, Thomson, Turrill, Vanderpoel, Wagener, Ward, Wardwell, Wayne, Webster, Whallon—114.

NAYS—Messrs. John Quincy Adams, Heman Allen, John J. Allen, Chilton Allan, Archer, Ashley, Banks, Barber, Barnitz, Barringer, Baylies, Beatty, James M. Bell, Binney, Briggs, Bull, Burd, Burges, Cage, Campbell, Chambers, Chilton, Choate, Claiborne, William Clark, Clayton, Clowney, Corwin, Coulter, Crane, Crockett, Darlington, Warren R. Davis, Amos Davis, Davenport, Deberry, Deming, Denny, Dennis, Dickson, Duncan, Ellsworth, Evans, Edward Everett, Horace Everett, Ewing, Felder, Fillmore, Foot, Foster, Philo C. Fuller, Fulton, Gholson, Gordon, Graham, Grayson, Grennell, Griffin, Hiland Hall, Hard, Hardin, James Harper, Hazeltine, Heath, Jabez W. Huntington, Jackson, William Cost Johnson, King, Lay, Lincoln, Martindale, Marshall, McCarty, McComas, McDuffie, McKennan, Mercer, Milligan, Moore, Pinckney, Potts, Ramsay, Reed, Rencher, Selden, William B. Shepard, A. H. Shepperd, William Slade, Sloane, Spangler, Stewart, William P. Taylor, Philemon Thomas, Tompkins, Turner, Tweedy, Vance, Vinton, Watmough, Edward D. White, Frederick Whittlesey, Elisha Whittlesey, Wilde, Williams, Wilson, Young—106.

Mr. WILDE called for a division of the question on the resolutions. Ordered.

The question on the first resolution, viz: that "The Bank of the United States ought not to be rechartered," was decided in the affirmative. Yeas 132, nays 82.

YEAS—Messrs. John Adams, William Allen, Anthony, Archer, Beale, Bean, Beardsley, Beaumont, John Bell, Blair, Bockee, Boon, Bouldin, Brown, Bunch, Bynum, Campbell, Cambreleng, Carmichael, Carr, Casey, Chaney, Chinn, Claiborne, S. Clark, Clay, Clayton, Clowney, Coffee, Connor, Cramer, Warren R. Davis, Davenport, Day, Dickerson, Dickinson, Dunlap, Felder, Forester, Foster, William K. Fuller, Fulton, Galbraith, Gholson, Gillet, Gilmer, Gordon, Grayson, Griffin, Joseph Hall, Thomas H. Hall, Halsey, Hamer, Hannegan, Joseph M. Harper, Harrison, Hathaway, Hawkins, Hawes, Heath, Henderson, Howell, Hubbard, Abel Huntington, Inge, Jarvis, Richard M. Johnson, Noadiah Johnson, Cave Johnson, Seaborn Jones, Benjamin Jones, Kavanagh, Kinnard, Lane, Lansing, Laporte, Lawrence, Lay, L. Lea, T. Lee, Leavitt, Loyall, Lucas, Lyon, Lytle, A. Mann, Joel K. Mann, Mardis, J. Y. Mason, Moses Mason, McIntire, McKay, McKinley, McLene, McVean, Miller, Henry Mitchell, Robert Mitchell, Muhlenberg, Murphy, Osgood, Page, Parks, Parker, Patterson, Dutee J. Pearce, Peyton, Franklin Pierce, Pierson, Pinckney, Plummer, Polk, Rencher, Schenck, Schley, Shinn, Smith, Speight, Standifer, Stoddert, Sutherland, William Taylor, Wm. P. Taylor, Francis Thomas, Thomson, Turner, Turrill, Vanderpoel, Wagener, Ward, Wardwell, Wayne, Webster, Whallon—132.

NAYS—Messrs. J. Q. Adams, Heman Allen, John J. Allen, Chilton Allan, Ashley, Banks, Barber, Barnitz, Barringer, Baylies, Beatty, James M. Bell, Binney, Briggs, Bull, Burges, Cage, Chambers, Chilton, Choate, William Clark, Corwin, Coulter, Crane, Crockett, Darlington, Amos Davis, Deberry, Deming, Denny, Dennis, Dickson, Duncan, Ellsworth, Evans, Edward Everett, Horace Everett, Fillmore, Foot, Philo C. Fuller, James Graham, Grennell, Hiland Hall, Hard, Hardin, James Harper, Hazeltine, Jabez W. Huntington, Jackson, William C. Johnson, Lincoln, Martindale, Marshall, McCarty, McComas, McDuffie, McKennan, Mercer, Milligan, Moore, Pope, Potts, Reed, Wm. B. Shepard, Augustine H. Shepperd, William Slade, Charles Slade, Sloane, Spangler, Philemon Thomas, Tompkins, Tweedy, Vance, Vinton, Watmough, Edward D. White, Frederick Whittlesey, Elisha Whittlesey, Wilde, Williams, Wilson, Young—82.

The question being taken upon concurring in the second resolution, "That the deposites ought not to be restored," it was decided in the affirmative—Yeas 118, nays 103, as follows:

YEAS—Messrs. John Adams, William Allen, Anthony, Beale, Bean, Beardsley, Beaumont, John Bell, John Blair, Bockee, Boon, Bouldin, Brown, Bunch, Bynum, Cambreleng, Carmichael, Carr, Casey, Chinn, Samuel Clark, Clay, Coffee, Connor, Cramer, Day, Dickerson, Dickinson, Dunlap, Forester, William K. Fuller, Galbraith, Gillet, Gilmer, Joseph Hall, Thomas H. Hall, Halsey, Hamer, Hannegan, Joseph M. Harper, Harrison, Hathaway, Hawkins, Hawes, Henderson, Howell, Hubbard, Abel Huntington, Inge, Jarvis, Richard M. Johnson, Noadiah Johnson, Cave Johnson, Seaborn Jones, Benjamin Jones, Kavanagh, Kinnard, Lane, Lansing, Laporte, Lawrence, Luke Lea, Thomas Lee, Leavitt, Loyall, Lucas, Lyon, Lytle, Abijah Mann, Joel K. Mann, Mardis, John Y. Mason, Moses Mason, McCarty, McIntire, McKay, McKinley, McLene, McVean, Miller, Henry Mitchell, Robert Mitchell, Muhlenberg, Murphy, Osgood, Page, Parks, Parker, Patterson, Dutee J. Pearce, Peyton, Franklin Pierce, Pierson, Plummer, Polk, Pope, Schenck, Schley, Shinn, Charles Slade, Smith, Spangler, Speight, Standifer, Stoddert, Sutherland, William Taylor, Francis Thomas, Thomson, Turrill, Vanderpoel, Wagener, Ward, Wardwell, Wayne, Webster, Whallon—118.

NAYS—Messrs. John Q. Adams, Heman Allen, John J. Allen, Chilton Allan, Archer, Ashley, Banks, Barber, Barnitz, Barringer, Baylies, Beatty, James M. Bell, Binney, Briggs, Bull, Burd, Cage, Campbell, Chambers, Chilton, Choate, Claiborne, William Clark, Clayton, Clowney, Corwin, Coulter, Crane, Crockett, Darlington, Warren R. Davis, Amos Davis, Davenport, Deberry, Deming, Denny, Dennis, Dickson, Duncan, Ellsworth, Evans, Edward Everett, Horace Everett, Ewing, Felder, Fillmore, Foot, Foster, Philo C. Fuller, Fulton, Gholson, Gordon, Graham, Grayson, Grennell, Griffin, Hiland Hall, Hard, Hardin, James Harper, Hazeltine, Heath, Jabez W. Huntington, Jackson, W. C. Johnson, King, Lay, Lincoln, Martindale, Marshall, McComas, McDuffie, McKennan, Mercer, Milligan, Moore, Pinckney, Potts, Ramsey, Reed, Rencher, Selden, William B. Shepard, Augustine H. Shepperd, William Slade, Sloane, Stewart, William P. Taylor, Philemon Thomas, Tompkins, Turner, Tweedy, Vance, Watmough, Edward D. White, Frederick Whittlesey, Elisha Whittlesey, Wilde, Williams, Wilson, Young—103.

The question being taken on concurring in the third resolution, it was decided in the affirmative—Yeas 117, nays 105, as follows:

YEAS—Messrs. John Adams, William Allen, Anthony, Beale, Bean, Beardsley, Beaumont, John Bell, John Blair, Bockee, Boon, Bouldin, Brown, Bunch, Bynum, Cambreleng, Carmichael, Carr, Casey, Chaney, Chinn, Sam'l Clark, Clay, Coffee, Connor, Cramer, Day, Dickerson, Dickinson, Dunlap, Forester, William K. Fuller, Galbraith, Gillet, Gilmer, Joseph Hall, Thomas H. Hall, Halsey, Hamer, Hannegan, Joseph M. Harper, Harrison, Hathaway, Hawkins, Hawes, Henderson, Howell, Hubbard, Abel Huntington, Inge, Jarvis, Richard M. Johnson, Noadiah Johnson, Cave Johnson, Seaborn Jones, Benjamin Jones, Kavanagh, Kinnard, Lane, Lansing, Laporte, Lawrence, Luke Lea, Thomas Lee, Leavitt, Loyall, Lucas, Lyon, Lytle, Abijah Mann, Joel K. Mann, Mardis, John Y. Mason, Moses Mason, McCarty, McIntire, McKay, McKinley, McLene, McVean, Miller, Henry Mitchell, Robert Mitchell, Muhlenberg, Murphy, Osgood, Page, Parks, Parker, Patterson, D. J. Pearce, Peyton, Franklin Pierce, Pierson, Plummer, Polk, Pope, Schenck, Schley, Shinn, Charles Slade, Smith, Speight, Standifer, Stoddert, Sutherland, William Taylor, Francis Thomas, Thomson, Turrill, Vanderpoel, Van Houten, Wagener, Ward, Wardwell, Wayne, Webster, and Whallon—117.

NAYS—Messrs. John Q. Adams, Heman Allen, John J. Allen, Chilton Allan, Archer, Ashley, Banks Barber, Barnitz, Barringer, Baylies, Beatty, Jas. M. Bell, Binney, Briggs, Bull, Burd, Burges, Cage, Campbell, Chambers, Chilton, Choate, Claiborne, William Clark, Clayton, Clowney, Corwin, Coulter, Crane, Crockett, Darlington, Warren R. Davis, Amos Davis, Davenport, Deberry, Deming, Denny, Dennis, Dickson, Duncan, Ellsworth, Evans, Edward Everett, Horace Everett, Ewing, Felder, Fillmore, Foot, Foster, Philo C. Fuller, Fulton, Gholson, Gordon, Graham, Grayson, Grennell, Griffin, Hiland Hall, Hard, Hardin, James Harper, Hazeltine, Heath, Jabez W. Huntington, Jackson, William C. Johnson, King, Lay, Lincoln, Martindale, Marshall, McComas, McDuffie, McKennan, Mercer, Milligan, Moore, Pinckney, Potts, Ramsay, Reed, Rencher, Selden, William B. Shepard, Augustine H. Shepperd, William Slade, Sloane, Spangler, Stewart, William P. Taylor, Philemon Thomas, Tompkins, Turner, Tweedy, Vance, Vinton, Watmough, Edward D. White, Frederick Whittlesey, Elisha Whittlesey, Wilde, Williams, Wilson, and Young—105.

The question was then taken on concurring in the fourth resolution, as follows:

"4. *Resolved*, That for the purpose of ascertaining, as far as practicable, the cause of the 'commercial embarrassment and distress complained of by numerous citizens of the United 'States, in sundry memorials which have been 'presented to Congress at the present session, and 'of inquiring whether the charter of the Bank of 'the United States has been violated, and also 'what corruptions and abuses have existed in its 'management, whether it has used its corporate 'power, or money, to control the press, to interfere in politics, or influence elections, and whether 'it has had any agency, through its machinery, 'or money, in producing the existing pressure, a 'select committee be appointed to inspect the 'books, and examine into the proceedings of the 'said bank, who shall report whether the provisions of the charter have been violated or not; 'and also what abuses, corruptions, or malpractices have existed in the management of said 'bank, and that the said committee be authorized 'to send for persons and papers, and to summon 'and examine witnesses on oath, and to examine 'into the affairs of the said bank and branches; 'and they are further authorized to visit the prin-

'cipal bank, or any of its branches, for the pur-
'pose of inspecting the books, correspondence,
'accounts, and other papers connected with its
'management or business; and that the said com-
'mittee be required to report the result of such
'investigation, together with the evidence they
'may take, at as early a day as practicable.''

And the fourth resolution was concurred in—
ayes 171, nays 42, as follows:

YEAS—Messrs. John Adams, H. Allen, John
J. Allen, William Allen, Archer, Ashley, Barrin-
ger, Baylies, Beale, Bean, Beardsley, Beaumont,
John Bell, James M. Bell, Blair, Bockee, Boon,
Bouldin, Briggs, Brown, Bunch, Burges, Bynum,
Cage, Campbell, Cambreleng, Carmichael, Carr,
Casey, Chaney, Chinn, Claiborne, Samuel Clark,
Wm. Clark, Clay, Clowney, Coffee, Connor, Cor-
win, Coulter, Cramer, W. R. Davis, Davenport,
Day, Deberry, Deming, Dennis, Dickerson, Dick-
inson, Duncan, Dunlap, H. Everett, Ewing, Fel-
der, Fillmore, Forester, Foster, P. C. Fuller, W.
K. Fuller, Fulton, Galbraith, Gholson, Gillet,
Gordon, Graham, Grayson, Grennell, J. Hall,
H. Hall, T. H. Hall, Halsey, Hamer, Hannegan,
Hardin, J. M. Harper, James Harper, Harrison,
Hathaway, Hawkins, Hawes, Heath, Howell,
Hubbard, A. Huntington, Inge, Jackson, Jarvis,
William Cost Johnson, R. M. Johnson, Noadiah
Johnson, Cave Johnson, S. Jones, B. Jones, Kav-
anagh, King, Kinnard, Lane, Lansing, Laporte,
Lawrence, Lay, L. Lea, T. Lee, Leavitt, Loyall,
Lucas, Lyon, Lytle, A. Mann, J. K. Mann, Mar-
tindale, Mardis, J. Y. Mason, Moses Mason,
McCarty, McComas, McIntire, McKay, McKin-
ley, McLene, McVean, Miller, H. Mitchell, R.
Mitchell, Moore, Muhlenberg, Osgood, Page,
Parks, Parker, Patterson, D. J. Pearce, Peyton,
P. Pierce, Pierson, Plummer, Polk, Pope, Ram-
say, Rencher, Schenck, Schley, Selden, A. H.
Shepperd, Shinn, William Slade, Charles Slade,
Sloane, Smith, Spangler, Speight, Standifer, Stew-
art, Stoddert, Sutherland, Wm. Taylor, Wm. P.
Taylor, F. Thomas, P. Thomas, Thomson, Tur-
ner, Turrill, Vanderpool, Vinton, Wagener, Ward,
Wardwell, Wayne, Webster, Whallon, F. Whit-
tlesey, E. Whittlesey, Wilde, Wilson—171.

NAYS—Messrs. J. Q. Adams, Chilton Allan,
Anthony, Banks, Barber, Barnitz, Beatty, Bin-
ney, Burd, Chambers, Chilton, Choate, Clayton,
Crane, Crockett, Darlington, Amos Davis, Denny,
Dickson, Evans, E. Everett, Gilmer, Gorham, Ha-
lsitine, Henderson, Lincoln, Marshall, McDuffie,
McKennan, Mercer, Milligan, Murphy, Pinckney,
Potts, Reed, W. B. Shepard, Tompkins, Tweedy,
Vance, Watmough, Williams, Young—43.

Mr. THOMAS, of Louisiana, inferred the
unanimous consent of the House to submit a motion that when the House adjourns it adjourn to
meet on Monday next; and the motion was
agreed to.

The committee of investigation was ordered to
consist of seven members.

Mr. WILDE offered as an amendment to the
resolutions a fifth resolution.

Mr. POLK moved an adjournment.

Mr. WILDE asked the yeas and nays on the
motion, and they were ordered.

The question being taken, it was decided in the
affirmative. Yeas 123, nays 7.

The House then adjourned, at half past seven,
to meet on Monday next.

IN SENATE.

MONDAY, *April* 7, 1834.

Mr. SILSBEE presented a memorial signed by
twelve hundred inhabitants of Salem, Massachusetts, praying Congress to make some arrangement for the regulation of the currency of the
country; to restore the deposites to the Bank of
the United States; and to recharter the bank. The
memorial was read, referred to the Committee on
Finance, and ordered to be printed.

Mr. WRIGHT presented the petition of the
heirs of the late Robert Fulton, deceased, praying
compensation for the construction of steam frigates, and other services; which was referred to
the Committee on Naval Affairs.

Mr. WRIGHT presented the petition of three
hundred and fifty-five citizens of Syracuse, New
York, praying the restoration of the deposites to
the Bank of the United States; which was read,

referred to the Committee on Finance, and ordered
to be printed.

Also, a memorial signed by eleven hundred and
forty-three citizens of Rochester, New York, sustaining the Executive, and praying that the deposites may not be restored to the Bank of the United
States, or that institution be rechartered. Read,
referred to the Committee on Finance, and ordered
to be printed.

Mr. KANE presented the petition of sundry
citizens of Illinois, praying aid from Congress to
construct a road from Chicago, in Michigan, to
Vincennes, in Indiana; which was referred to the
Committee on Roads and Canals.

Mr. FRELINGHUYSEN presented the preamble and resolutions of a large meeting of the democracy of Essex county, New Jersey, adverse to
a recharter of the Bank of the United States, opposed to a restoration of the deposites, and declaring the unlimited confidence of the meeting in the
National Executive. The proceedings were read,
referred to the Committee on Finance, and ordered
to be printed.

Mr. WHITE, from the Committee on Indian
Affairs, reported a bill for the relief of James
Brown, and a bill for the relief of Alexander J.
Robertson.

Mr. TIPTON presented the petition of Samuel
Hardesty, of Indiana; which was referred to the
Committee of Claims.

Mr. BIBB presented a memorial, signed by upwards of 1000 inhabitants of Shelby county, Kentucky, praying a recharter of the Bank of the
United States, and a restoration of the public deposites to that institution; which was read, referred to the Committee on Finance, and ordered to
be printed.

Mr. MORRIS presented a series of resolutions
of the Legislature of Ohio:

1. Asking grants "of lands for the benefit of
schools. Referred to the Committee on Public
Lands, and ordered to be printed.

2. Disapproving of the Military Academy at
West Point, and recommending its abolishment.
Referred to the Committee on Military Affairs,
and ordered to be printed.

3. Asking aid from Congress for the construction of the Ohio and Pennsylvania canal. Referred to the Committee on Roads and Canals, and
ordered to be printed.

4. Recommending an appropriation of lands for
the benefit of officers and soldiers of the late war.
Referred to the Committee on Military Affairs,
and ordered to be printed.

Mr. MORRIS presented the petition of Daniel
Taylor; which was referred to the Committee on
Claims, and ordered to be printed.

Mr. BIBB, from the Committee on the Judiciary, reported a bill for the better organization of
the district courts of Alabama.

Mr. BIBB presented the petition of Moses
Archer; which was referred to the Committee on
Pensions.

Mr. BROWN presented the proceedings of a
meeting of inhabitants of the town of Tarborough
and its vicinity, in the county of Edgecombe, North
Carolina, opposed to a recharter of the Bank of
the United States, and against a restoration of the
deposites to that corporation. Read, referred to the
Committee on Finance, and ordered to be printed.

THE SPECIAL ORDER,

Being Mr. CLAY's resolutions relative to the
Executive power of removal from office, was postponed, on his motion, and made the order of the
day for this day fortnight.

Mr. PRESTON offered the following resolution:

Resolved, That the Secretary of the Treasury be
directed to communicate to the Senate the name
of any agent, or agents, employed by him, to
transact the business of the treasury with the
banks selected for the deposite of the public funds;
the nature of the duties performed by said agent,
or agents; the amount of compensation paid for
the discharge of the said duties, and by whom;
and from what fund the said compensation is paid,
and whether the said agent or agents have been
appointed in pursuance of law.

Mr. EWING presented a memorial signed by
50 inhabitants of Muskingum county, Ohio, praying the abolition of slavery in the District of Columbia.

Mr. EWING said that although the memorial
merited respectful consideration, yet, under existing circumstances, any legislation on the subject
by Congress, at present, and probably for some
time to come, he thought, would be unwise and
inexpedient.

On his motion, the memorial was referred to the
Committee on the District of Columbia.

Mr. CALHOUN gave notice that he should, on
Wednesday, move to take up his motion for the
repeal of the Force bill.

ORDERS OF THE DAY.

The several resolutions submitted on Friday
last, were considered and adopted.

The following bills were read a third time and
passed:

A bill for the relief of William S. Anderson.

A bill for the relief of Garrigues Flaujac.

The bill for the relief of Elihu Hall Bay being
under consideration, a debate ensued, in which
Messrs. WHITE, POINDEXTER, WAGGA-
MAN, KANE, and BLACK, participated.

Mr. BLACK moved to lay the bill on the table.

Yeas 14, nays 14.

The debate was resumed by Messrs. FOR-
SYTH, FRELINGHUYSEN, PRESTON,
WHITE, and SPRAGUE, when Mr. PORTER
renewed the motion to lay the bill upon the table,
which prevailed.

The bill appropriating $350,000 for the construc-
tion of a lateral branch of the Baltimore and Ohio
railroad, coming up, on its final passage—

Mr. HENDRICKS said, he thought this was a
bill containing some provisions which ought to be
attended to. The bill appropriated $350,000, or
$30,000 a year for twenty years, for carrying the
mail. It was a general principle not to charge the
Government for the transportation of the mail on
common roads, and he thought the principle a
proper one in this case. He therefore moved to
recommit the bill to the Committee on the District
of Columbia.

Mr. GRUNDY was in favor of the motion. It
was very doubtful whether the principle in the bill
suggested by the gentleman from Indiana [Mr.
HENDRICKS] ought to be established. He did not
think Congress should bind itself to pay a stipulated sum for the performance of a specific duty.
It was impossible now to say what, in twenty
years, it might be expedient for the Government
to do in regard to the transportation of the mail.
The proposed arrangement might do very well
now, but something might occur, before that time,
which might prove that the arrangement was not
a desirable one for the public interest. He would
rather give the company a much larger sum, and
let them carry the mail free of charge as long as
the Government chose.

Mr. SPRAGUE observed that the Chairman of
the Committee on the District of Columbia was
absent, and to recommit the bill to the committee,
would seem like an expression of opinion that it
ought to be amended; he preferred, therefore, that
the bill should be laid on the table; which was
agreed to.

The following bills were read a third time and
passed:

A bill for the relief of Thomas Fillebrown, jr.

A bill for the relief of John A. Webster.

A bill for the relief of Hishe Homs, otherwise
called Captain Red Pepper.

The resolution of Mr. POINDEXTER, authorizing the printing of 1000 copies of the Journals of
the old Congress, being called up, it was, upon his
motion, laid upon the table.

On motion of Mr. FORSYTH, the Senate proceeded to executive business, and, after spending
some time therein, adjourned.

HOUSE OF REPRESENTATIVES.

MONDAY, *April* 7, 1834.

The CHAIR announced the following as the
Committee of Bank Investigation, under the
resolution adopted by the House on Friday last:
Messrs. THOMAS of Maryland, (chairman,) EVER-
ETT of Massachusetts, MUHLENBERG, of Pennsylvania, MASON of Virginia, ELLSWORTH of Connecticut, MANN of New York, LYTLE of Ohio.

Mr. BURGES presented a memorial from sun-

dry citizens of Bristol county, Rhode Island, together with a letter enclosing it; the reading of which he asked.

The CHAIR said the letter could only be read by unanimous consent.

An objection being made, the letter was not read.

The memorial was, on motion of Mr. BURGES, read, laid on the table, and ordered to be printed.

Mr. BURGES moved a restoration to the files of the House of certain letters, read on the last petition day by his colleague.

The CHAIR said it could be done only by unanimous consent, and even then it would be irregular.

Mr. PEARCE presented the resolutions and proceeding of a numerous and highly respectable meeting of the Democratic Republicans of the city of Providence, convened on the 26th ultimo, approving of the measures of the Executive in relation to the Bank of the United States and the deposites.

Also, the proceedings of a meeting of the working-men of that city, approving of the same measures.

Also, the proceedings and resolutions of a numerous meeting of citizens recently held in North Providence, against a recharter of the United States Bank, and the restoration of the deposites.

[The following communications addressed to him he asked leave to present, but as they could not be presented without the unanimous consent of the House, (they not being, in form, memorials,) and some few individuals objecting to their presentation, we give them to the public through our columns:

BRISTOL, *March* 19, 1834

SIR: Without deeming it advisable at the present time to call a public meeting upon the subject, and without soliciting additional names, or making known to others this expression of our sentiments, we wish individually to express our approbation of your present course in Congress, particularly in relation to the recharter of the United States Bank and the restoration of the deposites. We do not mean to say that embarrassments in business are not felt here as in other parts of the country, but it seems to us idle to pretend that the removal of the deposites could of itself have caused them without the effective agency of the bank. We do not know that the removal was necessary at the precise time when it was made; but if a new lease is not to be given to this institution, they must have been removed sooner or later, and can see no reason why the time selected was not as favorable to the object as any other time. In our opinion, the bank has pursued a systematic plan of operations against the Executive, and a return of the deposites would be a triumph of the bank—a triumph over the Executive and the Government. We daily hear arguments advanced as proof of the necessity of a bank, but in this vicinity no reasons are offered to our knowledge for the continuance of the present one. We regard all great moneyed institutions of this kind as dangerous in republican governments, and if necessary, are necessary evils; and in our view their dangerous tendency is greatly increased by duration, by the foothold they gain, the additional power, and the nature of independent perpetual corporations, they acquire by successive recharters. We are aware that a few individuals in this place, who have an interest in it, are friendly to the present bank, but we assure you that the friends of the Administration here, generally, are opposed to its recharter. We could not reasonably expect that it would die without a struggle for life, be the consequences of that struggle to the country what it may, and if the present embarrassments are general and serious, it is a proof that it can be a terrific engine of evil. Yet, holding that temporary pecuniary interests and particular instances of individual distress are light and trifling in comparison with the purity and permanency of our republican institutions, we wish not to see our representatives flinch and falter at the first exertion of its power. We therefore beg you, sir, to accept our hearty thanks for the firm and manly tone with which you have suported the patriotic views on this subject of the Chief Magistrate of the nation

We are, sir, very respectfully, your obedient servants. Signed:

JOHN D'WOLF,
JOHN GLADDING, jr.,
P. BORDEN,
H. POTTER DIMOND,
D. A. MORRIS,
H. C. WARDWELL,
JACOB BABBITT,
ICHABOD DAVIS,
JOSEPH M. BLAKE,
GREENWOOD REYNOLDS.

HON. DUTEE J. PEARCE.

To the Hon. Dutee J. Pearce:

SIR: The undersigned, who constitute a portion of your constituents, take this mode briefly to address you, and to offer some suggestions on the present agitated state of the public mind on the bank question. Waiving a detail of reasons with which you are already familiar, we are of opinion that, under present circumstances, the Bank of the United States cannot, will not, and ought not to be rechartered, "because the proof is abundant, clear, and irresistible, that it has fallen into abuses of its trust, manifold, high-handed, and alarming."

We are further of opinion that the present embarrassment of trade, for want of money, is principally owing to the feverish state of the public mind, occasioned more by political intrigue than all other causes put together.

The experience of the world fully proves, that in all commercial and manufacturing countries, the ebbs and flows of the money market are as certain, though not so regular, as those of the ocean tides, and that, in time, either is certain to produce the other.

Our opinion also is, that a bank, whose operations could be extended throughout the whole nation, has heretofore been, and if continued, or another created by Congress, would hereafter be highly beneficial to the country, not only as a fiscal agent of the Government, and a safe and convenient deposite of the funds of the treasury, but also an efficient aid in the operations of the mercantile and other business classes of the community.

Such a bank, we think, should be entirely above question or doubt as to its constitutionality, which is not the case with the present United States Bank, some of the ablest statesmen of the country having insisted on the contrary—and, in our opinion, it should be located somewhere within the exclusive territorial jurisdiction of the General Government.

The bank should be authorized to establish its branches in any, or all of the States of the Union, provided it could be done by an amicable arrangement with the State Governments, paying to the several States, where the same might be established, a reasonable tax, uniform, and as nearly equal as possible, so as to yield an income to the States, but to be subject to no requisition for money to the General Government.

These suggestions we offer to your consideration in the nature of advice, as we do not at all presume to dictate. They are made to you individually, with our permission, however, that you lay them before Congress, should you deem it advisable to do so, but not expressing any wish of our own in the last respect.

We are, very respectfully, your friends and fellow citizens.

[*Signed by one hundred and one names.*]

NEWPORT, R. I., *March* 12, 1834.

Petitions were presented by Messrs. YOUNG and ELLSWORTH.

Mr. HEMAN ALLEN presented a memorial from sundry citizens of Vermont, praying Congress to adopt measures to restore a sound currency. Read, laid on the table, and ordered to be printed.

Mr. SLADE presented resolutions adopted at a meeting of the citizens of Rutland county, praying the restoration of the deposites, and condemning their removal, &c. Read, laid on the table, and ordered to be printed.

Mr. LANSING presented a memorial from sundry citizens of Albany, against the recharter of the bank, and the restoration of the deposites. Read, laid on the table, and ordered to be printed.

Mr. PIERSON rose and said—

Mr. SPEAKER: I am charged with the presentation of a memorial and certain resolutions expressive of the sentiments of my constituents in relation to the agitating question which has so long occupied the attention of this House. A convention of delegates chosen by the people in their primary assemblies throughout my district, adopted this memorial and these resolutions without a dissenting voice. At this convention more than two hundred delegates thus chosen were assembled; and it is fair to presume that a majority of my constituents entertain the sentiments conveyed to this House through this memorial and these resolutions. I have before me the proceedings of some of the meetings in the county towns at which these delegates were chosen, expressive of the same sentiments, but in stronger language. I should have contented myself with the bare presentation of these proceedings without a single remark, if I had not perceived that they had been publicly arraigned before I had an opportunity of presenting them here. I have perceived also, that in the remarks made on the presentation of another memorial from my district in the other branch of Congress, I have been publicly charged with misrepresentation. I owe it to this House, as well as to myself, to make an explanation, and I ask permission, Mr. Speaker, to do so.

Leave being granted—

Mr. P. proceeded. Before I avail myself of this indulgence, it is proper that I should briefly state the character of this convention and the substance of the memorial and resolutions. I have already made mention of the number of delegates that attended this convention. I need not add that they were highly respectable. The people who chose them in their primary assemblies, have given you a sufficient guarantee of their respectability. It may sometimes happen that, in the circulation of memorials for signatures, fictitious names may be placed upon the roll, or genuine ones obtained, by fraud and misrepresentation; but it rarely happens that delegates, chosen directly by the people, will dare to deceive or misrepresent them. Sir, it is with some degree of pride that I acknowledge a personal acquaintance with most of these delegates. There are few, very few, among them, who are wealthy; but there are many, very many of them, who, by honest industry, have acquired a competency, which they are, no doubt, desirous of preserving, but which they will cheerfully surrender, if necessary, in defence of public liberty. They are engaged in all the great departments of human industry. A large proportion of them are employed in agriculture; an employment which forms the foundation of national wealth—I had almost said of national virtue. Some of them are engaged in commerce and manufactures, and many of them are mechanics and artisans, whose skill and industry is unsurpassed by any other people in any other section of our country.

Sir, in order that I may not be again charged with misrepresentation, let me not be misunderstood as to the political character of this convention. It was not composed of no-party men, nor was it an assemblage of persons without distinction of party. We have such meetings in the State of New York by name, but there is too much intelligence in the main body of the people, to be deceived by them. We know, then, that when a call of a meeting without distinction of party is made, it is to be composed chiefly, if not exclusively, of the opponents of the Administration. The friends of the Administration have never disguised or concealed their political names. They are republicans—they avow themselves such. This convention was a republican convention. It was called and convened by that name. It adopted the proceedings I am about to present by that name; and however odious the name may now be to certain politicians, it will never become obsolete, so long as we preserve our present form of government. Let New York and New York politicians be abused ever so much, a political party will exist there. It has existed ever since the formation of our Government. It existed when Mr. Jefferson was first elected President. His political principles are still fondly cherished in New York by a political party; and it is this party, which, at this trying time, will be found, as it always has been, opposed to a national bank; and, as a matter of course, opposed to the restoration of the deposites.

The substance of the memorial that I am about to present, may therefore be inferred. The memorialists tell you, in the most respectful language, that, "in common with a great majority of the people of the United States, they had viewed, with unfeigned alarm, the power of this bank. They tell you, too, that they had deemed the result of the last presidential canvass a decisive expression of the public will that this dangerous institution should not be perpetuated. They tell you, moreover, that they were aware that the charter of so great a monopoly would not be suffered to expire without a struggle—that they anticipated all its movements to excite public alarm, derange the currency, and prostrate individual credit.

But they tell you notwithstanding that they approve of the measures of the Administration in relation to this institution, and that they are convinced that its demands for a recharter should be refused, for the purpose of effectually resisting this war of the bank upon public and individual credit. In conclusion, they tell you that they are opposed to the recharter of the bank, and to the restoration of the deposites. Their resolutions are expressive of the same sentiments in bolder language.

Sir, I have felt myself called upon to say thus much of this convention and their proceedings, and I will now notice what has been publicly said against them.

I have before me a paper published by the printers to this House, which contains the publication of a letter written in my district, and read in the Senate, an extract of which I beg leave to read here. It is in these words:

"Ere this arrives, you will have heard of certain 'resolutions passed in a county convention, called 'by the office-holders and their creatures, to attend 'through the power of party discipline, approba'ting the course of the President. But such can'not be the sober sense of the county. The meet'ing, we presume, was got up in consequence of 'our memorial."

This letter, as is said, was signed by nine or ten citizens of Troy, and at the head of the list was the mayor of the city. Their names are not published, though I am informed they were made public when the letter was read. They have been reported to me. If correctly, (and I have no reason to doubt it,) I know them well. Some of them are men of great wealth, and all of them of great respectability. But most, if not all of them, have been known as belonging to a political party which Mr. Jefferson has most faithfully described, and whose principles and motives he detected at an early period in the history of our Government. In short, sir, they are Federalists. At this day, there are very few persons in the district I represent who will avow themselves such; but from the sentiments expressed in this letter, it may be taken for granted these nine or ten gentlemen are not averse to such avowal. "This convention," say they, "was called by the office-holders and their creatures;" ay, "creatures," Mr. Speaker. This is not an uncommon expression. It is often applied indiscriminately to the democracy and yeomanry of my district. I do not intend to rebuke those gentlemen for the remark. It was not a casual expression—it was deliberately made; it undoubtedly conveys the "sober sense" and meaning of these nine or ten gentlemen. They believe, no doubt, as an eminent statesman and leader of their party believed and said, before the adoption of our Constitution, "that all communities divide themselves 'into the few and the many: the first are rich and 'well born; the other, the mass of the people. The 'people are turbulent and changing—they seldom 'judge or determine right; give, therefore, to the 'first class a distinct and permanent share in the 'Government." Sir, those gentlemen carry out this principle. "This meeting," say they, "we presume was got up in consequence of our memorial." Thus we see that those nine or ten very worthy, very wealthy, and very respectable gentlemen, claim as their memorial, one that has heretofore been presented to both branches of Congress, signed, as it was said, by seventeen hundred and thirty of the citizens of Troy, without distinction of party.

Sir, I have a few words to say of this famous "Troy memorial," inasmuch as what I have hitherto said in relation to it has been the subject of much comment and some misrepresentation.

That memorial was originally transmitted to an honorable Senator from the State of New York, for presentation. Before he presented it, he was kind enough to submit it to my inspection, presuming, no doubt, that inasmuch as it came from my district, I was better acquainted with the memorialists than himself. I stated to the honorable Senator that the memorialists were highly respectable—that I was personally acquainted with many of them, and had information of others upon which I could rely. I did not state to him, as has been reported in one or more of the papers published in this city, that I was personally acquainted with nineteen-twentieths of them. The honorable Senator neither understood nor reported me as saying so; I do not believe there is any one man living who is personally acquainted with that proportion of them. My knowledge of the memorialists was founded upon acquaintance with, and information of them. I so said, and was so understood at the time. But I did state to him that I did not believe that more than one hundred of the memorialists were the friends of the Administration. I did not think or intimate that the memorial was entitled to less weight or credit because it came from the opponents of the Administration; and it will be perceived, that in the remarks made by the gentleman charged with the presentation, not a word was said of the political character of the memorialists, until another honorable Senator insisted that it had been signed by the citizens of Troy, without distinction of party. Then, and not till then, was the information I had given made public.

Sir, I certainly ought not to express my regret that my political opponents attach so much importance to the fact that a few of my political friends signed that memorial. It was a perfect non-committal production. It said nothing about the recharter of the bank or the restoration of the deposites, and I believe neither the United States Bank or the deposites were at all mentioned. Sir, I would permit my political opponents to claim among the memorialists any number of my friends they choose, if they would leave unmolested those of my constituents who did not sign it, and my humble self.

It was but a day or two after that memorial was presented, that another letter from a gentleman in my district was made public. This last letter asserted, that the aforesaid memorial was signed by the citizens of Tory, without distinction of party, "except a few whole-hog collar-men." I speak from recollection, for I have not the report of this last letter now before me. I am not mistaken, however, in the quotation of this last delicate expression.

At this day the expression is so common and so general in its intended application both here and elsewhere, that it has ceased to be reproachful. It seems to be applied by political opponents to all the friends of the Administration without discrimination. It is applied to every representative who will not betray the trust reposed in him by a confiding people. If he will violate the pledges he has given to his constituents, then, and not till then, he becomes uncollared, and unshackled, and is hailed as an independent representative. Sir, permit me to say, that I, for one, aspire to no such honor or distinction.

Mr. Speaker, I have a few words to say in vindication of myself, and I have done. "These nine or ten respectable citizens, with the Mayor at the head of the list," say, in the communication from which I have read an extract, that "our memorial," as it has been called, "was presented to the citizens of Troy without distinction of party, and that of the 1730 citizens who signed it, it is found on a critical examination, recently made, that at least four hundred are, or have been Administration men."

Sir, when I read this report, I almost feared that I had been too hasty in my examination of the names of the memorialists, and that I had been incautious, if not incorrect, in the statement I had made. I knew, to be sure, that I had seen the call of the meeting at which that memorial was adopted. I had seen the names of the persons appended to that call reported to be eleven hundred in number. I had received communications from constituents whose veracity was never questioned, asserting, that of those eleven hundred signatures, there were only thirty-one of the friends of the Administration. I have now before me a paper, published in my district, in which this assertion has since been made public, and which I have never seen contradicted. I had seen most, if not all, of the names appended to the call of that meeting, appended also to the memorial. I know, both from acquaintance with, and information of the residue of these memorialists, that they were generally of the same political character. I knew, moreover, that I had intended to make a liberal allowance when I stated the number at one hundred; still I feared I had been mistaken. I was willing publicly to correct the mistake if I could become satisfied that I had made one; I therefore procured a copy of the names subscribed to that memorial, and transmitted it to my constituents for information. They cheerfully instituted an investigation, and have communicated the result of it to me. Their communication I am willing should be made public. I ask that it may be read by the Clerk. [It was ordered to be read, as follows:]

"TROY, (N. Y.,) *March* 29, 1834.

"*Hon. J. Pierson:*

"DEAR SIR: After a patient investigation and examination of the names appended to the memorial sent from this city in February last, to Congress, only ninety-five of those names have been found known by either of us, the subscribers, to be friends of the general Administration; ninety-seven are aliens, sixty-seven are minors, and upwards of five hundred are not found on the city directory. It is probable that the number of each of the above may be somewhat larger, as there are names unknown to any of us. There are also names known to be non-residents, and some are presumed to be fictitious. Several of the subscribers hereto have seen many of those who have signed the said memorial, and who are friends of the Administration, and they state that they are opposed to the recharter of the United States Bank, and approve of the course which the Administration has pursued in relation to the same, and that if the memorial had been for a recharter of the said bank they would not have signed the same."

This letter (said Mr. P.) is signed by twenty-three citizens of Troy. They are not only gentlemen of great respectability, but intimately and extensively acquainted with the people of that city. I hazard nothing in saying that they are as well (if not better) acquainted with the political character of the citizens as any other equal number of gentlemen in that place. They are all well known throughout my district, and some of them throughout the State of New York. They have stood, and still stand, high in the confidence of the people—too high, indeed, to require the tribute of my poor praise.

Sir, I have not made this explanation or exposure in a spirit of unkindness towards those nine or ten gentlemen who have seemed desirous of wounding my feelings. I have made it in self-defence. I do not question the integrity of those gentlemen. They have, no doubt, stated what they believed. They predicated their statement or averment, (call it what you please,) as well upon information as their personal acquaintance. Sir, they should have had the charity to believe I did the same thing. If I were in fact mistaken, surely such mistake might have been deemed by them of too little importance to be the subject of correspondence with an eminent statesman. But, sir, I do not intend to complain. I shall leave all those who have been engaged in this controversy against me in the quiet enjoyment of all the honors they have acquired in a warfare that is novel, if not unprecedented.

Mr. SELDEN presented a memorial from eight hundred and eighty-one working-men, citizens of Troy, praying the restoration of the deposites and the recharter of the bank.

Read, and ordered to be printed, and laid on the table.

Mr. SELDEN presented a memorial from certain citizens of Albany, representing their situation in relation to the commerce of the State of New York, and of the great West, and the embarrassed condition of that commerce; and praying the establishment of a national bank for the regulation of the currency, &c.

Read, and ordered to be printed, and laid on the table.

Mr. FILLMORE presented a memorial from certain young men, citizens of Troy, condemning the measures of the Government in relation to the United States Bank, &c. Read, ordered to be printed, and laid on the table.

Messrs. GILLET, HAZELTINE, TURRILL, and BEARDSLEY, presented private petitions.

Mr. BEARDSLEY presented a memorial from 600 citizens of Utica, protesting against the restoration of the deposites, and the recharter of the United States Bank. Read, ordered to be printed, and laid on the table.

Messrs. HATHAWAY and VANDERPOEL presented private petitions.

Messrs. SCHENCK, PARKER, and DICKERSON, presented petitions.

Mr. BINNEY presented the memorial of the Select Council of Philadelphia, condemning the course of the Government on the subject of the deposites. Read, ordered to be printed, and laid on the table.

Mr. WATMOUGH presented a petition from a committee of the officers who served in the late war, praying a grant of land. Referred.

Mr. MUHLENBERG presented memorials signed by 5480 citizens of Berks county, in Pennsylvania, praying that the United States Bank may not be rechartered, and that the public deposites may not be restored, and denying the existence of great distress in that neighborhood. The language of the memorial was respectful. It was signed chiefly by farmers, mechanics, and laborers—the yeomanry of Berks county—men distinguished for the morality of their habits, and their attachment to the institutions of the country. Their opinions were entitled to respect at home, and throughout the State, because they speak a united and powerful voice through the ballot-box, and he hoped they would be respected here; for here the opinion of every citizen was entitled to respect, whether Federalist or Democrat, bank or anti-bank. He asked the reading of one of the memorials. The memorials were ordered to be printed, with the names, and laid on the table.

Mr. McKENNAN presented a memorial from citizens of Washington county, Pennsylvania, disapproving of the measures of the Government in relation to the United States Bank. Ordered to be printed, and laid on the table.

Mr. DARLINGTON presented a memorial from citizens of Delaware county, Pennsylvania, praying the restoration of the deposites, and the recharter of the Bank of the United States, as the only means of restoring confidence and relieving the present distress. Read, laid on the table, and ordered to printed.

Mr. DARLINGTON presented the proceedings of a public meeting on the same subject, and same character, held in the county of Delaware; which was read, ordered to be printed, and laid on the table.

Mr. SUTHERLAND presented the proceedings of a Democratic meeting of citizens, held in Delaware county, decidedly supporting the measures and views of the Administration in relation to the United States Bank. He read some of the resolutions, as a reply to the resolutions from a meeting in the same county, which had just been read. The resolutions were ordered to be printed and laid on the table.

Mr. SUTHERLAND also presented the memorial of sundry citizens of Blockley township, Pennsylvania, opposing the restoration of the deposites and the recharter of the bank. Ordered to be printed.

Mr. S. also presented the memorial of the Democratic citizens of Southwark, approving of the course of the Administration in relation to the United States Bank. Read, ordered to be printed, and laid on the table.

Mr. S. also presented a memorial from citizens of the third congressional district of Pennsylvania, sustaining the course of the Administration in relation to the United States Bank. The memorial was signed by two thousand eight hundred and seventy-nine voters of the district, which, in addition to those heretofore forwarded, was stated to make three thousand one hundred and seventy-nine names, and many more were coming. Read, laid on the table, and ordered to be printed.

Mr. WAGENER presented a memorial from a number of Democratic citizens assembled at Northampton, with certain resolutions, against the recharter of the bank and restoration of the deposites.

Mr. BEAUMONT presented four memorials from sundry persons, amongst them, one from 1118 citizens of Northumberland county, against the restoration of the deposites, and against the recharter of the bank.

Mr. B. also presented one of a different tenor from one hundred citizens of Muncy, Lycoming county.

Mr. GALBRAITH presented a memorial from sundry citizens of Franklin, Venango county, against the restoration of the deposites and recharter of the bank.

Mr. POTTS, sundry memorials in favor of the restoration of the deposites and the recharter of the bank, from the inhabitants of Chester county.

Mr. MILLER presented the proceedings of a meeting of the citizens of Adams county, in Pennsylvania, held at Gettysburg on the 22d of last month. Mr. M. said that the gentlemen who had enclosed the proceedings to him, had authorized him to say that the meeting was large and respectable. He said he knew a number of the gentlemen himself whose names appeared in the proceedings, and he knew them to be not only respectable, but intelligent. The proceedings are in relation to the Bank of the United States and the public deposites. They are opposed to the recharter of that institution, and approve of the measures of the Administration in removing the public moneys from it. They have also referred to several political topics, not immediately connected with legislation, but relating to a national convention, and the nomination of candidates for the first offices in this Government. On all of which subjects, (Mr. M. said) they had expressed their sentiments so much more fully, and so much better than he could in any condensed remarks he might make, that he would ask for their reading.

The hour being late, the motion for reading was withdrawn, and the proceedings were ordered to be printed, and laid on the table.

Mr. BARNITZ, a memorial from inhabitants of York county, in favor of the restoration of the deposites and recharter of the bank.

Mr. THOMAS, a memorial from Washington county, in Maryland. Also, from the Presidents and Directors of three banks in Frederick county, Maryland, in favor of, and certain resolutions entered into by the Legislature of Maryland, protesting against, a restoration of the deposites, &c.

Mr. CARMICHAEL, a memorial from inhabitants of Prince George's county, in favor of the restoration of the deposites.

Mr. TURNER, from 328 citizens of Baltimore county, in favor of the restoration of the deposites, &c.

Mr. BEALE, from Rockingham county, and Shenanhoah county, Virginia, against the restoration of the deposites.

Mr. BEALE said: Mr. Speaker, I present to you the resolutions of a people, who, in Virginia, in all the great struggles for political freedom, have been denominated the tenth legion of its democracy. Their resolutions approve of the withdrawal of the public money from the Bank of the United States, declare the unconstitutionality, illegality, and irresponsibility, of the Bank of the United States, and as therefore dangerous under a Government of limited powers.

It has been common upon the presentation of memorials and resolutions here, to say that they come from persons of all parties; not so here, those from a part of the county of Rockingham were unanimous—those from the county of Shenandoah were opposed by one dissenting voice, to one of the resolutions, amidst the affirmative sanction of hundreds of its bold yeomanry. But, Mr. Speaker, this large majority were of a particular party; they were of that party, and of that people and their descendants, who, in the days of the Revolution, fought against the British, the Indians, and the Tories, and aided in establishing upon a firm basis the rights of our race. They were of that party, who, under the auspices of Mr. Jefferson, effected the great civil revolution of 1800. They were of that party who sustained the Administration in the late war made for the rights of our sailors, and the liberties of the seas, and who did not then hold out false lights to the enemies of our country, and who in more modern times have rallied under no banner but that of the Union.

The SPEAKER, from Luray, in relation to the deposites.

Mr. WISE, from James City, complaining of the removal of the deposites, which they allege to be an unlawful assumption of power on the part of the President, and praying their restoration.

Mr. HALL, of North Carolina, from inhabitants of Washington, Beaufort county, for, and also one from Edgecombe county against, the restoration of the deposites.

Mr. BYNUM, from Halifax county, protesting against the restoration of the deposites and recharter of the bank.

Mr. CHILTON ALLAN, from Lexington, Ky., for the restoration of the deposites and recharter of the bank.

Mr. CHILTON, from inhabitants of his district, in favor of the restoration of the deposites.

Mr. HENDERSON presented the proceedings of a meeting held at Bellefonte, Centre county, Pennsylvania.

Mr. H. said this meeting was acknowledged to have been the largest ever convened in this county, and composed of the professional man, the substantial farmer, the manufacturer, and the mechanic. Amongst the many respectable names which he recognized was that of our distinguished fellow-citizen, the Hon. Andrew Gregg, whose name alone, at least in his own State, will command for those proceedings a respectful attention. He would only add, that it was highly gratifying to him to find that his course here, upon this all-absorbing question, had met with the approbation of so large a portion of his fellow-citizens, and that, without doing violence to his own opinions, he could cheerfully obey their mandates..

Mr. H. also presented the proceedings of a meeting adverse to those last presented.

Mr. H. said, though differing as he did, in many of the sentiments contained in these resolutions, he could cheerfully bear testimony to the respectability of the men whose names were signed to the paper; some of whom were too well known to require this humble tribute.

Mr. POPE presented a memorial and resolutions of 1083 inhabitants of Shelby county, Kentucky, deprecating the removal of the public deposites from the Bank of the United States, ascribing the present distress of the people to that cause, and resolving in favor of their restoration to that bank, and in favor of a recharter thereof, with such modifications as will meet the general sense of the people.

Mr. P. observed, that the signatures were evidently not the autograph of the memorialists, but were copied, he presumed, from the originals. He had no doubt, however, that it had been fairly done, inasmuch as the gentlemen who had forwarded the memorial to him, were of high character and worth. He had received the memorial on last Wednesday, and would have been much pleased if he could have presented it before the vote on the subjects of the memorial had been taken; but he was precluded from doing so by the rules of the House, which only permitted their presentation on Mondays. He said the people of Shelby county, as a body, were eminently respectable, industrious, and intelligent, and so were the memorialists as far as he knew them, and he regretted that he could not concur with them in all their views. He moved that the memorial be laid upon the table and printed.

Mr. LEAVITT presented sundry memorials for and against the restoration of the deposites, &c., from Harrison county, Ohio; also, one from Jefferson county, against the restoration of the deposites.

Mr. SPANGLER, from Tuscarawas county, Ohio, in favor of the restoration, &c.; and

Mr. CORWIN, from Warren county, in favor of the restoration, &c., praying Congress to take measures to restore the currency from its present state of depreciation.

Mr. MITCHELL, from inhabitants of twelfth congressional district, Muskingum county, in favor of the restoration of the deposites.

All the above memorials in relation to the deposites were laid on the table, and ordered to be printed.

Mr. BOON asked the unanimous consent of the House to submit a resolution to fix the day of adjournment for the present session.

A member objecting—

Mr. B. moved the suspension of the rule, to enable him to offer it. He subsequently withdrew it, but gave notice he would hereafter submit this resolution.

Mr. ASHLEY obtained leave to offer a resolution instructing the Committee on Commerce to inquire into the expediency of making Port Independence, in the county of Jackson, Missouri, a port of entry. Agreed to.

Mr. LYON, of Michigan, presented a letter from his Excellency Governor Porter, enclosing resolutions of the Legislative Council of that Territory, relative to taking a census of the people there, and praying Congress to authorize an extra session of the Legislative Council of thirty days, during the present year. Referred to the Committee on the Territories.

Mr. LYON also presented a memorial of the Legislative Council of Michigan, expressive of the views which that body entertain of the establishment of the southern boundary of that Territory. Ordered to be printed.

And on motion of Mr. WARD,
The House then adjourned.

IN SENATE.

TUESDAY, April 8, 1834.

Mr. HENDRICKS moved that the bill and amendment reported by the Committee on Roads and Canals, extending and repairing the Cumberland road through the States of Ohio, Indiana, and Illinois, be printed; which was so ordered. He gave notice that he should call the bill up for consideration on Thursday next.

Mr. SMITH, from the Committee on the Judiciary, reported a bill for the relief of Jonathan Blaisdell; which was read the first time, and ordered to a second reading.

Mr. SOUTHARD presented the proceedings of a meeting held in Clinton, Hunterdon county, New Jersey, approving of the course of the Executive with regard to the removal of the deposites from the Bank of the United States, ascribing the distress which prevails in the community to the action of that institution, and recommending that the deposites should not be restored, or the corporation rechartered.

Also, the proceedings of a meeting held on the same day, and at the same place, of a counter character.

Also, the proceedings of a meeting of citizens of the town of Morris, same county, of like tenor.

Also, a meeting of inhabitants of Cape May county, of a similar character.

Also, the proceedings of a meeting in Salem, New Jersey, of like import.

The first of which was read, and the reading of the others, on motion of Mr. PRESTON, was dispensed with, and the whole referred to the Committee on Finance, and ordered to be printed.

Mr. SILSBEE presented the memorial of sundry merchants of Boston, relative to the warehouse system; which was referred to the Committee on Commerce.

Mr. SILSBEE presented a memorial from New Bedford, Massachusetts, asking a restoration of the deposites to the Bank of the United States; which was referred to the Committee on Finance, and ordered to be printed.

Mr. SILSBEE, from the Committee on Commerce, reported a bill for the erection of a marine hospital in the city of Charleston, South Carolina.

Mr. TYLER presented the petition of Elizabeth Scott, which was referred to the Committee on the Judiciary.

Mr. TOMLINSON presented the petition of Peter Bradley; which was referred to the Committee on Claims.

Also, the petition of Carey Clark; which was referred to the Committee on Pensions.

Mr. McKEAN presented the memorial of the City Council of Philadelphia, praying a restoration of the deposites to the Bank of the United States.

Also, a memorial, of a similar character, from the county of Delaware, Pennsylvania.

The memorials were read, referred to the Committee on Finance, and ordered to be printed.

Mr. WHITE, from the Committee on Indian Affairs, reported a bill for the adjustment of the northern boundary line of the State of Missouri.

Mr. BLACK presented the petition of Charles Flinn; which was referred to the Committee on Public Lands.

Mr. KING, of Alabama, submitted the following resolution:

Resolved, That the Committee on the Judiciary be instructed to inquire into the expediency of authorizing the accounting officers of the treasury to credit the account of David McCord, late receiver of public moneys at the land office at Cahawba, in the State of Alabama, with the amount of money received by said McCord for the sale of public lands; and what was lost by Alexander Pope, by the burning of the steamboat Florida, while taking the same to Mobile, to deposite it in the Branch Bank of the United States, according to orders received from the Secretary of the Treasury.

The resolution was considered and adopted.

Mr. KING, of Alabama, presented the petition of Francis Stringer; which was referred to the Committee on Private Land Claims.

The VICE PRESIDENT communicated a letter from the Commissioner of the Land Office, transmitting a statement of patents for lands prepared for the signature of the President of the United States, in compliance with a resolution of the Senate to that effect.

Mr. KENT presented the petition of Charles Key; which was referred to the Committee on Pensions.

Mr. WHITE rose and moved (the morning business being disposed of) that the Senate proceed to the consideration of executive business.

Mr. CLAY hoped not. He thought there was nothing so urgent before the Senate as to make it necessary to omit going on with the business on the table.

Mr. WHITE said it was with great reluctance he would press the motion to the prejudice of the business of any gentleman. But situated as some of the executive business was, he thought he could not postpone it. Some of it required to be acted on; and on looking to the ordinary business for to-morrow, he feared, if he did not press the motion now, he might not have an opportunity of doing so for some days. The Senate knew what that business was, and if they believed there was any other business which ought to be preferred, he would acquiesce.

The motion was agreed to, on a division, 19 to 15.

When the doors were opened,

Mr. CLAYTON moved the consideration of the resolution providing a new rule of the Senate in reference to the presentation of petitions and reports, when called for in the order of the States.

Mr. CLAYTON urged the resolution to save the consumption of time and confusion resulting from several members rising at the same time.

Mr. CLAY, Mr. CALHOUN, Mr. KING of Alabama, and Mr. SPRAGUE, objected to the rule, as subjecting the President of the Senate to the tedious form of calling over all the States, which would cause as much delay as arose from the present mode of transacting the business of the Senate.

Mr. CALHOUN moved to lay the resolution on the table; which was disagreed to—yeas 17, nays 19.

Mr. CLAY moved an amendment, that after the reading the Journal the President should call for petitions and then for reports.

Mr. KING, of Georgia, expressed a hope that the elder members of the Senate would withdraw their opposition to the resolution, as it seemed to come principally from them, which he thought was to be attributed to superior skill and tact which they had acquired by long experience.

Mr. EWING then moved an adjournment, with a view of having a more full attendance of the Senate in considering the resolution. The motion was agreed to:

Yeas 21, nays 17.

The Senate then adjourned.

HOUSE OF REPRESENTATIVES.

TUESDAY, April 8, 1834.

Mr. CAVE JOHNSON reported a bill for the relief of Benjamin Oden; which was read twice, and committed.

Mr. R. M. JOHNSON, from the Committee on Military Affairs, reported the following resolution, which was agreed to:

Resolved, That, in consequence of the time which has elapsed since the establishment of the present system of discipline for the army and the improvements which have taken place in military science, it is expedient to have a revision of said system, and, therefore, that the Secretary of War be directed to cause a revision thereof to be made, and the same to be reported to Congress at its next session.

Mr. J. also reported a bill to allow further time to complete the issuing and locating of military land warrants to sundry officers engaged during the late war with Great Britain.

Mr. TOMPKINS, a bill for the relief of Simeon Meacham, of New York;

Mr. CAMBRELENG, a bill for the relief of Dominick Lynch; and

Mr. CHANEY, a bill for the relief of Francis St. Cyr;

All which bills were read twice, and committed.

Mr. CARR, from the Committee on Private Land Claims, reported a bill for the relief of Jacques Portier and others; which was read twice, and ordered to be printed.

Mr. CARR, from the same committee, reported a bill for the relief of the legal representatives of Isaac Williams, deceased; which was read twice, committed to a Committee of the Whole House, made the order of the day for to-morrow, and ordered, with the report, to be printed.

Mr. MASON, of Virginia, from the Committee on Public Lands, to which was referred the petition of sundry half-breed Indians, of the Sac and Fox tribes, in Missouri, reported a bill granting to them the reversionary interest of the United States in certain reservations of land occupied by them, and lying between the Mississippi and Des Moines rivers; which was read twice, and ordered to be engrossed for a third reading to-morrow.

Mr. WILLIAMS, a bill authorizing the President of the United States to run and mark the line dividing the territory of the United States from the State of Missouri; and

Mr. VINTON, a bill to renew the patent of Thomas Blanchard; which bills were read twice, and committed.

The House suspended the rule, to enable Mr. McKENNAN to submit the following resolution, which lies one day on the table for consideration:

Resolved, That the Secretary of War be instructed to furnish the House with a detailed estimate for the repairs of the Cumberland road, east of the Ohio river.

The House then took up the resolution submitted by Mr. MARDIS, in relation to the deposites.

Mr. CORWIN resumed his remarks. He adverted to the recent votes of the House, by which they had resolved that the Bank of the United States ought not to be rechartered, or the deposites restored to it, as showing some inconsistency with the vote appointing the committee of investigation into its affairs, and he argued that this must lend to a belief that the majority could not have intended to determine that their votes were to be considered as having made a final disposition of these several subjects; that, in fact, the charges brought against the bank would not amount to the crime of murder, but would settle down to one merely of assault and battery. Having reviewed the reasons of the Secretary of the Treasury until the expiration of his hour, he gave way, without concluding, to a motion by Mr. BRIGGS, for the special order of the day, being

The bill to provide for the settlement of certain revolutionary claims, commonly called the commutation bill.

Mr. CRAMER resumed, and concluded his remarks in support of it. After which,

Mr. CRANE, having obtained the floor, moved that its further consideration should be postponed,

and made the special order of the day for Thursday next; which motion prevailed.

On motion of Mr. POLK, the House went into Committee of the Whole on the state of the Union, Mr. HUBBARD in the chair, upon the bill making appropriations for the civil and diplomatic expenses of the Government for the year 1834.

The item appropriating $20,000 for clerkships in the State Department, having been read,

Mr. McKAY made some objections to it, and stated that, at a subsequent stage in the progress of the bill, he should move to reduce the appropriation to what it was last year.

Mr. POLK explained, that an allowance was made last year for extra clerkship, which was comprehended in this sum.

The item appropriating $500 in addition to the present salary of the chief clerk of the State Department, was read.

On motion of Mr. POLK, this item was stricken out.

Mr. VINTON, of Ohio, moved, under the instruction of the Committee on Patents, an amendment, adding to the salary of the machinist of the Patent Office $500, and to the messenger of the same office, $300.

Mr. VINTON represented that the duties of the machinist were more important than those of any officer in the Patent Office. His duties were of a higher grade than those of a mere copying clerk, and he proposed, therefore, to put him on a footing of a twelve hundred dollar clerk. The machinist was employed, not only in repairing and preserving the models, but in explaining their principles, and in giving information as to inventions made here and in foreign countries. Every member of Congress had had occasion, at some time, to visit the Patent Office, and the high qualifications of Mr. Keller, the present machinist, were well known to the House. The present salary of seven hundred dollars was fixed many years ago, when the business of the office was very small.

Mr. BURGES was sorry to differ from the gentleman from Ohio; but he could not consent, at this time of general embarrassment, to increase any salaries. The best machine makers in New England, at this time, if they can get employment at all, cannot obtain one dollar a day for their labor.

Mr. VINTON said that the embarrassments of the country had not diminished the expenses of living in Washington. If so, he had himself, in his own case, not had the good fortune to find it out.

Mr. McKENNAN asked a division of the motion.

Mr. WARDWELL spoke in favor of the amendment, and Mr. WILLIAMS in opposition to it.

The question being taken on the motion to increase the salary of the machinist, it was ascertained that a quorum had not voted, 61 voting in the affirmative, and 51 in the negative. The question being again put, the motion was lost; 58 to 71. The motion to increase the salary of the messenger was also rejected.

The next item was read, appropriating $1,400 as the salary of a clerk, to be employed in arranging the archives of the department.

A letter was read from the Secretary of State, explaining the object and importance of the appropriation.

Mr. J. Q. ADAMS moved to strike out the clause, on the ground, that, in an appropriation bill, no provision should be made for objects not authorized by special laws. He also objected to the clause, that it would be merely an entering-wedge to a new clerkship. If the chairman of the Committee of Ways and Means would bring in a bill to provide an additional clerk in the State Department, to be called the Keeper of the Archives, he would not say that he would not vote for it.

Mr. POLK said that it was not the practice of the early Congresses to introduce in the appropriation bills any new objects; but for the last twenty years it had been the constant practice. He alluded to many cases of the kind. A permanent clerk was not wanted for the object in view.

After some remarks from Mr. HALL, of North Carolina, and Mr. EVERETT, of Massachusetts, Mr. PARKER, of New Hampshire, said, that the proposition was to employ a person to do what the regular clerks of the office had neglected to do;

to have an industrious man to do what the clerks were too lazy to do. He would suggest to the Secretary of State the propriety of requesting his present clerks to go to the office at early hours, and do the business themselves. He had always found that the more laborers you employ, the less work you have done.

Mr. WILLIAMS opposed the amendment, and said that, with due diligence, the present clerks would do the duty, and save the expense.

Mr. R. M. JOHNSON spoke in favor of the appropriation. When we ask an uncommon diligence from others, said he, we should set the example ourselves. What had we done? We had taken our own compensation, and provided for no one else. After sitting four months, we had disposed, in part, of one question, and the disposition of the balance would probably take four months more. He expressed the hope that the House would proceed, to despatch business, without unnecessary debate, and be prepared to adjourn, at least at the end of six months from the commencement of the session.

After some remarks from Messrs. WAYNE, J. Q. ADAMS, MERCER, CHILTON, POLK, CAMBRELENG, HARPER of Pennsylvania, CROCKETT, EWING, and EVERETT of Vermont—

Mr. BROWN said an apprehension had been expressed, in the course of the discussion, that the adoption of the item under consideration, in its present form, might finally lead to the permanent establishment of another clerkship in the Department of State. He proposed to remove this objection to the form in which the appropriation was made in the bill, by offering an amendment, so that the 14th, 15th, and 16th lines should read as follows: "For arranging and preserving the archives of the Department of State, one thousand four hundred dollars."

After some remarks from Messrs. McKAY, Q. ADAMS, BURGES, and POLK,

Mr. GRENNELL moved that the committee do now rise, as it was evident that the House would not settle the question to-day. The motion was agreed to, 78 to 71, and the committee rose, and reported progress.

Mr. VANCE asked the consent of the House to submit a motion to lay on the table and print an amendment to the bill, which he proposed to offer at a subsequent stage of its progress. An objection being made,

Mr. VANCE moved a suspension of the rule; upon which motion the yeas and nays were ordered.

The question being taken, it was determined in the negative—yeas 105; nays 67, (not two-thirds;) and,

On motion of Mr. ANTHONY,
The House adjourned.

IN SENATE.
WEDNESDAY, April 9, 1834.

A message was received from the President of the United States, by Mr. DONELSON, his Private Secretary, upon executive business; and also a message from the President, transmitting a communication from the Commissioner of the General Land Office, responsive to an inquiry by resolution of the Senate of the 29th of March, relative to a treaty with the Choctaw Indians at Dancing Rabbit.

On motion of Mr. POINDEXTER, the message and documents were ordered to be printed, and referred to the Committee on Public Lands.

Mr. PRESTON called up his resolution relative to the treasury agent employed to examine into subjects connected with the removal of the deposites from the Bank of the United States; which, after being modified by the mover, was adopted.

Mr. TOMLINSON, from the Committee on Pensions, reported a bill, without amendment, from the House of Representatives, for the relief of David Page.

Mr. MOORE, in pursuance of notice, asked and obtained leave to introduce a bill for the relief of William Smith, administrator of John Taylor, deceased; which was read, and referred to the Committee on Public Lands.

THE FORCE ACT.

Mr. CALHOUN moved to take up for consid-

eration his bill to repeal the act of last session, commonly called the force act; which was agreed to.

Mr. CALHOUN then took the floor, and spoke at length in support of the bill; contending that, although the act would soon expire by its own limitation, yet that it contained principles which were entirely unconstitutional—principles which tended to consolidation, and ultimate despotism, and which it was disgraceful should remain on the statute book. When Mr. C. concluded,

Mr. CLAY and Mr. FORSYTH followed, in opposition to the repealing bill; and concluded by moving its reference to the Judiciary Committee.

Mr. PRESTON and Mr. POINDEXTER rejoined, in support of the bill; when the motion to refer was agreed to.

Mr. MANGUM then moved an adjournment. Which motion prevailing.

The Senate then adjourned.

HOUSE OF REPRESENTATIVES.
WEDNESDAY, April 9, 1834.

The following resolution, submitted yesterday by Mr. McKENNAN, was taken up, and agreed to:

Resolved, That the Secretary of War be instructed to furnish the House with a detailed estimate for the repairs of the Cumberland road, east of the Ohio river.

Mr. HEATH moved the suspension of the rules to enable him to offer a resolution in relation to the laws regulating the custom-houses. Negatived.

The House resumed the consideration of the resolution relative to the deposites, submitted by Mr. MANN.

Mr. CORWIN resumed his remarks, and spoke, without concluding, till the expiration of the hour.

On motion of Mr. POLK, the House proceeded to the

ORDERS OF THE DAY.

Several bills from the Senate were twice read, and referred.

On motion of Mr. POLK, the House went, by unanimous consent, into Committee of the Whole on the state of the Union, (Mr. HUBBARD in the chair,) upon the bill making appropriations for the civil and diplomatic expenses of the Government for the year 1834.

The question being on the motion of Mr. BROWN, of New York—

Mr. DICKSON spoke against the appropriation. Though small in itself, yet it was momentous in its consequences. The bill purported to be an appropriation bill, but, in fact, went on to create a number of new offices. Some of these offices he probably would be in favor of, if they were brought forward in a separate bill. He adverted to the clause in the bill providing for additional clerkships in the Pension Office, and contended that they were unnecessary. Thirty thousand applications had been decided upon by the Commissioner during the last two years, and therefore (he said) it must be supposed that the present number of clerks was sufficient to attend to three thousand applications, which, according to his calculation, were all which remained to be made. The amendment of his colleague did not do away with the objections urged against the entire clause, and in fact rendered it more objectionable, as it placed more of the disposal of the Secretary of State without any particular restrictions as to the manner of the appropriation.

Mr. JARVIS said it appeared to him that we had better confine this discussion to the matter immediately before us, which is the employment of an additional clerk in the Department of State, for which confirms confidence and for a specific object. These provisions respecting other departments were not now under consideration. The Secretary of State has applied to this House, through the proper committee, for a clerk to take charge of the archives of the office, and put them in order. And he tells you that it is necessary that they should be put in order. Not relying exclusively upon this statement, he had himself visited the department the morning, and satisfied himself that what was de-

sided by the Secretary was essential to the public interest. The evil represented by the Secretary was a growing one, and one of long standing. He imputed no blame to any one for this state of things; it probably existed originally from the want of sufficient force in the office.

Mr. J. also said that he had seen the Secretary, and conversed with him on the subject. He says that the present force in the department is barely equal to its amount of business. There was reason to believe that the work proposed could be done in one year. From what he saw, he should think that one clerk, in one year, working six hours a day, could do the business. It remained to be decided by the House, whether the papers should remain as they were, or whether they should be put in proper order.

Mr. LINCOLN opposed the clause entirely. He adverted to the language which the Secretary employed in his letter. He found, he says, the papers in the office in great confusion. The Secretary might have been contented with assigning his reasons for the appropriation, without reproving his predecessors for negligence of duty. He considered the remark of the Secretary as gratuitous, uncalled for, and ungenerous. It would have been enough for him to say, that there was a press of business in the office, without saying that he "found the office in a state of confusion." Mr. L. suggested that the time of some of the present clerks might be usefully employed in the business referred to. We had enough of political retainers on public bounty. Until we had men in office who adopt some other motto than that has belongs to the successful party, as the spoil of victory, &c., we should take care not to multiply offices. He was opposed to the creation or continuance of any office which was not indispensably necessary for the continuance of the administration of the Government. If work had been neglected, this was not the time to bring it up. It was wait a few months, and work will be cheaper. Clerks can be got at a lower salary. The work may be better done, and honest men better paid. This was no time for increasing the expenses of the Government. The revenue of the country is likely to prove inadequate to its wants. The Post Office Department was in debt, and its debts to be paid; in what manner, he left it to the advocates of strict construction to say. He would call the attention of the House to some facts which will show that the present was not a time to increase the burdens of the people. In a letter which had before him, from a town in Ohio, wheat was stated to be but fifty cents a bushel, and flour, two dollars and a half a barrel, could not find a market; one of the canal boats would stop running for want of freight. In another quarter of the State, there was the same depression of business. In the town of Worcester, Massachusetts, there was last year imported 10,000 barrels of southern corn, and 17,000 bushels of southern corn; also, a quantity of meat and grain from the West, of cotton from the South. Sixteen of the cotton mills which created the demand for this supply, had already stopped, and others were about

Mr. L. would be obliged (he said) to vote for proposition indicated yesterday by the gentleman from Ohio [Mr. VANCE] for the reduction of salaries of civil officers. His duty to the people would require him—though the calamity was expected—to vote for the reduction of his own as a member of the House. He feared that should be obliged to suggest another amendment to this bill. A committee was to go forth to ascertain where our money is. He hoped they would find, in the course of their investigation, the Bank of the United States was still a safe proper depository of the public funds, and they would so report to the House. He should, therefore, beg the chairman of the Committee of Ways and Means to consent to an amendment to fill, by adding the words "deposited in the United States Bank," after the words " to be paid of any money in the treasury not otherwise appropriated." If the bank, after a fair investigation, should be found trustworthy, the House will mainly agree that it is a proper depository for public money. He should not move this amendment with a view to delay the result of the investigation. He hoped the bank was prepared

to meet it, and that it would result satisfactorily. In the mean time, he thought the appropriations which are made ought to be subject to the same disposition as heretofore. He would not go into the question now. Before the subject was ultimately disposed of, he should take an opportunity to offer his views at large in regard to it.

Mr. HAWES was sorry (he said) that the gentleman from Massachusetts had taken this occasion to launch out in opposition to the measures of the Government. He admitted that the gentleman had been in a situation where he should have learned something of the forms of business, and this was the only thing in the gentleman's remarks in which he concurred. The sum of his whole argument was, not that the appropriation is unnecessary, but that the Secretary of State, in asking for it, cast a slur on former Secretaries. Mr. H. pointed to instances in which extra clerks were provided for in the State Department, in the appropriation bill, while that department was under the direction of the very gentleman [Mr. ADAMS] who made the motion to strike out this appropriation. But the gentleman had travelled out of his argument in order to attack the Postmaster General. He hoped that gentlemen would not make this attack here, without they were prepared to sustain it. If there was a deficit in the Post Office Department, the Postmaster General was not liable for it. It was owing entirely to gentlemen on this floor and in the Senate. The very members who abuse the Postmaster General here, are found every day cringing to him, and begging additional mail facilities for their respective neighborhoods. The accommodations which have been extended to the country by the Post Office Department, for a few years past, far exceeded those of former years. He would repeat, that not the Postmaster General, but the representatives of the people, were to be blamed for the increase of the expenditure of the department. The gentleman said that he would vote for the reduction of the compensation of the members of Congress. I hope (said Mr. H.) that I shall always be ready to vote for any salutary reduction. But when the gentleman comes out in advance, and says that he will vote a reduction which is not under consideration, he induces us to suppose that he would not make the declaration, if he thought the measure would pass.

He should not have made these remarks if the gentleman had not gone out of his way to attack the Postmaster General. The time would come when the people of this country would feel grateful to Mr. Barry for the liberal and intelligent manner in which he had administered the affairs of the Post Office.

Mr. LINCOLN rose to explain that he had not alluded, in any manner, to the Postmaster General. He spoke only of the debts of the department, without saying whether this House or the Postmaster General had involved it in debt.

Mr. WARD said that he rose for the purpose of submitting a simple remark on the subject under consideration, with the view of making the honorable gentleman from Massachusetts acquainted with the fact, that the subject in relation to arranging and making indexes of the archives in the Department of State, was submitted to the House of Representatives, in the first instance, by Mr. Livingston, the late Secretary of State, in compliance with a call made upon this House, and not by the present Secretary of State, as that honorable gentleman supposes.

Mr. W. said that a resolution was introduced into this House, some two or three years ago, according to the best of his recollection—he did not remember the precise date, requiring the Committee of Ways and Means to inquire into the expediency of such a measure. That the committee thereupon addressed letters to the heads of departments, requesting their opinions upon the subject. In answer thereto, they gave it as their deliberate opinion that such a measure was absolutely necessary. At that time, the sum of $6,000 was inserted in the appropriation bill, to be applied to that object, which, as was stated yesterday by the honorable gentleman from Massachusetts, [Mr. EVERETT,] was lost in the Senate by reason of one of the members of the committee to whom the subject had been referred, having moved to strike it out, under the impression that the same item of appropriation was twice inserted in the same bill.

He said he had no doubt but that the Secretary of State was induced, from that circumstance, to ask for the appropriation at this time, and he considered that the honorable gentleman from Massachusetts [Mr. LINCOLN] had done great injustice to the Secretary of State, by observing that he had cast a reflection upon his predecessors in office, in his letter to the Committee of Ways and Means, which had been read. That letter does not cast the slightest reproach upon any of the gentlemen who have heretofore filled that high office, and the distinguished gentleman now at the head of the Department of State is incapable of making such a charge against any individual.

The attention of the late Secretary of State was drawn to this subject more particularly in consequence of the act of the 5th of May, 1833, which authorized the publication of the diplomatic correspondence from 1783 to 1789, and which, by a recent resolution of this House, is directed to be distributed. The voluminous papers from which the selections were made, had been deposited in the garret rooms of the Department of State in files once arranged and labelled; but from accidents and removals, the researches of historians, and the mistakes or neglect of those who from time to time had access to the papers, in restoring them to the proper files, a perfect sense of confusion existed, and no man living could tell what papers were in the garret rooms or what were missing. They were therefore obliged to open every bundle of papers, with little regard to their labels, and from the vast mass, to select everything which bore upon the diplomacy of the country for that period.

During the progress of this work an act of Congress was passed authorizing the publication of the Documentary History of the United States, which will embrace a large proportion of the revolutionary papers. These must be selected and prepared for the press. A contract has been made with Messrs. Clarke and Force by the late Secretary of State to edit and publish the work, and unless the proper documents, most of which are now in the Department of State, are arranged or put in some order, the work cannot progress with the required facility, and the papers, old and worn as they now are, will sustain great damage without the contemplated arrangement and binding up in volumes. Among these papers, transcripts of which are now required for the Documentary History, are comprised not only the letters of the officers and agents of the government, civil and military, but a mass of other papers of infinite importance to the finances of the country. The reports of all the various committees of Congress from 1775 to 1789 on public affairs, and upon the applications of individuals, of which there is no record, and excepting a few printed reports, nothing exists but the original drafts of the reports of those committees. Of the same character are the letters and reports of the Board of War, letters and reports of the Board of Treasury and of the Superintendent of Finance, wherein a multiplicity of claims growing out of the revolutionary contest, were reported or decided upon, and some of which are kept alive to the present day. There is no record, nor are there duplicates of those papers. By arranging these papers and binding them in volumes, with suitable indexes, they will be preserved to future generations. Several volumes have been so arranged; but if the remainder are left as they now are, a few years more must ensure their decay and entire loss.

The honorable gentleman from Massachusetts [Mr. LINCOLN] seems to think that our finances are not in a situation to warrant this expenditure. This objection, a few years ago, might have been urged with some force, when we were indebted a hundred millions of dollars; but the expenditure of the small sum of $400 dollars, now that the debt is extinguished, for an object so laudable, and which all admit to be necessary, can carry but little weight with it.

The objection against its being inserted in the appropriation bill, might have been urged with greater plausibility, if this had been the first time appropriations had been made in this manner; but as similar provisions have been inserted in the course of the appropriation bills heretofore passed, Mr. W. said he should therefore record his vote in favor of it.

He said he would take this occasion to observe,

that he regretted that gentlemen should, in the course of their remarks upon almost every question before Congress, deem it necessary to cast reflections upon New York—a State which he was proud to call his native State, and one which he had the honor, in part, to represent. In the remarks made in the House yesterday, by the honorable gentleman from Indiana, [Mr. EWING,] he stated, in answer to some observations made by his worthy colleague, [Mr. CAMBRELENG,] that he presumed the appropriation was intended for some clerk to be appointed from New York; for that State, he said, came in for all the "loaves and fishes," which might account, he said, for his (Mr. CAMBRELENG's) being in favor of it.

[Here Mr. EWING explained.]

Mr. WARD said he could not believe that the remarks of the honorable gentleman had been made in any spirit of unkindness towards that State; but as he was in favor of the appropriation, he felt himself called upon to disclaim being governed by any such considerations, and be believed that his honorable colleagues were as free from any bias of the kind as himself.

Mr. W. said, that during the present discussion, he had ascertained from the "Blue Book," an official publication of the Department of State, and which contains a register of all officers and agents, civil, military, and naval, in the service of the United States, and which, in conformity with a joint resolution, is transmitted biennially to Congress, the remarkable fact, that the number of persons in office at the seat of Government from the great State of New York, does not exceed nine, and the aggregate of their salaries $12,000. The officers and clerks now employed in the several departments at Washington, have been appointed from the respective States as follows:

From Massachusetts	21	From Delaware	7
N. Hampshire	10	Virginia	53
Connecticut	10	N. Carolina	5
Vermont	1	S. Carolina	3
R. Island	1	Georgia	3
N. York (12,000)	9	Kentucky	6
N. Jersey	15	Tennessee	3
Pennsylvania	45	Ohio	2
Maryland	97		

It is, therefore, manifest, from this statement, that the State of New York, which contains nearly one-sixth of the whole population of the United States, and which pays into the treasury more than one-half of the revenue of the Government, has not a fair proportion of its citizens in office, and, instead of being censurable and obnoxious to the charge made against them by that honorable gentleman, have just cause of complaint; but he was happy to see that the patriotic and intelligent people of that State require no prompting from personal feeling or party considerations to do their duty to their State and to their country.

Mr. ARCHER said the gentleman from Massachusetts could not have well considered the effect of the observations which he had made as to the remark in the letter of the Secretary. That officer was one of the most high-minded and honorable men in the world, and was utterly incapable of casting a slur upon any of his predecessors in office. Mr. A. also remarked, that the object of the appropriation was not simply to arrange the papers, but to index them. This was necessary, not only for the accommodation of the department, but of the members of this House, and every one who had occasion to consult the papers in the department. He hoped some other occasion than that which was presented by this item would be taken for waging that ruthless war which was to be commenced upon the appropriation bills.

Mr. CHAMBERS spoke in opposition to the appropriation, on the ground that it was unnecessary and irregular.

Mr. POLK rose to call the attention of the House back to the question. To the objection that the bill would create offices, he replied by showing that it had been the usage of the Government to make temporary appropriations for extra clerk hire. The books were full of cases of this kind. The gentleman from Virginia [Mr. ARCHER] had saved him the trouble of vindicating the Secretary of State from the charge made against him. It had never entered the mind of the Secretary of State to cast censure upon any one on account of the condition of the office, and the remark in his letter could bear no such construction. The gentleman from Massachusetts insinuated that the appropriation bill would be made the occasion of another general bank discussion, by moving an amendment providing that all moneys appropriated should be paid out of the United States Bank He had rumors of this before. Does the gentleman speak his individual sentiments, or those with whom he acts? Are we to discuss the bank question again on this bill? He would not go into the subject yet, for it was not now before us. He hoped that on this single item the House would not indulge in a general discussion. If the item was approved, let us go on, and if not, let us strike it out, and go on with the bill. He was gratified to find that the gentleman from Virginia was in favor of making appropriations in the regular way, as heretofore.

Mr. BINNEY considered, that, as this service was one peculiarly called for by the Department of State, and upon grounds which could not apply to the other departments, he could see no good ground for reflecting upon the department for asking it at this period. He wished, however, that its language would be made more precise, to guard against any doubt of the intention being not to create a permanent office, but simply to do that which was at present matter of necessity. As it would be of public benefit, he wished to strike out the word "preserving," and insert, "for making indexes to."

After a few remarks from Mr. MANN, of New York, and Mr. HARDIN—

Mr. BROWN said that the question under consideration was upon the amendment which he had the honor to submit yesterday. That amendment applied to the form, and did not touch the principle of the appropriation. He was convinced that the proposition which the honorable gentleman from Pennsylvania [Mr. BINNEY] said he intended hereafter to offer, would carry out the views he entertained upon the subject more effectually than the amendment now before the committee. He would, therefore, withdraw his motion to amend, in order to afford the honorable gentleman an immediate opportunity to submit his proposition.

Mr. R. M. JOHNSON bore testimony to the efficiency with which, in his opinion, the various clerks in the departments performed the duties assigned them; for whenever he had come in contact with them, it was impossible, as he could say from his own experience, to find a set of men who were possessed of superior intelligence, capacity, and integrity.

Mr. FOOT said there was one objection to the appropriation, which was not to be overcome. It should be recollected, that this was the third session since a resolution had been adopted, calling on the Secretary to state the number of clerks, and distribute the labor to be performed. They had no answer to this; and, until that was given, he could not consent to vote for any increase to the number of clerks in that department.

Mr. McINTIRE said he would vote for the motion to strike out, because he believed the clerks were numerous enough, if called upon, to do the duty that was requisite. He had been acquainted with them and the nature of their duty for five years, and he thought they did not perform one-half the labor that might be done by the number of clerks employed. He would vote against both this appropriation and the one to increase the salary of the chief clerk.

Mr. CROCKETT complained that there was not the retrenchment under the Administration that was expected when it was brought into power, and he could see no necessity for making appropriations at all, whilst the law remained, or authorized the President to control the public funds.

Mr. BINNEY proposed his amendment, to strike out the words "preserving," and insert, "for making indexes to."

Mr. POLK said he hoped the amendment would prevail, as it was only meeting the views of the Committee of Ways and Means.

Mr. HARPER, of Pennsylvania, and Mr. POLK, mutually explained.

Mr. CAMBRELENG said, he hoped the amendment would be adopted. He desired to correct a misconception as to some remarks which he had made the previous day. What he then meant to say, was, that it was not in the power of the members, when in committee, to give to the subjects brought before them, the same full attention which they could bestow on them when in Committee of the Whole on the state of the Union.

The amendment of Mr. BINNEY was adopted.

Mr. CHILTON proposed another amendment, in substance, to provide that the amount in the item should not be paid, unless, in the opinion of the Secretary of State, the duty of the clerks could not be performed by them by devoting six hours, out of the twenty-four hours in each day.

Mr. VINTON remarked, that as it was evident the subject could not be then disposed of, he would move that the committee do rise.

The motion was negatived:

Ayes 72, noes 88.

The question being on Mr. CHILTON'S amendment—

Mr. BARRINGER said that he could not agree that it was proper the Secretary should be set as a watch over his clerks. He did not think the House should legislate in that small way; this he did not mean to say, from any feeling of disrespect to the honorable gentleman who proposed the amendment. But he desired that a law should be passed which would radically cure the evils complained of by the inefficiency—which he admitted in its fullest extent—of the present clerks. They were every day to be seen in the Hall of the House, on the avenue, and everywhere, but where they ought to be—in their offices.

Mr. CHILTON remarked, that the object of his amendment was mistaken by the honorable gentleman. It would be recollected, that the office hours of the clerks was from ten till three o'clock; his amendment only proposed to compel them to remain at their duties one hour longer. His main objection to the present appropriation was not so much to the amount, as it was on account of the principle involved, and which, if sanctioned, would go to multiply permanent offices under the Government, by means of appropriation bills.

The amendment of Mr. C. was negatived.

The question then recurring on the motion submitted by Mr. ADAMS, to strike out the item from the bill—

Mr. WILLIAMS said that as the amendment proposed by Mr. BINNEY, and which was adopted, did not substantially change the provision of the appropriation, or touch what he principally opposed it for—the amount appropriated by it—his objections were not removed, and he would vote to have it stricken out.

Mr. ADAMS rose to reply to the arguments adduced in opposition to his motion, and said that, as his objection was to both the form as well as the substance contained in the item, he regretted exceedingly that the member from Pennsylvania, [Mr. BINNEY,] for whom he had the highest respect, had, by his amendment, left the principle, which violated all the laws which had hitherto been observed in making appropriations, untouched. He contended that this was, in effect, giving extraneous aid to the bill making appropriations for the service of Government, and he warned the House, that if they sanctioned the principle of permitting items to be inserted which were foreign to the purport of their bills, that they should not be surprised if still more unconstitutional propositions should be made; from which he argued many manifest evils and abuses must inevitably ensue.

Mr. WILLIAMS moved that the Committee rise.

Mr. POLK opposed it.

The motion was negatived, yeas 68, nays 98 after which,

The question then being put on the motion of Mr. ADAMS, to strike out the 14th, 15th, and 16th lines, the motion prevailed:

Yeas 89, nays 70.

Thereupon the committee rose and reported progress.

And the House (at five o'clock) adjourned.

IN SENATE.

THURSDAY, *April* 10, 1834.

A message was received from the President of the United States, upon executive business, by Mr. DONELSON, his Private Secretary.

Mr. KANE, from the Committee on Private Land Claims, reported a bill for the relief of the heirs of William G. Christopher, and a bill for the relief of Antoine Cruzal.

Mr. MANGUM presented a memorial, signed by 103 inhabitants of Tyrrel county, North Carolina, praying a restoration of the public deposites to the Bank of the United States; which was read, referred to the Committee on Finance, and ordered to be printed.

The VICE PRESIDENT presented a communication from the Secretary of War, transmitting a report of the Commissioner on Indian Affairs, relative to the Choctaw treaty of the 3d of March last; which, on motion of Mr. GRUNDY, was ordered to be printed.

Mr. SHEPLEY presented a memorial, signed by 634 inhabitants of the towns of Gardiner and Pittston, in Maine, praying the interposition of Congress in regulating the currency of the country, and also the passage of a law creating a Bank of the United States. The memorial was read, referred to the Committee on Finance, and ordered to be printed.

Mr. CLAYTON, from the Committee on the Judiciary, reported a bill for the relief of Tench Ringgold, formerly marshal of the District of Columbia.

The resolution offered by Mr. LINN was taken up, modified on motion of Mr. POINDEXTER, and adopted.

The report of the Select Committee, to whom was referred the contested election of the Hon. ASHER ROBBINS, one of the Senators from Rhode Island, being called up, it was, on motion of Mr. POINDEXTER, laid upon the table, and made the order of the day for Thursday next.

The report of the Committee of Claims, unfavorable to the petition of Joseph Clark, was read and concurred in.

The bill for the better organization of the Treasury Department, was, on motion of Mr. TYLER, laid upon the table.

The bill for the relief of John McCarty, of Madison county, Alabama, was taken up; when Mr. MAUDAIN requested that the report of the committee might be read, and then moved an indefinite postponement of the bill. Upon this question, the yeas and nays were ordered, and are as follows:

YEAS—Messrs. Clay, Clayton, King of Georgia, Knight, Leigh, Naudain, Smith, Southard, Sprague, Swift, Tomlinson—11.

NAYS—Messrs. Black, Brown, Ewing, Frelinghuysen, Grundy, Hendricks, Hill, Kane, Kent, King of Alabama, Linn, McKean, Mangum, Moore, Morris, Poindexter, Porter, Prentiss, Preston, Robbins, Robinson, Shepley, Silsbee, Tallmadge, White, Wilkins, Wright—27.

So the motion for indefinite postponement was lost, and the bill ordered to be engrossed and read a third time.

SPECIAL ORDER.

The Senate then took up, for consideration, Mr. CLAYTON'S resolution, adding an additional rule to the rules of the Senate, relative to the presentation of petitions and reports.

Mr. CLAY'S modification was adopted; when Mr. POINDEXTER moved a further amendment, that every petition and memorial, when presented, shall be referred, of course, without putting the question for that purpose, unless the proposed reference be objected to.

Mr. KING, of Alabama, then moved to lay the resolution on the table; which was not agreed to. The question recurring on the amendment, it was agreed to; and the resolution, as amended, was then adopted.

The bill authorizing a change in the location of the 16th section of the public lands in the several States and Territories, for the benefit of schools, was read a second time, and ordered to be engrossed for a third reading.

The following bills from the House of Representatives were ordered to be engrossed, and read a third time:

A bill for the relief of John L. Lobdell.
A bill for the relief of the legal representatives of James Morrison, deceased.
A bill for the relief of Mrs. Eliza, widow of Captain Paschal Hickman, deceased.
A bill for the relief of Whitford Gill.

The bill for the relief of William Walker and the heirs of Samuel Brown, deceased, was, on motion of Mr. KANE, laid upon the table.

On motion of Mr. EWING,
The Senate adjourned.

HOUSE OF REPRESENTATIVES.

THURSDAY, April 10, 1834.

Mr. ASHLEY reported a bill for the relief of Peter Elba and his assignees.

Mr. CHANEY, for the relief of Joseph Meade.

Mr. CONNOR, from the Committee on the Post Office and Post Roads, to which was referred the bill from the Senate entitled "An act authorizing the Governors of the several States to transmit by mail certain books and documents," reported the same without amendment; which bills were read twice and committed.

On motion of Mr. CHANEY,
Resolved, That the Committee on Roads and Canals be instructed to inquire into the expediency of granting to the State of Ohio a quantity of the unsettled lands in the counties of Fairfield, Hocking, Athens, and Washington, for the purpose of aiding the State in the construction of the Hocking Valley railroad, from Lancaster to the Ohio river.

On motion of Mr. OSGOOD,
Resolved, That the Committee on the Post Office and Post Roads be instructed to inquire into the expediency of establishing a post road from Ipswich, through Rowley, New Rowley, and West Bradford, to Haverhill.

On motion of Mr. SPANGLER,
Resolved, That the Committee on the Post Office and Post Roads, to which has been referred a petition praying for the establishment of a mail route from Cambridge, in Guernsey county, Ohio, through Liberty, in said county, to Plainfield, in Coshocton county, Ohio, be instructed to inquire into the expediency of extending said proposed mail route from Plainfield, in said county of Coshocton, to Coshocton, in the same county.

On motion of Mr. HEATH,
Resolved, That the Committee on Commerce be instructed to inquire into the expediency of changing the present custom-house regulations, in relation to mortgages of vessels, so as to require the collectors of the several ports to have recorded in the respective custom-houses such papers relating to vessels as may be deemed necessary to remedy any defect that now exists, and to guard purchasers from future impositions, should they be attempted.

On motion of Mr. BEAUMONT,
Resolved, That the Committee on the Post Office and Post Roads be instructed to inquire into the propriety of establishing a post-route from the borough of Wilkesbarre, by the way of the State road to Conyngham, and thence to Tamaqua, in Pennsylvania.

On motion of Mr. BURD,
Resolved, That the Committee on Military Affairs be instructed to inquire into the expediency of establishing a national armory in the counties of Bedford, Cambria, Huntingdon, Centre, or Mifflin, in Pennsylvania, as to said committee appear best.

On motion of Mr. WATMOUGH,
Resolved, That the Committee on Commerce be directed to inquire into the expediency of making an appropriation for the erection of a public hospital at Pittsburg, Pennsylvania.

On motion of Mr. J. J. ALLEN,
Resolved, That the Committee on the Post Office and Post Roads be instructed to inquire into the expediency of establishing a post road from Wright's mills in Jackson county, Virginia, by the way of Muse's Bottom, and up the Ohio river, to Bellville in Wood county, Virginia.

Resolved, That the Committee on the Post Office and Post Roads be instructed to inquire into the expediency of establishing a post road, from Hereford's ferry, in Mason county, Virginia, to Jackson Court-house in the State of Ohio, passing through Sim's Creek settlement.

Resolved, That the Committee on the Post Office and Post Roads be instructed to inquire into the expediency of establishing a post road from Everton, in the county of Lewis, by the way of the mouth of Leading Creek and Steward's Creek to Charlestown, in the county of Kenawha, Virginia

Resolved, That the Committee on the Post Office and Post Roads be instructed to inquire into the expediency of establishing a post road from Huttonsville, in Randolph county, Virginia, by the way of Clover Lick, to Huntersville in Pocahontas county, Virginia.

On motion of Mr. WILSON,
Resolved, That the Committee on Invalid Pensions be instructed to inquire into the expediency of extending, for a further term of five years, the half-pay pension heretofore granted by the act of the 16th April, 1816, to the widows of persons killed, or who died in the land service of the United States during the late war.

On motion of Mr. WILDE,
Resolved, That the Clerk of this House do cause to be arranged and digested the returns of the different State banks for the last year, so far as the same may be attainable; and that they, together with the abstracts and estimates herewith submitted, after the additions and calculations thereof are verified, under the direction of the said Clerk, shall be printed for the use of Congress.

On motion of Mr. BYNUM,
Resolved, That the Committee on Commerce be instructed to inquire into the expediency of making a survey of the harbor of Beaufort, North Carolina, a port of entry; and to provide for the appointment of an inspector thereof.

On motion of Mr. OSGOOD,
Resolved, That the same committee be instructed to inquire into the expediency of extending aid to a pier on Badger's Rocks to Salisbury Head, near the mouth of the Merrimack river.

On motion of Mr. GRENNELL,
Resolved, That the resolutions of the Legislature of Massachusetts, in 1831, in favor of the passage of a law by Congress for the more perfect organization of the militia of the several States, be referred to the Committee on the Militia, and that the said committee be directed to inquire into the expediency of exempting from the performance of militia service, as soldiers, in time of peace, all persons under twenty-one, and over thirty-five years of age.

Mr. WARDWELL submitted the following, which lies over one day for consideration:
Resolved, That the Secretary of War be requested to report to this House the persons employed in directing and superintending the construction of the Delaware breakwater, the compensation allowed, the services actually performed by each, from the commencement of the work until the present time.

Mr. LANE offered the following resolution:
Resolved, That the Committee on Public Lands be instructed to inquire into the expediency of aiding in the construction of a railroad from Lawrenceburgh, on the Ohio river, to Indianapolis, in the State of Indiana, by appropriating one or more sections of the unappropriated refuse land, situate in the counties through which said road will pass, and adjacent to said road, for each mile thereof; provided the same shall have been offered for sale and subject to entry for the period of fifteen years or more.

On motion of Mr. MERCER,
Resolved, That the Committee on the Judiciary be instructed to inquire into the expediency of prohibiting by law the sale of lottery tickets in the District of Columbia.

On motion of Mr. SPEIGHT,
Resolved, That the Committee on the Post Office and Post Roads be instructed to inquire into the expediency of establishing a post route from Newbern to the house of James Riggs, on Big River, in the county of Rowan.

On motion of Mr. BARRINGER,
Resolved, That the same committee inquire into the expediency of establishing a post route from Hillsborough, by Mount Willing, Rock Creek, Long's Mill, to Asheborough, in Randolph county, North Carolina.

On motion of Mr. CONNOR,
Resolved, That the Committee on Military Affairs be instructed to inquire into the expediency of authorizing, agreeably to a resolution of the Congress of 1781, the appropriation of $500 for the erection of a monument to the memory of Brigadier General Davidson, of North Carolina.

On motion of Mr. DEBERRY,
Resolved, That the Committee on Revolutionary

Pensions be instructed to inquire into the expediency of so amending the pension act of the 7th June, 1832, as to provide for such persons as were employed as artizans in the army, while in the militia or regular service of the United States.

Mr. W. R. DAVIS submitted the following resolution, the consideration of which, was postponed:

1. *Resolved*, That the powers of the Executive department of the Federal Government have been enlarged beyond the authority of the Constitution.

2. That the powers of the Executive department of the Federal Govenment are increasing, and ought to be diminished.

3. That the patronage of the President of the United States has increased, is increasing, and ought to be diminished.

On motion of Mr. GAMBLE,

Resolved, That the Committee on the Post Office and Post Roads, be instructed to inquire into the expediency of changing the mail route from Savannah to Augusta, so as to make it pass through Waynesborough, in Burke county.

On motion of Mr. TOMPKINS,

Resolved, That the same committee inquire into the expediency of establishing a post route from Franklin, in the county of Simpson, Kentucky, to Scottsville, in the county of Allen.

On motion of Mr. R. M. JOHNSON,

Resolved, That the Committee on Public Lands be instructed to inquire into the expediency of amending the law which authorizes scrip for land bounty, so as to provide for claims granted to revolutionary services, and located, surveyed, and patented in the State of Kentucky, and which claims have been taken by prior or better claims by the judgment of the highest judicial tribunal in that State, according to the construction put upon the original law by the Secretary of the Treasury, which embraced those claims.

On motion of Mr. R. M. JOHNSON,

Resolved, That the Committee on Pensions be instructed to inquire into the expediency of repealing that law which requires two witnesses to establish a pension for wounds received during the revolutionary war, placing all such cases upon proof satisfactory to the Secretary of War, as in other cases.

On motion of Mr. R. M. JOHNSON,

Resolved, That the Committee on the District of Columbia be instructed to inquire into the expediency of abolishing imprisonment for debt within this District, and particularly as respects small sums *under fifty dollars, and as it respects all females.*

On motion of Mr. DAY,

Resolved, That the Committee on Invalid Pensions be instructed to inquire into the expediency of placing the names of William Baden and James Harrington on the roll of invalid pensions.

On motion of Mr. MARTINDALE,

Resolved, That the Committee on the District of Columbia be instructed to inquire and report to •the House whether any, and if any, what provision ought to be made by law, for cleaning and keeping clean Pennsylvania Avenue.

Mr. MILLER submitted the following resolution, which was ordered to lie on the table:

Resolved, That the Committee on Revolutionary •Pensions be instructed to inquire into the expediency of granting pensions to the widows of such deceased soldiers of the Revolution as would, if living, be entitled to the benefit of the act of 1832: Provided they were the wives of the said soldiers at any time they were in service. And also to inquire into the expediency of granting the benefits of the said act to those who were engaged in the wagon service during the Revolution.

On motion of Mr. DENNY,

Resolved, That the Committee on the Judiciary be instructed to inquire into the expediency of making an appropriation to aid in the erection of suitable buildings in Pittsburg, for the accommodation of the United States Court in and for the western district of Pennsylvania.

On motion of Mr. LYON, it was

Resolved, That the Committee on Revolutionary Pensions be instructed to inquire into the expediency of establishing an agency for paying pensioners west of Green river, in Kentucky.

On motion of Mr. HARDIN, it was

Resolved, That the Committee on Revolutionary Pensions be instructed to inquire into the expedi-

---

ency of putting the names of Joseph Brown, of Bullit county, and Henry Shauntee, on the roll of revolutionary pensioners, and that the documents evidencing said claims be referred to said committee.

Mr. CHILTON submitted the following resolution, which lies one day for consideration:

Resolved, That in view of the general distress of the people of the United States and that commercial embarrassment which is carrying ruin to the door of the agricultural portion of our citizens, the President of the United States be respectfully requested to submit to the House a plan for a Bank of the United States, competent to all the duties which may be required by the Government, and which may be so organized as not to infringe on our own delegated powers, or the reserved rights of the States, and comprising all the advantages, and may not be subject to the objections to which the present Bank of the United States is liable in his judgment.

On motion of Mr. DICKINSON, it was

Resolved, That the Committee of Claims be instructed to inquire into the expediency of making compensation to George Brandon and Stephen White, citizens of Tennessee, for property lost during the last war.

On motion of Mr. WHITTLESEY, of Ohio,

Resolved, That the Committee on Commerce be instructed to inquire into the expediency of making further provision by law to compensate the collectors of the customs for their services at the ports on Lake Erie, and to equalize their pay.

On motion of Mr. VINTON,

Resolved, That the Committee on the Judiciary be instructed to inquire into the expediency of reviving the law for granting copy-rights to authors, so far as relates to the reports of the judicial decisions of the courts of the United States and of the several States, and of distributing the reports of the judicial decisions of the Supreme Court of the United States along with the acts of Congress wherever the latter are required by law to be annually sent.

On motion of Mr. LEAVITT,

Resolved, That the Committee on Roads and Canals be instructed to inquire into the expediency of authorizing a survey of a north-western national road from Washington, Pennsylvania, upon the most eligible route to some point on the Maumee bay, or its vicinity.

Also, that the Committee on the Post Office and Post Roads be instructed to inquire into the expediency of establishing a mail route from St. Clairville, in the county of Belmont, by way of Uniontown, Flushing, Morsfield, Freeport, and West Chester, to Port Washington, on the Ohio canal, in the State of Ohio; and from Knoxville, in Jefferson county, to Tunnell-hill Mill.

On motion of Mr. PINCKNEY,

Resolved, That the Committee on Naval Affairs be instructed to inquire into the expediency of providing by law for the abolition of the use of ardent spirits in the navy; also, to establish a naval depôt at Charleston, South Carolina.

On motion of Mr. CROCKETT, it was

Resolved, That the Committee on the Post Office and Post Roads be instructed to inquire into the expediency of establishing a post route from Totten's Wells, in Dixon county, by Seth Bradford's, to Troy, in Tennessee.

ADJOURNMENT.

Mr. BOON submitted the following resolution, the consideration of which was postponed:

Resolved, That the President of the Senate, and the Speaker of the House of Representatives, close the present session of Congress by an adjournment of their respective Houses on Saturday, the 31st of May next.

On motion of Mr. CAVE JOHNSON,

Resolved, That the Committee on the Post Office and Post Roads be instructed to inquire into the expediency of establishing a post route from Clarksville, Tennessee, to Cadiz, in the county of Trigg, Kentucky.

On motion of Mr. CAVE JOHNSON,

Resolved, That the Committee on Ways and Means be instructed to inquire into the propriety of making a further additional appropriation for removing obstructions from the Cumberland river.

On motion of Mr. DICKINSON,

Resolved, That the Committee on the Post Office and Post Roads be instructed to inquire into the expediency of establishing a post route from Readyville, in the county of Rutherford, by way of Hoover's Gap, to Beach Grove, in Bedford county.

On motion of Mr. BELL, of Ohio,

Resolved, That the Committee on the Post Office and Post Roads be instructed to inquire into the expediency of establishing a mail route from Senecaville, through Senecaville, to Zanesville, Ohio.

On motion of Mr. PATTERSON,

Resolved, That the Committee on the Post Office and Post Roads be instructed to inquire into the expediency of establishing a post route from Sandusky City, Huron county, by York Cross Roads, Seneca Reservation, Tiffin, and Ristoa, to Findlay, the seat of justice of Hancock county, Ohio.

On motion of Mr. MITCHELL, of Ohio,

Resolved, That the Committee on Military Affairs be instructed to inquire into the expediency of establishing a national armory on the waters of the Muskingum, Ohio.

On motion of Mr. SPANGLER,

Resolved, That the Committee on the Post Office and Post Roads be instructed to inquire into the expediency of making an appropriation of money to aid in the construction of a bridge across the Muskingum river, between the towns of Coshocton and Roscoe, for the purpose of facilitating the transportation of the United States mail. Also for the construction of a bridge across Vernon river, near the town of Mount Vernon, for the same purpose.

On motion of Mr. WHITE, of Louisiana,

Resolved, That the Committee on Commerce instructed to inquire into the expediency of making an appropriation to erect a light-house at the entrance of Bayou St. John, in Louisiana. Also, providing a salary and office-rent for the receiving of Port Ponchartrain, Louisiana.

On motion of Mr. KINNARD,

Resolved, That the Committee on the Post Office and Post Roads be instructed to inquire into the expediency of establishing a post route from Martinsville, Morgan county, via Lyons's, Mooresville, Bellville, Danville, and Lebanon, Frankfort, in Clinton county, Indiana; and to Shelbyville, via Greenwood post office, Port Royal and Mooresville, and thence to the house of vid Lindley, in Monroe township, Morgan county, Indiana.

On motion of Mr. CASEY,

Resolved, That the Committee on Roads and Canals be instructed to inquire into the expediency of making an appropriation for the improvement of the great post road from the bank of the Wabash river, opposite Vincennes, Indiana, by Palestine, Darwin, Paris, and Danville, to Chicago, on Lake Michigan, in Illinois.

On motion of Mr. DUNCAN,

Resolved, That the Committee on Invalid Pensions be instructed to inquire into the expediency of establishing a pension agency in the northern part of Illinois, and of granting pensions for years to the widow and heirs of each officer soldier killed in the late Indian war. Also, the Committee on Post Roads be instructed to inquire into the expediency of establishing a route from Danville to Dixon's Ferry, on the river, from Rushville to Pittsfield, and from Bluington to Springfield, Illinois.

On motion of Mr. McKINLEY,

Resolved, That the Committee on the Post Office and Post Roads be instructed to inquire into the expediency of establishing a post route from Benton to Pikeville, by way of Warren's, on Red road, and Samuel J. Wilson's, late Burleson's settlement, in the State of Alabama.

On motion of Mr. MURPHY,

Resolved, That the Committee on Commerce instructed to inquire into the expediency of making a further appropriation to improve the pass the harbor of Mobile, known by the name of Choctaw Pass, by widening the channel which been already opened under appropriations tofore made; that the improvement of the said may be completed.

Also, that the Committee on the Public be instructed to inquire into the expediency of making such changes in the land districts of calcosa and Demopolis, as may render the

offices more convenient to the purchasers of public lands.

Also, that the Committee on the Post Office and Post Roads be instructed to inquire into the expediency of establishing a mail route from Claiborne, by Rocky Mount, Gainstown, to Captain Cherry's in the fork of the Alabama and Tombigbee rivers.

On motion of Mr. MARDIS,

Resolved, That the Committee on Indian Affairs be instructed to inquire into the expediency of appropriating a sum of money sufficient to extinguish the title of the Creek Indians (in Alabama) to all undisposed of reservations to which they may be entitled by the treaty of June, 1832.

On motion of Mr. ASHLEY,

Resolved, That the Committee on Indian Affairs be instructed to inquire into the expediency of compensating Shubael Allen for damages sustained by the depredations of Indians committed upon his property.

Mr. BULL submitted the following resolution, which lies on the table one day for consideration:

Resolved, That the Secretary of War be requested to inform this House what part, if any, of the sum of thirty-nine thousand one hundred dollars was expended in 1832, in improving the navigation of the Missouri river, and that of the Mississippi river, above the mouth of the Ohio river.

On motion of Mr. BULL,

Resolved, That the Committee on the Post Office and Post Roads be instructed to inquire into the expediency of establishing a post route from Jefferson City, Missouri, to the county seat of Pulaski county.

On motion of Mr. LYON, of Michigan,

Resolved, That the Secretary of War be requested to communicate to this House the report of Captain Andrew Talcott, of the result of observations made by him during the past season, for the purpose of ascertaining the latitude and longitude of the several places in the vicinity of the northern boundary of the State of Indiana and Illinois.

Mr. SEVIER submitted the following resolution, the consideration of which was postponed:

Resolved, That this House will, on the 4th Tuesday of this month, proceed to consider such bills in the order in which they stand on the calendar, as relate exclusively to Territorial concerns.

A resolution heretofore submitted by Mr. WHITE, of Florida, calling on the President of United States for correspondence in relation to invasion of Florida, in 1812, '13, and '14, was read, considered, and laid on the table.

On motion of Mr. PEYTON,

Resolved, That the Committee on Revolutionary pensions be instructed to inquire into the expediency of allowing the legal representatives of James in compensation for a piece of artillery furfor the United States service during the revnary war.

BEATTY submitted the following resolution lies on the table one day for consideration:

olved, That the Committee on Roads and be instructed to inquire into the expediency instructing the Secretary of War to send an er to extend the examinations of the Cumriver from Nashville up to the falls on said with instructions to report to the next sesof Congress the result of his examination as practicability and utility of improving the ation of said river.

motion of Mr. MILLIGAN,

olved, That the Secretary of War be instructfurnish to this House a copy of Captain eld's report on the condition of the harbors Delaware river, accompanied by an estimate a repair and preservation of the same.

motion of Mr. JARVIS,

olved, That there be a select committee apd to examine and report to this House r the directions contained in the joint reso-of April 27, 1826, and July 14, 1832, have omplied with in the compilation of the Bi-Register, and whether any measures can be by which the intention of Congress, as by said resolutions, may be more effectuized; and also to inquire into the expe-having the Register published annually, biennially.

HILTON ALLAN submitted the follow-tion, which lies on the table one day for tion:

Resolved, That the Secretary of the Treasury be directed to report to this House the amount of appropriations made since the 6th April, 1832, (to include all from a report of that date,) under the following heads, viz. fortifications, light-houses, public debt, revolutionary and other pensions, internal improvements, including the building of piers and breakwaters, preservation of ports and harbors, removing obstructions in rivers and creeks, &c., and the support of light-houses, including all incidental expenses, the amount disbursed in each year, and in each State and Territory.

Mr. EWING submitted a project for a national bank, which was ordered to be printed.

COMMUTATION BILL.

The commutation bill was, on motion of Mr. CRANE, postponed, and made the special order of the day for Wednesday next.

The House, on motion of Mr. POLK, resumed, in Committee of the Whole on the state of the Union, (Mr. HUBBARD in the chair,) the consideration of

THE GENERAL APPROPRIATION BILL.

Mr. VANCE offered an amendment, to be inserted after the second line.

Mr. POLK considered it was not in order to do so now, or until the clauses in the bill were all gone through. This was the rule of the House.

Mr. VANCE understood that the rule applied to the sections in the bill, not to the clauses; and that it would not be in order to turn back, if the section was passed.

Mr. POLK read the rules of the House.

The CHAIRMAN decided that the bill should be taken up and progressed with where they last left off.

Mr. WILLIAMS considered it was always in order to amend a bill before the House. He dissented, therefore, from the views of the Chair.

After a desultory conversation as to the point of order,

Mr. VANCE offered an amendment to the bill, as follows:

Be it further enacted, That from and after the passage of this act, instead of the compensation now allowed by law, there shall be paid to the within named officers, the following sums per annum:

To each of the Secretaries, of State, Treasury, War, and Navy, four thousand dollars. To the Postmaster General, three thousand five hundred dollars. To each Assistant Postmaster General, eighteen hundred dollars. To each of the Comptrollers of the Treasury, two thousand dollars. To each of the Auditors of the Treasury, two thousand{dollars. To the Solicitor of the Treasury, two thousand dollars. To the Register of the Treasury, two thousand dollars. To the Treasurer, two thousand dollars. To the Commissioner of Indian Affairs, two thousand dollars. To the Commissioner of the General Land Office, two thousand dollars.

And that there be deducted from the compensation now allowed by law to the clerks in the Departments of State, Treasury, War, and Navy, including those in the General Land Office, at the rate of thirty-three and one-third per centum per annum.

That from all officers of the custom, by whatever name designated, or in whatever manner employed, there shall be deducted from the compensation now allowed to them by law, at the rate of thirty-three and one-third per centum per annum.

That from all officers connected with the system of the public lands, either as surveyors general, registers, receivers, or clerks, there shall be deducted from the compensation now allowed them by law, at the rate of thirty-three and one-third per centum per annum.

That from all the clerks in the General Post Office, deputy postmasters, their assistants, and clerks, there shall be deducted from the compensation now allowed to them by law, at the rate of thirty-three and one-third per centum per annum.

That from all persons connected with the Indian department, as superintendents, agents, sub-agents, interpreters, agents for removals, commissioners, or in whatever other manner employed,

there shall be deducted from the compensation now allowed them by law or regulation, at the rate of thirty-three and one-third per centum per annum.

That to the members of the Senate and House of Representatives, instead of the compensation now allowed by law, they shall receive six dollars per day, and six dollars for every twenty miles travel to and from the seat of Government. And that from and after the expiration of the present presidential term, the salary of the President of the United States shall be fifteen thousand dollars per annum.

Mr. VANCE said he was not in the habit of making speeches, and should not long detain the House. The measure which he proposed was his own, and maturely considered. From the present derangement of the currency, and the general depression of business, the salaries of the officers of the Government were actually increased in value to the amount of the reduction which he proposed. If we are coming to a specie currency, it can be proved, by arithmetic, that in ten years the office-holders would possess themselves of the whole wealth of the country, if they are not reduced. The office-holders ought, he thought, to sympathize with the people in their distresses and embarrassments. The price of all the property in the country was reduced 40 or 50 per cent. The President, with his salary of $25,000, which he was sorry we could not touch during his term, could now purchase, with his $25,000, $50,000 worth of the property of his confiding constituents. He wished to teach the men who have monopolized all the offices that they ought not to tamper with the interests of the community. He even thought that we ought to reduce our own pay, though he knew that the representatives in Congress were worse paid than any officers under the Government, and he was aware that it was advisable to keep the members above the reach of Executive influence. His own constituents did not depend upon office for support, and their whole industry was paralyzed. He had offered the measure without concern with any individual.

Mr. POLK hoped the House would vote upon the amendment at once.

Mr. WARDWELL offered the following amendment to the amendment:

From the compensation now allowed to the printers of the two Houses of Congress, there shall be deducted thirty-three and a third per centum.

Mr. VANCE said the public printing depended upon contract, but he would not object to it now.

Mr. PARKER hoped we should take the question first upon reducing our own pay.

Mr. BURGES said that the President and his friends in office had, by their measures, augmented their salaries fifty per cent., as every commercial men in the country knew. We could not reach the President, but we could reach those who were loudly vociferous in the praise of the measures which enabled them to possess themselves of the produce of the country at half its value. He was opposed to the reduction of the daily pay of members of this House. The pay of members was actually less now than the salary of a clerk, in proportion to our expenses. While we were here, we were obliged to support our families at home. It would be a discouragement to the middling interest man, whom he considered as the best legislator, to come to this House. The printers he would not touch, because with them we had a contract.

Mr. CHILTON asked that the question should be taken upon each clause of the amendment.

The question on reducing the salary of the President was first taken, and decided in the negative—Yeas 60, nays 88.

The question on reducing the salaries of the heads of departments was taken, (the members passing through tellers,) and determined in the negative—Yeas 54, nays 90.

The clause relating to the salary of the Attorney General was rejected, by a vote of 56 to 79.

The clause relative to the Postmaster General being under consideration—

Mr. VANCE would merely state, he said, in relation to this clause, that $3,500 was the compensation of the Postmaster General until a few years ago, when it was raised to $6,000, for the benefit of the man, not the office.

Mr. MERCER said, by raising this salary,

though he was *particeps criminis*, we had done great injury to this Government. It had caused the transfer of that officer to the Cabinet.

Mr. HIESTER moved to fix the salary at $4,000; which Mr. VANCE accepted as an amendment.

The question was then taken on the clause as modified, and negatived. Yeas 68, nays 89.

The clause relative to the Assistant Postmaster General was rejected without a count.

The clause relative to the Comptrollers was rejected, 58 to 77.

The clause relative to the Auditors was rejected without a count.

The clause relative to the Solicitor of the Treasury was rejected by a vote of 67 to 78.

The clause relative to the Register of the Treasury was rejected, by a vote of 53 to 76.

The clause relative to the Treasurer was rejected without a count.

The clause relative to the Commissioner on Indian Affairs being under consideration—

Mr. WILLIAMS asked what was the salary of this officer, and what were his duties?

Mr. VANCE stated that the salary of the officer was 3000 dollars, and that the duties were formerly performed by a clerk, Mr. McKenny, for a salary of 1600 dollars.

Mr. MASON, of Virginia, said he should vote for this amendment, for some reasons which he gave.

Mr. POLK remarked, that it was evident that an appropriation bill would necessarily be much embarrassed if we undertook to reduce and fix all the salaries. The proper way, according to the doctrines we heard yesterday, would be to refer the subject to a committee for examination and a report. He had voted against every clause, and should continue so to vote.

Mr. FOOT said a few words in defence of his doctrines on this subject, which he had maintained ever since he came to this House, when he was a member of the Radical Committee.

Mr. DENNY said that the gentleman from Tennessee was voting against the doctrines which he advocated yesterday.

Mr. CHILTON remarked that the subject, if referred at all to a committee, according to the suggestion of the gentleman from Tennessee, would necessarily go to the Committee of Ways and Means. There was no way to get a vote on the question, but the way which had been taken.

Mr. VANCE said he had not been here for thirteen years without knowing how this matter was going. There was a solid phalanx which would vote down every proposition, in order to keep the yeas and nays out of the House. Now, if the chairman of the Committee of Ways and Means would agree that he should have a vote on each of those items, in the House, by yeas and nays, he and his friends would not say another word on the subject. He saw how it would be. Gentlemen would meet the subject before the people by saying that the subject could not be introduced into an appropriation bill, at the same time acknowledging that the salaries ought to be reduced. Mr. V. said he was in Congress in the famous times of retrenchment, when the gentleman from New York near him, [Mr. CAMBRELENG,] and his associates, denounced the existing Administration for profligacy of expenditure. He went on to compare the expenditures of the last Administration with the present. He maintained, also, that the most salutary retrenchments which were ever made in this country, were made by amendments to the appropriation bills.

Mr. BEARDSLEY did not doubt the patriotism of the movers of the mover, but he regretted that he had taken an appropriation bill for offering his motion. There were many of the proposed reductions which he approved of; but he would not vote them as amendments to the appropriation bill. In the outset he had almost determined to vote for one item, the reduction of our own pay, which seemed to be hardly palatable to the mover himself. But he had determined not to vote for that as an amendment to this bill. He hoped that the House would proceed to vote on the several clauses of the amendment, without discussion.

Mr. MASON, of Virginia, made some explanations of his former remarks. He was in favor of all proper reductions, but he thought it improper

to embarrass an appropriation bill with the subject.

Mr. WATMOUGH wished (he said) to establish a strong and vivid sympathy between officeholders and the people, and he should therefore vote for every one of the proposed reductions. An appropriation bill was, he contended, the most proper opportunity for the people to take to make a stand in favor of the liberties which they had left. It was the only way in which a restoration of the Constitution would be effected. Mr. W. alluded to the principles on which the present Administration came into power, and to the promises of retrenchment, and called upon gentlemen to redeem their pledges. The people he represented would support him in refusing a single dollar of appropriation until the Administration retraced its steps.

Mr. LANE spoke at considerable length against the amendment proposed.

Mr. POLK rose, not to enter into the question, but to call the attention of the House to the fact, that the appropriation for the salary of the Superintendent of Indian Affairs was not provided for in the present bill. This showed the impropriety of attempting to fix a sweeping scale of reduction as an amendment to an appropriation bill. We had now been here two days engaged on this bill, a circumstance which was unprecedented since his recollection. We had, as yet, got only to the fourth clause of the bill, and at this rate we should be occupied with it two months.

Mr. BATES said he would agree to waive all discussion if the gentleman would consent to suffer the yeas and nays to be taken upon the amendment in the House. He spoke at some length in support of the amendment. He was not in favor of reducing salaries, but he thought that two dollars were now worth as much as three dollars were last year.

Mr. CHILTON spoke in reply to the gentleman from Indiana, [Mr. LANE.]

Mr. LANE explained and rejoined.

Mr. BATES made a few observations; when Mr. FILLMORE moved that the committee do now rise.

Mr. POLK hoped the committee would not rise until the vote was taken on the clause under consideration.

The motion to rise was rejected—77 to 84.

The question was then taken on the clause relative to the salary of the Commissioner of Indian Affairs, and determined in the negative—yeas 56, noes not counted.

Mr. MERCER moved that the committee do now rise.

The motion was agreed to—ayes 91, noes 73.

The committee rose, and reported progress.

The House then adjourned, at a quarter past four o'clock.

IN SENATE.

The VICE PRESIDENT presented the following communication from the Secretary of the Treasury; which was ordered to be printed:

TREASURY DEPARTMENT,
April 11th, 1834.

SIR: In obedience to the resolution of the Senate, of the 9th instant, directing the Secretary of the Treasury "to communicate to the Senate the 'name of any agent or agents employed by him 'to transact the business of the treasury with the 'banks selected for the deposite of the public funds; 'the nature of the duties performed by said agent 'or agents; the amount of the compensation paid 'for the discharge of the said duties, and by whom; 'and from what fund the said compensation is 'paid; and in pursuance of what law the said 'agent or agents have been appointed," I have the honor to state, that, for many years past, it has been the duty of one of the clerks of this department to attend to the business of the treasury with banks. The clerkship to which that duty is assigned has been filled for upwards of four years by Samuel M. McKean. He is appointed under the act of Congress of 20th April, 1818, and the salary to which he is entitled under that act is $1600 a year; and since the deposites have been removed, as well as before, he has continued to attend to the business of the department with

banks, without any additional compensation for such services.

If this clerk in the department is not to be considered as embraced in the call made by the Senate, no agent has been employed by me to transact the business of the treasury with the banks selected for the deposits of the public funds.

I have the honor to be, sir, very respectfully, your obedient servant, R. B. TANEY, *Secretary of the Treasury.*

Hon. MARTIN VAN BUREN, *Vice President of the United States and President of the Senate.*

PETITIONS.

The VICE PRESIDENT then declared (under the rule adopted yesterday) that petitions were in order.

Mr. TYLER presented the petition of Lieutenant Washington Seawell, of the Engineer corps; which was referred to the Committee of Claims.

Mr. TOMLINSON presented a petition, signed by inhabitants of the States of Connecticut, New York, and Massachusetts, interested in the commerce of Long Island Sound, praying an appropriation for the improvement of Black Rock harbor. Referred to the Committee on Commerce.

Mr. McKEAN presented a memorial, signed, and the proceedings of a meeting held by citizens of Blockley, Philadelphia county, sustaining the Executive in removing the deposits from the Bank of the United States, praying that they may not be restored, and that the corporation may not be rechartered; which was read, referred to the Committee on Finance, and ordered to be printed.

Mr. PRENTISS presented a memorial, signed by 1619 citizens of Rutland county, Vermont, praying a restoration of the deposites to the Bank of the United States, and a recharter of that institution; which was read, and the usual order of reference and printing made.

Mr. EWING presented a memorial signed by upwards of 2000 inhabitants of Franklin county, Ohio, and a memorial signed by 4310 inhabitants of the city of Cincinnati and county of Hamilton, in the same State, praying a restoration of the deposites to the Bank of the United States, and a recharter of said bank; which were read, referred to the Committee on Finance, and ordered to be printed.

REPORTS OF COMMITTEES.

Mr. POINDEXTER, from the Committee on Public Lands, reported, without amendment, the following bills from the House of Representatives:

A bill for the relief of Nicholas D. Coleman.

A bill for the relief of William Haslett.

A bill for the relief of James Kitchens.

A bill for the relief of the heirs of Crocker Samp-son.

A bill for the relief of William Enos.

A bill for the relief of William Hazard.

A bill for the relief of William O'Neal.

Mr. BIBB, from the Committee on Naval Affairs, reported a bill from the House of Representatives, for the relief of Andrew Armstrong, without amendment.

Mr. NAUDAIN, from the Committee of Claims, made an unfavorable report upon the petition of Archibald W. Hamilton; which was laid upon the table and ordered to be printed.

Mr. WRIGHT, from the same committee, made a similar report upon the petition of Samuel Lewis jr., upon which a similar order was made.

Mr. CLAY submitted the following:

Ordered, That the Secretary of the Senate be directed to cause to be ascertained and reported to the Senate, the aggregate numbers of all who have, or shall have, on the day of his report, presented petitions, memorials, or other proceedings to the Senate, in pursuance of what law the said agents or agents have been appointed, distinguishable the number appertaining to each petition, memorial, or other proceeding.

Modified as follows, at Mr. POINDEXTER's suggestion: "And specifying the city, town, county, and State from which the memorial or petition was received."

Mr. CLAY said he was desirous that this service should be performed, because it was of importance to have collected in one view the number of our fellow-citizens, pro and con, who have come here soliciting relief.

THE CONGRESSIONAL GLOBE.

PRINTED AND PUBLISHED AT THE CITY OF WASHINGTON, BY BLAIR & RIVES.

| 23d Congress, 1st Session. | SATURDAY, APRIL 19, 1834. | Vol. I........No. 20. |

Mr. WRIGHT said there were many considerations which would make this a very delicate duty to be performed by the Secretary. One he would name, which would be recollected by the Senate. A short time since, a memorial was presented by an honorable Senator, coming from the city of Albany, and he [Mr. WRIGHT] also presented another from the same city. The Senate ordered the names to these memorials to be printed. They came in from the printer the day before yesterday, and the one which was said to have been signed by 2900 citizens of Albany, was found to contain the names of but 1316. Where this mistake existed, he did not know; but there was a great mistake somewhere. Again, if such an order should be executed, the report ought truly to represent the classification and business of the signers. Further, the gentleman from Kentucky said himself had presented memorials from the city of Troy. He [Mr. W.] had also information from that country that mistakes of an important character existed there too. He mentioned this to show the necessity of gentlemen examining the names to the memorials which they presented. The Albany memorial which he presented, he said at the time, contained the signatures of 1700 persons; and he had since found that it had only 1606 appended to it, and therefore he would suggest to the gentleman, whether it would not be better, in view of these difficulties, to lay the subject on the table for a few days, with a view to some further investigation of it.

Mr. CLAY said he was aware entire precision was not attainable in the execution of the order; but an approximation was possible, and a mistake of some four or five hundred either way was of no material consequence. He believed there would be some difficulty in distinguishing all the fictitious names, or erasing them from the memorials. He was willing to take them all together. The gentleman alluded to the mistake in the memorial from Albany. But was it not possible that it might turn out that a portion of one memorial had been detached from it and added to his? Something like this had recently occurred in Philadelphia, where a long memorial had been got up relative to the incorporation, by the State of Pennsylvania, of the Dyotville Glass Company. A portion of that list of signatures had been cut off and attached to a deposite memorial, and sent here. As to mistakes, they would be corrected by the adoption of the order.

Mr. WRIGHT took leave to say that the gentleman from Kentucky did him injustice in the imputation that he had any agency in cutting off any part of the memorial alluded to.

Mr. CLAY disclaimed any allusion to the honorable gentleman; he only intimated that such a thing might be done.

Mr. WRIGHT resumed. He believed he understood the remark as it was meant. He never, since he had been a member of the Senate, made any reflection upon any petition or name upon one. He thought, however, that the report ought to give the names in classes according to their several occupations; he had no objection to the order with such an explanation going with it. If there was such a mistake as he had mentioned in the Albany memorial, should it not be explained?

Mr. KING, of Alabama, said the gentleman from Kentucky must be aware that it was not proper to act now on this subject. Many of these memorials had been referred to the Committee on Finance, where they would remain until their report was brought back, and they were therefore not within the control of the Secretary. If the object were, not to act on the subject till the committee reported, he had no objection. If it was only to extend to the printed memorials, it might be done, but not to those which had been referred.

Mr. CLAY observed that there was always such free intercourse between the committees and officers of the Senate, that there would be no difficulty in having access to the papers, and ascertaining all that was in them.

The order was adopted.

The CHAIR presented a communication from the Secretary of War, transmitting a statement of the expenditures made in the year 1833, at the national armories.

On motion of Mr. POINDEXTER,

The Senate took up the resolution submitted by him a few days since, for the printing of one thousand copies of the Journal of the Old Congress, with a compendious index for the use of the Senate.

Upon this resolution a debate of some length ensued, in which Messrs. SOUTHARD, KING of Georgia, POINDEXTER, EWING, BIBB, and SHEPLEY participated, when, without taking the question, at four o'clock.

Mr. MORRIS moved an adjournment, but gave way to

Mr. POINDEXTER, upon whose motion, it was ordered, that when the Senate adjourn, it adjourn until Monday.

On motion of Mr. MORRIS, the Senate then adjourned.

HOUSE OF REPRESENTATIVES.

Friday, April 11, 1834.

Mr. ELISHA WHITTLESEY, from the Committee of Claims, made unfavorable reports on the cases of William Jett and John Kutts; and

Mr. EVANS, from the Committee on Invalid Pensions, on the case of John Perham; which were read and laid on the table.

Mr. ADAMS, of New York, from the same committee, reported a bill granting a pension to Luke Voorhies.

Mr. CAVE JOHNSON reported a bill for the relief of James Caulfield.

Mr. CHILTON reported a bill for the relief of Colonel Gideon Morgan.

Mr. PINCKNEY, from the Committee on Commerce, to which was referred the memorial of the City Council of Charleston, South Carolina, reported a bill for the repair and completion of the United States marine hospital, in the city of Charleston.

All which bills were severally read and committed.

The House resumed the consideration of the resolution offered by Mr. MARDIS, in relation to the deposites; and

Mr. CORWIN resumed and continued his remarks in opposition to it.

Mr. POLK moved the suspension of the rules, in order to move that the House resume the consideration of the civil and diplomatic appropriation bill.

Mr. WARD said he considered that the public business ought to be the first attended to, and therefore, he called for the yeas and nays on the motion.

Mr. WHITTLESEY, of Ohio, spoke of the urgent importance of the private business; and

Mr. POLK urged the necessity of going on with the appropriation bill.

The question being taken, the motion was negatived: ayes 92, noes 93.

The SPEAKER announced the order of the day to be the motion to reconsider the vote rejecting the bill for the relief of David Kilbourne.

On motion of Mr. WHITTLESEY, of Ohio, the further consideration of the motion was postponed till Friday next.

On motion of Mr. WHITTLESEY, of Ohio, the further consideration of the bill for the relief of Edmund Brooke, was read a third time.

Mr. ADAMS, of Massachusetts, opposed the bill.

Mr. WHITTLESEY, of Ohio, moved the postponement of the further consideration of the bill till Friday next.

A quorum not voting,

Mr. WHITTLESEY said there was manifestly a quorum in the House, and he hoped that the day would not be wasted.

Mr. HARPER, of New Hampshire, moved the indefinite postponement of the bill.

Agreed to, 92 to 65.

The following bills were read a third time and passed:

A bill for the relief of Francis Ogden;

A bill for the relief of the representatives of William Rogers, deceased;

A bill for the relief, in part, of the crew of the brig Sarah George.

The bill for the relief of Gaetano Carusi was taken up and further postponed.

The bill for the relief of Susan Decatur, being the order of the day, it was postponed.

The House went into Committee of the Whole on the bill to provide for the payment of property lost and destroyed while in the military service of the United States, during the late war with Great Britain, and for other purposes.

Mr. WHITTLESEY explained the object of the bill.

Mr. FILLMORE desired that the bill be read by sections.

Some discussion followed, in which Messrs. WARDWELL, HARDIN, WHITTLESEY of Ohio, FILLMORE, WILLIAMS, and STODDERT, participated.

Mr. HARDIN proposed an amendment, to restrict the granting of any compensation, unless in cases where the buildings were solely occupied by the military when destroyed.

Mr. DICKSON opposed this, and said he was inclined rather to enlarge than restrict. When in order, he would propose to alter the phraseology, so as to grant compensation where the houses had been occupied by the United States troops thirty-six hours previous to their destruction.

Mr. BEALE proposed to amend the amendment of Mr. HARDIN.

After further debate by Mr. MARSHALL and Mr. WHITTLESEY—

Mr. EVANS moved that the committee do rise.

The motion was negatived: Ayes 42, noes 57. No quorum.

Mr. VINTON moved that the committee rise and report the fact, that there was no quorum in attendance.

The CHAIRMAN having ascertained that there was a quorum in the Hall—

A motion that the committee do rise having been put, prevailed; whereupon

The committee rose, reported progress, asked and obtained leave to sit again,

And the House adjourned.

HOUSE OF REPRESENTATIVES.

Saturday, April 12, 1834.

On motion of Mr. KAVANAGH,

Ordered, That the Committee on the Post Office and Post Roads be discharged from the further consideration of the resolution of the Legislative Council of the Territory of Florida, respecting a road from St. Augustine to Cape Florida, and that the same be referred to the Committee on Roads and Canals.

On motion of Mr. CONNOR,

Ordered, That the same committee be discharged from the further consideration of the case of Matthew W. Mountfort, and that it be laid on the table.

Mr. WILLIAMS, from the Committee on Territories, reported a bill establishing the territorial Government of Huron; and

Mr. ADAMS of New York, a bill for the relief of Benjamin Leslie.

All which bills were read twice, and committed.

The House resumed the consideration of the resolution submitted by Mr. MARDIS in relation to the deposites.

Mr. CORWIN resumed, and concluded his remarks, by moving to amend the said resolution by striking out all after "resolved," and inserting in lieu thereof, the following:

"That the reasons of the Secretary of the Trea-

ury for the removal of the public deposites from the Bank of the United States are insufficient, and that it is inexpedient to enact a law requiring the Secretary of the Treasury to deposite the public moneys in the State banks."

Mr. CLAY rose and said, that as the House had, by their recent votes, expressed their decided opinion on the subject involved in the original resolution, as well as upon the amendment now proposed, it was surely unnecessary to revive a second discussion upon these subjects. He desired to have the attention of the House directed to the vast accumulation of other business yet to be disposed of, for which purpose, and with the perfect assent of his colleague, he now moved that the resolution be laid on the table.

Mr. VINTON demanded the yeas and nays on this motion; which were ordered.

Mr. McKENNAN said he must appeal to the courtesy of the honorable member from Alabama to withdraw his motion, in order to give those members who were successively cut off by the motions for the previous question, an opportunity of expressing their sentiments.

Mr. CLAY, however unwilling to refuse such a request, felt compelled, under the circumstances which he had stated, to decline withdrawing his motion.

Mr. CARR moved for a call of the House.

Mr. WILLIAMS demanded the yeas and nays on the call. Ordered.

The House having directed the call, yeas 152, nays 11—after some time spent therein—

Mr. WHITTLESEY, of Ohio, remarked, that as the hour (twelve o'clock) had arrived at which private bill business should commence on this day, by the rule, further proceedings on the call would not be of any service to the motion pending.

The proceedings under the case were then suspended. So the question on the resolution of Mr. MARDIS stands over.

The House having resolved itself into Committee of the Whole, (Mr. CLAY in the chair,) on the bill to provide for the payment of claims for property lost, captured, or destroyed, by the enemy, while in the military service of the United States, during the late war with Great Britain, and the Indian wars subsequent thereto, and for other purposes,

Mr. HARDIN proposed an amendment to the ninth section of said bill, which section was as follows:

"That any person who, in the time aforesaid, has sustained damage by the destruction of his or her house or building by the enemy, while the same was occupied as a military or naval deposite, or for barracks, under the authority of an officer or agent of the United States, shall be allowed and paid the amount of such damage: *Provided*, That it shall appear that such occupation was the cause of its destruction."

Mr. HARDIN proposed so to amend the ninth section, as to have it read, "occupied as a place of deposite for military stores belonging to the United States, or as barracks for soldiers, by order of an officer of the United States army." The amendment was agreed to by the committee.

Mr. WARD, of New York, then proposed by way of an amendment, a provision to extend the benefits of the bill to those who had sustained similar losses in the war of the Revolution.

This was resisted by Messrs. WHITTLESEY, WILLIAMS, HARDIN, FILLMORE, STODDERT, and PARKER, on various grounds—that the amendment could not with propriety be attached to this bill, without further very important modifications; in relation to the testimony which should be received by the Auditor in support of said revolutionary claims—that a measure for the liquidation and adjustment of this description of claims should come from the Committee of Revolutionary Claims, and contain all the safeguards which would be necessary for the security of the Government—that more than half a century has elapsed since these claims originated, and that without the most precautionary measures, the adoption of the amendment might produce great imposition and fraud—that by the resolution of the old Congress, this class of claims was rejected; and that, with the exception of a single case, Congress had not assumed, by its legislation, the adjustment and payment of claims for losses, &c., incurred during the war of the Revolution.

The amendment was sustained by the mover, Mr. WARD, and Messrs. EVERETT of Massachusetts, and HUBBARD of New Hampshire. It was urged that there was no good reason for the distinction between claims growing out of the last war, and claims growing out of the Revolution. The war of the Revolution was prosecuted for the benefit of the common country. That independence was attained by the treasure and by the power of every member of the Confederacy. That services were rendered for the whole country—that disabilities were incurred in sustaining the common cause of the Republic—and for these services, and for these disabilities, Congress have made provision. And that the principal reason why provision has not been made for remuneration for losses then necessarily sustained, must have been owing to the poverty of the national treasury, more than to the resolution of the Continental Congress, which has been referred to—that claims which existed for losses during the Revolution are as just and as honest as any claims for losses during the last war—and that no good reason exists why provision should not be made as well for the one as for the other—the length of time which has elapsed should not operate to bar them.

The amendment was, however, rejected by vote of the committee.

Upon his presenting amendments to the 10th section of a bill reported by the Committee on Claims, to provide for the payment of claims for property lost, captured or destroyed by the enemy while in the military service of the United States, during the late war with Great Britain, and the Indian wars subsequent thereto, and for other purposes, which 10th section of the bill, as reported by the committee to the House, provides, "That 'any officer, field or staff, volunteer, ranger, cav'alry, or other persons engaged in the campaign 'of eighteen hundred and eighteen against the 'Seminole Indians, or against any other Indians 'in the time of war since, who have sustained 'damage, without any fault or negligence on their 'part, respectively, by the loss of a horse, or neces'sary equipage, in battle, or by the loss of a horse 'that was wounded in battle, and afterwards died 'of said wound, while in the service:"

Mr. CARR proposed to amend that part of the 10th section above referred to, and cause it to read as follows: "That any officer, field or staff, volun'teer, ranger, cavalry, or other persons engaged in 'the campaign of eighteen hundred and eleven, on the Wabash, against the Indians, or against any 'other Indians in the time of war since, including 'the campaign of eighteen hundred and eighteen, 'against the Seminole Indians, and also the six 'companies organized by virtue of the act of Con'gress, approved the 13th of June, one thousand 'eight hundred and thirty-two, for the protection 'of the northwestern frontier; who have sustained 'damage, without any fault or negligence on their 'part, respectively, by the loss of a horse or neces'sary equipage, in battle, or by the loss of a horse 'that was wounded in battle, and afterwards died 'of said wound while in the service, or was stolen 'by the Indians and not returned, or otherwise 'lost, without any fault or negligence on the part 'of the owner," should be paid for in pursuance of the provisions of the bill as reported by the committee.

Mr. C. said, the reasons which influenced him to ask the adoption of the amendment which he proposed, were, that, upon examining the bill, he had seen what he considered an omission in the bill, in not providing for the payment of property lost by a very meritorious portion of our troops, who performed military service previous to the declaration of the late war, during the war, and subsequent to the close of the war with Great Britain.

It should be recollected that the campaign on the Wabash in the year 1811 was performed previous to the declaration of the late war; that the amendment which he proposed provides for the payment of property lost by individuals on that memorable campaign, which has not heretofore been provided for by law. Mr. C. said it was true that a law had passed, he believed in the year 1812, which provided for the payment of horses killed in the battle at Tippecanoe in November, 1811; but did not, he believed, provide for the payment of property lost by individuals at other periods of that campaign, while in the service of their country. Mr. C. said that the act of Congress approved the 9th of April, one thousand eight hundred and sixteen, providing for the payment of property lost, captured, or destroyed by the enemy, while in the military service of the United States, in the late war, did not provide for the payment of property for which his amendment proposed to provide; nor did the act of Congress, approved the third of March, one thousand eight hundred and seventeen. That act provided for the payment of any horse, mule, &c., lost while in the military service of the United States, when it shall appear that the loss was without any fault or negligence on the part of the owner, and extended to cases of property lost in the wars with the Indian tribes subsequent to the 18th February and prior to the 1st of September, 1815.

Mr. C. said he could not discover the reason why those individuals who had sustained loss of property in the campaign in the year 1811 upon the Wabash, should not be as fully and amply provided for as to their losses as those who had sustained loss at any period during the late war, and subsequent thereto. He believed that the services of those in the campaign of 1811 were as essential, and their achievements as beneficial to the security of the western frontier against a savage foe, as were the services of any portion of the troops in the late war. He believed that their services had been recognised by the Government, that those who had received wounds in the battle of Tippecanoe were entitled to receive pensions in proportion to their disabilities, and that the widows and orphans of those who fell in the battle were provided for in like manner with those who fell in the battle during the late war.

Mr. C. said his amendment also provided for the payment of losses sustained by sundry individuals who had belonged to and performed service in certain companies of mounted rangers, which had been organized by laws of Congress, passed during the war, and subsequent thereto, for the protection of the frontier. He said that those companies to which he alluded, who had done service in the late war, were composed mostly of citizens of the then Territories of Missouri, Illinois, and Indiana; that those troops furnished their own horses, and subsistence for them; they also furnished their own provisions, their own arms, ammunition, and all necessary equipage; and that these troops, for a term of two years, and some of them a longer period of active service, underwent many hardships and privations; were exposed to all kinds of weather; swimming creeks and rivers; encamping in the woods for days, weeks, and months, in bark camps, or under tents made of blankets. It was by the citizens of the thin and scattered settlements of the Territories of Missouri, Illinois, and Indiana, and under circumstances like these, that a frontier of some hundreds of miles in extent were mainly guarded, protected, and sustained, without whose exertions and vigilance that vast frontier must have been laid waste, and become a prey to savage violence.

It was a portion of these troops, with other citizen volunteers of the then Territories of Missouri, Illinois, and Indiana, who defeated and dispersed the Indians on the Illinois river in the late war. It was the rangers of Missouri, Illinois, and Indiana, who performed the task of hauling, with their own hands, some distance, every picket and stick of timber, out of which Fort Clark was built on the Illinois river, at Peoria Lake. After this service was performed, a part of those rangers were ordered to ascend the river in keel boats, for the purpose of destroying the Indian villages on the banks of the river. Being thus separated from their horses, which were running at large, being some hundreds of miles in the wilderness, where forage could not be obtained, several of them were stolen by the Indians or otherwise lost to their owners. On the return of those troops to their respective frontiers, two of these companies were ordered to pass through the wilderness, from near Fort Clark to Vincennes, on the Wabash; they left Fort Clark with seven days' provisions, and arrived at Vincennes on the seventeenth day after their departure from Fort Clark, subsisting on fall grapes and hazelnuts, for the greater part of ten days; that their

march was impeded by high waters; their horses having been without forage for several months, worn down with fatigue and starvation, several of them perished and were wholly lost to their owners.

Mr. C. said that these rangers were stationed, most of the time in which they were in the service of their country, at places distant from any settlement where forage could be had. That although the strictest vigilance was observed to keep secure their horses, yet a number of them were either stolen by the Indians, or lost without any fault or negligence on the part of their owners.

Mr. C. said, he thought it was doing nothing more than justice demanded, to pay those individuals who served as rangers in the late war, as well as those who served in the six companies organized in the year 1832, for the protection of the north-western frontier, for horses stolen by the Indians, died in the service, or were otherwise lost by unavoidable accident, without any fault or negligence on the part of the owner. It was for losses of this character that his amendment proposed to provide. He said that it was not on account of lucre or gain, in a pecuniary point of view, which influenced many of these individuals to leave their homes and their families, and volunteer in the service of their country. He observed that he thought he was tolerably well acquainted as to the claims which would be presented, if the amendment which he proposed were adopted, and was of the opinion that a very few thousand dollars would liquidate the whole of them; that although the sum would be small, and would not be felt by the Government, yet it would be of great benefit to very many worthy citizens, who had sustained losses, and whose constitutions (at least some of them) were much shattered, in consequence of the exposure and hardships which they endured while in the service of their country.

After various amendments were made to it, the committee rose and reported the bill, as amended, to the House.

The SPEAKER laid before the House a letter from the Secretary of War, transmitting a statement of the expenditures incurred, and the arms manufactured, in the national armories in the year 1833, prepared in conformity to the act of April 2, 1794.

Also, a copy of the map and report furnished the War Department by Lieutenant Allen, who accompanied H. L. Schoolcraft, Esq., to and beyond the sources of the Mississippi river, on a visit to the North-western Indians, in 1832.

Which letters were severally read, the report ordered to be printed, and laid on the table.

On motion of Mr. BARRINGER,

The House adjourned.

IN SENATE.

Monday, *April* 14, 1834.

PETITIONS.

Mr. CLAY rose, and said he was charged with the presentation to the Senate of the proceedings of a meeting of young men of the city of Troy, New York, and also a memorial from the city of Schenectady, in that State. The city of Troy was one of the finest of that succession of beautiful cities which decorate the banks of one of the noblest rivers on the globe—a city which had sprung up with astonishing rapidity, and at the time he visited it, he had never witnessed a more respectable, intelligent, and prosperous community than existed there. But the scene was now most sadly changed, and changed, too, by no fault of the population which inhabit that city; by no visitation of Providence upon it, but solely by the folly and wickedness of the rulers of the country. The resolutions describe the true causes of their distress, which we all know.

But there are other expressions of feeling and sentiment in these resolutions, which he estimated much more highly than those in relation to the pressure upon the community: they exhibited the spirit of freemen, indignant at Executive usurpation; and if the liberties of the country and our rights of property are sacrificed, he would ask of what estimate are our free institutions? These young men call for the times of Washington and Madison, and denounce that union of the purse and the sword which they have witnessed—a union which they say they would not tolerate in the Father of his Country, much less in any living mortal man. The memorial signed by the mechanics of the city of Schenectady, bore the signatures of eight hundred individuals, and a more skilful intelligent body of mechanics exist nowhere. It was brief, but it distinctly pointed out the causes of the distress, and asked Congress for the restoration of the deposites and the recharter of the Bank of the United States. By their letter to him, they said they were, in truth, what they represented themselves to be—working-men.

And now he desired to make a few observations upon the present state of things in the country. At the beginning of the present session of Congress, we found the Chief Magistrate of the nation in the uncontrolled and unlimited possession of the public purse; and at as early a period as was found convenient, resolutions were offered—one relating to the violation of the Constitution and laws, and the insufficiency of the Secretary's reasons for the removal of the deposites. Upon these resolutions a protracted debate ensued, which continued for three months, during which period honorable gentlemen were found sustaining the most dangerous and alarming doctrines, and amusing Congress by contending that the question presented was a question of bank or no bank. It was in vain that one gentleman after another rose in his place, and protested that it was a much higher question. It was in vain that member after member declared he would vote against the bank, but in favor of the restoration of the deposites. These resolutions were put to vote here, and the result was well known.

At the commencement of the session, the alleged distress was stoutly denied; it was said to be all panic; that there was no real suffering existing. But in the course of a very few weeks, gentlemen disowned these declarations, and members in their places were compelled to confess that they were mistaken; that deep and abiding distress did exist. But they said, take courage; let the question be settled, let the discussion cease, and tranquillity and prosperity will be restored to the country. Well, the question has been settled in some sort of way. In another House it has been evaded—merged in the previous question; and they have not met the true question at all. That branch of Congress which is regarded by the people as the especial guardians of the public purse, have evaded the real question, and, without determining on the sufficiency of the reasons given for the removal of the deposites, they have passed a resolution ratifying the uncontrolled will of the Executive authority. Did not every man know, that upon the doctrines which were urged here, there was but one hand, but one will, which governed, directed, and issued the public money?

But we were now told that all was settled; and yet what had occurred within one week after the settlement of this great question? Three banks in this District, all within sight of the dome of this Capitol, have blown up, producing a loss to the Government, by the bank in Alexandria, it is said, of some $30,000; and that sacred fund, the pension fund, had sustained a loss of $20,000 within a stone's throw of the Capitol. But the Executive was not satisfied with this. He had appointed a Secretary of the Treasury, who had been retaining his office three months, in defiance and in contempt of the Senate, not having deigned to send in his nomination for its consideration. When had such a thing ever occurred before? He ventured to say, never from the 4th of March, 1789, down to the present time. It was a most lamentable state of things, but one for which there was no remedy but that which was in the hands of the people themselves; and he warned those friends of the Executive who upheld his measures, to take heed from the things which had recently occurred, and retrace their steps. Recent events furnished a well-grounded hope that the virtue, intelligence, and patriotism of the people will prompt them to the rescue of their Constitution and laws, and he took the occasion to congratulate the presiding officer of the Senate upon the recent triumph of the Whigs over their opponents in the largest and most important city in the Union; they had obtained a victory, a most glorious victory, by the most important test—the ballot box. Eighteen months ago, the majority was 6000 one way—now that majority had melted almost entirely away. In a community of thirty-five hundred office holders, struggling between life and death, controlled by one will, and under one command, they had been defeated and prostrated. It was a triumph, a glorious triumph. And it was not the least pleasing thing to him, (Mr. C.,) and correct in historical accuracy, that it was a question between Whigs and Tories. When we looked back to the conflict between our fathers and our British ancestry, we saw on one side the expansion of Executive power, to the inculcation of the detestable doctrines of non-resistance and passive obedience; and what was the denomination of the other party? That party which was sustaining the cause of liberty, of equal rights, and opposing the gigantic strides of royal prerogative? The Whig party. And if we turned our attention to our own times, they would show that they were fully authorized in giving the same term to the party who opposed the new-fangled doctrines which were now engrossing all executive power in one hand. What were we contending for at this day? For the empire of the Constitution against that power which, if it prevail, will absorb the whole powers of the Government. It is the parental, watchful character of the Government, which gives it its true character, and he rejoiced at the recent event which tended so powerfully to give it that character. He would say persevere, and place your fine city at the head of the cities of the Union for the predominance of liberty and freedom, as it is at the head of commerce, the commercial emporium of the country, for without liberty you can have no safe or secure commerce. And he would also express a hope that the countrymen of Emmet, Macneven, and Sampson, will consider and review the course which they have taken, and not contribute to the establishment of a practical despotism here, which they have fled from in their own country.

And now he begged to say a few words to ourselves. We, as a Senate, can do no positive good, but we have it in our power to prevent much evil and to do a vast deal of negative good. Let it be a settled principle hereafter, that we will give our approbation to no nomination of a member of Congress to office, or at least till the Constitution and the laws shall be restored. He did not know whether any member of Congress was an expectant, and therefore he made no imputation upon any member of either House; but the maxim had been held by those in power, when they were out of power, and had been more signally disregarded since they came in power, than in any instance he had ever known; and as the best means of securing purity of purpose, he would never, while he remained here, or until the Constitution and laws be asserted, agree to the appointment of any member of Congress to any office, either at home or abroad, nor for any man who was a known, active partisan and electioneerer. Every incumbent in office had a right to enjoy the elective franchise, but he had no right to embody himself into any political corps. He would vote for no man who prostituted his office to procure a result in politics; and he hoped gentlemen would join him in opposing all approximations of usurpation and of power, and act worthy of an American Senate, and of American freemen, and hold up to freemen throughout the world one unextinguished light, steadily burning, in the cause of the people—in the cause of the Union—in the cause of the Constitution.

Mr. CLAY concluded by moving that the papers be read, printed, and referred to the Committee on Finance; which was agreed to.

Mr. SPRAGUE presented the petition of James Thomas; which was referred to the Committee on the Judiciary.

Mr. SILSBEE presented the proceedings of a meeting held in Salem, Massachusetts, sustaining the Executive in removing the deposites from the Bank of the United States, and opposed to the recharter of that institution; which was read, referred to the Committee on Finance, and ordered to be printed.

Mr. KING, of Alabama, presented a memorial of a citizen of South Carolina, engaged in the cultivation of the vine, and stating that the pine lands in Alabama, bordering on Mobile Bay, are well

adapted to the growth of the vine, and asking a small appropriation of these lands in order to test the experiment.

The memorial was referred to the Committee on Public Lands.

REPORTS OF COMMITTEES.

Mr. CLAYTON, from the Committee on the Judiciary, reported a bill to authorise the Secretary of the Treasury to compromise and settle the accounts of the United States with the Alleghany Bank of Bedford, Pennsylvania.

Mr. TOMLINSON, from the Committee on Pensions, reported a bill for the relief of George Lynch and others.

Mr. SILSBEE, from the Committee on Commerce, asked to be discharged from the further consideration of the petition of James H. McCulloch and others; which was agreed to.

Mr. MOORE, from the Committee on Revolutionary Claims, reported a bill from the House of Representatives for the relief of Margaret Ricar, without amendment.

Mr. BENTON, from the Committee on Military Affairs, reported a bill for the relief of John Hunter.

Mr. EWING submitted the following resolution:

Resolved, That the Secretary of the Treasury be directed to report to the Senate whether any of the banks which have recently failed in the District of Columbia had in deposite, or otherwise in their possession, any of the public money; and, if any, how much, at the time of their failure.

ORDERS OF THE DAY.

The resolution offered by Mr. POINDEXTER to print one thousand copies of the old Journals of Congress was laid upon the table.

The report of the Committee on the Judiciary relative to the President's message with regard to the pension agency, was laid upon the table, and made the special order of the day for Monday next.

The report of the Committee on Contingent Expenses on the subject of Mr. MANGUM's resolution repealing the order authorizing the purchase of documents printed by order of the House of Representatives, was agreed to.

The report of the Committee on Indian Affairs was, on motion of Mr. WHITE, laid upon the table.

The following bills from the House of Representatives were read, and appropriately referred:

A bill for the relief of Francis B. Ogden;

A bill for the relief of a part of the crew of the brig Sarah George;

A bill for the relief of the legal representatives of William Rogers, deceased.

The following bills were read a third time, and passed:

A bill for the relief of the legal representatives of James Morrison, deceased;

A bill for the relief of John L. Lobdell;

A bill for the relief of Whitford Gill—yeas 16, nays 14;

A bill for the relief of John McCartney;

A bill for the relief of the administratrix of Captain Paschal Hickman.

The bill authorizing a change in the location of the 16th section of public lands granted for the use of schools was laid upon the table, on motion of Mr. CLAY, by the following vote:

YEAS—Messrs. Calhoun, Clay, Clayton, Ewing, Frelinghuysen, Kent, King of Ga., Knight, Leigh, Mangum, Naudain, Prentiss, Robbins, Silsbee, Smith, Southard, Sprague, Swift, Tomlinson, and Wilkins—20.

NAYS—Messrs. Benton, Black, Grundy, Hendricks, Hill, Kane, King of Alabama, Linn, Moore, Morris, Porter, Robinson, Shepley, Tallmadge, Tipton, and White—16.

The following bills were ordered to be engrossed and read a third time:

A bill granting compensation to Charles Burkham, Thomas Moore, and others, for services rendered during the late war as spies.

A bill for the relief of John Clark and others.

A bill for the relief of Henry Oakes.

A bill for the relief of the heirs and legal representatives of John Ross, deceased.

A bill for the relief of John Shackford.

A bill making an appropriation for the construction of a road from a point opposite Memphis, Tennessee, to Little Rock, in Arkansas Territory.

A bill for the relief of John Maguire.

A bill for the relief of Thomas Ap Catesby Jones.

A bill for the relief of John Webber.

The following bills were laid upon the table:

A bill for the relief of Elizabeth Magruder of Mississippi, and

A bill for the relief of Abraham Forbes.

On motion of Mr. BLACK, the Senate adjourned.

HOUSE OF REPRESENTATIVES.

MONDAY, *April* 14, 1834.

Mr. BEAN, of New Hampshire, presented a memorial from Dover, New Hampshire, on the subject of the currency and the stagnation of business.

Read, laid on the table, and ordered to be printed.

Mr. EVERETT, of Massachusetts, presented a memorial from 1935 citizens of Salem, praying the interposition of Congress for the restoration of a sound currency. Also, a memorial of the same character from the town of New Bedford.

Which were laid on the table, and ordered to be printed.

Mr. BATES, of Massachusetts, presented a memorial from sundry citizens of the town of Springfield, Massachusetts, praying the restoration of the deposites. Laid on the table, and ordered to be printed.

Petitions were presented by Messrs. REED and J. Q. ADAMS.

Mr. OSGOOD presented the report and resolutions of a large meeting of citizens of the town of Lowell, in Massachusetts, on the subject of a national currency. Laid on the table, and ordered to be printed.

Mr. OSGOOD presented a report and some resolutions adopted at a meeting of the citizens of Lowell opposed to a recharter of the United States Bank, called without distinction of party. This report (said Mr. O.) was adopted by the citizens of a town which is known by reputation at least to every member of this House. No man who is all acquainted with the present condition of the northern portion of this Confederacy, as it regards the business and pursuits of its inhabitants, can be ignorant of the extraordinary growth, the rapid increase, and the unexampled prosperity of the great manufacturing town of Lowell. It is now scarcely more than eleven years since the first blow was struck, in laying the foundation of those works, which in that short period have raised up this town to be the manufacturing capital, not of Massachusetts only, but of all New England. During that brief interval of time, it has been changed from being the site of a few scattered tenements, into a wealthy, thriving, and populous city, embellished with all the arts, and abounding in all the comforts of life. It now contains more than twelve thousand inhabitants. Its population is of a kind to be deeply interested in the great question which now agitates the country. The importance of a well-regulated currency cannot fail to be perceived by those, whose daily subsistence depends upon an adequate supply of a sound circulating medium, and the profits of whose capital must be sensibly and immediately affected by the same cause. It seems to me, then, that this report is deserving of the deliberate consideration of this House. Without pledging myself to the adoption of all its views, I think I may safely say that it contains many sentiments which will be regarded with universal approbation, and some of the most important of them I will briefly notice.

It begins, sir, with the plain and undeniable proposition that the value of property and the prosperity of the community are intimately connected with the condition of the circulating medium; and that whatever affects the circulating medium must, to a certain extent, affect every article of commerce and every species of property. From hence, it deduces the high obligation of Government to regulate the currency by law, to put it beyond the power of irresponsible corporations to expand and contract it at pleasure, disturbing all the elements of commercial intercourse, sending ruin and distress through the community, and making men rich or poor as they choose. It then goes on to say that it is of the highest importance to the community to place the currency upon a firm and solid basis; that it should be sufficient at all times to supply the wants of a healthy business, but that it should not be so abundant as to tempt to overtrading, and to bring about, by natural and inevitable consequence, a scarcity of money, and those unfortunate reactions in business which so often afflict the country. It further states, sir, that gold and silver form the true basis of a currency; and that every departure from that basis tends to render the circulating medium unsafe. But it adds, what almost every one will be willing to allow, that it is impossible, under present circumstances, to adopt wholly, or even chiefly, a metallic currency; and that the only means now to be adopted, is one that will restrain the substitute for a metallic currency within proper bounds—that shall lead to a gradual increase of the metallic basis to such an extent as will place the currency of the country upon a safe footing. The report considers the establishment of a national bank upon proper principles, and cautiously guarded, as a measure highly beneficial to the country, in its present situation; and goes on to describe what it considers to be the proper business of such an institution. Its objects are stated to be of a two-fold nature—first, the collection and distribution of the public revenue; and, secondly, the facilitating exchange between different parts of the country. The State institutions are not considered adequate to the accomplishment of these objects; but they are considered in this report to be sufficient for all the purposes of a local currency. It is the opinion of those who adopted this report, that Congress ought not to invest the bank with greater powers than are absolutely necessary to carry into effect the objects for which it is to be created; that especial care should be taken that it be so guarded as not to interfere with the polices of the country; and that, in order to secure this great end, its charter should be limited to a term of fifteen years, and its capital should be less than half that of the present bank, which they think would be sufficient to meet the wants of the country, in relation to those objects for which it is to be instituted.

They think the bank ought to be located in the city of Washington, with power to establish offices of deposite and exchange in such places as the business of the country and the convenience of the Government may require; that no bonus be paid, and no interest allowed by the bank upon the public deposites; but that all the profits above six per cent. per annum upon the capital stock, shall be paid into the national treasury; that the Government shall have the right to subscribe for one-fifth of the capital, and the President, with the consent of the Senate, shall appoint one-fifth of the number of the directors.

These, sir, (said Mr. O.,) are some of the principal views taken in this report; and he now moved that it be laid upon the table, and to view hereafter, if there should be a committee appointed to consider the expediency of establishing a national bank, of calling it up, and moving its reference to that committee.

The motion was agreed to.

Mr. EVANS presented a memorial from the town of Gardiner, Maine, praying the restoration of the deposites. Read, ordered to be printed, and referred to the Committee of Ways and Means.

Mr. BURGES presented a memorial from the citizens of the town of Providence, protesting against the removal of the deposites. Laid on the table, and ordered to be printed.

Mr. PEARCE, of Rhode Island, presented a memorial, signed by sixteen hundred and sixty inhabitants of the city of Providence and its vicinity, approving of the course of the Administration in regard to the United States Bank and the removal of the deposites. He said that he had received the memorial since he came to the House from a highly respectable gentleman, which he received with the memorial, that all the signers are

inhabitants of the county of Providence, nearly all freeholders and voters; that they are the very backbone of the Democracy of the country; and, in point of intelligence and moral worth, would not suffer in comparison with the same number of signers of any memorial presented to Congress at the present session. Mr. P. said, since the memorial was put into his hands, he had examined the list of signers, many of whom he knew, and fully believed that what was said of all of them was correct.

Mr. P. also presented a memorial, signed by a great number of the citizens of Bristol, Rhode Island, approving of the course of the Administration in the removal of the deposites, and adverse to the recharter of the United States Bank.

He took occasion to say, that he had now a memorial in such a form as would be received by the House, that it was headed by a venerable gentleman, John D'Wolf, in every way as respectable as the Hon. James D'Wolf, his brother, whose name was at the head of the memorial from the county of Bristol, presented by his colleague on Monday last; that this memorial was also signed by Jacob Babbitt and Parker Borden, men highly respectable, who are (as is John D'Wolf) presidents of banks in the State of Rhode Island. He moved that these memorials be read, laid upon the table, and printed.

The SPEAKER presented a memorial from the town of Stratford, Connecticut, approving of the removal of the deposites, and protesting against the recharter of the bank.

On motion of Mr. HUNTINGTON, the memorial was read, laid on the table, and ordered to be printed.

Petitions were presented by Messrs. SLADE and EVERETT of Vermont, WARD, DICKSON, FULLER, and LAWRENCE.

Mr. BEARDSLEY presented a memorial from the town of Pittsford, Monroe county, New York, approving of the course of the Government in regard to the United States Bank, protesting against its recharter, and denying the existence of any public and general distress in that vicinity or within their knowledge. Read, ordered to be printed, and laid on the table.

Mr. LANSING asked leave to present certain resolutions adopted by the inhabitants of the town of Coeymans, in the county of Albany, and State of New York, in their annual town meeting assembled, against rechartering the Bank of the United States, and against the restoration of the public deposites to that bank.

Mr. L. said, before those proceedings are read, I ask the indulgence of the House, while I submit a few remarks in reply to, and explanatory of, some observations made by my honorable colleague [Mr. Selden] from the city of New York, when, a few days since, he presented a memorial of a different character from a portion of the inhabitants of the city of Albany.

The honorable member felt himself authorized to state, upon that occasion, that the memorial he then presented was signed by two thousand eight hundred persons. Mr. Speaker, I have been permitted to examine the original of that memorial upon the files of the Senate, and have myself counted the number of signatures found upon it. I now state to the House, from my own knowledge, thus derived, that no more than thirteen hundred and sixteen names are signed to the paper, as it now appears in possession of the Secretary of the Senate. Where my honorable colleague gets the additional fourteen hundred and eighty-four names which he purported to represent in the presentation of that memorial, he may, perhaps, be able to inform the House.

My honorable colleague (said Mr. L.) felt authorized further to state upon that occasion, that the memorial he then presented spoke the language and opinions of the people of the district from which it came, in opposition to the opinions and action of their representative here, and was the language of the constituents opposed to the act of their agent. I cannot believe, Mr. Speaker, (said Mr. L.) that the respectable committee who bore that memorial from Albany to this place, and who chose to make my honorable colleague their organ in its presentation to this House, authorized these representations as to the congressional district I have the honor to represent here; and I therefore consider the expressions wholly gratuitous, and as the opinions, or perhaps I might better say, the wishes, of the honorable member from whom they come.

Simultaneously with the presentation by my honorable colleague of the memorial before spoken of, I had the honor to present to the House a counter memorial, signed by fourteen hundred of the republicans of Albany, fully approving of the course of the Executive in the removal of the deposites, and against the rechartering of the Bank of the United States. I am personally acquainted with many of the signers of both memorials, and I recognise among the names upon each, individuals as respectable, intelligent, and responsible, as any of the citizens of that ancient city. I will not detain the House to go into minute particulars as to the individuals who have signed those memorials, but I will take the occasion to say, that with very few exceptions, the politics of the memorialists who sign both, are shown by the respective papers to be now what they were in 1832, the time of the last congressional election.

The district from which I come, is composed of the city of Albany and of nine country towns. The aggregate population of the district at the last census was 53,560; of this number of souls, 24,238 was the population of the city, and 29,322 the population of the towns. At the canvass in 1832, my opponent received a majority of about 100 of the votes of the city, and I obtained my election in the district by a majority of 182. Such was the evidence of the feeling of the district at that period. Within a few weeks past, town elections have been held in all the towns of the county composing my district, and those elections rather show an increase of strength on the part of the friends of the National and State Administrations, than any change unfavorable to them. These facts I have considered it a duty to myself and my district, to state explicitly, and having done so, I most cheerfully leave to the judgment of the House to say what credit is due to the declarations of my honorable colleague, that the language and opinions of the people of my district are opposed to the course and action of their representative in this body. To the judgment of *that* one of my colleagues I should be unwilling to submit the question, as he and myself might differ much more as to the obligations of the representative to those who elected him, than it is likely I shall differ with my most respected constituents, either as to what is my duty or their wishes.

Mr. LEE presented a memorial from citizens of Salem county, New Jersey, representing the distress growing out of the removal of the deposites, and praying the recharter of the bank. Laid on the table, and ordered to be printed.

Mr. WARD, of New York, presented the petition of Calvin Pollard, Lafever and Gallier, Isaiah Rogers, and Seth Green, praying for compensation for the draft of plans for the new custom house in New York.

Mr. SCHENCK presented the proceedings and resolutions of large and respectable meetings, held in the counties of Somerset and Hunterdon, New Jersey, approbatory of the general policy pursued by the Administration; also, praying that the United States Bank be not rechartered, and that the public moneys be not restored to that institution. Mr. S. said:

Mr. Speaker, in presenting these testimonials of public opinion, I beg leave to state, that with many of the gentlemen who composed the convention of Somerset, and with some of those who convened at the public meeting in Hunterdon, I have the pleasure of a personal acquaintance; and from what I know by reputation of others, I feel justified in assuring the House, that for intelligence, integrity, and patriotic attachment to the Constitution and laws of their country, they will suffer no disparagement by a comparison with an equal number of their fellow-citizens in any part of the Union.

The independent electors who constituted the meetings above referred to, are engaged in various pursuits. Many of them are farmers, who, with their own hands, cultivate the soil of which they are proprietors; and with manly independence, enjoy, as the reward of their industry, a comfortable competence. Enterprising mechanics have also embraced those occasions to declare their wishes and express their feelings upon this exciting topic—men, sir, whose hands are hard with useful labor, and whose hearts are warm with love of country, and who cheerfully earn their bread by the sweat of their brow, animated by the proud consciousness that they are American freemen. Professional men also united in manifesting their anxiety for their country's best interests. They know, from the history of former ages, that the inordinate desire of gain, and the accumulation of money in the hands of a few, have proved the bane of former republics. Seeing the same dangers impending over us, they are solicitous to avert the evil from our yet happy land. Mingling with the meeting, and excited with all the ardor of youthful aspirations for the welfare of their country, were to be seen the time-worn patriots and veterans of the Revolution, living witnesses of those deeply interesting scenes which transpired at that eventful period "which tried men's souls." They remembered, with profound concern, the great price which had been paid for American liberty; and they firmly resolved that the inestimable blessings which had been gained by heroic valor, undaunted courage, and unyielding perseverance, should not be sacrificed to sordid selfishness or pestiferous venality.

But, sir, it is not deemed necessary to detail the various interests represented at those assemblies of the people. It is enough to say, that men, highly reputable and personally interested in the various avocations which occupy the attention, and call into exercise the industry, of the community, participated in the patriotic deliberations of the respective conventions; men, sir, who are conversant with the occurrences of the day, and necessarily acquainted with the pecuniary condition of that part of the country in which they reside, so far as it can be ascertained by the usual intercourse between individuals, were convened upon those occasions. And, sir, they make no lamentation, nor do they utter a single expression indicative of a chilling panic or overwhelming pecuniary embarrassment in the resolutions which they designed to have presented for the consideration of the House.

If, sir, the amount of money in circulation be less than it was a few months ago, the people are apprized of the source of the evil, and will justly appreciate the motives of an institution which will thus unfeelingly exercise its power for the purpose of inflicting distress upon the community, in the hope of extorting an assent to recharter a corporation which the people have already condemned, and which they have determined shall not be tolerated. The decision expressed in the resolutions on the much-agitated subject of the United States Bank, I believe to be the deliberate and fixed opinion of a decided majority of the citizens of New Jersey. And, sir, I feel persuaded they will not be diverted from their purpose either by the fallacious promises of better times if the deposites be restored, or the menaces of want and ruin if the bank be not rechartered.

The issue of bank or no bank was fairly joined and distinctly understood by all the political parties of the country previous to the last presidential election. The reasons assigned by the President in his message returning the bill rechartering the United States Bank, was definitely submitted to the people. They canvassed with strict scrutiny that luminous document, and after full deliberation, rendered their verdict at the polls. The fact is notorious, that those opposed to the reëlection of the present Chief Magistrate reminded their fellow-citizens, in their speeches and through the press, that if the incumbent were sustained in the high office he then filled, the bank must go down. The intelligent freemen of this great Republic were, therefore, called upon by all parties to declare their wishes upon this subject, and they responded to the call by reëlecting that distinguished individual by an overwhelming majority. The conclusion is therefore irresistible, that the people, in their election franchise, indicated unequivocally their opinions and their wishes with regard to this institution.

I feel persuaded, sir, that a majority of the citizens of New Jersey have unabated confidence in the integrity and ability of the Chief Magistrate. And while they contemplate, in the history of his

past administration, the soundness of his political principles, the wisdom which has directed and the benefits which have resulted from his measures, they recognise in the course which he has pursued towards the United States Bank a patriotic solicitude to maintain the energy of the Constitution, preserve unimpaired the free institutions of our country, and avert those evils necessarily incident to large moneyed incorporations. Power is always more inimical to the freedom of individuals and the political privileges of the community when it is wielded by men either in their individual or corporate capacity when they are irresponsible to the people. Associations of individuals favored with peculiar privileges never fail to enlarge the sphere of their action by every means within their reach. Hence it follows they are impatient of control and ambitious for power, and when such influence is to be required by money, the direct tendency is to debase the moral feeling, by creating and cherishing a spirit of cupidity incompatible with patriotic disinterestedness, or the independence of freemen.

The constitutional power of Congress to incorporate a company of private individuals to make a monetary system to control the currency of the country, and locate their offices at pleasure throughout the States, without the concurrence of the State Legislatures, has been justly doubted by our most enlightened statesmen and ablest expounders of the Constitution, at every period of our history.

There cannot, I think, be any doubt entertained, at this time, that a large majority of the American people believe this potent corporation to be a dangerous excrescence on the body politic, originating in the idea of financial convenience, growing out of implication, and cherished by political expediency, until it has acquired a magnitude which threatens, by its contaminating influence, to corrupt public virtue, disturb social intercourse, pervert our political institutions, and paralyze the action of the General Government.

Sir, the facts which were developed by the committee appointed by the House of Representatives in 1832, to investigate the affairs and inquire into the conduct of that institution, created a "*vehement suspicion*" in the minds of the people, that the United States Bank did not confine its operations in the exercise of its corporate powers alone for the good of the community, by "*inoffensive usefulness*." And, sir, facts since disclosed have fixed the conviction deep in the public mind, that this institution, which was designed to be a fiscal agent of Government, and a source of accommodation to the commercial and trading portions of our fellow-citizens, has transcended its legitimate authority, and from being an agent, has employed its influence and pecuniary means to control public sentiment, and acquire supremacy and sway. Such a power, sir, is derogatory to our republican institutions, dangerous to our liberties, and will not be tolerated or sustained by an enlightened people, jealous of their high privileges, and tenacious of their independence.

Petitions were presented by Messrs. PARKER, POTTS, HIESTER, and BANKS.

Mr. HENDERSON presented resolutions from sundry inhabitants of Mifflin county, Pennsylvania, remonstrating against the policy of the Administration in regard to the United States Bank, and praying the restoration of the deposites and the recharter of the bank. Read, laid on the table, and ordered to be printed.

Mr. STEWART presented three memorials from citizens of the county of Fayette, praying the restoration of the deposites.

Also, seven memorials signed by 675 inhabitants of the same county, approving of the removal of the deposites, and deprecating a recharter of the Bank of the United States.

Also, the proceedings of a meeting held in the same county, with resolutions approving of the course of the Government in regard to the bank. All which were ordered to be printed, and laid on the table.

The SPEAKER presented a letter from George Wolf, Governor of Pennsylvania, transmitting the resolutions of the Legislature of that State on the subject of weights and measures. Read, laid on the table, and ordered to be printed.

The SPEAKER presented a memorial from Benjamin Phillips, on the subject of steam.

Mr. WHITE, of Louisiana, had (he said) read the memorial, and had personal knowledge of the memorialist, as a man of science, genius, and application. He moved the reference of the communication to a select committee. Agreed to.

Mr. ANTHONY presented the memorial of 324 citizens of Turbot township, Northumberland county, Pennsylvania, against the restoration of the deposites to the Bank of the United States, and praying a speedy decision of the question; which was read, laid on the table, and ordered to be printed.

Also, the proceedings of a large meeting held in Muncy, Lycoming county, Pennsylvania, approving of the course pursued by the National and State Administrations, in relation to the Bank of the United States, and deprecating the recharter of that institution, and the restoration of the deposites; which were read, laid on the table, and ordered to be printed.

Mr. BINNEY presented a memorial from 487 inhabitants of Union county, stating that they are laboring under great embarrassment, and praying Congress to adopt measures for the restoration of their former prosperity. Read, laid on the table, and ordered to be printed.

Mr. MILLIGAN presented the memorial of 736 citizens and legal voters of Kent county, Delaware, representing the unhappy influence which the removal of the deposites has had upon their business and pursuits, and praying their restoration. Also, resolutions to the same effect from citizens of the same county. Read, laid on the table, and ordered to be printed.

Mr. McKIM rose and said: I have been requested to present the proceedings of a meeting held in the 5th congressional district of Maryland, as also instructions to me, signed by 3715 voters of said district. As I admit the right of instruction, by the majority, when that majority can be well ascertained, the only inquiry which I deemed it necessary to make when I received these instructions, was, whether they were sanctioned by the signatures of a majority of the legal and qualified voters of the district; and this could only be known by an accurate investigation of the poll books. For that purpose, I proceeded immediately to Baltimore, as I did not feel at liberty to vote on any question affecting the instructions, while such documents as had been presented remained uninvestigated by me. That investigation has been made at my instance, and, in part, under my particular inspection. The result is, that of the 3715 signatures on the proceedings and instructions, there are 1802 of the names of the signers to the same which are not to be found on the poll books at the election held in October last, at which election sheriffs were elected for all the counties in the State. A difference of this remarkable character leaves me at liberty to make no other conclusion, consistent with what I believe to be the accuracy of the examination had in this affair, than that I am not instructed by a majority of the legal and qualified voters of the district, otherwise than by my election. I consider it my duty further to state, that if I had not received the instructions prior to the vote being taken on the resolutions reported by the Committee of Ways and Means respecting the Bank of the United States and the deposites, I should have voted with the majority on all the resolutions. I forbear all further remark, and ask that the proceedings and instructions be read, and laid on the table.

The papers were accordingly read, and laid on the table.

Mr. HALL, of North Carolina, presented some memorials from his constituents in relation to the deposites, which were laid on the table and ordered to be printed.

Mr. GRAHAM rose to present a memorial with resolutions, adopted at a meeting of the inhabitants of Burke county, North Carolina, held at Morgantown on the 27th of March last, which he then moved to have read, laid on the table, and printed.

The resolutions were in approval of the conduct of Mr. Senator Mangum for his prompt and manly vindication of them as signers of a former petition for the restoration of the deposites, &c., from offensive imputations which were cast on them by a Senator from Georgia; and they condemned the conduct of Mr. Senator Brown, for representing that these former proceedings came before Congress "in a questionable shape," &c. They resolved, "that the opprobrious epithets cast upon 'the proceedings of the meeting in January last, 'by the Honorable John Forsyth, a Senator from 'Georgia, a gentleman of known courtesy in de'bate, can only be accounted for by supposing the 'honorable Senator was more than ordinarily ex'hilarated, but whether from the influence of 'a 'pot-house' or the palace, this meeting deem im'material," and they approve of the bill for extending the charter of the Bank of the United States.

Mr. McKINLEY remarked that some of the matter contained in the resolutions was of such a character that the papers ought not to be received.

Mr. WAYNE suggested the propriety of having the motion to lay on the table withdrawn by the member from North Carolina.

Mr. GRAHAM withdrew his motion, for the purpose of giving members an opportunity to debate the subject.

The SPEAKER said the House were to determine, as the proceedings had been read, what disposition should be given to the papers.

Mr. WAYNE said it was the wish of many members that they should be again read, and he concurred with them in this desire, as it was his intention to move afterwards that the paper should not be received by the House.

The memorial and resolutions were read a second time.

Mr. WAYNE expressed his desire that the gentleman from North Carolina would withdraw the papers, or postpone any action upon them, as any debate which must arise would interfere with the presentation of other petitions.

Mr. GRAHAM said he could not accede to this, for he had a duty to perform to his constituents, who had a right to insist that their petition should be presented by him, and taking the usual course, that it should be laid on the table. The only words, as it appeared to him, at which offence could be taken, was the word "pot-house." This was a word the petitioners had understood was used by the honorable Senator from Georgia, in his place in the Senate, when he stated there that petitions were got up in such places. The petitioners, in using it, therefore, only throw the word back to the place from whence it came. It was not a word of their coinage——

The SPEAKER interposed. It was not in order to refer to the language used in the Senate.

Mr. GRAHAM renewed his motion to have the memorial laid on the table, &c.

A desultory conversation, as to the disposition to be made of the papers then arose, in which Mr. WILLIAMS, Mr. MERCER, Mr. WAYNE, and Mr. McKINLEY participated.

Mr. WAYNE finally moved that the papers should not be received.

Mr. McKINLEY moved to lay this motion on the table; which motion was agreed to.

So the question of the reception of the papers stands over for further debate.

Mr. GAMBLE rose to present a memorial from merchants in Savannah, against the removal of the deposites; and was proceeding to state at large the objects and contents of the memorial, when

The SPEAKER reminded him of the necessity of conforming to the rules of the House—which restricted members to a brief statement of their contents.

Mr. GAMBLE moved a suspension of this rule.

The House refused—ayes 56, noes 49. (No quorum.)

A motion to adjourn was negatived—ayes 48, noes 71. (No quorum)

Mr. PLUMMER moved a call of the House. Rejected.

Mr. WAYNE then renewed the motion to adjourn; which having prevailed, (the memorial stands over until next petition day,)

The House adjourned.

IN SENATE.

TUESDAY, *April* 15, 1834.

After the Journal had been read, a message was received from the House of Representatives, by

Mr. FRANKLIN, their Clerk, giving information of the death of LITTLETON PURNELL DENNIS, a member of the House from the State of Maryland; when

Mr. KENT rose and said: The message which has been just read, announces to you and to the Senate the death of the late Mr. Dennis, one of the Representatives from the State of Maryland, in the other branch of Congress. Already, Mr. President, our feelings have been repeatedly agonized by the sudden death of several of our associates in the legislative labors of the session, and the one that has just been made known to us is little less sudden than those that have preceded it.

But a few days since, and the deceased was busily engaged in the attentive discharge of the duties of his station, and he is now numbered with the dead! He is gone to "that bourn from whence no traveller returns." Truly has it been said that "in the midst of life we are in death!"

The deceased was a native of Somerset county, Maryland; a prominent member of a highly respectable family, in the fiftieth year of his age, and, although of a delicate constitution, was justifiable in looking forward yet to many years of usefulness and happiness. He was a member of the bar, justly esteemed in his profession, and always in possession of the confidence of his countrymen. His modest, unassuming, and retiring habits, could not conceal from them his good sense and high attainments; and early in life he was returned as a Delegate to the General Assembly of Maryland, and has been continued in the discharge of his legislative labors, with but little interruption, to the period of his decease.

Mr. K. concluded by moving the adoption of the following resolutions:

Resolved, That the Senate will attend the funeral of the late LITTLETON P. DENNIS from the Hall of the House of Representatives to-morrow at 12 o'clock.

Resolved, That as a testimony of respect for the memory of the deceased, the members of the Senate will wear crape on their left arm for thirty days.

The resolutions were adopted; when, on motion of Mr. KENT,

The Senate adjourned.

HOUSE OF REPRESENTATIVES.
TUESDAY, April 15, 1834.

After the Journal was read, Mr. STODDERT, of Maryland, rose and announced the decease of his colleague, the Hon. LITTLETON P. DENNIS, in the following terms:

Mr. Speaker: In announcing the death of LITTLETON PURNELL DENNIS, a Representative on this floor from the State of Maryland, I discharge a sad and solemn duty. Not a week has elapsed since he mingled in the deliberations, and cooperated in the active duties of this House: he now sleeps the sleep of death. What an impressive illustration of the instability of human life—" of what shadows we are, and what shadows we pursue." The deceased stood to me, air, in the double relation of colleague and friend. I knew him long and well. He was a useful, benevolent, and estimable man, and has finished his course in honor. He was no tame and ordinary character; and although his modesty may have delayed the development of his faculties for public service during his brief connexion with this House, his State is not left without proof of his legislative prudence and skill. He served her in both branches of her Legislature for many years, with honor and ability. He was well gifted by nature, well educated, and well principled. His native sagacity, sound judgment and decision, and purity of purpose, made him what he was, a capable and honest public agent. The brave, generous, open, and manly qualities of his nature, secured him the confidence and affection of the people among whom he lived, and made it their delight to honor him.

He is gone hence, sir, but his memory will survive, embalmed in the kindly regards of those who knew and appreciated his noble and manly qualities. An unembittered and untarnished by a single act of meanness, injustice, and oppression. He died, as he had lived, deserving and possessing the

warm-hearted esteem of many, the ill will of none. As the last act of respectful duty which it remains for friendship to perform, I move you, sir, the following resolutions:

Resolved, That the members of this House will attend the funeral of the late LITTLETON P. DENNIS, at twelve o'clock, m., to-morrow.

Resolved, That a committee be appointed to take order for superintending the funeral of LITTLETON P. DENNIS, deceased, late a member of this House, from the State of Maryland.

Resolved, That the members of this House will testify their respect for the memory of LITTLETON P. DENNIS, by wearing crape on the left arm for thirty days.

On motion of Mr. STODDERT, the usual notification was ordered to be sent to the Senate.

On motion of Mr. STODDERT,
The House then adjourned.

IN SENATE.
WEDNESDAY, April 16, 1834.

After the Journal was read, the Senate, on motion of Mr. KENT, adjourned.

The Senate then, preceded by the Sergeant-at-Arms, and headed by the Vice President, moved in procession to the Hall of Representatives to attend the funeral obsequies of the Honorable LITTLETON PURNELL DENNIS, late a Representative in Congress from the State of Maryland.

HOUSE OF REPRESENTATIVES.
WEDNESDAY, April 16, 1834.

The House met, pursuant to adjournment, for the purpose of attending the funeral obsequies of the Hon. LITTLETON PURNELL DENNIS, late a Representative in Congress from the State of Maryland.

The remains having been brought, under the charge of the Committee of Arrangements, to the Hall of the House, the usual services were performed.

At twelve o'clock, meridian, the funeral procession moved from the Hall of the House of Representatives to the place of interment, in the following order:

The Chaplains of both Houses.
Physicians and Clergymen who attended the deceased.
Committee of Arrangements:
Mr. Stoddert, Mr. Johnson of Maryland, Mr. McKennan, Mr. Coffee, Mr. Baylies, Mr. Wise, Mr. Fillmore.

Pall Bearers.		Pall Bearers.
Mr. Hubbard,		Mr. Huntington,
Mr. Allen, of Va.,		Mr. Briggs,
Mr Ashley,		Mr. Evans.

The family and friends of the deceased.
The members of the House of Representatives and Senators from Maryland, as mourners.
The Sergeant-at-Arms of the House of Representatives.
The House of Representatives, preceded by their Speaker and Clerk.
The Sergeant-at-Arms of the Senate.
The Senate of the United States, preceded by the Vice President and their Secretary.
The President of the United States.
The Heads of Departments.
Foreign Ministers.
Citizens and Strangers.

IN SENATE.
THURSDAY, April 17, 1834.

Several messages were received from the President of the United States by Mr. DONELSON, his Private Secretary, among them the following

PROTEST:
To the Senate of the United States:

It appears by the published Journal of the Senate that on the 26th of December last a resolution was offered by a member of the Senate, which, after a protracted debate, was on the 28th day of March last modified by the mover, and passed by

the votes of twenty-six Senators out of forty-six,* who were present and voted, in the following words, viz:

" Resolved, That the President, in the late Executive proceedings in relation to the public revenue, has assumed upon himself authority and ' power not conferred by the Constitution and ' laws, but in derogation of both."

Having had the honor, through the voluntary suffrages of the American people, to fill the office of President of the United States during the period which may be presumed to have been referred to in this resolution, it is sufficiently evident that the censure it inflicts was intended for myself. Without notice, unheard and untried, I thus find myself charged on the records of the Senate, and in a form hitherto unknown in our history, with the high crime of violating the laws and Constitution of my country.

It can seldom be necessary for any department of the Government, when assailed in conversation or debate, or by the strictures of the press or of popular assemblies, to step out of its ordinary path for the purpose of vindicating its conduct, or of pointing out any irregularity or injustice in the manner of the attack. But when the chief Executive Magistrate is by one of the most important branches of the Government, in its official capacity, in a public manner, and by its recorded sentence, but without precedent, competent authority, or just cause, declared guilty of a breach of the laws and Constitution, it is due to his station, to public opinion, and to a proper self-respect, that the officer thus denounced should promptly expose the wrong which has been done.

In the present case, moreover, there is even a stronger necessity for such a vindication. By an express provision of the Constitution, before the President of the United States can enter on the execution of his office, he is required to take an oath or affirmation in the following words:

"I do solemnly swear (or affirm) that I will ' faithfully execute the office of President of the ' United States, and will, to the best of my ability, ' preserve, protect, and defend, the Constitution of ' the United States."

The duty of defending, so far as in him lies, the integrity of the Constitution, would indeed have resulted from the very nature of his office; but by thus expressing it in the official oath or affirmation, which, in this respect, differs from that of every other functionary, the founders of our Republic have attested their sense of its importance, and have given to it a peculiar solemnity and force. Bound to the performance of this duty by the oath I have taken, by the strongest obligations of gratitude to the American people, and by the ties which unite to my every earthly interest with the welfare and glory of my country, and perfectly convinced that the discussion and passage of the abovementioned resolution were not only unauthorized by the Constitution, but in many respects repugnant to its provisions, and subversive of the rights secured by it to other coördinate departments, I deem it an imperative duty to maintain the supremacy of that sacred instrument, and the immunities of the department intrusted to my care, by all means consistent with my own lawful powers, with the rights of others, and with the genius of our civil institutions. To this end, I have caused this, my solemn protest against the aforesaid proceedings, to be placed on the files of the Executive Department, and to be transmitted to the Senate.

It is alike due to the people, the Senate, and the people, that the views which I have taken of the proceedings referred to, and which compel me to regard them in the light that has been mentioned, should be exhibited at length; and with the free-

* YEAS—Messrs. Bibb, Black, Calhoun, Clay, Clayton, Ewing, Frelinghuysen, Kent, Knight, Leigh, Mangum, Naudain, Poindexter, Porter, Prentiss, Preston, Robbins, Silsbee, Smith, Southard, Sprague, Swift, Tomlinson, Tyler, Waggaman, and Webster—26.

NAYS—Messrs. Benton, Brown, Forsyth, Grundy, Hendricks, Hill, Kane, King of Alabama, King of Georgia, Linn, McKean, Moore, Morris, Robinson, Shepley, Tallmadge, Tipton, White, Wilkins, and Wright—20.

dom and firmness which are required by an occasion so unprecedented and peculiar.

Under the Constitution of the Unitted States, the powers and functions of the various departments of the Federal Government, and their responsibilities for violation or neglect of duty, are clearly defined, or result by necessary inference. The legislative power, subject to the qualified negative of the President, is vested in the Congress of the United States, composed of the Senate and House of Representatives. The executive power is vested exclusively in the President, except that in the conclusion of treaties, and in certain appointments to office, he is to act with the advice and consent of the Senate. The judicial power is vested exclusively in the Supreme and other Courts of the United States, except in cases of impeachment, for which purpose the accusatory power is vested in the House of Representatives, and that of hearing and determining, in the Senate. But although, for the special purposes which have been mentioned, there is an occasional intermixture of the powers of the different departments, yet, with these exceptions, each of the three great departments is independent of the others in its sphere of action; and when it deviates from that sphere, is not responsible to the others, further than it is expressly made so in the Constitution. In every other respect, each of them is the coequal of the other two, and all are the servants of the American people, without power or right to control or censure each other in the service of their common superior, save only in the manner and to the degree which that superior has prescribed.

The responsibilities of the President are numerous and weighty. He is liable to impeachment for high crimes and misdemeanors, and, on due conviction, to removal from office, and perpetual disqualification; and notwithstanding such conviction, he may also be indicted and punished according to law. He is also liable to the private action of any party who may have been injured by his illegal mandates or instructions, in the same manner and to the same extent as the humblest functionary. In addition to the responsibilities which may thus be enforced by impeachment, criminal prosecution, or suit at law, he is also accountable, at the bar of public opinion, for every act of his Administration. Subject only to the restraints of truth and justice, the free people of the United States have the undoubted right, as individuals or collectively, orally or in writing, at such times, and in such language and form as they may think proper, to discuss his official conduct, and to express and promulgate their opinions concerning it. Indirectly, also, his conduct may come under review in either branch of the Legislature, or in the Senate when acting in its executive capacity; and so far as the executive or legislative proceedings of these bodies may require it, it may be examined by them. These are believed to be the proper and only modes in which the President of the United States is to be held accountable for his official conduct.

Tested by these principles, the resolution of the Senate is wholly unauthorized by the Constitution, and in derogation of its entire spirit. It assumes that a single branch of the legislative department may, for the purposes of a public censure, and without any view to legislation or impeachment, take up, consider, and decide upon, the official acts of the Executive. But in no part of the Constitution is the President subjected to any such responsibility; and in no part of that instrument is any such power conferred on either branch of the Legislature.

The justice of these conclusions will be illustrated and confirmed by a brief analysis of the powers of the Senate, and a comparison of their recent proceedings with those powers.

The high functions assigned by the Constitution to the Senate, are, in their nature, either legislative, executive, or judicial. It is only in the exercise of its judicial powers, when sitting as a court for the trial of impeachments, that the Senate is expressly authorized and necessarily required to consider and decide upon the conduct of the President, or any other public officer. Indirectly, however, as has already been suggested, it may frequently be called on to perform that office. Cases may occur in the course of its legislative or executive proceedings, in which it may, be indispensable to the proper exercise of its powers, that it should inquire into, and decide upon, the conduct of the President, or other public officers; and in every such case, its constitutional right to do so is cheerfully conceded. But to authorize the Senate to enter on such a task, in its legislative or executive capacity, the inquiry must actually grow out of, and tend to, some legislative or executive action; and the decision, when expressed, must take the form of some appropriate legislative or executive act.

The resolution in question was introduced, discussed, and passed, not as a joint, but as a separate resolution. It asserts no legislative power; proposes no legislative action; and neither possesses the form nor any of the attributes of a legislative measure. It does not appear to have been entertained or passed with any view or expectation of its issuing in a law or joint resolution, or in the repeal of any law or joint resolution, or in any other legislative action.

Whilst wanting both the form and substance of a legislative measure, it is equally manifest that the resolution was not justified by any of the executive powers conferred on the Senate. These powers relate exclusively to the consideration of treaties and nominations to office; and they are exercised in secret session, and with closed doors. This resolution does not apply to any treaty or nomination, and was passed in a public session.

Nor does this proceeding in any way belong to that class of incidental resolutions which relate to the officers of the Senate, to their Chamber, and other appurtenances, or to subjects of order, and other matters of the like nature—in all which either House may lawfully proceed, without any coöperation with the other, or with the President.

On the contrary, the whole phraseology and sense of the resolution seem to be judicial. Its essence, true character, and only practical effect, are to be found in the conduct which it charges upon the President, and in the judgment which it pronounces on that conduct. The resolution, therefore, though discussed and adopted by the Senate in its legislative capacity, is, in its office, and in all its characteristics, essentially judicial.

That the Senate possesses a high judicial power, and that instances may occur in which the President of the United States will be amenable to it, is undeniable. But under the provisions of the Constitution, it would seem to be equally plain that neither the President nor any other officer can be rightfully subjected to the operation of the judicial power of the Senate, except in the cases and under the forms prescribed by the Constitution.

The Constitution declares that "the President, 'Vice President, and all civil officers of the United 'States, shall be removed from office on impeachment for, and conviction of treason, bribery, or 'other high crimes and misdemeanors"—that the House of Representatives "shall have the sole power of impeachment"—that the Senate "shall have the sole power to try all impeachments"—that "when sitting for that purpose, they shall be on oath or affirmation"—that "when the President of the United States is tried, the Chief Justice shall preside"—that "no person shall be convicted 'without the concurrence of two-thirds of the 'members present"—and that "judgment shall 'not extend further than to removal from office, 'and disqualification to hold and enjoy any office 'of honor, trust, or profit, under the United 'States."

The resolution above quoted, charges in substance that in certain proceedings relating to the public revenue, the President has usurped authority and power not conferred upon him by the Constitution and laws, and that in doing so he violated both. Any such act constitutes a high crime—one of the highest, indeed, which the President can commit—a crime which justly exposes him to impeachment by the House of Representatives, and upon due conviction, to removal from office, and to the complete and immutable disfranchisement prescribed by the Constitution.

The resolution, then, was in substance an impeachment of the President; and in its passage, amounts to a declaration by a majority of the Senate, that he is guilty of an impeachable offence. As such, it is spread upon the journals of the Senate—published to the nation and to the world—made part of our enduring archives—and incorporated in the history of the age. The punishment of removal from office and future disqualification does not, it is true, follow this decision; nor would it have followed the like decision, if the regular forms of proceeding had been pursued, because the requisite number did not concur in the result. But the moral influence of a solemn declaration, by a majority of the Senate, that the accused is guilty of the offence charged upon him, has been as effectually secured, as if the like declaration had been made upon an impeachment expressed in the same terms. Indeed, a greater practical effect has been gained, because the votes given for the resolution, though not sufficient to authorize a judgment of guilty on an impeachment, were numerous enough to carry that resolution.

That the resolution does not expressly allege that the assumption of power and authority, which it condemns, was intentional and corrupt, is no answer to the preceding view of its character and effect. The act thus condemned, necessarily implies volition and design in the individual to whom it is imputed, and being unlawful in its character, the legal conclusion is, that it was prompted by improper motives, and committed with an unlawful intent. The charge is not of a mistake in the exercise of supposed powers, but of the assumption of powers not conferred by the Constitution and laws, but in derogation of both, and nothing is suggested to excuse or palliate the turpitude of the act. In the absence of any such excuse, or palliation, there is only room for one inference: and that is, that the intent was unlawful and corrupt. Besides, the resolution not only contains no mitigating suggestion, but on the contrary, it holds up the act complained of, as justly obnoxious to censure and reprobation; and thus as distinctly stamps it with impurity of motive, as if the strongest epithets had been used.

The President of the United States, therefore, has been, by a majority of his constitutional triers, accused and found guilty of an impeachable offence; but in no part of this proceeding have the directions of the Constitution been observed.

The impeachment, instead of being preferred and prosecuted by the House of Representatives, originated in the Senate, and was prosecuted without the aid or concurrence of the other House. The oath or affirmation prescribed by the Constitution, was not taken by the Senators; the Chief Justice did not preside; no notice of the charge was given to the accused; and no opportunity afforded him to respond to the accusation, to meet his accusers face to face, to cross-examine the witnesses, to procure counteracting testimony, or to be heard in his defence. The safe-guards and formalities which the Constitution has connected with the power of impeachment, were doubtless supposed by the framers of that instrument, to be essential to the protection of the public servant, to the attainment of justice, and to the order, impartiality, and dignity of the procedure. These safeguards and formalities were not only practically disregarded, in the commencement and conduct of these proceedings, but in their result, I find myself convicted by less than two-thirds of the members present, of an impeachable offence.

In vain may it be alleged in defence of this proceeding, that the form of the resolution is not that of an impeachment, or of a judgment thereupon; that the punishment prescribed in the Constitution does not follow its adoption, or that in this case no impeachment is to be expected from the House of Representatives. It is because it did not assume the form of an impeachment, that it is the more palpably repugnant to the Constitution; for it is through that form only that the President is judicially responsible to the Senate; and though neither removal from office nor future disqualification ensues, yet it is not to be presumed that the framers of the Constitution considered either or both of those results, as constituting the whole of the punishment they prescribed. The judgment of guilty by the highest tribunal in the Union; the stigma it would inflict on the offender, his family, and fame; and the perpetual record on the journal, handing down to future generations the story of his disgrace, were doubtless regarded by them as the bitterest portions, if not the very essence of that punishment. So far, therefore, as some of its most material parts are concerned, the passage, recording, and promulgation of the resolution, are an attempt to bring them on the President, in a

manner unauthorized by the Constitution. To shield him and other officers who are liable to impeachment, from consequences so momentous, except when really merited by official delinquencies, the Constitution has most carefully guarded the whole process of impeachment. A majority of the House of Representatives must think the officer guilty, before he can be charged. Two-thirds of the Senate must pronounce him guilty, or he is deemed to be innocent. Forty-six Senators appear by the Journal to have been present when the vote on the resolution was taken. If, after all the solemnities of an impeachment, thirty of those Senators had voted that the President was guilty, yet would he have been acquitted; but by the mode of proceeding adopted in the present case, a lasting record of conviction has been entered up by the votes of twenty-six Senators, without an impeachment or trial; whilst the Constitution expressly declares that to the entry of such a judgment, an accusation by the House of Representatives, a trial by the Senate, and a concurrence of two-thirds in the vote of guilty, shall be indispensable prerequisites.

Whether or not an impeachment was to be expected from the House of Representatives, was a point on which the Senate had no constitutional right to speculate, and in respect to which, even had it possessed the spirit of prophecy, its anticipations would have furnished no just grounds for this procedure. Admitting that there was reason to believe that a violation of the Constitution and laws had been actually committed by the President, still it was the duty of the Senate, as his sole constitutional judges, to wait for an impeachment until the other House should think proper to prefer it. The members of the Senate could have no right to infer that no impeachment was intended. On the contrary, every legal and rational presumption on their part ought to have been, that, if there was good reason to believe him guilty of an impeachable offence, the House of Representatives would perform its constitutional duty, by arraigning the offender before the justice of his country. The contrary presumption would involve an implication derogatory to the integrity and honor of the representatives of the people. But suppose the suspicion thus implied were actually entertained, and for good cause, how can it justify the assumption by the Senate of powers not conferred by the Constitution?

It is only necessary to look at the condition in which the Senate and the President have been placed by this proceeding, to perceive its utter incompatibility with the provisions and the spirit of the Constitution, and with the plainest dictates of humanity and justice.

If the House of Representatives shall be of opinion that there is just ground for the censure pronounced upon the President, then will it be the solemn duty of that House to prefer the proper accusation, and to cause him to be brought to trial by the constitutional tribunal. But in what condition would he find that tribunal? A majority of its members have already considered the case, and have not only formed, but expressed, a deliberate judgment upon its merits. It is the policy of our benign system of jurisprudence to secure, in all criminal proceedings, and even in the most trivial litigations, a fair, unprejudiced, and impartial trial. And surely it cannot be less important that such a trial should be secured to the highest officer of the Government.

The Constitution makes the House of Representatives the exclusive judges, in the first instance, of the question whether the President has committed an impeachable offence. A majority of the Senate, whose interference with this preliminary question has, for the best of all reasons, been studiously excluded, anticipate the action of the House of Representatives, assume not only the function which belongs exclusively to that body, but convert themselves into accusers, witnesses, counsel, and judges, and prejudge the whole case—thus presenting the appalling spectacle, in a free State, of judges going through a labored preparation for an impartial hearing and decision, by a previous *ex parte* investigation and sentence against the supposed offender.

There is no more settled axiom in that Government whence we derived the model of this part of our Constitution than, that "the Lords cannot impeach any to themselves, nor join in the accusation, *because they are judges.*" Independently of the general reasons on which this rule is founded, its propriety and importance are greatly increased by the nature of the impeaching power. The power of arraigning the high officers of Government, before a tribunal whose sentence may expel them from their seats, and brand them as infamous, is eminently a popular remedy—a remedy designed to be employed for the protection of private right and public liberty, against the abuses of injustice and the encroachments of arbitrary power. But the framers of the Constitution were also undoubtedly aware, that this formidable instrument had been, and might be abused; and that from its very nature, an impeachment for high crimes and misdemeanors, whatever might be its result, would in most cases be accompanied by so much of dishonor and reproach, solicitude and suffering, as to make the power of preferring it, one of the highest solemnity and importance. It was due to both these considerations, that the impeaching power should be lodged in the hands of those who, from the mode of their election and the tenure of their offices, would most accurately express the popular will, and at the same time be most directly and speedily amenable to the people. The theory of these wise and benignant intentions is, in the present case, effectually defeated by the proceedings of the Senate. The members of that body represent, not the people, but the States; and though they are undoubtedly responsible to the States, yet, from their extended term of service, the effect of that responsibility during the whole period of that term, must very much depend upon their own impressions of its obligatory force. When a body, thus constituted, expresses, beforehand, its opinion in a particular case, and thus indirectly invites a prosecution, it not only assumes a power intended for wise reasons to be confined to others, but it shields the latter from that exclusive and personal responsibility under which it was intended to be exercised, and reverses the whole scheme of this part of the Constitution.

Such would be some of the objections to this procedure, even if it were admitted that there is just ground for imputing to the President the offences charged in the resolution. But if, on the other hand, the House of Representatives shall be of opinion that there is no reason for charging them upon him, and shall therefore deem it improper to prefer an impeachment, then will the violation of privilege as it respects that House, of justice as it regards the President, and of the Constitution, as it relates to both, be only the more conspicuous and impressive.

The constitutional mode of procedure on an impeachment has not only been wholly disregarded, but some of the first principles of natural right and enlightened jurisprudence, have been violated in the very form of the resolution. It carefully abstains from averring in *which* of "the late proceedings in 'relation to the public revenue, the President has 'assumed upon himself authority and power not 'conferred by the Constitution and laws." It carefully abstains from specifying *what laws* or *what parts* of the Constitution have been violated. Why was not the certainty of the offence—"the nature and cause of the accusation"—set out in the manner required in the Constitution, before even the humblest individual, for the smallest crime, can be exposed to condemnation? Such a specification was due to the accused, that he might direct his defence to the real points of attack—to the people, that they might clearly understand in what particulars their institutions had been violated; and to the truth and certainty of our public annals. As the record now stands, whilst the resolution plainly charges upon the President at least one act of usurpation in "the late executive proceedings in relation to the public revenue," and is so framed that those Senators who believed that one such act, and only one, had been committed, could assent to it; its language is yet broad enough to include several such acts; and so it may have been regarded by some of those who voted for it. But though the accusation is thus comprehensive in the censures it implies, there is no such certainty of time, place, or circumstance, as to exhibit the particular conclusion of fact or law which induced any one Senator to vote for it. And it may well have happened, that whilst one Senator believed that some particular act embraced in the resolution, was an arbitrary and unconstitutional assumption of power, others of the majority may have deemed that very act both constitutional and expedient; or if not expedient, yet still within the pale of the Constitution. And thus a majority of the Senators may have been enabled to concur, in a vague and undefined accusation, that the President, in the course of "the late executive proceedings in relation to the public revenue," had violated the Constitution and laws; whilst, if a separate vote had been taken in respect to each particular act, included within the general terms, the accusers of the President might, on any such vote, have been found in the minority.

Still further to exemplify this feature of the proceeding, it is important to be remarked, that the resolution as originally offered to the Senate, specified, with adequate precision, certain acts of the President which it denounced as a violation of the Constitution and laws; and that it was not until the very close of the debate, and when, perhaps, it was apprehended that a majority might not sustain the specific accusation contained in it, that the resolution was so modified as to assume its present form. A more striking illustration of the soundness and necessity of the rules which forbid vague and indefinite generalities, and require a reasonable certainty in all judicial allegations, and a more glaring instance of the violation of those rules, has seldom been exhibited.

In this view of the resolution it must certainly be regarded, not as a vindication of any particular provision of the law or the Constitution, but simply as an official rebuke or condemnatory sentence, too general and indefinite to be easily repelled, but yet sufficiently precise to bring into discredit the conduct and motives of the Executive. But whatever it may have been intended to accomplish, it is obvious that the vague, general, and abstract form of the resolution, is in perfect keeping with those other departures from first principles and settled improvements in jurisprudence, so properly the boast of free countries in modern times. And it is not too much to say, of the whole of these proceedings, that if they shall be approved and sustained by an intelligent people, then will that great contest with arbitrary power, which had established in statutes, in bills of rights, in sacred charters, and in constitutions of Government, the right of every citizen, to a notice before trial, to a hearing before conviction, and to an impartial tribunal for deciding on the charge, have been waged in vain.

If the resolution had been left in its original form, it is not to be presumed that it could ever have received the assent of a majority of the Senate, for the acts therein specified as violations of the Constitution and laws were clearly within the limits of the Executive authority. They are the "dismissing the late Secretary of the Treasury, because 'he would not, contrary to his sense of his own 'duty, remove the money of the United States in 'deposite with the Bank of the United States and 'its branches, in conformity with the President's 'opinion; and appointing his successor to effect 'such removal, which has been done." But as no other specification has been substituted, and as these were the "Executive proceedings in relation to the public revenue," principally referred to in the course of the discussion, they will doubtless be generally regarded as the acts intended to be denounced as "an assumption of authority and 'power not conferred by the Constitution or laws, 'but in derogation of both." It is therefore due to the occasion that a condensed summary of the views of the Executive in respect to them, should be here exhibited.

By the Constitution, "the executive power is vested in a President of the United States." Among the duties imposed upon him, and which he is sworn to perform, is that of "taking care that the laws be faithfully executed." Being thus made responsible for the entire action of the Executive Department, it was but reasonable that the power of appointing, overseeing, and controlling those who execute the laws—a power in its nature executive—should remain in his hands. It is, therefore, not only his right, but the Constitution makes it his duty, to "nominate, and by and with the advice and consent of the Senate appoint," all "officers of the United States whose appointments are not in the Constitution otherwise provided for,"

with a proviso that the appointment of inferior officers may be vested in the President alone, in the Courts of Justice, or in the heads of departments.

The executive power vested in the Senate, is neither that of "nominating" nor "appointing." It is merely a check upon the executive power of appointment. If individuals are proposed for appointment by the President, by them deemed incompetent or unworthy, they may withhold their consent, and the appointment cannot be made. They check the action of the Executive, but cannot, in relation to those very subjects, act themselves, nor direct him. Selections are still made by the President, and the negative given to the Senate, without diminishing his responsibility, furnishes an additional guarantee to the country that the subordinate executive, as well as the judicial offices, shall be filled with worthy and competent men.

The whole executive power being vested in the President, who is responsible for its exercise, it is a necessary consequence that he should have a right to employ agents of his own choice to aid him in the performance of his duties, and to discharge them when he is no longer willing to be responsible for their acts. In strict accordance with this principle, the power of removal, which, like that of appointment, is an original executive power, is left unchecked by the Constitution in relation to all executive officers, for whose conduct the President is responsible, while it is taken from him in relation to judicial officers, for whose acts he is not responsible. In the Government from which many of the fundamental principles of our system are derived, the head of the executive department originally had power to appoint and remove at will all officers, executive and judicial. It was to take the judges out of this general power of removal, and thus make them independent of the Executive, that the tenure of their offices was changed to good behavior. Nor is it conceivable why they are placed, in our Constitution, upon a tenure different from that of all other officers appointed by the Executive, unless it be for the same purpose.

But if there were any just ground for doubt on the face of the Constitution, whether all executive officers are removable at the will of the President, it is obviated by the cotemporaneous construction of the instrument, and the uniform practice under it.

The power of removal was a topic of solemn debate in the Congress of 1789, while organizing the administrative departments of the Government, and it was finally decided that the President derived from the Constitution the power of removal, so far as it regards that department for whose acts he is responsible. Although the debate covered the whole ground, embracing the Treasury as well as all the other Executive departments, it arose on a motion to strike out of the bill to establish a Department of Foreign Affairs, since called the Department of State, a clause declaring the Secretary "to be removable from office by the President of the United States." After that motion had been decided in the negative, it was perceived that these words did not convey the sense of the House of Representatives in relation to the true source of the power of removal. With the avowed object of preventing any future inference that this power was exercised by the President in virtue of a grant from Congress, when in fact that body considered it as derived from the Constitution, the words which had been the subject of debate were struck out, and in lieu thereof a clause was inserted in a provision concerning the chief clerk of the department, which declared that "whenever the said 'principal officer shall be *removed* from office by 'the President of the United States, or in any other 'case of vacancy," the chief clerk should, during such vacancy, have charge of the papers of the office. This change having been made for the express purpose of declaring the sense of Congress that the President derived the power of removal from the Constitution, the act as it passed has always been considered as a full expression of the sense of the legislature on this important part of the American Constitution.

Here, then, we have the concurrent authority of President Washington, of the Senate, and the House of Representatives, numbers of whom had taken an active part in the convention which framed the Constitution, and in the State conventions which adopted it, that the President derived an unqualified power of removal from that instrument itself, which is "beyond the reach of legislative authority." Upon this principle the Government has now been steadily administered for about forty-five years, during which there have been numerous removals made by the President or by his direction, embracing every grade of executive officers, from the heads of departments to the messengers of bureaus.

The Treasury Department, in the discussions of 1789, was considered on the same footing as the other Executive departments, and in the act establishing it, the precise words were incorporated indicative of the sense of Congress, that the President derives his power to remove the Secretary from the Constitution, which appears in the act establishing the Department of Foreign Affairs. An assistant Secretary of the Treasury was created, and it wac provided that he should take charge of the books and papers of the department, "whenever the Secretary shall be *removed* from office by the President of the United States." The Secretary of the Treasury being appointed by the President, and being considered as constitutionally removable by him, it appears never to have occurred to any one in the Congress of 1789, or since, until very recently, that he was other than an executive officer, the mere instrument of the Chief Magistrate in the execution of the laws, subject, like all other heads of departments, to his supervision and control. No such idea as an officer of the Congress can be found in the Constitution, or appears to have suggested itself to those who organized the Government. There are officers of each House, the appointment of which is authorized by the Constitution, but all officers referred to in that instrument, as coming within the appointing power of the President, whether established thereby, or created by law, are "officers of the United States." No joint power of appointment is given to the two Houses of Congress, nor is there any accountability to them as one body; but as soon as any office is created by law, of whatever name or character, the appointment of the person or persons to fill it, devolves by the Constitution upon the President, with the advice and consent of the Senate, unless it be an inferior office, and the appointment be vested by the law itself "in the President alone, in the courts of law, or in the heads of departments."

But at the time of the organization of the Treasury Department, an incident occurred which distinctly evinces the unanimous concurrence of the first Congress in the principle that the Treasury Department is wholly executive in its character and responsibilities. A motion was made to strike out the provision of the bill making it the duty of the Secretary "to digest and report plans for the improvement and management of the revenue, and for the support of public credit," on the ground that it would give the executive department of the Government too much influence and power in Congress. The motion was not opposed on the ground that the Secretary was the officer of Congress and responsible to that body, which would have been conclusive, if admitted, but on other grounds which conceded his executive character throughout. The whole discussion evinces an unanimous concurrence in the principle, that the Secretary of the Treasury is wholly an executive officer, and the struggle of the minority was to restrict his power as such. From that time down to the present, the Secretary of the Treasury, the Treasurer, Register, Comptrollers, Auditors, and Clerks, who fill the offices of that department, have, in the practice of the Government, been considered and treated as on the same footing with corresponding grades of officers in all the other executive departments.

The custody of the public property, under such regulations as may be prescribed by legislative authority, has always been considered an appropriate function of the Executive department in this and all other Governments. In accordance with this principle, every species of property belonging to the United States, (excepting that which is in the use of the several coördinate departments of the Government, as means to aid them in performing their appropriate functions,) is in charge of officers appointed by the President, whether it be lands, or buildings, or merchandise, or provisions, or clothing, or arms and munitions of war. The superintendents and keepers of the whole are appointed by the President, responsible to him, and removable at his will.

Public money is but a species of public property. It cannot be raised by taxation or customs, nor brought into the treasury in any other way, except by law; but whenever or howsoever obtained, its custody always has been, and always must be, unless the Constitution be changed, intrusted to the Executive department. No officer can be created by Congress for the purpose of taking charge of it, whose appointment would not, by the Constitution, at once devolve on the President, and who would not be responsible to him for the faithful performance of his duties. The legislative power may undoubtedly bind him and the President by any laws they may think proper to enact; they may prescribe in what place particular portions of the public money shall be kept, and for what reason it shall be removed, as they may direct that supplies for the army or navy shall be kept in particular stores; and it will be the duty of the President to see that the law is faithfully executed—yet will the custody remain in the Executive department of the Government. Were the Congress to assume, with or without a legislative act, the power of appointing officers independantly of the President, to take the charge and custody of the public property contained in the military and naval arsenals, magazines, and storehouses, it is believed that such an act would be regarded by all as a palpable usurpation of executive power, subversive of the form, as well as the fundamental principles of our Government. But where is the difference in principle, whether the public property be in the form of arms, munitions of war, and supplies, or in gold and silver, or bank notes? None can be perceived—none is believed to exist. Congress cannot, therefore, take out of the hands of the Executive department, the custody of the public property or money without an assumption of executive power, and a subversion of the first principles of the Constitution.

The Congress of the United States have never passed an act imperatively directing that the public moneys shall be kept in any particular place or places. From the origin of the Government to the year 1816 the statute-book was wholly silent on the subject. In 1789 a treasurer was created, subordinate to the Secretary of the Treasury, and through him to the President. He was required to give bond, safely to keep, and faithfully to disburse the public moneys, without any direction as to the manner or places in which they should be kept. By reference to the practice of the Government, it is found that from its first organization the Secretary of the Treasury, acting under the supervision of the President, designated the places in which the public moneys should be kept, and specially directed all transfers from place to place. This practice was continued, with the silent acquiescence of Congress, from 1789 down to 1816, and although many banks were selected and discharged, and although a portion of the moneys were first placed in the State banks, and then in the former Bank of the United States, and upon the dissolution of that were again transferred to the State banks, no legislation was thought necessary by Congress, and all the operations were originated and perfected by Executive authority. The Secretary of the Treasury, responsible to the President, and with his approbation, made contracts and arrangements in relation to the whole subject-matter, which was thus entirely committed to the direction of the President, under his responsibilities to the American people, and to those who were authorized to impeach and punish him for any breach of this important trust.

The act of 1816, establishing the Bank of the United States, directed the deposites of public money to be made in that bank and its branches, in places in which the said bank and branches thereof may be established, "unless the Secretary of the Treasury should otherwise order and direct," in which event he was required to give his reasons to Congress. This was but a continuation of his pre-existing powers as the head of an executive department, to direct where the deposites should be made, with the superadded obligation of giving his reasons to Congress for making them elsewhere than in the Bank of the United States and its

branches. It is not to be considered that this provision in any degree altered the relation between the Secretary of the Treasury and the President, as the responsible head of the executive department, or released the latter from his constitutional obligation to "take care that the laws be faithfully executed." On the contrary, it increased his responsibilities, by adding another to the long list of laws which it was his duty to carry into effect.

It would be an extraordinary result if, because the person charged by law with a public duty is one of the Secretaries, it were less the duty of the President to see that law faithfully executed than other laws enjoining duties upon subordinate officers or private citizens. If there be any difference, it would seem that the obligation is stronger in relation to the former, because the neglect is in his presence, and the remedy at hand.

It cannot be doubted that it was the legal duty of the Secretary of the Treasury to order and direct the deposites of the public money to be made elsewhere than in the Bank of the United States, *whenever sufficient reasons existed for making the change*. If, in such a case, he neglected or refused to act, he would neglect or refuse to execute the law. What would then be the sworn duty of the President? Could he say that the Constitution did not bind him to see the law faithfully executed, because it was one of his Secretaries, and not himself, upon whom the service was specially imposed? Might he not be asked whether there was any such limitation to his obligations prescribed in the Constitution? Whether he is not equally bound to take care that the laws be faithfully executed, whether they impose duties on the highest officer of State, or the lowest subordinate in any of the departments? Might he not be told, that it was for the sole purpose of causing all executive officers, from the highest to the lowest, faithfully to perform the services required of them by law, that the people of the United States have made him their Chief Magistrate, and the Constitution has clothed him with the entire executive power of this Government? The principles implied in these questions appear too plain to need elucidation.

But here, also, we have a cotemporaneous construction of the act, which shows that it was not understood as in any way changing the relations between the President and Secretary of the Treasury, or as placing the latter out of Executive control, even in relation to the deposites of the public money. Nor on this point are we left to any equivocal testimony. The documents of the Treasury Department show that the Secretary of the Treasury did apply to the President, and obtain his approbation and sanction to the original transfer of the public deposites to the present Bank of the United States, and did carry the measure into effect in obedience to his decision. They also show that transfers of the public deposites from the branches of the Bank of the United States to State banks, at Chilicothe, Cincinnati, and Louisville, in 1819, were made with the approbation of the President, and by his authority. They show, that upon all important questions appertaining to his department, whether they related to the public deposites or other matters, it was the constant practice of the Secretary of the Treasury to obtain for his acts the approval and sanction of the President. These acts, and the principles on which they were founded, were known to all the departments of the Goverument, to Congress, and the country; and, until very recently, appear never to have been called in question.

Thus was it settled by the Constitution, the laws, and the whole practice of the Government, that the entire executive power is vested in the President of the United States; that as incident to that power, the right of appointing and removing those officers who are to aid him in the execution of the laws, with such restrictions only as the Constitution prescribes, is vested in the President; that the Secretary of the Treasury is one of those officers; that the custody of the public property and money is an executive function, which, in relation to the money, has always been exercised through the Secretary of the Treasury and his subordinates; that in the performance of these duties, he is subject to the supervision and control of the President, and in all important measures having relation to them, consults the Chief Magistrate, and obtains his approval and sanction; that the law establishing the bank did not, as it could not, change the relation between the President and the Secretary—did not release the former from his obligation to see the law faithfully executed, nor the latter from the President's supervision and control; that afterwards, and before, the Secretary did in fact consult, and obtain the sanction of, the President, to transfers and removals of the public deposites; and that all departments of the Government, and the nation itself, approved or acquiesced in these acts and principles, as in strict conformity with our Constitution and laws.

During the last year, the approaching termination, according to the provisions of its charter, and the solemn decision of the American people, of the Bank of the United States, made it expedient, and its exposed abuses and corruptions, made it, in my opinion, the duty of the Secretary of the Treasury to place the moneys of the United States in other depositories. The Secretary did not concur in that opinion, and declined giving the necessary order and direction. So glaring were the abuses and corruptions of the bank, so evident its fixed purpose to persevere in them, and so palpable its design, by its money and power, to control the Government and change its character, that I deemed it the imperative duty of the executive authority, by the exertion of every power confided to it by the Constitution and laws, to check its career, and lessen its ability to do mischief, even in the painful alternative of dismissing the head of one of the departments. At the time the removal was made, other causes sufficient to justify it existed; but if they had not, the Secretary would have been dismissed for this cause only.

His place I supplied by one whose opinions were well known to me, and whose frank expression of them, in another situation, and whose generous sacrifices of interest and feeling, when unexpectedly called to the station he now occupies, ought forever to have shielded his motives from suspicion, and his character from reproach. In accordance with the opinions long before expressed by him, he proceeded, with my sanction, to make arrangements for depositing the moneys of the United States in other safe institutions.

The resolution of the Senate, as originally framed, and as passed, if it refers to these acts, presupposes a right in that body to interfere with this exercise of executive power. If the principle be once admitted, it is not difficult to percive where it may end. If, by a mere denunciation like this resolution, the President should ever be induced to act, in a matter of official duty, contrary to the honest convictions of his own mind, in compliance with the wishes of the Senate, the constitutional independence of the executive department would be as effectually destroyed, and its power as effectually transferred to the Senate, as if that end had been accomplished by an amendment of the Constitution. But if the Senate have a right to interfere with the executive powers, they have also the right to make that interference effective; and if the assertion of the power implied in the resolution be silently acquiesced in, we may reasonably apprehend that it will be followed, at some future day, by an attempt at actual enforcement. The Senate may refuse, except on the condition that he will surrender his opinions to theirs and obey their will, to perform their own constitutional functions: to pass the necessary laws; to sanction appropriations proposed by the House of Representatives, and to confirm proper nominations made by the President. It has already been maintained (and it is not conceivable that the resolution of the Senate can be based on any other principle) that the Secretary of the Treasury is the officer of Congress, and independent of the President; that the President has no right to control him, and consequently none to remove him. With the same propriety, and on similar grounds, may the Secretary of State, the Secretaries of War and the Navy, and the Postmaster General, each in succession, be declared independent of the President, the subordinates of Congress, and removable only with the concurrence of the Senate. Followed to its consequences, this principle will be found effectually to destroy one coördinate department of the Government, to concentrate in the hands of the Senate the whole executive power, and to leave the President as powerless as he would be useless—the shadow of authority, after the substance had departed.

The time and the occasion which have called forth the resolution of the Senate, seem to impose upon me an additional obligation not to pass it over in silence. Nearly forty-five years had the President exercised, without a question as to his rightful authority, those powers, for the recent assumption of which he is now denounced. The vicissitudes of peace and war had attended our Government, violent parties, watchful to take advantage of any seeming usurpation on the part of the Executive, had distracted our counsels; frequent removals, or forced resignations, in every sense tantamount to removals, had been made of the Secretary and other officers of the Treasury; and yet in no one instance is it known that any man, whether patriot or partisan, had raised his voice against it as a violation of the Constitution. The expediency and justice of such changes, in reference to public officers of all grades, have frequently been the topic of discussion; but the constitutional right of the President to appoint, control, and remove the head of the Treasury, as well as of all other departments, seems to have been universally conceded. And what is the occasion upon which other principles have been first officially asserted? The Bank of the United States—a great moneyed monopoly—had attempted to obtain a renewal of its charter, by controlling the elections of the people and the action of the Government. The use of its corporate funds and power in that attempt was fully disclosed; and it was made known to the President that the corporation was putting in train the same course of measures, with the view of making another vigorous effort, through an interference in the elections of the people, to control public opinion and force the Government to yield to its demands. This, with its corruption of the press, its violation of its charter, its exclusion of the Government directors from its proceedings, its neglect of duty, and arrogant pretensions, made it, in the opinion of the President, incompatible with the public interest and the safety of our institutions, that it should longer be employed as the fiscal agent of the Treasury. A Secretary of the Treasury, appointed in the recess of the Senate, who had not been confirmed by that body, and whom the President might or might not, at his pleasure, nominate to them, refused to do what his superior in the executive department considered the most imperative of his duties, and became, in fact, however innocent his motives, the protector of the bank. And on this occasion it is discovered, for the first time, that those who framed the Constitution misunderstood it; that the first Congress and all its successors have been under a delusion; that the practice of near forty-five years is but a continued usurpation; that the Secretary of the Treasury is not responsible to the President; and that to remove him is a violation of the Constitution and laws, for which the President deserves to stand forever dishonored on the Journals of the Senate.

There are also some other circumstances connected with the discussion and passage of the resolution, to which I feel it to be, not only my right, but my duty, to refer. It appears, by the Journal of the Senate, that among the twenty-six Senators who voted for the resolution on its final passage, and who had supported it in debate, in its original form, were one of the Senators from the State of Maine, the two Senators from New Jersey, and one of the Senators from Ohio. It also appears by the same Journal, and by the files of the Senate, that the Legislatures of these States had severally expressed their opinions in respect to the executive proceedings drawn in question before the Senate.

The two branches of the Legislature of the State of Maine, on the 25th of January, 1834, passed a preamble and series of resolutions in the following words:

"Whereas, at an early period after the election 'of Andrew Jackson to the Presidency, in accord'ance with the sentiments which he had unformly 'expressed, the attention of Congress was called 'to the constitutionality and expediency of the re'newal of the charter of the United States Bank: 'And whereas, the bank has transcended its char'tered limits in the management of its business

transactions, and has abandoned the object of its creation, by engaging in political controversies, by wielding its power and influence to embarrass the administration of the General Government, and by bringing insolvency and distress upon the commercial community: And whereas, the public security from such an institution consists less in its present pecuniary capacity to discharge its liabilities than in the fidelity with which the trusts reposed in it have been executed: And whereas, the abuse and misapplication of the powers conferred have destroyed the confidence of the public in the officers of the bank, and demonstrated that such powers endanger the stability of republican institutions: Therefore,

"*Resolved*, That in the removal of the public deposites from the Bank of the United States, as well as in the manner of their removal, we recognise in the Administration an adherence to constitutional rights, and the performance of a public duty.

"*Resolved*, That this Legislature entertain the same opinion as heretofore expressed by preceding Legislatures of this State, that the Bank of the United States ought not to be rechartered.

"*Resolved*, That the Senators of this State in the Congress of the United States be instructed, and the Representatives be requested, to oppose the restoration of the deposites and the renewal of the charter of the United States Bank."

On the 11th of January, 1834, the House of Assembly and Council, composing the Legislature of the State of New Jersey, passed a preamble and a series of resolutions in the following words:

"Whereas the present crisis in our public affairs calls for a decided expression of the voice of the people of this State: And whereas we consider it the undoubted right of the Legislatures of the several States to instruct those who represent their interests in the councils of the nation, in all matters which intimately concern the public weal, and may affect the happiness or well-being of the people: Therefore,

"1. *Be it resolved by the Council and General Assembly of this State*, That while we acknowledge with feelings of devout gratitude our obligations to the great Ruler of Nations for his mercies to us as a people, that we have been preserved alike from foreign war, from the evils of internal commotions, and the machinations of designing and ambitious men, who would prostrate the fair fabric of our Union; that we ought, nevertheless, to humble ourselves in His presence, and implore His aid, for the perpetuation of our republican institutions, and for a continuance of that unexampled prosperity which our country has hitherto enjoyed.

"2. *Resolved*, That we have undiminished confidence in the integrity and firmness of the venerable patriot who now holds the distinguished post of Chief Magistrate of this nation, and whose purity of purpose and elevated motives have so often received the unqualified approbation of a large majority of his fellow-citizens.

"3. *Resolved*, That we view with agitation and alarm the existence of a great moneyed incorporation, which threatens to embarrass the operations of the Government, and, by means of its unbounded influence upon the currency of the country, to scatter distress and ruin throughout the community; and that we therefore solemnly believe the present Bank of the United States ought not to be rechartered.

"4. *Resolved*, That our Senators in Congress be instructed, and our members of the House of Representatives be requested, to sustain, by their votes and influence, the course adopted by the Secretary of the Treasury, Mr. Taney, in relation to the Bank of the United States and the deposites of the Government moneys, believing, as we do, the course of the Secretary to have been constitutional, and that the public good required its adoption.

"5. *Resolved*, That the Governor be requested to forward a copy of the above resolutions to each of our Senators and Representatives from this State in the Congress of the United States."

On the 21st day of February last, the Legislature of the same State reiterated the opinions and instructions before given, by joint resolutions, in the following words:

"*Resolved by the Council and General Assembly of the State of New Jersey*, That they do adhere to the resolutions passed by them on the 11th day of January last, relative to the President of the United States, the Bank of the United States, and the course of Mr. Taney in removing the Government deposites.

"*Resolved*, That the Legislature of New Jersey have not seen any reason to depart from such resolutions since the passage thereof; and it is their wish that they should receive from our Senators and Representatives of this State in the Congress of the United States, that attention and obedience which are due to the opinion of a sovereign State, openly expressed in its legislative capacity."

On the 2d of January, 1834, the Senate and House of Representatives composing the Legislature of Ohio, passed a preamble and resolutions in the following words:

"Whereas there is reason to believe that the Bank of the United States will attempt to obtain a renewal of its charter at the present session of Congress: And whereas it is abundantly evident that said bank has exercised powers derogatory to the spirit of our free institutions, and dangerous to the liberties of these United States: And whereas there is just reason to doubt the constitutional power of Congress to grant acts of incorporation for banking purposes out of the District of Columbia: And whereas we believe the proper disposal of the public lands to be of the utmost importance to the people of these United States, and that honor and good faith require their equitable distribution: Therefore—

"*Resolved by the General Assembly of the State of Ohio*, That we consider the removal of the public deposites from the Bank of the United States as required by the best interests of our country, and that a proper sense of public duty imperiously demanded that that institution should be no longer used as a depository of the public funds.

"*Resolved, also*, That we view, with decided disapprobation, the renewed attempts in Congress to secure the passage of the bill providing for the disposal of the public domain upon the principles proposed by Mr. Clay, inasmuch as we believe that such a law would be unequal in its operations, and unjust in its results.

"*Resolved, also*, That we heartily approve of the principles set forth in the late veto message upon that subject; and,

"*Resolved*, That our Senators in Congress be instructed, and our Representatives requested, to use their influence to prevent the rechartering of the Bank of the United States; to sustain the Administration in its removal of the public deposites; and to oppose the passage of a land bill containing the principles adopted in the act upon that subject, passed at the last session of Congress.

"*Resolved*, That the Governor be requested to transmit copies of the foregoing preamble and resolutions to each of our Senators and Representatives."

It is thus seen that four Senators have declared, by their votes, that the President, in the late executive proceedings in relation to the revenue had been guilty of the impeachable offence of "assuming upon himself authority and power not conferred by the Constitution and laws, but in derogation of both," whilst the Legislatures of their respective States had deliberately approved those very proceedings as consistent with the Constitution, and demanded by the public good. If these four votes had been given in accordance with the sentiments of the Legislatures, as above expressed, there would have been but twenty-two votes out of forty-six for censuring the President, and the unprecedented record of his conviction could not have been placed upon the Journals of the Senate.

In thus referring to the resolutions and instructions of the State Legislatures, I disclaim and repudiate all authority or design to interfere with the responsibility due from members of the Senate to their own consciences, their constituents, and their country. The facts now stated belong to the history of these proceedings, and are important to the just development of the principles and interests involved in them, as well as to the proper vindication of the executive department; and with that view, and that view only, are they here made the topic of remark.

The dangerous tendency of the doctrine which denies to the President the power of supervising, directing, and removing the Secretary of the Treasury, in like manner with the other executive officers, would soon be manifest in practice, were the doctrine to be established. The President is the direct representative of the American people, but the Secretaries are not. If the Secretary of the Treasury be independent of the President in the execution of the laws, then is there no direct responsibility to the people in that important branch of this Government, to which is committed the care of the national finances. And it is in the power of the Bank of the United States, or any other corporation, body of men, or individuals, if a Secretary shall be found to accord with them in opinion, or can be induced in practice to promote their views, to control, through him, the whole action of the Government, (so far as it is exercised by his department,) in defiance of the Chief Magistrate elected by the people, and responsible to them.

But the evil tendency of the particular doctrine adverted to, though sufficiently serious, would be as nothing in comparison with the pernicious consequences which would inevitably flow from the approbation and allowance by the people, and the practice by the Senate, of the unconstitutional power of arraigning and censuring the official conduct of the Executive in the manner recently pursued. Such proceedings are eminently calculated to unsettle the foundations of the Government, to disturb the harmonious action of its different departments, and to break down the checks and balances by which the wisdom of its framers sought to ensure its stability and usefulness.

The honest differences of opinion which occasionally exist between the Senate and the President, in regard to matters in which both are obliged to participate, are sufficiently embarrassing. But if the course recently adopted by the Senate shall hereafter be frequently pursued, it is not only obvious that the harmony of the relations between the President and the Senate will be destroyed, but that other and graver effects will ultimately ensue. If the censures of the Senate be submitted to by the President, the confidence of the people in his ability and virtue, and the character and usefulness of his Administration will soon be at an end, and the real power of the Government will fall into the hands of a body, holding their offices for long terms, not elected by the people, and not to them directly responsible. If, on the other hand, the illegal censures of the Senate should be resisted by the President, collisions and angry controversies might ensue, discreditable in their progress, and in the end compelling the people to adopt the conclusion, either that their Chief Magistrate was unworthy of their respect, or that the Senate was chargeable with calumny and injustice. Either of these results would impair public confidence in the perfection of the system, and lead to serious alterations of its framework, or to the practical abandonment of some of its provisions.

The influence of such proceedings on the other departments of the Govenment, and more especially on the States, could not fail to be extensively pernicious. When the judges in the last resort of official misconduct, themselves overleap the bounds of their authority, as prescribed by the Constitution, what general disregard of its provisions might not their example be expected to produce? And who does not perceive that such contempt of the Federal Constitution, by one of its most important departments, would hold out the strongest temptation to resistance on the part of the State sovereignties, whenever they shall suppose their just rights to have been invaded? Thus all the independent departments of the Government, and the States which compose our confederated Union, instead of attending to their appropriate duties, and leaving those who may offend to be reclaimed or punished in the manner pointed out in the Constitution, would fall to mutual crimination and recrimination, and give to the people confusion and anarchy, instead of order and law; until at length some form of aristocratic power would be established on the ruins of the Constitution, or the States be broken into separate communities.

Far be it from me to charge, or to insinuate, that the present Senate of the United States intend, in the most distant way, to encourage such a result. It is not of their motives or designs, but only of the tendency of their acts, that it is my duty to speak. It is, if possible, to make Senators themselves sensible of the danger which lurks under the precedent set in their resolution; and at any rate to perform my duty as the responsible head of one of the co-equal departments of the Government, that I have been compelled to point out the consequences to which the discussion and passage of the resolution may lead, if the tendency of the measure be not checked in its inception.

It is due to the high trust with which I have been charged; to those who may be called to succeed me in it; to the Representatives of the people, whose constitutional prerogative has been unlawfully assumed; to the people and to the States; and to the Constitution they have established, that I should not permit its provisions to be broken down by such an attack on the Executive department, without at least some effort "to preserve, protect, and defend" them. With this view, and for the reasons which have been stated, I do hereby SOLEMNLY PROTEST against the aforementioned proceedings of the Senate, as unauthorized by the Constitution, contrary to its spirit, and to several of its express provisions, subversive of that distribution of the powers of Government which it has ordained and established; destructive of the checks and safeguards by which those powers were intended, on the one hand, to be controlled, and on the other to be protected; and calculated, by their immediate and collateral effects, by their character and tendency, to concentrate in the hands of a body not directly amenable to the people, a degree of influence and power dangerous to their liberties, and fatal to the Constitution of their choice.

The resolution of the Senate contains an imputation upon my private as well as upon my public character; and as it must stand forever on their Journals, I cannot close this substitute for that defence which I have not been allowed to present in the ordinary form, without remarking, that I have lived in vain if it be necessary to enter into a formal vindication of my character and purposes from such an imputation. In vain do I bear upon my person enduring memorials of that contest in which American liberty was purchased—in vain have I since periled property, fame, and life, in defence of the rights and privileges so dearly bought—in vain am I now, without a personal aspiration, or the hope of individual advantage, encountering responsibilities and dangers, from which, by mere inactivity in relation to a single point, I might have been exempt—if any serious doubts can be entertained as to the purity of my purposes and motives. If I had been ambitious, I should have sought an alliance with that powerful institution, which even now aspires to no divided empire. If I had been venal, I should have sold myself to its designs. Had I preferred personal comfort and official ease to the performance of my arduous duty, I should have ceased to molest it. In the history of conquerors and usurpers, never, in the fire of youth, nor in the vigor of manhood, could I find an attraction to lure me from the path of duty; and now, I shall scarcely find an inducement to commence their career of ambition, when gray hairs and a decaying frame, instead of inviting to toil and battle, call me to the contemplation of other worlds, where conquerors cease to be honored, and usurpers expiate their crimes. The only ambition I can feel, is to acquit myself to Him to whom I must soon render an account of my stewardship, to serve my fellow-men, and live respected and honored in the history of my country. No; the ambition which leads me on, is an anxious desire and a fixed determination, to return to the people, unimpaired, the sacred trust they have confided to my charge; to heal the wounds of the Constitution and preserve it from further violation; to persuade my countrymen, so far as I may, that it is not in a splendid Government, supported by powerful monopolies and aristocratical establishments, that they will find happiness, or their liberties protection, but in a plain system, void of pomp—protecting all, and granting favors to none—dispensing its blessings like the dews of Heaven, unseen, and unfelt, save in the freshness and beauty they contribute to produce. It is such a Government that the genius of our people requires—such an one only under which our States may remain for ages to come united, properous, and free. If the Almighty Being who has hitherto sustained and protected me, will but vouchsafe to make my feeble powers instrumental to such a result, I shall anticipate with pleasure the place to be assigned me in the history of my country, and die contented with the belief that I have contributed, in some small degree, to increase the value and prolong the duration of American liberty.

To the end that the resolution of the Senate may not be hereafter drawn into precedent, with the authority of silent acquiescence on the part of the Executive department; and to the end, also, that my motives and views in the executive proceedings denounced in that resolution may be known to my fellow-citizens, to the world, and to all posterity, I respectfully request that this message and protest may be entered at length on the Journals of the Senate.

ANDREW JACKSON.

April 15th, 1834.

The protest having been read—

Mr. POINDEXTER said he did not rise to discuss at this time the several topics touched upon in this extraordinary paper, nor to express the feelings of indignation which the paper had excited, and ought to excite in his bosom, and in that of every honorable member of the Senate, and which it must excite in that of every patriotic citizen. He would leave that for another and more suitable occasion. His present object was to protest against the reception of this paper, and he now moved that the paper be not received.

He would go as far as any man in paying due respect to an executive communication, coming within the constitutional range of the executive authority; but when the Chief Magistrate departs from that constitutional range, and makes the Senate the medium through which to make popular appeals, and fulminate charges against the character of the Senate itself, he, for one, would resist such a course of practice. The paper, in its allusions to the resolutions of the gentleman from Kentucky, was most novel and unprecedented in its character; and if so, what appellation could be found suitable for this most singular paper?. Was such a thing ever dreamed of before? Was there an instance on the Journals of Congress, from the origin of the Government up to the present time, like it? It was not an executive message, but a paper which the President had no authority to send here—it was a mere paper, signed Andrew Jackson, nothing else; and if we refused to receive it, it would not be the first instance of a paper signed Andrew Jackson being refused a hearing here. On a former occasion, another paper, which his best friends were ashamed of, was presented here, and sent back to him—the offensive parts in it were struck out, and then it was received. Mr. P. regarded this as an attempt to bring this branch of the Government, standing between the liberties of the people and the vast strides of arbitrary power, into utter disrespect and contempt. Was there any power which the Executive did not now claim? He contended there was not one, except that which belonged to the Court of King's Bench in England, going upon the bench of the Supreme Court and presiding there.

We have here, to be sure, a qualified veto, by which we can overrule him by two-thirds, but with the patronage of the Blue Book, what measure was there that he could not be supported in? But what use had he made of his power of the veto? Why, that he would exercise it in considering any law which he could not approve in his capacity as a member of Congress. And what then became of the legislative power? We were mere drudges—we might prepare bills, discuss, amend and pass them, and when passed we may go to the imperial head, and he will tell us whether they shall be laws or not. He might as well go to the Judges of the Supreme Court, and direct them what judgment they should give. The Representatives of the States were held in mere mockery—the whole legislative power of the Goverment was placed in the hands of one man—he claims the power of removal from office, and being the commander-in-chief of the army and navy, and having unlimited control over the treasury, was there any other power remaining, that he did not possess? Perhaps he has the power of removal, and perhaps he ought to have it; and upon this basis he claims the right to exercise a legitimate power for illegitimate purposes; so that there was now no power in the Constitution which might not be perverted to the supremacy of the Executive will. Taxes may be constitutionally laid on the people, but if they be laid for the purpose of maintaining the clergy, it would be unconstitutional. He has the power of appointment and removal; but can he exercise this power, which is given him, for the purpose of attaining a power and authority which is not given him? He kicks one Secretary of the Treasury out of office because he would not do the duty enjoined on him, and thus he marches up to the treasury, and scatters the funds of the people abroad among his political friends, which, by the by, is a good deal needed these hard times. Mr. P. contended that this was the exercise of a power which might overturn the Constitution itself. Suppose the Constitution should give the Secretary of the Treasury the power of appointing his own clerks—it would be constitutional. The Secretary makes out his list of clerks—the President has another list made out by his under-workers, which he sends in to him. But the Secretary may say, I have the power of making all my clerks, and I prefer my own; to which the President would respond, I do not dictate to you; you must exercise your own judgment; but if you don't appoint my list, I will turn you out of office.

This is no message; it is merely a paper signed Andrew Jackson; and much more dangerous in its tendency than the paper which the same man sent here in 1819, and which the Senate kicked out of doors. Then, he held the military power only—now, he holds both the civil and military. This, Mr. P. said, was a measure calculated to produce no general good. It was merely an attack on this body. It would make a good article for a certain official journal; but it was unfit for the serious consideration of the Senate. He would spurn it from the Senate; it was an attempt to use the Senate as the medium through which to assail the body itself—this body which stands as a barrier between the people and the encroachments of Executive power—upon which liberty may repose, without danger, to the remotest posterity. Destroy this branch, and, with the aid of the Blue Book, no limit can be set to the extent of Executive power. It is a most miserable attempt to sustain that power. But it is nothing more than the Executive has said in his private chamber, and what appears daily in the columns of the Executive journal itself.

Mr. P. concluded by moving that the paper be not received.

Mr. SPRAGUE rose to make but a very few observations upon this most extraordinary paper. And what he would say was more in grief than in anger; for whatever other feelings, on ordinary occasions, he might have, on such an occasion as this, the paper, coming from such a source, and being calculated, if sustained, to produce such an injurious effect upon the institutions of the country, that all other feelings must be merged in that of deep regret. The claims of Executive authority and power, in this document, leave no other department in the Government than a single Executive will. He says all Executive power is vested in him; that he is responsible for the acts of every Executive officer, and that all the powers given by law are vested in him as the head and fountain of all; that he is the sole Executive, and that all executive power is merged in him individually. In what language does he speak of the Secretary of the Treasury? He speaks of his power over *his* Secretary, and repeats the President's control over *his* Secretary, and thus he is the Secretary of the President, and not the Secretary of the laws, or of the Treasury, and if so, every head of every department is his Secretary. Your Major General is *his* Major General, and all the officers of the country are his officers. He then has forty thousand officers, who are all his officers; and this corresponds well with the expression to the Philadelphia committee, that this is "*My Government.*"

But what more does he say? He has gone beyond what has ever been claimed here by his most ardent friends, and supporters of executive power. He has said that, by the Constitution, he must have possession of the public money and public

property, and that Congress cannot take from the Executive the control of the public money. Is this the possession of the public purse, or is it not? Gentlemen here admitted, on the deposite question, that Congress had the control of the public moneys; but now the President tells us that the Constitution gives him the possession and control of them. And with all this, what further? Why, the gentleman from Mississippi said that the President had no power to send such a message to Congress. But the gentleman did not observe that this power was claimed in a part of the Constitution never before claimed by any other President, to wit: his oath of office. He gives this as the foundation from which he derives his power, and claims it to be his duty to see the Constitution preserved inviolate. He says the Senate has violated the Constitution, and that it is his duty to go to the Senate and correct that violation. With the sword and the purse in his hand, and his oath to see that the Constitution is not violated, where is the limit of his power? And he is to sustain the Constitution, under his oath of office, as he understands it: not as the judiciary may expound it, or as Congress may declare it, but as he individually understands it. And because the Senate have passed a resolution expressive of their opinion, he says that it is a violation of the Constitution and acting judicially, and that he cannot be touched but by impeachment. Impeachment of the Executive with all the powers he claims! The expression of opinion by the Senate the President translates into a judicial sentence, passed without trial, and yet the same President has passed the same opinion on the Senate, and we have not heard that this is unconstitutional. In the Executive message sent to the Senate in March, 1833, he says that the Senate have acted unconstitutionally, and yet the Senate can do no act restraining his power. We cannot say he has used the money of the people. Ours is only a judicial power. Is not the document saturated throughout with denunciations of the Senate, charging this body with having violated the Constitution? And now it is a matter of grievous complaint that the Senate have dared to express similar opinions. The resolution offered by Mr. Branch, of North Carolina, when a Senator here, was not complained of as an unconstitutional exercise of power, and yet the resolution of the gentleman from Kentucky is complained of as an unconstitutional resolution, because it is not joint, and not intended as the foundation of legislative action. How did the President know that it was not intended as the foundation of a bill for the restoration of the deposites? Yet, he assumes it, and says the Senate cannot pass the resolution. The preamble declares that it is asserted, lest it should be drawn into precedent; and was it not the duty of the Senate to declare it, to prevent a silent acquiescence.

Mr. S. said he might cite the resolution relative to the Seminole war, and the resolution in the House of Representatives relative to the Panama mission, but it was unnecessary. There was one thing, however, upon which he would say a word. The President had seen fit to set forth in this document certain legislative proceedings, for the purpose of having a bearing on certain individual members of the Senate, and he had done him (Mr. S.) the honor to refer to his vote on the passage of the resolutions, and then detailed the resolutions of the Legislature of Maine, giving him instructions on that subject. Now, all that he (Mr. S.) need say to the tenant of the White House was, that if the Secretary of the Treasury was *his* Secretary, he (Mr. S.) was not *his* Senator. He recognised no right in the President to lecture him upon his duty as a Senator here. Whatever power he might have over *his* officers and men, and the officers of *his* Government, he was not *his* officer; and so long as the Government was confided to him to the extent of the part he took in it, it should not be *his* Government. Mr. S. said he recognised no right in the President to say whether he should act in accordance with his will or otherwise. In his spirit of dictation, what had we heard? Members had said they were elected as Jacksonmen, and therefore they had no discretion but to vote as Jacksonmen. He was not so situated. He owed no fealty to President Jackson; he was not elected as a Jacksonman. He submitted to no control of his—he never bowed the knee to Baal. He was elected to act on his convictions of duty, upon mature deliberation, upon such subjects as should come before him. He never would acknowledge the right of the Executive, or of any individual, to dictate to him, or to rebuke Senators here. He was aware there was a disclaimer accompanying this part of the document; that he said he gave it only as a matter of history, and he was the mere historian. But he might have given something more interesting, for this had been nothing more than what was in the official journal for the last three months.

The President closes this paper by an appeal to his own services in behalf of the people; the same process by which the people have been called on in all ages to confer unlimited power. He points to his wounds, to his past services, and appeals to the people if they can refuse anything to such a benefactor. And how (Mr. S. asked) is "my Government" now felt like the dews of heaven? Look abroad through the land; cast your eyes over the country; behold your green fields withered; listen to the cries of distress of the widow and the orphan, rising almost in execrations of the exercise of that power which has blasted their hopes and reduced them to despair. And yet, says this document, Government is only to be known as the dews of heaven in its operations. Such is the moral—such is the example.

Mr. FRELINGHUYSEN considered this as a most extraordinary proceeding—one which would form an era in American history. When the busy hum of industry was silenced, when the laborer was in want of employment, when banks were breaking in every direction, and the cries for relief from the unrelenting hand of power were heard everywhere around us, what did we see before us? A lecture of an hour and a half to the Senate for daring to interfere with the Executive power and authority—an interference which, he says, has a direct tendency to interrupt the harmony which should subsist between the various coördinate branches of the Government. He charges us with having ascribed to him encroachments upon the Constitution, and yet in every successive page he has charged the Senate with the same thing. And now (Mr. F. thought) our only course to preserve that harmony was, to refuse to receive the paper. He viewed this as an unauthorized Executive interference with the legislative action of the Senate. The President alleges that these resolutions lead to no legislation. How does he know this? Why does he conjecture what may or may not be the action of Congress? We allege that the Secretary of the Treasury was responsible to Congress; that if he removed the deposites, he was bound to report his reasons to Congress. Well, he did remove them, and gave his reasons for the act, and on their very face it appears that the Secretary was induced to do the act by the order of the President; and when the act refers him over to Congress, and we find that the Secretary may found himself on his own reasons or the Executive orders, have we no right to express our opinion, and say that the Executive had no authority, or that the reasons are insufficient? The House of Representatives had not come up to the question whether the reasons for the removal of the deposites were sufficient and satisfactory, and what do we now find? The President interfering between us and our future legislation. He founds himself on his power of removal, and while he leases himself on forty years construction, he forgets the country's experience for forty years of the necessity and utility of the Bank of the United States. The legislative consequences of our action were direct and immediate, for until Congress approved of the reasons of the Secretary, he was not sustained; and yet the President takes all this as a matter of history, and takes leave to record his protest against it.

But Mr. F. maintained that we had a right to administer official rebuke, in spite of his *sic volo, sic jubeo*. When we think he is making use of his popularity to destroy the liberties of the people, we have a right to say that the President is on the way to it, and if those liberties are not rescued by the ballot-boxes they will inevitably be lost. He could not consent to receive this paper, if for this reason alone. The allusion to the resolutions of the Legislature of New Jersey were unworthy of the Chief Magistrate of this great nation as the chronicler of the times. And if four Senators here have dared to meet the frowns of their constituents in their zeal for their country and the love of liberty by voting against these usurpations of Executive power, it was some evidence of the existence of these evils. He did not bow his knee to these instructions, and he appealed to the great Judge of all things for the honesty and uprightness of his intentions. He had but one word to say of these instructions. The people of New Jersey have their servants at home, and they have their servants here, and they have distinctly said that they consider it pure arrogance in their servants at home to dictate to their servants here.

Mr. BENTON rose and said that the public mind was now to be occupied with a question of the very first moment and importance, and identical in all its features with the great question growing out of the famous resolutions of the English House of Commons in the case of the Middlesex election in the year 1768, and which engrossed the attention of the British empire for fourteen years before it was settled. That question was one in which the House of Commons was judged and condemned, for adopting a resolution which was held by the subjects of the British Crown to be a violation of their Constitution, and a subversion of the rights of Englishmen. The question now before the Senate, and which will go before the American people, grows out of a resolution in which he (Mr. B.) believed that the Constitution had been violated—the privileges of the House of Representatives invaded—and the rights of an American citizen, in the person of the President, subverted. The resolution of the House of Commons, after fourteen years of annual motions, was expunged from the journal of the House; and he pledged himself to the American people to commence a similar series of motions with respect to this resolution of the Senate. He had made up his mind to do so without consultation with any human being, and without deigning to calculate the chances, or the time of success. He rested under the firm conviction that the resolution of the Senate, which had drawn from the President the calm, temperate and dignified *Protest* which had been read at the table, was a resolution which ought to be expunged from the journal of the Senate; and if anything was necessary to sustain his sense of duty in making a motion to that effect, and in encouraging others after he was gone, in following up that motion to success, it would be found in the history and termination of the similar motion which was made in the English House of Commons to which he had referred. That motion was renewed for fourteen years—from 1768 to 1782—before it was successful. For the first seven years, the lofty and indignant majority did not condescend to reply to the motion. They sunk it under a dead vote as often as presented. The second seven years they replied; and at the end of the term, and on the assembling of a new Parliament, the veteran motion was carried by more than two to one; and the gratifying spectacle was beheld of a public expurgation, in the face of the assembled Commons of England, of the obnoxious resolution from the journal of the House. The elections in England were septennial, and it took two terms of seven years, or two general elections, to bring the sense of the kingdom to bear upon their representatives; the elections of the Senate were sexennial, with intercalary exits and entrances; and it might take a less or a longer period, he would not presume to say which, to bring the sense of the American people to bear upon an act of the American Senate. Of that, he would make no calculation; but the final success of the motion in the English House of Commons, after fourteen years' perseverance, was a sufficient encouragement for him to begin, and doubtless would encourage others to continue until the good work should be crowned with success, and the only atonement made, which it was in the Senate's power to make, to the violated majesty of the Constitution, the invaded privileges of the House of Representatives, and the subverted rights of an American citizen.

In bringing this great question before the American people, Mr. B. should consider himself as addressing the calm intelligence of an enlightened community. He believed the body of the American people to be the most enlightened community upon earth; and, without the least disparagement

to the present Senate, he must be permitted to believe that many such Senates might be drawn from the ranks of the people, and still leave no dearth of intelligence behind. To such a community, in an appeal on a great question of constitutional law, to the understandings of such a people, declamation, passion, epithets, opprobrious language, would stand for nothing. They would float, harmless and unheeded, through the empty air, and strike in vain upon the ear of a sober and dispassionate tribunal. Indignation, real or affected; wrath, however hot; fury, however enraged; asseverations, however violent; denunciations, however furious,—will avail nothing. Facts—inexorable facts—are all that will be attended to; reason, calm and self-possessed, is all that will be listened to. An intelligent tribunal will exact the respect of an address to their understandings; and he that wishes to be heard on this great question, or being heard, would wish to be heeded, will have occasion to be clear and correct in his facts; close and perspicuous in his application of law; fair and candid in his conclusions and inferences; temperate and decorous in his language; and scrupulously free from every taint of vengeance and malice. Solemnly impressed with the truth of all these convictions, it was the intention of himself (Mr. B.)—whatever the example or the provocation might be—never to forget his place, his subject, his audience, and his object!—never to forget that he was speaking in the American Senate, on a question of violated Constitution and outraged individual right, to an audience comprehending the whole body of the American people, and for the purpose of obtaining a righteous decision from the calm and sober judgment of a high-minded, intelligent, and patriotic community.

The question immediately before the Senate was one of minor consequence; it might be called a question of small import, except for the effect which the decision might have upon the Senate itself. In that point of view it might be a question of some moment; for, without reference to individuals, it was essential to the cause of free Governments, that every department of the Government, the Senate inclusive, should so act as to preverve to itself the respect and the confidence of the country. The immediate question was upon the rejection of the President's message. It was moved to reject it—to reject it, not after it was considered, but before it was considered! and thus to tell the American people that their President shall not be heard—should not be allowed to plead his defence—in the presence of the body that condemned him, neither before the condemnation, nor after it! This is the motion, and certainly no enemy to the Senate could wish it to miscarry. The President, in the conclusion of his message, has respectfully requested that his defence might be entered upon the Journal of the Senate—upon that same journal which contains the record of his conviction. This is the request of the President. Will the Senate deny it? Will they refuse this act of sheer justice and common decency? Will they go further, and not only refuse to place it on the journal, but refuse even to suffer it to remain in the Senate? Will they refuse to permit it to remain on file, but send it back, or throw it out of doors, without condescending to reply to it? for that is the exact import of the motion now made! Will Senators exhaust their minds, and their bodies also, in loading this very communication with epithets, and then say that it shall not be received? Will they receive memorials, resolutions, essays, from all that choose to abuse the President, and not receive a word of defence from him? Will they continue the spectacle which has been presented here for three months—a daily presentation of attacks upon the President from all that choose to attack him, young and old, boys and men—attacks echoing the very sound of this resolution, and which are not only received and filed here, but printed also, and referred to a committee, and introduced, each one, with lauded commentary of set phrase? Are the Senate to receive all these, and yet refuse to receive from the object of all this attack one word of answer? In this point of view—as a question concerning the Senate itself—it may become material to the Senate, in a country and in an age when no tribunal is too high for public opinion to reach it, it may become material to the Senate, in such a country and such an age, to reject and throw out of doors, the calm and temperate defence of the President, in the midst of the reception of a thousand memorials and resolutions, condemning him for the very act which he is not allowed to defend. Is he to be the only citizen who is not to be heard by the Senate? Him whom it seems to be lawful for every one whose education and manners qualify him for the application of Billingsgate rhetoric, to lavish it upon him. Rejected or not, that communication cannot be secreted from the eyes of the American people. It has been read, and will be printed. An independent press will carry it to the extremities of the country, and hand it down to succeeding generations. It will be compared with speeches, delivered for three months in this Capitol, against this President; and an enlightened and upright community will decide between the language of the defence, and the language of the accusation; between the temper of the accusers, and the temper of the accused; between the violent President who has violated the Constitution and the laws, and the meek and gentle Senators who have sat in judgment upon him for it. The people will see these things—will compare them together—will judge for themselves; and that judgment, in this free and happy land, will be the final and supreme award, from which there is no appeal.

The great question (Mr. B. said) which was to go before the American people, and to claim from them that intense and profound consideration which the English people gave to the conduct of the House of Commons in regard to the Middlesex election, is the constitutionality of the Senate's conduct in adopting the resolution which condemned the President for a violation of the laws and of the Constitution of his country. It was the conduct of the Senate which would now be on trial; and that conduct deserved to be tried, and, as far as it depended upon him, should be tried, UPON THE FACTS OF THE CASE ALONE—upon the facts which our own journal contains—upon the resolutions as offered, and adopted, here—upon the authentic speeches which the supporters of these resolutions have published to the world, and which show the sense in which they understood the proceeding which they carried on. The proceeding he (Mr. B.) held to be an impeachment, without the forms of an impeachment—a conviction, without the form of a trial—a sentence of condemnation for a high crime and misdemeanor against the Chief Magistrate of the Republic, without evidence, without hearing, without defence, without the observance of a single form prescribed for the trial of impeachments; and this by the very tribunal which is bound to try the formal impeachment for the same matter, if duly demanded by the grand inquest of the nation in their Hall of Representatives. This was the question which the country would have to try, and in the trial of which, furious passion, reckless denunciation, bold, or even audacious assertion, will stand for nothing. The record! the record! will be the evidence which the country will demand. The facts! the facts! will be the data which they require! The speeches! the speeches! delivered on this floor will be the test of the spirit and intention with which these proceedings were pursued and consummated; and, without animadverting upon the *manner* in which the President's message and *protest* has been received here, and which has presented such an extraordinary scene in the American Senate, he should proceed to lay before the people the authentic evidence, in the calmest manner, which it will be their business to weigh in the formation of their opinions on this momentous subject. The first evidence which he should submit, was the series of resolutions which were presented to the Senate, before one could be framed which could unite the votes of the twenty-six Senators who finally voted together in the adoption of one of them. He said he should present the *series* of these resolutions; for in the metamorphosis which they underwent, there was much for anxious reflection; the first one containing specifications, which were omitted in the second and third; while the second and third notoriously rested upon the specifications omitted, and which could not be retained on the face of the record!

Mr. B. then read the resolution as first offered by Mr. CLAY at the commencement of the debate. It was in the following words:

"*Resolved*, That, by dismissing the late Secretary of the Treasury, because he would not, contrary to his sense of his own duty, remove the money of the United States in deposite with the Bank of the United States and its branches, in conformity with the President's opinion; and by appointing his successor to effect such removal, which has been done, the President has assumed the exercise of a power over the treasury of the United States not granted to him by the Constitution and laws, and dangerous to the liberties of the people."

He then read the resolution as amended, or altered, by the same gentleman, and offered again to the Senate towards the close of the debate. It was as follows:

"*Resolved*, That in taking upon himself the responsibility of removing the deposites of the public money from the Bank of the United States, the President of the United States has assumed the exercise of a power over the treasury of the United States not granted to him by the Constitution and laws, and dangerous to the liberties of the people."

He then read the third edition, revised, amended, and altered, of the same resolution, as finally submitted to the Senate by the original mover, and adopted by the vote of the Senate:

"*Resolved*, That the President, in the late executive proceedings in relation to the public revenue, has assumed upon himself authority and power not conferred by the Constitution and laws, but in derogation of both."

Mr. B. then remarked upon the alteration which these resolutions had undergone, and begged it to be well remembered that none of these *alterations* were *amendments* made by the Senate, but were the voluntary and successive changes introduced by the mover himself. He remarked, *first*, upon the nature of these changes; *secondly*, upon the design which induced them: and, *thirdly*, upon the effect of making them. The first change consisted in dropping the specification on which the general charge of violating the laws and the Constitution rested, and retaining the formal impeachment conclusion, of *dangerous to the liberties of the people*. The second change consisted in the omission of the specification, and in the suppression of that regular impeaching clause—*dangerous to the liberties of the people!* Now, (said Mr. B.,) when were these alterations made? Certainly it was after the objection had been fully taken in the Senate that this resolution contained impeachable matter! It was after the original resolution had been denounced as a virtual impeachment of the President of the United States, and after the suppressed passages had been pointed out as proving and identifying the impeachment character of the resolution. It was after all this that the alterations were made. Having showed the time when the alterations were made, Mr. B. next showed the *design* with which they must have been made; and that evidently was to get rid of the criminal aspect of the proceedings, and to avoid a trial before the people on those specifications, on which, possibly, the twenty-six could not unite here, nor go to trial upon anywhere! He remarked, in the third place, upon the *effect* produced in the character of the resolution, and affirmed that it was nothing. He said that the same charge ran through all three. They all three imputed to the President a violation of the Constitution, and of the laws of the country—of that Constitution which he was sworn to support, and of those laws which he was not only bound to observe himself, but to cause to be faithfully observed by all others. A violation of the Constitution and of the laws, (Mr. B. said,) were not abstractions and metaphysical subtleties. They must relate to persons or things. The violations cannot rest in the air; they must affix themselves to men or to property; they must connect themselves with the transactions of real life. They cannot be ideal and contemplative. In omitting the specifications relative to the dismission of one Secretary of the Treasury, and the appointment of another, what other specifications were adopted or substituted? Certainly none! What others were mentally intended? Surely none! What others were suggested? Certainly none! The general charge, then, rests upon the same specification; and so completely is this the fact, that no supporter of the resolutions has thought it necessary to make the least alteration in his speeches

which supported the original resolution, or to say a single additional word in favor of the altered resolution as finally passed. The omission of the specification is, then, an omission of form and not of substance; it is a change of words, and not of things; and the substitution of *a derogation of the laws and Constitution, for danger to the liberties of the people*, is a still more flagrant instance of change of words without change of things. It is tautologous and nonsensical. It adds nothing to the general charge, and takes nothing from it. It neither explains it nor qualifies it. In the technical sense it is absurd; for it is not the case of a statute in derogation of the common law, to wit, repealing a part of it. In the common parlance understanding it is ridiculous; for the President is not even charged with defaming the Constitution and the laws; and, if he was so charged, it would present a curious trial of *scandalum magnatum* for the American Senate to engage in. No! (said Mr. B.,) this derogation clause is an expletion! It is put in, to fill up! The regular impeaching clause, *of dangerous to the liberties of the people*, had to be taken out. There was danger, not to the people certainly, but to the character of the resolution, if it staid in. It identified that resolution as an impeachment, and, therefore, constituted a piece of internal evidence, which it was necessary to withdraw; but in withdrawing which, the character of the resolution was not altered. The charge for violating the laws and the Constitution still stood; and the substituted clause was nothing but a stopper to a vacuum—additional sound, without additional sense, to fill up a blank, and round off a sentence.

After showing the impeaching character of the Senate's resolution from its own internal evidence, Mr. B. had recourse to another description of evidence, scarcely inferior to the resolutions themselves, in the authentic interpretation of their meaning: he alluded to the speeches made in support of them, and which had resounded in this chamber for three months, and were now circulating all over the country in every variety of newspaper and pamphlet form. These speeches were made by the friends of the resolution to procure its adoption here, and to justify its adoption before the country. Let the country then read. Let the people read what has been sent to them for the purpose of justifying these resolutions which they are now to try! They will find them to be in the character of prosecution pleadings against an accused man, on his trial for the commission of great crimes! Let them look over these speeches, and mark the passages: they will find language ransacked, history rummaged, to find words sufficiently strong, and examples sufficiently odious, to paint and exemplify, the enormity of the crime of which the President was alleged to be guilty. After reading these passages, let any one doubt, if he can, as to the character of the resolution which was adopted. Let him doubt, if he can, of the impeachable nature of the offence which was charged upon the President. Let him doubt, if he can, that every Senator who voted for that resolution, voted the President to be guilty of an impeachable offence, an offence for the trial of which this Senate is the appointed tribunal, an offence which it will be the immediate duty of the House of Representatives to bring before the Senate, in a formal impeachment, unless they disbelieve in the truth and justice of the resolution which has been adopted.

Mr. B. said there were three characters in which the Senate could act, and every time it acted, it necessarily did so in one or the other of these characters. It possessed executive, legislative, and judicial, characters. As a part of the executive, it acted on treaties and nominations to office; as a part of the legislative, it assisted in making laws; as a judicial tribunal, it decided impeachments. Now, in which of these characters did the Senate act when it adopted the resolution in question? Not in its executive character, it will be admitted; not in its legislative character, it will be proved; for the resolution was, in its nature, wholly foreign to legislation. It was directed, not to the formation of a law, but to the condemnation of the President. It was to condemn him for dismissing one Secretary, because he would not do a thing, and appointing another, that he might do it; and certainly this was not matter for legislation; for Mr. Duane could not be restored by law, nor Mr. Taney be put out by law. It was to convict the President of violating the Constitution, and the laws; and surely these infractions are not to be amended by laws, but avenged by trial and punishment. The very nature of the resolution proves it to be foreign to all legislation; its form proves the same thing; for it is not joint, to require the action of the House of Representatives, and thus ripen into law; nor is it followed by an instruction to a committee to report a bill in conformity to it. No such instruction could even now be added without committing an absurdity of the most ridiculous character. There was another resolution with which this must not be confounded, and upon which an instruction to a committee might have been bottomed: it was the resolution which declared the Secretary's reasons for removing the deposites to be insufficient and unsatisfactory; but no such instruction has been bottomed even upon that resolution; so that it is evident that no legislation of any kind was intended to follow either resolution, even that to which legislation might have been appropriate, much less that to which it would have been an absurdity. Four months have elapsed since the resolutions were brought in. In all that time, there has been no attempt to found a legislative act upon either of them; and it is too late now to assume that the one which in its *nature* and in its *form*, is wholly foreign to legislation, is a legislative act, and adopted by the Senate in its legislative character. No! This resolution is judicial; it is a judgment pronounced upon an imputed offence; it is the declared sense of a majority of the Senate, of the guilt of the President of a high crime and a misdemeanor. It is, in substance, an impeachment—an impeachment in violation of all the forms prescribed by the Constitution—in violation of the privileges of the House of Representatives—in subversion of the rights of the accused—and the record of which ought to be expunged from the Journal of the Senate.

Mr. B. said the selection of a tribunal for the trial of impeachments was felt by the convention which framed the Constitution as one of the most delicate and difficult tasks which they had to perform. Those great men were well read in history, both ancient and modern, and knew that the impeaching power—the usual mode for trying political men for political offences—was often an engine for the gratification of factious and ambitious feelings. An impeachment was well known to be the beaten road for running down a hated or successful political rival. After great deliberation—after weighing all the tribunals, even that of the Supreme Court—the Senate of the United States was fixed upon as the body which, from its constitution, would be the most impartial, neutral, and equitable, that could be selected; and with the check of a previous inquisition, and presentment of charges by the House of Representatives, would be the safest tribunal to which could be confided a power so great in itself, and so susceptible of being abused. The Senate was selected; and to show that he had not over-stated the difficulties of the convention in making the selection, he would take leave to read a passage from a work which was canonical on this subject, and from an article in that work, which was written by the gentleman whose authority would have most weight on this occasion. He spoke of the Federalist, and of the article written by General Hamilton on the impeaching power.

"A well-constituted court for the trial of impeachments, is an object not more to be desired 'than difficult to be obtained, in a Government 'wholly elective. The subjects of its jurisdiction 'are those offences which proceed from the misconduct of public men, or, in other words, from 'the abuse or violation of some public trust. They 'are of a nature which may, with peculiar propriety, be denominated POLITICAL, as they relate 'chiefly to injuries done immediately to the society 'itself. The prosecution of them, for this reason, will seldom fail to agitate the passions of the 'whole community, and to divide it into parties, 'more or less friendly or inimical to the accused. 'In many cases it will connect itself with the preexisting factions, and will enlist all their animosities, partialities, influence, and interest, on one 'side or on the other; and, in such cases, there 'will always be the greatest danger that the decision will be regulated more by the comparative 'strength of parties than by the real demonstrations of innocence or guilt. The delicacy and 'magnitude of a trust, which so deeply concerns 'the political reputation and existence of every 'man engaged in the administration of public 'affairs, speak for themselves. The difficulty of 'placing it rightly in a Government resting entirely on the basis of periodical elections, will as 'readily be perceived, when it is considered that 'the most conspicuous characters in it will, from 'that circumstance, be too often the leaders, or the 'tools of the most cunning or the most numerous 'faction; and, on this account, can hardly be expected to possess the requisite neutrality towards 'those whose conduct may be subject of scrutiny.

"The division of the powers of impeachment 'between the two branches of the legislature, assigning to one the right of accusing, to the other 'the right of trying, avoids the inconvenience of 'making the same persons both accusers and judges; 'and guards against the danger of persecution from 'the prevalency of a factious spirit in either of 'those branches."

Mr. B. said there was much matter for elucidation of the present object of discussion in the extract which he had read. Its definition of an impeachable offence covered the identical charge which was contained in the resolution adopted by the Senate against the President. The offence charged upon him possessed every feature of the impeachment defined by General Hamilton. It imputes misconduct to a public man, for the abuse and violation of public trust. The discussion of the charge has agitated the passions of the whole community; it has divided the people into parties, some friendly, some inimical, to the accused; it has connected itself with preëxisting parties, enlisting the whole of the opposition parties under one banner, and calling forth all their animosities—all their partialities—all their influence—all their interest; and, what was not foreseen by General Hamilton, it has called forth the tremendous moneyed power, and the pervading organization of a great moneyed power, wielding a mass of forty millions of money, and sixty millions of debt! wielding the whole in aid and support of this charge upon the President; and working the double battery of seduction on one hand, and oppression on the other, to put down the man against whom it is directed. This is what General Hamilton did not foresee. But the next feature in the picture he did foresee, and most accurately describe, as it is now seen by us all. He said that the decision of these impeachments would often be regulated more by the comparative strength of parties than by the guilt or innocence of the accused. How prophetic! Look to the memorials, resolutions, and petitions, sent in here to criminate the President: so clearly marked by a party line, that when an exception occurs, it is made the special subject of public remark! Look at the vote in the Senate, upon the adoption of the resolution! also as clearly defined by a party line as any party question can ever be expected to be.

To guard the most conspicuous characters from being persecuted,—Mr. B. said he was using the language of General Hamilton,—to guard the most conspicuous characters from being persecuted by the leaders, or the tools of the most cunning, or the most numerous faction,—the convention had placed the power of trying impeachments, not in the Supreme Court, not even in a body of select judges, chosen for the occasion, but in the Senate of the United States, and not even in them without an intervening check to the abuse of that power, by associating the House of Representatives, and forbidding the Senate to proceed against any officer until that grand inquest of the nation should demand his trial. How far fortunate, or otherwise, the convention may have been in the selection of its tribunal for the trial of impeachments, it was not for him (Mr. B.) to say. It was not for him to say how far the *requisite neutrality towards those whose conduct may be under scrutiny*, may be found, or has been found, in this body. But he must take leave to say, that if a public man may be virtually impeached—actually condemned by the Senate of an impeachable offence—without the intervention of the House of Representatives, then has the Constitution failed at one of its most vital points, and a ready means found for doing a thing which had filled other countries with persecution, faction,

THE CONGRESSIONAL GLOBE.

PRINTED AND PUBLISHED AT THE CITY OF WASHINGTON, BY BLAIR & RIVES.

23D CONGRESS, 1ST SESSION. SATURDAY, APRIL 26, 1834. VOL. I........No. 21.

and violence, and which it was intended should never be done here.

Mr. B. called upon the Senate to recollect what was the feature in the famous court of the STAR CHAMBER, which rendered that court the most odious that ever sat in England. It was not the mass of its enormities, great as they were; for the regular tribunals which yet existed exceeded that court both in the mass and in the atrocity of their crimes and oppressions. The regular courts, in the compass of a single reign—that of James the Second; a single judge, in a single riding—Jeffries, on the western circuit—surpassed all the enormities of the Star Chamber in the whole course of its existence. What, then, rendered that court so intolerably odious to the English people? Sir, (said Mr. B.) it was because that court had no grand jury—because it proceeded without presentment, without indictment, upon information alone; and thus got at its victims without the intervention—without the restraint—of an accusing body. This is the feature which sunk the Star Chamber in England. It is the feature which no criminal tribunal in this America is allowed to possess. The most inconsiderable offender in any State of the Union must be charged by a grand jury before he can be tried by the court. In this Senate, sitting as a high court of impeachment, a charge must first be presented by the House of Representatives, sitting as the grand inquest of the nation. But if the Senate can proceed without the intervention of this grand inquest, wherein is it to differ from the Star Chamber, except in the mere execution of its decrees? And what other execution is now required for delinquent public men than the force of public opinion? No! (said Mr. B.;) we live in an age when public opinion, over public men, is omnipotent and irreversible!—when public sentiment annihilates a public man more effectually than the scaffold! To this new and omnipotent tribunal all the public men of Europe and America are now happily subject. The fiat of public opinion has superseded the axe of the executioner. Struck by that opinion, kings and emperors in Europe, and the highest functionaries among ourselves, fall powerless from the political stage, and wander, while their bodies live, as shadows and phantoms over the land. Should he give examples? It might be invidious; yet all would recollect an eminent example of a citizen, once sitting at the head of this Senate, afterwards falling under a judicial prosecution, from which he escaped untouched by the sword of the law, yet that eminent citizen was more utterly annihilated by public opinion, than any execution of a capital sentence could ever have accomplished upon his name. What occasion, then, has the Senate, sitting as a court of impeachment, for the power of execution? The only effect of a regular impeachment now, is to remove from office, and disqualification for office. An irregular impeachment will be tantamount to removal and disqualification, if the justice of the sentence is confided in by the people. If this condemnation of the President had been pronounced in the first term of his Administration, and the people had believed in the truth and justice of the sentence, certainly President Jackson would not have been elected a second time; and every object that a political rival, or a political party, could have wished from his removal from office, and disqualification for office, would have been accomplished. Disqualification for office—loss of public favor—political death—is now the object of political rivalship; and all this can be accomplished by an informal, as well as by a formal, impeachment, if the sentence is only confided in by the people. If the people believed that the President has violated the Constitution and the laws, he ceases to be the object of their respect and their confidence; he loses their favor; he dies a political death; and that this might be the object of the resolution, Mr. B. would leave to the determination of those who should read the speeches which were delivered in support of the measure, and which would constitute a public and lasting monument of the temper in which the resolution was presented, and the object intended to be accomplished by it.

It was in vain to say there could be no object, at this time, in annihilating the political influence of President Jackson, and killing him off as a public man, with a Senatorial conviction for violating the laws and Constitution of the country. Such an assertion, if ventured upon by any one, would stand contradicted by facts of which Europe and America are witnesses. Does he not stand between the country and the bank? Is he not proclaimed the sole obstacle to the recharter of the bank? and in its recharter is there not wrapped up the destinies of a political party, now panting for power? Remove this sole obstacle—annihilate its influence, kill off President Jackson with a sentence of condemnation for a high crime and misdemeanor, and the charter of the bank will be renewed, and in its renewal a political party, now thundering at the gates of the Capitol, will leap into power. Here, then, is an OBJECT for desiring the extinction of the political influence of President Jackson! An *object* large enough to be seen by all America, and attractive enough to enlist the combined interest of a GREAT MONEYED POWER, and of a GREAT POLITICAL PARTY.

Mr. SOUTHARD thought he felt, notwithstanding the warning given him by the gentleman who had just taken his seat, [Mr. BENTON,] the solemnity of the occasion which we were called upon to act; though he felt we should act with calmness and consideration, he feared he would not be able to school himself into all that degree of moderation so necessary for the occasion. He would call the Senate's attention to the position in which we were at the time we received this message from the Executive of the United States. For, in his opinion, the President had grossly perverted that position. When we came here we found the public treasure removed from the institution where it had been placed by law, to places not known to the law; and removed, too, by the President and Secretary of the Treasury. It was our duty, then, to inquire how and why it had been removed. The Secretary had given us his reasons for the act, and the President himself had also shown the grounds on which he acted. Mr. S. asked, therefore, if we could have avoided making the inquiry, and, having done so, could we avoid saying whether those reasons were sufficient? He apprehended we could not. The order of the President, and the reasons of the Secretary, were both before the Senate, and unless we overlooked both, without affirming or denying the validity of the reasons, we were bound to act as we had done. One of the resolutions expressed the insufficiency of the Secretary's reasons; but had we stopped there, it might have been said that the Secretary was under the necessity of obeying the orders of the President, who had the entire control of the public money. Therefore, he thought the position of the Senate had been grossly perverted by the President of the United States. The resolution says:

"*Resolved*, That the President, in the late executive proceedings in relation to the public revenue, has assumed upon himself authority and power not conferred by the Constitution and laws, but in derogation of both."

He defied human language to furnish terms more mild expressing the idea that the act of the President was unconstitutional; that he had not the authority to do what he had done. We said that it was in derogation of the laws of the country; and if we had said he had no rightful authority, we should have said precisely the same thing. The position taken by the Executive struck at all the legislative power of the Senate, and if the President was correct, we stood here as monuments of the folly of our ancestors who gave us no powers other than those which were necessary to record the executive proceedings. This paper of the Executive asserted that the resolutions were not intended to be the foundation of legislative action. Sir, (said Mr. S.,) the Executive has pronounced what is not true. It is an impertinent interference with the rights of the Senate. He (Mr. S.) said he had exhibited a falsehood. Mr. S. said it was intended as the foundation of legislative action. We meant it to be so, and he knew it to be so. Sir, how could we get at legislative action? Must we not first have decided the act to be wrong? We must first decide and then legislate. Before we undertake to restore the laws, we must first see that the laws have been violated. He said on his responsibility as a Senator, and would not allow it to go out without a contradiction, that it was intended as the foundation of legislative action.

There were many things in this protest, in its details, as well as in its great features, which certainly deserved comment. But he would not detain the Senate by noticing them all. But he would refer to some. The President, after perverting the act of the Senate, says, that the resolution was an accusation against his personal character. This was not so. Where was the attack made which should authorize him to send us a eulogy on his own life? The resolution was a mere declaration that the President had assumed powers upon himself not granted by the Constitution. He denied that that was such an impeachment of his private character as would justify him in coming to the Senate to speak of his revolutionary services. He had never heard his name mentioned in the history of these times, and if he and his friends were right, he must have been but a boy of thirteen years old at the time of the Revolution. He had heard of wounds he had received, but never at the head of a battalion or regiment.

The President said the question before the American people had been settled by a vast majority of that people. When and what question was it that had been passed on by the people? Was it the constitutionality of a United States Bank? No. If it had been passed on by the people, he (Mr. S.) was ignorant of the history of it. To prove that it had been settled in his election to the presidency, he must show how many of those who voted for him did so on account of his hostility to the bank; how many of them voted for the spoils of victory; how many of them voted for that reform which had been given us in an increase of office-holders and their salaries; how many of them voted for him on account of his revolutionary services, founded on fiction or poetry, but not on fact. Take away all these, and how many were given for the sole purpose of breaking down the bank? Where was the solemn decision of the people of the United States that the bank was unconstitutional? When the President came here to make us the medium through which to operate on the people, we ought to take nothing but facts. Shall we, by receiving this paper, place ourselves in an attitude which will compel us to enter into a contest with the Executive of the United States? Our resolution was a mere declaration of opinion, and being so, what right had the President to send us a message, presuming a different act, and giving us a plain warning to proceed no further? We have made a preparatory act, and the moment we have done so, we have received, not from Charles the First, or Cromwell, or Napoleon Bonaparte, but from a man combining the characters of the whole of them together, a warning to cease our further proceedings.

The message, in a gross and most impertinent manner, alluded to the relations subsisting between himself and his colleague and the State they represented. But he says he has adverted to it only as a mere matter of history. Would he have inserted it there had it been a mere matter of history? When he tells us so, I do not believe him. It was an impertinent interference with his rights as a Senator. He (Mr. S.) had been quoted in certain journals as having pledged himself to obey the will of the Legislature. It was a gross and base falsehood. He had been quoted by giving one half the sentence, and leaving out the other half, which explained the context. If the whole had been given, it would have proved the very reverse

of what was charged. He said when he began that he feared he could not treat the subject with that moderation which it required and demanded, and he now hoped some Senator would move an adjournment, or to lay the motion of the gentleman from Mississippi on the table, that it might receive a more calm and deliberate consideration. If we receive this mandate of the Executive, commanding us not to proceed, and if we submit to it, there is but one thing more: and that is, a company of soldiers to drive us from our seats.

Mr. KING, of Alabama, said he had hoped, from the declaration of the Senator from New Jersey, that "he would school his feelings, and discuss the subject with temperance," that the Senate would have been spared the reiteration of violent denunciation, and the most abusive epithets applied to the Chief Magistrate of the nation. Mr. President, we have heard the President of these United States, charged by a Senator in his place, before an American Senate, and in the face of the world, with giving utterance to falsehoods, knowing them to be false. Sir, the veracity and honor of General Jackson, are too well established by a long life spent in his country's service, in which his truth had never been questioned, nor his honor tarnished, to be now effected, even by the high authority of the Senator from New Jersey. But let us examine, Mr. President, upon what ground it is that the Senator has thought proper to bring this debasing charge against the President of the United States. Why, sir, he has stated in the message now under consideration, that the adoption of the resolution condemning him for having violated the Constitution and the law, was not designed as a foundation for legislative action. Now, sir, I put it to the Senator from New Jersey upon his conscience as a man, and his honor as a Senator, to say whether he did, or does now believe, that further legislation was expected to be founded on that resolution, by those who adopted it? [Mr. SOUTHARD said he did.] Sir, this is the first intimation I have heard of any such intention: I am bound to believe the Senator, yet I can but think few, if any, here, will agree with him: for myself, sir, I never for a moment believed there was any such design. I considered it to be a political movement, and that gentlemen supposed that by this condemnatory sentence, they would shake the confidence of the people in the purity and integrity of their President, impair the weight and influence of the Administration, and thus be enabled to pull down political opponents, and to elevate political friends. I may have been mistaken, but this, sir, was my firm belief. Will my veracity be called in question for stating it? I presume not; and yet, sir, the President of the United States, for stating what he believed to be true—what I believe to be true—and most of those around me believe also, has been charged over and over again with wilful falsehood. I am not permitted, Mr. President, to give utterance here to the feelings of deep indignation, which such a charge is calculated to excite, and I will pass over this part of the Senator's remarks with but one observation more, and that is, that the language he has felt himself justified in using, is as unusual as it is unbecoming in this body, never before indulged in to my recollection, but by one other individual, and approved of, I trust and believe, by no one, be his political and party feelings what they may.

We are told, sir, that the President has seized on this occasion to trumpet forth his own praises; to eulogize his services. Sir, attacked as he has been as a violator of the Constitution, a tyrannical usurper of powers not delegated by that instrument; for trampling under foot the rights and liberties of the people, could he, in the just pride of conscious rectitude, do less than recur to those events in his most eventful life, calculated to show most conclusively that such early devotion to the principles of liberty, such sacrifices, privations, and perils, sustained and encountered by him in defending his country's rights, must, with every unprejudiced mind, free him from imputations as illiberal as unjust? Mr. President, it is not for me to defend Andrew Jackson against the charge of having attempted to claim credit for services never rendered. Those services are known to the whole American people—detraction itself cannot lessen them. Sir, the fame of that man will live in the grateful recollections of a republican people throughout this widely extended empire, when the little politicians of the day shall sink into oblivion, and be remembered no more forever.

Mr. President, the Senator from Mississippi has said, that the receipt of this paper had filled every honorable Senator with indignation. Now, sir, I feel no such indignation, and if the Senator—

[Here Mr. POINDEXTER rose to explain; he said he did not say that every honorable Senator did feel indignant, but that he ought so to feel.]

Sir, I must be permitted to judge for myself as to what should excite my indignation; and not till I stand in need of the opinions of that Senator to regulate my feelings, on this or any other subject, shall I be in the slightest degree influenced by them.

Why, sir, the Senator from Mississippi gravely complains that the President asserts the power of appointment and removal from office: and why should he not, sir? Does not the Constitution expressly delegate to the President the right to nominate, and by and with the consent of the Senate, to appoint to office? And has it not been settled for more than forty years, that the absolute right of removal was also vested in the President, acted upon unquestioned under every Administration, until the present time, when new light seems to have burst upon the hitherto benighted minds of honorable Senators here, and they have all at once discovered that this power of removal from office never has existed, and that the exertion of it was a violation of the Constitution of the land? Most fortunate must it be for the country, Mr. President, that we have in these our days, men within these walls, who comprehend the provisions of the Constitution so much better than those who framed it; and who are determined, if practicable, to rescue that instrument from violation on the part of the present President—who has the hardihood to do what had been done by Washington, Adams, Jefferson, Madison, and all others who have heretofore discharged the executive duties of this Government.

But the President has exerted the veto power vested in him by the Constitution, to arrest what he on his conscience believed to be laws enacted in violation of that instrument, or calculated greatly to impair the general interest: and for this he is now arraigned as having usurped all the powers of legislation. Sir, it is somewhat amusing to see the changes produced on the minds of honorable Senators by the force of party feeling, condemning to-day what yesterday met with their most hearty support. The President, by his veto on the Maysville road bill, arrested the action of the General Government on works of internal improvement—put down, as far as in him lay, the claim which had been set up, to an unlimited exercise of power over such subjects; and thus, not only prevented the expenditure of nearly one hundred millions of dollars, then in progress of appropriation or contemplated on surveys then making, but, sir, by his patriotic devotion to the true principles of our Government, preserved from violation the sacred charter of our rights. How many, now in my eye, then applauded the act, who are now ready to condemn the exercise of the veto, and pronounce it an usurpation of all legislative power? How can those, Mr. President, who saw in the bill of the Senator from Kentucky, for the distribution of the proceeds of the sales of the public lands, the destruction of the best interests of the new States of the west and southwest, if not a violation of the Constitution itself, condemn the exercise of the veto, which alone saved us from that ruinous measure? Or will Senators, opposed to the Bank of the United States upon constitutional grounds, suffer their party feelings to lead them to the condemnation of a man who interposed the shield of that Constitution to protect the country from the blighting influence of this immense moneyed institution? Executive usurpation! I firmly believe, Mr. President, we now have, and ever have had, more to fear from legislative, than executive usurpation upon the rights of the people, and in violation of the Constitution. Sir, look at the tariff act of 1828, laid not for the purposes of revenue, but expressly and avowedly for protection. Few will be found in the southern section of our country who will not pronounce a tariff for protection alone, a violation of the Constitution. Its withering effects upon the prosperity of that whole section, I need not depict; they are known to all who hear me. Remonstrance was vain; an inexorable majority, who were filling their pockets with the spoils, turned a deaf ear; all the influence of this much-abused President, abused by those he was laboring to relieve, was exerted without effect; message after message recommended the reduction of duties to the revenue standard; bill after bill was introduced, prepared by the Secretary of the Treasury, under his direction, so to regulate the duties as to relieve the suffering portions of the country, and bring down the revenue to the lowest wants of the Government. Interest, regardless of the Constitution, still prevailed in the legislative halls, and these just bills were defeated. Tell me not, then, that it is executive usurpation from which we have most to fear.

Sir, the Senator from Maine [Mr. SPRAGUE] urges that the claims set forth by the President in this message, leaves no power in any other department of the Government. Sir, if I understood that paper, as read by the Secretary, the Senator is altogether mistaken. I am confident he had no design to misrepresent. The power claimed is a supervisory power, to see that the agents of the Government faithfully carry into effect the laws which may be passed for their control. This, and no more, is the extent of the claim set forth, and which now is denounced as an unheard-of assumption of power. Mr. President, the American people selected General Jackson as their President, because they believed him honest, patriotic, and possessed of a firmness of spirit, which would not be turned aside, for fear of consequences, from compelling all within the sphere of his legitimate control, to discharge their duty to that people; nor will they be induced to withdraw their confidence, however strongly he may be censured by politicians, should he continue steadily to pursue that course—for they will not be alarmed by the cry of *usurpation*, or *tyranny*, although it should come from this, or the other Chamber of this building.

It has been strongly urged, Mr. President, that never before, in the history of this country, has a President of the United States felt himself justified in making a communication to the Senate, complaining of the action of this body. Sir, a case precisely similar to this never has occurred; for, sir, never before has the Senate adopted a resolution condemning the President for a violation of the Constitution, which he had solemnly sworn to support, and placed that sentence of condemnation on the archives of the nation, as an enduring record of his disgrace—as far, at least, as their act could affix that stigma on his name. But, sir, a case somewhat similar did occur at an early period—in the Administration of that man whom we all delight to honor as the Father of his Country. Sir, General Washington was in the habit of coming down to the Senate, taking the seat you now occupy, and presenting his nominations for their confirmation. On one occasion it pleased the Senate to withhold its approbation from a nomination of a General Fishburn, of Savannah, Georgia. General Washington felt aggrieved; left the chair; and on a subsequent day, made a nomination, in writing, of another individual, for the same office, accompanied by a message complaining of the rejection of General Fishburn, and assigning his reasons for having nominated him. [Here Mr. K. read the message.] Sir, on this occasion General Washington felt himself authorized to send a communication to the Senate, to justify himself in making a nomination which they had rejected: not to procure the favorable action of that body upon the individual named—for he was not nominated, but another in his place; but to free himself from the implied censure which such rejection was supposed to convey. But now, sir, when the President attempts to free himself from the unprecedented censure passed upon him by the Senate by stating the grounds of his action, with the reasons which influenced him, and asks that it shall be placed on the same Journal on which the resolution of his condemnation stands, he is met with a degree of vituperation and denunciation which has astonished, if it has not disgusted, the most of those who heard it.

Mr. President, I am obliged to the Senator from Maine for calling our attention to another message which he considers insulting to the Senate. Wh

sir, gave rise to that communication? A resolution adopted by the Senate restricting the constitutional power of the President in nominating for office. It was adopted without reflection, at the instance of a Senator from Mississippi, with the design to protect the new States from having persons from other States sent within their limits to hold offices which he and most of us supposed citizens of the State where the office was located could be found as well qualified to discharge the duties. The motive was a good one; but the restriction was in derogation of the constitutional power vested in the President. He so viewed it, and determined not to be thus deprived of his legitimate right; hence the message which the Senator has declared to be an insult to the Senate. Why, sir, the Senate itself, on reëxamination, coincided in opinion with the President, and repealed the obnoxious resolution. I now ask the Senator if he will risk his reputation, as a sound constitutional lawyer, by denying that the President was right in refusing to be so restricted?

Sir, a resolution offered by a Senator from North Carolina (not now a member of this body) pending the famous Panama question, has been read to justify the Senate in adopting this. Mr. President, they are entirely dissimilar. There the then President had made known his intention to institute a new mission, without the advice of the Senate or the approbation of Congress. The Senate, as his constitutional advisers, believed it their duty to interpose and prevent the adoption of a measure then in a train for execution, opposed, as they believed, by the plainest principles of the Constitution. It was advice, sir, salutary advice, not censure: can the same be said of this resolution, charging the President with a violation of the Constitution and of law?

Mr. President, the Senator from Maine boasted that he is no Jackson man—that he will not bow the knee to Baal. Sir, this is not the first time the friends of the Administration have been taunted with subserviency to Executive views. I have heretofore disdained to notice it. Sir, I was known to those who placed me here as the personal and political friend of General Jackson. I have given to his Administration a firm and zealous, if not able support, whenever, in my judgment, the measures proposed were calculated to advance the general interests; but, sir, it has been my fate, in the discharge of what I conceived to be my duty, to stand arrayed against one of his most important measures: I allude to the bill of the last session, known generally as the Force Bill. Was subserviency manifested then? Sir, on other occasions I have differed with the views of the President, and frankly made known to him that difference—and little do those know him who suppose that thus to act either lessens his respect or diminishes his friendship for the individual. No, sir, high-minded and honorable himself, he fully appreciates these qualities in others. Base subserviency can never win his respect nor command his favor. Sir, the Senator from Maine informs us, he obeys no mandates. So it seems, sir, neither here nor elsewhere—here it is not desired; elsewhere it may be expected; but, sir, I leave the gentleman to settle it with those who may conceive they have a right to command.

Mr. President, this communication has been stigmatized by the Senator from Mississippi, and others, as a feeble, miserable production, not calculated to produce any effect on the country. If such, sir, be its character, why is it so violently assailed before it has fairly made its appearance in the Senate? Why is the proposition now made to refuse its reception? Does it not seem as if gentlemen were conscious that the resolution they have adopted will not bear the test of fair examination? But, sir, be that as it may, I am surprised at the proposition of the Senator from Mississippi. Has he not suffered his "indignant feelings," as he terms them, to hurry him into an indiscretion, which his vigorous intellect will condemn? Sir, this paper cannot be smothered; the very attempt to do so, will give to it increased importance in the eyes of the country. It will go forth—it will be read with avidity; ours are an intelligent, reflecting, sober people—denunciation and abuse of the President, even by those occupying seats in this august assembly, will not turn them aside from a calm examination of the whole matter. Yes, sir, not only this paper, but the resolution also will be scrutinized—the motive for its adoption will be canvassed, and understood; and gentlemen will find that they must abide the decision—there can be no escape.

Mr. LEIGH said there was one sentiment expressed by the honorable gentleman from Missouri [Mr. BENTON] in which he entirely concurred. It was the solemnity and importance of the present occasion. He declared before his God, that upon the fate of these resolutions and the disposition of this question, he believed depended the permanency of the Constitution handed down to us by our fathers. But there should be nothing done but in a spirit of calmness and moderation, and upon full deliberation; and yet he felt that he could not now discuss this question without giving utterance to feelings of passion, which would be thought by others unbecoming the occasion and his station—feelings which he now felt boiling in his bosom. He believed he felt the dignity and importance of the station he filled here, and never would he do aught to impair that dignity. He therefore moved that the Senate do now adjourn.

The Senate then adjourned.

HOUSE OF REPRESENTATIVES.

THURSDAY, *April* 17, 1834.

Mr. E. WHITTLESEY reported a bill for the relief of Anne Haliday.

Mr. CRANE, a bill for the relief of the legal representatives of Colonel Willis Reddick.

Mr. ELLSWORTH, a bill to authorize a writ of error in certain cases relating to patent rights to the Supreme Court of the United States.

Mr. WILLIAMS, a bill to authorize an extra session of the Legislative Council of the Territory of Michigan.

All which were read twice and committed.

Mr. ASHLEY reported a bill for the relief of John Wilson; which was read twice and ordered to be engrossed for a third reading.

Mr. MERCER, from the Committee on Roads and Canals, to which was referred, on the 14th instant, the memorial of the Chesapeake and Ohio Canal Company, made a report thereon, of its state, condition, finances, &c., which he moved to have committed, and printed for the use of the members.

Mr. STEWART, of Pennsylvania, moved the printing of 3000 extra copies.

The usual number were ordered to be printed, and the report having been committed, the motion for printing an extra number stands over.

Mr. HUBBARD, from the Committee on the subject of the Militia, reported a bill to provide more effectually for the national defence by organizing, arming, and establishing an uniform militia throughout the United States, and to provide for the discipline thereof; which bill was read twice and committed.

Mr. CHILTON moved to suspend the rule, in order to take up the following resolution submitted by him:

Resolved, That in view of the general distress of the people of the United States, and that commercial embarrassment which is carrying ruin to the door of the agricultural portion of our citizens, the President of the United States be respectfully requested to submit to the House a plan for a Bank of the United States, competent to all the duties which may be required by the Government, and which may be so organized as not to infringe on our own delegated powers, or the reserved rights of the States, and, comprising all the advantages, may not be subject to the objections to which the present Bank of the United States is liable in his judgment.

The House refused—Yeas 50, nays 112.

Mr. JARVIS renewed a motion, made and rejected by the House in the early part of the day, for a similar suspension, in order to take up a resolution submitted by him for an inquiry into the cause of the suspension of specie payments by the banks in the District of Columbia.

The SPEAKER said it was not then in order, as the House had already refused this motion.

Mr. JARVIS then gave notice that he should move to have the resolution taken up to-morrow.

The House resumed the consideration of the resolution submitted by Mr. MARDIS, with the amendment moved by Mr. CORWIN.

The motion pending thereon being to lay the resolution and the amendment on the table—

Mr. CLAY said, as he found it was desired by many members that this apparently interminable discussion should be proceeded with, notwithstanding the House had decided the questions involved by it, he would not oppose this wish for discussion, and he would, therefore, withdraw his motion to have the resolution laid on the table.

Mr. McKENNAN then obtained the floor, and the subject was postponed by unanimous consent.

The bill granting compensation for property burnt and destroyed during the last war, reported with amendments from the Committee of the Whole, was read twice, and ordered to be engrossed for a third reading.

The consideration of the military commutation bill was further postponed, on motion of Mr. CRANE, until Thursday next.

The House then resolved itself into a Committee of the Whole on the state of the Union, (Mr. HUBBARD in the chair,) on

THE GENERAL APPROPRIATION BILL.

The question pending being on the amendment submitted thereto by Mr. VANCE, to reduce the salary to be paid to the Commissioner of the Land Office to $2,000—

The motion was rejected: Ayes 55, noes 77.

The question then being taken on the amendment of Mr. VANCE, to deduct from the compensation now allowed by law to the clerks in the Departments of State, Treasury, War, and Navy, including those in the General Land Office, at the rate of 33½ per centum per annum. It was rejected: Ayes 43, noes 85.

The question being stated to make a similar deduction from all officers of the customs, (25 per cent. per annum,)

Mr. VANCE went into a comparative statement of the number of custom-house officers, and the salaries paid them in 1802, with the establishment in 1832—the whole number in the former year being only 577 officers throughout the United States, whilst in 1832 the number was 1600, and of which there was employed in New York alone 332, being nearly as many there, and receiving as much money as it had cost the whole country in the Jeffersonian times. Thirty of these officers received salaries in the aggregate amounting to $80,437, and the 332 in the whole receiving $408,791 21 annually. He referred to this, as it had been said in the former discussion, that if any of these officers could be shown to be too largely paid, members would vote for a reduction. Twenty individuals he now found received amongst them $115,000—which would give to each of these $5,000 and upwards; and if this statement did not bring to those honorable members a conviction that such salaries would bear the reduction he sought for by his amendment he knew not what else would. Seventy-three others had in the aggregate $218,054 43 paid them, which he also supposed would bear to be reduced. These statements were to be found in the Blue Book, to which he would refer, and in which he found that whilst in 1802 the salaries paid in Boston were $47,454, in Philadelphia $56,115 75, and in New York $62,-347 45—a total amount of $166,289 92, for these three cities; the annual expense in 1832, for Boston was $129,234 44, in New York $408,-791 28, and in Philadelphia $99,867 57—an aggregate amount of $637,873 26; leaving an excess over that paid formerly of $471,610. He referred gentlemen to the Blue Book for the perpetual increase in number and salaries which had accrued. This was to be found in the post office and civil list, as well as the customs. What he proposed, therefore, by his amendment to deduct twenty-five per cent. from this establishment, would amount to................$206,320 90

From the customs................328,860 43

From the civil list................450,139 43

Total................$985,320 96

How much further the reduction would make

he had not precisely ascertained—but having stated its general effects, he would cheerfully leave the disposition of the subject to the pleasure of the House.

Mr. CAGE said that he was as desirous as any person could be to maintain a rigid economy in every department of the Government; but he could not agree that the course now proposed by the member from Ohio [Mr. VANCE] was the most appropriate to effect his object. It was not true economy to cut down the salaries of individuals so low that none but incompetent persons might be found to fill up these situations of trust. He considered the best mode would be rather to curtail the number of those employed, than the amount of salaries.

Mr. BARRINGER proposed to amend the amendment by graduating the sums to be paid to the officers as follows, viz:

The sum to be paid to the collectors, in all, not to exceed	$3,000
To surveyors and inspectors	2,500
To weighers, agents, and other persons, not exceeding (fees included)	2,000

Leaving the principle of fees untouched, but putting limits to the amount of the salaries of these respective officers.

Mr. B. regretted if this amendment would have the effect of embarrassing the bill, but unless there was a prospect of getting a select committee raised, to inquire into the whole subject, that thus there would be some prospect of a reduction, he would feel compelled to press these amendments.

Mr. VANCE accepted this, and modified his amendment accordingly.

Mr. CAMBRELENG assured the honorable member from North Carolina, that he should have his most cordial vote, whenever such a committee of inquiry should be proposed, because he agreed with him, that the most rigid economy in the expenditures of the Government was become necessary. When formerly on the Committee of Commerce, the inequality in the salaries of various departments was so generally acknowledged, that repeated calls had been made on the Secretary of the Treasury, for the time being, for a report from him on these salaries, with a view to having some action on the subject; but it so happened, the information had not then been presented, or in time for the House to have it for this purpose. The inequality and injustice of subordinate officers receiving higher salaries than those in places of trust, was always felt; and he complained that it was rather increased by the acts of 1832 and 1833. He would, however, remark, that in many instances where salaries were supposed to be larger than they ought to be; for instance, in the case of inspectors, they were obliged, from the quantum of business they had to dispose of, to employ hands at their own expense, to help them. He would be at all times willing to aid in having an inquiry into the salaries of custom-house officers, with a view to place them on a more equal footing. The member from Ohio, who referred to the increased expenditures in New York, should not forget the vast amount of business that was done there, and which made the number of officers and the amount paid in salaries possibly only commensurate with the duties to be performed, and the amount of revenue collected in that port.

Mr. BARRINGER remarked, that if he thought there was any hope of having a committee of investigation raised, he should be glad to try it; he would give notice of a motion to raise a committee to reduce as well as to equalize the salaries, to-morrow morning.

Mr. PARKER was opposed to the amendment, as out of place in bills making appropriations, although he agreed there was much inequality, &c., in the duties and payments to various officers. The reduction, he admitted, was a good thing in itself; but the difficulty was, to find a good place to do a good thing; not that he complained there was such an excess at present over that of 1802 as to warrant a sweeping reduction; for he would undertake to say, that if the number of officers, &c., as stated by the member from Ohio, was deemed necessary for the duties to be performed at that time, the present increase of business would, if in the same ratio, make two thousand five hundred officers, instead of sixteen hundred, necessary. New York now collected more than half the revenue of the country, and if there was a comparative statement gone into of the number employed there, and the number employed in all the other parts of the United States, it would be found below a proportionate number. He adverted, at some length, to the great expenses to which public officers were subject; to the trifling benefit the Postmasters generally enjoyed from their salaries; and contended that a sufficient number ought to be employed, so as that their duties could be properly performed. At a proper time, he avowed he was in favor of a general system of economy, and should be now in favor of the proposition for the reduction of the pay to members.

Mr. REED said he felt gratified in observing that there was a general disposition apparent in the discussion to reduce and equalize the salaries of all their public officers. The great inequality that arose in them, he considered, was owing to the system which was commenced of paying them from fees. The great cities, now absorbing the great proportion of the business of the country, the fees increased there, whilst they decreased so much in the outposts, that many of the officers had scarcely anything to depend on, although it is absolutely necessary they should be maintained at these places, or the country would be inundated with smugglers. He wished the member from New Jersey [Mr. PARKER] would show him, however, when a good place was to be found to do what he acknowledged was a good thing. He had been for five years looking for it. He did not augur any good to arise from the action of any committee, considering the Secretary of the Treasury, who had the regulation and control of these officers, to be the most competent person to report their state, if not to redress the grievances felt from the present system.

Mr. LOVE regretted he must differ, on this occasion, from those with whom he usually felt pleasure in voting; but he could not either agree that this was a proper bill to introduce any reduction, or that the salaries were shown to be too large for the duties to be performed. He well remembered what was formerly said as to the subject of reform and retrenchment; but he considered that all that was said was merely pretence, and for the object of putting down one Administration to build up another. If the motive for all this was, in his opinion, bad then, it was equally bad now, and he would not, for any object, now consent to follow a hypocritical practice, which was always, to him, objectionable. He contended that the services of good public officers were only to be attained by the nation paying them on a scale commensurate with the duties and trusts reposed in them for faithful performance; and he did not desire to have such a class of officers employed in any department, who could not shut one eye and keep the other open; he wanted to have none who would blink or wink at any iniquities. The bad effects of reducing improperly the salaries of official personages was strikingly exemplified in Kentucky, when in a time of great party excitement the salaries to their State judges was so reduced that the administration of justice had fallen into incompetent hands, for no lawyer of any standing in his profession could be now found to give up his emoluments for the pittance afforded to the bench. He could not agree that the public desired the pay of the members to be reduced, for he believed that there would not be a person who would say that the member voting such a reduction did so from any other motive but the hope to create effect at home. In this, members, he thought, would find themselves mistaken. The people knew their own interest, and they desired to see their public officers well paid. He desired to see the inequality complained of remedied, but he could not therefore consent to revive the old cry of retrenchment, for he considered the best reform would be had by employing good men; and if the clerks did not do enough of service for the money they received, this could be better remedied by increasing the time at which they should labor, than in reducing the amount of their salaries.

Mr. CHILTON defended the motives with which he had originally introduced the resolution for retrenchment, alluded to by the gentleman, and said that although no person could feel more regret than he did at the result which the resolution produced, none felt more than he did the perverted use which was made of it; yet he hoped the time was not now far distant when the country would have their eyes opened, as he acknowledged his was, to the measures of the Administration, who had rode upon the cry of reform into their present high places, and they would take care how their credulity would be a second time practised upon. They would enforce upon the Government the same policy which was necessary to be observed by individuals, and thus keep their expenditure within their income, or they could not get along.

Mr. FILLMORE insisted that as the measures of the Government had the effect of raising the value of money, whilst, on the opposite side, they depreciated the means of subsistence, it was only acting justly to the people from whom these salaries were derived, to place them on a similar footing, in these points, with themselves; and he contended that if *three* dollars could now purchase those articles which formerly it would have taken *four* to do, the salaries of their public officers, with the reduction now contemplated by the amendment, would be practically as high as they had been. The objection as to the time of making these reductions, did not appear to him to be so essentially important when the necessity of doing so was so generally conceded. He found that there were propositions in the bill granting increased compensations. If it was proper, then, in the estimation of the committee, thus to alter the salaries for offices fixed by law, he could not see the force of any objection to their reducing the amount. He referred to the salaries paid in the State of New York as instances how much more economically the highest offices in that State were filled in comparison with those under the General Government; from which he inferred, that as these offices were all well filled, and the appointments to them not only not objected to, but sought for, on the score of emolument, by the most competent men in the State, one or the other of the rates of paying for public services may be unjust. Mr. F. referred to the fact that the judges of the Supreme Court in New York receive but $2000 a year. He desired to have a reduction now, instead of waiting the result of an inquiry, for another reason. It would become the interest of those whose salaries were reduced, and which they could never do in any other case, to come forward and oppose the effects upon them, and in this way only could they expect that any inquiry could be promoted with any hope of a good result. For these reasons, then, although he would have preferred making the reduction in any other shape than by the present appropriation, yet, it was clearly their duty that they should be made. He would vote for the amendment.

Mr. McKINLEY had hoped that the bill would have been got through without the lengthened discussion which now seemed so inevitable. It seemed to him that the great object which honorable members aimed at—reduction in the salaries of the officers—could not be effected in the way which they proposed. The offices themselves having been fixed by law with certain salaries, they could not be reduced without repealing the law which created them. He said that if the people were to be relieved, it must be by a reduction of the taxes. Would the reduction of salaries effect that object? If the suffering complained of was produced by the state of the currency, does not every citizen suffer? Are not expenses as high now as they ever were? Which of the boarding-houses of this city are cheaper than they were formerly? If he understood the object of gentlemen, it was not to relieve the people, but to punish the office-holders. What agency have the officers of the Government had in producing the evils complained of? What had the clerks done? Had the officers in the customs in New York any agency in producing distress, if it had been produced? The individual who was said to be the prime mover of this mischief, could not be reached by the proposed measure. Then you attempt to punish the innocent, not the guilty. Is this justice? It is said that five or six years ago, a scheme of reform was devised for political effect, and it failed. Why did it fail? Because it was ascertained that the Government could only be administered in the same manner in which it had been formerly. He thought this subject had consumed time enough in the committee. It was the last of all subjects which gentle-

men could handle successfully for political effect. He was not to judge for others; but this was the last mode which he would resort to for political effect. He hoped we should now go into the House with the bill. Here, so far as he was concerned, he would cheerfully assent to the yeas and nays on each item in the amendment. But no one had a right to give a pledge for others. In answer to the repeated demand upon the chairman of the committee for a promise to permit the yeas and nays to be taken in the House, he would say that no one should give pledges for him. Representing an independent people, he could not, he would not, suffer any one to pledge him to any particular course.

Mr. HORACE EVERETT said, that if time could be well spent upon any subject it was upon the appropriation bill. He was aware that the subject of reform and retrenchment had fallen into disrepute, on account of the failure of former attempts to render it a political hobby. But this would not deter him from voting for the proposition. He should vote for the reduction on the ground that money is worth much more at the present time than before. At the commencement of the session he would not have considered the present salaries as too large, but those salaries were now enhanced by the increased value of money at least twenty-five per cent. Every one would see that it was idle to send this subject to a committee for a report, at this stage of the session.

Some gentlemen had remarked that if we wished to relieve the people we must reduce the taxes. But there was no expectation that the revenue would be too large for the wants of the Government; and, on the contrary, it was his belief that the Committee of Ways and Means would be under the necessity of proposing an increase of the tariff in order to raise a sufficient revenue.

Mr. GALBRAITH opposed the proposition, and pointed out the inequality and injustice of the operation of the rule of reduction proposed. The reduction of prices on which the revenue was founded, he entirely denied. Flour was seven dollars a barrel when we came here, and it is seven dollars now. He was very willing to consent to an investigation by a committee, of the facts in regard to the sufficiency of the different salaries, but he would not agree to vote for a sweeping proposition as an amendment to another bill.

Mr. HARDIN said, that it had been objected to the reduction proposed that it was a breach of faith not to appropriate money for a salary which was fixed by law. This objection would be avoided by adding to the bill a clause repealing all acts and parts of acts heretofore passed on the subject. But there was a more serious objection with him. He had voted against the allowance of two thousand dollars to Doctor Beaumont and against the appropriation of fourteen hundred dollars for an extra clerk in the State Department, for the reason chiefly that he was opposed to the introduction of any extraneous matters into an appropriation bill. But he was not entirely satisfied that the salaries ought to be reduced. Some of them ought, perhaps, and he would not, without further examination, tell which. He was, besides, opposed to the principle of raising or reducing salaries according to the fluctuations of the currency. It was true that the minority could not originate any proposition, as in each committee they had but two, or at most three members. But he would not break through the established rules on account of the peculiar organization of the House. As to the revenue which had been spoken of, there would be no surplus by the remission of which we could relieve the people. We had now an unavailable fund of 450,000 dollars, to which we might add 50,000 more from the failure of banks in this District, and by December next, 500,000 dollars more by the failure of other banks to pay every officer of the Government amply and sufficiently.

Mr. VANDERPOEL remarked that his colleague [Mr. FILLMORE] had urged his support of this proposition on the ground that a reduction had taken place in all the expenses of living. But was it true that any such reduction had taken place? Was it true that money had lately so much increased in value, and every article of comfort or luxury depreciated in the same proportion? Had his colleague's landlady become conscience-smitten, so as to reduce her price of board below ten or twelve dollars a week, or whatever it was according to his original contract with her? If he, from the considerations he here urges, should feel disposed ultimately to exact from her an abatement of her price, I would, in justice to her, advise him to accompany her to market on one of these calm and delightful mornings, (and if she is pretty, I am sure, from my colleague's known gallantry, it will give him great pleasure to do so,) and see her pay from four to six York shillings for a pair of chickens, and from three to four shillings per pound for butter, and for every other article in the same proportion, and then let him determine whether a dollar will go so much farther now than it would before the panic-makers began their mischievous business. He would further refer to the prices current in the late New York papers for proof that the prices of many products had not fallen; and he would particularly refer him to an extract from a paper, so orthodox now, in the estimation of his colleague, that he would not, he was sure, dispute its accuracy as to matters of this sort. He referred to the New York Courier and Enquirer, as containing abundant evidence that stocks and produce, of almost every description, had lately very much advanced in price. There was no evidence of the fact that a dollar would command much more now, than it did six months ago. For his part, he (Mr. V.) had had but sorry evidence or experience of this alleged diminution of prices. On his way to this city, last fall, he gave five dollars for a hat; now he had had the good luck to pay six dollars for the same kind of article. Let the gentleman go to his tailor and see whether *his* prices are reduced. In the little intercourse which he (Mr. V.) had lately had with the craft, he had not found that they were more merciful now than formerly. If he might be permitted to use an expression which the newspapers had often represented him as being very partial to, he would say, that this cry about the reduction of prices in the articles of living, was all "*a humbug.*"

His colleague had drawn a portion of his argument from New York. Two thousand dollars, he said, was the salary of a judge in that State; and that, he said, was enough in all conscience; but the gentleman had remembered to forget to state how much the judges received under the old constitution, in the days of our Kents, our Thompsons, and our Spencers. Judicial salaries were then sometimes as high in New York as $4,500; but a reform took place, and the old judges were removed by the new constitution. Eight circuit judges were appointed, with salaries of only $1,250 a year. The chancellor and judges of the supreme court received but $2,000. Reputable and competent men, to be sure, took these offices; but it was with the expectation, at that time generally entertained, that the Legislature of New York would soon increase this very inadequate, he would almost say *petit larceny*, compensation. The Senate, year after year, with a promptness that did them honor, had passed a bill to increase these judicial salaries, but it always failed in the lower House; and sometimes gentlemen had been magnanimous enough to vote against it, on the ground that one of the judges of the supreme court, and one of the circuit judges, had been members of the convention, and had advocated the clause in the constitution of that State, restricting the compensation of members of the Legislature to three dollars per day! His colleague, (with whom Mr. V. was proud to say he had served in the Legislature of his native State,) and the party to which his honorable colleague belonged, had uniformly opposed the increase of judicial salaries, and generally based their opposition upon *the broad ground of principle*, which was found in the unfortunate speeches of the aforesaid judges. Mr. V. did not mean to question the *disinterestedness* or *patriotism* of such opposition. The result of this policy had been injurious to the interests of that great State, which he had the honor in part to represent. Its chancellor had been driven by it from the capital, where he ought to reside, into the country, where he is now to be sought for by those who had business with him, at great expense and loss of time.

Be assured, Mr. Chairman, that our judicial salaries now are not the boast of New York. As evidence that these salaries were generally regarded as inadequate by most of the reflecting men of that State, he need only mention the fact, that within the last six years, a court of common pleas had been created by law for the city of New York, with three judges, who, with the perquisites allowed them, received over $3,000 a year. It was in no spirit of pride that he mentioned this gross inconsistency.

But the ethics of his colleague appeared to him (Mr. V.) at least dubious. He says that some salaries are not too high, but that others are; that we shall never secure the necessary information as to those that are too large, till we make one sweeping and indiscriminate reduction; that then, and not till then, the secret will be let out. Sir, is this just—is it moral? It is proposed to do injustice to the meritorious, in order to ferret out those who receive too much. This, sir, is like punishing the innocent in order to detect the guilty; and comports well with the principles and policy of those gentlemen who would refuse to give a reasonable compensation to other officers of the Government, merely because the constitution had prohibited them from increasing their own pay. It strikes me, indeed, sir, that the argument drawn from New York is an unimportant one for the gentleman, and that the one based upon the alleged reduction of prices in the expenses of living is equally unavailable, because it is not supported *by fact*.

Mr. FILLMORE spoke in reply to his colleague, [Mr. VANDERPOEL,] and in support of the proposition to reduce salaries.

Mr. POLK rose to implore the House to proceed with the bill. This was the annual appropriation bill, one which was seldom delayed, even in times of high party excitement, by a general discussion. This was the fourth day on which this bill had been discussed, and we had got no further than the fourth clause of it, when we were met by a proposition to reduce all salaries from the sums fixed by law.

Mr. CHILTON ALLAN spoke in reference to the revenue of the country, which, he said, would suffer from the failure of the banks in which the public money was deposited. The Government (he said) had lost $100,000 by the failures of four banks within sight of the Capitol.

Mr. POLK here interrupted the gentleman from Kentucky, by asking him what authority he had for his assertion. Would the gentleman permit the member from Maine to introduce the resolution which he proposed this morning, for an inquiry into the causes of the failure of these District banks? and whether they stopped payment involuntarily or purposely, and from contrivance?

Mr. C. ALLAN said the question was an extraordinary one. When our money was scattered about in irresponsible State banks, what means had we of ascertaining how much of our money was lost? He had spoken from mere rumor. But he would say that the public money was in unsafe hands, and he here pledged himself, in the face of the House and the nation, to prove that the banks selected as the depositories of the Government could not now honor the draft of the Government for the amount of money held by them. He challenged gentlemen to give him a committee and let him try the fact, instead of taunting him with a petty question as to what motives a bank had in stopping payment.

Mr. POLK said, if he understood the gentleman rightly, he had at first made his assertion in an unqualified manner. He had asked the gentleman for his authority, because he did not wish to permit the assertion to go out to the public as a fact. It now appeared that the gentleman's statement was founded on conjectures about as solid as the statements made elsewhere on the same subject. Not one of the banks selected by the Secretary of the Treasury had failed. Some banks in this District had failed voluntarily, purposely, and with the view of operating here and elsewhere. There was a small deposite in the Bank of Alexandria, not one dollar of which will be lost, as it was well secured. But the Bank of Alexandria was not a deposite bank selected by the Secretary of the Treasury. Since the year 1787 there had been a small deposite left there.

Mr. ALLAN asked what sum was deposited in the Bank of Alexandria, and how it was secured; also, whether there were not Government deposites in the other banks which had stopped payment.

Mr. POLK replied, that the sum was $20,000; the nature of the security taken he did not know. The Secretary had made no deposites in any of the other banks. What deposites the disbursing officers might have made he did not know. But the effect of the explosion of these little concerns was a matter of after consideration. The gentleman had gone out of the question before the House, and indulged in a discussion of matters foreign to the question. An extraordinary attempt was making to embarrass this bill. If it was the purpose of gentlemen to defeat by delaying the passage of the bill, let them avow it, and we shall then know how to meet them. If the object is to perfect the bill, that is another thing. He hoped the House would proceed with the bill with an earnestness indicative of an intention of going through with it.

Mr. BEARDSLEY said, that the character of a Representative here was of some importance. He wished to know whether the gentleman from Kentucky [Mr. ALLAN] staked his character as a Representative on common rumor; and, if not, what authority he had for the assertion that he could prove that one or more, or all of the selected banks were unable to pay their deposites at this time.

After some remarks from Mr. HARDIN,

Mr. ALLAN replied, that if the House would give him a fair committee, an unpacked jury, he would prove to the nation that the banks which hold the public money were unable to repay it. Let it be tried, and before to-morrow he would prove it. But he did not acknowledge the right of the gentleman to interrogate him as to the foundation which he had for this charge. It was for the gentleman to say whether he would permit the trial. Let him give me a fair committee, and if I do not redeem my pledge, then I will agree to come under the censure of this House. He made the assertion on his own responsibility, and on his own information.

After some remarks from Mr. DENNY,

Mr. WILLIAMS intimated a desire to speak upon the question, but being unable from exhaustion to proceed now, he moved that the committee rise. Lost, 79 to 82.

After a few further remarks from Mr. BEARDSLEY and Mr. ALLAN,

Mr. GILMER said it was evident that the House was not now in a temper to decide this question, and he therefore moved that the committee rise. Agreed to.

The committee rose and reported progress; and

The House then adjourned.

IN SENATE.

FRIDAY, *April* 18, 1834.

The VICE PRESIDENT presented a communication from the Governor of Pennsylvania, transmitting resolutions of the Legislature of that State, in favor of the speedy establishment by Congress of a uniform standard of weights and measures.

PETITIONS.

Mr. KENT presented a memorial from inhabitants of Prince George's county, Maryland, praying a restoration of the deposites to the Bank of the United States, and a recharter of that institution; which was read, referred to the Committee on Finance, and ordered to be printed.

Mr. MOORE presented additional documents relative to the heirs of Major General Lord Stirling; which, on his motion, were ordered to be printed, and referred to the committee who have charge of the memorial.

Mr. WRIGHT presented the petition of Archibald W. Hamilton; which was referred to the Committee on Claims.

Mr. WRIGHT presented memorials from Pittsford, Monroe county, New York; Seneca Falls, Seneca county, New York; Rockland county, New York; and Rensselaer county, New York; against the restoration of the deposites to the Bank of the United States and the recharter of that corporation.

On motion of Mr. EWING the memorials were laid upon the table.

BILLS.

The bill for the relief of Elijah Simmonds was read a first time, and committed.

REPORTS OF COMMITTEES.

Mr. SOUTHARD, from the Committee on Naval Affairs, reported a bill for the relief of the officers and crew of the private armed vessel Fox.

Mr. LINN, from the Committee on Private Land Claims, reported a bill relative to the location of lands in the State of Missouri.

Mr. WILKINS gave notice that immediately after the Senator from Virginia [Mr. LEIGH] had concluded his remarks to-day that he should move the Senate to go into Executive business upon a subject involving our foreign relations.

On motion of Mr. POINDEXTER, it was ordered that when the Senate adjourned it should stand adjourned until Monday next.

The Sanate then proceeded to the

SPECIAL ORDER,

being Mr. POINDEXTER's motion that the Protest of the President upon the resolutions of the Senate be not received.

Mr. LEIGH rose and said he was quite sure that this document was not altogether unexpected here. He was prepared to expect a public declaration of war shortly ensuing the passage of the resolutions alluded to. Here it was, and he was free to admit that it had nothing in its language, which had been described as moderate and temperate, that offended him. It was moderate and temperate in the sense in which those phrases were applied in modern declarations of war. It was not the usual course of nations at this day to use abusive language in waging war against each other. It was the character of the paper, the actual design, the plain, manifest object of it, which raised feelings of indignation in his breast, but which he carefully endeavored to suppress. He could not wander with the gentleman from Alabama [Mr. KING] in good humor, which characterized his remarks, among the ruins of the Constitution, nor yet approach the subject with the feelings of wo which seemed to possess the gentleman from Maine, [Mr. SPRAGUE.] But he desired to enter into a grave, calm consideration of the question, and to use those arguments only which appeared properly to belong to the subject.

What was the character of the act, its design, and its object? The gentleman from Missouri [Mr. BENTON] said, yesterday—and he was manifestly apprized of the contents of the paper, because he was prepared with authorities and references for remarks upon it, which he could not have had, if he had not been fully aware of its approach—that gentleman said that it was an appeal to the American people against the Senate of the United States. And Mr. L. contended that it was the first instance of the kind ever known in the history of any free government. It was a direct appeal to the people for the trial of the Senate, for its life or death. It was an appeal, in a quarrel causelessly raised by the President, in which he proposes a trial between his popularity and the constitutional powers, rights, and authority of the Senate of the United States. And from what motive did it all spring? From that passion for conquest and arbitrary power, which, through his whole life, had been his constant characteristic. He had conquered the Bank of the United States—that monster lay dead at his feet; and the next object, suitable for his attack, was this Senate, and when this body should be conquered, there would be nothing more left worthy the hostility of this greatest captain of modern times, except the Constitution of the United States, which the people thought he would preserve, protect, and defend. And he (Mr. L.) predicted that if the people sustained him in this, the next thing we should hear would be a proposition to reduce the term of service of the Senate, and subject them to the recall of the State Legislatures, at their pleasure. He would not inquire into the pernicious or beneficial effects of such an amendment, but it would take away the only balance against sudden excitement in the popular branch of the Legislature, as it would against the encroachments of the Executive department. Whether this change would be for good or evil, it was not his design to inquire. But that would be the inevitable consequence of sustaining this appeal to the people; and if it was not sustained, it would be followed by another consequence far more important in the eyes of the President himself: his popularity will be proven to be unequal to his enterprise; and the Constitution will not only remain unimpaired, but its form and substance will be preserved. But Mr. L. would give the President's design in his own language. In the Protest, he says:

"But if the Senate have a right to interfere with 'the Executive powers, they have also the right 'to make that interference effective; and if the assertion of the power implied in the resolution be 'silently acquiesced in, we may reasonably apprehend that it will be followed, at some future day, 'by an attempt at actual enforcement."

The Senate may refuse; but if we fail to confirm his proper nominations, that is, all his nominations—and fail we surely shall, if some of the rumored nominations shall be made—then comes the denunciation against the Senate, that we have been interfering with the Executive powers. But again, the President says:

"If the censures of the Senate be submitted to 'by the President, the confidence of the people in 'his ability and virtue, and the character and usefulness of his Administration, will soon be at an 'end, and the real power of the Government will 'fall into the hands of a body, holding their offices 'for long terms, not elected by the people, and not 'to them directly responsible. If, on the other 'hand, the illegal censures of the Senate should be 'resisted by the President, collisions and angry 'controversies might ensue, discreditable in their 'progress, and in the end compelling the people to 'adopt the conclusion, either that their Chief Magistrate was unworthy of their respect, or that 'the Senate was chargeable with calumny and injustice. Either of these results would impair 'public confidence in the perfection of the system, 'and lead to serious alterations of its framework, 'or to the practical abandonment of some of its 'provisions."

First, his weight, and influence, and the popularity of his Administration, put in the one scale, and in the other the Constitution of the United States and its very existence. More—he indicates to us that these consequences will either impair confidence in the system, or lead to a practical abandonment of some of its provisions. What provisions? He means a practical abandonment of the constitution of this Senate. Let the people judge from this appeal, which party is right. But if they are to have these pernicious effects, why has the President sought them? for he has sought them. Now, when the Government is formed, the people act through their constitutional authorities; and when one member of those authorities appeals to the people against another, the appeal is of a revolutionary character, and revolutionary in its effects, and it is made, too, in expectation that the people will take sides with one or the other party, and alter or abolish the form of Government entirely. And to make this appeal, the President has sought a quarrel with this body. After a debate of three or four months, the Senate came to a resolution, which has acquired the singular denunciation of the Executive. And by his reading of it, he is guilty of a wilful violation of both the Constitution and laws. Mr. L. thought the resolution was worded by his colleague, [Mr. TYLER;] but, upon examination, the Senate would see how cautiously it had asserted that the President had assumed upon himself authority and power not warranted by the Constitution and laws, but in *derogation* of both, meaning that the force and effect of both was impaired. And how does the President make out that it is a criminal charge against him? He says:

"That the resolution does not expressly allege 'that the assumption of power and authority, 'which it condemns, was intentional and corrupt, 'is no answer to the preceding view of its character and effect. The act thus condemned, necessarily implies volition and design in the individual 'to whom it is imputed; and being unlawful in its 'character, the legal conclusion is, that it was 'prompted by improper motives, and committed 'with an unlawful intent. The charge is not of 'a mistake in the exercise of supposed powers,

'but of the assumption of powers not conferred 'by the Constitution and laws, but in derogation 'of both; and nothing is suggested to excuse or 'palliate the turpitude of the act. In the absence 'of any such excuse, or palliation, there is only 'room for one inference; and that is, that the 'intent was unlawful and corrupt. Besides, the 'resolution not only contains no mitigating sug-'gestion, but, on the contrary, it holds up the act 'complained of as justly obnoxious to censure 'and reprobation; and thus as distinctly stamps it 'with impurity of motives, as if the strongest 'epithets had been used."

Now, wherever a criminal charge was laid, a criminal intent was necessary; but in the absence of a criminal intent, the President says, that it is an arraignment of him for a crime; and how does he make it? Believing himself infallible as a constitutional judge, it is not possible that he could have transgressed the Constitution and laws. Sir, (said Mr. L.,) are not opinions daily given here by Senators in their places of other gentlemen sustaining unconstitutional acts, and are they not retorted upon as being perfectly constitutional? And yet is there any charge of wilful violation? None, sir, none. No one but the President of the United States would think that a charge of a violation of the Constitution was a charge of wilful violation. To satisfy him, there is but one example in this world which the Senate could have pursued; and that is, a certain collared editor, who thinks this act unconstitutional, but qualifies it by saying that the President acted from the purest and most patriotic motives, and therefore the measure was to be supported.

There is another thing in this most extraordinary message. The appeal to the people is not only for what the Senate has done, but for what it has not done—for a resolution which was proposed here, but which was not passed. The Protest says:

"Still further to exemplify this feature of the 'proceeding, it is important to be remarked, that 'the resolution, as originally offered to the Senate, 'specified, with adequate precision, certain acts of 'the President, which it denounced as a violation 'of the Constitution and laws; and that it was not 'until the very close of the debate, and when, 'perhaps, it was apprehended that a majority 'might not sustain the specific accusation contained 'in it, that the resolution was so modified as to as-'sume its present form. A more striking illustra-'tion of the soundness and necessity of the rules 'which forbid vague and indefinite generalities, 'and require a reasonable certainty in all judicial 'allegations, and a more glaring instance of the 'violation of those rules, has seldom been exhib-'ited."

Now Mr. L. humbly supposed that any thinking man, much more a charitable, pious man, as the President would have us believe him to be, would give us credit for not adopting the resolution as originally shaped, and charge us only with the resolution which we did adopt. But this was brought in to bear in this great appeal to the people of the United States. What was the character of this singular document? The Senate has no right to express an opinion of the unconstitutionality of the President's conduct, but he has the right to make the same charge against us. He lectures us and rebukes us, and undertakes to hint to us that our powers will soon be assailed, and that he will put the Constitution of the United States on the issue which he has sought. These are his pretensions, and not only these, but he claims a supervisory control over the treasury, and, not stopping at this, with the control of the army and navy, he claims an executive control over our proceedings here, and that *he* is to judge, not *we*, when we are within the pale of our constitutional duty.

But another thing. The President is of opinion that when the resolution is not coupled with the intent to found some legislative act upon it, that it is unconstitutional; and that hereafter, when resolutions are proposed as the foundation of a principle, a silent acquiescence in this would cause it to be claimed as a precedent. To him, (said Mr. L.) it appeared that whether legislative action on the resolution would ensue, depended on the action and proceedings in the House of Representatives. But the President says there *can not* be legislative action upon it, and, therefore, that we were acting judicially. Sir, (said Mr. L.,) have you not heard of resolutions being introduced into the British House of Commons, declaring a principle on which no legislative action took place, or was intended? If the President figured in the Revolution, as he says in a part of this paper, Mr. L. hoped he had read the history of those times, and if he did, he would remember Lord Dunning's resolution in the House of Commons, on which Lord North's administration was first defeated, and the power of the crown diminished. Did George the Third then send a message complaining of that act as unconstitutional? Mr. L. supposed every man who had read anything had read Junius's letters. In the year 1769, during the second year of the administration of Lord Chatham, a resolution was passed by the House of Lords, declaring that the crown possessed no right to suspend any law of the land. Was this legislative action, or designed as the foundation for it? And yet did George the Third complain that the House of Lords had transcended its duty, and assumed an unconstitutional power, by declaring his proclamation to be illegal? No, sir. Did William Pitt, the proudest minister that ever England had, go before his country and appeal to the people of England against the House of Lords, and complain that the House of Lords had condemned him in violation of the Constitution of his country? Did it alarm his pride? No, sir, no. No man but Andrew Jackson ever thought of such a thing. Mr. L. said he had no enmity against the President. On the contrary, he wished his Administration to be as successful as his best friends expected it to be. But he had a presumption which no mortal man had ever before been cursed with, which no monarch, since the days of King Henry the Eighth ever claimed before.

Sir, (said Mr. L.,) was there no necessity for the passage of this resolution, or rather was there not a palpable necessity for it? Remember the history out of which these extraordinary transactions had grown. The President published a paper, which he read to his Cabinet as the reasons for removing the public deposites from the Bank of the United States, and said that the measure was done upon his own responsibility; that the measure itself was his own; and then comes his Secretary of the Treasury, who assigns a series of what he is pleased to call *reasons* for the removal of the deposites; and the first of these resolutions condemns those reasons as unsatisfactory and insufficient. But over and above the reasons which the Secretary gave, stood the other reason that the President *ordered* the Secretary to remove the deposites; and that, Mr. L. ventured to say, was the sole reason for the act; for if Roger B. Taney had dared to do this deed, or if the President of the United States should now remove his hand from his support for having done the deed, such a torrent of indignation and obloquy as would fall on his head, from all parts of this wide-spead nation, the unhappy White himself never suffered. The President had given the order, and therefore this House was bound to say whether he was right or not. But why did he infer hostility from our language? If it could be interpreted as hostile, what would the world infer from his hostility, and the language he daily held in his house? Does he infer that our whole object was to put him down, and put up another in his place? If he did, Mr. L. said, it was not true in him, however it might be in others. Now let us see if the resolution be true, and let us see if an avowal of the principle contained in it, be not warranted by the Constitution and laws; and let us take the language of the President, in his own Protest:

"The custody of the public property, under 'such regulations as may be prescribed by legisla-'tive authority, has always been considered an ap-'propriate function of the Executive department 'in this and all other governments. In accord-'ance with this principle, every species of property 'belonging to the United States, (excepting that 'which is in the use of the several coördinate 'departments of the Government, as means to aid 'them in performing their appropriate functions,) 'is in charge of officers appointed by the Presi-'dent, whether it be lands, or buildings, or mer-'chandise, or provisions, or clothing, or arms and 'munitions of war. The superintendents and 'keepers of the whole are appointed by the Presi-'dent, responsible to him, and removable at his 'will.

"Public money is but a species of public pro-'perty. It cannot be raised by taxation or cus-'toms, nor brought into the treasury in any other 'way, except by law; but whenever or howsoever 'obtained, its custody always has been, and always 'must be, unless the Constitution be changed, in-'trusted to the executive department. No officer 'can be created by Congress for the purpose of 'taking charge of it, whose appointment would 'not, by the Constitution, at once devolve on the 'President, and who would not be responsible to 'him for the faithful performance of his duties. 'The legislative power may undoubtedly bind him 'and the President, by any laws they may think 'proper to enact; they may prescribe in what place 'particular portions of the public money shall be 'kept, and for what reason it shall be removed, as 'they may direct that supplies for the army or 'navy shall be kept in particular stores; and it will 'be the duty of the President to see that the law 'is faithfully executed—yet will the custody re-'main in the executive department of the Govern-'ment. Were the Congress to assume, with or 'without a legislative act, the power of appointing 'officers independently of the President, to take 'the charge and custody of the public property 'contained in the military and naval arsenals, mag-'azines, and store-houses, it is believed that such 'an act would be regarded by all as a palpable 'usurpation of executive power, subversive of the 'form as well as the fundamental principles of our 'Government. But where is the difference in prin-'ciple, whether the public property be in the form 'of arms, munitions of war, and supplies, or in 'gold and silver, or bank notes? None can be 'perceived—none is believed to exist. Congress 'cannot, therefore, take out of the hands of the 'executive department the custody of the public 'property or money, without an assumption of 'executive power, and a subversion of the first 'principles of the Constitution."

This was the principle upon which these proceedings were founded, and which we think are not warranted by the Constitution. Sir, no one has the custody of the public money. It has been dispersed abroad; and let two-thirds of both Houses of Congress, or let a unanimous vote of both Houses, declare that the control of the public money properly belongs to Congress, and still the President will appeal to the people and put in the balance his prerogative, and depend upon the result of the decision, with the same confidence of success he now does. But where has the President discovered his right to hold the custody of the public treasure? Look to the enumerated powers in the Constitution, and see if you can find it. Not at all. The very highest powers under the Government are claimed for him, and the most trivial precedents are adduced to sustain him, powers which, if yielded, will destroy the just balance of the Constitution, if we do not stand by and sustain it. Now, the President claims the power of removal of every marshal of every court of the United States; and if he possesses it, may he not compel or retard the execution of process issuing from those courts at his own will and pleasure? There never was so enormous a stretch of executive power claimed in any free Government; and yet he appeals to the good people of this country to sustain him in it. Mr. L. desired to give very briefly his opinion of the powers inherent in the executive department. He admitted that all the powers which Congress should, in addition to those he derived from the Constitution, vest in him, he might exercise; but to claim all executive powers, is, to convert this Government into a mere monarchy. Whether elective for four years or not, it is the principle of a monarchy, and nothing else. For observe, the President says, that Congress has no power over the public purse. Now suppose the case of the Commissioners of the sinking fund: the Chief Justice of the United States is one of those officers, the Vice President is another—all placed beyond the reach of the President. They apply vast sums of money in extinguishment of the public debt; and can the President interfere with them in discharge of that duty?

But Mr. L. would inquire, by what authority does the President send this protest to us? There is one paragraph in the Constitution of the United

States which says, "he shall from time to time 'give to the Congress information of the state of 'the Union, and recommend to their consideration 'such measures as he shall judge necessary and 'expedient: he may, on extraordinary occasions, 'convene both Houses, or either of them; and in 'case of disagreement between them, with respect 'to the time of adjournment, he may adjourn them 'to such time as he shall think proper." And this provision is the only one in which the President is authorized to hold intercourse with either House, except in executive business. What, then, is this resolution of which he complains? It is a resolution which is either passed or revocable. If it is passed and gone by, find us an instance which authorizes this proceeding, and this right to take up our journals, and make an appeal to the people upon them, and it will open the door to look into our journals in high party times, and seize upon anything for such purposes. But if the resolution is not irrevocable—if future action may yet take place upon it, and the gentleman from Missouri [Mr. BENTON] should submit his resolution to expunge it from our journals, or if an act should be based upon it—then this protest is a direct and palpable violation of the rights and privileges of this House. Let a proposition be made to rescind this resolution, and we act on the principle of it, and this violation of our privileges is equally palpable.

But a precedent has been found for this act. The precedents of the administration of General Washington, if in point, he would always respect, and if he did not coincide in opinion with them, would depart from them with great reluctance; for never was there, and never will there be, a man in this country so well fitted for President of these United States. Mr. L. held him in the highest respect; but instead of a just comparison between his act and this, there is an awful contrast. President Jackson rebukes us for an exercise of our powers, and makes an appeal to the people of the United States to sustain him. General Washington, having differed with the Senate in the power of appointment in one instance, where the power was vested in him jointly with the Senate, sent to the Senate the nomination of another man, and in the kindest and most modest tone, communicated the reasons which induced him to believe that the person whom he first recommended was worthy the appointment. It was simply an annunciation, in his own excuse and apology; and this is adduced here as a precedent for this act! He hoped the gentleman from Alabama [Mr. KING] would bring some more precedents for reference to these times from the days of Washington, Jefferson, and Madison.

But the President had found out another source of his power and authority. He has found in his oath of office a substantive grant of executive power. He says:

"In the present case, moreover, there is even a 'stronger necessity for such a vindication. By an 'express provision of the Constitution, before the 'President of the United States can enter on the 'execution of his office, he is required to take an 'oath or affirmation, in the following words:

"'I do solemnly swear (or affirm) that I will 'faithfully execute the office of President of the 'United States; and will, to the best of my ability, 'preserve, protect, and defend the Constitution of 'the United States.'"

"The duty of defending, so far as in him lies, 'the integrity of the Constitution, would indeed 'have resulted from the very nature of his office; 'but by thus expressing it in the official oath or 'affirmation, which, in this respect, differs from 'that of every other functionary, the founders of 'our Republic have attested their sense of its importance, and have given to it a peculiar solemnity and force. Bound to the performance of this 'duty by the oath I have taken, by the strongest 'obligations of gratitude to the American people, 'and by the ties which unite my every earthly interest with the welfare and glory of my country, 'and perfectly convinced that the discussion and 'passage of the above-mentioned resolution were 'not only unauthorized by the Constitution, but in 'many respects repugnant to its provisions and 'subversive of the rights secured by it to other co-ordinate departments, I deem it an imperative 'duty to maintain the supremacy of that sacred instrument, and the immunities of the department 'intrusted to my care, by all means consistent 'with my own lawful powers, with the rights of 'others, and with the genius of our civil institutions. To this end, I have caused this, my '*solemn protest* against the aforesaid proceedings, 'to be placed on the files of the executive department, and to be transmitted to the Senate."

In virtue of this oath, he asserts the source of authority under which he sends this protest, and that oath gives him just as much right to protest against an unconstitutional act of the Supreme Court as against this. If the Supreme Court were to pass a judgment upon an unconstitutional act of the President, he might send a protest to them and ask to have it placed upon its record. The Legislature of Virginia have expressed an opinion against his acts, and he might as well have sent a protest to them. But the State of New Jersey having passed a resolution approving of his act, all are entitled to join in songs of praise to the demagogue who is raised far above himself. The man is absolutely intoxicated with the power he possesses; his vanity, the most innocent of all faults, is inflamed by the flattery which he is daily drinking in, and he is maddened by the burst of uncontrolled domination. And it is out of this spirit that comes this protest, this appeal to the people.

The gentleman from Alabama [Mr. KING] had given great credit to the President for the happy termination of the tariff controversy of last session. Mr. L. yielded him no credit for that act, because he voted for the act of 1824; but the fortunate termination of that question was due to another and very different person. And as he was not in his seat, he might now say of him what might be thought to be flattery if he were present. It was to the patriotism and talent of Henry Clay, that he paid all his gratitude for that act, aided by Mr. Letcher of the House of Representatives.

At this stage of his speech, there was much clapping and hissing in the gallery; when (Mr. L. having paused) the VICE PREIDENT ordered them to be cleared; and while the officers were proceeding to execute the order, the interruption was resumed, and much increased.

Mr. BENTON then moved that the Sergeant-at-Arms be directed to take the offenders into custody.

Mr. MOORE said that before it was attempted, he would inquire whether it was practicable for the officer to do it.

Mr. BENTON insisted on his motion; contended that the Senate had been insulted; and asked the yeas and nays upon the question.

Mr. CLAYTON thought there was no occasion for the proceeding—there was no ground for the Senate arraying itself against the people of the country.

Mr. BENTON replied that he had no reference to the people who committed the first disorder. He knew how to make allowances for a sudden ebullition of feeling, and would go as far as any gentleman to excuse it. His motion applied not to those who were guilty of the first disorder, but to those who perseveringly repeated it, long after the order to clear the gallaries had been given.

Mr. BELL moved that the Senate adjourn.

The VICE PRESIDENT decided the motion to be out of order, as a motion was pending.

A member asked if it was in order to move to lay the motion on the table.

The VICE PRESIDENT said it was not; the order to clear the gallaries being in progress of execution.

Mr. POINDEXTER said, if the honorable member would designate the persons who had been guilty of the disorder, he would vote for the warrant to arrest. It was unconstitutional to issue a general warrant of arrest. The persons to be arrested must first be designated; otherwise the whole city might be brought up here on the warrant, or all the persons who had been in the galleries.

Mr. EWING was inclined to think we had power to arrest in the Senate Chamber for an actual interruption in the Senate, without a warrant, but not out of the Senate chamber without a warrant. Nor could a warrant be issued, without designating the individuals to be arrested. The galleries had now all been cleared, no person remained, except privileged individuals. He would not give his consent to a general warrant to arrest individuals.

The VICE PRESIDENT remarked that the order to clear the galleries having been executed, he was of opinion the motion to lay on the table was now in order.

Mr. BIBB said that no one regretted more than he did himself, the disorder which had occurred. He regretted the order to clear the galleries, because they were attended generally by persons who were unacquainted with the rules of order of the Senate. The galleries were now cleared, but it had gone further. An order to the Sergeant-at-Arms to arrest persons generally, was moved for. And from time immemorial, in England, it was contrary to every principle of liberty to issue general warrants. Such was the rule in courts of justice, and if so there, it was equally fit to apply here. We should get into greater difficulties if we were to attempt to arrest on such general powers. He would always vote, in case of interruption, for a motion to clear the galleries, but beyond that was a dangerous exercise of power.

Mr. BENTON asked what was the motion before the Senate.

The VICE PRESIDENT replied that it was his motion to order the Sergeant-at-Arms to take the offenders into custody.

Mr. BENTON observed that the persons who were in the galleries had all gone. He would, however, remark, that he made no motion for a general warrant; his motion was to take into custody the persons who were over his head, not to send the officer in pursuit of any one. It was to arrest *them* instanter. He would allow no one to say that he moved for, or was in favor of, a general warrant of arrest. But the business was now at an end. If one party commenced applause, it followed, of course, that the other would respond by hissing, and his motion applied as well to the one as the other. And he trusted that no one who was now taking notes of our remarks here would represent him as being in favor of issuing general warrants. He would withdraw his motion, because the people in the galleries were all gone.

Mr. LEIGH resumed—

The justice which he thought he owed to Mr Clay, he was happy to give him. But he returned to the protest of the President of the United States. He spoke of the life he had devoted in the service of his country; of his scars obtained in that service; of his advanced age; and of the hopes which he now cherishes, directed to the Throne of Grace, before which he thinks he shall shortly appear. His gray hairs are addressed to the people of the United States to sustain his protest, and these are the only efficient reasons he has given. Mr. L. said he did not know of the President's scars, but he would not doubt them, if he said they were upon his person. He knew this individual at one time personally, and he knew him well; he had attentively watched his official life, both before and since his elevation to the Presidency of the United States, and he confidently declared that he was a man of undoubted veracity. But not having found his revolutionary services recorded in the history of the times, unless those services are handed down in the papers of the times, they will be lost. As to his public services, and his only services, they were the victory of New Orleans. In regard to that, he would say nothing of the facts, or what he thought of the President in a constitutional point of view; he would sink all that, for under all the circumstances in which the country was placed at that time, the victory of New Orleans was one of the most important victories on record. But Mr. L. affirmed that never had a hero, in any age, obtained such a mass of military renown from a single victory, as the President had received for that; and he ventured to say, that he would find five hundred brigadier generals in the revolutions of France who had equally distinguished themselves. As to the President's gray hairs, on which he draws inspirations of heavenly blessings, he (Mr. L.) knew him too well to believe that the frosts of age had quenched the boilings of his bosom. He rather reminded him of Mount Etna, whose summit was capped with eternal snow, but which was always vomiting forth its liquid fire.

Mr. L. said he had intended saying a good deal more, but the late interruption had driven away his thoughts on the subject. He concluded by expressing a hope that the course which the Sen-

say would pursue upon this subject would be adopted in that spirit of moderation and temperance which should characterize this body.

Mr. EWING then rose, and expressed a wish to be heard, but yielded the floor to

Mr. WILKINS, who moved to lay the subject on the table, and that the Senate proceed to the consideration of executive business.

Mr. CLAYTON said he was opposed to the motion, and hoped the Senate would go on with the debate on this question. He was in favor of adopting an illustrious example in England so early as the year 1641, in the early part of the reign of Charles the First, upon a question of kingly prerogative, where the rights of the Parliament had been asserted. He hoped the Senate would go into no executive business, nor confirm any executive nominations, till we asserted the rights and privileges of the Senate, as well as our dignity and the dignity of the States we represented. He denied all right in the Executive to send such a message here. Let us not at his bidding pass upon any appropriation bills for the support of the country, or upon any Executive nominations, until this great question of right and privilege is decided.

Mr. CALHOUN heartily concurred with the gentleman from Delaware, [Mr. CLAYTON.] The paper was a palpable breach of the rights and privileges of the Senate, and until this question was settled he did not know whether to consider this body as a more dependant part of the Government or a coördinate branch of the Government.

Mr. WILKINS said the gentleman from Delaware was mistaken in the object of his motion. He gave notice this morning that he would make this motion. The business he alluded to was of great importance—it was in reference to a treaty which that gentleman understood connected with our foreign relations.

Mr. CLAYTON said that all other business was immaterial—there was none more important than the vindication of the dignity of the Senate, and he would oppose going into the consideration of any other business till that was decided on.

Mr. SPRAGUE said,/that although it was desirable that the business should be acted on soon, it was not necessary to-day or to-morrow.

Mr. WILKINS then withdrew the motion, and gave notice that he would renew it again on Monday, after the gentleman from Ohio [Mr. EWING] should have concluded his remarks.

On motion of Mr. EWING,
The Senate adjourned.

HOUSE OF REPRESENTATIVES.

FRIDAY, April 18, 1834.

Mr. BELL, from the Committee on the Judiciary, reported an amendment to the bill amendatory of the several acts in relation to the relief of insolvent debtors; which was agreed to, and the bill, as amended, was ordered to be read a third time to-morrow.

Mr. ARCHER, from the Committee on Foreign Relations reported a bill supplementary to an act to carry into effect the treaty between the United States and the King of the Two Sicilies; which was read twice, and committed.

Mr. ARCHER, from the same committee, reported a bill for the relief of Benjamin Hewitt. Read twice, and committed.

Mr. ALLEN, of Virginia, from the Committee on the District of Columbia, reported a bill for the relief of James Young. Read twice, and committed.

Mr. ALLEN, from the same committee, reported a bill for the relief of Henry Offut. Read twice, and committed.

Mr. CLAYTON, from the Committee on Public Lands, reported a bill for the relief Samuel Armstrong Bailey. Read twice, and further consideration postponed.

Mr. E. EVERETT, from the Committee on the Library, reported a joint resolution from the Senate for the purchase of a certain number of copies of the Laws of the United States, with an amendment.

On motion of Mr. DUNCAN, three thousand xtra copies of the report of Lieutenant Allen, who accompanied Mr. Schoolcraft in his tour through Louisiana, &c., were ordered to be printed.

Mr. HEATH moved a suspension of the rules of the House, in order to enable him to offer the following resolution:

Resolved, That the Secretary of the Treasury be directed to deposite in the Bank of the United States and its branches, from the first day of May next, and until the expiration of its charter, all the accruing revenues of the Government.

Mr. BURGES asked the mover to alter the last word to "nation," instead of "Government."

The CHAIR said that when the House had determined to receive the resolution, it might be modified or amended.

Mr. WILLIAMS asked the yeas and nays on the motion, and they were ordered.

The question being taken, the motion was rejected—Yeas 83, nays 89, as follows:

YEAS—Messrs. John Quincy Adams, Heman Allen, John J. Allen, Chilton Allan, Archer, Ashley, Barber, Barnitz, Bates, Baylies, J. M. Bell, Briggs, Bull, Burges, Cage, Campbell, Chambers, Chilton, Claiborne, William Clark, Clayton, Corwin, Coulter, Crane, Crockett, Darlington, W. R. Davis, Amos Davis, Davenport, Deberry, Denny, Dickson, Ellsworth, Evans, Edward Everett, Horace Everett, Ewing, Felder, Fillmore, Foot, Philo C. Fuller, Fulton, Gamble, Garland, Gholson, Gordon, Grennell, Hiland Hall, Hardin, James Harper, Hazeltine, Heath, Hiester, Jabez W. Huntington, Jackson, William Cost Johnson, King, G. W. Lay, Lincoln, Love, Martindale, McComas, McKennan, Milligan, Moore, Potts, Ramsay, Reed, Selden, William B. Shepard, William Slade, Stewart, W. P. Taylor, Philemon Thomas, Tweedy, Vance, Vinton, Watmough, Frederick Whittlesey, Elisha Whittlesey, Wilde, Williams, Wilson, Wise, Young—83.

NAYS—Messrs. John Adams, William Allen, Anthony, Beale, Bean, Beardsley, Beaumont, Bodle, Boon, Bouldin, Bunch, Cambreleng, Carr, Casey, Chaney, S. Clark, Coffee, Cramer, Day, D. W. Dickinson, Dunlap, Forester, Fowler, W. K. Fuller, Galbraith, Gillet, Gilmer, Joseph Hall, Halsey, Hannegan, J. M. Harper, Harrison, Hathaway, Howell, Hubbard, Abel Huntington, Cave Johnson, Kavanagh, Kinnard, Lane, Laning, Laporte, Lawrence, L. Lea, T. Lee, Leavitt, Loyall, Lyon, Lytle, J. K. Mann, Moses Mason, McIntire, McKay, McKim, McKinley, McLene, McVean, Murphy, Osgood, Page, Parks, Parker, Patton, Patterson, Pearce, Peyton, Pierce, Pierson, Plummer, Polk, Pope, Schenck, Schley, C. Slade, Speight, Standifer, Stoddert, W. Taylor, F. Thomas, Thomson, Turrill, Vanderpoel, Van Houten, Wagener, Ward, Wardwell, Webster, Whallon, C. P. White—89.

Mr. LINCOLN moved the suspension of the rules, in order to offer a resolution requiring information from the Post Office Department, which, he said, would be of use when the debate was resumed on the appropriation bill.

The motion was rejected.

Mr. JARVIS moved the suspension of the rules in order to allow him to offer a resolution for inquiring into the causes of the suspension of specie payments by the Bank of Washington, the Bank of Alexandria, the Patriotic Bank, and the Farmers' and Mechanics' Bank of Georgetown; and thereupon he asked the yeas and nays, which were ordered.

Mr. HARDIN said if the mover of the resolution would modify it so as to embrace an inquiry into the situation of each of the banks in the District, he would cheerfully support it.

Mr. WILDE asked if the motion could be postponed.

The CHAIR replied that a motion to postpone could not be in order.

Mr. ARCHER asked the mover if he was willing to extend the inquiry.

The CHAIR stated that when the resolution was before the House it could be modified or amended.

Mr. JARVIS said he was willing to make the resolution as comprehensive as any member might wish.

The question being taken by yeas and nays, it was determined in the affirmative, 149 to 23.

The resolution being received, it was read as follows:

Resolved, That a committee be appointed to investigate the situation of the Bank of Washington,

the Farmers' and Mechanics' Bank of Georgetown, the Patriotic Bank, and the Bank of Alexandria, situated in the District of Columbia, and to inquire into the causes which have led to the recent suspension of specie payments by the aforesaid banks, with power to send for persons and papers, and that the committee be directed to report the result of their proceedings to this House.

Mr. HARDIN offered the following amendment to the resolution, to be added after the last clause: And to inquire into the present condition of the Bank of the Metropolis; and also what is the amount of its debts and obligations, and the means it has to pay them; and particularly the species of property it possesses, and what amount is due to the bank from its officers or any of them.

Mr. JARVIS then moved to suspend the rules of the House, which set apart this day for the consideration of private business, in order to proceed to the consideration of the resolution. The motion was rejected.

Mr. POLK moved that the rules of the House be suspended, in order to take up the general appropriation bill, but withdrew it at the suggestion of Mr. ARCHER, in order to dispose of some bills on the table.

The bill for the relief of David Kilbourn being taken up, on motion of Mr. POLK, it was postponed.

The bill for the relief of Gaetano Carusi being taken up, and some debate being likely to arise,

Mr. POLK renewed his motion to suspend the rules, in order to proceed to the consideration of the appropriation bill.

Mr. McKIM asked for the yeas and nays, and they were ordered.

The question being taken, the motion was lost: Ayes 92, noes 65, (not two-thirds,) as follows:

YEAS—Messrs. John Adams, John J. Allen, William Allen, Anthony, Beale, Bean, Beardsley, Beaumont, Bockee, Bodle, Boon, Bunch, Cambreleng, Carr, Casey, S. Clark, Coffee, Connor, Day, D. W. Dickinson, Dunlap, Forester, Fowler, W. Fuller, K. Fuller, Garland, Gillet, Gorham, J. Hall, T. H. Hall, Halsey, Hannegan, J. M. Harper, Harrison, Hathaway, Hawkins, Hazeltine, Howell, Hubbard, A. Huntington, Noadiah Johnson, Cave Johnson, B. Jones, King, Kinnard, Lane, Lansing, Laporte, Luke Lea, T. Lee, Leavitt, Loyall, Lyon, Lytle, A. Mann, J. K. Mann, Mardis, Moses Mason, McIntire, McKay, McKim, McKinley, McLene, McVean, Osgood, Page, Parks, Parker, Patterson, D. J. Pearce, Peyton, F. Pierce, Pierson, Polk, Pope, Ramsay, Schenck, Smith, Speight, Standifer, William Taylor, Thomson, Turner, Turrill, Vanderpoel, Van Houten, Wagener, Ward, Wardwell, Webster, Whallon, and C. F. White—92.

NAYS—Messrs. John Q. Adams, H. Allen, C. Allan, Archer, Ashley, Barber, Barringer, Bates, Beatty, James M. Bell, Briggs, Bull, Burges, Chaney, Chilton, Claiborne, William Clark, Clayton, Corwin, Crane, Darlington, A. Davis, Denny, Dickson, Duncan, H. Everett, Ewing, Fillmore, Foot, P. C. Fuller, Graham, Grennell, Griffin, H. Hall, Hardin, James Harper, Heath, Hiester, J. W. Huntington, William Cost Johnson, Lincoln, Love, Martindale, McCarty, McKennan, Moore, Murphy, Pinckney, Potts, Reed, Selden, W. B. Shepard, Sloane, Spangler, P. Thomas, Tweedy, Vance, Vinton, Watmough, Edward D. White, F. Whittlesey, E. Whittlesey, Wilde, Williams, Wise, and Young—65.

The SPEAKER communicated a letter from the Secretary of War, transmitting a report of the Chief Engineer, respecting the expense of repairing the Cumberland road; also, a report from the same, in relation to the improvement of the navigation of the Monongahela; which were severally referred.

Mr. WISE, of Virginia, asked the unanimous consent of the House, to submit resolutions relative to the extent and limits of the legislative power, in relation to the custody and control of the public money.

An objection being made,

Mr. WISE moved the suspension of the rule, and thereupon asked the yeas and nays; which were ordered.

Mr. LOVE moved a call of the House, which was ordered and commenced.

Upon going through with the roll, 140 members

answered to their names, and the call was proceeded with.

Upon the second call 163 members answered to their names.

The Clerk proceeded to call the absentees.

Mr. BINNEY'S name being called, Mr. WATMOUGH offered in excuse for the absence of his colleague, that he was carried to Philadelphia by business, and moved that he be excused. Agreed to.

Mr. BROWN'S name being called, Mr. CRAMER stated that he was absent on account of the sickness of his family.

Mr. BROWN was excused for his absence.

Mr. WARD moved to suspend the further proceeding in the call.

Mr. WILLIAMS opposed the motion, and it was lost.

Mr. CARMICHAEL was excused, it being stated that he was confined at home by illness.

Mr. CHOATE and Mr. C. C. CLAY were excused for similar reasons.

Mr. DICKERSON was excused, it being stated that he was absent on business.

The following members were excused for various reasons—Messrs. GRAYSON, HAMER, and HARD.

Mr. LANE moved that all further proceedings in the call be suspended, and that the doors be opened. Rejected.

The following gentlemen were excused: Messrs. HENDERSON, HAWES, CHINN, LEWIS, LAY, McDUFFIE, MILLER, MITCHELL, MILLIGAN, SUTHERLAND, TOMPKINS, JACKSON, and WAYNE.

Several other members were excused; when Mr. MANN moved to suspend all further proceeding in the call. Rejected.

After rejecting an excuse offered for the absence of Mr. HARDIN, the House again refused to suspend the call.

Mr. PLUMMER moved that the members now in the Capitol be allowed to enter the Hall.

The CHAIR stated the motion was not in order, according to the 55th rule.

Mr. PLUMMER moved that Messrs. KAVANAGH and DENNY, who were in sight in the gallery, be admitted.

The CHAIR stated that the motion was not in order.

The CHAIR stated that one hundred and seventy members were now in attendance, and that ten or fifteen more were in the Capitol, as he was informed by the doorkeeper.

Mr. MARSHALL moved that the doors be opened for the purpose of admitting those members who were now at the doors of the House, without being taken into custody under the rule. Agreed to.

Mr. BEARDSLEY moved that all further proceeding in the call be stopped. Rejected.

The absentees having been again called, Mr. CONNOR moved that the Sergeant-at-Arms be directed to bring the absentees before the House.

Mr. BURGES suggested the expediency of postponing the motion till to-morrow at twelve o'clock.

Mr. POLK said that he recollected one instance in which the call of the House had proceeded one step beyond that which it had gone to-day, and then messengers were sent to the absentees informing them that the House had called and requested their attendance, without taking them into custody, and he suggested that this course be now pursued.

Mr. CONNOR modified his motion according to the suggestion of Mr. POLK, and it was agreed to.

Mr. VINTON moved that the House do now adjourn.

Mr. HUBBARD called for tellers; and the question being taken, the motion was lost—ayes 74, nays 78.

Mr. GILLET moved to suspend all further proceedings on the call, and to open the doors.

Mr. WARDWELL asked for the yeas and nays, which were refused.

The motion was agreed to by a vote of 90 to 76.

So all further proceeding in the call was suspended, and the doors of the House were ordered to be opened.

The question then recurred on the motion of Mr. WISE, of Virginia, to suspend the rules of the House for the purpose of enabling him to offer his resolutions.

The question being taken by yeas and nays, the motion was rejected—yeas 103, nays 93, as follows:

YEAS—Messrs. John Q. Adams, Heman Allen, Chilton Allan, William Allen, Archer, Ashley, Banks, Barnitz, Barringer, Bates, Bayliss, Beale, Beaty, Jas. M. Bell, Bouldin, Briggs, Bull, Burges, Bynum, Cage, Campbell, Chambers, Chilton, Claiborne, William Clark, Clayton, Clowney, Connor, Corwin, Coulter, Crane, Crockett, Darlington, Warren R. Davis, Amos Davis, Deberry, Denny, Dickson, Duncan, Ellsworth, Evans, Edward Everett, Horace Everett, Ewing, Fillmore, Foot, Foster, Philo C. Fuller, Fulton, Gamble, Garland, Gholson, Gilmer, Gordon, Gorham, Graham, Grennell, Griffin, Hiland Hall, Hardin, James Harper, Hazeltine, Heath, Heister, Jabez W. Huntington, William C. Johnson, King, Lay, Lewis, Lincoln, Love, Martindale, Marshall, John Y. Mason, McCarty, McComas, McKennan, Mercer, Moore, Patton, Patterson, Dutee J. Pearce, Peyton, Pinckney, Potts, Ramsay, Reed, Selden, Augustine H. Shepperd, William Slade, Sloane, Spangler, Stewart, Stoddert, William P. Taylor, Philemon Thomas, Tweedy, Vance, Vinton, Watmough, Elisha Whittlesey, Wilde, Williams, Wilson, Wise, and Young—103.

NAYS—Messrs. John Adams, Anthony, Bean, Beardsley, Beaumont, Blair, Bockee, Boon, Bunch, Cambreleng, Carr, Casey, Chaney, Samuel Clark, Clay, Coffee, Cramer, Day, Dickinson, Dunlap, Forester, Fowler, William K. Fuller, Galbraith, Gillet, Joseph Hall, Thomas H. Hall, Halsey, Hannegan, Joseph M. Harper, Harrison, Hathaway, Hawkins, Howell, Hubbard, Abel Huntington, Inge, Jarvis, Richard M. Johnson, Noadiah Johnson, Cave Johnson, Seaborn Jones, Benjamin Jones, Kavanagh, Kinnard, Lane, Lansing, Laporte, Lawrence, Luke Lea, Thomas Lee, Leavitt, Loyall, Lucas, Lyon, Lytle, Abijah Mann, Joel K. Mann, Mardis, Moses Mason, McIntire, McKay, McKim, McKinley, McLene, McVean, Milligan, Murphy, Osgood, Page, Parks, Parker, Franklin Pierce, Pierson, Plummer, Polk, Pope, Schenck, Schley, Smith, Speight, Standifer, William Taylor, Thomson, Turrill, Vanderpoel, Van Houten, Wagener, Ward, Wardwell, Webster, Whallon, and Campbell P. White—93.

Mr. WISE gave notice that he should renew the motion every day during the session.

Mr. PEYTON rose and said: Mr. Speaker, the honorable gentleman from Virginia has notified the House that he will offer the resolutions which have just been rejected, every day during the session, unless they are received. I voted for the suspension of the rule, to enable the gentleman to bring forward his resolutions, because I intended to offer an amendment in lieu of the whole of those resolutions. I now, sir, notify the House, and that gentleman, that I shall offer the resolutions which I hold in my hand, as a substitute, whenever the honorable member from Virginia shall offer his resolutions. I move, Mr. Speaker, that the rule be suspended for the reading of the resolutions which I send to the table.

The SPEAKER informed Mr. P. that it was not in order to offer a substitute for resolutions which were not received by the House.

Mr. PEYTON. Then, Mr. Speaker, I offer them as original resolutions, and ask for a suspension of the rule. If we are to have the question, let us meet it fully.

The reading of the resolutions was called for, and they were read, as follows:

Resolved, That the President of the United States, in the late executive proceedings in relation to the public revenue, has not assumed "upon himself authority and power not conferred by the Constitution and laws," but that he has acted in conformity to both.

Resolved, That the Senate of the United States, in a late resolution passed by that body, in the words following, to wit: "Resolved, That the 'President, in the late executive proceeding in re-'lation to the public revenue, has assumed upon 'himself authority and power not conferred by 'the Constitution and laws, but in derogation of 'both'"—have, by that resolution, adopted not

with a view to legislative action, but as a solemn censure upon the President, infringed upon the rightful and legitimate powers and prerogatives of the House of Representatives.

Resolved, That Congress has the power, by law, to select the places of depositing the public money, and providing for its safe-keeping.

The SPEAKER was proceeding to a count of the House, when, at the suggestion of several of Mr. PEYTON's friends, he observed that he would withdraw his resolutions for the present, pledging himself to bring them forward as a substitute for the resolutions of the gentleman from Virginia, whenever they were presented.

The resolutions having been read—

Mr. PEYTON withdrew, for the present, his motion, stating that he should renew it when the resolution of the gentleman from Virginia [Mr. WISE] should be offered.

On motion of Mr. LANE,

The House adjourned.

HOUSE OF REPRESENTATIVES.

SATURDAY, April 19, 1834.

Mr. R. M. JOHNSON, from the Committee on Military Affairs, presented a report with a bill to provide for the printing of five thousand copies of "Cavalry instructions for the use of the militia of the United States," and

Mr. WILLIAMS, a bill for increasing the salaries of the judges of the United States for the Territories of Arkansas, Michigan, and Florida; all which bills were read twice and committed, and ordered to be read a third time.

Mr. CLAYTON asked the unanimous consent of the House to submit the following:

Resolved, That a special committee be appointed for the purpose of inquiring into the expediency of equalizing and reducing the salaries of officers and all other expenses of Government in every department thereof, where the same can be constitutionally done; and also, to abolish such offices as may be deemed unnecessary; and that they have power to report by bill or otherwise.

Some members objecting,

Mr. CLAYTON moved a suspension of the rule, to enable him to offer it, on which motion the yeas and nays were ordered: yeas 127, nays 16. And the resolution having been submitted—

Mr. JARVIS proposed an amendment, which he hoped the member from Georgia would accept as a modification, viz: to insert after the word "unnecessary," and also of increasing the compensation of officers, whose salaries or emoluments are inadequate to the services performed by them.

Mr. CLAYTON accepted it.

Mr. EWING demanded the yeas and nays on the resolution as modified. Ordered.

Mr. PARKER said, that as he presumed this amendment was intended as a substitute for that which was already presented to the House by the gentleman from Ohio, [Mr. VANCE,] he desired that it should not be immediately adopted until members should ascertain whether it might not be made more general. He moved to postpone the further consideration of the resolution until Monday next.

Mr. BEARDSLEY inquired if the suspension of the rule entitled the subject to be considered in preference to other resolutions before the House?

The SPEAKER responded in the affirmative.

Mr. PARKER then said, in compliance with the opinion of the Speaker, he would withdraw his motion to postpone.

Mr. VANCE said he felt it necessary to state, in answer to the remarks of the gentleman from New Jersey, [Mr. PARKER,] that he adhered to his amendment; he had no knowledge of, or any understanding with, the gentleman from Georgia, [Mr. CLAYTON,] and did not know he had even an intention of presenting such a resolution; but notwithstanding that this was the first intimation which he had of it, he would vote for it cheerfully. Mr. PARKER, in explanation, said that he misconceived by the gentleman from Ohio. He had not said that there was any understanding of the subject between the two gentlemen. The resolution, it would be observed, would have the same effect, and only brought the subject up in a more tangible shape.

Mr. PLUMMER proposed to add the following, as an amendment to the resolution:

"And also into the expediency of reducing the compensation of the members of Congress."

Mr. CLAYTON said, if the resolution he proposed was examined into, it would be found to provide for reduction into all salaries derivable under the Government, and which would include the pay to members. He would remark, that what had been stated by the gentleman from Ohio was strictly correct. He had not had any conversation with him as to this proposition. He had been prompted to make it, solely from having ascertained, from many members, that if such a resolution should be proposed, they would support it. He believed the sense of the House had been sufficiently expressed, and that as the attempt of the gentleman from Ohio to procure retrenchment, through the medium of the bills making appropriations for the salaries of public officers, would prove abortive, he desired to bring up the subject in a shape unconnected with any appropriation bill, and if his proposition was adopted, he should desire that the amendment proposed by the gentleman from Ohio should cease. This whole matter was, in fact, unpremeditated on his part.

Mr. HARDIN hoped that the member from Mississippi would modify his amendment so as to include with the pay of members that which was paid them in the shape of "mileage."

Mr. PLUMMER assented, and

Mr. CLAYTON agreed to modify his resolution so as to include these amendments.

The resolution, as modified, was then agreed to—yeas 183, nays 2.

Mr. WISE, of Virginia, then asked the unanimous consent of the House to offer the resolutions presented by him yesterday, as follows:

Resolved, That the custody and control of the public moneys of the United States not appropriated by law, and not disbursed under appropriations by law, are, by the Constitution, placed under the order and direction of the Congress of the United States.

Resolved, That no change of the Constitution of the United States is necessary, to authorize the Congress of the United States to intrust the custody of the public money, not appropriated by law, and not disbursed under appropriation by law, to other agency than that of the executive department, and that the custody of the public money must not be necessarily, under the Constitution, intrusted to the executive department.

Resolved, That Congress can take out of the hands of the executive department, the custody of the public property, or money, without an assumption of executive power, or a subversion of the first principles of the Constitution, by the repeal and enactment of such laws as may be necessary to that end.

An objection being made—

Mr. W. then moved a suspension of the rule, and asked the yeas and nays on the motion, which were ordered, and the House refused to suspend, yeas 79, nays 91, (not two-thirds.)

Mr. PEYTON rose to remark, that he also must request a suspension of the rule, to again offer the resolutions presented by him, (inserted in our paper of Saturday;) for it was inevitable that the question involved in them must come up before the House.

Mr. WILDE demanded the yeas and nays on the motion to suspend. Ordered.

Mr. MOORE rose to a question of order. He desired to know if it was not a violation of order to propose resolutions of this character in allusion to the other branch of the legislature?

The SPEAKER remarked that this was a subject for discussion when the House should suspend its rules, and not on a motion to suspend them.

Mr. ELLSWORTH inquired whether there was any objection made to the resolutions? He believed not.

The SPEAKER. It was not for him to make this inquiry of every individual member.

After a remark from Mr. MERCER, as to the point of order—

The question on suspending the rules was put, and required—yeas 96, nays 99.

The House refused to suspend the rules for the purpose of enabling Mr. STEWART to take up a motion made by him on Thursday, for the print-

ing of an extra number of copies of the report presented on the condition, &c., of the Chesapeake and Ohio Canal.

MR. WISE'S RESOLUTIONS.

Mr. ALLEN, of Ohio, asked the unanimous consent of the House, to permit him to give some explanation in reference to a vote given by him on the motion made by the member from Virginia [Mr. WISE] yesterday, and which he considered it was necessary for him to make, in consequence of some comments which appeared, relating to the subject, in one of the city papers, [the Intelligencer.]

Objections having been made,

Mr. R. M. JOHNSON moved a suspension of the rule.

The SPEAKER inquired what rule?

Mr. R. M. JOHNSON. All the rules; so as to let the member have an opportunity to explain.

The SPEAKER. The explanation can only be given by unanimous consent; and this has been withheld.

Mr. R. M. JOHNSON and Mr. THOMSON, of Ohio, appealed to the House to withdraw the objections under the circumstances.

They were, however, repeated; and the House proceeded to the order of the day—being the consideration of private bills.

The bill for the ,relief of E. Brooks was postponed.

The bill for the relief of John Wilson, and the bill to compensate for property lost, burnt, or destroyed by the enemy during the last war, were read a third time and passed.

The House resolved itself into Committee of the Whole, (Mr. CONNOR in the chair,) and resumed the consideration of the bill to compensate Susan Decatur and others.

Mr. HUBBARD spoke at length, and with much zeal and ability, in support of the bill.

Mr. PARKER offered an amendment to the bill; which was rejected.

Mr. HARPER, of New Hampshire, offered an amendment, which was also rejected.

The bill was then, on motion of Mr. ARCHER, laid aside, and the next taken up, viz: the bill for the relief of the representatives of Richard W. Meade, deceased.

After some conversation on the subject of the latter bill,

On motion of Mr. POLK, the committee rose, reported progress, and obtained leave to sit again upon the bill for the relief of Susan Decatur, and the bill for the relief of the representatives of Richard W. Meade, deceased.

On motion of Mr. CHILTON,

The House adjourned.

CORRECTION.—It was erroneously stated in our report of the proceedings in the call of the House on Friday, that Messrs. KAVANAGH and DENNY were the members referred to as being in sight in the gallery. They both answered to the first call, and Mr. DENNY was present during the whole proceeding.

IN SENATE.

MONDAY, April 21, 1834.

The following message, explanatory of the Protest sent on the 17th instant, was received from the President of the United States, by Mr. DONELSON, his Private Secretary:

To the Senate of the United States:

Having reason to believe that certain passages contained in my message and protest transmitted to the Senate on the 17th instant may be misunderstood, I think it proper to state, that it was not my intention to deny in the said message the power and right of the legislative department to provide by law for the custody, safe-keeping, and disposition of the public money and property of the United States.

Although I am well satisfied that such a construction is not warranted by anything contained in that message, yet aware, from experience, that detached passages of an argumentative document, when disconnected from their context, and frequently when disconnected from previous intimations, and the particular positions they were intended to refute or to establish, may be made to bear a con-

struction varying altogether from the sentiments really entertained and intended to be expressed, and deeply solicitous that my views on this point should not, either now or hereafter, be misapprehended, I have deemed it due to the gravity of the subject, to the great interest it involves, and to the Senate, as well as to myself, to embrace the earliest opportunity to make this communication.

I admit, without reserve, as I have before done, the constitutional power of the legislature to prescribe, by law, the place or places in which the public money or other property is to be deposited, and to make such regulations concerning its custody, removal, or disposition, as they may think proper to enact. Nor do I claim for the Executive any right to the possession or disposition of the public property or treasure, or any authority to interfere with the same, except when such possession, disposition, or authority, is given to him by law. Nor do I claim the right in any manner to supervise or interfere with the persons intrusted with such property or treasure, unless he be an officer whose appointment is, under the Constitution, and laws, devolved upon the President, alone, or in conjunction with the Senate, and for whose conduct he is constitutionally responsible.

As the message and protest referred to may appear on the journals of the Senate, and remain among the recorded documents of the nation, I am unwilling that opinions should be imputed to me, even through misconstruction, which I do not entertain, and more particularly am I solicitous that it may not be supposed to claim for myself, or my successors, any power or authority not clearly granted to the President by the Constitution and laws. I have therefore respectfully to request that this communication may be considered a part of that message; and that it may be entered therewith on the Journals of the Senate.

ANDREW JACKSON.

April 21st, 1834.

After the message had been read—

Mr. POINDEXTER rose and said, he desired to make the same motion in regard to this, that he had made relative to the original message; he moved to lay this on the table, and would send to the Chair certain resolutions which he offered as a modification of his original motion, that the paper be not received, and which he moved to print.

The resolutions were read as follows:

1. Resolved, That the President, in transmitting the paper which he did to the Senate on the 17th instant, which he requested to be placed on its journals, as an executive protest, against a resolution not authorized by the Constitution, nor warranted by that mutual interchange of communications which the discharge of official duties renders necessary and proper between the legislative and executive departments.

2. Resolved, That the President, in the paper above referred to, assumes powers in relation to the Senate not authorized by the Constitution, and calculated in its consequences to destroy that harmony which ought to exist between the coördinate departments of the General Government; to interfere with the Senate in the discharge of its duties; to degrade it in the public opinion, and, finally, to destroy its independence, by subjecting its rights and duties to the determination and control of the Chief Magistrate.

3. Resolved, That the communication of a paper of such a character, with the declaration that accompanied it, is a plain and open breach of the constitutional rights and privileges of the Senate; that it cannot be received by this body without a surrender of the just powers confided to it by the Constitution, in trust, to secure the liberty and promote the prosperity of these States, and which its members are bound to maintain, under the sacred obligation of an oath.

4. Resolved, therefore, That the paper be not received by the Senate.

A debate of some length then ensued upon the supplemental message of the President and Mr. POINDEXTER's motion, in which Messrs. PRESTON, FORSYTH, EWING, POINDEXTER, CLAYTON, WEBSTER, and CLAY, participated.

The supplemental message was then laid on the table, and the Senate proceeded to the

SPECIAL ORDER OF THE DAY,

Being the motion of Mr. POINDEXTER, that the President's protest be not received, as modified by his resolutions.

Mr. EWING then took the floor, and spoke at length in support of the motion and the resolutions; and when he concluded,

Mr. KANE rose to speak upon the question, but expressed his readiness to yield the floor to Mr. WILKINS, if he wished to move to go into the consideration of executive business.

Mr. WILKINS then made that motion, accompanied by another to lay the subject under discussion on the table.

The motion was disagreed to.

Mr. FORSYTH said, before the Senator from Illinois [Mr. KANE] proceeded, he wished to move an amendment to the resolutions: after the words "passed by the Senate," in the first resolution, insert "in the words following, to wit:"

[Here inserting the protest at length, and also the supplemental message.]

Mr. LEIGH asked whether he was to understand that the mere motion of the gentleman from Georgia, would have the effect of spreading the protest on the Journal?

The presiding officer [Mr. KING] replied that it would.

Mr. BIBB then objected to the motion as being out of order, inasmuch as it went to defeat the very intention of the resolution.

Mr. CALHOUN thought it a very novel case. The object of all rules was to carry into effect the intention of the body, and the very point under debate was, whether the paper should go on the journals. He therefore submitted whether the main object could thus be defeated by a side movement.

Mr. FORSYTH desired to incorporate the true character of the message into the resolutions, in order that both might be presented together.

Mr. CALHOUN then insisted that Mr. FORSYTH'S motion be reduced to writing in accordance with the rules.

Some conversation then took place between Mr. CLAYTON, Mr. CLAY, and the Secretary, about certain alterations alleged to have been made in the protest after it had been presented to the Senate—the printed copy not being identical with the manuscript message.

The SECRETARY being called on to explain that matter, stated that the Private Secretary of the President, Mr. Donelson, called on him the day following the presentation of the message, and desired to make a few verbal corrections of errors, which he said existed in the message. But the Secretary believing that he had no authority to allow any, the least alteration to be made in the paper, told Mr. Donelson so, who was perfectly satisfied with the answer. The Secretary afterwards made pencil marks of the corrections suggested by Mr. Donelson, above the words in the manuscript proposed to be struck out, which now appear on the paper.

Mr. FORSYTH then sent to the Chair the original paper, as his motion reduced to writing, in accordance with the requisition of Mr. CALHOUN to that effect.

Mr. POINDEXTER and Mr. CALHOUN then objected that the document itself could not be so used—that it was out of order.

The CHAIR decided that it was in order.

Mr. CALHOUN then appealed from the decision of the Chair.

Mr. WEBSTER approved of the appeal. If the motion was rejected, the gentleman from Georgia might put the document in his pocket, and move off with it. It was our own document, not that he had any particular desire to have it, but he would rather have it in our own power. The gentleman had no right to the document of the Senate.

Mr. PRESTON said it was remarkable how gentlemen contrived to make one document perform so many offices. One day it was a protest, another an answer. And while in discussion here it assumes another shape by the interposition of the Private Secretary of the President, and now it is an amendment to a resolution.

Mr. CALHOUN said he would not hesitate to withdraw his objection, if the gentleman from Georgia would withdraw his motion, and send the paper back where it came from.

Mr. FORSYTH said he might suppose from the manner in which his motion had been treated, that gentlemen intended to deprive him of his right to have his proposed amendment on the journals. The rules of the Senate did not require him to have his motion written out expressly for the purpose; for if he should be required to copy the message, it would take him several hours, and the time for offering it would pass away. The gentlemen were to use it as a means of invective against the President, and he (Mr. F.) was not to be permitted to use it in his defence. As respects the alleged alterations, he would say, that the paper was the President's till it was received by the Senate, and he had a right to alter it till it was received by the Senate. And what were the alterations? Was there any attempt at fraud or covertly effecting them? The President did not desire, nor was he inclined to shrink from anything that he had ever said or done, either here or elsewhere.

Mr. FRELINGHUYSEN then moved that the Senate adjourn; which was agreed to, on a division, of 19 to 18.

The Senate adjourned.

HOUSE OF REPRESENTATIVES.

MONDAY, *April* 21, 1834.

REMOVAL OF THE DEPOSITES.

The unfinished business of the last petition day, being a motion submitted by Mr. EVANS, of Maine, to correct a memorial and certain resolutions presented by him from a large number of citizens of the towns of Gardiner and Pittston, (and which represented they were laboring under great embarrassments from an unexampled scarcity of money, &c.) and referred to the Committee of Ways and Means, with instructions to report a resolution declaring that a Bank of the United States is necessary, expedient, and ought to be established—

Mr. EVANS advocated his motion, on the ground that as the sufficiency or insufficiency of the reasons given to the House by Mr. Secretary Taney in justification of the removal of the deposites had not been reported upon, the people of the United States, if this was not done, would have a right to suppose that this question had been purposely evaded, instead of having been fairly met—as he contended it should have been—the former resolutions reported by the Committee of Ways and Means, and upon which the House had voted, not having touched the sufficiency or insufficiency of the reasons, which must be considered as the main question by them. He then went at large into the general bank subject; dwelling upon the utility of the present or a similar institution; and deprecating any substitution of the State banks in its place, to transact the business of the Government and of the nation. He reviewed the reasons of the Secretary, and argued from them, that as they were not sufficient to justify him in "the experiment" which was now bringing disastrous consequences to the country, the removal of the deposites ought not to have been attempted without these consequences having been foreseen, and, as they ought to have been, avoided. He censured the whole conduct of the President, as arising from a determination on his part to put down the bank at any hazard, although forewarned of the consequences, if this design should be carried out. He contended that the interests of the country demanded, instead of waiting for the experiment to work its own cure, that the Government should retrace its steps. Powers were now daily assumed and claimed which were at variance with the Constitution, and it therefore became necessary for Congress to take the subject up, as proposed by him, being the only means now left to avert ruin from every interest in the land—as well as with a view to check further unauthorized assumptions of power on the part of the Executive and his subordinates.

Mr. SMITH, of Maine, stated that he desired to reply to some of the remarks of his colleague; and he had also a petition to present. He moved the postponement of the further consideration of the resolutions, that they might not interfere with the presentation of petitions. When they came up in order, he should take occasion to make some remarks in reply to his colleague.

Mr. WISE moved, as additional instructions to the committee, the following resolutions:

Resolved, That the custody and control of the public moneys of the United States, not appropriated by law, and not disbursed under appropriations by law, are, by the Constitution, placed under the order and direction of the Congress of the United States.

Resolved, That no change of the Constitution of the United States is necessary to authorize the Congress of the United States to intrust the custody of the public money, not appropriated by law, and not disbursed under appropriations by law, to other agency than that of the executive department, and that the custody of the public money must not be necessarily, under the Constitution, intrusted to the executive department.

Resolved, That Congress can take out of the hands of the executive department the custody of the public property, or money, without an assumption of executive power, or a subversion of the first principles of the Constitution, by the repeal and enactment of such laws as may be necessary to that end.

Mr. HARDIN remarked that he had understood that the President had sent in to the Senate a withdrawal of his claim to the public money.

Mr. EVANS accepted the resolutions as a modification of his own.

Mr. PEYTON, of Tennessee, offered the following resolutions as a substitute for the instructions moved.

Mr. PEYTON was unwilling that the House should spend weeks and months in the discussion of a subject which he deemed unworthy of this body, and which would tend to increase the excitement which was said to prevail throughout the country. Gentlemen talk about a revolution, and of the spirit stirring abroad in the country which threw the tea overboard. They say it is a good spirit, and that liberty delights in a storm. At these sentiments his blood recoiled. Must American liberty live in a storm? Must our Government be resolved into its original elements? The friends of the President asked no aid from this House: but if the question was to be forced upon the House, he wished to have it fairly presented for their decision. The resolutions offered by the gentleman from Virginia, were said to be mere abstractions, mere truisms. Was it necessary to legislate upon a truism? It did not require a law to establish a truism. The tendency of the gentleman's resolutions—what their object was he knew not—was again to try the President of the United States, without notice, without a hearing, without arraignment.

The CHAIR here pronounced the range of remark taken, to be out of order.

Mr. PEYTON looked upon it as unprecedented and inexpedient for the two Houses to engage in censuring or praising each other.

The CHAIR said this was not a subject before the House.

Mr. PEYTON said, the course pursued would involve us in the controversy between the President and the Senate. That controversy we had nothing to do with—it should be left for the people. The people were just, and would pronounce a judgment which would stand to all time. Sir, I say that it is unjust for us to arraign or try the President. He is struggling against an institution which would crush any other man, and against an array of party strength more powerful than any ever witnessed in this country; and we are asked to cease our legislative pursuits, and join the Senate in hunting him down.

Mr. WISE followed in some remarks, vindicating his motives in offering his resolutions.

Mr. TURRILL said he did not rise for the purpose of answering the arguments of the gentleman, [Mr. WISE,] who declares himself to be in a state of "*betweenity*," but to a question of order. He wished to know whether resolutions relating to subjects not before the House, and not referring to the memorials to which they were attached, were in order.

The CHAIR said, the resolutions had been received by the House, and it was too late to make the point of order.

Mr. TURRILL moved to lay the whole subject on the table; upon which the yeas and nays were ordered.

Mr. EVANS withdrew the resolutions, with the exception of his original proposition.

Mr. TURRILL withdrew the motion to lay the resolutions on the table.

Mr. SMITH moved to postpone the further consideration of the subject till Monday next.

Mr. FILLMORE renewed the motion to lay the subject on the table.

Mr. CRAMER moved that the House adjourn; upon which Mr. SMITH called for the yeas and nays; which were refused.

Mr. FILLMORE withdrew the motion to lay on the table, and Mr. BOON renewed it.

Mr. SMITH moved to postpone the subject till Monday next.

The question being taken on the motion to lay the memorial on the table, it was determined in the affirmative, yeas 107, nays 91.

The House then adjourned.

IN SENATE.

TUESDAY, *April* 22, 1834.

A message was received from the President of the United States, by Mr. DONELSON, his Private Secretary, transmitting certain private bills which he had approved and signed.

The VICE PRESIDENT presented a communication from the Treasury Department, transmitting the report of the Register of the Treasury, giving the amount of foreign commerce during the year 1832 and 1833.

On motion of Mr. SILSBEE, fifteen hundred copies were ordered to be printed for the use of the Senate.

PETITIONS.

Mr. WEBSTER said, that before he left his seat some days since, he had presented a memorial from the city of Albany, New York, and was authorized to say, and did say, that it contained about two thousand eight hundred signatures of qualified voters, exercising the right of suffrage in that city. He saw afterwards in the public prints a contradiction of this statement, and one of the Senators from New York [Mr. WRIGHT] had taken notice of a deficiency in the number of signatures. The notice that that Senator had taken of it had attracted the attention of the memorialists, and it was then ascertained that one of the rolls of names attached to the memorial had been accidentally omitted by the individuals charged with its transmission to the seat of Government, but it had been found, and now here it is, (said Mr. W.,) with affidavits made in due form of law, and here are 1485 names, making up the deficiency; and if they are not sufficient, but little would be hazarded in declaring that four or five hundred more might be obtained in Albany. Sir, in one of Mr. Burke's glowing speeches, (said Mr. W.,) he remarked that no regard should be paid to the number of the inhabitants of the United States from the census which might be taken, because, before it could be completed, the numbers would be beyond it. So, sir, with regard to these memorials reprobating the acts of the Government: before you get through the consideration of them, others are continually swelling the aggregate.

On motion of Mr. W., the papers were referred to the Committee on Finance; and

On motion of Mr. WRIGHT, the additional names were ordered to be printed.

Mr. WEBSTER presented a memorial from a number of citizens of Adams, Berkshire county, Massachusetts, opposed to the measures of the Executive, and praying a restoration of the deposites to the Bank of the United States; which was referred to the Committee on Finance, and ordered to be printed.

Mr. BIBB presented the proceedings of a meeting of citizens of Hopkinsville, Kentucky, of like tenor, and upon which the same order was made.

Mr. CALHOUN presented a memorial, signed by Louis Bonaparte and others, in behalf of the Polish exiles lately arrived in this country in the two Austrian frigates at New York, praying Congress for a grant of land, under such stipulations as that body may think expedient.

The memorial was read, referred to the Committee on Public Lands, and ordered to be printed.

Mr. MANGUM presented a memorial from a number of inhabitants of Lenoir, one of the lower counties of North Carolina, praying a restoration of the public deposites to the Bank of the United States; which was read, referred to the Committee on Finance, and ordered to be printed.

Mr. FRELINGHUYSEN presented the proceedings of a county meeting, held at Somerville, Somerset county, New Jersey, approving of the course of the Executive with regard to the Bank of the United States, and opposed to the restoration of the deposites, and against the recharter of that institution.

Also, a memorial signed by inhabitants of the town of Princeton, and of residents of the counties of Somerset and Middlesex, in the vicinity of that town, in favor of a restoration of the deposites to the Bank of the United States; together with another from the county of Middlesex and city of New Brunswick, of like tenor.

After a debate, in which Messrs. FRELINGHUYSEN, SOUTHARD, and BENTON participated, the memorials were read, referred to the Committee on Finance, and ordered to be printed.

SPECIAL ORDER.

After the morning business had been finished, the Senate resumed the consideration of Mr. FORSYTH's motion to amend Mr. POINDEXTER's resolutions, assigning the reasons why the President's protest should not be received by reciting the protest itself in the first resolution.

Mr. CALHOUN having withdrawn his appeal from the decision of the Chair—

Mr. POINDEXTER submitted a general proposition in writing, as a point of order, designed to reach this particular case.

The CHAIR (Mr. KING, of Alabama, presiding) said, that whether he decided for or against the proposition, it would not affect Mr. FORSYTH's right to propose an amendment to either of the resolutions.

Mr. POINDEXTER said he designed his resolutions as one entire motion. The three first resolutions were the basis of the fourth; and they stated the reasons for coming to the fourth; they all went to but one point, which was, that the paper be not received. If the principle were established, which would be the consequence of receiving the motion, it would enable any member to offer any paper or memorial, however offensive in its terms; and thus, by saying "in the words following," (then inserting the paper,) impair the dignity of the Senate. All amendments, whether passed or rejected, should leave the original proposition where it stood before they were offered.

Mr. CLAY said the gentleman from Georgia offered the original paper itself as part of his proposition, and then the question arose whether he could so use it, which, being decided in the affirmative, the gentleman from South Carolina appealed from the decision of the Chair. That appeal he had since withdrawn, in order that the preliminary question, whether the amendment of the gentleman from Georgia was in order, might come up.

Mr. WEBSTER was afraid there might be some misapprehension on the subject, which he was desirous should be avoided. There were two objections now made: the first was, that the motion of the gentleman from Georgia was not in writing. The other was, that a proposition being made to exclude the President's message, this motion was made with a design to avoid that exclusion. He was anxious to get at the main question of order, whether the motion itself thus to amend, was in order.

Mr. CHAMBERS thought the true question was, whether a proposition could be made which would defeat the original proposition. If this could obtain, forty-seven Senators might gravely determine that a paper should not be placed on the journal, and the very proceeding in which this conclusion was endeavored to be arrived at, indicated that it was attained, in defiance of their will, by the instrumentality of the other forty-eighth Senator alone. It could not be; such a paper, from the very nature of the business in which the Senate was engaged, must be excluded.

Mr. POINDEXTER then withdrew his written proposition.

Mr. WRIGHT said he felt himself quite unskilled in points of order, but the question seemed to him a plain one. When the communication came from the President, we had the motion which was now embraced in four separate forms, that the paper be not received. These resolutions were an expression upon the character and contents of the paper itself, and upon the sentiments and principles contained in it; and should we be required to record our votes, without recording our reasons also, for those votes? How could any man hereafter determine the correctness of our judgment upon the paper, without having the paper itself? Why should we go on and make an expression of our sentiments, and then say that the paper should not come before us? It must either be considered or not, and was it not proper, and also the right of any Senator to have the paper spread on the journal along with the judgment, as evidence of the conclusion which was come to? Ought not the journal to carry along with it the evidence of the vote of every Senator?

Mr. CLAY replied, that the President had sent this paper here, for the sole purpose of having it recorded on our journals. It was not designed for any legislative or ultimate action; and therefore the only question was, whether it could be received or not. An amendment was then offered, which went to incorporate in itself every word of the document, and thus to effect the very object which the President wished, which the Senate was deliberating on, and which they might not decide according to his wishes. Then the question was, whether the motion was, or was not, in order; and common sense decided that it was not. It was possible to vote knowingly as to its contents, without its being on the journals. How many bills were put on the journals *in hoc verba*? None. He denied that it was necessary to go on the journal, in order to consider and vote upon it. It was already, to a certain extent, in the possession of the Senate; and the resolutions ought to be passed, in order to let the President know why, in view of our constitutional rights and privileges, we would not receive it. He was in favor of treating the paper with the utmost respect; and would, at any time, receive from the President any paper which he was ready to send for ultimate action by the Senate. But he declined receiving any protest upon any question, which led to no practical results.

Mr. FORSYTH said, if he understood the point of the objection, it was, that the effect of his motion would be to place the messages on the journal; and honorable gentlemen said that it was out of order, because it would defeat the object of the Senate. How could the Senate decide the question of order till they had decided the question which was now raised? The motion could not go on the journals till the *ayes* and *noes* were ordered. Honorable gentlemen were in favor of using the rules of order for common sense purposes, but their mode of using them was by the majority to defeat the rights of a minority. Here the Senate had received a message from the President—it had been read, and had been the subject of a three days' discussion, and propositions had been made as to the character of the paper, and yet honorable gentlemen had *not received it*. We had got it, and how could we *unget* it. Mr. F. did not know how you could make the President receive it, if it were your good pleasure to send it back to him again, and he should deny it. The paper was here, and it must be considered. Each resolution founded upon it was distinct in itself, and you could make a proposition to alter, amend, or negative either or all of them, and the Senate might still do what they chose with the message, if his amendment went on the journal. Gentlemen professed great respect for the President. He must be answered, but the message must not be spread on the journal. We had been told that nothing was so baneful in the eyes of power as simple truth, and Mr. F. thought the maxim applied as well to legislative majorities as to executive power. Mr. F. said his object was to incorporate the paper with the resolutions, in order that its character might be seen with reference to the resolutions. He contended that the motion was perfectly in order until one-fifth of the Senators present had decided that the yeas and nays should be taken. As an objection had been made to his offer of the original paper as his amendment, he now withdrew that, and sent to the Chair a copy of that paper, and asked the yeas and nays on the question of order.

Mr. BLACK then read the views which he took of the question, and came to the result, that a Senator might offer any amendment he chose, but it was competent for the Senate to make what disposition of it they pleased.

Mr. CALHOUN and Mr. BIBB contended that one-fifth of the Senate could not be permitted to control the majority, and thus effect an object indirectly, which the majority were opposed to.

The CHAIR then decided that the motion of Mr. FORSYTH was in order; whereupon,

Mr. POINDEXTER appealed from the decision; but before the question was taken,

On motion of Mr. WEBSTER,

The Senate adjourned.

HOUSE OF REPRESENTATIVES.

TUESDAY, *April* 22, 1834.

Mr. ASHLEY, from the Committee on Public Lands, made a report on the petition of Henry Stoker, accompanied by a bill for his relief. Read twice and committed.

Mr. CAMBRELENG rose to ask the unanimous consent of the House to present a memorial. He felt assured that gentlemen would, with one accord, grant him leave, when he stated that it was the petition of the Polish exiles.

Leave being unanimously granted—

Mr. C. said he took great pleasure in presenting to the Representatives of a free people, the memorial of the Polish exiles. Driven from their native land, these pilgrims of liberty come to worship at our altars. The memorialists are but a small portion of some 100,000 Poles, who have been exiled from their country. Some few found refuge in Europe; but most of them were banished to the wilds of Siberia. I trust, sir, we shall never violate those rules of public law, so necessary to protect the rights of nations, and to preserve the peace of the world, which prohibit us from interfering with the political affairs of other countries. But I know of no national obligation to prevent us from extending to these exiles our hospitality and our sympathy. Nor can the rigid rules of public law restrain the friends of freedom, in every land, from taking a deep interest in the struggles of patriots, wherever they may occur. Though the cause of unhappy Poland may not be the cause of nations, it is intimately associated with the cause of mankind.

[The SPEAKER stated that it was not in order to go further into the question, than to state the contents and object of the memorial.

Sir, (said Mr. C.,) I am aware that it is not in order, without the consent of the House; but I would not, in such a case, insult their patriotism by deeming it necessary to ask leave to submit a few brief remarks, in presenting the memorial. I repeat, sir, the cause of Poland is closely associated with the cause of mankind. Liberty mourns over her fate, and the children of every enlightened land learn her story, and weep over her calamities. Public law cannot blind us to the actual condition of the political world. The social elements of civilized nations are in commotion—antagonist principles are in active and general war. The history of the last twenty years—the fundamental changes in the Governments of Great Britain, France, and Spain, prove that a spirit of reform is silently revolutionizing the plan and form of ancient Governments. Western Europe is animated with this spirit; and absolute monarchies are giving way to constitutional and representative governments. It must be evident that the eastern and western portions of that continent cannot long remain in peace—the conflict between antagonist principles of government must come on. Yes, sir, the question must sooner or later be determined, whether all who contend for the rights of man shall be banished to our free land, or whether the white eagle of Poland is destined to wave triumphantly over the battlements of Warsaw.

I am sure, Mr. Speaker, it is not necessary for me to recount the sufferings of the Polish exiles, to excite the sympathies or to solicit the favor of the House. There is, there can be, but one sentiment from the Canadian to the Mexican frontier. The voice of the nation, from the ocean to the wilderness, will welcome them to our shores, and proclaim their right to demand our hospitality. The countrymen of a Kosciusko and of a Pulaski will find an eloquent advocate in the heart of every American. A debt of gratitude can never be cancelled. The claim of the memorialists is also sustained by the laws of hospitality and the usage of nations. They ask for a grant of land, that they may end their days in peace and security. Let us grant an asylum to these exiles, and while they mourn over the fate of the unhappy land of their nativity, may they be consoled with the reflection that the brave Pole can never be an exile in a land of liberty.

It has been usual heretofore to refer memorials of this character to the Committee on Public Lands. It was my wish in this case to ask for a select committee; but I know the members of the former would contend for the honor of favorably considering it, and I cannot deprive them of the opportunity of doing so.

The memorial was read, ordered to be printed, and referred to the Committee on Public Lands.

Mr. CLAYTON, from the committee appointed on the 19th instant, offered the following resolution, which was agreed to:

Resolved, That the committee appointed for the purpose of inquiring into the expediency of equalizing and reducing the salaries of officers, and for other purposes, contained in a resolution passed by this House on the 19th instant, be authorized to send for persons and papers in executing the objects of said resolution.

Mr. JARVIS moved the suspension of the rules, in order to call up for consideration the following resolution, with Mr. HARDIN's amendment, which he had adopted as a modification, which he offered last week:

Resolved, That a committee be appointed to investigate the situation of the Bank of Washington, the Farmers' and Mechanics' Bank of Georgetown, the Patriotic Bank, and the Bank of Alexandria, situate in the District of Columbia, and to inquire into the causes which have led to the recent suspension of specie payments by the aforesaid banks, with power to send for persons and papers; and that the committee be directed to report the results of their proceedings to this House.

And Mr. HARDIN's amendment to the resolution, to be added after the last clause:

"And to inquire into the present condition of 'the Bank of the Metropolis; and also what is the 'amount of its debts and obligations, and the 'means it has to pay them; and particularly the 'species of property it possesses, and what amount 'is due to the bank from its officers or any of 'them."

The question being on the adoption of the resolution—

Mr. EWING said he was convinced that we had talked long enough of existing evils; and though he was in favor of the inquiry, he thought it time to look to some definite action on the subject of the currency. He offered an amendment to the resolution, raising a committee of twenty-four, to report a plan for a national currency of a uniform value.

The motion was decided to be out of order.

Mr. BEARDSLEY said he was desirous of knowing what anthority we had for investigating the concerns of the banks in the District which had not suspended specie payment. This authority, as respects those banks which had thus suspended payment was, he learned, derived from their charter. In respect to them he had no doubt as to the power; but as to one bank named in the resolution, he would ask gentlemen to put their finger on the authority for interfering with it in any manner. He made the suggestion that gentlemen who had given their attention to the subject might inform him what was the ground on which we were proceeding. If we trusted to rumors, he would say we had some reason to doubt the solvency of the Bank of the Metropolis. But he presumed no gentleman in the House would hazard the suggestion that that bank was not as solvent as any other in the Union. Now, sir, I have reason to believe that the Bank of the Metropolis would have no objection to furnish the information sought for, and his only difficulty was, as to the authority on which we proceeded. As to the pretence that, because this is a deposite bank of the treasury, it is the right and duty of this House to make an inquiry into its concerns, &c., would be out of the question. He would not himself give way to the prejudice, and to the worse than idle clamor, that a bank, because it is a selected bank, is not solvent. Nor, because some other banks in the District had broken down, by pre-arrangement among themselves, and, as he believed, by pre-concert with another bank, by which they were probably to be indemnified, would he minister to the panic, by putting a solvent bank along with the rotten banks. He was very sorry that the gentleman from Maine had introduced this bank into his inquiry, merely because it was a deposite bank. He alluded to the declaration made some days ago by the gentleman from Kentucky, [Mr. ALLAN,] that the insolvency of the deposite banks could be proved, and remarked that it was a bare assertion, wholly unsupported by any facts. He repeated, that he would not lend himself to the gratification of party feelings around this Capitol by countenancing the supposition that the deposite banks were insolvent, because they were depositories of the public money. If the gentleman who moved the resolution has a fact showing that the Bank of the Metropolis is of doubtful solvency, let us have it; but do not let us make the impression that, in our opinion, the Bank of the Metropolis is just as solvent as the broken banks, and no more. The effect of such an impression would be to break the bank by clamor, if it could not be broken in any other way. He believed that this bank was a safe, solvent, and well-conducted institution; and if it had not been, that excellent and much abused officer at the head of the treasury would not have selected it. Every effort of the public press and of the party opposed to the Administration had been made during the last six months to break down the credit of the local banks. That had been the ruling motive of the party.

Mr. LANE regretted, he said, that he was compelled to differ from the gentleman from New York. No man had more confidence than himself in the Secretary of the Treasury, but he was in favor of inquiring into the concerns of any selected bank, whenever it was desired. He would not inquire whether the power was derived from the contract or from the charter. But he would say, that no bank should hold the deposites, for one moment, with his vote, which was not willing, at any time, to submit to this inquiry. He had confidence in the solvency of the bank referred to, and for that reason would he be willing to vote for the proposed inquiry. He wished to convince the people of its solvency, and allay the panic. If the bank was not prepared to submit to the investigation, it ought not to be a deposite bank.

Mr. HARDIN said he believed the Bank of the Metropolis was in that situation, that if the investigation of its affairs was committed to an unpacked jury, according to the suggestion of his colleague, it would be proved to be insolvent. He then went into some statements as to the condition of the bank, as derived from its last statements, and inferred that it was solvent, provided its bills and notes under discount were taken into consideration, but without them, it was insolvent. It so happened, that these discounts had been made to gentlemen in this vicinity, who were not able to pay, very promptly, their debts, and that this fund could not be very readily converted into specie, in the present embarrassed state of business. Every bank in the District was solvent, if this item be included, and without it, no bank in the District was solvent. He also stated, that he had been that the stock of the Bank of the Metropolis was worth only sixty-four dollars for a hundred.

On motion of Mr. BOON, the House proceeded to the

ORDERS OF THE DAY.

Mr. POLK, from the Committee of Ways and Means, made the following report:

The Committee of Ways and Means, in pursuance of the third resolution of their former report upon the subject of the Bank of the United States and the public deposites, which was adopted by the House, submit the following

REPORT:

The House, by its vote, having decided "that 'the State banks ought to be continued as the places 'of deposite of the public money, and that it is ex'pedient for Congress to make further provision, b

'law, prescribing the mode of selection, the securities to be taken, and the manner and terms on which 'they are to be employed," the committee deemed it proper, in a measure of so much importance, to ascertain from the Secretary of the Treasury his opinion and views, in regard to the regulations proper to be adopted in the employment of the State banks as the depositories of the public money, and the fiscal agents of the Government; and also for his views in regard to the probable effects which would be produced upon the currency by such regulations. They accordingly addressed a letter to the Secretary, requesting to be furnished with the information desired, and herewith report the answer which has been received.

In determining upon the mode in which the deposite banks shall be selected, the committee are of opinion that a due regard to the public interests will make it proper to leave the selection, in the first instance, to the head of the Treasury Department, or to some other person designated by law; but when once selected, to put it out of the power of the Executive to discontinue such depository without the sanction and approbation of Congress. Should it, however, be deemed expedient for Congress themselves to designate by law the banks which shall hereafter be employed as depositories, instead of delegating the power of selection, in the first instance, to an executive officer, there could be no objection to that mode, provided it be deemed practicable to make the selection in such manner as to protect and preserve the public funds to be deposited therein.

The bill which they report prescribes, first, the mode in which, and by whom, the State banks hereafter to be employed as the public depositories shall be selected; secondly, the terms and conditions upon which they shall be employed, the duties and services they shall perform, and the securities which they may be required to give, in order effectually to protect the Government against possible danger of loss; and, thirdly, it provides that, when once selected, they shall be placed beyond the power and control of the executive department, except as far as the safe and prudent management of the public revenue may render such control indispensable.

The bill restricts the discretion of the Executive, and places it out of the power of that department to discontinue the selected banks as places of public deposite to cases of failure on the part of said banks to comply with the terms and conditions on which they may be employed, or to cases in which any of said banks may become unsafe depositories of the public money, and reserves to Congress the ultimate control over the whole subject. By its provisions the Secretary of the Treasury cannot during the session of Congress dismiss from the service of the treasury any bank of deposite without having first obtained the sanction and approbation of Congress; and if during the recess of Congress any bank shall fail or refuse to comply with the terms and conditions upon which it has been employed, or if, from the periodical returns of its condition and business, or otherwise, the Secretary of the Treasury shall deem it necessary, in order to protect and preserve the public interest, to discontinue any of said banks as public depositories, he is authorized to issue such order temporarily, but is required at the commencement of the next session to report to Congress the reasons and the evidence upon which he has ordered such discontinuance, reserving to Congress the right to approve or reverse such order. Thus all apprehension that the power of the Executive over the selected banks may be used as a governmental patronage or for corrupt purposes, is effectually removed. So long as the selected banks shall continue to perform the duties required of them by the provisions of the bill, (should it become a law,) so long as they shall continue so to conduct their business as to keep the public funds deposited therein secure, they cannot be discontinued at the will of the Executive, but will be entitled to their custody as matter of right, unless it shall be the pleasure of Congress to withdraw them, or change the place of deposite.

The committee concur with the Secretary of the Treasury in the views which he has presented in his letter, in regard to the importance of banishing from circulation bank notes of the smaller denominations, and of substituting gold and silver coins in their place. This may, doubtless, to some extent, be encouraged and effected through the collection and management of the revenue. Congress possesses no power to restrict the State institutions from issuing small notes; but they have the power to impose as a condition upon which any bank shall be employed as a depository, that it shall first stipulate not to issue or use, after a given future day, notes of the smaller denominations, in the course of its business; and they have a right to refuse to receive in payment to the United States the notes of any bank which shall not cease, after a given future day, to issue small notes. The bill, accordingly, contains a provision to this effect, designed to induce the State banks to coöperate in banishing from circulation all notes of a less denomination than five dollars, after a given future day. In several States such a prohibition already exists, and in those States a metallic circulation has been found to take the place of the small notes which have been withdrawn. It may be necessary, hereafter, for Congress to extend the prohibition to the issue of notes below the denomination of ten or twenty dollars. But the committee do not deem it expedient, at this time, to recommend that the prohibition should be extended to notes above the denomination of five dollars. Should it hereafter be deemed proper, Congress can adopt further legislative provisions upon the subject.

It will be perceived from the letter of the Secretary of the Treasury herewith reported, that further legislation in relation to the coins, constitutes an important part of his scheme of the currency. The committee concur in opinion that it is important that further legal provision should be made regulating the value of foreign coins, and making the foreign gold and silver coins a tender in the payment of debts, and also regulating the standard of value of our own coins.

They have, however, reported no bill upon the subject of the coins, because bills upon that subject have already been brought before the House by a select committee, to whom this particular branch of the subject had been referred by the House. They concur in opinion that it is important they should be acted on at the present session of Congress.

Treasury Department,
April 15, 1834.

Sir: I have the honor to acknowledge the receipt of your letter of the 7th instant, and proceed to reply to the inquiries made by the Committee of Ways and Means.

In my report to Congress at the commencement of the present session, assigning my reasons for removing the deposites from the Bank of the United States, I expressed the opinion that a corporation of that description was not necessary, either for the fiscal operations of the Government, or the general convenience of the people.

One of the arguments most frequently urged in favor of the expediency of a Bank of the United States is the salutary influence which it is supposed to exert in securing to the country a sound currency. It is said the State banks have a constant tendency to over-issues, and that a superior power is necessary to keep them in check, and to control them in this particular—and the argument is constantly and earnestly pressed, that a Bank of the United States is the fit and appropriate means to accomplish this object. If there be any force in this argument, the paper currency furnished by the State banks, as well as that issued by the Bank of the United States, ought now to be in a sound state.

The Bank of the United States has been in existence seventeen years, and must have already exerted all the influence in relation to the currency, which can ever be expected from such an institution. And if it exercises a wholesome and salutary control over the conduct of the State banks, and restrains them within proper bounds, it has had full time and opportunity to exert that power, and the notes of the State banks, as well as those of the Bank of the United States, ought now to be found in a safe condition. For it must be admitted that we have gained but little by chartering the Bank of the United States, if only the comparatively small portion of the paper currency furnished by itself, is sound, while the great mass of the circulating medium is inherently vicious, and liable to be disordered at any moment. It is believed that more than three-fourths of the present paper currency is furnished by the State banks, and if so large a portion of our circulating medium is unsafe and unworthy of credit, then the Bank of the United States is either incapable of exercising the salutary control claimed for it, or it has failed to perform its duty to the public. In either event it is time to look for some other remedy.

Judging from the best information which the department has been able to obtain, the paper of the various banks (including the Bank of the United States) in actual circulation in ordinary times, amounts to at least eighty millions of dollars. Of this sum the Bank of the United States furnishes less than twenty millions, and the various State banks more than sixty millions; the specie in the vaults of the same banks, to support this extensive credit, does not probably exceed twenty-five millions.

In estimating the amount of specie, I confine myself to the coin supposed to be in possession of the banks. In some of the States, the circulation of bank notes below five dollars is prohibited by law, and in these States there is a considerable amount of specie passing from hand to hand, and forming a part of the ordinary circulating medium. It does not, however, probably exceed four millions of dollars. This metallic circulation lessens by so much the amount of paper, and to that extent it diminishes the evil occasioned by the great disproportion between the paper superstructure and its metallic basis. But the coin which is thus circulating, cannot be brought in aid of the paper currency, when a panic, or any other cause, suddenly throws it back upon the bank for redemption. It cannot, therefore, be estimated as a part of the means to secure the payment of the actual paper circulation. It takes the place of so much paper in the mass of the circulating medium, and thereby lessens the amount to be redeemed. But it will never find its way into the banks when their notes are rapidly returning upon them. They must rely upon the amount actually in their vaults—and it is with this amount that we must compare the paper circulation, in order to decide whether it is in a safe condition. It is evident that the chief part of the paper currency of the United States must always be furnished by the State banks. No Bank of the United States could provide a sufficient amount for the whole nation, without giving to it a capital of such enormous and startling magnitude, that no one, it is presumed, would seriously propose it.

And if Congress are to legislate, with the view of securing to the people of the United States a sound paper currency, the condition of the notes of the State banks is of much more importance to the community, than that of any Bank of the United States. The notes of the different local banks form the ordinary circulating medium for the great body of our citizens; and it would be unjust to them, to disregard its condition. The whole currency of the country should be placed in a sound and healthy state, as far as the legitimate authority of the United States will enable them to accomplish that object.

Under the authority delegated to Congress by the Constitution of the United States, they have no power to establish by law a paper currency; and the influence which they may lawfully exercise in securing its soundness, is altogether incidental. In legislating within the admitted scope of their authority, they may, without assuming powers not granted, look to the effect which their laws will produce upon an interest of so much importance as that of the paper circulation now floating through the country.

Taking this view of the subject, the first inquiry is, what is the present condition of the ordinary circulating medium of the United States? Is the great mass of the paper currency in a sound and healthy condition? If it is, we must endeavor to find means to preserve it in its present state, when the Bank of the United States shall cease to exist. But if it is not, then it is obvious that the creation of a Bank of the United States will not accomplish this desirable object; and that, even on the score of expediency, without reference to constitutional objections, some other plan should be devised.

If the estimate I have made of the proportion between the paper circulation and the specie in

possession of the bank be correct, or nearly so, the condition of the currency is obviously such, that the nation should not be content with it, nor desire to continue it in its present state. It is an immense superstructure of paper, resting on a metallic foundation too narrow to support it. It has never been sustained by its own inherent strength, but by public confidence. When every one firmly believes that the notes of the banks will, on demand, be paid in coin, they readily circulate and answer all the purposes of money. But the moment that confidence is impaired, they lose their value as a part of the circulating medium, and are returned upon the banks for redemption in specie, and the disproportion between the paper circulation and the coin prepared to redeem it, is so great, that it is constantly liable to have its chief support, *public confidence*, withdrawn from it.

In speaking of the dangers to which the currency is exposed, I do not mean to intimate that the State banks are unable to pay the amount of notes they have issued. On the contrary, I am persuaded that, with very few exceptions, they are as safe as the Bank of the United States. For that bank has never been in a condition to redeem its notes in specie, if they were all suddenly thrown back upon it. My object in inviting the attention of the committee to this subject is, not only to show the real condition of the currency, but to mark the utter inconsistency of the argument, which urges the recharter of the Bank of the United States, on the ground that it has furnished a sound currency to the nation, and at the same time attempts to discredit the notes of the State banks. Both parts of the argument cannot be true. The Bank of the United States has not furnished the nation with a sound paper currency, and has produced no salutary effect on the great mass of it, unless the issues of the State banks are now in a safe and healthy condition.

The diffiulty under which the State banks are laboring at this time does not prove that they are unsound, and that they have been worse managed than the Bank of the United States; when reports injurious to the credit of the State banks are industriously and widely circulated, some degree of embarrassment is unavoidable; especially when it is generally supposed to be in the power of the Bank of the United States to stop them at its pleasure. The evil is, however, in its nature, temporary, and will soon pass away. And the intelligence of the citizens will readily discover that the present difficulty is the offspring of useless alarm, and of a deliberate design to destroy the credit of the State banks. And when the real object of the excitement, and unfounded rumors which are daily circulated, shall be understood by the people, confidence will soon be restored, and business resume its usual channel. The stoppage of a bank from any cause naturally produces a run on the banks in its neighborhood, and if pains are taken to increase the excitement and alarm, the evil will be more extensively felt than it would be in ordinary times.

The dangerous expansion of the paper circulation, compared with its specie basis, shows that there is something essentially vicious in the whole system; and the mischief, so far from being corrected or lessened by a Bank of the United States, is more probably aggravated by such an institution. The great amount of paper afloat proves that the quantity depends more on the discretion and judgment of those who make the paper, than on their ability to redeem it whenever it is called for.

The dominion which a Bank of the United States must always exercise over the smaller corporations of the States, vests in it the entire discretion of expansion or contraction. If it discount and issue its paper freely, the State banks are induced, by the hopes of profit, to follow its example. If it suddenly curtails, they must curtail also, or become the victims of their own imprudence. And if, by any means, the conduct of that bank disturbs the public confidence in the safety of the State banks, their notes will be returned upon them with such rapidity as to endanger even the best managed institutions; and while such a power remains in the hands of a single corporation, the country will be constantly liable to sudden agitations and excitements from the alternate expansion and contraction of the currency; and those engaged in commerce will, in the years of abundance, be led into an extension of their business, which must, in the succeeding years of scarcity, inevitably result in bankruptcy and ruin. In a time of pressure, confidence is easily shaken; and whenever it becomes the interest of the Bank of the United States to excite alarm in the country, its great money power will most commonly enable it to effect the object, and by destroying confidence and credit, in a few months throw the whole business of the nation into confusion. A system of currency thus liable to constant fluctuations, and always in danger of being entirely overthrown, is certainly one of the worst that can be devised. Every species of property is unstable and insecure, unless the currency which is to be exchanged for it shall be steady in its value, and not liable to be seriously disturbed by accident or design. And the danger and evil is abundantly manifested by the history of the United States, since the establishment of the present bank. Years of hollow prosperity have been succeeded by years of pressure and suffering; and the present condition of things demonstrates how readily a concerted effort to excite a panic and destroy confidence, may endanger the great mass of the circulating medium, and injure most extensively the property and industry of the country.

The great evil of our present currency is the disproportion between the paper in circulation and the coin prepared to redeem it. The remedy is, to diminish this proportion, and to give to the paper currency a broader and firmer metallic foundation. Can this object be best accomplished with or without a Bank of the United States?

I do not perceive that a Bank of the United States, upon any plan, is likely to diminish the evil.

It may perhaps be supposed that a restriction on the bank, which would prevent it from issuing notes below twenty dollars, would tend to accomplish the object. But the only effect of such a restriction would be to substitute the notes of State banks of the lower denominations, in the place of the notes of the Bank of the United States.

Gold and silver will never circulate where banks issue notes which come in competition with them. For it will invariably happen that when the circulating medium is composed of different kinds of money, and one of them is less valuable than the other, but not sufficiently depreciated to be discredited, the inferior will, after a time, become the general currency, and the more valuable will entirely disapper. This is obvious in the States where the banks issue notes as low as one dollar. For silver dollars are never found in circulation where paper ones are freely issued by the banks. In order, therefore, to bring the precious metals into use, the rivalship of paper must be effectually taken away. We must not only remove the notes of the Bank of the United States, but also the notes of the State banks.

And to create a Bank of the United States, and restrict its issues, as above suggested, would be to invite the State banks to issue largely that description of paper which will not be interrupted by the competition of the Bank of the United States. The paper circulation would not be diminished, nor would the proportion of the metals be increased. Paper dollars would still be manufactured in the same abundance; they would still come in competition with gold and silver, and drive them from circulation.

The restriction therefore on the issue of the smaller notes, cannot be effectual, unless the several States shall be willing to coöperate with the legislation of Congress. They could hardly be expected to prohibit the issue of notes under twenty dollars by their banks, while a Bank of the United States was in existence with all the advantages it would possess over the State institutions. And if they could be induced to unite in such a plan, the inevitable result would be to put an end to the State banks; for their circulation of larger notes would be so much restrained by the competition and superior advantages of the notes of the Bank of the United States, that the small State corporations would probably soon find their charters of no value, and be compelled to wind up their concerns. The field for paper currency would then be left entirely to the Bank of the United States. Their notes being receivable everywhere in payment for debts due the Government, would give them a credit beyond their real value. The temptation under such circumstances to over-issues of paper would be almost irresistible. And after closing, by this course of legislation, the doors of the State banks, we should soon find ourselves with a paper currency equally liable to depreciation with the present one, from the great disproportion the paper would bear to the specie provided to redeem it. In a plan which would lead to such results, we could hardly expect the States to come in aid of the legislation of Congress, but we might count on their cordial coöperation in efforts to place the whole circulating medium of the country on a safe and durable foundation, when it can be done without injustice to their own citizens who are interested in the State institutions.

The first step towards a sound condition of the currency is, to reform the coinage of gold. The present gold coin is more in silver than its nominal value. It is therefore never seen in the ordinary exchanges of the country, and it is worse than useless to continue the expense of coining it at the mint, unless it is intended for circulation. It will never make its way into general circulation, until the relative value of silver and gold is observed, as near as may be, in the pieces coined of the respective metals. It has been truly said that gold is the antagonist of paper. Silver is too heavy to be transported from place to place, in large sums, without inconvenience. Some other circulating medium of general currency is therefore necessary, even for the expenses of a journey from one State to another. There must be either a paper currency of general credit, or gold must be introduced. And it is essential that in its standard value as coin, it should be placed on its proper footing in relation to silver, before a paper currency of general credit can be conveniently dispensed with. The charter of the Bank of the United States, by making its paper receivable everywhere for debts due to the Government, furnishes a paper currency not equal to gold or silver, but yet of sufficient credit for common use, and for the purposes of travelling from place to place. This will continue until the 3d of March, 1836. It is desirable, therefore, that provision should be made at the present session of Congress for the reform of the gold coins. The coinage will require time, and as this general paper currency is gradually retiring from circulation, the gold should be prepared to take its place. We produce gold to a large amount in the United States, and the product is increasing every year. The greater part of it is now exported as bullion, and this will continue to be the case until the value of the gold coin is changed. Even if the change should be made at the present session, there would not, perhaps, be a sufficient supply of our own gold coins to meet the demand for a circulating medium of general credit, at the expiration of the charter of the bank. But if foreign gold coins should be made a legal tender at their real value, there would doubtless be enough of that metal, at the time above mentioned, to meet the wants of the public. And there can be no sufficient reason for throwing out of circulation the foreign coins of gold or silver, which are current in other parts of the commercial world. Indeed, as a measure of immediate relief in the present state of things, it is necessary that the foreign coins, both of gold and silver, should be made a legal tender, in payment of debts, according to their intrinsic value. Very large importations of the foreign coins are continually arriving in the United States, and if they can be used by the State banks to discharge their engagements, they will probably remain here, and become a part of our circulating medium. And if they were made a legal tender in payment of debts, it would enable the State banks to extend their issues, and to redeem their notes with greater facility. I respectfully invite the early attention of Congress to this subject, and regard the proposed alteration in our laws as peculiarly necessary in the present exigency, and calculated to produce immediate and extensive benefit. As the Bank of the United States withdraws its circulation, it is of the first importance that the State banks should be enabled to extend their issues and to supply immediately, by their notes, the place which was filled by the Bank of the United States.

THE CONGRESSIONAL GLOBE.

PRINTED AND PUBLISHED AT THE CITY OF WASHINGTON, BY BLAIR & RIVES.

23D CONGRESS, 1ST SESSION. SATURDAY, MAY 3, 1834. VOL. 1........No. 22.

With the reform of the gold currency, it is proper to associate measures to prevent the issue of small notes. The only step which Congress could with propriety take, in relation to the notes of the State banks, would be to provide that no bank should be a depository of the public money, nor should the notes of any bank be receivable in payment of debts to the United States, which issued notes below a certain denomination. We may safely rely on the coöperation of the several States to impose upon their banks the restrictions necessary to aid in this desirable change in the state of the currency. The alteration proposed, should, however, be gradual. A day might be fixed after which the restriction above mentioned should go into operation, as relates to notes below five dollars. A further restriction, so as to affect notes, under ten dollars, would hereafter be advisable, and ought to be regarded as a part of the plan now proposed to be adopted. But it is not desirable, at this time, to name a definite day for that purpose. A great proportion of the issues of the State banks consists of five-dollar notes. Any measure calculated to impair the currency of notes of this description, about the time the Bank of the United States is going out of existence, would be injurious to the public. When the Bank of the United States is withdrawing its notes from circulation, the void must be filled up by gold and silver, or by the notes of the State banks, or the currency will be injuriously contracted. And if notes of five dollars were then put out of circulation, the diminution of the currency would perhaps be severely felt. And no measure should be adopted, calculated to impede their circulation, until it shall be manifest that the country is relieved from any inconvenience arising from the withdrawal of the notes of the Bank of the United States. But as soon as that period arrives, and it is apparent that gold and silver can be provided for the ordinary circulation below ten dollars, it would be advisable to extend the restriction to notes of that denomination. For we can never be safe from the fluctuations of the currency until all notes below ten dollars are banished from circulation. And it will be still more secure when the restriction is carried up to notes of twenty dollars, so as to substitute the gold eagles in the place of ten-dollar bank notes.

It will be seen from this statement, that it is no part of the proposed plan to dispense with the State banks. It obviously is not in the power of Congress (if it desired to do so) to take any measures for that purpose, without an amendment to the Constitution; and the States would not, and ought not, to surrender the power of chartering banking companies. The State banks are now so numerous, and are so intimately connected with our habits and pursuits, that it is impossible to suppose that the system can ever be entirely abandoned. Nor is it desirable that it should be. They are often abused, like all other human institutions; yet their advantages are many, and under proper regulations, and with the metallic basis now proposed for their paper issues, they will be found of much public advantage.

If there were no State banks, the profitable business of banking and exchange would be monopolized by the great capitalists. Operations of this sort require capital and credit to a large extent, and a private individual in moderate circumstances would be unable to conduct them with any advantage. Yet there is perhaps no business which yields a profit so certain and liberal as the business of banking and exchange, and it is proper that it should be open as far as practicable, to the most free competition, and its advantages shared by all classes of society. Individuals of moderate means cannot participate in them unless they combine together, and by the union of many small sums, create a large capital and establish an extensive credit. It is impossible to accomplish this object without the aid of acts of incorporation, so as to give to the company the security of unity of action, and save it from the disadvantage of frequent changes in the partnership, by the death or retirement of some one of the numerous partners. The incorporated banks, moreover, under proper regulations, will offer a safe and convenient investment of small sums to persons whose situations and pursuits disable them from employing their money profitably in any other mode. It is not more liable to be lost when vested in the stock of a bank than when it is loaned to individuals. The interest on it is paid with more punctuality, and it can be sold and converted into cash whenever the owner desires to employ it in some other way, and if a larger portion of the metals are infused into the circulation, the business of banking will become more sound and wholesome, and less liable to the disasters from which it has suffered under our extravagant and ill-organized system of paper issues. It will render investments in banking companies entirely safe and secure to the holders, and afford them the almost absolute certainty of a reasonable profit, without endangering the capital invested in it. For this reason, it is neither practicable nor desirable to discountenance the continuance of the State banks.

They are convenient and useful also for the purposes of commerce. No commercial or manufacturing community could conduct its business to any advantage without a liberal system of credit, and a facility of obtaining money on loan when the exigency of their business may require it. This cannot be obtained without the aid of a paper circulation founded on credit. It is therefore not the interest of this country to put down the paper currency altogether.

The great object should be to give to it a foundation on which it will safely stand. A circulating medium composed of paper and gold and silver in just proportions, would not be liable to be constantly disordered by the accidental embarrassments or imprudences of trade—nor by a combination of the moneyed interest for political purposes. The value of the metals in circulation would remain the same, whether there was a panic or not, and the proportion of paper being less, the credit of the banks could not be so readily impaired or endangered.

The state of the currency then, which is proposed in the foregoing resolutions, would provide silver and gold for ordinary domestic purposes and the smaller payments, and the banks of the different States would easily be able to furnish exchanges between distant places, according to the wants of commerce. There cannot, therefore, be any necessity for a paper circulation of general credit throughout the country. Funds are more conveniently and safely transferred from place to place by drafts and bills of exchange than by bank notes. The immense operations between different parts of the United States are now chiefly carried on by this means, and it is only in particular places, and for comparatively small amounts, that notes are used; and the local institutions would, without doubt, in a very short time make arrangements among themselves to furnish the exchanges which commerce requires; and the competition among many would reduce the rate of exchange to its proper level. Besides, they would find it their interest to make agreements among themselves to honor each other's notes to a certain extent, and thus furnish, as far as might be necessary, a paper currency of general circulation, in such places as would be likely, from their intercourse with each other, to require such a convenience. But the establishment of such a paper currency ought not to have any aid, direct or incidental, by legislative provisions. While it rests upon mutual arrangements among the banks themselves, they will keep the issues of each other within proper bounds. But when they are able to extend their credit by any legal provisions, in favor of their notes, the temptation is constantly presented to avail themselves of this advantage; and over-issues and over-trading are the necessary consequences. If, however, a different policy should be deemed advisable, the advantages now given by law to the Bank of the United States might easily be extended to the notes of the depository banks, and if their notes were made receivable in payment of all debts to the Government, their currency and general credit would be quite equal to that now enjoyed by the Bank of the United States. Believing, however, that such a provision would be calculated to increase the issues of paper, I cannot recommend it. The chief object of the plan I propose is to increase the proportion of the metallic currency without diminishing inconveniently the general mass of the circulating medium, and any provision tending to enlarge the proportion of paper beyond what the public convenience requires should be studiously avoided.

The advantages of the proposed plan over the present currency will not be confined to the superior stability of the paper circulation.

The laboring classes of the community are now paid their daily, or weekly wages, in bank notes of the smaller denominations, and if there are any in circulation of doubtful value and depreciated in public estimation, they are too often used in payments to the poorer and more helpless classes of society. They are not always judges of the value or genuineness of the notes offered to them, and consequently, are often imposed upon, and their small earnings still more diminished, by the depreciated character or entire worthlessness of paper in which they are paid. If the alteration suggested should be adopted, the smaller notes would soon be banished from circulation every where, and the laborer would, therefore, be paid in gold and silver, and that portion of society which is most apt to suffer from worthless or depreciated paper, and who are least able to bear the loss, would be guarded from imposition and injustice. It is time that the just claims of this portion of society should be regarded in our legislation in relation to the currency. So far we have been providing facilities for those employed in extensive commerce, and have left the mechanic and the laborer to all the hazards of an insecure and unstable circulating medium.

It may be objected to this plan, that in giving to the executive department, the power of selecting these fiscal agents from among the State banks, an undue influence may be exercised over them, and the power be used for improper and corrupt purposes. The answer to it appears to be a plain one. The States in which these institutions are situated, can at all times control them, and would effectually interpose to prevent such abuses of power. Besides, with the diminished revenue which will hereafter be collected, on the reduced tariff of duties, it is impossible to imagine that the gains to be derived from the public deposites, when distributed, as they must be, among so many banks, and among so many stockholders in each bank, can ever be sufficiently important to tempt them to swerve from their duty, or to influence, in any respect, their conduct or opinions.

But it is proper, no doubt, in all cases, to restrict political power within certain and defined limits, and it will be advisable, therefore, to regulate the selection in such a manner as to remove all apprehensions of its abuse. The following are respectfully suggested for consideration:

If the danger of abuse is considered by Congress as one of any magnitude, and as likely to produce improper influence, it may be effectually removed, by making it the duty of the Secretary of the Treasury to divide the deposites among all the incorporated specie-paying banks of the place where the revenue is collected, in proportion to their respective capitals actually paid in, provided they are all willing to receive them upon the terms prescribed by law; and if they are not all willing, then among so many as would agree to take them.

Every danger of abuse in the selection will, by this mode, be taken away; and the safety of the money could be secured, by authorizing the Secretary of the Treasury to demand security from any of these banks, when, in his judgment, the public interest required it; and there might also be a prohibition against removing the money to any place, except where it was immediately necessary for the purpose of disbursement.

This mode would somewhat complicate the operations of the department. Yet I do not perceive that it would produce any serious inconvenience to the public service. It might, and probably would, make it necessary to employ one or two more clerks in the department. But that would be but a small consideration, if it be deemed advisable to take from the Executive all discretion over the subject.

If, however, Congress should agree with me in supposing that the danger apprehended from this discretion is more imaginary than real, I would then respectfully propose the following regulations:

1. That the Secretary of the Treasury should annually, at the beginning of each session, report to Congress the banks which had been used by him during the year, as the depositories of the public money.

2. That the banks once selected as the depositories of the public money, should be continued as such, unless, in the judgment of the Secretary of the Treasury, the public interest required the depository to be changed; in which case, he should report to Congress, at its next session, the reason of the change.

3. That, in all cases where there were two or more banks at the same place where the revenue is to be deposited, at least two should be employed as the depositories of the money of the United States, if they are willing to receive it, and give the security that may be required.

4. Where there shall be no banks at the places where the revenue is received, the money shall be deposited in such places as the Secretary shall direct, subject to the same obligation to report to Congress.

5. No bank to be selected as a depository of the public money, or continued as such, which shall deal in any stocks, except those of the State in which it is situated, or of the United States.

6. After the third of March, eighteen hundred and thirty-six, no bank to be used as the depository of the public money, which shall issue or pay out notes below five dollars, and the notes of no bank to be received in payment of debts due to the United States, which shall issue or pay out notes of a less denomination than that above mentioned, after the time aforesaid, nor shall any bank be a depository of public money which does not pay specie on demand for its notes.

7. Each bank selected for the deposite of the public money shall return a statement of its affairs to the Secretary of the Treasury once a month, or oftener, if required. Such statement shall show the aggregate amount loaned to its own officers and directors, and also the amount loaned on its own stock.

With these limitations it is believed that the public money will be safe; and that even the possibility of abuse will be taken away.

In submitting this view of the currency and the plan of improving it, I have endeavored to provide against the danger of a too sudden contraction of the present circulating medium. I am not prepared to say that the amount in circulation is at this moment greater, or even so great, as the convenience of the country requires. I think it is not. For it has been rapidly and injuriously diminished, and it is to be regretted that the pains taken to destroy confidence in the great mass of the circulating medium, has so far succeeded as to bring upon the community the inconvenience and suffering which a rapid reduction of the circulating medium unavoidably occasions. The great object now in view is to terminate forever the evil of the present system, and to place the currency on a foundation so stable that it cannot again be shaken.

If a broad and sure foundation of gold and silver is provided for our system of paper credits, we need not hereafter apprehend those alternate seasons of abundance and scarcity of money suddenly succeeding each other, which has so far marked our history, and irreparably injured so many of our citizens.

These remarks are respectfully submitted for the consideration of the committee.

I have the honor to be, sir, very respectfully, your obedient servant, R. B. TANEY, Secretary of the Treasury.

Hon. JAMES K. POLK, Chairman Committee Ways and Means of the House of Representatives.

Mr. EWING asked, if it was in order, to move to recommit the bill with instructions.

The CHAIR said it was not in order.

Mr. EWING asked if he could move its recommitment to a standing or select committee.

After some conversation as to the question of order,

Mr. EWING submitted a motion to commit the bill to a select committee, with instructions, and obtained leave of the House to express his views on the subject. After speaking some time, Mr. E., at the suggestion of Mr. POLK, yielded the floor, with the understanding that he should have an opportunity hereafter to continue his remarks.

Mr. BURGES then moved an amendment to the motion to commit, instructing the Committee of the Whole on the state of the Union to provide in the bill that every deposite bank should pay three and a half per cent. per annum for all public money which it shall have in possession for two months or longer.

After some remarks from Messrs. POLK, REED, BURGES, BINNEY, and FELDER,

Mr. BURGES withdrew his amendment, and the bill and report were committed to the Committee of the Whole on the state of the Union, and ordered to be printed.

The SPEAKER communicated to the House the annual statements of the commerce and navigation of the United States.

On motion of Mr. CAMBRELENG, ten thousand extra copies were ordered to be printed.

The House then resolved itself into Committee of the Whole on the state of the Union, (Mr. HUBBARD in the chair,) and resumed the consideration of

THE GENERAL APPROPRIATION BILL.

The question on the amendments submitted by Mr. VANCE, viz: to reduce the salary and compensation to be paid to the Commissioner of the Land Office; the Collector, Inspector, and other officers of the Customs; the clerks, &c. in the Post Office; the compensation to be given to the next President of the United States; to the clerks in the House of Representatives, and the pay, &c., of members, were severally put and negatived.

The pay for clerks, machinist, and messenger in the Patent Office, $5,400, was agreed to.

The question being on the item for incidental and contingent expenses of the Department of State, including the expense of publishing and distributing the laws, $25,000,

Mr. McKAY proposed an amendment thereto, substantially to prevent any payments being made by the departments for extra clerical service, out of the contingent fund, except for recording and settling the papers therein. This practice of employing extra clerks, and paying them out of the contingent fund, he considered ought not to be permitted.

Mr. POLK remarked that part of the expense which had been incurred under the head of extra clerical service, was in consequence of a resolution of the Senate calling on the department to furnish various returns and statements of the comparative increase per centum of the white population, of slaves, of aliens, and of the militia throughout the United States. He was not aware that these returns had been completed, but for the present he would not object to the amendment.

Mr. HARDIN objected, as this was already a question which had been decided by the House.

Mr. J. Q. ADAMS wished to have the expense of distributing the laws accurately known, and presented separate from the incidental and other expenses of the department.

Mr. POLK said that the expense of distribution varied according to the length of the session, and in other causes it was impossible to be precise in the expense to be incurred. The amount expended in 1831, was $14,900; in 1832, $19,300; whilst in 1833 it was but $11,477. This showed a variance of $8,000, but which might be attributed to the discontinuance of the practice used formerly of employing special agents for the distribution. The conveyance by mail was now used for this purpose. The same objection, on the score of principle, might be laid for the fuel, and they might be called on to specify the quantity used for years past, and to appropriate, pro rata, for each department. The practice would be seen to prove

inconvenient, and he should hope, as the appropriation was the usual one, the member from Massachusetts would be satisfied.

Mr. ADAMS pressed his amendment, so as to grant $5,000 for incidental expenses, &c., and $20,000 for expense of distributing the laws.

After some remarks from Mr. McKAY, Mr. ADAMS, and Mr. FOOT,

Mr. POLK said the House could not know whether the precise amounts designated would be sufficient for the objects contemplated for each.

The question on the amendment of Mr. A. was then put and negatived: Ayes 43, noes 53. No quorum.

The CHAIRMAN having ascertained there were only 111 members present,

Mr. J. Q. ADAMS moved that the committee do rise and report the fact to the House.

The motion was rejected.

Mr. POLK desired to have a call of the House.

The CHAIRMAN informed the committee that although they had refused the motion to rise, yet, that no business could be transacted until a quorum was in attendance.

Some members having in the interim come into the Hall,

Mr. H. EVERETT rose and advocated the amendment.

And after some explanatory remarks from Mr. ARCHER and Mr. POLK, the question was a second time put, and the amendment was rejected: Ayes 50, noes 74.

The question recurring on the amendment proposed by Mr. McKAY,

Mr. WATMOUGH opposed it, as not sufficiently coming up to the professions of those who claimed to belong to the old Jefferson school.

Mr. CHILTON rose to propose an amendment to the amendment, viz: to strike out "the exemption in favor of clerks for arranging the records." He would oppose the practice that prevailed, of giving any power to the heads of departments, at their pleasure to employ extra clerks for any purpose, in addition to the number which was fixed by law. If the clerks were encouraged in this instance, they would look for extra service in every other case to help them in duties they were themselves capable of performing, as naturally as a horse would look to find corn in the trough out of which he was accustomed to feed.

The amendment was further opposed by Mr. HARPER, of Pennsylvania, and Mr. GRENNELL.

Mr. McKAY defended the propriety of his amendment, and advocated its necessity, as fixing some limits to the employment of the contingent fund, and rendering it imperative in the Secretary of State to cause the alteration in his office to be put in order.

After some remarks from Messrs. SHEPHERD, HARDIN, and HALL, of North Carolina, in which the propriety of supplying the clerks in the department with newspapers, Niles's Register, and other papers, was incidentally discussed—

Mr. ADAMS explained that it had been the usual practice to have fifty copies of Niles's Register supplied for the use of our ministers abroad.

Mr. BATES complained of the increased expenses to which the department was subjected, and inquired for information in relation to them from the chairman of the Committee of Expenditure in the Department of State. The expense for hardware and furniture was enormous.

Mr. SHEPHERD replied that it was his intention, he could assure the gentleman, to wade through all these matters which were the subject of complaint.

Mr. FULLER, of New York, desired to have some information on the subject of the unexpended balances of salaries to the clerks.

Mr. ARCHER explained.

The amendment proposed by Mr. CHILTON was rejected: Ayes 55, noes 81.

After some remarks from Mr. ADAMS, of Massachusetts, and Mr. McKAY,

Mr. BURD said that, in his opinion, the clerks should labor, and labor faithfully; that in summer they should go to their work at six o'clock in the morning, and labor till breakfast, at eight o'clock; and again from nine till two, and at three return to their offices and work till six. He was in favor of

paying them amply for their services, if faithfully performed.

The question being taken on Mr. McKAY'S amendment, it was rejected.

Mr. McKAY moved to strike out $1,300 in the 3d line, and insert $650; which was rejected.

The following clause being under consideration:

"For the Documentary History of the American Revolution, per act of the 2d March, 1833, $35,000"—

Mr. McKAY said that, in duty to his country, he must oppose this provision, and he would show the House that it might involve the country in an expenditure of a million of dollars. If the House was disposed to listen to the facts regarding the contract with the late Secretary, he would show that he had exceeded his authority in making the contract, and as the hour was late, he moved that the committee rise. Rejected.

Mr. McKAY went into some statements on the subject, and moved that the item be stricken out; when

Mr. EVANS moved that the committee do now rise. Lost—72 to 84.

The amendment proposed by Mr. McKay was negatived.

Mr. ARCHER moved an amendment, appropriating $25,000 for the purchase of the original correspondence and other papers of General Washington.

After some remarks from Mr. HALL, of North Carolina, the report from the Committee on Foreign Relations, recommending the purchase, was read, and several documents were also read with respect to the value of the papers, and some conversation took place, in which Messrs. ADAMS, CAMBRELENG, and HALL, took part.

Mr. ARCHER then withdrew the amendment, with a view to offer it again, in another form, hereafter.

Mr. FOOT moved to strike out the item appropriating $750 for additional watchmen, and an increase of the compensation of watchmen of the northeast executive building, in addition to the usual appropriation.

Mr. VINTON moved that the committee rise. Rejected—63 to 82.

The question being taken on the motion to strike out, it was determined in the negative.

Mr. FOOT moved to amend the bill, by striking out the item reimbursing the fund for the contingent expenses of the northeast executive building, &c. Mr. F. spoke against the clause, and in favor of specific appropriations. The motion was negatived.

Mr. J. Q. ADAMS, moved to amend the item making appropriations for two additional clerks in the 3d Auditor's office, by striking out a portion as surplusage Agreed to.

Mr. DICKSON moved that the committee rise. Lost—yeas 54, nays 59.

The item for supplying book-cases and fire-bags for the purpose of placing the title papers, &c. in a place of security, in case of fire, was, on motion of Mr. POLK, struck out.

The item for the contingent expense of the office of the Commissary General was reduced from $3600 to $2500.

The other items preceding these having been gone through—

Mr. POLK moved to strike out of the item for additional clerk hire, the words "for the first half of," so as to make it read for 1834, in order to carry into effect the act of the 7th of January, 1832, granting revolutionary pensioners $5000.

Mr. J. Q. ADAMS inquired how this became necessary.

Mr. POLK replied.

Mr. EVANS thought as this was an item that would require more discussion than could be given to it at this late hour, he would move that the committee rise.

Mr. POLK said, the subject could be fully examined into when the bill should be before the House.

Mr. EVANS said he was perfectly aware of the gentleman's anxiety to get this subject into the House. He also knew, when it was there, how soon his anxiety for the public service would induce him to take means to get it passed there.

Mr. POLK said, if the gentleman would be so

courteous as to permit him to answer him, he would make the motion for the rising of the committee.

Mr. EVANS declined.

The motion for the committee to rise was negatived—ayes 37, noes 78. (No quorum.)

The CHAIRMAN thereupon rose and reported that fact to the House.

Mr. EVANS moved an adjournment.

Mr. POLK called for the yeas and nays. Ordered.

Mr. CHILTON hoped the hour of six o'clock would be inserted.

The motion to adjourn was negatived—yeas 53, nays 87.

The House again went into committee.

Mr. ADAMS said, as the subjects to arise were of high importance, he would move that the committee rise, with a view to have a call of the House.

Mr. POLK said he had no objection to the committee rising, if the honorable member from Massachusetts would agree to take up the bill tomorrow, and go through with it, without wasting further time.

On the motion that the committee rise, the vote stood—

Yeas 36, nays 80. (No quorum.)

The CHAIRMAN rose and reported the fact to the House.

Mr. J. Q. ADAMS moved an adjournment; on which motion,

Mr. BEARDSLEY demanded the yeas and nays.

The motion to adjourn was not decided when we were obliged to go to press.

The motion made by Mr. J. Q. ADAMS to adjourn, at thirty-five minutes past six o'clock, being pending—

The yeas and nays were demanded by Mr. BEARDSLEY, and ordered.

The motion was rejected—yeas 39, nays 86.

So the House refused to adjourn.

Mr. J. Q. ADAMS rose to move a call of the House.

Mr. SPEIGHT (Speaker pro tem.) decided that he had no right to receive the motion.

Mr. ADAMS appealed from this decision.

Mr. SPEIGHT considering that there was a quorum in the House, his duty was to resign, and The House to resolve itself into Committee of the Whole on the state of the Union, in which condition they had been, when the committee rose to report the fact that there was not a quorum in attendance.

The motion accordingly went again into committee, Mr. HUBBARD in the chair.

Mr. MOORE rose to a point of order; he considered it was the duty of the Speaker to have put the question on the motion made by the member from Massachusetts.

Mr. SPEIGHT, (in the House,) explained, and maintained that his decision had been in strict conformity to the former practice of the House. That a committee having reported that a quorum was not in attendance, and if having in the interim been ascertained that a quorum was present, then it was the duty of the Speaker to vacate his seat, and reinstate the committee.

Mr. ADAMS denied that this was the practice of the House, and insisted upon his right, as well as that of every other member, to have the question put to the House upon any motion they should present.

Mr. WILLIAMS moved the committee rise.

The motion was rejected. Yeas 59, nays 72.

The item for additional clerk hire, with the amendment proposed by Mr. POLK, so as to make it read for 1834 to carry into effect the act of the 7th January, 1832, granting revolutionary pensions, $5,000 was then agreed to.

After some other items were gone through—

Mr. CHILTON ALLAN appealed to the House not to persist, at so late an hour (then half past seven o'clock) in proceeding with a bill of this importance, and which contained appropriations of an increased amount, beyond that of former years.

He moved that the committee rise.

The vote on this motion stood, yeas 37, nays 61. No quorum.

The CHAIRMAN rose and reported the fact to the House, after which,

Mr. EVANS moved an adjournment, which prevailed, and

The House adjourned.

IN SENATE.

WEDNESDAY, *April* 23, 1834.

PETITIONS.

Mr. McKEAN presented two memorials from the county of Chester, Pennsylvania. Also, the proceedings of a public meeting in Mifflin county, Pennsylvania, both in favor of the restoration of the deposites to the Bank of the United States, and in favor of a recharter of that institution; which were read, referred to the Committee on Finance, and ordered to be printed.

Mr. McKEAN presented the petition of W. J. Caldwell, and another; which was referred to the Committee on Finance.

Mr. SOUTHARD presented the petition of A. A. Nicholson, a first lieutenant of marines, praying to be compensated for his services as acting assistant quartermaster in the marine corps;

The petition of Stephen Oats; and

The petition of James Buchanan;

Which were severally referred to the Committee on Naval Affairs.

Mr. SOUTHARD presented a memorial from the city of Trenton, New Jersey, and another from the county of Warren, in favor of a restoration of the deposites to the Bank of the United States, and a recharter of that corporation; which were read, referred to the Committee on Finance, and ordered to be printed.

Mr. SOUTHARD presented the proceedings of a convention of delegates from the several counties of New Jersey, appointed at public meetings, recommending a restoration of the public deposites to the Bank of the United States, and a recharter of said bank.

SPECIAL ORDER OF THE DAY.

The Senate then resumed the consideration of the special order, being Mr. FORSYTH'S amendment to Mr. POINDEXTER'S resolutions, and Mr. POINDEXTER'S appeal from the decision of the Chair, which was, that the amendment was in order.

The question on sustaining the decision of the Chair was taken, and determined as follows, viz:

YEAS—Messrs. Benton, Black, Forsyth, Grundy, Hill, Kane, King of Alabama, King of Georgia, Linn, McKean, Morris, Robinson, Shepley, Tipton, White, Wilkins, and Wright—17.

NAYS—Messrs. Bell, Bibb, Calhoun, Chambers, Clay, Clayton, Ewing, Frelinghuysen, Hendricks, Kent, Leigh, Mangum, Moore, Poindexter, Prentiss, Preston, Robbins, Silsbee, Smith, Southard, Sprague, Swift, Tomlinson, Tyler, Waggaman, and Webster—26.

So the decision was reversed, and the amendment was declared not to be in order.

Mr. FORSYTH then asked a division of the question upon the resolutions.

Mr. CLAY rose and submitted the following resolutions, which he hoped Mr. POINDEXTER would accept as a substitute for his, as the variations were not material:

1. *Resolved*, That the protest communicated to the Senate on the 17th instant, by the President of the United States, asserts powers, as belonging to the President, which are inconsistent with the just authority of the two Houses of Congress, and inconsistent with the Constitution of the United States.

2. *Resolved*, That while the Senate is, and ever will be, ready to receive from the President all such messages and communications as the Constitution and laws, and the usual course of public business, authorize him to transmit to it, yet it cannot recognise any right in him to make a formal protest against votes and proceedings of the Senate, declaring such votes and proceedings to be illegal and unconstitutional, and requesting the Senate to enter such protest on its journals.

3. *Resolved*, That the aforesaid protest is a breach of the privileges of the Senate, and that it be not entered on the Journal.

After some conversation between Messrs. POINDEXTER, CALHOUN, CLAYTON, and PRESTON, the point of which was, whether it was not

better to receive the protest, and proceed to the consideration of the paper itself,

Mr. POINDEXTER accepted Mr. CLAY's resolution as a substitute for his own.

Mr. BIBB then proposed to amend the resolution by striking out all that follows the words "United States," in the first resolution, and insert the words "be not received."

Mr. KANE then obtained the floor, and moved an adjournment.

And the Senate adjourned.

HOUSE OF REPRESENTATIVES.

WEDNESDAY, *April* 23, 1834.

After the reading of the Journal—

Mr. J. Q. ADAMS said, some circumstances which occurred on the preceding day, which were incorrectly recorded, made it necessary for him to move to expunge the following words from the Journal: "After some time spent therein," and insert, "And the Speaker resumed the chair, and 'Mr. HUBBARD reported that the committee had, 'according to order, had the said bill under consideration, and finding itself without a quorum, 'had risen, and directed him to report that fact to 'the House." And again, to strike out, in another place, "Mr. HUBBARD resumed the chair of the 'Committee of the Whole on the state of the 'Union," and insert, "The House again resolved 'itself into Committee of the Whole House on 'the state of the Union, and proceeded in the consideration of the said bill; and after some time 'spent therein, the Speaker again resumed the 'chair, and Mr. HUBBARD reported that the committee, finding itself again without a quorum, had 'risen, and directed him to report that fact to the 'House."

Mr. A. said there were other matters connected with this, which made it imperative on him to require these corrections. He had made a motion for a call of the House, which was refused by Mr. SPEIGHT. He had appealed from this decision, and he had refused also to entertain this motion. There was no motion made for the chairman to go into Committee of the Whole on the state of the Union. Mr. HUBBARD, the chairman, had done so incorrectly; and when he ascertained that there was not a quorum, he called on the member from North Carolina [Mr. SPEIGHT] to fill the Speaker's chair in the House. He did not believe he was authorized to appoint any one. The appointment was not according to precedent. The statements on the Journal showed that the proceedings were informal. After stating at length several cases which authorized him to correct the proceeding, he said if this were not a mere matter of form, if the practice itself had not a tendency to lead to scenes of the grossest disorder, he would have passed the occurrences over, as that which might naturally arise after a long debate, when members were excited or fatigued, after a patient attention to the duties of the House. But this state of things was so interwoven and connected with an attempt, on the part of a portion of the House, to drive through it a bill, second to none in importance—he meant the general appropriation bill—that he could not pass it over. It was evidently the design of a portion of the House to drive, force it, without discussion, or permitting any amendment to be made. To such a length was this carried, that the honorable chairman of the Committee of Ways and Means formally proposed to make the motion for the rising of the committee a matter of bargain—ay, sir, a matter of bargain, whether he would or not object to my motion to this effect. It is true, the honorable chairman was arrested in the course of these remarks, and called to order.

Mr. BOON rose to order. He desired to know if it was in order to impute such improper motives as were implied by the language of the honorable member from Massachusetts to the chairman of the Committee of Ways and Means, and to a portion of the House.

The SPEAKER. No improper motives should be attributed by any member to others.

Mr. ADAMS maintained that he had a perfect right to allude, not personally, but historically, to the transactions of the previous day in the House. He had not made any personal reflection on the chairman, or any portion of the House. He trusted that at this day, when the House was full, that a different course would be followed, and that he would be permitted to speak, as he had a right to do, of their proceedings, as matter of history, when a direct proposition, a bargain, was attempted to be made, that if he would agree to sit out the bill to-morrow, the member and those whom he commanded——

The SPEAKER called the member to order.

Mr. ADAMS. Is it not in order, then, to speak the truth?

Mr. POLK. What the honorable member states is not correct; it is not true.

Considerable excitement and confusion was observed in the House.

Mr. ADAMS was proceeding, and used some language which was not distinctly heard by the reporters; for which,

Mr. POLK rose and called him to order.

The SPEAKER desired Mr. A. to take his seat.

Mr. VINTON inquired for what?

The SPEAKER said, for having transgressed the rules of debate, acting in a disorderly manner.

Mr. VINTON appealed from the decision of the Speaker to the House; and he would make this a question, whether one member had not a right to accuse another?

The SPEAKER. Not on a motion of this kind, or in an indirect manner.

The SPEAKER here read from the rules the part enjoining upon members that they should avoid personality in debate; and said that he had called the member from Massachusetts to order for not having confined himself to the question, and for making a direct and personal attack upon a member of the House. The member having been called to order, has taken his seat; the House will take what order in the proceedings they think proper.

Mr. WILLIAMS hoped the member from Massachusetts would be permitted to proceed with his remarks.

Mr. VINTON here withdrew his appeal.

Mr WATMOUGH desired to know what was the charge against the member from Massachusetts.

The SPEAKER said, for not debating the question, and for making a personal allusion to the chairman of the Committee of Ways and Means, in stating he wanted to make an improper use of his privilege, by making a bargain.

After some remarks from Mr. WATMOUGH,

Mr. ADAMS having obtained leave to make an explanation, he declared he had no intention to make any charge against the honorable chairman. It was true he had used the word "bargain," but not in an offensive sense. He would state the circumstances, and the House would then be able to judge for themselves. It would be in their recollection, that after a motion to adjourn was negatived, that he had moved a call of the House. Upon that occasion, the chairman of the Committee of Ways and Means rose in his place, looked forward to him, and said he would agree to adjourn, if he (Mr. A.) would pledge himself to take up the appropriation bill the following (this) day, and go through with it. In these remarks he was stopped by the chairman of the committee. If the honorable chairman of the Committee of Ways and Means did not understand that this proposition was a bargain, or the House so understood it, then it would be an improper word. Had he been permitted to answer, he must have said that he could not answer for more than himself in such a bargain, and although that honorable member might be satisfied that by the mere lifting of his finger, other members would follow him, and that he could carry his object, yet he would not have influence over any member, and therefore could not make such a bargain. This was his explanation. He left the proper use of the word to be decided upon by the House.

Mr. POLK rose, but gave way to

The SPEAKER, who said he owed it to himself to explain the circumstances under which he had been in the habit of appointing the Speaker *pro tem.* to preside in his absence. He did not consider, by the rule, that he was bound to nominate by name to the House the individual whom he selected. It was not a fact that the chairman of the committee had nominated Mr. SPEIGHT in his absence. It was a fact that he was nominated by himself; and having been suffering under some indisposition, he had, previous to his leaving the House, who were then in committee, informed the clerk the person whom he had named. After referring to the practice and usage of the British Parliament, on the matters involved, he concluded by saying it was competent for the House to express their decision on them.

Mr. POLK hoped that he should be permitted an opportunity to repel the personal attack that had been made upon him.

Mr. WILLIAMS rose to order. He maintained that the gentleman from Massachusetts had the right to the floor.

The SPEAKER said he had relinquished it, and then the member from Tennessee having rose, was entitled to it.

Mr. WILLIAMS. If he had, then he had nothing more to say; but he considered that he had sat down upon being directed to do so.

Mr. ADAMS said he had not yielded the floor, he had taken his seat when called to order. The explanation which he had given was to disclaim having made a personal attack; in doing this, he had not yielded the floor. He then proceeded to contend against the explanation, and particularly against the power claimed by the Speaker, to appoint a locum tenens, without naming him to the House. He referred to the perilous consequences that might ensue to the House and the nation, if with a bare quorum, any member making the motion, should not be permitted to have either a call of the House, or a motion to adjourn. He had sat in his place until seven o'clock, impransus, and was willing to do so at any personal inconvenience, for want of subsistence, if it had been the pleasure of the House to do so; that is, of the House properly constituted, for he had thought there was a design, from what took place, to deprive the members of their rights on such an important bill as that which was under discussion. He denied the right of the Speaker to nominate a person to act for him, without the sanction of the House, for, as he got his own authority from them, he had not the right to transfer it. The motions he made were strictly in order, he believed. If the Speaker was present, he would not have refused, as the member from North Carolina did, either to receive his motion, or refuse his right to appeal. He only desired the correction of the journal, that it might be in conformity to truth and right.

Mr. POLK said, as he was not willing to detain the House from the more important business before it, he would not follow the example of the member from Massachusetts. He only desired to notice the severe animadversions which had been made, and in such impassioned language, by that honorable member, upon a majority of the House. He also desired to notice the allusions which he had chosen to make with respect to himself. What was the substance of the gentleman's complaint? He charged, that a majority of the House, a great portion, were attempting to drive through it the appropriation bill, in an improper manner. Sir, said Mr. P., I deny the fact; and before I proceed further, I must ask, in what situation have we been placed with respect to the appropriation bill, to which so frequently, and in vindictive strains, the member from Massachusetts recurs? Have we not been engaged in it for nearly seven whole days and what had been our progress in it? Scarcely any, until yesterday. We have been met in all and every of its items, with obstructions purposely thrown in our way; I may add, with embarrassments improperly raised, to defeat a bill actually necessary for the public service at this moment.

What were we to do with a bill of this character, we who deemed it all-important to hasten through, when, according to the rumors that were more than intimated on this floor, as elsewhere, it was the intention to oppose it all through and to withhold the supplies for the service of the nation? Were we to sit still, fold our arms or come to the conclusion which we did, to endeavor to have it passed, and in the only way that we could accomplish that passage, by resolving to remain patiently in our seats, hear and discuss objections that should be started, and consider them in order to obviate them? Sir, it was with that determination I and a number of members, who are to be stigmatized for so doing, came to the House yesterday, and not to rise until we should g

through with it. The gentleman from Massachusetts, however, whose objects this is calculated to defeat, is not pleased, and he complains that the minority cannot control the majority. This is not our fault. It is a subject of congratulation to me that there are those who evinced their determination to carry through a bill which is for the benefit of the country. But all this may not doubtless please the gentleman, who, always voting for an adjournment at four o'clock, may thus, by causing delay, for aught I know, accomplish his purpose of defeating the bill. Sir, I will speak plainly——

Mr. ADAMS rose to order. The gentleman imputes to me that I always vote for an adjournment, and says, that by so doing, it is for the object of defeating the bill, of withholding the supplies.

The SPEAKER did not understand that this imputation was made.

Mr. POLK disclaimed it.

Mr. ADAMS said he was satisfied so far. He wished explanation as to the charge for voting always to adjourn, for he believed there was not any member less liable to the charge of desiring to adjourn to the injury of his constituents.

Mr. POLK. I leave this matter to be settled between the gentleman and his constituents. I have no explanation to give about it.

Mr. ADAMS. I appeal to the Chair. I am insulted; I have asked for an explanation on a charge of violating my duty as a member in this House.

The SPEAKER. Such a charge was improper.

Mr. PATTON here rose to order, and to ask if it was in order to impute to an individual member an intention to defeat a bill by voting for an adjournment, what he could not do directly? He wished also to know if it was in order to talk of a majority in that House who could be led, by one member, to vote by the lifting up of his finger? He witnessed these altercations and remarks with regret, and he must call on the Speaker to arrest them.

The SPEAKER said the parties had been called to order. They had taken their seats in consequence.

Mr. POLK resumed, and said that he was about to say that, regarding the despatch of the bill through the committee as all important to the public service, he wished to proceed with it, and when the motion was made to adjourn, he had voted against it. In regard to the charge of proposing to make an improper bargain to effect this, although the charge was qualified——

Mr. ADAMS called to order.

The SPEAKER. The member from Massachusetts has disclaimed that he intended anything personal.

Mr. POLK then said, that not to tire the House with a continuance of this subject, he would say once for all, that, placed as he was, with some responsibility, as the organ through whom some of these measures were proposed to the House, he would be perfectly satisfied, if no greater offence should be charged upon him than that of sticking to his seat; for it he should be acquitted to his constituents and to his conscience. He would repel the charge that a majority of the House had a desire to drive the bill through.

Mr. ADAMS had not said a majority of the House had such an object; he said a majority of those present at the time to which he alluded.

Mr. POLK said, constantly as he was interrupted by the gentleman, he would relieve the House from the unpleasant discussion. He desired that they should go on with the bill; avowing that he would not be deterred by sitting here late, from that object, by any such complaint as that there was a refusal to adjourn.

Mr. HUBBARD said, he felt it a duty to state, that having been called to the chair, in the Committee of the Whole on the appropriation bill, by the kindness of the Speaker, it was his purpose to act in that situation with impartiality; and if he committed any error, it should not be designed. He was aware that the member from North Carolina had been named by the Speaker to fill the chair, if occasion should arise for it, in consequence of his absence.

Mr. REED regretted the course this subject had taken; he could not allow that the Speaker had the right to leave the chair, or appoint a successor, unless by leave from the House. He was opposed to the course taken by the presiding officer.

Mr. FOOT supported the course taken as strictly within the rule. It was always understood, that the moment a committee rose, in consequence of there not being a quorum, when it was ascertained that there was one, the committee were from that moment reinstated in their former condition.

Mr. SPEIGHT justified his course when in the chair, as that which was according to the former usage of the House. He denied that he had any unkind feeling to the member from Massachusetts, and would, therefore, forbear noticing further the spirit with which he conducted this discussion.

After a remark or two from Mr. BRIGGS—

Mr. BINNEY contended that there ought to be some power in the House to compel the attendance of members in the Committee of the Whole, in order that a minority of the House might not control the proceedings of the committee.

Mr. MERCER suggested that, after all, this might be a question of fact and not of order. He had been informed by the gentleman who was in the chair when the member from Massachusetts made his motion and appeal, that he did not entertain them because he was in the act of surrendering, or had surrendered the chair to the chairman of the Committee of the Whole.

Mr. WAYNE suggested the expediency, with a view to enable the House to get rid of the question, of appointing a committee to examine the facts, and correct the journal accordingly.

Mr. SUTHERLAND said he had never known the question to be put on returning into the Committee of the Whole, when a quorum was ascertained to be present in the House. He considered the question as unimportant, and was anxious that the House should dispose of it in one way or other.

Mr. McKINLEY considered it as a matter of importance that the journal should be made to speak the facts as to the proceedings in the House. He contended, in regard to the second proposition of the gentleman from Massachusetts, that the House was necessarily obliged to return into the committee, when it was ascertained that there was a quorum, as when a message is received, while the House is in Committee of the Whole, the Speaker takes the chair to enable the House to receive the message, after which the House immediately returns to the committee.

Mr. CHILTON supported the amendment.

Mr. BOON believing (he said) that nothing was to be gained by a continuance of this debate, and wishing to enable the House to proceed to more important business, moved to lay the amendment on the table.

Mr. ADAMS asked the yeas and nays on the motion, and they were ordered.

The question being taken on the motion, it was decided in the affirmative: Yeas 100, nays 89.

Mr. ADAMS then moved the following amendment to the Journal:

"Mr. J. Q. ADAMS moved that there be a call 'of the House. The Speaker refused to put the 'question; upon which Mr. ADAMS appealed from 'the decision of the Speaker, who refused to entertain the motion, and left the chair, which was immediately resumed by Mr. HUBBARD, as chairman 'of the Committee of the Whole."

Mr. BOON moved to lay the motion on the table, upon which the yeas and nays were ordered.

The question being taken, it was decided in the negative: Yeas 94, nays 95.

Mr. ADAMS thanked the House for their determination to entertain the proposition, which, of the two he had offered, was infinitely the more important. He hoped the House would now suffer the journal to be so altered as to show what actually did take place. The decision of the House to lay his former motion on the table he was willing to consider as a decision that the House was a legitimate House, though a minority of the House constituted an actual majority of the Committee, rejecting all amendments to the bill, and endeavoring to force its passage. He did not charge the majority of the House with the attempt to drive the bill through, for the attempt was made by a minority. He stated that he himself made no motion to amend the bill, except one which the chairman of the Committee of Ways and Means accepted. Most of the motions rejected were made by the gentleman from North Carolina, [Mr. McKAY,] who was an ardent supporter of the Administration. He reminded the House that from the commencement of the session he had earnestly pressed upon the House his opposition to the insertion of any provision in the appropriation bills which was not warranted by previous laws. If the gentleman from Tennessee had adopted his principle when he first made the motion to strike out the provision for an additional clerkship in the State Department, there would have been little delay of the bill, but the gentleman himself resisted that motion for two days. He utterly disclaimed any unkind feeling towards the chairman of the Committee of Ways and Means, or the chairman of the Committee of the Whole, and whatever excitement he might show here in discussing facts, he left it at the door of the House when be left it, and the moment he left the door he would feel willing to take any member of the House by the hand.

Mr. BRIGGS offered a further amendment, specifying that Mr. SPEIGHT, and not the Speaker, was in the chair.

Mr. POLK said it seemed probable that this debate would prevent the House from taking up, to-day, the important bill which the gentleman from Massachusetts had so often referred to, and he trusted that he would not be held responsible by that gentleman for this delay. The gentleman held him responsible for delaying the bill two days. He appealed to the House whether he did not make every effort to avoid debate. Very often he had, perhaps impatiently, importuned the House to proceed with the bill. At the close of the second day, the gentleman from Massachusetts made a long speech on the subject, what he should call a set speech. He could hardly account for the circumstance that the gentleman could scarcely rise in his place without animadverting, in some way, upon him.

He (Mr. P.) discharged the duty of an individual member, and could not imagine what object any one could have in representing him as influencing others in the discharge of their duties. The gentleman from Massachusetts makes assaults upon every one, lashes all around the House, and then seeks to retreat by saying that if he had hurt any body's feelings, he did not intend it. He insisted that there was no one provision of this bill which was out of the usual course, and trusted that he would be acquitted of any unnecessary consumption of time. But why did the gentleman consume the time of the House by dragging this question before it? He proposes to amend the journal, and he goes off and charges the majority of the House with improper conduct, and repeats the remarks which he had already made before. Thinking it necessary that we should transact the public business, instead of consuming time in political discussions, which were intended for effect abroad, and ended in no legislation, he hoped the House would go on with the appropriation bills, sitting late and working hard, till we had got through with them. He hoped we should not sit here, to hear the same speeches delivered over and over again, for the benefit, as a member of this House used to say, of the people of Buncombe. He was sorry to consume even the time occupied by these remarks. He hoped the House would go on to transact its business, without that excitement which the gentleman from Massachusetts so much manifested, and yet deprecated—that we should do as he says, and not as he does.

Mr. LANE opposed the amendment, as not stating the facts as he understood them. The Speaker, he said, had left the chair, and was half way off from the platform, before the gentleman from Massachusetts made his motion.

After some remarks from Mr. EVANS,

Mr. SPEIGHT said, it was true that he was in the act of leaving the chair, when the motion was made; but candor required him to state, that had he remained in the chair, he should not have considered that he had a right to receive the motion for the call of the House. He also stated, that in his course, he had no design to interfere with the rights of any member of the House; and further observed, that it would be no cause of mortification to him if his name should be handed down to posterity as having made a wrong decision in this House.

Mr. BYNUM said he had voted to lay the amendment of the honorable gentleman from Massachusetts on the table, and should now vote against its passage, unless a motion was again made for it to lay on the table.

He thought its passage would be an act of injustice to his honorable colleague, who had occupied the chair at the time alluded to, as the motives and reasons by which the decision of which complaint had been made, would be handed down to posterity unexplained, and would certainly subject to the suspicion and censure of all who should in future observe the proceedings of the House, the conduct of his colleague. The amendment which had just been proposed by another honorable member from Massachusetts, [Mr. Briggs,] he thought made the whole still more objectionable. That honorable member proposed to insert the name of his colleague, who occupied temporarily the chair, and thereby made the censure more express and direct, which would inflict additional injustice on the occupant of the chair. He believed the conduct of his colleague while in the chair was not only innocent, but strictly correct. It appeared to him, from the different expositions that had been made in the House, that his colleague had taken the chair, as Speaker, while the House was in Committee of the Whole, for a special purpose, and his duties were restricted either to adjourn it, or to ascertain whether or not there was a quorum, on the commission of either of which his colleague thought his functions and powers immediately expired, and he did not, therefore, deem himself at liberty to entertain the motion of the honorable gentleman from Massachusetts; but after ascertaining the fact that there was a quorum, he immediately relinquished the chair, and the House, by its very nature, was resolved back into a Committee of the Whole. It did appear to him (said Mr. B.) that this decision was perfectly correct, as upon the very ascertainment of the fact of the existence of a quorum, the nature of the House was changed into a Committee of the Whole, and the functions of the Speaker of the House, he thought, necessarily ceased to exist, immediately after the announcement of the fact of the existence of a quorum, which forthwith, without motion, converted the body from the House into a Committee of the Whole; and he thought his colleague perfectly right in believing he had no power, as Speaker, to entertain the motion of the honorable gentleman from Massachusetts, [Mr. Adams,] and hoped he would be sustained in the decision he had made.

After some remarks from Messrs. FILLMORE and CHILTON,

Mr. BEARDSLEY moved that the motion to amend be laid upon the table; which was agreed to: Yeas 98, nays 90.

Mr. R. M. JOHNSON moved the suspension of the rules, in order to submit the following:

Resolved, That the several bills, viz:

No. 262. Making appropriations for the civil and diplomatic expenses of the Government for the year 1834;

No. 221. Making appropriations for continuing the Cumberland road in Ohio, Indiana, and Illinois, and repairing certain part of the Ohio, and continuing certain Territorial roads;

No. 269. Making additional appropriations for the improvement of certain harbors and removing obstructions in the mouths of certain rivers;

No. 109. Making appropriations for the Indian Department;

No. 182. Making appropriations for Indian annuities, and other similar objects;

No. 181. Making appropriations for certain fortifications for the year 1834;

Be the standing order of the day for Thursday, the 24th instant, at twelve o'clock, and on each succeeding day, (Saturdays excepted,) at the same hour, until the said bills shall be disposed of; and that till the hour of twelve o'clock on each day the business of the House shall proceed in the order prescribed by the rules of the House: Provided, that it shall be in order to present memorials and petitions on Mondays.

Mr. VINTON moved an adjournment. Rejected.

The question being taken by yeas and nays, on Mr. Johnson's motion to suspend the rules, it was

decided in the negative: Yeas 108, nays 83. [Not two-thirds.]

YEAS—Messrs. John Adams, William Allen, Beale, Bean, Beardsley, Beaumont, John Bell, Blair, Bockee, Bodle, Boon, Brown, Bullard, Bunch, Burd, Bynum, Cage, Cambreleng, Carr, Casey, Chaney, Chinn, Samuel Clark, Clay, Coffee, Connor, Cramer, Day, Dickerson, Dickinson, Duncan, Dunlap, Ewing, Forester, Fowler, Wm. K. Fuller, Galbraith, Gillet, Joseph Hall, Thomas H. Hall, Halsey, Joseph M. Harper, Harrison, Hathaway, Hawkins, Hazeltine, Heath, Howell, Hubbard, Abel Huntington, Jarvis, Richard M. Johnson, Cave Johnson, Benj. Jones, Kavanagh, Kinnard, Lane, Lansing, Lawrence, Luke Lea, Thomas Lee, Leavitt, Loyall, Lyon, Joel K. Mann, Mardis, Moses Mason, McIntire, McKay, McKennan, McKim, McKinley, McLene, McVean, Robert Mitchell, Osgood, Page, Parks, Parker, Patton, Patterson, D. J. Pearce, Franklin Pierce, Pierson, Polk, Pope, Schenck, Schley, Augustine H. Shepperd, Shinn, Charles Slade, Smith, Speight, Standifer, Stewart, Stoddert, Sutherland, William Taylor, Philemon Thomas, Thomson, Turrill, Vanderpoel, Van Houten, Wagener, Ward, Ward well, Wayne, Webster, Campbell P. White, Frederick Whiteley, Wilson, Wise—108.

NAYS—Messrs. John Quincy Adams, Heman Allen, Chilton Allan, Archer, Ashley, Banks, Barber, Barnitz, Barringer, Bates, Baylies, Beatty, James Bul. Binney, Bouldin, Briggs, Bull, Burges, Campbell, Chilton, Claiborne, William Clark, Clayton, Clowney, Corwin, Crane, Crockett, Darlington, Amos Davis, Davenport, Deberry, Denny, Dickson, Evans, Horace Everett, Fillmore, Foot, Foster, Philo C. Fuller, Fulton, Gamble, Gholson, Gilmer, Gorham, Graham, Grennell, Hiland Hall, Hannegan, Hardin, James Harper, Hester, Jabez W. Huntington, Jackson, Seaborn Jones, King, Lay, Lewis, Lincoln, Love, Martindale, Marshall, McComas, Milligan, Moore, Pinckney, Potts, Ramsay, Reed, Rencher, Selden, William Slade, Sloane, Spangler, Tweedy, Vance, Vinton, Watmough, Whallon, Edward D. White, Elisha Whittlesey, Wilde, Williams, Young—83.

On motion of Mr. POPE, the House adjourned.

IN SENATE.

A message upon executive business was received from the President of the United States, by Mr. Donelson, his Private Secretary.

Mr. CHAMBERS having obtained the unanimous consent of the Senate, introduced the following joint resolution, which was adopted.

Resolved, by the Senate and House of Representatives in Congress assembled, That the Commissioner of Public Buildings cause the Pennsylvania avenue, from Capitol Hill to the President's square, to be watered in such manner as to prevent the inconveniences now experienced.

Mr. GRUNDY presented a memorial, signed by the members of the Nashville bar, praying that the terms for holding the United States courts in Tennessee, may be changed. The memorial was referred to the Committee on the Judiciary.

Mr. WEBSTER presented a memorial, signed by four or five hundred inhabitants of Union county, Pennsylvania, praying a restoration of the deposites to the Bank of the United States, and a recharter of that institution.

Mr. CLAYTON presented a similar memorial, signed by seven hundred and thirty-six citizens of Kent county, Delaware.

Mr. ROBBINS presented a like memorial, from a number of the inhabitants of the city of Providence, Rhode Island, and the adjacent islands.

Which memorials were read, and ordered to the Committee on Finance, and ordered to be printed.

Mr. LEIGH presented the petition of William Mann; which was referred to the Committee on Claims.

Mr. HENDRICKS presented the petition of the Trustees of the Indiana Teachers' Seminary, praying a grant of land to promote the objects of said Institution. Referred to the Committee on Public Lands.

Mr. TYLER presented the petition of Charles J. Catlett; which was referred to the Committee on Finance.

Mr. CHAMBERS presented the petition of Jo-

seph Forrest; which was referred to the Committee on the Judiciary.

Mr. C. also, presented the petition of the widow of the late Colonel Moore, an officer in the Revolution; which was referred to the Committee on Pensions.

Also, the petition of the Provident Association of Clerks, in the District of Columbia; which was referred to the Committee on the District of Co. lumbia.

REPORTS OF COMMITTEES.

Mr. POINDEXTER, from the Committee on Public Lands, reported a bill for the relief of William Smith, administrator of John Taylor, deceased.

Mr. HENDRICKS, from the Committee on Roads and Canals, reported a bill to improve the navigation of the river Mississippi, near the city of St. Louis; which was read, and the documents accompanying the report ordered to be printed.

SPECIAL ORDER.

The Senate then proceeded to the special order, being Mr. Bibb's amendment to Mr. Poindexter's resolutions relative to the reception of the protest of the President of the United States of the 17th instant.

Mr. KANE spoke at length against the resolutions, and in favor of receiving the protest, and spreading it upon the journal of the Senate.

Mr. BIBB rose to address the Chair, but gave way to

Mr. WILKINS, upon whose motion the resolutions and amendment pending were laid upon the table, and made the special order of the day for to-morrow.

On motion of Mr. WILKINS, the Senate proceeded to executive business, and when the doors were opened—

Mr. HENDRICKS offered the following motion:

Resolved, That for the remainder of the present session, Fridays and Saturdays of each and every week shall be devoted to the consideration of bills.

Mr. CHAMBERS moved that the Senate now adjourn; which motion was negatived. Yeas 5, nays not counted.

The bill from the House of Representatives, authorizing the Secretary of the Treasury to issue a register for the brig America, of Savannah, was read a third time and passed.

On motion of Mr. FORSYTH, at half-past four o'clock,

The Senate adjourned.

HOUSE OF REPRESENTATIVES.

Mr. WHITE, from the Committee on Naval Affairs, reported a bill for the relief of Benjamin Hewett. Read twice and committed.

The following bills from the Senate were read a second time, and referred:

An act for the relief of John McCartney.

An act for the relief of the legal administrators of Captain Paschal Hickman.

The House resumed the consideration of the following resolution, offered some weeks ago, by Mr. Mardis, of Alabama:

Resolved, That the Committee of Ways and Means be instructed to inquire into the expediency of reporting a bill requiring the Secretary of the Treasury to deposite the public moneys of the United States in the State banks; and, also, as to the expediency of defining by law all contracts hereafter to be made with the Secretary for the safe-keeping, management, and disbursement of the same.

Together with the substitute offered by Mr. Corwin, of Ohio, declaring that the reasons offered by the Secretary of the Treasury, for the removal of the public deposites from the United States Bank, are insufficient, and unsatisfactory.

Mr. McKENNAN, who was entitled to the floor when the subject was last taken up, spoke in support of the substitute, and against the course of the Administration in regard to the United States Bank, till twelve o'clock, when the hour assigned to the consideration of resolutions expired.

Mr. ARCHER, from the Committee on Foreign Relations, reported a bill to enable the Secretary

of State to purchase the books and papers of General Washington. Read twice, and committed.

The following bills were read a third time, and passed:

A bill for the relief of Thomas Blanchard.

A bill for the relief of John S. Flemming.

A bill amendatory of the several acts for the relief of insolvent debtors of the United States.

The House resumed, in Committee of the Whole, (Mr. HUBBARD in the chair,) the consideration of the bill making appropriations for the diplomatic and civil expenses of the Government for the year 1834.

Mr. McKAY said there was so much confusion when this bill was last before the Committee of the Whole, that he could not draw the attention of the committee to all the points in the bill which he objected to. He now proposed to go back, and moved to strike out the following items:

For the salary of a clerk in the Topographical Bureau, $1,000.

For the salary of a clerk in the Clothing Bureau, $700.

Mr. POLK explained that the object of the first item was to increase the salary of a clerk already employed, and that the second was not an additional charge upon the Government, as a clerk had been discontinued in the Purchasing department, his business having been chiefly transferred to the Clothing bureau.

Mr. ADAMS, of Massachusetts, wished to know how long it had been the practice here to make provision for "bureaus?" He did not know that any were authorized in this Government by law.

Mr. POLK remarked, the designation of bureaus was given to the heads of the departments. The word had been used in former bills.

Mr. ADAMS moved to strike out the word bureaus wherever it occurred. If we sanctioned the division of the department into bureaus, we must necessarily add to the number of offices, by adding an appendage of clerks, &c., to each bureau. He was not averse to an increase of public offices, if rendered necessary by the increase of business; but he would have every office constituted and organized by law. He would have the heads of departments to understand, that if they recognize their departments so as to multiply offices, they should at least inform us what new organization they had adopted. He spoke in ignorance of the matter, not having any means of information before him.

Mr. CAMBRELENG remarked, that the division of duties made in the departments was convenient and economical.

Mr. McKINLEY said, whether the name was appropriate or not, he did not know; but the division of duties adopted was indispensable to the convenient despatch of business. The distribution of labor was left by law entirely to the heads of departments.

Mr. HORACE EVERETT said, if the appropriation bill had been confined to appropriations authorized by previous laws, there could have been no delay of its passage. As soon as it was ascertained that an expense would be allowed as a matter of course. The framers of the bill having made it the means of the creation of new offices, must bear the responsibility of the delay occasioned by objections to it. He went on to urge objections against this mode of establishing offices. He would like himself to see affixed, in every appropriation bill, to every item, the law authorizing it.

Mr. FOOT suggested that there would be no hesitation in passing the items in the appropriation bill, if those which were inserted for new offices, or for increased amount, were withdrawn. Otherwise, the honorable chairman of the Committee of Ways and Means must not be surprised at the opposition, and consequent delay, that should be given to the bill.

Mr. POLK explained.

Mr. McKAY considered that much of the expense arose from the great number of offices into which the bureau was divided, and the practice which prevailed of appointing to them officers of the army, who ought rather to be left at their respective posts. He proposed to the member from Tennessee, that he would agree to the increase of

the compensation to be given to the Commissary General of Purchases to what it was last year, if he would consent to strike out the item for the clerk's salary. This would obviate the objection there was to bringing the officers of the army from their posts, and would not militate against a proper supply being voted for clothing.

The discussion on this item was continued by Messrs. VANCE, JOHN Q. ADAMS, and PARKER.

And the question having been put on the motion to strike out the appropriation for a salary of a clerk in the Topographical Bureau, the motion was rejected: Ayes 63, noes 67.

The question then being put on the second item, the motion to strike out was rejected: Ayes 61, noes 63.

The next item being for contingencies in the office of the Commissioner of Pensions, $7,000.

Mr. McKAY was opposed to the number of extra clerks employed in the office, and desired to know what cause there was for an increase. There was another item for salaries of additional clerks, 10,600 dollars. This, he thought, was wrong. The Executive had no right to create additional offices; it belonged to the legislative department exclusively; and if this was agreed to, it was placing this large sum at the disposition of the President, who might employ as many or as few, to receive this amount, as he pleased. Was this right? Unquestionably not. It was contrary to the spirit of the Constitution, which provided that the President only had the right "to make appointments to offices established by law." How did it happen that, as the Secretary of War had not asked $5,000 in his estimates, it was now become necessary?

Mr. POLK, in reply, read a letter from the Secretary of War, stating that this sum was deemed necessary. He would also state that $40,332 were appropriated last year, whilst only $29,400 were proposed for this year. The appropriation of $5000 is to cover arrearages, and is not required for this year; therefore, it was not proper to include it in the others. He read a statement from the Commissioner of the Pension Office, showing the amount of duties and the office to perform them, with their increase from 1822 to 1834. Also, one with respect to the arrearage from the Comptroller of the Treasury, which explained that the amount asked for had been adjusted, and the department was responsible for it. He intended to move to reduce the item from $7000 to $6,500; which he was led to believe would suffice.

Mr. WILLIAMS said, although it had been necessary, heretofore, to employ the number of clerks, it was not now. He wished to know what number of applicants were now before the office for pensions; for if the number was not large, there was no necessity for additional clerks.

Mr. POLK replied, there were thirty thousand claims yet undecided upon; and read a further statement, showing the necessity which existed for the appropriation.

Mr. FOOT inquired as to the propriety of the appropriation for $5000 for additional or temporary clerk hire.

Mr. POLK read various statements to sustain the application for it.

Mr. FOOT had thought much of the increased appropriations for the Pension Office might have been owing to the change of the pension agency from the Bank of the United States—one of the strongest acts of executive assumption of unauthorized power that came within his knowledge. He desired, therefore, to know whether any of the increase was owing to this?

Mr. POLK. Not one dollar has been increased on that account.

Mr. J. Q. ADAMS desired to know what was the extraordinary pressure that had arisen since the estimates were first made.

Mr. POLK replied, that it was impossible to ascertain, from the accumulation of business, what the precise amount would be when the estimates were made in October. The members had, on coming to Congress, brought with them various and numerous claims, which the commissioner could not have had any knowledge of. He considered that the very nature of the business of the office rendered it impossible to tell the precise force, and it was incumbent on the office not to delay

payments to these aged and poor pensioners, but who could not receive them until additional clerks were employed to investigate the justice of their claims.

Mr. J. Q. ADAMS concurred, as much as any member could, in the propriety of attending to these claims. He was disposed, from the personal attention, the personal knowledge which he had of the gentleman at the head of the office, to pay full credit to any and everything he should state. But his inquiry not being answered, he would move to strike out the item, in order to give the chairman of the Committee of Ways and Means an opportunity of procuring better information as to the reason why this necessity was not anticipated or discovered before. If the Commissioner of Pensions, or the Secretary of War, could satisfy him of the necessity, he would not oppose it; but it was necessary to have full information whether the acts of the Executive, as alluded to by the honorable member from Connecticut, [Mr. FOOT,] had any share in producing the increased expense.

Mr. GRENNELL asked that action on the items in relation to the office should be suspended, considering that the information on which Congress were called on to make appropriations was of too general a character, whilst it should be in detail. He desired to know how many of these additional clerks had been employed on account of depriving the Bank of the United States of the agency?

Mr. POLK desired 'to correct a misstatement which he had made. The expenditure last year was $45,332, instead of $40,332. The saving this year was $16,000. It was impossible to ascertain precisely. Some allowance should be made for those who evinced their desire. The gentleman from Massachusetts had proposed if he would agree to strike out, he would—

Mr. ADAMS. No, sir. I said to the House—

Mr. POLK. The gentleman smells out what I was about to say—

Mr. ADAMS. The gentleman alludes to the bargain. I desired not a bargain. I only want information.

Mr. POLK. Our situations, although I made no bargain, and I say it in perfect good humor, were similar: he says he will do one thing, if I will do another. So I said the last evening, and such things may be done without any improper imputation upon the motives of any gentleman.

After some further remarks from Messrs. McCOMAS, McKAY, CAMBRELENG, GRENNELL, SUTHERLAND, DICKSON of New York, FOOT, and ADAMS,

Mr. WILLIAMS moved that the committee do now rise: Lost, 55 to 89.

The debate was continued by Messrs. WILLIAMS and SUTHERLAND; when

Mr. WATMOUGH moved that the committee rise: Lost, 52 to 94.

The question was then taken on the motion to strike out the item appropriating $5,000 for additional clerk hire in the Pension Office. It was determined in the negative.

Another motion was made for the committee to rise, and rejected.

Some conversation here took place between Messrs. ADAMS, POLK, and FOSTER, in regard to the items making appropriations for contingencies in the Pension Office.

Mr. POLK's motion to reduce from $7,000 to $6,500, also some verbal amendments proposed by Mr. ADAMS to the appropriation for arrearages and contingencies of the Pension Office, were agreed to.

Mr. BRIGGS moved that the committee do rise.

The motion was rejected: Ayes 57, noes 82.

The item for additional clerk hire for 1833 ($21,731 44) being under consideration—

Mr. HARDIN referred to the great increase which had taken place in the Post Office, as shown in an evident tendency on the part of the Administration to increase the number of office-holders. He desired to have some information on the subject.

After a remark or two between him and Mr. SUTHERLAND, which excited much merriment,

Mr. POLK rose and presented a statement from

the Post Office Department, which, he said, would afford every information that was desired.

The letter was read; after which,

Mr. VINTON made an earnest appeal, at half past five o'clock, to the majority of the House not to persist in trying, by wearing down the members by late sittings, to carry through this bill. He averred that such a practice would recoil upon themselves, and could do no good, even in hastening the passage of the bill, as there was so much other business before the Senate it was not to be expected that they could abandon it and proceed to this. He moved that the committee rise, but withdrew his motion in favor of

Mr. R. M. JOHNSON, who remarked, that he must press upon the House a choice of the bills that were essentially necessary for them to act upon, otherwise he must join with those who were determined to sit until this bill was got through.

Mr. CHILTON disclaimed any design on the part of the opposition to embarrass the bill by unnecessary discussion. It was now six o'clock. He moved the committee rise.

The motion prevailed: Ayes 75, noes 71.

Thereupon the committee rose and reported progress.

Mr. POLK submitted a resolution that the general appropriation bill, now in the Committee of the Whole, be taken up to-morrow at twelve o'clock, and each succeeding day, except Saturday and Monday, at the same hour, until the same shall be disposed of finally.

Objections having been made—

Mr. EVANS moved an adjournment. Rejected—ayes 72, noes 81.

Mr. POLK moved a suspension of the rules, to enable him to offer his resolution. Upon which motion the yeas and nays were ordered.

Mr. VINTON moved an adjournment; which prevailed—ayes 71, noes 69.

The House adjourned.

IN SENATE.

FRIDAY, *April* 25, 1834.

The VICE PRESIDENT presented a communication from the Department of War, transmitting a report of the Commissioner of Indian Affairs, in compliance with a resolution of the Senate of the 3d of March, 1834.

Mr. WEBSTER presented a memorial, signed by about three thousand citizens of Ontario county, New York, in favor of the restoration of the deposites to the Bank of the United States, and recharter of that institution.

Mr. W. said that this paper was signed by merchants, mechanics, and agriculturists, of the county of Oneida. They complained of a great fall in the price of produce and land in that neighborhood; all of which they attributed to the recent measures of the Government. Mr. W. thought that a new omen of union was presenting itself—persons of hitherto opposite sentiments on political subjects were now uniting, and were speaking with one voice of the evils which threatened the country. Two or three days since, we had heard a strong rebuke from the gentleman from Georgia, of the cries and factious clamors in Baltimore. These, however, had been repeated, and we had another cry from the same quarter. He (Mr. W.) thought the people were roused, and they would teach their rulers that the expression of their opinions was not treason, either legal or moral, and that they were not factious.

Mr. FORSYTH said, he had not seen the Baltimore papers, and therefore he could not say whether the same thing of which he (Mr. F.) spoke, had occurred. He thought however, it could not well be. A Sabbath day had not intervened since, so as to afford them the occasion. He was not in his seat yesterday, at the time the gentleman from Massachusetts made some remarks upon the presentation of a memorial from Union county, in Pennsylvania, but he would take this occasion to allude to them. (Here Mr. F. read Mr. W.'s remarks, as reported in the Intelligencer.) Now Mr. F. took it for granted, the report was correct; and if so, the gentleman had done him very great injustice. He had never found fault with any of the citizens of the United States for memoralizing Congress, nor had he ever said that meetings for such purpose were offensive in their character. His remarks referred to a meeting in Baltimore, and was confined simply to those who were *celebrating* the Sabbath day in that city, in a particular way. He thought that meeting was noisy and clamorous, and prompted by a spirit of faction, and that nothing but political feeling could have caused it. He believed it had been stated that one of the speakers on that occasion, had endeavored to avoid that violation of decorum, but was called out by the people to address them. Now, this was noise and clamor, and his remarks applied only to those who were assembled on that day. Another remark of the honorable gentleman, was complimentary to Governor Snyder, of Pennsylvania. And when, he would ask, had Governor Snyder become a favorite with the honorable gentleman? It was not long since the party the gentleman was connected with considered him a stupid Dutchman—that he was chosen by a community of stupid Dutch. Mr. F. spoke only of treasonable threats, and he did say that exertions were making to urge the people to the commission of treason against, not the President, but the Congress of the United States. The good newspapers of this city of Washington did not always tell the truth of what was done in this Hall. Some omitted to state what fell from gentlemen here—others suppressed it—while others put sentiments into our mouths which we never entertained, and never expressed. But it would not do to complain of it, because it would seem like interfering with the liberty of the press. But ought we not ourselves to be a little more regardful of what we say of each other? Now, these remarks of the honorable gentleman were calculated to do him a great deal of injury. Some time since, he was abused in the public papers for the expression of sentiments which he never uttered or dreamed of. And a petition had been sent to the other House, containing threats against him for saying what he never did say; and these remarks of the honorable gentleman were calculated to place him in actual danger if he should go to Baltimore. Now, he rose on this occasion to say, that his former remarks applied to the people of Baltimore who assembled on Sunday last in the afternoon, and no others.

Mr. WEBSTER said the honorable gentleman from Georgia should not complain of his remarks, because he was a volunteer upon the occasion alluded to. He voluntarily spoke of the transactions of Baltimore. The memorial then under consideration had certainly nothing to do with them; the memorial was from the State of New Jersey. The gentleman, however, took occasion to leave New Jersey and roam to Baltimore, in order to introduce a transaction in which a member of this body took part. Mr. W. said he wished to do that gentleman no manner of injustice. He remarked upon nothing in reply, but what had been said by the honorable gentleman of the citizens of Baltimore who chose to assemble in the streets and at the wharves, by dozens, by hundreds, and by thousands!

Mr. FORSYTH replied, that whether a volunteer or not, did not seem material. He found the subject in his way, and thinking it appropriate, he had used it. But the gentleman from Massachusetts should remark that his observations applied to *memorialists*. And although it might do him no injury here, yet persons at a distance would think that he had reference to meetings in Baltimore of a treasonable character, in which designs were formed against the acts of the Government. He did not say the acts of persons in the streets of Baltimore were of a treasonable character, on the occasion alluded to, but he contended that they had been misled by their feelings to do acts which were not creditable to them.

Mr. WEBSTER alluded to the warm feelings of the Senator from Georgia, [Mr. FORSYTH,] and thought he had better refrain from indulging in them. He had spoken of Governor Snyder, of Pennsylvania. He (Mr. W.) had never known that gentleman personally. He had retired from public life before Mr. W. had commenced his humble political career; but he had always heard of him as an ardent friend of civil liberty; a man of strong sense, and of straightforward course, and possessed of a warm and good heart; and if his descendants partook of his qualifications, they had his highest respect and esteem.

Mr. LEIGH did not like to take part in this conversation, but he could not forbear referring to a striking feature in the "signs of the times." He saw, or thought he saw, a parallel between Charles I and Cromwell, when religion was invoked in aid of the views of the Protector. We now hear of Sabbath breaking, and other infringements upon religious tenets. Is not the resemblance very strong? The President of the United States is a very religious man. The gentleman from Georgia, [Mr. FORSYTH,] is a very religious man; and it did not become him to interfere between those gentlemen and their God any more than it became the gentleman to interfere with a portion of the citizens of Baltimore, and their God. He would take leave to relate a story. A clergyman in conversation with another gentleman, refrained from expressing himself upon certain offences as strongly as the gentleman thought he ought to have done. The gentleman replied with some warmth, asking him "Sir, have you any religion?" The reply was, "None to *talk* of."

Mr. FORSYTH said he knew nothing of the religion of the President of the United States, and consequently should say nothing about it. Of his own religion, he felt himself at liberty to speak. He was sorry, very sorry, that the Senator from Virginia [Mr. LEIGH] was in error. He was not a religious man. He did not comprehend the allusion of the honorable gentleman in drawing a parallel between the acts of the reign of Cromwell, of Charles I, and the present times.

The memorial was then referred to the Committee on Finance, and ordered to be printed.

Mr. CLAY presented the proceedings of a meeting and a memorial from the district of Hanover, county of York, Pennsylvania, praying a restoration of the deposites to the Bank of the United States, and a recharter of said bank.

Mr. C. dilated upon the beautiful country, and the high respectability of the inhabitants from whence the memorial had emanated. He animadverted in severe terms upon the political flexibility of Governor Wolf, of Pennsylvania, and took occasion to advert to the success of the opposition party in Hanover county, Virginia, as a strong coincidence with that of the presentation of the present memorial. He said that Hanover—the good old Hanover—was the place of his nativity; that it was there the spirit of the Whigs of the Revolution was first aroused; and it was from that county that the grandsire of a gentleman over the way [Mr. TYLER] marched to Williamsburg, at the head of a company of volunteers, and rescued the public property from the grasp of Lord Dunmore. He said that upon the late occasion, the Whigs of the present day had proved triumphant, defeating one of the most potent politicians of that region, the descendant of that justly celebrated jurist, Spencer Roane. He remarked that there were six precincts in that county, where votes were polled, and from three information had been obtained. At those polls, the protest could find no reception. They had yet to learn what favor it had found at Negro Foot, Hell-town, and Long-and-Hungry—the names of the remaining precincts.

Mr. FORSYTH thought it was not fair to censure the Governors of the States here, for acts done in their official capacity. No doubt the gentleman from Kentucky did not like the act of the Governor of Pennsylvania, because it was a damper; but it was very irregular to take up the official conduct of the Governors of the States, and make it the subject of detraction here. But the Governor of Pennsylvania had proved that he understood the interests of the State he presided over, and the stand taken by him had procured the funds necessary for the great and magnificent system of internal improvements in which the State was engaged, in spite of his denunciations against the Bank of the United States. But would honorable gentlemen blind themselves to what had produced the change in the mind of Governor Wolf against that institution? If it was man-worship, they had done him great injustice. But the gentleman from Kentucky had spoken of the elections in Hanover, Virginia, and it was true they were turning there to *Clay*. Well, if the gentleman could take consolation from such small things, he (Mr. F.) could have no objection to it. And the honorable gentleman had made some allusion to the names of

districts in that county. Would the gentleman tell us near which of these he was born? But the gentleman had spoken of a restoration of the violated Constitution and the laws; and Mr. F. asked why did not those having the power do something to restore the Constitution and laws? Why appeal to the minority here? The only measure that had been submitted here for that purpose, was the bill of the gentleman from Massachusetts; but it sleeps upon your table in silence and quiet. Let us do our duty, and let the result, if it be a failure, fall on those who prevent it. These appeals to the people were unjust till the laws were passed. The gentleman complained that the President did not retrace his steps. Did any one doubt that the President of the United States was satisfied that the best interests of the country demanded the course which he pursued? and did not everybody know that it was not possible for mortal man to induce him to do other than what he believed his duty to his country required him to do?

Mr. CLAY said it had been a long time since he was born. He thought that he was nearly as old as the gentleman from Georgia, [Mr. Forsyth,] but from a reference made the other day by that gentleman to a revolutionary incident, in which General Washington, the father of his country, was an actor, he supposed he was some years his senior. He was born near the Court-house, at Black Tom Slash, near the Merry Oaks, and close to St. Paul's Church, where he went to school. The gentleman from Georgia had said, he thought it was not decorous to animadvert upon the conduct of Governors of States, but he would tell that gentleman that he must be permitted to think for himself of what was decorous. The gentleman supposed that the Governor's message was a damper here, but when he chose to shoot his arrows here for political effect, and against his former sentiments, had he not a right to make his comments upon them? Napoleon had said that he was the State, and the inhabitant of the White House had said that he was both the Government and the State. Mr. C. said, what could we do for the restoration of the laws, when we can have no coöperation by other departments of the Government? The gentleman had said the President would not retrace his steps. Who is he, and what is he, that he will not retrace his steps? Governor Wolf had abandoned the tariff, internal improvements, the bank, and all—all had been taken from him. It reminded him (said Mr. C.) of an anecdote which occurred at the White Sulpher Springs, in Virginia. A gentleman, after he had retired to his cottage for the night, and had gone to bed, but had not closed his eyes for sleep, saw glide into his room a thief, who marched directly up to his clothes, and deliberately take from them the gentleman's purse. The next morning, when the company had assembled at the general rendezvous, (the spring,) the gentleman related his loss and the manner of it; some persons asked him if he was awake, and would submit thus to be robbed before his eyes? He said it was all true; and he had not only apprehensions of losing his money and his clothes, but really feared, from the impudence of the rascal, that he should even be robbed of his shirt. It is thus with the Governor of Pennsylvania. He has lost all but his shirt; and doubtless he is in expectancy of having that stripped from his back. Mr. C. further related an anecdote of an interview with a Kentuckian and a North Carolinian, of Buncombe county. "What's the news," inquired the Carolinian, "in Kentucky?" "Oh, nothing particular," rejoined the other, "save that all our people have repented of the error of their ways, and have become religious. We have had great revivals, great rejoicings; and the devil has been driven out of the State." "And where has he been driven to?" anxiously inquired the other. "Why, to Buncombe, in North Carolina," responded the Kentuckian. And I suppose the protest of the President will also find refuge in Buncombe, North Carolina.

Mr. McKEAN asked for the reading of the resolution that alluded to the Governor of Pennsylvania, which the Secretary read as follows:

"*Resolved*, That while we disapprove the vacillating or time-serving policy of the Governor of Pennsylvania, with regard to the Bank of the United States, we highly commend the course pursued towards that institution by Daniel Webster, Henry Clay, John C. Calhoun, Horace Binney, and Mr. McDuffie, and their associates in Congress."

Mr. McKEAN said he was aware that the public opinions of public men were public property, and fair subjects of public animadversion; and if, in these times of indiscriminate crimination and recrimination, it became necessary for political effect, to include the name of the "*unassuming*" Governor of "*unassuming Pennsylvania*," with the other distinguished names in the resolution, even though the Governor should be characterized as vacillating and time-serving, he would not give himself much uneasiness on that account. True, the Senator from Kentucky had enlarged upon the expressions in the resolution, and even with that he was not disposed to find fault; it was the gentleman's province to do so. The Senator from Virginia on his right, [Mr. Leigh,] said the other day, that he would not defend Virginia, for the very fact of an attempt to defend implied defect of character. He was pleased with the maxim, and would adopt it on this occasion. The character of the present Governor of Pennsylvania could not suffer from imputations cast upon it by gentlemen here or elsewhere. There was, however, one allusion upon which he wished to say a word: it was said that Governor Wolf held different opinions at different periods in reference to the Bank of the United States. Mr. McK. said, at the time first alluded to, he stood in a relation to the Governor which gave him an opportunity of understanding minutely his opinions on the question of rechartering the Bank of the United States, and it was almost the only one upon which they differed. However, he was at that time opposed to the bank—and he stated, as a matter of his own knowledge, that Governor Wolf was then, and is now in favor of a national bank, and he believes the fiscal concerns of the Government cannot get along without it. He does think, however, that recent developments in relation to the management of that institution are sufficient to create doubts as to its influence upon the public morals.

Mr. BROWN said, if his Satanic majesty had, at any time, left Kentucky and taken refuge in Buncombe county, North Carolina, it was certain he had not always remained there since; for when gentlemen, who had for some years past, and until very recently, stood as opposite to each other politically as the antipodes, had been grouped together, in one of the resolutions which had just been read, (Messrs. Clay, Calhoun, Webster, McDuffie, and Binney,) and had by name received the strong approbation of the public meeting whose proceedings were then before the Senate, he thought that some supernatural agency must have been employed to effect so miraculous a result.

The attack of the honorable gentleman upon the Governor of Pennsylvania, was entirely out of place and uncalled for. The Governor of that State was accountable to those from whom he derived his official authority, and to none others. The Senator from Kentucky had made it a serious cause of complaint against that gentleman that he should continue to support a President who had done much to arrest the internal improvement system, and who had aimed a destructive blow against the tariff. Mr. B. was happy to hear justice done to the President on this subject. It had been attempted, here and elsewhere, to deprive the President of the merit, which the honorable gentleman had very properly awarded him; and the declaration which he had made, on this occasion, should be received, now and hereafter, as evidence to establish the claims of the present Administration to the credit of having done that for which they were entitled to the highest commendation. The course of the Governor of Pennsylvania, in opposition to the bank, had done him immortal honor. The stand which the patriotic State of Pennsylvania had taken, had added another just cause of gratitude and admiration to the many others furnished by her history, for the disinterested and noble example which she has set. Elevated above those mercenary feelings, which but too often influence human action, she was opposed to cherishing in her bosom a proud and corrupt moneyed monopoly, which aspires to bring the country under its arbitrary control. The honorable gentleman had congratulated his political friends on the success of the anti-administration party in Hanover, a small county in Virginia. Mr. B. said, if the friends of constitutional liberty were destined to witness the overthrow of those principles, in quarters from which they might have expected a voice animating and cheering them in the great contest which was now waging in opposition to the mighty power of the bank, it was a source of the highest satisfaction to perceive that the spirit of the great Democratic party, in our country, continued firm and invincible, and that the great body of the people were on the side of the country and against the bank.

The honorable gentleman had, in the course of his remarks, appealed to what he had been pleased to call the *Whig party*, and urged them to exertion in the great contest which was now going on between the parties which divide the country.

Mr. B. would recur for a few moments to the history of parties in England and in this country, to show what claim this newfangled and *self-styled Whig party* had to the appellation which they were about to assert an exclusive title to. In England, if his memory did not much deceive him as to the history of parties, the high tory party had generally been among the strongest supporters of the great moneyed monopoly which had so long existed in that country, and which had been a part of that formidable government machinery whose power and influence had been so effectually and successfully exerted to keep the *many* in subjection to the will of the *few*. In the writings of the illustrious Jefferson, published since his death, he expresses the opinion that the Secretary of the Treasury, in 1791, favored the introduction of a national bank in the United States, with a view of placing in the hands of the Government a powerful engine to subserve party purposes, and to assimilate our Government, in its practical operation on the people, still more to the English system of government.

Mr. B. said that two great epochs had occurred in our history, between which and the present period, he thought he could perceive many points of resemblance. When the people of this country had solemnly determined to throw off the yoke of the British Government, there was a party then who endeavored to alarm and intimidate them, by depicting the ruin and distress which would ensue from it; but instead of listening to those panic-makers and alarmists, they were willing to encounter any degree of danger and distress rather than surrender their rights as freemen. They persevered, and finally triumphed, when, if they had listened to those who were continually proclaiming ruin and *distress*, they would have remained in inglorious bondage. In the late war with England, the same attempts were made by the opposition party as now, to overawe the Government and the people, by representing the distress which an attempt to vindicate the rights of the country would bring on its citizens. The farmers and planters were told by the advocates of submission, that they would be overwhelmed in ruin if the Government went to war, but the whig republicans of that day, as in the Revolution, resolved not be alarmed by panic-makers. They again persevered, and were crowned with the most brilliant success. At the present day there was a party in our country which had endeavored to alarm the people into submission to the bank by the same course and same cries of distress. He had briefly endeavored to trace the parallel between those who had appealed to the fears of their countrymen by sketching the most gloomy pictures of distress at the two great epochs alluded to, and the party which was now endeavoring to accomplish their objects by like appeals. If party designations were to be given, he left it to others to make the application which the points of resemblance indicated by him would in a great degree justify.

Mr. B. said he felt gratified that the condition of the State of North Carolina was such as in a great degree placed her citizens above the reach of the great efforts which had been for some months made, to destroy confidence throughout the country, to produce general embarrassment, and by means such as these, to effect a political change in favor of the party now out of power. Most of the information which he had received from that State confirmed him in the opinion that the condition of her citizens, generally, in relation to pecuniary affairs, was sound and healthful, and that the prosperity of her independent farmers and planters

never rested on a more solid basis than at this time.

He had been informed from sources in which he placed the most implicit reliance, that drafts on the North could readily be obtained from the Bank of Cape Fear at the small premium of a quarter per cent., that being on terms as favorable as the United States Bank had ever transacted business of that kind, so far as he was informed. This fact afforded abundant proof, not only of the entire competency of the State banks to conduct the fiscal concerns of the Government, but of their ability to afford the same facilities to the commercial interests in carrying on the business of exchange between distant portions of the Union, as those afforded at any time heretofore by the Bank of the United States.

Mr. B. said that every means which ingenuity could devise, had been industriously seized on and dexterously used by political partisans, to withdraw the true question at issue, and to make erroneous impressions on the public mind. The opponents of the Administration, well aware that the conduct of the bank cannot stand the test of scrutiny before the public eye, with that skill and address which have often been resorted to with advantage in military operations, seek on every occasion which presents itself to make a diversion in favor of the bank, by attacking the acts of the Executive, and misrepresenting both his conduct and his motives. Mr. B. said, that for himself, he should keep steadily in view the great question which he considered really at issue, which was, whether the pretensions set up by an arrogant moneyed aristocracy, and the political party supporting it, should prevail in the conflict, or whether the cause of the country, and the Chief Executive Magistrate who was defending the citadel of our liberties against the most dangerous assaults, should be sustained.

On motion of Mr. WILKINS, the memorial was laid upon the table.

REPORTS OF COMMITTEES.

Mr. POINDEXTER from the Committee on Public Lands, reported a bill from the House of Representatives, for the relief of John C. Naylor, without amendment.

Also, a bill from the House, authorizing the Secretary of the Treasury to make additional compensation to the register and receiver of the land office at Tallahassee, Florida, with an amendment.

Mr. P., from the same committee, reported a bill for the relief of the heirs and legal representatives of John Girault; which was read, and ordered to a second reading.

Also, a bill for the relief of Absalom Lynch; which was read, and ordered to a second reading.

Mr. WHITE, from the Committee on Indian Affairs, reported a bill from the House of Representatives, without amendment, granting relief to certain citizens on the frontiers, who had suffered depredations by Indians.

Mr. WHITE, from the Committee on Revolutionary Claims, reported a bill from the House of Representatives, without amendment, for the relief of Lieutenant Robert Wilmott.

Also, a bill from the House, without amendment, for the relief of the heirs and legal representatives of Fuller Claiborne, deceased.

Also, a bill from the House, for the relief of the heirs and legal representatives of Thomas Wallace, deceased, with an amendment.

Also, a bill for the relief of the widow and heirs of Captain William Royall, deceased; the report accompanying which was ordered to be printed.

Also, a bill for the relief of Bissel Phelps; the report accompanying which was ordered to be printed.

Mr. TOMLINSON, from the Committee on Pensions, reported a bill from the House of Representatives for the relief of Judith Thomas and Daniel Palmer, without amendment.

Mr. TOMLINSON, from the same committee, asked to be discharged from the further consideration of the petition of Josiah Hopkins, and that the same be referred to the Committee on Naval Affairs.

The Senate then proceeded to the

SPECIAL ORDER,

Being Mr. BIBB's amendment of Mr. POINDEX-

TER's resolution, relative to the Protest of the President of the United States.

Mr. BIBB rose and addressed the Senate at length, in support of his amendment, and against the protest of the President; when, without concluding, he gave way to

Mr. POINDEXTER, upon whose motion it was

Ordered, That when the Senate adjourn, it would adjourn until Monday.

The Senate then adjourned.

HOUSE OF REPRESENTATIVES.

FRIDAY, *April* 25, 1834.

Mr. CAMBRELENG reported a bill for the relief of John Fraser & Co., of Charleston, South Carolina.

Mr. CAGE, a bill for the relief of William R. Harmer.

Mr. CHINN, a bill to extend the charter of the Alexandria Fire Insurance Company.

Mr. CRAMER, a bill for the relief of William Baker; and

Mr. POPE, a bill for the improvement of the harbor of St. Louis, Missouri.

All which bills were read twice, and committed.

Mr. JARVIS asked the unanimous consent of the House to take up the resolution offered by him for a select committee to inquire into the cause of the suspension of specie payments by the banks in the District which have suspended, as well as for an inquiry into the condition of the Bank of the Metropolis.

Objections having been made,

Mr. JARVIS moved a suspension of the rule, to enable him to have the resolution considered.

The motion prevailed—ayes 89, noes 34.

Mr. HARDIN, who had the floor from the previous day, resumed. He disclaimed having said, as he was represented to have done, in some remarks on this subject, made in one of the newspapers, that all the banks, including the Bank of the Metropolis, were insolvent. What he had said was, that if reference was had to the security of the notes and bills discounted by each of them, each was solvent; but that apart from that, neither they nor the Bank of the Metropolis could be considered solvent. Concurring entirely, he said, in the propriety of what fell from the honorable member from Indiana, [Mr. LANE,] that no bank should be continued as a depository of the public money, into whose affairs there would be any hesitation on their part, to permit inquiry; he proceeded to read from the report of the Secretary of the Treasury on this subject, a statement of the public money deposited in the several State banks since their removal, and a statement of their sources, which, he argued, went to show that they had not means in specie to discharge the calls that might be made upon them, in the proportion of one dollar in five, and generally that it would be impossible for them to do it, without making calls upon their debtors—which calls, in these embarrassed times, were not much to be relied upon; hence, he maintained, it became proper on the part of Congress to examine into their condition. He referred to the statement presented of the resources of the Bank of the Metropolis, and stated that much of them which was set forth as good, could not be considered so, when the depreciation upon corporation property, &c., was taken into account. He complained that in the item of stocks, which was represented as one of their resources, a large amount consisted of a number of shares of their own stock, which the bank had bought up at a discount. Thus, the Government money was proved to be placed in a bank whose stock was only worth seventy-five per cent., and the last account of their condition showed that in February, 1834, there was $181,541 in this way stated to be a part of their means, whilst, in fact, it was far too much a substraction from their means to meet the public engagement. He desired, however, to be distinctly understood, not as saying that any bank in the district was insolvent, but he would say from this, that no bank could be in a more tottering condition than this. For, if the stockholders and directors, with the public money in their possession, went on buying up

their own stock, consuming their tangible means, where was the residue to come from? It was, in fact, an anticipation of payment to themselves, even at a depreciation, which, however valuable might be their other assets, it was reprehensible in them to make. What security was there then, having made these purchases, they would stop there? He went on to comment upon the remarks of the honorable member from New York, [Mr. BEARDSLEY,] and to defend the directors of the bank from having, as charged, failed by precaution, or with the object of being well paid by the United States Bank for so doing, &c. He considered there could not have been a more flagitious charge upon them. He did not know them, but he would venture to say their character would be found to stand as high as that of any member in the House, and that to make such a charge, was hazarding a great deal. He would have risen on this subject, were it only to repel the attack which was made on his colleague [Mr. C. ALLAN] for having said, that with an impartial jury he would prove the insolvency of the deposite banks. This he, also, would engage to do, and would be willing to take the honorable member from New York himself—for that person whom the State of New York had appointed to be one of her judges, he would not object to as a juror on such an issue.

Mr. CHILTON rose for the purpose of using a fact, which he considered of some importance on the consideration of this resolution. Objection was raised by the member from New York [Mr. BEARDSLEY] to its adoption, he believed, on the ground that Congress had no power to investigate into the affairs of the Bank of the Metropolis. If this was so, he should like to know what power Congress had over the other banks, which did so equally extend, by the charters, to it. He called on him to turn to the charter, and show how or where it was, that the power was made contingent only in certain events. He contended that it would appear, on examination of the charters granted by Congress, that the powers were not contingent; and unless the terms that of the Bank of the Metropolis having been selected as one of the favorite banks of the Government, gave it such an exemption from investigation into its affairs, Congress had the power to make it. But this surely would not be contended. He would put this question for the honorable member to answer—whether the very circumstance of being selected as a depository for the public money, did not furnish the strongest of all possible arguments that Congress should make the inquiry. The country was more deeply interested in its stability than in that of the others, and it was important for them to examine whether, as was alleged of all the deposite banks, it was unable to meet demands upon it. So much as to the power. How he referred to the provisions in the charter, (upon which he was about to comment,) as containing an important fact, when he was obliged to suspend, without concluding his remarks, in consequence of the expiration of the hour allotted for morning business.

The joint resolution from the Senate, directing the Commissioner of the Public Buildings to water the Pennsylvania Avenue, was referred to the Committee on the District.

Mr. DUNCAN asked, and obtained leave of the House, to lay on the table, and have printed, "A bill to modify and extend an act to incorporate the subscribers to the Bank of the United States, with certain limitations and conditions;" which bill, he gave notice, he intended to offer as a substitute for a bill reported from the Committee of Ways and Means to regulate the deposites of the public money in the State and local banks, when that bill should be considered in the Committee of the Whole.

Mr. POLK asked the unanimous consent of the House, by which this day was set apart for the consideration of bills, for the purpose of going into committee on

THE APPROPRIATION BILL.

Mr. J. Q. ADAMS objected.

Mr. POLK moved a suspension of the rule for this purpose.

Mr. R. M. JOHNSON called for the yeas and nays. They were ordered, but he subsequently withdrew the call and the motion prevailed. Yeas 129.

The House then resolved itself into Committee of the Whole on the state of the Union, (Mr. Hubbard in the chair,) and resumed the consideration of the bill.

The item for additional clerk hire for 1833 ($31,731 44) being pending—

Mr. CONNOR read a letter from Judge McLean, the former Postmaster General, to show that he had found the business of the office so much on the increase that he was obliged to employ additional clerks, or otherwise the public business could not have been performed. It was owing to this increase that the appropriation was asked. He begged to state that the appointment of "agent" in the office was coeval with the department, and his duties are general throughout the Union.

Mr. SMITH, of Maine, rose to inquire if it would be in order to reduce the appropriation when before the House?

The CHAIRMAN responded in the affirmative.

Mr. LINCOLN said the present was a proper occasion to discuss the affairs of the Post Office Department, and he hoped that the chairman of the Committee of Ways and Means would not resort to the threats which he had announced on a previous occasion, of sitting to unseasonable hours, for the purpose of forcing the bill through the committee without permitting that attention to be given to it which it would demand. This subject, as well as the item for foreign missions, would require it; for if no other member would do so, he would move to strike out the appropriations where the appointments had not been made in conformity to the Constitution—that is, by the President by and with the consent of the Senate. It might also, from the discussion of the morning upon the condition of the banks selected as depositories, turn out to be necessary to insert a clause that every appropriation in the bill should be paid in the notes of the Bank of the United States. With these important matters, then, before them, he hoped that the minority—although he did not, in giving these intimations, mean to say that he acted in concert with any other member in the House—would be permitted time to discuss the various items in the bill. It was his intention to move that the item now under discussion be stricken out of the bill.

The chairman of the Committee of Ways and Means (said Mr. L.) came into this House when we had got only to the 45th line of this bill, with the declaration that he was determined to press this bill through before the House adjourned. We were in consequence kept here eight or nine hours without refreshment, and exhausted by the fruitless efforts of the honorable chairman to accomplish his purpose. He asked whether the minority had not a right to complaim of such a declaration, and of the arrangements which were made to carry it through. He hoped the honorable chairman of the committee would now suffer us to discuss, calmly and dispassionately, the various grave matters presented by this bill, and after we had spent a reasonable time in the discussion, that he would permit us to go home, that we might return invigorated and refreshed to our duties.

Mr. L. contended at length, that the Postmaster General had no right to employ clerks, without authority of law. These clerks, in his opinion, were unnecessarily numerous; and many of them, he said, were as useless to the department as its old mail bags. He wished to know what were the employments of all these clerks. He had offered a resolution formerly, which the House was not disposed to entertain, inquiring what were the duties of these clerks severally, and how they were paid. He was aware that the rejection of this appropriation would not affect the clerks themselves, for they had been paid. He wished to know where the Postmaster General got the money. Let us know if the Postmaster General takes the discretion of multiplying officers as he pleases, and of converting the funds of the department to this purpose, and then applies to this House to extricate him from his difficulties. Mr. L. said the department was from $800,000 to $1,000,000 in debt. He was warranted in saying that it had borrowed $300,000 from banks, had overdrawn on deposites $150,000, and was greatly indebted to mail contractors. To the discredit of the nation, the contractors were every day supplicating payment, and were driven away, by threats that their claims, if they continued their importunity, should be balanced in forfeitures, for failing to comply with the terms of their contracts. They were also threatened with the loss of their contract itself; for the Postmaster General made a most convenient provision in all his contracts, that they should be discontinued at his pleasure. These facts he challenged any one to deny.

Mr. POPE observed, that he was as ready as any one to enter into a full examination of the department. He was in favor of full discussion and thorough investigation. But he was unwilling to refuse the necessary supplies for that branch of the Government, unless it appeared that it was improper to do so. He said that the gentleman from Massachusetts had, in common with others, complained that the majority were disposed to hurry the appropriation bill through Congress without proper consideration. Such, he stated, was not the fact. But that if they did entertain such a wish, the fact that the gentleman from Massachusetts had made a long and labored speech, one half of which had no earthly relation to the subject, was their apology.

Mr. P. stated he would not have risen had not the gentleman from Massachusetts wandered from the question to assail the head of that department in a most unwarrantable manner. The gentleman had charged the Postmaster General with having placed men in his office not for the public good—that the clerks in the department were worthless and idle—that they were to be seen loitering about the city, and that they would do nothing and could do nothing. He asked the gentleman for his authority for this charge. The gentleman had stated that his professional education taught him the necessity of having authority for his assertions. Mr. P. called upon him to produce his authority. He knew, however, he could not produce it, for the charge was untrue.

The gentleman had also asserted, that the mail routes had become sinuous—that they were not established as channels of communication. Mr. P. observed, that it was right and proper that they should be sinuous, that the farmers of the country should receive the news, and enjoy all seasonable mail facilities, as well as the citizens of Boston and *Lowell*—that they contributed to the support, and were the prop and aid of the Government—that he was in favor of sending information to every hill and every valley, so that those concerned might be kept fully acquainted with their public affairs. Mr. P. repelled the charge, that the village postmasters were not worthy of their offices. So far as he knew them, they were highminded and honorable men, as much so as the gentleman from Massachusetts, or any one else. He also repelled the charge, that the mails went lumbering along with what ought not to be in them. This was an unfounded charge; and he called upon the gentleman from Massachusetts to furnish that authority, which his *professional education* ought to teach him was necessary.

Mr. P. stated that he had felt it his duty thus to notice the unjustifiable accusations of the gentleman from Massachusetts. Mr. Barry was one of Kentucky's most favored and gifted sons. His eloquence, his genius, and his spotless integrity, had won him the respect and attachment of his friends. He was an honest man, and utterly incapable of official delinquency. Mr. P. stated he had no doubt of the honor or integrity of the gentleman from Massachusetts; but he considered the gentleman would be most fortunate indeed, if his public or private life was as little blemished or stained as that of the Postmaster General.

[Mr. Lincoln here interposed, and disclaimed any impeachment of the personal character of Mr. Barry.]

Mr. POPE proceeded. He regretted very much an expression that had fallen on yesterday from his colleague, [Mr. Hardin.] That gentleman had stated that one of the clerks in the Department, [Mr. Loughborough,] held, he suspected, a sinecure office. He did not know the duties of that clerk. Mr. Barry and that clerk once practised law in Kentucky in conjunction, but he would not say that this was the *cause* of his appointment. Mr. P. said, he regretted that his honorable colleague had so expressed himself, because it appeared to be a covert insinuation, calculated to make an unfavorable impression on the public mind. He hoped his colleague intended to make no prejudicial insinuation, because he must be aware that that clerk was a gentleman of great worth, and as incapable of receiving, as was the Postmaster General of granting, a sinecure office. He had understood, in fact the chairman of the Committee on the Post Office and Post Roads had just informed the committee, that the gentleman alluded to was now absent on official duty.

Mr. P. concluded by stating that Mr. Barry, in this matter, only pursued the steps of Mr. McLean; that the business of the department had greatly increased, and that, consequently, more clerks were required to discharge the duties of the department, which necessarily increased its expenses. He considered the desired appropriation just and proper, and should, therefore, vote for it.

Mr. LINCOLN said he had not impugned the correctness of the conduct of the Postmaster General. He distinctly disclaimed any charge upon the Postmaster General. He supposed that he was led into error by misrepresentations.

Mr. REED had no accusation, he said, to make against the head of the Post Office Department. But the question was, is the department well managed? He was constrained to say that it was not well managed. He knew that it could not pay its debts to the contractors.

Mr. PARKER did not wish to take up the time of the committee by following the gentleman from Massachusetts, but he felt compelled to notice some of his remarks. He complains of the number of insignificant post offices, and requires that the mails should go on the direct and principal routes. He would stop the streams of information, which, through these channels, flow to the people. Though the revenue of some of these offices was but twenty-five cents, yet their expenses only consisted in the folding up newspapers and tying them up. The question before the committee is, whether we shall make any allowance for expenses of the Post Office not authorized by a previous law? Now, he would undertake to say that we had no express law, yet we had precedents which bound us to make the appropriation asked for. He went back as far as 1806, and showed that by an act then passed, certain provision was made for clerks in the Post Office Department, and in the year 1809, the appropriation act provided a further sum to pay for clerks employed in addition to those authorized by the act of 1806. He referred to many other similar acts as precedents for this.

Mr. EVANS spoke in favor of the motion to strike out, and wished that gentlemen should be suffered, on this floor, to express their dissatisfaction at the administration of public affairs, without being reproved for making a personal attack upon public officers. It was, he contended, admitted that the Post Office Department was in a deranged state. It was admitted in the report of the Postmaster General himself. The gentleman from Massachusetts excused the Postmaster General on the supposition that he acted upon misrepresentation of facts. He could point out some instances in which he knew that the Postmaster General was deceived. He instanced the appointment of Norton to the post office of old Hartford, which was revoked in a few days after it was made. He went on to point out what he considered as mismanagement on the part of the Post Office.

Mr. POLK went into a full statement of the former course in regard to the employment of clerks in the Post Office Department. The constant growth of the business of the department rendered it necessary continually to increase the number of the clerks. In consequence of this, the actual appropriations before the end of the year, fell short of the necessary expenses of the department, and, for more than fifteen years, it had been customary for the Postmaster General to employ additional clerks, when they were wanted, and rely upon Congress subsequently to provide for the expense. He did not consider it proper or pertinent, while considering this clause, to go into a full view of the whole administration of the Post Office. Mr. P. said he thought the fault was in Congress. He thought that Congress ought to create by law a sufficient and ample force for the department, in anticipation of its necessities. He was willing to do this now. But the course adopted by Mr. Barry was justified by precedent and law.

We had, from year to year, said, in effect, to the Postmaster General, we know your force is not sufficient for the business of your office; employ additional aid when it is wanted, and we will make the necessary appropriations.

Mr. HORACE EVERETT said that for contingent services the Postmaster General was authorized to employ additional clerks, but for the permanent annual service of the department, he ought to apply for an appropriation. He thought that the extra clerks ought now to be provided for, for the ensuing year, instead of making another appropriation for arrearages next year.

Mr. CONNOR said, he hoped the House would pardon him for again trespassing a short time on their patience. Standing in the relation in which he did to the Post Office Department, he felt it to be not only necessary, but his duty, to explain and correct many misapprehensions that gentlemen had fallen into. He was disposed, at all times, to economise and retrench in this or any other department of the Government, and if gentlemen would show that it is necessary and proper to reduce this item in the bill, he would go with them most cheerfully. But from his knowledge of the affairs of the Post Office Department, having been for the last six or seven years a member of the Committee on the Post Office and Post Roads, such had necessarily been his intercourse as to have made him familiar with its business and labors; and he unhesitatingly said that he believed the number employed has been absolutely necessary to the proper performance of the duties of the office; and that the Postmaster General, in employing extra clerks, had done so with a strict eye to economy. It may not, and perhaps is not known to gentlemen, that many of those clerks receive only $400, and several as low as $200.

The gentleman from Massachusetts [Mr. LINCOLN] says the Postmaster General is not authorized by law to employ extra clerk hire. He is correct. There is no such law; but to do so has grown into law by usage; from necessity it must be so, and cannot be otherwise. Such has been the practice for fifteen years, and has been at all times sanctioned by Congress, and must so continue until that department has reached its greatest height. The exact force necessary cannot be ascertained by any one. Any number of clerks which are sufficient at this time, will not be able to perform the labor six months hence. Judge McLean expresses that opinion in a letter to Mr. Barry, and which he read when up before. The gentleman speaks of disposing of one-half of this tribe. He knew not what the gentleman meant when he speaks of the clerks as a tribe, whether intended as an expression of reproach or otherwise. But he begged to say to him, his acquaintance with those clerks justifies him in saying they were honorable and meritorious, who were always to be found at their posts, and laboring early and late, as their business may require. And if the gentleman will go to the department, and go through it, and examine for himself, he must become satisfied that his opinions of the requisite labor are erroneous. Sir, the duties of solicitor, examiner, and office of appointments, the gentleman inquires what they are, as if to afford himself an opportunity of answering his own questions, and does answer them in his own way. Mr. C. said, if he would allow him, he would give to him correctly what are the duties of those bureaus, if permitted so to call them. "The duty of the solicitor is, to 'attend to the final settlement or closing of all accounts; the collection of all balances; the commencement of suits; and the correspondence with 'United States district attorneys and others, in 'relation thereto; also, the correspondence concerning the past accounts of postmasters." "The 'examiner's office is that which is charged with 'the crediting and examining all postmasters' accounts; the correspondence connected therewith; 'receiving and depositing in bank such remittances 'as are specially authorized; returning what is not 'receivable, and with notifying and reporting delinquents." The duties of the office of appointments consists in the examination and endorsement of memorials, letters, and reports; obtaining and noting information from the book-keepers and the office of mail contracts, filing papers in appropriate parcels and cases; notifying charges against postmasters and assistants, and complaints of the location of offices; writing references of cases, &c. &c. They also prepare abstracts of cases; register and attest commissions; and enter the changes, discontinuances, and appointments in the bond book, with the penalties of the bonds; inspect all bonds after execution, and return them for correction when required. He might go through the whole organization of the department, and show its properties substantially the same as has always existed; and without such assignment of duties, no department or other extensive establishment could get on.

The gentleman [Mr. LINCOLN] speaks of routes abused, and contracts by men not worthy of confidence. Does the gentleman not know that the Postmaster General has nothing to do with the establishment of routes—that they are established by Congress, and that his duty is afterwards to put a mail on those routes? Can the gentleman put his finger on any such unworthy contractor in his district or section of country? He cannot. I suppose the gentleman alludes to the extra allowances that have been made, the extras and stars in the Blue Book, that has made so much noise in the other end of the Capitol—charged by many as being improper, and no one will venture to ask to have them discontinued. As to his own section of country, as well as other of the older States, they obtained in their original contracts their full share, and all that was desired. If there be any such unworthy contractors as the gentleman seems to suppose, I know them not. There may be routes that should be discontinued—and whenever a bill has been presented for the establishment of new routes, there has also been a number with it reported for discontinuance, by the Postmaster General; but it has been rare that the members have permitted those or any of them to be discontinued.

The gentleman says the department is plunged irrecoverably in debt, and is insolvent from 800,000 to $1,000,000; and his colleague over the way [Mr. REED] says the department is unable to pay, which means, that it is insolvent, as I understand him. He will answer both these gentlemen at the same time, by saying to them, they are mistaken; such is not the fact. Mr. C. said, he would take the responsibility of here saying that the amount due by the Post Office Department does not exceed $300,000 beyond their available means, and that during the next year, they will be free from debt, and very shortly thereafter will be prepared to grant facilities, in the shape of extras, if it be necessary, for the accommodation of the people. Sir, as to that department's becoming insolvent, a moment's reflection must satisfy any and every gentleman how perfectly idle it is to suppose such a state of things. Congress establishes the post roads—the Postmaster General is required to put a mail on them. The power and manner of transporting that mail, either by horse or coach, weekly, twice or thrice weekly, or daily, is vested solely in him, and he could, if necessary or proper, discontinue every coach in the United States from its service, and have the mails transported, the cheaper way, on horseback.

The gentleman has said something about contractors applying for their pay and its being refused, and they threatened by the department if they did not go away they would be paid in forfeitures. The gentleman has been incorrectly informed. It is not so. No such case has ever occurred. If the pay of a contractor has been withheld, there is some other cause, some difficulty in relation to the performance of his duties; and he called on the gentleman to name any one of those if he could.

[Here Mr. L. said he would reply after the manner of a Yankee, by asking another question: Had not contractors often been at the department and been refused their pay, and were told they were defaulters?]

Mr. C. said no contractor had applied at the department for their pay, that did not receive what was due to him. He had but a moment before expressed a belief that there must be some cause for a refusal, if any such there was. He had touched the right chord—the gentleman's inquiry explains it—he has heard of some one who was a defaulter, complaining, and that's all. Forfeitures can only be charged against a contractor after they occur and are so reported to the department.

He would beg now to say a word or two to the gentleman from Maine, [Mr. EVANS,] who complains that contractors in his State have been paid with post notes, and have lost four or five per cent. in the sale or exchanging of them. Why, sir, those post notes were on specie-paying banks, and what better could the gentleman expect? When his constituents enter into a contract with the Postmaster General, no particular kind of money is required or specified—the contractor expects good money, and the department expects to give good money, and does give him such. As far as the amount collected in each State, in the shape of postage, goes, it is paid to the contractors. When that falls short, the department pays in drafts or post notes of banks where they may have deposites, always those being on specie-paying banks; and such, I presume, is the fact with Maine—as with many other States—the receipts of the whole State are not equal to the expenditures by 20 or 25 per cent. made in that State; and this may account for the reason why the gentleman's constituents were paid off in post notes. Sir, the post office in the city of New York alone yielded, the year ending in 1833, $179,000; in Philadelphia, $112,000, and thus in a single post office, the amount received is greater than that yielded by three or four States together. The department must, from necessity, transfer the money from those States, where there is a surplus, to those where there is a deficiency and want. As to the inquiry, sir, why the Committee on the Post Office and Post Roads have not examined and reported in relation to this department, he could only say, the facts had been reported to the House by the Postmaster General in his annual report, that no call has been made on this committee that has not been promptly answered, and they have been ready promptly to answer any that might be made on them by order of this House.

The motion to strike out was rejected.

Mr. REED moved that the committee rise—ayes 69, noes 77.

Mr. LINCOLN moved to reduce the item to $17,000.

Mr. EWING advocated the reduction, and spoke at length upon the necessity of reforming the abuses to which the Post Office had lent itself in electioneering. He disavowed any imputation upon the character of the man at the head of the department.

Mr. POLK here rose to a point of order: that the motion to reduce the item was not in order, the motion to strike out having been rejected. He referred to the rules, from which he quoted the rule to amend.

Mr. LINCOLN said he had some doubts about it himself; but he had handed it to the Chairman, and it received his sanction.

The CHAIRMAN decided that as there was no objection made at the time the amendment was offered, he took for granted that the committee received the motion by unanimous consent, which they had a right to do.

Mr. POLK. The mover himself admits its irregularity.

The CHAIRMAN decided that unless he withdrew it, the objection was too late.

Mr. LINCOLN declined to withdraw.

Mr. EWING then resumed, and asserted that men possessing intelligence, integrity, and worth, had been removed from the offices in Indiana, and men of a contrary character placed in their situations.

Mr. HANNEGAN said, however this might have been the case in the gentleman's district, it was not the fact with respect to his own. There, the offices were filled with men of the highest worth.

Mr. EWING said he knew of instances where men were appointed solely for being whole-hog Jackson men, and of an appointment being given in Bloomfield to a man who could not read his commission when appointed.

Mr. HANNEGAN rejoined.

And the question having been taken, the motion to reduce was rejected:

Ayes 53, noes 85.

Mr. POLK moved to strike out the item for additional clerk hire to bring up the arrearages in the Surveyor General's Office, ($3,500.)

Agreed to.]

Mr. WILLIAMS moved that the committee rise, and the motion prevailed: ayes 72, noes 64.

The committee thereupon rose and reported progress, and

The House adjourned.

HOUSE OF REPRESENTATIVES.

Saturday, *April* 26, 1834.

The resolutions heretofore offered by Messrs. Wardwell and Reed, for information from the War Department, were taken up, by consent, and agreed to.

The resolution heretofore offered by Mr. Stewart, for printing 3,000 extra copies of the report on the subject of the Chesapeake and Ohio Canal, was taken up, by consent, and agreed to.

Mr. CHINN, from the Committee on the District of Columbia, reported the joint resolution from the Senate for watering the Pennsylvania Avenue, without amendment.

Mr. FILLMORE moved the suspension of the rules, in order to proceed to the consideration of the resolution now.

The question being taken, it appeared that there was no quorum.

Mr. MANN, of Pennsylvania, asked for the yeas and nays on the motion; and, on division, it appeared that there was still no quorum.

Mr. HARPER, of New Hampshire, moved a call of the House. Negatived.

The motion for the yeas and nays was again put, and prevailed.

The question being then taken on the motion to suspend the rule, for the purpose of taking up for consideration the joint resolution for watering the Avenue, it was decided in the negative—ayes 84, noes 54—(not two-thirds.)

ADJOURNMENT.

Mr. BOON moved the suspension of the rules in order to take up for consideration the following resolution, some time ago offered by him:

Resolved, That the President of the Senate and the Speaker of the House of Representatives close the present session of Congress by an adjournment of their respective Houses on Saturday the 31st of May next.

Mr. BOON asked the yeas and nays, and they were ordered.

The question being taken on the motion, it was determined in the negative—yeas 91, nays 57; (not two-thirds.)

Mr. WHITE, of Louisiana, from the Select Committee on the memorial of Benjamin Phillips, reported "A bill authorizing experiments on steam engines."

Read twice and committed.

Mr. POLK moved the suspension of the rules in order to take up the appropriation bill, but withdrew it at the request of

Mr. THOMSON, who moved that the House take up the motion to reconsider the vote rejecting the bill for the relief of David Kilbourne.

The motion to reconsider prevailed; and, on motion of Mr. THOMSON, the further consideration of the bill was postponed to the first Monday in December next.

Mr. POLK renewed his motion to suspend the rules, in order to take up the appropriation bill, and, on division, the motion was rejected, by a vote of 92 to 60—(not two-thirds.)

The House went into the Committee of the Whole, Mr. Conner in the chair, on the bill to compensate Susan Decatur and others.

Mr. LANE, who had the floor from Saturday last, stated that he was unable, in consequence of indisposition, to proceed in the discussion to-day, and therefore relinquished the floor.

Mr. PARKER spoke in favor of the bill, and moved to strike out $31,418, and insert $25,000 as the portion of Mrs. Decatur.

Mr. McKINLEY moved a division of the question; but the Chair decided that it was not divisible.

The question being taken, the motion was lost.

Mr. ARCHER moved an amendment providing that the share of Mrs. Decatur be vested by the secretary of the Navy in public stocks, the income of which shall be paid to Susan Decatur during her natural life, and two-thirds of the principal there-

after paid to the heirs and legal representatives of the late Commodore Decatur, the other third being subject to Mrs. Decatur's disposition by will.

Mr. PEARCE, of Rhode Island, moved to strike out the enacting clause.

The motion was rejected—ayes 53, noes 80.

That amendment proposed by Mr. ARCHER prevailed—ayes 72, noes 61.

Mr. HARPER, of New Hampshire, proposed an amendment to strike out all after the enacting clause, and inserting a new distribution (in which $10,000 was to be given to Mrs. Decatur.)

The amendment was rejected.

After which, on motion of Mr. McKENNAN, the committee rose, and reported the bill to the House; which was ordered to be printed as amended; and

The House adjourned.

IN SENATE.

Monday, *April* 28, 1834.

A message was received from the President of the United States, upon executive business, by Mr. Donelson, his Private Secretary.

Mr. TYLER presented the proceedings and resolutions of a public meeting of young men of the city of Richmond, and town of Manchester, Virginia, condemning the course of the Executive, and recommending the restoration of the deposites to the Bank of the United States.

Mr. LEIGH presented a memorial from inhabitants of the county of Gloucester, Virginia, of a similar character.

Both the proceedings of the meeting and the memorial, were read, referred to the Committee on Finance, and ordered to be printed.

Mr. McKEAN presented a memorial of certain citizens of Pennsylvania, remonstrating against the imposition of duties upon foreign coal; which was referred to the Committee on Finance.

Mr. CHAMBERS presented the petition of George W. Howard; which was referred.

Mr. SILSBEE presented the petition of John Ames, paper manufacturer; which was referred to the Committee on the Judiciary.

Mr. TOMLINSON presented a memorial from a number of importing merchants of the city of New York, praying that the unexpected excess of the act of 2d of March, 1833, may be refunded. The memorial was referred to the Committee on the Judiciary.

Mr. WAGGAMAN presented the petition of Andre Frederick Paisseau and others, of Louisiana: which was referred to the Committee on Public Lands.

Mr. KING, of Alabama, presented the memorial of John Walker, in behalf of Edmund P. Folsome, an orphan child of the Choctaw nation, asking that a quarter section of land be set apart for him in conformity with the provisions of the treaty with the Choctaw nation.

The memorial was referred to the Committee on Indian Affairs.

Mr. WEBSTER presented a memorial signed by more than six thousand inhabitants of the city of Utica, and the county of Oneida, New York, praying the restoration of the deposites to the Bank of the United States, and asking Congress to take such measures as their wisdom may suggest, to restore the currency of the country to a healthful condition.

The memorial was accompanied by a few remarks by Mr. WEBSTER, and was then read and referred to the Committee on Finance, and ordered to be printed.

Mr. WILKINS presented a memorial of a large number of the inhabitants of Huntingdon, Huntingdon county, Pennsylvania, approving of the course of the President of the United States with regard to the Bank of the United States, approving the course of the Hon. William C. Rives, late a Senator from Virginia, and differing with certain Senators for not obeying instructions sent them by the Legislatures of their several States.

Mr. WILKINS said that he fully concurred with the gentleman from Massachusetts in the sentiment expressed by him. He, also, was not laboring under any political despondency, nor did he despair of the Republic, though he confessed he

despaired of anything being done at the present session of Congress to relieve the country, owing to the great contrariety of opinion prevailing here, in the House of Representatives, and out of doors. If it was possible for us, seeing so much of public sentiment, to ascertain what that sentiment was, we ought to endeavor to abide by it, and adopt something in accordance with it, in aid of the people. But he despaired of ascertaining it by the presentation of the proceedings of public meetings. He had many such expressions in his possession; but we could not ascertain from them the real state of public sentiment, in the excited situation of the country. It was to be presumed that all petitioners were equally interested in the prosperity of the institutions of the country, and in preserving the Constitution and laws, and they were therefore entitled to credit for their exertions. They were all equally respectable, and all interested in their country's welfare. Mr. W. had determined to present no more of these proceedings, but he had had in his possession, for some time past, the proceedings of a public meeting held at the Court-house in the town of Huntingdon, in Huntingdon county, Pennsylvania, which he would present. That county was in a central situation, upon the products of industry were at high prices. They admitted in these proceedings, that everything was paralyzed, but they attributed it all to the monster; and after this depression, when they have arrived at the point of killing, they say it is better—he thought it a practice which would not relieve the patient. All knew that the crops were short, and times low. But we were told that the bank was grinding down the people; but by their official reports we perceive that they have not been curtailing at all; and yet they must now curtail; and if the monster should thus go on calling in its debts, how was it possible for the pressure to go off. Common sense was against it.

Mr. CLAY rose to say, that as allusion had been made to his name as a retained counsel of the bank, in terms which were not to be misunderstood, he would not contradict it, out of respect to himself, but that he would be glad if the gentleman from Pennsylvania would return the memorialists his thanks for their notice of him. The assertion was not true. He had no professional connexion with the Bank of the United States for the last nine years.

Mr. WILKINS replied, that the Senate would recollect that on one occasion he gave an opinion that our fellow-citizens had a right to be heard by us, in any language they chose to use. We could not examine strictly the language in which they chose to present themselves here, for that would be infringing upon the rights guarantied to them in the Constitution. It was for the Senate, after the presentation of a paper, to say what they would do with it. He was aware that the language of a portion of this paper—that part which alluded to the gentleman from Kentucky—was exceptionable, and of which he disapproved. But he asked that gentleman when he (Mr. W.) had ever uttered a sentiment disrespectful either to him or any other gentleman of the Senate? [Mr. Clay said, never.] But when a paper was sent to him to present, Mr. W. said he felt no right to object to it. The gentleman from Kentucky would have a right to rebuke him whenever he should find him using language of his own, disrespectful to him or any other member.

The gentleman from Maryland [Mr. Chambers] had called up to his recollection an early period of his (Mr. W.'s) made at an early period in this discussion, but he had made it too general. He never denied that there was distress and pressure

on the people. In the month of January, he did deny that there was distress prevailing in the city of his residence. He did use the phrase, but he qualified it in a way to justify it, and he was justified now. He then said that he had no paper giving him evidence of distress in Pittsburg; but after this expression had gone to Pittsburg, a public meeting was held in consequence of it, and one of the resolutions there adopted, admitted that they had kept their complaints to themselves; that the cry of distress had not gone from Pittsburg, and in their expressions pointed particularly to the future. He acknowledged that distress did overspread the land, to the utter condemnation of the Bank of the United States; and he confessed, that in this respect, he was disappointed as to the power and disposition of the bank to cause distress. As regarded the Oneida memorial, the difference was in relation to the bank, whether the Government or the bank was the immediate cause of the prevailing distress. With respect to agricultural products, we knew that they were all looking up in price. Look at the article of flour in the markets of Philadelphia and Baltimore.

But allusion has been made to the Senators from New Jersey, and he regretted that it was there. But it only spoke of the question, whether those gentlemen were representing the sentiments of their constituents; they did not decide the question; and Mr. W. said his own wish was that they might represent them. But on the side of the Administration we have *prima facie* evidence in the instructions of the New Jersey Legislature, that they did not represent them. And this was combated by those gentlemen by giving the proceedings of meetings in New Jersey. He made no comments upon this subject; these men made their own conclusions, in relation to the present situation of public affairs, and time only would tell which party was right.

Mr. WEBSTER observed, that the gentleman from Pennsylvania said that there were so many memorialists that he did not know what they wanted. But could any reasonable man say that he doubted what the opinion of the people was at this time? Why, what was the question? It was on the propriety of the removal of the deposites, and he believed, the number of memorialists here was as twenty to one against it. And would any man say he doubted whether the majority of the people approved or disapproved of this measure? He could not think any man would say it was doubtful. He knew many gentlemen supported the Administration in the measure, but was the thing itself the object of their approbation? He was at a loss to know whether the gentleman from Pennsylvania had selected this paper for the decorum of its language, or the closeness or pertinency of its reasoning. He contended, however, that Congress was bound to furnish a remedy for the people for the grievances they labored under, before their adjournment.

Mr. WILKINS rose to correct an error of the gentleman from Massachusetts. He did not admit that he could not make up an opinion upon the present state of affairs, but he said there was such a variety of opinion as to retard any measures of relief. He had no doubt on which side public sentiment was in relation to the removal of the deposites, and the action of the Administration on the finances of the country; and he said that public sentiment was with the Administration. He admitted that in our commercial cities the Administration had lost ground, for the commercial community went with the moneyed interest of the country. But the sentiments of the commercial cities was not a fair test to ascertain the sentiments of the mass of the people—of the yeomanry of the country. In Philadelphia we had lost ground; but Philadelphia had always been opposed to the Administration; and in the city of the West we had also lost some ground; and he had no doubt he had been stripped of a portion of the favor which he had had the honor of enjoying; and on his return home, he doubted not, he should be met with some coolness for the course which he had taken; a course which, before God he could say his conscience dictated to him as the proper one. But as to the dominant party, the yeomanry of Pennsylvania, he had no doubt that their spirits were up; that they were sensitive and compact; that they stood together, and were unmoved by the operations of the Bank of the United States. And what must have been the mischievous conduct of that bank which could have weaned from it so unanimous an opinion of friendship as existed in Pennsylvania a short time ago! Such was its flagrant conduct, that a total change had now taken place against it. What, then, was the rule by which we were to judge of the state of public opinion? Will you take the elections since October last, as the touchstone? Take the elections since the removal of the deposites, and what must be the sentiment of every impartial man? The removal of the deposites was the subject of conversation on every election ground in Pennsylvania. And yet what was the consequence? We should judge of that act by the effects which followed, not immediately, but by the subsequent conduct of the bank. The gentleman from Louisiana, [Mr. PORTER,] was elected to the Senate by only one vote. And what was public sentiment in Missouri, Illinois, and Indiana? In favor of the Administration. In Ohio, where the elections took place on the second Tuesday of October, we had *prima facie* evidence, from the instructions of the Legislature, what that sentiment was there. In Pennsylvania, a large majority of the Senate and House of Representatives was decidedly so. In New Jersey, we had the same *prima facie* evidence, in the instructions of her Legislature. In New York, it was sufficient to say, that we had not been beaten. In the commercial emporium, where the greatest power and influence of the bank was brought to bear on the election, to a degree that perhaps will never be repeated, it had terminated in a defeat. These were the facts from which Mr. W. said he drew his conclusions. In Virginia, the contest was not yet over; but had the Administration gained or lost there? That was the question. Then, as to relief, no one was more disposed to legislate, and to do anything to restore harmony to the country than himself. He was willing to act at any moment, to quiet the public mind on this vexed question.

After some further remarks by Mr. PORTER, in which he said he was elected by a majority of *two* votes, instead of *one*, as had been observed by the gentleman from Pennsylvania, the paper was referred to the Committee on Finance, and ordered to be printed.

Mr. BROWN presented the proceedings and resolutions of a large meeting of citizens of Edgecombe county, North Carolina, approving of the course of the Executive with regard to the Bank of the United States, and recommending that the deposites be not restored to that institution, and the same may not be rechartered.

The proceedings were read, referred to the Committee on Finance, and ordered to be printed.

Mr. CLAY submitted the following resolutions, the immediate consideration of which he asked; and leave being obtained, the resolutions were considered, and after being slightly modified, on motion of Mr. MOORE, were adopted:

Resolved, That the Secretary of the Treasury be directed to report to the Senate the gross amount of the proceeds of the sales of the public lands, and the number of acres which have been sold during the year 1833, including the last quarter of the year, and distinguishing the amount received, and the number of acres sold in each State and Territory.

Resolved, also, That he report to the Senate the manner in which has been ascertained at the Treasury, from time to time, the "twentieth part of the net proceeds of the lands lying within the said State [Ohio] sold by Congress from and after the thirtieth day of June next, [1802] after deducting all expenses incident to the same," which by the compact with Ohio was set apart for laying out and making public roads; and the manner in which the like allowance made to other new States has been ascertained at the treasury, showing especially the deductions made from the gross amount to ascertain the net proceeds.

REPORTS OF COMMITTEES.

Mr. CLAYTON, from the Committee on the Judiciary, reported a bill for the relief of James Thomas; which was read, and the report accompaying it ordered to be printed.

Mr. CLAYTON, at the same time, on leave, presented a memorial praying indemnification for expenses incurred in the District during the cholera; which was referred to the Committee on the District of Columbia.

Also, the petition of the Rev. Mr. Wiltbank, chaplain of the navy yard, Philadelphia, praying compensation for services rendered; which was referred to the Committee on Naval Affairs.

Mr. WILKINS, from the Committee on Finance, reported the following bills from the House of Representatives, without amendment:

A bill for the relief of William B. Doliber and others;

A bill for the relief of Stephen Kingston;

A bill for the relief of Samuel B. Walker;

SPECIAL ORDER.

The Senate then proceeded to the consideration of the special order, being the amendment of Mr. BIBB to Mr. POINDEXTER's resolution relative to the protest of the President of the United States.

Mr. BIBB resumed and concluded his remarks against the reception of the protest, and the doctrines promulgated by that paper.

Mr. GRUNDY then took the floor; when, on his motion, at half-past four o'clock,

The Senate adjourned.

HOUSE OF REPRESENTATIVES.

MONDAY, *April* 28, 1834.

The Hon. RICE GARLAND, elected a member from Louisiana, in the room of the Hon. H. A. BULLARD, resigned, appeared, was qualified, and took his seat.

Mr. BINNEY rose to state that he had been informed by Mr. FRANKLIN, the Clerk of the House, that he had received the afflicting account of the death of his father. This event occurred on Saturday last; and there were circumstances connected with it, which rendered his going to Philadelphia indispensable. Under such circumstances, he had been informed that an absence of three or four days would not be objected to by the House. He asked leave, therefore, to submit a motion to this effect.

Leave having been given, the motion of Mr. B. that Mr. FRANKLIN have leave of absence for four days, was unanimously agreed to.

Mr. HALL, of North Carolina, who had presented sundry memorials in relation to the bank and the removal of the deposites, from his constituents, on the last petition day, called up his motion to print the same; and thereupon spoke at length, in explanation of his views.

The memorials were, on motion of Mr. HALL, laid on the table, and ordered to be printed.

Mr. GRAHAM moved to lay on the table the memorial from Burke county, North Carolina, presented by him on a former day. Agreed to.

Mr. GAMBLE called up a memorial from citizens of Savannah, respecting the United States Bank and the deposites, presented by him on a former day, and proceeded to discuss the facts alleged by the memorialists. The facts embodied in the memorial were, he believed, true, and were believed to be true by a majority of the people of Georgia, and the people of the United States. They estimated the loss on the cotton crop of Georgia, produced by the removal of the deposites, at one million of dollars, and of the whole cotton crop of the South, at six or eight millions. The number of the memorialists was small, being only two hundred, but they were men of intelligence, high character, and extensively engaged in business.

On motion of Mr. G. the memorial was read: and the motion to refer and print the same being under consideration,

Mr. WAYNE rose to make some remarks, but a question of order having been made, he yielded the floor.

The motion to refer and print was then agreed to.

Mr. WAYNE presented a memorial signed by 680 citizens and legal voters of the city of Savannah and county of Chatham, expressing their approbation of the course of the Government in relation to the United States Bank. He moved that the memorial be received, at the same time intimating an intention to call it up for the purpose of submitting some views on the subject at a future time.

Mr. W. also presented two private petitions.

Mr. FOSTER obtained leave to present a resolution relative to a post route; which was referred.

Mr. POPE presented the proceedings of a public meeting held in the city of Louisville, in the State of Kentucky, on the 3d of April, 1834. He observed, that the address and resolutions had been received by him more than two weeks ago; that he would take this occasion to observe, (so that it might be known to his constituents,) that the rules of the House prohibited the presentation of memorials and petitions on any other day than Monday; that the two last Mondays had been occupied with the presentation of memorials from other States; and this was the very *first opportunity* that had offered for the purpose.

Mr. P. said that, so far as he could learn, the persons composing the meeting were gentlemen of fine practical sense, of character, of substance, and whose interests were intimately identified with the growth and prosperity of Louisville; that bad government and unwise legislation would affect their interests as soon as it would those of any other class of men of any other city. He said that he had understood that the meeting was composed of at least six hundred persons; and that they were animated with unwonted enthusiasm, and had adopted with acclamation the address and resolutions which he had the honor to present. They deprecate, in the strongest terms, the course pursued by the Bank of the United States; protest against its being rechartered; justify the removal of the public deposites from its custody; testify to the sufficiency of the reasons assigned by the Secretary of the Treasury for the act; and deny the assertions of a late public meeting in that city, that there was a great reduction in the price of produce and other articles, and intimate that they could only have proceeded from a desire to alarm and agitate the public mind. Mr. P. concluded by moving that the proceedings be read, laid upon the table, and printed.

Mr. R. M. JOHNSON presented two private petitions; also, a memorial from 330 citizens of Grant county, in favor of the restoration of the deposites, and complaining of a general depression of business and prices; which was ordered to be printed.

Mr. MARSHALL presented a private petition.

Mr. CHILTON presented a memorial from citizens of the town of Brandenburg, praying the interposition of Congress for the relief of the country from present embarrassments. Laid on the table and ordered to be printed.

Mr. DAVIS presented a memorial from citizens of Lawrence and Greenup counties, on the subject of the Bank of the United States. Laid on the table and ordered to be printed.

Mr. THOMSON, of Ohio, presented the proceedings of a numerous meeting of the Democratic Republicans of Salem and its vicinity, with resolutions expressing their approbation of the course of the Government in regard to the deposites and the United States Bank; which were read, ordered to be printed, and laid on the table.

Mr. MITCHELL presented the petition of Abraham Boring; which was referred to the Committee on Public Lands.

Also, a memorial from citizens of the twelfth congressional district of Ohio, disapproving of the measures of the General Government in removing the deposites from the Bank of the United States.

Also, a memorial from the same district, in favor of the late action of the Secretary of the Treasury in removing the public funds from the Bank of the United States, and against its recharter.

Mr. CASEY presented the petition of sundry citizens of Edgar county, Illinois, praying the establishment of a post route; which, on his motion, was referred to the Committee on the Post Office and Post Roads.

Mr. CORWIN presented a memorial from citizens of Clinton county, in favor of the restoration of the deposites.

Mr. VANCE presented memorials from citizens of Champaign county, in favor of the restoration of the deposites.

Mr. LEAVITT presented a memorial from citizens of Harrison county, protesting against the recharter of the bank, and approving of the removal of the deposites.

All of which were laid on the table, and ordered to be printed.

Mr. WHITE, of Louisiana, presented memorials from citizens of Louisiana, representing the existence of much embarrassment and distress in that State, and disapproving of the course of the Administration in relation to the United States Bank. Read, laid on the table, and ordered to be printed.

The SPEAKER presented a memorial from sundry citizens of Louisiana, praying grants of land. Referred to the Committee on Public Lands.

Mr. HANNEGAN presented a petition.

Mr. EWING moved a suspension of the rules to permit him to offer a resolution. Negatived.

Mr. KINNARD presented the petition of sundry inhabitants of Bartholomew county, Indiana, for the establishment of a post route from Shelbyville, via Morran, Newhope, and Newbern, to Geneva post office, Jennings county.

Mr. CAGE presented several private petitions and memorials.

Petitions were presented by Messrs. CASEY and MARDIS.

Mr. MURPHY presented the memorial of sundry citizens of Dallas county, Alabama, praying Congress to restore the deposites, and charter a Bank of the United States, in such a manner as to render it acceptable to the nation. Read, laid on the table, and ordered to be printed.

Mr. ASHLEY presented several petitions.

Mr. WATMOUGH asked the unanimous consent of the House to take up the joint resolution from the Senate, to direct the Commissioner of Public Buildings to water the Pennsylvania Avenue.

Objections having been made—

Mr. W. moved a suspension of the rule, to enable him to offer it.

The House refused, yeas 80, nays not counted.

Mr. MERCER presented some papers in relation to the Potomac Bridge; which were laid on the table, and ordered to be printed.

Mr. OSGOOD asked leave to present some resolutions passed at a meeting of delegates from several towns in his district, and also a memorial, signed by a large number of the legal voters in said district, relating to the present situation of the country in regard to the currency, and asking a restoration of the deposites to the Bank of the United States. As these resolutions, and this memorial, were accompanied by a letter of instructions to Mr. O., he asked leave of the House to present some remarks in presenting them to the consideration.

The question having been taken on Mr. O.'s motion, the vote stood—ayes 80, noes 23. (No quorum.)

Mr. CONNOR moved an adjournment; which was rejected, yeas 66, nays 81.

On a second motion for leave to permit Mr. OSGOOD to explain, the vote stood 89 to 16—no quorum.

Mr. WARDWELL renewed the motion to adjourn; which prevailed, and

The Senate adjourned.

IN SENATE.

TUESDAY, *April* 29, 1834.

The VICE PRESIDENT presented a report from the Secretary of the Senate, stating that he had, in compliance with the resolution of the Senate of the 11th instant, prepared a list of the signatures to memorials, both for and against the removal of the deposites from the Bank of the United States.

Mr. CLAY moved that one thousand copies of the report of the Secretary be printed, but withdrew his motion, upon the suggestion of Mr. FORSYTH, with an intimation that he would renew it to-morrow.

PETITIONS.

Mr. BELL presented a memorial, signed by about 450 inhabitants of Somersworth, and another, signed by about 500 citizens of Dover, in New Hampshire, praying that the deposites may be restored to the Bank of the United States, and that that institution may be rechartered.

After some remarks by Mr. BELL, the memorials were read, referred to the Committee on Finance, and ordered to be printed.

REPORT OF COMMITTEES.

Mr. POINDEXTER, from the Committee on

Public Lands, reported a bill granting an entire township of land, to be located in the State of Illinois or Territory of Michigan, to be divided among the two hundred and thirty-five Polish exiles sent to the United States by the Emperor of Austria. The report and bill were read, and, together with the petition, ordered to be printed, and made the special order of the day for Thursday week.

RESOLUTIONS.

The following resolutions were submitted:
By Mr. CHAMBERS:

Resolved, That the Secretary of the Treasury be directed to inform the Senate whether any other Treasury drafts, called at the department " transfer drafts," on the United States Bank, have been drawn since his report of the 11th December, 1833, and the purposes to which the amount of such drafts, if any, have been applied.

By Mr. SWIFT:

Resolved, That the Committee on Pensions be instructed to inquire into the expediency of extending to Ebenezer Hart, of Vermont, a revolutionary soldier, the benefits of the act of Congress of June 7th, 1832, granting pensions to the officers and soldiers of the revolutionary army.

On motion of Mr. WILKINS, the Senate took up the memorial, presented some days ago, from the district of Hanover, York county, in Pennsylvania, on the subject of the removal of the deposites.

Mr. WILKINS spoke at length, in answer to Mr. CLAY's remarks upon the late conduct of Governor Wolf, in relation to the Bank of the United States; a full report of which will be given in a few days.

Mr. W. was followed by Mr. CLAY and Mr. MANGUM, in a few incidental remarks.

Mr. WEBSTER gave notice that he should to-morrow move the consideration of an appropriation bill from the House of Representatives, which required the immediate action of the Senate.

Mr. WEBSTER also gave notice that, after the transaction of the morning's business, he should move the Senate to proceed to executive business.

SPECIAL ORDER.

The Senate then proceeded to the consideration of the special order, being Mr. BIBB's amendment of Mr. POINDEXTER's resolutions on the protest of the President of the United States.

Mr. GRUNDY rose, and addressed the Senate until four o'clock, against the amendment and resolutions; when

Mr. CLAY obtained the floor, and after a few remarks in reply, moved an adjournment, but gave way to

Mr. MANGUM, to make an explanation; when,

On motion of Mr. CLAY,

The Senate adjourned.

HOUSE OF REPRESENTATIVES.

TUESDAY, *April* 29, 1834.

Mr. LINCOLN moved the suspension of the rules in order to offer a resolution proposing a series of inquiries in relation to the Post Office Department; and thereupon he asked the yeas and nays, which were ordered.

The question being taken, the motion was agreed to, yeas 103, nays 50.

The resolution was then submitted, and is as follows:

Resolved, That the Postmaster General be directed to lay before this House a statement of the number and names and dates of the appointments respectively of the clerks, agents, and other officers and persons employed in his department, (other than postmasters and persons employed in the respective post offices,) and of the distribution and assignment of the appropriate duties of each; and especially of the character of the services required of the Solicitor and clerks of the Solicitor's office; and the duties and official employment of each of the persons who in the register of the offices and agents of the Government called the " Blue Book," are denominated clerks of *appointments*; that he has also inform the House from what *fund* or *appropriation*, all the officers and persons employed in his department have received their compensation. And that he be further directed to state to this House to what corporations or individuals (if any) the Post Office

Department is indebted for money borrowed, and to what amount to each of such corporations or individuals respectively, and at what rates of interest such loans have been obtained; whether the department has overdrawn the amount of deposites to its credit in any bank or banks, and if so, in what balances it is now indebted to such banks; in what instances, if any, and to what amount, the department has anticipated its revenue by draft on post offices in advance of the current quarter; and whether there are arrearages due to any contractors, according to the terms of their contracts, either executed or continuing, for the conveyance of the mails, and to whom, and to what amount respectively; and what is the aggregate amount of the indebtedness of the department, beyond its present means and resources to discharge all its pecuniary obligations in time, and according to its engagements and liabilities.

Mr. LINCOLN asked the unanimous consent of the House to the consideration of the resolution; but an objection being made, he moved a suspension of the rule which required the resolution to lie one day on the table, in order that it might be considered now.

Mr. ADAMS, of Massachusetts, asked the yeas and nays thereon, and they were ordered.

The question being taken, the House rejected the motion to consider now, yeas 110, nays 66, (not two-thirds.)

Mr. MERCER obtained the consent of the House to submit the following resolution, which lies on the table one day of course:

Resolved, That the Secretary of the Treasury be directed to lay before this House a communication of the 6th of October, 1833, from a civil engineer of Pennsylvania, on the subject of the contemplated bridge across the Potomac, at the city of Washington.

On motion of Mr. GILMER, a report from the War Department, in relation to the death of Hardiman Owens, was taken up for reference.

Mr. CLAY said the subject related to the law, and the administration of the law, and he therefore moved its reference to the Committee on the Judiciary.

Mr. GILMER said that the most important part of the report related to the conduct of an officer of the army. It was due from the Government to the people to investigate the subject. It did not properly belong to the Judiciary Committee, but, as he thought, to a select committee.

After some words from Messrs. CLAY, WILLIAMS, GILMER, and McKINLEY,

Mr. POLK moved that the House proceed to the orders of the day, and it was agreed to.

The House went into Committee of the Whole, Mr. HUBBARD in the chair.

Mr. WHITE, of New York, moved that the committee proceed to the consideration of the bill regulating the value of foreign silver coins in the United States.

Mr. WHITE assured the chairman and the committee, that nothing but his duty to the commercial community would induce him to ask the favor, at this moment, when a great public measure (the appropriation bill) was before them; but, as its necessity was urgent, and as it could not occupy any great portion of time, he asked that it be now taken up.

Mr. POLK said, if it would not create debate, nor occupy much time, he would assent to its consideration now.

After some words from Mr. McKAY,

Mr. WHITE withdrew the motion for the present.

On motion of Mr. POLK, the committee proceeded to the consideration of the bill making appropriations for the civil and diplomatic expenses of the United States during the year 1834.

Mr. VANCE moved to strike out the following item:

For additional clerk hire, in order to bring up the arrears, and transcribing the field notes of said office, for the purpose of having them preserved at the seat of Government, $1,000.

After some explanations from Messrs. McKINLEY, POLK, LYON of Michigan, C. C. CLAY, and ASHLEY, and a few remarks from Messrs. VANCE and LANE,

The amendment was rejected.

The next item, being for the compensation to the Surveyor General of Arkansas, $1,500—

Mr. WILLIAMS moved that the question should be taken on each item, and not passed over without a vote being taken for the concurrence.

Mr. POLK suggested that the most convenient course was to move to strike out such items as were objected to.

Mr. WAYNE approved of the motion of the honorable member from North Carolina.

The question was then taken on several items; which were agreed to.

Mr. ASHLEY proposed an amendment to the item for additional clerk hire, authorizing the Secretary of the Treasury to provide for some surveys that should be found necessary, many which, he explained, had been overlooked in various places.

Mr. DUNCAN concurred in the propriety of the amendment.

Mr. POLK regretted that he must object to the amendment being proposed to this bill, where it was evidently out of place.

Mr. ADAMS objected to it, because it gave a discretionary power to the Secretary of the Treasury, to increase or grant compensation.

Mr. ASHLEY finally withdrew his amendment.

Mr. VANCE moved to strike out the next item, as he considered that these officers were perfect sinecures:

For enabling the respective surveyors general to furnish the several land offices, commencing under the credit system, with renewed township plats, under the direction of the Secretary of the Treasury, in cases where those previously furnished have been defaced, or become materially injured by use, $10,000.

The votes on the amendment to strike out, stood ayes 45, noes 53. No quorum.

The CHAIRMAN having ascertained there were one hundred and twenty-six members, being a quorum, present—

Mr. McKINLEY explained the necessity that existed for the appropriation.

It was opposed by Messrs. H. EVERETT, FULLER of New York, and BURGES.

Mr. POLK read a statement from the Commissioner of the Land Office, which went to show that much evil had accrued for the want of these maps; he, however, left it to the committee to say whether the appropriation should be reduced in amount.

After some remarks from Mr. BARRINGER and Mr. FULLER,

Mr. DUNCAN moved to reduce the appropriation to one half, viz: $5,000.

The CHAIRMAN said this was not in order.

Mr. WILLIAMS opposed the appropriation altogether.

Mr. POLK said he should not oppose the reduction.

Mr. PLUMMER bore testimony to the necessity that existed in the land offices in Mississippi, to have these maps renewed. It was all-important to the interest of his constituents that they should be supplied; and as Mississippi had paid into the treasury large sums, he hoped so small an appropriation would not be refused.

The motion to strike out was rejected: Ayes 57, noes 67.

Mr. ASHLEY moved to strike out $10,000, and insert $5,000.

Mr. BULL moved to insert $9,500.

The amendment was rejected.

And the amendment proposed by Mr. ASHLEY was agreed to: Ayes 92, noes not counted.

For compensation to the Secretary appointed by the President to sign all patents for lands sold or granted under the authority of the United States, per act of second March, eighteen hundred and thirty-three, including arrears of salary not paid for eighteen hundred and thirty-three, the sum of $2,750.

For compensation to the Commissioner of Public Buildings in Washington city, $2,000.

For the purchase of books for the Library of Congress, $5,000.

Mr. J. Q. ADAMS moved to amend this, by increasing the amount to $10,000, which, he said, was to carry out the recommendation of the Libra-

ry Committee, at the time there was a conference deemed necessary on account of the former disagreement existing between the two legislative branches on the subject of printing.

The amendment was rejected.

Several items of the bill were then read, and concurred in.

When the following item was read—

For compensation and mileage of the members of the Legislative Council, pay of the officers of the Council, fuel, stationary, and printing, for the Michigan Territory, $11,448—

Mr. POLK moved to amend this, by inserting $4,000 to pay up arrearages which occurred for the same objects during the past year.

Mr. McKAY objected.

Mr. LYON and Mr. POLK quoted the estimates to sustain the appropriation, which was finally agreed to.

For compensation to the Governor, Judges, and Secretary of the Arkansas Territory, including additional compensation to the Judges, under the act of twentieth April, eighteen hundred and thirty-two, at $800 each, from the sixteenth March, eighteen hundred and thirty-three, to thirty-first December, eighteen hundred and thirty-four, $13,500.

Mr. McKAY moved to amend, by inserting, in lieu of $800, $533.

Mr. POLK quoted the estimates.

Mr. SEVIER advocated it.

The amendment was rejected.

For incidental expenses of the Legislative Council of said Territory, per act of twenty-fourth May, eighteen hundred and twenty-eight, omitted last year, seven hundred and twenty dollars.

Mr. BELL proposed to amend the foregoing, at the recommendation of the Committee on the Judiciary, by inserting a paragraph to defray the expenses of digesting and printing the laws of the Territory, $3,000.

Mr. HARDIN did not see that any necessity existed for the General Government digesting and printing the local laws of any Territory, which could not be voluminous enough to require it. He hoped that no new items of expenditure would be inserted, but that the appropriation would be made only in reference to offices previously established by law.

Mr. BELL said he made the recommendations by desire of the committee, in consequence of a memorial to that effect from the Legislative Council. He could not agree that the principle alluded to was established, although he desired that it should, believing it to be a bad course of legislation, but the practice was well known to have prevailed in consequence of peculiar circumstances, which generally led to it, and which seemed almost impossible to avoid.

Mr. SEVIER maintained that the principle of inserting this amendment was as justifiable as others which found their way into the bill.

The motion of Mr. BELL was agreed to, 73 to 49.

Mr. BRIGGS, at the request of the Delegate from Florida, who was not now present, moved to strike out $11,300, as the appropriation for the Governor, judges, &c., of the Territory of Florida, and to insert $13,000. Rejected.

Mr. BRIGGS moved one or two other slight amendments, which were adopted.

Mr. SELDEN moved an amendment proposing a limitation to the fees of the district attorneys, by preventing them from dividing their actions against individuals.

Mr. POLK opposed the motion, and after some remarks from Messrs. McKAY, FILLMORE, PARKER, WAYNE, BRIGGS, and BEARDSLEY.

Mr. LANE moved to amend the amendment, by providing that the district attorney shall embrace in the same suit, the several demands which he may have in his hands for prosecution against an individual at any one time.

Mr. SELDEN spoke against the motion to amend.

Mr. WILLIAMS moved that the committee rise.

Ayes 91, noes not counted.

The committee then rose and reported progress and,

On motion of Mr. HUBBARD,

The House adjourned.

THE CONGRESSIONAL GLOBE.

PRINTED AND PUBLISHED AT THE CITY OF WASHINGTON, BY BLAIR & RIVES.

23d Congress, 1st Session.   SATURDAY, MAY 10, 1834.   Vol. I........No. 23.

IN SENATE.

WEDNESDAY, *April* 30, 1834.

A message was received from the President of the United States, upon executive business, by Mr. DONELSON, his Private Secretary.

Mr. WEBSTER, from the Committee on Finance, reported a bill from the House of Representatives, making appropriations for the War Department, without amendment. On his motion, the bill was recommitted to the same committee.

PETITIONS.

Mr. SPRAGUE presented a memorial from inhabitants of Hallowell, Maine, in favor of the restoration of the deposites to the Bank of the United States, and praying a recharter of that institution.

Mr. SPRAGUE said, that these memorialists complain of the prevalence of deep distress in their community, owing to the belligerent attitude assumed by the President of the United States towards the bank, as developed in the recent measures of Government; and they protest, against it, and say, that the power over the treasury, which the Executive has claimed is the protest, rightfully belongs to the Congress of the United States. He knew that it was said by some that the supplement had retracted the claim set up in the protest, but Mr. S. said, he believed it was only ambiguous, and left the claim of power just where it was, and where it might be put forth in all its rigor, or disclaimed according to circumstances. He says all the officers of Government are his officers, are executive officers, and under the control of the Executive; and in the supplement, he says he don't mean to control the money, but he is accountable for the conduct of the officers, and, therefore, he has the possession and custody of the public money. He says, Congress may designate the place where the money is to be kept, but that he is the keeper of the key. These petitioners are citizens of this most Democratic county in the State of Maine, and they speak with but one voice. They have not yet had their entire fields swept over by the dark and bitter waters of Jacksonism, but they say they wish this experience not so wide, that this confiding and generous, yet brave people, may be driven to despair.

Mr. SHEPLEY said, it was not his desire to enter into this question upon the presentation of memorials; but as some remarks had been made in relation to his State, which seemed to call for a remark, he would say a word or two. His colleague had said that but one voice proceeded from Kennebeck. True; and if that one voice was the memorials presented here, there was but one voice from Maine. These persons who believe the conduct and measures of the Administration to be correct, never take the trouble to present memorials or resolutions. The State of Maine now gives more than 70,000 votes; and a short time ago it gave 20,000; and yet, here are evidences of opinion from Maine, notwithstanding resolutions approbatory of the conduct of the whole Administration passed one branch of the Legislature by a vote of 119 to 53, and 22 to 2 in the other branch. These are, to be sure, the only exhibitions of public sentiment on that side. The State of Maine rests on her own quiet dignity; her people feel that her Legislature has expressed their opinions, and that they have not been done by disorderly, tumultuous expressions of public meetings. He is willing that they shall be heard, but constitutionally heard, through the ballot boxes. And what was this public expression, so much relied on? All this show was some 2600, out of 60,000 or 70,000, and yet we hear intimations thrown out as if there was some great expression of opinion from Maine, which would induce a belief that the expression of the Legislature was not truthful.

Mr. S. presented these views only in show, not what might at some future day be her opinions, for be pretended not to pronounce what they might be in future times, but what they were now. It was sufficient for him to look at the expressions of opinions as they were, and as they were ex-

pressed in the legitimate mode. But he understood that there was a new mode of electioneering adopted—new here, at least; and he, for one, would not have believed that this assembly would have been so occupied for five months past. Not a petition had been presented, but it was accompanied by some remarks of an electioneering tendency, and so avowed. Whether the people will think the Senate so constituted are conforming to their duty, they will judge. Mr. S. supposed this body was designed for different purposes. It seemed now that reason was no longer to be operated on, but excitement, appeals to the passions and prejudices of the people, and intimations of some strange events about to occur, was the order of the day. This was the new mode of electioneering; and the whole system was to be a new one—all for good, no doubt; and it was not more true that it was a new system than that new names were devised, and new systems applicable to particular districts of the country. Mr. S. said, he could not perceive that Kennebeck was especially distinguished by marks of Democracy; and if she was entitled to that appellation, in any other sense than in the sense of the new name which had been given her, he differed in opinion as to the justness of it. But this was not the time for investigating the paper which was the subject of so much remark. He hoped a fair, full, and deliberate investigation would be given to it; but until the paper should be received, he would withhold any comments he had to make.

The memorial was read, and referred to the Committee on Finance.

Mr. SMITH presented a memorial, signed by about 300 inhabitants of Coventry, Connecticut, praying that Congress would make an appropriation to erect a monument to the memory of Captain Nathan Hale, of the revolutionary army, who was despatched by General Washington on secret service, to the British camp, and after having successfully performed the objects of his mission, was arrested on his return, tried, condemned, and executed as a spy.

The memorial was referred to the Committee on Military Affairs.

Mr. WHITE presented the petition of Theodorick B. Rice; which was referred to the Committee on Military Affairs.

Mr. MOORE presented the petition of William Walker and others; which was referred to the same committee.

Mr. KENT presented a memorial of sundry citizens of Baltimore in support of the established merit of the warehouse system; which was referred to the Committee on Finance.

Mr. NAUDAIN presented the petition of Boyd Reilly, stating that he had invented and patented an improvement in the use of vapor baths, which he conceived would be important to the army and navy, and desiring Congress to purchase a right. Referred to the Committee on Military Affairs.

Mr. BENTON presented the petition of the Right Reverend Bishop Rosati, of St. Louis, Missouri, and others, praying to be released from the payment of duties, amounting to upwards of $600, which accrued on a set of bells imported from Havre, in France, for the Roman Catholic Cathedral in St. Louis. Referred to the Committee on Finance.

Mr. BENTON presented the petition of Colonel A. R. Woolley, praying an appropriation to cover a sum due him for pay and emoluments while settling his accounts, and which sum is not included in any appropriation yet made. Referred to the Committee on Military Affairs.

Mr. POINDEXTER, from the Committee on Public Lands, asked to be discharged from the further consideration of the resolution in reference to public lands, as affecting Galena, Illinois. Agreed to.

Mr. POINDEXTER, from the same committee, reported unfavorably upon the petition of Benjamin S. Polk; which report, on motion of Mr. MOORE was laid upon the table.

Mr. McKEAN, from the Committee on Pensions, asked to be discharged from the further consideration of the petition of James McFarland. Agreed to.

Mr. WRIGHT, from the Committee of Claims, made an unfavorable report upon the petition of Samuel Hardesty. The report was ordered to be printed.

Mr. SMITH, from the Committee on the Judiciary, reported a bill in favor of David Beard; which was read, and the report ordered to be printed.

Mr. NAUDAIN, from the Committee on Claims, reported a bill from the House of Representatives for the relief of Francoise Suzone, without amendment.

SPECIAL ORDER.

The Senate then proceeded to the consideration of the special order, being Mr. Bibb's amendment to Mr. POINDEXTER's resolutions with regard to the President's protest.

Mr. CLAY spoke at length in favor of the resolutions, when

Mr. WRIGHT obtained the floor, and, upon his motion,

The Senate adjourned.

HOUSE OF REPRESENTATIVES.

WEDNESDAY, *April* 30, 1834.

Mr. J. Q. ADAMS obtained leave to notify to the House, that on to-morrow he would ask leave to present a bill to restrict the Corporations of Alexandria, Georgetown, and Washington, from issuing notes of a less denomination than ten dollars.

Mr. WAYNE reported a bill for the relief of Alexander Scott, and

Mr. PARKER, a bill for the relief of James Tucker and John Judge; which bills were read twice and committed.

Mr. R. M. JOHNSON reported, from the Committee on Military Affairs, a joint resolution, giving a right of way at Harper's Ferry to the railroad company, through lands the property of the United States, and a report in relation thereto; which, on his motion, was ordered to be printed. The joint resolution, by the rule, lies on the table one day for consideration.

Mr. BELL, of Tennessee, reported a bill further to amend the judiciary system of the United States; which was read twice, committed, and ordered to be printed.

Also, a bill for the relief of Thomas McClelland; which was read twice, and committed.

Mr. WILLIAMS reported a bill to equalize the representation from the Territory of Florida; which was ordered to be printed, and the consideration postponed until to-morrow.

Mr. PARKER, of New Jersey, obtained leave to submit the following resolution:

Resolved, That the Committee on the Post Office and Post Roads be instructed to inquire into the expediency of establishing a post route from Camden, by way of Amboy, to New York.

The resolution was agreed to.

The House resumed the consideration of the resolution submitted by Mr. MARDIS:

Resolved, That the Committee of Ways and Means be instructed to inquire into the expediency of reporting a bill requiring the Secretary of the Treasury to pay creditors the public moneys of the United States in the State banks; and, also, as to the expediency of defining by law all contracts hereafter to be made with the Secretary for the safe-keeping, management, and disbursement of the same.

Together with the substitute offered by Mr. CORWIN, of Ohio, declaring that the reasons offered by the Secretary for the removal of the public deposites from the United States Bank are insufficient and unsatisfactory.

Mr. McKENNAN resumed, and spoke at length

in favor of the amendment submitted by Mr. Corwin.

Mr. GALBRAITH then obtained the floor, but was obliged to postpone his remarks.

The SPEAKER presented various accounts from the Comptroller of the Treasury.

The military commutation bill was postponed until to-morrow.

The motion submitted by Mr. Mercer, in relation to the Potomac bridge, was agreed to.

The House then, on motion of Mr. POLK, resolved itself into Committee of the Whole on the state of the Union, (Mr. Hubbard in the chair.)

On motion of Mr. C. P. WHITE, the bill to regulate the value of foreign coins was taken up and considered.

On motion of Mr. WAYNE, the bill to extend the time allowed to discharge the duties of the commissioners employed to carry into effect the convention with France being taken up and read—

Mr. WILLIAMS said he had heard no good reason why this time should be extended to this board of commissioners. He must, therefore, oppose it.

Mr. ARCHER suggested to the honorable member that this opposition should be postponed until the bill was before the House.

It was then laid aside, and ordered to be reported to the House.

On motion of Mr. ARCHER, the bill to extend the time to carry into effect the convention with the King of the Two Sicilies, was also taken up and considered.

The consideration of the appropriation bill was then resumed.

The amendment proposed by Mr. Selden, to restrict the district attorneys of the United States from bringing separate actions on custom-house bonds, and to compel them to consolidate them, to prevent unnecessary expense thereon, being pending—

Mr. DICKERSON submitted an amendment in lieu thereof, in substance to provide that no money shall be paid as costs to the district attorneys, unless the courts shall certify that the costs were justly due.

Mr. SELDEN entered into an explanation, to show that this would not fully meet the evils which he wished to remedy.

Mr. S. said his proposition was, that no more costs should be paid to the district attorney than if they had consolidated all the claims which could be consolidated. This threw the burden of proof upon the attorneys. He did not charge the attorney of the southern district of New York with any improper conduct. He presumed he had followed the example set him by his predecessors in office. In Philadelphia he knew of a case in which seven hundred indictments were prosecuted on seven hundred chests of tea improperly taken from the custom-house. Other abuses of the same kind were practised under the present law.

Mr. WAYNE said, the gentleman from New York seemed to go upon the ground that there were abuses to be corrected. If the gentleman would suspend his measure, he would pledge himself that the subject should be properly investigated by the Judiciary or some other committee, and proper means resorted to, to correct any existing abuses. For reasons which he referred to, he considered the appropriation bill as an improper place for introducing the measure.

Mr. GILLET opposed the amendment, and stated that the bill did not make any provision for costs in civil suits, and the amendment would, therefore, be inapplicable and inoperative.

Mr. HUNTINGTON advocated the amendment. If the amendment passed, no matter whether the bill provided for costs in civil suits or not, no Solicitor of the Treasury would pay costs except in cases where it appeared that the suits were properly brought, being joined in one action, where they could legally and properly be joined.

Mr. DICKERSON did not think, he said, that an appropriation bill afforded a proper occasion for regulating the mode of conducting suits, but he was willing to carry into effect the laws as they exist. He would remind the attorneys and the courts that it was their duty to see that suits were properly brought.

Mr. BEARDSLEY said this was a very proper subject to be sent to a committee for inquiry as to the existence of abuses and the means of correcting them. But he did not think the proposition of his colleague would remedy the evil, even if it could be properly introduced in an appropriation bill.

Messrs. HORACE EVERETT, SELDEN, CAMBRELENG, GILLET, BURGES, and TURRILL, made some remarks upon the question; after which the amendments to the amendment were rejected; and the question being taken on the original amendment proposed by Mr. SELDEN, it appeared that a quorum had not voted.

Mr. ADAMS, of Massachusetts, suggested to the gentleman from New York, [Mr. Selden,] the expediency of bringing the subject of his amendment before the Judiciary Committee, with a view to its permanent settlement.

The question being again taken, the amendment was rejected.

Mr. McKAY stated that he should, in the House, move an amendment restricting the appropriations for the courts of the United States, in the Territories, to cases arising under the laws of the United States. The estimate of the expenses for the courts in the Territory of Florida, for the year, was $27,000, more than was expended in twelve of the sovereign States of this Union. This happened from the fact that the money was expended upon the cases arising under the local laws of the Territory. His amendment would also apply to the courts in the District of Columbia, where $42,000 were, according to the estimates, to be expended this year, more than was expended in the fifteen or sixteen States of the Union. It was high time, he said, that this monstrous abuse should be corrected.

Mr. VANCE moved to strike out the following clause:

For the salaries of registers and receivers of land offices where there are no sales, $3,500.

After a few words from Messrs. POLK, McKAY, VANCE, and BURGES, the motion was put and rejected.

Mr. ASHLEY moved to amend the bill, by inserting the following:

For surveying the lands in the southwestern part of Missouri, lately purchased from the Catawba tribe of Indians, $30,000.

Mr. FOOT opposed the bill, as sixty thousand dollars was already proposed to be given for the surveying of public lands, in addition to the unexpended balance of former appropriations, he would move to strike out the words " in addition to," and insert " including," so as to put limits to the amount to be granted for this purpose.

Mr. ASHLEY sustained his amendment; which was finally agreed to.

Mr. WHITE, of Florida, opposed the amendment proposed by Mr. Foot, as, he said, if it was adopted, it would press more severely on the Territory which he had the honor to represent, than any other. The acquisitions made from the Indians recently, which required to be surveyed, made it necessary, from a due regard to the interest of the United States.

Mr. POLK explained the amount of unexpended balances on hand. After which,

Mr. FOOT consented to withdraw his amendment.

The following items were then severally agreed to:

For surveying the public lands, in addition to the unexpended balance of former appropriations, sixty thousand dollars.

For the salaries of two keepers of the public archives in Florida, one thousand dollars.

For compensation to the recorder, two commissioners, and translator, for the final adjustment of private land claims in Missouri, per act of ninth July, eighteen hundred and thirty-two, including an unexpended balance of former appropriations of eight hundred and ninety-five dollars and seventy-two cents, the sum of five thousand one hundred and seven dollars and twenty-eight cents.

For contingent expenses and office rent of said board, five hundred dollars.

For contingent expenses of said board, for eighteen hundred and thirty-four, including compensation to the agent employed to convey the annual report of the board to the seat of Government,

including also expenses incurred by commissioners in taking testimony, and for payment of balance of claims admitted in due course of settlement at the treasury, one thousand nine hundred and thirty-eight dollars and sixty-two cents.

For stationery and books for the offices of the commissioners of loans, one thousand two hundred dollars.

For registers of ships and vessels, and lists of crews, two thousand three hundred dollars.

Mr. McKAY inquired why the amount for miscellaneous claims should be increased to 20,000 dollars?

Mr. POLK moved to reduce the amount to 12,000 dollars. Agreed to.

For the salaries of the ministers of the United States to Great Britain, France, Spain, and Russia, 36,000 dollars.

Mr. FOOT moved to strike out " Great Britain and Russia," and to reduce the amount to 18,000 dollars.

Mr. F. said, as an appropriation of this nature had been made last year for ambassadors to these courts, where there had been no ambassadors, the amount ought to be at present in the treasury, and was therefore unnecessary.

Mr. ARCHER said the statement was incorrect; that although the appropriations were made, they had been exhausted for the objects which they were intended. He presented an account of the expenditures out of these appropriations for charge d'affaires, and other expenses of these courts.

Mr. FOOT inquired by what authority a specific appropriation was applied to other objects by the department, from one object to another.

Mr. ARCHER considered that the appropriations were made to the ministers to foreign countries, whether going there as ambassadors, charge d'affaires, or other designation.

Mr. FOOT remarked that there was a distinction kept up in the bill, by which separate appropriations for all the grades employed——

Mr. ARCHER meant to say that there was no power in the House to dictate to the President what grade of ministers he should send to foreign courts. He maintained that the appropriations having been employed, as he had shown them to be, was not an improper transfer of money appropriated from one object to another.

After some remarks from Mr. WAYNE,

Mr. J. Q. ADAMS condemned the practice of sending ministers abroad for a short period, to receive the salary and outfit of a whole year, as well as that of substituting charges, or other minor grades, to do the duties of the higher grades, as leading to much expense, and lessening the importance of the country in the eyes of foreigners. He would vote for the amendment proposed by the honorable member from Connecticut, as he did not know there would be any minister appointed to Great Britain, at least until a nomination was made, otherwise he feared it would be only encouraging the practice of making such appointments during the recess. With respect to the Court of Russia, he doubted whether it was necessary to have a minister there.

Mr. DAVIS, of South Carolina, seconded the proposition to strike out, on the ground that, by the Constitution, until the officers were appointed, by and with the consent of the Senate, they were not authorized to make the appropriation. If was contrary to the whole diplomatic system of the Government, on the ground of economy, and asked what object was there in sending ministers to England, whilst there was no business to be transacted there which could not be as well done by consuls? These officials, he contended at length, would suffice for all the purposes of commerce, and in a well-regulated republic there should not be any other want.

Mr. ARCHER replied to the arguments of the members who preceded him, and maintained that there was no misapplication of the sums appropriated, or any violation of the usage heretofore observed. The House had no constitutional power to interfere with the Executive. He was surprised from the statement expressed by the honorable member from Massachusetts, from him who had himself represented his country at this very court, with so much ability, that there was any necessity for a minister there. Was it not become the first, the most powerful court in the world? Was it not

our most constant and most steady friend for years past? He rather thought Government were to be censured for not having a minister there at all times; and the honorable member was the last person from whom he expected to hear such a declaration. He was authorized, in answer to the ideas thrown out that there was no appointment to be made this session, to state explicitly, that it was the intention of the President to nominate to these courts, during the present session, unless, in the mean time, circumstances should occur, which, in his judgment, should render it unnecessary.

Mr. WAYNE maintained that the present practice was not different from that which had been whilst the gentleman from Massachusetts was connected with the Government. If it was at all different, then he would admit he had some reason for his complaints. But the gentleman from Massachusetts ought to have known the salaries were paid in proportion to the time the persons are employed abroad and returning back to this country. Although it had occurred that a large sum was paid for the Russian mission in the case of Mr. Randolph, yet as that arose from his indisposition or misfortune, which could not be averted, it might occur to any Administration. They were not therefore censurable. He referred to the various nominations made to England, and the circumstances connected with the recall of Mr. Van Buren by the Senate, as having added to the expenditure, but not reflecting on the Executive, or warranting this to be made to him a matter of insinuation or reproach.

Mr. POLK briefly remarked that the appropriations now made were of the usual character, and upon estimates prepared by the department, which was the usual way in which the Executive intention of making these appointments was known to Congress.

Mr. DAVIS rejoined, and said that as far as his vote was concerned, he would support the rights vested in him as a representative, by withholding the appropriations to all nominations not filled up, as he contended, according to the Constitution, and thus say to the President, you shall comply with its provisions.

Mr. ADAMS rose to make some explanation, but gave way to

Mr. MERCER, who said, as this amendment was not to be disposed of lightly, and it was then close upon six o'clock, he would move that the committee rise.

The motion prevailed.

Thereupon, the committee rose.

The bills laid aside early in the day, were reported to the House, with the progress in the appropriation bill; after which,

The House adjourned.

IN SENATE.

THURSDAY, *May* 1, 1834.

A message upon executive business was received from the President of the United States, by Mr. DONELSON, his Private Secretary.

Mr. McKEAN presented the memorial of two hundred and sixteen inhabitants of the town of Milton, and county of Northumberland, Pennsylvania;

The memorial of between twelve and thirteen hundred inhabitants of Susquehanna county, Pennsylvania;

And the memorial of about sixteen hundred citizens of Bradford county, Pennsylvania;

Praying a restoration of the deposites to the Bank of the United States, and a recharter of that institution.

The memorials were read, referred to the Committee on Finance, and ordered to be printed.

Mr. McKEAN presented the proceedings of a Jackson and Wolf meeting of a large number of the inhabitants of Northampton county, Pennsylvania, approving of the course of the Executive in removing the deposites from the Bank of the United States, and opposed to the recharter of said bank.

The proceedings were read, referred to the Committee on Finance, and ordered to be printed.

Mr. CLAY presented a memorial signed by citizens of Bald Eagle township, Centre county, Pennsylvania, in favor of the restoration of the deposites to the Bank of the United States; which was read, referred to the Committee on Finance, and ordered to be printed.

Mr. CHAMBERS presented the proceedings of a meeting of citizens of Baltimore, in opposition to some of the doctrines of the protest of the President of the United States to the resolutions of the Senate with regard to the removal of the deposites.

Mr. CHAMBERS rose and said, he was requested by the officers of a large public meeting, just held by the Whigs of Baltimore, to present its proceedings to the Senate. The meeting was held in consequence of the invitation of the President in his appeal to the people. They had maturely considered it, and passed sentence upon the various questions which were the subject-matter of it, and now, here it was in the shape of a special verdict, in which the people of Baltimore have set forth their opinions. The gentleman from Tennessee [Mr. GRUNDY] might suppose that this allusion to Whig principles implied the opposite of it in his party, and that this coverlet or blanket was not broad enough to include us all; but, at all events, they were so well satisfied with this covering, that they did not mean to be disrobed of it. Mr. C. then commented at large on the President's protest, condemning the doctrines contained in it. He alluded to the Panama mission, and the opinions communicated to the Senate by Mr. Adams, when President, of his power to send a minister there in the recess, and that gentlemen who now sustained the Administration condemned those opinions.

Mr. C. concluded, by moving that the proceedings be read, and take the usual reference.

Mr. GRUNDY said he had carefully abstained from saying anything in the discussions upon these memorials. His constituents had sent none here, and he was inclined to leave them to the expression of their own sentiments in their own time and way. He was now called up for sentiments delivered on another occasion, and he regretted to find his opinions questioned on the presentation of a bank memorial. Between himself and the gentleman from Maryland [Mr. CHAMBERS] the same feeling existed as among all other citizens. We were all patriots and whigs—and all admitted it. But this new name the gentleman was pressing as if it was of some service to him; and he referred to the Panama mission, and says that the opponents of executive usurpation are Whigs. But was the gentleman from Maryland a Whig then—was he of the party then for which he now claims this name? Mr. G. ventured to say that the gentleman then voted for this very power, which was then claimed by the Executive, and about to be exercised. Well, if those who support it now are not as good as their opponents, he could say that the gentleman had improved in his whigism. And whether this was owing to a change in his condition, was matter for his own consideration. But a word in regard to the difference of position which they now occupied. What had Mr. Adams done at that time? Nothing but to give his opinion that he had a right to send such a mission, and therefore he submitted the subject to Congress. The Senate then took it up, as it was their duty to do, and pronounced their opinion. But was Mr. Adams charged with a violation of the Constitution and laws of the country? No, the Senate only differed with him in opinion in regard to the power which he intimated he possessed. Now, the President was directly charged with a violation of the Constitution and laws. Here was something clear, positive, palpable, and tangible. In the other instance there was nothing but an error in judgment imputed.

Mr. G. had no objection whatever that the gentleman from Maryland should call his friends Whigs. All he (Mr. G.) contended against was the assumption that they were the exclusive Whigs, for they were not deserving of the title. If the name was significant of the old tenets upon politics, Mr. G. hoped that the Whigs would include ninety-nine hundredths of the people. Whigs they were, but there was no class exclusively so. Mr. G. admitted that among the friends of the Administration there were a great variety of opinions on various subjects, but that fact only showed that they did not yield their opinions to the opinions or will of one man. We (the friends of the Administration) stood, in our humble judgment, on the principles which were upheld in '99, and which were carried down to the present day. And between the gentleman from Maryland and himself, Mr. G. said there was not so much difference after all. Here was a cover under which we could both get, and, therefore, in regard to their whigism there was not so much difference as the gentleman thought. Mr. G. believed they were Whigs, and we were Whigs, but he hoped the gentleman would not throw the correlative of the term on him, for he thought he did not deserve it; and if the gentleman would be willing to let us all go on as Whigs no inconvenience would result from from it. But when he excludes us who are as true Whigs as any, then we feel an insurrectionary spirit, and we are not quite satisfied with the treatment. These citizens of Baltimore, then, have taken the name of Whigs, and there are none more deserving of it. But when they get a new name, and they make a great boast of it, it seemed like claiming what they never had before. Now, they were Whigs long before this new assumption of the name. They were Whigs in the Revolution, and also in the last war, and the citizens of Baltimore were not doing themselves justice to claim just now what they had borne for the last half century, and it was not right for their friends to put this garment on them as if it were new, when it is an old one, and long worn by them, and is none the worse for wear. He therefore objected to the friends of the Whigs of Baltimore putting this mantle on as for the first time, for they had it before; it was no new invention, or new thing.

But, sir, we go under a name, and a good old one, too, which distinguished us from all others. In the struggle between the elder Adams and Mr. Jefferson, the friends of Mr. Jefferson were called democrats, and the friends of Mr. Adams aristocrats, by way of derision, and the name of republican was assumed. This was significant as to the powers of the General Government and its different branches. Now, this term Whig, will not do as a designation of party, because it includes a majority of all parties. Gentlemen have found out, that the term National Republican will not answer their purpose, because it cannot be spread broad enough to embrace a majority. The *Whigs* would cover everybody; and therefore Mr. G. wanted the gentleman to find some name that would do. National Republican would not cover the South—it would not cross the Potomac. You might build your contemplated fine bridge across that river, and still it would not cross it for the South, not even so far as Virginia or North Carolina; and as to South Carolina, it could not get within sight of it. South Carolina was fond of a name which she would not swap for it, because these *Nullifiers* of the South wanted to establish their own principles. Well, the time was, when they could not get out of the limits of South Carolina with them; and they were quite pent up there—but they seem to have expanded since. Mr. G. said he had not read, but he had heard much talk of the nullifying gentlemen lately visiting north of this place; and they were taken to the bosom by men who, twelve months ago, were ready to denounce them as traitors. In Philadelphia, too, these gentlemen were received not only with impunity, but with applause. This only showed how changeable we are, and he could not say how it might all be six months hence, for if fifteen thousand men in Baltimore twelve months ago considered that almost treason which they were now hugging to their bosoms as patriotism, we did not know what it might be twelve months hence. They had given us their opinions to-day, and by that time they might change them, and therefore he could not calculate where they might be found hereafter. Now, he took no exception whatever to all this, and yesterday, or the day preceding, when the gentleman from Kentucky [Mr. CLAY] was lecturing Governor Wolf about changing his opinions, it was saying nothing more than what was applicable to the gentleman himself. Governor Wolf was formerly in favor of the bank, and now he was against it, no doubt from the most honest convictions; the Senator himself had changed his own opinion on the same subject; therefore, no censure could attach to gentlemen for entertaining one opinion to-day, and on further consideration, changing it, and acting on it. So, some of the citizens of Baltimore were once friends of the President; they had now

changed, but might they not come back? Mr. G. did not think it strange that there should be changes in our large cities. They were suffering distress, and they had been told that the President was the cause of it; but when they examined this matter, they might find out that the cause of it was of a very different nature. Mr. G. thought the answer of the gentleman from Kentucky to his speech was sufficient, and yet the gentleman from Maryland comes in and adds a new codicil to the will, and the codicil (a thing that is very uncommon) is longer than the will itself. Mr. G. said, he did not like personal remarks. He knew himself to be weak, vulnerable, and very imperfect, and therefore he did not like to be assailed.

Mr. CHAMBERS inquired what he had said which had grieved the honorable member?

Mr. GRUNDY replied, that he had not been grieved at anything the honorable member had said. The burden he had imposed on him was light, and easy to be borne. But what he said in his speech had been answered, and he took exception to having it answered over again. But he would add nothing more upon these memorials; but if they came from his State, he would endeavor to do them justice. These memorialists had taken up a subject, and decided that, in the absence of all legislative purposes, where there is no design, avowed or implied, of legislative action, either House of Congress has a right to take up the conduct of any individual, discuss it, and decide upon it. If we should adopt this course, we would have but little time for legitimate legislation. We should try the President, and condemn him, and then the Secretary of State, and then take up Governor Wolf, if you please, and decide on him; and so go on and decide upon all other officers in the Government against whom we may entertain prejudices. Then we should take up the Governor of South Carolina, and Mr. G. thought he would be in a very bad way; he would probably be hung by the sentence of this body. We should then proceed to examine all the public men in the country. Well, this might all be right, but he thought we should not have full time to make all these examinations. He thought we came here to make laws, and provide for the public good and general welfare; but if we were to give opinions on all the public men in the country—it might be a more pleasant employment, and perhaps, in the opinions of some gentlemen, redound more to the good of mankind to censure public men, than make laws—we should do little else. He would not, therefore, subscribe to the doctrine that we have a right merely to express an opinion, and especially for the Senate, because we are the ultimate triers of all officers of the General Government; and if we have a right, beforehand, to enter judgment, impeachment is a mere matter of form. He could not, therefore, concur in the sentiments expressed by the citizens of Baltimore.

Mr. CHAMBERS here expatiated at some length upon the cognomen of Whig, adopted by the parties in opposition to the Administration.

Mr. GRUNDY replied that he yielded to the gentleman from Maryland entirely, as a soldier of age and experience, for he would not enter the ranks with him. But the gentleman said that he (Mr. G.) had entered into the ranks of the Jackson party, and must soon leave the name; for Jackson must die, and with that event the name. But (Mr. G. remarked) the Jefferson party did not expire with his administration or his life. It has grown up since into three or four parties. Were there not three or four Jefferson dinners given lately? He (Mr. G.) was invited to one of them in Philadelphia, although he did not go, and what was perhaps worse, neglected to send an apology. But the gentleman from South Carolina [Mr. Preston] was there; and the gentleman near me [Mr. Forsyth] was at another of them, the one to which he (Mr. G.) had been invited; so that he did not know how it might be at the death of General Jackson. Now he (Mr. G.) would say no more on this occasion—the gentleman from Maryland did not understand him, and he could not make him understand him. These memorialists were Whigs, and Mr. G. would not deny it. But good things were not made exclusively for any set of men, they were made for all mankind. And when a man was making a monopoly of a good thing, he did not think he was doing right. So, if one man, or party of men, shall, by force, appropriate the whole territory of a nation to himself or themselves, and refuse the rights of appropriation to others, it would be wrong. Now, Whig belongs to all friends of their country in common. The term Christian includes a variety of religious sects; yet, if one sect should set themselves up and say that we alone are Christians, would it not look like crowding the others out? In the same sense Mr. G. understood the term Whig; and let us all stand together as Whigs, and let our particular or peculiar political tenets be judged of by our country.

Mr. CLAY said the gentleman from Tennessee had alluded to the change of his opinions in favor of the bank. That change was made upon the most mature deliberation and conviction of the necessity of a bank, and he was willing to leave it to posterity to judge of the sufficiency of his reasons for changing. He was opposed to the bank in 1811, and in 1816, the experience of the war resulted in the establishment of the present Whig bank. No public man had a right to change but upon long deliberation and good reason, but Governor Wolf had changed in three days, and without any alteration in the state of the case.

Mr. GRUNDY replied that he had no doubt of the sincere honesty which produced the change in the gentleman from Kentucky in reference to the bank, and he need not look to posterity to do him justice. Some of his political adversaries already did him justice, more than others would do General Jackson, if he were brought before us for an infraction of the Constitution and laws. Governor Wolf was convinced of the propriety of his course. He had no acquaintance with Governor Wolf. He had heard the gentleman from Pennsylvania [Mr. McKean] say he had acted with him in Congress for six years; he was the Secretary of the Commonwealth while Governor Wolf was the Chief Magistrate of Pennsylvania; and that he was a man of great firmness and decision. It did not always depend on time whether a man should change his opinions or not, but upon surrounding circumstances. A state of things might exist which would teach his judgment the necessity of changing. But it was said that he (Mr. G.) had delivered a speech in favor of nullification. He did not know how that was, but if he did, he had been severely punished for it, and if he had now abandoned it, he stuck closely to State rights. He had been pressed so hard upon nullification, that he found it dangerous ground to stand on, and he had just moved a little off to the State-rights ground. But he repented sincerely, and the citizens of Tennessee generously and magnanimously forgave him for the temporary dereliction, if indeed he was guilty of any. And now, he was not willing to call the Nullifiers traitors, because they loved their country. But this Whig bank of 1816—Mr. G. said it was the first time in all his life that he had heard a bank called a Whig. Now, what were the principles of the Whigs of the time of Charles II, when it was said the party originated? Why they were against royal prerogative and against corporate rights of every kind. And if we were in favor of prerogative we were not in favor of great moneyed monopolies. If we have prerogative on one side they have monopolies on the other.

Mr. McKEAN thought these untimely desultory discussions had at least produced one beneficial result. It had, on this occasion, taught us that, when we were laying snares for our neighbors, how liable we were to get caught ourselves. The two honorable Senators from Kentucky and Tennessee [Messrs. Clay and Grundy] had succeeded admirably in fixing on each other the charge of inconsistency, if an honest change of opinion could thus be characterized. This had grown out of the introduction of the name of Governor Wolf into the debates upon the presentation of memorials. The honorable Senator from Kentucky seemed to think, if a certain degree of inconsistency could be fixed on him, he might then consent to be associated with Governor Wolf. After what has been exhibited, whether the gentleman would think that further proof of his qualifications were necessary, he would leave for him to decide; and much as the Governor and his friends might desire the association, it would not become them to solicit the connexion. But it seemed now that the degree of consistency was to be estimated by the length of time it took to change an opinion. The gentlemen had both changed on the subject of the bank, but they had taken more time to do so than Governor Wolf had, as had been alleged. But he denied that there was any positive proof that Governor Wolf had changed. He, however, did not pretend to doubt that Governor Wolf's opinions of the present bank had undergone some change. But he (Mr. McK.) had stated on a former occasion as a matter of his own knowledge, and would now repeat, that Governor Wolf's opinions as to the utility and necessity of a national bank had not changed. His principal object, however, in rising, (Mr. McK. said,) was to take notice of an assertion made the other day by the Senator from Kentucky, and which he had in substance repeated to-day, viz: that he [Mr. Clay] could prove in a court of justice that Governor Wolf, three days prior to the 26th of February last, promised to send a message to the Legislature of a directly opposite character to that which he communicated on that day. He did not doubt that the Senator had been so informed; therefore, what he intended to say could not be considered as alluding personally to the honorable gentleman, and it was not probable the gentleman would have an opportunity of adducing his proof in a court of justice: he would put the question directly at issue, and would now assert that he questioned the veracity of any man who would make such a declaration, and from this point he would not be driven by anything but the testimony itself.

Mr. CLAY said the Senator from Pennsylvania would, he presumed, do him the justice to say, that he had not, on this occasion, introduced the name of the Governor of Pennsylvania. It was introduced by the Senator from Tennessee, [Mr. Grundy;] but with regard to the promise of the Governor, Mr. C. said he had it from a gentleman of respectability, whose word would be as readily believed as Governor Wolf's.

Mr. McKEAN said, then I repeat my assertion, in unequivocal terms, that I question the veracity of any man who has, or may make such a declaration, and I challenge the gentleman to produce his proof.

Some further remarks were made by Mr. CLAY and Mr. GRUNDY; when, on motion of

Mr. POINDEXTER, the memorial was laid upon the table.

At half past four o'clock, on motion of

Mr. WEBSTER, the Senate proceeded to the consideration of executive business, and, after some time spent therein,

The Senate adjourned.

HOUSE OF REPRESENTATIVES.

Thursday, May 1, 1834.

Mr. J. Q. ADAMS, agreeably to notice, asked leave of the House to introduce a bill to prohibit the corporations of Georgetown, Alexandria, and Washington, from issuing promissory notes of any denomination less than ten dollars. Leave being granted, the bill was, on motion of Mr. Adams, referred to the Committee on the District of Columbia.

Mr. LINCOLN rose and said he had just seen in the official paper, published in this city, some aspersions cast upon an honorable colleague of his and himself. Mr. L. was proceeding to make some remarks, when he was called to order by the Chair, who stated that the subject to which he referred was not before the House.

Mr. LINCOLN then asked the unanimous consent of the House to take up, for consideration, a resolution which he submitted on Tuesday last, making sundry inquiries in relation to the administration of the Post Office Department.

An objection being made, Mr. L. moved a suspension of the rule, and thereupon called for the yeas and nays, which were ordered.

The question being taken, it was determined in the negative: Yeas 93, noes 62. (Not two-thirds.)

Mr. ASHLEY reported a bill providing for certain surveys of the public lands; which was read twice.

Mr. A. moved the engrossment of the bill, and

Mr. CONNOR its commitment to the Committee of the Whole, in the regular course.

After some conversation, on motion of Mr.

ASHLEY, the bill was committed to the Committee of the Whole on the state of the Union.

Mr. WHITE, of New York, called up the bill to legalize certain foreign silver coin; and it was ordered to be read a third time.

The following bills were ordered to be engrossed for a third reading:

The act to extend the time for carrying into effect the treaty with France; and the act to extend the time for carrying into effect the convention with the Two Sicilies.

APPROPRIATIONS.

On motion of Mr. POLK, the House went into Committee of the Whole on the state of the Union, (Mr. HUBBARD in the chair,) upon the general appropriation bill.

The question being upon Mr. FOOT's motion to strike out Great Britain and Russia, and to insert eighteen instead of thirty-six in the following clause:

For the salaries of the ministers of the United States to Great Britain, France, Spain, and Russia, thirty-six thousand dollars,

Mr. J. Q. ADAMS rose (he said) to explain the grounds on which he supported the motion, and to reply to some remarks which had fallen from the gentlemen from Virginia [Mr. ARCHER] and Georgia [Mr. WAYNE.] The gentleman from Virginia expressed his surprise that I should underrate the importance of the mission to Russia. I do not (said Mr. A.) underrate it. I know, and ought to know better than any other member, how highly important that mission has been to the interests of this country. He did not attach the same importance to our relations with that Power now, but still he considered them as sufficiently important to require the retention of a minister of the first grade at that court. He objected to the appropriation of salaries for ministers at courts where in fact we had only chargés des affaires. There ought not, he thought, to have been an interval of a month in the missions of the first grade to Great Britain and Russia. Year after year we had made the appropriations, all the money had been expended, and no ministers had been appointed. He had yesterday objected to sending ministers for short terms, with full outfits and salaries, and had remarked that one was sent for the term of six weeks. In the course of the debate the gentleman from Georgia had attempted to convert that remark into a personal reflection upon an individual who was now in his grave. That circumstance would alone have sealed his lips forever in relation to his conduct in that mission. He did not refer to the circumstances of that mission with a view to censure that individual, for he was now far beyond the reach of his censure; but he did mention it as one of the faults of this Administration. The gentleman from Georgia had brought before the House the great objects which these ministers had accomplished. He had alluded to the number of treaties which had been made, and the importance of the negotiations carried through.

Sir, were I to admit that these negotiations were as honorable to the country as he supposes them to have been, would that be any answer to the objection that the salaries of these Ministers are doubled and trebled by the short term of their appointment, and that they spend their time at watering places, &c., instead of spending it in the duties of their mission? Allusions were made to the arrangement with Great Britain. He regretted that this subject had been brought into the discussion. Was there not a gentleman in the other wing of this building, and another gentleman holding a high office in this city, whose honor was concerned in this question, and who could not be here to answer him on this floor? He would barely, therefore, on this subject, say, that if we judged of these marvellous missions by their effects, he would send gentlemen down to that part of the Union which was most interested on this subject, and ask what have been the effects of the colonial arrangement upon their interests. Not as it would affect himself, but as it affected others who were absent, was he unwilling to go into this discussion.

Mr. A. here referred to the annunciation yesterday made by the chairman of the Committee of Ways and Means, of the intention of the President to nominate ministers to these courts, during the session, unless it should be deemed unnecessary. He thought the qualification had much meaning in it. The annunciation appeared to him to be oracular.

Mr. ARCHER rose to explain. If the gentleman would allow him, he would let the House understand why he used the words of the Secretary of State, in communicating to the House information on this subject. If he had answered in any other manner, he might have committed either the Administration or himself. There was evidently a reservation implied in the reply, but he would not call it an improper reservation. He did not choose to put the reply in his own words, and therefore used the words of the Secretary of State, who had said to him that the President would make nominations to Great Britain and Russia, during the session, unless circumstances should arise which would render it unnecessary. He gave the message as it was given to him.

Mr. ADAMS. Precisely so. The honorable chairman has acted with perfect prudence and propriety. What I simply say is, that what he gave to the House is an oracle. It is not my fault, nor that of the honorable chairman, that it is not understood. The oracle was not intended to be understood. He took it for granted that these circumstances would in due time happen, and that the nominations would not be made. Whenever the chairman was authorized to say that the nominations would be made, his objections to the appropriations would fall to the ground. He would vote cordially and heartily for them, if he could have a pledge that they would be made. Mr. A. concluded with some further remarks, of a desultory character.

Mr. WAYNE had no desire or intention of occupying the time of the House by pursuing the course taken by the gentleman from Massachusetts, [Mr. ADAMS.] Did he consider it to be proper or necessary, it would not be a difficult task to show that the present Administration, in its negotiations, particularly with Great Britain, had accomplished what the former one had not done. The gentleman declines going into the particulars of the negotiation with Great Britain, because two distinguished gentlemen who were engaged in them under appointments by the present Administration were not present in this House to defend their conduct. He had only to say, that the conduct of those gentlemen on that subject, was part of the public history of the country. Individual statements from those gentlemen were, therefore, totally unnecessary. Their conduct was upon paper, and had become a part of our political annals. No consideration of delicacy towards those persons, as being absent, should prevent the fullest discussion that was necessary to throw light upon their conduct of this negotiation. The gentleman had introduced this subject, on the preceding day, by insinuating that the ministers appointed by the present Administration had remained but a very short time at the places of their mission. In referring to the case of Mr. Randolph, it was natural to recollect that of Mr. King, who had been sent to negotiate with Great Britain, respecting the colonial trade, without his instructions. The gentleman had not been pleased to allude to the sending of Mr. Gallatin, who was directed by the former Administration to abandon the principles which had been persisted in by our Government for a long series of years, and which were the basis of the instructions given to Mr. Rush in 1824. Ministers, he believed, had been sent quite as often by the former Administration as the present. He did not allude to this circumstance as a matter of reproach; but it would have been at least desirable that the ministers sent by the former Administration should have been furnished with the necessary instructions. They might possibly, in that case, have closed the negotiations which were not finished until it was done by the successor of Mr. Barbour.

If he understood the grounds of apprehension now expressed by gentlemen, they were, that a minister might be sent to England without the consent of the Senate. The House had the authority of the gentleman from Massachusetts [Mr. ADAMS] that a minister at London was necessary. Why, then, strike the provision for his salary out of this bill? Is it upon suspicion that the President will not do his duty? Suspicions of that kind were, perhaps, suitable for newspaper discussions, but he could not regard them as furnishing any basis for legislative action. The gentleman stated, in the former debate, that the interests of the country required the appointment of a minister to London; that a chargé d'affaires was not capable, from his inferior rank, to afford adequate protection to the interests of the country at that court; and he now advocates the motion for striking out the proposed salary for a minister, and proposes to substitute the salary of a chargé. He did not understand the consistency of this course, any more than he did the criticism upon the reply which had been made to the inquiry of the chairman of the Committee of Foreign Affairs. That reply had been called oracular. He could not imagine why it should be so called in an offensive sense. He did not know what other answer could be given to the inquiry than what had been made. It was a subject upon which, from the nature of things, a precise answer could not, and ought not, to be given. It might be absolutely necessary to have a minister sent to England forthwith. The customary appropriation for the salary should not therefore be withheld. On the other hand, a question deeply important to the territorial extent of one of the States of the Union, might induce that State to request that no minister be sent at this time. He disclaimed knowing anything relative to these affairs which was not equally well known to others. As to these inquiries, he deprecated any attempt to go beyond the constitutional rights of the House. If it was rightful to require official information relative to the intention to send a minister, it was equally so to know who is the person intended to be sent; then the question, as to the propriety of the appropriation, might turn upon a discussion of the character and fitness of the individual proposed to be nominated. Such signs of the times he deprecated.

As to one of the insinuations of the gentleman from Massachusetts, that a minister had been appointed with permission to go wherever he pleased, what minister had been so appointed? In the case of Mr. Randolph, no latitude had been taken which common reason would not justify. We are daily granting permission to the members of this House to leave their duties, upon less pressing grounds than those upon which Mr. Randolph absented himself for the benefit of his health. To the other topics alluded to by the gentleman, he felt capable of making conclusive replies, but did not feel justified in trespassing any further upon the time of the committee.

Mr. COULTER was anxious that the question might be divided so as to separate the appropriation for a minister to Russia, which he was willing to support, from that to England, which he was not willing, after having voted in favor of such an appropriation formerly, and no minister had been appointed. Congress have placed upon the statute book their opinion that a minister of the highest grade should be sent to London. The Executive has decided otherwise. The dignity and character of the House now required that the overture which had been slighted should not be repeated without a change of circumstances. Mr. C. concluded by moving to amend the amendment by striking out England.

Mr. EVANS obtained the floor, but gave way to

Mr. W. R. DAVIS, who proposed to amend the bill by adding a proviso, that no minister be appointed to Russia or England, without the consent of the Senate.

Mr. FOOT withdrew his original motion to strike out, and accepted Mr. DAVIS'S substitute.

Mr. EVANS then proceeded into a prolonged explanation upon the question of the colonial trade, which he contended the negotiations under the present Administration had left worse than it was found.

Mr. WAYNE, in reply to the gentleman from Maine, [Mr. EVANS,] went into a historical account of our controversy with Great Britain on the subject of colonial intercourse, and contended that the arrangement made by Mr. McLane was more favorable to our interests than any which we ever had before, and that it came nearer to the point of our claims than any which we ever had, or, perhaps, ever can have. We had, he said, established

principles under that arrangement, for which we had been contending for thirty years, and which ultimately would be of high advantage to the country.

Mr. CAMBRELENG rose to speak on the subject, but calls being made for the question, he yielded the floor.

Mr. HORACE EVERETT rose to ask whether the power was claimed by the President to make appointments during the recess? His object was to have a disclaimer of this power from the friends of the Administration. He put the question to the chairman of the Committee on Foreign Relations.

Mr. ARCHER said it was not for him to say how others construed the Constitution. He construed it for himself, and the gentleman from Vermont construed it for himself. But thinking that the Executive had no right to make appointments during the recess, he was bound to think that he would not attempt to exercise the right. He believed it was the intention of the President, as he had stated to the House, to make nominations during the session, if nothing occurred to render it unnecessary, and he could not even imagine the occurrence of any circumstances which would render it unnecessary. He expressed the hope that the gentleman from South Carolina [Mr. Davis] would withdraw his amendment. We had the right to refuse appropriations, but not to annex conditions to them.

Mr. DAVIS said, that after the declaration on the part of the Administration, his amendment would imply no want of confidence in the Executive. The gentleman, he thought, was mistaken in supposing that we could not restrict appropriations. What was the meaning of specific appropriations? Was it not appropriations limited to specific objects? He had used the language which was always used to effect limitations.

Mr. BINNEY was sorry, he said, to see the proposition of the gentleman from South Carolina substituted for that of the gentleman from Connecticut. It was not customary to qualify our appropriations. We made no appropriations for salaries, unless upon the supposition that they are to be made use of for constitutional appointments. The condition proposed could not be introduced, unless we believed that the money would be expended for salaries of ministers unconstitutionally appointed; and, if so, the best way would be to strike out the appropriation altogether. He should vote against the amendment, and renew the proposition of the gentleman from Connecticut. He went into some remarks in opposition to the appropriations.

Mr. BEARDSLEY said it was admitted by the gentlemen from Massachusetts and Pennsylvania, that we ought to be represented at the Court of St. James by a minister of the first grade. He did not understand any one on this floor as controverting this opinion, except the gentleman from South Carolina, who, in his remarks yesterday, expressed the opinion that we needed no minister there; but from his remarks to-day, and his amendment, he inferred that even he was desirous of having a minister appointed to Great Britain, provided he should be appointed by the President, with the advice and consent of the Senate. As far as he could collect the sentiment of the committee, it was, that we should have a minister. What, then, he would ask, was the duty of this House? Is it not to provide the salary? Are we to look beyond that, and ask whether the President will appoint a proper person, or make the appointment in a proper manner? Were we to withhold the appropriation, because the President may appoint a minister in an improper way, or a way which we may consider unconstitutional? This was a ground never taken before—not in the discussion on the Panama mission. Mr. B. thought that if we performed our own duty—if we determined that we would have a minister, and made the proper appropriation, we might well leave it to the President and the Senate to perform their duty. What had we to do with the appointments? Nothing. In reference to the amendment of the gentleman from South Carolina, he remarked, that we might, with equal propriety, ingraft a similar qualification on all other appropriations—on those for the heads of departments and their subordinates, and refuse them all any compensation, unless they are appointed by and with the advice and consent of the Senate. Was there any precedent for such a course? We might say that we would not pay them, unless they were constitutionally appointed. But there were two constitutional ways of making appointments—one with, and another without, the consent of the Senate. Where was the precedent for such a limitation? It was altogether new. As to the annunciation from the State Department, it appeared to him to be merely to the effect, that if the President should think the public interest required that a minister should be sent to England, he would do his part, by making the nomination. This was the fair, if not the strict, construction of the words—words which were taken down, not by the Secretary of State, but by the chairman of the Committee on Foreign Relations. We had, then, the assurance that the President would act.

But it was said that we have facts and circumstances to show that his design was, to refrain from performing his duty till the Senate adjourned, to the end that he might then exert the power of appointment free from the control of the Senate. If he did believe this, he would still vote for the appropriation. He would perform his own duty, and leave the President to perform his, in good faith or in bad faith; and if the President performed it in bad faith, he would hold him responsible for it to this House. After some further remarks, Mr. B. expressed the hope, that not only the amendment of the gentleman from South Carolina would be rejected, but any other which contemplated a qualification or refusal of the appropriation, if the House believed that we ought to have a mission to England.

Mr. CHILTON rose, amidst loud calls for the question, and spoke at some length against the appropriations for the missions to England and Russia.

Mr. LANE said it was not his intention to detain the committee by making a speech, nor would he follow the example of the gentleman from Kentucky, [Mr. Chilton,] by saying he would not make a speech, and then speak a half hour and say nothing about the subject.

It was his object to call the attention of the members of the committee, and particularly those who had taken part in the debate, to the position in which they stand. The bill contains an appropriation for the pay of ministers to England and Russia. The motion is to amend by striking it out.

Spread the arguments of gentlemen in favor of this motion upon the canvass, and what (said Mr. L.) is the picture? It is admitted by all, that such ministers should be appointed as are called for by the honor and the best interest of this Government, and due to the last of these courts. It is also admitted that before such appointment can be constitutionally made, the appropriation must be granted by this House. To accomplich this object, the same gentlemen, in the same arguments, and in the same breath, urge the striking the appropriation from the bill. This (said Mr. L.) is the picture as drawn by gentlemen themselves, and he would now call upon the committee, and particularly those who had contributed to the draft, to look upon it, if they can, without a blush.

One word (said Mr. L.) for his honorable and eloquent friend from Pennsylvania, [Mr. Binney.] This honorable gentlemen had said he would vote for the appropriation, provided he could be assured that the President would send the nominations to the Senate during the present session of Congress.

A letter is read from the Secretary of State by the honorable chairman of Foreign Relations, stating it was the intention of the President of the United States to make these nominations during the session. And behold, the gentleman says this is both satisfactory and conclusive to his mind, that the President will wait till after the close of the session, and then make the appointments, without the advice and consent of the Senate. This, to his mind, (said Mr. L.,) was a strange conclusion, even "passing strange." It brought to his recollection (said Mr. L.) the story of a young, artless, but credulous girl. A young gentleman, for whom, in the sequel of the story it appeared, she had some kind tender thoughts, made her a visit. They walked out in the evening; the silence was broken by his saying the moon was full and bright. Not the least objection to marry you, sir, was the ready reply. So fond of her lover, so willing to marry, that she took moon for marry. So with the honorable gentleman. He is so fond of opposition—so willing to rate at the appropriation, that when the President says he intends to nominate during the session, he is understood to say *he will* not.

Mr. J. REED briefly replied to Mr. Beardsley and Mr. Adams, expressed the grounds of his objection to the amendment moved by Mr. Davis, who modified his amendment, and made a few remarks in reply to Mr. Adams.

The question was then taken, and negatived, without a division.

Mr. FOOT renewed his motion to strike out the words "Great Britain and Russia."

On the call of Mr. COULTER, the question on striking out was put separately, and negatived. Yeas 69, nays 101.

The item appropriating $58,500 for salaries of chargés d'affaires to Portugal, Denmark, Sweden, Holland, Turkey, Belgium, Brazil, Buenos Ayres, Chili, Peru, Mexico, Central America, and New Grenada, having been read—

Mr. ADAMS, after some remarks, wished to inquire what information had been communicated as to the mission to the eight places last named.

Mr. ARCHER rose to reply, but gave way to

Mr. PATTON, who moved the committee rise, which was carried; and

The House adjourned.

IN SENATE.

Friday, *May* 2, 1834.

PETITIONS.

Mr. PRENTISS presented the proceedings of a convention of delegates from the several towns of Windsor county, Vermont, and also a memorial signed by fifteen hundred and fifty-one inhabitants of that county, in favor of the restoration of the deposites to the Bank of the United States, and in favor of the recharter of the said institution; which were read, referred to the Committee on Finance, and ordered to be printed.

Mr. SWIFT presented a memorial, of a similar character, from inhabitants of Addison county, Vermont, upon which a like order was taken.

Mr. WEBSTER presented a memorial from a large number of citizens of Boston, on the subject of the existing state of the coins of the country. Mr. W. said the memorialists complained that the disparity in the real value of the gold and silver coins compared with their nominal value, and also the expiration recently of certain laws making foreign coins a legal tender in payment of debts, had produced considerable inconvenience in the commercial world. Mr. W. moved the reference of the memorial to the Committee on Finance; and he would use the occasion to say that the committee had had a bill under consideration and in preparation for some weeks past, applicable to this subject, and the same matter was also under consideration in the other end of the Capitol. So that the memorialists would perceive that their wishes had been anticipated in a great measure by Congress.

The memorial was referred.

Mr. EWING presented a memorial, signed by about seven hundred and fifty inhabitants of Ross county, Ohio, and another signed by about one hundred citizens of Vermillion township, Richland county, Ohio, both in favor of the restoration of the deposites and the recharter of the Bank of the United States.

REPORTS OF COMMITTEES.

Mr. POINDEXTER, from the Committee on Public Lands, asked to be discharged from the further consideration of the petition of certain Choctaw chiefs, and also to be discharged from the further consideration of the petition of the Trustees of the Indiana Teachers' Seminary; which was agreed to.

Mr. MOORE, from the Committee on Revolutionary Claims reported a bill from the House of Representatives, with an amendment, for the relief of the legal representatives of Joseph Torry, deceased.

Also, a bill from the House, with an amend-

ment, for the relief of the legal representatives of George Hurlbert, deceased.

Mr. CLAY, from the Committee on Public Lands, reported a bill appropriating, for a limited time, the proceeds of the sales of public lands to the several States. A portion of the report was read by Mr. C., who moved that five thousand copies be printed, and the bill made the order of the day for Monday week.

Mr. CLAY having read a part of the report, a motion was made to dispense with its further reading.

Mr. FORSYTH said he did not know whether it was practicable for gentlemen to express their opinions hereafter upon the character of this report. If it could be done on the bill, he had no wish to say anything now. He could not vote for the printing; and therefore it was that he wished to hear it read; and he asked the yeas and nays on the question.

Mr. CLAY replied, that undoubtedly there would be ample opportunity to refute the reasons in the report, upon the discussion of the bill. Five thousand copies of the message of the President, to which this was an answer, had been printed, and it was but fair that an equal number of this report should be printed for distribution. The bill was similar to that of last session.

Mr. MOORE would not oppose the printing, but he would take the occasion to say, that he was opposed to the bill and the report in the committee; and he moved now to lay the motion to print on the table till to-morrow, with a view to give an opportunity to examine the report.

Mr. FORSYTH said, from the explanation given by the gentleman from Kentucky of the bill, it was obvious that no vote hereafter would test the correctness of the doctrines broached in the report—it could only be done now. He had not heard it all read, but from what he heard of it, it was respectful, and the character of the committee from which it came was a warranty for that. But he held that the first part of the report, which had been read, was erroneous, and calculated to make an incorrect impression as to the character of the President of the United States; and if the report were allowed to pass quietly, Mr. F. feared it would be taken for granted that we were of the same opinion. It states that the President ought to have returned the bill, that we might have had an opportunity to act on it. There was a provision in the Constitution under which the President would not have done his duty under the circumstances, by returning it. The bill was presented to him on the last day but one of the last session, and perhaps not before four o'clock in the day; he could scarcely have read the bill through, and all knew how business was transacted on the last day of the session, in consequence of the dilatory manner in which business is done, and the disregard of our rules. The President, at such times, is obliged to read by proxy, for it is impossible for him to do his duty to the public, by reading all the bills presented to him. He is obliged to submit minor matters to his cabinet officers—he uses their eyes and their understandings, and he is obliged to do so, in compliance with his constitutional duties. Now, to expect the President to have taken up this bill, examine it, and return his objections to it in so short a space of time, was very unreasonable. If there was any fault at all, it was in Congress. We should provide against this abuse, as it was called, of the executive power. Reference had been made in the report to Mr. Madison, and a contrast instituted between the conduct of the President and that of Mr. Madison on the bonus bill. But Mr. F. was satisfied that much more time was given to Mr. Madison in that instance. The single point presented there was a constitutional one alone—the message occupied but a single sheet. But the gentleman from Kentucky says, Mr. Madison sent his objections because his successor could not act. Mr. F. did not know his opinions on that subject, but he recollected there were some doubts on the subject, and he understood it to be asserted here as correct doctrine, that one President might limit the power of his predecessor. Mr. F. thought the successor possessed the same power and right as if he was in office the day before, and therefore he thought the opinion of the committee was wrong. It supposed an interregnum in the Presidential office—this was wrong, for Mr. F. thought the Constitution supposed the Presidency always to exist. In the case of a bill, it was the duty of the successor to examine it, and to act in the same way as the predecessor would have done. He believed it was Mr. Monroe's opinion that a President coming into office had the same right as to bills presented to him that his predecessor possessed. If this paper went out to the people, it would make a false impression in regard to this dogma of the committee.

The yeas and nays, on the question of printing, were ordered.

Mr. POINDEXTER said the President must have known the provisions of this bill several months, perhaps a year before it passed, and he had then made it the subject of a specific message to mislead the judgments of the people. It was a measure of immense importance to the new States, and the course pursued by the President was most extraordinary; it was not such a message as he had a right to present, because, we could not originate any new measure on it. Why should the new States ask for appropriations for public improvements and education, when they set their faces against the measure which would effect it?

Mr. BLACK was unwilling his vote on the question of printing should become the test on this question. He voted last year against its passage, but not because Congress had not plenary powers, but because it distributed the gross proceeds and not the net proceeds; and next, that it distributed them among the States entirely.

Mr. PORTER viewed this as nothing but a question of fair dealing between the President and a majority of the Senate, or the committee at least; and as five thousand copies of the message had been printed, he thought an equal number of the report ought to be printed.

Mr. KING, of Alabama, did not rise to discuss the principles of the bill—that was not necessary or proper now; but he wished to do some little justice to the President of the United States. He was surprised at the allusion to the non-return of the bill, made by the gentleman from Kentucky, when he knew, and every Senator knew, that the bill was not presented to the President till the last moment of the session. The President could not have known what the provisions of the bill were, because it underwent various amendments. Was it fair, then, to charge on the President a wilful retention of this important bill, when he had hardly a moment to consider it? But was it correct in fact, that two-thirds of the Senate and the House would have passed the bill if it had been returned? The majority on its passage was only three, and how then could it be supposed that it would pass, the President not having time in discharging the duty which the Constitution devolved on him seriously to consider it? And it was not possible for him to say what form it would assume; he, therefore, examined it, and under the Constitution, returned it with his objections, which the gentleman from Mississippi thought a most extraordinary thing, and he was so fond of rejecting Presidential communications, that he wished to reject this also. Gentlemen had a great disposition to find fault, but there was not the least occasion or room for fault-finding on this subject, as the people would see by looking at it. He had not examined the paper, but so far as it was read, no justice had been done to the President, and Mr. K. said, he must read it before he could agree to send out to the country a paper commenting so unfairly on the President. He differed entirely from the gentleman as to the benefit the new States would derive from the bill. He never wished to withhold information, and it was with great reluctance that he opposed the printing the extra numbers; but if the gentleman would postpone the matter till to-morrow, he would examine the paper, and if it was at all tenable he would vote to print.

After a few further remarks by Mr. CLAY, Mr. FORSYTH, and Mr. CALHOUN, the motion to print was agreed to by the following vote:

YEAS—Messrs. Bell, Black, Calhoun, Chambers, Clay, Clayton, Ewing, Frelinghuysen, Hendricks, Kent, Knight, Leigh, Linn, McKean, Mangum, Moore, Naudain, Poindexter, Porter, Prentiss, Preston, Robbins, Shepley, Silsbee, Smith, Southard, Sprague, Tipton, Tomlinson, Tyler, Waggaman, and Webster—32.

NAYS—Messrs. Benton, Brown, Forsyth, Grundy, Hill, King of Alabama, King of Georgia, White, and Wright—9.

RESOLUTIONS.

The following resolutions were submitted by Mr. SOUTHARD:

Resolved, That the Secretary of the Treasury be directed to communicate to the Senate the weekly and monthly reports and statements of the Bank of the United States, and also those of the banks which have been selected as places of deposite for the public moneys, which have been received at the Treasury Department since the 1st day of February last, and that he be further directed to communicate to the Senate such reports and statements of said banks which he shall hereafter receive, as soon as conveniently may be, after the same shall have been received.

Resolved, That the Committee on Finance be directed to inquire whether any, and which of the banks selected by the Secretary of the Treasury for the deposite of the public moneys, have stopped payment; the amount of public moneys deposited in them at the time of the suspension, if any; that they inquire also into the circumstances attending their selection, and the security taken by the Secretary; and whether the public moneys are safe in the places where they are now deposited; and that they have leave to send for persons and papers.

By Mr. WEBSTER:

Resolved, That the Secretary of the Treasury communicate to the Senate a copy of an opinion of the Attorney-General of the United States, in 1829, 1830, or 1831, on the subject of a proposed transfer of appropriations, if such opinion be on file, or on record, in the Department of the Treasury.

By Mr. TOMLINSON:

Resolved, That the Secretary of War be directed to communicate to the Senate the report of the officer designated, under the act of March 2, 1829, to survey Norwalk harbor, with a view to its improvement.

Mr. FRELINGHUYSEN gave notice that he should, to-morrow, ask leave to submit the following resolution:

Resolved, That the Secretary of the Senate be directed to procure thirteen copies of the American State Papers, now in the course of publication by Messrs. Gales & Seaton, for the use of such members of the Senate as are not now entitled to them.

Mr. CHAMBERS moved that when the Senate adjourn, it should stand adjourned to Monday. Lost: yeas 17, nays 21.

Mr. SOUTHARD, from the Committee on Naval Affairs, reported a bill for the relief of James Buchanan, a purser in the navy;

Also, a bill for the relief of the executor of Lieutenant Colonel Smith, late of the marine corps;

And moved that the committee be discharged from the further consideration of the petition of Josiah Hopkins; which was agreed to.

Mr. TOMLINSON, from the Committee on Pensions, reported a bill for the relief of Moses Archer. The report accompanying it was ordered to be printed.

Mr. CHAMBERS, from the Committee on Naval Affairs, reported a bill for the relief of Commodore John Rodgers, of the United States navy. The report was ordered to be printed.

Mr. SILSBEE, from the Committee on Commerce, reported a bill from the House of Representatives, relative to drawbacks, with an amendment

Mr. TIPTON, from the Select Committee, reported a bill, with an amendment, for the admission of Michigan and Arkansas Territories into the Union.

Mr. TIPTON, from the same committee, reported a bill for the relief of William Mann. The report was ordered to be printed.

Mr. SHEPLEY, from the Committee on Revolutionary Claims, made unfavorable reports upon the petitions of Colonel George Gibson, Lieutenant Gabriel Green, and William Asher.

The reports were ordered to be printed.

Mr. SHEPLEY, from the same committee, reported the following bills from the House of Representatives, without amendment:

A bill for the relief of Captain Ephraim Whitaker;

A bill for the relief of William Minor; and

A bill for the relief of the heirs of Dr. William Johonnot.

On motion of Mr. WEBSTER, the Senate proceeded to executive business; and, after spending some time therein,

Adjourned.

HOUSE OF REPRESENTATIVES.

FRIDAY, *May* 2, 1834.

Mr. JARVIS called up the resolution heretofore presented by him, providing for the appointment of a committee to inquire into the causes of the failure of the Bank of Washington, and Patriotic Bank, with the amendment proposed by Mr. HARDIN, extending the inquiry into the state of the Bank of the Metropolis.

No objection being made, the resolution was read.

Mr. CHILTON, who was entitled to the floor from a previous day, consumed the hour appropriated to morning business, in an animated speech in favor of the amendment, in which he contended that the Bank of the Metropolis had violated its charter by issuing notes of a less denomination than five dollars. Before he had concluded his remarks—

Mr. BOON called for the orders of the day.

SPECIE TENDER BILL.

The engrossed bill for making certain foreign silver coins a legal tender in the United States was read a third time.

Mr. FILLMORE objected to the provisions of the bill as he understood them. Its object was to provide that in payment of all sums over one hundred dollars certain foreign coins should be a legal tender, according to their weight and fineness. Now, in practice it would be very inconvenient for the person making a payment not only to weigh but assay the coin. He thought it should be provided, that if the coin bore a certain recognised stamp, the burden of showing its inferiority to the standard of that stamp should be cast upon the objecting party. Besides, the weighing was very inconvenient. He would much prefer having foreign coins made a legal tender by tale, as they were now in the ordinary circulation of the country.

Mr. C. P. WHITE said the making foreign coins a tender by tale would entirely defeat the object of the bill, which was to give such coins currency in large payments only at their intrinsic value, keeping the general circulation of the country supplied with our own coinage.

Mr. BURGES thought the bill provided for going back into the practice of ancient times when gold and silver was current only by weight. In modern times metallic currency is stamped and passes from hand to hand by tale. He was totally opposed to the making of mere bullion a lawful tender. This was the practical effect of the bill.

Mr. CAMBRELENG. If gentlemen will recur back a few years, they will perceive the necessity for this bill. Formerly the Spanish milled dollars formed nearly the whole metallic currency of the country, and were a legal tender. The countries where these dollars had been coined had thrown off their dependence on Spain, and now issued the republican dollar of Mexico and the South American States, which, with the five franc pieces, formed a great portion of our metallic currency. This bill merely proposes to make these coins a legal tender at their actual value. He could perceive no substantial grounds for objection to this. These coins now circulated by common consent. Most of them were better than our own in point of business. He hoped the bill would pass.

Mr. FILLMORE apprehended his objection was not understood. These coins were in general circulation. He could therefore see no reason why they should not be made a tender for small debts as well as large, and by tale. The stamp should be *prima facie* evidence of the fineness of coins.

Mr. GORHAM said the inconvenience to be obviated by this bill was to provide that large debts might be paid by the foreign coins, instead of their being merely pieces of silver without legal value. It was not proposed to lessen the circulation of our own coinage. That was still exclusively to be used in small payments. But our coinage was insufficient to meet all the large commercial transactions. Besides, the Mexican dollars were in fact actually worth about one-half per cent. more than our own.

Mr. BURGES contended that the public would never be satisfied with the operation of this bill, unless it provided that the dollar should pass by tale.

Mr. WILDE had formerly bestowed some attention to this subject, at a time when he belonged to the committee with the gentleman from New York, [Mr. C. P. WHITE,] and when it had also been his fortune to introduce a resolution respecting the gold and silver currency of the country. He was fully satisfied that the present bill ought to pass. The coins of all the South American States and Mexico were still coined in their original weight and fineness, except Colombia. In fact they were half per cent. better than our own coins. A person who carries ninety-nine of these dollars and one half dollar to the mint is entitled to receive two hundred American half dollars. All the expense he is subjected to is the delay of coinage. It will be better to make these coins a tender at their intrinsic value, than to subject the country to the expense of recoinage.

After a further explanation by Mr. GORHAM, in reply to Mr. BURGESS,

Mr. COULTER contended that the subject was of so much importance, that further examination should be given to it. He could not consent to a law which, to all practical purposes, provided that a debt of 100 dollars might be discharged by 99 dollars and a half dollar. This was giving too much privilege to the banks, who would redeem their bills in such coin alone.

Mr. SELDEN observed that considerable hostility was unexpectedly manifested to this bill, and it seemed to him without adequate cause. His attention had been directed to its provisions more particularly, in consequence of receiving information from some of his constituents of the necessity of enlarging the quantity of silver coin which might be used as a legal tender.

The propriety of adopting the dollars of the republics of South America and Mexico and the five franc pieces, for the purpose, had been examined by gentlemen who had a correct knowledge of the purity and value of these coins, and the benefit and necessity of rendering them available in the payment of debts. They had, with a good deal of solicitude, urged the subject upon the attention of many members of this House.

When the immense disproportion between the amount of debts to be paid and the medium wherewith they can be legally paid is considered, few can doubt the necessity of some legislation in the matter. Although it is pretty well ascertained that there are upwards of twenty millions of specie in the United States, yet it is said that not more than four millions consist of coins which constitute a legal tender under our laws, the balance consists principally of the dollars and coin referred to in this bill. It is estimated that the contracts to be fulfilled and paid by and to banks and money corporations alone, amount, in this country, to four hundred millions of dollars, which would allow one dollar of legal currency for one hundred dollars of debt. Add the immense amount of engagements existing between individual and individual, and we cannot but perceive the difficulties now existing, and the necessity of correcting them so far as we can.

The objections taken to some of the provisions of the bill, do not appear well founded. The first, is that suggested by the gentleman from Pennsylvania. He thinks, as some of these coins are a half per cent. above the actual value of the dollar of the United States, and as they are to pass by weight, and not by tale, that an individual who holds a hundred dollars of bank notes, and presents them for redemption, will receive only ninety-nine pieces of these coins and one of our own half dollars in full; and that, as they are not a legal tender for sums under one hundred dollars, he cannot pay them out at the rate at which he was compelled to receive them. It may be suggested to the honorable gentleman, that his constituents would avoid the difficulty entirely by presenting to the bank less than one hundred dollars of bills at a time. Divide the bills into different parcels, less than $100, and for each of them these coins are not a legal tender, either by weight or tale. Payment must be made in other coins, dollar for dollar. This operation may render the bill less extensive in effect than is now anticipated. Yet it is only intended for large transactions, such as balances between banks.

Another objection is started, not pressed, by my colleague, [Mr. CAMBRELENG.] He knows of no reason why the tender should not apply to debts less than $100. The answer seems plain, inasmuch as these coins are to pass by assay and weight, and not by tale, the difficulty of ascertaining their value renders them unfit to be used as a legal tender in the minor contracts. The inconvenience would be too great. For small sums, our own coins will supply the deficiency.

Again, it is asked, why does not the bill provide for making these coins a tender at once by tale? The answer is at hand. We shall be exposed to the effect of a depreciation of the value, either by diminution or adulteration of the coins. In other words, we would give the Governments of these countries the power of diminishing the value or standard of our circulating medium. This will never do. The object of this bill is to increase the quantity of silver which may be used in payments. It gives no increased value to these coins beyond the actual value of silver. The bill selects from the mass of bullion in circulation in the world a portion of it stamped at certain value, prepared by Governments in which we have a general confidence, and with which our commercial relations are extensive; the bullion, divided up into pieces of portable, convenient dimensions, thus stamped and divided, the bill provides that it may be used in the payment of debts at its actual value, to be ascertained by weight and purity.

The last objection which he shall notice, is one stated by another colleague from New York. It relates to a question of evidence; that is, who, under this law, must make proof that the coins are of the weight or fineness required: must the individual who offers to pay make proof that they are of the description required, or must the individual to whom payment is to be made show the contrary? His friend seems to think, under this bill, the presumption of law will be against the quality and quantity of silver in the coin; the contrary strikes him as the true construction. By the bill they are made current, their assay annually at the mint is provided for.

We can scarcely apprehend much difficulty; few will refuse to receive those coins, lest they should be adulterated, in payment of any debt; the weight can easily be determined. The objection that those who have debts due them over one hundred dollars, and owe debts under that sum, may be compelled to receive in payment a coin which they cannot pass away in payment, is an objection, but it is certainly a very slight one—those thus situated can always exchange with others having large debts to pay.

In conclusion, the effect of this bill will be to increase the quantity of silver in circulation by enabling the banks to rely upon these foreign coins as the means for redeeming their bills, and release the coins of our own country from their vaults. All agree that an increase of the precious metals will prove beneficial; this bill has a tendency to produce such a result.

Mr. JONES said that though he had objections to the bill, both as to the limitation of time, and the sums for which these coins might be a tender, still he considered it so important to have further metallic legal currency to satisfy the immense debts which were due, that he should feel bound to support it in its present shape. The facts stated by the gentleman from New York [Mr. SELDEN] were sufficient to convince any one of the absolute necessity for this measure.

Mr. H. KING contended that the effect of the bill would be to raise the value of foreign coins, as well as make them a legal tender.

Mr. C. P. WHITE in reply, stated that the bill expressly avoided interfering with the value of the coins, except according to their weight and fineness. To illustrate the necessity for this measure, he stated that a demand of $50,000 was made upon the branch bank at New York, having at the time

two millions in foreign gold and silver coins in its vaults. The individual holding the claim refused to accept fifty thousand Mexican dollars, which were of greater intrinsic value than so many of our own dollars. The bank was, in consequence, obliged, with two millions of specie on hand, to send to another institution for means to pay this demand. Unless this bill should pass, the commercial community would be exposed to great inconvenience.

Mr. DENNY had no objection to the bill, as far as it went, but was anxious to see some further provision added to it.

Mr. WILDE said the subject of coins and currency was among the most abstruse questions in the abstruse science of political economy. To give gentlemen further time for consideration, as he was anxious that the measure should be supported by a strong vote, he moved to postpone the subject until Tuesday next; which was agreed to.

Mr. POLK asked the consent of the House to proceed to the consideration of the appropriation bill.

Mr. ADAMS, of Massachusetts, wished, he said, before the House resumed the subject, to obtain some information on the item now under consideration, and objected to the motion.

Mr. POLK moved to suspend the rules, for the purpose of proceeding to the consideration of the bill, and it was agreed to.

The House then went into Committee of the Whole on the state of the Union, (Mr. HUBBARD in the chair,) upon the general appropriation bill, the following clause being under consideration:

For the salaries of the chargés des affaires to Portugal, Denmark, Sweden, Holland, Turkey, Belgium, Brazil, Buenos Ayres, Chili, Peru, Mexico, Central America, and New Grenada, fifty-eight thousand five hundred dollars.

Mr. J. Q. ADAMS made some remarks upon the clause, and objected to it that some of the countries named were too inconsiderable to require the establishment of permanent diplomatic intercourse with them. The House, he thought, ought to be informed what are the relations with those powers which render it necessary that we should maintain permanent missions there. There were some other powers not named here which were as important, in reference to their relations with us, as those which are named. The Republic of Switzerland was a nation with whom we ought to sympathize more than with any other nation of Europe, because, like ourselves, it is republican; but we never had any mission there, though Switzerland holds diplomatic intercourse with all the nations of Europe.

There had been times when we held no diplomatic intercourse with some larger powers, Sweden, Denmark, and Prussia. With these we had occasional intercourse, but no permanent missions had ever been established there. The principle of this Government has been, not to have missions unless there was a special call for them; and this principle was founded on economy, which we had not, he hoped, entirely abandoned. We had restricted the number of our missions, heretofore, on the score of economy only, for, in point of expediency, it might be very well to hold intercourse with every power.

He referred to the proceedings of the Government at its first organization, to show that no diplomatic mission was established, unless there was special occasion for it. He referred to the missions to Belgium and Central America, as wholly unnecessary. In reference to Buenos Ayres, he wished to know what had become of our quarrel with that power, and whether there was any occasion for reëstablishing diplomatic relations with it. He addressed these inquiries to the chairman of the Committee of Foreign Relations, because (he said) he had ascertained that he could not obtain the information elsewhere.

Mr. ARCHER understood the honorable gentleman from Massachusetts as making an inquiry of an extent so large as to go into all the diplomatic relations of the country, excepting those embraced in the clauses of the bill disposed of yesterday. The inquiry which the gentleman made last night and to-day, went to this extraordinary extent, embracing all the plans and views of the Administration on the subject of our diplomatic relations.

Mr. A. considered that, in relation to a large portion of these missions, the onus rested upon us to show that they were unnecessary. And why? Because this is not the department to which the Constitution has assigned the right and duty of establishing diplomatic missions. We are not participants in the responsibility of selecting the Powers with which we shall have diplomatic intercourse. The gentleman from Massachusetts, on the contrary, goes on the ground that before any diplomatic mission can be established, it must be approved by us. Is that the theory of our Constitution? Suppose a mission has been in existence for years, are we to say that it has been improperly established? He trusted that it was sufficient to say, in relation to all but two of these missions, that they were established constitutionally, that ministers had been appointed and sent to fill them, and were now in the discharge of their duties. Was the doctrine to prevail that every year we are to demand proof of what has already been sufficiently well proven, that a particular mission is necessary?

The gentleman admitted that it would be expedient to establish missions elsewhere; and in this he agreed with him. He thought himself that it would be highly proper to establish a diplomatic intercourse with Austria, one of the most important Powers in Europe—a Power with which we have a commercial treaty, and with one of whose ports to which we have access, we have a valuable and growing commerce.

It was with unaffected surprise that he found the honorable gentleman from Massachusetts disposed to sweep away all our diplomatic intercourse. What was the main object of our diplomatic intercourse? We were not concerned in the altercations of all these Powers. Our object was solely to maintain and extend the high and important interests of our commerce. Under our institutions, we gave to every man the exclusive fruits of his industry; but of what use was this, unless we gave him facilities for making this privilege available? Unless for this principle, we had very little reason to sustain any diplomatic relations at all. Shall we be told that a nation as rich as this—the richest on the globe except Great Britain—cannot afford to protect its commerce with any foreign nation, at the expense of four thousand five hundred dollars a year? In relation to those Governments, where we have had for a long time a permanent mission, and with which we had a valuable commerce, he trusted that it was unnecessary to say anything more. The gentleman asks why we have a mission to Belgium, a new State, and recently connected with Holland? Because (he replied) if the whole of our commerce with the Netherlands was worthy of preservation, one-half of it was. At least it was worthy of preservation at the expense of a few thousand dollars a year. This new and important state sought the establishment of diplomatic relations with us; and he asked what the gentleman would have said if the President had refused, on the score of economy, to reciprocate the disposition of the Government of Belgium? With this power, which possessed one of the most important ports in Europe, we had a valuable and a growing trade. If her overture had been refused, she would have been justified in refusing to us any commercial facilities whatever, or at least in raising her tariff to our disadvantage. If this consequence had followed the refusal or neglect of the President to nominate a minister to Belgium, the gentleman would have pronounced upon the President his unqualified censure.

Mr. A. went into a view of our object in establishing a diplomatic intercourse with the States of South America. Were we now to abandon those objects for which, after long and mature deliberation, we established these relations? And for what purpose should we abandon them? To avoid an expense of $4,500? After all the parade we had made, in relation to the concerns of South America, were we to renounce our connexion with them, merely for the sake of a small saving to this rich country? One of our objects was to establish a favorable intercourse with these States, and to guard it from the effects of European rivalry. Was it not important to us to procure our share of this vast and rapidly-increasing trade; and must we sacrifice it to the rivalry of foreign Powers for the sake of the important sum of $4,500 a year?

Mr. A. here entered into a full statistical statement in relation to the trade of different States of South America.

Mr. ADAMS here interrupted the gentleman from Virginia, by asking him how it happened that, in this appropriation, Colombia was overlooked? It would seem that, since its important port was found, the State itself was lost.

Mr. ARCHER replied, that Colombia was now divided into three Powers: Venezuela, New Granada, and Ecuador. At New Granada, we had now a minister, a citizen of Kentucky. We had an extensive trade with all three of these countries, and, in his opinion, we ought to have a minister in each of them. He suggested reasons, in connexion with the unsettled state of the Governments of South America, which rendered it more important for us to maintain diplomatic relations with them than with any European Governments.

In relation to the mission to Buenos Ayres, he explained that when our relations with that Government were suspended, it was communicated to us officially that the negotiation would be renewed here, and that a minister would be soon sent to us for that purpose. A short time back, another communication was received from the Government of Buenos Ayres, stating that a minister might be immediately expected by our Government. Under these circumstances, it would not be proper to refuse the Administration the means of reciprocating the disposition of the Government of Buenos Ayres. Having made the explanations which the gentleman from Massachusetts required, he would repeat, that when a mission had been established by the President, with the assent of the Senate, this House could not, with propriety, interpose any objections to it, unless something should come to our ears showing that some abuses existed in relation to it. Before the President and Senate had acted, we might undoubtedly demand the reasons for which our money was required.

Mr. POLK said he presumed the committee would bear in mind that this clause in the bill did not provide for any new mission. They had all been established in the usual constitutional manner. He was anxious that the committee might get through with the bill and report it to the House. There a distinct vote could be taken upon each item. He therefore hoped the bill might be proceeded in without any unnecessary delay in its present stage. In the House the whole ground might be gone over.

Mr. J. Q. ADAMS said, his object in making the inquiry which had been responded to by the chairman of the Committee on Foreign Relations [Mr. ARCHER] was, to obtain information which might govern his vote upon this appropriation. It was but justice to say, that the greatest part of the explanation of the gentleman was of a satisfactory character. But as to the mission to Buenos Ayres, to which his inquiries had been specially directed, the explanation was not satisfactory. Before he alluded further to that subject, he would notice the opinion expressed by the gentleman, that the *onus probandi*, when negotiations were made by the Executive, lay upon the members of the House who objected to them. The gentleman was the last individual from whom he expected to hear such a doctrine.

It was not consonant to the settled principles of our Government. In the discussions arising out of the treaty with Great Britain, (commonly called Jay's treaty,) the relative rights of this House and of the President and Senate were brought up under circumstances which interested the whole country. When the appropriations necessary to carry the treaty into effect were called for by President Washington, this House demanded that the instructions under which the negotiation had been effected should be laid before them, in order that the propriety of making the appropriation might be determined. President Washington refused to furnish the House with those instructions. A resolution was then adopted, declaring that the House, so far as regarded the appropriation of money required by a treaty, were not foreclosed by its ratification by the President and Senate. The doctrine of this resolution had been adhered to ever since, and had become a settled principle.

This principle applied with far more force to the appointment of a minister abroad. In the case of a treaty, a foreign power was concerned as a party, and many considerations should have weight,

which did not exist in the case of the appointment by the President and Senate of one of our own citizens to a mission abroad.

Mr. A. went at length into the arguments which had been employed against the appropriation for the Panama mission, to show that the House was not precluded from a decision whether a mission was necessary or otherwise. As to the proposed appropriation for a chargé d'affaires at Buenos Ayres, the explanation was not satisfactory. He was in possession of a publication in the Spanish language, made by the Government of that Republic, containing the correspondence between the gentleman who had been charged with our interests there and that Government, which contained observations requiring further explanation than had been given. He therefore moved to strike out the items providing for an outfit and salary for a chargé d'affaires at Buenos Ayres out of the bill.

Mr. WAYNE rose, but gave way to

Mr. MERCER, who moved the committee rise, which was negatived:

Ayes 66, noes 81.

Mr. WAYNE proceeded to say that the impatience of the committee, at hearing a speech at so late a period of the day, admonished him of the propriety of permitting the question to be taken. But the earnest manner in which the gentleman from Massachusetts [Mr. ADAMS] had urged his objections, induced him to submit one or two observations in reply to his views upon the power of the House to examine into the necessity and propriety of foreign missions which had been established in the usual form. In the cases put by the gentleman, he believed there was no member of the House who doubted the right of the House to interpose their opinions. But a broad distinction existed between those cases and the present: here was a mission, established and recognised year after year by the House. In these cases nothing of that kind existed. The principle of the resolution introduced by the gentleman from Tennessee [Mr. POLK] upon the 1st of April, 1826, relative to the Panama mission, which had been alluded to, could not be extended to the present case. The object of that mission was not the usual diplomatic intercourse recognised by the laws of nations. It was there proposed to send ministers to a congress of nations: here it is merely proposed to continue a mission long since established.

Mr. W. replied to the other positions taken by Mr. ADAMS, with much force; when the question was taken, and the motiop to strike out negatived: ayes 19, noes 102.

The item providing outfits for a minister to Russia, and a chargé to Buenos Ayres, having been read—

Mr. ARCHER moved to amend the clause by inserting outfits for chargés des affaires to Chili and Brazil; which, after a brief explanation from that gentleman, was agreed to.

The item for salaries for agents of claims at London and Paris having been read—

Mr. W. R. DAVIS suggested that the office of agent for claims at Paris being no longer necessary, it would be better to change the name of the allowance to that of salary to the consul.

Mr. POLK, after an explanation on the subject, said that if any change of phraseology was regarded as important, it could be done when the bill came before the House.

When the items providing appropriations for completing custom-houses at New London, Middletown, New Bedford, Newburyport, and Baltimore, were read—

Mr. McKAY stated at length the various sums appropriated heretofore for these objects, and the estimates made for their completion, and contended that in some instances the amounts named in the bill were larger than were necessary. After moving to reduce the amount at Middletown, which was carried, Mr. McK. said he was extremely unwilling to detain the committee at so late an hour, but believing, as he did, that a profuse expenditure had been gone into on these subjects, he would suspend the further motions he had proposed to make until the bill came into the House.

Mr. POLK said there were a few amendments which he had in charge from the Committee of Ways and Means to offer, which he should do *pro forma*, in order that they might come up in the House. Mr. P. accordingly proposed several additional items to the bill, some of which were adopted and others rejected.

Mr. ARCHER said he was instructed by the Committee on Foreign Affairs to move two or three amendments, which he would now do, without intending to discuss them at this time. They were accordingly proposed and adopted.

On motion of Mr. POLK, the committee then rose and reported the bill and amendments to the House.

Mr. POLK moved that the bill, as amended, be printed.

Mr. EVANS suggested the propriety of printing also the amendments which had been proposed and rejected, to which Mr. POLK assented, and it was ordered accordingly.

Mr. PINCKNEY, by consent, moved that when the House adjourns it adjourn to meet on Monday next; which was agreed to.

The House then, at nearly eight o'clock,

Adjourned.

IN SENATE.

SATURDAY, *May* 3, 1834.

PETITIONS.

Mr. SILSBEE said he desired to present a memorial from that section of New England which was extensively engaged in the fishing business; they complained of great pecuniary distress and pressure, and injury to their commerce, owing to the removal of the deposites. He moved the usual reference of the memorial, and, after being read,

Mr. FORSYTH said he thought he understood that this memorial came from a district of country engaged in the business of fishing, complaining of the destruction of their commerce. We had heard much of distress in the country, and we had memorials presented on the subject every day, and honorable gentlemen here proclaimed that great distress, and reductions in the prices of various products was produced by the late measures of the President. As to other great objects of industry, the prices current showed how correct they were. He would ask the gentleman who presented this memorial what the price of oil was?

Mr. SILSBEE replied, that he had not taken much time to inform himself. He believed that oil was *from* 70 to 75 cents a gallon; what the ordinary price was, he could not say. It sold at from 90 to 100 cents by the small quantity, and he would tell the gentleman that ships employed in the whale fishing had depreciated 25 per cent. He also hoped the gentleman from Georgia did not mean to say that he (Mr. S.) had occupied much time in discussions upon presenting memorials.

Mr. FORSYTH did not intend charging the honorable gentleman with having occupied the time of the Senate by speaking upon memorials. He would do him no such injustice; but he alluded to all the gentlemen on that side of the house. As regarded the distress of the people of New Bedford, he thought the memorial said that ten thousand seamen were affected by the act of the Executive, and the honorable member told us that the object for which the sailors were employed bore the ordinary price. Mr. F. said that from his experience and observation, 70 to 76 cents was a very living price for fish oil, and while it stood at that, the sailors would be engaged in the business. But it was said that the equipments of vessels was much reduced in price, and that a deficiency in the value of ships of 25 per cent. had taken place. But Mr. F. thought, that upon examination, it would be seen that this was not founded in fact. The cries of distress were got up, not in the sections from which these memorials came, but elsewhere. The heaviest cry came from Baltimore, and there the pressure was extreme. He held in his hand the prices current in Baltimore, and from that it would seem that the prices were good. Fish, shad, were $6 50, and herring $3 50 per barrel; flour, sales of Howard street at $5 per barrel. The article of sugar he would advert to for the benefit of the gentleman from Louisiana, [Mr. PORTER;] it was $7 to $8 50, and he had heard a very large crop was sold lately in Philadelphia at 8 cents. Tobacco $3 50, cotton 12½ to 13—holders firm, and expecting better prices. Mr. F. hoped gentlemen would look at the prices current from the various parts of the country from which these memorials come. He believed that persons doing business on credit might be suffering embarrassment, but he denied that there was any distress pressing on the great objects of the country.

Mr. WEBSTER said, that the theory of the honorable member from Georgia was fictitious, and not real. But he thought the slightest reference to the great interests of the whale fisheries, would convince any man that it must be most affected by causes disturbing the general credit of the country, owing to the long credits which the business required, and therefore the gentleman was mistaken in applying his remarks to the people of New Bedford; the fishing business was almost the sole business of New Bedford and Nantucket, and the time was, when, with no other trade, they had from seventy to eighty ships engaged in it beyond the capes of Good Hope and Horn—they must therefore deal on credit, and their cry was not false clamor. But we were told by honorable gentlemen that when this question was settled, prosperity would revive. Well, a decision had been made a month ago, by a majority of half a hundred votes, that the bank should not be rechartered, and yet the country is not settled, but is farther from it than ever.

Mr. FORSYTH replied, that he had not said that there was no cause of distress in the country, and that all the complaints sent here were false clamor. He admitted there was distress in some portions of the country, arising from the abridgment of banking accommodations, and the derangement of the exchanges of the country. He believed that distress did exist among business men whose accommodations had stopped, and where runs had been made upon banks, having no metallic basis to support them. What he said was this—that there was no foundation for the cry of distress, when we looked to the prices of the products of labor upon the forest, the ocean, or the earth. And what were they? All the prices showed them to be as high now as they were this time last year, or higher than they were at the time when, according to the statements of honorable gentlemen, the country was overflowing with prosperity. The prices current were so over the whole United States. In Boston, on the 28th April, in the article of coffee, the prices were rising. [Mr. F. here read from the newspaper report of prices current.] Now, as to the article of cotton, in Boston, four thousand bales were sold on manufacturer's account. So that all the manufactories were not stopped yet. New Orleans cotton, thirteen to fifteen; flour in demand and scarce, and he hoped when the news of the flour market reached New Orleans, it would rise there. Fish and molasses, as high as last year; sugar, prices firm, and supplies limited. Now, gentlemen said that the great necessaries of life were high, because the people must eat; but here all the prices were given. The lumber trade, too, stood in the same condition as it did this time last year, when we were enjoying the most unbounded prosperity.

But the gentleman from Massachusetts said that he (Mr. F.) was mistaken in regard to the New Bedford people. What he (Mr. F.) stated was, that the persons engaged in the whale fishing, if it be admitted that the article of their pursuit in business is as high as usual, cannot be suffering distress. But the gentleman from Massachusetts tells us of great rivalry existing in the New Bedford and Nantucket fisheries. And what were the elements of this rivalry? Let us examine the subject a little. The people of New Bedford and Nantucket are, beyond all doubt, unrivalled by the world, in nautical skill and enterprise. But the case is different in other parts of the world, where the expenses of an outfit, &c., are very great. There they are much cheaper. But the gentleman from Massachusetts said, that their business was deranged, because they purchased on a credit. The materials were all there; and the only difference was, that those who had not capital, could not get it. Mr. F. said, his remarks applied to the sailors in that service, as the memorial referred to ten thousand sailors, who were injuriously affected by the measures of the Administration. He believed that the sailors engaged in those voyages for a share in the profits of the voyage. Well, how

were they affected? The returns of former voyages were here, and the object of their enterprise was at the same price. Was there any difficulty in making investments, when the materials were 25 per cent. less in price than formerly?

But the honorable gentleman had referred to our predictions, that when this agitating question was settled, relief and tranquillity would be restored to the country. And he told us that it was settled by the other branch of Congress. Did that gentleman so consider it? Could he calculate that it was settled? What was the object of these memorials, and the speeches delivered upon them? Why, that it should be unsettled until it could be settled in a particular way. If honorable members had been satisfied with the judgment of the House of Representatives, and turned their attention to the adoption of measures for the general good, it would have been settled; but they have entered into the drama before the people with the House of Representatives, and none with respect to this question than the honorable gentleman from Massachusetts, that the country must and should be agitated. But as far as it could be settled under the circumstances, it had been produced. Had not a manifest change for the better, in the money market, taken place? Had not stocks risen? Had not exchange risen? Were there complaints in the city market? No. And this was owing in part to the fulfilment of the prophecy by us; and when the people saw that the wishes of the gentleman could not be accomplished, gentlemen would cease to agitate the public mind, which would not have been agitated by the measures of the Executive but for the interposition of extraneous causes. Some further remarks were made by Messrs. KNIGHT, PORTER, SILSBEE, CHAMBERS, EWING, SPRAGUE, FORSYTH, and POIN-DEXTER, when

The memorial was referred to the Committee on Finance, and ordered to be printed.

Mr. HENDRICKS moved that the special orders be postponed in order to take up the resolution submitted by him some days ago, setting aside Fridays and Saturdays for the consideration of private business. The motion was lost: Yeas 15, nays 18.

The following resolution was submitted by Mr. HENDRICKS:

Resolved, That the Committee on Military Affairs be instructed to inquire into the expediency of making an appropriation to pay for blankets furnished the militia of Michigan in the late war against Black Hawk and his followers, which blankets were not charged on the company muster rolls and deducted from the pay of the soldiers who received the same.

This resolution was agreed to.

By Mr. POINDEXTER:

Resolved, That until the special order of the day, on the protest of the President of the United States, shall be finally disposed of, the Chair shall announce the order on each day immediately after the journal shall have been read.

By Mr. SPRAGUE:

Resolved, That the Secretary of the Treasury be directed to communicate to the Senate a statement of the amount of fees accruing in each collection district in the United States, in each year, since January 1, 1829; the amount of fees paid at the Treasury, in each year, by those collectors whose fees have amounted to more than the maximum allowed them by law; the names and number of clerks and deputies employed by each collector who has received such excess of fees; the time when they were employed, and the amount paid each in each year. Also, a statement of the contingent expenses of each office where such excess of fees has been received, whether any allowances have been made to officers of the customs for travelling expenses; and if so, the names of such officers, and the times when such expenses were incurred. And also, a statement of the names of persons who hold, or have held, several offices in the customs at the same time, since January 1, 1829, with the date and time of continuance of such appointment, and the amount of pay which they have received from each office which they have so held during the period aforesaid.

Mr. BENTON, from the Committee on Military Affairs, asked to be discharged from the further consideration of the petition of Dr. Boyd Reilly, in order that the memorialist might have the benefit of a more suitable reference. Agreed to.

Mr. TYLER made an unsuccessful motion to take up a number of bills from the other House; when,

On motion of Mr. FORSYTH,
The Senate adjourned.

IN SENATE.

MONDAY, May 5, 1834.

A message upon executive business was received from the President of the United States, by Mr. DONELSON, his Private Secretary.

The VICE PRESIDENT presented a communication from the Treasury Department, transmitting a report from the Commissioner of the General Land Office, detailing the gross amount of the sales of public lands, in compliance with the resolution of the Senate of the 28th April.

On motion of Mr. CLAY, the report was ordered to be printed.

The Senate then took up the resolution submitted by Mr. POINDEXTER, requiring all business to give way to the consideration of the special order, being the President's protest.

Mr. HENDRICKS moved to amend, by inserting "except Fridays and Saturdays in each and every week, which days shall be devoted to the consideration of bills."

The amendment was advocated by Messrs. HENDRICKS, KING of Alabama, KING of Georgia, KNIGHT, and TIPTON; and opposed by Messrs. CLAY, CLAYTON, EWING, POIN-DEXTER, SPRAGUE, and WEBSTER; and was adopted by the following vote:

YEAS—Messrs. Bell, Benton, Black, Clay, Clayton, Ewing, Frelinghuysen, Grundy, Frelinghuysen, Grundy, Hendricks, Hill, Kane, King of Alabama, King of Georgia, Knight, Linn, McKean, Prentiss, Shepley, Swift, Tallmadge, Tipton, White, Wilkins, Wright—20.

NAYS—Messrs. Bell, Benton, Black, Clay, Clayton, Ewing, Leigh, Moore, Naudain, Poindexter, Porter, Preston, Robbins, Silsbee, Smith, Sprague, Tomlinson, Tyler, Webster—19.

Mr. POINDEXTER then proposed to withdraw the resolution; but this not being in order, he then moved that the resolution and amendment be laid upon the table; which was decided in the affirmative, by the following vote:

YEAS—Messrs. Bell, Benton, Black, Clay, Clayton, Ewing, Frelinghuysen, King of Alabama, King of Georgia, Knight, Leigh, Moore, Naudain, Poindexter, Porter, Preston, Robbins, Silsbee, Smith, Sprague, Swift, Tomlinson Tyler, Wagaman, Webster, White—26.

NAYS—Messrs. Brown, Forsyth, Grundy, Hendricks, Hill, Kane, Linn, McKean, Prentiss, Shepley, Tallmadge, Tipton, Wilkins, Wright—15.

The VICE PRESIDENT presented a communication from the War Department, transmitting the amount of expenditures in that department for 1833; which,

On motion of Mr. WHITE, was ordered to be printed.

RESOLUTIONS.

The following resolutions were severally considered, and adopted:

By Mr. TIPTON:

Resolved, That the Committee on the Judiciary be instructed to inquire into the expediency of allowing to the heirs of Antoine Peltier, deceased, the amount of their claim adjusted and allowed by the State of Virginia, for moneys advanced by said Peltier to the regiment of General George Rogers Clark, in the Illinois country.

By Mr. PRESTON:

Resolved, That the laws of the Territory of Florida be referred to the Committee on the Judiciary.

By Mr. KING, of Alabama:

Resolved, That the Committee on Finance be instructed to inquire into the expediency of authorizing the Secretary of the Treasury to credit the accounts of Uriah G. Mitchell, receiver of public moneys for the Cahawba land district, in the State of Alabama, with the sum of one hundred dollars, which was received by said Mitchell at the land sales in a counterfeit bill on the Bank of the United States.

Mr. TALLMADGE presented the petition of Thomas Harrison; which was referred to the Committee on Pensions.

Mr. TOMLINSON presented the petition of Eli Mitchell; which was referred to the same committee.

Mr. TOMLINSON presented the petition of Daniel Tomlinson, praying the passage of an act extending his rights as a patentee of some invention in the currying knife; which was referred to the Committee on the Judiciary.

GENERAL ORDERS.

The resolutions submitted at various periods for several days past by Messrs. CHAMBERS, PRENTISS, and SOUTHARD, were taken up and adopted.

SPECIAL ORDER.

The Senate then proceeded to the consideration of the special order of the day, being Mr. BIBB's amendment of Mr. POINDEXTER's resolutions on the protest of the President of the United States.

Mr. WRIGHT then took the floor, and spoke in support of the President's protest, and in favor of receiving and recording it on the journal; after which

Mr. CLAY made some explanatory remarks upon the condemnatory resolutions, and the several modifications which were made of them.

Mr. CALHOUN then rose and expressed a wish to be heard on the subject, and moved an adjournment; but withdrew the motion at the request of

Mr. POINDEXTER, who gave notice that, with a view to bring this discussion to a speedy close, he would, every day at one o'clock, move to proceed to the special order of the day, and postpone any other business, even to the interruption of speaking; and that he would for one, resist any motion to adjourn hereafter till five o'clock.

Mr. WEBSTER coincided in opinion with Mr. POINDEXTER; and said he had several memorials which he wished to present after the discussion had terminated.

The Senate, on motion of Mr. POINDEXTER, proceeded to the consideration of executive business; and, after some time spent therein,
The Senate adjourned.

HOUSE OF REPRESENTATIVES.

MONDAY, May 5, 1834.

This being the day for the presentation of petitions, the memorial presented from citizens of Georgia, by Mr. WAYNE, on Monday last, was taken up, and, on motion of Mr. W., its further consideration was postponed till next Monday.

The memorial of a convention held in the third Congressional district of Massachusetts, in favor of the restoration of the deposites of the public moneys to the Bank of the United States, which was presented last Monday, and was not then disposed of, being taken up—

Mr. OSGOOD said it was always an unpleasant task for a Representative to oppose the wishes of any portion of his constituents. Considering himself as the organ of their will, he cannot, without many painful sensations of regret, find his own sentiments in opposition to theirs. But the diversity of human opinion, while mankind remain constituted as they are, must often render it necessary for him to gratify the wishes of one part of his constituents at the risk of displeasing the rest. Nor will he always be able to find out what the wishes of a majority of his constituents really are. As to the general course of his official duties, if he has openly avowed his adherence to a political party, if he has been chosen with a knowledge on the part of his constituents of his political predilections, he may safely conclude that a concurrence with the measures of his party will not be obnoxious to those who elected him. But a new state of things may arise, unexpected events may happen, unforeseen measures may be proposed, a different course of policy may be instituted, and the vote that sanctioned his adherence to his party at the time of his election may fail to sustain him in this new juncture of events, and he will be com-

pelled to resort to some other criterion to determine the wishes of his constituents. If, under these circumstances, the measure proposed be one which excites little interest in the public mind—if, although it may involve consequences of great magnitude to the republic, it immediately affects neither the persons nor the property of his constituents, he may be left almost without any manifestation of public sentiment to guide him in his conduct. And if, on the other hand, the measure be one which excites an interest equal to, or perhaps even beyond its importance, if it touch the feelings of any particular class in the community, or rouse into opposition the adherents of a political party, he will be liable to be led astray by the overheated exertions of its opponents, and to mistake the noisy clamor of a few zealous partisans for the real, sober, and permanent sense of the community. And when the excitement has passed away, and the momentary passions which created it have subsided, he will find, to his mortification and regret, that in obeying the instructions of self-constituted conventions, and in listening to the dictations of interested memorialists, he has overlooked the opinions of the less obtrusive, but not the less enlightened portion of his constituents—that he has gone contrary to the wishes, and, what is more, to the welfare, of his district.

To come, then, to my own case, sir: for however unpleasant it may be, we are almost all of us compelled, at one time or another, to speak of ourselves upon this floor. I was chosen, with a knowledge on the part of my constituents, that I should vote against a recharter of the bank. At any rate, if they did not know it, it was not my fault, as I openly everywhere declared it. The recharter of the bank had been vetoed by the President long before my election. I was nominated by the friends of the Administration; I was supported by the friends of the Administration; and I was finally chosen as an open and avowed friend of the Administration. The recharter of the bank was a question that could not have escaped the attention of those who were at that time about to choose a representative in Congress. My own party, so far as I knew anything of their opinions, were unanimously opposed to a recharter. Those of the opposite party with whom I happened to converse, and who afterwards, from some local difficulties in my district, threw their votes for me, expressed much indifference as to the fate of the bank. They said it was a mere scramble for money, and they cared nothing about it. They elected me, knowing that I should vote against a recharter of the bank, and therefore virtually gave me liberty to vote against it.

If, under these circumstances, a part of my constituents, or a majority, if you please, had undertaken to instruct me to vote for a recharter of the bank, would any man say that I was bound to obey such instructions? Might I not have turned round upon them and said, a year has not yet elapsed since you elected me, with a knowledge that I should vote against the bank, and now you instruct me to vote for it? How long must I suppose that these your new instructions will remain valid? Have I any assurance that you will not change your minds again before the vote is taken? And if you do, must I change with you? Must I veer about with every current of wind that happens to strike the political weathercock in my district?

The gentlemen, sir, who composed the convention that adopted these resolutions, and this memorial, and the letter of instructions, saw this thing in its true light. They would not undertake to instruct me upon a point upon which my opinions had already been sanctioned by a vote of my district. They knew that this would be carrying the doctrine of instructions beyond the bounds of reason; that it would go to the destruction of all consistency, I might almost say, of all decency of conduct on the part of the representative. Well, sir, tacitly acknowledging the truth of these sentiments, they would not undertake to instruct me to vote for a recharter of the bank. But they have instructed me to vote for a restoration of the deposites. The restoration of the deposites, I suppose they would say, is a new question. The deposites were not removed at the time of your election. The sentiments of your district have never before been declared upon the subject; this memorial,

these resolutions, and this letter of instructions, form the only means by which you can come at a knowledge of the sentiments of your constituents upon this point; and now, through these, they speak to you in a language that can neither be disregarded nor disobeyed.

Well, sir, the question of a restoration of the deposites is undoubtedly, in some respects, a distinct question from a recharter of the bank. In the nature of things, there is no sort of connection or similarity between them. But it may often happen, that questions totally dissimilar in their nature, may, by the force of circumstances, be made dependent the one upon the other. And such I took to be the case with these two questions of a recharter of the bank, and a restoration of the deposites. It is not that a man might not very consistently, upon abstract principles, vote for the one, and against the other; nor that many members here may not have done it with the purest intentions. But I will leave it to the candor of any man to say, whether, if a resolution for a recharter of the bank had been carried through this House by a triumphant majority, it would not have tended to bring about a recharter of the bank.

But, air, according to this very memorial and letter of instruction, I am at liberty to vote against a recharter of the bank. For either my constituents don't want the bank rechartered, and so have not instructed me to vote for it; or if they do want the bank rechartered, they thought that, under all the circumstances of the case, it would be neither liberal nor manly, nor honorable, to instruct me to vote for a recharter. But what they have not done directly, they have done indirectly. What they have virtually acknowledged they had no right to do in one way, they have done in another. If they don't want the bank rechartered, they ought not to have instructed me to vote for a measure which would tend to bring about a recharter, and defeat their own views; and so give me instructions against instructions, in the very same letter. Or, if they do want the bank rechartered, but thought I was so delicately situated that they ought not to instruct me to vote for it if they do want it, then they ought not to have instructed me to vote for a restoration of the deposites. Having given me the liberty of accomplishing a certain end, they ought not to attempt to embarrass me in the means necessary to accomplish that end. Am I to understand that my constituents are unwilling that I should judge of the effect of measures upon this floor? Do they rate their representation so low that they are unwilling he should judge of the means necessary to accomplish the ends they have sanctioned? Is he to exhibit to this House and to the nation the mortifying spectacle of a man who is obliged to defeat his purposes by his own votes? Is he to adopt a crooked, vacillating, inconsistent, contradictory course; to go blundering on from one vote to another, without any regard to their ultimate effect upon the object he intends to accomplish? It is as much the interest of my constituents to preserve my influence and my dignity unimpaired upon this floor, as it is my interest and my duty, and I will add, my pride and my pleasure too, to preserve theirs. Whatever they may do to affect my influence here must affect their own in an equal degree. I shall endeavor to preserve both theirs and my own, as well as I can.

If I had believed that the removal of the deposites had been effected by a violation of the Constitution, if I had supposed that the President had assumed any unconstitutional powers in this transaction, I would have willingly waived any right I may have reserved to myself at the time of my election upon this great question of the bank. I would have said with the friends of the bank, let us vindicate the violated Constitution, let us avenge the insulted laws, let us show to the country and the world that we will do justice, be the consequences what they may. But such was not my opinion. After all the exertions of the friends of the bank, they utterly failed to prove, in my apprehension, any assumption of unconstitutional powers on the part of the President. When the heat of this controversy has passed away, gentlemen will wonder that they could have ever carried their views to such an extent upon this point. They will wonder they ever could have denied that the Treasury Department is an executive department,

or the head of that department an executive officer. They will see that the Constitution has placed the executive power in the hands of the President, and that if Congress were to undertake to exercise any part of that power, it would be in violation of the Constitution. Now, air, the raising and appropriating of money is clearly a legislative act, and as such, has been wisely intrusted by the Constitution to Congress; but the paying over this money, to the several objects to which it is appropriated, is as clearly an executive act. It is simply carrying into execution a law of Congress, and as such belongs to the executive branch of this Government. Now, in order to be able to pay over this money to the several objects to which it is appropriated, the officer who is to pay it over, must have it in his possession; he must be the keeper of the public money, and the keeper of the public money must be an officer to prove this, as we have here seen, keep it and pay it over according to the laws of Congress. But that does not alter the nature of his duty. It does not make it different from any other executive duty. The Executive is bound to execute all laws, in obedience to the will of Congress, if he execute them at all. We need not go to Montesquieu, nor Sidney, nor Locke, nor anybody else to prove this, as we have here some times taunted by our opponents. It results from the nature of our Government, and the different branches into which it is divided.

But the Secretary of the Treasury, it was said, is bound to report to Congress. Well, air, if we were to make a law to-morrow, compelling the Secretary of State, the Secretary of the Navy, the Secretary of War, to report to Congress, would that alter the nature of their respective offices? Congress had done professedly and by what gentlemen say has been done in reality, it had baptized this department by the name of Legislative, if it had called it the Legislative Department of the Treasury—the absurdity would have appeared upon the very face of it.

It seemed to us, sir, during this discussion, that the great error of gentlemen lay in supposing that because the Treasury Department might be called, been constituted in just the same terms, upon the same principles, or with just the same powers of the other executive department. Why, it was not an executive department. Why, begging gentleman's pardon, I thought that nothing to do with the question. The true question was, as I thought, what is the nature of the duties the Secretary is bound to perform? makes no difference whether they are few or many, whether they are limited or enlarged; whether Secretary is bound to report to the President or Congress. What is the nature of his duties, as I thought, the only question to be answered. Now, it was well said, that they must be of these three kinds: they must be either legislative, judicial, or executive. Well, sir, what legislative duties? They must clearly relate to the power of making laws. Nobody will pretend the Secretary of the Treasury has anything with that power. Is he a judicial officer? man will believe it. He must, then, be an executive officer. Why, sir, this department was established for the very purpose of carrying into execution the laws of Congress in relation to the public money, and, as such, is an executive department.

Now, as to the degree of control which Congress may have reserved to itself over this department, that does not alter the nature of the Those departments are all the creatures of Congress. It called them into existence, and it can extinguish them in a breath. It can make things called departments, of the power of carrying into execution the laws of Congress their respective officers become executive officers, and the Constitution having intrusted the superintendence of the executive branch of the Government to the President, they become responsible to him, and he becomes responsible for them, the people, for the faithful discharge of their duties. We were told, air, that the Secretary of the Treasury is the agent of Congress. To be sure he are the duties this agent is bound to perform? carry into effect the laws of Congress. But doing, he is performing those very duties

the Constitution has intrusted to the superintend-ence of the President. He is an executive officer, and Congress cannot make him anything else. This requires no illustration. Gentlemen may talk till doomsday, but they never can argue us out of reason and common sense. But I must do them the justice to say, that this has been the most desperate contest between the subtleties of lawyers and common sense that ever I had the good or bad fortune to witness.

Now, sir, as to this union of the purse and sword, of which we have heard so much. What is a union of the purse and the sword? When the same branch of the Government has the right of raising armies and of raising money to support those armies. Has the President claimed the right of enlisting a single soldier, or of raising a single dollar of money by way of taxation, but under the sanction of the laws of Congress?

Mr. Speaker, the gentlemen on the other side will, in their cool moments, be ready to acknowledge another thing—that the Secretary of the Treasury had a right to remove the public deposites from the Bank of the United States for good and sufficient reasons, and that he has a right to judge in the first instance of the sufficiency of those reasons. Well, sir, if this be true, it was all I wanted to direct me in the vote I was about to give. For if the President has assumed no unconstitutional powers in this transaction, if the Secretary of the Treasury had a legal right to remove the deposites, then I thought the question of their restoration was a question of expediency on the part of Congress. For, granting, by way of argument, that the removal was inexpedient, it did not follow that the restoration ought to take place. If the President or the Secretary had committed a foolish act, it did not therefore follow that Congress ought to commit another folly. Let us suppose for a moment that the deposites had been removed for a notoriously insufficient reason; but that after the removal, and before the restoration, a sudden calamity had befallen the bank, by which it had become an unsafe place of deposite for the public money: Would Congress be bound to restore the deposites under such circumstances? Certainly not. It might censure the Secretary if it might give the bank damages for the injury done to it, but it would not throw away the public money by placing it in an insolvent institution. The question of a restoration was, then, as I thought, a distinct one from that of the removal. And if the bank was not to be rechartered, I thought the deposites ought not to be restored. For, under such circumstances, a restoration could be of no benefit to the bank, and would tend to increase rather than relieve the distresses of the country. Why, sir, I was willing to take the story of the bank itself upon this question. What did the bank and the advocates of the bank tell us? That, unless the bank was to be rechartered, it must go on from day to day, from week to week, and from month to month, curtailing its business and contracting its accounts, in order to be able to wind up its affairs at the end of its charter. Well, sir, what, under such circumstances, would have been the effect of a restoration of the deposites? Would it have enabled the bank to enlarge its business by extending its discounts? Certainly not, sir, if what the bank said was true, that it must continue to contract its accounts, if it was not to be rechartered; unless, indeed, it has the very singular faculty of enlarging and contracting its discounts at the same time.

What, then, would have been the effect of a restoration? It would have been simply taking the deposites away from banks where they can be disbursed upon, and, where they are, to a certain extent at least, discounted upon, and putting them back into an institution where they could not be discounted upon, but where they could be locked up in its vaults, and withdrawn from the use of the commercial community. How, then, could a restoration of the deposites, if the bank was not to be rechartered, have tended to relieve the distress of the country? Shall we be told that it would have effected this object by restoring public confidence? Public confidence is a plant of a very delicate nature, and sometimes of a very slow growth. Gentlemen have been very successful in destroying it. Whether they can make it revive and germinate again at pleasure, remains to be proved. A

restoration of the deposites could only tend to restore public confidence, in so far as it would be a measure of relief to the community, and that it could produce no such relief I have already shown.

Again, if the deposites were to be restored without a recharter of the bank, they would have to be removed again at the end of the charter, and thus the country would suffer under the pressure of a double removal.

It seemed to me, sir, that the discussion upon this question was one of a very extraordinary character. We were told that the whole country was upon the verge of bankruptcy and ruin; that darkness and gloom had settled down upon our present prospects, and that a still heavier cloud of disaster and dismay was hanging over the horizon of our future hopes. We were told that the country had been plunged at once from the heights of prosperity into the lowest depths of wo; that our merchants are broken; that our commerce is ruined; that our manufactures are abandoned; that the arts are paralyzed; that labor is without its rewards; that industry has become no better than idleness; and that all about us is one wide-spreading scene of desolation and ruin. Nay, more, sir, we were told that the worst of the evils have not yet happened; that the portentous signs of a revolution are shaking their horrid tresses in the sky; that the elements are becoming convulsed; that the earth is quaking under our feet; and that, ere long, the fires of the volcano will burst forth, carrying, in their awful train, destruction and death. And what, sir, have we been told is the cause of all these calamities? Is it that Heaven, provoked at our ingratitude, and wearied out with our obstinacy and crimes, is withholding its blessed influences from us? Are the fountains of the waters dried up, and have the fruits of the earth been blasted and shrivelled under the burning influence of the sun? Has pestilence walked abroad through our land, and changed the countenance of health into paleness? No, sir. No disease is destroying the health, no famine is consuming the lives of our citizens. The spring again returns to us in its loveliness, and the earth is reviving in beauty. Has, then, a foreign foe invaded our soil? Have the minions of despotism come from beyond the Atlantic to ravage our fields, to burn our cities, to slaughter our countrymen, and to trample our liberties and Constitution in the dust? No, sir. No foreign foe has invaded our soil, and the sound of the trumpet is not heard in our land. Is it, then, civil dissensions and internal commotions that have produced all these evils? Sir, the very fear of them had long since passed away. What is it, then, what is it, that thus, as it were in a moment, in the twinkling of an eye, has plunged us at once into this gulf of wo? It is, say the advocates of the bank, it is the act of one bold, bad man. It is he, who, with more than the cruelty of a despot, and the power of a monarch, has changed this scene of happiness into one of misery.

And what remedy has been proposed for all this evil? How is the violated Constitution to be vindicated? How are the insulted laws to be avenged? How are our liberties to be rescued from the grasp of this remorseless usurper? By restoring the public deposites to the Bank of the United States. Good heavens, Mr. Speaker, is this high-sounding prologue to a tragedy, thus to be followed by the contemptible scenes of a farce? Is it thus that the violated Constitution is to be vindicated? When the barriers of the law are broken down, and the usurper is riding in triumph over the field, are we to sit here deliberating and coolly resolving that these things ought not so to be? When the foundations of the Republic are shaking, and the Constitution trembling under our feet, shall we cling hold of the Doric pillars of the bank, and hide ourselves in its vaults for safety? If gentlemen really believed what they said, why did they not propose some measure worthy of themselves and the country? Was there not one among them all, sir, who dared devote himself to his country, and, like the Roman of old, jump into this yawning chasm, to propitiate her angry deities? Shall I be told that the President has a veto beyond all majority in this House, who will sanction all his measures? Has, then, the patriotism of the gentlemen come to this, that they will not propose a measure, which, ac-

cording to their own principles, ought to be proposed and carried through this House, simply because they doubt its success? I will give the gentlemen more credit for their patriotism. If they really believed the Constitution had been violated, and that our liberties had been taken from us, they would not have stopped to calculate the consequences, to reckon the probabilities of success; they would have rallied around the standard of our liberties and the Constitution, with a determination to rescue them from the grasp of the usurper, or perish in the attempt.

It seems to me, sir, that the course pursued by the opposition, on this momentous question, has been a very disastrous one for the country; and I do not believe it will turn out to be a very fortunate one for themselves. If one-half of what we have been told, both in and out of Congress, be true, no measure has been proposed at all adequate to the occasion. If the Constitution has been violated, and our liberties invaded, then the first measure ought to have been the punishment of the usurper. But gentlemen have not chosen to occupy that ground. They have abandoned the high and honorable course which, according to their own principles, was open to them, and have descended to fight the battles of the bank, instead of the Constitution. Well, sir, if the removal of the deposites has been effected by a violation of the Constitution, their restoration, by a vote of two-thirds of both Houses, would show the disapprobation of Congress of the act of the Executive, if he be as bad as they represent him, he will abuse again? Well, sir, having abandoned that ground, the gentlemen have proposed a restoration of the deposites. The restoration of the deposites has been the great end, and they have urged the violation of the Constitution as the means to accomplish that end. The bank has been the first consideration with the gentlemen, to which the Constitution is but secondary and subservient. They have not attempted to impeach the President; and why? Because, I suppose, they will tell us there is a majority in this House who will support him in his measures. What, then, have they done? Why, they have tried to get a restoration of the deposites, and to relieve the distresses of the country. Do they suppose the nation to be so blind as not to see through all this? Do they think to hide their designs by so thin a disguise? It is nothing but the old story of the ins and the outs. They have dragged forth the old fashioned, lumbering state coach of the opposition, newly gilded and varnished up; they have painted the bank arms upon its panels; they have mounted the bank coachman upon the box; and they have placed the bank footman, in livery, behind. And they are driving on, sir, at a very merry rate, amid the huzzas of the town. All this old admirably well, as long as they are going over smooth pavements and macadamized streets. But when they have once fairly got out of sight of the exchange; when they have passed the bounds of the city, and left the suburbs behind; when they have come out into the rough, uneven roads of the country, give me leave to tell the gentlemen passengers that, their good-for-nothing, crazy old vehicle, will break down, and leave them floundering in the mud. Nothing but the people's line will run them.

The memorial which I have the honor to present to the House is signed by about 4,000 inhabitants, principally legal voters in my district. They state that the commercial and manufacturing portions of the district are suffering under great pecuniary embarrassments, which they attribute to the hostility of the Executive to the Bank of the United

States Well, sir, I will not deny that such embarrassments exist. When my constituents come here to memorialize Congress through me their Representative, that they are suffering under pecuniary difficulties, I will not stand up here to deny the fact. I will not pretend to know their own business better than they know it themselves. No, sir, I rather sympathize with them in their distress, and will coöperate in every measure which I may deem expedient for their relief. But when this distress is not of a local, but a general nature, when it pervades not one district of the country only, but the whole country, I must entertain my own opinion as to its causes. It is not, sir, that I have any want of respect for the opinions of the gentlemen who have instructed me. Some of them I know personally—many of them I know by reputation—and I will not pretend to put my judgment in comparison with theirs. But our opinions do not always depend upon ourselves, nor can we change them as we will.

I know, sir, that in having refused to obey these instructions, I have exposed myself to the attacks of those who will be ready to assail my motives, and to denounce me as the hireling instrument of a party. I shall endeavor to bear up against all such attacks, with that equanimity which it becomes every public man to exercise in the discharge of those duties which must always, more or less, subject him to reproach. But if the gentlemen who have condescended to mark my course upon this floor for reproof, and to instruct me in my duty here, shall suppose that I am insensible to their wishes, or that I have lightly and inconsiderately disregarded them, give me leave to say they will do me a manifest injury. If motives of self-interest had dictated my conduct, I should have pursued a very different course. No man, sir, can envy me the position in which I have placed myself, by disregarding these instructions. I have been obliged to go counter to the wishes of many valued personal friends. Alone, without legislative experience, I have been obliged to oppose myself to my colleagues in office—to a delegation, which, in point of abilities, of eloquence, of learning, of every liberal and manly accomplishment, will not suffer in comparison with that of any other State upon this floor; and with whom, whatever difference of political sentiment there may be between us, I shall always esteem it an honor to have been connected in the discharge of my duties here. But there are considerations above all feelings of personal affection, and personal respect. And if, after having deliberately formed my opinion upon a great question of public policy, after having maintained it for a long time through evil report and through good report—having refused to give it up in prospect of office, or rather having made the liberty of acting freely upon it the condition of accepting office—after all this, I could basely yield it up in apprehension of loss of office, I should sink myself in the estimation of those very men, who have now, as I think, somewhat unwarily, I will not say unkindly, urged me to do it.

I believe the House will do me the justice to say, that I have not very early intruded myself upon their notice. And, now that I am up, I will detain them with only one or two remarks more. I should be the last man to infringe upon the freedom, or even the latitude of debate, on this floor. It is due to the representatives of the people, as well as to those who sent them here, that they should have the right of discussing all questions of public policy, and the conduct of public men, with a perfect freedom and plainness. As a friend to the institutions and the rulers of my country, I would not shrink from any attack that might be made on the principles of the one, or the conduct of the other. If they cannot stand attacks, if they cannot bear discussion, let them go down together, and be consigned over to the ignominy and contempt of mankind. But while everything must be yielded to the right of discussion on this floor, something may be expected of gentlemen, if not on the ground of courtesy, at least upon the score of decency and self-respect. And if they will undertake to brand the rulers of their country with all the epithets which the phrensy of a mad ambition may suggest, they must be content if they only render themselves ridiculous, instead of injuring the object of their attack.

Especially would it become those who have themselves been denounced as maintaining doctrines subversive of the fundamental principles of this Government—doctrines tending to anarchy, sedition, and civil war—to exercise a little charity towards those who differ from them in the construction of constitutional questions; to learn a little moderation at least, if not humility, from their own sad experience. It was a rule with the ancient critics, that in his fictitious representations the poet should make the language used by his characters correspond with their situation:

> "Telephus et Peleus, cum pauper et exsul, uterque,
> Projicit ampullas et sesquipedalia verba,
> Si curat cor spectantis, tetigisse querela."

But in the theatrical declamations upon this floor, this ancient rule seems to have been wholly forgotten. If the gentlemen who have maintained those doctrines would condescend to bring down their language to correspond with the position they occupy in the eyes of the American people, we should be much more likely to be affected by their arguments.

But, sir, if it were true, as has been often asserted here, that a Tiberius, a Caligula, or a Nero, did in reality preside over the destinies of this nation, instead of the Chief Magistrate who now sways its councils with so much vigor, he would not be thus denounced and held up to public reprobation. Before such an event could happen, the spirit of liberty would have departed from this House and from this nation. The suppliant accents of slaves would have been substituted for the bold language of freemen, and we should no longer deserve our liberty, for we should not have the courage to assert it. Such was the case in Rome, under Cæsar; in England, under Cromwell; and in France, under Bonaparte.

But, if gentlemen will still have it that they are suffering under the evils of despotism; if, in spite of all the ribaldry and party abuse which is daily suffered to be poured forth against the rulers of their country, they will still insist upon it that they are subjected to the sway of an arbitrary monarch, I have one thing more to say. From my soul I abhor despotism in all its forms. By feeling, by education, by habit—in common, I trust, with every citizen of this republic,—I loathe the very name of despotism, in whatever alluring garb, or in whatever specious shape it may be presented to my view. But bad as it is, and deeply as I should deprecate its remotest approaches to the rulers of my country, there is one thing, in my opinion, still worse, and still more deeply to be deprecated; that is, a subjection to a proud moneyed aristocracy. If it should ever be my misfortune to choose between them, I should not be long in making up my mind. After having tried every expedient that patriotism could suggest or prudence dictate, to avoid the evil—if, after all, the calamity could not be averted, I would say, give me the man who has raised himself to power, although it be upon the ruins of the liberties of his country, but who, at the same time, has encircled that country with the glories of an illustrious name—who has stamped the impress of his own genius upon her arts, her arms, and her laws, and who has raised her up to be the admiration and terror of the world; give me him, tyrant, usurper, despot, though he be, rather than a subjection to a proud moneyed aristocracy, who have no ambition above the level of their own sordid trade; who make their power the pander of their avarice; who oppress their country when living, and who, when dead, leave no other memorials of their inglorious existence than the sighs, the tears, and the groans, of their fellow-citizens.

Mr. Speaker, I have finished all I intended to say in presenting this memorial. It has been a very painful duty to me, sir, for the first time that I ever had the honor of addressing any legislative, and, I may add, any public assembly, to be obliged to stand up here in defence of my own conduct. But circumstances have compelled me to do it, and if I have trespassed too far upon the indulgence of the House, my peculiar situation must form my apology. But if, in the sentiments I have uttered, or in the language I have used, I have been betrayed by too much warmth of feeling into expressions which may seem to some to bear too hardly upon my political opponents, I can only say, I trust the House knows how to distinguish between personal and political hostility. For the former, I shall offer no excuse; for I feel that I need none. From the latter, I do not wish to be considered exempt. But we may all of us have something to forget and forgive. The angry clouds which have been so long gathering in the national sky, have flashed their terrific lightnings athwart this Hall, and involved us in the horrors of the tempest. But these temporary convulsions of the elements may, perhaps, be but the salutary purifications of our political atmosphere; and though now the fears of the timid may be excited—though clouds upon clouds may close in the prospect, and settle down upon us in the gloom of an impenetrable night; yet, ere long, the light will break forth—the thunders will die away in the distant horizon, and the mild evening-star of peace and conciliation rise over these troubled waters of strife. And when we go forth to behold the wrecks of the storm, though we may, perhaps, find some old oak torn up by the roots, or even a whole forest laid prostrate by the blast; though the labors and the habitations of men may have been swept away by the violence of the tempest—we shall find, if I mistake not, nature reviving in fresh vigor and beauty; we shall find our liberties safe, the Constitution unimpaired, and the great principles of freedom springing [illegible] in luxuriant abundance, over the whole land.

Mr. O. concluded by moving that the memorial [illegible] laid on the table, and printed, with the names.

Mr. OSGOOD presented a memorial from [illegible] thousand seven hundred and sixty-two citizens [illegible] Boston, approving of the removal of the deposites, and protesting against their restoration; which [illegible] read, and, on motion of Mr. O., laid on the [illegible] and ordered to be printed, with the names.

Mr. GORHAM presented a memorial from [illegible] dry citizens, merchants of Boston, inviting [illegible] legislation of Congress on the subject of gold [illegible] silver coins. Referred to the select committee [illegible] that subject.

Mr. G. also presented two memorials of [illegible] Jarvis, of Boston, in the State of Massachusetts, counsellor at law: the one setting forth that he [illegible] invented an improvement in the construction [illegible] boilers for steam engines; the other setting [illegible] that he has invented a mode of ventilating [illegible] war and merchant ships; which memorials [illegible] referred to the committee on Naval Affairs.

Mr. J. Q. ADAMS presented a memorial of [illegible] zens, merchants, mechanics, and others, [illegible] in Detroit, condeming the measures of the Administration in respect to the Bank of the United States, and representing their effects as [illegible] jurious to the interests of the Territory of [illegible] gan. Read, laid on the table, and ordered [illegible] printed.

Mr. BURGES presented the memorial of [illegible] dry mechanics and citizens of Rhode Island [illegible] the subject of the currency and the United [illegible] Bank, and resolutions adopted by the same. [illegible] memorial was read, laid on the table, and [illegible] to be printed.

Mr. PEARCE presented several memorials [illegible] different towns in Rhode Island, approving [illegible] course of the Administration in reference [illegible] United States Bank, which were ordered [illegible] printed and laid on the table.

Mr. PEARCE also presented resolutions [illegible] ed at a meeting held in Centreville, county of [illegible] Rhode Island, on the subject of the currency [illegible] the depression of business. Read, laid on the [illegible] and ordered to be printed.

Mr. HUNTINGTON presented a memorial [illegible] the subject of the currency, from a number of [illegible] zens of Newtown, Connecticut; which was [illegible] ordered to be printed, and laid on the table.

Mr. HALL presented a memorial from a [illegible] tion of his constituents, of various occupations [illegible] professions, disapproving of the measures [illegible] Administration in reference to the bank, and [illegible] resenting them as injurious in their effects [illegible] the currency and the political rights of the [illegible] Ordered to be printed and laid on the table.

Mr. SLADE presented a memorial signed [illegible] 1948 citizens of the 2d Congressional district [illegible] State of Vermont, on the subject of the currency, with some introductory remarks. Ordered [illegible] printed and laid on the table.

Mr. ALLEN presented the memorial of [illegible] young men, citizens of Burlington, stating that [illegible] are distressed in consequence of the removal of [illegible] deposites, and praying their restoration and [illegible]

renewal of the charter of the Bank of the United States. Read, ordered to be printed, and laid on the table.

Mr. DICKSON presented a memorial from three or four thousand citizens of Ontario county, New York, on the subject of the currency and the United States Bank, and intimated an intention to call up the paper on Monday next, for the purpose of making some remarks upon it.

Mr. LAWRENCE presented a memorial from sundry young men of the city of New York, praying the restoration of the constitutional currency. Ordered to be printed and laid on the table.

Mr. CLARK, of New York, rose and said:

Mr. PRESIDENT: I am requested to present to the House the proceedings of a meeting held in the town of Seneca Falls on the 29th day of March last. The village in which the meeting was held is one of the most flourishing in Western New York. Its extensive milling and manufacturing establishments necessarily feel the pressure, which the memorialists admit is somewhat severe.

Unlike many of the petitions and memorials which have been presented here, claiming to be of a no-party character, this meeting was composed exclusively of the friends of the Administration. Numerous resolutions were reported by a committee of highly respectable gentlemen, all of whom I know; and I will embrace the opportunity here afforded me to say, that from the amount of business in which they are engaged, and their general intelligence, they are well calculated both to feel the full extent of the pressure and justly to appreciate its cause. One of the gentlemen composing this committee is the sheriff of the county, another, Mr. Bayard, who presented the resolutions to the meeting, is extensively engaged in the manufacture of flour, an article which, it is said by the friends of the bank, has suffered most by what they are pleased to call the ruinous measures of the Administration. The report of the committee was unanimously adopted.

In pursuance, Mr. Speaker, of the duty enjoined by the rules of this House, I will very briefly state the contents of such of the resolutions as apply most directly to the question which has agitated Congress and the nation from the commencement of the session to the present time. They resolve that the Bank of the United States ought not to be rechartered;

That the deposite of public moneys ought not be made in the Bank of the United States nor in any of its branches;

That, in their estimation, the State banks are fully adequate to discharge the duties of fiscal agents of the Government;

That they have full confidence in the resources of this country, and believe that its prosperity is not dependent on the existence of any moneyed institution;

That the firmness and patriotism of Andrew Jackson at this crisis deserves the lasting gratitude of the American people.

They further resolve that the restoration of the deposites or the recharter of the bank would, in their opinion, be equivalent to a surrender of their liberty, and that they believe the patriotic people of New York will be ready to endure any pecuniary privation rather than submit to the dictation of a great moneyed power;

That the only currency recognised by the Constitution is the hard-money currency, resting on the broad basis of the precious metals, and that a paper currency, subject as it is, of necessity, to a perpetual fluctuation, is but the scourge of honest industry and the pander of a pampered aristocracy;

That the efforts of partisan leaders and presses produce a panic among business men, a scarcity of money, and generally to derange the currency, a species of political warfare peculiar to the advocates of a great moneyed monopoly, and deserve the execration and punishment of a civilized community;

That the recent combined attack upon the safety-fund banks of that State, while it demonstrated their title to public confidence, was an unwarrantable assault, which, though severely felt by the people of that State, was chiefly designed to affect distinguished statesman under whose auspices safety-fund banks were associated together for protection of the public;

That the present pressure and scarcity of money

are not justly attributable to the removal of the deposites, and would have been more severe but for that timely measure; that they have proceeded, in some degree, from the tariff act of 1833, but more especially from the course and conduct of the bank itself; the speeches and efforts of its partisans and presses, all laboring with the common design of creating a political and fiscal necessity for the renewal of the charter of the bank.

These, sir, are the sentiments of freemen, who would not violate the integrity of the Constitution, to prolong the existence of a dangerous moneyed monopoly, and who will not permit pecuniary considerations to control their judgments and actions, on a question involving the prosperity of our free institutions.

Subsequently to the period when these resolutions were adopted, I have received information on which I can rely with certainty, that confidence is again in a great measure restored; the different kinds of produce rapidly rising in value; that wheat, the staple production of that section of country, was selling at 87½ cents a bushel, and that a further advance was warranted by the price of flour in the city of New York; that the large amount of business doing on the canals, justified the belief that the toll this season will exceed that of any former year.

The citizens of New York having recovered from the pecuniary embarrassment under which they labored for a short period, will now have leisure calmly to examine into the cause of the pressure. If, upon that examination, they shall become satisfied, as I believe they will, that it was produced solely for the purpose of effecting a recharter of the United States Bank, that institution, with its leading political friends, who have used it for party purposes, will receive the unanimous condemnation of an indignant and injured people.

Mr. FULLER presented a memorial from citizens of Livingston county, New York, praying Congress to interpose for the relief of the country from its present embarrassments by the restoration of the deposites, and the renewal or continuation for a time, of the charter of the Bank of the United States. Read, laid on the table, and ordered to be printed.

Petitions were presented by Mr. WARD, and Mr. C. P. WHITE.

Mr. WILLIAM TAYLOR presented a memorial from a large and respectable meeting of the citizens of Onondaga county, New York, approving of the course of the Government in relation to the Bank of the United States, introducing it with some remarks. Read, ordered to be printed, and laid on the table.

Petitions were presented by Messrs. MARTINDALE and SELDEN.

Mr. SELDEN presented a memorial, signed by six thousand inhabitants of the county of Oneida, praying the interposition of Congress for their relief from existing embarrassments, occasioned by the derangement of the currency, and recommending the restoration of the deposites, and the recharter of the United States Bank. Mr. S., after some remarks, moved the reference of the memorial to a select committee, with instructions to report a plan, in the form of a bill, for the establishment of a safe and uniform currency; which motion he submitted as a resolution.

Mr. BEARDSLEY replied at length to the statements of Mr. SELDEN; after which, without taking the question,

The House adjourned.

IN SENATE.

TUESDAY, May 6, 1834.

Mr. TYLER presented the petition of the heirs of Colonel William Campbell, a brigadier-general in the army of the Revolution, asking that a law may be passed allowing to them the pay and emoluments due their ancestor. The petition was referred to the Committee on Revolutionary Claims.

Also, the petition of Zachariah Cox, asking indemnity for property of which he was deprived by their official character. Referred to the Committee on the Judiciary.

And the petition of Jacob Weaver, praying remuneration for certain lands granted by the State of Georgia, and afterwards sold by the United

States. Referred to the Committee on Public Lands.

Mr. TIPTON presented the petition of the chiefs of the Potawatomie nation; which was referred to the Committee on Indian Affairs.

Mr. KENT presented the petition of the widow of Richard Waters, of Baltimore; which was referred to the Committee on Claims.

The following resolutions were submitted:

By Mr. KANE:

Resolved, That the Committee on Finance be instructed to inquire into the expediency of refunding to Pierre Menard and Louis Valle, the amount of duties wrongfully exacted from them upon goods imported into New Orleans in the ship Mars, in the month of July, 1829.

This resolution was agreed to, and, together with the documents, was referred to the Committee on Finance.

By Mr. EWING:

Resolved, That the Secretary of State be directed to transmit to the Senate copies of his orders to the superintendent of the Patent Office of the 17th of October and the 10th of December last. Also, a copy of certain charges exhibited to him by William P. Elliot, against said superintendent, for malconduct in office; with a copy of all the evidence taken by the commissioner appointed to investigate said charges; a copy of said commissioner's report; and a copy of a letter addressed to said superintendent, by said Secretary of State, dated the 28th March, 1834, touching said investigation.

By Mr. TIPTON:

Resolved, That the daily hour for the meeting of the Senate shall be eleven o'clock, till otherwise ordered.

REPORTS.

Mr. ROBBINS, from the Library Committee, reported a joint resolution, accepting the colossal statue of Jefferson, from Lieutenant Uriah P. Levy, of the United States navy, and designating the spot at which it shall be placed. The resolution was ordered to a second reading.

Mr. ROBBINS, from the same committee, reported a joint resolution in relation to the transmission by mail of the laws of the United States; which was ordered to a second reading.

♦ GENERAL ORDERS.

The resolution setting aside Fridays and Saturdays in each week for the consideration of private bills, the Senate refused to adopt: Yeas 13, nays 16.

The other resolutions lying upon the table, submitted by Messrs. WEBSTER, TOMLINSON, SPRAGUE, and PRESTON, were adopted.

The report of the Committee of Claims, unfavorable to the petition of Archibald W. Hamilton, was agreed to.

The report of the same committee, unfavorable to the petition of Samuel Newell, was agreed to.

The report of the Committee on Revolutionary Claims, unfavorable to the petition of Bissell Phelps, and a similar report upon the petition of the heirs of Gabriel Green, were agreed to.

Mr. NAUDAIN, adverting to the report of the Committee on Military Affairs which led to their being discharged from the further consideration of the memorial of Doctor Boyd Reilly, moved that the memorial, which was agreed to, be referred to a select committee; which was agreed to. Whereupon, the Senate proceeded to ballot for the committee, when the following gentlemen were elected, viz: Messrs. NAUDAIN, LINN, KENT, ROBBINS, and PRENTISS.

The following bills from the House of Representatives were read a first and second time, and referred:

A bill adjusting the claims of certain persons for the loss of property in the late war with Great Britain, and the war with Black Hawk and his Indians;

A bill for the relief of John Wilson;

A bill for the relief of John S. Fleming, administrator de bonis non of John Syme, deceased;

A bill amending the several acts in reference to the insolvent laws;

A bill authorizing the renewal of patent for the benefit of Robert Black; and

A bill for the relief of Henry Oakes.

The following bills were read a third time, and passed:

A bill for the relief of Captain Thomas Ap Catesby Jones;
A bill for the relief of John H. Maguire; and
A bill for the relief of John Webber.

SPECIAL ORDER.

At a quarter before the usual hour, (one o'clock,) Mr. POINDEXTER stated that the Senate seemed averse to the consideration of any legislative business until the protest had been disposed of, and moved to proceed to the consideration of the special order; which was agreed to.

PRESIDENT'S PROTEST.

The Senate resumed the consideration of the special order, being Mr. BIBB's amendment to Mr. POINDEXTER's resolution.

Mr. CALHOUN having the floor from the previous day, spoke at length against the protest of the President; and on concluding,

Mr. BIBB withdrew his amendment, " that the protest be not received."

Mr. FORSYTH then spoke in reply to Mr. CALHOUN, in defence of the course of the President, and in justification of the protest, and moved to strike out all after the word resolved in the resolutions, and insert the following:

1. *Resolved*, That the message of the President, protesting against the resolutions of the Senate of the 28th of March, be entered on the Journals, according to his request.

2. *Resolved*, That leaving to the States, to whom the Senate is alone responsible, to judge whether the resolution complained of is, or is not, within the constitutional competency of this body, and called for by the present condition of public affairs, an authenticated copy of the protest, and moved with a list of the ayes and noes, of the President's message, and of those resolutions, be prepared by the Secretary, and transmitted by the Vice President to the Governor of each State of the Union, to be by him laid before the Legislatures, at their next session, as the only authority authorised to decide upon the opinions and conduct of the Senators respectively.

Mr. FORSYTH, however, withdrew the amendment for the present, to enable Mr. CALHOUN to offer the following, as an amendment to Mr. POINDEXTER's resolution:

Resolved, That the President of the United States has no right to send a protest to the Senate against any of its proceedings.

Resolved, That the Senate do not receive the protest of the President.

Upon these propositions, Mr. CALHOUN asked the yeas and nays; which were ordered.

Mr. PRESTON then spoke at some length against the principles contained in the protest, but in favor of receiving the document.

Mr. WEBSTER also followed briefly on the same side, and moved that the questions be taken separately on Mr. CALHOUN's propositions.

Mr. CLAYTON then expressed a wish that Mr. CALHOUN would withdraw his second resolution.

This Mr. C. yielded to, but it was opposed by Mr. FORSYTH; and as it required the unanimous consent of the Senate to withdraw—

Mr. CLAY moved to lay the resolution on the table.

The motion was decided to be out of order, (Mr. KING, of Alabama, in the chair,) on the ground that the two resolutions were one amendment.

Mr. CLAY appealed from the decision of the Chair; and

Mr. FORSYTH asked the yeas and nays on the appeal; which were ordered, and are as follows:

YEAS—Messrs. Bell, Benton, Black, Brown, Calhoun, Ewing, Forsyth, Frelinghuysen, Grundy, Hendricks, Hill, Kane, Kent, King of Georgia, Knight, Leigh, Linn, McKean, Poindexter, Porter, Prentiss, Robbins, Shepley, Silsbee, Smith, Swift, Tallmadge, Tipton, Tomlinson, Tyler, Webster, White, Wilkins, Wright—34.

NAYS—Messrs. Clay, Clayton, Naudain, and Sprague.—4.

So the decision of the Chair was sustained.

The question recurring on Mr. CALHOUN's first resolution, was then taken, and decided in the affirmative, as follows:

YEAS—Messrs. Bell, Bibb, Black, Calhoun, Clay, Clayton, Ewing, Frelinghuysen, Kent, Knight, Leigh, Naudain, Poindexter, Porter, Prentiss, Preston, Robbins, Silsbee, Sprague,

Smith, Swift, Tomlinson, Tyler, Waggaman, Webster—25.

NAYS—Messrs. Benton, Brown, Forsyth, Grundy, Hendricks, Hill, Kane, King of Alabama, King of Georgia, Linn, McKean, Shepley, Tallmadge, Tipton, White, Wilkins, Wright—17.

The question then recurring on the second resolution, was decided in the negative, as follows:

YEAS—Messrs. Calhoun, Clayton, Ewing, Leigh, Naudain, Poindexter, Robbins—7.

NAYS—Messrs. Bell, Benton, Black, Brown, Clay, Forsyth, Frelinghuysen, Grundy, Hendricks, Hill, Kane, Kent, King of Alabama, King of Georgia, Knight, Linn, McKean, Moore, Porter, Prentiss, Preston, Shepley, Silsbee, Smith, Sprague, Swift, Tallmadge, Tipton, Tomlinson, Tyler, Webster, White, Wilkins, Wright—34.

The question coming up on Mr. FORSYTH's resolution,

Mr. FORSYTH made a few remarks in support of it; when the question on its adoption was taken, and decided in the negative, as follows:

YEAS—Messrs. Benton, Brown, Forsyth, Grundy, Hendricks, Hill, Kane, King of Alabama, King of Georgia, Linn, McKean, Shepley, Tallmadge, Tipton, White, Wilkins, Wright—17.

NAYS—Messrs. Bell, Bibb, Black, Calhoun, Clay, Clayton, Ewing, Frelinghuysen, Kent, Knight, Leigh, Moore, Naudain, Poindexter, Porter, Prentiss, Preston, Robbins, Silsbee, Smith, Sprague, Swift, Tomlinson, Tyler, Webster—25.

The question recurring on Mr. POINDEXTER's resolution,

Mr. WEBSTER rose, and expressed a wish to be heard; whereupon,

On motion of Mr. POINDEXTER,
The Senate adjourned.

HOUSE OF REPRESENTATIVES.

TUESDAY, May 6, 1834.

Mr. MITCHELL reported a bill for the relief of John Adams. Read twice and committed

Mr. STEWART reported a bill for the improvement of the steamboat navigation from Pittsburg to Brownsville, Pennsylvania; which was read twice and committed.

Mr. BURGES reported a bill for the relief of Ephraim F. Gilbert; which was read twice and committed.

Mr. GARLAND, of Louisiana, by unanimous consent, presented several memorials and petitions relative to individual claims; which were referred to the appropriate committees.

Mr. HIESTER reported a bill to incorporate the Friendship Benevolent Society of the City and County of Washington; which was read twice and committed.

Mr. CAVE JOHNSON reported a bill directing the running out and marking the line of the Chickasaw nation; which was read twice and committed.

On motion of Mr. WILLIAMS, the House, by unanimous consent, took up the bill heretofore reported from the Committee upon Territories, for regulating the election of the Legislative Council of Florida, and for other purposes; which was read and ordered to be engrossed for a third reading.

The resolution heretofore presented by Mr. MARDIS, declaring that provision should be made by law for the deposite of public money in the State banks, then came up, upon the amendment proposed by Mr. JONES, declaring that the deposite of public money should be restored to the Bank of the United States.

Mr. GALBRAITH, who was entitled to the floor from a former day, addressed the House in support of the original resolution, and in opposition to the amendment. Mr. G. went into a vindication of the proceedings of the Legislature of Pennsylvania, and of the views expressed by Governor Wolf, in reply to the views heretofore expressed by Mr. McKENNAN upon this subject. Before Mr. G. had concluded, the hour appropriated to morning business expired, and, on motion of Mr. BOON, the House proceeded to the order of the day.

CONTESTED ELECTION FROM KENTUCKY.

Mr. SEABORN JONES, from the Committee of Elections, made a report relative to the contest-

ed seat in the House between R. P. LETCHER and T. P. MOORE, in which the facts relative to the election were stated in detail. The report concludes that Mr. MOORE has a majority of either 44 or 49 votes, according as a certain principle should be recognised or rejected, and recommends the adoption of two resolutions, importing, in substance—

1. That THOMAS P. MOORE is entitled to the seat in the House, from the Fifth Congressional District of Kentucky.

2. That R. P. LETCHER shall be entitled to the compensation of a member of Congress during his attendance on the House the present session.

After the report had been read—

Mr. JONES moved that the further consideration of this subject be postponed until Tuesday next, and that the report be printed.

Mr. BANKS moved to amend the proposition to print, by ordering the evidence to be printed.

The SPEAKER inquired whether the gentleman from Georgia, [Mr JONES,] would accept the amendment as a modification of his motion?

Mr. JONES said he could not, agreeably to his instructions from the Committee of Elections, as to the amendment. The evidence in this case amounted to 1800 pages. If this amendment was adopted, judging from the progress of the printing ordered by the House, the papers would not be printed, and the case prepared for investigation, during the present session. The evidence might be printed by the commencement of the next session, but it would not be possible for the members of the House to investigate the testimony during the next session. He felt justified in making the statement from the time taken in the investigation of their objections, the committee had not found themselves able to report until this time. If it is expected that the members should wade through this immense mass of papers, he could not perceive the advantage of referring the question to the committee at all. Almost the whole of the session had been spent in ascertaining the facts which are stated in the report. He could not consent to put the nation, under these circumstances, to the great expense of printing these papers.

Mr. HARDIN said, though there were eighteen hundred pages of manuscript, he had satisfied himself that it would not make more than two hundred and fifty printed pages. The gentleman from Georgia [Mr. JONES] had some days past appointed his; that it was not proposed by the committee to commend the printing of the testimony. He inquired of the printer of, the House how long it would require to have this testimony printed, and received the reply that it could be done at the rate of one hundred pages a day. The whole might, therefore, be printed in less than three days. It appeared by the report that many votes had been excluded upon principles, the application of which depended upon contested facts. There were questions of residence, of infancy, of double voting, and a variety of matters of fact which could not properly decided without knowing the testimony. One person might take one view of it, another person another view. He was not to take upon trust. He most examine these papers for himself. This question had agitated the State of Kentucky from one end to the other. It involved the most important right of the citizen—the right of suffrage. It could not be properly decided, unless the documents were furnished, upon which decision was to be made. And he must be permitted to say that, among the various parties on which the House was divided—of which he enumerated six or seven—there was upon the amendment no individual of the party to which he either belonged.

Mr. HARDIN inquired of the Clerk whether the evidence had been reported?

Mr. JONES remarked that the evidence had not been reported, but it was in the committee room and could be brought down for the inspection of gentlemen.

The remainder of the day was occupied in discussing the question of printing all the documents connected with the subject, which prevailed, and the subject was postponed to Tuesday next.

The House then adjourned.

THE CONGRESSIONAL GLOBE.

PRINTED AND PUBLISHED AT THE CITY OF WASHINGTON, BY BLAIR & RIVES.

| 23d Congress, 1st Session. | SATURDAY, MAY 17, 1834. | Vol. 1........No. 24. |

IN SENATE.

WEDNESDAY, May 7, 1834.

The VICE PRESIDENT presented a communication from the Secretary of the Treasury, transmitting a statement of the salaries and compensation allowed to officers in the collection of the revenue, in compliance with a resolution of the Senate.

The letter and accompanying documents were, on motion of Mr. SILSBEE, ordered to be printed.

PETITIONS.

Mr. PORTER presented a petition from Captain Henry M. Shreve, the inventor of steam snagboats. The petitioner states that he had been successfully engaged in removing obstructions in rivers flowing through the valley of the Mississippi, and had opened a navigation in Red river, particularly, thought to be impracticable, at a comparatively trifling expense. He stated that a premium of one thousand dollars had been offered by the Government to the inventor of a boat calculated to effect these purposes; and that sum had been paid to an individual for a machine which had proved utterly useless. The petitioner did not ask the reward for his successful invention in money, but merely for the privilege of locating near the theatre of his own enterprise, 25,000 acres of land at the Government price of one dollar and twenty-five cents per acre. This petition was referred to the Committee on Public Lands.

REPORTS.

Mr. SHEPLEY, from the Committee on Engrossed Bills, made a report.

GENERAL ORDERS.

The following bills were read a third time, and passed:

A bill for the relief of John Shackford;

A bill appropriating $20,000 for a road commencing opposite to Memphis, in the State of Tennessee, to Little Rock, in Arkansas Territory;

A bill for the relief of the heirs and legal representatives of John Rose, sen., deceased; and

A bill for relief of Charles Burkham and others.

RESOLUTIONS.

The following resolutions were submitted by Mr. CLAY, and adopted:

Resolved, That the Secretary of the Treasury be directed to report, as soon as practicable, to the Senate, the amount of duties received and accrued on foreign imports during the first quarter of the year 1834, with a table showing the corresponding quarter of the year 1833, and distinguishing between the amounts accrued or received at each port.

Resolved, That he communicate to the Senate whether anything has happened since his annual report was made at the commencement of the present session of Congress, to vary, in his opinion, the estimate contained in the said report, of the proceeds of the duties on foreign imports for the year 1834.

SPECIAL ORDER.

On motion of Mr. FRELINGHUYSEN, the Senate proceeded to the consideration of the special order, being Mr. POINDEXTER's resolution, as amended by Mr. CALHOUN.

Mr. WEBSTER spoke at length in favor of the resolutions as amended by Mr. CALHOUN's resolutions.

Mr. BENTON then rose and spoke in reply, and against the resolutions and amendment.

Mr. POINDEXTER said he had intended to have delivered his sentiments upon this occasion, but declined doing so from a wish to get at the legislative business of the Senate, and asked that the question might be taken.

Mr. WEBSTER asked that the question might be taken by yeas and nays; which were ordered.

Mr. FORSYTH asked that the question might be taken separately; and before doing so, he wished to make some remarks in reply to the gentleman from Massachusetts, [Mr. WEBSTER.]

Mr. BROWN then, at a quarter past 4 o'clock, moved that the Senate adjourn; and upon this question

Mr. CLAY asked for the yeas and nays, which were ordered, and the motion for adjournment negatived by the following vote:

YEAS—Messrs. Benton, Bibb, Brown, Grundy, King of Alabama, King of Georgia, Linn, McKean, Shepley, Tallmadge, White, Wright—12.

NAYS—Messrs. Bell, Black, Calhoun, Clay, Clayton, Ewing, Frelinghuysen, Hill, Kent, Knight, Leigh, Moore, Naudain, Poindexter, Prentiss, Preston, Robbins, Silsbee, Smith, Southard, Sprague, Swift, Tipton, Tomlinson, Tyler, Waggaman, Wilkins—27.

Mr. FORSYTH then spoke at some length in reply to Mr. WEBSTER, to which Mr. W. rejoined, when the question was taken on the adoption of the first resolution, to wit:

Resolved, That the protest communicated to the Senate by the President of the United States, asserts powers as belonging to the President which are inconsistent with the just authority of the two Houses of Congress, and inconsistent with the Constitution of the United States.

And decided in the affirmative by the following vote:

YEAS—Messrs. Bell, Bibb, Black, Calhoun, Clay, Clayton, Ewing, Frelinghuysen, Knight, Kent, Leigh, Moore, Naudain, Poindexter, Porter, Prentiss, Preston, Robbins, Silsbee, Smith, Southard, Sprague, Swift, Tomlinson, Tyler, Waggaman, Webster—28.

NAYS—Messrs. Benton, Brown, Forsyth, Grundy, Hendricks, Hill, King of Alabama, King of Georgia, Linn, McKean, Shepley, Tallmadge, Tipton, White, Wilkins, Wright—16.

The question recurring on the following resolutions, to wit:

Resolved, That while the Senate is, and ever will be, ready to receive from the President all such messages and recommendations as the Constitution and laws and the usual course of public business authorize him to transmit to it, yet it cannot recognise any right in him to make a formal protest against votes and proceedings of the Senate, declaring such votes and proceedings to be illegal and unconstitutional, and requesting the Senate to enter such protest on its journals.

Resolved, That the aforesaid protest is a breach of the privileges of the Senate, and that it be not entered on the journals.

Resolved, That the President of the United States has no right to send a protest to the Senate against any of its proceedings.

Was decided, yeas 27, nays 16; being determined by the same vote taken upon each resolution separately, which was given upon the first resolution.

The following resolution was submitted by Mr. HENDRICKS:

Resolved, That, for the remainder of the session, the Fridays and Saturdays of each and every week shall be devoted exclusively to the consideration of bills.

Mr. POINDEXTER gave notice that he should, on Friday, call up the report of the committee on the Rhode Island contested election.

On motion of Mr. WAGGAMAN, at 5 o'clock, The Senate adjourned.

HOUSE OF REPRESENTATIVES.

WEDNESDAY, May 7, 1834.

Mr. WHITTLESEY, of Ohio, from the Committee of Claims, which was instructed to inquire into the expediency of making compensation to certain contractors for work done on the Cumberland road, west of Zanesville, in the State of Ohio, made a report, in part, which was read; when it was

Resolved, That the Committee of Claims be instructed to inquire into the expediency of making compensation to certain contractors who have ap-

plied to the Secretary of War for that purpose, for work done on the Cumberland road, east of Zanesville, in the State of Ohio, or for materials furnished for said road. And, also, that the papers furnished by the Engineer Department, in certain cases enumerated, be referred to said committee.

Mr. EVANS reported a bill, granting a pension to Isaac Carter, and a bill granting a pension to John Iredell. Read twice and committed.

Mr. GAMBLE obtained leave to submit the following resolution:

Resolved, That the Secretary of War be directed to communicate to this House the whole number of cadets that have been admitted to the Military Academy at West Point since its first organization to the present time; how many are there at present; the number that have graduated; how many have been commissioned, and are now in commission in the army, and the number that is necessary to be kept there to supply the vacancies that ordinarily occur in the army; also, the number of supernumerary cadets with the rank of lieutenant who are in the pay of the Government and not in command.

Mr. EWING asked the unanimous consent of the House to submit a resolution calling upon the Secretary of War for information relative to pensions; and an objection being made, he moved the suspension of the rules; which motion was rejected.

Mr. MERCER, from the Committee on Roads and Canals, reported a resolution directing that the report of Charles Elliott, engineer of the State of Pennsylvania, in relation to the plan of the proposed bridge across the Potomac, be referred to that committee and printed. Agreed to.

The House resumed the consideration of the resolution submitted by Mr. MARDIS in relation to the deposites, together with the amendment offered by Mr. CORWIN, declaring the reasons of the Secretary of the Treasury for removing the deposites to be unsatisfactory and insufficient.

Mr. GALBRAITH resumed his remarks in reply to his colleague, [Mr. McKENNAN,] and in support of the course of the Administration in respect to the Bank of the United States. Mr. G. spoke, without concluding, till the expiration of the hour, when the House proceeded to the orders of the day.

The bill equalizing the compensation in the Territory of Florida, and for other purposes, was read a third time, and passed.

The bill from the Senate to revive an act to grant preëmption rights to certain settlers was taken up and postponed till Tuesday next.

The bill to regulate the value of certain foreign silver coins was postponed till Tuesday next, and made the special order for that day.

The bill to relinquish the reversionary interest of the United States to certain Indian reservations was postponed.

The bill for the relief of Samuel Armstrong Bailey was read a third time, and passed.

A joint resolution for watering the Pennsylvania Avenue was taken up.

Mr. POLK moved its postponement till Tuesday, as the avenue had been well watered lately. Agreed to.

CLAIMS ON FRANCE.

The bill to extend the time for enabling the commission to carry into effect the convention with France was taken up.

Mr. ARCHER explained the object of the bill. The term for which the commission was instituted was about to expire, and, as its business was incomplete, it was necessary to extend it. He recommended the House, for a view of the state of the business of the commission, to a report from their secretary, which, at his request, was read from the Clerk's table. At the same time, he felt bound to inform the House that information was this morning received that the French Chamber

of Deputies had rejected the bill making appropriations for carrying the convention into effect. The vote was a very nice one, and so far from rendering this bill unnecessary, it augmented its necessity. We ought not to present loose and indefinite claims to the French Government, but have them ascertained and proved in the most satisfactory manner.

Mr. REED supported the bill, on the ground that it was necessary to enable claimants to procure papers from France, which were necessary to the establishment of their claims.

Mr. HUNTINGTON could, he said, speak with confidence of the assiduity of the commission in their application to business. It was indispensable to the claimants to be allowed time to procure documents from France.

Mr. McKAY said he could satisfy the House that the bill was unnecessary. We had information, by letters from New York, that the French Chamber of Deputies had refused the appropriation by a vote of 168 to 176, and that two of the French Ministry had thereupon resigned. If this was true, and there was no doubt of it, would it be proper for us, on our part, to go on and attempt to prove the claims? It was also ascertained that a number of papers necessary to the prosecution of the claims, and which, by the convention, the French Government was bound to furnish, had been refused to us. Now, if the French Government had refused to fulfil two of the most essential articles of the treaty, it was equivalent to a declaration on their part, that they would execute no part of the treaty. He hoped the subject would be postponed for ten days, to see whether our information was true. If it should be ascertained that the French Government have refused to execute the treaty, there would be no propriety in continuing the commission.

Mr. BURGES said, that one fact was disclosed by the proceedings in the French Chamber of Deputies on this subject, and that was, that it was absolutely necessary to ascertain the amount of the claims. The ground taken by the opponents of the appropriation in France was, that the sum of twenty-five millions of francs was too large for our claims. It would be found, through the commission, that the amount of the claims was three or four times larger than the sum allowed, even without interest, and that objection to the appropriation would be silenced.

Mr. BARRINGER concurred entirely, he said, with his colleague, [Mr. McKay,] in his views of the subject. We had acted prematurely in instituting a commission, before we had got possession of the materials upon which it was to act. For want of materials, the commission had not been in session half of the time since it was established. If we had first collected the materials, and then established the commission, its business would have been despatched in twelve months; whereas it has now been two years in existence, and the papers were still to be got. He would like to know what assurance we had that it would be any better two years hence if we passed this bill. His opinion was, that we ought to suspend the commission until France was ready to execute the treaty, and until the claimants were ready to present their claims, and then it could be revived, and the business completed in from three to six months. He moved to postpone the further consideration of the subject till Tuesday next, when he hoped the House would suspend instead of extending the commission.

Mr. WILDE said we might as well take the question now as next Tuesday; for nothing in the interval was likely to transpire which would alter the opinion of the House.

The motion to postpone was rejected.

Mr. WILLIAMS moved to recommit the bill, with instructions to limit the term of extension to six months. What assurance had we that the French Government would give up the papers at all? Next year we might have the same argument for the prolongation of the commission, as now. It was useless for us to go on until it was ascertained whether France would execute the treaty or not.

Mr. WILDE explained that the papers referred to were in possession of the Council of Prizes, and it was not to be expected that they would give up the originals. But they did not refuse copies. The whole contest between us and the French Government, on this point, was, at whose expense the copies should be furnished.

Mr. WAYNE said the true question was, whether we should deprive ourselves of one of the means of coercing the payment of these long outstanding claims. If we suspended our action on the subject, we would enable the Chamber of Deputies or the King to say that it was unnecessary for them to hasten their action. He was unwilling to do anything which would give countenance to the supposition, on the part of France that the American Congress had abandoned the pursuit of these claims. The reason for the rejection of the appropriation by the Chamber of Deputies, had reference, he said, to the state of parties in that body, the party opposed to the King and the ministry having the majority.

Mr. ARCHER remarked, that there was no difficulty with the executive department of the French Government on this subject, for it had manifested every disposition to comply with its engagements. He did not consider that we were authorized, by a mere rumor that the Chamber had refused the appropriation, to suspend our action in relation to the treaty. The rumor was an additional reason for passing the bill. It was not expedient to give the French Government an opportunity to say that it was useless to send the document, because the board is suspended by our act.

Mr. ADAMS said, the extension of this commission, either for six months or twelve months, was a small matter compared with the importance of pursuing the proper course. The information which had been given as to the vote of the Chamber of Deputies, furnished strong additional reasons for pursuing this course. In the intercourse between nations, relative to their difficulties, that nation which has right on its side must always presume that justice will be done. Especially it must be presumed that no nation will violate a solemn treaty. The proceedings of the Chamber of Deputies, which had been referred to, were not a violation of the treaty. It was only a refusal on the part of one branch of the French Government to furnish the money to pay the indemnity at this time. Is this a sufficient reason for refusing to ascertain the extent of the losses of our citizens? On the contrary, it was a strong additional reason, because if the French Government shall persevere in refusing to carry the treaty into effect, it gives us a right to demand indemnity for the whole losses of our citizens, which would probably amount to a hundred millions of francs, instead of the twenty-five proposed to be paid by the treaty. The course of the Chamber of Deputies, therefore, afforded the strongest reason for ascertaining the amount. He would prefer increasing the time to two years, rather than limiting it to six months. The difficulties which had arisen with regard to evidence, would probably be disposed of, as well as all the other difficulties arising upon this subject. In the intercourse between nations, there are *mollia tempora fandi*, when they are induced to extend that justice to each other, which at other times may have been refused. He concluded by expressing his hope that the amendment would not be adopted.

Mr. WILLIAMS said, he had no doubt but the commissioners had faithfully discharged their duty, so far as lay in their power. But it seemed there was a difficulty for want of evidence, which the French Government had refused to furnish. The gentleman from Virginia [Mr. Archer] intimates that it was no part of the duty of the Chamber of Deputies to furnish this evidence. This was true; but how was the obligation on the part of the Executive Government of France?

Mr. ARCHER said, he was not aware that any obstacle had been interposed by the Government of France to the procuring of evidence. A question had been raised whether the French Government, or our own, should bear the expense of transcribing the archives necessary, but nothing prevented individuals from obtaining evidence but the expense.

Mr. WILLIAMS. If the Government of France was not to blame, the individual claimants were, for the delay, in not furnishing evidence. The question before the House was, whether the time should be prolonged by the bill six months or twelve months. His object was not to interpose any delay, but to carry the whole subject forward to the next session of Congress, when the facts will have been fully ascertained. Where the blame for delay belongs can then be known.

Mr. REED said that in the law under which these commissioners were appointed as it was originally reported, the time was fixed at three years. At the solicitation of the claimants, it was reduced to two years. They had always been anxious to avoid delay. The truth was, there was no blame anywhere. It was impossible to tell until the cases were stated together, what evidence would be necessary. Sometimes there were a dozen or twenty separate claims arising out of different shipments by the same vessel. Each of these claimants could not ascertain beforehand whether the proof of condemnation was sufficient.

The question was then taken upon the motion of Mr. Williams, which was lost without a count.

The bill then passed without a division.

The bill supplementary to the act for carrying into effect the convention between the United States and the King of the Two Sicilies, was read a third time and passed.

Various bills and resolutions upon the Speaker's table were postponed; when the House took up the

APPROPRIATION BILL.

Upon concurrence with the various amendments which had been made in Committee of the Whole.

The amendment striking out the additional allowance of $500 proposed to be given to the Chief Clerk in the Department of State, was concurred in without a division.

The item providing for an additional clerkship in the Department of State, which had been struck out in committee, was then read.

Mr. JARVIS expressed a hope that the House would not concur with the committee in this amendment.

Mr. ADAMS said he had no inclination to resume the debate which had occupied so much time in committee, but would ask the yeas and nays; which were ordered.

The amendment striking out the item was carried—yeas 90, nays 62.

Various amendments of phraseology were also concurred in.

The item appropriating $2,600 for supplying book-cases and fire-bags for placing papers in, in the Land Office in a situation to be secured in case of fire, having been struck out in committee, the House concurred in the amendment.

The item appropriating $2,500 for additional clerk hire, to bring up arrears, &c., in the office of the Attorney General, in Ohio, Indiana, and Michigan, which was struck out in committee, having been read—

Mr. POLK said the item was struck out on his motion, but subsequent information had satisfied him that the appropriation was necessary. He therefore hoped the House would not concur in the amendment.

After a few remarks from Messrs. CLAY and VANCE, the question was taken, and the amendment non-concurred in without a division.

The item appropriating $3000 for compiling and printing the laws of the Territory of Arkansas, which was inserted in committee, having been read—

Mr. HARDIN objected to its adoption, and demanded the yeas and nays; which were ordered.

After a few remarks from Messrs. DUNCAN, E. WHITTLESEY, JOHN Q. ADAMS, and WHITE, the question was taken, and the amendment concurred in—ayes 126, noes 35.

The amendment made in committee to the item appropriating $24,400 for expenses of intercourse with the Barbary Powers, providing "that the commercial agent at Algiers be paid the same salary as is now paid to the consuls on the Barbary coast," was read.

Mr. McKAY opposed this allowance. Algiers was now a colony of France, and no reason existed for paying a consul or commercial agent there.

Mr. J. Q. ADAMS inquired under what authority this appointment was made?

Mr. ARCHER said, that by the existing laws

a consulate was established at Algiers, with a salary of $4,000 per year. The appointment of such an officer would have been within the strict letter of the law. But the condition and government of Algiers having changed, there was no necessity for this officer, and an agent was appointed under the authority which had always been exercised by the Executive. He had been allowed $1,200 per annum, instead of the $4,000 provided for the consulate by law. The agent who was appointed by the Executive for making the informal negotiations with the Ottoman Porte, which resulted in a treaty with that Power, had been appointed by the same authority.

Mr. ADAMS said this officer not having been appointed with the advice and consent of the Senate, was not constitutionally appointed. The intention of this proviso is to give this officer a legal existence. The practice of appointing informal agents was co-existent with the Government; but this was not such a case.

Mr. CHINN advocated the amendment at length. He contended that the appointment took place in the usual course, was necessary, and the proposed allowance was entirely reasonable in point of amount.

Mr. JARVIS conceived the object of the amendment was to raise the salary of an officer, who now received $1,200 per year, to $2,000. He was opposed to it in every point of view.

Mr. WISE insisted that the appointment of this officer was not warranted by law, and was in violation of the Constitution. Whatever might have been the practice heretofore, this officer could not be sustained upon principle. He was, therefore, opposed to the amendment.

Mr. BINNEY spoke in opposition to the continuation of this clause in the bill.

Mr. ARCHER hoped the House would not concur with the Committee of the Whole in the amendment.

The question being taken, the committee refused to concur.

The amendment appropriating $5,000 for an additional payment for the statue of Washington, was concurred in.

The amendment for the payment of the balance found to be due on settlement at the treasury to the legal representatives of John W. Smith, deceased, being under consideration—

Mr. McKAY opposed it, and after explanations from Mr. POLK, the clause was laid aside for the present.

The next amendment, reducing the appropriation for completing the custom-house at New London, from $12,000 to $9,000, was taken up.

After some discussion, in which Messrs. HUNTINGTON, POLK, McKAY, PEARCE of Rhode Island, REED, CAMBRELENG, OSGOOD, McKIM, BARBER, ELISHA WHITTLESEY, and PARKER, took part,

Mr. H. EVERETT moved to amend the amendment, by striking out $9,000, and inserting $5,000; which motion was rejected—73 to 79.

The question being then taken on concurring with the Committee of the Whole in the amendment, it was decided in the affirmative.

The next amendment, reducing the appropriation for creating a custom-house at New Bedford from $13,000 to $8,000, was concurred in.

The next amendment, reducing the appropriation for erecting a custom-house at Newburyport, was concurred in.

Mr. HIESTER moved an adjournment. 'Lost.'

The House then concurred in the following amendments, without debate:

To supply a deficiency in the contingent fund of the House of Representatives, five thousand dollars.

For completing the compilation of the laws of the Territory of Florida, two thousand five hundred dollars.

For compensation to Robert Mills, one thousand dollars.

For the completion of the marine hospital in Charleston, one thousand one hundred dollars.

For compensating the legal representatives of John W. Smith, deceased, nine hundred and ten dollars and twenty-four cents.

The amendments made in Committee of the Whole having been gone through with—

Mr. VANCE renewed the amendment, reducing the compensation of all the civil officers of the Government, and of the members of Congress, which he had offered in committee, and had been rejected—

When a motion was made to adjourn; but withdrawn, to permit

Mr. MERCER to offer a resolution.

Mr. M. asked the unanimous consent of the House to offer a resolution that the House adjourn from Thursday over to Monday, for the purpose of cleansing the Hall, and substituting matting for the carpets.

An objection being made, the motion was not received.

Mr. CONNOR moved an adjournment; which was agreed to—85 to 73.

The House then adjourned.

IN SENATE.

THURSDAY, *May* 8, 1834.

After the journal had been read—

Mr. KANE rose and asked leave to record his vote on the resolutions passed yesterday in relation to the President's protest. Mr. K. said he was necessarily absent from his seat, not supposing the question would have been taken.

Mr. CLAYTON remarked that he would be disposed to accede to the wishes of the gentleman from Illinois, but he thought important and injurious consequences might flow from it. The same request was made last session by a Senator from Virginia, to record his vote on the force bill, and was refused.

Mr. MOORE also objected. He was refused liberty to record his vote on the same bill last session.

Mr. KANE'S request, requiring the unanimous consent of the Senate, was refused.

PETITIONS.

Mr. BENTON presented a memorial from the city of Boston against rechartering the Bank of the United States, and against the restoration of the deposites, and expressing the opinion that the affairs of the bank might be wound up without necessarily producing general embarrassment, or any evils the apprehension of which should prevent the National Legislature from discharging a great debt to the present age, and to posterity, by permitting that institution to expire upon the limitation of its charter. He said that the memorial was very numerously signed, the letter which accompanied it stating the number at upwards of three thousand; and, from his information and belief, comprised a mass of intelligence and respectability which entitled the opinions expressed to the highest regard. Mr. B. said that he fully concurred in all the sentiments expressed by the memorialists, but that he would only avail himself of the present occasion to present some considerations in favor of the concluding sentiment expressed by the memorialists.

That sentiment was the expression of a belief that the affairs of the bank might be wound up, upon the expiration of its charter, without, *necessarily*, producing any general embarrassment to the community. The belief, thus expressed, by a body of citizens so numerous, so intelligent, so respectable, inhabiting a great city, and possessing ample means to judge of the subject, and solemnly addressed to the National Legislature, was itself an argument, and a very strong one, in favor of the truth of their position. It was, however, susceptible of being sustained by extrinsic arguments; and of these, he would present one or two to the consideration of the Senate.

The winding up of the affairs of the bank (Mr. B. said) would affect the community at two points, namely, the collection of debts due the bank, and the retirement of its notes from circulation. He spoke first of the collection of these debts, and said, that, in addition to the two years allowed by the charter for the bank to use its corporate faculties in collecting its debts, and closing its affairs, the institution might take as much more time as it pleased, by having recourse to the ordinary and well-known alternative of all corporations on the eve of dissolution—that of creating trustees, and putting its affairs into their hands. All corporations acted in this way that chose to do so. The first Bank of the United States had done so, and had not finished the collection of its notes in a dozen years after its dissolution. The present bank might act in the same manner, and was certainly bound to do so after the extraordinary manner in which that institution had increased its loans after it began to have reason to believe that its charter might not be renewed. There could, therefore, be no *necessity* for oppressing the debtors to the bank by forcing them to pay up their loans at the expiration of the charter. The available means of the bank would enable it to pay up its deposites, and redeem its circulation, and the debts would chiefly be used for the reimbursement of capital to the stockholders; and as these debts, when secured, would be bringing an interest to the stockholders, they would have no other inducement than other creditors have, to proceed harshly and rigorously against its debtors.

On the next point, the withdrawal of the notes of the bank from circulation, he (Mr. B.) believed that the community need not to fear any *necessary* embarrassment from that measure. The amount withdrawn would probably be much less than was generally imagined, and the void, if any, might be filled—ought to be filled—and probably would be filled, with something very preferable to any description of bank notes whatsoever. The bank had about seventeen millions of notes in circulation, and it had about eleven millions specie in its vaults. The difference was about six millions; so that a diminution of six millions was all that the community had to apprehend, as the eleven millions of specie now in the bank would all be paid out, either in refunding deposites, taking up notes, or returning the capital to the stockholders. A diminution of six millions is all, then, that will have to be provided for; and we have the facts in hand (said Mr. B.) which authorize us to affirm that this diminution will be far more than provided for by the importations of foreign specie. These importations in the last five months—he might say *four* months, for some of the custom-house returns, especially that of New Orleans, were only to the first of April—these importations for that brief period, amounted to near eight millions of dollars. Upon this point, he (Mr. B.) had the satisfaction to speak with certainty and precision; for the Secretary of the Treasury, Mr. Taney, with a view to ascertain the specie resources of the country, had given orders for weekly returns of specie imported and exported since the first of December last. These returns presented the gratifying result of about seven millions eight hundred thousand dollars imported, and less than a quarter of a million, to wit, $229,918 exported. Here, then, was the void filled at once, or rather provided for, before it occurred; and long before the expiration of the charter, the importations of specie, and the product of our own gold mines, now estimated at two millions per annum, will make up the deficiency, not once, but three or four times over. Mr. B. said that a brief measure of legislation from Congress, if Congress could only find time to legislate, would supply the country with an adequate currency of gold and silver; he alluded to the palpable object of raising the standard of gold, and making foreign coins current at their fair *money* value. These measures, the work of a few days' legislation—if we could only spare a few days to the business of the people—would fill the country with gold and with silver. They would increase the importations, great as the importations now were, and would retain in the country a great part of what was imported; they would also detain for circulation the mass of our native gold, the whole of which was now exported. Mr. B., therefore, held that the memorialists from Boston were well justified in expressing the opinion that the dissolution of the bank, and the winding up of its affairs, would not, *necessarily*, produce any general embarrassment to the people of the United States. After a few more remarks, to show that the Bank of the United States had diminished the quantity of circulating medium, especially in the South and West, by collecting and carrying off more specie than she furnished notes, Mr. B. concluded by making the usual motion, to read, print, and refer the memorial.

Mr. EWING replied to Mr. BENTON. Mr. B. rejoined, and a conversational debate ensued between them. The substance of Mr. BENTON'S remarks was as follows:

Mr. BENTON. He complained of the bank dealing in coin, first, because it was a breach of the charter; secondly, because it was a positive injury to the country, converting the bank into a great shaving shop for specie, and enabling it, by its capital and organization, to monopolize that article, to raise its price, to convert it into a commodity of merchandise, and to export it from the country. This was what the bank had done. Up to 1832 it had collected above forty millions of specie from the States where she had branches, and sold or exported a large portion of it. It had collected the greatest part of this sum from the South and West, say twenty-three millions up to May, 1832, and several millions since. In place of this specie carried off from the South and West, the bank had issued small notes and checks, chiefly five and ten dollar notes, and these had fallen into the current of trade, and flowed to the northeast; so that the South and West lost both their specie and their paper by the operation of this bank. It may have issued fifteen or twenty millions of paper in the South and West, of which very little now remained in those sections of the Union, perhaps not more than three or four millions, while the specie taken away certainly amounted to twenty-three millions two years ago, and probably amounted to thirty millions now.

Certain it was, that near a million of specie was taken from New Orleans last winter, which certainly depressed the money market there, and contributed to that depression in the price of flour and bacon, which the Senator from Ohio [Mr. EWING] mentioned a few days ago. Mr. B. did not complain of the specie which went from New Orleans and the West in the course of trade; what was incident to commerce must be borne with, and is not to be counteracted by law; but he complained of the Bank of the United States for adding its vast operations to those of commerce, and carrying off twelve or fifteen millions from New Orleans, which that city ought itself to use and distribute through the channels of its own trade. These twelve or fifteen millions, thus taken off by the bank, diminished the ability of the city of New Orleans to purchase western produce, and was thus an injury to the whole West. It also diminished the supply of specie at that place, from which place the western country received those metals. Mr. B. repeated, it was not of the operation of commerce that he complained, but of the operations of the bank, which had engaged in the specie trade in violation of its charter, and by its capital and organization, had deprived the South and West of probably thirty millions of specie, substituting a large issue of small notes and checks in place of that specie; these notes and checks had chiefly gone off to the Northeast; and thus the South and West, by the operations of the bank, had suffered an actual diminution of more than twenty millions of their circulating medium.

Mr. CLAYTON moved to reconsider the vote refusing leave to Mr. KANE to record his vote upon the resolutions of Mr. POINDEXTER, as amended by Mr. CALHOUN.

Upon this motion some conversation occurred between Messrs. CLAYTON, MOORE, FORSYTH, and EWING, advocating the motion, and Messrs. PRESTON and CALHOUN, opposed it.

Mr. CALHOUN objecting, leave was not granted.

On motion of Mr. HENDRICKS, the special orders were laid upon the table; and the Senate took up, in Committee of the Whole, the bill for the improvement and extension of the Cumberland road.

This bill appropriates $652,000 to effect the object contemplated, and was discussed at length by Messrs. SOUTHARD, PRESTON, and HENDRICKS, upon the general principles of the bill.

Mr. SWIFT offered an amendment to the fourth section "that as soon as the money hereby appropriated shall have been expended and the road 'put in repair, it shall be surrendered to the several States through which it passes, and the United States shall not be subject to any further 'expenses for its repair."

The amendment was agreed to.

The bill was then passed as in committee of the whole and reported to the Senate, and the question being on ordering the bill to be engrossed for a third reading—

Mr. PRESTON asked the yeas and nays, which were ordered, and are as follows:

YEAS—Messrs. Benton, Ewing, Frelinghuysen, Grundy, Hendricks, Kane, Kent, Linn, McKean, Poindexter, Porter, Prentiss, Robbins, Silsbee, Smith, Southard, Swift, Tallmadge, Tipton, Tomlinson, Webster—21.

NAYS—Messrs. Black, Brown, Forsyth, Hill, King of Alabama, King of Georgia, Leigh, Moore, Naudain, Preston, Shepley, Tyler, White—13.

REPORTS.

Mr. SMITH, from the Committee on the Judiciary, reported a bill without amendment, for the relief of Thomas Blanchard.

Mr. MOORE moved that the memorial of the Legislature of Alabama, on the subject of school lands, be printed; which was agreed to.

On motion of Mr. CLAYTON, the Senate proceeded to the consideration of executive business, and after spending some time therein,

The Senate adjourned.

HOUSE OF REPRESENTATIVES.

THURSDAY, *May* 8, 1834.

Mr. WATMOUGH, from the committee to which had been referred the subject of equalizing the pay of the army and navy, moved that the bill, and report heretofore made, be recommitted to the same committee; which was agreed to.

Mr. E. WHITTLESEY asked the consent of the House that several bills which had been sent from the Senate, and lay upon the Speaker's table, be read, and referred to the appropriate committees; which was agreed to.

The bills were read, and referred accordingly.

Mr. SCHLEY, from the Committee on Invalid Pensions, reported a bill granting a pension to Samuel Shelmerdine; which was read twice, and committed.

Mr. C. P. WHITE, from the Committee on Naval Affairs, reported the following resolution:

Resolved, That one thousand additional copies of the amended Rules and Regulations of the Navy, communicated by the President of the United States on the 2d May, 1834, be printed for the use of this House.

Which resolution, by the rules, lies one day on the table.

Mr. PEARCE, from the Committee on the Post Office and Post Roads, reported a bill for the relief of the sureties of Thomas F. Green; which was read twice, and commited.

Mr. CHINN laid before the House a presentment of the Grand Jury of the county of Washington, relative to the county jail; which was referred to Committee on the District of Columbia.

The resolution, heretofore offered by Mr. MARDIS, relative to the deposites of the public money, with the amendment of Mr. CORWIN, then came up.

Mr. GALBRAITH continued his speech, in reply to the arguments of his colleague, [Mr. McKENNAN,] until the expiration of the hour appropriated to morning business.

THE GENERAL APPROPRIATION BILL.

The amendments proposed to this bill by Mr. VANCE, for reducing the salaries of the President, heads of departments, and clerks in the public offices, heretofore discussed in Committee of the Whole, again came up.

Mr. VANCE was not disposed to interfere with the duties of the committee which had been raised upon the resolution of the gentleman from Georgia, [Mr. CLAYTON,] relative to the duties and salaries of public officers. He must state that he did not expect much from it. He had seen five committees raised for this purpose, but had not seen the salary of a single officer reduced. He believed the only mode of effecting this object was through the appropriation bills. This is the only way in which retrenchment can be effected. In 1822 a committee was raised called the retrenchment committee The labors of the committee resulted in nothing. But at the same session a clause was added to the appropriation bill by a gentleman from Tennessee, providing that the salaries of officers indebted to the Government should not be paid until their accounts were balanced. This additional clause has had a far more important effect than the labors of any committee on reform. The ground upon which he placed this proposition to reduce the salaries of officers of the Government was the increased value of money in consequence of the interference of the Government with the currency of the country. Had not this been done he would have been the last person to have proposed this reduction. He was satisfied that the amounts which would be received under the proposed amendment would be quite as valuable as the amounts received twelve months ago. Mr. V. then went into a comparative statement of the expenses of the four years of Mr. Adams's administration with those of the present Administration, and contended that an increase of eighteen millions had taken place, and that the increase was going on.

Mr. WARDWELL felt obliged to make a few remarks when assertions were made so entirely variant from the facts as they had come under his observation. If the proposition had been to reduce the salaries of such officers as now received too much compensation, as he was satisfied there were some such, he would most cheerfully support it. But here an indiscriminate reduction of all salaries, whether adequate or inadequate, of from twenty-five to thirty-three per cent. is proposed to be made by a sweeping amendment to this bill, not because they were too high six months ago, but that the price of money has been raised. It has been stated, as the main fact upon which this proposition is based, that two-thirds of the amount of a salary is now equal as compensation to the whole six months ago. Do gentlemen believe this statement? Can a single article of living be named which can be purchased cheaper than it could be six months ago? This ground of the amendment was not true. The gentleman from Ohio [Mr. VANCE] had compared the expenses of Government for several years. This had nothing to do with the amendment. The officers whose salaries were included in the amendment were paid no more than they had been under the former Administration. For himself, he was satisfied that though some officers were paid too much, yet on full examination, he believed there would be found necessarily rather an increase than a diminution of the salaries of the public officers here. He hoped the committee to which the gentleman from Ohio [Mr. VANCE] belonged would thoroughly examine this subject. He could not, because a few individuals possibly received more than they were entitled to, support a proposition for a general reduction of the compensation of officers, some of whom were not probably sufficiently paid. He believed the principle upon which the gentleman from Ohio [Mr. VANCE] had proceeded was a mistake. If that gentleman would inquire into the facts, he would find that money, instead of being worth more, was not worth so much as at many former periods, and that the articles of living were dearer instead of cheaper.

Mr. LEAVITT said the proposition of his colleague [Mr. VANCE] was one of so much magnitude and interest that he could not pass it by in silence. The amendment proposed a general and indiscriminate reduction of salaries. He considered this proposition as objectionable both with regard to the time and circumstances. This was an appropriation bill for the support of the Government. Its consideration, for reasons which it was not necessary to state, had been delayed to this late period of the session. The functions of the Government are in danger of being obstructed for the want of means for carrying them on. Under such circumstances a general and indiscriminate reduction is proposed. To investigate such a proposition in a manner which its importance requires, would occupy weeks, if not months of discussion. There had been no previous inquiry—no report from any committee. However powerful the intellectual endowments of gentlemen, it was impossible for them to arrive at a correct decision upon such a question, without knowing the facts. No one could say whether a public officer received too much salary, without knowing his duties, and the expenses to which he was subjected. For one, he rejoiced that a committee had been raised for the purpose of ascertaining the facts. This committee were now engaged in their duties. He would congratulate his collegue [Mr. VANCE] in holding a place upon this committee. On this subject, at least there will be no cause for complaint that his

views will be fully represented. Before he could vote intelligently upon this proposition, the report of this committee was necessary. But if a reduction of salaries was to be made upon a general hypothesis, without ascertaining the facts, why was it not extended to the judiciary, and the officers of the army and navy? Why did not his colleague carry out the principle? It was not possible to go into the details of the effect of the amendment. He would take the first item, proposing to reduce the salary of the President, as soon as it may be constitutionally done, to $15,000. This salary was fixed at $25,000 in 1789. Is the pressure of the times greater now than in 1789, when we had just emerged from the war of the Revolution? The sages of that period of gloom and depression did not consider $25,000 to be too great an allowance for the Chief Magistrate of the nation. Never, from that period until the present time had an proposition been made to reduce it. If such a reduction was necessary, there had been times when this necessity was more obvious and pressing than at this time. He did not propose going through the items of the amendment. He had no doubt but there were instances in which salaries should be reduced, but without information he was not prepared to act. It was necessary to avoid paying too much on the one hand and too little on the other. Gentlemen might seek to acquire popularity by arguments in favor of reducing salaries, but the people will not fail to understand that if salaries are fixed at too low a rate, none but men of fortune can afford to accept them. Office would, in this mode, be thrown into the hands of the rich. We had been told, as the ground of this amendment, that an extraordinary depression in the value of all kinds of property had been caused by the act of the Administration. He did not propose to take issue upon these matters of fact, as he did not know the sources of information possessed by his colleague. So far as his own knowledge went, the depression stated did not exist.

Mr. L. then went into a detailed reply to the statements of Mr. Vance, as to the increased expenditure of the Government. He expressed his surprise that his colleague, who had been a member of this House for thirteen years past, had not, when his friends were in power, effectually enforced his views of reducing the salaries of public officers. He imputed no unworthy motive to his colleague. But he could upon former occasions have introduced the principles of this amendment with much greater effect, while his political friends composed a majority of the House and the Government.

Mr. VANCE briefly replied to his colleague. The reason that he had not extended his proposition to the army and navy, was, that bills were already pending for regulating their pay; and he had not extended it to the judiciary because the Constitution did not permit us to do it, and, moreover, because he had no wish to do it. He intimated an intention, as we understood him, to retire from public life, and declared he had no desire to be Governor of Ohio, or to obtain any other office. He wished and intended to devote the remainder of his life to his occupation as a farmer.

Mr. BATES expressed a disposition to continue to public officers as good a compensation as they had heretofore received; but if money had appreciated, as he contended it had, it was proper to reduce the salaries to the extent of that appreciation.

Mr. MILLER opposed the amendment at length.

Mr. EWING spoke, at some length, in support of the amendment.

Mr. BYNUM was induced to believe, he said, that gentlemen who proposed this amendment were not in earnest, and if they were, they certainly presumod much upon the ignorance of the House. The proposition was to curtail the salary of almost every officer of the Government. It was very probable that some salaries were too high, and it was equally probable that others were too low; but it was proposed, at one blow, to reduce both those that were too high and those that were too low. But he doubted whether the gentlemen were in earnest, because we had appointed a committee to inquire into facts as to each office the salary of which is proposed to be reduced. The fact of the appointment of that committee, superseded the necessity of this amendment. They were appointed to inquire what salaries were too large, and what were too small, and, if any were found to be either too large or too small, he would cheerfully vote for their increase or reduction. But notwithstanding the appointment of this committee, this amendment was pressed upon us, before the result of its inquiry was laid before the House.

Much had been said about the extravagance of this Administration. And from whom did these charges come? If he was not mistaken, they came from one political party; and their object was to produce political effect. When those salaries were established, the country was as much depressed as it now is, for then we had just emerged from a long war, and had not recovered from its depression and embarrassments. In the judgment of the whole world, the country was never more happy than it is at the present time. Gentlemen must have more regard for their consistency, if they wish to preserve their influence with intelligent people. He could not assent to the correctness of their position, as to the present state of the country compared with its former condition. But for the agitations of politicians, we should be the happiest people and least in need of making reductions in salaries, than any other in the world. Gentlemen told us that one dollar now was worth as much as two dollars were last year. He could not believe it was so. Had any member here found any reduction in his expenses? Were the products of the country much reduced in price? The article of cotton, which was the staple product of his part of the country, was as high as its average price for several years past. Pork, bacon, and corn were also as high now, within a cent or two, as usual. Much had been said, in regard to the increase of the expenditures of the Government. The increase of population must necessarily increase the expenses of the Government. The addition of forty members to this House showed how rapidly the population of the country and its public expenditures must have increased. Look at our acquisitions of territory and say whether that has not called for increased expenditures. Twenty thousand miles had been added to the post office routes. Was this extravagance? Was it not called for by the necessities of the people, and was it not ordered by them, through their representatives? How could gentlemen come forward with charges against the Administration on account of these expenditures?

Gentlemen ask on what principles the present Administration came into power. He would tell gentlemen what were the principles on which it was supported in his part of the country, and would assure them that, in respect to those principles, it had fully met the expectations of its friends. It was expected that it would put a stop to the ruinous extravagance of the system of internal improvements; and it had done it. It was expected that it would reduce the tariff; and it had been done. All had been done in this respect which could be done, and more than he had expected would be done. It was expected to put a stop to the dangerous usurpations of the United States Bank, and had it not done it? There were many who encouraged the President in his first opposition to the bank, and owed their popularity to it, who were now backing out. These were the principles on which the Administration came into power. Never, in any part of the country, did he hear it objected to the late Administration that the salaries of public officers were too high, and never was it promised, or demanded, that the present Administration should reduce them. He could not conceive how gentlemen who had acquired popularity by lauding the veto, could come here and denounce the President for the very measures which they had approved.

The gentleman from Massachusetts had lugged in the old cry about distress, the wonderful distress of the country. Perhaps there might be more distress in the gentleman's neighborhood than in his. It seemed that all the minority were distressed. But if the majority of the people were satisfied with the operations of the Government, why should we change them? It was extraordinary for the minority to ask the majority to yield up their opinions and the government of the country to them. The opponents of the Administration were alone distressed, and it was their interest to make it appear that the country is distressed. The subject of the amendment was too important to be hastily decided upon. Believing that it was altogether an improper time to act on the subject, and that it was rendered unnecessary by the appointment of a committee to examine the subject, he should vote against the amendment.

Mr. LINCOLN considered the proposition as too broad, and he could not vote for it. He was ready, however, to reduce such salaries as might be found to be too high. For many reasons it was his opinion that this bill ought to be laid on the table, to wait for some further legislation. If the bill passed, under present circumstances, the whole pecuniary concerns of the Government would be left at the caprice, not the discretion, of one individual in the Government. Until it was ascertained, by law, where the treasury is, he was unwilling to vote for the passage of this bill. He would not consent to reduce the salary of the Vice President, but he would reduce the salaries of the Secretaries to the same sum which the second officer of the Government receives. If the question must be whether the amendment, as a whole, shall be adopted or rejected, he would vote for its rejection.

Mr. CHILTON rose to inquire of the gentleman from North Carolina, whether he meant to say that the President of the United States had made the various pledges which he spoke of to the country pending his election? He understood the gentleman to say that the President had pledged himself to the South to abolish internal improvement, to reduce the tariff, and to put down the United States Bank. He listened to the declaration with surprise, because the views of the President on those subjects were very differently represented by his friends in the West. He referred particularly to General Jackson's letter to Governor Rea. Mr. C. proceeded at some length, and concluded by remarking that he had nothing to say on the subject of the amendment.

Mr. BOON rose to correct the gentleman as to a matter of fact. The letter to which he referred was addressed, not to Governor Rea, but to the Senate of Indiana.

Mr. BURD spoke briefly in opposition to the amendment. He wished to pay the public officers amply and liberally. There ought not to be a clerk in the Post Office without a salary of one thousand dollars.

Mr. HARPER, of New Hampshire, did not rise to continue the debate. The economy and comfort of the House required that the question should be disposed of. He regretted that there was no way, according to the rules of the House, of getting the question on this amendment, without cutting off the subsequent amendments. He moved the previous question, but subsequently withdrew the motion.

Mr. McKAY said he was in favor of an economical administration of the Government, but he should vote against the amendment, because it was inconsistent with other parts of the bill, and unnecessary, inasmuch as a committee of the House was engaged in inquiries as to the expediency of reducing salaries, and would, in due time, report.

Mr. BARRINGER called for the question on each separate clause of the amendment. He was in favor of some of the items, but would not vote for the whole indiscriminately. Mr. B. explained that he had been misunderstood, as having made, when he formerly spoke on this subject, the charge against the clerks, as a body, of inefficiency and idleness. He had never made any such charges against the clerks, as a body.

Mr. VANCE said he had no wish to fish for minnows. If he could not get hold of the six and seven thousand dollar gentlemen, he would withdraw the proposition. The question on the first clause, reducing the compensation of the Vice President and heads of departments was then taken, by yeas and nays, and determined in the negative: Yeas 48, nays 141.

Mr. VANCE withdrew that part of the amendment relative to clerks, and called for the question on the next clause of his amendment, which proposes to limit the emoluments of the collectors and other officers of the customs.

Mr. SUTHERLAND said it was in contemplation to equalize the emoluments of the collectors

of the customs. The Committee on Commerce would present a plan upon that subject at the next session of Congress.

Mr. BARRINGER expressed himself in favor of this amendment in strong terms.

Mr. PARKER said, this limitation would extend only to a very few of the most important and responsible officers, and would not touch the great mass of custom-house officers. There was a strong necessity for a revision of the system of compensation. The emoluments of these officers should be such as to command the services of men of responsibility and high character. He considered this proposition as totally inadequate.

Mr. GILLET thought the proposed amendment out of place in the bill, which did not refer to the compensation of these officers in any manner whatever.

Mr. VINTON was satisfied that limitations and restrictions should be placed upon the bill. The expenditures of the last year had greatly exceeded the estimates.

Mr. VANCE did not propose, by the amendment, to affect the emoluments of any officer whose receipts were less than $2,000.

Mr. CAMBRELENG said the gentleman from Ohio [Mr. VINTON] had alluded to the excess of expenditure over the estimates. If that gentleman would take the trouble to examine into the subject, he would find that the House had added between three and four millions to the estimate, and that nearly four millions had been expended in pensions and other objects not embraced in the estimate. As to the proper compensation for officers of customs, care should be taken that it be not fixed so low as gradually to introduce a system of frauds upon the revenue, as in some countries in Europe.

Mr. HARPER, of Pennsylvania, went into a detailed statement relative to the unnecessary officers attached to the custom-houses, and the exorbitant compensation they received.

Mr. HARPER, of New Hampshire, was satisfied that a system for regulating the officers of custom-houses should be adopted; but believing this was not the proper occasion, and that no further time could be spent in this discussion, he demanded the previous question; which he afterwards withdrew.

Mr. GAMBLE moved that the House adjourn; which was negatived: Ayes 75, noes 89.

Mr. WILLIAMS moved the House adjourn; which was lost.

Mr. J. M. HARPER then renewed the call for the previous question; which was not sustained: Ayes 64, noes 101.

On motion of Mr. McKENNAN, The House adjourned.

IN SENATE.
FRIDAY, May 9, 1834.

Mr. KNIGHT presented the memorial of 2228 mechanics and others of the State of Rhode Island, praying the restoration of the deposites to the Bank of the United States, and the recharter of said institution.

After some remarks by Messrs. KNIGHT and ROBBINS, the memorial was read, and referred to the Committee on Finance, and ordered to be printed.

Mr. WEBSTER, from the Committee on Finance, reported the bill from the House of Representatives making appropriations for the army for the year 1834, with two amendments; and moved that the Senate proceed to its consideration; which was agreed to.

The amendments were an appropriation of $2,000 to certain Michigan militia, to compensate for the expenses of the late war with Black Hawk.

Also, $700 to Captain McGeorge's company of Indiana militia, for services in the same war.

The bill being considered as in committee of the whole, these amendments were agreed to.

Mr. BENTON then offered an amendment, appropriating $366 79 for arrearages of pay and subsistence to Colonel A. R. Woolley.

Mr. WEBSTER had no objection to the item; but he thought it a case of claim, and preferred that it should be made the subject of a private bill.

Mr. TIPTON was not opposed to the allowance,

but he was unwilling to embarrass the military appropriation bill with a claim.

Mr. BENTON explained the nature of the case. It was not properly a claim, but arrearages of pay, to supply an outstanding deficiency; and it had been submitted by the Military Committee, in accordance with the recommendation of the Secretary of War, to incorporate it in the general appropriation bill.

The amendment was disagreed to on a division: Yeas 11, nays 16.

The rules being suspended, and the bill having been ordered to be engrossed, it was read a third time, and passed.

The bill for the preservation and repair of the Cumberland road was then read a third time, and passed.

The VICE PRESIDENT presented a communication from the Department of State, stating, that in compliance with the resolution of the Senate of the 17th February last, transmitting a report from the Commissioner of Pensions; which was referred to the Committee on Pensions.

Mr. CLAYTON, from the Committee on the Judiciary, reported a bill upon criminal jurisprudence, authorizing the courts of the United States, in sentencing convicts in their courts to the several State penitentiaries, to order that their treatment and discipline shall be the same as prisoners in the several institutions in which they may be sentenced to undergo confinement. The bill was read a first and second time.

Mr. CLAYTON, from the same committee, reported a bill from the House of Representatives, with an amendment, relative to insolvent debtors; which amendments were ordered to be printed, and Mr. C. gave notice that he should, at an early day, move to take it up, probably Monday next.

Mr. TOMLINSON, from the Committee on Pensions, reported a bill for the relief of John Hagey.

Mr. FRELINGHUYSEN, agreeably to notice, called up the joint resolution authorizing the purchase of thirteen copies of American State Papers, published by Gales & Seaton; which was read a second time.

Mr. SHEPLEY, from the Committee on Roads and Canals, reported a bill for the relief of Walter Loomis and Able Gay.

Mr. BENTON gave notice that he should tomorrow ask leave to introduce a bill for the relief of Colonel Woolley.

The Senate then took up the resolution to meet at eleven o'clock for the remainder of the session.

Mr. GRUNDY objected to the adoption of the resolution. The Post Office Committee, of which he was chairman, were engaged in a most laborious and extensive investigation, and the time now afforded them was scarcely sufficient for the purpose; and if they were compelled to meet in session at eleven, it would be impossible for them to do what was necessary, or expected of them by the Senate.

Mr. TIPTON'S object was to facilitate business, and he thought most of the business now to be acted on was in the form of bills; but he had no objection that the resolution should be laid on the table.

On motion of Mr. EWING, the resolution was laid on the table.

The resolution setting apart Fridays and Saturdays during the remainder of the session for the consideration of private bills exclusively, was taken up for consideration; and after some conversation between Mr. WEBSTER and Mr. HENDRICKS, it was adopted.

The resolution of Mr. EWING, calling for information from the State Department, with regard to the Superintendent of the Patent Office, was taken up and adopted.

The Senate then proceeded to consider the bill authorizing the people of Michigan Territory to form a separate State Government.

Mr. EWING moved to lay the bill on the table,

as the Senate was thin, and the subject was important.

Mr. TIPTON urged its consideration without delay, and asked the yeas and nays on the motion; which were ordered, and are as follows, to wit:

YEAS—Messrs. Brown, Calhoun, Clayton, Ewing, Frelinghuysen, Knight, Naudain, Porter, Prentiss, Robbins, Silsbee, Smith, Southard, and Sprague—14.

NAYS—Messrs. Bell, Benton, Black, Grundy, Hendricks, Hill, Kane, Kent, King of Georgia, Linn, McKean, Shepley, Swift, Tallmadge, Tipton, Tomlinson, Webster, White, Wilkins, and Wright—20.

So the motion was decided in the negative; and the bill, and also an amendment submitted as a substitute for the whole bill, were then considered.

Mr. TIPTON said he would not disguise the fact, that he felt more than an ordinary solicitude for the passage of the bills permitting the people of Michigan and Arkansas Territory to form constitutions, and for their admission into the Union of the States. His anxiety was increased by having had charge of their applications from an early day in the session.

It would be recollected by the Senate that he introduced bills, for their admission, some months ago. These bills were referred to a select committee, of which he had the honor to be chairman. The committee was divided in opinion, and the subject was suspended by circumstances beyond his control, for months, and finally a majority of the committee instructed him to report an amendment to strike out the bill from the enacting clause, and insert an amendment authorizing the taking of the census. The census thus taken is to be laid before Congress at its next session.

This amendment, if adopted, would be dilatory in its effects, and would postpone the decision one year. To this he hoped the Senate would not give its sanction. He had prepared an amendment authorizing the taking of the census by the United States marshals for each Territory; and if there are 47,700 inhabitants, federal numbers, in both or either Territory, the Governor is to lay off districts, and order an election of delegates to form a constitution. What could be said in favor of one of these Territories might as truly be said of the other, and his amendment, if adopted, placed the admission of both on equal grounds, depending on the contingency of each Territory having a like number to a Representative in Congress from the other States. He was at a loss to see how the Senate could reject a proposition, in itself so just. The ordinance of July, 1787, for the government of the territory northwest of the Ohio river, may be called the foundation of good government in that country. This ordinance provides the means of education, regulates the descent of property, and holds out inducements to young men to emigrate to the West. Article five provides that the northwest territory shall be divided into not less than three, nor more than five States, as Congress might deem proper. The western State to be bounded by the Mississippi, the Ohio, and Wabash, and a due north line from post St. Vincennes to the Canada line. The middle State bounded by the north line, the Wabash, the Ohio, and a line drawn due north from the mouth of the Great Miami. The eastern State by the last-mentioned north line, the Ohio, Pennsylvania, and the Canada line, and each State to be not less than 100, nor more than 150 miles square. The ordinance also provides that Congress shall change the boundaries of these States, if found expedient, and to form one or two States north of an east and west line drawn through the southern extremity of Lake Michigan. And whenever any of the said States shall have 60,000 inhabitants, it shall be admitted into the Union on an equal footing with the original States in all respects whatever. This ordinance also goes on to say, that so far as it may be consistent with the general interest of this Confederacy, States may be admitted at an earlier period, and with less number, than 60,000. In 1805, the Territory of Michigan was organized north of an east and west line drawn through the southern point of Lake Michigan. The three first-mentioned States, Ohio, Indiana, and Illinois have been admitted; and in forming the State of Indiana, ten miles were taken off the south of the

Michigan Territory, and added to Indiana. The bill now proposed to admit Michigan and Arkansas both at the same time. In 1832, the question of applying for admission was submitted to the people of Michigan; they decided by a very large majority in favor of establishing a State government.

I find, on examining the population of other Territories that have been admitted, that the territory south of the Ohio, now State of Tennessee, had a population of

Population.	Year.	Admitted.
Tennessee.........35,791	1796	1796
Ohio.............45,365	1800	1803
Louisiana.........30,845	1810	1812
Indiana, about,....50,000	1816	1816
Mississippi......40,352	1810	1818

Kentucky, Alabama, Maine, and Missouri, when admitted, had less than Michigan and Arkansas. Five Territories were admitted on less population than these Territories have, and four had a greater population.

Arkansas had 41,000 one year ago, and Miller county was not included.

It is not matter of surprise that the people of the Territories should be anxious to form State Governments. This is always the case. The Federal officers in the Territories depend upon the President and Congress for office and for emolument, and not on the real sovereign, the people; and, in his opinion, the people acted wisely in submitting to the burden of State Government, for the dearest rights of freemen, that of choosing their rulers.

The people of that Territory made application to the last Congress, but it was not acted on. Their Legislative Council sent us a memorial, and Mr. T. hoped the Senate would not longer neglect to do these people justice.

The tide of population, like the tide of our Mississippi, (he said,) was continually rolling westward—nothing could prevent it. We might retard the growth of the West, by refusing them the protection of our laws, but it would progress westward to and beyond the Rocky Mountains.

A large proportion of the emigrants of this day were graduates from your colleges in the eastern States, and nothing was so animating to a young adventurer, as to know that as soon as he locates in a western Territory, it will be admitted into the Union, and that he will be eligible to the highest office in the State.

Mr. T. said we might as well undertake to stay the hand of time as to prevent the growth and power of the freemen that will inhabit the valley west of the Allegany Mountains, and between the great lakes and the Gulf of Mexico.

Already a settlement on the west bank of the Mississippi, north of the State of Missouri, have laid on our tables a petition praying Congress to extend the protection of our laws over that country.

We owe it to our constituents, to our country, and selves, that our legislation should keep pace with our population and the extension of our settlements; and he hoped, before Congress adjourns, we will authorize the admission of Michigan and Arkansas, and form the Territorial Government of Wisconsin. In this Territory the Indian title has been extinguished to twelve millions of acres of land that will soon be in market.

Mr. CLAYTON said he had no objection to the bill, but the question of settling the northern boundary line of Ohio was before the Judiciary Committee, and he thought this bill ought not to be passed till that was settled.

Mr. BLACK said he saw no provision in the bill exempting the public lands from taxation for five years. There were also some other amendments not in the bill, which he deemed it very proper should be put in it.

Mr. TIPTON said he had no objection to any amendments which might be thought proper.

On motion of Mr. CLAYTON, the bill was then laid on the table for the present.

EXILES FROM POLAND.

The Senate then proceeded to consider the bill granting a township of land to certain Polish exiles.

Mr. POINDEXTER moved to amend the bill by requiring one settler for every five hundred acres, instead of three hundred, as provided for in the bill; which was agreed to.

Mr. LINN then moved an amendment to insert "Missouri," so as to authorize the location in that State, if the President shall think proper.

Mr. POINDEXTER said that these exiles preferred a location in a non-slaveholding State.

Mr. LINN remarked that his wish was not to restrict these persons; he rather wished to give them a greater latitude for their choice.

The amendment was not agreed to.

Mr. KANE was opposed to the bill. In its present form, it would authorize a location on the Unitea lead mines. He did not approve of the preference given to these people over our own citizens, and he, for one, was unwilling to make the discrimination. He therefore moved an amendment, confining the location "to lands subject to sale at private entry."

The amendment was not agreed to.

Mr. HENDRICKS was opposed to the bill. He was willing to sell these persons the land at a minimum price, on a long credit, but not to give it to them. A case of foreigners, similarly circumstanced, existed in Indiana. A large number of emigrants from the cantons of Switzerland, settled there, in the most abject poverty, and having devoted themselves to the cultivation of the vine, by industry and economy they had accumulated a respectable property. He merely suggested the plan of sale, on extended credit, to the chairman of the Committee on Public Lands.

Mr. PRESTON and Mr. SHEPLEY made a few remarks, the former in favor, and the latter against the bill; when it was ordered to be engrossed for a third reading.

GENERAL ORDERS.

The bill changing the boundary lines of land districts in the Territory of Michigan, was read, and referred.

The bill supplementary to the act entitled "An act to carry into effect the convention between the United States and his Majesty the King of the Two Sicilies, concluded at Naples, on the 14th of October, 1832," was referred to the Committee on Foreign Relations.

The bill to extend the time allowed for the commission to carry into effect the convention with France, was, on motion of Mr. WEBSTER, laid on the table.

The bill to equalize the representation of the Legislative Council of the Territory of Florida, was read and referred.

The following bills were considered in Committee of the Whole, and reported to the Senate:

A bill for the relief of Luther L. Smith; and

A bill for the relief of Coleman Fisher.

[Here Mr. LINN made an unsuccessful motion to postpone the previous orders, and take up the bill for the relief of sundry citizens of the United States who have lost property by the depredations of certain Indian tribes.]

The bill to provide for the legal adjudication and settlement of the claims to land therein mentioned, was taken up.

Upon the consideration of this bill a considerable debate ensued.

Mr. SHEPLEY moved to amend the bill, by allowing testimony to be taken in courts of justice; upon which the yeas and nays were ordered.

YEAS—Messrs. Forsyth, Grundy, Hendricks, Hill, Kane, King of Alabama, King of Georgia, Linn, Moore, Preston, Shepley, Tipton, Tyler, White, Wilkins, Wright—16.

NAYS—Messrs. Benton, Black, Clayton, Ewing, Frelinghuysen, Kent, Naudain, Poindexter, Porter, Prentiss, Robbins, Smith, Southard, Sprague, Swift, Tallmadge, Tomlinson, Waggaman, Webster—19.

The question was then put upon ordering the bill to be engrossed, and decided by yeas and nays, as follows:

YEAS—Messrs. Benton, Black, Calhoun, Clayton, Ewing, Frelinghuysen, Grundy, Hendricks, Kane, Kent, King of Alabama, King of Georgia, Knight, Linn, Naudain, Poindexter, Porter, Prentiss, Preston, Robbins, Silsbee, Smith, Southard, Sprague, Swift, Tomlinson, Waggaman, Webster, Wilkins—29.

NAYS—Messrs. Brown, Forsyth, Hill, Moore, Shepley, Tallmadge, Tipton, Tyler, White, Wright—10.

The bill for the relief of Joseph Clift, of Arkan-

sas, was, on motion of Mr. POINDEXTER, under instructions from the Committee on Public Lands, indefinitely postponed.

On motion of Mr. CALHOUN, it was Ordered, That when the Senate adjourn, it would adjourn to meet on Monday.

On motion of Mr. HENDRICKS, The Senate adjourned.

HOUSE OF REPRESENTATIVES.

FRIDAY, May 9, 1834.

Mr. H. EVERETT moved that the Committee of the Whole on the state of the Union be discharged from the further consideration of the bill to provide for the appointment of agents and subagents for the Indians, and that it be referred to the Committee on Indian Affairs.

Mr. BARRINGER objected, for the reason that a quorum was not present; and remarked, that he would either move a call of the House or an adjournment. He moved that the House adjourn; upon which the yeas and nays were ordered.

The question having been taken, the motion to adjourn was rejected, yeas 12.

Mr. H. EVERETT'S motion was then put, and prevailed.

Mr. HAWKINS obtained the consent of the House to present four memorials, signed by a large number of the inhabitants between Oxford, in the county of Grenville, and State of North Carolina, and Clarksville, in the State of Virginia, praying the establishment of a post route; which on his motion, were referred to the Committee on the Post Office and Post Roads.

Mr. H. EVERETT moved that the Committee on Indian Affairs have leave to sit during the sittings of the House next week. Agreed to.

Mr. ASHLEY obtained leave to present several private petitions.

Mr. REED, on leave, offered a private petition.

Mr. PARKER, on leave, offered a resolution relative to a post route; which was agreed to.

Mr. McINTIRE, from the Committee of Claims, reported a bill for the relief of William Baker. Read twice, and committed.

Mr. ALLEN, of Virginia, from the Committee on the District of Columbia, reported a bill further to amend the act incorporating the Chesapeake and Ohio Canal Company. Read twice and committed.

Mr. WHITE, of New York, from the Committee on Naval Affairs, reported a resolution for the printing of one thousand extra copies of the Rules and Regulations of the Navy, communicated to the House by the President on the 2d of May.

Mr. McKAY asked what reason there was for printing an extra number? He also remarked that he was opposed to this system of giving up to the President authority to make laws.

Mr. WHITE replied that a joint resolution was passed at the last session, requesting the President to prepare rules and regulations for the navy, and they were prepared under the direction of a board constituted for the purpose. The object of printing them was to distribute copies among the officers of the navy, that we might learn their views upon what so nearly concerns their interest and comfort.

Mr. McKAY moved the postponement of the resolution till Saturday. Lost.

Mr. J. G. ADAMS asked whether an extra number had not been ordered to be printed when the message was received?

Mr. WHITE said that only the usual number had been ordered to be printed. An extra number was proposed for the information of the officers generally.

Mr. ADAMS asked whether it was intended to act on the subject at the present session?

Mr. WHITE replied that it would be acted on, if practicable.

Mr. ADAMS did not think (he said) that the views of the officers could be obtained in sufficient time to be available for the present session. If there was any use in printing the copies, he would not object to it. There was a law once passed here, in three lines, adopting a code of regulations for the army, before a single member of the House had read a word in the code. The consequence was that, at the next session, the law was repealed. He hoped Congress would not act in the same

manner in the present case. He hoped the affairs of the navy would be taken into the serious consideration of the House, and unless we suspend our action on this subject till the next session, there would be no use in printing the extra copies.

Mr. REED said, many of the officers had written to members of the House for copies of the proposed regulations, and he thought they ought to have them. The object was important and the expense small.

Mr. WILLIAMS was as anxious, he said, as his colleague could be, to prevent unnecessary expense, and would concur with him in opposing the exercise of legislative authority by the Executive, but this was not now the question. It was necessary that every officer should have a copy of these rules, and it was improper to put them at the expense of printing them for themselves. They were not yet adopted, but it was probable that they would be, without much further alteration. He felt that he could discharge his duty better on the subject, after learning the opinions of the officers of the navy

Mr. WHITE read the act under which the rules and regulations had been proposed.

After which, the resolution was agreed to, without a division.

On motion of Mr. GAMBLE, the House took up his resolution, calling for information concerning the Military Academy, for consideration, when Mr. G. proposed a modification of the resolution.

Mr. CONNOR suggested that the same information had been called for on motion of the gentleman from Kentucky, [Mr. JOHNSON.]

Mr. GAMBLE said, the same information in substance had been called for, but by a resolution which had not been acted upon.

The SPEAKER said, the resolution was not, therefore, in order.

Mr. GAMBLE withdrew the resolution.

Mr. BANKS, from the select committee on elections, made a report on the part of the minority of that committee, and counter to the report of the majority. Ordered to be printed.

Mr. VINTON, from the select committee on patents, reported a bill to erect a fire-proof building for the Patent Office, and for other purposes. Read twice, and committed.

Mr. WHITE, of Florida, on leave, presented a private petition.

Mr. CAVE JOHNSON moved the reconsideration of the vote by which the bill for the relief of Samuel A. Bailey was passed; which was agreed to.

Mr. JOHNSON offered an amendment to the bill; which was agreed to.

Mr. POLK asked the unanimous consent of the House to proceed to the consideration of the general appropriation bill; and an objection being made, Mr. P. moved that the rules be suspended for the purpose of taking up that bill; which motion prevailed.

The question being on the following clause of the amendment offered by Mr. VANCE—

"And in no case shall the compensation, by salary, fees, or otherwise, be permitted to exceed—
' of a collector, three thousand dollars per annum;
' of surveyors and inspectors, two thousand five
' hundred dollars per annum; and of weighers,
' gaugers, markers, appraisers, and all others con-
' nected with the collectors 'of the customs, two
' thousand dollars per annum'"—

The yeas and nays were ordered.

The question being taken, it was determined in the affirmative: Yeas 85, nays 79.

So this clause was adopted.

Mr. VANCE then withdrew the remainder of his amendment.

Mr. WHITE, of Florida, moved to amend the bill, by inserting an appropriation for the compensation of the judges of Florida Territory, for special duties in the adjudication of land claims, under the act of May, 1828, for the years 1833 and 1834, $3,900.

Mr. W. explained the grounds of this amendment.

Mr. POLK, the chairman of the Committee of Ways and Means, explained the provisions on this subject already embraced by the bill—

When a discussion arose upon the propriety of making the allowance contemplated by the amendment, in which Messrs. WHITE of Florida, Mc-

KAY, WAYNE, WILDE, and GAMBLE, participated; when

Mr. WHITE modified his amendment, so as to include the extra allowance for the judges of the middle and western districts for 1833, $1,600, and a contingent allowance for 1834.

Mr. GAMBLE moved to amend the amendment, by striking out the contingent clause.

Mr. WHITE accepted the modification.

After some further discussion between Messrs. McKAY and WHITE, the amendment was adopted, as amended:

Ayes 84, noes 48.

Mr. WHITE also moved to amend the bill, by adding an item appropriating $1,000 to defray the costs of certain suits against the United States.

After some explanation between Messrs. McKAY and WHITE, the amendment was adopted without a division.

Mr. SUTHERLAND moved that the following section be added to the bill:

"And be it further enacted, That the Secretary of ' the Treasury be, and he is hereby, authorized to ' pay to the collectors, naval officers, surveyors, ' clerks, gaugers, weighers, provers, markers, and ' measurers, of the several ports of the United ' States, out of any money in the Treasury not ' otherwise appropriated, such sums as will give ' to the said officers, respectively, the same com- ' pensation in the year one thousand eight hundred ' and thirty-four, according to the importance of ' that year, as they would have been entitled to ' receive, if the act of the fourteenth July, eigh- ' teen hundred and thirty-two, had not gone into ' effect."

Mr. S. felt that a few remarks, by way of explanation, were necessary, after the vote which had been given this morning. He was able to satisfy any gentleman, that unless this provision was made, the collector of Philadelphia, instead of receiving $3,000 per annum, to which he was restricted by the amendment which had been adopted, would, in fact, be more than $3,000 out of pocket. That collector was allowed by law a commission on the duties of three-eighths of one per cent., which amounted the past year to $6,500. The official fees amounted to $2,900. These together amount to $9,200. Now, the collector is obliged to pay in clerk hire $12,300, and $700 for stationery. Unless, therefore, this provision be adopted, the collector of Philadelphia would not get any compensation whatever. He mentioned this as an illustration of the necessity for the amendment. It has been the desire, for some time past, of the Committee on Commerce, to arrange a general system of regulation on this subject. A mass of materials had been collected for this purpose, which had been unfortunately burnt. Papers were now in the progress of being obtained, which would shed the necessary light on this important branch of our revenue system, to enable a proper law to be framed.

Mr. CLAYTON said, it was well known that the House had raised a committee in consequence of a resolution introduced by himself, for the purpose of inquiring into the propriety of reducing salaries and abolishing offices. During a recent visit to New York, he was informed of certain facts relative to the collection of the customs there, which induced him to warn the House not to grope in the dark. There had been a great increase of officers there since 1828. Mr. C. gave way to

Mr. SUTHERLAND, who said that more care, vigilance, and circumspection, was necessary to be exercised, when part of a cargo consisted of goods free of duty. The officers of customs, in this country, were men of high character and respectability. He hoped no measure would be taken, which might, by any possibility, tend to lower this standard, and place them on a footing of those in Europe. Unless a fair compensation is given them, they cannot discharge their duties. If the revenue is not collected, there will be no occasion for inquiring where the treasury is. Mr. S. went into a detailed statement showing the prosperity of the amendment.

Mr. POLK requested that a letter from the Secretary of the Treasury, dated 30th April last, on the subject of the compensation of custom-house officers, might be read; which having been done, Mr. P. said, a provision on this subject would

have been introduced into the bill, had this letter been received in sufficient season.

Mr. CLAYTON said it was impossible to foresee the consequences of adopting this amendment. There had been a great increase of custom-house officers in New York since 1828, which he enumerated. The annual expense had increased from $150,000 to $300,000. Before any such measure as this is adopted, there should be a full investigation on the subject.

The additional section proposed by Mr. SUTHERLAND was so modified as to apply only to collectors, naval officers, and surveyors.

Mr. S. said he would vote for the amendment in its altered state, though it was not in the shape he originally proposed.

After some remarks from Mr. J. W. HUNTINGTON in opposition to the amendment, as modified,

Mr. GORHAM said he was opposed to the amendment as it originally stood, extending as it did to the officers appointed by the collector, as well as to those appointed by the President and Senate. But, as modified, he saw no objection to its adoption. Unless something of this kind was done, it was uncertain whether the three officers now included in the amendment would receive any compensation whatever. The amounts had all been limited by the vote upon the amendment by the gentleman from Ohio; at the principal ports he was in favor of compensating them up to the amount of the limitation, indeed going beyond it, for the limitation adopted this morning had not received his vote.

Mr. HARPER, of Pennsylvania, went into a statement of the compensation of certain subordinate officers of the customs under the amendment as it originally stood.

The CHAIR apprized him of the modification.

Mr. H. intimated that he had no objection to the amendment as it now stood.

After some remarks from Messrs. SELDEN and JARVIS relative to the emoluments of officers of the customs—

Mr. VANCE moved an amendment to the amendment, directing a certain proportion of the officers of the customs of New York to be dismissed.

Mr. V. said, after these officers had been dismissed, the House would not get any compensation whatever. The gentleman from New Jersey [Mr. PARKER] had stated a few days since that the tariff of 1828 had given rise to so much smuggling as to render an increase of custom-house officers necessary. If the high duties were a sufficient reason for increasing the officers, the reduction of duties should be a sufficient reason for cutting down their number.

Mr. CAMBRELENG said he must be permitted to say this was an extraordinary mode of proceeding upon a subject which required so careful an examination of facts. The gentleman from Georgia [Mr. CLAYTON] had referred to the increase of officers at New York. He hoped the gentleman would do the collector the justice to ascertain the number of vessels which entered and cleared at that port, examine into the amount of the revenue collected, and satisfy himself whether it was collected so economically at any other port of the United States. He was entirely willing to support any well digested and practicable arrangement of these offices. The amendment, as it had been originally moved, was the same as was proposed on this session by the then chairman of the Committee of Ways and Means—a gentleman who resided in the city of New York, and who had also drawn the report in favor of the United States Bank.

Mr. PARKER said the amendment to the amendment did not go far enough. It only proposed to dismiss a part of the custom-house officers. It should have gone to dismiss the whole. He had frequently had occasion to go to the custom-house in New York. He was entirely convinced that the officers there employed could be dispensed with. He had never seen in his life individuals more busily employed. Gentlemen appeared to suppose that because the rate of duties had been lessened there was less employment for custom-house officers. He would inform that gentleman that everything required before to be

done was necessary now. In fact, some portion of employment was greatly increased. The abstruse mode of calculating duties required by the Compromise law was calculated sometimes to puzzle even an expert accountant. The gentleman from Ohio [Mr. VANCE] had alluded to his remark that the high tariff of 1828 had increased the propensity for smuggling. This was notoriously the fact, and rendered more officers essential to the protection of the revenue; and one of the most unfortunate consequences of the system of high duties is, that when men under the temptation of fifty per cent. have been induced to smuggle, they will not leave it off when duties are reduced to twenty-five per cent. It must also be remembered that the trade of New York has nearly doubled since 1828. It had swallowed up that of many other places, and it might be said of almost all other places of the United States. That a large increase of officers, under these circumstances, was necessary, was not a matter of surprise.

Mr. BROWN said, the amendment offered by the gentleman from Ohio [Mr. VANCE] proposes to strike from existence one hundred and twenty-one of the officers employed in the collection of the revenue in the city of New York. As one of the delegation from that State, he could not feel indifferent to the fate of this extraordinary proposition; and unwilling as he was to occupy the attention of the House, he must be permitted to make a few observations upon the subject. Gentlemen seem to argue this question as if the revenue officers and the Government alone were interested in its decision. He begged to correct this impression, if he was right in supposing such existed in the minds of honorable members. There was another class whose interests might be prejudiced by the event; that class was the merchants; those concerned in the vast commerce of the city, which led them to transact business with the custom-house. What information is there before Congress that the officers employed in that branch of the public service were too numerous? Were there more than the public interest and convenience required? None whatever, sir. The facts communicated by the gentleman from Georgia [Mr. CLAYTON] does not touch the question. He would, at a proper time, and upon a proper occasion, go with gentlemen in any reasonable effort to reduce the number of revenue officers, or the salaries of revenue officers, whenever such reduction can be made without injury to the public service, or diminishing the facilities for the transaction of commercial business. What particular reason exists for the application of this proposition to the city of New York alone, the House had not been informed, nor could he conjecture. Gentlemen were sometimes inclined to find fault with New York politics, and New York influence, but he hardly expected, while the general appropriation bill was under consideration, that the number of her citizens engaged in the collection of the revenue should be made the special subject of animadversion. New York has much to be proud of besides her well-spread commerce, which it might not become her Representatives to enumerate here. And she had as little to fear from the most searching scrutiny into her political affairs on any other branch of her public concerns, as any other portion of the Union. He hoped gentlemen might have an opportunity to see her as she really was; and when they felt inclined to speak of the number of officers employed within her limits in the preservation and collection of the revenue, he begged they would not forget her commerce, and the vast amount of revenue she brought yearly into the public treasury.

The gentleman from Connecticut [Mr. HUNTINGTON] seemed to think that the extent of service rendered in carrying into effect the revenue laws, and the collection of the impost duties, depended upon the amount realized by the Government; and that the operation of the last tariff law has taken away the necessity for the same number of custom-house officers. This opinion, he apprehended, was not true, to the extent which the gentleman seemed to suppose, and the observations of his colleague [Mr. CAMBRELENG] were so full and satisfactory, that he would not trouble the House further with that branch of the subject. Although, as a general rule, he was opposed to legislating upon offices or salaries in an appropriation bill, further than to provide means for the payment of those already created, still, rather than leave collectors, surveyors, and naval officers without an adequate compensation, he would so far depart from this rule as to vote for the amendment making provision for that purpose.

Mr. PEARCE, of Rhode Island, spoke in opposition to the motion, and in reply to Messrs. VANCE and CLAYTON.

Mr. VANCE said, as the House was impatient for the question, and as the gentleman from New York [Mr. CAMBRELENG] did not wish his amendment to be encumbered, he would withdraw his motion.

Mr. FILLMORE being solicitous, as he said, that this amendment should not be considered as inconsistent with the clause adopted on motion of the member from Ohio, [Mr. VANCE,] moved to amend the amendment, by adding to it the provisions, that in no case should the compensation of a collector exceed three thousand dollars, nor that of the surveyor and naval officers twenty-five hundred dollars each.

Mr. SUTHERLAND accepted the amendment as a modification, in order to prevent further delay, declaring, at the same time, that he was opposed to the reduction of the emoluments of those officers.

After some remarks from Mr. CLAYTON, in which he opposed the amendment, on the ground that the whole subject of salaries was before the Committee on Retrenchment,

Mr. HUNTINGTON called for the yeas and nays on the question; and they were ordered.

The question being taken, it was decided in the negative; yeas 78, nays 116.

YEAS—Messrs. John Adams, Heman Allen, William Allen, Anthony, Banks, Beale, Bean, Beardsley, Bockee, Bodle, Boon, Brown, Bunch, Burns, Bynum, Cambreleng, Samuel Clark, Clay, Day, Dickerson, Dickinson, H. Everett, Fowler, Galbraith, Gillet, Gorham, Joseph Hall, Halsey, Hannegan, Jos. M. Harper, Harrison, Hathaway, Henderson, Howell, Hubbard, Abel Huntington, Richard M. Johnson, Cave Johnson, Benjamin Jones, Kavanagh, Lane, Lansing, Laporte, Luke Lea, Thomas Lee, Leavitt, Loyall, Joel K. Mann, Mardis, McKim, McVean, Robert Mitchell, Murphy, Osgood, Page, Parks, Parker, Dutee J. Pearce, Franklin Pierce, Pierson, Plummer, Polk, Selden, Shinn, William Slade, Charles Slade, Speight, Standifer, Sutherland, William Taylor, Thomson, Turrill, Vanderpoel, Van Houten, Ward, Wayne, Webster, Whallon—78.

NAYS—Messrs. J. Q. Adams, John J. Allen, Chilton Allan, Archer, Ashley, Barber, Barnitz, Barringer, Bates, Baylies, Beatty, Beaumont, James M. Bell, Binney, Blair, Bouldin, Bull, Burd, Burges, Cage, Casey, Chambers, Chaney, Chilton, Chinn, William Clark, Clayton, Clowney, Coffee, Connor, Corwin, Coulter, Crane, Darlington, W. R. Davis, Amos Davis, Davenport, Deberry, Deming, Denny, Dickson, Duncan, Dunlap, Evans, Ewing, Forester, Foster, Philo C. Fuller, William K. Fuller, Fulton, Gamble, Garland, Gholson, Gilmer, Gordon, Graham, Griffin, Hiland Hall, T. H. Hall, Hardin, James Harper, Hawkins, Hazeltine, Hiester, Jabez W. Huntington, Jarvis, William Cost Johnson, Noadiah Johnson, Kinnard, Lay, Lincoln, Love, Lucas, Lyon, Martindale, Marshall, Moses Mason, McCarty, McIntire, McKay, McKennan, McLene, Miller, Milligan, Moore, Patton, Peyton, Pinckney, Pope, Potts, Ramsay, Reed, Rencher, Schley, W. B. Shepard, A. H. Shepperd, Sloane, Smith, Spangler, Stewart, Wm. B. Taylor, Philemon Thomas, Tompkins, Turner, Tweedy, Vance, Vinton, Wagener, Wardwell, Watmough, Edward D. White, Fredrick Whittlesey, Elisha Whittlesey, Wilde, Williams, Wise, Young—116.

So the amendment was rejected.

Mr. POLK moved to strike out $850, and insert $1250, as the compensation of the superintendent and watchmen of the northeast executive building.

The amendment was agreed to.

Mr. J. Q. ADAMS renewed the motion made in the Committee of the Whole, and there rejected, to strike out "Great Britain and Russia," and insert "eighteen," instead of "thirty-six" in the following clause:

"For the salaries of the Ministers of the United States to Great Britain, France, Spain, and Russia, thirty-six thousand dollars."

Mr. A. recapitulated the arguments which he had urged in the Committee of the Whole, in favor of this amendment, and called for the yeas and nays on the motion, which were ordered.

Mr. WAYNE briefly replied.

After some remarks from Messrs. BARRINGER, WILLIAMS, and FOSTER, the question was taken, and determined in the negative; yeas 69, nays 123.

YEAS—Messrs. John Quincy Adams, Heman Allen, Chilton Allan, Ashley, Banks, Barber, Bates, Beatty, James M. Bell, Binney, Briggs, Bull, Burd, Chambers, Chilton, William Clark, Clayton, Clowney, Corwin, Coulter, Crane, Darlington, Warren R. Davis, Amos Davis, Deming, Denny, Dickson, Evans, Horace Everett, Foster, Gamble, Garland, Gilmer, Gorham, Grennell, Hiland Hall, Hard, Hardin, James Harper, Hazeltine, Hiester, Jabez W. Huntington, Jackson, William C. Johnson, Lay, Lincoln, Lucas, Martindale, Marshall, McKennan, Milligan, Potts, Reed, Selden, William Slade, Sloane, Philemon Thomas, Tompkins, Turner, Tweedy, Vance, Vinton, Watmough, Frederick Whittlesey, Elisha Whittlesey, Wilde, Williams, Wise, Young—69.

NAYS—Messrs. John Adams, John J. Allen, William Allen, Anthony, Barringer, Baylies, Beale, Bean, Beardsley, Beaumont, John Bell, Blair, Bockee, Bodle, Boon, Bouldin, Brown, Bunch, Burns, Bynum, Cage, Cambreleng, Casey, Chaney, Chinn, Samuel Clark, Clay, Coffee, Connor, Davenport, Day, Deberry, Dickerson, Dickinson, Duncan, Dunlap, Felder, Forester, Fowler, Philo C. Fuller, William K. Fuller, Gholson, Gillet, Graham, Joseph Hall, Thomas H. Hall, Halsey, Hannegan, Joseph M. Harper, Harrison, Hathaway, Hawkins, Henderson, Howell, Hubbard, Abel Huntington, Jarvis, Richard M. Johnson, Noadiah Johnson, Cave Johnson, Benjamin Jones, Kavanagh, Kinnard, Lane, Lansing, Laporte, Luke Lea, Thomas Lee, Leavitt, Love, Loyall, Lyon, Joel K. Mann, Mardis, Moses Mason, McCarty, McIntire, McKay, McKim, McLene, McVean, Miller, Robert Mitchell, Moore, Murphy, Osgood, Page, Parks, Parker, Patton, Dutee J. Pearce, Peyton, Franklin Pierce, Pierson, Pinckney, Plummer, Polk, Pope, Ramsay, Rencher, Schley, William B. Shepard, A. H. Shepperd, Shinn, Charles Slade, Smith, Spangler, Speight, Standifer, Stewart, Sutherland, William Taylor, William P. Taylor, Thomson, Turrill, Vanderpoel, Van Houten, Wagener, Ward, Wardwell, Wayne, Webster, Whallon, Edw. D. White—123.

Mr. WISE moved that the House do now adjourn; which was negatived.

Mr. JARVIS moved to reconsider the vote by which the amendment of Mr. VANCE, which goes to limit the compensation of certain officers of the customs, was adopted, on the ground of the thinness of the House when that amendment was carried.

Mr. J. Q. ADAMS advocated the reconsideration of the vote, and wishing to propose a further amendment to the bill, moved an adjournment; which was negatived.

Mr. J. W. HUNTINGTON demanded the yeas and nays; which were ordered.

The motion to reconsider was lost; ayes 86, noes 94.

YEAS—Messrs. John Q. Adams, John Adams, William Allen, Baylies, Beale, Bean, Beardsley, Blair, Bockee, Bodle, Briggs, Brown, Bunch, Burns, Bynum, Cage, Cambreleng, Chinn, Samuel Clark, Clay, Coffee, Day, Philemon Dickerson, Fowler, William K. Fuller, Gillet, Graham, Thomas H. Hall, Halsey, Hannegan, Hard, Hardin, Joseph M. Harper, Hathaway, Hawkins, Howell, Hubbard,* Abel Huntington, Jarvis, Richard M. Johnson, Noadiah Johnson, Cave Johnson, Benjamin Jones, Kavanagh, Kinnard, Lane, Lansing, Luke Lea, Thomas Lee, Leavitt, Loyall, Joel K. Mann, Martindale, Moses Mason, McIntire, McKim, McLene, McVean, Murphy, Osgood, Page, Parks, Parker, Patton, Dutee J. Pearce, Franklin Pierce, Pierson, Pinckney, Plummer, Polk, Schley, Selden, Shinn, William Slade, Speight, Standifer, Sutherland, William Taylor, Thomson, Turrill, Vanderpoel Van Houten, Ward, Wardwell, Wayne, Whallon, and Wise—86.

NAYS—Messrs. Heman Allen, John J. Allen, Chilton Allan, Anthony, Banks, Barber, Barrin-

ger, Bates, Beaty, Beaumont, James M. Bell, Binney, Boon, Bull, Burd, Casey, Chambers, Chaney, Chilton, William Clark, Clayton, Clowney, Connor, Corwin, Coulter, Crane, Darlington, Warren R. Davis, Amos Davis, Davenport, Deberry, Deming, Denny, Dickson, D. W. Dickinson, Dunlap, Evans, Horace Everett, Ewing, Felder, Forester, Foster, Philo C. Fuller, Gamble, Garland, Grennell, Hiland Hall, James Harper, Harrison, Hawes, Hazeltine, Henderson, Heister, Jabez W. Huntington, Jackson, William C. Johnson, Laporte, Lay, Lincoln, Love, Lyon, Marshall, Mardis, McCarty, McKay, McKennan, Miller, Milligan, Robert Mitchell, Moore, Peyton, Pope, Potts, Ramsay, Reed, Rencher, William B. Shepard, Augustine H. Shepperd, Charles Slade, Smith, Spangler, Stewart, William P. Taylor, Philemon Thomas, Tompkins, Turner, Tweedy, Vance, Wagener, Watmough, Webster, Elisha Whittlesey, Wilde, and Young—94.

Mr. DAVIS moved to add the following proviso after the item making appropriation for the salaries of ministers abroad:

"Provided that so much of the sum herein appropriated for the payment of the salaries of the ministers to Great Britain and Russia shall not be expended unless the appointment of said ministers shall have been made with the consent and advice of the Senate."

A discussion arose upon this amendment, in which Messrs. DAVIS, BYNUM, LANE, H. EVERETT, and EWING took part, when Mr. WISE moved to amend the amendment, by adding "unless vacancies shall happen during the recess of the Senate.".

Mr. SELDEN suggested the propriety of substituting "occur," or "arise," for the word "happen," which had been settled by the highest authority to include existing vacancies, as well as those which might hereafter take place.

Mr. WISE considered the word "happen" to be the only appropriate term, being that used in the Constitution.

Mr. PATTON explained at length the grounds upon which he should feel bound to vote against the amendment to the amendment; to whom Mr. WISE replied.

Mr. BEARDSLEY stated his objection to the amendment and the amendment to it. It was worse than useless to reënact the Constitution in an appropriation bill.

Mr. DAVIS explained his views in offering the amendment, in reply to Mr. BEARDSLEY.

Mr. FOSTER suggested a modification of the amendment; which was not accepted.

Mr. COULTER moved an adjournment; which was negatived.

Mr. DAVENPORT moved a call of the House; upon which he demanded the yeas and nays; which were ordered.

Mr. GAMBLE moved an adjournment; which was negatived—yeas 49, noes 95.

The question was taken on the call of the House; which was refused—yeas 41, nays 127:

YEAS—Messrs. John Quincy Adams, Heman Allen, Banks, Barber, Barringer, Bates, Beatty, Binney, Campbell, Chambers, Chilton, William Clark, Clowney, Coulter, Darlington, Warren R. Davis, Davenport, Deming, Denny, Evans, Horace Everett, Ewing, Foster, Garland, Griffin, Hard, James Harper, Hawes, J. W. Huntington, William C. Johnson, Lay, Lincoln, Martindale, Rencher, William Slade, Sloane, Spangler, Watmough, Frederick Whittlesey, Wilde, and Young—41.

NAYS—Messrs. John Adams, John J. Allen, William Allen, Anthony, Bayliss, Beale, Bean, Beardsley, Beaumont, Blair, Bockee, Bodle, Boon, Bouldin, Brown, Bull, Bunch, Burd, Burns, Bynum, Cage, Casey, Chaney, Chinn, Samuel Clark, Clay, Clayton, Coffee, Connor, Amos Davis, Day, Deberry, Dickson, Dickinson, Dickinson, Dunlap, Forester, William K. Fuller, Fulton, Gamble, Gillet, Graham, Hiland Hall, Halsey, Hamer, Hannegan, Hardin, Joseph M. Harper, Harrison, Hathaway, Hawkins, Hazeltine, Henderson, Heister, Howell, Hubbard, Abel Huntington, Jackson, Jarvis, Richard M. Johnson, Noadiah Johnson, Cave Johnson, Benjamin Jones, Kavanagh, King, Kinnard, Lane, Lansing, Luke Lea, Thomas Lea, Leavitt, Lewis, Love, Loyall, Lyon, Joel K. Mann, Mardis, Moses

Mason, McCarty, McIntire, McKay, McKim, McLene, Miller, Robert Mitchell, Moore, Murphy, Osgood, Page, Parks, Parker, Patton, Dutee J. Pearce, Peyton, Franklin Pierce, Pierson, Pinckney, Plummer, Polk, Pope, Potts, Ramsey, Schley, Augustine H. Shepperd, Shinn, Charles Slade, Smith, Speight, Standifer, Stewart, Sutherland, William Taylor, Thomson, Turner, Turrill, Tweedy, Vance, Vanderpoel, Van Houten, Wagener, Ward, Wardwell, Whallon, Edward D. White, Elisha Whitlesey, and Wise—127.

The amendment to the amendment having been negatived—

The question was then taken on Mr. DAVIS's amendment; which was lost: Yeas 45, nays 122.,

YEAS—Messrs. Heman Allen, Banks, Barber, Beatty, Burd, Campbell, Chambers, Chilton, William Clark, Clayton, Clowney, Darlington, Warren R. Davis, Amos Davis, Deming, Denny, Dickson, Evans, Horace Everett, Ewing, Foster, Fulton, Gamble, Griffin, Hiland Hall, Hard, James Harper, Inge, William Cost Johnson, Lay, Lewis, Lincoln, Martindale, Milligan, Pinckney, Selden, Sloane, William P. Taylor, Francis Thomas, Philemon Thomas, Turner, Tweedy, Vance, Watmough, Elisha Whittlesey, Wise, Young—45.

NAYS—Messrs. John Quincy Adams, John Adams, John J. Allen, William Allen, Anthony, Barringer, Bayliss, Beale, Bean, Beardsley, Bean, mont, Binney, Blair, Bockee, Bodle, Boon, Bouldin, Briggs, Brown, Bull, Bunch, Burns, Bynum, Cage, Casey, Chaney, Chinn, Samuel Clark, Clay, Coffee, Connor, Coulter, Davenport, Day, Deberry, P. Dickerson, D. W. Dickinson, Dunlap, Forester, Philo C. Fuller, William K. Fuller, Gillet, Graham, Halsey, Hamer, Hannegan, Joseph M. Harper, Harrison, Hathaway, Hawkins, Hawes, Hazeltine, Henderson, Hiester, Howell, Hubbard, Abel Huntington, Jarvis, Richard M. Johnson, Noadiah Johnson, Cave Johnson, Benjamin Jones, Kavanagh, King, Kinnard, Lane, Lansing, Luke Lea, Thomas Lea, Leavitt, Love, Loyall, Joel K. Mann, Mardis, McCarty, McIntire, McKay, McKim, McLene, Miller, Robert Mitchell, Moore, Murphy, Osgood, Page, Parks, Parker, Patton, D. J. Pearce, Peyton, Franklin Pierce, Pierson, Plummer, Polk, Pope, Potts, Ramsay, Rencher, Schley, A. H. Shepperd, Shinn, Slade, Smith, Spangler, Speight, Standifer, Stewart, Sutherland, William Taylor, Thomson, Turrill, Vanderpoel, Van Houten, Vinton, Wagener, Ward, Wardwell, Whallon, E. D. White—122.

Mr. J. Q. ADAMS moved to amend the bill by striking out the appropriation for salaries and outfit for a chargé d'affaires to Buenos Ayres; upon which he asked the yeas and nays; which were ordered.

Mr. A. explained the grounds of his motion at length; when the question was taken, and lost: Yeas 59, nays 101.

YEAS—Messrs. John Quincy Adams, Heman Allen, Banks, Barber, Barringer, Bates, Beatty, Binney, Bull, Campbell, Chilton, William Clark, Coulter, Darlington, W. R. Davis, Amos Davis, Deberry, Denny, Dickson, Evans, Philo C. Fuller, Garland, Griffin, Hiland Hall, Hard, Hardin, James Harper, Hawes, Hazeltine, Hiester, William Cost Johnson, King, Lewis, Lincoln, Love, Lyon, Martindale, McKay, Milligan, Potts, Reed, Selden, William Slade, Sloane, Speight, Turner, Tweedy, Vance, Watmough, Frederick Whittlesey, Wilde—52.

NAYS—Messrs. John Adams, John J. Allen, William Allen, Anthony, Beale, Bean, Beardsley, Beaumont, Blair, Bockee, Bodle, Boon, Bouldin, Brown, Bunch, Burd, Burns, Bynum, Cage, Casey, Chaney, Chinn, Samuel Clark, Clay, Clayton, Coffee, Connor, Day, Dickerson, Dickinson, Dunlap, Forester, William K. Fuller, Gillet, Graham, Halsey, Hamer, Hannegan, Joseph M. Harper, Harrison, Hathaway, Hawkins, Henderson, Howell, Hubbard, Abel Huntington, Jarvis, Richard M. Johnson, Cave Johnson, Seaborn Jones, Benjamin Jones, Kavanagh, Kinnard, Lane, Lansing, Luke Lea, Thomas Lea, Leavitt, Loyall, Lyon, Joel K. Mann, Mardis, Moses Mason, McIntire, McKay, McKim, McLene, Miller, Robert Mitchell, Moore, Murphy, Osgood, Page, Parks, Parker, Patton, Pearce, Peyton, Franklin Pierce, Pierson, Plummer, Polk, Pope, Ramsey, Schley, Augustine H. Shepperd, Shinn, Smith, Speight, Standifer, Stewart, Suther-

land, William Taylor, Turrill, Vanderpoel, Van Houten, Wagener, Ward, Wardwell, Webster, Whallon, E. D. White, Wise, and Young—101.'

Mr. LINCOLN moved to strike from the bill the item making appropriation for additional clerk hire in the General Post Office for 1833.

Mr. L. explained the object of this amendment at length, to whom Mr. CONNOR replied.

Mr. WILDE demanded the yeas and nays upon the motion; which were ordered.

Mr. McKAY could not vote to support this appropriation, unless a proviso was added that the appropriation should not sanction the employment of additional clerks hereafter. Mr. McK. explained his views on this subject.

The amendment of Mr. LINCOLN was debated at length by Messrs. BATES, CONNOR, E. WHITTLESEY, PEARCE, McKAY, WILDE, REED, and HAWES, when Mr. CAVE JOHNSON demanded the previous question, which was afterwards withdrawn.

Mr. WISE moved an adjournment; upon which Mr. CAMPBELL asked the yeas and nays; which were ordered.

The motion to adjourn lost: yeas 46, nays 97.

YEAS—Messrs. J. Q. Adams, Heman Allen, Banks, Barringer, Bates, Beatty, Binney, Briggs, Burd, Campbell, William Clark, Darlington, Deberry, Deming, Denny, Evans, Ewing, Foster, Philo C. Fuller, Gamble, Garland, Griffin, Hiland Hall, James Harper, Hazeltine, Hiester, Jabez W. Huntington, Jackson, William Cost Johnson, King, Lay, Lincoln, Milligan, Pinckney, Potts, Ramsay, Reed, Sloane, Spangler, Vance, Vinton, Watmough, Edward D. White, Frederick Whittlesey, Wilde, Wise, and Young—46.

NAYS—Messrs. John Adams, John J. Allen, William Allen, Anthony, Beale, Bean, Beardsley, Beaumont, Blair, Bodle, Bouldin, Bull, Bunch, Burns, Cage, Casey, Chaney, Chilton, Chinn, S. Clark, Clay, Connor, Amos Davis, Day, Dickson, Philemon Dickerson, David W. Dickinson, Dunlap, Forester, Fowler, William K. Fuller, Gillet, Halsey, Hamer, Hannegan, Joseph M. Harper, Harrison, Hathaway, Hawkins, Hawes, Henderson, Howell, Hubbard, A. Huntington, Jarvis, R. M. Johnson, Cave Johnson, Seaborn Jones, Benjamin Jones, Kavanagh, Kinnard, Lane, Lansing, Luke Lea, Thomas Lea, Leavitt, Loyall, Lyon, Joel K. Mann, Mardis, Moses Mason, McIntire, McKay, McKim, McLene, Miller, Robert Mitchell, Moore, Murphy, Osgood, Page, Parks, Parker, Patton, D. J. Pearce, Peyton, Franklin Pierce, Pierson, Plummer, Polk, Pope, Ramsey, Schley, Standifer, Stewart, Sutherland, William Taylor, Francis Thomas, Thomson, Turner, Turrill, Van Houten, Wagener, Ward, Wardwell, Webster, Whallon, and Elisha Whittlesey—97.

Mr. McKAY's motion was further continued by Messrs. WILDE, E. WHITTLESEY, McKAY, and LINCOLN, when the question was taken, and the motion was negatived:

Ayes 56, noes 97.

Parks, Parker, Patton, Patterson, Dutee J. Pearce, Franklin Pierce, Peyton, Pierson, Plummer, Polk, Pope, Schley, A. H. Shepperd, Shinn, Speight, Sundifer, Stewart, Sutherland, William Taylor, Thomson, Turrill, Vanderpoel, Van Houten, Wagener, Ward, Wardwell, Webster, and Whalley—97.

Mr. WILDE moved to strike from the bill the item which provides for the compensation and expenses of an agent to Havana to procure the archives of Florida. Mr. W. stated the grounds of his motion. There was no law creating this office, and no appointment by the confirmation of the Senate of any such officer.

Mr. POLK held in his hand the correspondence of the Secretary of State and Attorney General on this subject. The archives in question involved the titles to public lands of immense value, and had been withheld in contravention of the treaty of 1819. Mr. P. went into an explanation of the object and duties of this agency, and referred to a former law sanctioning the appointment.

After some remarks from Messrs. WILDE and McKAY, in reply, the motion to strike out was lost—yeas 49, nays 91.

YEAS—Messrs. John Quincy Adams, Heman Allen, John J. Allen, Berringer, Bates, Beaty, J. M. Bell, Binney, Campbell, Chilton, Chinn, Corwin, Crane, Darlington, Amos Davis, Denny, Dickson, Evans, Ewing, P. C. Fuller, Garland, Griffin, Hiland Hall, Hardin, James Harper, Hawes, Hazeltine, Hiester, Jabez W. Huntington, Jackson, Seaborn Jones, King, Lay, Lewis, Lincoln, McKay, Milligan, Pinkney, Potts, Selden, Augustine H. Shepperd, Sloane, Spangler, Turner, Watmough, Elisha Whittlesey, Wilde, Wise, Young—49.

NAYS—Messrs. John Adams, William Allen, Anthony, Beale, Bean, Beardsley, Beaumont, Blair, Bodle, Briggs, Bunch, Burd, Burns, Casey, Cheney, Clark, Clay, Connor, Coulter, Day, Deberry, Philemon Dickerson, David W. Dickinson, Dunlap, Horace Everett, Forester, Fowler, William K. Fuller, Gamble, Halsey, Hamer, Hannegan, Joseph M. Harper, Harrison, Hathaway, Hawkins, Henderson, Howell, Hubbard, Abel Huntington, Jarvis, Richard M. Johnson, Cave Johnson, Benjamin Jones, Kavanagh, Kinnard, Lane, Lansing, Luke Lea, Thomas Lee, Leavitt, Loyall, Joel K. Mann, Mardis, Moses Mason, McIntIre, McKim, McLene, Miller, Robert Mitchell, Murphy, Osgood, Page, Parks, Parker, Patton, Dutee J. Pearce, Franklin Pierce, Peyton, Pierson, Plummer, Polk, Ramsay, Schley, Shinn, Smith, Speight, Sundifer, Stewart, Sutherland, William Taylor, Thomson, Tompkins, Turrill, Vanderpoel, Van Houten, Wagener, Ward, Wardwell, Webster, Whallon, Frederick Whittlesey—91.

Mr. McKAY then moved his proposed proviso to the appropriation for additional clerks in the General Post Office, declaring that it was not intended to sanction the employment of clerks not provided for by law hereafter.

It was opposed by Messrs. HARDIN and CONNOR, and was negatived without division.

The bill was then ordered to be engrossed, and had a third time on Monday.

The House then, at one o'clock, a. m., adjourned over to Monday.

IN SENATE.
Monday, May 12, 1834.

A message upon executive business was received from the President of the United States, by Mr. Donelson, his Private Secretary.

A message was received from the House of Representatives, by Mr. Franklin, their Clerk, stating that they had passed the general appropriation bill for the civil and diplomatic expenditures of the Government for the year 1834; and also the army appropriation bill for the same year.

PETITIONS.

Mr. WEBSTER presented the memorial of near fourteen hundred citizens of Rochester, New York, praying a restoration of the deposites to the Bank of the United States, and a recharter of said institution. Also, a memorial of a similar character from Mifflin county, Pennsylvania; and the proceedings of a meeting of citizens of Detroit, Michigan Territory, of a like nature.

All of which were referred to the Committee on Finance, and ordered to be printed.

Mr. McKEAN presented the memorial of ninety-six inhabitants of Chester county, Pennsylvania, in favor of the restoration of the deposites to the Bank of the United States, and a recharter of that institution.

Also, the proceedings of a meeting in Cumberland county, Pennsylvania, of a similar nature.

And a memorial of inhabitants of Luzerne county, Pennsylvania, sustaining the Executive in the course pursued towards the Bank of the United States, praying that the deposites may not be restored to that institution or that the same be re-chartered.

All of which were referred to the Committee on Finance, and ordered to be printed.

Mr. WRIGHT presented the memorial of one thousand seven hundred and ninety-six inhabitants of Livingston county, New York, praying a recharter of the Bank of the United States and a restoration of the deposites to the same.

Also, a memorial of six hundred and ninety-eight inhabitants of Warren county, New York, sustaining the Executive, and against a recharter of the bank or a restoration of the deposites.

And the memorial of eight hundred and ten citizens of Schenectady county, New York, of a like character of the preceding.

All of which were referred to the Committee on Finance, and ordered to be printed.

Mr. HENDRICKS presented the petition of John T. Towers, praying to be compensated for medical services rendered during the prevalence of the cholera in the city of Washington, in 1832; which was referred to the Committee on the District of Columbia.

REPORTS.

Mr. POINDEXTER, from the Committee on Public Lands, to whom it had been recommitted, reported a bill with amendments, to authorize the relinquishment of the 16th sections, being lands set apart for the benefit of schools, and to enter other lands in lieu thereof. The bill, on motion of Mr. POINDEXTER, was laid on the table.

Mr. POINDEXTER, from the same committee, reported a bill reviving the act of 3d March, 1817, to authorize the sale of four sections of land in Alabama to certain French emigrants, for the cultivation of the vine and olive.

Mr. TOMLINSON, from the Committee on Pensions, reported a bill without amendment, granting pensions to certain persons therein named.

Mr. BELL, from the Committee on Claims, reported a bill without amendment, for the relief of John S. Fleming.

Mr. BELL, from the Committee on the Judiciary, reported a bill extending the patent right of John Ames, for certain improvements in the manufacture of paper.

And also, a bill from the House of Representatives for the relief of Francis B. Ogden.

Mr. CLAYTON, from the Committee on the Judiciary, reported a bill adjusting the northern boundary line of the State of Ohio. The report was read; when, on motion of

Mr. EWING, one thousand extra copies were ordered to be printed.

Mr. CLAYTON, from the Committee on the Judiciary, reported a bill equalizing the representation in the Territory of Florida, without amendment.

Mr. TYLER, from the Committee on Finance, reported a bill for the relief of part of the crew of the brig Sarah George.

Mr. WEBSTER, from the Committee on Finance, reported a bill from the House of Representatives, authorizing the Secretary of the Treasury to remit certain duties chargeable to Aaron Baldwin, on part of the cargo of the brig Despatch.

Mr. WEBSTER, from the same committee, reported a bill without amendment, for the relief of Ezekiel Foster and Company.

Mr. TALLMADGE, from the Committee on Naval Affairs, reported a bill for the relief of the administrator of Micheal Hogan, deceased. The report was ordered to be printed.

Mr. MORRIS made a report from the Committee on Engrossed Bills.

Mr. BENTON, agreeably to notice, introduced a bill for the relief of Col. A. R. Woolley; which was read, and ordered to a third reading.

The following resolutions were submitted:
By Mr. McKEAN:

Resolved, That the Committee on Pensions be directed to inquire into the expediency and justice of granting a pension to Thomas Bradford, of Philadelphia, a captain in the revolutionary war.

By Mr. PORTER:

Resolved, That the Committee on Commerce be directed to inquire into the expediency of causing a survey and examination to be made of the Bull Pass, at the mouth of the Bayou La Fouche, in the State of Louisiana, in order to ascertain the practicability and cost of deepening the same and rendering it navigable.

By Mr. KANE:

Resolved, That the Committee on Claims be instructed to inquire into the expediency of refunding to Pierre Menard the amount of discount and interest by him paid to the Bank of the United States on money by the said bank advanced for the service of the United States.

The last resolution was agreed to, and the accompanying documents referred to the same committee.

GENERAL ORDERS.

The bill from the House of Representatives making appropriation for the civil and diplomatic expenses for the year 1834, was read by its title, and, on motion of Mr. WEBSTER, referred to the Committee on Finance.

The following bills were read a third time and passed:

A bill for the relief of Luther L. Smith;

A bill for the relief of Coleman Fisher;

A bill condemning convicts in the courts of the United States, when sentenced to confinement in the jails and penitentiaries of the several States, to similar treatment as convicts confined in those prisons;

A bill to provide for the legal adjudication and settlement of the claims to land therein mentioned;

A bill authorizing the Polish exiles, lately arrived in this country, to locate a township of land in the State of Illinois or Territory of Michigan.

[On the passage of this bill, Mr. WAGGAMAN asked for the yeas and nays, which were ordered, and are as follows:]

YEAS—Messrs. Benton, Calhoun, Clay, Clayton, Ewing, Frelinghuysen, Kent, King of Georgia, Knight, McKean, Moore, Morris, Naudain, Poindexter, Porter, Prentiss, Preston, Robbins, Silsbee, Smith, Tallmadge, Tipton, Tomlinson, Webster, Wilkins—25.

NAYS—Messrs. Black, Brown, Grundy, Hendricks, Hill, Kane, King of Alabama, Robinson, Shepley, Swift, Tyler, Waggaman, White, Wright—14.

SPECIAL ORDER.

The bill to authorize the people of the Territory of Arkansas to form a Constitution and State Government, and for the admission of such State into the Union upon an equal footing with the original States, in all respects whatsoever, was taken up.

Mr. EWING moved that the bill be laid upon the table; which motion was taken by yeas and nays, and decided in the affirmative, as follows:

YEAS—Messrs. Bell, Calhoun, Clay, Clayton, Ewing, Frelinghuysen, Kent, King of Georgia, Knight, Moore, Naudain, Poindexter, Porter, Prentiss, Robbins, Silsbee, Smith, Sprague, Swift, Tomlinson, Waggaman, Webster—22.

NAYS—Messrs. Benton, Brown, Black, Grundy, Hendricks, Hill, Kane, King of Alabama, McKean, Mangum, Morris, Robinson, Shepley, Tallmadge, Tipton, Tyler, White, Wilkins, Wright—19.

The report of the committee on the Rhode Island election was then taken up.

Mr. WRIGHT intimated a wish on the part of Mr. Porter, who contests the seat of Mr. Robbins, that the subject should be postponed to Monday next, and the Senate complied with the request.

Mr. BIBB called up his resolutions amending the Constitution of the United States; when, on his motion, the resolutions were made the order of the day for Thursday next.

The report of the Committee of Claims, unfavorable to the petition of Samuel Hardesty; and

The report of the Committee on Commerce,

unfavorable to the petition of the owners of the schooner Fair Lady:

Were severally read, and concurred in.

On motion of Mr. WILKINS, the Senate proceeded to ballot for a member of the Committee on Foreign Relations, vacated by the resignation of the Honorable WILLIAM C. RIVES; whereupon Mr. CLAY was chosen.

THE PENSION FUND.

Mr. CLAYTON moved to take up for consideration the report of the Judiciary Committee on the message of the President relative to the United States Bank and the pension fund; agreed to.

Mr. CLAYTON made some remarks in favor of adopting the report, and concluded by moving an amendment to the resolution, that the Secretary of War has no authority to appoint a pension agent, except when specially authorized to do so by act of Congress; which was agreed to.

Mr. WRIGHT then expressed a wish to give his views upon this subject, and moved to postpone it till to-morrow; which was agreed to.

The Senate then took up the joint resolution reported by the Library Committee, accepting the bronze statue of Thomas Jefferson, presented by Lieutenant Levy, and directing it to be placed in the centre of the public square east of the Capitol.

On motion of Mr. ROBBINS, the report was concurred in, and the resolution adopted.

The resolution authorizing the purchase of thirteen copies of the American State Papers was taken up for consideration.

The resolution was supported by Messrs. FRELINGHUYSEN and EWING, on the ground that the work was indispensable to members of Congress in the performance of their legislative duties; that the work was already printed, and the object was only to supply those new Senators who had not obtained them.

Mr. KING, of Georgia, opposed the resolution on constitutional grounds—that it was taking money out of the treasury for the purchase of books for the private libraries of members, without an appropriation by law; and that any other works might, with the same propriety, be purchased, and to any amount and extent. He admitted that works might be purchased which were necessary for the use of the members in the performance of their public duties, but that they should be confined to the office, and not be given as an absolute property to the officer.

Mr. K. moved to lay the resolution on the table for the balance of the session; which was disagreed to.

Mr. K. then moved an amendment, that the books should be left in the hands of the Secretary of the Senate, by the Senate, at the termination of their service, for the use of their successors; which was negatived.

The question recurring on the adoption of the resolution, Mr. K. asked the yeas and nays; which were ordered, and are as follows, to wit:

YEAS—Messrs. Bell, Bibb, Clay, Ewing, Frelinghuysen, Hendricks, Kent, Knight, McKean, Moore, Naudain, Poindexter, Prentiss, Robbins, Robinson, Silsbee, Tallmadge, Tipton, Tomlinson, and Wilkins—20.

NAYS—Messrs. Benton, Black, Calhoun, Grundy, Hill, Kane, King of Alabama, King of Georgia, Linn, Mangum, Morris, Shepley, and White—13.

So the resolution was agreed to, and it was then ordered to be engrossed and read a third time.

On motion of Mr. POINDEXTER, the Senate then proceeded to the consideration of Executive business; when, after spending some time therein, Adjourned.

HOUSE OF REPRESENTATIVES.

MONDAY, *May* 12, 1834.

The memorial of sundry citizens of Savannah, heretofore presented by Mr. WAYNE, having been postponed to this day, came up.

Mr. PATTON, in consequence of the absence from his seat of the gentleman from Georgia, moved that the further consideration of this subject be postponed to Monday next.

Mr. DUNCAN wished to get rid of discussion on the subject, and moved to lay the memorial on the table, and print.

Mr. E. WHITTLESEY appealed to the gentleman from Illinois, whether, in the absence of the gentleman who had charge of this memorial, courtesy did not render it proper to withdraw his motion to lay on the table.

Mr. DUNCAN declined.

The motion to lay on the table was negatived.

The further consideration of the memorial was then postponed to Monday next.

The consideration of the memorial from citizens of Ontario county, New York, which had been postponed to this day, was further postponed, on motion of Mr. DICKSON, to Monday next.

GENERAL APPROPRIATION BILL.

The consideration of the memorial from citizens of Oneida county, which Mr. SELDEN moved to refer to a select committee, which had been postponed from last Monday, having come up—

Mr. SELDEN, who was entitled to the floor, said he was willing, at the request of the chairman of the Committee of Ways and Means, to suspend his remarks until the third reading of the appropriation bill could be gone through with.

Mr. POLK hoped the House, by unanimous consent, would take up and dispose of the appropriation bill.

It being objected to—

Mr. POLK moved the rules of the House be suspended, in order that the engrossed appropriation bill might now be read a third time.

The motion to suspend the rules was carried: Ayes 101, noes 31.

The engrossed bill making appropriations for the civil and diplomatic expenses of Government for the year 1834 was then read a third time, and passed.

ARMY APPROPRIATION BILL.

Mr. POLK moved that the House consent to take up the bill for the support of the army for 1834, which had been returned from the Senate with amendments, in order that it be recommitted.

The House, by unanimous consent, took up the bill.

Mr. POLK said the amendments made in the Senate introduced a small appropriation for certain militia employed against Black Hawk and his followers, which had been submitted to the Committee of Ways and Means, and was assented to by every member of that committee. As it was necessary, by the rules, that the amendment pass through the Committee of the Whole, he hoped the House would refer the bill to the Committee of the Whole on the state of the Union, and for a moment go into that committee, in order to dispose of the amendment.

The motion of Mr. POLK to that effect having been agreed to—

The House resolved itself into a Committee of the Whole on the state of the Union, (Mr. BRIGGS in the chair.)

The amendments having been read—

Mr. POLK and the Committee of Ways and Means had examined the papers upon which these amendments were founded, and had unanimously agreed to recommend a concurrence with them.

The Committee of the Whole agreed to the amendments without a dissenting voice, when the committee rose, and reported the bill to the House as amended.

The House then concurred in the amendment without a division.

On motion of Mr. STEWART, the bill from the Senate for the repair of the Cumberland road was, by unanimous consent, taken up, twice read, and referred to the Committee on Roads and Canals.

Mr. ASHLEY offered the following resolution, by consent of the House:

Resolved, That the Secretary of War be required to furnish this House with a report of the officer of the corps of Engineers, who, as it appears from the annual report of the Chief Engineer, was instructed to make an inspection of the Cumberland road and its concerns in Illinois, in 1833.

Which by the rule lies one day.

The following resolution, heretofore offered by Mr. SELDEN, in connexion with the memorial of sundry citizens of Oneida county, in the State of New York, came up:

Resolved, That a committee, consisting of one member from each State, be appointed to consider

and report, in form of a bill, a plan for a safe and uniform currency, under the authority of the United States, and that the memorial of the citizens of the county of Oneida be referred to that committee.

Mr. SELDEN said he had become satisfied, after examination of the report of the Committee of Ways and Means, that the plan proposed by the majority of that committee was not fitted to carry their objects relative to the currency into effect. Mr. S. discussed some of the features of the report, and replied at length to the remarks made by Mr. BEARDSLEY, when this subject was before the House on Monday last. His colleague (he said) had stated that it would have afforded him pleasure to have presented the memorial. It was proper for him to state, that the gentleman had an opportunity of presenting this memorial, and had declined doing so. Mr. S. then referred to exertions which had been made by his colleague to procure the establishment of a branch of the Bank of the United States at Utica.

Mr. BEARDSLEY said it was unequivocally untrue that he had ever made such exertions.

Mr. SELDEN said he had stated what was generally reported and believed to be true on that point. Mr. S. went at length into the propriety of having a digested plan relative to the currency, prepared in case the bill reported by the Committee of Ways and Means did not become a law. His constituents (he said) were of opinion that the financial concerns of the nation required the institution of a national bank.

Mr. BEARDSLEY said the remarks of his colleague, [Mr. SELDEN,] relative to his agency in the establishment of a branch of the Bank of the United States at Utica, in 1830, rendered it proper for him to make a few remarks. He had never before heard of any such agency being laid to his charge. He had certainly heard and seen in newspapers a great many things, but it had never had his fortune to meet with this statement before. Entirely new as it was to him, he did not doubt but his colleague had both seen and heard what he had stated to the House. He would frankly say all he knew or had heard, which had this much to recommend to the subject. Two years ago a honorable member of the House from Pennsylvania, [alluding to Mr. WATMOUGH,] showed him a paper purporting to be a copy of a petition for the establishment of a branch bank at Utica, and which was dated in or about the year 1834, and to which his name was attached. Mr. B. said he informed the gentleman from Pennsylvania at that time that he had no recollection of signing any such paper, nor did he believe he aver did sign it; that as he could pretend to recollect his views at that time, he was satisfied he could not have signed it; that he desired the gentleman from Pennsylvania to procure the original, but from that day to this, (Mr. B. said,) he had neither seen nor heard anything further about the copy or the original.

My colleague (said Mr. B.) seems to regard as extraordinary that I should say it would have given me pleasure to present this memorial, and had been forwarded to me for that purpose; regards as the honorable gentleman thinks it remarkable, inasmuch as I had, as he says, severely criticised the memorial. Sir, I would gladly have presented this memorial: it was from my constituents, and shall certainly ever be ready to present their views here, although I may not be able to agree with the views which are expressed by the memorialists. It is true that my honorable colleague did see to me that he had received a memorial from my district, and he inquired whether he should present it, or whether I should. He certainly did not suggest to me that those who had sent it to him had expressed any wish or willingness that it should be handed to me for presentation. I regarded only as an act of civility on his part, and was courtesy required me to decline. I could not for such circumstances, think of taking it out of his hands, but very willingly left it for the honorable gentleman to present. I could not but have felt that those who had sent the memorial to him, did it because they felt a greater confidence in him than myself, and I could not think of breaking off this relation by thrusting myself between the honorable gentleman and those who had communicated with him.

My colleague infers that those who established

the branch at Utica, could not have had any political objects in view in arranging the board of directors, because, as he says, they were willing and desirous of placing in that board influential members of the democratic party. Sir, that is what I stated. I referred to that as evidence of the wish to draw in that class of individuals to sustain the bank. All experience proves that nine-tenths of those who are in any way drawn into a management of the concerns of the bank or its branches, slide into its political views and are found arrayed against the Democracy of the country and politically in favor of the bank. This the bank knew, and acted upon it; it failed, however, in a great degree, in that object, maugre all its efforts, for those who were selected could not be prevailed upon to lend themselves for any such purpose.

But the lever could not have been got up and sustained by the bank, as it broke down in a few months! It would have cost, says the honorable gentleman, but $1500 a year, a sum which the bank would not have regarded: it is certain, therefore, that it could not have been the creature of the bank. I know (said Mr. B.) that the bank cares little about $1500; but where that sum is so invested as to yield no adequate return, in money or influence, the bank, able as it is, would certainly prefer to save the $1500. Sir, I might inform the House that there are papers in judicial proceedings which establish very satisfactorily the connexion between a part of the bank direction and the lever; but I choose not to occupy the attention of the House further upon this part of the subject.

My colleague understands me to have made a censorious remark about the gentlemen whose names are annexed to the printed circular which was read when the memorial was presented a week since. My remarks are in print and must speak for themselves. I deem it only proper, however, to state unequivocally that my colleague has totally misapprehended my object and purpose: I had no design to animadvert upon the gentleman referred to, although I deemed their circular a fit subject for comment. That will also speak for itself, and I am willing to submit it, with my comments, to the judgment of the public.

This memorial, sir, has been presented and commented on elsewhere, and it was there stated that the county of Oneida was "largely interested 'in manufactures, both of woollen and cotton; 'which were in active operation until the Executive began its experiment; and as the experiment 'has gone on, one of these establishments after 'another has stopped." This statement was said to have been made on the authority of gentlemen who were "incapable of misrepresentation." I know not who should have been referred to as the originators of this statement, but I feel it to be my duty to state, that I have direct information on that subject from Oneida county, and that down to the 8th instant (several days after the statement had been made) no such failure or failures had occurred; nothing had at any time taken place to warrant any such statement or suspicion of the failure of any one manufacturing establishment in that county. The gentleman who made the statement, I cannot doubt, had what he regarded as good authority for what he said; but it is equally certain that the statement is without foundation; it is made by some one out of whole cloth.

The memorial represents the county of Oneida as in the most deplorable condition. Now, sir, I cannot pretend to be furnished with all the indications which in fact exist, of the actual situation of its business population; but I have one evidence of the prosperity of Utica, which is very convincing to my mind. The Erie canal passes through Utica, and a toll office is established in that city. Now, sir, although the tolls have been greatly reduced during the last winter, upon some property twenty per cent., and on the residue ten per cent., yet a greater amount of toll was collected in Utica during the month of April than in either of the two last years! It is true, the canal opened this year five days earlier than the last; but taking the number of days which it had been open, down to the 4th of this present month, a greater amount had been received than in an equal number of days at the commencement of the last year. This is a very substantial indication of individual and general prosperity. And, as to the whole State, the aggregate of the tolls received in the month of April this year exceeded that of the last. In fact, sir, I apprehend that the State at large was never more thriving and prosperous.

My honorable colleague objects to a former remark of mine. I did say that I would sooner see the State institutions prostrated than submit to the corrupt control of the United States Bank. This does not seem to accord with the views of my colleague; he is for submission; he is for yielding to the bank, let the consequences be what they may. In this we differ. My constituents do not, in this matter, as I believe, agree with the honorable gentleman more than I do; they have hearts and arms as I trust, to resist at all hazards every effort to bring them in passive obedience to the bank.

But the bank, in the language of my colleague, "seems to have the power of making political enemies, not friends." This is, indeed, a new idea. Will the honorable gentleman look at New York, Philadelphia, Baltimore—indeed, in any part of the Union? Has the bank made political enemies only? None but enemies here or elsewhere? Have its unprecedented efforts only resulted in making political enemies? Has it not almost denationalized the feelings of a considerable proportion of our countrymen? Have not, in many instances, the firmness and spirit of American freemen sunk under the influence of the bank? "Give us the bank," is the cry, although at the price of degradation and servitude; this is the impassioned expression of its followers and partisans.

The bank only make "political enemies, not friends!" Is not its influence seriously impairing the respectful reverence due to our moral and religious institutions? Have we not recently seen in a neighboring city, a factious mob, assembled in defiance of both human and divine law, for the purpose of hearing inflammatory harangues in support of the bank on the Sabbath day? Are not the efforts which are now making to control the population of our cities in favor of the bank, calculated to weaken, if not to eradicate, sound and correct principles of conduct among the mass of their citizens?

Sir, I have done. I will not trouble the House with any suggestions as to what my constituents may think of my remarks upon this memorial. I hope nothing has been said by me which can deserve their reprehension; but that point my honorable colleague and myself will leave to be adjusted between the constituents and their representative.

The resolution having been read—

Mr. BROWN moved to lay it on the table.

Mr. WILLIAMS called for the yeas and nays; and they were ordered.

Mr. CLAY moved a call of the House; which was rejected.

The question was then taken, on the motion to lay the resolution on the table, and it appeared that there was a *tie:* Yeas 89, nays 89, as follows:

YEAS—Messrs. William Allen, Bean, Beardsley, Beaumont, Bockee, Bodle, Boon, Bouldin, Brown, Bunch, Burns, Bynum, Cambreleng, Chaney, Chinn, Samuel Clark, Clay, Clayton, Cramer, Day, Philemon Dickerson, Dunlap, Felder, Forester, Foster, Fowler, William K. Fuller, Galbraith, Gamble, Gholson, Gillet, Gilmer, Gordon, Joseph Hall, Thomas H. Hall, Halsey, Hamer, Harrison, Hathaway, Hawkins, Hawes, Howell, Abel Huntington, Jarvis, Noadiah Johnson, Seaborn Jones, Benjamin Jones, Kavanagh, Kinnard, Lane, Lansing, Luke Lea, Thomas Lee, Loyall, Joel K. Mann, Mardis, Moses Mason, McIntire, McKay, McKim, McKinley, McVean, Miller, Robert Mitchell, Page, Parks, Parker, Patton, Patterson, Peyton, Franklin Pierce, Pinckney, Plummer, Polk, Schenck, Schley, Shinn, Standifer, Sutherland, William Taylor, Wm. P. Taylor, Thomson, Turrill, Van Houten, Wagener, Wardwell, Webster, Whallon, C. P. White—89.

NAYS—Messrs. John Q. Adams, John Adams, Heman Allen, John J. Allen, Chilton Allan, Anthony, Ashley, Banks, Barber, Barnitz, Barringer, Bates, Baylies, Beatty, Binney, Briggs, Bull, Burges, Cage, Campbell, Chambers, Chilton, W. Clark, Clowney, Connor, Corwin, Coulter, Crane, Darlington, Davenport, Deberry, Deming, Denny, Duncan, Horace Everett, Fillmore, P. C. Fuller, Fulton, Garland, Gorham, Graham, Griffin, H. Hall, Hard, Hardin, James Harper, Hazeltine, Henderson, Hiester, Jabez W. Huntington, William Cost Johnson, King, Laporte, Lincoln, Love, Lucas, Lyon, Martindale, Marshall, McCarty, McKennan, Mercer, Milligan, Moore, Murphy, Osgood, Potts, Ramsey, Reed, Rencher, Selden, William B. Shepard, Wm. Slade, Charles Slade, Sloane, Spangler, Stewart, Philemon Thomas, Turner, Tweedy, Vance, Vinton, Watmough, E. Whittlesey, Wilde, Williams, Wilson, Wise, and Young—89.

The SPEAKER voting in the affirmative, the motion was agreed to.

Mr. PARKER presented the proceedings of a State convention, held at Trenton, in New Jersey, on the 2d of April last, disapproving the conduct of the Executive in relation to the removal of the deposites from the United States Bank, and in favor of the charter of a Bank of the United States; approving the conduct of the Senators from that State, and disapproving the course taken by their Representatives in Congress. Mr. P. stated that these proceedings had been already printed by order of the Senate. He therefore moved that they be read, and laid on the table.

Mr. P. also presented the proceedings of a meeting of the citizens of Middlesex county, New Jersey, held at New Brunswick in March last, approving the conduct of the President in removing the deposites, and opposing a recharter of the bank; which was read, and ordered to be printed.

Mr. P. also presented the memorial of 1,443 citizens of the county of Middlesex, and State of New Jersey, approving the removal of the deposites, and supporting the Legislature of that State in their instructions to their Senators and Representatives. Read, ordered to be printed, and laid on the table.

Mr. HENDERSON presented the proceedings of a meeting of the citizens of Huntingdon county, Pennsylvania, friendly to the Administration of the General Government; which was read, and ordered to be printed.

Also, the proceedings of a meeting of the citizens of Mifflin county, Pennsylvania, approving of the course, and strongly expressive of their confidence in the present Administration; which was ordered to be printed.

Mr. CHAMBERS presented the proceedings of a meeting of citizens of Adams county, in favor of the restoration of the deposites and the recharter of the United States Bank.

The above memorials were severally laid on the table, and ordered to be printed.

Mr. ANTHONY presented a memorial from citizens of Lycoming county, on the subject of the bank and the state of the currency, and asked leave to address the House on the subject.

Mr. E. WHITTLESEY called for a count of the House.

The CHAIR, having consented, stated that there were 95 members present. Not a quorum.

Mr. J. Q. ADAMS moved an adjournment; which was agreed to.

IN SENATE.

Tuesday, *May* 13, 1834.

A message upon executive business was received from the President of the United States, by Mr. Donelson, his Private Secretary.

After the presentation of various petitions, reports, &c.

On motion of Mr. CLAYTON, the special orders were suspended, and the Senate took up the bill equalizing the representation of Florida Territory, and for other purposes.

The bill was considered in Committee of the Whole, and ordered to be engrossed for a third reading.

PENSION AGENCY.

The Senate then resumed the consideration of the report of the Judiciary Committee, upon the message of the President, in relation to the Pension agency, and the Bank of the United States.

Mr. WRIGHT having the floor, reviewed, at length, the various acts of Congress, from the year 1789 down to 1828, granting pensions, and establishing pension agencies, and contended, that as the Secretary of War had the power of designating the places where disbursements should be made, he had also the power of appointing the disbursing agents.

Mr. CLAYTON then expressed a wish to give

his views of the subject at length, but, as the hour was late, and the Senate thin, he moved to postpone the subject, and make it the special order for to-morrow; which was agreed to.

The Senate then, on motion of Mr. BENTON, proceeded to the consideration of executive business; and, when the doors were opened,

The Senate adjourned.

HOUSE OF REPRESENTATIVES.

TUESDAY, *May* 13, 1834.

The report from the Committee of Elections, in the case of the election contested between THOMAS P. MOORE and ROBERT LETCHER, was taken up as the special order for this day.

Mr. JONES said, that as the report of the minority of the committee was not yet printed, and as it is desirable that it should be before the House, he would move the postponement of the subject till Monday next. The motion was agreed to.

Mr. STEWART, from the Committee on Roads and Canals, reported, without amendment, the bill from the Senate, for continuing the Cumberland road; which was committed.

Mr. ASHLEY reported a bill, granting the preemption right to certain lots of land in the town of Louisiana, in the State of Missouri, for the use of schools. Read twice and committed.

Mr. WISE, on leave, presented a memorial from sundry inhabitants of York county, Virginia, praying Congress to carry into effect a resolution passed in 1781, for the erection of a monument on the spot where the British army, under Cornwallis, surrendered, and moved its reference to a select committee of five members. The motion was agreed to.

Mr. WISE also presented a memorial from the citizens of Gloucester county, Virginia, praying Congress to take measures to establish a uniform currency; and moved its reference, with instructions, to a select committee of seven, giving notice that he would call up the motion on Monday next.

Mr. DEMING reported a bill for the relief of Joseph Gilbert; which was twice read and committed.

Mr. CARR, from the Committee on Private Land Claims, made an unfavorable report on the petition of Louis Tesson, alias Honoré; which was ordered to lie on the table.

ADJOURNMENT.

Mr. BOON moved the suspension of the rules in order to call up for consideration the resolution heretofore submitted by him for the adjournment of Congress on the 31st of May, viz:

Resolved, That the President of the Senate, and the Speaker of the House of Representatives, close the present session of Congress, by an adjournment of their respective Houses, on Saturday, the 31st day of May next.

Mr. BOON gave notice, that if the motion prevailed, he would modify the resolution so as to fix upon the 16th day of June as the day of adjournment. He called for the yeas and nays on the motion, and they were ordered.

The question being taken, it was determined in the affirmative—yeas 152, nays 12.

Mr. BOON said, before he proceeded to discuss the resolution, he would take leave to repel an unfounded attack made upon him in a public print in reference to his introduction of the resolution. It was contained in the Telegraph of April last, and purported to be an extract from a letter written from this House. [Mr. B. here read the letter at length.] The writer of it, he said, was unknown to him; but whoever he might be, he pronounced it to be a false, base calumny, with malice aforethought written. When he first submitted the resolution, it was suggested to him by a friend that the House was thin. He accordingly withdrew it, at the same time distinctly stating that he would not then press it on account of the thinness of the House, and that he would take an early opportunity to renew the motion. The idea intimated by the letter-writer, that he was "subservient to the kitchen or to an imperial master" was unworthy of reply. It was too contemptible for notice, and he should not have noticed the writer at all, were it not to repel the insinuation that he was actuated by an insidious motive in proposing the resolution. He held himself responsible to no authority but that of his constituents. He sent his proposed modification of the resolution to the chair.

The resolution as modified was then read as follows:

Resolved, That the President of the Senate, and the Speaker of the House of Representatives, close the present session of Congress, by an adjournment of their respective Houses, on Monday the 16th day of June next.

The yeas and nays were ordered on the motion.

Mr. HARPER moved to strike out the 16th, and insert the 14th. He was no great stickler for the Sabbath; but it was evident that if Monday was fixed, we must sit on Sunday, which, he thought, ought to be avoided.

The motion was rejected.

Mr. WARDWELL moved to strike out Monday and insert Tuesday. Agreed to.

Mr. EWING moved to amend the resolution by adding the following—"provided the essential business of the people shall by that time be disposed of."

Mr. ANTHONY asked who should determine the question, we or the people?

Mr. EWING made a remark in reply, which we did not hear, and called for the yeas and nays on the motion, which were refused.

The motion was then put and rejected.

Mr. DENNY considered, he said, that it was our duty to remain in session till every hope of relief was extinguished.

Mr. VINTON inquired of the honorable chairman of the Committee of Ways and Means whether it was his intention, at the present session, to call up the bill for the regulation of the contracts with the deposite banks.

Mr. POLK replied that, so far as he was concerned, or those who united with him in reporting the bill, and indeed so far as he could learn the sentiments of those with whom he commonly acted, he would say that it was intended to call up that bill for action at the present session. He further would state that he would call the bill so soon as the necessary appropriation bills were acted upon.

Mr. ARCHER expressed the hope that the honorable chairman would give notice to the House of the time when he would call up that bill.

Mr. POLK replied that he would do so; and in answer to some inquiries from those around him, he said there were five appropriation bills reported from the Committee of Ways and Means, which he was desirous to have speedily acted upon, viz: one making appropriations for the Indian Department; one for certain fortifications for the year 1834; one for Indian annuities, and other similar objects; one for continuing the Cumberland road, in Ohio, Indiana, and Illinois, and repairing said road east of the Ohio, and continuing certain territorial roads; and one making additional appropriations for the improvement of certain harbors, and removing obstructions in the mouths of certain rivers. There was a bill in relation to West Point Academy, and others of importance, from other committees, (said Mr. P.,) yet to be acted upon; he therefore hoped that the House would be disposed to immediately consider and act promptly upon the appropriation bills.

Mr. VINTON said the bill referred to by him was of such importance to the country, that the House would not be justified in adjourning until it was disposed of. He should vote against the resolution.

Mr. HARDIN said he had received some time since a memorial from his constituents which he had not yet had an opportunity to present. It was highly probable that before the middle of June or July it would come to his turn to present it. In it he was expressly requested to oppose any adjournment of Congress until something was done for the relief of the country, by the establishment of a bank or the renewal of the charter of the present bank.

Mr. CHILTON remarked that as no benefit could be expected to result from a protracted session, he should vote for the resolution.

Mr. PLUMMER called for the orders of the day, and the question being put thereon, it was decided in the affirmative by a vote of 84 to 64.

The SPEAKER communicated to the House a letter from Samuel A. Foot, transmitting his resignation of his seat in this House.

The SPEAKER announced, as the special order of the day, "the bill to provide for the settlement of certain revolutionary claims."

Mr. CRANE, who was entitled to the floor when the bill was last under consideration, rose and supported the provisions of the bill in a speech of an hour and a half, and was followed by

Mr. H. ALLEN, who expressed himself to be favorably inclined towards revolutionary claims, but pointed out several objections to the provisions of the bill, which he explained at length.

Mr. TURRILL said: Mr. Speaker, if I had succeeded, as I had hoped to do, in obtaining the floor at an earlier day, it was my purpose to have examined somewhat minutely the several resolutions and statutes which have been passed by Congress in relation to the commutation of pay by the officers of our revolutionary army, together with the reasons which led to their passage, and from such examination to have demonstrated that these meritorious men possess both legal and equitable claims against the United States, and that rigid justice requires that these claims should be referred to some competent office for settlement. But, Mr. Speaker, this whole subject has been so fully and so ably discussed by the honorable gentleman from Ohio, [Mr. CRANE,] who has to-day addressed the House in favor of the bill, that I know I should be trespassing too far upon the patience of the House were I to occupy the time by entering upon such an examination of this subject. I do not, therefore, now rise for the purpose of entering into a full discussion of the merits of this bill, or with a view of answering the various objections which have been, or which may yet be, urged against it, but merely to state, in as brief a manner as possible, some of the most prominent reasons which induced me to agree to the bill in the committee, and which will now govern my vote on the question before the House; in doing which, I will detain the House but for a very short time.

It is matter of history, sir, that during the war of the Revolution, this country was suffering under great pecuniary embarrassment. The Government could not procure the necessary means to clothe and feed the army, much less to pay the officers and soldiers. As the war proceeded, the difficulties increased, the country became more and more embarrassed, and so great and so threatening were our dangers, that the stoutest hearts began to tremble for the result; the friends of liberty were engaged in a glorious, but a most unequal struggle. The pecuniary means, which were indispensable to a successful prosecution of this great undertaking, could not be obtained. At this crisis Congress resorted to the only expedient in its power to maintain the cause of the country and keep its army in the field. Full compensation was promised to those who should stand by their country to the end of that eventful contest, and provision was also made for the widows of those who should die in the service. The resolution passed in May, 1778, secures to "all military officers commissioned by Congress," who continued in the service of the United States "during the war," seven years' half pay. In August, 1780, Congress declared "that the resolution of May 15th, '1778, granting half-pay for seven years to the 'officers of the army who should continue in the 'service to the end of the war, be extended to the 'widows of those officers who have died, or shall 'hereafter die, in the service." In October, 1780, Congress declared by resolution, "that the officers 'who shall continue in the service to the end of 'the war, shall also be entitled to half-pay during 'life, to commence from the time of the reduction." Here, then, Mr. Speaker, was an express agreement, on the part of the United States, to give those officers who should serve to the end of the war half-pay during life. And this solemn national pledge was given at the urgent request of General Washington, whose powerful and patriotic mind was deeply impressed with the necessity, as well as the justice, of the measure. It was soon discovered, however, that this arrangement, though manifestly just and expedient, awoke associations and prejudices among the people, which rendered it very unpopular in many of the States, insomuch that the officers of the Revolution, although they had faithfully performed their part of the contract, and were justly entitled to half-pay for life, for t

war was then virtually at an end, with characteristic disinterestedness, drew up a memorial, and sent it to Congress, requesting them to remove all objections, by granting a compensation for a limited period, or a compensation in gross. In consequence of this memorial, Congress passed the resolution of 1783, "granting to the officers of the 'army five years' full pay, instead of the half-pay '*promised* for life." The preamble to the resolution, Mr. Speaker, contains, in a succinct form, the views of the officers, as well as of Congress, upon that application; and as it is short, I beg the indulgence of the House while I read it:

"Whereas the officers of the several lines under 'the immediate command of his excellency General Washington, did, by their late memorial, 'transmitted by their committee, represent to Congress, that the half-pay granted by sundry resolutions, was regarded in an unfavorable light by the 'citizens of some of these States, who would prefer a compensation for a limited term of years, or 'by a sum in gross, to an establishment for life; 'and did on that account solicit a commutation of 'their half-pay for an equivalent in one of the two 'modes above mentioned, in order to remove all 'subjects of dissatisfaction from the minds of their 'fellow-citizens:

"And whereas Congress is desirous, as well of 'gratifying the reasonable expectations of the officers of the army, as of removing all objections 'which may exist in any part of the United States 'to the principle of the half-pay establishment for 'which the faith of the United States hath been 'pledged; *persuaded that those objections can only 'arise from the nature of the compensation, not from 'any indisposition to compensate those whose services, 'sacrifices, and sufferings, have so just a title to the 'approbation and rewards of their country:* therefore, '*resolved*," &c.

Thus, Mr. Speaker, these brave, these generous men, who were entitled, richly entitled, to half-pay for life, voluntarily submitted the whole subject to the wisdom of Congress. They had entered the service of their country to conduct her to freedom, to independence; and they could not consent to receive anything for their "*services, sacrifices, and sufferings*," which was not freely granted by their fellow-citizens. Mr. Speaker, shall we perform this contract? Shall we pay what we have thus solemnly promised to pay? Shall we discharge a debt, the creation of which secured to us our free institutions? Or will this rich, this powerful nation, shield itself behind the statutes of limitation? Why were not these demands paid when they became due, and when many of the meritorious officers were suffering for want of the money? The reason is obvious. At the close of the war, this nation was not in a situation to pay a single dollar; and I am not aware that it has at any time since that period offered to pay these demands.

And will it be seriously urged by gentlemen on this floor, that we ought not to perform this contract, made in the hour of our necessity, because those entitled to commutation have been kept out of the use of their money, until the amount has become large? I trust not, sir. I am aware, sir, that certificates were tendered to the officers. But did those certificates in the slightest degree increase the liability of Government? No, sir. They were only additional evidences of prior indebtedness. Many of the officers did not think it an object to be at the trouble and expense of obtaining them. It was natural they should entertain such feelings, for at that time the credit of the Government was at such a low ebb, as to preclude all rational hope of obtaining money for them. In the language of my honorable colleague, [Mr. Vanderpoel,] who addressed the House in opposition to the bill, "these certificates were scarcely worth the rags from which the paper was made." Those "who obtained them, were compelled to sell them for a mere song."

To the claims of a portion of the Virginia troops, lapse of time cannot be an objection with any one. That State resisted the claims of those officers; suits were instituted, and a decision was had against the claimants. That decision operated as an effectual bar to all that class of cases, until 1830, when, upon full argument, that decision was overruled, and the halls of justice again thrown open.

Sir, for the last twenty years, Congress has been giving commutation under these resolutions; and it is too late now, I apprehend, to interpose the statute of limitations against righteous claims unrighteously denied.

The act of 1828 does not, as has already been clearly shown by the honorable gentleman from Pennsylvania, [Mr. Muhlenberg,] in any way affect the claims for commutation. It leaves those claims precisely as they were. They still exist in all their justice, and in all their sacred obligation.

If, then, sir, these claims are to be paid, to what tribunal, I ask, shall they be referred for settlement? Shall we send them to a responsible officer, everyway competent, from long experience in investigations of a similar character—an officer who will have in his possession all the documentary evidence extant, to show who were in the service, how long each officer continued in the service, and what officers have been paid, either by the State of Virginia or by the United States? Or shall we continue to legislate in detail upon each individual case? This is the main question presented to the House by the bill on your table. Let it be remembered that the proceedings in these cases are in their nature strictly judicial. There is no legislative discretion whatever to be exercised. Everything depends upon the proof. If that be sufficient to bring a claim within the resolutions, it must be allowed, as a matter of course. It cannot be resisted or denied, without partiality and oppression, nor is there any place for the exercise of discretion as to the amount. It is not a gratuity; it is a claim, and the amount is fixed and certain.

For myself, Mr. Speaker, I am convinced, from the little experience I have had upon this floor, that *this* is not the proper place for the settlement of such demands. Your committees to which these applications are referred, are not in possession of the documentary evidence necessary to their decision. They have not the records and vouchers to show what officers have been paid; and unless your committees are extremely vigilant and industrious—nay, more, sir, unless they take it upon themselves to send off and hunt up testimony in each case submitted to them, bills will often be reported in favor of those who have already received their commutation; and when once reported, being accompanied by the necessary proof of service, there will be nothing to impede their passage through the House.

Sir, the argument of the honorable gentleman from Vermont, [Mr. Allen,] in which he endeavored to show the facility with which bills granting commutation pass through the House, is, to my mind, one of the strongest reasons that can be urged in favor of referring these claims for settlement to a different tribunal.

If a claim is rejected by one committee, those interested renew the application year after year, until, in some way or other, they succeed in obtaining a favorable report.

I believe it to be much easier, Mr. Speaker, to get an unfounded claim allowed here than it would be to obtain for it the sanction of a judicial decision by a competent officer. Congress is more liable to be imposed upon. Here all the testimony is *ex parte*. It is furnished by the applicants themselves, and the rules of evidence are not as rigidly applied here as in a judicial tribunal. The proof is not as thoroughly examined or as accurately weighed.

Mr. Speaker, as a matter of economy, I would refer these claims, as proposed by the bill. Instead of increasing, I have no doubt but that it would diminish the draft upon your treasury. If we undertake to legislate upon each individual case, all that have merits will be allowed as a matter of course, and we shall, in that case, be compelled to pay many which have no merits, and which, were they submitted to the ordeal of a judicial investigation, would never be allowed.

Sir, it appears to me that there can be no well-founded objection either to the payment of these claims, or to the proposition to refer them for settlement to a competent officer. Gentlemen may differ as to the rules of evidence by which that officer shall be governed in making his investigations. That is a matter for the consideration and decision of the House. It is not my purpose, sir, now to enter into a defence of the rules contained in the bill. The reasons for introducing them have already been submitted to the House by other members of the committee. I will simply remark, however, that they are the same rules which have regulated the proceedings of your committee and this House for years, and if we continue to legislate upon this subject, the same rules of evidence will, I have no doubt, continue to regulate our proceedings, except, perhaps, they may gradually become more and more relaxed.

Mr. Speaker, I will not detain the House longer. If these demands are referred for settlement in the manner proposed by the bill upon your table, Congress will be relieved from a large portion of business; justice will not much longer be delayed; the old soldier who is entitled to commutation will then obtain a speedy hearing, and your treasury, sir, will be more effectually barred against all unfounded claims.

Mr. YOUNG also spoke in favor of the bill.

After a debate, in which Messrs. GILMER, YOUNG, VANDERPOEL, BATES, and WISE, took part—

Mr. BRIGGS moved that the House adjourn.

Mr. POLK requested him to withdraw it till the vote was taken on the question pending.

Mr. BRIGGS said he saw no prospect of a vote.

The motion to adjourn was rejected.

The question being on the motion of Mr. GILMER to recommit—

Mr. MARSHALL spoke at some length in opposition to it.

The discussion was continued by Messrs. VANDERPOEL, WISE, WARD of New York, MARSHALL, and BATES; when

Mr. McKINLEY moved that the House adjourn; which motion was negatived.

The question was taken on the motion to recommit, and it was determined in the affirmative, on division, by a vote of 88 to 76.

The House then adjourned.

REMARKS OF MR. TAYLOR,

OF NEW YORK.

In the House of Representatives,

May 5, 1834.

On presenting the resolutions of a meeting held in Onondaga county, New York.

Mr. Speaker: I have received, and am requested to present to this House, the proceedings and resolutions of a meeting held in the county of Onondaga, New York, chiefly relating to those important political questions which have long occupied the time and attention of Congress, and which have agitated the public mind throughout the whole country. I do not say, sir, a meeting composed of all political parties, as has been frequently asserted here of other meetings called for similar purposes, though I apprehend of not less distinctive political character, but a meeting of the friends of the Administration, of such as belong to a political party, a party uniformly known and distinguished as the republican party. In presenting these resolutions, I trust I shall be indulged in a few brief remarks as to the population and business of this county, the circumstances under which the meeting was called, and the character of the resolutions. [Leave being granted by the House, Mr. T. proceeded.] The county of Onondaga contained at the last census a population of 58,974, probably at this time more than 60,000. It is an agricultural and particularly a wheat-growing county. It is also, to some extent, a manufacturing county, in which are situated several cotton and woollen factories, flour mills, and a variety of other manufacturing establishments, besides the extensive salt works at Salina, where are manufactured annually more than a million and a half bushels of salt, being more than one-third of all the salt manufactured in the United States. It will readily be seen, that this, together with the mercantile transactions for such a business and population, and the purchase of the produce of that section of country on the line of the canal that extends through the county, must require a large amount of capital. This statement, sir, is made only for the purpose of showing that such a population and business must necessarily be affected by any causes deranging or materially affecting the moneyed affairs of the country.

It has, sir, been common for gentlemen, when presenting memorials or resolutions of meetings,

to speak of the intelligence and patriotism of their constituents; but, sir, my constituents require of me no compliment of this sort. Like the people of other sections of the country, they very well understand the bearing and effects upon their own interests, the permanent interests of their country and its political institutions, of any measure of Government, or of any power seeking an extraneous influence over the action of the Government, or the interests and liberties of the people; and I trust, sir, they have patriotism enough to resist any *such* influence, by proper means, even should it require a temporary sacrifice of individual interest or convenience.

The meeting which adopted these resolutions was held at a favorable time to pronounce a just judgment upon the topics which they had met to deliberate upon. It was not suddenly called together under the influence of a panic, which had been excited throughout the whole country, promoted and urged on by certain presses, political partisans, and interested individuals, and which, to say the least, was not diminished by those speeches which were distributed through the country, in which imagination had depicted in glowing colors, the wide-spread ruin and distress which was to come upon the people, and which was charged in advance to the policy of the Administration. I say, sir, this meeting was not suddenly called under such circumstances. They had waited, deliberated, witnessed the panic, felt the pressure, and carefully investigated the cause; and then, sir, they assembled to give an expression of opinion thus maturely and deliberately formed. This meeting was also called immediately after the elections had been held in the several towns of the county, at which the people had indicated their political sentiments, by electing town officers friendly to the Administration in fourteen out of seventeen towns of which the county is composed; and in perhaps every town, resolutions had been passed by the people, expressing their views upon the political questions of the day. It was, sir, under such favorable circumstances for forming a correct judgment, and of knowing public sentiment, that the Republicans of the county of Onondaga convened and adopted these resolutions, as the deliberate sense, not only of that meeting, which was largely attended, but also of a majority, a respectable majority, of the people of the county, as was evident from the recent elections. And, sir, instead of that change of political sentiment which is said to have taken place in the public mind, we find them reiterating the opinions which they have expressed on former occasions, approving the policy of this Administration, and particularly as relates to the United States Bank. And in reference to the removal of the Government deposites from the bank, believing that the curtailment of its discounts which was in rapid progress, if with the view of winding up its affairs at the expiration of its charter, rendered the deposites useless to the bank, and advantageous to the local institutions in affording the necessary accommodations to the public; or, if with the view of oppressing the people, and coercing a compliance with its wishes, the deposites ought not to remain in the hands of an institution with such dangerous power, and alarming designs upon the interests and independence of the people—designs rendered the more certain by subsequent events; they have resolved, "that the removal of the Government deposites 'from the United States Bank, was dictated by a 'wise forecast of events, rendering such a measure 'necessary."

They have observed, sir, the general policy of this Administration; the vigilant care with which the Executive has endeavored to guard the Constitution from encroachments, and the example of moral courage displayed in his endeavors, on the one hand, to preserve the Union from the disorganizing effects of that construction of the Federal compact, which finds in the sovereign power, and "reserved right" of any one State, "the rightful remedy," for what a majority of its citizens might deem an unconstitutional law; and on the other, to prevent the dangerous effects of that liberal construction, which, by implication, would concentrate all power in the hands of the Federal Government. And notwithstanding, sir, he has been denounced both here and elsewhere for the part he has taken relative to the recent disposal of the Government deposites, as having usurped authority and violated law, and the free use of the terms *despot, tyrant, usurper*, &c., they have not been able to discover, that in the removal of a Secretary of the Treasury, who differed with the President on prominent measures of his Administration, intimately connected with that policy which had most clearly received the sanction of the people, and the appointment of one of well known different views, and who, in the exercise of that power intrusted solely to his discretion, by the act incorporating the bank, has carried into effect that which, according to the dictates of his own judgment, and in the opinion of the Executive, the public good required, by ordering and directing the deposites to be made in the local banks; I say in all this, they have not been able to discover any violation of law, or usurpation of power; and they have resolved that, among other enumerated reasons, "the Chief Magistrate is entitled to the gratitude of his countrymen for his observance of the Constitution, and the just limits of Executive power."

They have resolved "that they do not find the power to create a bank incorporation granted in the Federal Constitution," and "that the existence of a great national banking institution is formidable and dangerous to liberty." The charges on which the bank, in the opinion of this meeting, "stands condemned at the bar of public sentiment," are expressed in one of their resolutions in clear, forcible, and concise terms, which, as I shall ask for the reading of the resolutions, I will not now repeat. It will be noticed, sir, that in one of their resolutions they speak of the "pressure and consequent prostration of business," as something that has been, but does not now exist. They say "the *late* pressure," &c.; and although they may not be entirely relieved from its influence, yet I understand, from sources entitled to the fullest credit, that the times are much improved, business has resumed its accustomed activity, and the produce of the country in Western New York, instead of being reduced one-third below its ordinary value, as was stated a few days since by my honorable colleague, [Mr. FILLMORE,] is now nearly or quite up to former prices. The fullest evidence of the activity of business may be found in the weekly statements of the amount of tolls collected on the canals of that State; from which it appears that during the first week of navigation $44,642 were received for tolls, notwithstanding the reduction of the rates of tolls of 25 per cent. on merchandise, and 10 per cent. on most articles of country produce, since last year. The following statement in the *Onondaga Standard*, of April 30, which I have just received, will show the activity and prospects of business in that section of the country, the predictions to the contrary notwithstanding: "Mr. 'Webster would blush for his credulity if he were 'here to witness, in person, the activity which 'prevails upon the canal. Instead of being re'duced, business is evidently greatly on the in'crease. The amount of tolls received at the office 'here, upon all other shipments except lumber, 'the most of which this season is cleared at Salina, 'is materially larger than for the same time last 'spring. For several days past, the crowd of 'boats near this village has been excessive, and all 'of them are deeply freighted. The quantity of 'merchandise coming up is increasing, and such is 'the *pressure* below, that a line, whose boats were 'designed to run no further west than this place, 'have taken freight through to Buffalo. *In short, 'no doubt can be entertained that the business of the 'season will be greater and more profitable than it ever 'has been.*" This statement of facts, about which there can be no mistake, is worthy of notice, as it exhibits a widely different and far more gratifying prospect, than might be apprehended from some other memorials and resolutions which have just been read.

It will be noticed that in one of these resolutions they have given us their opinion of the causes of that pressure and embarrassment in business, which has been experienced. And, sir, not being able to comprehend how the removal of the Government deposites, from the United States Bank, where, under the curtailment of its discounts which was going on, they were not needed and would not be used as a basis for discounting, and placing them in those banks that would, and that have used them for this purpose, could produce any pressure, but on the contrary, believing it was calculated to afford relief; they have looked for other and more natural causes, and have assigned reasons which appear to me much more just, satisfactory, and correct. They tell us that they "believe the late pressure and consequent prostration of business, has been caused principally by the policy of the bank, designedly seizing upon a period when overtrading and a change from credit to cash duties, favored its wicked purpose of coercing, through the distresses of the country, the renewal of its charter."

I shall not detain the House to notice but one other resolution adopted at this meeting, and that is, an approval of the measure recently recommended by the Governor of that State, and which has already become a law, whereby the credit of the State is to be pledged, if needful, for the preservation of confidence, and for the protection of its citizens against any measures, on the part of the bank, that might embarrass them, or obstruct a successful prosecution of business. This measure I should not here have noticed, but from the fact, that it seemed to give the honorable gentleman from Ohio, [Mr. CORWIN,] and some others, much serious alarm. But, sir, I must confess that in this most judicious and patriotic measure, which has met the approbation of this meeting, and, I believe, of a vast majority of the people of that State, I have not been able to discover anything that need excite alarm in the breast of that honorable gentleman, or any one else, except, indeed, it be such as might feel alarmed for those political prospects that would be liable to be darkened by the restoration of confidence, the subsiding of the panic, and the active and prosperous renewal of business. Such, and such only, as see, or fancy that they see, their political or party prospects brighten in proportion as the distresses of the country increase, might, perhaps, in this respect, justly see in this measure some cause of alarm. But, sir, I apprehend that many who have not taken the trouble to inform themselves upon the subject, entertain the erroneous impression that this measure is designed to sustain what is generally called the safety-fund banks of that State, which were supposed to be in imminent danger. If so, I beg leave to say, that the safety and solvency of these banks is not, and has not been questioned by the people of that State, and the most perfect security is felt by the holders of their notes, a security and confidence never so generally felt before the establishment of that system. But, in consequence of the attitude assumed by the United States Bank, its official declaration of ability to crush the local banks, and the evident indications of a disposition to make a demonstration of its power upon the institutions of that State, has rendered it prudent, on the part of the banks to diminish their circulation and curtail their discounts, in order to be prepared for the worst. This has necessarily deprived the people of their ordinary banking accommodations, and produced a scarcity of money. To enable the city banks to afford the necessary facilities for the transaction of its extensive business, and to meet any emergency that may arise, as well as to preserve public confidence, and to render to the people of the State at large such aid as circumstances may possibly require, the credit of the State is to be pledged for the loan of six millions of dollars, four millions of which is to be loaned to the banks of the city of New York, if, in the opinion of the Board of Commissioners constituted to conduct this business, "the public exigencies shall require it," and the remainder to pass into the hands of the Commissioners of Loans in the several counties of the State, to be by them loaned to individuals on security of real estate, if the board of supervisors in the several counties shall "determine that their citizens require it." But, sir, it is hoped, and even believed, that this loan may not be called for or required; for, seeing confidence restored, business resuming its accustomed channel and activity, and the ægis of State protection cast over the enterprise, the business and the institutions of the State, the bank will hardly be disposed to make a demonstration of its power in that quarter, if it has so designed; and, relieved from all embarrassing apprehensions of this sort, the local banks are amply sufficient for all the wants of the enterprise and the business of the people.

THE CONGRESSIONAL GLOBE.

PRINTED AND PUBLISHED AT THE CITY OF WASHINGTON, BY BLAIR & RIVES.

23d Congress, 1st Session.   SATURDAY, MAY 24, 1834.   Vol. I........No. 25.

IN SENATE.

Wednesday, May 14, 1834.

Two messages were received from the President of the United States, by Mr. Donelson, his Private Secretary.

1. Communicating a copy of a treaty of commerce between the United States and his Majesty the Emperor of all the Russias, ratified May 11th, 1833.

2. Communicating a copy of the convention between the United States and his Majesty the King of the Two Sicilies.

On motion of Mr. WILKINS, the messages were referred to the Committee on Foreign Relations.

PETITIONS.

The VICE PRESIDENT presented the proceedings of a meeting of delegates from Newcastle county, Delaware, approving the course of the Executive relative to the Bank of the United States, and protesting against the restoration of the deposites, or the recharter of that Institution.

After some remarks by Messrs. NAUDAIN and CLAYTON, on motion of the former gentleman, the proceedings were referred to the Committee on Finance, and ordered to be printed.

Mr. SMITH presented the petition of a number of citizens of Connecticut, remonstrating against the renewal of the patent of John Ames, for an improvement in the manufacture of paper; which was laid on the table.

Mr. CLAY presented a memorial signed by a number of the inhabitants of Louisville, Kentucky, in behalf of Jacob Lewis, who is desirous of establishing a pottery for the manufacture of Queensware, at the confluence of the Ohio and Mississippi rivers, and praying that a grant of land at that site may be made to him at the Government prices. The petition was referred to the Committee on Public Lands.

Mr. BIBB presented the memorial of a number of the inhabitants of Nelson county, Kentucky, praying a restoration of the deposites, and a recharter of the Bank of the United States; which was read, referred to the Committee on Finance, and ordered to be printed.

Mr. CHAMBERS gave notice that he should, on Friday next, move to take up the bill making an appropriation for the construction of a lateral branch of the Baltimore and Ohio railroad to the District of Columbia.

Mr. CHAMBERS presented a memorial in favor of repairing the Cumberland road. A bill for that purpose having passed the Senate, the memorial was laid upon the table.

Mr. PRENTISS presented a memorial of inhabitants of Vermont, remonstrating against the extension of the patent of John Ames for an improvement in paper making; which was laid on the table.

Mr. POINDEXTER presented the petition of Francis Surget and others; which was referred to the Committee on Public Lands.

Mr. MORRIS presented the proceedings of a large meeting of the inhabitants of Seneca county, Ohio, sustaining the Executive in his course towards the Bank of the United States, and approving of the removal of the deposites, and averse to a recharter of that corporation. The proceedings were read, referred to the Committee on Finance, and ordered to be printed.

Mr. MORRIS also presented the proceedings of a public meeting held in Columbiana county, Ohio, of the same tenor.

Mr. M. observed that the county of Columbiana was one of the largest counties in the State of Ohio, and was formerly, of itself, one congressional district. The proceedings of this meeting, he had no manner of doubt, were expressive of the opinions of the people of Ohio. There was one resolution among this number, however, the language of which he did not entirely approve of. It was clothed in strong and expressive terms, in relation to the resolutions lately adopted by a ma-

jority of the Senate censuring the conduct of the President of the United States. But the presiding officer of the meeting was a highly respectable citizen, and therefore he could not withhold the proceedings on account of but one resolution, the terms of which were somewhat objectionable, but the conclusion of which he approved. At no former period had public (political) excitement been at a greater height in Ohio than it was at present, and the current of public opinion was strong against the Bank of the United States, and in favor of the Administration. It was under the influence of these feelings and views that they expressed themselves in strong language. He moved that the proceedings be read, printed, and take the usual reference.

Mr. POINDEXTER objected to the reception of the paper, unless the honorable gentleman from Ohio would strike out the offensive resolution.

Mr. FRELINGHUYSEN asked whether the resolution was in respectful language, as that seemed to be the rule adopted.

Mr. MORRIS replied that it spoke in strong language, but it was not disrespectful. If he had drawn the resolution, however, he would have expressed the same views in different language.

Mr. BROWN said he did not like the practice of condemning without a hearing, either in this or any other matter—he hoped the paper would be read.

Mr. EWING and Mr. CLAY were also in favor of its being read.

After some further conversation, the proceedings were read, and the question being on the motion to print, (the reference being a matter of course,)

Mr. POINDEXTER was opposed to printing, as the paper had already been printed in a newspaper.

Mr. FRELINGHUYSEN was also opposed to printing, as other parts of the proceedings reflected, in most disrespectful terms, upon the gentleman's colleague, [Mr. Ewing.]

Mr. MORRIS contended that the constituents of himself and colleague had a right to express their sentiments in any language they pleased, as it respected their public conduct as Senators. Ought we, here, to shield ourselves from the reach of the people? If we misrepresent the opinions and wishes of our constituents, ought we not to be told that we do? If the private conduct of his honorable colleague had been assailed or reflected on, it would be unjustifiable. But there was a great difference between his public and private conduct, and this resolution arraigned his political course only; they attributed to him no improper motive; they regretted his course here, and had they a right to say that they viewed it in this light? It seemed to him (Mr. M.) that they had a right to do so, in any way and manner they pleased. If they had not, there was an end of all accountability on the part of the representative to those he represented.

Mr. FRELINGHUYSEN then moved to lay the paper on the table; upon which motion

Mr. MORRIS asked the yeas and nays; which were ordered, and are as follows, to wit:

YEAS—Messrs. Bell, Bibb, Calhoun, Chambers, Clay, Clayton, Frelinghuysen, Hendricks, Knight, Mangum, Moore, Naudain, Poindexter, Porter, Prentiss, Robbins, Silsbee, Smith, Swift, Sprague, Tomlinson—21.

NAYS—Messrs. Black, Brown, Forsyth, Grundy, Hill, Kane, King of Alabama, Linn, McKean, Morris, Preston, Robinson, Shepley, Tipton, Waggaman, White, Wilkins, Wright, —19.

So the proceedings were laid on the table.

Mr. EWING presented a memorial from citizens of Athens county, Ohio, complaining of great pecuniary distress and reduction in the price of agricultural products, which they ascribe to the removal of the deposites; and praying, as the only remedy, a restoration of the deposites to the Bank of the United States and the recharter of the bank.

Mr. MORRIS observed that these memorialists

complained of a depression in the prices of agricultural products, to the ruin of the citizen. This memorial came from a southern county, in the State of Ohio; not a very populous, although a respectable one. But it had heretofore ranked in opposition to the Administration; it was chiefly represented in the Ohio Legislature by men of that political character, and was now represented in the House of Representatives here, by a member in the opposition. But he (Mr. M.) thought that these memorialists were mistaken in what they said with regard to the prices of the staple articles of Ohio. He held in his hand a letter from a respectable and intelligent man, informing him that wheat, in Muskingum county, adjoining the county of this memorialist, was now at sixty-two and a half cents a bushel. [Mr. M. here read the letter.] This letter was signed by Major James Cochran, of Zanesville, who said that the bank question being considered settled, the prices were becoming fixed, so that things were not quite so bad as they were represented to be. Sixty-two and a half cents was a good living price for wheat; a fair price at this period, the fear crops having been very abundant.

After some remarks by Mr. EWING and Mr. MORRIS, the memorial was referred to the Committee on Finance.

Mr. KING, of Alabama, presented the memorial of the judges, attorney, and marshal, of the eastern district of Florida, praying an appropriation for the purchase of the building which is now occupied by the district court of the United States; which was referred to the Committee on Finance.

SPECIAL ORDER.

The Senate then proceeded to the consideration of the resolution reported by the Committee on the Judiciary on the President's message, in reference to

THE PENSION FUND.

Mr. CLAYTON having the floor, commenced a speech in support of the resolution, and in reply to Mr. Wright; when, at a quarter past three o'clock, without concluding, he gave way to

Mr. EWING, upon whose motion,

The Senate adjourned.

HOUSE OF REPRESENTATIVES.

Wednesday, May 14, 1834.

Mr. GARLAND moved that the bills which had been sent from the Senate and lay upon the Speaker's table, be read a first and second time, for the purpose of referring them.

Unanimous consent being given, various bills were read, and referred to the appropriate committees.

Mr. E. WHITTLESEY, from the Committee of Claims, reported the following resolution:

Resolved, That the Committee of Claims be discharged from the further consideration of the claims of Henry Develen and others; and that the same be referred to the Secretary of War.

Which, after a brief explanation from Mr. W., was adopted.

Mr. JARVIS, from the Committee on Foreign Affairs, reported a bill for the relief of the legal representatives of John Mullowny; which was read twice, and committed.

Mr. CAVE JOHNSON, from the Committee on Private Land Claims, reported a bill in favor of Thomas B. Clark, James Bradford, and John Fruge. Severally read twice, and committed.

Mr. WAYNE moved that a communication from the Secretary of State, relative to the publication of the diplomatic correspondence, be referred to the Library Committee; which was agreed to.

The motion heretofore offered by Mr. Mardis, in relation to the deposites of public money, with the amendment proposed by Mr. Corwin, came up.

Mr. GALBRAITH resumed his remarks in reply to Mr. McKennan, which he continued, until out concluding, until the expiration of the hour

allotted to morning business had expired; when, on motion of

Mr. McKINLEY, the House proceeded to the orders of the day.

Mr. BOON gave notice that to-morrow morning he should request the House to take up and dispose of the resolution heretofore submitted by him fixing the day for the adjournment of Congress.

Mr. POLK expressed a hope that the House would, by unanimous consent, dispose of the appropriation bills referred to the Committee of the Whole on the state of the Union.

No objection being made—

The House, on motion of Mr. POLK, went into Committee of the Whole on the state of the Union, (Mr. SPEIGHT in the chair.)

The bill making appropriations for the Indian department for 1834 was taken up.

Mr. POLK moved to strike the word "clerks" from the item making appropriation for Interpreters, translators, &c., at the several agencies; which was agreed to.

At the instance of Mr. POLK, a letter from the Secretary of War relative to the employment of blacksmiths, &c., was read, when that gentleman moved to strike out the words "treaty stipulations" and $16,000 from the item referring to the employment of blacksmiths among the Indian tribes, and insert the sum of $6,480 instead. Mr. P. explained the object to be, that such portion of the original sum proposed to be appropriated as was called for by treaty should be stricken from this bill and added to that making appropriations for Indian annuities. The motion was agreed to.

The item appropriating $5,000 for the purchase of iron, steel, &c., having been read—

Mr. POLK moved to strike out $5,000, and insert instead $1,465; which was agreed to.

The item making appropriations for the expense of transportation and distribution of annuities having been read—

Mr. POLK said the item more properly belonged to the Indian annuities bill, and moved it be stricken out; which was agreed to.

Mr. LEWIS moved that two additional items be added to the bill. The first making an appropriation of $8,000 for the expenses of negotiating with the western Pawnees, the other appropriating $11,160, being the amount due to certain Creek Indians, followers of McIntosh.

Mr. GRENNELL asked an explanation of these items.

Mr. LEWIS said the first item was proposed by the Committee on Indian Affairs, at the suggestion of the Indian commissioners, in consequence of the loss of property which had been occasioned by the Pawnees west of the Mississippi, who were totally out of the reach of our military force. The other item was proposed by the same committee, to carry into effect the stipulations of a treaty.

Mr. FILLMORE inquired whether this provision did not more properly belong to the bill for carrying those treaties into effect?

Mr. LEWIS had no objection to proposing the item as an amendment to that bill, and accordingly withdrew it. The other item was agreed to.

Mr. L. then moved to add to the bill an item appropriating $10,000 for the purchase of provisions for the support of such Creek Indians in Alabama as were destitute of provisions. Mr. L. said this appropriation had been recommended by the Secretary of War. Their situation was represented to be one of extreme destitution.

Mr. BATES wished to understand, before he voted upon this appropriation, how these Indians happened to be reduced to this state of starvation.

Mr. LEWIS said he might not be able to satisfy the gentleman as to the various reasons which prevented these Indians from being in a flourishing condition. Many of them, not aware that the policy of the Government, as to individual emigration, had changed, had depended upon leaving their country and had made no crops. Their habitual improvidence had thrown them into great distress.

Mr. GILMER did not consider the reason assigned a sufficient one. It was three years since the last Indians had been sent over the Mississippi individually. He was satisfied that the distribution of provisions among these Indians would only encourage idle habits among them and increase the distress under which they labored. This was the opinion of the more intelligent among them. The truth is, that a portion of these Indians are always starving. This was an inevitable consequence of their mode of life, and had always been the case since they had been known. Besides, these Indians are understood now to be within the jurisdiction of the State of Alabama. If the State had assumed jurisdiction over them, they had taken off the obligation of maintaining them from the United States.

Mr. LEWIS said there had been enrolments for emigration more recently, though the last emigration of individual Indians was three years ago, and this fact had undoubtedly produced habits of improvidence among a certain class. The gentleman from Georgia [Mr. GILMER] had stated that distress always existed among a certain portion of these Indians. He should not dispute this. The proposition for this appropriation was not his. It was made by order of the Committee on Indian Affairs, at the instance of the Secretary of War. As to the obligation of the State of Alabama to support these Indians as her own paupers, it could not be recognised so long as the Government continued to make treaties with them and place them on a footing different from the other citizens of that State.

Mr. VINTON requested the letter of the Secretary of War requesting this appropriation might be read.

Mr. LEWIS had not expected this bill to come up this morning, and the papers were not in the House.

Mr. VINTON contended that we were under obligations to support these Indians. He wished to know the facts relative to their actual condition. The main ground of opposition to the policy heretofore pursued by the Government in relation to these people, was that it must inevitably reduce them to poverty and distress. Whether these apprehensions had been verified, he wished to learn. He would also be glad to be informed why the law had not been executed which provided for the transportation of such as had enrolled themselves for emigration.

Mr. LEWIS said he had no information on the subject.

Mr. BURGES said, it appeared from the statement of the gentleman from Georgia, [Mr. GILMER,] that the policy of the Government had thrown the Indians back upon their old habits of precarious subsistence.

Mr. GILMER said he had made no such statement.

Mr. BURGES. The gentleman certainly said something. What it was, he would not undertake to repeat. It was clear, from the grounds on which the amendment was moved, that these Indians are in a state of great distress. It did not appear that they had ever been in such a condition before. It was not owing to the removal of the depositos, but to the policy which proposed to carry them over the Mississippi, and then begin in the condition of man when he first begins to walk on his hind legs. Whether this Government was bound to them by any obligations to provide for their support, he did not know. All the State of Alabama wants is their lands. After they had been cheated out of that, she was not bound to support them any more. If they had been wronged out of his property, compelling those who had got it to maintain him? It may be supposed, that as the measures adopted by the United States had led to their present distress, some relief should be afforded. But he could not consent to place money for that purpose in the hands of agents, to be disbursed without vouchers. He would never vote for the payment of Indian annuities so long as they were to be paid to individual Indians, without means of ascertaining the fact whether they were paid or not. He would vote no money under such circumstances.

Mr. VANCE was convinced that these Indians were in a suffering condition. He had been informed from a source which satisfied him, that the Shawnees, which had emigrated from the State of Ohio, were suffering for want of subsistence. He therefore moved to amend the amendment by adding $5,000 for the purchase of provisions for the Shawnees Indians.

Mr. GILMER had never understood that a single Indian had been thrown out of his ordinary means of subsistence by enrolling himself for emigration. None of them could have been driven, pointed in being permitted to remain, for the policy of individual emigration had been given up in 1830. He believed the principal cause of individual enrolment since that time had taken place among the Cherokees, which had been done at their own suggestion. He had never understood that any of the Creeks had been enrolled since 1830, excepting the peace of Chilly McIntosh, who had engaged one or two hundred Creeks to emigrate who had not gone. As to the mode of making payments to the Indians, a bill had been drawn by the Committee on Indian Affairs, which would be reported in a day or two, directing the payments of annuities to be made to the chiefs of tribes in their national councils, and not to individuals, which would remove the objection suggested by the gentleman from Rhode Island, [Mr. BURGES.] The starvation and distress of the Indians were inseparable from their habits and propensities. Similar improvidence and distress existed among them when they were first known.

Mr. LEWIS said the proposition of the gentleman from Ohio would introduce an entirely new feature into the system of Indian affairs. They had never been supported after the expiration of a year from their emigration. As to the obligations of Alabama to support the Indians within her limits, let them be either an independent people, capable of making treaties, or citizens of that State, and dependent on her protection. So long as this Government recognised them as independent, the State could not support them.

After some further debate, in which Messrs. LEWIS, H. EVERETT, GILMER, and MARDIS took part,

Mr. POLK suggested that the provision could be added to the annuity bill.

Mr. LEWIS then withdrew his amendment.

Mr. H. EVERETT moved to amend the bill by inserting a provision for paying the expenses of the treaty with the Wyandots; which was agreed to.

Mr. LEWIS asked whether the committee did not intend to propose a similar appropriation in relation to the Creek Indians.

Mr. EVERETT said no estimate had as yet been obtained of the expenses.

Mr. LEWIS moved the amendment, with a view to enable him to bring it up in the House.

Mr. ASHLEY moved an amendment, appropriating 1,000 dollars as the salary of a clerk in the office of the superintendent of Indian Affairs. Agreed to.

Mr. ASHLEY also moved to strike out 17,000 dollars and insert 16,500. Agreed to.

Mr. ASHLEY moved to strike out 20,000 dollars, in the 20th line, and insert 18,920. Agreed to.

On motion of Mr. POLK, the committee then took up for consideration the bill "making appropriations for Indian annuities, and other similar objects, for the year 1834."

On motion of Mr. POLK, an amendment was adopted, giving $6,754 to the Wyandots, instead of $5,900.

Mr. POLK moved to strike out $1,100 for the Eel River Indians, and insert $2,070.

Mr. McKAY opposed the motion, and it was supported by Messrs. POLK and HUBBARD; when the motion was rejected.

Mr. POLK moved to increase the allowance of the Chippewas, Ottawas, and Potawatomies to $16,995, and of the Menomonies to $1,940, of the Kanzas to $5,945; which was agreed to.

Mr. POLK moved to increase the allowance of the Osages to $19,040; which was negatived; and the sum then agreed upon was $11,070.

Mr. POLK moved to strike out the appropriation for the Kaskaskias of $1,000, to reduce that of the Kaskaskias and Peorias to $2,030, to strike out the Weas, to increase the allowance of the Delawares to $7,870, and of the Shawnees to $4,680. Agreed to.

Mr. HUBBARD moved to amend the bill by inserting a provision allowing $3,500 to carry into effect the 4th article of the treaty with the Apalachicola Indians. Agreed to.

Mr. POLK moved to amend by increasing the allowance for the expenses of distributing annui-

tion, salt, implements, &c., from $20,000 to $29,-500; which, after some debate, in which Messrs. BATES, POLK, and SEVIER, took part, was agreed to.

Mr. POLK moved to strike out $8,000, and insert $15,223, for the expenses of locating reservations and certifying contracts under the Creek treaty of the 24th March, 1832. Agreed to.

On motion of Mr. POLK, the clause appropriating $500 for compensation to a commissioner to value the improvements of the Brothertown Indians, was stricken out.

On motion of Mr. HUBBARD, a clause was adopted allowing $2,000 for running a line between the Sacs and Foxes.

A great number of amendments were adopted on motion of Mr. POLK and Mr. HUBBARD.

Mr. POLK moved an additional clause appropriating $241,000 for the removal of five thousand Creeks west of the Mississippi, and $27,520 for furnishing them with blankets, implements, &c., according to the stipulations of the treaty for their removal.

Mr. SEVIER proposed to amend the amendment by adding a proviso that the Indians should be removed under an authorized agent of the United States.

After some remarks from Messrs. POLK and MARDIS, Mr. SEVIER withdrew his motion, and the motion of Mr. POLK was agreed to.

On motion of Mr. POLK, an amendment was adopted, appropriating $68,325 for the expenses of the removal of the Cherokees to the west of the Mississippi.

Mr. VINTON asked whether the Cherokees were to be removed from Tennessee or Georgia?

Mr. POLK said from Georgia.

Mr. VINTON said so far as the appropriation related to the Cherokees in Georgia, he should not object to it. He moved a proviso, confining the appropriation to the Indians residing in Georgia and Alabama.

Messrs. WAYNE, POLK, and WILLIAMS, opposed the proviso, and it was supported by Messrs. VINTON and BATES; when it was rejected.

The motion of Mr. POLK was then agreed to.

On motion of Mr. POLK, some further amendments were adopted.

Mr. HAWES moved an amendment, the object of which was to provide that all payments of moneys under this bill, should be made to the Indians directly.

Mr. H. EVERETT suggested a modification, providing that the payments should be made to the chiefs of the tribes respectively.

Mr. HAWES accepted the amendment.

Mr. MARDIS said that this amendment would prevent the Creek Indians now living east of the Mississippi from receiving their annuity till they go west, because their government was dissolved.

Mr. PLUMMER was of the opinion that the money ought to be paid to the individuals of the tribe directly. The chiefs and captains now get all, and the poor and ignorant Indians none.

Mr. H. EVERETT suggested a further modification of the amendment, adding to it, "or to such persons as the tribes shall appoint."

Mr. HAWES said his object was to provide that the poor Indians should receive their share, and that this Government should not be held responsible for the money.

Some discussion followed, in which Messrs. VANCE, SEVIER, FILLMORE, and EWING, took part.

Mr. ASHLEY proposed an amendment to the amendment, providing that the agent should see the amount paid to the heads of families entitled to the same.

Mr. ASHLEY, in support of this proposition, remarked that last year forty or fifty thousand dollars was paid to the chiefs on the Mississippi, no part of which was paid to the Indians, but was delivered by the chiefs to an individual without opening the boxes, and were placed in one of the banks at St. Louis.

The amendment was further debated by Messrs. PARKER, PLUMMER, LANE, and H. EVERETT.

When the question was taken on Mr. ASHLEY's amendment to the amendment, which was adopted: Ayes 68, noes 57.

The question was then taken on the amendment as amended, which was lost without a count.

Mr. LEWIS moved to amend the bill by adding an appropriation of $11,500 for certain Creek Indians, followers of McIntosh.

After a brief explanation by Mr. LEWIS, the amendment was adopted.

The committee then rose, and reported the bills to the House, with the amendments.

The SPEAKER laid before the House a message from the President, enclosing a copy of a convention with the King of the Two Sicilies;

And another message, enclosing a copy of a convention with the Emperor of Russia; the ratification of both having been exchanged.

The SPEAKER also laid before the House several communications from the departments, in reply to resolutions calling for information.

Mr. HAWES moved to reconsider the vote by which the commutation bill was recommitted to the Committee of the Whole on the state of the Union.

Before the question was taken,
The House adjourned.

IN SENATE.

Thursday, May 15, 1834.

A message was received from the President of the United States, by Mr. Donelson, his Private Secretary, transmitting a copy of a treaty of peace, amity, and commerce, between the United States and the Republic of Chili.

The VICE PRESIDENT presented a communication from the Navy Department, relative to the naval asylum of Philadelphia.

The VICE PRESIDENT presented a communication from the Treasury Department, transmitting a report from the register and receiver of the land office at St. Stephens, in the State of Alabama.

The VICE PRESIDENT communicated a letter from the Secretary of War, enclosing a report from the Chief Topographical Engineer, in compliance with the resolution of the Senate of the 14th instant, relative to the harbor of Norwalk, Connecticut; which, on motion of Mr. TOMLINSON, was ordered to be printed.

PETITIONS.

Mr. NAUDAIN presented the proceedings of a meeting of inhabitants of Wilmington, Delaware, censuring the doctrines advanced in the protest of the President of the United States to the resolutions of the Senate of the 17th of April.

Mr. N. said that he viewed these proceedings in the light of an appeal—a response of the people to the President's paper. He said that he should not detain the Senate many minutes, but he would take occasion briefly to animadvert upon this remarkable paper, called the President's protest. He viewed it as an encroachment upon the rights of the Senate, and the liberties of a free and magnanimous people. It had no parallel in history. Representative Government might be overturned by executive encroachment; and mark it, sir, said Mr. N., this very protest is pregnant with such assumptions as are utterly repugnant to the genius of the Constitution. It seems, sir, that we must meet the rebuke of the President, when we call into question his motives. Mr. N. said that he had thought that what was done in this and the other House, was not to be called in question, and he thought it was time that the people should condemn this encroachment upon the privileges of a coördinate branch of the Government. Mr. N. said he should like to know whether an encroachment of this character was not calculated to call down the rebuke of the people? Is liberty of speech to be infringed, and this blot out the beams of discussion? He hoped the American people would respond to the appeal, both far and near. The second resolution was worthy of a free people. It utterly denies the right of the President to make the officers of the Government his agents, and entirely repudiates the idea of a President's claiming to be the Lord Protector and Dictator of the Commonwealth, and makes the officers of the Government obedient to his will.

Mr. N. thought the citizens of Delaware had a right to animadvert upon the paper, as promulgated by the Globe, the official journal. The paper (the protest) was an unwarrantable assumption of

the rights of the Senate, in its legislative character. The President claims the right, in that paper, to appoint and remove, to and from office, at his mere will and pleasure. Mr. N. thought this to be utterly subversive of the rights of the Senate. What! shall the President create vacancies when he pleases, a kind of irresponsible responsibility? Mr. N. referred to the history of 1825, when the President first came into power. He removed many and faithful officers, because he did not choose to be responsible for their acts. He would instance an honorable member on this floor, [Mr. Smith,] who had been appointed and confirmed by the Senate, as district attorney for the State of Connecticut, and had been unceremoniously ejected from office. To carry out the inference, he might nominate to office, the Senate might confirm the nomination, and directly they adjourned, though they should sit until July, the President revokes the appointment and places another incumbent to discharge the duties of the office; perhaps obnoxious to the Senate, the constitutional advisers of the President. Mr. N. said he did not wish to impress the Senate with the belief that he thought this abuse had been carried out into actual practice. He believed that consummation had not yet arrived.

Mr. N. was satisfied that the Globe spoke from authority, and he usually gave credence to any assertion of that paper, comprehending executive policy, and consequently believed that the President, as suggested by an article in that paper, would shortly send in certain nominations. He was satisfied that the President, in the doctrines of the protest, had cast off all pretensions to limitations of power. Who, sir, (said Mr. N.,) is to control this man, characterized in the resolution as the Lord Protector and Dictator of the Commonwealth? Sir, I believe it; I do believe it, that we have arrived at a most alarming era in our history. What is there left for us? The President claims all right; what check remains? He has placed his hands upon the public treasury, he says, upon his responsibility. What is responsibility? Impeachment? No President, sir, can be impeached. No, sir; no, sir. Any Executive who may attempt encroachment, lays his plans deep and broad. I mean not to impute any impure motives to the present Chief Magistrate; but I would ask, sir, what is to forbid him from taking the treasury of the people to bribe the people? Think you a man who is determined to usurp power is regardful of checks? The President says to his Secretary of the Treasury, "Mr. Secretary, I take the responsibility." Mr. Secretary says, "Sir, the responsibility is mine; and I can't surrender the trust." "Get out of office, then, sir," responds the Executive; and there are men supple and pliant enough to take his place.

Mr. N. then expatiated upon the cognomen lately adopted, of Whig; stated that the party had good reason to adopt that venerable and highly regarded name; and he was glad that a portion of his constituents, the good people of Wilmington, had adopted the appellation, and he hoped that the sentiments they promulgated in their resolutions would be adopted throughout the country.

Mr. SMITH rose to correct an error in the remarks of the gentleman from Delaware, [Mr. Naudain.] In his remarks, just delivered, that gentleman had appealed to him, (Mr. S.,) as affording an instance of the exercise of arbitrary power on the part of the President of the United States. This was a matter of great surprise to him; for he had never supposed the act alluded to to be so. He was not conscious of any injustice having been done towards him by the President, in the instance alluded to; nor had he ever before heard of his not done many other things in the course of his administration much more exceptionable than this, he would have found him among his supporters. He objected to the inference made from this fact by the honorable gentleman from Delaware.

Mr. NAUDAIN said he was not mistaken as to the facts. He stated them correctly; and he had a right to draw the inference, that the President had used an unwarrantable stretch of power. He did not think the gentleman [Mr. Smith] was aggrieved, but he thought that the nation was, by an arbitrary display of Executive prerogative.

Mr. FORSYTH said he would be glad to know

why gentlemen wished this paper printed. He did not perceive what use could be made of it. No legislative action, or reference of it, was proposed.

Mr. NAUDAIN replied that he desired it on account of the high respectability and intelligence of the people who sent the memorial here. It was their response to the appeal of the President, and he thought it but respectful on the part of the Senate to print it.

Mr. FORSYTH held the reasons to be entirely unsatisfactory, that the paper ought to be printed under the idea that it was respectful to the citizens who sent it here. We had no authority to expend the public money in this way. We had a sum of money placed at our disposal, to be appropriated to defraying the contingent expenses of the Senate; not for the purpose of administering to our own vanity. The protest of the President of the United States was disposed of; it was not before us; it was not printed, not out of respect to the people or the President of the United States. Why, then, encumber our tables with this new matter?

Mr. CHAMBERS said he had presented the first expression of the people upon the protest which was laid on the table. The President had appealed to the people on an issue of his own, and rumor said that forty thousand copies of them had been printed and circulated through the country. The Senate had responded to that paper as it thought proper, and this was the verdict of the people coming back to us, and gentlemen wished to put it on the table to sleep. He asked the gentleman from Georgia what useful information was to be derived from printing memorials. The subject to which they applied was put to rest, and yet we were daily printing them.

Mr. FORSYTH said, the gentleman from Maryland [Mr. CHAMBERS] would recollect that all memorials were sent to a committee, and they were proposed to be the subject for legislation. The printing of memorials stood upon an entirely different footing from this: they might be wanted. But he begged to know who wanted to refer to this paper. The gentleman said it was the verdict of the people upon the protest of the President; and suppose one hundred thousand of them should come here, would they make any difference in the direction of popular opinion in the issue between the President and the Senate! It could give the public no information to print it. If we were to multiply the number, it might. But it could be of no utility to print, except to put money into the hands of our printer. It was right that the paper should be received, read, and referred to, by honorable Senators who see their own images reflected in it. It was for the majority, however, who delighted in such exhibitions, to say whether it should be printed or not.

Mr. CHAMBERS replied, that yesterday the gentleman from Georgia voted against laying the Ohio memorial on the table, and he (Mr. C.) did not perceive how he could justify a vote against printing a paper on the same subject.

Mr. CLAYTON said that this was not only a protest against the President's protest, but it was an expression of the sentiments of a portion of the people on the restoration of the deposites and other agitating subjects. He wanted to know the sentiments of the people of Delaware and to have them for reference to.

Mr. KANE remarked, if it was just and proper to print this paper, the motion ought to be amended, so as to include the printing of the President's protest. And he appealed to the candor of the Senate, whether, if this paper was to be printed and to go among the documents and be preserved, the protest ought not to be preserved with it. That paper had existence, but not among the documents of the Senate. Any one who might hereafter take up the charge of certain individuals, could not see whether the charge was true or false. It was very unfair to give an opportunity to individuals to make this charge, without placing the instrument by the side of the charge, as its refutation. He was willing to vote to print, if the antidote could be permitted to go with the poison; he therefore moved an amendment that the protest be printed with the memorial.

Mr. CLAY thought the amendment was not in order. The protest was already pretty well circulated—forty thousand having been distributed from the Globe office.

The CHAIR decided that the amendment was in order.

Mr. CHAMBERS appealed from the decision of the chair; and after some conversation between Mr. CLAY, Mr. CLAYTON, and Mr. CHAMBERS, he withdrew the appeal.

Mr. FORSYTH said he should vote against the amendment, on the same ground that he would vote against printing the paper, not out of disrespect to the people of Delaware. The paper was deserving of respect from the number and character of the signers of it. He opposed the printing, simply on the ground that it was utterly useless. Honorable gentlemen could make themselves masters of its contents at the clerk's desk. No legislation was designed to be founded on it. The question was settled. The protest was no longer a subject of consideration for us. This memorial belonged to that large class of papers which were to be printed out of respect to our constituents; and on this ground he would vote against both the amendment, and the motion to print the paper. It was no respect to the President of the United States to put the protest on our printed files. Its only use was for reference. The gentleman from Kentucky referred to the uncontradicted story of forty thousand copies of the protest having been printed at the Globe office; and he thought the silence of the friends of the Administration was an admission of the truth of the fact. Now he, Mr. F., denied the justness of any such inference. But suppose it were true, he would ask if it had been done at the people's expense? Our documents were printed at the public expense; but as to this story, if they were printed, it was at the expense of the President himself. But he did not believe it was true. Indeed, he ventured to assert that not a single cent of the expense incurred for printing the protest came out of the public treasury. All the presses here had printed matter in support of their own parties.

Mr. KANE remarked that he did not say that the protest was misquoted, for he did not know whether it had been or not. All he said was that the doctrines of the protest were misrepresented. These persons had erred in their opinions of what the protest was. He thought that neither should be printed; but it was both unfair and improper to print an attack on the President and not print the protest itself. The effect which it would have would be unjust, and if either should be printed, both should.

Some further remarks were made by Mr. PRESTON, Mr. POINDEXTER, and Mr. FORSYTH, when the amendment was negatived, and the motion to print was agreed to.

Mr. CLAYTON asked the suspension of the orders, and called up the bill providing for an equal representation in the Legislative Council of the people of the Territory of Florida. The rule being suspended, the bill was read a third time and *passed*.

Mr. POINDEXTER requested the consideration of his resolution for printing the Journals of the Old Congress, which being agreed to, the resolution, on his motion, was referred to the Committee on the Judiciary.

Mr. CHAMBERS, from the Committee on the District of Columbia, reported a bill to incorporate the Washington Horticultural Society, with an amendment.

PENSION AGENCY.

Mr. CLAYTON resumed his argument on the resolutions of the Judiciary Committee on the pension agency of the Bank of the United States. Before he proceeded, he submitted the following resolutions as an amendment to those reported by the committee:

Resolved, That the act of Congress for the relief of certain officers and soldiers of the Revolution, passed on the 15th of May, 1828, and the act supplementary to that act, passed on the 7th of June, 1832, are properly acts providing for the payment of military pensions.

Resolved, That no power is conferred by any law, upon the Department or Secretary of War, to remove the agency for the payment of pensioners, under the said act of the 7th June, 1832, and the funds, books, and papers, connected with that agency, from the Bank of the United States, and to appoint other agents to supersede that bank in the payment of such pensioners.

On concluding his argument,

Mr. KANE took the floor and spoke in reply to Mr. CLAYTON, and in opposition to the resolutions, and after proceeding a short time, gave way to a motion by Mr. WRIGHT for an adjournment; which prevailed.

The Senate then adjourned.

HOUSE OF REPRESENTATIVES.

THURSDAY, *May* 15, 1834.

Mr. HARPER, of New Hampshire, reported a bill for the relief of Joseph W. Greer and others. Read twice and committed.

Mr. MERCER reported, from the Committee on Roads and Canals, a resolution for printing a number of copies of a treatise on roads and canals; which was agreed to.

ADJOURNMENT.

Mr. BOON asked the unanimous consent of the House to take up for consideration the following resolution:

Resolved, That the President of the Senate and the Speaker of the House of Representatives close the present session of Congress by an adjournment of their respective Houses on Monday the 16th day of June next.

An objection being made, Mr. BOON moved the suspension of the rules, and thereon asked the yeas and nays; which were ordered.

The question being taken, the motion was agreed to; yeas 126, nays 23.

Mr. HARDIN moved to strike out the 16th of June, and insert the 30th day of June.

Mr. H. presumed, he said, that neither the honorable member from Indiana, nor any member of the House, was more anxious for an early adjournment than he was. Business, both of a public and private nature, demanded his return home. But he was unwilling to fix upon so early a day as the 16th day of June. It would leave but twelve parliamentary days for the despatch of the public business. The two last petition days we occupied in getting through New York and into Pennsylvania. Another day we might get as far as North Carolina, and by that time there would be distress enough at the north to occupy another day. Fridays and Saturdays were set apart for local and private business. Who could believe that we can leave here on the 16th of nexth month, and despatch the public or private business which is most pressing? There were five appropriation bills to be acted upon, besides the commutation bill, the bill giving pensions to those who were engaged in the Indian wars, the Potomac bridge bill, the Chesapeake and Ohio Canal bill, the Cumberland road bill, the bill regulating the Indian Department, and the bill for the regulation of the Post Office Department. All these bills were of the most urgent importance. He knew not how many days the House were to be engaged in the unpleasant election contest which would be taken up next week, but certainly it could not be disposed of in less time than three or four days. The Judiciary Committee, to which he belonged, had reported a number of bills to the House which require immediate action, and not one of them had yet been taken up. It was true that we had been five months in session, and that owing to the situation of the country and the state of parties, the time had been unprofitably spent. The next session, it must be recollected, is restricted in length by the Constitution, and must terminate on the 3d day of March. It was, therefore, the more important that we should despatch as much business as possible at the present session. It was improper, too, in reference to the business of the Senate to fix an early day. The body would have important business to despatch in relation to nominations, and they have not yet acted upon the appropriation bills, or upon the bill for the payment of lost property. In a spirit of liberality, we ought not to force them to take the responsibility of fixing a day different from that proposed by the House. He hoped the mover would strike out the 16th of June, and insert the 30th of June.

Mr. CAMBRELENG rose, he said, to make a suggestion to the gentleman from Indiana, who had brought forward this measure. It was evident that the House was not prepared to-day to fix upon the time of adjournment. He hoped we should agree, on all sides, to pass some important

measures. The House, he hoped, would not adjourn till the coin bills were acted upon. The attention of the House would also be necessarily drawn to the new, extraordinary, and unexpected attitude assumed by the Bank of the United States. He hoped the gentleman from Indiana would consent to the postponement of the further consideration of the resolution till this day fortnight, and he made that motion.

Mr. H. EVERETT did not wish to prolong the session of Congress, but he was not now ready to fix the day of adjournment. Some bills relative to the Indian Department, which was well deserving of the attention of the House, would be reported on Monday next. He hoped, therefore, the resolution would be postponed.

Mr. WILDE said the extraordinary unanimity with which the motion to suspend the rules of the House in order to take up this subject, had been carried, clearly indicated that the House were disposed to act on the subject at once. Whatever individual feeling he might entertain in favor of an early adjournment, there were considerations, of a public character, which rendered a precipitate adjournment highly inexpedient. But still, he was disposed to be governed by the majority of the House. If we were not to act upon the highly important subject of the currency, we might dispatch all the other business of importance by the time proposed in the resolution. Whether we should or should not act definitively on that subject, rested with the majority of this House. In the present temper of the two bodies, it was obvious that, whatever time might be spent on the subject, its fate was certain. If there was no intention to do anything in reference to the subject of the currency, there was no necessity for postponing the resolution. After we had passed it, the Senate could amend or postpone it as they pleased. It was a law of politics, as well as of nature, that no two great epidemics could prevail at the same time. No matter what subject we may take up, the currency question must run into it. If we did not intend to act upon it, we might as well adjourn.

Mr. MERCER rose to support the motion of the gentleman from New York. The calendar which he held in his hand, contained four hundred and fifty bills, of which we had not touched more than fifty. The Committee of the Whole on the state of the Union, had before it the unprecedented number of thirty-nine bills, every one of which was important.

Mr. BEARDSLEY recollected, he said, only one session which was prolonged beyond the middle of June, and that was the last long session. Two subjects of great moment, the bank and the tariff, were then before Congress. The time of adjournment was at first fixed four or five weeks before the day on which the adjournment finally took place. He felt satisfied that it was the wish of his constituents, and of the country at large, that we should pass a few of the bills of general interest and go home. It was not desired by the people that we should stay here during the summer, and every one knew that, after the 1st of June, we could not continue in session, without hazarding our health. He would grant that little business had been done by this Congress, and he would undertake to say that if we sat three months longer, we should not pass more than half a dozen general bills. He fully believed that our constituents wished us to close the session after passing the appropriation bills and a few others of a general nature.

Mr. BURGES was in favor of the motion to postpone; but would prefer to postpone the resolution to the time when this House should consent to do something for the relief of the country.

Mr. FILLMORE hoped that a time would be fixed for the adjournment, in order that we might begin to select and set upon the most important business before the House. He did not care what time was fixed; but he hoped it would be fixed at once.

Mr. DICKSON moved the previous question, but withdrew it at the request of

Mr. BOON, who wished, he said, to reply to some of the remarks which had been made. When he introduced this resolution, he was of the opinion that, in a time of profound peace, six months was long enough for the despatch of the business of Congress, and he thought so now. If gentlemen would act, instead of debating, the business of the House would soon be despatched. But nothing could be said or done here which had not some immediate reference to the United States Bank; and unless the House would fix the day of adjournment, this kind of debate might last five or six months longer. This resolution was introduced in the ordinary way. It was not usual for the House to appoint a committee to report what business it was necessary to act upon until the day of adjournment was fixed.

We had been here five months speech-making, President-making, and Vice President-making; it had been entirely a political session, and not a session for business. To continue here was only to continue the excitement which had been got up in the country. He was sorry that he could not accept the modification proposed by the gentleman from Kentucky. There was a difference of opinion among his friends as to the time proper to be fixed, some wishing as early a day as the 31st of May, and others a day as late as the 1st of July, but he had fixed upon the middle of June, and now left it to the majority of the House to dispose of it as they pleased.

Mr. LOVE thought (he said) that the minority in the House acted injudiciously in opposing the proposition to adjourn. If the country suffers in consequence of a premature adjournment, the majority were responsible for it. Upon them, and not upon us, would fall the responsibility of leaving the country in its present condition in regard to the currency. He was willing to remain here if anything could be done. He denied, so far as he was concerned, the charge of President or Vice President making. At a former time the charge might have been true as to the business of this House, but at present the House, as well as the country, was agitated by questions of vastly greater importance.

Mr. R. M. JOHNSON said there was time enough before the day fixed in the resolution to transact the whole of the public business of importance, and go away with less confusion than they have done at any former period except that when we received our salary of $1500. That was the only session in which Congress ever did all its business and adjourned without confusion. If by prolonging the session for two months all the business could be done he would consent to it, but we could not expect to clear the whole legislative docket even if we sit to the 4th of March next. By fixing a day now for our adjournment we should be able to do ten times as much business as we should otherwise do. He considered that the tendency of this contest now was to decide the question whether the session of Congress should be made perpetual or not. The argument that all the business before Congress must be transacted at every session supposes the necessity of perpetual sessions. He would not be one to hold up the idea to the people that Congress ought to sit all the year. The Constitution did not contemplate such sessions. Further, he would remark, that a session longer than the middle of June was inconsistent with the comfort and health of the members of this body, and that the pallid countenances of many of them already indicated the prejudicial effect of their labors upon their health. He hoped that the House would fix the day of adjournment now, as it was evidently its temper to do. The Senate, as was usual, would probably take a little more time, if it was necessary.

Mr. CHILTON ALLAN had made up his mind to vote for an adjournment as soon as he should become convinced that nothing would be done for the relief of the people. He was almost convinced, by the recent rejection of the broad and liberal proposition of the member from New York, [Mr. SELDEN,] that it was determined by the majority not to do anything. It had been suggested that the bill reported from the Committee of Ways and Means would occupy some time; but he could not believe that a proposition to divide the public money among local banks, to legalize usurpation, and to repeal the Constitution, would occupy a moment's time.

The CHAIR called the member to order, for not confining his remarks to the question.

Mr. ALLAN said he would vote for the postponement, in order to give the majority time to reflect upon the responsibility they were about to assume.

Mr. EWING intended (he said) before he consented to adjourn, to attempt to bring before the House some of the business which it was its duty to transact. He was willing to leave here on the 16th of June, or at any time when Congress shall have done the necessary business of the West and the country at large. Not a bill affecting the interests of the West had yet been acted upon. We had done nothing but to make appropriations for office-holders.

Mr. CHILTON was not only in favor of an adjournment, but of an adjournment at the earliest day which had been named. His zeal to do something to quiet the agitation of the country was unabated; but he would ask gentlemen what desirable end was to be obtained by continuing the session during the summer? If there was a single gleam of hope that we should be able to effect anything for the public benefit, he would consent to prolong the session. But it was evident that we should be able to do nothing except to promote and keep up the excitement which prevails in the country. The question before the country could never be settled but by referring it back to the people. His experience had convinced him that business was much facilitated by fixing the day of adjournment. He was well satisfied that the country would see that the minority had done everything which was required of them to do, and that the responsibility rested upon the majority, who were willing to meet it.

Mr. MILLER should vote (he said) against the proposition to postpone the resolution, for the reason, that by fixing the day, we should facilitate the despatch of business. He had come to the conclusion that it was impracticable for Congress, at this session, to act on the subject of the currency; for which opinion he was about to offer some reasons, when

The CHAIR stated that the member could not go into that question.

Mr. MILLER hoped the day of adjournment would be fixed, in reference to other subjects than that of the currency, for he believed that the prospect of obtaining the definite action of Congress on that subject was very remote.

Mr. STEWART moved that the House proceed to the orders of the day.

Mr. BRIGGS demanded the yeas and nays on the question; which were ordered.

Mr. STEWART then withdrew his motion, and demanded the previous question, which was not sustained.

Mr. BELL had no desire to protract this discussion. He would, however, suggest that it might be expedient, in view of various circumstances which might arise, to prolong the session beyond the time which might now be fixed. He was not for putting it out of the power of the House to do this. Within two or three weeks, a disposition to despatch business had been manifested. Several important measures had been acted on. There were many other important measures which required the action of the House. He would never consent to put an end to a session of Congress on the ground that the House was not competent or willing to decide upon every measure required by the public interest. For some years past, it had been the fortune of the country that some great and absorbing question had seized upon almost exclusive attention, at each session of Congress. He was not willing to overlook any matter of public importance. At this time he was not prepared to decide when the House would be able to get though with such business as was necessary to be done. Two weeks hence, an opinion may be formed. It might be that the 16th of June would then receive his support as the day of adjournment. But at this time he could not fix upon that or any other precise day.

Mr. MANN said he was in favor of an early day of adjournment. He had little doubt but the House would be able to act upon all subjects of public interest by the 16th of June. But he was unable to see the force of the argument which had been urged in favor of fixing upon that day at this time. A strong disposition had been manifested by the House recently to go forward with the business. He hoped such measures as were most important—particularly those in which his own

State was interested—would be disposed of before the 16th June; but he could perceive no necessity on the part of the House for committing itself as to the precise day at this time.

Mr. BURD addressed the House at considerable length, and was understood to support the motion for postponement.

Mr. CAMBRELENG was quite as anxious as the gentleman from Kentucky [Mr. Johnson] could be to terminate the session. But when gentlemen recur to the situation of a portion of the important subject which demand the attention of Congress, they will be satisfied that the period has not yet arrived for fixing the time of adjournment. It should be recollected that the message of the President, sent to the House at the commencement of the session, was still in Committee of the Whole on the state of the Union. It had been stated that the majority of the House was responsible for the transaction of public business. If so, the majority should beware of fixing the day of adjournment before the necessary business could be completed.

After some further remarks from Messrs. BOON, EWING, and BURGES,

Mr. WAYNE said, the question was one upon which no difference of opinion ought to exist. What were the facts as to the situation of the business of the House? He had taken pains to make an abstract from the records, and it appeared that 478 bills had been originated, and were now ready for the disposal of the House; 169 had been definitely acted on by the House; and 34 bills from the Senate had been acted on. There was, therefore, no ground for any imputation of negligence upon the House. As to the discussions upon the great principles of our Government, he neither expected nor desired that they should cease. It was obvious, from the history of our Government, that the practical operation of every provision in the Constitution was not entirely foreseen. Discussion upon these subjects was, in his opinion, exceedingly profitable; and though he differed from many gentlemen in the views they had expressed, he hoped their arguments would convince the country that the public time devoted to them had not been improperly spent. He believed the people had regarded them with interest, and would fully sustain the decision of the House upon them. Our free institutions require that the fullest discussion should be given to such topics. There were several measures before both Houses of Congress which required its action before a final decision on the question of adjournment could with propriety be taken.

Mr. LANE said he regretted to differ in opinion with gentlemen with whom he usually acted, and none more so than his honorable colleague, who had introduced the resolution.

Sir, (said Mr. L.,) did he consult his own wishes or interest, he would vote for the earliest possible day of adjournment. But there were (said Mr. L.) considerations of a higher character than private interest or desire—the public good.

Mr. L. said he would not determine the question of adjournment by what had been done in the business of legislation; but from what remained to be done for the public and private interest. A postponement of the resolution does not, as some gentlemen had considered, necessarily extend the period contemplated by the resolution for the close of the session. On the contrary the House will then be able to act more advisedly upon the question.

Mr. L. said, no western gentleman could, in his opinion, consistently with the interest of his constituents, vote for the resolution, when not a bill in which the West was interested had yet been acted upon. Sir, the bill to reduce and graduate the price of the public lands—a bill in which the western people had more at stake, and felt a more lively interest in than any other—is undecided. There is another bill, until acted upon, he would never agree to leave the House—the one reported by the Committee of Ways and Means in relation to the public deposites. Every consideration of public duty required action upon the subject. There was (said Mr. L.,) another objection. By the passage of this resolution the House placed itself in the power of the Senate, to do which he would not consent, however great his confidence in that body might be, while so many bills of vast importance remained to be disposed of.

Mr. VANDERPOEL said he was sorry that he could not vote for the motion of his friend and colleague, [Mr. CAMBRELENG,] for whose opinions and views upon this floor he cherished that respect which was due to much greater experience in matters of legislation than he (Mr. V.) could boast; but he (Mr. V.) was decidedly in favor of fixing upon some day certain for the adjournment of Congress. Mr. V. would not say that he would prefer the day proposed by the resolution to any other day earlier or more remote; but he believed that it would conduce to the acceleration of the public business, to the dispensation with, or, at all events, to the abbreviation of many speeches with which gentlemen were still laden, if we now prescribed to ourselves a certain period within which our duties here must be executed. We would then be more apt to stop speaking, when we had finished thinking; and would, practically, pay more respect than we had been accustomed to pay to the maxim, that "Brevity is the soul of wit." After all, (said Mr. V.,) with all our vaunted wisdom, we are nothing, Mr. Speaker, but full-grown boys; and all experience teaches us that both boys and men will invariably execute more within a given period, when they are stinted, than when they are at liberty to dispose of matters at their leisure; and if we fix upon a day when our labors here are to terminate, we will inevitably redouble our diligence, and accomplish all that the interest of our constituents requires us to execute.

The gentleman from Georgia [Mr. WAYNE] has, to be sure, presented us with a pretty formidable calendar of unfinished business, and protests at the same time against the inference that we have not hitherto been diligent. Mr. V. said he should not regret it, if we were to go home without acting upon a majority of those bills; that he had long believed that excessive legislation in this country was an evil, and that, as an ordinary rule, if a balance were struck at the end of each session, the sins of commission, of legislative bodies, would much overbalance their sins of omission. Mr. V. said he was happy to perceive, from recent indications here, that there was a growing disposition to go about and execute the business that our constituents sent us here to transact, instead of spending the time with interminable panic speeches. Yes, (said Mr. V.,) it has become rather an uphill business to make a panic-speech here now; and the spirit is disinclined to grind out their grists. Would the number of petitions for further legislation cease, if we sat here till doomsday? But most anxious to bring the business of the session to a close, and return to his family, and no one could personally have lost to gain by postponing the period of adjournment, then he had. The close of a session of Congress, experienced by many to be one of the most important since the organization of the Government, was a question in which public duty must prevail over private gratification. It was almost five weeks to the 16th of June, the day of adjournment named in the resolution, and if we refused to postpone, and adopted the resolution, it was an act which we could not recall, and we thereby put ourselves entirely in the power of the other branch of the Legislature, who might, or might not, concur with us, as its members saw fit. His objection was not to the proposed time of adjournment, (he hoped and believed the House would be in a situation to adjourn by the 16th of June;) his objection was to fixing the day five weeks in advance, when the time could be determined two weeks hence, with far greater safety to the public interest than at this moment. Public events of great magnitude and moment might occur in the course of two weeks, which might lead us to regret our hasty and premature action. Gentlemen had intimated their determination not to adjourn until something shall be done to relieve the country. This idea of relieving the country so often repeated and reiterated, both here and elsewhere, was quite a vexed question, upon which a wide difference of opinion prevailed, and probably would prevail, until it was finally and effectually decided (as he trusted it would be) by the people. If gentlemen meant by "relieving the country," a restoration of the public deposites, or a recharter of the Bank of the United States, he would ask, what hope was there of accomplishing either of those purposes short of a new expression of the popular will? What hope was there of reversing the opinions and votes of those who, in resisting both those measures, believed, and honestly believed, they were fulfilling an obligation which they owed to their constituents and the country, and which would ultimately be sanctioned and sustained by the voice of public approbation? He would not transgress the order of the House by departing from the question of postponement under consideration. He would therefore vote for the motion of his honorable colleague, [Mr. CAMBRELENG,] in the hope that, at the expiration of two weeks, the day of adjournment might be settled for the 16th of June, the earliest day proposed.

Mr. HARDIN did not assent to the statement of his colleague, [Mr. LANE,] that the responsibility of not acting upon the measures before the House rested upon the majority. Upon a great portion of the most important questions, dividing the party was involved, and the responsibility of neglecting such measures rested upon both sides.

A further explanation was made by Messrs. EWING, BOON, and BURGES.

Mr. WARD was in favor of adjourning at the earliest possible day, but it was impossible to say whether the essential business could be completed by the 16th of next month. The most important business was generally postponed until near the end of the session. Investigation and arrangement was necessary before business could go forward. Twelve days before the close of the last session, only ten bills had been passed. On the last day, one hundred bills were passed.

After a remark from Mr. BEARDSLEY against the motion to postpone, the question was taken, and carried by the following vote:

YEAS—Messrs. Heman Allen, Chilton Allan, Anthony, Barnitz, Barringer, Beaumont, John Bell, Jas. M. Bell, Blair, Bouldin, Brown, Bull, Bunch, Burges, Cambreleng, Chambers, Chinn, William Clarke, Clay, Cleaveland, Coffee, Connor, Corwin, Cramer, Crane, Crockett, Davenport, Day, Deberry, Denny, Dickerson, Duncan, Dunlap, Evans, Horace Everett, Ewing, Philo C. Fuller, Fulton, Galbraith, Gillet, Gilmer, Gordon, Graham, Joseph Hall, Hamer, Hardin, Joseph M. Harper, Hathaway, Hawes, Howell, Abel Huntington, Jackson, Jarvis, William Cost Johnson, Noadiah Johnson, Seaborn Jones, King, Klenard, Lane, Laporte, Thomas Lee, Lincoln, Lewis, Lucas, Abijah Mann, Joel K. Mann, Martindale, Marshall, John Y. Mason, Moses Mason, McCarty, McKay, McKennan, McLene, McVean, Mercer, Joseph Hall, Hamer, Hardin, Joseph M. Harper, Morris, Murphy, Osgood, Patton, Parks, Patton, Patterson, Peyton, Franklin Pierce, Peyton, Pinckney, Plummer, Polk, Potts, Reencher, Schley, Shinn, William Slade, Charles Slade, Sloane, Spangler, Standifer, Sutherland, F. Thomas, Philemon Thomas, Thomson, Tompkins, Turner, Vance, Van Houten, Wayne, Whallon, Edward D. White, Wm. Williams, and Wise—116.

NAYS—Messrs. John Quincy Adams, John J. Allen, William Allen, Archer, Ashley, Barber, Bates, Beylies, Bean, Beardsley, Binney, Bodle, Boon, Briggs, Burns, Byron, Cage, Carr, Casey, Chaney, Chilton, Choate, Samuel Clark, Clayton, Coulter, Darlington, A. Davis, Deming, Dickson, Dickinson, Edward Everett, Felder, Fillmore, Foster, Fowler, William E. Fuller, Gamble, Garland, Gholson, Gorham, Grey-

son, Grennell, Griffin, Hiland Hall, Halsey, Hannegan, Hard, James Harper, Harrison, Hawkins, Hazeltine, Henderson, Hiester, Hubbard, Jabez W. Huntington, Richard M. Johnson, Cave Johnson, Benjamin Jones, Kavanagh, Lansing, Lay, Lane Lea, Lincoln, Love, Loyall, Lyon, Mardis, McComas, McIntire, McKim, McKinley, Miller, Milligan, Muhlenberg, Parker, Pierson, Pope, Ramsey, Reed, Schenck, William B. Shepard, Smith, Speight, William Taylor, Wm. P. Taylor, Turrill, Tweedy, Vanderpoel, Vinton, Wagener, Ward, Wardwell, Webster, Campbell P. White, Elisha Whittlesey, and Wilson—98.

The SPEAKER laid before the House a communication from the Secretary of the Treasury, covering certain returns relative to public lands; which was laid on the table, and ordered to be printed.

Also, a communication from the Secretary of the Navy, enclosing rules and regulations respecting naval hospitals; which was laid on the table, and ordered to be printed. And

A message from the President, enclosing a copy of a treaty with the Republic of Chili; which was referred to the Committee on Foreign Affairs.

INDIAN AFFAIRS.

The bill reported from the Committee of the Whole on the state of the Union, making appropriations for the Indian department for 1834, came up, on concurring with the amendments made in committee.

The amendments, excepting that appropriating $6,000 for the expense of forming a treaty with the western Pawnee, were concurred in.

That amendment having been stated—

Mr. ASHLEY said he was totally opposed to the appropriation of money for the purpose of buying peace with the Indians. There was no necessity for it. If they were disposed for hostilities, Congress, at its last session, had provided ample means for putting them down. The corps of dragoons had been raised to meet exigencies of this kind. If we should give them $6,000 for peace this year, it would require $16,000 next year, and the demands upon us would go on in that ratio.

Mr. LEWIS said, the object of the appropriation was, to enable the commissioners to redeem the prisoners they had taken. This tribe resided at the extreme west of our territory, and he had been informed by Governor Stokes that they possessed the fleetest horses perhaps in the world. The only way in which our fellow-citizens could be liberated, was to redeem them.

Mr. VANCE entirely concurred in the views expressed by the gentleman from Missouri, [Mr. ASHLEY.] If prisoners taken by Indians are redeemed, it will prove the most effectual inducement for them to capture our citizens. In his view, it would be one of the worst acts that could be done.

Mr. ASHLEY said he required to learn, from the authority of one of the commissioners, of the fleetness of these Indian horses. He professed to have some knowledge of these matters, and had generally found these Indian horses vary inferior animals. But, whatever their horses might be, he was opposed to the principle of the appropriation. The officer who commanded the regiment of dragoons was an exceedingly competent man to arrange all difficulties with these Indians, without this appropriation.

The question was then taken upon the amendment, and it was non-concurred in, and consequently struck from the bill. The bill was then ordered to be engrossed for a third reading.

On motion of Mr. STEWART, the House then went into Committee of the Whole on the state of the Union, Mr. J. Q. ADAMS in the chair.

Mr. McKIM moved that the committee take up the bill for continuing and repairing the Cumberland road, and for continuing several Territorial and military roads for 1834.

Mr. STEWART suggested the propriety of taking up the bill from the Senate relative to the Cumberland road.

Mr. McKIM assented to the proposition, as it embraced a portion of the same objects. The bill was read, and no amendment being proposed, it was laid aside.

Mr. HUBBARD moved that the harbor bill be then taken up.

The bill was read.

Mr. HUBBARD moved sundry amendments, among them $10,000 for the harbor of Mobile, and $50,000 for Savannah river.

After some remarks from Messrs. H. EVERETT, SPEIGHT, HUBBARD, MERCER, WILLIAMS, WAYNE, CAMBRELENG, McKAY, E. WHITTLESEY, and HALL, the question being then taken on the amendment to the amendment, it was rejected.

The question being taken on the amendment, it was carried.

Mr. HUBBARD moved an amendment, submitted on the 18th February, making appropriations for continuing, completing, and securing different works and improvements in different harbors and rivers, principally on the lakes.

The question being on the first clause of the amendment, "For continuing and securing the works at Oswego harbor, New York, $30,000"—

Mr McKAY made some objections to it, and Mr. E. WHITTLESEY spoke at some length in its support.

Mr. McKINLEY then moved that the committee rise, and report the Cumberland road bill, but Mr. McKAY objecting,

Mr. McKINLEY moved that the committee rise; which was agreed to.

The committee rose, and reported progress, and The House adjourned.

IN SENATE.
FRIDAY, May 16, 1834.

Under a rule of the Senate, Fridays and Saturdays are appropriated to the consideration of bills. A bill supplementary to an act entitled "An act to alter and amend the several acts imposing duties on imports," approved July 14, 1832, was ordered to be engrossed for a third reading.

On motion of Mr. NAUDAIN, the Senate suspended the previous orders, and took up bill No. 61, for the relief of Elizabeth Robinson, daughter of Lieutenant Richard Wilde, of the army of the Revolution.

[This was a claim for arrears of half-pay by the heir of Lieutenant Wilde, who was wounded at the battle of Germantown, and who died in 1786. The only question was whether interest should be allowed on the claim, Lieutenant Wilde not having brought himself within the provisions of the resolution of Congress of 1776, requiring the claim to be presented.]

Messrs. NAUDAIN and CHAMBERS advocated the allowance of interest, and Messrs. WHITE, SMITH, SHEPLEY, and CALHOUN, opposed it.

Mr. NAUDAIN offered an amendment to allow the interest; upon which Mr. WHITE asked the yeas and nays; which were ordered, and are as follows, to wit:

YEAS—Messrs. Chambers, Clayton, Kent, McKean, Naudain, Robbins, Silsbee, Wilkins—8.

NAYS—Messrs. Bell, Benton, Bibb, Brown, Calhoun, Forsyth, Frelinghuysen, Grundy, Hendricks, Hill, Kane, King of Alabama, King of Georgia, Knight, Linn, Mangum, Moore, Morris, Poindexter, Porter, Prentiss, Preston, Robinson, Shepley, Smith, Sprague, Swift, Tallmadge, Tomlinson, Tyler, White, Wright—32.

Mr. CLAYTON then offered an amendment granting two thousand dollars in lieu of all claims for the revolutionary services of said Wilde.

Upon this amendment Mr. WHITE asked the yeas and nays; which were ordered, and are as follows, to wit:

YEAS—Messrs. Chambers, Clay, Clayton, Frelinghuysen, Hendricks, Kent, McKean, Naudain, Poindexter, Porter, Prentiss, Robbins, Silsbee, Tipton, Wilkins—15.

NAYS—Messrs. Benton, Bibb, Brown, Calhoun, Forsyth, Grundy, Hill, Kane, King of Alabama, King of Georgia, Knight, Linn, Mangum, Moore, Morris, Preston, Robinson, Smith, Shepley, Swift, Tallmadge, Tomlinson, Tyler, White, Wright—25.

The bill was then ordered to be engrossed for a third reading, by the following vote, to wit:

YEAS—Messrs. Bell, Chambers, Clay, Clayton, Frelinghuysen, Hendricks, Kent, Knight, Linn, Moore, Naudain, Poindexter, Porter, Prentiss,

ties, Robbins, Silsbee, Smith, Sprague, Swift, Tipton, Tomlinson, White, Wilkins—23.

NAYS—Messrs. Benton, Bibb, Brown, Calhoun, Forsyth, Grundy, Hill, Kane, King of Alabama, King of Georgia, Mangum, Morris, Preston, Robinson, Shepley, Tallmadge, Tyler, Wright—18.

On motion of Mr. TYLER, the bill for the relief of John S. Flemming, the administrator of John Byne, deceased, was considered as in Committee of the Whole, and ordered to be engrossed for a third reading.

On motion of Mr. WILKINS, it was Ordered, That when the Senate adjourn it shall stand adjourned until Monday next.

Mr. CHAMBERS moved to take up the bill appropriating $250,000 for constructing a lateral railroad from the Baltimore and Ohio railroad to Washington; which was agreed to.

Mr. CHAMBERS then moved an amendment as a proviso to the second section, allowing the Postmaster General to transport the mail in any other way he may think proper, than on this road, and then terminate the compensation.

While the question was pending, Mr. BENTON, at five o'clock, moved that the Senate adjourn; which was agreed to.

The Senate then adjourned.

HOUSE OF REPRESENTATIVES.
FRIDAY, May 16, 1834.

Mr. CHILTON moved to suspend the rules of the House, to enable him to offer a resolution providing that during the remainder of the session the hour of meeting of the House shall be ten o'clock, A. M.

The motion was lost without a division.

Mr. SEABORN JONES, on leave, presented a petition for the establishment of a post route; which was referred to the Committee on the Post Office and Post Roads.

Mr. CHINN by leave presented a presentment of the grand jury of the county of Alexandria; which was referred to the Committee on the District of Columbia.

Mr. DEMING, from the Committee on Claims, reported a bill for the relief of the widow of Samuel Sutherland; which was read twice and committed.

Mr. C. P. WHITE, from the Committee on Naval Affairs, reported a bill providing for the rebuilding of the frigate Congress; which was read twice and committed.

MR. MARDIS'S RESOLUTION.

The resolution heretofore submitted by Mr. MARDIS, relative to the public deposites, and the proposition of Mr. CHAMBERS, to amend, was then taken up.

Mr. GALBRAITH then resumed his speech, in reply to Mr. McKENNAN, which he continued until the expiration of the hour appropriated to morning business.

Mr. PLUMMER moved to suspend the rules, in order to enable Mr. G. to conclude his remarks business. The motion was carried—ayes 101, noes 44.

Mr. G. then proceeded, and finished his remarks about one o'clock.

Mr. STEWART rose and said, at the rate this debate had gone on, it would probably occupy the whole session. As the Committee of Ways and Means had reported upon this subject, the necessity for the resolution was entirely superseded. He therefore moved to lay the resolution on the table.

The CHAIR suggested that the question could not be entertained unless the rules were suspended, this day being appropriated to private business.

Mr. BOON moved the suspension of the rules for that purpose.

This motion was carried—ayes 115, noes 93.

After a discussion upon a question of order, in which Messrs. PLUMMER, J. Q. ADAMS, and CLAY, took part.

Mr. STEWART withdrew the motion, which was renewed by Mr. MOORE.

Mr. PLUMMER objected that the motion could not again be made, the rules having been specially suspended to enable Mr. STEWART to make it.

After a discussion on the point of order, in

which Messrs. ADAMS, CLAY, and PLUM-
MER, took part—

The CHAIR (temporarily occupied by Mr.
HUBBARD) decided that the rules had been suspended to enable this motion to be made generally,
without personal reference to the gentleman from
Pennsylvania.

Mr. ADAMS appealed from this decision.

Mr. VANCE moved to reconsider the vote sus-
pending the rules—which was decided by the
Chair not to be in order pending the appeal of Mr.
Adams.

. The appeal was discussed by Messrs. ADAMS,
PLUMMER, EVANS, VINTON, and HUN-
TINGTON—

When Mr. MOORE withdrew the motion to lay
on the table—which was immediately renewed by
Mr. CLAYTON.

The discussion on the point of order was continued by Messrs. WAYNE, VINTON, VANCE,
BRIGGS, PLUMMER, WILLIAMS, and
GRENNELL, when the question was taken on
the appeal.

The yeas and nays having been ordered, the
decision of the Chair was sustained—yeas 149,
nays 13.

Mr. VANCE'S motion to reconsider the vote by
which the rules were suspended, then came up.

This motion was negatived: yeas 57, nays 105.

The question of laying the resolution on the
table, then came up. Having been stated—

Mr. McKENNAN called for a division of the
question.

The CHAIR decided that the question was not
divisible by the rules of the House.

Mr. McKENNAN appealed.

The appeal was discussed by Messrs. EVANS,
WILLIAMS, FILLMORE, and BURGES, when
Mr. McKENNAN withdrew the appeal.

The question having been stated upon laying
the resolutions and amendment upon the table—

Mr. CORWIN withdrew his amendment to the
resolution—when

Mr. MARDIS said the subject of the resolution
having been reported on, he withdrew the resolution.

On motion of Mr. POLK, the House went into
Committee of the Whole on the state of the Union,
upon the harbor bill, the Cumberland road bill,
and the bill making appropriations for fortifications, Mr. JOHN Q. ADAMS in the chair.

The question being upon the motion of Mr.
MERCER, to reconsider the vote adopting an
amendment to the harbor bill, making an appropriation of $15,000 for connecting the waters of
La Plaisance bay with those of the river Raisin,
some debate took place, in which Messrs. MER-
CER, EVANS, E. WHITTLESEY, SUTHER-
LAND, LYON of Michigan, and HUBBARD,
took part; when the motion to reconsider was rejected—41 to 84.

Mr. LOVE moved that the committee rise.
Lost.

The question then being upon the amendment
submitted by Mr. HUBBARD, for continuing,
completing, and securing the works and improvements in certain rivers and harbors,`

. Mr. EVANS called for further information from
the gentleman from New Hampshire in regard to
each item of the amendment.

Mr. HUBBARD made explanations, at some
length, on the subject.

After further discussion, in which Messrs.
EVANS and FILLMORE took part, the amendment was agreed to.

Mr. MERCER moved to amend the bill by inserting the following clause: " For defraying expenses for surveys, under the act of 30th May,
1824, $30,000.''

Mr. HUBBARD named $12,000 as the estimate
made by the War Department for surveys.

Mr. STEWART moved to amend the amendment by adding $5,000 for geological surveys;
which was rejected.

Mr. HUBBARD moved to add to the amendment the words, " including arrearages for 1833,''
which was adopted as a modification of the amendment, and the amendment was then adopted.

Mr. POPE moved to amend the bill by adding
the clause, " For the improvement of the harbor of
St. Louis, $40,000.''

Mr. ASHLEY supported the amendment, and,

after a few remarks from Mr. HUBBARD, the
question was put and the amendment was rejected.

Mr. HUBBARD offered an amendment, appro-
priating $29,000 for the improvement of Deep
Creek, the northern outlet of the Dismal Swamp
Canal; which was agreed to.

Mr. CAVE JOHNSON moved an amendment,
making an appropriation for removing obstructions
in the Cumberland river.

Mr. CROCKETT moved an amendment to the
amendment; which was pronounced out of order.

The question being taken, the amendment was
negatived.

Mr. BEATTY moved to amend the bill by
inserting a clause appropriating $50,000 for im-
proving the navigation of Cumberland river to
the highest point of steamboat navigation.

Messrs. CHILTON, C. ALLAN, and PEY-
TON, supported the amendment, and Mr. PAR-
KER opposed it.

The amendment was lost: ayes 60, noes 65.

Mr. CROCKETT offered an amendment, appropriating $60,000 to improve the navigation of
Forked, Deer, Hatchie, and Obion rivers, to be
expended equally on each.

Mr. CROCKETT supported the amendment at
length.

The amendment was rejected without a division.

Mr. HAWES moved an amendment, appropriating $25,000 to improve the navigation of Green
and Big Barren rivers, in the State of Kentucky.

Mr. H. explained his proposition.

The amendment was rejected without a division.

Mr. LANE moved an amendment for improving
the navigation of White Otter river, in the State of
Indiana, $10,000.

The amendment was rejected.

Mr. MANN moved the committee rise, and report the bill to the House; which was carried—
ayes 86, noes 58.

The committee accordingly rose, and

Mr. THOMSON moved that the vote by which
the time of adjournment was yesterday postponed
two weeks, be reconsidered, and that the question
be postponed until Tuesday next.

Before the question upon postponement was
decided—

The House adjourned.

HOUSE OF REPRESENTATIVES.

SATURDAY, May 17, 1834.

Mr. WATMOUGH, from the Select Committee,
to which was referred the bill to equalize the pay
of the officers of the army and navy, reported the
bill with an amendment; and, on his motion, it was
committed to the Committee of the Whole on the
state of the Union, and, together with the report
and accompanying documents, ordered to be printed.

Mr. WATMOUGH asked leave to notify the
House that, with their permission, he desired to
bring up the bill for consideration on Tuesday
next.

Mr. DUNCAN, from the Committee on Public
Lands, reported a bill to authorize the heirs and
representatives of James Latham, deceased, to
correct an erroneous entry of land. Read twice,
and postponed till Tuesday next.

Mr. PINCKNEY, from the Committee on Commerce, reported a bill, in addition to an act passed
on the 30th of July, 1832, concerning the tonnage
duty on Spanish vessels. Read twice, committed
to the Committee of the Whole on the state of the
Union, and, with the report, ordered to be printed.

Mr. CHILTON moved that the Committee of
the Whole be discharged from the further consideration of the bill extending the provisions of the
pension act of 1832 to those who served in the Indian wars, and refer the same to the Committee of
the Whole on the state of the Union. Lost.

The CHAIR stated the question before the
House as undecided yesterday, was, on the motion of the gentleman from Ohio, [Mr. THOMSON,]
to postpone the consideration of his motion to reconsider the vote by which the House postponed,
till the 29th instant, the consideration of the resolution for the adjournment of Congress.

Mr. THOMSON modified the motion so as to
postpone the consideration of the motion till Thursday.

Mr. BOON being in favor, as he said, of the im-

mediate consideration of the subject, asked for the
yeas and nays, and they were ordered.

Mr. EVANS said we had spent much time in
the consideration of this subject, and it had been
decided by a large majority; and we were now
likely to spend two or three hours upon it; he
moved to lay the motion on the table.

Mr. BRIGGS asked the yeas and nays on the
motion to lay on the table, and they were ordered.

The question being taken, it was determined in
the negative: yeas 77, nays 87.

So the House refused to lay the motion on the
table.

Mr. THOMSON said, as it was evident that
much time would be occupied by the subject, he
would withdraw the motion to reconsider.

Mr. R. M. JOHNSON rose to a point of order.
Can a member, he asked, who had moved a reconsideration, in which other members are interested, and which motion other members would
have made, rise up and withdraw it?

The CHAIR. He can, sir. A member may
modify or withdraw his motion until the House
amends it, which takes it out of the power of the
member.

Mr. JOHNSON. Is it in order for any other
member to renew the motion?

The CHAIR. No. The time has passed.

On motion of Mr. MERCER, the joint resolution, giving to the Winchester Railroad Company
the right of way through the United States land
at Harper's Ferry, was taken up, amended, and
passed.

The bill for the relief of Samuel A. Bailey was
read a third time and passed.

On motion of Mr. HUBBARD, the House went
into Committee of the Whole on the state of the
Union on the harbor bill, Mr. J. Q. ADAMS in the
chair.

Mr. DENNY moved to amend the bill by providing an appropriation of $25,000 for the im-
provement of the navigation of the Ohio from Louisville to Pittsburg, and advocated the motion at
some length.

Mr. DENNY, after some remarks, suggested
a modification of the amendment, providing that
$10,000 of the sum shall be expended in the re-
moval of obstructions from the Missouri river.

After some discussion, in which Messrs. MER-
CER, HUBBARD, VINTON, and POPE took
part,

Mr. DENNY modified his amendment, by providing that the Secretary of War should expend
such part of the sum of $75,000, appropriated for
the improvement of the navigation of the Mississippi, Missouri, and Ohio rivers, as he might think
proper, upon the removal of obstructions from the
harbor of St. Louis.

The debate was continued by Messrs. REED,
POPE, MERCER, and ASHLEY.

Mr. DENNY withdrew the modification of
his amendment in relation to the harbor of St.
Louis.

The question was then taken on Mr. DENNY'S
amendment. It was rejected.

Mr. SEVIER moved an additional clause, appropriating $30,000 for the improvement of the
navigation of the Arkansas river. Lost.

Mr. MILLIGAN asked information from the
committee who reported the bill, why the bill did
not appropriate for the Delaware breakwater the
whole sum which was recommended by the War
Department.

Mr. HUBBARD replied, that the department
recommended an appropriation of $380,000, but
the committee did not think it proper to appropriate more than the same sum which was appropriated last year; and they believed that a larger sum
than $270,000, the sum appropriated, would not
be necessary for carrying on the work during the
present year.

After a few remarks from Messrs. MILLIGAN,
SUTHERLAND, and HUBBARD,

Mr. MILLIGAN moved to strike out $270,000,
and insert $380,000.

Mr. HARPER, of Pennsylvania, supported the
amendment. He had been told by the superintendent, (he said,) that half a million of dollars a
year might be advantageously expended on the
work; and he urged the policy of finishing the
work as speedily as possible, both in reference to

economy and to the safety of our navigation. He
stated that the work would be completed at an expense within the amount of the original estimate,
which was two millions, one million of which had
been expended.

Mr. WARDWELL wished (he said) to see the
report on the resolution calling for information as
to the manner in which the large sums appropriated for this work had been expended.

Mr. CHILTON ALLAN would (he said) take
a hint in favor of economy, in application to this
subject, from the gentleman who had just voted
against an appropriation of $25,000 for the west-
ern waters. The amendment was rejected.

Mr. ASHLEY moved to amend the following
clause: " For improving the navigation of the Ohio,
' Missouri, and Mississippi rivers, fifty thousand
' dollars," so as to read as follows:

For improving the navigation of the Ohio, Missouri, and Mississippi rivers, *including the improvement of the harbor of St. Louis*, seventy-five
thousand dollars.

The amendment was rejected.

Mr. HUNTINGTON moved to add a clause to
the bill appropriating $30,000 for improving the
navigation of the Thames river, between New London and Norwich. Rejected.

Mr. H. also moved to amend, by inserting the
clause following: " For the improvement of the
harbor of Westbrook, in Connecticut, $20,000."
Lost.

Mr. WHITE, of Louisiana, moved to add $20,-
000 to the appropriation of $50,000 for the improve-
ment of the navigation of Red river.

Mr. ASHLEY was sorry that the gentleman
had not moved a hundred thousand dollars. The
removal of the raft from the Red river would improve the health of the country, facilitate its settlement, and increase the amount of the sales of the
public lands to millions. One hundred thousand
dollars now appropriated at once, would remove
the obstruction; but if we appropriated a smaller
sum yearly, it would cost more. The raft, which
was a collection of trees, &c., extending for a
hundred and fifty miles, was every year increasing.
He moved to increase the appropriation to a hundred thousand dollars.

After some remarks from Messrs. MERCER,
SEVIER, BINNEY, HUBBARD, and GAR-
LAND, the amendment was adopted—ayes 66,
noes 66.

Mr. WATMOUGH moved to add $10,000 for
the erection of piers at Delaware city, on the river
Delaware; which was negatived.

Mr. EWING offered an amendment appropriating $1,000 for the survey of White Outer river,
Indiana.

Mr. E. explained the amendment.

The question was taken, and the amendment

Mr. CARR moved an amendment to appropriate $25,000 to improve the Indian Chute through
the falls of the Ohio river.

Mr. CARR explained the object of the amendment, which he regarded as extremely important
to the navigation.

After a few remarks in opposition to it by Mr.
MERCER, the question was taken, and the amendment was negatived.

The bill was laid aside, and ordered to be revised, with the amendments.

FORTIFICATION BILL.

Mr. POLK moved that the committee take up
a bill making appropriations for certain fortifications for the year 1834.

Mr. POLK moved to strike out $34,770 for the
reservation of Castle Island and repair of Fort
Independence, and insert $17,594.

Mr. POLK explained that the sum proposed
to be proposed on the ground that the work was
to be reconstructed, but repaired, and was believed to be sufficient for that purpose.

Mr. GORHAM opposed the amendment, explained the condition of Boston harbor, and inquired what was proposed to be done as to the
work on George's Island.

Mr. POLK said that of a former appropriation
$25,000 only between $1,000 and $2,000 had
been expended for the fortification on George's
land. As the public interest will not probably
far, he should propose to strike out the appro-

priation in the present bill, in order that the subject might be taken up at another session.

Messrs. PARKER, GORHAM, and R. M.
JOHNSON, went into a prolonged discussion on
the fortifications of Boston harbor; when

Mr. P. THOMAS moved, the committee rise;
which was carried.

The Cumberland road bill and the harbor bill
were reported to the House, with the amendments,
and progress upon the fortification bill.

Mr. POLK moved the bills reported be printed,
with the amendments; which was agreed to.

Mr. MERCER moved to suspend the rules, to
enable him to offer a resolution for adjourning
over from Thursday next to the ensuing Monday,
in order to give an opportunity to purify and place
matting on the floor of the House; which was carried: Ayes 99, noes 35.

Mr. PARKER was opposed to making preparation for a summer session.

Mr. HAWES supported the resolution; which
was adopted: Ayes 95, noes 39.

The House then adjourned.

IN SENATE.

MONDAY, *May* 19, 1834.

The VICE PRESIDENT communicated the following documents from the Treasury Department:

1. Transmitting a statement of the amount of
public deposites in the Bank of Alexandria, at the
time when it suspended specie payments.

2. A communication in compliance with a resolution of the Senate making inquiry as to a supposed opinion given by the Attorney General to
the Secretary of the Treasury in the year 1829,
1830, or 1831.

3. A report in compliance with the resolution of
the 5th instant, on the subject of transfer drafts.

4. Transmitting the weekly and monthly reports
of the Bank of the United States, and the State
banks selected as the depositories of the public
funds.

These communications were, on motion of Mr.
CLAY, referred to the Committee on Finance, and
ordered to be printed.

PETITIONS.

The VICE PRESIDENT presented a memorial
from inhabitants of Bergen county, New Jersey,
in favor of the Executive measures in reference to
the Bank of the United States; which was read,
and, on motion of Mr. FRELINGHUYSEN, was
referred to the Committee on Finance, and ordered
to be printed.

Mr. PRENTISS presented the remonstrance of
certain citizens of Vermont to the bill renewing a
patent of John Ames, paper-maker;

Mr. SILSBEE presented a similar remonstrance
from inhabitants of Massachusetts; and

Mr. CHAMBERS one from citizens of Maryland; all of which were laid upon the table.

Mr. TYLER presented the memorial of sundry
ship-owners and others, praying the establishment
of a naval hospital at City Point, Virginia; which
was referred to the Committee on Commerce.

Mr. WRIGHT presented the petition of A. D.
Ostrander; which was referred to the Committee
on Naval Affairs.

Mr. McKEAN presented a memorial from some
citizens of Pennsylvania, praying an alteration in
the patent laws; which was referred to the Committee on the Judiciary.

Mr. McKEAN presented a memorial from inhabitants of Dauphin county, Pennsylvania, praying the establishment of a post route; which was
referred to the Committee on the Post Office and
Post Roads.

Mr. MOORE presented the petition of Henry
Smith; which was referred to the Committee on
Public Lands.

Mr. SPRAGUE presented the petition of John
How; which was referred to the Committee on the
Judiciary.

Mr. TOMLINSON presented the petition of
Edward Blake; which was referred to the Committee on Pensions.

Mr. EWING presented a memorial from certain inhabitants of Belmont county, Ohio, praying
a restoration of the deposites to the Bank of the
United States, and a recharter of that institution;
which was read, referred to the Committee on Finance, and ordered to be printed.

Mr. KENT presented the memorial of John
Kurtz, surviving partner of Bowie & Kurtz; which
was referred to the Committee on Claims.

Mr. BENTON presented the petition of Mary
McNair; which was referred to the Committee on
Pensions.

REPORTS.

Mr. CHAMBERS, from the Committee on the
District of Columbia, asked to be discharged from
the further consideration of the petitions of Noble
Young and others, and John Thomas Towers;
which was agreed to.

Mr. POINDEXTER, from the Committee on
Public Lands, reported a bill without amendment
from the House, relative to public lands in Michigan Territory.

Mr. POINDEXTER, from the same commit-
tee, asked to be discharged from the further consideration of the petitions of Charles Vandiford,
and Andre Frederick; which was agreed to.

Mr. WILKINS, from the Committee on Finance, reported a bill remitting the duties on a set
of bells, imported from France for the use of the
Roman Catholic Church in St. Louis, Missouri.

Mr. BENTON asked the Senate to take up and
pass the bill at this time, as it had undergone the
examination of the committee, and the passage of
such bills was generally a matter of course.

The bill was taken up for consideration, when

Mr. WILKINS stated that the committee
had examined the subject, and that there were
numerous precedents on the statute book to justify
the remission of the duties in this instance. The
bells were not obtained on speculation, but were
presented by a French gentleman to the Roman
Catholic Church in St. Louis, and it was believed
by the citizens of that city that they would be
found a useful accession to them.

The bill was passed to a third reading.

Mr. PRENTISS, from the Committee on Pensions, reported a bill for the relief of Carey Clark.

The bill was read, and the report ordered to be
printed.

Mr. SHEPLEY, from the Committee on Revolutionary Claims, reported bills—

For the relief of the heirs of Everard Meade,
with amendments;

For the relief of William Rogers; and

For the relief of General John H. Stone.

Mr. TOMLINSON, from the Committee on
Claims, reported a bill from the House for the relief of Benedict Alford and others; and stated
that he was instructed by the committee, when the
bill was called up, to move its indefinite postponement.

The following resolutions were submitted:

By Mr. BIBB:

Resolved, That the Committee on Military Affairs be instructed to inquire into the expediency
of giving suitable testimonials to Major George
Croghan, (now a colonel in the army of the United
States,) and to the officers and soldiers under his
command, for their gallantry and good conduct in
defending Fort Sandusky against the attack by the
combined forces of British and Indians, during the
last war.

By Mr. BIBB:

Resolved, That the Committee on the Judiciary
be instructed to inquire into the expediency of providing for recording the opinions of the Judges of
the Supreme Court of the United States before
they are delivered to the reporter.

The resolutions of Mr. B. were considered and
agreed to.

By Mr. LINN:

Resolved, That the Committee on Commerce be
instructed to inquire into the expediency of making
an appropriation for the building and support of a
marty hospital, to be erected in the town of Cape
Girardeau, or city of St. Louis, in the State of
Missouri.

By Mr. LINN:

Resolved, That the Committee on Claims be instructed to inquire into the expediency of making
compensation to the recorder of land titles at St.
Louis, Missouri, for extra clerk hire, office rent,
fuel for office, and plating instruments, furnished
and paid for by said recorder, between October
13th, 1830, to the 30th September, 1832.

By Mr. LINN:

Resolved, That the Committee on the Post Office

and Post Roads be instructed to inquire into the expediency of establishing a post route from Jefferson City, in the State of Missouri, to pass through the seats of justice of Morgan, Pulaski, and Green counties, in said State, to the seat of justice of Washington county, Arkansas Territory.

By Mr SPRAGUE:

Resolved, That the commissioners under the late treaty with France be requested to communicate to the Senate the amount of the claims which have been presented to them, specifying the number of vessels and cargoes; the number of memorials; and distinguishing into classes those memorials which have been accepted; those which have been suspended; those which have been rejected for defects in form; those which have been rejected for defects in substance; and specifying the amount of principal and interest claimed by the memorialists, in each class; also, the number of cases that have been acted and adjudicated upon, distinguishing those that have been adjudged good, from those that have been finally rejected.

GENERAL ORDERS.

The resolutions heretofore submitted by Messrs. WAGGAMAN and McKEAN were taken up and adopted.

The bill granting compensation to J. & W. Beeson and others, was read a first and second time.

The bill making appropriation for the Indian Department was read a first and second time, and referred to the Committee on Indian Affairs.

The resolution authorizing the purchase of thirteen copies of the American State Papers, published by Gales & Seaton, was read a third time and passed.

The bill modifying the laws relative to insolvent debtors, was ordered to be engrossed for a third reading.

On motion of Mr. POINDEXTER, the contested election of Rhode Island was made the order of the day for Monday next.

SPECIAL ORDER.

The Senate resumed the consideration of the bill to provide for the construction and use of a lateral branch of the Baltimore and Ohio railroad within the District of Columbia.

Mr. CHAMBERS withdrew the amendment requiring the mail to be carried for twenty years, at $3,000 per year, and substituted another, obliging the company to carry the mail free of charge for twenty years.

Mr. GRUNDY was in favor of the amendment at all events, whether the bill was enacted or not. He said, we were gaining considerably by the amendment, and if the honorable gentleman would carry it on a little further, we should get to what was right. If the bill could be placed on such a footing as to make this a fair contract, between the Government and this company, then Congress might deliberate upon it. But there was a principle in the bill which presented a most serious difficulty to his mind. The principle of collecting only so great an amount of taxes as the necessities of the Government might require, was settled on the passage of the compromise bill of the last session. Now, if we opened the avenues of expenditure in this way, (Mr. G. said,) we should create the necessity of further taxation. The principle in the bill was, that Congress gave the money of the General Government to a company incorporated in a different State. The company was incorporated in Maryland, and the circumstance of its coming into the District of Columbia made no difference. By incorporating the company to make the road, obtained jurisdiction over the soil upon which it was laid, and we might as well give this money to a company in any other place. What difference was there between this and a corporation in New York? And if we gave this sum because the object was in the District of Columbia, why not to any other road pointing to this District? Mr. G. thought it was better to go into partnership with them, and partake of the profits. It was a strange thing if Congress could give away the money of the people for any purpose whatever. He could find such authority nowhere in the Constitution or practice of the Government. If the sum was reduced, so that the transportation of the mail would be a fair equivalent, he would vote for it.

Mr. HENDRICKS said that if the bill was to

pass, we ought to adopt a principle that the United States mail should be carried forever free of cost, or make it a jointstock concern. Mr. H. though he could show from a statement of the chief engineer, that the company could afford to carry the mail forever without charge.

Mr. CHAMBERS'S amendment was agreed to.

Mr. HENDRICKS then moved to strike out twenty years, and insert "during the continuance of the charter." He contended that the consequence of making this road would be, that the existing road would fall into dilapidation, and then the United States would be at the mercy of this company for the transportation of the mail. Some security ought to be provided in the bill against the great monopoly of this company.

[Mr. H. then read extracts from the engineer's report, to show the estimated expense of transporting the mail.]

Mr. CHAMBERS observed that the calculation adverted to, showed that there was ample equivalent given. What the Government was to obtain for this $350,000, would cost it not less than $100,050,000. Many and extensive drafts had been made in favor of the western country, and he knew of no reasons ever having been received from them—he had never seen any; and now the gentleman from Indiana [Mr. HENDRICKS] wanted an equivalent for every cent given. No company would assume an obligation of interminable duration for a service, the character of which could not be appreciated. It could not be done for an equivalent in money. The error of the gentleman from Tennessee [Mr. GRUNDY] was, that he considered this as a Maryland road. It was a road authorized by Congress, and under the jurisdiction of Congress, and could not go on but by the authority of Congress. The bill looked no further to a Maryland corporation than as it was connected with an improvement within the District line. The mail was to be carried twice a day, and in a space of time not exceeding three hours—an improvement which could be obtained in no other way. There was no equivalent which the Government could obtain for a donation like this.

Mr. GRUNDY replied, that he might be mistaken in the principle, but he did not see where it lay. We possessed jurisdiction over this Ten Miles Square, and we have declared that a considerable sum should be appropriated to the repair of Pennsylvania avenue. We had a right to do so; but it was done that every citizen should have the benefit of it. But what was the case as to a railroad? You give money to a set of individuals for their benefit, to the exclusion of all others. It was not for the benefit of the United States, or of the citizens of the United States; but for the exclusive benefit of individual subscribers to the corporation. So in regard to the Chesapeake and Ohio Canal Company. You subscribed to the stock, and expected a dividend; and who now believed that this money was well laid out? The profit which the General Government would derive from this appropriation was only the transportation of the mail; a very inconsiderable profit, compared to that derived by the State of Maryland. The principle was involved, whether you would subscribe to a company in this way, and give away the public treasure, when you promised to raise no more taxes than an economical administration of the Government required.

Mr. HENDRICKS made some further remarks in support of his amendment; and

Mr. PRESTON spoke at length against the bill, chiefly on constitutional grounds.

Mr. CLAYTON then moved an amendment to the amendment, to insert "thirty years," during which time the mail was to be carried free of charge.

Mr. BIBB, Mr. KENT, and Mr. SMITH, spoke in favor of the bill, and Mr. KING of Georgia against it.

The amendment to the amendment was then disagreed to.

The question recurring on the amendment,

Mr CHAMBERS asked the yeas and nays; which were ordered, and are as follows, to wit:

YEAS—Messrs. Bell, Benton, Bibb, Black, Brown, Calhoun, Ewing, Forsyth, Frelinghuysen, Grundy, Hendricks, Hill, Kane, King of Alabama, King of Georgia, Knight, Linn, Mangum, Morris, Naudain, Porter, Prentiss, Preston, Rob-

bins, Robinson, Shepley, Silsbee, Smith, Sprague, Swift, Tallmadge, Tomlinson, Tyler, Waggaman, Webster, White, and Wilkins—37.

NAYS—Messrs. Chambers, Clay, Clayton, Kent, McKean, and Tipton—6.

So the amendment was agreed to.

And on the question, Shall the bill pass?

Mr. GRUNDY asked the yeas and nays; which were ordered, and are, yeas 22, nays 20, as follows, to wit:

YEAS—Messrs. Bell, Chambers, Clay, Clayton, Ewing, Frelinghuysen, Hendricks, Kent, Knight, McKean, Naudain, Porter, Prentiss, Robbins, Robinson, Silsbee, Smith, Sprague, Swift, Tomlinson, Waggaman, Webster, Wilkins—23.

NAYS—Messrs. Benton, Black, Brown, Calhoun, Forsyth, Grundy, Hill, Kane, King of Alabama, King of Georgia, Linn, Mangum, Morris, Preston, Shepley, Tallmadge, Tipton, Tyler, and White—19.

So the bill was passed.

The Senate then adjourned.

HOUSE OF REPRESENTATIVES.

MONDAY, May 19, 1834.

The memorial from Savannah, relative to the deposites of public money in the United States Bank, heretofore presented by Mr. WAYNE, was laid on the table, and ordered to be printed.

Mr. DICKSON, who heretofore presented a memorial from 3,006 electors of Ontario county, New York, relative to the deposites, and which his remarks had been compressed into a day, proceeded in an extended explanation of the condition of that county, and an argument on the powers of the executive over the Treasury Department, the removal of Mr. Duane, and rights of the Bank of the United States, which it occupied two hours and a half.

On motion of Mr. D., the memorial was laid on the table, and ordered to be printed.

Mr. ANTHONY, who last Monday presented a memorial from citizens of Lycoming county, Pennsylvania, approving the course of the Administration in reference to the Bank of the United States, and obtained leave of the House to express his views thereupon, rose, and spoke at considerable length in vindication of the removal of the deposites, &c.

[We shall endeavor to give Mr. A.'s speech length to-morrow.]

Mr. WISE, who heretofore presented a memorial on the subject of the currency from Gloucester county, Virginia, and submitted a resolution for the reference of the same to a select committee with instructions, the consideration of which was postponed to this day, being now entitled to the floor, rose and said, that as the day was nearly expired, he would, with the permission of the House, propose that the memorial and resolution be postponed, and taken up this day week, if they would have precedence.

On motion of Mr. W., the subject was accordingly postponed till Monday next.

Mr. ANTHONY presented a memorial from sundry citizens of Northumberland county, Pennsylvania, praying Congress to restore the deposites. &c. Laid on the table, and ordered to be printed.

Mr. GALBRAITH presented several memorials on the subject of the Bank of the United States; laid on the table, and ordered to be printed.

Mr. LAPORTE presented a memorial of one thousand two hundred and sixty-eight citizens of Susquehanna county, Pennsylvania, praying for a restoration of the public deposites to the Bank of the United States, and a recharter of the institution.

Mr. L. said, this memorial, with other similar tenor from Bradford county, had been to him some three or four weeks since, and this was the first opportunity that he had had to present them to the House.

He also presented a memorial, signed by a thousand and forty-three of the citizens of Bradford county, in favor of the restoration of the deposites, and the recharter of the Bank of the United States.

He also presented another memorial signed by about four hundred citizens of Bradford county, in favor of the restoration of the deposites to the Bank of the United States.

The memorials were read, ordered to be printed, and laid on the table.

He also presented the proceedings of seven public meetings held in the 17th Congressional district of Pennsylvania, four of them held in Tioga, two in Bradford, and one in Susquehanna county; all of them opposed to the restoration of the deposites, and the recharter of the Bank of the United States.

Mr. L. said, he would not take up the time of the House by asking that all of the proceedings should be read, but would content himself by only asking for the reading of the resolutions passed at one of the meetings.

The whole of the proceedings were ordered to be printed, and laid on the table.

Mr. BURD presented the proceedings of a large and respectable meeting of citizens of Cambria county, Pennsylvania, opposed to the restoration of the deposites and the recharter of the bank. Read, ordered to be printed, and laid on the table.

Mr. BINNEY presented the memorial of sundry citizens of Lycoming county, Pennsylvania, praying the recharter of the United States Bank. Read, ordered to be printed, and laid on the table.

Mr. HIESTER presented the proceedings of a meeting held in the county of Lancaster, by citizens opposed to the course of the Administration in reference to the Bank of the United States. Read, ordered to be printed, and laid on the table.

Mr. RAMSAY presented the memorial of the Bank of the United States; which was laid on the table, and ordered to be printed.

Mr. STEWART presented a memorial from sundry citizens of Fayette county, Pennsylvania, against the recharter of the bank; which was laid on the table, and ordered to be printed.

Mr. MILLER presented a memorial which he said was signed by three hundred and ten intelligent and respectable citizens and voters of the county of Adams, in the State of Pennsylvania. They are opposed to the renewal of the charter of the Bank of the United States, and state that they view with deep concern the struggles that are now making to effect that object. They attribute any derangement that exists in the currency to the extent to which the present paper system has been carried, by reason of which specie has been driven out or prevented from coming into circulation. They pray Congress to adopt some measure to remedy this evil, and state that they apprehend there is no way in which it can be so effectually accomplished as by raising the value of gold so as to prevent its exportation and secure its circulation among us.

Mr. DENNY presented the proceedings of a convention, held at Pittsburg, by individuals opposed to secret societies, approving of Mr. Adams's "suppressed speech," and disapproving the President's protest, of the removal of the deposites, and of the course of the Administration, and the influence of masonic societies generally. Read, laid on the table, and ordered to be printed.

Mr. BEAUMONT presented the proceedings of a meeting of the citizens of Luzerne county, on the subject of the Bank of the United States. Laid on the table and ordered to be printed.

Mr. BEAUMONT also presented a memorial on the same subject from citizens of the State of Mississippi.

Mr. PLUMMER moved the postponement of the memorial till Monday next. Lost.

Mr. PLUMMER moved that the memorial be referred to the Committee of Ways and Means, with instructions to report a resolution sustaining the course of the Administration, in relation to the removal of the deposites. After some conversation, Mr. B. withdrew the memorial.

Mr. BARNITZ presented a memorial from sundry citizens of York county, on the subject of the bank.

Mr. McKIM presented instructions from certain citizens residing in the first five wards of the city of Baltimore, addressed to him on the subject of the bank; which, on his motion, were read, ordered to be printed, and laid on the table.

Memorials were presented by Messrs. STODDERT and TURNER.

Mr. LUCAS presented a memorial from sundry citizens of Jefferson county, on the subject of the embarrassments of business, &c.; which was laid on the table, and ordered to be printed.

The CHAIR presented the proceedings of a meeting held in Newcastle, in Delaware, on the subject of the bank and the currency. Ordered to be printed.

Memorials were presented by Messrs. W. P. TAYLOR, DAVENPORT, and LOYALL.

Mr. SPEIGHT presented several memorials from citizens of North Carolina on the subject of the bank and the currency. Laid on the table and ordered to be printed.

Messrs. PINCKNEY, CLAYTON, WAYNE, and GAMBLE presented private petitions.

Mr HARDIN presented a memorial from sundry inhabitants of his district on the subject of the public distress and embarrassment, and protesting against the adjournment of Congress before something be done for the relief of the country. Read, laid on the table, and ordered to be printed.

Mr. LOVE presented a memorial from citizens of Garrard county, praying the restoration of the deposites; which was laid on the table, and ordered to be printed. Mr. L. took the occasion to say, for the information of his constituents, that, had he been present when the vote was taken on the resolution reported from the Committee of Ways and Means, he should have voted with the minority on the four first resolutions, and with the majority on the fifth resolution.

Mr. CHILTON ALLAN presented a memorial on the subject of the bank. Laid on the table and ordered to be printed.

Mr. POLK presented some private petitions.

Mr. VANCE presented a memorial from sundry citizens of Greene county, Ohio, and twenty-one memorials from citizens of Clarke county, Ohio, praying the restoration of the deposites. Laid on the table and ordered to be printed.

Mr. SLOANE presented a memorial from certain citizens of Ohio, on the subject of the public distress, &c. Read and ordered to be printed.

Mr. E. WHITTLESEY presented a memorial signed by 1500 citizens of his district, on the subject of the bank; which was laid on the table and ordered to be printed.

Mr. PATTERSON presented the proceedings of a meeting in Vermillion township, Richland county, Ohio, with a memorial signed by one hundred persons, disapproving of the removal of the public deposites, and praying for a recharter of the United States Bank. Also, the proceedings of a meeting held in Tiffin, Seneca county, Ohio, accompanied by a memorial from sundry citizens of said county, approving of the course pursued by the Secretary of the Treasury in the removal of the deposites and opposing the recharter of the United States Bank. Also, the proceedings of a public meeting held in Norwalk, Huron county, Ohio, approving of the removal of the public deposites, and opposing the recharter of the United States Bank. Mr. P. also had the claims of Platt Brush, late register of the land office in the Bucyrus district, in Ohio, referred to the Committee on Public Lands.

Mr. VINTON presented several memorials from citizens of Ohio, on the subject of the bank and the currency; which, on his motion, were postponed to Monday next.

Mr. CORWIN, of Ohio, presented the proceedings of a public meeting of the friends of the Administration, held in Warren county, Ohio. He said he had received the paper containing the proceedings of the meeting some time since in a blank envelope. That he had no written information concerning it, but was very sure it was intended to be presented to the House. One of the resolutions on the face of the paper requires it to be so disposed of. He said he could not say with certainty anything as to the numbers composing the meeting; the printed accounts of it which he had noticed, spoke of it as numerous. He said the paper contained an elaborate view of the question so much discussed everywhere, and in his opinion combined very happily and forcibly all the legitimate arguments against the United States Bank. The meeting approves the conduct of the President and Secretary of the Treasury in the removal of the public deposites. They remonstrate against the recharter of the United States Bank; argue, as I have said, against the power of Congress to create a bank. They insist that hard money is the only constitutional currency. He said he recognised amongst the officers of the meeting some of his oldest and most valued friends, with whom it gave him pain to differ, even on this question, where such diversity of opinion prevailed. It is proper that I should inform the House, that some of the gentlemen who composed this meeting had been honored by the confidence of their fellow-citizens often, by being placed in stations of high political trust. He moved that the proceedings be laid on the table, and printed.

Mr. BELL, of Ohio, presented a memorial from fourteen or fifteen hundred voters of Belmont county, Ohio, disapproving of the removal of the deposites; and on motion of Mr. B., the further consideration of the memorial was postponed till Monday next.

Mr. CHINN presented a memorial of the Provident Association of Clerks, in the civil department of the Government of the United States, in the District of Columbia, praying for pecuniary aid from the Government, to enable said association to accomplish the benevolent objects for which it was formed and incorporated by Congress; which memorial was referred to the Committee on the District of Columbia.

Mr. WEBSTER presented the petition of Isaac Mills, praying an invalid pension; which was referred.

Mr. MITCHELL presented memorials from Muskingum county, sustaining the course of the Administration; which, on his motion, were laid on the table, and ordered to be printed.

Mr. THOMSON presented a memorial from Columbiana county, Ohio, in favor of the Administration, and against the bank; which, on his motion, was read, laid on the table, and ordered to be printed.

Mr. GARLAND presented several memorials; which were referred.

Mr. McCARTY presented a memorial relative to the bank; which, on his motion, was postponed to Monday next.

Mr. PLUMMER presented several memorials from Mississippi, opposed to the United States Bank; which were laid on the table, and ordered to be printed.

Mr. DUNCAN presented memorials for and against the Bank of the United States; which were laid on the table, and ordered to be printed.

Petitions and memorials were also presented by Messrs. CASEY, SLOAN, MARDIS, CLAY, MURPHY, LYON, and WHITE.

Mr. MURPHY, by consent, offered the following resolution, which was adopted:

Resolved, That the Committee on Public Lands be instructed to inquire into the expediency of so amending the act of 23d May, 1828, entitled "An act for the relief of purchasers of public lands that have reverted for non-payment of the purchase money," and the act amendatory thereto, passed 9th May, 1832, as to carry into more complete effect the relief contemplated to be given by the said acts.

Mr. ASHLEY, by leave, presented the following resolution, which was adopted:

Resolved, That the Committee on Public Lands be instructed to inquire into the expediency of providing by law for issuing a patent, in the name of Wilson P. Hunt for a tract of land to which he is entitled.

The following resolution, offered by Mr. BEATTY, was adopted:

Resolved, That the Committee on the Post Office and Post Roads be instructed to inquire into the expediency of extending the mail route to Monticello, in the State of Kentucky, which now passes from Monroe, in Overton county, to Jamestown, Fenton county, in the State of Tennessee, where it now stops, passing Abraham Van Winkle's.

The following resolution, submitted by Mr. GARLAND, was adopted:

Resolved, That the Committee on Roads and Canals be instructed to inquire into the expediency of making an appropriation of public land in the State of Louisiana, or of money, for the purpose of removing the raft in the Bayou Pigeon, one of the outlets of the Mississippi river, and removing other obstructions to the navigation of that stream.

The SPEAKER laid before the House a letter from CORNELIUS W. LAWRENCE, of New York, resigning his seat in the House; which was laid on the table.

When the House adjourned.

IN SENATE.

TUESDAY, *May* 20, 1834.

Mr. WILKINS presented the proceedings of a meeting of certain citizens of Pittsburg, Pennsylvania, the resolutions of which were at variance with free masonry—the policy of the removal of the deposites—against the doctrines contained in the President's protest—and in favor of the principles avowed in the speech intended to have been delivered by the Hon. John Q. Adams, of the House of Representatives. The proceedings were read, ordered to be printed, and referred to the Committee on Finance.

Mr. WEBSTER presented the proceedings of a meeting of citizens of the borough of Columbia, Lancaster county, Pennsylvania, in favor of the restoration of the deposites and a renewal of the charter of the Bank of the United States; which was read, referred to the Committee on Finance, and ordered to be printed.

Mr. BROWN presented the proceedings of a public meeting in Wake county, North Carolina, sustaining the Administration with regard to its policy in reference to the Bank of the United States, averse to a restoration of the deposites, and against a recharter of that corporation. The proceedings were read, referred to the Committee on Finance, and ordered to be printed.

Upon the presentation of this memorial, a protracted debate ensued, in which Messrs WEBSTER, BROWN, and MANGUM participated.

Mr. MANGUM presented a memorial from a number of citizens of Raleigh, North Carolina, in favor of the restoration of the deposites, and the recharter of the Bank of the United States; which was read, referred to the Committee on Finance, and ordered to be printed.

REPORTS.

Mr. MOORE, from the Committee on Revolutionary Claims, reported a bill from the House of Representatives, for the relief of the heirs of John Taylor, deceased.

Also, a bill for the relief of the heirs of Francis Nash, deceased.

Mr. LINN reported a bill for the relief of John Wilson.

SPECIAL ORDER—PENSION AGENCY.

Mr. KANE having the floor, rose and observed, that as the hour was late, he moved to postpone the special order until to-morrow; which was agreed to.

Mr. CLAYTON presented the memorial of the principal chiefs of the Cherokee Nation, asking the interference of Congress in securing to them the payment of annuities under treaties made by the United States with the said tribes; which he moved to refer to the Committee on Indian Affairs.

Mr. FORSYTH expressed the hope that the memorial would not be referred without consideration. These people (he said) represented themselves as an independent Government, and measures for redress in such cases must first arise between ourselves. He wished to know what authority the gentleman from Delaware [Mr. CLAYTON] had for representing these people as an independent nation.

Mr. CLAYTON replied that the paper had been handed to him by John Ross, a person who was known as the principal chief of the Cherokee nation, and presenting themselves as having the serving the protection of this nation. They represented their annuities as being withheld from them, which was a proper subject for the consideration of the Committee on Indian Affairs; and if they were injured, it was the duty of Congress to grant them redress.

Mr. FORSYTH said he would raise the question he desired to arrive at, by moving that the paper be not received, because they presented themselves in a character in which they could not be heard. As to the authority given by the honorable gentleman, we know that it comes from John Ross. But Mr. F. would like to know by what authority this individual was presenting himself here, as the head of an independent nation, complaining against the Government of the United States. Was it not a departure from the practice of Congress and parliamentary usage, for the head of a sovereign tribe to come here and ask us to interfere against an independent branch of the

Government? Suppose any petty chief of a South American province, or of Africa, should present himself here, and enter a complaint against the Government, what gentleman of the Senate is there who would not brand it with audacity and presumption? And yet here is a complaint presented by the chief of the Cherokee nation. If they came to us as subjects of the United States, they would have a right to be heard. But they had no right to present themselves here as a sovereign Power.

Mr. CLAY contended that these people were not to be considered as a sovereign power, and that the only ground on which we could refuse to receive their petition was, that the Executive had the control of the subject, independent of Congress.

Mr. SPRAGUE thought if we could not do these Indians justice, we ought, at least to hear their petitions. The laws of the State of Georgia had been extended over them, and their annuities had been refused payment. It was a subject properly within the cognizance of Congress.

Mr. FORSYTH replied, that the gentleman from Maine [Mr. SPRAGUE] was mistaken in point of fact; the laws of Georgia had not been extended over the tribe. As to the fact that they were not presenting themselves as a foreign Government, they came here as the Cherokee nation; and what was a foreign Government, he would inquire? This was an independent Government, or they represented themselves to be so, appealing against the Executive—they were appealing to one branch of the Government against another. This very subject had been in discussion here for two years. There was no refusal, and there could be no refusal to do them justice; and honorable gentlemen could possess themselves of everything which could give them information in relation to this subject, by the usual proceeding of resolution, calling on the Department of War. He objected to having an independent member of this Union, which he had the honor of representing in part, thus arraigned before the Congress of the United States by an insolent Cherokee. Attempts like this had been made twice before. One of which he (Mr. F.) recollected in the House of Representatives, when he was a member of that body. The House refused to receive the complaint; and afterwards, when the political character which the complainants had assumed was dropped, their representations were heard, and justice was done to them, as the nature of their case seemed to require. This could be done here. He moved that the paper be not received.

Some further remarks were made by Messrs. FRELINGHUYSEN, BIBB, CLAYTON, TIPTON, WEBSTER, and FORSYTH, when the yeas and nays on his motion; which were ordered; and are as follows, to wit:

YEAS—Messrs. Bell, Bibb, Brown, Calhoun, Clay, Clayton, Ewing, Frelinghuysen, Hendricks, Hill, Kent, Knight, Leigh, Linn, McKean, Mangum, Naudain, Prentiss, Preston, Robbins, Robinson, Shepley, Silsbee, Smith, Sprague, Swift, Tipton, Tomlinson, Tyler, Webster—30.

NAYS—Messrs. Benton, Forsyth, White—3.

Mr. PRESTON presented the petition of Duff Green, praying remuneration for recording the opinions of the Supreme Court; which was referred to the Committee on the Judiciary.

Mr. EWING gave notice that he should, on to-morrow, ask leave to introduce a bill explanatory of an act for the relief of Payne & Arnold.

Mr. WHITE gave notice that he should to-morrow, at as early an hour as practicable, move the Senate to go into executive business.

The following resolution was submitted by Mr. EWING:

Resolved, That the Committee on the Post Office and Post Roads be instructed to inquire into the expediency of placing the postage on periodical pamphlets and newspapers on the same footing.

Mr. TIPTON, from the Committee of Claims, reported a bill with an amendment relative to remuneration for losses sustained during the late war with the northwestern Indians.

Mr. LINN, from the Committee on Private Land Claims, reported a bill for the adjustment of land titles in the State of Missouri, providing for the extension of the provisions of a statute on the subject for one year, from the 1st of October, 1834.

On motion of Mr. FRELINGHUYSEN, at a quarter before eight o'clock,
The Senate adjourned.

HOUSE OF REPRESENTATIVES.

TUESDAY, *May* 20, 1834.

Mr. E. WHITTLESEY reported a bill for the relief of Daniel Whittle; which was read twice and committed.

Also, a bill for the relief of Ann Blodget; which was read twice and committed.

Mr. FOSTER reported a bill for the relief of Thomas Cooper; which was read twice and committed.

Mr. POLK reported a bill for the relief to the restoration of an unexpended balance of a former appropriation for the payment of Georgia militia claims; which was read twice and referred to the Committee of the Whole House on the state of the Union.

Mr. CHINN reported a resolution providing that Friday and Saturday, the 6th and 7th instant, be set apart for business relative to the District of Columbia; which lies on the table.

Mr. H. EVERETT reported the following bill; which, together with a detailed report accompanying them, were committed to the Committee of the Whole House on the state of the Union:

A bill to provide for the organization of the Department of Indian Affairs.

A bill to regulate trade and intercourse with the Indian tribes and to preserve peace on the frontier and of the minority of the committee relative to the Western Territory, and for the security and protection of the Indian tribes therein.

On motion of Mr. ALLEN, of Ohio, ten thousand extra copies of the report accompanying these bills were ordered to be printed.

Mr. HEATH reported a bill for the erection of a marine hospital in Baltimore; which was read twice and committed.

KENTUCKY CONTESTED ELECTION.

Mr. JONES, from the Committee of Elections, reported a resolution providing that Robert P. LETCHER and THOMAS P. MOORE, Esquires, be heard at the bar of the House, in defence of their respective claims; which resolution was agreed to.

On motion of Mr. JONES, the report of the majority of the committee, with the resolutions accompanying it, were read:

Resolved, That THOMAS P. MOORE, Esq., be titled to the seat in this House, to represent the 5th Congressional District of the State of Kentucky.

Resolved, That ROBERT P. LETCHER, Esq., entitled to compensation at the rate of eight dollars for every twenty miles travelling.

Mr. JONES rose and said, I move, sir, the adoption of the first resolution.

Mr. BANKS, a member of the Committee of Elections, moved that the reports of the majority and of the minority of the committee be read, which Mr. JONES asked the year and nays which were ordered.

The question being taken, it was determined in the negative—yeas 54, nays 106.

YEAS—Messrs. John Quincy Adams, Heman Allen, John J. Allen, Chilton Allan, Banks, Barnitz, Barringer, Bates, Beatty, M. Bell, Binney, Briggs, Bull, Burd, Chambers, Chilton, William Clark, Clayton, Corwin, Coulter, Crockett, Darlington, Warren Davis, Amos Davis, Davenport, Deberry, Dickson, Ellsworth, Evans, Everett, Felder, Fillmore, Foster, Philo C. Fuller, Gamble, Garland, Gilmer, Gordon, Gorham, Greenleaf, Griffin, Hiland Hall, Hardin, James Harper, Hazeltine, Heath, Hiester, Jackson, Laporte, Lay, Lewis, Lincoln, Love, Martindale, McComas, McKennan, Milligan, Moore, Potts, Ramsay, Reed, Rencher, Slade, Sloane, Spangler, William P. Taylor, Philemon Thomas, Tompkins, Tweedy, Vinton, Wattmough, Edward D. White, Whittlesey, Wilde, Williams, Wise, and Young—84.

NAYS—Messrs. William Allen, Bean, Beardsley, Beaumont, Blair, Bockee, Boon, Brown, Bunch, Burns, Cambreleng, Carr, Casey,

Caney, Chinn, Samuel Clark, Clay, Coffee, Camer, Day, Dickinson, Duncan, Dunlap, Forester, Fowler, Wm. K. Fuller, Galbraith, Gholson, Gillet, Joseph Hall, Thomas H. Hall, Halsey, Lamer, Joseph M. Harper, Harrison, Hathaway, Hawkins, Hawes, Henderson, Howell, Hubbard, Huntington, Inge, Jarvis, Noadiah Johnson, Cave Johnson, Seaborn Jones, Benjamin Jones, Cavanagh, Kinnard, Lane, Lansing, Luke Lea, Thomas Lee, Leavitt, Loyall, Lyon, Joel K. Mann, Mardis, Moses Mason, McIntire, McKay, McKim, McKinley, McLene, McVean, Miller, Mitchell, Muhlenberg, Murphy, Osgood, Page, Parks, Parker, Patton, Patterson, D. J. Pearce, Peyton, F. Pierce, Pierson, Polk, Pope, Schenck, Shley, William B. Shepard, A. H. Shepperd, Sinn, Charles Slade, Smith, Speight, Standifer, Suddert, Sutherland, William Taylor, Thomson, Turner, Turrill, Vanderpoel, Van Houten, Wagner, Ward, Wardwell, Wayne, Webster, C. P. White, and Wilson—106.

Mr. BANKS offered the following as an amendment to the resolution under consideration. Mr. — said that this was the first of a series of propositions which he should bring before the House.

Mr. STEWART expressed a hope that the House would proceed to the orders of the day, and made a motion to that effect; which was negatived.

Mr. DICKSON called for the reading of the report of the minority of the committee; and on objection being made, the yeas and nays were called on the motion by Mr. VANCE, and ordered. The objection was then withdrawn, and the report was read.

The question then being on the following amendment offered to the first resolution by Mr. BANKS—After resolved, insert, " that the legal votes which were received in Lancaster, (Garrard county,) whilst Moses Grant, esq., acted as one of the judges, on the first morning of the election in August last, and those of a like character, given in the second day of the election, in the casual absence of the sheriff, ought to be estimated in ascertaining the results of the election;"

Mr. BANKS rose and addressed the House at length in its support. He contended that it was proof that a majority of votes were given to Mr. Letcher, and that was therefore elected, unless it could be proved that the votes were illegal, or was illegally. The votes were to stand unimpeached, until they were proved to be bad. Mr. B. explained the provisions of the laws of Kentucky, and insisted that the votes referred to in his argument were properly received, and ought to be counted. The argument was filed with reference to the printed evidence, as well as to cases of statutes which require recourse to the notes of a speaker to make up an intelligible report of a speech, which went over the whole ground, and occupied a little more than an hour in its delivery.

Mr. SEABORN JONES followed in opposition to the amendment, and in support of the original solution of the committee. Mr. J. contended that the whole current of the decisions upon contested elections in the House, as to establish the position that votes not taken at the time, in the manner, and at the place, required by law, could not be counted. That the right of suffrage was a political and not inherent right. The qualifications of voters were fixed by law, and must be exercised according to law. He went on to show that the temporary appointment of a judge of election, to take votes for the hour preceding the time fixed by law for commencing the election in Lancaster on the first day, was illegal, and that, agreeably to various precedents which he read, the votes so taken could not be counted. He also contended that the law of Kentucky positively requiring the presence of the sheriff, the votes received in his absence on the second day, could not be reckoned. Mr. J. referred to those States which require a property qualification, and contended that a decision, according to law, as well as the whole current of decisions, should reject the amendment.

Mr. MARSHALL followed in support of the amendment, till after four o'clock; when, without concluding, he gave way to a motion to adjourn; and, on motion of Mr. CHILTON ALLAN, The House adjourned.

IN SENATE.
WEDNESDAY, May 21, 1834.

Mr. WEBSTER presented memorials from inhabitants of Otsego, New York; citizens of Brockport, Monroe county, New York; and citizens of Pittsford, in the same county.

Mr. EWING, who, the other day, presented a memorial from inhabitants of Athens county, Ohio, introduced an additional memorial. Also, a memorial from Boon county, Ohio; and another from Greene county, Ohio.

Mr. McKEAN, a memorial from Luzerne county, Pennsylvania.

Mr. LEIGH, a memorial from Jefferson county, Virginia.

Mr. CLAY, six memorials from Huntingdon county, Pennsylvania. Also, one from Doylestown, Bucks county, Pennsylvania; and another from Seneca Falls, New York.

All of which were in favor of the restoration of the deposites to the Bank of the United States, and the recharter of that institution.

Upon the presentation of the last-named memorial, a long and animated debate ensued, in which Messrs. CLAY, WRIGHT, WEBSTER, FORSYTH, TYLER, BENTON, and LEIGH, participated.

The several memorials were referred to the Committee on Finance, and ordered to be printed.

Mr. McKEAN presented a memorial from inhabitants of Susquehannah county, Pennsylvania, against the restoration of the deposites and the recharter of the Bank of the United States; which was referred to the Committee on Finance, and ordered to be printed.

A message upon executive business was received from the President of the United States, by Mr. Asbury Dickins.

On motion of Mr. EWING,
The Senate adjourned.

HOUSE OF REPRESENTATIVES.
WEDNESDAY, May 21, 1834.

KENTUCKY CONTESTED ELECTION.

The report of the Committee of Elections upon the contested election between T. P. Moore and R. P. Letcher, being the unfinished business of yesterday, came up immediately after the journal was read.

Mr. MARSHALL resumed his speech in opposition to the report, and in favor of the amendment moved by Mr. BANKS, which proposed to declare that the votes taken at Lancaster, in Garrard county, before the hour for opening the polls, and in the absence of the sheriff, shall be counted.

Mr. M. stated the general principles and adjudged cases, as well as the peculiar facts relative to this election, and contended at length that the amendment should be adopted. After speaking two hours, he was followed by

Mr. CLAYTON, who rose to address the House on the question, though, he said, he felt discouraged in the attempt by the inattention of the House to those who had preceded him in the discussion. But, nevertheless, he would attempt to discharge his duty, believing that he would be heard elsewhere, if not here. He supposed that the question would occupy more of the time of this House than any other which had come before it; for it was a question affecting the right of representation —a question whether this is a representative Government or not. The Constitution gave to the States the right to fix the time, place, and manner of holding elections, and to those particulars was confined the power of the States over the subject. In the case before us, there was no dispute as to the time or place of the election; and we had only to inquire whether the manner in which it was conducted was legal.

Mr. C. went on, at great length, to argue that the manner in which the election was held there was nothing which essentially violated the law of Kentucky, or which authorized the committee to set aside the votes taken in Garrard county.

Mr. JONES, of Georgia, made a brief explanation on a point in which his argument had been misapprehended by his colleague.

Mr. HARDIN followed in support of the amendment, and in further reply to the gentleman from Georgia, [Mr. JONES.]

The question being on the motion to amend the resolution, by striking out all after the word resolved, and inserting the following:
" That the legal votes which were received in
' Lancaster, (Garrard county,) whilst Moses Grant,
' Esq., acted as one of the judges, on the first morn-
' ing of the election in August last, and those of
' a like character, given on the second day of the
' election, in the casual absence of the sheriff,
' ought to be estimated in ascertaining the results
' of the election"—

Mr. GILMER called for a division of the question on the amendment, so as to take the question separately on the legality of the votes taken the first day in Garrard; which was pronounced by the Chair to be in order.

Mr. BOON wished the question to be first taken on the motion to strike out; which the Chair pronounced to be out of order.

Mr. GRIFFIN asked the yeas and nays on the question; which were ordered.

Mr. JONES, of Georgia, spoke a considerable length in rejoinder to the several gentlemen who had replied to him.

Mr. HAMER took the floor; but yielded it to a motion to adjourn; and
The House then adjourned.

IN SENATE.
THURSDAY, May 22, 1834.

Mr. SMITH presented a remonstrance of certain citizens of Connecticut, against the renewal of the patent of John Ames, paper maker.

Mr. McKEAN presented the memorial of 662 inhabitants of Cumberland county, Pennsylvania.

Mr. CLAY the memorial of inhabitants of Montgomery county, Pennsylvania, both in favor of the restoration of the deposites and the recharter of the Bank of the United States.

The two preceding memorials were referred to the Committee on Finance, and ordered to be printed.

Mr. TYLER presented the petition of Christopher P. Carter; which was referred to the Committee on Claims.

A message upon executive business was received from the President of the United States, by Mr. Asbury Dickins.

On motion of Mr. WHITE, the Senate proceeded to executive business.

After spending some time therein, when the doors were opened, it was
Ordered, That when the Senate adjourn, it would adjourn until Monday next.

SPECIAL ORDER.

The report of the Committee on the Judiciary on the pension fund, being called up, on
Mr. KANE'S motion, it was laid upon the table, and made the special order for Monday next.

GENERAL ORDERS.

Mr. BIBB'S resolution, proposing an amendment to the Constitution of the United States as it respects the election of President and Vice President of the United States, was, on his motion, postponed until Monday next.

The following bills were read a third time and passed:

A bill to revive and amend an act for the relief of insolvent debtors of the United States;

A bill for the relief of Elizabeth Robinson, daughter of Lieutenant Richard Wilde, of the army of the Revolution;

A bill supplementary to an act entitled "An act to alter and amend the several acts imposing duties on imports," approved July 14, 1832; and

A bill relinquishing the duties on a set of bells imported from France for the use of the Roman Catholic Church at St. Louis, Missouri.

The resolutions offered during the week, with the exception of one offered by Mr. LINN, which was laid on the table, were taken up and agreed to.

The following resolution, submitted by Mr. ROBINSON, was considered, and agree to:
Resolved, That the Committee on Engrossed Bills, when they have examined a bill or resolution, shall deliver the same to the Secretary of the Senate, who shall, as heretofore, enter upon the Journal that the same has been correctly engrossed.

A bill for the relief of Samuel Armstrong Bailey

and others, was read a first and second time, and referred to the Committee on Public Lands.

The following bills were considered in Committee of the Whole, read a second time, and ordered to be engrossed for a third reading:

A bill for the relief of William Mann, late deputy marshal of the eastern district of Virginia;

A bill for the relief of Colonel A. R. Woolley;

A bill for the relief of the administrators of Bolitha Laws, deceased;

A bill for the relief of Henry Waller;

A bill for the relief of Martha Bailey and others;

A bill for the relief of the heirs and legal representatives of Frances Barham, deceased, and her husband, Fielding Barham;

A bill for the relief of George K. Jackson;

A bill to remove the office of Surveyor General of the public lands in Ohio, Indiana, and the Michigan Territory;

A bill for the relief of the legal representatives of Joseph Rowe, deceased;

A bill for the relief of Charles J. Hand;

A bill for the relief of John Yantis;

A bill for the relief of Asa Hartfield, his assignee, or legal representative;

A bill for the relief of Lieutenant Archibald S. Campbell; and

A bill for the relief of Captain Wolcott Chauncey.

The Senate, at a quarter before five o'clock, on motion of Mr. SOUTHARD, adjourned

HOUSE OF REPRESENTATIVES.

THURSDAY, May 22, 1834.

The resolution yesterday reported from the Committee on the District of Columbia, to set apart Friday and Saturday, the 6th and 7th days of June next, for the consideration of business relative to the District of Columbia, was taken up for consideration.

Mr. WILLIAMS moved to amend the resolution by providing that Thursday the 5th day of June be set apart for the consideration of business relative to the Territories; and when the motion was put, it was ascertained that a quorum was not present.

The question being again put, the motion was agreed to, and the resolution, as amended, was adopted.

The following resolution, heretofore offered by Mr. McCOMAS, was taken up and agreed to:

Resolved, That the Committee on Roads and Canals be instructed to inquire into the expediency of subscribing stock to the James River and Kanawha Company, in the State of Virginia.

Mr. E. WHITTLESEY, from the Committee on Claims, reported a bill for the relief of George Rendes; read twice, and committed.

Mr. C. C. CLAY reported a bill to authorize the sale of lots in the town of St. Marks; read twice, and ordered to be engrossed for a third reading.

On motion of Mr. WAYNE, 2,000 extra copies of the bill, with the accompanying report, to fix the pay of the officers of the navy, were ordered to be printed.

Mr. CONNOR reported a bill to establish certain post roads and for other purposes; read twice and committed.

Mr. WAYNE submitted a joint resolution, on leave, for supplying the new members of the present Congress with two copies each of the returns of the last census of the United States; which was read twice and ordered to be engrossed.

Mr. STODDERT, from the Committee on the District of Columbia, reported, without amendment, the bill from the Senate to authorize the construction of a lateral railroad, within the District of Columbia; which was committed to the Committee of the Whole House.

Mr. THOMAS submitted, on leave, a resolution relative to the erection of a light-house on lake Ponchartrain.

On motion of Mr. LANE, the House suspended the rule to consider the resolution heretofore offered, for an inquiry into the expediency of making an appropriation of refuse lands in aid of the construction of a railroad from Lawrenceburg, on the Ohio, to Indianapolis, and it was adopted.

Mr. CAMBRELENG moved a suspension of

the rules, in order to introduce a resolution granting the use of the Hall of Representatives on Monday night next for a public meeting in favor of the exiled Poles; which was agreed to, and the resolution was offered and adopted.

KENTUCKY CONTESTED ELECTION.

The question before the House was the resolution reported by the Committee of Elections, that THOMAS P. MOORE was entitled to the seat in the House from the Fifth Congressional District, as proposed to be amended by Mr. BAKER, by declaring that the votes taken in Garrard county, in the absence of the judge of election appointed by the county court on the first day, and in the absence of the Sheriff on the second day, be counted.

Mr. HAMER, who was entitled to the floor from yesterday, addressed the House at length against the amendment, in support of the report of the Committee of Elections, and in reply to the arguments heretofore urged by Mr. HARDIN, Mr. MARSHALL, and Mr. CLAYTON. He contended that an election was the expression of the voice of a majority of the people in the mode prescribed by the Constitution and laws—that both those who give, and those who receive the votes, must possess the qualifications required—that when principles clearly laid down for the government of such questions are departed from upon fancied grounds of equity, or because a hard case is presented, the consequences could not be foreseen. It was contended in the report of the minority that if votes were received by judges of election who were mere usurpers without any legal authority whatever, such votes ought to be counted. This doctrine he denied. Mr. H. then went on to establish that the appointment of Mr. Grant by the Sheriff to receive votes before the hour at which the polls were to be opened by law, was contrary to law and void. On this point he replied to the arguments of Messrs. HARDIN and MARSHALL at length, as well as upon the other point relative to the votes taken on the second day in the absence of the Sheriff. After speaking about an hour, Mr. H. finished, and was followed by

Mr. BINNEY, in support of the amendment, and in opposition to the report of the committee. He contended that the prescription of time, place, and manner of election was not intended to restrain, but to promote the exercise of the right of suffrage; that these were not essential, but circumstantial forms; and that the House was bound to give effect to the voice of the people, whether those forms were observed or not. Mr. B. illustrated his views by a great variety of analogies and cases, and contended that upon the facts presented, the votes referred to in the amendment ought to be taken into the computation. Mr. B. also contended that the votes of the theological students at Danville, rejected by the committee, ought to have been allowed to Mr. Letcher, which, with those referred to in the amendment, would give that gentleman a majority of two votes over Mr. Moore. These positions were argued at length upon the laws and constitution of Kentucky, which alone were, he said, applicable to the case. The precedents and cases determined by the House had no bearing, the House being, by the Constitution, made judge of the qualifications of the elected, but not of the electors—which belongs exclusively to the State.

BANK INVESTIGATION REPORT.

After Mr. B. had concluded—

Mr. THOMAS, of Maryland, from the Select Committee appointed to investigate the concerns of the Bank of the United States, rose and asked leave to submit a report.

Mr. WATMOUGH objected to the reception of the report at this time. We had, he said, subjects enough of excitement before us for the present. He hoped the business of the House would not be interrupted.

Mr. WATMOUGH was aware, he said, that he was not at liberty to submit the report without the leave of the House, and he would, with the consent of the House, give some reasons for submitting the report at the present time.

Mr. WATMOUGH said that to prevent any debate, he would withdraw his objections.

Mr. THOMAS then made the report, and moved that it be printed, postponed to Tuesday week, and made the special order for that day.

Mr. SELDEN hoped the motion would be denied, and taken first on printing. He would not assent to make it the subject of a special order for Tuesday week.

Mr. GALBRAITH called for the reading of the report; which the Chair said was not in order.

Mr. WATMOUGH said was very desirous, he said, that this subject should be brought before the House, but there was much business of a pressing character to be disposed of. He moved to postpone the consideration of the report to two day two weeks.

Mr. CLAY remarked, that when the report came up, if the House was not prepared to act upon it, they could postpone it further.

Mr. E. WHITTLESEY said the majority of the House could take up the report when they chose, and, therefore, there was no necessity to assign any day. He was unwilling to postpone the appropriation bills in order to take up the bank question.

Mr. VANCE did not, he said, think it well while to throw any obstacle in the way of its support. He hoped it would come before the House as soon as the House was ready to act upon it.

Mr. WATMOUGH, understanding that the other business of the House was not to be interfered with, withdrew his motion.

The motion to print and postpone till Tuesday week was then agreed to.

Mr. E. EVERETT rose, and begged leave to press their views in the form of a minority report.

Leave being given, he moved that the report be printed, and take the same direction with the majority report; which was agreed to.

Mr. CLAYTON moved that the House adjourn; upon which, on call of Mr. BEARDSLEY, the yeas and nays were ordered.

The question being taken, the motion to adjourn was negatived, yeas 87, nays 92.

Mr. MILLER moved the suspension of the rules, in order to move the printing of so many number of copies of the bank report and report.

The CHAIR pronounced the motion to be out of order, as a subject was before the House.

Mr. MILLER moved to postpone till Tuesday next the further consideration of the subject before the House.

Mr. JONES called for the yeas and nays upon the motion.

Mr. MILLER withdrew the motion to postpone and moved to lay the resolutions from the Committee of Elections on the table.

Mr. McKINLEY moved that the House do now adjourn, upon which the yeas and nays were ordered.

Mr. GHOLSON demanded that the hour (twenty minutes past four) be entered on the Journal.

Mr. CLAY rose to a point of order.

Mr. CLAY withdrew his point of order.

Mr. BRIGGS said the point of order could not be raised after the yeas and nays had been ordered.

Mr. CLAY withdrew his appeal.

The question being taken on the motion to adjourn, it was decided in the affirmative: yeas 84. The House then adjourned.

REPORT

Of the Secretary of the Treasury in compliance with resolution of the Senate.

TREASURY DEPARTMENT, May 14, 1834.

SIR: In pursuance of the resolution of the Senate, dated the 5th instant, directing the Secretary of the Treasury to report to the Senate whether any of the banks which have recently failed, the District of Columbia had on deposite, or otherwise in their possession, any of the public moneys, or, if any, how much, give the time of their care, I have the honor to state, that the Bank at Alexandria has been used as the depositing bank, the revenue collected at the port of Alexandria many years past, and at the time it stopped payment had in possession on deposite to the credit of the treasury of the United States the sum of forty-seven thousand five hundred and twenty-seven

dollars and eighty-four cents, ($27,528 84,) and to the credit of the collector of the customs for the district of Alexandria the sum of two thousand eight hundred and nineteen dollars and thirty-four cents, ($2,819 34.)

There appears to be, however, no ground for apprehending that any part of this sum is in danger of being lost. The bank, it is understood, has abundant means out of which the debt may be satisfied, and measures will be taken to recover it, if satisfactory security be not promptly given by the bank. But assurances have been given by the cashier to the district attorney that the security required will be placed in the possession of the department without delay.

It is proper to add, that a few days before the Bank of Alexandria stopped payment the sum of $3,487 50 was deposited in the bank to the credit of the Treasurer of the United States, by the corporation of Alexandria, on account of the loan made to the corporations of this District under the act of May 24, 1828. But as the draft of the Treasurer on that bank in favor of the Bank of the Metropolis for this money was not paid, it is believed that the United States are not responsible for it, and it is therefore not included in the sum above mentioned.

The Farmers and Mechanics' Bank of Georgetown had on deposite, to the credit of the Treasurer of the United States, at the time it stopped payment, the sum of sixty thousand dollars, ($60,000.) But a like sum has been advanced by that bank to the paymaster of the Harper's Ferry armory, to enable him to pay the workmen and carry on the works at that place, in anticipation of the regular appropriation. As that appropriation has now been made, the Farmers and Mechanics' Bank are entitled to receive the money they have so advanced, so that there is nothing due from that bank, as appears by a copy of the letter of the Secretary of War, herewith transmitted.

There was no public money on deposite, or otherwise, to the credit of the Treasurer, in any of the other banks in this District which have recently stopped payment.

The report of the Treasurer, hereunto annexed, will show that $14,000, belonging to the navy pension fund, was invested in the stock of the Bank of Washington, at the time that bank stopped payment; and it appears by the letter of the Secretary of the Navy, herewith transmitted, that this investment was made in the years 1811 and 1817.

I have the honor to remain, very respectfully, your obedient servant,

R. B. TANEY,
Secretary of the Treasury.

The Hon. the PRESIDENT OF THE SENATE.

REMARKS OF MR. CRAMER,

OF NEW YORK,

IN THE HOUSE OF REPRESENTATIVES,

April 8, 1834,

On the Revolutionary Commutation Bill.

The time which this subject has already occupied the attention of the House, and the distinguished talent and ability with which all the provisions of this bill have been sustained by the committee who reported it, admonish me that nearly all has been said which was necessary and proper, and that I ought not to trespass upon the patience of the House by obtruding my views upon it, conscious as I am that my proper prov- is rather to listen to, and receive instruction, to endeavor to impart it to others. But a sense of the justice of these claims, a settled iction of the entire propriety and expediency e provisions of this bill, and more especially anner in which it has been assailed by one of honorable colleagues, must be my apology for y presenting the reasons which have contrib- to the formation of my judgment; not that I the vain hope thereby to influence the a solitary member of this House, but with to a clear and succinct statement of the case resents itself to my own mind. I would , what were the services rendered by the ners? And on what equitable grounds is nsation demanded? If I have understood claims rightly, they are based on the solemn of the nation, given at a crisis when it had g else to pay in but its faith and its depreciated credit, and made for services the most important, appalling, and hazardous, that can be imagined. Yes, sir, the men for whom this bill proposes compensation, entered and continued in the service of the country, literally with a hangman's noose around their necks. For what, I ask, would have been their condition if they had proved unsuccessful in the final issue? No one need be told that the most of them, in all human probability, would have been tried, condemned, and executed as rebels. Congress, therefore, conscious of this fearful exposure, and as an additional inducement for them to remain in the service of their country, promised them the little pittance of half pay for life, on condition that they continued in the service to the close of the war, and this was predicated on a still more uncertain contingency, well understood by both parties, viz: that they should be victorious in the dreadful and unequal contest in which they had embarked. This agreement or contract was consummated by a resolution of this House, recorded 21st October, 1780; it was afterwards, in March, 1783, on the magnanimous request of the officers interested, commuted for a much less sum than the original amount, namely, five years' full pay in money, or in securities bearing an interest of six per cent. per annum.

Thus we have the services performed, and the pledged compensation; and what are the objections to the fulfilment of the contract, or in other words, to the passage of the bill under consideration? One which was urged by my honorable friend from New Hampshire is, that it erects a new and a different tribunal to ascertain whether the claimants bring themselves within the letter or spirit of the resolution of 1783. And is this objectionable? I confess I listened with attention to the gentleman who made it, and heard no satisfactory reason assigned to sustain the objection. Is it not evident that action on these claims would be more uniform and expeditious if they shall be settled by the Secretary of the Treasury under a general law, than if investigated and adjudicated by a committee of this House; fluctuating and changing as that body must necessarily be. Surely it must be admitted that the proposed arrangement would be infinitely more just, as the same rule, by the same officer, would be applied to all claimants, with leisure sufficient carefully and critically to examine all the proof. In addition to this, it would save much of the time of this and the other House, and also prevent unnecessary delay and expense to the applicants. It would, therefore, promote true economy, as well as expedite justice; for it must be recollected and admitted that the individuals here claiming are creditors of the Government, and if we pay at all, we must, or ought, to pay interest at the rate stipulated in the resolution to which I referred, for the entire period these settlements have been referred.

Another objection which has been made against the bill is, that the rule prescribing the proper testimony to substantiate the time and extent of this service, is too favorable to the applicants. This, however, is an assumption which is not warranted by the facts, nor by the established rules of evidence, as applicable to ancient covenants. But this objection, has been so fully discussed, and so triumphantly refuted by gentlemen who have preceded me in this debate, that I will not tax the patience of the House with any additional reason to demonstrate its fallacy.

The third objection which has been taken to the provisions of this bill is, that some may possibly be thereby included who have already received compensation, and perhaps others who were not originally entitled to any; and therefore it is gravely inferred, that because we may possibly do wrong, we must not do that which is clearly and manifestly right. This is proving too much. It would extend to the total exclusion of all legislation; for I defy human sagacity to frame a law so that injustice might not sometimes be consequent on its enforcement. But I cannot perceive, from the face of this law, nor from any legitimate reason which has been presented to the consideration of the House, that such consequences would necessarily, or even probably, follow, unless gentlemen are disposed to maintain the position, (which I regret to say some have too broadly intimated,) that these claimants were so destitute of moral rectitude, so sordid, so superannuated, and so indistinct in their reminiscences, that, in order to effect their own or others' designs on the treasury, they would affirm to any statement of facts which any artful, unprincipled scrivener might indite. But, in charity to the gentleman from New York, who intimated this, I will not suppose that it was seriously intended as being peculiarly applicable to these venerated relics of our nation's pride and boast. But be it as some gentlemen will have it—that occasional frauds may and will be practised, still I am for the law; for I insist that these claims are more sacred, and of a higher order, than any others which can be presented to the consideration of this House; and, for one, I hope I may be spared the painful retrospect of having uttered any sentiment derogatory to the character of these claimants, or of having, from false notions of economy, withheld that which was justly due to any man, who, in that momentous struggle, rallied around the sinking standard of his country. Yes, sir, I conscientiously contend that it is better, far better, in this case, that some should even receive Benjamin's portion, than that any should go unsatisfied.

But is it correct that frauds would be more successfully practised on a vigilant, intelligent public officer, than on the members of this House? So far as my experience extends, the reverse of this position is true. I therefore maintain that if gentlemen who are opposed to this bill are solely intent on carefully and honestly guarding the treasury, this is the proper and most effectual mode of doing it. But, for myself, sir, I am not disposed in this case to bar the treasury of the Union, at the hazard of doing injustice to those revolutionary veterans who, in the most gloomy and agonizing period of our nation's emancipation, stood in the front ranks in many a bloody and embattled field. No, let that eagle-eyed vigilance to protect the funds of the nation be reserved for a proper subject and a fit occasion; let it be rigorously observed and enforced in all cases of doubtful constitutional prerogative to make appropriations either on the ground of construction, expediency, or precedent—the most villanous and still the most successful subterfuge heretofore resorted to, to rob your treasury and sap the foundations of your Government. I will go all lengths with the gentlemen on this point, and here I will assure them is an ample and a glorious field for curtailment. Nay, I will go with them for retrenchment and economy on all proper occasions. But for heaven's sake let us not commence this system by doing an act of violence and gross injustice to the warworn veteran, or to his lineal descendants. No, sir, parsimony here would be prodigality; for we should be squandering and dissipating that which dollars and cents could not compensate for: I mean our national character; for I assert that it is an undeniable proposition that these are just dues, growing out of a national compact for services the most adventurous and important ever performed by man. And will any one have the hardihood to affirm, that in this case the laborer is not worthy of his hire; or, in other words, his promised reward? If any one doubts, let him estimate, if he can, the value of our independence, of our exalted and happy condition, as a people, contrasted with any or all other nations on the face of the globe. Nay, let him estimate, if possible, the value of our Union. Yes, our Union, and then let him say, if he can, that the men who achieved this by their valor and patient endurance of every deprivation and danger, shall go unpaid, and be denied the trifling bounty which was their due by solemn contract, because, forsooth, it will take a few thousands, nay, millions, if you please, to liquidate and cancel these claims. For one, I deprecate all such miserable miserly suggestions; such contracted, sordid reasons; and pity the mind that can be influenced by them. What! refuse to pay for services, but for which we should not now be here, legislating in this magnificent Hall, for a great, independent, and magnanimous nation? No, sir, we should have been spared that proud satisfaction, for we should still have been the humble vassals of some foreign prince, for such a race of patriots and heroes has not appeared on the American stage since that eventful period.

For one, sir, (said Mr. P.,) I never will be satisfied until every man who fought and bled in the

revolutionary struggle is paid the last cent which is legally or equitably his due. No, sir, I never shall feel as though enough had been done for those men who have done so much for us individually, for the nation, and for the world—until all, from the least to the greatest, are paid the uttermost farthing. Let it not be said of this republic, as it has been truly said of all the ancient republics, that they were ungrateful to their best benefactors. No; the Government, in this case, should act as an honorable man would act: invite all its just creditors to come and receive their pay, subjecting them to no unnecessary expense or delay. What should be said of an individual who should render the same excuse—interpose the same plea in bar to the payment of his creditors, which has on this occasion been urged by honorable members in avoidance of these claims on the part of the nation? I ask, what would be said of an individual who should refuse to pay a class of hardy, adventurous laborers, to whom he was principally indebted for an immense estate, because he, on his own volition, unauthorized by their consent, had appointed a time when he would pay; and inasmuch as, through inadvertence or ignorance, they had not attended to his call at the time specified; and who should therefore assume that he was exonerated from all liability, that now the door of justice was closed, that the day of retribution was past, and that he would not pay? And still more: suppose that he should interpose this other plea, which has here been urged in behalf of the Government, that there were many of these claimants, and, if he paid one, he could not refuse to pay others; and that the amount, although just, would be too large, and therefore he could not and would not pay? Would not every honorable man condemn such an excuse, and despise the wretch that made it? And shall the Government do that which no man possessing a correct moral sense would dare to justify in his friend?

Sir, I trust for the honor of the country that such principles will never be sanctioned as the deliberate sense of this or any future Congress. These claimants came not here, sir, as most others do, praying extra compensation for extra services rendered, or perhaps services never rendered. They come not here, sir, praying remuneration for real or pretended losses, but they do come with the nation's bond in their hands, sealed with their own blood, or the blood of their sires, and they ask us, as their faithful guardians, and the executors of our fathers' will, to cancel it. They come not here, sir, supplicating favors; but they come here literally and emphatically demanding rights. And will you turn them away from this Capitol, as a knave would from his counting-house, with the rogue's plea—the statute of limitations? Yes, sir; it is literally the rogue's plea in this case; for I contend that Government has no moral right beyond what an individual has to vary a contract, without the mutual consent of the contracting parties.

I trust there is too much honor and integrity, too much of the spirit of '76 in this House, to sanction such an unjust judgment.

REMARKS OF MR. TIPTON,
OF INDIANA,

In Senate, Tuesday, May 20, 1834,

On the motion of Mr. Clayton to refer and print the memorial of the Cherokee Chiefs.

Mr. TIPTON rose, and was in favor of receiving and referring this paper to the Committee on Indian Affairs. He would hear the complaints of the humblest individual, no matter of what color, if he was an individual entitled, as the Cherokees were, to the protection of our Government. But, sir, I am opposed to incurring the expense of printing the voluminous documents accompanying the memorial, until after it is examined and reported on by a committee of the Senate, who could judge correctly what consideration it is entitled to from this body.

I am confident (said Mr. T.) that it is right and proper to protect the poor Indians. No member of the Senate feels a deeper interest than I do in their preservation and prosperity; and it will be found much more difficult to shield the poorer class of Indians from combinations of dishonest chiefs, and their co-workers of mischief and oppression, than to protect them against the impositions of the officers of the Indian Department.

The policy adopted five years ago by this Administration, of paying the annuity to the heads of families, and not to the chiefs, is both just and proper. It not only shields the poor Indians from the impositions of dishonest chiefs, but enables the President to detect dishonest agents of the Indian department. The Secretary of War knows, or should know, the number of Indians in each tribe, and the amount to be paid to them by the Indian agents; and if the Indian agents were instructed to transmit, with their accounts for settlement, an abstract, showing the number of heads of families in each tribe, and the number of individuals in each family, with the amount of money paid to each, and this abstract should be certified by two witnesses, known to be entitled to credit for veracity, should the payment not have been made in the utmost fairness, to all persons belonging to the tribe. The President should dismiss every agent neglecting to do his duty agreeable to instructions.

The honorable Senator from Delaware [Mr. Clayton] has told us how oppressive it was for a poor Indian to travel fifty miles to receive fifty cents, when the chiefs could bring them their money without cost, as was the case under former Administrations. The honorable Senator is mistaken as to facts.

There is no law directing in what manner the annuity shall be paid; it is, as it should be, left to the President, and the mode complained of is the only just one. It is the duty of the agents to count the money due to each individual, or head of family, and to show each man what he is entitled to for himself, his wife, and each child, and not suffer the chiefs to cheat them out of a portion of the money due to them from the Government. It is true, that if all the chiefs were honest, this would change the case. Sir, said Mr. T., I have heard of Ross, the memorialist; his name and character have not made a favorable impression on my mind. I have no doubt but he, and others acting with him, will subtract 25 per cent. from the annuity, if it is put into their hands. The chiefs, most generally, are traders, and will pay the people in goods or whiskey, and keep the money, and the poor Indians never see a dollar.

There have been cases, said Mr. T., where the chiefs, and a few others, prevented the common Indians from receiving the money due them from the Government; although the agents would count and offer them their annuities, they would not receive it, fearing the displeasure of the chiefs; and the chiefs and traders want to coerce the Government to make the payment in such manner as to favor their interested and dishonest motives.

This chief, [Ross,] I understand, claims $3,000 to defray his expenses in coming here, and he wants the United States to pay this expense; and if Congress refuse this request, I do not doubt that Ross will never let the annuities pass from his grasp, until he wrings from the poor people of his tribe the price that he wants us to pay for coming here to annoy the President and Congress.

Sir, I am anxious to have a report on the facts of this case from the Committee on Indian Affairs. Let us know all the facts, and I have no doubt that we shall find that the chiefs, and a few others, actuated by selfish motives, are waiting upon this most just and proper measure of their Administration. When we understand all these facts, I hope that the Senate will sustain the Administration in this measure.

I know that many honest men, who are misled by such clamors, coming from interested men, are imposed on, and under a mistaken state of the facts, are aiding this chief, Ross, and others. I am sure that, so soon as better informed, they will change their course, and lend us their support.

Letters from Havre state that the French Government had despatched a sloop of war from Brest for the United States, with despatches from our Government, of such a character as it was presumed would be satisfacto y.—New York Evening Post.

THE CONGRESSIONAL GLOBE.

PRINTED AND PUBLISHED AT THE CITY OF WASHINGTON, BY BLAIR & RIVES.

23d Congress, 1st Session. | SATURDAY, MAY 31, 1834. | Vol. I........No. 26.

IN SENATE.

Monday, *May* 26, 1834.

A message upon executive business was received from the President of the United States, by Mr. Donelson, his Private Secretary.

The VICE PRESIDENT presented a communication from the Department of State, transmitting the information called for by the resolution of the Senate of the 9th instant, relative to the superintendent of the Patent Office; which, on motion of Mr. EWING, was for the present laid on the table.

PETITIONS.

Mr. SMITH presented the remonstrance of R. Watson and others, and Charles Hunt and others, against the renewal of the patent of John Ames; which was laid upon the table.

Mr. WRIGHT presented a memorial signed by the principal officers of eighteen of the banks in the city of New York, praying Congress to pass a law regulating the gold and silver coin of the United States, and the value of foreign coin.

Mr. WRIGHT moved its reference to the Committee on Finance.

Mr. WEBSTER said it was not to be supposed that this subject had escaped the attention of that committee during the session. The subject seemed to consist of two parts: to make foreign silver coins a tender in payment of debts, and a restoration of the relative value of our own gold and silver coins. This subject was before the other House, and was under the care of a gentleman from New York in that body. Mr. W. hoped the honorable member from New York [Mr. Wright] would use what exertions he could to induce a speedy action on the bill in the House of Representatives.

Mr. WRIGHT said he was aware that the subject was before the other House. These memorialists had connected distinct propositions in reference to the gold and silver coin, and they had done so because they were apprehensive that the measure before the House might not pass, and they believed their propositions were presented in a more simple form. Mr. W. said this, that the memorial might receive, as he was sure it would receive, the respectful attention of the committee.

Mr. WEBSTER observed that unless the bill in the House of Representatives should be progressed in to a conclusion during this week, he now gave notice that he should introduce the proposition now before the Committee on Finance on this day week.

Mr. CLAY presented several memorials from citizens of Huntingdon county, Pennsylvania, praying a restoration of the deposites to the Bank of the United States and the recharter of that corporation, under certain modifications; which was referred to the Committee on Finance, and ordered to be printed.

Mr. CLAY presented the petition of Hugh S. Gatewood, of Indiana, praying a grant of land for services rendered by his ancestors in settling the State of Kentucky; which was referred to the Committee on public lands.

Mr. HENDRICKS presented a memorial from citizens of Switzerland county, State of Indiana, praying that the deposites may be restored to the Bank of the United States, and that that institution may be rechartered.

Mr. H. said that the memorial was numerously signed by all political parties, and by men of every pursuit and occupation in life; that this was a county in which the friends of the present Chief Magistrate were numerous and the party strong; but that in this instance, all other considerations had been buried in oblivion, and this subject taken up because the people felt what they said; that this memorial was not to be viewed as a party production, but as the expression of an honest, intelligent people, truly representing the condition of their country, the causes which had produced it, and the remedy, in their opinion, proper to be adopted. This county (said Mr. H.) is situated on the Ohio river, above the falls. It is of the second class of counties in size and population, but in the peaceful industry, the virtue and intelligence of its population, it is second to none. It is a mixed population, grouped together from every quarter of the Union, and from almost every quarter of the world, chiefly, however, from Kentucky, Ohio, Pennsylvania, New York, and New England. This county, too, contains the Swiss settlement emigrants from the cantons of Switzerland, in Europe, who, at an early period, settled on the Ohio river, where they still live, and where they have long been successfully engaged in the culture of the vine.

Mr. H. said that the pursuits of this people were mainly agricultural; that they were the exporters as well as the growers of their produce; their market was New Orleans, to which they carried a heavy export trade every year. They had as little direct interest in the Bank of the United States as any people of the Union; they dealt not in stocks or in banks; they seek not accommodations in banks; but in the prosperity of the Bank of the United States they had a deep interest; for having no State banks as yet in operation, the paper of that bank had largely entered into the circulating medium of that section of the country. The present state of things had withdrawn rapidly from circulation the paper of that bank, and its place was but partially supplied with the paper of other banks, in which the people had less confidence than in the Bank of the United States.

The people of Switzerland county (said Mr. H.) tell you that past experience demonstrates the convenience and necessity of a paper circulating medium, convertible into specie, to supply the want of sufficient metallic currency. They believe that a sufficient quantity of gold and silver does not exist to form a circulating medium, and that a sudden change, or attempt at change, could not fail to prostrate the best interests of the country. They believe that the country cannot get along without a national bank of some kind; that without such institution, the currency cannot have either soundness or stability, nor can the exchanges of the country be equalized or regulated. And in these opinions Mr. H. entirely concurred. He believed we could not get along without a national bank, or a national currency. He said he was no advocate for the present bank, and believed it had no paramount claim for a recharter; he would prefer a new bank, one located in the city of Washington. He knew there were many objections to this location, but they were not insurmountable. By this location, the constitutional difficulty would be done away, for all admit the power of Congress to charter a bank here. He would not charter so large a capital as $35,000,000, for if, as so often alleged, the present bank had exercised too much power, and become dangerous, it was on account of its great capital. He would distribute the bonus among the States, and would permit it to locate branches in the States, only by permission of the State Legislatures; nor would he deprive Congress of the power, at a future day, if the public interests should require, of modifying such charter, or of chartering another bank. Such bank, although it could not go into operation till the expiration of the present charter, would give prospective stability to the currency, would at once inspire confidence, and that was all that was wanting.

Mr. H. said that no one regretted the removal of the deposites more than himself. It was an unfortunate measure for the country. He had never doubted the power to remove them, nor the correctness of the motive which had induced the removal, but he had always regretted the measure as deleterious and injudicious. He had said by his vote, that the reasons of the Secretary were unsatisfactory and insufficient; but he had carefully avoided any vote, or any act, having a tendency to increase excitement, which in his opinion was but increasing the distress complained of. He had voted against every measure having a tendency to prolong or imbitter the deep agitation of the country. His object was the tranquillity of the country, at this time too much disturbed; the prosperity of the country, which could not be restored unless the excitement be allayed.

Mr. H. moved that the memorial be read, printed, and referred to the Committee on Finance.

Mr. BENTON said he would add his testimony, if necessary, to that of the Senator from Indiana, [Mr. Hendricks,] in favor of the respectability of the population which furnished the subscribers to the memorial just presented. He knew their industry, enterprise, and sincere devotion to their country, and had no doubt but that they fully believed in all the distresses which they mentioned; but their petitions only recited what had been alleged on this floor for the last four or five months; and the reason why petitions were so late in coming from that distance must be because the petitioners were so far off from the source of alarm, so far off from this chamber, where the cry of distress was first raised four or five months ago. The petitioners speak of the scarcity of money in consequence of the disappearance of the United States Bank notes. Now (said Mr. B.) the petitioners doubtless thought there had been a great diminution of this kind of currency, because they heard it proclaimed from all quarters. But he (Mr. B.) would ask the Senator from Indiana himself, [Mr. Hendricks,] what was the real amount of these notes withdrawn from circulation?

Mr. HENDRICKS said, that he had not before him any statistical tables, showing him the condition of the Bank of the United States, neither monthly reports nor those of any other period, and his recollection did not furnish him with an answer to the question propounded. He presumed the Senator from Missouri was much more familiar with that subject than himself. Nor did it go to the point in question, whatever the facts might be. He presented the memorial of a portion of his constituents, men of intelligence, who well understood the fact which they stated to the Senate. What was that fact? The want of an adequate circulating medium, and the rapid disappearing of the United States Bank paper in that section of the country. This is a fact intimately connected with their business—a fact which they see and feel. They make no statement of this kind for any other portion of the country, but undertake to represent the condition of their own. Now, to them it makes little difference how much or how little may be the amount of notes withdrawn from circulation by the Bank of the United States. It is the effect of the existing derangement of the currency upon themselves of which they complain.

Mr. BENTON resumed. It was right to be a little statistical in this case. The statistics would show that, in point of fact, there was very little diminution of the circulation of the United States Bank notes. There was about sixteen or seventeen millions of those notes now out, and that lacked but little of the quantity out last year before the deposites were removed, and which was usually about seventeen or eighteen millions. Still the petitioners were no doubt right in the fact that these notes were scarce in the part of the country in which they lived; for the law of bank circulation, which he (Mr. B.) explained on another occasion, carried them off to the Northeast.

Mr. B. spoke of the prices of produce in New Orleans, and quoted from Benjamin Levy's Price Current, of the most recent date. From this, it appeared that western produce bore a good price; cotton higher than it was at this time last year; pork, beef, bacon, flour, corn, &c., about as high as usual, and in good demand. He also read a letter from Cincinnati, showing that steamboat business, both freight and passage, was better than it had been for three years past; that money was as plentiful as usual, prices as good as usual, people contented as usual, and panic-makers only out of business. Mr. B. then took up a New York paper, the *Times*, just received, and which gave the value of different bank notes at the broker's board in that city, and showed that the southern banks had nearly recovered their ancient rates in that market. The Carolina banks only about three per cent.

discount; the Virginia banks, even those which were reported dead, only about two per cent. discount; and the pet bank of this District, (the Metropolis,) which had been the subject of so many melancholy predictions, was at the rate of one per cent. discount, and no more! All is going on well, (said Mr. B.) It was nearly " the last of pea time" with distress memorials; and as the cry of distress began in the Senate, he presumed it would end in the Senate; and that, henceforth, nothing more would be heard than the faint and lingering accents of dying out an exanimate alarm.

Mr. HENDRICKS repelled the idea that the memorial which he had just presented to the Senate had been produced in any degree by the panic which pervades the country, or that it had been gotten up for political effect. The people of Switzerland county were not panic-makers, nor were they more liable to alarm from danger at a distance than the people of other portions of the Union. In this instance, he believed they were much less liable to alarm than many others. They stated facts connected with their own business. The produce business, in which many of them are engaged, is deeply affected by the distracted and depressed condition of the currency. They see, and they feel, and they cannot be mistaken in the facts they state. He had referred, when up before, to the condition of the New Orleans market, to the fact that bankruptcies, unparalleled in number and extent, had taken place in that commercial city, and that it was believed the means of receiving and paying for the produce of the upper country was not to be found there. In that reference he had allusion, among other things, to a letter which he had seen in the hands of a Senator on the floor, and such information was generally more to be relied on than the prices current. That letter did speak of unparalleled failures in that city; and that information accorded well with the experience of many who had recently been engaged in the produce business on the Ohio and Mississippi rivers.

Mr. H. repeated that this memorial had not been gotten up for political effect. He would remind the Senate of a remark he had made when first up, that the memorial was signed indiscriminately by men of all parties. He would venture the assertion, that there were many names on that paper of persons as warmly devoted to the present Chief Magistrate and his Administration, as any individual within the sound of his voice; men who, although they disapprove of the removal of the deposites, and of the measures which have produced the present state of things, yet have undiminished confidence in the purity and integrity of the motives which induced the measure—men who indulge in no denunciations, who believe the President of the United States to be an honest man, an ardent patriot, and one who would make, for the perpetuity of our free institutions, as great sacrifices as any other. It is not for political effect that such men make such statements as are contained in the memorial just presented. All their political feelings are on the other side of the question.

Mr. SILSBEE presented a remonstrance of citizens of Massachusetts against the renewal of the patent of John Ames; which was laid on the table.

Mr. WEBSTER presented a similar remonstrance from other citizens of that State. Same order.

REPORTS.

Mr. WEBSTER, from the Committee on Finance, reported a bill making appropriations for the Indian Department, and gave notice that he should call it up to-morrow, with a view to its passage.

Mr. WHITE, from the Committee on Indian Affairs, made unfavorable reports upon—

The petition of John Walker;

The petition of Henry Weirick; and

The petition of Mrs. McNair, widow of Alexander McNair.

All of which were read, and concurred in.

BILLS.

The following bills were read a third time, and passed:

A bill for the relief of Martha Bailey, and others;

A bill for the relief of the legal representatives of Joseph Rowe, deceased;

A bill for the relief of the heirs and legal representatives of Frances Barham, deceased, and her husband, Fielding Barham;

A bill for the relief of George K. Jackson;

A bill granting the right of preemption to John Yantis;

A bill for the relief of Asa Hartfield, his assignee or legal representative;

A bill for the relief of Henry Waller;

A bill for the relief of Charles J. Hand;

A bill for the relief of the administrators of Bolitha Laws, deceased;

A bill to remove the office of surveyor general of the public lands in Ohio, Indiana, and the Michigan Territory;

A bill for the relief of Lieutenant Archibald S. Campbell;

A bill for the relief of Capt. Wolcott Chauncey;

A bill for the relief of William Mann; and

A bill for the relief of Colonel A. R. Woolley.

A bill for the repair of the Mars' Hill military road, in the State of Maine, was, on motion of Mr. TIPTON, laid upon the table.

PENSION FUND.

The Senate then proceeded to the consideration of the special order, being the report of the Committee on the Judiciary relative to the conduct of the Bank of the United States in relation to the pension fund.

Mr. KANE resumed and concluded his remarks against the report of the committee, and in support of the message of the President. He was followed by Messrs. CLAYTON, WRIGHT, BIBB, FORSYTH, PRESTON, and KING of Alabama.

The question was then taken on the following resolution, offered as an amendment to the resolution reported by the committee:

Resolved, That the act of Congress for the relief of certain officers and soldiers of the Revolution, passed on the 15th May, 1828, and the act supplementary to that act passed on the 7th June, 1832, providing for any arrears acts providing for the payment of military pensions—

And decided by the following vote:

YEAS—Messrs. Bell, Bibb, Black, Calhoun, Chambers, Clay, Clayton, Ewing, Forsyth, Frelinghuysen, Kent, King of Georgia, Leigh, Mangum, Naudain, Poindexter, Porter, Preston, Robbins, Shepley, Silsbee, Smith, Southard, Sprague, Swift, Tomlinson, Waggaman, Webster—28.

NAYS—Messrs. Benton, Brown, Grundy, Hill, Kane, King of Alabama, Linn, McKean, Morris, Robinson, Tallmadge, Tipton, White, Wilkins, Wright—15.

The question was then taken on the following resolution, as a further amendment to the resolution reported:

Resolved, That no power is conferred by any law upon the Department or Secretary of War to remove the agency for the payment of pensions, under the said act of the 7th June, 1832, and the funds, books, and papers connected with that agency, from the Bank of the United States, and to appoint other agents to supersede that bank in the payment of such pensions.

Which was agreed to by the following vote:

YEAS—Messrs. Bell, Bibb, Black, Calhoun, Chambers, Clay, Clayton, Ewing, Frelinghuysen, Kent, King of Georgia, Leigh, Mangum, Naudain, Poindexter, Porter, Preston, Robbins, Silsbee, Smith, Southard, Sprague, Swift, Tomlinson, Waggaman, Webster—26.

NAYS—Messrs. Benton, Brown, Forsyth, Hill, Grundy, Kane, King of Alabama, Linn, McKean, Morris, Robinson, Shepley, Tallmadge, Tipton, White, Wilkins, Wright—17.

The question recurring on the following resolution, as amended by the foregoing, to wit:

Resolved, That the Department of War is not warranted in appointing pension agents in any State or Territory where the Bank of the United States or one of its branches have been established, except when specially authorized by act of Congress:

It was decided in the affirmative.

The Senate then, on motion of Mr. MANGUM, adjourned.

HOUSE OF REPRESENTATIVES.

MONDAY, May 26, 1834.

The further consideration of the memorial heretofore presented by Mr. WISE, which had been

postponed to this day, was, on motion of Mr. E. WHITTLESEY, in consequence of the absence of Mr. WISE, postponed to Monday next.

The memorial from the citizens of York county, Pennsylvania, presented last Monday by Mr. BARNITZ, and postponed to this day, came up.

Mr. B. meant at length into an argument against the removal of the deposites, and the policy of the Administration relative to the Bank of the United States. After going on a little more than an hour, Mr. B. moved that the further consideration of the subject be postponed to Monday next, upon which the question was taken and carried: Ayes 73, noes 42.

The memorial of the citizens of Norfolk county, Virginia, presented by Mr. LOYALL on Monday last, and postponed to this day, came up.

Mr. L. went into an exposition and defence of his course upon this question, in reference to the views of his constituents, which occupied about an hour. In conclusion, he moved that the memorial be laid on the table, and printed; which was agreed to.

The memorials from Washington and other counties in Ohio, presented on Monday last by Mr. VINTON, and postponed to this day, came up. Mr. V. moved the following resolution:

Resolved, That the memorial from the counties of Washington and others, in the State of Ohio, be referred to the Committee of the Whole on the state of the Union, to which has been referred the bill "to regulate the deposite of the moneys of the United States in certain local banks," with instructions to strike from said bill all after the enacting clause, and insert in lieu thereof a bill directing the deposite of the money of the United States to be hereafter made in the Bank of the United States, and for the renewal of the charter of said bank, with such modifications thereof as said committee shall deem expedient.

Mr. V. supported the resolution in a very ardent speech, after concluding which, he withdrew his resolution, and moved to refer the memorials to the Committee of the Whole on the state of the Union, and that they be printed; which was agreed to.

The memorial from sundry inhabitants of Belmont county, Ohio, presented on Monday last, by Mr. BELL, of that State, and postponed to this day, came up.

Mr. BELL, after a few preliminary remarks, moved that the memorial be read, laid on the table, and printed; which was agreed to.

The further consideration of the memorial presented on Monday last from citizens of Wayne county, Indiana, by Mr. McCARTY, was, on motion of that gentleman, postponed until Monday next.

The resolutions passed at a public meeting of the citizens of the county of Jones, in the State of Mississippi, held at the court-house, presented by Mr. PLUMMER on the 19th instant, being under consideration—

It was read and said, that a voice had at length been heard from the workingmen of Mississippi. His predictions on this floor a few weeks ago had been verified. The Democracy of that State (he said) had risen in their might, and resolved to live free or die. They have resisted the temptations held out to them by the bank. They have indignantly refused to sell their liberties, so dearly purchased by the blood of their fathers, to a moneyed corporation, for a few millions of rag-money dollars. They have, like the patriots of the Revolution, borne the pressure of the times until the last turn of the screw, without a murmur or a groan, and then, as if by enchantment, large asunder the whole machinery by which the United States bank would enchain them; and added another chapter to the evidence already adduced to prove that the people are the source of all power. The voice of that portion of the people of Mississippi, who had at all times stood by him and sustained him in his efforts to put down the aristocracy of the State and raise the standard of equal rights and equal privileges on its ruins, had at length been raised, (said Mr. P., and the echo has reached the halls of the National Legislature. The citizens of the county of Jones in that section of the State of Mississippi where there was as much patriotism, as much love of lib

erty, as much devotion to our free institutions, and he would venture to assert without the fear of contradiction by any one who knew the people as well as he knew them, in that section of the State, where the people were more ready to defend from violation the principles of that Constitution handed down to them by the sages of '76, and more ready to resist the encroachments of power upon their rights and liberties than any portion of the people of the Union, convened at the court-house on the 19th day of March last, and resolved that they had unshaken confidence in the integrity, firmness, and patriotism of the present Chief Magistrate, who has so often received the unqualified approbation of a large majority of his fellow-citizens. And that the course which he has pursued in relation to the United States Bank, particularly as evidenced by the removal of the deposites from that institution, increases and strengthens his claims upon the gratitude and admiration of his countrymen. That they approve of the course pursued by the Secretary of the Treasury (Mr. Taney) in removing the public deposites, and that the removal of the people's money from an institution so dangerous and corrupt, was but an act of justice to the outraged moral sentiments of an abused and unsullied people. That they viewed with contempt the conduct and course pursued by the bank party at a public meeting lately held at Natchez, which they conceive to be a prelude to worse times, if the bank should succeed in obtaining a recharter. That the recharter of the United States Bank was in their opinion dangerous to our present democratical form of government—to the rights and privileges of the people—and should be opposed by all good men. And they further resolved that they viewed with regret that some of their *public men* had become like cattle in the field, subject to be *bought* and *sold*.

The working portion of the community, he said, were the last to become excited upon a question of great national importance, and the last to make a movement towards expressing their sentiments in relation to the affairs of Government; but when they do move, said Mr. P., their course is like the rushing of the mighty winds; their might is like that of the waves of the ocean; the force of their opinions is like the power of the boisterous hurricane, driving everything before it and humbling to the dust the haughty oaks of the political forest that refuse to bow submission to their opinions. There is no power on earth that can withstand their influence. Neither the officers of a free Government, "clothed with a little brief authority," nor the monarch on his throne, with absolute sway, can resist their mandates. There was (he said) a Latin maxim which he had often heard quoted by those who had a knowledge of that language, the meaning of which he understood to be, "The voice of the people is the voice of God." If such (said he) is the power of the people, who can stand out against their expressed opinions? It is true, sir, (said Mr. P.) we hear those who set themselves up as the rulers of the people, but who in fact are their mere servants, declare their intention "to discard everything like party action, when they shall be called to decide upon the great leading principles of Government;" notwithstanding however their declarations and professions, when they see the expressions of the workingmen of the country written on the wall, they will tremble before the omnipotent political power of the people, and their knees will smite together like Belshazzar's. Standing, as he did, by himself, in opposition to the aristocracy of the State, professing to advocate the principles of the workingmen, at a time when it seemed that the bank had purchased the liberties of the people, so far as individuals could be found to sell themselves, and had forced others by the exercise of her all-controlling influence, to bow submission to her mandates; it was (he said) gratifying to his feelings to find, when opposed, abused, persecuted, and nullified by the advocates of the bank, and frowned upon by the blind followers of men disregarding principle and professing to support the measures of the present Administration, that he was sustained by those who had stood by him in all of his political struggles for principle, in opposition to the combined influence of National Republicanism, Nullification, and Jacksonism.

The name of Jones county, and her old and faithful representative, (Samuel Ellis,) the chairman of the meeting with whom he fought side by side, in the legislative councils of the State, for those Democratic principles now recognised as the constitutional law of Mississippi, operated on him (he said) like a charm; was music to his soul, and encouraged him to redouble his exertions in support of the efforts of the Chief Magistrate to relieve the people from the rag-money bondage of the bank, and the haughty power of an irresponsible moneyed corporation, calculated to prostrate the rights of the States and destroy the liberties of the people. The people who composed that meeting are no men worshippers; they are not the blind followers of any man or set of men; they support the measures of the Administration when right, and oppose them when wrong; they have decided that the body politic has not become so debilitated, nor the energies of the people reduced so low, that the Government cannot continue to exist without a moneyed monopoly to lean upon for support. They have said that they are not prepared for slavery; they have shown themselves worthy of that rich inheritance handed down to them by the patriots of the Revolution; they have declared themselves capable of self-government.

Public meetings (Mr. P. said) had been held by the people, in different parts of the State, got up by the aristocrats, the national republicans, nullifiers, tariffites, and those indebted to the bank, denouncing the Administration and its course on the bank question, and sustaining the rest of the delegation. False representations have been made to enlist the people on the side of the bank. Public meetings have also been called by the office holders, office seekers, and the Jacksonian aristocrats, and men worshippers, self-styling themselves the Democratic Republicans of the State, condemning the whole delegation, without distinction of persons. But this (he said) was the first movement made by the *bone and sinew* of the country, uninfluenced by partisan feelings or sinister motives for the purpose of approving of the course pursued by the Administration in relation to the United States Bank. The people have been excited to action against the political moves put in motion by the panic-makers of the bank, and nothing can appease their wrath, or calm the troubled waters, short of a total abandonment of the unconstitutional and oppressive banking system adopted by the General Government.

A few weeks ago, the most of the leading politicians of the State had taken a stand in opposition to the course pursued by the President, or seemed to hesitate on which side to enlist, whether on the side of the people or the bank. But one man among the literati of the State (he said) had had the firmness and independence to encourage him to stand firm in the course he had taken during the present session, and the office-holders and man-worshippers had even succeeded in destroying the confidence of the Executive in him. Things were, (he said) however, getting right. The leaders would be compelled to bow in submission to public opinion. The citizens of Jones county are not office-seekers. They have no other object in view than the good of their country. They have spoken the honest convictions of their hearts, without fear, favor, or affection of men, and without any reward, hope, or promise thereof. They have spoken the language of freemen, and the sentiments of the Democracy of Mississippi.

These things (he said) were not confined to the State he had the honor in part to represent. They are spreading to the remotest corners of the Union. The workingmen of Massachusetts are awakening from their lethargy. The Democracy of the ancient Commonwealth, who were the first to resist the tyranny of Great Britain, are resolved not to be the last to resist the encroachments of a purse-proud aristocracy. The Republicans of Berkshire, the Congressional district represented by the honorable gentleman before him, [Mr. BRIGGS,] which he (Mr. P.) claimed as his birth-place, were determined (he said) not to be outdone by their sister States in the race of patriotism, on the great question now convulsing the nation. They, too, as well as the people of the South, have discovered that the tide of moneyed influence has been for many years undermining their original principles, and washing away those rights and privileges guarantied to them by the magna charta of their liberties, before the foundations of the republic have crumbled from beneath them; and while it is yet in their power to redress their wrongs by legal and constitutional means, they, too, are resolved not to sleep, while the chains of domestic slavery are being riveted on their limbs by a haughty moneyed aristocracy. They, too, have discovered, that the day is fast approaching, when, to assert their rights as freemen, will subject them to the stigma of traitors, and punishment of rebels; and that they are already denounced as tories and enemies to their country. He said he held in his hand a letter, received a few days since from a friend and relative, dated at Richmond, Massachusetts, on the sixth instant. The writer (he said) was a Democrat of the old school, dyed in the wool. He is (said Mr. P.) a workingman in principle as well as practice. He is a carpenter and house-joiner by trade; and by the fruits of his industry, has been enabled, for a few years past, to cultivate a farm, the proceeds of which he depends upon to support his family. He is no office-seeker, no political juggler, and has nothing but the good of his country at heart. Although the letter was not intended for the public eye, it accorded so well with his own opinions, that he could not refrain from reading some extracts therefrom, believing, as he did, that it spoke the language of the workingmen of old Berkshire. Mr. P. then read the following extracts:

"Permit me to return you my sincere thanks for the favors shown in sending me public documents. It has furnished me with some interesting intelligence, which I could not otherwise have obtained. You will excuse me for the liberty I take; I am neither a writer nor a politician; that you know by my writing; therefore it would not become me, as a plain farmer, or a laboring man, to write to a gentleman in the Congress of the United States, giving my views on any particular subject which they have in their trust; but having confidence, sir, that you will make allowance for my inabilities and not expose them, I will give a few ideas of my own, however they may differ from any one else. I have just read the President's protest against the usurpation of the Senate. It is noble, patriotic; like all other of his writings, worthy of the highest place in the pages of our history. I am not master enough of language to give it the exalted station it merits. That, together with the veto, ought to be engraved in large letters of gold, and raised so high in the heavens that it can be read by every individual that inhabits this globe. I have read a small pamphlet which was sent to my friend, pretending to prove that credit is preferable to coin. When our farmers read anything that is trying to substitute paper or credit in place of gold and silver, there is a kind of inaction and gloom upon their faces, which renders them very unpleasant. But when they read of a scheme that will do away small bank notes, and substitute specie in their stead, there seems to be a lively action, and their countenances are like the spring, blossoms after a long winter.

"People in this place, I think I may safely say, are getting more and more in favor of the measures pursued by the President in relation to the bank. His most bitter enemies say they do not like so powerful an institution as that of Mr. Biddle's bank, and that it ought not to exist any longer, but do not wish that President Jackson should have the honor of pulling it down under his Administration. As I view the subject, I hope and implore the goodness of Almighty God, that so powerful, overbearing, and corrupt an institution, that can give into the hands of a small class of people, the power, as well as influence, to distress a whole nation, might in this our day be purged from our Republic. If those are not your views, permit me, sir, as you have a better opportunity to form a more correct knowledge of the subject, to ask of you to give me a slight view, by way of letter.

"Perhaps, sir, you may think I take a great interest in this bank concern for a man in my capacity and occupation of life. I certainly do. There has never been, since 1816, in my opinion, a subject brought up before the people of the United States that ought to wake up and call the attention of every individual citizen like this. I hope that institution which has been called by

'the name of the United States Bank, will never
' be rechartered for any term of time, however
' short, upon any conditions or modifications what-
' soever; for I do not think that that institution
' was ever properly entitled to 'that name. My
' reasons for this are, the people generally have
' not been led to the inquiry of the principles and
' situation of their bank, as they otherwise would,
' had it not been called by that name. Our good
' honest farmers have supposed, until very lately,
' that bills on the United States Bank were as safe
' to be locked up in their chests as the gold and
' silver—supposing the United States accountable
' for all the bills issued from that bank, and would
' redeem them at any future day. Now they be-
' gin to see their trust is in the hands of a class of
' individual speculators. Let every institution be
' called by the name of its proper owners. Just
' as I was about to close my scribbles, Mr. ——
' called on me; after passing the usual compliment,
' I inquired how the Administration stood in his
' estimation? (not expecting any very favorable
' answer, knowing that he had been, ever since
' Jackson's election, violently opposed to his Ad-
' ministration) he said, he supposed I had reference
' particularly to the removal of the public moneys
' from the United States Bank. Thus far, said he,
' I can say, the people of the United States will yet
' bless Old Hickory for the decided measures he
' has taken with that bank. If that institution can
' cause so great a pressure, and create such a panic,
' throughout the whole United States at this time,
' what could it not do in a few years more? He
' not only spoke his own mind, but the minds of
' many others of the same stamp. These sayings
' confirm what I have already said."

Such language might not be very acceptable to
those who differ with him in opinion, and those
who charged every one that sustained the Administration, on the bank question, with being under
the influence of improper motives, and particularly to those who intimate that all who support this
measure of the Executive, are the "slaves and
vassals of Andrew Jackson, and that they were
ready to exchange the Constitution and the law for
the will of a weak old man." Such language
needed no reply. It was, in his opinion, unworthy of that character which every gentleman on
that floor ought to maintain. It was not, he said,
the voice of prudence and discretion, aiming at the
good of the country, but it was the language of
mad ambition, reckless of the interests of the people, and everything else save the prostration of
the popularity of the present Administration, the
elevation of their political God to power, and a
division of the "loaves and fishes" among the
hungry curs of their party. They are the fulmina-
tions of a crazed brain, distracted by being disappointed in his political aspirations. They are the
ravings and rantings of that party who threaten
one day to destroy the Union, rather than submit
to an unconstitutional and oppressive system of
taxation, which they themselves are the authors of,
and the next day attempt to excite the people to
rebellion, because they will not bow submission to
an irresponsible corporation, about to enslave a
free country, which they themselves admit to be
in violation of the Constitution.

The proceedings of a public meeting at Holmesville, Pike county, which were heretofore presented by Mr. PLUMMER, and postponed to this
day, came up.

Mr. PLUMMER went into too extended an
exposition upon the subject for to-day's paper.
In conclusion, he moved that these proceedings
be laid on the table and printed.

Mr. EVANS presented a memorial and series of
resolutions adopted by sundry citizens of Hallowell, Maine, in opposition to the course of the Administration relative to the Bank of the United
States; which, after an explanation, he moved to
lay on the table and have printed. Agreed to.

Mr. HALL presented a memorial praying for a
post route: which was referred.

Mr. MILLER, by leave of the House, moved
that 30,000 copies of the reports of the majority
and minority of the Investigating Committee into
the concerns of the United States Bank, with the
accompanying documents and correspondence, be
printed.

Mr. HIESTER suggested that 15,000 was sufficient.

Mr. KING moved that ten thousand copies be
printed.

Mr. BRIGGS inquired whether upon this motion the reports would be sent out together?

Mr. MILLER said, his view was that they
should be printed separately, but that the correspondence, which was the most important portion
of the papers, should be annexed to each. He
thought it would be more convenient to gentlemen
on all sides of the House, to have the reports separate. As to the number, which might appear to
be large, it would afford the members but about
one hundred and fifty each for distribution.

Mr. BRIGGS move to amend the motion of the
gentleman from Pennsylvania, (Mr. MILLER,) so
that the majority and minority reports be printed
together.

Mr. EVANS raised a question of order—
When the motion to print was, agreeably to the
rules of the House, laid on the table until to-morrow.

Petitions and memorials were presented by
Messrs. OSGOOD, LINCOLN, BRIGGS, and
GRENNELL, of Massachusetts.

Mr. BURGES presented certain proceedings of
the House of Representatives of Rhode Island;
which, on his motion, was postponed to Monday
next.

Memorials and petitions were also presented by
Mr. D. J. PEARCE, of Rhode Island;

Messrs. BARBER and YOUNG, of Connecticut;

Mr. DEMING, of Vermont;

Messrs. PIERSON, BROWN, DICKSON,
ADAMS, BEARDSLEY, and CLARK, of New
York; Messrs. H. KING, LAPORTE, STOD-
DERT, MOORE, HAWES, BEATY, CHIL-
TON, and LEA.

Mr. BURD offered the following resolution,
which was agreed to:

Resolved, That the Committee on Roads and
Canals be instructed to inquire into the expediency
of causing a survey and examination to be made
by a competent engineer, of the route between
Cumberland, Maryland, and Newry or Hollidaysburg, in Huntingdon county, Pennsylvania, with
a view to connect the Chesapeake and Ohio Canal
and the Pennsylvania Canal, by a turnpike or
railroad, as may appear most expedient.

Mr. WATMOUGH presented several memorials from Montgomery county, on the subject of
the removal of the deposites; the consideration of
which were postponed till Monday next.

Mr. CLAY presented the petition of Isaac Wellborn, jr., asking the confirmation of his title to a
tract of land reserved to Thomas Harrison, under
the treaties of 1817 and 1819, between the United
States and the Cherokee tribe of Indians; which
was referred to the Committee on Public Lands.

The bill to revise and amend the act for the relief
of insolvent debtors, passed by the House of Representatives, and amended by the Senate, was
taken up, and, on motion of Mr. E. WHITTLE-
SEY, referred to the Committee on the Judiciary.

The bill for the relief of Matthew Daly, as
amended by the Senate, was taken up, and the
amendment concurred in.

The bill from the Senate, supplementary to the
act to alter and amend the several acts imposing
duties on imports, approved July 14, 1832, was
read twice, and referred to the Committee of Ways
and Means.

Several private bills from the Senate were read
twice, and referred.

The following message was received from the
President of the United States, by the hands of
Mr. DONELSON, his Private Secretary:

To the House of Representatives
of the United States:

I transmit a letter from the Marquis de Rochambeau, to the Minister of the United States in
France, referring to the petition of certain descendants of the Count de Rochambeau, which
was communicated to the House of Representatives, with my message of 22d February, 1833.
Extracts from the despatches of Mr. Livingston
to the Secretary of State, respecting the same subject, are also sent.

I likewise transmit for the consideration of the
House, a petition from the heirs of Baron de
Kalb, (accompanied by a note from General La-

fayette,) praying remuneration for services rendered by the Baron, to the United States, during the
war of the Revolution.

ANDREW JACKSON.
Washington, 12th May, 1834.

On motion of Mr. E. EVERETT, the above
message, with the accompanying papers, was referred to the Committee on Foreign Relations, and
ordered so be printed.

On motion of Mr. WARD,
The House adjourned.

IN SENATE.
TUESDAY, May 27, 1834.

A message upon executive business was received
from the President of the United States, by Mr.
DONELSON, his Private Secretary.

PETITIONS.

Mr. SMITH presented the remonstrance of a
number of the inhabitants of Connecticut against
the renewal of the patent of John Ames, paper-
maker.

Mr. EWING presented the memorial of 1163
inhabitants of Washington county, Ohio, praying
a restoration of the deposites to the Bank of the
United States, and the renewal of the charter of
that institution. Referred to the Committee on
Finance, and ordered to be printed.

Mr. WEBSTER rose and said, that in the intelligent and philanthropic community in which it
was his pleasure to reside, great efforts had been
made, and pains taken to improve the condition
and elevate the moral character of the sailors in
the mercantile marine of the United States. Exertions had been made to educate them, and to
teach them the value of property, by means of
saving institutions. These means had been promoted and assisted by a clergyman coming from
the class itself, and it was hoped that much progress had been made in the substantial improvement of the sailor. A large number of the citizens
of Boston had united in a memorial to Congress
on this subject, and they were of opinion that a
portion of the revenue arising from the commerce
of the country, which the sailor contributes essentially to promote and increase, could not be better
applied than to establish the means of giving him
intellectual and moral improvement. This memorial he held in his hand, and it was signed by persons in various public stations: first, by the municipal officers of Boston; next by clergymen; then
by merchants, ship owners, seamen, and others.
Mr. W. said it was well known that this class of
persons were always the objects of the particular
care of Government. They were so in the United
States. Hence the means which had been provided for the support and maintenance of sick and
disabled seamen. And perhaps it would be as
extravagant extension of this charity to provide
the means of their education. This, however, was
a subject for the consideration of the committee to
whom this memorial would be referred.

Mr. W. moved his reference to the Committee
on Commerce; which was agreed to.

REPORTS.

Mr. TOMLINSON, from the Committee on
Pensions, reported a bill to amend an act entitled
"An act for the relief of the surviving officers,
non-commissioned officers, and soldiers of the Revolution," passed in 1832. The bill was read, and
ordered to a second reading.

Mr. SHEPLEY, from the Committee on Revolutionary Claims, made a report unfavorable to the
petition of Major George Gibson; which was concurred in.

The report of the Committee on Indian Affairs,
unfavorable to the petition of John Walker, was
concurred in.

Mr. WEBSTER gave notice that he should, to-
morrow, move that the Senate proceed to executive business.

Mr. CLAY gave notice that on to-morrow he
would move for leave to introduce a joint resolution, the object of which would be to request
what the Senate had asserted in a resolution of
its own, that the reasons of the Secretary for the
removal of the deposites, were unsatisfactory and
insufficient; and to provide, that after the first of
July next, all deposites of the public revenue shall
be made in the Bank of the United States and its

branches, according to the 16th section of the bank charter.

The following resolution was submitted by Mr. PRESTON:

Resolved, That the Secretary of War report to the Senate a statement showing the names of the several pensioners who are now or may have been heretofore placed on the pension rolls, designating their rank, annual allowance, the sums which they have severally received, the laws under which their pensions have been granted, the date when placed upon the roll, their ages, and the States and counties in which they severally reside; also, the names of the pension agents who have received compensation as such, and the amount of such compensation, and the act under which it was allowed; the names of the clerks who are, and who have been, employed in the Pension Office, and the sums paid them as compensation, with an aggregate statement of the whole sum disbursed on account of pensions.

By Mr. POINDEXTER:

Resolved, That the Secretary of the Treasury be directed to communicate to the Senate copies of the several reports made by the agents appointed to examine into the condition of the land offices for the sale of the public lands, and the conduct of the several registers and receivers during the year 1833, together with the documents and other evidence annexed to said reports.

RHODE ISLAND ELECTION.

On motion of Mr. POINDEXTER, the several orders of the day were suspended, and the Senate took up the report of the select committee in the case of the contested election of Messrs. ROBBINS and POTTER.

On motion of Mr. POINDEXTER, the report of the majority was read; after which the report of the minority [Mr. WRIGHT] was also read.

The question was then taken on the adoption of the resolution submitted by the majority, to wit: "That ASHER ROBBINS is duly and constitutionally elected a Senator of the United States, to 'represent the State of Rhode Island for six years 'from the fourth of March last," and determined in the affirmative, by the following vote:

YEAS—Messrs. Bell, Bibb, Calhoun, Chambers, Clay, Clayton, Ewing, Frelinghuysen, Hendricks, Kent, Knight, Leigh, McKean, Mangum, Naudain, Poindexter, Porter, Preston, Silsbee, Smith, Southard, Sprague, Swift, Tipton, Tomlinson, Waggaman, and Webster—27.

NAYS—Messrs. Benton, Brown, Forsyth, Grundy, Hill, Kane, King of Alabama, King of Georgia, Linn, Morris, Robinson, Shepley, Tallmadge, White, Wilkins, and Wright—16.

ELECTION OF PRESIDENT AND VICE PRESIDENT.

The Senate then proceeded to consider the resolution of Mr. BIBB, proposing an amendment to the Constitution of the United States as it respects the election of President and Vice President of the United States.

Mr. BIBB then addressed the Senate in explanation of the mode of election which he proposed. He condemned the present mode by electors, and supported and advocated an election of the President immediately by the people. He deprecated an election devolving, in any instance, on the House of Representatives, and was in favor of providing, that whenever it should happen that no candidate for the presidency obtained a majority of the whole number of votes given, the election should return to the people, and so *toties quoties* whenever such was the result.

Mr. B., at four o'clock, gave way, without concluding, to Mr. MANGUM, on whose motion,

The Senate adjourned.

HOUSE OF REPRESENTATIVES.

TUESDAY, *May* 27, 1834.

Mr. E. WHITTLESEY reported a bill for the relief of Nathaniel P. Tatem; read twice, and committed.

Mr. BELL, of Tennessee, reported the bill to alter and amend the act for the relief of certain insolvent debtors of the United States, recommending the concurrence of the House in the amendments made thereto by the Senate.

The House having agreed to take up the bill for consideration, the amendments of the Senate were concurred in.

Mr. BELL also reported the bill from the Senate entitled "An act in addition to an act to provide for the more effectual punishment of certain crimes against the United States," without amendment; and on his motion, the further consideration of the bill was postponed till to-morrow.

Mr. ELLSWORTH moved that the Committee of the Whole on the state of the Union be discharged from the further consideration of the bill to authorize the issue of writs of error from the courts of the United States, in certain cases, relative to patent rights, so as to bring it into the House.

Mr. BATES opposed the motion, and it was negatived.

Mr. WATMOUGH asked the unanimous consent of the House to take up the bill to regulate the pay of the army and navy of the United States; which was objected to.

Mr. BEARDSLEY, from the Committee on the Judiciary, reported a bill for the relief of Abel Wood; read twice, and committed.

Mr. MILLER moved the suspension of the rules of the House, in order to enable him to call up the motion submitted by him yesterday, to print an extra number of the bank investigation report; which was agreed to.

The motion being to print thirty thousand copies of the report of the committee, with the accompanying documents, and also the same number of copies of the report of the minority of the committee, with the documents accompanying it,

Mr. BRIGGS moved to amend the motion, by requiring that the reports of the majority and of the minority of the committee be attached to each other. He advocated the motion on the ground of economy, and of the expediency of enabling the public to see both sides of the question at once. He said that if the two reports are printed separately, the accompanying documents must be twice printed; whereas, if the reports were united in one pamphlet, one set of the documents would answer for both.

Mr. LANE said, while he agreed with the honorable gentleman from Massachusetts [Mr. BRIGGS] that the object of printing extra numbers of the reports was to disseminate correct information among the people—to make them acquainted with the action of this House, and to enlighten the public mind—he should vote against the amendment proposing to have the report of the majority and the appendix, and the report of the minority, printed and attached, in order that they shall be placed in the same hands at the same time, as he did not believe that mode best calculated to produce that result. That he desired them separate; they could then be circulated to the best possible advantage. The majority report, and the appendix by which it is sustained, can be forwarded to one individual, the minority report to his neighbor. Each would read, and each would be desirous to see and read the other; and the ambition of each would be increased to have the one he had read seen by his neighbor, in direct proportion to the excitement of his political feelings, or the desire he might feel to arrive at truth, and have others possess the same advantage. Whereas to place both in the hands of the same person, he would have it in his power to suppress the one or the other, at his pleasure; and, therefore, to print and distribute them separate, to his mind, had the advantage, as two to one; and this is the more desirable, when we take into consideration the fact that to publish the highest number proposed—thirty thousand—will furnish to each member but one hundred and twenty-seven copies, and those to be distributed among fifty thousand persons.

Mr. L. said he had another objection to uniting the reports. To which would the appendix be affixed, the majority or the minority—to the report of the committee of the House, or to the *bank* report. From what we have seen, the evidence would be affixed to the bank report, and withheld from the other by the printer of this House. For, said Mr. L., on examining it—those printed and laid upon our tables—that course has been adopted; for what reason, he knew not. He would, therefore, vote against the motion to amend.

Mr. ELLSWORTH would hardly believe (he said) that there was a single member of the House who was unwilling to send out the views of the minority on the subject. He rose principally to say, that it was a mistake to suppose that the omission of the publication of the appendix to the report of the majority was the fault of the printer of this House. If he was correctly informed, the report of the majority could not be found by the public printer in the Clerk's office, and it did not reach him till he saw it in the columns of the Globe. The report of the minority falling into his hands, was published with the appendix. But the appendix to the report of the majority was not published in the Globe, and was not considered by them as an essential part of the report. He did not know that it was the intention of the majority to publish the correspondence. The House would not judge that the public printer had neglected his duty, and he wished that the editor of the Globe had done his. He had looked very anxiously in the Globe this morning for the report of the minority, and he did not find it there. It was now recommended to us to pursue the same course, and publish the report separately. He protested against this as an *ex parte* movement.

Mr. BARRINGER said his object in rising was simply to say, that he was casually present when a note was received by the public printers from a member of the majority of the committee, in which it was stated that the appendix was not considered as a part of the report, and had not been ordered to be printed.

Mr. MUHLENBERG. The note spoke of the journal of the committee, not of the appendix.

Mr. BARRINGER. Perhaps it was so.

Mr. THOMAS had endeavored (he said) to get the floor before this debate was indulged in, believing that he could satisfactorily explain this matter. As to the question whether the reports should be printed separately or united, he was perfectly indifferent how the House decided it. He should feel very little confidence in the conclusions of the majority of the committee if he thought that the report of the minority was of a character which could, in the slightest degree, shake or impair those conclusions. Not one fact stated by the majority was contradicted by the report of the minority. As to the inferences from these facts, there might be a difference of opinion. He apprehended no difficulty from joining the two reports. It appeared to be supposed that by uniting the documents some little expense might be avoided. But it was not so. The appendix of the majority report would not suit that of the minority. It was differently arranged, and contained different selections from that prepared by the minority. Whether the reports were published together or separately, no expense would be saved, even if that should be considered an important object.

Again, he was indifferent whether the reports were united or not, because, if any member should wish to send one without the other to a constituent, he would greatly lack in ingenuity if he could not cut the piece of twine which unites them, and then send them separately. Of the propriety of separating or uniting them, each member must judge for himself, and consult the wishes of his constituents.

Another matter was connected with this which he was sorry to see brought into the debate by one of the gentlemen [Mr. ELLSWORTH] who was his colleague on the committee. We were told that the public printer could not obtain access to the report of the majority. He had been applied to, as a member of the committee, for a copy of the report for publication in the Globe, in order that it might be published immediately. Being himself inexperienced in regard to the usage in such cases, he consulted others, who told him that it was proper and usual to give a copy for publication. The documents, he knew, must soon reach the public eye, and it did not appear to him that any inconvenience could arise from granting the request. With the consent of the other four members of the committee, who had assented to the majority report, he applied to Mr. Burch, one of the clerks of this House, and requested him to have a copy made out under his direction, for the Globe; but asked him to have it done by one of the clerks in his office, and not to permit the original to be taken from under his control. Some of his colleagues,

during his absence, had, it was said, informed the printers that the appendix was not considered a part of the report. There was some mistake in this. With whom it originated he knew not. Most certainly his colleague, [Mr. MANN,] who had, during Mr. T.'s absence, undertaken to superintend the publication of the report, had stated to the foreman in the office of the National Intelligencer, that the appendix was to be attached to the report. On his return to Washington on Monday, Mr. T. was surprised to find the report of the majority published without an appendix, while the appendix designed for the minority report was attached to it. He went to the office of the National Intilligencer for an explanation. He there learned that the appendix to the majority report had been omitted by mistake. It had now been properly arranged, and the House would no doubt have possession of it to-morrow. Mr. T. said he did not understand the motive for the introduction of this small matter into this debate by the gentleman from Connecticut. It could not certainly affect the merits of the grave questions which the House would soon be called to deliberate on. When they arose it would be time enough to enter on this discussion.

Mr. E. EVERETT wished, he said, to make a short explanation in defence of individuals who were absent, and were accused of negligence of duty. He meant the public printers.

Mr. THOMAS explained that it was far from his intention to impute any negligence of duty to the public printers.

Mr. EVERETT did not understand any grave charge to be made; but that one was left to be inferred. It had not been ordered by the committee that the journal should be printed. It was sent down with the appendix, and the business of setting up the types of the journal was commenced. Happening to be at the printing office, he suggested to the printers that it was not intended to publish the journal, but told them not to rely upon his impression, but to consult one of the majority of the committee. This was done, and his impression was fully confirmed. The fact was ascertained that the journal was not ordered to be published. By a subsequent determination, the printer was ordered to print the journal; and we now had it on our tables.

The gentleman says that the appendix of the report of the majority would not suit that of the minority. He did not know whether to consider this remark as exceptionable or not. The appendix of the minority was not extracted from the journal. It was a series of communications between the two committees, arranged in chronological order. He had supposed that the order and rule of the House would require both of these reports to be printed in one pamphlet, whether it was so directed in the resolution or not. The views of the minority were a part of the report. He had been a member of two committees—the retrenchment committee in 1828, and the committee on the apportionment bill; and he well recollected that the views of the minority of those committees formed a part of the report. He had understood that, in 1828, the Clerk was requested by the majority of the retrenchment committee to separate their report from that of the minority, but he said it was a thing unheard of, and he refused to do it without the special order of the Speaker. The Speaker was applied to for the order, and did not give it. Whichever way the question was decided, the people should hear both sides from him. In order to facilitate his labor in sending the reports to his constituents, he wished to have but one packet to hold and but one address to write.

Mr. THOMAS remarked, that it was erroneously supposed that he intended to reflect upon the printer of the House. He had said that no inconvenience had resulted from his having given a copy of the original report for publication, and no error had been committed by the printer of the House in consequence of that circumstance. The public printer had a copy both of the appendix and the journal, but he seemed to be at a loss to conceive why the appendix should be printed, as it consisted of extracts from the journal. This error of the printer had not, as the gentleman from Connecticut supposed, grown out of the fact that a copy of the report had been furnished to the Globe.

Mr. MANN said that having had something to do with the transaction, he felt called upon to explain what part he bore in it. If there was any error or mistake at all on the subject, it had sprung from two editorials in the Intelligencer, which he regarded as idle and pestiferous wind, knowing that as they applied to himself they were unmerited. It became necessary that there should be a copy of the original report, and that it should be corrected for the press. He was himself, in the absence of the chairman, laboriously engaged on Friday in performing this duty. When it was completed, he carried the report and documents, and the journal, to the office of the public printer on Friday evening. He did not find him there, and the next morning he carried them again, and left them with a person in the office. Will the public printer say that they had not the documents in time to print them and lay them on our tables? The printer, he also said, knew very well that the original report was in the hands of the clerk who was copying it, for he was there. The young man labored diligently until twelve o'clock on Friday in the work, when he [Mr. MANN] assisted him to finish it, and corrected it in the Globe. The censure of the gentleman from Connecticut must fall upon him for the inconvenience which he supposed the public printer to have suffered from the detention of the papers.

Mr. ELLSWORTH said the gentleman was wrong in supposing that he wished to cast any censure on him. He had spoken of a circumstance which to him appeared surprising, that a document, which the House ordered to be printed on Thursday morning——

Mr. MANN. Thursday evening, sir.

Mr. ELLSWORTH. On Thursday afternoon. It was surprising to him that the document then ordered to be printed, did not reach the public printer till Saturday morning. The original papers were taken away and detained till Saturday. It did appear to him as if some pains had been taken that the report should appear in the Globe, without the correspondence and without the report of the minority.

Mr. MILLER said, that if the gentlemen had all made their explanations, he would submit a few remarks, although he regretted to protract a debate at this important period of the session. As related to the mistake that had occurred in regard to the printing of the appendix, annexed to the report of the majority of the committee, he did not believe that much censure ought to be attached to any one. He understood that some mistake had occurred, by which the journal of the committee had been blended unintentionally with the correspondence between the committee of this House and the representatives of the bank. That it was subsequently discovered, when the type were partly set, and the correction of this error had caused the delay. Such mistakes may occur without any blame being attached to any person. With regard to the question immediately before the House, that of ordering both documents to be printed in one pamphlet, he viewed it as of very little importance. For himself, if they were printed separately, he would send them both together to such of his constituents as the number printed would enable him to supply. He was not afraid to trust them with both sides of the question. He presumed that other gentlemen would pursue the same course.

The present motion appeared to have no other object than that of compelling members to send them both together. He thought this matter might be trusted to the discretion of gentlemen themselves, and if members were disposed to separate them they could do so, notwithstanding they were bound together with a small cord.

In point of fact they were separate documents and had separate appendixes. This he knew when he made the motion; and that had induced him to submit the motion in the form he had.

He thought if the House printed an equal number of each report it ought to be sufficient to repel the charge of a disposition to print and circulate partial information at the expense of the nation. According to strict parliamentary proceedings, the views of the minority were not considered a report, and leave would have to be obtained to present them to the House. A different practice, however, had prevailed in the House, and he was not disposed to disturb it. It was, perhaps, one that was founded in good sense. But as the reports were separate and distinct documents, he could see no obligation on the part of the House to unite them. The decision that the House might make on the question was to him unimportant. He would, therefore, not trespass on the attention of the House.

Mr. BURGES was surprised, he said, that gentlemen who considered this motion so unimportant, should yet be so much opposed to it. It was the usage of the House to print in one view the reports of every member of a committee. The people wished to have the truth, and the whole truth. No one could vote against this motion without wishing to separate the allegations against the bank directors from their defence, &c.

Mr. CHILTON supported the amendment of Mr. BRIGGS—when

Mr. MILLER said he had no intention of sending forth garbled information to the people. Where reports had been printed separately, as was the case with the majority and minority reports of the Committee of Ways and Means the present session, he had felt it his duty to send them together. He had no idea that his motion would give rise to so much debate, and was perfectly willing to accept the amendment as a modification of his motion.

The question having been stated upon filling the blank with the highest number proposed,—thirty thousand.

Mr. PINCKNEY was in favor of printing the largest number of both reports; he was particularly anxious that the minority report should be extensively circulated, as it contained, as far as it went, sound and constitutional views.

Mr. MASON inquired whether it was in order to discuss the contents of either of the reports upon the motion before the House?

The CHAIR replied, upon a question of printing a document, the subject of it was open to discussion to a certain extent.

Mr. PINCKNEY proceeded: He wished to assign his reasons for voting to print the largest number. They were, perhaps, not the same reasons which would influence other members. The only objection he had against the report of the minority was, that it did not go far enough in its constitutional views. But it went far enough to show the monstrous powers arrogated by this House, which involve the liberties of the people. They will see in the measures which may be adopted—unless the people themselves fly to the rescue—the fetters which were forging for them; and if they had a particle of regard for their liberties left, they would rise and repel this attempt to subjugate them. He was anxious that the report of the minority of the committee might be extensively circulated in the State of Pennsylvania. It was that State which had placed General Jackson in the presidential chair. He wished that State to see this proposition to prostrate her sovereignty and drag fourteen of her most respectable citizens before the bar of this House. Her citizens would be able, by this attempt to degrade that State, to understand the tyranny of the Administration. The people of that State already know that every class is involved in unprecedented distress by its measures—they had seen the attempt made by the President to disgrace the Senate——

The SPEAKER called the gentleman to order.

Mr. P. said he was assigning the reasons why he should vote for printing the largest number of this document. The citizens of Pennsylvania might not know that it was now proposed to give this House power over the personal libesty of her citizens. They well knew their property was at the disposal of Congress—they might not be aware that their personal liberty was also at our disposal. They know that her meritorious sons, Messrs. Ingham and Duane, had been ignominiously dismissed from office without cause; but they may not know that it was contemplated to drag fourteen of her most distinguished citizens as criminals before this House. He wished the people of that State to read the reports and determine whether they would permit this to be done—whether that State will not interfere and rescue the personal rights and liberties of her citizens from being invaded in the manner proposed——

The CHAIR interposed. This was a question

of printing merely—the debate at large on the subject was postponed until Tuesday.

Mr. P. said he would not pursue the topic at this time. The grounds taken by the House, in the adoption of the resolution, ought to be understood. The people should know the flagrant violation of their rights that had been committed by the House.

The CHAIR said, no reflections upon the proceedings of the House were in order.

Mr. PATTON hoped the gentleman would be permitted to proceed, and that an opportunity would be afforded for reply.

The CHAIR said, that order must be preserved.

Mr. PINCKNEY wished the doctrines in these documents to be disseminated universally throughout the State of Pennsylvania, that her citizens might determine whether the proceedings of this House, and the measures proposed by this committee, do not involve an assumption of power which it was the duty of that State to resist. If her citizens should be brought to the bar of the House, under the resolution reported by the committee, he could not say which idea would be most mortifying to him: that the House should have so far transcended its authority, or that the State of Pennsylvania should have tamely submitted to such a usurpation.

Mr. MASON had not seen the report of the minority of the committee; but had no manner of objection that it should accompany the report of the majority. He trusted the example of the gentleman from South Carolina [Mr. PINCKNEY] would not be followed. He was not disposed to forestall public opinion as to the merits of either of these reports. As to his own share in the proceedings, he was prepared to abide the severest scrutiny to which his conduct could be subjected. A day had been assigned for the consideration of this subject; when that arrived, he hoped a full discussion would be gone into; at this time, he hoped the question would be taken, without going into any further irregular discussion.

Mr. BYNUM said he was sorry that the honorable gentleman from Pennsylvania had consented to accept of the amendment of the honorable member from Massachusetts, as he conceived that amendment to have a partial reflection on a certain party in this House. He was prepared to vote for the original motion of the gentleman from Pennsylvania. He stood on his own responsibility, and held himself amenable to no earthly power for his acts, except to that portion of the people whom he alone directly represented here.

[Mr. B. was about to enter into an argument on the merits of the amendment, when the SPEAKER stated the amendment had been acted on, and his remarks in relation to it would be out of order.]

Mr. B. then said, his principal object in rising had been to reply to the extraordinary remarks of the honorable member from South Carolina, [Mr. PINCKNEY,] who had just taken his seat, and asked if it would be in order to reply to some remarks that had just fallen from that honorable member?

The SPEAKER replied it would, and asked Mr. B. to proceed.

Mr. BYNUM then said, that it was strange that the gentleman had been guilty of the very thing that he, and the party with which he acted, had just complained of. It had been said, that the object of the majority of the committee, in their report, was to forestall public opinion. Now, he asked, what was the object of the gentleman in denouncing in advance the report of the majority of the Bank Committee? What was it done for by the gentleman, if it were not to prejudge it? The report of the committee was not now under consideration. The gentleman must have had an object in doing what he did, then; if it was a reasonable object, it certainly was to prejudice beforehand the people of the country against that report. He considered such a course unfair and unjustifiable.

The honorable gentleman had called on Pennsylvania to wake up, and resist the outrageous usurpations about to be practised on her citizens. He had no doubt that the poor, ignorant, benighted Pennsylvanians, would be greatly obliged to that honorable gentleman for taking charge of their interest on this floor, and for the great solicitude that he had expressed to have for them—poor, ignorant creatures, unenlightened, uninformed, as they were of the course they ought to pursue, as was thought by the intelligent gentleman from South Carolina. He asked if a poor farmer had treated with contempt the mandates of the Representatives of this House, if there would be, in all probability, so many *tears* shed by gentlemen, when the simple process of arrest was proposed by this House to be served on him? He doubted very much if he might not be dragged here, without a single sympathy of honorable gentlemen, who now manifested so much sensibility with regard to Nicholas Biddle and his bank associates.

It was now evident, and it was unnecessary to attempt to conceal it longer, that there were only two great parties in this country—one arrayed in favor of the government of the bank, and the other in favor of the government of the people. Gentlemen had shown their cloven foot too plainly to be misunderstood by any intelligent mind; their object was to defend the bank, and protect it in whatever course it might pursue. His object was the reverse; he was determined to defend and protect, as far as he was able, the Government and the people, in defiance of the bank and its mercenary advocates. He bowed to and recognised no tyrants nor tyrannical institutions, but to the tyrant, people; they were the only tyrants to whom he would bow or obey.

The gentleman from South Carolina had, in his usual course, denounced the President as a tyrant and usurper. Indeed, if a stranger were present, and not accurately acquainted with the proceedings of this House, and with the nature of the subject before it, he would take it for granted that the President had drawn up the tyrannical report of the majority of the bank committee. What had the President to do with that committee or its report? He really did not see in what manner the gentleman could reasonably make the President guilty of the tyranny and usurpation which had been committed on the bank by the enlightened and intelligent committee, appointed by an overwhelming majority of this House, to investigate its concerns. The gentleman had said, too, that the President had made war on the Senate. He denied it. It was the reverse. The Senate had made war—[here the Speaker said that he called the gentleman from South Carolina to order, when he made that remark, and it was out of order to reply to it.] Mr. B. then said that there was a desperate, reckless party, that not only in this House, but in other places, had seized every occasion, however irrelevant, to abuse and denounce the President of the United States as a tyrant and usurper. It was done to produce a revolution in public sentiment, with the sole purpose of bringing into power those reckless persons who were ready to produce any revolution, in order to turn themselves uppermost. Yes, they were willing to see the fairest and happiest country the world ever saw, deluged in blood and desolation, to wreak their vengeance on that venerable old patriot who now occupied the White House, to their exclusion. But for him, they thought their unbridled ambition might have been long since gratified. He was the only barrier between them and the great object of their ambition. Mr. B. said that the President had been placed there by the people—by a most overwhelming majority—and he hoped, in spite of the efforts of such a party, and their bank government to aid them, the people would sustain him, so long as he so nobly adhered to their rights and interests, in defence of which he was now willing to sacrifice his all.

He was glad that the gentleman had thought fit to arraign this House for the exercise of tyranny and usurpation towards the bank government. Yes, the representatives of the whole people had also been guilty of usurpation and tyranny towards the bank. But who were those that had been guilty of this usurpation? The members of this House, and many of them the warmest friends of the bank; for many of them voted to clothe this very committee with the very power that they had exercised, and proposed now to exercise. Were they, then, not as culpable as the committee, who only proposed to execute the powers granted them by the House? Certainly, he thought that those who gave the powers to the committee were the persons guilty of the usurpation, and among them was, he believed, a majority of the warmest friends of the bank in the House. But the cry of usurpation and tyranny had been set afloat to gull and impose on the poor ignorant people, no doubt, as gentlemen thought, and he expected next year to hear that the people themselves had become the tyrants and usurpers of the powers and rights of this precious monopoly—of this most arrogant and corrupt institution, that is now bidding defiance to the Government of the whole nation and its authority. The gentleman from South Carolina seemed much alarmed as to the power of the House to arrest a citizen in Pennsylvania and bring him here to testify before this body. He thought there was no more cause for alarm than there should be in case the court of the United States were to issue a subpœna to arrest an individual to appear before it in this city. The same power that had given this right to the court of the United States had given it to this body, as a collateral branch of the Government. He could not, then, see why such extraordinary sensibility should be felt by honorable gentlemen on the present occasion, except for the extraordinary interest taken on behalf of the bank and its officers.

What had we heard? (said Mr. B.) Had not the gentleman called upon the good people of Pennsylvania to resist the civil authorities of the Government? Had he not here, on this floor, endeavored to excite the good people of that patriotic State to rebellion?—yes, sir, to rebellion?

Mr. PINCKNEY rose to explain, and said he had not called on the people of Pennsylvania to resist the civil authorities of the Government.

Mr. BYNUM said he was very glad that the gentleman had disavowed his assertion, as he certainly understood him to have said what he had stated most distinctly; but he was glad that the gentleman had now qualified his remarks on that subject. He hoped no member of this House was capable of wishing to excite rebellion in this country, however desperate might be the fortunes of their political party.

Mr. WATMOUGH rose and called Mr. BYNUM to order.

Mr. LYTLE asked Mr. WATMOUGH to state the exceptionable words.

Mr. WATMOUGH declined.

The SPEAKER decided that Mr. BYNUM was not out of order.

Mr. B. continued. He should like to know why such alarm should be felt at the proposition of the committee, simply to arrest persons at a distance, and have them brought here to testify, when almost every judicial tribunal in the country, of any consequence, had exercised this power almost a thousand times over, without the least alarm or complaint being made in any quarter. Were the persons connected with this bank to have superior privileges to any other class of citizens of this country? He hoped not. He hoped that the freemen of America would never consent that a few bankers should be more exempt from arrests, or any other regular process of the laws of this country, than any other plain men of the community. He saw nothing in the report of the majority of the committee that had alarmed him in the least. The powers which it proposed to be exercised, had been exercised by bodies of much inferior dignity, a hundred times over, without prejudice to the citizen, or material injury to any one. He thought the charge against the committee, of usurping arbitrary power, of the same class with those that had been so profusely made against the Executive; both of which were equally, he thought, unfounded, and coined with the same intent. The people were not so blind, he hoped, as not to see through the game that certain political jugglers were endeavoring to play on them here and elsewhere. It was in vain to try to screen the conduct of the bank by attempting to draw off from it the attention of the people, by setting up a cry of tyranny and usurpation against all who dare to question the purity of its conduct, and who will not consent to bow before its golden *altar*. The keen-sighted people would never be diverted from their object by such shifts to avoid a strict investigation into the conduct of the bank; and those who expected to succeed by resorting to such means, his life upon it, would be wofully deceived when fairly confronted before the mass of the great body of the American people. The honorable gentleman and his party deceived themselves, if

they thought that they were to succeed by imposing on the honest freemen of this country philippics and bitter denunciations of all who presumed to differ with them, as being the advocates of tyranny and usurpation. The people were not so ignorant as not to require proof of such charges, before they proceed to condemn some of the best and purest of men.

He had submitted his views in reply to the honorable gentlemen, simply to let him know that there were others in this House who entertained opinions directly at variance with those the honorable gentleman entertained, and who were as tenacious and as conscientious of them as the honorable member could possibly be of his.

Mr. HAWES said, from appearance, if this discussion was not stopped, it would occupy the whole day. There was other important business before the House. He therefore moved that the motion be laid on the table.

This motion was lost without a count.

Mr. LYTLE felt an imperative obligation to make a brief explanation for the satisfaction of the House as well as himself. The committee were unanimously of opinion that both reports should be printed in the same volume. Every individual expressed an entire willingness that the views of both sides should be presented together. He had been amazed and confounded at the course of this debate. The House had been told that the majority of the committee had desired to "forestall" public opinion.

The CHAIR said no such charge had been made to the understanding of the Chair.

Mr. LYTLE said such a charge had been made by the gentleman from Rhode Island [Mr. BURGES.]

The CHAIR said it only could have been stated hypothetically, or that gentleman would have been called to order.

Mr. LYTLE said that between the Speaker and himself an honest difference of opinion might exist, but the obvious tendency and design of the remark of the gentleman from Rhode Island was to make that charge. If it was not, he could deny the fact. He threw the charge back with scorn and contempt from whatever source it might emanate, as a gross libel upon the motives and conduct of the committee. So far from any portion of the committee desiring to "forestall public opinion" by printing these reports separately, it was their unanimous opinion that they should be printed together. If the public printer has printed separately the copies designed for the use of the members, it was a matter which, so far as he knew, rested entirely between the clerk and the printer. He fully agreed with the gentleman from South Carolina [Mr. PINCKNEY] that the largest number proposed should be printed. He wished the people of this country to understand the position which had been taken by the bank. A true and distinct issue has been formed. It was no longer a mere question of bank or no bank. It was one of infinitely greater importance: whether a moneyed corporation was stronger than the Government which gave it existence, and whether the representatives of the people did or did not possess the right of examination, expressly reserved in the charter. This was the true issue which had been raised by the directors of this corporation. It had afforded the gentleman from South Carolina [Mr. PINCKNEY] an opportunity of urging upon the minds of the people of Pennsylvania the odious doctrines of nullification. It would, no doubt, be exceedingly agreeable to that gentleman, to associate Pennsylvania with South Carolina in such a case. But if he expected to effect this, he had misconceived public opinion. The effervescence of feeling which had been displayed upon a late festive occasion, was limited and superficial, and can be traced to causes altogether distinct from political partialities or sympathies, on the part of the people of that great State. The State of Pennsylvania was still sound to the core. She could not be deluded or seduced from her devotion to the Constitution. She was still the key-stone of the Union—bank or no bank. He did not propose to go into a discussion of the report at this time, but was prepared to defend every inch of ground taken by the committee. The report was a naked chronicle of their proceedings, concluding with resolutions, which were intended as a mere synopsis of what the committee considered necessary, in order to vindicate themselves and

this House from the insults heaped upon them by the managers of the bank.

The attempt that had been made soon after the appointment of the committee to "forestall" public opinion by the bank organ in this city, he should consider to be a proper subject of future inquiry. The conductors of the National Intelligencer had dared to asperse the motives and conduct of this committee. As the official organs of the bank, they had, "by authority," (he quotes from memory) announced to this House that it should be protected, through the well-known purity and elevated character of the President and Directors of the bank, from the unworthy scrutiny and nefarious designs of the committee of their own appointment. Thus it appears, that the first attempt to "forestall" public opinion was made by the printers to Congress, and we all know that the same line of conduct has been industriously pursued by the other pensioned presses of the bank throughout the Union.

He hoped the two reports, in accordance with the opinion of the committee, would be printed together, and that the largest number would be printed.

Mr. SUTHERLAND said he felt very thankful so far as he was concerned, as an humble member from the State of Pennsylvania, to the gentleman from South Carolina [Mr. PINCKNEY] for the interest he had expressed for the diffusion of intelligence among her citizens. If that gentleman had reflected that the motion to print had come from the State of Pennsylvania, he might have spared himself some portion of his sympathy.

Mr. PINCKNEY wished to explain. It was not Pennsylvania alone which he wished to enlighten, but the whole United States. He was not before aware that the motion to print had originated with a member from Pennsylvania.

Mr. SUTHERLAND said it was not in order to debate the general question. He should not have risen, but from the appeals which had been made in behalf of poor Pennsylvania. The gentleman from South Carolina [Mr. PINCKNEY] would do well to look at home. The people of South Carolina would not suffer from an increase of useful information.

Mr. HAWES again moved to lay the motion to print on the table; which was negatived without a division.

After some remarks by Mr. COULTER, the question was stated on filling the blank with the highest number, 30,000.

Mr. PINCKNEY moved to fill the blank with 40,000; which was negatived without a division.

The question was then taken on filling the blank with 30,000; which was carried—ayes 93, noes 89.

The motion to print 30,000 copies of both reports was then adopted without a division.

REVOLUTIONARY COMMUTATION BILL.

The motion to reconsider the vote by which the commutation bill had been recommitted to the Committee of the Whole on the state of the Union, then came up.

The question was debated by Messrs. GILMER, MARSHALL, VANDERPOEL, MASON, BURGES, and F. PIERCE, when the question was taken, and determined in the negative—yeas 76, nays 104.

The bill to regulate the value of certain foreign silver coins was taken up, and read a third time.

Mr. KING, of Pennsylvania, called for the yeas and nays on the passage of the bill, which were ordered.

Some discussion arose, in which Messrs. BURGES, WHITE of New York, DENNY, GORHAM, McKIM, SELDEN, CLAYTON, COULTER, KING of Pennsylvania, JONES of Georgia, BEARDSLEY, CAMBRELENG, and HARPER of Pennsylvania, took part.

Mr. BOON moved the previous question, but it was not seconded by the House.

The question was taken by yeas and nays on the motion of Mr. GORHAM, to recommit the bill, with instructions to strike out all after the enacting clause, and insert a section providing that the dollars of Peru, Chili, Mexico, and Central America, shall be a legal tender, at the rate of 100 cents each, when they are not below a certain weight and fineness, and that the five-franc pieces of France shall be a legal tender at ninety-three

cents each, and decided in the affirmative—yeas 86, nays 89.

On motion of Mr. WHITE, of New York, the House then resolved itself into a Committee of the Whole on the state of the Union, upon the above bill, to regulate the value of certain foreign silver coins, (Mr. BASCO in the chair.)

The committee rose and reported the bill, with the amendment moved by Mr. GORHAM.

The amendment having been concurred in, the bill, as amended, was ordered to be engrossed for a third reading. Read a third time and passed.

The House then adjourned.

IN SENATE.

A message upon executive business was received from the President of the United States, by Mr. DONELSON, his Private Secretary.

A message was received from the House of Representatives, by Mr. FRANKLIN, their Clerk, stating that they had passed a bill regulating the value of foreign coin, in which they asked the concurrence of the Senate.

PETITIONS.

Mr. CHAMBERS presented a memorial from sundry citizens of the second election district of Frederick county, Maryland, praying for a restoration of the deposites to, and the recharter of, the Bank of the United States; which was referred to the Committee on Finance, and ordered to be printed.

Mr. FRELINGHUYSEN presented two memorials from citizens of New Jersey, remonstrating against the renewal of the patent of John Ames, paper maker; which were ordered to be printed.

REPORTS OF COMMITTEES.

Mr. WEBSTER, from the Committee on Finance, reported a bill modifying the act regulating imports—repealing so much of it as relates to the importation of hardware, copper, and brass; which was read, passed to a second reading, and ordered, together with the documents, to be printed.

Mr. TOMLINSON, from the Committee on Pensions, asked to be discharged from the further consideration of the petition of the administrator of Robert Henry Dyer; which was agreed to.

Mr. TOMLINSON, from the same committee, asked to be discharged from the further consideration of the petition of James Smith; which was concurred in.

RESTORATION OF THE DEPOSITES.

Mr. CLAY, agreeably to notice given yesterday, asked leave to introduce the following resolutions:

Resolved by the Senate and House of Representatives of the United States of America in Congress assembled, That the reasons communicated by the Secretary of the Treasury, in his report to Congress of the 11th day of December, 1833, for the removal of the deposites of the money of the United States, from the Bank of the United States and its branches, are insufficient and unsatisfactory.

Resolved, therefore, That all deposites of the money of the United States which may accrue or be received, on and after the 1st day of July, 1834, shall be made with the Bank of the United States and its branches, in conformity with the provisions of the act entitled "An act to incorporate the subscribers to the Bank of the United States," approved the 10th April, 1816.

Mr. CLAY said, it would be perceived that the first of these resolutions was a mere reaffirmance of the resolution passed by the Senate a short time since. That was a separate resolution intended as the basis of future legislation, if it should be found necessary; and the question of which, by the Senate, without any further action on the subject. To the resolution adopted by the Senate it was objected that it was a mere abstract resolution, which could lead to no practical consequences. Mr. C. thought there was nothing in this objection; but to prevent any one from being misled, he thought proper to present these resolutions. The second, it would be perceived, provided for the restoration of the deposites to the Bank of the

United States, and the effect of its adoption would be to leave the Treasury Department to continue its experiment to the 1st of July, and leave the revenue already accrued in the deposite banks to be expended in the ordinary course of disbursement. It provided, in prospective, for the deposite of the revenue accruing after that period in the Bank of the United States, and for the restoration of the laws to their just authority. But it might be said that we had no right to expect the sanction of the House of Representatives to this measure. But whatever its fate might be, it was not a matter which ought to have any influence on the Senate. The Senate owed it to itself and to the country to discharge its whole duty—let others discharge theirs according to their own views of duty or not. He was unwilling to return to his constituents without having made every effort in his power to regain the lawful custody of the public treasure; and he thought that there was but this resolution left for this purpose; and the decision upon it would determine whether the public money should be left in the will and disposition of one man or not. To-morrow would be one year since any head of the Treasury Department had been appointed by and with the advice and consent of the Senate. Gentlemen had said, why this anxiety for these nominations? He answered, no other reason but because the Constitution required them to be made. Gentlemen asked if we wanted to reject them. Mr. C. said he did not acknowledge a right to make such an inquiry into motives; but if it might be made, he might, with equal propriety ask, were they withheld from a fear of their being rejected?

Mr. CLAY concluded by asking leave to introduce the resolutions, expressing a hope that they might be acted on immediately, passed, and sent to the other House.

Mr. BENTON deemed the present moment to be the most objectionable time that could have been selected for proposing to restore the public deposites to the United States Bank Such a proposition might have been a proper proceeding at the commencement of the session. A joint resolution at that time would have been the proper mode; it could have been followed by action; and, if constitutionally passed, would have compelled the restoration of these deposites. But the course was different. A separate resolution was brought in and passed the Senate, and there it stopped. It was a nugatory resolution, leading to no action. It was such a one as a State Legislature or a public meeting might adopt, because they had no power to legislate on the subject. But the Senate had the power of legislation; and, six months ago, when the separate resolution was brought in, the Senate, if it intended to act legislatively on the subject at all, ought to have proceeded by joint resolution, or by bill at that time. But it thought otherwise. The separate resolution was adopted; after adoption no instruction was given to a committee to bring in a bill; nothing was done to give legislative effect to the decision of the Senate; and now, at the end of six months, the first attempt is made to move in our legislative capacity, and to pass a joint resolution—equivalent to a statute—to compel the restoration of these deposites. This is the state of the proceedings; and, Mr. B. must be permitted to say, and to give his reasons for saying, that the time selected for this first step, in our legislative capacity, in a case so long depending, is most inappropriate and objectionable. Mr. B. would not dwell upon the palpable objections to this proceeding, which must strike every mind: the advanced stage of the session—the proposition to adjourn—the quantity of business on hand—the little probability that the House and the President would concur with the Senate, or that two-thirds of the two Houses could be brought to pass the resolution, if the President declined to give it his approbation,—these palpable objections must strike every mind, and make it appear to be a useless consumption of time for the Senate to pass the resolution. Virtually, it included a proposition to recharter the bank; for the most confidential friends of that institution admitted that it was improper to restore the deposites unless the bank charter was to be continued. The proposition to restore, then, virtually included the proposition to recharter; and that was a proposition which, after having been openly made on this floor, and leave asked to bring in a bill to that effect, had been abandoned under the clear conviction that the measure could not pass.

Passing from these palpable objections, Mr. B. proceeded to state another reason, of a different kind, and which he held to be imperative of the course which the Senate should now pursue: he alluded to the state of the questions at this moment depending between the Bank of the United States and the House of Representatives, and the nature of which exacted from the Senate the observance of a strict neutrality, and an absolute non-interference between those two bodies. The House of Representatives had ordered an inquiry into the affairs and conduct of the bank. The points of inquiry indicated misconduct of the gravest import, and had been ordered by the largest majority, not less than three or four to one. That inquiry was not yet finished; it was still depending; the committee appointed to conduct it remains organized, and has only reported in part. That report is before the Senate and the public, and shows that the directors of the Bank of the United States have resisted the authority of the House—have made an issue of power between itself and the House—for the trial of which issue a resolution is now depending in the House, and is made the order of the day for Tuesday next. Here, then, are two questions depending between the House and the bank; the first, an inquiry into the misconduct of the bank; the second, a proposition to compel the bank to submit to the authority of the House. Was it right for the Senate to interpose between those bodies while these questions were depending? Was it right to interfere on the part of the bank? Was it right for the Senate to leap into the arena, throw itself between the contending parties, take sides with the bank, and virtually declare to the American people that there was no cause for inquiry into the conduct of the bank, and no ground of censure for resisting the authority of the House? Such would, doubtless, be the effect of the conduct of the Senate, if it should entertain the proposition which is now submitted to it. That proposition is one of honor and confidence to the bank. It proceeds upon the assumption that the bank is right, and the House is wrong, in the questions now depending between them; that the bank has done nothing to merit inquiry, or to deserve censure; and that the public moneys ought to be restored to her keeping, without waiting the end of the investigation which the House has ordered, or the decision of the resolution which affirms that the bank has resisted the autherity of the House, and committed a contempt against it. This is the full and fair interpretation—the clear and speaking effect—of the measure now proposed to the Senate. Is it right to treat the House thus? Her resolutions, adopted with the greatest unanimity, imply the worst of misconduct to the bank. Certainly the House would not order an inquiry, unless they believed there was ground for it—grave and serious ground for it. The specified points of inquiry went to malpractices and abuses, to corruptions and oppressions, to violations and forfeiture of the charter! If true, they not only showed the bank to be unworthy of keeping the public moneys, but unworthy of existence—a criminal institution, ripe for the stroke of justice, and awaiting the sentence of the law! Was it right for the Senate, by adopting a resolution of honor and confidence to the bank, to make a virtual declaration, that the bank was innocent, and the House culpable, for proceeding against her? That the inquiry directed by the House is frivolous and unfounded, unworthy of consideration, and not fit to arrest, for a moment, the full current of honor and confidence from the Senate to the bank?

In the front of these inquiries (said Mr. B.) stood the prominent subject of the public distress; that distress which had been the subject of so many meetings, the burden of so many memorials, and the pregnant topic of so many woful speeches on this floor. The first subject of inquiry was, into the cause of this distress. The committee were directed to ascertain whether the bank, through its money, or through its management and influence, had contributed to produce the distress which the innumerable memorials presented to Congress so bitterly complained of; and they were directed to search for the evidence of that fact in the bank itself. Will the Senate, by its act, virtually affirm the frivolity, or the untruth, of this inquiry? Will the Senate virtually, intelligibly, and practically, acquit the bank, when the bank will not acquit itself? will not suffer its innocence to be tested by the recorded voice of its own books, and the living voice of its own directors? These directors have refused to testify; they have refused to be sworn; they have refused to touch the book; because, being directors, and corporators, and therefore parties, they cannot be required to give evidence against themselves. And this refusal, the public is gravely told, is made upon the advice of eminent counsel. What counsel? The counsel of the law, or of fear? Certainly no lawyer—not even a junior apprentice to the law—could give such advice. The right to stand mute does not extend to the privilege of refusing to be sworn. The right does not attach until after the oath is taken; and is then limited to the specific question, the answer to which might inculpate the witness, and which he may refuse to answer, because he will say, upon his oath, that the answer will criminate himself. But these bank directors refuse to be sworn at all. They refuse to touch the book; and in that refusal, commit a flagrant contempt against the House of Representatives, and do an act for which any citizen would be sent to jail by any justice of the peace in America. And is the Senate to justify the directors for this contempt? to get between them and the House? to adopt a resolution beforehand—before the day fixed for the decision of the contempt, which shall throw the weight of the Senate into the scale of the directors against the House, and virtually declare that they are right in refusing to be sworn? If it does, (said Mr. B.,) it may find itself confronted by the authority of the bank, as well as by the stern voice of the law. The bank itself—the directors individually, and the corporation as a board—have heretofore admitted and declared the right of the people to have the evidence which is now demanded. He did not speak of the former examinations, in which directors were sworn, and books examined. Strong as these cases were, he passed them over, to get at cases stronger still, and which should exhibit the present directors themselves—the same men, individually and corporately, upon their oaths, and upon their honors, in their most solemn and authentic acts, contradicting and condemning their present pretensions, and acknowledging the right of the people to have the evidence of their books, and of their oaths, to elucidate any question, either of abuse of powers, corruption of conduct, or violation of charter, which may be charged upon them. Mr. B. said that the present President of the bank had, heretofore, sworn to the right of Congress to know everything that the bank did. It was in the investigation of 1832, and in relation to a loan, which, at the uttermost, could only amount to malpractice, abuse or corruption, and could not work a forfeiture of the charter. It was the case of the first loan to Noah & Webb. This loan of $15,000 had not been entered upon the books of the bank. Nine months after it was made, it was for the first time put upon the books. The reason of this was stated by Mr Biddle, in his examination before the committee. It will be seen at page 86 of the report of that committee. A committee of the House of Representatives were coming to investigate the affairs of the bank. This loan was not upon the books; but at the approach of the committee, Mr. Biddle ordered it to be put there, and declares his reason to be this: "I THOUGHT IT RIGHT THAT EVERY-'THING *done by the bank should* ALWAYS *be* '*distinctly* KNOWN *and* AVOWED. I therefore '*gave the notes to the chairman of the committee, Mr.* '*Thomas P. Cope, who entered them on the books.*" Mr. B. said that he referred to this testimony of Mr. Biddle, not for the transaction to which it related, but for the sentiment which it declared; a sentiment sworn to, and acted upon, in 1832, and denied and repudiated by the same men in 1834! He had no comment to make upon this contradiction, the glaring nature of which would strike every mind.

Mr. B. proceeded to the next piece of evidence, emanating from the bank itself, to prove the acknowledgment of their obligation to submit the operations of the bank to the judgment of the people. Everybody (said Mr. B.) has heard of the resolutions of the bank, adopted at the Board of Directors, and confirmed and extended by successive

boards, for putting the funds of the bank, without limitation of amount, at the disposition of the President, to spread information before the people. Now, what were those resolutions, either in language, or in import, but authentic declarations of the right of the people to be made acquainted with the operations of an institution in which they are partners to the amount of seven millions of the stock, and whose notes enter so largely into the currency of the country, and the revenues of the Union? The words of the resolutions are, *to cause information to be communicated to the people in regard to the nature and operations of the bank*. The President of the bank was to execute the resolution, and has executed it at an immense expense, every fifth dollar of which is the money of the people. The operations of the bank have thus been made the subject of communication to the people by the bank itself. The Board of Directors—the very men now directing the bank, have admitted the right of the people to be made acquainted with the nature, and with the operations of the bank; they have filled newspapers and periodicals with their communications, intended to influence the opinions of the people; and now, when the Representatives of the people send a committee to obtain a little more of that information, and to find out whether the communications already made contain the truth, the whole truth, and nothing but the truth, they are unblushingly denied the privilege!

Mr. B. proceeded to a third piece of testimony to convict the bank, upon its own evidence and its own acts, of self-contradiction, in refusing to give testimony before the committee, and refusing to permit copies to be taken from the bank books: it was in the fact, that these identical directors, the same who now refuse to be sworn, had already appeared as volunteer witnesses, in their own persons, in the very case, and to the selfsame points, in many instances, to which they now refuse to testify. Here (said Mr. B.) is the proof, [holding up a printed pamphlet.] It is a little book of forty pages, drawn up by a committee of the bank, adopted by the board of directors, five thousand copies ordered to be printed, and universally received by the friends of the bank as the evidence of its correctness and upright dealings. It is dated December, 1833, and imports to be an answer "*to 'a paper signed* Andrew Jackson, *purporting to 'have been read to a Cabinet on the* 18*th of September, and to another paper, signed H. D. Gilpin, J. 'T. Sullivan, Peter Wager, H. McElderry, bearing 'date August* 19, 1833." Now, what were these papers here answered by the bank, but the very papers, on the charges contained in which the committee of the House was raised? The paper signed by Mr. Gilpin and the other Government directors, charged the bank with a long list of malpractices, amounting to abuses, corruptions, and violations of charter. The paper read by the President to his Cabinet, was founded upon the communication of the Government directors; and to these papers the bank directors publish an answer of forty pages, consisting of their own statements, and of extracts from their books, and contradicting or explaining the charges of the Government directors. To this the Government directors made a rejoinder of fifty pages; and the whole came before Congress and the nation. Upon these charges and answers, the committee of the House was raised. It went to Philadelphia to investigate the very points which had been brought before the public—the very points to which the bank directors had been testifying before the public, and publishing extracts from their books! Yet they refuse to be sworn! refuse to swear! refuse to testify! refuse, in the very case in which they had appeared as volunteer witnesses! refused to testify on the very points which fill their own pamphlet; that pamphlet of which they ordered five thousand copies to be printed, and the contents of which have formed the basis for all those speeches in favor of the bank, of which so many myriads of copies are distributed from this capital, and, as it is well believed, at the expense of the bank and of the people, who pay every fifth dollar of the money expended by the bank! This is the conduct of these directors: refusing to be sworn to the truth of their own statements; refusing to appear as witnesses before a committee of the House of Representatives, after having appeared as volunteer witnesses at the bar of the public, and given evidence upon the identical matters in controversy! Mr. B. held, upon these facts, that the bank directory were self-convicted of their contumacy to the House of Representatives, and as good as convicted of all the matters laid to their charge; and that it was assuming an immense burden upon itself, for the Senate to go on to vote a restoration of the public deposites to the bank! a vote which implies honor and confidence! which treats as frivolous or unfounded the charges against the bank! which virtually pronounces the opinion of the Senate on all the questions depending between the House and the bank, and throws the weight of that opinion into the scale of the bank!

Mr. B. called the attention of the Senate to another point in which the body of the directors, in their answer to President Jackson's cabinet paper, had made a charge against him, which, if true, would not only degrade and dishonor him personally, but entirely annihilate the influence of his name and opinions against the Bank of the United States. It was a charge of having attempted to make the bank subservient to his political views, and then turning against it because he could not thus use it. The charge was specific, with time and place, and would be read: "*It was in the midst 'of this career of inoffensive usefulness* (of the bank) '*when soon after the accession to power of the present 'Executive, the purpose was distinctly revealed, that 'other duties than those to the country were required—'and that it was necessary for the bank, in administering its affairs, to consult the political views of 'those who had now obtained the ascendant in the 'Executive. It is understood, that soon after that 'event, a meeting was held in Washington, of the 'principal chiefs, to consider the means of perpetuating their new authority, and the possession of the 'bank was among the most prominent objects of the 'parties assembled.*"

This is a charge (said Mr. B.) put forward by the present directors of the bank, in their pamphlet of December, 1833. It is put forward with a specification which admits of proof. The time, the place, the object, and the parties to the meeting, are all stated; and upon this statement an immense superstructure of accusation has been raised against the President. Now, the statement is either true or false; if true, it degrades and dishonors the President; if false, the people ought to know it. If the directors had submitted to be sworn, they would have been examined on this point; by refusing to be sworn, they have escaped the examination; and the people remain without proof on a point of the utmost materiality to their confidence in the administration of the Government. Mr. B. called upon all honorable men to say, whether the bank directors, after having made such a charge, and with circumstantiality of time and place, had a right to draw back, and refuse to be sworn to what they had stated.

Mr. B. then concluded with a motion to postpone the further consideration of Mr. Clay's resolution for a week, to give time to the House of Representatives to decide the question of contempt depending against the bank directors.

Mr. BENTON asked the yeas and nays on his motion; which were ordered, and are as follows, to wit:

YEAS—Messrs. Benton, Black, Brown, Forsyth, Grundy, Hill, Kane, King of Alabama, King of Georgia, Linn, McKean, Morris, Robinson, Shepley, Tipton, White, Wilkins, Wright—18.

NAYS—Messrs. Bell, Bibb, Calhoun, Chambers, Clay, Clayton, Ewing, Hendricks, Kent, Leigh, Mangum, Moore, Naudain, Poindexter, Porter, Preston, Robbins, Silsbee, Smith, Southard, Sprague, Swift, Tomlinson, Waggaman, Webster—25.

Leave was then granted, and the resolutions passed to a second reading.

The Senate then, on motion of Mr. WEBSTER, proceeded to the consideration of executive business; in which they were engaged until five o'clock, when

The Senate adjourned.

HOUSE OF REPRESENTATIVES.

Wednesday, *May* 28, 1834.

Mr. J. Q. ADAMS, by consent, moved that the use of the Hall of Representatives be granted to-morrow evening, for the purpose of holding therein a public meeting for the relief of the Polish exiles; which was agreed to.

Mr. FOSTER reported a bill to refund the fine imposed upon the late Matthew Lyon, under the sedition law, to his legal heirs and representatives. Read twice and committed.

Mr. R. M. JOHNSON reported the bill from the Senate, without amendment, for the relief of Colonel A. R. Woolley; which was committed to the Committee of the Whole, and made the order of the day for to-morrow.

Mr. CHILTON moved the suspension of the rule, in order to offer a resolution fixing the hour of meeting for the remainder of the session at ten o'clock A. M.; and thereupon asked the yeas and nays; which were refused.

Mr. CHILTON then withdrew the motion, in order to modify the resolution.

KENTUCKY CONTESTED ELECTION.

The House resumed the consideration of the resolution reported from the Committee of Elections, declaring Thomas P. Moore to be entitled to a seat in this House from the fifth Congressional district of Kentucky. The question being on the amendment offered as a substitute by Mr. Banks, that the votes given in Garrard county before ten o'clock on the first day of the election, while Moses Grant, Esq., acted as one of the judges, and the votes given on the second day, in the absence of the sheriff, ought to be counted in ascertaining the result of the election.

Mr. VANDERPOEL, a member of the Committee of Elections, took the floor and spoke at length in support of the views of the committee, and in reply to the argument of the gentleman from Pennsylvania, [Mr. Binney.]

Mr. POPE followed in opposition to the amendment. Upon the constitution and laws of Kentucky, he contended that the three votes of deaf and dumb persons allowed Mr. Letcher, in the report of the committee, ought not to have been counted. Those theological students at Danville, who had no *animus manendi*, were not legal voters at the place of their education. These positions Mr. P. argued and illustrated by the practice of the State. He supported the views of the committee in the rejection of the votes taken at Lancaster, referred to in the amendment, at length.

Mr. AMOS DAVIS spoke at some length in opposition to the views of the majority of the committee, and in reply to the remarks made by the gentleman from Kentucky, [Mr. Pope,] and others.

Mr. JONES, of Georgia, offered the following amendment to the amendment proposed by Mr. Banks, which is in these terms:

"That all the legal votes which were received 'in Lancaster, Gerrard county, whilst Moses 'Grant, Esq., acted as one of the judges, on the 'first morning of the election, in August last, and 'those of a like character, given on the second 'day of the election, in the casual absence of the 'sheriff, ought to be estimated in ascertaining the 'result of the election."

Strike out "legal" and insert "qualified" voters, and striking out the word "casual."

His object was, he said, to bring fairly before the House the question which the gentleman from Pennsylvania [Mr. Banks] wished to present. If the votes were legal, they ought to be counted, and if they were not legal, they ought not to be counted. If the voters were qualified, according to the law of Kentucky, they were legal. He also replied to the argument of the gentleman from Kentucky, [Mr. Davis.]

When Mr. J. had concluded,

The House adjourned.

IN SENATE.

Thursday, *May* 29, 1834.

A message upon executive business was received from the President of the United States, by Mr. Donelson, his Private Secretary.

PETITIONS.

Mr. McKEAN presented the petition of John and Sarah Addison, of Prince George's county, Maryland, representatives of Andrew Leitch, a major of the Revolution, praying for seven years'

half-pay, agreeably to the resolution of Congress of the 24th of August, 1780. The petition was referred to the Committee on Revolutionary Claims.

Mr. CHAMBERS presented the petition of William F. Giles, administrator of Philip Moore, deceased; which was referred to the Committee on the Judiciary.

REPORTS.

Mr. POINDEXTER, from the Committee on Public Lands, asked to be discharged from the further consideration of the petition of Hugh S. Gatewood: which was agreed to.

Mr. POINDEXTER, from the same committee, reported a bill from the House of Representatives, with an amendment, for the relief of Samuel Armstrong Bailey.

Mr. TOMLINSON, from the Committee on Pensions, reported a bill for the relief of John S. Workman; which was read, and ordered to a second reading.

Mr. MANGUM, from the Committee on Finance, reported a bill from the House of Representatives, without amendment, for the relief of the owners of the brig Liberator.

Also, a bill from the House, without amendment, for the relief of the owners of the schooner Joseph and Mary.

GENERAL ORDERS.

The resolution of Mr. POINDEXTER, calling for the reports of agents of land offices, was taken up and adopted.

The following resolution submitted by Mr. PRESTON on Tuesday last, was taken up for consideration:

Resolved, That the Secretary of War report to the Senate a statement showing the names of the several pensioners who are now, or may have been heretofore, placed on the pension roll, designating their rank, annual allowance, the sums which they have severally received, the laws under which their pensions have been granted, the date when placed upon the roll, their ages, and the States and counties in which they severally reside; also, the names of the pension agents who have received compensation as such, and the amount of such compensation, and the act under which it was allowed; the names of the clerks who are and have been employed in the Pension Office, and the sums paid them as compensation, with an aggregate statement of the whole sum disbursed on account of pensions.

Mr. PRESTON then spoke at length in explanation of his reasons for desiring this information, and was followed by Messrs. WEBSTER, FRELINGHUYSEN, SPRAGUE, EWING, CHAMBERS, WRIGHT, FORSYTH, CALHOUN, and KEPLEY.

In the course of the debate, Mr. FRELINGHUYSEN suggested an enlargement of the resolution, requiring "the State or continental line in which the pensioners served;" and also an amendment by Mr. CHAMBERS, that "the Secretary of War report the regulations which have been adopted in relation to the proof necessary to entitle the applicant to a pension under the act of July, 1832," which were both accepted as modifications by Mr. PRESTON.

Mr. FORSYTH then suggested a doubt that the objects of the resolution could be accomplished during the present session of Congress. He suggested, therefore, in order to attain the end desired, to change the mode of arriving at it, by making it the duty of a committee to make the investigation.

This was objected to by Mr. PRESTON, as it would not meet his views. He wished the information in detail, so that it might be printed and sent to every county in the United States, for public investigation.

After some further conversation between Mr. FORSYTH, Mr. CALHOUN, and Mr. PRESTON, the resolution was laid on the table for a day or two, to afford further time to inquire into the subject.

The CHAIR presented a communication from the Postmaster General, transmitting a statement of the contracts during the past year; which, on motion of Mr. GRUNDY, was referred to the Committee on the Post Office and Post Roads, and ordered to be printed.

The Senate, on motion of Mr. CLAYTON, proceeded to executive business, and after some time spent therein,

The Senate adjourned.

HOUSE OF REPRESENTATIVES.

THURSDAY, *May* 29, 1834.

Mr. J. Q. ADAMS obtained leave to lay the following resolutions on the table, and moved that they be printed, intending to move them as a substitute for the resolutions appended to the report of the Committee of Investigation, when that subject should come up:

Resolved, That the Select Committee of this House, appointed on the 4th of April last, to investigate the proceedings of the Bank of the United States, be discharged from the further consideration of the subject referred to them.

Resolved, That in the transactions of the said committee with the President and directors of the Bank of the United States, as set forth in the reports of the committee, and in the correspondence annexed to the same, no contempt of the lawful authority of this House has been offered by the said President and directors of the bank, or by any one of them.

Resolved, That any order of this House to the Sergeant-at-Arms to arrest and bring to the bar of the House the President and directors of the Bank of the United States, or any one of them, to answer for an alleged contempt of the authority of the House, as proposed by the concluding resolution offered by the report of the majority of the said Select Committee, would be an unconstitutional, arbitrary, and oppressive abuse of power.

The motion to print was agreed to.

The House, on motion of Mr. BOON, by unanimous consent, took up the following resolution:

"*Resolved*, That the President of the Senate, and 'the Speaker of the House of Representatives, 'close the present session of Congress by an ad'journment of their respective Houses on Monday 'the 16th day of June next."

The resolution having been read as modified by Mr. BOON, fixing the 16th of June as the day of adjournment—

Mr. POLK was satisfied that the day of adjournment of the two Houses of Congress ought to be fixed at the earliest day compatible with the important public business which remained undisposed of. He was apprehensive that the 16th of June was too early. When this subject was before the House a fortnight ago, he had voted to postpone its consideration for two weeks, with the hope that the House would, in the mean time, have disposed of much of the most pressing business, and that, by this time, a more definite and correct opinion might be formed as to the proper time to end the session. The fortnight had passed off, and scarcely any business had been disposed of. The only bill, of general importance, which had been passed, was the coin bill. He was satisfied that while the subject was kept open, the House would not proceed in the despatch of the necessary measures with that industry and earnestness which they would do if the day should be fixed. There were three important appropriation bills not yet passed; the Indian annuity bill and the harbor bill were before the House upon their engrossment, and the fortification bill had not yet been reported from the Committee of the Whole on the state of the Union. It was his intention, at the earliest possible period, to ask the House to go into the consideration of the bill reported from the Committee of Ways and Means, regulating the deposites of the public money. With these important measures before the House, and the election from Kentucky undisposed of, he thought the House could not safely fix upon so early a period of adjournment as the 16th of June. He would suggest to the mover of the resolution the propriety of prolonging the time for a fortnight—to fix upon the 30th of June instead of the 16th.

Mr. BOON said he had already prolonged the time from the 31st May to the 16th June, and he would now leave it in possession of the House. If any gentleman preferred a longer day, he might propose to modify the resolution by amendment.

Mr. ELLSWORTH entirely concurred with the gentleman from Indiana, [Mr. BOON.] He was anxious to fix upon the earliest possible day which would be satisfactory to the House. He was satisfied that the earlier the day was, the better. There were subjects of paramount importance, upon which he had hoped the House would act; but he was convinced they would not be acted on. The indispensable business of the House could be settled within the shortest period. He was for fixing on that period. He had hoped that the House would have expressed its opinion, as was its bounden duty, upon the reasons for removing the deposites from the United States Bank. The House was called on by the President—by the Secretary of the Treasury—by the Bank—by the Constitution, and by the whole country, to express this opinion. He had also hoped that the House would have fixed upon some regulation respecting the deposite of the public money. There was another subject of great importance which he had hoped to have seen settled—the disposal of the public domain. But he was convinced that nothing effectual would be done on any of these great questions, and was willing to vote for the earliest day of adjournment, if it was but ten days hence. We might as well go home then, as to stay until September.

Mr. HARDIN wished to substitute the 30th June for the 16th. The House owed it to themselves, as well as to the nation, to dispose of the measures mentioned by the gentleman from Tennessee, [Mr. POLK,] in addition to other indispensable measures. The gentleman from Connecticut [Mr. ELLSWORTH] states it to be the duty of the House to express its opinion upon the measures of the Administration relative to the bank, and to act upon the great question of the national domain, and yet desires to adjourn in a fortnight from this time. Was that gentleman afraid of the dog-days? For one, he was willing, if it was necessary, to wait and see if the dog-star would become ascendant in the House. If we adjourned at the time advocated by that gentleman, how many days of business should we have at our disposal? We have the appropriation bills, and the bill regulating the deposites, referred to by the gentleman from Tennessee, [Mr. POLK,] and we also have the report of the committee of investigation into the affairs of the bank, which would not, probably, be disposed of in a single day. He should be glad to have the benefit of the views and calculations of the mover of this resolution as to the time necessary to dispose of these important measures. In that case he might change his opinion, but acting upon the best means of information in his power, he was satisfied that the House ought not to adjourn short of four weeks from this time. Gentlemen should recollect that these measures must be acted on by the Senate. He was unwilling to throw the whole responsibility of fixing the period of adjournment upon that body.

Mr. BEARDSLEY said the House had been assured, when this subject was before them a fortnight ago, that at this time we should be able to fix upon a suitable period of adjournment. Have we any further light than we then had? Has anything in effect been done since that time in accomplishing the necessary business of the session? We have, to be sure, caused the carpets to be taken up, and matting substituted on the floor of this Hall. Some gentlemen had been to Harper's Ferry, others to Virginia, and others have attended the Baltimore races; but no important public business had been done, and he was satisfied that until the day of adjournment should be fixed, very little would be done. In fixing that day, the only question in his view was, what time is necessary to dispose of the business intended to be transacted by the House? We could not undertake to settle any such question for the Senate. That body can best judge of its own duties. They can change the day which may be fixed on by the House to one more agreeable to themselves. The sole question before the House is, how much time is indispensable to discharge its necessary duties? If the time should be wasted as it has been, neither the 16th nor the 30th of June would find much business accomplished. But if gentlemen were disposed to attend strictly to the business of the House, not more than three or four days were necessary to dispose of the appropriation bills. As to the Kentucky election, if the candidates should state their views of their respective rights, and the House would come up to the mark, that

might be disposed of in two or three days more. If the earliest period named should be fixed on, there would then be eight or ten days for other measures. The bill regulating the deposites of public money would not probably find its way through the other end of the Capitol; but he trusted the House did not require any great length of time to perform its duty to the country on that question. The gold coin bill would not, he believed, be a subject of debate, and might be disposed of in a few hours. These and other important measures might be disposed of by the 16th of June. Allusion had been made to the proceedings of the committee for investigating the bank. All he desired was the opinion of the House upon the report. He presumed every gentleman present had fully made up his mind upon the subject. If a general debate was to be gone into, the 30th of June was too short a period—the 30th of July would be too short—the 31st of December would be too short. If that subject was to be debated in the manner of which the House had had many instances, the first of January would not afford sufficient time. He should not vote on this question with a view of giving time for such a debate. The gentleman from Connecticut [Mr. Ellsworth] thinks it necessary that the House should express its opinion upon the removal of the deposites. Does the gentleman wish to travel over that question again? That gentleman had shown the fertility of his invention in finding reasons why a certain great corporation should not speak out. Reasons quite as strong might be found why the House should not. The privileges of that corporation seem to be one thing, and those of the House quite a different thing. But the House has expressed its opinion upon the removal of the deposites. If the gentleman doubts the fact, he begged him to examine the proceedings of the House. Unless the refusal of the bank to speak in reply to the inquiry of the House had commended it to the good opinion of gentlemen, he presumed no different decision would be made by the House upon that question. In view of all circumstances, he hoped the earliest day would be determined on.

Mr. CHAMBERS had hoped the House would not adjourn until some relief had been afforded against the ruinous policy of the Government. For that purpose he was willing to remain until September. But we had been here six months—our tables had been loaded with memorials on the subject—and no legislation had been accomplished upon the great interests of the country. For his own part, he despaired of any, and was now content to fix a day of adjournment. He would prefer that named by the gentleman from Tennessee, [Mr. Polk,] as it would give the House time to act upon several important subjects. The bill regulating the deposites of public money ought to be acted on, connected with the resolution of the gentleman from Massachusetts, [Mr. Adams,] inquiring into the state of the deposite banks. In his opinion, it would be precipitate to fix upon a day so early as the 16th of June.

Mr. PARKER proposed to amend the resolution, by fixing the 23d of June, instead of the 16th.

Mr. BURGES had been willing to protract the decision upon this question, in the hope that some accident, propitious to the welfare of the country, might have intervened, and induce the House to retrace its steps. But he had become satisfied that the moment the indispensable business was done, the session should be ended. He had hoped that when distress and desolation were covering the land, the House would have done its duty. But the people must take the matter into their own hands. Whenever the bill placing the deposites of public money into the State banks should pass, a revolution would commence, and ought to commence. As to the resolutions reported by the investigating committee, no person dared to vote for that which proposed to drag freemen before the House, for a constructive contempt. There was not a tribunal in the civilized world which would enforce such a proposition. The only object in making it, was to take the eyes of the public from that individual who was grasping at the liberties of the people. Would the House adjourn and leave the public treasure in the hands of those marauders who have got possession of it? Would the House sit here thirty days longer and not vindicate its rights?

Mr. H. EVERETT wished to bring to the notice of the House some important measures which had not been referred to. There was a variety of important business before the House, some portion of which was of a political character. That to which he alluded was not of that description. It was the bills which had been recently reported by the Committee on Indian Affairs. Whenever the attention of the House should be directed to them, he presumed the House would not be willing to adjourn without passing them. He hoped the House would devote a week to the consideration of these bills, and for that purpose would propose the 7th of July as the day of adjournment.

Mr. E. then moved to refer the resolution to a select committee, with instructions to report what public business was necessary to be acted on, and on what day the House might adjourn.

Mr. BOON asked to modify the resolution so as to fix on the 23d of June instead of the 16th, as the day of adjournment.

Mr. E. EVERETT would have no objection to the motion of his friend from Vermont, [Mr. H. Everett,] if it would effect any practical purpose. But his experience on such a committee as was proposed to be raised, as well as in the House, had taught him that much time would be spent in the committee in a struggle between favorite measures, which would be repeated in the House.

The result would be, that the consideration of what ought to be done would occupy the time which should have been spent in doing it. He was in favor of an early day, and was willing to agree to the resolution as now modified, and hoped the House would go effectually about the transaction of its necessary business.

Mr. SPEIGHT presumed that the mind of every gentleman present was made up on this subject; he therefore moved the previous question; which was not sustained: Ayes 87, noes 88.

Mr. BEARDSLEY moved to strike out the 23d and insert the 16th June, in the resolution as modified.

The CHAIR (temporarily occupied by Mr. Hubbard) decided that the motion to commit was first in order; if that should be negatived, the propositions would be taken up in their order, the longest day first.

Mr. H. EVERETT then withdrew his motion to commit, and moved that the 7th day of July be fixed as the time of adjournment.

Mr. BATES requested his friend [Mr. H. Everett] to withdraw the proposition. For himself he should vote for the earliest day named. The responsibility of fixing the time should rest upon the majority, and he hoped the gentlemen, with whom he usually acted, would not interpose in the matter at all.

Mr. H. EVERETT could not comply with the request. He did not regard this as a party question. It was a business question; and the responsibility of its decision rested upon every individual, according to his vote.

Mr. SEABORN JONES was opposed to fixing any day of adjournment until some of the important measures before the House should be settled; particularly that regulating the deposites of the public money. He did not understand the argument that fixing the day was necessary for the despatch of business. The proper mode of hastening the day of adjournment was to sit and do the business necessary, and which the country required to be done.

After a few remarks from Mr. BURD,

Mr. S. JONES moved that the further consideration of the resolution be postponed for a fortnight.

This motion was negatived without a count.

Mr. DAVENPORT moved that it be postponed for a week; upon which he demanded the yeas and nays, which were not ordered.

Mr. JONES demanded tellers, which were ordered; eleven only voted in the affirmative.

The question was then stated on fixing the 7th July as the day of adjournment, which was decided in the negative as follows: Yeas 28, nays 173.

YEAS—Messrs. Heman Allen, Barnitz, Blair, Burd, Carmichael, Clowney, Denny, Dunlap, H. Everett, P. C. Fuller, Gilmer, Graham, Hannegan, Hardin, Jarvis, William Cost Johnson, Kinnard, Lane, Lewis, Lytle, McCarty, McKim, McLene, Parks, Pearce, Plummer, Philemon Thomas, and Vance—28.

NAYS—Messrs. John Q. Adams, John Adams, John J. Allen, Chilton Allan, William Allen, Anthony, Archer, Ashley, Banks, Barber, Barringer, Bates, Baylies, Bean, Beardsley, Beaty, Beaumont, John Bell, Bockee, Bodle, Boon, Bouldin, Briggs, Brown, Bull, Bunch, Burges, Burns, Bynum, Cage, Cambreleng, Campbell, Carr, Casey, Chambers, Chaney, Chilton, Choate, S. Clark, William Clark, Clay, Clayton, Coffee, Connor, Corwin, Coulter, Cramer, Crockett, Amos Davis, Davenport, Day, Deberry, Deming, Dickson, Dickerson, Dickinson, Ellsworth, Edward Everett, Ewing, Felder, Fowler, William K. Fuller, Fulton, Galbraith, Gamble, Garland, Gholson, Gillet, Gordon, Gorham, Grayson, Grennell, Griffin, Joseph Hall, Hiland Hall, Halsey, Hamer, Hard, Joseph M. Harper, James Harper, Harrison, Hathaway, Hazeltine, Heath, Henderson, Hiester, Howell, Hubbard, Jabez W. Huntington, Abel Huntington, Inge, Jackson, Richard M. Johnson, Noadiah Johnson, Benjamin Jones, Seaborn Jones, Kavanagh, Lansing, Laporte, George W. Lay, Luke Lea, Thomas Lee, Leavitt, Lincoln, Love, Loyall, Lucas, Lyon, Abijah Mann, Joel K. Mann, Martindale, Marshall, Mardis, John Y. Mason, Moses Mason, McComas, McIntire, McKay, McKennan, McKinley, McVean, Miller, Robert Mitchell, Moore, Muhlenberg, Murphy, Osgood, Page, Parker, Patton, Patterson, Peyton, Pierce, Pierson, Polk, Pope, Potts, Ramsey, Schenck, Schley, William B. Shepard, A. H. Shepperd, Shinn, Wm. Slade, Charles Slade, Sloane, Smith, Spangler, Speight, Standifer, Stoddert, Sutherland, William Taylor, Wm. P. Taylor, Francis Thomas, Thomson, Tompkins, Turner, Turrill, Tweedy, Vanderpoel, Van Horten, Vinton, Wagener, Wardwell, Wayne, Webster, Whallon, Edward D. White, Frederick Whittlesey, Elisha Whittlesey, Wilde, Williams—173.

The question being on the motion to insert the 30th day of June—

Mr. VANCE said he should vote for this day, although he was in favor of a later day. No one could look at the state of our calendar without being convinced that, by the 23d, we could not act upon the ordinary business of the session, to say nothing of the bill respecting the deposites. What was the condition of the appropriation bills? The general appropriation bill, which occupied six weeks in its discussion here, had not yet been taken up in the Senate, and it could not be supposed that the Senate would finally act upon it by the 23d inst. Some of the appropriation bills would be lost if the 23d inst. should be fixed.

Mr. CAMBRELENG, in a few words, signified his concurrence in the proposition to fix upon the 30th of June, and he expressed the hope that there would be such a majority in favor of the motion as would evince an intention, on the part of the House, at least, to make an effort to despatch the public business.

The question being then taken, it was decided in the negative: yeas 97, nays 109.

YEAS—Messrs. Heman Allen, William Allen, Anthony, Ashley, Barnitz, Barringer, Beaumont, James M. Bell, Blair, Bouldin, Burd, Bynum, Cambreleng, Carmichael, Chambers, Chaney, William Clark, Clowney, Coffee, Connor, Amos Davis, Day, Denny, Duncan, Dunlap, Evans, H. Everett, Ewing, Forester, Fulton, Galbraith, Gillet, Gilmer, Gordon, Graham, Grayson, Hamer, Hannegan, Hardin, James Harper, Harrison, Heath, Henderson, Howell, Abel Huntington, Jarvis, Seaborn Jones, Benjamin Jones, Kavanagh, Kinnard, Lane, Laporte, Leavitt, Lewis, Lyon, Lytle, A. Mann, Joel K. Mann, Marshall, McCarty, McIntire, McKay, McKennan, McKim, McLene, McVean, Miller, Robert Mitchell, Moore, Murphy, Osgood, Parks, Patton, Patterson, Dutee J. Pearce, Franklin Pierce, Polk, Potts, Shinn, William Slade, Charles Slade, Standifer, Stoddert, Sutherland, Francis Thomas, Philemon Thomas, Thomson, Tompkins, Turner, Vance, Van Horten, Vinton, Webster, Edward D. White, Wilson, Wise—97.

NAYS—Messrs. John Quincy Adams, John Adams, John J. Allen, Banks, Barber, Bates, Baylies, Bean, Beardsley, Beaty, Bockee, Bodle, Boon, Briggs, Brown, Bull, Burges, Burns, Cage,

Campbell, Carr, Casey, Chilton, Choate, Samuel Clark, Clay, Clayton, Corwin, Coulter, Cramer, Crockett, Warren R. Davis, Davenport, Deberry, Deming, Dickson, Dickerson, Dickinson, Ellsworth, Edward Everett, Felder, Fowler, William K. Fuller, Gamble, Garland, Gholson, Gorham, Grennell, Griffin, Joseph Hall, Hiland Hall, Halsey, Hard, Joseph M. Harper, Hathaway, Hazeltine, Hiester, Hubbard, Jabez W. Huntington, Inge, Jackson, William C. Johnson, Richard M. Johnson, Noadiah Johnson, Lansing, Lay, Luke Lea, Thomas Lee, Lincoln, Love, Loyall, Martindale, Mardis, John Y. Mason, Moses Mason, McComas, McKinley, Muhlenberg, Page, Parker, Pierson, Pope, Ramsay, Schenck, Schley, Selden, William B. Shepard, A. H. Shepperd, Sloane, Smith, Spangler, Speight, William Taylor, William P. Taylor, Turrill, Tweedy, Vanderpoel, Wagener, Ward, Wardwell, Wayne, Whallon, Elisha Whittlesey, Frederick Whittlesey, Wilde, Williams—109.

The question then being on the motion of Mr. BEARDSLEY to strike out the 23d and insert the 16th—

Mr. POLK rose to express the hope that the motion would not prevail. He did entertain the opinion that we ought not to fix upon an earlier day of adjournment than the 30th of June, and the day now proposed could not be fixed upon with any propriety in reference to the despatch of the public business.

Mr. BOON hoped, he said, that the gentleman from New York would withdraw the motion.

Mr. WILDE said, before he voted for the proposition, he would ask the chairman of the Bank Investigation Committee, what time would be requisite, according to his judgment, to bring the business of which that committee had charge to a final close. He was unwilling to give a vote which looked to the suppression of an ample consideration of that subject. The reasons which governed him when he gave his views on this subject on a former occasion, still existed. He was then, and still was, desirous for fixing the earliest day for adjournment, if there was no probability of any action upon the great subjects before us. He should not have made these remarks but for the imputation which had been thrown upon the minority, of a desire to protract the session unnecessarily, and to embarrass the public business. He repeated that he was in favor of the earliest day which had been named.

Mr. THOMAS, of Maryland, rose, he said, to respond to the inquiry cheerfully and readily. It was not for him to prescribe a rule of action to others in this House. But, without disrespect to others, he might undertake to answer the question which had been propounded. The Committee of Investigation, he said, were disposed to call up the resolutions reported by them in good faith, and with a sincere, earnest, and unequivocal determination to carry them through. The gentleman from Georgia could anticipate as well as any one, the length of time which a subject embracing so wide a range of topics would occupy. So far as his own opinion went, he must say that he thought it utterly impracticable to undertake to act upon the questions involved in the bank report, together with other business before the House by the 16th instant. There were many appropriation bills to be disposed of, in two of which, the canal and national road bill, his immediate constituents had great interest. Besides, there was other indispensable business which would occupy the whole time of the House prior to the day named. It would be almost ridiculous to take up the subject of the bank report, and attempt to dispose of it, if the House fixed the 16th of June as the day of adjournment. He had had some conversation with his colleagues of the committee on the subject, and some of them concurred with him in the opinion that if that day was fixed on for the day of adjournment, it ought to be considered as an unequivocal declaration by the House of a determination not to act upon the bank report. It would be impossible, in that case, to consider the subject, unless all other business should be postponed till the next session. He was bound to suppose that the resolutions would be adopted, and that would elicit some discussion. If they were adopted, the measures consequent upon it would occupy some time. The fifth resolution proposed to authorize an attachment against twelve or fourteen individuals who had refused to testify, and committed other contempts against the authority of the House of Representatives. It would perhaps take the marshal or sergeant-at-arms a week to execute the process. Could it be imagined, then, that the House could dispose of so grave a subject in the time limited by the resolution, and transact also the business before it that could not be postponed? Every one of the members was as capable as he was of judging how long the subject would be discussed. The report comes up on Tuesday next. He should, therefore, think if the House fixed upon the 16th instant for the adjournment it ought to be laid upon the table.

Mr. WISE said he could not yet see land, and he would not throw the lead until he saw the land ahead. He moved to lay the resolution on the table; which was negatived. Yeas 65, nays 146.

Mr. SPEIGHT was inclined (he said) to vote for the 16th, but he was now in favor of fixing upon the 23d. He moved the previous question.

Mr. BEARDSLEY withdrew the motion to insert the 16th, and said that he should certainly vote for the previous question.

Mr. WILDE hoped the motion for the previous question would be withdrawn, as we were still in the dark.

The question being taken, the House refused to second the previous question.

Mr. SPANGLER renewed the motion to strike out 23d and insert 16th June.

Mr. WILDE hoped the motion would not prevail. If, by fixing the 23d, an opportunity would be afforded to take up the report of the bank committee, he would vote against the 16th. If it was true, as gentlemen on one side supposed, that the authority of the House had been contemned by a body of individuals, a just sense of duty and dignity should prevent the House from adjourning, bearing upon its character such a stain. What court ever adjourned over to its next term with a contemptuous witness unpunished, and the subject uninvestigated. He was unwilling to adjourn until the question was examined. He was unwilling that a grave question, affecting the honor of the House, should be laid over. If the gentleman from Maryland [Mr. THOMAS] supposed that the 23d would afford the necessary time, he would vote for that day, though he had intended to vote for the 16th.

Mr. CROCKETT was very anxious that we should fix on the 16th, because the proposition had come from a quarter which was accustomed to take responsibility. He never believed gentlemen to be in earnest in this bank report. They had proved it, and the proof was at hand. Their object was to get away and leave the question open, in order to keep up an excitement.

Mr. CLAYTON understood the gentleman from Maryland [Mr. THOMAS] to say, that if the 16th was adopted, he should consider it an indication that the House did not intend to consider the report of the committee of investigation. Believing it important that the subject should be considered, he had changed his opinion as to the time of adjournment, and moved a reconsideration of the vote by which the House refused to fix the 30th June.

Mr. LYTLE felt bound to vote for the longest day, both in reference to the report of the committee, and other important business before the House. He did not believe it practicable to adjourn at either of the periods which had been proposed. Work had been cut out which would last beyond all of them. He was for meeting the questions presented by the report of the committee, and hoped no one of the party with whom he usually acted would obstruct it. He alluded to the circumstance that distinguished gentlemen in the other House at one time expressed the opinion that Congress ought not to adjourn even if the present session was run into the next. But as soon as a committee of the House was sent to investigate the affairs of the Bank, their tone was entirely changed, and they declared themselves in favor of an early adjournment. He had observed, both in Congress and in certain presses throughout the Union, a similar change of tone. There was an evident disposition to shrink from the question. He was satisfied that an early adjournment was inconsistent with the inquiry which the state of that institution required.

Mr. R. M. JOHNSON was in favor of the 16th, but would vote for the 23d, because it seemed to be the prevailing opinion that the session should be so far prolonged. Should Congress remain here through June and July, he would hazard the opinion that few important measures would be concluded. He had been here twenty-seven years, and never yet saw a Congress which would give up talking, and go to work before the day of adjournment was fixed. We knew very well that nothing would be agreed on relative to the great subject before the House.

Mr. CHILTON, in reply to the gentleman from Ohio, [Mr. LYTLE,] denied that he, for one, was disposed to skulk from any examination into the affairs of the bank. He had voted against the resolution ordering the investigation, because he thought the country would derive no benefit from it. If we now entered upon that subject, it would occupy the whole summer, and no practical good would result from it. He was disposed to settle the whole matter by adjourning as soon as the appropriation bills were passed.

Mr. BURGES, so far from shrinking from the bank question (he said) he would stay here till the snow fell, rather than offer any obstacle to its consideration. If gentlemen wished to bring the bankers here, his voice should not be lifted against it. He would make no speeches on the one side or the other, and would do nothing which should obstruct their wishes. The question before the House was, shall we give time to the committee to arraign the president and directors of the bank? His reply to the question was yes, though there was not a man in the House more anxious to get home than himself. He hoped every gentleman who wished to afford the committee an opportunity to bring up that subject, would vote for the reconsideration.

Mr. LANE said he had given several silent votes upon the subject of the adjournment of the session. That it was not his intention to detain the House by saying anything that shall invite a reply, or add to the present excitement. On the contrary, he would desire to allay every unpleasant feeling, and banish from the Hall all party spirit—all thoughts of who should or should not hereafter fill high places.

Mr. Speaker, as yet we have done but little, while all the important bills in which the public interest is concerned, remain to be disposed of. He did not believe gentlemen would be disposed to destroy the important business of the House. A different feeling seems now to be manifested by all.

Sir, from the various important bills referred to by several honorable gentlemen, it is evident that the 23d of June will be too limited to accomplish that which all admit to be of public and private importance.

There is, however, one bill upon the files, regulating the deposites of the public money, (said Mr. L.,) he would never agree by his vote to adjourn until finally acted upon. However great his confidence in the Secretary of the Treasury, and unbounded in the Executive, every consideration of public duty demanded it. As we regard ourselves and respect the wishes of our constituents, and the reputations of those individuals, and the honor of the country, we will dispose of this delicate and all exciting subject. It is called for as we regard the public fears, to restore public and private confidence, and to relieve, as far as possible, the public embarrasment.

The objection made by the gentleman from Kentucky [Mr. CHILTON] is not a sound one, that, if we pass the bill, it will fail in the other House. However exceptionable the bill in its present form to the notions of that honorable gentleman, like all others, it may be altered and amended, until it might even fill the wishes of the gentleman himself. The other branch, in their wisdom, will also be at liberty to mould it to their sense of propriety and duty.

Mr. Speaker, my honorable friend from Kentucky [Mr. JOHNSON] says, twenty-seven years' experience has taught him that this House will never do anything until the day of adjournment is fixed. Granted; but does that prove that a reasonable time ought not to be given between the time of fixing and the day of adjournment? And that in doing this, we ought not to be influenced by the business to be transacted?

' There is another bill which seems to him here overlooked by all save the honorable gentleman at my left, [Mr. CHILTON.] I refer to the bill placing the soldiers of the West upon the pension list with those of the Revolution. Mr. Speaker, I may forget myself, but I will never forget the war-worn soldiers of the valley of the Ohio. No, sir, nor will I cease to vindicate their characters, and urge their claims upon the nation, while I shall be honored with a seat upon this floor.

Sir, my honorable friend at the right [Mr. JOHNSON] says his constituents desire to see him. Of this there can be no doubt. All who know him, desire to see him.

The gentleman says, this is the popular branch of the Government—the last hope of freedom. To this sentiment I respond most heartily. Yes, Mr. Speaker, in this Hall, I have no doubt, the last voice in defence of liberty and law will be heard—in this Hall, that eagle will make its last flutter—that banner for the last time be unfurled. Here shall liberty bid her last adieu. Yes, sir, in this Hall will the last smile be dashed from the lips of that fair goddess by some ambitious tyrant, bursting these doors with swords and body guards, bidding the Representatives of the people depart. Heaven grant that day shall be distant; far, far distant.

Mr. ANTHONY said it was difficult to bring so many opinions together upon any one time; but the 23d was, perhaps, the safest and best period to fix. The question had now been debated four hours, and he hoped the House was now ready for a decision. He called for the previous question.

The CHAIR informed the House that the main question was the motion of Mr. CLAYTON to reconsider the vote refusing to fix the 30th of June as the day of adjournment.

The previous question was seconded; yeas 106; and the main question ordered to be put, without a division.

The question of reconsideration was carried by the following vote:

YEAS—Messrs. J. Q. Adams, Heman Allen, William Allen, Anthony, Ashley, Barnitz, Bates, Beaumont, John Bell, James M. Bell, Blair, Bouldin, Bull, Bunch, Bund, Burges, Cambreleng, Carmichael, Chambers, Chaney, William Clark, Clayton, Clowney, Coffee, Connor, W. R. Davis, Amos Davis, Davenport, Day, Deberry, Denny, Duncan, Dunlap, Evans, H. Everett, Ewing, Forester, Fulton, Gillet, Gilmer, Gordon, Graham, Joseph Hall, Hamer, Hannegan, Hardin, Jos. M. Harper, James Harper, Harrison, Heath, Henderson, Howell, Abel Huntington, Inge, Jarvis, Seaborn Jones, Benjamin Jones, Kavanagh, King, Kinnard, Lane, Laporte, Lay, Leavitt, Lewis, Loyall, Lucas, Lyon, Lytle, Abijah Mann, J. K. Mann, Martindale, Marshall, John Y. Mason, Moses Mason, McCarty, McIntire, McKay, McKennan, McKim, McLene, McVean, Mercer, Miller, Milligan, Henry, Mitchell, Robert Mitchell, Moore, Muhlenberg, Murphy, Osgood, Parks, Patton, Patterson, Dutee J. Pearce, Peyton, Franklin Pierce, Plummer, Polk, Potts, Schenck, Selden, William B. Shepard, Shinn, Wiliam Slade, Charles Slade, Sloane, Standifer, Stoddert, Sutherland, Francis Thomas, Philemon Thomas, Thomson, Tompkins, Turner, Vance, Van Houten, Wagener, Watmough, Wayne, Edward D. White, Elisha Whittlesey, Wilde, Wilson, Wise, Young—120.

NAYS—Messrs. John Adams, John J. Allen, Chilton Allan, Banks, Barber, Baylies, Bean, Beardsley, Beaty, Bockee, Bodle, Boon, Briggs, Brown, Burns, Bynum, Cage, Campbell, Carr, Casey, Chilton, Choate, Samuel Clark, Clay, Corwin, Coulter, Cramer, Crockett, Deming, Dickson, Dickinson, Ellsworth, Edward Everett, Felder, Fowler, William K. Fuller, Gamble, Garland, Gholson, Gorham, Grayson, Grennell, Griffin, Hiland Hall, Halsey, Hard, Hathaway, Hazeltine, Hiester, Hubbard, Jabez W. Huntington, Jackson, Wm. Cost Johnson, Richard M. Johnson, Noadiah Johnson, Cave Johnson, Lansing, Thomas Lee, Lincoln, Love, Mardis, McComas, McKinley, Page, Parker, Pierson, Pope, Ramsay, Schley, A. H. Shepperd, Smith, Spangler, Speight, William Taylor, W. P. Taylor, Turrill, Tweedy, Vanderpoel, Vinton, Ward, Wardwell, Whallon, Frederick Whittlesey, Williams—85.

The question being on fixing upon the 30th of June—

Mr. J. Q. ADAMS said he would detain the House a moment with an explanation of his vote. From the day of the introduction of the resolution, he had uniformly voted for the shortest time. He had presumed that the bill regulating the deposites was not to be touched. All other important business might be despatched by the 16th. But having found it to be the intention of the chairman of the Committee of Ways and Means to bring up that bill, which would be necessarily a subject of discussion, he was in favor of a longer period. If the report of the bank committee was to be taken up, the 30th June was the very shortest time for its consideration. He hoped the House would reflect on its character. This is new matter. The House had sent a committee to investigate the affairs of the bank. Have they done it? Not one word on that subject is to be found in the report. It contains no information as to the affairs of the bank. The committee had returned with a charge against the bank, of having three times violated its charter; and for the punishment of those offences, the committee propose to bring the offenders to the bar of the House—to bring to our bar fourteen respectable individuals, to be punished as criminals. We are to send our Sergeant-at-Arms to arrest fourteen men.

Mr. CAMBRELENG rose to order. He inquired if that question was before the House.

The CHAIR (Mr. HUBBARD) did not consider the gentleman out of order.

Mr. ADAMS resumed. He was assigning reasons for changing his vote. He hoped every vote he should give would be given on principle; and he felt responsible to the House and to his constituents for an alteration of his vote. We are told that we are disposed to shrink from this subject, by an early adjournment. He was willing to stay for years, sooner than adjourn, if he thought the dignity of the House had been insulted, in order that it should be sustained. Was he out of order when he said that he had changed his vote, because of this new matter—because it was proposed to bring fourteen men in chains to our bar, to answer as criminals? We had not a soldier to enforce our orders. He recollected the anecdote of the man who took three prisoners by surrounding them; he supposed we should send our Sergeant-at-Arms to surround these fourteen individuals. He should admire to see that sight. But a grave question arises as to the right of the House to send into a State and arrest citizens and bring them here. This House is not a court of justice. We are to try these men upon an accusation brought by ourselves, and we are to punish them ourselves, with the whole power of our vindictive justice. Does any one suppose that this question is to be settled without much deliberation?

Mr. THOMAS said, the character of the remarks to which he had just listened impelled him to speak. During his absence from his seat, on another occasion, an act of the majority of the committee, of which he was one, had been most unjustly, he would not say falsely, characterized. They had been charged with authorizing a publication of this report, with a view of forestalling, improperly, the public judgment. The transaction he had heretofore, frankly, explained, and he could not feel the least respect for the opinion of any member who would, thereafter, impute to him or his colleagues, the slightest impropriety of motive. But what has this House witnessed from another quarter. The gentleman from Rhode Island [Mr. BURGES] has embraced every opportunity, in season and out of season, to speak slightly of the report of the bank committee. When it was first presented to the House, and again to-day, he had sought to excite popular prejudice against its authors and the measure they had recommended for the adoption of the House. Notwithstanding these proceedings from that and from other quarters, he had never attempted a vindication of the report, because he felt it did not need much vindication against mere declamatory assaults. But the gentleman from Massachusetts has now entered the arena. His remarks are too well calculated to forestall the judgment of the country to be passed unnoticed. The high character of the honorable gentleman for distinguished attainment, and the estimation in which his opinions are held by that large portion of the people who believe he has done signal service to his country in the important stations he has held, forbid that his remarks should pass unnoticed.

Why has this House been repeatedly told by him that the directors of the bank whom we propose to attach, are distinguished for talents, and especially for financial skill and judgment? Are we to take it for granted that the bank, under their control, is judiciously and wisely managed, solely because they are skilful financiers? However men may act, no one will admit that to be their principle of action. The gentleman mistakes much the character of this House and of their constituents, if he supposes the financial skill of the directors would suffice of itself to satisfy them that there is not good cause to inquire into the manner in which they have discharged a high trust. The gentleman also greatly misconceives the true character of the House and the genius of our institutions, if he imagines that the intellectual attainments and high character in other respects, of these persons, who had defied the authority of this House, would shield them from responsibility. That man who is to be deterred from discharging his duties here, because he may, by so doing, be compelled to encounter the displeasure of any man or set of men, no matter how high their station, or how great their intellectual powers, is unworthy to be esteemed the representative of freemen. For one, he had a very different rule for his conduct. He assented to the declaration that all men are created equal, and he was ready to act up to the theory on which our institutions are founded. All men are not only created equal in the eye of the law, but they exist as equals. With such rules for his guide, he would enforce the laws against the highest and most powerful, as readily as he would against the most humble; against the Chief Magistrate of the country, as cheerfully as against the most humble citizen. Our laws were made by all as a rule of conduct for all; and they are over and above all persons whatsoever. He went for the supremacy of the laws; and when convinced as he was in this instance, clearly and conclusively, that an important and essential principle of the laws had been contemned—one, without the enforcement of which, this House, the great sheetanchor of our Government, was deprived of one of its most important powers—he stood prepared to arrest or attach any being but the dread God who made him.

The gentleman has told us that the right to attach for contempt of the authority of this House is a most mysterious power. The memory of the distinguished gentleman must be more treacherous than his, and more forgetful than that of other persons present. He had the honor to serve with the gentleman in the preceding Congress. During its session, Governor Houston, of Tennessee, was arrested for an assault upon Mr. Stansbury, then a member of the House. No difficulty was then felt in discovering the existence of this "mysterious power." The resolution for the arrest of Houston was passed by the vote of all the members of the House, except thirty-five. The offence he had committed was of a character very different from the one now complained of. He had committed an assault on a member in the streets of this city, who was not engaged in the discharge of any duty imposed on him by this House. In that case, the gentleman acted with those who had not only the inclination, but found readily the law which authorized them to punish for a supposed contempt. In the present instance, it must be admitted by all, there is less doubt of the power of the House than in the case of Houston. Here we allege that the directors of the bank have contemptuously disregarded the legal process of this House, by refusing to submit to it. They have resisted the mandates of the House, made by a committee duly authorized to make them. It is not a contest between the committee and the directors. We have no personal affronts to avenge. We have no personal feelings to gratify. We were the officers of this House. They ordered that to be done which the directors will not permit to be done. The House must then surely do one of two things: either back out, repeal the resolution under which the committee has been appointed, and discharge the committee from the duty imposed, or enforce its will by attachment or other compulsory process. Gentlemen are mistaken if they suppose the committee feel peculiar responsibility on this subject. Those members of the committee who voted

for the original resolution of the House, are ready to vindicate its legality, justice, and propriety; and for that purpose have recommended, most respectfully, the only measure which appeared to them consistent with those principles. They are not in fear of the judgment of their constituents. Gentlemen may talk for effect of the arrest of distinguished citizens, and may pompously parade before the public mind these fourteen gentlemen in custody of our Sergeant-at-Arms. This scene cannot deter any man in the performance of his duty. No one has ever attended the session of a county court who has not witnessed similar proceedings. There, if a witness refuses to obey a summons, he is attached for contempt, and fined: I repeat, must be the judgment of this court. There, a sheriff or juror is liable to the service of the same process.

But, what shall we say of another portion of the remarks of the distinguished gentleman, with whose opinion alone, let it be understood, I am contending? Towards him personally I will, to manifest, what I feel, a sincere respect. But what, I repeat, must be the judgment of this House and of the public, on the attempt to ridicule the idea that our Sergeant-at-Arms can arrest fourteen men? Are we, then, to conclude that gentlemen are prepared to resist the lawful authority of the House? He inquires, too, will the State of Pennsylvania permit fourteen of her citizens to be summoned to the bar of this House? Sir, (said Mr.), the people of Pennsylvania are not ready to set at the will of any man or set of men. They will not be prepared to resist the laws at the bidding, or to promote the ulterior purposes of any party. Let but an insurrectionary spirit display itself, and every man who loves the institutions which have shed their benign influence upon every act of this noble Confederacy, will stand forth to defend the supremacy of the laws. Mr. T. said, he hoped the House would pardon the remarks. He was sensible they would be inappropriate when the reports of the bank committee came up for consideration. He disliked seriously the practice which prevailed here [discussing questions not immediately before the House,] but he could not consent to have his own view, and a measure of which he decidedly approved, done injustice to in this debate, without reply. He hoped the House would not adjourn till the 30th of June, and before that day would it candidly and correctly on the questions which were involved in the bank report, and on other highly important measures not yet disposed of.

Mr. SUTHERLAND moved the previous question, but immediately withdrew it.

Mr. HIESTER renewed the call for the previous question, which was not sustained by the House. The question was then taken on striking out and inserting the 30th of June, as the day of adjournment. This was carried by the following:

YEAS—Messrs. John Q. Adams, Heman Allen, William Allen, Anthony, Archer, Ashley, Banks, Barringer, Bates, Beaumont, John Bell, James M. Bell, Bouldin, Bull, Bunch, Burd, Burges, Bynum, Cambreleng, Carmichael, Chambers, Casey, William Clark, Clayton, Coffee, Connor, Corwin, Davis, Day, Deberry, Deming, Duncan, Dunlap, Evans, Horace Everett, Ewing, Forester, Philo C. Fuller, Fulton, Galbraith, Gillet, Gilmer, Gorham, Graham, Grayson, Joseph M. Harper, James Harper, Harrison, Heath, Henderson, Howell, Huntington, Jarvis, Cave Johnson, Seaborn Jones, Benjamin Jones, Kavanagh, King, Kinnard, Lane, Laporte, Luke Lea, Leavitt, Lewis, Lincoln, Lucas, Lyon, Lytle, Abijah Mann, Joel K. Mann, Marindale, Marshall, Moses Mason, Cart, McIntire, McKay, McKennan, McKim, Lee, McVean, Mercer, Miller, Robert Mitchell, Moore, Murphy, Osgood, Parks, Patton, Patterson, Duncan J. Pearce, Peyton, Franklin Pierce, Pinckney, Plummer, Polk, Potts, Selden, William Shepard, Shinn, William Slade, Charles Slade, Speight, Standifer, Stoddert, Sutherland, Francis Thomas, Philemon Thomas, Tompkins, Turner, Turrill, Vanderpoel, Van Houten, Vinton, Watmough, Wayne, Webster, Whallon, Edward D. White, Elisha Whittlesey, Wilde, Wilson, and Young—130.

NAYS—Messrs. John Adams, John J. Allen, Chilton Allan, Banks, Barber, Baylies, Bean, Beardsley, Beaty, Bockee, Bodle, Boon, Briggs, Brown, Burns, Cage, Campbell, Carr, Casey, Chilton, Choate, Samuel Clark, Clay, Corwin, Coulter, Cramer, Crockett, Davenport, Deming, Dickson, Dickerson, Dickinson, Ellsworth, Edward Everett, Felder, Fowler, William K. Fuller, Gamble, Garland, Gholson, Gorham, Grennell, Griffin, H. Hall, Halsey, Hathaway, Hazeltine, Hiester, Hubbard, Jabez W. Huntington, Jackson, Wm. C. Johnson, R. M. Johnson, Noadiah Johnson, Lansing, Thomas Lee, Lincoln, Love, Mardis, John Y. Mason, McComas, McKinley, Muhlenberg, Page, Parker, Pierson, Pope, Ramsey, Schenck, Schley, Augustine H. Shepperd, Smith, Spangler, Speight, William Taylor, William P. Taylor, Turrill, Tweedy, Wagener, Ward, Wardwell, Frederick Whittlesey, and Williams—83.

The resolution, as amended, was then adopted without a division.

Mr. S. JONES gave notice, that to-morrow he should ask leave to take up the report on the contested Kentucky election.

The House then adjourned.

IN SENATE.

FRIDAY, May 30, 1834.

A message upon executive business was received from the President of the United States, by Mr. DONELSON, his Private Secretary.

A message was received from the House of Representatives, by Mr. FRANKLIN, their Clerk, stating that the House had passed a joint resolution fixing the time for the adjournment of Congress, in which they asked the concurrence of the Senate.

The bill from the House of Representatives regulating the value of silver coin was read a first and second time, and referred, on motion of Mr. WEBSTER, to the Committee on Finance.

The bill for the better organization of the United States marine corps was taken up in Committee of the Whole, and which led to a discussion of onwards of three hours between Messrs. SOUTHARD, FORSYTH, PRESTON, CHAMBERS, CALHOUN, CLAY, LEIGH, PORTER, and BIBB. The bill was amended, on motion of Mr. BIBB, so as to abolish the brevet rank in the army and marine corps, save when merited by services rendered in action, and also excepting those now entitled to it after having rendered ten years' service.

The bill as amended was ordered to be engrossed and read a third time.

Mr. CLAY moved to take up for consideration the joint resolution submitted by him relative to the deposite of the public moneys in the Bank of the United States.

Mr. BROWN remarked that these resolutions were very important in their character; he therefore thought, as several seats were vacant, it would be very improper to take them up at this time. He was ready to give his vote at any time upon them, but it was hardly treating absent gentlemen fairly to pass them now.

Mr. WRIGHT asked whether it was in order to take up a subject of a public nature, this being a day set apart for the consideration of private bills.

Mr. CLAY said he had no wish to take advantage of the absence of other members. His only wish was, that the resolution might be ordered to be engrossed for a third reading, and then let the subject lie over till Monday.

Mr. WRIGHT asked the Secretary to read the order which had been adopted, setting apart Fridays and Saturdays exclusively for private business.

The order was read.

The CHAIR remarked that it was not aware that this was Friday. From the terms of the order, it seemed that the rule would prohibit the consideration of the resolutions.

Mr. CLAY then gave notice, that on Monday next, whoever were absent or whoever were present, he would press the resolutions to a final passage.

BILLS.

The following bills were considered in committee of the whole, and ordered to a third reading:

A bill for the relief of the town of Fayetteville, in the Territory of Arkansas;

A bill for the relief of John Chandler and William Johnson.

The Senate then considered the bill to enable South Hanover College, in Indiana, to establish an asylum for teaching the deaf and dumb.

Messrs. HENDRICKS and POINDEXTER advocated, and Messrs. SOUTHARD, GRUNDY, CLAY, SPRAGUE, and PORTER, opposed the bill:

When, on Mr. POINDEXTER'S motion, the bill was laid on the table.

The Senate then (at five o'clock) adjourned.

HOUSE OF REPRESENTATIVES.

FRIDAY, May 30, 1834.

Mr. SPEAKER STEVENSON rose and informed the House that he had taken the chair this morning, though still laboring under severe and continued indisposition, for the purpose of opening the House and preventing any delay in its business, and likewise for the purpose of announcing his determination of resigning the Speaker's chair and his seat in Congress. This he proposed doing on Monday next at eleven o'clock. He had formed this resolution under a deep sense of duty, and because his state of health rendered it impossible for him (as must be apparent to the House) to discharge in person the laborious duties of the Chair; and he had, therefore, deemed it respectful and proper to give this early notice of his intention to retire.

Mr. CHILTON moved the suspension of the rules in order to offer a resolution providing that, for the residue of the session of Congress, the House shall take a recess from two to four o'clock, and meet daily at ten o'clock A. M.

Mr. R. M. JOHNSON asked the yeas and nays on the motion, which were ordered.

The question being taken on the motion to suspend the rules, it was determined in the negative. Yeas 57, nays 89.

Mr. CHINN, from the Committee on the District of Columbia, reported a bill for the benefit of the town of Alexandria.

Mr. HEALTH, from the Committee on Commerce, reported a joint resolution for the purchase of one hundred copies of Barry's Laws of Exchange; read, and ordered to a second reading.

KENTUCKY CONTESTED ELECTION.

The House resumed the consideration of the resolution reported from the Committee of Elections, declaring THOMAS P. MOORE, Esquire, to be entitled to a seat in this House, as a representative from the fifth Congressional district of Kentucky, together with the following amendment offered by Mr. BANKS:

"That all the legal votes which were received in 'Lancaster, Garrard county, whilst Moses Grant, 'Esq., acted as one of the judges on the first morn-'ing of the election, in August last, and those of a 'like character, given on the second day of the 'election, in the casual absence of the sheriff, ought 'to be estimated in ascertaining the result of the 'election."

Mr. BANKS accepted as a modification the motion of Mr. JONES, to amend the amendment, by substituting the word "qualified" for "legal," and striking out the word "casual."

Mr. BANKS also modified his amendment by adding to it the following:

"That the votes of David McKee, Alfred W. 'Buford, Elijah Mount, Clayton Fitzpatrick, W. 'R. Preston, R. L. Berry, B. Lefler, R. McKeown, 'G. M. Ormond, and Lewis L. Mason, given in 'Mercer county, be counted; the first nine for R. P. 'Letcher, and the last one for T. P. Moore."

"That the votes of John McHan, Reuben Young, 'Vincent Inge, Jacob Coffman, William Jenkins, 'and the Rev. D. Robinson, be taken from the num-'ber of votes allowed by the majority of the com-'mittee to Moore, in Mercer county, and added to 'those counted for Letcher.

"That the votes of Eli Williams and Wade 'Dawson, of Anderson county, and that those of 'William Comer, Charles Welsh, Thomas Harns, 'Montgomery Vanlandingham, Joseph Murrin, Levi 'Nunnery, Richard Oard, Anderson Hulet, Hick-'man Evans, Henry Wood, and Richard White, of 'Jessamine county, be counted for R. P. Letcher."

ROBERT P. LETCHER, Esq., addressed the House, by permission, in defence of his claim to the seat.

Mr. L. proceeded till twelve o'clock in his remarks; when

The CHAIR announced that this day, being Friday, was set apart, by the rules, after the morning business, for despatch of private business; but, with the unanimous consent of the House, the gentleman could proceed.

No objection being made—

Mr. LETCHER resumed, and continued his remarks till after three o'clock. He concluded by expressing his thanks to the House for the patient attention which they had afforded him, and by stating that he was perfectly well satisfied that the committee, in making a report adverse to his claim, were not governed by any feeling of unkindness to him. He also wished to say, not however with a view to influence the vote of any member on this question, that he should respectfully decline the pay and mileage of a member, proposed by the committee, in case the House should determine that he was not entitled to the contested seat.

Mr. HAMER rose (he said) merely to make a motion, and there were too reasons why he made it. The first was, that the gentleman who had just closed his remarks had referred to, and read, a part of the testimony which related to a great number of voters, and that it seemed necessary that the gentleman who was to follow him [Mr. MOORE] should have some time allowed to him. The other reason was, that, as his health was infirm, he doubted whether he would have sufficient strength to enable him to go through with his reply this evening.

Mr. H. therefore thought it proper to move an adjournment.

The motion was agreed to; and

The House adjourned.

A sketch of the remarks of MR. CARR, *upon offering an amendment to the Harbor and River Bill.*

MAY 17, 1834.

Mr. CARR proposed an amendment to the bill for an appropriation of the sum of $25,000 to improve the navigation in the Indian Chute through the Falls of the Ohio river.

Mr. C. in a very brief and explicit manner earnestly urged the propriety and utility of improving the navigation in the falls. He stated that a survey had been made; that the Committee on Roads and Canals had called on the department for a copy of the survey, and also for an estimate of the amount necessary to make the improvement asked for. Mr. C. said he had been informed that the department had requested Captain Shreve to make an estimate of the probable amount which it would cost to improve the navigation through the falls to an advantage, but that he had not been informed whether this estimate had been made and forwarded to the Committee on Roads and Canals or not. Mr. C. said he had deemed it his bounden duty to offer at this time the amendment which he had proposed. If the estimate had not yet been made, he presumed that it would be done immediately. If so, it would be presented to the House for its action previous to the engrossment of the bill. Mr. C. said, that, in frequent conversations which he had had with Captain S. on this subject, (in whose judgment he confided much,) he had given it as his opinion, that with the sum of twenty-five thousand dollars, the obstruction which now impeded safe and easy navigation through the falls could be, in a great degree, removed. It was also the opinion of other gentlemen of experience in matters of this sort, that with the sum asked for, the navigation might be so improved as to render the passage of flat-bottomed boats, and other vessels of ordinary tonnage, safe through the falls throughout the greater portion of the year.

Mr. C. adverted to the vast commerce which was carried on upon the Ohio river, and of the deep interest which was felt by the agricultural community and others, in relation to the contemplated improvement—he spoke of the large number of flat-bottomed boats which annually descended the Ohio, laden with the productions of the cultivators of the soil, and of the enormous tax which the owners of them were liable to pay for a passage through the canal. Mr. C. was of opinion, that one half the amount which the owners of boats which descended the Ohio river, are liable to pay, within the term of one year, in the way of tolls, if they all passed through the canal, would so far remove the obstruction which now impedes the navigation, as to make the navigation both safe and easy through the falls, at least so far as the flat-bottomed-boat navigation, and boats of ordinary tonnage of other descriptions, are concerned. Mr. C. said, it was the opinion of many persons with whom he had conversed, some of whom were gentlemen of much experience, to improve the navigation of the falls in the manner in which he understood it was contemplated to be done, and depositing the rock which would have necessarily to be removed from the channel, so as to be improved in a proper manner, that so far from injuring the canal in the slightest degree, it would have the contrary effect; that the condition of the canal would be improved by it.

Mr. C. said, that as this was a matter of so much interest, to so large a portion of the country, he hoped the small sum asked for would be granted.

HOUSE OF REPRESENTATIVES.

APRIL 26, 1834.

Mr. EDWARD D. WHITE, from the select committee to which was referred the memorial of Benjamin Phillips, of Philadelphia, made the following report:

The object of the memorialist is to invite the attention of Congress, and of the public generally, to certain improvements devised by him in the use and structure of the steam engine. The model of his apparatus, accompanied by drawings and diagrams illustrative of its principles, have been submitted and examined. Whatever other advantages may be supposed to be combined in the scheme, the committee have considered it chiefly, if not exclusively, in reference to its comparative safety, or exemption from the danger of explosion.

It seems to be a point conceded by scientific observers, that among the primary causes of explosion in steam boilers, one of the most prominent may be traced to the want of a constant and regular supply of water, while the engine is in action. The usual means employed, as the committee are advised, both for supplying the consumption of the boiler, and for ascertaining the quantum of water in that receptacle, are inadequate and uncertain. The forcing pump is liable to derangement; and when the water has fallen so low as to superinduce the circumstances of danger, neither the common gauge cock, nor the common safety valve, can be relied on for an accurate indication of the state of things so essential to be known. By the plan submitted, these defects appear to be remedied. A constant and uniform supply of water, and a test water gauge, indicating to the eye, at any moment, the precise level of the fluid in the boiler, form a part of the melioration suggested.

But what appears to the committee to be the distinguishing feature of the plan, is, that it contemplates the employment of the steam at any given pressure, without a corresponding stress on the boiler. This result is obtained by generating the steam at a very moderate pressure on the boiler, from whence it is conveyed for use, to one or more receivers, in which, before it is applied as the momentum to the engine, it may be raised, by flues heated from a separate furnace, to any required degree of elasticity.

The committee are of opinion, that if the scheme be feasible, of which THEY DO NOT DOUBT, it must, of itself, be an important step towards the grand desideratum. Confined in a separate reservoir, not in immediate connexion with the boiler, the steam, however rarified, would not be liable to be suddenly injected with water, a process which all concurring experience proclaims to be the proximate cause of many of the most dreadful accidents that have occurred.

The form and position of the contemplated receiver is believed to present another condition of security. Placed vertically on the deck, with different chambers or compartments, connected by valves, the steam at its greatest tension, naturally rushing through the valves into the upper chambers of the recipient, if ever explosion should take place, it would be a mere effusion of steam, and not of heated water; and the discharge would be upwards, into the open air, leaving untouched the passengers and the property embarked in the vessel.

There are other particulars in the mechanism, of the usefulness of which practical engineers alone are competent to form an accurate estimate. It will suffice to say, that, as a whole, the committee consider the contrivance as reflecting credit on the science and ingenuity of the proprietor, and that his plan is worthy of a full and fair experiment.

On the question as to the power and the expediency of aid and coöperation on the part of the Government in experiments of the kind, the committee have come to an affirmative conclusion. When it is considered how intimately the subject matter connects itself with the general welfare, looking to the protection of the lives and property of the whole people that it involves considerations of naval and national defence, as well as the general interests of commerce; it is not thought that any valid opposing argument can be drawn from the want of power, much less can objection be raised on the score of policy.

The committee have thought proper to recommend a small sum to be placed at the disposal of the Secretary of the Navy to test the improvements in this branch. It is believed that a reasonable expenditure of the public money for this object would coincide with the universal sense and meet the applause of the nation. The knowledge of the mode of controlling and directing with safety, this powerful, but hitherto dangerous agent in the affairs of men, would be cheaply purchased at the cost of millions.

THE CONGRESSIONAL GLOBE.

PRINTED AND PUBLISHED AT THE CITY OF WASHINGTON, BY BLAIR & RIVES.

23d Congress, 1st Session.　　　　　　　　　　SATURDAY, JUNE 7, 1834.　　　　　　　Vol. 1.......No. 27.

IN SENATE.
Saturday, *May* 31, 1834.

Mr. WEBSTER gave notice that he should, on Monday next, move to print an additional number of copies of the Biennial Register.

On motion of Mr. EWING, the bill settling and establishing the northern boundary line of the State of Ohio, was taken up, and made the special order of the day for Wednesday next.

Mr. KING, of Alabama, on leave obtained, introduced a bill for the relief of Duncan L. Clinch, which was read twice, and referred to the Committee on Public Lands.

Mr. CLAYTON moved that the Senate take up the bill for the relief of the legal representatives of Moses Shephard, deceased. Lost. Yeas 12, nays 16.

Mr. CLAYTON, from the Committee on the Judiciary, introduced a bill for the relief of the legal representatives of Philip Moore, deceased; which was read, and ordered to a second reading.

On motion of Mr. KING, of Alabama, the bill for the relief of Mountjoy Bayly was taken up.

Mr. MOORE moved to recommit the bill to the Committee on Revolutionary Pensions. The principle involved was an important one. It was one of interest or commutation, which had always been reported against by the committee.

Mr. BLACK thought the principle of interest was different from that supposed by the gentleman from Alabama, [Mr. Moore.] It was on the principle of the funding act, which he thought was decided by yeas and nays at the last session. The interest was universally allowed, and was not questioned till this session.

Mr. POINDEXTER, Mr. BELL, and Mr. CHAMBERS, made some remarks against the recommitment.

Mr. MOORE then withdrew his motion, contenting himself to let the principle be settled on the passage of the bill.

Mr. PRELINGHUYSEN opposed the bill, on the principle that such claims of interest alone would exhaust the whole treasury.

Mr. BELL denied that the claim was one of interest. It was this belief which led gentlemen to the misapprehension. The claim was for fifty years of half-pay, and nothing more.

Mr. WHITE said, the object of this bill was to give interest on five years' full pay. He had looked into this claim, and had come to the conclusion that the applicant was entitled neither to the principal nor the interest. In the year 1831, he applied to Congress for his five years' full pay, instead of his half-pay for life, which was granted to him on producing proof to satisfy the Secretary of War. And Mr. W. thought that no satisfactory proof had ever been produced of his serving to the end of the war. Whether the Senate should decide for or against the principle of allowing interest in such cases, he protested against its being allowed in this case.

Some further remarks were made by Messrs. TYLER, BELL, BIBB, CHAMBERS, and KING of Georgia, in favor of the bill, and by Messrs. LEIGH, WHITE, and SMITH, in opposition to it.

The question being on the passage of the bill, Mr. BIBB asked the yeas and nays, which were ordered, and are as follows, to wit:

YEAS—Messrs. Bell, Bibb, Black, Chambers, Clay, Hendricks, Kent, King of Alabama, McLean, Poindexter, Porter, Robbins, Silsbee, Sprague, Tomlinson, Tyler—16.

NAYS—Messrs. Benton, Brown, Calhoun, Ewing, Forsyth, Frelinghuysen, Georgia, Leigh, Linn, Mangum, Moore, Morris, Prentiss, Robinson, Smith, Swift, Tipton, White, Wright—22.

The bill granting to General P. Thomas, of Louisiana, a tract of land in consideration of the military services rendered by him in taking possession of that portion of West Florida included the district of Baton Rouge, was considered as

in Committee of the Whole, and ordered to be engrossed for a third reading.

On motion of Mr. FORSYTH, the Senate adjourned.

HOUSE OF REPRESENTATIVES.
Saturday, *May* 31, 1834.

Mr. E. WHITTLESEY, from the Committee of Claims, reported sundry bills from the Senate; which were referred to the Committee of the Whole.

Mr. MERCER, from the Committee on Roads and Canals, reported a bill authorizing examinations, surveys, and estimates, for the construction of certain roads, and the improvement of certain harbors and rivers; which was read twice, and committed.

Mr. MERCER, from the same committee, reported the following resolution:

Resolved, That the Secretary of War be directed to lay before the House, any information in his department, respecting the cost of constructing the contemplated embankment across the swamp and water courses between a point on the Mississippi, opposite Memphis, in Tennessee, and the high ground west of St. Francis river, and to report whether the road beyond the same, leading from Memphis to Little Rock, requires a further sum for its completion, and what amount is deemed sufficient therefor.

Mr. M. requested that the House now act upon this resolution, as the information sought was important for the action of the House. The resolution was taken up by unanimous consent, and adopted.

Mr. SCHLEY, from the Committee on Invalid Pensions, reported a bill for granting a pension to Thomas Morton; which was read twice, and committed.

Mr. BELL, from the Judiciary Committee, reported a bill giving the assent of Congress to an agreement or compact entered into between the States of New York and New Jersey, respecting the territorial limits and jurisdiction of those States.

Mr. B. said it was regarded as a matter of great importance by these States that this bill should be passed the present session; there being, so far as he was apprised, no objection from any quarter to its provisions, he hoped the House would consent to its being read at length, with a view to move its engrossment for a third reading.

The bill was read accordingly.

Mr. J. Q. ADAMS wished this bill would take the ordinary course. The provisions of this bill were extremely important; and he presumed they had been duly considered by the Judiciary Committee. But he wished for time to look into them for himself, in order to ascertain if the rights of the United States were properly guarded. As understood the bill, it appeared to assert that the two States of New York and New Jersey had entire jurisdiction over the waters mentioned in the agreement. The United States, in his opinion, had important rights, which had not been noticed. He did not wish to disturb the agreement, so far as referred to territorial boundaries; but the paramount right of the United States ought not to be conceded.

Mr. BELL said the committee, in their examination of the subject, had not perceived that any thing was contained in the agreement which could in any way infringe the rights of the United States. If the gentleman from Massachusetts [Mr. ADAMS] felt any apprehension in that respect, he was perfectly willing to add a proviso saving all the rights of the United States. This would cure all objections of that kind. If the gentleman desired it, he had no objection to postpone the question of engrossment until the bill could be examined.

Mr. ADAMS hoped the bill would be printed.

Mr. BELL had no objection.

Mr. PARKER explained the circumstances which led to the necessity of settling the boundaries between the two States at length. The agree-

ment had been unanimously entered into between the commissioners of the two States, and had been confirmed unanimously by the Legislatures of both States. It was an agreement between the States relative to a matter belonging to the States exclusively.

Mr. BELL moved that the further consideration of the bill be postponed until Wednesday next, and that the bill be printed.

Mr. GILLET suggested the propriety of making it a special order for that day; which was agreed to.

Mr. BELL for the relief of the sureties of George Wheeler, et al.; which was read twice and committed.

Mr. BELL, instructed by the same committee, moved that the report upon the petition of James McCally be recommitted to that committee; which was agreed to.

Mr. DEMING, from the Committee on Revolutionary Pensions, reported a bill for the relief of Timothy Jordan; which was read twice and committed.

Mr. GARLAND, by unanimous consent, submitted the following resolution, which was adopted:

Resolved, That the Committee of Private Land Claims be instructed to inquire into the expediency of confirming, by law, all the claims for land in favor of individuals which were recommended for confirmation by the register of the land office at Opelousas, in the State of Louisiana, in his report of 1st October, 1825, which are excepted from the provisions of the act of Congress of 16th May, 1826, entitled "An act to confirm certain claims to lands in the district of Opelousas, in Louisiana;" and also, all claims in favor of individuals recommended for confirmation by the register and receiver of the land district south of Red river, in Louisiana, in their report of 1st November, 1824, upon the land claims situated between the Rio Honda and the Sabine, which are excepted from the provisions of the act of Congress of 24th May, 1828, entitled "An act to confirm claims to lands in the district between the Rio Honda and Sabine river, founded on habitation and cultivation."

KENTUCKY CONTESTED ELECTION.

The report of the Committee of Elections upon the contested election for the fifth Congressional district then came up.

Mr. MOORE addressed the House in support of his claim to the seat, and in reply to the argument urged yesterday by his competitor, Mr. Letcher, which occupied the attention of the House until nearly three o'clock. When Mr. Moore had concluded—

Mr. LEAVITT rose, and after some preliminary remarks on the state of business before the House, moved the previous question.

Mr. HARDIN asked if the previous question would cut off the amendments offered by the minority of the Committee on Elections?

The CHAIR stated that it would cut off all amendments.

The question being put, the House refused to second the previous election for the fifth Congressional district then came up.

Mr. HARDIN took the floor, and spoke at considerable length in support of the claim of Mr. Letcher to the seat.

Mr. McKINLEY rose and remarked that he did not think it would be right to give his vote on this question without giving his views in regard to it. He was willing to proceed now, and to remain here till the question was determined, or to adjourn.

Mr. McKINLEY yielded the floor to

Mr. J. Q. ADAMS, who moved an adjournment.

The question being taken by yeas and nays, it was contested election in the negative: Yeas 81, nays 121.

Mr. McKINLEY addressed the House upon the resolution and the amendment of Mr. Banks, in a speech of about half an hour; and was followed by

Mr. C. ALLAN, who supported the amendment for a short time, when he gave way to

Mr. WILLIAMS, who moved an adjournment; but the yeas and nays having been ordered, he withdrew the motion.

Mr. ALLAN then proceeded again, for a short time, when he moved the House adjourn, upon which the yeas and nays were ordered.

Motion to adjourn negatived; yeas 92, nays 106.

Mr. ALLAN then moved a call of the House, which was ordered, ayes 96, noes 58.

The roll was called, and 210 members answered to their names.

Mr. DICKSON moved the call be suspended, upon which Mr. MERCER demanded the yeas and nays, which were ordered.

Mr. DICKSON then withdrew the motion, until the list of absentees should be called through.

Mr. WARD moved that the call be suspended, which was agreed to.

Mr. BURD moved the House adjourn, which was negatived without a division.

The CHAIR stated the question as follows: Resolved, That THOMAS P. MOORE, Esquire, is entitled to the seat in this House, to represent the Fifth Congressional District of the State of Kentucky;

Which was moved by Mr. BANKS to be amended by striking out the whole after the word resolved, and inserting instead thereof—

"That all the legal votes which were received in 'Lancaster, Garrard county, whilst Moses Grant, 'Esq., acted as one of the judges, on the first 'morning of the election, in August last, and those 'of a like character, given on the second day of 'the election in the casual absence of the sheriff, 'ought to be estimated in ascertaining the result of 'the election."

The amendment was required to be divided.

A question arose as to the effect of striking out and inserting a part of the amendment, when

Mr. BEARDSLEY, as a means of obviating the difficulty, moved the previous question—

Which was negatived: ayes 89, noes 108.

Mr. MOORE proposed to add, after the resolution reported by the committee, the first member of the amendment proposed by Mr. BANKS, instead of moving to strike out the resolution; which was assented to by Mr. BANKS.

Messrs. ADAMS and MARSHALL debated the effect of this amendment.

The question was then taken, and carried by the following vote: yeas 112, nays 102.

The question upon the second member of the amendment, providing that the votes taken on the second day during the absence of the sheriff should be counted, was then taken and carried: yeas 131, nays 84.

The question was then taken on the next clause of the amendment, providing that the votes of the Theological Students at Danville, by name, should be counted.

Mr. GILMER moved the question be so divided as to take the question upon those students who belonged out of the State of Kentucky separately.

The question was first taken on counting the votes of all excepting Blackburne Leffler and G. M. Ormond. This was carried. Yeas 119, nays 96.

The question was then taken on counting the votes of Blackburne Leffler and G. M. Ormond; and was carried—yeas 112, nays 103.

The question was then taken on the votes contained in the next clause, containing five voters, who were originally certified as voting both for Letcher and Moore.

After an explanation by Messrs. HARDIN and S. JONES, it was carried—yeas 119, noes 95.

The question was taken on the next clause of the amendment relating to the voters who were struck from Letcher's poll, as being unknown.

After some remarks in explanation of the facts, relative to this proposition, from Messrs. HARDIN, GHOLSON, CHILTON ALLAN, ELLSWORTH, POPE, and BANKS,

Mr. MUHLENBERG moved to adjourn.

Which was carried, and the House, at nine o'clock, adjourned accordingly.

IN SENATE.

MONDAY, June 2, 1834.

Mr. SILSBEE presented the memorial of citizens of Massachusetts;

Mr. McKEAN, of citizens of Pennsylvania; Mr. BELL, of citizens of New Hampshire; Mr. WRIGHT, of citizens of New York; and Mr. HENDRICKS, of citizens of Indiana, remonstrating against the renewal of the patent right of John Ames, for an improvement in the manufacture of paper; all of which were laid upon the table.

Mr. McKEAN presented the proceedings of a meeting styled the Democratic Whig Association of the Third Ward of the Northern Liberties, Philadelphia, opposed to an adjournment of Congress, until something should be done to settle the currency of the country. The proceedings were read, referred to the Committee on Finance, and ordered to be printed.

Mr. WRIGHT presented, the petition of Nathaniel Niles, late temporary representative of the United States at Paris; which was referred to the Committee on Foreign Relations.

Mr. SPRAGUE presented the memorial of four hundred and fifty citizens of Augusta, Maine; and

Mr. CLAY, the memorial of citizens of Bourbon county, Kentucky—both in favor of the restoration of the deposites, and the recharter of the Bank of the United States. Referred to the Committee on Finance, and ordered to be printed.

Mr. SOUTHARD presented the memorial of citizens of Gloucester county, New Jersey, in favor of the course of the Executive with regard to the United States Bank, and praying that Congress will not enact a law rechartering that institution, or directing the public deposites to be restored to it. The memorial was referred to the Committee on Finance, and referred to be printed.

Mr. SOUTHARD presented the proceedings of a meeting of democratic citizens of Hunterdon county, New Jersey, in favor of the proceedings of the President with regard to the bank; disapproving of the course of the Senate in refusing to spread upon its journals the protest of the President against the Senate's passing judgment upon him without trial; and in favor of the doctrines embodied in that document.

Mr. SOUTHARD also presented the proceedings of the Democratic State Convention, composed of upwards of four hundred delegates, from every part of New Jersey, similar in character to that from Hunterdon county.

Mr. S. said he had some difficulty in his own mind, as to the proper course for him to pursue in regard to these memorials. The one last alluded to was couched in indecorous language towards the Senate, and also spoke in terms of reprehension of himself and colleague. He, however, moved that the resolutions be printed, and take the usual reference.

Mr. CLAYTON opposed the printing, on the ground of improper language used towards the Senate, and moved to lay the proceedings on the table.

Mr. FORSYTH hoped the motion would not be pressed. A memorial from another New Jersey convention was received some time ago from the other party, and this was but a response to that. This was just like the other. That denounced the President of the United States, and the minority of the Senate, though not by name, yet in effect. He hoped this would meet with the same disposition which that received.

Messrs. CLAYTON, EWING, POINDEXTER, and FRELINGHUYSEN, made some further remarks against printing the proceedings.

Messrs. FORSYTH and CHAMBERS in favor of the motion.

Mr. CLAY said, in order to have an opportunity of getting up his resolutions for consideration, he moved to lay the whole subject on the table.

Mr. FORSYTH observed, as it seemed to him that this course would be a final disposition of the matter, he asked the yeas and nays on the motion; which were ordered, and are as follow, to wit:

YEAS—Messrs. Bell, Bibb, Chambers, Clay, Clayton, Ewing, Kent, Knight, Leigh, Moore, Naudain, Poindexter, Porter, Prentiss, Robbins, Silsbee, Smith, Sprague, Swift, Tomlinson, and Webster—21.

NAYS—Messrs. Benton, Brown, Forsyth, Grundy, Hendricks, Hill, Kane, King of Alabama, King of Georgia, Linn, Morris, Preston, Robinson, Shepley, Tipton, White, Wilkins, and Wright—18.

So the question was determined in the affirmative.

Mr. WEBSTER, from the Committee on the Judiciary, reported a bill suspending for a time the payment of certain revenue bonds executed by William D. Ross, for duties due upon iron.

Mr. POINDEXTER, from the Committee on Public Lands, asked to be discharged from the further consideration of the petition of Henry Smith; which was agreed to.

Mr. GRUNDY, from the Committee on the Post Office and Post Roads, to whom was referred a resolution of inquiry, reported a bill placing the postage upon periodical pamphlets upon the same footing as newspapers; which was read, and ordered to a second reading.

Mr. CHAMBERS, from the Committee on the District of Columbia, asked to be discharged from the further consideration of the memorials of inhabitants of the District of Columbia and State of Maryland, praying Congress to purchase the Eastern Branch bridges, in order to make them toll free; which was agreed to.

Mr. CHAMBERS, from the same committee, reported a bill for the relief of the managers of the Female Orphan Asylum of Georgetown, District of Columbia; which was read, and ordered to a second reading.

Mr. TOMLINSON, from the Committee on Pensions, reported a bill from the House of Representatives, without amendment, for the relief of James B. Folsom, and gave notice that, when the bill was called up, he was instructed by the committee to move its rejection.

Mr. TOMLINSON, from the same committee, asked to be discharged from the further consideration of the petition of Charles King; which was agreed to.

Mr. BROWN then moved to take up for consideration the resolution of the House of Representatives, fixing a day for the adjournment of the present session of Congress.

The CHAIR said that the special order had precedence of other business.

SPECIAL ORDER.

The Senate then resumed the consideration of Mr. BIBB's resolution for an amendment relative to the election of President and Vice President of the United States.

Mr. BIBB then resumed and concluded his remarks in favor of his proposed amendment, when

Mr. BENTON moved to recommit the resolution to a select committee of five members; which, not being objected to by Mr. BIBB, was agreed to.

The Senate then balloted for the committee, when the following gentlemen were chosen: Messrs. BIBB, BENTON, WEBSTER, CALHOUN, and FORSYTH.

REMOVAL OF THE DEPOSITES.

Mr. CLAY then moved to suspend the orders of the day and take up the joint resolutions submitted by him, disapproving of the removal of the public deposites, and requiring them to be placed, after the 1st of July next, in the Bank of the United States.

Upon this motion, Mr. BROWN asked the yeas and nays; which were ordered, and are as follows:

YEAS—Messrs. Bell, Bibb, Calhoun, Chambers, Clay, Clayton, Ewing, Frelinghuysen, Hendricks, Kent, Knight, Naudain, Poindexter, Prentiss, Robbins, Silsbee, Smith, Southard, Sprague, Swift, Tomlinson, Tyler, Webster—24.

NAYS—Messrs. Benton, Black, Brown, Forsyth, Grundy, Hill, King of Alabama, King of Georgia, Lien, Mangum, Morris, Robinson, Shepley, Tipton, White, Wilkins—16.

So it was determined to suspend the orders, and the Senate proceeded to the consideration of the resolutions.

Mr. BENTON moved that the resolutions be postponed for the purpose of giving the Senate an opportunity of considering the following resolution:

Resolved, That the Senate will not consider any proposition to restore the public moneys to the keeping of the Bank of the United States, or to renew the charter of that bank, until after it shall have submitted to a full examination of its affairs

by a committee of one of the Houses of Congress, and especially into the part which the bank may have acted, if any, in producing the late commercial embarrassments and distresses.

Mr. B., in support of his motion, spoke somewhat at large in vindication of the right of Congress to examine into the conduct and affairs of the bank, and its duty to do so before it would entertain any proposition of honor or confidence to that institution. The right to make this examination (he said) rested upon many grounds. A clause in the charter reserved this right, and reserved it without limitation or restriction, without forms or conditions; and it was not to be endured that this unconditional right, reserved by Congress, should be defeated and nullified by the interposition of forms and conditions, restrictions and limitations, prescribed by the bank itself, and which would put it into the power of that institution to be examined or not, just as it pleased. Besides this chartered right to examine the bank, Mr. B. said that the United States was a partner in the institution, and possessed the natural and equitable right of all partners to know how the partnership concerns were managed. Every partner has a right to examine the books and papers of the concern; dormant partners possess this right as well as active partners; and if the members of the concern who have charge of these books and papers refuse to submit them to the inspection of the other partners, a court of equity will interfere, upon the application of the injured party, and place the books and papers where every partner can have free access to them. This is the natural right, and equitable law of partnerships; and the people of the United States, who are partners to the amount of seven millions of dollars in this bank, have a right to see how it has been managed, and their representatives are the proper persons to exercise that right. A committee of Congress is the proper organ to examine for the people; and if such a committee should be repulsed from the door of the bank, then the rights of the people, as partners in the institution, are resisted and violated.

A third ground on which Mr. B. bottomed the right of the Government to examine the affairs of the bank, resulted from the nationality of the institution—from its national character, in contradistinction to its mere banking character—and the consequent liability which it incurred with all other national institutions, to undergo the supervision of the power which created it. On this point he quoted General Hamilton, and showed that that eminent man, when he was first recommending a Bank of the United States in the year 1791, openly asserted the right and the duty of the Government to examine the institution as often as it thought fit, and declared that an objection to such an examination would imply mismanagement. Here he read the following paragraph from General Hamilton's report of 1791:

"If the paper of a bank is permitted to insinuate 'itself into all the revenues and receipts of a country; if it is even to be tolerated as the substitute 'for gold and silver, in all the transactions of business; it becomes, in either view, *a national concern 'of the first magnitude.* As such *the ordinary rules 'of prudence* require that the GOVERNMENT should '*possess the means of ascertaining*, WHENEVER IT 'THINKS FIT, *that so delicate a trust is executed with 'fidelity and care.* A RIGHT of this nature is not 'only desirable as it respects the Government, but 'it ought to be equally so to all those concerned in 'the institution, as an additional title to public and 'private confidence, and as *a thing which can only be 'formidable to practices that imply mismanagement.*"

All this has happened, said Mr. B. The paper of the Bank of the United States has insinuated itself into the receipts and revenue of the country; it has become a substitute for gold and silver; it has entered into all the transactions of business between man and man; and thereby this bank has become a national concern, and a concern of the first magnitude. The branch of the Government immediately representing the people have thought it to order an investigation into the affairs of the bank; and that investigation has been resisted and defeated by the bank. In the language of General Hamilton, this resistance implies mismanagement; and that mismanagement ought to stimulate the Government to an exertion of all its powers to enforce the examination to which it is entitled:

A fourth ground upon which Mr. B. placed the right of the Government to examine the affairs of the bank, related to the restoration of the deposites and the renewal of the charter. If the bank were culpable, it would have no claim to the further keeping of the public moneys, and it ought to submit to have that question of culpability tried by the evidence of its own books. If it had abused the powers granted to it, it can have no claim for further favor or confidence. On this point, he took a decisive stand, independent of the charter, and independent of all legal rights, and resting upon the great principle, that the Government had a right to know how the bank had been managed during its present existence, before it would renew to it another term of existence. This was a condition precedent in the hands of the Government. It was a condition which it had a right to prescribe, and which, under present circumstances, it was eminently its duty to prescribe. It had a right to say to the bank, we wish to know how you have exercised the great powers we have granted to you, before we renew those powers; we wish to examine your own books, to see what your conduct has been; and until you submit to that examination, we will not entertain, or consider, any proposition to renew your extraordinary privileges. This was what the Government had a right to say. It was what was done in England in relation to all great corporations—the East India Company, as well as the Bank of England. A committee of forty-eight members had thoroughly investigated the affairs of the East India Company before its charter was renewed; a committee of thirty-two members had also thoroughly examined the affairs of the Bank of England before its charter was renewed at the last session of Parliament. Lord Althorpe, in the House of Commons, in 1831, felt almost as an imputation upon him the question put by Sir Henry Parnell, whether he meant to ask for a renewal of the bank charter, before a committee of the House had investigated the affairs of the bank. He declared that there should be full inquiry; and full inquiry there was, without limitation, restriction, condition, or formality, on the part of the bank. Mr. B. said it was the right and the duty of Congress to act in the same way towards the Bank of the United States.

Even if no misconduct was imputed to it, it would be right to examine, and see if no misconduct had occurred. It should be a preliminary step of prudence and precaution, before such large powers should be granted again. But there was misconduct imputed to it; and dropping all other imputations, he would point out the one which stood first on the list of inquiries ordered by the House of Representatives—which was alluded to in the resolution which he proposed to submit, if the postponement took place which he moved for—and which went to ascertain whether the Bank of the United States was the author of the distresses which had prevailed in the country during the past winter. This he held to be a most vital inquiry, and one that should never be abandoned until the true authors of that distress were made known to the people. An immense number of memorials presented to Congress, charged it upon the President; a great number of others charged it upon the bank. The truth of these charges the people ought to know; and certainly the bank ought not to shrink from the evidence of its own books. A strong presumptive case of guilt was made out against it; and that presumption was ripening into full proof and absolute conviction, under the conduct of the bank in refusing to submit to the test of its own books. The Government directors, in their memorial addressed to Congress, had strongly inculpated the bank, and gone into a statement of facts to show that the directors refused every proposition to conduct the curtailment of the bank debts on a plan of equality and impartiality, and put the whole business of the curtailment into the hands of a subaltern committee, appointed by the President of the bank alone, and exempted even from the small restraint of reporting to the board of directors,—affirming that the late pressure in the money market had been occasioned by the bank itself—that the curtailment had been conducted by a secret committee, and had been partial, unequal, and unnecessary. Mr. B. went on to read several extracts from the memorial of the Government directors, to prove what he said. At page 16 of their memorial, he read a resolution submitted by the Government directors to the board, proposing a systematic reduction, to be gradual in its operation, and to bear upon all sections of the country, and all classes of debtors, in the same degree and proportion. This plan, the memorialists say, would have prevented an oppressive, sectional, and partial curtailment, and would have confined the business of curtailment to the board of directors, and given to every director a voice in what was done. This plan was rejected. No, worse than that: the imperious board refused even to consider it; and forthwith adopted a series of resolutions for reducing the business of the institution, and gave authority to the committee of the offices to modify these resolutions as they should deem expedient, and peremptorily refused to require this committee, thus invested with unlimited power over the great and delicate business of curtailment—refused to require them even to report to the board of directors. This Mr. B. considered to be a flagrant breach of the charter, which expressly enacts that not less than seven directors shall constitute a board to transact business. The reduction of a debt of sixty-odd millions was certainly a piece of business. It was the most important piece of business ever transacted by the bank; and has been so transacted as to fill this Hall with cries of ruin and distress from various quarters of the country.

The Government directors expressly charge, at page 17 of their memorial, that "*We attribute to 'them the excessive curtailment in the business of the 'institution, which has been so sudden and oppressive, and which was not necessary either to the extent to which it was carried, or in the manner in 'which it was made to bear on the community.*" Having read these extracts, Mr. B. commented upon them as containing a direct charge, *first*, of a breach of the charter in committing the proper business of the board to a subaltern committee of three members; and, *secondly*, of a partial, sectional, unnecessary, and oppressive curtailment of the debts of the institution. These were the charges; charges made by the Government directors, and not in newspapers, but in a memorial to Congress. True, these directors have been rejected by the Senate; but, equally true, the House of Representatives have ordered an inquiry into the conduct of the bank, and have put this charge of the Government directors at the head, and in the very front of the subjects to be inquired into by their committee. True again, that the charter reserves to either House of Congress the right, through a committee, to inspect the books, and to examine the proceedings of the bank, to see whether the charter has been violated. But what has happened? The committee of the House, sent to Philadelphia to inspect the books, and examine the proceedings of the bank, have been resisted and repulsed! They return without accomplishing their mission! and a loud cry is set up in one general chorus, by the bank and all its friends, in Congress and out of Congress, that the Government must go to law with the bank! that the directors are not bound to criminate themselves! that a *scire facias* must issue, and then they will answer in court! Thus refusing to abide the evidence of their own books! thus refusing to let a committee of Congress inspect their books, and examine their proceedings, to ascertain whether the bank was innocent or guilty of a wanton oppression of the community during the past winter.

Mr. B. said that since the distresses of the South Sea scheme in England, at the commencement of the last century, there had not been in any country so loud and pervading a cry of distress as has been heard in this country during four or five months past. The cries of the English people had been carried to Parliament, as the cries of the American people have been brought to Congress. What did the English Parliament do? Immediately raised a committee; sent them to examine the directors of the South Sea Company; received their report; ordered all the directors to the bar; interrogated them in the face of all England; convicted them of practices which had distressed, alarmed, and injured the community; and sent them to jail, loaded with the curses of an outraged kingdom. This is what Parliament did in a similar case to what has now happened in our America. Mr. B. would not ask what Congress had

done. That question was yet to be tried in the House of Representatives; he would not anticipate the issue; it was not his business to do so. But what had the Senate done? Had it ascertained the truth of the charges made by the Government directors before they were rejected? Not at all. Had they ascertained the truth of these charges before they proposed to restore the public deposites to the keeping of the bank? Not at all! Nothing is inquired into—nothing ascertained—all taken for false, or frivolous, that is alleged against the bank; and even her cry adopted, of, Go to law! Mr. B. remarked upon this cry for a *scire facias*, so suddenly adopted in the Senate here. It had broke out to-day, and now resounded from all quarters. Whence this cry? It comes from Philadelphia! It is brought back by the minority of the bank committee; it is put in their report; and forthwith it becomes the cry of the whole bank party. But what a contradiction is exhibited, and exhibited here to our faces! What a change in a few brief days! For four months we heard nothing else but of this responsible bank, subject to the control of Congress! this creature of our own creation, over which we had ample control! Yes, ample control! that was the word! this fiscal agent, which was responsible to Congress, to the President! and which was right in resisting all amenability to the President, because it was to Congress that the charter made it responsible! This was the language, in this Senate, for four months! What is it now? Why, that it is not Congress, but the Judiciary to which it is liable. It is the court—the court—to which it will submit. She will go to law with Congress, but will not submit to be examined by a committee. Congress may send a *scire facias*, but no committee of investigation. Such is the new refuge or subterfuge of the bank. When the President asks for information through the Government directors, his authority is resisted, because the bank is responsible to Congress, and not to him! When Congress asks the same information, then Congress is resisted, because the bank is responsible to the Judiciary, and not to Congress! Such are the contradictions, such the subterfuges, such the tricks played off in our faces, and in the view of the whole American people. In the face of such evidences of guilt—in the face of such a strong presumptive case to convict the bank of being the author of the distresses which have been complained of in the memorials to Congress, is it right to give her marks of favor and confidence? Is it right either to restore to her the keeping of the public moneys, or to grant her a renewal of her charter? Mr. B. thought not, and that the proper course for the Senate to follow was indicated in the resolution which he had read, and which he would submit for the consideration and action of the Senate, if the present proceedings should be postponed.

Mr. CLAY asked the yeas and nays on the motion; which were ordered, and are as follows, to wit:

YEAS—Messrs. Benton, Brown, Forsyth, Grundy, Hill, Kane, King of Alabama, Linn, Morris, Shepley, White, Wilkins, Wright—13.

NAYS—Messrs. Bell, Bibb, Black, Calhoun, Chambers, Clay, Clayton, Ewing, Frelinghuysen, Hendricks, Kent, McKean, Mangum, Naudain, Poindexter, Porter, Prentiss, Preston, Robbins, Robinson, Silsbee, Smith, Southard, Swift, Tipton, Tomlinson, Tyler, Waggaman, Webster—29.

So the motion to postpone was disagreed to.

Mr. BENTON then moved to strike out all after the word resolved, in the first resolution, and insert, as an amendment, the bill reported in the House of Representatives by the Committee of Ways and Means, providing for the deposite of the public moneys in the State banks, and making regulations for its security in those institutions.

Mr. B. accompanied his motion by some remarks in support of the amendment, and was followed by Mr. CLAYTON, Mr. WRIGHT, Mr. CLAY, and Mr. SHEPLEY.

Mr. CLAY asked the yeas and nays on the amendment; which were ordered.

Mr. FORSYTH then moved an adjournment, but withdrew it at the instance of

Mr. TIPTON, who moved that the vote given on Saturday, rejecting the bill for the relief of Mountjoy Bayly, be reconsidered. The motion was laid on the table.

Mr. FORSYTH then renewed the motion to adjourn; which was disagreed to, on a division—yeas 18, nays 23.

After some further conversation, the question was taken on the amendment, and decided as follows, to wit:

YEAS—Messrs. Benton, Brown, Forsyth, Grundy, Hill, Kane, King of Alabama, Linn, Morris, Robinson, Shepley, White, Wilkins, Wright—14.

NAYS—Messrs. Bell, Bibb, Black, Calhoun, Chambers, Clay, Clayton, Ewing, Frelinghuysen, Hendricks, Kent, Knight, Leigh, Mangum, Moore, Naudain, Poindexter, Porter, Prentiss, Preston, Robbins, Silsbee, Smith, Southard, Sprague, Swift, Tomlinson, Tipton, Tyler, Waggaman, Webster—31.

Mr. BENTON then moved, with a view to test the sense of the Senate directly upon the expediency of continuing the deposites in the State banks, to commit the resolutions to the Committee on Finance, with instructions to report an amendment regulating the deposites of the public money in the State banks.

Mr. CLAY asked the yeas and nays on the motion; which were ordered, and are as follows, to wit:

YEAS—Messrs. Benton, Brown, Forsyth, Grundy, Hill, Kane, King of Alabama, Linn, Morris, Shepley, White, Wilkins, Wright—13.

NAYS—Messrs. Bell, Bibb, Black, Calhoun, Chambers, Clay, Clayton, Ewing, Frelinghuysen, Hendricks, Kent, Knight, Leigh, McKean, Mangum, Moore, Naudain, Poindexter, Porter, Prentiss, Sprague, Swift, Tomlinson, Tipton, Tyler, Waggaman, Webster—22.

Mr. FORSYTH then moved to divide the question on the resolutions, the two propositions being different in their character, so that a distinct vote might be taken on each.

This, Mr. CLAY assented to.

Mr. FORSYTH said, that as honorable gentlemen had expressed a great willingness that a *scire facias*, or other proceeding, should be instituted, with a view to inquire into the proceedings of the bank, and to ascertain whether it had violated its charter, he would make a proposition, if he could obtain any encouragement from the opposite side, which should effect that object. He proposed to offer the following, as a substitute for the resolutions, to follow the word *resolved*:

"That a *scire facias* be issued by the proper officer, to try immediately if the charter of the Bank of the United States has been forfeited.

"1st. Because the corporation has advanced money to a foreign Government, without being previously authorized to do so by act of Congress.

"2d. Because the whole power over the management of the institution has been placed, by resolution, in the hands of a few persons, and has not been exercised by the board of directors as required by the charter.

"3d. Because the bank has failed to perform its duties under the pension laws, not having transmitted money placed in its possession to pay pensioners, when required by proper authority.

"4th. Because the corporation has refused, under various pretexts, to submit to an examination of its books and proceedings, by a committee of the House of Representatives of the United States, specially appointed for that purpose.

"5th. Because the money of the corporation has been loaned to individuals and expended in disseminating pamphlets and speeches throughout the United States, to influence popular elections and to procure a renewal of its charter.

"6th and lastly, For any other causes operating a forfeiture that can be established by evidence, in the belief of the district attorney of the United States, whose duty it is to issue the said *scire facias*."

Mr. FORSYTH said, that he and the honorable gentlemen desired the investigation, he thought they ought to accede to this course. If they would not agree to it, he would not formally offer what he proposed as a substitute.

The resolutions were then separated at Mr. Poindexter's suggestion, and the question being taken on each separately, they were ordered to be engrossed for a third reading; and, at half past six o'clock,

The Senate adjourned.

HOUSE OF REPRESENTATIVES.

Monday, June 2, 1834.

After the Journal was read, Mr. Speaker STEVENSON addressed the House as follows:

Gentlemen: I have attended in person to-day, for the purpose of resigning, as I now do, the office of Speaker of this House, with which I have been honored for the last seven years, and of announcing to you the fact, that I have this day communicated to the Executive of Virginia my resignation as one of the Representatives from that State in the present Congress.

The dissolution, perhaps forever, of the intimate associations that have existed so long between us, is calculated to excite sentiments of a painful character. I feel it, myself, deeply and unaffectedly; and in quitting a station in itself so honorable, and so repeatedly conferred on me and in a manner so flattering, a station endeared to me by so many considerations of a private and a public nature, I hope I may be pardoned in availing myself of this fit occasion of taking my leave of it and of you, a person, of offering my cordial and best wishes for your individual prosperity and happiness, and of pressing publicly, and for the last time, my grateful acknowledgements for the kindness and confidence by which I have been so long distinguished and honored! Few, probably, that have ever filled this chair, have enjoyed more of this kindness and favor than myself; none have received, or will cherish it, with feelings of warmer or more devoted gratitude. My obligations, gentlemen, are indeed deep to this House; and the value I may, or in whatever situation I may be placed, I shall continue, to the last hour of my life, to preserve and cherish those sentiments of profound respect and affectionate gratitude, which your long continued and unchanging kindness have so deeply impressed upon my heart, and which never cease to be impaired. The duty of presiding over a great deliberative assembly like this is no easy task. The high and distinguished character of such a trust, and the arduous and important functions, cannot fail to inspire any incumbent with a just sense of his own abilities and qualifications, whatever they may be.

My administration of its duties, for seven years, has not only taught me to know and feel this, but likewise to know how difficult, nay, impossible, it is, for any man to free himself from error or censure, in this chair, or give unqualified satisfaction to render this station one of more than ordinary delicacy and embarrassment, and of increased responsibility and labor. How assiduously I have struggled to discharge the duties of this chair in a manner worthy of it and of myself, with what sincere zeal I have devoted my time to my talents, and even my health, to your service, I leave for others to decide. But this I hope I may be pardoned for saying, in justice and fairness to myself, and under a deep conviction of its truth, that I have earnestly endeavored to discharge my duty, not only with temper, justice, and moderation, but with a just regard for your feelings, rights and feelings, the character and dignity of the House, and my own honor. This was all that I promised when I came to this chair, and this I have endeavored to do. With what success you have to say, and to your country to determine.

I am very sensible, gentlemen, that in such a long course of public service, and in an undiscerning discharge of the arduous and complicated duties of this chair, regardless of whom it might please or displease, my conduct may sometimes have been thought too harsh and rigorous, and may often, unintentionally, have wounded the feelings of individual members upon this floor.

and incurred their censure and displeasure. Under such circumstances, and while man continues what he is, we know that *personal resentments* are too apt to be indulged and to remain, and often, perhaps, difficult to be extinguished, even in the noblest minds; but revenge will not harbor there. Higher principles than *resentment*, and better principles than *revenge*, will animate men whose thoughts and hearts are liberal and enlarged, and especially where there is high intellectual ability and moral integrity. If, then, under the influence of momentary excitement and passion, if, in the eagerness of controversy or the commotion of debate, anything unkind or harsh should have been said or done, either on my part or on yours, let us, I pray you, forgive and forget it, and let us separate in the spirit of peace and good will. Let not this moment of our final separation be poisoned or imbittered by feelings of personal resentment or political hostility. Let the spirit of peace and charity shed its holy calm around us, refreshing alike to the affections and the intellect, and let us blot from our minds and hearts every feeling of personal or party resentment, and separate like brethren of one household, and as the representatives of a free and virtuous people. I have myself no injuries to complain of, and no memory for them, if I had; I came to this chair to gratify no private friendships, to indulge no personal hostility, and all that I have now to ask of you is, to do justice to the motives which have influenced and governed my conduct; and when I am gone, to protect my character as the presiding officer of this House, which may now be regarded, in some measure, as the property of my country, from all unjust and unworthy imputations. To those who have known me longest, and have known me best—to the liberal and just of all parties, and on all sides of this House—this appeal, I flatter myself, will not be made in vain. One word more, and I have done.

Although I am about to leave you, gentlemen, and in all probability forever, I shall never cease to regard this House, and everything connected with it, with feelings of the deepest solicitude and affection.

I need not remind you of the character and station which this House holds in the eyes of the American people. They justly regard it as the sanctuary of liberty, and law, and order; and justly repose on it with unlimited confidence and affection. In its deliberations and proceedings is essentially involved the security of our free institutions. How much, gentlemen, will depend upon the manner in which its high duties shall be performed!

Nor is it needful, I am sure, that I should admonish you, that you are the representatives of our whole country, and not of a part; that our Confederation can only exist and prosper, under the influence of a wise, equal, and just system of legislation; by the ties of common interest and brotherly affection; by a spirit of mutual forbearance and moderation, and by cherishing a hallowed devotion to that liberty and union secured to us by the blood of our common fathers. These are the foundations upon which alone our safety and security can rest.

Although our country, of late, gentlemen, has been deeply and painfully excited, and our councils too greatly divided, may we not hope that the causes of excitement are daily passing off, and subsiding, and that peace and tranquillity will again be restored to us. At such a time, and under such circumstances, is it not the duty of every wise, and liberal, and good man, in public or private life, without distinction of party, to unite for the purpose of healing these divisions, and giving peace and repose to the public mind? and should not those especially, who wield the public councils, pour oil upon this stormy sea, and still its troubled waters?

I invoke you, gentlemen, to peace and harmony; to union and action for the common good.

The people expect it; the prosperity and happiness of your country demand it.

God grant that you may prove yourselves worthy of the high trust, and equal to the crisis; and that your labors may ultimately prove successful in giving peace and repose to our beloved country.

This is the last time that I shall ever address you from the chair.

We separate this day, many, very many of us, to meet no more.

I pray to God to protect and bless you and our country; and I tender to you this, my last and affectionate farewell!

On motion of Mr. MERCER, the House agreed to proceed to the choice of a Speaker.

The Clerk appointed Messrs. McKINLEY, E. WHITTLESEY, MUHLENBERG, BYNUM, SCHLEY, and FORESTER, tellers.

The following table exhibits the result of each of the ten balloting which took place:

	1.	2.	3.	4.	5.	6.	7.	8.	9.	10.
Wilde	64	64	59	49	37	24	16	11	11	11
Polk	42	53	57	59	67	67	73	78	76	78
Sutherland	34	30	26	25	16	16	10	9	4	2
Bell	30	39	47	49	57	65	76	97	104	114
Speight	18	16	8	4	3	1	3	3	2	1
Wayne	15	13	15	25	30	36	26	13	8	6
Williams	4									
E. Everett	3	1								
Chilton	2									
Hubbard	2	1	1	2	1					
Gamble	1	1								
Gilmore	1	1								
Blanks	4	2	4	7	5	5	10	7	6	6
J. Q. Adams						2				
Hardin		1								
Lane		1								
Marshall				1						
Archer			1							
Crockett			1							
Coulter					1					
Binney								1		
Total	220	223	219	221	219	214	215	219	211	218

On the tenth ballot 218 votes were given—110 necessary to a choice.

JOHN BELL, of Tennessee, having 114, was declared duly elected Speaker of the House, and was conducted to the chair by Messrs. J. Q. ADAMS and R. M. JOHNSON. After taking the chair, the Speaker elect made the following address:

Gentlemen of the House of Representatives:

With the greatest sincerity I declare to you, that although I am duly and gratefully impressed by this mark of the partiality and confidence of the House, and by no means insensible to the distinction intended to be conferred on me, it is not without some distrust of the wisdom of my course in accepting this station, which your choice has assigned me. Without the slightest experience in the chair, it may be justly apprehended that your selection of a presiding officer has been too much influenced by personal kindness and friendship. And I shall be quite happy if the public interest shall suffer no detriment through a defective administration of the duties of the chair. In ordinary times, and under ordinary circumstances, I could flatter myself, that by diligent application I might be able in a short time to supply the want of experience, and to justify in some degree the confidence indicated by the House. That more than usual embarrassments must be encountered at this moment by any incumbent of the chair, will be admitted by all. The impatience, not to say irritation—the natural result of a protracted session—the excitement growing out of those sharp conflicts of opinion upon questions of public policy—conflicts exasperated and embittered at the present moment in an extraordinary degree—all present themselves to increase the difficulties, and call forth the exertions of a new and unpractised incumbent of the chair. And I feel, gentlemen, that whatever exertions may be made on my part must be vain, without your forbearance; nay, that they must fail altogether, without your cordial support and coöperation. When I reflect how great are the interests connected with this House, its character and action—interests not of a day or of a party, but of all time, of posterity, and of all the parties which are or ever will be arrayed against each other; and when I further reflect how much the character and action of this House depends on a skilful, firm, and impartial administration of the duties of the chair, I confess I feel the deepest solicitude.

It is not so generally understood, I regret to believe, as it should be, in how great a degree the measures of a legislative assembly are modified and influenced by the manner of its deliberations. All will concede that if it shall ever happen that this body shall fall into disrepute, and fail to command the respect and confidence of the people, our institutions will be in the greatest peril. Not only the character of the House, the wisdom and efficiency of its action, but the existence of our admirable frame of polity itself, may be said to depend, in some degree, upon the order and dignity of the deliberations of this House. While, then, I entreat the indulgence of the House to my own defects, I earnestly invoke the assistance of every member of it in endeavoring to maintain and preserve, so far as depends upon the proceedings of this body, those great and primary interests of constitutional Government and freedom, in support of which, I am sure, whatever difference of opinion there may be upon points of construction, policy, or administration, there is not a heart here, nor an American heart anywhere, that does not beat high.

On motion of Mr. BARRINGER,

The House then adjourned.

IN SENATE.

TUESDAY, *June* 3, 1834.

Mr. McKEAN said, a committee of thirty citizens, of the first respectability, from various sections of Pennsylvania, all of whom, he believed, were now in the lobby of the Senate, had honored him by putting into his charge a memorial to be presented to the Senate, signed by more than two hundred delegates from the different counties of that State, who assembled at Harrisburg, the seat of government, on the 27th ultimo, to consult as to the cause of public distress and mode of relief. And though, he said, a difference of opinion, as well as on questions of abstract expediency, existed between a portion of the memorialists and himself, it was nevertheless his desire to represent them fairly, and it was no less his pride than his duty to say, that this convention comprised as much of respectability, talent, and weight of public and private character, as any convention of men that had assembled anywhere within his knowledge, and whose experience entitled their opinions to the most respectful consideration.

He had been furnished with a statement showing the general, as well as political, complexion of the convention, and he took occasion to say, that the latter was corroborated by his own knowledge of the facts as stated. The whole number of delegates present was two hundred and nine; of this number, seventy-five were original Jackson men, about thirty of whom supported General Jackson in 1832. Delegates were appointed from forty-eight counties, and delegates were in actual attendance from forty-four counties, including the city of Philadelphia, accidents having prevented the attendance from the other four. He had been particularly instructed to say, that the entire proceedings had been distinguished for harmony, unanimity, and zeal, and the whole character of the convention furnished the strongest evidence of a great political change in Pennsylvania, and a growing opposition to the recent measures of the present Administration of the General Government. The memorial was written with great force and ability, and condemns, in *toto*, the conduct of the Executive branch of the Government in reference to the bank; to which cause they ascribe all the present distresses of the country, and ask Congress for relief.

Mr. McKEAN then presented the memorial, and moved that it be read, referred to the Committee on Finance, and printed, with the names.

Mr. WEBSTER rose, and asked, Is this the true voice of Pennsylvania? That was the question in which not only Pennsylvania, but every State in this Union, was at this moment interested. If it be, we might hope that a day of relief to the country, a day of restoration of the Constitution and laws, was at hand. When we looked at the great central States of the Union, we saw a population so numerous and so powerful, who, if they chose to come to the relief of the country and succor of the Constitution, might come, and it would be relieved and succored. He believed the

sentiments in this memorial were the sentiments of a majority of the people of Pennsylvania. The proofs were both in and out of the State—her position in relation to the great subjects now agitating the country, was a most interesting one, and her course might be a decisive one. Pennsylvania was well known as an early and ardent friend of the present Executive; and our great difficulty was in making known our condition to the President of the United States. It was matter of opinion, but he believed that the bottom of all our present difficulties, in obtaining relief, lay in the quarter he had mentioned. He could see no reason for such unyielding adhesion to personal opinion against urgent solicitation from all. Whatever was said of distress, was assigned to panic-makers; partisans at bottom. And then the bank was the monster that did it all.

Mr. W. thought that those who wished to know the truth had better look to this meeting and its result for their relief. Here was a convention of two hundred and fifty members of various political classes. A zealous and active party, called the anti-masonic party, of strong and unyielding purpose; and then those who assumed the name of Whig, a name which he hoped they would not relinquish, were of the number. And one third of the whole of these persons were among the original friends of the present Chief Magistrate. Who, then, could see these men assembled at this busy season of the year and say that it was the result of bank partisanship and panic-making? In the chair of the convention he perceived the name of Joseph Lawrence, of Washington county—a man of the simplest habits—a farmer; a man who tilled his own soil with his own hands; a man whom all the banks in the world could not buy. And the next was General Frick; a gentleman, he believed, of great experience, who had been several years in the State Legislature. He believed the honorable member from Pennsylvania, who had expressed himself with great fairness and candor on presenting this memorial, knew Mr. Frick. He belonged to the class of thousands who had every inducement to be silent; but who, with other persons, felt it their duty to partake of the deliberations of this assembly. The society of Friends, too, had stepped forward, who, Mr. W. was sorry to say, had heretofore, he thought, taken too little part in political affairs—they understood their interest and rights, and were determined to exercise them.

This memorial said, that the markets for the produce of the country were crippled, and they gave the instance of Pittsburg, a city of some thirty thousand inhabitants, that possessed, but a short time ago, a well-employed population. Their looms and forges were now stopped, and labor was seeking employment there. If these statements would not satisfy the Senate and the Executive, what should be proved? But he (Mr. W.) entertained but faint hopes of relief until the great movements of public opinion should bring it about. A change of agents was the only effectual mode of effecting a change in the system. He supposed that no persuasion would change the determination of those who administered the Government, and a change of councils was the only hopeful remedy for the people; and he believed the people of Pennsylvania were awake to the great question. He invoked and implored her to attend to it, to contemplate the future; and if she saw the danger and felt the evil, to bring to the crisis her power and her intelligence. She was a great manufacturing State, first and foremost in domestic industry and American labor. If she surrendered these interests who were to uphold them? He would ask her farmers and whole population to consider the political doctrines of the present day; to look and see if they breathed the spirit of American liberty. We were now approaching the end of the session, and yet we had done nothing—the Government had proposed nothing for relief. What was there which they intended to try? Should we do nothing? All depended upon the decision of one man! Mr. W. said he did not know where to begin or to end when speaking of the broken laws of the country. He would fain bring gentlemen to practical measures which he and they knew would relieve the country in an hour. But the danger of going home without doing anything, he deeply deplored.

Mr. FORSYTH said there was no doubt that the distress which had occasioned the speech of the honorable gentleman from Massachusetts, and which had produced this memorial, would continue till the remedy which the gentleman had suggested as the only and proper one, should be applied—till the men who now administered the Government of the United States were changed. The honorable gentleman referred to this memorial as being sufficient to satisfy Congress that it was the voice of the people of Pennsylvania. How did it differ from the memorial presented yesterday from the convention of the people of the State of New Jersey? Did the honorable gentleman admit that that memorial expressed the sentiments of the people of that State? It was presented here as coming from the people of the State of New Jersey in convention, as coming from a political party. And how was it with regard to the memorial now before us? They tell you that they were obeying the voice of the people of Pennsylvania. [Here Mr. F. read a passage from the published proceedings.] Here the impression was made on Congress, and the people of the United States, that the whole people of the State of Pennsylvania had united together, and appointed delegates to assemble together and consider the grievances under which they labored. Now, Mr. F. would not say that this was intended, because it was false; and he would not attribute to those gentlemen a desire to make a false impression. But how was the fact? The statement of the memorial supposed all the people of the State to be suffering alike. They called themselves a "convention of delegates from the citizens of Pennsylvania opposed to Executive usurpation." It was a party convention, assembled for the purpose of carrying out the sentiment of the gentleman from Massachusetts—to effect a change in the public agents. And what was it worth? As the voice of Pennsylvania, it was worth nothing—absolutely nothing. It was worth nothing, except so far as the facts stated were true, and the deductions from them were logical.

Mr. F. begged leave to call attention to some of the sentiments in this memorial. "Nay, the 'very delegates of the people of the United States 'instructed to bear the President a statement of 'their grievances, have either been refused ad'mission into the palace of their Cæsar, or, when 'admitted, have been denied the opportunity of 'making known their views." And therefore, they had applied directly to the Legislature, as they were denied access to the President of the United States. When? where? how? Mr. F. said he had yet to learn that any citizens had united and sent a memorial to the President of the United States. He knew very well that some individuals came here and presented a memorial to Congress, and called on the President, not by the authority or on the requisition of those who sent them, but merely of their own will and pleasure. Well, they had a conversation with the President, and went back and reported it to the people of Philadelphia, the memorialists, and said they had complied with their duty, and out of *respect* to the President, they called on him, to tell him what they knew of the distresses of the country. They were individuals who went of their own free will to make representations to the President. It was so with all the rest; and the reports they made of conversations held with him were not true; and great injustice had been done the President by their representations. When the committee called on the President, who were said to have been denied access to him, what did he say? Gentlemen, as delegates, as representatives of others, I cannot receive you. False statements have been made by others under similar circumstances, of my conversations with them. As gentlemen, as citizens, I will receive you with pleasure; and if you have anything to say from those you represent, I will receive it in writing, and answer it fully and respectfully. And this was the whole foundation of the remarks of these honorable gentlemen of the convention at Harrisburg. Suppose these honorable persons were to apply to us to be heard at the bar of the Senate in person, to represent the distress under which they were suffering, and to give us their views of the Constitution and laws of the country. They would be refused. But we should say to them, our doors are open to your memorials in writing. And they would then go back to Harrisburg, and say the Senate and House of Representatives have refused to hear our representations of your distress, and have turned us away from their doors. Was there any man here who would not be shocked at such a proceeding—who would not be startled at the audacity of those who would go back to those who sent them, making such representations of their reception? And yet here was the very case, only reversing the persons. They report that the President refuses to hear their memorials, because they were not in writing.

The object of these individuals was very intelligible, and a part of it, undoubtedly, was to remove the distress, and effect a change of the public councils in the process. The State of Pennsylvania was a most important power in the operation. She was generally very decided in her acts, and what she did would *tell*. He trusted in God that the State of Pennsylvania would do its duty; he was sure the people of that State would do what they thought was right, and he trusted they would do what was best. Should he anticipate what that would be? He thought he could see the light ahead; and that the result would be favorable to the condition of public affairs as administered on the principles which had been heretofore approved by the people of Pennsylvania. It was very true that it was an important question—one of great magnitude. It was a battle between the Bank of the United States, the House of Representatives, the Senate, and the President of the United States, and it was for the good people of Pennsylvania and others, to decide between us. But, (Mr. F. said,) he thought he saw in Pennsylvania indication of the real state of public opinion. The opinion, as it regarded the recharter of the Bank of the United States, had changed. Indications of hostility, not to be mistaken, against that institution, were manifest in Pennsylvania, and he thought the recent action of the bank, braving public opinion, by resorting to hollow pretexts to avoid an investigation of its affairs, was not calculated to make it more popular there. He could not believe that the bank would be justified by the people of Pennsylvania, when it set up pretensions at variance with those which it had before supported here. We had seen the facility of changing ground by those who were supporting the bank, but he thought the people were not so blind as not to see it. What a strange spectacle was presented by the bank. A complete revolution had taken place in the United States upon the subject of the institution. A half dozen years ago it was thought the control of the Government was complete over it. That it possessed power sufficient to detect all abuses, to correct any criminality of conduct, and impurity of purpose, and of laying bare the policy of its conduct in all branches of its business, as a means of preventing any excesses of a political or pecuniary character. How was it now? What power was there, which before was admitted to be retained, which was not now denied, and the justice of the denial supported and defended by the bank? Mr. F. would turn attention to a singular matter, as illustrative of this position. He alluded to the recent attempt to investigate the condition of the bank. This was resisted on two grounds. First, that no committee had a right to inspect the conduct of the bank, but with a view to the issuing of a *scire facias*, and that it had a right to the precise charge on which the *scire facias* was to be founded. Or, in other words, that they were to be approached with a bill of indictment, containing a precise specific charge. And a long argument had been entered into by a part of the committee in defence of this position. It assumed that the bank had no right to refuse to submit to an investigation, unless a distinct specification of abuses charged, was made out. But a few days before, these were the views held by a portion of that committee:

"Whereas this committee is now organized, and the directors of the bank have made known that they are prepared to submit their books for inspection:

"2. *Resolved*, That the committee take into consideration the several subjects referred to them, and that they proceed to inspect the books and examine the proceedings of the bank, as authorized

by the charter, touching the matters referred to them, and in the order in which they are arranged by the House of Representatives, viz:

"1. The cause of the commercial embarrassment and distress complained of by numerous citizens of the United States in sundry memorials which have been presented to Congress at the present session.

"2. Whether the charter of the bank has been violated.

"3. What corruptions and abuses have existed in its management; whether it has used its corporate powers or money to control the press, interfere in politics, or influence elections, and whether it has had any agency, through its management or money, in producing the existing pressure."

"To these resolutions the following were offered as an amendment by Mr. Ellsworth, and accepted by Mr. Everett:

"*Resolved*, That the committee on behalf of the directors of the bank be directed to submit to our inspection, at their banking house, the books and papers of the institution, as they shall be respectively called for.

"*Resolved*, That, in taking testimony, the committee will proceed according to those general rules of evidence which are adopted in courts of judicial inquiry.

"The question being taken on Mr. Everett's substitute, with the amendment, those who voted in the affirmative were, Mr. Everett, Mr. Ellsworth; in the negative, Mr. Thomas, Mr. Mason, Mr. Muhlenberg, Mr. Mann, Mr. Lytle."

This was a proposition held by two individuals of the committee who afterwards agreed to the unjust pretensions of the bank. And under what circumstances was this change made? It was a committee representing the power and authority of the House of Representatives, and treating the institution with respect. But the bank assumed as the basis of its refusal, to question the honor and the motives of every member of the committee. It assumed, as the basis of its refusal, that the committee came to the investigation as a political party; not as a committee of investigation. Mr. F. asked the honorable gentleman from Massachusetts, if the people of Philadelphia, or the people of any other part of Pennsylvania, were so blind as not to see the cause of all these refusals and these pretexts. If they were so, they were much more so than they had proved themselves to be on ordinary occasions.

Mr. WEBSTER said he did not perceive the full applicability of the honorable member's remarks. It was enough for him (Mr. W.) to say, that the bank investigation had nothing to do with the Harrisburg Convention. The laws were open, and why did not the honorable gentleman from Georgia advise a *scire facias*, if the bank was guilty? Mr. W. said the question would go on to trial, if the House of Representatives chose; it was not his business, but theirs. Whether this memorial was like the one from New Jersey, which was presented here yesterday, depended on the facts and circumstances of the two cases. Were the members of that convention, or any part of them, former opponents of the Administration? These thirty gentlemen would persuade the honorable member, and all other gentlemen, of the truth of their representations. But when the facts were stated here, we heard nothing but the bank and the monster. Mr. W. regarded the bank as nothing but an instrument of Government, and yet the honorable member from Georgia raised it to the rank of a department of the Government. Mr. W. would not agree that the bank was a party to the great contest which agitated the country. There was no party in it but the people themselves. They, it was true, were divided on the subject; but he went on the ground that the people of the United States would correct the existing evils, believing them to be competent to self-government. The honorable gentleman, he knew, had very great political sagacity—as much so as any person he knew in the United States; and the gentleman said that all the changes in Pennsylvania were against the bank. It all came to this, that the bank was a creature of Government, responsible to the law, and if the distress was owing to a violation of its charter, why did not the Government bring it to trial? The gentleman argued as though it was above the Government. If a redress of public grievances required that the bank should receive a blow, why withhold it?

Mr FORSYTH replied, that he had only to repeat what he had said yesterday, that he was not an adviser of the President of the United States. He would do his duty according to his opinions of what was right and proper. As to himself, Mr. F. said he was not favorable to the issuing of a *scire facias*, because it would but aggravate the public distress. The bank would expire in twenty months, and all knew its power to protract a decision of the question until that period. The honorable gentleman from Massachusetts gave him great credit for foresight and political sagacity, and he was sorry he could not return the compliment to the honorable gentleman. He was a gentleman of very extended views, but heretofore he had been exceedingly unsuccessful in his predictions, at least since he (Mr. F.) had known him. Let us appeal to time, then, and rest confidently on the sagacity of those we appeal to. The honorable gentleman had said that the bank was complained of as a monster, that it was the constant theme of remark. Well, the memorial from the Pennsylvania convention concluded by praying relief by a restoration of the deposites to—the bank. They asked a recharter of—the bank. And they prayed Congress to adopt measures to curb the Executive in his hostility to—what?—the bank. The bank, the bank, was the beginning and the end of the theme. But for the popularity and influence of the bank in Philadelphia, we never should have heard of this convention. The bank was not a party to it; but did not everybody know that it was a powerful party in the country? Did we not know that everybody in the country who were enlisted on that side were assailing the Executive for daring to touch its immaculate deposites? Honorable gentlemen might struggle to avoid it as a party, but they must adhere to it as a party, and rise or fall by it. And who were the master spirits who had managed this great concern? The managers of the bank, among whom was the distinguished gentleman whose name stands at the head of this committee, and who had always pursued the most incessant, he might say vindictive, hostility towards the Executive of the United States—an individual who was a candidate for the second office in the gift of the people, and in whose favor the bank had poured out its treasures in full stream, and poured them out in vain.

Mr. CLAY said the gentleman from Georgia, who was a firm supporter of the Executive, admitted that it was a question of change of agents. And it was that question. It ought to be a struggle for a change which should make principles predominant, and should cause the interests of the people to be looked to and the mandates of the Constitution observed. He was glad the question of a successor was put by, and it was left for the people to say who should administer the government of the country. As to this convention, there was no body of men in the country combining more of integrity and patriotism. The gentleman from Georgia referred to the Globe, (a paper of which he had not always spoken in the kindest terms,) for contradictions of the reports of conversations held by committees with the President. Mr. C. said, if reports were to be believed, the President could not have recollected what was said to him, and it was unjust to say that, because the people of Baltimore misrepresented him, he would not receive others from Philadelphia or New York. The convention was right, therefore, in saying that he had denied access to him, and imposed conditions on them which he had no right to prescribe. He had denied admission to his fellow-citizens, folding himself up in the East room, in all the ostentation of eastern magnificence, saying, present your complaints in writing, and I will answer you. The Lord Mayor of London would not have done so to the citizens of that city; the King of England would not have dared to prescribe such terms to his subjects.

Mr. BROWN said it was not without some surprise he had heard gentlemen, who seemed to approve the course of the bank, assert their willingness for an investigation into its conduct. How little did this declaration, made at this late period, comport with their acts in the early part of the present session. It would be remembered that the honorable Senator from Missouri [Mr. BENTON] had, at an early period of the present session, introduced a resolution in the Senate, proposing an examination into the conduct of the bank; but where then was the zeal of honorable gentlemen for an investigation? They had had ample opportunity for its manifestation on that occasion; but the Journals of the Senate would show that the resolution to which he alluded did not meet even the usual treatment required by parliamentary courtesy. A motion for indefinite postponement was made against it, by a Senator in opposition, he believed, on the day after its introduction, which was carried, chiefly by the votes of those in opposition to the Administration.

Honorable Senators in opposition had, with an air of triumph, asked why a *scire facias* had not been resorted to against the bank; and had defied the friends of the Administration to resort to a judicial inquiry into its acts. Mr. B. said he thought it would be difficult to suggest any course which would receive the sanction of those who defended the bank. To elude inquiry, and to defeat investigation, seemed to be a primary object. The course of the bank most clearly indicated that no mode of investigation was acceptable to that institution. It had been objected by it, that the Executive had no right through the Government directors to obtain information of its situation. The cry of Executive tyranny had been raised on that occasion, and the Executive charged with having invaded the sanctity of private accounts. The House of Representatives had passed resolutions authorizing a committee of that body to investigate the condition and affairs of that institution. This mode of inquiry, the right to which is explicitly given in the charter, and which has, on two other occasions, been acquiesced in by the bank, without the slightest objection, so far as he was informed, had encountered obstacles from the President and directors in the recent attempt to investigate its affairs, which went effectually to destroy the power of Congress to examine into its acts, and was tantamount to a declaration of entire independence of that branch of the Government. Thus, it was most apparent *that no mode* by which the bank is to be brought to justice, will prove acceptable to its friends; and when it had been said that a *scire facias* was the proper remedy, he was forcibly reminded of the story of a criminal offender, who, when suffering the penalty of the law from the hands of the officer of justice, thought one blow too high and another too low. The report of the Government directors was thought to be an outrage by the friends of the bank. An examination into its affairs by the committee was suddenly discovered to be another great outrage; and now, a *scire facias* is said to be the only true and proper remedy. If, sir, (said Mr. B.) this course had been resorted to by the President, or by Congress, the same clamor about hostility against the bank, and an arbitrary invasion of its rights, would, no doubt, have been heard, which has almost deafened the ear of the public for the last six months. Mr. B. considered this as a mere subterfuge, which was intended to shelter the bank from the indignation of an insulted people.

Mr. B. said the honorable gentleman from Kentucky [Mr. CLAY] had alleged, in justification of the political alliance which was formed of such heterogeneous materials, against the Administration, the example of the Allied Powers of Europe, who had united their arms to effect the overthrow of Napoleon. It was true (said Mr. B.) that the paper system of Great Britain had no doubt a powerful agency in conducting the allies to Paris; but he trusted that the unconquerable spirit of the freemen of this country would prevent the Bank of the United States from carrying the great political allies, now struggling for ascendency, in triumph to the American Capitol. The vigorous spirit of republican freemen was not so easy of conquest as the subjects of old and decayed monarchs. The power of the Holy Alliance in Europe had been constantly exerted to smother and crush the spirit of freemen. It was a name of evil omen, and should warn the people of the United States against alliances, either holy or unholy.

The honorable gentleman had censured, in most unmeasured terms, the President of the United States, for having declined any further interviews with committees.

He believed that no Chief Magistrate in this

country had been more accessible to his fellow-citizens, or had, in his personal intercourse, shown more courtesy and respect, than the present President of the United States. The resolution which he had formed to receive communications from committees only in writing, no doubt grew out of the great injustice with which he had been treated in the reports of some of those committees. Mr. B. sincerely believed, that the conversations of the President had been greatly misrepresented in some of the instances to which he had alluded. In more tranquil times than the present, party prejudices were but too apt to influence the opinions and actions of men; and at this period of unprecedented party excitement, that individual would stand but little chance of having justice done him, whose opinions were promulgated to the world by political opponents, colored by all their party prejudices, and liable to all the distortions which enmity and bitterness so well understood the use of.

The memorial (said Mr. B.) described the distress in the State of Pennsylvania, as pervading every branch of industry, which was attributed to the removal of the public moneys from the Bank of the United States. He did not doubt that some of those who composed the committee charged by the convention with bringing hither the memorial, were distressed. That portion of them who were stockholders, as he was informed some of them were, felt, no doubt, a great repugnance to the discontinuance of an institution which had yielded them large profits, and by the recharter of which, their stock would have risen greatly in value. Avarice submits, most reluctantly, to the discontinuance of its accustomed profits, and to the extinction of its hopes for the enhanced value of its stocks. Ambition, on the other hand, surrenders with keen pain, and only when compelled, the great political lever which this powerful corporation furnishes. Mr. B. was not sufficiently informed of the present condition of the people of Pennsylvania, to give an opinion as to the extent of the distress, which the memorial represented as existing in that wealthy and respectable Commonwealth; but he thought it by no means a necessary consequence, that all its great interests were distressed, because those who happened to be interested in the Bank of the United States might so imagine it, or so represent it. He, on the contrary, heartily subscribed to the sentiment expressed by Mr. Rush, a distinguished citizen of that State, at a public meeting held not long since in Philadelphia, that it is a libel on the free people and republican institutions of this country, to say that they are indebted for their prosperity to the Bank of the United States, but that the causes of their happiness and prosperity are to be found in our excellent system of Government, in the enterprise and industry of its citizens, and in the abundant and varied resources of our country.

Mr. B. said that the honorable gentleman from Massachusetts had most earnestly invoked the citizens of Pennsylvania to look to their interests, and to unite in producing a change in the measures of the Administration. Mr. B. said that the invocation of the honorable gentleman was not, he presumed, at all necessary to induce the people of that State to take proper care of their own interests. They had always shown their entire competency to do so, the most signal proofs of which were to be found in looking at her present condition.

Mr. B. said that the conduct of the bank had, for the last two or three years, been marked by a series of measures and bold pretensions, so hostile to a republican form of government, that to submit to its demands, and to restore the public moneys to its keeping, would be to acknowledge its superiority, and become a lasting subject of national reproach. It had boldly thrown itself into the party contests of the day, and thereby contributed to pollute the purity of our free system of government. It had, as he most sincerely believed, done much to inflict distress upon the country, to compel its citizens to come into its measures. It had disregarded an express provision in its charter, and closed its doors against the investigation ordered by the representatives of the people. After having thus boldly contemned the authority of the representatives of the people, and through them, the people themselves, he should deem it as humiliating to the nation to yield to their demands, and replace the public moneys in their custody, as he should consider it unworthy the national spirit to yield to an invading enemy who demanded the submission of the country.

Mr. FORSYTH replied that the gentleman from Kentucky said he had come to the support of the Executive. He was not a defender of the Executive, or of all his measures. True, he had had occasion to defend the President of the United States from what he considered unjust assaults upon him; and he knew very well that his motives would be assailed by those who were incapable of doing justice to him or to any other person in his situation. He intended to say nothing of the characters of these gentlemen of the convention. He knew some of them personally, and he knew them to be respectable; but he had no respect for their opinions.

Honorable gentlemen said they were willing and desirous to have an investigation of the bank. But there would be some preliminary matters to be settled before that could take place. First, would the majority of the committee be of those who believed the bank to be guilty? He did not offer the proposition for the *scire facias*. He said he would not take the responsibility of offering it, but that if gentlemen persisted that the bank was calumniated, he offered them a substitute for the resolution; this they refused. But honorable gentlemen admitted that the object of their pursuit was power—to get hold of the offices of Government—to correct the President of the United States. We were contending for the administration of the Government. What was the principle of gentlemen in desiring a seat in Congress, often at immense sacrifices, both personal and pecuniary, but ambition? A desire for higher places in serving the people, and to prove to the people that they deserved higher places. These were high and honorable purposes. A desire to possess power to administer the Government for the benefit and happiness of the people, for our own glory, and for the glory of the nation, and that our names may descend to posterity in connexion with its greatness and renown. We had been told, over and over again, that this was not a question of bank or no bank, and the honorable gentleman from Kentucky said that it was a question of law and the Constitution; but, notwithstanding, he concluded with the necessity and importance of—the bank. After eulogizing the committee, he concluded with the old threadbare subject of—the bank—the bank—the bank. We had heard appeals to General Washington as authority for—the bank. The authority of the elder Adams, of Madison, and of Monroe, to sustain—the bank. And the experience of forty-five years of prosperity to prove that the country cannot do without—the bank.

But one word as to these committees of memorialists, visiting the President. He (Mr. F.) denied that memorials had ever been sent to the President. Committees were sent to Washington with memorials to present to Congress, and of their own mere will, went to see the President out of—respect to him. He denied that they had ever been refused by the President, or that he had ever declined a personal interview with such persons. He had refused to hear them in their official character, and told them to give him in writing what they had to say and he would hear it and answer it. The honorable gentleman from Kentucky said that a king of England would never refuse an interview with his subjects in the manner the President had done. That he sat in the East room, folding himself up in all the pomp of eastern magnificence, and refused to see his humble subjects but upon prescribed terms. Well, all this was very pretty—very pretty indeed, and very poetic. But how was the fact. This ostentatious despot asked his fellow-citizens to come and see him as a farmer, laying aside official forms and ceremonies. He says, represent to me what you please, and I will give you a frank, candid answer. This, to be sure, was very much like the ostentation of a prince!

In regard to the gentleman's allusion to the Globe, Mr. F. said he did not recollect ever saying anything of that paper which could justify the honorable gentleman's remark. He had said that he did not altogether like the manner in which it was conducted; but it was a sheet of white paper in comparison with the papers on the opposite side. The honorable member made some further remarks which he (Mr. F.) had forgotten, and if he did not answer them, he hoped the honorable gentleman would forgive him.

On motion of Mr. BENTON, the resolution submitted by him proposing an amendment to the Constitution of the United States, as it respects the election of President and Vice President of the United States, was referred to the select committee to whom was committed a similar resolution offered by Mr. BIBB.

GENERAL ORDERS.

The joint resolution from the House of Representatives, fixing upon the day of adjournment, was taken up.

Mr. PORTER moved to lay the resolution on the table.

Mr. BROWN asked for the yeas and nays; which were ordered, and are as follows:

YEAS—Messrs. Benton, Bibb, Chambers, Clay, Clayton, Ewing, Grundy, Hendricks, Kent, Naudain, Porter, Robbins, Silsbee, Tyler, Waggaman, Webster, White—17.

NAYS—Messrs. Bell, Black, Brown, Calhoun, Forsyth, Frelinghuysen, Hill, Kane, King of Alabama, King of Georgia, Knight, Leigh, Linn, McKean, Mangum, Moore, Morris, Poindexter, Prentiss, Preston, Robinson, Shepley, Smith, Southard, Sprague, Swift—25.

After some conversation between Messrs. BROWN, CLAY, GRUNDY, and BIBB,

Mr. CLAY moved that the further consideration of the resolution be postponed until Monday next.

Mr. BROWN asked the yeas and nays; which were ordered, and are as follows:

YEAS—Messrs. Benton, Bibb, Chambers, Clay, Ewing, Grundy, Hendricks, Kane, Kent, Knight, Mangum, Moore, Naudain, Poindexter, Porter, Preston, Robbins, Silsbee, Southard, Sprague, Tomlinson, Tyler, Waggaman, Webster, White—25.

NAYS—Messrs. Bell, Black, Brown, Calhoun, Clayton, Forsyth, Frelinghuysen, Hill, King of Alabama, King of Georgia, Leigh, Linn, McKean, Morris, Prentiss, Robinson, Shepley, Smith, Swift, Tipton, Wilkins, Wright—22.

Mr. CLAY then moved that the Senate take up his resolutions; which was agreed to.

The resolutions being separated, and the question being on the passage of the first—

Mr. FORSYTH asked the yeas and nays; which were ordered, and are as follows:

YEAS—Messrs. Bell, Bibb, Black, Calhoun, Clay, Clayton, Ewing, Frelinghuysen, Hendricks, Kent, King of Georgia, Knight, Leigh, Mangum, Naudain, Poindexter, Porter, Prentiss, Preston, Robbins, Silsbee, Smith, Southard, Sprague, Swift, Tomlinson, Tyler, Waggaman, Webster—29.

NAYS—Messrs. Benton, Brown, Forsyth, Grundy, Hill, Kane, King of Alabama, Linn, McKean, Morris, Robinson, Shepley, Tipton, White, Wilkins, Wright—16.

The question recurring on the adoption of the second resolution, which provides for the deposite of the public moneys in the Bank of the United States after the 1st July next.

Mr. FORSYTH, after intimating a wish to address the Senate on the subject, moved to postpone the question till to-morrow; which was agreed to.

BILLS.

The following bills were read a third time, and passed:

A bill for the relief of John Chandler and William Johnson;

A bill for the relief of the town of Fayetteville, in the Territory of Arkansas;

A bill for the better organization of the United States Marine Corps, and to abolish brevet rank in the Army.

[Upon this bill the yeas and nays were demanded by Mr. FORSYTH; which were ordered, and are as follows:

YEAS—Messrs. Bell, Bibb, Black, Chambers, Clay, Clayton, Ewing, Frelinghuysen, Hendricks, Kane, Kent, Linn, Mangum, Poindexter, Prentiss, Preston, Robbins, Silsbee, Southard, Sprague, Smith, Swift, Webster, Wilkins, Wright—25.

NAYS—Messrs. Brown, Forsyth, Grundy, Hill, King of Georgia, McKean, Moore, Morris, Robinson, Shepley, Tipton, White—12.]

A bill granting to General P. Thomas, of Louisana, a tract of land, in consideration of the military services rendered by him in taking possession of that portion of West Florida included in the district of Baton Rouge.

[Mr. FORSYTH moved a reconsideration of the vote passing this last bill, and demanded the yeas and nays; which were ordered, and are as follows:

YEAS—Messrs. Black, Forsyth, Hill, Kent, King of Alabama, King of Georgia, McKean, Shepley, Swift, Tomlinson, White, Wilkins—12.

NAYS—Messrs. Benton, Bibb, Brown, Chambers, Clay, Frelinghuysen, Grundy, Hendricks, Kane, Linn, Moore Poindexter, Porter, Prentiss, Preston, Robinson, Silsbee, Smith, Southard, Tipton, Webster—21.

So the Senate refused to reconsider the vote.]

REPORTS.

Mr. WHITE, from the Committee on Revolutionary Claims, reported a bill for the relief of Francis Preston and wife; which was read, and ordered to a second reading.

Mr. KANE, on leave, introduced a bill to admit free of duty, books and apparatus intended for colleges and other literary institutions; which was read twice, and referred to the Committee on Finance.

Mr. WEBSTER moved that the Senate take up for consideration the Indian appropriation bill; which was agreed to.

After the usual number of readings, the bill was passed and returned to the House; and the Senate then, on motion of Mr. FRELINGHUYSEN, Adjourned.

HOUSE OF REPRESENTATIVES.
TUESDAY, June 3, 1834.

Mr. C. P. WHITE, from the Committee on Naval Affairs, reported bills for the relief of John H. Aulick and Silas Duncan; which were read twice and committed.

Mr. E. WHITTLESEY, from the Committee of Claims, reported bills for the relief of Henry Knowles, sen., and of John Pollock; which were read twice, and committed.

Mr. STODDERT, from the Committee on the District of Columbia, reported a bill prohibiting the Corporations of Washington, Georgetown, and Alexandria, in the District of Columbia, from issuing promissory notes of a less denomination than ten dollars, after the period therein mentioned; which was read, and,

On motion of Mr. VINTON, was postponed to Friday next, being the day set apart for business of the District.

Mr. SMITH offered the following resolution, by consent:

Resolved, That the Secretary of War be directed to communicate to this House a copy of the report of the survey recently made of the harbor of Portland, Maine, by Colonel Anderson, with a copy of the map and profile of the said harbor and breakwater proposed to be constructed therein. Also, copies of each preceding survey which has been made of said harbor, and now on file in the department.

Which, by the rules, lays one day upon the table.

KENTUCKY CONTESTED ELECTION.

The CHAIR announced the business in order to be the unfinished business of Saturday, being the Kentucky election.

Mr. ADAMS said, the business of yesterday had occupied the only day in the week set apart by the rules for the reception of petitions and memorials. As the session drew towards its close, it was important that the wishes of the people should be laid before the House with the utmost facility. He therefore hoped the House would consent to receive memorials this day, and made that motion.

Mr. WILLIAMS said, the important business now pending rendered it incumbent on him to object to the motion.

Mr. DENNY moved the suspension of the rules, to enable the motion to be made.

Mr. MANN inquired how many speeches were adjourned over from the previous petition day?

The CHAIR stated that six petitions had been postponed from the Monday of the preceding week.

The question was then taken on suspending the rule, and was negatived without a division.

The CHAIR then stated the question before the House to be the fifth branch of the following amendment, proposed by Mr. BANKS, to the resolution reported by the Committee of Elections:

"That all the legal votes which were received in Lancaster, Garrard county, whilst Moses Grant, Esq., acted as one of the judges, on the first morning of the election, in August last, and those of a like character, given on the second day of the election, in the casual absence of the sheriff, ought to be estimated in ascertaining the result of the election."

Mr. BANKS accepted as a modification the motion of Mr. JONES, to amend the amendment, by substituting the word "qualified" for "legal," and striking out the word "casual."

Mr. BANKS also modified his amendment by adding to it the following:

"That the votes of David McKee, Alfred W. Buford, Elijah Mount, Clayton Fitzpatrick, William R. Preston, R. L. Berry, B. Leffler, R. McKeown, G. M. Ormond, and Lewis L. Mason, given in Mercer county, be counted; the first nine for R. P. Letcher, and the last one for T. P. Moore.

"That the votes of John McHan, Reuben Young, Vincent Inge, Jacob Coffman, William Jenkins, and the Rev. D. Robertson, be taken from the number of votes allowed by the majority of the committee to Moore, in Mercer county, and added to those counted for Letcher.

"That the votes of Eli Williams and Wade Dawson, of Anderson county, and that those of William Conner, Charles Welsh, Thomas Harris, Montgomery Vaniandingham, Joseph Murrain, Levi Nunnery, Richard Curd, Anderson Hulet, Hickman Evans, Henry Wood, and Richard White, of Jessamine county, be counted for R. P. Letcher."

Mr. BANKS modified this part of the amendment by striking out the names of Harris, Nunnery, and Curd.

Mr. B. then advocated this branch of the amendment at length.

Mr. S. JONES replied to the statements and arguments of Mr. BANKS.

The debate was continued by Messrs. MARSHALL, POPE, and HARDIN; when,

Mr. HANNEGAN moved to amend the balance of the amendment, by striking out the whole which had not been adopted by the House, and inserting instead a clause providing that the names of Benjamin Higbee and Carey A. Wiley be stricken from the poll of Mr. Letcher.

Mr. HARDIN objected that the amendment to the amendment was not in order.

The CHAIR sustained the proposition in point of order, but suggested that it would present the question in a more direct and intelligible manner to offer it at a subsequent stage.

Mr. HANNEGAN assented to this course, and then argued the principles of the amendment before the House at length.

He was followed by Messrs. VANDERPOEL, CLAYTON, PEYTON, PARKER, BURGES, MOORE, HAMER, CHILTON, WILLIAMS, MANN, BEATY, CHILTON ALLAN, GAMBLE, and HARPER of Pennsylvania.

Mr. HUBBARD remarked that it had been his intention to have submitted at length his views upon the main resolution; but for the last six weeks, such had been his situation, that it had not been in his power to have participated in the debate; and he would assure the House that he had not risen at this hour of the day, and at this stage of the proceeding, to go into any general discussion of the subject. He merely wished, in as brief a manner as practicable, to present a few considerations upon the immediate question before the House. It is now proposed to amend the main resolution reported by the committee, by adding to the list in favor of Mr. Letcher, the votes which appear to have been given for him in Anderson county by two persons who were entered upon the poll book, one by the name of Williams, the other

by the name of Dawson; which votes had been rejected by the committee, on the ground that they were given by persons who had no legal residence in that county on the first Monday of August last, the time when the election took place. And, sir, disguise it as you may, the real and the only question in touching this point, does the evidence adduced satisfy our minds that no persons bearing those names could have had, at the time of the election, a legal residence in the county where they voted? Were there any such persons then residing within the limits of that county? If not, most clearly the committee did right in rejecting the votes which were given by them.

There is no member of this House who will not readily agree to this proposition. It is too plain to require argument; and if such a fraud has been practised upon the right of suffrage, it became the bounden duty of the Committee of Elections to detect it, and to prevent its injurious operation in the case before the House. They have attempted to do this, and they have done it in a way and manner that leaves not a particle of doubt upon his mind, that their finding, in this particular, ought to be confirmed by the House. He had examined, with some attention, the reports of the majority and of the minority of the committee, and he had endeavored, from the arguments of the parties litigant, and from all the lights which had been shed upon the case, to form for himself an opinion. He had so done; and he felt no embarrassment whatever upon the immediate question now under consideration. What is the evidence? It is admitted that the names of Williams and of Dawson are to be found on the poll book, and that these votes stand entered as having been given for Mr. Letcher; but is this fact conclusive? Is it not competent to contradict it by parol evidence? Is a poll book a record of such a description that you cannot controvert it—that you cannot impeach it—that you cannot destroy its force by other testimony? Sir, those who contend for such a doctrine, would find it difficult to sustain themselves. The law is not so. He would most freely admit that the record (as it is called)—the poll book—the mere entry of the names of the voters, is evidence, and evidence which, if uncontradicted, must satisfy the mind of every person, that such proceedings did take place, in the way, and in the manner, and by the persons, as the record purports to show; but it is not absolute—it is not conclusive evidence of the facts. It is evidence of a prima facie character; and not, as the gentleman from Pennsylvania, was understood to say, beyond the power of being explained and controverted. It is evidence; but it is evidence which may be impeached—which may be wholly destroyed by other testimony; and air, it has been so treated—it has been so admitted, by most of the gentlemen who have taken part in this discussion. It should be so considered. Well, then, what is the amount of evidence of personal identity resulting from the poll book?

It is nothing more and nothing less than that two persons, calling themselves by such names, appeared at the place of election, and claimed the right of voting. The right was granted—they did vote, and they did vote for Mr. Letcher. And here he would remark, that notwithstanding the positive requirements of the statute of Kentucky—notwithstanding it was the duty of the judges, in case the individual applying for liberty to vote should not be personally known, to administer to such applicant a particular oath, wherein the individual declares his qualifications as a voter, and his right to vote—notwithstanding such is the language of the law, he had understood that in practice, the oath was seldom administered, except in cases where the right of the person offering to vote was not challenged.

In the two cases before us, the individuals, beyond all doubt, voted as a mere matter of course. And he asked with confidence whether they could longed, or that they were sworn on the occasion. And he asked with confidence whether they could have been personally known to the judges of the election. He had come to an entirely different conclusion from the evidence adduced. With such a record, made as it was, and preserved as it had been, he could not doubt that two persons did actually appear, and did assume the names of Williams and Dawson, and did claim the right to vote, and did enjoy that right. But the inquiry

now is, were there in truth any such persons who were then legal residents in the county of Anderson, or were the judges imposed upon?—or, in other words, was there a fraud committed? If so, and that can be made to appear, it vitiates the whole proceeding—it destroys the whole effect of the record: and he could not doubt that all this was very competent and proper to show. And the question now is, whether the evidence which had been offered was sufficient to rebut the evidence resulting from the fact that these names appear upon the record. The latter is presumptive evidence, but it may, nevertheless, be impeached by testimony of a like character. Well, then, he would ask, what evidence has been adduced by Mr. Moore, tending to impeach the evidence resulting from the record? For he could not, for a moment, believe, that if Major Moore had brought forward the affidavit of every inhabitant in the county, and it should appear that no knowledge was had of any such persons as Williams and Dawson, that the record would be set aside at once as wholly unworthy of confidence.

The House, then, is bound to weigh all the evidence, and to see whether the weight of testimony is not now decidedly against the record. Mr. Moore had taken the deposition of the sheriff and of certain constables—men whose business led them through the county—men who would be likely to know the legal inhabitants of their counties, and they had testified unqualifiedly that persons of those names were not known to them—that they did not believe that any such persons resided within the limits of the county. But it has been asked, why has not the testimony of the judges of the election been taken?—that they had the means of knowing better than the deponents. To this remark he could not yield his assent. He, for one, did not believe that these judges could know the resident citizens of their county as well and as generally as sheriffs or as constables. They were men who, from the nature of their office, from their usual avocations, did not mix with the members of the community to the extent that sheriffs and officers of that character necessarily must. Judges were found in their studies, and confined to the discharge of such official duties as must necessarily limit their personal acquaintance with, and knowledge of, their fellow-citizens, while sheriffs and constables, from the very nature of their employments, extended their acquaintance into every village and neighborhood. He differed, therefore, from the gentleman from North Carolina, that Major Moore should have obtained the testimony of the judges of the election rather than the testimony of the sheriff and of the constables. He was of the opinion that the evidence procured was entitled to more consideration than the evidence of the judges alone would have been. But the testimony of the witnesses is not all the evidence which has been offered going to show that there were no such persons residing in the county in August last as Williams and Dawson. The books of the commissioners have been examined, and of those whose duty it is in each spring to make a perfect list of all the inhabitants in the county with reference to such personal taxation, and upon such books and upon such lists the names of Williams and Dawson cannot be found. Here, then, is not only the positive declaration of living witnesses who have the means of knowledge, but here are the books of the county commissioner, the lists of the tax-payers, all going to show that no such persons as Williams and Dawson were residing in the county on the day of election. And he would ask, is not all this sufficient to do away the force of the evidence resulting from the mere fact that the names of two such persons were found on the poll-book? He contended it was, and that the committee did entirely right in rejecting these votes. The presumption arising from all this testimony is, that no such persons were there; that a wrong has been done; and the burden of proof is changed. It is now the duty, and certainly is in the power of Mr. Letcher, according to the suggestions of the gentleman from Kentucky, [Mr. CHILVES,] to put this matter beyond all doubt. That gentleman has said that the lists of the constables of the county being ten or twelve in number, that the militia rolls would put this matter to rest—that they would be conclusive on this subject, and he has been pleased to add, that Major Moore should have

looked to those quarters for satisfactory evidence on this point. He differed in this particular from that gentleman. Mr. Moore had done all that was incumbent on him to do, and it devolved on the other side to give us further light; and it was not an arduous or a difficult duty to perform, for it would seem, from the remarks of the gentleman from Kentucky, that if these men were honest voters, were actual residents at the time, it can be shown, it can be made to appear. He would then ask, why has not Mr. Letcher gone to the constables, and to the militia officers, and put this matter at rest? Why has he not done it—it was clearly in his power, if the authority of the gentleman from Kentucky can be relied upon. The answer is at hand—the evidence which would come from those quarters would go only to confirm the testimony already taken. It is fair to presume this; and if the judges of the election would be able to give any different color to this transaction, their testimony would have been produced—it was within the reach of Mr. Letcher. And after all that Mr. Moore had shown in evidence, it was not to be required that he should go further—the burden was changed. The duty had devolved on Mr. Letcher. Inasmuch, then, as no attempt has been made by Mr. Letcher to satisfy the mind on this point, to make this matter clear, is it not fair to presume that no evidence does exist, or can be obtained, which will go to change the evidence offered by Mr. Moore, and now in the case? When the inquiry was made by the honorable gentleman from Georgia, [Mr. GAMBLE,] whether time had been allowed to Mr. Letcher, he thought the answer was not so full as it should have been. He presumed there was no disposition to mislead; but he would say, in further answer to the inquiry of the gentleman from Georgia, that the testimony by Mr. Moore was taken about the 20th of November last—six weeks before the first of January, beyond which point of time he believed no testimony was allowed to be taken, and that the testimony was taken in the presence of Mr. Letcher's agent. His counsel was there. Mr. Letcher, too, was present. All was open, and all was fair. Here was evidence taken (if properly regarded) which could not fail to destroy the force of the record—unexplained, it was conclusive. And this evidence was taken in the presence of Mr. Letcher's agent—at a time fully sufficient to enable him to explain it, and do it away by other evidence, if such evidence could be found. And as there has been no attempt whatever to impeach the testimony of Mr. Moore's witnesses, it did follow, to his mind, that the report of the committee, on this point, ought to be confirmed by the House.

The debate was further continued by Messrs. WAYNE, J. Q. ADAMS, and BRIGGS.

Mr. LANE took the floor, and intimated an intention to address the House on the subject, but, as the hour was late, he moved an adjournment; which was agreed to, and

The House adjourned.

IN SENATE.

WEDNESDAY, June 4, 1834.

Mr. McKEAN presented a memorial from inhabitants of Northampton county, Pennsylvania, praying a restoration of the deposites to the Bank of the United States, and a recharter of that institution; which was referred to the Committee on Finance, and ordered to be printed.

Mr. TOMLINSON presented the petition of George Reed; which was referred to the Committee on Public Lands.

Mr. BENTON presented the petition of Joseph and George Phelps; which was referred.

REPORTS.

Mr. POINDEXTER, from the Committee on

Public Lands, reported, without amendment, a bill from the House of Representatives for the relief of Duncan L. Clinch; which was read, and ordered to a second reading.

Mr. PRENTISS, from the Committee on Invalid Pensions, reported a bill for the relief of Eli Mitchell.

NEXT SESSION OF CONGRESS.

Mr. POINDEXTER gave notice that he should ask leave to introduce a bill to-morrow, fixing the meeting of the next session of Congress on a day anterior to the first Monday in December next.

GENERAL ORDERS.

The report of the Committee on Revolutionary Claims, adverse to the petition of Thomas Mott, wether, was, on motion of Mr. TYLER, laid upon the table.

RESTORATION OF THE DEPOSITES.

The second resolution of Mr. CLAY, requiring the public deposites to be made in the Bank of the United States and its branches after the 1st of July next, was taken up.

Mr. FORSYTH moved that when the question upon the adoption of this resolution should be taken, that it should be by yeas and nays; which were ordered.

Mr. FORSYTH, who was entitled to the floor, rose and said that he had intended to have addressed the Senate upon this subject, but that he had thrown out yesterday many of the points he had in contemplation to make, and as his colleague [Mr. KING] had expressed a wish to make some remarks upon the subject, he would yield the floor to him.

Mr. KING then spoke at length in explanation of the vote he intended to give against the passage of the resolution, and to avoid the charge of inconsistency in giving that vote, Mr. K., in the course of his remarks, digressed for a short time to the politics of South Carolina, and, on concluding, was followed by

Mr. PRESTON and Mr. FORSYTH.

Mr. BENTON then spoke briefly against the passage of the resolution.

Mr. McKEAN desired to say a word or two only, before the vote was taken. After more than six months outcry about the pecuniary distress of the country, he said this was the first opportunity given to any Senator to vote upon a proposition savoring of relief. His opinions on the great question which was agitating the public mind, had undergone no change. He, nevertheless, intended to vote for this resolution, not because he had much faith in the relief it would produce, but because a vast majority of his constituents, who had spoken on the subject, complained bitterly of extreme pecuniary distress, and prayed for the adoption of this very measure as a sure means of relief. He considered it a question of mere expediency, and one which he had no doubt many of his constituents were qualified to judge of, more correctly than himself. They asked for the measure, and he did not feel himself at liberty to oppose their will.

The question being on the final passage of the resolution, it was decided in the affirmative by the following vote:

YEAS—Messrs. Bell, Bibb, Black, Calhoun, Clay, Clayton, Ewing, Frelinghuysen, Kent, Knight, Leigh, McKean, Mangum, Naudain, Poindexter, Porter, Prentiss, Preston, Robbins, Silsbee, Smith, Southard, Sprague, Swift, Tomlinson, Tyler, Waggaman, Webster—28.

NAYS—Messrs. Benton, Brown, Forsyth, Grundy, Hill, Kane, King of Alabama, King of Georgia, Linn, Morris, Robinson, Shepley, Tipton, White, Wilkins, Wright—16.

NORTHERN BOUNDARY LINE OF OHIO.

The Senate then took up the bill fixing the northern boundary line of the State of Ohio.

Mr. CLAYTON, chairman of the Committee on the Judiciary, who reported the bill, spoke at length in explanation of its provisions.

Mr. KANE followed in reply, but, expressing a wish to make some examination into the subject, moved an adjournment; but gave way to

Mr. WRIGHT, who submitted the following resolution:

Resolved, That the Committee on the Judiciary be instructed to inquire into the expediency of

allowing the usual daily pay and mileage to the Honorable Elisha R. Potter, from the commencement of the present session up to the time of the decision of the contested election of a Senator from Rhode Island.

The Senate adjourned.

HOUSE OF REPRESENTATIVES.

WEDNESDAY, June 4, 1834.

Mr. E. EVERETT, from the Library Committee, reported a joint resolution for the distribution of the continuation of the Diplomatic Correspondence; which was read twice, and the question being on its engrossment—

Mr. CLAYTON said, he understood that it was proposed to give a copy of the work to such persons, including members of Congress, as have formerly received the work of which this is a continuation. He was opposed to this, and demanded the yeas and nays; which were ordered.

Mr. E. EVERETT said, the work was already published, and the only question was upon the mode of distribution.

The question being taken, it was determined in the affirmative—ayes 110, noes 57.

Mr. MERCER, from the Committee on Roads and Canals, reported a resolution for printing a communication from A. C. Flagg, Esq., respecting the New York canals; which was agreed to.

KENTUCKY CONTESTED ELECTION.

The House resumed the consideration of the subject of the election contested between Robert P. Letcher and Thomas P. Moore—the question being on the fifth amendment (as divided) to the resolution reported from the Committee of Elections, providing that the names of Eli Williams and Wade Dawson be counted for Mr. Letcher.

Mr. LANE, who was entitled to the floor, stated that it had been intimated to him, by the friends of the claimants, that they were very desirous to have the main question taken to-day, and he would therefore willingly waive the opportunity to make any remarks.

Mr. PARKER moved an amendment to the amendment, which was accepted as a modification by Mr. BANKS, who further modified the amendment so as to read as follows: "That the names 'of Eli Williams and Wade Dawson, of Anderson 'county, rejected by the committee upon the de-'position of the sheriff and others, that such per-'sons in the county were unknown to them, be 'counted for Mr. Letcher."

Mr. JONES, of Georgia, spoke at some length in opposition to the amendment.

Mr. J. Q. ADAMS spoke briefly in reply.

Mr. SUTHERLAND opposed the amendment. He also remarked that the House had already spent nearly two days on these two names. What was to become of the great interests of the country, if we went on in this whittling and quibbling way? He thought, himself, that the amendment might not to have been received, it being contradictory to the main proposition. In this way, we might go on trying Moore and Letcher, and Letcher and Moore, till the end of the session. He hoped the House would come to the question at once, which of the two claimants was entitled to the contested seat. Nothing, in his judgment, was to be gained by further delay.

Mr. POPE moved to amend the amendment, by adding the following words:

"There being no other evidence, but the fact that such names appear on the poll-books, that such men ever did live in the county."

After some remarks from Messrs. JONES of Georgia, BARRINGER, HARDIN, and a word two of explanation between Messrs. HUBBARD and SUTHERLAND, respecting the operation of the amendment moved by Mr. BANKS, the former while in the chair, the amendment offered by Mr. POPE was rejected.

The question now being taken by yeas and nays, counting the votes of E. Williams and Wilson for Mr. Letcher—a division of the question having been called for, and decided in the native—yeas 98, nays 115.

The question then recurring upon the balance the fifth amendment, Mr. McD. MOORE asked have the question first taken upon the names of Montgomery Van Landingham, Joseph Murrain, Holloman Evans, separately;

Mr. MERCER explained his views upon this branch of the amendment, referring to his experience in Virginia.

Mr. J. Y. MASON replied, stating at length the practice at elections in that State, and the rules adopted by the Legislature of Virginia, as to the proof of qualifications of voters.

Mr. HARDIN explained the practice of Kentucky; when

Mr. MERCER made a further explanation; and was followed by

Mr. LANE, who made a brief explanation of his views.

Mr. H. EVERETT inquired relative to the name of Joseph Murrain, and was replied to by

Mr. S. JONES, who also made some remarks in reply to Mr. MERCER.

The debate was continued by Messrs. HARDIN, H. EVERETT, BEATY, S. McD. MOORE, and HAMER; when the question was taken, and decided in the affirmative: Yeas 103, nays 100.

The question was then stated on counting the residue of the names in the fifth branch of Mr. BANKS's amendment, being those of William Conner, Richard White, Anderson Hulet, and Henry Wood.

Mr. J. Q. ADAMS inquired what difference existed between these names and those just decided?

Mr. S. McD. MOORE explained; and was followed by

Mr. S. JONES, who also explained the presumption against these votes; no such persons being known in the county.

After a few remarks from Mr MARSHALL, the question was taken, and decided in the negative: Yeas 89, nays 116.

Mr. POPE moved the following amendment to the amendment:

Resolved, That the votes of A. Kavenaugh, Geo. Elliott, Jr., Moses Bryant, John Shipman, Shelton Harris, John Floyd, Jeremiah Anderson, Garrit Vorris, John D. Stone, M. B. Moseley, William Wooley, Cornelius Naves, James Moorman, Robert Figg, John Cornett, and George Cadett, be stricken from Mr. Letcher's poll, it having been proved that they were minors at the time of the election.

Resolved, That the votes of Wm. Quinn, John McCoy, and William Wright, who voted in Garrard and Lincoln counties; and of Greenbury Peyton, and William Welsh, who voted in Jessamine county, and Elijah Carlson, who voted in Mercer county, be stricken from Mr. Letcher's poll; it having been proved that they were not citizens of Kentucky at the time of the election.

Resolved, That the vote of Rowland Shields ought to be counted for Mr. Moore on the Lincoln poll-book, it having been wrongfully stricken off by the judges of the election.

Resolved, That the vote of John Brady be taken from Mr. Letcher's poll, and counted on that of Mr. Moore, on the ground that he had, in the first instance, bona fide, and without mistake, voted for Mr. Moore.

Mr. POPE went into a detailed explanation relative to these voters, upon the testimony in the case, showing that each of those in the first item were under twenty-one years at the time of the election, and that the others were upon to the objections stated.

Mr. BURGES said it was not possible for him to go through with all the points of the gentleman's argument to-night, and he therefore moved that the House do now adjourn.

Mr. VANDERPOEL called for the yeas and nays on the motion, and they were ordered.

The question being taken, it was determined in the affirmative. Yeas 194, nays 89.

The House then adjourned.

IN SENATE.

THURSDAY, June 5, 1834.

Mr. McKEAN presented the memorial and documents of John Whitehead and others, asking for indemnity in consequence of the island of Key West, by orders of Commodore Porter and others, having been in part appropriated to public use, and part of the property of the memorialists consumed by the forces of the United States; referred to the Committee on Naval Affairs.

Mr. CLAY presented the memorial of citizens

---

of Scott county, Kentucky, praying the restoration of the public deposites to the Bank of the United States, and the recharter of that institution; which was referred to the Committee on Finance, and ordered to be printed.

Mr. WILKINS presented the remonstrance of sundry citizens of Pennsylvania against the renewal of the patent of John Ames, paper-maker; which was laid on the table.

NEW BILLS.

Mr. POINDEXTER, agreeably to notice, having obtained leave, introduced a bill anticipating the next session of Congress. The bill provides that when Congress shall this session adjourn sine die, it shall meet on the —— day of November next, instead of the first Monday in December, and that all unfinished business shall be taken up as though no adjournment had taken place. The bill was read twice, and made the special order of the day for Monday next.

Mr. BLACK, agreeably to notice, having obtained leave, introduced a bill for the removal of the land office from Clinton to Jackson, in Mississippi. The bill was read twice, and referred to the Committee on Public Lands.

GENERAL ORDERS.

The resolution of Mr. WRIGHT, providing for the compensation of the Hon. Mr. POTTER, of Rhode Island, was taken up, and agreed to.

The bill to grant to the State of Ohio certain lands for the support of schools in the Connecticut Western Reserve, was considered in committee of the whole, and ordered to be engrossed for a third reading.

The bill to amend an act for the payment of horses and arms lost in the military service of the United States against the Indians, on the frontiers of Illinois and the Michigan Territory, passed the 19th of February, 1833, was, on motion of Mr. TIPTON, laid upon the table.

Mr. TIPTON moved to suspend all the previous wagons, &c., in the late Indian war with Black Hawk; which was agreed to.

After some conversation between Mr. TIPTON and Mr. POINDEXTER,

Mr. ROBINSON, in reply to Mr. POINDEXTER, said: The reasons for the passage of this bill would be perfectly obvious when it was recollected, that the law of 1816, and all subsequent laws upon the same subject, had a limitation, prescribing the time within which the claims were required to be presented. [He here cited the several limitations.] During the time prescribed, many claimants were prevented, from various causes, from presenting for examination and payment, claims clearly allowable and just. The losses sustained during the war with the Indians in 1832, on the frontiers of Illinois and Michigan Territories, are almost wholly unprovided for. True, a law was passed at the last session, intending to make provision for their payment; but under the construction, as given to that law by the Third Auditor, the law was, in a very great degree, rendered nugatory—a construction which he would not, at this time, stop to examine, but which was such as to require the actual death of the horse to be proven. To make such proof, in the major part of the cases, was utterly impossible, both from the nature of the service, and the character of the losses. The service was chiefly in a frontier country, and part of the time as much as two hundred miles beyond the outer settlements; without roads, without any bridges, causeways, or any other of the ordinary facilities for the passage of the innumerable rivers and swamps, over, or rather through, which they had to pass; the former deep, wide, and often swimming; the latter, bog and miry, very extensive, and of the most difficult and dangerous passage. The service was a very hard one, occasionally making forced marches, when, if not wholly, unparalleled; and that, too, without any forage whatever—during a whole three months' tour of service, not the first feed for the horses was furnished by the United States. The consequence was, they were turned loose to graze, and this too with the approbation of the officers; indeed it could not be otherwise, for there was no other possible means of subsisting them. It often so happened, that the rider was dismounted, and separated from his

horse. Now it cannot but be obvious to every one, that the losses, under these circumstances, must have been very many, and without the slightest fault or negligence on the part of any one, and to make proof of the actual death wholly without the range of possibility. Where the loss happened in battle, it is not even in all cases possible to adduce such proof as is required under the rules adopted in the examination and allowance of these claims. Cases are in existence, and such have been presented and disallowed, where the owner or rider was killed in battle, his horse wholly lost and never afterwards heard of; but no proof is or can be had of the actual death of the horse. Yet the injury is as great, and the justness of the claim no less than if such proof was at hand and actually made. Under the construction, as given by the officer charged with the administration of the law of last session, not one case in twenty of losses will be paid for, judging from the few which have been allowed, and the many which have been rejected. Why, sir, in many cases where horses have been found, since the termination of the campaign, they have been claimed for the United States, and taken and disposed of as such, and the owner unable, under any law now in force, to get his just due. I hope the necessity of such a law as the one under consideration, with these explanations, and the report accompanying the bill, will be so apparent to all as to secure its speedy passage.

On motion of Mr. CALHOUN, the bill was laid upon the table, and made the special order of the day for Friday week.

The joint resolution from the House of Representatives, giving the right of way over property belonging to the United States, at Harper's Ferry, to the Winchester and Potomac Railroad Company, was read twice, and referred, on motion of Mr. CHAMBERS, to the Committee on Roads and Canals.

The resolution to print and circulate, under the direction of the Joint Library Committee, the diplomatic correspondence between the years 1783 and 1789, was read twice, and referred, on motion of Mr. ROBBINS, to the Library Committee.

The bill authorizing the sale of public lots in the town of St. Marks, by the register of the land office at Tallahassee, Florida, was read twice, and referred to the Committee on Public Lands.

On motion of Mr. PRESTON, the Senate proceeded to the consideration of the following resolution, submitted by him some days ago:

Resolved, That the Secretary of War report to the Senate a statement showing the names of the several pensioners who are now, or may have been heretofore, placed on the pension roll, designating their rank, annual allowance, the sums which they have severally received, the laws under which their pensions have been granted, the date when placed upon the roll, their ages, and the States and counties in which they severally reside. Also, the names of the pension agents who have received compensation, as such, and the amount of such compensation, and the act under which it was allowed, the names of the clerks who are and have been employed in the Pension Office, and the sums paid them as compensation, with an aggregate statement of the whole sum disbursed on account of pensions.

Mr. FORSYTH remarked that he had made some inquiry at War Department, on the subject of this resolution, and was informed that it could not be answered during the present session. By the next session it could be done, by an expenditure of some $1,000 or $1,500. By a calculation of the number of pensioners on the roll, it would be seen that it could not be answered at the present session. And he thought that the purpose of the honorable gentleman in desiring the information, was in effect accomplished, inasmuch as no person could be placed on the pension list under the late law, but by going into the county where he resided, and first announcing his claim there. The necessary expense of the printing would be too great for the advantages which were expected to be derived from it. He thought it could not be less than six or seven thousand dollars. He would have no objection to this, if it would result in anything good; and to avoid this expense in the first instance, he suggested the reference of the resolution to a committee to inquire into the subject.

Mr. PRESTON said, he knew no better mode of ascertaining what he wished to arrive at, and he thought the expense over-estimated. He thought the whole expense would not cost over $4,000 for printing 10,000 copies. He therefore adhered to his original proposition.

After some further conversation between Messrs. BELL, EWING, FORSYTH, and PRESTON, Mr. FORSYTH moved to refer the subject to the Judiciary Committee, which was negatived on a division, 17 to 18.

And the resolution was then agreed to.

SPECIAL ORDER.

The bill establishing the northern boundary line of the State of Ohio was taken up.

Mr. POINDEXTER moved that the bill be laid upon the table, and made the special order of the day for Thursday next. This motion having been withdrawn—

Mr. CLAYTON, who reported the bill, rose in explanation of its details.

Mr. EWING spoke at length in favor of the bill.

Mr. TIPTON followed in opposition, and concluded his remarks by moving its indefinite postponement.

Mr. LEIGH argued at considerable length against the postponement, and in favor of the bill, contending that it was a question of political expediency, that this matter should be settled in favor of the State of Ohio.

Some further conversation occurred between Messrs. TIPTON, LEIGH, and CLAYTON, when the question was taken by yeas and nays, and decided as follows:

YEAS—Messrs. Benton, Black, Brown, Grundy, Hill, King of Alabama, McKean, Swift, Tipton—9.

NAYS—Messrs. Bell, Bibb, Calhoun, Chambers, Clay, Clayton, Ewing, Frelinghuysen, Hendricks, Kane, Kent, Knight, Leigh, Linn, Mangum, Morris, Naudain, Poindexter, Porter, Prentiss, Robbins, Robinson, Shepley, Smith, Southard, Sprague, Tomlinson, Waggaman, Webster, White—30.

So the Senate refused to indefinitely postpone the bill.

Mr. TIPTON then offered an amendment, changing the boundary line between Ohio and Michigan; which was negatived.

The bill was then ordered to be engrossed and read a third time.

Mr. BIBB, from the Select Committee to whom was referred the resolutions relative to altering the Constitution in the manner of choosing the President and Vice President, made a report, being a substitute for the resolutions; which was ordered to be printed.

The following bills were considered in Committee of the Whole, reported to the Senate, and ordered to be engrossed for a third reading:

A bill for the relief of the owners and crew of the late privateer Roger Quarles, master;

A bill for the relief of John Percival, master commandant in the United States navy;

A bill further to extend the term of certain pensions chargeable on the privateer pension fund; and

A bill supplementary to the act authorizing the Territory of Florida to open canals between Chipola river and St. Andrew's bay, and from Manganese to Halifax river, in said Territory, approved March 3d, 1832.

Mr. TIPTON moved to take up the bill, to enable the people of the eastern division of the Territory of Michigan to form a Constitution and State Government, and for the admission of such State into the Union on an equal footing with the original States, and for other purposes.

Mr. T. subsequently withdrew the motion, and moved that the Senate adjourn. Lost: 17 to 17—the Chair (Mr. KING of Alabama) voting in the negative.

The bill to amend the several laws respecting the Post Office Department, was, on motion of Mr. GRUNDY, laid on the table.

On motion of Mr. SHEPLEY, The Senate adjourned.

HOUSE OF REPRESENTATIVES.

THURSDAY, June 5, 1834.

Mr. E. EVERETT, asked the consent of the House to read the third time the joint resolution providing for distributing the Diplomatic Correspondence from 1783 to 1789; which was agreed to.

The resolution was read a third time, and passed.

Mr. CHINN, from the Committee on the District of Columbia, reported a bill for regulating the rates of toll for crossing the Eastern Branch bridge; which was read twice, and committed.

Mr. ASHLEY, from the Committee on Public Lands, reported a bill granting to Henry M. Shreve the right of preemption to eighteen sections of land lying on Red river, in the State of Louisiana; read twice, and committed.

Mr. DUNCAN, from the Committee on Public Lands, reported a bill granting a quantity of public land in the State of Illinois, to assist in the construction of a road from a point on Wabash river, opposite to Vincennes, to Chicago; which was read twice, and committed.

Mr. McKENNAN, from the Committee on the District of Columbia, reported a bill for the relief of the heirs and legal representatives of Bailey E. Clarke; which was read twice, and committed.

Mr. J. HALL, from the Committee on the Expenditures of the Navy Department, made a report. Laid on the table, and ordered to be printed.

Mr. LEAVITT, from the Committee on Public Lands, reported a bill granting the right of preemption of certain lots of public lands in the town of Parryburg, in the State of Ohio; which was read twice, and committed.

Mr. J. ADAMS, from the Committee of Invalid Pensions, reported a bill for increasing the pension of Origen Eaton. Read twice and committed.

On motion of Mr. WHITE, of Florida, the House, by consent, took up the bill authorizing the President to direct the sale of certain public lots in the town of St. Marks; which was read a third time and passed.

On motion of Mr. McKIM, the House took up the joint resolution granting the right of way to the Winchester and Potomac Railroad Company at Harper's Ferry. Read a third time and passed. The House then proceeded to the special order, being the

BILLS CONCERNING THE TERRITORIES.

Mr. WILLIAMS moved the House go into committee upon the bills embraced in the special order; which was agreed to, Mr. WAYNE in the chair.

On motion of Mr. WILLIAMS, the bill repealing certain acts of the Legislative Council of Florida, was taken up.

The bill and report having been read—

Mr. WHITE, of Florida, moved an amendment providing for the election of two additional members of council which was agreed to.

After an inquiry by Mr. FILLMORE, and a reply from Mr. WHITE, on motion of the latter gentleman, the 3d section of the bill providing that the amount of the taxes illegally assessed, be refunded from the Treasury of the United States, was stricken out.

The bill was then laid aside.

The bill increasing the salaries of judges of the United States for the Territories of Michigan, Arkansas, and Florida, was then read.

Mr. WHITE moved an amendment limiting the increased allowance to those judges of Florida who do not receive extra allowance for deciding land claims under the treaty with Spain.

Mr. McKAY moved to include Arkansas in the amendment; which was agreed to.

The amendment was then adopted, and the bill laid aside.

On motion of Mr. SEVIER, the bill to establish an additional land office in Arkansas, was taken up and read.

After an amendment relative to the boundaries of the district, moved by Mr. SEVIER, was adopted, and some explanation by Messrs. KAY, CLAY, and MASON, the bill was laid aside.

On motion of Mr. WHITE, the bill for the relief of certain inhabitants of East Florida, was taken up and read.

Mr. McKAY inquired what was the amount of the claims provided for by this bill?

Mr. WHITE said they would not exceed $40,000.

Mr. WILLIAMS called for the reading of the report of the committee, relative to these claims.

Mr. WHITE said he could explain these claims in less time than the reading of the report would

inquire. Mr. W. went into a statement of the occupation of East Florida by the United States in 1811, and the nature of the claims arising out of this occupation.

After a few remarks between Messrs. McKAY and WHITE, the bill was laid aside.

On motion of Mr. LYON, the bill providing for the creation of certain land districts, &c., was taken up and read.

Several verbal amendments were adopted on motion of Mr. LYON.

Mr. CLAY moved an additional section, authorizing registers and receivers at land offices to administer oaths relative to the business of their offices; which was agreed to.

On motion of Mr. SEVIER, the bill from the Senate, authorizing the President to cause certain roads to be opened in the Territory of Arkansas, was taken up and read.

After some explanations between Messrs. McKAY and SEVIER, the bill was laid aside.

On motion of Mr. WHITE, the bill authorizing a road to be cut out from the northern boundary of Florida to the town of Appalachicola, was taken up and read.

Mr. WHITE moved an amendment, providing for the survey of a road from Tallahassee to Cape Florida, and a survey of the harbor of Appalachicola.

After an explanation from Mr. WHITE, the bill was laid aside.

On motion of Mr. SEVIER, the bill to mark and open a road from Columbia to Little Rock, in Arkansas, was read and laid aside.

On motion of Mr. WHITE, the bill from the Senate, providing for the construction of certain territorial roads in the Territory of Michigan, was read and laid aside.

A bill supplementary to the act authorizing the President to run and mark the dividing line between the Territory of Florida and Georgia, was taken up for consideration.

Mr. FOSTER moved an amendment, directing that the boundary line between Georgia and Florida be run according to the treaty of 1783, which he supported in a speech of some length.

Mr. WHITE, of Florida, opposed the motion, and it was supported by Mr. GILMER; when, the question being taken, the motion was lost.

The bill for running and marking the boundary line in the State of Missouri, was taken up, and amended, on motion of Mr. BULL, so as to direct the line to be run up the Missouri river till it reaches a parallel with the rapids of Des Moines river.

Mr. WILLIAMS moved a reconsideration of the vote, by which the amendment was adopted, but withdrew it after a discussion, in which Messrs. BULL, WILLIAMS, GAMBLE, H. VERETT, and ASHLEY, took part. A further amendment was offered by Mr. BULL, which rejected.

he bill for the relief of certain persons employed as spies by General Clark, was considered.

lso, a bill for the relief of Peter Alba and his assigns.

so, a bill for the survey of certain rivers and , and for the improvement of a harbor in the rritory of Michigan.

The bill for the relief of sundry citizens of Arsas, who lost their improvements in consemos of a treaty with the Choctaw Indians, was en up for consideration.

After some discussion, by Messrs. DUNCAN, AY, HUNTINGTON, McKAY, FILLDRE, H. EVERETT, MASON, WARDSLL, and SEVIER, on the general policy of bill——

an amendment was, on motion of Mr. H. EVETT, adopted, restricting the application of act to such persons as abandoned their improvets before the first day of June, 1898.

he bill to authorize the Legislative Council of higan to hold an extra session was taken up, after some explanations from Mr. LYON, of higan, was directed to be reported to the see.

he bill to authorize the President of the United es to cause the lead mines in the State of ois and the Territory of Michigan to be sold, for other purposes, was taken up for considera-.

Mr. PARKER and Mr. WILLIAMS opposed the consideration of the bill at this time, and Mr. DUNCAN expressed the hope that the committee would proceed with the consideration.

After some conversation upon the question, whether it was in order to consider the bill this day,

Messrs. ASHLEY, DUNCAN, GAMBLE, and R. M. JOHNSON briefly advocated the bill, and Messrs. REED, WARDWELL, FILLMORE, and PARKER, opposed it.

Mr. WILLIAMS moved to amend the bill so as to provide that six months' notice should be given of the sale; which was agreed to.

The discussion was further continued by Messrs. J. Q. ADAMS, DUNCAN, VINTON, CLAY, and LYON of Michigan, when the bill was amended, on motion of Mr. VINTON, and directed to be reported to the House.

On motion of Mr. LYON, the committee rose, and reported the above bills to the House.

Mr. LYON moved that the House go into Committee of the Whole on the state of the Union, for the purpose of considering certain bills relative to the Territories, which had been referred to that committee; which motion, after some conversation, he withdrew.

The several bills carried through the committee were ordered to be engrossed, and read a third time to-morrow, excepting——

The bill for the relief of sundry citizens of Arkansas who lost their improvements in consequence of a treaty with the Choctaw Indians——that authorizing the President to run and mark the line dividing the Territories of the United States and the State of Missouri——the bill authorizing the sale of the lead mines, and the bill authorizing the President to run and mark the dividing line between Georgia and Florida; all of which were postponed until to-morrow.

The House then adjourned.

IN SENATE.

FRIDAY, June 6, 1834.

The following bills were read a third time, and passed:

A bill granting to the State of Ohio certain lands for the support of schools in the Connecticut Western Reserve;

A bill further to extend the term of certain pensions chargeable on the private pension fund;

A bill for the relief of John Percival, master commandant in the United States Navy; and

A bill fixing and establishing the northern boundary line of the State of Ohio.

The following bills were considered as in Committee of the Whole, reported to the Senate, and ordered to be engrossed for a third reading:

A bill for the relief of Hannah Stone; and

A bill for the relief of Aaron Bellamy.

The following bills, upon being announced in their turn upon the calendar, were laid upon the table:

The bill establishing the territorial government of Wisconsin;

[On the motion by Mr. POINDEXTER to lay this bill on the table,

Mr. TIPTON said: The country called Michigan proper, the peninsula between lakes Erie and Michigan, was that intended for the State of Michigan. That portion of country intended to form the Wisconsin Territory, was all the country that was now included in the Michigan Territory lying west of Lake Michigan, and east of the Mississippi and Missouri rivers, a territory which would be sufficient very soon to form two large States, as is extended up the Missouri to White Earth river, in Wisconsin. Mr. T. said there must be at this time at least ten thousand inhabitants in that territory. About three thousand of these people were settled west of the Missouri river, and north of the State of Missouri, who claimed the protection of our laws. They were settling in the neighborhood of Dubuque's mine, on the lands purchased from the Sac and Fox Indians. Mr. T. asked that he would have no objection to lay the bill on the table until the Senate could act on the bill for the admission of Michigan into the Union.]

The bill supplementary to the act authorizing the Territory of Florida to open canals between

---

Chipola river and St. Andrew's bay, and from Matanzas to Halifax river, in said Territory, approved March 2, 1839;

The bill for the relief of the owners and crew of the late privateer Roger, Roger Quarles, master; and

The bill for the relief of Sebastian Butcher, and the heirs and legal representatives of Bartholomew Butcher, Michael Butcher, and Peter Bloom.

[The discussion upon the merits of the last bill gave rise to a conversation of a personal character between Mr. POINDEXTER and Mr. LINN, when, in order that the Senate might be in possession of the entire facts connected with the case, on motion of Mr. CLAY, the documents accompanying the bill were ordered to be printed.]

The bill granting pensions to certain persons therein named, was, on motion of Mr. TOMLINSON, made the special order of the day for to-morrow.

On motion of Mr. PRESTON, all the previous orders were postponed, and the Senate took up the bill to increase and regulate the pay of the surgeons and assistant surgeons of the army; which was ordered to be engrossed for a third reading.

The bill for the relief of the owners and crew of the privateer Roger, previously laid upon the table, was, on motion of Mr. BIBB, again taken up, considered, and rejected.

Mr. TIPTON moved to take up the bill for the repair of the Mars' Hill military road, in the State of Maine; but, before the question was taken, on motion of Mr. MOORE,

The Senate adjourned.

HOUSE OF REPRESENTATIVES.

FRIDAY, June 6, 1834.

Mr. POLK, from the Committee of Ways and Means, reported a bill making additional appropriations for the armory at Harper's Ferry, for the year 1834. Read twice, and committed.

Mr. POLK, from the same committee, reported a bill from the Senate, entitled "An act supplementary to an act entitled 'An act to alter and amend the several acts imposing duties on imports,'" approved July 14, 1832; which was committed, and made the order of the day for to-morrow.

Mr. LEAVITT, from the Committee on Public Lands, reported a bill for the relief of Jacob L. févre. Read twice, and committed.

Mr. JARVIS moved that the Committee of the Whole on the state of the Union be discharged from the consideration of the "bill making appropriations for the public buildings and grounds, and for other purposes," and that the same be referred to the Committee of the whole House; which was agreed to.

The bill from the Senate, to aid in the construction of certain roads in the Territory of Michigan, came up: the question being on its third reading,

Mr. WILLIAMS made some objection to the bill, and called for the yeas and nays on its engrossment; which were ordered.

Mr. MERCER briefly supported the bill.

Mr. McKINLEY imagined, he said, that it would be difficult for any member of the House to tell why those roads were making in various places. After considerable examination of the subject, he could not tell. No committee had made a report on the subject of the roads; and we had no information respecting them, from the Territory of Michigan. His own State derived no benefit from the appropriations. No roads were made by the United States, in Alabama, nor in those other States; but here several hundred thousand dollars were to be given for making roads in Territories. We allowed 3 per cent. from the sale of public lands for roads within the new States and Territories; and 2 per cent. for making roads to these States and Territories; but it would be found that the appropriations vastly exceeded the amount of those funds. He thought the whole system was unjust and partial in its operation. Gentlemen who were the other day talking about economy, and of reducing the salaries of clerks, had an opportunity now to carry out their system without any difficulty.

Mr. MERCER said it was not in the power of the Territories to make these roads, and if it was,

it would be extremely unjust to require them to do it. The United States, being the proprietor of the lands, was bound to make the roads. If the gentleman would point out any particular road which was unnecessary, he would consent to strike it out. He vindicated the system from the objection made by the gentleman from Alabama, that it was unequal and unjust. The gentleman was mistaken in supposing that Alabama had not received her due share of aid from the Government. The largest appropriation ever made to any Territory, was made to Alabama when a Territory. Mr. M. also went into a defence, generally, of the system.

Mr. WHITE, of Florida, stated some facts, showing that the public treasury had received four times as much from the sale of lands, in consequence of these improvements, than it would otherwise have received. The Government was the landholder in the Territories, and it was the interest of the landholder to open an avenue to emigration.

Mr. CHINN called for the special order of the day, being the business relating to the District of Columbia.

Mr. POLK submitted a motion to suspend the rule, in order to take up the unfinished appropriation bills.

Mr. E. WHITTLESEY suggested that, in the course of the day and to-morrow, there was time to act on the District business, and the appropriation bills also.

The question being taken, the motion to suspend the rules was lost.

Mr. CHINN moved that the House go into Committee of the Whole on the bills reported from the Committee on the District of Columbia.

Mr. MERCER expressed a hope that the gentleman would include the Potomac bridge bill.

Mr. JARVIS hoped, he said, that the bills reported from the Committee on Public Buildings would be included.

Mr. CHINN objected to taking up any other business than that which was embraced in the resolution setting apart this day and to-morrow for District business. If the District business was not attended to soon, it would not be acted upon at all.

The motion of Mr. CHINN was agreed to, and the House went into Committee of the Whole, (Mr. BRIGGS in the chair.)

The bill for the improvement of the Pennsylvania Avenue was considered.

Mr. PARKER objected to the item appropriating two hundred dollars for removing mud and dust from the surface of the Pennsylvania avenue. Congress, he said, had made the road as good a one as any in the United States, and it was the duty of the Corporation to keep it clean.

Mr. CHINN moved to reduce the sum to $143 73.

Mr. STODDERT said, the road was not made for the benefit of the city, but for the accommodation of the Government, and of the people of the United States having business with the Government. If it was proper to make a road for such a purpose, it was proper to keep it in order.

Mr. HARPER, of Pennsylvania, was unwilling, he said, to make a provision which would form a precedent, but, he had no objection to pay the expense which had already been incurred. He would not vote for any item in the bill which would go to establish the principle that the Government should make an annual appropriation for the improvement and cleansing of the streets in this city.

Mr. WARDWELL, proposed to amend the item, so as to make it read " for expenses already incurred in removing mud and dust," &c., which Mr. CHINN accepted as a modification of his amendment; and the amendment offered by Mr. CHINN was agreed to as modified.

Mr. PARKER objected to the item as amended, and moved to strike it out.

Mr. FILLMORE supported the amendment.

After some words from Mr. McKINLEY, Mr. EWING, and Mr. WATMOUGH, the motion to strike out was negatived.

Mr. PARKER moved to amend the item, by altering it so as to show that the expense was incurred by direction of the Committee on the District of Columbia; which was negatived.

Mr. HARDIN objected to the item appropriating four hundred dollars for the repair of Pennsylvania Avenue.

Mr. CHINN made some explanations.

Mr. HARDIN said he had examined and measured the Pennsylvania Avenue, and had ascertained that the work done upon it ought to have cost, and might have been done for, thirty thousand dollars; but it had actually cost one hundred and thirty thousand dollars. It would cost one about fourteen thousand dollars, according to his estimate, to make a good road of it. All that was necessary to do this was to put a coat of four feet of limestone rock upon it. Unless this was done every particle of the road would be blown away by next November. But he should make no motion respecting it.

Mr. McKINLEY moved to strike out the appropriation of four hundred dollars for repairing the Avenue; which was negatived.

Mr. McKINLEY objected to the item appropriating twelve hundred dollars for the arch over the Tiber; and moved to reduce it one-half.

Mr. WARDWELL hoped the gentleman would withdraw the motion. He was surprised himself that three thousand dollars was not demanded for the work, considering that the Avenue had cost $130,000, though in fact it was not worth three hundred dollars. If we could get off with twelve hundred dollars, without having any arrearages to pay, we should do well.

After some words from Messrs. MERCER and CHINN, the question was taken on the amendment, when it appeared that 43 voted in the affirmative, and 58 in the negative. (No quorum.)

Mr. McKINLEY withdrew his motion to amend.

Mr. McKAY commented upon the item in the bill appropriating $3,720 for arrearages for the improvement of Pennsylvania Avenue, and insisted that the appropriation ought not to be made unless the committee had fully investigated the expenditures which had been made for that object, and stated that he should look into the item when the bill came into the House, unless a satisfactory explanation should be made.

The bill was then laid aside.

The bill to organize the several fire companies in the District of Columbia, was then taken up and read.

Mr. CHINN moved an amendment to the first section providing that a company possessing an apparatus costing not more than $500 should not exempt more than fifty men from military duty, and that one possessing apparatus costing $1,000 might exempt seventy-five men.

Mr. C. also moved to amend the second section of the bill so as to provide that an inspector be appointed by the corporate authorities of each city, whose duty it shall be to inspect and report the state of the apparatus, &c.

Mr. C. also moved some verbal amendments; which were agreed to.

The bill was then laid aside.

The bill to incorporate the Washington National Monument Society was then read.

Mr. MANN moved an additional section, giving to Congress power to alter, amend, or repeal, the act, when, in their judgment, the public interests may require it.

Mr. SELDEN opposed this amendment; which was advocated by Mr. MANN; when the question was taken, and the amendment carried.

Mr. WARDWELL moved to strike out the eighth section, which provides for appointing collectors in the several States, which were divided into four districts.

After some remarks from Messrs. WARDWELL, McKENNAN, PARKER, BURGES, and CHINN—

Mr. HARDIN made some observations upon the object of the bill, which he considered to be simply to divide the United States into four great begging districts, and to furnish profitable employment for four persons as collectors. He moved to strike out the first section of the bill.

Some remarks were made by Messrs. FILLMORE, ADAMS, D. J. PEARCE, MANN, CHINN, MERCER, McDUFFIE, MOORE, STEWART, and CHILTON, when it was discovered that this bill had not been committed, and, of course, had not been properly taken up.

The bill to extend the charter of the Fire Insurance Company of Alexandria was then taken up; and, after an amendment proposed by Mr. CHINN, was laid aside.

The following bill, for the benefit of the city of Washington, was then taken up:

A BILL for the benefit of the city of Washington.

Be it enacted by the Senate and House of Representatives of the United States of America in Congress assembled, That the Secretary of the Treasury be, and he is hereby, authorized to pay out of any unappropriated money in the treasury, a sum not exceeding sixty thousand dollars annually, in quarterly instalments, for the period of three years from the passage of this act, to the mayor of the city of Washington, to be applied under the direction and authority of the Boards of Aldermen and Common Council, to extinguish so much of the interest annually accruing on their public debt.

Mr. STODDERT called for the reading of the report relative to this bill; which was done.

Mr. MANN was opposed (he said) to the passage of this bill, and was under the necessity of moving to strike out the enacting clause. He knew of no principle of justice, equity, or policy, whereby the nation ought to be required to pay the debt which this corporation, in their providence or improvidence, have contracted. If we assumed the payment of the interest, we should soon be compelled to pay the principal also. The report, which he characterized as an able one, had not convinced him that the Government, although it was located here, was bound to relieve this bankrupt corporation from its difficulties. We were not to be called upon, in our representative capacity, to dispose charities, but to transact the public business.

Mr. STODDERT, in reply, contended that the Congress, having exclusive jurisdiction within the limits of the District, exercised over it the same authority and guardianship which a State Legislature had over a State. The committee did not intend this bill as an entering wedge, and that had expressly stated in their report, and provided in the bill, that the appropriation should be continued only three years. The measure which had produced this embarrassments of the corporation ought not to be characterized as improvident or extravagant. They were such as were approved by the most prudent and enlightened men. Be the question was, whether it was our duty to provide for the works of this District. He held in his hand the deeds of cession, from which it appeared that the land was given to the Government in trust to be used for the benefit of the city, and not to be applied to public and national ones. The Government now held in the city land to the value of one million of dollars, and had received from the sale of land over seven hundred thousand dollars, and had appropriated for the city $735,000, of which $476,000 were for public and federal uses, viz: for the penitentiary $106,000, for the canal $150,000, and for the avenue $140,000. The appropriations now proposed ($156,000) would, if made, still leave a large sum in the public treasury, which had no right to use for any other purpose than for the improvement of the city. There could be no possible doubt as to our power or duty in this matter, and we had no alternative but to permit the city to sink beneath its embarrassments or to relieve it.

Mr. HARDIN took a different view, he said, of the provisions of the deed of cession from that presented by the gentleman from Maryland. The proprietors gave one-half of the land with a view to enhance the value of the rest, and Government was to pay twenty-five pounds an acre for such part of the lands as they purchased. The lands were not given in trust for the people of the District, but for the people of the United States. In no city of the United States was so much public money expended as in this. Taking one year with another, the Government expended here from fifteen hundred thousand to two millions a year. We were asked if we would suffer a city having the name of Washington to go down. There was not a State in the Union which had not a town or county called Washington. If all sink, the name of Washington would not be lost, whether this city should rise or fall. He admitted that the report was ably and eloquently drawn; but it could not persuade him that the

city was "an enterprising city." It was an abuse of words to call this an enterprising city, where nobody labored more than four hours a-day. The people of the city had no reason to complain of any want of liberality to it on the part of Congress. We had given one hundred and fifty thousand dollars for a canal, the only earthly purpose of which was to bring wood to their doors; we swept their streets for them; and even went to the expense of building frames to protect their shade trees. We had given a hundred thousand dollars for a trough across the Potomac; and we had a bill before us for another hundred thousand for the same purpose. We had given a million for the ditch, and had a bill now to give a million more. It was time, he thought, to stop.

Mr. MERCER had never, he said, known any subject to be discussed here relating to the city of Washington, without an attempt on the part of some members to build up a popularity elsewhere, by abusing and making a sport of the unfortunate citizens of the District. Mr. Mercer went on to argue, that every capital in Europe had been built up at the expense of the Government. The policy which was proposed in regard to the District was, therefore, neither new nor extraordinary. The Chesapeake and Ohio Canal, for which the city had contracted a heavy debt, was a work which was every way entitled to the aid of the Government. He would refer the gentleman from New York to the example of his own State. The Delaware and Hudson Canal stock was, at one time, worth little or nothing. The company applied to the State for relief. The State loaned to the company its credit; the canal was completed; and now its stock is greatly above par. Mr. M. went into many statements to prove that the Chesapeake and Ohio Canal, when completed, would be more productive than any similar work in the United States or in Europe, and that in reference to the perpetuity of the Union, it was more important than any other work in the Union.

After some further debate, in which the bill was opposed by Messrs. HARDIN and MANN, and supported by Messrs. CHINN, WARDWELL, and STEWART—

Mr. VINTON moved the committee rise; which was carried: ayes 62, noes 60.

The committee accordingly rose, and the bills passed through the committee, were reported to the House, and progress on the last bill.

The House then adjourned.

IN SENATE.

THURSDAY, *May* 29, 1834.

Debate on the resolution submitted by Mr. Preston, calling for information from the Secretary of War relative to the pensioners of the United States.

Mr. PRESTON said, it was of importance to ascertain with precision the number of claims which would probably be made upon the Government. His object was to follow up the resolution when the information should be obtained upon it, by ordering the publication of the names in the various counties of the United States, where the applicants for pensions, or the pensioners, reside, and thus, by publishing them, prevent frauds upon the Government. In his judgment, there was some radical mistake, mismanagement, or fraud, in the pension system, which called on Congress to look minutely into it. He came to this conclusion from the fact that there were thirty-six thousand pensioners of the Revolution on the pension roll. And so far from decreasing, since the adoption of the present gigantic system, it had annually increased, and was increasing, equal to the calculation made at the time of its decrease. There was an actual increase of 25 per cent., from which it would seem that these revolutionary heroes increase in numbers. When the system was adopted, an elaborate report was made as to the probable and possible number which would be put on the roll from it. The estimate was made on the maximum of numbers which would apply. The calculation then was, that it could not add more than ten thousand to the pension roll. [Mr. P. here read extracts from the report of the committee which reported the act of July, 1832.] The aggregate amount of revolutionary soldiers were supposed to have been 328,000, and at the time of the report, that ten thousand might, by possibility, have been alive. But instead of ten thousand, in eighteen months, the applications had amounted to twenty-four thousand six hundred, of which the Secretary of War reported that about one thousand would probably be rejected. Up to this time, then, the calculation had been more than trebled, and thirty-six thousand were now on the roll. Mr. P. said, it struck him as incredible, that at this time there should be so vast a number alive. It was well known that our pension system was more extensive than it was in any other country; agents were appointed in every part of the country to collect claims, and bring them before Congress; many were pushed too far, and sustained throughout by fraudulent testimony. Mr. P. related a striking instance of this to sustain a claim for a pension by a person who served on board the frigate South Carolina during the Revolution. The present result on the pension books he considered impossible, and therefore it demanded scrutiny.

Mr. P. then proceeded, at length, to show, from various statistical statements and tables of longevity, that so great a number of pensioners could not now be alive. He took the estimated population of the United States at the Revolution, calculated the proportion of fighting men, and assuming the average age at thirty, he came to the conclusion, upon the ordinary tables of longevity, that there could not be one-third the number of old soldiers now in existence that were represented to be living. Mr. P. argued, also, that fraud must exist, from the fact that a large proportion of the pensioners now on the roll, were in States which produced no soldiers in the war of the Revolution, while those States which furnished the fighting men, had comparatively few pensioners. Mr. P. believed no one was aware of the immense expenditure which was annually made to pensioners, and that we could not calculate the amount to which it would extend, if it went on two or three years more. He thought it would be five or ten millions.

Mr. WEBSTER said he presumed no member had any objection to the resolution of inquiry. If fraud had been practised, or mistake had occurred, in the administration of the pension laws, which was of so much importance as to make an inquiry necessary, why, this course was the correct one on which to commence reform. But while he concurred with the honorable gentleman in this, he would repeat a suggestion he made the other day, that the state of facts from which the gentleman reasoned, did not conduct him to the disproportions to which he arrived. He had shown a great apparent disproportion between the population of different States and the pensioners in each State, and from the longevity of the South, he came to the conclusion that the proportion should be the other way. But Mr. W. would submit to the honorable member, how frauds should exist in a greater proportion in one part of the country than in another; at least to so enormous an extent? It could not be. We must, therefore, look to other causes for an explanation of the difficulty. And it might be explained by reference to one or two considerations. The disproportion in the emigration from different States, and the change in the population. No fact in the whole range of statistics was more easily explained than the disproportion of pensioners in New York and Massachusetts. What was New York in the Revolution? It certainly was not to be compared to Massachusetts at that period. What made the population of New York? Half a million of its population went to that State after the war. The fighting men rushed to New York after the peace, and the same thing took place after the Canadian war, as at the peace of '83.

Mr. FRELINGHUYSEN said that the rules of longevity of the honorable gentleman from South Carolina were not correct or applicable; that the latitude given by the act of 1832, to those who had served but six months, must multiply the number of pensioners; he thought a child of seven years old, at the commencement of the war, might have served his six months before the peace, and not be a very aged man now. He did not believe the most jealous scrutiny into the matter would disclose any material frauds. He was astonished, after the passage of the act of 1832, on his return home, to see so many old worthies applying to the court for pensions.

Mr. WRIGHT said it was not his object to offer any opposition to the resolution. On the contrary, he hoped it would pass. He thought the statements which had been made upon the present and a former occasion, when this subject was before the Senate, and the suspicions of frauds which were shown to be entertained, had satisfied every member of the body that some inquiry should be made, which would correct the public mind, detect frauds, *if* frauds exist, and allay suspicion as to honest applicants. He said he would go with the honorable Senator to any extent to detect and punish any frauds which might be found to exist, and he would much rather engage in such an inquiry in his own State than in any other, because his motives would not then be suspected, nor could he be accused of designing to cast unjust imputations anywhere. He also owed it to himself to remark, that upon a former occasion, when this subject was under consideration, he should have made the observations which it was now his purpose to make, had it not been for the fact that an honorable Senator from Massachusetts, [Mr WEBSTER,] made explanations, in answer to the Senator from South Carolina, which were perfectly satisfactory to him, and he had no disposition to protract the debate, or to consume the time of the Senate.

The argument of the honorable Senator from South Carolina, [Mr. PRESTON,] was based upon premises which he (Mr. W.) considered unsound, and calculated to lead to error. These premises were comparisons of the present number of pensioners from each State upon the pension rolls, made under the several pension laws, with the number of troops furnished by each State during the revolutionary war. These comparisons, as made by the honorable Senator, had no reference to the present population of the States, and here, (Mr. W. said,) he considered was the radical error.

New York had been made, by the honorable Senator, very prominent in the comparisons he had presented, formed upon the basis just mentioned, and which he (Mr. W.) believed he could satisfy the Senator himself, and the Senate, was unsound. New York, at the time of the Revolution, when compared with some other States, was small in population; and her quota of troops was small in proportion to her population. The inhabited portions of New York, at that early period, were a narrow tract of country along the Hudson river, small settlements upon the borders of Lake Champlain and Lake George, and a limited portion of the lands upon each side of the Mohawk river, extending westwardly from Albany some hundred miles, more or less. These were the portions of the State then embracing nearly all of the white population.

Mr. W. said he spoke from recollection, and from a very bad recollection as to statistical facts; but he believed that, at the commencement of the revolutionary war, the population of New York and South Carolina were not greatly variant, and that the troops, both regulars and militia, furnished by these States, were not widely different. How was it now? He would assume the population of New York to be 2,000,000, and for all the purposes of the pension law of 1832, the number must be below the fact; and he believed the population of South Carolina, of all descriptions, to be now about 500,000. Is it then fair to compare the number of pensioners upon the various pension rolls, residing within these two States, to determine the fairness of the pension applications, or the absence of fraud in the grants of pensions made to the citizens of each State? Mr. W. said he could not so consider the argument. The population of New York had increased since the revolutionary war, and before the passage of the act of 1832, more than three times its amount at the time of the war. It had not been so with the population of South Carolina. The increase in New York had not been solely from the increase of its original population. It was not true that the population of New York, existing at the time of the Revolution, had multiplied so much more rapidly than that of South Carolina; but the difference had been occasioned by emigration into New York from the old States. That emigration was principally from the eastern States; it commenced soon after the war, and continued until western New York was principally settled.

Mr. W. said his residence was in the county of St. Lawrence, the extreme northwestern county of the State. His recollection was, that settlements were commenced in that county at about the year 1800, and that the county was organized between that time and 1804. It was not now a large county in population, relatively speaking, and during the war of the Revolution, he did not suppose there was an armed white man in it. Still it now presented a somewhat numerous list of revolutionary pensioners. He had been informed that at the first Court of Record held in the county, after the passage of the act of 1832, about seventy of the venerable survivors of that glorious struggle, assembled in that new county to make their applications for the pensions granted by it. He did not know the fact, but he presumed that of the number assembled there would not have been found five who claimed to have served either in the New York line, or the New York militia. The county is almost exclusively settled from the States of Massachusetts and Vermont, and the pensioners now residing within it, are nearly all emigrants from those and other States. Inasmuch as this county had no white population during the war, if the premises of the gentleman be sound, it should have no pensioners now, and his reasoning is, that the fact that it has, raises the presumption that the applications have been sustained by fraud.

Mr. W. said, he knew the honorable Senator would not contend that this was true as to all these cases, but he seemed to think it must be as to a large portion of them. If the gentleman was as well acquainted as himself with the population, and the progress of settlement of the western portions of New York, he would change his opinions. Where, he would ask the honorable Senator, was now the population of New York? Of its 2,000,000 of inhabitants, he felt confident he should be within the fact, when he said that at least 1,000,000 was to be found in portions of the territory of the State where there was no white population at the close of the revolutionary war. The county of Oneida, the most populous county of the State, the city and county of New York alone excepted, was a wilderness, inhabited by the savages exclusively, until long after the conclusion of that war. He believed it was true that there might have been a block-house or two, or some slight works, erected for defence against the Indians, within its territory during or before the termination of the war, but the county was unsettled and uninhabited by the whites until after that period. Now, he believed, if a line were drawn across the State as far east as the east bounds of this county, nearly, if not quite, the one-half of the white population of the State would be found west of such line. The most of this population, too, would be found to consist of emigrants from other States since the Revolution, and they had brought with them a full share, he thought he could say a large share, of the soldiers of the Revolution. Was it unnatural that it should be so? Who so likely to emigrate from the thickly settled portions of the old States to the great West, to the unexplored wilderness, as the soldiers of that war? They undoubtedly come out of that war, as most of them went into it, poor, and unable to purchase the cultivated and valuable land of the old States.

Mr. W. said it was not the rich, but the poor men of a country, in any war, who constituted its soldiery and filled the ranks of its armies; and it was not the rich, but the poor men of a country who constituted the pioneers of its wilderness, and first swept away its forests and cultivated its soil. This would always be the work of those whose pecuniary circumstances compel them to earn their living by the labor of their own hands, and who can only acquire homes where land is cheap and can be made valuable by their own improvements. Such were the soldiers of the Revolution, and vast numbers of them left their residences in the settlements, and pushed their way into western New York.

Mr. W. said he would remind the honorable Senator that the counties of Westchester and Saratoga, perhaps more emphatically than any other portions of New York, except the city, were the seat of war, and still he could not be mistaken in supposing that Oneida, and many other of the comparatively new counties, would be found to be the places of residence of a greater number of revolutionary pensioners than either of the counties he had first named. The reason was obvious. Their populations were much greater, and were composed as much of those who lived and acted in the scenes of that war, as the people of those counties. Indeed, many, who served in the army as citizens of those counties, were now to be found at the West, as emigrants from the old to the new parts of the State. A proper consideration of these facts, he was sure, would convince the honorable Senator that his mode of reasoning was unjust and must lead him to erroneous and unjust conclusions. The supposition that the population of the States had maintained their proportions from the time of the Revolution to the present day, was inadmissible, as contradicting known facts, and to suppose that the soldiers of that seven years' war had remained more stationary than any other equal portion of the population of the States was equally against probability and fact.

Mr. W. said he was glad that the amendment offered by the honorable Senator from New Jersey, directing the call to embrace the line or corps in which each pensioner served, had been adopted, because that would show where these veterans of each State now reside. He was perfectly willing that any proper scrutiny, as to the pensioners residing within his State, should be had, and he had no fear that the call, as now made, would show a greater number of those pensioners from the New York line, or the New York militia, than the proportion which the numbers of those corps, actually in service, would be found to bear to the whole army.

Mr. W. said he felt sure the honorable Senator had not selected New York, so peculiarly, for the purpose of his comparisons, from any invidious motive. He had expressly disavowed any such intention, and he (Mr. W.) should not have been able to convince himself of the existence of such a motive, if the disavowal had not been made. But he must say, it did appear to him, if it had been the sole object of the Senator, reasoning from the premises he had chosen to assume, to have shown the palpable disparity between the troops in service from each State, and the number of pensioners now residing within it, that he might have obtained much stronger instances than that between South Carolina and New York, by turning his attention to the new States of the West. He had told the Senate that the troops furnished by New York and South Carolina were nearly equal, and that the pensioners residing in New York at the present time were eighteen times as many as those residing in South Carolina. If the honorable Senator had taken Ohio, how would his comparison have resulted? Mr. W. said he had not looked at the report to which the gentleman had referred, but he presumed that Ohio now returned a number of pensioners equal to that of South Carolina. [Here Mr. Preston remarked *four times* as many.] Then (said Mr. W.) Ohio has within it four times as many revolutionary pensioners as South Carolina, and Ohio did not furnish a soldier for the service—Ohio did not contain a white man, till years after the war. South Carolina, therefore, furnished just as many more men for the service than Ohio, as the whole number of men she sent into that great struggle, and still Ohio presents four times as many pensioners from that service, as are presented by South Carolina. Here (Mr. W. said) the gentleman had a comparison, not counting in tens, but in thousands, and he would not attempt to establish the rate per cent. advantage to Ohio, but would leave it with the other calculations of the Senator. He must, however, be permitted to suppose that the honorable gentleman would see, from this instance, the palpable injustice of his comparisons, and the erroneous impressions they would be likely to create. According to his positions, Ohio, Indiana, Illinois, Missouri, and the new States at the southwest, ought not to present a pensioner, as they were not inhabited at the time of the war, and therefore presented no troops for the service. Still it was admitted that they all did present pensioners, and surely the gentleman would not contend that the single fact of their not having sent troops into the revolutionary army was proof that all the pension applications from those States were false and fraudulent. On the contrary, the error was, that the honorable Senator had not made allowance for the great changes of location of the inhabitants of the old States, and reflection would satisfy him that the grounds he had assumed, and the conclusions he had drawn, from erroneous premises, were manifestly unjust to some of the States.

Mr. PRESTON replied at length to Mr. Wright and others, commenting extensively upon the whole pension system; and, in the course of his remarks, compared the number of pensioners in New York with those in Ohio, and compared also the populations of the two States, to show that the population of the latter was half that of the former, while the number of persons receiving pensions residing within the latter, was but about one-fifth of the number appearing to reside within the former. Hence he inferred that Mr. Wright's mode of accounting for the great number of pensioners residing in New York, by the emigration to that State from other States, was not supported by facts.

Mr. WRIGHT rejoined. He said he should not be led by the gentleman into a discussion of the pension system; that the resolution before the Senate was a call for information, and he had no disposition to discuss the questions which might arise, when the information should be obtained, in anticipation, or upon a supposed state of facts. He should be ready to meet those questions when the facts were settled, but he must decline wholly attempting to settle them upon hypotheses, and especially in considering a call for the facts. His object, therefore, in rising, at this time, was simply to answer the remarks of the Senator as to the disparity in the number of pensioners between Ohio and New York, and, this done, he would detain the Senate no longer. The answer seemed plain to his mind, and, upon its being suggested, he thought it would be equally plain to the Senate. The revolutionary soldiers were the early emigrants from the old States. They were not modern emigrants, as their ages must necessarily satisfy every gentleman. Western New York was opened to them immediately after the peace of 1783, and they soon began to form settlements there. The territory now composing the State of Ohio was then beyond the reach of settlement, and it was many years after, and when western New York had become measurably full, that the emigration flowed over it into Ohio. Before that period had arrived, most of these old soldiers had fixed themselves down in permanent abodes nearer to the settlements of the old States. Hence, when the tide set most strongly to Ohio, there would have been among the emigrants a much less proportionate number of revolutionary soldiers.

Even now (Mr. W. said) their descendants from western New York were beginning to move on, not into, but beyond, Ohio, into the States of Indiana, Illinois, and Missouri; but few, very few, of these aged patriots would be found among the emigrants. They remained at the homes they had established in their younger days. The weight of years had become too heavy upon them to render them willing again to seek the wilderness, and again to encounter the hardships of a new country. This seemed to him a sufficient reason for the diminution in the number of pensioners as the emigration was followed west.

The discussion was further continued by Messrs. SPRAGUE, EWING, CHAMBERS, PRESTON, FORSYTH, and CALHOUN.

The vacancies on the Committee of Commerce, occasioned by the election of Mr. Foot Governor of Connecticut, and Mr. Lawrence Mayor of New York, have been filled by the appointment of Mr. Gillet and Mr. Lincoln.

The Hon. M. T. Hawkins, who has been absent some eight or ten days at Philadelphia, to consult Dr. Physick, resumed his seat yesterday; and we are gratified to learn that his health is much improved.

THE CONGRESSIONAL GLOBE.

PRINTED AND PUBLISHED AT THE CITY OF WASHINGTON, BY BLAIR & RIVES.

23D CONGRESS, 1ST SESSION.   SATURDAY, JUNE 14, 1834.   VOL. I........No. 28.

IN SENATE.

SATURDAY, June 7, 1834.

A communication was received from the Treasury Department, transmitting a report from the commissioners under the treaty concluded by the Hon. William C. Rives, late Minister to France; which was ordered to be printed, and referred to the Committee on Foreign Relations.

BILLS.

The following bills were read a third time, and passed:

A bill for the relief of Aaron Bellamy;
A bill for the relief of Hannah Stone; and
A bill to increase and regulate the pay of the surgeons and assistant surgeons of the army.

The following bills were considered in committee of the whole, and ordered to be engrossed for a third reading:

A bill for the relief of Francis Barnes;
A bill for the relief of Lucy Loomis;
A bill for the relief of the heirs or legal representatives of Dr. John Berrien, deceased;
A bill for the relief of General James Taylor, late quartermaster general and district paymaster, of the army of the United States;
A bill for the relief of the widow and children of George Ludlum, deceased;
A bill providing for the final settlement of the claims of States for interest on advances to the United States during the last war.

Upon ordering this bill to be engrossed, the yeas and nays were ordered, and are as follows:

YEAS—Messrs. Bell, Chambers, Clay, Clayton, Ewing, Frelinghuysen, Hendricks, Kent, Knight, Leigh, McKean, Naudain, Porter, Preston, Robbins, Shepley, Silsbee, Smith, Sprague, Tomlinson, Webster, and Wilkins—22.

NAYS—Messrs. Benton, Bibb, Black, Calhoun, Grundy, Hill, King of Alabama, King of Georgia, Mangum, Moore, Morris, Preston, Robinson, Tallmadge, Tipton, White, and Wright—17.

A bill for the relief of Andrew Armstrong;
A bill to remunerate Stephen C. Phillips for the support and transportation of shipwrecked American seamen; and

A bill for the relief of Aaron Fitzgerald.

The following bills were laid upon the table:

A bill for the relief of Thomas J. Mortee;
A bill for the relief of Oliver M. Spencer; and
A bill for the relief of the heirs of Alexander Boyd, deceased.

On motion of Mr. CALHOUN,
The Senate adjourned.

HOUSE OF REPRESENTATIVES.

SATURDAY, June 7, 1834.

The following resolution, heretofore offered by Mr. BELL, was adopted:

Resolved, That the Secretary of War be requested to inform the House what part, if any, of the sum of thirty-nine thousand one hundred dollars was expended in the year 1832, in improving the navigation of the Missouri river, and that of the Mississippi above the mouth of the Ohio river.

The following resolution, heretofore offered by Mr. J. Q. ADAMS, was then taken up:

Resolved, That the Secretary of the Treasury be directed to lay before this House the names of the presidents, cashiers, directors, and stockholders, lawyers and solicitors, of all the banks selected by him as depositories of the public moneys, in the place of the Bank of the United States and its branches, together with the amount and stock in said banks, held by each stockholder, and the amount of debt due by each president, cashier, and director, of each of the banks, to said bank, at the time when it was selected as a depository, and at his time.

Mr. CAMBRELENG suggested the propriety of modifying the resolution so as to call for information as to the aggregate amount due from the officers of each institution, without a detailed statement of the debts due from each individual,

which he thought would not promote the public object professed by the gentleman from Massachusetts.

Mr. ADAMS declined making the modification. In many banks the directors had not, in point of fact, a dollar of interest. Shares stand in their names, but they owe the institution the full amount. He wished to ascertain the actual state of these banks, and how their officers stand connected with them in point of interest.

Mr. STEWART moved to amend the resolution by striking out the names of the lawyers and solicitors of these banks. No public object could be promoted by this information. Another reason why he wished this part of the resolution to be struck out was, he was not apprized of the manner in which the Secretary was to be informed of the names of every person who might be employed by these institutions.

Mr. POLK did not perceive the precise object of the information requested by the gentleman from Massachusetts [Mr. ADAMS.] That gentleman had in view, no doubt, a public object. In order to act with perfect fairness in the matter, similar information should be obtained relative to the Bank of the United States. He did not care how far examination was made into the condition of the local banks who were depositories of the public money, if information was obtained *pari passu* from the Bank of the United States. While the proposition of the gentleman from Pennsylvania [Mr. STEWART] was pending, it would not be in order to move the following amendment, which he would send to the Chair, and wished it might be read. He should move it as soon as the proposition before the House was disposed of:

"And that he also communicate to this House the amount of debts due by the president, cashier, and directors of the Bank of the United States, at the time, or at any time within one year last past; and, also, the names of the lawyers and solicitors of the Bank of the United States and branches, and the amount of debt due by each to said bank at this time, and at any time within one year last past."

Mr. COULTER felt no great solicitude as to the amendment proposed by his colleague, [Mr. STEWART,] but should not vote in its favor. These State banks had been made fiscal agents, and, being such, should communicate their condition to the proper authority as well as the manner of their management. If this information was not in the power of the Secretary, it ought to be in his power, as he had made them the agents of the Government. He should regret the adoption of the amendment suggested by the gentleman from Tennessee, [Mr. POLK,] as the question was now before the House in another shape.

Mr. EWING said the object of the modification suggested by himself relative to the lawyers and solicitors, which had been accepted by the gentleman from Massachusetts, [Mr. ADAMS,] was to obtain the names of the individuals who had been bribed to cry down a sound currency, and to promote one of mere rags. When illustrious names are attacked with regard to their connexion with the Bank of the United States, he was anxious to see who were connected with institutions which had been miscalled State banks.

Mr. MILLER trusted the House would adopt the resolution in the shape in which it was presented. He had been glad to perceive that no friend of the Administration had opposed its adoption. He would vote for obtaining this information relative to the State banks; and he hoped the friends of the Bank of the United States would not object to obtaining the same information relative to that institution; he therefore hoped that neither the original resolution, nor the amendment proposed by the gentleman from Tennessee, [Mr. POLK,] would meet with opposition.

Mr. GILLET said he hoped the amendment of the gentleman from Pennsylvania, to strike out so much of the resolution as related to lawyers, solicitors, &c., would not prevail. He wished that

part retained; and hoped to see the proposition of his friend from Tennessee, [Mr. POLK,] which extended the inquiry to the United States Bank, as well as the deposite banks, adopted. It would be recollected that there was on the Speaker's table a proposition to restore the public deposites to the Bank of the United States; and before this House could act understandingly upon that proposition, it ought to be in possession of the information sought for by the proposed amendment. This amendment required the same information of the United States Bank, as the mover of the resolution desires of the deposite banks. He understood it to be conceded, if the information asked for by this resolution should be withheld or denied, or if the facts disclosed should show the public moneys to be in unsafe depositories, that then other depositories should be selected. It seemed to him to be equally important to ascertain the same facts in relation to the United States Bank, before we placed the public money in that institution. The vote on the deposite question might be materially influenced by the information asked for. He could not vote to change the depositee from banks that invite scrutiny, to one that should avoid it, or refuse to give us all the information desired. He desired *all* the facts in relation to the real condition of both the deposite banks and the United States Bank. If either used its funds to aid politicians, and to promote the interest of party, he wished to know it, that the seal of reprobation might be affixed upon it.

Mr. G. said, we had once called for information as to these deposite banks, and our call had been promptly and fully responded to. He believed it would be so in this instance. We ask the same information of the United States Bank. The question is distinctly put to the friends of that bank, will you give us the same information in relation to it that you ask of the deposite banks? He desired the same information from both. We have an equal right to ask of both, and it was our duty to obtain it of both, before we acted on the question of restoration. The reason for desiring the information is equally strong in both cases. We have large sums of money in both, and both are named as the future depository of the public treasure.

Mr. G. said, the friends of the United States Bank had affirmed that the concerns of that institution had been managed with great ability and integrity; and that *all* its transactions were above reproach; and they had expressed the contrary opinion of the deposite banks. On the other hand, the friends of the deposite banks had made equally confident assertions against the United States Bank, and in favor of the selected banks, and had invited the severest scrutiny into their affairs. Here were issues fairly and distinctly made up, and he hoped both would be tried at the same time, and by the same ordeal. Should either refuse the information sought, he should take that refusal as evidence against the bank so refusing. He should esteem every such bank unworthy of public confidence.

Have we not quite as much reason for desiring information of the United States Bank as the others? Information of the United States Bank done so? Has the United States Bank done so?

Mr. G. said, members would bear in mind that the deposites had been removed on charges against the bank of interfering in political affairs, and corrupting the press, &c. And how stands the case as to those charges? This House, by a vote of 174 to 41, had sent a committee to Philadelphia to investigate the truth of these charges. And what had been the result? The committee had returned, and reported to us that they had not been permitted to examine the books of the bank; that the officers of the bank refused to testify; and that they were refused all information sought by the resolutions of this House appointing the committee. Mr. G. inquired, are we to go on blindly, under such circumstances, and give that institution the custody of the public treasure?

28

Do gentlemen who are friendly to the bank expect, in the present situation of affairs, that the nation will presume all is fair, honest, and above impeachment? Do they desire us, with such evidence before us, to vote in the dark? This effort to avoid all scrutiny into the affairs of this bank must have a tendency to confirm all the charges made against it. There could be no other conclusion than that its affairs would not bear the scrutiny of open day.

The friends of the deposite banks do not ask us to vote in the dark. They ask both to be placed upon the same footing, as to inquiries into their management.

If the United States Bank is conducted with as much ability and purity of purpose as its friends allege, certainly neither the bank nor its friends can wish to bar the proposed scrutiny. He should more naturally expect them to challenge the most rigorous investigation into all its transactions. He must express the hope that the friends of the bank would not shrink from the proposed inquiry nor attempt to avoid it, by withdrawing the resolution. Should either be done, he must be at liberty to believe that bank to be unworthy of confidence, and that its doings would not bear the test of public scrutiny. Conscious innocence always invites scrutiny, while guilt avoids it. The bank has in its own possession the evidence which is to decide the charges made against it. If it is innocent of the charges, let us have the proof which is in the custody of the bank. If the bank and its friends refuse us the information asked for, it will be a virtual concession of the guilt of the former, and the people will unhesitatingly condemn it. The proposition to place both banks on the same footing, is a liberal and proper one, and cannot be objected to by either, if all is as it should be. Mr. G. said, no bank ought to have the custody of the public money, which should refuse the information asked for. The friends of the deposite banks challenge the inquiry.

The question was then taken upon Mr. Stewart's proposition to strike out, which was lost without a division.

Mr. POLK then moved the foregoing amendment.

Mr. ADAMS said if the gentleman would make his inquiries precisely coextensive with that proposed by the resolution, he would accept it as a modification. But he could not consent to make inquiries as to the debts due by the lawyers and solicitors of the Bank of the United States, as he had proposed no such inquiry relative to the State banks.

Mr. BEATY moved to amend the amendment proposed by Mr. Polk, by adding the following:

"*Be it further resolved*, That the Secretary also 'inform the House, whether the President of the 'United States, heads of departments, and Treasurer, have been in the habit of keeping their private accounts in the Branch Bank of the United 'States in the city of Washington; and at what time 'did they, or either of them, cease to keep their 'accounts in said branch bank."

Mr. SELDEN suggested to the gentleman from Tennessee, [Mr. Polk,] that the amendment, in its present shape, would prevent the information sought for from being furnished within any reasonable time. It would be necessary to state the balances of each account for every day during an entire year. By introducing the words "United States and its branches," immediately after the banks referred to in the original resolution, the information called for would be coextensive with regard to each class of institutions.

Mr. ADAMS said if the amendment should take that shape, he would accept it as a modification.

Mr. POLK said the question before the House was not upon his amendment, but upon the proposition to amend it moved by the gentleman from Kentucky, [Mr. Beaty.] Had that proposition covered the whole ground, he would not object to it. There was no reason why this inquiry should be confined to the executive officers. Such an inquiry should not be made by piecemeal. He would extend it, not simply to the executive officers, but to the judicial and legislative officers of the Government—not only as to their credit at the bank, but into the state of their indebtedness to the bank. In reply to the objections made to his amendment, he had only to say that, instead of reducing the inquiry in the manner suggested, he would propose to extend the inquiry in the original resolution into the indebtedness of the lawyers and solicitors of the deposite banks to those institutions.

Mr. P. was apprized by the Chair that the hour allotted to morning business had elapsed. His remarks were accordingly suspended.

DISTRICT OF COLUMBIA.

Mr. HUBBARD moved the House go into Committee of the Whole, in execution of the special order of the day; which was agreed to, (Mr. Briggs in the chair.)

The bill for the benefit of the city of Washington, which was under consideration when the committee rose last evening, was again taken up, upon the motion of

Mr. MANN, to strike out the enacting words.

Mr. PARKER supported the motion at length. He felt every disposition to relieve the Corporation and citizens of Washington from the burdens under which they complained of laboring, but could not do it upon the principles on which the passage of this bill had been urged. He could not recognise the right of the Corporation of Washington to value and tax the public property. This Corporation had improvidently involved itself in debt. It was in fact insolvent, and could pay neither principal nor interest. This state of things did not change the relations between the Corporation and the Government. Mr. P. went into an explanation of the original foundation of the city, and of the amount of the expenditures of public money here, and contended that the Corporation had no claim to be relieved from the debts which had been improvidently contracted. But if any constitutional plan should be proposed for a loan to the city by the United States, he would assent to that course, even if the money should never be repaid.

Mr. STODDERT replied in detail to the argument of Mr. Parker. One of the great causes of the embarrassments of the Corporation, was the magnificence of its plan, by which the original proprietors and their descendants have been involved in ruin. This plan was not devised by them, but was imposed on them by Congress. It was projected for the benefit of the Union; and the improvements which had been made were for the benefit of the public. The tax-paying citizens do not exceed in number that of the officers of Government. It was only equitable, that as the expenditures were incurred for the public benefit, that a portion of the expense should be borne by the public.

Mr. SUTHERLAND advocated the bill, and opposed the motion. This city was emphatically the city of the Union. Every portion of the United States felt a deep interest in its prosperity. It concerned very nearly our national pride. When the British, during the last war, undertook to assault our national honor in its tenderest point, the attack was made here. In sustaining this city, the House only supported our country, and our country's honor. When the Father of his country was about to leave this world, he had founded this city, which had been separated from all dependence upon the States, for the exclusive use of the Government. It was never intended to have been built up by the handful of men who followed the Government here. Its extensive plan and broad avenues show this. That glorious city which he in part had the honor to represent, had not been laid out upon a plan of such magnificence. To sustain this great plan had impoverished the corporation. Mr. S. appealed to the memory of Washington, of whom this city was the most worthy monument, in support of his views, and contended that this was not a local, but a national question, upon which the House was bound to vote, not in view of their personal feelings, or private convenience, but in reference to the honor and glory of the country.

After a few words from Mr. McKENNAN, the question was taken on striking out the enacting words; which was lost—yeas 51, nays 80.

Mr. PARKER moved to amend the bill by providing that the money should be applied only to the payment of the interest of the canal debt; but withdrew it, saying that he would offer it in the House.

The bill was then laid aside to be reported.

The bill to subscribe one hundred thousand dollars in aid of the completion of the lateral branch of the Chesapeake and Ohio Canal to Alexandria, was taken up, and explained and advocated by Messrs. STODDERT, EVANS, MERCER, THOMAS of Louisiana, and VINTON, and opposed by Mr. CHILTON, who moved to strike out the enacting clause

The question being taken on the motion, there were, yeas 30, nays 63—not a quorum.

Mr. CHILTON withdrew the motion, and the bill was laid aside to be reported.

The bill to prevent the Corporations of Washington, Georgetown, and Alexandria, from issuing promissory notes of a less denomination than ten dollars, and providing for the withdrawal from circulation of all such notes, was taken up, amended on motion of Mr. CHINN, and laid aside to be reported.

The bill further to amend the act incorporating the Chesapeake and Ohio Canal Company, was taken up, and verbally amended, on motion of Mr. ALLEN, of Virginia.

Mr. W. C. JOHNSON moved to lay aside the bill, in order to bring before the House a memorial which he had received on the subject, and which he hoped would be taken into consideration, together with the bill.

Mr. MERCER suggested that the amendments required by the memorialists, might be offered in the House.

Mr. ALLEN, of Virginia, remarked, that he had no disposition to press the bill, without full consideration.

Mr. JOHNSON withdrew the motion, and the bill was laid aside to be reported.

The bill to incorporate the Washington Insurance Company, was considered, and laid aside to be reported.

The bill to incorporate the Clerks' Saving Company, was considered, and laid aside to be reported.

The bill to amend the charter of the Potomac Fire Insurance Company, of Georgetown, was considered, and laid aside to be reported.

The bill to incorporate the Georgetown Savings Institution, was considered, and laid aside to be reported.

The bill for the relief of Henry Awkward was considered, and laid aside to be reported.

The bill subscribing three hundred and fifty thousand dollars for the construction of a lateral railroad within the District of Columbia, was then taken up.

Mr. MANN, of New York, hoped, he said, that some gentleman would explain the object and policy of this bill. But as he was unwilling, at this time, to bring on a discussion, he would make his objection to the bill in the House.

The bill was then laid aside. to be printed.

On motion of Mr. CHINN, the committee rose, and all the above bills were reported to the House.

On motion of Mr. MERCER, the House went into the Committee of the Whole, on the "bill authorizing the construction of a bridge across the Potomac, and repealing all acts already passed in relation thereto," and other bills, (Mr. Hubbard in the chair.)

The bill being taken up, Mr. STODDERT moved an additional section, making the Aqueduct and Navy Yard bridges free; which was lost.

The bill was then laid aside, to be reported.

The bill "making appropriations for the public buildings and grounds, and for other purposes," being taken up—

Mr. PARKER moved to amend the bill by striking out the enacting clause, but withdrew the amendment.

Mr. E. EVERETT moved an amendment, providing for the removal of the naval monument to some place in the eastern square of the Capitol.

Mr. S. JONES opposed the motion.

After some remarks from Mr. VINTON,

Mr. E. EVERETT modified his motion so as to remove the monument to the Botanic Garden.

Mr. S. JONES would inquire where the Botanic Garden was? To which it was replied that it was somewhere below the Capitol.

The motion was lost.

Mr. MERCER moved to strike out the provision for enclosing the Botanic Garden; which was agreed to.

Mr. PARKER moved to strike out the word "MacAdamizing" in the clause for MacAdamiz

ing the foot and carriage ways north of the President's house.

After a few words from Messrs. STODDERT, FULLER, J. Q. ADAMS, FILLMORE, and HARPER of Pennsylvania, the amendment was agreed to.

Mr. FILLMORE moved to amend the clause, so as to provide for the flagging of the foot-way and paving the carriage-way.

After a few words from Messrs. STODDERT, PARKER, LYTTLE, HARPER of Pennsylvania, JARVIS, MARTINDALE, MERCER, and E. EVERETT, the amendment was negatived.

Mr. PARKER moved to insert "gravelling," so as to provide that the carriage-way should be gravelled; which was agreed to.

Mr. PARKER moved to reduce the appropriation from $13,000 to $10,000; which was lost.

Mr. VINTON moved to amend by inserting $5,000 for the extension of the square west of the Capitol.

After a few remarks from Messrs. VINTON and J. HARPER, the motion was negatived.

Mr. J. HARPER moved to strike out the item for enclosing the ground between the President's House and the canal.

Some remarks were made by Messrs. J. HARPER, S. JONES, and MERCER; when the question was taken, and the motion was carried.

Mr. HARPER made some remarks upon this item appropriating $3,000 for trees for the public grounds; which were replied to by Mr. JARVIS.

The reading of the bill was proceeded in.

Mr. WATMOUGH moved an amendment for applying a deficiency in the appropriation for the public vault at the Congressional Burying-ground; which was agreed to.

The item appropriating $6,000 for additional furniture for the President's House having been read,

Mr. SCHLEY moved to strike out the item.

Mr. WATMOUGH made some remarks in support of the item, and a further explanation from Messrs. JARVIS, EWING, and WARD, when Mr. SCHLEY withdrew the motion.

Mr. E. EVERETT moved an item for restoring the Speaker's chair and seats of the House to the position they were in previous to the late change, $3,000.

After some remarks from Messrs. CLAY, E. EVERETT, EWING, BURD, E. WHITTLESEY, SUTHERLAND, PARKER, MERCER, R. M. JOHNSON, and HARDIN, the proposition was negatived.

Mr. J. Q. ADAMS moved an item, appropriating $1,000 for erecting a monument over the remains of General Jacob Brown; which, after a brief explanation from Mr. A., was agreed to.

The committee then rose, and reported the bills to the House.

The House then adjourned.

IN SENATE.

MONDAY, June 9, 1834.

Mr. ROBBINS presented resolutions adopted by the Legislature of Rhode Island, recommending the restoration of the deposites, and the recharter of the United States Bank.

Mr. McKEAN presented a memorial of like character, signed by 158 inhabitants of Cambria county, Pennsylvania.

Mr. BIBB presented the memorial of inhabitants of Warren county, Kentucky, of a similar nature; all of which were referred to the Committee on Finance, and ordered to be printed.

Mr. WRIGHT presented the memorial of 1831 inhabitants of Ontario county, New York, approving of the course of the Executive in ordering the public deposites to be removed from the Bank of the United States, and opposed to the recharter of that corporation.

Mr. SHEPLEY said he had a distress memorial, signed by a single individual, which he desired should be read. The memorial was signed by Seth Pitts, a soldier of the Revolution, who stated that he did not wish to die until he had atoned for an error that he was forced into, without knowing what he was about; and requested that his name might be erased from a memorial sent to the Senate. He had signed a petition urging Congress to have the deposites restored, and the bank rechartered, when, in truth, he was opposed to the corporation;

thought the Secretary of the Treasury right in the direction that his duty admonished him to give in removing the public funds from the bank; and felt it to be his duty to correct an error, which would relieve him from a load of sin, which would be burdensome to carry across Jordan.

The memorial was referred to the Committee on Finance, and ordered to be printed.

Mr. CHAMBERS presented the petition of A. A. Vanbibber, administrator of the late Purser Garretson, asking that certain allowances may be made in the settlement of the accounts of the deceased.

Mr. CHAMBERS also presented the memorial of Master Commandant George Burd of the navy, asking a pension, on account of a wound received in service; which was referred to the Committee on Naval Affairs.

Mr. WRIGHT asked if it would be in order to make a report from the Committee of Claims. No objection being made, Mr. W. reported that the committee wished to be discharged from the further consideration of the petition of Archibald W. Hamilton, which was agreed to.

Mr. EWING, from the majority of the Committee on the Post Office and Post Roads, made a report condemning the administration of the department, and closing with resolutions censuring the officers engaged in that office.

After the report had been read,

Mr. GRUNDY asked whether it was in order to present to the Chair a paper containing the opinions of two members of the committee, differing very widely in many particulars from that presented by the majority. He proposed to lay before the Senate the opinions of the minority of the committee upon most of the subjects treated of in that paper. He moved that it be received and read, and remarked that he thought each would be better understood after both had been heard.

Mr. EWING said the minority gave the chairman of the committee information of the several subjects designed to be treated of by them in their report. The object was to arrive at truth, and he hoped the views of the minority would be received.

Mr. GRUNDY remarked that the statement of the gentleman from Ohio was correct as to the course pursued in the investigation. The report he had never seen or heard read, chiefly because he had no desire to hear it, but he found from hearing it read now that two or three cases of contracts were alluded to which he (Mr. G.) must have forgotten, for he had not noticed them in his paper.

Mr. G. then presented the views of the minority, not as a report, but as a paper; which was received and read.

After some conversation between Messrs. EWING, GRUNDY, and FORSYTH, the printing of the two documents was ordered.

Mr. SOUTHARD moved that fifteen thousand extra copies of the report be printed for distribution; which was opposed by Mr. FORSYTH; and upon which the yeas and nays were asked by Mr. WRIGHT.

Mr. CHAMBERS moved that the Senate adjourn; which was negatived; when

The motion to print the extra copies was, on motion of Mr. SWIFT, postponed till to-morrow.

ADJOURNMENT OF CONGRESS.

The joint resolution from the House of Representatives, fixing upon the 30th of June for the adjournment of Congress, was then taken up for consideration.

On motion of Mr. McKEAN, the resolution was amended by striking out "30th of June," and inserting "30th instant;" which was adopted.

The resolution as amended was then concurred in.

Mr. POINDEXTER then moved to take up the bill providing for the meeting of the next session of Congress prior to the first Monday in December; which was agreed to.

After some conversation between Messrs. POINDEXTER, CLAY, WEBSTER, and CALHOUN,

Mr. POINDEXTER moved to lay the bill on the table; which was agreed to.

Mr. WILKINS gave notice that he should move on Thursday next to take up the bill authorizing a subscription to several copies of the Diplomatic Code, published by Jonathan Elliot, of this city.

Mr. CLAY moved that the additional names of subscribers to petitions, for and against the removal of the deposites and the renewal of the charter of the Bank of United States, which had been received posterior to the former order of the Senate, requiring their classification, should also be made out by the Secretary; which was adopted.

Mr. POINDEXTER, from the Committee of Public Lands, asked to be discharged from the further consideration of the petition of Edward and George Phelps and George Weed. Agreed to.

Mr. POINDEXTER, from the same committee, reported a bill for the removal of the Land Office from Clinton to Jackson, in Mississippi; which was read a first time, and ordered to a second reading.

On motion of Mr. CHAMBERS,
The Senate adjourned.

HOUSE OF REPRESENTATIVES.

MONDAY, June 9, 1834.

Mr. MILLER asked the unanimous consent of the House to take up the resolution submitted by the gentleman from Massachusetts, [Mr. J. G. ADAMS,] calling for information in relation to the deposite banks.

Objections having been made—

The House resumed the consideration of the memorial from citizens of York county, Pennsylvania, praying for a change of measures on the part of the Government, in relation to the United States Bank and the currency, presented on the last petition day.

Mr. BARNITZ spoke at some length in support and explanation of the views of the memorialists; when the memorial was laid on the table.

Mr. POLK rose to ask the consent of the House to take up the appropriation bills on the table, which, in his opinion, were of more importance than the presentation of memorials at this late stage of the session.

Objections being made—

Mr. POLK moved to suspend the rules setting apart this day for the reception of memorials, in order to take up the appropriation bills.

Mr. WISE hoped (he said) the gentleman would withdraw his motion, and if he did not, he should make it a question of order. He had made a motion, three weeks ago, to refer a memorial on the subject of the deposites to a select committee, with instructions to report certain resolutions, and he had hoped to be permitted to obtain for that motion the consideration of the House.

Mr. POLK said he should not withdraw the motion, but if the House chose to hear speeches on an old and trite subject, in preference to proceeding with the public business, they would refuse to suspend the rules.

Mr. WISE remarked that his resolution related to a subject entirely new.

Mr. DENNY said, that the reception of memorials was as important as any business which could be transacted, and he asked the yeas and nays on the motion; which were ordered.

Mr. PARKER said, that if the House did not sustain the motion, we must spend the whole day in presenting memorials, and hearing speeches.

Mr. WILLIAMS remarked, that the object in setting apart this day, was not to make speeches, but to present memorials and petitions, which was a constitutional right. The speeches were incidental to the presentation of the memorials.

The CHAIR stated that the memorial presented by the gentleman from Virginia, [Mr. WISE,] on a former day, was first in order. Next to that, memorials and petitions were in the order of proceeding. The motion to suspend the rule was strictly in order.

Mr. BURGES said a word or two against the motion.

The question being then taken on the motion to suspend the rules, it was determined in the negative—yeas 113, nays 66, (not two-thirds.)

Mr. MILLER moved the suspension of the rules, in order to take up for consideration the resolution submitted by the gentleman from Massachusetts [Mr. ADAMS] respecting the deposite banks.

The CHAIR pronounced the motion to be out of order, as no business had intervened between the motion and the refusal of the House to sus-

pend the rule on the motion of the gentleman from Tennessee.

The House proceeded to consider the memorial of sundry citizens of the county of Gloucester, in the State of Virginia, protesting against the removal of the deposites, together with the following resolutions, submitted by Mr. WISE:

Resolved, That the custody and control of the moneys of the United States, not appropriated by law, and not disbursed under appropriations by law, are, by the Constitution, placed under the order and direction of the Congress of the United States, which order and direction must be made by law in the form of bills or joint orders, votes or resolutions, upon which the President of the United States has simply the power of a negative, subject to a vote of two-thirds of each House of Congress.

Resolved, That no change of the Constitution of the United States is necessary to authorize the Congress of the United States to intrust the custody of the public money, not appropriated by law, and not disbursed under appropriations by law, whenever or howsoever obtained, to other agency than that of the Executive Department, and that the custody of the public money must not be necessarily, under the Constitution, intrusted to the Executive Department.

Resolved, That Congress can take out of the hands of the Executive Department the custody of the public property or money, without an assumption of Executive power, or a subversion of the first principles of the Constitution.

And that said committee be further instructed to report such measures as it may deem necessary and proper to provide for the future safe-keeping, control, and disposition of the public property and moneys, and to assert, maintain, and protect the constitutional powers of Congress over the public property and public purse.

Mr. WISE proceeded to address the House for about two hours and a half upon the general principles asserted in the resolutions. When he had concluded—

Mr. PEYTON replied at length to several of the positions taken by Mr. WISE in his speech, and concluded by moving the amendment heretofore offered by him, as follows:

Resolved, That the President of the United States, in the late executive proceedings in relation to the public revenue, has not assumed "upon himself authority and power not conferred by the Constitution and laws," but that he has acted in conformity to both.

Resolved, That the Senate of the United States, in a late resolution passed by that body, in the words following to wit: "*Resolved*, That the 'President in the late executive proceedings in 'relation to the public revenue, has assumed upon 'himself authority and power not conferred by the 'Constitution and laws, but in derogation of both'" —have, by that resolution, adopted, not with a view to legislative action, but as a solemn censure upon the President, infringed upon the rightful and legitimate powers and prerogatives of the House of Representatives.

Resolved, That Congress has the power, by law, to select the placeas of depositing the public money, and providing for its safe-keeping.

Mr. MILLER moved to lay the whole subject on the table.

Mr. WISE moved a call of the House; which was ordered.

After the call had been some time proceeded in—

Mr. E. WHITTLESEY moved a suspension of the call; upon which

Mr. CLAY asked the yeas and nays; which were ordered.

Mr. E. WHITTLESEY withdrew his motion to suspend the call.

The Clerk then proceeded a second time to call the names of the absentees.

Mr. WILDE moved a suspension of the call, upon which the yeas and nays were ordered.

Mr. W. said, as his object was to save the time of the House, and not to waste it, he would withdraw the motion.

The call was again proceeded in.

Mr. MANN, of Pennsylvania, moved to suspend the call, upon which the yeas and nays were ordered.

Mr. M. withdrew the motion, and the call was proceeded in.

Mr. WILDE renewed the motion—to suspend the call; upon which,

Mr. MANN, of New York, demanded the yeas and nays; which were ordered.

The question being taken, it was determined in the affirmative: Yeas 117, nays 63.

So the call of the House was suspended.

Mr. BEARDSLEY moved that the House do now adjourn; upon which the yeas and nays were ordered.

The motion was lost: Yeas 79, nays 115.

The question being on Mr. MILLER's motion to lay the resolution, with the amendment, on the table, it was taken by yeas and nays, and determined in the affirmative: Yeas 105, nays 97.

On motion of Mr. WHITE, of New York, The House adjourned.

IN SENATE.

Mr. SOUTHARD presented a memorial from inhabitants of Hunterdon county, New Jersey, in favor of a restoration of the deposites to the Bank of the United States, and the recharter of that corporation.

Mr. WEBSTER presented a memorial from Mercer county, Pennsylvania, of similar import; both of which were referred to the Committee on Finance, and ordered to be printed.

Mr. BLACK presented a memorial from the members of the Mississippi bar, praying that the district court of the United States may be removed from Natchez to Jackson; which was referred to the Committee on the Judiciary.

Mr. SILSBEE, from the Committee on Commerce, reported a bill extending the limits, as a port of entry, of the Northern Liberties of Philadelphia: which was read a first and second time.

Mr. EWING presented a memorial from the county of Hamilton, Ohio, stating that the Senate, agreeably to the Constitution, possessed appointing powers as well as the Executive. The memorial was ordered to be printed, and laid on the table.

Mr. BIBB, from the Committee on the Judiciary, reported a bill in favor of James and Samuel Smith; which was read, and ordered to a second reading.

Mr. TIPTON, from the Committee on Military Affairs, asked to be discharged from the further consideration of the memorials of officers of the army asking compensation of land for services rendered during the late war; which was agreed to.

Mr. WEBSTER, from the Committee on Finance, asked to be discharged from the resolution of Mr. WRIGHT, compensating Mr. Potter, who was returned a member of the Senate by the Legislature of Rhode Island, but refused a seat. The committee was discharged.

Mr. WRIGHT offered the following resolution: Whereas the Hon. Elisha R. Potter did, at the commencement of the present session of Congress, come to be laid before the Senate a commission from the Governor of the State of Rhode Island, duly authenticated, and constituting the regular *prima facie* evidence to enable him to a seat in the Senate; and whereas the contest for the seat obtained by Mr. Potter was not finally decided by the Senate until the 27th of May, now last past, when the said seat was awarded to Mr. Asher Robbins:

Therefore *Resolved*, That the said Elisha R. Potter is entitled to the compensation of mileage allowed by law to members of Congress, for his travel from his place of residence, in the State of Rhode Island, to the Capitol, and returning, and

also to the per diem allowance of a member of Congress for the time he actually attended at the city of Washington during the contest pending before the Senate, in relation to the seat claimed by him and occupied by the Hon. Mr. Robbins.

Mr. WRIGHT, from the Committee of Claims, asked to be discharged from the further consideration of the petition of Archibald W. Hamilton; which was agreed to.

Mr. CHAMBERS, from the Committee on the District of Columbia, reported a bill for the relief of Georgetown and Alexandria, giving each of those cities $15,000 annually, for three years; which was read twice.

Mr. HENDRICKS, from the Committee on Roads and Canals, reported a bill granting the right of way to the Winchester and Potomac Railroad Company through the public property at Harper's Ferry. Read twice.

Mr. TOMLINSON, from the Committee on Pensions, reported a bill for the relief of Noah Miller.

Mr. ROBBINS, from the Committee on the Library, reported a bill providing for the erection of the statue of Jefferson, presented to his countrymen by Lieutenant Levy, of the navy, in the public square, east of the Capitol.

The bill for the relief of Oliver M. Spencer, being under consideration, a debate of some length ensued.

The principle in this bill was to refund a sum of money paid by Oliver M. Spencer for a tract of land bought of the Government, which fell short of the quantity about fifty acres; the survey by the Government officer being admitted to have been erroneous.

The bill was opposed on the ground that the rule of *caveat emptor* should apply in full force; and that to relax the rule would open the door to endless applications of disappointed purchasers for redress.

On the other side, the bill was supported on the ground that the injury done to Spencer was entirely the result of mistake on the part of the officer of Government, and the person having purchased and paid his money on the representation of the Government, and the deficiency not being at the time known, every principle of law and equity required that he should be refunded the excess of purchase money.

Messrs. POINDEXTER, MOORE, and PRENTISS, spoke in favor of the bill, and Messrs. BLACK, FORSYTH, BIBB, CLAY, EWING, KING of Alabama, PRESTON, and CHAMBERS, in opposition to the bill.

After some immaterial amendments, the question being on the engrossment of the bill for a third reading—

Mr. MOORE asked the yeas and nays; which were ordered, and are as follow, to wit:

YEAS—Messrs. Benton, Clayton, Ewing, Frelinghuysen, Grundy, Hendricks, Kane, King of Alabama, Knight, Linn, Moore, Poindexter, Prentiss, Robinson, Southard, Tyler, Waggaman—11.

NAYS—Messrs. Bell, Bibb, Black, Brown, Calhoun, Chambers, Clay, Forsyth, Hill, King of Georgia, Leigh, Mangum, Morris, Naudain, Preston, Robbins, Shepley, Smith, Sprague, Swift, Tallmadge, Tipton, Tomlinson, White, Wilkins—25.

So the question was determined in the negative, and the bill was rejected.

The special orders being postponed, the Senate resumed the consideration of the motion made yesterday by Mr. SOUTHARD, to print thirty thousand extra copies of the reports of the Post Office Committee.

Messrs. SOUTHARD, EWING, CLAYTON, and WEBSTER, spoke at length in support of the motion and the report of the majority of the committee, who were followed by

Mr. GRUNDY, chairman of the committee, in support of the views of the minority, expressing his willingness to vote for six thousand extra copies of the reports, that being the highest number of any other report for which he had ever had the printing of thirty thousand extra copies.

He thought useless and extravagant.

Mr. FORSYTH spoke in opposition to printing so large and useless a number, which he estimated would cost $17,500. Mr. F. did not justify the borrowing of money by the department.

ant authority of law; but contended that it was not without precedent in the history of the Government. That two instances of the sort had occurred, which made two Presidents of the United States. He alluded to a sum of $250,000 borrowed by Mr. Monroe, when Secretary of War, on the responsibility of that department, and remitted it to General Jackson at New Orleans, at that important crisis which resulted in the victory of New Orleans. He contended, however, that in both instances, the loans were for the use of the respective departments—but that a report of the sums borrowed should have been made to Congress.

Before any question was taken on the motion to print—

On motion of Mr. PRESTON, at five o'clock, The Senate adjourned.

HOUSE OF REPRESENTATIVES.

TUESDAY, June 10, 1834.

The following resolution, offered by Mr. GARLAND, by consent, was adopted:

Resolved, That the Committee on the Post Office and Post Roads be instructed to inquire into the expediency of establishing a post route from Opelousas, in the State of Louisiana, by the Bayou Large, and the Atchafalaya, in connexit with the principal mail route from New Orleans to Natchez, such point as may be deemed most convenient by the Postmaster General.

The following resolution, also presented by Mr. GARLAND, was adopted:

Resolved, That the Committee on Commerce be directed to inquire into the expediency of making an appropriation for the purpose of replacing the buoys that were placed on the coast of Louisiana, to mark out the channel from the vicinity of the Lighthouse on Point au Fer into Atchafalaya Bay, which have been sunk or destroyed.

ADJOURNMENT OF CONGRESS.

Mr. HUBBARD moved that the resolution fixing the day of adjournment, returned by the Senate, with an amendment, be taken up:

Mr. WILDE objected.

Mr. HUBBARD moved the suspension of the rules for the purpose.

Mr. SPEIGHT suggested that there was no necessity for suspending the rules, as the resolution could soon come up in order.

Mr. HUBBARD persisted in his motion; which was agreed to.

The amendment of the Senate, which was substituting the word "instant," instead of "next," in connexion with the 30th of June, the day designated as that on which the two Houses should adjourn, was then concurred in without a division.

Mr. ASHLEY moved that the Committee of the Whole be discharged from the consideration of the bill to establish an additional land office in Missouri, and that it be brought into the House; which was agreed to.

Mr. McINTIRE, from the Committee on Claims, reported a bill for the relief of Daniel Homans; which was read twice, and committed.

Mr. POLK, from the Committee of Ways and Means, reported a bill from the Senate for the relief of the Roman Catholic Church at St. Louis, Missouri, with a recommendation that the same be rejected. The bill was referred to the Committee of the Whole.

Mr. C. P. WHITE, from the Committee on Naval Affairs, reported a bill to provide for the instruction of three steam-batteries; which was read twice, and committed.

Mr. PARKER, from the same committee, reported a bill establishing the ration for the navy; which was read twice, and committed.

Mr. MERCER, from the Committee on Roads & Canals, reported the following resolutions:

Resolved, That the Committee of the Whole, which was referred the bill authorizing a subscription to the stock of the Chesapeake and Ohio canal, be discharged from the further consideration thereof, and that it be referred to the Committee of the Whole on the state of the Union.

Resolved, That the report and estimate of the cost of improving the chute through the Great falls of the Ohio, be referred to the Committee on Roads and Canals, and be printed.

Mr. MERCER obtained permission to lay the following additional rule on the table:

"When any motion is depending before the 'House, whether of the nature of an original reso-'lution, a bill, or an amendment thereof, it shall 'be in order for any member entitled to the floor 'to move ' that the debate on such motion shall 'cease;' and if this motion be seconded by a ma-'jority of the House, it shall be put without fur-'ther debate; and if adopted by the House, the 'motion depending shall be put without further 'delay; provided that a call of the House may be 'moved prior to the final vote thereon."

Mr. HEATH moved to suspend the rules, in order that the joint resolution authorizing a subscription to Barney's Chart of Bills of Exchange be taken up.

The motion was negatived without a division.

Mr. R. M. JOHNSON moved that the bill extending the time for locating land warrants for military services during the late war be taken up.

The House having assented, the bill was read.

After a verbal amendment, made on suggestion of Mr. E. WHITTLESEY, the bill was ordered to be engrossed.

Mr. VINTON presented an amendment, providing for the suppression of lottery offices in the city of Washington, which he proposed to move when the bill prohibiting the issuing of small notes within the District shall come up; which he moved be laid on the table, and printed.

KENTUCKY CONTESTED ELECTION.

The order of the day being the contested election, it was then taken up.

The question was upon the amendment moved by Mr. BANKS to the resolution reported by the Committee of Elections, as proposed to be amended by Mr. POPE, as follows:

Resolved, That the votes of A. Kavenaugh, Geo. Elliott, jr., Moses Bryant, John Shipman, Shelton Vorris, John D. Stone, M. B. Moseley, William Wooley, Cornelius Naves, James Moorman, Robert Figg, John Cornett, and George Catlett, be stricken from Mr. Letcher's poll, it having been proved that they were minors at the time of the election.

Resolved, That the votes of Wm. Quinn, John McCoy, and William Wright, who voted in Garrard and Lincoln counties; and of Greenbury Peyton and William Welsh, who voted in Jessamine county, and Elijah Carlton, who voted in Mercer county, be stricken from Mr. Letcher's poll; it having been proved that they were not citizens of Kentucky at the time of the election.

Resolved, That the vote of Rowland Shields ought to be counted for Mr. Moore on the Lincoln poll-book, it having been wrongfully stricken off by the judges of the election.

Resolved, That the vote of John Brady be taken from Mr. Letcher's poll, and counted on that of Mr. Moore, on the ground that he had, in the first instance, bona fide, and without mistake, voted for Mr. Moore.

Mr. POPE proposed to modify his amendment by adding several names to those whom he proposed, by the amendment, to strike from the poll of Mr. Letcher.

Mr. BANKS, who was entitled to the floor when this subject was last under consideration, replied, in detail, to the argument heretofore made by Mr. Pope in support of his amendment.

Mr. P. DICKERSON said: Mr. Speaker, I must ask the indulgence of the House for but a few minutes, whilst I express my views of the subject now under discussion. It is now proposed further to amend the original resolution, by striking out of the list of voters the names of some persons who are alleged to have been minors at the time of the election. I shall vote against this amendment for the same reason that I have heretofore voted against all the amendments which have been proposed.

The object of the present inquiry and discussion, is, to ascertain the person entitled to represent the Fifth Congressional District of Kentucky upon this floor. The result of that inquiry should be a resolution declaring the person entitled to the seat. The committee have reported such resolution, declaring that Thomas P. Moore is entitled to the seat. And I contend that, according to the correct

course of proceeding, and to all precedents, no proper amendment can be proposed to that resolution, except to strike out the name of Mr. Moore, and insert that of Mr. Letcher. I therefore have voted against all the amendments which have hitherto been proposed, and shall continue to vote against all of a similar character that may be hereafter proposed.

Before I can vote for an amendment to any resolution, I must be first satisfied, not only that the principle contained in the proposed amendment is correct, but that it is proper to add it, by way of amendment, to the original resolution. The term amendment, implies that the proposition proposed to be amended is imperfect, either in form or substance. It cannot be pretended that the present resolution is defective in form; and if it be wrong in substance, it is in respect to the person named therein, and not otherwise. I therefore insist that no sufficient reason can be shown, why the several amendments which have already been adopted, or that which is now proposed, should be attached to the original resolution reported by the committee in this case.

Permit me to call the attention of the House to the form which their resolution, with the amendments, will present, when completed according to the present plan. The original resolution declares, that one of the candidates is entitled to his seat. This settles the question fully and definitively, and concludes the whole subject. We shall then have, by way of amendment, a number of propositions containing the very matter which should be the basis of the arguments in support of the original resolution, but which to my view appear entirely misplaced when used as amendments to that resolution.

As to precedent, I have examined the journals of the proceedings of this House, from the formation of our Government to this time, and I believe that no precedent can be found to justify the present course of proceeding. In similar cases, the resolutions are almost all reported, and adopted in the simplest form, declaring who is entitled to the seat.

I find, however, two cases in which efforts were made to attach to the resolution some qualification of a similar character to those now proposed. In the case of the contested election in 1807, between William McCreery and Joshua Barney of Maryland, the Committee of Elections made a report in these words:

"Resolved, That William McCreery, having 'the greatest number of votes, and being duly qualified, 'agreeably to the Constitution of the United States, is 'entitled to his seat in this House."

The Committee of the Whole House, after argument, struck out the words, "having the greatest number of votes, and being duly qualified agreeably to the Constitution of the United States," by a vote of 70 to 37. A motion was then made to insert the words, "by having the qualifications prescribed by the laws of Maryland," after the words William McCreery, but it was negatived by a vote of 92 to 8; and the resolution, in its simple form, was adopted by a vote of 88 to 18. In this case, the matter which was proposed by way of amendment, must have been true, and yet the House decided, and I think correctly, that it should not form a part of the resolution, nor be inserted by way of amendment to the same.

A similar course was pursued in the case of Philip B. Key, of Maryland, whose election was contested by some of his electors in 1808. In that case the resolution reported was, "That Philip B. Key, having the greatest number of votes and being qualified agreeably to the Constitution of the United States, is entitled to his seat in this House." The House struck out the words "having the greatest number of votes," &c., by a vote of 79 to 28, and, judging the resolution in its most simple form, which was adopted by a vote of only 57 to 52. These two cases show the practice in this House, and I think establish the true rule: that the resolution in such cases should express only the result of the investigation, and not the grounds or arguments which have led to that result. These are my views upon the subject, and such as have governed my votes upon this occasion. But as it appears that a majority of the House are disposed to adopt a different course, and in fact to argue this ques-

tion by taking the ayes and noes, I certainly do not feel disposed to interfere with their views. But I would respectfully submit, that a due respect to former precedents, and to the form of your resolution, would require, that after the House shall have finished the discussion by taking the ayes and noes upon the several proposed amendments, they will restore the resolution reported by the committee to its original simplicity of form, either by the operation of the previous question, or by such other course as may better suit the feelings of the House.

Mr. HARDIN opposed the amendment by a few remarks.

Mr. POPE made a further explanation of his views in offering the amendment. The House having, by its former votes, gone behind the doings of the committee in favor of one party, should give similar benefit to the other. For himself, he was originally opposed to the course. But it having been adopted, the principle ought to be impartially applied. Mr. P. went into an explanation relative to the names contained in his proposition, by referring, in detail, to the printed testimony. Mr. P. concluded by modifying his amendment, by striking of three names contained in his amendment, as originally offered.

Mr. MARSHALL, after some remarks, moved to amend the amendment by striking off certain names from the poll of Mr. MOORE.

Mr. MOORE, of Virginia, suggested that the question had better be taken first on the proposition of the gentleman from Kentucky [Mr. POPE.]

After some conversation between Messrs. POPE, HARDIN, MARSHALL, and C. ALLAN, as to the mode of proceeding,

Mr. MARSHALL withdrew his amendment.

Mr. JONES, of Georgia, made some statements and explanations relative to the names of voters in the amendment.

Mr. MOORE mentioned certain votes upon which he wished the question to be taken separately.

Mr. SUTHERLAND, after adverting to the late period of the session, the press of important business, and the impossibility of arriving at any result this session, if we went on in this way, strongly urged the House to meet the question at once, and decide, from the facts before them, which of the claimants is entitled to the seat.

Mr. BURGES suggested that if the previous question was resorted to, we should have to decide, without farther investigation, whether Mr. Letcher was elected by a majority of twelve votes or not. The gentleman from Pennsylvania did not probably intend to invite the House to vote Mr. Letcher in, and it would be still more extraordinary if he wished them to vote for Mr. MOORE.

Mr. FOSTER wished, he said, to decide the question to-day, and he would sit here, with a majority of the House, till midnight for that purpose. Let us, said he, appoint two tellers, and take the question on each individual vote. In this way we could ascertain who was elected. We could not vote upon all the names in mass. That would be to guess at a result.

Mr. SUTHERLAND made a few remarks in support of his previous suggestions.

Mr. MARSHALL submitted a substitute for the proposition of Mr. Pope, including in the substitute the several names proposed to be excepted by himself and by his colleague [Mr. POPE.]

Mr. FILLMORE suggested that the readiest mode of arriving at a correct result would be to take the question upon each name separately.

Mr. LANE said, it was perfectly apparent that we might go on till the end of the session with this discussion, without obtaining a decision of the question. As few gentlemen appeared now to be prepared to act on this subject, he moved the postponement of its further consideration till to-morrow week.

Mr. LYTLE said, the discussion had gone to an extent which must satisfy any one that the House, having left the principles of the committee, will take at least three months before they arrived at a conclusion. Believing that the House was as well prepared now as it would ever be to decide the question, he called for the previous question.

Mr. WILDE asked what would be the effect of the previous question?

The CHAIR stated that the effect would be to

obtain the question on the original resolution reported from the committee, as amended by the House.

Mr. HUBBARD made some remarks on the point of order.

Mr. MANN, of New York, asked whether the Chair had decided that the previous question would not cut off the amendments which had been adopted?

The CHAIR had so decided.

Mr. MANN hoped, then, that the motion for the previous question would be withdrawn.

Mr. LYTLE said he would withdraw it for the present.

Mr. LANE withdrew the motion to postpone.

The question then being on the substitute offered by Mr. MARSHALL—

Mr. MARSHALL said he would withdraw it, and offer it in paragraphs, as amendments to the proposition of his colleague, [Mr. POPE.]

The question being then on Mr. POPE's amendment, it was taken separately on each name.

The question on striking off the name of A. Kavenaugh from the poll of Mr. LETCHER was taken by yeas and nays, and decided in the affirmative—yeas 151, nays 50.

The names of George Elliott, jr., Moses Bryant, John Shipman, and L. Harris, were also severally stricken off.

The question being taken, by yeas and nays, on striking off the name of John Floyd, it was determined in the negative—yeas 48, nays 143.

The question was then taken upon striking off the name of Jeremiah Anderson.

After some observations by Messrs. HARDIN, FILLMORE, LANE, S. JONES, MERCER, J. HARPER, VINTON, McKINLEY, and GILMER,

Mr. LYTLE moved the previous question.

Mr. HUBBARD inquired what was the main question, and whether it was divisible?

The CHAIR stated the main question to be upon the adoption of the resolutions reported by the Committee on Elections, and expressed how far it was divisible.

The previous question was not seconded—yeas 100, nays 102.

Mr. BURGES moved the House adjourn; but, on the yeas and nays being ordered, he withdrew the motion.

Mr. ANTHONY renewed the motion to adjourn, on which the yeas and nays were ordered.

The motion was lost—yeas 66, nays 145.

Mr. S. JONES demanded the yeas and nays on striking out the name of Anderson; which were ordered.

The motion to strike out was negatived—yeas 99, nays 103.

The previous question was again demanded by Mr. LYTLE.

Mr. McKENNAN inquired whether, if the previous question was sustained, it would be in order to substitute the name of R. P. Letcher for that of T. P. Moore in the resolution.

The CHAIR explained, that if the House negatived the resolution declaring Mr. Moore entitled to the seat, it would be competent to offer another, declaring Mr. Letcher entitled to it.

The call for the previous question was sustained: Yeas 105, nays 96.

Mr. MARSHALL moved a call of the House.

The call was ordered: Yeas 119, nays 85.

The call was ordered, and sixteen members answered to their names.

Mr. WARD moved the suspension of the call.

Mr. HARDIN demanded the yeas and nays.

Mr. WARD then withdrew his motion.

The call then proceeded.

After various members had been excused—

Mr. MANN moved the call to be suspended; on which

Mr. HARDIN called for the yeas and nays; which were ordered.

The suspension of the call was carried: Yeas 123, nays 85.

The question, "Shall the main question be now put?" was propounded.

Mr. HARDIN moved that the House adjourn, and demanded the yeas and nays; which were ordered.

The motion to adjourn was negatived: Yeas 29, nays 152.

Mr. MERCER moved to reconsider the vote he had given to strike out sundry votes from the poll of Mr. Letcher.

The CHAIR decided the motion was not in order, the House having sustained the previous question, which the higher order of privileged questions.

Mr. MERCER appealed from the decision of the Chair, and supported his appeal at length.

Mr. W. R. DAVIS inquired whether the vote, the reconsideration of which was moved, had been given before or after the previous question was moved.

The CHAIR said, the vote was given before the previous question was moved.

Mr. E. EVERETT asked for the reading of the 41st rule; which was done accordingly.

Mr. CLAY supported the decision of the Chair, and called for the reading of the 35th rule of the House; which was read.

Mr. LYTLE made some remarks, which was replied to by Mr. MERCER.

The question was further debated by Messrs. WILDE, THOMAS, VINTON, SPEIGHT, FOSTER, LYTLE, and McKENNAN; when

Mr. MERCER withdrew the motion to consider and his appeal.

Mr. McKENNAN asked if it was in order to call the attention of the House to the fact that, according to the amendments adopted by the House, Robert P. Letcher had a majority of the votes, and was therefore elected.

The CHAIR pronounced that it was not in order.

The reading of the resolutions as amended was called for, and they were read.

Mr. MARSHALL asked that the statements of the deductions from votes, &c., should be read from the report of the Committee of Elections. [Loud cries of order.]

The CHAIR decided that it was not in order, as it was in the "nature of an argument."

Mr. MARSHALL appealed from the decision of the Chair.

The question being taken on the appeal, the decision of the Chair was sustained.

The question then being, "Shall the main question be now put?" it was taken by yeas and nays, and determined in the negative—yeas 108, nays 112.

Mr. HARDIN moved the House adjourn; which was carried.

The House then adjourned.

IN SENATE.

WEDNESDAY, June 11, 1834.

Mr. EWING presented the petition of Ralph Vanhorn, of Indiana, a mail contractor, complaining that the department has not paid him the sum due for carrying the mail; which was referred to the Committee on the Post Office and Post Roads.

Mr. McKEAN presented the proceedings of a public meeting held in Crawford county, Pennsylvania, recommending a restoration of the deposites to the Bank of the United States, repudiating the right of the President to send a protest to the Senate; complaining of the Executive's removing bank directors who had been rejected; remonstrating against the withholding information condemning the course of the President in refusing to hold interviews with committees of the people, and finding fault that no legislative course of action to settle the currency has been proposed. The proceedings were referred to the Committee on Finance, and ordered to be printed.

Mr. PRESTON presented the petition of Hannah Grobbes, which was laid upon the table.

Mr. PRESTON presented resolutions adopted at a meeting of citizens of Chester District, South Carolina, recommending a restoration of the deposites to the Bank of the United States, and disapproving of the protest of the President lately sent to the Senate. The resolutions were referred to the Committee on Finance, and ordered to be printed.

REPORTS.

Mr. KANE, from the Committee on Private Land Claims, reported a bill, without amendment,

from the House of Representatives, confirming certain land claims in the district of St. Stephens, in Alabama; which was ordered to be engrossed for a third reading.

Mr. SMITH, from the Committee on the Judiciary, asked to be discharged from the further consideration of the petition of Elizabeth Scott; which was agreed to.

Mr. BENTON, from the Committee on Military Affairs, reported a bill for the relief of Captain William Monroe; which was read, and ordered to a second reading.

Mr. TOMLINSON, from the Committee on Pensions, reported a bill for the relief of Captain James Hamilton, which, agreeably to instructions, he moved should be indefinitely postponed; which was agreed to.

Mr. TALLMADGE, from the Committee on Pensions, asked to be discharged from the further consideration of the petition of Edward Blake; which was concurred in.

Mr. MOORE, from the Committee on Public Lands, reported a bill for the relief of Susan Marlow; which was read, and ordered to a second reading.

Also, a bill for the relief of Samuel Smith and others, upon which the same order was taken.

Mr. ROBBINS, from the Committee on the Library, reported a resolution for the distribution of the Diplomatic Correspondence; which was read, and ordered to a second reading.

On motion of Mr. BIBB, all the orders were postponed, and the Senate proceeded to the consideration of the report of the select committee relative to the election of

PRESIDENT AND VICE PRESIDENT.

The question being on the adoption of the amendment reported by the select committee, in lieu of the resolution submitted by Mr. Bibb at the commencement of the session—

Mr. BIBB said it was his desire to avoid discussion upon the subject. The session was far advanced, and he thought the minds of gentlemen must be made up in relation to it.

Mr. FORSYTH asked that the resolution and amendment might be read; which was done.

Mr. LEIGH made a few observations in opposition to any consideration of this subject at this time. He thought the proposed amendment in the system of choosing a President and Vice President would be productive of much more confusion and inconvenience than the present. Almost every State in the Union had the vanity to think that some one of its citizens was qualified for the office of President of the United States, and the consequence would be, that each State would have its candidate, and those of the largest States would invariably have the best prospects of success. He thought the system of management, which prevailed to some extent, would fall into the hands of the small politicians, instead of the large ones, if the amendment prevailed, and he preferred its being in the hands of the large politicians, if it must be at all. He thought this subject of the most magnitude and importance, and requiring deliberate investigation and discussion, for which there was not sufficient time at the present session. He hoped it might be permitted to lie on the table, and be brought forward early in the next session.

Mr. BIBB remarked, that this subject, with a view of preventing the election of a President from going into the House of Representatives, had agitated the country since 1816. It was now settled that the machinery of electors was both useless and cumbersome, preventing the separation of the question of President from that of Vice President. At present, the election of both was in the hands of the petty politicians of the country, and he thought the proposed system would place it in the hands of the people themselves. He thought the objection, that each State would have its own candidate, under the new system, ought to be abandoned. He admitted there were many distinguished men in the several States who might be thought worthy of elevation to the presidency; but he had so much respect for the opinions of the people, that he believed they would perceive who were the most prominent candidates before them, and that they would generally choose from them. His great object in pressing this resolution at this time was, that the proposed amendment might be acted on by the respective State Legislatures, and, if approved of by the requisite number, the amendment might be made before the next presidential election, and thus avoid any recurrence to the House of Representatives to effect a choice at that time.

Mr. BENTON explained the proposition. It contained three points. 1. To refer the election of President and Vice President to a direct vote of the people. 2. To take the election out of the House of Representatives. 3. To abolish the general ticket system, and introduce a uniform system of districts.

He said that the theory of the Constitution had failed with respect to the electors. They were intended to choose the President and Vice President, and to follow their own will in the choice. This theory had failed. Electors now had no choice. They were pledged to particular candidates, and could not vote otherwise without treachery to a sacred trust. They had become, therefore, a useless piece of machinery, which might do harm, but could do no good. In the election of Vice President, these electors must sometimes obstruct the will of a part of the people. It would happen in the case where two voters agreed about the President, but disagreed about the Vice President. They must both vote for the same elector to secure their choice for the first office; the elector could only represent *one* of them in voting for the second office.

The two other principles, Mr. B. said, depended upon one another. They rested on compromise. The great States complained of the equal right of the small ones in the House of Representatives; and the small ones complained of the general ticket system, which enabled the majority in a great State to press the minority into their service, and make them vote against their choice, and thus overwhelm the small States with masses, which masses might contain many votes which would be given to the candidate supported by the small States, if the voters were free, under the district system, to support whom they pleased. In yielding to this compromise, each class of States gained an object dear to it, and parted with a right more specious than valuable. The right of the small *States* to vote in the House of Representatives, was an illusion. In practice it belonged to the representative, and not to the *State;* for the *State* had no way to enforce her will or to recall the vote of her representative, if given contrary to her will. The general ticket system was unfriendly to the rights of the people; it enabled the majority to impress the votes of the minority, and that ought to condemn it in a country of equal rights.

Mr. B. explained the nature of the proposition to amend the Constitution. He considered it a mere question of reference. It was not for Congress to decide upon the amendment; that was to be done by the State Legislatures, and the vote of Congress merely referred the amendment to them for their adoption or rejection. He thought that members should not be reluctant to make these references, seeing that they were not laws binding upon the people, but propositions for the people to decide; and that all a member had to decide was, whether he was willing that his State should decide upon the amendment *for itself,* he being one of the people to make the decision himself at the final question.

Mr. B. explained the practical operation of the amendment. It provided for a second election by the people if the first failed. He presumed there would be frequently two elections, and that the first one would operate as a nomination, and would propose the real candidate for the actual election. Thus the people were to meet in August and vote for President and Vice President. If no one had a majority of the whole number, then a second election would take place in November or December between those having the two highest numbers. Mr. B. said that the first or preliminary election would stand in place of the caucuses and conventions now used for nominating Presidential candidates, and would supersede those caucuses and conventions. It would enable the people themselves to propose the candidates—to make the nominations—and afterwards make the election out of these nominations. In answer to the suggestions of the Senator from Virginia, over the way, [Mr. Leigh,] that the large States would always have the foremost on the list, Mr. B. said there would be danger of that consequence if the general ticket system prevailed; but the amendment proposed the district system, and it would be difficult for any eminent man to obtain the vote of every district in his State.

Mr. B. was anxious for a vote upon the proposition. It was the oldest subject before the House, for it stood No. 1 on the calendar. It was an old subject before the people, and it was probable that the public mind was now ready to decide it. If referred to the people now and adopted, it will be in time for the next Presidential election, and will supersede the necessity for a caucus or a convention. He thought the two Houses of Congress could not open it at once and without formal debate. Whoever was agreed to the principles might concur in the details, for they had been well digested. They were the work of two committees, one an extraordinary committee of nine members, from which it was first reported; the other, the select committee of five members to which it had been referred by the order of the Senate, and which had reëxamined it, and had given the present details the sanction of their approval. Mr. B. believed that the details and the phraseology were as perfect as could be made; and that every member who was in favor of the principles, or rather every member who was willing to give his constituents an opportunity of voting upon these principles, might safely adopt it.

Mr. TYLER was in favor of laying this subject on the table. He preferred the original proposition for which this substitute of the select committee was proposed as an amendment. He preferred it because this provided for dispensing with the whole district system, and providing for the exercise, in its fullest force, in each State, of the general ticket system. This proposition, however, divided the whole of the United States into districts; it broke up all the boundary lines of the States; and the consequence was, that we must vote by districts. He concluded by moving to lay the whole subject on the table; which was agreed to.

The VICE PRESIDENT presented a communication from the Treasury Department, relative to one of the land districts in Alabama; which, on motion of

Mr. POINDEXTER, was referred to the Committee on the Public Lands.

SPECIAL ORDER.

The Senate then resumed the consideration of the special order, being the motion made by Mr. SOUTHARD to print 30,000 copies of the reports of the Committee on the Post Office and Post Roads.

A protracted and desultory debate ensued upon the proposition to print 30,000 copies of the reports of the majority and minority of the Committee on the Post Office and Post Roads, in which Messrs. WEBSTER, GRUNDY, HILL, CLAYTON, LEIGH, SOUTHARD, BIBB, FORSYTH, EWING, KNIGHT, SPRAGUE, SHEPLEY, MANGUM, BROWN, and WILKINS, participated.

The question being taken on Mr. WRIGHT'S request, by yeas and nays, was determined in the affirmative by the following vote, to wit:

YEAS—Messrs. Bell, Bibb, Calhoun, Chambers, Clayton, Ewing, Frelinghuysen, Grundy, Kent, Knight, Leigh, Linn, Mangum, Naudain, Poindexter, Preston, Robbins, Robinson, Silsbee, Smith, Southard, Sprague, Swift, Tomlinson, Tyler, Webster—26.

NAYS—Messrs. Benton, Black, Brown, Forsyth, Hendricks, Hill, King of Alabama, King of Georgia, Morris, Shepley, Tallmadge, White, Wilkins, Wright—14.

The Senate, at a quarter before nine o'clock, adjourned.

HOUSE OF REPRESENTATIVES.

Wednesday, *June* 11, 1834.

Mr. E. WHITTLESEY reported a bill for the relief of the legal representatives of Jacob Ireland. Read twice, and committed.

Mr. GILLET reported a bill to provide for the seizure and sale of property imported in violation of the laws of the United States. Read twice, and committed.

Mr. MITCHELL, on leave given, presented additional evidence in support of the claim of Adam Smith, for work and labor done on the Cumberland road, west of the Muskingum river; and, on motion, had the original papers recommitted to the Committee of Claims.

Mr. WATMOUGH obtained the consent of the House to submit a resolution setting apart Friday and Saturday next for the consideration of the naval pay bill.

Mr. VANCE thought, he said, we should scarcely have time at this session to attend to the appropriation bills; but, if we should pass the bill regulating the pay of the navy, to the exclusion of all other business, there would not be time for the Senate to act upon it.

Mr. GILLET objected to the motion.

Mr. LOVE moved to amend the resolution, by adding, "and the bill to re-organize the marine corps."

On motion of Mr. MARDIS, the resolution was laid on the table.

Mr. WAYNE moved a suspension of the rule, in order to take up the resolution for distributing copies of the census of 1830 among those members who have not received them; which was agreed to.

The resolution referred to was taken up and agreed to.

On motion of Mr. SMITH, the resolution recently submitted by him, calling for certain information from the War Department, was taken up and agreed to.

The House proceeded, by consent, to the consideration of the resolution moved by Mr. LYON, on the 10th of April, calling for information relative to the longitude and latitude of several places in the vicinity of the nothern boundary of the States of Ohio, Indiana, and Illinois; and the said resolution being read, was agreed to.

The bills from the Senate, lying on the Speaker's table, were severally read and referred.

The bill from the Senate, to fix the northern boundary line of Ohio, had its first reading.

Mr. ALLEN, of Ohio, moved to postpone the consideration of the bill till Thursday next, and to make it the special order of the day for that day.

Mr. LYON, of Michigan, objected to this motion, and hoped the bill would take the regular course. He moved its reference to the Committee on the Judiciary.

Mr. ALLEN, of Ohio, opposed at length the reference to the committee, as unnecessary, and hazarding the passage of the bill at this session, to the great injury of the interests of Ohio.

Mr. LYON rose to reply, but his remarks were overruled by the Chair, who announced the special order of the day, the

KENTUCKY CONTESTED ELECTION.

The House resumed the consideration of the report from the Committee on Elections on the election contested between Robert P. Letcher and Thomas P. Moore. The question being on the amendment moved by Mr. Pope to the resolution reported from the committee.

Mr. McKINLEY said it was out of the question that the whole of this session should be given up to this subject, however important it might be to the State and the individuals concerned. We must take up the subject with a determination to get through with it, in order to attend to some other business. If it was not finished to-day, he should move the postponement of its further consideration to Wednesday next.

Mr. HARDIN moved to amend the amendment of Mr. Pope, by striking off certain names from the poll of Mr. Moore, and inserting the names previous to those in Mr. Pope's amendment.

The CHAIR decided that the proposition was not in order, as it was not in effect so much an amendment to the pending amendment, as a motion to exclude the balance of the amendment from consideration.

After some remarks from Mr. FOSTER, Mr. HARDIN withdrew his motion.

The question being on striking from Mr. Letcher's poll the name of Gerrit Vorhis, it was taken and determined in the affirmative.

The question was taken on striking off the name of John D. Stone, and decided in the negative.

The question was taken on striking off the name of William Wooley, and decided in the negative.

The question being on striking off the name of James Moorcan, it was decided in the negative.

The question being on striking off the last name (Robert Figg) in the first resolution of Mr. Pope's amendment—

Mr. MARSHALL moved to amend the amendment by striking off several names from the poll of Mr. Moore, they being, as he contended, proved to be minors.

The question being then taken on striking off the name of Robert Figg, it was agreed to.

Mr. GILLET, with a view, he said, to save time and bring the subject to a close, moved a substitute for the resolution and amendments, and inserting, that ___, of the 5th Congressional district of Kentucky, is elected to a seat in this House.

The CHAIR decided that the motion was not in order.

Mr. GILLET appealed from the decision of the Chair.

Mr. SPEIGHT supported the decision of the Chair.

Mr. GILLET withdrew the appeal, intimating that when the amendments under consideration were disposed of, he should renew his motion.

The question then being on striking from the poll of Mr. Moore certain names embraced in the amendment of Mr. MARSHALL, the following names were severally stricken off: Richmond West, Archibald Gordon, Anthony Long, and Joseph Henley.

The question was taken upon striking out the name of David B. Hughes, after considerable discussion, and was determined in the negative: Yeas 79, nays 105.

Mr. WISE had taken no part in the contest, and had become sick of the delay which it had occasioned. For the purpose of putting an end to the difficulty in which the House was involved, he offered a resolution declaring the election for the 5th Congressional district of Kentucky to be void, for irregularity and uncertainty, and directing a new election to be held.

The CHAIR (occupied temporarily by Mr. SPEIGHT) decided the resolution to be not in order.

Mr. MILLER inquired whether it would be in order to postpone the resolution and amendments now before the House, and take up this resolution?

The CHAIR decided it would not be in order.

Mr. WISE inquired whether a motion to lay the resolution and amendments on the table would be in order?

The CHAIR replied in the affirmative.

Mr. WISE made that motion.

Mr. MARSHALL moved a call of the House.

Mr. WISE then withdrew his motion.

Of H. N. Horine; which was carried—yeas 116, nays 38.

Of Joshua Grimes; which was negatived, without a division.

Of H. H. Thurman; which, after a long discussion, was negatived—52 to 67.

The question then recurred upon the second branch of Mr. Pope's amendment; striking off the names of certain voters from the poll of Mr. Letcher, on account of non-residence.

The first name, (that of William Quinn,) after the reading of the testimony, the House refused to strike off.

The House also refused to strike off the name of John McCoy.

The question was then on striking off the name of Greenbury Peyton, which was agreed to; and of William Welsh, which was negatived.

Mr. MARSHALL then moved to amend the above part of Mr. Pope's amendment, by adding certain names to be stricken from Mr. Moore's poll, for non-residence.

Mr. McKAY rose and said it was evident that it was now time to bring this subject to a close, as we had spent a long time upon it, and still seemed to have no prospect of arriving at a result. For several days past we had been engaged in the examination of individual votes. Were members bound by these votes? He thought not. He voted against the admission of the students; the House voted otherwise. Must he be bound to vote for Letcher because the House had made that decision? Certainly not. Each member was bound to decide upon the case according to his view of the whole. He moved to commit the report of the committee, with all the amendments, to the Committee of the Whole House, with instructions to report a resolution declaring that the election of representative to Congress, in the fifth Congressional district of Kentucky, in August, 1833, is void, from uncertainty and irregularity, and that neither of the claimants is entitled to a seat.

Mr. E. EVERETT made some objection to the reception of the motion, on a point of order.

The CHAIR decided that the motion was in order.

Mr. HARDIN wished the question on the motion to be taken in a full House; and he therefore moved a call of the House; which was ordered.

After the call had been proceeded in for some time.

The Sergeant-at-Arms was directed to notify the absentees.

Mr. DAVENPORT moved to suspend all further proceedings in the call, in order to admit the absentees at the door; which was agreed to.

Mr. WILDE moved that all further proceeding in the call be suspended; which was agreed to.

The question recurring upon the motion of Mr. McKAY, it was modified by the mover so as to commit the subject to the Committee of the Whole House, with instructions to report a resolution requiring a new election to be held in the Fifth Congressional district of Kentucky, it being impossible for the House to determine who was elected at the election held in August last.

Mr. GILMER opposed the motion. He did not conceive that there was any difficulty in ascertaining which of the claimants received a majority of qualified votes. He was at a loss to discover the uncertainty, in this case, which was talked of. Mr. Letcher came here with forty-nine more votes than Mr. Moore, and there could be no uncertainty until forty-nine votes were stricken from Mr. Letcher's poll. There was informality, no doubt, in the manner in which some of the votes were taken, but not such informality as justified us in excluding the votes. According to his calculation, Mr. Letcher had a majority of thirty votes, after excluding the nineteen votes taken on the second day in Garrard county, and two students who were not citizens of Kentucky.

Mr. WISE said he should vote for the proposition. The irregularity and informality of the proceedings, during the election, could only be equalled by the irregularity and informality of the manner which had been adopted by the House. We were now precisely where the case had originally started, excepting that the House had decided that a few votes should, and a few others should not, be counted for the respective candidates. One of the candidates alleges that there are no poll books before the House, and the gentleman from Georgia [Mr. Gilmer] alleges that by the poll books, Mr. Letcher has a prima facie majority of forty-nine. Has the House been willing to receive the prima facie evidence on either side? The case has been sent to a committee of the House, who had reported the result of a most laborious examination. The House had neither ratified nor confirmed that result. If the principles adopted by the committee were carried out, with all deductions which seemed to be reasonable, Mr. Moore has a majority of twelve or thirteen votes. On the other hand, taking the copies of the books produced by Mr. Letcher, and making the necessary deductions, there was about a similar majority for that candidate. For himself, he felt perfectly indifferent upon the question. He had entered into no party feelings on the subject. From the commencement he had been of opinion that the election should be sent back, and he would take upon him to say, that any moment, when the friends of either candidate thought he won in danger, they would have been ready to have given their support to that proposition.

Mr. CLAYTON opposed the motion to commit. Had the sheriff of Lincoln county done his duty,

Mr Letcher would have taken his seat under a regular certificate. Mr. C. made some comments upon the remark of Mr. McKay, that he did not feel bound by the votes which had been decided by the House. We had gone through on one side, and we ought now to go through the other. He was willing to meet the result. We now ought to go through the other. He would cheerfully acquiesce in the result.

Mr. ANTHONY said he had hitherto been a listener to the discussion which had grown out of this contest, and would ask the indulgence of the House, while he stated his accordance with the views of the gentleman from North Carolina, as he had been for some time convinced of the impracticability of coming to a satisfactory conclusion upon the large mass of contradictory testimony which had been taken in this case. He stated that there were upwards of eleven hundred pages before him, out of which the conclusion was to be drawn who was entitled to the seat; that the majority on either side was not contended to be more than ten or a dozen votes; the evidence was so doubtful and conflicting, that he had found it utterly impossible to satisfy his mind, without neglecting those other important duties which devolved on him as a representative. From the manner in which other members had voted upon several questions relating to the matter, it was obvious that many were in a similar situation.

The immense mass of testimony compelled gentlemen to take the facts, to a certain extent, upon trust; they had to rely upon the faith which they had in the statements of those who had examined the evidence, and although it might with propriety be said that "faith without works is dead, being alone," yet he candidly appealed to other gentlemen to say whether they had carefully read these 1100 pages, so that they were enabled to determine who was legally and duly elected a member of the fifth Congressional district of Kentucky, or whether they had pinned their faith on the sleeves of the Committee of Elections on the one side, and on certain members who attentively considered the subject on the other?

The honorable gentleman from Georgia had remarked, that the questions in dispute were matters of law, and not of fact. To a certain extent he was correct, but many questions involved in the decision were of complicated doubtful facts, about which there was a variety of evidence on both sides, and it was extremely difficult to arrive at the truth.

He admitted the propriety of counting the votes taken at the Garrard poll before ten o'clock on the first day and during the absence of the sheriff on the second, when he was attending to the highest of all earthly duties, the sick bed of a dying wife, was a question of law, which did not involve any controverted facts; yet the votes of the students at Danville college, the Salvisa votes, as well as those of minors, non-residents, &c., which had occupied the House for some days, were no more or less than sheer questions of fact; and until members agreed on the fact, it was impossible to determine the law in such cases. It was only necessary, in order to show how difficult it was to arrive at a just conclusion, to state, that on the proposition to deprive Mr. Letcher of nineteen votes, given during the sheriff's absence on the second day, the gentleman from Georgia was in a small minority; and yet that gentleman was willing to take the opinion of the House on that point, and forego his own; because, as he said, it was a question of law. For his part, he agreed that in law, the rule *stare decisis* should usually prevail; but in this case, he would vote according to the best of his judgment on every question made, and would not consent that a majority of the House should, by their decision on isolated points, control the ultimate vote he might give.

Mr. A. said that on a question involving, as this does, the right of suffrage, party feelings ought to be altogether discarded. That so far as he knew himself, he could conscientiously declare that he was influenced by no such feelings; and he had voted to give Mr. Letcher the votes taken in Lancaster before ten o'clock, and those given in the absence of the sheriff. He had voted against the admission of those which were given by the college students; yet he was free to acknowledge that he had some doubt as to the correctness of all the votes he had given, principally on account of the uncertainty of the facts. On the several questions relating to minors, non-residents, &c., he had endeavored to vote as he deemed right, without the least regard to either of the parties; but he could not pretend to say that he had perfect confidence in the conclusions at which he had arrived. Whether in the majority or the minority, he had always found himself among gentlemen of high legal attainments, eminent talents, and in every respect much better qualified to decide than himself.

Such being his situation, he was perfectly indifferent whether Mr. Moore or Mr. Letcher obtained his seat; he had no predilections to gratify; they were both gentlemen of the highest respectability and stood on an equal footing; either of them, he had no doubt, would do honor to themselves as well as the district. Should the resolution of the member from North Carolina prevail, the candidates would return to the district unprejudiced by this investigation. Mr. Letcher, on the one hand, would have the "*prima facie*" evidence in his favor, of which he was deprived by the improper and highly exceptionable conduct of the deputy sheriff of Lincoln. While on the other hand, Mr. Moore would have the report of the Committee of Elections in his behalf, and which every gentleman of this House would admit, afforded a strong presumption that he was duly elected, after the long time and assiduous attention that talented and respectable committee had devoted to the investigation.

Mr. A. said that the session was now drawing rapidly to a close; we had but a few days before us, and were we to proceed in canvassing all the contested votes, when would this matter end? We had much important business, indispensable to be acted on, and little more than two weeks remained. Would it not, he asked, be the fairest, the safest, the most correct course, to send back the election to the people—the source of all power? They are capable, they are doubtless willing, to settle this controversy. That Congressional district can gain little or nothing by either of those gentlemen taking his seat for the few remaining days of this session. If they return home to their constituents, the qualified voters will decide between them, and this House will be spared the necessity of deciding a question, which, to say the least of it, is one of a very doubtful character.

Mr. A., in conclusion, observed, that if a majority of the members believed they understood this case thoroughly, and were prepared to decide it, he would be perfectly satisfied that they should reject the proposition now before the House, but if, like himself, they could not come to a satisfactory conclusion in their own minds who was duly elected, the proper course, in his opinion, was to declare the election void, for uncertainty and irregularity, and to let the people of the fifth Congressional district determine who should be their representative.

If he were compelled to decide the main question, although he would do it with great reluctance, as it was so intricate as even to puzzle a Philadelphia lawyer, yet he would not shrink from the performance of that duty, according to the best light which he had before him. He would not say that he should be guided in his vote by the report of the committee; but certainly, as it came from a standing committee of this House, who had been elected for their talents, their industry, their respectability, and impartiality, it was entitled to great consideration.

Hoping, however, that he would be spared the necessity of a decision between those honorable gentlemen, he should have no hesitation to send them home, and leave this vexed, this intricate, this perplexing and uncertain question, to the determination of their constituents.

Mr. MANN moved the House adjourn, which he immediately withdrew.

Mr. ADAMS regarded the motion of Mr. McKay as an unconstitutional proposition—as the House was made the judge of the election of its members. The House could not constitutionally evade the question. It must judge of the election. The proceedings of the Committee of Elections, as well as the House, have gone on the ground that an election has been made. Most of the principles introduced have been settled. If the House should go a little further, there will be no difficulty. Instead of sending it to the Committee of the Whole, with instructions, he hoped the House would sit until it decided whether Mr. Letcher or Mr. Moore is entitled to the seat.

Mr. McKINLEY said it was true the House was to judge of the election of its members; but it cannot be said that this House is a court and must be governed by the rules of a court of justice. In giving his final vote he could not be controlled by the decisions which had been made by the House upon individual cases. He was responsible for his own vote. What the result would be upon a computation founded on the decisions of the House, he could not say; but he could say that he was very much dissatisfied with some of the decisions, and he believed that most gentlemen were in the same situation. We have had questions of nonage, upon which decisions, diametrically opposite, have been made. Almost every principle which had been recognised had been contradicted by other votes of the House. We had undertaken to be governed by the laws and constitution of Kentucky.

But the application of the principles of the laws and constitution of Kentucky had been ridiculed, and we have been told that we should only regard the rules of substantial justice. The great question in his mind was, Will the decision of the House do justice to the candidates and to the people? That had been his desire from the beginning. He was willing to send the subject back to the people, and would be contented with their decision.

Mr. BINNEY supposed this would be the closing argument, which was his apology for a few remarks. After spending many days upon this subject, it is now proposed for the House to say that it has found a decision of the case impracticable. Every gentleman who votes in the affirmative so says to himself, though he has been called on by every consideration of duty, to make a decision. As to the difficulties which had been suggested by gentlemen in coming to a satisfactory decision, all they had to do was to adhere to the principles on which they had voted. If they could not remember on what principles they had voted, that reason should be assigned. After the laborious investigation of the candidates, and the thorough examination of the committee, all that was not brought into doubt should be regarded as established on either side. The ground was therefore greatly circumscribed. Gentlemen had no right to stultify themselves. The constitution and their constituents had made the members of this House judges of this election. There can be no question more simple than that before the House. It is said there is a mass of evidence. Does this render a decision impracticable? It is only so to those who shrink from the labor of investigation.

Mr. SUTHERLAND believed he had shown from the commencement a willingness to meet the question. He should support the proposition without intending to stultify himself. He was willing to repose the power of deciding this question with the great fountain of power—the people themselves. The people of the fifth Congressional district could settle it more accurately than this House could. They are better acquainted than we can be with both candidates and witnesses. We had a question arising as to the relative truth of two brothers by the name of Horine. The people of Kentucky know all about these Horines. They also know the sheriff whose conduct has given rise to so much remark. Not being afraid to meet the people, he was for sending it back. If either candidate should receive a seat he would not retain it twenty days. He would tell them to go home to their friends and lay the case before the people, in whose decision every confidence could be placed.

Mr. WISE made some remarks in reply to Mr. Binney. It was no difficulty as to principles, but doubt as to facts, which rendered a correct decision by the House impracticable. Twenty or thirty votes depended upon conflicting evidence, which it was impossible to decide upon.

Mr. LINCOLN opposed the proposition to commit, on the ground that the House was bound to discountenance the proceedings of the sheriff who withheld the poll-book, whose object was to send the election back to the people. He was unwilling

that the House should be made an instrument in promoting the design.

Mr. McKAY, after a few remarks, expressed a willingness to modify his proposition by striking out the reason assigned in the resolution.

The yeas and nays having been ordered—

The question was taken on the motion to commit to the Committee of the Whole, with instructions, and carried—yeas 113, nays 109.

Mr. FILLMORE moved an adjournment; which was negatived—yeas 100, nays 103.

Mr. McKAY moved that the House resolve itself into Committee of the Whole.

Mr. MARSHALL opposed the motion. The subject was not before the House—it had been committed, and there were many orders standing in Committee of the Whole before this.

Mr. EVANS also contended, that being committed to the Committee of the Whole, it must take its rank among the orders of the day. It was not now in the power of the House to reach it.

Mr. CLAYTON, Mr. MERCER, and Mr. WAYNE, also expressed their opinion on the question of order.

Mr. WAYNE moved an adjournment.

Mr. JONES of Georgia, and Mr. WISE, submitted that the motion to adjourn was not in order.

The CHAIR overruled the objection.

The House then adjourned.

IN SENATE.

Thursday, June 12, 1834.

A message upon Executive business was received from the President of the United States, by Mr. Donelson, his Private Secretary.

PETITIONS.

Mr. TOMLINSON presented the memorial of citizens of the town of Lynn, New London county, Connecticut, in favor of the restoration of the deposites and the recharter of the Bank of the United States; which was referred to the Committee on Finance, and ordered to be printed.

Mr. WEBSTER presented a similar memorial, signed by 937 citizens of the county of Tompkins, New York; which took the same course as to reference and printing.

Mr. McKEAN presented a remonstrance of citizens of Chambersburg, Pennsylvania, against the renewal of the patent of John Ames, paper maker.

REPORTS.

Mr. TALLMADGE, from the Committee on Naval Affairs, reported a joint resolution for the relief of John S. Stiles; which was read and ordered to a second reading.

Mr. SOUTHARD, from the same committee, asked to be discharged from the further consideration of the memorial of John Whitehead, and recommending the reference of the same to the Navy Department; which was agreed to.

Mr. SOUTHARD, from the same committee, reported a bill for the regulation of vessels propelled, in whole or in part, by steam; which was read.

Mr. NAUDAIN, from the select committee, reported a bill granting to Boyd Reilly $5000, for the use of his patent for the application of sulphur and other irrespirable vapors to the human body; which was ordered to a second reading.

Mr. WEBSTER, from the Committee on Finance, reported the general appropriation bill with amendments; which, with the documents and amendments, were ordered to be printed.

Mr. CHAMBERS, from the Committee on the District of Columbia, reported a bill appropriating $70,000 annually, for three years, to the city of Washington, to be applied to the payment of the interest of the corporation debts.

The resolution compensating the Hon. Mr. Porter for his attendance and mileage, was postponed until to-morrow.

The resolution for the distribution of the Diplomatic Code, offered by Mr. Wilkins, was read a first and second time.

Mr. TIPTON called up his resolution changing the hour of the meeting of the Senate from twelve until eleven o'clock, until otherwise ordered; which was agreed to—yeas 18, nays 12.

Mr. MOORE, from the Committee on Revolu-

tionary Claims, reported a bill from the House, without amendment, for the relief of John Emerson, and moved its indefinite postponement; which was concurred in.

The following bills were read a third time and passed:

A bill for the relief of Francis Barnes:

A bill for the relief of the heirs of Alexander Boyd.

On motion of Mr. WILKINS, the Senate proceeded to executive business, when the doors were opened, it adjourned.

HOUSE OF REPRESENTATIVES.

Thursday, June 12, 1834.

Mr. E. WHITTLESEY, from the Committee of Claims, reported a bill for the relief of Washington Sewall; which was read twice, and committed.

The question of referring the bill settling the boundaries between Ohio and Michigan to the Judiciary Committee, which was arrested by the expiration of the hour appropriated to morning business yesterday, again came up.

Mr. LYON, who made the motion to refer, supported it at length in reply to the arguments urged yesterday by Mr. ALLEN, of Ohio. The controversy had arisen in 1802 or '3, when Ohio was admitted into the Union. It had frequently come before the House and its committees, and the pretensions of Ohio had been uniformly disregarded. During the present session the subject had come before the Committee of Territories, who had reported against the claim of Ohio. It was impossible for the House to make the necessary investigation; but it should be referred to one of the standing committees, for their report upon the law and facts.

Mr. VINTON said the arguments on the part both of Ohio and Michigan, had been reported by the Committee of Territories three months ago. It was highly important that the subject be disposed of during this session. The situation of the Judiciary Committee of the House was such as rendered it exceedingly improbable that it would report immediately. The location of a part of the line of canals now in progress by Ohio, depends upon the settlement of this controversy. Mr. V. related the course of the bill before the Senate, in reply to the reasons stated by Mr. LYON, and insisted that the commitment of the bill, under existing circumstances, was equivalent to a rejection of the bill for the present session.

Mr. EWING advocated the motion to commit, at length.

Mr. WILLIAMS contended that the House should postpone the bill to a day certain, and make it the special order agreeably to the motion heretofore made by Mr. ALLEN. A decision of the controversy was important, which would not probably be done during the present session, if the bill was referred to the Judiciary Committee.

Mr. VANCE would propose the reference of the controversy to a select committee, composed of a member from each State. It was exceedingly important that the question be settled before Michigan was admitted.

Mr. LANE said, the internal improvements in the States of Indiana and Ohio, rendered the immediate settlement of this controversy necessary.

Mr. LYON had no objection to the reference proposed by the gentleman from Ohio [Mr. VANCE.] The committee would be rather large, and Ohio would have the advantage, as one of her members would be on the committee.

Mr. VANCE said that Ohio might be omitted.

Mr. GAMBLE advocated the reference of the bill to a select committee, as it involved questions of very considerable intricacy and importance.

Mr. G. explained the action of the Committee on Territories on this subject, and stated various facts to show the propriety of referring the bill.

Mr. BOON denied that the order of the day—

On which the CHAIR called up the unfinished business of yesterday:

THE KENTUCKY CONTESTED ELECTION.

The CHAIR stated that the House having committed the subject to the Committee of the Whole, with instructions, it was competent to fix the time when it should be made the order of the day.

Mr. SUTHERLAND moved that the subject be made the order of to-day.

Mr. STEWART moved that it be made the order for Monday next.

The latter question being the first in order, was taken and negatived.

The motion of Mr. SUTHERLAND was carried without a division.

The House then, on motion of Mr. SUTHERLAND, went into committee in exercise of the order, (Mr. HUBBARD in the chair.)

Mr. McKAY moved two resolutions, declaring that neither candidate was entitled to the seat, and that the Executive of the State be notified, in order that a new election be made.

Mr. WILDE contended that the resolutions were not in order, inasmuch as they varied from the instructions given by the House to the committee.

Mr. McKAY contended that the resolutions were a substantial compliance with the instructions. If any gentleman could present the resolutions in a form more accordant with the instructions, he would accede to the proposition.

Mr. SUTHERLAND proposed a resolution, in the words of the instructions, as follows:

Resolved, That there be a new election for a member of this House from the fifth Congressional district in Kentucky—it being impracticable for this House to determine with any certainty who is the rightful representative of said district.

Mr. McKAY withdrew his resolutions.

Mr. WILDE inquired whether the resolution was in the same terms with the instructions?

The CHAIRMAN said it was substantially so.

Mr. WILDE said it must be literally so.

The instructions and resolutions were then read.

Mr. SUTHERLAND moved that the committee rise, and report the resolution to the House; which was agreed to.

The committee rose and reported the resolution accordingly.

The SPEAKER resumed the chair, and the resolution having been reported.

Mr. CLAYTON moved a preamble to the resolution, which (he said) contained a naked statement of the facts relative to the votes received by the House, which showed that Letcher had a clear majority of eleven votes, and that various other votes being in controversy which were given to T. P. Moore, therefore,

Resolved, That there be a new election, &c.

Mr. MARDIS could regard the proposition as no other light than an insult to a majority of the House. If in order, he would move to lay the proposition on the table.

Mr. CLAYTON said it was the first time he ever heard that the truth could be regarded as an insult. The proposition contained nothing but the truth.

The CHAIR decided the motion to lay a part of the subject on the table was not in order.

Mr. WILDE suggested to his colleague the propriety of withdrawing his proposition and substituting a modification of the resolution before the House, declaring that R. P. Letcher was duly elected, and entitled to a seat in this House, from the fifth Congressional district of Kentucky.

Mr. CLAYTON assented, and moved the foregoing as an amendment.

Mr. SUTHERLAND raised a question of order. No question subject could be introduced under color of amendment.

The CHAIR decided the amendment to be in order.

Mr. HARDIN then went into a general argument upon the case, which was replied to by Mr. POPE.

Mr. MOORE moved a call of the House, in order that this question might be settled, and the House proceed to other business.

The call was ordered without a division, and was proceeded in for some time, when it was found there were twelve absentees.

Mr. BOON moved to suspend all further proceedings in the call, upon which

Mr. HARDIN demanded the yeas and nays.

Mr. BOON withdrew the motion.

Mr. J. K. MANN moved the suspension of the call; upon which

Mr. McKENNAN demanded the yeas and nays; which were ordered.

The question being then taken, the House determined to suspend the call, by a vote of 148 to 65.

The question then being on the amendment to the resolutions reported, it was taken by yeas and nays, and determined in the negative—yeas 113, nays 114.

YEAS—Messrs. John Quincy Adams, Heman Allen, John J. Allen, Chilton Allan, Archer, Ashley, Banks, Barber, Bernitz, Barringer, Baylies, Beaty, James M. Bell, Binney, Briggs, Bull, Burd, Burges, Cage, Campbell, Chambers, Chilton, Choate, William Clark, Clayton, Clowney, Corwin, Coulter, Crane, Crockett, Darlington, Warren R. Davis, Davenport, Deberry, Deming, Denny, Dickson, Duncan, Evans, Edward Everett, Horace Everett, Ewing, Felder, Fillmore, Foster, Philo C. Fuller, Fulton, Gamble, Garland, Gholson, Gilmer, Gordon, Gorham, Graham, Grayson, Grennell, Griffin, Hiland Hall, Hard, Hardin, James Harper, Haselting, Heath, Hiester, J. W. Huntington, Jackson, William C. Johnson, King, Kinnard, Laporte, Lay, Lewis, Lincoln, Love, Martindale, Marshall, McCarty, McComas, McKennan, Mercer, Milligan, Moore, Patton, Pinckney, Potts, Ramsay, Reed, Roncher, Selden, William B. Sheppard, Augustine H. Sheppard, William Slade, Sloane, Spangler, Steele, Stewart, William P. Taylor, Philemon Thomas, Tompkins, Turner, Tweedy, Vance, Vinton, Wardwell, Wayne, Edward D. White, Frederick Whittlesey, Elisha Whittlesey, Wilde, Williams, Wilson, Young—112.

NAYS—Messrs. John Adams, William Allen, Anthony, Beale, Bean, Beardsley, Beaumont, Blair, Bockee, Bodle, Boon, Bouldin, Brown, Bunch, Burns, Bynum, Cambreleng, Carmichael, Carr, Casey, Chaney, Chinn, Samuel Clark, Clay, Coffee, Connor, Coomer, Day, Dickerson, Dickinson, Dunlap, Forester, Fowler, William K. Fuller, Galbraith, Gillet, Joseph Hall, Halsey, Hamer, Hannegan, Joseph M. Harper, Harrison, Hathaway, Hawkins, Hawes, Henderson, Howell, Hubbard, Abel Huntington, Inge, Jarvis, Richard M. Johnson, Noadiah Johnson, Cave Johnson, Balwin Jones, Benjamin Jones, Kavanagh, Lane, Lansing, Luke Lea, Thomas Lea, Leavitt, Loyall, Lyon, Lytle, Abijah Mann, Joel K. Mann, Martindale, John Y. Mason, Moses Mason, McIntire, McKay, McKim, McKinley, McLene, McVean, Miller, H. Mitchell, Robert Mitchell, Muhlenberg, Murphy, Osgood, Page, Parks, Parker, Patterson, Dutee J. Pearce, Peyton, Franklin Pierce, Pierson, Plummer, Polk, Pope, Schenck, Schley, Shinn, Charles Slade, Smith, Speight, Standifer, Stoddart, Sutherland, William Taylor, Francis Thomas, Thomson, Turrill, Vanderpool, Van Houten, Wagener, Ward, Wardwell, Webster, Whallon, C. P. White, Wise—114.

So the House refused to adopt the amendment.

Mr. J. Q. ADAMS moved that the last clause of the resolution be stricken out.

Messrs. LANE and WISE opposed the motion. The question being loudly called for, was then taken, and decided in the negative without a division.

Mr. CLAYTON then moved the preamble to the resolution, which he before suggested.

Whereas, by the returns of the election for a Representative of the fifth Congressional district, in the House of Representatives, it appears that Robert P. Letcher had a majority of forty-one votes; that the said election was contested by Thomas P. Moore; and the Committee of Elections, to whom the case was referred, reported to this House, that there was an election, and that T. P. Moore was elected by a majority of forty-five votes, of all the legal votes in said district; and whereas this House, by sundry resolutions, had added to and abstracted from the votes of each party in the following manner, to wit:

From the majority as reported by the committee 44

They have restored the votes given on the first day before Graves—

To Letcher 39
Moore 3
      — making maj.   19

They have restored the votes on the second day in the absence of the sheriff 45

To Letcher 39
Moore 13
      — making maj.   19

Restored to Letcher the votes of the theological students 9
Moore 1
             —   8

Making Letcher's majority 2
Restored to Letcher the Salvisa vote, which had been taken from him and given to Moore 5
Taken from Moore the same 5
            —   10

Restored to Letcher the votes of Jessamine.. 3
            —   15

Taken from Letcher, on Mr. Pope's amendment, June 10 5
            —   10

Taken from Moore, on Mr. Pope's amendment, June 11 4
            —   6

Taken from Moore, on Mr. Marshall's amendment, to be added to Letcher............ 5
            —   11

Whereby it appears that Robert P. Letcher received a majority of eleven votes of all the legal votes in said district, and whereas it appears by motions now pending before this House, that sundry other votes are yet in controversy between the parties, and the House having stopped the investigation upon these votes which were alleged to have been illegally received by Thomas P. Moore:

Mr. SUTHERLAND asked whether the motion was in order—it being contradictory to the resolution.

The CHAIR decided that it was in order.

Mr. WISE said he should vote against the amendment, because it did not state the whole truth, and stated a falsehood. It suppressed the truth, inasmuch as it did not give the votes of members, and suggested a falsehood in representing that, because the House had given a majority to one of the parties, they would give the seat to neither.

Mr. THOMSON made a point of order upon the motion to amend. He thought the vote should first be taken upon the resolution.

The CHAIR decided otherwise.

After a few words from Messrs. CLAYTON and BURGES, in reply to the gentleman from Virginia, [Mr. Wise,]—

Mr. JONES, of Georgia, suggested an amendment to the preamble, stating that the House had determined that Robert P. Letcher was not entitled to the seat.

Which was accepted by Mr. CLAYTON as a modification.

After some remarks from Messrs. WISE, ANTHONY, and CLAYTON—

Mr. HARDIN expressed a wish that the gentleman from Georgia would withdraw the amendment, as it was incorrect in figures.

Mr. MARSHALL pointed out an error of two votes in the figures, and moved an amendment rectifying it; which was accepted as a modification.

Mr. CLAYTON said, that in compliance with the request of several of his friends, he would withdraw the amendment.

Mr. GARLAND renewed the same motion to amend, and thereupon demanded the yeas and nays; which were ordered.

The question being taken on the motion, it was determined in the negative: Yeas 72, nays 137.

The question being on concurring with the Committee of the Whole in the resolution reported, it was taken by yeas and nays, and determined in the affirmative: Yeas 114, nays 103.

So the resolution, as reported, was agreed to.

Mr. CHILTON ALLAN rose to ask whether it was in order to offer a resolution relative to the conduct of the sheriff, Alfred Hocker, in withdrawing the poll-book of Lincoln county.

The CHAIR said it would not be, without the suspension of the rule.

The bill for the relief of Edmund Brooke was read a third time; and the question being on its passage,

Mr. J. Q. ADAMS moved its postponement to the first Monday in December next.

Mr. CHINN opposed the motion.

Mr. WARDWELL moved to lay the bill on the table, and thereupon asked the yeas and nays; which were ordered.

The question being taken, it was determined in the negative.

Mr. J. Q. ADAMS asked the yeas and nays on the passage of the bill, which were ordered.

After some discussion, in which Messrs. MERCER, CALDWELL, FILLMORE, PARKER, STODDERT, CHINN, PEYTON, BEARDSLEY, BOULDIN, MANN of New York, and STEWART, took part,

Mr. CLAY, believing (he said) that no good could come from the discussion, moved the previous question; which was ordered.

The main question was then ordered to be put, and the yeas and nays were ordered upon it.

The question being then taken upon the passage of the bill, it was determined in the affirmative: Yeas 106, nays 47.

The bill to continue the act to grant preemption rights to certain settlers on the public lands was taken up on its third reading.

Mr. VINTON made a few remarks in opposition to the bill, and was replied to by Mr. CLAY.

On motion of Mr. VINTON,
The House adjourned.

IN SENATE.

FRIDAY, June 13, 1834.

The VICE PRESIDENT presented a communication from the Treasury Department, transmitting a report from the agents appointed to examine the land office, agreeably to the resolution of the Senate of the 27th ultimo; which,

On motion of Mr. POINDEXTER, was referred to the Committee of Public Lands, and ordered to be printed.

Mr. POINDEXTER, from the Committee on Public Lands, reported a bill for the benefit of the town of St. Mark's, Florida.

Mr. SILSBEE, from the Committee on Commerce, reported a bill establishing the city of Natchez, Mississippi, as a port of entry.

Mr. CHAMBERS asked to suspend the previous orders, and was replied to by Mr. KING of Alabama, believed the rule setting apart Friday and Saturday for private business a good one, and thought the regular way the best.

Mr. WEBSTER concurred with the honorable Senator from Alabama; and without a division the motion was lost.

Mr. WRIGHT gave notice that he should on Monday morning ask the Senate to decide upon the resolution submitted by him, granting compensation to the honorable Elisha R. Potter, while attending here with the commission of the Governor of Rhode Island, as one of the Senators of that State.

BILLS.

The following bills were considered in Committee of the Whole, and ordered to be engrossed for a third reading:

A bill for the relief of James Fife, a Creek Indian.

[Upon this bill a discussion ensued between Mr. TIPTON, Mr. WHITE, and Mr. KING of Alabama.]

A bill to create two additional land districts in the State of Illinois, and two new land districts north of said State, in the Territory now attached to Michigan, which lies between Lake Michigan and the Mississippi river.

A bill for the relief of William Duer, John Duer, and Beverly Robinson, trustees of the estate of Sarah Alexander, deceased, granddaughter of General Lord Stirling, of the army of the Revolution.

[This bill authorized the issuing of scrip for a quantity of public land, to the amount of eighteen thousand dollars, to the trustees of the heir of the late Lord Stirling, and who were descendants of that officer, for services rendered by him in the revolutionary war. The State of New Jersey (Lord Stirling being an officer of the line of that

State) issued to him a certificate of the debt, for which the United States became liable. This claim was for principal and interest.]

Messrs. WHITE, MOORE, SMITH, PORTER, LEIGH, SOUTHARD, CLAY, and FRELINGHUYSEN, supported the bill; Messrs. FORSYTH and KING of Georgia made some remarks in opposition to the bill.

Mr. SPRAGUE moved to strike out the allowance of scrip for land, and to insert in lieu of it a grant of eighteen thousand and fifty-one dollars and thirty-one cents; which was agreed to.

The debate was further continued by Messrs. SHEPLEY and WHITE.

A bill for the repair of the Mars Hill military road, in the State of Maine, was ordered to be engrossed, and read a third time.

SPECIAL ORDER.

The Senate took up the bill for the satisfaction of claims due to certain citizens for spoliations committed on their commerce prior to the 30th of September, 1800.

Mr. FORSYTH said, that as there could be but little expectation of the passage of this bill the present session, with a view to test the sense of the Senate, he moved to postpone it to the second Monday in December next.

Mr. CHAMBERS objected to the postponement, if it was ever intended to act on the bill. It had already been seven years in Congress, and was a subject of great importance.

After some further observations between Messrs. FORSYTH, WEBSTER, and CHAMBERS—

Mr. POINDEXTER suggested a postponement to some day next week.

Mr. FORSYTH asked the yeas and nays on his motion; which were ordered, and are as follows, to wit:

YEAS—Messrs. Benton, Bibb, Black, Brown, Calhoun, Forsyth, Grundy, Hendricks, Hill, Kane, King of Alabama, King of Georgia, Tallmadge, Tyler, White, and Wright—16.

NAYS—Messrs. Bell, Chambers, Clay, Clayton, Frelinghuysen, Kent, Knight, Leigh, Linn, McKean, Moore, Naudain, Poindexter, Prentiss, Preston, Robbins, Robinson, Shepley, Silsbee, Smith, Southard, Sprague, Swift, Tomlinson, Webster, and Wilkins—26.

Mr. POINDEXTER then moved the postponement of the bill to next Tuesday. Agreed to.

The bill granting pensions to certain persons therein named was, on motion of Mr. CLAYTON, laid upon the table.

Mr. TOMLINSON gave notice that he should move, to-morrow morning, to take up the bill, as there were several very meritorious cases comprehended in it.

The bill to amend an act for the payment of horses and arms lost in the military service of the United States against the Indians, on the frontiers of Illinois and the Michigan Territory, passed the 19th of February, 1833, came up next in order.

Mr. KING, of Alabama, moved to strike out the first nine sections of the bill; when, after some conversation between Messrs. TIPTON, ROBINSON, CLAYTON, POINDEXTER, and KING of Alabama,

Mr. ROBINSON moved to postpone the bill till to-morrow; which was agreed to.

On motion of Mr. PORTER, the Senate then proceeded to the consideration of executive business; and when the doors were opened,

The Senate adjourned.

HOUSE OF REPRESENTATIVES.

FRIDAY, *June* 13, 1834.

The CHAIR communicated to the House a letter from the Secretary of War, transmitting an answer to a resolution of the House on the subject of the navigation of the Mississippi and Missouri rivers; which was laid on the table.

Mr. H. EVERETT gave notice that immediately after the appropriation bills were disposed of, he should call up the bills in relation to the Indian department, in the hope that one of them, at least, would be acted upon before the close of the session.

The House resumed the consideration of the following resolution, offered by Mr. JOHN Q. ADAMS:

Resolved, That the Secretary of the Treasury be directed to lay before the House the names of the presidents, cashiers, directors, and stockholders, lawyers and solicitors, of all the banks selected by him as depositories of the public moneys, in the place of the Bank of the United States and its branches, together with the amount and stock in said banks, held by each stockholder, and the amount of debt due by each president, cashier, and director, of each of the banks, to said bank, at the time when it was selected as a depository, and at this time.

To which the following amendment was offered on a former day by Mr. POLK:

"And that he also communicate to this House 'the amount of debts due by the President, cash-'iers, and directors of the Bank of the United 'States at this time, or at any time within one 'year last past; and also, the names of the lawyers 'and solicitors of the Bank of the United States 'and branches, and the amount of debt due by 'each to said bank at this time, and at any time 'within one year last past."

And the following amendment to the amendment, by Mr. BEATY:

"*Be it further resolved*, That the Secretary also 'inform the House whether the President of the 'United States, heads of department, and treasurer, 'have been in the habit of keeping their private ac-'counts in the Branch Bank of the United States in 'the city of Washington; and at what time did 'they, or either of them, cease to keep their ac-'counts in said branch bank."

Mr. BEATY withdrew his amendment.

The question recurring on the amendment offered by Mr. POLK, Mr. J. Q. ADAMS expressed the hope that the gentleman from Tennessee would withdraw it; without it, the House would, he believed, adopt the motion without debate. It was in the gentleman's power to obtain his object by a separate proposition. Let the condition of the United States Bank be what it might, it had no reference to the question before us. The immediate question was, whether the selected banks were safe depositories of the public money? The matter introduced by the gentleman from Tennessee was extraneous, and calculated to embarrass the resolution. He objected also to the amendment, that it proposed a more extensive inquiry than was proposed by the resolution, and demanded information which the House had no right to demand. The House had once ordered this inquiry into the condition of the United States Bank, and the bank had, in defiance of the House, refused to submit to the investigation. The House had labored a long time under this contempt, without exhibiting any disposition to maintain its assumed authority. He alluded to the demand made by the Committee of Investigation upon the Bank of the United States, of its correspondence with members of Congress; the object of which, he intimated, was to prove the assertion of the President, that if the last Congress, at its first session, had sat three weeks longer, it would have been bribed to recharter the bank by a vote of two-thirds. The inquiry ordered by the House (he contended) exceeded its powers, and was legally resisted by the bank. He hoped, therefore, that the gentleman from Tennessee would cease his inquisitiveness, and that he would suffer the resolution to pass without the proposed incumbrance.

Mr. POLK replied that he had no expectation, when he came to the House this morning, of being drawn into a discussion of this subject. The gentleman had commenced and ended his remarks with an expression of a wish that he would withdraw his motion to amend the resolution, and in the interval, had chosen to make some observations which it might be proper for him to answer. He should do it in a few words, premising that he should not comply with the gentleman's request by withdrawing the amendment. The gentleman avowed his object in calling for the information to be to ascertain whether the public money was safe in its present places of deposite. I, said Mr. P., proposed a similar inquiry in regard to the United States Bank, where the Government has two or three millions in deposites, and seven millions of stock. It was more important to require the proposed information from the Bank of the United States than from the local deposite banks, for the reason that the Government was a stockholder, as well as a depositor in the United States Bank, and was more peculiarly proper to require it from the United States Bank, because that bank had set itself up in antagonist position to the Government, had denounced the Executive as a tyrant, usurper, and despot, and more recently, had denounced and insulted the representatives of the people, because they sustained him in his measures. But, according to the gentleman, this immaculate and inoffensive Bank of the United States must not be looked into, though the affairs of the State banks must be thoroughly probed. Again, he thought it more peculiarly proper to carry the inquiry into the concerns of the United States Bank, because a committee of the House, appointed to investigate its affairs, by a vote of one hundred and seventy members, had gone to Philadelphia with the very inquiries which were now proposed to be made into the State banks, and had been insultingly repulsed.

The bank was requested, by resolution of the committee, "to furnish the particular items, and 'the aggregate of all fees and compensation paid 'during each year to attorneys, counsellors, or 'lawyers, since the establishment of the bank; 'stating the amount paid to each person employed, 'together with the residence, the times when the 'payments were made, and the particular services 'rendered for each charge paid; also, whether the 'same has been paid at the parent bank or branches, 'and at which, designating them; also, of all sums 'paid as a general or annual fee or salary to coun-'sellors for the bank, specifying the names of such 'persons, the amounts, and times, and places of 'payment; and, also, whether such sums were 'paid by the order, in each case, of the board of 'directors, or how otherwise paid; designating such 'sums as have been paid in cash, and such as may 'have been passed to the credit of such persons or 'others, in payment of any debt or debts due to 'said bank."

To the series of resolutions of which this was one, the board of directors replied, by a resolution, unanimously adopted:

"That the board do not feel themselves at liberty 'to comply with the requirement of the resolutions 'of the Committee of Investigation of the 29th 'ultimo, and 1st instant, and do not think they are 'bound to do so, inasmuch as, in respect to a part 'of the papers called for, the effect would be the 'same as the surrender of their books and papers 'to a secret and *ex parte* examination, which they 'have already refused to consent to."

I do not conceive, then, said Mr. P., that the amendment is improper or inexpedient. The gentleman's request he could not comply with. It would be more reasonable that he should ask the gentleman to modify his own resolution by extending his inquiries to the United States Bank. Mr. P. then adverted, in terms of great severity, to a semi-official exposé of the bank, published in the National Gazette, as a reply to the report of the Committee of Investigation.

The bank, he said, in this paper, which was evidently prepared under its own directions, defied and insulted the House of Representatives. After setting itself up in opposition to the Government, assuming to construe the powers of the Executive, and to dispute what authority he should and should not exercise, it now abuses and denounces the House.

Mr. J. Q. ADAMS. Will the gentleman give us proof that what he is about to read came from the bank?

Mr. POLK. The paper furnishes intrinsic evidence of its authorship, for it contains a letter from a member of the committee which could not have been procured but from the bank. Yes, sir, the bank, which was so scrupulous in regard to private correspondence, has not hesitated to avail itself of a private letter, with a view to assail members of this House. Mr. P. then read some paragraphs from the paper, as follows:

"The House of Representatives, it cannot be 'dissembled, has lost much of the confidence of 'the country, and has lost it by inattention to its 'own character. They have been much too ser-'vile—have permitted themselves to be the dupes 'of political jugglers. It is a fact perfectly noto-'rious, that a very large portion of the House, 'outside of the bar, acknowledge the improper 'conduct of the Executive—yet step forward a few 'feet, and vote to support the very measures they 'disapprove. The House ought to be ashamed of 'such conduct. There are really many honest

'and well-meaning men in that body, and they 'ought to revolt at the humiliation to which the 'Kitchen Cabinet subjects them. The present 'feeling of the country towards the House is one 'of surprise and pity—surprise, that a popular 'body should be so indifferent to popular rights; 'and pity, that it should suffer the control of these 'political jugglers. If, therefore, that body should 'be despised, it will only be because it has made 'itself despicable. If it be treated with contempt, 'it will be because it is contemptible."

Mr. J. Q. ADAMS. Will the gentleman read the letter of which he spoke?

Mr. POLK. The gentleman can read the letter himself, if he pleases. I am not bound to read for the gentleman's edification or amusement. I choose to proceed with my remarks, in proper temper, I hope, having read enough of this bank bulletin. Right or wrong, sir, (continued Mr. P.) whatever the bank does, the board of directors assert the legal right to do what has been done. As an answer to my objection to the course of the bank, it is said that the board of directors approve it.

He did not wish to evade the investigation into the concerns of the local banks, but he wished also to carry it into the affairs of the Bank of the United States—an institution which some regard as the sole agent of the Government. The bank issues its bulletin, and declares that you have no power; that they stand above your reach; and you are now requested modestly to decline asking the bank any more questions. He shrunk from no scrutiny into the affairs of the local banks, and had no objection to the object of the resolution of the gentleman from Massachusetts.

Mr. WAYNE objected, he said, to the passage of the resolution of the gentleman from Massachusetts, and also of the amendment of the gentleman from Tennessee, and he believed he could convince the House that we had no power to pass either, and that it would be impolitic to exert the power if we had it. What coercive power had we in case the information should be refused? If we attempted to coerce the local banks by withdrawing the deposites from them, we put it into the power of the Secretary of the Treasury to exercise an undue influence through the means of these institutions. We assumed in the resolution that we had a right to investigate the condition of the local banks generally; a power which, he contended, belonged to the respective States alone. We had sufficient security for our interests in the weekly statements of the selected banks and their standing in the commercial world. He was opposed to the amendment of the gentleman from Tennessee, as unnecessary, because the measures of the Government in relation to the Bank of the United States would not be changed—certainly not with his vote; and as illegal, because the powers reserved to either House of Congress, under the twenty-third section of the charter, could not be delegated to any functionary of the Government. If we were to assert the power, he would do it in a way in which it would be effective. Would that information be given to an officer of the Government, which had been denied to a committee of this House? He was aware that another refusal of the bank to give the information, would be deemed another instance of contumacy on the part of the institution; but he asked no such aid as this. He was willing to leave the question where it was. We had put the bank in the wrong, and he wished to keep her there.

The CHAIR here arrested the remarks of Mr. WAYNE—the hour assigned to the consideration of resolutions, having expired.

The House proceeded to the orders of the day.

The bill establishing the northern boundary line of the State of Ohio, which laid over from yesterday, came up, upon the respective motions of Mr. ALLEN, of Ohio, to postpone to Thursday next, and make it the special order of that day, and of Mr. VANCE, to refer to a select committee.

Mr. LYON expressed his concurrence in the proposition to refer to a select committee. The interests of Michigan required important information to be considered, which, in so large a body as the House, it would be difficult to communicate in detail. He had heretofore laid before one of the standing committees some views upon the legal principles involved; but the question of expediency, which was of the most vital consequence to the Territory of Michigan, had not been gone into. He wished for an opportunity to do this before a committee.

Mr. ALLEN, of Ohio, begged the House to bear in mind that the reference of this bill to a committee amounted, in effect, to its rejection.

The question was then taken on the motion to postpone, being the first in order, which was negatived—ayes 63, noes 68.

The motion to refer to a select committee was then agreed to without a division.

Mr. VANCE moved that the committee consist of seven members; which was ordered accordingly.

Mr. LYON inquired whether the gentleman from Ohio, who made the motion, would be of the committee?

Mr. VANCE hoped he would be excused from serving.

REMOVAL OF THE DEPOSITES.

The joint resolution of the Senate, disapproving of the removal of the deposites from the Bank of the United States, came up on its first reading.

Mr. POLK moved to lay the resolution on the table.

Mr. E. WHITTLESEY suggested that probably no objection would be made to laying the resolution aside for the present, until the other bills on the table were disposed of, and hoped the motion to lay on the table would be withdrawn.

Mr. POLK declined.

Mr. CROCKETT moved a call of the House; which was ordered.

After the call had proceeded for some time,

Mr. R. M. JOHNSON moved all further proceedings on the call be suspended.

The yeas and nays having been ordered on this motion, it was withdrawn.

The CHAIR having stated, in answer to an inquiry, that 211 members had answered,

Mr. ANTHONY renewed the motion to suspend the call.

Mr. HIESTER demanded the yeas and nays, which were ordered.

The question on suspending the call was carried—yeas 107, nays 76.

The resolution having been read, on motion of Mr. CHILTON,

Mr. W. R. DAVIS wished to inquire of the gentleman who moved to lay the resolution on the table, whether this course was intended for a final disposition of the question, or merely temporary?

Mr. POLK said it was in the power of the House only to answer that question.

Similar inquiries having been made by Messrs. CHILTON and DENNY,

The CHAIR stated that the question, by the rules of the House, was not debatable. That it would be competent, whenever the motion was in order, for a majority of the House to take up the resolution.

On motion of Mr. BURGES, the resolution was again read, when the motion to lay on the table was carried by the following vote:

YEAS—Messrs. John Adams, William Allen, Anthony, Bean, Beardsley, Beaumont, Blair, Bockee, Bodle, Boon, Bouldin, Brown, Bunch, Burns, Bynum, Cambreleng, Carmichael, Carr, Casey, Chaney, Chinn, Samuel Clark, Clay, Coffee, Connor, Cramer, Day, Dickerson, Dickinson, Dunlap, Forester, Fowler, William K. Fuller, Gillet, Gilmer, Joseph Hall, Halsey, Hamer, Joseph M. Harper, Harrison, Hathaway, Hawkins, Hawes, Henderson, Howell, Hubbard, A. Huntington, Inge, Jarvis, Richard M. Johnson, Noadiah Johnson, Cave Johnson, Seaborn Jones, Benjamin Jones, Kavanagh, Kinnard, Lane, Lansing, Laporte, L. Lea, T. Lee, Leavitt, Loyall, Lyon, Lytle, Abijah Mann, Joel K. Mann, Mardis, Moses Mason, McIntire, McKay, McKim, McKinley, McLene, McVean, Miller, Henry Mitchell, Robert Mitchell, Muhlenberg, Murphy, Osgood, Page, Parks, Parker, Patton, Patterson, Dutee J. Pearce, Franklin Pierce, Pierson, Plummer, Polk, Pope, Schenck, Schley, Shinn, C. Slade, Smith, Speight, Stoddert, Sutherland, William Taylor, Francis Thomas, Thomson, Turrill, Vanderpoel, Van Houten, Wagener, Ward, Wardwell, Wayne, Webster, Whallon, and C. P. White—114.

NAYS—Messrs. John Quincy Adams, Heman Allen, John J. Allen, C. Allan, Archer, Ashley, Banks, Barber, Barnitz, Barringer, Baylies, Beaty, Bell, Binney, Briggs, Bull, Burd, Burges, Cage, Campbell, Chambers, Chilton, Choate, William Clark, Clayton, Clowney, Corwin, Coulter, Crockett, Darlington, W. R. Davis, Deberry, Deming Denny, Dickson, Duncan, Evans, E. Everett, H. Everett, Ewing, Felder, Fillmore, Foster, Philo C. Fuller, Fulton, Gamble, Garland, Gholson, Gordon, Gorham, Graham, Grayson, Grennell, Griffin, Hiland Hall, Hard, Hardin, James Harper, Hazeltine, Heath, Hiester, Jabez W. Huntington, Jackson, William Cost Johnson, Lay, Lewis, Lincoln, Love, Martindale, Marshall, McCarty, McComas, McKennan, Mercer, Milligan, Moore, Pinckney, Potts, Ramsay, Reed, Rencher, Selden, Augustine H. Shepperd, William Slade, Sloane, Spangler, Steele, Stewart, Philemon Thomas, Tompkins, Turner, Tweedy, Vance, Vinton, Edward D. White, Frederick Whittlesey, Elisha Whittlesey, Williams, Wise, and Young—101.

The joint resolution of the Senate directing the deposites of the public money to be made in the Bank of the United States and its branches, was read the first time.

Mr. POLK moved to lay this resolution on the table.

Mr. CHILTON demanded the yeas and nays; which were ordered.

Mr. MARTINDALE called for the reading of the resolution, when the question was taken to lay it on the table, which was carried, as follows:

YEAS—Messrs. John Adams, William Allen, Anthony, Bean, Beardsley, Beaumont, Blair, Bockee, Bodle, Boon, Bouldin, Brown, Bunch, Burns, Bynum, Cambreleng, Carmichael, Carr, Casey, Chaney, Chinn, Samuel Clark, Clay, Coffee, Connor, Coulter, Cramer, Day, Dickerson, Dickinson, Dunlap, Felder, Forester, Fowler, William K. Fuller, Gillet, Joseph Hall, Halsey, Hamer, Joseph M. Harper, Harrison, Hathaway Hawkins, Hawes, Henderson, Howell, Hubbard, A. Huntington, Inge, Jarvis, Richard M. Johnson, Noadiah Johnson, Cave Johnson, Seaborn Jones, Benjamin Jones, Kavanagh, Kinnard, Lane, Lansing, Laporte, Luke Lea, Thomas Lee, Leavitt, Loyall, Lyon, Lytle, A. Mann, Joel K. Mann, Mardis, Moses Mason, McIntire, McKay, McKim, McKinley, McLene, McVean, Miller, H. Mitchell, Robert Mitchell, Muhlenberg, Murphy, Osgood, Page, Parks, Parker, Patton, Patterson, D. J. Pearce, Peyton, F. Pierce, Pierson, Plummer, Polk, Pope, Schenck, Schley, Shinn, Charles Slade, Smith, Speight, Standifer, Stoddert, Sutherland, William Taylor, F. Thomas, Turrill, Vanderpoel, Van Houten, Wagener, Ward, Wardwell, Wayne, Webster, Whallon, and Campbell P. White—118.

NAYS—Messrs. J. Q. Adams, H. Allen, John J. Allen, C. Allan, Archer, Ashley, Banks, Barber, Barnitz, Barringer, Baylies, Beaty, James M. Bell, Binney, Briggs, Bull, Burd, Burges, Cage, Campbell, Chambers, Chilton, Choate, William Clark, Clayton, Clowney, Corwin, Crane, Crockett, Darlington, W. R. Davis, Deberry, Denny, Dickson, Duncan, Evans, E. Everett, H. Everett, Ewing, Filmore, Foster, Philo C. Fuller, Fulton, Gamble, Garland, Gordon, Gorham, Graham, Grayson, Grennell, Griffin, Hiland Hall, Hard, Hardin, James Harper, Hazeltine, Heath, Hiester, J. W. Huntington, Jackson, W. C. Johnson, King, Lay, Lewis, Lincoln, Love, Martindale, Marshall, McCarty, McComas, McKennan, Mercer, Milligan, Moore, Pinckney, Potts, Ramsay, Reed, Rencher, Selden, A. H. Shepperd, Wm. Slade, Sloane, Spangler, Steele, Stewart, P. Thomas, Tompkins, Turner, Tweedy, Vance, Vinton, E. D. White, F. Whittlesey, E. Whittlesey, Williams, Wise, and Young—98.

The bill from the Senate to revive the act entitled "An act to grant preëmption rights to settlers on public lands," approved 29th May, 1830, was taken up on its passage.

After the reading of a letter from Mr. Graham, former Commissioner of the Land Office, at the clerk's table—

Mr. VINTON opposed the passage of the bill at length. The system under which the public lands are sold, requires that after they are surveyed they shall be first exposed to public auction. The reason is, that in every tract of country there are sections which have advantages of water power,

or of a position in reference to commercial advantages, which are worth more than the minimum Government price. This bill proposes that individuals who may have gone upon such tracts contrary to existing law, however valuable they may be, shall be entitled to such lands at $1 25 per acre. The law which it was proposed to revive, was passed at midnight on the last day of the session, on the ground that it was essential for the protection of the poor who had settled upon, and should receive at the Government price, a little pittance of land. Some such cases have undoubtedly arisen—but he was satisfied that the great majority of those who had availed themselves of the former law, were capitalists and speculators. A large sum had been appropriated for removing the raft of the Red river, which would lay open a large tract of the finest cotton lands in the United States. The increased value of these lands would amply repay the amount expended in these improvements. But if this bill passes, instead of bringing ten or fifteen dollars an acre, not a single section of this land will bring more than $1 25 per acre.

Mr. V. called for the reading of a letter published in the printed documents, relative to the outrages committed in Alabama by settlers on the public lands, to prevent bidding at the public sales; which being done, Mr. V. illustrated his position by the facts shown by these documents, and contended that it was contrary to every principle of public policy to encourage such conduct. Mr. V. alluded to the lead mines on the Mississippi, and the effect of this law upon these lands, which had been ordered to be sold. The individuals who had intruded themselves into these lands against law, had caused two Indian wars, which had cost from one to two millions of dollars. This was substantially a bill to benefit speculators.

Mr. CLAY replied at length to the arguments of Mr. VINTON. Unless this measure was adopted, the hardy individuals who had opened the way into the forest would have their houses sold over their heads, being out-bid at the public sales by speculators, and would be obliged to purchase their homes by paying these capitalists a profit of from fifty to one hundred per cent. Mr. C. went into an extended explanation of the effect of the law which it was proposed to revive, and contended that the auction sales made before the passage of it very little exceeded the minimum price. The sales of cotton lands in Mississippi averaged only two cents and a fraction above the minimum price. Deducted from these must be the increased expense of sales by auction, and the result is that the actual receipt was not greater than the Government price.

Mr. WHITE, of Florida, also combated the arguments of Mr. VINTON. There was no law which prohibits settlements upon the public lands. There had been a law passed, on the recommendation of Mr. Jefferson, prohibiting persons entering into possession of land in Louisiana under pretended French and Spanish titles. This law did not reach to settlements without claim of title. The object of the bill is to enable those who had made improvements to purchase the land of the Government, without paying speculators for not bidding against them at the public sales.

Mr. McCARTY supported the provisions of the bill, in reply to Mr. VINTON. To obviate the objections which had been suggested, he proposed to add a proviso, requiring the person claiming to enter land under a preëmption right, to make oath to certain facts which would place his right within the intent of this law.

Mr. LEWIS, also, supported the bill. It was necessary to protect the honest settler against the speculator, under the auction system. It was a mistake to say that the bill now proposed to be revived had been passed at midnight; it was opposed at every stage of its progress by the gentleman from Ohio, and was finally passed in broad daylight. The person whose letter had been read relative to the proceedings in Alabama, was a speculator, who was anxious to preserve the former system, and who felt that the passage of the bill would destroy his profits. He was sensible that too much discussion would defeat the bill; he hoped its friends would confine themselves to explanation.

Mr. POLK was in hopes that this bill, introducing no new principle, simply reviving an existing law—

Mr. VINTON said, it not only revived the former law, but provided that those rejected under the former law should be allowed.

Mr. POLK said, no person could obtain any lands, unless by paying for them at $1 25 cents. The State from which he came was not interested in the question, but his observation of the evils of the former system had convinced him of the necessity of this bill. Nothing prevented him from discharging his duty in moving that the appropriation bills which were undisposed of, be taken up, but a strong reluctance to interfere with the only measure which had come up during the session for the general benefit of the people of the western country.

After a brief explanation from Mr. CLAY—

Mr. H. EVERETT opposed the provisions of the bill. The necessity for this law, which had been referred to, had arisen out of our prior legislation. There should be some permanent principle adopted instead of passing these temporary laws. If the country was prepared to take the broad ground of permitting settlers to enter lands at the minimum price, as soon as they go upon them, he should not oppose it. But unless such a measure should be adopted as a principle of general policy, he could not support it.

Mr. DUNCAN had often advocated the position suggested by the gentleman from Vermont, [Mr. H. EVERETT.] He had long been convinced that it was the true policy of the Government.

Mr. PLUMMER advocated the provisions of the bill. There was a clause in the Choctaw treaty prohibiting settlements until after the removal of the Indians. But the Indians themselves, the surveyors, and all parties interested, petitioned in favor of permitting settlers to go upon these lands. Sales and surveys could not otherwise be made. These pioneers were necessary to furnish with provisions the surveyors and other persons who wish to examine the lands.

Mr. LANE supported the bill, in reply to the objections of Mr. VINTON. There was no competition at a public sale where there was a thousand tracts for each purchaser. The sales, therefore, rarely exceeded the minimum price. The public treasury had lost nothing from the original law, and would lose nothing from this extension of it.

Mr. CLAYTON resided in a State which had no public lands in it; but, on a careful investigation of the subject, he was satisfied that the interests of the Government would be promoted by the passage of this bill. If Government did not give this privilege of preëmption, speculators would sell it. He thought the Government should take the credit to itself.

Mr. EWING obtained the floor, but gave way to

Mr. VINTON, who thought it extraordinary that his remarks, which were considered as having no force, should call out a dozen answers, and gentlemen were not satisfied.

Mr. ASHLEY made some remarks in support of the bill.

Mr. STEWART moved the previous question.

Mr. WILLIAMS hoped the gentleman from Pennsylvania would withdraw his motion; if not, he should be under the necessity of moving a call of the House.

Mr. STEWART withdrew the motion for the previous question.

After some discussion, in which Messrs. McKAY and PEYTON took part—

Mr. PEYTON moved to recommit the bill, with instructions to report a resolution, providing that all the lands remaining unsold in the State of Tennessee, be sold at twenty-five cents an acre.

Mr. SPEIGHT moved the previous question; which was seconded, by a vote of 91 to 54.

The main question, being the passage of the bill, was then ordered to be put.

Mr. BEARDSLEY suggested the expediency of adopting, by consent, the amendment moved by the gentleman from Indiana.

To which Mr. VINTON objected.

The question being taken on the passage of the bill, it was decided in the affirmative—yeas 124, nays 53.

So the bill was passed.

Mr. POLK asked the House to take up the bill making appropriations for the payment of Indian annuities, which would not, he thought, take up twenty minutes.

Mr. WILLIAMS moved an adjournment; which was negatived.

The bill was then taken up for consideration.

Mr. POLK moved that the House non-concur in certain amendments made in the Committee of the Whole, making additional appropriations for blacksmiths, in several tribes; which was agreed to.

Mr. POLK moved to strike out $27,825 for rifles, and insert $28,875; which was agreed to.

On motion of Mr. POLK, the amendments made in the Committee of the Whole were severally concurred in, with the exception of the amendment authorizing the use of the Seneca fund for the payment of annuities, on which some remarks were made by Messrs. J. Q. ADAMS, POLK, FILLMORE, and PARKER; when

Mr. BINNEY moved to add a proviso declaring that the right of the Seneca Indians to the amount of that fund shall not be impaired.

Messrs. PARKER, J. Q. ADAMS, and LINCOLN, opposed the amendment with the proviso, and Mr. BINNEY made an explanation of his views, when the proviso was agreed to.

The amendment as amended was then carried.

The amendment moved in committee by Mr. HAWES, providing that the annuities paid under this act shall be made to the chiefs of the tribes, or to such persons as the tribes shall appoint, was negatived.

The bill was ordered to be engrossed and read a third time to-morrow.

The House then adjourned.

REPORT

Of the Committee of the House of Representatives, appointed to investigate the affairs of the Bank of the United States; presented by Mr. Thomas, of Maryland, May 22, 1834.

The committee appointed in pursuance of a resolution of the House of Representatives, passed on the 4th day of April, by which it was

Resolved, That for the purpose of ascertaining, as far as practicable, the cause of the commercial embarrassment and distress complained of by numerous citizens of the United States, in sundry memorials which have been presented to Congress at the present session, and of inquiring whether the charter of the Bank of the United States has been violated, and also what corruptions and abuses have existed in its management; whether it has used its corporate power or money to control the press, to interfere in politics, or influence elections; and whether it has had any agency, through its management or money, in producing the existing pressure, a select committee be appointed to inspect the books and examine into the proceedings of the said bank, who shall report whether the provisions of the charter have been violated or not; and, also, what abuses, corruptions, or malpractices, have existed in the management of said bank; and that the said committee be authorized to send for persons and papers, and to summon and examine witnesses on oath, and to examine into the affairs of the said bank and branches. And they are further authorized to visit the principal bank, or any of its branches, for the purpose of inspecting the books, correspondence, accounts, and other papers connected with its management or business: and that the said committee be required to report the result of such investigation, together with the evidence they may take, at as early a day as practicable—

Respectfully submit the following report, in part, of their proceedings, so far as they have found it practicable to discharge the duties devolved on them.

Charged, particularly, to examine into the conduct and condition of the Bank of the United States, they have endeavored most anxiously to ascertain correctly the true character of that highly responsible and delicate trust.

To judge rightly of the proceedings of the House of Representatives, and of its committee, towards the bank, it must be borne constantly in mind that that corporation differs essentially from an ordinary banking company, incorporated for private

benefit. The Bank of the United States was chartered for great public purposes, as an agent deemed necessary to the Federal Government, in the efficient exercise of its high prerogative, to fix the value of money, and thereby secure the benefits of a sound circulating medium to the Confederacy.

It was designed to aid the Treasury Department to collect conveniently and disburse the national revenue. Of its stock the United States hold seven millions of dollars, and its notes are by law made receivable, at par value, in payment of all dues to the Government. Concede, as we must, that the bank was established for great public ends, and that the House of Representatives is the grand inquest of the Union, and as such has power to visit and inspect all departments of the Federal Government, to correct their abuses, reform their errors, and confine the exercise of their powers within the limits prescribed by law to each, and it follows that the House has power to appoint a committee to make a minute and full inquiry into all the multiform operations of this powerful corporation.

But that there might be no doubt of the existence of the power here contended for, it has been expressly reserved in the 23d section of the charter of the bank, which provides, "That it shall be at 'all times lawful for a committee of either House 'of Congress appointed for that purpose to inspect 'the books and examine into the proceedings of 'the corporation hereby created, and to report 'whether the provisions of its charter have been 'violated or not."

The language in which this authority of the House is described is so plain and so full, that an attempt to illustrate it appears to be supererogatory. The committee to be appointed are to "inspect the books and examine into the proceedings of the corporation," without exception. The section contains no reserved power to the bank to designate the place where or the persons in whose presence the examination shall be made. These modes of exercising the main power are necessarily, as its incidents, dependent on the discretion of the sovereign with whom it is lodged. A contrary construction would make either or both Houses of Congress dependent on the agents whose conduct is to be the subject of inspection.

If the bank can attach any conditions to its exercise not found in the charter, then it could render nugatory the power by which it was intended it should be checked and controlled. That the great conservative purposes for which such committees of investigation were to be appointed might not be thus defeated, the extent and character of their inquiries are rightly made to depend on the wisdom, patriotism, and justice of either House of Congress.

The only restriction to be found in that clause of the bank charter which we are considering, is that which relates to the committee, and not to the House; and has reference, not to the extent of the examination, but to the character of the report to be made. The committee is directed to report, amongst other things, "whether the provisions of its charter have been violated or not." The object of this specific requirement is to be found in another clause of the same section of the charter, which provides, "whenever any committee as aforesaid, shall find and report, or the President of the United States shall have reason to believe, that the charter has been violated, it may be lawful for Congress to direct, or the President to order, a *scire facias* to be sued out of the circuit court of the district of Pennsylvania, in the name of the United States, calling on the said corporation to show cause wherefore the charter hereby granted, shall not be declared forfeited."

But if there ever had been a well-founded doubt as to the true and fair construction of this reserved power of the House, the committee did suppose it had been long since yielded.

In 1818, Mr. Spencer, of New York, offered to the House of Representatives a resolution providing for the appointment of a committee to inspect the books, and examine into the proceedings of the bank. In the debate to which that resolution gave rise, the opinions now entertained by your committee were well expressed by many distinguished gentlemen. For presenting short extracts from one of the speeches then made, no apology, it is supposed, will be needed. Mr. Lowndes said he had no "*apprehension* of defect of power in the 'House to prosecute the inquiry in the terms proposed. He had *no doubt* of the power of the 'House, if the public interest required it, to direct 'a committee to make such a report. The nation '(said he) has a deep interest in the conduct and 'management of the bank; our duty to the people 'whom we represent, the nation's interest, as 'owners of a large portion of the stock, its interest in the revenues being wholly payable in the 'notes of the bank, will justify a constant and vigilant attention to its proceedings. If there had '*been a doubt whether the conduct of the bank had 'been* PROPER OR NOT, *the House was fully justified 'in investigating into the facts, and inquiring whether* 'ABUSES *had been committed or not*. He would vote 'for any inquiry in its broadest shape."

The resolution of Mr. Spencer was adopted, and a committee appointed, who visited the principal bank at Philadelphia, and some of its branches. They had free, unrestrained access to the books and papers of the bank. They were furnished by the officers with such extracts and copies from the books and papers as they called for. They summoned before them the directors and officers of the bank, and examined them on oath touching their conduct and proceedings. And the committee made to the House, on the 16th January, 1819, an elaborate report, from which we learn that their inquiries had been chiefly directed "*to the* GENERAL *management of the bank and the conduct of its officers*." The transactions of private citizens with the bank were then freely and fully examined. Individual transactions of the President and directors of the bank, in the purchase of its stock, were fully investigated, and those officers sworn, and required to testify before the committee. Though deeply affected, personally and officially, by these developments, they never hesitated or objected to obey the process, or to give their testimony.

The names of the borrowers from the bank were published without scruple, with the amount of money due from each, whenever, and not otherwise, such a publication was deemed *necessary* to illustrate the improper conduct or mal-administration of its officers.

This precedent, to which the committee of 1832 strictly conformed, is entitled to high respect, from the eminent character of those by whom it was established, and who have justly enjoyed high reputations for purity of purpose and distinguished attainments.

If any additional reason for deference to this contemporaneous construction of the twenty-third section of the charter be necessary, it may be found in the fact, that the directors of the bank, in 1819, themselves assented to it. They conceded to the committee of the House the right to inspect *all* their books and papers, in such manner as that committee thought just and proper. Besides, those who now have the management of the bank, in 1832, without question of right, without hesitation, without protest, produced for the inspection of the committee of the House, all their books, papers, correspondence, and accounts, and appeared when summoned, and testified on oath touching the transactions of the institution under their control. With these preliminary observations, for which, it is believed, ample apology, if any be required, will be found in the subsequent portion of this report, the committee will proceed with a brief analysis of their proceedings in the execution of the duty devolved on them, showing the unexpected obstacles interposed by the managers of the bank to the progress of the examination, and their repeated refusals, in violation of their charter, and in contempt of the authority of the laws and of the House of Representatives, to permit their books or papers to be inspected, or their proceedings to be examined.

The purposes for which your committee were appointed, are stated so distinctly in the resolution of the House, that they have experienced no embarrassment in deciding on the character of the duties imposed. They were required, 1st, to ascertain, if practicable, the cause of the commercial embarrassments and distress complained of by numerous citizens of the United States, in sundry memorials which have been presented to Congress at the present session, and whether the bank has had any agency, through its management, or money, in producing the existing pressure.

2d. To inquire whether the charter of the Bank of the United States has been violated, and what corruptions and abuses have existed in its management.

3d. To examine whether the bank has used its corporate power or money to control the press—to interfere in politics, or influence elections.

The powers designed to be conferred on the committee, if they could have been exercised, are adequate to the performance of the duties enjoined; they were authorized to send for persons and papers; to summon and examine witnesses on oath; to visit, if necessary, the principal bank and its branches; and to inspect the books, correspondence, accounts, and other papers connected with its management. Such are the duties and the powers of your committee, conferred on them by the House with extraordinary unanimity, and which your committee felt bound to regard, as consistent with the chartered rights of the corporators and their debtors.

Under a deep sense of respectful obedience to the decision of the House of Representatives thus solemnly expressed, and feeling that they had no right to question its justice or propriety, your committee proceeded to Philadelphia on the 22d of April, to commence the performance of their duties.

On the 23d of April, their chairman addressed to the President of the bank, a communication, enclosing a copy of the resolution of the House of Representatives, and notifying him of the readiness of the committee to visit the bank on the ensuing day, at any hour agreeable to him. In reply, the President informed the committee that the papers thus received should be submitted to the Board of Directors, at a special meeting to be called for that purpose. It appears, in the journal of the proceedings of the committee, herewith presented to the House, that this was done, and that the directors appointed a committee of seven of their board, to receive the committee of the House of Representatives, and to offer for their inspection such books and papers of the bank, as may be necessary to exhibit the proceedings of the corporation, according to the requirement of the charter. In the letter of John Sergeant, Esq., as chairman of the committee of directors, communicating the proceedings of the board, he says that he was directed to inform the chairman of this committee, that the committee of the directors "will immediately direct the necessary arrangements to be made for the accommodation of the committee of the House of Representatives," and would attend at the bank to receive them the next day, at eleven o'clock. Your committee attended, and were received by the committee of directors. (Appendix A.)

Up to this period, nothing had occurred to justify the belief that a disposition was felt, on the part of the managers of the bank, to embarrass the proceedings of the committee, or have them conducted differently from those of the two preceding committees of investigation. On assembling, however, the next morning, at the bank, they found the room which had been offered for their accommodation, pre-occupied by the committee of the board, with the president of the bank, as an *ex officio* member, claiming the right to be present at the investigations and examinations of this committee. This proceeding the committee were not prepared to expect. When the appointment of the committee of seven was first made, it was supposed that that measure, however designed, was not well calculated to facilitate the examination.

The officers of the bank were believed to be the most appropriate agents of the board of directors to exhibit their books and papers. By them the entries in the books are made, and by them such entries are most readily explained. It is their duty, too, to be daily at the banking house, and on that account they could assist in the examination more readily than the committee of directors.

These objections to the special agents of the board, were felt and expressed, but they were waived, and no disposition had been manifested or felt by your committee, to conduct the examination in any manner not entirely acceptable to the board.

Under these circumstances, your committee did think that a decent respect for their rights and privileges, and much more for the dignity of that body from which all their powers were derived, might have induced the committee of directors to forbear to make them feel an entire want of control over their own room. With a previous determination to be present when their books were to be inspected, they could have waited to avow it until these books were called for, and the attempt made to inspect them in their absence. These circumstances are now reviewed, because they then excited an apprehension, which the sequel formed into conviction, that this committee of directors had been appointed to supervise the acts and doings of your committee, and to limit and restrain their proceedings, not according to the directions contained in the resolution of the House but the will and judgment of the board of directors. Your committee have chosen to ascribe the claim of the committee of directors, to sit conjointly with them, to the desire to prevent them from making use of the books and papers for the purposes pointed out by the resolution of the House. They are sensible that this claim to be present at all examinations, avowed prematurely, and subsequently persisted in with peculiar pertinacity, could be attributed to very different motives; but respect for themselves, and respect for the gentlemen who composed the committee of directors, utterly forbids the ascription to them of a feeling which would merit compassion and contempt much more than resentment.

This novel position, voluntarily and deliberately taken by the committee of the directors, predicated on an idea of equality of rights with your committee, under your resolution, rendered it proper and in some measure necessary, that your committee should express its opinions of the relative rights of the corporation and the House of Representatives. To avoid all misunderstanding, and future misrepresentations, it was desirable that each question should be decided separately. Contemplating an extended investigation, but unwilling that an apprehension should exist of improper disclosures being made of the transactions of the bank and its customers, your committee, following the example of the committee of 1832, adopted a resolution declaring that their proceedings should be confidential, until otherwise ordered by the committee, and also a resolution that the committee would conduct its investigations "without the presence of any person not required or invited to attend."

Copies of these resolutions were furnished to the committee of directors, in the hope that the executive control of a room at the bank, during its hours of business, would thereafter be conceded to your committee, while the claim of the committee of directors to be present when their books were submitted for inspection, should be postponed for decision, when the books were called for and produced by them. (App. A.)

On the 28th ult., this committee assembled at the banking house, and again found the room they expected to find set apart for their use, preoccupied by the committee of directors, and others, officers of the bank. And instead of such assurances as they had a right to expect, they received copies of two resolutions adopted by the board of directors, in which they were given to understand that their continued occupation of the room must be considered a favor, and not a matter of right; and in which the board indulge in unjust commentaries on the resolution of the House of Representatives, and intimate an apprehension that your committee design to make their examinations secret, partial, unjust, oppressive, and contrary to common right. (App. A.)

When this communication had been read, your committee adjourned to meet at their own chamber, at the North American Hotel. Notwithstanding all that had occurred, the correspondence with the committee of directors was continued. If in so doing an error was committed, let it be imputed to the belief that great forbearance well became the committee of the immediate representatives of the people. (App. A.)

While it was thus doubtful whether a room could be obtained in the banking-house, without conditions being attached derogatory to the rights and dignity of the House, and a concession in advance of a claim set up by the bank, which might seriously incommode your committee in their business, they determined to execute your resolution, if practicable, without intruding on the directors of the bank; they therefore required of the president and directors, in writing, to submit, for the inspection of the committee, at their committee room, on the 3d day of May, certain books and papers of the bank, which might have been thus produced without interruption to the ordinary business of the bank. The requisition, in terms, implied the presence of the directors or their committee.

On the day named, the board addressed a written communication to the committee, declaring "that they cannot comply with that part of the 'resolution of the committee of investigation which 'requires that certain books of the bank be sent to 'the North American Hotel, this day, at eleven 'o'clock." (App. B.)

Your committee are of opinion that this refusal of the board of directors to submit the books of the bank to the inspection of your committee, is a violation of the bank charter, and a contempt of the laws and authority of the House of Representatives.

The reasons for this opinion need not be here repeated or enlarged.

It has been maintained, and is insisted, that the right to inspect the books of the bank carries with it the power to perform that office out of the banking house, if it cannot be done conveniently and effectually therein; and your committee cannot perceive that just ground of complaint exists against a claim of power, in a committee of either House of Congress, which, by the laws, and with a wise regard to the public interests, is conceded to the judicial tribunals of both the Federal and State Governments.

The facts already stated demonstrate that a room could not be procured in the bank for the use of the committee, without a concession not to be recalled, which would have made your committee dependent on the courtesy of the directors of the bank at every step of the inquiry, and the various communications received from the directors and their committee, annexed to this report, will fully corroborate this statement.

Having failed to accomplish the object of procuring the books of the bank for inspection, at their committee room, your committee felt it to be their duty to demand their submission for that purpose, at the bank, of the president and cashier of the bank, the usual and general agents of the corporation. For that purpose, on the 5th day of May, having apprized the committee of directors of their intention, at one o'clock they repaired to the bank, and then required the president and cashier, each of them respectively, to produce certain of the books of the bank for inspection of the committee. This was refused by each of those officers, for reasons stated in writing, and to be found in the appendix to this report. (App. C.)

In this refusal, your committee believe there was a substantial violation of the bank charter, and a contempt against the authority of the House committed.

They are of opinion, that your committee were under no obligation of right to recognise any agent of the bank other than those generally known as such, and make their duty and right to inspect the books depend on the convenience or caprice of such deputation.

If such be the fact, then the examinations of the bank will, in all cases, depend on the disposition of the directors to have their proceedings examined.

Having been thus denied, by the officers of the bank, and having been informed by the directors, that they were not aware of having declined to furnish a room for the exclusive use of the committee, your committee, sincerely desirous to meet the wishes and directions of the House, believed it to be their duty to seek another interview with the committee of directors, and by arrangement, met the committee of the board, at the bank, on the seventh day of May, at an hour fixed by themselves.

Your committee then and there, in writing, required the committee of the board, to produce to your committee, for inspection, certain books and papers of the bank, to enable your committee to inquire into the truth of representations made by the Government directors to the President of the United States and to Congress; and to ascertain whether the board of directors had violated the charter of the bank, by authorizing the exercise of illegal powers by their committees or officers, and whether the bank had any agency, through its management or money, in producing the present pressure, or has used its corporate power or money to control the press, to interfere in politics, or influence elections.

Without giving a specific answer to these calls for books and papers, the committee of directors presented a written communication, which was said to be "indicative of the mode of proceeding deemed right by the bank."

The committee of the board in that communication, express the opinion, that the inquiry can only be rightfully extended to alleged violations of the charter, and deny virtually the right of the House of Representatives to authorize the inquiries required in the resolution.

They also required of the Committee of Investigation, "when they asked for books and papers, 'to state specifically in writing, the purposes for 'which they are proposed to be inspected; and if 'it be to establish a violation of the charter, then 'to state specifically in writing, what are the al'leged or supposed violations of the charter, to 'which the evidence is alleged to be applica'ble."

To this extraordinary requirement, made on the supposition that your committee were charged with the duty of crimination, or prosecution for criminal offence, and implying a right on the part of the directors to determine for what purposes the inspection should be made, and what books or papers should be submitted to inspection, your committee replied, that they were not charged with the duty of criminating the bank, its directors, or others; but simply to inquire, amongst other things, whether any prosecution in legal form, should be instituted, and from the nature of their duties, and the instructions of the House of Representatives, they were not bound to state specifically in writing any charges against the bank, or any special purpose for which they required the production of the books and papers for inspection.

A specific answer was required to the calls which had been made.

The committee of the board, after deliberation, made a communication to your committee, in writing, in which they announced their purpose to adhere to their resolution, and refused to submit the books and papers of the bank, required by your committee to be produced for their inspection.

These calls were made in the bank, and in the presence of the committee of the board, and then and there a compliance with them was refused. Not feeling authorized to regard this unexpected and unequivocal refusal as the act of the board of directors, your committee submitted the proceedings of their committee to the board, and they were by the board "fully approved and sanctioned." (App. D.)

In this act of refusal, which nothing that had occurred had prepared them to anticipate, your committee are of opinion, that the charter of the bank was violated, and a contempt of the authority of the House of Representatives committed.

Your committee, acting under the instructions of the House of Representatives, without power to modify or enlarge them, charged to inquire, and not authorized to accuse or to arraign, except in their report to the House itself; armed with but the limited authority of a committee, unauthorised to punish, were necessarily compelled to the conclusion, that, in the face of the obstructions already detailed, they could not efficiently prosecute the inquiries with which they were charged, without the aid of the power of the House of Representatives.

Anxious, however, to perform their duty without complaint to the House, and in conformity with the proceedings of the committee of investigation of 1819 and 1832, your committee called on the bank, in a series of resolutions, to furnish statements, and certain extracts and copies from their books and papers, which, in the opinion of your committee, were all intimately connected with their duties, and many of them indispensabl

THE CONGRESSIONAL GLOBE.

PRINTED AND PUBLISHED AT THE CITY OF WASHINGTON, BY BLAIR & RIVES.

23D CONGRESS, 1ST SESSION. SATURDAY, JUNE 21, 1834. VOL. I........No. 29.

to afford to the House of Representatives the information which they had directed your committee to obtain.

The first of these was responded to by the committee of directors, and the information furnished. Though useful, it was comparatively unimportant.

The board of directors, after deliberation, refused to comply with the other calls, for reasons which will be found in their resolution in the appendix, and which reasons deserve examination, as manifesting the deliberate purpose of the directors to resist all attempts to examine into the proceedings of the corporation in the latitude required by your resolution. (App. E.)

They say that the board of directors do not feel themselves at liberty to comply with the requirement of the committee of investigation, because "part" of the copies called for "relate to matters over which the board have no control."

This reason, it is plain, cannot have had much weight in producing the decision of the board. If only a part of the information desired was beyond the control of the board, that fact could have been stated, and this committee would have cheerfully received the residue.

2d. The board say, they cannot comply, because it would be impossible for them to do so "within any reasonable time, having ascertained 'by a careful examination, that the copies and 'statements called for by the resolutions of the '29th ultimo alone, would require the uninter-'rupted labor of two clerks for at least ten months."

This reason, it is also fair to presume, could not materially have influenced the decision of the board. If, in truth, an entire compliance with all the resolutions would require great labor, still that did not justify the refusal to comply with any one of them. Besides, the whole objection could have been obviated by the employment of more clerks than two, the compensation to whom, if paid either by the bank or this committee, would have been well expended in gratifying the requirement of the House of Representatives.

3d. The board say they cannot "comply, inas-'much as in respect to a part of the papers called 'for, the effect would be the same as the surrender 'of their books and papers to a secret and *ex parte* 'examination."

Who can read this last reason for refusing, given by the directors, and fail to peceive that this committee is justified in declaring that, without the aid of *compulsory process*, they cannot obey the directions of the House? If extracts from their own books, made by their own clerks, will not be furnished, because they *might* be used to conduct an *ex parte* examination, what benefit could this committee expect to derive by access to the books themselves?

Permission to take extracts for themselves could, and probably would, be denied for the same reasons; and a committee of the House, without power to compel obedience to its demands, would have power to make no use of the books, which were not approved by the directors themselves. And the House will be at no loss to determine what attitude they would be willing to give their inquiries. And, without authentic extracts, such as were unhesitatingly furnished by the bank to both the former committees of investigation, your committee could very imperfectly convey to the House the grounds of their conclusions or the result of their inspection and examination.

In what condition, then, is your committee placed? The House have commanded them to inquire "what corruptions and abuses have existed in the management of the bank;" whether it has used "corporate power, or money, to interfere in politics, or influence elections."

To do this they have attempted to use the only means that can, by possibility, enable them to fulfil this duty; and they are refused by the directors access to those means which are in their custody, and which, by their charter, they are bound to furnish.

Because, say they, the inquiry this committee has been charged to make, "can only be rightfully extended to alleged violations of the charter." And even these violations of charter are not to be inquired of until the board is furnished with "a specification of all the charges intended to be inquired into." Should supposed violations of charter be specifically charged, then the directors are to decide whether the facts, if true as stated, would amount to technical violations of charter, and then, and not till then, will your committee be permitted to "proceed with them in order as stated." It must be said, that these pretences, by which the bank would justify its bold disregard of the provisions of its charter, are in themselves, derogatory to the dignity, and contemptuous to the authority of the House, to which it in part owes its being.

The committee believe that these proceedings of the bank directors, denying vital and essential powers to the two Houses of Congress, and asserting, in effect, a paramount and controlling authority over both in executing a power devised as a check upon the bank itself, would justify a more extended comment. But confiding in the disposition of the House to maintain its own rights and dignity, and to sustain your committee in the faithful discharge of their duty, they present, as a part of this report, the various resolutions adopted by your committee, with those received from the agents of the bank, as an appendix, declaratory of the powers believed to be possessed, and the purposes of your committee.

They believe that these resolutions will, of themselves, vindicate their conduct and proceedings from all those imputations which are to be found in the various communications of the directors, and their committee, and will serve to show that they have afforded no justification whatever for the extraordinary position ultimately taken by the committee of directors and the board. But that their determination not to permit any conduct of theirs not involving breach of charter, to be investigated, must have been entertained long before it was made known to your committee—and that it was not communicated until every other means of preventing the examination had proved unavailing. But for this conduct, which your committee cannot regard as distinguished by frankness and candor, the absence of your committee from their duties in this House would have been of much shorter continuance.

Believing they had now exhausted, in their efforts to execute the duty devolved upon them, all reasonabe means, depending solely upon the provisions of the bank charter, to obtain the inspection of the books of this corporation, your committee were at last reluctantly compelled to resort to the subpœnas which had been furnished to them under the seal of this House, and attested by its Clerk. They, thereby, on the 9th instant, directed the marshal of the eastern district of Pennsylvania to summon Nicholas Biddle, (President,) and thirteen other persons, directors of the bank, to attend at their committee-room on the next day, at 12 o'clock, at noon, to testify concerning the matters of which your committee were authorized to inquire, and to bring with them certain books, therein named, for inspection. The marshal served the summons in due form of law; and at the time appointed, the persons therein named appeared before the committee, and presented a written communication, signed by each of them, as the answer of each to the requirements of the subpœna, (which is in the appendix marked F.) In this paper they declare "that they do not 'produce the books required, because they are not 'in the custody of either of us, but, as has been 'heretofore stated, of the board," and add, "con-'sidering that as corporators and directors, we 'are parties to the proceeding, we do not consider 'ourselves bound to testify, and therefore respect-'fully decline to do so."

Your committee will not dwell long to answer these technical excuses for this contempt of the lawful mandate of the House. They are to be found at large in the written document above referred to. Most of them, it is believed, have been already satisfactorily answered. The two novel excuses herein set forth cannot but be condemned as insufficient. The first is founded on a very refined distinction between the power of the directors as persons and as corporators. The same persons have and have not power to submit the books. As corporators, the custody of the books is in them; but as individuals, although collectively assembled, the same books are not under their control. Thus, by an attenuated technicality, the lawful authority of the House is to be defied. If in one room of the bank, they must be esteemed as "individual citizens," who may lawfully disregard the *subpœna duces tecum*, because they have not the book demanded—if, in another room of the same house, by a transmigration not known to heathen philosophy, their identity is gone—they have become mere ideal creatures, on which not even a *subpœna ad testificandum* can be served. To make this excuse still more extraordinary, let it be remembered that seven of the gentlemen by whom it is offered had been appointed by the board of directors to exhibit the books of the bank for inspection, and of course must have had the right to their exclusive possession for that purpose.

The reason assigned for the refusal to be sworn is parallel with that which has just been considered. They claim that, as corporators and directors, they are parties to the proceedings of the House, and therefore not bound to give testimony. It is a humane rule, to be found in the criminal law, which declares that no man shall be compelled to criminate himself, and one which this committee would be unwilling, under any circumstances, to deny; but your committee are not aware of any principle of evidence which will excuse a person for refusing to give testimony, simply because it may subject him to a civil action.

There are provisions in the bank charter, making the directors liable to a civil suit if proved to have participated in certain transactions therein mentioned. But it ought not to be supposed that anything can be found on the books of the bank that would subject the directors to a criminal prosecution. Even if the latter supposition be not entirely without foundation, still it is insisted that a witness called on to testify, must do so, unless the court or other tribunal before which he appears, shall adjudge that he is interested. That question the witness cannot be permitted to decide for himself, otherwise evidence might be withheld without good cause. As to the supposition that the directors, or the corporation under their control, are to be considered parties to the inquest this committee was directed to institute, it has already been answered in this report, and needs no further reply. If the inquest had been prosecuted, and had satisfied Congress or the President that a *scire facias* ought to issue, then, and not till then, could the bank directors become parties to the proceeding, and under that principle, attempt to conceal transactions known only to themselves; and even then their books might be used as evidence against them. Justice requires us to add, that the directors, while they protested against our right to examine them, declared they had had no knowledge, which, if a necessary regard to their duty and the rights of others permitted, they would not willingly expose without reserve.

Under such circumstances, it is to be regretted that they have not imitated the course of the directors of 1819 and 1832, by waiving their supposed technical rights, and inviting an unrestrained examination of their proceedings. Such conduct could not but have gained public approbation; and it is humbly conceived, could not have been reasonably objected to by any persons having business with the institution. If such had been the course of the directors, the committee hope to be pardoned for saying it was their purpose to have endeavored to have performed the duties which had been enjoined, thoroughly, impartially, and with a rigid adherence to the immutable principles of truth and justice.

Thus, your committee conclude, the just power and authority of the House of Representatives have been set at naught, defied, and contemned.

Thus, the charter of the Bank of the United States has been deliberately violated, by repeated refusals of the directors of that corporation to submit their books and papers to the inspection of this committee.

Thus have the just expectations of the House and of their constituents been disappointed, and all means of obtaining the best and most accurate information concerning the operations of a controlling moneyed institution, been cut off and denied.

It remains for the House and the country to decide how far this conduct of that directory has been dictated by their solemn duty, as declared, to protect the interests of others committed specially to their protection. How far it conforms to those principles of action which are based on conscious integrity and uprightness of purpose, which defies scrutiny, and invites investigation; and how far it shall be received as a plea of guilty to the high misdemeanors which they insist have been charged against the corporation of which they have the management and control.

These grave questions, with others growing out of the transactions and proceedings, are left to be decided by the House of Representatives.

To elicit those opinions, the following resolutions are most respectfully submitted:

1. *Resolved*, That, by the charter of the Bank of the United States, the right was expressly reserved to either House of Congress, by the appointment of a committee, to inspect the books, and to examine into the proceedings of the said bank, as well as to ascertain if at any time it had violated its charter.

2. *Resolved*, That the resolution of the House of Representatives, passed on the 4th of April, 1834, for the appointment of a committee with full powers to make the investigations embraced in said resolution, was in accordance with the provisions of the charter of said bank and the power of this House.

3. *Resolved*, That the President and Board of Directors of the Bank of the United States, by refusing to submit for inspection the books and papers of the bank, as called for by the committee of the House of Representatives, have contemned the legitimate authority of the House, asserting for themselves powers and privileges not contemplated by the framers of their charter, nor in fairness deducible from any of the terms or provisions of that instrument.

4. *Resolved*, That either House of Congress has the right to *compel* the production of any such books or papers as have been called for by their committee, and also to *compel* said president and directors to testify to such interrogatories as were necessary to a full and perfect understanding of the proceedings of the bank at any period within the term of its existence.

5. *Resolved*, That the Speaker of this House do issue his warrant to the Sergeant-at-Arms to arrest Nicholas Biddle, President, Manuel Eyre, Lawrence Lewis, Ambrose White, Daniel W. Cox, John Holmes, Charles Chauncey, John Goddard, John R. Neff, William Platt, Matthew Newkirk, James C. Fisher, John S. Henry, and John Sergeant, Directors of the Bank of the United States, and bring them to the bar of this House, to answer for their contempt of its lawful authority.

IN SENATE.

SATURDAY, *June* 14, 1834.

Mr. WEBSTER, from the Committee on Finance, to which was referred the bill from the House of Representatives, regulating the value of foreign silver coins, reported the same, with amendments, and which bill (he said) he should ask the Senate to take up early next week.

Mr. WEBSTER gave notice that on Monday next he should move to take up the general appropriation bill; and if its details could not be gone through with on that day, he should again move that it be taken up on Wednesday, as Tuesday had been set apart for the consideration of the French spoliation bill.

BILLS.

The bill from the House of Representatives, to enable Edmund Brooke, of Georgetown, to bring into the District certain negro slaves from Virginia, was read a first and second time, and referred to the Committee on the District of Columbia.

The bill for the relief of the legal representatives of James P. Hainesworth, deceased, was ordered to be engrossed and read a third time.

The bill granting pensions to certain persons therein named was taken up, and on an amendment proposing to strike out the name of William Shaler, a debate ensued, in which Messrs. TOMLINSON, EWING, PRENTISS, KANE, and CHAMBERS, participated.

The amendment finally prevailed by the following vote:

YEAS—Messrs. Bell, Bibb, Black, Calhoun, Frelinghuysen, Grundy, Hendricks, Hill, Kane, King of Alabama, King of Georgia, Knight, Leigh, Linn, McKean, Mangum, Moore, Morris, Poindexter, Porter, Prentiss, Preston, Robinson, Shepley, Silsbee, Smith, Swift, Tipton, Tomlinson, Tyler, Webster, White, Wilkins, and Wright—34.

NAYS—Messrs. Chambers, Clayton, Ewing, Kent, Naudain, Robbins, Southard, and Waggaman—8.

After some other amendments, striking out the name of William P. Shaw and others, the bill was ordered to be engrossed, and read a third time.

Mr. HENDRICKS made an ineffectual effort to take up the bill to improve the navigation of the Wabash river.

The following bills were read a third time, and passed:

A bill for the relief of the widow and children of George Ludlum, deceased;

A bill for the relief of Lucy Loomis;

A bill for the relief of the heirs and legal representatives of Dr. John Berrien, deceased; and

A bill for the relief of General James Taylor, late quartermaster general and district paymaster in the army of the United States.

The bill providing for the final settlement of the claims of States, for interest on advances to the United States made during the last war, being under consideration,

Mr. HILL said:

This bill is for the payment of interest on the claims of the several States, for money advanced and services rendered during the late war with Great Britain. Not only does it introduce a new principle in the computation of interest, but it opens accounts which have been settled many years since, and which most of the States had considered as finally closed.

It is to be remarked, that in settling the several claims of the States, a uniform principle of allowance was pursued at the Treasury Department; that the claims passed the scrutiny of the accounting officers, under the superintendence of agents especially appointed on behalf of the States; and that the claims, about which there was little doubt, were allowed at once, or as soon as they could be examined. In making these settlements, more or less of the claims were disallowed. The claims were not, in all instances, for money advanced by the States. Volunteer militia frequently turned out in cases of alarm, and were in service for a short period only. These and other services were performed in many instances with no expectation of charging either the State or the United States. But, as was natural, when it was understood that payment would be assumed by the General Government, the several States made up their accounts, embracing services and expenses of every kind, including as well those expenditures that were unauthorized, as those that were authorized by the General Government. It is believed that the allowances ultimately made were considered by most of the States to be very liberal.

It will be remarked, that these State claims do not present as strong an appeal to the public justice as do the claims of individuals, which were settled on similar principles. The services were in many instances made for the defence of the States themselves; and on the subject of military defences, the several State Governments had a joint interest with the Government of the United States. It was not expected, in those cases where the service was not especially ordered by the General Government, that the United States would assume this expense as a matter of course. It was a matter of grace that the United States paid any part of such claims. Now, if interest is to be allowed on these claims, how strong must be the claims of individuals who have had accounts settled on the same principles? In many cases the sums allowed to States were the claims of individuals—the States as such had never advanced anything; but, after the allowances were made to the States, these individuals for the first time received their pay. Now, if the accounts shall be reopened, and further allowances shall be made, will the States pay those individuals, according to their several claims, or will they retain the whole amount?

Let us for a moment reflect what will be the effect of the precedent presented by this bill. If interest must be allowed to the States for expenditures in which the States had an equal interest with the United States; if settlements made fifteen or twenty years ago with the States, are to be opened at this time for the purpose of allowing such interest—can we hereafter deny to individuals who have had settlements made, and allowances paid, the reopening of their accounts? If we allow those settlements with States to be opened for services during the last war, shall we not be bound to reopen the accounts of individuals for any and every service and expenditure made by private individuals from the commencement of the war of the Revolution to the present moment? We have, Mr. President, but commenced the payment of our national debt, if the principle adopted in this bill shall prevail. A hundred millions of dollars will not satisfy all the claims that may be made perhaps with equal justice as those which are allowed in this bill.

As to how much will be immediately taken from the treasury if this bill shall become a law, after diligent inquiry, I have not been able to ascertain the amount. Two years ago, that vigilant and faithful officer who has had much to do in the settlement of these accounts, the Third Auditor, was requested to make a calculation what would then be the amount which would be due on the bill allowing the State interest which then passed both Houses of Congress. He answered that it was impossible to tell, as there was no data in his department by which it could be ascertained at what time interest should commence. He did, however, attempt a rough estimate, and from this he supposed the amount in that bill then due, would exceed ONE MILLION THREE HUNDRED THOUSAND DOLLARS. His estimate, undoubtedly was below the mark.

There are some claims in most of the States which have been rejected by the rules adopted for the settlement of the army accounts. It is believed that the Government has been extremely liberal in allowing these claims, and that the States have little cause to complain of those parts of their claims which have been denied. This law, Mr. President, will reverse the usual order of things—it will place those claims which are of doubtful merit in a better position than those about which there is no doubt; because those claims which have been longest delayed, are the claims which will be best paid.

Since the commencement of the present Administration, a portion of the claim which has long been preferred by Massachusetts, amounting to something like half a million of dollars, has been allowed by Congress, and paid. If interest shall be allowed on that allowance, the amount to be paid will be greater than that which has been already paid. But this is not all: Massachusetts holds behind a still greater amount of claim. I believe her demand is now about half a million of dollars more; and her interest account at this time will be greater than the principal.

It is well recollected that the State of Massachusetts refused to call out her militia during the late war with Great Britain, as they were required by a law of the Government. When that State was invaded by a foreign enemy, she held herself back—she failed to drive that enemy from her borders when it was in her power to do it. Nay, it seemed for a time that her real intention in calling out troops was rather to turn her arms against our own Government, than against the foreign enemy. The moral sentiment of the country was shocked at the conduct of that State, sustained as the course of

her Executive was by both her legislature and her judiciary. But on the principle of this bill, her claim will be better treated in the end than that of any other State. If she had obtained the moneys years ago, she would not have had it in her power to invest it at par in Government six per cent. stock; and of course it is better that until this time she has never been paid, if she shall get her whole claim in the end.

I cannot consent, Mr. President, to pay Massachusetts the enormous amount which this bill will give her. The amendment proposed by a Senator from that State [Mr. Silsbee] contemplates interest not only on what she has obtained, but on all she shall obtain hereafter.

The bill which passed the Senate two years ago, and was vetoed by the President, is, I believe, similar to the bill now under consideration. Had that bill become a law, not only would millions have been drawn from the treasury to pay the interest on the principal sums which had already been allowed, but the States would have pressed the several items of account that had been justly disallowed. The State of Massachusetts, having seized with greedy eagerness on her half a million for interest on that part already allowed, would have further pressed her great claim, long held back, for the purpose of taking principal and interest on that also.

I am myself a native of Massachusetts, and never in my life did I converse with a sensible, honest Democrat and friend in his country, belonging to that State, on the subject, who did not confess that the Government would be right never to allow a dollar of her claim. The friends of this bill, is it the system of the opposition who make up the majority of this body, to support every extravagant expenditure, that the treasury may become bankrupt? Does this opposition wish to see the tax on tea and coffee, on salt and other necessaries and conveniences of life which have been taken off, again put on, that "American industry" may be encouraged? If, at a time when, according to the stories which have daily dinned our ears for the last six months, business of every kind is prostrated and the country is ruined—if, at such a time, the great manufacturers at Lowell can divide, as they lately have divided, at the rate of twelve per cent. per annum profit on their capital, do we want further taxes on the people for the protection of manufactures?

I ask gentlemen if the estimate of the Secretary of the Treasury, which anticipated that the receipts might equal the expenditures during the present year, included the items of nearly a full million of dollars for the Cumberland road—three hundred and fifty thousand dollars for the Baltimore railroad company—a million of dollars additional subscription to the Chesapeake and Ohio canal company—an annual half million of dollars for the payment and relief of the District of Columbia, besides some three hundred thousand dollars paid, in this year, principally for extra publications, to pet opposition printers within the District—an unlimited amount of money for French claims, prior to the year 1800—and now two or three millions of dollars, as the first fruits of this interest bill? If these items, and others of a kindred character, have not been anticipated by the head of the treasury, what can we expect but bankruptcy in that department, before another year shall come round?

Taking up the National Intelligencer of this morning, I observe the following paragraph, commenting on the very decisive proposition, in another place, of certain resolutions relating to the deposites, that not long since passed the Senate:

"The public money, therefore, will remain in the local banks, where it is now, or wherever else it may be, until the next session of Congress at least, unless it should be the pleasure of the 'President of the United States, in the plenitude 'of his omnipotential authority, to transfer its 'custody elsewhere. We shall be agreeably disappointed if, by the time Congress gets together 'again, there will be much of the public treasure accessible to deposites or to transfer anywhere."

Very complacent, to be sure! Can anything exceed the insolence of these bloated parasites and panders of a corrupt monopoly, who are not only feasting on the fruits of their corruption, but who have thrown themselves upon the treasury, in opposition to the will of the people, and are actually receiving between one and two hundred thousand dollars of the public money in the very year in which they anticipate a bankrupt treasury? Is it for contemning the people that these men are fed from the public crib? They anticipate that there will not be much of the public treasure accessible after the present year! Well indeed would it have been for the people if there had been no surplus money in the treasury to pay them for extra jobs, surreptitiously authorized by resolutions smuggled through one or the other branch of Congress, as a mere matter of favor to them. If there be no other advantage in an empty treasury, that of preventing the waste of hundreds of thousands on opposition printers will be some consolation to an abused people.

Taunted as we are by the printers of the bank, and by others in Congress, with the prospect of an empty treasury, I trust that neither this bill, nor some others of a like character, will be suffered to pass both branches of Congress at the present session.

The debate was continued by Messrs. PRESTON and BIBB, in opposition, and by Mr. CHAMBERS in support of the bill, and was, on motion of Mr. PRESTON, recommitted by the following vote:

YEAS—Messrs. Benton, Bibb, Black, Brown, Calhoun, Forsyth, Grundy, Hill, Kane, King of Alabama, King of Georgia, Leigh, Linn, Mangum, Moore, Morris, Preston, Robinson, Shepley, Tallmadge, Tipton, Tyler, Waggaman, White, and Wright—24.

NAYS—Messrs. Chambers, Clay, Clayton, Ewing, Frelinghuysen, Hendricks, Kent, Knight, McKean, Naudain, Poindexter, Porter, Prentiss, Silsbee, Smith, Sprague, Swift, Tomlinson, and Webster—19.

The following bills from the House of Representatives were read twice, the first referred to the Committee on Finance, and the last to the Committee on the Public Lands:

A bill providing for the payment of Indian annuities for the year 1834;

A bill for the relief of the legal representatives of Leonard Holley.

The following bills were read a third time and passed:

A bill to remunerate Stephen C. Phillips, for the support and transportation of shipwrecked American seamen;

A bill for the relief of General James Taylor, late quartermaster general and district paymaster in the army of the United States;

A bill for the relief of Aaron Fitzgerald;

A bill confirming certain land claims in the district of St. Stephen's, Alabama;

A bill for the relief of Andrew Armstrong;

A bill to create two additional land districts in the State of Illinois, and two new land districts north of said State, in the Territory now attached to Michigan, which lies between Lake Michigan and the Mississippi river;

The bill for the relief of James Fife, a Creek Indian;

[Upon a proposition made by Mr. POINDEXTER to indefinitely postpone this bill, a debate upon its merits occurred, in which Messrs. TIPTON, WHITE, MOORE, and FRELINGHUYSEN, advocated the bill; and Messrs. POINDEXTER, and KING of Georgia, opposed it.

The question on indefinite postponement was negatived by the following vote:

YEAS—Messrs. Bell, Black, Brown, Calhoun, Hill, King of Alabama, King of Georgia, Leigh,

Mangum, Poindexter, Preston, Robbins, Wright —13.

NAYS—Messrs. Benton, Bibb, Chambers, Clay, Frelinghuysen, Grundy, Hendricks, Kent, Knight, Linn, McKean, Moore, Naudain, Porter, Prentiss, Robinson, Shepley, Silsbee, Smith, Southard, Swift, Tallmadge, Tipton, Tomlinson, Waggaman, White —36.]

The bill for the repair of the Mars Hill military road, in the State of Maine;

The bill for the relief of William Duer, John Duer, and Beverly Robinson, trustees of the estate of Sarah Alexander, deceased.

On motion of Mr. POINDEXTER, the Senate proceeded to executive business; and, after remaining some time therein,

Adjourned.

HOUSE OF REPRESENTATIVES.

SATURDAY, June 14, 1834.

Mr. ARCHER, from the Committee on Foreign Affairs, reported a bill to carry into effect the convention between the Government of the United States and Spain; which was read twice, and committed.

Mr. ARCHER, from the same committee, reported a bill for the relief of David Leslie; which was read twice, and committed.

Mr. LYON presented the following resolution; which was adopted:

Resolved, That the Clerk of this House cause to be prepared and printed as early as practicable, a correct map of the northern boundary line of the State of Ohio, as surveyed, marked, and designated under the act of Congress of the 30th May, 1832, together with as much of the northern part of that State and the State of Indiana, and also so much of the southern portion of the Territory of Michigan as may be necessary fully to understand the question of boundary line now existing between Ohio and Michigan.

On motion of Mr. CONNOR, the Committee of the Whole was discharged from the consideration of a bill for the relief of the heirs of Leonard Holley, a soldier of the late war; which was agreed to. The bill was ordered to be engrossed and read a third time to-day.

On motion of Mr. POLK, the Indian annuity bill was, by consent, read a third time.

Mr. WILLIAMS remarked, that he had inquired, while this bill was in Committee of the Whole, with regard to the expenditure of $500,000 by the Indian bill of 1830, and was answered by the chairman of the Committee of Ways and Means that it would be found in.

Mr. POLK said that he had been informed by the Secretary of War that the whole of that sum had been disbursed agreeably to law. Soon after the inquiry was made, he found, by recurrence to the printed documents, that the sum had been accounted for, and at that time could have probably satisfied the gentleman by pointing out the evidence on that subject; but as this time the books were not at hand.

Mr. WILLIAMS said he would have been better satisfied had the details of the disbursements been shown.

Mr. POLK moved that the House, by consent, go into Committee of the Whole on the state of the Union, upon the remaining appropriation bills.

Mr. W. R. DAVIS could not consent to make any appropriations while the public moneys remained in the illegal custody in which they were now placed. He would inquire of the chairman of the committee whether any provision by law was contemplated upon that subject?

Mr. POLK said he proposed to go into committee generally. After the appropriation bill had been gone through with, he should propose to take up the bill regulating the public deposites, now in that committee.

The House then went into Committee of the Whole on the state of the Union, Mr. GHOLSON in the chair.

In taking up the bill making appropriations for fortifications for 1834, was taken up on motion of Mr. POLK.

Mr. P. says to that, in the House, he should move to reduce or strike out the appropriations for

forts on George's Island, Grand Terre, and Throg's Neck.

Mr. WHITE, of Florida, moved to amend the bill by adding an item for repairing the fortifications at St. Augustine, $50,000.

Mr. W. explained the necessity of this appropriation.

Mr. POLK said the amendment had not been before any committee of the House, so far as he knew, and it was unprecedented for the House to make such an appropriation without previous examination.

The question was taken on the amendment; which was lost.

Mr. PARKER moved to strike out the appropriation of $100,000 for a fort on Throg's Neck, East river.

The question was taken, and the motion to strike out was lost.

Mr. GORHAM moved an amendment striking out the proposed appropriation for Castle Island and George's Island, and inserting the sum of $125,000 for those objects.

Mr. G. said, the appropriation in the bill for these purposes was $137,000 in two separate items; he proposed, in accordance with the opinion of the engineer, to unite them, and reduce them to the proposed sum.

Mr. POLK was not disposed to be driven into a discussion of the amendments here and again in the House.

The question was taken on the amendment, which was lost.

The item appropriating $50,000 for fortifications in Charleston harbor, having been read—

Mr. PINCKNEY moved an amendment confining the appropriation to the preservation and repair of Castle Pinckney and Fort Moultrie.

The amendment was lost.

The bill was then laid aside.

Mr. POLK moved the committee to take up the bill making a re-appropriation for certain Georgia militia claims.

The bill was read, and no amendment being proposed, was laid aside.

Mr. POLK moved the committee take up the bill making appropriations for the National Armory, at Harper's Ferry.

Mr. ARCHER moved to amend the bill by adding an additional sum of $5,598 16 for completing certain works there.

Mr. POLK said the sum required was only $3000, which was contained in the bill.

Mr. ARCHER withdrew his amendment and the bill was laid aside.

Mr. SUTHERLAND moved that the bill making appropriations for building light-houses, light-boat beacons, and monuments for the year 1834, be taken up; which was carried.

After the bill was read—

Mr. SUTHERLAND moved an amendment appropriating $3,500 for a monument or beacon on Deer Island Point in Boston harbor; which was agreed to.

Mr. PEARCE moved an amendment changing the location of the light-house proposed to be built for the harbor of Bristol, Rhode Island; which was agreed to.

Mr. WARDWELL moved an amendment designating with more exactness the location of a light-house on Lake Ontario; which was agreed to.

Mr. VANDERPOEL moved an appropriation for a light-house in Hudson river, in place of one carried away by ice, $5,000; which was agreed to.

Mr. SUTHERLAND moved $10,000 for two light-houses in Pennsylvania; which was agreed to.

Mr. DUNLAP moved $5,000 for a light-house at Memphis, on the Mississippi river; which was agreed to.

Mr. ALLEN, of Ohio, moved $3,000 for a light-house at the mouth of the Scioto river; which was negatived.

Mr. SUTHERLAND moved $5,000 for a light-house at the mouth of Pearl river; which was agreed to.

After filling various blanks, the bill was laid aside.

Mr. BINNEY moved to take up the bill making appropriations for the Military Academy at West Point.

The bill having been read—

Mr. BINNEY moved to amend the bill by striking out the 2d section, making provision for the salary of Mr. Leslie as drawing master, which was agreed to.

Mr. J. Q. ADAMS asked what was the meaning, force, and effect of the words et cetera, in the 2d clause, providing for "repairs," &c. It was rather a comprehensive word; and he would move to strike it out, unless some explanation was given of it.

Mr. BINNEY said the word was useless, and of no effect; and moved to strike it out; which was agreed to.

Mr. BINNEY moved an amendment, authorizing the settlement of the claim of Colonel Thayer, for the purchase of philosophical apparatus for the academy, under an order from the Secretary of War; which was agreed to.

Mr. THOMAS moved an amendment, providing that the benefit of the act shall not extend to any cadet who shall not graduate, or who, having graduated, shall not serve five years in the army.

This subject, he said, was to prevent young men from going to the academy for the purpose of an education at the public expense, without intending to devote themselves to the public service.

Mr. EWING said, that if the object of the gentleman was to destroy the institution, it could not be better attained in any way than this. The West was now beginning to derive some benefit from the academy.

Mr. THOMAS withdrew the amendment for the present, in order to modify it.

Mr. DICKINSON, of Tennessee, spoke against the general principle and policy of the bill. If we were surrounded by hostile nations, as Austria or Prussia is, we might need such an institution; but this would never be the case, until the Union was dissolved. He was opposed to the institution, as countenancing an inequality of principles, contrary to the principles of free government, and he moved to strike out the enacting clause of the bill.

Mr. WARD, of New York, spoke about one hour in support of the bill, and in favor of the continuance of the institution.

Mr. SMITH, of Maine, expressed a wish to bring the institution back to its original object, which was merely to educate engineers. This bill provided for expenses incurred during the last six months, and it was necessary that the appropriation should be made. If the gentleman from Tennessee would withdraw his amendment, he would propose one, which he thought would better meet the feeling of those who are opposed to the institution. He would move an amendment, repealing the second section of the act of 1803, fixing the military peace establishment, and the second, third, and fourth sections of the act of 1819, increasing the number of cadets and instructors. Also, an amendment striking out the appropriations for additional buildings.

Mr. DICKINSON said his proposition was intended to test the sense of the House on the subject, and he wished to have a vote taken on it.

Mr. BROWN said, the motion of the honorable gentleman from Tennessee [Mr. DICKINSON] to strike out the enacting clause of the bill, and the amendment which the honorable member from Maine [Mr. Smith] declared he would hereafter submit, involves not only the fate of the bill under consideration, but the existence of the military academy itself. He rose to express his regret that this important question should be discussed at this time; and he would ask his honorable friends to pause before they proceed further. The military academy has been established more than thirty years. Its establishment had been repeatedly and earnestly recommended to Congress by General Washington, while President of the United States. It has been sanctioned and sustained by every Administration, (commencing with that of Mr. Jefferson,) down to the present time; and he ventured to say, it had at all times enjoyed the confidence and approbation of a large majority of the American people. He would remind honorable gentlemen that the faith of the nation was concerned in the duration of the institution for some time yet to come. Did they mean to deprive its professors and teachers of the places to which the Government had invited them, and for which their

learning and attainments so eminently qualified them, without a moment's notice, or the slightest opportunity for preparation? Did they mean to cast loose upon the world two hundred and fifty young men, selected from every part of the Union, whose education and hopes of future usefulness had been committed to the care and guardianship of the nation? He trusted he knew too well the high motives and generous impulses which guided the action of honorable gentlemen upon this floor, to believe for a moment they could be sensible of such a gross and flagrant violation of the public faith, as these propositions (if adopted) would most surely accomplish.

He begged it might not be forgotten that the bill under consideration, was one of the usual annual appropriation bills. And had not the House over and over again, in the course of the session, repudiated the practice of creating or destroying offices by means of bills of this character? And if the practice was pernicious when applied to offices alone, he begged to know if it would not be dangerous and pregnant with mischief, when applied to the long-settled and permanent institutions of the country? It had been his fortune to reside in the immediate vicinity of West Point during the greater part of his life. It was within sight of his home, and formed a part of the district which he had the honor to represent. And he hoped he would be pardoned when he declared he felt an unfeigned and anxious solicitude for the preservation of an institution which he regarded as a necessary and essential part of our system of public defence and an honor and an ornament to the nation. If the question must now undergo discussion, whether a military school for the instruction of our officers in the elementary principles of military science should exist hereafter, he must insist upon his right to be heard, reluctant as he was to examine so grave a question within the last fourteen days of the session. He wanted the subject examined (as it should be) upon a bill or resolution introduced expressly for the purpose. And he would respectfully assure honorable gentlemen that the friends of the academy would not shrink from nor shun the inquiry. He would forbear to say more at present, since he was whether the honorable gentleman from Tennessee would not withdraw his motion to strike out, and suffer the bill to pass through the committee. And should the discussion be renewed hereafter, he trusted the House would afford him an opportunity to be heard.

After a few words from Messrs. DICKINSON, JOHNSON of Kentucky, and McKAY, the question was taken, and the amendment rejected.

Mr. HAWES renewed his motion in a modified form.

Mr. SMITH moved to amend it by substituting for it the provisions suggested by him, as above mentioned.

Mr. EWING opposed the amendment.

After a few words from Messrs. McKAY and SMITH, the question was taken on the amendment to the amendment, and decided in the negative, without a division.

The amendment offered by Mr. HAWES was then rejected.

Mr. HAWES then moved to amend the bill by providing that each cadet should, upon his appointment, give bond, with security, to refund to the United States the expense of his education in case he should not remain in the service; which motion was rejected.

Mr. BURD moved an amendment, providing that each cadet shall give bond to refund the expense of his education to the Government, in case he shall not serve in the Government from thirty years; which motion was rejected.

Mr. DUNCAN moved to amend the bill, by providing that no one should be appointed and the number of cadets be reduced to sixty; which was rejected.

Mr. PINCKNEY moved to amend, by providing that after the 1st of January next the Military Academy shall be abolished; which was rejected.

The bill was then laid aside to be reported.

Mr. ASHLEY moved to take up the bill for the continuation of the Cumberland road; which was negatived—63 to 55.

On motion of Mr. WHITE, the committee took up for consideration the following bills, which were laid aside without amendment:

A bill regulating the value of certain foreign gold coins in the United States, and a bill concerning the gold and silver coins of the United States, and for other purposes.

On motion of Mr. POLK, the committee then rose and reported all the above bills.

The bill re-appropriating the unexpended balance for the payment of the Georgia militia, and the bill making appropriations for a canal, in connexion with the works at Harper's Ferry, were read a third time, and passed.

The House then adjourned.

IN SENATE.

Monday, June 16, 1834.

The VICE PRESIDENT presented a communication from the Secretary of the Treasury, in compliance with a resolution of the Senate of 11th March last, transmitting a statement of the Comptroller, relating to additional compensation allowed to mail contractors since the 30th of September, 1825.

On motion of Mr. GRUNDY, the communication and report were referred to the Committee on the Post Office and Post Roads, and ordered to be printed.

The VICE PRESIDENT also presented a communication from the Secretary of the Treasury, transmitting the amount of duties upon foreign imports during the first quarter of the year 1834, and furnishing estimates of the probable receipts of the remaining quarters of the year.

The report was as follows:

TREASURY DEPARTMENT,
June 16th, 1834.

SIR: In compliance with the resolution of the Senate, of the 7th of May last, directing the Secretary of the Treasury " to ' report as soon as practicable, to the Sen-'ate, the amount of duties received and ' accrued on foreign imports, during the ' first quarter of the year 1834, with a table ' showing the comparative amount of that ' quarter, and the corresponding quarter ' of the year 1833, and distinguishing be-'tween the amounts accrued or received ' at each port." Also, " whether anything ' has happened since the annual report was ' made at the commencement of the pres-'ent session of Congress, to vary, in his ' opinion, the estimate contained in the ' said report, of the proceeds of the duties ' on foreign imports for the year 1834 ;" I herewith transmit the statement required by the first resolution abovementioned, by which it appears that the duties which accrued from customs in the first quarter of 1833, amounted to the sum of $5,798,-114 87, and in the corresponding quarter of 1834, to the sum of $5,344,540 40, and that the actual receipts into the treasury from the same source in the former quarter, amounted to $6,966,437 09, and in the latter, to $4,435,386 13. A few of the minor ports have not been heard from; but they an not materially vary the result.

In answer to the second resolution I ave the honor to state, that estimating he duties on foreign imports in the anual report made at the commencement of the present session, it was assumed as he basis of the estimate, that the imports f the present year would be nearly equal to those of 1832. This estimate was higher than the average imports of the five or six receding years; but, as stated in that report, it was considered as a safe one; because, although the imports of 1831 and 1832 had been unusually large, those of 1833 had gone still higher, and the general state of commerce and the situation of the country, justified the belief that there would be no serious diminution in the present year. .

From the comparative statement of the amount of duties which accrued in the first quarter of the present year, and the corresponding quarter of 1833, it appears that the amount of foreign imports in the first quarter of 1834, must have exceeded that of the corresponding quarter in the preceding year. Several articles which form important items in our ordinary imports, and paid duty in the first quarter of 1833, were free from duty in the first quarter of 1834, and the rate of duty was reduced on others ; and the difference between the amount of duty which accrued in these two quarters, would have been greater if the importations in the latter had not exceeded those of the former.

In some instances, without doubt, importations, which in the ordinary course of our foreign trade would have been made in the last quarter of 1833, were delayed until the first quarter of the present year, in order to obtain the benefit of the reduced tariff, which took effect on the first of January last; and this circumstance has enlarged, in some degree, the imports of the first quarter of 1834. But after making a due allowance for the increase which may have arisen from this cause, and which would be peculiar to the first quarter of the year, the amount of duties which accrued in the quarter, are sufficient to show that the imports of the present year will most probably exceed the amount at which they were estimated in the annual report, and be fully equal to those of 1833, which were unusually large. If this expectation should be realized, the proceeds of the customs will exceed the amount at which they were estimated by more than 1,000,000 dollars. The difference in the comparative receipts of the two first quarters as shown by the statement herewith transmitted, does not arise from any fluctuation in commerce or diminished importations, but is chiefly occasioned by the alterations in the times of payment, introduced by the act of 14th July, 1832.

The receipts of the first quarter, and the bonds already taken, confirm the opinion that the income from customs will be greater than the estimate presented at the commencement of the session. The actual receipts into the treasury from customs for the first quarter of the present year, amounted to the sum of $4,435,386 13, and the duties secured by bonds payable in the second quarter, amount to the sum of $4,003,368 77. After making a fair deduction from these amounts for return duties, which may yet be called for, and for debentures and expenses of collection, the net income of these two quarters may be safely estimated at $7,500,-000. And if the third and fourth quarters should be only equally productive with the two first, the receipts will equal the amount at which they were estimated in the annual report. But under our present system of duties, the receipts from customs in the ordinary course of commerce will always be greater in the two last quarters of the year than in the two first. The woollen goods which form so large a portion of our imports, are for the most part brought into the country in the third and fourth quarters of the year. The high duties with which they are charged, render them a very productive source of revenue; and being now payable in cash, they enter into the receipts of the third and fourth quarters in which these goods are imported. The receipt of these two quarters of the year, will, therefore, generally exceed those of the two preceding ones by at least one million of dollars.

Although not embraced in the resolution, it will no doubt be gratifying to the Senate to learn that the receipts from the lands are equally encouraging, and will more than equal the amount at which they were estimated. The receipts into the treasury, from this source, during the first quarter of the present year, amount to the sum of $1,398,506 16, while in the corresponding quarter of 1833, they amounted only to $668,526 66, and from the returns already received for the present quarter, the receipts of the two first quarters of this year from lands, may be safely estimated at more than $2,-000,000. In the annual report, the receipts for the whole year were estimated at $3,000,000. The information above stated, shows that the anticipated income from this source, as well as from the customs, will be more than realized.

Upon the whole, the information received since the annual report on the finances was made to Congress, affords satisfactory evidence that the extent of our foreign commerce has been fully sustained, and gives strong reasons for believing that the receipts into the treasury during the present year will be greater than the amount which they were estimated at the commencement of the present session.

I beg leave to repeat what I have already said in the annual report from this department, that as the receipts of each year, under the present system of short credits and cash duties, must mainly depend on its own importations, the estimates for the year can never be made with as much certainty as under the former system, when the receipts chiefly depended on the duties which had accrued in preceding years, and which were ascertained and secured by bonds before the time the estimates were presented.

And as all calculations on the amount of revenue hereafter to accrue, must be more or less uncertain, and are liable to be affected by unforeseen contingencies, it would hardly be proper to appropriate on a scale of expenditure fully equal to the expected income. There is, however, no reason for apprehending that the resources of the present year can fall short of the estimate contained in the annual report. And it is believed, that appropriations may be made with entire safety according to that estimate.

I have the honor to be, sir, very respectfully, your obedient servant,

R. B. TANEY,
Secretary of the Treasury.

Hon. MARTIN VAN BUREN,
*Vice President United States,
and President of the Senate.*

The Secretary of the Senate commenced the reading of the report.

Mr. WEBSTER moved to dispense with the reading, and refer it to the Committee on Finance.

Mr. BENTON demanded the reading.

The Secretary of the Senate resumed the reading, and completed it.

Mr. WEBSTER moved to refer, and print it.

Mr. BENTON rose, and said that this report was of a nature to deserve some attention, before it left the chamber of the Senate, and went to a committee, from which it might not return in time for consideration at this session. It had been called for under circumstances which attracted attention, and disclosed information which deserved to be known. It was called for early in May, in the crisis of the alarm operations, and with confident assertions that the answer to the call would prove the distress and the suffering of the country. It was confidently asserted that the Secretary of the Treasury had over-estimated the revenues of the year; that there would be a great falling off—a decline—a bankruptcy; that confidence was destroyed—enterprise checked—industry paralyzed—commerce suspended!—that the direful act of one man, in one dire order, had changed the face of the country, from a scene of unparalleled prosperity to a scene of unparalleled desolation! that the canal was a solitude, the lake a desert waste of waters, the ocean without ships, the commercial towns deserted, silent, and sad; orders for goods countermanded; foreign purchases stopped! and that the answer of the Secretary would prove all this, in showing the falsity of his own estimates, and the great decline in the revenue and importations of the country. Such were the assertions and predictions under which the call was made, and to which the public attention was attracted by every device of theatrical declamation from this floor. Well, the answer comes. The Secretary sends in his report, with every statement called for. It is a report to make the patriot's heart rejoice! full of high and gratifying facts; replete with rich information; and pregnant with evidences of national prosperity. How is it received—how received by those who called for it? With downcast looks, and wordless tongues! A motion is even made to stop the reading! to stop the reading of such a report! called for under such circumstances! while whole days are given up to reading the monotonous, tautologous, and endless repetitions, of distress-memorials, the echo of our own speeches, and the thousandth edition of the same work, without emendation or correction! All these can be read, and printed too, and lauded with studied eulogium, and their contents sent out to the people, freighted upon every wind; but this official report of the Secretary of the Treasury upon the state of their own revenues, and of their own commerce, called for by an order of the Senate, is to be treated like an unwelcome and worthless intruder; received without a word—not even read—slipped out upon a motion—disposed of as the Abbe Sieyes voted for the death of Louis the Sixteenth, *mort sans phrase!* death, without talk! But he (Mr. B.) did not mean to suffer this report to be despatched in this unceremonious and compendious style. It had been called for to be given to the people, and the people should hear of it. It was not what was expected, but it is what is true, and what will rejoice the heart of every patriot in America. A pit was dug for Mr. Taney; the diggers of the pit have fallen into it; the fault is not his; and the sooner they clamber out, the better for themselves. The people have a right to know the contents of this report, and know them they shall; and if there is any man in this America whose heart is so constructed as to grieve over the prosperity of his country, let him prepare himself for sorrow; for the proof is forthcoming, that never, since our America had a place among nations, was the prosperity of the country equal to what it is at this day!

Mr. B. then requested the Secretary of the Senate to send him the report and comparative statement; which being done, Mr. B. opened the report, and went over the heads of it, to show that the Secretary of the Treasury had not overestimated the revenue of the year; that the revenue was, in fact, superior to the estimate; and that the importations would equal, if not exceed, the highest amount that they had ever attained.

To appreciate the statements which he should make, Mr. B. said it was necessary for the Senate to recollect that the list of dutiable articles was now greatly reduced. Many articles were now free of duty, which formerly paid heavy duties; many others were reduced in duty; and the fair effect of these abolitions and reductions would be a diminution of revenue, even without a diminution of imports; yet the Secretary's estimate, made at the commencement of the session, was more than realized, and showed the gratifying spectacle of a full and overflowing treasury, instead of the empty one which had been predicted; and left to Congress the grateful occupation of further reducing taxes, instead of the odious task of borrowing money, as had been so loudly anticipated for six months past. The revenue *accruing* from imports in the first quarter of the present year, was $5,344,540; the payments actually made into the treasury from the custom-houses for the same quarter was $4,435,386; and the payments from lands for the same time was $1,398,206. The two first months of the second quarter were producing in a full ratio to the first quarter; and the actual amount of available funds in the treasury on the ninth day of this month, was ELEVEN MILLIONS TWO HUNDRED AND FORTY-NINE THOUSAND FOUR HUNDRED AND TWELVE DOLLARS The two last quarters of the year were always most productive. It was the time of the largest importations of foreign goods which pay most duty—the woollens; and the season also for the largest sale of public lands: it is well believed that the estimate will be more largely exceeded in those two quarters than in the two first; and that the excess for the whole year, over the estimate, will be full two millions of dollars. This (Mr. B. said) was one of the evidences of public prosperity which the report contained; and which utterly contradicted the idea of distress and commercial embarrassment, which had been propagated from this Chamber for the last six months.

Mr. B. proceeded to the next evidence of commercial prosperity; it was in the increased importations of foreign goods. These imports, judging from the first five months, would be seven millions more than they were two years ago, when the Bank of the United States had seventy millions loaned out; and they were twenty millions more than in the time of Mr. Adams's Administration. At the rate they had commenced, they would amount to one hundred and ten millions for the year. This will exceed whatever was known to our country. The imports, for the time that President Jackson has served, have regularly advanced from about seventy-four millions to one hundred and eight millions.

The following is the statement of these imports, from which Mr. B. read:

1829	$74,492,527
1830	70,876,920
1831	103,191,124
1832	101,029,266
1833	108,118,311

Mr. B. said that the imports of the last year were greater in proportion than in any previous year; a temporary decline might reasonably have been expected; such declines always take place after excessive importations. If it had occurred now, though naturally to have been expected, the fact would have been trumpeted forth as the infallible sign—the proof positive—of commercial distress, occasioned by the fatal removal of the deposites. But, as there was no decline, but, on the contrary, an actual increase, he must claim the evidence for the other side of the account, and set it down as proof positive, that commerce is not destroyed; and, consequently, that the removal of the deposites did not destroy commerce.

The next evidence of commercial prosperity which Mr. B. would exhibit to the Senate, was in the increased and increasing number of ship arrivals from foreign ports. The number of arrivals for the month of May, in New York, was 223, exceeding by 36 those of the month of April, and showing not only a great, but an increasing activity in the commerce of that great emporium—he would not say of the United States, or even of North America—but he would call it that great emporium of the two Americas, and of the New World; for the goods imported to that place were thence distributed to every part of the two Americas, from the Canadian lakes to Cape Horn.

A third evidence of national prosperity, was in the sales of the public lands. Mr. B. had, on a former occasion, adverted to these sales, so far as the first quarter was concerned, and had shown that instead of falling off, as had been predicted on this floor, the revenue from the sales of these lands had actually doubled, and more than doubled, what they were in the first quarter of 1833. The receipts for lands, for that quarter, were $668,926; for the first quarter of the present year they were $1,398,206; being two to one, and $60,000 over! The receipts for the two first months of the second quarter, were also known, and would carry the revenue from lands, for the first five months of this year, to two millions of dollars; indicating five millions for the whole year; an enormous amount, from which the people of the new States ought to be, in some degree, relieved, by a reduction in the price of lands. Mr. B. begged, in the most emphatic terms, to remind the Senate that at the commencement of the session the sales of the public lands were selected as one of the criterions by which the ruin and desolation of the country was to be judged. It was then predicted, and the prediction put forth with all the boldness of infallible-prophecy, that the removal of the deposites would stop the sales of the public lands; that money would disappear, and the people have nothing to buy with; that the produce of the earth would rot upon the hands of the farmer. These were the predictions; and if the sales had really declined, what a proof would immediately be found in the fact to prove the truth of the prophecy, and the dire effects of changing the public moneys from one set of banking houses to another! But there is no decline, but a doubling of the former product; and a fair conclusion thence deduced that the new States, in the interior, are as prosperous as the old ones on the seacoast.

Having proved the general prosperity of the country from these infallible data: flourishing revenue—flourishing commerce—increased arrivals of ships, and increased sales of public lands, Mr. B. said that he was far from denying that actual distress had existed. He had admitted the fact of that distress heretofore, not to the extent to which it was charged, but to a sufficient extent to excite sympathy for the sufferers; and he had distinctly charged the whole distress that did exist, to the Bank of the United States, and the Senate of the United States—to the screw and pressure operations of the bank, and the alarm speeches in the Senate. He had made this charge, and made it under a full sense of the moral reponsibility which he owed to the people, in affirming anything from this elevated theatre. He had, therefore, given his proofs to accompany the charge; and he had now to say to the Senate, and through the Senate to the people, that he found new proofs for that charge in the detailed statements of the accruing revenue, which had been called for by the Senate, and furnished by the Secretary of the Treasury.

Mr. B. said he must be pardoned for repeating his request to the Senate, to recollect how often they had been told that trade was paralyzed; that orders for foreign goods were countermanded; that the importing cities were the picture of desolation; their ships idle; their wharves deserted; their mariners wandering up and down. Now, (said Mr. B.,) in looking over the detailed statement of the accruing revenue, it was found that there was no decline of commerce, except at places where the policy and power of the United States Bank was predominant! Where that power or policy was predominant, revenue declined; where it was not predominant, or the policy of the bank not exerted, the revenue increased, and increased fast enough to make up the deficiency at the other places. Mr. B. proceeded to verify this statement by a reference to specified places. Thus, at Philadelphia, where the bank holds its seat of empire, the revenue fell off about one-third; it was $797,316 for the first quarter of 1833, and only $542,498 for the first quarter of 1834. At New York, where the bank has not been able to get the upper hand, there was an increase of more than $120,000; the revenue there for the first quarter of 1833, was $3,122,1[illegible]; for the first of 1834, it was $3,249,786. At Boston, where the bank is again predominant, the revenue fell off about one-third; at Salem (Massachusetts) it fell off four-fifths; at Baltimore, where the bank has been defeated, there was an increase in the revenue of more than $70,000; at Richmond the revenue was doubled, from $12,034 to $25,[illegible]; at Charleston, it was increased from $69,5[illegible] to $102,810; at Petersburg, it was slightly increased; and throughout all the region south of the Potomac there was either an increase, or the slight falling of

which might result from diminished duties without diminished importations. Mr. B. said he knew that bank power was predominant in some of the cities to the south; but he knew, also, that the bank policy of distress and oppression had not been practised there. That was not the region to be governed by the scourge. The high mettle of that region required a different policy: gentleness, conciliation, coaxing! If the South was to be gained over by the bank, it was to be done by favor, not by fear. The scourge, though so much the most congenial to the haughty spirit of the moneyed power, was only to be applied where it would be submitted to; and, therefore, the whole region south of the Potomac was exempted from the lash. Mr. B. paused to fix the attention of the Senate upon these facts. Where the power of the bank enabled her to depress commerce and sink the revenue, and her policy permitted her to do it, commerce was depressed, and the revenue was sunk, and the prophecies of the distress orators were fulfilled; but where her power did not predominate, or her policy required a different course, commerce increased, and the revenue increased; and the result of the whole is, that New York and some other anti-bank cities, have gained what Philadelphia and other bank cities have lost; and the Federal treasury is just as well off, as if it had got its accustomed supply from every place.

This view of facts, Mr. B. said, must fasten upon the bank the odium of having produced all the real commercial distress which has been felt. But at one point, at New Orleans, there was further evidence to convict her of wanton and wicked oppression. It was not in the Secretary's reports, but it was in the weekly returns of the bank; and showed that in the beginning of March, that institution had carried off from her branch in New Orleans, the sum of about $800,000 in specie, which it had been collecting all the winter by a wanton curtailment, under the pretext of supplying the amount of the deposites taken from her at that place. These $800,000 were collected from the New Orleans merchants in the very crisis of the arrival of western produce. The merchants were pressed to pay debts, when they ought to have been accommodated with loans. The price of produce was thereby depressed; the whole West suffered from the depression; and now it is proved that the money was not wanted to supply the place of the deposites, but was sent to Philadelphia, where there was no use for it, the bank having more there than she can use; and that the whole operation was a wanton and wicked measure to coerce the West to cry out for a return of the deposites, and a renewal of the charter, by attacking their commerce in the market of New Orleans. This fact, said Mr. B., would have been proved from the books of the bank, if they had been inspected. Failing in that, the proof was intelligibly found in the weekly returns.

Mr. B. had a further view to give of the prosperity of the country, and further evidence to show that all the distress really suffered, was factitious and unnatural. It was in the great increase of money in the United States during the last year and a half. He spoke of money; not paper promises to pay money, but the thing itself—real gold and silver—and affirmed that there was a clear gain of from EIGHTEEN to TWENTY MILLIONS OF SPECIE, within the time that he had mentioned. He then took up the custom-house returns to verify this important statement, and to let the people see that the country was never so well off for money as at the very time that it was proclaimed to be in the lowest state of poverty and misery. He first showed the imports and exports of specie and bullion for the year ending the 30th of September, 1833. It was as follows:

Year ending September 30, 1833.

	Imports.	Exports.
Gold bullion..	$48,267..........	$26,775
Silver bullion.	297,840	-
Gold coin....	563,585..........	495,890
Silver coin,...	6,160,676..........	1,722,196
	$7,070,368	$2,244,861

Mr. B., having read over this statement, remarked upon it, that it presented a clear balance of near five millions of specie in favor of the United States on the 1st day of October last, without counting at least another million which was brought by passengers, and not put upon the custom-house books. It might be assumed (he said) that there was a clear accession of six millions of specie to the money of the United States on the morning of that very day which had been pitched upon by all the distress orators in the country to date the ruin and desolation of the country.

Mr. B. then showed a statement of the imports and exports of specie and bullion, from the first of October, 1833, to the 11th of June, instant. It was as follows:

From October 1st to June 11th.

	Imports.	Exports.
Gold bullion..	$304.491.........	$11,177
Silver bullion..	256,617.........	1,376
Gold coin.....	410,907.........	87,570
Silver coin	10,156,909.........	898,638
	$11,128.924	$998,761

Mr. B. remarked, upon this statement, that it presented a clear gain of more than ten millions of dollars. He was of opinion that two millions ought to be added for sums not entered at the custom-house, which would make twelve millions; and added to the six millions of 1833, would give eighteen millions of specie of clear gain to the country in the last twenty months. This (he said) was prosperity. It was wealth itself; and besides, it showed that the country was not in debt for its large importations, and that a larger proportion of foreign imports now consisted of specie than was ever known before. Mr. B. particularized the imports and exports of gold; how the former had increased, and the latter diminished, during the last few months; and said that a great amount of gold, both foreign and domestic, was now waiting in the country to see if Congress would raise gold to its fair value. If so raised, this gold would remain, and enter into circulation; if not, it would immediately go off to foreign countries, for *gold* was not a thing to stay where it was undervalued. He also spoke of silver, and said that it had arrived without law, but could not remain without law. Unless Congress passed an act to make it current, and that at full value as money, and not at the mint value, as bullion, it would all go off.

Mr. B. recapitulated the evidences of national prosperity—increased imports—revenue from customs exceeding the estimate—increased revenue from public lands—increased amount of specie—above eleven millions of available funds now in the treasury—domestic and foreign commerce active—the price of produce and property fair and good—labor everywhere finding employment and reward—more money in the country than ever was in it at any one time before—the numerous advertisements for the purchase of slaves, in the papers of his city, for the southern market, which indicated the high price of southern products—and affirmed his conscientious belief that the country was more prosperous at this time than at any period of its existence; and inveighed in terms of strong indignation against the arts and artifices, which, for the last six months, had disturbed and agitated the country, and done serious mischief to many individuals. He regretted the miscarriage of the attempt to examine the Bank of the United States, which he believed would have completed the proof against that institution for its share in getting up an unnatural and factitious scene of distress, in the midst of real prosperity. But he did not limit his invective to the bank, but came directly to the Senate, and charged a full share upon the theatrical distress speeches delivered upon the floor of the Senate, in imitation of Volney's soliloquy over the ruins of Palmyra. He repeated some passages from the most affecting of these lamentations over the desolation of the country, such as the Senate had been accustomed to hear about the time of the New York and Virginia elections. "*The canal a 'solitude. The lake a desert waste of waters. That 'populous city, lately resounding with the hum of busy 'multitudes, now silent and sad. A whole nation, in 'the midst of unparalleled prosperity, and Arcadian 'felicity, suddenly struck into poverty, and plunged 'into unutterable woe, by the direful act of one wilful 'man.*" Such, said Mr. B., were the lamentations over the ruins, not of the Tadmor in the desert, but of this America, whose true condition you have just seen exhibited in the faithful report of the Secretary of the Treasury. Not even the "*baseless fabric of a vision*" was ever more destitute of foundation than those lamentable accounts of desolation. The lamentation has ceased; the panic has gone off; would to God he could follow out the noble line of the poet, and say, "*leaving not a wreck behind.*" But he could not say that. There were wrecks! wrecks of merchants in every city, in which the bank tried its cruel policy, and wrecks of banks in this District, where the panic speeches fell thickest and loudest upon the ears of an astonished and terrified community!

But, continued Mr. B., the game is up; the alarm is over; the people are tired of it; the agitators have ceased to work the engine of alarm. A month ago he had said it was "*the last of pea time*" with these distress memorials; he would now use a bolder figure, and say, that the Secretary's report just read, had expelled forever the ghost of alarm from the chamber of the Senate. All ghosts, said Mr. B., are afraid of the light. The crowing of the cock—the break of day—remits them all, the whole shadowy tribe, to their dark and dreary abodes. How, then, can this poor ghost of alarm, which has done such hard service for six months past, how can it stand the full light, the broad glare, the clear sunshine of the Secretary's report? "*Alas, poor ghost!*" The shade of the "*noble Dane*" never quit the stage under a more inexorable law than the one which now drives thee away. This report, replete with plain facts, and luminous truths, puts to flight the apparition of distress, breaks down the whole machinery of alarm, and proves that the American people are, at this day, the most prosperous people on which the beneficent sun of Heaven did ever shine!

Mr. B. congratulated himself that the spectre of distress could never be made to cross the Mississippi. It made but slow progress anywhere in the Great Valley; but balked at the King of Floods. A letter from St. Louis informed him that an attempt had just been made to get up a distress meeting in the town of St. Louis, but without effect. The officers were obtained, and according to the approved rule of such meetings, they were converts from Jacksonism; but there the distress proceedings stopped, and took another turn. The farce could not be played in that town. The actors would not mount the stage.*

Mr. B. spoke of the circulation of the Bank of the United States, and said that its notes might be withdrawn without being felt, or known by the community. It contributed but four millions and a quarter to the circulation at this time. He verified this statement by showing that the bank had twelve millions and a quarter of specie in its vaults, and but sixteen millions and a half of notes in circulation. The difference was four millions and a quarter; and that was the precise amount which that gigantic institution now contributed to the circulation of the country! Only four millions and a quarter. If the Gold Bill passed, and raised gold 16 to 1, there would be more than that amount of gold in circulation in three months. The Foreign Coin Bill, and the Gold Bill, would give the country many dollars in specie, without interest, for each paper dollar which the bank issues, and for which the country pays so dearly. The dissolution of the bank would turn out twelve millions and a quarter of specie, to circulate among the people; and the sooner that is done the better it will be for the country.

The bank is now a nuisance, (said Mr. B.) With upwards of twelve millions in specie, and less than seventeen millions in circulation, and only fifty-two millions of loans, it pretends that it cannot lend a dollar, not even to business men, to be returned in sixty days; when, two years ago, with only six millions of specie and twenty-two millions of circulation, it run up its loans to seventy millions. The president of the bank then swore that all above six millions of specie was a surplus! How is it now, with near double as much specie, and five millions less of notes out, and twelve millions less of debt? The bank needs less specie than any other banking institution, because its notes are receivable, by law, in all Federal pay-

* About the same time a similar failure took place at Crawfordsville, Indiana.

ments; and from that circumstance alone would be current, at par, although the bank itself might be wholly unable to redeem them. Such a bank is a nuisance. It is the dog in the manger. It might lend money to business men, at short dates, to the last day of its existence; yet the signs are for a new pressure—a new game of distress for the fall elections in Pennsylvania, New York, and Ohio. If that game should be attempted, (Mr. B. said,) it would have to be done without excuse, for the bank was full of money; without pretext, for the deposite force is over; without the aid of panic speeches, for the Senate will not be in session.

Mr. B. said, that among the strange events which took place in this world, nothing could be more strange than to find, in our own country, and in the nineteenth century, any practical illustration of the ancient doctrine of the metempsychosis. Stranger still, if that doctrine should be so far improved as to take effect in soulless bodies; for, according to the founders of the doctrine, the soul alone could transmigrate.* Now corporations had no souls; that was law, laid down by all the books; and of all corporations, moneyed ones especially; and above all, the Bank of the United States, was most soulless. Yet the rumor was, that this bank intended to attempt the operation of effecting a transfer of her soul; and after submitting to death in her present form, to rise up in a new one. Mr. B. said he, for one, should be ready for the old sinner, come in the body of what beast it might. No form should deceive him; not even if 'k condescended, in its new shape, to issue from Wall street, instead of Chestnut!

A word more, and Mr. B. was done. He had a word to those gentlemen whose declarations, many ten thousand times issued from this floor, had deluded an hundred thousand people to send memorials here, certifying what these gentlemen so incontinently repeated, that the REMOVAL of the DEPOSITES had made the DISTRESS; and nothing but the RESTORATION of the DEPOSITES, or the RENEWAL of the CHARTER, could REMOVE the DISTRESS! Well! the deposites are not restored, and the charter is not renewed; and yet the distress is gone! What is the inference? Why, that gentlemen are convicted, and condemned, upon their own argument! They leave this chamber, to go home, self-convicted upon the very test which they themselves have established; and after having declared, for six months, upon this floor, that the removal of the deposites made the distress, and nothing but their restoration, or the renewal of the bank charter, could relieve it, and that they would sit here until the dog-days, and the winter solstice, to effect this restoration, or renewal; they now go home in good time for harvest, without effecting the restoration or the renewal; and find everywhere, as they go, the evidences of the highest prosperity which ever blessed the land. Yes! repeated, and exclaimed, Mr. B. with great emphasis, the deposites are not restored—the charter is not renewed—the distress is gone—and the distress speeches have ceased! No more lamentation over the desolation of the land now; and a gentleman who should undertake to entertain the Senate again in that way, in the face of the present national prosperity—in the face of the present report from the Secretary of the Treasury—would be stared at, as the Trojans were accustomed to stare at the frantic exhibitions of Priam's distracted daughter, while vaticinating the downfall of Troy in the midst of the heroic exploits of Hector.

After some remarks by Mr. WEBSTER and Mr. CHAMBERS,

Mr. WEBSTER modified his motion to refer to the Committee on Finance, and moved that the communication be laid on the table and printed; which was agreed to.

PETITIONS.

Mr. BIBB presented the proceedings of a meeting of citizens of Harrodsburg, Kentucky, remonstrating against the right of the President in sending his late protest to the Senate, disapproving of his withholding important nominations, and approving of his sending other nominations after the rejection of the former directors of the Bank of the

* From the Greek; meta, again; en, in, psyche, the soul, i. e. The soul again in.

United States. The proceedings were referred to the Committee on Finance and ordered to be printed.

Mr. LEIGH presented a memorial signed by about seven hundred inhabitants of the county of Kenawha, Virginia, in favor of the restoration of the deposites to the Bank of the United States; which was referred to the Committee on Finance, and ordered to be printed.

Mr. BELL presented the memorial of sundry citizens of New Hampshire, remonstrating against the renewal of the patent of John Ames, for his improvement in the manufacture of paper; which was laid upon the table.

FOREIGN SILVER COIN.

On motion of Mr. WEBSTER, the Senate proceeded to the consideration of the bill from the House of Representatives, regulating the value of foreign silver coin, as in Committee of the Whole.

On motion of Mr. WEBSTER, the recommendation of the director of the mint to insert in the bill the weight of the respective coins which it provides shall be received as a legal tender, was adopted.

The bill was then reported to the Senate as amended, and without any opposition to its passage, was ordered to be engrossed for a third reading.

Mr. BIBB, on leave obtained, presented the petition of the sureties of George Harrison; which was referred to the Committee of Claims.

REPORTS.

Mr. SMITH, from the Committee on the Judiciary, asked to be discharged from
The petition of Thomas Tenant and others;
The petition of Henry H. Burr; and
The petition of William Hunter; which was agreed to.

Mr. ROBBINS, from the Committee on the Library, reported a joint resolution for the relief of the heirs and legal representatives of the late Robert Fulton; which was read, and ordered to a second reading.

Mr. CHAMBERS, from the Committee on the District of Columbia, reported a bill, without amendment, to authorize Edmund Brooke to introduce two slaves into Georgetown; which was ordered to a second reading.

Mr. SMITH, from the Committee on Revolutionary Claims, asked to be discharged from the further consideration of the petition of Richard Wall; which was agreed to.

Mr. SHEPLEY, from the same committee, reported the following bills:
A bill for the relief of Captain James Craine, with an amendment;
A bill for the relief of the heirs of William Teas, with an amendment;
A bill for the relief of the heirs of Lucy Bond, Hannah Douglass, Elizabeth Goodwin, and Temperance Holmes, with several amendments;
A bill for the relief of Philip Turner, without amendment.

[Mr. S. gave notice that he was instructed by the committee, when the bill was taken up, to move its indefinite postponement.]

Mr. SHEPLEY, from the same committee, asked to be discharged from the further consideration of the petition of Captain John Harris; which was agreed to.

COMPENSATION TO MR. POTTER.

The resolution submitted by Mr. WRIGHT, to compensate the honorable Elisha R. Potter for his attendance while claiming a seat in the Senate, under the authority of a certificate of the Governor of Rhode Island, was taken up.

Mr. WRIGHT then made some observations in favor of the resolution.

It was opposed by Messrs. POINDEXTER, CLAY, and WEBSTER.

Mr. BIBB moved to strike out the words "is entitled to receive his compensation," and to insert in lieu thereof, "ought, under the circumstances, to be paid," which

Mr. WRIGHT accepted as an amendment.

Mr. CLAY then moved to refer the resolution to the Judiciary Committee.

Mr. WRIGHT expressed himself favorable to the reference, and the motion was agreed to.

GENERAL APPROPRIATION BILL.

Mr. WEBSTER then moved to take up the bill from the House of Representatives making appropriations for the civil and diplomatic expenses of the Government for the year 1834.

Mr. POINDEXTER hoped the bill might be postponed till to-morrow, the day being pretty far advanced.

Mr. WEBSTER reminded the gentleman from Mississippi that to-morrow was assigned to an other purpose. He thought we might make considerable progress in the bill to-day. There were many things in it against which there could be no objection.

Mr. PRESTON said he would rather take up the bill early in the day. He begged leave to suggest to honorable gentlemen that he was by no means certain that in the present state of the business of the country the bill ought to be taken up at all. Where was the treasury of the United States? Floating about, nobody knew where. He would suggest the propriety of refusing to take up the bill at all till something was done to restore the treasury of the United States to a place of safe custody.

Mr. WEBSTER said, to be sure, if that subject was to be agitated again, some time might be necessary. He would give notice, then, that to-morrow morning, after the reading of the Journal, he would move to take up the bill.

Mr. PRESTON did not mean to say that such a discussion would or ought to ensue. But he threw it out as a suggestion, whether it was proper to discuss this bill when the public treasure was in its present condition.

Mr. FORSYTH suggested to the gentleman from South Carolina, [Mr. PRESTON,] that if such a question was to be agitated, it was as well to urge it on the final passage of the bill as now. If we should proceed to the consideration of the bill to-day, the only question would be on the amendments reported by the Committee on Finance. The bill was postponed till to-morrow.

The bill making additional appropriation for unexpired balances upon Georgia militia claims, during the years 1792, 1793, and 1794, was read and referred to the Committee on Finance.

The bill making additional appropriations for the United States Armory at Harper's Ferry, for the year 1834, was read, and referred to the same committee.

The resolution authorizing the Secretary of the Senate to procure 150 copies of Elliot's Diplomatic Code, was read, and referred to the Committee on the Library.

The resolution providing for the distribution of additional copies of the returns of the last census, was ordered to be engrossed for a third reading.

The following bills were read a third time, and passed:

The bill to extend the time to carry into effect the convention between the United States and France;

The bill supplementary to the act entitled "An act to carry into effect the convention between the United States and his Majesty the King of the Two Sicilies, concluded at Naples on the 14th of October, 1832;"

The joint resolution providing for the distribution of the Diplomatic Correspondence between the years 1783 and 1789;

The bill granting pensions to certain persons therein named;

The bill for the relief of the legal representatives of James P. Haineworth, deceased.

ORDERS OF THE DAY.

The following resolution submitted by Mr. CLAY was taken up, modified by extending the time for the report to be made, and adopted:

Resolved, That the Secretary of the Treasury be directed to report to the Senate, at the next session of Congress, the total quantity of the several classes of scrip issued under the act entitled "An act for the relief of certain officers and soldiers of the Virginia line, and navy, and of the continental army, during the revolutionary war; and under the subsequent acts containing appropriations for land to the same object; also, the number of certificates, the quantity in each, and to whom granted, distinguishing the line of service to which the officer or soldier belonged, to whom or to what

representatives the same was granted; and like-wise the names of the several agents who present-ed the warrants and obtained the certificates of scrip. And the said Secretary is further directed to report a similar statement in respect to all war-rants which have been filed or officially presented, but upon which certificates of scrip have not yet been issued.

The resolution from the Committee on the Judi-ciary, asking to be discharged from the petition of the executor of Abner L. Duncan, deceased, was agreed to.

The resolution from the Committee on Naval Affairs, asking to be discharged from the memo-rial of John Whitehead and others, and that the same be referred to the Secretary of the Treasury, was taken up and agreed to.

On motion of Mr. CLAY,
The Senate adjourned.

HOUSE OF REPRESENTATIVES.

MONDAY, June 16, 1834.

Mr. POLK asked the unanimous consent of the House to take up the appropriation bills lying on the Speaker's table.

Mr. GRENNELL objected, remarking that this was the last day on which an opportunity would be afforded for the presentation of petitions and memorials.

After further objections from Messrs. HARDIN and BURGES,

Mr. POLK moved to suspend the rules by which Monday was appropriated for the reception of petitions and memorials, for the purpose of act-ing upon the appropriation bills on the Speaker's table.

After a remark from Mr. BURGES, in opposi-tion to the motion—

The question was taken, when it appeared that a quorum was not present.

Mr. POLK then moved a call of the House; which was ordered.

After the call had been proceeded in for some time,

Mr. BURGES moved to suspend it; which was negatived.

The call was further proceeded in, for some time; when, on motion of Mr. DICKSON, it was suspended.

Mr. POLK modified his motion, suspending the rule, so far as to take up the appropriation bills at half-past one o'clock.

Messrs. HARDIN and VINTON opposed the motion.

Mr. CHILTON expressed the hope that the gentleman from Tennessee would withdraw the motion, with the understanding that no debate should be allowed upon any memorials which might be presented.

The question being taken, the motion of Mr. POLK was agreed to.

The memorial of 1841 citizens of Indiana, pray-ing the restoration of the deposites and the rechar-ter of the United States Bank, with certain restric-tions, which was presented on a former day by Mr. McCARTY, being taken up for consideration,

Mr. McC. explained the views of the memorial-ists, and his reasons for differing from them in opinion on the subject; at the same time declaring his willingness to receive and obey it as the voice of his constituents, and moved the printing and reference of the memorial.

Mr. WARDWELL observed that he had not, during this protracted session, occupied the time of the House by saying a word upon the subject of the bank and of the distresses of the country; and he would not, at this time, trouble the House with any remarks, were it not for a most singular communication which he had received from a highly respectable constituent.

This memorial from the State of Indiana states, in substance, that there is unexampled distress throughout the country in consequence of the re-moval of the public deposites from the Bank of the United States. If this be the case, the people whom he had the honor to represent must be subject to the same calamity. But they had not sent their com-plaints here—the district gave a majority of votes against General Jackson at the last Presidential election, yet he had not received a single petition memorial complaining of the removal of the de-

posites, or in favor of the bank. He had, it is true, received letters, stating that the district was liber-ally supplied with speeches and reports in favor of the bank and against the Administration, and that for two or three months past there had been much excitement in that section of the country; he had no doubt but that this excitement was, in some measure, produced by the unexampled exertions of political partisans, who, no doubt, were anxious to make the people believe that they were really distressed.

The manner in which he had reason to believe the names of some of his constituents were obtain-ed, for the purpose of furnishing them with these political papers in favor of the bank, he would now state to the House. By this morning's mail, he had received, in a letter from a gentleman of the first respectability, and in whose statements the most implicit confidence may be placed, a printed paper or circular, which he would now read to the House. [Here Mr. W. read a paper, dated in February last, at the city of New York, and signed by J. N. Bolles, and two others, requesting the names of the ministers of the Gospel, exhorters, elders, deacons, and of moral, influential, public-spirited, and benevolent persons, for the purpose of transmitting to them a paper containing a circu-lar, which they wished to send through the State. Mr. W. read also an extract from the letter which enclosed the circular, stating, that to the persons whose names had been furnished agree-ably to the request contained in the circular, there were forwarded from time to time, and franked by members of Congress, the speeches of Mr. Clay and Mr. J. Q. Adams, and the report of Mr. Web-ster, in the Senate, February 5, 1834, from the Committee on Finance.]

From these facts, gentlemen can draw their own conclusions. He knew nothing of the matter him-self. He only stated the facts as received by him. He could vouch for the respectability, high char-acter, and moral worth of the individual who sent him the circular. All may be right. Doubtless it was, so far as the name of members of this House are concerned.

As to distress in his district, he would state that he could say nothing of his own knowledge. He had, however, received letters recently, stating that many kinds of property sold by farmers had not brought a better price since the year 1817. He would state further, that at the last session of the Legislature of the State of New York, a bank was incorporated and located at Sackett's Harbor, in his district, with a capital of $200,000; and such was the eagerness to obtain stock, that nearly $600,000 were subscribed. This shows most con-clusively that there is some money left in the dis-trict, notwithstanding the removal of the deposites.

Mr. FULLER said he had sent documents into the gentleman's district, at the urgent request of two gentlemen residents of that district, who had furnished him with a list of names for the pur-pose. As to the circular, he knew nothing about it, nor of the religious people to whom it was sent.

Mr. GRENNELL said, as the controversy was changed from State to church affairs, he would move to lay the memorial on the table, but with-drew it at the request of

Mr. SELDEN, who said he had little to do with the church—less than he ought to have. He was requested in this city, last winter, by a gentleman from the county of Jefferson, to send some docu-ments into it, and a list of names was given to him for the purpose. He had sent some, and was very sorry that he could not send more. He would, with pleasure, furnish the gentleman with a list of names of his constituents, if he would un-dertake to supply them with information; and if the gentleman was unwilling or afraid to trust his own constituents with the truth, he would also furnish them with information, so far as it might be in his power.

Mr. WARDWELL replied that he had not com-plained that the gentleman had sent documents into his district, but of the manner in which it was done. He had read a circular issued from the city of New York, requesting the names of the re-ligious people in his district, and had stated the fact, that the documents were sent to them under the frank of "D. Selden" and "P. C. Fuller." The franks might be forgeries, for aught he knew; but the documents were sent in the manner he had

mentioned. He was perfectly willing that the gentleman should send information into his dis-trict; but he (Mr. W.) was unable to furnish doc-uments to the gentleman's constituents. He would furnish them with pleasure, if he could get them without paying for them, as he presumed the gen-tleman did.

Mr. SELDEN now understood the gentleman (he said) to convey the charge further than he did at first. He had insinuated that he, sent blank franks to New York, or left them there, which he unequivocally denied. If the gentleman intended to make this insinuation, it was a matter between him and the gentleman. He would ask him to point out any proof of any kind in support of the charge.

On motion of Mr. GRENNELL, the memorial was ordered to be printed, and laid on the table.

The memorial from citizens of Franklin, Mas-sachusetts, presented on a former day, being taken up—

Mr. GRENNELL spoke in explanation and support of the memorialists, and moved that the memorial be printed and laid on the table; which was agreed to.

The resolutions condemning the removal of the deposites, &c., from the lower House of the General Assembly of Rhode Island, being taken up—

Mr. BURGES spoke on the subject about an hour.

Mr. PEARCE, of Rhode Island, moved the postponement of the further consideration of the resolutions till Monday next.

The CHAIR said they would lie over of course.

Various bills from the Senate were read the first and second time, and referred to the appropriate committees.

The bill from the Senate for continuing the Cum-berland road through the States of Ohio, Indiana, and Illinois, reported by the Committee of the Whole on the state of the Union, was read.

Mr. POLK said this Senate bill contains appro-priations greater than the bill reported by the Com-mittee of Ways and Means by the sum of $477,000, and contains appropriations $670,000 greater than was appropriated last year. As half the year had elapsed, he believed it was the opinion of the de-partment that the amount contemplated by this bill could not be profitably expended during the present year. He should therefore move to reduce the appropriations. As to that portion of the bill providing for the repair of the road east of the Ohio, Mr. P. explained the various propositions for repairing and renewing this road, and stated that the Committee of Ways and Means were of opinion that $300,000 were sufficient to repair the road in a proper manner. This bill contemplated an expenditure for this road of $1,102,000. Upon this scale, applied to the other public works, not only the present, but the future, revenue of the Government would be inadequate. He should move to reduce the appropriations to the scale of the last year. He moved to strike from the third section of the bill the sum of $652,000 for repair-ing the road east of Ohio, and insert $300,000. This sum would be sufficient to enable the depart-ment to comply with the conditions required by the States. In the present stage of this measure, he did not propose going into a discussion of the general principles involved with it. He concluded his explanation by asking that the report of the committee on this subject be read.

The report having been read—

Mr. STEWART called for the reading of the report of the Secretary of War on this subject.

Mr. E. WHITTLESEY appealed to the friends of the measure, whether it would be best to accede to the proposition of the chairman of the Commit-tee of Ways and Means?

Mr. STEWART persisted in requiring the re-port to be read; which was read.

Mr. S. then explained, and supported the neces-sity of the appropriation as it passed the Senate. The simple question was, whether the plan of the department should be carried out. A great por-tion of the road had been taken up, and sound economy required that the plan be executed. If this was done, he would pledge himself that the road would cost the United States nothing here-after.

Mr. W. R. DAVIS inquired how often that

pledge had been made in the House when former bills had been passed?

Mr. STEWART. No such pledge could be made until this time, when the States have resolved when the road shall be put in repair, they will erect gates to preserve it.

Mr. McKENNAN inquired whether the chairman of the Committee of Ways and Means proposed to strike out the limitation in the next section?

Mr. POLK did not. He was of opinion that the sum proposed by him was amply sufficient for the complete repair of the road. The gentleman from Pennsylvania [Mr. STEWART] was mistaken in supposing the plan of repair had been settled, as he had stated. The Secretary of War, during the present session, had submitted this subject to the committee. He was unwilling to vote more than $300,000 at this session, or any other. Two years ago, $150,000 was appropriated to put this road in repair, in order that the States might accept this road; the last session $154,000 was voted for the same purpose. Since the States were to accept the road, $304,000 had been expended. Now $652,000 more were asked. This was monstrous. If $300,000 would not repair the road, he never would vote another dollar to that object.

Mr. McKENNAN said this appropriation, beyond $300,000, did not come from the friends of the road, but from those who wished to see the end of the expenditure.

Mr. McKAY was opposed, in principle, to the bill altogether; but he would vote in favor of appropriating $300,000, or even $600,000, if it could be entirely got rid of. He well remembered that in 1832 the gentleman from Pennsylvania near him, [Mr. McKENNAN,] pledged himself to the House that $328,000 would fully repair this road, and that after that sum had been expended, the road would maintain itself. After explaining the provisions of the laws of Pennsylvania, Maryland, and Virginia, Mr. McK. proposed a proviso, which he should offer, that not more than $100,000 should be expended until those States should agree to take the road when the amount should be expended. Unless a guarantee should be given, he would not vote to expend either sum.

Mr. THOMAS, of Maryland, said the interests of his immediate constituents forbade he should remain silent and permit the House to decide on the pending amendment under the erroneous impression which the remarks of the chairman of the Committee of Ways and Means were well calculated to produce. That gentleman had read an extract from the documents on our file from the War Department. The House ought to know that this extract did not appear in the report of the Secretary of War made to this House at the commencement of the session; nor in the annual report from the Engineer Department. It was to be found in the estimates of the War Department for the expenditures of the year 1834. In that paper, the Secretary of War requires an appropriation of $300,000 for continuation of the repairs of the Cumberland road east of the Ohio river, provided the mode in which the department prefers these repairs should be made meets the approbation of Congress.

Now, the House will perceive that this estimate for the year 1834 must not be its guide in deciding on the propriety of passing the bill from the Senate under consideration. That bill proposes an appropriation of $652,000—not to be expended in 1834, but to *complete* the repairs of the Cumberland road now in progress. It is well known that the Senate refused to make an appropriation for prosecuting these repairs until an estimate had been furnished from the Engineer Department, showing the whole sum which would be required to complete them. In so doing, Mr. T. thought the Senate had acted wisely. The experience of the past ought to satisfy every member that these partial appropriations were inexpedient.

At the first session of the last Congress, the laws of Maryland and Pennsylvania, relating to this road, had been assented to by the United States. They proposed that this Government should repair the Cumberland road within the limits of those States, and then surrender all claim to jurisdiction over it to them. In which event, they agreed to appoint superintendents to collect a sum sufficient in toll from travellers thereon to keep that road ever thereafter in good repair.

In pursuance of this compact between the United States and the States of Maryland and Pennsylvania, to which Virginia subsequently assented in part, two of the appropriations were made by the last Congress at its several sittings to prosecute this improvement. In November last, those appropriations were exhausted, and from that time to the present, the officers of this Government employed to superintend these repairs had been idle, although they had a right to expect their salaries would be continued. The road, too, had been left in such a condition that it would now cost several thousand dollars more to repair it than would have been necessary if the work had progressed without interruption. These facts were made known to the Senate, and to avoid such a state of things hereafter, that body had rightly determined to appropriate a sum sufficient to exempt this Government from all further demands for this object.

The sum proposed to be given, is that which is demanded by the War Department, if the first of these several plans of repair mentioned in the annual report of the Chief of the Engineer Department, meets our approbation. Mr. T. here read extracts from the report in confirmation of his views. He then invited the House to turn its attention to the only question which ought to be agitated in connexion with this bill. Are the estimates of the War Department unreasonable? Is the mode of improvement on which those estimates are predicated the one which Congress ought to sanction? Mr. T. said, from his personal knowledge of the country, he had no difficulty in answering both these questions in the affirmative. It would, he thought, be useless, worse than useless, to make a defective or partial repair of this great highway. If it is to be done, let it be well done, and in a manner creditable to the United States and beneficial to the people of the great valley of the Mississippi, for whose particular accommodation it was originally designed.

Mr. T. made some statements concerning the nature of the chief material which had been used in the original construction of the road, to show that we ought to profit by experience and now use the limestone, which alone was calculated to make the road permanent. He also explained the defective manner in which the road had been originally constructed, and insisted that the MacAdam plan now proposed by the War Department ought to be preferred.

In reply to statements which had been made showing the large sums of money heretofore expended on this road, Mr. T. appealed to the House, and entreated them not to permit such exhibitions to prejudice their minds. What have we to do with the errors of the Administrations which have preceded this? It is certain that Mr. Jefferson's administration committed one error in not providing for the continued repair of the national road in some economical manner. And the Administration which succeeded his, erred also in attempting to keep this road in repair by annual appropriations from the national treasury. But are we to permit these things to create a prejudice against the present measure. We now propose to make a good road, to reject the worthless material heretofore used, and then to erect toll-gates to collect a sum sufficient to relieve the treasury from this drain.

What, said he, are we reminded, too, of the very large sum which this road originally cost! He agreed the sum expended was enormous and was at a loss to know how so much money could have been honestly expended for such a purpose. But are we to refuse an appropriation asked for by the present head of the War Department, solely because his predecessors or their subordinate agents, under former Administrations, have wasted or misapplied appropriations made by Congress. He hoped not. He hoped the House would examine the estimates now furnished, and if they were, as he believed they were, reasonable and accurate, he trusted the whole sum of $652,000 would be given.

Mr. T. said the House need not be alarmed at the suggestion of the gentleman from Tennessee, that this sum would embarrass the Treasury Department. It was now well understood, that the receipts from the customs for the year 1834 would exceed considerably the estimated receipts made by the Secretary of the Treasury at the commencement of the present Congress. Besides, the whole sum asked for cannot be expended within the year. It was most probable not more than $150,000 or $200,000 would be actually drawn from the treasury during the year 1834. So that the only difference between the bill from the Senate and the bill, if amended as proposed by the gentleman from Tennessee, would be this: if we make now an appropriation of $300,000, we shall be called next year for more money; we shall waste time again in a long debate, and perhaps suffer the repairs to be again suspended. On the contrary, if we sanction the bill from the Senate, we shall place at the disposal of the War Department a sum sufficient to relieve us from all further applications, and accomplish the object which the friends of the road desire.

Mr. SUTHERLAND moved to amend the amendment so as to provide that no larger sum than $300,000 be appropriated for the object this year.

After some further remarks from Messrs. E. WHITTLESEY, ARCHER, and STEWART,

Mr. CHILTON moved that the further consideration of the bill be postponed to Thursday next, with a view to proceed to other business.

Mr. MERCER hoped the bill would not be postponed. We should want time on Thursday next as much as now.

Mr. VANCE opposed the postponement. If it was to be passed, he hoped it would be passed at once.

Mr. SELDEN was in favor of the postponement, in order that the friends of the bill might unite their own views in regard to it.

Mr. EWING opposed the postponement.

Mr. CHILTON withdrew the motion, in the hope that the question would be taken without further debate.

After some further discussion, in which Messrs. MERCER, POLK, SUTHERLAND, THOMAS of Maryland, CHAMBERS, and BEARDSLEY, participated,

Mr. W. R. DAVIS, in order to test the principle of the bill, moved to strike out the enacting clause.

Mr. MANN, of New York, could not, he said, vote for any of the propositions. We had expended four millions of dollars in making a road which we could neither give away nor use, without very great additional expense. He would vote to reduce the appropriation to $300,000, and to strike out the enacting clause, or for any proposition by which we could get clear of the burden of this road.

Mr. VANCE did not see (he said) how gentlemen could get along without this road. Without it, they would have no chance to make speeches every year in favor of economy, State rights, &c. If this was out of the way, gentlemen would be obliged to look out for some other subject for retrenchment speeches. They would be driven to talk about the $600,000 for the New York custom-house, the half a million for the repair of navy yards, the million for repairs and contingencies for the navy, &c. We would have to look for some of the heavy expenditures made on our seaboard. He remembered the time when there was no commerce between the East and the West by this route. If gentlemen chose to cut off the commerce which had since grown up, and which had led to the settlement of the western States, let them do it by refusing to keep up this road. All the money which had ever been expended upon this road would not amount to three cents a pound on the merchandise which had been transported upon it. The whole sum expended on the road did not amount to as much as the sums expended for repairs on your little navy yards and dock yards. Yet, inasmuch as the money had been expended for the benefit of the West, in common with the rest of the country—although it was the only expenditure which had been made for the benefit of the West—it was the constant theme of declamation for the friends of economy and retrenchment, as if all the revenue which had for the last twenty or thirty years been collected had been expended upon the Cumberland road.

The debate was continued by Messrs. GHOLSON, CHINN, GILLET, VINTON, POLK, F. THOMAS, SUTHERLAND, McKINLEY, and S. JONES, who, after an explanation of his views, moved to lay the bill on the table.

Mr. HAWES demanded the yeas and nays; which were ordered.

The motion to lay on the table was lost: Yeas 65, nays 133.

Mr. J. Q. ADAMS moved to amend the amendment by striking out the reference to the acts of Pennsylvania, Virginia, and Maryland, which he deemed unnecessary and improper, as he conceived those States were not bound under the qualified assent of Congress to accept the road.

Mr. W. C. JOHNSON explained his views upon the question raised by this motion; when the question was taken on the amendment to the amendment; which was lost.

The question was then stated on Mr. POLK'S motion to strike out $659,000 and insert $308,000.

Mr. McKINLEY demanded the yeas and nays; which were ordered.

Mr. MERCER made explanations relative to the expense of repairing the road.

The question was then taken on the amendment moved by Mr. POLK; which was negatived: Yeas 91, nays 92.

Mr. SUTHERLAND moved an amendment providing that not more than $300,000 should be drawn from the treasury for repairs during the present year.

Mr. P. DICKERSON proposed to amend the amendment by providing that not more than $300,-000 should be expended, unless the States of Maryland, Pennsylvania, and Virginia, should agree to take charge of the road, when the whole sum of $659,000 should be expended.

Before the question was taken,

The House adjourned.

IN SENATE.
TUESDAY, June 17, 1834.

A message upon executive business was received from the President of the United States, by Mr. DONELSON, his Private Secretary.

BILLS.

The bill making a reappropriation of unexpended balances for Georgia militia claims, during the years 1792, 1793, and 1794;

The bill making appropriation for the year 1834, for the United States Armory, at Harper's Ferry, Virginia;

And the bill concerning the Orphans' Courts for the counties of Washington and Alexandria, District of Columbia—were severally ordered to be engrossed for a third reading.

REPORTS.

Mr. TOMLINSON, from the Committee on Pensions, to whom was referred the memorial of the Legislature of Indiana, in behalf of William Bilsland, asked to be discharged from the further consideration of the same; which was agreed to.

Mr. TOMLINSON, from the same committee, made a similar report upon the petition of Adrian Peters; which was concurred in.

Mr. BIBB, from the Committee on the Judiciary, reported a bill granting additional compensation to the United States judge of the western district of Florida; which was read, and ordered to a second reading.

Mr. LINN, from the Committee on Private Land Claims, reported a bill from the House of Representatives, without amendment, for the relief of George Gordon.

PETITION.

Mr. BIBB presented the memorial of Thomas Law and others, citizens of Washington, District of Columbia, on the subject of a national currency, to be issued by the United States, loaned to the States, and by the States to be loaned out; receivable in all dues and payments to the treasury; intended to substitute notes of the Government of the United States, instead of bank notes, and thereby to protect the community against the evils of the banking system. The memorial was referred to the Committee on Finance, and ordered to be printed.

RESOLUTION.

The following resolution was submitted by Mr. PRAGUE, considered, and agreed to:

Resolved, That the Secretary of the Treasury be requested to report to the Senate an answer to the resolution of the Senate of the 6th day of May

last, in relation to officers of the customs, so far as may now be in his power.

ORDERS.

The bill concerning the duties on lead was then taken up.

Mr. FRELINGHUYSEN offered the following proviso to the bill: "That it shall not extend to or affect the existing duties on red and white lead, shot, and litharge."

Mr. CALHOUN said he had no objection to any provision which should be necessary to prevent frauds upon the revenue; but he was opposed to going any further, and adopting anything under the guise of preventing frauds, which should be in effect an increase of duties. He therefore moved to lay the bill on the table till to-morrow, that he might have an opportunity of looking into it. He, however, withdrew the motion at the request of

Mr. FRELINGHUYSEN, who observed that all the provisions of the bill had for their object the prevention of frauds, except one. That was a section laying a duty of two per cent. per pound on lead ore; it was inserted at the suggestion of one of the honorable Senators from Missouri, who thought such a provision necessary for our own lead mines, which were sufficient to produce much more lead than was necessary for our own consumption.

Mr. CLAY said, enactments to prevent frauds were usual. He thought the provision laying a duty of two per cent. on lead ore ought to be stricken out. But the bill to protect the revenue against frauds ought to pass.

Mr. PRESTON said, it was always desirable that frauds should be prevented, and he would be sorry if the motion of his colleague to lay the bill on the table should prevent its passage. He was opposed to the two per cent. duty, but he suggested that the provision to prevent frauds might be made to conform to that which had been adopted to prevent frauds on the importation of sugar, which had been melted down abroad, and afterwards imported in the shape of syrup.

Mr. CALHOUN then renewed his motion to lay the bill on the table; which prevailed.

The bill for the relief of the legal representatives of Moses Shepherd, deceased, being upon its passage,

The merits of the bill were argued in some instances, at length, by Messrs. BLACK, HENDRICKS, LEIGH, KING of Alabama, SMITH, SHEPLEY, FORSYTH, TYLER, BIBB, and POINDEXTER; when it was lost by the following vote, viz:

YEAS—Messrs. Chambers, Clay, Ewing, Frelinghuysen, Hendricks, Knight, Leigh, McKean, Naudain, Poindexter, Porter, Prentiss, Robbins, Robinson, Silsbee, Smith, Tallmadge, Tomlinson, Tyler, and Webster—20.

NAYS—Messrs. Bibb, Black, Brown, Calhoun, Forsyth, Grundy, Hill, Kane, King of Alabama, King of Georgia, Linn, Mangum, Moore, Morris, Preston, Shepley, Southard, Swift, Waggaman, White, and Wright—21.

Mr. CALHOUN then moved to take up the bill concerning the duties on lead, which was agreed to; when the proviso offered by Mr. FRELINGHUYSEN was adopted.

Mr. CALHOUN moved to strike out that part of the bill imposing duties "on all lead, in whatever shape imported," and insert in lieu of it, that the article which shall be subject to a duty of "double the value of the raw material;" which was adopted.

On Mr. C.'s motion, the bill was further amended, by striking out the duty of two per cent. per pound, inserted by the House; when, after some conversation between Messrs. CLAY, LINN, and CALHOUN, the bill was ordered to be engrossed for a third reading.

On motion of Mr. TYLER, the Senate proceeded to the consideration of executive business.

When the doors were opened, the Senate proceeded to the consideration of the special order of the day.

FRENCH SPOLIATION BILL.

The bill to provide for the satisfaction of claims due to certain citizens for spoliations committed on their commerce prior to the 30th day of September, 1800,

After the adoption of several unimportant amendments,

Mr. CHAMBERS spoke at length in favor of the bill, and was followed by Mr. FORSYTH against the bill, and Mr. WEBSTER in favor of it; who both declined going at large into the merits of the bill, reserving their views for another occasion.

Mr. FORSYTH then moved that the further consideration thereof be postponed to Thursday next, and that it be made the special order for that day; which was agreed to.

The bill authorizing the distribution of copies of the late census to members of Congress;

The bill making reappropriations of unexpended balances for Georgia militia claims for the years 1792, 1793, and 1794;

On motion of Mr. WHITE,

The Senate adjourned.

HOUSE OF REPRESENTATIVES.
TUESDAY, June 17, 1834.

Mr. CLAY, from the Committee on Public Lands, reported the following resolution:

Resolved, That the Committee of the Whole on the state of the Union be discharged from the further consideration of the bill No. 92, to reduce and graduate the price of public lands; and that said bill be made the special order of the day for the 20th instant.

Mr. VINTON said, the bill brought up the whole subject of the disposition of the public domain, and was a counter project to the measure which passed the Senate at the last session. At this stage of the session it was obviously impracticable to give the subject the consideration its importance demanded.

Mr. CLAY said, the gentleman was mistaken in supposing this was a project counter to the measure referred to, or had been got up merely to defeat it. On the other hand, it was a subject which had been before Congress for ten or twelve years past. It did not contemplate the disposition of the public domain, excepting such refused lands as had been in market, some of them from ten to twenty years. The subject had been brought to the attention of the House by memorials from various sections of the country, and from the Legislatures of all the new States. And he hoped Congress would be able to dispose of it during the present session.

Mr. ELLSWORTH said, there was no subject in which his constituents felt a deeper interest than this—and it was obvious that sufficient time did not remain during the present session to dispose of it. The gentleman from Alabama [Mr. CLAY] suggests that it only applies to a portion of the public lands. This might be true as to its immediate application, but if the bill passed, it would soon embrace the whole public domain. He should be unwilling to see a measure of so much importance taken up at this period of the session.

Mr. H. EVERETT hoped the whole day would not be consumed in determining what should be done. With a view of testing the opinion of the House on this question, he moved to lay the resolution on the table.

Upon which question, the yeas and nays were ordered.

Mr. PATTON, considering this a most important question, moved a call of the House; which was negatived.

The question was then taken on laying on the table; which was carried: yeas 82, nays 50.

Mr. ELLSWORTH, from the Committee on the Judiciary, reported a bill authorizing the Secretary of the Treasury to grant a right of way in the city of New York; which was read twice, and ordered to be engrossed for a third reading.

Mr. LEAVITT, from the Committee on Public Lands, reported a bill for the relief of William W. Stevenson, of the Territory of Arkansas; which was read twice and committed.

Mr. S. JONES moved the rules of the House be suspended, in order that certain joint resolu-

tions relative to the management of the Post Office, might be laid on the table and printed.

Mr. CONNOR suggested that a bill comprehending the provisions contained in these resolutions, as well as several others, was now depending in the other end of the Capitol.

After a brief explanation from Mr. JONES, the motion was negatived.

Mr. STODDERT, from the Committee on Patents, reported a bill to renew the patent right of William Perkins; which was read twice, and committed.

CUMBERLAND ROAD BILL.

The House then proceeded to the unfinished business of yesterday, being the bill for the continuation and repair of the Cumberland road.

Mr. GILMER moved to reconsider the vote by which the motion of Mr. Polk to reduce the appropriation for repairing the road from $652,000 to $300,000 was yesterday rejected.

Mr. STEWART said the friends of the bill would vote in favor of the amendment if the restriction in the next section should be stricken out. If the supporters of the amendment would intimate their willingness to accede that proposition, no objection would be made to the amendment.

Mr. HAWES hoped no such intimation would be given. He was opposed to the whole system. Unless an end was put to the log-rolling which prevailed in this House in relation to internal improvements, it would be necessary to increase the tariff to keep the treasury from bankruptcy. The immense amount of appropriations which had already passed the House were sufficient, he believed, to exhaust the treasury.

Mr. BROWN said he voted yesterday against the proposition of the honorable gentleman from Tennessee, [Mr. Polk,] and, upon reflection, he now thought the vote was wrong. It had been his intention to move for a reconsideration this morning, but it gave him pleasure to find he had been anticipated by the honorable gentleman from Georgia, [Mr. Gilmer.] He was not unfriendly to such an appropriation as would finish the road when he considered the compact made by the Government; but he doubted very much whether the treasury would be able to bear so large an appropriation of the public money for this single purpose during the present year. He hoped the observations of the honorable member from Kentucky [Mr. Hawes] would not be entirely lost upon the House. He hoped honorable gentlemen would look about them and see where all these immense appropriations will ultimately lead us. He admitted to a certain extent the obligation of the Government to complete this road, and he would willingly, at the proper time, vote for such a sum as would finish and put it in a condition to be surrendered to the several States through which it passes, and thus rid the nation forever from these continual, and what seemed to him extravagant and never-ending expenditures of the public money. Unless he was much mistaken, the friends of the bill admitted that no more than $300,000 could be expended upon the road during the present year, and he therefore, upon reflection, deemed it most prudent to limit the present appropriation to that sum. He should vote for the reconsideration of the motion to amend, and should it prevail, he would then record his vote in favor of the sum proposed by the honorable gentleman from Tennessee.

Mr. EWING opposed the reconsideration at length.

Mr. HARDIN went at length into an explanation of the obligation resting upon the United States to make this road. Mr. H. expressed his alarm at the amount of the appropriations for various works of internal improvement contained in the bill already reported, which he estimated to be twenty millions. With regard to this road, he thought the $2,500,000 which had been expended upon it solely to enable Baltimore to compete with Philadelphia was quite enough. If a road to the west was necessary, why not make a road by the White Sulphur Springs and the Kenawha, which was a hundred miles nearer! If the friends of the bill were not satisfied with the $300,000 proposed by the amendment, he hoped they would not obtain more by the vote of the House.

Mr. F. THOMAS replied in detail to the arguments and suggestions of Mr. Hardin. Mr. T. expressed his willingness to accede to the propositions of Messrs. Sutherland and Dickerson, providing that only $300,000 should be expended during the present year, and that no further sum should be laid out upon the road until the States should signify their assent to take and maintain the road when the whole should be expended; and hoped the House would fairly meet the question, whether the road should be fully and finally repaired by the United States, or should be abandoned; which he considered to be involved in this motion to reconsider, unless the limitation was struck from the bill.

Mr. BURGES opposed the motion to reconsider, and explained his views of the mutual and relative interests of the eastern and western States at length.

Mr. CAMBRELENG concurred in opinion with the gentleman from Virginia, [Mr. Archer.] He was willing to vote for almost any sum that would enable us to get rid of the road, and transfer it to the States through which it passed; but he feared it would be as difficult for us to rid ourselves of the Cumberland road, as it would be for certain gentlemen to abandon another unprofitable concern. He was by no means opposed to the object in view; but the appropriation should be made with reference to the actual condition of the revenue, whatever amount might be applied during the present year. It was not so much with a view to this single object that he had risen, but to notice all extraordinary appropriations, and to ask gentlemen before they proceeded further in authorizing expenditures not included in the annual estimate submitted by the Treasury, to inquire into the condition of the revenue for 1834. He concurred entirely with the gentleman from Kentucky, [Mr. Hardin,] that the state of the treasury did not authorize such extraordinary expenditures. The sum of eleven hundred thousand dollars was appropriated by this bill. We had bills amounting to about three millions for expenditures in this District and the neighborhood. There were bills now before us embracing appropriations amounting to more than five millions, for objects which were not included in the treasury estimates; which bills, it was expected by gentlemen, we should act upon. Before we do so, we should look into the state of the treasury for 1834. The balance in the treasury, and the estimated receipts for the year, from all sources, amount to twenty-six millions and a half—the expenditures of the year, embracing only those included in the estimates, and allowing an equal amount for unexpended balances of appropriations at the beginning and at the end of the year, amount to twenty-three millions and a half, including five millions for the public debt and interest—leaving a surplus of three millions. If we make the same extraordinary appropriations at this as at the last session, of three millions and a half, there would be a deficit of half a million at the end of the year. He had no doubt that the receipts of the year would equal the estimate of the Secretary of the Treasury—they might perhaps exceed it—but we should recollect how much the resources of the year had been diminished. At the commencement of 1833, we had of available revenue bonds, twenty-one millions and a half, while on the 1st of January last, we had but seven millions and a half, making a difference of fourteen millions, and we commenced the year with a reduction of about two millions in our revenue from imports—making the resources for 1834 below those of 1833, sixteen millions. With this knowledge we were not authorized to make large appropriations for extraordinary objects; if we did so, this House, and not the treasury, would be held accountable for any deficiency.

We hear much of the increase of Government expenditures, but we overlook the causes—it is in this hasty legislation, at the close of the session, when millions are appropriated without proper examination, in our presidential contests, when millions are authorized under political influences, in the great struggle between the tariff and anti-tariff sides of the House—the former endeavoring to increase the expenditures to sustain a large revenue, the latter struggling to bring down the revenue to a just and moderate measure of national expenditure—these were the causes—and the measures laying the foundation of new and heavy additions to our annual expense, were uniformly hurried through the House during the last week of the session—and too frequently on the very last night. This was the great cause of our recent increase of expenditures. It originated with the legislative, and not with the executive branch of the Government—and the corrective should begin here—in this House. There never could be any comprehensive, effectual, or substantial system of retrenchment of the expenditures of Government, till this habit of authorizing extraordinary expenditures, in the gross, at the close of the session, was reformed. As long as it is continued, our Federal expenditures must go on rapidly increasing; and it is not the executive branch of the Government, but this House, which should be held accountable to the country for this steady increase of the expenses of Government. During the last night of business of the last session, we appropriated eight hundred thousand dollars for this District. We had now before us bills amounting in their ultimate consequences to more than three millions for this District alone. In 1829 we laid the foundation for an expenditure of many millions at the mouth of the Delaware. It was in this way that almost all our increase of Federal expenditures was justly to be ascribed to legislative and not to executive origin. It was not from opposition to this bill particularly that he had made these remarks. He should pursue the same course in regard to all other expenditures not indispensably required for the service of the year. He should, when the question came before us, support the motion which the gentleman from Tennessee [Mr. Polk] promised to make, to strike out the appropriations for fortifications not yet commenced. He would do so for another reason—in the hope that, before the next session, the subject would attract the attention of the War Department; and that a system would be proposed, similar to that adopted in regard to the navy—appropriating a fixed sum annually for the gradual enlargement of fortifications, furnishing them with ordnance, &c., to be placed under the direction of able officers to be distributed to one object or another as they might deem most fit for the national interest. Without such a system, some of our fortifications never would be supplied with ordnance, while our appropriations for fortifications would go on annually increasing and be annually contested. He hoped that no expenditure, not absolutely required, would be authorized for this or any other purpose, and that gentlemen would unite, on all sides, in arresting the progress of our annual expenditures and in an attempt to diminish those Government expenses which had originated in measures of our own, hastily adopted and too generally growing out of political causes. With regard to this measure, he hoped the sum of eleven hundred thousand dollars, the aggregate proposed in the different sections of the bill, would be reduced to an amount corresponding to the state of the treasury.

Mr. THOMAS, of Maryland, contended that the proposed expenditure was taken into account in the treasury estimates.

Messrs. CHILTON and DUNCAN spoke in support of the bill, and in opposition to the motion to reconsider.

Mr. PARKS said he had heard of the Cumberland road for many years, and every year we had been told that the sum asked would be the last which would be wanted. It appeared, from statements made here this morning, that one hundred and thirty-two miles of the road had cost two and a half millions of dollars, which was equal to 19,774 dollars a mile. It should be recollected, too, that this road, which had cost so much, run through one of the most fertile regions of this country. He would now call the attention of the House to the expense of road-making in the State of Maine. A few years ago, a military post having been established on the northeastern frontier, it was thought expedient to make a road to it, for the conveyance of stores, troops, &c. The distance was seventy miles, the whole lying in an uninhabited and entangled forest, and the provisions used by the laborers were brought from this very Ohio country. But this road cost only twenty-one hundred dollars a mile; and he assured the House that the greater part of—for he was over it last fall—was as solid, smooth, and perfect, as the

Pennsylvania avenue from the Capitol to the President's House. Further: he would state that the State of Maine, in taking the road from the Government, asked only six thousand dollars to put it in complete repair, and this sum the delegation from Maine thought would be amply sufficient. To be sure, this was not a Macadamized road, but it was as good a road as any in New England. He thought we had better abandon the road which was to cost $20,000 a mile, and build one on a less expensive plan.

Mr. VANDERPOEL said that he was one of those who voted for the larger sum on yesterday, but that subsequent reflection had satisfied him that the sum of six hundred thousand dollars was too large, and he would therefore vote for a reconsideration, with a view ultimately to vote for the minor sum. He was satisfied that the condition of the treasury would not justify the appropriation of the enormous sum proposed. Considering the compact that had been adverted to in this debate, and the fact that the Federal Government had already fathered this child for so many years, he (Mr. V.) had no constitutional scruples to embarrass him, in relation to this particular matter; and was therefore at liberty of viewing it as a *mere matter of justice;* of justice, so far as it regarded the whole nation, which was proposed to be taxed, and of justice, also, as it regarded the claims of that section of country which the road accommodated; and viewing it solely under considerations of expediency and justice, he was constrained to say, that the larger amount proposed to be appropriated, was unreasonable and extravagant. Give your New England Yankees six hundred thousand dollars, and they would be able to construct with it a perfect *Appian way* over the whole of New England. They knew the value of money, and had the talent to disburse it to the best possible advantage. He had been told that nearly, or over, three millions of dollars had already been appropriated for this road. He could not say that he regretted even this enormous expenditure, because it had perhaps tended very much to the population and prosperity of that magnificent valley, where, at no distant period, would be the majority of our population. As an American citizen, looking to the good of *the whole country*, he should not deplore such a result, for mankind would always go where nature presented the strongest attractions; but there were reasons why we should at this crisis, keep an eye to economy. We had heard a great deal on this floor about the enormous expenditures of this Administration; and from the formidable appropriations he (Mr. V.) had already witnessed here, he was convinced that the Executive was made the scapegoat for the uniform prodigality of this House in making appropriations. Some of the most ardent friends of this bill, had been most loud and vehement in their denunciations of the alleged extravagance of this Administration; and he (Mr. V.) could not but observe, that when some gentlemen had dilated upon this, their *favorite topic*, they always took good care to forget, that the legislation of Congress had contributed most essentially to the expenditures of this Administration; that upon this Administration had fallen the enormous calls made upon your treasury under the pension laws of 1828 and of 1832, and other claims created by Congress, too numerous to mention; and if we now, in the fulness of our affection for our western brethren, were to appropriate this formidable sum of six hundred thousand dollars, it was difficult to say how long it would be before one of the friends of the bill would animadvert "*upon the startling aggregate expenditures of* 1834," without mentioning the amount disbursed upon the Cumberland road, as a constituent part of the sum total of this year's expenditure. Mr. V. therefore thought, that we were admonished, not only by a consideration of what was reasonable, but by the facility with which, not we, sir, but the head of the executive department, might in future be reproached for extravagance, not to grant the enormous sum appropriated by the vote of yesterday.

Mr. V. said, though he should vote for the minor sum, he desired to have it distinctly understood that he had not been converted to the measure by the speech made yesterday by the gentleman from Ohio, [Mr. VANCE.] That gentleman must have supposed that my colleague [Mr. MANN] was the mouthpiece of the New York delegation, or he certainly would not have indulged in a train of remark so illy calculated to propitiate the good will, and secure the votes of New York. Sir, (said Mr. V.,) it is the good or ill fortune of gentlemen from New York, sometimes to differ in opinion as to the subjects that here come before us, and, for my part, I can freely say, that I am too often annoyed with the question, "How will the New Yorkers go upon this subject?" I cannot accord to the gentleman from Ohio, or any other gentleman, the right to infer that the entire New York delegation intend to go *for* or *against* a particular measure, because one of its number indicates his course in regard to it. I repeat, sir, that I am not unfriendly to the bill, if it contains a reasonable sum, nor to the section of the country which it is designed to benefit; but I will here remark, that if the appropriation is to be supported in the spirit which characterized the speech of the gentleman from Ohio, [Mr. VANCE,] then the measure might well exclaim, "*Oh save me from my friends, and I will take care of my enemies.*" Why had the gentleman alluded so cavalierly to the appropriation for the New York custom-house, and for the navy-yard at Brooklyn? What was there in the history and career of New York, to justify the spirit which such remarks evinced? Was she justly chargeable with a spirit of meanness and parsimony to our western brethren? Had New York been a leech upon your treasury? Had she ever received anything to aid her in her magnificent works of internal improvement? No, sir. She applied to you for aid, and you refused it. She asked for bread, and you gave her a stone; for, after she had completed her grand work, which was an ornament not only to that *great State*, but to the country, and to the age in which we lived, you, sir, (I mean this Federal Government,) attempted to subject her canal boats to your custom-house regulations. I believe, sir, that you appropriated some three or four thousand dollars to make a military road somewhere in the neighborhood of Sackett's Harbor, to enable you to transport your own cannon to the frontier; and that, sir, tells the whole story of your munificence to New York, by way of aiding her in her schemes of internal improvement. Mr. V. said he did not know why this facility to attack New York. Was it because she was great—because she had over two millions of population—because her resources were immense—and because she had her great commercial emporium, where was collected most of the revenue of this Government? He mentioned these things in no spirit of boasting, for he was fully persuaded, from the short time he had already been here, that these circumstances were not much calculated to commend her to an undue share of favor here. If New York had a commercial emporium that required custom-houses, and all the facilities for the collection of revenue, and if she had a harbor, accessible at all times, and well fitted as a naval depôt, he could not perceive that these advantages, which nature had secured to her, warranted taunting allusions to her, or furnished any argument in favor of this formidable appropriation for the Cumberland road.

Mr. BEARDSLEY said he did not rise to discuss the character of the New York delegation. An opinion might be formed of that delegation without their speaking of themselves, and as one of the number, he chose to avoid that subject. Neither did he rise to say anything in reply to the remarks of the gentleman from Ohio, [Mr. VANCE,] for he had heard nothing from him to which he took exception, or which he thought should be regarded as offensive by any member from New York. But he had risen to entreat the House to drop the subjects upon which they had been occupied the last two hours, and to vote upon the bill before them, in order that they might take up some other of the important business of the session. The House, he thought, would not be greatly benefited or improved by remarks upon the character of any delegation, and he hoped the question about that of New York would be laid on the table, and the motion for reconsideration disposed of without further debate.

Mr. McKENNAN spoke earnestly in opposition to the motion to reconsider. He considered the reduction of the sum as tantamount to the destruction of the bill itself.

Mr. LOVE followed on the same side.

Mr. HARDIN opposed the bill, and the whole system of which it was a part. The system of internal improvements, he viewed as unconstitutional, and as enabling the Federal Government to swallow up the States. The interests of the West, he thought, were wholly mistaken on this subject. He believed it would be more for the interest of the West, if mountains, higher than the Andes, and capped with eternal snows, were between the western and the Atlantic States. The trade of the West would then pass through its natural channel—New Orleans. Now, the imports of the West were made from the Northeast, and her exports through the Southwest—the two points being thousands of miles distant.

Messrs. LOVE, STEWART, and THOMAS, of Maryland, followed in opposition to the motion to reconsider.

Mr. POLK advocated the motion, and insisted, that as only $200,000 could be beneficially used this year for the work, it was unnecessary to deprive the Government of the use of three times that sum. He also contended, that though the revenue of the year would exceed the estimates by two millions of dollars, yet we had appropriated, and were likely to appropriate, such large sums for different objects, that the treasury would not be able to meet them.

Mr. WAYNE made some remarks in support of the motion to reconsider, and in opposition to the bill.

Mr. D. J. PEARCE moved the previous question.

Mr. LANE earnestly requested him to withdraw it, as he wished to make a few remarks.

[Loud cries of "no," "no," and "question," "question."]

The previous question was seconded, and the main question was ordered to be put, without a division.

Mr. THOMAS, of Maryland, moved a call of the House; which was negatived.

The question on the motion to reconsider was then taken by yeas and nays, and determined in the affirmative:

Yeas 101, nays 96.

The amendment offered by Mr. POLK, reducing the appropriation for the repair of the road east of the Ohio, from $652,000 to $300,000, was then agreed to without a division.

Mr. McKENNAN moved to amend the bill by striking out the words "entire completion of," in third section, and the whole of the 4th section of the bill; which was divided.

The question on the former being taken first—

Mr. ELLSWORTH opposed the motion. He should hesitate to vote for any appropriation for repairs, unless it was provided that this should be the last appropriation for that object. He would not therefore, vote to strike out the words "entire completion of."

Mr. BEARDSLEY had voted against the motion to reconsider, and would vote against this motion. He wished the action of the House now to be final and conclusive.

Mr. McKENNAN remarked, that if the words were stricken out, the bill would stand exactly as it was reported from the Committee of Ways and Means.

The question being taken, the motion to strike out the words "entire completion of," was negatived—yeas 93, nays 115.

The question was then stated on striking out the fourth section.

Mr. GHOLSON moved to amend the section by adding a declaration that after the money appropriated by this act shall be expended, Congress will abandon all further jurisdiction of the road.

After some remarks from Messrs. GHOLSON, BEARDSLEY, W. COST JOHNSON, ELLSWORTH, and MERCER,

Mr. EWING offered an amendment to the amendment, providing that the States of Indiana, Ohio, Illinois, and Missouri, shall not be prohibited from taxing the public lands after the relinquishment of this road takes effect.

Mr. GILMER proposed a substitute for the amendment of Mr. GHOLSON, which he wished that gentleman to accept, before it was decided between them.

Mr. McKIM moved the previous question; which was seconded.

The CHAIR stated the main question would be on the third reading of the bill as amended.

The question on the third reading was carried; yeas 127, nays 78.

The bill was then read a third time and passed.

The House then adjourned.

IN SENATE.

WEDNESDAY, *June* 18, 1834.

A message upon executive business was received from the President of the United States, by Mr. DONELSON, his Private Secretary.

The VICE PRESIDENT presented a communication from the War Department, transmitting a statement relative to Indian tribes; which, on motion of Mr. TIPTON, was ordered to be printed.

The VICE PRESIDENT also presented a communication from the Treasury Department, transmitting, in compliance with a resolution of the Senate, a statement of the monthly accounts of the Bank of the United States, and the State banks where the public moneys are deposited.

Mr. SMITH presented a petition signed by 736 citizens of Tolland county, Connecticut, praying a restoration of the deposites to the Bank of the United States, and the recharter of said institution, or another, under certain modifications.

Mr. SMITH prefaced the presentation of the memorial with a few remarks relative to the distress complained of, and its causes.

Mr. McKEAN said he did not rise to interfere with the prerogative of the honorable Senator from Connecticut, nor would he obtrude upon the Senate his opinions of the merits or demerits of the memorial just presented by the honorable gentleman. He had generally found it to be the best policy to mind his own business; but he considered the present a legitimate occasion, in parliamentary order, as connected with the same subject, to correct some misstatements which were going the newspaper rounds, in reference to himself. It had, he knew not how, got into print that he should have said in his place as a Senator, that a majority of the citizens of Pennsylvania were opposed to the removal of the deposites. Now, he averred, in the face of the whole Senate, that he had never, publicly or privately, said any such thing; nor should he now presume an opinion the one way or the other. What he had said on the subject was strictly confined to the opinions of the petitioners whose memorials he was at the time about to present; and then only in cases where he had been by letter, or otherwise, requested to do so. Why, sir, (said Mr. McK.,) it might be considered presumptuous, if not impertinent, for a Pennsylvania Senator to venture an opinion on this floor, as to the general political character of that State, when there are so many other gentlemen on either side of the question who seem to understand precisely, not only what the present sentiment of the people of Pennsylvania now is, but what it will be in all time to come: and from these erroneous statements, it had been ungenerously inferred that he (Mr. McK.) was not quite as good a Jackson man as he ought to be. It was not, he said, because he was apprehensive, if this should reach the ears of the Executive, that it would deprive himself and family of their daily bread, that he noticed it; but he did not like to risk the injurious effects that might result to his State and constituents, by thus insidiously frittering away *his well-known influence with the present Administration*. He had, on another occasion, said he would vote to restore the deposites; not because he believed the restoration would afford the desired relief, but because a very large majority of his constituents, who had expressed any opinion on the subject, had asked for the restoration of the deposites as a measure of relief; and for so doing he had been proscribed and denounced as a traitor, by a certain well-disciplined corps, who had ceased not, day nor night, to pursue him since a certain period in 1829. He did not complain of this; very far from it. He ought rather to rejoice. For though he could, in truth, boast of as true and faithful friends as any man ever had, he had long been convinced that his enemies had rendered him more essential service than his friends.

But, (said Mr. McK.,) how stands this case? He held in his hand a statement, made by one of the under secretaries, from the Senate files, showing the number of individuals from Pennsylvania who had petitioned that body to restore the deposites, and also the number of those who had remonstrated against the restoration. This included all who had actually signed memorials, on both sides, which had been presented to the Senate during the present session from Pennsylvania, and stands thus: from the counties of Union, Cambria, Northampton, Cumberland, Montgomery, Adams, Mifflin, Northumberland, Bradford, Susquehanna, Chester, Delaware, Lycoming, Huntingdon, Lancaster, Franklin, Schuylkill, Berks, Alleghany, Philadelphia county and city, Pittsburg, Moyamensing and Southwark, Oxford, Byberry, Germantown, Waynesborough, Tamaqua, Bristol, Pottsville, and Muncy creek, (towns and villages,) forty different memorials, signed by *thirty-eight thousand and seven hundred* freemen of Pennsylvania, complaining of distress, and praying for the restoration of the deposites; and opposed to this, from Pennsylvania, are six, and only six, memorials from Philadelphia, Pittsburg, and the county of Schuylkill, signed by only *five hundred and seventy-one* individuals, who remonstrate against the restoration of the deposites; exhibiting a disparity of more than sixty-seven to one, and an aggregate majority of thirty-eight thousand one hundred and twenty-nine in favor of restoring the deposites. What is the duty of a faithful representative of the people under such circumstances? Shall he, because all have not complained, turn a deaf ear to thirty-nine thousand, who have laid their petitions at his feet? In giving his vote for the restoration of the deposites, he had not consulted the mere will of the Executive, nor that of any other individual; nay, he had not consulted his own will.

He was what he professed to be, the sincere friend of Andrew Jackson, though he detested many of the reptiles that were basking in the beams of his effulgence, and, without an authority, presuming to act and speak in his name. But he was also on that floor the humble representative in part of the people of Pennsylvania; and if he understood their interest, and knew their will on questions of mere expediency, he would advocate the one, and obey the other, please or displease whom it might. He was a party man as far as conscience would permit. He abhorred and condemned alike, a captious opposition, and a blind and sycophantic devotion to any Administration.

He desired to examine this a little further. He had another statement, made out by the same officer, from the files of the Senate, which showed that there have also been presented to the Senate from Pennsylvania resolutions and proceedings of thirty-five meetings of the people in their primary assemblies. Also, eleven corporate bodies, and resolutions and proceedings of one general State convention, making in all forty-seven—all recommending that the public deposites be restored; and, on the other side, there have been only resolutions of twelve meetings of citizens opposed to the restoration presented to the Senate from Pennsylvania.

Supposing the question be tested exclusively on party ground, and let the friends of General Jackson only be heard, he was certainly within bounds when he said, that of the 38,700 petitions, there were at least 8,000 of them General Jackson's sincere friends, and very many of them his most active supporters; and several of them, as well as himself, were members of the electoral college in 1832, and gave him their votes. Then we have 8,000 against 571—about fourteen Jackson men in favor, to one Jackson man opposed, to the restoration. So, consider it in what light you please, either as a question of general expediency, or as a purely party question, his vote was correct—if the will of the people, as expressed, was to be considered at all binding upon the representative. He had conscientiously listened to the complaints of the people; and if that be treason, let his enemies make the most of it.

The memorial was then referred to the Committee on Finance, and ordered to be printed.

Mr. CLAY presented the following memorials:

From the inhabitants of Huntingdon county, Pennsylvania;

From citizens of the town of Cannonsburg, Washington county, Pennsylvania; also,

The proceedings of a meeting of inhabitants of Boon county, Kentucky; and

The proceedings of a meeting of the citizens of Bowling Green, Kentucky;

All in favor of a restoration of the deposites to the Bank of the United States, and the recharter of that institution; which were referred to the Committee on Finance and ordered to be printed.

Mr. KNIGHT presented a memorial, signed by 400 inhabitants of the county of Kent, Rhode Island, of a similar character, and upon which the same order was taken.

Mr. BROWN presented the proceedings of a meeting of citizens of Wake county, North Carolina, held at Holly Spring. The resolutions approve of the course of the Administration in removing the deposites from the Bank of the United States, sustain the reasons of the Secretary of the Treasury, are averse to a recharter of that institution, and approve of the acts of the Administration generally. The proceedings were read, referred to the Committee on Finance, and ordered to be printed.

REPORTS.

Mr. PRESTON, from the Committee on Military Affairs, reported the following joint resolution:

Resolved by the Senate and House of Representatives of the United States of America in Congress assembled, That the President of the United States be requested to cause a gold medal to be struck, with suitable emblems and devices, and presented to Colonel Croghan, in testimony of the high sense entertained by Congress of his gallantry and good conduct in the defence of Fort Stephenson; and that he present a sword to each of the following officers engaged in that affair: to Captain James Hunter, Lieutenants Benjamin Johnson, Cyrus A. Buyler, and John Meeks, Ensigns Edmund Ross and Joseph Duncan.

BILLS.

The bill concerning the duties on lead, and

The bill concerning the Orphans' Courts of the counties of Washington and Alexandria, District of Columbia, were severally read a third time and passed.

Mr. SOUTHARD moved a reconsideration of the vote upon the bill for the relief of the legal representatives of Moses Shepherd, deceased, but consented that the motion should lie on the table.

GENERAL APPROPRIATION BILL.

On motion of Mr. WEBSTER, the Senate proceeded to the consideration of the bill making appropriations for the civil and diplomatic expenses of the Government for the year 1834.

A lengthened and desultory debate then ensued upon a proposition by Mr. PRESTON to postpone the further consideration of the bill to Tuesday next, on the ground that no legislative provision had been made relative to the custody of the public treasure.

In this debate, Messrs. PRESTON, WEBSTER, FORSYTH, CLAY, and GRUNDY, participated; and it terminated by Mr. PRESTON'S withdrawal of the proposition to postpone; and the Senate proceeded in the consideration of the bill.

The amendments reported by the Committee on Finance being first taken up—

The recommendation to reduce the salary of the additional watchman of the northeast executive building from 750 dollars to 300 dollars, was adopted.

The amendment to give the messenger of the library 500 dollars instead of 700 dollars, was then agreed to.

The amendment appropriating 70,080 dollars for mileage and pay of members of Congress, in addition to the appropriation of the 11th February, 1834, was also agreed to.

The amendment appropriating 7,000 dollars for the necessary apparatus to establish a refinery of gold and silver at the mint, came up next in order, and after some explanation of its object from Mr. WEBSTER,

Mr. BENTON said he was not opposed to the appropriation, but it was his wish, and he believed the general object, to make gold a part of the currency of the country; and he would only remark, that he would consider the vote upon this proposition as expressing the sense of the Senate upon

the question of making gold a part of the currency of the country.

The amendment was agreed to.

The appropriation of $40,000, to compensate for documents ordered to be printed by Gales & Seaton, after some conversation between Mr. FORSYTH and Mr. WEBSTER, was agreed to.

The appropriation of $49,960, for printing and engraving maps and documents relating to the public lands, ordered to be printed by the Senate, came up next in order.

Upon a request for some explanation of this item by Mr. FORSYTH, the estimates were read; when

Mr. FORSYTH asked the yeas and nays on the passage of the amendment; which were ordered, and are as follows:

YEAS—Messrs. Bibb, Calhoun, Chambers, Clay, Clayton, Ewing, Frelinghuysen, Hendricks, Kane, Kent, King of Alabama, Knight, Linn, McKean, Mangum, Naudain, Poindexter, Porter, Prentiss, Preston, Robbins, Robinson, Silsbee, Smith, Southard, Swift, Tomlinson, Tyler, Webster, and Wilkins—30.

NAYS—Messrs. Brown, Forsyth, Hill, King of Georgia, Shepley, Tipton, Waggaman, White, and Wright—9.

The question was determined in the affirmative.

The appropriation of $46,294 to the contingent expenses of the Senate, was then agreed to on a division—yeas 30, nays not counted.

The appropriation of $5000 to enable the Secretary of the Treasury to carry into effect the act for the relief of certain insolvent debtors, approved June 7th, 1834, was also agreed to.

The next amendment was to strike out the second section in the bill limiting the salaries of the collectors of customs to $3000, the naval officers to $2500, and the weighers, gaugers, markers, appraisers, and all others connected with the collection of the customs, to $3000 each, and to insert in lieu thereof—

That these officers and their respective clerks shall receive such sums as will give them respectively, the same compensation in the year 1834, according to the importations of that year, as they would have been entitled to receive if the act of July, 1832, had not gone into effect, and that they shall be paid for the year 1833 as if they had been specifically included in the third section of the general appropriation bill of 1833. Provided, That the compensation of weighers, gaugers, measurers, or appraisers shall in no case exceed, either by fees or salaries, $2000 each per annum. And Provided also, that no officer shall receive, under this act, a greater annual salary or compensation than was paid to such officer for the year 1832.

A debate then ensued, in which Mr. WEBSTER, Mr. WRIGHT, and Mr. PORTER, supported, and

Mr. CLAY and Mr. SILSBEE opposed the amendment, the latter of whom were in favor of the provision inserted in the bill by the House.

Mr. PORTER then offered a proviso to the amendment, that the number of officers in the custom-houses shall not be augmented beyond those now in service.

Mr. WEBSTER made some further remarks in favor of the amendment, and expressed his willingness, for himself, to accept the proviso.

After some further remarks from Mr. WRIGHT and Mr. CLAY—

Mr. FORSYTH moved an adjournment; which was agreed to—18 to 15.

At six o'clock the Senate adjourned.

HOUSE OF REPRESENTATIVES.
WEDNESDAY, June 18, 1834.

The Committee of the Whole, on motion of Mr. HARDIN, were discharged from the bill ceding the right of the United States to certain land in the city of New Orleans, and the same was referred to the Committee of the Whole on the State of the Union.

Mr. MERCER, from the Committee on Roads and Canals, reported a bill authorizing the construction of certain roads, and the improvement of certain harbors of the United States; which was read twice, and committed.

Mr. MERCER moved to suspend the rules, in order that the additional rule, proposed by him

some days since, might be taken up; which was negatived.

Mr. VINTON, from the Committee on Patents, reported a bill for the relief of James Jones; which was read twice and postponed until Tuesday next.

Mr. P. DICKERSON moved to reconsider the vote by which the resolution proposed by Mr. CLAY, making the bill for the graduation of the price of public lands the special order for the 20th instant, was yesterday laid on the table.

Mr. CLAY requested the bill might be read; which was done.

Mr. REED called for the reading of the amendment proposed to this bill, which was, substantially, the land bill of the Senate of the last session; which was done.

Mr. PATTON said, it must be manifest that the consideration of the bill and amendment, must bring up all the various projects relative to the disposal of the public lands in the different sections of the Union. All gentlemen, he thought, would admit that questions of so much importance should not be brought up at the heel of the session. He therefore moved to lay the motion to reconsider on the table.

Mr. WILLIAMS moved a call of the House; which was ordered.

After the call had proceeded through the first stage, on motion of Mr. WILLIAMS, it was suspended.

Mr. GRENNELL called for the yeas and nays on the question of laying the motion to reconsider on the table; which were ordered.

The motion was carried, yeas 111, nays 87.

The SPEAKER laid before the House a communication from the Secretary of War, covering a report from the officer at the head of the Topographical Bureau, relative to the survey of the harbor of Portland, Maine.

On motion of Mr. SMITH, the papers were laid on the table, and ordered to be printed.

The bill making certain foreign silver coins a legal tender, as amended by the Senate, came up.

Mr. C. P. WHITE moved that the House concur in the amendment of the Senate. Agreed to.

The bill authorizing the Secretary of the Treasury to grant a right of way in a certain case in the city of New York, was read a third time and passed.

Mr. POLK moved to suspend the rules in order that the bills relative to the public service—the appropriation bills, and the coinage bill, might be taken up; which was carried, yeas 121, nays 34.

The bill making additional appropriations for certain harbors, and removing obstructions from the mouth of certain rivers for 1834.

The amendment made in committee, lessening the appropriation for improving the navigation of Red river from $30,000 to $100,000, was read.

Mr. THOMAS, of Louisiana, moved to amend the amendment, by reducing the appropriation to $50,000.

Mr. GARLAND opposed the amendment. He was not aware of any reason why the amount fixed by the committee should be reduced. The amount was required to complete the work, and lessening the appropriation would only obstruct its progress. The raft increased annually about three miles in length, and delay only increased the expense of removing it.

Mr. THOMAS withdrew his motion.

Mr. HUBBARD was unwilling to go into a discussion of this subject. The sum proposed by the department to be applied to this object was $25,000. The committee concluded to increase it to $30,000. This sum, he believed, was all that could be profitably expended before the end of the next session of Congress. The object of the committee was to carry on the works commenced. He was opposed to increase appropriations upon individual statements, it would, be treading on unsafe ground.

Mr. POLK said the amendments added in the committee, proposing additional appropriations which had never been examined by any committee, amounted to $350,000. We had the estimate of the Engineer Department, calling for $25,000. This was from a responsible source; and the views of individuals, however respectable, could not be compared with this estimate as the basis of action by the House.

Mr. HAWES hoped that every gentleman who

wished to see the obstruction removed would, on every principle of economy, support the amendment. This amount was now sufficient, but hereafter it might require double the amount from the continued increase of the obstruction.

Mr. VINTON had voted for the amendment, but should vote against concurring in it. The improvement was not for commercial purposes, but it is intended to bring a large body of the best cotton land in the United States into the market. Instead of bringing a price according to its value, by the bill granting preëmption rights, passed a few days since, this land will not fetch more than one dollar and twenty-five cents per acre. All the motives for supporting the amendment had been destroyed by that bill. He should, therefore, vote against the amendment.

Mr. McKINLEY was not in favor of large appropriations generally, but sometimes sound economy required it. From the statements of Mr. Shreve, whose practical acquaintance with this subject rendered his opinions far more valuable than those of any other engineer in the service, he should support the amendment.

Mr. McK. replied at length to the arguments of Mr. VINTON as to the effect of this improvement.

Mr. LANE supported the amendment in committee, and should vote for it again, believing it to be called for by good policy and economy, upon which he explained his views relative to this measure.

Mr. EWING supported the amendment at length.

Mr. SUTHERLAND thought it was much better, if it was intended to pass the bill, to act upon it. These arguments had been heard in the Committee of the Whole. Unless the bill could be acted on and sent to the Senate, it was futile to take it up. Gentlemen should recollect that there were but few days of the session left, and act accordingly.

Mr. VINTON rose in a further defence and explanation of his views in opposition to the amendment.

Mr. McKIM asked for the yeas and nays on the motion; which were ordered.

After some further discussion, in which Messrs. THOMAS of Louisiana, GARLAND, ASHLEY, and HUBBARD, took part, the question was taken on concurring with the Committee of the Whole in the amendment, and decided in the negative: Yeas 60, nays 121.

Mr. GARLAND moved to insert $60,000; which was negatived.

The question being on concurring in the amendment appropriating ten thousand dollars for improving the harbor of Mobile, in removing the bar at the entrance of the harbor, called the Choctaw Pass—

Mr. MURPHY spoke in support of the amendment, and the question being taken, it was concurred in.

The question being on the amendment appropriating fifty thousand dollars for the improvement of the navigation of the river Savannah, and in removing the obstructions in said river, from the city of Savannah to its mouth—

Mr. WAYNE moved to amend the amendment, by striking out fifty and inserting twenty thousand dollars; which was agreed to, and the amendment, as amended, was concurred in.

The question being next upon the amendment appropriating thirty thousand dollars for continuing and securing the works at Oswego harbor, New York—

Mr. McKINLEY opposed the amendment, and called for the yeas and nays thereupon; which were ordered.

After some debate, in which Messrs. TURRILL, McKENNAN, McKINLEY, GILLET, POLK, E. WHITTLESEY, WARDWELL, MANN of New York, STEWART, BEARDSLEY, BURGES, SELDEN, HUBBARD, and McKIM, took part—

Mr. McKINLEY moved to amend the amendment made in Committee of the Whole, by striking out thirty thousand dollars and inserting eight thousand dollars.

The debate upon the item was continued by Messrs. GARLAND, SUTHERLAND, MERCER, and EWING;

When the question on the amendment to the amendment was taken, and it was negatived; yeas 41, nays 97.

The question was then taken on concurring with the Committee of the Whole in the amendment; which was carried.

The amendments added in Committee of the Whole, for $15,000 for Big Sodus Bay, $20,000 for Genesee river, $12,000 for Black Rock harbor, $20,000 for Buffalo harbor, $4,000 for Dunkirk harbor, $20,000 for Presque Isle, $13,350 for Cleaveland harbor, $10,000 for Grand river, $5,000 for Black river, $6,700 for Huron river, $5,000 for [Ashtabula creek, were all concurred in.

The item appropriating $30,000 for surveys, added in committee, then came up on the question of concurrence.

Mr. ARCHER said he was a member of the House in 1834, when this appropriation was first made. It had been continued from that time to the present; and with ordinary care in its expenditure, surveys enough would have been accumulated to last for a thousand years. He would ask the chairman of the Committee of Ways and Means for an explanation of this item.

Mr. POLK said this was replied by the Committee of Ways and Means, who deemed it unnecessary and improper to continue this appropriation. It had been moved in the Committee of the Whole by the gentleman at the head of the Committee of Roads and Canals, [Mr. MERCER,] and was there inserted in the bill. After an explanation upon the subject at some length, Mr. P. expressed his decided opposition to the amendment.

Mr. MERCER supported the amendment at some length; and was followed by

Mr. J. Q. ADAMS, who advocated with great earnestness the system of internal improvement.

Mr. ARCHER replied, and Mr. ADAMS rejoined; when the question was taken, and the amendment was negatived—yeas 90, nays 103.

The item for improving the branch of Elizabeth river, called Deep Creek, $29,000, was then read.

Mr. LOVE moved the House adjourn; which was negatived.

Mr. MILLER called the previous question.

Mr. H. EVERETT moved to lay the bill on the table; on which the yeas and nays were ordered.

After

Mr. WILLIAMS moved an adjournment; which was lost; yeas 74, nays 106.

Mr. MILLER withdrew the previous question.

Mr. EVERETT withdrew the motion to lay on the table.

The motion to lay on the table was renewed by Mr. BEATY.

Mr. MERCER moved the House adjourn, on which he demanded the yeas and nays; which were ordered.

The motion to adjourn was lost.

Mr. GARLAND moved a call of the House; which was negatived.

Question to lay on the table lost: Yeas 66, nays 122.

The question was then stated on concurring in the amendment appropriating $29,000 to improvement of Deep Creek.

Mr. BEATY moved to amend the amendment by adding $50,000 to the improvement of the Cumberland river.

Mr. B. went into an explanation of the proposition.

Mr. PEYTON also supported the amendment to the amendment at length.

Mr. MILLER explained the motives upon which he had moved the previous question.

Mr. LANE moved the House adjourn; which was carried.

And the House adjourned.

IN SENATE.

THURSDAY, June 19, 1834.

A message was received from the President of the United States, transmitting despatches received from our Minister to France, covering a letter from Captain Ballard, of the frigate United States, detailing a fatal accident, at Toulon, which led to the death of some French seamen, in firing a salute, three of the ship's guns being charged with ball. The message recommended Congress to grant pensions

to the heirs of the deceased, and to the wounded seamen, at the same rate as is allowed in similar cases in the naval service of the United States.

On motion of Mr. WAGGAMAN, the message and documents were referred to the Committee on Foreign Relations, and ordered to be printed.

The VICE PRESIDENT presented a communication from the Secretary of the Senate, enclosing a supplemental list of petitions, public meetings, &c., both for and against the removal of the deposites and the recharter of the Bank of the United States, since the 18th of May.

On motion of Mr. CLAY, one thousand copies were ordered to be printed.

Mr. BIBB, from the Committee on the Judiciary, to whom was referred the memorial of members of the Mississippi bar for removal of the district court of the United States from Natchez to Jackson, reported the same as inexpedient.

Mr. CLAYTON, from the Committee on the Judiciary, to which was referred the resolution providing for the compensation of the Hon. ELISHA R. POTTER, reported the same to the Senate, with a request that the committee be discharged from the further consideration of the subject.

Mr. C. then explained the reasons why the committee reported against the allowance of compensation to Mr. Potter.

After some conversation between Mr. WRIGHT, Mr. KING of Alabama, and Mr. CLAYTON, upon a point of order, the committee was discharged.

Mr. WRIGHT then submitted an amendment to the resolution, with a view of testing the sense of the Senate as to the allowance of pay to Mr. Potter, instructing the Committee on the Judiciary to report a bill making the allowance, upon which he asked the yeas and nays; which were ordered.

Mr. CLAY and Mr. CLAYTON opposed the amendment.

Mr. WEBSTER thought Mr. Potter was entitled to one day's pay and mileage, which ought to be provided by law.

Mr. WRIGHT briefly supported the amendment.

Mr. KNIGHT was in favor of allowing an equitable compensation to Mr. Potter, to be provided for in an appropriation bill.

After some further remarks from Mr. BIBB, Mr. KNIGHT, Mr. CLAY, and Mr. TALLMADGE, the question on the resolution, as amended, was determined in the affirmative by the following vote:

YEAS—Messrs. Benton, Bibb, Brown, Chambers, Grundy, Hendricks, Hill, Kane, King of Alabama, Knight, Linn, McKean, Moore, Morris, Preston, Robinson, Shepley, Silsbee, Tallmadge, Tyler, Waggaman, White, Wilkins, Wright—24.

NAYS—Messrs. Bell, Black, Clay, Clayton, Ewing, Forsyth, Frelinghuysen, Kent, King of Georgia, Leigh, Mangum, Naudain, Poindexter, Porter, Prentiss, Smith, Southard, Sprague, Swift, Tipton, Tomlinson, Webster—22.

CUMBERLAND ROAD.

The bill making appropriation for the repair of the Cumberland road was taken up, and on motion of Mr. HENDRICKS, the amendments of the House of Representatives were concurred in.

The following bills from the House were read twice and referred:

A bill authorizing the Secretary of the Treasury to grant the right of way in certain cases in New York;

A bill repealing certain acts of the Legislative Council of Florida;

A bill increasing the salaries of the judges of the Territories of Michigan, Arkansas, and Florida;

A bill for the relief of certain inhabitants of East Florida;

A bill establishing an additional Land Office in Arkansas.

Mr. CHAMBERS, agreeably to notice, introduced a bill for the relief of Gad Humphreys; which was read twice, and referred to the Committee on Indian Affairs.

FRENCH SPOLIATIONS.

The Senate then resumed the consideration of the

bill making compensation to claimants for French spoliations previous to the year 1800.

Mr. FORSYTH said as it was obvious we were not able to pass this bill at the present session, he moved to postpone it to the next session of Congress.

Some discussion ensued on this motion, when the question was determined in the affirmative by the following vote:

YEAS—Messrs. Benton, Bibb, Black, Brown, Calhoun, Clay, Forsyth, Grundy, Hill, Kane, King of Alabama, King of Georgia, Leigh, Linn, Mangum, Morris, Poindexter, Porter, Robinson, Swift, Tallmadge, Tyler, White, Wright—24.

NAYS—Messrs. Bell, Chambers, Clayton, Ewing, Frelinghuysen, Kent, Knight, McKean, Moore, Naudain, Prentiss, Robbins, Shepley, Silsbee, Smith, Southard, Sprague, Tipton, Tomlinson, Webster, Wilkins—21.

GENERAL APPROPRIATION BILL.

The Senate then resumed the consideration of the bill making appropriations for the civil and diplomatic expenses of the Government for the year 1834.

The proviso offered by Mr. PORTER to the amendment, relative to the fees to be allowed to custom-house officers, was adopted.

Mr. SOUTHARD then offered the following amendment to the amendment:

"And provided further, that the said collectors, naval officers, and surveyors, shall render an account quarterly to the treasury; and the other officers herein named or referred to, shall render an account quarterly to the respective collectors of the customs where they are employed, to be forwarded to the treasury, of all the fees and emoluments whatever by them respectively received, and of all expenses incident to their respective offices; which accounts shall be rendered on oath or affirmation, and shall be in such form, and be supported by such proofs to be prescribed by the Secretary of the Treasury, as will, in his judgment, best improve the provisions of this section, and show its operation and effect."

Which was adopted without opposition.

Mr. CLAY then moved to strike out all the first part of the amendment, in the following words:

"That the Secretary of the Treasury be authorized to pay the collectors, naval officers, surveyors, and their respective clerks, together with the weighers and markers, of the several ports of the United States, such sums as will give to said officers, respectively, the same compensation in the year 1834, according to the importations of that year, as they would have been entitled to receive, if the act of 14th July, 1832, had not gone into effect; and that the clerks employed by the respective collectors, &c., together with the respective collectors &c., together with the respective collectors of ports, shall be paid for the year 1833, as if they had been specifically included in the third section of the general appropriation act of the year '33."

After some discussion, in which Messrs. CLAY, WRIGHT, BIBB, SILSBEE, SHEPLEY, WILKINS, and TALLMADGE, participated, at the suggestion of Mr. WEBSTER,

Mr. CLAY withdrew his proposed amendment.

Mr. SILSBEE then moved to strike out of the amendment "weighers, gaugers, markers, measurers, or appraisers," and insert " that in no case shall the compensation of any other officer, collectors, naval officers, and surveyors, whether by salaries, fees, or otherwise, exceed the sum of $3000 each per annum," which was agreed to; and the amendment reported by the Committee on Finance, as amended, was agreed to.

Several other amendments were offered, which will be given in the subsequent proceedings on the bill.

Mr. WILKINS gave notice that he should, to-morrow, move the Senate, at as early an hour as practicable, to go into executive business.

On motion of Mr. MANGUM,

The Senate adjourned.

☞ Congress having fixed Monday, the 30th instant, for the day of adjournment, the next number of the Congressional Globe will not be published until Tuesday, the 1st of July; and the proceedings of the last day of the session will be given in it.

THE CONGRESSIONAL GLOBE.

PRINTED AND PUBLISHED AT THE CITY OF WASHINGTON, BY BLAIR & RIVES.

23d Congress, 1st Session.   SATURDAY, JUNE 28, 1834.   Vol. 1........No. 30.

HOUSE OF REPRESENTATIVES.

Thursday, June 19, 1834.

The message received from the President of the United States, yesterday, transmitting an extract of a despatch from Mr. Livingston, and the copy of a communication made to him by Captain Ballard, commander of the frigate United States, by which it appears that in firing a national salute from that ship, at Toulon, in honor of the birthday of the King of the French, two men were killed, and four others wounded, on board the French ship of war Suffren, with a recommendation that such provision be made by law for the sufferers and their families, as would be made for American seamen killed or wounded in battle, was read.

On motion of Mr. E. EVERETT, the message and accompanying documents were ordered to be printed and referred to the Committee on Foreign Relations.

Mr. J. Q. ADAMS called for the reading of the papers.

Mr. ELLSWORTH, from the Committee on the Judiciary, reported a bill to authorize the issuing of writs of error in certain cases of patents, which was postponed to, and made the order of the day for, Saturday.

Mr. H. EVERETT, from the Committee on Indian Affairs, reported a resolution for setting apart Tuesday for the consideration of the bills relative to the Indian department.

Mr. POLK moved to strike out Tuesday and insert Wednesday; which was agreed to, and the resolution as amended, was adopted.

Mr. W. C. JOHNSON reported a bill authorizing an appropriation for a turnpike between Rockville and Monocacy creek in Maryland; read twice and committed.

Mr. CHINN reported a bill to extend the time for completing the Washington city canal and for other purposes; read twice and committed.

Mr. LEAVITT reported a bill for the survey and sale of certain reservations of land in Ohio; which was read twice and ordered to be engrossed.

Mr. CLAY moved to take up the bills relative to the Territories; which was agreed to.

The bill to create two additional land districts in the State of Illinois, and two new land districts north of said State, in the territory now attached to Michigan, was read a third time and passed.

The bill repealing certain acts of the Legislative Council of Florida, was read a third time and passed.

The bill to increase the salaries of the Judges of the Territories of Florida, Michigan and Arkansas, was read a third time, and opposed by Messrs. McKAY, HAWES, McCARTY; and supported by Messrs. LYON of Michigan, EWING, GAMBLE, WILDE, and SEVIER; when the bill passed.

The bill to establish an additional land office in Arkansas, was read a third time and passed.

The bill for the relief of certain inhabitants of East Florida, was read a third time and passed.

Mr. POLK moved to take up the orders of the day, at the same time giving notice that he would to-morrow morning ask the House to take up for consideration the bill regulating the deposites.

The bill making appropriations for fortifications for the year 1834 being taken up—

Mr. BEARDSLEY moved to lay it on the table, and thereupon called for the yeas and nays; which were ordered.

The question being taken, it was decided in the negative—yeas 77, nays 102.

Mr. POLK moved to reduce the appropriation for Castle Island, from $34,000 to $17,000; which was agreed to.

Mr. P. moved to strike out the clause, " for a harbor at George's Island, $100,000."

The motion was supported by Mr. POLK and Mr. W. R. DAVIS, and opposed by Messrs. GORHAM, E. EVERETT, and GRENNELL; when

Mr. CROCKETT made some desultory remarks in opposition to the Executive Government; and was replied to by Mr. DUNLAP, who opposed the general principle of this bill, as well as the internal improvement system generally.

Mr. CROCKETT briefly rejoined.

The opposition to Mr. Folk's motion was continued by Messrs. SELDEN, BEARDSLEY, FILLMORE, and REED; and it was supported by Messrs. POLK, HAWES, and McKINLEY; when

Mr. PEYTON, after some remarks in opposition to the system of fortification generally, moved to strike the enacting clause from the bill.

Mr. S. JONES supported this proposition at length.

Before the question was taken,

Mr. LANE moved that the House adjourn; which was carried.

IN SENATE.

Friday, June 20, 1834.

The VICE PRESIDENT presented a communication from the Secretary of the Treasury, transmitting a report of the Register relative to officers of the customs.

REPORTS.

Mr. CHAMBERS, from the Committee on Naval Affairs, reported a bill for the relief of Isaac Garretson, late a purser in the navy.

Also, a bill placing Master Commandant George Budd upon the invalid pension roll.

Mr. CHAMBERS moved that the report of the Secretary of the Treasury, made yesterday, relative to the accounts of the deposite banks, and the Bank of the United States, be printed; which was agreed to.

Mr. SOUTHARD, from the Committee on Naval Affairs, reported a bill to authorize the Secretary of the Navy to cause provisions, and other stores, to be transferred from one depôt to another; a bill changing the title of Master Commandant, to Commander; and Sailing Master, to Master; a bill to establish a naval academy; a bill to regulate navy rations; a bill relative to the enlistment of boys in the navy;

a bill to establish a fund for the benefit of the widows and orphans of commission and warrant officers of the navy; and

a bill granting pensions to French subjects accidentally killed by discharging a salute from the United States frigate United States, in the harbor of Toulon.

Mr. SOUTHARD requested that this bill might be read a second time, in order that it might be ordered for engrossment; which was agreed to.

Mr. BIBB submitted an amendment, that the pensions allowed should be double the amount of what was given to American seamen who were killed or wounded in battle, and for like periods; which, after some further remarks from Messrs. CLAY, BIBB, SOUTHARD, TALLMADGE, and MANGUM, was adopted, and the bill, as amended, was ordered to be engrossed for a third reading.

B. Ostrander.

Mr. WHITE, from the Committee on Indian Affairs, made a report upon the memorial of John Ross, and other delegates of the Cherokee nation, relative to the disposition of their lands in the State of Georgia; which report was ordered to be printed, and the consideration thereof postponed until the next session.

Mr. CLAY, from the Committee on the Judiciary, reported a bill granting the right of way in a certain case in the city of New York.

Mr. WEBSTER, from the Committee on Finance, reported a bill from the House of Representatives, making appropriations for the payment of Indian annuities, and gave notice that he should move that it be taken up to-morrow.

Mr. W. also gave notice, that to-morrow he should ask the consideration of the bill repealing so much of the tariff law of 1832 as relates to hardware.

Mr. SMITH, from the Committee on the Judiciary, reported a bill regulating the weight of interest in the bill providing for the final settlement of the claims of States for interest on advances to the United States during the last war.

Mr. WAGGAMAN submitted the following resolution:

Resolved, That the Committee on Military Affairs be instructed to inquire into the expediency of making an appropriation to complete the erection of towers, barracks, and store-houses, in the vicinity of New Orleans, for the use of the United States.

Mr. BENTON presented the memorial of Francis P. Blair, responding to certain portions of the report of the Committee on the Post Office and Post Roads, in which the memorialist felt himself implicated; which was laid on the table.

The Senate then, on motion of Mr. WILKINS, proceeded to the consideration of executive business.

When the doors were opened, the Senate had adjourned.

HOUSE OF REPRESENTATIVES.

Friday, June 20, 1834.

The SPEAKER laid before the House a communication from the Secretary of War, covering the report of Captain Talcott, relative to the boundary of Ohio, Indiana, and Illinois; which was laid on the table, and ordered to be printed.

Mr. POLK, from the Committee on Ways and Means, reported a resolution for discharging the Committee of the Whole on the state of the Union from the bill regulating the deposite of the public money of the United States in certain local banks, and that the same be made the special order for this day at twelve o'clock.

Mr. E. WHITTLESEY suggested that Friday and Saturday being set apart by the rules for private bills, it was not competent for that committee to take up public business on either day.

The CHAIR decided, that unless the rules were suspended, this day could not be devoted to public business by a special order.

Mr. POLK moved to suspend the rules, for the purpose of taking up the bill to-day; on which

Mr. CLAY demanded the yeas and nays; which were ordered.

After some conversation as to the most expedient course, the question was taken on suspending the rules, and carried: Yeas 114, nays 54.

Mr. S. JONES moved to amend the resolution, by striking out "this day at twelve o'clock," and inserting "Monday next, at twelve o'clock;" which was negatived.

Mr. WATMOUGH moved to amend, by striking out this day, and inserting Tuesday next; which was negatived.

Mr. CHILTON moved to amend the resolution, by adding the joint resolutions of the Senate, relative to the deposites, which have been heretofore laid on the table.

The CHAIR decided that the amendment was not in order, the rules having been suspended for the purpose of considering the bill reported by the Committee of Ways and Means. If the gentleman from Kentucky should offer a suspension of the rules, the amendment might be moved.

Mr. ADAMS. Do I understand the Chair to decide, that, the rules of the House having been suspended for the purpose of taking up a resolution, that resolution cannot be amended?

The CHAIR had not so decided. The rules were suspended for a definite purpose, which was stated and understood by the House when the question was taken on the suspension of the rules. It was not in order to take up a distinct and independent subject, by way of amendment to the resolution, unless a further suspension of the rules of

the House was obtained. This decision was made agreeably to the uniform practice of the House, as the Chair understood it.

The decision of the Chair, after some conversation, was acquiesced in.

The resolution offered by Mr. POLK was then adopted without a division.

The bill to amend an act passed 29th May, 1830, for the relief of sundry owners of vessels sunk for the defence of Baltimore, was then taken up, and ordered to be engrossed for a third reading.

The bill from the Senate for the relief of Charles Burnham and others, was read.

After an explanation from Mr. E. WHITTLESEY, the bill passed.

The bill for the relief of Peter Alba, his heirs and representatives, was read a third time, and passed.

The bill creating additional land districts in the States of Illinois and Missouri, and in the territory lying north of Illinois, attached to Michigan, was read a third time, and passed.

The resolution to provide for watering Pennsylvania Avenue was laid on the table.

The act authorizing the President to cause a road to be cut in the Territory of Florida, and making appropriations for certain surveys therein, was read.

After a brief explanation by Mr. WILDE, in favor of the bill, the question was taken, and a quorum not voting—

Mr. CHINN moved a call of the House; which was negatived.

Mr. WILDE moved an adjournment, and demanded the yeas and nays; which were ordered. The motion was negatived; yeas 28, nays 130.

Mr. E. WHITTLESEY, from the Committee of Claims, reported a bill for the relief of Jane Taylor, and others. Read twice and committed.

Mr. CHILTON, from the Committee on Invalid Pensions, reported a bill granting a pension to John W. Potts. Read twice and committed.

Mr. ARCHER, from the Committee of Foreign Affairs, reported a joint resolution authorizing the President to make suitable provision for the families of those killed on the occasion of firing a salute in the harbor of Toulon, and for the wounded survivors; which was read twice.

Mr. J. Q. ADAMS objected that appropriation of money could only be made by law, and not by resolution, and moved that it be committed to the Committee of Foreign Affairs; which, after a few words from Mr. ARCHER, was agreed to.

The House then proceeded to the consideration of the special order.

THE DEPOSITE BILL.

The bill was read as reported.

Mr. POLK addressed the House a little more than an hour, in explanation and defence of the provisions of the bill.

He was followed by Mr. FOSTER, in opposition to the bill.

After a brief explanation between Messrs. GILMER and FOSTER—

Mr. WILDE addressed the House at length. The debate was further continued, and was not concluded when the House adjourned.

IN SENATE.

SATURDAY, June 21, 1834.

A message upon executive business was received from the President of the United States by Mr. DONELSON, his Private Secretary.

Mr. HENDRICKS submitted the following resolution; which was considered and adopted:

Resolved, That the Committee on Pensions be instructed to inquire into the expediency of placing the name of William Warner on the invalid pension roll.

GENERAL APPROPRIATION BILL.

On motion of Mr. WEBSTER, the Senate resumed the consideration of the appropriation bill for the year 1834.

Several immaterial amendments to the bill suggested by Mr. KNIGHT, Mr. HENDRICKS, and Mr. WEBSTER, were adopted.

Mr. FORSYTH then moved to strike out the appropriation of $35,000 to Clark and Force, for printing the Documentary History of the American Revolution, authorized to be executed by a contract made with them by the late Secretary of

State, (Mr. Livingston,) and insert an appropriation of $15,000, to remunerate those persons for expenses incurred in preparing to execute the contract. The amendment also provided that the further prosecution of the work should henceforth be suspended.

Mr. F. was induced to offer this proposition from a sense of justice to the late Secretary of State, (Mr. Livingston,) who, it was clear, had misconceived his authority under the act of Congress. It seemed to him that there was no limitation to it—that it might run up to one or two millions of dollars; and even by the arrangement of the Finance Committee, it would be reduced to not less than $400,000. His object was to make an appropriation sufficient to cover all the expenses which these gentlemen have been subjected to, and if any damage should be done them, they could be compensated for it at the next session of Congress.

Mr. CHAMBERS was afraid the proposed publication was not very well understood. These gentlemen preferred their memorial to Congress, proposing this publication. After due consideration, Congress passed an act authorizing the compilation, and prescribed the tribunal to which the work should be submitted. The Secretary of State was selected as this tribunal, and the work was directed to be executed under his exclusive superintendence. The publishers were willing that Congress should prescribe just what materials they chose for the work, and they were to publish no other than useful documents relative to the history of this country, and they were to receive an equivalent for it equal to the lowest scale of compensation known to the Government for such work.

Mr. C.'s remarks were here suspended, by the introduction of the Clerk of the House of Representatives, who communicated the following joint resolution, passed by the House:

Resolved, by the Senate and House of Representatives of the United States of America, in Congress assembled, That a committee be appointed, on the part of this House, to join such committee as may be appointed by the Senate, to consider and report by what token of respect 'and affection it may be proper for the Congress of the United States to express the deep sensibility of the nation on the event of the decease of General Lafayette.

Mr. CHAMBERS said, as he was disposed to manifest the highest sense of respect for the memory of General Lafayette, he moved that the appropriation bill be laid on the table for the present, this joint resolution; which was agreed to.

The resolution was then read; when

Mr. WEBSTER moved that the Senate concur therein.

The motion was immediately agreed to.

Mr. CHAMBERS suggested that the committee consist of one Senator from each State.

Mr. WEBSTER thought the number too large.

Mr. POINDEXTER suggested nine members.

Mr. FORSYTH hoped the President might appoint the committee; which was assented to.

Mr. FORSYTH expressed a hope that the committee might consist of thirteen, as there were peculiar associations connected with that number.

The committee was then ordered to consist of thirteen.

[The committee was not announced when the Senate adjourned.]

The Senate then resumed the general appropriation bill: when, at the request of

Mr. CHAMBERS, a communication from Messrs. Clarke and Force, making some explanations relative to, this work, was read.

Messrs. SOUTHARD, FRELINGHUYSEN, and CHAMBERS, made some further remarks in support of the appropriation, and against the amendment.

Messrs. KING of Georgia, and HILL, spoke at length in opposition to the further prosecution of the work, and in favor of the amendment.

Mr. MANGUM then moved an amendment to the amendment, to strike out "$15,000 to remunerate," and insert in lieu thereof "$30,000 to pay the Secretary of State to settle with Messrs. Clarke and Force."

Mr. FORSYTH accepted the proposition as a modification of his amendment.

After some further remarks from Messrs. FOR-

SYTH, WEBSTER, PRESTON, WILKINS, and MANGUM,

Mr. BIBB moved a proviso to 'the amendment, "that nothing herein contained shall be taken as a sanction of the contract made under the act of Congress by the late Secretary of State, on the 9th March, 1833."

The proceedings of the Senate were here suspended by the introduction of Mr. DONELSON, Private Secretary of the President, who presented the following message:

To the Senate and House of Representatives:

The afflicting intelligence of the death of the illustrious LAFAYETTE has been received by me this morning.

I have issued the General Order enclosed, to cause appropriate honors to be paid by the army and navy to the memory of one so highly venerated and beloved by my countrymen; and whom Providence has been pleased to remove so unexpectedly from the agitating scenes of life.

ANDREW JACKSON.

WASHINGTON, June 21, 1834.

After the message had been read—

On motion of Mr. FORSYTH, it was referred to the Joint Committee appointed on this subject.

The Senate then resumed the consideration of the appropriation bill; when

Mr. FORSYTH accepted Mr. BIBB's proviso.

And after some further remarks from Messrs. KING of Georgia, KING of Alabama, CLAY, LEIGH, CLAYTON, WEBSTER, EWING, and CALHOUN,

Mr. FORSYTH asked the yeas and nays on the passage of the amendment; which were ordered, and are as follows:

YEAS—Messrs. Bibb, Black, Brown, Calhoun, Forsyth, Grundy, Hendricks, Hill, Kane, King of Alabama, King of Georgia, Linn, McKean, Mangum, Morris, Preston, Robinson, Shepley, Tallmadge, Tipton, White, Wilkins, Wright—23.

NAYS—Messrs. Bell, Benton, Chambers, Clay, Clayton, Ewing, Frelinghuysen, Kent, Leigh, Naudain, Poindexter, Porter, Prentiss, Robbins, Silsbee, Smith, Southard, Sprague, Tomlinson, Tyler, Waggaman, Webster—22.

So the amendment was adopted.

Mr. BIBB then offered a further amendment, appropriating four hundred dollars for the purpose of recording the opinions of the Supreme Court; to which

Mr. FORSYTH objected, as being an useless expense, although it was a small one. Copies of the opinions of the judges could at all times be obtained from the Clerk of the Court, and the opinions of the Court delivered, were already published.

Mr. CLAYTON made a few remarks in favor, and Mr. SMITH against the proposition; when it was negatived.

Mr. BIBB then moved a further amendment, to insert "eight hundred dollars each to the Judges of the Superior Courts of the eastern and southern districts of the Florida Territory, for additional compensation."

After some conversation between Messrs. FORSYTH, BIBB, and KING of Alabama, the amendment was agreed to.

Mr. POINDEXTER then offered an amendment to the bill, "that no payment shall be made under this or any other act passed at the present session of Congress in any other bank notes than those which are at par value at the place where such payment is made."

Mr. FORSYTH remarked that he thought it a very fair proposition and a very just one, yet he would suggest that some difficulty might arise in its operation from the circumstance that the notes of the Bank of the United States we were bound to receive in payment of dues to the Government, but all the notes of that bank were not everywhere at par. For instance, the notes of the New Orleans branch were not at par in Philadelphia.

Mr. POINDEXTER said that a large portion of the revenue was collected in New York, and the notes of many of the local banks there were not at par everywhere, and if the paper of those banks was not to a distance for disbursement, it would occasion a loss to the person to whom it was paid. His object was, when payments were made, that it should be dollar for dollar.

Mr. WILKINS observed, that no bank notes

were a legal tender in payment of debts, and he presumed it was not the object of the gentleman from Mississippi to make them so. It was always optional with the persons receiving money to take notes or specie, whichever they pleased.

Mr. BENTON was opposed to the amendment in its present form. We had gone a great way in encouraging the paper system, and he could not assent to anything which went to make notes receivable at all. All persons knew that they were not bound to receive notes of any kind which might be offered them. But soldiers, for example, seeing this law, would think they were bound to receive them. He was against a paper system altogether, but especially was he opposed to payments in dues from the United States. Every person having a warrant from the treasury for a sum of money had a right to the specie for it, and he was at liberty to refuse anything else. Mr. Gallatin, when he provided for the deposites of the public moneys in the State banks, made an arrangement by which they were to take in deposite par notes and pay out in specie.

The bill he (Mr. B.) offered a fortnight ago for the regulation of the public moneys in the local banks embraced a similar provision. That was not adopted here, and it was now under discussion in the other House. He was therefore against any measure legalizing, or tending to legalize paper; but he was ready to vote for a provision requiring that every warrant from the treasury on a deposite bank should be paid in specie. He therefore moved to amend the amendment by a provision to that effect.

Some further remarks were then made by Mr. SHEPLEY, who explained why he would vote for Mr. Benton's motion, and then against the amendment, whether the motion prevailed or not. Messrs. BENTON, PORTER, and WEBSTER, made some further observations, when

Mr. SHEPLEY asked the yeas and nays on the amendment to the amendment; which were ordered, and are as follows, to wit:

YEAS—Messrs. Benton, Bibb, Forsyth, Grundy, Hill, Kane, King of Alabama, Morris, Robinson, Shepley, Sprague, Tallmadge, Tipton, White, Wilkins, Wright—16.

NAYS—Messrs. Brown, Clayton, Ewing, Frelinghuysen, Hendricks, Kent, Leigh, McKean, Mangum, Naudain, Poindexter, Porter, Prentiss, Robbins, Southard, Swift, Tomlinson, Tyler, Webster—19.

So the motion was negatived.

The question recurring on the amendment—

Mr. WRIGHT desired to state, in few words, why he was opposed to it. The law required the local banks to receive the paper of the United States Bank and its branches, and this amendment went to compel the banks to pay out the revenue in a better currency than that which they received; this was his only objection. He knew that United States Bank notes were not always at par. He knew that the bills of the parent bank were refused by the branch in New York, when tendered in payment of debts due the branch.

Some further discussion ensued on this proposition, in which Messrs. WEBSTER, CALHOUN, POINDEXTER, SPRAGUE, and BIBB, participated; when

Mr. POINDEXTER demanded the yeas and nays on the amendment, which are as follows:

YEAS—Messrs. Black, Chambers, Clay, Clayton, Ewing, Frelinghuysen, Mangum, Naudain, Poindexter, Porter, Prentiss, Robbins, Robinson, Silsbee, Sprague, Waggaman, Webster—17.

NAYS—Messrs. Benton, Bibb, Brown, Calhoun, Forsyth, Grundy, Hendricks, Hill, Kane, Kent, King of Alabama, King of Georgia, Leigh, Linn, McKean, Morris, Shepley, Swift, Tallmadge, Tipton, Tomlinson, Tyler, White, Wilkins, Wright—25.

So the question was determined in the negative.

Mr. POINDEXTER gave notice that he would renew the amendment when the bill should be read in the Senate.

Mr. CHAMBERS then moved to strike out the provision for the salaries of the Secretary of State, the Secretary of the Treasury, and the Attorney General, on the ground that those officers were not nominated to the Senate; but at

Mr. WEBSTER'S suggestion, he did not press his motion, and no further amendment being pro-

posed, the bill was reported to the Senate, and on motion of Mr. WEBSTER, it was postponed to Monday next.

The bill for the relief of the legal representatives of Philip Moore, deceased;

The bill granting a pension to Moses Archer;

And the bill to establish a port of entry at Natchez, Mississippi;

Were severally ordered to be engrossed and read a third time.

The bill granting pensions to the legal representatives of the French seamen killed at Toulon, and to those who were wounded by the accidental firing of shotted guns from the frigate United States, while engaged in a salute, was read a third time, and passed.

On motion of Mr. PRESTON,

The Senate (at five o'clock) adjourned.

HOUSE OF REPRESENTATIVES.

SATURDAY, June 21, 1834.

After the Journal of yesterday was read—

Mr. J. Q. ADAMS rose and said, that on entering the Hall, a few minutes since, he had been for the first time informed, that intelligence had been received of the great calamity which had lately befallen the friends of the rights of man throughout the world, by the death of a most distinguished and venerable individual in France. Since he had received the information, he had not had time to propose any definite proposition for the action of the House; but it was an occasion which rendered it proper for Congress to adopt some measure to express the sense this nation entertained of the character and services of the great man whose loss we were called on to deplore. It had occurred to him (Mr. A.) that the most proper mode of paying the respect due to his memory, would be to refer the subject to the consideration of a joint committee. He would, therefore, as soon as he could draw up such a resolution, move that a joint committee of the two Houses of Congress be charged with reporting the proper mode of testifying the respect which this nation entertained for the memory of General Lafayette.

In a few minutes Mr. ADAMS prepared and presented the resolution, which, after undergoing some modification, on suggestion of Messrs. CAMBRELENG and WAYNE, was adopted, as is given above in the Senate proceedings.

Mr. CLAY, from the Committee on Public Lands, reported a bill confirming certain conflicting certain land claims in the District of St. Stephen's, Alabama. Read a third time and passed.

Mr. ARCHER, from the Committee on Foreign Affairs, reported a bill making provision for the families of those killed on the occasion of firing a salute at Toulon, and the wounded survivors; which was read twice, and committed to the Committee of the Whole on the state of the Union.

Mr. E. EVERETT, from the Joint Committee on the Library, reported a joint resolution for distributing Livingston's Penal Code.

The resolution was adopted.

Mr. POLK, from the Committee of Ways and Means, reported a bill for carrying into effect certain Indian treaties recently ratified by the Senate; which was read twice and committed.

Mr. JARVIS, from the Select Committee on that subject, reported a joint resolution requiring the Secretary of State to compile and publish an annual list of all the officers in the service of the United States.

Mr. J. Q. ADAMS objected that this measure should not have been thrown into the shape of a resolution, but of a bill.

Before the subject was disposed of—

Mr. POLK called for the orders of the day.

The CHAIR named the orders of the day were, agreeably to the rules of the House, the private bills on the calendar.

Mr. POLK moved to suspend the rules, to take up the deposite bill.

Mr. DICKSON demanded the yeas and nays; which were ordered.

The motion was lost, by the following vote, (not two-thirds):

YEAS—Messrs. Adams, John J. Allen, William Allen, Beale, Bean, Beardsley, Beaumont, Blair, Bockee, Bouldin, Brown, Burns, Bynum, Cambreleng, Carmichael, Carr, Casey, Chambers,

Chinn, Samuel Clark, Clay, Connor, Coulter, Cramer, Davenport, Day, Denny, Dickerson, Dickinson, Duncan, Ewing, Felder, Forester, Fowler, William K. Fuller, Fulton, Gholson, Gillet, Gilmer, Gordon, Graham, Grayson, Griffin, Joseph Hall, Halsey, Joseph M. Harper, Harrison, Hathaway, Hawkins, Hawes, Henderson, Howell, Hubbard, Abel Huntington, Inge, Richard M. Johnson, Noadiah Johnson, Seaborn Jones, Kavanagh, Kinnard, Lane, Lansing, Laporte, Luke Lea, Thomas Lee, Leavitt, Abijah Mann, Joel K. Mann, Moses Mason, McCarty, McComas, McIntire, McKay, McKim, McKinley, McLene, McVean, Miller, Robert Mitchell, Muhlenberg, Murphy, Osgood, Page, Parks, Parker, Patton, Patterson, Dutee J. Pearce, Franklin Pierce, Pierson, Polk, Rencher, Schley, William B. Shepard, A. H. Shepperd, Shinn, Charles Slade, Smith, Speight, Standifer, Stoddert, Sutherland, William Taylor, Francis Thomas, Thomson, Turrill, Van Houten, Wagener, Ward, Wardwell, Wayne, Webster, Whallon, C. P. White, Wilde—136.

NAYS—Messrs. John Quincy Adams, Heman Allen, Anthony, Archer, Ashley, Barnitz, Barringer, Bayliss, Beaty, Bell, Binney, Bull, Burd, Chilton, William Clark, Corwin, Crockett, Darlington, Deberry, Dickson, Ellsworth, Evans, Edward Everett, Horace Everett, Fillmore, Foster, Gamble, Garland, Gorham, Grennell, Hiland Hall, Hardin, James Harper, Hazeltine, Heath, Hiester, Jabez W. Huntington, Jackson, William C. Johnson, Lay, Lincoln, Love, Lytle, Mercer, Milligan, Potts, Ramsay, Reed, Selden, Sloane, Spangler, Steele, Stewart, Philemon Thomas, Tompkins, Turner, Tweedy, Vance, Vinton, Watmough, E. D. White, Frederick Whittlesey, Elisha Whittlesey, Williams, Wilson, Wise, and Young—89.

The House then proceeded to consider the

GOLD COINAGE BILL.

Mr. WHITE, of New York, moved to strike out all after the enacting clause of the bill, and to insert a substitute, which was read.

Mr. BINNEY remarked, that he understood the proposal to dispense altogether with the subsidiary coins, to enhance the value of gold, in relation to silver, to the proportion of one to sixteen.

Mr. WHITE assented, and entered into a detailed explanation of the principles and provisions of the amendment.

Mr. SELDEN moved to amend the amendment, so as to establish the value of gold, in relation to silver, at the rate of one to fifteen and five-eighths, as originally proposed by the committee. Mr. S. spoke at great length in support of his proposition.

The discussion was further continued by Messrs. CLOWNEY, GORHAM, JONES of Georgia, GILLET, BINNEY, EWING, CAMBRELENG, McKIM, REED, and SELDEN, when the question was stated on Mr. SELDEN'S amendment to the amendment, and it was negatived—yeas 53, nays 127.

Mr. GORHAM moved so to amend the amendment, as to make the proportion between gold and silver 15.825 to 1, instead of 16 to 1, as contemplated by the amendment.

This proposition was negatived—yeas 69, nays 112.

Mr. BINNEY inquired whether there was a similar clause in this bill so securing the accuracy of the coinage as was contained in the present law?

Mr. WHITE presumed that the present law on that subject would reach the coinage proposed by the bill.

Mr. BINNEY read the provision of the law, and presented a correspondent section to be added to this bill, which was accepted by Mr. WHITE as a modification.

The amendment, as modified, was then agreed to without a division.

The bill, as amended, having been engrossed, was read a third time, and the question stated on its passage.

Mr. WILDE demanded the yeas and nays; which were ordered.

Messrs. ADAMS, ARCHER, and GORHAM, assigned the reasons why they should vote in favor of the bill, though not perfectly satisfied with the proportion fixed by it; and Messrs. ELLSWORTH and WILDE each made a remark as to the grounds of their voting against it.

The question was carried—yeas 145, nays 36. So the bill was passed.

The bill to regulate the value of foreign gold coins within the United States, as reported by the Committee of the Whole, was taken up.

Mr. C. P. WHITE moved an amendment making the valuation of these coins conform to the bill just passed relative to American coinage; which was adopted.

The bill having been engrossed, was read a third time, and passed without a division.

On motion of Mr. H. EVERETT, the House, by consent, went into committee on the bill for the relief of John Bruce, and on the bill for the relief of John Gardner, Mr. STEWART in the chair.

These bills were read in committee, and reported to the House without amendment.

The bill for the relief of Bruce was read a third time and passed, and the bill for the relief of Gardner was also passed.

The bill from the Senate granting pensions to certain citizens or subjects of France, was, on motion of Mr. ARCHER, taken up.

The House went into Committee of the Whole on the state of the Union, Mr. WARD in the chair, on that bill, which was reported to the House without amendment.

The bill having been read a third time, a discussion arose as to its phraseology, and the general principles involved in it, in which Messrs. J. Q. ADAMS, ARCHER, PINCKNEY, FOSTER, and SEABORN JONES took part, when, on the suggestion of

Mr. E. EVERETT, that the bill reported by the Committee of Foreign Affairs, was free from some of the objections stated to this bill,

Mr. BEARDSLEY moved that the further consideration of the bill be postponed till Monday; which was agreed to.

The SPEAKER laid before the House the messages of the President relative to the death of General Lafayette, and the claim of the heirs of Count Rochambeau, which may be found in the Senate proceedings. They were laid on the table and ordered to be printed.

The House then adjourned.

IN SENATE.

MONDAY, June 23, 1834.

A message upon executive business, was received from the President of the United States, by Mr. DONELSON, his Private Secretary.

Mr. HENDRICKS presented the petition of John P. Hedges; which was referred.

Mr. EWING presented a memorial from inhabitants of Portage county, Ohio, asking a restoration of the deposites to the Bank of the United States, and a recharter of that institution; which was referred to the Committee on Finance, and ordered to be printed.

Mr. WEBSTER, from the Committee on Finance, made a partial report on the subject submitted to that committee on the 5th of May last, in reference to the currency, gold and silver coin, and other purposes. He gave notice that he should, in a day or two, ask the consideration of the report, and would move that the committee be discharged from the further consideration of the same.

Mr. HILL presented certain resolutions of the Legislature of New Hampshire, expressive of the opinions of that State in reference to the course of the Administration.

The resolutions were laid on the table.

The following bills were read a third time, and passed:

The bill establishing Natchez as a port of entry;

The bill for the relief of the legal representatives of Philip Moore, deceased;

The bill for the relief of Moses Archer;

The bill changing the boundaries of the Michigan land district;

The bill granting the right of way through certain property of the United States, to the Winchester and Potomac Rail Road Company, at Harper's Ferry, Virginia;

The bill to amend an act for the relief of William Burris, of Mississippi, approved February 19, 1831;

The bill for the relief of the schooner Three Sisters, of Saybrook;

The bill for the relief of Philip Bessom.

The committee apppointed to meet a similar committee of the House, to devise a most suitable means of testifying respect to the memory of the illustrious Lafayette, were announced as follows: Messrs. Webster, White, Calhoun, Clay, Forsyth, Wilkins, Tyler, Benton, Poindexter, King of Alabama, Chambers, Brown, Shepley.

The following resolutions were submitted by Mr. SPRAGUE:

Resolved, That a committee of five members be appointed to examine the condition and proceedings of the Post Office Department, with power to send for persons and papers, and to take the position of witnesses, either by personal examination, or on commission, with permission to sit in the recess of Congress, and to report at the next session.

Resolved, That the Postmaster General be directed to communicate to the Senate all the papers in his department relative to the investigation of the conduct of James Curtis, late postmaster at Eastport, Maine.

GENERAL APPROPRIATION BILL.

The Senate then resumed the consideration of the bill making appropriations for the civil and diplomatic expenses of the Government for the year 1834.

Mr. SOUTHARD moved to strike out the amendment inserted in the bill when considered as in Committee of the Whole, for discontinuing the publication of the Revolutionary History by Clarke and Force, and to insert the following:

For the Documentary History of the Revolution, per act of March 2d, 1833, $30,000; and it shall be the duty of the Secretary of State to examine the contract entered into by Edward Livingston, late Secretary of State, with Clarke and Force, for the prosecution of this work, and make a special report thereon to the next session of Congress, setting forth the nature and character of the materials of which the work is to be composed, the progress made on the work, the number of volumes which will be required to complete it, and an estimate of the money which will be necessary to complete it.

After some remarks from Mr. SOUTHARD, in favor of the amendment,

Mr. FORSYTH opposed its adoption, and demanded the yeas and nays; which were ordered, and are as follows:

YEAS—Messrs. Bell, Chambers, Clay, Clayton, Ewing, Frelinghuysen, Kent, Knight, Leigh, Moore, Naudain, Poindexter, Porter, Prentiss, Preston, Robbins, Silsbee, Smith, Southard, Swift, Sprague, Tomlinson, Tyler, Waggaman, Webster—25.

NAYS—Messrs. Benton, Bibb, Black, Brown, Calhoun, Forsyth, Grundy, Hendricks, Hill, Kane, King of Alabama, King of Georgia, Linn, Mangum, Morris, Robinson, Shepley, Tallmadge, White, Wright—20.

So the amendment was agreed to.

Mr. CLAYTON then moved a further amendment, appropriating $275,000 to carrying on the Delaware breakwater.

After some conversation between Messrs. CLAYTON, GRUNDY, NAUDAIN, WEBSTER, and CLAY,

Mr. CLAYTON withdrew the motion, with the intention of offering it to-morrow, in case the harbor bill should not be passed through the House by that time, with an appropriation for that object contained in it.

Mr. PRESTON renewed the motion offered by Mr. Bibb, to insert an appropriation of $400 for recording the opinions of the Supreme Court, which was briefly supported by Mr. PRESTON, Mr. BIBB, Mr. CLAYTON, Mr. EWING, Mr. GRUNDY, and opposed by Mr. CHAMBERS, Mr. SMITH, Mr. FORSYTH, and Mr. SHEPLEY, who asked the yeas and nays on the motion, which were ordered, and are as follows:

YEAS—Messrs. Bibb, Calhoun, Clayton, Ewing, Grundy, Kane, King of Georgia, Linn, Mangum, Poindexter, Prentiss, Silsbee, Tyler, Webster—15.

NAYS—Messrs. Bell, Benton, Black, Brown, Chambers, Clay, Forsyth, Frelinghuysen, Hill, Robbins, King of Alabama, Knight, Leigh, Naudain, Robbins, Robinson, Shepley, Smith, Southard, Sprague, Swift, Tallmadge, Tomlinson, Waggaman, White, Wilkins, Wright—27.

So the amendment was not agreed to.

Mr. CLAYTON, from the Judiciary Committee, agreeably to the instructions of the Senate, offered an amendment, providing for paying the honorable E. R. Potter the mileage and daily pay of a member up to the period when the election of the box, orable Mr. Robbins was decided by the Senate, accompanied with the expression of his opinion against the amendment. Mr. C. thereupon asked the yeas and nays upon the amendment, which were ordered.

Mr. WEBSTER submitted an amendment to the amendment, to allow Mr. Potter mileage and one day's pay.

Mr. CLAY, Mr. CLAYTON, and Mr. POINDEXTER, opposed the allowance of anything to Mr. Potter.

Mr. WEBSTER'S proposition was rejected.

The question recurring on Mr. CLAYTON'S motion, was determined in the affirmative, by the yeas and nays, to wit:

YEAS—Messrs. Benton, Bibb, Brown, Chambers, Grundy, Hendricks, Hill, Kane, King of Alabama, Knight, Linn, Preston, Robinson, Shepley, Silsbee, Tallmadge, Tyler, White, Wilkins, Wright—20.

NAYS—Messrs. Black, Clay, Clayton, Ewing, Forsyth, Frelinghuysen, Kent, King of Georgia, Leigh, Mangum, Naudain, Poindexter, Prentiss, Porter, Smith, Southard, Sprague, Tomlinson, Webster—19.

Mr. POINDEXTER then made his motion to prohibit the payment of any appropriation to a bank notes which shall not be of par value where such payment shall be made, upon which he asked the yeas and nays, which were ordered, and are as following, to wit:

YEAS—Messrs. Bibb, Black, Chambers, Clay, Clayton, Ewing, Frelinghuysen, King of Georgia, Knight, Mangum, Naudain, Poindexter, Porter, Prentiss, Robbins, Silsbee, Southard, Sprague, Smith, Tomlinson, Waggaman, Webster—22.

NAYS—Messrs. Benton, Brown, Forsyth, Grundy, Hendricks, Hill, Kane, Kent, King of Alabama, Linn, Morris, Preston, Shepley, White, Wilkins, Wright—16.

So the amendment was agreed to.

The Senate then proceeded to the consideration of executive business, and when the doors were opened, the Senate had adjourned.

HOUSE OF REPRESENTATIVES.

MONDAY, June 23, 1834.

Mr. CHINN, from the Committee on the District of Columbia, asked the consent of the House to submit a motion to set apart this day, after 1 o'clock, for the consideration of those bills relating to the District of Columbia.

Objections being made—

Mr. CHINN moved a suspension of the rules; which was negatived.

Mr. E. EVERETT, from the Committee on the Library, reported a Senate bill for procuring a marble bust of the late Chief Justice Ellsworth, without amendment.

Mr. MITCHELL, of Ohio, obtained the consent of the House to submit the following resolution:

Resolved, That the Secretary of War be directed to communicate to this House the several reports of the board of visiters to the Military Academy for the present year.

Mr. BEARDSLEY, from the Committee on the Judiciary, reported a bill to carry into effect the judgments of the district courts of the United States; which was read twice, and laid on the table till to-morrow.

Mr. GAMBLE, from the Committee on Territories, reported a bill attaching the territory of the United States west of the Mississippi, north of the State of Missouri to the Territory of Michigan; which was read twice and ordered to be engrossed.

On motion of Mr. GAMBLE, the Committee of the Whole were discharged from the further consideration of the bill authorizing a census of the inhabitants of the Territories of Michigan and Arkansas, and the case was referred to the Committee of the Whole on the state of the Union.

Mr. POLK moved that the rule setting apart this day for the consideration of memorials be so

far suspended as to permit the bill regulating the deposites to come up after two o'clock.

Mr DENNY opposed the motion, and asked a division of the question, but withdrew it.

Mr. D. called for the yeas and nays; which were ordered.

Mr. E. WHITTLESEY called for a division of the question.

Mr. J. Q. ADAMS moved to amend the motion so as to fix five o'clock instead of two o'clock. He would be willing to sit till midnight upon the deposite bill; but he thought, as this was the last petition day of the session, it was due to the people to devote a part of it to the reception of petitions.

The amendment was rejected without a division.

The question being then taken on the motion to suspend the rules, it was determined in the affirmative—yeas 127, nays 61.

The question being on the second branch of the motion, to take up the deposite bill at two o'clock, Joseph Swartwood. Read twice, and referred.

Mr. DENNY moved to amend the motion by substituting for the deposite bill the bills relative to harbors and fortifications.

After some discussion on the question of order, Mr. DENNY withdrew the motion.

The question being then taken on the motion to take up the deposite bill at two o'clock, it was determined in the negative: Yeas 124, nays 65—not two-thirds.

Mr. MITCHELL, from the Committee on Military Pensions, reported a bill for the relief of Joseph Swartwood. Read twice, and referred.

Mr. SUTHERLAND moved to suspend the rules, in order to lay on the table a memorial; which was negatived.

Mr. FILLMORE moved the suspension of the rules, in order to move to postpone the consideration of the memorials lying on the table, until after the memorials were presented.

The CHAIR decided that the motion was not in order, the gentleman from Rhode Island [Mr. PEARCE,] being entitled to the floor on the last petition day.

The resolutions heretofore presented by Mr. BURGES, from the lower house of the Rhode Island Assembly, having come up in order—

Mr. PEARCE, who was entitled to the floor, addressed the House at length in reply to the observations made by Mr. Braxes last week.

Mr. BURGES addressed the House in answer to his colleague, and concluded by moving that the resolutions be referred to the Committee of the Whole on the state of the Union, with instructions to report a resolution declaring the reasons of the Secretary of the Treasury for removing the deposites to be insufficient.

Mr. PEARCE rejoined at length, and after some conflicting remarks between the two gentlemen—

Mr. DENNY moved to lay the papers on the table; which was agreed to.

The resolutions heretofore presented by Mr. YOUNG were, on his motion, laid on the table, and ordered to be printed.

The prior unfinished business (the harbor bill) then came up.

The question was upon the amendment moved by Mr. MERCER, inserting $29,000 for the expenses of surveys, the vote rejecting which was reconsidered last week.

Mr. SMITH opposed the amendment. It was intended to provide by it for $17,000, which had already been expended.

Mr. POLK said the statement which had been made on that subject was incorrect; the correct amount of arrearages was $7,000.

After some debate, the question being taken by yeas and nays on the motion to add $29,000 for surveys, it was decided in the affirmative: Yeas 103, nays 87.

Mr. MARSHALL withdrew the motion to lay the bill on the table, which had been carried some days ago and reconsidered.

Mr. BEATY moved to amend, by appropriating $25,000 for the improvement of the navigation of Cumberland river to the highest point of steamboat navigation.

The question being taken by yeas and nays, was negatived: Yeas 85, nays 95.

Mr. ASHLEY moved to amend, by inserting an appropriation of $100,000 for improving the harbor of St. Louis, in Missouri.

After some remarks from Messrs. POLK and ASHLEY, the question was taken on the amendment, by yeas and nays, and decided in the negative: yeas 72, nays 96.

Mr. HAWES moved to amend by inserting a clause for the improvement of the navigation of Green river and Big Beaver river, in the State of Kentucky, $25,000; whereupon he asked the yeas and nays, which were ordered.

After some remarks from Messrs. POLK, HARDIN, CHILTON, TOMPKINS, and MERCER, the question was taken, and the amendment was negatived.

Mr. DENNY moved to amend the bill by inserting $25,000 for the improvement of the navigation of the Ohio river between Louisville and Pittsburg, to be commenced this year, under the direction of the Secretary of War. Negatived.

Mr. EWING moved to insert an appropriation for improving the navigation of the Wabash river, $30,000.

Messrs. KINNARD and EWING supported the proposition; which was negatived—ayes 43.

Mr. CARR moved an amendment for improving the navigation in the Indian Chute, through the Falls of the Ohio, $26,000.

This amendment was negatived.

Mr. CROCKETT moved to amend the bill by inserting $30,000 for improving the navigation of Hatchee, Forked Deer, and Obion rivers, to be distributed equally to each; which was negatived.

The amendment for improving the navigation of Deep creek, near the Dismal Swamp canal, $29,000, as amended by the addition of Mr. Mercer's amendment, appropriating $29,000 for surveys.

Mr. HAWES demanded the yeas and nays; which were ordered.

Messrs. HUBBARD, BEATY, MERCER, MASON, SUTHERLAND, WISE, HAWES, and FILLMORE, discussed this amendment at length, when the question was taken, and it was carried—yeas 92, nays 82.

Mr. SEVIER moved to amend the bill by appropriating $30,000 for completing the navigation of Arkansas river; which was negatived.

Mr. WATMOUGH moved an appropriation of $10,000 for the erection of piers in Delaware river; which was negatived without a division.

Mr. WISE moved to lay the bill on the table—on which he asked the yeas and nays.

The motion to lay on the table was lost—yeas 66, nays 109.

Mr. SUTHERLAND now moved that the bill be engrossed; which was carried.

The bill having been ordered to be read a third time—

Mr. PARKS moved a call of the House; which was negatived.

Mr. HAWES moved the House adjourn; which was negatived.

The bill having been read a third time—

Mr. POLK called for the yeas and nays; which were ordered.

The bill was passed: Yeas 107, nays 48.

After various bills from the Senate were read the first and second time, and referred to the appropriate committees, the House adjourned.

IN SENATE.

TUESDAY, June 24, 1834.

A message was received from the President of the United States, upon executive business, by Mr. DONELSON, his Private Secretary.

Mr. MORRIS presented memorials from the counties of Hamilton, Warren, Muskingum, Belmont, and Columbiana, Ohio, approving of the course of the Administration, and opposed to the recharter of the Bank of the United States or the restoration of the deposites to that institution.

The memorials were referred to the Committee on Finance, and ordered to be printed.

Mr. TOMLINSON presented the petition of sixteen hundred citizens of Windham county, Connecticut, in favor of a restoration of the deposites, and the recharter of the Bank of the United States; which obtained the same reference and order.

Mr. TOMLINSON also presented the proceedings of a meeting of the same county, of a similar character.

Mr. HILL moved that the Senate take up for consideration the resolutions from New Hampshire, which were laid on the table yesterday.

After some remarks upon a point of order, in which Messrs. BENTON, CLAY, CLAYTON, HILL, and EWING, participated,

Mr. HILL asked the yeas and nays upon taking up the resolutions; which were ordered, and are as follows, to wit:

YEAS—Messrs. Benton, Brown, Forsyth, Grundy, Hendricks, Hill, Kane, King of Alabama, King of Georgia, Leigh, Linn, Morris, Robinson, Shepley, Tallmadge, White, Wilkins, Wright—18.

NAYS—Messrs. Bibb, Calhoun, Chambers, Clay, Clayton, Ewing, Frelinghuysen, Kent, Knight, Mangum, Moore, Naudain, Poindexter, Porter, Prentiss, Preston, Robbins, Silsbee, Smith, Southard, Sprague, Swift, Tomlinson, Tyler, Waggaman, Webster—26.

Mr. BROWN, from the Committee on Claims, wished to be discharged from the further consideration of the petition of William Duncan; which was agreed to.

Mr. HILL, from the Committee on Revolutionary Claims, made a report upon the petition of Pizarro Herbert, and others, favorable to the memorialists.

Mr. CLAYTON, from the Committee on the Judiciary, reported a bill from the House without amendment, repealing certain acts of the Legislative Council of Florida.

Mr. POINDEXTER'S resolution, authorizing the Committee on Public Lands to pursue their investigation into alleged frauds, was taken up and considered; when

Mr. WRIGHT offered an amendment, the substance of which was, that the persons implicated should have due and timely notice, so as to enable them to contradict and rebut the charges made against them.

The resolution and amendment were then ordered to be printed.

Mr. SILSBEE submitted the following resolution:

Resolved, That the Secretary of the Treasury be directed to report to the Senate, at the commencement of the next session of Congress, the amount of revenue collected, and the amount of tonnage entered, at each of the custom-houses of the United States; the amount and rate of commissions charged by each of the collectors on the revenue collected by him, and the amount of fees received at each of the custom-houses for each of the two last years. Also, the number of officers of every description employed at each of the custom houses; the amount of emoluments of every kind received by each of those officers, and the expenses incident to their respective offices, for each of the two last years; stating whether such emoluments arise from commissions, salaries, or fees, and how much from each of those sources; and stating, also, whether any, and, if any, such of these offices, or officers, as may be dispensed with without injury to the public service.

The following resolution, submitted by Mr. SOUTHARD, was agreed to:

Resolved, That, for the balance of the session, the Senate will convene at ten o'clock, and take a recess from two to four o'clock.

Several private bills were received from the House, and referred to the appropriate committees; when,

Mr. WILKINS moved that the Senate proceed to the consideration of executive business; which was agreed to.

After some time spent with closed doors, The Senate adjourned.

HOUSE OF REPRESENTATIVES.

TUESDAY, June 24, 1834.

The SPEAKER laid before the House a letter from the Clerk of the House, stating that the digest of the returns of State banks, required by a resolution of the House, had been prepared, so far as the means had come into his possession.

Mr. WILDE said, he had examined the work in the course of its progress, and was satisfied that it contained information of the greatest importance relative to the institutions to which it referred

Mr. C. P. WHITE moved that 3,000 additional copies be printed; which was agreed to.

Mr. PARKER asked the consent of the House to present the proceedings of a State convention, held at Trenton on the 21st of May last, relative to the present posture of public affairs.

Mr. WATMOUGH objected.

Mr. PARKER moved that the rules be dispensed with, to enable him to present the proceedings.

This motion was negatived, two-thirds not supporting it.

Mr. EVANS, from the Committee on Invalid Pensions, reported a bill granting arrearages of pension to Edward Lincoln; which was read twice, and committed.

Mr. CHINN, from the Committee on the District of Columbia, reported a resolution making the bills on the Speaker's table relative to the District the special order from and after five o'clock to-morrow.

After a remark from Mr. WILDE, The resolution was lost.

Mr. CARR reported bills for the relief of Daniel Smith and Zachariah McGirth; which were read twice, and committed.

Mr. GRAYSON, from the Committee on Naval Affairs, reported a bill to provide for the establishment of a navy-yard at Charleston, S. C.; which was read twice, and committed.

Mr. SUTHERLAND, from the Committee on Commerce, reported a bill authorizing the removal of the custom-house from Magnolia to St. Marks, in Florida; which was read twice; when

Mr. WATMOUGH moved that the bill enlarging the limits of the port of entry of Philadelphia be added to the bill.

Mr. SUTHERLAND said, having charge of the bill which it was proposed to add to the present bill, he had intended, at the next meeting of the committee, to propose to add the bill, and two or three others similarly situated, to the Senate bill recently referred to the committee, which would ensure it a better chance of passing.

Mr. WATMOUGH withdrew his motion to amend. The original bill was then ordered to be engrossed.

Mr. WAYNE, by consent, presented the petition of sundry citizens of Florida, praying that a certain road might be made, which would greatly facilitate the communication between the Atlantic States and New Orleans.

The petition was referred to the Committee on Roads and Canals.

The engrossed bill to attach the territory west of the Mississippi river, and north of the State of Missouri, to the Territory of Michigan, was read a third time, and passed.

The engrossed bill to amend an act passed 29th May, 1830, for the relief of sundry owners of vessels sunk for the defence of Baltimore, was read a third time, and passed.

The engrossed bill for making a road from the northern boundary of Florida to Apalachicola, was read a third time, and passed.

The engrossed bill authorizing a road to be cut out from Columbia to Little Rock, in the Territory of Arkansas, was read a third time and passed.

The bill from the Senate for the relief of the town of Fayetteville in the Territory of Arkansas, was read a third time and passed.

The bill for the survey of certain roads and the improvement of certain harbors in the Territory of Michigan, was read a third time and passed.

The bill to authorize an extra session of the Legislative Council of the Territory of Michigan, was read a third time and passed.

The bill to allow further time for issuing and locating military land warrants for services during the late war, was read a third time and passed.

The bill for the relief of the relatives of certain French seamen killed in firing a salute at Toulon, and for the wounded survivors, came up on its third reading—

Mr. ARCHER moved that the bill be recommitted for the purpose of amendment. Agreed to.

The House then went into committee on this bill, Mr. WARD in the chair.

Mr. ARCHER moved to strike out the whole bill after the enacting clause, and insert a substitute which he proposed.

Mr. ELLSWORTH preferred the original bill,

which provided a direct indemnity to the sufferers, to this amendment, which authorized the President to enter into a treaty with the French Government on the subject.

Mr. POLK hoped the discussion on this point would be deferred till the bill came into the House.

The amendment was adopted, and the committee rose and reported it to the House, where the amendment was concurred in, and the bill ordered to be engrossed as amended.

The bill making appropriation for fortifications for 1834, came up—

Mr. POLK moved to postpone this bill until to-morrow, in order that the deposite bill might be taken up.

Mr. REED demanded the yeas and nays on the motion; which were ordered.

The motion to lay the bill on the table, was agreed to—yeas 119, nays 68.

Mr. LANE moved to reconsider the vote laying the bill on the table; and, on his motion, the motion to reconsider was postponed till to-morrow.

THE DEPOSITE BILL.

The House resumed the consideration of the " bill regulating the deposites in the local banks."

Mr. DUNCAN offered, as a substitute for the bill, an amendment continuing in force the charter of the Bank of the United States, which he submitted on the 25th of April last.

Mr. COULTER, who was entitled to the floor, when the subject was last up, spoke at considerable length in opposition to the bill.

Messrs. LANE and McVEAN spoke in favor of the bill.

Mr. DUNCAN made some remarks in favor of the amendment which he had offered as a substitute for the bill.

Mr. STEWART spoke in opposition to the bill, and was followed by Messrs. JONES of Georgia, and MILLER, on the other side.

Mr. CHILTON rose and said, he hoped the question would be brought to a decision. He understood, from the friends of the bill, that they had made it as perfect as possible; and, as much business was to be done, he hoped the bill would be passed at once, if it was to be passed; though he should certainly vote against it himself. He, therefore, was constrained, though reluctantly, to move the previous question.

Mr. ELLSWORTH hoped the gentleman would withdraw the motion.

Mr. BOON said, if it was withdrawn, he should certainly renew it.

Mr. CHILTON said he could not withdraw it, consistently with what he believed to be his duty. The motion for the previous question was seconded.

Mr. BROWN moved a call of the House; which was ordered.

Seventy-six members were ascertained to be absent.

Mr. R. M. JOHNSON moved the suspension of all further proceeding on the call; but the yeas and nays being called for, he withdrew it.

After some time, the call was suspended, on motion of Mr. GAMBLE.

The question being, " Shall the main question be now put?"

The yeas and nays were ordered on the call of Mr. H. EVERETT.

The question being taken, the main question was ordered to be put: Yeas 117, nays 77.

The question being on the engrossment of the bill, it was taken by yeas and nays, and decided in the affirmative: Yeas 111, nays 86.

The question, When shall this bill be read the third time? having been propounded—

No objection having been made, it was ordered accordingly.

Mr. E. EVERETT insisted that the bill making provision for the wounded French sailors at Toulon, had been previously ordered to be read a third time.

After some remarks from Mr. POLK,

The CHAIR decided that the House having ordered the deposite bill to be read, and it being the business now in hand, it would be gone through with before any other business should be taken up.

The bill having been engrossed, the Clerk began to read it; when

Mr. WATMOUGH objected to the bill being read.

The CHAIR decided that the objection came too late. It should have been made when the time of the third reading was propounded to the House.

The bill was read a third time.

Mr. GHOLSON wished to make a personal explanation as to his course on this question. He had disapproved of the removal of the deposites from the bank, but had voted to lay the whole resolutions on the table, because he believed the bank had lately violated its charter in resisting the examination of the committee of the House. He would have preferred the amendment of his colleague, [Mr. Gholson,] but that having been cut off by the previous question, he would vote for this bill, because he considered it a question between this law and no law on the subject.

Mr. BURD opposed the bill in a speech at length.

Mr. McKENNAN demanded the yeas and nays on the passage of the bill; which were ordered. The bill was passed—Yeas 112, nays 96.

YEAS—Messrs. John Adams, William Allen, Anthony, Beale, Bean, Boardsley, Beaumont, Blair, Bockee, Bodle, Boon, Bouldin, Brown, Bunch, Burns, Bynum, Cambreleng, Carmichael, Carr, Casey, Chaney, Chinn, Samuel Clark, Clay, Coffee, Connor, Cramer, Day, Deming, Philemon Dickerson, D. W. Dickinson, Dunlap, Forester, Fowler, William K. Fuller, Galbraith, Gholson, Gilmer, Joseph Hall, Halsey, Hannegan, Joseph M. Harper, Harrison, Hathaway, Hawkins, Hawes, Howell, Hubbard, Abel Huntington, Inge, Jarvis, Jabez W. Johnson, Noadiah Johnson, Cave Johnson, Seaborn Jones, Benjamin Jones, Kavanagh, Kinnard, Lane, Lansing, Laporte, Lea, Leavitt, Thomas Lee, Lyon, Lytle, Abijah Mann, Joel K. Mann, John Y. Mason, Moses Mason, McIntire, McKay, McKim, McKinley, McLene, McVean, Miller, Robert Mitchell, Muhlenberg, Murphy, Osgood, Page, Parks, Parker, Patton, Patterson, Dutee J. Pearce, Franklin Pierce, Pierson, Plummer, Polk, Pope, Schenck, Schley, Augustine H. Shepperd, Shinn, Smith, Speight, Standifer, Stoddert, Sutherland, William Taylor, Francis Thomas, Thomson, Turrill, Tweedy, Vanderpoel, Van Houten, Wayne, Ward, Wardwell, Webster, Whallon, Campbell F. White—112.

NAYS—Messrs. John Q. Adams, Heman Allen, John J. Allen, Archer, Ashley, Barber, Barnitz, Barringer, Baylies, Beaty, Binney, Bull, Burd, Cage, Campbell, Chambers, Chilton, William Clark, Clayton, Corwin, Coulter, Darlington, Davenport, Deberry, Denny, Dickson, Duncan, Ellsworth, Evans, Edward Everett, Horace Everett, Ewing, Felder, Fillmore, Foster, Philo C. Fuller, Fulton, Gamble, Garland, Gorham, Graham, Grennell, Griffin, Hiland Hall, Heath, Hardin, James Harper, Hazeltine, Heath, Hester, Jabez W. Huntington, Jarvis, Jackson, William Cost Johnson, Lay, Lewis, Lincoln, Love, Martindale, Marshall, McComas, McKennan, Mercer, Milligan, Moore, Pinckney, Potts, Ramsey, Reed, Rencher, Selden, William B. Shepard, William Slade, Charles Slade, Sloane, Spangler, Stewart, Philemon Thomas, Tompkins, Tracy, Vinton, Watmough, Edward D. White, Frederick Whittlesey, Elisha Whittlesey, Wilde, William Wilson, Wise, Young—90.

DEATH OF GENERAL LAFAYETTE.

The following are the resolutions reported by the joint committee of the Senate and House of Representatives:

Resolved, &c., That the two Houses have received with the profoundest sensibility intelligence of the death of General Lafayette, the friend of the United States, the friend of Washington, and the friend of Liberty

Sec. 2. And be it further resolved, That the national honors and efforts of this illustrious person in the cause of our country during her struggle for independence, and the affectionate interest which he has at all times manifested for the success of her political institutions, claim from the Government and people of the United States, an expression of condolence for his loss, veneration for his virtues, and gratitude for his services.

Sec. 3. *And be it further resolved*, That the President of the United States be requested to address, together with a copy of the above resolutions, a letter to George Washington Lafayette, and the other members of his family, assuring them of the condolence of this whole nation in their irreparable bereavement.

Sec. 4. *And be it further resolved*, That the members of the two Houses of Congress will wear a badge of mourning for thirty days, and that it be recommended to the people of the United States to wear a similar badge for the same period.

Sec. 5. *And be it further resolved*, That the Halls of the Houses be dressed in mourning for the residue of the session.

Sec. 6. *And be it further resolved*, That John Quincy Adams be requested to deliver an oration on the life and character of General Lafayette, before the two Houses of Congress, at the next session.

The resolutions were read twice, and ordered to be engrossed for a third reading by a unanimous vote.

The engrossed bill authorizing the President to make an arrangement with the French Government respecting the French seamen killed and wounded by firing a salute at Toulon was read.

After some remarks from Messrs. McKINLEY, ARCHER, J. Q. ADAMS, and FELDER, the bill was passed: Yeas 133, nays 14.

On motion of Mr. POLK, the vote postponing the reconsideration of the fortification bill was carried, when he withdrew his motion to lay it upon the table, and the bill now remains upon the Speaker's table.

On motion of Mr. HARDIN,
The House then adjourned.

IN SENATE.

Wednesday, June 25, 1834.

The VICE PRESIDENT laid before the Senate a communication from the Secretary of the Treasury, relative to the operations of the mint for the past year.

Mr. WHITE, from the Committee on Revolutionary Claims, reported a bill from the House for the relief of Ann M. Barron.

Mr. NAUDAIN, from the Committee on Claims, reported a bill from the House of Representatives, to amend an act for the relief of the owners of vessels sunk during the last war, for the defence of Baltimore; which, on motion of Mr. N., was read, and ordered to be engrossed for a third reading.

Mr. POINDEXTER moved that the Senate take up the bill to establish an additional land office in Arkansas; which was agreed to, and the bill was read, and ordered to be engrossed for a third reading.

The bill for the better organization of the district courts for the district of Alabama was read, and ordered to be engrossed for a third reading.

The Senate took up the bill which was lying on the table, for confirming to G. Hodges, his heirs or legal representatives, and H. Masters, his heirs or legal representatives, certain lands in the State of Missouri; which, after undergoing an amendment offered by Mr. Kane, was ordered to be engrossed for a third reading.

Mr. HILL, from the Committee on Revolutionary Pensions, made unfavorable reports upon several private petitions; from which the Committee were discharged.

Mr. TYLER, from the Committee on Revolutionary Claims, asked to be discharged from the further consideration of the petition of Francis A. Talbot and others; which was agreed to.

The bill to provide for the payment of claims for property lost, captured, or destroyed by the enemy, while in the military service of the United States during the late war with Great Britain, and the Indian wars subsequent thereto, and for other purposes, was taken up on motion of Mr. KING, of Alabama.

After some conversation between Messrs. KING of Alabama, CALHOUN, and TIPTON,

On motion of Mr. CALHOUN, the bill was laid upon the table—yeas 19, nays 16.

Mr. WEBSTER, from the Joint Committee on the subject of paying suitable respect to the memory of General Lafayette, made a report. The resolutions are the same as those adopted in the House.

Mr. WEBSTER, from the Committee on Finance, reported a bill from the House, without amendment, relative to foreign gold coin and the gold coins of the United States; which was read a first and second time.

On motion of Mr. WEBSTER, the Senate took up for consideration the bill providing Indian annuities for the year 1834.

The reading of the bill being dispensed with,

Mr. FRELINGHUYSEN offered an amendment to be inserted at the close of the bill, providing that the money to be paid to the Indians shall be paid to the chiefs of the respective tribes, or to the persons whom the respective tribes shall appoint to receive it,

After some remarks from Mr. PRELINGHUYSEN and Mr. SPRAGUE, in favor of the amendment, and from Mr. WHITE in opposition to it,

Mr. FRELINGHUYSEN consented to modify the amendment to extend it only to those Cherokees who reside east of the Mississippi.

Mr. FORSYTH and Mr. TIPTON opposed the amendment, and Mr. FRELINGHUYSEN and Mr. SPRAGUE supported it, when

Mr. CHAMBERS suggested a further modification of it, to extend it to the Cherokees generally, both east and west of the Mississippi, which Mr. FRELINGHUYSEN accepted.

Mr. FORSYTH submitted a further amendment to the amendment, to pay the money to the persons whom a majority of the tribes should direct.

Mr. FRELINGHUYSEN opposed the proposition, and Mr. FORSYTH supported it; when it was negatived.

The question recurring on the amendment,

Mr. FORSYTH asked the yeas and nays on its adoption; which were ordered, and are as follows:

YEAS—Messrs. Bibb, Calhoun, Chambers, Clay, Clayton, Ewing, Frelinghuysen, Kent, King of Georgia, Knight, Linn, Mangum, Moore, Naudain, Poindexter, Porter, Prentiss, Preston, Robbins, Shapley, Silsbee, Smith, Southard, Sprague, Swift, Tomlinson, Tyler, Webster—28.

NAYS—Messrs. Benton, Black, Brown, Forsyth, Grundy, Hill, Kane, King of Alabama, Morris, Robinson, Tallmadge, Tipton, Waggaman, White, Wright—15.

So the amendment was agreed to, and the bill, as amended, was ordered to be engrossed for a third reading.

The joint resolution, reported by the committee appointed to inquire by what means the Congress of the United States can best testify the respect of the nation for the memory of Lafayette, was taken up for consideration, and unanimously adopted.

The bill from the House of Representatives regulating the deposite of the public moneys in the State banks, was read; and on motion of

Mr. WEBSTER, referred to the Committee on Finance.

The bill granting pensions to the French seamen who were killed at Toulon, was taken up, with the amendments of the House thereto, and, on motion of Mr. SOUTHARD, they were referred to the Committee on Naval Affairs.

On motion of Mr. SPRAGUE, the Senate took up for consideration the resolution submitted by him, authorizing the Committee on the Post Office and Post Roads to pursue their investigations into the affairs of that Post Office Department during the recess of Congress.

The resolution was briefly supported by Mr. SPRAGUE, and opposed by Mr. FORSYTH, who asked the yeas and nays on its adoption; which were ordered, and are as follows, to wit:

YEAS—Messrs. Benton, Bibb, Black, Calhoun, Chambers, Clay, Clayton, Ewing, Frelinghuysen, Grundy, Hendricks, Kane, Kent, Knight, Linn, Mangum, Moore, Naudain, Poindexter, Porter, Prentiss, Robins, Shepley, Silsbee, Smith, Southard, Sprague, Swift, Tomlinson, Tyler, Waggaman, White—33.

NAYS—Messrs. Brown, Forsyth, Hill, King of Alabama, King of Georgia, Morris, Robinson, Tallmadge, Tipton, Wright—10.

So the resolution was agreed to.

Mr. CLAYTON then asked to be excused from serving on the committee, urging personal considerations as a reason for the request.

Mr. C. was then excused.

The bill to repeal certain provisions of "An act to alter and amend the several acts imposing duties on imports," approved the 14th July, 1832, was read a third time and passed.

The resolution submitted yesterday by Mr. SPRAGUE, relative to James Curtis, postmaster at Eastport, Maine, was, on motion of Mr. WEBSTER, laid upon the table.

The resolution submitted by Mr. SILSBEE, calling for information relative to the amount of revenue collected, the amount of tonnage, and a list of entries and clearances at the several custom-houses in the United States, was considered, and adopted.

The bill providing for the payment of Indian annuities, and for other similar purposes, was then read a third time and passed.

The following bills were read a third time, and passed:

The bill authorizing the selection of certain Wabash and Erie canal lands, in the State of Ohio;

The bill to amend an act entitled "An act for the relief of William Burris, of Mississippi," approved February 19, 1831;

The bill for the relief of the owners of the schooner Three Sisters, of Saybrook;

The bill establishing an additional land office in the Territory of Arkansas;

The bill for the relief of Philip Bessom; and

The bill to amend the act for the relief of sundry individuals, owners of vessels sunk for the defence of Baltimore.

The resolution requesting the President of the United States to furnish information relative to the extinguishment of the Cherokee land claims in the State of Georgia, was taken up.

Mr. FORSYTH spoke at length against the adoption of the resolution; when the hour of two having arrived, the Senate took a recess until four o'clock.

EVENING SESSION.

Mr. WHITE spoke briefly in reply to Mr. FORSYTH, and in support of the resolution.

After some further conversation between Mr. FRELINGHUYSEN, Mr. POINDEXTER, and Mr. FORSYTH,

Mr. CLAY moved to lay the whole subject on the table; which was disagreed to: Yeas 16, nays 17.

Mr. FORSYTH then moved an amendment, "that the President be requested to ascertain upon what terms the claims of the citizens of the State of Georgia may be extinguished, and communicate the same to the Senate at the next session of Congress."

Mr. PORTER then renewed the motion to lay the whole subject on the table, and asked the yeas and nays on the motion; which were ordered, and are as follows, to wit:

YEAS—Messrs. Black, Brown, Calhoun, Clay, Forsyth, Hill, Kane, Kent, King of Alabama, King of Georgia, Linn, Mangum, Moore, Poindexter, Porter, Preston, Robinson, Shepley, Tallmadge, Tyler, Webster, Wright—22.

NAYS—Messrs. Benton, Chambers, Clayton, Ewing, Frelinghuysen, Grundy, Hendricks, Knight, Naudain, Robbins, Smith, Southard, Sprague, Swift, Tipton, Tomlinson, White—17.

So the motion was agreed to.

GENERAL APPROPRIATION BILL.

On motion of Mr. WEBSTER, the Senate resumed the consideration of the bill making appropriations for the civil and diplomatic expenditures of the Government for the year 1834.

Mr. WEBSTER then moved an amendment to increase the appropriation from $4,000 to $8,000, for the erection of a custom-house in Newburyport, Massachusetts; which was agreed to; after which, no further amendment being proposed, the bill was ordered to be engrossed for a third reading.

The following bills were read a third time and passed:

The bill for the relief of Pearson Freeman;

The bill authorizing the Secretary of War to appoint an agent in the town of Decatur, in the State of Alabama, and to provide for the paying of certain pensioners in said town of Decatur;

The bill making appropriations for the civil and

diplomatic expenses of the Government for the year 1834.

On motion of Mr. FORSYTH, the memorial of certain Cherokee Indian Chiefs was ordered to be printed.

A message upon executive business was received from the President of the United States, by Mr. DONELSON, his Private Secretary.

Mr. WRIGHT moved that the Senate adjourn; which was agreed to.

The Senate, at eight o'clock, adjourned.

HOUSE OF REPRESENTATIVES.

WEDNESDAY, June 25, 1834.

On motion of Mr. E. WHITTLESEY, it was ordered that, for the remainder of the session, the House meet at ten o'clock, a. m., and take a recess from two to four o'clock.

Messrs. VANCE, CHILTON, and PARKS, obtained leave to present petitions.

The SPEAKER laid before the House the communications from the Secretary of the Treasury, covering documents relative to the Mint; and in reply to a resolution of the House, showing the amount of proceeds of sales of lands included in the Louisiana purchase; which were laid on the table and ordered to be printed.

Mr. E. EVERETT, from the Joint Committee on the Library, reported a bill making provision for the purchase of the fac similie of Washington's accounts; read twice and committed.

Mr. THOMAS, of Maryland, submitted a resolution setting apart Friday next and each succeeding day of the session thereafter, till the subject was concluded, for the consideration of the report of the committee appointed to investigate the affairs of the Bank of the United States.

Mr. WATMOUGH demanded the question on the consideration of the resolution.

The question being taken by yeas and nays on the consideration of the resolution, it was decided in the affirmative—yeas 95, nays 65.

Mr. WILDE proposed that, if the question should be taken up, the House should go into the Committee of the Whole upon it, in order that a full discussion might be had.

Mr. ELLSWORTH was opposed (he said) to the resolution, if it was intended, after a partial discussion, to arrive at a conclusion by means of the previous question.

Mr. MILLER moved the orders of the day.

Mr. H. EVERETT moved that the House proceed to the consideration of the special order of the day, the Indian bills.

Mr. THOMAS requested the gentleman to suspend his motion, as it was highly important that the House should know whether this subject was to come up or not.

Mr. EVERETT felt bound (he said) to persist in his motion.

Mr. CLAYTON asked permission of the House to make a report from the Committee on Retrenchment.

Leave being granted, Mr. C. reported a resolution granting leave to three of the members of the committee to continue their investigations during the recess, and report to the House at the next session.

The resolution and report were ordered to be printed.

On motion of Mr. H. EVERETT, the House then resolved itself into a Committee of the Whole House on the state of the Union, Mr. WILDE in the chair, and took up for consideration the bill to provide for the organization of the Indian Department.

The bill having been read by sections, and amended in some unimportant particulars, was laid aside to be reported.

The House then proceeded to consider the bill to regulate trade and intercourse with the Indian tribes, and to preserve peace on the frontiers.

The bill having been read by sections—

Mr. GARLAND moved to strike out the words "Indian agent or sub-agent" in the second section, so that the Superintendent of Indian Affairs shall alone be authorized to issue licenses to persons to trade with the Indians.

After a few words from Messrs. EVERETT and ASHLEY, the amendment was agreed to.

Various amendments were proposed to the bill

by Mr. EVERETT, which were adopted, and the bill was laid aside.

The committee then took up the bill to provide for the establishment of the Western Territory, and for the security and protection of the emigrant and other Indian tribes therein.

After the bill had been gone through with, and various minor amendments made,

Mr. J. Q. ADAMS said, this was a very extraordinary bill. We often had constitutional objections raised to bills, but he had never seen a bill which would give occasion to a greater number. He would be glad to learn where the committee propose to find power to authorize Congress to erect a government of Indians, and give them the privilege of sending a delegate to this House?

Mr. H. EVERETT said, the objections suggested had not escaped the attention of the committee. He did not propose going into the discussion here, but would defer it till the bill came into the House. The express power given to regulate intercourse with the Indian tribes, and to manage the public lands, was believed by the committee to cover the whole provisions of this bill.

On motion of Mr. EVERETT, the committee rose, and reported the three bills to the House.

The amendments of the bill providing for the organization of the Department of Indian Affairs were concurred in, and the bill ordered to be engrossed.

The amendments to the bill to regulate trade and intercourse with the Indian tribes, and to preserve peace on the frontiers, were all concurred in, excepting that striking out "agent or sub-agent," in connexion with the power of granting licenses to trade with the Indians, which was so amended, on motion of Mr. GILMER, as to leave "agents" in the bill.

Mr. ASHLEY moved that the twenty-ninth section, providing for the appointment of commissioners to make treaties with the Indians, be stricken out.

Mr. A. contended that the Indian agents were the most suitable persons to negotiate treaties, and the appointment of commissioners was totally unnecessary.

Mr. H. EVERETT said the argument would have been forcible, were it not the fact, that we willing to adopt any provision, to prevent this contingent power from being a source of corrupt or improper patronage; but unless the section was retained, occasions would undoubtedly arise where it would be necessary to give the power in each particular case.

Mr. WILLIAMS supported the proposition to strike out. If it was necessary to ask for an appropriation to hold a treaty, power could be given to appoint commissioners.

Mr. WAYNE said it sometimes happened that the negotiations were, of necessity, in advance of the appropriations.

Mr. EVERETT would not insist on retaining the section in the bill.

The section was struck out without a division. After a modification at the instance of Mr. FILLMORE, the bill was ordered to be engrossed.

The bill providing for the establishment of the Western Territory, &c., came up on the amendments reported from the committee; which were concurred in.

Mr WILLIAMS moved that the House take a recess till half past four o'clock. A quorum not having voted,

Mr. DAVENPORT moved a call of the House; which was negatived.

The motion for a recess was then carried.

EVENING SESSION.

The bill providing for the establishment of the Western Territory, &c., being before the House, on the question of engrossment,

Mr. H. EVERETT said, he perhaps attached more importance to the bill than other members,

but he regarded it as of the highest consequence. The object of the committee had been to provide ample protection for the Indians, and the counsel toe supposed it had been done in a manner satisfactory to the Indians themselves and in the only efficient manner. Mr. E. went into a detailed explanation of the several provisions of the bill in reply to the remarks of Mr. VINTON. Mr. E. also expressed his opinion upon the constitutionality of the provisions of the bill in reply to the doubts suggested by Mr. J. Q. ADAMS in Committee of the Whole.

Mr. ADAMS thought the consideration of the bill should be postponed till the next session. It was one of the most important measures which had been brought up during the present session. He would acknowledge that his attention had been so much devoted to subjects of less moment, that he had neither read the bill or report until to-day. It was not only proposed to place our relations with the Indians upon an entirely new footing, but it looked forward to admitting this Territory into the Union.

He believed Congress had no power to pass a bill containing such provisions as are found in this bill. It stood on grounds entirely distinct from our laws relating to Territories. No authority could be found for admitting a Territory containing an Indian population exclusively into the Union. Another important consideration was, that the whole bill proposes to divest Congress of all power over the regulation of this Territory and to transfer it to the President of the United States. Mr. A. went into a detailed commentary upon the several provisions of the bill. Mr. A. concluded, by moving to lay the bill on the table, but immediately withdrew it.

Mr. GILMER believed, from the course of the argument adopted by the gentleman, [Mr. ADAMS,] that he had entirely misunderstood the provisions of the bill. He contended there was nothing in the bill which referred to the admission of a Territory, inhabited by an Indian population, into the Union; the expressions in the bill only went to secure to the Indians their title to their lands. Mr. G. went into an explanation of the other provisions contained in the bill objected to by Mr. ADAMS.

Mr. ARCHER considered the bill as one of such momentous character that it ought not to be hastily acted upon. He did not think that, at this late stage of the session, the bill ought to have been taken up. He opposed the bill, not, he said, because it established an independent Indian government in the territory of the United States, but because it established a military despotism, under the authority of the United States, within the territory which we guaranty to the Indians. At the very time that we propose to protect them and respect their rights, we subject them to a proconsular government. The bill professes to call the government a territorial government of the United States. Had it not, then, at a proper time, and under proper circumstances, a right to demand admission into the Union?

Mr. FILLMORE suggested several objections to the bill. But he hoped it would be amended so as to render it less objectionable. He anticipated no difficulty from seeing a Representative from that Territory on this floor.

Mr. WILLIAMS perceiving, he said, that this bill would occasion much debate, moved to lay it on the table; which was agreed to.

On motion of Mr. H. EVERETT, the House resolved itself into a Committee of the Whole—Mr. CASEY in the chair—on the bill to carry into effect the 4th article of the treaty of 1821 between the United States and the Creek Indians.

The bill was reported, without amendment, and the question being on its engrossment,

Mr. WILDE explained the provisions of the bill. The object of it was to indemnify citizens of Georgia for Indian depredations committed upon them.

Mr. J. Q. ADAMS asked the gentleman from Georgia, who last addressed the House, how many times these claims had been paid for?

Mr. WILDE. Never.

Mr. ADAMS said he was not entirely satisfied with that answer. He wished to know how often the Government has, after a full examination, settled these claims. They were old acquaintances

of his. ' If he was not mistaken, these were a residue of claims which had been sifted over and over again, and paid for more than once.

Messrs. LEWIS, GILMER, MASON of Virginia, H. EVERETT, WILDE, JONES of Ga., and WAYNE, advocated the propriety of passing the bill, and it was opposed by Messrs. MANN of New York, and PARKER; when Mr. ADAMS moved to lay the bill on the table.

The question being taken, the motion to lay the bill on the table was negatived, yeas 62, nays 86.

Mr. FILLMORE having moved to strike out so much of the bill as relates to the allowance of interest, some further discussion took place, between Messrs. WILDE, HARDIN, FOSTER, LEWIS, HARPER of Pennsylvania, McKAY, and PATTON, when

Mr. HUBBARD moved that the bill be postponed until to-morrow, expressing his wish to address the House on the bill.

Mr. S. JONES resisted the motion to postpone, and it was negatived.

Mr. PATTON suggested a modification of the clause under discussion, which was agreed to.

Mr. HARDIN read the provisions of the treaty under which this claim was set up, and contended that they had been strictly complied with.

The question was taken on Mr. FILLMORE'S amendment, and was negatived—ayes 53, noes 67.

Mr. HUBBARD moved to strike out the whole bill, after the enacting clause, and insert a substitute which provided that a commissioner be appointed by the President to investigate the claims.

Mr. H. called for the reading a report formerly made upon this subject, which was done.

After a brief explanation by Mr. HUBBARD, the question was taken, and the amendment lost.

The question was then taken on the engrossment of the bill; which was carried.

Various bills from the Senate were referred to appropriate committees.

The bill making appropriations for the civil and diplomatic service of the year 1834, as amended by the Senate, was referred to the Committee of Ways and Means.

Several Senate bills were read a third time and passed, and the House at a late hour adjourned.

IN SENATE.

Thursday, June 26, 1834.

Mr. BENTON, from the Committee on Military Affairs, reported a bill without amendment for the relief of Amos W. Brown.

Mr. HENDRICKS, from the Committee on Roads and Canals, reported several bills for the construction of Roads in Michigan Territory.

Mr. BROWN, from the Committee on Claims, asked to be discharged from the petition of Simeon Gerron, and the petition of Benjamin Crisman, and others, which was agreed to.

Mr. NAUDAIN, from the Committee on Claims, asked to be discharged from the further consideration of the petition of William Tharp. Agreed to.

Mr. WILKINS, from the Committee on Foreign Relations, reported a bill for the relief of sundry inhabitants of East Florida; which was ordered to be engrossed and read a third time.

Mr. WILKINS, from the same committee, made a report upon the memorial of Mary O'Sullivan, widow of John O'Sullivan, deceased, concluding with a resolution referring the case to the Secretary of the Treasury, and requiring a report at the next session of Congress; which was concurred in.

Mr. CLAYTON, from the Committee on the Judiciary, reported, without amendment, the bill authorizing the establishment of a territorial government west of Missouri.

Mr. TOMLINSON, from the Committee on Pensions, asked to be discharged from the further consideration of the memorial of Henry Le Mountain; which was agreed to.

Mr. KING, of Alabama, from the Committee on Military Affairs, asked to be discharged from the further consideration of the petition of Samuel Dale; which was agreed to.

Mr. SOUTHARD, from the Committee on Naval Affairs, reported, without amendment, the bill extending the time for the payment of pensions to the widows and orphans of persons who died in the naval service of the United States. The bill was ordered to be engrossed for a third reading.

Mr. SOUTHARD was elected to supply the vacancy in the Committee on the Post Office and Post Roads, occasioned by Mr. CLAYTON's being excused from longer service upon the committee.

Several bills were read a first and ordered to a second reading.

The following resolution was submitted by Mr. SILSBEE, considered, and adopted:

Resolved, That the Secretary of the Treasury be directed to report to the Senate, at the commencement of the next session of Congress, the amount of "hospital money" which has been received at each of the custom-houses of the United States in each year, since the passage of the act of July, 1798, and the amount of these receipts which has been expended in each district for the relief of sick and disabled seamen since the date of said act.

Also, the number of marine hospitals which have been built in the United States, with the cost of each of them, and where they are located.

Mr. BIBB, from the Committee on the Judiciary, obtained leave to introduce a resolution authorizing the printing of the Executive Journal of the Senate, with an index, separately from the Legislative Journal.

Several bills were considered in Committee of the Whole, and ordered to be engrossed for a third reading.

Mr. POINDEXTER moved to take up the bill authorizing the relinquishment of the sixteenth sections granted for the use of schools, and the entry of other land in lieu thereof.

After some conversation between Mr. POINDEXTER, Mr. MOORE, and Mr. PORTER, the motion was negatived: Yeas 18, nays 19.

The Senate, at two o'clock, took a recess until four.

EVENING SESSION.

The Senate reassembled at four o'clock.

A message upon executive business was received from the President of the United States, by Mr. DONELSON, his Private Secretary.

Mr. TIPTON asked the indulgence of the Senate to take up the bill providing for the admission of the Territory of Arkansas into the Union, intimating his intention to move to take up the bill for the admission of Michigan also.

Some objections being urged by Mr. CLAYTON,

Mr. TIPTON said his only object was that the people of the Territory might be authorized to have the census taken, preparatory to their final admission. He had been waited on by the delegates from the Territories, and requested that these bills might be acted on; and as they were not represented here, he was desirous of showing the people of the Territories that he had not neglected their interests. He therefore asked the yeas and nays upon the motion to take up the bill; which were ordered, and are as follows, to wit:

YEAS—Messrs. Benton, Black, Chambers, Grundy, Hendricks, Hill, Kane, King of Alabama, Linn, Robinson, Shepley, Swift, Tallmadge, Tipton, White, Wilkins, Wright—17.

NAYS—Messrs. Bibb, Calhoun, Clayton, Ewing, Kent, King of Georgia, Porter, Preston, Robbins, Silsbee, Smith, Southard, Sprague, Tomlinson, Waggaman, Webster—16.

So the Senate determined to consider the bill; which, having been read in part,

Mr. WEBSTER moved to lay the bill on the table; which was disagreed to: Yeas 15, nays 16.

Some further progress was made in reading the bill and amendment.

Mr. SPRAGUE renewed the motion to lay the bill on the table. Agreed to: yeas 17, nays 14.

GENERAL APPROPRIATION BILL.

Mr. WEBSTER moved that the Senate consider the bill making appropriations for the civil and diplomatic expenses of the Government for the year 1834; which was agreed to.

The Senate then receded from their amendment to the bill not-concurred in by the House, and concurred in the amendment of the House, increasing their contingent fund to $35,000, made to the Senate's amendment.

So the bill was finally passed.

The following bills were read a third time, and passed:

The bill for the relief of James Noble;

The bill prolonging the time for the payment of pensions to the widows and children of officers, seamen, and marines, who have died in the naval service;

The bill for the relief of the heirs of Henry Eckford;

The bill authorizing a sum of money to be distributed among the officers and crew of the late privateer General Armstrong;

The bill for the relief of John E. Tholozan and William Russell;

The bill for the relief of William Purcell;

The bill for the relief of D. and E. Robinson and the heirs of J. and J. Robinson;

The bill for the relief of P. H. Green and W. Emerson;

The bill to improve the navigation of the Wabash river;

The bill limiting the time of advertising the sales of the public lands;

The bill for the relief of Christian Ish's heirs;

The bill for the relief of Michael Gratz's administrators;

The bill to exempt merchandise, imported under certain circumstances, from the operation of the act of the 19th of May, 1828, entitled "An act in alteration of the several acts imposing duties on imports;"

The bill to provide compensation for the Governor and judges of the Michigan Territory, for services rendered by them under the act of Congress of the 21st of April, 1806, entitled "An act to provide for the adjustment of titles to land in the town of Detroit;"

The bill for the relief of John Peck.

The following bills were considered in Committee of the Whole, and ordered to be engrossed for a third reading:

The bill supplementary to the act entitled "An act to carry into effect the convention between the United States and his Majesty the King of the Two Sicilies," concluded at Naples on the 14th of October, 1832;

The bill confirming claims to land in the State of Missouri, and for other purposes;

The bill for the payment of a debt due to Pierre Menard;

The bill for the relief of the widow and heirs of Captain William Royall, deceased;

The bill for the relief of Frances Preston and Sarah B. Preston, representatives of the late General William Campbell, deceased;

The bill for the payment of a debt due to Joseph Bogy; and

The bill for the relief of the legal representatives of Francis Nash.

Mr. CHAMBERS moved that the Senate take up, for consideration, the bill for the benefit of the city of Washington; which was agreed to.

Mr. CLAY moved to amend by reducing the grant to one year.

The question of limiting the appropriation of $70,000 to one year, was then agreed to.

The question recurring on the engrossment of the bill for a third reading,

Mr. WRIGHT said he could not give his support to it, and as he was desirous of recording his vote against the bill, he asked the yeas and nays; which were ordered, and are as follows, to wit:

YEAS—Messrs. Chambers, Clay, Clayton, Ewing, Frelinghuysen, Hendricks, Kent, Moore, Naudain, Poindexter, Porter, Robbins, Silsbee, Southard, Sprague, Swift, Tipton, Tomlinson, Waggaman, Webster, and Wilkins—21.

NAYS—Messrs. Benton, Black, Brown, Calhoun, Grundy, Hill, King of Georgia, Leigh, Linn, Mangum, Morris, Prentiss, Preston, Robinson, Shepley, Smith, Tallmadge, Tyler, and Wright—19.

So the question was determined in the affirmative. At a subsequent stage of the day's proceedings, the bill was read a third time, and passed.

The bill supplementary to an act entitled "An act for the relief of the city council of Charleston, South Carolina," passed May 20, 1830, was read a second time, and, on motion, laid on the table.

The bill for the relief of Tench Ringgold was then taken up.

Upon the consideration of this bill a desultory conversation ensued between Messrs. CHAMBERS, CLAYTON, SHEPLEY, BIBB, PORTER, BLACK, and SOUTHARD.

Mr. SHEPLEY proposed an amendment striking out an appropriation for the costs expended by Mr. Ringgold in a suit in the Supreme Court of the United States; upon which the yeas and nays were ordered, and are as follows:

YEAS—Messrs. Bibb, Black, Ewing, Forsyth, Grundy, Hendricks, Hill, King of Alabama, King of Georgia, Leigh, Mangum, Morris, Preston, Robinson, Shepley, Swift, Tallmadge, Tomlinson, Tyler, Webster, White, and Wright—22.

NAYS—Messrs. Chambers, Clay, Clayton, Kent, Knight, Poindexter, Porter, Robbins, Southard, and Tipton—10.

The bill, as amended, was ordered to be engrossed for a third reading.

Mr. BLACK made an unsuccessful motion to adjourn.

On motion of Mr. HENDRICKS, the Senate took up the bill to enable the people of the eastern division of the Territory of Michigan to form a constitution and State Government, and for the admission of such State into the Union on an equal footing with the original States.

But, without making any progress therein—
On motion of Mr. CLAY, at 8 o'clock—
The Senate adjourned.

HOUSE OF REPRESENTATIVES.

THURSDAY, June 26, 1834.

The SPEAKER laid before the House a communication from the First Comptroller of the Treasury, with a list of balances, in conformity to law.

Mr. F. THOMAS, by consent, presented various petitions and memorials; which were referred.

Mr. POLK, from the Committee of Ways and Means, reported the general appropriation bill, as amended by the Senate, with a recommendation that the House concur in all amendments excepting some two or three which were specified. The bill, as amended, was referred to the Committee of the Whole on the state of the Union.

Mr. ADAMS, from the Committee on Manufactures, reported, in relation to the resolution of the Legislature of Vermont, that the subject be postponed to the next session.

On motion of Mr. ELLSWORTH, the Committee on the Judiciary was discharged from all subjects before them, which had not been acted on.

Mr. CLAY moved that the Committee on Public Lands be discharged from all the subjects before them which had not been reported on; which was agreed to.

Mr. CONNOR, from the Committee on the Post Office and Post Roads, reported the following resolution, which was adopted:

Resolved, That a committee be appointed to examine the condition and proceedings of the Post Office Department, with power to send for persons and papers, and to take the depositions of witnesses either by personal examination, or on commission, with permission to sit in the recess of Congress, and to report at the next session.

The question was taken upon the number seven for the committee; which was negatived.

It was then ordered that the select committee consist of five persons.

Mr. CHINN moved to suspend the rules, in order that several bills relating to the District of Columbia be taken up.

Mr. POLK hoped the House would first take up the appropriation bills, which remained undisposed of, which must, by the rules, be sent to the Senate to-day.

The question being stated on Mr. CHINN's motion—

Mr. MERCER moved so to amend it as to include the bill relative to the construction of the Washington bridge.

Mr. MERCER'S amendment was adopted.

The question was then taken on Mr. CHINN's motion as amended, and it was negatived.

Mr. POLK moved to suspend the rules, in order to proceed directly to take up the appropriation bills.

Mr. C. P. WHITE moved to amend the motion by adding the bill reported by the Committee on Naval Affairs.

The question was then taken on Mr. POLK's motion; which was carried.

The House then, on motion of Mr. POLK, went into Committee of the Whole on the state of the Union, for the purpose of taking up the bill making appropriation for Indian annuities, and the general appropriation bill, (Mr. SPEIGHT in the chair.)

The Indian annuity bill was read in committee.

Mr. POLK explained the provisions of the bill. Its object was to carry into effect sundry treaties which had been ratified by the Senate during the present session. The items were made in accordance with the treaties which he had in his possession, and if any objection was made, he would refer to the provisions. An estimate had been made for certain objects not embraced in the present bill, but were included in one before the Senate, which, for the purpose of facilitating a decision upon it, he now moved as an amendment to this bill.

The various items of this amendment were read.

Mr. POLK went into an explanation of some of the items, particularly that of $139,000 for the Cherokee improvement, abandoned under treaty, which had been recently valued in pursuance of its provisions. He did not propose to detain the House, unless explanation in detail was desired by any gentleman.

Mr. E. WHITTLESEY desired an explanation of the last item in the amendment, being $450 to pay certain counsel fees in the case of Brunetti against Street and Kearney—

Which was given by Mr. POLK.

The question was taken on striking out the item; which was agreed to without a division.

The amendment proposed by Mr. POLK was then adopted.

Mr. McKINLEY moved an amendment, providing for the expense of holding certain treaties, &c., with Indians. After a brief explanation by Mr. McK.

Mr. WILLIAMS called for a division of the question.

The various items were adopted, excepting that appropriating $3,400 for the expenses of a treaty appropriating $3,400 for the Cherokee nation in June, 1834.

Mr. WILLIAMS contended that it was irregular to call for appropriation for a treaty not before the House. He wished to learn with which of the delegations the treaty had been made.

Mr. McKINLEY said there were two delegations from the Cherokees—one from the east, and the other west of the Mississippi. A treaty had been made with those from east of the Mississippi. It was not proposed to appropriate money to carry the treaty into effect, but simply to pay the delegates, in conformity with the invariable practice of the Government, for their expenses.

Mr. WILLIAMS did not wish to be understood as opposing any Indian treaty; but being of opinion that the delegates were not authorized to make the treaty, he should not vote in favor of appropriation for that object.

Mr. McKINLEY said the Government were bound to pay the delegates. The questions arising upon the treaty were not before the House.

The amendments were then adopted.

Mr. WHITTLESEY said that since the item relative to the counsel fees in the case of Brunetti and Kearney and Street had been struck out, he had examined the report of the Committee of Claims more fully, and found that a bill was reported to indemnify them for the judgment, but it did not appear that counsel fees were provided for. He proposed to refer that subject to the Secretary of War, and proposed an amendment to that effect; which was agreed to.

The bill was then laid aside.

On motion of Mr. POLK, the committee then took up for consideration the bill making appropriations for the civil and diplomatic expenses of the Government for the year 1834.

The amendments of the Senate were read and agreed to, with the exception of the amendment in relation to the compensation of the judges in Florida, which was disagreed to.

On motion of Mr. POLK, the bill was amended so as to add $35,000 to the appropriation for the contingent fund of the House.

The bills were then reported to the House with the amendments.

The House took up the "the bill making appropria-

---

tions for carrying into effect certain Indian treaties and for other purposes," and, the amendments being concurred in, the bill was passed.

The House then took up the civil and diplomatic appropriation bill, and the question being on concurring in the amendment relative to the emoluments of the collectors, &c., some discussion took place; after which the amendment was concurred in.

The amendment relative to the publication of the Diplomatic Correspondence, was concurred in.

The amendment providing that no bank notes should be received under this bill, except those which are of par value at the place where they are paid, was objected to by Mr. McKINLEY, and supported by Mr. DENNY, was it was concurred in.

The amendment authorizing the payment to E. R. POTTS of mileage and pay as a member, for each day's actual attendance, preceding the decision of the Senate on the election contested by him, was opposed by Mr. McKINLEY, and supported by Messrs. PEARCE of Rhode Island, ADAMS of Massachusetts, and BURGES, when the question being taken by yeas and nays, the amendment was concurred in: Yeas 86, nays 56.

The amendment increasing the contingent fund of the House was concurred in.

All the other amendments were concurred in.

The House then took a recess till four o'clock.

EVENING SESSION.

Several bills from the Senate were referred to the appropriate committees.

The House then went into Committee of the Whole on various bills, which having been gone through with, were reported to the House.

Various bills from the Senate were read twice, and referred to the appropriate committees.

The bill to provide for the organization of the department of Indian Affairs was read a third time, and passed.

The bill to regulate trade and intercourse with Indian tribes, and to preserve peace on the frontier, was read a third time, and passed.

The bill providing for the payment of certain claims of citizens of Georgia against the Creek Indians, was read a third time.

Mr. J. Q. ADAMS wished to make a few remarks; but it was so late, and the House so thin, it seemed to him most proper to adjourn.

The motion was negatived.

Mr. ADAMS said the allowance of interest in this bill was precisely the principle which was vetoed by the President, in the bill giving interest to the States for advances during the war. If the bill passed both Houses, it could not receive the approbation of the President. He wished to make some observations on the bill, and moved its postponement till to-morrow; on which the question was taken; but no quorum voting,

The House adjourned.

IN SENATE.

FRIDAY, June 27, 1834.

The VICE PRESIDENT presented a communication from the Department of State, in compliance with the resolution of the Senate of the 26th February, 1833, in reference to the classification of the inhabitants of the United States, showing the proportion of whites to blacks, and also a response in part to the resolution of the 29th of March, 1834, of a similar character.

On motion of Mr. BIBB, three thousand copies were ordered to be printed.

Mr. KNIGHT presented a resolution allowing extra compensation to some of the officers of the Senate; which was considered and adopted.

The VICE PRESIDENT presented the memorial of Mountjoy Bayly. Read and referred.

Mr. NAUDAIN, from the Committee on Claims, reported a bill for the relief of John E. Pies.

Mr. NAUDAIN, from the same committee, moved to be discharged from the further consideration of business referred to them, and not acted upon; which was agreed to.

The bill from the House granting pensions to the representatives of the French sailors, killed at Toulon, was amended, opposed, and sent to the House for concurrence.

On motion of Mr. CLAYTON, the orders were

postponed, and the bill to organize a territorial government north of Missouri and west of the Mississippi, was taken up. The bill was considered in Committee of the Whole; ordered to be engrossed for a third reading, and subsequently read a third time and passed.

On motion of Mr. EWING, the Senate took up the report and resolutions of the Committee on the Post Office and Post Roads.

Mr. KNIGHT took the opportunity to make some comments upon the memorial of F. P. Blair.

Mr. FORSYTH remarked, that as time was pressing, he thought it advisable to proceed to the consideration of the report; which was agreed to.

Mr. EWING then spoke at length in support of the resolutions reported by the committee; when, without concluding, the hour of two having arrived, the Senate took a recess until four o'clock.

EVENING SESSION.

The Senate resumed its session at four o'clock.

A message upon executive business was received from the President of the United States, by Mr. DONELSON, his Private Secretary.

Mr. EWING resumed and concluded his remarks in support of the resolutions of the Committee on the Post Office and Post Roads.

Mr. BENTON, from the Committee on Military Affairs, made a report upon the memorial of the inhabitants of Tolland county, Connecticut, relative to the removal of the remains of Captain Nathan Hale, hung by the enemy as a spy during the revolutionary war. Ordered to be printed.

Mr. GRUNDY then took the floor, and spoke at length in reply to Mr. EWING. Upon concluding, Mr. WRIGHT made a few remarks upon the necessity of proceeding to the business on the calendar, and concluded by moving to lay the resolutions on the table, upon which he asked the yeas and nays, which were ordered, and are as follow, to wit:

YEAS—Messrs. Benton, Brown, Forsyth, Grundy, Hendricks, Hill, Kane, King of Alabama, King of Georgia, Morris, Robinson, Shepley, Swift, Tallmadge, Tipton, White, Wilkins, and Wright—18.

NAYS—Messrs. Bibb, Calhoun, Clay, Clayton, Ewing, Frelinghuysen, Kent, Knight, Naudain, Poindexter, Porter, Prentiss, Preston, Robbins, Smith, Southard, Sprague, Tomlinson, Tyler, Waggaman—20.

So the question was determined in the negative.

Mr. CLAYTON then proceeded to reply to Mr. GRUNDY, and in support of the resolutions.

Some further conversation occurred; when Mr. WEBSTER asked for the yeas and nays, which were ordered upon the first resolution, and intimated his intention to move that the remaining resolutions lie upon the table.

The first resolution, to wit:

Resolved, That it is proved and admitted, that large sums of money have been borrowed at different banks by the Postmaster General, in order to make up the deficiency in the means of carrying on the business of the Post Office Department, without authority given by any law of Congress; and that, as Congress alone possesses the power to borrow money on the credit of the United States, all such contracts for loans by the Postmaster General are illegal and void—

Was decided by the following vote:

YEAS—Messrs. Benton, Bibb, Black, Brown, Calhoun, Chambers, Clay, Clayton, Ewing, Forsyth, Frelinghuysen, Grundy, Hendricks, Hill, Kane, Kent, King of Alabama, King of Georgia, Knight, Linn, Mangum, Moore, Naudain, Poindexter, Porter, Prentiss, Preston, Robbins, Robinson, Shepley, Silsbee, Smith, Southard, Sprague, Swift, Tomlinson, Tyler, Waggaman, Webster, White, Wright—41.

Mr. WEBSTER then moved to lay the remaining resolutions on the table; which was agreed to.

The resolution from the House rescinding the joint resolution, so as to allow the action upon original bills up to post 3 p. m. of this evening, was, on motion of Mr. WEBSTER, laid upon the table.

The Senate then, on motion of Mr. POINDEXTER, proceeded to executive business; when, after remaining therein until half-past nine o'clock, the Senate adjourned.

HOUSE OF REPRESENTATIVES.
FRIDAY, *June* 27, 1834.

Messrs. J. K. MANN, McKIM, HUBBARD, VINTON, CRANE, HIESTER, DENNY, and CONNOR, by consent, presented sundry memorials, which were laid on the table and ordered to be printed.

Mr. THOMSON, on leave of the House, presented three petitions from sundry citizens of the State of Ohio, praying for the establishment of a mail route from North Union, Carroll county, by Kilgore, and Shakers' Mills, to Springfield, Jefferson county.

Also, a petition praying for a mail route from Gnadenhutten, by Urick's Mills and One Leg, to Leesville, in the county of Carroll; all of which were referred to the Committee on the Post Office and Post Roads.

Mr. T. likewise presented the proceedings of a democratic meeting which was held on the 17th of May last at the district school-house in Poulkstown, St. Clair township, in the county of Columbians, and State of Ohio; which was laid on the table and ordered to be printed.

Mr. E. EVERETT, from the Joint Library Committee, reported the following joint resolution:

Resolved by the Senate and House of Representatives of the United States of America in Congress assembled, That the bronze statue of Thomas Jefferson, presented to the people of the United States by Lieutenant Levy, be placed in the square on the eastern front of the Capitol.

Mr. ARCHER said, that besides the objection that no statue ought to be placed in the Capitol before that of General Washington, it was the opinion of many of the most competent judges, that the statue in question was not such as should be placed in the Capitol at all. None should be entitled to that distinction excepting those which possessed the very first order of merit. He would move to lay the resolution on the table, but from his willingness to hear any explanation on the subject that gentlemen might be disposed to give.

After a few remarks from Messrs. EVERETT, MERCER, LANE, and CLAY, the question was taken on the engrossment of the resolution, which was carried.

The bill from the Senate limiting the time of advertising the sales of the public lands, reported from the Committee of Public Lands, by Mr. MASON, was read a third time and passed.

The bill of the Senate for the relief of William Russell, and another reported from the same committee, were read a third time and passed.

Mr. JARVIS, from the Committee on Public Buildings, reported the following resolution:

Resolved, That the Clerk of the House be directed to pay to John Vanderlyn, out of the contingent fund of the House, $1500 as additional compensation for the full-length portrait of Washington, executed by him, to be placed in the hall of Representatives, in pursuance of a resolution of this House of 17th February, 1832.

After a brief explanation from Mr. JARVIS, the resolution was adopted.

The bill to carry into effect the 4th article of the treaty of 1821, between the United States and the Creek Indians, was read a third time; and after some remarks from Mr. J. Q. ADAMS, the House took a recess till four o'clock.

EVENING SESSION.

The House took up the bill respecting the jurisdiction and limits of the State of New York and New Jersey, and it was read a third time and passed.

Mr. MERCER moved to take up the bill in relation to the Potomac bridge. Lost.

The House then resumed the consideration of the bill to carry into effect the fourth article of the treaty of 1821, between the United States and the Creek Indians—the question being on its passage, and

Mr. J. Q. ADAMS renewed his remarks in opposition to the bill.

Mr. CAMBRELENG spoke briefly in reply to the gentleman from Massachusetts.

After a few words from Mr. LINCOLN, the previous question was called for and seconded.

The main question was ordered to be put, and the question being taken on the passage of the

---

bill, it was determined in the affirmative—yeas 99, nays 60.

So the bill was passed.

The fortification bill was then read a third time and passed.

The light-house bill was read a third time, and the question being on its passage,

Mr. POLK stated the reasons why he considered its passage, this year, unnecessary, and called for the yeas and nays; which were ordered.

After a few remarks from Messrs. ELLSWORTH and SUTHERLAND, the question was taken and determined in the affirmative—yeas 105, nays 81.

So the bill was passed.

The bill making appropriations for the support of the Military Academy at West Point, during the year 1834, was read a third time, and the question being on its passage, Mr. DICKINSON asked the yeas and nays; which were ordered.

The question being taken, it was determined in the affirmative—yeas 119, nays 55.

So the bill was passed.

Various bills were ordered to be engrossed, when

Mr. WILDE moved an adjournment; which was carried.

IN SENATE.
SATURDAY, *June* 28, 1834.

On motion of Mr. CLAY, the Senate rescinded the order for a recess from two to four o'clock.

On motion of Mr. GRUNDY, the Committee on the Post Office and Post Roads were discharged from the consideration of all subjects referred to them, with the exception of the resolution requiring them to investigate the affairs of the Post Office Department during the recess.

On motion of Mr. WEBSTER, the Senate took up the resolution rescinding the 16th joint rule, so as to admit the presentation of bills up to two o'clock of this day; which was agreed to.

Mr. POINDEXTER moved to take up the resolution making inquiry into frauds upon the public lands.

Some conversation ensued between Messrs. POINDEXTER, WRIGHT, WEBSTER, CLAY, and KING of Alabama; when

Mr. POINDEXTER withdrew the motion.

The following bills were read a third time and passed:

A bill making additional appropriation for the improvement of certain harbors, and the removal of obstructions in certain rivers;

A bill for the relief of Tench Ringgold;

A bill for the payment of a debt due to the heirs of Antoine Peltier;

A bill to authorize the correction of erroneous selections of land granted to the State of Indiana for the purpose of constructing the Michigan road;

A bill for the relief of James Ord;

A bill for the relief of Jonathan M. Blaisdell;

A bill regulating the payment of certain Indian annuities;

A bill authorizing the removal of the custom-house from Magnolia to St. Marks in Florida.

Mr. CLAY moved to rescind the rule setting apart Fridays and Saturdays for the consideration of bills.

The consideration of this motion being objected to, it was agreed to—yeas 19, nays 16.

The resolution was then adopted without a division.

Mr. CLAYTON, from the Committee on the Judiciary, reported the bill from the House giving the consent of Congress to the compact between the States of New Jersey and New York, respecting the territorial limits and jurisdiction of said States; which received its several readings and was ordered to be engrossed, and finally passed.

The Senate considered the resolution of the Joint Library Committee for placing the bronze statue of Thomas Jefferson, presented by Lieut. Levy, in the square east of the Capitol.

After some remarks from Messrs. CLAY, TYLER, CALHOUN, POINDEXTER, and PORTER, the resolution was laid on the table.

Mr. WEBSTER, from the Committee on Finance, reported the bill from the House making appropriations for the Military Academy of the United States for the year 1834.

The bill, òn motion of Mr. WEBSTER, received its several readings, and was passed.

The following bills were read a third time, and passed:

A bill for the relief of Terence Le Blanc;
A bill for the relief of William Weedon;
A bill for the relief of Jeremiah Worsham;
A bill for the relief of the legal representatives of John Thompson, jr., late of Louisiana;
A bill for the relief of Samuel Gibbs's heirs;
A bill granting pensions to certain persons therein named;
A bill for the relief of the heirs of Arnold Henry Dohrman;
A bill for the relief of Elijah Lincoln;
A bill for the relief of Marguerite Baron, widow of J. P. Ledoux;
A bill for the relief of George Douglass and others;
A bill further to provide for the location of certain land claims in the Territory of Arkansas;
A bill for the relief of Asel Wilkinson;
A bill in reference to preemption rights in the southeastern district of Louisiana;
A bill for the relief of the representatives of B. Bird and G. Pomeroy;
A bill for the relief of B. Jacobs and S. Bayard, surviving executors of John Bayard, deceased, and of the executors of Joseph Falconer, deceased;
A bill confirming the title of Samuel Vail in a certain tract of land in the parish of East Baton Rouge;
A bill for the relief of John Allen;
A bill for the relief of John Winslett;
A bill for the relief of Frederick Raymer;
A bill for the relief of George Elliott;
A bill for the relief of the representatives of Walter Livingston, deceased.

GOLD BILL.

On motion of Mr. WEBSTER, the Senate proceeded to the consideration of the bill regulating the value of the gold coins of the United States.

After some debate the question was taken on ordering the bill to be engrossed for a third reading, and determined in the affirmative by the following vote:

YEAS—Messrs. Benton, Bibb, Black, Brown, Calhoun, Ewing, Frelinghuysen, Grundy, Hendricks, Hill, Kane, Kent, King of Alabama, King of Georgia, Leigh, Linn, Mangum, Morris, Poindexter, Prentiss, Preston, Robbins, Robinson, Shepley, Smith, Swift, Tallmadge, Tipton, Tomlinson, Tyler, Waggaman, Webster, White, Wilkins, Wright—35.

NAYS—Messrs. Chambers, Clay, Knight, Porter, Silsbee, Southard, Sprague—7.

The bill was then read a third time and passed.

The Senate took up, for consideration, the bill regulating the value of certain foreign gold coins within the United States, and after undergoing some immaterial amendment, it was ordered to be engrossed, and was then read a third time and passed.

EVENING SESSION.

The Senate having assembled, after the recess, and the VICE PRESIDENT having left the chair,

Mr. WEBSTER moved that the Senate proceed to the choice of a President pro tem.

The motion was agreed to; and on the third ballot,

Mr. POINDEXTER, having received a majority of the whole number of votes given, was declared duly elected President pro tem., and having been accompanied to the Chair by Mr. CHAMBERS, made his acknowledgments for the honor conferred upon him.

A message was then received from the President of the United States by Mr. DONELSON, his Private Secretary.

Mr. FRELINGHUYSEN, from the Committee on Indian Affairs, reported the bill from the House, to preserve peace on the frontiers, and to regulate intercourse with the Indian tribes, with two amendments.

Also, the bill from the House, to provide for a department of Indian affairs, with one amendment.

Mr. WILKINS, from the Committee on Foreign Relations, reported the bill authorizing the Secretary of State to purchase the books and papers of General Washington; which, on his motion, was taken up, considered, ordered to be engrossed, and then read a third time and passed.

The amendments of the House to the bill repealing the duties upon certain articles of hardware, were concurred in.

Mr. CHAMBERS, from the Committee on the District of Columbia, reported a bill from the House making appropriation for the public buildings and grounds, and for other purposes, with amendments, and, on his motion, the Senate adopted the amendments; when the bill was ordered to be engrossed for a third reading.

The following bills were considered as in Committee of the Whole, ordered to a third reading, and having been so read, were passed:

A bill granting pensions to certain persons therein named;

A bill for the relief of Horatio N. Crabb;
A bill for the relief of John G. Reynolds;
A bill making certain allowances and granting certain arrearages to the captains and subalterns of the United States corps of marines;
A bill for the relief of Robert Reynolds;
A bill for the relief of Henry Sewall and Robert Sewall;
A bill granting pensions to persons therein named; [Francis Jacobs and others;]
A bill for the relief of George Bowen;
A bill for the relief of Henry Whitney;
A bill for the relief of Jonathan Walton and John J. De Graff;
A bill for the relief of Alexander J. Robinson;
A bill for the relief of the legal representatives of James Brown;
A bill for the relief of Antoine Cruzat;
A bill for the benefit of the heirs at law of the representatives of William G. Christopher, deceased;
A bill for the relief of Wm. Enos, of Arkansas;
A bill for the relief of William K. Pauling;
A bill for the relief of William Haslett;
A bill for the relief of Margaret Riker;
A bill for the relief of sundry citizens of the United States, who have lost property by the depredations of certain Indian tribes;
A bill for the relief of Buller Claiborne, deceased.

FORTIFICATION BILL.

On motion of Mr. WEBSTER, the Senate took up for consideration the bill making appropriations for certain fortifications within the United States for the year 1834.

Mr. BENTON, in pursuance of the instructions of the Military Committee, submitted an amendment, appropriating $107,040 for finishing towers, barracks, and storehouses, at New Orleans, for the use of the United States troops; which was agreed to; after which the bill was ordered to be engrossed. It was then read a third time, and passed.

The following bills were read a third time, and passed:

A bill for the relief of the heirs of Thomas Wallace, deceased;
A bill for the relief of John C. Naylor;
A bill for the relief of Judith Thomas and Daniel Palmer;
A bill for the relief of Samuel D. Walker;
A bill for the relief of Stephen Kingston;
A bill for the relief of the widow of William B. Doliber and other owners, and the heirs of the crew of the schooner Mary and Hannah;
A bill for the relief of François Suzone;
A bill making appropriations for certain fortifications for the year 1834;
A bill for the relief of Thomas Minor;
A bill for the relief of the legal representatives of George Hurlbut, deceased;
A bill for the relief of the legal representatives of Joseph Torry, deceased;
A bill for the relief of the legal representatives of Everard Meade, deceased;
A bill for the relief of the heirs and legal representatives of John Taylor, deceased; and
A bill for the relief of Lieutenant Robert Wilmott.

Mr. CHAMBERS, from the Committee on the District of Columbia, reported the bill to construct a bridge over the river Potomac at the city of Washington, and to repeal all other acts in rela-

tion thereto, which he moved that the Senate proceed forthwith to consider. Agreed to.

After an amendment offered by Mr. WEBSTER, providing for the adjustment of the expenditures of Mr. Dibble, a contractor under the law of last session, the bill was passed on its third reading.

Mr. WILKINS, from the Committee on Foreign Relations, reported the bill to carry into effect the convention between the United States and Spain, with amendments; which he moved that the Senate consider forthwith. Agreed to.

Mr. WHITE moved to lay the bill on the table till the next session; which was agreed to.

Mr. CLAY moved to reconsider the vote indefinitely postponing the bill making appropriations to light-houses, beacons, &c.; which was agreed to. The bill was then recommitted to the Committee on Commerce.

The bill from the House concerning tonnage duty on Spanish vessels was read a first time, and referred to the Committee on Commerce on motion of Mr. PRESTON.

The following bills were read a third time, and passed:

A bill for the relief of Ephraim Crane;
A bill for the relief of Ann Mortimer Baron;
A bill for the relief of the legal representatives of John M. Gregory;
A bill for the relief of the heirs of Hannah Douglass, and others;
A bill for the relief of John Emerson;
A bill for the relief of Ephraim Whitaker, an officer of the Revolution; and a subaltern of Burton at the capture of General Prescott.

On motion of Mr. SWIFT, the Senate proceeded to consider the bill to establish the department of Indian Affairs, as in Committee of the Whole.

The bill was ordered to be engrossed for a third reading, and, by unanimous consent, was read a third time, and passed.

A bill for the relief of John Bruce was considered, ordered to be engrossed, and read a third time, and passed.

Several bills were received from the House with slight amendments; which were agreed to.

A bill for the relief of the Polish exiles, with an amendment by the House, taking away the gratuity in the Senate's bill, was disagreed to on that account.

The Senate, at eleven o'clock, proceeded to the consideration of executive business, and after remaining some time therein,

Adjourned until nine o'clock, Monday morning.

HOUSE OF REPRESENTATIVES.
MONDAY, June 28, 1834.

Mr. POLK moved to suspend the rules, to enable him to offer a joint resolution suspending the operation of the 16th joint rule of the two Houses, which prohibits the sending bills from one to the other during the three last days of the session, so far as to permit the sending of those bills which had already been passed by the House.

The suspension was agreed to; and after some remarks from Messrs. SELDEN, POLK, E. WHITTLESEY, J. Q. ADAMS, and HAWES, the resolution was adopted.

Mr. R. M. JOHNSON asked the consent of the House to submit a vote of thanks to the late Speaker STEVENSON.

Mr. CROCKETT objected.

Mr. JOHNSON moved the suspension of the rules, to enable the resolution to be submitted.

Mr. BURGES called for the yeas and nays; which were ordered.

The motion to suspend was lost: Yeas 59, nays 49, (not two-thirds.)

The joint resolution of the House relative to the suspension of the joint rules respecting sending bills between the two Houses, as amended by the Senate, came up for concurrence and was agreed to.

A bill authorizing the heirs and representatives of James Latham deceased, to withdraw and re-locate a land warrant was read a third time, and passed.

The bill to authorize a suit of error in certain cases relating to patent-rights, to the Supreme Court of the United States, was read a third time.

Mr. HARDIN explained the abuses to which the country were exposed from patentees and speculators under them, and opposed the provisions of the bill.

Mr. ELLSWORTH replied.

The bill was passed.

The bill supplementary to the act to amend the several acts respecting copy rights, was read a third time and passed.

The bill authorizing the running out and marking the northern boundary line of the country purchased of the Chickasaw nation was read a third time.

Mr. J. Q. ADAMS objected to the words "directed" as applied to the President. It was an unconstitutional assertion of superiority on the part of Congress which was totally unprecedented. He moved these words be struck out; which, by unanimous consent, was done.

The bill was then passed.

The bill to prohibit the corporations of Washington, Georgetown, and Alexandria, from issuing promissory notes, or bills of any denomination less than ten dollars, was read a third time, and passed.

The bill for completing the improvement of Pennsylvania Avenue, was read a third time and passed.

The bill authorizing the construction of a bridge across the Potomac, and repealing all acts already passed in relation thereto, was read a third time and passed.

The bill making appropriations for the public buildings and grounds, and for other purposes, was read a third time and passed.

The bill carrying into effect the convention between the United States and Spain, was read a third time and passed.

The bill to enable the Secretary of State to purchase the manuscripts and books of General Washington, was read a third time and passed.

The bill authorizing the purchase of the live oak frames for a frigate and sloop of war, and for other purposes, was read a third time and passed.

The bill to provide for rebuilding the frigate Congress, was read a third time and passed.

The bill to authorize the President to direct the transfer of appropriations for naval service under certain circumstances, was read a third time and passed.

A bill making appropriation for the improvement of the navigation of the Hudson river, and for other purposes, was read a third time.

Mr. HAWES demanded the yeas and nays on the passage of this bill; which were ordered.

The bill was passed: Yeas 95, nays 62.

Various bills from the Senate were read twice, and committed to the appropriate committees.

A bill from the Senate authorizing the correction of erroneous selection of lands granted to the State of Indiana, was read a third time and passed.

The bill making provision for the individuals wounded, &c., in firing the salute at Toulon, as amended by the Senate, came up on the question of concurrence.

The amendment was concurred in.

The House went into Committee of the Whole on the state of the Union, upon the amendments to the harbor bill made by the Senate, (Mr. WILDE in the chair.)

The amendments were all agreed to, and the bill, as amended, reported to the House; where the amendments were concurred in.

The amendment of the Senate to the bill making appropriation for carrying into effect certain Indian treaties was read, providing for the payment of the expenses of thirteen delegates from the Eastern Cherokees.

On motion of Mr. POLK, the House went into Committee on this amendment, (Mr. CASEY in the chair.)

The amendment was opposed by Messrs. CLAY and McKINLEY;

And supported by Messrs. WILLIAMS, BURGES, and HUNTINGTON; when the amendment was agreed to.

The bill, as amended, was reported to the House; where the amendment was concurred in.

Mr. HEATH moved that the House take up the bill making appropriations for a marine hospital in the city of Baltimore, and for other purposes; which was agreed to.

. The amendments were concurred in; and the bill ordered to a third reading, read, and passed.

The bill granting an additional quantity of land for the satisfaction of revolutionary land warrants, was taken up; and the amendments having been concurred in, the bill was ordered to a third reading, read a third time, and passed.

Mr. C. P. WHITE moved to suspend the rules, in order to take up the bill authorizing the Secretary of the Navy to make experiments in regard to the steam engine; which was agreed to, and the bill was read a third time, and passed.

The bill to remit the duties on locomotive steam engines, &c., was taken up, and

Mr. MARTINDALE moved to lay it on the table.

The question being taken by yeas and nays, the motion was negatived: Yeas 67, nays 77.

Mr. DICKERSON made some remarks in opposition to the bill; when the bill was amended so as to limit its operation to one year.

Mr. H. EVERETT moved to strike out the second section, considering it (he said) as trenching upon the principles of the compromise act, and thereon he demanded the yeas and nays; which were ordered.

The question being taken, the motion to strike out was agreed to: Yeas 76, nays 67.

The bill was then ordered to be read a third time, read, and passed.

A bill in addition to an act passed 13th July, 1832, entitled "An act concerning tonnage duty on Spanish vessels," was taken up.

Mr. McKIM moved to lay the bill on the table; which was negatived.

The bill was then read a third time, and passed.

On motion of Mr. SMITH, the 16th rule was suspended, so far as to permit the last mentioned bills to be sent to the Senate for concurrence.

EVENING SESSION.

On motion of Mr. WHITE of Louisiana, it was ordered, that additional compensation be given to the watchmen of the Capitol.

Mr. SPEIGHT moved a resolution of thanks to the late Speaker, [Mr. STEVENSON.]

Mr. WHITTLESEY objected to the consideration of the resolution. He said it was understood that the House would devote this evening to bills, of which a great number remained to be acted upon.

The CHAIR decided that the motion did not require a vote of two-thirds.

Mr. WHITTLESEY requested the gentleman from North Carolina to withdraw the motion; which was declined.

Mr. EWING asked the yeas and nays on the motion; when it appeared that there was no quorum.

Mr. SPEIGHT moved a call of the House; which was ordered.

Upon the first call, 162 members answered to their names.

On motion, all further proceeding in the call was suspended.

Mr. SPEIGHT then submitted the following resolution:

Resolved, That the thanks of this House be presented to the honorable ANDREW STEVENSON, late Speaker, for the firmness, dignity, skill, and impartiality with which he filled the office of Speaker during the present session.

Mr. READ desired the yeas and nays; which were ordered.

The question being taken, the resolution was agreed to: yeas 97, nays 49, as follows:

YEAS—Messrs. John Adams, John J. Allen, William Allen, Bean, Beardsley, Beaumont, Blair, Bockee, Bodle, Boon, Bouldin, Bunch, Cage, Cambreleng, Carmichael, Carr, Casey, Chaney, Chinn, Samuel Clark, Clay, Coffee, Connor, Cramer, Davenport, Day, Dickerson, Dickinson, Dunlap, Felder, Forester, Fowler, William K. Fuller, Gholson, Gillet, Gilmer, Joseph Hall, Halsey, Hamer, Hannegan, Joseph M. Harper, Harrison, Hathaway, Hawkins, Hawes, Heath, Henderson, Abel Huntington, Inge, N. Johnson, Kavanagh, Kinnard, Lane, Lansing, Laporte, Thomas Lee, Luke Lea, Leavitt, Lyon, Lytle, Abijah Mann, John Y. Mason, Moses Mason, McDuffie, McIntire, McKay, McKim, McKinley, McVean, Miller, Muhlenberg, Murphy, Osgood, Page, Parker, Patton, Patterson, D. J. Pearce, Franklin Pierce,

Polk, Schenck, Schley, Shinn, Charles Slade, Smith, Speight, Stoddert, Sutherland, William Taylor, Francis Thomas, Thomson, Vanderpoel, Wagener, Ward, Wardwell, C. P. White—97.

NAYS—Messrs. John Quincy Adams, Heman Allen, Archer, Barber, Binney, Burges, Campbell, Chambers, Denny, Duncan, Evans, Edward Everett, Horace Everett, Ewing, Fillmore, Garland, Grayson, Griffin, Hiland Hall, Hardin, James Harper, Hazletine, Hiester, Jackson, Jarvis, William C. Johnson, King, Lewis, Lincoln, Martindale, McKennan, Mercer, Milligan, Pinckney, Potts, Reed, Rencher, Selden, William B. Shepard, Spangler, Steele, Tweedy, Vinton, Williams, Watmough, Wilde, E. D. White, F. Whitlesey, E. Whittlesey—49.

A bill regulating the value of foreign gold coins, returned from the Senate with an amendment, was taken up and the amendment concurred in.

An act compensating certain diplomatic services and for other purposes, was read a third time and passed.

A bill from the Senate, entitled an act to repeal certain provisions of an act to alter and amend the several acts imposing duties on imports, was read a third time, amended, on motion of Mr. DICKERSON, and passed.

Mr. POLK submitted the customary resolution for allowing extra compensation for the messengers of the House; which was agreed to.

A bill from the Senate for the construction and use of a lateral branch of the Baltimore and Ohio Railroad, within the District of Columbia, was taken up.

Mr. HAWES moved to postpone the consideration of the bill till the first Monday of December next; upon which

Mr. HEATH asked the yeas and nays; which were ordered.

After some remarks from Mr. H. in earnest support of the bill,

Mr. HAWES moved to lay it on the table; upon which the yeas and nays were ordered.

The question being taken, the motion to lay the bill on the table, was carried—yeas 106, nays 49.

A bill entitled an act in addition to an act for the punishment of certain crimes against the United States, was read a third time and passed.

A bill to aid in the construction of certain roads in the Territory of Michigan was taken up, and after some remarks in support of it from Mr. LYON of Michigan,

Mr. POLK moved to lay it on the table; which was negatived.

The bill was then read a third time, and passed.

A bill authorizing the President of the United States to open roads in the Territory of Arkansas, was read a third time, and passed.

The House went into Committee of the Whole on the amendment of the Senate to the bill granting pensions to certain persons therein named, (Mr. MILLAR in the chair.)

The amendments were agreed to, and reported to the House, and the House concurred in the amendments.

A bill for the relief of Hannah Stone was read a third time, and passed.

A bill for the relief of Wolcott Chauncey was read a third time, and passed.

A bill for the relief of the representatives of James P. Hainesworth was read a third time, and passed.

A bill to amend an act for the relief of William Burris was read a third time, and passed.

A bill confirming to Gilbert Hodges and Henry Masters & Co. certain lands in Missouri was read a third time, and passed.

The House went into Committee of the Whole on the state of the Union, (Mr. E. EVERETT in the chair,) on various Senate bills.

The bill to establish a port of entry at Natchez, in the State of Mississippi, was taken up.

Mr. SUTHERLAND moved an amendment establishing various ports of delivery, and extending the limits of the port of Philadelphia, &c.

The amendment was agreed to, and the bill laid aside.

The bill granting a township of land to certain exiles from Poland was taken up.

The amendments proposed by Mr. CLAY, from the Committee on Public Lands, were read; after an explanation by Mr. CLAY in support of

amendment, they were adopted, and the bill laid aside.

The bill for the better organization of the marine corps was taken up, and, having been read, was laid aside.

The bill for the settlement of claims therein mentioned, was taken up upon the amendments proposed by the Committee on Public Lands.

Some discussion took place between Messrs. WILDE, CLAY, BINNEY, and C. JOHNSON. The amendments were adopted.

The bill to regulate the pay of surgeons in the army was taken up.

Mr. McKAY moved an amendment, which was opposed by Mr. BURGES, and was adopted, and the bill laid aside.

The bill for the repair of Mars Hill military road, in the State of Maine, was taken up, read, and laid aside.

The bill to complete the road from Memphis to Little Rock was taken up, read, and laid aside.

The bill concerning the duties on lead was taken up, read, and laid aside.

The bill concerning naval pensions and the navy pension fund was taken up, read, and laid aside.

The bill authorizing the selection of certain Wabash and Erie canal lands, in the State of Ohio, was taken up, read, and laid aside.

The bill to improve the navigation of the Wabash river, was taken up, read, and laid aside.

A bill to procure a bust of Chief Justice Ellsworth, was taken up, read, and laid aside.

The committee then rose and reported the foregoing bills to the House, which were severally ordered to a third reading, excepting the bill for the settlement of certain claims therein named, relative to the Bartrop and Maison Rouge claims, in Louisiana, which, after a discussion, in which Messrs. CLAY and J. Y. MASON supported the bill, and Messrs. C. JOHNSON and BEARDS-LEY opposed it, was rejected: Yeas 64, nays 96.

Progress was reported on the bill to exempt certain imports from the operation of the act of 15th May, 1828; it remains under reference to the Committee of the Whole on the state of the Union.

A bill making appropriations for the public buildings, and grounds, and for other purposes, as amended by the Senate, came up on the question of concurrence.

The House went into Committee of the Whole on the state of the Union, on this bill, Mr. MASON in the chair. The committee rose and reported their disagreement to part of the amendment and agreement to the other, and were concurred in by the House.

A bill making appropriation for fortifications for 1834, returned from the Senate with amendments, came up on the question of concurrence.

The House went into Committee of the Whole on the state of the Union, on the amendments, Mr. WARD in the chair.

Mr. POLK moved that the House disagree with the amendment appropriating $107,000 for barracks, &c., at New Orleans, on the ground that no estimate had been furnished from the proper authority; which was carried without a division.

The other amendments were agreed to, and the bill reported to the House; when the proceedings of the committee were concurred in.

The House then went into committee on various private bills from the Senate, (Mr. MASON in the chair,) which were gone through with, and reported to the House, and read a third time.

A bill for the relief of Thomas Rhodes and Jeremiah Austill, was rejected.

A bill for the relief of John A. Webster, and the legal representatives of John H. Morton, was passed.

A bill to increase the salary of the collector of the port of Franklin, District of ———, was passed.

A bill for the relief of the widow of Clement B. Penrose, was passed.

A bill granting a tract of land to General Philemon Thomas, was passed.

A bill for the relief of William Mann was passed.

A bill authorizing a sum of money to be distributed among the officers and crew of the late private armed brig Gen. Armstrong, was passed.

A bill for the relief of George Read, was passed.

A bill for the relief of John Kirkpatrick, was passed.

A bill for the relief of Phineas Sprague and others was passed.

A bill for the relief of the representatives of Thomas H. Boyles was passed.

A bill to confirm the selection and survey of two sections of land to Francis Lafontaine & Son was passed.

A bill for the relief of Lawrence Milligan was passed.

A bill for the relief of James Fife was passed.

A bill for the relief of Hugh McGinnis was passed.

A bill for the relief of Peter Mills was passed.

A bill for changing the term of the district court for the western district of Louisiana was passed.

A bill authorizing the Governors of the several States to transmit by mail certain books and documents, was read a third time and passed.

A bill for the relief of Andrew Armstrong was passed.

A bill to remunerate Stephen C. Phillips, &c., was read a third time and passed.

A bill for the relief of Elizabeth Robinson, daughter of Lieutenant Richard Wilde, deceased, was read a third time and rejected.

Mr. J. Q. ADAMS notified the House that the Senate had adjourned to meet early on Monday morning, and that it was now nearly twelve o'clock. He moved that the House, when it adjourns, adjourn to meet at nine o'clock on Monday morning; which was agreed to.

Mr. CAMBRELENG called the attention of the House to the mass of business now before it, and to the necessity of having a quorum on Monday morning.

Mr. E. WHITTLESEY moved that two be added to the special post office committee; which was agreed to.

Mr. J. Q. ADAMS moved that the House do now adjourn; which was negatived.

Mr. WARD, of New York, submitted a resolution for the payment of the Chaplain of the House an additional compensation of one hundred dollars, on account of the length of the session.

A motion was then made that the House adjourn; which was lost, no quorum voting.

The bill for the relief of the sureties of John H. Morton was read a third time and passed.

The bill for the relief of John McConkey was read a third time and passed.

Mr. ADAMS moved that the House do now adjourn. Lost.

A bill for the relief of the administrators of Captain Paschal Hickman was taken up, and laid on the table.

A bill for the relief of Thomas Fillebrown, jr., was read a third time, and, on its passage, rejected.

A bill for the relief of the heirs of John Rose, deceased, was read a third time and passed.

Mr. HALL, of Maine, moved that the House do now adjourn. Lost.

A bill for the relief of Hishe Homa, alias Capt. Redpepper, was read a third time, and passed.

Mr. ADAMS, when the question was taken, objected that gentlemen voted on both sides.

Mr. J. Q. ADAMS moved that the House do now adjourn; which was negatived.

Mr. A. gave notice that, on Monday morning, he should move a call of the House, and require the absentees to be noted.

Mr. ASHLEY stated that he should be here on Monday morning, and in the meantime, should interpose no obstacle to the business of the House.

A bill for the relief of Col. A. R. Woolley was read a third time, and passed.

A bill for the relief of the administrators of Rolitha Laws, deceased, was read a third time, and passed.

A bill for the relief of Charles J. Hand was read a third time, and passed.

A bill for the relief of the Roman Catholic church in St. Louis, Missouri, was read a third time.

Mr. POLK moved to lay the bill on the table; upon which it was found that a quorum had not voted.

Mr. E. EVERETT moved that the House do now adjourn. Lost.

Mr. ASHLEY moved to postpone the further consideration of the bill till Monday. Agreed to.

The bill for the relief of John Chandler and William Johnson, was read a third time, and passed.

The bill for the relief of William Doer and others, trustees of Sarah Alexander, deceased, was read a third time and passed.

The bill for the relief of Aaron Fitzgerald, was read a third time, and passed.

The bill for the relief of Moses Archer was read a third time, and passed.

The bill for the relief of Philip Moore was read a third time, and passed.

The bill authorizing a sum of money to be distributed among the officers and crew of the late privateer armed brig General Armstrong was read a third time, and passed.

The bill confirming certain land claims in the State of Missouri, and for other purposes, was read a third time.

Mr. E. WHITTLESEY called for an explanation of its provisions, when some remarks were made by Messrs. ASHLEY, CAVE JOHNSON, MASON, GARLAND, and PLUMMER; when Mr. WARDWELL moved to lay the bill on the table; which was carried.

The bill for the relief of the representatives of Philip Moore was passed.

The bill for the relief of Stephen Pleasonton was rejected.

A bill to provide for the compensation of the Governor and judges of Michigan Territory, for certain services, in adjusting land titles at Detroit, was rejected.

A bill for the relief of William D. Acken was passed.

A bill for the relief of the representatives of Francis Nash was passed.

A bill for the relief of the widow and heirs of Captain William Royall, deceased, was passed.

A bill for the relief of John Peck was passed.

A bill for the relief of James Ord was passed.

The bill for the relief of Jonathan M. Blundel was passed.

The bill for the relief of James Noble, was passed.

The amendment of the Senate to the bill for the relief of Thomas Minor, was concurred in.

The House then adjourned.

IN SENATE.

MONDAY, June 30, 1834.

The bill to regulate the trade and intercourse with Indian tribes was amended, read a third time, and passed.

The following bills, which had passed the Senate, were returned by the House with amendments; which were concurred in:

A bill for the relief of John A. Webster;

A bill for the relief of P. Sprague and others;

A bill for the relief of Clement B. Penrose;

A bill for the relief of Gen. McGinniS;

A bill for the relief of James Fife, a Creek Indian;

A bill for the relief of George Read;

A bill for the relief of Andrew Armstrong;

A bill for the relief of William Mann;

A bill for the relief of the owners and crew of the privateer General Armstrong.

The resolution submitted by Mr. SOUTHARD, to authorize the Committee on Finance to sit during the recess, for the purpose of investigating the affairs of the Bank of the United States, and for other purposes, was considered and adopted by the following vote:

YEAS—Messrs. Bibb, Chambers, Clay, Ewing, Frelinghuysen, Knight, Leigh, Mangum, Moore, Naudain, Poindexter, Porter, Robbins, Silsbee, Smith, Southard, Sprague, Tomlinson, Waggaman, Webster—20.

NAYS—Messrs. Grundy, Hendricks, Hill, Kane, King of Alabama, King of Georgia, Robinson, Shepley, Tallmadge, Tipton, White, and Wright—12.

On motion of Mr. WRIGHT, the Senate proceeded to the consideration of the bill for the improvement of the navigation of the Hudson river, in New York.

Some conversation ensued, in which Messrs. WRIGHT, CALHOUN, TOMLINSON, WEBSTER, SMITH, and TALLMADGE, participated.

Mr. CALHOUN moved to lay the bill on the table, and asked for the yeas and nays; which were ordered, and are as follows:

YEAS—Messrs. Benton, Bibb, Black, Calhoun, Grundy, Hill, King of Georgia, Leigh, Linn, Mangum, Moore, Preston, Shepley, Tyler, and White—15.

NAYS—Messrs. Clay, Ewing, Frelinghuysen, Hendricks, Kane, Knight, Naudain, Poindexter, Robbins, Robinson, Silsbee, Smith, Southard, Tallmadge, Tipton, Tomlinson, Waggaman, Webster, and Wright—19.

The bill was then read a third time, and passed by the following vote:

YEAS—Messrs. Clay, Ewing, Frelinghuysen, Grundy, Hendricks, Kane, Naudain, Poindexter, Robbins, Robinson, Silsbee, Smith, Southard, Sprague, Tallmadge, Tipton, Tomlinson, Waggaman, Webster, Wilkins, and Wright—21.

NAYS—Messrs. Bibb, Black, Calhoun, Hill, King of Alabama, King of Georgia, Leigh, Linn, Mangum, Moore, Preston, Robinson, Tyler, and White—14.

On motion of Mr. FRELINGHUYSEN, the vote upon the bill to regulate the trade and intercourse with the Indian tribes was reconsidered, amended by crossing an officer to be called the Superintendent of the Western Territory, and passed.

The bill for the relief of the owners of the schooner Admiral was read a third time, and passed.

Mr. WILKINS, from the Committee on Foreign Relations, made a report, the nature of which was not stated; and, on motion of Mr. CHAMBERS, it was ordered to be printed.

The bill to carry into effect the fourth article of the treaty with the Creek Indians, so far as regards the claims of Georgia, was read the third time and passed.

The bill appropriating 500,000 acres of land to satisfy the claims of the officers and soldiers of the Virginia Continental Line was taken up.

A debate of some length ensued, in which Messrs. TYLER, CLAY, LEIGH, HENDRICKS, PRESTON, BIBB, KNIGHT, and CALHOUN, participated.

On motion of Mr. HENDRICKS, the bill was laid upon the table by the following vote:

YEAS—Messrs. Black, Clay, Ewing, Frelinghuysen, Hendricks, Hill, King of Alabama, King of Georgia, Knight, Naudain, Porter, Robbins, Shepley, Silsbee, Smith, Sprague, Tallmadge, Tipton, and Tomlinson—19.

NAYS—Messrs. Benton, Bibb, Calhoun, Grundy, Kane, Kent, Leigh, Linn, Mangum, Moore, Poindexter, Preston, Robinson, Tyler, and White —15.

The following bills were considered in Committee of the Whole, and subsequently read a third time and passed:

A bill to renew the patent of Thomas Blanchard;

A bill for the relief of Ezekiel Foster & Co., of Eastport, State of Maine;

A bill for the relief, in part, of the crew of the brig Sarah George;

A bill for the relief of Francis and Judith Taylor;

A bill for the relief of Atwater & Daggett, and others, owners of the brig Hannah.

The Senate agreed to a conference with the House relative to the disagreement on the amendments offered to the bill constructing a bridge across the river Potomac. Messrs. CHAMBERS, TOMLINSON, and KING of Georgia, were appointed the committee on the part of the Senate.

The following bills were read a third time and passed:

A bill for the relief of John Wilson;

A bill to refund the extra tonnage duties paid on the brig Liberator;

A bill to refund to certain owners of the schooner Joseph and Mary the sum paid into the treasury by reason of the condemnation of said vessel;

A bill for the relief of the heirs of James Bell, deceased;

A bill to authorize the sale of lots in the town of St. Marks, in Florida;

A bill to authorize Edmund Brooke, of Georgetown, to remove two slaves into the District of Columbia.

On motion of Mr. SILSBEE,

The Senate proceeded to the consideration of the

bill authorizing the construction of light-houses, and placing buoys in certain rivers and harbors.

Several amendments reported by the Committee on Commerce were adopted, when the bill was read a third time, and passed.

A bill for the relief of the legal representatives of Leonard Holley, deceased;

A bill for the relief of James March;

A bill for the relief of George Gordon, assignee and representative of the heirs of Matthew Ramsey, deceased;

A bill to authorize the Secretary of the Treasury to grant the right of way in a certain case in the city of New York;

A bill repealing certain acts of the Legislative Council of Florida, and adding two delegates thereto;

A bill to increase the salaries of the judges of the United States in the Territories of Michigan, Arkansas, and Florida;

A bill for the relief of Amos W. Brown;

A bill for the relief of Samuel A. Edmonson;

A bill to authorize a road to be cut out in the Territory of Florida;

A bill to mark out and open a road from Columbia to Little Rock, in Arkansas Territory;

A bill to authorize an extra session of the Legislative Council of the Territory of Michigan;

A bill to authorize the purchase of live oak frames for a frigate and sloop of war, and for other purposes;

A bill to authorize the President of the United States to make a transfer of appropriations in the naval service under certain circumstances, and for other purposes;

A bill to authorize the Secretary of the Navy to make experiments for the safety of steam engines;

A bill to provide for the rebuilding of the frigate Congress;

A bill supplementary to an act concerning copyrights;

A bill to complete the improvements on the Pennsylvania Avenue;

A bill concerning tonnage duty on Spanish vessels;

A bill authorizing the legal representatives of James Latham, deceased, to withdraw and relocate a land warrant;

A bill granting compensation for certain diplomatic services, and for other purposes;

A bill forbidding the corporations of Washington, Alexandria, and Georgetown, in the District of Columbia, from issuing any promissory notes under the denomination of $10, and for the gradual withdrawal of the present circulation of corporation notes;

A bill relinquishing the reversionary interest of the United States in certain Indian reservations between the rivers Mississippi and Des Moines;

A bill to provide for the payment of claims for property lost, captured, or destroyed by the enemy, while in the military service of the United States, during the late war with Great Britain, and the Indian wars subsequent thereto, and for other purposes;

Were severally read a third time, and passed.

A message upon executive business was received from the President of the United States, by Mr. Donelson, his Private Secretary.

Mr. CHAMBERS, from the committee on conference on the bill relative to the Washington bridge, made a report that the joint committee had agreed to a compromise; which was concurred in by the Senate.

The following bills were laid upon the table:

A bill for the relief of the heirs of Peter Albin;

A bill for the survey of certain rivers and roads, and the improvement of certain harbors in Michigan Territory;

A bill for the relief of the heirs and legal representatives of Captain William Thornton;

A bill for the relief of Maria Brooke;

A bill to regulate the public deposites in State banks;

A bill to establish the northern boundary line of the country purchased of the Chickasaws;

A bill making appropriations for the erection of marine hospitals at Baltimore and other places.

The resolution submitted by Mr. Preston, calling for information relative to pensions, was considered and rejected.

The resolution empowering the chairman of the Committee on Public Lands to issue commissions for taking depositions in alleged frauds in the land office, during the recess of Congress, was considered, and an amendment offered by Mr. Wright, changing the character of the inquiries, was negatived by the following vote:

YEAS—Messrs. Benton, Black, Grundy, Hendricks, Hill, Kane, King of Alabama, King of Georgia, Linn, Robinson, Shepley, Tallmadge, Tipton, White, Wright—15.

NAYS—Messrs. Bibb, Calhoun, Chambers, Clay, Ewing, Frelinghuysen, Kent, Knight, Mangum, Moore, Poindexter, Porter, Prentiss, Smith, Southard, Sprague, Tomlinson, Waggaman, Webster—19.

The resolution was then agreed to, without a division.

The resolution submitted by Mr. Moore, calling for information from the War Department, was agreed to.

The several standing committees, on motion made by their several chairmen, were discharged from the further consideration of subjects referred to them.

On motion of Mr. BENTON, the communication from the Secretary of the Treasury relative to the amount of specie imported into the United States, was ordered to be printed.

The bill incorporating the Colombian Horticultural Society of the District of Columbia, was laid upon the table.

Mr. HENDRICKS presented a memorial of certain citizens of Indiana, in favor of a restoration of the deposites to the Bank of the United States, and the recharter of that institution; which was ordered to be printed.

The bill for the relief of Samuel Armstrong Bailey, was read a third time and passed.

The resolution authorizing the printing of the Executive Journal of the old Congress, was laid upon the table.

The resolution calling for information from the War Department, relative to pensioners, and which had been rejected during the morning, was, on motion of Mr. FRELINGHUYSEN, reconsidered and adopted.

The resolution authorizing the purchase of six copies of Elliot's American Diplomatic Code, was agreed to.

The following resolution, submitted by Mr. BIBB, was considered and agreed to:

Resolved, That the use of the report made to the Senate from the Department of State, in obedience to the resolution of the Senate of the 23d of March, 1834, be referred to the Department of State, for the purpose of completing the statistical report, by States and Territories; and that, from time to time, as the same shall be arranged by States and Territories, that the Secretary of State transmit the parts to the Secretary of the Senate, to be printed.

Mr. BENTON submitted a resolution to expunge the resolutions of Mr. Clay, with regard to the removal of the deposites, passed in March last, the consideration of which (being objected to) was postponed to the next session.

The Senate, at half past three o'clock, proceeded to the consideration of executive business, and spent upwards of two hours therein.

When the doors were opened—

Mr. BENTON asked leave to withdraw the following bills:

The bill to graduate the price of public lands, referred to the Committee on Public Lands 18th December, 1833, and

The bill to grant a township of land to Louisiana, Indiana, Illinois, and Missouri, referred to the Committee on Public Lands February 6, 1834.

Leave was refused.

The yeas and nays having been demanded, were ordered, and are as follows:

YEAS—Messrs. Benton, Hendricks, Hill, Kane, Linn, Robinson, Shepley, Tallmadge, Tipton, White, Wright—11.

NAYS—Messrs. Bibb, Black, Calhoun, Chambers, Clay, Frelinghuysen, Kent, Knight, Leigh, Mangum, Poindexter, Porter, Preston, Robbins, Silsbee, Smith, Southard, Sprague, Tomlinson, Webster—20.

Mr. GRUNDY, from the committee appointed to wait on the President of the United States, reported that the committee had discharged that duty

and that they had been informed by the President that he had signed all the bills presented to him with the exception of the bill for the improvement of the Wabash river, and that he should hold that bill up for future advisement, and if constitutional objections did not intervene, he should sign the bill within the time allowed by law, and that he had no further communication to make.

The two Houses having exchanged the usual messages,

On motion of Mr. GRUNDY,
The Senate then adjourned, *sine die.*

HOUSE OF REPRESENTATIVES.

Monday, June 30, 1834.

The following was announced as the special committee for the investigation of the Post Office Department: Messrs. Connor, Polk, E. Whittlesey, H. Everett, Beardsley, Waymough, and Hawes.

Mr. SELDEN presented memorials from Osego and Tompkins counties, in New York, on the subject of the currency. Laid on the table.

Mr. SELDEN, from the Committee on Commerce, to which was referred the memorials praying authority by law to import spirits in casks of a smaller size than those now allowed by law, and to divide the same into smaller casks for exportation, without losing the debenture, reported that the committee was favorable to the object of the memorials, and would report all accordingly at the next session, if it should be found practicable to guard the revenue.

Mr. J. Q. ADAMS moved that the Committee on Manufactures be discharged from all further consideration of the subjects committed to it; which was agreed to.

On motion of Mr. POLK, the Committee of Ways and Means were discharged from the further consideration of all business referred to it.

Several private bills which had passed the House, and been returned with amendments from the Senate, were taken up, and the amendments concurred in.

The House took up for consideration the bill from the Senate granting lands to the Polish exiles, together with the amendments of the House to the same, requiring that the Government price of the land should be paid by the grantees at the end of ten years, in which amendment the Senate had refused to concur.

A debate arose upon this bill; and after an ineffectual motion to lay it on the table,

Mr. McKIM moved the previous question; which was seconded.

The main question, which was on the motion to insist, was then ordered to be put, and being taken by yeas and nays, was determined in the affirmative: Yeas 88, nays 62.

So the House insisted on their amendment.

The bill authorizing the construction of a bridge across the Potomac, and repealing all laws passed in relation thereto, came up on the question of concurrence with the amendment of the Senate, which strikes out the second section, providing for the construction of a bridge at an expense not exceeding $130,000, and instead of making an appropriation directly for the indemnity of Mr. Dibble on a settlement by the Secretary of the Treasury, provides that a report shall be made on the subject to the next session of Congress.

Mr. MERCER made an explanation on the subject, and moved that the House disagree to that part of the amendment striking out the second section, and concur in the balance, with an amendment which he proposed.

The question having been divided, the House disagreed to the striking out the second section.

A debate arose upon the balance of the amendment, in which Messrs. FILLMORE, MERCER, E. WHITTLESEY, A. MANN, PEYTON, STEWART, J. HARPER, CHINN, and CHAMBERS, took part; when,

Mr. WARDWELL moved the previous question; which was sustained.

The question of concurrence was then taken, and negatived: yeas 46, nays 87.

So the House disagreed to the whole amendment.

Mr. POLK said he perceived, from reading the journal this morning, that he was placed as a member of the Select Committee appointed to sit during the recess of Congress to examine into the condition of the General Post Office. Mr. P. said he had never shrunk from the performance of any duty assigned to him since he had been a member of the House. It was well known to the House that he had, during the present session, been a member of a most laborious committee, the duties of which he attempted to perform. He had been at all times willing to give his whole time and attention, while Congress was in session, to the business of the House. This committee was, however, to sit at Washington during the recess. The state of his private affairs, he said, would render it very inconvenient for him to be at Washington earlier than the meeting of the next session of Congress. He must, therefore, respectfully ask the favor of the House to excuse him from serving as a member of this committee.

Mr. P. was excused accordingly.

On motion of Mr. E. WHITTLESEY, the House went into committee upon the bill for the relief of John Shackford, Mr. Ward in the chair.

The bill was taken up, read, reported without amendment, read a third time and passed.

The SPEAKER laid before the House a communication from the Postmaster General in answer to resolutions of inquiry; which, on motion of Mr. CONNOR, was laid on the table.

Amendments made by the Senate to several bills, were concurred in.

The Senate having requested a conference upon the bill relating to Washington bridge, Messrs. MERCER, FILLMORE, and W. C. JOHNSON, were appointed managers on the part of the House.

On motion of Mr. ASHLEY, the bill for the relief of the Roman Catholic Church, St. Louis, Missouri, was taken up, and after debate, in which Messrs. HARDIN, PARKER, and JOHN Q. ADAMS, took part—

Mr. PARKER moved to lay it on the table; which was negatived.

Mr. POLK opposed the bill upon the principle laid down by Mr. Madison in his veto message in 1811, which he read.

Mr. HARDIN read the act of 1833, remitting duties on articles imported by Bishop Flaget, of Bairdstown.

The bill was supported by Messrs. SUTHERLAND, CAMBRELENG, HORACE EVERETT, BURD, J. Q. ADAMS, BEARDSLEY, and opposed by Mr. POLK—

When the previous question was ordered.

Mr. POLK demanded the yeas and nays on the passage of the bill; which were ordered.

The bill was passed: Yeas 67, nays 58.

Mr. ASHLEY moved that the House take up the bill confirming land claims in the State of Missouri, and for other purposes; which was negatived.

The amendments of the Senate to the light-house bill being taken up for consideration were severally concurred in.

The amendments of conference, to which was referred the disagreement between the two Houses in regard to the bill for the continuation of the Potomac bridge, reported in favor of insisting upon the disagreement of the House to the amendment, striking out the second section of the bill, and of concurring in the other amendment; which report was agreed to.

Mr. H. EVERETT moved to take up the resolution granting the Chaplain of Congress additional compensation of an hundred dollars; which was agreed to.

The order of the House for recess from two to four o'clock, was, on motion, rescinded.

Mr. HIESTER offered a resolution requiring the Clerk of the House to compile certain information relating to canals, &c.; which was rejected.

Mr. JARVIS moved a call of the House; which was ordered.

It appeared that 88 members only were present.

Mr. CLAY moved that all further proceeding in the call be suspended. It was out of order, in his opinion, to enforce a call of the House on the last day of the session. The call was suspended.

Mr. J. Q. ADAMS moved a call of the House; and supported the motion at length; and

Mr. WILLIAMS followed on the same side.

Mr. CLAY explained his views in opposition to the motion; and was followed by

Mr. E. WHITTLESEY on the same side.

Mr. HARDIN contended that the House could do nothing without a quorum.

Messrs. BAYLIES and DUNCAN made some brief remarks against the motion for a call, when

Mr. HAWES said gentlemen had been anxious for opportunities for making speeches during the whole session. He hoped any gentleman having that desire would now proceed.

Mr. ADAMS said he accepted the invitation, and accordingly went into an extended disquisition upon the duties of members of Congress; insisting, in the course of his remarks, that whenever a quorum appeared, so that the House could proceed to business, he would take his seat. When he had concluded, some remarks were made by Mr. CLAY, and

Mr. ADAMS withdrew the motion for a call.

The question was taken on the amendment to the bill providing for payment for property lost and destroyed in the late Indian campaign; which was concurred in.

The amendments made by the Senate to the bill to complete the improvements on Pennsylvania Avenue, came up.

The amendments were concurred in.

The amendments to the bill imposing a tonnage duty on Spanish vessels, were agreed to.

The bill for the relief of Samuel Armstrong Bailey came up on the amendment of the Senate; which was concurred in.

On motion of Mr. JARVIS, it was

Resolved, That a committee be appointed on the part of the House, to join such committee as might be appointed on the part of the Senate, to wait upon the President, and inform him, that if he had no further communication to make to them, the two Houses, having completed their business, are ready to close the session by an adjournment.

Mr. FULTON, from the Committee appointed on the part of the House, reported that the committee had, in pursuance of the resolution, waited on the President, who had informed them that he had signed all the bills presented to him, excepting that for the improvement of the Wabash river; respecting which he made the following statement:

The bill entitled an act to improve the navigation of the Wabash river has been presented to me at so late a period of the session, with so many others that call for immediate action, that I have not been able to give to it the full consideration which its importance merits. I have strong doubts whether I can approve this bill consistently with the opinions I entertain as to the power of the Government on subjects of this description; but my respect for the decision of the two Houses of Congress, and for the large body of my fellow-citizens who are interested in this improvement, induces me to hold the bill for the present, that I may, during the period allowed to me by the Constitution for that purpose, give to it the most careful and deliberate consideration; and that he had no further communications to make during the present session.

The House then adjourned, to meet on the first Monday of December next.

This number concludes the "Congressional Globe" for the first session of the 23d Congress. It will be published again the next session for the same price; namely, weekly during the session, for *one dollar a copy, in advance.* The next session being limited to three months, we can afford to print some extra numbers, containing a few leading speeches on the most important subjects that may be discussed. At the end of the next session an Index will be made to both sessions, and sent to all who may subscribe for it during the second session.

THE

CONGRESSIONAL GLOBE,

CONTAINING

SKETCHES OF THE DEBATES AND PROCEEDINGS

OF THE

TWENTY-THIRD CONGRESS.

BLAIR & RIVES, EDITORS.

SECOND SESSION......VOLUME II.

CITY OF WASHINGTON:
PRINTED AT THE GLOBE OFFICE FOR THE EDITORS.

1835.

INDEX

TO THE SECOND VOLUME OF THE CONGRESSIONAL GLOBE.

SENATE.

HOUSE OF REPRESENTATIVES.

CONGRESSIONAL GLOBE.

BY BLAIR & RIVES. ——WEEKLY—— PRICE $1 A SESSION.

2d Sess........23d Cong.   MONDAY, DECEMBER 8, 1834.   Volume 2........No. 1.

TWENTY-THIRD CONGRESS:

SECOND SESSION.

IN SENATE.

Monday, December 1, 1834.

This being the day fixed by the Constitution for the meeting of both Houses of Congress,

The VICE PRESIDENT took the Chair and called the Senate to order.

A quorum of members being present—

Mr. WHITE submitted the following motion:

Ordered, That the Secretary acquaint the House of Representatives that a quorum of the Senate is assembled and ready to proceed to business; which was agreed to.

Mr. WHITE submitted the following resolution:

Resolved, That a Committee be appointed, on the part of the Senate, to join such committee as may be appointed by the House of Representatives, to wait on the President of the United States, and inform him that Congress is ready to receive any communication he may be pleased to make. The resolution was agreed to.

Mr. CLAY then moved that the Senate waive balloting for the committee, and that the Presiding Officer appoint the same; which was agreed to; and Messrs. WHITE and SWIFT were appointed.

Mr. KNIGHT offered the following resolution, which lies one day on the table:

Resolved, That each Senator be supplied, during the present session, with three such newspapers, printed in any of the States, as he may choose, provided the same be furnished at the usual rate for the annual charge of such papers; and provided, also, that if any Senator shall choose to take any newspapers other than daily papers, he shall be supplied with as many such papers as shall not exceed the price of three daily papers.

Mr. GRUNDY, from the Committee on the Post Office and Post Roads, offered the following resolution:

Resolved, That the 34th Rule of the Senate, so far as respects the Committee on the Post Office and Post Roads, be suspended; and that the present Committee on the Post Office and Post Roads be continued, with all the powers vested in them, and subject to all the duties enjoined on them, by the resolution of the Senate of the 28th day of June, 1834

Mr. GRUNDY remarked, that the resolution was one which he could find no precedent to sanction. But he offered it at this time, owing to the peculiar situation of the committee. They had been assiduously engaged, for some time past, collecting testimony and other evidence connected with their duties, but they would not be able to make a satisfactory report for some time to come. Some of the witnesses for examination would be here to-morrow, and he was therefore desirous that the Senate should suspend the rule which requires the Standing Committees to be balloted for at the commencement of each session, so far as the same applies to the Committee on the Post Office. He asked the immediate consideration of the resolution; which was agreed to, and it was then adopted.

A message was received from the House of Representatives, by Mr. FRANKLIN, their Clerk, stating that a quorum of members of that House was present, and that a Committee had been appointed to join the Senate Committee, for the purpose of informing the President of the United States that the two Houses were organized, and ready to receive their communications.

The Senate then adjourned.

HOUSE OF REPRESENTATIVES.

Monday, December 1, 1834.

At 12 o'clock the Speaker took the Chair, and called the House to order.

The Clerk then proceeded to call the Roll,

whereupon the following members answered to their names:

Maine.

Joseph Hall.   Rufus McIntire.
Leonard Jarvis.   Gorham Parks.
Edward Kavanagh.   Francis O. J. Smith.

New Hampshire.

Benning M. Bean.   Henry Hubbard.
Robert Burns.   Franklin Pierce.
Joseph M. Harper.

Massachusetts.

John Quincy Adams.   Edward Everett.
Isaac C. Bates.   George Grennell, Jr.
William Baylies.   Gayton P. Osgood.
George N. Briggs.   John Reed.

Rhode Island.

Dutee J. Pearce.

Connecticut.

Noyes Barber.   Samuel Tweedy.

Vermont.

Horace Everett.   William Slade.
Hiland Hall.

New York.

John Adams.   Gerrit Y. Lansing.
Samuel Beardsley.   George W. Lay.
Abraham Beckee.   Abijah Mann, Jr.
John W. Brown.   Henry C. Martindale.
C. C. Cambreleng.   Charles McVean.
Samuel Clark.   Henry Mitchell.
John Cramer.   Sherman Page.
Rowland Day.   Job Pierson.
John Dickson.   William Taylor.
Millard Fillmore.   Joel Terrill.
William K. Fuller.   Aaron Vanderpoel.
Ransom H. Gillett.   Isaac B. Van Houten.
Nicoll Halsey.   Aaron Ward.
Gideon Hard.   Daniel Wardwell.
Samuel C. Hathaway.   Reuben Whallon.
Abel Huntingdon.   Campbell P. White.
Noadiah Johnson.

New Jersey.

Philemon Dickerson.   James Parker.
Thomas Lee.   Ferdinand S. Schenck.

Pennsylvania.

Joseph B. Anthony.   Henry King.
Charles A. Barnitz.   John Laporte.
Andrew Beaumont.   Thos. M. T. McKennan.
Horace Binney.   Joel K. Mann.
George Chambers.   Jesse Miller.
William Clark.   Henry A. Muhlenberg.
Edward Darlington.   David Potts, Jr.
Harmer Denny.   Robert Ramsay.
James Harper.   Joel B. Sutherland.
Samuel S. Harrison.   David D. Wagener.
William Hiester.   John G. Watmough.
Joseph Henderson.

Delaware.

John J. Milligan.

Maryland.

James P. Heath.   John T. Stoddert.
William Cost Johnson.   Francis Thomas.
Isaac McKim.   James Turner.

Virginia.

John J. Allen.   William McComas.
James M. H. Beale.   Charles F. Mercer.
Nathaniel H. Claiborne.   Samuel McD. Moore.
Thomas Davenport.   John M. Patton.
William F. Gordon.   William P. Taylor.
George Loyall.   Edgar C. Wilson.
Edward Lucas.

North Carolina.

Daniel L. Barringer.   Abraham Rencher.
Henry W. Connor.   William B. Shepard.
Edmund Deberry.   Augustine H. Shepperd.
Thomas H. Hall.   Jesse Speight.
Micajah T. Hawkins.   Lewis Williams.
James McKay.

South Carolina.

William K. Clowney.   John K. Griffin.
William J. Grayson.   Henry L. Pinckney.

Georgia.

Augustin S. Clayton.   George R. Gilmer.
John Coffee.   William Schley.
Thomas F. Foster.   James M. Wayne.
Roger L. Gamble.   Richard H. Wilde.

Kentucky.

Chilton Allan.   Richard M. Johnson.
Martin Beaty.   James Love.
Thomas Chilton.   Chittenden Lyon.
Amos Davis.   Thomas A. Marshall.
Benjamin Hardin.   Patrick H. Pope.
Albert G. Hawes.   Christopher Tompkins.

Tennessee.

Samuel Bunch.   Cave Johnson.
David W. Dickinson.   Luke Lea.
William C. Dunlap.   James K. Polk.
John B. Forrester.   James Standifer.
William M. Inge.

Ohio.

James M. Bell.   Jonathan Sloane.
John Chaney.   David Spangler.
Benjamin Jones.   John Thomson.
Jeremiah McLene.   Joseph Vance.
Robert Mitchell.   Samuel F. Vinton.
William Patterson.   Elisha Whittlesey.

Louisiana.

Philemon Thomas.

Indiana.

Ratliff Boon.   George L. Kinnard.
John Carr.   Amos Lane.
John Ewing.   Jonathan McCarty.

Mississippi.

Harry Cage.

Illinois.

Zadok Casey.

Alabama.

Clement C. Clay.   John McKinley.
Samuel W. Mardis.

Missouri.

William H. Ashley.   John Bull.

The following members severally appeared, were sworn, and took their seats:

Massachusetts—S. C. Phillips.

Connecticut—E. Jackson, P. Miner, J. Trumbull.

New York—C. G. Ferris, J. J. Morgan.

Virginia—J. Robertson.

Kentucky—R. P. Letcher.

Ohio—D. Kilgore.

Louisiana—H. Johnson.

Illinois—W. L. May, J. Reynolds.

A message was received from the Senate, informing the House that a quorum of the Senate had assembled, and were ready to proceed to business.

On motion of Mr. McKINLEY, the following resolutions were adopted:

Resolved, That a message be sent to the Senate, informing that body that a quorum of the House of Representatives has assembled, and that the House is ready to proceed to business.

Resolved, That a Committee be appointed on the part of this House, jointly with such Committee as may be appointed by the Senate, to wait on the President of the United States, and inform him that a quorum of the two Houses is assembled, and that they are ready to receive any communication he may be pleased to make.

The SPEAKER appointed Messrs. McKINLEY and LANSING, on the part of the House.

The usual resolutions for furnishing the members with newspapers, and with regard to the hour of meeting, were adopted.

On motion of Mr. CONNOR,

The House adjourned.

IN SENATE.

Tuesday, December 2, 1834.

The Hon. Mr. MORRIS, one of the Senators from Ohio, appeared, and took his seat.

Mr. WHITE, from the Committee appointed to wait upon the President of the United States, in conjunction with a similar Committee from the House of Representatives, to inform him that the two Houses of Congress were organized, and ready to receive any communication he may be pleased to make, reported that they had performed the duty assigned to them, and that the President gave information that he would make a communication to both Houses this day at 12 o'clock.

The following Message was then received from the President of the United States, by A. J. Donelson, Esquire, his Private Secretary:

Fellow-citizens of the Senate
and House of Representatives:

In performing my duty at the opening of your present session, it gives me pleasure to congratulate you again upon the prosperous condition of our beloved country. Divine Providence has favored us with general health, with rich rewards in the fields of agriculture and in every branch of labor, and with peace to cultivate and extend the various resources which employ the virtue and enterprise of our citizens. Let us trust that, in surveying a scene so flattering to our free institutions, our joint deliberations to preserve them may be crowned with success.

Our foreign relations continue, with but few exceptions, to maintain the favorable aspect which they bore in my last annual message, and promise to extend those advantages which the principles that regulate our intercourse with other nations are so well calculated to secure.

The question of the northeastern boundary is still pending with Great Britain, and the proposition made in accordance with the resolution of the Senate for the establishment of a line according to the treaty of 1783, has not been accepted by that government. Believing that every disposition is felt on both sides to adjust this perplexing question to the satisfaction of all the parties interested in it, the hope is yet indulged that it may be effected on the basis of that proposition.

With the Governments of Austria, Russia, Prussia, Holland, Sweden, and Denmark, the best understanding exists. Commerce, with all, is fostered and protected by reciprocal good will, under the sanction of liberal conventional or legal provisions.

In the midst of her internal difficulties, the Queen of Spain has ratified the Convention for the payment of the claims of our citizens arising since 1819. It is in the course of execution on her part, and a copy of it is now laid before you for such legislation as may be found necessary to enable those interested to derive the benefits of it.

Yielding to the force of circumstances, and to the wise counsels of time and experience, that power has finally resolved no longer to occupy the unnatural position in which she stood to the new governments established in this hemisphere. I have the great satisfaction of stating to you that in preparing the way for the restoration of harmony between those who have sprung from the same ancestors, who are allied by common interests, profess the same religion, and speak the same language, the United States have been actively instrumental. Our efforts to effect this good work, will be persevered in while they are deemed useful to the parties, and our entire disinterestedness continues to be felt and understood. The act of Congress to countervail the discriminating duties, levied to the prejudice of our navigation, in Cuba and Porto Rico, has been transmitted to the Minister of the United States at Madrid, to be communicated to the Government of the Queen. No intelligence of its receipt has yet reached the Department of State. If the present condition of the country permits the Government to make a careful and enlarged examination of the true interests of these important portions of its dominions, no doubt is entertained that their future intercourse with the United States will be placed upon a more just and liberal basis.

The Florida archives have not yet been selected and delivered. Recent orders have been sent to the agent of the United States at Havana, to return with all that he can obtain, so that they may be in Washington before the session of the Supreme Court, to be used in the legal questions there pending, to which the Government is a party.

Internal tranquillity is happily restored to Portugal. The distracted state of the country rendered unavoidable the postponement of a final payment of the just claims of our citizens. Our diplomatic relations will be soon resumed, and the long subsisting friendship with that Power affords the strongest guarantee that the balance due will receive prompt attention.

The first instalment due under the convention of indemnity with the King of the Two Sicilies, has been duly received, and an offer has been made to extinguish the whole by a prompt payment—an offer I did not consider myself authorized to accept, as the indemnification provided is the exclusive property of individual citizens of the United States. The original adjustment of our claims, and the anxiety displayed to fulfil at once the stipulations made for the payment of them, are highly honorable to the Government of the Two Sicilies. When it is recollected that they were the result of the injustice of an intrusive power, temporarily dominant in its territory, a repugnance to acknowledge and to pay which would have been neither unnatural nor unexpected, the circumstances cannot fail to exalt its character for justice and good faith in the eyes of all nations.

The Treaty of Amity and Commerce between the United States and Belgium, brought to your notice in my last annual message, as sanctioned by the Senate, but the ratifications of which had not been exchanged, owing to a delay in its reception at Brussels, and a subsequent absence of the Belgian Minister of Foreign Affairs, has been, after mature deliberation, finally disavowed by that Government as inconsistent with the powers and instructions given to their minister who negotiated it. This disavowal was entirely unexpected, as the liberal principles embodied in the convention, and which form the ground-work of the objection to it, were perfectly satisfactory to the Belgian representative, and were supposed to be not only within the powers granted, but expressly conformable to the instructions given to him. An offer, not yet accepted, has been made by Belgium to renew negotiations for a treaty less liberal in its provisions, on questions of general maritime law.

Our newly established relations with the Sublime Porte promise to be useful to our commerce, and satisfactory in every respect to this Government. Our intercourse with the Barbary Powers continues without important change, except that the present political state of Algiers has induced me to terminate the residence there of a salaried consul, and to substitute an ordinary consulate, to remain so long as the place continues in the possession of France. Our first treaty with one of these powers—the Emperor of Morocco—was formed in 1786, and was limited to fifty years. That period has almost expired. I shall take measures to renew it with the greater satisfaction, as its stipulations are just and liberal, and have been, with mutual fidelity and reciprocal advantages, scrupulously fulfilled.

Intestine dissensions have too frequently occurred to mar the prosperity, interrupt the commerce, and distract the governments of most of the nations of this hemisphere, which have separated themselves from Spain. When a firm and permanent understanding with the parent country shall have produced a formal acknowledgment of their independence, and the idea of danger from that quarter can be no longer entertained, the friends of freedom expect that those countries, so favored by nature, will be distinguished for their love of justice and their devotion to those peaceful arts, the assiduous cultivation of which confers honor upon nations and gives value to human life. In the mean time I confidently hope, that the apprehensions engendered, that some of the people of these luxuriant regions may be tempted, in a moment of unworthy distrust of their own capacity for the enjoyment of liberty, to commit the too common error of purchasing present repose by bestowing on some favorite leaders the fatal gift of irresponsible power,—will not be realized. With all their Governments, and with that of Brazil, no unexpected changes in our relations have occurred during the present year. Frequent causes of just complaint have arisen upon the part of the citizens of the United States,—sometimes from the irregular action of the constituted subordinate authorities of the maritime regions, and sometimes from the leaders or partisans of those in arms against the established Governments. In all cases, representations have been, or will be made, and as soon as their political affairs are in a settled position, it is expected that our friendly remonstrances will be followed by adequate redress.

The Government of Mexico made known in December last, the appointment of Commissioners and a Surveyor, on its part, to run, in conjunction with ours, the boundary line between its territories and the United States, and excused the delay by the reasons anticipated—the prevalence of civil war. The Commissioners and Surveyor not having met within the time stipulated by the treaty, a new arrangement became necessary, and our Chargé d'Affaires was instructed, in January last, to negotiate, in Mexico, an article additional to the pre-existing treaty. This instruction was acknowledged, and no difficulty was apprehended in the accomplishment of that object. By information just received, that additional article to the treaty will be obtained, and transmitted to this country, as soon as it can receive the ratification of the Mexican Congress.

The re-union of the three States of New Granada, Venezuela, and Equador, forming the Republic of Colombia, seems every day to become more improbable. The Commissioners of the two first are understood to be now negotiating a just division of the obligations contracted by them when united under one Government. The civil war in Equador, it is believed, has prevented even the appointment of a Commissioner on its part.

I propose, at an early day, to submit in the proper form, the appointment of a diplomatic agent to Venezuela. The importance of the commerce of that country to the United States, and the large claims of our citizens upon the Government, arising before and since the division of Colombia, rendering it, in my judgment, improper longer to delay this step.

Our representatives to Central America, Peru, and Brazil, are either at, or on their way to, their respective posts.

From the Argentine Republic, from which a Minister was expected to this Government, nothing further has been heard. Occasion has been taken, on the departure of a new Consul to Buenos Ayres, to remind that Government, that its long delayed Minister, whose appointment had been made known to us, had not arrived.

It becomes my unpleasant duty to inform you that this pacific and highly gratifying picture of our foreign relations, does not include those with France at this time. It is not possible that any Government and People could be more sincerely desirous of conciliating a just and friendly intercourse with another nation, than are those of the United States with their ancient ally and friend. This disposition is founded, as well on the most grateful and honorable recollections associated with our struggle for independence, as upon a well grounded conviction that it is consonant with the true policy of both. The People of the United States could not, therefore, see without the deepest regret, even a temporary interruption of the friendly relations between the two countries—a regret which would, I am sure, be greatly aggravated, if there should turn out to be any reasonable ground for attributing such a result to any act of omission or commission on our part. I desire, therefore, the highest satisfaction from being able to assure you, that the whole course of this Government has been characterised by a spirit so conciliatory and forbearing, as to make it impossible that our justice and moderation should be questioned, whatever may be the consequences of a longer perseverance, on the part of the French Government, in her omission to satisfy the conceded claims of our citizens.

The history of the accumulated and unprovoked aggressions upon our commerce, committed by authority of the existing Governments of France, between the years 1800 and 1817, has been rendered too painfully familiar to Americans to make its repetition either necessary or desirable. It will be sufficient here to remark, that there has, for many years, been scarcely a single administration of the French Government by whom the justice and legality of the claims of our citizens to indemnity, were not, to a very considerable extent, admitted; and yet near a quarter of a century has been wasted in ineffectual negotiations to secure it.

Deeply sensible of the injurious effects resulting from this state of things upon the interests and

character of both nations, I regarded it as among my first duties to cause one more effort to be made to satisfy France, that a just and liberal settlement of our claims was as well due to her own honor as to their incontestible validity. The negotiation for this purpose was commenced with the late Government of France, and was prosecuted with such success, as to leave no reasonable ground to doubt, that a settlement of a character quite as liberal as that which was subsequently made, would have been effected, had not the revolution, by which the negotiation was cut off, taken place. The discussions were resumed with the present government, and the result showed, that we were not wrong in supposing, that an event by which the two governments were made to approach each other so much nearer in their political principles, and by which the motives for the most liberal and friendly intercourse were so greatly multiplied, could exercise no other than a salutary influence upon the negotiation. After the most deliberate and thorough examination of the whole subject, a treaty between the two Governments was concluded and signed at Paris on the 4th of July, 1831, by which it was stipulated that "the French Government, in order to liberate itself from all the reclamations preferred against it by citizens of the United States, for unlawful seizures, captures, sequestrations, confiscations, or destruction of their vessels, cargoes, or other property, engages to pay a sum of twenty-five millions of francs to the United States, who shall distribute it among those entitled, in the manner and according to the rules it shall determine;" and it was also stipulated on the part of the French Government, that this twenty-five millions of francs should "be paid at Paris in six annual instalments of four millions one hundred and sixty-six thousand six hundred and sixty-six francs and sixty-six centimes each, in to the hands of such person or persons as shall be authorized by the Government of the United States to receive it." The first instalment to be paid "at the expiration of one year next following the exchange of the ratifications of this convention, and the others at successive intervals of a year, one after another, till the whole shall be paid. To the amount of each of the said instalments shall be added interest at four per centum thereupon, as upon the other instalments then remaining unpaid, the said interest to be computed from the day of the exchange of the present convention."

It was also stipulated, on the part of the United States, for the purpose of being completely liberated from all the reclamations presented by France on behalf of its citizens, that the sum of one million five hundred thousand francs should be paid to the Government of France, in six annual instalments, to be deducted out of the annual sums which France had agreed to pay, interest thereupon being in like manner computed from the day of the exchange of the ratifications. In addition to this stipulation, important advantages were secured to France by the following article, viz: "The wines of France, from and after the exchange of the ratifications of the present Convention, shall be admitted to consumption in the States of the Union, at duties which shall not exceed the following rates by the gallon, (such as it is used at present for wines in the United States,) to wit: six cents for red wines in casks; ten cents for white wines in casks; and twenty-two cents for wines of all sorts in bottles. The proportions existing between the duties on French wines thus reduced, and the general rates of the tariff which went into operation the first January, 1829, shall be maintained, in case the Government of the United States should think proper to diminish those general rates in a new tariff.

In consideration of this stipulation, which shall be binding on the United States for ten years, the French Government abandons the reclamations which it had formed in relation to the 8th article of the treaty of cession of Louisiana. It engages, moreover, to establish on the *long staple* cottons of the United States, which, after the exchange of the ratifications of the present Convention, shall be brought directly thence to France by the vessels of the United States, or by French vessels, the same duties as on *short staple* cottons."

This treaty was duly ratified in the manner prescribed by the constitutions of both countries, and the ratification was exchanged at the City of Washington on the 2d of February, 1832. On account of its commercial stipulations it was, in five days thereafter laid before the Congress of the United States, which proceeded to enact such laws favorable to the commerce of France as were necessary to carry it into full execution; and France has, from that period to the present, been in the unrestricted enjoyment of the valuable privileges that were thus secured to her. The faith of the French nation having been thus solemnly pledged, through its constitutional organ, for the liquidation and ultimate payment of the long deferred claims of our citizens, as also for the adjustment of other points of great and reciprocal benefits to both countries, and the United States having with a fidelity and promptitude by which their conduct will, I trust, be always characterized done every thing that was necessary to carry the treaty into full and fair effect on their part, counted, with the most perfect confidence, on equal fidelity and promptitude on the part of the French Government. In this reasonable expectation we have been, I regret to inform you, wholly disappointed. No legislative provision has been made by France for the execution of the treaty, either as it respects the indemnity to be paid, or the commercial benefits to be secured to the United States, and the relations between the United States and that power, in consequence thereof, are placed in a situation threatening to interrupt the good understanding which has so long and so happily existed between the two nations.

Not only has the French Government been thus wanting in the performance of the stipulations it has so solemnly entered into with the United States, but its omissions have been marked by circumstances which would seem to leave us without satisfactory evidences, that such performance will certainly take place at a future period. Advice of the exchange of ratifications reached Paris prior to the 8th April, 1832. The French Chambers were then sitting and continued in session until the 21st of that month, and although one instalment of the indemnity was payable on the 2d of February, 1833, one year after the exchange of ratifications, no application was made to the Chambers for the required appropriation, and in consequence of no appropriation having then been made, the draft of the United States Government for that instalment, was dishonored by the Minister of Finance, and the United States thereby involved in much controversy. The next session of the Chambers commenced on the 19th November, 1832, and continued until the 25th April, 1833. Notwithstanding the omission to pay the first instalment, had been made the subject of earnest remonstrance on our part, the treaty with the United States, and a bill making the necessary appropriations to execute it, were not laid before the Chamber of Deputies until the 6th of April, nearly five months after its meeting, and only nineteen days before the close of the session. The bill was read and referred to a committee, but there was no further action upon it The next session of the Chambers commenced on the 26th of April, 1833, and continued until the 26th of June following. A new bill was introduced on the 11th of June, but nothing important was done in relation to it during the session. In the month of April, 1834, nearly three years after the signature of the treaty, the final action of the French Chambers upon the bill to carry the treaty into effect, was obtained, and resulted in a refusal of the necessary appropriations. The avowed grounds upon which the bill was rejected, are to be found in the published debates of that body, and no observations of mine can be necessary to satisfy Congress of their utter insufficiency. Although the gross amount of the claims of our citizens is probably greater than will be ultimately allowed by the Commissioners, sufficient is, nevertheless, shown, to render it absolutely certain that the indemnity falls far short of the actual amount of our just claims, independently of the question of damages and interest for the detention. That the settlement involved a sacrifice in this respect was well known at the time—a sacrifice which was cheerfully acquiesced in by the different branches of the Federal Government, whose action upon the treaty was required, from a sincere desire to avoid further collision upon this old and disturbing subject, and in the confident expectation that the general relations between the two countries would be improved thereby.

The refusal to vote the appropriation, the news of which was received from our Minister in Paris about the 15th day of May last, might have been considered the final determination of the French government not to execute the stipulations of the treaty, and would have justified an immediate communication of the facts to Congress, with a recommendation of such ultimate measures as the interest and honor of the United States might seem to require. But with the news of the refusal of the Chambers to make the appropriation, were conveyed the regrets of the King, and a declaration that a national vessel should be forthwith sent out, with instructions to the French Minister to give the most ample explanations of the past, and the strongest assurances for the future. After a long passage the promised despatch vessel arrived. The pledges given by the French Minister, upon receipt of his instructions, were, that as soon after the election of the new members as the charter would permit, the legislative Chambers of France should be called together, and the proposition for an appropriation laid before them; that all the constitutional powers of the King and his Cabinet should be exerted to accomplish the object; and that the result should be made known early enough to be communicated to Congress at the commencement of the present session. Relying upon these pledges, and not doubting that the acknowledged justice of our claims, the promised exertions of the King and his Cabinet, and above all, that sacred regard for the national faith and honor for which the French character has been so distinguished, would secure an early execution of the treaty in all its parts, I did not deem it necessary to call the attention of Congress to the subject at the last session.

I regret to say that the pledges made through the minister of France have not been redeemed. The new chambers met on the 31st July last, and although the subject of fulfilling treaties was alluded to in the speech from the throne, no attempt was made by the King or his Cabinet to procure an appropriation to carry it into execution. The reasons given for this omission, although they might be considered sufficient in an ordinary case, are not consistent with the expectations founded upon the assurances given here, for there is no constitutional obstacle to entering into legislative business at the first meeting of the chambers. This point, however, might have been overlooked, had not the chambers, instead of being called to meet at so early a day that the result of their deliberations might be communicated to me, before the meeting of Congress, been prorogued to the 29th of the present month—a period so late that their decision can scarcely be made known to the present Congress prior to its dissolution. To avoid this delay, our Minister in Paris, in virtue of the assurance given by the French Minister in the United States, strongly urged the convocation of the Chambers at an earlier day, but without success. It is proper to remark, however, that this refusal has been accompanied with the most positive assurances, on the part of the Executive Government of France, of their intention to press the appropriation at the ensuing session of the Chambers.

The executive branch of this government has, as matters stand, exhausted all the authority upon the subject with which it is invested, and which it had any reason to believe could be beneficially employed.

The idea of acquiescing in the refusal to execute the treaty will not, I am confident, be for a moment entertained by any branch of this government; and further negotiation is equally out of the question.

If it shall be the pleasure of Congress to await the further action of the French Chambers, no further consideration of the subject will, at this session, probably be required at your hands. But,

if, from the original delay in asking for an appropriation, from the refusal of the Chambers to grant it when asked, from the omission to bring the subject before the Chambers at their last session, from the fact that, including that session, there have been five different occasions when the appropriation might have been made, and from the delay in convoking the Chambers until some weeks after the meeting of Congress, when it was well known that a communication of the whole subject to Congress at the last session, was prevented by assurances that it should be disposed of before its present meeting, you should feel yourselves constrained to doubt whether it be the intention of the French Government in all its branches to carry the treaty into effect, and think that such measures as the occasion may be deemed to call for, should be now adopted, the important question arises what those measures shall be.

Our institutions are essentially pacific. Peace and friendly intercourse with all nations, are as much the desire of our Government as they are the interest of our People. But these objects are not to be permanently secured, by surrendering the rights of our citizens, or permitting solemn treaties for their indemnity in cases of flagrant wrong, to be abrogated or set aside.

It is undoubtedly in the power of Congress seriously to affect the agricultural and manufacturing interests of France, by the passage of laws relating to her trade with the United States. Her products, manufactures, and tonnage, may be subjected to heavy duties in our ports, or all commercial intercourse with her may be suspended. But there are powerful; and, to my mind, conclusive objections to this mode of proceeding. We cannot embarrass or cut off the trade of France, without, at the same time, in some degree, embarrassing or cutting off our own trade. The injury of such a warfare must fall, though unequally, upon our own citizens, and could not but impair the means of the Government, and weaken that united sentiment in support of the rights and honor of the nation which must now pervade every bosom. Nor is it impossible that such a course of legislation would introduce once more into our national councils, those disturbing questions in relation to the tariff of duties which have been so recently put to rest. Besides, by every measure adopted by the Goverument of the United States with the view of injuring France, the clear perception of right which will induce our own people, and the rulers and people of all other nations, even of France herself, to pronounce our quarrel just, will be obscured, and the support rendered to us in a final resort to more decisive measures, will be more limited and equivocal. There is but one point in the controversy, and upon that the whole civilized world must pronounce France to be in the wrong. We insist that she shall pay us a sum of money, which she has acknowledged to be due; and of the justice of this demand, there can be but one opinion among mankind. True policy would seem to dictate that the question at issue should be kept thus disencumbered, and that not the slightest pretence should be given to France to persist in her refusal to make payment, by any act on our part affecting the interests of her people. The question should be left as it is now, in such an attitude that when France fulfils her treaty stipulations, all controversy will be at an end.

It is my conviction, that the United States ought to insist on a prompt execution of the treaty, and in case it be refused, or longer delayed, take redress into their own hands. After the delay on the part of France of a quarter of a century in acknowledging these claims by treaty, it is not to be tolerated that another quarter of a century is to be wasted in negotiating about the payment. The laws of nations provide a remedy for such occasions. It is a well settled principle of the inter-national code, that where one nation owes another a liquidated debt, which it refuses or neglects to pay, the aggrieved party may seize on the property belonging to the other, its citizens or subjects, sufficient to pay the debt, without giving just cause of war. This remedy has been repeatedly resorted to, and recently by France herself, towards Portugal, under circumstances less unquestionable.

The time at which resort should be had to this, or any other mode of redress, is a point to be decided by Congress. If an appropriation shall not be made by the French Chambers at their next session, it may justly be concluded that the Government of France has finally determined to disregard its own solemn undertaking, and refuse to pay an acknowledged debt. In that event, every day's delay on our part will be a stain upon our national honor, as well as a denial of justice to our injured citizens. Prompt measures, when the refusal of France shall be complete, will not only be most honorable and just, but will have the best effect upon our national character.

Since France, in violation of the pledges given through her minister here, has delayed her final action so long that her decision will not probably be known, in time to be communicated to this Congress, I recommend that a law be passed, authorizing reprisals upon French property, in case provision shall not be made for the payment of the debt, at the approaching session of the French Chambers. Such a measure ought not to be considered by France as a menace. Her pride and power are too well known to expect any thing from her fears, and preclude the necessity of a declaration that nothing partaking of the character of intimidation is intended by us. She ought to look upon it as the evidence only of an inflexible determination on the part of the United States, to insist on their rights. That Government, by doing only what it has itself acknowledged to be just, will be able to spare the United States the necessity of taking redress into their own hands, and save the property of French citizens from that seizure and sequestration which American citizens so long endured without retaliation or redress. If she should continue to refuse that act of acknowledged justice, and in violation of the law of nations, make reprisals on our part the occasion of hostilities against the United States, she would but add violence to injustice, and could not fail to expose herself to the just censure of civilized nations and to the retributive judgments of Heaven.

Collision with France is the more to be regretted, on account of the position she occupies in Europe in relation to liberal institutions. But in maintaining our national rights and honor, all Governments are alike to us. If by a collision with France, in a case where she is clearly in the wrong, the march of liberal principles shall be impeded, the responsibility for that result, as well as every other, will rest on her own head.

Having submitted these considerations, it belongs to Congress to decide, whether, after what has taken place, it will still await the further action of the French Chambers, or now adopt such provisional measures, as it may deem necessary and best adapted to protect the rights and maintain the honor of the country. Whatever that decision may be, it will be faithfully enforced by the Executive, as far as he is authorized so to do.

According to the estimate of the Treasury Department, the revenue accruing, from all sources, during the present year, will amount to twenty millions six hundred and twenty-four thousand seven hundred and seventeen dollars, which with the balance remaining in the Treasury on the first of January last, of eleven millions seven hundred and two thousand nine hundred and five dollars, produces an aggregate of thirty-two millions three hundred and twenty-seven thousand six hundred and twenty-three dollars. The total expenditure during the year for all objects, including the public debt, is estimated at twenty-five millions five hundred and ninety-one thousand three hundred and ninety dollars, which will leave a balance in the Treasury on the first of January, 1835, of six millions seven hundred and thirty-six thousand two hundred and thirty-two dollars. In this balance, however, will be included about one million one hundred and fifty thousand dollars of what was heretofore reported by the Department as not effective.

Of former appropriations it is estimated that there will remain unexpended at the close of the year, eight millions two thousand nine hundred and twenty-five dollars, and that of this sum there will not be required more than five millions one hundred and forty-one thousand nine hundred and sixty-four dollars, to accomplish the objects of all the current appropriations. Thus it appears that after satisfying all those appropriations, and after discharging the last item of our public debt, which will be done on the first of January next, there will remain unexpended in the Treasury an effective balance of about four hundred and forty thousand dollars. That such should be the aspect of our finances is highly flattering to the industry and enterprise of our population, and auspicious of the wealth and prosperity which await the future cultivation of their growing resources. It is not deemed prudent, however, to recommend any change for the present in our impost rates, the effect of the gradual reduction now in progress in many of them, not being sufficiently tested, to guide us in determining the precise amount of revenue which they will produce.

Free from public debt, at peace with all the world, and with no complicated interests to consult in our intercourse with foreign powers, the present may be hailed as that epoch in our history the most favorable for the settlement of those principles in our domestic policy, which shall be best calculated to give stability to our Republic, and secure the blessings of freedom to our citizens. Among these principles, from our past experience, it cannot be doubted, that simplicity in the character of the Federal Government, and a rigid economy in its administration, should be regarded as fundamental and sacred. All must be sensible that the existence of the public debt, by rendering taxation necessary for its extinguishment, has increased the difficulties which are inseparable from every exercise of the taxing power; and that it was, in this respect, a remote agent in producing those disturbing questions which grew out of the discussions relating to the tariff. If such has been the tendency of a debt incurred in the acquisition and maintenance of our national rights and liberties, the obligations of which all portions of the Union cheerfully acknowledged, it must be obvious, that whatever is calculated to increase the burdens of Government without necessity, must be fatal to all our hopes of preserving its true character. While we are felicitating ourselves, therefore, upon the extinguishment of the national debt, and the prosperous state of our finances, let us not be tempted to depart from those sound maxims of public policy, which enjoin a just adaptation of the revenue to the expenditures that are consistent with a rigid economy, and an entire abstinence from all topics of legislation that are not clearly within the constitutional powers of the Government, and suggested by the wants of the country. Properly regarded, under such a policy, every diminution of the public burdens arising from taxation, gives to individual enterprise increased power, and furnishes to all the members of our happy Confederacy, new motives for patriotic affection and support. But above all, its most important effect will be found in its influence upon the character of the Government, by confining its action to those objects which will be sure to secure to it the attachment and support of our fellow-citizens.

Circumstances make it my duty to call the attention of Congress to the Bank of the United States. Created for the convenience of the Government, that institution has become the scourge of the People. Its interference to postpone the payment of a portion of the national debt, that it might retain the public money appropriated for that purpose, to strengthen it in a political contest—the extraordinary extension and contraction of its accommodations to the community—its corrupt and partisan loans—its exclusion of the public directors from a knowledge of its most important proceedings—the unlimited authority conferred on the President to expend its funds in hiring writers, and procuring the execution of printing, and the use made of that authority—the retention of the pension money and books after the selection of new agents—the groundless claim to heavy damages, in consequence of the protest of the bill drawn on the French Government, have, through various channels, been laid before Congress. Immediately after the close of the last session, the Bank, through its President, announced

its ability and readiness to abandon the system of unparalleled curtailment, and the interruption of domestic exchanges, which it had practised upon from the 1st of August, 1833, to the 30th June, 1834, and to extend its accommodations to the community. The grounds assumed in this annunciation, amounted to an acknowledgment that the curtailment, in the extent to which it had been carried, was not necessary to the safety of the Bank, and had been persisted in merely to induce Congress to grant the prayer of the Bank in its memorial relative to the removal of the deposites, and to give it a new charter. They were substantially a confession that all the real distresses which individuals and the country had endured for the preceding six or eight months, had been needlessly produced by it, with the view of affecting, through the sufferings of the People, the legislative action of Congress. It is a subject of congratulation that Congress and the country had the virtue and firmness to bear the infliction; that the energies of our people soon found relief from this wanton tyranny, in vast importations of the precious metals from almost every part of the world; and that at the close of this tremendous effort to control our Government, the Bank found itself powerless, and no longer able to loan out its surplus means. The community had learned to manage its affairs without its assistance, and trade had already found new auxiliaries; so that on the first of October last, the extraordinary spectacle was presented of a National Bank, more than one half of whose capital was either lying unproductive in its vaults, or in the hands of foreign bankers.

To the needless distresses brought on the country during the last session of Congress, has since been added the open seizure of the dividends on the public stock, to the amount of one hundred and seventy thousand and forty-one dollars, under pretence of paying damages, cost, and interest, upon the protested French bill. This sum constituted a portion of the estimated revenues for the year 1834, upon which the appropriations made by Congress were based. It would as soon have been expected that our collectors would seize on the customs, or the receivers of our land offices on the moneys arising from the sale of public lands, under pretences of claims against the United States, as that the Bank would have retained the dividends. Indeed, if the principle be established that any one who chooses to set up a claim against the United States, may, without authority of law, seize on the public property or money wherever he can find it, to pay the claim, there will remain no assurance that our revenue will reach the Treasury, or that it will be applied after the appropriation to the purposes designated in the law. The paymasters of our army, and the pursers of our navy, may, under like pretences, apply to their own use moneys appropriated to set in motion the public force, and in time of war leave the country without defence. This measure resorted to by the Bank is disorganizing and revolutionary, and if generally resorted to by private citizens in like cases, would fill the land with anarchy and violence.

It is a constitutional provision, that "no money shall be drawn from the Treasury but in consequence of appropriations made by law." The palpable object of this provision is to prevent the expenditure of the public money, for any purpose whatsoever, which shall not have been first approved by the Representatives of the People and the States in Congress assembled. It vests the power of declaring for what purposes the public money shall be expended, in the Legislative Department of the Government, to the exclusion of the Executive and Judicial, and it is not within the constitutional authority of either of those Departments, to pay it away without law, or to sanction its payment. According to this plain constitutional provision the claim of the Bank can never be paid without an appropriation by act of Congress. But the Bank has never asked for an appropriation. It attempts to defeat the provision of the constitution, and obtain payment without an act of Congress. Instead of awaiting an appropriation passed by both Houses, and approved by the President, it makes an appropriation for itself, and invites an appeal to the Judiciary to sanction it. That the money had not technically been paid into the Treasury, does not affect the principle intended to be established by the constitution. The Executive and Judiciary have as little right to appropriate and expend the public money without authority of law, before it is placed to the credit of the Treasurer, as to take it from the Treasury. In the annual report of the Secretary of the Treasury, and in his correspondence with the President of the Bank, and the opinions of the Attorney General accompanying it, you will find a further examination of the claims of the Bank, and the course it has pursued.

It seems due to the safety of the public funds remaining in that Bank, and to the honor of the American People, that measures be taken to separate the Government entirely from an institution so mischievous to the public prosperity, and so regardless of the Constitution and laws. By transferring the public deposites, by appointing other Pension Agents, as far as it had the power, by ordering the discontinuance of the receipt of Bank checks in payment of the public dues after the first day of January next, the Executive has exerted all its lawful authority to sever the connexion between the Government and this faithless corporation.

The high-handed career of this institution imposes upon the constitutional functionaries of this Government, duties of the gravest and most imperative character—duties which they cannot avoid, and from which I trust there will be no inclination on the part of any of them to shrink. My own sense of them is most clear, as is also my readiness to discharge those which may rightfully fall on me. To continue any business relations with the Bank of the United States that may be avoided without a violation of the national faith, after that institution has set at open defiance the conceded right of the Government to examine its affairs; after it has done all in its power to deride the public authority in other respects, and to bring it into disrepute at home and abroad; after it has attempted to defeat the clearly expressed will of the people by turning against them the immense power intrusted to its hands, and by involving a country otherwise peaceful, flourishing, and happy, in dissension, embarrassment, and distress—would make the nation itself a party to the degradation so sedulously prepared for its public agents—and do much to destroy the confidence of mankind in popular governments, and to bring into contempt their authority and efficiency. In guarding against an evil of such magnitude, considerations of temporary convenience should be thrown out of the question, and we should be influenced by such motives only as look to the honor and preservation of the republican system. Deeply and solemnly impressed with the justice of these views, I feel it to be my duty to recommend to you, that a law be passed authorizing the sale of the public stock; that the provision of the charter requiring the receipt of notes of the Bank in payment of public dues, shall, in accordance with the power reserved to Congress in the 14th section of the charter, be suspended until the Bank pays to the Treasury the dividends withheld; and that all laws connecting the Government or its officers with the Bank, directly or indirectly, be repealed; and that the institution be left hereafter to its own resources and means.

Events have satisfied my mind, and I think the minds of the American People, that the mischiefs and dangers which flow from a National Bank far overbalance all its advantages. The bold effort the present Bank has made to control the Government, the distresses it has wantonly produced, the violence of which it has been the occasion in one of our cities famed for its observance of law and order, are but premonitions of the fate which awaits the American People should they be deluded into a perpetuation of this institution, or the establishment of another like it. It is fervently hoped, that, thus admonished, those who have heretofore favored the establishment of a substitute for the present Bank, will be induced to abandon it, as it is evidently better to incur any inconvenience that may be reasonably expected, than to concentrate the whole moneyed power of the Republic in any form whatsoever, or under any restrictions.

Happily it is already illustrated that the agency of such an institution is not necessary to the fiscal operations of the Government. The State Banks are found fully adequate to the performance of all services which were required of the Bank of the United States, quite as promptly, and with the same cheapness. They have maintained themselves, and discharged all these duties, while the Bank of the United States was still powerful, and in the field as an open enemy; and it is not possible to conceive that they will find greater difficulties in their operations, when that enemy shall cease to exist.

The attention of Congress is earnestly invited to the regulation of the deposites in the State Banks, by law. Although the power now exercised by the Executive Department in this behalf, is only such as was uniformly exerted through every Administration from the origin of the Government up to the establishment of the present Bank, yet, it is one which is susceptible of regulation by law, and, therefore, ought so to be regulated. The power of Congress to direct in what places the Treasurer shall keep the moneys in the Treasury, and to impose restrictions upon the Executive authority, in relation to their custody and removal, is unlimited, and its exercise will rather be courted than discouraged by those public officers and agents on whom rests the responsibility for their safety. It is desirable that as little power as possible should be left to the President or Secretary of the Treasury over those institutions—which, being thus freed from Executive influence, and without a common head to direct their operations, would have neither the temptation nor the ability to interfere in the political conflicts of the country. Not deriving their charters from the national authorities, they would never have those inducements to meddle in general elections, which have led the Bank of the United States to agitate and convulse the country for upwards of two years.

The progress of our gold coinage is creditable to the officers of the mint, and promises in a short period to furnish the country with a sound and portable currency, which will much diminish the inconvenience to travellers of the want of a general paper currency, should the State banks be incapable of furnishing it. Those institutions have already shown themselves competent to purchase and furnish domestic exchange for the convenience of trade, at reasonable rates, and not a doubt is entertained that, in a short period, all the wants of the country in bank accommodations and exchange, will be supplied as promptly and cheaply as they have heretofore been by the Bank of the United States. If the several States shall be induced gradually to reform their banking systems, and prohibit the issue of all small notes, we shall, in a few years, have a currency as sound, and as little liable to fluctuations, as any other commercial country.

The report of the Secretary of War, together with the accompanying documents from the several bureaux of that Department, will exhibit the situation of the various objects committed to its administration.

No event has occurred since your last session rendering necessary any movements of the army, with the exception of the expedition of the regiment of dragoons into the territory of the wandering and predatory tribes, inhabiting the western frontier and living adjacent to the Mexican boundary. These tribes have been heretofore known to us principally by their attacks upon our own citizens and upon other Indians entitled to the protection of the United States. It became necessary for the peace of the frontiers to check these habitual inroads, and I am happy to inform you that the object has been effected without the commission of any act of hostility. Col. Dodge, and the troops under his command, have acted with equal firmness and humanity, and an arrangement has been made with those Indians, which it is hoped will assure their permanent pacific relations with the United States and the other tribes of Indians upon that border. It is to be regretted that the prevalence of sickness in that quarter has deprived the country of a number of valuable lives, and particularly that General Leavenworth, an officer well known and esteem-

ed for his gallant services in the late war, and for his subsequent good conduct, has fallen a victim to his zeal and exertions in the discharge of his duty.

The army is in a high state of discipline. Its moral condition, so far as that is known here, is good, and the various branches of the public service, are carefully attended to. It is amply sufficient, under its present organization, for providing the necessary garrisons for the sea-board and for the defence of the internal frontier, and also for preserving the elements of military knowledge, and for keeping pace with those improvements which modern experience is continually making. And these objects appear to me to embrace all the legitimate purposes for which a permanent military force should be maintained in our country. The lessons of history teach us its danger, and the tendency which exists to an increase. This can be best met and averted by a just caution on the part of the public itself, and of those who represent them in Congress.

From the duties which devolve on the Engineer Department, and upon the Topographical Engineers, a different organization seems to be demanded by the public interest, and I recommend the subject to your consideration.

No important change has, during this season, taken place in the condition of the Indians. Arrangements are in progress for the removal of the Creeks, and will soon be for the removal of the Seminoles. I regret that the Cherokees east of the Mississippi have not yet determined, as a community, to remove. How long the personal causes which have heretofore retarded that ultimately inevitable measure, will continue to operate, I am unable to conjecture. It is certain, however, that delay will bring with it accumulated evils; which will render their condition more and more unpleasant. The experience of every year adds to the conviction, that emigration, and that alone, can preserve from destruction the remnant of the tribes yet living among us. The facility with which the necessaries of life are procured, and the treaty stipulations providing aid for the emigrant Indians in their agricultural pursuits, and in the important concern of education, and their removal from those causes which have heretofore depressed all and destroyed many of the tribes, cannot fail to stimulate their exertions and to reward their industry.

The two laws passed at the last session of Congress on the subject of Indian affairs, have been carried into effect, and detailed instructions for their administration have been given. It will be seen by the estimates for the present session, that a great reduction will take place in the expenditures of the department in consequence of these laws. And there is reason to believe that their operation will be salutary, and that the colonization of the Indians on the western frontier, together with a judicious system of administration, will still far her reduce the expenses of this branch of the public service, and at the same time promote its usefulness and efficiency.

Circumstances have been recently developed, shewing the existence of extensive frauds under the various laws granting pensions and gratuities for Revolutionary services. It is impossible to estimate the amount which may have been thus fraudulently obtained from the national treasury. I am satisfied, however, it has been such as to justify a re-examination of the system, and the adoption of the necessary checks in its administration. All will agree, that the services and sufferings of the remnant of our Revolutionary band, should be fully compensated. But while this is done, every proper precaution should be taken to prevent the admission of fabricated and fraudulent claims. In the present mode of proceeding, the attestations and certificates of judicial officers of the various States, form a considerable portion of the checks which are interposed against the commission of frauds. These, however, have been, and may be, fabricated, and in such a way as to elude detection at the examining offices. And independently of this practical difficulty, it is ascertained that these documents are often loosely and sometimes, even blank certificates have issued; sometimes prepared papers have been

signed without inquiry; and, in one instance at least, the seal of the court has been within reach of a person most interested in its improper application. It is obvious that, under such circumstances, no severity of administration can check the abuse of the law; and information has, from time to time, been communicated to the Pension Office, questioning or denying the right of persons placed upon the pension list, to the bounty of the country. Such cautions are always attended to, and examined. But a far more general investigation is called for. And I therefore recommend, in conformity with the suggestion of the Secretary of War, that an actual inspection should be made, in each State, into the circumstances and claims of every person now drawing a pension. The honest veteran has nothing to fear from such a scrutiny, while the fraudulent claimant will be detected, and the public treasury relieved to an amount, I have reason to believe, far greater than has heretofore been suspected. The details of such a plan, could be so regulated as to interpose the necessary checks, without any burthensome operation upon the pensioners. The object should be two-fold:

1. To look into the original justice of the claims, so far as this can be done under a proper system of regulations, by an examination of the claimants themselves, and by inquiring, in the vicinity of their residence, into their history, and into the opinion entertained of their revolutionary services.

2. To ascertain, in all cases, whether the original claimant is living, and this by actual personal inspection.

This measure will, if adopted, be productive, I think, of the desired results, and I therefore recommend it to your consideration, with the further suggestion, that all payments should be suspended till the necessary reports are received.

It will be seen by a tabular statement annexed to the documents transmitted to Congress, that the appropriations for objects connected with the War Department, made at the last session, for the service of the year 1834; excluding the permanent appropriation for the payment of military gratuities under the act of June 7, 1832, the appropriation of two hundred thousand dollars for arming and equipping the militia, and the appropriation of ten thousand dollars for the civilization of the Indians, which are not any ally renewed, amounted to the sum of nine millions three thousand two hundred and sixty-one dollars, and that the estimates of appropriations necessary for the same branches of service for the year 1835, amount to the sum of five millions seven hundred and seventy-eight thousand nine hundred and sixty-four dollars, making a difference in the appropriations of the current year over the estimates of appropriations for the next of three millions two hundred and twenty-four thousand two hundred and ninety-seven dollars.

The principal causes which have operated at this time to produce this great difference, are shown in the reports and documents, and in the detailed estimates. Some of these causes are accidental and temporary, while others are permanent, and aided by a just course of administration, may continue to operate beneficially upon the public expenditure.

A just economy, expending where the public service requires, and withholding where it does not, is among the indispensable duties of the Government.

I refer you to the accompanying report of the Secretary of the Navy, and to the documents with it, for a full view of the operations of that important branch of our service, during the present year. It will be seen that the wisdom and liberality with which Congress have provided for the gradual increase of our navy material, have been seconded by a corresponding zeal and fidelity on the part of those to whom has been confided the execution of the laws on the subject, and that but a short period would be now required to put in commission a force large enough for any exigency into which the country may be thrown.

When we reflect upon our position in relation to other nations, it must be apparent, that in the event of conflicts with them, we must look chiefly to our navy for the protection of our national

rights. The wide seas which separate us from other governments, must of necessity be the theatre on which an enemy will aim to assail us, and unless we are prepared to meet him on this element, we cannot be said to possess the power requisite to repel or prevent aggressions. We cannot, therefore, watch with too much attention this arm of our defence, or cherish with too much care the means by which it can possess the necessary efficiency and extension. To this end our policy has been heretofore wisely directed to the constant employment of a force sufficient to guard our commerce, and to the rapid accumulation of the materials, which are necessary to repair our vessels, and construct with ease such new ones as may be required in a state of war.

In accordance with this policy, I recommend to your consideration the erection of the additional Dry Dock described by the Secretary of the Navy, and also the construction of the Steam Batteries to which he has referred, for the purpose of testing their efficacy as auxiliaries to the system of defence now in use.

The report of the Postmaster General, herewith submitted, exhibits the condition and prospects of that Department. From that document it appears that there was a deficit in the funds of the Department, at the commencement of the present year, beyond its available means, of three hundred and fifteen thousand five hundred and ninety-nine dollars and ninety-eight cents, which on the first of July last had been reduced to two hundred and sixty-eight thousand ninety-two dollars and seventy-four cents. It appears, also, that the revenue for the coming year will exceed the expenditures about two hundred and seventy thousand dollars, which, with the excess of revenue which will result from the operations of the current half year, may be expected, independently of any increase in the gross amount of postages, to supply the entire deficit before the end of 1835. But in this calculation is based on the gross amount of postages which had accrued within the period ending March, 1833, it was extended to members of Congress throughout the whole year. It is believed that a revision of the laws relative to the franking privilege, with some enactments to enforce more rigidly the restrictions under which it is granted, would operate beneficially to the country, by enabling the department at an earlier period to store the mail facilities that have been withdrawn, and to extend them more widely as the growing settlements of the country may require.

To a measure so important to the Government, and so just to our constituents, who ask to enjoy privileges for themselves, and are not willing to concede them to others, I earnestly recommend the serious attention of Congress.

The importance of the Post Office Department, and the magnitude to which it has grown, both in its revenues and in its operations, seem to demand its re-organization by law. The whole of its receipts and disbursements have hitherto been placed entirely to Executive control, and individual discretion. The principle is as sound in relation to this as to any other Department of the Government, that as little discretion should be left to the Executive officer who controls it, as compatible with its efficiency. It is therefore earnestly recommended that it be organized with an Auditor and Treasurer of its own, appointed by the President and Senate, who shall be branches of the Treasury Department.

Your attention is again respectfully invited to the defect which exists in the Judicial System of the United States. Nothing can be more desirable than the uniform operation of the Federal Judiciary throughout the several States, all of which, standing on the same footing as members of the Union, have equal rights to the advantages and benefits resulting from its laws. This object is not attained by the judicial acts now in force, because they leave one-fourth of the States without Circuit Courts.

It is undoubtedly the duty of Congress to place all the States on the same footing in this respect, either by the creation of an additional number of associate judges, or by an enlargement of the circuits assigned to those already appointed, so as to include the new States. Whatever may be the difficulty in a proper organization of the judicial system, so as to secure its efficiency and uniformity in all parts of the Union, and at the same time to avoid such an increase of judges as would encumber the supreme appellate tribunal, it should not be allowed to weigh against the great injustice which the present operation of the system produces.

I trust that I may be also pardoned for renewing the recommendation I have so often submitted to your attention, in regard to the mode of electing the President and Vice President of the United States. All the reflection I have been able to bestow upon the subject, increases my conviction that the best interests of the country will be promoted by the adoption of some plan which will secure, in all contingencies, that important right of sovereignty to the direct control of the People. Could this be attained, and the terms of those officers be limited to a single period of either four or six years, I think our liberties would possess an additional safeguard.

At your last session I called the attention of Congress to the destruction of the public building occupied by the Treasury Department. As the public interest requires that another building should be erected, with as little delay as possible, it is hoped that the means will be seasonably provided, and that they will be ample enough to authorize such an enlargement and improvement in the plan of the building as will more effectually accommodate the public officers, and secure the public documents deposited in it from the casualties of fire.

I have not been able to satisfy myself that the bill entitled "an Act to improve the navigation of the Wabash river," which was sent to me at the close of your last session, ought to pass, and I have therefore withheld from it my approval, and now return it to the Senate, the body in which it originated.

There can be no question connected with the administration of public affairs, more important or more difficult to be satisfactorily dealt with, than that which relates to the rightful authority and proper action of the Federal Government upon the subject of Internal Improvements. To inherent embarrassments have been added others resulting from the course of our legislation concerning it.

I have heretofore communicated freely with Congress upon this subject, and in adverting to it again, I cannot refrain from expressing my increased conviction of its extreme importance, as well in regard to its bearing upon the maintenance of the Constitution and the prudent management of the public revenue, as on account of its disturbing effect upon the harmony of the Union.

We are in no danger from violations of the Constitution by which encroachments are made upon the personal rights of the citizen. The sentence of condemnation long since pronounced by the American People upon acts of that character, will, I doubt not, continue to prove as salutary in its effects as it is irreversible in its nature. But against the dangers of unconstitutional acts which, instead of menacing the vengeance of offended authority, proffer local advantages, and bring in their train the patronage of the Government, we are, I fear, not so safe. To suppose that because our Government has been instituted for the benefit of the People, it must therefore have the power to do whatever may seem to conduce to the public good, is an error, into which even honest minds are too apt to fall. In yielding themselves to this fallacy, they overlook the great considerations in which the Federal Constitution was founded. They forget that in consequence of the conceded diversities in the interest and condition of the different States, it was foreseen, at the period of its adoption, that although a particular measure of the Government might be beneficial and proper in one State, it might be the reverse in another—that it was for this reason the States would not consent to make a grant to the Federal Government of the general and usual powers of Government, but of such only as were specifically enumerated, and the probable effects of which they could, as they thought, safely anticipate: and they forget also the paramount obligation upon all to abide by the compact, then so solemnly, and, as it was hoped, so firmly established. In addition to the dangers to the Constitution springing from the sources I have stated, there has been one which was perhaps greater than all. I allude to the materials which this subject has afforded for sinister appeals to selfish feelings, and the opinion heretofore so extensively entertained of its adaptation to the purposes of personal ambition. With such stimulants it is not surprising that the acts and pretensions of the Federal Government in this behalf should sometimes have been carried to an alarming extent. The questions which have arisen upon this subject have related—

1st. To the power of making internal improvements within the limits of a State, with the right of territorial jurisdiction, sufficient at least for their preservation and use.

2d. To the right of appropriating money in aid of such works when carried on by a State or by a company in virtue of State authority, surrendering the claim of jurisdiction; and

3d. To the propriety of appropriation for improvements of a particular class; viz. for light-houses, beacons, buoys, public piers, and for the removal of sand bars, sawyers, and other temporary and partial impediments in our navigable rivers and harbors.

The claims of power for the General Government upon each of these points certainly present matter of the deepest interest. The first, is however, of much the greatest importance, inasmuch as, in addition to the dangers of unequal and improvident expenditures of public moneys, common to all, there is superadded to that the conflicting jurisdictions of the respective governments. Federal jurisdiction, at least to the extent I have stated, has been justly regarded by its advocates as necessarily appurtenant to the power in question, if that exists by the constitution. That the most injurious conflicts would unavoidably arise between the respective jurisdictions of the State and Federal Governments, in the absence of a constitutional provision marking out their respective boundaries, cannot be doubted. The local advantages to be obtained would induce the States to overlook in the beginning the dangers and difficulties to which they might ultimately be exposed. The powers exercised by the Federal Government would soon be regarded with jealousy by the State authorities, and originating as they must from implication or assumption, it would be impossible to affix to them certain and safe limits. Opportunities and temptations to the assumption of power incompatible with State sovereignty, would be increased, and those barriers which resist the tendency of our system towards consolidation greatly weakened. The officers and agents of the General Government might not always have the discretion to abstain from intermeddling with State concerns; and if they did, they would not always escape the suspicion of having done so. Collisions, and consequent irritations would spring up—that harmony which should ever exist between the General Government and each member of the Confederacy, would be frequently interrupted—a spirit of contention would be engendered—and the dangers of division greatly multiplied.

Yet we all know, that notwithstanding these grave objections, this dangerous doctrine was at one time apparently proceeding to its final establishment with fearful rapidity. The desire to embark the Federal Government in works of internal improvement, prevailed in the highest degree, during the first session of the first Congress that I had the honor to meet in my present situation. When the bill authorizing a subscription on the part of the United States for stock in the Maysville and Lexington Turnpike Companies, passed the two Houses, there had been reported, by the Committees of Internal Improvements, bills containing appropriations for such objects, exclusive of those for the Cumberland road, and for harbors and light-houses, to the amount of about one hundred and six millions of dollars. In this amount was included authority to the Secretary of the Treasury to subscribe for the stock of different companies to a great extent, and the residue was principally for the direct construction of roads by this Government. In addition to these projects, which had been presented to the two Houses, under the sanction and recommendation of their respective Committees on Internal Improvements, there were then still pending before the committees, and in memorials to Congress, presented, but not referred, different projects for works of a similar character, the expense of which cannot be estimated with certainty, but must have exceeded one hundred millions of dollars.

Regarding the bill authorizing a subscription to the stock of the Maysville and Lexington Turnpike Company as the entering wedge of a system, which, however weak at first, might soon become strong enough to rive the bands of the Union asunder, and believing that if its passage was acquiesced in by the Executive and the People, there would no longer be any limitation upon the authority of the General Government in respect to the appropriation of money for such objects, I deemed it an imperative duty to withhold from it the Executive approval. Although, from the obviously local character of that work, I might well have contented myself with a refusal to approve the bill upon that ground, yet, sensible of the vital importance of the subject, and anxious that my views and opinions in regard to the whole matter, should be fully understood by Congress, and by my constituents, I felt it my duty to go further. I therefore embraced that early occasion to apprize Congress, that, in my opinion, the Constitution did not confer upon it the power to authorize the construction of ordinary roads and canals within the limits of a State, and to say respectfully, that no bill admitting such a power could receive my official sanction. I did so in the confident expectation that the speedy settlement of the public mind upon the whole subject would be greatly facilitated by the difference between the two Houses and myself, and that the harmonious action of the several departments of the Federal Government in regard to it, would be ultimately secured.

So far at least as it regards this branch of the subject, my best hopes have been realized. Nearly four years have elapsed, and several sessions of Congress have intervened, and no attempt, within my recollection, has been made to induce Congress to exercise this power. The applications for the construction of roads and canals, which were formerly multiplied upon your files, are no longer presented; and we have good reason to infer that the current of public sentiment has become so decided against the pretension as effectually to discourage its re-assertion. So thinking, I derive the greatest satisfaction from the conviction, that thus much at least has been secured upon this important and embarrassing subject.

From attempts to appropriate the national funds to objects which are confessedly of a local character, we cannot, I trust, have any thing further to apprehend. My views in regard to the expediency of making appropriations for works which are claimed to be of a national character, and prosecuted under State authority, assuming that Congress have the right to do so, were stated in my annual message to Congress in 1830, and also in that containing my objections to the Maysville Road Bill.

So thoroughly convinced am I, that no such appropriations ought to be made by Congress, until a suitable constitutional provision is made upon the subject, and so essential do I regard the point to the highest interests of our country, that I could not consider myself as discharging my duty to my constituents in giving the Executive

tion to any bill containing such an appropriation. If the People of the United States desire that the public Treasury shall be resorted to for the means to prosecute such works, they will concur in an amendment of the constitution, prescribing a rule by which the national character of the works is to be tested, and by which the greatest practicable equality of benefits may be secured to each member of the confederacy. The effects of such a regulation would be most salutary in preventing unprofitable expenditures, in securing our legislation from the pernicious consequences of a scramble for the favors of Government, and in repressing the spirit of discontent which must inevitably arise from an unequal distribution of treasures which belong alike to all.

There is another class of appropriations for what may be called, without impropriety, internal improvements, which have always been regarded as standing upon different grounds from those to which I have referred. I allude to such as have for their object the improvement of our harbors, the removal of partial and temporary obstructions in our navigable rivers, for the facility and security of our foreign commerce. The grounds upon which I distinguished appropriations of this character from others have already been stated to Congress. I will now only add that at the first session of Congress under the new constitution, it was provided by law, that all expenses which should accrue from and after the 15th day of August, 1789, in the necessary support and maintenance and repairs of all light-houses, beacons, buoys, and public piers, erected, placed, or sunk before the passage of the act, within any bay, inlet, harbor, or port of the United States, for rendering the navigation thereof easy and safe, should be defrayed out of the Treasury of the United States; and further, that it should be the duty of the Secretary of the Treasury to provide by contracts, with the approbation of the President, for rebuilding when necessary and keeping in good repair the light-houses, beacons, buoys, and public piers in the several States, and for furnishing them with supplies. Appropriations for similar objects have been continued from that time to the present without interruption or dispute. As a natural consequence of the increase and extension of our foreign commerce, ports of entry and delivery have been multiplied and established, not only upon our sea-board, but in the interior of the country, upon our lakes and navigable rivers. The convenience and safety of this commerce have led to the gradual extension of these expenditures; to the erection of light-houses, the placing, planting, and sinking of buoys, beacons, and piers, and to the removal of partial and temporary obstructions in our navigable rivers, and in the harbors upon our great lakes, as well as on the seaboard. Although I have expressed to Congress my apprehension that these expenditures have sometimes been extravagant and disproportionate to the advantages to be derived from them, I have not felt it to be my duty to refuse my assent to bills containing them, and have contented myself to follow in this respect in the footsteps of all my predecessors. Sensible, however, from experience and observation, of the great abuses to which the unrestricted exercise of this authority by Congress was exposed, I have prescribed a limitation for the government of my own conduct, by which expenditures of this character are confined to places below the ports of entry or delivery established by law. I am very sensible that this restriction is not as satisfactory as could be desired, and that much embarrassment may be caused to the Executive Department in its execution, by appropriations for remote, and not well understood objects. But as neither my own reflections, nor the lights which I may properly derive from other sources, have supplied me with a better; I shall continue to apply my best exertions to a faithful application of the rule upon which it is founded. I sincerely regret that I could not give my assent to the bill entitled "An act to improve the navigation of the Wabash river;" but I could not have done so without receding from the ground which I have, upon the fullest consideration, taken upon this subject, and of which Congress has been heretofore apprized, and without throwing the subject again open to abuses which no good citizen, entertaining my opinions, could desire.

I rely upon the intelligence and candor of my fellow-citizens, in whose liberal indulgence I have already so largely participated for a correct appreciation of my motives in interposing, as I have done, on this, and other occasions, checks to a course of legislation which, without, in the slightest degree, calling in question the motives of others, I consider as sanctioning improper and unconstitutional expenditures of public treasure.

I am not hostile to internal improvements, and wish to see them extended to every part of the country. But I am fully persuaded, if they are not commenced in a proper manner, confined to proper objects, and conducted under an authority generally conceded to be rightful, that a successful prosecution of them cannot be reasonably expected. The attempt will meet with resistance where it might otherwise receive support, and instead of strengthening the bonds of our confederacy, it will only multiply and aggravate the causes of disunion.

ANDREW JACKSON.

December, 1, 1834.

The message having been read—

Mr. WHITE moved that five thousand copies thereof, and fifteen hundred copies of the accompanying documents, be printed for the use of the members of the Senate; which was agreed to.

The resolution submitted yesterday by Mr. KNIGHT, relative to authorizing a subscription for newspapers for the use of the members, was taken up for consideration.

Mr. KING, of Georgia, said, that, upon inquiry, he found that resolutions similar to the present, and for the same object, had been frequently passed by both Houses of Congress, and with so little interruption heretofore, that it now constituted a regular practice. At one time, it was admitted that it was a very improper one, and, notwithstanding the continuance of the practice, it was still equally so. He hoped that some gentleman who was in favor of it, would show some reasonable connexion between the propriety of the practice of printing the documents of the Senate and subscribing for the various newspapers of the day, or any of the fashionable novels, the Waverly novels, or the romances of Mrs. Radcliffe. It was true that the newspapers and periodicals might contain speculations of the editors on political subjects, but so did the works of Bolinbroke, and a variety of other authors. They might also contain a republication of the proceedings of this body, and notices of subjects connected with the legislation of Congress, but they did not necessarily contain them. They were unconnected with every branch of this Government. Honorable gentlemen, he thought, should show some reasonable connexion between the printing of documents and subscribing for newspapers. To admit the power was no argument in favor of the utility or expediency of exercising it. We should never exercise power merely to show that we possess it. A few thousands could not be expended more uselessly than in this way. Many flourishes might be made about the amount of useful information which the members would derive from the subscriptions to newspapers, but was there a single individual member, either of this or the other House, who was qualified for a seat in Congress, who was not a subscriber to more papers than he had leisure to read? He ventured to say there was none, and he defied contradiction. The expenditure contemplated was therefore useless, and not necessary. What must be the reflection on seeing grave Senators seated at their desks looking over the Mirror, the Lady's Book, &c. and afterwards folding them up and again throwing them on Mr. Barry to send to their wives, their daughters, and their sweethearts. The mail was improperly burthened with such things. A majority of the Senate, at the last session, looked at the same principle involved in another subject, and corrected it. He, Mr. K. opposed the principle then, but he took no credit to himself for it, because he usually acted with the party who had no power in this body, and therefore he gave all the credit of the measure he alluded to, to the opposition. He concluded by moving that the resolution be laid on the table.

The motion was disagreed to, and the resolution was then adopted.

Mr. POINDEXTER offered the following resolution, which, on his motion, was considered and adopted:

Resolved, That the 34th rule of the Senate, so far as respects the Committee on Public Lands, be suspended; and that the present Committee be continued with all the powers vested in them, and subject to all the duties enjoined on them by the several resolutions of the Senate, at the last session, relative to frauds in the sale of the public lands.

The Senate then adjourned.

HOUSE OF REPRESENTATIVES.

TUESDAY, Dec. 2, 1834.

The following members appeared in addition to those who answered to their names on Monday: Messrs. Edward Howell, Henderson, Banks, Young, Fowler, Shinn, Jackson of Massachusetts, Wise, Philo C. Fuller, Bouldin, Hazeltine, Allen of Ohio, Leyall, Chinn, Coulter and Galbraith.

H. F. Janes, a new member from Vermont, appeared, was sworn, and took his seat.

Mr. McKINLEY, from the Joint Committee, appointed yesterday to wait on the President of the United States, reported that they had performed that duty, and that the President had informed them that he would send a communication, in writing, to each House, at 12 o'clock this day.

A Message was received from the President of the United States, by the hand of Andrew J. Donelson, Esq. his Secretary, which will be found in another part of this paper.

After the reading of the Message from the Clerk's table,

On motion of Mr. CONNOR, it was ordered that it be referred to the Committee of the Whole on the state of the Union, and that 10,000 copies of the message and accompanying documents be printed.

On motion of Mr. BOON, the House then adjourned.

IN SENATE,

WEDNESDAY, December 3, 1834.

The Hon. Mr. BROWN, of North Carolina, Mr. TOMLINSON, of Connecticut, and Mr. SPRAGUE of Maine, appeared and took their seats.

A message was received from the President of the United States, communicating the annual report of the Treasury Department.

On motion of Mr. BENTON, the reading of the report was dispensed with, and the usual number of copies was ordered to be printed.

The VICE PRESIDENT laid before the Senate a communication from the Treasury Department, containing the receipts and expenditures of that Department for the year 1833.

Mr. POINDEXTER submitted the following resolutions:

Resolved, That the Commissioner of the General Land Office be directed to communicate to the Senate a list of the purchasers of the public lands at the Land Offices in Columbus and Chocchuma in the State of Mississippi, specifying the name of each original purchaser, and of the assignee or assignees to whom the certificate of purchase may have been endorsed, the quantity of land purchased by each, and the price per acre paid for each tract respectively, between the first day of October, 1833, and the first day of January, 1834.

Resolved, That the said Commissioner be directed to report to the Senate the aggregate number of acres of the public lands offered at public sale by proclamation of the President of the United States, at each of the Land Offices in the State of Mississippi, from the first day of January, 1833, up to the present time.

Mr. EWING gave notice that on to-morrow he would ask leave to introduce a bill to settle and establish the Northern boundary line of the State of Ohio.

Mr. MOORE gave notice that on Monday next he would ask leave to introduce the following bills:

A bill authorizing the relinquishment of the 16th

sections granted for the use of schools, and the entry of other lands in lieu thereof;
A bill for the relief of Elijah Simmons;
A bill for the relief of Eli Robinson;
A bill for the relief of Samuel Smith, Linn Mc-Ghee, and Le Moice, Creek Indians: and
A bill for the relief of Susan Marlow.

On motion of Mr. GRUNDY, so much of the President's Message as relates to the Post Office Department, was referred to the Committee on the Post Office and Post Roads.

The Senate then adjourned.

HOUSE OF REPRESENTATIVES,
WEDNESDAY, DEC. 3, 1834.

The following members appeared:
Messrs. ALLEN of Vermont, FULTON of Virginia, BLAIR of Tennessee, HANNEGAN of Indiana, GHOLSON of Virginia, GRAHAM, of North Carolina, STEWART of Pennsylvania, CRANE of Ohio, and CORWIN of Ohio.

Mr. CASEY, of Illinois, rose, he said, to offer a resolution to the House expressive of the respect of the members of this body for the memory of the Hon. CHARLES SLADE, late one of the Representatives from Illinois on this floor. In submitting the resolution which I now have the honor to do, for the consideration of the House, it is not my purpose to trespass on its time or attention by a labored eulogy on the character of my late distinguished colleague and much esteemed friend now no more. He died near Vincennes, Indiana, of that scourge of nations, cholera, on his way home from attending the last session of Congress. His amiable manners, his mild and benevolent disposition, his sound sense, and untiring devotion to his legislative duties while here, has made a lasting impression on all who knew him. He had a heart that responded to every advance of sympathy and benevolence; a heart formed for the most ardent attachments; open and undisguised, the prominent traits of his character were always before the world.

But, suffice it to say, that though the dust of CHARLES SLADE now sleeps with that of his fathers, he still lives in the hearts of hundreds and thousands of his countrymen who, with sincerity, deplore his death.

I therefore respectfully ask the members of this House to concur with me in this humble, this last, tribute of respect to his memory.

Mr. CASEY then offered the following resolution, on which was adopted.

Resolved, unanimously, That the members of this House will testify their respect for the memory of CHARLES SLADE, deceased, late a member of this House from the State of Illinois, by wearing crape on the left arm for one month.

Mr. JANES addressed the Chair as follows:
It has become my melancholy duty to announce to this House the death, since the last session, of another of your then members. The Hon. BENJAMIN F. DEMING, of Vermont, departed this life on the 11th of July last, on his way from this place to his home in that State. The deceased had been but a short time a member of this body, at long had held a distinguished place in the councils of his native State, and was there, and wherever he was known, universally esteemed and beloved as an enlightened and honest statesman, as an amiable citizen, as a christian of pure and unsullied morals. However flattering it may be to hold a seat on the floor of this House, to me it is deeply affecting that as one I have the honor of occupying has been made vacant by the death of an able legislator; by the removal from his family of an affectionate husband, a kind parent; and from me, a wise and constant friend. But if we permitted to gather hope from the public as I rate worth—the rectitude of moral character— daily christian deportment of man—few, if any, we left more comforting, more enduring evidences than the deceased, that he has now a crown of immortality, an eternal rest.

Mr. J. then offered the following resolution, which was agreed to:
Resolved, unanimously, That the members of this House will testify their respect for the memory of BENJAMIN F. DEMING, deceased, late of

---

the State of Vermont, by wearing crape on the left arm for one month.
On motion of Mr. HUBBARD,
The House then adjourned.

IN SENATE.
THURSDAY, December 4, 1834.

The Hon. Mr. LEIGH, one of the Senators from Virginia, appeared, and took his seat.

The following Message was received from the President of the United States, by the hands of A. J. DONELSON, Esquire, his private Secretary:

To the Senate of the United States:
I transmit to Congress a communication addressed to me by Mr. George Washington Lafayette, accompanying a copy of the Declaration of Independence, engraved on copper, which his illustrious father bequeathed to Congress, to be placed in their Library, as a last tribute of respect, patriotic love, and affection, for his adopted country.

I have a mournful satisfaction in transmitting this precious bequest of that great and good man, who, through a long life, under many vicissitudes, and in both hemispheres, sustained the principles of civil liberty asserted in that memorable declaration, and who, from his youth to the last moment of his life, cherished for our beloved country the most generous attachment.

ANDREW JACKSON.

The bequest accompanies the message to the House of Representatives. A. J.
4th December, 1834.

THE LETTER ENCLOSED IN THE ABOVE.]

PARIS, JUNE 15, 1834.

SIR: A great misfortune has given me more than one solemn and important duty to fulfil, and the ardent desire of accomplishing with fidelity my father's last will, emboldens me to claim the patronage of the President of the United States, and his benevolent intervention, when I am obliged respectfully and mournfully to address the Senate and Representatives of a whole nation.

Our forever-beloved parent possessed a Copperplate, on which was inscribed the first engraved copy of the American Declaration of Independence: and his last intention, in departing this world, was, that the precious plate should be presented to the Congress of the United States, to be deposited in their Library, as a last tribute of respect, patriotic love, and affection, for his adopted country.

Will it be permitted to me, a faithful disciple of that American school, whose principles are so admirably exposed in that immortal Declaration, to hope that you, sir, would do me the honor to communicate this letter to both Houses of Congress at the same time that, in the name of his afflicted family, you would present to them my venerated father's gift.

In craving such an important favor, sir, the son of General Lafayette, the adopted Grand-Son of Washington, knows, and shall never forget, that he would become unworthy of it, if he was ever to cease to be a French and American patriot.

With the utmost respect, I am, sir, your devoted and obedient servant,

GEORGE W. LAFAYETTE.
To the PRESIDENT of the United States.

In pursuance of notice yesterday, Mr. EWING, introduced a bill to settle and establish the Northern boundary line of the State of Ohio.

The resolutions submitted by Mr. POINDEXTER yesterday, were considered and adopted.

On motion of Mr. KANE,

Ordered, That when the Senate adjourns it adjourn over to Monday next.

Mr. TIPTON submitted the following resolution:
Resolved, That the Committee on Roads and Canals be instructed to inquire into the expediency of an appropriation to improve the navigation of the Wabash river.

This resolution lies on the table one day.
On motion of Mr. EWING,
The Senate adjourned (to Monday.)

HOUSE OF REPRESENTATIVES.
THURSDAY, Dec. 4, 1834.

On motion of Mr. WHITTLESEY, of Ohio, it was ordered, that the Standing Committees of the House be appointed.

On motion of Mr. GRENNELL,
Resolved, That two Chaplains, of different denominations, be elected by Congress, one by each House, to serve during the present session, who shall interchange weekly.

The SPEAKER laid before the House the Annual Report of the Secretary of the Treasury on the state of the Finances; which, on motion of Mr. POLK, was laid on the table, and 10,000 copies ordered to be printed.

The SPEAKER laid before the House a communication from the Secretary of the Treasury, enclosing a copy of the Receipts and Expenditures of the Government for the year 1835; which, on motion of Mr. POLK, was laid on the table.

The SPEAKER also laid before the House a communication from the Secretary of the Treasury, enclosing a Report of the Register and Receiver of the Land Office at St. Stephens, Alabama; which, on motion of Mr. CONNOR, was laid on the table and ordered to be printed.

A Message was received from the President of the United States, transmitting a communication from GEORGE WASHINGTON LAFAYETTE, which will be found in the Senate's proceedings.

On motion of Mr. E. EVERETT, the communication was referred to the Committee on Foreign Affairs.

The SPEAKER laid before the House a letter from the Clerk, enclosing his Annual Report of the disbursement of the Contingent Fund of the House for the year 1835; which, on motion of Mr. CONNOR, was laid on the table, and ordered to be printed.

The SPEAKER laid before the House a letter from the Secretary of the Treasury, containing the Annual Estimates of Appropriations for the year 1835; which, on motion of Mr. POLK, was laid on the table, and directed to be printed.

The SPEAKER laid before the House the Annual Report of the Treasurer of the United States; which was laid on the table, and ordered to be printed.

Mr. WARDWELL submitted the following resolution, which lies one day for consideration:

Resolved, That the Secretary of the Navy be directed to report to this House, the amount expended in erecting the Ship House at Navy Point, in the county of Jefferson, and State of New York, and the expense of keeping the same in repair. Also, the like information in relation to the vessel built and lately sold at Storr's Harbor, in said county, and the amount of compensation allowed to the officer or officers, person or persons, who have from time to time had charge of the same. Also, the reasons, if any exist, for the further preservation of the vessel and Ship House at Navy Point. Also, that he report the amount heretofore paid for the use and occupation of the land now belonging to the State of Henry Eckford, dec. at Navy Point and Storr's Harbor, on which the vessels New Orleans and Chippewa were built, and also the terms of any contract which may have been made with the Government, or its authorized agent, for the use and occupation of such land.

On motion of Mr. WHITE, of Florida, a report made by the Engineer Department at the last session, in relation to the Canal between Pensacola and Mobile Bays, was ordered to be printed.

On motion of Mr. MANN, of New York, it was ordered that when the House adjourns, it will adjourn to meet again on Monday next.

On motion of Mr. MANN, of New York,
The House then adjourned.

REPORT
Of the Secretary of the Treasury on the state of the Finances.

TREASURY DEPARTMENT, December 2d, 1834.

The Secretary of the Treasury respectfully presents the following Report, in obedience to the "Act supplementary to the act to establish the Treasury Department."

He would invite the attention of Congress—

1st. *To the Public Revenue and Expenditures.*

The balance in the Treasury, on the 1st of January, A. D. 1832, was - - $4,502,914 45
The actual receipts into the Treasury during the year 1832, from all sources, were - - 31,865,561 16

Making the whole amount in the Treasury in that year, $36,368,475 61
The actual expenditures during the same year, including the public debt, were - - - 34,356,698 06

The balance in the Treasury on the 1st of January, A. D. 1833, was, therefore, - - - 2,011,777 55
In addition to this balance, the receipts during the year 1833, were, from all sources, 33,948,436 25

Viz. from—
Customs, - $29,032,508 91
Lands, - - 3,967,682 55
Dividends on Bank Stock, 474,985 00
Sales of Bank Stock, 135,300 00
Incidental items, 337,949 79

These made, with the above balance, an aggregate of 35,960,203 80
The expenditures during A. D. 1833, were - - 24,237,298 49

Viz. on the Civil List, Foreign Intercourse, and Miscellaneous subjects, - $3,716,245 93
Military Service— including Fortifications, Ordnance, Indian Affairs, Pensions, Arming Militia, and Internal Imports, 13,096,152 43
Naval Service, including Gradual Improvement, 3,901,356 75
Public Debt, 1,543,545 38

Thus a balance was left in the Treasury, on the 1st of January, 1834, amounting to - 11,702,905 31
The receipts into the Treasury, ascertained and estimated, during A. D. 1834, are computed to be 20,624,717 94
Of these, the receipts during the first three quarters are ascertained to have been - - 16,324,717 94

Viz. from
Customs, - $12,740,872 25
Lands, - - 3,076,475 50
Dividends on Bank Stock, ⎫
Sales of Bank Stock ⎬ 507,370 19
Incidental Items ⎭

$16,324,717 94
And those, during the fourth quarter, it is expected, will be 4,300,000 00

Thus, with the balance on the 1st of January, 1834, they form an aggregate of - - 32,327,623 25
The expenditures of the whole year are ascertained and estimated to be - - - - 25,591,390 91
Of these, the expenditures during the first three quarters, are ascertained to have been - 16,545,342 92

Viz. on Civil List, Foreign Intercourse, and Miscellaneous, - $3,475,527 08

Military Service, including fortifications, &c. 8,349,400 06
Naval Service, including, &c. 2,913,183 12
Duties refunded, 108.546 19
Public Debt, 1,698,686 47

The expenditures for the 4th quarter, including $4,462,330 99, on account of the public debt, it is supposed, will be about - 9,046,047 99
Thus leaving on the 1st of January, 1835, an estimated balance of 6,736,232 34

This balance includes what has before been reported by this Department as not available, the sum of about $1,400,000, but which is now ascertained to be reduced to about the sum of $1,150,000; making the computed available balance on the 1st of January, 1835, to be - 5,586,232 34

It is estimated, that of former appropriations, there will remain unexpended at the close of this year, the sum of $8,002,925 13.

Of this amount, it is supposed that only $5,141,964 27 will be required to accomplish the objects intended by the current appropriations—leaving the sum of $999,742 93, applicable afterwards under permanent appropriations, and that of $1,523,308 79, to be applied in aid of the appropriations for the ensuing year, without re-appropriation—as will be seen in the estimates when submitted, and the balance of $337,909 14, which has not been required at a l, or seasonably, for the objects contemplated in its appropriation, and will, thereafter, be carried to the surplus fund. In the examination of this result, as to outstanding appropriations, it should be noticed, that one small amount of unclaimed interest on the public debt, and another of unfunded debt, though chargeable on the Treasury, are not included. Embracing these and the amount applicable afterwards to permanent appropriations, there would not be money enough in the Treasury to pay, at once, every claim outstanding. But, excluding them, it will be seen that the effective, unexpended funds on the 1st January, 1835, will be $5,586,231 34, to meet what will be required for the remaining and unexpended appropriations, being $5,141,964 27; or, in other words, that our *available* means then on hand to discharge all the old and existing claims on the Treasury, with the exceptions before named, will be about $444,268 07 more than their actual amount.

The next subject deserving consideration is the condition of

2. The Public Debt.

All the four and a half per cents, outstanding at the commencement of the present year, have been redeemed, except the sum of $443 25. Money sufficient to meet the whole balance was placed in the United States Bank and its branches, as commissioners of loans, in May last, and that portion not yet paid to the holders of the debt still remains in these depositories. A part of the five per cent. stock, created in March, A. D. 1821, amounting to $4,712,060 29, was all of the 123 millions of debt existing in A. D. 1816, and of the subsequent additions to it which was left to be redeemed. It did not become payable till the 1st of January, 1835; but as there was sufficient money in the Treasury for the purpose, and it having been considered beneficial to the public to save, as far as practicable, all the accruing interest, early in July last, agents were employed by this Department to purchase, at par, if possible, the whole of the remaining debt. Between that time and the 30th ult, the Department had succeeded in redeeming about $491,253 35 of it, and additional purchases are constantly making. In October last, the undersigned gave notice that the whole of this debt unredeemed after the first of January next, would cease to bear interest, and would be computed by paid, after that date, on application to the commissioners of loans in the several States. Under authority from the commissioners of the sinking fund, this Department has since placed and made arrangements to place, seasonably, in those offices ample funds, for the above purpose.

Thus, before the close of the year, the whole will either be paid, or money provided to pay it—and the United States will present that happy, and, probably, in modern times, unprecedented spectacle, of a People substantially free from the smallest portion of a public debt.

Considering these facts, it was deemed proper to charge the whole amount of the remaining debt to the expenditures of the present year. Interest on all not paid before the 30th ult., has been computed till the 1st of January next, the time being so short; and the account for the payment of the public debt, during the year, will then stand as follows:

All the disbursements on account of the public debt, during the year 1834, will be, as before shown, - - - $6,161,017 46
Of which there will have been applied to principal, 5,964,774 93
And to interest, 196,242 53

The stocks, which will have been redeemed by the application of this sum during the year, are of the residue of the exchanged 4½ per cent. stock, issued under the act of the 26th of May, 1824, - - - $1,232,625 99
The residue of the 5 per cent. stock, issued under the act of the 3d March, 1821, - - 4,712,060 29
Certain portions of unfunded debt, 38 74
Treasury notes, - - 50 00

Making in all the principal before named, $37,733 95
There is an unfunded debt of about $37,733 95
Consisting of claims registered prior to 1798, for service and supplies during the revolutionary war, of about - 27,437 96
Treasury notes issued during the last war, 5,975 00
And Mississippi stock, 4,320 09

Nothing has been paid on any of these during the present year, except $88 74. But should the application of the rest be presented, which is not very probable as to many of them, the means undoubtedly will always exist for their payment at the Department.

3. The estimate of the *Public Revenue and Expenditures for the year* 1835, *next require attention, and are as follows:*

The receipts into the Treasury from all sources during the year 1835, are estimated at the sum of $20,000,000

Viz. From
Customs, - 16,000,000
Public Lands, - 3,500,000
Bank dividends and miscellaneous receipts, 500,000

To which add the balance of available funds in the Treasury on the 1st of January, 1835, estimated at, - - - 5,586,232 34

And they make together the sum of, - - - $25,586,232 34
The necessary appropriations for the year 1835, including those under new and permanent acts, are estimated at $15,660,232 73.

But the whole expenditures for the service of that year, are estimated to require the additional sum of $1,523,308 79, which has before been appropriated and mentioned as applicable to the wants of 1835, without a re-appropriation, making together, $17,183,541 52

Viz. on
Civil, Foreign Intercourse, and Miscellaneous items, - 2,788,225 35
Military service, &c., Pensions, and the appropriations under the act of 7th June, 1832, 9,672,654 50
Naval service, and gradual improvement, 4,672,661 17
Unclaimed interest on Public Debt, 50,000

To this add, as a contingent expen-

diture, about half the amount of the average excess of appropriations beyond the estimates during the last three years,   2,600,000 00

And they make the sum of, $19,683,541 52

Leaving an available balance in the Treasury, at the close of the year 1835, or on the 1st of January, 1836, estimated at, $5,902,690 82

But should the whole amount of former appropriations, current and permanent, that will be outstanding on the 1st of January, 1835, and be needed to complete the services of former years, amounting in all, as before shown, to the sum of $6,141,707 20 be actually called for during the year 1835, there would be an apparent deficiency in the Treasury on the 1st of January, 1836. It usually happens, however, that of the new and the old appropriations, a sum of five or six millions remains uncalled for at the commencement of each year, and hence no real deficit is then anticipated, as much, if any, excess, after defraying all the expenditures then chargeable to the Treasury.

This estimate of receipts is formed on the supposition, that the value of imports during the ensuing year, and especially of those paying duties, will not differ essentially from the average during the last three years. Though our population has, within that period, probably increased over one million, yet our manufactures and internal trade have probably increased nearly in an equal proportion—and this circumstance, coupled with the greater caution and frugality practised during the past year, and still continuing, will, it is believed, tend to prevent any considerable augmentation in the consumption or importation of foreign articles.

The imports during the year ending September 30th, 1834, are estimated in value at $123,093,351—being, compared with the preceding year, an increase of $14,101,541. Those during the three past years have, on an average, been about $111,038,142.

The Exports, during the same year, are estimated at $97,318,724; of which $74,444,429 were in domestic, and $22,874,295 in foreign products—being, compared with the preceding year, an increase of $6,655,321; of which $3,802,399 were in articles of domestic, and $2,852,922 in those of foreign products. The average exports during the last three years have had about $91,719,690; of which $69,407,976 are the average in articles of domestic products, and $22,311,714 in those of foreign.

It will thus be seen, that the imports of the last year varied in amount $12,055,209, from the average of the three past years, and those paying duties are believed to have varied much less. It is, therefore, in connexion with the reasons before named, considered safe to infer, that the imports of the ensuing year may not differ materially from that average. Should they not so differ, the revenue from customs will probably correspond in substance with that of the past year, except so far as it may be changed by the whole amount of all the importations when compared with the above average.

Because the classes and value of articles paying duty, for aught which is known, will probably be similar, and the rate of duties on them will not, by existing laws, be essentially altered till the 31st of December, A. D. 1835.

The revenue from the sale of Public Lands, has been estimated at half a million more than the amount it was estimated for the current year, and one million more than the proceeds for 1833. This estimate would have been made still larger, had not the sales of the Chickasaw lands, which will probably exceed half a million of dollars, been pledged by treaty to other purposes, and not to the general revenue of the Government. This large computation is founded on the facts of the progressive increase for some time evinced; the sum actually received during the past year; the great quantity of new and saleable lands coming into market, the enlarged demand for them to satisfy the necessary wants of our growing population, and of the emigrants from Europe, and

the high prices which their produce fortunately obtains both at home and abroad.

The revenue from Bank Dividends has been estimated at somewhat less than heretofore, in consequence of the sales of our Bank stock under the act of July 10th, 1832, for the investment of the accruing income of the Navy Pension and Hospital Funds—having already amounted to $656,600, and on which the Treasury can now receive no dividends applicable to general purposes. It might perhaps be advisable to deduct a still further sum to meet any contingency, like that of the present year, in which the United States Bank, without the consent of this Department, or the sanction of Congress, and without any forewarning of its intention, seized on about $170,041 of the estimated revenue from this source, and has since withheld it from the public Treasury.

Copies of the opinions of the Attorney General, and the whole correspondence on this subject between the Department and the Bank, which took place previously to the request for these opinions, are annexed, for the consideration and action of Congress. It may be proper to add, that within a few days past a new communication in relation to this transaction, has been received from the Bank, and when a reply is finished, both will be submitted, if desired.

No foundation appears to have existed in law or equity for the great claim of damages made by the Bank on account of the protest of what has been called, in common parlance, the bill of exchange, drawn on the French Government by this Department. It is believed that the bill, when protested, ought, by our agents abroad, had they acted with due regard towards their principal, to have been taken up for the credit of that principal, which was the United States, rather than for the credit of the Bank; or, at the farthest, if similar and conflicting relations existed between them and the Bank, they should have pursued the equitable course of taking it up for the credit of both the United States and the Bank, or the more liberal one of giving the preference to the Government, which was the drawer; and in either of these events, no further difficulty, by this extraordinary claim, would probably have been left. But as these agents preferred a different course, thereby justly impairing the further confidence of the Government in their discretion, it would seem that the Bank in the next place, having long been the general fiscal agent of the Government, and the primary one in importance, should have returned the bill, and made no charge against its principal, the United States, except for the actual advances, and the actual costs and expenses it had incurred in the transaction. The actual advances, by the Bank, when the bill was originally received, had only been a matter of form, and were nothing. The money, in fact, never belonged to this Department, except in trust for the merchants, or their widows and orphans, who had suffered by French spoliations; and a sum exceeding the whole amount of it having been left in the Bank and its branches, and no part of the money having ever been brought into the Treasury by my warrant, it was immediately, on notice of the protest, restored in form, and a willingness was expressed to make remuneration to the Bank for all reasonable costs and expenses. But the temptation of an opportunity to obtain more from its principal, by a novel species of litigation, through a virtual judicial prosecution for damages, against the Government of the Union, seems to have been too strong for resistance; and the Bank concluded to depart from the above equitable rule, and by some technical regulation of strict law between individuals, to attempt to procure a large sum, as mere constructive damages, and by the extraordinary mode of seizing on the dividends which had been declared by the Bank itself to belong to the United States, and of withholding them till made the ordinary contingencies of a lawsuit.

It seems to have preferred this unprecedented course, rather than to pursue the usual mode of a petition addressed to the Justice of Congress, though Congress is well known to be the customary and only tribunal for adjusting controverted claims against the Government, when no suit is

pending by the United States, and the only tribunal which, under the constitution, is empowered to appropriate money to discharge any claim whatever. After applying to this Department, and being, so long as a year ago last June, informed of its inability to admit or authority to discharge the damages demanded, it is remarkable that the Bank should have continued to pay over the accruing dividends, and not till after the last session closed, and when any deficiency in the current revenue could not be provided for, should, without any prior application to Congress, have resorted to this unusual proceeding, and sought to have its claim against the United States, adjudicated by the Judiciary, when the United States are not amenable to any citizen or corporation, high or low, before the Judiciary, for the decision of any claim, unless they have, of their own accord, been pleased to resort to that tribunal by a previous action against them; and, in which event only, is a set off, under certain limitations, authorized to be pleaded, as either equitable or legal. But, here the United States had instituted no such action against the Bank and had no intention or foundation to institute one; and yet, the Bank, not in the case provided in the charter where dividends might be withheld, but by an unfaithful act, as an agent, and as a public corporation, towards its principal and the community, proceeded to seize their dividends in a case entirely different and most questionable in equity as well as law and refused to fulfil the duty imposed by its charter, and by civil and moral obligations of paying over those dividends promptly to the Treasury. In the adoption of this reprehensible rate violation of its obligations. The further attempt appears to be made in this way to take from Congress and the Executive, the constitutional power, on their high official responsibility and deep sense of duty, to make or withhold appropriations to discharge all controverted demands against the United States, and to enable the Judiciary instead of them, indirectly and unconstitutionally to make these appropriations, in all cases of citizens or corporations, who possess doubtful claims, and are unscrupulous enough to commit, in order to prevent their adjudication by Congress, a deliberate attack on the property of their acknowledged dues.

In every such and more detailed views on this extraordinary case, a reference is made to the whole correspondence and opinions annexed, without the discussion of any topics, which the power and the wisdom of Congress are able to select for evincing its opinions on this outrage, whether, by withdrawing indulgences from the Bank as to the receipt of its notes for public dues, or by adopting some other measure on the subject, which the nature of the transaction, the rights of the United States, and the constitutional authority of Congress, may be thought to justify and demand.

Believing that a similar seizure was not likely to be repeated by the Bank in 1835, under the other pretence of satisfying claims for damages, in consequence of the removal of the deposites, as set up in its second letter, this Department has estimated the probable revenue the ensuing year from this source, at the usual rate of dividends lately made on all our stock in the Bank, remaining after the shares which have taken place for the investment of the Navy Pension and Hospital funds. But should Congress, on a full examination of the subject, think otherwise, it may be provident to supply some other equivalent for this portion of the estimated receipts.

The estimate of revenue from miscellaneous sources, has been computed a little below the ac-

tual receipts of the current year; because the dividends applicable to general purposes, will be on a less amount of Bank stock, and the anticipated sales of such stock to meet the further wants of the before mentioned funds, will be much reduced.

In this explanation of the estimate of the receipts during the coming year, it is hoped that satisfactory reasons have been assigned, to show its general accuracy. This estimate being one and a half millions larger than that of last year, it is more likely to exceed, than, like that, to fall short of the actual result. That estimate proved to be less than the actual receipts, probably about $2,000,000, or from customs about $1,200,000, from lands nearly $800,000; and the residue chiefly from larger sales of Bank stock as before named, than was anticipated. As the first deduction of 10 per cent. from the excess of duties on goods imported, and paying over 20 per cent. ad valorem, took effect on the 31 of December last, it was not practicable to fix beforehand with much certainty the amount of the diminution on account of it from the revenue of the year, as the same value of merchandise might not be imported as in any previous year, which should be selected for a guide in forming the estimate; and the particular kinds of merchandise thus imported, whether free, or paying a duty, might greatly fluctuate. To these uncertainties in the whole value, and in the kinds of goods imported, were to be added the circumstances that the system of reduction, going into operation, was almost entirely new in practice; and that the cash duties substituted for credit on some articles, tended to render former means of calculation still more inapplicable and doubtful.

It is hoped that, as the ensuing year is exposed chiefly to only one of these sources of uncertainty, which is the whole value of dutiable goods imported, the estimate made for the income from customs, will not vary essentially from the amount of receipts which time may prove to be correct.

In relation to the excess of revenue received from lands over the estimate made for the year 1834, the amount from that source happened to be unprecedented, and as full returns of the very large sales in December, 1833, had not then been received, it was entirely unexpected. But the actual excess, this year, though not so large as in the previous one, coupled with circumstances before named, has induced the department to submit a larger estimate, under this head, than has heretofore been made.

The estimates for the expenditures of the ensuing year, have been graduated and modified by the following circumstances: the actual expenditures for the year 1833, did not differ much from the expectations expressed concerning them in the last annual report, except that the residue of the 4½ per cent. stocks, although charged to 1833, was not in fact all reimbursed, or the money paid to the Commissioners of Loans for that purpose, within that year, but only $13,198 of them were redeemed in the residue of 1833. Between the 1st of January and May, 1834, about $497,697 more was redeemed, and afterwards the sum of $759,271 was advanced to the commissioners of loans to meet the balance which was then outstanding. Partly from this cause, therefore, reducing the actual expenditure in the fourth quarter of 1833 about a million below the estimate, and partly from an increase in the revenue of nearly two millions beyond the estimate of that quarter, from causes before enumerated, the actual *available* amount in the Treasury on the first of January, 1834, was greater than the estimate; having been $10,302 905, instead of the estimated sum of $7,983,790. The expenditures in 1834, on account of the public debt thus became increased beyond the estimate about $1,256,968. Another source of expenditure, increased during the past year, beyond the estimates, was the sum of $75,407 for interest on the public debt, which had before been unclaimed, but which has since been demanded and discharged, and to meet which, probably from adhering to the usage of former years, or from an impression it would remain uncalled for, no money had been specifically set aside, nor any charge made to the expected expenditure of the year. Besides these unexpected calls during the present year, the appropriations in money, by new acts of Congress, and by former permanent acts, still in force, have been computed to be about $21,000,000. These constituted a new burthen, in addition to a balance of public debt which remained to be paid, amounting to about six millions, and a balance of old appropriations liable to be called for, amounting to about five millions more. The whole appropriations thus chargeable for expenditures to the year, did not vary much from thirty-one millions of dollars in money, besides a number of grants of land of considerable extent and value, that were voted by Congress. Having presented this explanation of the principal expenditures which have been charged to the present year, and defrayed to the extent required, a basis has been laid for showing the reasons upon which this Department has proceeded to reduce its estimates for new appropriations for expenditure the ensuing year to the extent of about six and a third millions of dollars below those of last year. This is about one and a third of a million less, independent of the amount then estimated to be needed towards the discharge of the public debt. In that sum of new appropriations, amounting to about 21,000,000 of dollars, there was no permanent charge that has been deemed likely to be much lessened for the ensuing year, such as the arming of the militia and the gradual improvement of the Navy. Nor, in the opinion of this department, will the great objects for expenditure, of a character general and somewhat fixed, such as those usually connected with civil and foreign purposes, the Navy and Army, including works classed as internal improvements, Indians and pensions, admit, immediately, of so great diminution in number or amount, as might be desired and is hereafter expected: but as large a reduction as practicable, without injury to the public interests and a neglect of important duties, has been made in the estimated expenditures for each of them, being in all, after allowing a small increase in some, about one and a third millions of dollars.

It is anticipated that with the valuable improvements of late years in steam, and the great advantages in using these improvements for harbor and maritime defence, some of the fortifications originally contemplated, may hereafter be wholly dispensed with, or be built on a different and reduced scale; and though it is thought that only about two millions can the following year be prudently retrenched from the expenditures connected with fortifications and harbors, Indians and pensions; yet it is manifest, that very soon the amount required for those public purposes must, by the completion of the most necessary defences, by the extinguishment of most of the titles of the Indians, and the removal of that unfortunate race beyond the Mississippi, and by the rapid march of death among pensioners, and the detection of numerous frauds among their professed agents, become still more diminished, and as our impost duties will be further reduced by the operations of the act of March, 1833, the reduction both in revenue and in expenditure, for these great objects, will, therefore, happily and conveniently for a time be likely very near to correspond. A more fixed amount for the ordinary peace establishment of the army, and some other expenditures connected with the Executive, Legislative, and Judicial Departments, would, like what now exists, with greater precision and uniformity in the expenses of the Navy, be a great desideratum in the permanent adjustment of our revenue system, and would tend, in many important respects, to useful retrenchment. The gradual increase required in some classes of expenditure, by the gradual increase of our population and wealth, and of those public establishments which fluctuate with them, such as some parts of the Judiciary, the Legislative; and Executive, could then be accurately foreseen and provided for; while any extraordinary and unexpected enlargement in expenses would then excite inquiry, and unless resting on clear and extraordinary causes, would justify opposition. When so resting, they would be met by the public cheerfully by means of increased taxes and revenue.

Another important circumstance deserves consideration in explanation of the new and contingent item of $2,500,000, now first added to the estimates for the ensuing year. It has been ascertained by a careful scrutiny and comparison, that much of the great expenditures of the last four years, beside the payment of the debt, have arisen from appropriations by Congress to a larger amount, under particular heads, than the general estimates for the year, submitted by the Treasury, and from large appropriations to objects not specifically included in any estimates. To illustrate this, an abstract of a table of the general estimates, appropriations, and expenditures, during the past two years, and of all these, but the expenditures during the past three years, has been prepared and is submitted, showing a difference between the estimates and appropriations, independent of the public debt, in 1832, of between five and six millions, in 1833 of nearly five millions, and in 1834 of about three millions. The largest portion of this great increase, amounting in the two first years, from one-quarter to one-third of the whole appropriations, it will be seen is under the civil and miscellaneous heads, and under items classed with the military establishment, such as harbors improved, pensions, &c. For the information of the public on a comparison deemed so very important, it is proposed to publish the detailed table from which this is compiled, and a similar one hereafter, appended to the annual exhibit of the receipts and expenditures. Should this practice of making appropriations so greatly exceeding the estimates be continued by Congress, it will not only prevent much reduction, particularly under the miscellaneous head, but it will be necessary to provide for the consequences of it by an augmented revenue, proportionate to these demands, or by a larger regular surplus in the Treasury to meet such unexpected increases of appropriations. It must be manifest, that it is not in the power of this Department to foresee and compute these increases with any degree of accuracy, as with the exception of some subsequent estimates, submitted after the annual ones, they depend almost wholly, in their inception, on the pleasure and discretion of Congress; and as they consist chiefly of miscellaneous public objects, and private grants, for almost numberless causes, they may vary greatly in different years. But it might be unfaithfulness in the undersigned, towards both Congress and the public, since the extent of the influence of this excess on the expenditures, though always something, has been ascertained to be very large during the last three years, not to bring it distinctly to their notice, and not to submit a contingent item in the estimates for the purpose of covering it. Whether that which the Department has now offered, reduced as it is nearly one half from the average of the actual excesses during the three past years, will prove correct or not, and whether the diminished estimates under some other heads, will correspond or not, with the actual amount of appropriations that may be made, and with our anticipated means to meet them, will depend much on the caution and policy Congress may deem proper to use in restricting appropriations more nearly within the estimates presented. On the presumption that they may be more restricted than heretofore, only the addition before mentioned has, on this account, been made to the whole estimated expenditures for the ensuing year. A reduction so much lower than the late actual average excesses, is supposed to be justified from two leading considerations. One of them is the circumstance, that during a short session of Congress, which now occurs, fewer bills of a miscellaneous character can generally be well examined and passed, than during a long session. Another is, that as our revenue diminishes, it is probable that greater vigilance will be exercised by all, in the allowance of very ancient and almost obsolete private claims, or of claims very doubtful in character as to either facts or principles, and in making further appropriations to some objects of public importance, which have already received liberal attention, and which from their nature, must be expected to diminish rather than increase in their demands on the public Treasury. Thus, in regard to light-houses, custom-houses, marine hospitals—not to comment on various objects connected with internal improve-

ment and public expenditure, within the District of Columbia—it is manifest that the sums appropriated for some years past, can be safely and judiciously diminished in several respects, and in others almost entirely discontinued. If this be done, as it doubtless will be, with discrimination and judgment, though some new objects will have to be added, and increases in some old ones computed, yet it is probable that the saving in expense to the public will not only be considerable, but at the same time, no object of a really commercial character, and of national magnitude, need be neglected, nor any power exercised, and treasure expended, in those doubtful cases of constitutional right in the General Government, which tend to alienate brethren of the same political family, and to perpetuate excitements unfavorable to useful legislation, and in some degree dangerous to our Union. It has been further considered, in the estimates and reductions for the ensuing year, that our whole expenditure on account of the public debt has in one sense ceased, either by completing the payment of it, or by a deposite of money with the commissioners of loans, or a readiness of it in the Treasury sufficient to pay all which remains, whenever the holders choose to receive it. But tho' all the principal and interest necessary for this object will, before the year closes, have been placed in the Bank and its branches as Commissioner of Loans, yet the practice is, to require the interest, if not called for seasonably, to be, after a certain period, returned to the Treasury, and the principal only to be retained by the Bank, till otherwise directed by the Commissioners of the Sinking Fund, or by Congress. The unclaimed interest, after having been once paid out of the Treasury and returned, does not at this time exceed $261,-538, or the money ready there for its discharge, after meeting all the outstanding current appropriations. Under this practice, it will be seen that its payment must constitute some annual charge on the Treasury till the whole is actually adjusted, and consequently, $50,000 for that purpose has been included in the estimated expenditure of the ensuing year. This will probably be nearly all the demands of any kind for the public debt, in any form which will then be made on the Treasury or the sinking fund. The rest of the sinking fund, if not abolished by Congress, could hereafter be applied for general purposes.

In substantial conformity to the proposition made last year by this Department, it would now seem still more imperative on Congress to provide that the money, whether principal or interest, drawn from the Treasury and placed in the Bank and its branches as Commissioners of Loans, and which shall not be called for by the public creditors before the close of the ensuing year, should be repaid into the Treasury and held under notice to creditors to receive it there; that the office of Commissioner of Loans be abolished, the duties of the Commissioners of the Sinking Fund, and the provisions as to the fund itself suspended—and such power devolved on this Department as may be necessary to a settlement of that part of the debt which may not then have been demanded; and as the Bank charter soon thereafter expires, to provide further that the books and other papers connected with the public debt should be returned, and deposited here to enable the Treasury to guard against mistakes and frauds. The whole amount unclaimed in possession of the Bank on account of the public debt has been reduced to $282,333, and though about to be augmented by the transfer of a sufficient sum to meet the whole residue of the outstanding debt, it will probably not remain much larger at the close of the ensuing year.

With a little legislation of this kind, every thing will be done by Congress which is deemed necessary to close up, it is hoped, forever all the once large public debt of these United States. By the payment of the whole of it with punctuality and fidelity, it is gratifying to reflect that our public credit as a nation has been raised to a high standing, and a large stock of confidence acquired from others, which in such future exigencies as are likely to happen sooner or later, in all countries, will aid us to procure ample and seasonable loans without ruinous discounts or delays.

In pursuing this honorable course, the government of the Union has not only shown good faith abroad to its foreign friends and allies, those who lent assistance when most needed; but it has redeemed, whether at home or abroad, the entire debt of both the revolution and the late war, paid the purchase money for Florida and Louisiana, and with a most scrupulous sense of moral as well as political obligation, administered in various ways to the wants and atoned for many of the losses of those, who perilled life and fortune in the struggle for independence, in which our public debt had its sacred origin. It is an additional source of gratification, that this has been effected without imposing heavy burthens on the People, or leaving their Treasury empty, trade languishing and industry paralised; but, on the contrary, with almost every great interest of society flourishing, with taxes reduced, a surplus of money on hand; valuable stocks and extensive lands still owned by the government, and with such various other financial resources at command as to give to our country in this respect a very enviable superiority.

When it is considered, that this has been effected by a young and at first not very numerous people, within about half a century, and who, during the same period, have provided such other and ample means to sustain their useful systems of Government, and to build up great and prosperous communities, we may well be proud of the illustration our country affords of the financial ability of free institutions, and of the high destinies in various respects, not appropriately noticeable on this occasion, but which may await our preservation of these institutions in their original vigor, purity, and republican simplicity.

From the views before taken of the probable wants during the ensuing year for expenditures, and of the probable receipts to meet them, it has been stated, that on the 1st January, 1836, it was estimated that there will remain a surplus of available funds of about $5,900,690. This result has been attained by considering the unavailable portion of our funds then and now on hand, at the reduced sum of about $1,150,000, instead of $1,400,000, as heretofore reported. But it may be desirable to Congress to know, that there is a prospect, during the ensuing year, of collecting some further portion of these funds. This will be accomplished, it is anticipated, by the appointment of some more active agents—by new compromises—and by more rigorous requirements in collections where property exists, so as to reduce farther the whole amount from $50,000 to $100,000, and if this hope be realized, the above named available balance will to that extent be increased. A minute analysis and examination of these unavailable funds have recently been completed, and will be submitted in the supplemental report, soon to be laid before Congress, on the present mode of keeping and disbursing the public revenue. But on the other hand, enlarged somewhat as this balance may happen to be from any causes, it should be remembered that on the 31st day of December, 1835, another reduction of 10 per cent. must, by the existing laws, be made from a part of the present tariff, and if the surplus in the Treasury, by a year from next January, should prove to be increased to two millions, it could not, with safety, be regarded as too great for meeting, with a reduced rate of imposts on importations, the probable wants of A. D. 1836. At all events, such is the uncertainty on that subject at this distance of time, that though something unusual in the latter part of A. D. 1836 may, in the way of final dividends on our portion of the capital of the bank stock, be received; yet it is not now possible to foresee the contingencies that may check either the present large importations of merchandise or large sales of land, and consequently reduce the revenue derived from them, or that may require an increase in our army or navy expenditures, arising from those unfortunate collisions to which all nations are liable, that feel disposed to sustain the faith of treaties, vindicate their public rights, and protect, efficiently, their commerce and citizens. No further reduction of the tariff, until that already provided for at the close of the ensuing year, would, therefore, seem to be prudent.

The reduction or increase of the Tariff is now referred to with a view to revenue alone, and not with a view to questions so much agitated heretofore, of protection, countervailing regulations, and the proper national policy to be pursued, as to the imported luxuries and necessaries of life. On those points, it is considered far better for the real manufacturers themselves, not engaged in mere speculative investments, as well as for commerce, agriculture, and the revenue, that a policy should be selected, not unjust to either great interest or either great section of the Union, and when once established, that frequent changes should be avoided, and the occasional increase or reduction of revenue, which may sometimes become proper for financial purposes, should be connected with articles wholly detached from the question of protection to manufactures. The Tariff as to these troublesome points, is regarded as now adjusted, by the act of March, 1833, till the year A. D. 1842, except in respect to such new regulations as may be required from time to time, for the due enforcement of the spirit of that act, or such other changes as new occurrences may satisfy the great mass of the community, are rendered proper for earlier modifications, without a departure from the spirit of the compromise then intended among the friends of free trade and of high protection.

A separate Report, on certain subjects relating to the due enforcement of the present Tariff being in preparation, only one of them will now be adverted to. It is the evasion of the present duty on silks from beyond the Cape of Good Hope, by their being first landed, and occasionally re-colored, or re-stamped, in Europe, before imported into this country. In this way, and by the present discrimination in favor of European silks, the revenue loses a very large amount. As some illustration of the loss by such discriminations, the recent one in favor of French silks alone amounted to over $300,000 a year; and that now in favor of French wines amounts to nearly $200,000 more; making a loss of over half a million a year on these two articles with only one nation.

But, while on the other points, independent of the spirit of the compromise of 1833, legislation may be regarded as still fairly open, it certainly ought not to be attempted on so delicate and difficult a subject, unless imperative cases for it shall occur, whether combined or not with any increase or reduction of the tariff that may become necessary as a mere question of revenue by the actual condition of our receipts and expenditures. So far from any increase being necessary at present, or prospectively, the balance now on hand in the Treasury, and the accruing revenue under existing laws, will, in the opinion of the Department, prove amply sufficient to answer all ordinary demands, and, united with our other resources, to answer any unexpected demands of no very extraordinary amount.

As appears by the documents annexed, the Government has about $6,343,400 subject to general use, invested in the United States Bank stock, and the sum of $1,882,500 invested in different canal stocks; and the proceeds of the sales of which, if authorised in any unexpected deficiency, would, in most cases, prove amply sufficient, without any resort to an increased tariff. On the contrary, neither of the available balances estimated to be on hand in 1835 or 1836, after deducting what will be wanted for outstanding appropriations, can probably exceed a million. Should the surplus, without that deduction, prove to be about six millions, as estimated, the undersigned respectfully submits that it will require no legislation, as that amount has been about the average usual balance retained on hand for many years—a balance that has furnished great facilities in meeting all claims, even at the remotest points, with punctuality and good faith, afforded much stability and elevation to our public credit, by providing seasonably the means for a punctilious fulfilment of contracts, and yielded so great security against sudden evils of every kind in financial affairs, as to render one of near that amount provident and economical; and especially so at this moment, when any surplus which may exist, will accrue under a permanent compromise of the Tariff, that contains within itself a provision to reduce still further the duties, and undoubtedly the whole

amount of our revenue after the close of the coming year.

It is a source of sincere congratulation, that from the general prosperity of our commerce, and from the peace, industry, and abundance which so widely prevail over our fortunate country, under its admirable institutions, that researches are obliged to be directed, rather to the due reduction or disposition of any occasional surplus that may happen to exist in the Treasury, than to obtain sufficient for public purposes by taxation and other burthens. But under our altered system as to duties, and the public debt, it will be prudent to calculate that deficiencies, as well as surpluses, may happen oftener than formerly. In the opinion of the undersigned, however, neither can be soon anticipated so as to require immediate legislation. But should Congress think differently, no harm could arise from vesting a power in the Treasury Department, in case of an unexpected deficiency occurring in the revenue from any cause whatever, to sell such portion of our public stocks as may be necessary to supply the public wants growing out of actual appropriations. In a contingency of that kind, against which, in the present system of our revenue, and without a large ordinary surplus to be applied as it can be spared or not, for the payment of a public debt, in the manner heretofore practised, it is difficult to guard effectually against not only the occurrence of a deficiency, but its usual evils, a delay, if not great embarrassment and injury to public creditors, and a violation of our plighted faith. At the same time, it might be expedient to provide, that whenever the collections of the revenue, permanently authorized, should prove to be in an excess not immediately needed, or useful as a proper surplus in the Treasury, that the Department should either obtain interest for it, of the Banks where the largest amounts are long deposited, or invest it temporarily in some safe stocks, till needed, or till the tariff is again changed. This would probably secure a due interest on it, while retained, instead of the present and past modes of obtaining interest on any occasional surplus, by applying it in discharge of the public debt, and which mode since the payment of the latter, can no longer be pursued.

Should facts occur, which appear to require legislation, such an arrangement, like a regulator in some large or complicated machinery, remedying any occasional irregularities, might operate more beneficially as to any considerable excess or deficiency, than yearly changes of the tariff, made to meet yearly vibrations in our revenue, or to meet yearly reductions or augmentations in our expenditures. This subject of interest from the deposite Banks, at some rate, and under some circumstances, was adverted to in a report by a committee in one House of Congress the last session, and would, at this time, be more fully examined in connexion with that report, and the subsequent intimation of the United States Bank, of its claim for damages on account of the late removal of the deposites, connected, it is apprehended, with the idea of a profit or interest derived from them, were it supposed that either point could, in the present condition of things, be considered of any practical importance. But the balance of money at present on hand, as before remarked, is merely the usual and convenient amount for current fiscal operations, and most of it is liable at any moment to be withdrawn to meet existing appropriations. While the intimation of the Bank, resting, as it probably must, on an impression that the *bonus* was paid instead of interest on the public deposites, is not believed to be supported by the language or spirit of the charter, which required the *bonus* "for the exclusive privileges and benefits conferred by this act on the Bank," and which *exclusive* favors, whether termed *privileges* or *benefits*, consisted principally in the sole right of banking for twenty years, and for which alone, Mr. Madison, in his veto of 1815, and Mr. Dallas, in his letter, Dec. 24. 1815, thought "that a bonus should be paid [illegible] Government." The latter further observed, "independent of the bonus here proposed to [illegible] exacted, there are undoubtedly many public [illegible]antages to be drawn from the establishment of [illegible] national bank, but they are generally of an incidental kind, and as *in the case of the deposites,* 'and distribution of the revenue, may be regarded 'in the light of equivalents, not for the monopoly 'of the charter, but for the reciprocal advantages of a fiscal connexion with the Government."

If the reasons should ever be presented to this Department in support of the late intimation of a demand for damages for the removal of the deposites, in a case where the bonus was claimed and paid on the above grounds, and where the right to remove the deposites was expressly reserved in the charter to the officer removing them—it will then probably be in season to enter more fully into this collateral question; or should the balance in the possession of the State Banks, at any time, become much larger than the current demands existing against the Treasury, it will, if Congress do not earlier think proper to act on it prospectively, nor to authorize any temporary investment of it, be then considered necessary and proper for this Department to examine in what cases, and under what circumstances, on what surpluses, and at what rate, interest could equitably be demanded, in addition to the useful duties performed by the selected Banks in behalf of the Treasury. On these points, however, it is hoped that this Department will not be understood as recommending that taxes should ever be imposed with a view to permit a large surplus, any more than a deficiency, to occur; but that, when the former unexpectedly and unintentionally happens, an income should be realized from it, by interest or an investment until, at the end of every few years, a thorough revision of the tariff would, in the pursuit of this policy be made, and so graduated as, during the next succeeding term, to be likely to correct any great irregularities, whether excesses or deficiencies, that had happened during the preceding term, and to lead to the sale and use of any interest or investments, which, in the mean time, had accumulated.

Those other questions, naturally connected with the present deposite Banks, and, indeed, with our whole existing system of finance, so far as regards the keeping and disbursing of the public money, might here be appropriately considered. Yet, without any desire to avoid, but rather from a wish to submit that full and frank discussion of them which their acknowledged importance and the exciting interest in them demand from the fiscal department of the Government, they will be postponed to a separate supplemental report, which will be confined exclusively to their consideration, and will soon be presented to Congress.

It appears to the undersigned, that a change in the commencement of the fiscal year, and of the time at which the annual appropriations begin, would be a great improvement in the financial operations of the Government. If the year was to commence after the last day of March, instead of September, and the annual appropriations begin from the same date, many delays and embarrassments would be avoided, and the information on the condition of the receipts and expenditures of the previous year, to be laid before Congress each session, could be much more full and accurate.

Upon the subject of the new coinage of gold, and the operation of the acts of the last session relating to it, and the value and tender of foreign coins, this Department does not, until further experience is had, contemplate offering many recommendations for new legislation. A particular suggestion, deemed proper, is that the one dollar gold coin, originally embraced in the late act, should be authorized. If found on trial to be convenient, as small gold coins have been found, some of less and some of little larger amount, in Portugal, Russia, Spain, Turkey, and Switzerland, it does not seem to comport with the interest and welfare of the community to prevent here its coinage and circulation; and if not found on trial to be useful, the sagacity of self interest will soon lead to the abandonment of its coinage, by making no demand for it. Thus the community can in no event sustain much, if any injury from it; while the facilities of the public, by having a coin of either metal, gold or silver, as small as one dollar, may be greatly increased. This kind of legislation with a view to provide a full supply and variety of coin, instead of bills below five and ten dollars, is particularly conducive to the security of the poor and middling classes—who, as they own but little in, and profit but little by Banks, should be subjected to as small a risk as practicable by their bills.

The wealthy and commercial, for whose benefit chiefly banks are instituted, will then chiefly use their bills, and suffer by them, if forged or depreciated; while the laboring classes, and men of small property will, by the justice and paternal care of the Government, generally be provided with a currency of hard money, not exposed to any risk of failures, and to be used for all dealings of such an amount as their daily or weekly wants may in most cases require.

The new coinage has as yet been confined principally to the half and quarter eagles, and has equalled in all about $3,114,090—or in four months more than four times the annual average coinage of gold for many years past. The demand for other coins has also been promptly met throughout the year. To aid in carrying the new law into efficient operation, this Department last August placed in the hands of the Director of the Mint, under the act of April 2d, 1792, twenty thousand dollars, and ten thousand more in September, as it was needed, and could be without inconvenience spared from the Treasury. By this course, many have been enabled at once to realize funds from their deposite of bullion or coin, and the mint to continue its operations uninterruptedly, and to supply promptly where desired coins already prepared for circulation. The strong disposition of the public to use the new coinage, has been observed with pleasure; and the liberal aid of many of the Deposite Banks, in assisting to increase its circulation, has proved very useful, and deserves commendation. As the new coinage commenced nearly in the middle of the year, and the date till next January could not, by law, be altered, so as to distinguish the new from the old coin, such other alterations were adopted by the Director of the Mint as the law permitted, and as were calculated to aid the community in readily discriminating between them.

After the next year begins, the new date alone will enable the public to distinguish the new coins; and such modifications only will be made in the former emblems as taste and convenience may, in the opinion of the Director, and without an omission of any thing required by Congress, appear to demand. His report, which it is expected will soon be received and presented, will, probably furnish every further particular connected with the concerns of the Mint that may be interesting. But it is considered proper to invite the attention of Congress to a change in the law respecting the organization of the Mint establishment, so as hereafter to prevent its operations in refining and coining for others, from being a tax on the Treasury, and any longer swelling the large amount of our annual expenditures. This could easily be effected by imposing a duty or seignorage of about one per cent. on the prompt coinage of silver, and one-fourth per cent. on that of gold, the present coinage of copper now defraying its own expense. This would be no more burthensome to the persons holding bullion than the delay now allowed for the recoinage, and which delay of forty days [or half per cent. discount if delivered in five days,] and consequent loss of interest could with such a seinorage, and the advantages now authorized from the Treasury, be without inconvenience reduced to eight or ten days, and the whole establishment be thus sustained by its own earnings, without much, if any, increased cost to either individuals or the public.

But, in such case, if the cost should ever be increased to individuals, some additional inducement will be held out to prevent either the exportation or melting of our coin, which have been so great hitherto, before the late change in the law, as to have left in deposite and circulation in this country an amount of it not exceeding that struck in two or three out of the forty years during which the Mint has been in operation. The expenses and labor of the Mint equalling, on an average, about [illegible] 000 dollars a year, or 800,000 dollars in all, including buildings, have thus, except for about two years, been entirely lost to the country.

It has been desirable to attempt some improve[illegible]

ners in the Revenue Cutter Service. With such a view, all its regulations have been revised and republished. By those, it has been endeavored to promote the cause of temperance, and thereby to increase the health and efficiency of the crews, and the safety of the public property and the public interests in this branch of service, by holding out a similar inducement to that now existing in the Navy, to discontinue the use of spirit on shipboard. Greater security has been provided for the prompt payment of their wages, and for official accountability. It has further been deemed expedient, not only to stop any contemplated increase in the Cutters, but to reduce the number of them, and of the persons employed in this service, as rapidly as the diminished temptation to smuggling will safely permit.

By several resolutions, appropriations, and acts of Congress, at the last and previous sessions, a variety of other subjects, not yet reported on, has been confided to the attention of this Department, such as the erection of a number of custom-houses, the building of a bridge over the Potomac river in this District, a compromise of the suits pending against the firm of Th. H. Smith & Son, an opinion on the validity of some private land titles in Missouri, a report on certain provisions in the tariff act of July 14th, 1832, some statements as to the marine hospital money, a re-organization of the Treasury Department, and a revision of the subject of salaries and fees to custom-house officers. These have received careful attention, and will form the subjects of separate reports to Congress, early in the present session.

In the report on the last of them, it is contemplated to offer such suggestions, by way of addition to this communication, as are appropriately connected with that inquiry, and as would otherwise have been mentioned here in respect to some changes deemed suitable in the whole amount of compensation to various custom-house officers, and the number of such officers, at various ports, and in relation to other changes in the system, which the great alterations in the existing duties seem to indicate as required for sound economy and the public convenience.

A few remarks concerning hospital money will be be postponed, and annexed to the statement requested in relation to that subject.

In the preparation of new weights and measures, the authority given in the act of 2d March, 1799, and on the principles set forth in a report on this department, of June 20th, 1832, concluded with the provision on this subject in the constitution, some progress has been made since the date of that report. But the difficulty in procuring the suitable materials from abroad, has retarded the completion of the work, and the present engagements of the distinguished gentleman specially employed to superintend this business, and which engross most of his time, in a survey of the coast, may, with the circumstance before named, prevent the final accomplishment of this desirable object another year. But it is hoped that then, either at the arsenal in this city, or at the mint, the natural and appropriate place, the new weights and measures will be satisfactorily finished, and greater uniformity and accuracy attained in a subject in which, both as to revenue and commerce, it is much needed, and will prove eminently useful to the public.

The survey of the coast before alluded to, has, in the last annual report, been transferred to the charge of the Navy Department, with which it has to be more intimately and appropriately connected. With this survey, the situation and pay of our present light-houses, already being in number, besides 20 light-boats, and the necessity for others, from time to time, would be too, be, in some degree, fitly associated. A measure likely to lead to economy, is not extending the establishment of light-houses beyond the real wants of the country, and in fixing their best localities, so important to the safety of our navigation and navy, it is respectfully recommended—that in the survey now in progress, Congress would require the latitude and longitude of every light-house to be carefully ascertained and published, the importance of its position to be inquired into, and that no new one be hereafter erected, till a report is made in respect to its public benefits by the two collectors and the commander of the Navy Yard nearest the proposed site.

The rebuilding of the Treasury edifice, on or near its former location, with the dimensions of the building enlarged so as to meet the wants of the department, and rendered fire-proof for the security of its papers, seems indispensable to the convenient operations, and to the safety of some of the most valuable records connected with the public archives.

The Report from the Commissioner of the General Land Office is annexed. Many of its suggestions are highly important, and some of the recommendations, as to changes in this branch of the collections of the public money, are respectfully, though earnestly, urged on the consideration of Congress.

The Indian titles having of late years been more extensively extinguished, the quantity of valuable lands brought into market has increased in amount, so as to place in the Treasury over three millions annually, instead of about one million, as was the case twenty years ago. Within the same period, the Land Offices have been augmented in number from about eighteen to fifty-three, have, in actual operation in 1834. These circumstances have added much to the business of that Bureau, and should clearly lead to a corresponding increase in its Clerks, or a separation from it of some of its present laborious duties; as the diminution in other business, in some other Bureaus, might lead to reductions in the number of their Clerks, to the extent proposed in the plan soon to be submitted, in the re-organization of the Treasury Department. Attempts have been made, during the past year, with some success, to simplify the mode of making entries in the General Land Office of the sales effected; some difficult and long-delayed questions of accounts have been decided; greater local accommodations and facilities furnished to the offices and increased convenience and promptitude, as far as practicable with the present force of the Bureau, have been introduced in the ascertainment of titles, and in the collection and disbursement of the large amount of revenue derived from this source. But new legislation can alone give entire relief, in the present condition of its enlarged duties, and at least $30,000 a year, for ten years, will be required to be expended, in additional Clerk-hire, to dispose of all the writing in arrear, and that may be hereafter rendered necessary by the additional sales of land.

It gives me great pleasure to state, that among more than fifty offices and one hundred Receivers and Registers connected with the present system of land sales, amenable to the Secretary of the Treasury, and under his control as to their collections, not one, during the last year, has proved to be a defaulter, although the money collected and paid over has probably exceeded four millions.

All which is respectfully submitted.

LEVI WOODBURY,
Sec'ry of the Treasury.

REPORT OF THE POSTMASTER GENERAL.

GENERAL POST OFFICE DEPARTMENT,
November, 1834.

To the President of the United States:

SIR: The Report which I had the honor to make on the 30th November, 1833, exhibited a balance due from this Department on the 1st July, 1833, beyond the whole amount of its available funds, of $195,208 40.

The expenses for the transportation of the mail necessarily continued undiminished till the close of the year 1833, prior to which date the retrenchments stated in that Report could not take effect; consequently the balance of debt against the Department continued to augment till that period.

The gross amount of postages was, from July 1 to December 31, 1833, $1,375,437 28

Compensation to Postmasters, including the contingent expenses of their offices during the

same period, amounted to $434,626 89

Incidental expenses of the Department during the same time, amounted to $47,797 29

The expense for transportation of the mail from July 1 to 31 December, 1833, was 1,013,402 68

Making the total expenses of the Department————————$1,495,826 86

This sum, after deducting the gross amount of postages for that period, leaves a deficit for the six months ending 31st December, 1833, of $120,391 58

To this sum add the deficit existing on the 1st July, 1833, 195,208 40

And the balance of the debt against the Department beyond the amount of its available funds, was, on the 1st of January, 1834 $315,599, 98

From the 1st of January, 1834, the retrenchments in the transportation of the mail, stated in my Report of last year, began to take effect; and from that period, the revenues of the Department have exceeded its expenses.

The gross amount of postages was, from January 1 to June 30, 1834 $1,448,269 69

Compensation to Postmasters, including the contingent expenses of their offices, within the same period, amounted to $461,433 64

Incidental expenses of the Department for the same time, amounted to 30,300 38

The transportation of the mail from January 1 to June 30, 1834, amounted to 909,028 43

Making the total expenses of the Department met for the half year ending the 30th of June, 1834 ————————$1,400,762 45

This sum deducted from the gross amount of postages for that period, leaves a revenue beyond the amount of expenses for the half year from January 1 to June 30, 1834, of 47,507 24

This sum deducted from the deficit existing January 1, 1834 315,599 98

Reduces the balance of debt which existed against the Department on the 1st July, 1834, to $268,092 74

Such was the financial condition of the Department on the 1st day of July last. The amount of this debt has been continually diminishing to the present time, and it continues to diminish in an increased ratio.

On the 1st of July, 1834, the balance of the account with Banks was $398,616 99 against the Department, consisting of loans, $275,000, and over-checks to the amount of $123,616 99.

In this statement, the difference between loans and over-checks is rather nominal than essential. When over-checks are mutually agreed upon to a certain definite amount as a standing order, they are called loans; but when they vary indefinitely as to time and amount, they are called over-checks. In either case they are debts due from the Department to Banks.

The amount of balance against the Department has been considerably reduced since the first of July last.

On the 1st day of the present month it stood as follows:

Amount due for loans from Banks $275,000 00
Amount of over-checks, November 1, 1834, 55,969 00

Making together the sum of $330,969
On the same day the balances of

Bank deposites in favor of the Department, constituting the amount of cash on hand, amounted to   82,031 34

Making the actual balance of the accounts with Banks, against the Department, on the 1st of Nov. 1834   248,937 75

The contracts for the southern section, including the States of Virginia, North Carolina, South Carolina, and Georgia, and the Territory of Florida, which will expire with the current year, have been renewed, to take effect from the 1st of January next, on such terms as will effect an annual saving from the amount now paed for transportation in that section, of about $120,000.

Additional retrenchments have also been made in the expense of transportation subsequent to my last report, to the annual amount of about $59,000. Making together an annual saving from the 1st of January next, of $179,000.

From the savings thus effected, together with the current excess of revenue in favor of the Department, it may be safely calculated, that without any reliance upon an increase in the gross amount of postages, the revenues of the Department will exceed its expenditures, during the ensuing calendar year, to the amount of $270,000.

From a careful estimate, it may be anticipated with entire confidence, that before the close of the year 1835, the whole balance of debt against the Department will be extinguished. No part of this debt was contracted upon the credit of the Treasury, nor upon any other credit or authority than that of the Department alone.

It was never regarded by either of the parties in the character of a debt of the Government, but a mere expedient to anticipate the resources of the Department, based upon the credit of those resources alone.

The means of its liquidation within a reasonable time were always within the legal control of the head of the Department; and no other means have at any time been sought or desired by the Department.

In my Report of November, 1833, the expense for transporting the mail, and for incidentals, from July 1 to December 31, 1833, was estimated at $1,061,644 71
The actual expense for that period, was   1,061,199 97

Varying from the estimate only $444 74
The nett proceeds of postages for the year ending 30th June, 1834, were then estimated at $2,037,410 81
The actual nett proceeds of postages for that year, were $1,927,644 44

Falling below the estimate by the sum of $109,766 37

Thus it appears that the expenses of the Department have not essentially varied from the estimates; but the nett revenue arising from postages has fallen short of the estimates then made, more than a hundred thousand dollars. This is believed to be, in a very considerable degree, attributable to the great increase of free letters. The progressive increase of population naturally brings with it an accumulation of business in the Executive offices, which tends, in some measure, to increase their correspondence; and in addition to this, a law passed in March, 1833, extending to members of Congress the privilege of franking during the whole recess. Every other year, this session of Congress is protracted to a much greater length than in the alternate year, when a Congress terminates.

The expenses for the delivery of free letters, at two cents each, have always amounted to a much greater sum during the year when the session is protracted, than during the alternate year. To make a fair comparison between the amount of free letters before and after the extension of the franking privilege, it is necessary to take two entire years. Thus: The allowance to Postmasters for the delivery of free letters for the two years ending July 30, 1832, (before the extension,) was $40,556 89

For the two years ending July 1, 1834, (after the extension,) was   54,158 88

Making, since the extension, an increase of $13,601 99
Or payment for the delivery of 680,099 free letters more than were delivered the two preceding years. But no allowance is made for the delivery of free letters at post offices where the Postmasters' commissions exceed $500 a quarter.

If the same proportion of free letters is delivered at offices where no allowances for them are made to Postmasters, as at the smaller offices, then the increase since the franking privilege was extended, is equal to 960,000 free letters more than what were delivered within the same period of time prior to that extension. The postage on each of these letters, if not free, would be from six cents to two dollars. The average, it is believed, would not be less than twenty-five cents each, exclusive of the Postmasters' commissions. If estimated at this average, they would amount to $240,000
To this add the allowance actually made for their delivery,   13,601 99

And the increase of free letters within the last two years has actually cost the Department $253,601 99
which is more than equal to the balance of debt at this time existing against the Department.

Estimates have been obtained from several of the Executive offices, of the amount of their official correspondence carried on through the Post Office establishment under the franking privilege of the officers by whom it is conducted; and it appears that from the Departments of State, Treasury, War, and Navy, including the sub-offices of the Treasury and Navy, the official correspondence by mail, on which no postage is paid, is estimated to be equal to 2,685,235 single free letters in a year, and that by far the greater proportion of them are sent the full distance for which the highest rate of postage would be chargeable. The average postage on those letters, if not free, is believed would be not less than 18⅓ cents each, which would amount to $303,481 36.

This estimate is exclusive of the offices of the Attorney General, Adjutant General, Commissary General, Inspector General, Quarter Master General, Paymaster General, and Superintendent of the Patent Office, all of whom have the privilege of franking. It is also estimated that the number of free letters passing under the frank of members of Congress, amounts to 8000 a day during the session.

If the correspondence of the offices above-mentioned, which are not embraced in the estimate, and the postages fairly estimated which would be chargeable on the correspondence of members of Congress, if not free, should be added to the statement, it is believed that the annual amount of free letters would not fall short of a million of dollars, exclusive of the correspondence of the Post Office Department itself.

This is an annual contribution by the Department to the Government.

Though the amount of revenue arising from postages, for the year ending June 30, 1834, did not equal the estimate, yet there was a considerable increase above the amount of the preceding year. The gross amount of postages for the year ending June 30, 1833, was $2,616,538 27
For the year ending June 30, 1834, it was   2,823,706 97

Making an increase in the gross amount of $207,168 70

The nett amount of postages, after deducting commissions to postmasters, and the contingent expenses of their offices, was, for the year ending June 30, 1833, $1,790,254 65
For the year ending June 30, 1834, it was   1,927,644 44

Making an increase in the nett proceeds of $137,389 79

The finances of the Department continue to be in an improving condition; and the solicitude which has been shown to obtain mail contracts, the reduced rates at which they bare been taken for the Southern Section, and the zeal with which contractors generally persevere in their services to the Department, furnish ample demonstration that its credit is unimpaired.

The number of post offices in the United States, was, on the 1st of July last, 10,693, being an increase of 566 over the number reported last year.

The annual amount of transportation has been but slightly varied since my last report. The mail is now carried in stages and steam-boats about 16,900,000 miles a year, and on horseback, and in sulkies, about 8,600,000 miles; making together about 25,500,000 miles a year.

The celerity of the mail should always be equal to the most rapid transition of the traveller; and that which shortens the time of communication, and facilitates the intercourse between distant places, is like bringing them nearer together. While it affords counteraction to mass of business, it tends to counteract local prejudices, by enlarging the sphere of acquaintance.

It perpetuates existing friendships, and creates new ones, by which the bonds of union are strengthened, and the happiness of society promoted. These considerations have always had their full weight upon my mind in making improvements in mail operations.

The multiplication of rail-roads in different parts of the country, promises, within a few years to give great rapidity to the movements of travellers, and it is a subject worthy of inquiry, whether measures may not now be taken to secure the transportation of the mail upon them. Already have the rail-roads between Frenchtown, in Maryland, and New Castle, in Delaware,- and between Camden and Amboy, in New Jersey, afforded great aid to important facilities to the transmission of the post Eastern mail. The rail-road between the city and Baltimore will soon be completed, and the distance from the post office in this place to that of Baltimore, will not be materially varied from the present road, 38 miles.

From Baltimore by Port Deposite, in Maryland, to Coatesville, in Pennsylvania, the line for a rail road is located, and the stock subscribed for its completion; and from Coatesville to Philadelphia a rail-road is made and in operation.

The distance between Baltimore and Philadelphia, on this road, will be 117 miles, about 11 miles greater than the present land route. From Philadelphia to Trenton bridge, about 30 miles, the rail-road is nearly completed; and from Brunswick, in New Jersey, to Jersey City, at the west side of the Hudson river, opposite the City of New York, 30 miles, the rail-road is in a state of progress. When these works shall be completed, the only interval will be between New Brunswick, about 26 miles, to complete the entire rail-road between this place and the City of New York; and it cannot be supposed that the enterprising State of New Jersey will long delay to perfect a communication so important, passing through most of her largest and most flourishing towns. When this shall be done, the whole distance between this city and New York by a continual rail-road, will not exceed 231 miles; and the journey may be performed at times with certainty, allowing ample time for stopping at important places on the road, in 12 hours, and ordinarily in a shorter period.

If provision can be made to secure the rapid transportation of the mail upon this, and other rail-roads which are constructing, some instances already finished, it will be of great utility to the public; otherwise, these corporations may become exorbitant in their demands, and prove eventually to be dangerous monopolies.

I have the honor to be, most respectfully, your humble servant,   W. T. BARRY.

Scarcity of Women.—A St. Louis editor remarking on the extreme scarcity of the gentler sex in and about the vicinity of that place, says that a man who dwelt in that desolate region lately walked twenty miles to obtain sight of a petticoat.—*Am. Paper.*

CONGRESSIONAL GLOBE.

BY BLAIR & RIVES.   ——WEEKLY——   PRICE $1 A SESSION.

2d Sess........23d Cong.   MONDAY, DECEMBER 15, 1834.   VOLUME 2........No. 2.

TWENTY-THIRD CONGRESS.

SECOND SESSION.

IN SENATE.

MONDAY, December 8, 1834.

The Hon. Messrs. WEBSTER of Mass., WAGAMAN of Louisiana, PRENTISS of Vermont, KING of Alabama, and CLAYTON of Delaware, appeared and took their seats.

The VICE PRESIDENT laid before the Senate a communication from the Secretary of the Treasury, in relation to the construction of the bridge over the Potomac at the city of Washington.

Also, the Report of the Secretary of the Treasury relative to a re-organization of the Treasury Department.

On motion of Mr. KANE, the reading of these communications was dispensed with, and they were ordered to be printed.

The Presiding Officer also laid before the Senate a letter from the Secretary of the Treasury, communicating information of the quantity of scrip issued upon bounty land warrants to the Virginia Continental lines; which, on motion of Mr. TYLER, was ordered to be printed, with the accompanying documents.

Also, another communication from the Treasury Department, relative to the case of Mary O'Sullivan; which, on motion of Mr. KANE, was ordered to be printed.

Also, another communication from the Treasury Department, showing the amount of funds in the Treasury applicable to the erection of Marine Hospitals, and the number of such hospitals in the United States, which, on motion of Mr. SILSBEE, was ordered to be printed.

The VICE PRESIDENT also laid before the Senate, a communication from Jacob Kern, President of the Convention of the Legislature of Pennsylvania, with a certificate of the election of JAMES BUCHANAN, to represent that State in the Senate United States, to supply the vacancy occasioned by the resignation of the Hon. WILLIAM WILKINS.

Also, a communication from the Secretary of the Senate, with a statement of the contingent expenses of the Senate for the past year.

Mr. WEBSTER gave notice that on to-morrow he would ask leave to introduce a bill to provide compensation to American citizens for spoliations their commerce prior to 1800.

Mr. TIPTON gave notice that on to-morrow he would ask leave to introduce a bill for the relief of Gad Humphreys.

The bill to settle and establish the Northern boundary line of the State of Ohio, was taken up its second reading, and on motion of Mr. EWING, it was laid on the table.

Mr. NAUDAIN gave notice that on to-morrow he would ask leave to introduce a bill authorizing a purchase, on the part of the United States, of the tent of Boyd Reilly, for applying certain irremovable guns to the human body, to be used in army and navy.

Mr. MOORE gave notice that on to-morrow he would ask leave to introduce a bill granting to the State of Alabama the two per cent. proceeds of sales of public lands, within the State, to be applied as the General Assembly may provide, the education of the children of those who are circumstances too indigent to furnish means of educating them.

Mr. MOORE, on leave given, introduced a bill the relief of Samuel Smith, Lynn Magee, and others, Creek Indians; which was read a first time, and ordered to a second reading.

Mr. MOORE, on leave given, also introduced a bill to authorize a relinquishment of the 16th section, and the granting of other lands in lieu thereof, for the use of schools; which was read a first time, and ordered to a second reading.

Also, a bill for the relief of Susan Marlow; which was read a first time, and ordered to a second reading.

On motion of Mr. WHITE, 1750 additional copies of the documents accompanying the President's Message, were ordered to be printed.

Mr. EWING submitted the following resolution:

Resolved, That the Secretary of War be directed to transmit to the Senate a copy of any communications received by him from the Commissioners appointed by the States of Maryland, Pennsylvania, and Virginia, to receive portions of the Cumberland Road lying within the limits of those States respectively, and to erect toll gates thereon; and if any money be necessary to complete the repairs of said road agreeably to the requirements of laws of said States which have received the assent of Congress; and that he furnish an estimate of the amount. Also, that he inform the Senate what is the condition of the masonry on that road; and how many inches of metal have been put on that part of it which has been located anew, and upon that part of it which lies between the Monongahela and Ohio rivers—and also what depth of metal is in his opinion necessary to make it a permanent and substantial road, upon the plan which has been adopted, in its repairs by the Department.

Mr. KING, of Alabama, gave notice that on to-morrow he would ask leave to introduce a bill for the relief of Theodore Brightwell.

Mr. TYLER gave notice that on to-morrow he would ask leave to introduce a bill authorizing a further issuing of scrip to holders of military bounty land warrants of the Virginia line.

Mr. EWING submitted the following resolution:

Resolved, That the Secretary of War be directed to transmit to the Senate copies of all surveys and documents that are in his Department, relative to the improvement of the harbour at the mouth of the river Rai in, in the Territory of Michigan.

Mr. SOUTHARD moved that on Wednesday next the Senate would proceed to the appointment of the Standing Committees.

Mr. CONNET rER suggested the postponement of the day till Monday next, as the Senate was not very full, and as it was desirable to have a full attendance of members.

Mr. SOUTHARD had no objection, with a view to consider the subject, that the motion be laid on the table, and moved to that effect; which was agreed to.

The Senate then adjourned.

HOUSE OF REPRESENTATIVES.

MONDAY, DEC. 8, 1834.

The following Standing Committees were appointed by the Speaker, pursuant to the order of the House:

Elections—Messrs. Claiborne, Griffin, Hawkins, Vanderpoel, Hannegan, Hard, Burns, Reynolds, K[i]more.

Ways and Means—Messrs. Polk, Wilde, Cambreleng, McKim, Binney, Loyall, McKinley, Hubbard, Gorham.

Claims—Messrs. Whittlesey of Ohio, Barbour, McIntire, Gholson, Forester, Stoddert, Banks, Fulton, Miner.

Commerce—Messrs. Sutherland, Harper of New Hampshire, Pinckney, Heath, Pearce of Rhode Island, Gillet, Phillips, Johnson of Louisiana, Morgan.

Public Lands—Messrs. Clay, Boon, Slade, Ashley, Lyon, Mason, Lincoln, Cavey, Clayton.

Post Office and Post Roads—Messrs. Connor, Kavanagh, Thomas of Louisiana, Briggs, Murphy, Lane, Laporte, Hall of Maine, Schley.

District of Columbia—Messrs. Chinn, W. B. Shepard, McKennan, Allen of Virginia, Hiester, Filmore, King, Vanderpoel, Steele.

Judiciary.—Messrs. Foster, Gordon, Beardsley, Thomas of Maryland, Hardin, Parks, Pierce of New Hampshire, Robertson, Moore.

Revolutionary Claims—Messrs. Muhlenberg, Crane, Bates, Standifer, Marshall, Young, Bayne, Turrill, Kinnard.

Public Expenditures—Messrs. Davenport, Ly-

---

on, Page, Clarke of Pennsylvania, Tweedy, McLene, Jackson of Massachusetts, Hazeltine, Ferris.

Private Land Claims.—Messrs. Johnson of Tennessee, Mardis, Carr, Galbraith, Mann of New York, Bull, Chambers, Davis of Kentucky, May.

Manufactures.—Messrs. Adams of Massachusetts, Denny, Dickerson of New Jersey, Martindale, McComas, Osgood, Clowney, Cramer, Jackson of Connecticut.

Agriculture.—Messrs. Bockee, Taylor of Virginia, Hathaway, Barnitz, Bean, Dunlap, Clowney, Turner, Beaty.

Indian Affairs.—Messrs. Gilmer, McCarty, Everett of Vermont, Graham, Allen of Ohio, Dickinson of Tennessee, Howell, Love of Virginia, Grennell.

Military Affairs.—Messrs. Johnson of Kentucky, Vance, Speight, Ward, Thompson, Coffee, Bunch, McKay, Anthony.

Naval Affairs.—Messrs. White of New York, Milligan, Watmough, Lansing, Reed, Grayson, Parker, Smith, Wise.

Foreign Affairs.—Messrs. Wayne, Everett of Massachusetts, Hall of North Carolina, Coulter, Jarvis, Pierson, Patton, Letcher, Peyton.

Territories.—Messrs. Allan of Kentucky, Potts, Johnson of New York, Wilson, Jones of Ohio, Ewing, Gamble, Cage, Trumbull.

Revolutionary Pensions.—Messrs. Wardwell, Barringer, Tompkins, Moore of Virginia, Lea of Tennessee, W. K. Fuller, Fowler, Bell, Lay. Adams.

Invalid Pensions.—Messrs. Miller, Beale, ams of New York, Schenck, Chilton, Chaney, Mitchell of Ohio, Brown of New York, Janes.

Roads and Canals.—Messrs. Mercer, Blair, Vinton, Stewart, Rencher, Johnson of Maryland, Lucas, Pope, Reynolds.

Revised and Unfinished Business.—Messrs. Dickson, Harrison, McVean, Sninn, Taylor of N. York.

Accounts.—Messrs. Mann of Pennsylvania, Lee of New Jersey, Mitchell of New York, Crockett, Curry.

The following Standing Committees of the House, appointed at the last session, remain through the Congress:

On Expenditures in Department of State.—Messrs. Allen of Vermont, P. C. Fuller, Harper of N., Spangler, Clarke of N. Y.

On Expenditures in Department of the Treasury.—Messrs. Allen of Vermont, P. C. Fuller, Harper of N., Spangler, Clarke of N. Y.

On Expenditures in Department of War.—Messrs. Whittlesey of N. Y., Doherty, Chambers, Webster, Halsey.

On Expenditures in Department of Navy.—Messrs. Hall of Maine, Huntington of N. Y., Ramsay, Sloane, Van Houten.

On Expenditures in Department of Post Office.—Messrs. Hawes, Fulton, Burns, Wagener, Lay.

On Expenditures on Public Buildings.—Messrs. Whallon, Darlington, Brown, Henderson, Hard.

R J MANNING and F. W. PICKENS, elect ed to fill vacancies in the South Carolina Delegation, appeared, were qualified, and took their seats.

Petitions and memorials were presented by:—Messrs. JARVIS and McINTIRE, of Maine; Messrs. HUBBARD, BEAN, and HARPER, of New Hampshire;

Messrs. ADAMS, BATES, and EVERETT, of Massachusetts;

Mr. BARBER, of Connecticut;

Mr. PEARCE, of Rhode Island;

Messrs. WARDWELL, TILMORE, BEARDS.

LEY, WARD, HALSEY, and MANN, of New York;

[Mr. WARD presented the petitions of Jonathan Ward; Samuel Young, and William A. Weaver.]

Mr. PARKER, of New Jersey;

Messrs. CHAMBERS, SUTHERLAND, and BEAUMONT, of Pennsylvania;

Mr. HEATH, of Maryland;

Messrs. CHINN, PATTON, LOYALL, and GHOLSON, of Virginia;

Mr. WAYNE, of Georgia;

Messrs. POPE, MARSHALL, LYON, JOHN-SON, and LETCHER, of Kentucky;

[Mr. POPE presented a petition of numerous citizens of Louisville, Kentucky, praying for the establishment of a District Court at that place; which was referred to the Judiciary Committee.

Also, the petition of Joseph Chilton and others; which was referred.]

Mr. VINTON, of Ohio;

Messrs. GARLAND and JOHNSON, of Louisiana;

Mr. CAGE, of Mississippi;

Messrs. CLAY and MARDIS, of Alabama;

[Mr. CLAY presented the memorial of the Tennessee Canal Commissioners, for the construction of a Canal around the Muscle Shoals, setting forth the progress already made in that work, and the necessity for a further appropriation to complete the same, which they request shall be made; which was referred to the Committee on Roads and Canals.

Mr. C. also presented the petition of Isaac Wellborn, Jr. praying the passage of an act to confirm his title to a tract of land, which was referred to the Committee on the Public Lands.

Mr. C. also presented the petition of John McCartney, praying compensation for property destroyed, or carried off Indian territory, by United States troops; which was referred to the Committee on Indian Affairs.

Mr. MARDIS presented the petition of sundry citizens of Pickens and Sumpter, praying for a repeal of so much of the existing pre-emption laws as restricts the right of occupants to convey their lands, &c.; which petition was referred to the Committee on Public Lands.]

Mr. ASHLEY, of Missouri;

[Mr. ASHLEY presented the petition of Mary McNair, praying remuneration for Indian depredations;

The petition of Thomas Bazzell, praying remuneration for a horse, lost in the service of the United States;

The petition of James Ruby, praying a donation of land. Referred.]

Mr. WHITE, of Florida.

The following resolution, submitted on Thursday by Mr. WARDWELL, was taken up:

Resolved, That the Secretary of the Navy be directed to report to this House, the amount expended in erecting the Ship House at Navy Point, in the county of Jefferson, and State of New York, and the expense of keeping the same in repair. Also, the like information in relation to the vessel built and lately sold at Storr's Harbor, in said county, and the amount of compensation allowed to the officer or officers, person or persons, who have from time to time had charge of the same. Also, the reasons, if any exist, for the further preservation of the vessel and Ship House at Navy Point. Also, that he report the amount heretofore paid for the use and occupation of the land now belonging to the heirs of Henry Eckford, deceased, at Navy Point and Storr's Harbor, on which the vessels New Orleans and Chippewa were built, and also the terms of any contract which may have been made with the Government, or its authorized agent, for the use and occupation of such land.

Mr. WHITE moved the following amendment, which was accepted by Mr. WARDWELL, and thus amended, the resolution was agreed to—viz.

" And any other information in possession of the Department relative thereto. "

On motion of Mr. EDWARD EVERETT,

Resolved, That a committee of three members be appointed on the part of this House, who, together with three persons to be appointed on the part of the Senate, shall direct the expenditure of the money appropriated for the Library of Congress.

On motion of Mr. CLAYTON,

Resolved, That the Committee of Ways and Means inquire into the expediency of establishing a branch of the Mint in some central position of what is denominated the Gold Region, lying between the States of Virginia and Alabama.

On motion of Mr. JARVIS,

Resolved, That a committee be appointed whose duty it shall be to consider all matters referred to

them touching the public grounds and buildings in the City of Washington, with leave to report by bill or otherwise.

On motion of Mr. HUBBARD,

Resolved, That the Committee on Revolutionary Pensions be instructed to inquire into the expediency of providing by law for the publication _semi-annually_, in those newspapers printed in the respective States, which from their location may be best calculated to give information, and which shall be designated for that purpose by the Secretary of War, for the time being, _the names and the residence_ of all those persons represented to be living in said States, who are on the rolls of the invalid and revolutionary pensioners and annuitants, under the several acts of Congress.

On motion of Mr. PEARCE,

Resolved, That the Committee on the Post Office and Post Roads be instructed to inquire into the expediency of establishing a post route from Wickford, in the State of Rhode Island, to Newport, in the same State, by the most direct course from one place to the other.

Mr. BEATY moved the following resolution, which was read and laid upon the table for one day:

Resolved, That the Secretary of the Treasury be requested to send to this House the aggregate amount of revenue collected on imported merchandise, tonnage, &c. in each State of this Union, for the year 1833.

Mr. HAWES offered the following resolution:

Resolved, That a Select Committee, consisting of one member from each State, be appointed, with power to inquire into the expediency of amending the laws relating to the Military Academy at West Point, in the State of New York, or whether it would not comport with the public interests to abolish said institution.

Mr. CLAYTON hoped that this inquiry would not be denied. An impression had gone abroad, that this institution was a nursery for the sons of members of Congress and the rich. If this impression was true, it ought to be abolished. Its benefits were said to be extended to the favored few, to the exclusion of the sons of poor soldiers and officers. He would not say, that these charges were true; but the suspicions which were in circulation demanded that a full inquiry into the subject should be made.

Mr. HAWES remarked, that the rumors referred to by the gentleman from Georgia, (Mr. Clayton) demanded this inquiry. The minds of his constituents were made up on this subject, and he believed the constituents of other gentlemen, felt a deep solicitude in relation to it. The institution had been held up as pure by its friends, and he trusted that no gentleman who had abused the Bank of the United States, because a full inquiry was denied to a Committee of this House, would oppose the investigation proposed in the resolution.

Mr. PARKER moved to amend the resolution, by striking out so much as related to abolishing the Academy, and also that the Committee should consist of one member from each State. He suggested that a Select Committee, composed of a more limited number would be sufficient, and that the clause in relation to the abolishment of the institution was unnecessary, as upon the report of the Committee, the House could take such steps as the facts disclosed might render proper.

Mr. SPEIGHT was in favor of the amendment, so far as regarded the abolishment of the Academy. He considered the inquiry necessary, and if the rumors afloat were true, the institution should be abolished. The committee would, however, have it in their power to recommend such a measure, if the facts warranted it. He was in favor of a large committee, and agreed with the gentleman from Kentucky, (Mr. Hawes,) that those who favored the investigation of the affairs of the Bank of the United States, ought not to oppose the contemplated inquiry. It was true, the subject had heretofore been referred to the Committee on Military Affairs but their complaint had been made, that in consequence of a majority of that committee being in favor of the West Point Academy, a full investigation into its affairs had not taken place. He considered the present a simple mat-

ter of inquiry, and he trusted all objection to its adoption would be withdrawn.

Mr. JOHNSON, of Kentucky, said, that the Committee on Military Affairs, at the last session, after a thorough investigation, had made a full report on this subject, but owing to the press of business, the did not believe that ten members of the House were either aware of this fact, or had read the report. He was sorry at all times to interpose any objection to motions made by his colleagues; but he was not in favor of abandoning the usual practice of referring subjects, which appropriately belonged to the Standing Committees to Select Committees. As regarded the proposition to raise a Select Committee, to consist of so large a number, it was unusual, and in the course of a long service in Congress, he did not recollect that such a course had been adopted on more than one or two occasions. He had no objection to a Select Committee of seven or nine members. It had been suggested that a majority of the Committee on Military Affairs were in favor of this Academy. If so, they could be instructed by the House. In relation to the rumors, which had been referred to, he knew nothing of them, and repeated all rumors as the idle wind. He was anxious the fullest investigation should result in nothing prejudicial to those who conducted the Academy, and that the greater the scrutiny into its affairs, it would be the more approved by the American people.

Mr. WILLIAMS said, that an inquiry might properly be made as to the propriety of abolishing the army. One was just as essential to the security of the other. If, however, abuses, injurious to the institution, were in circulation, it was proper that they should be inquired into. If true, and abuses existed, they should be corrected. If untrue, they should be refuted. The Committee on Military Affairs was the proper one to make this investigation. That Committee was technically and practically better acquainted with the subject. He doubted whether the present rule for the admission of persons into the Academy was a good one, and if this was changed, it was probable that all objections would cease. He would vote for the resolution in any shape; but viewing the Military Committee as the proper one to make the investigation, he moved to amend the resolution by so referring it.

Mr. BROWN hoped the amendment of the gentleman from North Carolina would prevail. He was the friend of the Military Academy, and he sincerely hoped that no one entertaining the sentiments would throw any obstacle in the way of a full, free, and searching inquiry into its affairs, and the administration of its affairs. A Select Committee of one member from each State could look at the institution standing separate and free, and unconnected with the army, of which it so most certainly a very essential part. It was also the foundation upon which in a great measure rested one system of public defence, and should be regarded and examined in connection with the whole subject. It therefore properly belonged to the Committee upon Military Affairs, which was raised by the rules of the House for the express purpose of investigating all questions of a military character. He should, therefore, prefer to have the inquiry made by that committee. The Military Academy was a national institution, and if there was any question or doubt in the public mind in any way to remove all such doubts was to make all the light and information which can be had bear upon the subject. He had approved that a reference be fully investigated—the Military Committee of which the honorable gentleman (Col. Johnson) from Kentucky, was Chairman, had in the last session a most able and elaborate report upon the nature and character of the institution at West Point, and he could hardly believe that any unprejudiced mind could rise from the perusal of that report without a perfect conviction of the utility and necessity of a military school for the instruction of our officers in the elements of that science. If, however, gentlemen desired a further investigation, and another report, he hoped a friend of the Academy would interpose the slightest opposition,

Mr. HARDIN considered this institution as essentially necessary to the military defence, as the arm is to the body. There was no specific charge alleged against it, and unless that was the case, he believed the proposed investigation uncalled for. If there was any blame, in regard to the appointment of Cadets, it rested with members of Congress, as their recommendations for their particular States, were generally confirmed by the Executive Department. He concluded by moving to lay the resolution and amendments on the table.

The question was then taken upon laying the resolution on the table, and decided in the negative, as follows:

YEAS.—Messrs. C. Allan, Archer, Ashley, S. Clark, Evans, E. Everett, Gorham, Hiester, Jarvis, R. M. Johnson, Love, Manning, Philips, Vance, Vinton, Ward, Wardwell, Whallon, Wilde.—19.

NAYS.—Messrs. J. Q. Adams, J. Adams, Wm. Allen, H. Allen, Banks, Barber,Barnitz, Barringer, Bates, Baylies, Beale, Bean, Beardsley, Beaty, Beaumont, Bell, Binney, Blair, Bockee, Briggs, Brown, Bull, Bunch, Burd, Burns, Cage, Cambreleng, Campbell, Carmichael, Carr, Casey, Chambers, Chaney, Chilton, Chinn, Claiborne, Wm. Clark, Clay, Clayton, Clowney, Coffee, Connor, Corwin, Cramer, Crane, Crockett, Darlington, A.‑ Davis, Davenport, Day, Deberry,Dickson, P. Dickerson, D. W. Dickinson, Dunlap, Horace Everett, Ewing, Ferris, Fillmore, Forester, Foster, Fowler, Philo C. Fuller, Wm. K. Fuller, Fuxton, Galbraith, Gamble, Gholson, Gillet, Gilmer, Gordon, Graham, Grayson, Grennell, Joseph Hall, Hiland Hall, Thos. H. Hall, Halsey, Hamer, Hannegan, Hard, Hardin, Joseph M. Harper, Jas. Harper, Harrison, Hathaway, Hawkins, Hawes, Hazeltine, Heath, Henderson, Howell, Hubbard, Huntington, Inge, E. Jackson, Janes, Noadiah Johnson, Cave Johnson, Henry Johnson, B. Jones, Kavanagh, Kilgore, King, Kinnard, Lane, Lansing, Laporte, G. W. Lay, Luke Lea, Thomas Lee, Letcher, Lewis, Lincoln, Loyal, Lyon, Abijah Mann, J. K. Mann, Martindale, Marshall, Mardia, J. Y. Mason, Moses Mason, McCarty, McComas, McIntire, McKay, McKim, McKinley, McLene, McVean, Miller, Miner, Henry Mitchell, Robert Mitchell, Moore, Morgan, Muhlenberg, Murphy, Osgood, Page, Parks, Parker, Patton, Patterson, D. J. Pearce, Peyton, Pickens, F. Pierce, Pierson, Pinckney, Polk, Pope, Potts, Ramsay, Reed, Rencher, Reynolds, Robertson, Schenck, Schley, A. H. Shepperd, Shinn, Slade, Sloane, Smith,Spangler, Speight, Standifer, Steele, Sutherland, Wm. Taylor, Wm. P. Taylor, P. Thomas, Thompson, Tompkins, Trumbull, Turner, Turrill, Tweedy, Van Houten, Wagener, Watmough, Wayne, White, F. Whittlesey, Williams, Wise, Young.—190.

Mr. HAWES knew but perhaps one member of the Committee on Military Affairs, (Mr. R. M. Johnson,) and there was no man on earth that he could sooner trust. He had as much confidence in the Military Committee as any other committee of the House; but the subject was one of so much importance, that he thought each State should have a voice in it. If the gentleman from New York, (Mr. Brown,) in whose district this institution is located, is so well satisfied that every thing is right, why is he so anxious again to refer the subject to the Committee on Military Affairs? It had been supposed that the resolution proposed to abolish the Academy. This was a mistake. It merely proposed an inquiry into its management, which might or might not eventuate in a recommendation that it should be abolished. One of his colleagues (Mr. Hardin) was adverse to the resolution, because nothing specific was alleged. He would furnish him and the House a specific allegation. One of the near relations of that gentleman (who was wealthy) had been appointed a cadet in this institution, to the exclusion of other worthy and indigent youths.

Mr. MANN of New York was in favor of the proposed inquiry. At the same time he wished it stended a little farther—to make it an extensive possible, He had no doubt of the mal-administration In the West Point Academy. He understood it cost the Government some five or six thousand dollars to qualify a young man for the

Army. He was in favor of the general principles of the institution, but was opposed to its abuses. But he wished this inquiry extended to another branch of the service. He wished to offer an amendment abolishing the office of " Commander-in-Chief" of the Army.

[The SPEAKER here reminded the gentleman that such an amendment was not now in order, there being then pending an amendment to an amendment.]

Mr. MANN resumed. He would propose his amendment at the proper time. He would, however, remark, that the pay, rations, &c. of the " Commander-in-Chief" of the Army, was understood to be about $10,000. He was friendly to this officer; but he was unwilling that he should receive a compensation so disproportionate to that of other officers, and which greatly exceeded the salaries paid to the Heads of Departments.

[The SPEAKER here reminded the gentleman that he was indulging in a course of remarks, not then in order.]

Mr. MANN continued. In relation to the immediate question before the House, he would, in general, perfer sending subjects to the appropriate standing committees. As, however, it had been suggested that the Military Committee had prejudged the case, he had no objection to a select committee, but preferred a smaller number than proposed by the original resolution.

Mr. WARD was a member of the Military Committee which had investigated the subject at a former session. If it was again to be inquired into, he would prefer a select committee. There being no specific charges, the Military Committee would have no new ground of inquiry, and they had already given to the subject the most thorough examination, and reported the result to the House.

The amendment of Mr. WILLIAMS was then disagreed to—Yeas 76, Nays 98.

The question recurred on Mr. PARKER'S motion to amend. A division of the question being called for, it was first put upon limiting the number of the Select Committee, and lost. Yeas 73, noes not counted.

The remainder of the amendment, to strike out that part of the inquiry in relation to the expediency of abolishing the West Point Academy, was also negatived.

Mr. MANN of New York, then moved to add to the resolution the following amendment:

" And that said committee be also instructed to inquire into the expediency of abolishing the office of Major General Commanding-in-Chief, and apportioning more equitably the pay, rations, and emoluments of the general officers of the army."

Mr. SMITH of Maine, said, he was entirely in favor of both the proposition contained in the original resolution of the gentleman from Kentucky, and the proposition of the amendment offered by the gentleman from New York. He was persuaded that both subjects merit the careful investigation of this House. But, said Mr. S., I am opposed to connecting them, as I believe they will but embarrass each other, and perhaps defeat the intention of the proposed investigation in relation to each. It must be apparent to every gentleman, that by connecting these subjects, the labors and difficulties incident to the investigation, will be possibly, if not probably, so much increased, as to prevent our having a report made at all, or if at all, at too late a period to be definitely acted upon by the House, during the present short session. While, therefore, I am in favor of the proposition of the gentleman from New York, in favor of each of the propositions made for investigation, and as much in respect to the one as to the other, I am constrained to vote against joining them together. If the gentleman from New York will withdraw his amendment, and propose his desired investigation in a distinct resolution, I pledge him that my vote shall be given in its support. As it is now presented, I trust it will not be adopted.

Mr. WISE remarked, that under the constitution, the President of the United States was the " Commander-in-Chief." He desired to know whether it was the object of the gentleman from New York to abolish the office of President?

Mr. MANN: By no means. The person to

whom he alluded had assumed the cognomen of "Commander-in-Chief," and if the gentlemen from Virginia would suggest a more proper term he would adopt it. He was not in favor of abolishing the office of President, although some gentlemen might think it expedient.

Mr. WISE suggested the term " General-in-Chief," which was accepted as a modification, when the amendment was rejected.

The original resolution was then adopted by the following vote:

YEAS—Messrs. John Quincy Adams, John Adams, Heman Allen, William Allen, Archer, Banks, Barber, Barringer, Bates, Baylies, Beale, Bean, Beardsley, Beaty, Beaumont, Bell, Blair, Bouldin, Briggs, Brown, Bull, Bunch, Burd, Burns, Cambreleng, Campbell, Carmichael, Carr, Casey, Chambers, Chaney, Chilton, Claiborne, William Clark, Clay, Clayton, Clowney, Coffee, Connor, Corwin, Crane, Crockett, Darlington, Amos Davis, Davenport, Day, Deberry, Dickerson, Dickinson, Dunlap, Evans, Horace Everett, Ewing, Fillmore, Forester, Foster, Fowler, Philo C. Fuller, William K. Fuller, Galbraith, Gamble, Garland, Gholson, Gillet, Gilmer, Gordon, Graham, Grayson, Grennell, Joseph Hall, Hiland Hall, Thomas H. Hall, Hamer, Hannegan, Hard, Joseph M. Harper, James Harper, Harrison, Hawkins, Hawes, Heath, Henderson, Hiester, Hubbard, Huntington, Inge, William Jackson, Ebenezer Jackson, Janes, Noadiah Johnson, Cave Johnson, Henry Johnson, Benjamin Jones, Kavanagh, Kilgore, King, Kinnard, Lane, Lansing, Laporte, Lay, Luke Lea, Thos. Lee, Lewis, Loyall, Lyon, Abijah Mann, Joel K. Mann, Martindale, Marshall, Mardia, John Y. Mason, Moses Mason, May, Mc-Carty, McComas, McIntire, McKay, McKim, Mc-Kinley, McLene, McVean, Miller, Milligan, Miner, Henry Mitchell, Robert Mitchell, Moore, Morgan, Muhlenberg, Murphy, Osgood, Page, Parks, Patton, Patterson, Pearce, Peyton, Pickens, Pierce, Pierson, Pinckney, Polk, Pope, Ramsay, Reed, Rencher, Reynolds, Robertson, Schenck, Schley, William B. Shepard, A. H. Shepperd, Shinn, Slade, Sloane, Smith, Spangler, Speight, Standifer, Steele, Sutherland, Wm. Taylor, William P. Taylor, Philemon Thomas, Thomson, Tompkins, Trumbull, Turner, Turrill, Tweedy, Vanderpoel, Van Houten, Wagner, Wayne, White, Whittlesey, Williams, Wise, Young—181.

NAYS.—Messrs. Chilton Allan, Ashley, Barber, Hockee, Samuel Clark, Cramer, Dickson, Edward Everett, Ferris, Halsey, Hardin, Hathaway, Hazeltine, Howell, Jarvis, Richard M. Johnson, Love, Manning, Parker, Pl.illips, Vance, Vinton, Ward, Wardwell, Whallon, Wilde—27.

On motion of Mr. WATMOUGH, the bill regulating the pay of the Navy of the United States was made the special order of the day for to-morrow week.

The SPEAKER laid before the House a letter from the Secretary of the Treasury, enclosing a report, made in pursuance of a resolution of the House at its last session, in relation to the re organization of the Treasury Department.

Mr. WAYNE moved to refer the report to a Select Committee of nine; which was agreed to; and on motion of the same gentleman, 5,000 extra copies were ordered to be printed.

The SPEAKER also laid before the House two communications from the First Comptroller of the Treasury, containing a list of balances due to the Government; which were laid on the table.

On motion of Mr. BRIGGS,
The House then adjourned.

IN SENATE.

Tuesday, December 9, 1834.

A joint resolution was received from the House of Representatives, by Mr. FRANKLIN, their Clerk, for the appointment of Chaplains of different denominations, to officiate during the session; which,

On motion of Mr. FRELINGHUYSEN, was concurred in.

Also, a joint resolution for the appointment of a joint Library Committee; which,

On motion of Mr. ROBINS, was concurred in.

The Senate then proceeded to ballot for the Committee on their part, when it appeared that

20

Mr. ROBINS, Mr. POINDEXTER, and Mr. BIBB, were chosen.

Mr. WEBSTER, in pursuance of notice, and on leave given yesterday, introduced a bill to provide satisfaction for certain American citizens for spoliations on their commerce, prior to September 30, 1800.

On motion of Mr. WEBSTER, the bill received its first reading, for the purpose of reference to a Select Committee.

On balloting for the committee, it appeared that Mr WEBSTER, Mr. PRENTISS, Mr. PRESTON, Mr. SHEPLEY, and Mr. GRUNDY, were chosen.

Mr. KING, of Alabama, on leave given, introduced a bill for the relief of Theodore Brightwell; which was read the first time, and ordered to a second reading.

Mr. TIPTON, on leave given, introduced a bill for the relief of Col. Gad Humphreys; which was read the first time, and ordered to a second reading.

Mr. TIPTON also gave notice, that on to-morrow, he would ask leave to introduce a bill for the relief of Hiram A. Hunter, of Indiana.

Mr. TIPTON also submitted the following resolution:

Resolved, That the Committee on Commerce be instructed to inquire into the expediency of establishing a port of entry at the town of Lafayette, on the Wabash.

Mr. SILSBEE presented a memorial praying compensation for spoliations upon American commerce prior to 1800; which was referred to the Select Committee chosen on that subject.

Mr. TYLER, in pursuance of notice given yesterday, asked and obtained leave to introduce a bill authorizing a further issuing of scrip to holders of military bounty land warrants; which was read the first time and ordered to a second reading.

Mr. MOORE, in pursuance of notice, introduced a bill for the relief of Elijah Simmons; which was read the first time and ordered to a second reading.

Mr. NAUDAIN, in pursuance of notice, introduced a bill authorizing the purchase of Boyd Reilly's patent apparatus for applying the irrespirable gases to the human body, to be used in the Army and Navy of the United States; which was read the first time and ordered to a second reading

Mr MOORE, in pursuance of notice, introduced a bill for the relief of Eli Robinson; which was read the first time, and ordered to a second reading.

Mr. KING, of Alabama, gave notice that on to-morrow he would ask leave to introduce a bill to provide for the better organization of the United Stat s District Court in Alabama.

The following resolution, submitted yesterday by Mr. EWING, was considered, and adopted:

Resolved, That the Secretary of War be directed to transmit to the Senate a copy of any communication received by him from the Commissioners appointed by the States of Maryland, Pennsylvania, and Virginia, to receive portions of the Cumberland road lying within the limits of those States respectively, and to erect toll gates thereon; and if any money be necessary to complete the repairs of said road agreeably to the requirements of laws of said States which have received the assent of Congress; and that he furnish an estimate of the amount. Also, that he inform the Senate what is the condition of the masonry on that road; and how many inches of metal have been put on that part of it which has been located anew, and upon that part of it which lies between the Monongahela and Ohio rivers; and also, what depth of metal is in his opinion necessary to make it a permanent and substantial road, upon the plan which has been adopted, in its repairs by the Department.

Mr. EWING'S resolution, relative to the improvement of the harbor of the river Raisin, submitted yesterday, was also adopted.

The bill for the relief of Samuel Smith, and other Indians, was read a second time, and, on motion of Mr. MOORE, was referred to the Committee on Public Lands.

The bill authorizing the relinquishment of the 16th section and granting other lands in lieu thereof for the use of schools, was read the second time, and,

On motion of Mr. MOORE, referred to the Committee on Public Lands.

The bill for the relief of Susan Marlow, was read the second time, and

On motion of Mr. MOORE, it was referred to the Committee on Public Lands.

The Vice President laid before the Senate a letter from the Secretary of the Treasury, with a statement relative to the Bank of the U. States and the deposite banks for the past years; which,

On motion of Mr. GRUNDY, was ordered to be printed, together with the accompanying documents.

Mr. SILSBEE gave notice that on to-morrow he would ask leave to introduce a bill to exempt certain merchandise from the operation of duties imposed by the tariff of 1828.

Mr. SOUTHARD gave notice that on to-morrow he would ask leave to introduce several bills on naval subjects, which had been reported at the last session.

Mr. TYLER gave notice that on to-morrow he would ask leave to introduce a bill to remit the duties on all locomotive steam engines intended for rail roads, and upon parts of such engines and wheels for rail-road cars, with their necessary appendages imported, or which may be ordered, prior to fourth of March next.

Mr. BENTON submitted the following resolution:

Resolved, That the Secretary of the Treasury be directed to communicate to the Senate any correspondence with the Bank of the United States on the subject of the branch drafts, and dividends withheld, not heretofore communicated. Also, to inform the Senate whether the Directors on the part of the Government have been refused access to the books and accounts of the institution.

The Senate then adjourned.

HOUSE OF REPRESENTATIVES.
TUESDAY, DEC. 9, 1834.

Petitions and memorials were presented by—
Messrs. LINCOLN, ADAMS, and JACKSON, of Massachusetts;

Messrs. WARD, of New York;

Messrs. BANKS, MUHLENBERG, BURD, and KING, of Pennsylvania;

Messrs. ARCHER, BOULDIN, CLAIBORNE, and GORDON, of Virginia;

Mr. CLAYTON, of Georgia;

Messrs. POPE, JOHNSON, and ALLAN, of Kentucky;

[Mr. Pope presented the petition of the administrators of Lieut. Elliott. Also, the petition of the heir of Samuel Smith—all praying for commutation pay; which were referred.]

Messrs BLAIR and DUNLAP, of Tennessee;

Mr. CRANE, of Ohio;

Mr. GARLAND, of Louisiana;

Mr. MARDIS, of Alabama;

Mr. ASHLEY, of Missouri;

Mr. SEVIER, of Arkansas Territory.

The said petitions were severally referred to the appropriate committees.

On motion of Mr. R. M JOHNSON, from the Committee on Military Affairs, several b lls emanating from said committee, were ordered to be printed.

Mr. CHILTON rose and said, it would he recollected that at the last session, a resolution had been adopted, on his motion, after a protracted discussion, directing an inquiry into the propriety of compensating the remnant of that band of revolutionary patriots, who were engaged in protecting the frontiers from the year 1782 to the treaty of Greenville, in 1795. The committee, under the resolution, had reported a bill, which remained for inquiry. His present object was to move that the Committee of the Whole be discharged from the further consideration of the bill referred to, and that it be committed to a Committee of the Whole on the State of the Union. If these venerable worthies were to receive any thing for their services and tolls, and if their last moments were to be soothed by any substantial token of their country's gratitude, speedy action was necessary

to effect so desirable an object. He accordingly made the motion indicated.

Mr. WARDWELL moved to amend the motion by adding to it the bill extending the provisions of the act supplementary to the act making appropriations for the relief of the surviving officers and soldiers of the revolution.

Mr. CHILTON accepted the amendment as a modification of his motion, and thus amended, the motion prevailed. Yeas 81, nays 74.

On motion of Mr. POLK, the reports of the Secretary of the Treasury on the state of the finances, and the estimated appropriations necessary for the year 1835, were referred to the Committee of Ways and Means.

On motion of Mr. CROCKETT, the bill to amend an act entitled "An act authorizing the State of Tennessee to issue grants and perfect titles to certain lands therein described, and to settle the claims to the vacant and unappropriated land within the same," passed 18th April, 1806, was made the special order of the day for to-morrow week.

On motion of Mr. JOHNSON, of Ky.

Resolved, That the Committee on Public Lands be instructed to inquire into the expediency of making a further appropriation to satisfy Virginia Military Land Warrants.

On motion of Mr. BEATY,

Resolved, That the Committee on Roads and Canals be instructed to inquire into the expediency of making a further appropriation to continue the improvement of the navigation of the Cumberland river

On motion of Mr. THOMAS, of La.

Resolved, That the Committee on Commerce be, and is hereby, instructed to inquire into the expediency of establishing a light-house at the pass between Lake Ponchartrain and Lakes Maurepas.

On motion of Mr. JOHNSON, of La.

Resolved, That the Committee on Commerce be instructed to inquire into the expediency of making an appropriation to remove the obstructions to the navigation of vessels over the bar at the mouth of the Mississippi river, and to deepen the harbor at that place.

On motion of Mr. GARLAND,

Resolved, That the Committee on Public Lands be instructed to inquire into the expediency of making an appropriation of land or money, for the purpose of making levees on the public lands on the Western banks of the Mississippi river, from the Northern boundary of the State of Louisiana as low down as the grand levee of Point Coupee; and on the Southern bank of Red river, from the mouth thereof as far up as may be necessary, to protect the country from the inundations of that river.

On motion of Mr. HANNEGAN,

Resolved, That the Committee on Commerce be instructed to inquire into the expediency of establishing a port of entry at the town of Lafayette, or some other suitable point above the rapids of the river Wabash.

On motion of Mr. CARR,

Resolved, That all the papers and documents heretofore referred to the Committee on Claims, on the subject of making provision by law for the payment of property lost by individuals in the Tippecanoe campaign, in the year 1811. Also, for the payment of property lost by the Rangers of Indiana, Illinois, and Missouri, in the late war with Great Britain; and the six companies of mounted Rangers, organized in the year 1832, for the protection of the Northwestern frontier, be again referred to the Committee on Claims, and that said committee be instructed to report by bill, or otherwise.

On motion of Mr. EWING,

Resolved, That the Committee on Canals and Internal Improvements be instructed to inquire into the expediency, in strict accordance with the policy heretofore pursued, of making an appropriation to improve the navigation of the Wabash river, from its junction with the canal, a few miles North of Tippecanoe, to its junction with the Ohio river.

On motion of Mr. McKINLEY,

Resolved, That the Committee on Roads and Canals inquire into the expediency of authorizing

the State of Alabama to lay and collect tolls on the navigation of the canal now construct ng round the Muscle Shoals, to be applied to keeping the Canal in repair, attending to the locks, and collecting the tolls, and the surplus, if any, to be applied in aid of the completion of the Canal.

On motion of Mr MARDIS,

Resolved, That the Committee on the Judiciary, be instructed to inquire into the expediency of establishing, in the State of Alabama, a third District of the United States Federal Court, to be held in the town of Tuscaloosa, to consist of the counties of Fayette, Walker, Pickins, Sumpter, Green, Perry, Tuscaloo a, Bibb, Shelby, Jefferson, St. Clair, Burton, Talladega, Chambers, and Randolph.

On motion of Mr. ASHLEY,

Resolved, That the Committee on Claims be instructed to inquire into the expediency of liquidating the claim of Messrs. Thompson and Ross, for supplies furnished the troops of the United States during the summer of 1832.

On motion of Mr. SEVIER,

Resolved, That the Committee of Ways and Means be instructed to inquire into the expediency of making a further appropriation to complete the improvement of the navigation of the Arkansas river.

The following resolution offered by Mr. JARVIS, was ordered to lie on the table for one day:

Resolved, That the President of the United States be requested to communicate to this House, any information he may possess respecting the burning of the building occupied by the Treasury Department in the year 1833.

On motion of Mr. SMITH, of Maine,

Ordered, That the Committee on Commerce be instructed to inquire into the expediency of an appropriation for the improvement of the harbor at Portland, in Maine, by the erection of a breakwater, pursuant to the recommendation and survey of Col. —— Anderson, of the Engineer Corps in 1832.

On motion of Mr. HUBBARD,

Resolved, That the Committee on Revolutionary Pensions be instructed to inquire into the expediency of amending the Act of Congress, approved February 19, 1833, in addition to the act for the relief of certain surviving officers and soldiers of the revolution, passed June 7th, 1832, so that all persons entitled to pensions for any disabilities incurred in the war of the revolution, shall have the right to claim and receive the same in addition to any pension or annuity to which they may be entitled under any act of Congress for revolutionary services.

On motion of Mr. PEARCE,

Resolved, That the petitions, resolutions, and documents presented and submitted to this House at the last session, praying for and relating to the erection of certain Marine Hospitals, at places in said petitions and resolutions named, and referred to the Committee on Commerce, be again referred to the same committee.

On motion of Mr. WHALLON,

Resolved, That the Committee on Commerce be instructed to inquire into the expediency of making an appropriation for building two light houses, the one on Split Rock Point, and the other on Cumberland Head, Lake Champlain.

On motion of Mr. MORGAN,

Resolved, That the Committee on Commerce inquire into the expediency of obliging all merchant ships, or vessels of the United States, over the burthen of two hundred tons, bound south of the equator, to have on board, as a part of their crew, two apprentices, at least, as a means of benefitting the naval and commercial interests of the United States.

On motion of Mr. ADAMS, of New York,

Resolved, That the Committee on Invalid Pensions inquire into the expediency of granting a pension to Lambert P. Van Valkenburgh, of the town of Lexington, county of Green, and State of New York.

On motion of Mr. MANN, of New York,

Resolved, That the Committee on Military Affairs be instructed to inquire and report upon the expediency of abolishing the office of Major-General-Commanding-in-Chief, and of providing for

a fixed allowance and for a reduction and more equitable distribution of th: pay, rations, and emoluments of the General and Staff Officers of the Army.

On motion of Mr. FILLMORE,

Resolved, That the Committee on Commerce be instructed to inquire into the expediency of establishing a Marine Hospital at the city of Buffalo, New York.

On motion of Mr. HENDERSON,

Resolved, That the Committee on the Post Office and Post Roads be instructed to inquire into the expediency of extending the present mail route from Bellefonte to Mill Hall. (Centre county,) to the town of Salina, a distance of three miles farther.

On motion of Mr. CHAMBERS,

Resolved, That it be referred to the Judiciary Committee to consider the expediency of reporting a bill limiting the liability of the sureties of deceased, removed, or resigned public officers of the United States.

On motion of Mr. MILLER,

Resolved, That the Committee on Revolutionary Pensions be instructed to inquire into the propriety of granting a pension to Andrew Lawshe, of act of Congress.

On motion of Mr. McKIM,

Resolved, That so much of the report of the Secretary of War as relates to the Joint Resolution of Congress passed at the last session, and providing for the construction of a rail road through the public grounds at Harper's Ferry, be referred to the Committee on Military Affairs.

On motion of Mr. DAVENPORT,

Resolved, That the petition and papers of John W. Godfrey, deceased, late of the State of Virginia, now on the files of this House, which have, at previous sessions of Congress, been referred to the Committee on Revolutionary Claims, and not finally acted on, be again referred to that Committee.

On motion of Mr. MASON, of Virginia,

Resolved, That the Committee on Commerce be instructed to inquire into the expediency of making an appropriation to erect a hospital at City Point in Virginia, for the reception of sick seamen.

On motion of Mr. MASON, of Virginia,

Resolved, That the Message of the President of the United States, on the subject of a present received by the Consul of the United States at Tangier, from the Emperor of Morocco, made to this House at the last session of Congress, be recommitted to the Committee on Foreign Affairs, with instructions to report a bill directing the sale of the lion and horses presented, and such application of the proceeds of such sale, as shall be deemed most appropria e. Also, to inquire into the expediency of making disposition of such other presents as have been made to officers of the Government, and deposited in the Secretary of State office, as being presented contrary to the constitution.

On motion of Mr. SPEIGHT,

Resolved, That the Committee on Commerce be instructed to inquire into the expediency of making an appropriation for the building of a light-boat, to be stationed at or near Harbor Island Bar, in the State of N. Carolina.

On motion of Mr. WILLIAMS,

Resolved, That the Committee on Revolutionary Pensions be instructed to inquire into the expediency of providing by law for the payment to the militia, of the same pensions that are paid to the soldiers and officers of the regular army.

On motion of Mr. GRAYSON,

Resolved, That the Committee on Commerce be instructed to inquire into the expediency of making an appropriation for erecting light-houses, and placing buoys at the entrance of the inlets of St. Helena and Port Royal, on the coast of South Carolina.

On motion of Mr. HUBBARD,

Resolved, That a committee be appointed on the part of this House, to join such committee as may be appointed on the part of the Senate, to consider and report the arrangements necessary to be adopted, in order to carry into effect the last resolution reported on the 26th June, 1834, by the

Joint Committee appointed at the last session of Congress, on the occasion of the death of General La Fayette.

The resolution moved by Mr. BEATY yesterday, was read, considered, and agreed to.

On motion of Mr WISE, the Committee of the Whole was discharged from the further consideration of a bill to carry into effect a resolution of 1781 for the erection of a marble column at York, in Virginia, and it was made the special order for Wednesday.

The resolution submitted yesterday by Mr. BEATY, was considered and agreed to.

The SPEAKER laid before the House a report from the Secretary of the Treasury, in the case of Thomas H. Smith & Son; which, on motion of Mr. McKIM, was referred to the Committee of Ways and Means.

PRESIDENT'S MESSAGE.

On motion of Mr. CONNOR, the House resolved itself into a Committee of the Whole on the state of the Union—Mr. SPEIGHT in the Chair—on the Message of the President of the United States.

Mr. CONNOR submitted the following resolutions:

Resolved, That so much of the President's Message as relates to the political relations of the United States with other nations, be referred to the Committee on Foreign Affairs.

Resolved, That so much of the said Message as relates to the commerce of the United States with foreign nations, be referred to the Committee on Commerce.

Resolved, That so much of said Message as relates to the finances, and to the Bank of the United States, be referred to the Committee of Ways and Means.

Resolved, That so much of said Message as relates to the Report of the Secretary of War, and the public interests intrusted to the War Department, be referred to the Committee on Military Affairs.

Resolved, That so much of said Message as relates to the Indian tribes, be referred to the Committee on Indian Affairs.

Resolved, That so much of said Message as relates to the " existence of extensive frauds under the various laws granting pensions and gratuities for revolutionary services, and the re-examination of those laws," be referred to the Committee on Revolutionary Pensions.

Resolved, That so much of said Message a relates to the Report of the Secretary of the Navy and the naval service, be referred to the Committee on Naval Affairs.

Resolved, That so much of said Message as relates to the Post Office Department, be referred to the Committee on the Post Office and Post Roads.

Resolved, That so much of said Message as relates to the extension of the Judiciary system of the United States, be referred to the Committee on the Judiciary.

Resolved, That so much of said Message as relates to the amendment of the Constitution, in relation to the election of President and Vice President of the United States, be referred to a Select Committee.

Resolved, That so much of said Message as relates to the destruction of the building occupied by the Treasury Department, and to the erection of a new building for the use of the Treasury Department, be referred to the Select Committee on the Public Buildings.

Resolved, That the said Select Committees have leave to report by bill or otherwise.

The resolutions having been read, Mr. CLAYTON proposed an amendment, in the following terms:

" That so much of the President's Message as relates to the Treaty [with France, concluded at Paris on the 4th day of July, 1831, be referred to the Committee on Foreign Affairs, with instructions to report that it is expedient to await the further action of the French Chambers on the question submitted to them, of granting the appropriations necessary to carry the Treaty into effect; inasmuch as the delay of consummating its terms seems to have proceeded more from the de-

licate and important character of the claims resting on voluminous documentary evidence, their long standing, and the peculiar complexity of the principles involved in their adjustment, than from any design, on their part, to impair the friendly relations which have so long and happily subsisted between the French and American Governments, or any desire to evade the performance of ample justice when the whole matter shall have been fully and fairly considered."

Mr. CLAYTON, in supporting the amendment he had offered, proceeded to say that he considered the question involved in the resolution, as perhaps one of the most important which would come before the House during the present session, and he wished it to be fully understood, that, in the few remarks he should offer, his purpose was to avoid every thing in the remotest degree connected with party feeling. He trusted he should be the last man to bring forward any thing to disturb the harmony of the House. The President, in submitting that portion of his message which related to this subject, had, he doubted not, done that which he honestly believed to be expedient and proper. He had nothing to censure in the proceeding, nor was it his design to cast any blame upon any one. The question, however, in all its weight and solemn responsibility, was by the message submitted to the consideration and decision of the legislative branch of the Government. The body whom he addressed were responsible for all the consequences attendant upon their decision; and when the extent of those consequences was taken into view, it was a consideration which could not but strike the mind of every individual in a most forcible manner. The People of the United States were now looking intently to the legislative body for what was to ensue.

It could not be disguised that the recommendation in the message amounted, practically, to nothing more or less than a declaration of WAR against France. That was the recommendation. And he trusted that gentlemen would not suffer themselves to be deceived into any other view of it. Let every gentleman ask himself whether, should that be done which the President advises, war must not be the natural and inevitable consequence? He was ready to admit that the time might come, nay, that it might, perhaps, be not distant, when war would be necessary; but he concluded that that time was not yet come. In the message, the House was presented with an alternative. "If," says the President, in his message, "it shall be the pleasure of Congress to await "the further action of the French Chambers, no "further consideration of the subject will, at this "session, probably be required at your hands." But if this course should not appear to Congress proper to be adopted, then the President submits the only other which, in his opinion, remained. "I recommend," says he, "that a law be passed, "authorizing reprisals upon French property, in "case provision shall not be made for the payment "of the debt at the approaching session of the "French Chambers." Mr. C. said, he would here appeal to the candor of the House to say, whether they believed that resorting to a measure of this character would not immediately place the United States in hostile relations with one of the proudest, most high-spirited, most warlike, and most wealthy, powerful, and formidable nations of the world? Let no gentleman deceive himself. The moment such a measure should be sanctioned by the legislative authority, all prospect of a friendly termination of our dispute with France was at an end.

It might, perhaps, be said, that before the House came to a decision of any kind, they ought to allow themselves ample time; as possibly the whole matter might have been decided before the message should reach France. But he would ask whether, should that be the case, gentlemen would wish to place that nation in such a condition as they would then occupy? Should the House, on the contrary, adopt the instructions he had had the honor to propose, would it not go far to show to the French People and their Government, that there existed in the American nation no unkind, no hostile feeling toward our ancient friends and allies. Al that sense of mutual mortification would be spared, which must be the inevitable result of having needlessly threatened those who were, without a threat, disposed to do us right. But supposing that the question should *not* have been settled, and the message containing the language he had read should arrive on the other side of the water, what would be the effect upon the French Chambers?

Had gentlemen read the debates in that body on the subject of our treaty? Had they seen what a high-minded, proud, lofty spirit pervaded and animated the speeches of the French orators, so exactly characteristic of that ancient and chivalrous people? Did any man believe, that, if such language was held when no threat had been uttered, those men would be disposed to yield our claims after the threat had been heard? If the Chambers hesitated now, from their view of the character of our demand, did any man believe that, after this Message of the President of the United States had reached them, they would be more disposed to yield us our rights? Mr. C. said, he might show from another portion of the message itself, what might be expected to be the temper and feelings of the French people in such circumstances. The President, speaking of the conduct of the Bank, observes:

"To the needless distresses brought on the 'country during the last session of Congress, has 'since been added the open seizure of the dividends on the public stock, to the amount of one 'hundred and seventy thousand and forty-one dollars, under pretence of paying damages, cost, 'and interest, upon the protested French bill.— 'This sum constituted a portion of the estimated 'revenues for the year 1834, upon which the appropriations made by Congress were based. It 'would as soon have been expected that our collectors would seize on the customs, or the receivers of our land offices on the moneys arising from 'the sale of public lands, under pretences of claims 'against the United States, as that the Bank would 'have retained the dividends. Indeed, if the 'principle be established, that any one who chooses may set up a claim against the United States, 'may, without authority of law, seize on the public property or money wherever he can find it, 'to pay the claim, there will remain no assurance 'that our revenue will reach the Treasury, or that 'it will be applied after the appropriation to the 'purposes designated in the law. The paymasters of our army, and the pursers of our navy, 'may, under like pretences, apply to their own 'use moneys appropriated to set in motion the 'public force, and in time of war leave the country without defence. This measure resorted to 'by the Bank is disorganizing and revolutionary, 'and, if generally resorted to by private citizens 'in like cases, would fill the land with anarchy 'and violence."

Here was a parallel case. If such an act as that of the Bank, in the case referred to, was felt by the President to be "revolutionary," and full of "violence," what effect would the language he held on the subject of reprisals be expected to exert in France? A proposition, while they were still deliberating on our claims, to take redress into our own hands, and seize at once upon their ships upon the high seas! As men felt, so nations would feel; and what was true of the one, would, to a great extent, be true of the other.

Gentlemen should not consider this question like that between France and Portugal. Portugal was a small nation, in a state of political distraction, and utterly unable to resist the demand made upon her, or to avenge aggressions on her property. France was a very different thing. She was not to be compelled, as Spain had been, to endure without resenting it, the language held to her. When the gentleman who now presided over the Department of State was our Minister near that Power, very different consequences must ensue, should language of a similar tenor be addressed to her. Reprisals were, in effect, acts of hostility; so soon as they should be authorized on our part by Congress, France would instantly retaliate, and order reprisals by her citizens; and what must be the consequence? Who did not see that the result must be war? Now, he did not believe that, as yet, we had justifiable cause of war with the French nation. He argued this question, and intended to argue it, as if the recommendation of the President was a recommendation of war. He trusted gentlemen would not so far deceive themselves as to view it in any other light. Indeed, it was very plain that the Secretary of the Treasury, in his Report, seemed to look towards such an event. The President did the same. The Secretary says:

"It is not now possible to foresee the contingencies that may check either the present large 'importations of merchandise or large sales of land, 'and consequently reduce the revenue derived 'from them; or that may require an increase in our 'army or navy expenditures, arising from those 'unfortunate collisions to which all nations are liable that feel disposed to sustain the faith of treaties, vindicate their public rights, and protect, 'efficiently, their commerce and citizens. No further reduction of the tariff, until that already 'provided for, at the close of the ensuing year, 'would therefore seem to be prudent."

In fact, the President and his minister had done, as it became a judicious Government to do; they had anticipated a possible state of war, and had provided against it. That such must be the natural consequence of the measure the President had recommended, he believed no candid man would for a moment deny.

Mr. C. said he had no hesitation in declaring his belief, that our claims on the French Government were perfectly fair and just: he believed that we had not asked a cent more than was justly due to us; that we ought to have the money; and that, should our demand be definitely postponed, the *refusal* would present *just cause of war*. But it had not been definitely refused. Whoever would take the pains to read the French debates, would find that the members of the French Chambers insisted on no other principles than we ourselves did. The French Constitution declared that the Chambers must act upon every grant of money required to fulfil the stipulations of a treaty, and their speakers stood upon this constitutional right. [Here Mr. C. quoted copiously from the speeches made in the French Chamber of Deputies.]

Now, if the matter debated there was mainly, or in part, a constitutional question, ought we to proceed to hasty and rash measures because they came to a different conclusion from that which we might think the right one? The question was to this day undecided in our own Government.— There were among us, as among them, two opinions as to the obligation of Congress to make appropriations of money to fulfil the stipulations of a treaty. The prevailing opinion was that Congress were not bound, but remained free to deliberate and to decide in view of circumstances. As an illustration of this:—were it to be held otherwise, how might the tariff question be at any time unsettled by the stipulations of our foreign negotiators? Should such a principle as this once be sanctioned, what consequences must follow? There would be an end to the power of Congress over the appropriation of public money. And, holding such views ourselves, ought we to complain if similar opinions were maintained in the French Legislative halls? The matter was not yet fully settled, either here or there. Should the decision of the Chambers be that they could not appropriate money for the treaty, we should then be referred back to the grounds of our original claim before any treaty existed: and then Congress must decide whether or not they would go to war to compel the payment of claims which had been left to negotiation for forty-five years.

The question, however, was still undecided: and, in the meanwhile, all the influence of the Crown and of the Cabinet was exerted in our behalf: it was all urged in favor of the fulfilment of the terms of the Treaty. Under such circumstances would it, he asked, be wise to go to war? The menace of the message was war. Gentlemen must be blind not to see that France would so receive it. If she was now the same proud and high-toned nation which the history of Europe had so fully evinced her to be, all thoughts of amicable negotiation, under such a menace, must be at an end. There were some things in the speeches of the Deputies which were calculated to startle our

pride. They referred to the days of their revolutionary struggle and of ours, and adverted to the great sufferings of both nations in the cause of free principles; especially in the maintenance of that principle so important in our estimation, that free ships made free goods: that the flag covered the cargo.

[Here Mr. C. again quoted from the French debates.]

Throughout these speeches, Mr. C. found no language or feeling of disrespect towards our Government. And let it be remembered, that the subject was one of great importance to the French Government. Let it be remembered that at the close of that great revolution in their affairs, which resulted in the exiling of Bonaparte to Elba, and the letting in all the harpies who accompanied what was called the Restoration, the French nation had to pay a thousand millions of francs, because she had been struggling for the principles of free trade and the rights of neutrals. Our Government, at that time, disclaimed all part or participation in the doings of those nations who combined together to force the Bourbons upon France—nations whose only purpose seemed to be to emulate each other in robbing the French Treasury. All parties in the Chambers agreed in conceding that something was due to us. The only question was as to the precise amount. Bonaparte's Government admitted that, on the very strictest principles of calculation, at least thirteen millions, and, on principles more liberal, eighteen millions of francs were due to the United States. The Restoration Government, when they were expelled by the French People, had been on the eve of settling with us for twelve millions; and the existing Government admitted, without hesitation, that a large debt was justly due. The difficult question to be settled, was, the true and just amount.

To fix this properly, was a work of difficulty itself of time: and surely it would be time well lost, should it result in preventing our conflict with one of the oldest and strongest and most warlike nations of Europe. What were two or three sessions of the Chambers? especially when our name was treated with the utmost respect in all their discussions, and while, though they had great difficulty in deciding on questions of their own, which were involved in the decision, they continued to manifest nothing but a friendly disposition and purpose toward this country? Some of their arguments were not without great weight. Some of them especially, seemed entitled to much consideration from a nation which respected its own laws. It was, that a part of our claim was for goods taken during the prevalence of our own embargo and non-intercourse laws, from citizens who were sailing the high seas, in open violation and defiance of those laws. They insist that, if our own citizens choose to take the risk of appearing on the ocean in direct disobedience to our authority, they ought to abide by the consequences. But he waived all this. He had stated enough to show that there did exist just cause for some delay. He would only add an extract from one speech, which insisted, that should our claim be allowed without rigid examination, the allowance of it could be placed only on the ground of gratuity. [Here Mr. C. quoted from one of the French orators.]

Mr. C. said, that it was his persuasion, after reading these debates, and recollecting that we had the whole weight of the Crown and the Cabinet thrown into our scale, that the ultimate decision would be what we asked that it should be.

But there was another aspect of the subject, and a very serious one. It was this: that, should we go to war at this time, we must do it upon a deficient Treasury. Not only was the Treasury of the Nation destitute of a dollar, but there was an actual scarcity of two millions and a half of dollars! This he was prepared to demonstrate. He did not consider that, however, as at present necessary. He had the vouchers ready to establish his position. Now, should the nation go to war on such a Treasury, what must be the consequence? He had risen with no wish to rouse jealousies, or awake angry feeling; but to make a speech pacific in all respects; and he hoped that

what he had yet to say would be received in no other spirit.

But it was plain that if we went to war, it would be, in effect, with all the world. The field of battle would be the high seas; and there we had a commerce afloat to the value of two hundred millions, viz. ninety millions outward, and one hundred and eleven millions inward; and this would immediately be subject to the vessels of all nations, provided they did but hoist the French flag. It would not only be a war with a nation numbering thirty millions of people, but it would subject us to attacks from all other quarters. Yet let him not be misunderstood. Let no gentleman suppose him to be unwilling to risk all this; yes, and ten thousand times more, on a question where the national honor was involved; but he never could consent to expose the property of his fellow citizens to such a hazard, until all proper measures of a pacific character had been tried in vain.

The nation was now said to be out of debt, and the fact was the envy and admiration of other governments, and the pride of our own. But if we went to war, we must instantly plunge into a new debt. And what would be the further consequence? As our commerce must be destroyed, the natural course of things would be to turn capital from commerce to manufactures, just as it had happened during the last war. Our citizens would, as soon as possible, withdraw their capital from the ocean, where it would be subjected to such a risk of destruction, and invest it in manufactures. And what next? Why, then we should have appeal upon appeal for protection, and the tariff must be raised. And then all the difficulties between the Northern and the Southern States must be aroused afresh. Could any gentleman look at such consequences, and not feel a desire to avert war, if it could be done with honor?

Mr. C. observed that it had been his purpose to say much more, but that he was physically unable. He had not risen with any desire to make a flourish, but to recall to the consideration of the House the pacific relations which had subsisted between this country and France for 45 years. The President seemed disposed to hurry Congress into a course which must forfeit at once all this mutual good understanding. It was not his wish to recall scenes that were past, although one of the French Deputies had done so, and had adverted to the time when the flags of France and America were dying in the same field, and joined in the same cause. He would only ask the House to look on that picture, (pointing to the portrait of WASHINGTON,) and then on that, (pointing to the likeness of LAFAYETTE.)

If the pictures of those great men could speak now, what would they say? While the House was engaged in deliberating on a war with France, it would be well to veil these portraits. He felt assured the American People would approve of no such war. Virginia would never do it. Mount Vernon would never allow it. Yorktown would not consent to it. All the South would oppose it. The nation was unprepared for it—the circumstances did not demand it.

Mr. CLAIBORNE, of Va., said he rose to support the motion made by the gentleman from Georgia (Mr. CLAYTON.) He said he could not refrain from mingling in the discussion of a question so vitally interesting to his constituents and to the world. Were he dumb, he would make an effort to break the bands of silence, to give utterance to his feelings upon this all important subject. Mr. C. said he spoke on this question without premeditation; relying upon the spontaneous feelings of his heart, and the best interests of his constituents, to direct both the matter and manner of his address. He said the winds of Heaven at this moment were wafting the President's Message to every portion of the civilized world. It had been asserted that the message contained no menace—no threat. But I fear, said Mr. C., it may be differently understood by the French people, and that they may look upon it as having received the sanction of the American nation. He said he believed the nation wanted, if possible, to live in peace with all foreign powers. It was their interest as well as duty. He said he had no hesitation in asserting that, as

far as he had been able to ascertain public opinion, it was averse to war. The people were disposed to live in peace with all the world, and especially with their ancient friend and ally, France. From this determination they would not depart, as long as they could adhere to it without a sacrifice of national honor.

Mr. C. asked, what did the President recommend? He recommended, in the event of a certain contingency, to wit, the French Chambers not making the necessary appropriations to carry into effect their treaty with us, that then, and in that event, he, the President, should be authorized by Congress to make reprisals on French property, to the amount of the sum stipulated to be paid the American Government in the treaty of the 4th of July, 1831. Yes, said Mr. C., to arm him with power to seize upon the property of innocent and unoffending individuals. If this power be conferred upon him, it will be virtually conferring upon the President unconstitutional power—a power to declare war. For, disguise the fact as gentlemen may, I can view it in no other light than a declaration of war. Is there any gentleman on this floor who does not believe that war will be the inevitable consequence of the measure? Yes sir, it will follow with the certainty that the peal of thunder succeeds the electric flash in the gathering storm. Sir, I am not afraid to express my sentiments on the present occasion. I am one of the representatives of the People, and a free man. I come here to advocate the people's interest. This is the goal that I direct all my efforts to. I will support the measures of the Administration when I think them right, and oppose them when I believe them wrong. I am no partisan, and if an imputation of that sort should be made against me, self-poised and self-sustained, I will stand conscious and erect. Gentlemen have read history to little effect, if they are ready to clothe a single individual with the power of making war. If we are to derive wisdom from experience and from the admonitions of history, we will withhold it. The granting of this power improvidently has carried the sword through the fairest provinces of the world, and brought ruin to the doors of millions. When cause of war shall exist, and the honor of the nation shall demand a declaration, I will, as the representative of a proud and chivalrous people, join in meeting its horrors; but, until dire necessity shall require it, I shall use all my efforts to avoid it. Policy, sound morals, every thing, tells me this is the proper determination.

But, Mr. Chairman, does the existing difference between the United States and France present such a case? In my humble judgment it does not. What, sir, is the state of the fact? Is it not the Executive Government of France making use of every exertion to obtain from the Chambers the necessary appropriations? Does it not already appear to every gentleman, who has given himself the trouble to read the debates in the Chambers, that a respectable portion of that body do not regard the treaty as binding until ratified by them, and the only constitutional power in the French Government to levy a tax upon the People? We should, in the examination of this question, have some regard to the existing state of affairs in that country. What would be our situation, if the President and Senate were to make a treaty, and in that treaty stipulate to pay a sum of money, and Congress was to refuse to grant the appropriations? The President would surely, in that case, recommend the disappointed nation to stay their hand a little, and give time to effect a change of public opinion. The Government of France and the Government of the United States are governments founded on public opinion, and sustained by popular sentiments and popular feelings. Who says nay to this proposition? None—no not one. It ought to be remembered, that a majority of eight only were against the necessary appropriation, at the time the question was first taken in the Chambers. It cannot be forgotten, that the King has pledged himself to present it at the next meeting of the Chambers, and again urge the necessity of the appropriation; and we know that it is his fixed purpose to do all in his power to have the claim adjusted. With a knowledge of these facts, shall

we indulge for one single moment in the language of menace, and provoke a war with France, our oldest and most steady friend? A people who stood by us in the hour of peril and danger, who mingled their blood and treasure with the blood and treasure of our fathers, in fighting for the liberties of our beloved country! This great citadel of republican government was erected by the joint efforts of our fathers and the French people. Were I to experience for a moment other than a wish for eternal peace between France and the United States, some ghost smeared with blood would rise from the plains of Monmouth to upbraid me. Do not draw wrong conclusions from what I say. I am the advocate of peace. An eloquent writer has well said—the heart that can mourn over the havoc and desolation of the fields of battle, is closely allied to the arm that is ever ready to protect innocence from outrage, and society from oppression. It is the emblem of moral courage—the daring to do what is right.

Sir, is it inconsistent with genuine courage, before you enter into a contest, either as private men or public functionaries, to calculate the consequences that will follow? Sir, ours is the most commercial nation on earth, except Great Britain; our merchant vessels are incessantly wafting the productions of our soil from the frozen belt that encircles the northern pole, to the sandy bars which environ the antarctic circle. At this moment the surface of the ocean is whitened with the sails which cover her millions of American property. Declare war tomorrow, and two months will not have elapsed before all the unemployed shipping of other countries would apply to France for letters of marque and reprisal, and under the French flag pounce down upon and sweep this vast commerce from the ocean. Then in a brief period would be presented to your eyes the melancholy spectacle of your commerce ruined, your surplus produce unsold, your seaport towns languishing, and every village and cottage from Maine to Georgia withering before the blighting effects of war. Mr. Chairman, let me here say to you, that the American People should be the last on earth to go to war, and for this plain reason: they have more at stake than any other. Our Government is the admiration of the whole world. No people among civilized nations enjoy a higher degree of freedom and happiness; none who have their civil and religious liberties better secured. This Government, administered in its purity, is an ample shield, behind which the people may stand in the full enjoyment of all the hopes of freemen; nor are we, Mr. Chairman, alone interested in the success of our Government: The enlightened and liberal in every portion of the earth pray for the preservation of our political institutions; already have foreigners come here to study our laws, and have gone home with their minds richly imbued with liberal principles, and have been enabled greatly to ameliorate the condition of their own countrymen.

Mr. Claiborne said he felt that the mild and philosophical principles he was enforcing were in perfect accordance with the principles of the American Government, and would receive the sanction of the enlightened district which he was proud to represent.

He said he felt certain that in the vote he should give, he should represent the feelings and wishes of his constituents. He was well satisfied that if the naked question was submitted to them, that their high sense of justice and morality would revolt at the idea of this Government seizing by force the private property of the citizens of France, to indemnify some speculating merchants for losses sustained under the Berlin and Milan decrees of France, made by way of self-preservation against the unlawful orders in council of Great Britain, in declaring not only the ports of France, but those of neutral nations, in a state of blockade. It would not be forgotten that the United States, by the passage of her non-intercourse law, adopted measures of retaliation, and thus lessened her claim to indemnification for spoliations under the Berlin and Milan decrees. They could justly claim indemnity for spoliations committed upon property after the repeal of those decrees by the French Government.

Mr. Chairman, I believe the French owe us fairly more than 25 millions of francs. You are aware, however, that the French Government, at no time before the establishment of the Government of July, acknowledged that they owed this Government more than two and a half millions of dollars, and against this sum that they claimed an offset for what they conceived a violation on the part of this Government of the 8th article of the treaty of 1803, between France and the United States, stipulating that French vessels should be received in the ports of Louisiana upon the terms of the most favored nations which they contend was violated when they were not put upon the same footing with those of Great Britain, after the treaty of Ghent. When such difficulties have grown up between us, said Mr. C., what is the course to be pursued? I answer and say, let us address the French Government in the language of friendship—let us say to them, we believe you owe us 25 millions of francs; you have agreed by treaty to pay us that sum. If you complain that you were under a misapprehension of facts—point out errors; we are ready to correct them—we want only our due, and we feel you are too magnanimous, when you are satisfied of the true amount due, to withhold it. The people of France certainly must desire to be in peace and amity with us—I have confidence that justice will be done us by the French Government—that the interruption of good feeling will be momentary, and will pass away, and be succeeded by days and years, and I hope centuries, of brotherly love. Good Americans and good Frenchmen desire this state of things; and that the peace now happily existing may exist forever, is my most ardent wish. I could, sir, have said a great deal more, but less was impossible.

Mr. WAYNE, Chairman of the Committee on Foreign Affairs, observed, that the amendment offered by the gentleman from Georgia to the proposition of the gentleman from North Carolina, to refer to the Committee on Foreign Affairs so much of the Message as relates to our concerns with foreign nations, was improper as to time, and in its matter. He thought discussion now upon the subject to which the amendment relates, would be premature, and might do much harm. Indeed, if the admissions made by the gentleman in his remarks, could in any event be taken as the sense of the House, or of any portion of the people of this nation, much injury would be done to those who were interested in the faithful and speedy performance by France of the stipulations of the treaty of the 4th July, 1831. But the gentleman's admissions would have no response in this nation. He proposes to terminate all inquiry into the affair, and to prevent any action by Congress upon the Message, by instructing the Committee to report that it is expedient to await the further action of the French Chambers—and his reason is, that the postponement of voting money for the payment of the instalments due by the treaty, has arisen from the delicate and important character of the claims referred, and the peculiar complexity of the principles involved in their adjustment. In other words, that the French legislators have been for two years and a half discussing principles which they do not understand, and still require time to enable them to come to a correct conclusion. And yet the gentleman, with nothing before him but a report of the discussions of the Chamber of Deputies, without any of the correspondence between the two Governments, since the failure upon the part of France to discharge her obligations under the treaty, had, in two or three short days, been able to unravel the intricacy of the whole affair, and so satisfactorily to himself, that he proposes to substitute the results of his happy ability for the examination of the committee and the more deliberate judgment of the House. It would have been well at least, and a prudent man would, either for censure or praise, as he might be disposed, have postponed his conclusion, until he had ascertained how far the message, relating to this affair, could be sustained by the correspondence between the two Governments since the ratification of the treaty. It would have occurred to another, that the affair, as presented to the nation by the message, imposed upon Congress the necessity of inquiring into facts, with the view of determining upon the propriety of the President's suggestions, and carrying them out, or of devising some other means to secure the rights of those for whose benefit the treaty had been made. Congress had now become the guardians of the rights of our citizens, vested in them by a treaty, which France must perform, or for which the United States, as a nation, must receive an indemnity, at some time or other, to the full extent of its original obligations, and all the consequences which may ensue from a refusal by any department of the French Government to fulfil the stipulations of the treaty. But the gentleman could only see in the message a declaration of war, and all the disasters which follow in the train of war. If his object had been to fall into the current which, for some days, has been flowing in a certain channel, to produce the impression upon the public mind that the President designed to provoke a war with France—the gentleman had taken the proper course to effect his intention—notwithstanding he had disclaimed any party feeling in his movement. There was nothing in the message of a warlike character or threat. All idea of menace is in terms denied, and the French character, government, and people, are treated with the respect and regard due from one nation to another—when either, by putting itself in the wrong, justifies the language of complaint. Nor is the message without a reference to those recollections which, if France will cherish, by doing us justice, the United States will never forget, nor cease to acknowledge. There is a difference between a firm attitude in the pursuit of acknowledged rights, and the language of menace. The President, after giving a narrative of all that had taken place since the treaty had been concluded, recommends, if an appropriation shall not be made by the French Chambers at their next session, that some legislation shall be enacted by Congress, to meet the predicament in which we shall be placed by the refusal of France to pay an acknowledged debt. In anticipation of that event, the rights of our citizens can only be sustained by prompt measures. But they are only to be contingent—until the refusal of France shall be complete. The refusal has already been as positive as it can be by one of the Departments of the French Government. The information received by us of that fact in May last, would have justified then some ultimate measure of redress; but the course of the King of the French called for our forbearance. Since that time, there has been another meeting of the Chambers; but no appropriation was made, nor was any effort made by the King or his Ministers to procure one. Then the Chambers were prorogued to the last week in December, and now it is only possible that we can have during this session of Congress, the result of the King's assurances that it was his intention to press the appropriation at the ensuing session of the Chambers. Almost three years have passed since the appropriation for the first instalment under the treaty should have been made, and since the ratification of the treaty there have been five sessions of the Chambers. With this procrastination in view, will any one, having a proper American feeling, and who appreciates government as he should do, by its ability to give happiness to its citizens at home and to obtain for them redress when wronged by foreign nations—complain of the President because he has expressed his confidence that no branch of this government will, for a moment, entertain the idea of acquiescing in a refusal to execute the treaty, or because he has said further negotiation is out of the question. Because, whilst deprecating the consequences of collision with France, he has said, in maintaining our national rights and honor, all governments are alike to us. Or for having recommended the mildest or only alternative short of war—when one nation obstinately refuses to pay to another a liquidated debt. The President has not asked that the power of authorizing reprisals should be put into his hands. He recommends reprisals, if another sitting of the Chambers shall be closed without definitive action upon the subject—but he does not attempt to prescribe or to intimate the time or manner of

its being done, and only assures Congress that its decision shall be faithfully executed, as far as it shall authorize him to act. By his language, Mr. W. understood, and so he believed the whole nation would understand the President to say—Not having shunned the responsibility of making the recommendation, I am sincere in the determination not to shun the responsibility of executing the decision of Congress, whatever that may be.

And as for having recommended reprisals in the event of the French Chambers again refusing to execute the stipulations in the treaty, those who may dislike such a course, should remember reprisals or a tame acquiescence in the refusal, is all that we shall have left to us—short of war. Reprisals, though sometimes leading to war, are more frequently the means of preventing it. In this case, will it not be so? For, besides the just cause which we shall have for resorting to it, we have the honor of the King of the three days, that he differs from the Chambers in his sense of the obligations imposed upon France by the treaty; and without a declaration of war by himself, it cannot be made by France. So much, Mr. W. deemed it right to say, in regard to the message, in reply to the misconceptions of it by his colleague, and in answer to his apprehensions of war.

But there were two points of view in which the subject was presented to the House; and from the mere intimation of them, it would be obvious that it should be sent to a committee, untrammelled by instructions. The first were the rights which our citizens had acquired under the treaty, and, secondly, what national honor would require from Congress, if the French Chambers persevered in refusing to execute it. If the amendment prevailed, it would be equivalent to a postponement by Congress of the rights of our citizens. The subject should be fully canvassed by a committee, and afterwards, upon its report, by Congress, that our merchants might feel and know, that their pursuits were under the vigilant guardianship of Congress, and that all the world might see, however long it may be delayed by circumstances, that there was to be a day of retribution for every outrage upon our commerce, under whatever pretence, or by whatever nation it might be committed. The sense of this security will give life to our enterprise in every clime, and confidence to our mariners upon every sea. In this instance, the subject should be sent to a committee without instructions, that it might deliberately inquire and report that course which Congress should take as the best fitted to induce France to fulfil her obligation, or what will most successfully accomplish the purpose, should it be thought advisable, now or hereafter, to redress ourselves. But I do not propose to argue this point, at this time. The intimation of it is enough to ensure the rejection of the amendment. As to what national honor would require, if France persevered in her course, and definitively refused to recognise our rights under the treaty, and also to make reparation for her delay in doing it, Mr W. was not mistaken when he said, there would be but one sentiment among the American People, as to the course to be pursued. It would no longer be a question of dollars and cents, but of national honor, demanding every sacrifice of money and of life to maintain it, with the superadded obligation to sustain all that the laws of nations required in regard to treaties. The cause would not only be ours, but that of every nation having treaties, or which may have to make treaties, with France. Mr. W. would not pursue this topic. He had thought it to be his duty, from the relation in which he had been placed to the House, to make some remarks upon the amendment proposed by his colleague, and upon his speech, that the public might be advised of the true state of our affairs with France, and to prevent the message from being misconceived by those who might read the remarks of his colleague. The ordinary course was, to refer subjects bearing on our foreign relations to the Committee on Foreign Affairs. Why do so, if the committee was to be locked up by instructions, which took from it the freedom of deliberation, and confined them to report the judgment of an individual. His colleague had expressed himself in a speech professing much benevolence, and full of apparent patriotism; but the course he proposed, if countenanced by the House, would compromise the interest of a large class of his fellow citizens, by adding to the foreign obstacles already in the way of the payment of their claims, all the prejudices of party at home. But he would say no more, for he was convinced the impropriety of his colleague's movement would be manifested by an almost unanimous rejection of the amendment, without further debate.

Mr. ARCHER suggested to the mover to withdraw his amendment. The present was not the proper time to discuss this subject. An opportunity would be afforded, when the committee should make a report. If the motion was pressed, he must vote against it.

Mr. CLAYTON rose in reply. He said he was sorry he could not accept the suggestion of the hon. gentleman from Virginia, for whom he entertained great respect. He considered this one of those occasions on which to be found in a minority of one, would be to occupy one of the proudest stations which any man could hold. He would leave it to the nation and to posterity to say, whether it was not well done, to endeavor to prevent that excitement, and the rousing of all those feelings of embittered hostility, which would be at once let loose should the House in any degree sanction the views suggested in the Executive communication. He would ask gentlemen whether they were not as well prepared now as they would be after a report was rendered, to judge on the expediency of the course proposed? The step he had taken was no unusual one. Two months of the last session had been occupied in debating a proposition introduced in precisely the same way. What, he asked, would be gained by sending this subject to the Committee on Foreign Affairs? Had not the House all the documents before them? Were they not printed, and on the table of every member? All the committee would have before them, the House had before it. There was no ambiguity of meaning; the whole case was as plain as the committee could make it.

He was willing so far to comply with the wishes of his friend from Virginia, as to postpone the subject for a week. But why wait for a long report when they could as well judge and act without it? If the House was ready at once to reject his proposition, the natural inference would be, that there was a majority in that House disposed and ready to go to war with France. The gentleman (his colleague) from Georgia, it seemed, could see nothing hostile, nothing of war, or warlike, in the Message of the President. But Mr. C. would appeal to the common sense of any man to say, whether the language of the Message did not contain a *menace:*

"I recommend that a law be passed, authorizing reprisals upon French property, in case provision shall not be made for the payment of the debt at the approaching session of the French Chambers."

Here the President insisted that but one session more of the Chambers shall be permitted to pass, till letters of marque and reprisal shall be issued by this Government. Who did not know that the first act of reprisal would be considered by France as an act of hostility, and met on her part with instant retaliation? As to the interest of the American claimants, to which the chairman of the Committee on Foreign Affairs had alluded, Mr. C.'s proposition was manifestly safer for them than the measure of the President. The moment we went to war, the claims were gone. When the clouds and smoke of war cleared away, the claims would all vanish with them. Whenever peace was proposed, the whole would be sacrificed. What he wanted, was to give to the People of France the evidence that the People of America were not disposed to go to war with them; that we respected them as friends, and desired them to remain friends. If he thought that a long report (however able) from the Committee on Foreign Affairs, would throw any new light upon the matter, he would willingly wait for it; but he could not believe but that the House was as ready now as it would be then. Could it be the wish, the design of any gentleman, to throw this agitating question abroad and rouse the national feeling into a state of perturbation? He trusted not. He was sorry that he could not withdraw his motion; he was willing, however, to defer the subject for a week, as he had said, or even for a fortnight, if gentlemen insisted; farther he could not go.

Mr. R. M. JOHNSON said, the gentleman from Georgia assumed at the threshold, that the recommendation of the President was a proposition to declare war. He certainly did not so consider it, nor did the President himself. The code of civilized nations expressly recognises the right of reprisal in a nation from which a just debt is withheld, as a mode of redress compatible with the continuance of peace. But the President does not propose even this redress short of war, but under circumstances, which the gentleman from Georgia says, would render an appeal to arms not only just, but indispensable to preserve the "*national honor*" for which he is prepared to make ten thousand times greater sacrifices than he has depicted as necessarily resulting from war. He says our claims on France are just—that we have not asked a cent more than is just—that the treaty stipulates for nothing more than is just—and that a refusal to execute it is "*a just cause of war.*" Well, the French Chamber of Deputies have definitively and positively refused to pay the money, which the nation has bound itself, by the most solemn of all obligations, to pay. The Chambers, after successive sessions of elaborate discussion and long deliberation, have defeated the stipulations of the treaty, by the rejection of the proposition of the King of the French, to provide for the payment of our demands. The President of the United States, however, in communicating this fact to Congress, does not call upon us to act upon this *peremptory refusal* as "*a just cause of war.*" He does not ask, that we should consider this violation of the faith of treaties and insult to our national honor, as making proper an immediate appeal for redress, to the remedy of reprisals, of which the late example of France, in regard to Portugal, affords a practical illustration. No—the President proposes a course of greater moderation than the principles avowed by the gentleman from Georgia, and the late precedent set by France herself most clearly justify and invite. The message would have us overlook the wrong already inflicted, and the affront offered in the first absolute refusal of the French Chambers to comply with the treaty. It proposes, in the event of a *second denial* of justice by the newly elected Chambers, that then only shall the violation of the treaty be regarded as conclusive, and as shutting the door against a hope of voluntary redress on the part of France; and even after this consummation of wrongs, which have remained twenty-five years unredressed, the President does not, in his communication to us, hold the strong language of the gentleman from Georgia, and say that it forms "*a just cause of war,*" but only insists that it is *a just cause for reprisals*—that is, that we should take possession of as much French property as would be sufficient to pay the sum stipulated in the treaty; and, after retaining it a sufficient length of time to give the French Government an opportunity to redeem it, by the payment of the sum acknowledged to be due to our citizens, that it should be confiscated, as the property of our people was by France twenty-five years ago.

It is premature, however, to enter into this discussion now. The House has before it a mass of documents. It was its duty, through its Committee, to sift them thoroughly, and look into all the bearings of the case. No man entertained more friendly feelings towards France, he said, than he did, and none would be more unwilling hastily to sever the ties of the ancient friendship which has existed between France and the United States. He would observe all the forms which are introduced into legislation, for the purpose of giving due deliberation to all proceeding in this delicate subject. The haste with which the gentleman would rush into a discussion and decision of the great and important subject, was neither respectful to those who administer the Government of France, nor to our own administration. The President, as we have seen, wishes the final action of this Government, to await the final determination of the French Chambers. And there can, therefore, be no motive for the precipitation with

which we are invited to express an opinion as to the intentions of the French government, and to adopt a course predicated upon our suppositions in this respect, when the final measure contemplated here, is to await the full development of the intentions of France in the overt acts of its Representative body. For the present, the usual course of delay, for the sake of deliberation, should (he thought) be taken by our councils. The subject should be submitted to the Committee on Foreign Relations. It was an able committee, and would, in its report, take a view of the whole ground. The question was too solemn to be sported with. He could not consent to vote for the instructions proposed, and yet he disliked to vote against the proposition of the worthy member from Georgia, towards whom he entertained the most kindly feelings. He had uttered the most patriotic sentiments and was actuated by the most honorable motives. The gentleman had thrown out a most excellent speech, which would go to balance the effect of the President's Message. But the gentleman had not examined the subject in extenso. He (Mr. Johnson) would therefore, avid his appeal to that which had already been made by the worthy member from Virginia (Mr. Archer,) that he would consent to withdraw his motion. He had listened to the excellent speech of this member with the greatest pleasure: and he always did listen to him, whenever his multiplied occupations would at all permit, with the greatest interest and satisfaction. The gentleman could not but be aware that the instructions, should they be adopted, though they might be nil the committee, would not bind the House. He trusted they would be withdrawn.

Mr. CLAYTON remarked, that the gentleman from Kentucky (Mr. Johnson) had flattered him, instead of reasoning with him. He would, therefore, withdraw his amendment.

The Committee then rose, the Chairman reported the resolutions to the House, and they were then adopted.

On motion of Mr. HUBBARD,

The House adjourned.

IN SENATE.

WEDNESDAY, December 10, 1834.

The Hon WM. C. PRESTON, of South Carolina, appeared and took his seat.

The VICE PRESIDENT laid before the Senate a communication from the War Department, accompanied by a Report from the Engineer Bureau, relative to the progress of the work on the Cumberland Road.

Mr. TIPTON'S resolution relative to the establishment of a port of entry at La Fayette, on the Wabash river, was taken up, and, on his motion, was laid on the table.

The resolution submitted by Mr. SOUTHARD, for the appointment of the Standing Committees on Wednesday, (this day,) was taken up for consideration.

On his motion the resolution was amended, so as to read Thursday next, (to-morrow,) at one o'clock; and it was then adopted.

The following resolution submitted yesterday by Mr. BENTON, was taken up for consideration:

Resolved, That the Secretary of the Treasury be directed to communicate to the Senate any correspondence with the Bank of the United States on the subject of the branch drafts, and dividends withheld, not heretofore communicated. Also, to inform the Senate whether the Directors on the part of the Government have been refused access to the books and accounts of the institution.

Mr. TYLER presumed that no gentleman could have any objection to the passage of the resolution—it was desirable that the information should be obtained. But he felt that it was due to the Committee on Finance to say that if the honorable gentleman who offered the resolution had waited a few days, the necessity of submitting it would have been entirely obviated. The subject of it had attracted the attention of the Committee. It was of considerable importance, and in a few days a full report would be made on the subject by the committee.

Mr. BENTON observed, that under the circumstance, he had no objection that the resolution lie on the table, and made a motion to that effect, which prevailed.

The bill for the relief of Theodore Brightwell, deceased, was taken up, as in Committee of the Whole, and,

On motion of Mr. KING of Alabama, was laid on the table.

The bill for the relief of Col. Gad Humphreys, was taken up as in Committee of the whole, and

On motion of Mr. TIPTON, was laid on the table.

The bill to authorize an issue of scrip to officers and non commissioned officers of the Revolutionary war, was taken up as in Committee of the Whole, and,

On motion of Mr. TYLER, was referred to the Committee on Public Lands.

The bill for the relief of Elijah Simmons was taken up as in Committee of the Whole, and

On motion of Mr MOORE, it was also referred to the Committee on Public Lands.

The bill authorizing an appropriation for purchasing the right to use Boyd Reilly's patent apparatus for applying the irrespirable and other gases to the human body, to be used in the Army and Navy, was taken up as in Committee of the Whole, and

On motion of Mr. NAUDAIN, it was referred to a Select Committee of five.

On balloting for the committee, it appeared that Messrs. NAUDAIN, ROBBINS, KENT, PRENTISS, and SPRAGUE, were chosen.

The bill authorizing a relinquishment of the 16th section, and the appropriation of other lands in lieu thereof, for the use of schools, was considered as in Committee of the Whole, and

On motion of Mr. MOORE, it was laid on the table.

Mr. WAGGAMAN gave notice that, on to-morrow, he would ask leave to introduce a bill to appropriate a sum of money to repair the United States Barracks at New Orleans.

Mr. TIPTON, on leave given, introduced a bill for the relief of Hiram A. Hunter; which was read the first time, and ordered to a second reading.

Mr. WEBSTER, from the Select Committee appointed on the subject, reported a bill to make compensation for spoliations upon American Commerce prior to 1800.

Mr. W. also gave notice that, on Wednesday next, he would call up the bill for consideration.

Mr. KING, of Alabama, on leave given, introduced a bill to amend the act organizing the United States Courts for the State of Alabama; which was read the first time, and ordered to a second reading.

Mr. BENTON gave notice that, on to morrow, he would ask leave to introduce a bill to grant a quantity of land to the State of Missouri for objects of internal improvement

Also, a bill to reduce and graduate the price of the public lands of the United States

On motion of Mr. KING, the Senate proceeded to the consideration of Executive business.

When the doors were opened, the Senate adjourned.

HOUSE OF REPRESENTATIVES.

WEDNESDAY, December 10, 1834.

Petitions and memorials were presented by .

Mr. HUBBARD, of New Hampshire;

Messrs. BRIGGS, PHILLIPS, OSGOOD, GORHAM, and REED, of Massachusetts;

Mr. PEARCE, of Rhode Island;

Mr. PEARCE, of Rhode Island, presented the petition of John N. Reynolds, lately returned from a voyage of exploration in the Pacific ocean, and on the Northwest coast, praying that an expedition may be fitted out to survey the islands and reefs in that ocean, and on that coast. The petition was recommended by both branches of the Legislature of Rhode Island; and Mr. Pearce stated that the Legislatures of several other States would join in the prayer of the memorial, as would the merchants and chambers of commerce in the principal cities of the Union. To show the importance of the object in view, Mr. Pearce stated that there were now engaged in the whale fishe-

---

ry 132,000 tons of shipping, that there were employed 10,000 seamen, and that the bottoms directly and indirectly employed 170,000 tons of shipping; and more than 12,000 seamen, that more than one-tenth part of our whole navigation was engaged in it, and the capital invested was 12,000,000 dollars. He further stated that the annual loss of property, upon the islands and reefs not laid down upon any chart, was fully equal to the expense of the expedition and survey requested.

Messrs. WHITE, CAMBRELENG, and CLARK, of New York;

Messrs. CHAMBERS, BANKS, WAGENER, HARPER, and MILLER, of Pennsylvania.

[Mr. MILLER presented the petition of Captain John Smith, of the borough of Carlisle, Pennsylvania, praying that his name be entered on the roll of the Pennsylvania line of the army of the revolution, as a first Lieutenant, and that he may be entitled to the benefit of the several acts of Congress, made for the benefit of the surviving officers of the army of the revolution, according to the said rank.]

Mr. HEATH, of Maryland;

Messrs. I'HINN, BOULDIN, ROBERTSON, LOYALL, GLAIBORNE, and FULTON, of Virginia;

Mr. WILLIAMS, of North Carolina;

Messrs. CLOWNEY and PINCKNEY, of South Carolina;

Messrs. POPE, CHILTON, and LETCHER, of Kentucky;

[Mr. POPE presented the petition of numerous inhabitants of Louisville, Kentucky, praying for the establishment of a District Court at that place; which was referred to the Judiciary Committee.]

Mr. BLAIR, of Tennessee;

Mr. CRANE, of Ohio;

Messrs. THOMAS and GARLAND, of Louisiana;

Messrs. LANE, EWING, and KINNARD, of Indiana;

[Mr. KINNARD presented the petition and claims of Andrew Hoover and Scioto Evans, for certain horses lost, while in the military service of the United States, during the late war with the Indians on the frontiers of Illinois and Michigan Territory, which were referred to the Committee of Claims.

Mr. KINNARD also presented the petition and claim of the heirs of Humphrey Barret, praying compensation for property pressed into the military service of the United States, during the war of the revolution. Referred to the Committee on Revolutionary Claims.

Mr. LANE presented the petition of Richard Oliver, of Dearborn county, Indiana, praying to be placed on the Pension Roll.]

Mr. LYON, of Michigan;

Which petitions and memorials were referred to the appropriate Committees.

Mr. CLAY, from the Committee on Public Lands, submitted the following resolution:

Resolved, That the " bill to reduce and graduate the price of the Public Lands," No. 92, reported at the late session, be made the special order of the day for the 1st Monday in January next.

Resolved, That the bill to reduce and graduate the price of Public Lands, reported at the late session, No. 92, and the report, No. 87, accompanying the same, be reprinted for the use of the House.

And, on motion of Mr. CLAYTON, of Georgia, 5,000 extra copies of said report were ordered to be printed.

Mr. EWING suggested, that there was an amendment to the bill, in relation to the public lands, and he desired that it should also be committed with the original bill.

Mr. CLAY had no objection. The amendment would go with the bill, as a matter of course.

The resolutions were then agreed to.

On motion of Mr. CLAYTON, 5,000 extra copies of the report of the Committee on Public Lands, on the subject of reducing and graduating the price of the public lands, were ordered to be printed.

Mr. GILMER from the Committee on Indian Affairs, moved that the bill "to provide for the establishment of the Western Territory," and for

the security and protection of the emigrants and other Indian tribes therein named," be made the special order of the day for the first Tuesday in January; which was agreed to.

On motion of Mr. GILMER, the foregoing bill and amendments, were ordered to be printed.

The following resolution, submitted yesterday by Mr. JARVIS, was considered and agreed to:

Resolved, That the President of the United States be requested to communicate to this House, any information he may possess respecting the burning of the building occupied by the Treasury Department in the year 1833.

The following resolution, offered by Mr. HUBBARD, was ordered to lie on the table for one day:

Resolved, That the Secretary of the Treasury be directed to communicate to the House of Representatives, as soon as practicable, copies of the correspondence, not heretofore communicated, which has taken place between him and the President of the Bank of the United States, on the subject of the Branch Drafts, and in relation to the claim made by the Bank for damages, and the course pursued by that institution on account of the protest of the bill drawn on the French Government by the Treasury Department.

On motion of Mr. WHITE, of New York,

Resolved, That the Committee of Ways and Means be instructed to inquire into the expediency of providing by law for the establishment of a branch of the Mint of the United States at the City of New York.

On motion of Mr. PARKER,

Resolved, That the Committee on Commerce be instructed to inquire into the expediency of making an appropriation for the survey of the river Pessaic, in the State of New Jersey, below the port of Newark, and of the channel of Newark Bay, and the Kill Vankull, to its termination in the Bay of New York, with a view to improve the navigation thereof.

On motion of Mr. WATMOUGH,

Resolved, That an additional number of copies of the amendment to bill No. 334, with the accompanying report, regulating the Pay of the Navy of the United States, be printed for the use of this House.

On motion of Mr. BURD,

Resolved, That the Committee on Roads and Canals be instructed to inquire into the expediency of causing a survey and examination of the ground from Cumberland, Md., via Bedford, to Hollidaysburg, in Huntingdon county, Pa., with a view of connecting the Chesapeake and Ohio Canal with the Pennsylvania Canal by a rail road or turnpike, between the points aforesaid, and if expedient, that said committee be instructed to report a bill making a suitable appropriation for said object.

On motion of Mr. W. B. SHEPPARD,

Resolved, That the Committe on Commerce be instructed to inquire into the expediency of placing a light boat in the thoroughfare between Albemarle and Pamlico sounds.

On motion of Mr. PINCKNEY,

Resolved, That the Committee on Commerce be instructed to inquire into the expediency of constructing a breakwater at Sullivan's Island, South Carolina, with a view to the preservation of the fort and other property thereon.

Resolved, That the Committee on Commerce be instructed to inquire into the expediency of erecting two small additional light-houses at the Bar of Charleston, South Carolina.

On motion of Mr. ALLAN, of Kentucky,

Resolved, That the Committee of the Whole on the state of the Union be discharged from the further consideration of the bill to establish the Territory of Huron.

Resolved, That the said bill be referred to the Committee on Territories.

On motion of Mr. DUNLAP,

Resolved, That the Committee on the Judiciary be instructed to inquire into the expediency of establishing a third Judicial District in the State of Tennessee, and of requiring the Judge of the District of East and West Tennessee to hold one dr more terms of said Court annually at the town of Jackson, in said State.

On motion of Mr. DICKINSON,

Resolved, That the Committee on the Post Office and Post Roads be instructed to inquire into the expediency of establishing a post route from Readyville, in Rutherford county, Tennessee, to Beech Grove, Bedford county.

On motion of Mr. PEYTON,

Resolved, That the Committee on Commerce be instructed to inquire into the expediency of establishing a port of entry at Portageville, at the mouth of Laurel, on the Cumberland river.

On motion of Mr. VINTON,

Resolved, That the Committee on Roads and Canals be instructed to inquire into the expediency of making an appropriation for the improvement of the navigation of the Ohio river between the City of Pittsburgh and the Falls of the Ohio.

On motion of Mr. MITCHELL, of Ohio,

Resolved, That the Committee on Military Affairs be instructed to inquire into the expediency of establishing a National Armory on the waters of the Muskingum river, in the State of Ohio.

Mr. JOHNSON, of Louisiana, moved the following resolution, which lies on the table one day:

Resolved, That the Secretary of the Treasury be directed to report to this House, the causes which have retarded the issuing patents in favor of claimants to lands in the State of Louisiana, which have been confirmed by virtue of the different acts of Congress, which have been passed for the adjustment of land claims within the said State.

On motion of Mr. GARLAND,

Resolved, That the Committee on the Post Office and Post Roads, be instructed to inquire into the expediency of establishing a post route from the town of Opelousas, in the State of Louisiana, to pass by Washington, Holmesville, and the Bayou Rouge, to intersect the principal mail route from New Orleans to Natchez, at such point as may be deemed most convenient by the Postmaster General.

On motion of Mr. GARLAND,

Resolved, That the Committee on Commerce be instructed to inquire into the expediency of making an appropriation for the purpose of replacing the buoys that were placed on the coast of Louisiana, to mark out the channel from the vicinity of the Light House on Point au Fer, into the Atchafayala Bay; which have sunk, or been destroyed.

On motion of Mr. HANNEGAN,

Resolved, That the Committee of the Whole be discharged from the further consideration of bill No. 349, being a bill to grant an additional quantity of land to the States of Ohio and Indiana, to aid in the construction of the Wabash and Erie Canal.

Resolved, That said bill be committed to the Committee of the Whole on the state of the Union.

On motion of Mr. CARR,

Resolved, That all the memorials, petitions, &c. together with an estimate made by Capt. Henry Shreeves, by order of the Secretary of War, of the probable cost of improving the navigation through the Falls of the Ohio river, and heretofore referred to the Committee on Roads and Canals, be again so referred, and that said Committee be instructed to inquire into the expediency of making an appropriation for the above-named purpose, with leave to report, by bill or otherwise.

On motion of Mr. LANE,

Resolved, That the Committee on the Post Office and Post Roads be instructed to inquire into the propriety of establishing a post route from Burlington, Boon county, Ky. to Versailles, in Ripley county, Indiana, by the way of the Rising Sun, in the county of Dearborn.

On motion of Mr. LANE,

Resolved, That the Committee on the Public Lands be instructed to inquire into the propriety of permitting any person not owners of land for actual settlement, and those who are cultivators and owners of land, to add to his or her farms, to enter any quantity of the public land, at fifty cents per acre, not exceeding one quarter section, provided such land sha'l have been offered at public sale, and been subject to entry for twenty years or upwards, and shall remain unsold at the time of such entry;

On motion of Mr. KINNARD,

Resolved, That the Committee on Claims be instructed to inquire into the expediency of amending the act entitled " an act to provide for the payment of claims for property lost, captured, or destroyed by the enemy, while in the military service of the United States, during the late war with the Indians on the frontiers of Illinois and Michigan Territry," approved 30th June, 1834, so as to apply the provisions of said act to property lost in said service, belonging to other persons besides " Volunteers, Rangers, and Cavalry."

The following resolution, offered by Mr. EWING, was ordered to lie on the table for one day:

Resolved, That the Secretary of the Treasury be directed to transmit, or cause to be transmitted to this House, a list of all such land claims heretofore noted by, or presented to the Commissioners authorized to receive and adjust the same, as may have been decided unfavorably, and not yet satisfied, in the Vincennes Land District, with the foundation of the claims and decisions in brief, and such documents in relation to the subject matter, as he may control, and deem proper.

On motion of Mr. CASEY,

Resolved, That the Committee of Public Lands be instructed to inquire into the justice and expediency of granting 320 acres of land, to the widow and heirs of each person killed by the Indians on the frontiers of Illinois and Michigan, in 1832.

On motion of Mr. MAY

Resolved, That the Committee on Public Lands be instructed to inquire into the expediency of establishing a Surveyor General's Office in the State of Illinois, and of appointing a Surveyor General whose duties shall be confined exclusively to that State.

On motion of Mr. REYNOLDS,

Resolved, That the Committee on Commerce be instructed to inquire into the expediency of making an appropriation, to establish a Marine Hospital at or near the mouth of the Ohio river, in Illinois.

On motion of Mr. CLAY,

Resolved, That the Committee on the Public Lands be instructed to inquire into the expediency of author zing Register and Receivers of Land Offices to administer all oaths connected with the sale or entry of the public lands.

On motion of Mr. MURPHEY,

Resolved, that the Reports No. 2, 3, and 4 of the Register and Receiver of the Land Office at St. Stephens and State of Alabama, acting as Commissioner under the third section of the act of Congress of the 2d of March, 1829, entitled " an act confirming the reports of the Register and Receiver of the Land Office for the district of St. Stephens, in the State of Alabama, and for other purposes," be referred to the Committee on Public lands.

On motion of Mr. MARDIS,

Resolved, That the Committee on Public Lands be instructed to inquire into the expediency of permitting all settlers on the public lands of the United States, who would have been entitled to enter their improvements at Government price under the provisions of the existing pre-emption laws, and who were prevented from so doing in consequence of the Government of the United States selecting their settlements to satisfy Indian claims to reservations, to enter one hundred and sixty acres of the public domain in the proper land district, free from charge, except office fees.

On motion of Mr. BULL,

Resolved, That the Committee on the Post Office and Post Roads be instructed to inquire into the expediency of establishing a mail route from the town of Richmond Bay county to Penniston's, on Grand river, in said county.

On motion of Mr. ASHLEY,

Resolved, That bill No. 451, providing for the improvement of the harbor of St. Louis, be made the order of the day for Thursday week, the 18th instant.

On motion of Mr. LYON, of Michigan,

Resolved, That the Committee on Roads and Canals be instructed to inquire into the expediency of making appropriations for connecting, by a ship canal, the navigable part of the River Raisin

with I ake Erie. and for remov'ng the bar at the mouth of Clin'on river, in Michigan Terr tory.

On motion of Mr. LYON, of Michigan, *Resolved*, That the Comm ttee on Commerce be instructed to inqu re into the exped ency of erecting a light-house at the mouth o' Detroit river, one at the mouth of Kalamazoo river, and one at the mouth of Grand river, in the Territory of Michigan

Mr. WHITE. of Florida, moved the follow.ng resolution, which lies on the ta'le one day:

Resolved, That the Secret ry of W ar be direct-ed.to r port to this House, wh t progress h s been made in the r pairs of the Fort, and the construc-tion of the sea-wall, at St. Augustine, Florida; and what further sum w ll be required to complete the same, w th the report and estimate of the Engineer charged wi h that work.

. Mr. FOSTER moved the following resolution, which lies on the table one day:

Resolved, That the President of the United States be requested to communicate to this House, (if not in his opinion incompatible with the public interest,) any communication or correspondence which may have taken place between our Min ster at Paris, and the Fr nch Government, or between the Minister from France to this Government, and the Secretary of State, on the subject of the re-fusal of the French Government to make provision for the execution of the treaty concluded betwe n the United States and France on the 4th of July, 1831.

On motion of Mr. JARVIS, *Resolved*, That the Committee on Commerce be instructed to inqu re into the expediency o' pro-viding by law, that the sh ps and vessels o' the United States be registered, enrolled, and l cens-ed anew, and that the reg sters, enrolments, and l censes under twen y tons, be required to conta n, in a blt on to the names of the owners o' the ves-sels, the share which each owner may have there-in. The said documents to be issued instea l of those now in use; without expense to the owners of of the vessels.

Mr POPE moved to discharge the Committee of the Whole House from the consideration of bill No. 342, "in relation to the Louis ille and Port-land (anal," and to refer the same to the Commit-tee of the Whole on the State of the Union

Mr. P observed, that his sole object in submit-ting the motion was to ensure a vote upon the bill at the present cession He disliked to tax the for-bearance of the House, but the measure was one of such vital interest to his constituents and the whole western country, that he felt compelled to sacrifice any scruples he might feel on that head to the demands of pu l c duty. He b iefly stated that the bill was reported at the last session of Con-gres , but like all others of the same nature, re-mained on calendar untouched. 1 he object of the bill was to enable the Secretary of the I reasury to purchase, in the name of the United States, the private stock in the Louisville and Portland Canal Company, and to relieve the navigation of the Canal from any tax or toll except what was necessary to keep it in good repair. He stat d that the Gov-ernment now owned near y one-third of the stock of the co pany, and he hoped to be able to show, on a fit occasion, that it should purchase the re-mainder. He would only say at this ti e. that thirteen Stat s (inc uding New York, Pennsylva-nia, Maryland, and Virginia, were deeply interested in the passage of this bill. He exp essed the hope, that inasmuch as the object of the bill was to re-lieve, f om injurious and distressing exactions, the commerce of so large a po tion of the United States, that the House would indulge him, by yiel ing its support to the motion he had made.

The motion prevai ed.

Mr. CHILTON submitted the following resolu-tion:

Resolved, That the Committee on roads and Ca-nals be instructed to inquire into the justice and expediency of making an appropriation of a por-tion of the public funds to a l the States of Ken-t cky an l Tennessee in th improvem nt of the road leading fr m the city of Loui vi le, in the State of K ntucky, to Nashville, in the State of Tenne see

A count being called for on agreeing to the res-olution, .

Mr. CHILTON said, that the object of his motion was p rhaps m sun l rstood by the House. It proposed only an inqui y, which the House was in the practice of g anting to every gentleman. The road from Louisville to Nashville, was perhaps one of greater importance than any other West of the Allegheny mountains. A most extensive com-merce was carrie l on between the cities indicate l in his resoluti n. and this road was one of the prin-cipal mail routes between Washington City and New Orleans It was connect d with t e National or Cumberland Road, an l its improvem nt was a matter of deep interest to the citiz ns of Kentucky and Tennessee. In times of low water an immense part of the trade of East Tenn see and the South-ern part of Kentucky, passed over the road in question. The proposed inquiry involved no new principle, and he trusted that there would be no objection to it.

The question was then taken, and the resolution was rejected. Yeas 72, nays 88.

The SPEAKER laid before the House a letter from the Secretary of War, enclosing a report from the Engineer Department, in relation to the re-pairs made upon the Cumberl nd Road; which, on motion of Mr. THOMSON, was lai i on the table, and ordered to be printed. .

On motion of Mr. SEVIER, the bill to provide for taking a census of the inhabitants of Michig n and Arkansas Te ritories, was made the special order of the day f r Thursday the 18th in t , an l Mr. 8 gave notice, that when the bill came up for consideration, he shoul l move to amend it. The amendment, on his motion, was ordered to be printed.

ELECTION OF CHAPLAIN.

The House, pursuant to order, proceeded to the election of Chapla n.

Mr. WARDWELL nominated the Rev. Mr. Smith.

Mr. POLK nom nated the Rev. Mr. Copp.

Mr. CHINN nominated the Rev. Mr. Slicer.

Mr THOMAS, of La. nominated the Rev. Mr. Ungerer.

Mr DEBERRY nom nated the Rev. Mr. Mc-Keever.

Messrs. WARDWELL, POLK, CHINN, THO-MAS of La., and DEBERRY, were appointed Teller, who, a ter counting the votes, announced the following result:

Mr. Copp,	-	-	-	52
Sl cer,	-	-	-	42
Smith,	-	-	-	32
Ungerer,	-	-	-	37
McKeever,	-	-	-	25
Palfrey,	-	-	-	5
Stockton,	-	-	-	2
Harrison,	-	-	-	1
S rgeant,	-	-	-	1
Mrs. Roya l,	-	-	-	2
Blanks,	-	-	-	5

There being no cho ce, the House proceeded to ballot a second time, previous to which, Mr. HAR-PER, of New Hampshi e, nominated the Rev. Mr Stockton. The following was the re ult:

Mr. Copp,	-	-	-	55
Sm th,	-	-	-	39
S licer,	-	-	-	30
Ungerer,	-	-	-	28
McKeever,	-	-	-	22
Stockton,	-	-	-	9
Palfrey,	-	-	-	4
Post,	-	-	-	1
Blank,	-	-	-	1

No per on hav ng a majority. the House pro-ceeded to ballot a thi d t me, when the vote stood as follows:

Mr. Copp,	-	-	-	59
Sm th,	-	-	-	59
Sl cer,	-	-	-	26
Ungerer,	-	-	-	14
McKeever,	-	-	-	14
Stockton,	-	-	-	4
Palfrey,	-	-	-	4
Blanks,	-	-	-	3

There at ll being no choice—

Mr. DAVENPORT moved an adjournment, which was lost.

The House then proceeded to ballot a fourth t me, wh ch re ulted a follow :

Mr. Smith,	-	-	-	99
Copp,	-	-	-	60
Slicer,	-	-	-	9
Palfrey,	-	-	-	4
Ungerer,	-	-	-	1
McKeever,	-	-	-	1
Blank,	-	-	-	3

Mr. Sm th, of Wash ngton City, having a majo-rity of votes, was declared by the SPEAKER, du ly elected Chapla n for the season.

On mo ion of Mr. McKIM, The House adjourned.

Selec' Committee to re-organize the Treasury De-partment.—Messrs. WAYNE, MASON of Va., M KENNAN, CAMBRELENG, RENCHER, EVANS, POPE, JARVIS, and McKAY.

IN SENATE.

Thursday, Dec. 11, 1834.

The Senate pr ceeded to the special order of the day, being the election of the Standing Com-mittee.

The VICE PRESIDENT announced that the several Chairmen would be first chosen, and the ballots being taken, the result was as follows:

For the Committee on Foreign Relations, Mr. Clay was elected.

For the Committee on Finance, Mr. Webster was elected.

For the Committee on Commerce, Mr. Silsbee was elected.

For the Committee on Manufactures, Mr. Pat-Lingohuyse was elected.

For the Committee on Agriculture, Mr. Brown was elected.

For the Committee on Military Affairs, Benton was elected.

For the Committee on the Militia, Mr. Robin-son was elected.

For the Committee on Naval Affairs, Mr. Southard was elected.

For the Committee on Private Land China, Mr. Black was elected.

For the Committee on Indian Affairs, Mr. White was e ected.

For the Committee on Claims, Mr. Bell was elected.

For the Committee on the Judiciary, Mr. Clay-ton was elected.

For the C mmit tee on Roads and Canals, Mr. Hendricks was elected.

For the Committee on Pensions, Mr. Tomlin-son was elected.

For the Committee on the District of Columbia, Mr. Tyler was elected.

For the Committee on Revolutionary Claims, Mr Moore was elected.

For the Committee on the Contingent Expenses of the Senate, Mr. Knight w av elected.

For the Committee on Engrossed Bills, Mr. Shepley was elected.

The Senate then proceeded to ballot for the remaining members of the several committees, when it appeared that—

For the Committee on Foreign Relations, Messrs. King of Georgia, Mangum, Sprague, and Tallmadge, were elected.

For the Committee on Finance, Messrs. Webster, Tyler, Mangum, and Ewing, were elected.

For the Committee on Commerce, Messrs. King of Alabama, Sprague, Waggaman, and Wright, were elected.

For the Committee on Manufactures, Messrs. Knight, Morris, Prentiss, and Tyler, were elected.

For the Committee on Agriculture, Messrs. Kent, Robinson, Morris, and Swift, were elect-ed.

For the Committee on Military Affairs, Messrs. Tipton, Clayton, King of Alabama, and Prea-ton, were elected.

For the Comm ttee on the Militia, Messrs. Hen-dricks, Waggaman, McKean, and Swift, were elected.

For the Comm tee on Naval Affairs, Messrs. Bibb, Robbins, Tallmadge, and Black, were elected.

For the Committee on Private Land Claims, Messrs. NAUDAIN, KANE, PORTER, and SHEPLEY, were elected.

For the Committee on Indian Affairs, Messrs. PRELINGHUYSEN, TIPTON, SWIFT, and SMITH, were elected.

For the Committee on Claims, Messrs. NAUDAIN, BROWN, TIPTON, and SHEPLEY, were elected.

For the Committee on the Judiciary, Messrs. LINN, PRESTON, SMITH, and BELL, were elected.

For the Committee on Roads and Canals, Messrs. KENT, ROBBINS, ROBINSON, and McKEAN, elected.

For the Committee on Pensions, Messrs. TALLMADGE, McKEAN, PRENTISS, and PRESTON, were elected.

For the Committee on the District of Columbia, Messrs. KENT, BIBB, TOMLINSON, and SOUTHARD, were elected.

For the Committee on Revolutionary Claims, Messrs. SMITH, WHITE, LEIGH, and FRELINGHUYSEN, were elected.

For the Committee on the Contingent Expenses of the Senate, Messrs. TOMLINSON and MORRIS were elected.

For the Committee on Engrossed Bills, Messrs. ROBINSON and MORRIS were elected.

Mr. CLAY gave notice, that on Mo-day next, he would ask leave to intro duce a bill to provide for the distribution of the sales of the public lands for a limited time, among the several States.

On motion of Mr. CLAY, so much of the President's Message as relates to Foreign Affairs, was referred to the Committee on Foreign Relations.

On motion of Mr. WEBSTER, so much of the message as relates to the Revenue, was referred to a Committee on Finance.

On motion of Mr. SOUTHARD, so much of the Message as relates to Naval Affairs, was referred to the committee on that subject.

On motion of Mr. SILSBEE, so much of the message as relates to Commerce, was referred to a committee on that subject.

On motion of Mr. TOMLINSON, so much of the Message as relates to Pensions, was referred to a committee on that subject.

On motion of Mr. HENDRICKS, so much of the message as relates to Internal Improvements, was referred to the Committee on Roads and Canals.

On motion of Mr. WHITE, so much of the message as relates to Indian Affairs, was referred to the committee on that subject.

Mr. POINDEXTER said he would move that much of the Message as relates to the Public Lands, be referred to the Committee on Public Lands, but there was nothing in the Message on the subject.

Mr. BENTON, on leave given, introduced a bill to grant a quantity of land to the State of Missouri for objects of Internal Improvement. Also, a bill to reduce and graduate the price of the public lands of the United States; which were severally read the first time, and ordered to a second reading.

Mr. BENTON gave notice, that on Monday next, he would introduce a proposition to alter the institution of the United States, as relates to the election of President and Vice President of the United States.

Mr. BENTON also gave notice, that on Monday next, he would ask leave to introduce a bill to set a township of Land to a University in Missouri.

Mr. EWING gave notice, that on Monday next, would ask leave to introduce a bill to improve harbour at the mouth of the river Raisin.

a motion of Mr. EWING, the bill to settle and blish the northern boundary line of the State of was taken up, and referred to the Judiciary Committee.

a motion of Mr. KING, of Alabama, the bill to organize of the U. States Courts for the State Alabama, was taken up, and referred to the Committee.

The Senate then adjourned to Monday next.

HOUSE OF REPRESENTATIVES.

THURSDAY, December 11, 1834.

Petitions and memorials were presented by Messrs. BATES and REED, of Massachusetts.

Mr. BURGES, of Rhode Island.
Mr. ALLEN, of Vermont.
Messrs. WHITE, CAMBRELENG, and DICKSON, of New York.
Messrs. WATMOUGH and McKENNAN, of Pennsylvania.
Messrs. JOHNSON and McKIM, of Maryland.
Mr. SPEIGHT, of North Carolina.
Mr. DAVIS, of Kentucky.
Messrs. POLK, DICKINSON, and JOHNSON, of Tennessee.
Messrs. MITCHELL and McLENE, of Ohio.
Mr. THOMAS, of Louisiana.
Mr. CAGE, of Mississippi.
Mr. REYNOLDS, of Illinois.
Messrs. LEWIS and MURPHY, of Alabama.
Which memorials and petitions were appropriately referred.

Mr. WATMOUGH, from the Committee on Naval Affairs, reported a bill for the relief of Elizabeth May; which was read twice and committed.

Mr. WHITE, of New York, from the Committee on Naval Affairs, reported a bill amendatory of the act in addition to the several acts for the organization of the Treasury, War, and Navy Departments; which was read twice and committed to a Committee of the Whole on the state of the Union.

Mr. WARDWELL, from the Committee on Revolutionary Pensions, reported a bill for the relief of Daniel Cage; which was read twice and committed.

The following resolutions, submitted yesterday, were considered and agreed to:

By Mr. HUBBARD:

Resolved, That the Secretary of the Treasury be directed to communicate to the House of Representatives, as soon as practicable, copies of the correspondence, not heretofore communicated, which has taken place between him and the President of the Bank of the United States, on the subject of the Branch Drafts, and in relation to the claim made by the Bank for damages, and the course pursued by that institution on account of the protest of the bill drawn on the French Government by the Treasury Department.

By Mr. WHITE, of Florida:

Resolved, That the Secretary of War be directed to report to this House, what progress has been made in the repairs of the fort, and the construction of the sea-wall, at St. Augustine, Florida; and what further sum will be required to complete the same, with the report and estimate of the Engineer charged with that work.

By Mr. JOHNSON, of Louisiana:

Resolved, That the Secretary of the Treasury be directed to report to this House, the causes which have retarded the issuing patents in favor of claimants to lands in the State of Louisiana, which have been confirmed by virtue of the different acts of Congress, which have been passed for the adjustment of land claims within the said State.

By Mr. EWING:

Resolved, That the Secretary of the Treasury be directed to transmit, or cause to be transmitted to this House, a list of all such lands as may heretofore not've by, or presented to the Commissioners authorized to receive and adjust the same, as may have been decided unfavorably, and not yet satisfied, in the Vincennes Land District, with the foundation of the claims and decisions in brief, and such documents in relation to the subject matter, as he may control and deem proper.

The following resolution, submitted yesterday by Mr. FOSTER, was taken up:

Resolved, That the President of the United States be requested to communicate to this House, (if not in his opinion incompatible with the public interest,) any communication or correspondence which may have taken place between our Minister at Paris and the French Government, or between the Minister from France to this Government and the Secretary of State, on the subject of the refusal of the French Government to make provision for the execution of the treaty concluded between the United States and France on the 4th of July, 1831.

Mr. FOSTER said that he understood the Committee on Foreign Affairs had recently received a communication from the Secretary of State on the

subject embraced in the resolution, and that additional information was expected by that Committee. He would, therefore, move to lay the resolution on the table for the present; which was agreed to.

On motion of Mr. JARVIS,

Resolved, That the Committee on Commerce be instructed to inquire into the expediency of providing by law that in the survey of the Coast of the Unit d Stctes, now in progress, the latitudes and longitudes of every Light house be carefully ascertained and published, and that no new Lighthouse shall hereafter be erected, till a report is made in respect to its public benefit by the two Collectors and the Commander of the Navy Yard nearest the proposed site, in conformity with the recommendation of the Secretary of the Treasury in his annual Report on the State of the Finances.

On motion of Mr. PEARCE,

Resolved, That the Committee on Commerce be instructed to inquire into the expediency of making an appropriation for a Light-house on Pawpaw Point, a place near to, but below the port of Bristol, in the State of Rhode Island, and that the petition and papers relative to the same, presented at the last session, be again referred to said Committee.

On motion of Mr. FILLMORE,

Resolved, That the report from the Secretary of the Treasury, in relation to the bridge across the Potomac, be referred to the Committee of Claims.

Mr. BURGES offered the following resolution, which, under the rule, lies one day:

Resolved, That the Secretary of the Treasury Department be directed to send to this House, in a tabular form, the amount of money paid into the Marine Hospital Fund by all seamen in the mercantile service in the District of Providence, in the District of Newport, and in the District of Bristol, respectively, in the Rhode Island District, from the commencement of the present Government of the United States, up to the time when that fund was by law placed at the disposal of the President. Also, the like amount, in like form, paid by said seamen after that time and before the commencement of the year 1828; and also, the like amount, in like form, paid since that time—together with the several sums expended in each of said Districts, for the relief of sick and disabled seamen—showing the balance due to or from said fund, in each of said Districts, respectively, at the several times aforesaid, if any, and how the same may have been disposed of.

On motion of Mr. HARD,

Resolved, That the Committee on Roads and Canals be instructed to inquire into the expediency of making an appropriation to construct a Pier in the Niagara River, near Young's Town, in the State of New York.

On motion of Mr. BINNEY,

Resolved, That the Committee on the Judiciary be instructed to inquire into the expediency of providing by law for designating jurors to serve in the courts of the United States, in each State, according to the mode now practised in the highest courts of law in the respective States.

On motion of Mr. BURD,

Resolved, That the Committee on Invalid Pensions be instructed to inquire into the expediency of increasing the pension of William Keiler, of Bedford County, Pennsylvania, late an officer of the Army of the United States, so as to grant him a pension from the time when he was wounded or to allow him the pension of a commissioned officer, wounded in said service.

The following resolution, offered by Mr. McKENNAN, was ordered to lie on the table one day:

Resolved, That the Secretary of War be directed to transmit to this House any communication he may have received from the Commissioner appointed by the States of Maryland, Pennsylvania, and Virginia, to receive portions of the Cumberland Road within the limits of those States respectively; and to erect toll gates thereon, and to furnish an estimate of the amount of money which may be necessary to complete the repairs of the said road, agreeably to the requisitions of the laws of said States, which have received the assent of Congress. Also, that he inform the House what

Mr. WHITE, of Florida;

Mr. LANE, of Indiana.

Which memorials and petitions were appropriately referred.

Mr. JOHNSON, of Kentucky, from the Committee on Military Affairs, reported a bill allowing further time for issuing and locating certain military land warrants; which was read twice and ordered to be engrossed and read a third time.

Mr. THOMSON, from the Committee on Military Affairs, reported a joint resolution in relation to the location of the Baltimore and Ohio Rail Road, in the vicinity of Harper's Ferry; which was read twice, and after some explanations by Messrs. THOMSON, MERCER, and McKIM, postponed to Monday.

Mr. BUNCH, from the Committee on Military Affairs, reported a bill for the relief of Thomas Buford; which was read twice and committed.

The resolution submitted yesterday by Mr. BURGES, was taken up, and its further consideration postponed till Monday next.

The following resolution, submitted yesterday by Mr. McKENNAN, was taken up:

Resolved, That the Secretary of War be directed to transmit to this House any communication he may have received from the Commissioners appointed by the States of Maryland, Pennsylvania, and Virginia, to receive portions of the Cumberland Road within the limits of those States, respectively; and to erect toll-gates thereon, and to furnish an estimate of the amount of money which may be necessary to complete the repairs of the same road, agreeably to the requisition of the laws of all States, which have received the assent of Congress. Also, that he inform the House what is the condition of the masonry on the road, how many inches of metal have been put on that part of it which has been located anew, under the act of Congress, and upon that part of it which lies between the Monongahela and Ohio rivers. And also what depth of metal is, in his opinion, necessary to make a permanent and substantial road upon the plan which has been adopted in its repair, by the Department.

Mr. McKENNAN submitted the following as a modification of his resolution, which was agreed to, and thus modified, the resolution was adopted:

"And also, that he furnish this House with a copy of the instructions which were given by the Department to the Superintendent as the manner in which the repairs upon that road should be made."

The following resolution, submitted yesterday by Mr. WILLIAMS, was taken up:

Resolved, That the Secretary of the Treasury be directed to communicate to this House, the number of land offices and land districts in the United States; the time when they were established respectively; the quantity of land sold or remaining unsold; and the amount of money received in each district; and the expense of keeping up the land system in each State where it exists.

Mr. WHITTLESEY, of Ohio, moved to amend the proposition by adding the words "and Territories" after the word "State," which was agreed to, when the resolution was adopted.

On motion of Mr. VINTON, it was ordered that when the House adjourns, it will adjourn to meet on Monday next.

Mr. PEARCE, of Rhode Island, offered the following resolution, which, under the rule of the House, lies one day on the table:

Resolved, That the Secretary of War be directed to communicate to this House the report of Calender Irvine, Commissary General of Purchases, made in October or November, 1829, upon the claim of David Cooke, of Philadelph a, for money furnished by said Cooke for p wder furnished by the authority of the United States.

On motion of Mr. WARDWELL,

Resolved, That the Committee on Commerce be instructed to inquire into the expediency of providing by law for the erection of a light house at Big Sandy Creek, in Lake Ontario, county of Jefferson, and State of N w York

On motion of Mr. HAZELTINE,

Resolved, That the Co mittee on Commerce be instructed to inquire into the expediency of making an appropriation for a beacon light at Silver

Creek harbor, on Lake Erie, in the State of New York, and that the petition and papers relative to the same, presented at the last session of last Congress, be again referred to said committee.

On motion of Mr. ADAMS, of New York,

Resolved, That the Committee on the Judiciary be instructed to inquire into the expediency of extending in all cases, to parties in suits, commenced in the Circuit Court of the United States, or in any District Court having jurisdiction of a Circuit Court, where rights claimed under patents issued under law of the United States shall come in question, the right to a writ of error or appeal.

On motion of Mr. GALBRAITH,

Resolved, That the Committee on Commerce be instructed to inquire into the expediency of establishing a port of entry at Olean Point, on the Allegany river, in the State of New York.

On motion of Mr. MERCER,

Resolved, That so much of the President's Message at the opening of the present session of Congress as relates to the subject of Internal Improvements, be referred to the Committee on Roads and Canals.

On motion of Mr. SPEIGHT,

Resolved, That the Committee on Commerce be instructed to inquire into the expediency of making an appropriation for the erection of a customhouse in the town of Newbern, North Carolina.

On motion of Mr. PINCKNEY,

Resolved, That the Committee on the Judiciary be instructed to inquire into the expediency of purchasing the building, in the city of Charleston, recently occup e as a banking-house, by the bank of South Ca olina, to be used as a federal courthouse—and that they also inquire into the expediency of increasing the compensation of the United States Attorney for the district of South Carolina.

On motion of Mr. BEATY,

Resolved, That the Committee on the Post Office and Post Roads be instructed to inquire into the expediency of changing the present mail route, leading from Williamsburg, Whitley county, to London, Laurel county, Kentucky, so as to pass through Portageville, at the mouth of Laurel, in the said county of Whitl y

On motion of Mr. HAWES,

Resolved, That the Committee on Commerce be instructed to inquire into the expediency of making improvements, on Green river, in the county of Butler, and State of Kentucky, a port of entry.

On motion of Mr. LYON, of Kentucky,

Resolved, That the Committee on Revolutionary Pensions be instructed to inquire into the expediency of establishing an agency, for paying pensions, south of Green river, in the State of Kentucky.

On motion of Mr. PEYTON,

Resolved, That the Committee on the Post Office and Post Roads be instructed to inquire into the expediency of establishing a post route from the town of Monroe, via Locust blade, in Overton county, Tennessee, Celina, in Jackson county, Tenn ssee, and by Garret Moore's, Tennesse , to Tompkinsville, Kentucky.

On motion of Mr. PATTERSON,

Resolved, That the petitions referred at the last session of Congress, to the Co mittee on Roads and Canals, praying for the construction of a road from Lower Sandusky to the boundary line established at the treaty of Greenville, be again referred to the said Committee, and that they be instructed to inquire into the expediency of making the same.

On motion of Mr. MURPHY,

Resolved, That the Committee of Ways and Means be instructed to inquire what further appropriation may be necessary to complete the improvement of the Choctaw Pass, in the harbor of Mobile.

Mr. LEWIS submitted the following resolution:

Resolved, That the Committee on Public Lands be instructed to inquire into the expediency of authorizing any settler on lands reserved by the Government in obedience to Indian treaties, or otherwise, who settled such lands before such reservation was selected, and who, by reason of such reservation, was deprived of the benefits of

the pre-emption law of 1834, to enter, with the proper officer in said Land District, two quarter s ctions of any public lands in such District, at the price of twenty-five cents per acre.

Resolved, That sa d Committee further inquire into the expediency of authorizing any person who has cultivated or improved public Lands, in the year 1834, to enter not exceeding two quarter sections of any public lands in his respective land district, by paying to the proper officer fifty cents per acre for such land, within five we months from the 4th of March next: Provided such individual shall desire to enter said land before the expiration of the proper Land Office by the first day of June next.

Resolved, That said Committee further inquire into the expediency of authorizing any citizen of the United States, making oath that it is his intention to settle any portion of the public lands, and who shall actually settle and improve the same before one year, at the end of such period to enter an exceeding two quarter sections, by paying his the Land Office fifty cents per acre. If such public lands have been offered for public sale within five years, and it it remain unsold, and twenty-five cents per acre, in case said lands have been offered for public sale, and have remained unsold for a l nger period than five years.

Mr. WILLIAMS sai l, that the whole subject embraced in the resolutions was already referred to a Committee of the Whole on the state of the Union, and made the special order for the first of January. He hoped, therefore, that the mover would consent to have his resolutions similarly committed.

Mr. LEWIS said, he had presented a new matter of inquiry, which, he hoped, would be permitted to take the usual course. He preferred that the subject should go to the Committee on Public Lands.

Mr. MERCER called for a division of the question upon the adoption of the resolution.

Mr. CLAY could see no objection to the adoption of the resolutions. A new practice, it seem d, was attempted, by referring every thing regarding the public lands broadly to the Committee of the Whole. He objected to such a course, unless the House should first abolish the Committee on the Public Lands. He did not understand the motive which seemed to govern gentlemen in this particular. This was certainly not the place for this subject to be first examined and discussed. It was unusual, and he hoped that the resolutions of his colleague would be adopted.

Mr. CHILTON viewed the subject as one of great importance. He was opposed to the adoption of the resolutions. If gentlemen were prepared to surrender the public domain, the proposition of the gentleman from Alabama (Mr. Lewis) would be found a very convenient stepping stone. It owed it to his constituents and his count y to oppose with m ght and main every measure of the kind. He was not opposed to the honest settlement, but he objected to the practice of squatting, who, in d fiance of law, enter d upon the public lands, with the view of obtaining from Congress undue advantages, to which they were entitled. He should vote f r referring the resolutions to the Committee of the Who e.

Mr. H. EVERETT said, the resolutions had three objects the first was a reduction of the price of the public lands; the second was an exemption right to actual settlers; and the third was to give a new class of cases—to grant pre-emption rights to those who signify an intention to become settlers. He considered the two former policies res ly properly referred, and as to the last object of inquiry, it ought not to be seriously entertained by the House. He therefore moved to lay the resolutions on the table; but withdrew the motion at the request of

Mr. CLAY, who desired to correct a misapprehension. The proposition of his colleague (Mr. Lewis) had been assimilated to the one of another colleague (Mr. McKinley) on yesterday. This was not the fact. The one proposed an inquiry, the other was an instruction to the Committee to bring a bill of a speed the character.

Mr. LEWIS had examined the several

[*To be continued in next Number.*]

CONGRESSIONAL GLOBE.

BY BLAIR & RIVES.	———WEEKLY———	PRICE $1 A SESSION.
2d Sess.......23d Cong.	MONDAY, DECEMBER 22, 1834.	Volume 2.......No. 3.

TWENTY-THIRD CONGRESS.

SECOND SESSION.

HOUSE OF REPRESENTATIVES.

Friday, December 12, 1834.

[*Continued from last Number.*]

tion which had already been referred, regarding the public lands. They were not identical with the one which he had proposed. He had proposed an inquiry in the usual mode. By voting for the inquiry no member would be committed in regard to the measures which might be recommended by the Land Committee. They would be at liberty to oppose any such measure. It was the only method whereby he could bring his proposition before the House. It had been said that one branch of the proposed inquiry, should not be entertained by the House. It was certainly no reflection upon this House, nor was it extravagant in its terms—not as much so as one which was presented yesterday. It had reference to lands which had already been offered for sale. He hoped that inquiry would not be stifled, and that courtesy at least would induce gentlemen to show his proposition to go to the Committee on Public Lands.

Mr. REED said the gentleman last up supposed that the adoption of his resolutions was the only mode by which he could reach his object. He was mistaken. The bill would bring up the whole subject; and if it did not suit the gentleman's views, he could offer an amendment embracing his present, or any other proposition. It was not consonary to ask a Committee to alter their own bill. The usual practice was to effect that object by offering amendments.

Mr. E. WHITTLESEY reminded the House that this day was set apart by the rules for the consideration of private bills. He therefore moved to proceed with the orders of the day, which was agreed to—yeas 99, nays 51.

The SPEAKER laid before the House a message from the President of the United States, enclosing (pursuant to a resolution of the House,) sundry documents in relation to the destruction of the late Treasury building by fire.

On motion of Mr. POLK, the said communication was referred to the Committee on the Public Buildings.

The SPEAKER also laid before the House the following communication from the Secretary of the Treasury.

Treasury Department, }
December 12th, 1834. }

In obedience to a resolution of the House of Representatives, passed the 11th instant,

"That the Secretary of the Treasury be directed to communicate to the House of Representatives, as soon as practicable, copies of the correspondence, not heretofore communicated, which has taken place between him and the President of the Bank of the United States, on the subject of the Bank for damages, and in relation to the claim made by the Bank for damages, and the course pursued by that institution on account of the protest of the bill drawn on the French Government by the Treasury Department."

I have the honor to report, that the only correspondence on those subjects not heretofore communicated to Congress, which has taken place between the President of the Bank of the United States and this Department, consists on his part of two letters, one received here on the 28th, and the other on the 30th ult.

That which related to the damages and the course pursued by the Bank on account of the protest of the bill drawn on the French Government, being deemed of most public importance, has been answered, and copies of his letter, and the reply of this Department, are herewith communicated.

The other letter related to the late Circular from the Treasury, declining to receive the branch drafts in payment of the public dues after the close of the present year—and as it wished the Department distinctly to "understand it is not at all against the *measure itself*, but only the reasons assigned for it, that any objection is made," there did not seem to be much public necessity for hastening a reply. But soon as the great pressure of the current business in this office may permit, one shall be completed, and copies of both transmitted to the House of Representatives.

I have the honor to be, very respectfully, your obedient servant,
LEVI WOODBURY,
Secretary of the Treasury.

Hon. John Bell,
Speaker of the House of Representatives.

—

Bank of the United States, }
Nov. 28th, 1834. }

Sir: Your favor of the 13th of July last reached the Bank during my absence, and finding on my return that my letters addressed to you at Washington, had been published in the newspapers of Nashville, it seemed useless to prolong a discussion which could only inflame the passions of the country in the midst of its elections. I have, therefore, forborne to answer your letter until the time had passed for the repetition of a similar appeal from the laws.

The whole case appears to be exceedingly simple. There is a difference of opinion between the Treasury and the Bank about the damages on a bill of exchange. This is a matter of account which depends on the existing laws, and the acts of Congress provide specifically before what tribunal and in what manner, the question must be tried. Thus by the act of the 3d of March, 1797, it is provided, that if any person, accountable for public money, fails to pay it, "it shall be the duty of the Comptroller, and he is hereby required to institute suit for the recovery of the same," and in such a suit "no claim for a credit shall be admitted, upon trial, but such as shall appear to have been presented to the Accounting Offic rs of the Treasury for their examination, and by them disallowed in whole or in part." The Bank has accordingly presented its account for damages, which has been disallowed. It has then retained a sufficient amount of public money for the purpose, and invited a suit by the Treasury so as to bring the subject before the court. It did this and so stated it "as the best if not the only mode" of settling the question. But as the money itself was an object of indifference to the Bank, which sought only to vindicate its own rights, and the retaining it was a mere form, to comply with the act of Congress, the Bank at the same time requested from the Secretary to know, whether there was "any other mode of submitting the rights of the respective parties to the judicial tribunals more acceptable" to him—and would instantly have released the money on any arrangement with the Treasury to bring the case before the courts.

There is a still more summary process of obtaining a decision. By the act of Congress of May 15th, 1820, if the public money be withheld, the first Comptroller of the Treasury can issue a warrant of distress against the party in default, who may then appeal to the Courts of the United States.

Either of these courses is open to the Executive. If it chooses neither, the Bank, having done its duty, is content. Before the proper tribunal, the Bank will always be ready to prove,

1. That the bill of exchange on the French Government was drawn without the slightest authority whatever from that Government to draw

2. That the Bank proposed to the Treasury to collect the money as its agent—and not to pay it until it was received from France, thus avoiding the very embarrassment which has occurred; but this offer was declined, and requested the immediate payment by the Bank as a purchaser.

3. That of the money so paid by the Bank, the whole was immediately appropriated by the Treasury, and a part used in the current expenses of the Government.

4. That when the bill was protested in Paris, as was inevitable, and the money paid by the agents of the Bank, to save the credit of the Treasury, the claim of damages by the Bank was an indispensable act of duty, as that alone would enable the Treasury to claim damages from the French Government, which, if the Treasury had any right to draw at all, was as much due as the principal.

5. That the universal and inflexible rule of the Treasury is to make every one pay damages; and as it had required of the Stockholders of the Bank to pay damages, when their bills sold to the Treasury have been protested, so should it now pay damages to those Stockholders, when they in turn have bought a bill from the Treasury which becomes protested.

All this will be made manifest whenever the Treasury resorts to the proper tribunal. Until then, it seems unjust to prejudge the question, and quite fruitless to discuss it.

I have the honor to be, very respectfully, yours,
(Signed) N. BIDDLE, *President.*

Hon. Levi Woodbury,
Secretary of the Treasury, Washington, D. C.

—

Treasury Department, }
December 11th, 1834. }

Sir: Your communication of the 28th ult. acknowledging the receipt of my letter of the 13th of July last, relative to the detention of the public dividends by the Bank of the United States, was duly received.

After a silence of more than four months, coupled with the hostile position the Bank had assumed, it was supposed that you did not contemplate entering into further correspondence in respect to this subject, and especially was it supposed, that a correspondence would not be resumed, with an avowed view to any explanations or new arrangements, at so late a period, that your communication could not reach this Department till the day previous to that session of Congress to which you had been early apprized a report would be made on the whole of the proceedings of the Bank in this extraordinary transaction.

Presuming, therefore, that the Bank ought to have felt all the reluctance expressed in your letter, "to prolong a discussion" on that *transaction*, which cannot but be admitted, from its unprecedented and unjustifiable character, was well calculated to "inflame the passions of the country," and that this circumstance might naturally have led to the postponement of a reply till after "the elections," yet no reason is assigned in your explanation, whatever may be the reason conjectured by others, for the failure to forward that reply immediately after the popular elections had terminated, and in season for a suitable examination of its contents before Congress convened.

But it would be unjust to the Bank not to return thanks for the reply now considerate sentiment expressed in your apology for the first delay—a wish not "to prolong a discussion which could only inflame the passions of the country in the midst of its elections." This Department regrets that so powerful a corporation—though perhaps unable to restrain, and therefore not so responsible for the harangues of some of its advocates, on whatever days, places, or occasions—had not, in its own resolutions, reports of committees, and essays and pamphlets, publish d by its President, under a vote "to cause to be prepared and circulated such documents and papers as may communicate to the people information in regard to the nature and operations of the Bank"—earlier used a little more effort to *practise* the same forbearance from attempting "to inflame the passions and operations of the Bank." How fitly the Bank can now become the censor of the President or this Department, for also communicating "to the people information on the nature and operations of the

Bank," and that information consisting only of official correspondence on both sides—must be left to others to decide.

Your last letter having at length been received, and having, as appears, been already sent to "the newspapers" by the Bank, without waiting for a reply, and before one, in the great pressure of business at this season, could be expected, its contents are in some particulars found to be so very extraordinary in their tone, in their allusions, and assertions, that, unpleasant as the task is, this Department has, under all the circumstances, felt constrained to submit such remarks in relation to them as are deemed appropriate, and as seem imperatively to be required. The Bank may therefore, sir, rest assured, that though your letter arrived so late as to prevent the submission of it to the President before preparing his annual message, or to the Attorney General before his opinion was requested on the case, and as to deprive the undersigned from offering any due comment on it in his report to Congress concerning this subject, yet, in relation to the affairs of which it treats, an "appeal from the laws" has never, as you appear to intimate, been made by this Department, nor is one in contemplation. Any such "appeal" is left to those who, without the sanction of an appropriation by Congress, or without a legal precept, seize upon the public property, and convert it to their private emolument. But, after a violation of the rights of the United States, and a diversion of its revenue from the Treasury and the public service, into the vaults of the Bank, if the latter expects that the Chief Executive Magistrate of the Union, or the Secretary of the Treasury, will be silent, and not communicate early and full information concerning the outrage, to the People and their Representatives—and that those public officers are to be deterred from this discharge of a solemn duty, because the Bank entertains an opinion, that such a course is an "appeal from the laws," you have yet to learn, that both the character of that Chief Magistrate, and the obligations of duty entertained by this Department, have been greatly misapprehended.

In proceeding to the other contents of your letter, is conceded with you, that "that the whole case appears exceedingly simple." The Bank sets up a claim against the United States. It is presented and disallowed by the accounting officers, because considered in itself neither equitable nor legal; because it had never received the sanction of the United States by an appropriation; and because, if just, no branch of the Government, except Congress, had any constitutional power to authorize its payment.

Thereupon, the Bank, instead of resorting to Congress for that sanction, proceeded without it, and without any legal precept, to seize on the dividends belonging to the United States, and to convert them to its private use. The vital error of the Bank on this subject, appears to have been, in supposing that the Treasury and its accompting officers were any thing but mere agents of Congress to superintend the settlement of what has been appropriated. If, on the solicitation of the Bank, or any individual, however powerful, they allowed or settled any thing else than what had been sanctioned by an appropriation, it would manifestly be conniving at peculation, or a misapplication of the public money. It must be well known to the Bank, that the first and proper inquiry at the Treasury to every applicant is, where is the appropriation to pay the claim? And next, where is the evidence of its correctness, under the appropriation? It seems rather unreasonable to insist, that the Treasury possesses almost unlimited power when the Bank wants favors, but to deny to it almost all power when apprehending danger from it.

Beside all the decisive reasons against the reprehensible conduct of the Bank in this transaction, which are contained in the late Message of the President, and in the opinion of the Attorney General, the Bank, if it possess, as has been intimated, another controverted claim against the United States, for the removal of the public deposites, might, on this principle, in order to discharge it, or atone for any other pretended wrong, not only refuse to pay over dividends, but refuse, to the amount claimed, the payment of its notes or bills received by the Treasury for the public revenue; and when this consideration is weighed, it will readily be seen that the whole operations of the Government, in war and in peace, while, by law, the notes of the Bank must be received for the public revenue, are liable, at the pleasure of the Bank, to be paralyzed, and the public faith thereby violated.

After these objections, and when the common, the equitable, and constitutional tribunal of Congress was, and still is, for the Bank, as for all other claimants against the Government, similarly situated, open for a resort to obtain damages—it is lamented, that the Bank was so inconsiderately advised as to appeal to this other course, so novel, dangerous, and unnecessary, of seizing upon the public revenue, as being in your opinion "the best, if not only course of settling the question." You state further, that this has been done by the Bank only "to vindicate its own rights," when no case is believed to exist where a person not receiving money as an officer or contractor of the Government, or money not previously granted by Congress under some special or general appropriation, (in which mode the Bank did not receive these dividends,) has ever been able to "vindicate" his supposed "rights," by retaining the money to meet any claims, however well founded, against the Government; and when application by the Bank for relief in this case, had never been presented to Congress, and refused, so as to furnish the slightest apology for being obliged, in order to procure redress, to resort to this unusual remedy.

But if the views of the Department on this proceeding be erroneous, much gratification would be derived from having the particular act and clause quoted by the Bank, on which it relies in making the assertion, that "the retaining of this money was a mere form to *comply* with the act of Congress." This Department has not been so fortunate as to discover any statute, and much less the one cited, of March 3d, 1797, which requires of a claimant against the Government, that he should, in a controverted case, seize its property in order "to comply with the act of Congress;" nor any statute which authorizes, recognises, or palliates such a seizure, in order to force the Government into a law suit, and thus, through the agency of the judiciary, attempt to effect the payment of doubtful claims, to which no money has been appropriated, nor legislative sanction given. The proposition of the Bank to make some arrangement to have this question brought "before the Courts," and the assurance now given, that, in such event, it "would immediately have released the money," would have deserved much more attention and stronger confidence, had this assurance been more promptly given, and that amicable disposition, now manifested, been earlier evinced by the Bank, in having at least requested such an arrangement before the dividends were withheld. Before committing that aggression, the Bank was not pleased even to notify the Treasury that it wished the question of damages settled by litigation, and it communicated not the slightest intimation of a desire to make any "arrangement with the Treasury to bring the case before the Courts." But the Bank having, on these points, preserved perfect silence, and the Department and Congress having thus been lulled into security till after the ajournment of the latter, then suddenly, and without previous notice, a portion of the accruing revenue, estimated and expected to aid in meeting the large appropriations which had just been made, and to pay the residue of the public debt, was withheld by the Bank, and was not offered to be restored till after the termination of a suit, probably protracted for many years. After committing that aggression, and still withholding in its possession the money of the United States, the Bank then, and not till then, "invited" this Department to bring the subject of the damages in some way before the courts, and thus indirectly to sanction the appeal of the Bank from the authority of Congress over this matter, and to acquiesce, till adjusted by litigation, in the Bank's unprecedented and ruinous course as to the public revenue—a course involving a principle which, under all the circumstances of this case, if once adopted, might disorganize our whole collections, by the seizure of them, without legal precept, under one pretence or another, and, as previously explained, place even our disbursements, so far as the public funds consist of United States Bank notes, at the sole mercy of an irritated and unscrupulous corporation. But this the Department could not sanction, however urgently "invited," without proving faithless to every principle of public duty and public safety. Late as even that invitation, it is remarkable that your letters expressed nothing about the money itself "being an object of indifference to the Bank," or that it "would instantly have released the money in any arrangement with the Treasury to bring the case before the courts." On the contrary, though some persons may for some time have apprehended from certain circumstances, that money was "an object of indifference to the Bank" in comparison with some other objects, yet it is difficult to discover "what rights" the Bank then sought to "vindicate," except its rights to the money, and why it should be so tenacious of its rights to the money, and so indifferent to the money itself. By your correspondence at that time, the money appears to have been withheld with the express view to force the Department into a consent to pay the controverted damages claimed, without any sanction by Congress, or into some arrangement to submit to the judiciary for decision, a question which, under the constitution and the circumstances of the case, belongs to Congress alone, and, after that decision, and not till then, if unfavorable, to make a restoration of the dividends, the Bank had so unexpectedly seized, in derogation of the laws. It was not "until the time had passed for the repetition of a similar appeal from the laws" by the Bank to cover its other intimated claim for damages, on account of the removal of the deposites, with any probable hope of public approbation in favor of its new mode of aiding the fiscal operations of the Government, and not till after those "elections" to which you refer, may, in your opinion, have terminated so disastrously to its hopes, that the Bank professed a perfect "indifference" about the money, and a willingness to release it, in case an arrangement was effected for a suit at law.

How a suit could still proceed, and the money be first released or repaid, must be left to the Bank for further explanation, as it is incomprehensible to this Department, unless effected through some fictitious case, to be agreed on, in order to deprive Congress of its constitutional power over appropriations to settle contested claims against the United States, and which agreement, you may rest assured, that this Department has as little inclination as it has legitimate power to make

It may be proper then to state further and distinctly, that the submission of the whole case to the wisdom and authority of Congress, appears to the Treasury to be the only suitable course, and that it cannot enter into any arrangement in relation to the subject, except to receive, as requested in its communication to the Bank in July last, the dividends due to the United States, and to refer the Bank, as is done with other claimants in similar cases, to the justice of Congress for any damages demanded on the bill of exchange beyond the actual expenses and costs incurred. The acknowledgments of this Department should not be omitted for your kindness in pointing out more than one mode that might be pursued in the Courts of law against the Bank; but, as the advice of an opposing party is not always safest, and as Congress is competent to give directions upon the claim of the United States, and is considered the proper tribunal for adjusting the claim of the Bank, your benevolent suggestions will, it is feared, prove unavailing: especially, since the summary process to which you now allude, beside being open to other objections, is in express terms and by a decision of the Courts, applicable to the case only of debtors, who, unlike the Bank in this instance, obtain possession of the public money, in their capacity of public officers. What may be the design now in making, "for obtaining a decision," a proposition, which would doubtless be if accepted, is best known to yourself and such "distinguished" counsel of the Bank as you cite

to this Department, in your other published letter of the 26th ult. It must be admitted, that the Bank, in the next place, evinces great frankness in proceeding to disclose, under five separate specifications, what it expects to prove on trial. Whether there is much likelihood that this expectation will ever be realized, others must decide: but the ingenuousness in stating beforehand to the opposite party what is to be proved against him, should not pass without due commendation, though it is regretted, that under all the circumstances, a suspicion—it may be an unjust one—has arisen, that the statement was made rather with a view to be immediately laid before the community by the Bank, either to "inflame the passions" or to forestall public opinion on those points before a reply was received from this Department.

In laying down the first position which the Bank asserts it "will always be ready to prove," viz. "that the Bill of Exchange on the French Government, was drawn without the slightest authority whatever from that Government," it is feared that the zeal of the Bank to vindicate a foreign Government, has led you to overlook the treaty, in which that Government expressly stipulates to pay "the sum of twenty-five millions of francs, at Paris, in six annual instalments, of four millions one hundred and sixty-six thousand six hundred and sixty-six francs and sixty-six centimes each, *into the hand of such person or persons as shall be authorized by the Government of the United States to receive it.*" The Bank appears, moreover, to have forgotten the written authority, under seal from the President of the United States, which accompanied the bill, and empowered the holder, as the person designated under the treaty and in pursuance of it, to receive the money, which had then become honestly due from the French Government, and should, notwithstanding your apology, have been promptly paid, according to every principle of national good faith. In your ardent defence of a foreign country, for a neglect to fulfil its treaties, and attack upon a Department of your own, "for acting without the slightest authority whatever," it also seems to have escaped notice, that the Treasury acted, not only under the authority before-named, from France, of a solemn stipulation to make the payment to any "persons" "authorized by the Government of the United States"—and that the holders of this bill were so specially authorized by this Department and the President; but that Congress had previously empowered and required the Secretary of the Treasury, by the act of July 13th, 1832, "to cause this money to be received from the French Government, and transferred to the United States, in such manner as he may deem best." If, notwithstanding all this, unfortunately for your own country, the Bank should be able to support the position, that "the bill was drawn without the slightest authority" from France, you certainly will deserve her acknowledgments for the aid thus rendered to get rid probably of the whole of a claim which she has appeared not very eager to discharge; because, if France was not liable, under all the circumstances, to pay it in that form, it is difficult to discover how she is liable to pay it in any form.

It is to be regretted, that in your professions of regard for "the credit of the Treasury," knowing then as now what its authority was for drawing the bill, you did not refuse entirely to take it, as the Bank must have foreseen and believed, that the money would not probably be paid on an instrument, if drawn without the slightest authority," and that the affair would probably end in a claim by it for large damages. Were it not for the solicitude, since expressed by the Bank, to accommodate the Treasury, and the "indifference" the Bank now professes "as to the money," it might be inferred by some, that possessing the before-mentioned opinions, and pursuing the before-mentioned course, it must have meditated originally a speculation as to the protest and expected damages.

What seems at first rather inexplicable, is, that the Bank, knowing, and being ready to prove that this Department drew the bill "without the slightest authority," and hence could not require France to pay any damages, if the bill was protested—should yet insist, that the claims of damages by the Bank, was "an indispensable act of duty, to enable the Treasury to claim damages of the French Government." This great kindness towards the Government of your own country, uninvited and voluntarily to seize on its revenue, and attempt to plunge it into a law suit at home, and a controversy abroad, to enable it to obtain large damages of another country, which it must, if obtained, immediately pay over to the Bank, certainly deserves all due acknowledgment. In fine, while the Bank is professing to give all this friendly advice for the benefit of the Treasury, and to feel, itself, "a great indifference about the money," its regard for the Treasury upon this particular subject seems, when stripped of all blandishments, to consist in urging the Government to demand, and, to hazard a new quarrel with France to obtain, large and vindictive damages, by asserting that they are as much due "*as the principal*," when in fact the United States are entitled from France to only the reasonable and actual damages sustained, and when large and vindictive ones are to be sought in behalf, not of the Treasury, but of the disinterested institution which is urging this indefensible measure; and when, if such aggravated damages are obtained, they are expected to go at once, and exclusively, not into the Treasury, but into the vaults of the Bank; or, which is virtually the same, are to supply the place of the great amount of public revenue the Bank has already on this account seized and withheld.

But notwithstanding this, if now, or at any other period, the Bank shall, as alleged, be ready to prove that "the money was paid by the agents of the Bank to save the credit of the Treasury," the favor will be cheerfully acknowledged by this Department, as in that event no right in the Bank to the aggravated damages claimed against the Treasury, and which has led to the outrage of seizing on the public dividends, could well be pretended to exist. It is hoped, as you profess to consider that "the claim of damages by the Bank was an indispensable act of duty," you will also not hesitate to perform another equally "indispensable act of duty," by furnishing, as early as practicable, the evidence to prove the point just mentioned; since, if such evidence is furnished, not only should the aggravated damages be relinquished, but the conduct of those agents and of the Bank in that particular, be duly appreciated.

In that event, they of course, did not pay the money for "the credit of the Treasury" for the purpose of exacting from it, on account of the professed favor, the large constructive damages of $150,000 or $170,000, but, it must be presumed, they paid it with a view to save the Treasury from exposure to such a claim by some foreigner who might be heartless or sordid, and whose pecuniary profit being alone concerned, might be so destitute of patriotic feeling for this country as to permit the bill not only to be protested abroad, and the "credit of the Treasury" to suffer, so as to have it returned home protested, but who might thereupon immediately make a demand on the Treasury beyond the actual damages and costs sustained, and even for great, and it may be properly added, penal damages, and to pursue this demand in so inexorable a spirit as not to wait for the decision of Congress upon it, but, without legal process or any previous notice of his design, to seize upon a large amount of the public revenue, for the purpose of discharging it.

In relation to your third head of proof, "that of the money so paid by the Bank, the whole was immediately appropriated by the Treasury, and a part used in the current expenses of the Government," it gives me pleasure to attempt a correction thus early of these misapprehensions.

This Department has, in the reports sent here monthly by the direction of the President of the Bank, statements, which show that the amount standing to the credit of the public in the Bank, which of course includes its branches, was at no time after the purchase of the French Bill on the 11th of February, 1833, until the formal return of the money to the Bank on the 18th of May, 1833, less than eight millions of dollars. That of this, at no time, was less than four millions left in the Bank and its branches, to the credit of the Treasurer, subject to draft for any purpose, and that the residue was deposited on account of the public debt, and of the public collecting and disbursing officers. So that whatever sum of money may have been "appropriated by the Treasury" or "used" between those periods, it still left in the vaults of the Bank and in its use, standing to the credit of the Treasurer, at the times of all your intervening returns, a sum from three to four millions beyond the amount of the bill, or from three to four times more than the amount which you had, in form only, paid to the Treasury, or passed to its credit, in trust for the numerous sufferers by French spoliations. And no part of the sum received on the bill was ever so "appropriated" or "used" by the Treasury as to be carried into it by warrant; or it could not, until Congress should have passed a new law, have refunded, as it did, the whole amount, the moment notice was given of the protest of the bill.

In regard to the practice which you cite of this Department in charging damages on ordinary bills of exchange bought of individuals who sustain no official relations with the Government, and who neglect to provide funds abroad to meet those bills and to pay punctually our creditors and officers in a foreign country, it is hardly necessary here to show the difference between the two cases, in both form and substance, after the preceding remarks, and after the views contained in the first opinion of the Attorney General, published with the late annual report from this Department. Still less is it necessary to show further that in none of those cases probably did the idea ever enter into the imagination of the officers of the Government, that they ought, in order to obtain the damages due and often actually accruing to the full amount received on protested bills, to resort, without either notice, lawful process, or a previous adjudication, to a seizure of the property or dues of the individuals who drew and sold them. As in conclusion you give assurances that "all" your allegations "will be made manifest whenever the Treasury resorts to the proper tribunals," this Department takes the liberty to renew the expressions of its opinion, that it has already resorted to the proper tribunal, in the first instance, by submitting this whole transaction to the consideration of Congress, where you will doubtless be indulged with an opportunity, if desired, to make all your charges "manifest." But the Bank may rest satisfied, that it will be long, unless otherwise directed by Congress, before this Department, however urgently "invited" by the Bank, will consent to enter into any arrangement, or to institute any proceedings, which, under existing circumstances, will, in their operation, be likely to take from Congress, and transfer to some other tribunal, the power to adjust controverted claims, when no law has been passed, nor appropriation made, to pay them; and which will be likely to break down those salutary checks and distinctions between the Legislative and Judicial Departments, as to the disposal of the public money, which the People and the States have, with much clearness and wisdom, established in the great charter of their Union. For ample views on the law and equity of the whole case, and for any further reply which may be proper to any of the principles advanced in your letter, in support of the extraordinary claims and proceedings of the Bank, you are referred to the late Annual Report from this Department, and to the opinions of the Attorney General that accompany it.

Had the Bank thought more of following, in its own example, the salutary advice it so frankly bestows on others, not to "prejudge" or "discuss" this question of its claim to damages, and had it omitted to "prejudge" or "discuss" it in the report of its committee last December, and in your letter now under consideration, the preceding remarks in relation to it would most cheerfully have been forborne. This Department has now, very reluctantly, but in the manner that seemed to be required by the tone and contents of your communication, replied to such portions of it as appeared to merit notice, and can sincerely conclude with the consoling reflection, uttered by yourself in

behalf of the Bank, that "having done its duty, it is content."

I have the honor to be, sir, very respectfully, yours, LEVI WOODBURY,
Secretary of the Treasury.
N. BIDDLE, Esq. President of the Bank of the U. S., Philadelphia.

On motion of Mr. HUBBARD, the communication was ordered to be printed.

ORDERS OF THE DAY.

On motion of Mr. PATTON, the bill for the relief of Mrs. Susan Decatur, was postponed to Friday next.

On motion of Mr. THOMSON, the bill for the relief of D. Kilgore, was postponed to Friday next.

The House then went into Committee of the Whole, Mr. WARD in the Chair, upon the following bills:

A bill for the relief of the legal representatives of Richard W. Meade;

For the relief of Samuel Bragdon, David Chase, and others;

For the relief of Charles Gordon and others;

For the relief of William McLain and others;

For the relief of William P. Zantzinger;

For the relief of Silas D. Fisher;

For the relief of the representatives of Colonel George Gibson, deceased;

For the relief of Lieut. Mervin P. Mix;

For the relief of Tufts and Clarke;

For the relief of Com. Isaac Hull;

For the relief of Humphrey B. Gwathney;

To amend an act for the relief of Robert C. Jennings, and of the executors of James Roddy, deceased;

For the relief of Robert Haile;

For the relief of the heirs of Evan Edwards;

For the relief of the heirs and representatives of William Graham;

For the relief of Samuel S. Lord;

For the relief of Samuel Huntt;

For the relief of Marcus Quincy and William Gorham, of Portland;

And a bill for the relief of Francis Lasselle, and others, Michigan volunteers.

Upon the bill for the relief of Commodore Isaac Hull, a lengthened discussion ensued, in which Messrs. PARKER, REED, PEARCE, MANN of New York, HARDIN, E. WHITTLESEY, and GARLAND, participated.

The committee then rose and reported the bills to the House, with the exception of those for the relief of the legal representatives of Richard W. Meade—for the relief of the representatives of Col. George Gibson—and for the relief of Lieut. Mervin P. Mix.

The House then adjourned to Monday.

Select Committee—to which was referred that part of the President's Message relative to the election of President and Vice President—Messrs. GILMER, ARCHER, BINNEY, BEARDSLEY, GORHAM, JOHNSON of Kentucky, SPEIGHT, HUBBARD, and CARR.

IN SENATE.

MONDAY, December 15, 1834.

The Hon. JAMES BUCHANAN, Senator elect from Pennsylvania, appeared, was qualified, and took his seat.

Messrs. CALHOUN, of South Carolina, BLACK, of Mississippi, PORTER, of Louisiana, and BIBB, of Kentucky, also appeared and took their seats.

The Hon. LEWIS F. LINN, of Missouri, also appeared, and after the reading of the certificate of his re-election, was qualified, and took his seat.

Petitions and memorials were presented by Messrs. WEBSTER, McKEAN, SHEPLEY, SOUTHARD, BENTON, TYLER, WAGGAMAN, KENT, SILSBEE, HENDRICKS, and WRIGHT.

On motion of Mr. FRELINGHUYSEN, the Senate agreed to proceed to the election of a Chaplain, on their part, to-morrow, at 1 o'clock.

Mr. SILSBEE, on leave given, introduced a bill ——empt merchandise, imported under certain instances, from the operation of the tariff of which was read the first time, and referred to committee on Finance.

Mr. SOUTHARD presented a memorial from the Corporation of Washington, praying for relief; which was referred to the Committee on the District of Columbia.

Mr. SOUTHARD, on leave given, introduced the following bills:

A bill to provide for the enlistment of boys in the naval service of the United States;

A bill to establish and regulate navy rations;

A bill to change the titles of certain officers in the navy;

A bill to provide for the regulation of vessels propelled in the whole, or in part, by steam;

A resolution to provide for the settlement of the claim of Jno. S. Stiles;

A bill for the relief of the representatives of Isaac Garrison, deceased;

A bill for the relief of George Budd, Master Commandant in the U. S. Navy;

A bill for the relief of the commanding officers of the navy of the United States;

A bill for the relief of Henry B. Tyler, executor of Col. Richard Smith, deceased;

A bill for the relief of McKean Buchanan;

A bill for the relief of William Hogan, administrator of Michael Hogan, deceased;

A bill for the relief of Lieut. Archibald S. Campbell;

A bill for the relief Loami Baldwin;

A bill for the relief of the officers and crew of the private armed vessel Neptune;

A bill for the relief of the heirs and representatives of Henry Eckford, deceased;

A resolution directing the adjustment of the claims of the heirs of the late Robert Fulton, deceased.

All these bills were referred to the Committee on Naval Affairs.

Mr. PORTER gave notice that on to-morrow he would ask leave to introduce a bill to provide for the legal adjudication of claims to certain lands therein mentioned.

Mr. POINDEXTER, from the Committee on Public Lands, reported the following bills:

A bill for the relief of Susan Marlow;

A bill for the relief of Elijah Simmons;

A bill authorizing the relinquishment of the 16th section, and granting other lands in lieu thereof, for the use of schools, &c.;

A bill for the relief of Samuel Smith Lynn Magee, and Lemoise, Creek Indians.

On motion of Mr. POINDEXTER, the depositions lately taken before the Committee on Public Lands, were ordered to be printed.

Mr. KANE introduced a bill, on leave given, to provide for organizing the Territorial Government of Wisconsin; which was read the first time, and ordered to a second reading.

Mr. EWING, on leave given, introduced a bill making appropriation to improve the harbor at the mouth of the River Raisin.

Mr. BENTON on leave given, introduced a joint resolution for an amendment of the constitution relative to the election of President and Vice President of the United States.

Mr. BENTON also introduced a bill granting a township of land for the endowment of the French University in St. Louis.

Referred to the Committee on Public Lands.

Mr. TYLER, on leave given introduced a bill to remit the duties on locomotive steam engines; which was read the first time and referred to the Committee on Finance.

Mr. KING, on leave given, introduced a bill for the relief of Duncan L. Finch.

Mr. MOORE, on leave given, introduced a bill granting two per cent. of the net proceeds of the sales of certain public lands for purposes of education in Alabama.

Mr. MOORE submitted the following resolution, which was considered and adopted:

Resolved, That the Secretary of the Treasury Department be directed to communicate to the Senate the amount of the two per cent. of the sales of public lands lying within the State of Alabama, reserved to be applied to the making of a road or roads, leading to the said State, under the direction of Congress; and also, if any, what amount of the three per cent. of the said proceeds of sales of public lands, reserved to

be applied to internal improvements within the State, be now due the State.

Mr. HENDRICKS submitted the following resolution:

Resolved, That the Committee on the Post Office and Post Roads be instructed to inquire into the expediency of establishing the following post roads in the State of Indiana, viz.

From Bedford, in Lawrence county, via Bloomfield, to Bowling Green, in Clay county.

From Connersville, in Fayette county, to Lewisville, in Henry county.

From Winchester, in Randolph county, via Mississinewa, to Fort Wayne, in Allen county.

From Greensbury, in Decatur county, via Edmon's Mill, Huntsville, Goshen, and Newburn, to Columbus, in Bartholomew county.

From South Bend, by Edwardsburg, Whitman ville, Volinia, Schoolcraft, Bronson, and Gus River Plain, to the Rapids of Grand river, in Michigan Territory.

From Lawrenceburg, in Dearborn county, to Versailles and Napoleon, in Ripley county, by way of Aurora, Wilmington, and Moor's Hill.

From Newcastle, in Henry county, to Mooretown; in Delaware county.

From Rising Sun, in Dearborn county, via Jones' Mills, Dellsborough, and Watts's Mill's, to Cross Plains, in Ripley county.

From Charlestown, in Clarke county, to New Providence, in the same county.

From Martinsville, in Morgan county, by way of Lyon's Mills, Mooresville, Danville, and Lebanon, to Frankfort, in Clinton county.

From Putnamsville, in Putnam county, via Dickson's Mills, Rockville, Montezuma, in Park county, and Hill's Green, in Vermilion county, to Bloomfield, in Edgar county, in the State of Illinois.

From Bowling Green, in Clay county, via New Brunswick and Caledonia, to Carlisle, in Sullivan county.

From Charlestown, in Clarke county, by way of Vienna, in Scott county, and Slate Ford, on the Wiscaticaw, to Rockford, in Jackson county.

From Napoleon, in the county of Ripley, Indiana, through Versailles, Cross Plains, Mount Sterling, Vevay, Ghent, and Owington, to Georgetown, in Scott county, in Kentucky.

Mr. ROBBINS introduced a joint resolution authorizing the purchase of five hundred copies of the History of Congress, published by Carey and Lea; which was referred to the Library Committee.

Mr. NAUDAIN, from the Select Committee appointed on the subject, reported a bill authorizing the purchase of Boyd Riley's patent apparatus for applying the irrespirable gases to the purity of the human body, for the use of the Army and Navy.

Mr. TIPTON, on leave given, introduced a bill to provide compensation for the Governor and Judges of Michigan Territory; referred to the Committee on Claims.

The bill for the relief of Hiram A. Hunter was also, on his motion, referred to the Committee of Claims.

The bill for the relief of Col. Gad Humphreys, was referred to the Committee on Indian Affairs.

Mr. CLAY, on leave given, introduced a bill to provide for the distribution, for a limited time, of the sales of the public lands among the several States, &c.; which was read the first time.

Mr. TIPTON submitted the following resolution:

Resolved, That the Committee on Commerce be instructed to inquire into the expediency of an appropriation for the construction of a harbor at Trail creek, Lake Michigan.

The VICE PRESIDENT laid before the Senate a communication from the Treasury Department relative to the purchase of sites for the erec-

tion of a Warehouse in Baltimore, a Custom-house in New York, and New Bedford, &c.

Also, a Supplement to the Annual Report of the Secretary of the Treasury; which, on motion of Mr. CLAY, was referred to the Committee on Finance, and ordered to be printed.

Also, a communication from the War Department, giving information relative to the improvement of the harbor at the mouth of t'e river Raisin; which was ordered to be printed.

Also, a communication from the Commissioner of the Land Office, relative to the sales of public lands in Mississippi; which was ordered to be printed.

On motion of Mr: KING, of Alabama, the bill for the relief of Theodore Brightwell, was referred to the Judiciary Committee.

The following Message was received from the President of the United States, by the hands of Mr. DONELSON, his Private Secretary:

To the Senate of the United States:

The joint resolutions of Congress, unanimously expressing their sensibility, on the intelligence of the death of General Lafayette, were communicated, in compliance with their will, to George Washington Lafayette, and the other members of the family of that illustrious man. By their request, I now present the heartfelt acknowledgements of the surviving descendants of our beloved friend, for that high.ly valued proof of the sympathy of the United States.

ANDREW JACKSON.

Washington, Dec. 10th, 1834.

A joint resolution was received from the House of Representatives, for the appointment of a committee to carry into effect the resolution of June last, relative to the death of Gen. Lafayette.

On motion of Mr. CLAY, the resolution was concurred in, and the committee on the part of the Senate was ordered to consist of five, and to be appointed by the Chair.

[The committee will be announced to-morrow.]

The Senate proceeded to the consideration of Executive business, and after spending some time with closed doors,

The Senate adjourned.

HOUSE OF REPRESENTATIVES.

MONDAY, December 15,1834.

Petitions and memorials were presented by—

Messrs. EVANS and PARKS, of Maine;

Mr. BURNS, of New Hampshire;

Messrs. BRIGGS, OSGOOD, and BATES, of Massachusetts;

Messrs. ALLEN and SLADE, of Vermont;

Messrs. BOCKEE, WARD, MITCHELL, WARDWELL, MARTINDALE, and HARD, of New York;

Messrs. KING, McKENNAN, STEWART, SUTHERLAND, and DENNY, of Pennsylvania;

[Mr. DENNY presented memorials asking an appropriation to aid in improving the road from Pittsburg, Pennsylvania, to the United States Arsenal, near that city.]

Mr. MILLIGAN, of Delaware;

Mr. JOHNSON, of Maryland;

Messrs. McCOMAS, ALLEN, CHINN, WILSON, WISE, MOORE, PATTON, and MERCER, of Virginia;

Messrs. POPE and JOHNSON, of Kentucky;

Messrs. MARDIS, LEWIS, and CLAY, of Alabama;

[Mr. CLAY, in behalf of the legal representatives of the late General John Brahan, presented the petition and accompanying documents of said Brahan, heretofore presented; which were referred to the Committee on the Public Lands.]

Mr. SEVIER, of Arkansas;

Mr. WHITE, of Florida.

Which petitions and memorials were appropriately referred.

Mr. MARSHALL, from the Committee on Revolutionary Claims, moved to discharge the Committee of the Whole on the state of the Union, from the further consideration of the bill to provide for the settlement of certain revolutionary claims, (commonly called the commutation bill,) and that the same be recommitted to the Committee on Revolutionary Claims. Mr. M. remarked, that although a majority of the House were sup-

posed to be in favor of the general principles of the bill, yet it was feared that a majority would not sustain it in its present shape. It was with a view to expedite the measure, and render it acceptable to the House, that his motion had been made. The motion was agreed to.

Mr. ALLAN, of Kentucky, from the Committee on Territories, reported, with an amendment, the bill for the establishment of the Territory of Huron. The bill was referred to a Committee of the Whole on the state of the Union.

Mr. PEARCE, of Rhode Island, from the Committee on Commerce, reported a bill making appropriations for the erection of a marine hospital in the city of Baltimore, and other places, which was read twice, committed to a Committee of the Whole on the state of the Union, and directed to be printed.

The joint resolution, giving the right of way through the property of the United States at Harper's Ferry to the Winchester and Potomac Rail Road Company, was read a third time and *passed.*

The following resolution, submitted by Mr. BURGES, on Thursday last, was taken up:

Resolved, That the Secretary of the Treasury Department be directed to send to this House, in a tabular form, the amount of money paid into the Marine Hospital Fund by all seamen in the mercantile service in the District, of Providence, in the District of Newport, and in the District of Bristol, respectively, in the Rhode Island District, from the commencement of the present Government of the United States, up to the time when that fund was by law placed at the disposal of the President. Also, the alike amount, in like form, paid by said seamen after that time and before the commencement of the year 1828; and, also, the like amount, in like form, paid since that time—together with the several sums expended in each of said Districts, respectively, for the relief of sick and disabled seamen—showing the balance due to or from said fund, in each of said Districts, respectively, at the several times aforesaid, if any, and how the same may have been disposed of.

Mr. FILLMORE moved to amend the resolution so as to extend the inquiry to all of the revenue Districts of the United States. He understood that the gentleman from Rhode Island was apprehensive that the adoption of his amendment would retard and delay an answer to his resolution. This objection would be obviated, when the gentleman was informed, that at the last session, the Senate had made a similar call for information, which the Department was probably prepared to furnish forthwith.

Mr. BURGES suggested to the gentleman from New York that his resolution called for a more minute detail of facts in relation to Rhode Island than the resolution of the Senate did; and the adoption of his amendment would certainly cause great and unnecessary delay, inasmuch as the information called for by the Senate was already prepared. It would, therefore, be rendered necessary by the proposed amendment, to again go over the whole ground, to obtain the specific information from all parts of the United States, which he only required in relation to Providence. If, however, the gentleman wished this specific information from all parts of the Union, and would offer a resolution to that effect, he would cheerfully co-operate with him. But he hoped his resolution would not be trammelled with the amendment.

Mr. FILLMORE said, as the gentleman still thought that his amendment would prejudice his call, he would withdraw it.

The resolution was then adopted.

The following resolution submitted on Friday last, by Mr. PEARCE, of R. I. was considered and agreed to:

Resolved, That the Secretary of War be directed to communicate to this House the report of Calender Irvine, Commissary General of Purchases, made in October or November, 1820, upon the claim of David Cooke, of Philadelphia, for money furnished by said Cooke for powder furnished by the authority of the United States.

The following resolutions submitted on Friday by Mr. LEWIS, were taken up:

Resolved, That the Committee on Public Lands

be instructed to inquire into the expediency of authorising any settler on lands reserved by the Government in obedience to Indian treaties, or otherwise, who settled such lands before such reservation was selected, and who by reason of such reservation, was deprived of the benefits of the pre-emption law of 1834, to enter, with the proper officer in said land District, two quarter sections of any public lands in such District, at the price of twenty-five cents per acre.

Resolved, That said committee further inquire into the expediency of authorising any person who has cultivated or improved public lands, in the year 1834, to enter not exceeding two quarter sections of any public lands in his respective land district, by paying to the proper officer fifty cents per acre for such land, within twelve months from the 4th of March next: *Provided,* such individual shall designate said lands before the Register of the proper Land Office by the first day of June next.

Resolved, That said committee further inquire into the expediency of authorising any citizen of the United States, making oath that it his intention to settle any portion of the public lands, and who shall actually settle and improve the same for one year, at the end of such period to enter not exceeding two quarter sections, by paying into the Land Office fifty cents per acre, if such public lands have been offered for public sale within five years, and still remain unsold, and twenty-five cents per acre, in case said lands have been offered for public sale, and have remained unsold for a longer period than five years.

The question being taken upon Mr. WILLIAMS'S motion to refer the resolutions to the Committee of the Whole, and Mr. MERCER having called for a division of the question, it was first put upon referring the first resolution to the Committee of the Whole, which was decided in the negative—yeas 72, nays 73.

The remainder of Mr. WILLIAMS'S motion was also disagreed to.

The resolutions were then rejected—yeas 37, noes not counted.

On motion of Mr. HUBBARD,

Resolved, That the Committee on Revolutionary Claims be instructed to inquire into the expediency of allowing to the heirs of Doct. William Cloggswell, deceased, (who was a hospital Surgeon of the army, during the war of the revolution,) the commutation pay granted to such officers in pursuance of the resolution of the Continental Congress of March, 1783.

On motion of Mr. SLADE,

Resolved, That the Committee on Invalid Pensions be instructed to inquire into the expediency of placing the name of *Justus Cobb,* a soldier of the late war, on the roll of Invalid Pensions.

On motion of Mr. HARD,

Resolved, That the Committee on Commerce be instructed to inquire into the expediency of making an appropriation to survey and construct a harbor at the mouth of Eighteen Mile Creek, in the county of Niagara, in the State of New York.

On motion of Mr. CHAMBERS,

Resolved, That the Committee for the District of Columbia be instructed to consider the expediency of reporting a bill prohibiting, under suitable penalties, the sale and purchase of lottery tickets within the District of Columbia.

On motion of Mr. DENNY,

Resolved, That the Committee on the Judiciary be instructed to inquire into the expediency of making an appropriation to aid in the erection of suitable buildings at Pittsburg for the accommodation of the United States Court, in and for the Western District of Pennsylvania.

On motion of Mr. COULTER,

Resolved, That the Committee on Invalid Pensions be instructed to inquire into the propriety of placing Richard Harden, a soldier of the late war, on the Pension roll.

Mr. McKIM submitted the following, which lies one day:

Resolved, That the Secretary of the Treasury be directed to have assayed at the Mint of the United States, all foreign gold and silver coins now in circulation throughout the United States, and to furnish this House with a statement of the quan-

tity of fine gold and silver contained in each of said coins, and their current value at the Mint, agreeably to the law passed at the last session of Congress, regulating the value of gold and silver coins.

Mr. THOMAS, of Md., submitted the following, which lies one day:

Resolved, That the Secretary of the Treasury be, and he is requested to communicate to this House, any information he has received, or can obtain, concerning the official proceedings of the Government Directors in the Bank of the United States.

On motion of Mr. MERCER,

Resolved, That the Secretary of the Treasury be directed to lay before this House a copy of any contract which may have been made since the last Session of Congress for the construction of a bridge across the Potomac, within the District of Columbia, and an estimate of the probable cost of the same, according to the terms of such contract.

On motion of Mr. ALLEN, of Va.,

Resolved, That the Committee on the Judiciary be instructed to inquire into the expediency of allowing Benjamin Reeder, late Marshal of the Western District of Virginia, to transfer to his successor in office, a warrant from the Treasury, placed in his name as in March, 1822, against Salathiel Curtis, Collector of the 5th District of Virginia, and his securities, which was levied, but a sale enjoined; and that said Committee also inquire into the expediency of allowing said Reeder his fees for levying, advertising, and attending to sell the property of the defendants, and that they have leave to report by bill or otherwise.

Mr. FULTON offered the following resolution, which, under the rule of the House, lies one day on the table:

Resolved, That five thousand copies of the "proceedings and discussions of the French Chamber of Deputies, on the subject of the treaty between France and the United States," be printed for the use of the members of this House.

On motion of Mr. GRAHAM,

Resolved, That the Committee on Ways and Means be instructed to inquire into the expediency of establishing a branch of the Mint in the gold region of North Carolina.

On motion of Mr. MASON, of Virginia,

Resolved, That the Committee on the Post Office and Post Roads be instructed to inquire into the expediency of establishing a post route from Hickaford, in Greenville county, Jerusalem, to Murfee's Ware-house, on the Portsmouth and Roanoke Rail Road, in Southampton county, Virginia, and of discontinuing the route from Cross Keys to Williams's Store, in Southampton county, and of extending the route from Cross Keys to Patterson's, in North Carolina.

On motion of Mr. A. H. SHEPHERD, of N. Car.

Resolved, That the Committee on the Post Office and Post Roads inquire into the expediency of establishing a post route from Greensborough, North Carolina, by Thompson's Store, to Roxborough, in Pearson county.

On motion of Mr. R. M. JOHNSON,

Resolved, That the Committee on Military Affairs be instructed to inquire into the expediency of extending the time of issuing Military Land Warrants to the officers and soldiers of the revolutionary army.

On motion of Mr. MARSHALL,

Resolved, That the Committee on Revolutionary Claims be instructed to inquire into the propriety of granting to Mrs. Mary Graham, widow of Reginald Graham, deceased, compensation for the services and advances of her deceased husband, during the revolutionary war.

On motion of Mr. HAWES,

Resolved, That that the Committee on Roads and Canals be instructed to inquire into the expediency of making an appropriation for the removal of obstructions to the navigation of Green and Big Barren rivers, in the State of Kentucky.

Mr. HAWES submitted the following, which lies one day:

Resolved, That the Secretary of War be instructed to furnish this House with a copy of the survey of the Falls of the river Ohio; also, the estimate made by Captain Henry Shrieve, of the probable

cost of improving the navigation through the Falls; as also his plan for doing the same.

On motion of Mr. JOHNSON, of Louisiana,

Resolved, That the Committee of Ways and Means be instructed to inquire into the expediency of providing by law for the establishment of a Branch of the Mint of the United States at the city of New Orleans.

On motion of Mr. HANNEGAN,

Resolved, That the Committee on Commerce be instructed to inquire into the propriety of making an appropriation for the construction of a harbor at the mouth of Trail creek, on Lake Michigan, in the State of Indiana.

Mr. LANE offered the following resolution, which was rejected:

Resolved, That the Committee on Roads and Canals be instructed to inquire into the expediency of appropriating the refuse lands belonging to the United States, which shall have been offered at public sale, and been subject to entry for 20 years and upwards, and shall remain unsold on the 1st day of June next, situated in the counties of Franklin, Dearborn, Ripley, Switzerland, and so much of Decatur as is attached to the Jeffersonville District, in the State of Indiana, for the purpose of constructing and improving a road from the town of Fairfield, in the said county of Franklin, by the way of Brookville, to Laurenceburgh, on the Ohio river, in Dearborn county; and a road from Rushville, in the county of Rush, by the way of Simmons, to the same point upon the Ohio river; and a road from Napoleon, in the county of Ripley, to Aurora, on the Ohio river, in the county of Dearborn; and from Napoleon to the Rising Sun, upon the Ohio river; and from Napoleon to Vevay, by the way of Versailles, in Switzerland county, on the Ohio river; and a road from Napoleon, aforesaid, to Laurenceburgh, aforesaid—to be sold in such manner, and by such persons, and at such times, and the money expended in such manner, as the President of the United States shall be pleased to order and direct.

On motion of Mr. McCARTY,

Resolved, That the Committee on the Post Office and Post Roads be instructed to inquire into the expediency of establishing the following post routes, to wit: From Oxford, in Ohio, by Fairfield, West Union, Columbia, and Danville, to Rushville, in Indiana; also, from Liberty by Brownsville, to Philometh, to Centreville; also, from Liberty, by New Boston, to Richland.

On motion of Mr. BULL,

Resolved, That the Committee on Commerce be instructed to inquire into the expediency of establishing a port of entry at Green's Landing, in the county of Marion, on Mississippi river, in the State of Missouri.

On motion of Mr. ASHLEY,

Resolved, That the Committee on the Public Lands be instructed to inquire into the expediency of correcting an error committed in issuing a patent for one hundred and fifty acres of land in part of Wm. Pennington, and granting to said Pennington the right to enter, in lieu of the land patented, the same quantity of any of the public lands subject to entry at private sale.

On motion of Mr. LYON, of Michigan,

Resolved, That the Committee on Public Lands be instructed to inquire into the expediency of appropriating a township, or some other quantity of the public lands in Michigan Territory, to aid in establishing an academy or school on the Island of Michilimackinac, in said Territory, for the purpose of educating Indian youth.

On motion of Mr. LYON, of Michigan,

Resolved, That the Committee on Commerce be instructed to inquire into the expediency of making Green Bay, in Michigan Territory, a port of delivery.

On motion of Mr. SEVIER,

Resolved, That the Committee on Private Land Claims be instructed to inquire into the expediency of authorizing the Register and Receiver of the proper Land District in Arkansas to receive proof of claimants of the validity of Spanish or French land claims, with a view to their final adjustment, and report the same as soon as practicable.

On motion of Mr. WHITE, of Florida,

Resolved, That the Committee on Roads and Canals be instructed to inquire into the expediency of making an appropriation for a road from Black Creek to Swanee River, and from the head of Pensacola Bay by Pittman's ferry on Choctawhatchie river to Campbellton, Jackson county, in the Territory of Florida.

On motion of Mr. WHITE, of Florida,

Resolved, That the Committee on Private Land Claims be instructed to inquire into the expediency of increasing the compensation of Deputy Surveyor for surveying private land claims in Florida.

The SPEAKER laid before the House the following Message from the President of the United States:

WASHINGTON, 10th Dec., 1834.

To the House of Representatives of the United States:

The joint resolutions of Congress, unanimously expressing their sensibility on the intelligence of the death of General Lafayette, were communicated, in compliance with their will, to George Washington Lafayette, and the other members of the family of that illustrious man. By their request, I now present the heartfelt acknowledgments of the surviving descendants of our beloved friend, for that highly valued proof of the sympathy of the United States.

ANDREW JACKSON.

On motion of Mr. E. EVERETT, the Message and accompanying documents were referred to the Committee on Foreign Relations.

The SPEAKER laid before the House a Report from the Secretary of the Treasury, in relation to the purchase of sites for the erection of Custom Houses, Warehouses, &c.; which, on motion of Mr. McKIM, was referred to the Committee on Commerce.

The SPEAKER laid before the House a Report from the Secretary of the Treasury, in response to a resolution containing the number of Custom-house officers, and their compensation, &c.; which was, on motion of Mr. PEARCE, referred to the Committee on Commerce.

On motion of Mr. SUTHERLAND, 2,000 extra copies of said Report were ordered to be printed.

The SPEAKER also laid before the House a supplemental Report from the Secretary of the Treasury, on the subject of keeping and disbursing the public revenue, with accompanying documents; which, on motion of Mr. POLK, was referred to the Committee on Ways and Means, and 10,000 extra copies were ordered to be printed.

The following bills, reported from the Committee of the Whole on Saturday, were ordered to be engrossed, and read a third time:

For the relief of Samuel Bragdon, David Chase, and others;

For the relief of Charles Gordon and others;

For the relief of William McLain and others;

For the relief of William P. Zantzinger;

For the relief of Silas B. Fisher;

For the relief of Tufts and Clarke;

For the relief of Humphrey B. Gwathney;

To amend an act for the relief of Robert C. Jennings, and of the executors of James Roddy, deceased;

For the relief of Robert Halle;

For the relief of the heirs of Evan Edwards;

For the relief of the heirs and representatives of William Graham;

For the relief of Samuel S. Lord;

For the relief of Samuel Huntt;

For the relief of Marcus Quincy and William Gorham, of Portland;

And a bill for the relief of Francis Lanelle, and others, Michigan volunteers.

On motion of Mr. GRENNELL, the bill for the relief of Robert C. Jennings, and of the executors of James Roddy, deceased, was recommitted to the Committee on Claims.

The bill to "allow further time for issuing and locating military land warrants during the last war," and the bill for the final adjustment of land claims in the State of Louisiana and Territory of Arkansas, were passed.

The bill authorizing an appropriation of $100,000 of stock in the Georgetown and Alexandria Canal and Aqueduct Company, was taken up:

Mr. HARDIN said, this bill, he thought, should be acted on with caution. He did not wish to deprive it of its place upon the docket, but he suggested that it should be laid aside for the present. Congress had already subscribed for $100,000 worth of the stock of the Alexandria Canal, where the Almighty had previously prepared a better canal than human art could achieve. He would ask how long Congress were disposed to go on in this headlong course? How much has that canal cost? How much will it cost? It has been asserted here that the formerly projected stone bridge across the Potomac would have cost at least three millions of dollars! Now if that were the fact, what must not this aqueduct cost. It must have stone abutments, arches, &c., and be in a great degree more expensive than the bridge would have been. It may, and probably will cost millions upon millions! As to estimates, Mr. H. said, he cared but little for them. Estimates were like the Doctor, feeling the sick man's pulse, they were sometimes *high*, and sometimes *low*. He had no confidence in them. He hoped the House would at all events pass the bill by for the present.

Mr. CHINN did not wish to press the bill, if gentlemen were not prepared to act on it at this time. He therefore moved to postpone its further consideration to this day three weeks; which was agreed to.

A bill to authorize the construction of rail roads and canals through the public lands, was taken up.

After a few remarks, of an explanatory character, by Messrs. FILLMORE and CLAY, the latter gentleman proposed an amendment, intended to guard more fully the rights of the United States.

Mr. BRIGGS, in view of the importance of the bill, then moved its postponement, until this day two weeks; which was agreed to.

The bill to incorporate the Washington National Monument Society, was, on motion of Mr. CHINN, postponed till the second Monday in January.

A joint resolution, directing contracts to be made for Historical Paintings for the Rotundo of the Capitol, was taken up—

Mr. ADAMS, of Mass., said he discovered that the resolution proposed that *four* artists be employed in the execution of the proposed paintings. He doubted whether four native artists could be found competent to the undertaking. The four paintings already placed in the Rotundo, were executed by *one*. If four or more were employed, he predicted the result would be the production of very indifferent work, unfit to be exhibited to the world. He moved to strike out the word *four*, so as to leave it optional to employ either one or more. He did not mean to say that the same individual should execute the whole of those paintings; he wished some discretion might be exercised, in order to procure worthy specimens of the arts.

Mr. JARVIS said, as Chairman of the Committee who reported this resolution, he felt bound to state the objects which governed them. There was no difference of opinion in the committee on this subject. He had no doubt that *four* American artists could be found fully equal to the task. It was desirable to prevent such a monopoly as produced the paintings already exhibited in the Rotundo, and he was sure there was nothing so admirable in those, as to disparage the idea of producing their equal. The difficulty would not be in finding four competent American artists, but in selecting from the multitude in the galaxy. He would not do the arts of his country the wrong to believe the proposed number could not be found.

Mr. WISE said, in reply to Mr. Adams, that he hoped the House would pardon a few observations from him on this resolution and amendment, as he felt a deep interest in the subject. The gentleman from Massachusetts says that he doubts whether *four* American artists can be found competent to execute these paintings. Sir, I am proud to say and believe, that this country—the great masters dead—is richer now in native talents in the fine arts than any country on the globe. Without meaning to be invidious in the naming of our artists, as an American, I will boast that Alston is the finest historical painter—Sully the finest portrait painter—and Greenough is the finest sculptor in the world. And to these I could add the names of twice the number *four*. One—Chapman—I know to have slept upon his easel during a stay of three years in Italy, before the works of the old masters in the Vatican, and to have had an historical painting engraved by the Academy of Fine Arts at Rome. The country is rich in artists. Though the fine arts are not encouraged here, they are indigenous to the country. The gentleman says that the result of employing *four* will be that the paintings will be indifferent. Sir, I cannot see how. There are four pannels in the Rotundo to be filled. By selecting an artist for each, you will enlarge the field of selection, develope as much native talent as possible, and by having more than one artist, you will insure success in the pictures, by competition. Such is the object of selecting *four*. The evil of a monopoly is now to be seen in the Rotundo. The precedent of Trumbull's paintings, instead of being quoted for the selection of *one* artist, should be cited for the selection of four. Does the gentleman from Massachusetts not know, that the piece of the signing of the Declaration of Independence was dubbed, by a former representative of Virginia, (Mr. Randolph,) the "painting of shins." It may be seen by any one who will look at them, that the faces in one are the *faces* of all four, and that all the faces in the same piece have all the same characteristics. There always will be too much *sameness* in any four pieces executed by the same hand, however different the subjects; and, therefore, there should be different hands to execute them. Contrast is wanted for effect, besides competition for success. If four are employed, four styles of American painting will be exhibited. I hope, sir, the resolution will pass in its original form.

Mr. WARD said, that the subject had been brought before the committee of which he was a member, at its last session, on the motion of the honorable gentleman from Virginia, (Mr. Wise,) and it had there been fully discussed. The committee, in reporting the resolution in its present shape, considered that it was due to American artists that these paintings should be distributed among them. He was proud to know that there were many American artists fully competent to this task. He spoke of *Sully*, *Allston*, *Vanderlyn*, *Morse*, *Chapman*, *Wier*, *Peale*, *Leslie*, *Trumbull*, *Agate*, *Osgood*, and others, as native artists, whose works would never discredit the Capitol of the nation. With this host before us, he thought it would be highly inexpedient to confine our selection to a less than that which the committee had proposed. There were, he did not doubt, many young artists in our country, where names were now, perhaps, unknown to fame, but who only wanted an opportunity to distinguish themselves. *Chapman* and *Wier*, he considered, were artists of no inconsiderable merit. They were destined, if generously cherished—if properly appreciated—to become, at no distant day, the most distinguished artists in this or any other country. Nature has endowed these youthful artists with a taste and genius that qualify either of them to adorn the walls of our Capitol with the bright deeds of American history, immortalized by American genius. There were many of our artists worthy and deserving of notice and of patronage, and he hoped some of them would have an opportunity of transmitting their names to posterity in this great work.

Mr. BURGES said, he could hardly understand what it was that was to secure the immortality of the host of youthful prodigies alluded to by the gentleman from New York, (Mr. Ward.) If we are so crowded with artists, said Mr. B., if we are so annoyed with their illimitable number, why not let them all have an equal chance for the prize. Let them select their subjects, produce their paintings, expose them to every eye, and let the public select such as are most worthy of selection. But what are to be the subjects of these paintings? He, for one, felt somewhat tenacious of having a vote on the question *what* subject should be represented in the Rotundo. He was opposed to running any bargains in this matter. He remembered to have seen some of the works of Mr. Austin, and he would have no objection to his being employed in the work, provided the subject was first declared by the House. The House had before tried in vain to come to a conclusion on this point, when a subject for exhibition was proposed to them, and that subject was the battle of New Orleans! A matter of thrilling interest, but one which, like many others, would involve some political feeling. There were many subjects which could not be painted so as to give unity to their appearance. He alluded to the declaration of independence, and showed wherein it was rendered a fit subject for a painting. He had seen many attempts to paint the deluge, but never saw them succeed. Without unity, a painting becomes a confusion—a rabble—a rout—a mob—and who could paint a mob? Nobody—unless it were to place one upon a stump to make a speech. Mr. B. said he had not yet so far adopted the theories of the day, that if our country contained an Angelo or a Corregio, he would not employ him for fear of the cry of monopoly. There was not quite so much democracy or agrarianism in him as to reduce genius to such an equality. If there were such a galaxy of painters in our country, there must be some ruling star, some bright luminary among them, more glorious than the rest. Let the artist select his subject and lay it before the House, and then let the House decide upon it.

Mr. WISE said, that it had been urged that this country is not rich enough in artists for four paintings, but he did not expect to hear the question which had been asked by the gentleman from Rhode Island (Mr. Burges,) "What is there to "call forth so much native talents in the fine arts "in this country?" In *this country*, sir? It is not only the richest in the fine arts now, but is the richest country in the world, *sir, in historical events* for the pencil of the painter! In historical events of the battle-field, and in the council chamber. Every inch of ground in this country is consecrated *to freedom*, by events great, holy, and sacred. Every State in the Union has events to be painted—even the little State of Rhode Island has a *great man* to be painted! But, sir, this was not the meaning of the gentleman. He did not mean to disparage his country as well as her artists. His meaning *peeped out* before he took his seat, and was not left smothered in his question. The gentleman appears to tremble lest the battle of New Orleans should be put upon canvass; lest some act or event of the President's life should be selected as the subject of one of these paintings. Sir, it is not contemplated by any one that I know of, certainly by no one of good taste, to make an event, however distinguished, as *late* as any of the *last* war, the subject of one of these paintings. No artist of good taste I know would select any recent event to be illustrated by a master-piece; for it is in painting as in novel-writing, sir—you must go back until you meet events hallowed by time, and magnified and mystified by antiquity. For this reason, sir, if the gentleman chooses to propose the amendment, I for one will agree to it, that the selection of subjects shall be confined to a date antecedent to the treaty of '83. The gentleman asks, though, why not leave it to the artists to select the subjects, finish the paintings, and then, if worthy, for the Government to purchase them? Sir, to every one who has given the least attention to the subject, the answer is easy. The fine arts are hot-house plants. In every country but this they are encouraged. Every court of Europe has a student at Rome, where there is an academy for the study of the old masters. No such institutions are maintained here by the States, the General Government has not the power of this patronage, and private patronage is alone inadequate. Does the gentleman know the magnitude of the undertaking of one of these paintings, the artist thus unaided? Sir, the artist must devote himself exclusively for years to the work—three, five, aye, ten years, are not too long to study, and finish a work to adorn your capitol. He must study anatomy; he must travel to Italy for his materials, and his composition. What artist in this country can bear the expense and sacrifice of his time, unles he has the government contract for his guarantee? None, unles his pock-

ets are lined with at least $5000, to spare and to risk. Besides, sir, above all sensitive men on earth, artists are the most sensitive. They will never consent to undertake such immense works, at so much risk to themselves of pecuniary loss, reputation, and feeling, without a certainty of compensation. They can never be brought by necessity to hazard fortune and fame upon a painting to be offered to this government—to be undervalued—criticised by every pretender who knows not fore-shortening from coloring—and then to be rejected, perhaps, as unworthy. Sir, you must encourage their efforts, before you enjoy the benefits of them, and before your country will be graced by their labors. The paintings now in the Rotundo, were voted for before they were executed: I agree with the gentleman from Rhode Island, that the selection of the subjects should be left to the artists themselves. No artist can paint well from the selection of another.—His picture must be of his own fancy he must burn with his own conception, or his painting will never please the eye of the imagination. And if the gentleman from Rhode Island had attended to the resolution, he would have seen that the selection of subjects is left to the artists themselves, subject to the judgment of a Select Committee. The gentleman asks, who could picture a mob? Hogarth, sir, pictured a mob, and if the gentleman will step into any bookstore having his engravings, he can see a fellow so maddened with the rage of a mob, that he is sawing himself down from the top of a sign-post. Sir, I scarcely know what the gentleman means by an "aristocratic painting," or by *agrarian* principles, in this discussion. One of the reasons why *four* artists are proposed to be employed is, that we know not who is really greatest of the corps. There is something *national* in making the trial. It is not to pull down the best to the common level, but to ascertain whether the favoritism of private patronage may not have distinguished some one undeservedly above the others. We have frequently employed *foreign* artists, sir, at great expense, and I now desire very much to see if America cannot bestow her favors and lawful patronage in such a manner, on American artists, as to nurture the finer arts, to illustrate, in their turn, the arms, the civic virtues, and the glorious deeds of this illustrious nation.

Mr. BURGES did not rise to follow the gentleman from Virginia (Mr, Wise) through all his *colorings* of the fine arts. He merely wished to contradict one of his assertions. The gentleman had said that his (Mr. Burges's) object had "*peeped out*"—that he was fearful that some incident connected with the life of the present Chief Magistrate, might form the subject of one of the proposed paintings. He was not in the habit of "peeping" at all, and where he could find language to express himself, he always used it. He had no desire to withhold from posterity the noble and glorious achievements of the Chief Magistrate; but he trusted in God that posterity would never be made acquainted with the actions and motives of some of those who were at times found in the rear, supporting the President, and at other times in front, harassing and attacking him.

Mr. WISE said in reply, that he could not conceive how he could be made, or how any thing he had said could make him the subject of the unworthy allusion of the gentleman from Rhode Island. I feel myself, sir incompetent to make a *proper* reply to him. Silence is, perhaps, the best that could be made, as *that* gentleman is notoriously a "*privileged character*," as he has been called on this floor. But, sir, I cannot conceive why he should, unless from constitutional weakness, as well as weakness of old age, go out of his way to spit at *me*, on this occasion, his habitual and characteristic venom and malig——

[Here the SPEAKER shook his head.]

Sir, I leave the blank to be filled by the House, who know him well. Sir, I know not, and I care not whether the President or any friend of his, desires the battle of N. Orleans, or any other event of his life, the subject of either of these paintings. As I before said, I would prefer the events of the revolution; but I care not what subjects are selected, so that American artists are chosen, and the subjects and the execution comport with the dignity of our national history, and the works tend to nurture the arts at home, and redound to the credit of our own country.

The question was then taken on the amendment, and carried—ayes 104, noes not counted.

After some conversation between Messrs. VINTON, ADAMS, WISE, and JARVIS, the resolution was so modified, on motion of the latter, as to confine the subjects of the paintings to incidents in the history of the country prior to the peace of 1781; but before the question was taken, on motion of Mr. CLAYTON,

The House adjourned.

IN SENATE.

TUESDAY, December 16, 1834.

Mr. BENTON, from the Committee on Military Affairs, reported a bill for the relief of Col. John Eugene Leitzendorfer; which was read the first time, and ordered to a second reading.

Mr. PORTER, on leave given, introduced a bill to provide for the legal adjudication of claims to lands in certain cases therein mentioned; which was read twice, and referred to the Committee on Public Lands.

Mr. POINDEXTER, on leave given, introduced a bill, granting to the borough of Michilimackinac a certain quantity of public ground. Read twice, and referred to the Committee on Public Lands.

Mr. SHEPLEY, on leave given, introduced a bill in addition to the act granting drawback on certain goods, wares, and merchandise, passed January, 1805. Read twice, and referred to the Committee on Commerce.

Mr. BENTON, on leave given, presented a statement from the Treasurer, of the imports and exports of specie for the past year up to 13th December; which was ordered to be printed.

Mr. WAGGAMAN submitted the following resolution:

Resolved, That thirty copies of the documents in relation to the public lands, now printing by order of the Senate, be distributed by the Secretary, as follows: ten copies to the Library of Congress; ten copies to the office of the Secretary of the Senate; ten copies to the office of the Clerk of the House of Representatives.

Mr. SOUTHARD, on leave given, introduced a bill relative to certain improvements in Florida; which was read twice, and referred to the Committee on Naval Affairs.

On motion of Mr. TIPTON, the Senate proceeded to consider the resolution submitted by him yesterday, for an inquiry into the expediency of an appropriation to improve the Wabash.

Mr. TIPTON said he was desirous of making another effort to obtain an appropriation to improve the navigation of the Wabash. It is with great reluctance, (said Mr. T.) that I obtrude myself upon the notice of the Senate, but this subject is of such vital importance to my constituents that I cannot let it rest without making another effort to serve them. Bills have passed both branches of Congress at different sessions appropriating money to improve that river, but to these bills the President of the United States has refused his sanction, I have no doubt, under a mistaken idea of the claims of the river, as well as the facts of the case. I consider it due to myself, and not disrespectful to the President of the United States, to say that I differ from him in opinion in relation to the power to appropriate money to improve the navigation of our rivers He does not feel authorized to sanction appropriations to improve rivers unless it be such as lead to a port of entry established by law, and he has more than once refused his sanction to bills to improve the Wabash river, upon that ground, as I understand him. I contend that the power exists to appropriate money to improve rivers in any part of the United States where the business of the country and the capacity of the river require such improvement, and I have no fears in trusting the money in the Treasury to the discretion of Congress and the President to be appropriated to such objects as the interest of the country may require: under the supervision and control that the People hold over their public servants through the ballot box all is then perfectly safe

The President in his annual Message, with which he returned the Wabash bill to the Senate, has signified that if a port of entry was established on the Wabash it would bring appropriations to improve that river within the rule that he has laid down for the government of his own action in such cases. Without being able to perceive either the wisdom or the justice of the rule I have determined to yield to the necessities of the case, and so far to conform to it as to ask the Senate to pass a bill establishing a port of entry at the town of Lafayette, and another appropriating money to improve the river, and hope that Honorable Senators will give both their support.

At the late session of Congress the bill for improving the Wabash was laid before the President on the 28th of June, two days before Congress adjourned; and on the 30th of that month, on the last day of the session, we received a verbal message through our committee, informing us that the President of the United States had approved and signed all the bills passed by the two branches of Congress at the then present session, except that for improving the navigation of the Wabash, and as that bill involved a question of importance, he had retained it for further consideration. In his message returning this bill to the Senate, the President stated that he had not been able to satisfy his mind that the bill ought to pass. He goes on to state his objections to extravagant appropriations for internal improvement, and argues over again the case of the Maysville road bill, but he says not one word of the merits or the demerits of the Wabash bill, against which I contend that no sound reasoning can be produced, drawn from the constitution or the practice of this Government from its foundation. Nor am I able to discover any necessary connexion between the Maysville road bill and the Wabash bill; the former provides for a local object, the construction of a road from one point to another within a State; the latter provides the means to improve an important river, the line of demarcation between two States, a reserved public highway, as I shall presently show.

The common phrase, internal improvements, is generally used in speaking of roads and canals; these may be local, and best constructed by the individual State within which they lie, because a road or canal can be constructed in any direction through a State or county. But sir, improving the navigation of our rivers is very different. The rivers of the United States are the common property of all, every body may navigate them without let or hindrance, and that the joint funds of the nation should improve them, cannot, in my judgment, be denied. This principle has been acted upon from our earliest history, and I know of no case where the general Government has refused to improve a river of so much importance to any portion of our country, as the Wabash is to the western States.

The appropriation now asked for is to be expended in connexion with other appropriations to open a line of communication by water from New York to New Orleans. It should be borne in mind that large appropriations have been made to improve the Hudson, the Mississippi, and the Ohio rivers; the N. York Canal connects the Hudson river with lake Erie at Buffalo; the Wabash and Erie Canal will connect lake Erie, through the Maumee bay, with the Wabash, at or near the town of Lafayette. This canal is upwards of 200 miles long, about 78 miles in the State of Ohio and 128 within the State of Indiana; this canal is now being constructed. Thirty-five miles of that portion of this work lying within the State of Indiana is finished, and ready to be filled with water next spring; forty miles more are under contract, and to be completed next fall; and it is in contemplation to put the balance within Indiana under contract next season, and there can be no reasonable doubt but that Ohio will finish her part of this noble work without unnecessary delay, and we look with confidence to the completion of the whole work within three years.

Following down the Wabash from the intersection of our canal at Lafayette to the Rapids, of White river, where the improvement contemplated by this motion is to be made, the distance is about 300 miles, and navigable for steam boats

most of the year; and from these rapids to the Ohio is 100 miles, also navigable. By improving these rapids, and the completion of our canal, we will open a water communication from New York to New Orleans, the shortest and the best that ever can be constructed across this continent. Is such a work not worthy the attention of the Government? Or is the door of appropriation now to be closed on the application of Indiana and Illinois for aid to complete this most important public work?

The Wabash is a reserved public highway, by a compact between the United States and the Commonwealth of Virginia, at the time that Virginia ceded the Northwestern Territory to the United States; and by an ordinance of Congress, of 13th July, 1787, the 4th article of this ordinance concludes thus. "The navigable waters leading into the Mississippi and the St. Lawrence, and the carrying places between the same, shall be common highways, and forever free, as well to the inhabitants of the said Territory as to the citizens of the United States, and those of any other State that may be admitted into the confederacy, without any tax impost or duty therefor." Here is an ordinance of Congress older than the constitution is embraced in, and has become part of the constitution; and it gives power to improve the rivers.

By an act of 2d March, 1827, Congress granted lands to aid in constructing a canal, to connect, at navigable points, the waters of the Wabash with those of Lake Erie, and reserved the right to the United States to transport troops and munitions of war on that canal free of any charge. This canal is now in rapid progress of construction. It lies within the limits of two States, occupying what was the principal carrying place, between the Mississippi and the St. Lawrence, at the time of forming the act of cession and ordinance above mentioned; the United States having reserved the right to use both our river and canal, free of any charge. Can it then be unreasonable or unconstitutional for the General Government to improve the navigation of the river? I think not.

At the point where this appropriation is to be expended, the Wabash is the line of demarkation, between the States of Indiana and Illinois. Each of these States has made an appropriation to aid in improving the rapids; but these young States have not the ability to complete the work. Indiana has contracted a debt of near half a million in the prosecution of her canal, and it will probably be necessary to double that debt within the present year, and our people very naturally, and I think very properly, look to the General Government, the great land-holder in the west, to re-improve these rapids with the money of the nation, as it will evidently benefit the whole country.

The State of Indiana pays into the United States Treasury as large a sum, as a tax or duty, on goods imported from foreign markets, and consumed by her citizens, as any State in the Union, of the same population, besides what her inhabitants pay for public lands bought for cultivation. She has no harbors to improve, except that of Trail Creek, on Lake Michigan; no breakwaters to draw millions from the Treasury in their construction. She asks nothing but the improving of her rivers. No session of Congress passes but other States are provided with money to improve their rivers—the Hudson, James, Savannah, Red river, and Cumberland, with a long list of less rivers that I will not detain the Senate to read, are all been improved at the expense of the General Government.

At the session of Congress of 1831-2, a bill passed which was approved, providing for improving the Muskingula, and other rivers, to places where there was no ports of entry; and the Globe, in speaking for that approval says: "If the purchase contemplated by Congress can be accomplished, and the three rivers mentioned, made navigable to the points in question, then ports of entry will of course be established at the head of navigation." I ask, why not be so liberal to the Wabash? It is a larger river than the Monongahela—watering a much more extensive territory, and the finest soil in the world, with a greater population to be provided for.

To show what has been done elsewhere, I have procured a statement showing the appropriations

---

of 1832 and 1834, for improving harbors and rivers. It is as follows:

Appropriations for improving rivers in 1832—Laws first session of Congress 1832, page 134.

Kennebec river, Maine,	$2,600
Pascagoula river,	15,900
Red river, Louisiana and Arkansas,	22,628
Berwick branch of the Piscataqua,	220
Entrance of the Genesee river,	16,000
Cape Fear river, below Wilmington, N. C.	28,000
Ohio, Missouri, and Mississippi rivers,	50,000

The President to extend the steamboat navigation from Pittsburg to the Cumberland road at Brownsville;* also the Missouri, from its junction with the Mississippi, to the mouth of the Kansas river; and also the Upper Mississippi, from St. Louis to Galena, with power to remove all obstructions in the channel, &c.

The Arkansas river,	15,000
The mouth of Conteaut Creek, Ohio,	7,800
Removing obstructions at the mouth of the Ashtabula Creek, Ohio,	3,800
Do. do. Grand river, Ohio,	2,600
To remove and bar at mouth Black river,	8,000
Mouth of Huron river,	1,200
Cumberland river,	30,000
Savannah river,	20,000

Appropriations for improving rivers, made in 1834. Laws first session of Congress, page 68:

Cape Fear river, below Wilmington, N. C.	$5,234
Ohio, Missouri, and Missippi rivers,	50,000
St. Mark's river, Florida,	4,650
Red river,	50,000
Savannah river, in removing obstructions from City of Savannah to its mouth,	30,000
Genesee river, for completing the works thereon,	29,000
Grand river, Ohio, for repairing and securing the works,	10,000
Black river, for securing the works,	5,000
Huron river, Ohio,	6,700
Ashtabula creek, Ohio,	5,000
Cumberland river,	30,000
Hudson river, (See page 103,)	70,000

This statement shows that millions upon millions are applied to improving rivers and small streams east of the mountains; if but 10, 20, or 50 miles long, you call them rivers, and we vote money to improve them. I do not mention this in a spirit of complaint, but to show the contrast. We have over 500 miles of Mississippi, 1000 miles of Ohio, and 2000 of Mississippi, these we think present equal claims to attention, and I feel it my duty to urge them upon the notice of Congress. All other rivers beside the Wabash have been improved by the United States, while bills for that river have been vetoed or withheld. Was this necessary for the public good, or is it just and proper? Do those in power think so? My constituents will remain forever silent under such circumstances? I do not mean, Mr. President, to charge the Chief Magistrate with intentional injustice; but only to say that he has acted under a mistaken apprehension of the facts, which has worked injustice to my constituents.

I have recently been taught that a system is practised to keep men silent that are disposed to speak out: When Congress adjourned last summer, I addressed a circular to my constituents, informing them of what had been done for their benefit, and what was left undone; but said nothing flattering of the treatment that the Wabash bill had met with, and concluded by advising the people to correct these wrongs at the ballot box. After the publication of my circular, the Globe, a newspaper printed in this City, devoted three or four of its long columns in abusing me, because I had dared thus to address my constituents. But, sir, I do not feel injured by this attack of the Globe. The writer in that paper must establish a character for truth and veracity among the people of Indiana, before they will take his word against one they have known long and known well. The writer of the article referred to, has mistaken his man. This appropriation is for the improvement of the Monongahela river, upon which there never has been any port of entry established.

---

if he thinks that I can be lashed into silence, for the power of the press, nor no other power, can intimidate or will keep me silent while the interest of Indiana is at stake, and in this case of the Wabash bill I contend that justice has not been meted out to her.

A President or other public officer, is but a transient being; here to-day, gone to-morrow; but the principles of justice upon which our government should be administered are immutable and will endure in all time to come. Every public man owes a heavy responsibility to his constituents—and I would have felt unworthy the trust reposed in me, if I had remained silent on a subject so deeply interesting to those I have the honor, in part, to represent here.

The term of service of the present Chief Magistrate is drawing to a close, what he has done, he has done: it must go down to posterity to form his political character, and God knows that I need not if I could, pluck a laurel from his brow; but, sir, this subject of improving our rivers cannot rest here, the People should take it into their own hands, and in selecting a successor for the present incumbent, before they cast their votes, they should ascertain whether he is for or against Internal Improvement. No sir, that is too broad a term, it can be explained away or construed to mean any thing or nothing; they should know whether the candidates are for or against improving the navigation of our rivers, and I aver that no men holding the opposite doctrine need expect one-fourth of our votes.

I hope sir, that this resolution will be adopted, and that both Congress and the President will agree that the United States should improve this river. I cannot believe, without more evidence than is now before me, that there is a disposition in either to prevent it when the question is properly understood.

[As Mr. TIPTON's remarks, made on the floor of the Senate, implicating the character of our press, have the advantage of a place in the Congressional Globe, as part of the Debate, we feel bound to submit the refutation through the same channel. If we cannot meet our honorable assailants where they take the privilege of making their attacks, they will at least allow us to reply in our own forum.—Editors of the Globe.

From the Daily Globe of December 18.

SENATOR TIPTON.

This gentleman, in a speech made by him in the Senate, which appeared in the Globe yesterday, as sent by himself for publication, makes the following remark:

"I have recently been taught that a system is practised to keep men silent that are disposed to speak out. When Congress adjourned last summer, I addressed a circular to my constituents, informing them of what had been done for their benefit, and what was left undone; but said nothing flattering of the treatment that the Wabash bill had met with, and concluded by advising the people to correct these wrongs at the ballot box. After the publication of my circular, the Globe, a newspaper printed in this city, devoted three or four of its long columns in abusing me, because I had dared thus to address my constituents. But, sir, I do not feel injured by this attack of the Globe. The writer in that paper must establish a character for truth and veracity among the People of Indiana, before they will take his word against one they have known long, and known well. The writer of the article referred to, has mistaken his man, if he thinks that I can be lashed into silence; for the interest of Indiana is at stake, and in this case of the Wabash bill, I contend that justice has not been meted out to her."

We have marked in Italics the passages in the above to which we would invoke the attention of the public. It will be seen that Mr. Tipton makes a

question of veracity with us, which he refers to its decision. We most cheerfully submit ourselves to its judgment, and will agree to stand forever branded as a calumniator, if a single honest man in the country shall say, that in the article to which Mr. Tipton alluded in the Senate, there is one false charge brought against him, or any thing like abuse.

We give below the whole article, on which the Senator from Indiana has based the charge, that we have " DEVOTED THREE OR FOUR OF ITS (the Globe's) LONG COLUMNS IN ABUSING HIM"—and we peremptorily deny, that there is a single line in that article, or that we ever wrote any other article in relation to Mr. Tipton, which will justify his assertion. On the contrary, it will be seen that although in his circular he has insinuated a strong impeachment of the President's motives in refusing his signature to the Wabash bill, yet, in our reply, which was intended to vindicate the Chief Magistrate from the aspersions of the Senator, we carefully abstained from making any remark which could be construed into retaliation, or savoring, in the slightest degree, of vindictive retort.

As General Tipton has so wantonly and unjustly assailed us on the floor of the Senate, as having abused him, and of violating truth in giving vent to the bad feeling which induced such a course; he will pardon us for stating some circumstances, which, we trust, will satisfy Mr. Tipton that our disposition towards him has been directly the reverse of that imputed.

Mr. Tipton was for many years and an Agent. He has acquired a great estate in the lands obtained by treaties from the Indians, while he held his agency. These lands lie upon the Wabash, and in the neighborhood of the route of the canal, through which the Senator proposes to unite the navigation of the Lakes with that of the Mississippi. One of the Representatives of Indiana had resolved to exhibit charges against Mr. Tipton. We entertained so good an opinion of Mr. Tipton as to believe him incapable of the wrong imputed, and interested ourselves personally to prevent the publication of the contemplated accusation against him. We still hope that there is some mistake in the grounds upon which the gentleman, to whom we alluded, intended to rest his charges—but when we find Mr. Tipton ready to assail our press, without cause, to gratify the malignity of the opposition in the Senate, and evidently with a view to conciliate their support to a measure calculated to advance the value of his lands, we must confess that we feel our faith in him somewhat diminished. What will not a man do, who is ready, without provocation, to sacrifice a friend to the *Moloch* opposition, to induce them to pander to his own personal interests?

But Mr. Tipton is ready to appeal to the ambition, as well as the malice, of the opposition leaders, to carry his measure in the Senate.

"This subject of improving our rivers cannot rest here, the People should take it into their own hands, and in selecting a successor for the present incumbent, before they cast their votes, they should ascertain whether he is for or against internal Improvement. No, sir, that is too broad a term; it can be explained away or construed to mean any thing or nothing; they should know whether the candidates are for or against *improving the navigation of our rivers, and I see that no men holding the opposite doctrine need expect one-fourth of our votes.*"

Mr. Tipton having thus in effect promised *three-fourths* of the State of Indiana to some candidate for the Presidency, in favor of "*improving the navigation of our rivers,*" Mr. Webster instantly takes him at his word, and responds—

"*With regard to the resolution under consideration, he had no objection to its adoption. He had no more doubt of the right of Congress to improve the navigation of the Wabash, than to appropriate money for the Delaware Breakwater, for the improvement of Boston harbor, to erect fortifications, to improve a harbor in Lake Erie, or to build a light-house at the mouth of the Balize.*"

So, it seems that the log-rolling system of voting away money raised by taxes on the people generally, to secure the influence of particular sections or States, is to be resumed, under the auspices of Messrs. Webster and Tipton. *This looks like a wedding!!!*

With one further remark, we dismiss the subject. Mr. Tipton says:

"*All other rivers have been improved except the Wabash, while bills for that river are vetoed or withheld.*"

Is this true? We deny it positively. The appropriations, applied under the direction of President Jackson, have all been confined to streams leading to ports of entry or delivery. Mr. Tipton instances the Monongahela as one to which an appropriation has been made, and on which no port of entry has been established. It is true that an appropriation was put at the disposal of the President, authorizing him to lay it out in improving the Ohio, Mississippi, and Monongahela. He exerted the discretion given him in the act, and applied it on the Ohio and Mississippi—and exclusively below the ports of entry on each.]

Mr. WEBSTER said he did not understand whether the subject matter of the present resolution was for an appropriation to improve the Wabash, or whether it was the resolution submitted some days ago by the Hon. member, (Mr. Tipton,) which directed an inquiry by a Committee, into the expediency of making a port of entry high up the Wabash.

[The resolution was again read at Mr. W.'s request.]

Mr. WEBSTER resumed. That resolution, as he understood it, was for the purpose of removing the constitutional objections urged by the President against the appropriation by Congress for the improvement of that river. He did not propose to argue the question involved in the objection at this tim-, though he proposed to do so when the question should come up. He would, however, only remark that he did not comprehend, if Congress did not possess the constitutional power to improve the navigation of a stream, how the power to do so could be acquired, by first establishing a port of entry upon the stream. As to the present resolution, he thought there could be no objection to it. He voted last year for the bill making the appropriation to improve the Wabash; and he entertained no more doubt about the constitutional power of Congress to do so, than he did of the power to construct a breakwater at the mouth of the Delaware—to erect fortifications—to improve Boston harbor, or the harbors in Lake Erie. He had no scruples whatever about it. He thought last year that the people of Indiana had claims, and therefore he voted for the bill. And if the honorable gentleman thought he had any prospect of obtaining the passage of a law for the purpose, he would support it again. He (Mr. W.) thought there was no reasonable prospect of success, so long as the councils of the nation were so much divided as they were at present on this subject.

Mr. TIPTON made a few other remarks, after which, the resolution was adopted.

The Senate then proceeded to the special order of the day, which was the election of Chaplain. The ballots having been taken, resulted as follows:

Iowa:

Mr. Hatch,	22
Perry,	7
Stockton,	1
Sloss,	6
Ungerer,	3
Brook,	2
Sargent,	1
Higby,	3

No person having a majority of votes, the board proceeded to a 2d ballot, when the following was the result:

Mr. Hatch,	22
Perry,	9
Slicer,	7
Tipton,	1
Higby,	1
Sargent,	1
Stockton,	1
Brook,	1
	45

Mr. Hatch having received a majority of all the ballots given, was declared duly elected Chaplain for the present session.

The resolution submitted yesterday by Mr. HENDRICKS, relative to certain post roads, and one submitted by Mr. TIPTON relative to improving the bank of Trail Creek, were adopted.

On motion of Mr. BENTON, the resolution submitted by him, relative to an alteration of the Constitution, were ordered to be printed, and were made the special order of the day for Monday next.

The bill to establish the territorial government of Wisconsin was read a 2d time, and, on motion of Mr. KANE, referred to the Judiciary Committee.

The bill granting a township of land to the French University, at St. Louis, was, on motion of Mr. BENTON, referred to the Committee on Public Lands.

Mr. CLAY moved that the bill introduced by him, to distribute, for a limited time, the proceeds of the sales of public lands among the several States, be taken up, and made the order of the day for Tuesday the 30th instant.

The Senate then adjourned.

HOUSE OF REPRESENTATIVES.

TUESDAY, December 16, 1834.

Petitions and Memorials were presented by Mr. HUBBARD, of New Hampshire; Mr. TRUMBULL, of Connecticut; Mr. HALL, of Vermont; Messrs. McVEAN, GILLET, and HUNTINGTON, of New York; Mr. McKIM, of Maryland; Messrs. CHINN, LOYAL, ALLEN, MASON, CLAIBORNE, and ROBERTSON, of Virginia; Mr. JOHNSON, of Kentucky; Mr. LEA, of Tennessee; Messrs. CORWIN and MITCHELL, of Ohio; Mr. EWING, of Indiana; Messrs. CASEY and MAY, of Illinois. [Mr. CASEY presented the petition of Gasten, widow of John Gasten, deceased, a soldier of the revolution, praying remuneration for services rendered, and losses sustained, during the revolutionary war; which, on his motion, was referred to the Committee on Revolutionary Claims.] Mr. WHITE, of Florida. Which petitions and memorials were referred to appropriate committees.

Mr. POLK, from the Committee of Ways and Means, reported the following bills:

A bill regulating the deposits of the money of the United States in certain local banks,

A bill to repeal so much of the act entitled "An act transferring the duties of Commissioner of Loans to the Bank of the United States, and abolishing the office of Commissioner of Loans," as requires the Bank of the United States to perform the duties of Commissioner of Loans for the several States;

A bill to authorize the sale of the Bank stock of the United States.

The said bills were read twice, and, on motion Mr. POLK, their further consideration was postponed to, and they were made the special orders of the day, for the first Monday in January.

Mr. POLK, from the same committee, reported a bill making appropriations for, the payment of revolutionary and other pensions of the United States, for the year 1835; which was read twice, and committed to a Committee of the Whole.

Mr. JOHNSON, from Kentucky, the Committee on Military Affairs, reported the following bills, which were read twice and committed, viz.

A bill for the better organization of the corps of Topographical Engineers;

A bill providing for the gradual increase of the corps of Engineers, and for other purposes;

And a bill to authorize the appointment of additional paymasters;

Mr. JOHNSON, from the same Committee, reported a bill extending the time for issuing military land warrants to the officers and soldiers of the revolutionary army; which was read twice, and directed to be engrossed for a third reading.

Mr. WAYNE, from the Committee on Foreign Relations, reported the following bills, which were read twice and committed:

A bill to authorize the allowance of certain charges in the account of the American Consul at ——;

And a bill to provide for the settlement of the heir of Mary O'Sullivan.

Mr. WHITE, from the Committee on Naval Affairs, reported a bill authorizing the enlistment of boys in the naval service; which was read twice and committed.

Mr. MERCER, from the Committee on Roads and Canals, reported the following resolution, which was agreed to:

Resolved, That the Committee on Roads and Canals be discharged from the further consideration of the resolution instructing them to inquire into the expediency of making an appropriation for the improvement of the road through the Pohitto Swamp, on the mail route from Natchez to New Orleans, and that the resolution be referred to the Committee of the Whole, to which has been referred a bill embracing the same object.

The following resolutions, submitted yesterday, were taken up and agreed to:

By Mr. McKIM:
Resolved, That the Secretary of the Treasury be directed to have assayed at the Mint of the United States, all foreign gold and silver coins now in circulation throughout the United States, and furnish this House with a statement of the quantity of fine gold and silver contained in each of said coins, and their current value at the Mint, as compared to the law passed at the last session of Congress, regulating the value of gold and silver coins.

By Mr. THOMAS, of Maryland:
Resolved, That the Secretary of the Treasury be, and he is requested, to communicate to this House any information he has received, or can obtain, concerning the official proceedings of the Government Directors in the Bank of the United States.

By Mr. MERCER:
Resolved, That the Secretary of the Treasury be required to lay before this House a copy of any report which may have been made since the last session of Congress, for the construction of a bridge across the Potomac, within the District of Columbia, and an estimate of the probable cost of the same, according to the terms of such contract.

By Mr. BLAIR:
Resolved, That the Secretary of War be instructed to furnish this House with a copy of the survey of the Falls of the river Ohio; also, the estimate made by Captain Henry Shriever, of the proba-

ble cost of improving the navigation through the Falls; as also his plan for doing the same.

The following resolution, submitted yesterday by Mr. FULTON, was taken up:

Resolved, That 5000 copies of the "Proceedings and Discussions of the French Chamber of Deputies on the subject of the treaty between France and the United States," be printed for the use of the members of this House.

After a short explanation by Messrs. E. EVERETT, FULTON, and FOSTER, the resolution was amended by striking out 5000, and inserting 10,000; when it was agreed to.

On motion of Mr. WILSON,
Resolved, That the Committee on Roads and Canals be instructed to inquire into the expediency of directing an appropriation to be made for the improvement of the Monongahela river, from Middletown, in Virginia, to Pittsburgh in Pennsylvania.

On motion of Mr. LOYALL,
Resolved, That the Committee on Invalid Pensions inquire into the expediency of granting to the heirs, or legal representatives of Josiah Hopkins, a seaman, who was wounded on board the U. States sloop of war Hornet, during the late war with Great Britain, arrears of pension to which he was entitled, from the 23d March, 1815, to the 5th September, 1833.

On motion of Mr. ALLEN, of Virginia,
Resolved, That the Committee on the Judiciary be instructed to inquire into the expediency of changing the time of holding the United States Court, for the western district of Virginia, at Clarksburg.

On motion of Mr. SPEIGHT,
Resolved, That the Committee on the Post Office and Post Roads be instructed to inquire into the expediency of establishing a post road from Kingston to Greenville, North Carolina.

Mr. CLAYTON submitted the following resolution:

Resolved, That the Committee of Ways and Means inquire into the expediency of reporting a law for the purpose of remitting the duties on locomotives engines, railroad car wheels, with rolled iron tires, axles, springs, &c. already imported, or which may hereafter be imported within two years.

Mr. DENNY moved to amend the resolution by striking out the "Committee of Ways and Means" and inserting the "Committee on Manufactures."

Mr. CLAYTON was opposed to the amendment. On former occasions, similar propositions had been referred as he proposed. Any thing having relation to the imposition or remission of duties, belonged peculiarly to the Committee of Ways and Means.

Mr. DENNY conceived it irregular to send to the Committee of Ways and Means a matter affecting the industry of the country, and which properly belonged to the Committee on Manufactures. This was not strictly a proposition of revenue, and he hoped his amendment would be agreed to.

Mr. SPEIGHT was in favor of the resolution as it was originally offered. He would not impugn the motives of the members of the Committee on Manufactures, but a majority of that committee was in favor of the protective principle. The Committee of Ways and Means were charged exclusively with the care of the revenue and the manner of raising it. They would, therefore, give to the subject an impartial investigation. As had been remarked, similar references had been heretofore made, and he hoped no attempt to stifle or smother this inquiry, would prevail.

Mr. PARKER did not regard this proposition as one of revenue or finance. It was not a question whether the revenue should be reduced, but whether it was good policy to admit certain articles free of duty, and how far such a measure might affect an important branch of home industry. The question was a simple one, and from its very terms, it was evident that the inquiry properly belonged to the Committee on Manufactures.

Mr. POLK referred to the practice heretofore in similar cases, to shew that the inquiry properly belonged to the Committee of Ways and Means.

He was indifferent as to the disposition which the House might make of the proposition.

Mr. H. EVERETT, presumed that the main object of the gentleman from Georgia, was a reduction of the revenue. He referred to the former practice of the House, and the precedents cited by the gentleman from Tennessee (Mr. Polk.) They were not in point, and were generally cases where articles had been already imported, and did not look to future importations, &c.

[The further discussion of the resolution was here arrested by a call for the orders of the day.]

The SPEAKER laid before the House a letter from the Secretary of the Treasury, in response to a resolution of the House of the 11th inst. calling for information in regard to the causes which had retarded the issuing of patents to lands in the State of Louisiana; which was laid on the table.

A joint resolution directing the Secretary of State to compile and cause to be printed an Annual Register of all persons employed in the civil and military service of the United States; was read a third time and passed.

The joint resolution granting the right of way through the public property at Harper's Ferry, to the Potomac and Winchester Rail Road Company, was read a third time and passed.

The following bills were read a third time and passed, viz.

For the relief of Samuel Bragdon, David Chase, and others;

For the relief of Charles Gordon and others;

For the relief of William McLain and others;

For the relief of William P. Zantzinger;

For the relief of Silas D. Fisher;

For the relief of Tufts and Clarke;

For the relief of Humphrey B. Gwathmey;

For the relief of Robert Haile;

For the relief of the heirs of Evan Edwards;

For the relief of the heirs and representatives of William Graham;

For the relief of Samuel S. Lord;

For the relief of Samuel Hunt;

For the relief of Marcus Quincy and William Gorham of Portland;

And a bill for the relief of Francis Lasselle, and others, Michigan volunteers.

On motion of Mr. WATMOUGH, the House resolved itself into Committee of the Whole (Mr. Briggs in the Chair) on the bill to equalize and regulate the pay of the officers of the army and navy of the United States, and the amendment reported to the same by the Select Committee, to whom the bill had been re-committed, (which amendment proposed to strike out the original, and insert in lieu thereof, a bill "to regulate the pay of the Navy of the United States.")

Mr. HARPER offered an amendment to that part of the amendment which fixed the compensation of the senior Captain, when commanding a squadron, at $6,500 per annum, so as to make the allowance $4,500.

Mr. H. thought the bill calculated to pamper and compensate too highly the higher grade of officers, while many of those in a subordinate station were not competently provided for, and went at some length into the merits of the entire subject.

Mr. WATMOUGH addressed the Committee in reply, and against the amendment of his colleagues. He went into a detailed explanation of the view of the committee which reported the bill. He dwelt with emphasis on the injustice which is done to many of the officers in the Navy of the United States, by the inadequacy of their pay.

Mr. MANN, of New York, next addressed the Committee, in reply to Mr. Watmough. In the course of which he commented at length upon the whole subject. He was in favor of equalizing the pay of the officers of the army and navy; but he preferred that this should be done by reducing the compensation of the officers of the army to that of the pay given to those engaged in the naval service. He believed that the salaries generally given to those engaged in the public service ought to be reduced instead of being increased. He had no objections to a proper increase of the pay of a Captain commanding a squadron on a foreign station, but not to the extent proposed. He concluded his remarks by moving to strike out the enacting clause.

The CHAIR decided the motion out of order; but on being referred to the rule of the House by Mr. SPEIGHT, the motion was entertained.

Mr. WARD briefly opposed the proposition of his colleague, (Mr. Mann,) when it was negatived.

After a few additional remarks by Messrs. HARPER and WATMOUGH,

Mr. WAYNE said, the subject had now been brought, by the discussion which had taken place, to the notice of the House. He trusted that, even the gentleman from New-York, (Mr. Mann,) when he had time for reflection, must be convinced of the propriety of the proposed measure, and in order to give further time for an examination of the subject, he moved that the Committee rise and report progress, which was agreed to, When the House adjourned.

IN SENATE.

WEDNESDAY, Dec. 17, 1834.

Petitions and memorials were presented by Messrs. TYLER, CLAYTON, ROBBINS, and PORTER.

The following bills from the House of Representatives were read the first time, and referred to the appropriate committees:

A joint resolution directing the Secretary of State to compile and cause to be printed an Annual Register of all persons employed in the civil and military service of the United States.

The joint resolution granting the right of way through the public property at Harper's Ferry, to the Potomac and Winchester Rail Road Company.

A bill for the relief of Samuel Bragdon, David Chase, and others;

For the relief of Charles Gordon and others;

For the relief of William McLain and others;

For the relief of William P. Zantzinger;

For the relief of Silas D. Fisher;

For the relief of Tufts and Clarke;

For the relief of Humphrey B. Gwathmey;

For the relief of Robert Haile;

For the relief of the heirs of Evan Edwards;

For the relief of the heirs and representatives of William Graham;

For the relief of Samuel S. Lord;

For the relief of Samuel Huntt;

For the relief of Marcus Quincy and William Gorham, of Portland;

And a bill for the relief of Francis Lasselle, and others, Michigan volunteers.

A bill to define the claims to land in Louisiana and Territory of Arkansas, was read a second time and referred to the Committee on Public Lands.

The bill to allow further time to complete the issuing and location of military land warrants during the late war, was also read a second time, and referred to the Committee on Public Lands.

Mr. POINDEXTER, from the Committee on Public Lands, reported a bill to provide for the legal adjudication of claims to lands therein mentioned.

Mr. POINDEXTER, on leave given, introduced the following bills, which were read twice and committed:

A bill for the relief of Calvin Smith,

A bill for the relief of Elizabeth Magruder,

A bill for the relief of Andrew Knox.

Mr. KING, of Alabama, on leave given, introduced a bill for the relief of Thomas Rhoads and Jeremiah Austen—read twice and committed.

Also a bill making an appropriation to complete a road from Lyme Creek to Chatahoochie—read twice and committed.

Mr. BELL, on leave given, introduced a bill for the relief of Peter H. Green; read twice and committed.

Mr. BENTON. from the Committee on Military Affairs, reported a bill for the relief of J. and W. Besson and others.

The following resolution submitted yesterday by Mr. CLAYTON, was considered and adopted.

Resolved, That the Committee on the Judiciary be instructed to inquire into the expediency of providing by law for the payment of a salary to the Marshal of the Delaware District.

Mr. SOUTHARD, on leave given, introduced bill for the completion of certain improvements in Florida; read twice and committed.

Mr. WEBSTER then moved that the Senate proceed to the consideration of the bill to make compensation for

FRENCH SPOLIATIONS.

On American Commerce, prior to 1800; which was agreed to.

Mr. WEBSTER said, that this subject had been so often before the Senate, and he trusted it was so well understood, that he should not repeat what he had said on a former occasion in regard to it. The case had been fully investigated before, and several reports had been made upon the merits of the claims proposed to be compensated, accompanied by various documents, statements, and estimates; these had been printed, and were familiar to the members of the Senate. At the last session, he entered into an examination of these claims, but he did-not intend to go at length into the subject now. He would only state, in very few words, an outline of the grounds on which the claims rested. The bill proposed to make satisfaction to an amount not exceeding five millions of dollars, for seizures, captures, and sequestrations, upon American commerce prior to the year 1800. The bill supposed, in the first place, that illegal seizures and captures were made on the vessels and property of the citizens of the United States before 1800. Secondly, that these acts of wrong were committed by such authors, and under such circumstances, as gave to the sufferers the right to demand indemnity therefor from France. The bill assumed one other position, and that was, that all such claims had an equity upon the United States, which called upon the Government of the United States to give them indemnity. These were the grounds on which the bill was framed. That many aggressions, confiscations, and acts of wrong, had been committed upon the property of the citizens of the United States, there was no doubt; and that they were committed under circumstances which gave them the right to claim from the French Government indemnification, was also doubtless. There were only two questions then presented. One was, on what question was it that the Government of the United States was answerable for the indemnity for wrongs committed prior to 1800. And the other was, to what extent were the United States bound. The answer to the first question was, because, by a treaty between the United States and France for a consideration valuable to the United States, the Government of the U. States discharged the Government of France from all liability for this indemnity. It went upon the ground of disputes arising between the parties, of a negotiation ratified, and ultimately of an offset of the respective claims, one against the other, and thus merging them forever—in short, that the result was, the treaty of commerce of 1798. There was a report some years ago upon this subject, giving this short view of it. It was then urged that the claim was worthless, by the operation of time, which gave no hope of indemnity from France, and under the accumulation of these objections, there was no hope, even if the Government had not released them, and therefore the Government ought not to pay them. But Mr. W. contended, we had advanced too far, at this time, to urge this hypothesis. Other claims, no less valid than these were, had been pressed upon France, and she had stipulated to pay, in satisfaction of them, twenty-five millions of francs. It had never been compensated out of this fund, because they had been released. Under the late treaty, a board of commissioners had been established to ascertain the extent and validity of the claims contemplated under its provisions, and the board had determined that this class of claims had no right to be paid out of that fund, but only those subsequent to 1800. These, Mr. W. said, were the claims. The United States had relinquished them and by this act of the Government, the citizens of the United States injured by it, had no right to apply to the Government of France for indemnity, not to be paid out of the twenty-five millions. The other question was, as to the amount. It might be asked, how we could fix the five millions. His answer was, that the amount in the bill, estimating the number of captures and con-

fiscations, vessels seized, burnt, and destroyed, compared with the claims against France, showed, did not meet the real amount due. But he did not wish or intend to go into a discussion of the bill at length, nor would he do so, unless a debate ensued which rendered it necessary.

Mr. TYLER said, that the subject was of great importance, both as regarded the amount involved in the bill and the principles involved in it. He had investigated it to some extent, and had come to the conclusion that the claimants had so just claim. He had listened attentively to the argument of the honorable member from Massachusetts, and however capable he was of stating his opinions and convictions on a question of law, he had not yet convinced him of his error on this subject. But he was not prepared to discuss the question now. I went back to the year 1796, and embraced a period up to 1800—he must therefore look into history of the times of that period. There had been repeatedly urged at that very time, one minister after another, of our Government upon France—every duty of pressing them had been discharged by this Government to every of its citizens. But the main ground upon which the claims rested, was, that we had entered into a convention with France, by which they were deprived of—this was the whole amount of it, and himself, he could not distinguish it from any ordinary treaty of peace. How could any American citizen come here and ask compensation because the Government of the United States compromised his claim by a treaty of peace? Well might an individual whose property had been captured by a British cruiser during the late war, come here and demand to be retributed for it, because his claim had been compromised by treaty of peace at Ghent. But there was another consideration. The best part of these claims went to the insurance companies, and if we were bound to retribute them for their losses, we were entitled to receive a share of their profits—premiums, it was well known, were recovered. He would like to see the account stated fairly—we take the losses, let us take the profits. T. said, he was willing thus to strike the balance for the most immense profits were made at that period, in trade; but he did not intend to argue the question; his design was simply to awaken attention to the subject.

Mr. BENTON said he was pleased to see the gentleman from Virginia (Mr. Tyler) opened the debate upon the true grounds—principle involved, and the amount approved in the bill. During 14 years that he (Mr. B.) had the honor of a seat on this floor, or rather during 10 years of that time, he had narrowly raised this bill. He had been constantly assisted by some gentlemen, competent to the task, would justice to it, and place the subject before American People in the point of view it ought to be placed. He (Mr. B.) had not had time to look into the question. We had a volume of 600 pages laid on our tables some years which was only an epitome,—no, it was not epitome, for that term implied that the whole subject was brought out, but it was only a small exhibition of the case, the papers being selected by the agent. Then reports had been made on the subject. He meant nothing unkind in that to them, but they had come forward, not in the form framed upon this ex parte document. He did complain of it; but he thought there ought to be a minority which should go into the whole matter. The Committee who reported the bill were composed of five, three of whom were in favor of the claim. One gentleman (Mr. Preston,) was not here, and the other (Mr. dy,) was literally swamped in the business of Post Office, from which he did not expect to be relieved until the middle of February. The committee was so framed as that it was impossible to bring the subject before the country. He (Mr. B.) had not time to examine it now, but if time was not to be galloped through at once, he would take it up, and try to make himself master of it. It was very glad the honorable gentleman from Virginia (Mr. Tyler,) had turned his attention to it. Mr. B. said his own convictions were strong.

ought not to pass, and he should feel himself culpable and regardless of the interests of his
country, if he omitted to give it his attention. The
so to which the claims related were not limited
1793, but went back to '76; they were not
used to acts of the revolutionary Government,
would include any that could be trumped up
under Louis XVI, or the first year of the consulate.
as there ever an instance of such an illimitable
it! It went back to the time when there
ght be a citizen of the United States, and the
or was opened as widely as possible for the admission of claims. Language could not be looser
in the phraseology of the bill. Was there any
of seizure, or capture, or of confiscation,
in '76, which could not be paid under this bill?
cases under which it was alleged compensa-
ly could be made, were widely different
in the last treaty with France. The claims un-
that treaty were ascertained by the negotiators
the utmost possible precision. 1st. For com-
mation for vessels seized at St. Sebastian, which
been invited there by the French General
ervenot, commanding.' 2d. For captures made
for the Berlin decree, before that decree was
wn. 3d. For captures made after its revoca-
and 4th, for vessels burnt at sea, to prevent
information of the movements of the French fleet,
being communicated to the British. But,
B. said, he did not rise now to go into the
but if the bill was not to be galloped
through, he begged to say, that he had some facts,
as to its principles and details, which he wish-
to lay before the Senate.

Mr. PRESTON said, that as the honorable gen-
man from Missouri had alluded to him in his re-
ks, he felt bound to say a word in explanation.
would be glad if that gentleman, and the hon-
member from Virginia, (Mr. Tyler,) would
a thorough investigation to this subject. He,
[Mr. P.,] had been placed on the committee, he
pered, in some sort, by accident, perhaps be-
be came from a section of country known to
opposed to extravagant expenditures of the
money. He had investigated the docu-
to which the gentleman alluded, and the
ble report of Mr. Livingston on the subject,
had formed his opinion of the merits of the
claims from them. He took the only report
was against them, and gave the whole his
ded attention, as a friend desirous of sup-
ng them. He had found them altogether un-
The amount of the claim was an obsta-
its passage, but he did view that as of any
quence, compared with the principle involv-
Whether it was five millions or five hundred
it made no difference with him. If the
or honesty of the nation was impli-
he cared not how much of blood or
it might cost, he would support it, whe-
it was for claims anterior or subsequent to
Many of these claimants were his consti-
widows and children, and therefore he felt
dly disposition towards them. But there
dangerous and delicate questions involved
which required deliberate and close atten-
The he was not able to give it now. As
led the treaty of '98, by which these claims
compromised, he did not consider them
tened by that act. We were willing to
given three times the amount specified in this
have bought ourselves from the trammels
treaty.

BENTON replied, that the gentleman from
Carolina (Mr. Preston) thought the magni-
of the claims presented an obstacle to the
of the bill. He believed that when that
an had more experience here, the course
legislation would convince him that it was
of vast magnitude which were most suc-
l, that precisely in proportion to the mass,
mentum was increased—its chance of get-
through was enhanced. It was the millions
rolled along rapidly, while the small claims
arrested and laid by in the mass of unfinish-
ness. When the honorable member had
as long here as he (Mr. B.) had been, he
not be surprised at what he now said. The
from South Carolina had alluded to Mr.
gston's report on the subject. And al-

though he, Mr. B. had the greatest respect for
that gentleman's talents and honor, yet in money
matters, he was a child. This claim, said Mr. B.
is in reality owned by assignees, who bought from
the original claimants for a few cents in the dollar, or insurers, who received their premium for
all the vessels they insured, whether lost or saved;
and is the United States to turn insurer for them,
and pay for every vessel lost. The Senator from
South Carolina (Mr. Preston) said, there were
widows and orphans in his State, who were claimants. Mr. B. said, the old certificate funding act
of '91 was plead in the name of old soldiers, who
had sold to speculators at two and six pence in
the pound, and to whom Congress voted thirty
shillings in the pound. The magnitude of this
claim was carrying it along, Mr. B. said, as the magnitude of the assumption bill carried that, for 25
millions; and the magnitude of the certificate
funding bill carried it. They got through immediately, while Amy Dardes's horse, at $150, did
not get through until forty years. He was opposed to voting millions to speculators, who buy
claims for a trifle on the Government; he would not
make the Federal Government insure the insurers.
He would resist this bill, though he might have
to study the folio volume of 1000 pages, which
contained its history; he would not be restricted
to the ex-parte document, compiled under the
direction of the agent; as he had been informed;
but would look to the whole case. He would defend the Treasury from this enormous attack upon it. He would do battle for his country, and
call upon others to help.

Mr. SHEPLEY said he had been alluded to as
a member of the Committee which had reported
this bill, that as he had never before been on this
committee, it would be readily supposed that he
had made up his opinion hastily on the subject.
But that he had, previous to the meeting of the
Senate, examined this question, not as a committee man, but as a Senator, in which capacity he expected to be called upon to act, and had prepared
himself accordingly. He had not come with materials for the fight; he had copies of the documents before him, from an examination of which
he had drawn his conclusions. But he could show-
the Senate how he had examined and where he
had found his materials. From sources of undoubted authority, from the printed documents
of this government, he had drawn his conclusions
and come to the conviction that those claims were
just and ought to be satisfied by this country.—
These claims against France were good and might
have been recovered of that government; that
they were worth as much as those for which we
had obtained indemnities from Spain, Denmark,
and other governments; that they were regarded
so in our negotiations with France. That if they
had been urged with the same perseverance, as
our claims upon other nations and under other circumstances have been, reparation would have been
made by France. But why were these claims neglected, why not pressed by this government till
allowed? The reason is obvious; because France set
up claims against us, claims, which we were bound
by solemn obligation to allow. We had guarantied to France her possessions in West India, in
the 11th article of the treaty, wherein she had
bound herself to obtain for us independence; also
other claims under the 17th and 22d articles of the
treaty of commerce. We had failed to fulfil
these stipulations; we had shrunk from the contest,
and left France to be robbed of her possession,
without raising a finger in her behalf. For these
infractions, France justly claimed of us some remuneration, some offset for the neglect of her interests and the losses she had sustained thereby.
She offered, nay, she urged the United States to
appoint a commission to investigate these claims,
and was ready to pay, to the utmost farthing, all
that could be justly brought against her. But
then she claimed of us more than the sum of our
claims upon her. The United States offered to
compensate her, if she would accept of 5,000,000
francs, for a release of our obligations under the
11th article of the treaty of alliance; but she would
not accept it, but offered to receive 10,000,000,
which we refused. But these claims of France
were finally set off against the claims of our citizens,

and thus the United States, in releasing France,
has bound herself to discharge the claims that our
citizens had upon France.

Mr. S. said, that it had been urged that the
opinions of the friends of this bill, had been
formed upon partial views of the subject. But
if the gentlemen wish for the proof, he could
show from official documents the facts to which
he alluded. He did not believe that official documents of this government presented too directly opposite and contradictory propositions. He relied on the documents—did not rise with a design
to enter into an examination of them page by
page and section by section, but would refer those
gentlemen, who were desirous of investigating
this subject, to them for proof of all he had advanced, and was willing to exhibit these proofs
from the public documents on to-morrow, or at
any other time when it should be the pleasure of
the Senate to hear him.

On motion of Mr. WEBSTER, the Senate adjourned.

HOUSE OF REPRESENTATIVES.

WEDNESDAY, DEC. 17, 1834.

Petitions and memorials were presented by—
Messrs. JARVIS and HALL, of Maine.

[Mr. JARVIS presented the petition of the Medical Faculty in the District of Columbia, on the
subject of certain low and marshy grounds in the
city of Washington, belonging to the General Government, which are deemed detrimental to the
health of the city—praying that Congress should
take such measures as may remedy the evil. The
petition was referred to the Committee on the
Public Buildings.]

Mr. REED, of Massachusetts.
Mr. PEARCE, of Rhode Island.
Messrs. WHITE, BEARDSLEY, PAGE, FER-
RIS, CAMBRELENG, and WARDWELL, of
New York.
Mr. HEATH, of Maryland.
Messrs. CHINN and PATTON, of Virginia.
Messrs. TOMPKINS, LYON, POPE, and
BEATY, of Kentucky.

[Mr. POPE again presented the petition of Robert G. Chappell, praying compensation for destruction of property, &c.: which was referred to
the Committee on Indian Affairs.]

Messrs. FORESTER and BELL, (SPEAKER,)
of Tennessee.
Mr. PATTERSON, of Ohio.
Mr. THOMAS, of Louisiana.
Mr. EWING, of Indiana.
Mr. CAGE, of Mississippi.
Messrs. MAY and REYNOLDS, of Illinois.

[Mr. REYNOLDS presented a memorial of the
Legislature of Illinois, praying that certain grants
of lands may be made to individuals, founded upon cultivation, and heads of families, &c.

Upon presenting the above mentioned memorial, Mr. R. said:

Mr. SPEAKER, I present to this House a memorial from the General Assembly of the State of Illinois. This memorial contains some cases of ancient settlers in Illinois, praying a confirmation to
certain land claims. These persons emigrated to
Illinois and became citizens of that country between the years 1780 and 1790. They also improved the soil to such extent as to entitle them
to an improvement right, so called, of 400 acres,
under the acts and resolves of Congress, and the
cession act of the State of Virginia. The Virginia cession act passed in the year 1784, and the
last act of Congress passed in 1791—all recognising and confirming those individuals in their possessions and rights, who improved and cultivated
the soil. These settlers resided in the country
between those dates, and made improvements,
and were, as I conceive, entitled to a confirmation
of their claims of 400 acres to each individual.

The Governor of the then Territories, Northwestern, and Indiana, who were authorised by
various acts of Congress to adjust these claims to
land, did not grant to each person named in this
memorial, who was by the Governor's own acts
entitled to such grant, the full quantity of 400
acres; and to obtain the balance of the 400 acres,
is the prayer of this memorial, and that of your
humble servant.

I personally know these claimants, and know them to be entitled in justice and equity to the quantity of land to make up to each the 400 acres.]

Which memorials and petitions were appropriately referred.

Mr. ASHLEY, by consent, submitted the following resolution:

Resolved, That bills Nos. 168 and 174, providing for the extension of the Cumberland road from Vandalia, Illinois, to the seat of Government of Missouri, be made the special order of the day for Thursday the 15th January next.

A count being called for on the adoption of the resolution—

Mr. ASHLEY said he hoped the proposition would receive the assent of the House. The subject to which his resolution had reference, had been long before the House, and in justice to the part of the country most interested, it should be disposed of. He had asked that it should be made the special order for the 15th January, in order to afford gentlemen time to examine it, and if they thought proper, to oppose it. Were he to ask the House to take up immediately some bill relating to fortifications or harbors, it would probably not be opposed, by those who now object to the consideration some thirty days hence, of a bill of the utmost importance to the section of country from whence he came.

The resolution was then agreed to—yeas 74, nays 50.

Mr. PEARCE, from the Committee on Commerce, reported a bill making an appropriation for a Custom House in the town of Newbern, North Carolina; which was read twice and committed.

The following resolution, submitted yesterday by Mr. CLAYTON, was taken up:

Resolved, That the Committee of Ways and Means inquire into the expediency of reporting a law for the purpose of remitting the duties on locomotive engines, railroad car wheels, with rolled iron tires, axles, springs, &c., already imported, or which may hereafter be imported within two years.

The question being on Mr. DENNY'S resolution to amend the resolution so as to substitute the Committee on Manufactures for the Committee of Ways and Means,

Mr. DICKERSON, of N. J. said, that at the first view of this subject he had been impressed with the belief that it properly belonged to the Committee of Ways and Means; but upon mature deliberation, he was convinced, it was more appropriately referable to the Committee on Manufactures. If the object (said Mr. D.) was to inquire whether the duties, which are already paid into the Treasury on Locomotive Engines were to be refunded, then it might be a proper subject for the Committee of Ways and Means. But, this is not the state of the question. It will not be contested here that it would come within the purview of the duties of that Committee to inquire what effect the abolition of these duties will have on our internal improvements, or our domestic industry. Yet, this is the very subject of investigation. It is not to inquire what effect the measure may have on the state of the Treasury—but on the object just alluded to; and also to ascertain how far our country has advanced in her improvements in these great objects. And, I apprehend, (said Mr. D.) the honorable chairman of the Committee of Ways and Means will be somewhat disappointed by the result of this investigation. Mr. D. concluded by reiterating his conviction that the subject should be referred to the Committee on Manufactures.

Mr. MASON of Va. said, this was a mere question of reference, although it had been argued as though the fate of the proposition was involved in the inquiry. He referred to the relative duties of the two committees, and contended that the subject peculiarly belonged to the Committee of Ways and Means. The proposition was one which regarded revenue. The Secretary of the Treasury had furnished estimates of the amount of accruing revenue to be derived from duties. The proposition before the House, proposed to allow a drawback on certain articles included in the Treasury estimate, and to admit them free of duty hereafter. It was, therefore, certainly the province of the Committee of Ways and Means to examine the subject. He could see no ground whatever for sending this inquiry to the Committee on Manufactures, and as propositions of a similar character had, at the last session been sent to the Committee of Ways and Means, he hoped the amendment would not prevail.

Mr. CLAYTON said, that the adoption of the amendment would, in effect, defeat his proposition. It was the duty of the House to take care of all the great interests of the country. For this purpose, there were committees of different grades, and who had the care of particular interests. The present was a proposition peculiarly affecting the great agricultural class of the country. We had a Committee on Agriculture, and yet we are asked to send this inquiry to the Committee on Manufactures. Were he to propose to send this subject to the former committee, he would be told that it was improper it should go to a committee who had the care of agriculture, and were interested, but he was denied this argument in reference to the Committee on Manufactures; and thus the great agricultural interest must knock at the door of the Committee on Manufactures for relief. What chance would there be for success from such a quarter? Some of the manufacturers, he believed, would rather have their eye-teeth drawn, than to submit to the loss of the profit on a four-penny nail. The Committee of Ways and Means, having the care of the revenue, was the proper one to judge between the two interests alluded to. The Government cannot do without revenue, and it was for the committee charged with that subject to examine how far the proposed measure would affect the finances of the country. He trusted that the amendment would not be adopted.

Mr. DENNY referred to the precedents of the last session, and contended that they were not similar to the present proposition. In the cases which had been referred to, the articles had already been imported, and the duties were either paid into or secured by the Treasury. It was proposed to remit those duties, and as a subject merely of revenue they were referred to the Committee of Ways and Means. The present proposition proposed a wider range; it went not merely to remit the duties on articles already imported, but to abolish the duties altogether on future importations, and thus to change the tariff, which was understood to be settled by compromise, for some time to come. But the gentleman from Georgia, (Mr. Clayton,) had spoken of this proposition as one of agriculture. There had been no memorial from the agricultural interest on the subject, nor had it been recommended by the Committee on Agriculture. It was then merely the application of an individual member. The gentleman believed that the manufacturers would rather have their eye-teeth drawn, than submit to the loss of the profit on a four penny nail, there were perhaps others, who would rather see the Union dissolved, than submit to pay a duty on a *British* four-penny nail, though at the same time an important branch of home industry was thereby fostered and encouraged.

Mr. SPEIGHT said, if this was a question involving the quantum of protection necessary to particular articles of manufacture, he might agree with the gentleman from Pennsylvania (Mr. Denny) that it should go to the Committee on Manufactures; but this was a question of quite a different nature. It proposed to allow a drawback on certain articles imported, and to permit others to be imported free of duty. It was a question affecting the revenue of the country. This was not the first time, when the question of jurisdiction had been raised, when a proposition had been offered affecting the peculiar interests of his constituents. As an agricultural community, his constituents labored under heavy disadvantages in carrying their articles to market, and he asked whether their grievances were to be entirely disregarded in order to favor the manufacturing interests? This doctrine ought not to prevail in a government of equality and justice. The gentleman from Pennsylvania (Mr. Denny) had referred to a certain compromise tariff act. He was not disposed to disturb it, and it was a measure which gave good grounds to the gentleman from Pennsylvania to rejoice.

If, however, in the progress of events, it became apparent that any part of that act, operated with undue oppression, it was certainly proper, that it should undergo revision, and amendment. Mr. S. read from the journal of last session, to show that on several occasions, subjects of a like nature to the present, had been referred, without objection to the Committee of Ways and Means, and that bills had been reported and passed in conformity to the recommendations of that committee. These bills, however, were intended to benefit a different section of the country. No question of jurisdiction was then raised. In the course of six years service in this House, he believed the universal practice had been to send all questions involving a reduction of duties, to the Committee of Ways and Means.

Mr. STEWART, said that upon this resolution of inquiry, it seemed the subject of the Tariff was to undergo a general discussion. If the gentleman from North Carol'na, (Mr. Speight,) desired that the compromise act, as it was called, should be repealed, he should have his hearty concurrence. If this subject was to be discussed on isolated points, he would ask, where would it end? The present proposition was said to involve the interests of agriculture. If so, why not extend it, and propose to abolish the duty on ploughs and harrows? In order to arrest what he conceived a most unnecessary discussion, and to test the disposition of the House on the subject, he moved to lay the resolution on the table.

Mr. CLAYTON demanded the yeas and nays, which were ordered, and were as follows:

YEAS—Messrs. J. Q. Adams, John Adams, H. Allen, William Allen, Joseph B. Anthony, J. Ba[...] Charles A. Barnitz, William Baylies, Martin Be[...] Andrew Beaumont, John Blair, Abraham Bo[...] John W. Brown, George Burd, Tristam Bu[...] George Chambers, John Chaney, Thomas C[...] William Clark, Richard Coulter, John Cr[...] David Crockett, Edward Darlington, Amos D[...] Harmar Denny, John Dickson, Philemon Dickson, George Evans, Edward Everett, Ho[...] Everett, Millard Fillmore, John B. Forester, [...] C. Fuller, Benjamin Gorham, George Grennell, Hiland Hall, Nicoll Halsey, Gideon Hard, Benj[...] Hardin, Samuel G. Hathaway, Abner Hazel[...] James P. Heath, Joseph Henderson, W[...] Hiester, Ebenezer Jackson, Henry F. Janes, [...]liam Cost Johnson, Cave Johnson, Henry Jo[...] Gerrit Y. Lansing, Thomas Lee, Chittenden L[...] Joel K. Mann, Henry C. Martindale, Rufus [...]tire, Thos. M. T. McKennan, Isaac McKim, Ch[...] McVean, Jesse Miller, Robert Mitchell, Jo[...] Morgan, Henry A. Muhlenberg, Gayton P. [...]good, James Parker, William Patterson, Dut[...] Pearce, Stephen C. Phillips, Job Pierson, P[...] H. Pope, David Potts, jr., Robert Ramsay, [...] Reed, Ferdinand S. Schenck, William N. S[...] William Slade, Jonathan Sloane, Francis [...] Smith, James Standifer, John N. Steele, An[...] Stewart, Philemon Thomas, John Thomson, [...] Turner, Samuel Tweedy, Isaac B. Van Ho[...] Samuel F. Vinton, David D. Wagener, [...] Ward, John G. Watmough, Taylor Webster, [...]erick Whittlesey, Elisha Whittlesey—92.

NAYS—Messrs. John J. Allen, Chilton [...] William S. Archer, Noyes Barber, Daniel L. [...]ringer, James M. H. Beale, Benning M. [...] Samuel Beardsley, Horace Binney, Geo[...] Briggs, John Bull, Samuel Bunch, Jesse A. B[...] Harry Cage, C. C. Cambreleng, Robert B. C[...]bell, Richard B. Carmichael, John Carr, [...] Casey, Joseph W. Chinn, Nath. H. C[...] Samuel Clark, Clement C. Clay, Augus[...] Clayton, William K. Clowney, John Coffee, [...] W. Connor, Thomas Corwin, Joseph H. [...] Thomas Davenport, Rowland Day, Edmun[...]berry, David W. Dickinson, William C. D[...] John Ewing, John M. Felder, Charles G. [...] Thomas F. Foster, William K. Fuller, J[...] Fulton, Roger L. Gamble, James H. G[...] Ransom H. Gillet, William F. Gordon, Ja[...]ham, William J. Grayson, John K. Griffin, [...] Hall, Thomas H. Hall, Edward A. H[...] Joseph M. Harper, Micajah T. Hawkins, [...]

Bowers, Edward Howell, Henry Hubbard, Abel Huntington, William M. Inge, William Jackson, Jabez W. Jarvis, Richard M. Johnson, Noadiah Johnson, Seaborn Jones, Edward Kavanagh, Daniel Kilgore, Henry King, George L. Kinnard, Amos Lane, Luke Lea, Dixon H. Lewis, Levi Lincoln, Gideon Love, George Loyall, Abijah Mann, jr., Edward J. Manning, Samuel W. Mardis, John Y. Mason, Moses Mason, jr., William L. May, Jonathan M cCarty, William McComas, John McKinley, Isaac McKim, F. Mercer, Phineas Miner, Henry Mitchell, Samuel McD. Moore, John Murphy, Sherman Page, Gorham Parks, Balie Peyton, Franklin Pierce, Henry L. Pinckney, James K. Polk, Abraham Rencher, John Reynolds, John Roberts on, Augus'e H. Shepperd, David Spangler, Isaac Southard, John T. Stoddert, William Taylor, Francis Thomas, Christo. Tompkins, Joseph Trumbull, Joseph Vance, Daniel Wardwell, Campbell P. White, Lewis Williams, Henry A. Wise—108.

So the House refused to lay the resolution on the table.

Mr. CHAMBERS then took the floor in support of referring the inquiry directed by the resolution, to the Committee on Manufactures, but after he concluded his remarks, the hour devoted to the discussion of resolutions had expired, and the House proceeded to the

ORDERS OF THE DAY.

The engrossed bill to extend the time for issuing Military Land Warrants to officers and soldiers of the revolutionary war, was read a third time and passed.

The House then resolved itself into a Committee of the Whole on the state of the Union on the bill reported by the Select Committee, of which Mr. WATMOUGH is Chairman, to equalize and reduce the pay of the officers of the Navy—Mr. BIGGS in the Chair.

The question being on the amendment offered by Mr. HARPER of Pa., to strike out the sum $5,500, as the compensation of a senior Captain commanding a squadron, and insert $4,500:

Mr. WATMOUGH regretted that it had been deemed necessary to make any motion for the amendment of this bill. If gentlemen would reflect deliberately on the subject, he felt assured they would convince themselves that such amendments were inexpedient. He dwelt upon the justice of allowing our naval officers a pay more adequate to their services, and such as should render them capable of supporting the honor and dignity of their country abroad, and the wants and necessities of their families at home. They, in the view of their duties, necessarily often come in contact with those of similar grade in European navies, and they are bound, by all those obligations prompting the honor of themselves and their country, to reciprocate those courtesies which are extended to an intercourse in civilized life. He did not remind the committee of the dangers and privations of a sailor's life—his struggles with the elements, and his noble daring, both in the tropics and the hyperborean seas. All this was well known. Mr. W. said this was a mere matter of fact, and not a subject for pictorial declamation. He therefore would conclude by expressing the hope, that it would not be deemed necessary to make any material amendment to the bill. With these brief remarks, he would leave the subject to the liberality and magnanimity of the committee.

Mr. SPEIGHT inquired if the bill, as reported by the Select Committee, did not, in some cases, lessen the pay of officers, as well as increase it in others?

Mr. WATMOUGH replied, and was understood to say there was, in effect, no reduction contemplated by the bill.

Mr. FILLMORE said, it appeared from the documents on the table, that when this subject was first introduced there, it embraced a proposition to equalize the pay of the officers of both the army and the navy. It now seemed that the committee had abandoned the subject of the pay of the army, and confined themselves to the navy. He had formerly been introduced by the committee, embracing both of these interests, but was now thrown aside, as he understood the matter, and this substituted in its place. Had we

gone on, and passed that bill (said Mr. F.,) we should have increased the pay of the officers of the army about $70,000, and that of the navy about $163,000. After some further structure on the present bill, Mr. F. concluded by expressing the necessity of supporting the amendment of his colleague, (Mr. Harper,) unless more reasons should be given for the present terms of the bill than had yet been advanced.

Mr. WATMOUGH again replied. He said it was true the committee had abandoned the equalization bill, from a conviction, both on the part of the committee and of the Department, of its utter impracticability. In the minds of the members of the Select Committee, that point had been definitively settled. To do away with emoluments in the army, was, in effect, to destroy its efficiency. In reporting the present bill, the committee had begun with the highest pay, at $5500, and gone down by regular and equitable gradation.

Mr. CONNOR said, I am for paying the officers of both the army and the navy well. They fight well—let us pay them well. I am for giving them an equitable—a liberal compensation; and I would also be willing they should be enabled to lay up something for their old age. But (said Mr. C.) let us not go too far, nor too fast. He thought this was too great a lift at one movement. To increase a salary, at once, from $2500 to $5500, was more than he could sanction. He was constrained to go for the amendment.

Mr. WARD supported the bill as reported. He said while various changes and modifications had been made in the arrangements of the army, none had taken place in the navy—which now remained as it was when first organized, and had been in every respect, most culpably neglected. He asked gentlemen to look at the changes and advances which had been made in the salaries of the officers of our Government. That of the Secretaries of State, &c. were, at its organization, $3500; they are now $6000 per annum. He did not complain of this increase—the state of the country demanded it—but did deprecate the principle which left our gallant naval officers with such inadequate compensation. If we would have our Government well administered, we should pay its officers with liberality. He asked, should this only free Government on earth—the only nation untrammelled with debt, show a niggardly and penurious disposition in recompensing its public servants? English and French Admirals's he declared, received $10,000 per annum, while we hesitate to give ours five! He contended that out of this sum it would be impossible for the officer to save more than a bare support for his family at home. He believed there was not an American citizen, however humble, who would not feel himself degraded did he believe that the officer bearing the proud flag of his country, did not reciprocate those civilities extended to him in a foreign port. Mr. W. declared his conviction, that there was not an officer in our service who had not received a large fortune by inheritance, who possessed a dollar to bequeath to his children! He hoped the amendment would not prevail.

Mr. SUTHERLAND followed in a speech of some length and energy. He said he was in favor of the advocate of our gallant navy as the gentleman who last addressed the committee (Mr. Ward,) or any other individual. He would not advocate the interest of the army against the navy, nor those of the navy against the army. They were the two great arms of the national defence, and he equally esteemed and respected both. But he stood here as the advocate of a class of men whom he conceived to be unfairly dealt by in the bill before the committee. He referred to gunners, whose pay, he contended, would be decreased by the passage of the bill as reported. He proceeded at length to advocate the claims of those fighting men in our gallant navy, whose rights he deemed to be neglected. He expressed his determination to vote for a reduction of the high officers, unless those of petty officers were correspondingly raised.

Mr. WATMOUGH explained, and Mr. SUTHERLAND briefly rejoined.

Mr. PARKER thought this discussion entirely

out of place. He wished to propose an amendment, by striking out all from the fifth to the tenth line, but this was decided not then to be in order.

After some few remarks from Messrs. FILLMORE and WARD, the question was taken on the amendment of Mr. HARPER, and carried—ayes 90, nays 55.

Mr. WATMOUGH then submitted a series of amendments graduating the pay of the other officers so as to correspond with the reduction in the pay of Captains by this vote decided on.

Mr. WISE also submitted an amendment, and after some further remarks from Mr. WATMOUGH, calling the attention of the committee to the nature and necessity of his amendments—

On motion of Mr. SPEIGHT, the committee rose, reported progress, and obtained leave to sit again.

When the Speaker again resumed the Chair, it was, on motion of Mr. WATMOUGH,

Ordered, That the amendments offered in committee, be printed for the use of the House.

And then, on motion of Mr. BRIGGS,

The House adjourned.

IN SENATE.

Thursday, December 18, 1834.

Petitions and memorials were presented by Mr. McKEAN and Mr. HENDRICKS.

Mr. SOUTHARD, from the Naval Committee, reported the following bills, to wit:

A bill for the relief of the legal representatives of Michael Hagan, deceased;

A bill for the relief of the heirs and legal representatives of Henry Eckford, deceased;

A bill concerning the commanding officers of the Navy of the United States;

A bill for the relief of Joseph Baldwin;

A bill for the relief of Henry B. Tyler;

A bill for the relief of the legal representatives of Isaac Garretson, deceased;

A bill to change the titles of certain officers in the Navy of the United States;

A bill providing for the enlistment of boys in the Navy of the United States;

A bill to regulate the issuing of licenses to vessels navigated in whole or in part by steam.

Mr. HIBB, on leave given, introduced the following bills:

A bill for the relief of Pierre Menard;

A bill for the relief of Joseph Bogey;

A bill for the relief of Antonie Peltier;

A bill to reduce the postage on periodical pamphlets, and to extend the franking privilege to the head of the Engineer Department.

The said bills were read twice and referred.

Mr. HENDRICKS, from the Committee on Roads and Canals, reported a bill making an appropriation for the improvement of the Wabash.

Mr. WEBSTER, from the Committee on Finance, reported a bill to exempt certain merchandise from the operation of the tariff of 1828, under certain circumstances.

Also, a bill for the relief of the owners of the brig Despatch.

Mr. WAGGAMAN, on leave given, introduced a bill making an appropriation to complete the military barracks at New Orleans; which was read twice and referred.

Mr. TYLER, from the Committee on Finance of last session, who were directed by a resolution of the Senate to investigate the condition of the

BANK OF THE UNITED STATES,

Made a report of great length, the reading of which occupied two hours and a half.

A motion being made to print it, Mr. BENTON rose, not to object to the printing, nor to go into an argument in answer to the report, which would come more properly at another time, but to correct some errors which claimed his attention. His own name was made to figure in that report, in very good company to be sure, that of President Jackson, Vice President Van Buren, and Senator Grundy. It seems that we have all, said Mr. B., been detected in something that deserves exposure,—in the offence of aiding our respective constituents, or fellow-citizens, in obtaining branches

banks to be located in our respective States; and upon this detection, the assertion is made that these branches were not extended to these States for political effect, when the charter was nearly run out, but in good faith, and upon our application, to aid the business of the country. Mr. B. said, it was true that he had forwarded a petition from the merchants of St. Louis, about 1826 or '27, soliciting a branch at that place; and he had accompanied it by a letter, as he had been requested to do, sustaining and supporting their request; and bearing the testimony to their characters as men of business and property which the occasion and the truth required. He did this for merchants who were his political enemies, and he did it readily and cordially, as a representative ought to act for his constituents, whether they are for him, or against him, in the elections. So far so good; but the allegation of the report is, that the branch at St. Louis was established upon *this* petition, and *this* letter, and therefore was not established with political views, but purely and simply for business purposes. Now, said Mr. B., I have a question to put to the Senator from Virginia, (Mr. Tyler,) who has made the report for the committee: It is this: whether the President or Directors of the Bank had informed him that Gen. Cadwallader had been sent as an agent to St. Louis, to examine the place, and to report upon its ability to sustain a branch?

Mr. Tyler rose, and said, that he had heard nothing at the Bank upon the subject of Gen. Cadwallader having been sent to St. Louis, or any report upon the place being made.

Then, said Mr. BENTON, resuming his speech, the committee has been treated unworthily,—scurvily,—basely,—by the Bank! It has been made the instrument to report an untruth to the Senate, and to the American People; and neither the Senate, nor that part of the American People who chance to be in this chamber, should be permitted to leave their places until that falsehood was exposed.

Sir, said Mr. B., addressing the Vice President, the President and Directors of the Bank of the United States, upon receiving the merchants' petition, and my letter, *did not send a branch to St. Louis!* They sent an agent there, in the person of General Cadwallader, to examine the place, and to report upon its mercantile capabilities and wants; and upon that report, the decision was made, and made against the request of the merchants, and that upon the ground that the business of the place would not justify the establishment of a branch. The petition from the merchants came to Mr. B. while he was here, in his seat; it was forwarded from this place to Philadelphia; the agent made his visit to St. Louis before he (Mr. B.) returned; and when he got home, in the spring, or summer, the merchants informed him of what had occurred, and that they had received a letter from the directory of the Bank, informing them that a branch could not be granted; and there the whole affair, so far as the petition and the letter were concerned, died away. But, said Mr. B., it happened just in that time, that I made my first demonstration—struck my first blow—against the Bank; and the next news that I had from the merchants was, that another letter had been received from the Bank, without any new petition having been sent, and without any new report upon the business of the place, informing them that the branch was to come! And come it did, and immediately went to work to gain men and presses, to govern the politics of the State, to exclude him (Mr. B.) from re-election to the Senate, and to oppose every candidate, from Governor to constable, who was not for the Bank. The branch had even furnished a list to the mother Bank, through some of its officers, of the names and residences of the active citizens in every part of the State; and to these, and to their great astonishment at the familiarity and condescension of the high directory in Philadelphia, myriads of Bank documents were sent, with a minute description of name and place, postage free. At the Presidential election of 1832, the State was deluged with these favors. At his own re-elections to the Senate, the two last, the branch Bank was in the field against him every where, and in every form; its directors traversing the State, going to the houses of the members of the General Assembly after they were elected, in almost every county, over a State of sixty thousand square miles; and then attending the legislature, as lobby members, to oppose him. Of these things Mr. B. had never spoken in public before, nor should he have done it now, had it not been for the falsehood attempted to be palmed upon the Senate through the instrumentality of its committee. But having been driven into it, he would mention another circumstance, which also he had never named in public before, but which would throw light upon the establishment of the branch in St Louis, and the kind of business which it had to perform. An immense edition of a review of his speech on the veto message, was circulated through his State on the eve of his last election. It bore the impress of the Bank foundry in Philadelphia, and was intended to let the people of Missouri see that he (Mr. B.) was a very unfit person to represent them: and afterwards it was seen from the report of the Government Directors to the President of the United States, that SEVENTY-FIVE THOUSAND copies of that review was paid for by the Bank of the United States! That looked bad enough, said Mr. B. but it was not all. That speech, of which the bank thought it worth while to get a review written, and to publish an edition of SEVENTY-FIVE THOUSAND copies, was not thought worthy to be put in the Register of Debates! that Register to which Congress is a subscriber, and which purports to be a true history of our debates. More; the replies to it were published in the same Register! He spoke of the speech on the veto message! There was another, on the final passage of the bank bill, not totally suppressed, but compressed into nothing; six hours' speaking put into a paragraph; and his main speech on the whole bill thus converted into what an unfortunate orator of Arkansas once said of his own in seeing the marrowless skeleton of his oration in the newspaper—"*a diminutive metamorphit!*" And as for a third speech, inserted for him in that same Register, it was an infamous falsification of the truth. Mr. B. had never mentioned these things publicly before, nor should he have done it now, except to show that the falsehood of which the Senate's committee has been made the organ, is a part of the system of the Bank, pervading our Congressional history even. It was his intention, at some proper time, to have a committee to report upon those publications, called Registers of Debates, so far as they have been published since the Bank of the United States has undertaken to wield the press. The one which he now had in his eye was that of Messrs. Gales and Seaton.

Mr. B. said that if he had had a line from the committee, (and he was within their reach all the summer,) he could have turned them to the inquiry which would have brought out the truth, with respect to the establishment of the St. Louis branch, and saved them from the imposition which the bank directory had practised upon them. As it was, he still wanted their help in a case which was now theirs, as well as his; it was to aid him in exposing the unworthy,—the scurvy,—and the base, trick of the Bank. He should submit a resolution, requiring the committee to obtain from the President of the Bank a copy of Gen. Cadwallader's report; a copy of the answer to the merchants; and a copy of the second letter, announcing the change of determination, and the immediate establishment of the branch. Until those copies came in, he should say no more on that point, but must be content to see his name figure in the myriad of copies of the report (the more the better) which would be printed, and which would give the village orators of the Bank an opportunity of astonishing the natives who came in from the heads of the creeks and the gorges of the mountains, with showing them what an inconsistent, and unprincipled fellow, this Mr. Benton is; and to admire the delicacy of the Bank which never publishes a private letter, nor exposes the names of public men.

Mr. B. said there was another thing which must be noticed now, because the proof to confound it was written in our own journals. He alluded to the "*hostility*" of the President of the United States to the Bank, which made so large a figure in that report. The "*vindictiveness*" of the President,—the "*hostility*" of the President, was often pressed into the service of that report, which he must be permitted to qualify as an elaborate defence of the Bank. Whether used originally, or by quotation, it was the same thing. The quotation from Mr. Duane was made to help out the argument of the Committee—to sustain their position—and thereby became their own. The "*vindictiveness*" of the President towards the Bank, is brought forward with imposing gravity by the Committee; and no one is at a loss to understand what is meant! The charge has been made too often not to suggest the whole story as often as it is hinted. The President became hostile to the President of the Bank because he could not manage him, and make him use the institution for political purposes! and hence his revenge, his vindictiveness, his hatred of Mr. Biddle, and his change of sentiment towards the institution. This is the charge which has run through the bank presses for three years, and is alleged to take date from 1829, when an application was made to change the President of the Portsmouth Branch. But how stands the truth, recorded upon our own journals? It stands thus: that for three consecutive years after the harboring of this deadly malice against Mr. Biddle, for not managing the institution to suit the President's political wishes—for three years, one after another, with this "*vindictive*" hate in his bosom, and this diabolical determination to ruin the institution, he nominates this same Mr. Biddle to the Senate, as one of the Government directors, and at the head of those directors! Mr. Biddle, and some of his friends with him came in, upon every nomination for three successive years, after vengeance had been sworn against him! For three years afterwards he is not only named a director, but indicated for the Presidency of the Bank, by being put at the head of those who came recommended by the nomination of the President, and the sanction of the Senate! Thus was he nominated for the year 1830, 1831, and 1832; and it was only after the report of Mr. Clayton's committee of 1832 that the President ceased to nominate Mr. Biddle for Government Director! Such was the frank, confiding, and friendly conduct of the President; while Mr. Biddle, conscious that he did not deserve a nomination at his hands, had himself also elected during each of these years, at the head of the stockholders' ticket. He knew what he was meditating and hatching, against the President, though the President did not! What then becomes of the charge faintly shadowed forth by the committee, and publicly, and directly made by the Bank and its friends? False! False as hell! and no Senator can say it without finding the proof of the falsehood recorded in our own journal!

Mr. B. was not now going into a general answer to the report, but he must do justice to an absent gentlemen—one of the purest men upon earth, both in public and private life, and who, after the manner he had been treated in this Chamber, ought to be secure, in his retirement, from Senatorial attack and injustice. The committee have joined a conspicuous issue with Mr. Taney, and they have carried a glorious bank victory over him, by turning off the trial upon a false point. Mr. Taney arraigned the legality of the conduct of the Exchange Committee, which, overleaping the business of such a committee, which is to buy and sell *real bills of exchange*, had become invested with the power of the whole board; transacting that business which, by the charter, could only be done by the board of directors, and by a board of not less than seven, and which they could not delegate. Yet this committee, of three, selected by the President himself, was shown by the report of the government directors to transact the most important business; such as making immense loans upon long credits, and upon questionable security; sometimes covering its operations under the simulated garb, and falsified pretext, *of buying a bill of exchange;* sometimes using no disguise at all. It was shown, by the same report, to have the exclusive charge of conducting the curtailment last winter; a business of the most important character to the country, having no manner of affinity to the proper functions of an exchange committee; and which they conducted in the most partial and in-

[Continued in next number.]

CONGRESSIONAL GLOBE.

BY BLAIR & RIVES. ———WEEKLY——— PRICE $1 A SESSION.

2d Sess.......23d Cong. MONDAY, DECEMBER 29, 1834. VOLUME 2.......No. 4.

TWENTY-THIRD CONGRESS.

SECOND SESSION.

IN SENATE.

THURSDAY, December 18, 1834.

[*Continued from last Number.*]

ustoms manner, and without even reporting to the board. All this the gov rnment directors communicated. All this was commented upon on this floor; yet Mr. Taney is selected! He is the one pitched upon; as if nobody but him had arraigned the illegal acts of this committee; and then he is made to arraign the existence of the committee, and not its misconduct! Is this right? Is it fair? Is it just thus to pursue that gentleman, and to nurse him unjustly? Can the vengeance of the Bank never be appeased while he lives and moves on earth?

Mr. B. had performed a duty, which ought not to be delayed an hour, in defending himself, the President, and Mr. Taney, from the sad injustice of that report; the report itself, with all its elaborate standing; for the Bank,—its errors of omission and commission,—would come up for argument after t was printed; and when, with God's blessing, and the help of better hands, he would hope to how that it was the duty of the Senate to recommit it, with instructions to examine witnesses upon oath, and to bring out that secret history of the institution, which seems to have been a sealed book to the committee. For the present, he would cling to light two facts, detected in the intricate maze of the monthly statements, which would fix a cross, both the character of the Bank and the character of the report; the Bank, for its audacity, recklessness and falsehood; the report, for its blindness, fatuity, and partiality.

The Bank, as all America knows, (said Mr. B.) filled the whole country with the endless cry which had been echoed and re-echoed from this chamber, that the removal of the deposites had set her under the necessity of curtailing her debts; and compelled her to call in her loans, to fill the vacuum in her coffers produced by the removal; and thus to enable herself to stand the pressure, which the "hostility" of the government was bringing upon her. This was the assertion for six months; and now let facts confront this assertion, and reveal the truth to an outraged and insulted community.

The first fact, (said Mr. B.) is the transfer of so moneys to London, to lie there idle, while pressed out of the People here during the panic and pressure.

The cry of distress was raised in December, at a meeting of Congress; and during that month the sum of $129,764, was transferred, by the Bank, to its agents the Barings. This cry waxed stronger till July, and until that time the monthly transfers were:

December,	-	$129,764
February,	-	355,253
March,	-	261,543
May,	-	34,749
June,	-	2,142,054
July,	-	501,950
		$3,425,313

Making the sum of near three millions and a half transferred to London, to lie idle in the hands of an agent, while that very money was squeezed out of a few cities here; and the whole country, all the halls of Congress, were filled with the deafening din of the cry, that the Bank was forced to curtail, to supply the loss in her own coffers on the removal of the deposites! And, worse still! The Bank had, in the hands of the same agents, a large sum when the transfers of these collections began, making in the whole, the sum of $4,261,301, on the first day of July last, which was lying idle in her agents' hands in London, drawing little or no interest there, while squeezed out of the hands of those who were paying 7 bank interest here, near seven per cent., and

had afterwards to go into brokers' hands to borrow at one or two per cent. a month. Even now, at the last returns on the first day of this month, about two millions and a half of this money (2,687,006) was still lying idle in the hands of the Barings! waiting till foreign exchange can be put up again to eight or ten per cent. The enormity of this conduct, Mr. B. said, was aggravated by the notorious fact, that the transfers of this money were made by sinking the price of exchange as low as five per cent. below par, when shippers and planters had bills to sell, and buying it 3 per cent. above par when merchants and importers had to buy; thus double taxing the commerce of the country—double taxing the producer and consumer—and making a fluctuation of thirteen per cent. In foreign exchange, in the brief space of six months. And all this to make money scarce at home, while charging that scarcity upon the President! Thus combining-calumny and stock-jobbing with the diabolical attempt to ruin the country or to rule it.

The next fact, Mr. B. said, was the abduction of an immense amount of specie from New Orleans, at the moment the western produce was arriving there; and thus disabling the merchants from buying that produce, and thereby sinking its price nearly one half; and all under the false pretext of supplying the loss in its coffers occasioned by the removal of the deposites.

The falsehood and wickedness of this conduct will appear from the fact, that at the time of the removal of the deposites, in October, the public deposites in the New Orleans branch, ware far less than the amount afterwards curtailed, and sent off; and that these deposites were not entirely drawn out for many months after the curtailment and abduction of the money. Thus, the public deposites, in October, were:

In the name of the Treasurer of the United States, $294,228 62
In the name of public officers, 173,764 64
$467,993 26

In all, less than half a million of dollars. In March, there was still on hand:
In the name of the Treasurer, $40,266 38
In the name of public officers, 63,671 80
$103,938 06

In all, upwards of one hundred thousand dollars; and making the actual withdrawal of deposites, at that branch, but $360,000, and that paid out gradually, in the discharge of Government demands.

Now what was the actual curtailment during the same period? It is shown from the monthly statements, that these curtailments, on local loans, were $788,904; being upwards of double the amount of deposites, miscalled *removed*; for they were not *removed*; but only paid out in the regular progress of Government disbursement, and actually remaining in the mass of circulation, and much of it in the Bank itself. But the specie removed during the same time! that was the fact, the damning fact, upon which he relied. This abduction was:
In the month of November, $334,647, *at the least*.
In the month of March, 808,084, *at the least*.
$1,142,731

Making near a million and a quarter of dollars, at the least. Mr. B. repeated, at the least; for a monthly statement does not show the accumulation of the month, which might be as sent off; and the statement could only be relied on for so much as appeared a month before the abduction was made. Probably the sum was upwards of a million and a quarter of hard dollars, thus taken away from New Orleans last winter, by stopping accommodations, calling in loans, breaking up do-

mestic exchange, creating panic and pressure, and sinking the price of all produce; that the mother Bank might transfer funds to London, gamble in foreign exchange, spread desolation and terror through the land; and then charge the whole upon the President of the United States; and end with the grand consummation of bringing a new political party into power, and perpetuating its own charter.

These, said Mr. B., are two, and only two, out of multitudes, of the astounding iniquities which have escaped the eyes of the committee, while they have been so successful in their antiquarian researches into ANDREW JACKSON'S and FELIX GRUNDY'S letters ten or twenty years ago, and into MARTIN VAN BUREN'S and THOMAS H. BENTON'S, six or eight years ago; letters which every public man is called upon to give to his neighbors, or constituents; which no public man ought to refuse, or, in all probability, ever did refuse; and which are so ostentatiously paraded in the report, and so emphatically read, in this chamber, with pause and gesture; and with such a sympathetic look for the expected smile from the friends of the bank; letters, which so far as he was concerned, had been used to make the committee the organ of a falsehood. And now, Mr. B. would be glad to know, who put the committee upon the scent of those old musty letters; for there was nothing in the resolution, under which they acted, to conduct their footsteps to the silent covert of that small game.

But, Mr. B. was done for the present. He was done for the present, but not for the future. Justice cannot be done upon this report of the committee until it is printed. The only object which he saw had in view was to vindicate some gentlemen, including himself, who were most unjustly treated; and to show the true character of the entire report, by exhibiting the minute diligence, and miraculous success of the committee in hunting out *things of nothing*, to be turned to the account of the Bank, and to the prejudice of its adversaries; while stone blind to such recent, and such enormous misconduct of the Bank as he had just detailed to the Senate, and which came within the precise letter of the resolutions under which they acted.

Mr. TYLER said he was perfectly willing that the report should go back to the committee, and that the honorable gentleman (Mr. Benton) should be placed upon the committee. There was not a single assertion in the report which did not rest upon proof, upon documentary proof, which could not be, and he invited the honorable gentleman's attention to it. There was sufficient in the report to satisfy the People upon the subject of the curtailment by the Bank—whether it was necessary or not. Here were their orders, and they were submitted to the Senate to say whether there was necessity for it or otherwise. If the gentleman from Missouri had looked to both the statements in the report, he surely would not have pronounced it an exparte report. Mr. T. said his deliberate opinion was, and he should declare it before the country, that the Bank was right in its controversy with the Government, and that its adversary was wrong. In regard to the charge committee, no false issue had been made. The report expressly referred to the argument of Mr. Taney, who contended that the exchange committee was in itself a positive violation of the charter of the Bank. With regard to the letter of Gen. Cadwalader, he knew nothing of it, nor did he think it of any consequence. The branch, however, was established at St. Louis—whether it came there by means of the honorable gentleman's influence or his blows. He knew that the bank had undergone frequent reviews by that gentleman, and that they had not been into all parts of the country, and no doubt they the'r due influence. But he declined adding any thing more, and concluded by moving that the report and documents be printed; which was agreed to—and then

The Senate adjourned over to Monday next.

HOUSE OF REPRESENTATIVES.

THURSDAY, December 18, 1834.

Petitions and memorials were presented by—

Mr. JARVIS, of Maine;

Mr. REED, of Massachusetts;

Mr. BARBER, of Connecticut;

Messrs. LEE and FOWLER, of New Jersey;

Messrs. BINNEY and SUTHERLAND, of Pennsylvania;

Messrs. McKIM and TURNER, of Maryland;

Messrs. LUCAS, MERCER, DAVENPORT, and PATTON, of Virginia;

Mr. MARSHALL, of Kentucky;

Mr. VANCE, of Ohio;

Mr. EWING, of Indiana;

Mr. SEVIER, of Arkansas.

Which petitions and memorials were appropriately referred.

On motion of Mr. MARDIS, by leave,

Resolved, That the Committee on the Post Office and Post Roads be instructed to inquire into the expediency of establishing a mail route from Wetumpka, via Coosa Court-House, Cillavoga, Mardisville, Taladega, to Benton Court-House, in the State of Alabama; and further, to inquire into the expediency of establishing a mail route from Taladega to Chambers Court-house, in the State of Alabama; and further, to inquire into the expediency of establishing a mail route from Tuscaloosa, via Sanders's Ferry, to Vienna, Tombecbee river, in the State of Alabama.

Mr. PEYTON, from the Committee on Foreign Affairs, reported a joint resolution, authorizing the sale of a Lion and two Horses, received as a present by the American Consul at Tangier, from the Emperor of Morocco; which was read twice, and ordered to be engrossed for a third reading.

Mr. PEYTON, from the same committee, asked to be discharged from the further consideration of a resolution of the House, directing the committee to inquire into the expediency of causing the other presents received from Foreign Powers, at various times, and now in the State Department, to be sold; which was agreed to.

Mr. CARR, from the Committee on Private Land Claims, reported a bill for the relief of Nicholas D. Coleman; which was read twice, and ordered to be engrossed.

Mr. CLAY, from the Committee on Public Lands, reported a bill authorizing the survey of certain lands adjacent to the canal on the Licking Summit, in the State of Ohio; which was twice read and committed.

Mr. CLAY, from the same committee, reported a bill to extend the time of issuing military land warrants to the officers and soldiers of the revolutionary army; which was read twice. A bill of a similar character having passed the House, of which Mr. C. was not aware, be therefore moved to lay the present bill on the table; which was agreed to.

Mr. CLAY, from the same committee, reported a bill to authorize the Registers and Receivers of public Land Offices to administer oaths connected with the entry and sale of lands; which was read twice, and after a short conversation between Messrs. CLAY, LANE, and PARKER, its further consideration was postponed to Monday next.

Messrs. CHAMBERS and MAY, from the Committee on Private Land Claims, made unfavorable reports in certain private claims referred to that committee.

The House resumed the consideration of the following resolution, offered by Mr. CLAYTON, of Georgia:

Resolved, That the Committee of Ways and Means inquire into the expediency of reporting a law for the purpose of remitting the duties on locomotive engines, railroad car wheels, with rolled iron tires, axles, springs, &c., already imported, or which may hereafter be imported within two years.

The question being on Mr. DENNY'S motion to amend by substituting the Committee on Manufactures for the Committee of Ways and Means—

Mr. CHAMBERS continued the remarks which he had commenced yesterday. The object of the resolution was intended to exempt from the payment of duty, certain articles, affecting materially the interests of the iron manufacturer of this country. It was not limited to any particular improvement or to any special company; but proposed to admit free of duty any quantity of articles, at all times, and for any body—for the space of two years. As a question of revenue, it was of small concern, and as such, the House was competent to decide upon it in whatever shape it might come before it. The importer cannot complain, inasmuch as he makes his importation under a knowledge of the existing law; but it was a matter of infinite concern to the manufacturer, who upon the faith of your statute, has embarked his capital to a large extent, in this branch of industry. As affecting this meritorious class, this inquiry should properly go to the Committee on Manufactures. It was for that committee to consider what was the nature of the compromise act of 1832—how far the American manufacturer was capable of supplying the demand for the articles in question—and whether, should the duty on them be remitted, the act might not be evaded, and importations be made of articles for other than rail road purposes—all these considerations, and others which might be mentioned, rendered this inquiry, in his opinion, the peculiar province of the Committee on Manufactures.

The gentleman from North Carolina, (Mr. Speight,) had remarked that his constituents were deeply interested in agriculture, which he supposed conflicted with the manufacturing interest. Mr. C. contended that these conflicting interests should not now be weighed—that it was done by the act of 1832, and there it must rest. The gentleman, it was true, disclaimed a disposition to interfere with the arrangement of 1832, yet, at the same time, he was advocating a resolution, which is intended to change the act of 1832, and to reduce the duties, and thus while the gentleman was unwilling to assail the compromise act as a whole, he was attacking it in detail. What would be the result of such a course? There were several other great interests, which, by the mode of proceeding proposed, might be destroyed, if brought separately before the House. He mentioned the woollens, the cotton, the glass, and the sugar interests, which might be thus assailed; and upon a memorial or resolution calculated to affect either of them, we were to be told that it was a mere question of revenue, belonging exclusively to the Committee of Ways and Means. He did not mean to impugn the motives of that highly respectable committee; but the House should not tolerate a course of proceeding so unusual and improper.

It had been said by the gentleman from Virginia, that it was merely proposed to allow a drawback on articles already imported, and consequently would not affect the home manufacturer. The resolution specified no particular company or rail road to be benefited, but was broad in its terms. It was evidently intended to place the foreign manufacturer on an equality with our own, and was a direct breach of the act of 1832. It had also been alleged, that these articles were not manufactured in this country. He believed the case was otherwise. It required no superior skill to manufacture a portion of them. This matter would, however, be a proper subject of inquiry by the Committee on Manufactures.

Mr. C. referred to the precedents of last session, which had been adverted to. They were of recent origin, and if, in these cases, the House had acted incautiously or inconsistently, should we now do the same thing, and even go further? Rather let us, said he, retrace our steps, and send this inquiry to that committee whose duties will lead to a proper and more mature consideration of the subject. There had been complaint in relation to the improper reference to the Committee of Ways and Means, at the last session, of matters not belonging to it. We had a legal committee; yet it would be recollected, that at the last session a judicial question, in relation to Pension Agencies, was referred to the Committee of Ways and Means, who, in their report, had furnished the House with a legal argument. Upon the whole, he hoped that the amendment of his colleague (Mr. Denny) would prevail, and that the inquiry would be sent to the Committee on Manufactures.

Mr. CAMBRELENG said, the House had been for three or four days, debating the question whether this resolution should be referred to the Committee of Ways and Means, or of Manufactures, and by degrees they were getting into a discussion of the tariff. Much of what the gentleman from Pennsylvania (Mr. Chambers) had said, would be very proper if we were about to adopt or reject the resolution; but it is merely one of inquiry, and the question is, to what committee that inquiry shall be submitted. All questions relating to remission or exemption from duty, had been uniformly submitted to the Committee of Ways and Means; and if they were now about to be transferred to another committee, without intending to lessen the importance of the manufacturing interest, he thought the commerce, agriculture, and internal improvements of the country, much more deeply interested in the question of facilitating internal communication. He concurred with the gentleman from Pennsylvania, that the tariff compromise ought not to be disturbed. He was therefore surprised to find an attempt now made to go back to the protecting system, when the very object of the compromise bill was to establish a system of revenue duties, and to restore all jurisdiction over the subject to the Committee of Ways and Means. As to the ability of our manufacturers to supply rails and locomotive engines, the gentleman from Pennsylvania must recollect, that even his own State, behind none for its devotion to the manufacturing interest, was compelled to import two thousand tons of rail road iron. Were we to depend on a domestic supply, you might graduate a road to the Alleghenies before you could procure rails or locomotives to put the first thirty miles in operation. Had the policy so strenuously contended for by some gentlemen, for some years back, been adopted, and the importation of rails and locomotives obstructed, it would have thrown the internal improvements of the country five years in the rear of similar improvements abroad. Whether locomotive engines should be free from duty, ought not to depend on the private interest of the rail road proprietor or the manufacturer. On that ground, it ought to be rejected; but we had nothing to do with their particular interests—the question rested on more elevated ground—on a policy which was as old as the constitution itself—the wise policy of removing every obstruction to the introduction into our country of the improvements made abroad—of allowing the importation of models of art and books of instruction—of encouraging, not by restrictions on, but by relieving from taxation, those objects of modern discovery which tended to our improvement in arts and sciences, or to better the condition, and to the universal advantage, of the country. It was only on that ground that the measure under consideration could be defended. He had, at the origin of this new improvement, advocated its free and immediate introduction into the country—and we had then adopted the policy. We were not now, however, called upon to decide on the propriety of adopting the measure proposed, or of continuing the policy of admitting these engines free of duty; but simply to determine whether the inquiry should be sent to the proper committee. That committee he believed to be the one charged with the revenue and general interests of the country, and not that which guarded the interests of any one particular branch of industry.

Mr. JACKSON, of Massachusetts, was decidedly friendly to the American System; but he was nevertheless firmly of opinion, that the proposed inquiry should go to the Committee of Ways and Means; and if the other friends of the Tariff could view the subject in a correct light, he was persuaded they would agree with him. This country was unable to manufacture the rail road apparatus which would be required for the next two years. If it was proposed to extend the time to ten years, he might question its propriety. He had some experience on this subject, and he was satisfied that we could not supply engines, &c. for rail roads already completed. He had himself made an effort to obtain an engine for one of these rail roads, but could not; and it became necessary to send to London for one. Besides, the dif

ference in the expense of an engine procured in England and this country, was two, or three, or four times as much as the amount of duty. You cannot, therefore, prevent their importation; nor will the continuation of the present duty at all benefit those engaged in their manufacture in this country. Great Britain had been longer engaged in the manufacture of those engines, &c., possessed more skill, and a more ample capital, and he inquired whether it was good policy to retard the progress of important public improvements, by burdening the railroad companies with unnecessary duties, which could be of no possible advantage to our own manufacturers? He referred to the great saving which resulted from the use of locomotive instead of horse power. There were millions of dollars invested in rail-roads, and rather than wait for months for the purpose of obtaining proper machinery in this country, it was matter of economy to obtain them at once from England. The companies would obtain these engines from abroad, were the duty double what it now is. If so, why send this inquiry to the Committee on Manufactures? By a remission of these duties, domestic industry would be more encouraged, and the public prosperity much more advanced than by permitting the duty to remain, or by increasing it. He combated the assumption that the rail-road corporations were wealthy, and adverted to the small dividends which they made, and concluded by hoping that the amendment would be disagreed to, and the original resolution adopted.

Mr. MILLER said, that he felt some doubt yesterday as to the proper disposition of this subject. He was ignorant in regard to the state of the manufacture of the articles in this country, and he had voted to lay the resolution on the table, under the impression that it was calculated to open the whole subject of the tariff. He now believed that the particular matter before the House needed investigation, and if he had any doubts before, the remarks of the gentleman from Massachusetts, (Mr. Jackson) had entirely satisfied his mind. As a subject of revenue, it was of little importance. The question of the difference in price and quality, and whether these articles could be supplied in this country, were proper subjects for the Committee on Manufactures to inquire into; and it was the peculiar duty of the Committee of Ways and Means to inquire into matters relating to the finances. The present proposition was a plain one, and he trusted it would be decided at once.

Mr. EWING next obtained the floor, and was proceeding to give his reasons for the vote which he should give on the proposition, when his remarks were arrested by a call for the orders of the day.

On motion of Mr. WATMOUGH, the House then resolved itself into a Committee of the Whole on the state of the Union, on the bill to equalise and regulate the pay of the officers of the Army and Navy of the United States, Mr. BRIGGS in the Chair.

The question being on the amendment offered by Mr. WISE to the amendment presented to the House by the Chairman of the Select Committee, Mr. WATMOUGH,

Mr. SPEIGHT said he did not rise to enter deeply into the discussion of this bill; but he would offer a remark upon an idea which was suggested by the observations of the gentleman from New York on his left, (Mr. Mann,) when the bill was last before the Committee. He could not subscribe to the doctrine that to equalise the pay of the officers in the two great branches of our national defence, it was essential to bring down that of the officers of the Army to a standard corresponding with the present inadequate pay of our naval officers. He agreed with gentlemen that they should go together—that their pay should be equalised—but not reduced in such a manner as to jeopard the right arm designed for the preservation of our liberties. He also dwelt on the importance of the naval service, in the protection of our commerce in peace and our national honor and safety in war. It was not, with him, and he trusted not with other members of the House, a calculation of dollars and cents. He would ask what gentleman of talents and honora-

ble ambition would sacrifice life, health, and comfort, for the mere pay and emoluments of an officer in the naval service? Mr. S. said he accorded with the sentiment already expressed, that the sums first proposed by the honorable chairman of the Select Committee, were rather too high; and with some slight alterations, he felt favorably disposed towards the amendment offered by the gentleman from Virginia, (Mr. Wise.) He had heard it advanced that it was a dangerous principle to countenance the raising of a salary. Why, there was a time when the highest class of vessels in our navy was a sloop of war. As our country and our navy increased, salaries must increase along with them. He suggested to his friend from Pennsylvania (Mr. Watmouth) the expediency of engrafting in his own amendment some of the provisions embraced in the amendment proposed by the gentleman from Virginia, (Mr. Wise.)

But this, it was decided by the CHAIR, would not be in order.

Mr. WATMOUGH observed that he was particularly desirous, and he believed a large portion of the members of the House were desirous that this bill should be disposed of in committee to-day, and laid before the House. His amendment was then read as follows:

" The senior captain, when commanding a squadron, four thousand five hundred dollars; when on other duty, four thousand dollars; when on leave, or waiting orders, three thousand five hundred dollars.

"All other captains, when commanding squadrons in chief, four thousand five hundred dollars; when commanding squadrons, and under the command of a superior officer, or when acting as Navy Commissioners, four thousand dollars; when of five years' standing, and commanding vessels for sea service, or navy yards, coast stations, or acting as captain of a fleet, three thousand five hundred dollars; when on other duty, three thousand dollars; when on leave, or waiting orders, two thousand five hundred dollars; when under five years, and commanding vessels for sea service, or navy yards, coast stations, or acting as captain of a fleet, three thousand two hundred and fifty dollars; when on other duty, two thousand eight hundred dollars; when on leave of absence, or waiting orders, two thousand five hundred dollars."

Mr. WISE then moved the following as an amendment to the above: " Strike out all after the word ' The,' in the first line, and insert—

" Captains, when commanding four thousand dollars; when on duty, three thousand seven hundred dollars; when waiting orders, three thousand and fifty dollars; when in command of a squadron, four thousand five hundred dollars."

Strike out from the 5th to the 27th line, inclusive, and insert the above.

Strike out from the 28th to the 34th line, inclusive, and insert,

Master commandants, when waiting orders, two thousand dollars; when on duty, two thousand five hundred dollars.

Strike out from the 36th to the 47th line, inclusive, and insert,

Lieutenants, when waiting orders, one thousand dollars; when on duty, one thousand five hundred dollars.

Strike out from the 99th to the 104th line, inclusive, and insert,

Sailingmaster, when waiting orders, eight hundred dollars; when on duty, one thousand three hundred dollars.

Strike out from the 112th to the 116th line, inclusive, and insert,

Passed midshipmen, waiting orders, six hundred dollars; when on duty, seven hundred and fifty dollars.

Strike out from the 122d to the 128th line, inclusive, and insert,

Midshipmen, waiting orders, four hundred dollars; when on duty, six hundred fifty dollars.

Strike out from the 136th to the 143d line, inclusive, and insert,

Boatswain, gunner, carpenter, sailmaker, and armorer, when waiting orders, seven hundred dollars; when on duty, eight hundred dollars.

Strike out from the 118th to the 131st line, inclusive."

The CHAIR here remarked, that inasmuch as

the chairman of the Select Committee (Mr. WATMOUGH) had introduced an amendment to his amendment, giving it the second degree, according to the strict letter of the rules of the House the amendment of the gentleman from Va. (Mr. Wise) would come under the third degree and be, therefore, inadmissible. But, if no objection was raised to the proceeding, he would entertain the motion.

No objection being made, the discussion proceeded.

Mr. SPEIGHT remarked that as there appeared to be but little difference in many points of the two amendments, and particularly as to the pay of a Captain in command of a squadron, he suggested to the gentleman from Va. (Mr. Wise) the propriety of leaving that point as it was in the amendment of the chairman of the select committee.

Mr. WISE said there was an essential difference in the two amendments. His amendment struck out the word "Senior," making no distinction of grade, in the rank of Captain.

Mr. REED spoke briefly in favor of retaining a distinction between the Senior and Junior Captains of the Navy.

After some remarks from Mr. WATMOUGH,

Mr. WISE, to prevent confusion and prolixity, proposed to substitute his amendment for so much of the amendment of the honorable Chairman of the Select Committee as relates to Captains.

Mr. WATMOUGH then followed in opposition to the amendment last offered, and in support of his own. He said the subject grade in question, he could not consent to relinquish. He asked who this new proposition came from? Not from such as fought our battles so gallantly at Tripoli and subsequently—With such he had consulted. It did not originate with the gentleman himself, (Mr. Wise,) for he was aware the subject was entirely new to the honorable member. He did not impugn the motives of that gentleman, but hoped he would not insist on this proposition, which he deemed fraught with the most detrimental consequences to the moral feeling and well-being of the naval service.

Mr. WISE replied. He had but one feeling in this matter, and that was a warm feeling of friendship for the general features of the bill, and for the benefit of the American service. He said it was true, this proposition did not originate with him. His attention had been called to the subject since he had belonged to the Naval Committee, by brave and worthy members of our naval service. He continued, at some length, to advocate and sustain the propriety of his amendment.

After some explanatory conversation between Messrs. HARPER, WISE, and SPEIGHT,

Mr. SPEIGHT called for information from the Chairman of the Select Committee (Mr. Watmough) by what law or authority such a distinction was made as that of Senior and Junior Captain in the naval service.

Mr. WATMOUGH said, he was happy to give the gentleman the information sought for, and referred to the law of 1799, and also a resolution of the Congress of 1776, in which a distinction was made between Captains of five years standing or less.

Mr. WISE contended that the law and resolution referred to did not bear the gentleman out in the creation of different grades in the rank of Captain. That was the highest rank in our navy, and there could be no promotion above it.

Mr. HARPER briefly expressed his conclusion, after mature deliberation, to support the amendment of his colleague (Mr. Watmough.)

Mr. MANN spoke at length, on the general principles of the bill, deprecating the course which had been pursued in bringing the subject in its present shape before the House.

[He was followed by Mr. REED, in favor of the amendment of the Chairman of the Select Committee, and by Mr. PEARCE; but the length of their remarks renders it impossible to present them in this day's paper.]

On motion of Mr. WARD, the Committee then rose, reported progress, and obtained leave to sit again.

When the House adjourned.

HOUSE OF REPRESENTATIVES.

FRIDAY, December 19, 1834.

Petitions and memorials were presented by—

Mr. BARBER, of Connecticut;

Messrs. MITCHELL, CAMBRELENG, HARD, and BEARDSLEY, of New York;

Messrs. CHAMBERS and GALBRAITH, of Pennsylvania;

Messrs. STODDERT and THOMAS, of Maryland;

Messrs. GORDON, TAYLOR, and MASON, of Virginia;

Mr. GRIFFIN, of South Carolina;

Messrs. BEATY and LETCHER, of Kentucky;

Messrs. DICKINSON and LEA, of Tennessee;

Messrs. MITCHELL and KILGORE, of Ohio;

[Mr. MITCHELL presented sundry depositions relating to the claim of Adam Smith, for work and labor done on the Cumberland road, West of Zanesville, accompanied with a sample of metal exhibited by him; all of which were referred to the Committee of Claims.]

Mr. KINNARD, of Indiana;

Mr. CAGE, of Mississippi;

Mr. MURPHY, of Alabama;

Mr. ASHLEY, of Missouri.

The SPEAKER laid before the House a memorial of a convention recently held in Baltimore, composed of delegates from the States of Virginia, Ohio, Pennsylvania, Maryland, and the District of Columbia, asking an appropriation of money in aid of the Chesapeake and Ohio Canal Company; which, on motion of Mr. MERCER, was committed to a Committee of the Whole on the state of the Union, and ordered to be printed

On motion of Mr. THOMAS, of Maryland,

Resolved, That the Committee of Ways and Means be instructed to inquire into the expediency of making an appropriation to pay the claim of Josiah Frost, of Allegheny county, Maryland, on account of his contract for the repairs of a portion of the Cumberland road.

On motion of Mr. LOVE,

Resolved, That the Committee on Revolutionary Claims be instructed to inquire into the expediency of allowing James Barnet, a lieutenant in the revolutionary army, half pay for life, allowing a a credit for what he has received as commutation.

On motion of Mr. HAMER, by leave,

Resolved, That the Select Committee to whom was referred so much of the President's Message as relates to the election of President and Vice President of the United States, be instructed to inquire into the expediency of so amending the Constitution as to provide for the election of President and Vice President by a direct vote of the People in districts; the number of districts in each State to be equal to the number of Senators and Representatives to which each State may be entitled in Congress, and each district having one vote; the election of said officers in no event to devolve upon Congress; no person who has been elected President to be again eligible to that office; and that no Senator or Representative shall be nominated or appointed to any office of trust, honor, or profit, under the authority of the United States whilst holding a seat in Congress.

On motion of Mr. WHITE, of Florida,

Resolved, That the Committee on Naval Affairs be instructed to inquire into the expediency of making an appropriation for deepening the Bar of Pensacola Bay, according to the report of the Engineers of the United States, and that of the Secretary of the Navy, made at the last session of Congress.

The following resolution, heretofore offered by Mr. CLAYTON, was again taken up:

Resolved, That the Committee of Ways and Means inquire into the expediency of reporting a law for the purpose of remitting the duties on locomotive engines; railroad car wheels, with rolled iron tires, axles, springs, &c., already imported, or which may hereafter be imported within two years.

Mr. EWING, of Indiana, continued the remarks which he commenced yesterday, but from the low tone of voice and the difficulty of hearing in the Hall, the Reporter is unable to give a connected view of what he said.

Mr. RENCHER desired to explain the reasons which would govern his vote. He was opposed to the resolution, mainly because the friends of the tariff objected to it. They look upon it as a direct blow aimed at the tariff—this was almost the only reason, which would induce him to vote for sending this inquiry to the Committee on Manufactures instead of the Committee of Ways and Means; and he would vote to lay the proposition on the table, but for the respect which he entertained for the mover (Mr. Clayton.) He was unwilling to do any thing which might endanger the harmony which prevailed on the subject of the tariff. So far as the resolution related to rail road iron already imported, the friends of the tariff could have no objection to it; but it went further, and looked to future importations, and in that view substantially changed the tariff and was a palpable departure from, and an infringement of the compromise act of 1832. Why, he inquired, should we remit the duties in order to favor these wealthy joint stock rail road companies? Why should they be exclusively exempted from the necessary burthens imposed by the government upon its citizens? Other portions of the community might thereby be subjected to even greater exactions.

It had been said that by the adoption of this measure we may promote the cause of internal improvements. He was opposed to it on that ground, because it was an attempt to do that indirectly which we have no power to do directly. His main objection to the resolution, however, was, that it was an invasion of the compromise act of 1832. He had received that compromise in good faith, and would not, therefore, do any thing to disturb it. For these reasons, he would vote to send the inquiry to that committee which was most acceptable to the friends of the tariff.

Mr. BEARDSLEY said, that this was a mere resolution for an inquiry, and therefore of a character usually favored by the House. On that ground he had voted the other day against laying it on the table. But, although it might be of some importance, it was not, in his estimation, sufficently so to authorize a protracted debate, to the exclusion of other subjects of much greater interest. It was now quite manifest, as well from the debate which had already taken place, as from the anxiety indicated this morning to address the Chair upon the subject, that a long discussion might be looked for before any vote could be had on the resolution. Under such circumstances he thought the proposition ought to be laid on the table, and he would make a motion to that effect. He was not actuated by any considerations connected with what was called the compromise act of 1832. He did not believe that the legislation of the country ought to be trammelled or controlled by that act, or that we are bound in honor to regard that measure as sacred. He was not disposed to disturb the act referred to; but he did not predicate his present motion upon any consideration having reference to its obligatory character upon the House. He repeated, in conclusion, that his object in moving to lay the proposition on the table, was to arrest an unnecessary and prolonged discussion.

Mr. CLAYTON asked the gentleman from New York (Mr. Beardsley) to withdraw his motion until he could reply to the remarks of the gentleman from North Carolina (Mr. Rencher.)

The motion was withdrawn.

Mr. C. said he would remind the House, that the resolution was merely one of inquiry, and that it could not possibly be known, until the inquiry was made, whether it did interfere with the compromise or not. He was free to say, that if it did, he would surrender the question; for he hoped he should be among the last men who would disturb the settlement of a matter entered into so solemnly, and that had quieted such distracting agitations. But it was not true, in his opinion, that it did disturb that question. Similar applications had come from the tariff interest itself. Rail road iron had been exempted from duties on their exclusive solicitation. A large proportion of the friends of the present measure, belonged to that side; let an inquiry therefore be made, and if it should appear that the object sought by the resolution so interferes with the tariff question, as to disturb the compromise, it will no longer have his support, but he should hope to hear no more from that side of the question about suspending duties upon objects that happen to suit their particular convenience, as in the case of railroad iron. Let us have no more applications for relief when it answers their purpose, and then a loud complaint when a measure precisely similar comes before the House.

The gentleman from North Carolina seemed to think that the resolution favored the very doctrines against which the South has been so long contending—namely, *Protection*. If he (Mr. C.) thought so, he surely would abandon it as quick as he could get away from it; but he thought he could convince the gentleman himself that that idea was erroneous. He did not consider the present duties on the objects contained in his resolution as revenue duties; they were not intended for the support of Government, but were exclusively designed to protect those articles. So far then, he considered he was assailing an unlawful, and he meant by that expression, an unconstitutional provision. He was only asking a simple repeal of a law which was passed in derogation of the great interest which he represented. If, when the law was about to be passed, it would be a good argument against it to say that it greatly prejudiced the agricultural interests of the South, that it was invading their rights, surely it was legitimate to come here and ask a suspension of the duties for a limited time in favor of those rights. He did not ask protection of those interests! he only asked a restoration of those privileges of which they had been robbed. This was the proper view of the question. But for these duties, that had been laid for the express purpose of a particular class, the great agricultural and planting South, could have gone on to erect rail roads, and procured the materials, necessary for that object, without taxation; and now that they ask to have these taxes suspended, it is conceived they are in favor of protecting certain interests in the country! No, sir, it is not protection, it is matter of right we ask; and the apparent disposition to refuse it, shows how soon that will be considered as a right, by an exclusive interest, which was originally yielded to it as a matter of favor. He repeated, that if he thought his motion went either to support the protective system, or to disturb the compromise, and in the compromise he considered the whole American System involved, not only the Tariff, but Internal Improvement, he should abandon it without delay; and if his resolution is rejected on either of these grounds, he shall be perfectly satisfied, and shall henceforth consider it as proof, assuming the authority of precedent, of the first solemn determination of Congress to sustain the compromise. Now, go it, which way it may, he would be content.

Mr. BINNEY said there were misapprehensions on the subject. It had been supposed that the resolution related in part to rail road iron. Such was not the fact. Another misapprehension, was that rail road iron was now subject to duty. This was also a mistake. That description of iron, when imported by corporations, was not dutiable under our statute. The simple question was whether this subject should be submitted for investigation to the Committee on Manufactures, or to that of Ways and Means. Some remarks which had fallen from various members of the House, rendered it imperative on him to express an opinion on the subject. Whatever that opinion might be, he did not conceive that it should involve any principle for or against the interests conserved, by either of those committees. In the first place, this same subject, at the last session of Congress, had been referred to the Committee of Ways and Means. He would now consider it a reproach to that Committee to take it out of its hands. The investigations of that Committee had already resulted in the production of a bill, bearing directly upon the subject in debate. Mr. B. contended that this was not a measure for giving money for the promotion of Internal Improvements, or the protection of American Manufactures. It was to take away a tax, levied by the revenue laws of the country, and he believed it strictly belonged to the Committee of Ways and Means. Mr. B. said

he had just received a communication from an individual engaged in the manufacture of Locomotive Engines for the use of Rail Roads, which he should, in due time, lay before the House. The communication of this individual, whom he had known for 30 or 40 years past, would, if no other consideration had, have convinced him of the propriety of referring this subject to the Committee of which he was a member—that of Ways and Means,—which he believed as capable as any other of acting and deciding on its general merits,—no matter what interests it might involve.

Mr. DICKERSON followed on the opposite side of the question—contending that the subject properly belonged to the Committee on Manufactures. He answered many of the arguments advanced by the gentleman from Pennsylvania, and concluded by remarking, that as it was evident this question was about to open the whole tariff question, he would move to lay the resolution on the table.

He, however, at the request of Mr. Burges, (who promised to renew it,) withdrew the motion.

Mr. BURGES strenuously contended that this was a proper subject for the Committee on Manufactures, and for that committee only. It had been frequently said in the course of this debate that this matter was liable to conflict with some provisions of what is at called the "Compromise." Sir, said Mr. B., I have little to say of this compromise. The People have not compromised; and the time must come when all such arrangements must be swept away by the loud voice of public opinion. Gentlemen might prepare themselves for that event, for come it must, and come it would. They might make up their minds for this event, for the labor of the country could not succumb to the interests of Europe, or the prejudices of the South. Mr. B. proceeded to a discussion of the relative strength of the cast and rolled iron of this country and of Europe; some of the latter of which, brought into this country under the name of rolled iron, was no better than cast—nay, it could be more properly compared to the ice that congeals from the roofs of your houses! He contended that the introduction of this European manufacture would peril the lives of our fellow-citizens, while we could have no legal redress for any accidents that might occur from the defect of the materials. He concluded, by again repeating, that he had nothing to do with that false and cowardly arrangement so often called the "compromise."

Mr. BURGES then renewed the motion to lay the resolution on the table; which was decided in the affirmative, as follows—ayes 123, noes 85:

YEAS.—Messrs. John Quincy Adams, John Adams, Heman Allen, Chilton Allan, William Allen, Banks, Barber, Barnitz, Bayliss, Beardsley, Beaty, Beaumont, Blair, Boon, Brown, Bull, Burd, Burges, Burns, Chambers, Chaney, Chilton, W. Clark, Corwin, Cramer, Crockett, Darlington, A. Davis, Day, Deany, Dickson, Dickerson, Evans, H. Everett, Fillmore, Fowler, Philo C. Fuller, Galbraith, Garland, Gillet, Grennell, J. Hall, H. Hall, Mahony, Hannegan, Hard, Hardin, Joseph M. Harper, Harrison, Hathaway, Hazeltine, Heath, Henderson, Heister, Howell, Ebenezer Jackson, Jarvis, Wm. Cost Johnson, Richard M. Johnson, Noadiah Johnson, Benjamin Jones, Kinnard, Lane, Lansing, Laporte, Lay, Thomas Lee, Love, Lyon, Abijah Mann, Joel K. Mann, Martindale, Marshall, Moses Mason, McKennan, McKim, McLene, McVean, Miller, Milligan, Miner, Henry Mitchell, Robert Mitchell, Morgan, Muhlenberg, Osgood, Page, Parks, Parker, Patterson, Pearce, Phillips, Pierson, Pinckney, Pope, Potts, Ramsay, Reed, Schenck, Shinn, Slade, Sloane, Smith, Standifer, Steele, Stewart, Sutherland, William Taylor, Francis Thomas, Thomson, Tompkins, Turner, Tweedy, Vanderpoel, Van Houten, Wagner, Ward, Webster, Whallon, F. Whittlesey, E. Whittlesey, Wilson, Young—123.

NAYS.—Messrs. John J. Allen, Archer, Ashley, Bevis, Bean, Binney, Briggs, Bunch, Bynum, Cage, Cambreleng, Campbell, Carr, Casey, Chinn, Claiborne, Clay, Clayton, Clowney, Coffee, Connor, Crane, Davenport, Deberry, Dickinson, Dunlap, Ewing, Felder, Ferris, Foster, William K. Fuller, Gamble, Gholson, Gordon, Graham, Gray-

son, Griffin, Hamer, James Harper, Hawkins, Hawes, Hubbard, Huntington, Inge, William Jackson, Kavanagh, Kilgore, King, Luke Lea, Letcher, Lewis, Lincoln, Loyall, Lucas, Manning, Mardis, John Y. Mason, May, McCarty, McComas, McKinley, Moore, Murphy, Patton, Peyton, Pickens, Pierce, Polk, Rencher, Reynolds, Robertson, William B. Shepard, A. H. Shepperd, Spangler, Speight, Stoddert, William P. Taylor, Philemon Thomas, Trumbull, Vance, Watmough, Wayne, Wilde, Williams, Wise.—85.

The SPEAKER laid before the House a letter from the Secretary of the Treasury, in response to a resolution of the 16th instant, relative to the bridge across the Potomac; which was laid on the table.

The joint resolution authorizing the sale of a lion and two horses, received as a present by the American Consul at Tangier from the Emperor of Morocco, was read a third time, amended on the motion of Mr. J. Q. ADAMS, and passed.

The bill for the relief of Nicholas D. Coleman, was read a third time, and passed.

The bill for the relief of D. Kilburn was taken up.

A lengthy discussion ensued, in which Messrs. E. WHITTLESEY, WARDWELL, THOMSON, BRIGGS, BURD, CHILTON, and BURGES, participated.

Before any question was taken on the third reading of the bill—

Mr. PARKS, by consent, moved that when the House adjourns, it will adjourn to meet again on Monday; which was agreed to.

The House then adjourned.

IN SENATE.
Monday, December 22, 1834.

Petitions and memorials were presented by Mr. HENDRICKS, SILSBEE, WRIGHT, HILL, McKEAN, BUCHANAN, SMITH, CLAY, and PORTER.

The VICE PRESIDENT laid before the Senate a memorial from the Convention lately assembled at Baltimore, praying further aid from Congress for the continuation and completion of the Chesapeake and Ohio Canal; which was referred to the Committee on Roads and Canals.

Mr. WRIGHT presented a memorial from a number of merchants and others in New York, requesting the aid of Congress in fitting out an exploring expedition to the South Seas; which was referred to the Committee on Naval Affairs.

The following resolutions were submitted:

By Mr. HILL:
Resolved, That the Secretary of the Treasury be requested to transmit to the Senate as early as may be practicable, the number and the amount of Navy and Military Virginia Revolutionary Land Warrants, now on file for scrip in the General Land Office—the names of the individuals who performed the service—and also the names of the persons or agents who filed the warrants, or are interested in the same.

Also, that the Secretary of the Treasury be further requested to inform the Senate the amount of superseded Navy and Military Virginia Revolutionary Bounty Land Scrip now lying in the General Land Office—the names of individuals who performed the service, and the names of the persons or agents now claiming said scrip, and the reasons for suspending the delivery of the same.

By Mr. LINN:
Resolved, That the Committee of Claims be instructed to inquire into the expediency of making an appropriation to compensate Augustus Jones, Marshal of Missouri, for services rendered the public, in detecting and breaking up bands of counterfeiters, who were flooding the country with spurious money; and that said Committee call on the Secretary for information relating to this subject.

By Mr. TOMLINSON:
Resolved, That the Committee on Revolutionary Claims be instructed to inquire into the expediency of compensating Phineas Taylor, of Banbury, in the State of Connecticut, for a horse, and other property, taken from him for public use during the revolutionary war.

By Mr. BLACK:
Resolved, That the Postmaster General inform the Senate whether so much of the act of Congress approved 25th June, 1832, as establishes a mail route from Burnt Corn, in the State of Alabama, by Claiborne, Clarksville, Coffeeville, Washington Court House, Winchester, Ellisville, Williamsburg, Monticello, and Meadville, to Natchez, in the State of Mississippi, has been carried into effect, and if it has not, what cause or causes have prevented it.

By Mr. POINDEXTER:
Resolved, That the Secretary of the Senate be directed to procure fifty copies of the American Diplomatic Code, to be retained for the use of the Senate.

This resolution was twice read, and referred to the Library Committee.

By Mr. KING:
Resolved, That the Committee on Indian Affairs be instructed to inquire into the expediency of authorizing the appointment of an agent to receive evidence of the losses sustained by the inhabitants of the now State of Alabama, by the invasion of a party of Creek Indians in the year 1814, when Fort Mims was taken, and those who fled there for protection, massacred.

By Mr. SWIFT:
Resolved, That the Secretary of War be directed to cause a survey to be taken of the channel between the islands of North and South Hero, in Lake Champlain, together with an estimate of the probable expense of removing obstructions to vessels in said channel, with a view of facilitating the navigation of said lake, by the removal of said obstructions; and that he make a report thereof to the Senate at the next session of Congress.

By Mr. KENT:
Resolved, That the Committee on Military Affairs inquire into the expediency of making an appropriation for the immediate commencement of fortifications on the Patapsco at the city of Annapolis, and at St. Mary's; all deemed essential by the Board of Engineers in their report, dated the 9th of February, 1821, for the security of the cities of Baltimore and Annapolis, and for the protection of the commerce of the Chesapeake Bay.

Mr. WRIGHT, from the Committee on Finance, reported a bill for the relief of Humphrey B. Gwathmey.

Mr. WRIGHT also gave notice that to-morrow he would ask leave to introduce a bill entitled "an act in addition to an act to provide more effectually for the settlement of the accounts of receivers of public moneys," approved March 3d, 1797.

Mr. LINN gave notice that to-morrow he would ask leave to introduce a bill authorising an appropriation to aid in improving the harbor at St. Louis.

Mr. SHEPLEY, from the Committee on Claims, reported a bill for the relief of Peter H. Green.

Mr. CLAYTON, from the Judiciary Committee, reported the bill to settle and establish the northern boundary line of the State of Ohio, without amendment.

Mr. CLAYTON said he would call up this bill for consideration at the earliest period which was offered him.

Mr. MOORE, from the Committee on Public Lands, reported the bill granting to the State of Alabama 3 per cent. of the net proceeds of the sales of public lands; amended to 2 per cent.

Mr. BENTON rose and asked the indulgence of the Senate for a moment, that he might try an issue with Messrs. Gales and Seaton, editors of the Congressional Register, by an inspection of the record. He had stated on Thursday last that they had, in their Register, suppressed two of his main speeches on the Bank of the United States, in 1832, and inserted a falsified account of another. This statement seemed to be denied in the National Intelligencer of this morning, and he had now brought in the Register, Vol. 8, part the first, for the session 1831-32, to verify what he had said. Mr. B. then turned to the Register, for the debates of June 8th and 9th, when, as the Senate would recollect, he spoke at large on the question to engross the bill; he spoke the afternoon of one day and the forenoon of the next. Of all this, about half a column is in the Register; and even

that attributed to him things which he had not
said, and which he disclaimed. The second sup
pression was on the return of the bill with the veto
Message, when he again spoke the afternoon of
one day, and some hours of the next. Of all this,
scarce a paragraph was to be found in the Register. It was a speech, however, which was well
known to the country at the time, and of which
the Bank of the United States had reviewed, and
SEVENTY-FIVE THOUSAND copies printed and circulated. Mr. B. said, the editors of the Intelligencer had undertaken to show there could be no
suppression, because they had inserted a great
many long columns of his speeches in their Register. He said it would not require a yard stick to
measure what they had inserted for him on these
two occasions, when he spoke part of two days at
each time; a barley corn would do for the measure.
They were about the length of a barley corn, as
they appeared in the Register. The third point
that he complained of was that of inserting under
his name a falsified account of an unpleasant altercation which grew out of the debate on the Veto
Message. He had qualified that account of that
altercation, by the epithets which it deserved, on
Thursday last, when he branded it as an infamous
falsification of the truth.

It was Mr. B.'s intention, at some suitable time,
to have a committee to examine into these Registers, and that with much larger views than would
relate to the personal injury done to himself. For
the present he had no object, but to try an issue,
by inspecting the record: he had done this, and
shown the volume and page, day and year, subject
and occasion, on which his speeches were suppressed, and falsified.

The bill from the House to extend the time for
issuing and locating military land warrants, was
read twice and referred to the Committee on Public Lands.

The joint resolution from the House, authorizing
the sale of the lion and horses presented to the
United States Consul at Tangiers, by the Emperor of Morocco, was read twice, when

Mr CLAY said, as there was no very appropriate committee to which the resolution could be
sent, he would move to refer the resolution to the
Committee on Agriculture.

Mr. KING, of Alabama, observed, that as the
presents appeared to be connected with our foreign relations, he thought the Committee on Foreign relations the most appropriate one for the resolution to be sent to.

Mr. CLAY objected to that reference, as the
animals, he was informed, were now in this city,
and the subject was not connected with our foreign
affairs.

Mr. KING replied, that if the Committee on
Agriculture desired to take charge of the subject,
(not being himself on the committee,) he had no
objection. But as it appeared that our consuls and
other public functionaries could receive no presents
from foreign powers, and in previous instances,
when induced to do so, rather than give offence to
those who presented them, they had been sent to
the Government, he thought the committee he had
indicated the most suitable one. But if the Agricultural Committee were desirous of using the
horses, he, Mr. K., had no objection.

The resolution was referred to the Committee
on Agriculture.

The bill for the relief of Samuel Smith, Lynn
Magee, and Lemoise, Creek Indians;

The bill authorizing the relinquishment of the
sixteenth section for the use of schools, and granting o her lands in lieu thereof; and

The bill for the relief of Susan Marlow;

Were read twice, as in Committee of the Whole,
and severally ordered to be engrossed for a third
reading.

A bill for the relief of Eliza Sims, was read and
referred.

Mr. WAGGAMAN called up the resolution
with regard to the distribution of the thirty copies of the documents relative to the public lands;
which was agreed to.

SPECIAL ORDER OF THE DAY.

The Senate then proceeded to the special order
of the day, the bill to appropriate 5,000,000 dol-

lars to satisfy claims for spoliations made upon
American commerce by France prior to 1800.

Mr. SHEPLEY said:

Mr. President: When I consider the importance
of the bill now under consideration, I cannot forbear asking again the indulgence of the Senate,
while I turn to the published documents of this
Government, and from them, attempt to show the
justice of the measure contemplated by this bill.

I am aware, that it will be but a very limited
and imperfect exhibition of the merits of the bill,
to occupy the time of the Senate by a dry recital
of State papers; and yet, that is nearly all that I
propose to do. I shall attempt to show from such
documents—

That the property of our citizens was illegally
taken from them by France.

That their right to have compensation from
France was recognised by the United States; that
it was also admitted by France.

That France had claims against the United
States, the justice of which, to some extent, was
not denied.

That compensation for these injuries might
have been obtained from France, if we had been
willing to institute a commission for mutual compensation for injuries. France offered this.

The right to compensation was not destroyed by
a state of war.

For the purpose of showing the character of the
injuries inflicted upon our commerce, it will be
necessary to examine the commercial relations between this country and France at that time.

By the treaty of amity of commerce of the 6th
of February, 1778, article 23d, it provided, that it
shall be lawful for the subjects of France and the
People of the United States, "to sail with their
ships with all manner of liberty and security, no
distinction being made who are the proprietors of
the merchandises laden thereon, from any port to
the places of those who now are, or hereafter shall
be, at enmity with the most Christian King, or the
United States." And this "not only directly from
the places of the enemy aforementioned to neutral places, but also from one place belonging to
an enemy to another place belonging to an enemy,
whether they be under the jurisdiction of the
same prince, or under several." "And it is hereby stipulated, that free ships shall also give a freedom to goods; and that every thing shall be deemed to be free and exempt," "although the whole
lading, or any part thereof, should appertain to the
enemies of either, contraband goods being always
excepted."

The 24th article enumerates the goods which
are to be regarded as contraband.

The 25th article prescribes, that in case either
party shall be engaged in a war, its ships and vessels "must be furnished with sea-letters or passports, expressing the name, property, and bulk
of the ship"—according to the form annexed to
the treaty. This was to be the evidence of the
property of the ship as respects its national character.

It was during the existence of this treaty, admitted by both parties to be then obligatory upon
the parties to it, that the first causes of complaint
arose.

By a decree of the National Convention of
France of the date of 9th May, 1793, it is declared: "Art. 1. The French ships of war and
privateers may arrest, and bring into the ports of
the Republic, the neutral vessels which shall be
laden wholly or in part, either with articles of
provisions belonging to neutral nations and destined
to an enemy's port, or with merchandises belonging to an enemy."

The same convention on the 23d of the same
month, declared by decree "that the vessels of
the United States or not comprehended in the dispositions of the decree of the 9th of May." This
decree of the 23d was repealed on the 28th of
May.

The Convention on the 1st of July again decreed that the vessels of the United States were
not comprehend in the decree of the 9th of May.

And the decree of the 27th July again "maintained the dispositions of that of the 9th of May."

The Executive Directory, on the 2d of July,
1796, declared "that neutral and allied powers
shall, without delay, be notified, that the flag of
the French Republic will treat neutral vessels,
either as to confiscation, as to searches or captures,
in the same manner as they shall suffer the English
to treat them."

And on the 2d March, 1797, the Directory decreed "That the French vessels of war and privateers may stop and carry into the ports of the
Republic, neutral vessels which may be found
loaded entirely or in part with merchandise belong to the enemy."

The French Minister of the Marine and of the
Colonies, on the 30th April, 1797, declares: "Every
American ship must have a passport and a (role
d'equipage) ship's roll—I mean a (liste d'equipage) crew list. Whereas, without these papers, she ought to be confiscated." And he gives
reasons for it—and yet the passport only was required by the treaty,— as was afterwards admitted
by France.

The Council of Five Hundred, on the 11th
January, 1798, decreed, that "The character of
the vessel, relative to the quality of neuter or
enemy, is determined by her cargo."

An extraordinary tribunal was made the organ
to decide upon prizes by a decree of 8th of
November, 1793, declaring "the validity or possibility of prizes made by privateers, shall be decided by way of administration by the Provisory
Executive Council."

All these decrees, and the proceedings under
them, were not only in direct violation of the
treaty and the articles recited, but so far that
depredations on our commerce took place before
the passage of the act of Congress of the 7th of
July, 1798, annulling the treaties.

The right of the citizens to have compensation
from France was, as I have said, recognised by
the United States.

The Secretary of State, Mr. Jefferson, in a circular letter addressed to the merchants, under
date of August, 1793, says. "I have it in charge
from the President, to assure the merchants of the
United States, concerned in foreign commerce or
navigation, that due attention will be paid to any
injuries they may suffer on the high seas or in
foreign countries, contrary to the law of nations,
or to existing treaties; and that on their forward-
ing hither well authenticated evidence of the same,
proper proceedings will be adopted for their
relief."

And in a letter to our Minister to Great Britain,
under date of April 26, 1797, the Secretary says
"that nearly all the vessels, or cargoes, or seizures
which are carried in by their privateers, are condemned by the civil officers on shore. Besides
when he, (Mr. Adet,) mentions unauthorized captures, he cannot refer to the multitude which we
complain of, as made in direct violation of our
treaty with France."

In the instructions to our Envoys to France,
under date of July 15, 1797, is this declaration:
"Indeed, the greatest part, probably nearly all
the captures and confiscations in question, have
been committed in direct violation of that treaty,
or of the law of nations."

The President of the United States in his speech
of the 8th of December, 1798, speaking of a decree of the Directory, says, "it enjoins them to
conform to all the laws of France, relative to
cruising and prizes; while these laws are themselves
the sources of the depredations of which we have
so long, so justly, and so fruitlessly complained."

So perfect was the right of the citizens to have
compensation regarded, that in the treaty of the
order date of 23d October, 1799, to our Envoys to
France, is this clause:—

"First—At the opening of the negotiation, you
will inform the French ministers, that the United
States expect from France an indemnity for the
dition of the treaty, a stipulation to make to the citizens of the United States, full compensation for
all losses and damages which they shall have sustained by reason of irregular or illegal captures,
or condemnations of their vessels and their proper-

ty, under color of authority or commissions from the French Republic or its agents."

It remains next to ascertain whether France did not admit her obligation to make compensation.

In the deliberations of the Executive Directory on the 31st July, 1798, it is stated, that such information has been received as to "leave no room to doubt, that French cruisers, or such as call themselves French, have infringed the laws of the Republic, relative to cruising and prizes."

And in a decree of the 18th March, 1799, the Executive Directory admits, that the former decree "in what relates to the roles d'equipages with which neutral vessels ought to be furnished, has had improper interpretations, so far as concerns the roles d'equipages of American vessels, and that it is time to do away the obstacles resulting therefrom, to the navigation of the vessels of that nation."

Our Envoys claiming compensation from France, find France also claiming a fulfilment on our part of the treaties; and in their letter of 17th May, 1800, to the Secretary of State, they say, "Our success is doubtful. The French think it hard to indemnify for violating engagements, unless they can thereby be restored to the benefits of them." The objection here then is not to making an indemnity, but to making it, without having the benefit of the same treaties, for the violation of which we claimed of them compensation.

The French Ministers in their proposal to the American Envoys, under date 11th August, 1800, say: "Thus, the first proposition of the ministers of France, is to stipulate a full and entire recognition of treaties, and the reciprocal engagement of compensation for damages resulting on both sides from their infraction."

If this is not accepted, they then propose "the abolition of ancient treaties," and in such case, "there would be no demand of compensation."

Here, then, is an offer of compensation for injuries to our citizens, made by France, but she claimed compensation from the United States for the non-fulfilment of the treaties, and that the compensation should be reciprocal.

These claims of France against the United States arose out of our neglect or refusal, as she alleged, to fulfil the spipulations of treaties. They were, first: the 11th article of the Treaty of Alliance of 6th February, 1778. This article stipulated the guarantee should be on the part of "the United States to his Most Christian Majesty, the present possessions of the crown of France in America, as well as those which it may acquire by the future treaty of France."

And, secondly—the 17th and 22d articles of the Treaty of Commerce, of the same date. By the first of these articles, the privateers and prizes of France might enter our ports and depart at pleasure, and the privateers and vessels of the enemies of France were excluded from our ports. And the latter article prohibited the privateers of the enemies of France from being fitted out in our ports, and sale of their prizes being made in them, or even provision furnished more than was necessary for their going to the next port.

The importance of the stipulations to France, will be readily acknowledged, when we remember that she was at war with England; that she had islands in the West Indies to be preserved; that by having a place of refuge in our ports for her armed vessels, she could greatly harass and injure the very extensive commerce of England in the West Indies; take her vessels, and retreat in safety with them to our ports.

Our Government, it is well known, determined to maintain a strict neutrality between the contending parties, and refused to France the advantages which these treaties gave her; and this course was the occasion of great complaint, and of a very sharp correspondence between the ministers of France and of this Government.

In the course of the negotiation to settle the difficulties between the two nations, our Ministers, not being authorized or willing to agree to "the reciprocal engagement of compensation for damages resulting on both sides" from the breach of the treaties as proposed by France, offered finally, in their letter of the 20th of August, 1800, that the ancient treaties should be renewed and confirmed, with certain modifications. These were, that the articles respecting privateers and prizes should be so modified as, upon payment of 3,000,000 francs within seven years, no greater rights than those of the most favored nations should exist. And that the mutual guarantee should, for the future, be considered as fulfilled, by affording aid to the amount of 1,000,000 of francs when either party was attacked; and that either party might "exonerate itself wholly from its obligation, by paying to the other, within seven years, a gross sum of 5,000,000 of francs, in money, or such securities as may be issued for indemnities;" and that "there shall be a reciprocal stipulation for indemnities, and these indemnities shall be limited *to the claims of individuals.*" It will be noticed here, that the United States Ministers do not offer to France any compensation for the injury to France, as a nation, for the claims respecting the guarantee and the privileges for privateers and prizes for the past.

The French Ministers, on the 25th of August, say that their proposal to confirm the ancient treaties, and for mutual compensation, "did away all idea of a modification," and that as the American Ministers had proposed an essential modification of the 17th article, "it is therefore evident that this note refers to the second part of the alternative, which consisted of a new treaty, without indemnity."

"The French Ministers therefore insist upon the condition, that all stipulation for indemnities be laid aside."

They make the following propositions to our Ministers:

"1st. The ancient treaties shall be continued and confirmed to have their full force, as if no misunderstanding between the two nations had ever occurred.

"2d. Commissioners shall be appointed to liquidate the respective losses.

"3d. The 17th article of the treaty of commerce of 1778 shall be continued in full force with a single addition, immediately after these words, to wit, 'And on the contrary, no shelter shall be given in their ports or harbors to such as shall have made prize of the subjects of his Majesty, or of the citizens of the United States,' there shall be added 'if it be not in virtue of known treaties on the day of the signature of the present, and subsequent to the treaty of 1778, and that for the space of seven years. The 22d article subject to the same reservation as the 17th article.

"4th. If during the term of seven years the proposal *to establish* the 17th and 22d articles be not made and accepted *without reserve*, the award for indemnities determined by the Commissioners shall not be allowed.

"5th. The guarantee stipulated by the treaty of alliance shall be converted into a grant of succor for two millions. But this grant shall not be redeemable unless by a capital of ten millions."

These proposals not being satisfactory to the American Ministers, the French Ministers made on the 4th of September, 1800, proposals anew:

"We shall have the right to take our prizes into the ports of America.

"A commission shall regulate the indemnities which either of the two nations may owe to the *citizens* of the other. The indemnities which shall be due by France shall be *paid by the United States*. And *in return for which*, France yields the *exclusive privilege* resulting from the 17th and 22d articles of the treaty of commerce, and from the rights of guarantee of the 11th article of the treaty of alliance."

The American Ministers answer on the 6th September, and say these proposals are inadmissible, "the nearest approach to them" is

"1st. The former treaties shall be renewed and confirmed.

2d. The obligations of the guarantee shall be specified and limited as in the first paragraph of their 3d proposition of the 20th of August.

3d. There shall be mutual indemnity and a mutual restoration of captured property not yet definitely condemned, according to their 5th and 6th propositions of that date.

4th. If at *the exchange of ratifications, the United States propose a mutual relinquishment of indemnity, the French Republic will agree to the same; and in such case the former treaties* shall not be *deemed obligatory*, except under the 17, and 22d articles of that of commerce, the parties shall continue forever to have for their public ships of war, privateers, and prizes, such privileges in the ports of each other, as the most favored nation shall enjoy. The American Ministers requested a conference to consider these propositions—and in their journal under 12th September, they say, "The 1st and 3d *were agreed to*, with some modification of the 3d as to the rules of evidence *which did not vary its principle.*" The 2d and 4th were considered together, as in some measure connected, and after considerable discussion, the French Ministers said, unless an option perfectly similar and reciprocal was assured to the French Republic, *the operation of which would enable her to get rid of the indemnities, by an offer of abandoning the exclusive privileges*," they could not agree to it.

Here it will be noticed that *it was agreed*, that upon the former treaties being confirmed, indemnities should be paid, but France would not yield *her exclusive rights under the treaties; but by payment being made to our citizens by their own Government, or by a relinquishment of indemnities.* Our Ministers were not authorized to relinquish the indemnities, or to provide for their payment by the United States—and hence they say on the 13th September in their journal, that "being now convinced that the door was perfectly closed against all hope of obtaining indemnities *with any modifications of the treaties*, it remained only to be determined, to attempt a temporary arrangement, which would extricate the United States from the war, or that peculiar state of hostility in which they are at present involved."

This is not an allegation that indemnity could not be obtained at all, but only that it could not be obtained without a performance on our part of the obligations into which we had entered by our treaties with France.

Here then let us contemplate the condition of the negotiation and state of facts admitted by both parties. We have seen that the proposals of the American Ministers, that the former treaties be confirmed, and that there should be mutual indemnities, were agreed to. But the French Ministers would not assent to the Americans only having the right to relinquish the indemnities as a consideration for their discharge from the 17th and 22d articles of the treaty of commerce. Let it be remembered, that the claims of France cannot be regarded as destroyed by the act of July 7th, 1798, annulling the treaties, even if we admit that one party to a treaty can annul it by a legislative act. Both parties to the treaties admitted their validity until that act of 1798 was passed. For five years before the treaties were declared by the United States to be annulled France had not had the benefit of the peculiar privileges secured to her. Not that the Administration of that day is blamed; it might be wise to refuse to grant these privileges, and rely upon making a proper recompense, or upon finding an excuse for refusing it in the wrongs done to us. Our government is a parental government. It was framed and exists for the promotion of the happiness of the People; for the protection and security of the rights and property of the citizens. It was bound by every duty to obtain indemnity for these citizens, if it could do so consistently with its duties to other citizens. It could have obtained compensation for them without imposing any heavier burthen upon other citizens, than a performance of the duties enjoined by existing treaties. Or it might have obtained indemnity for these classes by causing their losses to be made good by all the citizens; that is, by the nation, as a consideration of a discharge from the treaty stipulations. Was it not just, that the consideration for the discharge of the treaty stipulations should be borne by the whole; and not by a portion, and an unfortunate portion of its citizens? This government cannot plead that it will not obtain an indemnity for its citizens of France, because France had claims against the United States of a national character to a like amount. It should keep the claims of the citizens against France separate from the claims of a nation-

al character against itself. If France had claims against the United States, those should have been satisfied by the whole People of the United States; and to make use of such claims against itself as an excuse for not obtaining compensation for losses incurred by a portion of its citizens, is to impose upon that small portion the burthen which should be borne by the whole. It is in effect to take private property for public uses without just compensation.

And if this has been done, the claimants are entitled to a fair compensation.

The indemnities were not abandoned by the negotiators, but they postponed the further discussion of the claims, on each side, to a future day, and on the 30th September concluded and signed a treaty, the second article of which is as follows:

"ART. 2d. The Ministers Plenipotentiary of the two parties not being able to agree at present respecting the treaty of alliance of the 6th of February, 1778, the treaty of amity and commerce of the same date, and the convention of the 14th of November, 1788, nor upon the indemnities mutually due or claimed, the parties will negotiate further on these subjects at a convenient time; and until they may have agreed upon these points, the said treaties and convention shall have no operation, and the relations of the two countries shall be regulated as follows."

On the 3d of February, 1801, the treaty was ratified by the Senate, "provided the second article be expunged," and by adding an article limiting the operation of the treaty to a term of eight years.

On the 31st of July, 1801, it was also ratified on the part of France, agreeing to the limitation, and to "the retrenchment of the second article, provided that by this retrenchment the two states renounce the respective pretensions which are the object of the said article."

On the 19th of December following, the treaty was again submitted to the Senate, which "resolved, that they considered the said convention as fully ratified."

This is the history of the final discharge of France from all obligation to compensate our citizens for losses. It was effected by the act of this Government, in expunging the second article of the convention, and regarding it as fully ratified, with the express provision annexed by France, that it was a renunciation, by each nation, of its claims. Thus, also, the United States were forever discharged from the onerous burthens of the ancient treaties, and from all claim of indemnity, for refusing to France the privileges which they secured to her.

And at the same time, and by the same act and instrument, these claimants were forever deprived of obtaining that indemnity from France, which if these claims had been kept separate and never had been connected with any subject of national grievance, they most certainly would have obtained.—The history of negotiation cannot shew a more direct surrender of an admitted claim, as a consideration of the release of an obligation. France always offered to set off one class of claims against the other; the Envoys of the United States refused it; the Senate and the French Government agreed to it, and accomplished it.

Nor was the right to compensation destroyed by a state of war. Neither nation regarded the right to claim, or the obligation to compensate, as destroyed on account of an existing war. The United States claimed an indemnity as an existing right; and France admitted the claim to be good.

It is true, that the United States authorized the capture of the vessels of France on the high seas, but they declared it to be only in defence of the persons and property of their citizens. War was not declared by either nation. And in the convention of 30th September, 1800, the claims on both sides were by the second article regarded as subsisting and valid. This would not have been done if war had destroyed the right to have a future negotiation and compensation. France in her negotiations declared, as our Envoys say, that her object was to avoid making compensation for these claims, because she would find herself too much exhausted by the war to satisfy them; and

yet anxious as she was, she never insisted upon a discharge because a state of war had existed.

On the 16th Aug. 1798, the Executive Directory declare their wish "to pursue the friendly habits of France towards a people whose liberty it defended." And at the same period the Minister of Marine says, "Our political situation, with regard to the United States citizen, not having as yet undergone any change which can affect the respect due to neutral nations," "no injury should be done to the safety and liberty of the officers and crews of any American vessels."

The French Ministers in their letter of the 6th of May, 1800, speak of the "misunderstanding" and "transient misunderstanding."

And in their letter of the 11th of August following, the French Ministers say, "that the treaties, which united France and the United States are not broken; that even war could not break them; but that the state of misunderstanding which has existed for sometime," "has not been a state of war, at least on the side of France." By saying the treaties are not broken, the French Ministers could not be regarded as intending to say, that they had not been in many instances violated, as they had both demanded and yielded to a compensation as proper for such violations.

The minister of Exterior Relations, Talleyrand, in a letter of August 26th, 1798, says, "Therefore, it never thought of making war against them, nor exalting civil commotions among them; and every contrary supposition is an insult to common sense."

On the part of the United States it is well known, that she always professed and determined to maintain a neutral position.

In the instructions to our Envoys, 22d October, 1799, it is said, "this conduct of the French Republic would have well justified an immediate declaration of war on the part of the United States, but desirous of maintaining peace, and still willing to leave open the door of reconciliation with France, the United States contented themselves with preparation for defence, and measures calculated to protect their commerce.

The American Ministers, in a letter dated 20th August, 1800, speaking of the act of Congress annulling the treaties, say, if it "had amounted to a cause of war; yet, as the wisdom of France recoucilled it to peace, its application on the principle of war to the extinguishment of claims, would be inexplicable.

Does it become the United States now to allege, that these claims should not be paid by her for other and different reasons than those which France used to avoid compensation?

France never seriously maintained that the claims were extinguished by war, and how can the United States now introduce such a defence?

As to the amount of compensation, there may not be any very certain and definite proof of it. It appears from a letter of the Secretary of State to a former Chairman of a Select Committee, under date of 22d January, 1827, that there were 444 cases then reported to that Department. I am informed that there were 175 cases filed before the Commissioners, under the Florida treaty, other and different from those comprising the 444 before named, making 619 cases, which are known. There are probably others. Five millions divided among the 619 cases, would give but little over 8000 to each case as an average.

It is probable the average value would be much greater than that sum.

There is an estimation of losses accompanying 88 out of the 444 cases; the aggregate of which is stated to be $2,235,702 59.

If all the cases were to exhibit losses as great as these, the amount of the losses would be more than eleven millions. But it is not supposed, that all the cases were as valuable.

The amount offered by the United States to France, to be released from the stipulations of the treaties, as we have seen, was 8,000,000 francs. France offered to receive 10,000,000 for the ex-

tinction of the guarantee, but would offer us some for the relinquishment of her exclusive privileges under the treaty of commerce.

It may be inferred from this, that both nations considered that the claims would amount to more than these sums—as France was anxious to set off the claims against the stipulations of the treaty, and the United States declined it, until it was done as before stated.

It may be proper to remark, that these 619 cases, are of an entirely different character, as it alleged to be so, from those for which recompense was obtained under the Louisiana treaty, or under the Florida treaty; and if they do not so prove to be, no compensation can be made by the bill, as it does not provide for such as were provided for under those treaties. Our debt is paid. Compensation has been secured by treaty for all, or nearly all, the injuries which our citizens have suffered from other nations. Can the high character of this nation for doing justice to all, at home and abroad, be maintained without making compensation for these injuries, which have been the consideration of procuring for her a discharge from every onerous obligation? If the bill may pass, the only great claim remaining will be satisfied, and the duties of the Government, to do justice to all, will have been fulfilled. If these claims are just, all fear for evil consequences to arise from their allowance, may be dismissed. Things are rightly so ordered here, that to do justice to all others, is to serve ourselves best.

When Mr. SHEPLEY concluded—

Mr. HILL took the floor and moved to adjourn; but afterwards withdrew the motion.

The Senate then proceeded, on the motion of Mr. POINDEXTER, to the consideration of Executive Business.

When the doors were opened—

The Senate adjourned.

HOUSE OF REPRESENTATIVES.

MONDAY, Dec. 22, 1834.

After the presentation of petitions and memorials—

Mr. BYNUM moved the following resolution, which lies one day:

Resolved, That the Secretary of War be instructed to lay before this House, a report of the progress of different works of internal improvement now carried on by the General Government in the State of North Carolina, and the amount of appropriations expended in the prosecution of the same.

On motion of Mr. DUNLAP,

Resolved, That the Committee on the Post Office and Post Roads be instructed to inquire into the expediency of establishing a post route from Balivar, Tennessee, by Nubbin Ridge, Simpson's Bridge, on Hatcher River, Cyprus, Cumberland Wolfe's Ferry, on Tennessee River, to William Lilly's, in Harden County, said State.

On motion of Mr. CLAY, of Alabama,

Resolved, That the Committee on the Post Offices and Post Roads, be instructed to inquire into the expediency of establishing a post route from Campbellton, Georgia, by way of Jacksonville, in Benton County, to Ashville, in St. Clair County, Alabama. And also a post route from Belfonte, in Jackson County, by way of Bellos and Nicholson's, in Will's Valley, and Children's Ferry, on Coosa river, to Jacksonville, in Benton County, Alabama.

On motion of Mr. EWING,

Resolved, That the Committee on Roads and Canals, be instructed to inquire into the expediency of making an appropriation to provide durable materials to construct a Bridge on the National Road over the river Wabash at Terre Haute, upon an approved plan, not impeding or obstructing the navigation thereof.

On motion of Mr. POPE,

Resolved, That the Committee on Commerce be instructed to inquire into the expediency of making an appropriation in aid of the support of the Marine Hospital, at the city of Louisville, in the State of Kentucky.

On motion of Mr. EWING, of Indiana,

Resolved, That the Committee on Military Affairs be instructed to inquire into the justice and

expediency of making provisions for the widows and orphans of such officers and soldiers in the service of the United States, as died on the frontier, in the late Indian war with Black Hawk.

On motion of Mr. MAY,

Resolved, That the Committee on Public Lands be instructed to inquire into the expediency of repealing so much of the law in relation to the sale of the public lands, which prohibits the actual settler from purchasing more than two tracts of 40 acres each.

On motion of Mr. LYON, of Michigan,

Resolved, That the Committee on Commerce be instructed to inquire into the expediency of erecting a Light-house on or near Point Wagoushance, on the Strait of Michillimackinac, in Michigan Territory,

The bill to authorise the Registers and Receivers of the Public Land Offices to administer oaths connected with the entry and sale of the public lands, was taken up, and read, as follows:

Be it enacted by the Senate and House of Representatives of the United States of America in Congress assembled, That it shall be lawful *for any Register or Receiver of any Land Office of the United States to administer any oath that may be necessary, or required by law, in the entry or purchase of public lands, and to receive therefor such compensation as now is, or may hereafter be, allowed for the administration of oaths or taking affidavits, by the laws of the State or Territory in which such service may be performed;* and such affidavit shall be filed in the proper Land Office, as now required by law.

Sec. 2. *And be it further enacted*, That any person who shall wilfully and corruptly take any false oath before any Register or Receiver of any Land Office of the United States, in any of the cases contemplated in the foregoing section, shall be held and deemed guilty of perjury, and, on conviction thereof, be punished as in other cases of wilful and corrupt perjury.

Mr. LANE moved to amend the bill by striking out the words in italics and inserting the following in lieu thereof:

"And it is hereby made the duty of the Registers and Receivers of the Land Offices of the United States to administer all such oaths and to fill up all such affidavits (as shall be furnished to such Register or Receiver from the proper department in the form of printed blanks) as shall, or may be necessary or required by law in the entry or purchase of the public lands, without compensation."

Mr. McCARTY said, he was opposed to the amendment offered by his colleague, (Mr. Lane.) He considered it would be unjust and illiberal on the part of the Government to require its public officers to perform these additional duties without compensation. He said he was in favor of the passage of the bill, for it contained provisions that would relieve the purchasers of the public lands in many districts from much trouble; instead of being under the necessity of hunting up a judicial officer to draw up the necessary affidavits and administer the oaths required by the existing laws, as is now the case, this bill contemplates the performance of this duty where it should be, at the register's office where the entry is made; he was, therefore, for the bill. He thought it ought to be amended, but that the amendment under consideration was objectionable. Mr. McC. said, he considered it improper to require either the payment of this additional expense by the purchasers of public lands, or the performance of the duties without compensation. It was the act of the Government that made it requisite that these affidavits should be taken; they should therefore pay the expense. He hoped the amendment under consideration would not be adopted, and concluded by asking the reading of an amendment which he sent to the Chair, providing for the payment of these additional services by the Government; which, if in order, he would offer when the amendment then before the House was disposed of.

Mr. LANE was opposed to the amendment of his colleague. It would greatly increase the salaries of these officers, who already received almost the best pay under the Government. They were offices which were eagerly sought after, and tenaciously held on to, under the present compensation. Those officers are now paid a salary of $500, and one per cent. on the amount of purchase money received by them for public lands. They are also furnished stationary. Many of them receive from $1500 to $3000 per annum; and if the amendment of his colleague prevailed, some of them would receive at least $5000 per annum, and the whole of them would obtain by it a greatly increased compensation. By his own amendment, he proposed that neither the purchaser nor the Government should pay the fees for administering the necessary oaths; but that the duty should be performed without fee by those who already receive the most ample salary.

Mr. McCARTY replied, that the reason urged by his colleague in support of his amendment was, in his estimation, a strong reason why it should not pass. It is urged, said Mr. McC., that if the officers who are required to perform these extra duties should be paid by the Government for the labor performed, it would increase their salary some one or two thousand dollars per annum, and that this would be too great a deduction from the proceeds of the land sales for the Government to tolerate. If this be true, which is denied, what kind of principle do you establish? Why, by the doctrine of the gentleman, you impose a duty upon your public agents, worth, in justice and good faith, $1000 or $2000 per annum to perform; but because he is well paid for performing other duties which you have required at his hands by previous laws, you will pay him nothing, though it may be necessary, in order to perform this duty, to pay away for clerk hire half his salary. This, Mr. Speaker, has not been the principle upon which this Government has ever acted; but I differ, said Mr. McC., very much from the statement of the gentleman in reference to the extent of this increase of salary by the payment of these extra duties. I have had something to do with this kind of service myself, and I will venture to say, that the compensation for these extra duties, by the allowance of the ordinary fees, will not increase the emolument of the officers of a single land office in the United States to exceed $200 or $300 per annum; but notwithstanding this fact, there were times immediately preceding a public sale, when pre-emption rights had to be perfected, when it would require more than one or two clerks to enable the register to keep pace with the demands upon his office, and this must be done with the greatest possible despatch, cost the officer what it may. I am not, said Mr. McC., in favor of increasing salaries, but the reverse; but when you demand the time and service of a citizen, you should pay him a reasonable compensation for the services you thus demand and receive. Mr. McC. was aware that his colleague was conversant with the transactions in a particular land office; his attention had upon a time been particularly directed that way, but the gentleman knows full well that the burthens of his amendment will not fall upon the officers of that office. No, sir, those duties will not have to be performed there; the burthen will fall elsewhere; for I doubt very much, said Mr. McC. whether it has ever in the period of twelve months, or whether it will within the same period to come, be necessary, unconnected with any other subject than the sales of the public lands, to take fifty affidavits at the office to which the gentleman has reference; therefore, these officers will have but a small portion of these extra duties to perform, and therefore, entitled to no extra pay. They, it is true, get high salaries, and they ought to be brought down, as well as many others, to a standard with those who have to devote their whole time and attention, and receive much less.

I am not sure, said Mr. McC. that my amendment can be entertained by the House, as it provides for the payment of money, until it is considered in committee. [The Speaker replied that it could not.] Then, (said Mr. McC.) I move to commit the bill to the Committee of the Whole House, in order that it may be properly amended.

Mr. CLAY hoped that the motion to commit would not prevail. The main object of the bill was to afford facility to the purchasers of the public lands, in making their entries and purchases. Neither of the amendments was important to those most interested, and they would prefer paying the fee of twenty-five cents to the defeat of the bill. In order to ensure the passage of the act, he had assented to the amendment of one of the gentlemen from Indiana (Mr. Lane.) He never could support the amendment of the other member from the same State (Mr. McCarty.) A commitment, unless to a day special, would be tantamount to a defeat of the measure, and he hoped it would not be done.

Mr. McCARTY proposed to commit the bill and make it the order for to-morrow.

Mr. LYON, of Michigan, was opposed to both amendments. As a matter of convenience, by the original bill the purchaser may either make oath before the Registers and Receivers, or before a Justice of the Peace. This was all they would require or expect.

Mr. ASHLEY thought it a trifling matter as it regarded the fee for administering the oaths. He had no objection to the amendment offered by one of the gentlemen from Indiana (Mr. Lane) In order, however, to prevent the delay or defeat of the bill, by the discussion of unimportant propositions, he would move the previous question.

Mr. ASHLEY subsequently withdrew his motion for the previous question, when the motion to commit was negatived.

Mr. J. Q. ADAMS said, he hoped the first amendment would be adopted, and that the amendment last offered, would be rejected. These officers, the Registers and Receivers of the public lands, owe their whole time to the public which employs and pays them If they were authorized to administer these oaths, it would be the public time, and not their own which would be devoted to that service. The last amendment offered, would operate as a reduction of the price of the public lands. Mr. A. said, there were already propositions enough before the House for reduing the price of the public domain, and for giving away the public lands. We hear them daily—propositions, he might more properly call them, for *robbing* the public of its lands. Mr. A. said, it should not be forgotten that these lands belonged to the whole Union, and yet we hear the monstrous doctrine almost daily advanced that the lands should belong to the States in which they are located! It was time for those States, who receive no part of the benefit derived from plundering the public domain, to look to their rights. He called upon members to hold on to, and guard sacredly the public purse-strings. The duties of the Registers and Receivers would not interfere with the administration of these oaths.

Mr. CLAY said, that the remarks of the gentleman from Massachusetts, (Mr. Adams,) would have been more strictly in order, if made upon an occasion in prospect, when the whole subject of the public lands would come up for discussion. The gentleman seemed to be excited, and spoke of the daily attempts on the part of the new States to rob the Government of its territory. Was this true? The applications made to this House, generally looked to a reduction of price on inferior lands, according to their diminished value. The propriety of complying with these requests would be a matter of inquiry at the proper time. But the gentleman complains that the old States receive no benefit from the disposition of the public domain. What, said Mr. C., becomes of the millions which are paid into the public Treasury by the purchasers of the public lands in the New States? Was not much the greater proportion of money thus paid into the Treasury, expended for the benefit of the old States? In relation to the present bill, its passage was of more importance to the purchasers, than any consideration connected with the subject of fees for administering the oaths referred to. The principal object was to relieve the purchasers from the trouble of hunting up a judicial officer for that purpose, and he trusted the question would be taken at once, and the bill be suffered to pass.

Mr. BOON said the amendment of his colleague (Mr. Lane) would operate unequally. By it, those Receivers and Registers who will have much the largest salaries, will have the least to

perform. He was anxious that the officers referred to should be put upon something like a footing of equality.

Mr. LANE said his colleague (Mr. Boon) was mistaken in supposing that the greatest amount of duty under this bill would fall to the lot of those who received the smallest salaries. He referred to the business of several of the land offices to show that in this particular, he was correct.

It was proper that some person acquainted with subject should administer these oaths, and hence the Receivers and Registers had been named; but what was most important, they were required to perform this duty without fee or reward. He agreed with the gentleman from Massachusetts, (Mr. Adams) that these officers owed their time to the country, and they were well paid for it.

Mr. MARDIS said the debate which was progressing he considered wide of the question. The bill proposes to substitute the Registers and Receivers of the Public Land Offices for judicial officers, before whom certain oaths or affidavits shall be made. It was also proposed to amend this proposition, and require this duty to be performed without charge to the person making oath: and upon this question of mere convenience or facility to the purchaser of the public lands, we are engaged in a discussion of the whole land subject. This was certainly not the time or the occasion, to enter into a debate upon the future disposition of the national domain; and he therefore hoped that the bill now before the House would be permitted to progress.

Mr. LANE'S amendment was then agreed to, and the bill ordered to be engrossed.

On motion of Mr. CONNOR, the Select Committee appointed at the last session to examine and report the situation of the Post Office Department, had leave to sit during the session of the House.

Mr. CHAMBERS, from the Committee on Private Land Claims, reported a bill for the relief of H. Bright; which was read twice and committed.

PAY OF NAVAL OFFICERS.

The House then resolved itself into a Committee of the Whole on the state of the Union, Mr. BRIGGS in the Chair, on the bill to equalise and regulate the pay of the officers of the Army and Navy of the United States, and the amendments thereunto proposed by Mr. Watmough, as Chairman of the Select Committee, and by Mr. Wise, a member of the Committee on Naval Affairs.

Mr. PEARCE said he had but few words to add to the remarks which he addressed to the Committee on Friday last. He would be brief; and he hoped the example would be followed. He professed no spirit of prophecy; but he deemed it no hazard to predict that if the bill was not passed through the Committee to-day, or at furthermost to-morrow, its fate would be greatly perilled by the delay. Mr. P. then proceeded to give the reasons which induced him to prefer the amendment offered by the gentleman from Virginia (Mr. Wise,) to that of the Select Committee. When he last addressed the committee, it appeared that he misconceived the nature of the duties of a gunner on board of ship. He supposed his station to be at the gun, but he was now informed that this officer had charge of the magazine, and was placed below to deal out the ammunition in time of action. Mr. P. said, however, he had nothing to take back in what he had said. The importance of the office, in his mind, was in no respect depreciated, but rather enhanced. A man who filled that very responsible station should be one of character and respectability, and his pay should be commensurate with his services. Mr. P. next spoke of the importance of the officer denominated the schoolmaster; or, by the amendment of the Select Committee, called the Professor of Mathematics. He contended that these should be as competent as any, of the Professors of our Universities, and have a corresponding compensation. There once was a project afoot, for the establishment of a Naval School in our country; but for his own part he had no hope of living so long as to see that object realised. When he reflected on the strong feeling—he might say prejudice—existing against our Military School at West Point,

he despaired of ever seeing one established for the Navy. Another difficulty was, that even if the project was a popular one, a Delegate in the Councils of the nation from Maryland would probably deem Annapolis a proper location for the School: —One from Pennsylvania, would think Philadelphia its most eligible site—while he himself would doubtless contend that the place of his own residence was preferable to all others. Under these circumstances the office of School master on board became doubly important in his estimation. He next spoke of the pay of Surgeons and their Assistants,—preferring the more liberal compensation offered by the amendment of the gentleman from Va. (Mr. Wise.) He understood these officers were compelled to furnish their own medicines—which rendered it necessary to expend two years' salary before the commencement of an ordinary voyage. Mr. P. said, he did not wish to curtail the pay of any officer in the service, but he could not understand what was meant by the continual reiteration of the importance of commanding officers being enabled to support their dignity, and the dignity of our government, while abroad. He wished to pay them liberally—to pay them all that was necessary. But he did not conceive it to be proper to take the pay of either French or British officers as a criterion to regulate that of our own. What might be necessary for the support of Admiral Nelson at Naples, he did not think would be required by Commodore Rodgers on the same station. The latter would not, like the former, have to defray the extravagant expenses of the lady of an English nobleman. Again, there were other disparaging circumstances in the service operating against the junior officers of the navy. They had not the same chances of promotion that their seniors have enjoyed, among which was the benefit of the wars in which our country had ever been engaged. Mr. P. said, he certainly could have no feeling conflicting with the interests of the Captains. To Commodore Rodgers he felt under peculiar obligations, as having done more for his State than any other officer in the navy. Captains Hull and Chauncey he looked upon as the next door neighbors of himself and his constituents, Captain Morris he considered as the joint property of Rhode Island and Connecticut. But some of the senior officers of the navy have already enjoyed an opportunity that probably will never fall to the lot of the juniors—that of making fortunes by the transportation of specie. The gentleman from New York, (Mr. Mann,) had advocated the reduction of the salaries of the officers of the army. This Mr. P. believed to be totally impracticable. He adverted to the advance which had been made in the pay of naval officers of the Government, particularly the Heads of Departments, all of which had been advanced at least one-third; while that of our naval officers has ever remained stationary. Attempts had often been made to reduce the pay of members of Congress; but gentlemen all knew how futile all such attempts were. Masters Commandant in our navy must remain fifty years in the service before their daily pay became equal to the boys—the pages and messengers of the House. These boys, be said, faithfully earned their money, perhaps more faithfully than many members did. But where was our liberality to old and faithful servants in the public employment? It certainly was not evinced in the pay of Masters Commandant. It was true, we sometimes paid them with compliments—with votes— and many with a sword. Mr. P. proceeded to compare the pay of the officers of the army and navy—contending that the latter should be raised, rather than the former reduced. He concluded by repeating his preference for the amendment of the gentleman from Virginia (Mr. Wise,) as the most equitable and satisfactory in all its details.

Mr. VANDERPOEL said, that the course which the debate had already taken, was such as every gentleman at all acquainted with the elements of which this House was, and from the nature of things ever must be composed, would naturally expect. The American Navy! A proposition to increase the pay of its officers!!! What charming themes to draw out on the one side the

soul-stirring effusions of those orators (and he so cognised one [Mr. Ward] in a most esteemed colleague) whose hearts were warmed, and whose tongues were inspired by the recollection of what our gallant Navy had done; and on the other, the more chilling lucubrations of those over-cautious sentinels, at the door of your Treasury, who over-estimate of one virtue, sometimes called economy, and sometimes parsimony, we are too apt to... might properly be called national justice. He would not say, that the remarks of another of his honorable colleagues, (Mr. Mann,) who had evinced such uncompromising hostility to this bill and its amendments, entitled him to a rank among these too faithful sentinels. The frank and bold manner in which he always stated his propositions, was an ample guarantee of his sincerity in what ever course he might take in relation to the various subjects that came here for our action and deliberation.

His colleague (Mr. Mann) seemed to be but a little troubled about the manner in which this bill came before us. It did not, in his opinion, come from the right source. It did not emanate from a Standing Committee of the House, and therefore, in his opinion, it ought not to be treated with much favor. For my part, said Mr. V., I care not how it came here; if it has only proceeded from one of the regularly constituted organs of the House, I will, if it has merit, adopt it. But the child charm and attraction enough to command it to our favor? Has it the charms of truth and justice? If so, why should we not embrace it? Why institute a most useless and unkind inquiry into its pedigree? But, if it were in this instance necessary to vindicate its parentage, or establish its legitimacy, he would not even despair of the task. Did the subject, referred to the committee which had reported the bill under consideration, peculiarly belong to either the Military or the Naval Committee? Not at all, sir. Both the army and navy were within the scope of the inquiry contained in the resolution which had originated the committee. They were required to inquire into the expediency of equalising the pay of the officers of the army and navy, and it was therefore emphatically fit and proper, that it should be referred to an amphibious committee, like the one which has reported this bill. The fallacy of his friend and colleague's objection to the bill spoke with great deference,) was excited only by the unsoundness of his views in relation to the substance.

In regard to the general question, whether its compensation of the naval officers ought to be raised, long speeches must surely be unnecessary, arguments for and against the proposition were very readily occur to every intelligent mind. It is very new or unknown facts could be disclosed— strikingly new principles could be developed in discussion. The only questions to be determined were—First. Is the labourer worthy of his hire; and secondly, what compensation do the obligations of justice, as well as the honor of the nation, require that we should render him. For his own part, Mr. V. said, he would freely acknowledge that until his attention was called to the bill, he was not aware (to borrow the very just and emphatic language of the Secretary of the Treasury) "how degradingly low!" was the compensation provided by law for the officers of the navy. He did not mean could doubt, that they were more meanly paid, than any other officer under the government. Was it not indeed surprising, that this prospect of such pitiful emolument, so many good and gallant men, who have wants like ourselves, could have been induced to enter the naval service! The love of country and the love of glory must indeed have been with them, what they should have been, paramount considerations. They must, however, be remembered, that many of most of the officers entered the naval service before they had arrived to manhood, and were induced by parents and friends to choose this wild and patriotic occupation. They grew up to such estate, and then found themselves in the naval service of their country. Their habits were formed, and their entire unfitness for any other pursuit in life, by which they could earn their bread...

*

wives and children, were as notorious and as well established, as that the fishes of the deep could subsist only in their native element. Emphatically given up, then, as they were, to their country, were they not the legitimate objects of the care, or at least the *justice* of that country? And yet, so low was the allowance upon which their stern parent had hitherto placed them, that parent whose interests they had ever been ready to vindicate, and whose honor they had so valiantly protected, that it would now be an insult to the understanding of intelligent and honorable gentlemen to attempt, by any labored process of reasoning to prove, that their present compensation could afford them aught but a mere *scanty subsistence*, that if true to the honor and dignity of that flag which floats over them, they could not, with their mere official earnings, make any provision for old age and decrepitude, or become able to bequeath to their children aught but *the glory of their achievements*, which was to be sure, in its way, very good food for a proud heart, but after all, a very poor guarantee against nakedness and hunger.

Mr. V. said, he would not enter upon a crusade against the army, but justice required that he should remind the house, that the present compensation provided for the army is vastly greater than that which you give to your navy. The report upon your table tells you, sir, that a Major General of the first-rank, who ranks with a Captain of the navy over fifteen years standing, receives $3,542 more than the navy Captain; that a Brigadier General, who ranks with a Captain over ten years standing receives $2,231 more than such Captain, and that a Colonel, who ranks with a Captain of the third rank, received $799 per year more than such Captain! He might go on to the end of the chapter, but he had already instituted comparisons enough to shew, that the inequality was most gross and shocking! And what was there in the nature of the two branches of the public service to justify such prodigious inequality in the standard of compensation allowed to them? There was nothing. But on the contrary, it was no injustice to the army to contend, that in time of peace, the claim to the highest compensation was vastly in favor of the navy. Yes—Commissions in the army in time of peace, were, comparatively, sinecures. Barring the toilsome and honorable expedition against Black Hawk, and an occasional chase after a few retreating and predatory savages, what has your army done, or rather, what has it had to do, since the peace of 1815? It had done all that had been required of it, but it could, in the nature of things, have but little or nothing to do. Not so with the navy—our vast and growing commerce must be protected, the pirate must be driven from the ocean, and peace and prosperity may smile over and gladden the land, but they bring to the gallant sons of the ocean no exemption from toil and peril.

And yet, *sir*, how has it happened, that when the pay of every other officer of the Government has been increased, your Secretaries, your Treasurer, your Register, your Auditors, and your Clerks in the Departments, those Clerks (he did not mean to speak disrespectfully of them as men, for he knew and esteemed many of them,) some of whom, as it regarded the nature of their duties, were mere machines, that did not require any more mind than the pens with which they copied the thoughts of others; how, he asked, had it happened, that their compensation had been increased and increased from time to time, until they were in the receipt of very comfortable, not to say formidable sums, when the pay of the officers of the Navy, the men who were the protectors of your commerce, and in some measure the guardians of your national honor, had not, as had all other compensations, "*grown with the growth*" of the nation? It was, sir, because those brave men were not able to be here, leaning over our bar, as others had an opportunity of being, to petition and beg for an increase of their remuneration. No. They were on duty, many of them far from their friends, their native land, and all the endearments of home. They were on their stations or cruising on distant seas.

"Their march is o'er the mountain wave,
"There home is on the deep."

And because such was the case, would Congress neglect them? He trusted not. It was, in fact, high time, that the rights of these meritorious men should be taken into consideration. He was no enthusiast, but he thought a very high responsibility rested upon us to foster this most important branch of our national defence. He would say, that when he looked over the statement of the salaries that were paid to our naval officers, and compared those of the two services, the army and the navy, together, and looked also at the sums paid to our civil officers, he blushed, yes, blushed to turn from that statement to the records of history, in which it was told, how much our navy had contributed towards the glorious results, which this country had attained, with what imperishable laurels it had decorated its brow!!

An argument against increasing the pay of the naval officers had been used by one of his honorable colleagues [Mr. Mann] which struck him as entirely unsound. He had observed, that the present compensation of Captains and Commanders of squadrons was much more than many gentlemen here can earn in their professions, and, therefore, it ought not to be increased. I fear, sir, that if this standard were applied to our own cases, it would be pretty sure to prove that many of us illy deserve our eight dollars per day. The gentleman no doubt alluded to lawyers and physicians. Now, sir, many of us but too well know that clients and patients in our respective vicinities are unkind enough to imagine that they can very comfortably dispense with our services, and as to such (he did not mean to insinuate that his esteemed colleague was one) it might truly be said, at the end of a long session, when their per diem and mileage make a pretty "*snug sum*," that their receipts here range far above the standard, which the gentleman has prescribed as a proper measure of compensation to public officers, viz. *the amount they could earn at home*. But, sir, ought not more elevated considerations to enter into the account in this matter than the mere estimate of what an attorney, in some quiet village, without any temptation or exposure to expense could possibly earn or would probably require for the support of himself and his family? Can those who measure the merits and the claims of the weather-beaten sons of the ocean by so contracted a standard, appreciate the perils and privations, to which they are constantly exposed, and the very important trusts that are confided to them? Do they recollect that they are not only doomed to grapple with the enemies of their country, when the war trump is sounding, but that the storm, the tempest, and the pestilence, are everlasting foes with which no truce can be effected; that they are in a great measure the guardians of your national honor abroad, and that to them is committed, to a great extent, the high trust of convincing the subjects of monarchs and despots, what they have so strenuously contended against, that a popular Government is not subversive of all those courtesies and civilities, and *that noble chivalry*, which serve to characterize the gentleman, and elevate civilization? These were duties and considerations which, in his humble estimation, elevated the standard of a naval officer's wants, above that of the sons of Esculapius or the disciples of Lord Coke. By saying this, he certainly meant no disparagement to those professions, of one of which he was an humble member.

He would, however, ask, why select any of the learned professions as furnishing a prop r measure of compensation for your naval officers? Why not take one of the mechanical branches; for surely, the mechanics were not inferior in respectability or national utility, to any of the professions which have been called in question. No sir; quite the contrary. The farmers and mechanics, the working and producing classes of the country, are indeed the salt of this nation. Blot them out, sir, and few and feeble indeed will be the hands to water that tree of liberty which took root with the revolution. Why not fix upon *their* earnings and *their* income, as furnishing a proper measure of compensation to those, who consent to be torn from their families, and all that is dear *in* "HOME" to fight the battles of your country? Why not say, that a journeyman mechanic can earn only $300 per year, and therefore your naval officers should not receive more? Gentlemen, while pursuing the course, the mischievous tendency of which I am attempting to demonstrate, should go the whole—(wrong, I mean.) They should not be obstructed *in*, or diverted *from* their course by the mole-hill impediments of national justice or national honor. He insisted upon the soundness of the principle, that there were some officers of the navy, whose compensation should be such as to enable them to extend and reciprocate those hospitalities which they will naturally receive when abroad. It had been very appropriately asked during this discussion, by an honorable gentleman from Massachusetts, (Mr. Reed,) why does your President receive $25,000 per year? This was truly a "pretty snug sum"—yes, it was a very large sum. Was it given to enable him to secure an inheritance for his children? No, sir. It was to enable him to extend those hospitalities which all men of liberal feelings have a right to expect, and do expect, from the Chief of a great, a free, and a wealthy nation. Your naval officers received civilities when abroad, and they would, as a general rule, dishonor the profession they had chosen, and that country whose stars and stripes they were so gallantly displaying, not to reciprocate them. This necessarily increased their expenses, and it was the occurrence of every year, that a high-minded officer, having done all, and no more, than the honor of his country required him to do, returned from a foreign cruise with empty pockets; yes, almost overwhelmed with debt and embarrassment. His proud spirit, sir, his love of country, could not brook the idea, that the men and the officers of foreign nations should, when his back was turned, tauntingly and exultingly say, among themselves, "There is a specimen of your free Governments—its officers afraid to accept of hospitalities abroad, because they are too stingy and too mean to return them." Sooner than expose the country which they loved, to such cutting, such humiliating reproach, they have ever proudly sustained the honor of that country, though want and poverty were its sure penalties. He would here take occasion to remark, that the interchange of those civilities, on the part of our naval officers, with the citizens of other nations, was, or might be, of great utility, independently of that courtesy, he should say *decency*, which required our officers to respect them. By this reciprocation of courtesies, our officers enjoyed the opportunity of becoming acquainted with the habits and manners of other nations. They acquired facilities to see, and to become acquainted with their harbors, their coasts, their public works, their resources, and with their vulnerable or their impregnable points—all which information might be of inestimable value in the event of a war with such nation. Every dictate of interest, combined with every consideration of national honor, to demonstrate the expediency of giving to our naval officers such compensation as would enable them to return, to a decent and reasonable extent, whatever civilities they might receive from the citizens of other countries.

But, said Mr. V., I have been at sea quite long enough. It was high time, that he anchored for a few moments to the amendments of the gentleman from Virginia, (Mr. Wise.) He should vote for those amendments, because the original bill, or rather the amendment of the gentleman from Pennsylvania, as well as the amendments proposed by the honorable Chairman of the Committee, (Mr. Watmough) introduced a new principle in our statute books.—Hitherto seniority of commission, had not given any claim to an increase of a compensation. It was true that by regulations established by the Secretaries of War and the Navy in 1818, with the approbation of the President, of the United States, it was established "that the rank and precedence of sea and land officers will take place according to the seniority of their respective commissions," but he was not aware that there had been any legislative sanction of this principle.

[Mr. WATMOUGH here referred Mr. V., to page 5 of the report, to shew that this regulation has been sanctioned.]

Mr. V. said if it were as the honorable gentleman had stated: He stood corrected. He had, however, another objection to the honorable gentleman's amendments. He thought, that in his very laudable

solicitude for the senior, he had not done justice to the junior office. He would instance the case of the lieutenants. They were in the first instance allowed $1500 when at sea, and $1200 when waiting orders. By the last amendments of the gentleman from Pennsylvania they were to be allowed $1200, when at sea, and $1000, when waiting orders.

There was in his opinion a vast disproportion between the junior and the senior offices. What was the present salary of a lieutenant? It amounted to $960 per year. This included rations and every allowance that they were entitled to. Now, when he considered, that many of them would probably have to wait and toil forty years, before they could be promoted—that they would have to serve six times as long as the Patriarch of old served for his beloved prize, before they could be elevated to a captaincy, he thought the sum they now receive most "degradingly low," and that the sum first mentioned could not be deemed too high. He had, until he had very recently inquired into the matter, supposed, that everything was provided for our naval officers, when at sea, that there were, what are commonly called "ship's stores," on board of our naval vessels, and that the officers, as well as the sailors, were provisioned at the national expense. He had discovered, however, that such was not the case, that the officers had to find their own provisions, and even their own table furniture, and cooking utensils. Now it was to be kept in remembrance, that many of these officers had wives and families, also, to provide for on shore. They had in fact two messes to support out of their incomes.

And when he considered how onerous, how highly responsible were the duties of a lieutenant, their claim to an increase of compensation would be greatly fortified. And what were those duties? As he understood, he had in time of action to direct and point the guns. Each lieutenant had charge of from 60 to 70 men—there being from 12 to 14 men stationed at each gun. These men, it was his duty to drill, and when the enemy has boarded, the lieutenant was, as he had learned from a source upon which he could rely, the first to board, unless a pike driven through his body prevented the execution of this hazardous piece of duty. He had, too, to take his turn on watch, and was held responsible for the general safety of the vessel. And what were his duties and obligations according to the naval code of nations, on coming into port? Because it might be said that he, at least, had not the necessity of reciprocating the hospitality of officers in foreign service.

But it was not so—according to the custom of naval life, the captains messed by themselves, and the subordinate officers by themselves; and if a lieutenant were entertained by an officer of the same grade in foreign service, on board ship, or on shore, he had to reciprocate the courtesy in like manner, by inviting him to the lieutenants' mess. He had asked a lieutenant how he managed to get along, having to comply with these customs, and having, besides, a wife and family to provide. And his answer was, that "when he left port, he always found himself confoundedly in debt; and when at sea, he worked for a dead horse, and there denied himself all the luxuries and many of the comforts of life." Is this, sir, the measure of American justice to public servants? He would not impugn the motives of the gentleman from Pennsylvania, (Mr. Watmough,) for he deserved much credit for what he had done in this matter, but he, nevertheless, thought that he had in some measure, overlooked the claim of these Lieutenants.

There was another heresy prevailing, which was in regard to the office and duties of gunner. A gentleman from Pennsylvania (Mr. Sutherland) had spoken with much eloquence in behalf of the gunners—now he (Mr. V.) had supposed that the gunner was the man who loaded and pointed and fired the guns; but he found that such was not the case, that they were not the "*men of fire and smoke*," that their station was in the magazine, below, comparatively—out of the reach of shot and danger, and that they smelled no other "smoke" than that of the lamp which lighted that magazine. Why not, he would ask, give the increase to the hardy tars who had to serve at the guns, who were exposed to all the danger?

[Mr. SUTHERLAND here observed that he had also pleaded for the sailors.]

Mr. V. said he had already detained the Committee much longer than he had intended when he rose, and hoped that he might, in conclusion, be permitted to say, without incurring the imputation of egotism, that he represented a strictly fresh water district; that he had had, in the course of his life, but little or no intercourse with naval officers, and did not know that a single one of them could be numbered among his constituents. He did not know that he had a single relative in the naval service, and the vote which he should give for a reasonable increase of the compensation of this important branch of service would be dictated solely by a sense of the vast importance of the navy to the interest and honor, if not the safety of the country, and of the strong claims which its too long neglected officers had to the justice, not to say the *liberality*, of this great, this just, and opulent nation.

Mr. R. M. JOHNSON, of Kentucky, said that in every discussion of a measure during this short session, it was the duty of all to remember how much business we had to transact and thus put a just value upon time, and to economize it. With this sentiment in his mind he would, on this important measure, indulge in a few general remarks. As to the Navy, it was a great favorite with the nation; and that favorable opinion was not without good reason—the history of our country would furnish ample cause why we were partial to the Navy—we would refer to our naval conflicts with the Barbary powers, Tropoli, and our quasi war with France, and particularly our late war with Great Britain—who does not recollect the feelings and gratitude of confidence, of patriotism, which swelled the bosom of every faithful citizen at the news of our splendid naval victories following each other in quick succession. Perry and McDonough on the lakes; Hull, Decatur, Lawrence, Porter, and others, on the mountain waves, on the ocean.

Our gallant Navy, therefore, was justly a favorite with the People. It had never excited the jealousy of the statesman or patriot. Its motto was, For our country, right or wrong for our country. This being the true state of the case, it was to him unaccountable and surprising that such opposition, such persevering opposition should have been made to every proposition for the last twenty years to make adequate provision for the Navy, and to assign proper grades of command to the officers. The People, by common consent, conferred upon our senior naval officers the honorary title of Commodore, yet our laws have conferred no such command. The highest grade of command in our naval service was that of Captain. He did not see any reason for such a state of things. It might have been correct when our Navy was in its infancy—when we had only a Captain's command—but now we had increased our Navy from necessity—it had increased with our commerce and our population—and it was correct to confer higher grades of command, as much so as to confer the command and grade of a Colonel to a Regiment, of a Major to a Battalion, and a Captain to a Company. But let us pass from this subject to that of the compensation. Adequate compensation was still more necessary and important to the service than grades of command. It was a very difficult subject to know precisely what compensation ought to be given. It was very easy to commence with the salary and compensation of the civil officers of Government, and where they get annually $3,000, to say they could live upon $2,000; and that members of Congress who now received $8 per day might live upon 6 or $4. In case of necessity, for our country, Mr. J. said we could all live upon half rations. But it should be recollected we were not fixing the compensation of the Navy upon any such principle. We were fixing it upon the principle of justice—of propriety. The laborer was worth his hire—the officers of the Navy, and all attached to the Navy were working men—hard-working men—and that man would find himself egregiously mistaken if he supposed that he could enter the naval service and sleep upon beds of down. If he supposed that he could sleep and slumber, and fold his arms together to sleep without trouble, without anxiety, he would find out his
culation. The reverse was his lot; it was
of toil, of suffering, of hardship, of danger.
the hour that a man enters the naval servic
country, until he is hurried to that bour
whence no traveller returns, he will learn
lot is one of privation, toil, anxiety, and
Mr. J. said he was a working man
hard working man, ever since he had grown
manhood—and his constituents were working
and reasonable men, and patriotic men—
is the reason why they have honored me
They know I will not squander the public m
they know I am not extravagant myself, and
will not vote for extravagant salaries. But
have always sustained me in voting for salarie
reasonable and just compensation, which wil
the officer easy in his circumstances; that
will enable him to live comfortably—not l
ously; that which will enable him to furnish
self and a small family with the necessari
comforts of life—but not with its superfluitie
which will enable him to live as a freeman
to live, in a free country—but not enough t
him wealthy. These are the principles by
he should be governed—these were the
by which his constituents wished him to be
ed; and they should govern in honor of the
in honor of his country, and in honor of
In fixing the compensation, Mr. J. said he
look at human life and society as he found
inquire what sum was required to place t
cers of the navy in the situation which he
scribed. He would then bring that
to govern his votes upon the compensat
posed.

Mr. J. expressed his regret that some
who had spoken in favor of the Navy, had
in the Army, and had made comparison
he did not consider useful or conclusive.
sidered all such arguments and comparis
evant. The army as well as the navy wa
rite with the American People. This
opinion was not without good reason. Th
of the late war would prove it, and he
vote to pull down the army to the condi
navy, nor should he vote to elevate the
any other principle than that of its ow
merit. He said it was not necessary
and he hoped upon no other occasion,
the gallantry of the army and navy,
Congress to do justice to either. For, if
the sacrifices which both have made
country—if we will do justice to the
both to their country—if we bring to our
the battles they have fought; the
have won; the gallantry they have dis
have glory enough for any army or n
nothing now is wanting for them but a
vision to make them respectable and
of the wants and frowns of fortune, and
themselves in readiness for any other crisis.

It should never be forgotten, that from the m
ment that any citizen enters the army or navy,
has to give up totally all other pursuits; he has
abandon every other prospect of gain; and a gr
portion of his time, he has to abandon
There is no man who knows the hardships a
sacrifices of a soldier's life, whether in the army
navy, but the man who has tried—who has m
the experiment—but as it is for his country
bears it cheerfully.

The real truth is, that in time of war, wh
every thing that is dear to freedom is at stak
when the country is suffering under all the cala
ties of war, and bleeding at every pore, we
disposed, if possible, to overrate the army and
navy, and particularly the merits of a brave
gallant officer. But in time of peace we are
as much inclined to underrate each, and to th
that they are a privileged corps, when in fact t
are the working men of the government—
drudges and dray horses for the country—they
working for their country all the time; and un
tunately, in free governments, the spirit of jealo
inclines us often to pull down, in time of pe
the pillars of strength, and to undermine the fo
dations of our greatness and security. An insta
of that kind is the opposition to the Military Ac
emy, the institution and favorite of Thomas Je

legislative business shall be suspended on that day.

That the oration shall be delivered at half past 12 o'clock in the Hall of the House of Representatives.

That the President of the United States, and the Heads of the several Departments, the French Minister and members of the French Legation, and all the other Foreign Ministers at the seat of Government, and the members of their respective Legations, be invited to attend on that occasion, by the Chairman of the Joint Committee.

That the President of the United States, the Heads of the several Departments, the French Minister and members of the French Legation, the other Foreign Ministers at the seat of Government, and the members of their respective Legations, and John Quincy Adams, be requested to assemble at half past 12 o'clock, P. M. in the Senate Chamber, and that they, with the Senate, shall be attended by the Joint Committee to the Hall of the House of Representatives.

That the galleries of the House, under the direction of its officers, shall be opened on that day for the accommodation of such citizens as may think proper to attend.

The resolution having been read—

Mr. CLAY remarked, that, as the other House were probably now acting on a similar resolution, reported by the Committee on their part, he moved that it lie on the table; which was agreed to.

Mr. CLAY said he held in his hand a resolution, to which he desired to call the attention of the Senate, for a moment. It would be recollected that that part of the President's annual message which applied to our French affairs, had been referred to the Committee on Foreign Relations. After this reference, the committee thought it necessary, to the proper discharge of their duty in this particular, to be put in possession of the instructions which had been given to our minister in France on this subject, and also, all the correspondence which had been exchanged between the two Governments with relation to it. Under this view of the case, a letter was prepared by direction of the committee, and transmitted to the Secretary of State, requesting that the necessary information might be communicated. This letter was very promptly replied to by the Secretary, covering the information sought for, but accompanied with a request that it should be considered confidential by the committee. But it seemed to the committee, that as the opinion and recommendation of the President on the subject, had been made public, the committee could not acts upon documents which were only confidentially communicated. The Secretary of State, in his letter, suggested an application to the President, in the usual way, and he had accordingly drawn up this resolution, but which he would not press upon the consideration of the Senate now, as a wish had been expressed to him to that effect, by a gentleman who desired to examine it.

Mr. CLAY then submitted the resolution, as follows:

Resolved, That the President be requested to communicate to the Senate, (if, in his opinion, it shall not be incompatible with the public interest,) the instructions which have been transmitted, from time to time, since the 4th of July, 1831, to the representatives of the United States at the government of France, relating to the execution of the treaty, which was signed on that day between the United States and France; and also all the correspondence which has passed at Washington or at Paris between the two governments respecting the execution of the said treaty.

The VICE PRESIDENT laid before the Senate a letter from the Treasury Department, communicating the information required by a resolution offered by Mr. MOORE, relative to the 3 per cents. of Alabama; which was laid on the table and ordered to be printed.

The VICE PRESIDENT also laid before the Senate a memorial from the territorial Government of Michigan, relative to the introduction of that Territory into the Union; referred to the Judiciary Committee.

Mr. CLAYTON, from the Judiciary Committee, reported a bill to increase the salary of the Marshal for the Delaware District.

Mr. POINDEXTER, from the Committee on Public Lands, reported the following bills.

A bill for the relief of Anson Lynch.

A bill to extend the time for issuing military Land warrants for services in the Revolutionary army.

A bill for the relief of Andrew Knox.

A bill to graduate the price of the public lands, to provide for the sales of those which have been longest in the market, and for other purposes.

A bill branting to the state of Missouri a quantity of land for purposes of internal improvement.

A bill granting a township of land for the endowment of the French University in St. Louis, Mo.

A bill for the relief of Robert Haile;

A bill for the relief of Evan Edwards;

A bill to remove the United States Land Office from Clinton to Jackson, Mississippi;

A bill for the relief of William Graham.

Mr. GRUNDY from the Committee on the Post Office, to which the same had been referred, reported the bill making an appropriation for the completion of the road from Lyme Creek to Chatahoochie.

Mr. WRIGHT, agreeably to notice given yesterday, and on leave, introduced a bill in addition to the act o provide more effectually for the settlement of the accounts of Receivers of Public Moneys; which was read twice and referred.

Mr. LINN, on leave given, introduced a bill making an appropriation to improve the Mississippi river, near St. Louis.

Also, a bill to confirm certain claims to land in Missouri and for other purposes; which were twice read and referred.

Mr. CLAY, from the Committee on Foreign Relations, reported a bill for the relief of the legal representatives of John Malony, late Consul at Tangiers; which, on his motion, was read three several time, and passed.

Mr. BROWN, from the Committee on Agriculture, to whom the subject had been referred, reported the bill authorizing the sale of the Lion and two Horses, presented to our Consul at Tangiers, by the Emperor of Morocco.

Mr. McKEAN presented the memorial of sundry citizens of Pennsylvania, praying Congress to fit out a nautical expedition to explore the Southern hemisphere; which was referred to the Committee on Naval Affairs.

On motion of Mr. BELL, the Committee on Claims was discharged from the further consideration of the resolution relative to increasing the compensation of the Judges and other officers of Michigan Territory, and the same was referred to the Judiciary Committee.

The same Committee was also discharged from the consideration of the petition of Somerville Pinckney, and the same was referred to the Committee on Foreign Relations.

Mr. POINDEXTER, on leave given, introduced a bill for the relief of Elihu Hall Bay, and others, of South Carolina; which was read twice, and referred to the Committee on Private Land Claims.

FINAL PASSAGE OF BILLS.

A bill for the relief of Elijah Simmons;

A bill for the relief of Susan Marlow;

A bill authorizing the relinquishment of the sixteenth sections for the use of schools, and granting her lands in lieu thereof;

A bill for the relief of Lynn Magee and Lemoise, Creek Indians—were severally read a third time and passed.

The following resolutions, submitted yesterday, were severally considered and adopted:

By Mr. HILL:

Resolved, That the Secretary of the Treasury be requested to transmit to the Senate, as early as may be practicable, the number and the amount of Navy and Military Virginia Revolutionary Land Warrants, now on file for scrip in the General Land Office—the names of the individuals who performed the service—and also the names of the persons or agents who filed the warrants, or are interested in the same.

Also, That the Secretary of the Treasury be further requested to inform the Senate the

amount of superseded Navy and Military Virginia Revolutionary Bounty Land Scrip now lying in the General Land Office—the names of individuals who performed the service, and the names of the persons or agents now claiming said scrip, and the reasons for suspending the delivery of the same.

By Mr. TOMLINSON:

Resolved, That the Committee on Revolutionary Claims be instructed to inquire into the expediency of compensating Phineas Taylor, of Banbury, in the State of Connecticut, for a horse, and other property, taken from him for public use during the revolutionary war.

By Mr. LINN:

Resolved, That the Committee of Claims be instructed to inquire into the expediency of making an appropriation to compensate Augustus Jones, Marshal of Missouri, for services rendered the public, in detecting and breaking up bands of counterfeiters, who were flooding the country with spurious money; and that said committee call on the Secretary for information relating to this subject.

By Mr. SWIFT:

Resolved, That the Secretary of War be directed to cause a survey to be taken of the channel between the Islands of North and South Hero, in Lake Champlain, together with an estimate of the probable expense of removing obstructions to vessels in said channel, with a view of facilitating the navigation of said lake, by the removal of said obstructions; and that he make a report thereof to the Senate at the next session of Congress.

Mr. KENT called up for consideration the following resolution submitted by him yesterday:

Resolved, That the Committee on Military Affairs inquire into the expediency of making an appropriation for the immediate commencement of fortifications on the Patapsco, at the city of Annapolis, and at St. Mary's, all deemed essential by the Board of Engineers in their report, dated the 9th of February, 1821, for the security of the cities of Baltimore and Annapolis, and for the protection of the commerce of the Chesapeake Bay.

Mr. KENT briefly explained his views of the necessity and importance of the fortifications indicated in the resolution, to the city of Baltimore. That city, he said, was even now in a more defenceless condition than it was at the last war. From its peculiar situation it was so accessible to an enemy that it could easily be captured by a very small force. He did not offer the resolution from any apprehension of war, although our relations to foreign powers was by no means so pacific as formerly. But it behooved a prudent Government "in peace to prepare for war." The resolution was then adopted.

SPECIAL ORDER OF THE DAY.

The CHAIR having announced the special order, being the bill to provide compensation for French spoliations committed prior to 1800,

Mr. HILL rose and said—

Mr. PRESIDENT: During the short time I have been a member of the Senate, I have discovered that claims preferred to Congress stand a much better chance of success than if preferred to almost any other tribunal. In fact it has become a matter of general remark, that when a claim on the public is before Congress, success depends less on its justice than on the perseverance with which it is pursued.

It is considered little discouragement that a flat denial by one committee is given to a claim: the same claim is frequently at the same session preferred in another branch of the legislature; and if it does not there succeed, it is sure to be followed up at a future session. The value of perseverance is demonstrated in more successful cases than that of Amy Darden's horse, which, after having been brought upon the journals year by year, for at least forty years, was finally paid in the generous year of 1832, when there was so great a desire to get rid of as much money as possible from the treasury, in order that high taxes might be continued for the benefit of *protecting* American manufactures!

The bill now under consideration proposes to take directly from the treasury the round sum of five millions of dollars; not that five millions of dollars will cover the whole amount that may be claimed, and ten times five millions would scarcely do that on the principle that certain commutation claims, principal and interest, had been allowed by Congress;—and this sum is to be appropriated in the first instance for the benefit of "such citizens of the United States, or to their legal representatives, as had valid claims to indemnity upon the French Government, arising out of illegal captures, detentions, forcible seizures, illegal confiscations, and condemnations, made or committed before the year 1800."

The claims for which the bill of the Senate proposes indemnity are of more than thirty-three years standing. Although, during the whole time since 1802, they have been before Congress, it is very remarkable that it was not until the year 1826, a report, in favor of their validity, could be obtained in either House of Congress. Such an instance of claim, just or unjust, it is believed is not presented on the face of your journals since the adoption of the Constitution.

That a portion of these claims was originally justly due from France, will not be disputed: nor will it be disputed that American citizens had equally valid claims to indemnity from the British Government, "arising out of illegal captures, detentions, forcible seizures, illegal condemnations, and confiscations, made or committed" under her orders in council, prior to the existence of the late war of 1812. The declaration of war, by the American Congress, in June, 1812, precluded the prospect of all remuneration from Great Britain for her illegal seizures, as did the declaration of war against France by successive acts of Congress, of May 28, July 7, and July 9, 1798, authorizing the capture of French armed vessels, and declaring such vessels to be good and lawful prize, and declaring the treaties theretofore concluded with France, to be no longer obligatory on the United States.

But however just might have been these claims on France, I flatter myself that it may be made abundantly apparent to every impartial and disinterested man, that the Government of the United States, in its own behalf, ought not to be, and is not, responsible for the payment of one cent of them.

In prosecuting the negotiation which terminated in the treaty of September 30, 1800, the United States accomplished more for American citizens than could ever have been reasonably anticipated; they saved an "immense property of our citizens then depending before the French Council of Prizes." The payment of even this was resisted by the French Government until it was provided for to be paid by the United States themselves in the Louisiana treaty

Urging these claims, appeals are made to motives of benevolence and humanity; they are said to belong to widows and orphans. Very little, it is apprehended, is due to considerations of this kind. In ninety-nine cases of a hundred, it is believed that those claims will go to swell the profits of speculators who have conditionally engaged to pay for them a mere trifle, or to add to the estates of a few men who have made immense wealth as underwriters, or to the enormous gains of insurance companies. Of the cases of seizure provided for in this bill, it is not probably going too far to presume that in nineteen of every twenty cases, the real owner of the property was not the loser. Although the commerce of the country, soon after the war in Europe, consequent on the French revolution, was much interrupted by seizures and spoliations, both by Great Britain and France, yet the period from 1793 to 1800 is often referred to by our merchants and ship-owners as being the time of all others, when they made most money. The Americans not only disposed of their produce at the highest rate, but they were to a great extent the carriers of the belligerent nations. The temptations presented in the facilities for making money were so great, that it is not to be wondered if the Americans frequently violated that strictly neutral character which should have protected their commercial intercourse and relations.*

Liable to constant capture or detention, it is presumed that few, very few, American ships went to sea without ample insurance against loss by capture or otherwise. The greatly increased profits of American business warranted the payment of a large insurance; and if the amount paid for insurance was lost in one voyage, it was more than made up in the profits of other voyages.

The underwriters and insurance companies at this time found their greatest harvest. The price of insurance was raised even greater in proportion than the risk—as high probably as fifteen, twenty, and in some instances fifty per cent. Now although these insurers, standing in the place of the insured, may have an equitable claim on their behalf upon the foreign nation that should illegally seize the property of a neutral individual, little right have they to exact from their own government what would amount to an entire cover of the whole risk. If the country should pay the entire loss, so should the country be entitled to the gains of the underwriters. That the underwriters of the time above referred to laid the foundation of immense fortunes by insurance of ships and property on the high seas, is abundantly proved by the condition of some of the most wealthy men in the northern States who have lived or still are living. These men have accumulated wealth under every treaty that has been made by this government procuring indemnity for spoliations; and it is such men, together with [illegible] wealthy speculators and corporations, who have bought up these claims for a trifle, who are [illegible] be benefited by the passage of this law. There are few poor widows or orphans that will derive advantage from any portion of the immense [illegible] that the bill appropriates. If one ship in three of every ship that sailed had been captured, neither were the underwriters or owners of such ships [illegible] losers—for the first received more than the full amount of loss, and the others made greater profits than they could in a time of profound peace [illegible] the advanced price of the merchandise ship[illegible]

Mr. President, there is little wonder that [illegible] claims for twenty-five years should have failed to obtain the favorable report of a committee. Should this bill pass, it need not be matter of surprise [illegible] other claims of a similar character should [illegible] them until it shall appear that the United States as yet have just begun to discharge the [illegible] debt. How many millions sacrificed by [illegible] controversies will the Government be not bound to discharge, if it justly owes the claims provided for in this bill?

I shall contend, in the first place, that the controversy with France giving rise to these claims terminated in war; and that as war ended all obligations of prior treaties, so there was on the part of the American Government nothing due France which could go for a consideration [illegible] equivalent for these claims.

The French Government resisted the payment of these claims when they were first presented on the ground that war had put an end to [illegible] Messrs. Ellsworth, Davie and Murray, the American negotiators, repeating the declaration of [illegible] President of the French commission, in the journal of Sept. 12, 1800, say, "He would "sooner resign than sign such a treaty (as "they proposed,) adding, that if the question "could be determined by an indifferent nation "he was satisfied such a tribunal would say, [illegible] "the present state of things was war on the [illegible] "of America, and that *no indemnities* could [illegible] "claimed. The other two commissioners [illegible] "similar declarations."

The same gentlemen, September 13, 1800, [illegible]

"The American Ministers, being now convinced "that the door was perfectly closed against "hope of obtaining indemnities with any [illegible] "cation of the treaties," they proceeded to [illegible]

---

*From *Washington's Proclamation of Dec.* 3, 1793.

"Whosoever of the citizens of the United States shall render himself liable to punishment or forfeiture under the law of nations, by committing, aiding, or abetting hostilities against any of the said powers, or by carrying to them any of those articles which are *deemed* contraband by the *modern* usage of nations, will not receive the protection of the United States against such punishment or forfeiture."

ate without. Now, if the door was closed against all hope, what sacrifice for the claimants did the American Government make by agreeing no further to prosecute them?

The treaty of September 30, 1800, was agreed upon as the best for American citizens suffering under French spoliations, that could be procured. The journal of Messrs. Ellsworth, Davie, and Murray, continues: "Nor is it conceived that the "treaties between the United States and France "have undergone a more nullifying operation "than the condition of war naturally imposes. "Doubtless the congressional act authorizing the "reduction of French cruisers by force, was an "*authorization of war*, limited indeed in its extent, "but not in its nature. Clearly, also, their subse- "quent act, declaring that the treaties had ceased "to be obligatory, however proper it might be for "the removal of doubts, was but declaratory of "the actual state of things. And certainly it was "only from an *exercise of the constitutional preroga- "tive of declaring war, that either of them derived "validity*. So that the treaties in question, having "had only the usual inoperation, might, without a "breach of faith, have the usual recognition."

Mr. Murray, (p. 662, Senate Documents 102,) speaking of the treaty which had then been just executed, says: "Indemnities which were *impossible*, together with the discussion about the abolished treaties and consular convention, to sleep till a more convenient time."

Mr. Murray again, (p. 676,) "But having no power to dispose of what may be considered as a ...able claim for the future, *although I do not consider it as worth a quarter per centum*," &c.

Again, same, (p. 682,) "If the Senate meant by striking out the second article of the treaty *to consider indemnity as worth nothing*, then the business, I presume, is closed."

Again, same page: "The absolute *want of value* the prospect of indemnities."

From these, and other like statements of the negotiators of the treaty of September 30, 1800, which was the most favorable for the United States and its citizens that could be obtained, it is evident that the treaty was negotiated on the basis of a war; that this state of things had discharged the French Government from all obligations to make restitution for captures and seizures, as it did the American Government from similar obligations to France; and that, as a natural consequence, the American Ministers considered the prospect of further indemnity to be worth nothing. The character of the negotiation was this: France was willing to consider that war had put an end to all prior treaties, and of course to indemnities for their infraction. If the treaties were in force, and indemnities for seizures and spoliations were due to the Americans, so also something was due to France from the United States, for their failure under the treaties. The result proved that no indemnity could be obtained from France, and therefore the negotiation terminated, on the admission of both parties, that as war existed, so indemnity on all hands was abandoned.

Yet, in compliance with instructions from the American Executive at home, the second section of the treaty left the question of indemnity open, or rather evaded the question. That section was in the words following:

"ART. 2. The Ministers Plenipotentiary of the two parties, not being able to agree, at present, respecting the Treaty of Alliance, of 6th of February, 1778, the Treaty of Amity and Commerce of the same date, and the Convention of the 14th November, 1788, nor upon the indemnities mutually due or claimed; the parties will negotiate further on these subjects at a convenient time; and until they may have agreed upon these points, the said treaties and convention shall have no operation; and the relations of the two countries shall be regulated as follows."

As the treaty was first concluded and ratified by the French Government, including this second article, all the objects of peace and reciprocal intercourse were secured without giving up any demand of our citizens for spoliations; and at the same time, an "immense property of our citizens ... depending before the French Council of Prizes" was secured to American citizens.

The treaty or convention, duly signed, was sent to the United States, and submitted by the President to the Senate. The Senate, February 3, 1801, consented to, and advised its ratification, provided *the second article* be expunged, and the following be added:

"It is agreed that the present convention shall "be in force for the term of eight years, from "the time of the exchange of the ratification." It was so ratified by the President.

Thus altered, the convention was sent back to France, where the First Consul, complaining of the alterations made by the Senate, agreed to ratify it by adding the following clause:

"The Government of the United States having "added to its ratification, that the convention "should be in force for the space of eight years, "and having omitted the second article, the Gov- "ernment of the French Republic consents to "accept, ratify, and confirm the above convention "with the addition, importing that the convention "shall be in force for the space of eight years, "and with the retrenchment of the second arti- "cle; *provided that, by this retrenchment, the two "States renounce the respective pretensions which "are the object of the said article*."

After these conditional ratifications and their exchange, President Jefferson submitted the convention anew to the Senate, who resolved that they considered it as fully ratified.

It is most obvious, that in expunging the second article of the treaty, the Senate had no idea of lessening the chance of securing any thing that might be legally due from France to citizens of the United States; and it is equally obvious, that in subsequently tacitly assenting to that article as finally altered by Bonaparte, neither President Jefferson or the Senate of the United States, for a moment, considered they were performing an act which should thereafter make the American Government responsible to individuals for French spoliations.

The act of expunging and otherwise changing the article, was performed in the last month of the elder Adams's administration. This first step opened the door for another change of the terms of the treaty by Napoleon; and the new administration of Mr. Jefferson, viewing even the terms of the altered treaty as highly favorable to American citizens—more favorable, probably, than any new negotiation could open to them—readily seized the opportunity of taking the treaty as it was, rather than to throw all the advantages gained at the mercy of future changes and vicissitudes.

Page 698 of the Senate Documents, before quoted, the French Minister, Talleyrand, repeats, as the suggestion of Mr. Murray, the American Minister, that the second article of the convention of September, 1800, was expunged by the American Senate, under the idea that, if retained, it would be "susceptible of producing "disquiets in future, by promising nothing but an "ulterior and discordant negotiation." And Mr. Madison, Secretary of State, in a letter to Mr. Livingston, before the Senate and President finally assented to the convention, (page 708,) says: "I "am authorized to state, that the President does "not consider the declaratory clause (last intro- "duced by Bonaparte) as more than a legitimate "inference from the rejection by the Senate of the "second article; and that he (the President) is "disposed to go on with the measures due under "the compact to the French Republic."

The American Government did go on to execute that compact. March 20, 1801, the Secretary of the Navy directed S. Higginson and Co. to restore the Berceau frigate, captured by Captain Little. The Vengeance and the Insurgente frigates were also restored; the latter, having been lost, by substitute. The convention provided for the restoration of public ships taken on both sides—also, that all ships and property captured, and not definitively condemned at the time of the negotiation, should be mutually restored. The Government of the United States, as stated by Mr. Madison, paid Mr. Pichon, the French Minister, on the general account, $140,841 25, and to individual French subjects $74,667 41. (See Doc. p. 720.)

But France delayed restitution, although solemnly bound by the convention of September 30, 1830, until the claims came to be thought of little value. Applications for payment were often made, and as often denied or evaded. Restitution was indeed made by the subsequent treaty of 1803, by which a title to Louisiana was acquired. This restitution would not, even then, have been made, had it not come in conveniently to France, as a part of the nominal price paid for the cession of that valuable territory. Of this price, Bonaparte, deprived as he was of the maritime force to protect it, considered the money actually paid as a full equivalent, without including the amount allowed for spoliations under the convention of 1800. He, in fact, set his own price to his Minister, Barbe Marbois, at fifty millions of francs, when the latter succeeded in obtaining of Messrs. Livingston and Monroe sixty millions of francs in cash, besides twenty millions, allowed for the spoliations. It was considered, at the time, that all which was gained to the American claimants for French spoliations and seizures in the Louisiana treaty, was to them clear gain. Their claims were believed to be hopeless, and the opposition to the American administration opposed the execution of the treaty on account of the alleged "outrageous price" paid for the territory ceded.

In the correspondence relative to the execution of the Louisiana treaty, the twenty millions of francs allowed and paid the claimants, are mentioned as "covering all the claims" of the Americans for *illegal* spoliations and seizures; and in these twenty millions other claims were included than those first comprehended in the list presented by the American Minister. [See Talleyrand's letter to Livingston, Doc. p. 829.]

Mr. Livingston says, sixteen millions would have covered "the debts confined to the words of the convention." Four millions, then, must have been paid to persons whose claims were not acknowledged by France to be legitimate.

Citizen Pichon, the French Minister, wrote that cases of capture by the French West India cruisers are included in the fourth article of the treaty, and are ordered to be restored.

Barbe Marbois (doc. p. 826) says, "the sum of twenty millions of francs had been determined on in order to extinguish *the whole American* claim and the interest up to the day of the treaty."

The restitution of property under the convention of April 30, 1803, applied to captures of which the Council of Prizes had ordered restitution—to debts contracted prior to the 30th September 1800, the payment of which had been claimed of the Government of France, and for which the creditors have a right to the protection of the Government of the United States; and it is expressly stated, that "it does not comprehend prizes whose condemnation has been or shall be confirmed."

Now it is quite apparent from the face of these exceptions, that they are precisely such as the French Government never would have paid if they had been left for negotiation, till doomsday: they were either such as had been adjudicated and condemned for a positive infraction of the laws of neutrality, or else they were such as were captured, tried, and condemned, under an actual state of war between the two nations.

It is remarkable that neither in the successive reports, from 1826 down to the present time, of committees friendly to these claims, nor in the elaborate essay of Mr. Walsh's Quarterly Review in their favor, are the indemnities provided for in the convention of April, 1803, mentioned as at all connected with the spoliations and seizures made by France prior to the year 1800. Why this omission?

I think I have not mistaken the character of the contest between this country and France prior to the treaty of September 30, 1800. That controversy was to all intents and purposes a war. I cannot present a more faithful account of that controversy and the subsequent events which have given rise to the bill now before the Senate, than by making quotations from the history of the cession of Louisiana to the United States, written by Barbe Marbois, the translation of which was first published in this country in the year 1830. That inflexible republican, like the illustrious La-

fayette, equally the friend of his own country and of this Republic, still lives at the advanced age of between eighty and ninety years, to witness the benefits his labors have bestowed on mankind, in being instrumental in ceding to the United States that extensive tract of country. In behalf of the the French Government, he was the sole negotiator with Messrs. Livingston and Monroe, of the Louisiana treaty. He says: (p. 234.)

"It is necessary to go back a few years in order to understand the object of this important part of the negotiation [the indemnity for spoliations].— The interests of commerce, colonial settlements, and navigation, have effected great changes in the reciprocal relations of the nations of Europe.— The independence of the United States has rendered them still more complicated. But such changes are not often remarked by statesmen themselves, till they have committed great faults, by persevering in old errors.

"The directory, led astray by false notions of the situation of the French colonies, had not remarked that their existence depended upon the preservation of a good understanding with the United States. Instead of re-establishing friendly relations with the American Union, it had, after more than once putting it in jeopardy, finally broken *the alliance* which had been the precious fruit of the policy of the councils of Louis XVI. Mutual discontent had not yet resulted in direct hostilities; but even in peace captures were made by privateers, bearing the French flag, which became the subject of great complaints on the part of the United States. It was likewise, at this period, that the first disasters of the French colonies led to the emigration of many families, who from great opulence had fallen into deep distress. Numbers of them took refuge in the United States. Never was hospitality more nobly exercised than under these circumstances; never were more sincere and effectual consolations offered to misfortunes by a grateful people. This generosity towards refugees, the objects of the persecutions of the directory, was not regarded by its members as a motive for reconciliation with the American republic. They had inherited the animosities of the convention, and the West Indian possessions were the victims of them. These colonies, prosperous in time of peace, are exposed to all sorts of calamities as soon as the war breaks out. Their intercourse is interrupted; a parent state, weak at sea, can neither supply them with provisions nor export their produce, and is most frequently incapable of defending them. If they resort to neutrals, the relaxation of the prohibitory system habituates the colony to privileges which make them look on the return of peace with indifference. The directory, in order to maintain their prohibitory laws, had permitted the local authorities to provide for the preservation of the colonies by arming privateers, and these agents encouraged them indiscriminately, to fall on all flags. They carried their disregard of the rules of justice and the laws of nations so far as to condemn, as lawful prizes, ships that had entered the ports with subsistence and provisions intended for the inhabitants of the islands that they governed. Victor Hughes, one of these colonial rulers, openly professed and put in practice the maxim, that "in time of want, all kinds of provisions are good prize." The American government, before commencing hostilities with France, wished to exhaust all pacific measures. It had sent thence ministers (Messrs. Pinckney, Marshall, and Gerry) to the directory towards the end of the year 1797. On their arrival at Paris, they were circumvented by all sorts of intrigues. Their correspondence is a monument of the base manner in which the French government at that time, managed their political affairs. "The most disgraceful cupidity," they wrote to their constituents, "was openly manifested at Paris." The American commissioners were told that "their government paid money to obtain peace with the Algerines and with the Indians; *and that it was doing no more to pay France for peace.*"

"This negotiation lasted for six or seven months: it was broken off when it was found impossible to continue it on such erroneous principles. * * *

"The animosity was still increasing in 1799;

when Congress, renouncing vain attempts at moderation, resolved that all intercourse with France should be suspended; that the treaties had ceased to be obligatory; and that the capture of French vessels was permitted."

Thus far the historian distinctly and conclusively states two important facts material to the question of indemnities: The one is that *the alliance* (treaties of 1778) *was broken by France*—the other —*that a state of actual war, from the action of Congress, existed between France and the United States.* M. Marbois continues—

"From the beginning of the Consular Government, a wise policy had put a stop to all reprisals; a convention had been signed on the 30th September, 1800; but, according to a stipulation, without which the reconciliation would have been impossible, indemnities were to be paid for all prizes unlawfully made. [Mark here the character of the indemnities, distinguishing those which were *unlawfully* from such as the French considered *properly* made.] Ministers had been subsequently interchanged, and the Envoy of the United States (Mr. Livingston) had calculated on prompt satisfaction. The communications which he addressed to his Government, authorized this hope; but the expectations were not realized, and in fact the finances of France had scarcely began to emerge from the chaos in which the bad Government of the Directory had plunged them.

"This part of the convention of 1800, therefore, remained unexecuted; and this contempt of the most ordinary rules of justice, carried the general irritation in the United States to its greatest height. The President and his Cabinet, compromitted by their moderation, were beginning to make their reproaches heard, and talked of doing themselves the justice that we refused them. The American Minister at Paris had received orders to make this discontent known, and his notes were drawn up with a firmness to which Bonaparte was not accustomed. If one of the continental powers of Europe had dared to employ similar language, the invasion of its territory would have been the consequence." * * * "At the notes of Mr. Livingston, the American Minister, remained unanswered, the injured merchants and ship owners lost their patience, and murmured against their Government. The enemies of France in the United States, attentive to the general discontent, hoped to avail themselves of it in order to force the Union into an alliance with England."

Here it will be observed that the sole object of complaint by the "injured merchants" was the non-execution of the convention of September 30, 1800, leaving it plainly to be inferred, that at this time they did not think of asking further indemnities than that convention provided.

The writer goes on to detail the events which accompanied the shutting up the port of New Orleans, producing strong excitement in the Western States, and creating an anxiety to secure the free navigation of the Mississippi on the part of the United States of the one side, and the perilous condition of this French colony in case war should break out and render it an easy prey to the British maritime superiority on the other side. Events were impending on both sides which rendered it not less desirable that the United States should acquire, than that France should dispose of the territory of Louisiana at much less than what has since proved to be its value. Accordingly at the same time Mr. Jefferson and his Cabinet were taking secret measures to purchase a part of Louisiana, and Mr. Monroe was sent to aid in the purchase, Bonaparte was urging his Minister to make preparations and force the sale to the United States of the whole right France possessed in the territory.

The historian continues, (p. 277,) "The conferences began the same day between Mr. Livingston and M. Barbe Marbois, to whom the First Consul confided this negotiation. But the American Minister had not the necessary powers. He had resided at Paris about two years. The first object of his mission had been indemnities claimed by his countrymen for prizes made by the French during peace." That is, indemnities under the convention of Sept. 30, 1800.

In the mean time, Mr. Monroe had arrived, bringing full powers to negotiate. As it is my object to confine myself to the subject of indemnities as much as possible, I omit a relation of conferences about prices offered and asked for the territory. The author proceeds: (p. 305.)

"The convention of the 30th of September, 1800, had for its object the securing of reciprocal satisfaction to the citizens of the two States, and the preventing as far as possible of any thing that could for the future affect their good understanding. We there find the principle, the vision, and the legality of which only one nation is the world disputes: 'that free ships make free goods, although they are the property of an enemy.'"

"A special promise had been given to pay the debts arising from requisitions, seizures, and captures, made in time of peace; but the execution of the agreement had not followed the treaty. For two years and a half the Minister of the United States had been reiterating his reclamation, and demanding in vain the reparation of these losses.

"The cession of Louisiana afforded the means of realizing promises that had been so long illusory. The Americans consented to pay eighty millions of France, on condition that twenty millions of this sum should be assigned for the payment of *what was due from France to the citizens of the United States.*

"The two Ministers fixed this condition of indemnity at twenty millions of francs, and they probably expected that they would be required to state the grounds of the estimate, in order that they might be discussed and a reduction effected. But no opposition was made, and it was instantly agreed that the amount should be deducted from that of the eighty millions. *The intention of distinguishing all former claims was sincere as his idea.* The round sum of twenty millions was evidently an estimate formed on reasonable conjectures, and could not be an absolute result established by documents. But, the American negotiators agreed that if there was any difference, the amount rather exceeded than fell short of the claims, and the French Plenipotentiary gave assurances that in no case should this excess be claimed by France. Thus the respective demands were easily agreed to."

Again: (p. 311.)

"The First Consul had followed, with a lively interest, the progress of this negotiation. It will be recollected that he had mentioned fifty millions as the price which he had put on the cession, but it may well be believed that he did not expect to obtain so large a sum. He learned that eighty millions had been agreed on; but that they were reduced to sixty, by the reduction stipulated for previously made for the settlement of the debt due by France to the Americans. Then forgetting, or feigning to forget, the consent that he had given, he said with vivacity to the French Minister, 'I would that these twenty millions be paid into the Treasury. Who has authorized you to dispose of the money of the State? The rights of the claimants cannot come before our own.' This first excitement was calmed as he was brought to recollect that he had previously consented to treat for a much smaller sum than the treaty would receive, without including the twenty millions indemnity for the prizes. 'It is true,' he said, 'the negotiation does not leave one sufficient to desire: sixty millions for an occupation that not perhaps last but a day! I would that France should enjoy this unexpected capital, and that it may be employed in works beneficial to her marine.'

"If we regard the statement of M. Marbois, containing the facts, we must believe it is the most interest chance in the world, that the American merchants ever did receive the indemnity of twenty millions of francs; Napoleon Bonaparte, the last moment of his life, while he was alive— [CONTINUED IN NEXT BURIAL.]

CONGRESSIONAL GLOBE.

BY BLAIR & RIVES.	——WEEKLY——	PRICE $1 A SESSION.
2d Sess........23d Cong.	MONDAY, JANUARY 5, 1834.	Volume 2......No. 5.

TWENTY-THIRD CONGRESS.

SECOND SESSION.

IN SENATE.

Tuesday, Dec. 23, 1834.

[Continued from last Number.]

the rest of Europe, would not have taken that sum out of his treasury to pay these claims. Sixty millions of francs, the sum paid into the French treasury, was all Bonaparte would have asked for Louisiana. The twenty millions paid was so much money of the American people generously and gratuitously bestowed by their Government, for which the underwriters, and others who profited by the boon, are scarcely disposed to thank us; and they would even wink this sum out of sight in their eagerness to grasp more for claims whose foundation, to say the least, is extremely doubtful.

But, Mr. President, if there was the least room to doubt that war had put an end to all right of indemnity from France, it will be easy to show, that the United States never *first violated* any engagement with France, in a manner that claimed from us an indemnity.

I see it asserted in a newspaper of this city, copied from a Boston newspaper, expressing the feelings probably of some of those interested in these claims, that thirty-four years ago, our own government *sold to the French government,* a great amount of claims of our own citizens on France, for indemnity, and received pay for them, and released France from all obligations to pay the claimants, whose demands were acknowledged *to be just* by both nations."

In the first place, I deny that this Government ever sold to the French Government the claims of our citizens. This Government had done its whole duty to the claimants—it had pressed the claims as far and as long as it was bound to do; and if, at length, it agreed to press them no further, it was to procure indemnity, not for itself, but for others, and many of the self-same claimants, which indemnity otherwise would have been utterly hopeless, and lost to them forever.

To the declaration that this Government received payment for these claims, I answer, that if no claims of citizens of the United States against France had existed, it is quite certain the United States would have procured as good a treaty with France, as that of the convention of September, 30, 1800; and that France would have laid in no claim whatever, for an alleged infraction of prior treaties on our part.

It is said these demands were acknowledged to be just by both nations. The Quarterly Review says—" The French Government did not deny the justice of these demands: they even offered to make arrangements to compensate the losses; but they had claims upon the Government of the United States, which they insisted upon taking into consideration, and they refused to enter into any agreement, unless these claims were provided for.

I have no where seen evidence that France at any time conceded these claims to be just. The statements of the Quarterly Review are fallacies. Was not the refusal to pay them—was not the first ratification of the treaty with the second article by Bonaparte, which made no provision for payment, tantamount to a denial and a rejection of these claims? To be sure, France would have no objection to making provision for the payment of just such a sum as the American Government might ask for these claims, provided the United States would agree to pay France an equal or greater sum for alleged infractions of prior treaties; and this is the whole amount of concession which France has ever made to these claimants.

If these claims, as preferred against the United States, possess any merit, it is, that the United States have received of France for them an equivalent. That equivalent is alleged to be the discharge by France of the prior obligations contained in sundry recited treaties.

One gentleman, (Mr. Webster) says that " by a

---

treaty of the U. States the government of the United States, *for a valuable consideration,* released France from these claims"—that the United States were relieved from " onerous stipulations" of the treaties of alliance and commerce with France of 1778"—that " these claims were relinquished for considerations which were valuable to the whole people of the United States"—that these claims were " released as a set-off against the infractions of the treaties of alliance and commerce with France."

Another Senator (Mr. Preston) says this claim on the American Government " is irresistible," because by the aid of the release of the claims on France " the American Government extricated itself from the most embarrassing circumstances"—that " this government offered *three times* the amount of this bill to be relieved"—that " we have used the property of these people for purposes of the government"—that " we have used the money for State purposes."

A third Senator, (Mr. Shepley) says he " can prove that the government might have obtained reparation for these claims of France if it had chosen to do so;" that payment was not obtained, " because France set up counter claims for alleged violations of her treaty of alliance," that " there cannot be found a more perfect set-off than in the set-off of these two claims."

The Senators may all rest assured that if these claims had never existed, in negotiating the treaty of Sept. 30, 1800, France never would have thought of preferring a claim for any infraction of her treaties of alliance and commerce. Neither if these claims had not been made, should we ever have heard that the contest subsequent to the act of Congress declaring the treaties at an end, was not war to all intents and purposes. Why, Congress by a solemn act declared the treaties of alliance and commerce to have been at an end; and yet gentlemen, to make out any plausibility to these claims on the United States, are obliged to declare those treaties to have been in force.

Mr. President, I will proceed to show that there was no infraction of the treaties by the United States; that there were no " onerous stipulations" violated by this Government; and by consequence, that there was no " valuable consideration" ever received by the United States as a set-off against these claims.

" Pacificus," No. 2, written by Alexander Hamilton, (and surely gentlemen will consider him good authority,) in justification of President Washington's proclamation of neutrality of April, 1793, says—(Federalist, p. 561:)

" The alliance between the United States and France is of the defensive kind. In the caption of the treaty it is denominated a " treaty eventual and defensive." In the body (article second,) it is called a defensive alliance. The words of that article are as follows :—" The essential and direct " end of the present defensive alliance, is to maintain effectually the liberty, sovereignty, and independence, absolute and unlimited, of the United States, as well in matters of government, " as of commerce."

" France then being on the offensive in the present war, and our alliance with her being *defensive* only, it follows that the *same foderis,* or condition of our guarantee cannot take place, and that the United States are free to refuse a performance of that guarantee, if demanded."

Gen. Hamilton contends that even if the war with Great Britain had not been an offensive war on the part of France, the United States, under the peculiar circumstances, would not have been bound by the guarantee. In favor of this position he says—p. 570:

" We may learn from Vattel, one of the best writers on the law of nations, that " if a State " which has promised succors, finds itself unable " to furnish them, its very inability is its exemption; and if the furnishing of succors would expose it to an evident danger, this is also a lawful

---

" dispensation. The case would render the treaty " pernicious to the State, and therefore not obligatory. But this applies to an imminent danger " threatening the safety of the State. The case of " such a danger is tacitly and necessarily reserved " in every treaty."

Taking this quotation from Vattel to be sound doctrine, it would be difficult to discover where were the " onerous stipulations" from which the United States obtained a discharge, by not consenting to prosecute claims which the American Ministers had in repeated instances pronounced to be hopeless, and of no value.

Even Mr. Madison, in his letters of " Helvidius," who espoused the side of the republican party, at that time in opposition to and in answer of the same letters of Hamilton, and took the ground most favorable to France, did not contend that the United States had violated the guarantee in the treaty of alliance by abstaining from the protection of the possession by France of her West India islands, &c. Indeed it does not appear either here or elsewhere, that France at any time specifically demanded the performance of the guarantee; and without such demand, it is abundantly evident no obligation was violated. What was complained of by the republicans who were friendly to the French revolution at the time, was the spirit of hostility to that revolution, and the partiality for neutrality between France and England—that was contended for by a set-off against hostility to that revolution, then contending single-handed, which was evinced by some of the leading members of the existing American administration.

" Veritas," a writer in the National Gazette of June, 1793, speaking of Washington's proclamation of neutrality, says:

" As the proclamation has not the most distant " allusion to the treaties existing between France " and the United States, there is room for surmising " that those treaties, from which we have long enjoyed important advantages, are now to be considered of no obligation; and this, I believe, is the " light in which many have construed the proclamation."

Washington's Proclamation was indeed worse than any thing charged at the time by its enemies, if it could be supposed that it placed the United States in the plight of having violated her most solemn treaty engagements; and she must have so conducted them, under this proclamation, if the allegations be true that she was, by the treaty of September 30, 18.0, ' extricated from the most embarrassing circumstances,' as is contended by one Senator, (Mr. Preston,) or if in that treaty we received that " valuable consideration" in full relief from " onerous stipulations," as is contended by another, (Mr. Webster.)

Dunlap's Daily Advertiser, published at Philadelphia, of April 29, 1793, says—

" The (French) National Assembly, in their " letter to Monsieur Genet, if we have a true copy, " appear to entertain the idea, that we are not so " situated as to be expected to participate in the " war. The government of France have not made " any requisition of the kind that we know."

A writer in the same paper, June 10, says— " There is not a single article in either of those (treaties) subsisting between the United States and France, wherein it is stipulated that we shall join France in her wars. Our alliance was of the defensive kind. The clause of guarantee implies not an agreement to enter into war, but only that the United States shall use their reasonable endeavors to maintain the French in their possessions."

Same paper: " Now, sir, this same minister, (Genet,) told you on his arrival, that it was not the wish of the nation he represents to involve us in the war."

Mr. Jefferson, in a letter, Aug. 16, 1793, says, that Citizen Genet assured the President, assured the citizens of Philadelphia, and repeated this assurance, " that on account of our remote situation and other circumstances, France *did not expect that we should become a party to the war,* but

wished to see us pursue our prosperity and happiness in peace.".

The French minister who negotiated the Louisiana treaty, confesses that France *first broke the alliance* between the two countries; and even the Quarterly Review says France armed against us, and seized immense amounts of our property, and was the first to violate existing treaties; and yet it was our violation of existing treaties that constitutes our obligation to her for the payment of which these claims are urged to be an offset!

The Convention of September 30, 1800, removed the evils of war which then existed; and this was the first object of that convention on the part of the United States. The American negotiators wished indemnity for all spoliations that took place prior to the several acts of Congress which authorized the capture and condemnation of French ships and property on the high seas, and which declared all existing treaties between the two countries to be at an end, and they made a distinction between the claims originating before, and those arising after the act of Congress nullifying the treaties with France; but the French Envoys would consent to no such distinction.

The first project of a treaty exhibited by the American envoys, proposed that "full and complete compensation" should be made for captures on both sides. Now, if the American Government is bound to make compensation to Americans because France was bound, and she stands in the place of France, on account of the alleged off-set, is not the American Government also bound likewise to make restitution to Frenchmen for its own captures? The Senate report of May 24, 1828, admits that eighty-four French ships were captured by the Americans, of which sixty-eight (valued at $600,000,) were condemned, one-half to the captors, the other to the United States. Was this property ever restored to France? If not, will it not be the duty of France to claim it, and our duty to pay it, after this Government shall have stood in her place to make restitution for the property she has taken from American citizens, under like circumstances?

It is said our Government appropriated these claims to its own use, by making them the "valuable consideration" for which it obtained a release from the obligations incurred by the early treaties with France; *but it is evident, from the fact that the treaty was fully ratified on the part of France, without a discharge of the claims, that the French Government placed no value whatever on the nominal obligations of the American Government, contained in those ancient treaties.*

Considering that the United States violated no obligation to France, and that if there was any violation, it was on the part of France, who first broke the alliance—where will the principle lead, if the American Government now makes restitution for the remaining claims on France, that were not provided for in the convention of 1800, and secured to be paid in the convention of 1803? If, by consenting no further to urge that portion of the claims which the French Government would never have allowed, this Government has become responsible itself for the claims—if, to purchase peace, and secure other claims to the amount of twenty-millions of francs, the United States, as for this "valuable consideration," became responsible—so is it clearly and equally responsible, hereafter, to make restitution for the thousand ships and millions of property seized by Great Britain under her orders in council, prior to the declaration of war by Congress, in 1812. Up to the last moment of the negotiation with Great Britain, the American Commissioners continued to insist on a restitution for those seizures. To obtain peace, however, I find they did give this up. Niles's Register of Feb. 18, 1815, presents, as taken from an English newspaper, the following, as one of the terms of peace:

"The Americans have waived any stipulation on the subject of maritime rights, as well as respecting *compensation for captures under the orders in council, or on any other account.*"

The British Government, however, did agree to make compensation for slaves, and other property seized on the land. It also recognised the treaty of peace of 1783, so far as related to possessions and boundary, with a single exception; and with equal truth might it be urged, that the treaty of peace of 1783 existed and was in force while war existed with Great Britain, as now it is urged that the treaties of alliance and commerce between France and the United States existed and were in force during the negotiation of the French Convention of September 30, 1800.

"Compensation for captures under the Orders in Council, or any other account," was waived by the American Commissioners at the treaty of Ghent. Here is even a stronger case than is presented in the treaty of September 30, 1800; for the American negotiators agreed at once to yield the millions of "valid claims" to indemnity, "arising out of illegal captures, detentions, forcible seizures, illegal condemnations, and confiscations, made or committed" by Great Britain in time of peace, for the "valuable consideration" of peace, which saved millions of blood and treasure to the country. Here is a "set-off" to American claims quite as complete, and much more direct, than the set-off in the French Convention; and why not at once make provision for the payment of all claims for British spoliations, as well as of all French claims, direct from our own Treasury? Of these British, as well as of the French claims, almost every Senator may say that "a portion of my constituents—some of them widows and children and grandchildren—are interested." Are these claims not indeed "irresistible?"

But an honorable Senator (Mr. Shepley) says, the United States once offered to pay five millions of francs to be released from the obligations of the ancient treaties—and that France once proposed to receive ten millions of francs for a part, and thirteen millions for the whole violation of plighted faith. It is easy to conceive how these offers might be made on either hand, although neither party should consider its claim as of real value. It amounts to nothing more nor less than this: The United States were willing to allow five millions of francs (less than a million of dollars) if France would consent to a restitution of all captures, seizures, and spoliations, on both hands; and by such an arrangement no doubt we should have been great gainers. France was willing to negotiate in a similar manner if the sum of nominal damage for alleged infraction of the ancient treaties might be raised so much as to bring her not greatly in our debt. As the parties could not be brought to agree, it was quite natural that the basis of actual war should be taken as the ultimate ground of negotiation, and *bona fide* captures (excepting public armed ships) were suffered to remain in the hands of the captors. For such captures, the bill provides restitution from our own Treasury. The principle that would allow them would allow restitution from our Treasury for any and every capture made in any maritime war that ever was waged.

The Senator from Maine says: "France offered to submit all claims," including her extraordinary claim for damages under the ancient treaties, "to a commission," and to abide by the award of that commission; but that the United States refused. This was perfectly natural, if the commissioners for the United States believed, as was the fact, that the French claim for damages was a mere finesse. They did as all prudent men would do, when they declined to leave that claim to be estimated and decided on by persons who might be interested against them, and who might place them under real obligations to pay for what was really no consideration at all.

It is said that "claims precisely circumstanced like these, have been pressed upon France until she has consented to pay us twenty-five millions of francs." The circumstances of the two cases, as was shown by the Senator from Missouri, [Mr. Benton,] are so different that in no two features are they alike. The claims specified under the four different heads of the treaty negotiated by Mr. Rives in 1831, bear a very near analogy to those which were provided for in the Louisiana treaty, but are entirely unlike those which were declared to be desperate by the negotiators of the treaty of September 30, 1800.

There is nothing in the fact, that should favor these claims, if it be true, as is alleged, that the board of commissioners under the last treaty with France has determined that this class of claims cannot come in under that treaty. The objects of restitution under that treaty are particularly specified under four different heads; and neither of those heads embraces claims that bear even a distant analogy to the claims under consideration.

The zeal with which our Government has, at all times, advocated the claims of its citizens, is in this instance urged as proof that the Government, admitting their justice, is responsible for their discharge. The Quarterly Review says—"As long as they were to be paid by France, no doubt was entertained of their validity." And again—"In performance of this duty (to procure redress for injuries done to our citizens) the Government of the United States invited its citizens to confide their claims to its management, and undertook to do every thing in its power to obtain satisfaction." So the Government of the United States, to the last end of the chapter, pressed on the Government of Great Britain the claims for remuneration under her illegal and unjust seizures and condemnations by the orders in council, until finding the prospect of remuneration absolutely hopeless, and finding peace of more value than further destruction of lives and property, this government, in both cases, consented to waive all further claims for illegal seizures and condemnations. There probably was never an instance of treaty with any foreign nation where this government did not press the claims for individual injury to the last moment.

The admission of our negotiators, that there was ground for pressing these claims on France, is taken for granted as an admission that the claims are now due by this government. Such an inference is gratuitous and fallacious. The history of diplomacy, in all ages, furnishes evidence that claims and pretensions are often set up to counteract other claims and pretensions, both of which in the end are yielded; and that these, although sometimes founded in justice, are yielded as an offset to those having really no foundation. The claim by the United States for remuneration of seizures and spoliations under the treaties of alliance and commerce, after the United States by act of Congress had declared those treaties at an end, was likely to be met by the best pretext for claim the French Government could find under the same treaties. As neither of the claims was perhaps tenable, under the practice of nations, to make no restitution where a state of war—call it, if you please, a "*quasi*-war"—had existed, so both nations at length were willing each to withdraw its respective pretensions under treaties which had been broken and declared to be void, and to offset each against the other, all the captures and condemnations that had occurred during the existing differences. And both nations did well for their citizens to make peace even on these terms, neither laid itself liable by consenting to waive the further pressing of individual claims for the payment of such claims. Negotiation and war could not reclaim them; and the nation was not bound further to compromit the welfare of its citizens by continuing a belligerant attitude on account of these claims.

Mr. President, my propositions are—

1. That a state of war between France and the United States effectually put an end to all obligation by France to make restitution for captures and spoliations beyond what they particularly specified in the treaty of September 30, 1800.

2. That the United States, after pressing France for a restitution of those claims so long as they could do it without a sacrifice of other paramount public and private interests, assumed no responsibility for their payment by consenting to press those peculiar claims no further.

3. That if the fact of the existence of war and the abrogation of prior treaties shall be denied, still the United States, having first violated no previous treaty, were under no obligation to France and owed her nothing for such infraction.

4. That as the United States owed nothing to France, so the claimants are entitled to no compensation from the United States for any alleged claims on France.

Mr. President, I listened with close attention to

the argument of the Senator from Maine, (Mr. Shepley) in favor of these claims. From the logical mind of that gentleman, I had anticipated much stronger reasons for passing the bill than he did present: from his known aptitude for thorough investigation, I had anticipated an array of facts giving color at least to the strong and positive statements which he had before promised to make so clear and apparent. In his argument I have been disappointed.

Because the government of the United States (when we say government we mean not all branches of the government, but only the Executive or its agents) because the agents of this government expressed a willingness and a wish to negotiate on the basis of the ancient treaties, and as if no war had existed, the Senator infers that no war did exist. He quotes the French ministers who negotiated the treaty of 1800, as saying that "*the treaties have not been broken*—that there has only been a misunderstanding"—that "they never thought of making war, nor of creating commotions" in the United States; and this he considers positive and conclusive proof that war had not existed, and that the treaties had not been broken. *But did the Senator recollect that in starting with his argument, he first labored to show that the French nation at the very commencement, had violated the treaties by ordering the seizure and arrest of neutral ships, and the ships of the United States with the rest?*

"The treaties have not been broken." Will the Senator take this ground to make the claims binding on the United States? Has it not been shown that the treaties were broken? The gentleman himself had first to insist that France broke the treaty when she directed the seizure of the neutral property—Barbe Marbois says France first *broke the alliance*: the very book of documents compiled to prove these claims, opens with complaints, that France had been the first to violate her treaty engagements.

The gentleman says the state of things that existed was not war; that neither nation set up that there was war; that France has never plead war as a release from these claims; that the annulling of treaties amounted only to *cause* of war. If both the American and French authorities at any time chose to negotiate on the basis of *status quo ante bellum*, or even to infer that a general capture of property and hard fighting on both sides was not war; the same authorities will rise in contradiction of this position. Messrs. Ellsworth, Davie, and Murray, in their Journal of Sept. 12, 1800, expressly say that the President of the French Commission declared (and the other two commissioners united with him in the declaration,) that he would sooner resign than sign a treaty with indemnities; that any impartial tribunal would declare the present state of things to be war; and that, being a state of war, no indemnities could be claimed.

The same American commissioners themselves, in so many words, declare that there was war; they say the treaties have undergone the nullifying operation that war imposes; that "doubtless the congressional act authorizing the reduction of French cruisers by force, was an authorization of war, limited indeed in its extent, *but not in its nature*," and that "clearly also, their subsequent act, that the treaties had ceased to be obligatory, however proper it might be for the removal of doubts, *was but declaratory of the state of things*; and certainly," they say—mark the expression!—"it was only from *an exercise of the constitutional prerogative of declaring war that either of them derived validity*."

Oliver Wolcott, Secretary of the Treasury, in his report to Congress, Jan. 23, 1800, after the consular government had directed a relaxation of the war operations, inferred a state of war to exist, as will be seen by the following extracts:

"That all exports to France or her dependencies were prohibited after the 1st day of July, 1798, (by law of Congress.)

"Vessels have been carried to the vicinity of French ports, where, as it is believed, they have been captured by French privateers, in consequence of preconcerted arrangements; other vessels have entered French ports on pretence of distress. Although the *vessels* have, in many instances, been liberated, yet the *cargoes* have been detained by order of government.

The Secretary continues: "The plea of *forcible exchange* cannot be admitted, without permitting the French government virtually to repeal our laws, by means of their own internal regulations; and if the United States refuse to submit to an insidious policy, and some of our citizens suffer losses, it is against the French and not the American government that their complaints ought to be directed."

I repeat, sir, if these claims had not been interposed, a state of war would never have been doubted; and it will be seen that the whole French commission repudiated the idea that the "state of things" was any thing else than war.

It was entirely unnecessary that the Senator so long dwelt on the proofs that the property for which restitution is claimed, was *illegally* seized. The illegal seizure is not doubted; and while he would urge this as a reason why the American government should stand in the place of France to make restitution, *we urge it as one of the proofs that the United States are exonerated from this restitution*; for if by these seizures France first broke the treaties, nothing was due from the United States even if it should be admitted that we afterward violated those treaties, as it cannot be contended that one party was bound to a rigid adherence to the treaties after the other party had repeatedly violated them, and persisted in her determination to continue their violation.

The Senator says, the United States in repeated instances acknowledged the goodness of these claims; that the negotiators on some occasions urged them on France as good and valid; and the Secretary of State declared that the captures were made "in direct violation of the treaties." Instructions also were given making it an "indispensable condition" that all captures shall be indemnified. The fact, that when the whole treaty-making power (not the negotiators alone, but the President and Senate,) was brought to act, indemnification was not "an indispensable condition," is better proof that the Government did not, than did consider this a debt good and of valuable consideration on their part.

But the Senator says, "France was willing to indemnify, provided we would acknowledge the treaties to be still in existence"—that she said "the parties on both sides ought to be compensated." Has France, since she threw up indemnities on both sides, ever made restitution to her citizens for the property which was captured and condemned by the Americans? Not a dollar! France, it is true, was willing to allow an indemnity, provided we would allow her a greater indemnity, or give her a chance to obtain one—she was willing to revive ancient treaties that had been declared null and void on both sides, if she could make a better bargain in the once case than she could in the other. But France, in the end, great as was the amount of her claim, was willing to make it a draw game.

The gist of the whole matter is, "the consideration," "the valuable consideration" received by the United States, for which we are bound to pay these claims.

The astute advocate of the claims in the American Quarterly Review, had said the claims of France on the United States "were indefinite, and from their nature, incapable of exact calculation; but they were not on that account less real, or less entitled to attention."

I had hoped the Senator from Maine would be more definite. The violation of the guarantee in the treaty of alliance is set up as giving France her principal claim on us. I have shown you, as I trust, that France never asked of the United States the performance of this guarantee, which would at once have thrown us into collision with England. It was for the interest of France itself that the United States should maintain a neutral position after she had declared war against England; and if it had not been her interest, the guarantee was binding on us only while France was engaged in a defensive, not an offensive war. In any event, she could not complain until she had at least made a formal request. Even had France requested, the reasoning of Gen. Hamilton, and his quotation from Vattal, most conclusively demonstrate that if the United States had promised succors to France by treaty, if the furnishing those succors would expose it to an evident danger, this danger is a lawful dispensation from the obligation.

The lengthy correspondence that took place between different envoys and agents, from 1793 to 1800, as well under the ever-changing administrations of the French Directory, as under the consular rule of Bonaparte, is full of evidence that neither the guarantee in the treaty of alliance, nor the obligations of the treaties of commerce, were at any time insisted on by France. Then Messrs. Pinckney, Marshall, and Gerry, in a letter to the Secretary of State, assign as the principal ground of complaint, that the French directory "wanted a loan" from the United States, which they had no authority to grant; and added, "the directory felt itself wounded by the different speeches of Mr. Washington and Mr. Adams."

Gen. Washington, accepting the command in chief of the armies of the United States, in 1798, at the time of the rupture or war with France, distinctly alleges the unfounded pretensions of the French directory as his principal reason for once again standing in the service of the country. He says he is induced to enter the service by "their disregard of solemn treaties and the laws of nations," and that "their demands on us amount to tribute."

The Senator has undertaken to show what were the claims of France on the United States, constituting the obligation of the United States to the present claimants. If I understood him right, they consisted entirely in the value of our obligations to France, under the several treaties of alliance and commerce of 1778. He says the mutual guarantee of one of the treaties, that one party should protect the other in trade with its own enemy, was a valuable property to France, inasmuch as it would have secured her a trade of incalculable amount.

To confront his exposition of these obligations, and even the allegation that the United States at any time violated the treaties, the volumes of published diplomatic papers furnish abundant testimony. You can scarcely open the books without falling upon them. One or two quotations to this point, at different periods, may suffice.

Gen. Washington, in his message to Congress, Dec. 5, 1793, speaking of the difficulties with France, says:

"In the mean time, I have respected and pursued the stipulations of our treaties, according to what I judged their true sense; and have withheld no act of friendship which their [the French] affairs have called for from us, and which justice to others left us free to perform."

And as covering nearly the whole ground of controversy, the following extract of a letter from the three American Envoys, Messrs. Pinckney, Marshall, and Gerry, to the French Minister of Foreign Affairs, dated Feb. 7, 1798, will serve to prove, that from the beginning to nearly the end of the chapter, the American Government had no idea it was violating any obligation to France by the neutral position it had assumed:

"America (say they) found herself at peace with all the belligerent powers: she was connected with some of them by treaties of amity and commerce, and with France by a treaty of alliance also. These several treaties were considered with the most serious attention, and with a sincere wish to determine by fair construction, the obligations which they really imposed. *The result of this inquiry was a full conviction that her engagements by no means bound her to take part in the war*, but left her so far the mistress of her own conduct, as to be at perfect liberty to pursue a real system of neutrality."

The Senator from Maine has not shown that this construction of the treaties by the eminent men then constituting the Government of the United States was a false construction. He must show this to prove that the United States were under any obligation to France for failing to perform any treaty stipulation. Will Senators at this day contend that Washington's proclamation of neutrality was indefensible?

The offer of the Envoys of the United States to a specific sum to release them from the obligations of these treaties, I consider in no other light than an offer to subtract that amount from claims on France, if she would consent to allow those claims. It was a diplomatic expedient to evade that state of things which really existed, and which, if admitted to exist, precluded all hope of restitution. It was a diplomatic expedient calculated to secure something for the claims of France, whereas without it, nothing could be had. Hence we find the American envoys offering to give eight millions of francs, while they utterly refused to leave any thing to the uncertain decision of a board of commissioners. If they considered this French pretension as of any value, they would have been equally willing as France to have submitted the whole question arising under the treaties to a board of commissioners.

President, of late years invention seems to be at the rack in devising ways and means to extract money from the public treasury; in proportion to the facilities of accumulating money an onerous system of duties and taxation the expedients for expending and making with the funds of the Government multiplied. Individual claimants are continually pressing on us for those antiquated claims, of the extent of which the claimants themselves were are until they obtained the information from speculator, whose whole business is to hunt up from musty records, and magnanimously for a moiety of what shall be recovered, to do business of obtaining them. Many a man in distant section of the country has unexpectedly received the offer of five, or ten, or twenty cent, for his chance of recovering a claim in of his father or grand-father, for something e or suffered in the days of the revolution, or e time of the quasi war with France, or at other period of national distress. Claims of kind, although thousands have been paid off, more numerous now than they have been at period within the last thirty years, and they continue to multiply. Success in procuring sums on claims which have little or no foundation, emboldens others to advance theirs; fraud forgery are sometimes brought in to aid in abetting the money of the treasury. It is made interest of the several States to procure each such as possible for its share of these allowances and even members of Congress, acting honestly for the local interests of their constituents, are themselves instrumental in contributing to common abuses.

be claims intended to be provided for in this small be allowed, the main part of them will go well the enormous wealth of a class of men owe their good fortune not to their patriotism, but to that cupidity which has often shown willing to sacrifice the country's best good at the altar of avarice. Who but the underwriters and insurers, and those who have ventured upon ocean in pursuit of an unauthorized trade—but those who have shown themselves willing advice "free trade and sailors' rights," and pardon their country in a great contest for rights and justice on the ocean—who but these, will be benefited by the passage of the bill? Nevertheless, I would pay dollar that is justly due these and all others I cannot believe the Government owes one of these claims; and, therefore, I oppose the passage of the bill.

Then Mr. HILL concluded Mr. ROBBINS took floor and moved an adjournment, which prevailed, and the Senate adjourned.

HOUSE OF REPRESENTATIVES.

Tuesday, December 23, 1834.

Petitions and Memorials were presented by—
HUBBARD, of New Hampshire;
BAYLIES, of Massachusetts;
BURGES, of Rhode Island;
JACKSON, of Connecticut;
ADAMS, HAZELTINE, LANSING, N. of New York;
VAT UR, of New Jersey;

Messrs. SUTHERLAND and HIESTER, of Pennsylvania;
Messrs. GORDON and MOORE, of Virginia;
Mr. PINCKNEY, of South Carolina;
Messrs. MARSHALL and BEATY, of Kentucky;
Mr. DICKINSON, of Tennessee;
Mr. KILGORE, of Ohio;
Mr. JOHNSON, of Louisiana;
Messrs. LANE and KINNARD, of Indiana;

[Mr. LAWS, of Indiana, presented the petition of the citizens of Rising Sun, in the county of Dearborn, praying the establishment of a post route from Versailles, in Ripley county, thence down the Valley of Lauchery Creek, by way of Watt's Mill, Dillsborough, James's Mills, Hartford, to Rising Sun, thence to Burlington, Boon county, Kentucky.

And a similar petition of the citizens of Decatur and Rush county, praying a mail route from Napoleon, in Ripley county, to Clarksburgh, in Decatur county, thence by way of Richland, New Salem, Dickson's Store, Smelser's Mills, in Rush county, to Louisville in Henry county, Ind.

Mr. KINNARD presented additional documents in support of the petition of James Calvin, an invalid soldier of the late war. Referred to the Committee on Invalid Pensions.]

Mr. MAY, of Illinois;

[Mr. MAY presented the petition of sundry inhabitants of the county of McLean, praying the establishment of a post route from Springfield, Illinois, to Chicago, in said State.]

Messrs. McKINLEY and MURPHY, of Alabama;
Mr. LYON, of Michigan;
Mr. THOMAS, of Maryland.

Which memorials and petitions were appropriately referred.

Mr. POLK, from the Committee of Ways and Means, reported the following bills, which were read twice and committed to a Committee of the Whole on the state of the Union:

A bill making appropriations for the support of the Army for the year 1835;

And a bill making appropriations for the current expenses of the Indian Department, for the year 1835.

Mr. POLK, from the same Committee, reported the following resolution, which was agreed to:

Resolved, That the Committee on Indian Affairs be instructed to inquire into the expediency of providing by law, for a clerk to be employed in the office of Superintendent of Indian Affairs at St. Louis.

Mr. WATMOUGH, from the Committee on Naval Affairs, reported a bill explanatory of the act of 20th June, 1834, making certain allowances and granting arrearages to officers of the United States corps of marines; which was read twice and committed.

Mr. CLAY, from the Committee on the Public Lands, reported a bill for the relief of Isaac Wellborne, jr. and William Wellborne; which was read twice and committed.

Mr. CLAY, from the same Committee, reported a bill supplementary to the act of last session, granting pre-emption rights in certain cases to the settlers on the public lands; which was read twice and committed.

Mr. CAMBRELENG, from the Committee of Ways and Means, reported an amendment to the bill "to exempt merchandise imported under certain circumstances from the operation of the act of 19th May, 1828;" which was ordered to be printed.

Mr. JOHNSON, of Kentucky, from the Committee on Military Affairs, reported a bill to revive and continue in force an act to provide for persons who were disabled by known wounds, received during the war of the revolution; which was read twice, and ordered to be engrossed.

Mr. HUBBARD, from the Select Committee appointed for that purpose, reported the joint resolution; which was read twice, and ordered to be engrossed. [*See Senate proceedings.*]

Mr. MERCER, from the Committee on Roads and Canals, reported the following resolution; which lies one day for consideration:

Resolved, That the Secretary of War be directed to lay before this House a report of the expenditure hitherto made in the improvement of the Cumberland river, and the effect thereof, with any information in his possession as to the extent to which such improvement can be carried up the said river, and at what cost.

Mr. BEATY, on leave, submitted a joint resolution, for an adjournment of the two Houses from the 23d to the 29th inst.

Mr. WATMOUGH moved to amend the motion by substituting the 24th inst. for the 23d.

Mr. POLK said, that the motion was unprecedented. He was not aware of a single instance in which a similar proposition had been adopted, and he saw no particular reason for departing from the usage of the House in this instance. He therefore moved to lay the resolution and amendment on the table.

Mr. WARDWELL demanded the yeas and nays on the motion to lay the subject on the table; which were ordered, and are as follows:

YEAS—Messrs. John Q. Adams, John Adams, Heman Allen, John J. Allen, Chilton Allan, Wm. Allen, Ashley, Banks, Barringer, Baylies, Bean, Boon, Bouldin, Briggs, Brown, Bull, Burges, Burns, Bynum, Cage, Cambreleng, Carmichael, Carr, Casey, Chambers, Chaney, Chilton, Claiborne, Samuel Clark, Clay, Clowney, Coffee, Coulter, Crockett, Darlington, Amos Davis, Davenport, Day, Denny, Dickson, Dickerson, Dickinson, Dunlap, Fillmore, Forester, Fowler, Philo C. Fuller, Wm. K. Fuller, Galbraith, Gamble, Gholson, Gillet, Gordon, Graham, Grennell, Griffin, Joseph Hall, Thomas H. Hall, Halsey, Hardin, Joseph M. Harper, Harrison, Hathaway, Hazeltine, Henderson, Hiester, Howell, Hubbard, Huntington, Ebenezer Jackson, Janes, Jarvis, R. H. Johnson, Noadiah Johnson, B. Jones, Kavanagh, King, Kinnard, Lane, Lay, Luke Lea, Thomas Lea, Letcher, Lewis, Lincoln, Loyall, Lucas, Lyon, Lytle, Abijah Mann, Joel K. Mann, Marshall, Martin, Moses Mason, May, McCarty, McComas, McIntire, McKay, McKennan, McKim, McKinley, McLean, McVean, Mercer, Miller, Miner, Robert Mitchell, Moore, Morgan, Muhlenberg, Murphy, Parker, Dutee J. Pearce, Franklin Pierce, Polk, Potts, Ramsay, Reed, Rencher, Reynolds, Robertson, Schenck, A. H. Shepperd, Shinn, Slade, Sloane, Smith, Stewart, Wm. Taylor, Francis Thomas, Philemon Thomas, Thomson, Tompkins, Turnbull, Turner, Tweedy, Vanderpoel, Van Houten, Wagener, Wardwell, Watmough, Webster, Whalon, Wilde, Williams, Wilson, Wise, Young—181.

NAYS—Messrs. Bates, Beale, Beaty, Campbell, Wm. Clark, Clayton, Corwin, Crane, Evans, Gorham, Heath, Wm. Jackson, W. C. Johnson, Cave Johnson, Henry Johnson, Lansing, Manning, Martindale, Milligan, Phillips, Pickens, Pierson, Pinckney, Spangler, Vance, Vinton, Frederick Whittlesey—28.

The following resolutions, submitted yesterday, were considered and agreed to:

By Mr. BYNUM:

Resolved, That the Secretary of War be instructed to lay before this House, a report of the progress of different works of internal improvements now carried on by the General Government in the State of North Carolina, and the amount of appropriations expended in the prosecution of the same.

By Mr. ALLAN, of Kentucky:

Resolved, That the Secretary of the Treasury be instructed to report to this House a statement of the disbursements and appropriations made since the 9th of April, 1832, under the following heads, viz. Fortifications, light-houses, public debt, revolutionary and other pensions, internal improvements, including the piers and breakwaters, preservation of ports and harbors, removing obstructions in rivers and creeks, and the support of light-houses, including all incidental expenses, showing as far as practicable the amount disbursed in each year, and in each State, and in each Territory. *Resolved further*, That the Secretary blend the report hereby required to be made, with the reports from his department to the House, dated on the 31st December, 1829, and April 9th, 1832, so as to exhibit at one view, the expenses of the Government from its commencement to the time under the heads designated.

By Mr. SLOANE:

Resolved, That the Secretary of the Treasury by directed to transmit to this House an estimate of the expense of erecting a beacon light at the mouth of the Black river, in the State of Ohio, and any report that accompanied said statement.

Mr. HUBBARD offered the following resolution which under the rule, lies one day:

Resolved, That the Secretary of the Treasury be directed to communicate to this House, copies of any correspondence which has taken place between himself or any of his predecessors in office since 1834, as far as practicable, with any of the officers of the Bank of the United States, or of any of its Branches, which may have any relation to the claim of the United States against the Bank of Columbia, and to communicate his opinion as to the probability of collecting the balance, or any part thereof, now due from the Bank of Columbia to the United States.

Mr. PEARCE, of Rhode Island, offered the following resolution, which lies one day:

Resolved, That the President of the United States be requested to communicate to this House, such information as he may have, and which in his opinion may be proper to be communicated, and not incompatible with the public interest, showing the steps which have been taken and the progress which has been made in effecting an adjustment and satisfaction of the claims of American Citizens upon the Mexican Government.

Mr. LINCOLN offered the following resolution, which, under the rule, lies one day:

Resolved, That the President of the United States be requested to lay before this House (if, in his opinion, it is not incompatible with the public interest) any communications which may have been had between the Government of the United States and that of Great Britain, since the rejection by the former of the advisory opinion of the King of the Netherlands in reference to the establishment and final settlement of the Northeastern boundary of the United States, heretofore in controversy between the two governments.

And that he also be requested to communicate any information he may possess of the exercise of practical jurisdiction by the authorities of the British Province of New Brunswick over the disputed territory within the limits of the State of Maine, according to the true line of boundary as claimed by the United States, and especially upon that part of the territory which has been incorporated by the government of Maine into the town of Madawaska; together with such representations and correspondence (if any) as have been had by the executive of that State with the Government of the United States, on the subject.

On motion of Mr. WATMOUGH,

Resolved, That the Committee on Naval Affairs be instructed to inquire into the expediency of establishing an Ordnance Department for the naval service.

On motion of Mr. WILSON,

Resolved, That the Committee on the Post Office and Post Roads be instructed to inquire into the expediency of establishing a post route from Knottsville, Monongahela county, Virginia, to Kingwood, in Preston county, Virginia, and from Brandonville to Smithfield, in Pennsylvania.

On motion of Mr. GRAHAM,

Resolved, That the Committee on the Post Office and Post Roads be instructed to inquire into the expediency of establishing a mail route from Ashville, in North Carolina, by Edysville and Mill's Gap, to Spartanburg Court-House, in South Carolina.

On motion of Mr. CHILTON,

Resolved, That the Committee on the Post Office and Post Roads be instructed to inquire into he expediency of establishing a Post Office at the White Sulphur Springs, in Grayson county, Kentucky; and that said committee further inquire into the expediency of establishing a post route from Brandonburgh, in Mead county, to Litchfield, in Grayson county, by way of the Post Office at Big Spring.

On motion of Mr. CRANE, of Ohio,

Resolved, That the Committee on the Post Office and Post Roads be instructed to inquire into the expediency of establishing a Post route from Dayton, in Montgomery county, Ohio, through Germantown and Jacksonburg, to Oxford, in Butler County, Ohio:

On motion of Mr. JOHNSON, of Louisiana,

Resolved, That the Committee on Commerce be instructed to inquire into the expediency of providing a salary and office rent for the Surveyor on Port Ponchartrain, in the State of Louisiana.

On motion of Mr. LANE, of Indiana,

Resolved, That the Committee on Military Affairs be instructed to inquire into the expediency of providing by law for the education, at the Military Academy, of the Junior Midshipmen now in service, and of such as may be hereafter appointed. The whole number of students not to exceed the number of Cadets allowed by the existing laws.

On motion of Mr. REYNOLDS, of Illinois,

Resolved, That the Committee on Commerce be instructed to inquire into the expediency of establishing a port of entry at Alton, in the State of Illinois.

On motion of Mr. CLAY, of Alabama,

Resolved, That the Committee on the Public Lands be instructed to inquire into the expediency of reporting a bill to relieve Wm. Walker, of Jackson County, Alabama, from the consequences of a mistake in the entry of a tract of land in that county.

On motion of Mr. DAVENPORT,

Resolved, That the Committee on the Post Office and Post Roads be instructed to inquire into the expediency of establishing a post route from Weldon, North Carolina, via Boydton, Charlotte Court-house, and Brookneal, to Green Hill, in the county of Campbell, Virginia.

On motion of Mr. WHITE, of Florida,

Resolved, That the Committee on the Judiciary be instructed to inquire into the expediency of providing by law for a new Judicial District in the Territory of Florida, the Judge of said District to reside at Apalachicola.

On motion of Mr. A. H. SHEPPERD,

Resolved, That the Committee on Indian Affairs be instructed to inquire into the expediency of making compensation to the society of Moravians, for the expenses incurred at their Missionary Establishments, within the limits of the Cherokee tribe of Indians.

On motion of Mr. KAVANAGH,

Resolved, That the Committee on Commerce be instructed to inquire into the expediency of making an appropriation for placing buoys in Damariscotta river, in the State of Maine.

On motion of Mr. BEAN,

Resolved, That the Committee on Invalid Pensions be instructed to inquire into the expediency of placing the name of John Kaime, of New Hampshire, on the list of Invalid Pensions.

On motion of Mr. READ,

Resolved, That the Committee on Commerce be instructed to inquire into the expediency of discontinuing one of the Light-houses in Chatham, Massachusett.

Mr. FOSTER asked the House to take up and consider the resolution submitted by him some days since, calling on the President of the United States for information connected with our relations with France; but at the suggestion of Mr. WAYNE, the motion to consider was withdrawn.

The SPEAKER laid before the House a report from the Commissioner of the Public Buildings, in obedience to the act of the 3d March, 1829, containing an account of the expenditures upon the improvement of the public grounds, which, on motion of Mr. JARVIS, was laid on the table, and directed to be printed.

The bill authorizing the Registers and Receivers of the public land offices to administer oaths connected with the entry and sale of the public lands, was read a third time and passed.

PAY OF NAVAL OFFICERS.

The House then resolved itself into a Committee of the Whole on the state of the Union, Mr. BRIGGS in the Chair, on the bill to equalize and regulate the pay of the officers of the Army and Navy of the United States, and the amendments thereunto proposed by Mr. WATMOUGH, as Chairman of the Select Committee, and Mr. WISE, a member of the Committee on Naval Affairs.

The discussion was resumed on the amendment offered by Mr. WISE, to increase the compensa-

tion of Boatswains, Gunners, Carpenters, and Sailmakers, and adding the office of Armorers to the list, allowing each seven hundred dollars while waiting orders, and eight hundred while on duty.

Mr. WATMOUGH briefly stated the objections which existed in his mind to the amendment. He repeated the ideas he had previously advanced, that was highly important to offer inducements for these officers to remain at sea rather than on shore; and hence the difference in the compensation in those situations. He was willing to allow them $750 when on board of a frigate, and $600 while on board a sloop, brig, or schooner; or while acting on shore. Further he could not consistently go.

Mr. WISE declined to accept this proposition, and stated the reasons which urged him to do so. These men, ho ding these very responsible stations, he was well informed could not live on shore with the compensation proposed for them. It was not to avoid duty at sea, that these men desired a fair compensation while they casually at home with their families. They may lay ask that they may live. He was well aware that the present inadequate pay brought only from their habits and abilities, were unworthy of the station—who required a thorough portion before they were competent to the performance of their important duties. The pay of these men, he contended, bore no fair comparison with that of other offices of the Navy, in proportion with their duties.

Mr. REED said these men could have no idea of absence, inasmuch as there was only on each of them attached to a vessel. He did deem it important to include the office of Armorer in the amendment.

Mr. WISE replied, contending that a ship not properly manned without an Armorer—one, too, more competent than a common blacksmith—one, probably, whose services could not be procured for a less sum than 25 cents per hour. Such was the information which he had been enabled to collect from authentic sources, in relation to this office.

Mr. WATMOUGH again explained, and urged some further objections to the amendment.

Mr. SUTHERLAND asked the gentleman saying one word in favor of these men. He plained that his former remarks upon this subject had been misunderstood or misrepresented. He only asked the committee to allow these officers a proper compensation while they were at home. His argument was, that while they were at home with their families, they should be taken care and not, as proposed by this unequal reduction, their wages on shore, be hurried off again to sea soon, almost, as their feet have touched the shore. He spoke particularly of Boatswains, and the importance of their services. He would make these men exiles from their homes, their wives, and children, under the penalty of having their pay reduced to the inadequate sum of per annum. These men pass and the same naval affections—the same strong feeling for their families, that others did. The carpenter, he added, was a very important man on board, and dwelt on the onerous nature of his duties. He said he was aware that his colleague (Mr. Watmough) came from a district where these working men—the bone and sinews of way—are numerous. The committee of which that gentleman was chairman, was constituted to equalize the pay of officers. He wished to see at least an equalization of the pay of those serving on board the same ship. After some further observations Mr. S. concluded with the remark, that all the experienced individuals with whom he had conversed, joined him in the views he had taken on this important point, of giving to these officers a more adequate compensation while on shore—while the bosom of their families—a blessing which so seldom enjoyed.

Mr. BATES said, he conceived this question a mere matter of fact, and not a subject for oratorical flourishes. He asked if the amendment embraced the views of the officers of the navy? If by their judgment and discretion, his own would be, in a great measure, controlled—

Mr. WISE replied, in effect, that it did.

Mr. BURGES wished this subject could be discussed without so much ardor. He thought the aim of these officers to their families once in two or three years, should be satisfactory to the gentleman from Pennsylvania, (Mr. Sutherland.) However that might be, he believed the laborer worthy of his hire. He was attached to that class of our fellow-citizens, and he hoped he never would forget the sympathy which he had ever felt and professed for the working classes. But it seemed that all at once this class were supposed possess extraordinary merit. They were even in advance of your Admirals and your Generals.

Mr. B. contended that the compensation contained in the bill was amply sufficient, and it was more than some of the individuals received to could get if following their occupations of the public service. He was willing to encourage bravery, but was not in favor of paying to men a sum so greatly disproportionate to the service rendered. He went at length into particulars connected with the pay, duties, &c. of the various individuals engaged in the naval service.

Mr. REED, of Massachusetts, referred to the report of the Secretary of the Navy on this subject, to show that the bill went as far as was recommended by the Department on the particular object of the amendment. He made no pretensions of exclusive friendship for the working men of the community or the navy; he was willing to do justice to all. The persons embraced in this amendment were seldom absent on leave. It was impossible to do without them on board particularly a ship of the largest class. Recompense had been made to the pay of seamen. He was in favor of giving that class of the service most ample compensation. He should have offered an amendment to that effect if he had not believed that it was not strictly proper to embrace them in the present bill.

Mr. FERRIS observed that he did not wish to trespass on the patience of the House or unnecessarily to prolong this exciting debate. But he would endeavor to answer an argument adduced the gentleman from Rhode Island, and deliver with so much ingenuity, ability, and eloquence, as to make an impression against the proposed amendment. The gentleman triumphantly asks, why a mechanic attached to the national service should be allowed more wages, than a mechanic of the same grade could earn on shore. It appeared to Mr. F. there were obvious reasons why there should be a greater allowance. The mechanic on shore had advantages over se in the service. They had the enjoyment of domestic fire side and the social circle. The advantages of forming connexions in society, and if he possessed talents and enterprise, he might by economy lay up a small capital, and with the assistance of friends establish himself in business, some a master mechanic and a man of fortune. Many of our most substantial citizens have risen in way, who look back with satisfaction upon enterprise, industry, and economy, which led them from small beginnings to comfort and affluence. The mechanic attached to the service is deprived of all these advantages—his sole dependence is on the provision his country has made him, and from the allowance proposed, he could lay up but a small pittance for that period, when age and infirmity shall render him unfit for service; and when he shall be compelled to linger out the remnant of his days in comparative penury and want without a cheering hope to animate him—that when be shall be called to that "bourn from whence no traveller returns," his wife and little ones would be left with the moderate means of living. There is another obvious reason why there should be a difference—The mechanic on shore ens, afterthe toils of the day, the comforts of family and fireside, while he at sea encounters perils of sea and battle—sustaining the flag the rights of this country.

Mr. F. would call the attention of the House to observation, applicable to the general provisions of this bill. The officers of all grades and are, when on shore, are obliged to live, on the Atlantic border, in the large cities—where house rent, fuel, and all necessary expenses for the support of a family, including the education of children, are extravagantly high, when compared to the expense of living in the fruitful west. If gentlemen would make a calculation of the necessary expenses to be deducted for the allowances made by this bill, and by this amendment, they would find that but a small sum could be saved by the most rigid economy, as a provision for their families, in case of death, or for coming age and infirmities. He should not detain the House by declaiming on the gallant deeds of the navy, or the imperishable glory it had shed on the country. But he felt it his duty to make these observations, from a due regard to the claims of that useful class of officers—the mechanics attached to the service—which the amendment proposes to relieve.

Mr. BURGES briefly replied, and explained his former remarks.

Mr. FERRIS rejoined, and also explained.

After a few additional remarks by Messrs. WATMOUGH and WISE, the question was taken on the amendment of the latter, in relation to the pay of boatswains, gunners, sail-makers, and carpenters, and rejected.

Mr. WATMOUGH moved an amendment intended to guard the rights and interests of surgeons, while absent; which was adopted.

Mr. MANN, of New York, said, he would now propose an amendment which would enable those gentlemen who were so extremely zealous in favor of the higher officers in service, to extend their sympathies to the common sailors; a class, in favor of whom no voice had yet been raised, and who were so important to the service. He would, therefore, move to increase the present pittance paid to the common sailor, at the rate of $3 per month.

After a few remarks by Messrs. WATMOUGH and CAMBRELENG, of an explanatory character, the amendment was rejected.

Mr. WATMOUGH offered an amendment to that part of the first section which specified that the compensation given in the bill should be full of all allowances, with certain exceptions; which was agreed to.

Mr. WISE moved a proviso that officers, commanding a squadron on a foreign station, should be entitled to fourteen rations per day; which was rejected.

Mr. GILLET proposed an amendment, providing that the specific pay to the officers of the Navy proposed in the bill, should be in full of all compensation, &c. &c.

Mr. WATMOUGH contended that the substantial part of this amendment was already incorporated in the bill, by the amendment he had just offered, and which was adopted.

Mr. GILLET said it was not his purpose, at the present time, to discuss at length the subject of this amendment. He had not taken part in the discussions relative to the amount to be paid to the officers respectively. His object was, to have the door shut against pay beyond the sum mentioned in the bill. If the sum proposed to be given was not large enough, let it be increased, and made what it should be. But he was decidedly opposed to leaving an opportunity for allowances. He was for giving, in one sum, all that could possibly be allowed. The People, and this House, would then know what was paid for services in the navy. It was, doubtless, true that some of the officers were not sufficiently paid, but his object was to close the almost boundless field of allowances.

He had understood the object of the Chairman of the Select Committee to be, to place the officers a gross sum, and cut off all allowances. He now invited him to aid in rendering that object certain. Then the country would know, with certainty, what was paid. Mr. G. said he hoped to have an opportunity in the progress of fully explaining his views on this subject, in which he hoped to have a concurrence of this House.

After a few additional remarks by Mr. WATMOUGH, the amendment proposed by Mr. GILLET was negatived.

Mr. GRENNELL moved to amend the bill by increasing the compensation proposed to be given to the first Clerk to a Commandant of a Navy Yard from $900 to $1150. Mr. G. said the duties which would be required of this Clerk were arduous, and required a person possessing skill and integrity. He instanced the case of a heavy fraud committed by a Clerk in the Navy Yard at Charlestown, Massachusetts, to show the necessity of having an honest and faithful individual to perform the duties required.

The amendment was rejected.

Mr. PARKER moved to strike out the second section, which is in the following words:

"Sec. 2. And be it further enacted, That the Secretary of the Treasury shall be, and be is hereby, authorized and directed to deduct from the pay hereafter to become due of the commission and warrant officers of the navy of the United States' three per centum of the amount thereof, and to pay the same to the Secretary of the Navy and the Navy Commissioners for the time being, who are hereby appointed a Board of Commissioners by the name and style of "Commissioners of the Navy Widows and Orphans' Fund," which, together with any other moneys to which the fund may become legally entitled, shall constitute a fund for the relief of the widows, children, " and relatives of the said commission and warrant officers of the navy of the United States, to be invested by said board, and the proceeds of it divided and disbursed in such manner as may be hereafter prescribed by Congress."

After a few remarks by Mr. WATMOUGH, the motion was disagreed to.

Mr. MASON moved to strike from the second section, the words " and relatives," printed in Italics.

This motion was discussed by Messrs. MASON, WATMOUGH, and CAMBRELENG, when Mr. REED moved to amend the amendment by inserting in lieu of the words " and relatives," the words " widows, children, and unmarried sisters."

The debate on this amendment was further continued by Messrs. REED, WATMOUGH, and MASON.

Mr. FILLMORE suggested to the mover of the amendment to the amendment, (Mr. Reed,) to include in his proposition, " widowed mothers."

Mr. REED assented to this modification, when the motion, as modified, was agreed to.

Mr. PARKER again addressed the committee, in opposition to the second section of the bill, and proposed to renew the motion to strike it out; but the CHAIR declared that such a motion was not in order.

The third section was read as follows:

"Sec. 3. And be it further enacted, That, from and after the passage of this act, it shall be the duty of every medical officer of the United States' navy to provide himself with all such instruments as are necessary in his profession, and that the sum of   dollars be, and the same is hereby, annually appropriated, out of any money in the Treasury not otherwise appropriated, to be applied, on an estimate to be furnished under the direction of the Secretary of the Navy, to the object specified in this act."

Mr. WATMOUGH moved to strike this section from the bill, which was agreed to.

Mr. JARVIS moved to add an additional section to the bill, providing that hereafter, in the distribution of prize money, it shall be done in proportion to the pay which each officer, &c. now receives. Mr. J. said that he wished the question taken on his amendment, and that when the bill should come up in the House, he would endeavor to prove that the present system of distributing prize money was unjust and improper. The amendment was agreed to.

The amendments having been gone through with, the Committee rose and reported the bill to the House as amended.

On motion of Mr. WATMOUGH, the bill and amendments were ordered to be printed.

The House then adjourned.

The VICE PRESIDENT laid before the Senate a letter from the Secretary of State in answer

to a resolution requiring him to communicate to Congress the situation of the contract made by Edward Livingston, Esq., late Secretary of State, with Clarke and Force, for the publication of the American Diplomatic Correspondence.

On motion of Mr. WEBSTER, the communication was ordered to be printed.

Petitions and memorials of a private nature were presented by Messrs. WEBSTER, WAGGAMAN, KANE, SPRAGUE, and TOMLINSON.

Mr. WEBSTER presented a petition from sundry citizens of Boston, praying the passage of a law allowing a drawback on the exportation of cordage; which was referred to the Committee on Commerce and ordered to be printed.

The Joint Resolution from the House of Representatives directing the mode of carrying into effect the resolution of June last, adopted on the occasion of the death of General Lafayette, was read, and

On motion of Mr. WEBSTER, concurred in.

Mr. KING, of Alabama, gave notice that on Monday next he would ask leave to introduce a bill for the relief of David McCall.

Mr. CLAYTON, from the Judiciary Committee, made two several reports upon the petitions of John Cutts and John Donnel; which were ordered to be printed.

Mr. CLAYTON, from the same Committe, reported a bill for the relief of Col. James Thomas; which was read the first time and ordered to a second reading.

Mr. POINDEXTER, from the Committee on Public Lands, reported the bill from the House granting to the borough of Mackinaw a lot of land, with an amendment; which was read the first time and ordered to a second reading.

He also gave notice that on Monday next he would ask leave to introduce a bill to provide more effectually against frauds in the sale of the public lands of the U. States.

The following resolutions were submitted:

By Mr. McKEAN:

Resolved, That the Committee on Commerce be instructed to inquire into the expediency of establishing a port of entry at Brownsville, on the Monongahela river.

By Mr. ROBINSON:

Resolved, That the Committee on the Post Office and Post Roads be instructed to inquire into the expediency of establishing a mail route from Golconda, in Illinois, by Walnut Grove, and Davidson's mills, to Frankfort, in the same State.

The following resolution, submitted yesterday by Mr. CLAY, was read and adopted;

Resolved, That the President be requested to communicate to the Senate, (if, in his opinion, it shall not be incompatible with the public interest,) the instructions which have been transmitted from time to time, since the 4th of July, 1831, to the representatives of the United States at the government of France, relating to the execution of the treaty, which was signed on that day between the United States and France; and also all the correspondence which has passed at Washington or at Paris between the two governments respecting the execution of the said treaty.

Mr. TIPTON moved the consideration of the resolution submitted by him some days since instituting an inquiry into the expediency of establishing a port of entry on the Wabash.

Mr. TIPTON said—

I have reason to fear that I will weary the patience of the Senate with motions to improve the navigation of the Wabash, and my remarks in supporting them; but, sir, the claims of that river to public consideration, the situation of the country, and the condition of the people that inhabit the Wabash and its tributaries, have been so much misunderstood elsewhere, that I owe it to the Senate, to the country, and to myself, to invite the attention of Congress to that subject once more; this I propose to do at this time, and promise to be as brief as I can to do the subject that justice its importance to the west demands.

This motion contemplates establishing a port of entry at Lafayette, on the Wabash. This town is situate about 400 miles by the river from the mouth of the Wabash, and 215 by our canal from the Maumee bay on Lake Erie, surrounded by a country unsurpassed in fertility of soil, becoming wealthy, and of immense resources. In proposing to establish a port of entry at the place mentioned, I have two objects in view; first, to invite and extend commerce to the interior of our country, and to remove the last objection that can be raised to an appropriation of money by Congress to improve the navigation of the river.

This proposition has nothing new or novel in it: the principle has been frequently acted on by Congress: ports of entry have been established high up on many of our rivers, and I am unable to perceive any good objection to this being done. It invites our merchants in the interior to become the importers of their own goods, direct from foreign markets, to such parts of our country as consume them, thereby saving to the merchants in the interior, the drayage, storage, commission, and other charges that they are subjected to when their packages have to be opened, goods stored, and duty, paid, in the ports of New York or New Orleans.

It is true that steamboats cannot pass the rapids at White river and ascend the Wabash to Lafayette and our canal, when the river is low. This was also the case with the Ohio before the construction of the Louisville and Portland canal. Steamboats could not pass the Falls of the Ohio, to ascend to Cincinnati and Pittsburg, unless the Ohio was high and ports of entry were established at both places. The United States contributed to aid the construction of the Louisville and Portland canal, and we expect them to improve the navigation of the Wabash.

The Wabash is equally as susceptible of navigation, above the rapids, near White river, as the Ohio from Marietta to Pittsburg, and better than Cumberland, and a port of entry has been established at Nashville; of this I do not complain: it is, in my judgment, right and proper. I ask no more for the Wabash than has been done for other rivers of similar claims, and I hope this will not be denied.

By the Blue Book, I find that ports of entry are established in several of the old States, at places where it was once thought necessary, that turn out to be rather unimportant. Some of these ports yield no revenue, but officers of the customs are appointed; and where no business is to be performed, no salary is paid. At other places, $150 or $180 are paid, where but little service is required. A port of entry at Lafayette cannot be less important than some of those are.

It is due to the intelligent and enterprising population invited by the wise policy of this Government to seek homes on the western waters, that a port of entry should be established among them, to encourage commerce. In 1827 a grant of land was made to aid in constructing a canal, to connect at navigable points the waters of the Wabash with those of Lake Erie. This grant consists of the one half of five miles on each side of the canal line, to be divided by alternate tiers of sections.

The State of Indiana rated her lands at 1st, 2d, and 3d rate. Those lands are sold at $1.50, $2.50, or $3.50 per acre. Agreeably to this rate, by thus rating the canal lands, we have raised the United States lands in that vicinity to a corresponding value; and a quantity of United States lands have been sold at these prices, that would have remained unsold for 20 years to come, if no public improvement had been begun in that country.

The United States received $693,522.40 for lands sold in Indiana last year from the extraordinary sales. I infer that these sales are owing to the improvements going on there, and that the grant of land to aid in the construction of the Wabash and Erie canal has been beneficial to the United States, and I challenge the most violent opponent of internal improvement to pass our rivers, lakes, and canals, from N. York to N. Orleans, and say, if he will, that these public works do not promote the best interest of our country.

After leaving the steamboat at Albany, the traveller will pass rapidly on the rail road to Schenectady, thence westward, he sees millions of tons of freight floating on the canal and lake to the far west. Continuing his journey southwest along the Maumee river, that part of the Wabash and Erie canal line not yet under contract, here the country is progressing slowly in population and cultivation; but when the traveller arrives at Fort Wayne, where the work is progressing on our canal, every body is engaged, all is bustle and business, and from Fort Wayne, crossing the summit between the Mississippi and the St. Lawrence, 75 miles of the canal is completed, or in a good state of forwardness; here is to be seen farms and villages springing up, as it were, by magic; nothing is wanting but a continuance of the fostering care of this government to make this a most desirable part of the country in a short time.

Emigrants are daily arriving among us from New York, Pennsylvania, and Ohio, men of wealth and business, who have been engaged as engineers or contractors on the public works in the old States that have been finished, go west with educated and intelligent families, seeking a permanent home. These present a very different appearance from that class of individuals that roams the western wilds after bear and deer.

Should a traveller stop for the night in one of our villages that are springing up at every ten or fifteen miles along the canal, where the work has been begun, and does not rise by twilight, he will be aroused by the sound of the hammer, the woodman's axe, or the mechanic's plane. This is the fruit of the wise policy heretofore pursued by this Government toward the new States in the west—its blessings cannot be too widely diffused.

I happened in conversation with one of the Postmasters last fall; he remarked that he was astonished to see the number of newspapers and pamphlets that passed his office for Huntington, and other villages on the canal. The people in these neighborhoods take more papers, said he, than many other places of twice their age and four times their population—and must be a reading people. This is, no doubt, true, and where we find a reading people we always find a moral and industrious people, who patronise schools and other institutions that enlighten the mind and elevate the character of man.

The population that are flocking to that country, are both enterprising and industrious. By their exertion they are opening farms, building towns, and constructing the canal. The face of the country is undergoing a wonderful change; what was but a few days ago a desert for wild beasts to roam through, has become the peaceful abode of civilized man. It is in that country, and for the benefit of these people, that I have endeavored to describe that I wish to establish a port of entry, and to improve the navigation of their river.

Strong inducements have been held out to the people to purchase and settle western lands. Men who have emigrated to the west, and divested themselves of the commercial facilities to which they were accustomed in the eastern states, look to the General Government to extend these facilities to their new homes; and the government owes it to the people, to diffuse its blessings to all parts of our country, where it can be done with convenience, as it can in this case.

I am not one of those that believe, that a law of Congress, establishing a port of entry, confers power to appropriate money to improve rivers;—all that has been said and written upon this subject, has not changed my mind. I entertain no doubt but the power exists to appropriate money to improve rivers in any part of the United States, or their Territories, where the business of the people require such improvement.

The eighth section of the first article of the constitution of the United States, granting powers, reads thus:

"The Congress shall have power to lay and collect taxes, duties, imposts, and excises; to pay the debts and provide for the common defence and general welfare of the United States."

The same section concludes as follows:

"To make all laws which shall be necessary and proper for carrying into execution the foregoing powers, and all other powers vested by this constitution in the Government of the United States, or in any department or officer thereof."

Here is a grant of power by the constitution itself, authorizing the Legislative Department of

the Government to make all laws necessary and proper for the public interest. The ordinance of Congress of 13th July, 1787, is older than the constitution, and binding on the parties to that instrument, (which has, unfortunately, been too much overlooked in this whole transaction.) The Wabash is a reserved public highway, free to all the People of the United States; and I propose to establish a port of entry on that river, and to improve this public highway. I can find no limitation on the power of Congress or the President, as regards appropriations to improve the navigation of rivers, and to establish ports of entry, beside their own discretion. Does not the constitution, and constant practice of the Government, authorise the improving of this river? And the terest of a large portion of our constituents seems demand it.

There is an additional reason for establishing a port of entry: it will remove a difficulty from certain quarter that I have found extremely inconvenient. It can cost nothing—it will violate no principle; and where it is within the power of Congress to do so much good, without violating the former practice of the Government, or creating new expenses, I think it will hardly be denied us.

It may be asked, why this motion was not made at year, before the Wabash bill passed? It was troduced by an honorable member of the other ranch of Congress, at the last session; but, owing ... the press of business in that House, did not get through. I am desirous to get an expression of the Senate on this proposition, at as early a day as may be convenient, that it may have an opportunity of becoming a law before we adjourn.

This motion looks to establishing a port of entry, and improving the river. Near half a million of people reside on the Wabash and its tributaries, all deeply interested in the steps taken here to extend to them commercial facilities. Every gentleman conversant with the New Orleans market for the upper country produce, will testify that the rise of the Wabash to let our boats pass the rapids of White river, has an influence upon the sales at New Orleans. Should not the river rise to let boats out early in the spring, our produce, consisting of flour, corn, pork, and beef, is locked up at home, and prices are high in the lower country. When the river rises, and boats get off, they are thrown all at the same time, into the market below. Our produce is mostly carried to market by our farmers, who, anxious to return to their farms, and dreading the disease of a Southern climate, in the sickly season, sell at great sacrifice. Many of our people fall victims to the disease, and find graves in that country. Hundreds of lives and thousands of dollars are sacrificed in that unhealthy climate every year. A portion of these can be preserved by the improvement proposed.

The Delegation are not urging this measure upon Congress of their own accord. Our Legislature has frequently memorialized Congress upon these subjects, and I have no doubt, will do so again at this session. We do no more than reiterate here the wishes of those we have the honor to represent, with a hope that a deaf ear may not be turned to our request.

In submitting a resolution to the Senate a few days ago, I alluded, in the most temperate language, to a publication made in the Globe last summer, as I then believed, to array the Jackson party in Indiana against me, for advocating the improvement, by the United States, of the navigation of the Wabash. For this I am again assailed, and insinuations made calculated to injure me, and to prejudice this measure. It is true, that I live on the Wabash, and like other men of industry, who settled there at an early day, own some land, but far from a great estate, as charged by the Globe. And were it true that I have a large estate, is that d ground for the Globe to oppose improving the r, and thereby injure the people of more than ...? State?

If any person have charges to prefer against me her in my public or private capacity, let them be ught forward, I stand ready to meet them at all es and places. I have no favors to ask. But if I expected to deter me from my duty by such ts, they are mistaken. I shall vote according

to my own sense of right, without being driven from my course by threats or insinuations.

[We open our columns to Gen. TIPTON to enable him to meet some remarks recently made by us in repelling an attack on this print, contained in a speech delivered by him on the floor of the Senate. We feel it due to ourselves, however reluctant to say a word more on the subject, to accompany General Tipton's notice with a brief comment.

In the first place, we aver that the publication alluded to, whatever General Tipton *"then believed," was not intended "to array the Jackson party in Indiana against him, for advocating the improvement by the United States of the navigation of the Wabash."* Our sole object was to vindicate the motives of the Chief Magistrate from the imputation of hostility to Indiana, in refusing his assent to the appropriation to the Wabash on which there was no port of entry, and of partiality to other States, because he had acquiesced in appropriations to other streams in which there are ports of entry established. This impeachment of the President's motives we considered distinctly made in the circular of Senator Tipton—and as we know that the President had proceeded altogether upon principles plainly laid down on several previous occasions, and not upon unworthy preferences, we considered it due to him to give the explanations contained in the publication complained of by General Tipton. We however insist that the explanation was given in the most decorous terms, and in the kindest spirit towards General Tipton, as is shown by the reference made in the beginning of the article of the firm support given by him to the Administration on another important subject.

Gen. Tipton has fallen into another error, in supposing that we have the slightest disposition to prejudice the measure he has proposed. The whole tenor of our article, on which Gen. Tipton commented, breathed a spirit favorable to the improvement of the Wabash, when circumstances would render it compatible with the principles laid down by the President; and, indeed, we suggested in it the very proposition which Gen. Tipton has now made to the Senate, for the purpose of bringing the Wabash, and its canal communication with the Lakes, within the description which can alone entitle it to be considered as of the class of navigable streams which are of national importance. If Congress resolve to unite the Lakes with the Ohio, through the channel of the Wabash, and make ports of entry and delivery upon it, then, undoubtedly, the river will be brought, not only in name, but in fact, within the President's principle. But while General Tipton adopts our suggestion of obtaining a recognition of the Wabash from Congress, as a channel of communication, important in a national point of view, how can he with propriety assume, that what he thus adopts on his own part, as friendly to his object, is evidence of hostility, on our part, towards it?

General Tipton's speech, as it appears in the National Intelligencer, has the following remark:

"He should avail himself always of the oppor-

tunity to express his sentiments, despite of the threat which had been held out by the Globe, of another attack, in addition to the one which was made a few days since on him.

"That print threatened the publication of charges made by one of his colleagues. He hinted the publication of all charges against his private and public conduct; and he flattered himself that he should have little difficulty in defending himself to the satisfaction of his constituents and all unprejudiced minds."

The speech, as it appears in the Globe to-day, having undergone the author's revision, and containing no such remark, we infer that the report in the Intelligencer cannot have his sanction. We, therefore, treat it as the Reporter's mistake when we give it a direct contradiction. We deny that " A THREAT" of attack upon General Tipton *" has been held out by the Globe."* We stated that attacks had been threatened from other quarters, and that we used our good offices to prevent them. We have never even *" threatened the publication of charges made by one of his colleagues."* We are not informed that any one of his colleagues have now the remotest intention of making the charges which we spoke of as having been once in contemplation. We speak of the *past* not the *future*, and meant to prove that we did not entertain the personal hostility to General Tipton, to which our article, purely defensive of the President's motives, had been ascribed.

We owe an apology to those however, of whose relations with General Tipton we had spoken, without using a name. There had been a frankness and boldness used by the party in question, that satisfied us it wish was entertained to conceal opinions held as to Gen. T. This we felt a sufficient justification to use facts known to several, to vindicate ourselves from the unjust imputation of acting in our public capacity from private malice, and that too, when vindicating the motives of the Chief Magistrate. The party alluded to, we trust, will consider the object we had in view of sufficient importance to justify the remote way in which he has been involved by our allusion. If there is any thing implied in the authentic speech published in the Globe to-day, calculated to lend support by inference to the interpretation of the Intelligencer, the above remarks will be as applicable to the one as to the other.]

The following resolution submitted yesterday by Mr. HENDRICKS, was taken up and adopted:

Resolved, That the Committee on the Post Office and Post Roads be instructed to inquire into the expediency of establishing a post route from Louisville, by way of Salem, Bond, Bedford, Bloomfield, and Bowling Green, to Terre Haute. Also a post road from Bedford through Mount Pleasant, to Portersville.

Also, from Danville, through New Maysville, Green Castle, Putnamville, Manhattan, Pleasant Garden, Bowling Green, Ramsay's mill, Clay County, and Caledonia, to Carlisle: Or so much of said route as may not heretofore have been established by law.

The following resolutions, lying [on the table] were taken up and adopted;

Resolved, That the Postmaster General inform the Senate whether so much of the act of Congress approved June 25th, 1832, establishing a mail route from Burntcorn, in the State of Alabama, by Claiborne, Clarksville, Coffeeville, Washington C. H., Winchester, Ellsville, Williamsburg, Monticello, and Meadville, to Natchez, in

State of Mississippi, has been carried into effect; and if it has not, what cause or causes have prevented it.

Resolved, That the Committee on the Post Office and Post Roads be instructed to inquire into the expediency of establishing a mail route from Augusta, in Perry county, Mississippi, by the bay of Belonti to Hancock C H, in the same State.

Resolved, That the Committee on Indian Affairs be instructed to inquire into the expediency of authorising the appointment of an agent to receive evidence of losses sustained by the inhabitants of the State of Alabama by an invasion of a party of Creek Indians, in 1814, when Fort Mims was taken, and those who fled there for protection massacred.

The bill from the House of Representatives to authorise the Registers an i Receivers of the Land Offices of the United States to administer oaths in all matters connected with their official duties, was read a second time and referred.

The bill for the relief of Col. John Eugene Leisendorfer, was considered as in Committee of the Whole.

[Col. Leisendorfer was one of the subordinate officers under General Eaton, when he marched from Egypt with the forces of the exiled Bashaw Caramolle, to co-operate with the naval expedition under Commodore Preble against Tripoli, in 1804.]

Mr. BENTON, in support of the bill, went into a brief but interesting detail of the services, sufferings, and the merits of Col. Leisendorfer.

Mr. POINDEXTER opposed the bill on the ground that it would be setting a bad precedent to increase the compensation of this individual. He objected also to the provision in the third section, pensioning him on the same ground, and contended that it would furnish a good precedent for the heirs of General Eaton to make a similar claim upon Congress.

Mr. BENTON said, that in running over the history of Gen. Eaton's life, he should judge that he had received no remuneration, and if an application should be made on the part of his heirs, it would stand with me on the same footing, relative circumstances considered, with the grant to Lafayette, and on a better footing than the grant to the Poindexters, for both of which he had voted with hearty good will. He also said that, in looking into the case of Gen. Eaton, in our State papers, which he had just done to make himself master of Col. Leisendorfer's case, he made up his mind that he was a meritorious and injured man.

Mr. POINDEXTER thought many instances of the kind might be found on the statute book.

Mr. PRESTON having objected to the third section,

Mr. BENTON said he had no objection to its being struck out of the bill; and it was accordingly done.

After some remarks from Mr. WEBSTER, relative to the high character and meritorious services of Gen Eaton,

The question was put on the engrossment of the bill for a third reading, and on a division being demanded by Mr. POINDEXTER, the bill was ordered tobe engrossed—yeas 19, nays 15.

Mr. WEBSTER then moved that when the Senate adjourn it will adjourn to meet on Saturday next; which was agreed to.

The Senate then adjourned.

HOUSE OF REPRESENTATIVES.

WEDNESDAY, DEC. 24, 1834.

Petitions and memorials were presented by—
Mr. YOUNG, Connecticut;
Mr. PARKER, New Jersey;
Messrs. HIESTR and BEAUMONT, of Pennsylvania;
Mr. THOMAS, Maryland;
Mr. POPE, of Kentucky;
Messrs. STANBERY and BELL, (Speaker,) of Tennessee;
Mr. LYON, of Michigan;
Mr. WHITE, of Florida;
Mr. WISE, of Virginia;
Mr. W. B. SHEPARD, of North Carolina.
Which petitions and memorials were appropriately referred.

The SPEAKER presented the following memorial, being the same as that presented by Mr. LYON, of Michigan:

EXECUTIVE OFFICE, ?
Detroit, December 12, 1834. 5

SIR: In obedience to a request of the Legislative Council of the Territory of Michigan, I have the honor to transmit to you a memorial of that body, praying the establishment of a separate Territorial Government for the district of country West of Lake Michigan.

I have the honor to be, very respectfully, your most obedient servant,
STEVENS T. MASON.

Hon. JOHN BELL,
Speaker of the H. R. U. States.

To the Senate and House of Representatives of the United States in Congress assembled:

At an extra session of the Legislative Council of the Territory of Michigan, held on the first Monday of September last, pursuant to an act of Congress of the 30th of June, 1834, an act was passed to provide for the taking a census of the inhabitants of that part of the Territory of Michigan which is situated to the eastward of the Mississippi river.

This duty has been performed by the sheriffs of the several counties, under oath, and nearly in the same manner as that which has been heretofore adopted by the General Government to obtain an enumeration of the citizens of the United States.

The population is found to amount to ninety-two thousand six hundred and seventy-three souls. The counties situated upon the Peninsula, and those lying north and west of Lake Michigan, contain the following numbers:

Wayne	16,638	Jackson	1,865
Washtenaw	14,920	Berrien	1,787
Oakland	13,844	Calhoun	1,714
Monroe	8,542	Branch	764
Lenaive	7,911	Michillimacinac	891
Macomb	6,055	Chippewa	526
Cass	3,280	Brown	1,957
St. Joseph	3,168	Crawford	810
Kalamazoo	3,124	Iowa	2,633
St. Clair	2,244		

In this enumeration, the inhabitants of the country which is situated between the Mississippi and Missouri rivers, and which was, for the purpose only of temporary government, attached to the Territory of Michigan, at the last session of Congress, is not embraced. They may be justly estimated at from five to eight thousand souls.

The population of *Western* Michigan, (now generally known as the Wiskonsin Territory,) may be stated at from twelve to fifteen thousand. And we would again respectfully ask of your honorable body to hear their complaints, and to grant to them speedily the relief for which they pray.

The country inhabited by that people, has been subjected, at various times, to different Governments; but, on all occasions the promise seems to have been held out to them, that their subjection to those governments should be but temporary. So remote indeed have been the seats of those Governments, that it is believed neither the laws of the United States nor of any Territory, actually had force west of Lake Michigan, until after the year 1820. About that time, a justice of the peace or notary public might be seen claiming and exercising his office there under a commission from the King of France.

The inhabitants between Lake Michigan and the Mississippi, have almost every year since their subjection to the Government of Michigan, in the year 1818, complained to Congress of the great evils under which they were suffering in consequence of this connexion. They are separated from the great majority of the inhabitants of the Territory, by one of the largest lakes upon this Continent, and it must obviously be very difficult, if not impracticable, to communicate with them during one-half of the year.

Their pursuits in life are also as widely different as their habitations are distant.

It is supposed that a very large proportion of the country which lies between lake Superior, Green Bay, and the Fox, Wisconsin, and Mississippi rivers, must continue for many years, as it is now, the hunting grounds of uncivilised Indian Tribes.

South of the Wiskonsin river, and within this Territory, and also in the counties of Dubuque and Demoine, West of the Mississippi, are situated the very extensive and valuable lead mines of the United States. The miners are the immediate tenants of the Government, pursuing a very laborious and hazardous business, and paying their rent to it as to a landlord. It is presumed they are, for these reasons, entitled to its special attention and protection. They compose more than two-thirds of the population of that part of the Territory, and they reside upwards of six hundred miles, (some as much as nine hundred miles) from the seat of Territorial Government.

The judiciary system in that section of the Territory, likewise, is so weak and inefficient, that the laws afford little or no protection to the virtuous, nor does their prompt and energetic administration, deter the vicious.

It is feared by that people, that these, and even greater evils, are about to be entailed upon them and their country, *forever,* by the formation of a State Government by the eighty-seven thousand two hundred and seventy-three people inhabiting the Peninsula of Michigan, and the counties north of the Peninsula, *for the whole of the Territory which lies north of the line drawn east through the southerly bend of Lake Michigan.*

It is to this unnatural union, so prejudicial to the best interests of the inhabitants of western Michigan, and destructive to their rights as American citizens, your memorialist would respectfully call the attention of your honorable body; and they do respectfully ask, on behalf of the citizens of the whole Territory, that Congress will, at its present session, establish a Territorial Government for the citizens inhabiting the territory lying west of a line drawn through the middle of Lake Michigan to the northern extremity, and thence north to the boundary line of the United States.

Your memorialists respectfully refer to the act to provide for taking a census of the inhabitants of Michigan, passed by the Council, September 6, 1834, together with the aggregate returns of the census taken under the said act, copies of which said documents, duly certified by the Secretary of the Territory, are herewith presented to your honorable body.

Resolved, That his Excellency the acting Governor, be, and he is hereby requested, to transmit copies of the preceding memorial to the President of the Senate, the Speaker of the House of Representatives, and to the Delegate in Congress from this Territory.

COUNCIL CHAMBER,
Detroit, December 12, 1834.
JOHN McDONELL,
President of the Legislative Council.

JOHN NORVELL,
Secretary.

Mr. REYNOLDS offered the following resolution, which, under the rule, lies one day:

Resolved, That here after, in all elections made by the House of Representatives for officers, the votes shall be given *viva voce* each member in his place naming aloud the person for whom he votes.

Mr. FORESTER, from the Committee of Claims, reported a bill for the relief of the heirs of Michael Henry, deceased; which was read twice and committed.

The joint resolution fixing a day, &c. for the delivery of an address by John Quincy Adams, on the life and character of Lafayette, was concurred in.

The following resolutions submitted yesterday, were taken up and agreed to:

By Mr. HUBBARD:
Resolved, That the Secretary of the Treasury be directed to communicate to this House, copies of any correspondence which has taken place between himself or any of his predecessors in office since 1834, as far as practicable, with any of the officers of the Bank of the United States, or of any of its Branches, which may have since taken to the claim of the United States against the Bank of Columbia, and to communicate his opinion as to the probability of collecting the balance, or any

part thereof, now due from the Bank of Columbia to the United States.

By Mr. PEARCE, of Rhode Island:

Resolved, That the President of the United States be requested to communicate to this House, such information as he may have, and which in his opinion may be proper to be communicated, and not incompatible with the public interest, showing the steps which have been taken and the progress which has been made in effecting an adjustment and satisfaction of the claims of American Citizens upon the Mexican Government.

The following resolution submitted yesterday by Mr LINCOLN, was taken up:

Resolved, That the President of the United States be requested to lay before this House (if, in his opinion, it is not incompatible with the public interest) any communications which may have been had between the Government of the United States and that of Great Britain, since the rejection by the former of the advisory opinion of the King of the Netherlands in reference to the establishment and final settlement of the Northeastern boundary of the United States, heretofore in controversy between the two Governments.

And that he also be requested to communicate any information he may possess of the exercise of practical jurisdiction by the authorities of the British Province of New Brunswick over the disputed territory within the limits of the State of Maine, according to the true line of boundary as claimed by the United States, and especially upon that part of the territory which has been incorporated by the goveenment of Maine into the town of Madawaska, together with such representations and correspondence (if any) as have been had by the executive of that State with the Government of the United States, on the subject.

Mr. PARKS, of Maine, said, that as the resolution was one particularly interesting to the State of Maine, and as no member of the delegation from that State, in either branch of Congress, had thought it necessary to call for information on that subject, he asked the honorable gentleman from Massachusetts what was his object in making the call, and more especially as regarded what was embraced in the two last parts of the resolution.

Mr. LINCOLN said, it would afford him pleasure to respond to the inquiry of the gentleman. The subject involved in the motion he had submitted, was one of deep interest to the people of Massachusetts, and he would be faithless to his trust, were he to suffer any opportunity to pass, to maintain and vindicate that interest. By the act of Massachusetts, whereby Maine had become a separate and independent State, there was a reservation of a right to enjoy in common, a moiety of the proceeds of the sales of unappropriated and uncultivated lands, situated within the boundary of the new State, amounting to about 5,000,000 of acres. The British Government had set up a strong pretension to these lands, under the treaty of 1783—in which Massachusetts was so largely interested. The matter in dispute was finally referred to the arbitrament of the King of the Netherlands, who had merely indicated an opinion adverse to the interests of Maine and Massachusetts. This opinion produced great excitement in the two States. The Legislature of Maine protested against it in strong language, and sent a Commissioner to the Legislature of Massachusetts, (who is now a member of this House, Mr. Parks,) calling upon that State to stand by her in preventing this encroachment upon her territory and sovereignty. Massachusetts did pledge her faith, that in all times and all circumstances, she would stand by Maine, in opposition to this decision of the King of the Netherlands, which, if carried into effect, would operate as a transfer of the citizens of a free country to the dominion of a foreign government, and a monarchy. These remonstrances were felt in the councils of the nation. [Mr. L. here read the resolutions which were submitted to the Senate of the United States on this subject.]

Mr. L. referred to the last annual message of the President, in order to show that the negotiations upon the subject of this boundary line were not re-opened. It was for the purpose of knowing whether this was intended to be done, and what was doing by the Government on this subject, that he had offered the resolution. He entered into a history of the negotiations which had taken place, and of the treatment which the citizens of Maine had received from the British authorities, particularly at Madawaska. The honor of Maine was not in his custody—but in abler hands. It was, however, time to know whether this controversy was to be setted, add in what manner. It was due to the States of Maine and Massachusetts, that they should be informed on this subject. Their respective Legislatures would assemble in a few days, and they should be made acquainted with the present state of the of this controversy. If he knew any thing of the temper of these Governments, they would not much longer submit to tardy negotiation on this subject. It was with these views, (and which he explained much more at length,) that he had been induced to offer the resolution.

Mr. PARKS in reply, said, that the House would by this time perceive that the resolution from the gentleman from Massachusetts, was of a most extraordinary character, and the reasons he had assigned for bringing it forward were (he must say) equally extraordinary. The gentleman gives as his reason why he interferes in a question touching the jurisdiction of another State, that Massachusetts, a part of which he represents on this floor, is interested in the property or ownership of the territory in dispute between the State of Maine and the United States on one side, and Great Britain on the other. It was true, that when Maine determined to assume the rank of a free, sovereign, and independent State, she was compelled by her *kind guardian mother*, Massachusetts, to pay well for her liberty, to purchase her freedom at a high price, by asserting that Massachusetts should be the owner with her in common of the wild lands then undisposed of within her territory; but she did not grant to Massachusetts any jurisdiction over the same. Maine will always recollect these circumstances. The *last*, the gentleman from Massachusetts seems to have forgotten, for he now comes forward to ask, as he is pleased to say, as a member from Massachusetts, interested in the *property*, to inquire whether the *jurisdiction* of *Maine* has been infringed upon, exhibiting a *kind parental* solicitude, as if she had no one on this floor or in the other House, to watch over her honor or protect her rights; and this too without any instructions from Massachusetts to move at all in the matter. If Massachusetts believes that Maine has violated her faith pledged to her by the solemn act that effected the separation, let her, as a State, call on Maine as a State, each in their sovereign capacities, for a breach of that compact, for by that compact alone has she any right of ownership in the territory in question, and with that compact, the federal government has nothing to do. When Maine fails to fulfil any of her obligations, then *she* will have a right to complain, and to take such measure, as a State, as she may think advisable, but even then she will have no right to come *here* for redress. The State of Maine is not to be called to the bar of this House to answer for her conduct to Massachusetts. I aver that the gentleman, in the capacity in which he makes this call, viz. as a *representative of Massachusetts*, has no right, on this floor, to interfere with the question of jurisdiction of Maine within her own limits. Thank God the time has passed by, when she has any legal right to interfere in our internal relations, or external either, excepting such as may regard our engagements with herself. But, further, sir, if she desires information upon this matter, she has the materials for it within herself. She has but to call upon her own land agent and she will get information much more correct and accurate than can be possibly in the possession of any department of this government. Her land agent traverses every portion of our extensive forests without let, hindrance, or control; he has as many deputies as he chooses to employ, and the honorable gentleman, from the official situations he has for so many years held as the Governor of Massachusetts, must know full well that no individual in this nation has more information upon that branch of his inquiry, than the gentleman who so honorably and faithfully fills the office of her land agent. But, sir, the honorable gentleman goes further, he calls for any correspondence that may have taken place between the government of Maine and the government of the United States, upon this same subject of jurisdiction, and this too, as I understand, likewise in his capacity as a member from Massachusetts. To this I answer, that to Massachusetts she is not accountable for any thing that may have taken place between her, as a State, and the general government. Whenever Massachusetts, as an individual owner of certain real estate within her limits, is injured by any act or conduct of hers, then she, like all other individuals, may seek her remedy from that State; but she must recollect she is but an individual proprietor, having a stake in the soil, and the soil only.

But, sir, let us suppose that the gentleman quits the position he assumed, as calling for this information as a member of Massachusetts, and that he calls for it in his relation as the representative of a part of the People of the United States on this floor—should it be granted? Neither of the members from Maine have desired it; nay, the honorable gentleman confesses that he did not consult any one of them upon the subject; neither has the Executive desired it, either for its own justification, or any other purpose. Neither of the parties interested, and only interested, have made any request on the subject; and yet, the gentleman from Massachusetts, out of his abundant regard and solicitude for the interests and honor of Maine, (for I can see no other reason,) wishes to know whether the *jurisdiction* of Maine has been infringed upon, and desires to see (if any) what correspondence has taken place between her and the General Government on the subject. Sir, it seems to me that such curiosity in a *stranger* to the parties is *improper*, if it is not *officious*. Sir, I do not object to this resolution because I fear that in any manner it will (if passed) implicate the honor of the State which, in part, I represent on this floor. I expressly disavow any such feeling. So far as the honor of the State is concerned, I should be perfectly willing to have every act done, every word written, and every thing proposed or intimated by that State, laid open to the world. I fear not that she would suffer by it. I object solely for two reasons; in the first place, that if, as from the President's message, a hope remains of a peaceable adjustment of this perplexing question, a [illegible] to the resolution *would* not do good, but might do harm. And secondly, because the call, coming as it does, is derogatory to the State, and to the members upon the floor of this and the other House, and among whom are some of the gentleman's most ardent political friends. I do not understand from the gentleman that he contemplates any legislative action of this House upon the subject, nor, indeed, can I well see how any can be had. If any communications have taken place between the government of Maine and the General Government, it must be in the character of the latter, as general guarantee to the individual States of their rights and territory and to the Executive in his capacity as a component part of the treaty-making power, through which all attempts at a *peaceable* adjustment of this controversy must be had. Does this House seek to intrude itself upon that power, and appropriate to itself rights which, by the constitution, are secured to different branches of the Government? But, sir, I principally oppose the resolution, because uncalled for as it is, either by the Executive Government on the one hand, and the State on the other. This House ought to have too much respect for the rights of States, to countenance this attempt of the gentleman from Massachusetts, the more especially as from his own statement he does not make the call in his capacity as a Legislator of the Union, but as a member of Massachusetts: which State, from common civility to her sister State, should have made the call, if necessary, directly upon her. I warn this House to be careful how they justify this course—how they approve this precedent. I ask what would have been the language of Georgia, for example, if, contrary to either her wishes or that of the General Government, the correspondence of her Executive with the Exe

he Un on, had been called for by a member from a differ nt State, wholly uninterested in the mat-er, what would have been the feelings of that State, or of any other State in the Union? I say hat a precedent for this call, made in this manner, annot be found in the whole leg slative history of his country; and I again warn the *real* friends of State Rights how they countenance it. It is dero-gatory to every member of both Houses of Con-gress from Maine, because it virtually premises hat they are forgetful of her honor and interest—

[Here Mr. LINCOLN disavowed any intention of rraigning Maine, or of interfering in any way with er honor or interest]

I am well aware, Mr. Speaker, that the honora-le gentleman expressly disavows any such intent, nd I am not the less aware, sir, that such is the in-erence that must be drawn from the resolution, iz. that the members from Maine are derelict to er honor and interests, and that they have to take ing and lodge themselves under the pro'ecting nd fostering care of Massachusetts. The gentle-an says, "Would to God I *could* speak for Maine this floor." Mr. Speaker, I well know that ssachusetts has a strong desire to take the *be-ided* people of Maine under her care and pro-ction, and that nothing prevents but the *indiffer-ence* of the people themselves, to profit by so *high honor*. I should have thought, sir, but for the olution of yesterday, that the people of the ate which the gentleman represents, must by s time have learned, by the frequent rejection of ir *kind* offices, and more particularly by the s of the last summer, that the people of Maine sider themselves as of *age*, and abondantly able of forming their own opinions on publ c ers, protecting their own rights and honor, and ing her own best interests The gentleman s the honor of Maine is not in his hands. True *it is not*. It is *here* in the hands of her Sena-and Representatives, and when they shall prove ant to, or insufficient for, the task confided em, he will recall them, and either send others r fitted for the trust, or *perhaps* call on the eman from *Massachusetts* for aid.

r. Speaker, I again repeat that I do not oppose passage of this resolution because I fear that developements that might be made, would promit the honor of my State. I believe it is re fear and above reproach;" if not—then r suffer for it. But, sir, I oppose it, as set-a precedent injurious, as I believe, to State , and as being an unauthorized interference e affairs existing between one of the sovereign of this Union and the general government, h will tend strongly, to say the least, to des-yall that parliamentary courtesy which ought to exist on this floor, between the represen-s of the people of different independant com-ies.

. EVANS was ignorant of the intention of en leman from Massachusetts (Mr. Lincoln) er the resolution under consideration. He nded that the motion was not only proper, ecessary. That information was requisite to e members from the State of Maine to act vote understandingly on this important sub-Massachusetts, he said, was no volunteer in atter; her aid had been asked by a special n from the State of Maine; and even if it not so, any member on that floor, let him from what State he might, had a right to ask e information required. Maine had invaria-ooked to the aid of Massachusetts in the pro-of this controversy. She had not looked in , and she had always felt grateful to that State e co operation and support which she had ved from that quarter. This was the first that he had ever heard Massachusetts re-ched for her determination to stand by Maine is contest.

r. PARKS explained. He did not reproach chusetts because she had consented to stand aine in this controversey. But he did not k Massachusetts for coming forward here with roposition on this subject, without consulting e or any one of her members on this floor.]

r. EVANS continued. His colleague did not hat because Massachusetts held an interest e property within the territory in dispute with Great Britain, that she had any right to interfere, and he had also stepped aside to assail the manner in which this right of property was acquired by Massachusetts. The separation of Maine from Massachusetts was a matter of compromise. There were a great many individuals in the present State of Maine, who were opposed to the separation, because, perhaps they were unwilling to part with the preponderating political influence of Massa-chusetts. His colleague was among the number who were decidedly opposed to the separation.

[Mr. PARKS again rose in explanation. He opposed the terms of separation, because the new State was required to surrender to Massachusetts so much of her territory, and not in consequence of any political consideration.]

Mr. E. said, he accepted the explanation. He did not pretend to know the precise motives which had actuated his colleague, and he begged his par-don if he had mistaken them.

But his colleague had argued that this call for information was unnecessary inasmuch as no legis-lative action was contemplated, or could necessa-rily grow out of it. How does he know this? If it should turn out that the government of Great Britain was exercising practical jurisdiction with-in the territory in dispute, contrary to a positive pledge to refrain from any such assumption, might not legislation on our part very properly flow from such a course of proceedings?

Mr. E. proceeded at some length to examine the history of the negotiations with Great Britain in relation to the matter in dispute, and contend-ed that Massachusetts held such an interest in the decision of the subject, as would completely justi-fy her in inquiring what was the present state of these negotiations. For aught she knows, a pro-position might be made by the British Government to pay a sum in money for the lands in dispute; and if so, had not that State a right to inquire what disposition had been, or was to be made of this money? He could not see how Maine could be degraded by such a step on the part of Massachu-setts. Perhaps his colleagues had some know-ledge touching the present state of the negotia-tions on the subject. He had none. He desired to have this information—he wished to know whether the negotiation was resumed upon a basis which would satisfy Maine. On this subject his colleague seemed content—he was not. It was true that Maine had been very quiescent for some time past. There had been no Minister in Lon-don, (where the negotiations were pending,) for about two years and a half. For several years this boundary question had formed a most excit-ing topic in Maine. Latterly there had been great apathy—hardly a whisper was heard. Those who formerly spoke the most and the loudest on this subject had become perfectly calm and indif-ferent.

In conclusion, Mr. E. said, that this was a ques-tion in which the whole Union should feel inter-ested. The disputed territory, although a part of the State of Maine, was also a part of the United States, and he conld see no impropriety in a mem-ber from any other State, propesing a call for in-formation, upon a subject in which the nation gen-erally was concerned.

Mr. LINCOLN said, that from the admonition he had received from the first member from Maine (Mr. Parks) who had addressed the House, it might hereafter be a question of consideration how far it would be proper for him to submit a proposi-tion here without first seeking a conference with that gentleman. He offered as an apology for what had been termed a gratuitous interference with the affairs of Maine, the peculiar interest which Massachusetts possessed in the subject. The member from Maine had evaded the true question, and had referred to motives. His mo-tives in offering the resolution were of a most dis-interested character. But the gentleman had com-plained of the terms upon which Maine had be-come an independent State. Was that complaint just? He thought not. Massachusetts, prior to the separation, was a first rate State in point of population and territory, and by the act of separation she was, in this particular, only a third rate State. Was it therefore unreasona-ble that she should seek to retain a part of the waste and uncultivated lands within the boun-dary of the new State, to be disposed of for her peculiar benefit! Was that act derogatory to her? Were not similar terms exacted upon the admis-sion of the other States into the Union? Had not Massachusetts as much right to claim this reserva-tion, as had the United States to retain wild and uncultivated lands, subject to her future disposi-tion, upon the formation of a new and indepen-dent State? This was no new principle. It was the first time that he had heard Massachusetts ac-cused of having agreed to the separation by im-posing hard and unfair terms upon Maine. There was a time, and there was record evidence of the fact, that quite a different feeling prevailed.

Mr. L. was at a loss to perceive any objection which could be properly urged against the pro-posed call for information. The subject to which it had reference, involved interests of great mag-nitude. No less than 5,000,000 acres of land, worth about $15,000,000, were in dispute. The question relative to French spoliations, was of far less importance, and even that question was now agitating the whole country. It had been urged that Massachusetts could obtain the desired infor-mation through her land agents in Maine. This was a mistake. They could not obtain it. Besides, they might be arrested by the British authorities. The gentleman said that no legislation was to fol-low upon the reception of this information. Who authorized him to make any such assertion? But it was contended that it was derogatory to go to the Department here for the correspondence with the Government of Maine; and it was asked why we do not seek it by applying to the latter? There was a reason why Massachusetts should not apply to Maine for information. The gentleman from Maine (Mr. Parks,) was appointed a Commissioner to seek the aid of Massachusetts in preventing a surrender of this disputed territory. Massachu-setts did pledge herself to stand by Maine in this controversy. What shortly followed this pledge? Why, the Legislature of Maine, with closed doors, received a proposition to surrender to the General Government the whole territory in dispute, to be negotiated away for money, and this, too, without informing Massachusetts that she had taken such a step. But this call did not propose to go back that far in the history of the transaction, and the gentleman need not fear that any thing would be furnished connected with the proceedings to which he had just referred. He intended no indignity to the government of Maine by his resolution. He had proposed a simple call for information which might be given, if not in-compatible with the public interest. He thought it important to the interests of those he represent-ed, that this information should be obtained, and it was with that view that he had submitted the motion.

Mr. FOSTER, in addressing the House, re-marked, that it was very annoying to be engaged in, or to interfere with *family quarrels*; but the po-sition taken, and allusions made by various mem-bers, would justify a few remarks from him. He could see no positive impropriety in the call on the President for information proposed in the re-solution. There appeared to him just as much propriety in a call upon the President for informa-tion in regard to a negotiation between the State of Maine and the General Government, as if that negotiation were pending between the latter and a foreign power. If this call had been made upon the State of Maine, it would, of course, have been inadmissible; and if gentlemen had called upon him for his opinion upon that point, it would freely have been given. The jurisdiction of the Federal Courts was operative in Maine as in other States. After a few other remarks, (inaudible to the Reporter,) Mr. F. said he heard from gentlemen on that floor words like "*the free, sove-reign, and independent State of Maine*." It was music to his ears, and sounded like the harbin-ger of the final predominance of correct princi-ples. It looked as if Maine, at least, was not only assenting to, but about again enjoying her sovereign and unalienable State rights. Mr. F. said it would be remembered that he had, at a former period had occasion to broach this doctrine on that floor; and he rejoiced to hear it boldly

proclaimed there, by the gentleman from Maine (Mr. Evans) that the General Government of the United States, possessed no power to dispose of any part of the territory of his State; and that if that general government did so, the act would be *null, unconstitutional*, and *void*. This very principle, said Mr. F. has heretofore been prostrated by the *force of—a name*. He would gladly, on all occasions, stand by the State of Maine, when she asserted these principles, so vitally important in the preservation of our free institutions. An allusion had been made to the fact that Maine had sent a Minister Plenipotentiary to Massachusetts to negotiate in reference to her rights. This was all considered perfectly justifiable on the part of Maine; but how long was it since another State was sneered at for a similar act? He held that the States, in their individual and sovereign capacities, had the right of treating with each other by Ministers, delegates, or otherwise. He referred to the resolutions passed some four or five years ago by the Legislatures of Maine and of Massachusetts on this northern boundary and State Rights question. He hailed them, and he hoped they would long be hailed as burning and shining lights to govern other States, who were seeking and struggling for their rights—those rights which were never delegated, and which were inherent only in themselves. He would warn such States that in these principles was the rock of their political salvation; and he rejoiced to see them spreading from one end of the Union to the other. He concluded by hoping that all opposition to the adoption of the resolution would be withdrawn.

Mr. GILLET here moved to lay the resolution on the table; which he afterwards modified by a call for the orders of the day.

The question on this motion was decided in the negative—ayes 69, noes 70.

Mr. SMITH said, if he were influenced by the feelings, or some of the prominent considerations which had been expressed by his honorable colleague, who had last spoken, (Mr. Evans,) in relation to the resolution of the honorable gentleman from Massachusetts, he certainly could not feel justified in giving the vote which his honorable colleague had indicated that he should give, nor in entertaining the conclusions which he does upon this subject.

The House will remark, sir, that my colleague commenced his observations with an expression of entire *indifference* as to the fate of the resolution which the gentleman from Massachusetts has offered. Sir, were I indifferent to a resolution, involving matters of such vast importance to the People of Maine, being one of her Representatives, I could not vote in favor of it.

But the gentleman next said, that he does not think any thing can come out of the resolution, if passed; that he has no idea that the Executive will answer it, or will answer it in any other way than by saying, that he has no information that can be communicated relative to the subject-matter of this resolution, without prejudice to the pending negotiation. Sir, if I entertained this conviction, I certainly should feel myself warring with my sense of duty to vote in favor of the resolution. Why pass it, with such an expectation?

Again the gentleman says, that he very much questions the propriety of the Executive's exposing the correspondence and other documents involved in the subject-matter of this resolution, at the present time, and while the negotiation is pending between this Government and Great Britain. Sir, could a better reason be given than such a conviction, to justify and demand that gentleman's vote *against* the resolution? I confess, I am unable to conceive of a stronger motive for opposing the resolution, than the gentleman himself has thus avowed. And yet he expresses his determination to vote in favor, and advocates the adoption of the resolution!

Sir, the gentleman has further told the House, and in this I think him correct to a considerable extent—that great apathy now prevails in Maine upon this subject. It is so, in one point of view. And is not this another most satisfactory argument against the adoption of the resolution? Why force such a call upon the Executive at this time, if the people themselves, who are immediately interested, are not anxious upon the subject? I repeat, sir, that if I were governed only by the arguments which the gentleman's own remarks furnish upon this subject, I could not with him vote in favor of the resolution. But it is true, there is a degree of apathy in Maine, and with the people of Maine, upon this subject, at the present time. Sir, the people of Maine take a proper view of its situation. They consider it in hands which are bound to control it. They consider it as still under negotiation, and in a state of progression. And while it is so, they do not desire to interpose obstacles to its right termination, nor to prejudice its progress. My colleague, as well as the gentleman from Massachusetts, knows, that the negotiation upon this subject is still pending between our Government and that of Great Britain, for the fact has been so announced in the opening message of the President to Congress at its present session, and the gentleman from Massachusetts has read to the House that part of the message.

But, says my honorable colleague, (Mr. Evans,) two years and a half have elapsed without any Minister of this Government at the Court of the British Government to attend to this negotiation. Sir, this is true. But, said Mr. S., I am greatly surprised that my honorable colleague should have mentioned this fact, either as a reproach upon the Executive of this nation, or a reason why this resolution for information should now pass. Whose fault has it been, let me ask, during these two years and a half to which the gentleman alludes, that our Government has been thus long without a representative in England? Has it been the fault of the Executive of this nation? Or of the State of Maine, or rather, I should ask, has it been the fault of *the people of Maine?* Does not my honorable colleague, as well as the honorable mover of this resolution, know full well, that two attempts certainly have been made by the Executive of this nation, to have our Government represented at the British Court, and that it is no fault of his that the interests of Maine and Massachusetts have not been attended to there? Sir, let me tell my colleague, and this House also, that the people of Maine understand right well, and most correctly, as I believe, that the want of a national representative at the British Court on the part of our Government, during those two and a half years past, has operated as a most serious, if not principal obstacle, in the adjustment of this most important boundary question, in which Maine is so deeply interested. They understand, also, that in this omission to be so represented abroad, the National Executive is free of all blame, and that upon other heads the censure should fall.

Sir, continued Mr. S. I can see no practical good to be accomplished by this resolution. I am equally ignorant, with the mover of it, and with my colleague, of the nature of any information which the Executive can possess upon the subject, proper to be communicated to this House, and to the public, at this time. The negotiation is pending still. But, the honorable gentleman from Massachusetts, says, that State is deeply interested in the negotiation—that Maine has heretofore sought the aid of Massachusetts in this matter, and that Massachusetts freely pledged herself to Maine, and most solemnly, to stand by her, and help to maintain her rights in this controversy, at all times and under all circumstances. And the gentleman here declares, that Massachusetts has been true to her pledges thus given, and he here renews those pledges of continued fidelity in every event to come. And it is with reference to the alleged interest of that State on this subject, to her past pledges and support of Maine, and to her pledges of continued fidelity, he has offered a resolution calling for certain information touching the immediate rights and interests of Maine, without intending any disrespect to any one. This call is also made subject to the very proper condition, which I will regard as made in sincerity, that the President shall communicate only such information, if any, as cannot prejudice the negotiation that is now pending. Sir, all this implies a suspicion that there may be information possessed by the Executive upon the subject-matter of the negotiation, which the President will think proper to communicate to this House and to the public at this time. I cannot conceive of its being so. I do not believe it is so. But as the gentleman from Massachusetts thinks otherwise, and is anxious to be informed how the fact is—as he alleges the deep interest of his State in the matter—as he has recapitulated her past pledges to Maine, and asserts her constant fidelity to them, and now renews them in the most solemn manner to stand by Maine in this controversy under all circumstances; as he is willing to appeal to the discretion of the Executive upon the propriety of communicating at this time either more or less, or none at all, of the supposed information upon the subject; and as he (Mr. Smith) also had entire confidence in the discretion of the President to communicate the documents sought, if any there be, or to withhold them, as the interests of Maine, Massachusetts, and the nation, may, in his opinion, require, he (Mr. S.) would, from these considerations alone, if the gentleman from Massachusetts persists in crowding his resolution upon the Executive at this time, vote for its passage. But, said Mr. S. I protest against the idea, that there is any thing in the possession of the Executive in connexion with this matter that could, if all were made known to the world, do dishonor to Maine, or to the National Government. The only reason existing at the present time, of which I could conceive, why the whole correspondence and documents relating to the matter might not be properly spread before this House and before the world at the present time, is, that a negotiation upon the subject of them is still pending between our Government and a foreign Government, and that this negotiation may be greatly prejudiced by such a premature publication. In all other respects I have no fears whatever. There is no concealment and no disguise upon the matter, which is not for the common benefit of all the States in the Union, all of which are interested in the pending negotiation.

As to the interference, sir, of Massachusetts with the affairs of Maine, and upon which one of my honorable colleagues has expressed himself in terms that he feels to be justly merited, I have (said Mr. Smith,) much of feeling. The contrary winds—the counter winds—the *political trade winds* of Massachusetts, which are felt occasionally sweeping over the affairs of Maine, like the counter and trade winds which are met with upon the natural ocean, serve a most salutary purpose. They admonish the yeomanry of Maine, with great accuracy, of the direction in which their true interests are to be pursued. And so long as Massachusetts will keep up this sort of interest, Maine will continue to be found, as she has been for years past, true to her real interests and principles. Sir, I am not sure, nevertheless, that there would not have been more propriety, and more honorable courtesy on the part of the gentleman from Massachusetts in this matter, if he had consulted with at least a portion of the delegation from Maine in relation to his resolution, before he proposed it. I did suppose, sir, that the honorable gentleman could have found, *one*, certainly, of that delegation, in whom he could have reposed confidence upon the matter. But even that one of my honorable colleagues entirely disclaims any knowledge of the honorable mover's interference before the resolution was offered; and the gentleman from Massachusetts admits, in fact, that he consulted none of the delegation from Maine in relation to it. To me, sir, it seems that in a matter of this character, there would have been more courtesy if the gentleman from Massachusetts had adopted a different course. I have not, however, on account of this, any strong feelings. But regarding the disposition and pledges of the State of Massachusetts upon this boundary question—regarding what she is said to have done, and is willing to do with Maine in relation to it hereafter, and altogether repudiating the idea that there is any thing in this whole subject-matter which needs be concealed, except upon the ground that the negotiation upon it is still pending between our Government and Great Britain—regarding, moreover, the gentleman's assurance, which is very properly embodied in his resolution, that he seeks nothing which the President may not deem

her proper to be communicated at this time, I willing, for one, that his resolution should pass. Mr. EVANS replied. He said his surprise now that his colleague (Mr. Smith) should take exception to the motives under the influence of which he was disposed to vote for the resolution, as the gentleman himself avows an intention to vote with him. That gentleman was welcome to benefit of the reasons which might induce him support the resolution, and he claimed the same defence for himself. The information called in the resolution he deemed extremely important, and if it was proper, it should be given to the Senate; he was anxious to receive it. His colleague (Mr. Smith) had expressed his surprise because he (Mr. E.) had advanced a doubt whether this information would be given, that we did ask for it! Mr. E. said he was one of those who would not be deterred from making due exposure by the existence of such a doubt. The facility of eliciting desirable information was silent inducement to him to command a trial. If also been said that the negotiation was in a state of progression; he would ask what sort of progression?—whether it was backward or forward? The gentleman had disavowed all desire of concealment, on the part of the opponents of the resolution; but, said Mr. E., this is the very gist of the matter. We do complain of concealment; we desire to know what is the progress and sort of this negotiation between the government of Maine and that of the General Government, and if the gentleman is sincere in his professions, let him join myself and others in bringing whole subject before the public. Mr. E. replied by an allusion to the remarks of the gentleman from Georgia, (Mr. Foster,) expressing surprise at now being denominated a nullifier. Mr. SMITH said that there was only a remark to of his honorable colleague to which he must advert. The gentleman says, there has a desire on the part of the Governor and Council of Maine, and of some others, to conceal proceedings which have been had in relation to a boundary controversy. The gentleman very careful to say, or rather not to say, that Governor and Council of Maine had ever been upon to disclose any portion of those proceedings. According to my recollection, and I think my honorable colleague's recollection confirm my own upon the subject—the Legislature of Maine have never made a call upon the Governor and Council of that State to disclose any proceedings.

Mr. EVANS here rose, and said, his recollection was not altogether distinct upon the subject, he believed such a call had been attempted, but not carried, it was voted down by the majority with whom his colleague (Mr. Smith) acted in Legislature of Maine.)

continued Mr. S., my honorable colleague a full well, that the People of Maine have called for such a disclosure of those proceedings. And whatever the Legislature of that State has done, and whatever those who have counsel that Legislature and the other official organ of the State, for years past, have done, in to, to this subject, has been most satisfactorily transparently sustained by the People of this State and it is manifest, that if there has been any prior concealment in the matter, of which I take nothing, my honorable colleague's remarks have struck at the People themselves, and their immediate representatives in the Legislature, whom they have sustained. And in that there is nothing for concealment, I might not be disclosed most creditably to, if there were no negotiation still pending Great Britain. Under any other condition of affairs, I could have no objection to spreading whole of the proceedings of Maine, and of all connected with her in it, as well as those of the General government, before this House and before world. When I addressed this House a short since, I remarked explicitly that I repudiated the idea that there was any thing to be concealed time upon any other ground than the fear of affecting the pending negotiation. And, I think, that, having entire confidence in the discretion of the Executive to determine rightly whe-

ther any information can be properly communicated at this time or not, and not fearing that any can be disclosed at any time discreditable to the State or nation, and regarding the alleged interests of Massachusetts in the subject, and her relationships to Maine in it, if the honorable gentleman from Massachusetts insists upon the passage of the resolution, I am willing for one, that it should pass, believing that to be the most judicious course under the circumstances of the case as now presented.

Mr. WARD moved (by consent) that when the House adjourn, it adjourn to Saturday next at 12 o'clock.

On this question Mr. BEATY asked for the yeas and nays—but the motion was not seconded by the House.

Mr. CHILTON then moved to amend the motion by substituting Friday for Saturday.

This was also negatived, and the motion of Mr. WARD was agreed to.

The House then adjourned, to meet again on Saturday, the 27th inst.

IN SENATE.

SATURDAY, Dec. 27, 1834.

Mr. SOUTHARD presented a memorial, signed by sundry citizens of the City of Washington, praying relief of Congress from the pecuniary difficulties in which the city is involved; which was referred to the Committee on the District of Columbia.

Mr. SOUTHARD, from the Committee on Naval Affairs, reported a bill for the relief of Purser W. B. Zantzinger.

Mr. SILSBEE, from the Committee on Commerce, reported a bill for the relief of Tuffts & Clark.

Mr. ROBINSON presented certain joint resolutions of the Legislature of the State of Illinois, instructing their Senators, and requesting their Representatives in Congress, to use their exertions to procure the passage of a law establishing ports of entry at Ottawa on the Illinois, Lafayette on the Wabash, and at Galena, in that State; which were referred to the Committee on Commerce.

On motion of Mr. BUCHANAN, the petition of Thomas Anderson, on the files of the Senate, was referred to the Committee on Foreign Relations.

Mr. BLACK, from the Committee on Private Land claims, reported the bill from the House of Representatives for the relief of Nicholas D. Coleman.

On motion of Mr. ROBBINS, the Senate then adjourned.

HOUSE OF REPRESENTATIVES.

SATURDAY, December 27, 1834.

The Hon ROBERT T. LYTLE, of Ohio, appeared, and was qualified.

Petitions and memorials were presented by—
Mr. EVANS, of Maine;
Mr. HARPER, of New Hampshire;
Mr. GORHAM, of Massachusetts;
Mr. JANES, of Vermont;
Mr. WARD, of New York;
Mr. GALBRAITH, of Pennsylvania;
Messrs. LOYALL and WILSON, of Virginia;
Messrs. TOMPKINS and JOHNSON, of Kentucky;
Mr. POLK, of Tennessee;
Mr. CHANE, of Ohio;
Mr. THOMAS, of Louisiana;
Messrs. CASEY, MAY, and REYNOLDS, of Illinois.

[Mr. CASEY introduced a resolution passed by the Legislature of Illinois, instructing the Senators, and requesting the Representatives from that State, to use their exertions to have ports of entry established on the Wabash, Illinois, and Peoria rivers; which, on his motion, was referred to the Committee on Commerce.

Mr. MAY presented the petition of a number of citizens of Sangamon and Morgan counties, praying the establishment of a post route from Beardstown, in Morgan county, to New Salem, in Sangamon county; which, on his motion, was referred to the Committee on the Post Office and Post Roads.

Also, the petition of John Scott, of McLean county, Illinois, praying compensation for property lost during the revolutionary war.]

Mr. WHITE, of Florida.

Which petitions and memorials were appropriately referred.

Mr. WARDWELL, from the Committee on Revolutionary Pensions, reported, a bill to continue the office of Commissioner of Pensions; which was read twice and committed.

Mr. BROWN, from the Committee on Invalid Pensions, reported a bill for the relief of John Moore; which was read twice and committed.

On motion of Mr. POTTS,

Resolved, That a Committee be appointed on Enrolled Bills.

On motion of Mr. STEWART,

Resolved, That the Committee on Commerce be instructed to inquire into the expediency of establishing a port of entry at Brownsville, in Pennsylvania.

Mr. BYNUM submitted the following resolution, which, under the rule, lies over one day:

Resolved, That the Executive be requested to cause to be laid before this House, as soon as practicable, such information in relation to the relative positions of the province of Texas, one of the United Provinces of the Republic of Mexico, and the Government of the United States of North America, as may be in possession of either of the Departments, not deemed incompatible with the interests of either of the two Governments.

Also, what progress has been made in distinguishing the boundary lines between the Governments and the Republic of Mexico, which were to be run in conformity with the stipulations made and entered into between the Government of Spain and that of the United States, as ratified by the latter in Congress on the 22d February, 1819.

Also, whether, if any subsequent regulations have been entered into between the Commissioners of this and the Government of Mexico, to carry into execution the conditions of the above mentioned stipulations, posterior to the recognition of the latter Government, as an independent Republic.

On motion of Mr. GARLAND,

Resolved, That the Committee of Ways and Means be instructed to inquire into the expediency of making a sufficient appropriation to complete the improvement on the Red river, in the State of Louisiana and Territory of Arkansas, in the course of the ensuing year.

On motion of Mr. ASHLEY,

Resolved, That the Committee on Roads and Canals be instructed to inquire into the expediency of providing by law for the construction of a road across the State of Missouri, on the county of New Madrid, in the State of Missouri, on the most eligible route from the Mississippi in the direction of Batesville, Arkansas Territory, and that an adequate quantity of the public land on said route be appropriated to effect that object.

On motion of Mr. LEA,

Resolved, That the Committee on the Post Office and Post Roads be instructed to inquire from the expediency of establishing a mail route from Marysville, in the State of Tennessee, by way of Montvall springs, so as to intersect the route from Madisonville, Tennessee, to North Carolina, at Hugh Gormley's, on Tennessee river.

Resolved, That the Committee on the Post Office and Post Roads be instructed to inquire into the expediency of establishing a mail route from Knoxville, in the State of Tennessee, by way of Low's Ferry, on Clinch river, to Richard Oliver's, in Anderson county.

Resolved, That the Committee on the Post Office and Post Roads be instructed to inquire into the expediency of establishing a mail route from Philadelphia, in Monroe county, Tennessee, by way of Witten's Store, on Pond creek, to Washington, in Rhea county, in said State.

On motion of Mr. LYON, of Michigan,

Resolved, That the Committee on Public Lands be instructed to inquire into the expediency of authorising the sale of certain lands at Toledo, in Michigan Territory, granted for the use of the University of said Territory.

On motion of Mr. BROWN,

Resolved, That the Committee on Revolutionary Claims be directed to inquire into the expediency of making provision by law for the payment to Joseph Morrill, assignee of John Carman, of certificate No. 12, 171, dated the 1st January, 1782, signed Timothy Pickering, Quartermaster General, to secure to the said John Carman, or his order, the payment in specie of 209 dollars, with interest at six per centum per annum, until paid; and that the papers heretofore submitted be again referred to said committee.

On motion of Mr. FOWLER,
Resolved, That the Committee on the Post Office and Post Roads be instructed to inquire into the expediency of establishing a mail route from Hamburg, via Franklin and Sparta, to Newton, in the county of Sussex, and State of New Jersey.

NORTHEASTERN BOUNDARY.
The following resolution, heretofore offered by Mr. LINCOLN, was again taken up:
Resolved, That the President of the United States be requested to lay before this House, (if, in his opinion, it is not incompatible with the public interest,) any communications which may have been had between the Government of the United States and that of Great Britain, since the rejection, by the former, of the advisory opinion of the King of the Netherlands, in reference to the establishment and final settlement of the northeastern boundary of the United States, heretofore in controversy between the two Governments. And that he also be requested to communicate any information he may possess, of the exercise of practical jurisdiction, by the authorities of the British province of New Brunswick, over the disputed territory, within the limits of the State of Maine, according to the true line of boundary as claimed by the United States; and especially upon that part of the territory which has been incorporated, by the Government of Maine, into the town of Madawaska, together with such representations and correspondence (if any) as have been had by the Executive of that State with the Government of the United States, on the subject.

Mr. PARKS said, he did not intend to occupy the time of the House by further debating this resolution. He merely rose to divest himself of the plumage which had been thrown over him by the gentleman from Massachusetts, (Mr. Lincoln.) He was not, as he had been stated, the author of the report and resolutions which had been adopted by the Legislature of Massachusetts on this subject. He was simply the agent appointed by the Legislature of Maine to carry to the Legislature of Massachusetts certain resolves of the former. The report and resolutions which had been alluded to, were written by a gentleman of high character, and who was now a member of the Legislature of Massachusetts. The gentleman from Georgia, (Mr. Foster,) seemed somewhat surprised to learn that the people of Maine were in favor of State rights. He could tell the gentleman that, however other States might oscillate from one extreme to the other, on the subject of State rights, the principles of Maine had always remained the same; and the gentleman was welcome, so far as he was concerned, to all the gratification which the annunciation of this fact could give him.

Mr. GILLET moved to lay the resolution on the table, which was decided in the negative, yeas 77, nays 79.
The resolution was then agreed to by the following vote:
YEAS—Messrs. John Q. Adams, Heman Allen, John J. Allen, Chilton Allan, Ashley, Banks, Bates, Bayles, Briggs, Chambers, Chilton, Samuel Clark, William Clark, Clowney, Corwin, Coulter, Crane, Crocket, Darlington, A. Davis, Davenport, Deberry, Denny, Dickson, Evans, Fillmore, Foster, Philo C. Fuller, Fulton, Gamble, Garland, Gholson, Gordon, Gorham, Graham, Grennell, Griffin, Joseph Hall, Hiland Hall, Hard, Hardin, Harrison, Hazeltine, Hiester, William Jackson, Ebenezer Jackson, James, William C. Johnson, Henry Johnson, Lay, Letcher, Lincoln, Love, Lucas, Manning, Martindale, Marshall, M. Mason, McCarty, McKay, McKennan, Miller, Miner, Muhlenberg, Phillips, Pickens, Pinckney, Pope, Potts, Ramsay, Reed, Robertson, A.H.Sheppard, Slade, Sloane, Smith, Spangler, Stew-

art, P. Thomas, Tompkins, Trumbull, Tweedy, Vinton, F. Whittlesey, Williams, Wilson, Wise—87.
NAYS—Messrs. John Adams, William Allen, Anthony, Bean, Beaumont, Bockee, Boon, Bouldin, Brown, Bunch, Burns, Bynum, Cambreleng, Carr, Casey, Claiborne, Clay, Day, Dickerson, Dunlap, Ferris, Forester, Fowler, William K. Fuller, Galbraith, Gillet, Thomas H. Hall, Halsey, Hamer, J. M. Harper, Hathaway, Henderson, Howell, Hubbard, Huntington, Inge, Jarvis, Richard M. Johnson, Noadiah Johnson, Benjamin Jones, Kavanagh, Kilgore, Kinnard, Lane, Lansing, Laporte, Lea, Lee, Loyall, Lyon, Lytle, J. K. Mann, Mardis, May, McIntire, McLene, R. Mitchell, Morgan, Murphy, Parks, Parker, Patterson, Pearce, Peyton, Pierce, Pierson, Polk, Reynolds, Schenck, Shinn, Standifer, Taylor, Thomson, Vanderpoel, Van Houten, Wagener, Ward, Wardwell, Webster—79.

The SPEAKER laid before the House the following letter from the Secretary of the Treasury:
TREASURY DEPARTMENT,
December 26th, 1834.
SIR:—In obedience to the first clause of the Resolution of the House of Representatives passed on the 11th instant, directing the Secretary of the Treasury "to communicate to the House of Representatives, as soon as practicable, copies of "the correspondence not heretofore communicat-"ed, which had taken place between him and the "President of the Bank of the United States, on "the subject of the Bank Drafts," &c. I have now the honor to submit a copy of a letter on that subject received from the President of the Bank of the United States, on the 28th ultimo and the reply thereto by this Department on the 24th instant.
In order to make the contents of both, more intelligible, and to include all probably embraced by the resolution, I have taken the liberty to precede them by a copy of the Treasury circular, issued by this Department on the 5th ultimo and to which these letters as frequently refer, with a copy of the communication of that date, transmitting it to the Bank.
I have the honor to remain, very respectfully, your obedient servant,
LEVI WOODBURY,
Secretary of the Treasury.
The Hon. the Speaker of the
House of Representatives.
Which letter, and the accompanying documents, on motion of Mr. HUBBARD, was laid on the table and directed to be printed.
Mr. HUBBARD said this correspondence was of an important character, he therefore (by consent) moved that 10,000 additional copies be printed.
After some conversation between Messrs. HUBBARD, FOSTER, MARTINDALE and GARLAND, the motion was, with the assent of the mover, laid over to Monday.
The SPEAKER laid before the House a communication from the Secretary of the Navy in answer to a resolution of the 8th inst. relative to the Ship House, &c. at Navy Point, New York; which was laid on the table.
The SPEAKER laid before the House a communication from the Secretary of War inclosing a copy of a survey of the Falls of the Ohio river; which was referred to the Committee on Roads and Canals.
The SPEAKER laid before the House a letter from the Secretary of War in response to a resolution of the 15th inst., inclosing a report of the Commissary General of Purchases, upon the claim of David Cook; which was referred to the Committee of Claims.
The SPEAKER laid before the House a Report from the Secretary of the Treasury, under the act for the relief of insolvent debtors; which was laid on the table, and ordered to be printed.
The SPEAKER also laid before the House a communication from the Secretary of the Treasury, in response to a resolution of the 17th inst. relative to the public lands; which was committed to a Committee of the Whole on the State of the Union and directed to be printed.
The following message from the President of the United States was received by the hands of Mr. Donelson, his private Secretary:

To the House of Representatives:
I transmit to the House a Report from the Secretary of State, together with the papers relating to the refusal of the French Government to make provision for the execution of the Treaty between the United States and France, concluded on the 4th of July, 1831, requested by their resolution of the 24th instant.
ANDREW JACKSON.
WASHINGTON, 27th Dec. 1834.
On motion of Mr. FOSTER, the message accompanying papers, were referred to the Committee on Foreign Affairs, and ordered to be printed.
On motion of Mr. REED, 10,000 extra copies of the report of the Secretary of the Treasury communicating the number, names, pay, &c., those persons engaged in the several custom houses in the United States, were ordered printed.
The House then adjourned.

IN SENATE.
MONDAY, December 29, 1834.
Petitions and Memorials were presented by SILSBEE, Mr. HENDRICKS, Mr. EWING, Mr. TOMLINSON.
Mr. EWING presented a memorial from Legislature of Ohio, praying the passage of an act by Congress, to adjust and settle the boundary line of the State of Ohio which was on the table, and ordered to be printed.
The VICE PRESIDENT laid before the Senate a communication from the Treasury Department, relative to the Insolvent Debtors of the United States.
Also, a memorial from citizens of Hillsboro Pennsylvania, praying an additional appropriation for the continuation and repair of the Cumberland road; which was referred to the Committee on Roads and Canals.
He also laid before the Senate a memorial of citizens of New York, praying Congress to make an exploring expedition to the South Seas which was referred to the Committee on Naval affairs.
Mr. KING, of Georgia, gave notice, that tomorrow he would ask leave to bring in a bill to establish a mail route in East Florida.
Mr. TOMLINSON gave notice, that he would ask leave to introduce a bill for the relief of Walter Lomax and Abiel Gay.
Mr. BELL, from the Committee on Claims reported a bill for the relief of Hiram A. Hunter.
Mr. BELL also reported unfavorably upon petition of George Bently and others.
Mr. KING, of Alabama, on leave given, introduced a bill for the relief of David McCord which was twice read and referred to the Judiciary mittee.
Mr. WHITE submitted the following resolution: Resolved, That the Committee on Revolutionary Claims be instructed to inquire into the expediency of providing by law for the payment of the commutation of five years' full pay to the heirs of Dixon, a Colonel in the North Carolina Continental establishment during the revolutionary war.
The Senate then adjourned.

HOUSE OF REPRESENTATIVES.
MONDAY, December 29, 1834.
Petitions and memorials were presented by Mr. HALL, of Vermont.
Messrs. CAMBRELENG, VANDERPOEL, MANN, WARDWELL, HUNTINGTON, HAZELTINE, of New York.
[Mr. MANN, of New York, presented the petition of sundry citizens of the State of New York, praying for the passage of a law to permit the introduction of Red Cedar timber prepared for roads, into the United States free of duty.]
Messrs. HARPER and McKENNAN, of Pennsylvania.
Mr. McKIM, of Maryland.
Messrs. MOORE, TAYLOR, WISE, PATTON, and LOYALL, of Virginia.
Mr. A. H. SHEPPERD, of North Carolina.
Mr. CLAYTON, of Georgia.
Messrs. TOMPKINS and BEATY, of Kentucky.
Messrs. CRANE and THOMSON, of Ohio.

Mr. GARLAND, of Louisiana.

Mr. MAY, of Illinois.

[Mr. MAY presented the petition of Josette Beaubien, praying permission to locate two sections of land in lieu of two sections reserved to her under the treaty of 1832, between the United States and the Pottawattamie Indians.

Also, the petition of B. M. Hays, praying remuneration for hospital stores furnished the troops during the late Indian disturbances, and for attendance upon the sick, whilst in the service of the United States.]

Messrs. McKINLEY and MARDIS, of Alabama.

Mr. LYON, of Michigan.

Mr. SEVIER, of Arkansas.

Mr. WHITE, of Florida.

Mr. Speaker BELL, of Tennessee.

Mr. PEARCE, of Rhode Island.

Which petitions and memorials were appropriately referred.

Mr. JARVIS, from the Committee on Foreign Relations, reported a bill for the settlement of the account of Edmund Roberts; which was read twice and committed.

Mr. JARVIS, from the same Committee, reported bill to carry into effect the convention between the United States and Spain; which was read twice and committed.

Mr. MITCHELL, from the Committee on Invalid Pensions, reported a bill granting a pension to Alson S. Morris; which was read twice and committed.

Mr. McINTIRE, from the Committee on Claims, reported a bill for the relief of Laurentius M. Eiler; which was read twice and committed.

Mr. ALLAN, of Kentucky, from the Committee on Territories, reported a bill to amend the several acts for the establishment of the Territorial government of Florida; which was read twice and committed.

Mr. BANKS, from the Committee on Claims, reported a bill for the relief of Moses Bliss; which was read twice and committed.

Mr. MAY, from the Committee on Private Land Claims, made a report adverse to the petition of the heirs of Francis Jarvis, deceased; which was laid on the table and directed to be printed.

Mr. MAY, from the same Committee, reported a bill for the relief of the heirs of James Latham, deceased; which was committed to a Committee of the Whole House, and made the order of the day for Tuesday next.

Mr. BROWN, from the Committee on Invalid Pensions, made an unfavorable report upon the petition of Rufus Parker; and the same was laid on the table.

Mr. KINNARD, from the Committee on Revolutionary Claims, made an unfavorable report on the petition of Charles C. Mill.

Favorable reports were also made by Messrs. ELLENBERG, MITCHELL of Ohio, BAYLAY, and WISE, from Standing Committees, upon petitions of various individuals, whose names were not heard by the reporter.

The following resolution, submitted on Wednesday last, by Mr. REYNOLDS, was taken up:

Resolved, That hereafter, in all elections made the House of Representatives for officers, the vote shall be given viva voce, each member in his turn naming aloud the person for whom he votes.

Mr. REYNOLDS remarked, that the resolution was of some importance, and that he did not wish to force it on the consideration of the House at this time, but wished the action on it at some future day; and that he perceived that there were many members absent from their seats; he therefore would move to postpone the further consideration of the subject until Tuesday week.

After some conversation between Messrs. REYNOLDS, HUBBARD, CLAY, McKENNAN, HARDIN, the motion to postpone was agreed to.

The following resolution, submitted on Saturday by Mr. BYNUM, was taken up:

Resolved, That the Executive be requested to lay before this House, as soon as practicable, such information in relation to the relative position of the province of Texas, one of the United Provinces of the Republic of Mexico, and the Government of the United States of North America, as may be in possession of either of the Departments, not deemed incompatible with the interests of either of the two Governments.

Also, what progress has been made in distinguishing the boundary lines between the Governments and the Republic of Mexico, which were to be run in conformity with the stipulations made and entered into between the Government of Spain and that of the United States, as ratified by the latter in Congress on the 22d February, 1819.

Also, whether, if any subsequent regulations have been entered into between the Commissioners of this and the Government of Mexico, to carry into execution the conditions of the above mentioned stipulations, posterior to the recognition of the latter Government, and as an independent Republic.

Mr. BYNUM said, that since he had offered the resolution, he had discovered that most of the desired information was contained in the annual message of the President, at the opening of Congress. He therefore moved to lay the resolution on the table.

Mr. SEVIER hoped the resolution would not be laid on the table, and that it would be permitted to pass, as full information on the subject was desirable.

Mr. BYNUM had no objection to the adoption of the resolution; but he repeated, that most of the information required, was already in possession of the House.

The resolution was then laid on the table.

The resolution to print 10,000 extra copies of the correspondence between the Secretary of the Treasury and the President of the Bank of the United States, was taken up.

After a few remarks of explanation by the mover of the resolution, Mr. HUBBARD, the motion was agreed to.

On motion of Mr. STEWART,

Resolved, That the Committee on Invalid Pensions be instructed to inquire into the expediency of placing Robert Dunsmore on the pension roll.

On motion on Mr. STEWART,

Resolved, That the Committee of Ways and Means be instructed to inquire into the expediency of making a further appropriation for the completion of the repairs and the erection of toll gates on the Cumberland road east of the Ohio river.

On motion of Mr. WHITE, of Florida,

Resolved, That the Committee on Roads and Canals be instructed to inquire into the expediency of making an appropriation for a canal between Pensacola and Mobile bays.

On motion of Mr. PEARCE, of R. Island,

Resolved, That the Committee on Revolutionary Pensions be instructed to inquire into the expediency of reporting a bill granting unto Benjamin Cornell, of Newport, in the State of Rhode Island, a soldier of the revolution, a pension.

On motion of Mr. WARD,

Resolved, That the Committee on Military Affairs inquire into the expediency of granting to the widow of the late General Leavenworth, deceased, a sum equal to his pay and emoluments from the time of his death to the thirty-first day of December instant.

On motion of Mr. DICKSON,

Resolved, That the Committee on Manufactures be instructed to inquire into the expediency of amending the several acts imposing duties on imports, that the same duties be imposed on all books imported hereafter and printed previous to the year 1814, as are now imposed by law on books imported and printed previous to the year 1775.

On motion of Mr. BEAUMONT,

Resolved, That the Committee on the Post Office and Post Roads be instructed to inquire into the expediency of establishing a mail route from Carbondale, Pennsylvania, through the townships of Greenfield, Abington, and Nicholson, to Tunkhannock.

Mr. PINCKNEY offered the following resolution, which, under the rule, lies one day:

Resolved, That the Secretary of War be, and he is hereby, requested to communicate to this House such information as may be necessary to explain the cause or causes of the suspension of the work at Fort Sumpter, in Charleston harbor, and whether any, and if any, what measures have been taken by the Department, in relation to the difficulty from which said suspension has arisen.

On motion of Mr. BEATY,

Resolved, That the Committee on the Post Office and Post Roads be instructed to inquire into the expediency of establishing a post route, leaving the present route, leading from Barboursville, in the county of Knox, Kentucky, to Williamsburg, in Whitly county, at Major Charles Rotchholt's, thence by the mouth of Laurel River, the Stone Coal Mines, Somerset, Mount Vernon, and Slaughter's Salt Works, to Richmond, in Madison county, Kentucky; and that the petitions and papers referred at the last session of Congress to said committee, in relation to so much of said contemplated route as lies between Richmond, in Madison county, and Somerset, in Pulaski county, be again referred to said committee, and that the petitions and papers referred to said committee, at the last session, relating to post routes from Monroe, Tenn., by Jamestown, to Monticello, Kentucky, and from Monroe, Tenn, by Locust Shade to Burkesville, Kentucky, and from Burkesville, Kentucky, to Gainsborough, Tennessee.

On motion of Mr. EVANS, of Me.,

Resolved, That the Committee on Invalid Pensions be instructed to inquire into the expediency of granting to Thankfull Randall, formerly the widow of Isaac Pisham, deceased, five years' half pay, to which she was entitled as the widow of said Pisham, he having died in the service of the United States, during the late war.

On motion of Mr. WHITTLESEY, of N. Y.

Resolved, That the Committee on Claims be instructed to inquire into the expediency of making compensation to Naaman Goodsell for services rendered by him to the United States under the direction of the Secretary of the Treasury.

On motion of Mr. THOMSON, of Ohio,

Resolved, That the Committee on Roads and Canals be instructed to inquire into the expediency of granting a quantity of the unsold unappropriated public land in the State of Ohio, to that State, to be by her sold, and the proceeds applied to the purchase of stock in the Sandy and Beaver Canal, which is ultimately intended to connect the Ohio Canal with that of Pennsylvania. If this plan should not be deemed advisable, to inquire into the expediency of a subscription by the United States for a portion of the said stock, or the granting of efficient aid in the construction of said canal in any other acceptable mode—and that the several acts of incorporation of said Canal company, the report of the engineers who surveyed and located it, together with the letters, and other papers accompanying them, be referred to said committee, and be printed for the use of the members of both Houses of Congress.

On motion of Mr. MITCHELL,

Resolved, That the Committee on Roads and Canals be instructed to inquire into the propriety of making an appropriation for clearing out the obstructions in the Muskingum river, in the State of Ohio, from the termination of slack water navigation at Zanesville, to its junction with the Ohio river.

On motion of Mr. CRANE,

Resolved, That the Committee on Roads and Canals be instructed to inquire into the expediency of improving the navigation of the Miami river of lake Erie, below the rapids of said river.

On motion of Mr. GARLAND,

Resolved, That the Committee on Commerce be instructed to inquire into the expediency of making an appropriation for the purpose of removing the obstructions to the navigation of the river Atchafylaya, and Bayou Pigeon, outlets of the Mississippi river, in the State of Louisiana.

On motion of Mr. KINNARD,

Resolved, That the Committee of Ways and Means be instructed to inquire into the expediency of making an appropriation on the Cumberland Road, in the State of Indiana, and of allowing the superintendent of said road in the States of Indiana and Illinois a per centage on the amount of money disbursed by him.

On motion of Mr. MARDIS,

Resolved, That the Committee on Roads and Canals be instructed to inquire into the expediency of causing a survey and estimate to be made for a rail road from the most eligible point on the Tennessee river, in the town of Tuscaloosa, and from thence to the Alabama river. And also to cause a like survey and estimate to be made for a rail road or canal upon the most eligible route from the Tennessee river, opposite the head of Wills' Valley to the Alabama river, so as to connect the waters of the former with those of the latter river.

Mr. SEVIER offered the following resolution, which, under a rule of the House, lies one day:

Resolved, That the President of the United States be requested, (if not deemed incompatible with the public interest,) to negotiate with Spain for her right and title to the country lying between the Sabine and Red Rivers, in Arkansas Territory.

On motion of Mr. REYNOLDS,

Resolved, That the Committee on Roads and Canals be instructed to inquire into the expediency of providing by law for the survey of the following routes, in the State of Illinois, to wit: Kaskaskia river, from its mouth to Vandalia. Big Muddy River, from its mouth to the bridge on it, near Frankfort; and Cash river, from its mouth to Vienna.

The report of the surveys, showing the amount of money necessary to their improvement and other necessary information, be made to the next Congress.

On motion of Mr. PINCKNEY, the bill establishing a Navy Yard in the city of Charleston, South Carolina, was made the special order of the day for Wednesday week.

The SPEAKER laid before the House the following communications:

A letter from the Secretary of the Treasury in answer to a resolution of the House of the 24th inst , in relation to the claim of the U. States upon the Bank of Columbia—referred to the Committee of Ways and Means.

A letter from the Secretary of the Treasury, in response to a resolution of the 16th instant, relative to the official proceedings of the Government Directors of the Bank of the United States—referred to the Committee of Ways and Means.

A report from the Secretary of the Treasury, in relation to the bridge across the Potomac, at Washington—referred to the Committee on Claims.

The following bills from the Senate, were read twice and committed:

A bill for the relief of Samuel Smith, Lynn McGee, and Semoine, Creek Indians;

A bill for the relief of Susan Marlow;

And a bill for the relief of Elijah Simmons.

An engrossed bill to revive and continue in force the act to provide for persons who were disabled by known wounds received in the revolutionary war, was read the third time and passed.

PAY OF NAVAL OFFICERS.

The House proceeded to the consideration of the bill to equalize and regulate the pay of the Officers of the Navy, as reported to the House with amendments, from the Committee of the Whole.

The first amendment, fixing the pay of senior Captains "at all times when in service at 4,500 dollars, and when on leave of absence, or waiting orders, at 3,500 dollars," was concurred in.

The next amendment, which fixes the pay of all other Captains, when commanding squadrons, on coast stations, and when acting as Navy Commissioners, at $4,500; when commanding Navy Yards $4,000; on other duty, $3,750; on leave of absence or waiting orders, $3,000, being under consideration,

Mr. PARKER, moved to strike out the words "coast stations, and when acting as Navy Commissioners."

Mr. WATMOUGH expressed a fervent hope that the amendment would not be adopted. The whole bill, with its numerous amendments, had been most elaborately discussed in Committee of the Whole, and he believed the sense of the House had been fully elicited. He did, therefore, particularly desire that the time of the House should not be wasted by further useless argumentation on

points which might already be considered as definitively settled.

After a few words from Mr. PARKER, in exculpation of the motives which induced the offer of the amendment, and from Mr. PINCKNEY, in opposition to it, the motion was rejected, and the amendment, as reported to the House from the Committee of the Whole, was concurred in.

The next amendment, which fixes the pay of Masters Commandant, and Commanders, when on sea service, at $2,500; on other duty, at $2,000; and while waiting orders, at $1,800; being under consideration,

Mr. FILLMORE moved to amend it by inserting after the words "waiting orders" the words "or on leave of absence," which was agreed to.

Mr. WATMOUGH said, he hoped the amendment agreed to in Committee of the Whole would not be concurred in by the House, and on the question being taken, the amendment was rejected.

The amendment relating to Lieutenants was next concurred in, as follows:

"Commanding, one thousand eight hundred dollars—on other duty; one thousand five hundred dollars—waiting orders, one thousand two hundred dollars."

The next two amendments concerning Assistant Surgeons, and Surgeons, were concurred in, after a debate on the motion to add " *Pursers*" to the provision made for the Surgeons.

The amendment reads:

" *Pursers*—when attached to vessels for sea service, or at navy yards, $1400. When on leave of absence or waiting orders, $900."

Mr. WISE asked for some information on the subject of the amendment.

Mr. WATMOUGH then explained the reason which had induced the committee to change the present regulations concerning Pursers. He stated that it had been deemed expedient to abolish the commissions of the Pursers on tea and sugar sold out to the sailors, and the additional salary to the Pursers was given to compensate him for his loss by this abolition of the commissions.

Mr. WISE stated that the fixed pay of Pursers at present was very small, and that he had 50 per cent. on the tea, sugar, tobacco, &c , which amounted to some thousands, and a commission of 23 per cent. on a secondary class of articles. The Captains, also, in consequence of their insufficient pay, are frequently obliged to borrow money of the Pursers. He adverted to practices of Purse a by which the sailors were heavily taxed. Articles had been purchased at Gibraltar, and, after the vessel had gone to sea, the sailors are compelled to receive these articles at double their cost, and as specie. He estimated the annual profit of a Purser on board a seventy-four at $14,000. He said he hop d the amendment would not be concurred in, although the Purser never received four times as much as a Captain, because he thought the regulation of their pay should be made the subject of a separate act.

Mr. PEARCE made a few remarks on the uncertainty of the passage of the bill referred to, and opposed the amendment.

Mr. PARKER hoped the House would reject the amendment, and remarked that the gentleman from Pennsylvania had, last session, introduced a bill under which he now admitted that the Pursers had been drawing four dollars a month from the poor seamen. He wished that there should be no increase of the pay of the Pursers.

Mr. WAYNE thought that the clause should be stricken out, and regretted that he must separate from the Chairman on this question.

Mr. WATMOUGH said, that it was the object of the provision to strike at these evils if they existed. He did not desire to increase, but he did desire to bring down the pay of the Pursers, and he had desired to make the bill specific on this point.

Mr. WAYNE said he should probably vote to reduce the pay of the Pursers at a proper time, for he desired that it should be regulated.

The House then refused to concur in the amendment.

The following amendments were next considered and agreed to:

Chaplains.—When attached to vessels for sea service, or at navy yards, one thousand two hundred dollars.

When on leave of absence, or waiting orders, eight hundred dollars.

Professor of Mathematics.—When attached to vessels for sea service, or in a yard, one thousand two hundred dollars.

Secretaries.—To commanders of squadrons, when commanding in chief, one thousand dollars.

To commanders of squadrons, when not commanding in chief, nine hundred dollars.

Sailingmasters.—Of a ship of the line for sea service, one thousand one hundred dollars.

When on other duty, one thousand dollars.

When on leave of absence, or waiting orders, seven hundred and fifty dollars.

Second Masters.—When attached to vessels for sea service, seven hundred and fifty dollars.

When on other duty, five hundred dollars.

When on leave of absence, or waiting orders, four hundred dollars.

Passed Midshipmen.—When attached to vessels for sea service, six hundred dollars.

When on other duty, five hundred dollars.

When on leave of absence, or waiting orders, four hundred dollars.

Warranted Masters' Mates.—When attached to vessels for sea service, or at navy yards, four hundred and fifty dollars.

When on leave of absence, or waiting orders, three hundred dollars.

Midshipmen.—When attached to vessels for sea service, four hundred dollars.

When on other duty, three hundred and fifty dollars.

When on leave of absence, or waiting orders, three hundred and sixty dollars.

Clerks.—Of a yard, nine hundred dollars.

First clerk to a commandant of a navy yard, nine hundred dollars.

Second clerk to a commandant of a navy yard, seven hundred and fifty dollars.

To commanders of squadrons, captains of fleet, and commanders of vessels, five hundred dollars.

Boatswains, Gunners, Sailmakers, Carpenters —Of a ship of the line, for sea service, seven hundred and fifty dollars.

Of a frigate, for sea service, six hundred dollars.

When on other duty, five hundred dollars.

When on leave of absence, or waiting orders, three hundred and fifty dollars.

Officers temporarily performing duties belonging to those of a higher grade, shall receive the compensation allowed to such higher grade, while actually so employed.

No officer shall be put on furlough but at his own request, and all officers so furloughed shall receive two-thirds only of the pay to which they would have been entitled if on leave of absence.

If any assistant surgeon shall have been struck from the United States, on duty, at the time of one of his date were examined, he shall, if rejected at a subsequent examination, be entitled to the same rank with them, and if from a y his relative rank cannot be assigned to him, will retain his original position on the register.

One ration per day, only, shall be allowed all officers when attached to vessels for service.

The compensation hereinbefore specified shall be in full for pay and subsistence, and for all allowances, in lieu of cabin furniture to commanders of vessels and squadrons, and for all accounts officers attached to navy yards, or employed any shore duty, except for the detention and maintenance on special service, for house rent, or other money where quarters or public accommodations be not provided, and for travel under orders for which sixteen cents per mile shall be allowed. And all acts or parts of acts inconsistent with provisions of this act, are hereby repealed.

On the question of concurring with the foregoing amendment, a debate sprung up. A motion of Mr. REED, to amend it by striking out the word " sixteen," and inserting " ten."

Mr. WARD moved to insert the word " twelve," and it was accepted as a modification.

Mr. FILLMORE moved to strike out the after

tion " for detention and employment on special service." He stated that, if the officer was not paid enough for his whole time, the pay should be increased.

Mr. WATMOUGH expl ined, that an officer was frequently transferred from one place to another at an additional charge to himself, and it was to compensate him for that that the provision was introduced.

Mr. McKINLEY was opposed to leaving a discretion in the hands of any Department on a subject which might lead to favoritism.

Mr. REED referred to the usages of the Department. These Captains were sometimes taken from their stations and placed on other duties, at great additional expense, and it had been usual for the Department to give extra allowances of from $1 to $3 a day. He was desirous to cut off all extra allowances.

Mr. VANDERPOEL said, it was well known that he was friendly to the increase of the pay of the naval officers, and it was in that spirit of friendship, that he should vote for the motion of his colleague to strike out the clause under consideration. He was against all extra allowances for special duties. He had regarded it as one of the greatest merits of the bill under discussion that it was simple and perspicuous, that it called things by right names, and paid the officers specific sums per annum, and no more. He was opposed to *et cetera,* *contingencies,* and extra allowances. The principle was wrong, and was, as he could have hoped, inconsistent with the spirit in which this bill was conceived, viz. a desire to make such provision for the naval officers, as that the People should always know and understand exactly what their servants received. If we paid them liberally per year, wh h he was certainly willing to do, if we paid them liberally when waiting orders, they ought not, to consider it a hardship to be put per annum once in the course of their lives on courts martial, or to be detailed for some other special duty, without receiving for it extra remuneration. He must confess that the amounts included in the bill should exclude all extra claims for what are denominated " *special duties.*" He was willing to allow them ten cents per mile for their travelling fees, when they went to and returned from the point where " such special service" was to be executed, but he was opposed to any per diem allowance, at the same time that their annual salary was going on.

Mr. MANN alluded to the scale of allowances made in the Army, when officers were sent on journeys to inspect provisions, &c. He thought the allowance ought to be fixed on the same scale, and should vote against the motion.

Mr. WAYNE was in favor of retaining this part of the amendment, as he wished to make the extra allowance adequate to the service to be performed. If the officer were sent on his own expense on a service which required expenditure, he would be induced to shorten the period of employment, although the public service might thereby be injured.

Mr. MASON, of Virginia, suggested that the better way would be to amend the clause, by inserting the words, " when absent on Court Martial," instead of striking out, as proposed.

Mr. BROWN said it was not his purpose to interfere in any manner with the details of the bill under consideration. And he should leave the arrangement of its provisions to those better qualified than himself for the examination of such questions. His honorable colleague (Mr. Fillmore,) would have submitted the amendment, and his honorable colleague (Mr. Vanderpoel,) who so earnestly advocated its adoption, were at a loss to know what the nature of the special service were for which provision was made in the bill. There was a single instance in his memory, (a trifling one, it true,) which might possibly have some influence upon the judgment of the House; and he therefore begged to state it. He happened to reside in the vicinity of one of the largest iron foundries in the country, where cannon had sometimes been manufactured for the use of the Government, and had known officers of the Navy (and amongst them a Midshipman,) detailed for the proof and inspection of those guns, preparatory to their delivery by the manufacturer. Now the present pay of Midshipmen, including rations, amoun'ed to the sum of 319 dollars and 25 cents yearly; and no one could reside for a few weeks in the vicinity of West Point (the place to which he alluded,) at a less expense than one or two dollars per day. This is but one instance (amongst the many thousands of far greater consequence ,) of extra duty performed by officers in the naval service, where an extra allowance must be made to enable them to meet their unavoidable expenses. They might be detailed upon Courts Martial, upon duties of inspection, and upon a thousand nameless and necessary services, both at home and abroad, which could not be executed without additional compensation. The House would see how impossible it was to define what those special services were; and that no legislation can possibly settle the amount of compensation. The discretion must, therefore, be lodged with the Navy Department, or not exercised at all—and the compensation, consequently, withheld altogether.

Mr. FILLMORE contended that the bill provided different grades of compensation for those who were on a foreign station, who commanded at a navy yard, or who were waiting orders The bill provided for the active services of the officers, among which services were included the sitting on Courts Martial, or any other incident al duty. If the pay was not sufficient, let it be increased, directly, but not in the manner proposed.

Mr. VANDERPOEL said, he had listened with great attention to the honorable gentleman from Georgia, (Mr. Wayne,) and to his friend and colleague, (Mr. Brown,) and he was constrained to say, that he had heard nothing to convince him that the first view he had taken of this matter was erroneous; and he would here take occasion to say, that if gentlemen had succeeded in convincing him that he had been in error, he would not have been so convinced " *against his will,*" for, certainly, if he had any sympathy as to indulge, they were in favor of the officers of the navy; if he had any wish to gratify, it was that they should be fairly paid for their services; but he had yet heard no satisfactory reason why, after providing for them a liberal compensation in the shape of specific sums, to be paid annually to each, they should be allowed any thing for any extraordinary or special duties, that might, by possibility, be required of them.

It was an old adage, that " straws show which way the wind blows," and something had occurred, in the course of this debate, that made him suspect, that some gentlemen were now in favor of retaining this provision for extra allowance, from no friendly disposition towards this bill. He confessed that the support which one of his honorable colleagues, (Mr. Mann,) who had so early opened his battery upon the bill, looked a little *ominous.* It was, he believed, fair play, according to the ethics of legislative halls, to charge a bill, in its first stages, with as much odious and unpalatable matter as possible, with a view to secure its final rejection. He did not know but his colleague had become a convert to the bill; but he must in candor confess, that he was a little jealous as to the motive that had induced him to support this proposition for extra allowance for special duties.

He did not think that the case which another of his honorable colleagues (Mr Brown) had put, was at all a fortunate one for the purpose for which it was adduced. He had told us, that midshipmen were frequently required to leave the Navy Yard at Brooklyn, and stationed for a few days at the cannon foundry at West Point, and that they could not live there for less than two dollars per day. He would ask, whether they would not be obliged to pay for their own living when at the Navy Yard? Most surely. How, then, would the account of profit and loss stand, when sent on such an expedition? They would receive, for mileage, six dollars for going, and six; and the same sum for returning—when the actual fare and expense of going up and returning would not exceed two dollars! Here, then, was a gain of ten dollars; and the idea, that it would cost one of these young gentlemen two dollars per day for living in the neighborhood of West Point, struck him as

being somewhat strange. What! the price of living, in the rich and fruitful county of Orange, so exorbitantly high! He was well aware that there was a small portion of that wealthy and respectable district, which his friend so ably represented, so sterile, that if Nebuchadnezzar had been turned out there, he would have starved to death. (He meant the Highlands.) But they included but a very small part of the gentleman's district. This was, perhaps, dwelling too long upon the case which the gentleman had put. He would only further observe, that he expected that the officers of the Navy should take a little of the " *bitter*" with " *the sweet,*" and that he would not, by authorizing these extra claims for special duties, expose them to the temptation of preferring claims that would induce uncharitable men to say, that what " *they love in dancing,*" they " *make up by turning around.*" Pay them so much per year, and then the people will know exactly what they are paid.

Mr. MANN, of New York, said, that his colleague was mistaken in supposing that by supporting the bill in this particular, he wished to render it odious. That he was undesignedly opposed to the bill, he readily admitted. He thought it quite possible, however, that it might become a law. With this belief, it was perhaps best, in order that the millions of public property which might in this way be confided to the officers, should be properly taken care of, that some additional compensation should be given as an incentive to a correct discharge of that duty.

Various propositions of amendment were suggested, but before any question was taken.

Mr. BOON said, the House was thin, and there was no likelihood that the bill would be disposed of at the present sitting. He therefore moved an adjournment, but withdrew the motion at the request of

Mr. HUBBARD, who asked the consent of the House to offer the following resolution:

Resolved, That the ladies be admitted to the privileged seats of the Hall of the House of Representatives on Wednesday next.

Objection being made, Mr. HUBBARD moved to suspend the rule; which was agreed to. Yeas 109, nays, 18.

The resolution was then submitted and agreed to.

The House then adjourned.

Petitions and memorials were presented by— Messrs. SWIFT, TALLMADGE, and KENT.

Mr. McKEAN presented the petition of John Randolph Clay, Charge d' Affaires at St. Petersburg, alledging that there was an error in the calculation of his account by the Committee on Foreign Relations, and praying relief.

Also, a preamble and resolutions of a meeting at West Alexandria, Pa. relative to the repairs of the Cumberland road.

A message was received from the President of the United States, by Mr. DONELSON, his private Secretary, communicating a report from the Secretary of State, and the papers relating to the refusal of the French Government to make provision for the execution of the treaty of July, 1831, between the United States and France. The message was in response to the resolution submitted by Mr. CLAY and adopted some days ago.

Mr. MANGUM moved that the papers be referred to the Committee on Foreign Relations, and that they be printed.

Mr. CALHOUN expressed a wish that the motion to print might include the debates of the French Chambers upon the subject of the treaty, and the letter of Mr. Rives, which was supposed to have caused some difficulty on the subject of

the appropriation. He wished that a full and complete view of the whole subject might be laid before the nation.

Mr. MANGUM said, there were also two or three other important letters which it was necessary to have printed—he would, however, confine his motion now, only to the reference, and withdraw the motion to print.

Mr. CALHOUN also withdrew his motion to print the debates, and expressed a hope that the honorable member, (Mr. Mangum,) would attend to it at the proper time.

The communication and documents were then referred.

Mr. POINDEXTER, from the Committee on Public Lands, reported a bill for the relief of Silas E. Fisher, which, on his motion, was taken up for consideration, and then laid on the table.

Mr. POINDEXTER, from the same Committee, also reported

A bill for the relief of Thomas J. Mertec, and

A bill for the relief of Charles Lynch; which were read the first time, and ordered to a second reading.

On motion of Mr. POINDEXTER, the Committee on Public Lands were discharged from the further consideration of the petition of Andrew A. H. Knox; which he reported against.

Mr. POINDEXTER, from the same Committee, reported the bill from the House of Representatives, to authorize Registers and Receivers of public moneys, for the sale of public lands, to administer oaths, &c.

Mr. P. gave notice, that when the bill should be called up for consideration, he would move for its indefinite postponement. He had been informed that the Commissioner of the General Land Office had himself prescribed an oath, which he required to be taken by all applicants for lands, before they could be allowed to make entry. They were required to swear that they had gone upon the lands applied for, and examined them, and that no one else was entitled to the right of pre-emption. This oath had given rise to very great inconvenience among settlers, and he believed there was no law or authority for it. He, therefore, proposed the following resolution, which he moved might be considered now:

Resolved, That the Commissioner of the General Land Office be directed to lay before the Senate a copy of any oath or oaths prescribed by the Department of the Treasury, to be administered to all persons who may become the purchasers of the public lands, subject to entry at private sale, and that the said Commissioner report to the Senate under what act of Congress the said oath or oaths was authorized and administered.

The resolution was then adopted.

Mr. POINDEXTER said he was instructed by the Committee on Public Lands, to offer the following resolution:

Resolved, That the Secretary of the Senate be and he is hereby directed to cause to be prepared and laid before the Senate, manuscript maps of the several States of Ohio, Indiana, Illinois, Missouri, Mississippi, Alabama, and Louisiana, and the Territories of Michigan, Arkansas, and Florida; which maps shall contain plats of the public lands, within the aforesaid States and Territories, which have been surveyed under the authority of the United States, marking upon the maps aforesaid, the lands the Indian title to which is not extinguished, and distinguishing by colors upon the maps aforesaid the lands granted to the army; the lands sold by the United States; the lands granted to each of the said States and Territories for the endowment of colleges, or reserved from sale for the use of schools; or confirmed to persons claiming under British, French, or Spanish titles; and also the lands surveyed as aforesaid, remaining unsold; stating likewise the computed number of acres of each of the enumerated classes of lands, and the number of acres which may have been surrendered to the United States under any law passed for the relief of the purchasers of the public lands. And that Charles Gordon, who was employed in making the aforesaid maps, under a resolution of the Senate, of the 28th of February, 1833, and who has made some progress in the work, be continued

in said service until the maps herein directed to be made out, are completed.

The VICE PRESIDENT laid before the Senate a further report from the Secretary of the Treasury relative to the bridge across the Potomac, at Washington.

Mr. SILSBEE, from the Committee on Commerce, reported, with an amendment, the bill from the House of Representatives for improving the harbor at the mouth of the river Raisin, in the Michigan Territory.

Mr. TIPTON from the Committee on Claims, reported a bill for the relief of William C. Easton; which was read the first time and ordered to a second reading.

Mr. TOMLINSON, on leave given, introduced a bill for the relief of Walter Lomax and Abel Gay; which was read twice and referred.

Mr. KING, of Alabama, gave notice that to-morrow, he would ask leave to introduce a bill granting pre-emption rights to certain persons therein mentioned.

Mr. BENTON, from the Committee on Military Affairs, reported a bill making an appropriation for the repair of the military barracks at New Orleans.

On motion of Mr. WAGGAMAN, the bill was taken up for consideration, as in Committee of the Whole, and ordered to be engrossed for a third reading.

The joint resolution from the House of Representatives, for the appointment of a joint committee on enrolled bills, was taken up for consideration, and, on motion of Mr. POINDEXTER, concurred in.

The committee being balloted for, Messrs. KING of Georgia, and LINN, were appointed.

The following resolutions, lying on the table, were taken up and adopted:

By Mr. ROBINSON:

Resolved, That the Committee on the Post Office and Post Roads be instructed to inquire into the expediency of establishing a mail route from Galena, in Illinois, by Walnut Grove and Davidson's Mills, to Frankfort, in the same State.

By Mr. WHITE:

Resolved, That the Committee on Revolutionary Claims be instructed to inquire into the propriety of providing by law for the payment of the commutation of five years' full pay to the heirs of Harry Dixon, a Colonel in the North Carolina line, or continental establishment, during the revolutionary war.

By Mr. McKEAN:

Resolved, That the Committee on Commerce be instructed to inquire into the expediency of establishing a port of entry at Brownsville, on the Monongahela river.

By Mr. HENDRICKS:

Resolved, That the Secretary of the Treasury be directed to communicate to the Senate the report of a survey made under authority of a law of Congress, fixing, designating, and marking, the northern boundary of the State of Indiana.

The bill for the relief of Col. John Eugene Leitzendorfer, was read a third time and passed.

The bill to provide for the adjudication and settlement of certain claims to land therein mentioned, was considered as in Committee of the Whole.

Mr. KING, of Alabama, expressed a wish for further time to examine this bill; it was one of much importance, and he moved that it be postponed to, and made the special order of the day for, Monday next.

Mr. PORTER was opposed to the postponement—the same bill had been passed by the Senate last year, and only failed in the House for want of time to act on it. The bill was then fully discussed—it provided for the adjudication and settlement of three disputed claims to lands in Louisiana; that of the heirs of Winthrop, the Marquis of Mason Rouge, and Baron Bastrop, who held under Spanish grants. Mr. P. contended that great injustice was done to the holders of these lands by the long continued refusal of Congress to provide for the settlement of their difficulties; that there was no ground for further delay, as the disputes must ultimately come before the judicial tribunals for determination, and the holders would not be contented with any thing short of it. Why,

he asked, should they be denied a resort to these tribunals?

Mr. KING replied that he moved the postponement with great reluctance; but a sense of duty compelled him to do so. To be sure, the bill was partially discussed at the last session. The Winthrop claim embraced a number of cases, which he would like to look into. The Mason Rouge cases, he knew, had found no favor here, and he believed the claimants already had the opportunity of bringing suits and testing their titles. He merely desired time to examine the subject.

After some further remarks from Mr. PORTER and Mr. POINDEXTER, the motion to postpone was disagreed to, and the bill was ordered to be engrossed for a third reading.

The following resolutions were presented by Mr. LINN:

Resolved, That the Committee on Claims be instructed to inquire into the expediency of making an appropriation to compensate Joseph Hertich for a boat impressed by an officer of the United States, during the last war with England, and put in the service of the General Government.

Resolved, That the Committee on Commerce be instructed to inquire into the expediency of making an appropriation for the purchase of a site, and the erection of a marine hospital, at St. Louis, Missouri.

Resolved, That the Committee on the Post Office and Post Roads be instructed to inquire into the expediency of establishing a post route from the City of Jefferson, State of Missouri, to pass through the seats of justice of Morgan, Pulaski, and Green counties, to Washington county, Arkansas Territory.

The special order of the day, the bill to provide compensation for French spoliations prior to 1800, having been announced,

Mr. CLAYTON suggested to the gentleman who had the floor, (Mr. Robbins) that as the day was advanced, if he had no objection, he would move to postpone the subject, so that the body might spend some time in the consideration of Executive business.

Mr. ROBBINS having yielded to the suggestion, the special order was postponed, and after having spent some time with closed doors,

The Senate adjourned.

HOUSE OF REPRESENTATIVES.

Tuesday, December 30, 1834.

Petitions and memorials were presented by Messrs. STEWART, McKENNAN, and BURD, of Pennsylvania.

Messrs. FULTON and MERCER, of Virginia.

Mr. CHILTON, of Kentucky.

Mr. Speaker BELL, of Tennessee.

Messrs. THOMSON, PATTERSON, HAMER and CRANE, of Ohio.

Mr. EWING, of Indiana.

Mr. MURPHY, of Alabama.

Mr. SEVIER, of Arkansas.

Mr. WHITE, of Florida.

Mr. WARD, of New York.

Which petitions and memorials were referred to the Standing Committees.

Mr. CLAY, from the Committee on the Public Lands, reported a bill for the relief of William Walker and the heirs of Samuel Brown, deceased which was read twice and postponed to Tuesday next.

Mr. CASEY, from the Committee on the Public Lands, reported a bill providing for the establishment of a Surveyor General's office in the State of Illinois, which was read twice.

Mr. CASEY stated that the establishment of a separate Surveyor General's Office for the State of Illinois was a matter of deep interest to the people of that State; he was therefore, exceedingly anxious that the bill should be acted upon at the present session of Congress, and hoped that the House would permit the bill to be committed to the Committee of the Whole on the state of the Union; and accordingly made a motion to that effect; which motion was agreed to.

Mr. C. ALLAN, from the Committee on Territories, reported a bill to establish a new Judicial District in Florida; which was read twice and postponed to tomorrow week.

Mr. FOSTER, from the Committee on the Judiciary, and Mr. BROWN, from the Committee on Invalid Pensions, made unfavorable reports upon petitions referred to said Committees.

The following resolution, submmitted yesterday by Mr. PINCKNEY, was considered and agreed to:

Resolved, That the Secretary of War be, and he is hereby, requested to communicate to this House such information as may be necessary to explain the cause or causes of the suspension of the work at Fort Sumpter, in Charleston harbor, and whether any, and if any, what measures have been taken by the Department, in relation to the difficulty from which said suspension has arisen.

The following resolution, submitted yesterday by Mr. SEVIER, was taken up:

Resolved, That the President of the United States be requested (if not deemed incompatible with the public interest) to negotiate with Spain for her right and title to the country lying between the Sabine and Red rivers, in Arkansas Territory.

Mr. SEVIER said—Mr. Speaker, it is my duty perhaps to explain to the House, the object I have in view in offering that resolution. There is, sir, a considerable tract of valuable country lying north of the Sabine and south of Red river, upon which many of our citizens have resided for years; a country, of which we have had the undisturbed possession, and over which we still exercise jurisdiction, that will, in all probability, be lost to us forever, if the boundary line, designated by the treaty of 1819 between this Government and Spain should be permanently established. I believe Spain to be the rightful owner of this tract of country; and of that Government, I presume, we can obtain it for a mere trifle. It is true Mexico claims this country; but I ask, what evidence has she of her title? Has she purchased it?—Has she conquered it? No; she has done neither; and as well might her cupidity and arrogance lead her to set up a claim for Cuba, as for the tract of country in question. Mexico never revolutionized the country north of the Sabine—she never marched a soldier into it—nor has she ever given a dollar for it. Our citizens have held the undisturbed possession of this country from 1806 down to the present day. It is true, we ceded it to Spain in 1819, for which she gave us the Floridas Has Spain ever parted with her right acquired by that treaty? Has she ever sold it? Has it been taken from her? No, sir, she has not sold it, nor has Mexico ever taken, it from her, or been in possession of it. Upon what technical, vain, and flimsy pretext is it then upon which she founds her claim to a country which she never acquired by arms, or treasure, or inheritance. Will any honorable gentleman be kind enough to inform me? Is it by *discovery*, backed by a bull from a Pope? A title thus acquired may have been good in the days of Cortes and Pizarro—it may yet be good where Indians alone are concerned; but I apprehend we are not prepared to recognise it as valid at this day in regard to ourselves. We, sir, have been for years negotiating with Mexico upon a subject, about which we ought never to have negotiated: and if I am correctly informed, we are still negotiating with her upon this same subject, when public policy and national dignity and justice should induce us to abandon it.

The conduct of Mexico in regard to this slip of country, brings forcibly to my mind a scrap of ancient history. We have been informed that the Devil met our Saviour upon the Mount, and told him if he would fall down and worship him, that he would give him the whole world. Now, I need not tell you, or the House, *I presume*, that his Satanic Majesty had no world to give. So with Mexico. She has had her agents among our citizens, possessed of extensive grants to land bordering upon the very banks of Red river, for the purpose of bribing them to abjure their own country, and by allegiance and expatriation, to become citizens of Mexico. These agents, to some extent, were successful. They induced, by their valuable bounties, some of our honest, hard-working, industrious citizens—citizens who were anxious to obtain land upon easy terms for themselves and children, to take the oath of allegiance to Mexico. They induced others to resist the execution of the civil authority of our country, and so prevalent was this spirit of resistance becoming, that the Governor of Arkansas, who chanced at that time to be in that part of the country, gave them a public address upon the impropriety of their conduct. He told them in his speech, that the Sheriff would be sustained in the execution of the civil authority of the country. He told them if their resistance should produce a civil war, that they would be vanquished, and that if taken in arms against their country, they would not be treated as prisoners of war, but hung up as traitors to the country. Now, sir, it is not for me to say what effect this speech had upon my constituents—but I can say, and do say it, with great pleasure, that, at this time, all things are going on as they should go on.

I did not rise to make a long speech. I hope the resolution will be adopted.

Mr. ADAMS, of Massachusetts, said this was a resolution of a peculiar character. It called upon President of the United States to negotiate with the Government of Spain for a portion of this continent to which the latter had no title—to dis-acknowledge the Government of Mexico, and to recognise the right of Spain to that which she had long since ceased to have any claim He concluded by moving to lay the resolution on the table; but withdrew the motion.

Mr. SEVIER said, in reply to Mr. ADAMS, that the gentleman seems to express some astonishment at my resolution, and thinks it highly improper to authorize the President to negotiate with Spain for the tract of country mentioned in the resolution, inasmuch as Spain owns no land upon the Continent. The gentleman himself made the treaty of 1819, (or at least he has the credit of it in our country,) by which the country in question was given to Spain in part payment for the Floridas. Now, sir, allow me to ask the honorable gentleman to tell me *when* Spain parted with the title to the country he himself, on behalf of his Government, ceded to her? I want to know who bought it, or what power took it from her? I state that she never parted with it—that she never sold it—and that it never was taken from her by force.

It is a country very desirable for us to own, and I suppose it can be had of her for "six and nine pence," or thereabouts.

We have been pursuing towards Mexico a coaxing, scratching, tickling policy long enough. It is time to talk to her manfully—to tell her to confine herself to her lawful territory—to give up her preposterous claims to a country she does not own—and above all, to cease tampering with our citizens, or else we will make her. Our partialities are all for Mexico against Spain, and yet I must confess, that I have yet to see any thing in the government of that fickle, jealous, and bigoted Republic, in any wise calculated to excite either my love or admiration. I hope the resolution will not be laid upon the table.

Mr. POLK said, the motion of the gentleman from Arkansas proposed, to say the least of it, an unusual course of proceeding. The House of Representatives formed no part of the treaty-making power. That power was vested in the President and Senate. The House had certainly no right to interfere in so grave and important a subject as the one contained in the resolution. He therefore renewed the motion to lay it on the table.

Mr. CAMBRELENG hoped that the motion to lay the resolution on the table, would be withdrawn, and that it would be rejected by a direct vote.

Mr. POLK withdrew his motion.

Mr. ARCHER suggested to the mover of the resolution, that by its adoption the object which he had in view would be frustrated. It would give just cause of offence to Mexico, and might induce that Government to break off all negotiations with the United States. It would be tantamount to a denial of the independence of the Mexican Government; and after offering this insult to that nation, it would not do for the United States to propose any further negotiations in that quarter.

Mr. MERCER hoped that the resolution would be withdrawn. He would not be satisfied with a simple vote of rejection. He wished to inform the Government of Mexico that a proposition of this character was not even entertained by this House. The proposition was in violation of our acknowledgment of the independence of that Government. He referred to the circumstance that the life of an American minister was endangered in Mexico, owing to a supposed interference in the politics of that country. From this consideration, and the commercial rivalry existing between the two governments, Mexico had perhaps good cause to suppose that we entertain unfriendly feelings towards her; and if the resolution was not withdrawn, he hoped it would be unanimously rejected.

Mr. SEVIER said, he had no idea that his resolution would have met with such opposition from so many quarters of the House. The gentlemen seem to suppose my resolution very unusual and extraordinary—that I am for taking of Mexico lands, to which her right is undoubted—and lastly, that it may produce much mischief, and no possible good. My object is not to produce mischief, or to embarrass the Administration, or to take of Mexico one inch of ground which belongs to her. And as such results seem to be apprehended by my friends, I will withdraw the resolution. But in doing this, let it be distinctly understood, that it is not because I am in favor of settling this slip of country with free blacks. We have difficulties enough already with our runaway slaves, and I am not disposed to increase those difficulties, by affording them a safer and more secure retreat. I withdraw the resolution.

Mr. FILLMORE offered the following resolution, which under the rule lies one day:

Resolved, That the Secretary of the Treasury be directed to report to this House the amount of Hospital money collected in the several collection districts of the State of New York for each year, from the year 1798, to the present time, and also the amount expended in each year during the same time in each of said districts, and for what purposes and objects such expenditures were made to the amount remaining unexpended at this time for each district, and also, the donations to said fund, and by whom made, and when, and on what condition, if any, and how the money or property given to said fund by donation has been disposed of or applied, and what compensation or portion of said fund has been expended or applied for collecting, receiving, or investing, or paying out the same, and to whom.

On motion of Mr. WHITTLESEY, of N. Y.

Resolved, That the Committee on Invalid Pensions be instructed to inquire into the expediency of continuing the pension of Levi H. Parish, or of granting him further relief.

Mr. GALBRAITH submitted the following resolution, which under the rule lies one day:

Resolved, That the Secretary of War be directed to furnish to this House a statement of the expenditures on the work at the harbor, at Presque Isle, during the past season, the amount paid for stone, giving the number of cords, and at what rate, the amount for timber and other materials, and at what rate, the amount paid for labor, to whom, and at what rate per day or month; the amount paid for superintendence, to whom, and at what rate per day; and the number of days charged for such service, as well as every other item of expenditure at the said harbor; also, whether the direction of Col. Totten with regard to taking frequent soundings in the way, have been attended to.

On motion of Mr. STEWART,

Resolved, That the Committee on Invalid Pensions be instructed to inquire into the expediency of placing Daniel O'Brien on the pension roll.

Mr. THOMAS, of Maryland, offered the following resolution, which, under the rule, lies one day:

Resolved, That the thirteenth rule of this House be amended, by inserting therein the word District Attorneys of the United States, after the words Judges of the United States.

On motion of Mr. JOHNSON, of Kentucky,

Resolved, That the Committee of Ways and Means be instructed to inquire into the expediency of making an appropriation to erect a bridge over the Ohio river at Wheeling, to connect the Cumberland Road on each side of the river.

On motion of Mr. WHITE, of Florida,

Resolved, That the Committee on Commerce be instructed to inquire into the expediency of making an appropriation to improve the harbor at St. Augustine, Florida, according to the report of the Engineer who made the survey in obedience to an act of Congress.

On motion of Mr. REED, of Mass.,

Resolved, That the Committee of Ways and Means be instructed to inquire into the expediency of making an appropriation to complete the custom-house at New Bedford.

On motion of Mr. BYNUM,

Resolved, That the Committee on the Post Office and Post Roads be instructed to inquire into the expediency of establishing a semi-weekly mail route from the town of Winton, through Pitch Landing, in the county of Hertford, via Colerain and Windsor, in the county of Bertie; thence through Williamston and Jameson, in the county of Martin, to the town of Washington, in the county of Beaufort, in the State of North Carolina.

On motion of Mr. STODDERT,

Resolved, That the Committee on Commerce be instructed to inquire into the expediency of authorising the Secretary of the Treasury to elect either Piney-point or the Potomac river (as the interests of navigation and commerce may dictate,) for the establishment of a light.

On motion of Mr. EVERETT, of Vt.,

Resolved, That the Committee on Revolutionary Pensions be instructed to inquire into the expediency of placing the name of Joseph Parker on the roll of Revolutionary Pensions—and that the testimony in his case, now on the files of the House, and the accompany testimony, be referre l to the same Committee.

The SPEAKER laid before the House a letter from the Secretary of the Treasury, in answer to a resolution of the 23d instant, relative to a beacon-light on Black river, in the State of Ohio; which was referred to the Committee on Commerce.

PAY OF THE NAVY.

The House resumed the consideration of the amendments proposed by the Committee of the Whole, to the bill to regulate the pay of the Navy of the United States.

The motion of Mr. FILLMORE, pending on the adjournment yesterday, to strike from that part of the amendment of the Committee relative to extra allowances to officers, the words "except for detention and employment on special service," being under consideration—

Mr. MINER addressed the House in opposition to the motion to strike out. While he was opposed in the general to granting discretionary powers to the Departments, he conceived that, in the present instance, some discretion was necessary.

The motion to strike out was then rejected.

Mr. WATMOUGH moved to amend the first section by inserting in the extra allowances to officers, after the words "chamber money," the words "for which two dollars per week shall be allowed."

After a short conversation of an explanatory character between Messrs. REED, WATMOUGH, BATES, HARPER, of Pennsylvania, McKINLEY, HARDIN, and WISE, the amendment proposed by Mr. WATMOUGH was agreed to.

Mr. BRIGGS moved to amend the first section by striking out from that part of the bill relating to extra allowances, the words "except for detention and employment on special service," and inserting in lieu thereof the words "two dollars per day when absent on courts martial, inspecting navy yards or vessels, and surveying the coast."

The amendment was agreed; and thus amended, the amendment of the Committee was concurred in.

The amendment of the Committee of the Whole to the second section, which proposed to strike out "relatives," and insert " widowed mothers and unmarried sisters," as the persons who shall re-

ceive the benefit of a fund to be constituted by reserving three per cent. out of the pay of commission and warrant officers of the Navy, was next considered.

Mr. WISE moved to amend the amendment, so as to make it read, " widows and children, and when there are no widows and children, widowed mothers."

After various suggestions of amendment, and some d scussion, in which Messrs. FILLMORE, CAMBRELENG, McKENNAN, WISE, ANTHONY, and WATMOUGH took part, the amendment proposed by Mr. WISE was rejected.

The amendment of the Committee of the Whole was then disagreed t to.

The next amendment of the Committee of the Whole, which proposed to strike out all of the third section after the enacting clause, and to insert a provision that hereafter the distrib tion of prze money to the officers, seamen, and ma ines, shall be in proportion to the pay which they respectively receive, was read,

Mr. WISE suggested a proviso, in substance that the marines should receive per capita the same as the sailors

Mr JARVIS propos d a provis , that in estimating the pay, the clothing of the marin s should be taken into consideration.

Mr. WISE accepted the modification proposed by Mr. JARVIS

Mr. HARPER opposed the amendment. He contended that the Marine was not the only individual on board our vessels of war who stood in a different position from the seamen. The service was necessarily divided into different classes, as seamen, ordinary seamen, landsmen, boys, and marines. These d stinctions were essential to the good order and well being of the service. Should it be deemed necessary to incorporate the amendment of the gentleman from Maine (Mr. Jarvis) he should feel constrained to vote against the whole amendment as submitted to the House from the Committee of the Whole.

Mr. BINNEY followed in opposition to the amendment proposed by Mr. Jarvis. He said it appeared to him that the whole section was out of place. It more properly belonged to a separate bill, for the government of the navy. The adoption of this section would introduce an entire new principle in that government, and he was not disposed to overthrow ancient systems for new ones, without mature reflection on the consequen. If the old regulations relative to prize money were not made with due reference to justice, let new ones be made, but let it be done by a separate bill, and with due deliberation. He asked gentlemen to reflect on the consequences involv. He said there were seven different classes included in our naval service. The distribution of prize-money should be regulated by the experi nce already acquired in our service, as well as in that of the nations of Europe. He proceeded to show that the proportion allowed by the amendment to the petty officers, seamen, and marines, was grossly disproportionate to that of the higher officers of the Navy, on whom so much responsibility rested. Remuneration for services, he said, had always been, and always must be correspondent to the accomplishments of mind, and the responsibilities assumed by the individual employed. He contended that the pay of officers was not a fair criterion to govern the division of prize money. A different rule must pre. ponderate in war from that which obtains in time of peace. In the moment of action, the greatest re sponsibility laid upon the commanding officer; and while he fully acknowledged the importance of the services of subordinates, he cou'd not consent to place them higher than their commanders. The great principle of rewarding merit began with the head, and went downwards, with judicious gradation. Sailing-masters, by this amendment, were placed inferior to all whom they commanded

Mr. JARVIS said he should feel discouraged in pressing the amendment which he had just submitted, from the distinguished forensic talent, so well known to be possessed by the Honorable member, (Mr. Binney) who opposed it; were it not that he felt that he had truth and justice on his side. It appeared that one gentleman would

oppose the whole section if this amendment was agreed to, and another wished the subject left for future legislation. He (Mr. J.) said he perfectly understood what was meant by this "future legislation." It meant t; give it " the go by," and nothing more would ever be done by Congress to establish the rights of subordinate officers and seamen, unless the provisions were incorporated in this bill. One gentleman (Mr. Binney) had contended that the whole merit of victory belonged to the commander.

[Mr. BINNEY said "A very considerable merit."]

Mr. JARVIS continued. He advocated the claims of the sailor and the subordinate. Higher individuals had higher motive—a marble monument, &c. It had been said that his amendment rendered the prize-money of a Master Commandant less than that of Lieutenants. It was also said that it would raise that of Surgeons to an equality with those who were placed in more hazardous situations in time of action. He asked where could be a more horrid scene than that which must be encountered by the Surgeon in battle. To him on deck, after the commencement of excitement, fighting became a pleasure. Not so with the Surgeon below, whose condition was the faint hope of saving the life of the mangled body presented to his care.

Mr. J. said, reference had been made to the customs of Europe on this point. He instituted such comparison for the regulation of our conduct, unless it were to avoid their dangerous example. His object was to secure the neglected rights of poor fellows who had too long received little more than hard knocks and salt junk. He had no disposition to take up the time of the House, but he conceived the present system fraught with evil, and abounding in radical defects.

Mr. WAYNE spoke in favor of leaving this subject for the future action of Congress. The attention of that b dy had already been called to it by the President, and was now under examination by the Naval Committee. He suggested to the gentleman from Maine (Mr. Jarvis) to withdraw his amendment, and not, by it, obstruct the passage of the bill.

Mr. JARVIS replied that he would freely do so, were it not that he was convinced that his was the only chance of incorporating these provisions in the b ll.

The question was then taken, and rejected—yeas 43, nays not counted.

The question on the amendment to the third section, proposed by Mr. WISE, was then taken, and also rejected.

On the next amendment, relating to the navy pension fund, Mr. PARKER moved to divide the question on striking out the section and adopting the amendment.

The question on striking out was then agreed to, and on the adoption of the amendment, t debate ensued, in which Messrs. CAMBRELENG, MANN, MASON, PARKER, CLAYTON, JOHNSON of Kentucky, and WATMOUGH, participated.

Before a final vote was taken,

The House adjourned.

IN SENATE.

After the Journal had been read, Mr. PRESTON moved that when the Senate adjourn, it will adjourn to meet on Friday next; which was agreed to.

The Committee on the part of the House of Representatives, appointed in pursuance of the Joint Resolutions relative to the delivery of an Oration upon the Life and Character of General LAFAYETTE, were then introduced, preceded by Mr. JOHN Q. ADAMS, and took the seats assigned to them.

The PRESIDENT OF THE UNITED STATES, accompanied by the several HEADS OF DEPARTMENTS, were t en introduced, an l took seats in front of the Presiding Officer's chair.

A portion of the Foreign Diplomatic Corps were also introduced, and took seats on the right of the President and Heads of Departments.

At half past 12 o'clock, on motion of Mr.

CLAY, the Senate withdrew to the Hall of the House of Representatives, agreeably to the order described by the Committee of Arrangement.

After the delivery of the Oration by Mr. JOHN J. ADAMS, the Senate, together with the VICE PRESIDENT, returned to their own Chamber—when The Senate adjourn d.

HOUSE OF REPRESENTATIVES.

WEDNESDAY, DEC. 31, 1834.

On motion of Mr. HUBBARD, it was

Ordered, That when the House adjourn, it will adjourn to meet again on Friday next.

GENERAL LAFAYETTE.

The SPEAKER announced, that under the joint resolution, the House would be considered as regularly in session, until adjourned in the usual manner, after the delivery of the contemplated eulogy on the Life and Character of Lafayette.

According to previous arrangement, the Senate, accompanied by the Vice President, the President, leads o' Departments, a portion of the Foreign Diplomatic Corps, the Joint Committee of Arrangements, and Mr. JOHN QUINCY ADAMS, entered the Hall of the House of Representatives half past 12 o'clock, P. M.

Mr. HUBBARD (the Chairman of the Committee of Arrangements on the part of the House,) conducted Mr. ADAMS to the Speaker's Chair, from which he rose and delivered an Address on the life and Character of General Lafayette, which occupied about three hours time.

When Mr. ADAMS had concluded, the Vice President and Senate retired to their Hall, the President of the United States, Heads of Departments, &c. &c. withdrew, and the House, on motion, adjourned over to Friday.

IN SENATE.

FRIDAY, JANUARY 2, 1835.

The VICE PRESIDENT laid before the Senate a communication from the Secretary of State, relative to the Diplomatic expenses of that Department for the past year.

Also, a communication from the Secretary of the Treasury in obedience to a resolution of the Senate, relative to the number of navy and military bounty land warrants which had been issued. Referred to the Committee on Public Lands.

Also, a letter from the Postmaster General, in obedience to a resolution of the Senate, submitted some days ago by Mr. BLACK, relative to the establishment of a direct mail route from Burnt Corn in Alabama, to Natchez in Mississippi.

The letter having been read—

Mr. BLACK said, that this was a very important mail route to the people of Mississippi, and particularly those of Natchez, which he thought would appear obvious when it was known that a very large number of respectable citizens of that State, as well as the Legislature thereof, had petitioned Congress expressly for its establishment. I was in consequence of these solicitations that he act of Congress was passed authorizing it, and he regretted greatly, that the act had not been carried into effect. The act required, that the route should be established for carrying the mail in four horse post coaches, as well for the convenience of passengers as the mail, and while extraordinary were granted in Alabama, this route was unattended to. He moved that the communication be printed and referred to the Committee on the Post Office.

Mr. GRUNDY said, that the people of the district of country alluded to, were already supplied with the mail. But it was proper to say, that the contracts for the transportation of it which existed at the time the act was passed, had not yet expired; and after they had expired, the route would be put in operation in the way prescribed by the law. But was it expedient or proper, he inquired, to put it in operation when the old contracts had not yet expired? There was one thing which was much to be regretted, and that was, that the transportation of passengers seemed, in most places, to have got the upper hand of the transportation of the mail, when, in fact, it should be entirely subordinate and secondary to that object. The use of post coaches for carrying passengers, it was true, was very convenient and desirable, but even

this would be done on the route alluded to, when the existing contracts had expired.

Mr. BLACK replied, that the honorable member from Tennessee was right in saying that the transportation of passengers should be subordinate to that of the mail. But he believed that the old contracts had all expired since the passage of the act of Congress establishing this route, and although there was a mail carried on it, yet the entire benefits of the law had been lost to that country by the communication not being kept up directly. Letters took an indirect course, sometimes above and sometimes below the route.

The motion to print and to refer to the Post Office Committee, was agreed to.

The VICE PRESIDENT also laid before the Senate a communication from the Treasury Department relative to the subordinate officers which may be dispensed with in the Custom-house; which was referred to the Committee on Commerce.

Petitions and memorials were presented by Messrs. WEBSTER, KNIGHT, PORTER, WAGGAMAN, WHITE, TOMLINSON, KENT, and SILSBEE.

Mr. WEBSTER, from the Committee on Finance, reported the bill for the relief of the legal representatives of Joseph White, deceased; which was read the first time and ordered to a second reading.

Mr. PORTER, from the Committee on Private Land Claims, reported a bill to confirm the title of a tract of land to the heirs of M. De La Carera.

The following resolution was submitted by Mr. ROBINSON, and adopted:

Resolved, That the Secretary of the Treasury be directed to lay before the Senate a copy of the report of the Commissioners of the survey and establishment of the northern boundary line of the State of Illinois, together with copies of all papers upon that subject.

Mr. KENT submitted the following resolution:

Resolved, That the Committee on Military Affairs inquire into the propriety of authorizing the Secretary of War to purchase the property adjoining Fort McHenry, now rented by the public for the accommodation of the garrison.

Mr. KING, of Georgia, pursuant to notice, on leave given, introduced a bill to establish a mail route in East Florida.

Mr. KING, of Alabama, pursuant to not ce, and on leave given, introduced a bill granting preemption rights to settlers on the public lands; both of which were read twice and referred.

Mr. KANE moved, that when the Senate adjourn it adjourn to me et on Monday next; which was agreed to.

The following resolution submitted by Mr. POINDEXTER on Tuesday last, was taken up for consideration:

Resolved, That the Secretary of the Senate be, and he is hereby directed to cause to be prepared and laid before the Senate, manuscript maps of the several States of Ohio, Indiana, Illinois, Missouri, Mississippi, Alabama, and Louisiana, and the Territories of Michigan, Arkansas, and Florida; which maps shall contain plats of the public lands, within the aforesaid States and Territories, which have been surveyed under the authority of the United States, marking upon the maps aforesaid, the lands the Indian title to which is not extinguished, and distinguishing by colors upon the maps aforesaid the lands granted to the army; the lands sold by the United States, the lands granted to each of the said States and Territories for the endowment of colleges, or reserved from sale for the use of schools; or confirmed to persons claiming under British, French, or Spanish titles; and also the lands surveyed as aforesaid, remaining unsold; stating likewise the computed number of acres of each of the enumerated classes of lands, and the number of acres which may have been surrendered to the United States under any law passed for the relief of the purchasers of the public lands. And that Charles Gordon, who was employed in making the aforesaid maps, under a resolution of the Senate, of the 28th of February, 1823, and who has made some progress in the work, be continued in said service until the maps herein directed to be made out are completed.

Mr. WRIGHT expressed a hope that this resolution might not be pressed this morning. It had not attracted his attention till now, and therefore he was not prepared to vote upon it. A similar resolution had been passed, he believed, some years ago, requiring the Secretary of the Treasury to form a similar work to that contemplated by the resolution, and some progress had been made in it. He, Mr. W., desired to inquire whether the Secretary of the Senate had it in his power to prepare it, and next, what the probable expense would be; he was ignorant of the effect which the resolution was calculated to have, and whether the work was proper to be performed.

Mr. POINDEXTER said, that the resolution was submitted at the instance of the Committee on Public Lands. It was to furnish a work, which should present a complete view of all the States and Territories, in which the public lands were situated, as well as of the several surveys and grants of lands made. The Secretary of the Treasury was not the agent of the Senate, and if done by the Secretary of the Senate, the expense of it would form a part of the contingent expense. He had no objection to the reference to the Secretary of the Treasury, but he thought the honorable member (Mr. Wright,) would perceive the importance of the resolution; he had no objection that it should lie for a short time; indeed, he had rather, it would take that course.

The resolution was laid on the table, and, on motion of Mr. POINDEXTER, it was ordered to be printed.

The following resolutions, submitted by Mr. LINN, and lying on the table, were taken up, considered, and adopted:

Resolved, That the Committee on Claims be instructed to inquire into the expediency of making an appropriation to compensate Joseph Hertich for a boat impressed by an officer of the United States, during the late war with England, and lost in the service of the General Government.

Resolved, That the Committee on Commerce be instructed to inquire into the expediency of making an appropriation for the purchase of a site, and the erection of a marine hospital, at St. Louis, Missouri.

Resolved, That the Committee on the Post Office and Post Roads be instructed to inquire into the expediency of establishing a post route from the city of Jefferson, State of Missouri, to pass through the seats of justice of Morgan, Pulaski, and Green counties, to Washington county, Arkansas Territory.

The Report of the Judiciary Committee against the petition of Thomas Cutts, was taken up for consideration; and after some remarks from Messrs. SHEPLEY, LEIGH, SMITH, CLAYTON, POINDEXTER, and PORTER, it was laid on the table.

The Joint Resolution from the House of Representatives, presenting the thanks of Congress to Mr. J. Q. ADAMS, for his Oration upon the Life and Character of General Lafayette, and requesting a copy thereof for publication, was taken up for consideration, on motion of Mr. CLAY, and concurred in.

On motion of Mr. POINDEXTER, all the special orders on the calendar were postponed to Monday next.

The bill making an appropriation for the repair of the military barracks at New Orleans, and

The bill to provide for the legal adjudication and settlement of claims to lands therein mentioned, were read a third time and passed.

The report of the Judiciary Committee against the petition of John Thompson, was taken up for consideration, and concurred in.

The following bills were considered as in committee of the whole, and ordered to be engrossed for a third reading, to wit:

A bill for the relief of J. & W. Gleason and others;

A bill to authorize the enlistment of boys in the naval service;

A bill to change the titles of certain officers in the navy;

The bill to regulate navy rations was taken up for consideration, and

On motion of Mr. POINDEXTER, was laid on the table.

The bill for the regulation of vessels propelled in the whole or in part by steam, having been taken up for consideration—

Mr. CLAY remarked, that the Chairman of the Naval Committee was absent, in consequence of indisposition, he therefore moved that all the navy bills be laid on the table, until the benefit of the Chairman's explanations could be obtained.

The motion was agreed to.

The bill to exempt merchandise imported under certain circumstances, from the operation of the tariff law of 1828, was considered as in Committee of the Whole, when some explanations were made by Mr. WRIGHT and Mr. SILSBEE, relative to the effects which would result from the passage of the bill.

The question being on the engrossment of the bill for a third reading.

Mr. HILL demanded the yeas and nays, which were ordered and are as follow, to wit:

YEAS—Messrs. Bell, Buchanan, Clay, Clayton, Ewing, Frelinghuysen, Hendricks Kent, Knight, Naudain, Poindexter, Prentiss, Robbins, Silsbee, Smith, Sprague, Swift, Tomlinson, Waggaman, Webster—20.

NAYS—Messrs. Benton, Bibb, Black, Brown, Calhoun, Grundy, Hill, Kane, King of Alabama, King of Georgia, Leigh, Moore, Morris, Robinson, Shepley, Tallmadge, Tipton, White, Wright—19.

So the question was determined in the affirmative.

The bill making an appropriation for the improvement of the river Wabash, being under consideration as in Committee of the Whole—

Mr. HENDRICKS said that the position he occupied in relation to the bill now before the Senate, as well as to former bills on the same subject, rendered it necessary and proper for him to say a few words on the present occasion; that duty and inclination alike impelled him to this course, and that if any apology should be thought necessary for obtruding himself on the attention of the Senate, it would be found on the table of every Senator, in the form of instructions to himself and his colleague, from the Legislature of the State they had the honor to represent. These accompanied the printed report recently made by the Committee on Roads and Canals, on the subject of this bill.

It would be recollected, said Mr. H., that at the last session, the bill to improve the navigation of the Wabash, about which so much had recently been said here and elsewhere, had been introduced by himself, on leave of the Senate. It would also be recollected, that, heretofore, himself and his colleague had been unsuccessful in endeavoring to have the improvement of this river classed with works of internal improvement already begun—however firmly they were of opinion, that the Wabash and Erie canal, a work now in rapid progress, and a work to which this Government had made large appropriations of public lands, was but a part and portion of this very work; and that that appropriation of public lands would fairly class the improvement of the Wabash with works already begun by the means of the Federal Government. They had, however, been foiled in their attempts to have it so considered by the Senate. This work—the improvement of the river, was then classed with new objects of internal improvement, and became an item in the harbor bill of 1832, which received the veto of the President. We all recollect, said Mr. H., that bill, and its history. This work, in the opinion of its friends, having such high claims to be considered a work of national importance, was only endangered in 1832, by the society in which it was found; for it was confidently asserted and believed, and especially by the friends of the present Administration, that this item, unconnected with others, would not have met the disapprobation of the President. Murmurs too were heard, somewhat loud and reproachful, of members of the delegation, who were supposed to have had this matter more especially in charge, for permitting it thus to be classified and defeated.

In this view of the case then, and that it might stand on its own basis and alone, I determined at the last session, said Mr. H., to present it in a separate bill, drawn up in the same language, and asking for the same amount, which had been sanctioned by both Houses, as an item in the harbor bill. In this form it was presented to the Senate. In this form it passed both Houses, and was presented for the signature of the Executive. I give this history of it, said Mr. H., to present it fairly before the Senate. It was my intention, had the resolution referring it to the committee, not been introduced by my colleague, to have asked leave of the Senate, and to have introduced the same bill; but the one form is as good as the other. The committee have reported the bill, and the result is the same.

The views of the President on the subject of internal improvement, I very much regret, because in their effects, they are in my opinion, injurious to the prosperity of the Union, and especially are they so, to that portion of it whence I come. With his views however, it is unnecessary on the present occasion to conflict; for this bill stands upon its own basis, and is not, as I believe, obnoxious to his objections. But I would here merely remark on the subject generally, that it does seem to me reasonable, that this Government being the great landhold r in the West, and in all the new States, should sustain a portion of the expense, in making the principal primary roads.— The owners of the soil in all the new States, whose property is supposed to be increased in value by roads when made, are taxed for making them; and why should the Government be exempt from the fair proportion of the assessment? But the case is still stronger in relation to rivers, which the General Government declared to be public highways, assume jurisdiction of, retain perpetually the ownership of, exclude them from the surveys, and thus prevent them from becoming private property of the citizens, or the property of the States through which they flow. If the Government of the Union has not power to improve them, where does it get the power of jurisdiction over them? For that power of ownership and jurisdiction, necessarily excludes the ownership and jurisdiction of the States. If the states have neither ownership nor jurisdiction, they surely have not the power of taking possession of them, even for the purpose of improving them. If they have no control over the bed of the river, how can they stop a channel here, and open another there, or drain the water into a feeder for the purpose of canals?

The Congress of 1787, by its ordinance, declared the river Wabash a navigable river, and this has been repeated, by numerous subsequent acts in relation to other streams of the new States. The rapids of the Wabash, below Vincennes, say for fifteen miles, will certainly be best improved, by a canal of that length, or perhaps longer. A few years ago, a corps of engineers were instructed to examine many places proposed for the location of a western armory. Now suppose this armory to have been located as I put in motion there, would this Government permit the States of Indiana and Illinois to withdraw the water of that river from a valuable public work, into the feeder of a canal? If the river belongs to the Federal Government, the States cannot, without permission of the Government, enter upon it, even for the purposes of improvement. The power of improvement, then, seems inseparably connected with ownership and jurisdiction. To say that the latter exists in this Government, and not the former, is to say that the improvement can never be made, without a compact on that subject between the Federal Government and that of the State; and no one would contend, that such compact could confer any power, which was not previously in the constitutions of the respective Governments. The power of improving the navigation of rivers, surely belonged to the States before the formation of the Union. It is since, either transferred to the Government of the United States, or not being so transferred, is reserved to the States, or by the formation of the constitution of the United States, it is entirely annihilated. Now, in the case of the Wabash, it is not reserved to the States; for, by compact and ordinance, Congress declared its power over it, declared it a common public highway, and guarantied its free navigation forever. The power, then, to improve this river, not being reserved to the States, it is in the Federal Government, or it is annihilated. That it is not annihilated, but remains in this Government, under the sanction of the constitution of the United States, is obvious and certain, by reference to the sixth article of that instrument itself.

I will now, Mr. President, said Mr. H., proceed to state some reasons for believing that this work of internal improvement, the navigation of the Wabash river, rests upon a basis essentially different from other ordinary objects, such as those chiefly comprised in the harbor bill of 1832. Indeed, I have great reason to believe that the President could not have been in possession of all the facts of the case, or he would have taken a totally different view of the whole matter. In the first instance, then, this is not a new work. It is emphatically an old work; commenced about two years ago, and now in successful progress. A work to which this Government has already appropriated a portion of her public lands, a portion of the very means by which the work is now carried on; for the canal is but an improvement of the river, in and through the State of Indians. And what is this work? It is a work which, when finished, will form a perfect inland navigation, between New York and New Orleans, or the shortest and most eligible route. It is true that the bill before the Senate is to improve the navigation of the Wabash river, and the appropriation, if made, will no doubt be chiefly expended in improving the rapids below Vincennes, possibly by a canal around them; for whether that mode of improvement be now adopted or not, it will no doubt be the mode ultimately adopted. The canal will rather pause than stop at the mouth of the Tippecanoe. So greatly important will be that bank the canals, which the Wabash is destined for a while to supply, that the canal will ultimately be constructed down the entire length of the Wabash, to the Ohio river. And, sir, what was the origin and what is the present condition of this work already begun, under the united auspices of the Federal Government, and that of the State of Indiana.

The origin of the Wabash and Erie Canal, said Mr. H., was a law of Congress of March, 1827, appropriating a quantity of the public lands, equal to five miles in width along its whole line, to aid the State of Indiana in constructing a canal to unite the navigable waters of the Wabash river, with those of Lake Erie. In addition to this important grant of lands, a corps of United States Engineers was detailed to locate the canal, the whole expense being paid by this Government. The canal was located from the Maumee bay, on Lake Erie, across the summit level near Fort Wayne, and down the Wabash river to the mouth of the Tippecanoe. The whole distance is 193 miles; 75 of which are within the limits of the State of Ohio, and the remaining 136, within the State of Indiana. The State of Ohio has, by compact with the State of Indiana, agreed to construct that portion of the canal which lies within her own boundaries; and the State of Indiana has relinquished to her a corresponding portion of the grant. The State of Indiana has entered with spirit on her part of the work. She has sold a portion of her lands, and made other large appropriations, and the work is going rapidly on. It is proper here to remark, that the river below the mouth of Tippecanoe, has also been surveyed by an officer of the Engineer corps, at the expense of the United States. An appropriation for this object was made in 1826. Capt. Smith, of the corps of Engineers, was detailed to the service in 1827, and made his report to the War Department in 1831.

This report, with estimates of that officer, will be found on the tables of this House.

Of the 136 miles spoken of, 70 are under contract, and about 35 at this moment finished. It is furthermore contemplated to finish the work to 1836 or 1837. The State of Ohio, we believe, will not be long after that period, in constructing her portion of it to the Maumee bay, and the idea of being premature then, as has been intimated in asking for this appropriation for the river, will no doubt be the last portion of the river done. It will, in all probability, be found when the canal shall be finished. This work

is vastly more important, than the improvement of any other river of its size. It is more important in the extent and magnitude of the navigation with which it is connected; it the greatness of the commerce which it creates and accommodates, and in the unparalleled extent and productiveness of the regions of country through which it passes.

Another reason why I believe that the improvement of the navigation of the Wabash has stronger claims upon this government than almost any other object presented, is, that the importance of this navigation seems to have been in view of the government, before the constitution was formed. It seems to have been provided for by the Congress of the confederation, and the provision thus made, to have been afterwards sanctioned by the constitution itself. I allude, said Mr. H. to the ordinance of Congress of July, 1787, which is declared to be a compact "unalterable unless by common consent" between the original States, and the People, and States in the northwestern territory, wherein the navigable waters of the Wabash and of the Miami of Lake Erie, and the carrying place between them, are declared to be common high-ways. The ordinance alluded to, is in these words:

"The navigable waters leading into the Mississippi and St. Lawrence, and the carrying places between the same, shall be common highways and forever free, as well to the inhabitants of the said territory, as to the citizens of the United States, and those of any other States, that may be admitted into the confederacy, without any tax, impost, or duty therefor."

Now sir, the people of the Northwestern Territory, at this time the people of the States of Ohio, Indiana, Illinois, and the Territory of Michigan, have never as yet requested any change in this ordinance. It remains now, as it was then. It secures to the people of the then Northwestern Territory, the free navigation of the rivers leading into the Mississippi and the St. Lawrence, as well as the carrying places between them; and although there is no positive stipulation, in so many words, that the Government of the Union shall improve and keep in the condition of usefulness which the country may need and require, those great highways of commerce, yet the implied intention and pledge of the Government to do so, has always appeared to me too strong to be resisted. Nor was the extent or binding obligation of this compact at all weakened, by the constitution of the United States, adopted afterwards; for in that very constitution, by its 6th article it is declared, that "all debts contracted, and engagements entered into, before the adoption of this constitution, shall be as valid against the United States under this constitution, as under the confederation." This ordinance, then, is sanctioned by the constitution itself.

In this view of the question, it has always appeared to me, that instead of constitutional objections to these works of internal improvement, there is a direct constitutional obligation to carry them on and complete them; and I have always thought, that instead of aiding the State of Indians in constructing the canal and improving the river, it was incumbent on the General Government to do both, without the interposition of the State. The carrying places referred to in that ordinance, are well known to have been, that at Fort Wayne, between the Wabash and the Miami of Lake Erie, and that at Chicago, between the waters of the Illinois river, and those of Lake Michigan. There may have been others of less note, but these were the principal ones. That at Fort Wayne was especially well known. Its advantages and importance were perhaps even magnified; and there is little doubt that it was in reference to this, more than to any other, that the clause in the ordinance just referred to, was framed and inserted. This carrying-place had been known and used by Indian traders before and during the Revolution. They had frequently passed over it in rainy and flood seasons of the year, in pirogues and canoes; and subsequent to that period, detachments of United States troops, with their baggage, have frequently passed this portage in the same way.

This, sir, said Mr. H., is not a view of this matter now presented to the Senate for the first time. It is now about nine years since the proposition to make an appropriation of public lands to aid the State of Indiana in improving the navigation of the Wabash and Maumee rivers, was first made by myself to the Senate; and in a report on that subject, which it became my duty to make, as a member of the Committee on Roads and Canals, the ground of obligation, on the part of the federal government, to improve this carrying place, and to aid in this chain of inland navigation, was distinctly taken and presented to the Senate. It was relied on as a strong ground, and one which shielded the application then made from the constitutional difficulty about internal improvements. This ground was then sustained by the Senate. An appropriation of public lands was made to this object in March, 1827; and by the united aid of this appropriation, and of the energies of the State, the canal is now in rapid progress.

The State of Indiana is unable at this time to prosecute and to accomplish this work. She has embarked largely considering her age and her resources, and the canal which she is now pushing rapidly on, is as much as ought to be expected from her at the present time. Where the interests of the General Government, as in the present case, is in unison with those of the States, the object is decidedly one of national importance; and where the obligations of the federal government, in the construction of this work, are paramount to all others, it does seem reasonable that an appropriation should be unhesitatingly granted, to aid in making this improvement; otherwise it must be left undone, till the State of Indiana shall have finished her canal, which canal must still remain, for a great portion of the year, comparatively useless till the river shall be improved.

The People of the western country, as a matter of necessity, consume foreign goods, almost to the entire amount of their surplus productions, and the landholder in that country is deeply interested in every facility of transportation to and from the country. That which diminishes transportation, adds to the value of his agricultural productions, as well as diminishes the cost of foreign goods. Every facility too of transportation, diminishes the difficulty and expense of emigrants in getting to the country; brings more means and more people into the country; saves more of their means to purchase public lands after they get there; increases the receipts into the land offices, and is of lasting benefit to the emigrating classes of the old States. In all ages of the world, of which history gives us any knowledge, whereso ever civilization and the arts of peace have flourished most, there internal improvements have been most fostered by the Government; there roads and canals have been made to subserve the great purposes of agriculture and commerce; and the most warlike nations of the earth have also made these improvements the means of national defence, and used them as the most important facilities in offensive war. But considerations of this kind might be multiplied to an unlimited extent, and I shall not dwell on them.

I have, said Mr. H. the most implicit confidence in the declaration of the President, in which he regrets that he could not give his assent to the Wabash bill. I believe that his feelings and inclination were wholly in its favor, and I sincerely regret that he had not taken the view of the case which I have endeavored to present. Had he taken this view, I cannot but think that he would have come to a different conclusion, and to this different conclusion it does seem to me he might have arrived without in the least receding from any ground he has heretofore taken on the subject of internal improvements.

The rule by which appropriations for the improvement of rivers are confined to places below ports of entry, established by law, has never been satisfactory to my mind, nor does it appear to be very satisfactory to the President himself. It seems to imply, that a work which is unconstitutional to-day, may become constitutional to-morrow, by the simple passage of a law establishing a port of entry at the head of supposed navigation, and that the constitution can be changed and new powers given to it by the legislative power; a power which it has created, prescribed, and limited.

A port of entry on some central position of this extensive navigation will be convenient and useful. It will, probably, soon be indispensable. It was moved in the other House at the last session, and conversations were had with the chairman of the Committee on Commerce here on the same subject. It was thought then to be premature; as the application for aid in improving the river, and constructing the canal had on previous occasions been considered. I am anxious to have the reasonable assistance of the government in perfecting this navigation; and the proper facilities created for using it when perfected. I am disposed then, as I was at the last session, that a port of entry or delivery should be established at Lafayette, upon the Wabash, and have at this time, this additional reason, that I doubt not, it would remove all objetions to an approval of the bill, if it should again pass both Houses. These objections, however, I hope will be done away by other considerations, in addition to those already named, by the rapid progress of the canal since the close of the last session of Congress, and by the advance already made towards a perfect inland navigation between the two commercial emporiums of the country, New York and New Orleans. Important facts exist in the case now, that did not exist at the close of the last session.

Then it was not a fact, that 35 miles of the canal had been finished, and that the water had been let in to the summit level section of the canal. Now, these facts exist. The waters of the St. Joseph, a tributary of the Maumee, already flow upon the summit level of the country and mingle with the waters of the Wabash. The water communication is now continuous, very imperfect to be sure, but it is continuous between the ports of entry and delivery which are numerous on Lake Erie, and those upon the Mississippi.

When Mr. HENDRICKS had concluded—

Mr. HILL remarked that as the Senate was not full, he thought the bill had better be laid on the table, and made a motion to that effect, which was disagreed to.

The question being on the engrossment of the bill for a third reading—

Mr. HILL demanded the yeas and nays, which were ordered.

Before the question was taken—

Mr. POINDEXTER said he had no difficulty whatever in giving his vote upon this bill. But he wished it to be understood, that he did not yield his assent to the distinction, on the score of constitutionality, taken by the President, between the improvement of a river which led to a port of entry, and one upon which there was no port of entry. He would, by no vote of his, sanction such a senseless distinction. The President had repeatedly signed bills for appropriations to improve rivers upon which there were no ports of entry. He had approved an appropriation to the Red river, where there was nothing but wolves and bears; and if a port of entry had been established there, he (Mr. P.) would be at a loss to know what wild annimal of the forest would be appointed there as the Receiver. The objection alluded to had neither the constitution nor common sense to support it. It was one of those refined distinctions which were peculiar to a certain party of the present day.

The question being on the engrossment of the bill, it was determined in the affirmative by the following vote:

YEAS.—Messrs. Benton, Clay, Clayton, Ewing, Frelinghuysen, Hendricks, Kane Kent, Knight, Linn, Naudain, Poindexter, Porter, Robbins, Robinson, Silsbee, Smith, Swift, Tipton, Tomlinson, Waggaman, Webster.—22.

NAYS —Bibb, Black, Brown, Buchanan, Calhoun, Grundy, Hill, King of Alabama, King of Georgia, Leigh, Mangum, Moore, Morris, Preston, Shepley, Tallmadge, White, Wright.—18.

Mr. LINN gave notice that on Monday next he would ask leave to introduce a bill to confirm titles to certain lands in Missouri.

On motion of Mr. WRIGHT,

The Senate adjourned.

HOUSE OF REPRESENTATIVES.

FRIDAY, January 2, 1835.

Petitions were presented by—
Mr. McKIM, of Maryland, and
Mr. WHITE, of Florida.

Mr. POLK, from the Committee of Ways and Means, reported the following bills; which were read twice and committed to a Committee of the Whole House on the state of the Union:

A bill making appropriations for certain fortifications of the United States, heretofore commenced, for the year 1835;

A bill making appropriations for the Naval service for the year 1835;

And a bill to authorize the proper officers of the Treasury Department to credit the account of the Treasurer of the United States with the amount of unavailable funds standing to his debit on the books of the Treasury; and to transfer the amount to the debit of the banks and individuals indebted for the same.

Mr. BANKS, from the Committee of Claims, reported a bill for the relief of the Springfield Manufacturing Company; which was read twice and committed.

Mr. FULTON, from the Committee of Claims, reported a bill for the relief of Davis S. Campbell; which was read twice and committed.

Mr. FULTON, from the same Committee, Mr. KINNARD, from the Committee on Private Land Claims, Mr. TOMPKINS, from the Committee on Revolutionary Pensions, and Mr. FOSTER, from the Committee on the Judiciary, made unfavorable reports upon various petitions, &c. referred to said committees.

Mr. MERCER, from the Committee on Roads and Canals, reported a bill to amend an act granting to the State of Alabama, certain relinquished and unappropriated lands for the purpose of improving the navigation of the Coosa, Black Warrior, and other rivers in said State; which was read twice and committed.

The following resolutions, submitted on Tuesday last, were taken up, and agreed to:

By Mr. FILLMORE:

Resolved, That the Secretary of the Treasury be directed to report to the House the amount of hospital money collected in the several collection districts of the State of New York for each year, from the year 1798 to the present time; and also, the amount expended in each year during the same time, in each of said districts, and for what purposes and objects such expenditures were made, and the amount remaining unexpended at this time for each district; and also, the donations to said fund, and by whom made, and when and in what conditions, if any, and how the money or property given to said fund by donations, has been disposed of or applied, and what compensation or portion of said fund has been expended or applied for collecting, receiving, or paying out the same, and to whom.

By Mr. GALBRAITH:

Resolved, That the Secretary of War be directed to furnish to this House—

A statement of the expenditures on the works at the harbor at Presque Isle, during the past session; the amount paid for stone, giving the number of cords, and at what rate; the amount for timber and other materials, and at what rate; the amount paid for labor, to whom and at what rate per day or month; the amount paid for superintendence, to whom, at what rate per day, and the number of days charged for each service; as well as every other item of expenditure at the said harbor; also, whether the direction of Col. Totten, with regard to taking frequent soundings in the Bay, have been attended to.

The resolution submitted on Tuesday by Mr. THOMAS, of Maryland, to amend the 13th rule of the House so as to include among those who are admitted to the privileged seats within the Hall, the District Attorneys of the United States, was taken up.

Mr. FOSTER remarked, that some of the District Attorneys, and particularly the one who resided in this City, had frequently important business to transact with the members of the Judiciary Committee, and from their exclusion from the Hall, they were compelled to have members call-

ed out of the House. By the adoption of the resolution, it would probably not add more than two persons at any one time to those who already possessed the privilege of the House.

Mr. PATTON moved to amend the resolution, by including also members of the State Legislatures.

Mr. BEATY suggested that the Judges of State Courts should be embraced in the proposition to amend.

Mr. PATTON modified his amendment as requested.

The amendment, as modified, was then disagreed to—yeas 68, nays 70.

Mr. HARDIN moved to lay the resolution on the table; but withdrew the motion at the request of

Mr. THOMAS, of Md., who explained the reasons which had induced him to offer the resolution, which were in substance the same as those which had been given by the gentleman from Georgia, (Mr. Foster.) He could not conceive how the adoption of the resolution could possibly incommode any gentleman, as a very limited number of persons would or could avail themselves of the privilege which it granted.

Mr. HARDIN was opposed to enlarging the rule on this subject. It had already been carried too far. He could not possibly see what business the Auditors, the Register of the Treasury, and some others could have in the House. He did not object to the resolution because it was opposed to the admission of the accomplished attorney for the District of Columbia, into the Hall; but because he was opposed to enlarging a rule which already had the effect of rendering it almost impossible for members to hear what was going on in the Hall. He was a member of the Judiciary Committee, and was not aware that the District Attorney for this District, had ever called on that committee on any business connected with his public duties. The fact was, innumerable applications were made to this House for claims, and the members were continually importuned by lawyers who resided in this city, who were paid a fee for so doing, by claimants. He submitted it as the gentleman from Maryland (Mr. Thomas) if this was not the leading motive which had caused this application on the part of the Attorney of this District.

[Mr. THOMAS said, he was not aware that such was the case. He believed it was not.]

Mr. HARDIN continued. He was satisfied this was one of the motives, if not the leading one, which had induced the application.

Mr. BURGES would have been gratified if the amendment which proposed to admit members of the Legislatures upon the floor of the House, had prevailed. As, however, they are to be excluded, he was not in favor of admitting the District Attorneys. He felt mortified, that this District, after all the liberality which had been extended to it by Congress, should think it necessary to send an attorney here to supervise the proceedings of this House.

Mr. VANDERPOEL remarked, that by a liberal construction of the rule, hereto ore, it was believed that members of the State Legislatures were entitled to the privilege of the House. By the vote on the amendment proposed by the gentleman from Virginia, (Mr. Patton,) a different construction had been given to the rule. As the members of the State Legislatures were excluded, he should feel bound to vote for the exclusion of the District Attorneys. If, however, the vote in relation to the former could be reconsidered, he would willingly vote to admit both classes to the privileged seats in the House.

Mr. MILLER concurred in the remarks of the gentleman from Rhode Island and New York. (Messrs. Burges and Vanderpoel.) He moved to amend the resolution so as to include members of the State Legislatures and District Attorneys, which varied from the amendment which had been rejected, by not including Judges.

Mr. HARDIN moved to lay the resolution and amendment on the table, which was agreed to—Yeas 108, Nays not counted.

On motion of Mr. EVANS,

Resolved, That the Committee on Revolutionary

Pensions be instructed to inquire into the expediency of granting to Abraham Pray, a Revolutionary Pension, and arrears of Pension withheld from him by the War Department, upon the alleged ground of not having perfected his proof reasonably—and that the papers heretofore presented to the House be referred to said Committee.

On motion of Mr. JARVIS,

Resolved, That the Committee on Naval Affairs be instructed to inquire into the expediency of reporting a bill authorizing the President of the United States to cause such experiments to be made by a board of Engineers to be by him selected, as shall test the practical utility of a fire ship invented by Uriah Brown, for harbor and coast defence, and making the necessary appropriations for that purpose.

On motion of Mr. HUBBARD,

Resolved, by the Senate and House of Representatives, That the thanks of Congress be presented to John Quincy Adams, for the appropriate oration delivered by him on the Life and Character of General Lafayette, in the Representatives Hall, before both Houses of Congress, on the thirty-first day of December, 1834, and that he be requested to furnish a copy for publication.

Resolved, That the Chairman of the Joint Committee appointed to make the necessary arrangements to carry into effect the resolution of the last session of this Congress, in relation to the death of General L. Fayette, be requested to communicate to Mr. Adams the aforegoing Resolution, receive his answer thereto, and present the same to both Houses of Congress.

On motion of Mr. WARDWELL,

Resolved, That the Committee on the Post Office and Post Roads be instructed to inquire into the expediency of providing for the publication of the maps the Post Office and Post Roads, and which are now being drawn by David H. Burr.

On motion of Mr. STEWART,

Resolved, That the Committee on the Judiciary be instructed to inquire into the expediency of making more effectual provision for the punishment of perjury committed under the Process Laws of the United States.

On motion of Mr. JOHNSON, of Md.,

Resolved, That a Select Committee be appointed to inquire into the propriety of establishing a National Foundry for the purpose of fabricating ordnance of various kinds, suitable to the wants of the general government, and report to this House by bill or otherwise.

On motion of Mr. HALL, of N. Carolina,

Resolved, That the Committee on the Post Office and Post Roads be instructed to inquire into the expediency of establishing a post route from Godly's Cross Roads, Beaufort county, to Cox's Cary's store, on South Dividing creek, so as to supply Post Office facilities to the population generally on the south side of Pamlico river, as far as may be required.

On motion of Mr. CLAYTON,

Resolved, That the Committee on Naval Affairs be instructed to inquire into the expediency of establishing a Naval Depot at Brunswick, in the State of Georgia.

Mr. GAMBLE submitted the following resolution:

Resolved, That the Secretary of the Treasury be directed to communicate to this House, whether, in his opinion, it is practicable or convenient for the Department to collect, and safely keep and disburse, the public moneys of the United States, without the agency of a Bank, or Banks, and, if so, to report to this House the best and in his opinion, by which that object can be accomplished.

Mr. GAMBLE asked a suspension of the rule which required his resolution to lie one day upon the table. His object was to receive the required information at as early a day as possible.

Mr. POLK said, if the gentleman would refer to the supplementary Report made by the Secretary of the Treasury, he would find the information which he desired. In that report, the Secretary of the Treasury had declared that some of the United States was necessary to facilitate the fiscal operations of the Government, that the

[CONTINUED IN NEXT NUMBER.]

CONGRESSIONAL GLOBE.

BY BLAIR & RIVES.	———WEEKLY———	PRICE $1 A SESSION.

2d Sess......23d Cong.	MONDAY, JANUARY 12, 1835.	Volume 2........No. 6.

TWENTY-THIRD CONGRESS.
SECOND SESSION.

HOUSE OF REPRESENTATIVES.
FRIDAY, Jan. 2, 1835.
[*Continued from last Number.*]

tem adopted by the Department was amply competent, and had proved entirely successful. From the facts and statements embraced in the Report to which he had referred, Mr. P. had no doubt that the plan adopted for the safe-keeping, of the public moneys, was so far completely successful, that it could no longer be denominated "an experiment." Under these circumstances, he could see no necessity for adopting the resolution.

Mr. GAMBLE said, his main object was to know whether any Bank whatever was necessary to be used as the fiscal agent of the Government. If we were to have an agent of this character, he preferred that it should be one emanating from the Government, and belonging exclusively to it. He was as much opposed to the plan of using the State institution for this purpose as he could be to the Bank of the U. States. The plan suggested by the President of the United States in his annual message in 1830, although at the time it met with' no countenance from any quarter, was one which he believed was more practicable, under existing circumstances, than any other—a Bank founded upon the Government deposites and responsibility, entirely disconnected from any State institution, or local stockholders, &c. The Bank of the United States it was conceded on all hands, must go down. Some new and permanent system upon the subject of the keeping and disbursement of the finances of the country must be adopted, and he was anxious to receive all the light which could be thrown on the subject, not only by the Secretary of the Treasury, but by the entire cabinet. The resolution which he had offered could do no harm, and might be beneficial. He therefore hoped it would be permitted to pass.

Mr. CAMBRELENG said, this was a question of considerable importance. The supplementary report of the Secretary of the Treasury would, however, be found entirely explicit in every point embraced in the resolution. He had no great objection to the resolution being sent to the Department, although it was probable the Secretary of the Treasury would refer the House to the report to which he had alluded for the information required. If it was possible to mature a plan to dispense with the agency of Banks in conducting the fiscal operations of the Government, he might not be opposed to it; it was, however, wholly impracticable to dispense with such an agency at this time. In regard to the establishment of a Government Bank, to which the gentleman from Georgia (Mr. Gamble) had alluded, such a project was not now likely to meet with many supporters from any quarter.

Mr. WHITTLESEY, of Ohio, said that as there seemed to be a disposition to discuss the resolution, he would move that the House proceed to the consideration of the orders of the day.

The motion prevailed.

The SPEAKER laid before the House a report from the Secretary of the Navy, pursuant to the act of 1809, in relation to the contingent expenditure of said Department; which was laid on the table.

The SPEAKER laid before the House a communication from the Secretary of War, in response to a resolution of the 11th ult., relating to the sea wall at St. Augustine, in Florida; which was laid on the table.

CLAIM OF DAVID KILBORN.

The Order of the Day being announced, the bill on the relief of David Kilbourn taken up,

Mr. THOMSON, of Ohio, said, he was about to have moved the postponement of the consideration of this bill, inasmuch as it was likely to elicit some further discussion; but from the solicitation of

several friends of the bill, he would withdraw that intention, and hoped the question would be taken on its engrossment.

On the question of engrossing the bill for a third reading, the yeas and nays were demanded, and the motion seconded by the House.

The question was then discussed by Messrs. THOMSON, of Ohio, BRIGGS, WARDWELL, and HUBBARD, in favor of the bill; and Messrs. WHITTESEY, of Ohio, HARDIN, GRENNELL, and LANE, in opposition to it.

Pending this discussion, an unsuccessful motion was made to lay the bill on the table.

The question was then taken by ayes and noes, on the engrossment of the bill, and decided in the negative, ayes 94, noes 97.

So the bill was rejected; and then

The House adjourned.

HOUSE OF REPRESENTATIVES.
SATURDAY, Jan. 3, 1835.

Mr. McINTYRE, from the Committee on Claims, and Mr. LAY, from the Committee on Revolutionary Pensions, made unfavorable reports upon petitions referred to said committees.

The following resolution, submitted yesterday by Mr. GAMBLE, of Georgia, was taken up:

Resolved, That the Secretary of the Treasury be directed to communicate to this House, whether, in his opinion, it is practicable or convenient for the Department to collect, and safely keep and disburse, the public moneys of the United States, without the agency of a Bank, or Banks; and, if so, to report to this House the best mode, in his opinion, by which that object can be accomplished.

Mr. CLAYTON addressed the House in favor of the passage of the resolution. He deemed the principle argument in its favor, the existence of the incontrovertible fact, that Congress did not possess the power to charter incorporations. For inasmuch as it would be incompatible with its constitution of that kind in Philadelphia, yet, by the present system of deposites, we make use of a corporation created by the State of Pennsylvania. He asked if we did not, by this course, do indirection, accomplish that which we could not, constitutionally, by direct means accomplish? The subject for inquiry was to see if we could not separate ourselves entirely, the Government, from all connexion with banking institutions—not only from the Bank of the United States, but from all local Banks also. We are told that the Bank of the United States, with its twenty-four branches, is incompetent to the discharge of the fiscal affairs of the Government. Not from pecuniary inability, but from legal and other sufficient objections. Headed why these same objections would not apply equally to the local institutions? He thought they clearly did. We have been told, said Mr. C. that this great moneyed monopoly—this monster—had interfered with the political affairs of the country—arraying itself in opposition to the Government itself. He would ask where such a moneyed influence could be placed to be more dangerous to the liberties of the People, than in the hands of their rulers? Mr. C. said, the resolution of his colleague (Mr. Gamble) was merely one of inquiry, whether the fiscal operations of the country could not be properly managed, and at the same time dispense altogether with Banks and banking institutions. The People of the South believed they could, and had ever been opposed to moneyed monopolies.

Mr. ALLAN, of Kentucky, said it was not usual to discuss a mere proposition of engrossing. There was, however, some misunderstanding upon this subject. He had read the supplementary report to which reference had been made, and it certainly did not contain all the information required by the resolution. The Report from the Department was elaborate, and recommended the State banks as the fiscal

agents of the Government. The Committee of Ways and Means had reported a bill, in accordance with the recommendations of the Treasury. The resolution, however, went further, and called on the Secretary to state whether his Department could be conducted, in reference to the keeping and disbursement of the public moneys, *without any bank agency whatever.* This information was the more desirable at this time, because of the determination which had been expressed in a certain quarter, to resort as speedily as convenient, to a hard money currency or circulation. If the plan which had been recommended by the Treasury and the Committee of Ways and Means, which proposed to employ the State banks as the fiscal agents of the Government, should be adopted, it would thwart the project of a metallic currency, as the amount of paper money would be thereby greatly increased instead of diminished; and its circulation would also be facilitated by the passage of the bill which had been presented to the Committee of Ways and Means. If the Secretary of the Treasury would present a plan whereby the agency of all banks in conducting the operations of that Department may be dispensed with, it would contribute more than any thing else, to check the issue of bank paper, which now, more than at any other time, was flooding the country, while it would, at the same time, be the best means of furthering the views of those who were in favor of a hard money currency.

Mr. POLK remarked, that there was a time when certain gentlemen on this floor contended that the fiscal operations of the government could only be conducted successfully by the Bank of the United States. A new light seemed to have broken in upon gentlemen, and for the first time they had discovered that no Bank whatever was necessary for this purpose.

[Mr. ALLAN explained. He gave no opinion on the subject. It had been contended by some that Bank agency was unnecessary. He wished to know' the views of the Treasury on this point.]

Mr. POLK continued. The gentleman from Kentucky would find that the precise information which he desired was contained in the report from the Department. In that document the Secretary says:

"After the charter shall expire, no difficulty is anticipated in having any of these duties, which may then remain, discharged by State Banks. But if any should occur, it will become necessary to devolve these duties on some responsible receiver or collector already in office, or on some safe agent not now in office, as has been the practice for years in this country, in paying pensions at convenient places, near which there was no State Bank or branch of the United States Bank, and as has long been the usage in some countries of Europe, by having the public revenue in certain districts chiefly received, kept, and transmitted, through private agents and brokers. *This kind of personal agency, however, is, in the opinion of the undersigned, to be avoided, in all practicable and safe cases, under our present system of selected Banks: because it would render the system less convenient, less secure, and more complex, if not more expensive. Hence it has not yet been resorted to.*

"But it was considered proper to mention this contingency, in order that its effects, if ever anticipated, may beforehand be duly weighed in the examination of the whole subject; and to add, that if th s contingency be extended to the whole establishment of State-Banks, as well as of the United States Bank, on the responsibility that they may all cease to exist, or may refuse to receive and manage the public deposites. However improbable the occurrence of such an event may be,) the fiscal operations of the Government could undoubtedly still proceed, through the personal agencies before mentioned. It is admitted, however, that it would be at some inconvenience, and some increase of expense, unless

remedied in a manner that may hereafter be developed, and would not, in the opinion of this department, and in the present condition of things, be so eligible a system as the present one. Because Banks, though exposed to some dangers and evils, and though not believed to be necessary for the fiscal purposes of any Government, and much less of one in the present happy financial situation of ours, are frankly acknowledged to be, in many respects, a class of agents economical, convenient, and useful."

It would be seen by these extracts, that the Secretary had responded directly and fully to that portion of the resolution upon which gentlemen were desirous of receiving information. In the bill reported by the Committee of Ways and Means, provision is made, in the event of the failure of the State Banks to answer the purposes contemplated, for the safe-keeping and disbursement of the public moneys. The adoption of the resolution was therefore wholly unnecessary, if not improper, as the proposed call upon the Department for a plan which it has not recommended, might have a tendency to delay the action of the House upon the bill reported by the Committee of Ways and Means, which would come up in a day or two as the special order. He was not disposed now to enter into a discussion of the constitutional question, which had been mooted by the gentleman from Georgia, (Mr. Clayton,) but he was prepared to prove, when the bill to which he had referred should come up, that the keeping and disbursing of the public moneys, under the present system, was as safe and convenient as any plan which had been heretofore adopted. Mr. P. concluded by declaring that he did not rise for the purpose of throwing any obstacles in the way of the passage of the resolution; but supposing it possible that amid the lumber on the tables of members, the Report of the Secretary of the Treasury, from which he had read extracts, had been overlooked, he had thought proper to refer to it, in order to show that all the material information sought by the resolution, was already in the possession of the House.

Mr. FILLMORE regretted the existence of this controversy, at the present time. He believed the members of the House were already in possession of all information on this subject that the Department could give. It was not usual, moreover, Mr. F. said, for this House to call upon a Department for a mere opinion—nor did he think it comported with its dignity to do so. The opinion had been advanced, from sources which he had been accustomed to respect, that the employment by the government of a corporation, was equivalent to the creation of such corporate body. From this opinion, he felt bound to dissent. He could see no propriety in the argument. Did it follow that because the government employed rail roads, steam boats, owned by chartered companies, &c. for purposes of transportation, government possessed the power to *create* those companies? Certainly not. The government held the power to create a navy, but it did not follow that it could not legally employ the vessels of companies for all necessary purposes. He thought there was a most palpable distinction between the power to *create* and to *employ*. He concluded by saying he had not contended that Congress had the power to incorporate banking institutions—but he objected to the reasons urged in support of that position. He was disposed to oppose the resolution as essentially unnecessary.

Mr. EWING said, if the Secretary of the Treasury possessed the power to act on this subject, he saw no reason for the interference of Congress. He did not believe that the system which had been adopted had or would prove successful. He referred to the agency which had been assigned to the Receivers of public moneys, as a part of the system adopted by the Department, and denied the utility of such an arrangement. He believed that Congress alone had the right to establish and regulate the depositaries of the public moneys. He was not the advocate of the Bank of the United States. It was known to the world that he had proposed a distinct *projet* on this subject, upon which he desired the action of Congress.—He would, therefore, move to amend the resolution by proposing in lieu thereof that a select committee of one member from each State be appointed, for the purpose of inquiring into the expediency of adopting a plan which he had presented at the last session for the establishment of an institution for the management of the fiscal concerns of the government.

Mr. S. JONES regretted that the resolution had been brought forward at this time; and hoped his colleague would withdraw it. It would lead to no beneficial results, and was calculated to renew the discussion of a question which had been mooted for months during the last session. The information sought could be of no service; and if it could, it would be found substantially in the supplemental report of the Secretary of the Treasury.

But he rose not so much to oppose the resolution as to notice some observations which had been made by those supporting it. His colleague seemed to suppose that, if we could employ the State Banks as fiscal agents, we necessarily had the right to create a bank for that purpose. He could not conceive by what process of reasoning his colleague had brought himself to that conclusion. The State banks had been created by the laws of the different States in the exercise of their rightful and constitutional powers. Congress had nothing to do with, and could not judge of the constitutionality of those institutions. We find them in existence, and the only question for us to determine in regard to them is, whether we will use them as fiscal agents for the collection and disbursement of the revenue of the United States. It is distinct from the question, whether we will create a Bank to act as a fiscal agent; and is entirely unconnected with and independent of it. The Secretary of the Treasury is the fiscal officer of the United States, and with him rests the discretion and responsibility of placing the public money in what depository he pleases. Congress has the power to direct in what places it shall be deposited, and upon what terms and conditions; but in the absence of all law upon this subject, the Secretary of the Treasury must exercise his own discretion, and act upon his own responsibility. And he would assure his colleague that he would at any time join him in limiting the discretion of that officer in passing a law which shall point out where the public money shall be deposited, and the terms and conditions on which the deposites shall be made. And, sir, both the gentlemen (Mr. Clayton and Mr. Ewing) seem to have fallen into another mistake: they contend, that by the establishment of State Banks, an attempt has been made by the States to regulate the currency; and we are told this belongs to Congress and not to the States. Never was there a greater error. Congress has the right to coin money, and regulate the value thereof. So far then from the Banks regulating the currency, the value and currency of Bank notes are regulated by the value of the coin. For, if any Bank does not pay its notes in specie, they must necessarily depreciate, and may become entirely valueless. The State Banks then cannot regulate the currency; nor can the Secretary of the Treasury, in selecting any of them as depositories of the public money, regulate the currency; nor can Congress, by any law in regard to it, regulate the currency.

This Government is and ought to be a hard money government. It was so until Congress, in chartering the Bank of the United States, authorized the payment of debts to the United States, to be paid in its bills, and it will be so again so soon as that charter expires. Congress may make such provision in favor of the State Banks, but never with his consent. No, sir, let the dues to this government be payable in gold and silver. I was opposed to any law which shall authorize the bills of any Bank to be receivable in payment of debts to the Government. Congress may go further, and say no bill of any bank shall be received in payment. But this would be useless. None will be taken, unless it can be redeemed in gold and silver; and while a bank is able and willing to redeem its bills in gold and silver, you may prevent their payment to the Government, but you cannot by any law prevent the people from taking them.

Nay more. Though you may require your collectors to demand gold and silver in payment, you cannot prevent the People from calling on those very Banks for the gold and silver, into which it will be again deposited by the collector, as soon as it is received. And to save all this trouble, the importer will deposite the bills in the Bank, for which it is bound to pay him specie, and he will take to the collector a certificate of the cashier that his check will be paid in gold and silver.

You may also prevent the State Banks from being made the depositories of the public money. But this, so far from proving a benefit, will prove an expense, useless and unnecessary. You must erect buildings suitable for such depositories, and you must employ guards to protect them. All this expense may be saved by the employment of State banks. If they will answer all the purposes of the Government as fiscal agents, there will be no necessity for a Bank of the United States. It will not then be a *necessary* and proper means for carrying into effect any of the powers granted by the constitution, and not being *necessary*, it cannot ever be pretended to be constitutional.

Mr. McKIM moved to lay the resolution on the table. He suggested that the House was already in possession of all the information required.

On this question Mr. GAMBLE called for the yeas and nays.

Mr. WHITTLESEY, of Ohio, called for the Order of the Day, but the call was rejected.

The yeas and nays were then ordered, and taken as follows. Aye 106, nays 87.

YEAS.—Messrs. J. Adams, H. Allen, Wm. Allen, Joseph B. Anthony, Banks, Bean, Blair, Bockee, Boon, Bouldin, Brown, Bunch, Burns, Bynum, Cambreleng, Carr, Casey, Chinn, S. Clark, Wm. Clark, Clay, Coulter, Cramer, Day, P. Dickerson, Ferris, Fillmore, Fowler, Philo C. Fuller, Wm. K. Fuller, Fulton, Gillet, Joseph Hall, E. Hall, Halsey, Hamer, Joseph M. Harper, Harrison, Hathaway, Hawes, Hazeltine, Henderson, Hiester, Howell, Hubbard, Huntington, Janes, R. M. Johnson, N. Johnson, Henry Johnson, S. Jones, B. Jones, Kavanagh, Kilgore, Kinnard, Lane, Lansing, Laporte, G. W. Lay, L. Lea, T. Lee, Loyall, Lucas, Lytle, Abijah Mann, J. K. Mann, Manning, Moses Mason, May, McIntire, McKay, McKim, McLene, McVean, Miller, R. Mitchell, Morgan, Murphy, Osgood, Parker, Patterson, F. Pierce, Polk, Pope, Reynolds, Schenck, Schley, W. B. Shepard, A. H. Shepperd, Shinn, Smith, Standifer, Stewart, W. Taylor, Thomson, Turner, Turrill, Van Houten, Wagener, Ward, Wardwell, Wayne, Webster, Wilson.—106.

NAYS.—Messrs. J. Q. Adams, J. J. Allen, C. Allan, Archer, Ashley, Barber, Barringer, Bates, Baylies, Beaty, Binney, Briggs, Bull, Burd, Burges, Cage, Chilton, Claiborne, Clayton, Clowney, Corwin, Crane, Crockett, Darlington, Amos Davis, Davenport, Deberry, Denny, Dickson, Evans, E. Everett, Ewing, Felder, Foster, Gamble, Garland, Gordon, Gorham, Graham, Grennell, Griffin, Hardin, James Harper, Heath, R. Jackson, W. C. Johnson, King, Letcher, Lewis, Lincoln, Love, Lyon, Martindale, Marshall, Mardis, J. Y. Mason, Maury, Moore, Patton, Phillips, Pickens, Potts, Ramsey, Reed, Rencher, Robertson, Slade, Sloane, Spangler, Steele, W. P. Taylor, P. Thomas, Tompkins, Trumbull, Tweedy, Vance, Vinton, Wilmough, Whittlesey, Wilde, Williams, Wise, Young.—87.

So the House concurred in the motion to lay the resolution on the table.

Mr. DICKSON laid a motion on the table to reconsider the vote of yesterday on the claim of David Kilbourn; the consideration of which was postponed to Friday next.

Mr. CHILTON submitted the following resolution:

Resolved, That the Committee on Roads and Canals be instructed to inquire into the subject, and report their opinion to this House, of the most equal and just mode of applying the revenues of the country to such works of public improvement within the respective States of this Union, as may be necessary for the facilitating of commerce with foreign nations, and among the several States. And that they moreover report their opinion of

the best and most practicable mode of ascertaining and determining the nationality and importance of such improvements as may be proposed within the said several States.

Mr. CHILTON remarked, that this day was set apart for the consideration of private bills; and if any gentleman would move to proceed to the consideration of the orders of the day, he would postpose the remarks which he desired to make in favor of the adoption of the resolution which he had presented.

Mr. E. WHITTLESEY moved that the House proceed to the consideration of the orders of the day; which was agreed to.

The SPEAKER laid before the House a resolution of the Legislative Council of Michigan Territory, relative to the boundary line between the State of Ohio and said Territory; and also a resolution relative to the construction of a harbor in the Territory aforesaid. Referred.

The SPEAKER laid before the House a communication from the First Comptroller of the Treasury, transmitting a list of balances on the books of the Fourth Auditor, for the last three years, &c.; which was laid on the table.

The following bills from the Senate were read twice, and committed:

A bill making appropriations for completing the Military Barracks at New Orleans;

A bill providing for the legal adjudication and settlement of the claims to land therein mentioned; And a bill for the relief of Col. John Eugene Leitensdorfer.

ORDERS OF THE DAY.

The bill for the relief of Mrs. Susan Decatur, and others, coming up as first in order—

Mr. VINTON moved to postpone its further consideration to Friday next.

Mr. PATTON hoped that the motion would not prevail. It was time that this bill was disposed of.

After some further remarks on the propriety of proceeding to the consideration of the bill, by Messrs. VINTON, CAMBRELENG, PATTON, and ARCHER, the motion to postpone was rejected.

Mr. GILLET said he presumed, in as much as this subject had been, for a series of years before Congress, that every member present was fully acquainted with its merits, and prepared to vote on it. He understood it had been here so long that the elder Reporters could report the speeches pro. and con. without hearing them. Further discussion could not, certainly, be necessary. In order that a vote might be now taken on the main question, he moved to lay the bill and amendments on the table.

Mr. HUBBARD said, as the motion of the gentleman from New York (Mr. Gillet) was a test question, and as there was a thin attendance of members, he would move a call of the House.

The motion was negatived.

The question recurring on the motion to lay the bill and amendments on the table, it was decided in the affirmative—Yeas 96, Nays 90. So the said bill was virtually rejected.

The following bills were read twice and ordered to be engrossed for a third reading:

A bill for the relief of James Gardiner;

A bill for the relief of the legal representatives of Bayley E. Clark;

A bill for the relief of Henry Awkward;

A bill to authorize the Secretary of State to issue letters patent to James Jones;

And a bill for the relief of the heirs of Nathaniel Tyler, deceased.

The bill for the relief of Commodore Isaac Hull, was taken up.

The question being upon an amendment reported by the Committee of the Whole, a discussion ensued in which Messrs. WARD, HARDIN, REED, BURGES, and PEARCE of Rhode Island participated. Before the latter gentleman had concluded his remarks, Mr. CLAY moved an adjournment which carried.

And the House adjourned.

IN SENATE.

MONDAY, Jan. 5, 1835.

Petitions and memorials were presented by Messrs. SILSBEE, WHITE, POINDEXTER, KANE, and TYLER.

Mr. ROBINSON presented joint resolutions from the Legislature of Illinois, praying Congress to establish a Marine Hospital on the western waters. :

The VICE PRESIDENT laid before the Senate a communication from the State Department with a list of patents, and the names of the several patentees which have expired for the year 1834.

He also laid before the Senate a letter from the Secretary of State, containing statistical tables of the property, population, taxes, &c., of the several States of the Union, not before communicated.

He also laid before the Senate joint resolutions of the Legislative Council of Michigan Territory; which were referred to the Judiciary committee.

He also laid before the Senate a communication from the War Department, with a report of the Commissioner of Pensions relative to the number of applications for pensions which have been rejected since the last annual report.

Mr. WHITE presented the petition of Samuel Martin, of Knox county, Tenn., on subjects in general which the petitioner thought of importance. Mr. W. said he was at some loss to designate the Committee to which the petition could be most appropriately referred; but as the first subject touched upon in it was perhaps considered by the petitioner of the greatest moment, and as that had relation to the navy, he moved to refer it to the Naval committee; which was agreed to.

On motion of Mr. POINDEXTER, the bill for the relief of Silas D. Fisher was taken up, and, on his motion, it was then referred with the documents, to the Committee on Public Lands.

The following resolutions were submitted:

By Mr. LEIGH:

Resolved, That the Secretary of the Treasury be requested to lay before the Senate, a copy of any letter or letters from his Department to the receivers of public moneys, or any of them, in the course of the last year, (if any such letter or letters have been written,) purporting to contain information and instructions to the said receivers, that for the mutual accommodation of the public officers and creditors in their neighborhood, of the receivers, and of the Treasury Department, he, the Secretary, proposed thereafter, to direct warrants in their favor to such receivers, for payment, when required by them; and further, that it would be in the power of such receivers, also before a warrant should be obtained by such public officers and creditors, and whenever such receivers should have confidence in their honesty and solvency, to take a draft or assignment by them in their own favor, of their supposed claim on the Treasury, to pay its amount, and, on its being forwarded to the Treasury, to receive a warrant in their own behalf, for the sum due; and that all the warrants paid in the manner first stated, or received in the name of such receivers, would be ample vouchers in their behalf on the settlement of their accounts. And that the Secretary of the Treasury, in case such instructions and authority, as are above mentioned, or any of like import, were in fact given by him to the said receivers of public moneys, be requested to communicate to the Senate the particular reasons, if any there were, not mentioned in the letters themselves, which induced him to give the same, and to state, moreover, to what receivers of public moneys such letters and instructions have been sent, and what has been the practice of such receivers, and of the Treasury Department, in consequence thereof.

By Mr. CALHOUN:

Resolved, That a Select Committee be appointed to inquire into the extent of Executive patronage; the circumstances which have contributed to its great increase of late; the expediency and practicability of reducing the same, and the means of such reduction; and that they have leave to report by bill or otherwise.

By Mr. LEIGH:

Resolved, That the Committee on Claims be instructed to inquire into the expediency and propriety of making an appropriation to compensate James Points, Marshal of the western district of Virginia, for extraordinary services, rendered by him to the public, in detecting, apprehending, and bringing to justice a band of counterfeiters, who were flooding the country with counterfeit

money, or bank notes; and to compensate George Smith, C. M. Varner, Peter Koremer, and others, who aided the Marshal in rendering the said services. And that the said Committee do call on the Secretary of the Treasury for information relative to this subject.

By Mr. WRIGHT:

Resolved, That the Secretary of the Treasury be requested to report to the Senate the progress which has been made in his department under the resolution of the Senate of the 28th of February, 1823, directing to be prepared and laid before the Senate, maps of the several States of Ohio, Illinois, Indiana, Mississippi, Alabama, and Louisiana, and of the Territories of Michigan, Arkansas, and Florida; whether the said maps or any number of them have been completed according to the direction of said resolution; what is the state of advancement upon such of said maps as have not been completed; whether the means are in the possession of the department to complete the said maps; and whether any of the said maps heretofore completed and laid before the Senate have been posted up so as to conform to the existing condition of the lands and to what date each map has been so posted up.

Mr. HENDRICKS from the Committee on Roads and Canals, reported the joint resolution from the House of Representatives giving the right of way to the Winchester and Potomac Railroad Company through the public ground at Harper's Ferry; which, on his motion, was taken up, considered as in Committee of the Whole, and ordered to be engrossed for a third reading.

Mr. HENDRICKS, from the same Committee, reported a bill to authorize the Tallahassee rail road company to locate their road through certain public lands of the United States; which was read the first time, and ordered to a second reading.

Mr. HENDRICKS, from the same Committee, also reported a bill for the completion of certain improvements in Florida.

The resolution submitted by Mr. KENT on Friday last, for an inquiry into the expediency of the Government purchasing Fort McHenry, was taken up, considered, and agreed to.

The bill authorizing the enlistment of boys in the Navy, and

The bill to change the titles of certain naval officers, were severally read the third time, and passed.

The bill to exempt merchandise imported under certain circumstances from the operation of the tariff act of 1828, being on its third reading—

Mr. BENTON rose to invoke the attention of the Senate to the principles which the bill involved, and the amount of money it might take from the Treasury. He said, when it was before the Senate on Friday last, and was ordered to be engrossed for a third reading, it had attracted so little attention, and caused so little to be said, that scarcely any one comprehended its magnitude, and to his knowledge two Senators sitting in the recess of a window, under the colonnade, and within his view at the time, did not even suspect that a bill which might take a million and a half of dollars from the Treasury, besides violating great principles, was passing its ordeal, and was ordered to be engrossed for a third reading. The remarks from the Senator from New York, (Mr. Wright,) was the only thing which awakened his own attention, and put him on his guard so far as to vote against it.

The bill, said Mr. B. violates the plainest principles, and lays the example of the most dangerous precedent. It was to grant relief against an act of Congress, passed on purpose, and with the full view to operate as it has done. There is no pretence of mistake, or fraud, but a naked attempt to give back money collected under a law of Congress, made on purpose, and after debates and votes, to collect that very money. Every Senator who was here, said Mr. B. in 1828, will recollect the strenuous efforts which we made to put off to some day beyond the 30th of June; the taking effect of the tariff act of that year; and how all these attempts were voted down, and only one section of the act, eventually allowed to be postponed. Mr. B. said, many Senators now present, could recollect all this, but, for the benefit of

others, come in since, he would read some passages from the Senate journal. Mr B. then read to show two motions made by General Smith, of Maryland, to postpone the taking effect of the bill, one of them to the 30th September, the other, on the failure of that motion, to the 15th of September. He read the yeas and nays upon both these motions, by which it was seen that both were rejected; and now, be said, the parties were reversed; those who voted against giving time to the importing merchants then, vote for giving money to them now; and those who voted for giving them time, of whom he was one, now voted against giving the money. And he did so upon the plain principle that the act was passed on purpose, and to operate just as it did; and to give back the money now, would be to introduce a principle under which the difference between the amounts of all tariff acts may be refunded at any indefinite period; for this bill for relief goes up the end of December, seven or eight months after the passing of the tariff act of 1828, and after which there is nothing in its principle to keep it from coming to the present day. Another unjust principle was, that the amount of the difference of duty was to be refunded to the importing merchants, and not to the consumers, who had already refunded them their duties, with their profit upon it.

The amount which might be taken from the Treasury, under the bill, next claimed Mr. B.'s attention. He thanked the gentleman from New York (Mr. Wright,) for the information that he had given on this point. It was, that from an answer given by the Secretary of the Treasury some time ago, upon a former presentation of this bill, which then only went up to the 30th of September, that about $450,000 would be withdrawn under it. Now, said Mr. B., this bill goes to the 31st of December, covers the great importations of the fall, and will probably take three times as much as it formerly would, say one million and a half. This was a great sum, Mr. B. said, and its greatness was getting it along. He believed it had been found necessary to enlarge the scope of the bill—to double, and more than double its grasp—to get it along—to extend it from two months to five months, and from the light importations of June and July, to the heavy ones of October. Another thing he disliked in this bill—it had a lobby member to nurse it! Mr. B. was against all the bills, in his first impulsions, which had lobby nurses. It was an attendance found objectionable in all the State Legislatures, and not less so here. The constitution of the United States had provided for the representation for the People. Every section of the Union had representatives on the floor; to have others in the lobby to push the great money claims, was unknown to the constitution, might be of evil effect; and be was against the practice.

Mr. B. said the Secretary of the Treasury ought to be consulted, to know how much money this bill might withdraw; whether he had the means to pay it; and if not, how would he provide for it? by loans, or by taxes, and the revival of the tariff? He said enormous bills were depending to absorb the revenues; not the bills which carry on the Government, but which members originate. He would name three alone in this Senate; this refunding bill, say of $1,500,000; the French spoliation bill $5,000,000; the divide-out land bill, $3,500,000. Here, he said, is ten millions of extra appropriations at once; which is half the whole annual revenue; while that whole revenue, with the exception of only about a quarter of a million to spare, was required by the ordinary appropriations. He said it was in vain to rejoice at the extinction of the public debt, if such enormous and wasteful projects as these could succeed.

Mr. WEBSTER said, he had no desire that the bill should pass without every member of the Senate understanding its principles as well as its details. When the bill was first reported, he thought that it was so well understood that there was no reason to enter into a further explanation of it. It was originally introduced in 1829 or '30, and the subject had been brought before the Senate by the Chairman of the Committee on Commerce, the member from Maryland, (Mr. Chambers,) in '32; that it was then fully discussed and understood as now explained by his colleague, (Mr. Silsbee.) That it was then reported to the Senate, and passed without opposition, in precisely the same form in which the Committee had now reported it. That it was not agreed to by the House of Representatives, and returned to the Senate. It was again acted upon at the last session, in its present form, and received the sanction of the Senate without a discussion. As no objection had been made to the features of the bill on former occasions, the Committee had now reported it without amendment, and in the same form in which it had received the former sanctions of the Senate. As the question was on the third reading, he was not disposed to enter at length into a discussion of the bill. If gentlemen wished for further information, if they wished to investigate more thoroughly the bearings of the bill, as the measure was an important one, one which would take a large sum from the Treasury, he would not object to the inquiry. But he saw nothing alarming in its appearance; it had often passed in the same form. He could recommend it generally; that the claims formed different classes, to be sure, in some of which the equity was clearer than in others.

Mr. BUCHANAN said he had the misfortune, on this question, to differ from the Senator from Missouri, (Mr. Benton.) He need not say he entertained a great respect for his judgment; but he would remark, that, to himself, the principle of the bill was perfectly clear. He had thought so on Friday last, when he voted for its engrossment, and still continued to be of the same opinion.

He inquired, what was the true principle of the bill? In all civilized countries, it was a uniform, cardinal principle, that all laws should be prospective, and never retrospective. It would be unjust, in the highest degree, to subject the citizens of a country to the operation of a law before it was possible that they could be acquainted with its existence. This was a principle of such manifest justice, that it could not be denied, or even doubted. Sufficient time ought always to be given to enable those whom the law was destined to effect to become acquainted with it, and to accommodate their conduct to its provisions. It was upon this very principle that France had agreed to indemnify American citizens for the captures made under the Berlin and Milan decrees, before they could have known of the existence of these decrees. This is the very principle upon which the present bill rests. Its object is to grant relief from the onerous effects of the tariff law of April, 1828, in cases in which our importing merchants were not and could not be acquainted with its existence in time to regulate their conduct by a knowledge of its provisions. This law had, consequently, operated retrospectively upon their interests, and, therefore, unjustly. What, then, was the object of the bill? It was to do no more than ought to have been done by the act of 1828. It was merely to correct the injustice which had resulted from our own legislation.

This bill seemed to be exceedingly well guarded against fraud No person could obtain relief under its provisions, until he had satisfied the Secretary of the Treasury, not only that he had ordered goods from a foreign country before he could have known of the passage of the act of 1828, but also that after he had been informed of its passage, it was too late to countermand the order. This was indispensable. But more than this was required. A person claiming relief, must, in addition, satisfy the Secretary of the Treasury, by his own oath, or other proof, that he had actually sustained a loss in consequence of his ignorance of the existence of the act; and an indemnity for this loss was all which could be demanded.

He was as desirous as any gentleman could be of taking care of the public money; but he was equally disposed to do justice. He would vote for a general re-commitment of the bill, because he thought that it might with propriety be confined to importations made at an earlier day than the 31st December, 1828, and he was willing to restrict its operation within the narrowest limits which justice would admit. But let the bill come before us when it may, he would vote for it; because he was unwilling to bind our citizens by a law with which they could not, by any possibility, have been acquainted in time to save themselves from injury. This injustice had been done by the act of 1828, and he was anxious to correct it, and thus relieve the character of our legislation from the odium which must attach to it by the passage of an act in its nature retrospective.

Mr. SILSBEE said there had been a palpable violation of justice, which this bill was going to remedy. The Senate had acted upon it three times already, and he was opposed to further delay. That the honorable Senator (Mr. Benton) had estimated the amount this bill proposed to refund at a million and a half, but it was all supposition—mere conjecture—he had not looked into the provisions of the bill; if he had, he would have found that the importer, in order to obtain the benefit of this act, would be obliged to show that the goods had been ordered in foreign countries, where the orders could not have been countermanded in reason to prevent the purchase, which was a difficult thing to show, and consequently the number of cases would be diminished. His only objection to the call for information was want of time. He was desirous it might be sent to the House at an early day.

Mr. KANE said he preferred the reference of the bill without the specific instructions. All laws affecting the interests of individuals should be prospective. Certainly France agreed to make indemnity for captures under the Berlin and Milan decrees, but then she fixed upon a time, beyond which compensation should cease—seventy days, he believed, after their promulgation. Laws, in order not to have a retroactive bearing, should have some time fixed for them to take effect. And with regard to this bill, if the 30th of September was inserted in the bill, he would vote for it. He wished the bill recommitted, more particularly for the purpose of calling the attention of the committee to the provision authorizing the merchant to be refunded who did not realize the ordinary profits. No human being could lay down a rule which could apply to such a case as this.

Mr. BENTON, in reply to the remarks (by Mr. Webster) that this bill had repeatedly passed the Senate, and with little opposition, said that he had been fourteen years a member of the Senate, and would have been but an inattentive observer not to have seen, and felt that the gentlemen here from the sea board, and great cities, deem it quite an act of supererogation for members from the interior,—from the heart of the forest,—to undertake to illuminate the Senate upon commercial, or financial subjects; therefore such members seldom spoke upon such bills; and as for the gentlemen from the commercial cities, they could not do it without seeming to attack their own constituents. The money is to go to their own constituents, and are they to stop it? Every gentleman knew, he said, that a money bill, the proceeds of which went to a member's constituents, was the most trying vote to which his firmness could be put. Even a small sum,—a few thousand dollars for a vile creek,—cannot be opposed without raising a cry against him. He has voted against his own constituents, would be the loud and incessant cry! Gentlemen from the great cities, then, cannot oppose this million and a half, without being subject to the cry of opposing their own constituents; gentlemen from the interior cannot without being stared at as obtrusive, and handling things not exactly within their sphere. Hence this bill had passed several times, and was on the point of passing again, without being noticed. But is silent passage an argument in favor of a bill? On the contrary was it not a maxim, that the worst measures are generally those which pass unanimously and silently? The resolution for a revolutionary history, by which a couple of gentlemen of this city might take from the treasury indefinite millions; did it not pass *sub silentio*? Was not every gentleman astonished at the last session when he heard what he had done? And is it not now thought to be a plume in the cap of the present Secretary of State, that he is trying to limit those millions to $400,000? But he trusted Congress, which could do, what the Secretary could not, would stop it altogether. He hoped the printing jobs were going to receive the attention

of the Senate and the people. The revolutionary pension bill, said Mr. B., of 1818, did not that pass in this good easy manner, and upon a calculation that it would take but $200,000 a year, and with regrets that it could only take it for a few years; while we have since seen it amount to five millions in a year, and is now costing us more money than ever was expended in any year of the revolution, and displays an army of revolutionary pensioners, at half a century after the war, greater than ever Washington saw during the war.

Mr. B. replied to the Senator from Pennsylvania, (Mr. Buchanan,) and concurred with him in the justice of all he had said, so far as his doctrine was general, but denied its applicability to this subject, because Congress in 1828 had considered the very point, and passed the law for the very purpose of making it take effect before it could be known; and they did so upon the ground that the importer would add the new duties to the price of his goods, and get it all back, with a profit, out of the consumer. Mr. B. said such laws, to take effect before they could be known, were condemned in all codes. The civil law, from the code of Justinian, to the code Napoleon, which was framed upon it, made a beautiful provision for the promulgation and taking effect of laws; they were to take effect one day after promulgation in the place where passed, and so on, in so many successive days in no many successive circles, around the capital, the days increasing with the distance, until the empire was embraced, and the law had time to reach its furthest boundary. To do otherwise, and make laws, especially penal ones, to take effect before they could be known, was to imitate the tyrant that posted his edicts, in small letters, on the tops of lofty columns, where nobody could read them—all this, said Mr. B. was urged against the early taking effect of this tariff act of 1828; but it was answered, that it was necessary to make it take effect immediately to catch the impending importations, and to prevent immense orders from being sent out to fill up the country with goods before the act would take effect, and thus defeat the relief that was intended for the manufacturers; and as to the merchants, it was said it made no difference to them; they would be reimbursed the additional duty, with a profit, from the consumer. And now, said Mr. B. what do we see? a complete reversal of arguments and votes! an absolute rally, which he would call rally No. 1, for it might be the first of a series, of the old high-tariff party, now standing together as one man in this chamber, to oppose and reverse what they did in 1828, and to take a course which must lead to debt, or taxes,—to loans, or the renewal of the high tariff!

Turning to the Senator from Massachusetts that sat nearest to him, (Mr. Silsbee,) Mr. B. said it was certainly true what he had stated, that goods had fallen, instead of rising under the tariff law of 1828. Mr. B. knew something about that. He had seen an order arrive in the West to march a regiment of infantry (Col. Leavenworth's) from the Missouri frontier to the Canada frontier; an order which interpolated a new practice in our military system, that of guarding the coast against smugglers, like French conscripts during the continental system; an order which announced the evil without curing it; for what could a regiment of infantry do to prevent smuggling upon a line of a thousand miles of lakes, rivers, forests? The smuggling had sunk the price of goods, and that was fixed at a thousand times before it took place.

Mr. WEBSTER rose again. He was not bound, he said, to make out the consistency of other Senators who had formerly voted on this subject.—There seemed to be a mistake occasioned by the manner in which the bill had passed. That act was started in the other House; that certain sections were limited to the 30th of June; but upon the amendment of the bill the 30th of June was stricken out, and the 30th of September inserted at such a way as to cause the error. That the power of the act had been unjust through inadvertency and mistake.

Mr. BENTON said, that as to himself, he certainly was under a mistake as to the amendment mentioned by the Senator from Massachusetts, [Mr. Webster,] and so far as any gentleman said the mistake deceived him, he certainly would not include such a gentleman under his remark; but he believed that the whole Senate of 1828 could not say that they were under a mistake in the amendment which postponed one section only of the act.

After some little conversation between Messrs. BENTON, KANE, WEBSTER, BIBB, and WRIGHT, with regard to the instructions, as part of Mr. Barrow's motion, the question being divided, the bill was recommitted, and the instructions laid on the table.

The Senate then proceeded to the consideration of the

SPECIAL ORDER,

Being the bill making compensation for French spoliations prior to 1800.

Mr. ROBBINS having the floor, spoke at length in support of the bill; but he was so imperfectly heard in the gallery, that we cannot give a report of his speech.

Without concluding, Mr. ROBBINS yielded the floor to Mr. KNIGHT, upon whose motion,

The Senate adjourned.

HOUSE OF REPRESENTATIVES.

MONDAY, January 5, 1835.

Mr. PLUMMER, of Mississippi, appeared and took his seat.

Petitions and Memorials were presented by—

Messrs. McINTIRE, HALL, and SMITH, of Maine;

Messrs. BRIGGS, PHILLIPS, EVERETT, and GRENNELL, of Massachusetts;

Mr. HALL, of Vermont;

Messrs. DAY, CAMBRELENG, FILLMORE, GILLET, and TURRILL, of New York;

Mr. PARKER, of New Jersey;

Messrs. MUHLENBERG, BANKS, CLARK, and MILLER, of Pennsylvania;

Messrs. McKIM, HEATH, and THOMAS, of Maryland:

[Mr. McKim said—I am requested to present the memorial of a number of citizens of Baltimore, praying that the Forts, recommended by a Board of Engineers many years past to be erected for the defence of Baltimore, may be commenced, or such other works as may be deemed necessary. Having the honor to represent, in part, the citizens of Baltimore on this floor, I ask leave of the House to say a few words in explanation and support of the memorial.

It is, I presume, well known, that Baltimore is the emporium of the State of Maryland, and now ranks as the third city in the Union, in size and population. In the late war with Great Britain, her citizens supported the rights of the nation with all their energy; and when a powerful British army, under the command of a successful General, landed at North Point, in 1814, to capture the city, her citizens, both old and young, marched to meet the invading foe. A battle ensued—the commanding General of the enemy was slain, and Baltimore had to deplore the loss of a number of her brave citizens. The enemy retreated, without accomplishing the object for which they came—peace took place shortly after, and the Government appointed a Board of Engineers to examine and report on such places as might require works of defence. The Board reported in 1821, and, among others, recommended two works, of the first and second class, to be erected for the defence of Baltimore. The first class to be commenced as soon as possible, and the second at a later period. Thirteen years have passed since this report was made, and, while a great number of the works recommended in the report have been commenced and nearly completed, I regret to state, that those mentioned for Baltimore have been entirely passed over. The cause I know not; but the fact is so. Surely the lives and property of the citizens of Baltimore are as much entitled to protection from this Government as those in any other part of the Union. The entire property at risk in Baltimore may be estimated at one hundred million of dollars, and only one Fort to protect the harbor, and that, as I am informed, not in so good a condition, at present, as at the close of the late war. The citizens of Baltimore place every dependence on the justice of Congress, and

expect that the same protection will be afforded to Baltimore as has been done to the neighboring cities, and other points of the Union.]

Messrs. ALLEN, PATTON, CHINN, TAYLOR, CLAIBORNE, and MOORE, of Virginia;

Messrs. WAYNE and GILMER, of Georgia;

Messrs. POPE, ALLAN, CHILTON, and JOHNSON, of Kentucky;

[Mr. POPE presented the petition of Thomas McIntosh, of Kentucky, praying to be placed on the pension roll.]

Messrs. PEYTON and DUNLAP, of Tennessee;

Messrs. CRANE, SLOANE, PATTERSON, SPANGLER, VINTON, and WEBSTER, of Ohio;

Mr. GARLAND, of Louisiana;

Mr. EWING, of Indiana;

Mr. MAY, of Illinois;

Mr. MARDIS, of Alabama;

Messrs. BULL and ASHLEY, of Missouri;

Mr. SEVIER, of Arkansas;

Mr. WHITE, of Florida.

Which petitions and memorials were appropriately referred.

Mr. MERCER, from the Committee on Roads and Canals, reported a bill to amend an act entitled an act authorizing the construction of a bridge across the Potomac, and repealing all other acts in relation to the same; which was read.

Mr. MERCER said, as the bill did not invoke an appropriation of money, and was intended merely to legalize a slight deviation from the plan which had been heretofore authorized for the construction of the bridge, he hoped the bill would be permitted to progress without being committed.

The bill was read a second time, and ordered to be engrossed.

Mr. MILLER, from the Committee on Invalid Pensions, reported a bill for the relief of George C. Seaton; which was read twice and committed.

Mr. MITCHELL, from the Committee on Invalid Pensions, reported a bill for the relief of John Bryan; which was read twice and committed.

Mr. JANES, from the Committee on Invalid Pensions, reported a bill granting a pension to James Swallow; which was read twice and committed.

Mr. FORESTER, from the Committee on Invalid Pensions, reported a bill for the relief of John Sanders and others; which was read twice and committed.

Mr. GORDON asked the consent of the House to submit and have printed an amendment to the bill reported by the Committee of Ways and Means, to regulate the deposites of the public money in the State Banks.

Objection being made, Mr. G. asked a suspension of the rule in order to enable him to make the motion indicated.

The motion to suspend the rule prevailed--

When Mr. GORDON offered an amendment to the bill referred to; which was ordered to be printed.

Mr. EWING offered the following resolution, which, under the rule, lies one day:

Resolved, That the President of the United States be requested to transmit, or cause to be transmitted, to this House, copies of every circular letter of instruction, emanating from the Treasury or War Departments, since the 30th day of June last, and addressed to either the receiving or disbursing officers stationed in States where land offices are established, or public work are constructing, under the authority of Congress.

Mr. GAMBLE offered the following resolution, which, under the rule, lies one day:

Resolved, That the Secretary of the Treasury be directed to digest and prepare and communicate to this House, a detailed plan by which the public revenue of the United States may be collected, safely kept, and disbursed, without the agency of a Bank or Banks, either State or National.

On motion of Mr. WHITTLESEY, of Ohio,

Resolved, That the report of the Secretary of War, relative to the extension and completion of the pier at Cunningham's Creek, in Ohio, with the documents that accompany the said report,

referred to the Committee on Roads and Canals, with instructions to inquire into the expediency of making the necessary appropriations for extending and completing said work.

On motion of Mr. CLAY,

Resolved, That the Committee on Roads and Canals be instructed to inquire into the expediency of relinquishing to the State of Alabama the two per cent. of the net proceeds of sales of the public lands, which have taken place since the first day of September, 1819, or may hereafter take place, by the terms of the contract between the United States and that State, on her admission into the Union, for making a road, or roads, leading to the said State, to be applied under the direction of the Legislature of Alabama in the construction of a rail road or canal to connect the waters of Mobile Bay with those of the Tennessee river; or to create a fund for the support of primary schools, as said Legislature may determine.

On motion of Mr. JOHNSON, of Louisiana,

Resolved, That the Committee on the Public Lands be instructed to inquire into the expediency of increasing the fees allowed to the Deputy Surveyor of the United States for the State of Louisiana, in those cases when it is found impracticable to procure the work to be executed for the present maximum fixed by law; and into the expediency of allowing to the Registers of the Land Offices of the United States for the State of Louisiana, an additional salary, instead of the fees payable by the claimants of lands, for issuing patent certificates and delivering patents.

On motion of Mr. WHITTLESEY, of Ohio,

Resolved, That the Secretary of War be directed to transmit to the House of Representatives a copy of the survey made by authority of the United States for a canal from the Portage Summit, in the State of Ohio, to Kearney's line, so called, in the State of Pennsylvania, and a map of the route, and an estimate of the cost of said canal.

On motion of Mr. EWING,

Resolved, That the Committee on Roads and Canals be instructed to inquire into the expediency of granting a suitable quantity of unsold and unappropriated land to the State of Indiana, to be by her disposed of at a price not below that of the public lands, and the proceeds to be invested in stock of the Evansville and Lafayette Rail Road, which is contemplated to connect the Wabash and Erie Canal with the Ohio river at that town. Also, into the expediency of granting, in like manner, a suitable quantity of public land, to construct a Rail Road or a Canal from New-Albany, on the Ohio, near Louisville, through Bedford, Lawrence county, and Greencastle, Putnam county, to the Wabash river, near the junction of the Wabash and Erie Canal. Also, into the expediency of granting, in like manner, a suitable quantity of public land, to improve the navigation of White river, and its two branches, from the Wabash river to the points declared navigable by law of that State.

The following resolution, submitted on Saturday by Mr. CHILTON, was taken up:

Resolved, That the Committee on Roads and Canals be instructed to inquire into the subject and report their opinion to this House, of the most equal and just mode of applying the revenues of the country to such works of public improvement within the respective States of this Union as may be necessary for the facilitating of commerce with foreign nations, and among the several States. And that they moreover report their opinion of the best and most practicable mode of ascertaining and determining the nationality and importance of such improvements as may be proposed within the said several States.

Mr. CHILTON rose and said, that the proposition which he had submitted to the House would be found on examination to consist of two parts. The first relates to the great principles of justice, which may be observed in making disbursements of public money from the Treasury for works of improvement. The second, to the character of the work proposed in the several States of the Union. He said he should like to confine his remarks to these two points. The first relates to the principle of distribution and includes the inquiry—What distribution will be just? This inquiry excludes any discussion with regard to so much of the revenue of the country as regards the necessary expense of the government. He was persuaded there would be found no difference of sentiment with regard to so much as relates to the necessary expense of the government. It is right that every American citizen should contribute so much, whether directly or indirectly, as are necessary for carrying on the operations of government. The difference of opinion that exists, relates to the remainder of the money in the Treasury after the expenses of government have been paid. In order to determine with regard to the distribution, what course will be proper and just. The answer involves two questions. Questions of fact in part and part of conventional agreement or constitutional law. Those of fact will be first. How is this fund created and from whence derived? and secondly, to whom does this fund belong? In answer to the first question—it is derived from a variety of sources, the principal of which are the duties on foreign productions and from the sale of public lands. He might advert to many more, to the Post Office and Patent Office, &c., but the aggregate would be found so inconsiderable that he would not take up the time of the House to enumerate them. He would confine himself to these two great and important sources of revenue, to the amount received from duties on the foreign article, and from the sale of the public domain of this nation. The duties on foreign articles are paid immediately by the importers, mediately by the consumers, and remotely by the foreign manufacturers. He did not consider the cost of the article was increased to the consumer in proportion to the amount of duties. He would put a single case in illustration. In 1828, when the tariff bill was passed, the Eastern members adopted the opinion that the cost of molasses would be reduced in proportion to the reduction of duty. By the act then passed, the duties were reduced. When Congress met next winter, he called on them to know if they had realized their fond hopes, and learned to his astonishment that the price was increased instead of being diminished. He inquired of them the cause, but they could not tell; neither was he able to find any one who could account for it to their own or his satisfaction, till he happened in company with an intelligent foreigner, who remarked that it was a matter very easily accounted for, that foreigners had their secret agents employed in all American markets. They knew as well as Americans themselves the price of the article and the extent of the demand, and when the duties were reduced here 5 cents per gallon, the price was increased five cents per gallon abroad. Mr. C. said, he had shown by this illustration, that the consumer was not relieved by a reduction of duties, but that the profits of the foreigner were increased. When you take into consideration the small extent of the territory of Great Britain, it is certain they cannot live by agriculture, but must be engaged in manufactures and commerce; they are compelled to sell the articles they manufacture whether they will command much or little. He said that the duties the citizen pays for the support of his own Government, would, but for those duties, be paid into the pockets of foreigners. Mr. C. proceeded with his remarks till arrested by a call for the orders of the day.

The SPEAKER laid before the House the following communications:

A letter from the Secretary of State, transmitting, in pursuance of law, a list of patents, &c.; which was laid on the table;

A letter from the Secretary of State covering a list of patents, which have expired during the last year; which was laid on the table.

A letter from the Secretary of war transmitting, in pursuance to a resolution of May 29th, 1830; a list of persons who have applied for pensions, and also, a list of those persons whose applications have been rejected; which was laid on the table and directed to be printed.

A letter from the Secretary of War, in response to a resolution of the House in relation to the Cumberland Road—referred to the Committee of Ways and Means.

A letter from the Secretary of War in answer to a resolution of the House, in relation to certain improvements and public works in the State of North Carolina; which was laid on the table and directed to be printed.

A bill for the relief of the City of Alexandria, was taken up, and, on motion of Mr. CHINN, its further consideration; was postponed to Thursday next.

The following bills were read a third time and passed:

A bill for the relief of James Young;

A bill for the relief of the heirs and legal representatives of Bailey E. Clark;

A bill for the relief of Henry Awkward;

And a bill to authorize the Secretary of State to issue letters patent to James Jones.

When the hour allotted for the consideration of morning business had elapsed—

Mr. CLAY, of Alabama, rose and reminded the Chair and the House, that, several weeks ago, the "Bill to reduce and graduate the price of the public lands" had been made the *special order* for this day. He inquired of the Chair, whether this bill would not have precedence over other special orders?

The SPEAKER replied in the negative—remarking that when the day arrived for the consideration of another special order, since that of the "Navy bill" had been pending, he had given his opinion, that the unfinished special order had precedence, and that the House had then acquiesced. The Speaker also mentioned the several *special orders* which had precedence over the bill mentioned by Mr. C.

Mr. CLAY remarked, that the decision heretofore pronounced by the Chair had (perhaps from inattention) escaped his notice; that he did not wish to interfere with other special orders, if he could avoid it, and would therefore, for the present, acquiesce in the course indicated as the proper one, by the Chair.

PAY OF THE NAVY.

The House then proceeded to the consideration of the unfinished special order, being the bill to regulate the pay of the navy of the United States.

The amendment pending at the hour of adjournment when the bill was last under discussion, offered by Mr. R. M. JOHNSON, of Kentucky, which raises the salaries of Past Midshipmen and Midshipmen, was read and agreed to, after being assented by the Chairman of the Select Committee, (Mr. Wrtmough.)

Mr GRENNELL proposed to amend the clause relating to Clerks of Navy Yards, by raising their pay from 900 to $1100 per annum.

Mr. GRENNELL said, he was not disposed to obstruct the passage of the bill, towards the general features of which he felt favorably disposed; but the more he had reflected on this point, the more firmly he was convinced of the justice of the amendment he had submitted. The office belonged to what might be properly called the civil department of the navy—a class too apt to be overlooked. Mr. G. said, he should go for the bill, though it contained some objectionable features—some of the salaries, he believed, were placed at rather too high a rate; but this important office, that of Clerk of Navy Yards was, in his view, disproportionately too low. The duties of that officer were onerous and responsible. He not merely kept the accounts of the yard, but had charge of the correspondence—not, as had been supposed, barely to *file* that correspondence, but was himself the *writer*, and should possess talents and receive a compensation correspondent to his duties. A Chaplain received $1200 per annum, while a Clerk's duties were certainly much more severe. He did not deny the importance of the duties of the former officer; but it would be admitted they were only required twice a week; while the Clerk must be in attendance every day, from sun-rise till sun-set; and even Sunday did not bring a Sabbath to him. Mr. G. here enumerated all the duties of Clerks; and appealed to gentlemen to admit that compensation was not in proportion to that given to other officers. He said it ought to be remembered that the salary of the Clerk in the yard at Washington had always been $1000 per annum, until the last year, when it was

reduced by the Navy Commissioners to $750. He hoped the amendment would prevail.

[Here Mr. LEWIS, of Alabama, obtained leave to lay a motion on the table to reconsider the vote of Saturday last on the bill for the relief of Susan Decatur, the consideration of which was postponed to Friday next.]

The question was then taken on the amendment of Mr. GRENNELL, and it was rejected without a division.

The question now being on the engrossment of the bill—

Mr. ALLEN, of Va. rose and said he should feel constrained, from various considerations, to move that this bill be committed to the Committee on Naval Affairs, for revisal. The increase in the pay of the officers by this bill, was more than $200,000. The whole pay of navy officers will thus cost the nation at least a million of dollars. No one could be more alive than himself to the glory which our naval officers had shed upon our name—but not even this consideration should induce him to support this bill in its present shape, contrary to his own ideas of right.

Mr. A. said, there was another view which should be taken of this subject. The officers destined to receive the additional compensation, were not generally those who so brilliantly distinguished themselves in the last war. Those engaged in that memorable contest, had most of them passed to their final reward. They belonged to the old school of economy, and were content with what their country awarded them, and the glory of achieving her victories. Mr. A. here went into a comparison between the relative pay and duties of the officers of the army and the navy. The disparity was not now so great as had been represented, to the disadvantage of the latter.—The bill did not equalize the pay of the two services. A certain class of officers in the navy, were to be paid at a much higher rate than those of a corresponding rank in the army. The pay of a Lieutenant in the navy was not only greater than that of a Colonel of the army—but nearly equal to that of a Brigadier General.—The laurels won by the army were as green as those gathered for us by the navy, and he asked if the former could not with reason complain of the injustice of the distinctions contained in this bill. What was it in the two services that justified this great disparity of pay. It had been said, that in time of peace the duties of the navy involved dangers and inconveniences which were not incident to the land service. This, he contended, was not the fact. He spoke of the hardships and dangers of frontier posts, and contrasted them with advantages which a naval officer has of visiting remote portions of the globe—advantages sought after with avidity by men of wealth. Again, the officers of the navy have the advantage of long furloughs—sometimes of two or three years, which is denied to those of the army. On the whole, he thought the advantages were altogether on the side of the navy. Mr. A. next adverted to the argument which had been advanced for raising these salaries, that the officers were unable, with their present pay, to reciprocate the civilities extended towards them in foreign parts. This argument could only apply to the commanding officers of squadrons, as it was them only that were interested. But Mr. A. said this was not the view in which this matter struck him. It did not tally with our former ideas of republicanism. He thought an American Commander could obtain more respect abroad, by the order and condition of his ship, and the discipline of his crew. The policy of our Government was economy, and not pompous display, while that of other countries was the reverse. Our subordinate officers, he contended, were better paid than those of any other nation on the globe; and the effect of the proposed advances, would be to make them chiefly the aim of the sons of the wealthy, to the exclusion of the hardy and deserving—thereby, he believed, decreasing the efficiency of the service. He warned the friends of this bill to beware, or the People would be aroused, and insist on a return to our ancient and popular Jeffersonian system of economy. Mr. A. objected to the bill on another account. He meant the establishment of a new and most unwarrantable system of *pensions*. He referred to the orphan and widows' pension fund, which he characterized at length, as leading to new and dangerous principles in our Government, leading to corruption of a most glaring character. He concluded by moving that the bill be committed to the Committee on Naval Affairs.

Mr. MANN moved to amend the motion by adding, "with instructions to prepare a bill for equalizing the pay of officers of the army and navy;" and then,

On motion of Mr. MANN, the House adjourned.

IN SENATE.

TUESDAY, Jan. 6, 1835.

Petitions and memorials were presented by Messrs. HILL, WRIGHT, BUCHANAN, and LEIGH.

The VICE PRESIDENT laid before the Senate a letter from the Treasury Department, transmitting six copies of the Navy Register for the year 1834.

Also, another letter from the same Department, in obedience to the act of June last, transmitting a copy of the report of the Director of the Mint relative to the assay of coins made at the Mint.

Also, another letter from the same Department, transmitting a report of the survey of the northern boundary line of the State of Indiana, made in obedience to a resolution of 30th December, 1833.

Mr. HENDRICKS, from the Committee on Roads and Canals, reported a bill making an appropriation to improve the Mississippi river, near the city of St. Louis.

On motion of Mr. SILSBEE, the Committee on Commerce was discharged from the further consideration of the petition of Elizabeth Scott.

Mr. ROBINSON, on leave given, introduced a bill to authorize the Secretary of the Treasury to compromise certain claims of the United States; which was twice read and committed.

Mr. WAGGAMAN gave notice that to-morrow he would ask leave to introduce a bill to give effect to the 8th article of the treaty with Spain.

On motion of Mr. WRIGHT, the Committee on Commerce was discharged from the consideration of the petition of James Nicholson, and the same was referred to the Committee on Claims.

On Mr. WRIGHT'S motion, the same committee was discharged from the consideration of the petition of Ludwig Ludwigson, and the same was referred to the Judiciary Committee.

Mr. TOMLINSON, on leave given, introduced a bill for the relief of Carey Clark; which was twice read, and referred.

Mr. POINDEXTER, from the Committee on Public Lands, made a report upon the report of the Secretary of the Treasury, relative to the issuing of Virginia military bounty land warrants; which, on his motion, was ordered to be printed.

Mr. POINDEXTER, from the same Committee, reported a bill for the relief of Silas D. Fisher.

FRENCH RELATIONS.

Mr. CLAY, from the Committee on Foreign Relations, to which had been referred that part of the President's message, appertaining to our relations with France, made a report, which concluded by a resolution, "That it is inexpedient at this time to pass any law vesting in the President authority for making reprisals upon French property, in the contingency of provision not being made for paying to the United States the indemnity stipulated by the treaty of 1831, during the present session of the French Chambers."

Mr. CLAY read the report from his seat, which occupied an hour and a half, and when he concluded, he submitted a proposition to make the report and the resolution the order of the day for Tuesday next, and that the report be printed, together with any of the documents which any gentleman might desire.

Mr. TALLMADGE suggested to the honorable Chairman the propriety of making the Report the special order for Tuesday, two weeks hence—and whilst he was up, lest it might be inferred, from the general language of the Report, that it had received the unanimous approbation of the Committee on Foreign Relations, he felt it his duty to express to the Senate his dissent from some portions of it. He concurred with the honorable Chairman (Mr. Clay) in many of the views which he had taken of this interesting subject; but there were others in which he could not concur—there were some of the premises, the arguments, and conclusions, which he could not approve. He believed that the President was fully justified and borne out by the correspondence, in the positions which he had assumed in his Message to Congress. He entertained no doubt of the binding obligation of the treaty on France, and the duty of the French Chambers to carry it into effect; and that a refusal on their part to make the necessary appropriation to meet the stipulations contained in it, would be a violation of the pledged faith of the nation. He dissented entirely from that part of the report in relation to the effect supposed to have been produced on the Chamber of Deputies, in the late rejection of the bill, by reason of the correspondence of Mr. Rives, the able and skilful negotiator of the treaty. He had no doubt of the power of Congress to pass a law at this session authorizing reprisals on French property, in the manner recommended by the President. But this was no time for discussion or argument on these or other matters of the report. He would only say, that with a knowledge that the French Chambers had been convened nearly a month earlier than was anticipated by the President, when he communicated his message to Congress, he was of opinion, when this subject was under consideration before the committee, that, as a matter of expediency, it were better that no report be made, until we had heard further of the action of the Chambers, and which we were in the daily expectation of hearing.

Mr. CLAY said it was true, that this subject, the report, and he regretted to say it, was not entirely co-incided in by all the members of the Committee; he did not know whether there was a concurrence in the resolution or not. It was true that it was not time to enter into the argument now, for the only thing was, what time should be chosen for the consideration. He thought that the sooner Congress manifested its will on this subject, the better—better for the country, its commercial operations, and the various insurances made. And he had a perfect persuasion that if it was the intention of Congress not to pass a law authorizing reprisals in the contingency iindicated by the President, the sooner it was known, as well on the other side of the Atlantic as on this, the better. He thought, therefore, that the postponement to the time suggested, ought not to prevail. He did not know what France might do; or what construction she would put upon the late message of the President, nor any thing about the view she might take of it. If she should fly into a passion on account of it, we might be involved in serious difficulties.—But if she was prudent, she would wait to see whether the message should be seconded by Congress. If Congress thought it expedient to pass no such law as that requested by the President, but that it was safest and wisest to wait for the action of France, he asked, would it not be likely to produce a better effect? He did not know whether a discussion would ensue upon the report or resolution. We hold the negative, said Mr. C. We are in favor of no law, and, therefore, there would probably be no discussion. It was only in the event of a proposition to pass a law, that a discussion could ensue. It was necessary to a good understanding between the two countries, that there should, at as early a period as possible, be an announcement of our intentions upon the measure suggested by the President. He was, therefore, opposed to the postponement for two weeks. He thought the document might be printed and on our tables in two days. The postponement to next Tuesday was agreed to.

Mr. CLAY then moved that the Report be printed; which was agreed to.

Mr. POINDEXTER moved that twenty thousand additional copies be printed for the use of the Senate.

Mr. CLAY had no objection to the number; but he thought five thousand were sufficient.

Mr. POINDEXTER replied that our c

relations with France were of the utmost importance to the nation; and he thought the views of the enlightened committee on the subject, should be fully spread before the country. Although they would probably be circulated by means of the public journals, yet that would not be done in sufficient time—twenty thousand, he thought, was not too much. Thirty thousand copies of the Report of the Post Office Committee had been printed last year, and spread over the whole country. This was not a less important document, since it would enable the People to witness any conflict that might take place between this branch of the Government and the President of the United States.

Mr. CALHOUN said he would vote for the largest number. He had heard it read with great pleasure; it contained all the documents upon a question which was of the utmost importance to the country. War was at all times to be avoided—and of all calamities which could befal this country, he considered a war with France would be the most unfortunate.

Mr. EWING said that he also would vote for the largest number. If he had the whole number of 25,000 copies, they would not be more than sufficient to give his constituents all the information they wished.

Mr. PORTER was also determined to vote for the largest number—he was extremely anxious that his constituents should be informed of the precise situation of this question. There could be no doubt that if the appropriation to carry the treaty into execution should not be made, the two countries were drifting to a position in which collision must inevitably ensue, and he wished to avoid it. We sympathised with public opinion, and it was important that opinion should be correct. The document would not be read in the newspapers, and there was no other way of its reaching the people.

The question being about to be put, on printing 20,000 extra copies,

Mr. HILL demanded the ayes and noes; which were ordered.

Mr. LEIGH said, he would vote for the largest number, but for a single reason, and that was, that if they were ordered, they could by no possibility be printed in less than four months.

Mr. PRESTON thought the document should be disseminated as widely as possible. We should avoid war by all just and honorable means, so long as it was possible, but, above all, a war with France. And he thought the views of the Committee would satisfy the nation that we could avoid a war with France. He concurred fully in the conclusions of the Committee that it was the duty of Congress to act on present circumstances—that we should not anticipate what France would do—and he concurred in the shadowing forth of the course which we might be compelled to take. He concurred with them that it was the duty of the nation to defend its honor, at any hazard or cost whatever, but not to plunge into a war except to defend its honor and maintain its rights. He was willing to disseminate this document as largely as possible, but he thought with the gentleman from Virginia, (Mr. Leigh,) that it was physically impossible, almost, to have the twenty thousand printed in time for distribution. He proposed some ten or fifteen thousand extra copies.

Mr. EWING said he was just informed by the printer of the Senate, that he could have the documents printed and on the tables in three days, and the additional number of copies in two weeks.

Mr. WRIGHT said he would vote against printing the 20,000 copies, not because he could possibly have any wish to prevent the distribution of the document, which would go through the country much more rapidly than we could send it, but because the people were not out of the reach of information till they could reach it from us. When so large a number of documents were ordered, they became so old that they were not read—the information went so far before them, that when they came from the printer, there was no inducement to read them, and it was incurring an expense without deriving any utility from it. His quota of the Post Office report which had been alluded to, did not reach him till the 1st of October

and at that period when he sent the document to his constituents, he received replies from them that they had seen it before. This subject was immensely important, and the press would distribute the report sooner than we could. He thought five thousand copies, the usual number. quite sufficient.

After some further remarks from Mr. PORTER, Mr. EWING, Mr. BIBB, and Mr. POINDEXTER, the question was taken on printing 20,000 additional copies, and decided in the affirmative by the following vote:

YEAS—Messrs. Bell, Bibb, Calhoun, Clay, Clayton, Ewing, Frelinghuysen, Hendricks, Kent, Knight, Mangum, Moore, Naudain, Poindexter, Porter, Prentiss, Robbins, Silsbee, Smith, Southard, Sprague, Swift, Tipton, Tomlinson, Waggaman, Webster—26.

NAYS—Messrs. Benton, Black, Brown, Buchanan, Grundy, Hill, Kane, King of Ga. Leigh, Linn, McKean, Morris, Preston, Robinson, Shepley, Tallmadge, Tyler, White, Wright—19.

Mr. POINDEXTER, from the Committee on Public Lands, reported a bill for the final adjustment and settlement of claims to lands in Florida and Arkansas Territories, with an amendment.

SPECIAL ORDER.

The bill to make compensation for French spoliations prior to 1800, coming up, at the suggestion of Mr. WRIGHT, the bill was passed over, and the Senate proceeded to the other special orders.

The resolutions offered yesterday by Mr. LEIGH were taken up and adopted.

The resolution offered yesterday by Mr. WRIGHT was taken up for consideration, and on his motion it was amended by making the following addition:

"And also to report the names of the several persons who have been employed by the department as draftsman upon the said maps, the dates from which to which each person has been so employed, and the rates of wages, and the amounts paid to each respectively for such service."

The resolution, as amended, was agreed to.

The following resolution offered yesterday by Mr. CALHOUN, was taken up and adopted.

Resolved, That a Select Committee be appointed to inquire into the extent of Executive patronage; the circumstances which have contributed to its great increase of late; the expediency and practicability of reducing the same, and the means of such reduction; and that they have leave to report by bill or otherwise.

On motion of Mr. CALHOUN, it was ordered that the Committee consist of six.

Mr. CALHOUN wished that the Committee might consist of two members from each of the political parties. For it is well known, said Mr. C. that there are different political interests in the Senate. That when he considered the extent of Executive patronage and influence, and its important effect upon our future prospects, he wished to go into its consideration free from all prejudices, and to give it an impartial consideration. He wished the committee might be immediately appointed.

Mr. POINDEXTER proposed that the election of the committee would be postponed till to-morrow morning.

Mr. CALHOUN objected.

And so the Senate proceeded to ballot for the committee, when Messrs. CALHOUN, SOUTHARD, BIBB, WEBSTER, BENTON, and KING of Georgia, were elected.

Mr. KENT, on leave, and agreeably to former notice, introduced a bill for making compensation for certain advances made to the Government during the last war; which was read twice and referred to the Committee on the Judiciary.

Mr. KENT also introduced a joint resolution for amending the constitution of the United States with regard to the election of President and Vice President.

On motion of Mr. FRELINGHUYSEN, the bill authorising the purchase of the right and apparatus of Boyd Reilly for applying irrespirable gas to the human system, to be used in the army and navy of the United States, was taken up and considered in Committee of the Whole, and without opposi-

tion, was ordered to be engrossed for a third reading.

On motion of Mr. CLAYTON, the bill establishing the northern boundary line of the State of Ohio, was taken up for consideration.

Mr. C. then observed, that it was important this bill should receive the immediate action of Congress, on account of its connexion with Michigan and the proposed new Territory of Wisconsin, that this line should be established before admitting Michigan into the Union. Mr. C. being Chairman of the committee that reported the bill, went on at some length to explain the views that had governed the committee in the formation of the bill.

Here a motion was made to adjourn, which did not prevail.

Mr. HENDRICKS then offered an amendment, which was agreed to.

After some further observations by Messrs. CLAYTON and HENDRICKS, Mr. ROBINSON offered another amendment, which was also received—

And the bill as amended was ordered to be engrossed for a third reading, without opposition.

On motion of Mr. HENDRICKS, the communication received this day from the Treasury Department on the subject of the northern boundary line of Indiana, was ordered to be printed.

And then the Senate adjourned.

HOUSE OF REPRESENTATIVES.
TUESDAY, January 6, 1835.

A message was received from the President of the United States, by Mr. DONELSON, his Private Secretary.

Mr. BROWN, from the Committee on Invalid Pensions, reported a bill for the relief of Jane Buckingham; which was read twice and committed.

Mr. CLAYTON, from the Committee on Public Lands, reported a bill confirming to the representatives of Thomas F. Riddick the title to 640 acres of land; which was twice read and committed.

Mr. CLAY, from the Committee on Public Lands, reported a bill granting an additional quantity of land for the satisfaction of revolutionary land warrants; which was read twice and committed.

Mr. CLAY, from the same Committee, reported a bill for the relief of James Moore and William Moore; which was read twice and postponed for one week.

Mr. CARR, from the Committee on Private Land Claims, reported a bill for the relief of Robert T. Archer; which was read twice and postponed for one week.

Mr. CARR (instructed by the Committee on Private Land Claims) moved that the Committee of the Whole be discharged from the further consideration of the bill for the relief of the heirs of James Latham, deceased; which was disagreed to.

Mr. JOHNSON, of Louisiana, moved to discharge the Committee of the Whole from the consideration of the bill supplementary to the act of July 4th, 1832, for the final adjustment of land claims in the southeastern district of Louisiana, and that the same be committed to a Committee of the Whole on the state of the Union. The motion was disagreed to.

Mr. THOMSON, from the Committee on Military Affairs, made a favorable report in relation to certain fortifications at St. Augustine, in Florida, which, on his motion, was referred to the Committee of the Whole, to whom the bill on the subject of fortifications had been committed.

Mr. FOSTER, from the Committee on the Judiciary, Mr. LAY, from the Committee on Revolutionary Claims, Mr. BOON, from the Committee on Public Lands, and Mr. ADAMS, of New York, from the Committee on Invalid Pensions, made favorable reports upon various petitions and subjects referred to said Committees.

Mr. HUBBARD, from the Joint Committee appointed on that subject, reported the following correspondence between the Joint Committee and JOHN QUINCY ADAMS, on the subject of the address delivered by the latter on the Life and Character of General Lafayette.

To the Hon. JOHN QUINCY ADAMS:

SIR: We have the honor to present to you special copies of the Joint Resolutions adopted . . .

Senate and House of Representatives on the 2d instant, expressing the thanks of Congress for the appropriate Oration de ivered by you in the Hall of Representatives on the 31st ultimo, on the life and character of General Laf yette, and authorizing a request to be made to you for a copy of it for publication.

Having shared the high gratification of hearing he Oration, we take pleasure, in pursuance of the second of the Joint Resolution, in requesting you o furnish a copy of the Oration for publication.

We have the honor to be, with great respect, four obedient servants,

HENRY CLAY, Chairman of the Committee on the part of the Senate.
HENRY HUBBARD, Chairman Committee on part of House.
Jan. 5th, 1835.

To Messrs. HENRY CLAY and HENRY HUBBARD, Chairmen of the Joint Committee of Arrangements of the Senate and House of Representatives of the United States, to carry into effect the resolutions of Congress in relation to the death of General Lafayette.

GENTLEMEN: I received with deep sensibility your communication of the joint resolutions of both Houses of Congress, upon the oration delivered before them on the Life and Character of Lafayette.

The kind indulgence with which they have accepted the endeavor to give effect to their purpose of paying a last tribute of national gratitude and affection to the memory of a great benefactor of our country, will be impressed upon my heart to the last hour of my life.

With this sentiment, I shall take pleasure in furnishing, as requested, a copy of the address for publication.

I am, gentlemen, with the highest respect, your fellow citizen and obedient servant,
JOHN QUINCY ADAMS.

Mr. HUBBARD remarked that the oration was now under the control of the House. It had been considered by the Joint Committee that it would a most proper for each House to act independent t in regard to having it printed, inasmuch as there was no printer to Congress. He asked leave to present the following resolution:

WHEREAS it was resolved at the last session of Congress, that JOHN Q. ADAMS be requested to deliver an Oration on the life and character of General LAFAYETTE, before the two Houses of Congress; and in pursuance of that resolution and thereby of these resolutions which have been subsequently adopted, Mr. Adams, on Wednesday, the 31st day of December, 1834, in the Hall of the House of Representatives, and in the presence f both Houses of Congress—and also in the presence of the President of the United States, and of Heads of the respective Departments of the General Government, and of a most numerous assembly of citizens, did deliver an Oration replete with those pure and patriotic sentiments which will be universally cherished by every true and English-eyed American: The House of Representatives was satisfied with the manner in which Mr. Adams has performed the duty assigned him, and worthy of her resolution of communicating, " through the medium f the press," those principles which have been f him so ably discussed, as well as their sentiments of respect for the distinguished character id their sentiments of gratitude for the devoted services of Lafayette, which have been by him on occasion so faithfully expressed, have come the following resolution:

Resolved, That —— copies of the Oration be printed for the use of the House.

Mr. PEARCE, of Rhode Island, moved to fill e blank in the resolution with 10,000 copies.
r. PINCKNEY proposed 20,000—Mr. BROWN moved 50,000—and Mr. MILLER 40,000.

The question was first put on the largest number, and carried—yeas 80, nays 61.

Mr. EVANS, of Maine, suggested that the motion ought to be printed on better paper, and with more neatness than the ordinary documents were ordered by the House. He therefore moved to amend the resolution, by directing that

---

the printing should be executed under the direction of the Committee appointed by the House.
The amendment was agreed to.

The resolution as amended, was then agreed to
-Petitions (on leave) were presented by)—
Mr. BOON, of Indians;
Mr. GILLET, of New York;
Mr. BLAIR, of Tennessee;
Mr. McCOMAS, of Virginia;
Mr. McKENNAN, of Pennsylvania;
Mr. THOMAS, of Maryland;
Mr. DICKINSON, of Tennessee.
On motion of Mr. PINCKNEY,
Resolved, That the Committee on the District of Columbia be, and they are hereby authorized and instructed to ascertain the amount of fuel that may be necessary for the immediate relief of the suffering poor of Washington, and to place the same at the disposal of the Corporation, for that purpose.
On motion of Mr. SEVIER,
Resolved, That the Secretary of War be instructed to report to this House the survey and estimate of Dr Hervard, the Engineer who surveyed so much of the Little Rock and Memphis road as lies between the St. Francis and Mississippi rivers.
On motion of Mr. LEA, of Tennessee,
Resolved, That the Committee on the Post Office and Post Roads be instructed to inquire into the expediency of establishing a post route from Campbell's Station, by the way of Low's Ferry and Holston river, to Marysville, Blount county, Tennessee.
Mr. BEATY offered the following resolution, which, under the rule, lies one day:
Resolved, That the Secretary of War be requested to report to this House whether the whole amount or what part of the $30,000 appropriated at the last session of Congress for the continuation of the improvement of the navigation of the Cumberland river, has been applied to that object, and whether its application was made under the direction of the said Secretary or the President of the United States, and whether the whole amount, or what part of said $30,000 was directed to be laid out upon said river below Nashville, and if any part of said sum be left, will it be laid out in continuation of the improvement of the river above Nashville, if not, the reasons for withholding it.
The following resolution, heretofore offered by Mr. CHILTON, was taken up:
Resolved, That the Committee on Roads and Canals be instructed to inquire into the subject and report their opinion to this House, of the most equal and just mode of applying the revenues of the country to such works of public improvement within the respective States of this Union as may be necessary for the facilitating of commerce with foreign nations, and among the several States, and that they moreover report their opinion of the best and most practicable mode of ascertaining and determining the nationality and importance of such improvements as may be proposed within the said several States.
Mr. CHILTON said that he had, in his remarks yesterday, stated that the revenues of the country were paid, in the first place, by the importers, and that they were subsequently paid by the American People to the importers. It is by no means difficult to understand the operation by which the importer is repaid the amount of duty which is paid by him into the Custom-house. The commission houses, when they sell, add not only the amount of duties paid, but a commission on them. Subsequently it is not difficult to see how the individual pays it. When he goes to the retail store, whether the article he buys cost much or little, he pays the amount that has been paid to the commission merchant or importer, by the retailer, together with the profits of the retailer. He said he had endeavored to show that the revenues of the country were paid by the People of the Union, and not by any select portion of it; where the greater proportion is consumed, the greater proportion is paid. He had disposed of the questions of fact. He now came to that of conventional agreement or constitutional law:—
Mr. C. was here interrupted by a call for the orders of the day—which prevailed.
The SPEAKER laid before the House the following communications:

A letter from the Secretary of the Navy accompanied by 275 copies of the Navy Register, for the use of the members of the House.

A letter from the Secretary of the Treasury, enclosing a report from the Directors of the Mint, pursuant to the acts of June last, in relation to foreign coins, &c., which was laid on the table and ordered to be printed.

A communication from the War Department, transmitting various documents in relation to the claims of Nimrod Farrow and Nathaniel Harris, which was referred to the Committee on Claims.

The SPEAKER laid before the House the following Messages, &c. from the President of the United States:

To the House of Representatives:

In answer to the resolution of the House of Representatives, passed on the 24th ultimo, I transmit a report from the Secretary of State upon the subject.
ANDREW JACKSON.

THE REPORT.
The Secretary of State, to whom was referred a resolution of the House of Representatives of the 24th ultimo, requesting the President " to " communicate to that House such information as " he may have, and which, in his opinion, may be " proper to be communicated, and not incompati- " ble with the public interest, showing the steps " which have been taken, and the progress which " has been made in effecting an adjustment and " satisfaction of the claims of American citizens " upon the Mexican Government," has the honor to report, that, in pursuance of instructions from this Department, various representations have been made to the Government of the United Mexican States, from time to time, by the Minister of the United States in that Republic, that owing to the condition of the country, they have hitherto been without success; but that in the Minister's latest despatch, date t the 20th October last, he expresses the opinion that the state of affairs will be such, after the then approaching meeting of the Mexican Congress in January, as will enable him to close in a satisfactory manner the negotiations now pending.
All which is respectfully submitted,
JOHN FORSYTH.
DEPARTMENT OF STATE,
Washington, 5th Jan., 1835.

To the House of Representatives of the U. States:
In answer to a resolution of the House of Representatives, passed on the 27th ultimo, I transmitted a report made to me by the Secretary of State on the subject, and I have to acquaint the House that the negotiation for the settlement of the Northeastern Boundary being now in progress, it would in my opinion, be incompatible with the public interests to lay before the House any communications which have been had between the two Governments since the period alluded to in the resolution.
ANDREW JACKSON.
Washington, 6th Jan. 1835.

REPORT TO THE PRESIDENT OF THE UNITED STATES.
DEPARTMENT OF STATE,
Washington, 5th January, 1835.
The Secretary of State, to whom was referred a resolution of the House of Representatives of the 27th ultimo, requesting the President to lay before the House, if in his opinion it is not incompatible with the public interest, any communications which may have been had between the Government of the United States, and that of Great Britain, since the rejection by the former of the advisory opinion of the King of the Netherlands, in reference to the establishment and final settlement of the Northeastern Boundary of the United States in controversy between the two Governments, and also requesting the President to communicate any information he may possess of the exercise of practical jurisdiction by the authorities of the British Province of New Brunswick over the disputed territory within the limits of the State of Maine, according to the true line of boundary as claimed by the United States, and especially upon that part of the territory which has been incorporated by the Government

of Maine into the town of Madawaska, together with such representations and correspondence (if any) as have been had by the Executive of that State with the Government of the United States on the subject, has the honor to report, that the Department has no information which has not already been laid before the House, of the exercise of practical jurisdiction by the authorities of the British Province of New Brunswick over the disputed territory within the limits of the State of Maine, nor any other representation or correspondence had by the Executive of that State with the Government of the United States on that subject. Representations were made to this Department in the latter part of the year 1833, by the British Minister at Washington, on the part of the authorities of New Brunswick, complaining of infractions of the understanding subsisting between the two Governments in regard to the disputed territory. These complaints, however, on being referred to the Governors of Maine and Massachusetts for explanation, were believed to be without just grounds. There was no complaint on the part of Maine, and the correspondence which took place on the occasion, is not supposed to be within the scope of the resolution of the House.

As the negotiation between the United States and Great Britain, which was commenced in accordance with a resolution of the Senate after the rejection of the advisory opinion of the King of the Netherlands, for the establishment of the North-eastern boundary, is now in progress, it is submitted to the President whether it would be compatible with the public interest to lay before the House any communications which have passed between the two Governments on the subject.

All which is respectfully submitted

JOHN FORSYTH.

PAY OF NAVAL OFFICERS.

The House then proceeded to the consideration of the unfinished special order, being the bill to regulate the Pay of the Officers of the Navy of the United States.

The question being on the motion of Mr. ALLEN, of Va. to commit the bill to the Committee on Naval Affairs, and the amendment thereto offered by Mr. MANN, of New York, to add the words "with instructions to prepare a bill to equalize the pay of the officers of the Army and Navy,"

Mr. MANN, of New York, rose and said, that having, before the House adjourned yesterday, moved to amend the motion of the honorable gentleman from Virginia, by adding instructions to the Committee to report a bill to equalise the pay of the Army and Navy, he would now endeavor, briefly as possible, to submit a few considerations in favor of the original motion, as he proposed to amend the same, and against the passage of the bill. We have (said Mr. M.,) professed to be an economical, republican, plain people. It has been said that our Government, in its practical operation, conferred a greater degree of benefit and protection upon the People, than any other known among civilized nations. Its theory, rejecting all privileged classes, all exclusive legislation in favor of the few at the expense of the many, proceeding upon the principle "that all men are created equal," has commanded alike the admiration of patriotism and philanthropy. Its practice thus far has mainly conformed to its theory. Occasional deviations from the republican track, will be found in our history; but he (Mr. M.,) trusted these would only form exceptions to general rules and principles, and not rules and principles themselves. If at any time, in our good nature, in our generosity, or if you please liberality, we overstep the bounds of prudence, and do violence to that justice which the nation owes equally to the most humble as the most exalted, we ought soon to expect to meet the corrective at the ballot box. Mr. Speaker, (said Mr. M.) the present era will form a bright page in our national history, unless by our own acts we shall wantonly cast a shade over it, which will grow darker by age, until the remembrance of the present shall become unwelcome to the recollections of men. By the economy and frugality of our republican habits, under an honest administration of our financial affairs, our national debt, (by some maintained to be a national blessing,) which in 1817 amounted to one hundred and twenty-three millions of dollars, has been paid off, and the anomaly in the history of the oppressions of the human race is now presented of a great nation out of debt, possessing accruing surplus revenues to an extent which may prove dangerous to its purity, and obnoxious to its safety. Are we (said Mr. M.) about to commence a system of extravagant legislation, creating high salaries, sinecures, perquisites, allowances, douceurs, and privileges, which will lay the foundation of a new national debt, to prove more cruel and enduring than has ever yet excited the fears of our people? There are those, sir, (said Mr. M.) in the atmosphere surrounding this Capitol, who will answer, "Never fear—the laborer is worthy of his hire, and his hire is not enough to supply his wants, and his necessary luxuries and entertainments—his respectability must be supported, or the nation is disgraced." Put the question (said Mr. M.) to our constituents; I do not mean the wealthy and luxurious of our large cities and towns; but the great planting and farming interest of the country; and if I have not grossly mistaken their opinions, their answer will be, "True, the laborer is worthy of his hire, and let that hire be reasonable, even liberal;" but they will be careful to add a warning against extravagance. This bill, sir, (said Mr. M.) may be considered as a pioneer to a system which the peculiar situation of our financial affairs, the generous and better feelings of our nature towards our gallant officers, invites and allures us—a system of prodigal expenditures of the public revenues, for the benefit of our favorites, to silence their clamors, and pamper their appetites, wholly inconsistent with a just sense of our duties to the country, the purity of its laws and administration, and destructive to its welfare. We have been reminded of our overflowing treasury, and that Republics are ungrateful,—we hear, spoken in eloquent accents—our national greatness, our bravery, our liberality, our justice, our honor, our debt of gratitude to those who protect and defend us from "perils by sea and by land;" but, sir, said Mr. M., pardon me for the apprehension, that this is the "siren" to our vanity, which lulls to security, and "deceives but to destroy."

I trust, sir, said Mr. M., that the lessons gathered from the history of European oppressions have not all been yet lost to the people, and that there is yet a spirit which may be awakened to a sense of danger—which will shield us from the evils that have been inflicted upon those nations, by the adoption of systems of bounties, pensions, and sinecures, which have turned all the property of those kingdoms out of the hands of honest industry, into the laps of luxurious idleness and vice.

Mr. Speaker, when this bill was under consideration before the Committee of the Whole, I had occasion to say that it was a little remarkable that a proposition to equalise the pay of the army and navy, should so readily have resolved itself into an effort simply to increase the pay of the navy, and I desired (said Mr. M.) to be informed by what process and for what reasons, the original object had been abandoned by the committee, and their efforts directed only to increase the pay of the navy. The Chairman of the Committee, (Mr. Watmough,) has contented himself by answering that it was found impracticable to undertake to reduce the pay of the army, without endangering the success of the principal object of raising the pay of the navy. Is it true, sir, (said Mr. Mann,) that the army and navy have already gained so much influence over our legislative counsels that it is impracticable to restrain their control? The very proposition is sufficiently alarming, but the admission of it upon this floor is astonishing! Does the gentleman mean to admit that it is impracticable to reduce the pay and emoluments of the swarms of officers of the army, because they are unwilling to be reduced, and that, therefore, we must abandon that branch of the subject, and comply with the demands of the officers of the navy, by raising their emoluments up to the standard of the army?

[Mr. WATMOUGH explained and said, he had made no such admissions or declarations that he was aware of, as the gentleman had supposed. He must have been misunderstood.]

Mr. MANN continued. He was confident the honorable gentleman had made such remarks in answer to his, (Mr. M.'s inquiry,) although perhaps the gentleman had forgotten himself, in the zeal with which he pressed this bill. Why, sir, said Mr. M., the course of proceedings of this committee seems to me to amount to such an admission, otherwise for what reason, I ask again, did the committee abandon their original object of equalizing the pay of the officers of the army and navy? I am aware sir, said Mr. M. that the 603 officers of the army are a more numerous, if not a more dangerous body, than Congress. They command 6595 men, that is an average of one officer for about ten men; from which it might be inferred that the men are under sufficient discipline for a peace establishment. Mr. M. hoped that the honorable gentleman had not taken counsel from his fears of this army in arriving at his conclusion, that it was impracticable to legislate as to the pay and emoluments of this branch of the public service. Will it be denied, sir, (said Mr. Mann,) that some remedial legislation, in regard to the emoluments of the officers of the army, would be beneficial to our finances, if not to the "morale" of the army itself. Let us look into this "ingratitude of Republics." The honorable gentleman from Virginia, (Mr. Allen,) who addressed the House yesterday on this subject, was mistaken in what he said in respect to the pay of the officers of the army. He might easily be mistaken, sir, (said Mr. M.) because in looking into the documents generally on this subject; although we have a bureau here for every division and subdivision of duty, there is confusion and uncertainty, I will not say a fraudulent suppression, in regard to the allowances and emoluments of the officers of the army. Sir, said Mr. M. the Blue Book, compiled every two years, pursuant to a law of Congress, under the direction of the Secretary of State, is required by law to "exhibit the amount of compensation, pay, and emoluments allowed to each officer or agent." Now, sir, in regard to the pay of the army, this document only shows the pay and allowances to your Major General $200 per month and 15 rations per day. A Brigadier General $104 per month and 12 rations, and thus through the different grades. Sir, said Mr. M. we shall soon learn that this celebrated Blue Book does not tell us half the truth. I do not know whose fault it may be, but, sir, in respect to the army, this book is not entitled to the least credit. In document marked B, accompanying the report of this bill, the pay and emoluments of a Major General are stated to be $6512 64, a Brigadier General $4422 48. In another document, sir, said Mr. M. accompanying the same report, called statement A, under the joint signatures of the Secretaries of the War and Navy Departments, I find the following statement, which I beg leave to read for the information of the House. Mr. M. read—

The following table exhibits the maximum amount of pay and stated allowances which the respective grades of the army can receive, and the overage amount actually received during the year 1832.

GRADES.	Actually received in 1832.	Maximum amount.
Major General,	$6,528 80	$6,674 [illegible]
Brigadier General,	4,265 20	4,515 [illegible]
Colonel,	2,678 65	3,014 [illegible]
Lieutenant Colonel,	2,329 80	2,457 [illegible]
Major,	2,099 40	2,221 [illegible]
Captain,	1,442 91	1,568 [illegible]
First Lieutenant,	1,103 57	1,443 [illegible]
Second Lieutenant,	1,027 40	1,383 [illegible]
Brevet Second Lieuts.	1,027 40	1,383 [illegible]
Cadets,	338 00	338 [illegible]

Sir, this statement does not agree with the statement first mentioned in any one item, yet it may be taken and deemed as authentic as any other, so far as it goes. It does not profess to ... allowances made to the officers of the ...

most circumstances, these officers are entitled tim, to double rations, fuel, quarters, stationery, transportation, or travelling allowance, besides a special extra average per diem allowance of two dollars on court martial or special duties. cannot learn, sir, (said Mr. M.) from any documents within my reach, what all this paraphernalia of allowances costs the country, or what is its value to the officers, and it is doubtful whether, at this time, any department of the Government can inform you what is the exact value and amount of the pay and allowances per annum to the general and staff officers of the army. The practice of brevets, which has obtained extensively, seems better adapted to the increase of pay than to any other object of the service. For instance, a brigadier General stationed at Washington, performing the duty of the head of the Bureau of the Engineer Corps may obtain a salary under a law giving him $104 per month and twelve rations per day, of $4,515. I do not take this example from any hostility to the respectable gentleman who has been so fortunate as to secure such snug quarters. I believe he is a good engineer; but his engineering is perhaps on a scale more expensive to the country than the scale of his salary.

These details (said Mr. M.) furnish a single example of how much abuse may be practised, under the guise of the public service; if not the public good. They show on the face of them the necessity of legislative correction, and if the committee had adhered to their original purpose, I could have entertained some hope of seeing our army of officers placed on a footing more just to the true interests of the country and the other branches of the public service. Unfortunately they have not done so, and therefore I am for the motion of the honorable gentleman from Virginia to commit this bill with instructions "to report a bill to equalise the pay of the army and navy," and I would add a provision to cut off all allowances.

Mr. Speaker (said Mr. M.) I come now to the examination of the dry details of this bill, and I must ask the indulgence of the House while I submit a few considerations against its passage. I will attempt to show that its provisions will increase the pay and emoluments of the navy, except in the highest grades, much beyond the maximum which the Secretary, or the navy board, or even its officers themselves, have as yet asked or desired. I will attempt to go further, sir, (said Mr. M.) and show by comparisons that the present pay and allowances to the American navy, except in the highest grades, are now, under our laws and regulations, greater than those of any other considerable navy in Europe. Some of the general provisions of this bill, sir, will also (said Mr. M.) claim our attention. The first thing (said Mr. M.) which presents itself to our attention is usually an unimportant part of a bill—its title "A bill to *regulate* the pay of the navy of the United States." I have (said Mr. M.) been brought up in the old schools where I learned to call things by their right names. Perhaps I am behind the intelligence and ingenuity of the age, but I should call this in plain English "a bill *to increase* the pay of the navy." When the honorable gentleman adopted his bill, he must have been influenced by the doctrine that "a rose by any other name would smell as sweet." But why not call it by its true name? Is it to be implied that its friends entertain some fears that it has rhubarb in its composition. Sir, (said Mr. M.) whatever you call it, the bill will still be a bill to *increase* the pay of the navy, instead of what it should have been "a bill to equalise the pay of the army and navy."

The first item in it seeks to establish a distinction between officers of the same grade, by designating "a senior captain," or a concealed Admiral, "Commander in Chief" of the navy. I confess myself a little jealous of "titles and dignities" under this Government. Perhaps, said Mr. M., it is owing to a defect of education in the school to which I have always been attached. Why, said Mr. M., do we propose to do things for the navy under *false colors?* That branch of the service has never given us such examples. Their banners have always been boldly hung out, inscribed with liberty and truth.

To this "senior captain" we propose by this bill to give, when in service, a salary besides some allowances of 4,500 dollars. "When on leave of absence or waiting orders, 3,500 dollars." In respect to "all other captains," the provisions of the bill are similar, except in some contingencies not likely to occur.

The ten captains of the navy, of over fifteen years standing, "when at sea," and when at shore stations, and as navy commissioners, now receive an average salary of 3,493 72, besides some other valuable allowances.

Is not this enough to satisfy all reasonable demands upon the gratitude of republics? We are answered in the negative, said Mr. M; and to show us simple republicans how far we are behind those great and oppressive aristocracies, we are referred to the precedents of the British and French navies, communicated to us (to my surprise) by the Secretary of the Navy, not, I am confident, for our imitation or adoption.

In those navies an Admiral—"*senior officer*"—receives from 7,500 dollars to 9,500 dollars, which is increased nearly fifty per cent. when they are on duty; or, in other words, the princely treasures of those kingdoms, "gathered from the mouths of famine," are opened to the rapacity of those who hold to the maxim of "taking care of the rich, and the rich will take care of the poor." These precedents, said Mr. M., cannot have been placed upon our records as examples for our adoption at the instance of any American citizen, and for myself, I cannot permit them to influence my judgement or action, in respect to any provision of this bill. To me, they are bad precedents, and the circumstance of their being before us, has, in no degree, disposed me in favor of the bill which accompanied them.

It will be legitimate, however, for me to refer to them again, for another purpose. Sir, said Mr. M., we are told that the pay of the officers of the navy, was established by a law passed in 1799, since which it has not been increased, while the pay in other departments of the public service has been enlarged, and this is urged as a reason why we ought now to show our liberality with the public treasures, and increase the pay of the navy. I am aware sir, said Mr. M. that our public servants immediately about the Capitol, are much in the habit of applying to the legislative power to give, give! And that in the better sympathies of our nature, we are too apt to yield to such importunities, forgetting the interests of those multitudes of our fellow-citizens, far removed from the scene of our action, but whose interests deserve the most of our care. It should not be forgotten, said Mr M. that in 1799 an administration existed, (under the elder Adams,) in this country, that whatever other objections arose against it, it was not guilty of being in favor of low salaries. The pay of the captains of the navy was raised at that critical period in our history, and in our finances, from $75 to $100 per month, and it is under that law now by which these captains, through allowances and perquisites, obtain the average before stated of $3493 per annum; except that in 1815 Congress passed a law to organize the Navy Board, and establishing their pay at $3500, besides some contingencies. Mr. Speaker, said Mr. M., I do not perceive the force of the reasoning, that because you have raised the pay in one branch of the service, that therefore you must raise another, or the whole. If admitted, it would lead to raising the pay under this Government (already in my judgment too high in every department) to a degree which would exalt the agent above the principal. The officers of the navy, sir, said Mr. M., in addition to pay and emoluments, in time of war, are entitled to prize money, which is usually the lion's part. This item during the late war amounted to $1,140,594, divided according to our prize laws, between the gallant officers and crews of the vessels so fortunate in capturing the enemy. When we reflect again, that these officers are not called into foreign sea service more than about one year in five, I am confident the country will be satisfied that there is no necessity of passing this bill, so far at least as the thirty-seven captains of the navy are concerned.

Mr. Speaker, the next item of this proposition "to regulate," raises the pay of the Masters Commandant, or in the more dignified language, to the title of this item "Commanders," (leaving the appellative Chief off for the present) They are to receive $2500 on sea service, on other duty, $2000. Waiting orders, (that is, engaged to do nothing,) $1800. There are at present 41 of these officers in the service. They are mostly its active and efficient officers. Their rank has not been *above actual service*, and I am frank to admit, that some of them have not heretofore obtained as much pay as their services may have merited when compared with other grades in the navy. There seems to be an extraordinary discrepancy in their pay and allowances at present, which I cannot well account for. For instance, those nine who are in actual sea service, receive $1356 25 each, while the nine commanding navy yards, receiving, or recruiting stations, obtain $2010 75 each. On the whole, sir, if their pay and emoluments were properly distributed, it would seem to me, that better justice would be done, and this class of officers more equally rewarded, if not better satisfied.

Sir, said Mr. M., I could go through the details of this bill, in every grade of the service, increasing the pay as it does, in every instance, to a degree not heretofore contemplated by even the officers themselves. The committee who reported it, has made two reports on the subject, each differing in principle from the other, and brought in three different bills for the same object, each varying widely from its immediate predecessor, and then the Chairman before the Committee of the Whole, accepts, virtually, a new bill, differing essentially from all the other propositions, and this is amended, until you find it, a deformity upon your table. After this exhibition, what confidence, sir, ought the House to repose in the doings of the committee? Why, sir, the honorable gentleman ought to suspect his own judgment, and distrust himself for having lent his ears too willingly, to those whose interests had got the better of their judgments. He has informed us that he diligently sought the most extensive information on this subject—but, sir, said Mr. M., although I will not question the gentleman's diligence, yet I am compelled to doubt his success in the pursuit, and oppose the use he proposes to make of his attainments. There are, however, several documents appended to his reports, from which I have compiled three brief statements, to prove to you the two propositions that this bill will increase the pay of the Navy far beyond the maximum which the Secretary and the Navy Board, acting in behalf of the interest committed to their direction, have asked or desired; and secondly, that the present pay of the Navy is, in all the grades except the higher, greater than in any other considerable navy in Europe. For this last purpose, I have used part of the precedents furnished to us, of the pay in the British and French Navies. Let me remark further, that the document furnished by the joint deliberations of the Secretaries of War and Navy, was drawn up in obedience to a resolution of the Senate of 3d March, 1833, requesting the President to "cause to be prepared and laid before the Senate, at the commencement of its session, a plan for equalising the pay of the officers in the Army and Navy, and providing for a fixed compensation for their services, in lieu of present allowances. After the Secretaries had prepared this document or plan, they submitted it to the Navy Board for their consideration; and they proposed some modifications, by increasing some grades and diminishing others, in a slight and unimportant degree. Thus, sir, this plan of increase in the pay of the Navy, has the sanction of the two Secretaries, the Navy Board, as the official representatives of the Navy, and of the President of the United States. It is therefore entitled to at least as much consideration as the opinion of the honorable gentleman, who has given us his three different opinions in the shape of bills.

Mr. Speaker, I have taken pains to compare the provisions of this bill with the pay thus proposed under the official sanction, of the high officers charged with this duty, and the pay provided by the bill exceeds that proposed in the plan, in every

single instance except one or two of the highest grades.

The brief statements which I present as examples, exhibit the present pay of the Navy as far as the same appears in the documents, the pay proposed by the Secretaries and Navy Board, the increased pay provided in this bill, and the comparative pay in the British and French Navies.

[Here Mr. M. read many of the details in the documents, and compared them with the provisions of the bill.]

GRADES.	Present average pay.	Pay proposed by See'y Navy and Navy Board.	Pay provided in the bill.
1. Senior Captain at sea	2,493 72	3,500	4,500
Ditto on leave of absence, &c.	1,940 00	3,000	3,500
2. Other Capt's Comd'g squadrons or acting as Navy Commissioners	3,500 00	4,200	4,500
3. Other Capt's Comd'g at sea and Navy Yards	3,466 00	3,500	4,000
On leave, or waiting orders	1,940 00	2,300	3,000
4. Masters Comd't at sea	1,356 25	2,000	2,500
Ditto on other duty	2,010 50	1,600	2,000
Ditto on leave, or waiting orders	1,176 25	1,400	1,800
5. Lieut's in command	1,296 25	1,500	1,800
On other duty	1,292 93	1,000	1,800
On leave, or waiting orders	945 00	800	1,200
6. Midshipmen at sea	319 25	250	400
7. Chaplains at sea	662 50	1,000	1,200
8. Schoolmaster		600	1,200

FRENCH NAVY—Pay of Flag Officers.

Admiral, - - - - $7,500 00
Vice Admiral, - - - 3,865 00
Rear Admiral, - - - 1,875 00
Capt. Ship of the Line, 1st class, 1,125 00
Do do do 2d class, 1,012 00
Do Frigate, 787 50

Allowances.—These vary at yards and at sea, amounting, in some cases, to as much as the pay of these classes of officers.

Lieut. of a ship of the Line, - $450 00
Do. Frigate, - - 337 50
Surgeon of the 11th class, - 562 00
Midshipmen 1st do - - 150 00

All vances to the under officers much less than in American navy.

Note.—The pay of the superior grades is increased nearly 50 per cent. when at sea.

BRITISH NAVY.

Rear Admiral, or Commodore of the 1st class, - - - $4,861 80
Captain of a Fleet, - - 4,861 80
Captain first rate, - - 3,542 08
Commander first rate, - - 3,542 08
First Lieut., 7 years standing, first rate, 663 78
All other Lieutenants, - 531 02
Master, - - - - 752 38
Chaplain, - - - - 708 03
Surgeons, - - - - 1,134 00
Assistant Surgeons, - 531 02
Midshipmen, - - - 138 52

Note.—Other grades conform to these rates, and this is the pay in first-rate vessels, which is generally diminished through all the other six classes of vessels belonging to the British Navy.

After Mr. M. had referred to the details of the pay in the British and French Navies, and was proceeding to show that in all the grades below Admiral, it was far lower than the present pay in the American Navy,

Mr. WATMOUGH explained, and said those precedents were incorrect, and that the gentleman was mistaken, because that pay was increased when in service 50 per cent., and that the officers obtained large allowances besides.

Mr. M. continued, and said that he was aware that the higher grades in the French service, when at sea, had such increase, but none of the lower grades. The honorable gentleman (said Mr. M.) has told us nothing new. Suppose I was mistaken 50 per cent. it will be easy to add that to the pay of those navies, and then you will not equal the pay of the lower grades in our navy. The honorable gentleman appends documents to his reports, for our consideration, and then says they are incorrect and cannot be relied on. Sir, (said Mr. M.) I should wish to know whether any of these documents are to be relied on; or whether the gentleman will also stultify the residue. If these documents, (said Mr. M.) are in any degree worthy of credit, then have I proved to you, the two propositions which I have before made; and now, sir, let me ask this House if it is prudent for us in the discrete discharge of our duties, to pass this bill thus increasing the pay to a greater extent than has been proposed by those officers who have had the subject under their careful revision? I might here pause, and ask whether the present pay of the navy is not now sufficiently large? Shall we outstrip in our career, the vices and oppressions of European aristocracies? But, Mr. Speaker, I have not yet spoken of the allowances now made to our officers, which will be found to exceed those in Europe. I have a little book compiled in 1832, by that most indefatigable and valuable officer, the Secretary of the Navy, while he was at the head of the Navy Department, which contains many things on this subject, not known generally to the public. The honorable chairman has not thought it advisable to make this book a part of the documents to his report. I will beg leave to read a few paragraphs.

"Allowance on bills drawn by commander of ships or squadrons. This was 2½ per cent., but ceased after the 10th November, 1826." I am informed that it is now established at 1 per cent., but I will not vouch for the truth of this. If it be true, sir, the allowance of 1 per cent. on the expences of a three year's cruise will sustain the dignity of the captain sufficiently for a republic.

"Allowance for cabin furniture. Commanders of vessels in commission will be allowed as follows, in lieu of cabin furniture:

"Commodore of a squadron $30 per month; captain of line of battle-ship $25 per month; captain of a frigate $20 per month; master commandant in command $15 per month; lieutenant commanding $10 per month."

"The following articles are deemed fixtures, and will be provided by the Government, viz. sofas, sideboards, secretaries, book cases, curtains, carpets, wash stands, basins, covers, and hanging lamps for the cabin."

"Allowance for chamber money. Two dollars per week to officers stationed where there are no quarters.

"Allowance for detention on special duty. $10 per day to judge advocates who do not belong to the navy; $3 per day to captains and master commandants; $2 per day to surgeons, lieutenants, and citizens generally; $1 50 per day to all others.

"The following articles of furniture are allowed by the Navy Department: Commandants' houses (giving items) $665, and oil cloths for passage and parlor, not to exceed $2 per yard; master commandants' houses (giving items) $319; besides like oil cloths; houses of lieutenants, sailing masters, surgeons, and pursers at yards (giving items) $178, besides like carpets." These, sir, are not yet all the allowances made, but I fear I go too far into detail. I will mention fuel, candles, and stationary, travel or transportation, (including constructive journeys,) which amount to an annual sum to each officer, greater than the people, or, perhaps, the Government are now aware of. Mr. Speaker, said Mr. M., looking at all this array of salaries, allowances in kind, or in money, I am constrained to call it "an abuse," for I will not use a harsher term. It needs no comment, and I forbear. Let us turn our attention, for a few moments, to some of the general provisions of this bill, which appear to me objectionable. By one of these provisions surgeons, ordered as fleet surgeons, are to have their pay increased one-half, and, "when appointed to perform the duties of Surgeon General, his pay shall be increased three-fourths." Now, sir, said Mr. M., I should like to be informed why it is that

we undertake to do things for the navy which we do not like to do directly and openly. Is it necessary that there should be concealment in any of our objects? Why so, said Mr. M., provide openly, under large capitals, they shall be appointed a new officer in the navy, (as you have in the army,) to be called a Surgeon General, with a salary and allowances of $3500. If such an officer is necessary to the service, let it be understood, and the reasons shown for it; and is there any doubt that it would be favorably considered, if those reasons were sufficient? If you pass this bill, said Mr. M., you will have such an officer added to the long list now in commission, and he will have a salary of 3,000 dollars.

Again, Mr. Speaker, we are about to lay the foundation of a naval school in the establishment of this "Professor of Mathematics"! If so, said he, let it be avowed, and let us understand openly and distinctly, the purpose. The honorable gentleman (Mr. Watmough,) has reported in favor of such establishment. I perceive by that report, that we have now some schoolmasters attached to the navy. At Boston there is one teacher stationed upon a salary of $981 73, besides allowances; he must be a gentleman of considerable importance, not addicted to labor in his vocation; he has (do not be surprised) as pupils! At New York there "two professors," and one has 73, and the other $662 39, with allowances; they both have fifteen pupils! At Norfolk, "professor," and thirty-one pupils. These must be rare foundations for naval schools! I will not now discuss whether we ought to fit our young men how to live at the public expence; yet, sir, this "professorship of mathematics," they may prove a germ, on which to engraft an establishment to educate hereafter, in exclusion to the community generally, under the disguise of preparing youth for the public service, which will correspond with that at West Point under the surveillance of the officers of the army. Before we adopt this "professor," I should like to be informed how many assistant professors are necessary to enable him to perform his duty; perceive that the "professor of mathematics" at West Point has four "assistant professors," that naval professors should require a like number; we might as well perhaps establish a corps of professors under the command of a bureau, with a salary of at least $4,513! This naval professorship, we are given to understand, has he established and being, copied from the English, a "professorship," but we are told that this appellation does not correspond with his "dignity," he being more often called "the Government of the United States," jealous of his rank and title. Now, sir, said Mr. M., I have yet to learn that the calling or occupation of a "schoolmaster" is either derogatory or degrading. If it be so, then, sir, I am obliged to confess I have borne this degradation in respect of many other gentlemen on this floor, and shall leave this "profession" with his humble origin of a "school master," without "grievance," and I am inclined to believe he will render good service as he will if you reduce these high sounding titles, which imply that he performs duties by deputy.

There is another provision (said Mr. M.) which should not escape notice. It contains the principles and has the modern objects of a "Brevet," which has obtained in the army. It provides that officers performing duties of a higher grade, shall be entitled to the pay and emoluments of that grade. If the House was prepared to establish the principle and practice of "brevets" in the organization of the navy, it is probable my objections to this complaint as to the difficulties and delays in its motion. Officers who have been hitherto contented in the performance of the duties appointed to their grade, will soon, like many others of the army, have two or three "brevets," and the end and the coxswain may "space the officer and play the Commodore." No provisions could be devised which would prove more hurtful to the discipline of the navy, more subversive of its best interests. Against it, I had occasion on the other day, that the second section provides, to set apart 3 per cent. of the pay of officers to "constitute a fund for the relief of un—

children of those officers," was virtually an annual appropriation out of the Treasury to grant annuities or pensions to those persons who have not heretofore come within the pension policy of this country. The Hon. gentleman from Virginia (Mr. Mason) said in reply, that I was mistaken in pposing it to be an appropriation out of the treasury; it was out of the pay of the officers, and he undertook to establish his position. Why, r. Speaker, who can fail to perceive that if you establish a rate of pay for your officers from which a deduct annually 3 per cent., you must make at pay 3 per cent. higher than you would other. we deem necessary. But sir, said Mr. M., I not add to what was said on this point, and so all said yesterday, by the Hon. gentleman (Mr. len) from Virginia. Mr. Speaker, my two Hon. league (Ward and Vanderpoel) for whom I certain feelings of habitual respect, have delivered to us some warm-hearted eulogiums upon character and services of our navy and its offi. rs. In all they have said in that respect, I most ly and sincerely concur; but, perhaps unfortu. ly, I have been obliged to consider the ques. a before us as one of entirely different character, ly disconnected with those brilliant achieve. who which have won so much favor and com. ded so much eloquent admiration. Sir, said M., there are at present 1007 officers attach. to the navy. Their present aggregate pay is 3,425 25. If you pass this bill, sir, their ag. will be $973,393 34, making an in. of $235,168 09. This statement may not entirely accurate, although it is derived from most correct official sources. The pay of these ers, sir, at present, is a sum sufficient to sup. t the civil administration of any three of the est State Governments in this Union, and the rd pay provided in this bill is a sufficient to support the government of either one m. We are then to decide, sir, not whe. the navy has acquired glory in deadly con. but whether we will enlarge the perma. expenditures of this Government (al. complained of in every quarter of the) by so large a sum annually, to be garnered the fruits of honest labor, in order to increase laries of the officers; not so much for those were connected with the glories of which my ues speak (for many of them have long made their beds in the "vasty deep") but who are to succeed, and who are now press. m every quarter of the country to gain ad. into the service. My friends alluded to of the higher grades in the British and navies, and I fear those precedents, in the ed moments of their warm-hearted zeal ds the brave may for once have caused to forget the interests of those whose utmost the heat and burden of the day, secures for but a limited protection, against the chills of nters of their lives. y, Mr. Speaker, continued Mr. M. we need little apprehension, that those who work for ited States will work for nothing; neither I we have our repose disturbed for fear they hot get enough. Let us remember that this ment derives all its revenues, as well as all wers, from the people; that it cannot act at ccept by agents whose self-interest, (an all ing spring of human action,) is alway against cipal, quickened by cupidity, and sharpen. avarice; and for one I conclude there is no on their side of the question. Sir, said I let me add that I have always been friend. the navy—I have appreciated its utility, with its gallantry. I would provide liber. sustain its real and true interests, its digni. reputation abroad, by suitable and general But do not sir, I beseech, charge the coun. so large a permanent expenditure to raise laries, and increase our luxuries, lest consequent effeminacy, we too soon the evils, which Spain found in the mines a new world. POPE said, that he had heretofore abstain. any interference in the progress of the re the House. He had, however, listened rely to the various propositions of gentle. and the remarks which had been made on

the subject. He was satisfied that the present compensation to those engaged in the naval service was too low. He was not to be deterred by any thing which might be urged, from doing entire justice to, and paying adequately those individuals who encountered the perils of the ocean, in sustaining and defending the flag and the honor of the nation. He believed that the bill was not altogether just in its details; but he would prefer taking it with its imperfections, than that no act on the subject should be passed. He would rather give too much than too little to those engaged in the naval service of the country. While he entertained these views, he was apprehensive that the bill, in its present shape, would not receive the assent of the House; and he appealed to the gentleman from Virginia, (Mr. Allen,) to withdraw his motion to commit, for the purpose of giving him (Mr. P.) an opportunity to submit a proposition which he indicated, to amend the bill, and which he considered necessary to ensure its passage.

Mr. WISE hoped his colleague would withdraw his motion to commit the bill, and enable its friends to remedy its defects, if any should be found to exist.

Mr. ALLEN of Va. said that inasmuch as his motion had been superseded, or varied by the instructions which had been proposed by the gentleman from New York, (Mr. Mann,) he had no objections to withdraw it.

The motion being withdrawn, Mr. POPE proposed to amend the bill by striking from the following clause, the words printed in italics:
" To captains, when commanding squadrons on coast stations, and when acting as Navy Commis. sioners, four thousand five hundred dollars."

Mr. PARKER suggested that the words "coast stations," be also stricken out.

Mr. POPE assented to the suggestion as a modification of his motion.

Mr. POPE further moved to amend the bill by striking out $3,700 as the compensation to Cap. tains "when on other duty," than specially stated, and inserting $3000;

Also, to strike from the bill all that part relat. ing to extra allowances, and to raising a fund by deducting three per cent. from the pay of the commission and warrant officers, for the relief of the relations, &c. of deceased officers.

Mr. WATMOUGH was anxious that this bill, which had occupied as much of the time of the House, should be disposed of. If gentlemen would be satisfied with the amendment as proposed by the gentleman from Kentucky, he would not oppose them, and was willing that they should be adopt. ed.

Mr. JARVIS remarked that the portions of the bill which it was proposed to change, having been amended in Committee of the Whole, and the House having concurred in the amendments thus proposed by the Committee, he did not think that the House could now, without a commitment en. tertain the proposition of the gentleman from Ken. tucky.

After some conversation between Mr. MASON of Virginia, and the CHAIR, (temporarily filled by Mr. Hubbard,) on the point of order raised by Mr. JARVIS—

Mr. JONES, of Georgia, moved to commit the bill to a Committee of the Whole on the state of the Union, with instructions to strike out all after the enacting clause, and insert in lieu thereof several sections, (which he sent the Clerk's table,) proposing to es ablish the ranks of Admi. ral, Vice Admiral, and Rear Admiral, in the naval service, and fixing various grades of compensation to the individuals employed in the same.

Mr. JONES moved that this amendment be printed.

Mr. GILLET hoped that the gentleman would include in his motion to print the bill before the House, together with all amendments which had been adopted. It was almost impossible to ascer. tain the precise shape which it had assumed.

Mr. JONES accepted the modification. The motion to print being put, there appeared, yeas 66, nays 63. A quorum not voting, The House adjourned.

Petit ns and memorials were presented by Messrs LINN and BIBB.

Mr. TYLER presented a petition from citizens of Georgetown, praying relief from Congress from the pecuniary embarrassments in which that city is involved. Referred to the Committee on the Dis. trict of Columbia.

Mr. HENDRICKS, from the Committe on Roads and Canals, reported a bill for the relief of Walter Loomis and Abel Gay.

The bill from the House of Representatives for the relief of the heirs of Nathaniel Tyler, was read twice and referred to the Committe on Pub. lic Lands.

Mr. PORTER, on leave given, introduced a bill supplementary to the act to authorize the people of Louisiana to enter certain back lands, which was read twice and referred.

Mr. WAGGAMAN, pursuant to notice, and on leave given, introduced the following bills:

A bill for the relief of Wyat Singleton and James Andrews.

A bill for the relief of James L. Stokes, and for other purposes.

A bill for the relief of Abraham Wrinkle.

A bill for the relief of Wm. L. Cockerel.

A bill for the relief of Paul Paisset.

Which bills were severally read twice and re. ferred.

Mr. LINN, on leave given, introduced a bill for the relief of Bartholomew Butcher and others, heirs of Peter Bloom; which was read twice and referred.

Mr. BLACK, from the Committee on Private Land Claims, reported a bill for the relief of Eliza. beth Magruder, without amendment.

The following bills, from the House of Repre. sentatives, were read the first time and ordered to a second reading:

A bill for the relief of James Young;

A bill for the relief of Henry Awkward;

A bill for the relief of Baily E. Clark;

A bill to authorize the Secretary of State to is. sue letters patent to James Jones.

The bill for the relief of J. W. Gleason and oth. ers, was read the third time and passed.

Mr. CLAY submitted the proceedings of the Joint Committee appointed in consequence of the death of Gen. Lafayette, together with the cor. respondence between the Chairmen of the Com. mittee and Mr. J. Q. Adams, on the subject of the Oration delivered by that gentleman upon the life and character of Lafayette, by which it appear. ed that Mr. Adams assented to the request to furnish a copy of the Oration for publication.

Mr. C. said, if he was guided by the opinion which he had formed of the Oration, or of its ex. traordinary merit, he could scarcely name any number of copies to be printed which would be too great. The House, however, had ordered 50,000 copies, and therefore not so many would be neces. sary to be ordered by the Senate. A number proportioned to that would be ten thousand, which he thought sufficient. He therefore moved that ten thousand copies of the Oration be ordered to be printed; which was agreed to.

The bill making an appropriation to improve the navigation of the river Wabash, came up on its third reading.

Mr. CLAY said he desired to make some ob. servations upon that part of the President's Mes. sage out of which this bill had grown.

He would vote with pleasure for the bill, and he hoped it would pass the Senate, and meet with a kinder fate in the House than it experienced last session. The President in his Message had stated a principle in relation to the power of Congress over Internal Improvements, which was so novel and so extraordinary in its character that he thought it ought not to pass without some obser. vation. What was that principle? It was this. That the limit given by the constitution to the power of Congress over Internal Improvements, was that limit which was furnished by tide water, and that such improvement could not be author. ized by Congress which should extend beyond a sort of entry, and they were generally confined to tide water. By this construction of the consti.

tution, the exercise of the power did not depend upon the grants in that instrument, but altogether on collateral circumstances. If this interpretation were correct, the constitution did not depend upon its own provisions to govern, but entirely upon the discretion of Congress, and he also complained of the effect of such an interpretation. What was it? It was to repudiate, and entirely to cut off from the benefits of Internal Improvements made under the authority of the General Government, the whole interior of the country which lay above tide water. Whatever might be the fate of this construction, it was impossible that the country should be contented with this limited extent of power. He had risen on this occasion solely for the purpose of entering his protest against such an interpretation of the power of Congress over Internal Improvements, as was held by the President in his message.

The question being on the final passage of the bill,

Mr. KING, of Alabama, demanded the yeas and nays; which were ordered, and are as follows, to wit:

YEAS.—Messrs. Benton, Clay, Clayton, Ewing, Frelinghuysen, Hendricks, Kane, Kent, Knight, Linn, McKean, Naudin, Porter, Prentiss, Robbins, Robinson, Silsbee, Smith, Southard, Swift, Tipton, Tomlinson, Webster—23.

NAYS—Messrs. Bibb, Black, Brown, Buchanan, Calhoun, Grundy, Hill, King of Ala., King of Ga., Leigh, Mangum, Moore, Morris, Preston, Shepley, Tallmadge, Tyler, White—18.

So the question was determined in the affirmative.

The joint resolution giving the right of way to the Winchester and Potomac Rail Road Company, through the public lands of the United States, at Harper's Ferry, and

The bill authorizing the purchase of Boyd Reilly's patent apparatus for applying the irrespirable gases to the human body, to be used in the navy and army of the U. States, were severally read a third time and passed.

The bill to settle and establish the northern boundary line of the State of Ohio, having been taken up on the third reading,

Mr. SHEPLEY said, he believed that, with regard to this bill, many gentlemen were acting under erroneous impressions. That, in order to give the delegate from Michigan an opportunity of laying before the Senate certain statements and facts, relating to this subject, he would move the suspension of the 19th rule of the Senate, which forbids the admission, upon the floor of this House, of any person interested in any discussion of the Senate. He moved the suspension of this rule, in order to have an opportunity of making another motion to admit the delegate from Michigan to be heard by the Senate on this important subject.

Mr. CALHOUN observed, that to dispense with a rule of the Senate, required unanimous consent.

Mr. KING, of Ala., said that the rules of the Senate had been then most flagrantly violated.—For it had been otherwise decided during the last session, when he contended that it required unanimous consent.

Mr. POINDEXTER said, he was disposed to extend as much indulgence as possible to the delegate from Michigan. That the bill was one of great importance to his constituents, and he would move, therefore, that the bill be laid on the table, in order to give the delegate time to lay his views before the Senate in writing or otherwise.

Mr. EWING did not object to hear the delegate; but did strongly object to laying the bill on the table. He was opposed to any delay. The subject had been before the Senate for two years already. The delegate had enjoyed the aid of an able executive officer in collecting facts on the point in dispute. That it rested more on statements than facts. He would not oppose rescinding the rule of the Senate. He wished to hear the arguments of the delegate, but he was opposed to all delay—he wished the bill sent to the other House in season to be fully discussed this session.

Mr. SHEPLEY replied, that he was informed ...rk which line, and Mr. Poin-

dexter) would prevail, and in a few days the maps might be here; that if the bill should pass the Senate by the middle of the month, there would still remain forty-five days for its passing through the other House.

Mr. CLAYTON explained the subject with respect to maps.

After some further discussion by Messrs. SHEPLEY, EWING, LEIGH, and BIBB, the question was put on Mr. SHEPLEY'S motion, and, on a division, was lost.

The bill was then read a third time and passed, the title having been first amended, to read " An act to settle and establish the northern boundary line of the States of Ohio, Indiana, and Illinois."

Mr. CLAY said, that in consequence of the resignation of Mr. Sprague, there was a vacancy in the Committee of Foreign Relations, and he moved that the Senate proceed to fill the vacancy, which was agreed to; when, on balloting for the member, Mr. PORTER was elected.

Mr. SILSBEE remarked, that by the same occurrence, there was a vacancy in the Committee on Commerce. He moved that the Senate proceed to fill the same; which was agreed to, when Mr. TOMLINSON was chosen.

The VICE PRESIDENT laid before the Senate a report from the Board of Commissioners appointed under the act for the adjustment of land claims in Missouri; which, on motion of Mr. POINDEXTER, was ordered to be printed, and referred to the Committee on Private Land Claims.

The VICE PRESIDENT also communicated a report from the Navy Department, made in obedience to the act of March, 1809, showing the amount of contracts of that Department for the last year.

SPECIAL ORDER.

The bill making compensation for French spoliations committed prior to 1800, being announced as the special order,

Mr. TALLMADGE rose and expressed a hope that the bill might not be further pressed to day. His colleague [Mr. Wright] was desirous of expressing his views upon the subject, but he was now diligently employed examining into it. Having heard yesterday that the debate was drawing to a close, he was prepared himself, and would be ready by tomorrow to deliver his sentiments.

Mr. WEBSTER said he was not authorised to put off the bill any longer, but felt himself bound to hold to more urgency on the subject than he had done. If the honorable member from New York could not address the Senate to-day, he hoped some other gentleman who intended to speak, if any designed doing so, would embrace this opportunity.

Mr. TALLMADGE here made some remarks directed towards Mr. Webster, which were not heard, and concluded by moving a postponement of the special order till tomorrow.

Mr. WEBSTER expressed himself anxious to have the question taken and the debate finished, if the gentleman from New York [Mr. Wright] would be likely to be the last to speak upon the bill, he had no objection to the postponement.

Mr. POINDEXTER remarked that there would probably be no amendment offered to the bill; and if not, he would suggest that it be allowed now to be engrossed for a third reading.

Mr. WEBSTER had no objection.

Mr. TALLMADGE thought there would probably be some objection to the details of the bill, and he was opposed to it being ordered to be engrossed now, as that course would cut off all amendments, when it came up on its final passage.

Mr. BIBB was unwilling at this time that the bill should be ordered to be engrossed. He thought the gentleman from New York [Mr. Wright] would have given his sentiments to day; which would have allowed him, Mr. B. a better opportunity of examining the documents.

Mr. WEBSTER said that the question involved, was a judicial one, strictly speaking, and one which required close and strict attention. He would be very glad to have the advantage of the experience and judgment of the hon. member from Kentucky [Mr Bibb] in a question of this sort, and he was willing that the postponement should take place, if it was understood that the

question on engrossing the bill could be taken tomorrow, or on Friday at farthest.

The motion to postpone was agreed to.

On motion of Mr. BENTON, the Senate then went into the consideration of Executive business, and after some time spent with closed doors, The Senate adjourned.

HOUSE OF REPRESENTATIVES.

WEDNESDAY, Jan. 7, 1835.

Petitions and memorials were presented on leave, by—

Mr. MILLER, of Pennsylvania;
Mr. MASON, of Virginia;
Mr. GILLET, of New York;
Mr. REYNOLDS, of Illinois.

[Mr. REYNOLDS, of Illinois said—I am requested to present to this House, most strange and singular petitions. They proceed from a race of human beings that much need the care and attention of the Government of the United States—they have it in all cases wherein the Government is informed of their situation. These petitions are signed by about four hundred and fifty families of Fox Indians, and pray the Congress of the United States to take their situation into consideration, relative to the payment of their annuities. The State, that they are poor, which I know to be true, and depend much on their annuities for support. They say furthermore, that they have some of them, received any of the annuity ever of this year, and the others have received only a part of the annuity for the year. These annuities were paid in Bank notes at St. Louis, which is a great distance from their residence—and paid to some chiefs, who handled the amount over to the American Fur Company—the petitioners were not present at the transaction. They pray, that the annuities may hereafter be paid to each individual, or head of a family, in their own villages, and notice given of the time and place, which was not given in this instance.

Mr. BARBER, of Connecticut;
Mr. ADAMS, of Massachusetts;
Which petitions and memorials were appropriately referred.

Mr. McINTIRE, from the Committee on Claims, reported a bill for the relief of Joel Sartain; which was read twice and committed.

Mr. POLK, from the Committee of Ways and Means, reported a bill making appropriations for the Civil and Diplomatic expenses of Government for the year 1835; which was read twice, and committed to a Committee of the Whole on the state of the Union.

Mr. CARR submitted the following resolution:

Resolved, That the Committee on the Public Lands be instructed to inquire into the expediency of granting to each fractional township which there is no school lands located, a quantity of land for school purposes, sufficient to make them equal with whole townships, in proportion to the quantity of land contained in said fractional townships.

Mr. CARR remarked that in all the new States he believed, by the act of Congress admitting them into the Union, the section numbered sixteen in every township, and where such section had been sold, granted or disposed, other lands equivalent thereto, and most contiguous to the same, granted to the inhabitants of such township for the use of schools. Mr. C. stated, that upon the Ohio river and elsewhere, there were fractional townships in which there are no lands set apart for school purposes, and there were also George Rogers Clark, and the officers and soldiers under his command, which is called the Illinois grant, in which fractional townships are no school lands. Mr. C. said, the township which he had submitted, had for its object to provide more ample justice, than to grant to the people of said fractional townships, where no school lands are not set apart, such quantity of land to make them equal with those residing in ships, and to whom school lands have been ceded. He presumed to this proposition no one could object.

The resolution was adopted.

Mr. EVERETT, of Mass. offered the following resolution, which, under the rule, lies one day:

Resolved, That the Secretary of War be directed to communicate to this House, a copy of the Report of the Board of Engineers of the 13th of March, 1834, relative to the repairs of Fort Independence in Boston harbor, together with his opinion of the expediency of executing the repairs proposed in the said report.

On motion of Mr. JOHNSON, of Maryland:

Resolved, That the Commmittee on the District of Columbia be instructed to inquire into the propriety of establishing a territorial government within the District of Columbia, and of reporting some mode of relief to the said District from its present embarrassments.

The following resolution was offered by Mr. BROWN, which, under the rule, lies one day:

Resolved, That the Secretary of the Navy be requested to furnish this House with a statement containing the yearly amount of compensation, to which the post captains, masters commandant, lieutenants, masters' surgeons, surgeons' mates, pursers, chaplains, teachers, midshipmen, boatswains, gunners, carpenters, sail makers, and clerks in the navy ot the United States are severally entitled and which they actually receive under the existing laws, and the rules and regulations of the Navy Department, designating particularly the sums allowed and paid for the pay and rations, of the several officers themselves, and for the pay, rations, and clothing of their servants, together with the sums allowed for house rent, fuel, candles, stationary, furniture, commissions upon disbursements, and upon bills of exchange, and also the additional compensation (if any) made to officers while in command of squadrons or single ships, upon a home or foreign station, or while in command of Navy Yards, or acting as Navy Commissioner, and the difference of compensation and allowances for services rendered at sea, from those which are rendered on shore, and also the several sums usually allowed and paid for travel, and for services and attendance upon Courts Martial, surveys and duties of inspection, and for all or any other duties and services not enumerated or particularly mentioned in this resolution, so far as the same can be ascertained by the Navy Department.

On motion of Mr. A. H. SHEPPERD, of North Carolina,

Resolved, That the Committee on the Post Office and Post Roads be instructed to inquire into the expediency of establishing a post route from Germantown to the Little Yadkin post office, in Stokes county, North Carolina.

On motion of Mr. PINCKNEY,

Resolved, That the Committee on Military Affairs be instructed to inquire into the expediency of making compensation to Dr. J. E. B. Finley and Dr. E. Harvy Deas, for professional services rendered to certain companies of United States troops, according to a contract made with them by Major Heileman, of the United States army, and that the papers accompanying this resolution be referred to the same committee.

On motion of Mr. PEARCE, of Rhode Island,

Resolved, That the Committee on Agriculture be instructed to inquire into the expediency of adopting measures to establish the growth and manufacture of Silk—

And also of introducing into each State in the Union, the practical improvements made by Gamaliel Gay in the reeling and weaving the same.

On motion of Mr. WHITE of Florida,

Resolved, That the Committee on Revolutionary Claims be instructed to inquire into the expediency of allowing to Jesse Potts, of Florida, a Captain in the Continental line, in the war of the Revolution, his commutation pay under the resolution of Congress of 1783.

Mr. HAMER, on leave, submitted the following resolution:

Resolved, That the Committee on the Judiciary be instructed to inquire into the expediency of amending the Constitution of the United States so as to limit the service of the Judge of the Supreme and inferior Courts to a term of years.

Mr. EVANS moved the question of consideration.

Messrs. HUBBARD and MARDIS asked, simultaneously, for the yeas and nays; which were ordered.

Mr. WILLIAMS moved a call of the House; which was negatived.

The question was then propounded, "Will the House consider the resolution?" which was decided in the negative by the following vote:

YEAS—Messrs. John J. Allen, William Allen, Bean, Beaty, Bockee, Boon, Brown, Bull, Burns, Bynum, Cambreleng, Campbell, Carmichael, Carr, Casey, Chaney, Chilton, Samuel Clark, Clay, Clayton, Clowney, Cramer, Day, Dickerson, Dunlap, Ferris, Forester, Foster, Galbraith, Gamble, Gillet, Joseph Hall, Thomas H. Hall, Halsey, Hamer, Hardin, Joseph M. Harper, James Harper, Harrison, Hathaway, Henderson, Howell, Hubbard, Huntington, Inge, Jarvis, Noadiah Johnson, Seaborn Jones, Kilgore, Kinnard, Lane, Lansing, Luke Lea, Lewis, Love, Lyon, Joel K. Mann, Mardis, Moses Mason, May, McCarty, McIntire, McKay, McKim, McLene, Miller, Robert Mitchell, Morgan, Muhlenberg, Osgood, Pierson, Plummer, Polk, Reynolds, Robertson, Shinn, Smith, Standifer, Turner, Turrill, Vanderpoel, Van Houten, Wardwell, Whallon—84.

NAYS—Messrs. John Q. Adams, Chilton Allan, Anthony, Archer, Ashley, Banks, Barber, Barnitz, Bates, Baylies, Briggs, Burges, Cage, Chambers, Chinn, Claiborne, William Clark, Coffee, Corwin, Coulter, Crane, Crockett, Darlington, Amos Davis, Davenport, Deberry, Denny, Dickson, Evans, Edward Everett, Ewing, Fillmore, Philo C. Fuller, Fulton, Garland, Gilmer, Gordon, Graham, Grennell, Hard, Hazeltine, Heath, Hiester, William Jackson, Janes, William C. Johnson, Henry Johnson, Laporte, Lay, Letcher, Lincoln, Loyall, Manning, Martindale, Marshall, John Y. Mason, McComas, McKennan, McVean, Miner, Murphy, Patton, Pickens, Pinckney, Pope, Potts, Ramsay, Reed, Schenck, Schley, Augustine H. Shepperd, Slade, Sloane, Spangler, Steele, William Taylor, Philemon Thomas, Tompkins, Trumbull, Tweedy, Vance, Vinton, Watmough, White, Frederick Whittlesey, Wilde, Williams, Wilson, Wise, Young—90.

So the House refused to consider the resolution.

The House resumed the consideration of the resolution heretofore offered by Mr. CHILTON.

Mr. CHILTON said, he had endeavored to sustain the position which he had assumed, viz. that the funds in the Treasury of this nation were paid by the People of this Union, and of course belong to them, and not to any particular State or section of the Union. I am sustained in this opinion by the President of the United States. In his last Annual Message, the President says, "my views in regard to the expediency of making appropriations for works which are claimed to be of a national character, and prosecuted under State authority, assuming that Congress have the right to do so, were stated in my annual message to Congress in 1830, and also in that containing my objections to the Maysville road bill. So thoroughly convinced am I that no such appropriations ought to be made by Congress, until a suitable constitutional provision is made upon the subject, and so essential do I regard the point to the highest interests of our country, that I could not consider myself as discharging my duty to my constituents in giving the Executive sanction to any bill containing such an appropriation. If the People of the United States desire that the public Treasury shall be resorted to for the means to prosecute such works, they will concur in an amendment of the the constitution, prescribing a rule by which the national character of the works is to be tested, and by which the greatest practicable equality of benefits may be secured to each member of the confederacy. The effects of such a regulation would be most salutary in preventing unprofitable expenditures, in securing our legislation from the pernicious consequences of a scramble for the favors of Government, and in repressing the spirit of discontent which must inevitably arise from an unequal distribution of treasures which belong alike to all." Having disposed of the questions of fact and of law referable to the same, he now came to the solution of the question, What distribution of public funds will be just and equal? He would not attempt to point out what mode should be adopted. Great injustice had been done to the western States, by what has been familiarly called the American system. A distinguished member from the western States had reported to this House a mode of distribution which he (Mr. C.) believed to be just; it was, that there should be a distribution of the amount remaining in the Treasury to the States, in proportion to their population or representation on this floor. But this was not adopted. Contributions had been made for public works in some sections of this Union, while they had been withheld from others which had as important works, and claims as strong on Government. It had been intimated, that an attempt would be made to dispose of this resolution by laying it on the table; but if gentlemen suppose to stifle inquiry in this way, they will find it will be the last argument that will satisfy the people. He would invite attention to that part of the President's message in which he attempts to explain the reasons which induced him to veto works of improvement. He says: "The desire to embark the Federal Government in works of internal improvement prevailed in the highest degree during the first session of the first Congress I had the honor to meet in my present station. When the bill authorizing a subscription, on the part of the United States, for stock in the Maysville and Lexington Turnpike Company, passed the two Houses, there had been reported by the Committee on Internal Improvement bills containing appropriations for such objects, exclusive of those for the Cumberland Road, and for Harbors and Light Houses, to the amount of about one hundred and six millions of dollars. In addition to those projects which had been presented to the two Houses, under the sanction of their respective Committees on Internal Improvements, there were then still pending before the Committees, and in memorials presented, but not referred, different projects for works of a similar character, the expense of which cannot be estimated with certainty, but must have exceeded one hundred millions of dollars." Why was it that the first year of General Jackson's administration was selected for the purpose of encouraging these works? Why was it that the numerous applications were made, on which the Committees reported favorably, allowing upwards of one hundred millions of dollars and others involving the country one hundred millions more? There might be those that had not taken the pains he had to ascertain the motives. Mr. C. said he was one of the original supporters of the Executive of the United States; he had frequently had occasion to refer to this before, but he never did it boastingly, because it was not what he was disposed to boast of. Mr. C. proceeded till the orders of the day were called for.

The SPEAKER laid before the House the following communications:

A letter from the Secretary of the Treasury, in answer to a resolution of the House of the 12th ult., transmitting a list of the Land Offices and Land Districts, and the amount of moneys which have been received in each; which, on motion of Mr. CLAY, was laid on the table, and ordered to be printed.

A letter from the Secretary of War, in answer to a resolution of the House in relation to the suspension of the works in the harbor of Charleston, South Carolina; which, on motion of Mr. PINCKNEY, was laid on the table, and ordered to be printed.

A letter from the Secretary of War, in relation to the canal route in the vicinity of the Licking Summit, &c., in the State of Ohio; which was laid on the table.

PAY OF NAVAL OFFICERS.

The House then proceeded to the consideration of the unfinished special order—being the bill to regulate the pay of the officers of the Navy of the United States.

The question being on the motion of Mr. JONES, of Georgia, to recommit the bill to a Committee of the Whole on the state of the Union, with instructions to strike out all after the enacting clause, and insert in lieu thereof, a bill providing for the establishment of the ranks of

Admiral, Vice Admiral, and Rear Admiral, and fixing various grades of compensation to the individuals employed in the service—

Mr. JONES, of Georgia, arose and stated, that having had a conversation with the gentleman from Kentucky, (Mr. Pope,) he did not feel disposed to press the consideration of his motion until that gentleman should have an opportunity to present his amendment. He, however, must be understood to retain the opinion, that the well-being of the naval service required the establishment of the higher ranks indicated in his own proposition. He was well aware that this was unpopular in the House; but when he connected with his own impressions the remarks and arguments of gentlemen on that floor in relation to the support of the dignity of the officer and of the country abroad, he was still more convinced of the propriety of adding these higher ranks to those already existing in the navy. They were calculated not only to obviate the difficulties alluded to, but, also, to place before the officer another object of ambition—another inducement for alacrity in the performance of his duties. Not that they had ever failed in such performance—far from it—their merits were well known to him—but as another reward for their faithful services, which they have not now in prospect. He then withdrew his proposition for the present, for the purpose of giving precedence to the introduction of the motion of the gentleman from Kentucky, (Mr. Pope,) whose amendment was then read and adopted by Mr. J. as a modification of his motion.

Mr. WISE said he was not disposed to offer any special objections to this course; but he feared, though he did not entertain that belief himself, that it would be construed by many into an act of hostility to the bill.

Mr. POPE disclaimed all such hostility.

Mr. GILLET said, he had understood the true question before the House, on the adjonrnment of last evening, to be on the printing of the bill and amendment.

The CHAIR explained. That motion had been withdrawn.

Mr. GILLET then moved the postponement of the consideration of the bill till to-morrow, with the view to have it printed; for he protested, he could not himself understand the situation in which it stood, and he believed a great number of members were in the same condition.

Mr. WATMOUGH said, the bill was essentially the same, with the amendments as that already printed. He deprecated delay. The friends of the bill had shown a disposition to make every possible sacrifice consistent with their deep sense of right for the purpose of facilitating its passage.

Mr. JONES, of Georgia, expressed a hope that the gentleman from New York, (Mr. Gillet,) would waive his motion to print, in order to go into a Committee of the Whole, and get the bill in a condition to be engrossed. It would then be time enough to have it printed for further examination and amendment.

Mr. GILLET said the difficulty could not thus be avoided. A disagreement existed between the Chairman of the Select Committee (Mr. Watmough,) and himself, as to the construction of some of the provisions already passed upon—particularly in relation to *allowances* to commanding officers at sea and on shore. He said he also had amendments to propose as well as the gentleman from Kentucky, (Mr. Pope,) and, in the present confused state of the bill, he was not sure that he could properly designate where they should come in, or what should be their exact purport.

Mr. WATMOUGH said the amendment of the amendment of the gentleman who last addressed the Chair, went to strike out *all allowances*—so he could see no difficulty in the way of the gentleman, which could require the delay incident to printing.

The question was then taken on the motion of Mr. GILLET, and rejected.

Mr. REED next addressed the House in opposition to the motion to recommit the bill. He saw no necessity for it. It was already sufficiently understood for the action of the House, and for all purposes of amendment. The importance of, and the great and stirring interest excited by the bill, had been dwelt upon by the gentleman from Virginia (Mr. Allen) with great coolness and moderation, and he might say, apathy. That gentleman had appealed to many voluminous authorities, and among the rest, the Blue Book, to prove the present pay of the navy equal to that of the army. He had been corrected by the gentleman from Pennsylvania on his right, (Mr. Watmough's,) but the same argument was repeated. That gentleman had also said that most of the heroes of the late war who achieved our naval victories, were dead. No, sir, said Mr. R., the greater part of those brave men who "plucked up drowned honors from the deep" for us, are still living, and others as gallant as they, are ready to imitate the deeds of noble daring of their predecessors. Mr. R. said he never had wished to see a comparison between officers of the army and navy. It served but to sunder the ties which ever had and ever should bind them together.' But if such a comparison must be made, the services and pay of each would certainly show no advantage possessed by the navy. He had been surprised to hear the gentleman (Mr. Allen) speak of a three years cruise, as a mere jaunt of pleasure—a visit to some watering place. It was a great hardship for some gentlemen to leave their families for six months, for much greater compensation. He believed there was not a gentleman on that floor who would take the three years tour and duty of the officer of the navy, for double the compensation proposed. He next adverted to what was denominated the pension-fund, and justified this part of the bill. But, said Mr. R., if the majority think proper, let it be rejected; he would still support the bill, for the other good it contained. The gentleman from New York, (Mr. Mann,) had threatened them with the ballot box. He hoped gentlemen would do their duty, without such fears before their eyes, leaving the consequences with their constituents. Those who rowed and looked back were in danger of upsetting the boat. That gentleman had next attacked the title of the bill. Though he acknowledges "a rose by any other name would smell as sweet." Yet, it is rhubarb to him. Sir, the fault is in his taste. Mr. R. said he thought the title a very proper one.

After some further remarks, Mr. R. contended for the justice of advancing the pay of naval officers, on the ground that all other officers of the Government had received an exception of pay. The Heads of Departments—the Postmaster General—the Custom-house Officers—our honorable selves—all, all have been advancing with the growth of the country and its business, excepting the naval officers, who have remained stationary for forty years. The gentleman (Mr. Mann) had made a comparison between the pay of subordinate officers in our navy and in that of Great Britain and France. Sir, said Mr. R., our under officers are superior to those of any other nation, in all their capacities, and deserve a correspondingly higher compensation. If the gentleman really felt such strong republican impulses, let him show it by supporting the rights and interests of these commoners and working men of the navy.—But the gentleman appeared to be opposed to all things—to the army, the navy, the Blue Book; all allowances, and all salaries. Sir, I really fear his zeal and his respect for the ballot-boxes, have entirely misled his judgment. From many positions taken by gentlemen, Mr. R. was inclined to fear that the bill had, in many points, been misapprehended; and if so, it might be necessary to have it recommitted. This remained with the House to determine. For his own part he was content with it as it stood. Mr R. said he was truly friendly to our gallant navy. It had been denominated an *arm* of our national defence. He would take leave to pronounce it the *right* arm. Our country was one, which must from its location, be defended by wooden walls. We were in fear of invasion by land—all attacks must come from the sea; and though we were happily at peace now, with all the world; yet the same passions of the human breast, which have heretofore produced wars, still existed,—and while they did exist, a state of preparation for its emergencies was the surest way of preserving the blessings of peace. Should war be our fate, said Mr. R., how important will a strong naval armament be for our defence, but if our country should continue to prosper under the benign influence of peace, the expense of its support will never be felt nor murmured at by a grateful and happy People. Mr. R. next dwelt on the importance of our navy in time of peace, in the protection of our commerce, the chastisement of pirates, and securing to our countrymen the trade of distant islands. Another argument for the increase of these salaries, was the great uncertainty and tardiness of promotion. Our Lieutenants might spend long lives in toilsome and dangerous service, and yet how very few could ever attain a higher rank? He concluded by a further defence of the appropriation of three per cent. out of the pay for the support of the relatives of the persons engaged in the service.

He was followed by

Mr JARVIS, who rose and offered an amendment, which was read by the Clerk.

Mr. JARVIS said he professed a friendship for the Navy, but he trusted it was an enlightened and judicious one. He wished to see some advance in the pay of naval officers; but he thought some of the provisions of this bill went beyond all reason. If passed, he believed it would tend to render that important arm of the national defence unpopular with the People—with whom it had always, up to this day, been extremely popular. He asked how their constituents would manage this thing, if it were placed directly in their own hands? Most members of Congress had also belonged to their several State Legislatures. There was not a State judicial office with a salary higher than $2,000. The Governors of five States received but $1000 per annum—five $1500—and five more not exceeding $2000. He could only attribute the liberality of Congress on these occasions to the zig-zag manner in which the expense was defrayed. In the collection of State taxes, the tax-gatherer meets you at your door, face to face, but not so with a tax collector through the customs. Mr. J. said he would venture to assert, that if these salaries were to be raised by direct taxation, not one member on that floor would record his vote for this bill, unless he expected to vacate his seat on that floor at the close of the session. The increase proposed was more than sufficient to cover the whole expenses of each of three-fourths of the States, and more than the average of that of the whole of them. Mr. J. here went into an examination of the increase proposed to the salary of each officer. He said it was alarming; it seemed like a determination to tap the *butt of* the Treasury at both ends, and knock out the bung hole.

After some further remarks from Mr. JARVIS, in support of his amendment,

Mr. CROCKETT said he did not know how the motion he was about to make would be received by the House, but his object was to come to a determination on this subject some way or other. The House had already spent two weeks on the bill, and, to all appearance, were likely to spend two or three more, unless some final stop was put to it. In the mean time, there was much important private business on the table, and, among it, some that greatly concerned his constituents. He therefore called for the *previous question*.

A majority of the House, however, did not second the motion.

Mr. WISE expressed a desire to address the House; but as the day was somewhat advanced, he moved an adjournment.

The motion was negatived.

Mr. WISE then said—

Mr. SPEAKER: I am in favor of the amendments proposed by the gentleman from Kentucky (Mr. Pope) and would sustain them, if I thought we could go into committee with safety to the bill. But believing that the motion to re-commit will be used, not by the gentleman himself, however, to defeat this bill entirely, I shall oppose the re-commitment, and support the bill as it is, rather than endanger its passage by attempting to amend its minor defects.

My colleague, (Mr. Allen,) who addressed the House the other day in opposition to the bill, de-

[CONTINUED IN NEXT NUMBER.]

CONGRESSIONAL GLOBE.

BY BLAIR & RIVES.	——WEEKLY——	PRICE $1 A SESSION.
2d Sess........23d Cong.	MONDAY, JANUARY 19, 1835.	Volume 2........No. 7.

TWENTY-THIRD CONGRESS.

SECOND SESSION.

HOUSE OF REPRESENTATIVES,
Wednesday, January 7, 1835.
[Continued from last number.]

trusted all legislation which appeals to prejudice or passion—to feelings of national pride or glory; to neither of which does this bill appeal so much as to an enlightened sense of national justice and policy and individual right, founded solely on the just law, "that the laborer is worthy of his hire," and that the faithful servant who labors much, risks much, is responsible for much, and deprived of much, in important public service, should be adequately paid in proportion to his labor, his risk, his responsibility, and his privation.

Sir, I fear there was no necessity to awaken distrust against this proposed increase of the pay of the navy. There was no manner of danger that this House was about to be carried away by any intemperate zeal—by any passion or prejudice—or by any feeling of national pride and glory for the navy.

Far, far from there having been too much feeling for this class of public officers—there has always been a total want of feeling or interest in their behalf. They have repeatedly come, and you have as repeatedly sent them away empty—they have cried, and you have heeded not their petitions. They have knocked, and the treasury has been closed against them; and this, too, when others have come, and you have loaded them with gold—when others have but whispered, and you have nodded your assent—when others have taken the key, and opened the door without knocking, and you have turned away your heads from the robbery of the Treasury, to keep from being State's evidence! The army pay has been increased—the Secretaries have been made couriers—their clerks, like candles, are yearly new lopped—one department has learned to take the public money without asking, and you have made all extra appropriations asked for besides—have put your own hands pretty deeply into the public purse—and the very messengers, too, men, "Columbia's white slaves," of you all, are richly larded with the very drippings of extravagant expenditures of the public money. And look at the Navy pay list! The very same it was in the time of Paul Jones, and the only pay list of any branch of your service not stained with wastefulness, but pale and meager with degrading parsimony. And you, forsooth, you are told not to let a sense of national pride and glory carry you away, in the midst of all this scene of extravagance on other objects, in preventing the elbows of your Cap from peeping through their coat sleeves on the quarter decks of your proudest ships on foreign stations! Sir, I do invoke the national honor and pride to remove injustice, to preserve something like equality of pay amongst all public servants, according to their duties and responsibilities. No one need invoke the glorious achievements of your navy, which has proved to be one of the most faithful public servants, to increase the pay of its officers for the purpose of gratifying pride merely, when your present Secretary of the Navy reports that their pay "is altogether inadequate to an honorable discharge of their duties." Yes, sir, "to an honorable discharge of their duties," and when, too, your own Committees have reported it to be "degradingly low."

It is with these reports and this evidence, they approach you—saying, proving that the inadequacy of their compensation is killing to their pride, their pride, their honor, and common honesty, weakening to the navy's strength, injurious and destructive to the public interest, by degrading and corrupting the country's fighting men. It is upon these topics of justice and interest, and of glory, though of national honor and pride as connected with justice and interest, that I mean to speak; though I cannot see the unfairness of a good and faithful servant's pointing to his well-doings, when he comes to ask justice at the hands of those whom he has nobly served, especially if he has been more than thrice ungratefully refused his just due. He should be paid in some gain, and not all in glory; and if in seeking his due he should happen to speak of his deeds, the solid argument of inadequate compensation should hardly be impaired in our minds by his stirring up the recollection of his past glorious services to the country.

Sir, I wish to present some facts to the House. The gross amount of the present pay of the commission and warrant officers, provided for in the bill, is in round numbers, - - - $770,000

The Se'ect Committee first proposed an increase of - - $116,000
By its second report, it proposed an additional increase of - 84,000
All the amendments in the Committee of the Whole and in the House, have increased the pay - - - 6,000

Making the whole increase, $206,000

The gross amount of pay as proposed by this bill, - - - $976,000

Relying then upon the reports of the Department and of the committee, that there should be some increase, the sole question is, whether this amount of increase is too much?

The present pay of the navy was fixed in the 18th century. The changes since then have been great in every point of view. Though articles of family and personal consumption are perhaps lower now than then, yet the wants of men have multiplied in a quadruple ratio. Respectable living is much higher to the officers. What was respectable living then is mean now, to almost every grade and class of society.

The navy itself has greatly increased, and its duties multiplied, the responsibilities of its service much more onerous than formerly, the living of officers, their duties and responsibilities then being to the living of the officers, their duties and responsibilities now, as a ship of war then would be to a line of battle ship now.

The present pay is said to be "degradingly low." I should think, then, that the sum of $20,000 was no very great increase to raise the pay of so many officers and men from such a condition to that of a respectable footing. This sum appears reasonable to me, especially when the whole list, with its increase, will gain by comparison with that of any other branch of service. And if the increase of pay is not in the aggregate too much, there is no reason for recommitting this bill on account of its form.

The officers of every grade more generally unite in approving the pay proposed, and its distribution, and are better satisfied with what they call the "equanimity" of this bill than with that of any other ever proposed. For this I have the authority of respectable officers of every grade. And the main object of the bill is not only to increase and regulate, but to equalize the pay of the officers—not to equalize the pay of the army and navy, but to equalize the pay of the navy by itself. It was found wholly impracticable to equalize the pay of the army with that of the navy. There can be no assimilation of the pay of the two, because there does not, and cannot exist any relation whatever of grades and duties between them, except by the mere arbitrary regulation of the two Departments, for the idle purposes of etiquette.

There is a want more generally among grades in the army than in the navy. And the duties of a sailor to those of a soldier can no more be assimilated than the fishes of the sea to the birds and beasts of dry land. But as a comparison was instituted by my colleague, I must beg leave to set him right as to certain errors of which he was guilty both as to the pay of the officers of the army, and as to the relative pay of army and navy. By regulation of the Departments alone, Commodores rank with Brigadier Generals; Captains with Colonels; Master Commandants with Majors; Lieutenants with Captains;

Now, sir, my colleague very honestly, no doubt, but very unjustly to the navy, took the pay of thirty-six Captains of the navy, (a Commodore is nothing more than a Captain,) and compared its gross amount with that of one Major General, two Brigadier Generals, and the Colonels of the army. The balance was large, of course, against the navy. But, sir, it was a false balance.

There is no grade of the navy as high or corresponding with that of Major General. Below him to the rank of Captain in the army, with whom a Lieutenant of the navy ranks, there is a most numerous list of superior officers, all ranking higher by brevet than their nominal grades, and some of them receiving the brevet pay.

In the navy, the highest rank is that of captain. There is no topmost higher to which a sailor may climb. Here promotion in the navy is damned up, and the number of this rank is, of course, comparatively much greater than that of the corresponding rank in the army. But, as the first grade of the navy ranks with brigadier generals and colonels, and the second grade with majors, we must compare the pay of the navy captains with that of all the officers of the army, from major generals down to majors, with whom masters commandant rank. How stands the comparison then?

From major general to majors, according to the report of the Secretary of War, there are 38 generals and colonels and lieutenant colonels, as officers to the 36 captains of the navy. How stands their relative pay?

Sir, I will not touch that blue book, a lie upon the calendar. I refer you, sir, to Adjutant General Jones's report to Congress in '32 '33. He makes the statement of the army pay under the present law,

Rank.	Total pay per year.
Major General - - -	$6,515 64
Brigadier General - -	4,422 32
Colonel - - -	2,941 32
Lt. Colonel - - -	2,372 32
Majors - - -	2,106 32

This table with the notes will enable us to ascertain very nearly what the army pay is.

"Note:—Officers are required to keep their "servants and horses, to entitle them to their al- "lowance."

"Double rations are allowed to officers when "commanding separate posts, and are to be added "to the above in such cases."

"Fuel and quarters are allowed by regulations "and paid through the Quartermaster's department, and are not included in this table."

The subsistence or rations of a Major General, per year amount to $1,095.

Double rations -	$2,180
House rent about -	800
Fuel not included,	
Double rations and rent -	$2,980

Excluding fuel and taking only single rations, the pay of Major General is $8,607 64
A Brigadier General's pay at a separate post, allowing $600 for house rent, and exclusive of fuel is $5,898 32
A Colonel's pay at a separate post, allowing $400 for quarters, exclusive of fuel, is $3,379 32
A Lieut. Colonel's pay, at a separate post, $350 for quarters, exclusive of fuel, is $2,805 32
A Major's under same circumstances, allowing $300 for rent, is $2,698 32
But this is not the worst of it. Nearly all of these grades, and many of the Captains have separate posts. Besides, the Brigadier Generals are Maj.

there are not more patrons of the navy who have drawn prize money in proportion to the number of all the crews seeking it, than persons who have drawn prizes in lotteries in proportion to the number of persons holding tickets. A vessel has *first to be fallen in* with—then be *captured*—then sent in safety to the United States, and there are nine chances to one of recapture before arriving in our ports, especially when the enemy are powerful at sea—which must always be the case with any nation we are likely to be at war with. If the capture arrives safely, however, the greater portion of the proceeds (after paying *double duties* to the United States for all dutiable articles on board, and, in case of an inferior force, *half the value* of vessel and cargo) is eaten up by the various expenses—enriching only District Attorneys, Marshals, auctioneers, and prize-agents—so that poor Jack and his officers get but *a small slice for their shares*. Many of our officers, who were thought to be very successful in taking prizes, realised only from $50 to $100 during their cruise; and many others were taken themselves, and continued *prisoners through the war*. But, again, before prize-money, there has to be *a war*; and then a long war, if at all. We are a nation of peace. Our whole policy is peace. It is now 20 years since officers and crews have had a chance for prize-money. In the execution of other duties, your officers have not unfrequently made captures, when they have been held liable for heavy costs, harassed in suits at law, and, in some instances, obliged to beg relief from Congress. The amount of prize-money received by the *most fortunate officer*, commanding during the last war with Great Britain, it is confidently believed would not exceed $10 per month during his whole term of service. The amount for the most fortunate *junior* officer would not be $3 per month.

"The ideas entertained in relation to prize-money are extremely erroneous—if acquired at all, it is hardly fought for and *dearly won*—adds glory to our flag, and has nothing to do with the pay and emoluments of officers, for *it never comes out of the pockets of the People*. The argument would hold equally good against reducing or giving less pay to officers of the customs in consequence of the possibilities or probabilities that may occur for them to detect goods *about being smuggled*—merely because they are entitled to half the net proceeds, when the goods shall have been *tried, condemned, and all expenses paid*. Men of war seldom deem it prudent to weaken the efficiency of their ships, by sending their men on board prizes, consequently the great bulk of prizes taken are *destroyed*." Such is the unanswerable manner in which the navy can reason for itself. In addition to this, I have the pointed authority of Lord Nelson for saying "that prize-money is a *s005ng* to the State." It is "a *s005ng* to the State," *taken from an enemy*, and, though *poor reward*, a sharp *stimulus* to the courage of crew and commander.

But, sir, such arguments as these would not have been required in the year 1816, just after the war. Your navy magnanimously deferred its application for increase of pay, then, because of the heavy burthen to the public debt, added by that war so gallantly and gloriously fought by sailors' arms "for free trade and sailors' rights." You have now celebrated the extinguishment of that debt, your Treasury is a Horn of Plenty, and *now*, if you *stint your navy and war does come*—

"Look on thy country
"And see the cities and the towns defac'd
"By wasting rule of the cruel foe."

Sir, I beg of you, *now, before hand*, to

"Strike these that hurt, and hurt not those that help!
"One drop of blood drawn from thy country's bosom
"Should grieve thee more than streams of foreign gore."

Mr. WAYNE said, that important questions, like the present, must frequently have their conclusion, upon the same principle which actuated the framers of the Government—in the principle of compromise. He was satisfied that the friends of the bill before the House, could only accomplish their main objects by a resort to the principle to which he alluded. He had risen for the purpose of moving to strike from the bill certain passages which appeared obnoxious to some gentlemen. They were the same, with one or two exceptions,

which were embraced in the proposition of the gentleman from Kentucky, (Mr. Pope.) His proposition, he conceived, would present a fair ground of compromise, and as no member, so far as he had understood, was opposed to giving adequate pay to those employed in the naval service, the House would, by mutual concessions, be enabled, he hoped, to come to a decision of the question without further difficulty. He, therefore, moved to amend the bill by striking out all that part relating to extra allowances, and to raising a fund by deducting three per cent. from the pay of the commission and warrant officers, for the relief of the relatives of deceased officers.

The SPEAKER stated that the motion required the unanimous consent of the House.

Mr. JONES, of Georgia, objected.

Mr. WAYNE moved a suspension of the rule, in order that he might be enabled to submit the motion.

The SPEAKER decided that the motion, under the circumstances in which it was presented (there being other motions pending) could only be made with the unanimous consent of the House.

After some conversation between the SPEAKER, and Messrs. WAYNE, JONES, of Georgia, CAMBRELENG, and HARDIN, in relation to the mode of proceeding upon the commitment and the several instructions which had been presented, the latter gentleman moved an adjournment, which carried.

The House then adjourned.

IN SENATE.

THURSDAY, Jan. 8, 1835.

Petitions and memorials were presented by Mr. PORTER and Mr. EWING.

On motion of Mr. TYLER, the memorial presented by him yesterday, from citizens of Georgetown, was ordered to be printed.

The CHAIR submitted a communication from the Secretary of State, transmitting a list of the officers employed in that Department, for the year 1834, with the compensation given to each.

The joint resolution recommending an amendment of the Constitution, so as to provide that when a bill shall be vetoed by the President, it may be passed into a law by a *majority only*, of both Houses, was taken up for consideration, and

On motion of Mr. KENT, was postponed to Thursday the 22d inst. and ordered to be printed.

Mr. ROBINSON, pursuant to notice, and on leave given, introduced a bill for the relief of Wilkinson Godwin, which was read twice and referred.

Mr. SOUTHARD, from the Committee on Naval Affairs, reported a bill for the relief of A. D. Ostrander.

Mr. SOUTHARD, from the same committee, reported a joint resolution for the settlement of the claim of John S. Stiles, under a contract for the supply of navy bread.

The bill for the relief of James Young was read a second time, and referred to the Committee on the District of Columbia.

The following bills were read a second time and referred:

The bill for the relief of Henry Awkward.

The bill for the relief of the heirs and legal representatives of Baily C. Clark.

A bill to authorize the Secretary of State to issue letters patent to James Jones, for an improvement in the manufacture of cotton fabrics.

Mr. CLAYTON, from the Judiciary Committee, reported a bill for the relief of William Tharp, which was read the first time, and ordered to a second reading.

Mr. EWING, pursuant to notice, and on leave given, introduced a bill for the relief of — Paine and Elias Arnold; which was read twice and referred.

Mr. KING, of Alabama, gave notice, that tomorrow, he would ask leave to introduce a bill authorizing George Whitman to import an iron steam boat in duty-free of parts, free of duty.

The following bills were read a second time, and ordered to be engrossed for a third reading:

A bill for the relief of Henry B. Tyler, executor of Lieut. Col. Richard B. Smith.

A bill for the relief of McKean Buchanan.

A bill for the relief of the administrator of Michael Hogan, deceased.

The bill providing for the regulation of vessels propelled in whole or in part by steam, and

The bill for the relief of — a purser in the navy, were severally taken up for consideration, and

On motion of Mr. SOUTHARD, were laid on the table.

SPECIAL ORDER.

The Senate resumed the consideration of the bill making compensation for French Spoliations prior to 1800; when

Mr. WRIGHT spoke at length in opposition to the objects and principles of the bill.

When Mr. W. concluded,

Mr. WEBSTER rose and remarked, that he hoped he should not be called on to speak, except to reply finally to all the gentlemen who intended speaking in opposition to the bill.

Mr. KING said, if the Senator from Massachusetts would pardon him, he would, before the question was taken on engrossing the bill, say something in justification of the vote he should give. He did not however propose to go fully into the subject. He had made no regular preparation with a view of doing so. But some of those friends with whom he had been very weak in the habit of acting, especially on questions requiring a defence of the public Treasury, had advocated the claims of those interested in the passage of the bill, with a degree of labor, zeal, and apparent earnestness of feeling which afforded the best possible evidence of their entire conviction of the propriety of the course they had adopted; and he therefore felt it a respect due to them, as well as a justification of himself, to give at least some of the reasons why he should side with them upon the present occasion.

Mr. K. said, he should be brief, for the reason first stated. In fact, he did not think the bill called for a very wide range of discussion. For although the history of the claims was a long one, and the facts and documents connected with them numerous, yet it would be seen from the discussion, so far as heard, that the facts necessary to be known and understood to direct our judgment upon the bill, were neither numerous or controverted; on the contrary, the difference in the minds of Senators upon the merits of the claims, would result from a difference of conclusion from the same admitted facts, and not from any controversy about the facts themselves.

What was the proposition, by the establishment of which the advocates of the bill sought to enforce upon the Senate the propriety of its passage? If he understood it, it was this: That France, on the 30th of September, 1800, was indebted to citizens of the United States, (the claimants) at least five millions of dollars. That the United States were at the same time under treaty stipulations to France; onerous to them, and valuable to France; and that the United States, having charge of the claims of their citizens, released those claims to France, in consideration of a release of their own treaty stipulations to that nation. Hence it was contended that the United States are liable to their own citizens for those claims of France, upon the same principle that an agent is liable to his principal if he appropriate the effects of the latter to his own use. The doctrine was sound enough, if the proposition were established. But, in prosecuting an inquiry into the truth of the proposition, we should inquire, and if possible ascertain—

1st. Whether in point of fact the government of France was, according to the existing rules of national law, indebted to the claimants five millions, or any other sum, on the 30th September, 1800?

2. Whether in point of fact the United States were at the same date bound by treaty stipulations onerous to them, and valuable to France, which would afford a consideration for the release of the claims?

And it might not be unimportant to inquire, in the third place, whether, if these claims once existed and were released by the acts of our government in its regular administration, any responsibility

ity should attach to the government for obeying the necessary exigencies of State policy?

Mr. K. returned to the first inquiry. Was France indebted to the claimants on the 30th September, 1800? That France had committed spoliations which made her liable at one time to claimants was not disputed on either side, but *insisted on* by both. The claims, he said, arose as well by a reckless violation of the laws of nations as by repeated and sometimes admitted infractions of the treaty of commerce between the two countries, dated the 6th February, 1778. Several of the articles of this treaty, connected with these claims, had just been read by his friend from New York (Mr. Wright.) The article most material, he Mr. K. read.

It is as follows: "Article 23d. It shall be lawful for all and singular the subjects of the Most Christian King and the citizens, people and inhabitants of the said United States to sail with their ships with all manner of liberty and security. No distinction being made who are the proprietors of the merchandise laden thereon, from any port to the places of these who now are or hereafter shall be at enmity with the Most Christian King, or the United States. It shall likewise be lawful for the subjects and inhabitants aforesaid to sail with the ships and merchandise aforesaid mentioned, and to trade with the same liberty and security from the places, ports and harbors of those who are enemies of both or either party, without any opposition or disturbance whatsoever, not only directly from the places of the enemy aforementioned to neutral places, but also from one place belonging to an enemy, to another place belonging to an enemy, whether they be under the jurisdiction of the same Prince, or under several. And it is hereby stipulated, *that free ships shall give a freedom to goods*, and that every thing shall be deemed to be free and exempt, which shall be found on board the ships belonging to the subjects of either of the confederates, although the whole lading or any part thereof should appertain to the enemies of either—contraband goods being always excepted. It is also agreed in like manner, that the same liberty be extended to persons who are on board a free ship with this effect, that although they be enemies of both or either party, they are not to be taken out of that free ship unless they are soldiers, and in actual service of the enemies."

Another article in the treaty provided that a sea letter *of a particular form, specified in the article*, should, on being exhibited, determine the neutral or friendly character of the vessel. This article was violated in the most flagrant manner, by an unexpected decree, requiring what they called a "role d'equipage," which took hundreds by surprise, who had prepared themselves with a letter in the form prescribed by the treaty. In short, France first violated the treaty, as seemed on all hands admitted, and continued her depredations from 1793 till the treaty of 1800. Nor was our Government remiss in attention to the claims of its citizens. Every effort was made to recover indemnity for them. Envoy after Envoy was sent to the French Court to negotiate on the subject; but they were subjected to the most degrading conditions as the price of the privilege of negotiating, and treated with a contempt only equalled by that which was paid to our flag; and at last virtually kicked out of the country. These indignities were submitted to until—nay, *long after* forbearance ceased to be a virtue, and finding negotiation hopeless, we determined to resort to force.

Mr. K. insisted that the spoliations which were the subject of the bill, had caused a war between the two countries,—a war, to be sure, of limited duration, but still a public war, by which the claims were extinguished. The acts of a hostile nature passed by Congress in 1798, had all just been read or referred to by his friend from New York, the most material of which were those authorising the capture of the armed vessels of France. On the 28th day of May, in that year, Congress passed an act authorising the armed vessels of the United States to capture any armed vessel of France which had committed depredations on our commerce, or which might be found cruising about our coasts for that purpose. This act has been called *defensive* barely in its character. Admit it to be so, said Mr. K., and what is to be said of the act of 9th July, 1798? This act authorizes the capture of French armed vessels *any where on the high seas*. In other words, it authorized a general maritime war with France.

And did these acts, inquired Mr. K., end in idle ceremony? Not at all, sir. The President, as authorized, issued his proclamation to carry them into effect; and from that time the armed forces of the two nations understood perfectly well the hostile relations in which their respective nations stood to each other, and acted accordingly.—When their ships met, they instantly cleared for action; some of the most desperate conflicts ensued—their masts were cut off by the dexterity of our gunners—their hulls were shattered into useless floating wrecks—their decks were drenched in the blood of their seamen—conquered, captured, carried into port, confiscated, sold, and distributed as prize. And yet, gentlemen say there was no war in this! The Senator from New York who had just taken his seat, in referring to this state of things, asked if it could be called peace? "Certainly," he was answered from the seat of the Senator from Massachusets. "Certainly," we may call things by what names we please, but, in nature, they are not changed by the names we arbitrarily give them. We may call a declaration of war a proclamation of neutrality. We may call a challenge to mortal conflict a love letter, or a billetdoux. Or a bloody war may be called, as in this case, "a mere misunderstanding." Yet, these things would remain unchanged in their natures and consequences by the names assigned to them.

But, inquired Mr. K., why is it that those hostilities, carried on by the authority of the Government, did not constitute war? He knew not what reason the Senator from Massachusetts (Mr. Webster) who was to conclude the discussion, might assign; but other Senators had assigned no other reason than that "the negotiators *said* there had been no war." They might as well have "said" that there never was a flood. They might as well have "said" that the battle of Waterloo was a friendly salutation between the contending armies. Their sayings could not change war into peace. But the truth was, said Mr. K., the French negotiators, when the claims were *first* presented, "said" *there had been war*, "and that any indifferent nation would say so," and that, consequently, "no indemnities could be claimed."

It makes but little difference, however, said Mr. K. what these gentlemen said in the politeness of their diplomacy, striving to forget the past, and mutually seeking the advantage in reviving an extinguished treaty. Mr. Vatel said, when he wrote his book on the law of nations, that "war is that state in which we prosecute our rights by force." Public war being that prosecuted by national authority. Were not these acts of hostility by national authority, and in the prosecution of our rights by force? Certainly they were. In fact, it was war in a very unqualified sense. *It was the forcible collision of the armed forces of the two nations, by authority of each.* The claimants then on the 30th September, 1800, had *no claim which we could with technical right insist on*, and France never surrended this right to disclaim them, *or offered* to surrender it, unless upon terms she thought advantageous to her.

But it was said that if these claims were extinguished by war, they were revived by negotiation. Mr. K. inquired how they could be revived by *mere negotiation?* The Envoys could not revive an extinguished claim by merely insisting on it, or taking it into notice in negotiating a treaty. They might as well have undertaken to revive the edict of Nantz. It was a matter they could not controul *without the approbation of the ratifying authority*. It was of no consequence upon what principle they *negotiated*, but we should inquire upon what principle the Senate *ratified*. But it is said they were recognised as a subject of negotiation in the 2d article of the treaty. Very well, sir, and did the Senate ratify the 2d article? Not at all. Their first act, when the treaty was presented, was to put the sponge upon it. They said, in effect, let the second article be blotted from the instrument. Could the Senate have disclaimed, more emphatically, the notice which had been taken of the subject? The negotiators had taken the subject into consideration, and it was necessary to dispose of it. They therefore said, in the 2d article, that "not being able to agree" upon the subject, they postponed it to a more convenient time. The 2d article expunged by the Senate, the treaty was sent back to Napoleon, and what did he do? Why he agreed to the retrenchment of the second article, "provided" —provided what, sir?—that the respective nations would pay the *claims* of their citizens respectively? Not at all, sir. He never thought of such a thing. For France had never paid its citizens for the claims they were at the same time setting up against us. But he agreed to the retrenchment of the second article, provided each party renounced the respective "*pretensions* which were the object of the second article." "Pretensions" was a very slighting term to use in reference to a valid debt. The pretensions in his mind most likely were the claims of mutual guaranty, and the privilege of neutrals; but whatever they were, this was only another mode for disposing of them as not sustainable. So we see, sir, that the *ratifying power* acted on the principle that the claims were extinguished by hostilities, whatever *the negotiators may* have said or done in the matter.

Mr. K. said, that after the second article was expunged, the matter stood precisely in the predicament in which it would have stood if the claims had not been noticed in the treaty. And he supposed it would hardly be contended that if national hostilities had existed, and peace restored by treaty, without noticing claims *which were the cause of hostilities*, that these claims would not be extinguished.

But it is said our own Envoys alleged that this class of claims was due, and insisted on its payment. Certainly they did, sir, and on many things else they did not obtain. He understood his friend from Maine, (Mr. Shepley,) who dwelt on this circumstance, had much of the confidence of his constituents as a lawyer, as well as a politician. If so, he would ask his friend if he had not often insisted strongly that thousands were due to his client when he knew there was not due to him one cent? Doubtless he had, and did only his duty in doing so. The Government and Envoys acted on a similar principle. They were representing American citizens, and they did the best they could for them; but not being able to recover indemnities from France, it was a little hard their very diligence should be used as a reason for charging the United States with the claim.

But it is further said that the French also acknowledged these claims. Yes, sir, said Mr. K., and how did they acknowledge them? They acknowledged them, always coupled with a condition that would at the same time extinguish them. They would negotiate for the payment of these claims, *provided* we would revive an extinguished treaty, and allow them to put their own price on its supposed obligations. What kind of acknowledgment was this? and they certainly never made any other. You, sir, said Mr. K., make claim on me for ten millions of dollars. Very well; I may safely answer, "your account is a false one, but I will acknowledge it, if you will permit me to produce a false receipt for it." "Your debt is barred or extinguished; but I have claims of greater amount against you of a similar character, and I have no objection to settle, if I can bring you in debt." Various offers were made on both sides, but they were all, when closely examined, of this nature; for they were always "to renew" the treaties, which implied their previous extinction; and these offers of renewal were always accompanied with modifications and conditions, thought advantageous to the proposer. The claims, then, Mr. K. insisted, had been extinguished by the hostile relations between the two countries, and had never been revived either by negotiation or acknowledgment.

Mr. K. then went into the second subject of inquiry. Were the United States, on the 30th September, 1800, bound by treaty stipulations to the Government of France, onerous to the one and valuable to the other? Mr. K. thought not. The

conduct of France had perhaps sufficiently discharged the United States from all the obligations of the treaties. But, to put the matter beyond doubt, in a judicial point of view, Congress, on the 7th of July, 1798, passed an act, declaratory on the subject by which (after reciting in the preamble as a justification of the act the frequent violations of the treaties by France) it was enacted, "That the United States are of right freed and exonerated from the stipulations of the treaties and of the Consular Convention heretofore concluded between the United States and France, and that the same shall not henceforth be considered as legally obligatory on the Government or citizens of the United States."

One would suppose, said Mr. K., that this act would settle the matter. But, to his utter astonishment, this right in the United States as an independent party to the treaty had been denied. It was said the consent of both parties must first be obtained. There might be some modification of the right, as between the United States and its citizens claiming the benefit of a treaty; or the right of Congress to repeal a treaty by ordinary legislation without reasons, might be questioned. But this was a judicial act of an independent sovereign power, containing the reasons for the decision, which reasons all acknowledged to be perfectly true. And when gentlemen were so general in their denial of the power of Congress on this subject, as to include the act in question, he scarcely knew how to treat such a position. What an extraordinary position we should be placed in! Having treaties of peace and commerce with all the world, any nation with whom we had made treaties might violate them at pleasure, drive our commerce from the ocean, and even bring war to the Capitol, and the United States could not move against the offender without breaking the faith of treaties! This would be a new principle to introduce into the law of nations.

From the time of Grotius up to the present time, it had, he thought, been acknowledged a universal principle of national law, that in cases of compact between independent nations, there being no common judge, each party had the right to judge for itself, "as well of the infraction as of the mode and measure of redress." This principle had been much quoted of late to sustain the rights of the States of the Union, to judge of an infraction of the constitution. He never could see the application of this principle to the rights of the States in their relation to the Federal Government; but when applied to the United States and France, two nations entirely independent in all their exterior relations, the principle was plain, and the application easy. Mr. K. said he had happily turned to one authority on national law, which he believed spoke the sentiments of all elementary writers on the subject.—[Mr. K. then read from Vattel, book 11, ch. 13, page 213.]

"Treaties contain promises that are perfect and reciprocal. If one of the parties fails in his engagements, the other may compel him to fulfil them. A perfect promise confers a right to do so. But if the latter has no other expedient but that of arms to force his ally to the performance of his promise, he will sometimes find it more eligible to cancel the promises on his own side also, and dissolve the treaty. He has undoubtedly a right to do this, since his promises were made only on condition, that the ally should on his part, execute every thing which he had engaged to perform. The party therefore, who is offended or impaired in those particulars which constitute the basis of the treaty, is at liberty to chose the alternative of either compelling a faithless ally to fulfil his engagements, or of declaring the treaty dissolved by his violation of it. On such an occasion, prudence and wise policy will point out the line of conduct to be pursued."

It cannot be necessary, said Mr. K. to insist that the United States possess the same rights on this subject with other independent nations; and he presumed it would not be denied that the reasons set forth in the act for dissolving the treaty are perfectly true, and constitute a legal justification of the measure. It might safely be submitted to the Senate as an original question, whether France had not, by her violation of the treaty, justified

its nullification by us? The author just quoted, said Mr. K. on another page, cites Grotius to prove that "every article of a treaty, carries with it a condition, by the nonperformance of which, the treaty is wholly cancelled." I ask senators then, said Mr. K. whether France did not first violate the treaty? That she did so, is the very first position established by them. And here the advocates of the bill found themselves in this strange predicament. That their first position to establish a claim against France, proved at the same time that the United States were not responsible for it. Mr. K. would not dwell longer on this branch of the subject. He considered the treaty clearly cancelled, as well by the acts of France, as by its nullification by the United States for sufficient causes. He therefore concluded that on the 30th of September 1800, the United States were not bound by treaty stipulations to France, and therefore could have received no consideration for the release of the claims in question.

But it is said the treaty stipulations were valuable at the date referred to, because the American negotiators offered for them 8,000,000 francs; and one would be led to think, said Mr. K., from the confidence with which gentlemen refer to this offer, that they had something almost equivalent to the promissory note of the Government for at least this amount. He had already remarked that these offers in negotiation determined nothing, unless reduced to treaty and ratified. But when we examined this "offer," what kind of an offer was it? It was an offer which, if accepted by the French Government, would have brought them eight or nine millions of dollars in debt! It is said we offered five millions of francs for a release from the stipulations of the 11th article of the treaty of 1778, which guaranteed to France her West India Islands; and three millions for the privilege of her privateers secured by the 17th article. The better to understand the value of this offer, said Mr. K., let us look to the instructions which preceded it, and with an evident reference to which it was made. These instructions say, "on the part of the United States, instead of troops or ships of war, it would be convenient to stipulate for a moderate sum of money, or quantity of provisions, at the option of France. The provision to be delivered at our ports in any future defensive war," &c. It was the opinion of our cabinet at that time, that the guarantee in the 11th article only extended to a defensive war, and no treaty renewing it on any other than this construction would have been ratified by the U. States. This offer, then, was to renew the mutual guarantee, but at the same time to settle its construction and its value. For the privileges under the 17th article we should have paid three millions, for those privileges were needed by us in our commercial relations with England. But the five millions were contingent upon a future defensive war. This part of the arrangement was as valuable to one party as the other, and in fact the contingency had not yet happened, which would have justified the claim. So then we see this valuable offer, said Mr. K., was an offer of three millions of francs certain, and five millions contingent, that we might receive fifty millions certain, by way of indemnities. Well might we propose to renew the treaties on such terms. It was not very surprising that France did not accept the generous offer.

Mr. K. said it only remained to inquire whether there was any just cause of complaint against the government because the attitude it assumed towards France may have released these claims. To admit this would allow individuals to control the policy of nations. If these claims were so released, it was only one of those individual sacrifices constantly made to State policy, in the necessary operations of government. We had done every thing that could be reasonably required to secure their claims. We had spent large sums in missions and negotiations before we resorted to hostile measures, which were of course attended with heavy expense. Perhaps, said Mr. K. if we were to enter into a strict account with these claimants we have spent more money in pursuit of their claims than the amount at which they are estimated, without computing the blood of our citizens which may be estimated beyond millions of

treasure. It is for this, among other reasons, said Mr. K. that war always relinquishes the claims for which it is declared. The blood of a single citizen satisfies millions of debt.

The attitude which the United States assumed then, was necessary to the permanent policy and honor of the country; and all private interests must yield to it. In fact, said Mr. K., it has been clearly shown by the Senator from New Hampshire, (Mr. Hill,) that their claims, under no circumstances, would ever have been worth one cent. It would be recollected that we did get the promise in the treaty of 1800, of indemnity for all prizes not definitively condemned. Did Bonaparte pay these claims, for which we held his bond in his treaty? Not at all, sir. Not a dollar of them would be paid to us; and we never should have got a dollar from him even for those acknowledged indemnities, had not Louisiana been forced as it were to suction, to prevent it from falling into the hands of the English. And not even then, sir, if we had not been cheated out of the amount by French diplomacy, by which it was gratuitously paid by our selves, and ten millions besides. Bonaparte told his Ministers to take fifty millions of francs. He obtained eighty, with the stipulation that treaty millions were to be deducted to satisfy indemnities under the treaty of 1800. Bonaparte was delighted at the bargain; but mark what he said to his broker, his agent, when the treaty was reported to him. "I would that these twenty millions be paid into the Treasury. Who authorised you to part with the money of the State?" He was reminded that he still would get ten millions more than he asked, besides satisfying the Americans. "Ah 'tis true," said he, "the treaty does not leave me any thing to desire. Sixty millions for an occupation that would not perhaps last a day," &c. Is it likely then, inquired Mr. K., that when he had uniformly refused to satisfy what he had solemnly promised to pay "for captures not definitively condemned," that he would have paid for captures every one of which had been condemned, and to which any treaty stipulation had been refused? Sir, said Mr. K., the claims were not worth a all in the dollar, at any time. Bonaparte paid no claims? No, sir. He, with his drum-headed justice, and gun-powder administration, robbed every body and paid no body. If these were to be, said Mr. K., however the claims may have been released, the claimants lost nothing, for France never would have paid any thing for these claims, every one of which had received the condemnation of her tribunals in some form or other, whether rightly or not. In the late treaty, we had to exclude all cases condemned, however just our complaint, of the proceedings under which the condemnations were made.

Mr. K. concluded, then, that France owed no part of these claims on the 30th September, 1800, which she ever would have paid, or that it simply could be insisted on.

That the United States, on the same date, were under no treaty stipulations to France, a release from which would afford a consideration for the claims. Claims and treaties, he said, had both extinguished, and no act had ever been done by the treaty making power in this country to revive them. These views he thought an entire answer to the claims.

As to the nature of these claims, said Mr. K. which had been already referred to, he must say, they were not such as appealed strongly to our sympathies. There were few, it was said, in the hands of the original losers, and they were mostly in the hands of Insurance Companies and underwriters. These, said Mr. K., are the weakest of all possible claims. It was known that in those days, profits were enormous, and increased by the risk, which was known to be great, and by the risk and profit regulated the premium, which were also excessively high. If then the loss should be returned, the insurer was enriched by his premium, whilst he had the loss returned to him. This, he thought, a tolerably fair business for insurers. We are told, to be sure, of "widows and orphans" who await the tardy justice of Government. He thought it likely these might be men, and some very rich ones too. The widows and orphans of the original losers, however, he thought

ed were few in number, and only thrust forward in the foreground of the picture, whilst rich in-surers, underwriters, and speculators, in greater numbers, lay back, concealed in its more remote and deepening shades.

Mr. K. said he had been unable to bring his mind to the support of this bill. It was but right, however, that he should confess, in conclusion, (although he could not say he was prejudiced) he had a powerful weight of presumptive evidence to get rid of, before he could look into details to get at the original merits of the claim. He said it might be safely assumed that no government in the world was more just to the claims of its citizens than that of the United States, and if at any time a claim was not allowed when pressed upon it, the refusal was a strong circumstance against it. This claim had been before Congress for thirty-four years and had not yet got through both Houses of Congress. And during a portion of that period it was known that we were not looking out for ways and means to defray the expenses of government, but actually looking out for ways and means to absorb an apprehended surplus. I would say, then, said Mr. K. that if this claim was refused by government from 1800 to 1824 it might reasonably be put down as doubtful. If from 1824 to 1832, we might put it down as very doubtful; and if it passed through the generous year of 1832, without being allowed, we might with much reason venture to consider it desperate and unworthy the attention of any tribunal or government. He had not, however, depended entirely upon these strong circumstances against the claims, but had listened attentively to the speeches for and against them, and had revived his recollection of the most material historical facts upon which they rested, and his first unfavorable impressions were fully confirmed, and he should vote against the bill. Though he fully concurred in the sentiments of the Senator from Carolina, that if, notwithstanding the age and amount of the claims, they were really just, and the honor of the government were involved in withholding them, the appropriation should be made, if it took the last dollar in the treasury, and forced us even to make new contributions to satisfy it.

When Mr. K. concluded,

Mr. BIBB rose and said, that he was desirous of giving his views on this question, but he was not prepared to do so now.

Mr. BIBB then yielded to a motion to adjourn, which was submitted by Mr. KING, of Alabama.

Mr. WEBSTER was opposed to the adjournment, unless the honorable member from Kentucky desired it.

Mr. BIBB said he certainly did, and

The Senate adjourned.

HOUSE OF REPRESENTATIVES.

THURSDAY, January 8, 1835.

Petitions and Memorials were presented, on leave, by

Mr. WILLIAMS, of North Carolina;

Mr. GORHAM, of Massachusetts;

Mr. BEATY, of Kentucky;

[Mr. BEATY presented the petition of James Smith, of Cumberland county, Kentucky, praying Congress to grant him a section of land which was referred to the Committee on Public Lands.]

Mr. WARDWELL, of New York;

Messrs. KINNARD, LANE, and EWING, of Indiana;

[Mr. KINNARD presented the application of John Griffith, to be placed on the revolutionary pension roll. Referred to the Committee on Revolutionary Pensions.

Mr. KINNARD presented additional documents in support of the petition of James Calvin. Referred to the Committee on Invalid Pensions.]

Mr. BOULDIN, of Virginia;

Mr. LYON, of Michigan;

[Mr. FORESTER presented the petition of James Frumtluer for a pension.]

Which petitions and memorials were referred.

Mr. KINNARD, from the Committee on Revolutionary Claims, made an unfavorable report on the petition of the heirs of Bernard Lipscomb, heir at law of Capt. Reuben Lipscomb.

Mr. HARDIN, from the Committee on the Ju-

diciary, reported a bill to alter the times and places for holding the Circuit and District Courts of the United States for the District of Kentucky; which was read twice, and committed.

Mr. FORRESTER, from the Committee on Invalid Pensions, reported a bill for the relief of Joshua Columber; which was read twice, and committed.

The following resolutions, heretofore offered, were, by consent, considered and agreed to:

By Mr. E. EVERETT:

Resolved, That the Secretary of War be directed to communicate to this House, a copy of the Report of the Board of Engineers of the 15th of March, 1834, relative to the repairs of Fort Independence, in Boston harbor, together with his opinion of the expediency of executing the repairs proposed in the said report.

By Mr. BEATY:

Resolved, That the Secretary of War be requested to report to this House whether the whole amount or what part of the $30,000 appropriated at the last session of Congress for the continuation of the improvement of the navigation of the Cumberland river, has been applied to that object, and whether its application was made under the direction of the said Secretary or the President of the United States, and whether the whole amount, or what part of said $30,000 was directed to be laid out upon said river below Nashville, and if any part of said sum be left, will it be laid out in continuation of the improvement of the river above Nashville; if not, the reasons for withholding it.

By Mr. EWING:

Resolved, That the President of the U. States be requested to transmit, or cause to be transmitted, to this House, copies of every circular letter of instruction, emanating from the Treasury or War Department, since the 30th day of June last, and addressed to either of the receiving or disbursing officers stationed in States wherein land offices are established, or public works are constructing, under the authority of Congress.

On motion of Mr. MERCER,

Resolved, That the Committee on the District of Columbia be instructed to inquire into the expediency of extending the jurisdiction of the corporation of Washington to the police of the bridge now constructing across the river Potomac; and that the said committee be also instructed to inquire into the expediency of devising by law some practicable mode of disposing of unappropriated or ungranted lands within the District of Columbia.

On motion of Mr. STEWART,

Resolved, That the Committee of Ways and Means be instructed to inquire into the expediency of increasing the annual appropriation for the improvement of the Ohio and Mississippi, to be expended between Brownsville and the falls of the Ohio, at Louisville.

Mr. LYON, of Michigan, offered the following resolution, which lies over one day:

Resolved, That the Secretary of War be requested to furnish this House with an estimate of the probable expense of prosecuting and completing with great accuracy, the astronomical observations, contemplated by the act of Congress of the 14th July, 1832, entitled an act for taking of certain observations preparatory to the adjustment of the Northern boundary line of the State of Ohio.

Mr. FULTON offered the following resolution, which, under the rule, lies one day:

Resolved, That the Secretary of the Treasury be requested to present to this House a list of all commutation and half pay claims paid at the Treasury Department of the United States, under any act or acts of Congress, providing for the payment of such claims; in which list shall be specially stated the amount of each claim, to whom originally due, to whom paid, and by what authority; whether paid to the claimant himself, or to his heirs, executors, administrators, or his or their attorney or attorneys in fact, with the names of the heirs, executors, administrators, attorney or attorneys in fact, as the case may be.

Mr. BYNUM offered the following resolution, which, under the rules, lies one day:

Resolved, That the Secretary of State be requested to inform this House, whether the commissioners or surveyors have been appointed on

the part of the Government, to lay off and run the boundary lines between the Government of the United States and the Republic of Mexico, than those appointed under the act of 1819, by the stipulations made and entered into with the Government of Spain.

On motion of Mr. TAYLOR,

Resolved, That the Committee on Revolutionary Pensions be instructed to inquire into the expediency of granting a pension to Joel Marshall, a soldier of the revolution.

On motion of Mr. ALLEN, of Virginia,

Resolved, That the Judiciary Committee be instructed to inquire into the expediency of authorizing the Judge of the western district of Virginia to prescribe by a rule of court the times of holding the several courts now directed by law to be held in said district.

On motion of Mr. PARKER,

Resolved, That the Committee on Commerce be instructed to inquire into the expediency of making an appropriation for securing Flat Beach, on Tucker's Island, at Egg Harbor, in the State of New Jersey, from further injury by inundations or otherwise, according to an estimate and survey made by Captain Hartman Bache, as reported to the War Department 6th March, 1830.

On motion of Mr. JOHNSON, of Louisiana,

Resolved, That the Committee on Roads and Canals be instructed to inquire into the expediency of granting to the State of Louisiana, a tract of land on each side of the route designated for a canal from lake Barataria to Berwick's bay, in said State, to aid the company organized for the purpose of executing the work in effecting the object.

Mr. E. EVERETT, on leave, introduced a joint resolution, authorizing Jared Sparks to retain for the present the papers and correspondence of Gen. Washington, now in his possession; and to authorise the Secretary of State to pay to George C. Washington the remainder of the purchase money due him by the Government for the paper and documents referred to; which was read twice, and ordered to be engrossed.

Mr. TAYLOR, of New York, moved to reconsider the vote of yesterday, whereby the House refused to consider the following resolution, submitted by Mr. HAMER, of Ohio:

Resolved, That the Committee on the Judiciary be instructed to inquire into the expediency of amending the constitution of the United States so as to limit the service of the Judge of the Supreme and inferior Courts to a term of years.

Mr. HARDIN said he was not in favor of limiting the tenure by which Judges of the Supreme Court held their offices to any number of years, but he was in favor of making such an alteration in the constitution as at the age of something like 70, or 65, or 75 years they might be compelled to quit the bench. He had no desire to make any particular reference to any of the Judges now presiding in the Supreme Court, but it was a fact well known, that two, at least, of those gentlemen were now between 80 and 90 years of age—perhaps nearer the last number—and one of them, he verily believed, had been unable to hear any argument for ten years past, though he was one who could be greatly profited by argument.

[The SPEAKER here reminded the gentleman from Kentucky, that the question pending being one of consideration, it was not debatable.]

Mr. HARDIN remarked, that he had said all that he desired to say on the subject.

Mr. MERCER hoped to be permitted to correct the gentleman in one particular. There was but one of the Judges to whom he had made reference who was over eighty years of age, and he was barely beyond that age.

Mr. WILLIAMS, of North Carolina, demanded the yeas and nays; which were ordered, and were as follows:

YEAS—Messrs. John Adams, John J. Allen, William Allen, Beale, Bean, Beaty, Beaumont, Boon, Brown, Bull, Bunch, Burns, Bynum, Cambreleng, Campbell, Carmichael, Carr, Casey, Chilton, Samuel Clark, Clay, Cramer, Day, Dickerson, Dunlap, Ferris, Forester, Foster, Fowler, Galbraith, Gamble, Gillet, Grayson, Griffin, Joseph Hall, Thomas H. Hall, Halsey, Hamer, Hardin Harrison, Hathaway, Henderson, Howell, Hub-

bard, Inge, Jarvis, Richard M. Johnson, Noadiah Johnson, Benjamin Jones, Kavanagh, Kilgore, Kinnard, Lane, Lansing, Luke Lea, Thomas Lee, Lewis, Love, Lytle, Abijah Mann, Joel K. Mann, Mardis, Moses Mason, May, McCarty, McIntire, McKay, McKinley, McVean, Miller, Robert Mitchell, Morgan, Muhlenberg, Osgood, Parks, Patterson, Peyton, Pierce, Pierson, Plummer, Polk, Rencher, Reynolds, Shinn, Smith, Standifer, William Taylor, Francis Thomas, Thomson, Turner, Turrill, Vanderpoel, Van Houten, Wagner, Wardwell, Webster, Whallon, Wise, Young—97

NAYS—Messrs. John Q. Adams, Heman Allen, Chilton Allan, Banks, Barber, Barnitz, Barringer, Bates, Baylies, Bouldin, Briggs, Burges, Cage, Chambers, Chinn, Clayton, Coffee, Corwin, Coulter, Crane, Crockett, Amos Davis, Davenport, Deberry, Denny, Evans, Edward Everett, Ewing, Felder, Fillmore, Philo C. Fuller, William K. Fuller, Garland, Gilmer, Gordon, Gorham, Graham, Grennell, James Harper, Hazeltine, Heath, Hiester, William Jackson, Ebenezer Jackson, Janes, William Cost Johnson, Henry Johnson, Laporte, Lay, Lincoln, Loyall, Manning, Martindale, Marshall, McComas, McKennan, Mercer, Milligan, Miner, Parker, Patton, Phillips, Pickins, Pinckney, Pope, Potts, Ramsay, Reed, Robertson, Schenck, Schley, William B. Shepard, Augustine H. Shepperd, Slade, Sloane, Spangler, Steele, William P. Taylor, Philemon Thomas, Tompkins, Trumbull, Tweedy, Vance, Vinton, Watmough, Wayne, White, Frederick Whittlesey, Wilde, Williams—92.

So the House reversed their vote of yesterday, and determined to consider the resolution.

Mr. HARDIN desired to propose an amendment to the resolution.

Mr. A. H. SHEPPERD rose to a question of order. He supposed that the vote which had just been taken placed the subject in the same position in which it was before the vote of yesterday was taken; the question then pending being that of consideration, it was not competent to move an amendment to the resolution until the House should first decide in favor of its consideration.

The CHAIR decided that the vote which had been just taken was tantamount to a decision that the House would consider the resolution, &c.

After some conversation upon the question of order between the CHAIR and Messrs. A. H. SHEPPERD, MERCER, and BRIGGS, the decision of the Chair was acquiesced in.

Mr. HARDIN moved to amend the resolution by directing the Committee to inquire at what age it would be proper to declare Judges incompetent to serve on the bench.

Mr. HAMER accepted the amendment as a modification of his motion.

Mr. VANCE moved to amend the resolution by directing the Committ e to inquire into the propriety of so amending the constitution as to prohibit the President of the United States from making removals from office unless by the consent of the Senate.

The hour allotted to morning business having expired, the House, on motion of Mr. PARKER, proceeded to the consideration of the orders of the day and the bills, &c., upon the Speaker's table.

Mr. SPEAKER laid before the House a letter from the Secretary of State, covering a list of the clerks in his department and the salaries paid to each: which was laid on the table and ordered to be printed.

A bill from the Senate to settle and establish the northern boundary line of the States of Ohio, Indiana and Illinois, was read twice, and, on motion of Mr. ALLEN, of Ohio, committed to a Select Committee of seven members.

The following bills from the Senate were read twice and committed:

A bill to provide for the enlistment of Boys in the Navy:

A bill to change the titles of certain officers of the Navy:

A bill for the relief of J. and W. Beeson, and others:

A bill to improve the navigation of the Wabash river:

And a bill for the benefit of Boyd Reilly.

The bill for the relief of the city of Alexandria, was read a third time.

Mr. MARDIS demanded the yeas and nays on its passage; which were ordered.

Mr. HARDIN had seen no report of the estimated cost of the canal, in the stock of which Congress was asked by the bill to subscribe 100,000 dollars The United States had heretofore given 100,000 dollars for the purpose of aiding in opening this canal between Georgetown and Alexandria. The corporation of Alexandria had added to the sum 50,000 dollars, and the citizens of that city 80,000 making in all 230,000 dollars, all of which was already expended on this canal. Neither the corporation nor the citizens of Alexandria, could render further aid in the future progress of this work. The city owed a debt of 250,000 dollars in Holland, to pay the interest on which, required a tax of seventy-five cents upon the hundred dollars worth of property, and it was evident, from the complete exhaustion of her means, that it would be impossible for Alexandria to prosecute this work. Under these circumstances, it was apparent that it would devolve on Congress alone, if they should deem it expedient, to finish this work. One question then, was, would the 100,000 dollars proposed to be subscribed by the bill, complete this canal? If not, how was the necessary sum to be raised? Is it expected that Congress will continue to vote appropriations for this object until it is finished. He had conversed with an intelligent gentleman from Alexandria, and from the data which he had received from him, (and which Mr. H. recapitulated) he was satisfied that instead of 100,000 dollars it would take more than one million. There must be some mistake in the estimates which had been made on the subject. At all events, he for one, was unwilling to give another 100,000 dollars in aid of this aqueduct and canal between Georgetown and Alexandria, particularly when the broad and beautiful Potomac afforded the most natural channel of communication between the two cities.

It had been said that this work was necessary to prevent Alexandria from going down. He should regret it. But he did not consider it of much importance to the citizens of the United States, whether a few merchants in Georgetown and Alexandria should be deprived of the opportunity of realizing a commission on a few barrels of flour If, however, Alexandria should go down, it would not be owing to a failure to finish the contemplated canal. The cause would be obvious. The commercial advantages of the large cities completely overshadowed the prosperity of the villages in their vicinity. You might as well expect corn and tobacco to grow and flourish under the expanded branches of an oak, as that such a city as Alexandria should enjoy great commercial prosperity while situated in the immediate neighborhood of Baltimore. Congress had appropriated some 130 or 140 thousand dollars to open a canal in the City of Washington, and he would ask, what great advantages had been derived from this improvement? You might, indeed, occasionally see a solitary boat floating upon this canal, with a few cords of wood or some stone, to be used in walling that part of the work which was unfinished, and now and then in the summer or spring a long-boat, laden with oysters and *white* cat-fish. Of other advantages, he was ignorant.

Mr. H. thought it highly improper that these extravagant appropriations of public money should be made. He thought that Congress should confine appropriations to the support of the army and navy, and the civil list. If a general system of internal improvements could be adopted in which all sections of the country could participate, he might not be found in opposition to it; but he did object to the partial, if not useless, appropriations of millions of dollars for the benefit of this District, or for purposes connected with the District; and he should also object to other partial appropriations, intended to benefit a particular section of the Union, while his own State received not a solitary cent. There were bills on the Clerk's table for appropriations to an amount sufficient to break it down, were it even placed upon it in bank notes.

Mr. CHINN said the gentleman from Kentucky (Mr. Hardin) would allow him to set him right on some points of fact. First, in regard to the length of the proposed aqueduct. It was true, the river at the place of its location, was fifteen hundred feet wide; but the abutments reduced that width to one thousand feet. The arches, too, instead of being, as represented by the gentleman, eighty-two feet span, were in number only eight or nine, and were about one hundred feet span. Engineers of great talent and experience had pronounced arches of more than one hundred feet perfectly safe and practicable. Authorities, demonstrative of this fact, he had before him, for the satisfaction of any gentleman who might wish to consult them. Mr. C. said that he was aware that estimates were generally received with many grains of allowance. They were so received by himself. But here we had demonstration before us; for, contrary to the position of the gentleman, the most difficult part of the work was already accomplished; of which any gentleman might convince himself by making a visit to the spot. Its practicability had been already clearly established, and the work had thus far been most judiciously and economically managed.

Mr. C. said, that it was not to be wondered at that Alexandria felt deeply upon this subject. Previous to the cession of this District to the U. States, she had been prosperous, commanding great commercial advantages. The very first act of legislation within the District of Columbia inflicted upon her a most serious and permanent injury. He referred to the measure of cutting a channel to Georgetown. In proof of this he adduced statistical estimates of her trade at the different periods. Mr. C. stated another fact, that the privilege had formerly been extended to Alexandria to open a channel for her own especial benefit. The reason why she had not effected this, was, that the privilege was granted about the time of the late war with Great Britain, and before she could complete the work, the term of limitation expired.

Mr. C. stated many other reasons which should induce the passage of this bill. He would come down to a later period. The history of that great work, the Chesapeake and Ohio Canal, would furnish some facts of a strong character, bearing upon this matter. That work was one of immense importance to the wealth and prosperity of the vast extent of country contiguous to it, from its commencement to the mouth of the Potomac. But it seemed that the People of Alexandria were a fated People. The lateral canal from Georgetown to Washington, had taken from them all the benefits they had anticipated from that work. Mr. C. was sorry the gentleman from Kentucky (Mr. Hardin) had found it necessary to refer to the enormous appropriations made by Congress for the benefit of this District. But since he had done so, he would ask how much of those appropriations had gone for the benefit of Alexandria. The entire appropriation of Congress amounted to 50,000 dollars. Alexandria was not alone to be benefited by this work. Every man, woman, and child in its vast vicinity were concerned—every man who put his produce on board a boat at the extremity of the canal, was interested in the appropriation provided for in the bill. The Government itself was most deeply interested; and if it were a truism that that work was most useful which spread the most general good, this commanded peculiar attention.

Mr. C. concluded by appealing to the justice of Congress to pass this bill, which he conceived to be so plainly due, not only to Alexandria, but to themselves. It was a last throe—a final struggle—to recover her commercial prosperity; and he trusted in God she would be successful. With her, indeed, it was a matter of life and death!

Mr. VANDERPOEL moved to postpone the further consideration of the bill till Monday next.

Mr. CHINN hoped not, since it had been already twice postponed, and he hoped the House would now act upon it.

Mr. VANDERPOEL said, if his memory served him aright, the same bill had undergone considerable discussion towards the close of the preceding session. The bill was an important one, in-

olving a large appropriation, and though he would be glad to gratify the gentleman from Virginia, yet, under the circumstances of the case, ublic duty compelled him to press his motion.

The motion to postpone was then put, and negatived.

Mr. MERCER said, he had listened to the ble, lucid, and to him convincing argument of s honorable colleague, (Mr. Chinn,) with great tisfac ion. Mr. M. entered into an elaborate atement of facts respecting the Potomac Bridge, ad the relative cost of that and the aqueducts, ae former of which would not amount, by the ew plan, to more than $250,000. The city of lexandria had some claims upon the liberality of ongress, for she contributed her full quota of ases during the war, and that without representation, contrary to the principle of our government, and yet had received nothing, or but little i return. Alexandria had suffered greatly by the ession, and had fallen from her former condition. he time was when one-twentieth part of the exorts of the whole United States, was cleared om the port of Alexandria alone. The first ank established South of the Potomac was there, ad it was within his recollection that the value of at stock was doubled in a short time. In the ays of the Father of his country, the collectorsp of that port was one of the best gifts in the ands of the General Government, and one of the eroes of the revolution had been rewarded with

All this was matter of history; that Mr. M. ould prove.

Mr. M. also advocated the appropriation, on the ound of the increased facility that would there- be afforded, whether in peace or war, by the ansmission of important despatches and express- and said that a delay of two days on the river d not unfrequently occurred. This also appl ed the march of armies, in case of war or invasion. ith regard to the permanency of the work, every surance was given, grounded on the most consive testimony and reasoning, that if the aqueict should be constructed on the plan proposed, would be indestructible. This was all that was ked for. The town of Alexandria did not ask ngress to complete the canal—they had themlves paid every instalment called for, which was ore than the other cities had done.

It had been said that the plan was erroneous, cause it proposed the construction of a canal on arly a parallel line with the river, but if similar ses were to be referred to, Young's Tour and the ientific works of the most celebrated engineers Europe, would show that a river, from the obructions it presented, and the continual variaas of the wind, had been abandoned. A referce to the great canal of the Duke of Bridgwar in Lancashire in England, would testify this t. Would any man believe it possible for a at to be managed through the floods of the tomac, on a surface of a mile in width, in all asons of the year? It could not. Yet this could done on a canal. To reject this bill would be le short of laying an edict upon Alexandria, d by whom? By that body from whom alone could expect relief. After some further remarks, d sundry details on the importance of the prosed measure, Mr. M. concluded by urging upon e House not to reject the bill.

Mr. MANN, of New York, alluded to the fact this bill having been before the House at the t session, advocated by the same gentleman, and the same principles as now. Mr. M. replied at gth to the arguments of Mr. Chinn. The ntleman from Virginia had the happy faculty of illustrating every subject on which he turned attention as to render it enchanting, but he ped the House would not be led away. The ntleman had urged many beautiful arguments, t Mr. M. must be excused for saying that they re of a character that ought not to weigh in tters of the kind now under deliberation. He heard the gentleman, as he always did, with culiar pleasure, because he was always clear, tinct, and lucid in his propositions, and he was ry, that on this occasion, he had not chosen ubject more worthy of his advocacy. What s the nature of this bill? It proposed that ngress should subscribe for one thousand shares, at a hundred dollars per share, in the stock of the Alexandria Canal Company. Now, Mr. M. would not for a moment question the principle that Congress had exclusive legislation in all cases whatsoever; but he begged to inquire where was the power, or upon what authority could Congress appropriate money for charitable purposes, for the measure proposed could be designated as nothing less than one of charity? If Congress could do so in one case, it could in another, and the whole revenue of the country might fall under the principle. They had been told by the honorable Chairman of the Committee (Mr. Chinn) that the legislation of Congress had been extremely injurious and detrimental to the City of Alexandria; but surely it was to be presumed that what had been done, had been done by the knowledge and consent of the inhabitants, if not at their request, and why should this charge be made upon Congress?

Mr. MERCER explained, as we understood, that it was within his knowledge that a large majority were oposed to the measures referred to.

Mr. MANN proceeded. The gentleman had stated that if this work were completed, 200,000 barrels of flour would pass through the city of Georgetown to Alexandria by way of this canal. But Mr. M. would ask what would this amount to? Why the profit on its carriage would not even pay the persons necessarily employed in taking care of the canal.

He had seen too much of such works to put any confidence in the reports of engineers. They had turned out to be totally fallacious—he could cite a greater number of cases than the time would allow of. He would ask what assurance we had that the persons who may be employed, would not come here and ask you to pay them extra allowances, in consequence of bad contracts. The claims for special allowance on contracts, on the New York Canals, amount to more than seven millions of dollars. He could see no good and substantial reasons why we should be called on to legislate on this floor for the benefit of Alexandria. The expenses that had been paid by the United States for criminal Courts had been very great.

Mr. M. said since he had been here, we had given for the District of Columbia, something like three millions of dollars. Then with what justice could it be said, that the District had suffered by the illiberality of Congress? If this bill could be passed in this House, you might expect that a bill would follow in a very short time, for an appropriation, not only to pay the interest on the debt of the City of Washington, but you would soon be asked to give another million for their support.—After some further remarks, Mr. M. concluded by saying, that every view he had been able to take of the subject, convinced him that this bill ought not to pass.

Mr. CHILTON said he inclined to the opinion, that this bill ought not to pass. He had no scruples as to the constitutional power of Congress to make appropriations for improving the country where they were necessary, but this he thought would be a useless waste of the public money.—Here was one of the finest streams in the world, running almost straight from Georgetown to Alexandria, possessing all the advantages for navigation that could be desired, and we were called on to construct a canal along side of it! Could any man acquit himself to his constituents, or to his own conscience, if he should vote to make a canal parallel with this beautiful stream? Besides there were works which had claims a hundred times as strong on the Government, the funds to complete which were insufficient, and if they passed the bill now under consideration, with what justice could they reject the others? Nor did the present work present any probable advantages which could authorize the appropriation.

After some further observations, Mr. C. declared his determination to vote against the bill, and he trusted it would be rejected.

The question on the passage of the bill was then taken by yeas and nays, and decided in the negative.

YEAS—Messrs. John Q. Adams, Heman Allen, John J. Allen, Anthony, Archer, Banks, Bates, Baylies, Beale, Binney, Briggs, Bull, Cage, Chambers, Chinn, Wm. Clark, Corwin, Coulter, Crane, Darlington, Denny, Evans, Edward Everett, Ewing, Galbraith, Garland, Gholson, Gorham, Grennell, Hiland Hall, Hard, Hiester, William Jackson, Ebenezer Jackson, Wm. C. Johnson, R. M. Johnson, Henry Johnson, King, Kinnard, Lane, Laporte, Lincoln, Love, Lucas, Martindale, McKennan, McKinley, Mercer, Milligan, Miner, Patton, Dutee J. Pearce, Phillips, Pope, Potts, Ramsey, Reed, Rencher, Wm. B. Shepard, Sloane, Spangler, Stewart, Francis Thomas, Philemon Thomas, Trumbull, Vance, Vinton, Watmough, Wayne, Fred'k Whittlesey, Wise, Young.—72.

NAYS—Messrs. John Adams, Chilton Allan, William Allen, Bean, Beaumont, Blair, Bockee, Boon, Bouldin, Brown, Bunch, Burns, Bynum, Cambreleng, Carr, Casey, Chaney, Chilton, Claiborne, Samuel Clark, Clay, Clowney, Coffee, Cramer, Amos Davis, Davenport, Day, Deberry, Dickson, Dickerson, Dickinson, Dunlap, Fehler, Ferris, Forester, Foster, Fowler, Philo C. Fuller, Wm. K. Fuller, Fulton, Gamble, Gillet, Gilmer, Gordon, Graham, Grayson, Griffin, Joseph Hall, Thomas H. Hall, Halsey, Hamer, Hardin, Joseph M. Harper, James Harper, Harrison, Hathaway, Hazeltine, Heath, Henderson, Howell, Huntington, Inge, Janes, Jarvis, Noadiah Johnson, Seaborn Jones, Benj. Jones, Kavanagh, Kilgore, Lansing, Lay, Luke Lea, Thomas Lee, Letcher, Lewis, Loyall, Lyon, Lytle, Abijah Mann, Joel K. Mann, Manning, Marshall, Mardis, Moses Mason, May, McCarty, McIntire, McKay, McLene, McVean, Robert Mitchell, Moore, Morgan, Muhlenberg, Murphy, Parks, Parker, Patterson, Peyton, Franklin Pierce, Pierson, Pinckney, Polk, Reynolds, Robertson, Schenck, Schley, Shinn, Smith, Standifer, Steele, Wm. P. Taylor, Thomson, Turner, Tweedy, Vanderpoel, Van Houten, Wagener, Wardwell, Webster, Whallon, White, Williams.—123.

The House then adjourned.

IN SENATE,

FRIDAY, January 9, 1835.

Mr. EWING presented a petition, praying a grant of land to the College at Columbus, Ohio.

Mr. GRUNDY, by direction of the Post Office Committee, moved that the committee have leave to sit during the sessions of the Senate; which was agreed to.

Mr. WAGGAMAN, pursuant to notice, and on leave given, introduced a bill to give effect to the 18th article of the treaty with Spain; which was read twice and referred.

Mr. SILSBEE, from the Committee on Commerce, to which was referred the bill for the relief of Samuel S. Lord and others, reported the same without amendment.

Mr. SILSBEE, from the same committee, reported a bill for the relief of Christopher C. Bailey.

Mr. POINDEXTER, from the Committee on Public Lands, reported a bill supplementary to the act authorising the State of Louisiana to enter the back lands.

Also, a bill for the relief of Wilkinson Goodwin, without amendment, but with an expression of opinion by the committee against its passage.

Also, a bill for the relief of Nathaniel Tyler, without amendment.

Also, against the petition of the trustees of the Willoughby University of Lake Erie, for a donation of land, and the committee were discharged from the further consideration of the same.

Also, against the petition of the trustees of the public school of the parish of Carroll, in Louisiana, for a donation of land.

Mr. BLACK, from the Committee on Private Land Claims, to which was referred the bill for the relief of Wyatt Singleton and James Andrews, reported the same without amendment.

Mr. TYLER gave notice that, on Monday next, he would ask leave to introduce a bill to provide a system of laws for the District of Columbia.

Mr. BENTON submitted the following resolution:

Resolved, That the Committee on Finance be instructed to obtain from the Bank of the United States a copy of all instructions, if any, to the branch banks, directing them to collect and remit

Spanish milled dollars to the mother bank; the number of such dollars annually remitted; the rates at which they sold at different periods, say at or about the beginning of each quarter of the year; whether the Bank of the United States has sold such dollars to the United States, and if so, how many and at what rates; how many it has sold to others or exported to foreign countries; also, a statement of the amount of gold coin; of the amount of silver coin; and the amount of bullion remitted to the mother bank, or elsewhere, by her order, annually since the 1st day of April, 1832; also, a statement showing the amount of silver coin and of gold coin remitted by the mother bank to each branch since that day; also, the amount of gold coin and the amount of silver coin annually sold or annually exported by the Bank, since the said first day of April; also, a statement of the amount of gold received from the United States Mint since the first day of August last; and a statement of the whole amount of gold on hand in the Bank and its branches, for each month from April 1, 1832, to the present time.

The following bills were read the third time and passed:

A bill for the relief of Henry B. Tyler, executor of Col. Richard Smith, deceased;

A bill for the relief of McKean Buchanan;

A bill for the relief of the administrators of Michael Hogan, deceased.

The bill for the relief of Lt. Archibald S. Campbell was called up for consideration, and

On motion of Mr. TALLMADGE laid on the table.

The bill for the relief of Loami Baldwin was taken up for consideration.

[The object of this bill was to make compensation to Mr. Baldwin for services rendered during the administration of Mr. Adams, as a civil engineer, in the construction of two dry docks at Charleston, South Carolina.]

Mr. HILL moved to lay the bill on the table; which was not agreed to.

Mr. HILL and Mr. BENTON then opposed the bill on the ground that Mr. Baldwin was an engineer in the employment of the Government at an annual salary of $4,000; that this allowance would be double pay for services rendered by a salaried officer; that the claim had been disallowed by the Secretary, and afterwards by the Auditor; and that if a contract had been made with Mr. Baldwin for this service, it was no doubt in writing, and ought to be shown.

Some further remarks were made by Messrs. SOUTHARD, FRELINGHUYSEN, CALHOUN, POINDEXTER, and CLAYTON, in favor of the bill.

It was said by them that an express contract was made with Mr. Baldwin by the then Secretary of the Navy (Mr. Southard) for the performance of this duty, which was an extra service; that he was not an officer of the Government, because he held no commission; but that if he was, it had been the usage of the Government to pay its officers extra compensation for any services which they were called on to render, out of the line of their ordinary duties. That the justice of this claim was enhanced in consequence of the contract which had been made with Mr. Baldwin to pay him $5 a day for the time employed in performing the duty assigned him.

The question being on the engrossment of the bill for a third reading.

Mr. HILL demanded the yeas and nays, which were ordered; but before the question was taken,

Mr. BENTON renewed the motion to lay the bill on the table, with a view to make some further examination into it.

The motion was then agreed to.

SPECIAL ORDER.

The Senate resumed the consideration of the bill making compensation for French spoliations prior to 1800.

Mr. BENTON then spoke at length in opposition to the bill. When he concluded,

Mr. WEBSTER rose, and said that if no other gentleman intended to address the Senate on this subject, he proposed to answer the objections which had been urged against the bill, so far as

---

the Senate would indulge him, either to-day, tomorrow, or on Monday.

[Some gentlemen suggested Monday.]

Mr. WEBSTER said as it seemed to be the wish of gentlemen that he should defer his remarks till Monday, he would move that when the Senate adjourn, it will adjourn to meet on Monday next.

The motion being received by unanimous consent, was agreed to.

On motion of Mr. CLAYTON, the Senate then proceeded to the consideration of Executive business, and when the doors were opened,

The Senate adjourned to Monday.

HOUSE OF REPRESENTATIVES.
Friday, January 9, 1835.

Petitions and memorials were presented on leave by Mr. EWING, of Indiana, and Mr. HEATH, of Maryland.

Mr. CASEY, of Illinois, asked leave to introduce the report of the engineer appointed by the commissioners of the fund appropriated by the States of Illinois and Indiana for the improvement of the navigation of the Wabash river.

On leave being granted, Mr. CASEY said, it would be recollected by the House that on yesterday the bill which had passed the Senate making an appropriation for the improvement of the navigation of the Wabash river, was referred to the Committee on Roads and Canals. By the last mail from the west, through the politeness of a friend, he had received the report of the engineer appointed by the commissioners of the fund appropriated by the States of Illinois and Indiana for the improvement of the navigation of the Wabash. It contained some valuable information in relation to the proposed improvement, and as it was desirable that the National Legislature should be in possession of every possible information on this subject, he thought it his duty to introduce this report. It was a subject of deep and abiding interest to the people of that section of the country, and he did hope that it would receive the favor and consideration of Congress. Mr. C. concluded by a motion to refer the report to the Committee on Roads and Canals, and that it be printed; which was agreed to.

[Mr. CLAY, of Alabama, presented a petition from certain members of the Legislature of Alabama, asking the establishment of a post route from Ashville, in St. Clair county, by way of Jacksonville, in Benton county, Alabama, to in Georgia, and sundry other routes through adjacent counties in Alabama—which was referred to the Committee on the Post Office and Post roads.]

Mr. CLAY, from the Committee on the Public Lands, reported, without amendment, the bill from the Senate, authorizing the relinquishment of the 16th sections of lands appropriated for the use of Schools, and the location of other lands in lieu thereof.

Mr. CLAY moved to postpone the further consideration of the bill until Monday next.

Mr. EVANS moved to commit it to a Committee of the whole.

The motion to commit was supported by Messrs. EVANS, WILLIAMS, and LANE, and opposed by Messrs. CLAY, EWING, and McKINLEY. The motion prevailed—yeas 91, nays 30.

Mr. FOSTER, from the Committee on the Judiciary, reported a bill to change the place of holding the District Court of the United States for the district of Mississippi; which was read twice and ordered to be engrossed for a third reading.

Mr. WARDWELL, from the Committee on Revolutionary Pensions, reported a bill to authorise the Secretary of War to appoint agents to examine pensions, in order to prevent frauds, and for other purposes; which was read twice and committed to a committee of the Whole on the State of the Union.

Mr. INGE, from the Committee on the Public Lands, made an unfavorable report upon the petition of R. Young and others; which was laid on the table.

Mr. CAMBRELENG, from the Committee of Ways and Means, reported a bill for the relief of

---

Chastelain and Pouvert, which was read twice and committed.

Mr. MERCER gave notice that he would on Tuesday next, move to take up the bill authorizing a further subscription in the stock of the Chesapeake and Ohio Canal Company.

Mr. BOON, from the Committee on the Public Lands, reported a bill for the benefit of Charles Caldwell, of Arkansas, which was read twice and ordered to be engrossed for a third reading.

Mr. CONNOR gave notice that he would on to take up, on the 27th instant, the bill to establish certain post routes, and to alter and discontinue others.

Mr. MARSHALL, from the Committee on Revolutionary Claims, reported a substitute for the bill to provide for certain revolutionary claims, which, together with the original bill, he moved to commit to a Committee of the Whole on the state of the Union, and that the same be made the special order for Friday the 3d of January.

After some remarks on the propriety of making the bill a special order, by Messrs. WARDWELL, MARSHALL, MILLER, and LANE, the bill was substituted for the 30th January, and the question agreed to—yeas 80, nays 44.

Messrs. MUHLENBERG, DAVIS of Kentucky, BOON, LEA of Tennessee, GRAHAM and McNELL, made (from various Standing Committees) unfavorable reports upon petitions, &c., which had been referred to them.

[Mr. KINNARD moved to discharge the Committee on Revolutionary Claims from the further consideration of the petition of Robert Morris, and to refer the same to the Committee on Private Land Claims, which was agreed to.]

On motion of Mr. ALLEN, of Virginia,
Resolved, That the Committee on Revolutionary Claims be discharged from the further consideration of the heirs of Isaac Israel, and that the petitioners have leave to withdraw their papers.

Mr. H. EVERETT, by consent, offered the following resolution, which was agreed to:
Resolved, That the Secretary of War be directed to communicate to this House a copy of the order given by him to the Commissioner of Pensions directing the suspension of the aforesaid pensions under the act of 7th June, 1832.

On motion of Mr. LYON, of Michigan,
Resolved, That the Committee on Public Lands be instructed to inquire into the expediency of establishing an additional land district for the sale of public lands in the Territory of Michigan.

On motion of Mr. CONNOR,
Resolved, That the Committee on the Post Office and Post Roads be instructed to inquire into the expediency of establishing a post route from Salisbury by Barringer's Mills, to Coleman's Store in Mecklenburg county.

Mr. ASHLEY offered the following resolution, which, under the rule, lies one day:
Resolved, That the Secretary of the Treasury be requested to return to this House, the report referred to him at the last session of the Commissioners appointed to examine and adjust Private Land Claims in Missouri, with such remarks as he may think proper to make thereon.

On motion of Mr. HEATH,
Resolved, That the Committee on Commerce be directed to inquire into the expediency of making an appropriation for defraying the expenses of a special mission to Europe for the purpose of endeavoring to obtain some modification of the quarantine regulations in force there.

On motion of Mr. TAYLOR, of New York,
Resolved, That the Committee on the District of Columbia be instructed to inquire into the expediency of disposing at public sale or otherwise, so much of the unoccupied public grounds in the City of Washington as may be consistent with the public interest and convenience in reference to public buildings, and appropriating the avails towards the payment of the interest and the extinguishment of the debt of the corporation of Washington, contracted pursuant to an act of Congress, entitled "an act to enlarge the powers of the several corporations of the District of Columbia, and for other purposes," approved 24th May, 1828.

The following Joint Resolution then came up in third reading:

Be it resolved by the Senate and House of Representatives of the United States of America in gress assembled, That the Secretary of State and he hereby is, authorized and directed, to ask Jared Sparks to retain the papers of General Washington, now in his possession, in virtue of contract and agreement with the late Bushrod Washington, until he shall have completed the location of the works of Gen. Washington, on which he is now engaged, or until otherwise ordered by Congress; and that the Secretary of State be authorized and directed forthwith to pay George C. Washington the balance of the money due to him, under the act approved on the first day of June, 1834, for the purchase of the manuscripts and papers of General Washington.

Mr. GILLET begged to inquire of the gentleman who reported the resolution (Mr. E. Everett) whether any intimation was given last year, when arrangement was made for the purchase of these manuscripts, that there was any lien upon them, or any right by which they could be withheld from the use of Government as soon as the appropriation was made?

Mr. E. EVERETT replied, that the whole circumstances and history of the case, and the precondition and situation of the papers, had fully spread before the House in the documents presented last year—the contents of which assumed to be within the knowledge of most present.

Mr. GILLET had perused those documents and report referred to by the gentleman; but he recollection of any thing in the nature of a upon those papers. The question then was led to their value and historical and documentary importance, and the purchase was made, by himself at least, as unconditional, without any contingencies. Not a word was about their being mortgaged, and Mr. lot's communication was confined to the subject of their value. Mr. G. said he considered it that any portion of the money should have paid until the Government had been in possession of all the papers. He believed Mr. is to be as honorable a man as lived; but his or many other circumstances, might tend to jeopardize their security. He was deeply of opinion that the resolution ought not to

Mr. E. EVERETT explained that more than half of the papers were already in the possession of the Government, and that the loan of the rest was asked for only till the completion of work in which Mr. Sparks was engaged, would, in all probability, not extend beyond a year—three-fourths of it being finished. He could see no objection to the passage of resolution, for the papers were as safe in Mr. lot's hands as they would be in the possession intended depository. All parties desired the Secretary of State, Mr. Washington, Sparks, and he hoped a majority of the

Mr. PARKER agreed with the gentleman from York, (Mr. Gillet,) and with him was ignorant of the authority of Mr. Sparks to detain these. They ought now to be in their proper place, and not at Boston, or any other part of united states. All that ought now to be asked the gentleman should be, that he might be asked at Washington to make such an examination of, and take such extracts from them, as be deemed necessary to the completion of work. Mr. P. raised this objection last year, as money should not be paid till the papers been delivered, and he trusted that the balance would be withheld till that had been done.

Mr. VANDERPOEL had voted last session in favor of the appropriation for the purchase of these and he did so, as he believed the majority of the understanding that they would come lately into the hands of the purchasers. I no idea that there existed a previous only by which they could be detained. They then told that the documents relative to revolutionary claims were alone worth double the

Mr. E. EVERETT explained, that all the papers on that subject were in the custody of the Department, and indeed were in the District of Columbia at the time the purchase was made.

Mr. VANDERPOEL was not previously aware of that, but still it appeared to him that the House ought not to pay away the money asked for without a full equivalent. He had been in favor of the appropriation first as relics of the Great Father of his country, and then because assurances were given that their possession would be the means of effecting a great saving of the public money. For these reasons, and others that might be urged, Mr. V. was unwilling to vote for the payment of the balance of the appropriation until the papers had been delivered up.

Mr. MERCER called the attention of the House to the fact, that Mr. Sparks had been engaged by the government in the compilation of the diplomatic history of the United States, and surely no one would conceive these papers to be insecure in such hands.

Mr. E. EVERETT would add, that Mr. S. was not only employed by the government to prepare this compilation, but he had been permitted to take out from the Department of State all the requisite revolutionary documents, and that he had arranged, indexed, and put them in regular order. All that was asked the House, was to grant the same permission that had been given by the late Judge Washington, whose reverence for his great relative would have prevented his placing them where their security would be hazarded.

Mr. SEABORN JONES begged to ask the gentleman from Massachusetts what amount of money had been already paid?

Mr. E. EVERETT said $200,000 out of $25,000, the sum agreed upon.

Mr. SEABORN JONES thought enough had been done, and he should be unwilling to pay any further sum until the papers had been delivered. There had been considerable discussion on this subject last year. The possessors of the papers first asked $20,000, and as soon as Congress agreed to give that sum, and a bill had been reported for the purpose, they then asked $25,000, and now we find that there is some contingency, or lien, by which they are withheld, and will be withheld, no one knew how long, even after the whole sum should be paid. Mr. J. said, he felt bound to vote against the resolution.

After a few further remarks from Mr. E. EVERETT, Mr. VINTON, and Mr. PARKER, who read the act of last session—

Mr. McVEAN said, he could not see what the House had to do with Mr. Sparks. The papers had been purchased of Judge Bushrod Washington, and to him they had to look for them, for there was no reservation in the contract that we were to receive them of Mr. Sparks. The question was, if they ought to pay the res due of the money until the papers were delivered up, and Mr. McV. was of opinion they ought not, and should vote accordingly.

Mr. MINER and Mr. BATES briefly supported the resolution.

Mr. CLAYTON said, if these papers were worth any thing to the United States, it was plain they had the right to them. From the contract made by the late Judge Bushrod Washington with Mr. Sparks, this gentleman might retain them as long as he pleased, for it was left entirely to himself to say when he had done with them. He might give them up whenever he thought proper, for Congress had no power to take them out of his hands, he having, by agreement, a prior claim to their possession. Mr. C. expressed his intention of voting against the passage of the resolution.

The yeas and nays having been ordered, the question was then taken, and decided in the negative. Yeas 87, nays 101.

So the resolution was rejected.

ALEXANDRIA CANAL.

Mr. BOULDIN said that he had yesterday voted under same misapprehension on the bill for the relief of the City of Alexandria. He was, like many of his constituents and colleagues, opposed, from principle, to the system of Internal Improvements, as a system; but if national legislation had inflicted local injury, he would be one of the first

to repair it. Such an injury he was convinced had been inflicted, by the obstructions of the channel of the Potomac. He moved to reconsider the vote of yesterday, and that it be postponed to the first Monday in February next.

The question being taken on the motion to postpone, it was decided in the negative—ayes 75, noes 76.

Mr. MERCER said, to avoid a long discussion on this subject, and at the same time give the House an opportunity for its mature consideration, he would propose that it be postponed to a fortnight from next Monday.

Mr. GILLET moved that it be indefinitely postponed.

Mr. WHITTLESEY, of Ohio, asked if this question did not require a vote of two-thirds of the House to decide upon it, according to the rules.

The CHAIR explained, and without taking the question on the subject of reconsideration, the House passed to the

SPECIAL ORDER OF THE DAY,

Being on the bill for the relief of Commodore Isaac Hull, and the amendment of the Committee of the Whole, striking out allowances for compensation as Navy Agent.

Mr. PEARCE, of R. Island, was in favor of the amendment, and in opposition to the allowances claimed.

Mr. BURGES followed in support of the claim.

Mr. PARKER opposed it, and

Mr. BINNEY stated that he wished to address a few remarks to the House on this subject, and was prepared to proceed, if it was the general wish longer to continue the sitting, but as the hour was somewhat advanced, to try the sense of the House, he would move an adjournment.

The motion was agreed to, and

The House adjourned.

HOUSE OF REPRESENTATIVES.

SATURDAY, January 10, 1835.

Mr. WATMOUGH, on leave, moved to print the bill to regulate the navy, together with the several pending amendments.

Mr. GILLET moved to include an amendment which he had offered in Committee, and which he contemplated submitting in the House.

Mr. WATMOUGH acquiesced, when the motion, as modified, was agreed to.

Mr. POLK, from the Committee of Ways and Means, reported the following bill:

A bill to suspend, conditionally, the receipt of the bills and notes of the Bank of the United States and its branches, in payment of debts to the United States.

Be it enacted by the Senate and House of Representatives of the United States of America, in Congress assembled, That, from and after the passing of this act, the bills or notes of the Bank of the U. States made payable, or which shall have become payable on demand, shall not be receivable in any payment to the United States: *Provided,* That if said Bank of the United States shall pay into the Treasury the full amount of dividends of property on the capital stock of said bank, owned by the United States, heretofore withheld from the Treasury by said bank, it shall, upon such payment into the Treasury, be the duty of the Secretary of the Treasury to authorize the receipt of such bills or notes in payments to the U. States for a period extending to the expiration of the chart of said bank on the 3d day of March, in the year 1836.

The bill was read twice, and committed to a Committee of the Whole on the state of the Union.

Mr. POLK, on leave, moved to print a statement prepared by the Secretary of the Treasury, of the rate of domestic exchange, as charged by the Bank of the United States and its branches, and the different local banks in the Union.

Mr. WHITE, of New York, moved to print 5,000 extra copies of the statements referred to.

The motion requiring the unanimous consent of the House, and Mr. BRIGGS objecting—

Mr. WHITE moved to suspend the rule, in order to enable him to submit the motion; which was agreed to.

Mr. WHITE then submitted the motion indicated.

Mr. McKINLEY moved to amend the motion by directing that 10,000 extra cop es be printed, instead of 5,000, which was agreed to; and, thus amended, the proposition to print was agreed to.

Mr. POLK gave notice that he would move, on Monday next, to proceed to the consideration of several appropriation bills—the Navy, Army, and Pension bills—and, if possible, some others.

Mr. POLK also stated that he was instructed by the Committee of Ways and Means to give notice that, on as early a day as practicable, a motion would be made to take up the several bills relating to the Bank of the United States. The Committee had hitherto abstained from pressing the consideration of the bills to which he had referred, from a disinclination to interfere with the necessary business of the House. He repeated, that the bills would be called up at the earliest possible period.

Mr. CARR presented a joint memorial from the Legislature of Indiana, soliciting aid from the General Government for the purpose of establishing Hospitals on the Ohio river, at such points as may afford relief to the sick and disabled persons who navigate said river, &c.; which memorial was referred to the Committee on Commerce.

Mr. MAY moved to discharge the Committee of the Whole from the further consideration of the bill for the relief of the heirs of James Latham, deceased, and that the same be engrossed.

The motion was advocated by Messrs. MAY and R. M. JOHNSON, and resisted by Messrs. LANE and EVANS, and disagreed to.

Mr. WHITE, of New York, from the Committee on Naval Affairs, reported, without amendment, the following bills:

A bill to alter the titles of certain officers of the navy: and

A bill to authorize the enlistment of boys in the navy of the United States.

The SPEAKER laid before the House a letter from the Secretary of War, transmitting, in obedience to a resolution of the House, additional information on the subject of the Cumberland Road, which was referred to the Committee on Roads and Canals.

The SPEAKER laid before the House a letter from the Secretary of the Navy, communicating the contracts entered into by the Navy Board, for the year 1834; which was laid on the table, and ordered to be printed.

A bill for the relief of Charles Caldwell, of Arkansas, was read a third time, and passed.

On motion of Mr. WILLIAMS,

Resolved, That the Committee on the Post Office and Post Roads be instructed to inquire into the expediency of establishing a post road from Wilkesborough, by Trap Hill, in North Carolina, to Grayson Court House, in Virginia, and that a petition to that effect from the citizens of Wilkes and Ashe counties, be referred to the same committee.

On motion of Mr. EVERETT, of Vermont,

Resolved, That the petition of Lydia Parkhurst, presented at the last session, with the accompanying papers, be referred to the Committee on Revolutionary Claims.

On motion of Mr. McCARTY,

Resolved, That the Committee on the Post Office and Post Roads be instructed to inquire into the expediency of establishing a post route from South Bend, by Laporte and the Upper Crossings of Salt Creek, in Indiana, to Ottowa, in Illinois.

On motion of Mr. REYNOLDS,

Resolved, That the Committee on the Judiciary be instructed to inquire into the expediency of authorizing a settlement of the claims of the United States on the Bank of Illinois upon such equitable and reasonable terms, as will enable the bank to make payment, and at the same time to resume her banking operations.

The following resolution, being the unfinished morning business, was again taken up:

Resolved, That the Committee on Roads and Canals be instructed to inquire into the subject and report their opinion to this House, of the most equal and just mode of applying the revenues of the country to such works of public improvement

within the respective States of this Union as may be necessary for the facilitating of commerce with fo e gn nations, and among the several States. And that they moreover report their opinion of the best and most practicable mode of ascertaining and determining the nationality and importance of such improvements as may be proposed within the said several States.

Mr. CHILTON resumed his remarks by disclaiming any personal hostility towards, or any intention or wish of assailing, from the line of discussion he had been compelled to pursue, the present Chief Magistrate of the United States. Mr. C. had been drawn into this discussion as the ardent friend of Internal Improvements. During the last session of Congress, he had taken occasion to give his sentiments on this subject, and to show that the views and hopes of the western country, in President Jackson, had been frustrated, and the pledges of that individual unredeemed. A very worthy gentleman, friendly to the Executive, and whom Mr. C. was proud to call his personal friend, (Mr. Bynum, we believe,) had then asserted that General Jackson had redeemed all his promises—which were, to put down the system of Internal Improvements, abolish the Tariff, and to put down the Bank of the United States. Mr. C. then took occasion to assert otherwise, and had met with no reply. The fact was, that it was in consequence of the expectations excited by the previous course, the declarations, and pledges of General Jackson, that as soon as that individual was exalted to the high station he now held, the table of that House was literally loaded with petitions and memorials from his friends west of the mountains, praying for appropriations for objects of Internal Improvement. The people of the west did consider that up to that time their claims had been disregarded by the course of the former occupier of the Presidential Chair. The day was reiterated, from day to day, and Mr. C. himself responded to it at the time, that gross injustice had been done the west, ern country, and their interests and welfare had been set aside in carrying on works of Internal Improvement, by the immediate predecessor of Gen. Jackson. Mr. C. then entered into a review of the course pursued by Mr. Adams, and drew a contrast between his Administration and that of the present Chief Magistrate in respect to the same subject, the former of whom, so far from striving to crush the system, did a'l in his power to foster and promote it.

Mr. C. then referred to the call made upon General Jackson by Governor Ray, of Indiana, previous to his first election, who invited him explicitly to give his sentiments on the subject, and, Mr. C. added, that if he failed in proving that the President had changed his opinions, and maintained the reverse of what he formerly did, he would immediately surrender his seat on that floor and consent to lose his character for consistency and truth. He considered himself bound to do this to contrast the opinions of General Jackson himself; for if he should be able to show that he held one set to-day, and another to-morrow, that he avowed principles one day which he repudiated the next, this sufferer would be produced, that whatever that individual's opinion might be, they were entitled to very little influence, or at least to less than they would have if they had been uniformly consistent and undeviating. Mr. C. would invite the attention of the House to the first act of General Jackson's administration on this subject, viz. his veto of the Maysville and Lexington road bill. In his last annual message, in justification of the course he had taken, what were the objections there made to that bill? That the improvement was local—that it began and ended in the same State. Mr. C. said, the same objection might be made to every internal improvement. Every improvement must be located somewhere; and it was in vain to expect an improvement to benefit all parts of the Union alike, in a country so extended and diversified, and with interests so various. Did the President entertain the same opinions when he was in the Senate of the United States, as when he voted the Maysville and Lexington road bill? Mr. C. adverted to this to show that he was but man, and might occasionally find

himself in error, and change, of course, just as other feeble mortals did.

Mr. C. here referred to the Senate Journal, second sess on of the 18th Congress, page 155, to show that Gen. Jackson voted in the affirmative on the bill authorizing a subscription to the stock of the Delaware and Chesapeake Canal Company, and that he also voted in the affirmative on an amendment offered to that bill authorizing a subscription for stock of the Dismal Swamp Canal Company. If appropriations for internal improvement, said Mr. C. were constitutional then, were not less so now, for not a solitary amendment had been made to the Constitution of the United States, since that time. The obligation to support the Constitution were as binding then as now. Here then is one of the votes to which the friends of Gen. Jackson in the west were referred when were called on to give him their suffrages, and offered a reason why so many applications were made ... for internal improvement, were presented ... during the first year of his elevation to the presidency. Let him not be astonished even, nor his friends here be astonished overmuch, a great many applications were made. It was proceeding when Mr. WHITTLESEY of ... called for the Order of the Day.

CLAIM OF COMMODORE HULL.

The House then resumed the consideration of the Special Order of the Day, being on that ... the relief of Commodore Isaac Hull, and ... amendment agreed to in Committee of the ... to strike out that part of the bill providing for ... payment of $6,300 for extra services as Agent at the Navy Yard at Washington, ... commanding the same.

Mr. BINNEY took the floor in opposition to ... amendment, and, in support of the claim ... tended that the duties of Navy Agent being performed by Com. Hull, and a spot of ... should impel the House to require the service rendered, by a fair compensation. In order to advocate the claim in an argumental length—going into a minute history of the ... of the office of Naval Agent, and the duties ... involved, at various periods, from the origin ... of the Government. He also examined the act of ... 1804, which provides for the government of the ... Navy Yard at Washington. That law here ... that "the Commandant of the Yard shall be a ... superintendence and care of the same—and form the duties of Navy Agent—and recover ... of a Captain commanding a squadron," the ... law of 1804, he contended, should be construed according to the true intent and meaning of the ... law-giver. It was designed to apply to the ... cumstances and exigencies of the times in ... was enacted, some 30 years ago. It had not ... otly considered inoperative up to 1823, when new law was enacted. It was unjust, he contended, to revive it now, under circumstances variant from those under which it was enacted, meant to apply. Mr. B. continued in remarks for more than an hour, and was followed by

Mr. McKINLEY, who opposed the claim ... thought there would be great danger in allowing the construction of the law contended for by the gentleman from Pennsylvania, (Mr. Binney,) opening the door to favoritism and corruption. Mr. McK. hoped the amendment of the Committee of the Whole would prevail.

Mr. HARDIN followed on the same side of the question. The language of the law was quite definite, and could not be mistaken. Rather than by its strict letter. In the course of his ... marks, Mr. H., produced a letter from the Fourth Auditor of the Treasury, stating that ... Hull, prior to his entering on the duties of ... office, was explicitly informed of the terms on ... all the duties required of him—and that, of this instance, he was allowed an extra clerk of his ... own selection, at a salary of $1,000 dollars ... and was afterwards raised to 1,500 dollars. ... said, this claim was but an entering wedge, ... would form a precedent of the most dangerous character. It would be far better to pay Commodore Hull one hundred thousand dollars ... gratuity, than to pass this bill.

Mr. REED again addressed the House in favor of retaining this claim in the bill, and the...

amendment of the Commi tee of the Whole to
be out th section, was then taken by yeas and
a, and decided in the affirmative as follows:
YEAS—Messrs. John Adams, Wm. Allen, An-
ay, Bean, Beaty, Beaumont, Blair, Bockee,
ada, Brown, Bull, Burns, Bynum, Cam-
ing, Campbell, Carmichael, Carr, Casey, Cha-
, Chilton, Chinn, Claiborne, Samuel Clark,
L Clark, Clay, Clowney, Coffee, Cramer,
es Davis, Davenport, Day, Deberry, Dicker-
Dickinson, Dunlap, Fillmore, Forester, Fow-
Philo C. Fuller, Wm. K. Fuller, Galbraith,
Ain, Gillet, Gilmer, Gordon, Graham, Gray-
Griffin, Joseph Hall, Thomas H. Hall, Halsey,
es, Hardin, Joseph M. Harper, Hathaway,
Kiss, Hawes, Heath, Biester, Howell, Hub-
l Inge, Wm. Jackson, Janes, Jarvis, Noadiah
Jon, S. Jones, B. Jones, Kavanagh, Kilgore,
urd, Lansing, Laporte, Luke Lea, Thomas
y Love, Loyall, Lytle, Abijah Mann, Joel K.
s, J. Y. Mason, Moses Mason, May, McComas,
sive, McKay, McKinley, McLene, McVean,
s, Miner, Robert Mitchell, Moore, Morgan,
henberg, Murphy, Osgood, Parks, Parker,
es, Patterson, Dutee J. Pearce, Peyton, F.
es Pinckney, Plummer Poll, Pope, Ramsay,
olds, Robertson, Schenck, Schley, A. H.
pard, Shinn, Smith, Standifer, Stoddert,
Taylor, Wm. P. Taylor, Francis Thomas,
ness, Turner, Turrill, Vance, Vanderpoel,
ner, Wardwell—128.
NAYS—Messrs. John Q. Adams, Heman Allen,
J. Allen, Archer, Banks, Barber, Bates,
ph, Binney, Briggs, Burges, Cage, Clayton,
i Darlington. Denny, Dickson, Evans, Ed-
Everett, H. Everett, Ewing, Ferris, Garland,
en, H. Hall, James Harper, Harrison, Hazel-
Henderson, Huntington, Ebenezer Jackson,
Johnson, Henry Johnson, King, Lane, Ley,
l Manning, Marshall, McKennan, McKim,
h, Milligan, Phillips, Potts, Reed, Rencher,
Spangler, Trumbull, Tweedy, Vinton,
Watmough, Wayne, White, E. Whittlesey,
s Williams, Wise, Young—61.
he claim was rejected. The bill was then
ed to be engrossed for a third reading on
y next, as amended, and then
House adjourned.

IN SENATE.
MONDAY, January 12, 1835.
KING, of Georgia, rose and stated, that the
LBERT CUTHBERT, Senator elect from
a, was present; that he had lost his creden-
s, the case was not without precedent, he
hat he be permitted to qualify and take his
The motion was agreed to, and Mr. CUTH-
was qualified according, and took his seat.
ions and memorials were presented by
TYLER, TALLMADGE, PRENTISS,
SR., WEBSTER, TIPTON, and MOORE.
ssage was received from the President of
ted States, communicating a report of the
of the Mint, with a statement of the ope-
of that institution for the year 1834.
tion of Mr. BENTON, the communica-
ordered to be printed.
VICE PRESIDENT laid before the Senate
nication from the Secretary of the Treasu-
edience to the resolution submitted on
t, by Mr. LEIGH, calling for the cur-
ance of that Department with the Receiv-
ublic Money, in the course of the last

BENTON remarked, that as the gentleman
rginia was not in his seat, he thought it
e in accordance with his wishes to move
communication be printed, and he moved
thousand extra copies be printed.
suggestion of Mr. KING, of Alabama, the
otion was laid on the table.
LEIGH having shortly afterwards taken his
subject was taken up, and on his motion,
N. was referred to the Committee on Fi-
with directions to consider the report, to
te the practice referred to, and whether
the and judicious, and if not, whether any
regulations be necessary to correct it.
CE PRESIDENT also laid before the Se-
rtificate of the re-election of JOHN M.

CLAYTON, a Senator from the State of Delaware
for six years from the 4th of March next.
Mr SMITH, from the Judiciary Committee, reported a bill for the relief of David McCord.
Also, a bill for the relief of Thomas L. Winthrop
and others; which was read the first time, and ordered to a second reading.
Also, a bill for the relief of David Beard; which
was read the first time, and ordered to a second
reading.
Mr SMITH, from the Committee on Revolutionary Claims, to which was referred the bill for
the relief of the legal representatives of Colonel
William Bond and Colonel William Douglass, reported the same without amendment.
Mr. SMITH, from the same Committee, reported a bill for the relief of Captain George Hurlbrook;
Also, unfavorably upon the petition of Lieutenant
John Taylor.
Mr. ROBBINS, from the Library Committee,
reported a resolution authorizing the purchase of
50 copies of the American Diplomatic Code, for
the use of the Senate.
Mr. ROBBINS, from the same Committee, reported the joint resolution for the purchase of 500
copies of Cary & Lea's History of Congress.
Mr. BENTON here rose and said, that as there
were applications now before Congress for a renewal of the charters of the Banks of this District, he begged leave to submit to the Senate by
way of notice, a paper containing the substance of
the amendments, which he intended to insist on
when the bills should come up for consideration.
I. That no application for a renewal of charter
should be entertained in favor of any bank which has
heretofore failed or suspended payment, until all
the circumstances attending such failure or suspension shall have been fully examined, and reported
upon by a Committee of one of the Houses of
Congress.
II. That Banks of circulation ought to be reduced in number, not increased.
III. That no charter ought to be renewed,
granted, or extended, except upon the following
fundamental principles, (among others:) 1st,
The Bank to pay all its currency in gold and silver;
the holder to have the right to require the one-half
in gold and the other half in silver; 2. No paper
currency to be issued, renewed, or paid out, of a
less denomination than $20; 3d: The stockhold-
ers, for the time being, to be liable, each to the
amount of his stock, for the circulation and deposites, on the failure of the Bank to redeem its
currency, or pay its deposites; with summary process for the recovery; and all sales and transfers of
stock to be void, which shall be adjudged, by a
jury, to have been made with intent to evade this
liability.
On Mr. BENTON's motion, the paper was ordered to be printed.
Mr. TYLER, pursuant to notice and on leave
given, introduced a bill to provide a system of laws
for the District of Columbia; which was read
twice and referred.
Mr. KING, of Alabama, pursuant to notice, and
on leave given, introduced a bill to authorize
George Bidwell to import an iron steam boat, in
detached parts, free of duty.
The following resolution, submitted by Mr.
BENTON, and lying on the table, was taken up
for consideration:
Resolved, That the Committee on Finance be
instructed to obtain from the Bank of the United
States a copy of all instructions, if any, to the
Branch Banks, directing them to collect and remit
Spanish milled dollars to the mother Bank; the
number of such dollars annually remitted; the
rates at which they sold at different periods, say at
or about the beginning of each quarter of the year;
whether the Bank of the United States has sold
such dollars to the United States, and if so, how
many and at what rates; how many it has sold to
or exported to foreign countries; also, a
statement of the amount of gold coin of the
amount of silver coin; and the amount of bullion
remitted to the mother Bank, or elsewhere, by her
order, annually since the first day of April, 1832;
also, a statement showing the amount of silver
coin and of gold coin remitted by the mother bank

to each branch since that day; also, the amount of
gold coin and the amount of silver coin annually
sold or annually exported by the Bank; since the
said first day of April; also, a statement of the
amount of gold received from the United States
Mint since the first day of August last; and a statement of the whole amount of gold on hand in the
Bank and its branches, for each month from April
1, 1832, to the present time.
Mr. TYLER said he desired to say but a word
on this subject. He had no sort of objection to
the inquiry, and wished to be so distinctly understood. The material allegation in the resolution
was in reference to the conduct which the Bank
had pursued relative to the currency and coin of
the United States; the call was for information
on this subject. And he begged leave to say
to the Senate, that this matter was made the subject of specific inquiry by the Committee of Investigation of 1832. The Committee on Finance, during the last summer, having ascertained that the subject was fully inquired into in
1832, carefully examined and analyzed the report, and he was ready now to affirm that the
counter report, which was then made, was no
conclusive that it had relieved the committee
from the labor of prosecuting their inquiries into
that subject. In reference to the Bank bartering in the currency of the country, he thought
that charge had been answered by the exhibit
appended to the report of the Committee on Finance. He thought that by that exhibit it was
shown, that this traffic could not have been carried on. But if the honorable gentleman from
Missouri thought that any thing could come out of
the inquiry, he had no objection to it. He (Mr.
T.) was ready to condemn the Bank in all things
in which it should have erred; he was no friend
of the Bank, and when we came to measure facts,
it would be seen that he stood so high in opposition to the Bank, that he was not to be shaken
by any thing which should yet take place. It
was not necessary for him to make this disclaimer, but it came in his way, and he had given utterance to it. But the honorable gentleman from
Missouri might have information which the committee did not possess, and he, Mr. T. was willing
it should be shown.
Mr. BENTON asked leave of the Senate to
amend the resolution, by correcting a date in it.
All the returns asked for, came up to the 31st
January, 1831. He wished to insert that day instead of the 1st of April. As to the subject matter of the call, he would only say, that it would be
hardly right to mention the information on which
he made the call. He might, to be sure, be mistaken in his information, and if it should so appear,
he would have no more to say on the subject. As
to the honorable gentleman's situation with reference to the Committee and the Bank, he (Mr.
B.) prayed God to grant him safe deliverance—
his situation seemed something worse than walking on eggs, (to use an old maxim,) or treading on
burning plough shares. But it was probable we
should be able to measure facts before long.
Mr. TYLER replied, that the honorable gentleman from Missouri need not feel the slightest concern for his deliverance. He was delivered from
Jacksonism—he thanked God he had got rid of
that. He had, from his mother's lap, been taught
an old adage, which he should cling to through
life, that, in all matters, political as well as others,
"honesty was the best policy."
Mr. BENTON did not doubt the disinterestedness and integrity with had always governed the
honorable gentleman from Virginia. He, Mr. B.,
had heard him make several speeches, during the
time on this floor, and in all of them the gentleman
commenced and ended in the same strain, upon his
own high-wrought integrity and divine exactness.
So with regard to this matter, of which there was
no occasion to have made any observations relative to his integrity. But an opportunity would
be afforded for measuring swords before long.
He took this occasion to make a public apology to
the honorable member from Kentucky just before
him, (Mr. Bibb,) which he had made the other day
privately. It was for addressing the Senate upon
the French spoliation bill, when that gentleman

Spanish milled dollars to the mother bank; the number of such dollars annually remitted; the rates at which they sold at different periods, say at or about the beginning of each quarter of the year; whether the Bank of the United States has sold such dollars to the United States, and if so, how many and at what rates; how many it has sold to others or exported to foreign countries; also, a statement of the amount of gold coin; of the amount of silver coin; and the amount of bullion remitted to the mother bank, or elsewhere, by her order, annually since the 1st day of April, 1832; also, a statement showing the amount of silver coin and of gold coin remitted by the mother bank to each branch since that day; also, the amount of gold coin and the amount of silver coin annually sold or annually exported by the Bank, since the said first day of April; also, a statement of the amount of gold received from the United States Mint since the first day of August last; and a statement of the whole amount of gold on hand in the Bank and its branches, for each month from April 1, 1832, to the present time.

The following bills were read the third time and passed:

A bill for the relief of Henry B. Tyler, executor of Col. Richard Smith, deceased;

A bill for the relief of McKean Buchanan;

A bill for the relief of the administrators of Michael Hogan, deceased.

The bill for the relief of Lt. Archibald S. Campbell was called up for consideration, and

On motion of Mr. TALLMADGE laid on the table.

The bill for the relief of Loami Baldwin was taken up for consideration.

[The object of this bill was to make compensation to Mr. Baldwin for services rendered during the administration of Mr. Adams, as a civil engineer, in the construction of two dry docks at Charleston, South Carolina.]

Mr. HILL moved to lay the bill on the table; which was not agreed to.

Mr. HILL and Mr. BENTON then opposed the bill on the ground that Mr. Baldwin was an engineer in the employment of the Government at an annual salary of $4,000; that this allowance would be double pay for services rendered by a salaried officer; that the claim had been disallowed by the Secretary, and afterwards by the Auditor; and that it a contract had been made with Mr. Baldwin for this service, it was no doubt in writing, and ought to be shown.

Some further remarks were made by Messrs. SOUTHARD, FRELINGHUYSEN, CALHOUN, POINDEXTER, and CLAYTON, in favor of the bill.

It was said by them that an express contract was made with Mr. Baldwin by the then Secretary of the Navy (Mr. Southard) for the performance of this duty, which was an extra service; that he was not an officer of the Government, because he held no commission; but that if he was, it had been the usage of the Government to pay its officers extra compensation for any services which they were called on to render, out of the line of their ordinary duties. That the justice of this claim was enhanced in consequence of the contract which had been made with Mr. Baldwin to pay him $5 a day for the time employed in performing the duty assigned him.

The question being on the engrossment of the bill for a third reading.

Mr. HILL demanded the yeas and nays, which were ordered: but before the question was taken,

Mr. BENTON renewed the motion to lay the bill on the table, with a view to make some further examination into it.

The motion was then agreed to.

SPECIAL ORDER.

The Senate resumed the consideration of the bill making compensation for French spoliations prior to 1800.

Mr. BENTON then spoke at length in opposition to the bill. When he concluded,

Mr. WEBSTER rose, and said that no other gentleman intended to address the Senate on this subject, he proposed to answer the objections which had been urged against the bill, so far as

the Senate would indulge him, either to-day, tomorrow, or on Monday.

[Some gentlemen suggested Monday.]

Mr. WEBSTER said as it seemed to be the wish of gentlemen that he should defer his remarks till Monday, he would move that when the Senate adjourn, it will adjourn to meet on Monday next.

The motion being received by unanimous consent, was agreed to.

On motion of Mr. CLAYTON, the Senate then proceeded to the consideration of Executive business, and when the doors were opened,

The Senate adjourned to Monday.

HOUSE OF REPRESENTATIVES.

FRIDAY, January 9, 1835.

Petitions and memorials were presented on leave by Mr. EWING, of Indiana, and Mr. HEATH, of Maryland.

Mr. CASEY, of Illinois, asked leave to introduce the report of the engineer appointed by the commissioners of the fund appropriated by the States of Illinois and Indiana for the improvement of the navigation of the Wabash river.

On leave being granted, Mr. CASEY said, it would be recollected by the House that on yesterday the bill which had passed the Senate making an appropriation for the improvement of the navigation of the Wabash river, was referred to the Committee on Roads and Canals. By the last mail from the west, through the politeness of a friend, he had received the report of the engineer appointed by the commissioners of the fund appropriated by the States of Illinois and Indiana for the improvement of the navigation of the Wabash. It contained some valuable information in relation to the proposed improvement, and as it was desirable that the National Legislature should be in possession of every possible information on this subject, he thought it his duty to introduce this report. It was a subject of deep and abiding interest to the people of that section of the country, and he d d hope that it would receive the favor and consideration of Congress. Mr. C. concluded by a motion to refer the report to the Committee on Roads and Canals, and that it be printed; which was agreed to.

Mr. CLAY, of Alabama, presented a petition from certain members of the Legislature of Alabama, asking the establishment of a post route from Ashville, in St. Clair county, by way of Jacksonville, in Benton county, Alabama, to in Georgia, and sundry other routes through adjacent counties in Alabama—which was referred to the Committee on the Post Office and Post roads.]

Mr. CLAY, from the Committee on the Public Lands, reported, without amendment, the bill from the Senate, authorizing the relinquishment of the 16th sections of lands appropriated for the use of Schools, and the location of other lands in lieu thereof.

Mr. CLAY moved to postpone the further consideration of the bill until Monday next.

Mr. EVANS moved to commit it to a Committee of the whole.

The motion to commit was supported by Messrs. EVANS, WILLIAMS, and LANE, and opposed by Messrs. CLAY, EWING, and McKINLEY. The motion prevailed—yeas 91, nays 30.

Mr. FOSTER, from the Committee on the Judiciary, reported a bill to change the place of holding the District Court of the United States for the district of Mississippi which was read twice and ordered to be engrossed for a third reading.

Mr. WARDWELL, from the Committee on Revolutionary Pensions, reported a b-ll to authorise the Secretary of War to appoint agents to examine pensions, in order to prevent frauds, and for other purposes, which was read twice and committed to a Committee of the Whole on the State of the Union.

Mr. INGE, from the Committee on the Public Lands; made an unfavorable report upon the petition of R. Young and others; which was laid on the table.

Mr. CAMBRELENG, from the Committee of Ways and Means, reported a bill for the relief of

Chastelain and Pouvert, which was read twice and committed.

Mr. MERCER gave notice that he would on Tuesday next, move to take up the bill authorizing a further subscription in the stock of the Chesapeake and Ohio Canal Company.

Mr. BOON, from the Committee on the Public Lands, reported a bill for the benefit of Charles Caldwell, of Arkansas; which was read twice and ordered to be engrossed for a third reading.

Mr. CONNOR gave notice that he would move to take up, on the 27th instant, the bill to establish certain post routes, and to alter and discontinue others.

Mr. MARSHALL, from the Committee on Revolutionary Claims, reported a substitute for the bill to provide for certain revolutionary claims; which, together with the original bill, Mr. M. moved to commit to a Committee of the Whole on the state of the Union, and that the same be made the special order for Friday the 30th January.

After some remarks on the propriety of making the bill a special order, by Messrs. WARDWELL, MARSHALL, MILLER, and LANE, the bill was substituted for the 30th January, and the motion agreed to—yeas 80, nays 44.

Messrs. MUHLENBERG, DAVIS of Kentucky, BOON, LEA of Tennessee, GRAHAM and GRENNELL, made (from various Standing Committees,) unfavorable reports upon petitions, &c., which had been referred to them.

[Mr. KINNARD moved to discharge the Committee on Revolutionary Claims from the further consideration of the petition of Robert Allen, and to refer the same to the Committee on Private Land Claims, which was agreed to.]

On motion of Mr. ALLEN, of Virginia,

Resolved, That the Committee on Revolutionary Claims be discharged from the further consideration of the heirs of Isaac Israel, and that the petitioners have leave to withdraw their papers.

On motion of Mr. EVERETT, by consent, offered the following resolution, which was agreed to:

Resolved, That the Secretary of War be directed to communicate to this House a copy of any order given by him to the Commissioner of Pensions directing the suspension of the allowance of pensions under the act of 7th June, 1833.

On motion of Mr. LYON, of Michigan,

Resolved, That the Committee on Public Lands be instructed to inquire into the expediency of establishing an additional land district for the sale of public lands in the Territory of Michigan.

On motion of Mr. CONNOR,

Resolved, That the Committee on the Post office and Post Roads be instructed to inquire into the expediency of establishing a post route from Salisbury by Barringer's Mills, to Cobourn's Store in Mecklenburg county.

Mr. ASHLEY offered the following resolution, which, under the rule, lies one day:

Resolved, That the Secretary of the Treasury be requested to return to this House the report referred to him at the last session, of the Commissioners appointed to examine and adjust the private Land Claims in Missouri, with reasons as he may think proper to make thereon.

On motion of Mr. HEATH,

Resolved, That the Committee on Commerce be directed to inquire into the expediency of making an appropriation for relieving the expense of a special mission to Europe for the purpose of devoting to obtain some modification of the quarantine regulations in force there.

On motion of Mr. TAYLOR, of New York,

Resolved, That the Committees on the District Co umbia be instructed to inquire into the expediency of disposing at public sale or otherwise, so much of the unoccupied public grounds in the City of Washington, as may be consistent with public interest and convenience in reference to public buildings; and appropriating the avails towards the payment of the interest and the extinguishment of the debt of the corporation of Washington, contracted pursuant to an act of Congress, e ntitled "an act to enlarge the powers of the several corporations of the District of Columbia, and for other purposes," approved May 1828.

The following Joint Resolution then came up on its third reading:

Be it resolved by the Senate and House of Representatives of the United States of America in Congress assembled, That the Secretary of State, and he hereby is, authorized and directed, to omit Jared Sparks to retain the papers of Gene-Washington, now in his possession, in virtue a contract and agreement with the late Bush-| Washington, until he shall have completed the lication of the works of Gen. Washington, on ich he is now engaged, or until otherwise ordered by Congress; and that the Secretary of te be authorized and directed forthwith to pay George C. Washington the balance of the mo-due to him, under the act approved on the h day of June, 1834, for the purchase of the &s and papers of Gen. Washington.

Mr. GILLET begged to inquire of the gentleman who reported the resolution (Mr. E. Everett) ther any intimation was made for the purchase of these ers, that there was any lien upon them, or any tract by which they could be withheld from the ds of Government as soon as the appropriation t made?

Mr. E. EVERETT replied, that the whole circumstances and history of the case, and the preposition and situation of the papers, had a fully spread before the House in the document presented last year—the contents of which presumed to be within the knowledge of most remen present.

Mr. GILLET had perused those documents and report referred to by the gentleman; but he no recollection of any thing in the nature of a upon those papers. The question then was fixed to their value and historical and documentary importance, and the purchase was re-ded, by himself at least, as unconditional, without any contingencies. Not a word was about their being mortgaged, and Mr. tts's communication was confined to the subject of their value. Mr. G. said he considered it strange that any portion of the money should have a paid until the Government had been in possession of all the papers. He believed Mr. tts to be as honorable a man as lived; but his view, or many other circumstances, might intervene to jeopardise their security. He was deeply of opinion that the resolution ought not to

Mr. E. EVERETT explained that more than half of the papers were already in the possession of the Government, and that the loan of the money was asked for only till the completion of work in which Mr. Sparks was engaged, would, in all probability, not extend beyond per year—three-fourths of it being finished. E. could see no objection to the passage of resolution, for the papers were as safe in Mr. ks's hands as they would be in the possession their intended depository. All parties desired The Secretary of State, Mr. Washington, Sparks, and he hoped a majority of the se.

Mr. PARKER agreed with the gentleman from r York, (Mr. Gillet,) and with him was ignorant of the authority of Mr. Sparks to detain these ers. They ought now to be in their proper ody, and not at Boston, or any other part of United states. All that ought now to be asked by the gentleman should be, that he might be sitted at Washington to make such an exact on of, and take such extracts from them, as t be deemed necessary to the completion of work. Mr. P. raised this objection last year, the money should not be paid till the papers been delivered, and he trusted that the balance would be withheld till that had been done.

Mr. VANDERPOEL had voted last session in r of the appropriation for the purchase of these ers, and he did so, as he believed the majority in the understanding that they would come mediately into the hands of the purchasers. had no idea that there existed a previous con-t by which they could be detained. They then told that the documents relative to re-sionary claims were alone worth double the ney.

Mr. E. EVERETT explained, that all the papers on that subject were in the custody of the Department, and indeed were in the District of Columbia at the time the purchase was made.

Mr. VANDERPOEL was not previously aware of that, but still it appeared to him that the House ought not to pay away the money asked for without a full equivalent. He had been in favor of the appropriation first as relics of the Great Father of his country, and then because assurances were given that their possession would be the means of effecting a great saving of the public money. For these reasons, and others that might be urged, Mr. V. was unwilling to vote for the payment of the balance of the appropriation until the papers had been delivered up.

Mr. MERCER called the attention of the House to the fact, that Mr. Sparks had been engaged by the government in the compilation of the diplomatic history of the United States, and surely no one would conceive these papers to be insecure in such hands.

Mr. E. EVERETT would add, that Mr. S. was not only employed by the government to prepare this compilation, but he had been permitted to take out from the Department of State all the requisite revolutionary documents, and that he had arranged, indexed, and put them in regular order. All that was asked the House, was to grant the same permission that had been given by the late Judge Washington, whose reverence for his great relative would have prevented his placing them where their security would be hazarded.

Mr. SEABORN JONES begged to ask the gentleman from Massachusetts what amount of money had been already paid?

Mr. E. EVERETT said $20,000 out of $25,-000, the sum agreed upon.

Mr. SEABORN JONES thought enough had been done, and he should be unwilling to pay any further sum until the papers had been delivered. There had been considerable discussion on this subject last year. The possessors of the papers first asked $20,000, and as soon as Congress agreed to give that sum, and a bill had been reported for the purpose, they then asked $25,000, and now we find that there is some contingency, or lien, by which they are withheld, and will be withheld, no one knew how long, even after the whole sum should be paid. Mr. J. said, he felt bound to vote against the resolution.

After a few further remarks from Mr. E. EVE-RETT, Mr. VINTON, and Mr. PARKER, who read the act of last session—

Mr. McVEAN said, he could not see what the House had to do with Mr. Sparks. The papers had been purchased of Judge Bushrod Washington, and to him they had to look for them, for there was no reservation in the contract that we were to receive them of Mr. Sparks. The question was, if they should pay the res due of the money until the papers were delivered up, and Mr. McV. was of opinion they ought not, and should vote accordingly.

Mr. MINER and Mr. BATES briefly supported the resolution.

Mr. CLAYTON said, if these papers were worth any thing to the United States, it was plain they had the right to them. From the contract made by the late Judge Bushrod Washington with Mr. Sparks, this gentleman might retain them as long as he pleased, for it was left entirely to himself to say when he had done with them. He might give th m up whenever he thought proper, for Congress had no power to take them out of his hands, he having, by agreement, a prior claim to their possession. Mr. C. expressed his intention of voting against the passage of the resolution.

The yeas and nays having been ordered, the question was then taken, and decided in the negative. Yeas 87, nays 101.

So the resolution was rejected.

ALEXANDRIA CANAL.

Mr. BOULDIN said that he had yesterday voted under same misapprehension on the bill for the relief of the City of Alexandria. He was, like many of his constituents and colleagues, opposed, from principle, to the system of Internal Improvements, as a system; but if national legislation had inflicted local injury, he would be one of the first

to repair it. Such an injury he was convinced had been inflicted, by the obstructions of the channel of the Potomac. He moved to reconsider the vote of yesterday, and that it be postponed to the first Monday in February next.

The question being taken on the motion to postpone, it was decided in the negative—ayes 75, noes 76.

Mr. MERCER said, to avoid a long discussion on this subject. and at the same time give the House an opportunity for its mature consideration, he would propose that it be postponed to a fortnight from next Monday.

Mr. GILLET moved that it be indefinitely postponed.

The CHAIR explained, and without taking the question on the subject of reconsideration, the House passed to the

SPECIAL ORDER OF THE DAY,

Being on the bill for the relief of Commodore Isaac Hull, and the amendment of the Committee of the Whole, striking out allowances for compensation as Navy Agent.

Mr. PEARCE, of R. Island, was in favor of the amendment, and in opposition to the allowance claimed.

Mr. BURGES followed in support of the claim.

Mr. PARKER opposed it, and

Mr. BINNEY stated that he wished to address a few remarks to the House on this subject, and was prepared to proceed, if it was the general wish longer to continue the sitting, but as the hour was somewhat advanced, to try the sense of the House, he would move an adjournment.

The motion was agreed to, and

The House adjourned.

HOUSE OF REPRESENTATIVES.

SATURDAY, January 10, 1835.

Mr. WATMOUGH, on leave, moved to print the bill to regulate the navy, together with the several pending amendments.

Mr. GILLET moved to include an amendment which he had offered in Committee, and which he contemplated submitting in the House.

Mr. WATMOUGH acquiesced, when the motion, as modified, was agreed to.

Mr. POLK, from the Committee of Ways and Means, reported the following bill:

A bill to suspend, conditionally, the receipt of the bills and notes of the Bank of the United States and its branches, in payment of debts to the United States.

Be it enacted by the Senate and House of Representatives of the United States of America, in Congress assembled, That, from and after the passing of this act, the bills or notes of the Bank of the U. States made payable, or which shall have become payable on demand, shall not be receivable in any payment to the United States: *Provided,* That if said Bank or the United States shall pay into the Treasury the full amount of dividends of property on the capital stock of said bank, owned by the United States, heretofore withheld from the Treasury by said bank, it shall, upon such payment into the Treasury, be the duty of the Secretary of the Treasury to authorize the receipt of such bills or notes in payments to the U. States for a period extending to the expiration of the chart r of said bank on the 3d day of March, in the year 1836.

The bill was read twice, and committed to a Committee of the Whole on the state of the Union.

Mr. POLK, on leave, moved to print a statement prepared by the Secretary of the Treasury, of the rate of domestic exchange, as charged by the Bank of the United States and its branches, and the different local banks in the Union.

Mr. WHITE, of New York, moved to print 5,000 extra copies of the statements referred to.

The motion requiring the unanimous consent of the House, and Mr. BRIGGS objecting—

Mr. WHITE moved to suspend the rule, in order to enable him to submit the motion; which was agreed to.

Mr. WHITE then submitted the motion indicated.

Mr. McKINLEY moved to amend the motion by directing that 10,000 extra cop es be printed, instead of 5,000, the proposition to print was agreed to, amended, the proposition to print was agreed to.

Mr. POLK gave notice that he would move, on Monday next, to proceed to the consideration of several appropriation bills—the Navy, Army, and Pension bills—and, if possible, some others.

Mr. POLK also stated that he was instructed by the Committee of Ways and Means to give notice that, on as early a day as practicable, a motion would be made to take up the several bills relating to the Bank of the United States. The Committee had hitherto abstained from pressing the consideration of the bills to which he had referred, from a disinclination to interfere with the necessary business of the House. He repeated, that the bills would be called up at the earliest possible period.

Mr. CARR presented a joint memorial from the Legislature of Indiana, soliciting aid from the General Government for the purpose of establishing Hospitals on the Ohio river, at such points as may afford relief to the sick and disabled persons who navigate said river, &c.; which memorial was referred to the Committee on Commerce.

Mr. MAY moved to discharge the Committee of the Whole from the further consideration of the bill for the relief of the heirs of James Latham, deceased, and that the same be engrossed.

The motion was advocated by Messrs. MAY and R. M. JOHNSON, and resisted by Messrs. LANE and EVANS, and disagreed to.

Mr. WHITE, of New York, from the Committee on Naval Affairs, reported, without amendment, the following bills:

A bill to alter the titles of certain officers of the navy; and

A bill to to authorize the enlistment of boys in the navy of the United States.

The SPEAKER laid before the House a letter from the Secretary of War, transmitting, in obedience to a resolution of the House, additional information on the subject of the Cumberland Road; which was referred to the Committee on Roads and Canals.

The SPEAKER laid before the House a letter from the Secretary of the Navy, communicating the contracts entered into by the Navy Board, for the year 1834; which was laid on the table, and ordered to be printed.

A bill for the relief of Charles Caldwell, of Arkansas, was read a third time, and passed.

On motion of Mr. WILLIAMS, *Resolved,* That the Committee on the Post Office and Post Roads be instructed to inquire into the expediency of establishing a post road from Wilkesborough, by Trap Hill, in North Carolina, to Grayson Court House, in Virginia, and that a petition to that effect from the citizens of Wilkes and Ashe counties, be referred to the same committee.

On motion of Mr. EVERETT, of Vermont, *Resolved,* That the petition of Lydia Parkhurst, presented at the last session, with the accompanying papers, by referred to the Committee on Revolutionary Claims.

On motion of Mr. McCARTY, *Resolved,* That the Committee on the Post Office and Post Roads be instructed to inquire into the expediency of establishing a post route from South Bend, by Laporte and the Upper Crossings of Salt Creek, in Indiana, to Ottowa, in Illinois.

On motion of Mr. REYNOLDS, *Resolved,* That the Committee on the Judiciary be instructed to inquire into the expediency of authorizing a settlement of the claims of the United States on the Bank of Illinois upon such equitable and reasonable terms, as will enable the bank to m.ke payment, and at the same time to resume her banking operations.

The following resolution, being the unfinished morning business, was again taken up:

Resolved, That the Committee on Roads and Canals be instructed to inquire into the subject and report their opinion to this House, of the most equal and just mode of applying the revenues of the country to such works of public improvement within the respective States of this Union as may be necessary for the facilitating of commerce with fo e gn nations, and among the several States. And that they moreover report their opinion of the best and most practicable mode of ascertaining and determining the nationality and importance of such improvements as may be proposed within the said several States.

Mr. CHILTON resumed his remarks by disclaiming any personal hostility towards, or any intention or wish of assailing, from the line of discussion he had been compelled to pursue, the present Chief Magistrate of the United States. Mr. C. had been drawn into this discussion as the ardent friend of Internal Improvements. During the last session of Congress, he had taken occasion to give his sentiments on this subject, and to show that the views and hopes of the western country, in President Jackson, had been frustrated, and the pledges of that individual unredeemed. A very worthy gentleman, friendly to the Executive, and whom Mr. C. was proud to call his personal friend, (Mr. Bynum, we believe,) had then asserted that General Jackson had redeemed all his promises—much were, to put down the system of Internal Improvements, abolish the Tariff, and to put down the Bank of the United States. Mr. C. then took occasion to assert otherwise, and had met with no reply. The fact was, that it was in consequence of the expectations excited by the previous course, the declaration, and pledges of General Jackson, that as soon as that individual was exalted to the high station he now held, the table of that House was literally loaded with petitions and memorials from his friends west of the mountains, praying for appropriations for objects of Internal Improvement. The people of the west did consider tha' up to that time their claims had been disregarded by the course of the former occupier of the Presidential Chair. The only was reiterated, from day to day, and Mr. C. himself responded to it at the time, that gross injustice had been done the western country, and their interests and welfare had been set aside in carrying on works of Internal Improvements, by the immediate predecessor of Gen. Jackson. Mr. C. then entered into a review of the course pursued by Mr. Adams, and drew a contrast between his Administration and that of the present Chief Magistrate in respect to the same subject, the former of whom, so far from striving to crush the system, did a'l in his power to foster and promote it.

Mr. C. then referred to the call made upon General Jackson by Governor Ray, of Indiana, previous to his first election, who invited him explicitly to give his sentiments on the subject, and, Mr. C. added, that if he failed in proving that the President had changed his opinions, and maintained the reverse of what he formerly did, he would immediately surrender his seat on that floor and consent to lose his character for consistency and truth. He considered himself bound to do this to contrast the opinions of General Jackson himself, for if he should be able to show that he held one set to-day, and another to-morrow, that he avowed principles one day which he repudiated the next, this effect would be produced, that whatever that individual's opinion might be, they were entitled to very little influence, or at least to less than they would have if they had been uniformly consistent and undeviating. Mr. C. would invite the attention of the House to the first act of General Jackson's administration on this subject, viz. his veto of the Maysville and Lexington road bill. In his last annual message, in justification of the course he had taken, what were the objections there made to that bill? That the improvement was local—that it began and ended in the same State. Mr. C. said, the same objection might be made to every internal improvement. Every improvement must be located somewhere; and it was in vain to expect an improvement to benefit all parts of the Union alike, in a country so extended and diversified, and with interests so various. Did the President entertain the same opinions when he was in the Senate of the United States, as when he vetoed the Maysville and Lexington road bill? Mr. C. adverted to this to show that he was but man, and might occasionally find himself in error, and change, of course, just as other feeble mortals did.

Mr. C. then referred to the Senate Journal, second sess on of the 18th Congress, page 132, to show that Gen. Jackson voted in the affirmative, on the bill authorizing a subscription to the stock of the Delaware and Chesapeake Canal Company, and that he also voted in the affirmative on the amendment offered to that bill authorizing a subscription for stock of the Dismal Swamp Canal Company. If appropriations for internal improvement, said Mr. C. were constitutional then, they were not less so now, for not a solitary amendment had been made to the Constitution of the United States, since that time. The obligation to support the Constitution were as binding then as now. Here then is one of the votes to which the friends of Gen. Jackson in the west were referred when they were called on to give him their suffrages, and offered a reason why so many applications for appropriations for internal improvement were made during the first year of his elevation to the Presidency. Let him not be astonished over and nor his friends here be astonished overmuch, a great many applications were made. He was proceeding when Mr. WHITTLESEY of Ohio called for the Order of the Day.

CLAIM OF COMMODORE HULL.

The House then resumed the consideration of the Special Order of the Day, being on the bill for the relief of Commodore Isaac Hull, and the amendment agreed to in Committee of the Whole to strike out that part of the bill providing for payment of $6,500 for extra services to the Agent at the Navy Yard at Washington, commanding the same.

Mr. BINNEY took the floor in opposition to the amendment, and in support of the claim. He contended that the duties of Navy Agent had been performed by Com. Hull, and a spirit of equity should impel the House to requite the services rendered, by a fair compensation. He continued to advocate the claim in an argument of some length—going into a minute history of the duties of the office of Naval Agent, and the duties involved, at various periods, from the earliest of the Government. He also examined the law of 1804, which provides for the government of the Navy Yard at Washington. That law holds that "the Commandant of the Yard shall have the superintendence and care of the same—and it shall form the duties of Navy Agent—and requires it of a Captain commanding a squadron," &c. The law of 1804, he contended, should be construed according to the true intent and meaning of the law-giver. It was designed to apply to circumstances and exigencies of the times in which it was enacted, some 30 years ago. It had been only considered inoperative up to 1829, when a new law was enacted. It was unjust, he contended, to revive it now, under circumstances so variant from those under which it was meant to apply. Mr. B. continued his argument for more then an hour, and was followed by

Mr. McKINLEY, who opposed the claim. He thought there would be great danger in altering the construction of the law contained by the gentleman from Pennsylvania, (Mr. Binney,) opening the door to favoritism and corruption. Mr. McK. hoped the amendment of the Committee of the Whole would prevail.

Mr. HARDIN followed on the same side of the question. The language of the law was clear and definite, and could not be construed other than by its strict letter. In the course of his remarks, Mr. H., produced a letter from the Auditor of the Treasury, stating that Commodore Hull, prior to his entering on the duties of this office, was explicitly informed of the nature all the duties required of him—and that, for that instance, he was allowed an extra clerk, at his own selection, at a salary of $1,000 dollars, which was afterwards raised to 1,300 dollars. He said, this claim was but an entering wedge, would form a precedent of the most dangerous character. It would be far better to present Commodore Hull one hundred thousand dollars gratuity, than to pass this bill.

Mr. REED again addressed the House in favor of retaining this claim in the bill, and the question

amendment of the Committee of the Whole to strike out this section, was then taken by yeas and nays, and decided in the affirmative as follows:

YEAS—Messrs. John Adams, Wm. Allen, Anthony, Bean, Beaty, Beaumont, Blair, Bockee, Brown, Bull, Burns, Bynum, Cambreleng, Campbell, Carmichael, Carr, Casey, Chaney, Chilton, Chinn, Claiborne, Samuel Clark, Clark, Clay, Clowney, Coffee, Cramer, Davis, Davenport, Day, Deberry, Dickerson, Dickinson, Dunlap, Fillmore, Forester, Fowler, Philo C. Fuller, Wm. K. Fuller, Galbraith, Gillet, Gillner, Gordon, Graham, Gray, Griffin, Joseph Hall, Thomas H. Hall, Halsey, Hardin, Joseph M. Harper, Hathaway, Hawes, Heath, Hiester, Howell, Hubbard, Inge, Wm. Jackson, Janes, Jarvis, Noadiah Jones, B. Jones, Kavanagh, Kilgore, Lansing, Laporte, Luke Lea, Thomas Love, Loyall, Lytle, Abijah Mann, Joel K. Mason, Moses Mason, May, McComas, McKay, McKinley, McLene, McVean, Miner, Robert Mitchell, Moore, Morgan, Murphy, Osgood, Parks, Parker, Patterson, Dutee J. Pearce, Peyton, F. Pinckney, Plummer Polk, Pope, Ramsay, Robertson, Schenck, Schley, A. H. Shinn, Smith, Standifer, Stoddert, Taylor, Wm. P. Taylor, Francis Thomas, Turner, Turrill, Vance, Vanderpoel, Wardwell.—128.

NAYS—Messrs. John Q. Adams, Heman Allen, J. Allen, Archer, Banks, Barber, Bates, Binney, Briggs, Burges, Cage, Clayton, Darlington. Denny, Dickson, Evans, Edward Everett, H. Everett, Ewing, Ferris, Garland, H. Hall, James Harper, Harrison, Hazeltine, Henderson, Huntington, Ebenezer Jackson, Johnson, Henry Johnson, King, Lane, Lay, Manning, Marshall, McKennan, McKim, Milligan, Phillips, Potts, Reed, Rencher, Spangler, Trumbull, Tweedy, Vinton, Watmough, Wayne, White, E. Whittlesey, Williams, Wise, Young.—61.

the claim was rejected. The bill was then ordered to be engrossed for a third reading on Friday next, as amended, and then the House adjourned.

IN SENATE.

Monday, January 12, 1835.

Mr. KING, of Georgia, rose and stated, that the ALBERT CUTHBERT, Senator elect from Georgia, was present; that he had lost his credentials; that the case was not without precedent, he asked that he be permitted to qualify and take his seat. The motion was agreed to, and Mr. Cuthbert was qualified according, and took his seat.

Petitions and memorials were presented by Mr. TYLER, TALLMADGE, PRENTISS, PORTER, WEBSTER, TIPTON, and MOORE.

A message was received from the President of the United States, communicating a report of the Bank of that institution for the year 1834.

On motion of Mr. BENTON, the communication was ordered to be printed.

The VICE PRESIDENT laid before the Senate a communication from the Secretary of the Treasury, in obedience to the resolution submitted on the 3d inst. by Mr. LEIGH, calling for the correspondence of that Department with the Receivers of Public Money, in the course of the last

Mr. BENTON remarked, that as the gentleman of Virginia was not in his seat, he thought it might be in accordance with his wishes to move the communication be printed, and he moved that a thousand extra copies thereof be printed. The suggestion of Mr. KING, of Alabama, the communication was laid on the table.

Mr. LEIGH having shortly afterwards taken his seat, the subject was taken up, and on his motion, the report was referred to the Committee on Finance, with directions to consider the report, to inquire into the practice referred to, and whether regular and judicious, and if not, whether any regulations be necessary to correct it.

The VICE PRESIDENT also laid before the Senate a certificate of the re-election of JOHN M.

CLAYTON, a Senator from the State of Delaware for six years from the 4th of March next.

Mr. SMITH, from the Judiciary Committee, reported a bill for the relief of David McCord.

Also, a bill for the relief of Thomas L. Winthrop and others; which was read the first time, and ordered to a second reading.

Mr. SMITH, from the Committee on Revolutionary Claims, to which was referred the bill for the relief of the legal representatives of Colonel William Bond and Colonel William Douglass, reported the same without amendment.

Mr. SMITH, from the same Committee, reported a bill for the relief of Captain George Hurlbrook;

Also, unfavorably upon the petition of Lieutenant John Taylor.

Mr. ROBBINS, from the Library Committee, reported a resolution authorizing the purchase of 50 copies of the American Diplomatic Code, for the use of the Senate.

Mr. ROBBINS, from the same Committee, reported the joint resolution for the purchase of 500 copies of Cary & Lea's History of Congress.

Mr. BENTON here rose and said, that as there were applications now before Congress for a renewal of the charters of the Banks of this District, he begged leave to submit to the Senate by way of notice, a paper containing the substance of the amendments, which he intended to insist on when the bills should come up for consideration.

I. That no application for a renewal of charter should be entertained in favor of any bank which has heretofore failed or suspended payment, until all the circumstances attending such failure or suspension shall have been fully examined, and reported upon by a Committee of one of the Houses of Congress.

II. That Banks of circulation ought to be reduced in number, not increased.

III. That no charter ought to be renewed, granted, or extended, except upon the following fundamental principles, (among others:) 1st, The Bank to pay all its currency in gold and silver; the holder to have the right to require the one-half in gold and the other half in silver; 2. No paper currency to be issued, renewed, or paid out, of a less denomination than $20; 3d; The stockholders, for the time being, to be liable, each to the amount of his stock, for the circulation and deposites, on the failure of the Bank to redeem its currency, or pay its deposites; with summary process for the recovery; and all sales and transfers of stock to be void, which shall be adjudged, by a jury, to have been made with intent to evade this liability.

On Mr. BENTON'S motion, the paper was ordered to be printed.

Mr. TYLER, pursuant to notice and on leave given, introduced a bill to provide a system of laws for the District of Columbia; which was read twice and referred.

Mr. KING, of Alabama, pursuant to notice, and on leave given, introduced a bill to authorize George Bidwell to import an iron steam boat, in detached parts, free of duty.

The following resolution, submitted by Mr. BENTON, and lying on the table, was taken up for consideration:

Resolved, That the Committee on Finance be instructed to obtain from the Bank of the United States a copy of all instructions, if any, to the Branch Banks, directing them to collect and remit Spanish milled dollars to the mother bank; the number of such dollars annually remitted; the rates at which they sold at different periods, say at or about the beginning of each quarter of the year; whether the Bank of the United States has sold such dollars to the United States, and if so, how many and at what rates; how many it has sold to others, or exported to foreign countries; also, a statement of the amount of gold coin; of the amount of silver coin; and the amount of bullion remitted to the mother bank, or elsewhere, by her order, annually since the first day of April, 1832; also, a statement showing the amount of silver coin and of gold coin remitted by the mother bank

to each branch since that day; also, the amount of gold coin and the amount of silver coin annually sold or annually exported by the Bank; since the said first day of April; also, a statement of the amount of gold received from the United States Mint since the first day of August last; and a statement of the whole amount of gold on hand in the Bank and its branches, for each month from April 1, 1832, to the present time.

Mr. TYLER said he desired to say but a word on this subject. He had no sort of objection to the inquiry, and wished to be so distinctly understood. The material allegation in the resolution was in reference to the conduct which the Bank had pursued relative to the currency and coin of the United States; the call was for information on this subject. And he begged leave to say to the Senate, that this matter was made the subject of specific inquiry by the Committee on Investigation of 1832. The Committee on Finance, during the last summer, having ascertained that the subject was fully inquired into in 1832, carefully examined and analyzed the report, and he was ready now to affirm that the counter report, which was then made, was so conclusive that it had relieved the committee from the labor of prosecuting their inquiries into that subject. In reference to the Bank bartering in the currency of the country, he thought that charge had been answered by the exhibit appended to the report of the Committee on Finance. He thought that by that exhibit it was shown, that this traffic could not have been carried on. But if the honorable gentleman from Missouri thought that any thing could come out of the inquiry, he had no objection to it. He (Mr. T.) was ready to condemn the Bank in all things in which it should have erred; he was no friend of the Bank, and when we came to measure facts, it would be seen that he stood so high in opposition to the Bank, that he was not to be shaken by any thing which should yet take place. It was not necessary for him to make this disclaimer, but it came in his way, and he had given utterance to it. But the honorable gentleman from Missouri might have information which the committee did not possess, and he, Mr. T. was willing it should be shown.

Mr. BENTON asked leave of the Senate to amend the resolution, by correcting a date in it. All the returns asked for, came up to the 31st January, 1831. He wished to insert that day instead of the 1st of April. As to the subject matter of the call, he would only say, that it would be hardly right to mention the information on which he made the call. He might, to be sure, be mistaken in his information, and if it should so appear, he would have no more to say on the subject. As to the honorable gentleman's situation with reference to the Committee and the Bank, he (Mr. B.) prayed God to grant him safe deliverance—his situation seemed something worse than walking on eggs, (to use an old maxim,) or treading on burning plough shares. But it was probable we should be able to measure facts before long.

Mr. TYLER replied, that the honorable gentleman from Missouri need not feel the slightest concern for his deliverance. He was delivered from Jacksonism—he thought God he had got rid of that. He had, from his mother's lap, been taught an old adage, which he should cling to through life, that, in all matters, political as well as others, "honesty was the best policy."

Mr. BENTON did not doubt the disinterestedness and integrity with had always governed the honorable gentleman from Virginia. He, Mr. B., had heard him make several speeches, during the time he had the pleasure of associating with him on this floor, and in all of them the gentleman commenced and ended in the same strain, upon his own high-wrought integrity and disinterestedness. So with regard to this matter, of which there was no occasion to have made any observations relative to his integrity. But an opportunity would be afforded for measuring swords before long. He took this occasion to make a public apology to the honorable member from Kentucky just before him, (Mr. Bibb,) which he had made the other day privately. It was for addressing the Senate upon the French spoliation bill, when that gentleman

up the bill making appropriations for the Indian Department for the year 1835.

Mr. ASHLEY moved to amend the bill by adding for the pay of a clerk for the office of superintendent of the Department of Indian Affairs at St. Louis, 1000 dollars.

Mr. POLK said he concurred in the propriety of the proposed item. A clerk was certainly necessary, and the reason of the omission in this bill by the Committee of Ways and Means, was because the subject had been referred to the Committee on Indian Affairs. He was willing that the amendment should be adopted, if the committee thought this bill the proper place for it.

Mr. GRENNELL suggested that this would be a departure from the usual practice, since it seemed to be the settled policy of the House that the Committee of Ways and Means should report appropriations only for existing laws and existing offices; and the effect of adopting the proposed amendment would be tantamount to creating a new office.

After a few remarks from Mr. ASHLEY, in explanation, the question on his amendment was taken, and lost—ayes 35, noes 89.

The bill was then ordered to be reported to the House, without amendment.

The Committee then took up the bill making appropriations for the support of the army for the year 1835.

Mr. MANN, of New York, begged to inquire of the hon. Chairman of the Committee of Ways and Means, whether any appropriations in this bill were greater than heretofore.

Mr. POLK. I can answer the gentleman: there were none of a greater amount than in former years, but, on the contrary, considerable reductions.

Mr. MANN would be glad to know what they were.

Mr. POLK referred particularly to the contingent expenses, which were last year $344,000, and this year $398,000. The aggregate decrease in the expenses of the army by the present bill would be $600,075. Mr. P. proceeded to refer to various other items which had been curtailed. He then moved to amend the bill by adding, after the eighth line, "for arrearages of the pay department of the army $5,6080 5," and produced various documents from the War Department, and from General McComb, which were read by the clerk, going to sanction the proposed amendment.

Mr. MANN thought this claim, which was for extra services rendered by Gen. McComb, had better be left to the ordinary and usual legislation of the House—the Committee on Claims—by which it would undergo careful and rigid examination. He disavowed all personal feeling or predilection on the subject, as he had no acquaintance with the individual whose interests were involved. It might be that the amount of arrearages proposed in the amendment was due; but he thought it required investigation. He, therefore, hoped the amendment proposed by the Honorable Chairman of the Committee of Ways and Means, (Mr. Polk,) in whose abilities and scrutiny he had the utmost confidence, would not be adopted. Mr. M. said there was another item in the bill which called for some animadversion. He referred to the pay of Surgeons in the army, which was 15,000 dollars more than the appropriation of last year. This, he understood, was done with a view to make a Surgeon rank with a Major. Mr. M. said this Government was going on with dangerous strides, year after year, with gradual though great increases, in salaries and allowances, until he did not know but that the recipient of them would soon tell us, as a certain Prince did the Parliament of England, " the Lord hath no further need of your services."

Mr. POLK remarked, that the gentleman's remarks did not apply to the present bill, but to one reported from the Committee on Military Affairs, and passed at a former session.

Mr. MANN made some further remarks, which were not distinctly heard; but reiterating the dangers which he apprehended from this constant increase of salaries and perquisites of office.

Mr. WILLIAMS opposed the amendment—not that he was in possession of any facts whether the

claim were just or not, but because (as we understood him to say,) it was presented in an irregular manner. Before the award should be made by the House, it should be investigated by one of its standing committees.

Mr. R. M. JOHNSON said the claim of Gen. McComb had been investigated by the Military Committee, who were convinced of its justice. He hoped it would not be rejected because it had not undergone all the requisite formalities, since it had been found correct and equitable both by the War Department and a committee of that House. Mr. J. thought the House should place some confidence in the officers of the Government; and they had reported favorably of this claim, and passed a high eulogium on the character of Gen. McComb.

Mr. WHITTLESEY, of Ohio, made a reference to the proceedings at different times by Congress, relating to the claim of Gen. McComb, and said he concurred with the gentleman from North Carolina, that the matter should come before the House from one of its standing committees.

Mr. POLK said the claim had been investigated, the War Department had asked for it, and the amendment was now a mere question of appropriation, and as such, within the duties of the Committee of Ways and Means. Mr. P. recommended that the vote be taken on it at once, so as to save time, and he would endeavor to produce all the information necessary by the time the bill came up for consideration in the House.

Mr. WHITTLESEY explained. The case was altogether a novel one, but if the gentleman wished the item to remain in the bill, he would offer no further opposition at that time, though he should vote against it.

The amendment was then put and rejected.

Mr. POLK then offered one or two other verbal amendments, which were adopted. The bill was then with the amendments, ordered to be reported to the House.

On motion of Mr. MANN, the Committee then, rose, and the chairman (Mr. Hubbard) reported the bills to the House.

The bill making appropriations for the Navy Department, for the year 1835, was then, on motion of Mr. POLK, taken up in the House, the amendments of the Committee agreed to, and the three bills ordered to be engrossed for a third reading tomorrow.

The House then adjourned.

IN SENATE.

TUESDAY, Jan. 13, 1835.

Petitions and memorials were presented by Messrs. HENDRICKS and TYLER.

Mr. HENDRICKS presented a memorial from the General Assembly of Indiana, praying an appropriation by Congress, for the establishment of a line of hospitals on the Ohio river; which was referred to the Committee on Commerce, and ordered to be printed.

Mr. WHITE, from the Committee on Indian Affairs, reported unfavorably upon the petition of the Sac and Fox Indians, complaining of the manner in which their annuities were paid.

Mr. WHITE said, that the Committee thought the laws in existence provided a sufficient remedy for any inconvenience which existed, with regard to the payment of Indian annuities, and on his motion the Committee were discharged from the further consideration of the subject, and the petition was referred to the Secretary of War.

Mr. WHITE, from the same Committee, reported unfavorably upon the petition of Charles Looman, and was discharged from the further consideration of the same.

Mr. WHITE, from the same Committee, to which was referred the bill for the relief of Col. Gad Humphreys, reported the same, and gave information that when the bill came up, he would move for its indefinite postponement.

Mr. FRELINGHUYSEN, from the Committee on Revolutionary Claims, to which was referred the bill for the relief of Col. John Thorn, John Henderson, and others, reported; which was read the first time and ordered to a second reading.

Mr. TYLER, from the Committee on Finance, reported a bill for the relief of Charles J. Catlett;

which was read the first time the same, and ordered to a second reading.

The following resolutions were submitted:
By Mr. WAGGAMAN:

Resolved, That the Committee on Commerce be instructed to inquire into the expediency of providing by law for the establishment of a marine hospital in the city of New Orleans.

By Mr. HILL:

Resolved, That the Secretary of the Navy be requested to communicate to the Senate, so much of the correspondence of his Department, with Loammi Baldwin, as relates to his compensation as Superintendent of Dry Docks and Inspector of Navy Yards, together with copies of all accounts rendered by him, connected with his services in the inspection of Navy Yards.

Mr. LEIGH, from the Committee on Revolutionary Claims, reported a bill for the relief of the legal representatives of Robert Joyce, deceased; which was read the first time, and ordered to a second reading.

Mr. POINDEXTER, from the Committee on Public Lands, to which was referred the bill for the relief of James I.. Stokes and others, reported unfavorably upon the same.

Mr. HENDRICKS gave notice that tomorrow he would ask leave to introduce a bill for the relief of William O'Neill.

The bill for the relief of the owners, officers, and crew of the private armed brig Neptune and Fly was taken up for consideration, and,

On motion of Mr. ROBBINS, was postponed till to-morrow.

The following bills were considered in the committee of the Whole, and ordered to be engrossed for a third reading:

A bill for the relief of Samuel Bragdon and David Chase.

A bill for the relief of Charles Gordon.

A bill for the relief of Humphrey B. Gwathmey.

A bill for the relief of Peter H. Green and William Emerson.

A bill to increase the pay of the Marshal of the District of Delaware.

The bill making an appropriation of $90,000 to complete the road from Lyme creek, in Alabama, to Chatahoochee, opposite Columbus, Ohio, for consideration.

Mr. KING, of Alabama, briefly explained the necessity which existed for this appropriation, that the road lead directly from the seat of Government to New Orleans, and was indispensable for the transportation of the great southern mail.

Mr. POINDEXTER made a few remarks in favor of the bill, when

Mr. KING, of Georgia, expressed a disposition to vote against the bill in its present shape, on the ground that the two per cent. fund, reserved for such purposes, was laying idle in the Treasury; this amounted to about $115,000. But he objected entering into an examination of the subject, and moved to lay the bill on the table, in order to prepare an amendment, requiring the appropriation to be taken out of the fund above.

Mr. KING, of Alabama, made some explanation of the nature of the two per cent. fund alluded to; but did not oppose the motion to lay the bill on the table; and it was then agreed to.

SPECIAL ORDER.

The Senate resumed the consideration of the bill making compensation for French spoliations prior to 1800.

Mr. BIBB commenced by observing that he agreed with the gentleman from Massachusetts (Mr. Webster,) that this question was only a financial question; one to be determined by the law of nations. He believed the justice of the claims turned wholly on the guarantee. That clause had large claims against us, justly due to the consequence of, and growing out of the guarantee, if these claims to France had been maintained. The claims of our citizens—if this was a state of the case, he would acknowledge the justice of the bill before the Senate. But he believed it could be maintained—he did not deny the rights of our citizens had been injured by the Government—he did not believe France had any just claims against us.

[CONTINUED IN NEXT NUMBER.

CONGRESSIONAL GLOBE.

BY BLAIR & RIVES.	——WEEKLY——	PRICE $1 A SESSION.
2d Sess......23d Cong.	MONDAY, JANUARY 26, 1835.	Volume 2........No. 8.

TWENTY-THIRD CONGRESS.
SECOND SESSION.

IN SENATE.
Tuesday, Jan. 13, 1835.

[Continued from last number.]

a guarantee. Mr. B. was well aware that the in rests of individuals ought to be supported by eir governments to a certain degree, but he did t think that Governments were bound to push ch interest to the extremity of war—he did not mit that the rights of the whole were to be oparded by the claims of individuals—the safety 'the community was paramount to the claims of rivate citizens. He would proceed to see if the terests of our citizens had been neglected by is Government. These claims have been urged, id Mr. B., from year to year, with all the earnest-ing from the guarantee. But they went from bad to worse, till negotiations were in vain. 'e then assumed a hostile position. During a year '98, more than twenty laws were seed by Congress upon this very subject—some raising troops—some for providing arms and mitions of war—some for fitting out a naval ree, and so on. Was this negotiating the claims of rotizens? We went as far as the interests of the tion would permit. We prosecuted these ims to the very verge of plunging into that tful war then desolating Europe. The Gov-ment then issued its proclamation of neutrality in non-intercourse. Mr. B. next proceeded to ow that France had no just claims upon us, ising from the guarantee. This guarantee, said a B. was not considered binding, even by rance herself, any further than was consistent th our relations with other nations; that it was eclared by her Minister; and, moreover, that he acknowledged the justice of our neutrality. hese treaties had been violated by France, and g United States could not surely be bound by ties which she had herself violated; and, con-quently, we were under no obligation on ac-nt of the guarantee. Mr. B. went on to show by the terms of the treaty of 1800, the debts e our citizens had not been relinquished— t the guarantee did not exist, and as the ims had not been abandoned, Mr. B. concluded these claims ought not to be paid by this Gov-ment. He was opposed to going back 34 rs to sit in judgment on the constituted au-ities of that time. There should be a stability Government, and he was not disposed to en the judgment of the man (Washington) has justly been called the first in war and the his peace. We are sitting here to rejudge the tions of the Government 34 years since.

Then, Mr. BIBB concluded:

Mr. SHEPLEY moved an amendment to the oviding that the five millions appropriated, be in full satisfaction of all the claims for ich appropriations prior to 1800.

Mr. WEBSTER said he saw no objection to amendment. The five millions in the bill was in arbitrary sum, but he thought it bore the proportion that the appropriation did for ortion of the Florida claims.

he amendment was agreed to.

Mr. PRENTISS said that as he was a member e Committee which reported this bill, it be expected that he would give an ex-n of his views upon the subject of it. He re to enter into the inquiry whether war ex-between the United States and France or not, e all this was superseded by the treaty of If we were bound to look to the basis on that treaty was finally concluded. He t the whole matter neither complex nor dit. The justice of the claims upon France, had been denied by that government, and fully proved, of a doubt existed on the sub-key the tone and language of the public jour-of the day. Having admitted them, France up counter claims on her part, and her claims

relative to the islands, gave rise to great uneasiness and trouble to the Government of the U. States. France continued to press her claims, until by the treaty of 1800, it was conceded the claims of both nations were subsisting. And the final consum-mation of the whole was that the release of the claims on the one side was a release of those on the other. This was Mr. Madison's opinion, and he was fully competent to form a correct judg-ment on the subject. No one, he thought, who would examine the documents on the subject, could deny the justice of the claims, and if they were released, it followed that the Government of the United States had appropriated private proper-ty to public use, and of course were bound to make compensation therefor. Mr. P. disclaimed any interest or partiality for the claims, as he did not believe that a single citizen of his State had one cent to receive from them should they be al-lowed. He believed they were founded in jus-tice, and therefore, he would vote for the bill.

Mr. WEBSTER said he did not wish to protract the debate. Some gentlemen who desired to vote upon the question were absent from indisposition, and therefore, he would move to postpone the fur-ther consideration of the bill to Monday next, with the expectation that a vote upon the question might be taken at that time.

The motion was agreed to.

FRENCH RELATIONS.

Mr. CLAY rose and said, that he had yielded to the solicitations of his friends, by moving to post-pone the consideration of the report and resolu-tion of the Committee on Finance upon our rela-tions with France, which was made the special or-der for this day, till to-morrow. His sense of the necessity of a prompt disposition of this subject was so strong, that he gave notice that he would then insist upon its being taken up.

The motion was agreed to.

On motion of Mr. WHITE, the Senate proceed-ed to the consideration of Executive business, after which

The Senate adjourned.

HOUSE OF REPRESENTATIVES.
Tuesday, January 13, 1835.

Petitions and memorials were, by consent, pre-sented by—

Messrs. LYTLE and CRANE, of Ohio;
Mr. HEATH, of Maryland; and
Mr. CHINN, of Virginia;

Which petitions and memorials were referred.

Mr. CLAYTON, from the Committee on the Public Lands, reported a bill for the relief of the heirs of John Brahan, late receiver of public mo-neys at Huntsville, Alabama; which was read twice and committed.

Mr. CORWIN, from the Committee of Ways and Means, reported a bill making appropriations for certain roads, and examinations for surveys for the year 1835; which was read twice and com-mitted.

Mr. CORWIN, from the Committee of Ways and Means, reported the following resolution; which was agreed to:

Resolved, That the Committee on Military Af-fairs be instructed to inquire into the expediency of purchasing six acres of ground adjoining Fort McHenry, in the State of Maryland, for the use of the United States.

Mr. BOON, by consent, submitted the follow-resolution; which was agreed to:

Resolved, That the Committee on the Post Of-fice and Post Roads be instructed to inquire into the expediency of establishing a post route from Proc-torville to Mount Prospect, in Crawford county, Indiana.

Mr. FOSTER, from the Committee on the Ju-diciary, reported a bill to authorize a writ of er-ror in certain cases relating to patent rights, to the Supreme Court of the United States; which was read twice, and postponed for two weeks.

Mr. EVERETT, of Massachusetts, from the Com-

mittee on Foreign Affairs, reported a bill author-izing the payment of an outfit, and to provide for certain expenditures of Nathaniel Niles; which was read twice and committed.

Mr. JOHNSON, of Kentucky, from the Com-mittee on Military Affairs, reported a bill to au-thorize the Secretary of War to purchase certain Land near Baltimore; which was read twice and committed.

Unfavorable reports upon petitions, &c. were made by Messrs. WILLIAMS, GILMER, and SLADE; which were laid on the table.

Mr. McCARTY moved to reconsider the vote of yesterday, rejecting the following resolution, sub-mitted by Mr. LANE:

Resolved, That the Committee on the Public Lands be instructed to inquire into the expediency of appropriating a portion of the refuse public land, to aid the State of Indiana in constructing a canal from the National Road in said State, down the Valley of White Water to Laurenceburg, on the Ohio river.

Mr. McCARTY remarked, that when this resolu-tion was offered yesterday, he was under the im-pression, as he suggested at the time, that the sub-ject matter embraced in it had been previously re-ferred to a standing committee. Upon examina-tion, he discovered that he was mistaken; and he had therefore moved a reconsideration of the vote; and hoped the resolution would be adopted.

Mr. LANE said, he regretted he could not, in justice to himself, accept the kind aid of his good feeling colleague, (Mr. McCarty,) in the motion he had made to reconsider the vote of yesterday, rejecting the resolution he had the honor of pre-senting to the House for adoption. That it was his intention to present it anew to the House, lo-cating its commencement.

That he had made no effort to carry the resolu-tion on yesterday, after the statement of his col-league, (Mr. McCarty,) "*that the subject embraced in the resolution had been heretofore referred to a Standing Committee.*" He supposed the state-ment true, for he had not supposed it possible for his colleague, or any other gentlemen on this floor, to hazard any statement of which he was not fully apprized. But on examination, said Mr. L., he had become satisfied that no such resolution, as sup-posed, had been referred.

The resolution under consideration, called for an inquiry into the propriety of appropriating a portion of the refuse public lands to aid the State in constructing a canal from the national road down the valley of White Water, to the Ohio, at Laurenceburg. The resolution of his colleague, (Mr. McCarty,) was an inquiry into the propriety of "*a grant of each alternate section of the unap-propriated lands on each side of a road, leading from Laurenceburg to Fort Wayne in Indiana.*"

Mr. L. said, that upon the route of the road in this resolution for the first 70 miles, so far as his information extended, there would not be on either side of said road, one acre of public land to set apart for the road.

That the resolution he had the honor of present-ing, and which had been rejected upon the ob-jection and statement of his colleague—was to aid the State in constructing a canal 'connecting the national road with the Ohio, passing through the valley of Whitewater, the richest, and oldest, and most populous portion of Indiana.

The question, said Mr. L., is with the House for their decision; but that he would prefer pre-senting the resolution anew to their reconside-ration.

The motion to reconsider the vote rejecting the resolution, was then negatived.

Mr. GAMBLE asked the consent of the House to take up a resolution, heretofore offered by him, calling upon the Secretary of the Treasury for a plan, if practicable, for the safe-keeping and dis-bursement of the public moneys, without the agency of a bank or banks.

Objections being made, Mr. GAMBLE moved

18th September, 1830, so as to include his plantation and expelling him from possession thereof. That he ascertain said facts and circumstances by the testimony of disinterested witnesses, and report the same to the Senate, with his opinion whether said Humphreys has sustained any loss for which he ought to be compensated, and to what amount.

The following resolutions were considered, which lie one day:

By Mr. WAGGAMAN:

Resolved, That the Committee on the Library be instructed to inquire into the expediency of purchasing for the President's House, certain oil paintings now on sale in this city—and also into character and value of said paintings.

By Mr. BLACK:

Resolved, That the Committee on Pensions be instructed to inquire into the expediency of placing on the pension list the names of Daniel McInnis and Francis Patterson, of the State of Mississippi.

By Mr. HILL:

Resolved, That the Secretary of the Treasury be requested to communicate to the Senate any information in his department in relation to the claims of the owners of the brig Despatch and cargo for restitution of the amounts paid by them for discriminating duties on the said brig and cargo, that may go to establish or invalidate said claim.

By Mr. HILL:

Resolved, That the Secretary of the Navy be requested to report on the claim of the owners, officers, and crews, of the private armed vessels Neptune and Fox, whether they were by losses entitled to the bounty of 25 dollars each upon 69 prisoners captured by said private armed vessels; and if so entitled, why said claim has not been admitted and allowed by said Department; also, any other information that may exist in the Department tending to elucidate the validity or invalidity of said claim.

By Mr. KANE:

Resolved, That the Secretary of the Senate do cause to be made out, and laid before the Senate, a statement, showing the amount of money paid in each year by order of the Senate, for printing, and the purchase of books for the use of the Senate, from the 1st session of the 18th Congress to this time; designating, in all cases where the amount paid shall exceed $500, the object for which, and the persons to whom, the money was paid. Also, a statement, showing the amount of printing ordered by the Senate, which has not been completed, and an estimate of the sum or sums of money which will be due when such printing shall be completed.

The bill for the relief of the legal representatives of Moses Shepperd, deceased, was taken up for consideration, when

Mr. HILL spoke briefly in opposition to the bill, and Mr. HENDRICKS supported it.

When the hour arrived for taking up the special order, Mr. CLAY moved to lay the bill on the table; which was agreed to.

FRENCH RELATIONS.

The Senate then proceeded to the consideration of the Report of the Committee on Foreign Relations, and the resolution appended, concerning our Relations with France, in the following words:

Resolved, That it is inexpedient, at this time, to pass any law vesting in the President authority for making reprisals upon French property, in the contingency of provision not being made for paying to the United States the indemnity stipulated by the treaty of 1831, during the present session of the French Chambers.

Mr. CLAY rose and said that it was not his purpose, at the present stage of the consideration of the resolution, nor, indeed, did he deem it necessary at any other stage of it, to enter into a protracted discussion of the subject; nor did he deem it necessary to say much to enforce the arguments embraced in the report in favor of the adoption of the resolution. In the present posture of our relations with France, it seemed to the Committee that the course proposed was the proper one—that it was most expedient to await the action of France at the present session of the Chambers; and, therefore, he thought it was not proper or necessary to go at large into a discussion of the questions embraced in the report. In all questions connected with our foreign relations, it was always necessary to present to the world the existence of undivided councils. Before the happening of a rupture, examination and discussion may be required; but after a rupture shall take place, whatever of unanimity and of influence we have, should be exerted to give to our arms the utmost vigor which the resources of the country are capable of. He was very certain that no such measures were at present necessary with France. That our claims were founded in justice, that we ought to pursue them by all just and honorable means, and that we must ultimately obtain satisfaction for them, were sentiments in which the Committee entirely coincided in opinion with the President, and he had no doubt that it was also the sentiment of the people of this country. The committee also entirely concurred with the President in his views relative to the treaty with France. But if the President had stopped after the expression of the statement of the case, and had abstained from the recommendation of the measures which he deemed necessary to be taken in the contingency indicated by him, there could have been no difference of opinion between him and the committee. But when he said that the the Executive of France was honest and sincere in his anxiety to obtain the appropriation, and when he disclosed his purpose of abiding by the action of the French Chamber, it seemed to the committee an inconsistency that there should be at the same time the recommendation of a measure, the execution of which could only be rendered necessary by a doubt of the ulterior purposes of France. Confidence and distrust were unnatural allies. Confidence should at all times be free, full, frank, and ingenuous, but to say that he confided in the sincerity of the King, and that he would suspend any recommendation of a hostile measure, and then suggest a measure of reprisal, appeared to the committee, with all respect to his patriotic purposes as the Executive of the U. S. Government, to be a course calculated to produce most mischievous results. It seemed necessary to the committee, therefore, that there should be some expression of opinion on the part of Congress after such an expression on the part of the President, which should be likely to meet any possible contingency likely to arise. 1st. It was possible that the French Chamber might make the appropriation before the receipt of the President's message. 2d. The appropriation might be made after its receipt and notwithstanding the tone and language of the message. 3d. The Chambers might, after the receipt of the message, refuse to make the appropriation until after that part of the message which might be exceptionable to them should be withdrawn or explained; or they might 4thly, altogether and absolutely refuse to pass the appropriation and again reject the bill. Now, in any one of these four contingencies, an expression of Congress was indispensably necessary to the passage of the bill and the payment of the money. But suppose the Chambers should pass the bill before the receipt of the message, and the money should be placed in the French Treasury, in pursuance of it, to meet the stipulations contained in the treaty, it would throw on the King a high responsibility if he should be required to pay the money till the recommendation in the message was explained. In the second contingency, by the passage of the resolution, we should take a course that would be highly gratifying to the feelings and the pride of France, which we ought to promote by all honorable means. If they then should pass the bill they would see that there was confidence reposed on the part of Congress, that there would be a compliance with the assurances of the French Government. It was indispensably necessary that such a measure should be adopted in reference to the other two contingencies he had supposed. But if the Chambers should reject the bill on this ground, they would place themselves in the wrong, because they had acted on the recommendation of one department of the Government before it was ascertained that the other departments concurred, and they would then hasten to repair the wrong. If they should speedily pass the bill, and afterwards should discover that Congress did not concur with the President, they would find that the recommendation of the President, although he maintained a strong hold upon the affections of the People, was an inchoate recommendation and not perfect. Under all circumstances and in every contingency, therefore, the resolution seemed adapted to the occurrence of any one of them, and seemed eminently calculated to secure the objects of the treaty. As he had premised that a protracted discussion was not necessary, he would resume his seat, expressing, however, a disposition to modify the resolution in any form which was consistent with the object he had in view, and he hoped that it would receive the unanimous consent of the Senate, as such a vote would have a most happy effect; but he would consent to no modification which did not say that Congress did not deem it expedient to legislate on the subject at this time.

Mr. KING, of Georgia, rose and submitted the following amendment as a substitute for the resolution reported by the committee:

"*Resolved*, That as the French Chambers have been convened earlier than was expected by the President of the United States at the opening of the present session of Congress, it is inexpedient to pass any law relating to the treaty of 1831, until further information shall be received from France."

The amendment having been read—

Mr. KING said he agreed perfectly with the honorable Chairman of the committee, that lengthy discussion was not called for, or perhaps justified. He also differed so little with the honorable Chairman on the subject of the report and resolution, that he should say but very little in favor of the trifling changes which he proposed to make in the form of the resolution offered for the adoption of the Senate. He had agreed in committee and still agreed, to the report, with a few trifling exceptions in its details; and he had, and still agreed to the general conclusion to which the committee come, that it was inexpedient at this time to legislate on the subject of the treaty of 1831. The tone and tenor of the report, with the exception referred to, met his decided approbation. Though he had reserved to himself the right which he now exercised, of offering amendments to the form of the resolution, and expressing his dissent to a few of the details of the report itself.

Sir, said Mr. K. what is the tone and character of this report? He did not believe that it was intended by the Chairman who drafted it, as a party paper. It was not proposed to the committee, or by the committee adopted, as a party paper. It was not presented to the Senate as a report of that character, and he did not believe it would be received by the People of the United States as a party paper, unless the public press and party politicians of the country should wrongfully succeed in stamping upon it that character. As just observed by the honorable Chairman, it sustained the most important positions of the President throughout. The President was treated with the most entire respect. The motives of the President were treated with full respect, and even his recommendation was treated with respect. So much so that the intimation is clear in the report that the difference between the President and the committee probably arose from the difference of time and of circumstances under which they deliberated. From the remarks he had made on the subject of the character of the report, the object of the first part of the amendment was sufficiently obvious. It was to connect more closely the report and the resolution, and sustain the appearance of harmony between the two branches of the Government, by referring to the probable reason of the difference between the recommendation of the President, and the action of Congress. There were, to be sure, several reasons that might be gathered from the report, but this was most prominent, and he selected it because it was the one more especially mentioned in the report. Mr. K. read from the report, page 18: "It is not impro-

bable to suppose that the President would have abstained from any such recommendation, if he had known what recent intelligence from France shows, that, in point of fact, the Chambers assembled on the 1st of December, instead of the 29th, the day on which it was believed by the President they would meet."

The object of the latter part of the amendment was also obvious. He did not wish to stand committed, or hold out the idea to France that we would, *under no circumstances*, take any steps during the present session of Congress, however we might be justified by future information received. He was very far from wishing to connect himself or the Senate to any future specific mode of action, or to any action at all. At present, we agree that legislation was inexpedient. But he was unwilling to commit ourselves to the inexpediency of legislation at this session, provided future information, before the adjournment, should call for legislation upon the subject.

Mr. CLAY replied that he was glad to see the honorable member from Georgia animated with the best spirit on this subject—that he was frank, open, and unreserved, in the expression of his sentiments; and he was happy to find in his resolution that there was no ground for serious difficulty between them. But he thought the gentleman's resolution was objectionable in two of its provisions. The report was an argumentative document, and it was not usual in resolutions appended to such papers, to reiterate the reasoning in the report. His first objection to the resolution was, that it assigned one of the reasons contained in the report, for the adoption of the resolution, and he thought that not the strongest one. If one of the reasons in the report might be drawn down, he thought all might, and each Senator might require the introduction into the resolution, of the reasons which governed his vote. The French Minister had said, in a part of the correspondence, that a bill would be prepared for the appropriation, and submitted to the Chamber the next day; but the Committee came to the conclusion that we ought not to reproach them for not doing so, because they were the most proper judges of what was the proper time for its presentation; he could not, therefore, assent to one of the reasons being introduced into the resolution. There was one other part of the resolution, "that it was inexpedient to act till further information should be received from France," an expression which he viewed in the light of a menace, and implied that "their further action was not of a satisfactory nature, then we were prepared to resort to the measure recommended by the President. Now he, Mr. C., would not say what he would do, if France would not make the appropriation at the present session of the Chambers: "Sufficient for the day is the evil thereof." Let us have all the circumstances before us: He was for having Congress free to deliberate upon war, open, undisguised war—upon commercial restrictions or reprisals, unfettered in the event of any contingencies. He was anxious for all the circumstances—whether they had abandoned the claim, or intended to go on pressing it—But if we looked further, it would be seen that the propriety of this course was more apparent when we considered that this Congress terminated on the 3d March, when a new Congress would come in—that they ought to remain so when the awful alternative of a rupture or submission to wrong shall be presented; he, therefore, moved to strike out the parts of the amendment which he had indicated as objectionable.

Mr. WEBSTER thought that the importance of unanimity on this subject was so great, and the practical difference between the two resolutions was so small, that pains should be taken to throw them into a shape that the resolution could be adopted. The prevailing sentiment seemed to be a concurrence in the views of the President, of the nature of the controversy with France, of the clear right of this country, and the utter impossibility that the councils of the United States can depart from the just expectation of a reasonable fulfilment of the stipulations by France. He thought there did seem to be an objection to the hon. member's amendment, because it placed the action of the Senate on one of several reasons, and left the inference that on other reasons given in the report, the action of the Senate might be otherwise. It founded the action of the Senate upon a reason which might cease to exist to-morrow. Suppose the Chamber should reject the bill, and the Executive Government of France should, for that cause, dissolve the Chambers and call a new one; he did not wish to form an opinion what the Government of the United States might do upon such an event occurring. It was, therefore, desirable to leave this Government free from any indication or intimation of what its action might be, in any event. The sentiment of the country was, that we were right, and that France was wrong; and this sentiment was not likely to be altered.

Mr. BUCHANAN said, he should be exceedingly rejoiced if we could adopt any form of words which would unite the vote of the Senate on this occasion. He would go as far as any man to make concessions, in any matter in which principle was not involved, for the purpose of presenting ourselves to the world as a united nation. However we might differ amongst ourselves, as to matters of internal policy, we ought always to exhibit a bold and united front to foreign nations in defending the interests and honor of the country.

Mr. B. felt great pleasure in doing justice to the frank and conciliatory spirit of the Report of the Committee on Foreign Relations. It was a statesman-like production, worthy of its distinguished author; but, he must be permitted to say, that if this were the proper occasion for such a discussion, he thought he could successfully controvert several of the positions which it contained, and show that they were founded in error.

He would greatly prefer that the resolution proposed by the Senator from Georgia (Mr. King,) should stand as he had introduced it. It contained upon its face the reason, and the only reason which would induce him to vote for any resolution of this character. It was simply because the French Chambers had been convened earlier than was expected by the President of the United States at the commencement of the present session of Congress, that he would give his support to any such resolution. He should, therefore, be gratified if this preamble could be retained.

France had, before the close of the last session of Congress, communicated to the President, that it was the unanimous determination of the King's Government to appear before the new Legislature with its treaty and its bill in hand, and that its intention was to do all that the charter allowed to hasten, as much as possible, the period of the new presentation of the rejected law. On the faith of this assurance, the President rested satisfied, and did not present the subject to Congress at its last session. How has France redeemed this pledge? Has that Goverament hastened, as much as possible, the presentation of the rejected law? At the first meeting of the new Legislature, the law was not presented; and, in the face of this engagement, the Chambers were prorogued, not to meet in the Autumn, as they might have done, but, on the 29th of December, the very latest day which custom had sanctioned. If this assurance had any meaning at all, it was that the Chambers should be convened at least so early in the season as to afford sufficient time to communicate the fact to the President before the meeting of Congress. The President, at the date of the message, was not aware that the Chambers would assemble on the first of the month. No such information had been communicated to him. The French Government had never informed him such was their intention. It now appears that they did assemble on that day; and, for his own part, he was willing to wait until the result of their deliberations could be known.

What effect this circumstance might have produced on the President's determination, he was not prepared to say. Every gentleman could judge for himself. He was not possessed of any information on that subject.

There is a point, said Mr. B., in the intercourse between nations, at which diplomacy must end, and a nation must either consent to abandon her rights or assert them by force. After having negotiated for a quarter of a century, to obtain a treaty to redress the wrongs of our injured citizens—and after the French Chamber has once deliberately rejected that treaty, will not this point have been reached, should the Chamber again refuse to make the appropriation? If this be so, is it not right, is it not fair, to present this alternative to France? Would she not have just cause to complain, if we did not adopt this very course? To inform her frankly and fairly that we have arrived at this point, I am solemnly convinced, is the best diplomacy to which we can resort, to redress the wrongs of the injured claimants. France will then have the alternative distinctly presented; and it will be for her to decide, whether she will involve herself in war with her ancient ally, rather than pay those claims which the Executive branch of her own government has determined to be just, by a solemn treaty. Such an attitude on the part of the United States, will do more to accomplish the execution of the treaty, than any temporising policy which we can adopt. I never was more clearly convinced of the truth of any proposition.

France, from the tone and language of the President, will have no right to consider this a menace. It is no more than to say, diplomacy has ended, and the treaty must be executed, or we shall, however reluctantly, be compelled to take redress into our own hands. We cannot, we dare not, abandon the just rights of our own citizens, however painful it may be for us to assert them. France is a brave and a chivalrous nation; her whole history proves that she is not to be intimidated, even by Europe in arms. But France is wise as well as warlike. To inform her that our rights must be asserted, is to place her in the serious and solemn position of deciding whether she will, for the sake of a few millions of francs, more or less, resist the payment of a just debt by force. Whenever she is convinced that this result is inevitable, the money will be paid; and although, I hope I may be mistaken, I believe it will never be paid before. France has never appeared to regard the question in this serious light.

It has been asked what would the American Congress do, placed in similar circumstances? Would they appropriate the money with a menace impending over their heads? I answer no, never. But it would be no menace, if, after Congress had twice refused to vote an appropriation to carry a treaty into effect, a foreign government, in the spirit of candor, in language mild and courteous, such as that used by the President, were to inform us they could not abandon their rights, and, however painful it might be, they should be compelled, by a sense of duty, to assert them by force.

Mr. B. concluded by saying he felt it due to himself thus to explain the vote which he intended to give.

Mr. CUTHBERT said, he had not arisen to enter into any exposition of his opinions on this subject, but simply to suggest that such phraseology might be used as should unite the votes of every honorable Senator, now separated only by a slight shade of difference. Mr. C. read the resolution, and said, if it was so worded as to express that, "under existing circumstances," or, "the state of circumstances now existing," it might meet the views of all parties, and enable the Senate to pass its unanimous vote upon the subject.

Mr. KING, of Alabama, congratulated the Senate upon the spirit and temper which appeared on both sides, and said, he was one of those who was not in favor of taking up this question at the present time; but the report having been made, it became necessary to act upon it. He wished for more information before any discussion should have arisen, and thus he was not prepared to say expressly what ought to be done, or what the Congress of the United States should do. What he desired now was, as far as practicable, to express an opinion in language that could not be misunderstood, either in this country or on the other side of the Atlantic, of our determination.

Mr. K. had hoped that his honorable friend from Georgia would have yielded in the spirit of concession, and that they might vote explicitly on the ground, that at this time it was inexpedient to pass any act upon the subject. Mr. K. [illegible] pressed a hope that every gentleman wo[illegible]

himself justified in voting for the proposed measure, so that it might go forth to the world as the unanimous voice of that body.

Mr. LEIGH wished to have both amendments read, in order that the Senate might see if there was any essential difference between them.

[The amendments were read accordingly.]

Mr. LEIGH resumed, by saying that he could perceive no, or very little difference between the propositions of the Senators from Kentucky and Georgia, (Mr. Clay and Mr. King,) if any, it was trifling, and of the two, he preferred that of the former gentleman. Both, however, came exactly up to his (Mr. L's) idea of what was wise, politic, and just, for the United States, and respectful towards France. They had been told by the gentleman from Pennsylvania that he was well satisfied the true mode of negotiation with France would be to indicate distinctly, that unless she did justice, we would take the matter into our own hands, and seek that redress which she ought to grant.

Mr. BUCHANAN explained. There was a period when negotiation must cease, and one or the other alternative must be adopted.

Mr. LEIGH continued. Then was he to understand the gentleman, that there was a period in diplomacy, and that that period or crisis had arrived? If that be the gentleman's opinion, Mr. L. must beg to differ with him entirely and absolutely. He was not prepared, at that time, to adopt the President's proposition, so far as he had heard it, nor did he believe any one was. What, then, was the mode most likely to accomplish this object? Either force must be resorted to, or we must confide in the justice of the French nation. The last was, in his opinion, the best. Mr. L. was, however, for making our expression as absolute and dignified as possible, and not to commit ourselves by declaring that there was no circumstances in which we will not hazard a war with France. On the contrary, he was for presenting a bold front.

After some further remarks to the same purport, Mr. L. said he concurred in the sentiment of the gentleman from Alabama, that it would be inexpedient to adopt any legislative measure "at this time;" mark that "at this time," for in that consisted the main sum and substance of his affirmative to the proposition.

Mr. CALHOUN expressed a hope that the question would be taken without further discussion, and that the phraseology might be so amended as to meet the views of every gentleman, so that the voice of the Senate might be unanimous.

Mr. KING of Georgia, said that to the various suggestions and propositions from different parts of the Chamber, he had only a word in reply. And that was that he was willing to accept any modification of the resolution that would unite a vote upon the subject. He would, however, whilst up, say a word in explanation of the amendment, and answer some objections which had been made to it. He said in answer to the Senator from Kentucky, he would say that he selected the one reason as that which separated the Committee from the President, not only because it was that mentioned in the report, but because it seemed to include all the rest. It had been said by the honorable Senator truly, that France had promised to do several things which she had not performed, besides an early assembling of the Chambers, some of which might with equal propriety be referred to. True; but the assembling of the Chambers being in general necessary for the performance of the other promises, we were led to hope that the Chambers being now convened, the performance of all her other promises would follow. And he wished further distinctly to convey the idea to France, that as the Chambers had assembled, we expected that they would do all that was necessary before they were prorogued, to fulfil, the execution of the treaty.

It was objected, he said, to the language of the amendment, that we seemed by it pledged to action, when further information might be secured from France. He had no such intention; and if such construction were found, he would be willing to change the language, and say, "unless farther information from France shall justify legislation," &c. He said there was not a Senator in the hall more unwilling to commit himself or the Senate to specific action on this subject than himself; but whilst he did not wish to commit himself to act, he did not wish to commit himself *not* to act, if action should be called for. He would not even at this time commit himself to hostile action, if there should be another simple refusal by the Chambers to make the appropriation. But he said there were a large portion of the people of the United States who thought that France had already treated us with much indignity, and if there should be another refusal, coupled with an acknowledged insult, he would not say even then what should be done. It would be time enough to decide upon the mode of action, when action might be thought necessary. But for the present he would say, that the United States were now out of the nursery, and although, as a nation, we may not have arrived at the years of maturity, we were at least in a condition to act for and take care of ourselves. He concluded by saying he had no material objection to the modification proposed, if it would unite both parties in the vote, and unless some gentleman objected, he should take it for granted that there was a general acquiescence.

Mr. CUTHBERT rose to explain the difference, in his own opinion, between the resolution proposed by himself, and that offered by his colleague, (Mr. King,) as amended. That resolution merely expresses the opinion, that it is inexpedient to pass a law on the subject at this time. It does not, said Mr. C. leave the Senate at liberty to change its opinion with a change of circumstances. If there be no difference, the gentleman from Virginia (Mr. Leigh) can have no objection to the amendment. He wished to have the subject presented in such a form that no one could object. We should kindle in our own bosoms, said Mr. C. the old American feelings that produced union amongst us—feelings that cure all the cancers of party strife. Whatever dissensions may divide us at home—however we may wrangle with each other—when the stranger steps in, let us be united; when the contest is with a foreigner, we should be one.

Mr. CLAYTON said, that he was not willing to adopt the amendment proposed by the gentleman from Georgia, (Mr. Cuthbert,) "that under present circumstances it is inexpedient." He should vote for the resolution as amended by the chairman of the Committee, (Mr. Clay.)

Mr. CLAY rose again, he said, not to prolong the discussion. He wished to acknowledge the commendation of the report, made by the honorable Senator, (Mr. Buchanan.) He would not now attempt to defend the errors mentioned by the gentleman, but at some future time he hoped to be able to establish any thing advanced in the report.

Mr. BUCHANAN said, he did not pretend to measure himself with the eloquent gentleman from Kentucky. But he was so well convinced of the truth and justice of the remarks in regard to the report, that he would not shrink from a contest, even with the distinguished Senator himself, rather than abandon the opinion he had formed.

Mr. TALLMADGE said he rejoiced to see the unanimity which seemed to pervade the Senate on the subject of our relations with France, and he was unwilling to introduce any topics into the discussion at this time, which would tend to interrupt the harmony which seemed to prevail. At the time the report was made to the Senate, he took the opportunity to express his approbation of some portions of it, and his dissent from other portions He was then of opinion that it were better that the committee should make no report, and that Congress should not act on the subject till further information was received from France, and that the whole matter be left, where it was left by the President's message. He was still of opinion that that would have been the better course. But the majority of the committee thought otherwise. The report is before the Senate, and must receive that consideration which is due to its importance. He was rejoiced to see the manifestation of a general disposition to adopt such a course as should tend to unite all parties, on this question, as it was there presented. He rejoiced to see, that however much we might differ about our own local and internal affairs, there was but one feeling when the honor of the nation was concerned.

It was a gratifying spectacle to witness the interest manifested by the citizens, who, on this occasion crowd this chamber, and still more gratifying to believe and know; that but one sentiment pervades the whole. It is an *American* feeling—a feeling which swallows up every other, when the question is one between our own and a foreign nation. No matter what may be our dissensions at home, the indications given here, this day, assure us, that they cannot be extended abroad. Let our motto be, *for our country always*.

Mr. T. said, in dissenting from some portions of the report, it was his intention, when a proper occasion presented, to enter fully and at large upon the discussion of those portions of it. He had supposed that this might be deemed a proper occasion, and was prepared to enter upon it at this time. But he was reluctant to do any thing to interrupt the harmony of the Senate on the important and leading matters of the report. He would, therefore, omit what he otherwise would have said, and reserve for a more fitting occasion, if one should offer, what he intended to have submitted to the consideration of the Senate at this time, under a full persuasion that he should be able to assign satisfactory reasons for his dissent from the majority of the Committee.

Mr. T. said he approved the resolution under consideration, as it had been amended, and should give it his support. He was desirous of leaving the whole matter open for the future action of Congress, when we should receive information from France to enable us to determine what that action should be. There might be a difference of opinion as to what measures ought to be adopted, if France should refuse to do us justice; but, it was best that each individual Senator, and the Senate as a body, should be left free to act as should be deemed most expedient when the time should arrive, and we should be imperiously called upon to act He would, therefore, detain the Senate no longer than briefly to remark upon the positions contained in the President's message and in the report of the committee. These documents agree entirely in the important points between the United States and France. They agree in the enormity of the aggressions upon the rights of our citizens, and of the outrages upon our commerce, for which indemnity has so long been sought. They agree in the fruitless efforts which have been made, for nearly a quarter of a century, to obtain redress of the grievances of which we have complained in vain. They agree as to the amount of our claims upon France—that our just claims far exceed the sum stipulated to be paid us by the treaty of 1831. They agree, also, that we will not look behind the treaty for any liquidation of the amount of our demands, other than what is contained in the treaty itself. And above all, they agree that the stipulations of the treaty must ultimately be performed. That the idea of non-performance on the part of France, is utterly out of the question. These are the important points to this momentous affair, and it is a matter of congratulation that on all these, there is no difference of opinion, as he believed, amongst the representatives of the American people, and he trusted no difference amongst the people themselves.

The difference, then, said Mr. T., between the Message and the Report is, comparatively, unimportant. This difference consists, *first*, as to the President's conclusion from the correspondence, that the French Government had engaged to present to the new Chambers, the bill making the appropriation to carry the treaty into effect, in time to enable him to communicate the result to Congress, at the commencement of the present session: *second*, as to the remedy to be pursued in case the Chambers should again refuse. As to the first, the chairman supposes that if the French minister, when the Secretary of State expressed to him this expectation of the President, had expressed his *assent* to it, then the engagement would have been complete. With all due deference, said Mr. Tallmadge, to the honorable chairman, he would take leave to say, that if, after

the Secretary of State had thus communicated the President's expectation to the French Minister, and he did not express his dissent, then the engagement became binding on the French Government, and should have been performed. But, he said, he would not pursue this subject, as it was not h s intention, at this time, to discuss it.

How, then, does the matter stand? The President is required, by the Constitution, to make such recommendations to Congress as he shall think the interests of the nation require. In the difficulties between the U. States and France, he has, in a certain court, recommended reprisals on French property, to satisfy the demands which are acknowledged by solemn treaty, to be due to our citizens. In making this recommendation, he has discharged his duty. It remains for Congress to discharge theirs. The President leaves the whole matter, as it was his duty to leave it, to the consideration and action of Congress. Mr. T. said, if he were to express his individual opinion, as at present advised, and from the best light now before us, he would be for adopting the measure recommended by the President in his message. But, said he, this is not the time to consider that or any other measure. When farther information should be received from France, and it shall be ascertained that the Chambers have deliberately determined that the stipulations of the treaty of 1831 shall not be carried into effect, he did not doubt, that the American Congress would adopt such measures as the interests of our citizens and the honor of the country require.

In conclusion, Mr. T. said, he felt it his duty to remark to the honorable Chairman, that whenever the opportunity presented for acting upon the controverted points of the report, he would undertake to vindicate the conduct of Mr. Rives, the distinguished minister who negotiated the treaty. He had not been able to discover the propriety of introducing this gentleman's name into the report in the manner in which it had been done, and he regretted, extremely, that the Chairman should have felt himself under the necessity of doing it, when to almost every unbiased mind, the propriety of the step would seem so very justifiable.

Mr. KING then adopted the suggestion of Mr. CLAY, with regard to his amendment.

The question being upon the resolution as amended, to wit:

Resolved, That it is inexpedient at present to adopt any legislative measure in regard to the state of affairs between the United States and France.

Mr. MANGUM asked the yeas and nays, which were ordered, and are as follows:

Yeas—Messrs. Bell, Benton, Bibb, Black, Brown, Buchanan, Calhoun, Clay, Clayton, Cuthbert, Ewing, Frelinghuysen, Grundy, Hendricks, Hill, Kane, Kent, King of Alabama, King of Ga., Knight, Leigh, Linn, McKean, Mangum, Moore, Morris, Naudain, Poindexter, Porter, Prentiss, Preston, Robbins, Robinson, Shepley, Silsbee, Smith, Swift, Tallmadge, Tipton, Tomlinson, Tyler, Waggaman, Webster, White, Wright—45.

So the resolution was unanimously adopted.

The bill from the House making appropriations for the support of the army for the year 1835, was read twice and referred.

The Senate then adjourned.

HOUSE OF REPRESENTATIVES.
Wednesday, Jan. 14, 1835.

Mr. CLAY, from the Committee on the Public Lands, reported a bill confirming certain claims in the district of St. Stephens, in Alabama; which was read twice, and its further consideration postponed for one week.

Mr. POLK, from the Committee of Ways and Means, reported, without amendment, the bill from the Senate making an appropriation in aid of the erection of military barracks, in the city of New Orleans.

The bill was committed to a Committee of the Whole on the state of the Union.

Mr. HARPER, from the Committee on Commerce, reported a bill for the relief of ——

Go, tt and others; which was read twice and committed.

Mr. BANKS, from the Committee on Claims, reported a bill for the relief of Captain John Downs, of the United States Navy; which was read twice and committed.

Mr. WHITE, from the Committee on Naval Affairs, reported a bill for the relief of the widows and orphans of the officers, seamen, and marines, of the United States schooner Wild Cat; which was read twice and committed.

Mr. CAMBRELENG, from the Committee of Ways and Means, and Mr. CHANEY, from the Committee on Invalid Pensions, made unfavorable reports upon petitions referred to said committees; which were ordered to lie on the table.

Petitions and memorials were submitted, on leave, by—
Mr. HAZELTINE, of New York;
Mr. CLAY, of Alabama;
Mr. GARLAND, of Louisiana;
Mr. MAY, of Illinois; and
Mr. PIERCE, of New Hampshire.

Which petitions and memorials were referred.

Mr. REYNOLDS rose and remarked, that some weeks since, he had offered a resolution, having for its object to change the rule of the House, in regard to the mode of electing its officers—requiring that the vote hereafter should be viva voce, instead of by ballot. He did not wish to urge this subject on the consideration of the House; but supposed that it would be as well to dispose of it at this as at any other time. It required no great deliberation to arrive at a proper conclusion on it. He therefore moved to take it up.

Mr. WILLIAMS objected.

Mr. REYNOLDS then moved a suspension of the rule, and on that question he demanded the yeas and nays, which were ordered, and were yeas 94, nays 87.

Two-thirds not voting in the affirmative, the motion to suspend the rule was therefore negatived.

The following resolutions, submitted on the 8th and 12th instant, were, by consent, taken up, and agreed to:

By Mr. LYON:
Resolved, That the Secretary of War be requested to furnish this House with an estimate of the probable expense of prosecuting and completing with great accuracy, the astronomical observations contemplated by the act of Congress of the 14th July, 1832, entitled an act for taking of certain observations preparatory to the adjustment of the northern boundary line of the State of Ohio.

By Mr. LYON:
Resolved, That the Secretary of the Treasury be directed to furnish this House with a copy of the decision of the Commissioners on all private land claims at Michilimackinac, Green Bay, and Prairie du Chien, together with connected plats and copies of the field notes of all such claims as have been surveyed at either of the aforementioned places.

On motion of Mr. FILLMORE,
Resolved, That the Committee on the Judiciary be instructed to inquire whether any further legislation be necessary to convict a person of perjury for false swearing under the act entitled "an act supplementary to the act for the relief of certain surviving officers and soldiers of the revolution," passed June 7th, 1832, and if, in their opinion, it be necessary, that they report a bill to effect that object.

On motion of Mr. HATHAWAY,
Resolved, That the Committee on Invalid Pensions be instructed to inquire into the expediency of granting a pension to Reuben Rounds, a soldier of the last war.

On motion of Mr. BYNUM,
Resolved, That the Committee on Public Lands be instructed to inquire into the expediency of amending the laws relative to the same, so as more effectually to expedite the surveying and running off such lots of claimants as have been agreed to in conform ty with the several acts of Congress appertaining thereto.

On motion of Mr. JARVIS,
Resolved, That the Committee of Ways and Means be instructed to inquire into the expediency of reducing the rate of duty upon wines of the

Cape of Good Hope, so that they may be allowed to enter into the consumption of this country.

On motion of Mr. SLADE,
Resolved, That the Committee on Revolutionary Pensions be instructed to inquire into the expediency of providing, by law, for the taking of testimony before Courts or Magistrates acting under State authority, in all cases arising under the law of the 15th May, 1828, for the relief of certain surviving officers and soldiers of the army of the revolution, and under the pension law of 7th June, 1832, and, also, for legalizing the testimony already taken in such cases, under such authority.

Mr. POPE, on leave, submitted a resolution, directing that the hour to which the House should stand adjourned, for the remainder of the session, should be 11 o'clock, A. M. instead of 12 o'clock, M. as at present.

Mr. C. P. WHITE asked for the yeas and nays on its adoption.

Mr. GARLAND suggested that the resolution should be so amended as to direct that it take effect on and after Monday next.

Mr. POPE accepted this amendment as a modification of his motion.

Mr. HARDIN moved to lay the resolution on the table; which was negatived. Yeas 70, nays 125.

Mr. BROWN moved to amend the resolution by fixing the first of February as the day on which the House would commence its sittings at 11 o'clock, A. M.

After a few remarks by Messrs. BROWN, POPE, and POLK, the amendment was agreed to.

The resolution as amended was then agreed to.

The SPEAKER laid before the House a letter from the Secretary of the Navy, transmitting a list of the clerks in his Department, and in the office, of the Navy Commissioners, and the salaries of each; which, on motion of Mr. WHITE, was laid on the table, and directed to be printed.

The SPEAKER laid before the House a communication from the Secretary of War, in response to a resolution of the 6th inst. relative to a road between Memphis and Little Rock; which, on motion of Mr. SEVIER, was laid on the table, and directed to be printed.

The bill making appropriations for the support of the Army for the year 1835, was read the third time and passed.

APPROPRIATION BILLS.

Mr. POLK moved to postpone the orders of the day for the purpose of moving that the House resolve itself into Committee of the Whole on the state of the Union, to take up the appropriation bills.

Mr. WATMOUGH hoped the motion would not prevail.

After some conversation between the CHAIR, Mr. POLK, Mr. WISE, and Mr. WATMOUGH, as to the effect of the motion, it was agreed to—ayes 73, noes 65.

The House accordingly resolved itself into a Committee of the Whole on the state of the Union—Mr. HUBBARD in the Chair, and took up the bill (No 600) making appropriations for forts and fortifications of the United States, heretofore commenced, for the year 1835.

Mr. E. EVERETT moved to amend the bill by inserting, instead of the eighth, ninth, and tenth lines, "for repairing the fortification on Gastle Island, in Boston harbor, according to the plan adopted by the Board of Engineers on the 2nd of March, 1834, in addition to the balance of the former appropriation, $75,000."

Mr. E. gave the reasons which induced the call for this appropriation at the present time. The only question seemed to be with reference to the proper time for commencing those repairs, as all would admit their great importance. No time appeared more propitious than the present, inasmuch as the fact was just announced, that the appropriation bill now on the table was reduced some $450,000 from that of last year, and the total amount of appropriations which it contained were but $439,000.

Mr. E. proceeded to advocate the amendment, by representing the importance of the repairs contemplated. He said there was not now a single piece of ordnance which could be brought to bear

in Boston harbor. The appropriation of $8000, now contained in the bill, was designed only for the repair of a sea-wall, and had nothing to do with the important repairs which he referred to. Mr. E. here called for the reading of a report of the Secretary of War, on this subject; which having been read by the Clerk,

Mr. POLK said, it would be seen by the document just read, that the Secretary did not himself decide on the most proper time for the reconstruction of Fort Independence. It was evident the work would be tantamount to rebuilding the fort, and the whole question with the House would be to decide whether they would now commence the reconstruction of these works, without being called upon in the usual manner to do so.

Mr GORHAM spoke in favor of the amendment. He contended that the appropriation was called for by the highest considerations of public interest. The fort was a very old one, and had not undergone any essential repairs for the last 40 years. The proper officers of government had also reported the necessity of the work. He asked why it was not done? The refusal on the part of Congress to make the appropriation, would look like a determination to abandon the work altogether. He knew of no time more suitable than the present for its accomplishment, and he would repeat the question—why should it longer be delayed? If the question was asked why it had been so long delayed, he would answer, because other appropriations, of large amount, took precedence. That excuse could not now avail. He said there were seven millions worth of property now exposed in Boston Harbor, without a gun to protect it.

Mr. DUNLAP said he thought with the gentleman from Massachusetts, (Mr. Gorham,) who had just taken his seat, that it was high time for the House to determine whether they would proceed to make appropriations for all the appropriations recommended by the Board of Engineers. This appropriation of $75,000, it appeared, was asked with a view of, in effect, commencing a new fort in the place of the old one—one which was now dilapidated. He could not consent to make appropriations for new works until the old ones were completed and equipped. It seemed to be the design to carry into effect splendid schemes of the Board of Engineers. During the war, that board was too small for the purposes of the country, and the exigencies of the times. But what, he would ask, was their occupation now, in their enlarged condition, in time of peace? It was to traverse this vast Union, and point out the means of expending the hundreds of millions which were drawn by taxation from the people. He asked, if the country was now in a situation to proceed with these gigantic works? It was but a few years since, a compromise had been effected on the tariff question. Should these works be allowed to progress, before their completion, it would probably be found necessary to levy a new tariff, notwithstanding the odium attach d to the other, among a large portion of our fellow citizens. Before we embarked in such vast works, it would be most prudent to know that we had the money in the Treasury to answer the expenditure. It was enough, he t'ought, for the present purposes of the Government, to finish and equip the fortifications which they had already commenced—some of them as early as the close of the last war. To be effective, these must all be armed and manned. He was opposed to the amendment.

Mr. EVERETT made a few observations in explanation and reply.

Mr. DICKERSON opposed the amendment on the ground that it was inexpedient to commence new fortifications until those already begun were finished and armed. When that was done, he would be willing to vote appropriations for new works, but not till then.

On the question being taken on the amendment, there appeared—Ayes 45, noes 61.

There being no quorum voting, after some delay, the SPEAKER resumed his seat, and the chairman (Mr. Hubbard) announced that fact to the House.

Mr. POLK moved a call of the House; which being agreed to, the call was proceeded in until

Mr. JOHNSON, of Kentucky, moved that the further proceedings in the call be suspended.

The motion was agreed to.

The question was then taken on the amendment offered by Mr. EVERETT, of Massachusetts, and decided in the negative—ayes 59, nays 77.

Mr. McKIM offered an amendment "for the repair of Fort McHenry, in Baltimore, and for keeping the same in order, $50,000."

Mr. McKIM called for the reading of a report of the Secretary of War, on this subject; which being done, he said he had no disposition to take up the time of the House in advocating the amendment. He would barely state that there were now one hundred millions worth of property exposed in Baltimore, while Fort McHenry could not boast the possession of one gun. It had three mortars, and was every way in a worse condition than during the last war. He thought a city which had defended itself so nobly on that occasion, should not be left entirely destitute of the means of defence.

Mr. POLK gave the reasons for not embracing this or a similar appropriation in the bill. The subject was already in the hands of the Military Committee, and to them, he thought, it properly belonged.

The question was then taken on the amendment, and lost without a division.

Mr. THOMSON, of Ohio, from the Committee on Military Affairs, said, he was instructed by that Committee to offer, as an amendment, "for the repair of Fort Marion, (formerly Fort St. Marks,) at St. Augustine, in Florida, $44,181."

The amendment was supported by Messrs. THOMSON and WHITE, of Florida, opposed by Mr. POLK, and negatived—yeas 61, nays 82.

Mr. PARKER moved to strike from the bill the following clause:

"For a Fort on Throg's Neck, East river, New York, in addition to the balance of former appropriations, $30,000."

Mr. PARKER advocated this amendment; and it was opposed by Messrs. FERRIS, POLK, and CAMBRELENG. It was disagreed to without a count.

After some conversation between Mr. SEVIER and Mr. POLK, in relation to a former item of appropriation for repairs of fort Gibson, in Arkansas Territory,

Mr. SEVIER moved to amend the bill, by appropriating $20,000 for the erection of a fort on the frontiers of Arkansas Territory, and the removal of the United States troops from fort Gibson to the same; which was negatived.

The bill was then ordered to be reported to the House.

The Committee, on motion of Mr. POLK, proceeded to consider the bill from the Senate, making an appropriation for the completion of the military barracks in New Orleans.

Mr. POLK briefly explained the nature of the appropriation; when the Committee rose and reported the two bills to the House, without amendment.

The bill from the Senate making appropriations for the completion of the military barracks at New Orleans, was then read a third time and passed, When the House adjourned.

IN SENATE.

THURSDAY, January 15, 1835.

Petitions were presented by Messrs. WEBSTER, TIPTON, and TYLER.

Mr. TOMLINSON, from the Committee on Pensions, to which was referred the bill to revive and continue the act providing pensions for persons disabled by known wounds received in the Revolutionary war, reported the same with an amendment; inserting one year, instead of six.

Mr. TOMLINSON, from the same committee, reported a bill to continue the office of Commissioner of Pensions.

The bill having been read the first time,

Mr. TOMLINSON said that it would be rejected by the Senate, that the office of Commissioner of Pensions would expire by the appropriation bill of 1832 '3. The office, he said, expired by its own limitation on the termination of the present Congress. It was necessary, therefore, in consequence of the great accumulation of business

in that department, that it should be continued. And he was desirous that prompt action should be had on the bill; that it might go to the other House, and become a law as speedily as was practicable, so that the President might have time to nominate a suitable person to the Senate to fill the office. The bill prescribed the same duties, the same salary, and the same franking privilege which the Commissioner of Pensions enjoyed under the former law. Mr. T. moved that the Senate take up the bill now; which was agreed to.

The bill was then considered as in Committee of the Whole, reported to the Senate, and ordered to be engrossed for a third reading.

Mr. PRENTISS, from the Committee on Pensions, to which was referred the bill for the relief of Carey Clark, reported the same without amendment.

The resolutions offered yesterday by Messrs. WAGGAMAN, BLACK, and HILL, were taken up, considered, and agreed to.

The resolution submitted yesterday by Mr. KANE, was taken up for consideration, and the following was offered by Mr. CLAYTON as a substitute therefor, and agreed to:

Resolved, That the Secretary of the Senate do cause to be made out, and laid before the Senate, a statement showing the amount of money paid in each year, from the first session of the 18th Congress to this time, by order of the Senate, for printing and the purchase of books for the use of the Senate; by order of the House of Representatives, for printing and the purchase of books for the use of that House; by order of Congress, for printing and the purchase of books for the use of Congress, or of any department or officer of the Government; and by order of each of the Executive Departments; designating, in all cases, the object for which, and the persons to whom the money was paid. Also, a statement showing the amount of printing ordered, which has not been completed, by whom the contracts for such printing was made, and an estimate of the sum or sums of money which will be due when such printing shall be completed.

Mr. KANE, pursuant to notice, and on leave given, introduced a bill for the relief of the heirs and legal representatives of James Latham, deceased; which was read twice and referred.

Mr. BELL, from the Judiciary Committee, reported a bill for the relief of James Barrow, which was read the first time, and ordered to a second reading.

Mr. McKEAN, pursuant to notice, and on leave given, reported a bill for the relief of Capt. William Morrow; which was twice read, and referred.

Mr. POINDEXTER, pursuant to notice, and on leave given, reported a bill granting a quantity of land for the satisfaction of certain revolutionary bounty land warrants; which was read twice and referred.

The following resolution was submitted by Mr. TIPTON:

Resolved, That the Secretary of War be requested to transmit to the Senate an estimate of the cost of constructing a bridge over the river Wabash, at the crossing of the Cumberland road; and also, a report as to the practicability of constructing said bridge on such a plan as not to obstruct the navigation of the river, at any stage of water; and, should the files of the Department not now furnish the information sought for by this resolution, that the Secretary will cause it to be procured and reported to the Senate, at an early day in the next session of Congress.

The bill to graduate the price of the public lands, and to provide for the sale of those which have been longest in market, was taken up for consideration, and on motion of

Mr. BENTON, it was postponed to, and made the special order for Wednesday next.

The bill granting a township of land to the French University at St. Louis, was taken up for consideration.

Mr. POINDEXTER said, he was instructed by the Committee on Public Lands, to move its indefinite postponement, but he would move, at present, that it be postponed to, and made the special order for Wednesday next, with the other bills signed for that day.

The bill for the relief of Anson Lynch of Mississippi, and

The bill for the relief of Andrew Knox, were severally ordered to be engrossed for a third reading.

The bill to change the place of holding the land office in Mississippi, from Clinton to Jackson, was taken up for consideration, when

Mr. POINDEXTER moved its indefinite postponement.

After some remarks from Mr. BLACK and Mr. KING, of Ala., Mr. MOORE moved to lay the bill on the table; which was agreed to.

The joint resolution, providing for the amendment of the Constitution, in relation to the election of President and Vice President of the United States, was taken up for consideration.

Mr. BENTON said, that the amendment proposed a change in the Constitution of the United States, in regard to the mode of election of the President and Vice President of the United States, and was in continuation of the proposition which do had the honor of making for ten years past. In the form which the amendment now wore, had been unanimously approved of by two committees of the Senate. It was drawn by a Select Committee, consisting of nine members, four or five years ago, specially elected for the purpose of considering the propriety of the amendment reposed, the members of which were taken one from each section of the Union? The proposition came unanimously from that committee of the Senate, and certainly (without intending to implicate himself,) it came recommended to a favorable consideration of the Senate, in the most imposing manner. But, this was not all; at the last session of Congress, the proposition was again submitted to a committee of five, appointed for the express purpose, and omitting simply, if they were entitled to the highest respect for the last mentioned committee made no amendment to the proposition, except that they perfected its phraseology, but left untouched the principles contained in it. He thought that we could not see an amendment in this respect which was in a purer form than that which was now presented. He said that the principles of the amendment were in a most unexceptionable manner. There are two great fundamental principles embraced in it. The first was to dispense with the intervention of electors in the choice of the two highest officers of the government altogether, and submit a choice directly to the People. The next was, to establish the district system throughout the whole United States. The majority to be taken in each district as one vote for President and one for Vice President. Another was, that in case no event, should the election devolve on the House of Representatives. But in the event two individuals having an equal number of votes, and no one having a majority, then the election to go back to the People. And, if after that, there should be no choice, a contingency which could never happen, an event scarcely within the verge of possibility, the choice should devolve upon the House of Representatives. These, said he, were the principles of the joint resolution. And he thought it better to state them to the Senate, than that they should be read over at the Secretary's table. The subject, however, I come up unexpectedly, several members were out of their seats, but the Senate was in possession of the principles embraced in the proposition, and it was his earnest wish that at the end of ten years, we might have a direct vote upon it. He was ready to await the action of the Senate. would not press the question to day, if gentlemen did not desire it, but he invited the new Senators to give it their consideration and examination. Mr. POINDEXTER said that this subject had for so long before the Senate, and had attracted a universal attention here, and among the people, that he would be gratified if a vote could be had upon it. He was disposed to vote for it, and he believed it was fully understood by the Senate and the People.

Mr. BUCHANAN said he might perhaps feel himself in a different situation from any other member of the Senate, in reference to this subject, having more recently come from the people

than any other gentleman present. He did not feel ready to vote upon the proposition, and would be glad to accept the polite invitation of the gentleman from Missouri. He suggested that the resolution might be permitted to lie over for a few days—the gentleman might choose his own time.

Mr. BENTON then moved that the resolution be laid on the table; which was agreed to.

The bill to distribute for a limited time, the proceeds of the sales of public lands, among the several States, &c. came up for consideration, and

On motion of Mr. POINDEXTER, was postponed to Wednesday next.

The following bills were ordered to be engrossed for a third reading.

A bill for the relief of Robert Hale.

A bill for the relief of Insle Edwards.

A bill to allow further time to complete the issuing of military bounty land warrants, for services during the last war.

A bill to extend the time of issuing military land warrants to officers and soldiers of the revolutionary army.

The bill for the relief of the heirs and legal representative of William Graham, was taken up for consideration, and

On motion of Mr. POINDEXTER, it was indefinitely postponed.

Mr. CLAYTON, from the Judiciary Committee, to which was referred the bill for the relief of Tench Ringgold, late marshal of the District of Columbia, reported the same without amendment.

Mr. CLAYTON, from the same committee, to which was referred the bill from the House of Representatives changing the place of holding the district courts of the United States for the State of Mississippi, reported the same without amendment.

The joint resolution authorizing the President of the United States to make sale of a lion and two horses, presented to the United States' consul at Tangiers by the Emperor of Morocco, was taken up for consideration.

Mr. PORTER objected to the bill, that there was no time specified in it, at which the sale should be made, and moved to amend it by inserting the fourth Saturday in February next, and the sale to be made at auction.

Mr. FRELINGHUYSEN moved to amend the amendment, so as to strike out all about the lion, and insert an authority to the President to present the animal to the proprietor of Peale's Museum at New York, and the horses to the Agricultural Society at New York.

Mr. PORTER inquired why the Hon. gentleman from New Jersey wished to give them to New York? If they were to be disposed of in the way he had indicated, he certainly would oppose sending them to New York. The Agricultural Society of Louisiana, he knew, would be very glad of them, particularly the horses. New York was already powerful enough; she had the largest population, the greatest commercial city, and all the Safety-Fund Banks—and why should she have the lion too?

Mr. FRELINGHUYSEN asked for a division of the question, to be taken on the lion first.

Mr. BENTON expressed himself decidedly in favor of presenting these animals to some public institution—it was much the most appropriate way of disposing of them.

Mr. MOORE was opposed to any proposition on this subject which came from the New York quarter. He was opposed to sending any lions there, or taking a lion from there.

Mr. CLAY said he had much rather see the bill amended so as to leave it to the President of the United States to dispose of these animals as he thought proper, and suggested such amendment.

Mr. POINDEXTER submitted an amendment, in writing, "that the lion be presented to Louis Phillippe, King of France, by the President of the United States."

Mr. BUCHANAN said he was decidedly opposed to that amendment, because it would be a declaration of war at once.

Mr. FRELINGHUYSEN here accepted the suggestion of Mr. CLAY, and modified his amendment so as to allow "the President to present them to such person or institution as he may designate."

Mr. SHEPLEY said that this was a very small affair for the Senate to be engaged in; but he would ask what authority we had to be giving away the property of the United States. If we had a right to make this donation, we could dispose of any other property of the United States, and to any amount, in the same way. The principle was the same.

Mr. FRELINGHUYSEN replied that, according to the common law principle, in order to have a property in a thing we must be able to hold up it. Now, as we could not hold the lion at all, it was better to get rid of him as soon as possible.

The question being on the amendment submitted by Mr. FRELINGHUYSEN, and modified by him, it was disagreed to on a division—yeas 14, nays 15.

Mr. POINDEXTER then moved an amendment, authorizing the animals to be presented to Captain James Kelly, to compensate him for his trouble and expense in transporting them to this country; which was disagreed to on a division—yeas 14, nays 19.

Mr. EWING then moved a further amendment to the bill, requiring the sale to take place in Washington City; which was agreed to, and the bill, as amended, was ordered to be engrossed for a third reading.

On motion of Mr. BENTON, the Senate proceeded to the consideration of Executive business, and when the doors were opened,

The Senate adjourned.

HOUSE OF REPRESENTATIVES.
THURSDAY, Jan. 15, 1835.

Mr. JOHNSON, of Kentucky, from the Committee on Military Affairs, reported a bill to provide for the widows and orphans of the militia who were killed or who died in the service during the late war with the Indians; which was read twice and committed.

Mr. JOHNSON, from the same committee, reported a bill for the relief of Col. Daniel Newnan; which was read twice and committed.

Mr. CARR, from the Committee on Private Land Claims, reported a bill from the Senate, with amendments, to provide for the legal adjudication and settlement of the claims to land therein mentioned; which bill was committed to a committee of the Whole on the state of the Union, and the amendments ordered to be printed.

On motion of Mr. CARR, the same committee were discharged from the further consideration of the petition of the heirs of Jacob Thomas, and it was ordered to lie on the table.

Messrs. DAVIS of Kentucky, CHANEY, and CHAMBERS, each made unfavorable reports upon petitions which had been referred to their respective committees.

Petitions and memorials were presented, on leave, by

Messrs. HARD, HOWELL, and TAYLOR, of New York;

Messrs. BOON and HANNEGAN, of Indiana;

Mr. PEARCE, of Rhode Island;

Mr. HALL, of Maine;

Messrs. McKENNAN and HIESTER, of Pennsylvania;

Mr. LYON, of Michigan.

Which petitions and memorials were appropriately referred.

On motion of Mr. SUTHERLAND, the "harbor bill" was recommitted to the Committee on Commerce.

On motion of Mr. CHANEY,

Resolved, That the Committee on the Post Office and Post Roads be instructed to inquire into the expediency of establishing a post route from Pickasington, in the county of Fairfield, by the town of Winchester, to Circleville, Ohio.

On motion of Mr. JOHNSON, of Kentucky,

Resolved, That the Committee on the Contin-

gent Expenses of the House be directed to audit the accounts of the members of the committee appointed by the House of Representatives on the 26th day of June last, for investigating the condition and proceedings of the Post Office Department, at the rate of compensation paid to the committee for preparing a code of laws for the District of Columbia, of which Philip Doddridge, Esq. was Chairman, viz. eight dollars per day during the recess, without any other allowance.

On motion of Mr. TRUMBULL,

Resolved, That the message of the President of the United States, communicated to the House of Representatives at a former session of Congress, recommending a compensation of the claim to title to the island in the Delaware on which Port Delaware is situated, together with the documents accompanying the same, be referred to the Committee on Military Affairs.

Mr. EWING offered the following resolution, which, under the rule, lies one day:

Resolved, That the Secretary of War be requested to cause the late annual report of the Engineer Department to be re-examined in relation to an alleged inaccuracy in the amount of unexpended appropriations heretofore made to construct the National Road in the State of Indiana, and transmit to this House, as speedily as may be practicable, the result, together with a statement showing the sum that now remains unexpended, and that which will actually be available for payment of labor on said road in Indiana, during the approaching season.

On motion of Mr. LEA,

Resolved, That the Committee on Revolutionary Pensions be instructed to inquire into the expediency of placing Peter Bowerman, of Blount county, in the State of Tennessee, on the roll of revolutionary pensioners, and that the documents in support of his claim be referred to said committee.

On motion of Mr. MANN, of New York,

Resolved, That the Committee on the Judiciary be instructed to inquire into the expediency of revising the statute laws of the United States, and for the purpose of instituting a commission to consist of —— members, to report to Congress such revision for its consideration and adoption.

Mr. WILLIAMS, by consent, submitted the following resolution:

Resolved, That the use of the Hall of the House of Representatives be granted to the Colonization Society on Monday evening, the 19th instant.

Mr. MARDIS demanded the yeas and nays. He was unwilling that the Hall should be given up for any such purpose.

The yeas and nays were ordered, and were yeas 123, nays 53.

So the resolution was agreed to.

The House resumed the consideration of the following resolution heretofore offered by Mr. CHILTON:

Resolved, That the Committee on Roads and Canals be instructed to inquire into the subject, and report their opinion to this House, of the most equal and just mode of applying the revenues of the country to such works of public improvement within the respective States of this Union as may be necessary for the facilitating of communication with foreign nations, and among the several States. And that they moreover report their opinion of the best and most practicable mode of ascertaining and determining the nationality and importance of such improvements as may be proposed within the said several States.

Mr. CHILTON resumed his remarks by referring to what he had said the other day on the subject of the two clauses of the constitution of the United States, and read a lengthy extract from a report made to the House of Representatives, January 7th, 1819, by Mr Calhoun, then Secretary of War, in answer to certain resolutions of the House on the subject of internal improvements. In this extract, Mr. Calhoun explicitly declared it to be his opinion that a judicious system of internal improvements, by roads and canals, constructed for the convenience of commerce and the transportation of the mails, offered one of the best and most efficient means for the complete defense of the country. Whatever difference of opinion might exist, said Mr. C. as to the gentleman's opinion on some subjects, every one gave him credit for possessing powerful talents, and integrity of purpose. Mr. C. said he was not one of those who advocated what had been designated as a "splendid scheme of internal improvements," by taxing the People of the country to effect it, because, in his opinion, it would be better to leave the taxes in the hands of the People of the States; his object was to expend the residue of the public treasure in such objects, after the needful demands of the government had been discharged. Surely, there was no gentleman there, who could not see the great importance of carrying on a national system of internal improvements, who would take a survey of the beautiful streams and rivers bestowed upon our country by the God of nature. He might, to be sure, upon constitutional scruples, but there were many who did not profess those scruples, and, to such he appealed, and asked them, how they could reconcile it to their consciences to abandon this system? There was no nation under the sun devoted to such high and exalted destiny as our own, and the present condition of the State of New York, where internal improvements had been fostered and carried out, contrasted with the condition of other States, was an illustration of this. Mr. C. offered his acknowledgments to the House for the courtesy which had been extended to him. There were a great many other points on which, if time had permitted, he would have touched. He had intended to have introduced divers propositions showing that the Experience had sanctioned one work and rejected another, both of which were identical in principle. He had also intended to have gone further in exhibiting to the House the flagrant injustice that had been done to the Western country. The State of Kentucky, which was the sixth State of the Union in its quota of militia, had never received a solitary dollar since the year 1798. If the West was of no consideration but in time of war, and fit only to fight the battles of the country, let it be at once avowed. He could assure gentlemen that more depended upon the decision of this question than they were perhaps aware of; and the course, not only of himself, but of others, might be regulated by its issue. Mr. C. was for equal justice. Here was a firm originally of thirteen partners, who were each entitled to an equal share of the benefits, but if one or two are to engross the whole, he was almost going as far as to say the sooner the firm was dissolved the better. He was almost going to say, he would nullify—though he was no nullifier; but he believed if ever this doctrine became popular, it would be on account of the gross injustice done to one part of the country to the advantage of another. Mr. C. concluded by saying this was the last report he probably should ever attempt to bring under the consideration of that body. The present session, in all probability, would close his labors on that arena, but he should never cease to feel a deep and lively interest on this subject. All that his resolution asked was, that the Standing Committee, to whom the subject had been referred, should "inquire into the subject, and report their opinion to this House, of the most equal and just mode of applying the revenues of the country to such works of public improvement as may be necessary," &c. and he did hope that the House would permit it to be adopted, and the inquiry made. Again expressing his acknowledgments for the courtesy with which the House had favored him, Mr. C. concluded by calling for the yeas and nays on the adoption of the resolution.

They were accordingly ordered.

Mr. ASHLEY said, he rose only to make a very brief explanation. The gentleman from Kentucky, in the course of his remarks the other day, had set down the State of Missouri as having received the sum of $24,000. Mr A. wished to correct this mistake, and to assure the gentleman from Kentucky, that he sympathized with him, for the State of which Mr. A. had the honor to be a representative, had received no such sum, but was in a similar situation to the honorable member's own State.

Mr. HARPER, of New Hampshire, moved to lay the resolution on the table.

Mr. CHILTON called for the yeas and nays, which were ordered.

Mr. McKIM asked for the reading of the resolution, which was read.

The question was then taken on laying the resolution on the table, and decided in the affirmative; yeas 122, nays 77.

YEAS—Messrs. J. Adams, J. J. Allen, Wm. Allen, Anthony, Archer, Barringer, Beale, Bean, Beaumont, Blair, Bockee, Boon, Brown, Bunch, Burns, Bynum, Cage, Cambreleng, Casey, Chinn, Claiborne, Samuel Clark, Clay, Clayton, Clowney, Coffee, Cramer, Davenport, Day, Deberry, Dickerson, Dunlap, Ferris, Philo C. Fuller, W. K. Fuller, Fulton, Gamble, Gholson, Gillet, Gordon, Graham, Grayson, Griffin, Thomas H. Hall, Halsey, Hamer, Joseph M. Harper, Harrison, Hathaway, Hawkins, Henderson, Howell, Hubbard, Huntington, Inge, Jarvis, Richard M. Johnson, Noadiah Johnson, Seaborn Jones, Benjamin Jones, Kavanagh, Kilgore, King, Lansing, Laporte, Lea, Loyall, Lucas, Abijah Mann, jr., Joel K. Mann, Manning, Mardis, John Y. Mason, Moses Mason, jr., McIntire, McKay, McKinley, McLene, McVean, Miller, Robert Mitchell, Moore, Muhlenberg, Murphy, Osgood, Parks, Patterson, Peyton, Pierce, Pierson, Polk, Pope, Ramsay, Reynolds, Robertson, Schenck, Schley, Shepperd, Shinn, Standifer, Sutherland, Taylor, Wm. P. Taylor, Vanderpool, Wagener, Wardwell, Whallon, White, Wise—122.

NAYS—Messrs. John Quincy Adams, Heman Allen, Ashley, Banks, Barber, Barnitz, Baylies, Beatty, Bell, Binney, Briggs, Bull, Burges, Chambers, Chilton, Wm. Clark, Corwin, Coulter, Crane, Crockett, Darlington, Denny, Dickson, Evans, E. Everett, Ewing, F. Ellmore, Gorham, Grennell, Hiland Hall, Hardin, Hazeltine, Heister, Jackson, E. Jackson, Janes, W. C. Johnson, Kinnard, Lane, Letcher, Lincoln, Martindale, Marshall, McCarty, McKennan, Mercer, Milligan, Miner, Phillips, Pinckney, Sloane, Spangler, P. Thomas, Thomson, Tompkins, Turner, Tweedy, Vance, Watmough, Webster, Whittlesey, Wilson, Young—77.

So the House determined to lay the resolution on the table.

Mr. MARSHALL from the Committee on Revolutionary Claims, reported a bill for the relief of the representatives of Col. Anthony W. White, which was read twice and committed.

The SPEAKER laid before the House a letter from the Secretary of the Treasury, transmitting a report of the Commissioners appointed to audit and adjust private land claims in the State of Missouri.

Mr. ASHLEY, by consent, submitted the following resolution in relation to the foregoing communication, which was agreed to:

Resolved, That the Report of the Secretary of the Treasury in relation to private land claims in Missouri, be referred to the Committee on Public Lands, with instructions to inquire into the expediency of providing by law for the confirmation of these claims.

The SPEAKER laid before the House a letter from the Secretary of War, in answer to a resolution of the 12th inst. respecting the improvement of the Arkansas river, which, on motion of Mr. SEVIER, was referred to the Committee on Ways and Means.

The following bills from the Senate, were read twice and committed:

A bill to provide for the compensation of a Marshal of the District of Delaware;

A bill for the relief of Peter B. Green and William Emerson.

APPROPRIATION BILL.

On motion of Mr. POLK, the House took up the report of the Committee of the Whole on the state of the Union, on the bill making appropriations for certain fortifications heretofore commenced, for the year 1835.

Mr. EVERETT moved, in the House, to amend

amendment which he had proposed in the Committee of the Whole, viz. "For repairing the fortification on Castle Island, in Boston harbor, according to the plan adopted by the Board of Engineers, on the 24th of March, 1834, in addition to the unexpended balance of the former appropriations, $75,000."

Mr. E. said, he would not take up the time of the House by repeating the observations he had yesterday addressed to the Committee. He would barely advert to one fact, which he deemed important. It had been stated by the honorable Chairman of the Committee of Ways and Means, (Mr. Polk,) that no call had been made from the Department for this appropriation. He proceeded to show that such a call had been made by the minutes of the Board of Engineers; and it was a estimates alone that all the appropriations in the bill were founded. Mr. E. here read an extract from a report on the subject from the Department, which declared the work to be 'necessary." He said there was another point which seemed to be misunderstood by some individuals he had spoken on the question. They were under the impression that the fortification on George's Island protected the whole harbor. This was not the fact, as there were two channels, and both fortifications were essential to their protection.

Mr. GORHAM followed in support of the amendment of his colleague, (Mr. Everett.) He said he would content himself by reading the report of the Board of Engineers on the matter in contest. Mr. G. here read extracts from that report.

Mr. POLK said, he would follow the example of the gentlemen from Massachusetts, (Messrs. Everett and Gorham,) and not again open the whole subject of discussion. He was merely to correct a statement which had been made, that this appropriation was authorized by the recommendation of the Department. The appropriation of $8,000 already contained in the bill, was the estimated amount for repairs; and no estimate had been made for reconstruction. The bill had provided all that the department had asked for, viz: $15,000 for Fort Warren, and $8000 for Fort Independence. After some further remarks, in explanation of the present situation of these works, he called on the House to endeavor to keep their appropriations down, at least to the estimates of the officer appointed to make them. He had long, with pain witnessed the fact that all excess of appropriation had originated in that House.

Some conversation here ensued between Messrs. GORHAM, EVERETT, and POLK, not distinctly understood.

Mr. PARKER, addressed the House a few minutes, in favor of the amendment. It was, he said, admitted that the work was important, and that it was in a state of dilapidation. It was also apparent that $8000 expended upon it, would be just so much money thrown away. As the question has presented itself, he was in favor of adopting the amendment, and on that question he asked for the ayes and noes, which were ordered.

Mr. POLK said as he regarded the vote which would be given on this question indicative of the ruling of the House on subjects of the most essentially vital importance, he deemed it essential to have a full House when it was taken. He therefore moved a call of the House.

A majority of the members present having seconded the motion, the call was proceeded in on the Clerk had once gone through the list, and was calling the names of the absentees the call was interrupted by a motion of Mr. HIESTER for a suspension, which was agreed to.

The amendment of Mr. EVERETT, of Massachusetts was then ready, and the question being taken by ayes and noes, there appeared, Ayes 89; noes 120.

So the House determined not to adopt the amendment.

Mr. McKIM then moved the amendment offered by him in Committee of the Whole yesterday, "for the repair of Fort McHenry, in the city of Baltimore, and for putting the same in a proper state of defence, $50,000."

Mr. McK. said he should not detain the House

---

by a lengthy argument of the reasons which induced him to move this item. All he should say was, that in the opinion of the War Department, it was thought expedient that Baltimore should be put in a proper state of defence; and there were papers before the House, which testified that its present defences were altogether inadequate. Mr. McK. read a letter from the Secretary of War to a similar purport, and referred to other papers.

Mr. POLK would only remark, that a memorial on this subject from the citizens of Baltimore, had been presented to the House, and referred to the Committee on Military Affairs, who had the whole matter at this time under investigation; and therefore, he did not think it proper to take it out of their hands. The same principle applied to this appropriation which applied to that for repairs in Boston harbor. The House had been furnished with no estimates

Mr. McKIM asked for the yeas and nays on his amendment; which were ordered.

The question was then taken and decided as follows: Yeas 65, nays 130.

So the House determined not to agree to the amendment.

Mr. THOMSON said, notwithstanding the two votes of the House just recorded, he still deemed it his duty to move the following amendment "for the repair of Fort Marion, formerly Fort St. Mark's, and the repair of the sea wall at St. Augustine, in Florida, $44,181." Mr. T. said, this was an object of a different character from either of the two last. It was for the repair of a Fort now sinking into a state of dilapidation, the original cost of which was said to have been two millions of dollars, and for arresting the progress of the ocean upon the sea walls which had been endangered by the conduct of the United States officers.

Mr. WHITE, of Florida, expressed his surprise at the opposition these items meet with from the Chairman of the Committee of Ways and Means, but he hoped he would see cause to withdraw his opposition to the present amendment. The gentleman objected to the appropriation for the city of Baltimore on the ground that the subject was before the Military Committee, and they had not yet acted upon it; now here was one recommended and introduced by that committee, not only of the present, but of a former session of Congress, when a distinguished gentleman from South Carolina (Mr. Drayton,) was its chairman. The gentleman objected that the Engineer had made no report, and that no recommendation had come from the War Department. But if we would ask if we were come to that pass, like a provision laid down in the French constitution, that no measure could be debated in the Chamber of Representatives, till it was recommended by a cabinet minister? He hoped not. Mr. W. made some further remarks in support of the proposed item, and hoped as the subject had been discussed in, and recommended by a standing committee of the House, that the amendment would prevail.

Mr. THOMSON called for the reading of the letter of the Secretary of War, which having been read by the Clerk—

Mr. POLK said, the letter contained no opinion of that origin of the Government, but merely transmitted certain documents referred to. What were the facts, and what was the information upon which the House was called upon to appropriate this money? The Fort at St. Marks, or Fort Marion, as it was then called, was built by the old Spanish Government when Florida was one of the colonies of that power, for what purpose, he believed few could imagine; for it was conceded on all hands, that an armed force could not possibly reach it. In the first place, the depth of water was never over nine feet; and Mr. P. had the authority of the War Department for the assurance that it was in every way unimportant for coast defence. (Mr. P. here read the document referred to.) Mr. P. denied that he was governed by the dictation of any Cabinet Minister, nor would he yield to the dictation of any Department of the Government, but he would gladly receive any information within the scope of their duty to give. Mr. P. made some further remarks in opposition

---

to the amendment, and asked for the yeas and nays; which were ordered.

Mr. WISE moved to adjourn; but, at the request of Mr. POLK, withdrew the motion.

The question was then taken on the amendment, and decided in the negative—yeas 67, nays 111.

So the House refused to agree to the amendment.

On motion of Mr. McKENNAN,
The House then adjourned.

Friday, Jan. 16, 1835.

Petitions and memorials were presented by Messrs. KING of Alabama, TYLER, and PRESTON.

Mr. TYLER presented a memorial from certain citizens of Georgetown, praying for the incorporation of a new Bank in that city, with the power of establishing branches in Alexandria and Washington; which was referred to the Committee on the District of Columbia.

Mr. BLACK, from the Committee on Private Land Claims, to which was referred the bill for the relief of Edward Paine, and Elias Arnold reported the same with an amendment.

Mr. BLACK from the same committee, to which was referred the bill for the relief of William L. Cocheral, reported the same with an amendment.

Also, the bill for the relief of Abraham Winkle, which had been referred to the same committee, with an amendment.

Mr. KNIGHT, from the Committee on Claims, made an unfavorable report upon the petition of Mountjoy Bailey.

Mr. POINDEXTER, from the Committee of Public Lands, to which was referred the following bills, reported them as follows:

A bill granting an additional quantity of land, in satisfaction of revolutionary bounty land warrants.

A bill for the relief of John Tice.

A bill from the House of Representatives for the relief of Charles Colwell. [The committee dissenting from the propriety of its passage.]

A bill for the relief of William O'Neill, which, on motion of Mr. POINDEXTER, was taken up for consideration, and then laid on the table.

Mr. TIPTON gave notice, that to-morrow he would ask leave to introduce a bill for the relief of Samuel and James Smith.

Mr. SILSBEE, from the Committee on Commerce, to which was referred the petition of Thomas Aspinwall, reported a bill authorizing certain allowances to be made to the United States Consul at London.

On motion of Mr. SILSBEE, the bill was taken up for consideration, and ordered to be engrossed for a third reading.

The following resolutions were submitted:

By Mr. TYLER:

Resolved, That the Committee on Revolutionary Claims be instructed to inquire into the propriety of allowing to the legal representative of Wm. Royall, deceased, in erest on the commutation pay allowed by an act passed at the last session of Congress.

By Mr. TIPTON:

Resolved, That the Committee on Pensions be instructed to inquire into the expediency of placing John Smith, of Indiana, on the roll of invalid pensioners, from the date of his first application for a pension, in the year 1817.

By Mr. BENTON:

Resolved, That the report of the Committee on Finance, under the resolution of the Senate, to investigate the affairs and conduct of the Bank of the United States, and which report was made on the 18th of December, 1834, be recommitted, with instructions to renew and complete the inquiries into the subjects mentioned in the resolution.

On motion of Mr. KING, of Alabama, the Senate took up for consideration the bill making an appropriation to complete the road from Lynn creek to Chatahoochie, opposite Columbus, in Alabama.

Mr. KING submitted an amendment to obviate the objection urged by Mr. POINDEXTER, when

the bill was under consideration on a former day, "that the appropriation shall be taken out of the 2 per cent. fund, which has been set apart for making roads in Alabama," which he supported by some remarks.

Mr. POINDEXTER was not altogether satisfied with the amendment, and proposed to amend the same further, by adding a proviso "that the Legislature of Alabama should give her assent to the appropriation.

Some remarks were then made by Messrs. KING, TIPTON, PORTER, MOORE, GRUNDY, in favor of the bill; and by Messrs. POINDEXTER, BLACK, and HENDRICKS against it.

The question being on the amendment to the amendment, Mr. POINDEXTER asked the yeas and nays, which were ordered; and the question was disagreed to by the following vote:

YEAS—Messrs. Knight, Moore, Poindexter, Webster.—4.

NAYS—Messrs. Benton, Bibb, Buchanan, Clayton, Frelinghuysen, Grundy, Hendricks, Hill, Kent, King of Ala., King of Ga., Linn, McKean, Mangum, Morris, Naudain, Porter, Robinson, Shepley, Smith, Southard, Swift, Tallmadge, Tipton, Tomlinson, Waggaman, White, Wright.—28.

The question recurring on the amendment, Mr. WRIGHT asked the yeas and nays thereon; which were ordered, and are as follows, to wit:

YEAS—Messrs. Benton, Black, Buchanan, Cuthbert, Grundy, Hill, Kane, Kent, King of Ala. King of Georgia, Linn, McKean, Morris, Robinson, Shepley, Tallmadge, Waggaman, White, Wright —19.

NAYS—Messrs. Clayton, Ewing. Frelinghuysen, Hendricks, Knight, Mangum, Moore, Naudain, Poindexter, Porter, Smith, Southard, Swift, Tipton, Tomlinson, Tyler, Webster—17.

So the question was determined in the affirmative.

The question then being on ordering the bill to be engrossed for a third reading, as amended,

Mr. MOORE moved that the bill be laid on the table till to-morrow; which was agreed to.

The CHAIR communicated a letter from the Treasury Department, accompanied by the returns made to that department by the Banks of the District of Columbia; which, on motion of Mr. WEBSTER, was referred to the Committee on Finance.

Also, another communication from the Treasury Department, showing the number of clerks employed in that department for the year 1834, and the compensation paid to each.

The following resolution, submitted yesterday by Mr. TIPTON, was taken up for consideration:

"Resolved, That the Secretary of War be requested to transmit to the Senate an estimate of the cost of constructing a bridge over the river Wabash, at the crossing of the Cumberland road; and also, a report as to the practicability of constructing said bridge on such a plan as not to obstruct the navigation of the river, at any stage of water; and, should the files of the Department not now furnish the information sought for by this resolution, that the Secretary will cause it to be procured and reported to the Senate, at an early day in the next session of Congress.

Mr. TIPTON said that this resolution proposed an inquiry into the practicability of constructing a bridge over the Wabash, where the national road crosses that stream. Several of the western States, and were interested in the execution of this bridge; and all the States west of the river, more deeply interested in it than was. The mail sent to all the States west river, would be transported in stages, and be much retarded in its progress, if there no other mode of crossing the river than in boats. The rise in the river in consequence its, rendered the crossing in boats dangerthe floating ice in the winter season obthe passage of boats, sometimes carryrac that of the mail and of travellers. was a large portion of Indiana, nearly of the State, and a portion of the State situated on the Wabash, above the national road, and all that country usly injured if a bridge should be so

erected as to have the effect of obstructing the navigation of the river at a high stage of the water; and his vote for an appropriation to erect this bridge, Mr. T. said, would depend upon the ascertainment of the fact, whether it would have this effect or not. He hoped and believed that a bridge could be constructed on such a plan, that the navigation would not be impeded or interfered with in any way, at any stage of the water; and if it should so turn out, the bridge ought to be erected. The inquiry could injure no one, and would be a great satisfaction to those immediately interested.

The resolution was adopted.

Mr. HENDRICKS, from the Committee on Roads and Canals, reported a bill to establish a mail route in East Florida, between the navigable waters of the St. Johns and the Suwanee rivers.

Mr. HENDRICKS, from the same committee, also reported a bill for the continuation and repair of the Cumberland road; which was read the first time, and ordered to a second reading.

The bill for the relief of the heirs of James Lath m, was read the second time and referred.

The following bills were read a third time and passed:

A bill for the relief of Robert Hale;

A bill for the relief of Etham Edwards;

A bill to allow further time for completing the issuing and locating of military land warrants during the late war;

A bill for the relief of Andrew Knox;

A bill to continue the office of Commissioner of Pensions;

A bill for the relief of Absalom Lynch.

The bill authorizing the sale of a lion and two horses, presented by the Emperor of Morocco to the United States Consul at Tangiers, also came up for a third reading; and, on motion of Mr. POINDEXTER, was laid on the table.

The following bills were read the second time, considered as in Committee of the Whole, and ordered to be engrossed for a third reading:

A bill for the relief of Francis Lasalle;

A bill for the relief of James Thomas;

A bill granting a township of land to the borough of Mackinaw;

A bill for the relief of William B. Zantzinger, late purser in the navy;

A bill for the relief of Tufts & Clark;

A bill for the relief of Nicholas D. Coleman;

A bill for the relief of Hiram A. Hunter;

A bill for the relief of Thomas J. Mortee.

On motion of Mr. WEBSTER, it was then Ordered, That when the Senate adjourns, it will adjourn to meet on Monday next.

On motion of Mr. CLAYTON, The Senate adjourned.

HOUSE OF REPRESENTATIVES.

Friday, January 16, 1835.

Petitions and memorials, by consent, were presented by—

Mr. GARLAND, of Louisiana;

Mr. GRAYSON, of South Carolina;

Mr. PHILLIPS, of Massachusetts;

Mr. WHITE, of Florida;

Mr. MERCER, of Virginia;

Which memorials and petitions were appropriately referred.

[Mr. MAY presented the petition of sundry citizens of Illinois, praying the establishment of a mail route from Terre Haute, Indiana, to Quincy, on the Mississippi river; which, on his motion, was referred to the Committee on the Post Office and Post Roads.]

Mr. WHITE, of Florida, offered the following resolution, which, under the rule, lies one day:

Resolved, That the Secretary of War be requested to cause an examination to be made into the present condition of Fort Marion in East Florida, and to report to the next session of Congress, whether the public interests would not be promoted by its repair and preservation for defence and barracks, with an estimate of the cost of the repairs, and that of the sea wall between it and St. Francis barracks; and also to present a report of the manner and objects to which the twenty thousand dollars appropriated has been expended.

On motion of Mr. DUNLAP, Resolved, That the Committee on Revolutionary Pensions be instructed to inquire into the expediency of authorizing the Secretary of War to establish a pension agency in the town of Jackson, in the State of Tennessee, and to provide for the payment of all the United States pensioners residing in the counties of Hardin, McNairy, Henderson, Fayette, Shelby, Tipton, Haywood, Madison, Henderson, Perry, Carroll, Gibson, Dyer, Obion, Weakly, and Henry, at said agency.

On motion of Mr. STEWART, of Pennsylvania, Resolved, That the Committee of Ways and Means be instructed to inquire into the expediency of making an appropriation to pay the salary of Valentine Geisey, late superintendent of the Cumberland road.

Mr. PINCKNEY offered the following resolution, which, under the rule, lies one day:

Resolved, That the President of the U. S. be requested (if not inconsistent with his opinion of the public interest) to communicate to this House any correspondence that may have taken place between the Government and that of Spain respecting the act of Congress, passed on the 30th day of June, 1834, entitled "an act concerning tonnage duty on Spanish vessels"—and also any information in his possession going to show whether there is any prospect that the commerce of the United States with the Island of Porto Rico, will hereafter be regulated upon principles of reciprocity, or whether it is in contemplation by the Spanish authorities to increase or reduce the discriminating duties of tonnage, and the discriminating duties on imports and exports now levied on American vessels and on American merchandise and produce.

Mr. WARDWELL, from the Committee on Revolutionary Pensions, reported a bill for the relief of Walter Phillips; which was read twice and committed.

Mr. HUBBARD, from the Committee of Ways and Means, reported a bill making appropriations for harbors, rivers, and the Delaware breakwater; which was read twice and committed.

Mr. CAMBRELENG, from the Committee of Ways and Means, reported a bill to prevent evasions of the revenue laws, and for other purposes; which was read twice and postponed to Monday.

Mr. SUTHERLAND, from the Committee on Commerce, reported a bill making appropriations for building light-houses, erecting beacon light, and making surveys for the year 1835; which was read twice and committed.

Mr. SUTHERLAND, from the same committee, reported a bill making appropriations for the improvement of certain harbors therein mentioned which was read twice and committed.

Mr. GILLET, from the Committee on Commerce, reported the following resolution, which was agreed to:

Resolved, That the Committee of the Whole be discharged from the further consideration of bill No. 526, and it be committed to the Committee of the Whole on the state of the Union.

Mr. BEALE, from the Committee on Invalid Pensions, reported a bill placing the name of Captain Cole on the pension roll; which was read twice and committed.

Messrs. FOSTER, HUBBARD, McINTIRE, ADAMS of New York, and MOORE, each made unfavorable reports upon petitions, &c. referred to their respective committees.

Mr. BLAIR, from the Committee on Roads and Canals, reported a bill to authorize the State of Alabama to apply the two per cent. of the proceed of the sales of public lands within that State, to opening a canal, or making a railroad, for the purpose of connecting the waters of the Tennessee and Coosa rivers; which was read twice.

Mr. BLAIR moved that the said bill be now engrossed for a third reading; and remarked, the bill on its face so clearly developed the object, that explanation would be unnecessary. He would however say, that by the terms of the compact under which the State of Alabama came into the Union, two per centum of the net proceeds of the sales of the public lands were reserved to make a road or roads leading to that

at the bill proposed, the contracting parties greeing thereto, to change the direction of that d and apply it to the constructing a rail road canal between the Tennessee and Coosa rivers. He said that inasmuch as no new appropriation of money from the Treasury was asked, and he necessity of speedily putting it in the power of labama to pass upon the proposed change, he ad obtained the unanimous cons nt of the seven embers in the committee, when the subject was rought before them, to the motion which he ad made. He said that, aware that some might bject that the Legislature of Alabama could ot c nstitutionally change the compact which ad been made by the convention, the bill was so orded as to obviate every scruple, by requiring the assent of the State of Alabama, before the change should be made. Mr. B. said that he ould foresee no possible objection to the proposition, inasmuch as there was no necessity for aking such roads to Alabama as were contemplated at the time of the compact. The Indian title has, generally, been extinguished in the adjoining States, and the territory settled up to her orders; what was then regarded as being necessary, is now wholly unnecessary. The improvement which is proposed, (Alabama consenting,) is one of the first importance. It will intersect three States, and unite waters flowing from through five of the States of this Union. It has been long a subject of examination by the Committee on Roads and Canals, and has as often as it has been brought forward, been favorably reported upon. He hoped the House would order the bill to be engrossed for a third reading, inasmuch as any other disposition of it would tend to defeat it at this stage of the session.

Mr. McKINLEY said, he was taken by surprise. He had never heard that it was intended to introduce such a bill. His constituents were interested in the disposition of this fund, and as this bill is not calculated to benefit them, he would move to lay it on the table.

Mr. McKinley withdrew the motion at the request of

Mr. CLAY, who entered into an explanation of the circumstances under which the bill had been reported. A resolution on this subject, adopted on his motion some time since, had been referred to the Committee on Roads and Canals. He had supposed that his colleague (Mr. McKinley) was aware of this fact. The committee, it was true, had reported a bill somewhat variant from his proposition; but he could not see how his colleague could have been taken by surprise by the introduction of the bill. In relation to the relinquishment of this fund, he would remark, that by the terms of the compact, two per cent. of the net proceeds of the sales of the public lands within said State, after her admission, was reserved to the State of Alabama, for the purpose of opening a road or roads *to* the State—not for making roads within the State. More than $100,000 had accrued under this compact—more than fifteen years had elapsed, and not a single dollar had been applied as contemplated. From the policy which had been adopted by the General Government, it was not likely that this sum would be so applied. Besides, it would go but a little way towards accomplishing the original object intended. The sole intention of the bill was so to change the compact, as to permit the State of Alabama to apply this money to another important, though different object—namely, the opening of a canal or rail-road to connect the waters of the Tennessee with Coosa river. He could see no possible objection to the passage of the bill, inasmuch as the State of Alabama was left, by its terms, *perfectly at liberty to accept, or reject*, the proposed relinquishment of the fund. Mr. C. said, it was true that his resolution contemplated giving a broader discretion to the Legislature—that was, the application of the fund to the construction of a rail-road or canal, connecting *the waters of Mobile Bay with those of the Tennesse river*, instead of naming any *particular river*, flowing into Mobile Bay—and he would still prefer the bill in that form. As the committee had thought proper to vary the terms of the relinquishment, however, still leaving it entirely to the election of Alabama to receive it or not, on those terms, and as, without the passage of this bill, the fund would continue to be inactive and unproductive, he hoped it would pass, and should give it his support. It would be better to get the benefit of the fund in the mode proposed, than to lose the advantage of it altogether, and he hoped his colleague would withdraw his opposition.

Mr. MERCER suggested to the gentleman from Tennessee, (Mr. Blair,) the propriety of permiting the bill to go to the Committee of the Whole on the state of the Union, where it would be open to amendment. He feared that it would be lost if pressed at this time, &c.

Mr. MARDIS was apprehensive that this subject was not understood by the House. The fund referred to, was not the property of the United States. The bill did not ask the appropriation of a single cent. It only asked a change of the disposition of a fund reserved to the State of Alabama, by compact—that it may be applied specially to the opening of a canal or rail-road, to connect the waters of the Tennessee and Coosa rivers. By applying this money in the mode proposed by the bill, it would open a steam communication between New Orleans to Maine, with the exception of about 300 miles. But his colleague, (Mr. McKinley) thought that his constituents would not be benefited by this improvement. He could not suppose his colleague acted upon the selfish principle that because it was not in his immediate district, his constituents would not be in favor of this great national improvement. But a very small portion of his constituents were immediately interested in this work; but its importance, in a general point of view, would induce him to give this measure his cordial support. He hoped, therefore, that the bill would be ordered to be engrossed, and, if nescessary, it would be postponed to such time as would allow gentlemen to examine it thoroughly.

Mr. McKINLEY repeated that he was taken by surprise on the introduction of this bill. He had held no conversation with either of his colleagues, or any other person, on the subject; nor was the resolution to which one of his colleagues (Mr. Clay) alluded calculated to apprise him of an intention to introduce any such measure as the present. The reason of his surprise was, that a bill of this character, affecting the interests of the people of Alabama, should be introduced without consultation with its representatives on this floor, and that it should be proposed to order its engrossment at the moment of its introduction. It was certainly not strange, that he should indicate a determination to protect the interests of his constituents.

Mr. BLAIR replied to Mr McKinley, and others, that, for twelve years, the connexion of the Tennessee and Coosa rivers had been, to his knowledge, before Congress; that it was, in his estimation, the most important improvement (involving the expenditure of a like amount of money) in the Union. It was of direct interest to five States of this Union. He had, as a member of the Committe and of the House, urged the appropriation of money to complete that object. When refused money, he had consented to take lands in its vicinity, as had been given to other States, when that was refused. He was ready to resort even to the expedient of making an appeal to the State of Alabama, to divert the two per cent. from useless roads, to the prosecution of that great work. Mr. B. said that the House had the subject before it, and would dispose of it as might be thought best, for his own part he would give no consent to refer the bill to a Committee of the Whole on the state of the Union. He preferred a vote on the subject, and if rejected, it would be done openly and directly—to refer to the committee at this stage of a short session, was voting to bury the bill under the mass of business then upon the table. As to the remark of the gentleman from Alabama (Mr. McKinley,) hat this State had not asked for the change, and that he had not been consulted—he could say that the measure had been pressed by others from his State, and Mr. B. had supposed that a perfect understanding had prevailed amongst the members of that delegation This he could say with truth, that Alabama has always regarded the connexion of the Tennessee and Coosa, as a work of importance, and the Legislature at its present session, had that subject before it in a proposition from a committee of that body to pledge the faith of the State for the repayment of a loan of one million dollars to perfect that improvement. And if Mr B. was not mistaken, the gentleman himself had subscribed to its importance in voting for the appropriation of the public lands to works of improvement in his State, of which this was one.

Mr. FILLMORE thought there were principles of considerable importance involved in the bill which rendered it proper that it should go to a committee. The House was called upon to vary a compact, or enter into a new one. He thought that the measure proposed was equivalent to an appropriation of money from the Treasury: He was not unfriendly to the bill; nor did he desire to throw any unnecessary obstructions in the way of its passage; but he considered it necessary that it should be committed.

Mr. BRIGGS inquired of the Chair, whether, under the rule, it was not indispensably necessary that the bill should be committed?

After some conversation between the CHAIR, Messrs. BRIGGS, CLAY, and McKINLEY, on the point of order, the bill, in obedience to the decision of the Speaker, was committed to a Committee of the Whole on the state of the Union.

Mr. GILMER, from the Committee on Indian Affairs, reported a bill to authorize the superintendent of Indian Affairs at St. Louis to employ a clerk; which was read twice. Mr. G. asked that it might be engrossed for a third reading.

Mr. GARLAND objected on the ground that the course was irregular, and gave a precedence over other bills heretofore reported. He referred to one or two in particular, in which many citizens of his own State were deeply interested, and on which it had been found impossible to procure the action of the House. He preferred that the business should progress in its regular order.

Mr. POLK moved to suspend the rule was satisfied that the bill ought to pass, a hoped it would be ordered to be engrossed time.

Mr. ASHLEY said there ought to be n ral rule without an exception. He thoug bill presented a case of that sort. A clerk w solutely necessary in the office of the superi ant of Indian Affairs at St. Louis. The bu of that office, unless a clerk was provided, have to be measurably suspended, and the su intendent would be compelled to employ on his own expense, or suffer the business to l glected, if this bill was not passed. He that the rule would be suspended, and th permitted to progress.

The question was then taken, and the Hous fused to suspend the rule—*yeas* 95, nays two thirds being necessary.

Mr. POLK moved to suspend the rule aside this day for the consideration of privat in order that the House should proceed w consideration of the appropriation bills; w was disagreed to.

The SPEAKER laid before the House from the Secretary of the Treasury, cove report, pursuant to a resolution, in relation to marine hospital fund, &c.; which was laid on table and ordered to be printed.

A bill for the relief of Richard T. Archer, ordered to be engrossed and read a third tim

On motion of Mr. ARCHER, the House r ed itself into a Committee of the Whol WARD in the Chair, and took up and con the bill for the relief of the legal represen of Richard W. Meade.

The bill having been read by the Clerk,

Mr. ARCHER called for the reading Report on the claim by the Committee on F Affairs. (Which was accordingly also read Clerk.) Mr. A. then supported the claim at length, going into a minute detail of all cumstances out of which it grew. Th ment of the United States had put it power of the claimant to collect this Spain, by the solemn stipulations of a t pursuance of these stipulations, our Go

had received a certain sum of money for various claims, including this, and paid out the whole amount to others than the present claimant

Mr. WHITE, of Florida, recapitulated the circumstances attendant on the execution of the treaty between the United States and Spain, by which Florida was ceded to the former. In answer to an inquiry of the gentleman from Virginia, (Mr. Archer,) Mr. W. said the United States did, by the terms of that treaty, assume the claims of our citizens against that government.

Mr. POLK regretted that some members of the committee had not prepared themselves to meet this bill. It was an old acquaintance in the House, and had long ago been rejected by a vote of more than two to one. Mr. P. opposed the validity of the claim at considerable length, and gave a succinct statement of the former proceedings both of Congress and of a commission appointed for the purpose several years ago, in reference to it. If the House adopted this bill, they would be re-opening a mass of claims to an amount of not less than thirty-nine millions of dollars, which would come under the same principle. Mr. P. also contended that there was no additional evidence presented at this time more than was before the Spanish commission, and on which they had heretofore adjudicated, and appealed to the Hon. Chairman of the Committee if this was not so.

Mr. ARCHER said if the bill should pass, he was given to understand that additional testimony would be adduced.

Mr. POLK said, then he was right; there was no evidence before the House than was before the commission, and by passing the bill, the House would be entertaining an appeal from a tribunal of its own creation, to the hazard of many millions of the public treasury. Mr. P. said if he could believe there was one dollar due to this individual claimant, he would cheerfully lend his feeble aid towards its recovery. He sincerely desired strict justice to every American citizen. He concluded by expressing a wish that the bill might not be decided upon to-day, but a farther time might be given for its investigation.

Mr. ARCHER asked for the reading of the bill, by which the House would perceive that it embraced no appropriation, but simply directed an investigation to be made by the Attorney General and two Auditors.

The bill having been read by the Clerk,

Mr. POLK called for the reading of the bill of 1828, which having been done, Mr. P. said the first two sections of both bills were the same, but the one before the House contained a provision for the payment of the claim, should a decision be made in its favor, which was not in the former one.

Mr. ARCHER said he was not aware before that the bill contained a clause for the payment of the claim. He moved that this clause be stricken out.

Mr. EVERETT, of Massachusetts, called for the reading of a document which had some bearing on the question. The report of the committee of 1826 was then read by the Clerk.

Mr. E. said it was true that the bill of 1828 was lost by a vote of two to one, but he would remind the House that in 1836 the same bill passed by a majority of not less than two to one, and the honorable gentleman from Tennessee voted in the affirmative.

Mr. POLK said the bill of 1826 was brought on at a late hour of the evening, at the heel of the session, and he would admit that he did vote, as others did, in the dark, as to the facts, without having given the subject due examination.

Mr. P. also remembered that his vote was not against him on occasion of the rejection of bill of 1828, and he then gave a similar explanation.

EVERETT continued to advocate the which, he contended, was founded in truth justice, and rested upon its own merits, with reference to the other claims alleged by the man from Tennessee, to be involved in the principle. He could see no evil that could mar its reference to a Board for investigation.

RDIN said, he regretted that business

of another character had compelled him to be absent during the greater part of this discussion; but he desired to give his sentiments on this claim, since it was one which he had investigated at a former session. He would proceed, if it was the pleasure of the Committee, but as the hour was late, he moved that the Committee rise.

The motion being agreed to, the Committee rose, reported progress, and obtained leave to sit again.

On motion of Mr. HUBBARD,
The House then adjourned.

HOUSE OF REPRESENTATIVES,

SATURDAY, January 17, 1835.

The bill to authorize the superintendent of Indian Affairs, at St. Louis, to appoint a clerk, was ordered to be engrossed for a third reading.

Mr. TURRILL submitted the following joint resolution, which was postponed to Monday next:

Resolved by the Senate and House of Representatives of the United States of America in Congress assembled, That the Secretary of State, whenever the same shall come into his possession, be authorized and required to deliver to the Secretary of War such of the documentary evidence and papers purchased of the heirs of General Washington, as will be serviceable in the adjustment of pension claims pending in the War Department.

Petitions on leave were presented by—

Mr. HANNEGAN, of Indiana.

[Mr. HANNEGAN, on leave, presented a memorial and joint resolution of the Legislature of the State of Indiana, relative to the establishment of a port of entry at the town of Lafayette, on the Wabash river in said State; and moved that the same be referred to the Committee on Commerce; which was accordingly done.]

Mr. SCHLEY, of Georgia.
Mr. ASHLEY, of Missouri.
Mr. SMITH, of Maine.
Mr. ADAMS, of Massachusetts.

Which were appropriately referred.

Mr. MANN, of N. Y., asked the House to consider two resolutions which he had (by permission) laid upon the table a few days since—requesting the Secretaries of the War and Navy Departments respectively, to furnish copies and statements of the items and aggregates of the compensation, allowances of the officers of the army and navy, including all stated and special allowances of every description, for the two last years, and showing, also, their travel, and grades, and where stationed, and what services they have performed.

Mr. said, that he had been informed, since, these resolutions have been laid upon the table, that it was not probable they could be answered in season to permit any action of the House upon the subject at this session, and wishing to afford the Departments ample time to make full and accurate reports, he would take occasion now to say, that on the coming in of such reports at the next session, he would ask for the appointment of a committee, to consider and thoroughly investigate the subject in the hope that ample, equal, and even liberal justice, might be done to all the officers engaged in those branches of the public service.

The resolutions were then taken up, modified by the mover, and adopted in the following form:

Resolved, That the Secretary of War be requested to communicate to this House an abstract of the items of all accounts and claims for the compensation and allowances of every kind for the two last fiscal years, distinguishing each year ending 30th September, 1834, of the generals, colonels, lieutenant colonels, majors and captains of the army, and also of all officers attached to the Engineer and Topographical departments, which have been actually paid and allowed, with a general statement showing also the aggregate pay and emoluments, including all stated and special allowances paid and allowed to each commission officer of the army, name and rank of every grade for each year aforesaid, and the aggregate of the whole; and showing, also, the places from and to which, and the computed distance between such places, and the amount for which transportation has been allowed and paid to each officer of the

army, and where stationed, and what services each has performed.

Resolved, That the Secretary of the Navy be requested to communicate to this House an abstract of the items of all the accounts and claims for compensation and allowances of every kind for the two last fiscal years, distinguishing each year, ending 30th September, 1834, of the captains, masters commandant, lieutenants, pursers, and navy agents of the navy, with a general statement, showing also the aggregate pay and emoluments, including all stated and special allowances actually paid and allowed to each commissioned officer of the navy, by name and rank, of every grade, and where stationed (excepting midshipmen) for each year aforesaid, and the aggregate of the whole; showing, also the places from and to which, and the computed distance between each, and the amount for which transportation or travel has been allowed and paid to each officer of the navy, and where each is stationed, and what services each has performed.

The following resolution submitted on Thursday last, by Mr. EWING, of Indiana, was considered and agreed to:

Resolved, That the Secretary of War be requested to cause the late annual report of the Engineer Department to be re-examined in relation to an alleged inaccuracy in the amount of the expended appropriations heretofore made to construct the National road in the State of Indiana, and transmit to this House as speedily as may be practicable, the result, together with a statement showing the sum that now remains unexpended, and that which will actually be available for payment of labor on said road in Indiana, during the approaching season.

On motion of Mr. HANNEGAN,

Resolved, That the Committee on Public Lands be directed to inquire into the expediency of extending the benefit of the pre emption law to all persons who were actual settlers, or had made improvements on the public lands with the intention of becoming settlers prior to the first day of January, 1835.

On motion of Mr. ALLEN, of Ohio,

Resolved, That the Committee on Public Lands be instructed to inquire into the expediency of granting to the State of Ohio a quantity of land equal to that which has been sold by the officers of the General Government within the limits of the grant formerly made by Congress to that State, to aid in the extension of the Miami Canal since the passage of the act making said grant. Also, a quantity equal to twenty-five sections, in addition to the original grant, the whole to be selected from the alternate sections now reserved from sale along the line of the Miami canal in that State.

On motion of Mr. JARVIS,

Resolved, That the Committee of Ways and Means be instructed to inquire into the expediency of regulating by law the number of clerks to be employed in the Departments of State, of the Treasury, of War, of the Navy, and of the Post Office, in such manner as to prevent the introduction into the appropriation bills of appropriations for extra clerk hire, or arrears of clerk hire not provided for in any existing laws.

On motion of Mr. MAY,

Resolved, That the Committee on Public Lands be instructed to inquire into the expediency of reporting a bill authorizing the county commissioners of Joe Davies county to purchase of the United States, at the minimum price of the public lands, for the use and benefit of the county aforesaid, the section of land embracing the town of Galena.

On motion of Mr. GARLAND,

Resolved, That the Committee on Commerce be instructed to inquire into the expediency of creating a collection district in the State of Louisiana, to include all the coast from the Perdido Bay, to the Sabine river, and also inquire into the Aure Bayou, where it empties into the Vermillion Bay, to the Sabine river, and also inquire into the expediency of establishing ports of entry or suitable points on the Bay, on Vermillion, and the river Mermentau, and Calcasieu, in said district.

On motion of Mr. CHINN,

Resolved, That the Committee on the Post Office and Post Roads be instructed to inquire into

he expediency of establishing a post route from arnlau Church, in Richmond City, Virginia, to Henderson's river, in Northumberland county.

On motion of Mr. ASHLEY,

Resolved, That the Committee on Claims be instructed to inquire into the expediency of liquidating the accounts of William Newland and D. M. ice for attendance on, and supplies furnished wo soldiers of the United States army, whilst sick and on furlough.

On motion of Mr. BEAUMONT,

Resolved, That the Committee on Revolutionary Pensions be instructed to inquire into the expediency of paying to Ann Wilson, widow of Valentine Wilson, a revolutionary soldier, the amount of his pension arrears from the 4th March, 1831, to the time of his death, 4th July, 1833.

On motion of Mr. CASEY,

Resolved, That the Committee on the Post Office and Post Roads be instructed to inquire into the expediency of establishing a mail route from Mount Carmel, by Coffington, Albion, Leech's ..., and Fairfield, to Salem, all in the State of Illinois.

Mr. REYNOLDS submitted the following resolution:

Resolved, That the Committee on the Judiciary be instructed to inquire into the expediency of extending the Federal Judiciary to all the States in the Union *alike*, and report thereon.

Mr. REYNOLDS remarked, that he did not pretend to be more patriotic and more able to bring this subject before the House than any other Representative from the new States; but he could not remain a disinterested spectator and see that the new States were not on an equal footing with the other States. He was raised in one of the new States, and knowing and experiencing the feelings and situation of them, in this respect, he could not rest satisfied on this subject until all enjoyed the *same* privileges and advantages. The new States could not tax the soil within their limits like the other States, and, in that, labored under many inconveniences which the latter did not. He conceived that the mere *mention* of this subject was sufficient to enable this enlightened body to do justice to the new States, and that was all he desired or asked.

Mr. ARCHER observed, that the subject was already brought before the Committee on the Judiciary by the Message of the President.

It being further suggested that a bill on this subject was in a state of preparation—

Mr. REYNOLDS remarked, that he was not heretofore aware of these facts. He knew that the President always did right on this subject—he did not allude to his late Message in particular. But as the subject was before the Committee on the Judiciary, the object was answered, and he would therefore withdraw the resolution; which he did.

The following resolution, which had been agreed to by the House, then came up for reconsideration, of which notice had been given on a former day:

Resolved, That the Committee on the Contingent Expenses of the House be directed to audit the accounts of the members of the committee appointed by the House of Representatives on the 26th day of June last, for investigating the condition and proceedings of the Post Office Department, at the rate of compensation paid to the committee for preparing a code of laws for the District of Columbia, of which Philip Doddridge, Esq. was Chairman, viz: eight dollars per day during the recess, without any other allowance.

Mr. MANN, of New York, moved to reconsider the resolution, for the purpose, as he stated, of offering an amendment thereto.

The motion was agreed to without a division.

Mr. MANN then said he had, with some little trouble, prepared an amendment to this resolution, which he begged to offer to the consideration of the House.

The amendment was then read by the Clerk as follows:

Strike out all after the word resolved, and insert, "That the Committee of Accounts of this House be directed to audit the accounts of the members of the Committee appointed by this House on the 26th day of June last, for investigating the condition and proceedings of the Post Office Department, and allow each member of such committee at the rate of 8 dollars per day, (including a reasonable time for their travelling respectively to the Seat of Government,) during the time they have actually been engaged at the Post Office Department, up to the commencement of the present session."

Mr. M. proceeded by saying, he would take this occasion to remark, that in a consultation with several gentlemen of the House, it had been suggested as a matter of justice to this committee, to allow them, in addition to what was proposed, their usual mileage for travelling expenses, and to that suggestion Mr. M. would yield, by a modification of his amendment, if any gentleman wished to propose it. He would do so for this reason, that when gentlemen were called away on public business, their affairs at home must necessarily suffer; and he was willing, upon principle, that they should be paid the same as in an extra session of Congress. The resolution as amended by him, would give each of these gentlemen about $550, which many of them, perhaps, would be disposed to consider as an inadequate compensation; but whether it would be deemed sufficient by the House, he was not prepared to say. He repeated, he would submit the amendment, and if any gentleman felt disposed to modify it, by allowing the usual travelling expenses of members, Mr. M. would accept the modification.

Mr. WILLIAMS, of North Carolina, was willing to grant the members of this Committee a full, adequate, and just compensation; for there could be no question that their duties had been many and arduous; but he was at a loss to perceive how this could be done in the manner proposed, conformable to the laws at present in force. The laws regulating the pay of members had not been repealed, and, until they were, he could not perceive how they could, constructively, allow this committee the extra pay of mileage. These gentlemen had not performed the journey twice; they came to this city but once, and he thought it neither reasonable nor proper that they should be twice paid. That they should be paid eight dollars per diem he thought just, but not double mileage.

Mr. GILLET would inform the gentleman from North Carolina, that he knew one of the members of the committee who did return home. He came to this city, spent a considerable time here, and returned to his family; so that one, at least, by the gentleman's own principle, would be entitled to his allowance of mileage.

Mr. MILLER said he could see no necessity whatever for the passage of this resolution. The law had fixed the compensation of members, and it was alleged that this committee met on the first of September. Well, that was nothing more than a prolongation of the session, or an anticipation of the meeting of Congress. Their duties were precisely similar to those they would have had to perform during the session, and nothing more, and he could see no necessity for giving them more than the law fixed, viz. eight dollars a day. This could be given them without the resolution proposed.

Mr. MANN, of New York, begged to make a single remark in reference to what had fallen from the gentleman from North Carolina, whose opinions, on such subjects, he was bound to treat with respect. Mr. M. had drawn this resolution, giving the members of the Committee eight dollars a day for the time they were *actually engaged*, and he only said, that it had been *suggested* to him by several gentlemen to give them the mileage, and he had said that if such a modification were proposed, he would accept it. That, having been engaged during the vacation, their necessary business at home must have been neglected, and this offered a reason for the extra pay, though it was not embraced in his amendment. The gentleman from North Carolina said, we could not do this without changing the law. Mr. M. knew the law was peremptory on this subject; but he had supposed it competent for the House to appropriate its own contingent fund, and it was upon that principle he relied.

As to the remark of the honorable member from Pennsylvania, (Mr. Miller,) that these gentlemen would be entitled to their pay of eight dollars a day, as a matter of right, without a resolution, Mr. M. had supposed it necessary, in consequence of its being a special expenditure, out of the ordinary course, and beyond the power of the Committee upon the contingent expences of the House; and he understood that that Committee had heretofore refused, or had, in the present instance, refused to audit these accounts.

Now, for the resolution as drawn up by himself. It would give the members of this Committee pay for sixty-nine days; their session commencing in this city on the first or second of September, exclusive of the time spent in travelling, amounting, in round numbers, to about five hundred and fifty dollars. The original resolution embraced the whole period of time, from the adjournment of the last session of Congress, on the 30th June.

Mr. M. said, he understood the practice had been settled heretofore, that Committees engaged in the business, and by order of the House, should be paid their necessary travelling expenses. Such was the case last session in regard to the Committee appointed to investigate the affairs of the Bank of the United States, who were paid their mileage between the seat of government and the city of Philadelphia, and no more; their wages as members of Congress went on; but they paid all their others, except travelling expenses. In conclusion, he would remark, that notwithstanding the objections of the gentleman from North Carolina, (Mr. Williams,) the House could appropriate as much of its own contingent fund as it thought proper. Mr. M would observe, that he was by no means particularly disposed to give those gentlemen an extraordinary or an unusual compensation, but he was disposed to treat them with liberality.

Mr. GILLET then offered the following amendment to the amendment:

"And that those who came to Washington on said business; and returned home before the commencement of the present session of Congress, be allowed their extra travel and their per diem allowance while attending on said committee, and no more"

Mr. HARPER, of Pennsylvania, said, he was opposed to both amendments, because he considered them unfair, unequal, and unjust in their operations. The reason assigned by one gentleman for allowing this extra compensation was, that the usual daily pay was insufficient. That might be true. They have doubtless attended there at an extra expense, and neglected their business, but he did not think this offered a satisfactory reason for double mileage. Besides, it should be remembered, that some of these gentlemen resided at comparatively a small distance from this city, and others at a very remote distance, and therefore, paying them in the way proposed would be drawing a great distinction in the cases, and be no criterion. One would receive very little, and another a great amount. It was well known that of the compensation received by members of Congress none was so ample as that of mileage. Some received no less than $3,000 mileage, in coming to, and returning from Washington, while that of others did not amount to a hundred dollars. This was the ground of his objection to the first amendment. With regard to the second—It seems that some one or more members of the committee took occasion to return home to attend to their private affairs, and it was proposed not only to pay them their $8 a day during their absence, but also their mileage for going and returning. This would be rewarding them, not for attending to their public duties, but for going home to attend to their private concerns, and abandoning the former. If additional compensation be necessary any where, it ought to be bestowed rather upon those who remained at their post than upon those who went away.

Mr. CROCKETT said, he should oppose both amendments, for he thought the usual pay of $8 a day ample. It was nonsense to talk about its being a sacrifice to come there, for if it was, they would not see so many grasping to be members of Congress. He considered $8 a day a sufficient remuneration for any man, let his business be what it may.

Mr. FILLMORE opposed the claim for extra mileage, and said it was nothing more than a protracted session, or an anticipation of the session, so far as the committee were concerned, and he was willing to give them what the law allowed, but no more.

Mr. MANN wished to offer a few words of explanation. The gentleman from Virginia, seemed to suppose that Mr. M's amendment proposed to pay the committee for all the time of the recess, this was not the case; it only proposed to give them $8 a day for the time they were actually engaged in the performance of their duty. He had said that if that should be considered inadequate, and any gentleman moved an addition, he would not oppose it, but would accept it as a modification. One of Mr. M's colleagues proposed to give them something for going home to attend to —their elections, for we might as well call things by their right names.

Mr. FILLMORE. It proposed to pay them $8 a day, including "a reasonable time for their travelling respectively to the seat of government," and Mr. F. would like to know what was meant by "a reasonable time?" Was it to be a day's pay for every twenty miles, for that was the principle fixed by the law? or how was it to be fixed? It was immaterial what the amount was, the principle was the same, and as he said before, it would be paying them, he would even say rewarding them, for going home to attend to their private business. He was disposed to act liberally, and was willing to allow them for the whole time from the commencement of their session, until that of Congress, whether they were occupied the whole time on the public business or not. His honorable colleague asked if Congress had not power to pay this extra allowance out of its contingent fund. Mr. F. would ask if these persons were to be paid as commissioners or as members of Congress? If as commissioners, an act of appropriation must be passed, if as members of Congress, the existing laws already regulated and fixed what was to be done. The case of the Bank Investigating Committee had been cited as a precedent, but it was not in point, since that committee had to travel out of their usual route; whereas in the case before us, the members travelled from their residences direct to this city, which they must have done if they had not been on the committee. Mr. F. declared his intention of opposing any proposition for extra allowance.

Mr. WARDWELL said, as this seemed to be a New York affair, he would make a few brief remarks. The gentleman who spoke last did not seem to understand what the law was. If Mr. W's recollection was correct, it was that no member of that House was entitled to any pay unless he attended, and if any member went away, without leave, he was also not entitled to pay. He could claim it only for actual attendance upon the duties of the House. Mr. W. said he was opposed to the amendment; not for the reasons assigned by the gentleman from Pennsylvania, who said that those who came from the greatest distance had the advantage. Mr. W. thought otherwise, and that those who lived near home, had the advantage, for they could have a holliday every week, and were not only near enough to give prompt orders about their private affairs, but they might go home every Saturday night. In this case, Mr. W. contended, the House had no power to order the extra mileage, or any more than the lawful $8 per diem. He even doubted whether they had power to pay them as a Committee, but at all events, he was decidedly opposed to paying them more than that.

Mr. R. M. JOHNSON said, it was his intention to submit a very few remarks to the House. He observed, that it was a proper occasion to state, emphatically, that he was opposed to the practice lately introduced of appointing committees to do in the recess what ought to be done during the session of Congress. He hoped that the practice would hereafter cease. It could not, in his opinion, be justified; nor did he think the people would sanction it, whenever the subject was investigated; but having been driven into the measure in self defence, on account of the committee created by the Senate, it had become our duty to fix the rate of compensation to the members, and he was for paying them neither more nor less than the per diem allowance of $8 per day, which all of the members received. Mr. J. said, that it was objected that the per diem allowance embraced the whole recess, and was not limited to the number of days which the committee had been engaged in this city. He understood that the duty of the committee was co-extensive with the confederacy, and not confined to this ten miles square. It extended alike to Maine and St. Louis, and beyond; our Post Offices existed every where; our mail stages and mail coaches were running every where; and he supposed that the committee extended to a minute examination of every thing which concerned the Department, of matters and things in general. The commission was not confined to this place, and if the committee had performed this arduous duty, they deserved pay for every day of the recess, and he would not suppose for a moment that any member of the committee had been deficient. He expected that every member of the committee had so devoted his time to his duty, wherever he was, that he could not, and did not, attend to any other business. It was an interruption of his time, and occupied his mind. If this was not the case, he would not be willing to give full wages. He recollected that during the last session, a sufficient mass of documents had been reported to require two months to examine and understand them. This, he understood, was performed by the committee—no doubt the mass of useless documents would be found to be pretty much like two grains of wheat in a bushel of chaff—yet they were documents, and required examination and close examination. He had conversed with several members of the committee, and he understood from them that they were fully as much employed during the recess as members of Congress during a session, for which we receive by law, and by the will of our constituents, eight dollars per day. Unless, therefore, a better mode of compensation could be devised, he should vote for the original proposition; and he wished to give so much by the day, and not allow mileage, or go into constructive journeys, or the contingent expenses of the committee. If we departed from the rule of paying what we all got while in session, we did not know what we should give, and he wished to know precisely the amount given, and then there was no deception or uncertainty.

Mr. J. said he should not trouble the House any longer on the subject. The whole amount would soon be expended in debate. The committee were willing to take whatever the House would grant, and he should be contented and satisfied, whatever it might be; but, for his part, he would vote for paying a reasonable compensation to the servants of the people, if those servants were faithful, which, in the present instance, he believed to be the case. For his part, he would say, that, while he would make any sacrifice for his country, if duty called for it, yet, for money, he would not have undertaken and executed what had been done by the committee, for double the amount proposed.

The discussion was here arrested by a call, (by Mr. Ashley,) for the orders of the day; which prevailed—yeas 86, nays 72.

The **SPEAKER** laid before the House the following communications:

A letter from the Secretary of the Treasury, in answer to a resolution of the 23d ultimo, transmitting the amount of expenditures heretofore made under certain specific heads, fortifications, internal improvements, light-houses, &c., &c.; laid on the table and ordered to be printed.

A letter from the Secretary of the Treasury, transmitting a list of the clerks in his Department and their compensation; laid on the table and ordered to be printed.

A letter from the Secretary of the Treasury, covering statements of the situation of the several Banks in the District of Columbia; referred to the Committee on the District of Columbia.

The following bills, from the Senate, were read twice and committed:

A bill for the relief of Absalom Lynch, of Mississippi; and

A bill continuing the office of Commissioner of Pensions.

The bill for the relief of Richard T. Archer was read a third time and *passed*.

The House then, on motion of Mr. ARCHER, went into Committee (Mr. WARD in the Chair) on the bill for the benefit of the representatives of Richard W. Meade, deceased.

Mr. HARDIN said, in rising to oppose this claim, he labored under many embarrassments. Among these, the most prominent were its presentation by one of the standing committees of the House, and that committee distinguished, perhaps above others, for the eminent standing and talents of its members. Another source of embarrassment might be found in the circumstance that the claim involved the essential interests of a widow and female orphans. This circumstance had no doubt operated on the generous feelings of various members; but he contended that in settling down on the propriety of allowing this claim, the subject must be divested of all such imposing aspects. Mr. H. here went into a history of the case under consideration. He said Mr. Meade was a resident of the city of Philadelphia until 1804, when he emigrated to Spain, and there embarked in very extensive commercial transactions, in which he was engaged until 1816, when he was thrown into prison by the authorities of Spain, and remained in durance until May, 1818. He that year, or the year after, arrived in the United States. The whole amount of the claim, Mr. H said, was about $491,000, composed of various items, growing out of the contracts existing between Mr. Meade and the Spanish Government; he having furnished that Government with flour and rice to the amount of $4,629,123, between the years 1809 and [illegible]. This vast amount was chiefly for the supply of the Spanish army, and the English troops under the command of Lord Wellington. Indeed, it was believed that those powers never could have sustained themselves against the forces of Napoleon, had it not been for the supplies furnished by Mr. Meade. Mr. H. next adverted to the investigation which this claim had received by the Board of Commissioners appointed to settle the claims of our citizens against Spain, and the opinion of Judge White, one of those Commissioners. [illegible] then proceeded to show, that, according to the laws of nations, Mr. Meade having domiciled himself in Spain, could claim no remedy from this Government, for the defalcation of Spain. But it had been said that by treaty we had given Spain a pretext for refusing to liquidate this claim. That because, by the treaty securing the cession of Florida, we had assumed the payment of five millions of dollars of Spanish claims, and paid out every dollar of the same on authenticated claims, we were bound to pay this claim also. Mr. H. could not subscribe to this doctrine. He protested against the principle of making this government furnish an indemnity for claims which she could not herself recover from the aggressing nation. She did her best to obtain justice for her citizens, and this was all that could reasonably be demanded of her. The proper evidence to substantiate this claim had not been produced to the commissioners, and they decided, (no doubt correctly) against it.

After quoting the opinion of a former Secretary of State, Mr. H. said, that in seeking this claim from the Spanish Government, Mr. [illegible] had said, in a letter to the King, that he was enthusiastic in the cause, for the support of which his supplies were furnished. That he had embarked heart and hand in the cause of Spain and Wellington against France. And what was the result? After the Eagles of France were driven from the soil of Spain, those very troops—the veterans of Wellington were sent over here to war with us. But he thanked God they met with a different reception. They knew not the American character; and dearly did those very men, sustained by the supplies of Mr. Mead, pay the price of their temerity. And now, forsooth, Mr. [illegible] comes forward and asks us to pay for the flour he furnished to Wellington's army—for feeding the enemies of the United States. Mr. H. [illegible] the language of the Secretary, just [illegible] thought this claim, of all others, should [illegible]

TWENTY-THIRD CONGRESS.
SECOND SESSION.

HOUSE OF REPRESENTATIVES.
SATURDAY, January 17, 1835.

to be countenanced on that floor. He concluded by moving to strike out the enacting clause of the bill.

Mr. SUTHERLAND said, some six or seven years ago this claim was before the House. He then examined it, and was fully convinced that it was founded in justice, and advocated it accordingly. From further examination he still retained the same opinion, and would again support it. He remembered also, that the gentleman from Tennessee (Mr. Polk) had opposed the bill on the former occasion. Mr. S. said he would briefly remark in relation to one of the arguments of the gentleman from Kentucky, (Mr. Hardin) against the American claimant; that Mr. Mead, that this point, during the whole discussion, had never been questioned. He was the American Consul at Cadiz, and both Spain and the United States had, on all occasions, conceded the fact, that he was an American citizen. But Mr. S. said he advocated the bill on other ground. It was not a bill to direct the payment of the claim. It did not even refer it to the adjudication of the supreme court. No, it was to be placed in the hands of your own officer for investigation. It was to be sent to the Attorney General, and two audit rs to be designated by the President. He asked if there was a man on that floor who doubted that Mr. Mead had just claim, without reference to its amount? He did not believe there was. It had not, indeed, heretofore been denied. The government, Mr. S. contended, was solemnly bound to permit this prosecution. He explained the reason why the legal vouchers were not produced to the commissioners, when they were investigating these claims. They were not supposed, at first, to be essential, and when they were found to be so, it was too late to procure them from Spain in time for the investigation, though every exertion was made to do so. And because the necessary evidence could not be procured to a specific time, did it become the duty and honor of that House to now plead the statute of limitation against an honest claim? Mr. S. said the present Secretary of State (Mr. Forsyth) was our Minister to Spain at the time the claim in question transpired, and was well acquainted with all the circumstances involved in it. And a gentleman, while a member of the Senate, only introduced a bill for the allowance of Mr. Mead's claim. He would present this fact against Mr. Mead's claim, and the learned argument that might be advanced on the subject. He asked if gentlemen were told to have this claim examined by impartial men of their own choice? After some further magnetic remarks, in the course of which he alluded to the sufferings of Mr. Mead in a Spanish lion's prison, in which he contracted a disease which finally bore him from this world to another, Mr. S. reiterated his solemn belief that this was a just and honest claim. He did not pretend to determine what should be its precise amount; but appealed to the House to suffer that point to be examined. Let us, said he, go into it with clean hands and a pure heart, and give to the widow of the orphan their just due.

Mr. ARCHER next took the floor in favor of a bill, and after addressing the House some fifteen minutes, on his motion the committee rose, reported progress, and obtained leave to sit again; when,

On motion of Mr. WARD, The House adjourned.

IN SENATE.
MONDAY, January 19, 1835.
Petitions and memorials of a private nature, were presented by Messrs. KING of Alabama, WAGER, KENT, BLACK, EWING, FRELINGHUYSEN, MANGUM, and CALHOUN.

Mr. TIPTON presented joint Resolutions from the Legislature of Indiana, relative to the establishment of a port of entry at Lafayette on the Wabash.

Mr. TIPTON, pursuant to notice, and on leave given, introduced a bill for the relief of Saml. and James Smith; which was read twice and ref rred.

The following resolutions, lying on the table, were taken up, considered and adopted:

By Mr. TYLER:
Resolved, That the Committee on Revolutionary Claims be instructed to inquire into the propriety of allowing to the legal representative of Wm. Royall, deceased, interest on the commutation pay allowed by an act passed at the last session of Congress.

By Mr. TIPTON:
Resolved, That the Committee on Pensions be instructed to inquire into the expediency of placing John Smith, of Indiana, on the roll of invalid pensioners, from the date of his first application for a pension, in the year 1817.

The resolution submitted by Mr. BENTON, to recommit the report of the Committee on Finance relative to the investigation made by the Committee into the affairs of the Bank of the United States, was taken up, and on motion of Mr. POINDEXTER, laid on the table till to-morrow.

Mr. GRUNDY, from the Committee on the Post Office, to which the same had been referred, reported without amendment, the bill reducing the postage on periodical pamphlets, and to extend the franking privilege to the Engineer Department.

Mr. WEBSTER, from the Judiciary Committee, to which the same had been referred, reported the bill making an appropriation to pay revolutionary and other pensioners of the United States, without amendment.

Mr. W. also gave notice that he would move to take up the bill to-morrow.

Mr. BELL, from the Committee on Claims, to which the same was referred, reported, without amendment, the bill for the relief of Henry Awkward.

Mr. BELL, from the Judiciary Committee, reported a bill for the relief of Joseph Grant; which was read the first time, and ordered to a second reading.

Mr. TOMLINSON, from the Committee on Pensions, to which the bill from the House of Representatives for the relief of Samuel Hunt was referred, reported the same, without amendment, and gave notice that when the bill came up for consideration, he would move for its indefinite postponement.

The following resolutions were submitted:
By Mr. PORTER:
Resolved, That the Committee on Roads and Canals be instructed to inquire into the expediency of making an appropriation to repair and complete the road leading from the northern boundary line of Arkansas, by Little Rock and Washington, to Fulton, on the north bank of Red river.

By Mr. TIPTON:
Resolved, That the Committee on Roads and Canals be instructed to inquire into the expediency of making an appropriation to repair the military road leading from Fort Jesup, in Louisiana, to Fort Towson, in Arkansas.

By Mr. BENTON:
Resolved, That the Committee on Military Affairs inquire into the expediency of appropriating a suitable sum of money in assisting the officers and soldiers of the army of the United States, at the several military posts, to obtain the services of chaplains.

Mr. WEBSTER, from the Committee on Finance, to which the bill to exempt merchandise imported under certain circumstances from the operation of the tariff law of 1828, had been recommitted, reported the same with two amendments.

Mr. WEBSTER said, that the amendments were

in truth but one amendment, in his view, and went to modify the bill so as to limit its operation to such imports as were made prior to the 30th of September instead of the 30th December, so as to place the act of 1828, in all its sections, upon the same footing as it is placed in the first section.

The bill was then taken up, on motion of Mr. WEBSTER, considered as in Committee of the Whole, and ordered to be engrossed for a third reading.

Mr. CLAYTON, from the Judiciary Committee, reported a bill to provide for the territorial government of Wisconsin.

The unfavorable reports of Committees upon the petitions of Charles Loosan and Simon Power, were severally considered and concurred in.

The following bills were then read the third time and passed:

A bill for the relief of William B. Zantzinger;

A bill for the relief of Tufts and Clark;

A bill for the relief of Francis Laselle, and others;

A bill authorizing the allowance of certain charges in the accounts of the American Consul at London;

A bill for the relief of Thomas J. Mortee.

A bill for the relief of James Thomas;

A bill granting a lot of land to the borough of Mich'limackinaw, for public purposes.

A bill for the relief of Hiram A. Hunter.

The bill to make compensation for French spoliations, prior to 1800, came up as the special order, and on motion of Mr. WEBSTER, was postponed till to-morrow.

The joint resolution, introduced by Mr. KENT, to amend the constitution of the United States, in relation to the veto power, came up for consideration, as in Committee of the Whole, and

On motion of Mr. KENT, was laid in the table.

The bill granting two per cent. of the proceeds of sales of public lands in Alabama, set apart for purposes of public improvement, to purposes of education within that State, was taken up for consideration as in Committee of the Whole.

A protracted and discursive debate ensued upon this bill, which was participated in more or less by Messrs. MOORE, WEBSTER, POINDEXTER, FRELINGHUYSEN, and PRENTISS, who supported the bill, and by Messrs. KING of Ga., KING of Ala., KANE, PORTER, and BLACK, who opposed it.

Mr. MOORE explained the principles of the bill, the object of which, he said, was to change the destination of the proceeds of sales which had been set apart for the construction of roads, to purposes of education, in Alabama. He commented at length upon the necessity of promoting and fostering education; that the fund allowed, proposed to be thus applied, amounted now to about $115,000, but that it was not proposed to change its destination without the assent of Alabama.

Mr. KING of Georgia, said he thought the bill a most extraordinary one. It proposed, virtually, that the rich and respectable State of Alabama should become a charity scholar to the Government of the Union. This two per cent. fund, he said, was as much the money of the nation, for the purposes for which it was originally destined as any other money in the Treasury. The principle of pouring out the money and property of the Union for the exclusive use of the new States was originally wrong, and became more and more as these States continued to progress in wealth and population.

He thought these *nurslings* of ours—the *minors* of the confederacy—had been in the long enough, and he, for one, was disposed the them as early as possible, at least he was was disposed to consider their *education* as He thought at least their proficiency in the branches of science could not be doubted, and in the modern science of political economy, excellence of this science consisted (as he believed

it did,) in securing the greatest possible amount of comfort from the smallest possible share of labor, all must admit them perfect in this branch at least. He said it was almost amusing to see with what apparent confidence gentlemen from these rich and independent States would rise and ask for the charity of the Government. His friend and namesake from Alabama, he said, rose gravely from his seat at the last session, without any suffusion in his countenance, that he recollected, in open day and open Senate, and gave notice that he would introduce a bill to appropriate, he did not recollect how much land, in the States of Alabama or Mississippi, for what purpose would any body guess? Why sir, said he, to educate *the young ladies* of these three rich and powerful States.

Why, sir, said Mr. K., the Senator speaks of educating the poor in Alabama—there was comparatively none there. The southwestern States were blessedly inhabited by Nabobs and Slaves. The slaves were not permitted to receive an education, and their masters were abundantly able to pay for it. If they would propose to take our lands for the education of the really poor of all the States, if there were no constitutional objections, he would seriously think of the proposition; but to be lavishing our gifts on the lords of Alabama, was like the Cormorant picking up crumbs from the Robin, they would do him no good, and yet the Robin might make a meal upon them. Just so he said in this case. These two per cents. and odd acres of the government, were of no consequence to our rich neighbors, but if properly distributed, the benefit of them would be felt. He hoped his friends would not mistake the spirit in which he had made these remarks, but he wished them to understand that he was very serious in his opposition to the bill, and when the Senator from Alabama had made a direct apology to the Senate for introducing such a bill, he should move to lay it on the table.

Mr. WEBSTER said that this fund was a reservation for the purpose of making roads, and this was an application to change the fund, and apply it to purposes of education, and if the State of Alabama preferred it, he saw no reason why we should oppose it. Mr. W. then enlarged on the subject of education, and suggested that two principles should be incorporated in this bill; first, that the schools should be free; that was, without charge; and next, that they should be common, so as to obviate the distinctions of rich and poor among the scholars. He, therefore, suggested an amendment to the bill, that the fund "should be a permanent fund, to establish free common schools," in conformity with his views of the subject.

Mr. POINDEXTER expressed himself satisfied with the amendment, but thought if it was adopted, individuals who were able to contribute something for the support of schools, might perhaps be prevented from doing so.

Mr. KING, of Alabama, was in favor of the amendment suggested by the gentleman from Massachusetts, but he was opposed to the bill. He doubted the power of Congress to change the destination of the fund. And the State of Alabama was not willing, so far as he was informed, that it should be changed. He objected to the bill, too, that it proposed to repeal the ordinance by which Alabama was admitted into the Union. He however, preferred the amendment which went to the establishment of free common schools, if the bill was to pass.

After some conversation between Messrs. EWING, MOORE, and KING, the amendment was agreed to.

Mr. POINDEXTER then moved further to amend the amendment, by striking out the second section, which repealed the ordinance admitting Alabama into the Union; which was agreed to, and the bill was reported to the Senate.

[illegible]ANE then urged as an objection to the the proposition to reserve the two per [illegible] made by Congress to the convention [illegible]sed the Constitution of Alabama, and [illegible]tion accepted it. If this were so, he [illegible] it a constitutional provision, which [illegible] not alter.

[illegible] replied to this objection, that the proposition was not a part of the constitution of the State, but was part of the ordinance. It was not, therefore, a matter of fundamental law, and Congress, with the consent of the State, was perfectly competent to change and modify it as they pleased.

After some further remarks,

Mr. POINDEXTER said that as the other House had a bill before them which was similar to this, he would move to lay the bill on the table, with a view of seeing what disposition should be made of that bill.

The motion was agreed to.

The bill from the House to authorize the Commissioner of Indian Affairs at St. Louis to employ a Clerk, was read the first time.

Mr. POINDEXTER moved to reconsider the vote of Friday last, by which the bill for the relief of William Graham was indefinitely postponed.

Mr. BLACK moved to take up the bill making an appropriation to the road from Lyme creek, in Alabama, to Catahoochie, opposite Columbus; which was agreed to.

Mr. BLACK then moved to reconsider the vote by which the appropriation was required to be taken out of the two per cent. fund, and the bill and motion were then laid on the table.

Mr. CLAY then moved to take up the bill for the relief of the heirs and legal representatives of Moses Shepperd, deceased.

The bill was supported by Messrs. SMITH, HENDRICKS, LEIGH, and TYLER, and opposed by Messrs. HILL, BLACK, and SHEPLEY.

The question being about to be taken, Mr. BLACK moved an adjournment; which was disagreed to on a division—yeas 15, nays 17.

The question being on ordering the bill to be engrossed for a third reading,

Mr. WRIGHT demanded the yeas and nays; which were ordered, and are as follow:

YEAS—Messrs. Clay, Clayton, Ewing, Frelinghuysen, Hendricks, Kent, Knight, Leigh, Linn, McKean, Moore, Naudain, Poindexter, Porter, Prentiss, Robbins, Silsbee, Smith, Southard, Tomlinson, Tyler, Webster—22.

NAYS—Messrs. Benton, Bibb, Black, Brown, Buchanan, Cuthbert, Grundy, Hill, Kane, King of Alabama, King of Georgia, Mangum, Morris, Preston, Robinson, Shepley, Swift, Tipton, Waggaman, White, Wright—21.

So the question was decided in the affirmative.

Mr. CLAY then gave notice that, to-morrow, he would move the Senate to go into the consideration of Executive business, and, on his motion,

The Senate adjourned.

HOUSE OF REPRESENTATIVES.

MONDAY, January 19, 1835.

Petitions and memorials were presented by—

Mr. KAVANAGH, of Maine;

Mr. EVERETT, of Massachusetts.

REMOVAL OF THE INDIANS.

Mr. E. EVERETT said he had been requested to present to the House a memorial from a council of Cherokee Indians, held at Running Water, in the Cherokee country, in behalf of those members of that tribe, who were desirous of removing from their present location to the country west of the Mississippi. The memorial had been intrusted to him by a delegation who were at this moment in attendance in the House. The signatures, he understood, were attached to the original memorial, to be presented to the other branch of the Legislature, the present being a certified copy thereof. The signatures were fif-seven in number, twenty of them being in the hand-writing of those whose names they purported to be, the remaining thirty seven being subscribed in the usual manner of persons who were themselves unable to write. It was accompanied by a certificate setting forth that it was adopted in open council, and he was satisfactorily informed, that the memorial was the unaided composition of one of the subscribers, Mr. John Ridge, well known to many members of the House as a highly distinguished individual of the Cherokee tribe. By that gentleman, and two of his associates, Mr. E. had been personally requested to present the memorial. He should further state, that it was also accompanied by a series of resolutions adopted at the same council, expressing, in a more precise and definite form, the principles set forth, somewhat at large, in the memorial.

Mr. E. supposed it would be in order, and indeed it might be expected, that he should ask for the reading of the memorial and accompanying resolutions *in extenso*, but as all the documents were of considerable length, and would occupy too much of the time of the House, he would content himself, in lieu thereof, with briefly stating their purport and substance. The memorialists set out by stating their undoubted conviction of their right to the soil on which they were born, and the injury that would be done them by the policy of removing them therefrom. Now, without in the least degree going into a discussion on this subject, for his purpose was very different, he would only say that he felt it due to himself to state, that in this view, he fully concurred with them. They then go on to state the astonishing improvements made in the arts of civilization in the Cherokee tribes. Improvements, said Mr. E., known to many members of this House, and to none, Mr. Speaker, better than to yourself, and which have excited the attention of philanthropists both in this country and in Europe. The memorialists then state their undoubted and sorrowful conviction that in the present state of affairs, it would be impossible for them to retain their national existence, or to carry on their progress in the arts of civilization and humanity, and in consequence of this much to be deplored state of affairs they have been led to turn their eyes to the West, to the countries now unoccupied, and they desire—and it is the object of their memorial to set forth that desire—that with the aid, and under the protection, of the United States of America, they hope to accomplish that object. In considering this subject, the memorialists state, that there are some interesting points which, in their opinion, are matters of legislation for both Houses of Congress. They wish to be furnished with some means to enable them to remove with greater comfort and convenience, as some compensation for the many and great sacrifices they must necessarily make in giving up and abandoning their lands and improvements, to be paid to them *not here*, but on their arrival in the region West of the Mississippi. They also think they may reasonably ask for further legislation on the part of Congress, to ensure to them those civil and political privileges which become the dignity and character of the United States to guaranty to them. It might be thought that some of those objects came more properly within the compass of the treaty-making power, but they had stated, and Mr. E. thought correctly, that some of those objects were within the province of Congress. They then go on to set forth, that in the present disastrous condition of their nation, it was exceedingly doubtful whether any treaty could be framed that would meet with the unanimous approbation of the members of the tribe. They also doubt whether, in their present situation, parties could be found whom this Government would be disposed to recognise. In this state of things they have thought their only resource would be to lay their real situation before—and to confide in the justice, the clemency, the liberality, and the indulgence of—the two Houses of Congress.

Mr. E. regretted to find that there were at this time two parties among the Cherokee tribe of Indians, whose views were greatly at variance on the great policy to be pursued; but with these matters he would not presume to interfere, one way or the other. He believed this was all he had need to say by way of setting forth the object and substance of the memorial.

Before taking his seat, Mr. E. said, he should move the reference of all these papers to the Committee on Indian Affairs. That committee very fairly represented all sides of the House upon this great, embarrassing, and delicate question, and he did not think it improper to state that the bills reported from that committee, together with the provisions of the one not yet acted on, were highly acceptable. If the committee should consider that these documents contained matter of legislation, as he firmly believed they did, for these

claimants, and if they should find that Congress can do any thing, as he also believed it could much—to restore harmony between the parties in the Cherokee nation, and to smooth the way for those now willing to emigrate—if they can do any thing to heal the wounds of the Indians, and to quiet their minds on the ground of political, social, and civil liberty, he was sure the House and the country both would sustain the committee.

Mr. E. continued. He certainly never thought, four years ago, that it would fall to his lot to present a memorial to that House, having for its object to facilitate the removal of an Indian tribe from the spot of their birth to the region west of the Mississippi. As little did it enter his mind, that he should ever be requested to present such a memorial from the Indians themselves, by the delegates and representatives of a great tribe, for that purpose. It had been handed to him by three individuals of high standing among their brethren, two of whom were well known by himself to have been among the most intelligent and active of their brethren, when the great stand was made in favor of what was understood by those on this side of the House to be the rights of the Indians, and the duties of the United States towards them. He believed it was the lesson of wisdom to yield to the force of circumstances, and it was Mr. E.'s conviction, and he believed of those friends who acted with him on that occasion, that it has become unavoidably necessary that the Indians should yield to the necessity of their condition. That opinion he had expressed in conjunction with those whose opinions were of far greater weight and influence than his own, even to the Indians themselves. He believed it would have been better—and he mourned it as much as any man could—but he believed it would have been better that they should have yielded at that time. He now believed it impossible for the Cherokees to enjoy their political, social, moral, and religious rights and privileges, by remaining where they were. He believed, moreover, that the longer they stayed, the more they would suffer, and further, that the time never would come in which they could make better terms with the government than at present. He was willing and anxious that all that was possible should be done to sooth their feelings, and prevent their rights from being infringed upon or subverted, and it was in the hope that it was not too late to effect this, that he had made it his duty, at the request of the memorialists, to present their memorial to the House. If any thing could be done for their relief, he was sure the House would do all in its power, and let us do all that we can, and Mr. E. we shall remain greatly the debtors of this unfortunate people. Mr. E. concluded by moving that the memorial and accompanying papers be referred to the Committee on Indian Affairs and printed.

The reference was made accordingly, and the motion to print was agreed to.

Petitions were further presented by—
Mr. BURGES, of Rhode Island;
Mr. YOUNG, of Connecticut;
Messrs. WHITE, CAMBRELENG, HAZELTINE, and WARD, of New York.

[Mr. WARD presented the petition of Clinton Roosevelt, of the State of New York, wherein he sets forth that he has discovered a mode of building steam vessels of war, which are capable of approaching an enemy's vessel of any force, and by means of a torpedo affixed to the prow projecting under water, to destroy the vessel attacked without endangering the steam battery. Mr. W. stated that the petitioner had furnished certificates from Professors Renwick and Hackley, of N. York, that they have examined the principle on which this improvement is founded; and that it appears to them to be feasible; that they were not aware of any important practical difficulties which would prevent its being carried into effect.

The petition and documents were referred to the Committee on Naval Affairs.]

Messrs. WAGENER, BINNEY, BANKS, McKENNAN, DENNY, and STEWART, of Pennsylvania.

[Mr. WAGENER presented the petition and documentary evidence of Christian Bixler Jacob

Weygandt, executor of Jacob Weygandt, deceased; William Brown, administrator of General Robert Brown, and Jacob Boyer, administrator of Jacob Dreisback, deceased, sureties of Nicholas Kern, collector of direct taxes and internal duties during the war of 1812—15, praying for a passage of a law to discharge them from all alleged liabilities under the said bonds. The purport of the petition is, that Nicholas Kern, during the late war, was appointed collector of direct taxes and internal duties, and the above persons became his sureties. That the accounts of N. Kern, were not settled until the year 1826, when it appeared he was a defaulter. Under a warrant from the Fifth Auditor, he was committed to jail, and was discharged by order of the President of the United States. Suits have now been instituted against the surviving sureties and the representatives of those deceased. From the evident gross neglect of the officers of government in permitting his accounts to be unsettled for ten years and upwards, and no notice given to the sureties of the debt, and the probability, had the sureties been apprised of the delinquency, in a reasonable time, much, if not all, might have been recovered, presents a strong equitable case for the interposition of Congress.]

Mr. MILLIGAN, of Delaware;
Messrs. THOMAS, McKIM, and CARMICHAEL, of Maryland;
Messrs. CHINN, BEALE, LUCAS, BOUSE, PULTON, GORDON, and WISE, of Virginia;
Messrs. GRIFFIN and FELDER, of South Carolina;
Messrs. SCHLEY, GILMER, and FOSTER, of Georgia;
Messrs. MARSHALL, ALLAN, and JOHNSON, of Kentucky;
Messrs. THOMSON, PATTERSON, KILGORE, VANCE, CRANE, and WHITTLESEY, of Ohio;

[Mr. PATTERSON presented three petitions from the citizens of the State of Ohio, one for the improvement of the harbor at the mouth of Vermilion river, one for the improvement of the harbor at port Clinton, and a third for a mail route from Perrysburgh, in Wood County, to Melmore in Seneca county.]

Messrs. McCARTY, HANNEGAN, and KINNARD, of Indiana;

[Mr. KINNARD presented the petition and report of the Levenworth and Bloomington Rail Road Company, in the State of Indiana.]

[Mr. McCARTY presented the petition of sundry citizens of Henry county, Indiana, for a post route from Knightstown to Pendleton, which, on his motion, was referred to the Committee on the Post Office and Post Roads.]

Mr. PLUMMER, of Mississippi;

[Mr. PLUMMER presented a memorial of the President and Directors of the West Feliciana Rail-road Company, asking the grant of a township of land to aid them in the construction of a road from St. Francisville, in Louisiana, to Woodville, in Mississippi; referred to the Committee on Public Lands.

A petition, signed by Wm. Rupe, President, and S. E. Godhard, Secretary, of a meeting of the settlers on the public lands, praying Congress to extend the provisions of the pre-emption act of June 19th, 1834, to all actual settlers prior to the first of January, 1835; referred to the Committee on Public Lands.

The petition of John Tucker, praying for a pre-emption right to enter a quarter section of land at the minimum price of $1 25 per acre; referred to the Committee on Public Lands.

The petition of Edward Mitchell, praying for a grant of land as a remuneration for services rendered by his wife, in 1810, in the employ of the Government, in teaching the art of spinning and weaving among the Choctaw Indians; referred to the Committee on Public Lands.

On motion of Mr. PLUMMER, the petition of Benjamin Roach, and accompanying documents, presented at the last session of Congress, praying permission to relinquish certain lands and locate others in lieu thereof, were referred to the Committee on Public Lands.

Mr. PLUMMER also presented additional testimony in support of the petition.

On motion of Mr. PLUMMER, the following petitions, memorials, and claims, heretofore presented to the House, were again referred:

The petition of Wm. L. S. Deming, to the Committee on Claims;

The petition of the heirs of Henry King, to the Committee on Revolutionary Claims;

The petition of Right Fore, to the Committee on Invalid Pensions;

The memorial of the President and Trustees of Mississippi College;

The memorial of the Trustees of Oakland College;

The claim of Zachariah Dixon; and

The claim of Edward Jones, to the Committee on Public Lands;

The petition of Joseph W. Hegemen;

The petition of John K. Goff;

The petition of the heirs of Col. John Ellis;

The petition of Woodson Wren; and

The petition of Silya la Vick, to the Committee on Private Land Claims;

The petition of John H. Horn, to the Committee on Indian Affairs.]

Messrs. MAY and REYNOLDS, of Illinois.

[Mr. REYNOLDS presented the case of the owners of lots in the village of Peoria, in the State of Illinois, with accompanying documents from the honorable the Secretary of the Treasury. Mr. R. observed, that this village was the first place settled in the Illinois country, and that the citizens had not yet obtained a right to their property in said village. The only request was for a small appropriation, to enable the Surveyor General to survey the lots, whereupon patents would issue.

He also presented the papers of Capt. Stacy McDonough, of Illinois, showing that he was entitled to a pension for his wounds received in the year 1793.]

Messrs. MARDIS and MURPHY, of Alabama;
Mr BULL, of Missouri;
Mr. RENCHER, of North Carolina.

Which petitions and memorials were appropriately referred.

Mr. POPE gave notice that he would on next Wednesday week, move the House to resolve itself into a committee of the whole on the state of the Union, for the purpose of considering bill No. 342, in relation to the Louisville and Portland Canal.

Mr. CHILTON gave notice that he would, on Monday next, move the House to go into committee, on the bill to extend the provisions of the act of 1832, granting pensions to the officers and soldiers of the revolution. Mr. C. presented an amendment to said bill, which was ordered to be print d.

Mr. PLUMMER, by consent, submitted the following resolutions, which were agreed to:

Resolved, That the Committee on Public Lands be instructed to inquire into the expediency of passing a law, authorizing Isaac Richmond, Jonah White, Conway Oldham, Daniel Richmond, David Clay, Ignatius Bankston, Samuel Hackenbury, Jefferson Clay, George Simmons, Samuel B. Parrish, Thomas C. McMackin, David Mobray, and John Ba'four, and others, persons who were entitled to pre-emption rights to eighty acres of land, under the provisions of an act of Congress, passed on the 2d day of March, 1833, entitled "an act supplementary to the several laws for the sale of public lands," and were prevented from making their entries under said act, in consequence of a decision of the officers of Government against their rights, to enter in lieu thereof the same quantity of unappropriated land elsewhere, within the same land district, at the minimum price of $1 25 per acre; and that the accompanying documents be referred to said Committee.

Resolved, That the Committee on Public Lands be instructed to inquire into the expediency of referring so much of the act entitled "An act supplemental to the several laws for the sale of public lands," approved April 5th, 1832, as provides that "no person shall be permitted to enter more than one half quarter section of land in quarter quarter sections or tracts of forty acres, and in no case, unless he intends it for cultivation, or for the use of his improvement." Also, into the expediency of repealing so much of said act as requires the

person applying to make an entry under its provisions, to file an affidavit before making the entry.

Resolved, That the Committee on Public Lands be instructed to inquire into the expediency of granting to the State of Mississippi a quantity of land equal to that granted to the other new States of the Union for purposes of Internal Improvement.

Resolved, That the Committee on the Post Office and Post Roads be instructed to inquire into the expediency of establishing the following post routes: From Memphis, in Tennessee, to Coffeeville, in Mississippi; from Lagrange or Bolivar, in Tennessee, by Point Veto, to Leflore, in Mississippi; from Tuscumbia, Alabama, to Point Veto, in Mississippi; from Doak's Stand, by Canton, to Clinton, in Mississippi.

Mr. MILLIGAN offered the following resolution, which, under the rule, lies one day:

Resolved, That the Secretary of War be instructed to furnish to this House a copy of Captain Delafield's report on the condition of the harbor in the river Delaware, accompanied by an estimate of the repair and preservation of the same.

On motion of Mr. BURGES,

Resolved, That the Committee on the Judiciary be directed to inquire into the expediency and economy of so altering and amending the laws of the United States, that thereafter all printing whatever, required to be done for the United States, in any part of the public service, shall be done and performed within the District of Columbia, and that no such printing shall be done by any person or persons who may be concerned in any way of emolument with a public journal or newspaper.

On motion of Mr. TURNER,

Resolved, That the Committee on the Post Office and Post Roads be instructed to inquire into the expediency of providing by law, that in future all contracts for carrying the mail shall be specific for each route, and that where the same contractor shall contract for more than one route, each route shall be distinctly designated, and the amount of compensation for each be distinctly and explicitly stated, with the number of miles in each route, and by what mode of conveyance the mail is transported on each route.

On motion of Mr. BYNUM,

Resolved, That the Committee on Commerce be instructed to inquire into the expediency of making the port of Williamston, in the State of North Carolina, a port of entry.

On motion of Mr. JOHNSON, of Louisiana,

Resolved, That the Committee on the Post Office and Post Roads, be instructed to inquire into the causes of the frequent failures in transporting the mail between Washington City and New Orleans.

On motion of Mr. McCARTY,

Resolved, That the Committee on the Public Lands be instructed to inquire into the expediency of granting to the State of Indiana, with a view to the construction of a rail road or canal in the valley of the White Water, such of the public lands lying within said State, in the Cincinnati Land District, as have been in market for twenty years, with such other grants in the adjoining districts, as the policy of the country and the advancement of such improvements may seem to said committee reasonable, just, and proper.

On motion of Mr. EWING,

Resolved, That the Committee on the Post Office and Post Roads be instructed to inquire into the expediency of establishing a post road from New Maysville, to pass thence through Bainbridge, Poplar Spring, Blakesburg, and Russellville, in Putnam county, to Rockville, Parke county, Indiana.

Mr. LYTLE, by consent, submitted the following joint resolution; which was read and ordered to a second reading:

Resolved by the Senate and House of Representatives, That the President of the United States be authorized to employ Hiram Powers, of Ohio, to execute in Italy, the Busts of the several Presidents of the United States, to be placed in the Rotundo of the Capitol, at such compensation as will bear a relative value to the sums heretofore paid and contracted to be paid to other artists, for work of similar character, and to make, from time to

time, such advances as may be necessary, in his judgment, for the progress and completion of the work.

Mr. JARVIS, from the Committee on Public Buildings, reported the following joint resolution:

Resolved by the Senate and House of Representatives of the United States in Congress assembled, That the Commissioner of Public Buildings be directed to cause the Statues executed by ing L. Persico, to be placed in the niches in front of the Capitol, for which they were originally intended.

The resolution was read a first and second time, when Mr. JARVIS moved its engrossment.

Objection being made, Mr. JARVIS moved a suspension of the rule; which was agreed to, Yeas 130, nays not counted.

After a short conversation between Messrs. PEARCE and JARVIS, the resolution was read a third time and passed.

Mr. FULTON, from the Committee on Claims, reported a bill for the relief the executor of Charles Wilkins, deceased; which was read twice and committed.

Mr. CARR, from the Committee on Private Land Claims, reported a bill for the relief of William O'Neal and Robert Morrison, of Indiana; which was read twice, and ordered to be engrossed and read the third time to-morrow.

Mr. CARR, from the same committee, asked to be discharged from the farther consideration of the petition of Eley Segura and others; which was ordered to lie on the table.

Mr. SUTHERLAND, from the Committee on Commerce, reported, with an amendment, the bill in relation to buoys, light-boats, &c.; which was ordered to be printed.

Mr. MILLER, from the Committee on Invalid Pensions, reported a bill for the relief of Benjamin Holland; which was read twice, and committed.

Mr. HARPER, from the Committee on Commerce, reported a bill for the relief of Isaac Champlin and others; which was read twice, and committed.

Mr. FOSTER, from the Committee on the Judiciary, reported a bill to allow additional compensation to the District Attorney of the United States for the District of South Carolina; which was read twice, and committed.

Messrs. GRENNELL, KINNARD, GILMER, and McINTIRE, each made unfavorable reports upon petitions, &c. which had been referred to their respective Committees; which were laid on the table.

[On motion of Mr. KINNARD, the Committee on Revolutionary Claims was discharged from the further consideration of the petition of the heirs of Ralph R. Horn; and the same was referred to the Committee on Revolutionary Pensions. Mr. K., from the Committee on Revolutionary Claims, made an unfavorable report on the petition of John Crooper, executor of Warren Ashley.]

On motion of Mr. POLK, the House proceeded to the consideration of the orders of the day and the bills upon the Speaker's table.

The following bills from the Senate were read a first and second time, and committed:

A bill for the relief of Thomas J. Morti e;

A bill to authorize the allowance of certain charges in the accounts of the American Consul at London;

A bill for the relief of James Thomas;

A bill granting to the borough of Mackinaw certain grounds, for public purposes;

A bill for the relief of Hiram A. Hunter;

And a bill for the relief of Andrew Knox.

An engrossed bill, authorizing the Superintendent of Indian Affairs at St. Louis to employ a Clerk, was read a third time, and passed.

The House resumed the consideration of the bill making appropriations for certain fortifications for the year 1836.

Mr. PARKER moved the same amendment to the bill in the House that he had previously offered in the committee of the whole on the state of the Union, to strike out the 12th, 13th, and 14th lines, making an appropriation of $50,000 for the fortification of Throg's Neck, near the city of New York.

Mr. PARKER repeated the objections which

he entertained against the appropriation. He wished Congress to examine and understand it, in the language of the homely adage, "look before you leap." He read several documents relative to the work which computed its cost at $577,000. He thought the great question was the House should be, whether the money could not be expended to better advantage in other fortifications. He considered all appropriations for this object, a waste of the public funds. He believed Hellgate to be a better and safer protection to the city of New York, from that point of the compass, than the fortifications on Throg's Neck could ever be. Mr. P. said he remembered that during the last war, no one anticipated an attack of the enemy from that quarter.

Mr. P. concluded by saying that he opposed this appropriation as a friend to the bill, and the general system of fortification. He deemed it not only useless, but calculated to excite ridicule.

Mr. MORGAN, of New York, said that the appropriation for the defence of New York harbor, now moved to be stricken out, was certainly not a large one. He had not expected, therefore, that any gentleman would move to have it stricken out; least of all had he expected that the gentleman from New Jersey would have made such a motion. The gentleman from New Jersey was our neighbor, our next-door neighbor, but it is true that he is our neighbor on the safe side. The gentleman resides on those pleasant shores of New Jersey which form the western boundary of New York harbor; and those shores, including the gentleman's residence, are well protected by the forts on Staten Island, and the other islands in that part of the harbor. But how is it in respect to the approach to the City of New York from the sea, on the other side; that is, by the arm of the sea, called the Sound, or East river? Very different indeed. There is not a gun mounted, nor a proper place to mount it on, between the sea and the city, and your Navy Yard. On this side, the City of New York is now exactly in the condition that a house would be, the owner of which, fearing an enemy, had secured one door with bolt and bars, and chains and locks, and entirely forgetting that there was another door to his house, had left it open to the assailant. Indeed, the gentleman who made the motion to strike out, ought to think that the formidable pass, which he called Hellgate, would be a sufficient defence to us. But, sir, even the terror of a name did not exist for our defence; for learned antiquaries and etymologists had shown, that the name of this pass it had gate—not Hellgate. In the olden time, the rocks producing the rapid and roaring currents of this pass, were indeed objects of terror, so terrible to our ancestors as were the Scylla and Charybdis of the Italian seas. But Scylla and Charybdis, have been alike stripped of their terrors, by the skill and enterprise of modern times. Sir, vessels of all sizes may go through this pass with perfect safety. There is not an hour of the day when it is not whitened by innumerable sails: the whole coasting trade, the largest steam boats are constantly passing through it. The first case, I believe, of the passage of a large ship through Hurlgate, occurred during the revolutionary war. A British fifty gun ship, commanded by a namesake of the honorable gentleman from New Jersey, the gallant Parker, pursued by a French squadron, was carried by his safety through this pass. During the last war between England and France, two French ships of the line, the Dido and the Cyane, pressed it, to avoid a British squadron at Sandy Hook. In the late war, our own frigates of the largest class went through its the President I believe did so—that ship which was lost to us, by carrying away part of her false keel in passing the bar of Sandy Hook, the entrance to New York harbor, which is acknowledged to be well fortified. There is not a doubt, Mr. Speaker, that the passage of the Sound, the defence of which has been so utterly neglected, is practicable to vessels drawing any depth of water; and that the city of New York Yard is attached to it, are utterly without defence against an enemy making his attack in that direction. And will this House leave that city exposed

this danger by striking out the appropriation. That city, sir, which is one of the greatest commercial marts, if not the greatest commercial mart in the world—that city where two thirds of your revenue are collected, and consequently, two-thirds of all imports from abroad are received—that city, which is daily receiving the rich freights of the South, and the innumerable cargoes of the East—that city, into which are pouring every hour of the day, by means of the Hudson, and by the Northern and Western canals, and by the Ohio canals, and the great lakes, the vast productions of the North and of the West. All these, sir, are constantly accumulating in this great market. And to whom do they belong? Not to New York city alone, but to the planter of the South, the farmer and manufacturer of the East, and of the North, and of the West. And is it not not the interest of the nation, and the duty of this House, to protect their property? But there is a more solemn duty than this imposed upon this House. The City of New York contains nearly three hundred thousand people;—if there be any use in fortifications at all: —if the men of this city are to have any thing more than their naked breasts to present to an enemy, come with what force, and in what manner he may, then have they a right to expect of you, the defence of their wives, their children, and their firesides, by this appropriation—and they do expect it.

Mr. FERRIS followed on the same side of the question, and dwelt at considerable length, on the preponderating commercial consequence of New York—the great proportion of revenue which she yields to the General Government, and the justice of that government securing to her an efficient protection from foreign aggression. Mr. F. went into an examination and review of the objections advanced by the gentleman from New Jersey (Mr. Parker,) to the appropriation, in the course of which he referred to various documents and reports from the Departments of the Government. He referred to the landing of General Howe and the British army under his command on this point during the war of the revolution, and glanced at some of the historical facts connected with that period. He said New York had contributed large and liberally to her own defence, and the question for the House was, whether this 300,000 of our people were entitled to this small appropriation in aid of their common defence.

Mr. POLK said he rose simply to repeat the facts under which this appropriation was placed in the bill. On a former occasion he had opposed an appropriation for this work, but then the House solemnly determined to proceed with the work. It was now inserted according to the estimate of the Department, and the question seemed to be whether this appropriation should be made or the money already expended on the work be thrown to the winds. Mr. P addressed some further explanatory remarks on the object of the appropriation, and

Mr. FERRIS supplied some omissions which he had made in his topographical description of the assailable points of the city and vicinity of New York.

Mr. BATES said he recollected that the other day when the proposition was made by his colleague (Mr. E. Everett) for an appropriation for Fort Independence in Boston Harbor, it met with opposition from a quarter where it was least expected. The amount of United States shipping and property in that harbor could not secure that appropriation. Now, (said Mr. B.) I am in favor of this appropriation, which is precisely analagous to that proposed for Fort Independence; and in order to show the consistency of gentlemen, on the question, he would ask for the ayes and noes.

They were ordered.

Mr. TRUMBULL spoke aginst the amendment and in favor of retaining the appropriation in the bill. He referred to the remark of the gentleman from New Jersey (Mr. Parker) in relation to the protection afforded by the danger of navigating the Hurlgate. That gentleman must be aware that at certain periods of the tide, that place was perfectly safe and harmless in navigation. It was navigated daily by vessels bearing the commerce of his own state, (Connecticut) and steamboats to and from the city of New York. He thought the fortification highly essential to his own constituents, as well as to the citizens of New York, and others."

Mr. PARKER explained. He had not denied, that at a certain state of the wind and tide, this place could be passed.

Mr. CAMBRELING, alluded to the remark of the gentleman from Massachusetts (Mr. Bates) who had demanded the yeas and nays in order to convict members of inconsistency. Mr. C. said there was an appropriation already passed in the bill, for the benefit of Boston Harbor, precisely analagous to this one. That proposed for the reconstruction of Fort Independence, could not properly be so considered.

Mr. BATES said, the only difference was, that one appropriation was contained in the bill as reported, and the other was not.

Mr. EVERETT, of Massachusetts, addressed the House for a few minutes in explanation of his views of these appropriations.

Mr. WARDWELL said, it seemed the gentleman from Massachusetts, (Mr. Bates,) had demanded the ayes and noes in order to test the votes of the N. York delegation. He did not regret this. He was free to confess that he voted against the proposition to rebuild Fort Independence because it had not come to the House recommended by the proper committee. With regard to the appropriation under discussion, it was not a matter of any peculiar personal interest to himself or his immediate constituents, as he came from the interior of the State. The subject, however, he was aware was vitally important to the commerce of Massachusetts and Connecticut—much more so than to the people of New York.

Mr. FERRIS rose to make a further reference to a report of the Board of Engineers, which he read.

Mr. E. EVERETT said he perfectly coincided with the gentleman from New York (Mr. Wardwell,) as to the importance of this work to his constituents, as well as to others; and he assured him that he should take pleasure in recording his vote in favor of the appropriation. He was not sorry the yeas and nays had been demanded. But the gentleman had said the appropriation for fort Independence in Boston harbor had not been recommended by a proper committee. He would ask what committee could be more appropriate for a military work than that on military affairs? They had recommended it; but it would be impossible to procure justice on this point, until Congress should determine to pay some respect to the recommendations of the engineers employed by the Government.

Mr. DICKINSON said, at the last session of of Congress there were some principles laid down by it, which he would now gladly see acted upon; one of which was to build no more forts until those which are already built and decaying, were armed. He said while there was a speck of war descernible in our political horizon, he thought it would better become the nation to look to her immediate and important points of defence, and equip her forts already erected, than to attempt new ones. He would choose too, to see both our army and navy composed of American citizens, which was far from being the case at present; particularly the latter, as he was credibly informed that from a boatswain downwards our navy consisted of three Englishmen to one native born citizen! He hoped the House would sustain itself in its former principles by rejecting not only this appropriation but that for Boston also.

Mr. WARD, of New York, said he should detain the House with only a few observations upon the amendment under consideration He would not have said a word on the subject, but for the remarks of the honorable gentleman from Massachusetts, (Mr. Bates,) which he considered as rather invidious towards the New York delegation. That honorable gentlemen had called for the yeas and nays on the question, for the purpose, he said, of showing the consistency of gentlemen on the question; most of the members from New York having, as he alleged, voted against the appropriation for Fort Independence, in Boston harbor. That opposition, the gentleman remarked, came from an unexpected quarter, and he now seemed desireus of ascertaining whether a question in which the State of New York is, in like manner, interested, the delegation from New York would vote for or against the proposition. This charge of inconsistency, Mr. W. said, would not apply to him, for he had voted for the appropriation alluded to, though, on reflection, he was led to doubt the propriety of that vote, for the reason that the appropriation had not been recommended by the Committee of Ways and Means, to which the investigation of the subject properly belonged. But, after hearing the argument on the subject, in the Committee of the Whole, he was induced to vote for it, chiefly by the consideration that it was highly important to put the city of Boston in a perfect state of defence. It was his wish that no distinction should ever be made betwixt one State and another, as to the fortification of our sea board. Mr. W. said, he would take this occasion to declare, that he would vote for no appropriation the sole object of which was merely to benefit a State by the expenditure of public money within its limits, and he had no doubt that every member of the House would join him in the declaration. The decision of this question, therefore, would not be governed by any such policy. The expenditure of $30,000, which is the whole sum proposed in the State of New York, was not an object, in that point of view, worthy of the slightest consideration. He believed that the completion of the fort at Throg's neck was essential to the defence of a city which was the acknowledged commercial emporium of our country, and for that reason alone, he should vote against the motion to strike out this appropriation. The honorable gentleman from Tennessee, (Mr. Dickinson,) seemed to think that we should go on to complete the works already commenced before we began any others, and that we should rely for our own defence from foreign aggression, not upon fortresses, but the stout hearts and strong arms of our citizens.

Mr. W. differed with his honorable friend. He considered, he said, that men of the strongest nerves, sometimes, and under certain circumstances, required a shelter from the enemy. It was, he thought, undisputed, that skilful and scientific fortifications were one of the cheapest, as well as most efficient modes of defence. By a proper system of fortifications, our cities and harbors would be defended at a less expense, both of life and treasure, than by the bare exposure to the enemy of the freeman's breast. The fort on Throg's Neck was not a new work, as the honorable gentleman supposed. It had already been commenced, and it belonged to the plan of fortifications recommended under a former Administration, for the defence of our commercial cities by a distinguished individual, now a member of the other branch of our national legislature, and then at the head of the War Department (Mr. Calhoun,) a plan which that gentleman and his friends have great reason to be proud of, and which, if ever carried into full effect, would secure our widely extended country from the insults and assaults of any foreign force. All that was left for Congress to do was to carry out the noble system which had already been begun, and in a few years our cities and harbors, with the vast amount of property always collected in them, in the security of which the citizens of every part of our country are deeply and directly interested, will be [illegible] beyond the reach of danger from foreign ho[illegible] whereas a neglect of these defences would [illegible] and facilitate aggression. It was said that we required no forts for our security. To this remark he would barely reply that it would be difficult to satisfy the enlightened representatives of a great and free People at this day, that we could, with safety dispense with these means of national defence.

He would not now enter into a discussion of the general question, whether fortifications were necessary to national defence, for it was sufficient to say that, from the earliest period of which we have any record, down to the present time, civilized nations have relied upon them in a [illegible] measure, for their security from invasion a[illegible]

sault. He adverted to the gallant and successful defence made by our brave troops, under the command of Col., afterwards General Hamilton, at Mud fort, in the Delaware, during the Revolutionary war, as an illustration of the advantage of such works. The advance of the B itish armament was impeded by that fort for a great length of time, thereby affording our army an opportunity to take up a secure position near the city of Philadelphia, which afterwards fell into the hands of the enemy. If the works on Throg's Neck, which had been commenced, should be now abandoned, all the money which had been expended there would be a total loss to the country. As a proof of the importance of this position to the security of New York, it had been stated, and, to his own knowledge, stated correctly, by his colleague, (Mr. Jarvis,) that General Howe selected this very point as the place for debarking the British army during the war of the revolution, with the view of dislodging the American army from the city and island of New York. During the whole of that war, it was considered as one of the most important, and one of the most assailable positions in the vicinity of New York; and such, he had no doubt, would again be the case in the event of another war. He, therefore, hoped the House would not strike out the appropriation, and more especially since it had undergone the scrutiny and received the sanction of the Committee of Ways and Means, to which the subject properly belonged.

Mr. MANN, of N. Y. said, if this was an original proposition, he should have no hesitation whatever in voting against it, but as it then stood, the case was different. Some gentlemen had made it a local matter, for the exclusive benefit of the city of New York, but the fact was, that Throg's Neck was situated at a distance of about twelve miles from that city, on Long Island. Moreover, in General Bernard's report, this place is made an object of especial attention, and was among the plans recommended by him in 1825, as worthy of being put in a situation of defence. Mr. M. said he should vote for no new works till those already in existence were fully armed. They had been told that the fortifications of Boston and Baltimore were not furnished with a single gun, and he thought it time for the House to turn its attention to armaments, and not to the erection of new works.

Mr. HEATH, of Maryland, also spoke in favor of the appropriation. He hoped the New York delegation would also show a liberal disposition towards important appropriations for the defence of the smaller States. We were one people—our interests were all essentially combined, and we should act as a band of brothers for the true interests of all. He hoped the appropriation would be retained.

The question was then taken on striking out the appropriation by yeas and nays, and decided in the negative, as follows: ayes 87, noes 114.

The bill was then ordered to be engrossed for a third reading to-morrow, without amendment.

On motion of Mr. EVERETT, of Massachusetts, The House adjourned.

IN SENATE.
TUESDAY, Jan. 20, 1835.

Petitions and memorials were presented by—Messrs. PRENTISS, HENDRICKS, PORTER, PRESTON, TIPTON, KING of Ala., BROWN, and WEBSTER.

Mr. HENDRICKS presented a memorial and joint resolutions from the Legislature of Indiana, praying for a donation of land, and an appropriation in aid of completing the Wabash Canal; which was referred to the Committee on Roads and Canals.

The VICE PRESIDENT laid before the Senate a communication from the Navy Department, transmitting the correspondence with Loami Baldwin, relative to his superintendency of dry docks, at Charleston, South Carolina, in pursuance of a resolution of the Senate for that purpose.

On motion of Mr. HILL, the communication ordered to be printed.

r. PRESTON gave notice, that to-morrow he ld ask leave to introduce a bill to prevent ids and impositions upon the pension laws.

Mr. KING, of Ala., gave notice, that to morrow he would ask leave to introduce a bill for the relief of Moses Beard and others.

Mr. TIPTON, from the Committee on Claims, reported a bill for the relief of Joseph Hardy; wh ch was read the 1st time, and ordered to a second reading.

Mr. LINN, from the Committee on Private Land Claims, to which the same was referred, reported a bill confirming claims to land in Missouri, and for other purposes, with an amendment.

Mr. POINDEXTER, from the Committee on Public Lands, to which a resolution on the subject was referred, reported a bill authorizing the investment of the two per cents. of Mississippi, reserved for making roads, in certain bank stocks; which was read the first time, and ordered to a second reading.

The following resolutions, lying on the table, were taken up, considered, and adopted:
By Mr. PORTER.
Resolved, That the Committee on Roads and Canals be instructed to inquire into the expediency of making an appropriation to repair and complete the road leading from the northern boundary line of Arkansas, by Little Rock and Washington, to Fulton, on the north bank of Red river.

By Mr. TIPTON:
Resolved, That the Committee on Roads and Canals be instructed to inquire into the expediency of making an appropriation to repair the military road leading from Fort Jesup, in Louisiana, to Fort Towson, in Arkansas.

By Mr. BENTON:
Resolved, That the Committee on Military Affairs inquire into the expediency of appropriating a suitable sum of money in assisting the officers and soldiers of the army of the United States, at the several military posts, to obtain the services of chaplains.

The following resolutions were submitted:
By Mr. WAGGAMAN:
Resolved, That the Committee on Roads and Canals be instructed to inquire into the expediency of constructing at the national expense, a rail-road from Jacksonville, on the St. John's river, to the mouth of Fuwaney river, at its entrance into Vacassaus Bay, on the side of the Gulf of Mexico, or to such other convenient point on said river as may be judged most expedient.

By Mr. HENDRICKS:
Resolved, That the Committee on Roads and Canals be instructed to inquire into the expediency of authorizing the several rail-road companies chartered by the State of Indiana, to construct roads from the Ohio river into the interior of the State, to use the timber of the public lands in the construction of their respective works; and also, to inquire into the expediency of making grants of the public land for the location of such roads, and to aid the companies in making them wherever the same may pass over any unsol'd lands of the United States.

The joint resolution from the House of Representatives, directing the Commissioner of Public Buildings to have the statues, executed by Persico, and now in the Rotundo, placed in the niches in front of the Capitol, for which they were designed, was read twice and referred.

The bill for the relief of Richard B. Archer was read the first time, considered as in Committee of the Whole, and ordered to a second reading.

The bill from the House of Representatives authorizing the Superintendent of Indian Affairs at St. Louis, to employ a clerk, was read twice and referred.

The bill for the relief of Charles Lynch; and the bill to exempt merchandise imported under certain circumstances, from the operation of the tariff of 1828, were severally read the third time and passed.

The bill for the relief of the heirs of Moses Shepperd, deceased, came up for a third reading.

Mr. HILL renewed his opposition to the bill, and submitted a motion, "That the bill be recommitted, with instructions to specify the several items on which allowances shall be made, the amount allowed on each item, and the aggregate amount on all the items; which amount shall be in full of all claims pertaining to the several con-

tracts made by Moses Shepperd for constructing any part of the Cumberland road."

Upon which Mr. H. asked the yeas and nays, and they were ordered.

After some remarks from Mr. HENDRICKS, in opposition to the motion, and in favor of the immediate passage of the bill, the question was taken on the recommitment and agreed to—yeas 34, nays 19—as follows:

YEAS—Messrs. Benton, Bibb, Black, Brown, Buchanan, Calhoun, Cuthbert, Grundy, Hill, Kane, King of Alabama, King of Georgia, Linn, McKean, Morris, Preston, Robinson, Shepley, Swift, Tallmadge, Tipton, Waggaman, White, Wright—24.

NAYS—Messrs. Bell, Clay, Clayton, Ewing, Frelinghuysen, Hendricks, Kent, Leigh, Moore, Naudain, Poindexter, Porter, Prentiss, Robbins, Silsbee, Smith, Tomlinson, Tyler, Webster—19.

On motion of Mr. CLAY, the Senate then proceeded to the consideration of Executive business, and after some time spent therein,
The Senate adjourned.

HOUSE OF REPRESENTATIVES.
TUESDAY, January 20, 1835.

Petitions and Memorials were presented, on leave, by—
Mr. PEYTON, of Tennessee.
Mr. GORHAM, of Massachusetts.
Mr. CARR and EWING, of Indiana.

[Mr. CLAS presented a memorial and joint resolution of the General Assembly of the State of Indiana, praying a further donation of the public domain, to assist in the completion of the Wabash and Erie Canal, and in the construction of and other works of internal improvement as will have a tendency to open a line of communication between the Wabash and Ohio rivers; which, upon his motion, were referred to the Committee on Roads and Canals, and ordered to be printed.]

Mr. GAMBLE, of Georgia.
Which petitions and memorials were presented.

Mr. BARRINGER, from the Committee on Military Affairs, reported a bill for the relief of James Taylor; which was read twice and committed.

Mr. WARDWELL, from the Committee on Revolutionary Pensions, reported, without amendment, the bill from the Senate to continue the office of Commissioner of Pensions; which was committed.

Mr. WHITE, from the Committee on Naval Affairs, reported the following bills; which was read twice, and committed to a Committee of the Whole on the state of the Union, viz.
A bill authorising the construction of a Dry Dock for the naval service,
And a bill to provide for constructing three steam batteries.

Mr. FOSTER, from the Committee on the Judiciary, reported, without amendment, the bill from the Senate increasing the compensation of the Marshal of the District of Delaware; which was committed.

Mr. CLAY, from the Committee on Public Lands, reported, without amendment, the bill from the Senate for the relief of Samuel Smith, Lynn Magee, and Semoiss, Creek Indians; which was committed.

Mr. CLAY, from the same committee reported a bill to extend the time of issuing scrip certificates on United States land warrants; which was read.

Mr. CLAY asked that the bill might be read a second time, with a view to its engrossment.

After a short discussion of an explanatory character by Messrs. VINTON, CLAY, E. M. JOHNSON, and DENNY, the bill was read a second time, and ordered to be engrossed for a third reading.

Mr. CLAY, from the same committee, reported a bill in relation to patents for public lands, sold by the United States, or for private land claims confirmed; which was read twice and postponed for one week.

Mr. CLAY, from the same Committee, reported a bill to authorize the City Council of St. Augustine to widen the streets of said city; which was read twice and ordered to be engrossed.

Mr. POPE, from the Committee on Roads and

Canals, reported an amendment to the bill "to construct certain roads and harbors, and to improve the navigation of certain rivers," and also an amendment to the bill "to authorize examinations, surveys, and estimates for the improvement of certain rivers and harbors," which amendments were ordered to be printed.

Mr. REYNOLDS, from the Committee on Roads and Canals, reported an amendment to the bill to authorize examinations, surveys, and estimates for the construction of roads, and for the improvement of certain rivers; which was ordered to be printed.

Mr. REYNOLDS, from the same Committee, reported, without amendment, the bill from the Senate, to improve the navigation of Wabash river, which, on motion of Mr. R., was committed to a Committee of the Whole on the state of the Union.

Mr. WILLIAMS, from the Committee on the Public Lands, reported, with an amendment, the bill from the Senate for the relief of Elijah Simmons; which was committed.

Mr. CHINN moved to take up a bill to organize the Fire Companies of Washington City, and a bill to extend the charter of the Fire Insurance Company of Alexandria.

Objection being made,

Mr. CHINN moved to suspend the rules of the House, for the purpose indicated; which was negatived.

Messrs. DICKINSON, CHANEY, CASEY, CLAYTON, FOSTER, GILMER, LAY, and MUHLENBERG, each made adverse reports upon petitions, &c., which had been referred to their respective committees; which were laid on the table.

On motion of Mr. JOHNSON, of Louisiana, *Resolved*, That the Committee on Public Lands be instructed to inquire into the expediency of providing fire proof buildings for the Surveyor General and Registers of the land offices of the United States, in the State of Louisiana.

On motion of Mr. McCARTY, the following resolution, offered by him on the 12th inst., was taken up:

Resolved, That the President of the U. States be requested to transmit to the House copies of all letters and correspondence of all Indian Agents and sub-agents, and other persons connected with the Indian Department, now in the Executive or War Department, or in the office of the Commissioner of the General Land Office, connected with or relative to the survey, location, sales, and transfer of all Indian reserves of lands since the year 1825, up to this time; and also, all the orders and communications from the Executive of the United States, through the War Department, or General Land Office, or otherwise, in reference to said surveys, locations, sales, and transfers of Indian reserves; together with maps and plots of said surveys, and of the tracts approved and confirmed by the President under said transfers and sales, and what remains unappropriated, that have been reported and submitted for his approval, together with the evidence of title.

Mr. McCARTY briefly explained the reasons which had induced him to offer the resolution; when, after a few remarks by Messrs. MILLER and CLAY, the latter moved to postpone the resolution for one week.

Mr. McCARTY objected to the postponement, but the further consideration of the subject was here arrested by a call (by Mr. Watmough) for the orders of the day; which prevailed.

The following bills were read a third time and passed:

A bill for the relief of William O'Neal and Robert Morrison;

And a bill making appropriations for fortifications for the year 1835.

On motion of Mr. POLK, the previous orders, &c. were postponed for the purpose of going into committee on the appropriation bills.

GENERAL APPROPRIATION BILL.

The House then, on motion of Mr. POLK, resolved itself into a Committee of the Whole on the state of the Union, Mr. SPEIGHT in the Chair, and proceeded to take up and consider

The bill (No. 616) making appropriation for the civil and diplomatic expenses of government, for the year 1835.

The bill was taken up by sections.

Mr. McKINLEY moved to insert after 149th line, an item for additional clerk hire, in the Bureau of Private Land Claims, to aid in the distribution of Private Land Claims, Recording Claims, &c. $2,000. Agreed to.

Mr. POLK moved to insert three items after the 172d line for the Superintendent of the Bureau of Indian Affairs, $3000, for Clerks in do. $570, and for contingent expenses, $800. Agreed to.

Mr. POLK also moved to strike out 3000 dollars and insert 4000 dollars, for the compensation of the clerks, &c., in the office of the Commissary General of Purchases, and to strike out the appropriation of 700 dollars for the Clerk of the Purchasing Department; agreed to.

Mr. POLK then moved to strike out 6400 dollars for the pay of temporary clerks in preparing statement under resolutions of the Senate of 6th and 30th June, 1834; agreed to.

On the item for the salary of the Superintendent of the southwest Executive, and Watchman,

Mr. PARKER moved to strike out $850 and insert $1200, and explained that a discrepancy existed in the pay for those persons and others performing the same or similar duties.

Mr. POLK said it was the same as in former years, but he saw no impropriety in making the compensation equal.

The amendment was then agreed to.

On the item for the appropriation for the Library of Congress being read—

Mr. E. EVERETT moved an additional item "for new articles of furniture for the Library of Congress $1500," which was agreed to.

On the appropriation to pay the expenses of the Legislative Council of Michigan, being read—

Mr. POLK moved to insert " for the pay and mileage of members of the legislative council of Michigan, and the officers thereof, and the incidental expenses of an extra session of the said council, held at Detroit, in the year 1834, $4268 81," which was agreed to.

The item for allowances to the law agent, assistant counsel, and district attorney, for settling private land claims in Florida, being under consideration,

Mr. WHITE, the delegate from Florida, moved to strike out "law agent," to insert $4060 instead of $5550, and to add a proviso that none of the money should be paid out of the Treasury till the claims had been adjudicated, and entered into an explanation of some length in support of his proposition.

Mr. POLK said, in reference to this item, information was asked from the department, and Mr. P. read a letter from the Secretary of the Treasury of the 14th January, setting forth that the appropriation was in conformity to an act of Congress of 1828. Mr. P. also recited the clause of that act, and cited the amounts of former years showing that it was less than heretofore. He saw no occasion for the reduction of the amount, or for adopting the proviso, nor could he perceive how it could be done consistently with the public interest—at least, not until the act referred to had been repealed.

After some further conversation between Mr. MERCER, Mr. POLK, and Mr. WHITE, of Florida, the question on tht amendment was taken and decided in the affirmative. Yeas 81, nays not counted.

On the item for the purchase of law books for the office of the Attorney General $3000,

Mr. POLK moved to insert $2000 instead of $3000.

Mr. J. Q. ADAMS wished to know at what period the principle for this appropriation was adopted?

Mr. POLK replied, when Mr. Berrien was Attorney General, an appropriation of $500 had been made. Mr. P. then sent to the Clerk's table, a letter from the present Attorney General, setting forth that there had been no provision consistent with the importance of the office, for a library, and that those officers had hitherto been compelled to resort to the library of Congress, or depend upon their private resources. Mr. Butler

had been favored with the use of Mr. Taney's private library, of which he would soon necessarily be deprived. If Congress would make an appropriation of three thousand dollars, it would hereafter only require three or four hundred dollar annually to supply the necessary new publications.

Mr. J. Q. ADAMS was unsatisfied, for he could see no reason why the Attorney General should be furnished with a library at the expense of the country. Mr. A. moved to strike out the whole clause.

Mr. FOSTER thought, on the contrary, that a library in the office of the Attorney General, was indispensable, and should be furnished at the public expense. Mr. F. advocated the propriety of the appropriation, with some energy, and said he thought it the most reasonable application ever made to that House.

Mr. D. J. PEARCE opposed the item and said, without some better cause than had been assigned, he saw no valid reason why the appropriation should be made. A considerable amount of the sum assigned for the purchase of books for the library of Congress was always expended in the purchase of books for the department of law, to which the Attorney General had at all times ready access.

Mr. POLK further explained.

The question was then taken on Mr. J. Q. Adams's motion to strike out the whole clause; which was negatived. Ayes 53, noes 72.

On Mr. POLK'S motion to amend the clause by inserting $2000 instead of $3000, was then agreed to without a division.

On the clause for compensation to the District Attorneys and Marshals being read—

Mr. FOSTER move1 an additional item, for compensation to the District Attorney of South Carolina, and for the Marshal of Delaware.

Mr. POLK inquired if this was in pursuance of any law.

Mr. FOSTER replied in the negative, but advocated the expediency of the appropriation.

Mr. POLK thought it could only be done under a special act, and suggested to Mr. Foster to withdraw his amendment, and a special bill might be introduced to meet the object.

Mr. FOSTER then withdrew his amendment, and the clause, as it stood, was adopted.

On the following item being read, appropriating $300,000 for defraying the expenses of the Supreme, Circuit, and District Courts of the United States, &c.

Mr. PARKER inquired how it was that this amount had increased from the amount of last year, which was then $260,000.

Mr. POLK said the increase of this item did escape the attention of the committee, who made the necessary inquiry of the Treasury partment, and it was founded on estimates w had been furnished by the Marshals of the eral States. Mr. P. then sent to the Clerk's ble a table of the various items, which was re and the clause was agreed to.

The clause "to make good a deficiency in the funds for the relief of sick and disabled seamen &c., 25,000 dollars" having been read—

Mr. J. Q. ADAMS asked how this deficiency had been created?

Mr. POLK explained, and produced a document from the Secretary of the Treasury, setting forth that the deficiency actually existed from an excess of expenditure.

Mr. J. Q. ADAMS said, though he should not move to strike out the clause, he deemed it a v improper one, since it led to the expenditure money without the authority of law.

Mr. CAMBRELENG said, the expenditure necessarily a fluctuating one. The gentle seamen abroad, who became disabled, law, be sent home by Consuls, and this amount could not be anticipated.

The conversation then dropped.

Mr. REYNOLDS moved to amend t providing for the survey of the publ adding, for " surveying lots in Peo $500."

Mr. R. said, he had made inquiry at the Ty

sury Department, and found that no provision had been made for this object.

The amendment was negatived without a division.

The clauses for salaries of Foreign Ministers, and Charges d'Affaires, then came under consideration.

Mr. J. Q. ADAMS asked, why it was that an appropriation was inserted for a Charge d'Affaires to Buenos Ayres? There was no such officer there. Mr. A. said, he had last year made a motion to strike out this item, on the ground that there not only was no such minister there, but under the then existing circumstances; he thought it highly improper that there should be. But that appropriation was passed, and if it had not been diverted to some other purpose, he again asked why this was inserted in the bill? Mr. A. also alluded to the outfit appropriated last year for a minister to London, where no minister had resided.

Mr. POLK said, in relation to the $9,000 appropriated last year for a minister to England, he would send to the table of the Clerk a letter from the Secretary of the Treasury, which accounted for the expenditure of $6,682 50, for the pay of a Charge d'Affaires at that Court, leaving a balance of $2,317 50, which was paid over to the surplus fund. With regard to the mission to Buenos Ayres, he had sought no information on the subject from the Department, and had therefore received none.

Mr. ADAMS said the explanation was not satisfactory. He wished the House distinctly to know what they appropriated money for, and how it was expended.

Mr. CAMBRELENG said, if the facts were as stated by the gentleman from Massachusetts, it ought to be stricken out, but he hoped the gentleman would permit it to go to the House, and there act upon it.

Mr. ARCHER agreed with the gentleman from Massachusetts in the propriety of striking out this appropriation. We had a right to suppose the money to be then in the Treasury; as the appropriation had been made, the Department had no right to divert it to another purpose. If such had been done, it was time to mark it with a distinct brand of reprobation.

Mr. POLK begged to inquire of the gentleman from Virginia if it was within his own knowledge that the money appropriated for this object had been expended in some other foreign mission?

Mr. ARCHER intimated that the question should be addressed, not to him, but to the gentleman from Massachusetts.

Mr. POLK then begged to inquire of that gentleman.

Mr. J. Q. ADAMS then said he inferred as much because it had not been expended in the manner and for the object directed by Congress.

Mr. POLK then said it was an inference—and and inference drawn without facts. The gentlemen were not authorized to draw a conclusion either that the money has been, or that it would be, expended in any object other than that for which it was intended. Mr. P. begged for leave to differ with the distinguished gentleman from Massachusetts—distinguished in his acquirements in foreign diplomacy; that the appropriation for the mission to England, had been diverted from its purpose. We had a Minister in Great Britain, of the second grade, who was entitled to half the salary given to one of the first grade. Congress had made an appropriation for a Minister of the latter grade, and from circumstances which needed not then to be adverted to, the Government could not pay a full Minister; but did it follow that we were to be unrepresented? Mr. P. made some further explanation on this point. With regard to the item for the charge at Buenos Ayres, he would only remark that it was submitted among the regular annual estimates, furnished by the head of the department, and after the very elaborate discussion of last year, he had not supped the question would have been again re-agi-
4. Mr. P. concluded by saying that if no good a could be assigned, why the item should be :en out, he hoped the Committee would suffer p remain as it stood. He would pledge him-

self that if additional information should be required, he would, when the bill came into the House, endeavor to procure it.

Mr. ARCHER said if he understood the duty of the Committee of Ways and Means, it was to be prepared to answer all interrogatories on the subjects introduced, and recommended by them. He asked what had become of the appropriation made last year, and he was answered that it was incumbent on the gentleman from Massachusetts to answer the inquiry. It was known that an appropriation was made for a Minister to Buenos Ayres last year, and it was not pretended that a Minister had been sent there, and he would ask what had become of the money? It certainly had not been applied to the use for which it was intended, and why were they called upon to make it again? Mr. A. was by no means disposed to bring a charge of malfeasance upon the administration, since it might be an oversight, but he was not disposed to vote an appropriation twice over for the same object. He hoped they were not yet limited to such subserviency. If the House should blindly vote on this item, the organ of the administration would only have to get up in his place, and propose any measure, and that would be a sufficient reason for its adoption.

Mr. CAMBRELENG hoped that no portion of the House were liable to the charge of subserviency.

Mr. ARCHER disclaimed having made any personal or general allusion to the members of the House.

Mr. CAMBRELENG continued. He thought the matter before them was one about which there ought to be no difference of opinion. It was certainly not one worthy of a long debate. The gentleman from Massachusetts had reminded the Committee that a similar appropriation was made last year, which still remained in the Treasury. With that knowledge, it certainly ought not to be appropriated again; but it ought not to be struck out upon the presumption that the appropriation had been misapplied by the Department. Whether it was struck out or not, was not important, as we should have the necessary information before it would be acted on in the House. He had hoped the gentleman from Massachusetts would have deferred his motion til this time, but it was not material.

After some further debate, the question was taken on the amendment of Mr. J. Q. Adams, to strike out all that part of the clause relating to Buenos Ayres, and agreed to.

Mr. POLK proposed an additional clause, making an appropriation for the outfit of a minister to Spain, $9,000.

He produced a letter from the Department, stating that the present minister to Spain had obtained leave to return home, and would doubtless avail himself of the opportunity. The amendment was agreed to.

Mr. POLK moved to insert "Portugal" in the provision "for outfits of the Charge d'Affaires to Prussia and Venezuela," and instead of "nine," insert thirteen thousand dollars.

Mr. J. Q. ADAMS asked whether this appropriation for a mission to Venezuela was not a new one?

Mr. CAMBRELENG answered he believed it was.

Mr. J. Q. ADAMS said, on a former occasion, a debate arose in the House, as to the location or existence of the Republic of Columbia. It was then settled down to New Grenada, and he wanted some further information on the subject of this government of Venezuela—whether it was recognised by the President, or whether it was of sufficient importance to command two missions.

Mr. CAMBRELENG said, he should leave the gentleman from Virginia to adjust the geographical question with the gentleman from Massachusetts, which had been raised last year, and with which he had nothing to do. But as it regarded the propriety of sending a minister to Venezuela, he would state his opinion that in a commercial view, a Charge d'Affaires to that government was far more important than to any one of the three into which Columbia had been divided. He hoped the provision would be retained.

Mr. ARCHER concurred in the opinion of the gentleman from New York, near him, [Mr. Cambreleng,] that an agent at Venezuela was of more importance to our commerce than to any other of the new South American States.

The amendment of Mr. POLK was then agreed to.

Mr. SEVIER moved to strike out two thousand dollars out of the appropriation for the Territory of Arkansas, making it nine instead of "eleven thousand dollars.

After some conversation between Messrs. SEVIER and POLK, the amendment was agreed to.

Mr. LYON, of Michigan, moved an additional appropriation for the expenses of that government, but the motion was lost.

Mr. PINCKNEY moved to amend the bill by making an appropriation of $20 000 for the purchase of a building in Charleston, for the use of the Federal Court, and for a jail.

Mr. FOSTER said he would merely remark, that this subject had been under consideration before the Committee on the Judiciary, and was then disapproved.

The question being taken, the amendment was lost.

The bill being laid aside,

The Committee then on motion of Mr. FOSTER took up the bill to make additional compensation to the District Attorney, for the District of South Carolina.

Mr. PINCKNEY moved an amendment, increasing the pay of the Attorney $400 instead of $200 as provided by the bill.—Negatived.

The bill was then laid aside.

The Committee, on motion of Mr. POSTER, proceeded to consider the bill allowing additional salary to the Marshal of the District of Delaware after which,

The Committee rose, reported the bills to the House (the former as amended,) when
The House adjourned.

IN SENATE.

Mr. TALLMADGE presented the memorial of the heirs of Noah Brown and others, praying remuneration for the depreciation of certain treasury notes; which was referred to the Committee on Claims.

Mr. FRELINGHUYSEN presented the memorial of John Ross and other head men of the Cherokee tribe of Indians east of the Mississippi.

Mr. F. said that the memorialists stated the situation of their affairs with the State of Georgia, that they had now reached that crisis which required the interposition of the Government of the United States. They proposed to Congress to purchase their territory, and cede the same to Georgia; and since this Government thing it, they proposed to submit to the laws of Georgia; that they had come to the deliberate determination not to remove west of the Mississippi, but intended to remain, and proposed, under certain guarantees, to become citizens of Georgia, and be entitled to all the privileges, political as well as others, to which citizens of that State were entitled. And they proposed to this Government to make such arrangements with Georgia as would secure to them these privileges. He moved the reference of the memorial to the Committee on Indian Affairs, and that it be ordered to be printed; which was agreed to.

The VICE PRESIDENT laid before the Senate a letter from the War Department, communicating the names of the Clerks employed in that Department for the year 1834, with the compensation paid to each.

Also, another letter from the War Department, transmitting a statement of the expenses for contingencies of the survey for the year 1834.

Also, another letter from the War Department, containing an abstract of all the licenses which have been granted to trade with the Indians; which communications were severally laid on the table, and ordered to be printed.

Mr. PORTER, from the Committee on Foreign Relations, reported a bill for the relief of ... O'Sullivan.

The following resolutions submitted yesterday, were taken up, considered, and agreed to:

By Mr. WAGGAMAN:

Resolved, That the Committee on Roads and Canals be instructed to inquire into the expediency of constructing at the national expense, a railroad from Jacksonville, on the St. John's river, to the mouth of the Suwaney river, at its entrance into Vicksburg Bay, on the side of the Gulf of Mexico, or to such other convenient point on said river as may be judged most expedient.

By Mr. HENDRICKS:

Resolved, That the Committee on Roads and Canals be instructed to inquire into the expediency of authorizing the several rail-road companies chartered by the State of Indiana, to construct roads from the Ohio river into the interior of the State, to use the timber of the public lands in the construction of their respective works; and also, to inquire into the expediency of making grants of the public land for the location of such roads, and to aid the companies in making them wherever the same may pass over any unsold lands of the United States.

The following resolution was submitted by Mr. HENDRICKS:

Resolved, That the Committee on the Judiciary be instructed to inquire into the expediency of May by law, the time of commencement and close of every succeeding session of Congress.

The unfavorable report of the Committee on the petition of Benjamin I. Heard, and the unfavorable report of the Committee on revolutionary Claims against the claim of the heirs of Col. Harry Dixon, deceased, were severally concurred in.

The joint resolution from the House of Representatives, directing the Commissioner of Public Buildings to have the statues, executed by Persico, and now in the Rotundo, placed in the niches in front of the Capitol, for which they were designed, was read the second time, as in Committee of the Whole, and ordered to be engrossed for third reading.

The bill for the relief of Richard P. Archer was read the second time and referred.

The bill authorizing the registers and receivers of public moneys to administer oaths, was taken up and considered as in Committee of the Whole.

Mr. POINDEXTER said, that several weeks ago he offered a resolution calling on the Commissioner of the General Land Office for copies of the law which had been prescribed to be taken by them prior to making entries of public land. A answer had yet been received from that office this resolution, and none, he presumed, would made to it. This bill was intended to cover a subtle violation of public law on the part of the Treasury Department, and as he wished an answer to the resolution, he would, with that view, move to lay the bill upon the table; which was read to.

The bill making an appropriation to improve harbor at or near the mouth of the river Raisin was considered as in Committee of the Whole, and ordered to be engrossed for a third reading.

The bill for the relief of William C. Easton was taken up and considered, as in Committee of the Whole.

After some remarks by Mr. TIPTON, in favor the bill, Mr. HILL moved to lay it on the table; which was agreed to.

The bill for the relief of William Pettiplace and others, heirs and legal representatives of Joseph Shue, deceased, was considered as in Committee of the Whole, and ordered to be engrossed for a third reading.

The bill for the relief of David Lynch and others, was taken up for consideration, and on motion of Mr. KING, of Ala., was laid on the table, with a view to allow some further examination to be made into its merits.

Mr. BENTON, from the Military Committee, reported a bill for the relief of Col. John Hudry, New Orleans.

The report having been made—

Mr. WAGGAMAN observed that Col. Hudry last night committed suicide.

Mr. BENTON expressed his astonishment and regret at so melancholy an occurrence, and took the opportunity to say that he was well acquainted with Col. Hudry at New Orleans, where he behaved with great gallantry during the late war, and sustained great pecuniary sacrifices. He also believed that the claim was perfectly correct and just.

Mr. PORTER remarked that a more melancholy event had rarely occurred within his recollection. He knew the individual well, and knew him to be a most estimable man, and every thing that had been said of him by the gentleman from Missouri was well merited. He did behave himself most gallantly at New Orleans, both on the 23d of December and the 8th of January, 1815, and expended there in various munitions of war from ten to fifteen thousand dollars from his private purse, for which he had never been compensated. That he came here last winter, pressing his claim, and there was no doubt it would have been allowed, but he last night put an end to his existence from utter despair of its recovery.

Mr. BENTON then suggested the propriety of a recommitment of the bill, with a view to its amendment, so as to allow the claim to the heirs and legal representatives of the deceased.

Mr. KING, of Alabama, remarked that he was a member of the Military Committee, and from the examination he had given the claim, he had no doubt of its being correct. But he suggested to the gentleman from Missouri, to take up the bill for consideration now, and amend it conformably to his proposition.

Mr. BENTON acceded to the suggestion, and on his motion,

The Senate proceeded to consider the bill, which was amended so as to make the allowance (about $4,366) to the heirs and legal representatives of Col. John Hudry.

The bill as amended, was then ordered to be engrossed and read a third time.

Mr. KING, of Alabama, pursuant to notice, and on leave given, introduced a bill to revive the act of 1824, for the relief of the heirs and legal representatives of John Donalson and Stephen Heard; which was read twice and referred.

Mr. LEIGH, from the Judiciary Committee, made an unfavorable report upon the petition of Sarah Yorke.

On motion of Mr. MOORE, the Senate resumed the consideration of the bill to remove the land office in Mississippi, from Clinton to Jackson; and the bill was ordered to be engrossed and read a third time.

Mr. PRESTON gave notice that he would, tomorrow, ask leave to introduce a bill for the relief of Thomas Cooper, of South Carolina.

Mr. PRESTON, pursuant to notice, and on leave given, introduced a bill to detect and punish frauds and impositions upon the pension laws; which was read twice and referred.

Mr. LINN, from the Committee to which the bill for the relief of Bartholomew Butcher and Peter Butcher had been referred, reported the same without amendment.

The bill making compensation for French spoliations prior to 1800, came up as the special order, when,

On motion of Mr. SHEPLEY, it was postponed till to-morrow.

The bill to distribute for a limited time the proceeds of the sales of the public lands among the several States, came up as the special order; and

On motion of Mr. CLAY, it was postponed to this day week.

The bill graduating the price of the public lands, and providing for the sale of those which have been long at in market, came up as the special order; when

Mr. BENTON moved that the Senate proceed to the consideration of Executive business, with a view to the despatch of business which remains unfinished.

Mr. CLAYTON remarked that there were several Senators unavoidably absent.

Mr. CLAY said he was very desirous that the Senate should engage in Executive business; and he came to the Senate Chamber to-day for that purpose, but there were several Senators absent who desired to be present at that time. He therefore suggested to put it off till to-morrow.

Mr. BENTON then waived his motion, and moved to postpone the bill to Wednesday next; which was agreed to.

Several other land bills lying on the table were postponed to the same day.

On motion of Mr. CLAY, the Senate resumed the consideration of the bill for the relief of Nicholas D. Coleman, and after some remarks by Mr. LEIGH and Mr. BLACK in favor, and by Mr. CLAY in opposition to the bill, it was negatived.

The joint resolution, directing the President of the United States to cause to be presented to Colonel Croghan and his under officers, medals, struck with suitable devices, as a testimony of national gratitude for their deeds of patriotism and valor in defence of Fort St. Stephens, being under consideration,

Mr. BIBB gave a brief outline of the history and events connected with that brilliant affair, and paid a handsome compliment to the officers and soldiers who fought in defence of that Fort.

The resolution was agreed to.

The following bills were considered as in Committee of the Whole, and ordered to be engrossed and read a third time:

A bill confirming the titles to certain lands in Florida to Gen Carara;

A bill authorizing the construction of a rail road through the Lands of the United States, from Tallahassee to St. Marks, in Florida;

A bill appropriating appropriation for completing certain improvements in Florida;

A bill appropriating 20,000 dollars for removing sand-bars in the Mississippi river, amended,

On motion of Mr. HENDRICKS, by adding a clause directing the appropriation to be extended under the direction of the Secretary of War.

A bill providing for the adjustment of certain land claims in Louisiana;

A bill for the relief of Elizabeth Magruder.

The bill, reported by the Committee on Public Lands, for the relief of Silas B. Fisher, was, on motion of Mr. POINDEXTER, laid on the table.

And then the Senate adjourned.

HOUSE OF REPRESENTATIVES.

WEDNESDAY, JAN. 21.

Mr. FORESTER, from the Committee on Claims, reported a bill for the relief of the heirs of Benjamin Gentry; which was read twice and committed.

Mr. FORESTER, by consent, submitted the following resolution:

Resolved, That a Select Committee consisting of —— members be appointed, to investigate the commutation claims and seven years half pay claims of the widows and orphans of those who died or were killed in the service of the revolutionary war, as well such commutation and seven years half pay claims as have been paid, as those which are still unpaid; and the half-pay claims authorized to be paid at the Treasury Department of the United States, under any act or acts of Congress providing for the payment of the same, as well those that have been paid, as those that have not, and that said committee be directed to inquire into the expediency of passing such laws as may be deemed expedient to prevent frauds against the Government and the claimants.

Mr. MILLER suggested that the adoption of the resolution would interfere with an important bill reported by the Committee on Revolutionary Claims, on a branch of the subject embraced in the resolution.

Mr. FORESTER had no wish to interfere with the bill to which reference had been made. His main object was to have a full investigation of the frauds which were known to exist, and to devise some means of preventing others in future, not only against the Government, but against individual claimants.

Mr. CHILTON was opposed to the adoption of the resolution. The whole subject was before the Committee on Revolutionary Claims. It would be a departure from the parliamentary rule, if not a reflection upon a standing committee of the House to attempt to wrest from it in this way, its legitimate functions and duties.

Mr. VANDERPOEL agreed with the gentleman from Kentucky, that it was unnecessary to

raise a Select Committee on this subject. He was willing to vote for a resolution sending the same inquiries to the Committee on Revolutionary Claims, inasmuch as he doubted whether that Committee was fairly in possession of the whole subject embraced in the present resolution. He referred to the practices resorted to by speculators, in order to defraud honest claimants of their rights, and was willing to aid in preventing those fraudulent practices. He was, however, opposed to raising a Special Committee, and preferred that the subject should be sent to the Committee on Revolutionary Claims. He concluded by moving to lay the resolution on the table; but withdrew the motion at the request of

Mr. BAYLIES, who remarked, that, as a member of the Committee on Revolutionary Claims, he did not view the resolution as a reflection upon the Committee to which he belonged. He referred to the objects contemplated by the resolution, and remarked, that the Committee on Revolutionary Claims were anxious to place this subject on a footing to avoid, as far as possible, special legislation—to produce, in regard to it, something like principle and uniformity of action. He could see no good reason for adopting the resolution.

Mr. MASON of Virginia, considered the proposed inquiry in some degree distinct from the regular and ordinary duties of the Committee on Revolutionary Claims. It was known that the most profligate frauds had been committed, not only upon the Government, but upon individual claimants. At the last session, he had offered a resolution calling for a list of persons entitled to commutation pay. Upon a consultation with the Third Auditor of the Treasury, he was apprized of the most profligate frauds which had been committed by speculators, and informed that it had been deemed expedient, in order, if possible, to prevent their recurrence, to withhold information touching these claims, except to those directly or indirectly interested. In consequence of this interview, he withdrew his resolution. The object of the present resolution was to raise a committee to devise the means, if possible, to protect the claims of the heirs of those who achieved our liberties, and to prevent the perpetration of frauds, not only against the Government, but against the meritorious claimants, to which reference had been made. If the object could be attained by a reference of the subject to the standing committee of the House, he hoped his friend from Tennessee would withdraw his motion for a select committee and let the subject go to the former.

Mr. FORESTER referred to the duties of the Committee on Revolutionary Pensions. The object which he had in view, went further than the ordinary business confided to that Committee. It proposed to investigate the whole subject, for the purpose of preventing speculators from seizing upon the bounty of the Government, which had been extended to the heirs of those who had fought the battles of the revolution. He intended no reflection upon the Standing Committee by his motion. Mr. F. referred to the fraudulent practices which existed on this subject. As things now stood, it was impossible for claimants to procure information which they could understand, while the hungry speculator makes himself acquainted with them. He wished to guard against all this. He wished to prevent these speculations upon the honest earnings of the ancestors of his constituents.

Mr. MILLER opposed the resolution, because the first branch of it withdrew from the Committee on Revolutionary Claims, a subject properly before that committee. He alluded to the commutation bill, which was made the special order for a future day. If this resolution was passed, it would commit the whole subject to this special committee, which he thought wholly unnecessary.

Mr. MUHLENBERG remarked that he was not in his seat during a portion of the time in which the motion had been discussed. He believed the gentleman would accomplish his object, when the general bill on the subject came up, which opened the whole question.

Mr. REED referred to the frauds and speculations which had taken place in reference to this subject; and he thought the proposed inquiry entirely proper.

Mr. GRENNELL was in favor of the resolution. Its object was patriotic and humane. He was in favor of a Select Committee, because the inquiry extended beyond the scope of the ordinary duties of the Committee on Revolutionary Claims.

Mr. TURRILL had heard no good reason assigned for the adoption of the resolution. He considered the whole subject already before the Committee on Revolutionary Claims.

Mr. EWING wished to ingraft a small amendment upon the resolution. He desired to give those who were rejoicing on account of the complete redemption of the public debt, real ground for rejoicing, by making provision for the redemption of the continental paper money. After a few additional remarks, Mr. E. moved the following amendment to the motion:

"Also, to inquire into the expediency of providing for the redemption of continental paper yet remaining unpaid, according to the principles of equity and justice."

Mr. FOSTER said, as only fifteen minutes remained of the time allotted to resolutions and reports, he would move to postpone the resolution for another week, in order that the committees might have an opportunity to make reports.

Mr. FORESTER had no object to postponing the resolution to the 30th inst., which would be beyond the time allotted for the disposition of the bill to which reference had been made.

Mr. FOSTER accepted the suggestion as a modification of his motion.

The resolution was then postponed to the 30th instant, and, on motion of Mr. BEATY, ordered to be printed.

Mr. POLK, from the Committee on Ways and Means, reported a bill making appropriations for Indian Annuities, and other similar objects for 1835; which was read twice and committed.

Mr. J. Q. ADAMS said, he was desirous of addressing a question to the chairman of the Committee on Foreign Relations, and he wished to inquire of the chair who was the chairman of that committee.

Mr. CAMBRELENG stated, in answer to the inquiry of the gentleman from Massachusetts, that the Committee had done him the honor to elect him their chairman.

Mr. J. Q. ADAMS said, he apprehended the gentleman's reply would be found to have involved something like the introduction of a new principle into that House, in the part taken by that committee. Mr. A. had felt some degree of embarrassment, as to the manner in which this subject should be introduced to the House, but upon giving it the deepest reflection, he had thought it best to apply to the Chair, because the usual authority from which he could learn who were the chairmen of the various standing and select committees of the House, were the Journals of the House, and they were under the care of the presiding officer. Now it was one of the rules of the House, that all standing committees should be appointed at the commencement of every session; and another rule was, that they should be appointed by the Speaker. He was unaware of any rule of the House, by which the Speaker named the chairmen of the several committees, but by usage, which had become almost universal, the person first named upon each standing or select committee, was considered as appointed by the Speaker *ex-officio*, the chairman of that committee, although a committee had power to elect its chairman, if they thought proper. As far, however, as he (Mr. A.) was acquainted with the practice of that House and its committees, the power of electing the chairmen of the latter had never been exercised,—or, if ever, it was believed only upon rare and extraordinary occasions. From what had been stated by the gentleman from New York, (Mr. Cambreleng,) it would be seen that this old and general usage, of considering the person first named on the committee as its *ex-officio* chairman, until another had been duly elected by the committee—and that in the event of the resignation of the person thus constituted the official chairman, the person next named was also *ipso facto* considered as chairman, it would be seen, he said, that this usage had been departed from. From the statement of the gentleman from New York, it appeared that the Committee on Foreign Relations had thought proper to elect a chairman of their own, and thereby displace the chairman appointed by the Speaker. If this had happened with respect to one the least important of the committees of the House, Mr. A. would still have thought the procedure [illegible] worthy of notice, but occuring as it had in one of the most important of the committees, consisting, or supposed to consist, of persons of the highest character, and owing the deepest responsibility to the House and to the nation—and its chairman also, a person under the heaviest responsibility, he considered it his duty to bring the matter before the House.

The CHAIR intimated that the debate had [illegible] on thus far by the indulgence of the House, [illegible] out any motion having been made, but if it [illegible] the pleasure of the House, the gentleman [illegible] proceed.—(Cries of "Go on, go on.")

Mr. ADAMS resumed. He was stating [illegible] certain events had taken place which called for the serious consideration of the House, and that he [illegible] under some embarrassment as to the mode and manner in which he should bring it under its notice. In order, however, to make the debate proper, and within the rules of order, it was his intention to conclude by a motion or resolution, the purport of which he would state to be, to [illegible] the name of the chairman of the Committee [illegible] Foreign Relations on the Journals of the House.

The main point, however, upon which he [illegible] ed to direct the attention of the House was [illegible] that here was a chairman of one of its most important and responsible committees acting, with[illegible] the House knowing any thing about it. This [illegible] say the least of it, was an incongruous proceeding as well as out of the usual form. It should [illegible] upon the journals, since, if it was desired to know who composed any committee, or who was [illegible] chairman, they offered the only record, and [illegible] them, would any one refer for ascertaining [illegible] fact. If it should turn out that the committee [illegible] question had elected a new chairman, for he would not dispute the word of the gentleman from New York, why, at least it ought to be entered upon the journals, so that every member of that House and every one in the nation, might know it. [illegible] in order to found some few observations he [illegible] ed to make in this case, as the gentleman from New York had told them he was the chairman [illegible] the committee, Mr. A. begged leave to put [illegible] other question to the gentleman, which he [illegible] answer or not as he pleased—it was, whether [illegible] gentleman was elected chairman by a majority [illegible] that committee, or by a minority?

Mr. CAMBRELENG said, that before [illegible] ing the inquiry of the gentleman from Massachusetts, he must apologize to the Speaker for [illegible] answered the first question of that gentleman. Not having heard the whole of his remarks, [illegible] was not aware that the inquiry was addressed [illegible] the Speaker; had he so understood him, he certainly should not have risen at all. He merely [illegible] the question, and stated the fact for the [illegible] tion of the gentleman. He sincerely regretted that the gentleman from Massachusetts (Mr. [illegible] erett,) and himself, should have been placed [illegible] awkward an attitude before the House. [illegible] he had differed with that gentleman politically, [illegible] had ever been on friendly, if not on [illegible] terms with him. In accepting the station [illegible] him by the Committee, he had supposed the gentleman from Massachusetts would be [illegible] from a position not agreeable to himself [illegible] particular crisis. The gentleman from [illegible] (Mr. Archer,) the former Chairman of the Committee on Foreign Affairs, had not, at this [illegible] doubtless from motives of propriety, [illegible] continue in that station in the present [illegible] state of our foreign relations. With regard [illegible] particular inquiry put to him by the gentleman from Massachusetts, he had merely to say, [illegible] vote of the Committee stood four to [illegible] gentleman from Massachusetts (Mr. E[illegible] and himself not voting.

Mr. J. Q. ADAMS. The gentlem[illegible] York has answered with perfect candor[illegible]

ble soever we learn that he was elected Chairman of the Committee not by a majority, but by a
minority of that body. Every member of the
Committee, nine in number, were present, and the
gentleman states that he received four votes, so
that he could not have been elected by a majority.
It was not, however, Mr. A's purpose, at that
time, to question the regularity of the procedure,
but to ask that the fact of the gentleman being
chairman of the Committee on Foreign Relations
may be entered on the Journals of the House.
He entreated the gentleman from New York, as
well as the House, to believe that the grounds upon
which he had brought this matter forward, did not,
in the slightest degree, involve the personal respect which he always had, and always should entertain towards that gentleman. If it had been
his pleasure of the Speaker to appoint him in
the usual manner, no one would have been more
satisfied with that appointment than himself. He
believed that in accepting the office, the gentleman believed he was relieving Mr. A.'s colleague and friend from a most awkward and unpleasant situation, but that was not the question.
In question was whether his honorable colleague
was in that situation, a situation of deep responsibility and high honor? Mr. A. thought the whole
procedure was one that ought to go before the
House, and that it should be known whether the
acts, orders, and acts of that House had been properly pursued by the committee. It was for that
reason that he had deemed it necessary to lay the
matter before the House for consideration. It
was a new thing, and he did not understand it to
have been done in consequence of any usage,
or of any established principle. In Jefferson's
Manual of Parliamentary Practice it is stated to be
a usage that "the person first named is generally permitted to act as Chairman; but this is a matter of courtesy; every committee having a right to
appoint their own chairman." That was stated as
a parliamentary usage of England, but so far
as being so in that House, he believed it would
be exceedingly difficult to adduce a single instance in which a committee had elected their
own chairman. He was aware that the practice
in the other House varied. Well, then, here
was a departure from usage, and a departure in a
very questionable, viz. a chairman elected
by a minority, instead of a majority of the body
of which he is to preside. In respect to the appointment of a chairman by a minority, he found
nothing in the Parliamentary Manual having any
bearing, but he was at a loss to see upon what
ground the committee had departed from the old rule.
There was a positive rule to the contra-
ry, and he would refer to a manual published in
Pennsylvania, by a member of that House, which
stated that the election should in all cases take
place by a majority of the members present. Mr.
A. concluded by reiterating that his object was,
in the election of chairman of the Committee on
Foreign Relations should be made a matter of record, and by entering upon the journals of the
House the that the chairman appointed by the Speaker
at the commencement of the session, had resigned,
and he made that motion accordingly.
Mr. E. EVERETT said he did not rise to discuss this matter, and he had to solicit the indulgence of the House under the circumstances upon
which he found himself compelled to make a
brief explanation. The honorable gentleman from
New York has said that Mr. E.'s respected colleague had placed him before the House in a very
embarrassing situation, and has justly alluded to
it. (Mr. E.) as one on whom he has long and
with proud upon a footing of intimate personal
friendship. It was natural perhaps that the gentleman from New York should think that his (Mr.
E.) colleague had placed him in an embarrassed
position, but Mr. E. thought it due to himself to
prove to avoid any erroneous inference, that he
had placed in that situation without any concurrence or co-operation on his part. His respected
colleague had consulted him, but had not made it
the substance of any request from him; on the contrary he had done nothing to induce his honorable
colleague to bring the matter before the House,
and no explanation was necessary to remove from
the mind of the gentleman from New-York, the

idea that he (Mr. E.) in any degree had prompted this movement. So much on that ground.
Another remark which fell from the same gentleman, seemed to require still more that Mr. E.
should say a word or two. The gentleman said that
he considered, instead of doing any thing unfriendly towards him—of which he had never charged
the gentleman, or designed to charge him—that
he had relieved Mr. E. from the situation in which
the delicate sense of honor of the gentleman from
Virginia, (Mr. Archer,) at the commencement of
the present session, had led him to relieve himself. Now, this would seem to lead to the inference that Mr. E. ought to have taken the same
step which the gentleman from Virginia did, and
not to have remained in a condition to receive the
votes of the members of the Committee. In the
first place he would say, that this was of all other the
last point on which he expected to have been called
upon to address the House this day. When his
friend from Georgia, (Judge Wayne)—he called him
his friend not from mere parliamentary courtesy—
retired from the office, Mr. E. felt the delicacy
of his situation, and at first intended to have declined acting in that capacity, and why? Because,
by the usage of the House, (a usage by no
means without exceptions,) the Chairman of the
Committee on Foreign Affairs was understood to
be politically friendly to the existing Administration; and that not being the case with himself, he
felt considerable delicacy on the subject, and advised with his friends as to what course he ought
to pursue. They stated, and gave reasons which
had great weight with him, that he ought not to
take the step which his private feelings preferred.
He also inquired of the honorable Speaker of the
House—he hoped he was not transcending the
line of propriety in adverting to this—whether he
considered him (Mr. E.) Chairman of the Committee, after the resignation of Mr. Wayne.
The Speaker said it was his impression that Mr.
E. should take the Chair without any hesitation.
But the governing principle upon his mind was,
that though not the political adherent of the present Administration, he did happen to be with the
majority of the committee on the great and all-important question before the country; and thus, by
taking the place of Chairman, he was not thrusting himself into an awkward and embarrassing position, it devolving upon him under long Parliamentary usage. Being in the majority, he saw
neither inconvenience nor impropriety in that
step. More than this, he thought, in the simplicity of his heart—and he still thought—that he took
a view of that subject, which would have been unanimously sustained by the committee and the House
likewise. With some misgivings he would confess, he did, acting under the specific advice of
the Chair, on the first meeting after the retirement of Mr. Wayne, take his seat as Chairman of
the Committee, conceiving his right to do so, and
remained there until he was removed by the action of the committee. He could assure the House
that no one could feel less regret than he did on
the subject, nor was there one who would more
cheerfully acknowledge the great merits of the
gentleman from New York, or would more readily than himself, do his duty, with that gentleman
as chairman. Mr. E. would conclude by repeating
that this matter had been introduced by his respected colleague, without his concurrence in the
slightest degree.
Mr. JARVIS said: Mr. Speaker, this really appears to me to be something like "much ado about
nothing." The whole amount of it is, whether a
committee has a right to elect its own chairman or
not—a point I never knew disputed before. As it
was through my instrumentality that the question
was brought up before the committee, I am willing,
perfectly willing, to take the whole responsibility
upon myself, "whether for good or for evil."
My principal object is to make it known, that is
very doing alone, and without consultation with
any member of the committee. I certainly wished
that it might have been done by some other gentleman of the committee, but as none other saw
fit to do it, I deemed it proper myself to bring the
question to their decision. Indeed, sir, I was in
hopes that it would have been done by the gentleman from Massachusetts himself, but the question

having been brought up in the committee, it was
perfectly understood, nor did any difference exist,
that the first named gentleman had the right
by courtesy, and that the committee had the right
to elect their own chairman. I regret that this
discussion has taken place, because it is on a subject which I had never before heard questioned—
the right of a committee of this House to elect its
own chairman.
We have been told that the present chairman
was elected by a minority of the committee; but
the honorable member from Massachusetts labored under a mistake when he made that assertion.
What are the facts? The committee consists of
nine members; at the first ballot there were eight
votes thrown—four for the gentleman who is now
chairman, and three for the other gentleman from
Massachusetts, (Mr. Everett,) and one for another
highly respectable member of the committee. At
the second ballot there were seven votes thrown,
four being a majority thereof, as many were given
in for the gentleman from New York, (Mr. Cambreleng,) and he was declared duly elected. Now,
sir, let me ask, what is the usage of this House?
Do we require a majority of the whole body to
elect any officer—not even excepting the Speaker? No, sir, we require only a majority of a quorum; and a majority of a quorum of the committee in the case under consideration elected their
chairman.
The gentleman from Massachusetts (Mr. Everett) gave us for a reason why he did not decline
the office, that he was with the majority of the
Committee in their views on the important question before the country. This, sir, is news to me.
I have attended every meeting of that Committee
save one, and at that one I believe no business was
transacted of any great importance, and I did not
know that the gentleman was in the majority—at
any rate, I knew that at the last meeting he was
in the minority on a question which he himself
brought before the Committee, and his wishes
were not acceded to, by a vote of five to four. I
know not whether there be anything in this matter requiring further observation.
The other gentleman from Massachusetts (Mr.
Adams) has made it a great point that the election
of Chairman of the Committee on Foreign Affairs
was not entered upon the Journals of the House.
Now, I will ask him where he will find a precedent
for it? So far from its being consistent with established usage, as the gentleman supposes, in my
opinion it would be a departure from it. I do
hope, Mr. Speaker, that the time of the House
will not longer be taken up in so fruitless a discussion.
Mr. E. EVERETT said, as the gentleman from
Maine (Mr. Jarvis) had positively contradicted the
statement made by Mr. E. in regard to the division
of the Committee, he would only say it was not possible that that gentleman and himself should differ
as to a matter of fact, on a question in which every
thing pertaining to it was well known to both!
Mr. E. did not say that upon every question agitated before the Committee he was with the majority, but only on the great and all-important one,
whether the Committee would recommend to the
House a decisive measure of reprisals or hostility
towards France, he stood with the majority, and
th t in the only question of great importance that
has taken place since the gentleman from N. York
presided, Mr. E. was in the majority, and that
gentleman in the minority.
Mr. CAMBRELENG said, if the gentle-
man referred to him, he could only say that he (Mr.
E.) had mistaken Mr. C.'s opinion, and mistook
the opinion of the Committee. He knew the gentleman did not design to mislead the House nor
the nation; but he would mislead both, if his remarks were suffered to pass uncorrected. The
majority of that Committee were neither in favor
of the gentleman's resolution, nor of the resolution of the gentleman before him, (Mr. Patton,)
nor, in other words, of one similar to that which
passed the other branch of this legislature a few
days ago.
Mr. POLK called for the orders of the day;
but the motion was not agreed to.
Mr. GILLET rose to a question of order, and after a few remarks on the point by the Chair—

Mr. PATTON then rose and said, Mr. Speaker, as a member of the Committee on Foreign Relations, and as a reference has been made to me, I feel it my duty to say a few words on the subject brought before us—brought before us, sir, without any participation of mine; but of which I take leave in the outset to say I do not complain. I was in the minority of the committee on the election of chairman, and voted against the dismission and displacement of the honorable and distinguished member from Massachusetts, from that position which, by usage, he occupied, and which I saw, and can now see, no just or proper reason why he should be removed therefrom. And, sir, I feel myself especially called upon to make this statement, because of the remarks made by the gentleman from New York, that considerations of declicacy and propriety demanded of the honorable member (Mr. Everett) that he should have retired from that situation, which reflects as much upon my course in voting that he should retain his position as it does upon that gentleman.

Mr. CAMBRELENG disclaimed all intention of applying his remark to the gentleman from Virginia, or to the gentleman from Massachusetts (Mr. Everett)—He had referred to the former Chairman of the Committee on Foreign Affairs (Mr. Archer) and to him alone.

Mr. PATTON. I understood the gentleman to say that the honorable member from Massachusetts should have retired from the situation in which he stood, and in which, in any humble judgment, he had a right to stand, from considerations of delicacy and propriety. Sir, my vote was given in order to retain him in a position which constituted a situation of delicacy and propriety; and I maintain that he had no just or proper grounds for retiring from it, that it was an elevated, an honorable, a distinguished situation to which he had arrived in due course; and that it devolved upon him high and important duties, which he would have been recreant if he had shrunk from the performance of. That gentleman had long been a distinguished ornament of that Committee; he was about to retire from the position he had so honorably and ably sustained; he was about to retire from Congress; and it seemed to me to be an uncalled for, an unjust, and therefore an improper act, calculated to mortify his feelings, that he should be thus displaced from the position he had held.

I readily admit that, under ordinary circumstances, and at the commencement of a session, a gentleman should be placed at the head of that committee friendly to the existing Administration; a committee, before which there was likely to come on questions of deep and vital importance; but that time had passed; the whole matters connected with the subject of our foreign relations of the slightest interest or importance to the country or the House, had long been before that committee, had been deliberated upon by that committee, and its solemn judgment given in relation to the most prominent and important question involved in our deliberations. And, sir, I again reiterate the statement made by the gentleman from Massachusetts, (Mr. Everett,) that, as I understood the complexion of the opinion of the committee, there is and was a majority concurring in the views which I understand that honorable member to maintain in relation to that subject, from any thing that he has offered in the shape of action in committee, but by his concurrence in the action I had myself proposed, and against which there has not yet been any decisive vote, and upon which there has been an expression of opinion as to its propriety from a majority of the committee. I ask, then, why it is, and upon what principle of delicacy and propriety it is, that the honorable gentleman was called upon to abandon that position, in order to place upon that committee a gentleman understood until now to be in the minority of the committee? It is news to me, to use the language employed by an honorable member from Maine upon that committee (Mr. Jarvis) "it is news to me," which has just been announced by the honorable member from New York—but most agreeable and acceptable news to me, that there is no member of that committee in favor of recommending reprisals at present! I rejoice to hear it. I trust it may be proclaimed throughout the land. I am glad to find there has undergone a change of opinion, with a portion of the committee, for certain it is that the time was that there was a considerable minority of that committee, which had grown, and which I confess I began to fear would grow so large, as to make the majority, in favor of an immediate and prompt recommendation of reprisals, in conformity with the recommendation of the President of the United States. Sir, I am glad, I am delighted, to hear that such is the state of things; and I do trust that a majority of this House will promptly second and confirm this now unanimous judgment of the committee, that that recommendation shall not be carried out. Trusting that this feeling, so much to be rejoiced at—that this unanimity, so much to be desired, may be found to prevail elsewhere, as well as in the committee, I shall, sir, if I can get permission of the House, upon the first opportunity, present a proposition that will enable the House to indicate that feeling.

There has been, and is now, a question before the committee, presented for action by myself—presented substantially three weeks ago, which was once rejected, and is now postponed—postponed—I know not with what view—to what end—with what design. But I wish the House and the country to understand, that the delay which has taken place, and the failure to act upon this important subject, about which the country is so much alive, and so anxious—one in which the country is so deeply interested—one in relation to which we have various and perpetual calls to know what we are going to do, and why we do not act, —I wish the House and the country to understand that it is a delay in which I have had no participation. There is no man upon that committee, no matter of what political party—and I say it in justice to those honorable gentlemen of that committee who belong to what is called the opposition party—no man disposed to pass censure upon the administration, but on the contrary, all are disposed to respond to the general tone of the President's Message, as prompted by a patriotic spirit, and a jealous regard for the rights of the country. It is one to which the voices of the representatives of the People of the U. S. ought to respond, and, at the same time, avoid doing any thing calculated to prevent the satisfactory adjustment of a matter involving the interests of the country. There ought to be a report made at once, so as to prevent the recurrence of any new difficulty.

As to this appointment of a Chairman, I feel no concern about it whatever. Individually, it is to me, as I should think it must be to every body else, a matter of not the slightest concern, who is at the head of the Committee—except as to personal feeling; for any other purpose it is, indeed, a quarrel about nothing. But, sir, I am perfectly willing that the House shall decide in some way that shall be final, what are the rights of the committee in relation to this subject, and whether the appointment by the Committee on Foreign Relations, be an authoritative and valid appointment. If it be, sir, I am content, and care nothing about it; let it stand. If it be not, then, sir, I hope the House will take it into their own hands, and elect their own chairman; and whenever such a question is presented to me—having not seen—not now seeing—any reason why a preference should be drawn against the honorable gentleman from Massachusetts, (Mr. Everett,) he shall have my vote here most cordially, as he had it there.

Mr. CAMBRELENG extremely regretted that he was compelled to rise again in a debate of this character; but the gentleman from Virginia, (Mr. Patton,) in repelling a presumed attack, had charged a majority of the Committee on Foreign Affairs with neglecting their duty to the House. When the proper time arrives for decisive action, he trusted that the Committee would not be backward in discharging its duty to the House, and its obligations to the country. He did not know that there was any member of the Committee in favor of proposing reprisals, or any other measure, at this time—that there was a majority of the
mittee, and he was authorised to state it—
the proceedings, of no committee could be
held from the House—who were of opinion
if we meant to do nothing, it was best to
thing. Some of the members of the Comm
and he was one of that number—believed
be the most dignified course. He thought
entirely compatible with the interest or h
the country, in the present attitude of ou
tions with France, to propose to the House
lution even of a negative or declaratory ch
He was opposed, in the peculiar state of o
tions, to taking any step which might be
strued to imply a disposition on the part
House to do homage to "the pride of F
Other gentlemen opposed immediate ac
other grounds. The gentleman who m
postponement of a resolution—similar
adopted by the Senate, and offered by the
man from Virginia (Mr. Patton)—made
tion, believing that the most effectual way
nothing, was to say nothing. A majority
Committee were decidedly opposed to an
whatever, at this time—but if the House
otherwise, the Committee could be instr
report such a resolution as the gentlem
Virginia and Massachusetts desired.

Mr. PATTON said either the gentlem
N. York was very unfortunate in hearing,
very unfortunate in giving expression
thoughts, if he understood me as mak
attack upon the majority of the
tee, or as intending to reflect upon them.
rather too much of self respect, even if I
what I hope I have, a proper share of re
this House, and for all its organs, to
what I certainly did not feel, any disre
any one of them. But the committees of th
are agents of this House, and under its
and in the House, when the proper occa
arrive, I will say exactly when, and in w
how far I differ in opinion with the m
the committee. I disagree to the correct
policy, and wisdom of the course pursued
majority; and I have indicated as much
deny the right of that committee to pre
House from expressing its opinion upon
which are matured for its judgment, be
committee do not choose to express thei
are now nearly at the close of the second
this short session of three months, and th
has been before us, before the House, a
the whole country, for upwards of six w
will any man upon that committee, o
House, say that he has not formed his j
upon these matters?

[Mr. BOON here rose to a question
and after some conversation thereon
CHAIR, Messrs. BOON, J. Q. ADAMS,
and BRIGGS,]

Mr. PATTON proceeded. He was a
his remarks were not strictly relevant to
tion before the House; but the remarks
the honorable chairman of the Committee
reign Relations had drawn him into a wi
thad he had intended. He had merely
that he conceived as soon as a committee
ed an opinion upon a subject-matter bef
was its duty to present it to the House.

Mr. COULTER said, in his opinion, th
of the gentleman from Massachusetts (
ams) was strictly parliamentary, and cal
the condition of the Committee on Fo
fairs. It was very true that in some old
on parliamentary law. it was stated, that
by usage and courtesy the first named on
mittee was the Chairman of that commit
was nevertheless in the power of that c
to constitute its own Chairman; but he
of no instance in which this practice had
served. He thought also, that in case o
tion of the first named individual, the s
the list of the committee became chair
rule being equivalent to, and commensur
the other. Therefore it was that when a
tee was announced, at the commencem
any other period of the session, it was sa
to the House and to the country, who
chairman of the same. But if the comm

ook to exercise the power which this old rule sed to confer upon them, it must become ne- ary so to i form the House, so that it might be red on the journals, and become generally wn. The motion under consideration was due e House and due to the gentleman from New k, and Mr. C. could perceive no objection in ting it. He would also state further, that the tion of the committee's right to elect a chair- was discussed there, and assented to unani- sly. They proceeded to the election, and the er chairman (Mr. Everett) himself announced e gentleman from New York that he was du- ected. Mr. C. must respond to the gentle- from Virginia that it was a matter of no con- ence further than as related to personal feel- , and he would say that a deep wound had been cted upon his own, but that was not a matter he House. When the question came up in roper shape, he should be prepared to give House the views he entertained upon it.

. ARCHER obtained the floor, but yielded the request of

. JARVIS, who said: Mr. Speaker, I should have thought of addressing the House again this subject, were it not for some observa- which fell from the gentleman from Virginia, one of the Committee on Foreign Affairs myself. The gentleman made an attack upon and upon the majority of that committee, in his reasons for voting as he did. I under- the gentleman to say he voted as he did, be- he considered it would be a violation of de- y and propriety to vote otherwise.

. PATTON disclaimed having used such lan- , and explained.

. JARVIS. The gentleman, however, did the words "uncalled for," "unjust," and proper," in reference to this subject. Now, majority of the committee do not seem to it was "uncalled for," because the ques- on going into the election of a chairman was mous. That it was neither "unjust" nor proper," in their opinion, may be inferred the course taken by the committee; and I state in a few words what it was that actuated . I consider that the chairman of the various mittees of this House ought to be men in a n degree in confidential relation with the ative branches of the Government, or at least as the latter may enter into confidential rela- with. I conceive that the chairman of a ittee ought not to be a man who has shown first to last an unrelenting hostility to the istration, and who, on every occasion, has avored to thwart it. The gentleman from ine, with his very delicate notions, may think per and right to embarrass the administra- by electing such a chairman; I do not think The gentleman has said, that if this election d come on in this House, he should again for the gentleman from Massachusetts (Mr. ett) as chairman of the committee. I am glad to know beforehand how that gentleman to vote. The gentleman says that a ma- concurred with the hon. member from Mass. is a point of fact upon which we are distinct- issue, for I repeat it was not so. There two distinct questions brought before the mittee, and both of them voted down. On first question the gentleman from Massa- tts and the gentleman from Virginia, in the majority; on the second ques- they voted in the minority. Sir, I voted st both propositions. I voted against the because I thought that at the present time at rather too far, and I voted against the se- because it did not go far enough—neither of met my views of policy, but if I had been d to determine between them, I should have nly preferred the epigram of the President madrigal of the gentleman from Virginia. latter gentleman brought his proposition a d time before the committee, and it was post- d. It was the opinion of the committee, that intended to do nothing, the proper course be to say nothing, and not issue a report to world which should enable the disaffected to speak any language they thought proper. was very glad to hear from that gentleman that it was not the intention of any one on the committee to do otherwise than respond to the sentiments embraced in the President's message. I am very happy to hear it, though I did not know that was the case, for I thought there was a disposition to give us something of the "milk and water" kind, which I believe the President has not been in the habit of giving us. The gentleman seemed to think that it was proper in the beginning of the session to have a chairman of the committee thinking with the administration; but he seemed to think it proper in the middle of the session, to have one who thought entirely different from the administration; what kind of a chairman the gentleman would wish to have at the end of it, we do not know.

Mr. PATTON. Not such a chairman as the gentleman from Maine would make, at any period of the session. There is one remark made by that gentleman, to which I beg leave to say a few words in reply. He says, or seems to say, or seems to wish it to be understood that he supposes that I desire the appointment of a Chairman who would throw embarrassment in the way of the Administration and for that end. Sir, events are too recent in the knowledge of this House and of this Congress, to give any point to such an imputation as that. I stood here during the last session, in a position, and pursued a course, which will prevent any insinuation of that sort from having any weight here or elsewhere. Sir, I stood here in vindication of this Administration from assaults of the most violent character, in opposition to two-thirds of the legislature of my native State. I made that vindication under circumstances which I knew at the time involved great personal sacrifices; I regarded all but "as dust in the balance" in the discharge of my public duty. Mr. Speaker, I have never stood here, nor ever will stand here, as long as those who send me shall continue to honor me with their confidence, either to throw embarrassment in the way of any administration, or to comply with base subserviency to all the edicts of this or any administration.

In the performance of my duty on this floor, I care not who or what the administration are. I come here to represent the people who sent me here; to sustain their rights and interests, and to vindicate the constitution of my country from assaults made upon it, whether they come from the administration or are aimed at the administration. Sir, I think in general it was best that the Chairman of the Committee on Foreign Relations, as of most of the Committees of this House, should concur, in general political sentiment, with the majority of the House, and especially that that should be the case in relation to so important a one as the Committee in question; because the Chairman of that Committee is supposed, by usage of the House, and perhaps by propriety itself, to be on terms of more confidential intercourse and communication with the Secretary on Foreign Affairs, who might make his communications through a gentleman who stood in that political relation. But this is a matter of little importance. I saw no necessity for cashiering our Chairman. Although that gentleman is a political opponent of the administration, I presume he is so conscientiously—and it gives me pleasure to say, that so far as I know, or have seen, he has conducted himself in opposition with the dignity and spirit of a gentleman. I did think, and do now think, that the gentleman from Massachusetts, as far as I could ascertain his views, did concur in opinion with a majority of the Committee.

The gentleman from Maine has undertaken to throw out another remark, which I suppose he considers witty and sarcastic. But he should bear in mind, that wit and sarcasm are always pointless unless sharpened by truth. I ask, what ground is there for the gratuitous and insolent insinuation—

The CHAIR here interposed and called the gentleman to order.

Mr. PATTON—for the insinuation that my opinions can never be known till I have voted. A frank disclosure of my opinions upon political questions has been my misfortune. It is not a fault. I have never waited, as some politicians do, to see which way the wind blows, for God knows, I am always willing to give a free and frank expression of any sentiments. It would be fortunate, perhaps, if we could know what some gentlemen's opinions were even *after they had voted*, for since we are giving the experience of the committee upon this subject, it may not be amiss, perhaps, to remind the gentleman from Maine, that he was one of those who voted againt the recommendation for reprisals, when the question was first put, and he himself afterwards moved to reconsider that vote. Whether that reconsideration was prompted by a change of opinion or not, I confess I have no means of knowing, except from the gentleman from New York, who informs us that the committee are unanimous that there ought to be no reprisals. Now, except as far as we can judge from the votes which the gentleman has given, and from information derived from the gentleman from New York, the gentleman from Maine left us at a loss to know what his opinion was when he first voted, and what his opinion may be now. I regret that any thing of a personal character should have been brought into this discussion; and before I sit down, I beg leave to discharge myself from any imputation of having in the slightest degree, any intention of making any reflection whatsoever upon the committee. I stated this explicitly at the outset of my remarks. They have precisely the same right to their opinion that I have to mine, and I have precisely the same right to my own opinions that they have to theirs. I intended no reflection upon them. I again, however, repeat, that I do not concur with the committee in their course, which I think was calculated to inflict a wound on the feelings of, and an unmerited reflection upon the gentleman from Massachusetts. If those who voted in the majority, did not think so in carrying out their view, they had so expressed their opinion.

Mr. ARCHER rose and said, he had not, thus far, taken any part in this discussion, which had taken a wide and unparalleled range; but circumstances seemed to call upon him for the expression of his opinion on some of the points which it involved. He would ask if any such office or officer as "Chairman of a Committee," was known or recognised by the House? He believed not. It was the whole Committee to which the House looked as one of its instruments or agents. Put the question on the strongest possible ground—suppose a Committee to be constituted in the usual manner, of which the gentleman first named is considered, by usage, the Chairman. Suppose the Committee to displace that individual, and elect another. Would it be contended that it was not competent for them to do so? Again—it being known that the duties of the Chairman of a Committee were much more onerous than those of any other member, suppose they should come to the humane conclusion that it was unfair to impose all those duties on one individual, and should agree that they should be performed consecutively by all the members of the Committee, each individual taking his regular turn in the chair; would any one on that floor contend that it was not competent for them to do so? But when there was a removal of the head of the Committee from his station—as was the case in the present instance, by the transfer of his esteemed friend from Georgia (Mr. Wayne) to another sphere of action—what was the evident and obvious course for the Committee to pursue? Precisely what it had done—to proceed to the election of another Chairman. They had a right to do so, and they had done it. That House had no cognizance of the acts and doings of Committees, further than they were reported to it.

Mr. A. said, gentlemen were mistaken when they averred that no precedent existed on this subject. Such a precedent did exist. He could not determine positively the year in which it occurred; but he distinctly remembered that a former colleague of his, (the late Mr. Randolph,) in consequence of some change in the political relations of the country, was, by one important standing committee of the House, in consequence of the occurrence of a vacancy, elected as their chairman. When you appoint a committee, you constitute an

organ capable of making its own subordinate regulations. Mr. A. said, he admitted with the gentleman from Pennsylvania (Mr. Coulter) that it was incumbent on the committee in this case, as that did in the case of the late Mr. Randolph, to report the fact of the election to the House. Had they done so, it would have superseded the necessity of this debate. It was still competent for them to do so, and he suggested to the gentleman from Massachusetts (Mr. Adams) the propriety of withdrawing his motion, in order to give the committee an opportunity to take this course.

Mr. ADAMS said, it would give him pleasure to gratify the gentleman from Virginia (Mr. Archer,) if he could, by that course attain his object. But he could not consent to withdraw his motion until he could ascertain who was Chairman of the Committee on Foreign Affairs. The gentleman from New York himself, (Mr. Cambreleng,) had admitted that he received only four votes, which was a minority of the committee. Mr. A. said, he had made a motion to that effect, and he wished to see it recorded on the journal of the House, that *Edward Everett*, of Massachusetts, or *Churchill C. Cambreleng*, of New York, was Chairman of the Committee on Foreign Affairs.

Mr. A. continued. When he first rose he had distinctly stated that his object in rising was to propound a question to the chairman of that committee. It became necessary for him, first to ascertain who that chairman was. Hence this inquiry. The subject on which he desired to propound his question, was the very important one so often alluded to in this debate. It related to our affairs with France,—that part of the President's *Message* being referred to that committee. He wished to know what that committee had done—what it was doing—and what it intended to do in relation thereto. But he was now unable to put that question. The gentleman from Virginia had said that every member of a committee could be its chairman—sometimes one and sometimes another. He knew no such rule or practice.

Mr. ARCHER explained. He had said that it was competent for committees to elect their own chairman, and he read Jefferson's Manual to that effect. In Standing Committees the gentleman first named thereon was considered as the chairman by courtesy, and discharged the duties accordingly.

Mr. ADAMS resumed. Such was not the rule of that House, and no such usage having obtained there, he had two objections to it. First, the displacement of a chairman, was, he would not say, an insult to the individual holding the station; but it evidently conveyed a censure on his conduct or opinions. Secondly, it was calculated to display an improper, dishonorable, and degrading subserviency on the part of that House towards the Executive or Administration. This doctrine was entirely new to him, and he thought it due to the dignity and honor of that House to repudiate it. He asked where was the rule by which committees of that House were to be made to coincide in and support all the views of the Administration? Especially when those views involved the great questions of peace and war? He knew of none—but he well knew of instances where a contrary practice had obtained. Mr. A. said that during the administration of Mr. Monroe, when he was himself at the head of the Department of State, the individual placed by the Speaker at the head of the House of Representatives as chairman of the Committee on Foreign Relations, was not only decidedly hostile to the Administration, but himself and that individual were not then on speaking terms. These facts, Mr. A. said, the Speaker at that time knew, but he had never entertained an idea of complaining that the Speaker had done injustice to the Administration in the selection. The business between the Department and the committee was as well transacted through the medium of other individuals. Mr. A. asked what must be the result of this principle, if carried out and persisted in? Evidently to place that House at the feet of the Executive.

Mr. ARCHER said the gentleman from Massachusetts (Mr. Adams) was correct in point of fact. The chairman of the Committee on For-

eign Affairs had been opposed to the Administration, prior to his own appointment to that station.

Mr. ADAMS was glad to hear the gentleman from Virginia (Mr. Archer) confirm the assertion. For his own part, he knew the fact. This new principle, he contended, was a most dangerous one—calculated to prostrate that House before Executive domination. He wished it be distinctly understood that he made no personal objection to the honorable member from New York. Let the chairman be ever so much a friend of the administration—it constituted no objection: but it was the *rule* that he must be of such particular political complexion, which he denounced as odious and inadmissible. He would have that House, in point of fact, as it was in name, one of the most dignified bodies on the face of the globe. He would have its committees appointed, neither with a view to their opposition or adhesion to any administration.

Mr. A. said, before he sat down, he felt that he ought to confirm the remark made by his honorable colleague (Mr. E. Everett), by stating that he had brought this subject before the House, without any recommendation or concurrence on his (Mr. E.'s part,)but rather in opposition to that gentleman's wishes. I had determined, (said Mr. A.,) as soon as I heard—(not from him, for it was common rumor)—of the change in the head of He Committee, to have the subject investigated. And when I reflected that the individual whose rights and feelings were more particularly implicated, was my colleague and friend, I came to the conclusion that it became peculiarly my duty to bring it before the House. I have accordingly done so. Mr. A. said he still adhered to the opinion, that the four votes given for the gentleman from New York (Mr. Cambreleng) were insufficient to elect him. He would be perfectly satisfied, however, if the House would insert the name of the chairman of that Committee on the journal. He knew not how else to get over the matter. He said he would conclude by repeating, that when he could ascertain officially, *who was* the chairman of the Committee on Foreign Affairs, he had a question to put to him.

Mr. LANE said he had not been able to comprehend the object of the distinguished member from Massachusetts, (Mr. Adams.) He admits the Committee on Foreign Relations have selected a Chairman. And the object of the motion as avowed by the mover is not to set aside that election, but to place the fact upon the Journal of the House.

The honorable gentleman from Virginia, (Mr. Archer,) requests his friend to withdraw the motion, that the Committee may report, which will place the House in the possession of all the gentleman desires.

To this request the gentleman from Massachusetts (Mr. Adams) responds that he will not withdraw the motion from the House, because he is not informed who the Chairman of that committee is that the gentleman from New York (Mr. Cambreleng) was not elected by a majority of the votes of the committee; that four votes did not constitute a majority of nine; that by the usage of the House, his honorable friend and colleague (Mr. Everett) was the Chairman of the Committee on Foreign Relations.

Sir, the gentleman seems to have forgotten the fact, that upon the ballot by which the Chairman claims to have been elected, but seven votes were cast, and that four is a majority of seven. That gentleman is eloquent upon the rights of the majority, and says they have been disregarded.

Mr. Speaker, that the majority ought, in all cases, to prevail, is a sentiment as democratical as it is patriotic; and it is a subject of national gratulation to hear it acknowledged even at this late period of our political history, by the honorable gentleman from Massachusetts, (Mr. Adams.) But, sir, while the sentiment is praiseworthy, for some individuals to invoke a discussion would be delicate, if not embarrassing. The day has been when a different principle was not only *held*, but *prevailed* in this House—when the minority formed for the *brief patriot of four years*, a Chairman of a committee constituted of the entire American People—a day when the *voice* of fifteen times forty

thousand freemen was disregarded. A day by *management*, and by means of which it us not to speak, eighty-*four* was made to over ninety-nine.

Sir, said Mr. Lane, the day has already spent in, it is true an interesting, but is aspects an unpleasant debate. The time House is the time and the money of the People. To spend it without any visible or valuable is a sacrifice of the public interest. To bring a close, Mr. Speaker, I move you to lay tion upon the table.

On this motion Mr. REED called for the ye and nays, which were ordered.

Mr. JARVIS appealed to the gentleman Indiana (Mr. Lane) to withdraw his motion one moment, as he was desirous of making gle remark on a point implicating his own al feelings.

After some hesitation, Mr. LANE withdrew motion to lay the subject on the table, as ing the pledge of the gentleman from Jarvis) that he would renew it.

Mr. JARVIS then said the gentleman girls, (Mr. Patton,) with whom he had ever on terms of the most friendly intercourse, progress of his remarks, and in the heat bate, had suffered an expression to escape which was at least unparliamentary, and he —indeed he had no doubt, on cooler he would not hesitate to qualify or retract.

The SPEAKER here interposed and that for the expression alluded to, the gentleman from Virginia (Mr. Patton) was called to order the Chair, and the Chair had considered it a tracted by the member in which that gentleman immediately qualified it.

Mr. JARVIS said, under these circumstances he had not another word to add.

Mr. PATTON rose, and said he had not ed his expression, nor did he consider it ed, while—

The SPEAKER again repeated that he considered it. He could countenance no debate.

Mr. JARVIS, according to his promise, renewed the motion of Mr. Lane to lay the lution on the table.

Messrs. ARCHER and ADAMS rose appealing for a withdrawal of the motion.

Mr. PULK rose to a question of order—the tion not being debateable.

Mr. JARVIS replied, that the motion to the gentleman from Indiana, (Mr. Lane,) could not be withdrawn without his consent.

The question was then taken by yeas and on the motion of Mr. LANE, and decided affirmative, as follows:

YEAS—Messrs. John J. Allen, Wm. Allen, thony, Beale, Bean, Blair, Bockee, Boon, Brown, Burns, Carmichael, Carr, Casey, S. Clark, Coffee, Conner, Cramer, Day, F. son, D. W. Dickinson, Dunlap, Ferris, K. Fuller, Galbraith, Gillet, Gillett, Grayson, Joseph Hall, Thomas H. Hamer, Joseph M. Harper, Harrison, Hawkins, Hawes, Henderson, Howell, Huntington, Inge, Jarvis, R. M. Johnson, Johnson, B. Jones, Kilgore, Kinnard, Lane, ning, Laporte, Lea, T. Lee, Loyall, Lyon, Abijah Mann, Joel K. Mann, Mardis, J. Y. Moses Mason, May, McIntire, McKay, McKinley, McLene, McVean, Miller, Robert chell, Morgan, Muhlenberg, Osgood, Parks, ker, Patterson, Dutee J. Pearce, Peyton, lin Pierce, Pierson, Pinckney, Plummer, Pope, Ramsay, Reynolds, Schenck, Sibley, Shepperd, Shinn, Smith, Speight, Standefer, therland, W. Taylor, Fran. Thomas, Thomas Turrill, Vanderpoel, Wagener, Ward, Webster, Whallon, White—109.

NAYS—Messrs. John Q. Adams, Heman Allen C. Allan, Archer, Banks, Barber, Barnitz, ger, Bates, Baylies, Beaty, Binney, Beggs, Burges, Bynum, Cage, Chambers, Clark, Crane, Darlington, Amos Davis, Davenport, berry, Deny, Dickson, Evans, H. Everett, ing, Felder, Fillmore, Foster, Philo C. Gamble, Gholson, Gordon, Gorham,

iffin, Hiland H. Hall, Hannegan, Hard, Hardin, mes Harper, Hazeltine, Heath, Hiester, Wm. ikson, Ebenezer Jackson, Janes, Wm. Cost hason, Henry Johnson, King, Lay, Letcher, wis, Lincoln, Love, Lucas, Manning, Martin- ie, Marshall, McComas, McKennan, Mercer, llgan, Miner, Moore, Patton, Phillips, Pickens, ths, Reed, Rencher, Robertson, W. B. Shep- l, Slade, Sloane, Spangler, Steele, W. P. Tay- r, Tompkins, Trumbull, Turner, Tweedy, Vance, ston, Watmough, F. Whittlesey, Williams, Wil- s, Young.—97.

So the House decided to lay the motion of Mr. ams on the table.

Mr. MERCER then rose and said he had, in mmon with the whole House, regretted to wit- ss a personal misunderstanding (the first that I occurred during the present session) between ne, of his respected members. In thus alluding to subject, Mr. M. said, he acted as the friend of h those honorable individuals. He had dis- stly heard his colleague, (Mr. Patton,) make s remark that he could not retract his expres- a while the language of the gentleman from ine, (Mr. Jarvis,) remained in full force. Be- rhng, as he, Mr. M. really did, that no personal respect was intended by the gentleman from ine, towards his colleague, he had sought and tained assurance of that fact. Those honora- gentlemen were now fully reconciled, and he as happy to be the organ to announce that intel- gence to the House.

On motion of Mr. MERCER, the House then ad- rned.

IN SENATE.

Thursday, January 22, 1835.

Petitions and memorials were presented by Mrs. TYLER, BLACK, and LEIGH.

Mr. FRELINGHUYSEN rose, after the reading the Journal, to make a correction which he rved two of the newspapers of the day had en into, in their report of his remarks upon presentation of the Cherokee memorial yes- y. He was represented as having said that Cherokees proposed to cede all their lands in egia to the Government of the United States. as particular he was misapprehended. They osed only to cede all those lands which were nded for their personal use and enjoyment; uost to be secured to them absolutely, together h equal political privileges with other citizens eorgia.

The VICE PRESIDENT laid before the Senate mmunication from the Secretary of the Trea- made in obedience to a resolution of the Se- e, transmitting a statement of the progress ch had been made in the preparation of maps rtain States, required to be prepared by a lion of 28th February, 1823.

Mr. LEIGH, from the Committee on Revolu- ry Claims, made an unfavorable report upon petition of Col. Vivion Brooking.

Mr. WEBSTER, from the Committee on Fi- ce, to which the same had been referred, re- ted the bill from the House of Representatives, king appropriations for the Indian Department the year 1835.

Also, the bill making appropriations for the port of the army for the year 1835.

Mr. WEBSTER moved that the Senate proceed the consideration of these bills, which was ted to, and the first-named was then consider- in Committee of the Whole.

Mr. HENDRICKS objected to a clause in the approp-riating $81,300 for the pay of one hun- and six supernumerary Lieutenants, gradu- of the Military Academy, and asked some ex- ation relative to this item from the Chairman the Finance Committee.

Mr. WEBSTER had he thought there was no propriation in the bill but what was authorized existing laws. He supposed these supernu- ries were attached to the army.

Mr. WRIGHT suggested that the item was in bill because these Lieutenants were attached the army and ready for duty.

Mr. WEBSTER said he would not press the bill this time, unless gentlemen were satisfied the correctness of it.

On his motion, the bill was then laid on the table.

The bill making appropriations for the support of the army for the year 1835 was read a second time, as in Committee of the Whole, and ordered to be engrossed for a third reading.

The following resolutions were submitted by Mr. SOUTHARD:

Resolved, That the Committee on the Library be instructed to inquire into the expediency of purchasing the copies of Walterston & Vanzandt's "Continuation of the Tabular Statistical Views of the United States," which remain unsold of the edition, for the use of Congress.

Resolved, That the Committee on Naval Affairs be instructed to inquire into the expediency of making an appropriation to deepen the Bar of Pensacola Bay, in Florida, so as to admit vessels of war of the largest class to the United States Navy Yard, establish'd there.

Mr. SOUTHARD, from the Committee on Na- val Affairs, made unfavorable reports upon the petitions of Captain Drinker and Samuel Martin.

Mr. LINN from the Committee on Private Land Claims, to which was referred a bill confirming the title of Joseph Sovin, alias La Rochelle, and those claiming under him, to a tract of land in Missouri, reported the same without amendment. The bill was read the first time, and ordered to a second reading.

The following resolution submitted yesterday by Mr. HENDRICKS, was taken up, considered, and agreed to:

Resolved, That the Committee on the Judiciary be instructed to inquire into the expediency of fixing by law, the time of the commencement and close of every succeeding session of Congress.

The bill from the House of Representatives making appropriations for certain fortifications for the year 1835, was read the first time, and or- d-red to a second reading.

Mr. KING, of Georgia, from the Committee on Foreign Relations, made an unfavorable report upon the petition of Somerville Pinckney.

The bill for the relief of William O'Neil, was read the second time and referred.

The following Senate bills were read the third time and passed:

A bill for the relief of the heirs or legal repre- sentatives of Col. John Hudrey, deceased.

A bill authorizing the construction of a rail- road from the public grounds near Tallahassee to St. Marks in Florida.

A bill for the relief of the heirs of General Carera.

A bill for the relief of William Pettiplace and —— White, legal representatives of Joseph White, deceased.

A bill to improve the navigation of the Missis- sippi river, in the vicinity of St. Louis.

A bill authorizing the removal of the land of- fice from Clinton to Jackson, in Mississippi.

A bill for the completion of certain improve- ments in Florida.

A bill for the relief of Elizabeth Magruder, of Mississippi;

A bill to improve the harbor at or near the mouth of the river Raisin;

Mr. PRESTON, pursuant to notice, and on leave given, introduced a bill for the relief of Thomas Cooper, of South Carolina; which was read twice, and referred to the Judiciary Commit- tee.

[This bill proposes to refund to Doctor Cooper the sum of $400, with interest from the year 1798, being the amount of a fine imposed upon him, un- der the old alien and sedition laws.]

Mr. PRESTON, from the Judiciary Committee, reported a bill authorizing the Secretary of the Treasury to compromise the claim of the United States upon the Bank of Illinois; which was read the first time, and ordered to a second reading.

The following bills from the House of Repre- sentatives, were read a third time and passed:

A bill to provide for the final adjustment of claims to land in the State of Louisiana;

The joint resolution requiring the statues exe- cuted by Persico to be placed in the niches in front of the Capitol, for which they were de- signed;

A bill making appropriations for the current expenses of the Indian Department, for the year 1835;

A resolution authorizing a gold medal to be struck and presented to Col. Croghan, and swords to the officers who were under his command, for their gallant conduct at fort Sandusky, during the late war.

The bill making compensation for French spo- liations prior to 1800, came up as the special or- der, and

On motion of Mr. ROBBINS, it was postponed to, and made the special order for Monday next.

Mr. CLAY rose and said, that in consequence of the indisposition of several Senators who were ab- sent, he would not make the motion which he in- tended yesterday, to make to to-day, to go into the consideration of Executive business.

Mr. FRELINGHUYSEN, from the Committee on Revolutionary Claims, reported a bill for the relief of David Brooks; which was read the first time and ordered to a second reading.

The bill for the relief of J. B. O'Strouder, was taken up for consideration, and, on motion of Mr. SOUTHARD, indefinitely postponed.

The Senate then proceeded to the general or- ders of the day, and the following bills were read a second time, considered as in Committee of the Whole, and ordered to be engrossed for a third reading.

A bill for the relief of William Clark;

A resolution for the relief of John S. Stiles;

A bill for the relief of Samuel S. Lord and others.

The bill for the relief of Walter Loomis and Abel Gay, was considered on second reading, as in Committee of the Whole, when some remarks were made by Mr. HENDRICKS and Mr. TOM- LINSON in favor, and by Mr. HILL and Mr. WRIGHT in opposition to the bill, when,

On motion of Mr. WRIGHT, it was laid on the table.

The bill granting military bounty land scrip to the heirs of Nathaniel Tyler, deceased, was con- sidered as in Committee of the Whole, and after some remarks by Mr. CLAY, Mr. LEIGH, and Mr. POINDEXTER, on motion of Mr. CLAY, was laid on the table.

On motion of Mr. HILL, The Senate adjourned.

HOUSE OF REPRESENTATIVES.

Thursday, January 22, 1835.

Petitions and memorials were presented by— Mr. PLUMMER, of Mississippi; Mr. PARKER, of New Jersey; Mr. GORHAM, of Massachusetts; Mr. TOMPKINS, of Kentucky; Mr. CHINN, of Virginia; Mr. MAY, of Illinois; Mr. KINNARD, of Indiana;

[Mr. KINNARD presented the petition of William Bowman, of Morgan county, Indiana, praying the correction of certain errors in the entry of land.]

Mr. WHITE, of Florida; Mr. SEVIER, of Arkansas; Mr. GRAYSON, of South Carolina; Mr. GILLET, of New York; Which memorials and petitions were appropri- ately referred.

Mr. THOMSON, from the Committee on Mili- tary Affairs, reported a bill for the relief of Docts. Findley and Meade; which was read twice and committed.

Mr. CLAY, from the Committee on the Public Lands, reported a bill supplementary to the act reviving the act granting pre-emption rights to settlers on the public lands, approved May 29, 1830; which was read twice and postponed to the first of February.

Mr. BOON, from the Committee on the Public Lands, reported a bill granting school lands to fractional townships; which was read twice and committed.

Mr. FOSTER, from the Committee on the Ju- diciary, reported a bill to authorize letters patent to be issued to Francis B. Ogden; which was read twice and ordered to be engrossed.

Mr. FOSTER, from the same Committee, re-

ported the following resolutions, which were agreed to:

Resolved, That a communication, with the accompanying document, from the Secretary of the Treasury to the Chairman of the Judiciary Committee, dated 31st December last, on the subject of the proposed discharge of Joseph L. Dias from a judgment obtained by the United States against him, in the Southern District of New York, be referred to the Committee on the Judiciary, with instructions to consider and report thereon.

Resolved, That the communication from the Secretary of State to the Chairman of the Judiciary Committee of the 15th January inst. relative to the punishment of consuls and commercial agents, and also relative to the commission of frauds in obtaining patents for inventions for which patents have already been obtained, be referred to the Judiciary Committee, with instructions to consider and report on the several subjects introduced in said communication.

Mr. ASHLEY, from the Committee on Public Lands, reported a bill to confirm private land claims in Missouri, which was read twice and committed. On motion of Mr. A., the documents on this subject not heretofore published were ordered to be printed.

Mr. INGE, from the Committee on Public Lands, reported a bill to authorize the settlement of the claims of deputy surveyors who have surveyed Spanish land claims in Florida, which was read twice and committed.

Mr. INGE, from the same Committee, reported a bill for the relief of James M. Tuttle, which was read twice and ordered to be engrossed for a third reading.

Mr. FOSTER, from the Committee on the Judiciary, reported a bill to regulate the sittings of the United States District Courts for the eastern and western districts of Tennessee, which was read twice and ordered to be engrossed

Messrs. BANKS, SLADE, FULTON, FOSTER, CLAYTON, YOUNG, and INGE, each made unfavorable reports upon petitions, &c. Referred to their respective committees.

Mr. CARR, from the Committee on Private Land Claims, moved that said committee be discharged from the consideration of the petition of Chad Miller, and that said petition be referred to the Committee on the Public Lands. The motion prevailed, and the petition so referred.

The resolution heretofore offered by Mr. TURRILL, was, on his motion, taken up, modified, and adopted.

The following resolution, heretofore offered by Mr. PINCKNEY, was taken up and agreed to:

Resolved, That the President of the U. S. be requested (if not inconsistent in his opinion with the public interest) to communicate to this House any correspondence that may have taken place between the Government and that of Spain respecting the act of Congress, passed on the 30th day of June, 1834, entitled "an act concerning tonnage duty on Spanish vessels"—and also any information in his possession going to show whether there is any prospect that the commerce of the United States with the Island of Porto Rico, will hereafter be regulated upon principles of reciprocity, or whether it is in contemplation by the Spanish authorities to increase or reduce the discriminating duties of tonnage, and the discriminating duties on American vessels and on American merchandise and produce.

On motion of Mr KINNARD,

Resolved, That the Committee on Private Land Claims be instructed to inquire into the expediency of allowing William Bowman, of Morgan county, Indiana, to relinquish to the United States, certain lands erroneously entered at the Land Office at Crawfordsville, and to enter certain other lands in lieu thereof, as shown by his petition and the papers on file in the office of the Commissioner of the General Land Office.

Mr. BOON moved to suspend the rule of the House for the purpose of calling the States, for resolutions; which was lost.

The following resolution, heretofore offered by Mr. JOHNSON, of Kentucky, was taken up:

Resolved, That the Committee on the Contingent Expenses of the House be directed to audit the accounts of the members of the committee appointed by the House of Representatives on the 26th day of June last, for investigating the condition and proceedings of the Post Office Department, at the rate of compensation paid to the committee for preparing a code of laws for the District of Columbia, of which Philip Doddridge, Esq. was Chairman, viz. eight dollars per day during the recess, without any other allowance.

When the resolution was last before the House, the following amendment was proposed by Mr. MANN, of New York:

Strike out all after the word resolved, and insert, "That the Committee on Accounts of this House be directed to audit the accounts of the members of the committee appointed by this House on the 26th day of June last, for investigating the condition and proceedings of the Post Office Department, and allow each member of such committee at the rate of eight dollars per day, (including a reasonable time for their travelling respectively to the Seat of Government,) during the time they have actually been engaged at the Post Office Department, up to the commencement of the present session."

To which latter proposition Mr. GILLET moved the following amendment:

"And that those who came to Washington on said business, and returned home before the commencement of the present session of Congress, be allowed their actual travel and their per diem allowance while attending on said committee, and no more."

Mr. LANE said he had been surprised to hear a difference of opinion expressed, by honorable members of the House, upon the subject of compensating the committees appointed at the last session, to investigate the Post Office Department in the recess of Congress.

That to his mind a plainer proposition could not be presented to the human understanding for decision. The Committee are members of this House, as much they were appointed to perform duties properly belonging to this House; as such will be their report, and as such ought to be their pay.

This admitted, and the question is determined. Suppose Congress had adjourned to meet in October. The travel and the pay would have been the same, except the per diem from Oct. to the 1st Monday in December.

Will any gentleman attempt to distinguish the one from the other.

The committee convened in October and continued their labors until the meeting of Congress. To pay them $8 per day from the time they respectively entered upon the duties assigned them, to the first Monday in October, is to pay them as members of Congress—all they have a right to expect, all they deserve, and all this House has the power under the law to allow.

The members of this committee, like every other member of this House, received their travelling pay to and from this *capital,* before or at the close of the last session. They will now, if not already done, draw their pay a second time.

And is there an honorable gentleman on this floor, who really believes the members of this committee, will have necessarily travelled the road to and from their respective places of residence more than four times. If not, for this they have or will receive, eight dollars for every twenty miles, to pay them more, would be to pay them for travelling expenses never incurred; to pay them other than for every day they have devoted to the public interest as members of the committee, would be to pay them for services never rendered.

That his honorable friend had, on the right, from Kentucky, (Col. Johnson,) had said, he would pay the committee from the close of the last to the commencement of the present session. That his constituents were *intelligent, patriotic,* and *bold,* and would sustain him in rewarding the public servants generously.

Mr. L. said while he fully acquiesced in the praises his friend from Kentucky (Col. Johnson,) had been pleased to bestow upon his constituents, he felt justified in claiming for himself the honor

of representing a People equally *intelligent, patriotic,* and bold, and at the same time more enterprising and industrious. That while he has no doubt they would sustain him in patronizing a just and adequate compensation to every public servant, he should consider he was paying a poor compliment to their intelligence and patriotism, could he entertain, much less express the belief they would, or ought to sustain him, should he vote for paying any one in or out of this House in travelling expenses never incurred, for services never performed, or for time in no wise devoted to the public interest. Pay the committee like every other member in the House, $8 for every 20 miles coming to and returning from the city, at each session, and for each day, upon the committee or in this House, and no more. For this purpose he sent an amendment to the chair.

The amendment of Mr. LANE, was then read as follows:

Strike out all after the word Department, and insert

"By allowing to each member of said Committee eight dollars per day, from the time said Committee met at Washington, until the commencement of the present session."

Mr. MANN, of New York, was willing to accept the proposition of the gentleman from Indiana.

The amendments proposed by Messrs. MANN and GILLET, were negatived.

The question recurring upon Mr. LANE'S amendment, Mr. PARKER moved to amend it by adding "the usual allowance of mileage to Washington City."

Mr. PARKER was of opinion that the members of this committee should receive something beyond the ordinary allowance. They were able and willing to leave their business at home unmolested, to . There were members residing at a distance particularly in the south, who, as a matter of choice, remained in this neighborhood, and who did not go home at the close of the session, who were nevertheless paid their mileage. The Post Office Committee were here in the recess by the direction of the House. Their duties were arduous and he hoped that the amendment submitted by him would prevail.

Mr. LANE suggested that the members of the committee, as a matter of course would receive the usual allowance for mileage. He was opposed to giving them double the amount provided by law.

Mr. PARKER'S amendment was disagreed to.

Mr. BEAUMONT, moved to amend the amendment of Mr. LANE, by adding the words "no more," which was negatived.

The amendment submitted by Mr. LANE, then concurred in, and thus amended, the motion was agreed to.

The following resolution, heretofore offered Mr. McCARTY, was again taken up.

Resolved, That the President of the U. S. be requested to transmit to this House copies of all letters and correspondence of all Indian Agents and sub-agents, and other persons connected with the Indian Department, now in the Records of the War Department, or in the office of the Commissioner or the General Land Office, connected with or relative to the survey, location, sale, and transfer of all Indian reserves of lands since the year 1825, up to this time; and also, all the deeds and communications from the Executive of the United States, through the War Department, or General Land Office, or otherwise, in reference to said surveys, locations, sales, and transfers of Indian reserves; together with maps and plots of said reserves, and of the tracts approved and confirmed by the President under said transfers and sales, and what remains unappropriate, that heretofore reported and submitted for this approval, together with the evidence of title.

Mr. McCARTY addressed the House in favor of the resolution, and in explanation of the reasons which had induced him to offer it.

Mr. PLUMMER moved an amendment to the resolution, to restrict the call for information "that not already communicated to the House under resolutions of that body, adopted at the last session."

BY BLAIR & RIVES. ——WEEKLY—— PRICE $1 A SESSION.

2d Sess......25d Cong.   MONDAY, FEBRUARY 2, 1835.   Volume 2......No. 10.

TWENTY-THIRD CONGRESS.
SECOND SESSION.

HOUSE OF REPRESENTATIVES.
[CONTINUED FROM LAST NUMBER.]
Thursday, January 23, 1835.

Before the amendment was disposed of, Mr. POLK called for the orders of the day, which was sustained by the House.

The SPEAKER laid before the House the following communications:

A letter from the Secretary of War, enclosing an abstract of the licenses granted to trade with the Indians—laid on the table, and ordered to be printed.

A letter from the Secretary of War in relation to the contingent expenses of his Department—laid on the table, and ordered to be printed.

A letter from the Secretary of War, in response to a resolution of the House, relative to an unappropriated balance for the construction of the Cumberland Road, in the State of Indiana; which was referred to the Committee of Ways and Means.

A letter from the Secretary of War, enclosing a list of the clerks in his Department, and their respective salaries; laid on the table and ordered to be printed.

Bills from the Senate of the following titles, were read twice and committed:

A bill for the relief of Charles Lynch, of Mississippi;

And a bill to exempt merchandise imported under the circumstances from the operations of the act of 19th May, 1828, in alteration of the several acts imposing duties on imports.

The following bills were read a third time and passed.

A bill to extend the time for issuing scrip upon School States land warrants;

And a bill to authorise the City Council of St. Augustine to widen the streets in said city.

GENERAL APPROPRIATION.

The House then took up the bill reported from the Committee of the Whole, making appropriations for the civil and diplomatic expenses of Government for the year 1835.

Several amendments of the Committee of the Whole were agreed to without amendment.

Mr. POLK moved to disagree to so much of an amendment to the item for law agent, &c. in Florida, as went to provide that no part of the money should be paid till the claims had been adjusted, and after some conversation between Messrs. POLK, WHITE of Florida, and GRENNELL, the motion was agreed to, and the remaining portion of the amendment concurred in by the House.

Mr. POLK then moved to concur in the amendment of the committee to strike out the appropriation for the salary of a Minister to Buenos Ayres. Mr. P. said he had made inquiry and he wished to be distinctly understood, that no portion of the money appropriated for this purpose last year had been drawn out of the Treasury. Its intention in the present bill, arose from its being the actual annual item; the fact of its not being expended having been overlooked. He was not only anxious but desirous that the amendment should be concurred in by the House.

It was agreed to.

Mr. POLK then said, an honorable member from Illinois, (Mr. Reynolds,) had proposed an additional item in the committee of $500, for the purpose of the survey of certain lots in Peoria, which had been rejected, and he now moved that it be agreed to. He had consulted the department, and found the appropriation called for. It was agreed to.

Mr. MERCER observed, that he should not reply a proposition which he had submitted in the Committee of the Whole, in relation to the fund appropriated for the suppression of the slave trade, in consequence of information which he had ob-

tained from the chairman of the Committee of Ways and Means, that a surplus of some $14,000 of that fund remained in the Treasury. Mr. M. observed, however, that he could not but express his surprise and regret at the conduct of the Government, in continuing our ships of war in idle parade in the Mediterranean, while that infamous traffic was rife on the African coast.

Mr. POLK replied, that he possessed no information in regard to the previous expenditure of this fund. The information he possessed, was to be found in the Annual Report of the Secretary of the Treasury, by which it would be seen that of the fund alluded to, there did remain the sum of $14,214 91 unexpended.

Mr. POLK then moved that the bill be engrossed for a third reading.

Mr. VANCE proposed to add a section to the bill repealing a portion of the 2d section of the bill of 1834, and re-enacting another part of the same, relating to the pay of collectors, naval officers, and surveyors of the several ports of the United States, out of any money in the Treasury not otherwise appropriated, such sums as will give to this said officers, respectively, the same compensation in the year 1835; according to the importations of that year, as they would have been entitled to receive, if the act of 14th July, 1832, had not gone into effect, &c.

Mr. VANCE addressed the House on the subject of the amendment, at some length, and was replied to by Messrs. POLK and SUTHERLAND.

A debate ensued, in which Messrs. GILLET, POLK, SUTHERLAND, VANCE, FILLMORE, HARPER, MINER and WILLIAMS, took part.

Mr. VANCE moved that the House adjourn. The motion was lost: ayes 63, noes 76.

Mr. GILLET offered an amendment to the amendment of Mr. VANCE, which was rejected.

After a protracted debate, Mr. WILLIAMS moved that the House adjourn. He however withdrew the motion, at the solicitation of Mr. WATMOUGH, in order to allow him to place an amendment on the table, to the bill to regulate the pay of the Navy, with a view to have it printed.

Mr. POLK objected to this proposition, and hoped the House would have the bill which was before it, engrossed, before it consented to adjourn.

Mr. WILLIAMS then renewed his motion for adjournment, and on this question,

Mr. PARKER called for the ayes and noes, which were ordered, and taken as follows: ayes 100, noes 85.

So the House adjourned.

IN SENATE.
Friday, January 23, 1835.

Mr. KENT presented the credentials of the Hon. ROBERT H. GOLDSBOROUGH, a Senator from the State of Maryland, elected to supply the vacancy occasioned by the resignation of the Hon. Ezekiel F. Chambers.

Mr. GOLDSBOROUGH having presented himself, the oath was administered, and he took his seat in the Senate.

Mr. HENDRICKS presented certain documents showing the comparative length of the several sessions of Congress, having application to the resolution submitted by him, for fixing a time for the adjournment of every succeeding session of Congress; which, on his motion, was referred to the Judiciary Committee, and ordered to be printed.

Mr. TOMLINSON, from the Committee on Pensions, made an unfavorable report upon the petition of Wm. Welsh.

On motion of Mr. WRIGHT, the report of the Secretary of the Treasury, relative to the progress made at that Department, in the preparation of maps, &c., of certain States, was ordered to be printed.

The following resolutions, submitted yesterday,

by Mr. SOUTHARD, were taken up, considered, and agreed to:

Resolved, That the Committee on the Library be instructed to inquire into the expediency of purchasing the copies of Watterston & Vanzandt's "Continuation of the Tabular Statistical Views of the United States," which remain unsold of the edition for the use of Congress.

Resolved, That the Committee on Naval Affairs be instructed to inquire into the expediency of making an appropriation to deepen the Bar of Pensacola Bay, in Florida, so as to admit vessels of war of the largest class to the United States Navy Yard, established there.

On motion of Mr. WEBSTER, the Senate then resumed the consideration of the army appropriation bill, as in Committee of the Whole.

Mr. WEBSTER said, that an objection had been urged yesterday by the honorable member from Indiana (Mr. Hendricks) against the item of appropriation to pay certain supernumerary Lieutenants. He (Mr. W.) then said, that he thought the provision was only in fulfilment of the exigency of the existing laws. Mr. W. here referred to the act of 1812, to show that when cadets were not attached they were to be provided for. That there were one hundred and six specified in the bill, which was a less number than was authorized by the law alluded to.

Mr. HENDRICKS said, he did not consider the act of 1812 as having any thing to do with the military academy. The provisions of that law were certainly as the gentleman from Massachusetts represented them to be, but he was unable to reconcile them with subsequent laws. The act of 2d March, 1821, to reduce and fix the military peace establishment, provided for the discharge of all supernumerary officers. He would not, however, persist in his opposition to the bill, but he objected to the provision alluded to, and thought it ought to be inquired into.

After some further conversation between Mr. WEBSTER and Mr. HENDRICKS, the bill was ordered to be engrossed and read a third time.

The bill making appropriations for certain pensioners of the United States for the year 1835, was read the second time, considered as in Committee of the Whole, and ordered to be engrossed for a third reading.

The bill authorizing a further issuing of scrip in satisfaction of military bounty land warrants, and the bill making appropriations for certain fortifications of the United States, for the year 1835, were read the second time and referred.

The following bills were severally read the third time and passed:

A bill for the relief of William Clark;

A resolution for the relief of John S. Stiles, upon a contract for Navy bread;

A bill making appropriations for revolutionary and other pensioners of the United States, for the year 1835;

A bill making appropriations for the Indian Department for the year 1835;

A bill for the relief of Samuel S. Lord and others.

Mr. PRESTON, from the Judiciary Committee, to which was referred the bill to prevent and punish frauds against the pension laws, reported the same without amendment.

Mr. ROBBINS submitted the following resolution:

Resolved, That the Secretary of the Senate be directed to furnish a copy of the Register of the Debates of Congress, published by Gales and Seaton, to each of the members of the Senate, who have been elected since the commencement of the present session, or who may be elected during the session.

Mr. ROBBINS asked the consideration of the resolution at this time.

The motion requiring unanimous consent,

Mr. HILL objected; and

Mr. ROBBINS then gave notice that he would call it up on Monday next.

Mr. CLAY rose and said, that in consequence of the continued indisposition of an absent Senator, he would not move to go into Executive session to-day, but as the business on the docket ought to be despatched, he gave notice, that on Monday next, whether there was any indisposition of members or not, he would make that motion. While up, he would move, that when the Senate adjourn, it will adjourn to Monday next, which was so ordered.

The bill for the relief of Wilkinson Goodwin was read the second time, considered as in Committee of the Whole, and,

On motion of Mr. POINDEXTER, indefinitely postponed.

The bill for the relief of Wyatt Singleton and James Andrews, was read the second time, considered as in Committee of the Whole, when

Mr. BLACK moved its indefinite postponement, but yielded to a motion by Mr. PORTER, that it be laid on the table; which was agreed to.

The bill for the relief of Thomas L. Winthrop and others was taken up for consideration as in Committee of the Whole, and,

On motion of Mr. SMITH, postponed to Wednesday next.

The bill for the relief of David Beard was read a second time, considered as in Committee of the Whole, and after some remarks from Messrs. HILL, SMITH, and CLAYTON,

Mr. SHEPLEY submitted an amendment; the substance of which was to refer the subject to the Secretary of the Treasury, to examine into the justice of the claim.

Mr. CLAYTON objected to the amendment, and, on his motion, the bill and amendment were laid on the table.

The following bills were read the second time, considered as in Committee of the Whole, and ordered to be engrossed for a third reading:

A bill for the relief of Christopher C. Bailey;

A supplement to the act authorizing the people of Louisiana to settle back lands;

A bill for the relief David McCord;

A bill in addition to the act for the relief of the legal representatives of Lucy Bond and Hannah Douglass, was read the second time, considered as in Committee of the Whole, and, after some remarks by Messrs. SMITH, TYLER, HILL, SHEPLEY, MOORE, LEIGH, and WHITE, the question being on the engrossment of the bill for a third reading,

Mr. HILL asked the yeas and nays, which were ordered, as I are as follows, to wit:

YEAS—Messrs. Bibb, Buchanan, Frelinghuysen, Gaisborough, Kent, Leigh, Linn, McKean, Moore, Naudain, Porter, Preston, Robbins, Shepley, Silsbee, Smith, Southard, Swift, Tomlinson, Tyler, Webster, White—22.

NAYS—Messrs. Benton, Black, Brown, Cuthbert, Grundy, Hendricks, Hill, King of Ala., King of Ga , Robinson, Tallmadge, Tipton, Wright —13.

So the question was determined in the affirmative.

On motion of Mr. BENTON,

The Senate adjourned.

HOUSE OF REPRESENTATIVES.

Friday, January 23, 1835.

Mr. CAMBRELENG, from the Committee on Foreign Affairs, reported, without amendment, a bill from the Senate for the relief of Thomas Aspinwall; which was committed.

Mr. CAMBRELENG, from the Committee of Ways and Means, reported, with amendments, the bill from the Senate to exempt merchandise imported under certain circumstances, from the operation of the tariff act of May, 1828. The amendments were read, and, together with the bill, committed.

Mr. THOMSON, from the Committee on Military Affairs, reported a bill to authorise a common mine to secure to the United States, Pea Patch Island, in the river Delaware; which was read twice committed.

FORRESTER, from the Committee on Claims, with an amendment, the bill from the for the relief of Hiram A. Hunter; which was committed.

Mr. CHINN, from the Committee on the District of Columbia, reported a bill to extend the jurisdiction of the corporation of the city of Washington; which was read twice and committed.

Mr. FULTON, from the Committee on Claims, reported, without amendment, a bill from the Senate for the relief of Henry B. Tyler, executor of Col. Richard Smith; which was committed.

Mr. REED, from the Committee on Naval Affairs, reported a bill for the benefit of Boyd Reilly; which was read twice and committed.

Mr. HARPER, of New Hampshire, from the Committee on Commerce, reported a bill for the relief of Reuben Colburn; which was read twice and committed.

Mr. McKINLEY, instructed by the Committee of Ways and Means, asked for the printing of a Report from the Treasury Department, in relation to the establishment of branches of the Mint; which was agreed to, and, on motion, 5,000 extra copies of the document referred to were ordered to be printed.

Messrs. BROWN and ANTHONY each made unfavorable reports upon petitions referred to their respective Committees.

The following resolution, heretofore offered by Mr. PEARCE, of Rhode Island, was considered, and agreed to:

Resolved, That the Secretary of the Navy be directed to communicate to this House a copy of the report made to the Navy Department by John N. Reynolds, October 9, 1829, describing a number of the islands, reefs, and shoals, in the Pacific Ocean, and on the northwestern Coast of America.

Mr. ANTHONY, by consent, offered the following resolution, which lies one day on the table:

Resolved, That the Secretary of War be directed to forward copies of the report and profile of Major Biche's survey of a route for a rail-road from Williamsport, Pennsylvania, to Elmira, New York, to the Governors of Pennsylvania and New York, with a request that they lay the same before the Legislatures of their respective States.

On motion of Mr. VANCE,

Resolved, That the Secretary of the Treasury communicate to this House the amount paid to the different Custom house offices of Boston, New York, Philadelphia, and Baltimore, under the provisions of the 3d section of the act making appropriations for the Civil and Diplomatic expenses of Government for the year 1834.

On motion of Mr. STANDIFER,

Resolved, That the Committee on the Post Office and Post Roads be instructed to inquire into the expediency of establishing a post route from Ten Mile Post Office, in Rhea county, by Gordon's Iron Works, through the Grassy Cove, to John Narremore's, on the Sparta road, in Tennessee.

Tyler, heretofore, the following resolution, heretofore offered by Mr. McCARTY, was taken up:

Resolved, That the President of the U. States be requested to transmit to this House copies of all letters and correspondence of all Indian Agents and sub-agents, and other persons connected with the Indian Department, now in the Executive or War Department, or in the office of the Commissioner of the General Land Office, connected with or relative to the survey, location, sale, and transfer of all Indian reserves of lands since the year 1825, up to this time; and also, all the orders and communications from the Executive of the United States, through the War Department, or General Land Office, or otherwise, in reference to said surveys, locations, sales, and transfers of Indian reserves; together with maps and plots of said surveys, and of the tracts approved and confirmed by the President under a transfer and sale, and what remains unappropriated, that have been reported and submitted for his approval, together with the evidence of title.

Mr. PLUMMER moved an amendment to the resolution, to restrict the call for information to " that not already communicated to the Senate under resolutions of that body, adopted at the last session."

The question being on the amendment—

Mr. PLUMMER said he had not yet had an opportunity of investigating this subject so fully as he ought to do, to justify recording his vote upon its adoption. He had, however, given it a partial

investigation yesterday, as much as the time would permit, and he had considerable doubts of the expediency or propriety of adopting it, in any form or shape whatever. At any rate, he certainly thought that the amendment he had offered should be appended to it, for this reason: at the last session of Congress, a call was made, by a resolution of the Senate, for, part, at least, of the information called for by the present resolution, and a report was made, comprising between two and three hundred pages of, matter. Subsequently to that, a call was made upon the same Department—the Bureau of Indian Affairs—for the

Mr. WILLIAMS asked for the yeas and nays; which were ordered.

The question was taken and decided as follows: yeas 71, nays 108.

The question then recurring on agreeing to the resolution as modified by the amendment, and

Mr. BATES called for the yeas and nays; which were ordered.

Mr. PLUMMER called for the orders of the day. Negatived—yeas 71, nays 83.

Mr. McKINLEY said he had been so unfortunate, thus far, as to have heard no satisfactory reason advanced for the adoption of this resolution. If such reason had been given by the mover, (Mr. McCarty) it had escaped his attention. If the friends of the resolution could produce any better reason for incurring the enormous expense of printing the document called for, than the mere gratification of an idle curiosity, he would be glad to hear it.

Mr. McCARTY said he did not presume the printing of the correspondence and documents would be so very expensive as gentlemen seemed to anticipate. The information sought for, he believed could be furnished in a few days. He had not a doubt that gentlemen were laboring under a great mistake on these points. He hoped no further obstacles would be thrown in the way of obtaining the information desired.

Mr. LOVE contended that the subject of expense should present no obstacle to the passage of the resolution. When the object was the detection of fraud, or where a mere suspicion of fraud existed, an investigation should be made, without reference to the secondary consideration of expense. He was not about to charge the Government with a participation in frauds; but if its faithless agents had abused the trusts reposed in them, by defrauding either the Indians or others, the nation had a right to know the facts—if those frauds were ever so light, or the expense ever so great. He hoped the resolution would be adopted.

Mr. McKINLEY again addressed the House. He could see no object to be obtained by the passage of this resolution. If frauds had been committed, would the publication of these documents tend to the punishment of the delinquents? He could not see how this extraordinary expense should have a tendency to correct the evil. It seemed to him to be only a publication of papers, to gratify the curiosity of individuals, without the least beneficial result to the country. If such were not his conviction, he would cheerfully lend his aid to sustain the inquiry.

Mr. BYNUM said he trusted he would be the last person in the House who would refuse an inquiry into a subject calculated to detect fraud or promote public good. But the proposition before the House seemed to him to be rather an extraordinary one. The mass of documents here proposed to be printed, he verily believed, would never be read by ten members on that floor, besides the honorable gentleman who introduced the resolution. It was admitted, Mr. B. said, that the expense of printing would be very great. But it had been said by the gentleman from Kentucky, (Mr. Love,) that the expense should not be taken into consideration. Sir, said Mr. B., I differ with the gentleman on this point, especially where the expense was greater than the losses sustained. If the gentleman would introduce a proposition for inquiry, which could result in any public benefit, without this enormous expense of perhaps fifteen or twenty thousand dollars, he would cordially cooperate with him. But under the present aspect, he could see the prospect of no benefit to any one, excepting it were to the public printers.

Mr. LANE said, the resolution called for extensive information, covering a period of ten years and the entire continent. To furnish it, would require the employment of several clerks for three or four months; and when obtained, could not be made the foundation of any action of this House. Is there any gentleman on this floor who can, for a moment, believe that any one who may have committed frauds upon the Indians, would have been so weak as to have placed it in any correspondence? This is not the manner frauds are perpetrated. The object of the resolution, as observed by the honorable gentlemen from Indiana, (Mr. McCarty,) and from Kentucky, (Mr. Love,) is, to obtain evidence of frauds which rumor has said have been perpetrated by Indian agents, in the sale of reservations. So far as private individuals are concerned in these alleged frauds, this is not the tribunal; the constitution has properly referred such inquiry for decision to courts of justice. To remedy this evil, then, the resolution is incompetent. If the object is as avowed, to bring to justice, and expose to public view and public condemnation, it is equally incompetent and improper. Let the mover of the resolution specify, put his finger upon the Indian agent, or *refer* it to a committee for inquiry; and if any frauds shall be discovered, call for all such papers as shall or may be necessary for the object, that the public interest, or the honor of the nation shall demand. If the gentleman will adopt this course, I will go as far as any one to bring all such agents to public justice.

Mr. LOVE said, it had been admitted that rumors had gone abroad, going to implicate officers of the Government in participating in immense frauds. He thought this a proper subject for the investigation of the Committee on Indian Affairs. He had no hesitation in declaring his conviction that the Executive Departments of the Government were entirely disconnected with these alleged frauds. He condemned the doctrine that the item of expense should have any weight in the detection of crime. He asked if the individual who stole $100 should be suffered to escape because it would cost $500 to convict him? It had been insinuated too, that it was his desire, in voting for the printing of these documents, to give the public printer a profitable job. Sir, said Mr. L., printers, under the present management of the press, are a sort of cattle that I have little or nothing to do with. After some further remarks, Mr. L. repeated, that he believed the Executive Departments had no participation in the frauds in question. Of this fact he was fully convinced.

Mr. MARDIS said that he had the honor to come from the State that the gentleman from Kentucky (Mr. Lane) considered so very delicately situated in reference to this question. That notwithstanding the declaration of the gentleman, he should, on this as upon all other propositions before the House, give free utterance to his sentiments (Mr. LANE said he was misunderstood; and that he did not intend to make any such insinuation.) Mr. M. resumed his remarks by saying, that after the explanation of the honorable gentleman, he had nothing further to say on that point. Mr. M. said that a thing proper in itself, should, nevertheless, be done in a proper manner. He had no objection to a thorough investigation of the conduct of all the public officers of this government whenever the public good would be promoted by such examination; he went further—he would, on a bare suspicion that a public agent had been guilty of fraud, or unfairness in the discharge of the duties of his office, cost what it might, expose his delinquencies. He held with the friends of the resolution, that it was of the utmost importance to the community, that all their agents should not only be honest, but above all suspicion, and did not agree with gentlemen, that the expenses of the proposed investigation should be taken into the account. But, Mr. Speaker, said Mr. M., I am not of the opinion that the resolution, i adopted, would accomplish the object that the honorable member seems to have had in view. The resolution asks for information, generally, in relation to the sale of Indian reservations. Fraud is imputed to some one connected with these sales—whether to the purchasers, or to the Secretary of War, or some sub-agent, or agents acting under him, we are not informed. If the object of the resolution be to ascertain whether or not the purchasers of Indian reservations have practised a fraud on the reserves, then he apprehended the House had no jurisdiction over the subject. The sale is an individual transaction, and Congress has not the power to erect itself into a Court of Chancery, for the purpose of passing upon these contracts. The validity of transactions of this nature are properly referable to the judicial tribunals of the country. If, however, the object of the gentleman from Indiana (Mr. McCarty) was, as he supposed, to convict some public functionary of malfeasance in office, then it seemed to him that it would be proper to raise a committee, vested with power to send for persons and papers, with a view that the facts might all be fully examined into, as well for as against the accused. This course appeared to him to be proper, in many points of view. First, because he held it to be correct doctrine, that no man should be condemned before an opportunity had been given him to be fully heard in his defence before his judges. Secondly, such a course recommended itself to the intelligence and justice of the members of this House. He therefore moved to amend the resolution so as to authorize the appointment of a committee, empowered to send for persons and papers, to be charged with the investigation of all the matters contained in the resolution. Mr. M. withdrew his motion to amend, with a view to send the subject to the Committee on Indian Affairs.

Mr. LOVE said, to avoid all further difficulty, he would move to committee the resolution to the Committee on Indian Affairs.

Mr. MARDIS then withdrew his proposition for a select committee.

Mr. McCARTY begged to make a brief explanation. He disclaimed any intention of casting a single imputation upon the officers of the Government in this city, and his motives have been egregiously mistaken, if such an inference has been drawn, there was nothing in the resolution to warrant any such inference, and such allusions were unjust and unfounded. He had no expectation that any thing improper on the part of the Executive, or either of the Departments mentioned in the resolution existed, that would be brought to light by the call. No man upon this floor has a higher opinion of the integrity of the Chief Magistrate than he had. In offering the resolution he had, he had done it from motives of public duty alone, to expose fraud, if any existed, and to exculpate the innocent, upon serious deliberation and reflection, and he would not be dictated to as to the manner in which he should discharge that duty.

Mr. MARDIS disclaimed having any such intention towards the honorable gentleman.

Mr. McCARTY contined, nor did he mean to cast any imputation upon the Executive, but he wished to show what he believed, that the Executive had been imposed upon by persons who endeavored to practise deception upon him, for the purpose of putting money into their own pockets, and then shielding themselves from investigation. Mr. McC. repeated, he was astonished to see objections to the resolution from any quarter of the House. The object of the resolution was to expose guilt and shield the innocent.

Mr. BARRINGER said there were strange rumors abroad—rumors not of to-day or of yesterday, involving charges of fraud and *mal-feasance*, and it was right that they should be investigated, and either proved or disproved, by that branch of the legislature. He would mention one or two of them. It was said that a stock company had been formed for the purchase of Indian reserves, consisting of a capital of $100,000 in shares of $1000 each, and that there was one individual who had subscribed $5000 in money, and another $5000 in services, by exercising his influence, and certifying that the transactions were fair and honorable. If there was ground for these rumors it was right that it should be known, and at any rate it was a matter worthy of investigation, that those who were guilty should be held up to the scorn and reprobation of the country, and meet the [illegible] ment they merited. Many gentlemen [illegible] floor had constituents who were impl[illegible] and he should imagine they would rejoice at [illegible] portunity of placing them before the cou[illegible] the garb of innocence; and he trusted ther[illegible] not one who would attempt, or desire to scre[illegible] guilty.

If the resolution be not broad enough to [illegible] the ground, it was perfectly competent [illegible] House to frame such a one as should mee[illegible] object desired, and be acted on promptly b[illegible] House. He must be permitted to say, th[illegible] thought the House had been hitherto too neg-

gent in regard to the management of the Indian lands. Charges of corruption and *mal-feasance* had been made, and reiterated again and again, against certain public officers, receivers, registers, &c. and yet no inquiry had been instituted there. That House had permitted such rumors to go abroad in the land, without attempting any investigation into the foundation of them. It was no excuse for them that the other branch of the legislature had acted in part. It was the duty of the Representatives of the People to step forward, and rip up these transactions. If they have been honest, let it be known; if corrupt, let it be exposed, and the sooner the better.

Much had been said about the expense of answering the call of this resolution. What, were we to set about an inquiry into the cost, when a great public defaulter is to be brought before us? When a public functionary was charged with a dereliction of duty and absolute commission of fraud, were they to stop and inquire how much it would cost? Who ever heard in a court of justice of a jury or of the public prosecutor stopping in the discharge of their duty by a consideration of cost? Did a judge ever pause at proceeding to trial from such a consideration? Mr. B. cared not what the cost might be in this case, he looked not to a *quid pro quo*, but to do justice in bringing a delinquent to justice. Let an example be made, and that promptly; for so long as they permitted such rumors to pass unheeded, so long did they hold out inducements to their public functionaries to abuse their trusts. How would it now appear, if the resolution should be rejected? Why, that those rumors to which he had referred, had been broadly and openly repeated upon the floor of the Representatives of the People, the assembled wisdom of the country; and in spite of that, no investigation was to take place, because, forsooth, it would cost money! He knew not what it would cost—he cared not—but if the fact were so that great frauds had been committed, he was for having them investigated; and when that was done, let punishment fall where it was due, be the cost what it might. Mr. B. had not intended to trespass upon the patience of the House, and he should conclude by hoping that the resolution would be adopted.

Mr. POLK made another attempt to call up the orders of the day; but the House refused—ayes 79, noes 94.

Mr. MILLER expressed his intention, from circumstances which had arisen during the debate, to support the resolution.

Mr. BOON demanded the previous question, but the motion was not seconded by the House.

Mr. EWING said he should vote for the resolution. He wished to see it passed in the form in which it was originally presented. When the proposition was made to publish the pension list, not a word was objected to that measure, though the expense was probably three times as great as that of this correspondence would be. Not a word was said against that printing; but when you come to investigate the conduct of Indian agents and land speculators, objections are abundant. It had been said the whole affair rested on vague rumors, and that "rumor was a pipe blown by surmises." He could not think all these rumors could be without some foundation in fact. It also had been contended that our action on this subject would not effect the punishment of the delinquents. Mr. E. contended that exposition was of itself a punishment of a high order. He thought the investigation due to the country.

Mr. CAGE said he felt it his imperious duty to himself and to his constituents to vote for investigation in its most extended form. He repelled the idea that this measure was got up for the purpose of implicating or casting censure on the Executive Department. It was the unworthy agents who had crept into the confidence of the Government. It was not alleged that that government had, in any instance, winked or connived at fraud.

Mr. WARDWELL said the speeches of gentlemen appeared to be all on one side. He really wished they would save the time of the House by taking the question.

Mr. ASHLEY said, his objection to the resolution was, that the information desired could not be obtained at the present session of Congress. If the gentleman would make his resolution more specific—pointing out the State or designating the individual office where the investigation should take place, he would second the proposition.

Mr. HAMER and Mr. BYNUM both addressed the House in opposition to the resolution in its present shape. They wished it to be made more specific—to make its objects more tangible, and they would then support it.

Mr. LANE said, he had risen to explain. He had opposed the resolution, and voted to lay it upon the table, believing, as he did, that the subject was not attainable by its adoption.

The course now given to it, by a reference to a committee for inquiry, accorded with his views. Believing as he did that the committee would first inquire if any frauds had been committed, by whom and where, and then call for such papers and information as should be alone indispensable.

One word, Mr. Speaker, said Mr. L. in defence of the people of Indiana, a part of whom he had the honor of being the immediate representative. Sir, a purer, more intelligent, high-minded, and honorable population than that of Indiana, cannot be found in any other State. That he had considered it his duty, to say this much in defence of the People, and the Indian agents, from the circumstance, that the resolution came from the State, and that two of his honorable colleagues, (Messrs. McCarty and Ewing,) had expressed their belief, that frauds had been committed in the sale, and transfer of Indian reservations—from an apprehension that some might be led to suppose, from this circumstance, that the frauds, which rumor had thrown upon the public, had taken place in Indiana. That he had been acquainted with all the Indian agents employed by the Government for the last 20 years, and he believed them to be honest and high-minded men and incapable of committing a fraud on the Government, an Indian, or any one else.

Mr. McCARTY said a few words in explanation.

Mr. PLUMMER regretted that his amendment should have given rise to so protracted a discussion. He would not now trouble the House with any additional remarks, farther than a mere explanation. His object in proposing the amendment which he did, was not to screen any branch of the Government, or any officer acting under the Government, from the most scrutinizing investigation; but it was to prevent the useless expense of obtaining and printing information, a part of which had been already laid on the table, and the residue of which would be laid before us in two or three days at farthest, on a call from the other end of the building, at an expense, according to a rough estimate, of upwards of $19,000. The gentleman who moved the resolution (Mr. McCarty,) had done him the honor to accept his amendment as a modification of his resolution. His objections to the resolution were therefore in a great measure done away. He desired a postponement only for the purpose of giving it an examination. He voted for the motion to lie on the table for the same reason. With regard to the certificates of fraud and depositions alluded to by the gentleman from North Carolina (Mr. Barringer) and others; and rumors in relation to the formation of companies for purposes of speculation, so far as his own State and constituents were concerned; instead of shrinking from an investigation, he invited it; he defied it; let it come; he was ready to meet it. He supposed that allusion was made to certain affidavits and rumors introduced into the other branch of the legislature at the last session of Congress. It is well known that the Committee on Public Lands in the Senate were at the last session authorized to investigate these alleged frauds with power to send for persons and papers. It is well known also that some of the certificates introduced into that body have been responded to by the persons implicated. It is furthermore well known that the Chairman of that committee was authorized to continue the investigation during the recess of Congress. This had been done through the aid of Commissioners appointed by the Chairman of the committee of that body. Some half a dozen persons had been selected in Mississippi, and how many in other States he would not pretend to say. A report had been made to the committee, and the committee, he was informed, had reported to the Senate. This report, he understood, was now in the hands of the printer, and would soon be laid on our tables. On the result of the investigation alluded to, he would not express an opinion, unless circumstances should make it his duty to do so. He hoped that gentlemen would not make further charges of fraud, and locate the charge in Mississippi, until the result of that investigation was known. If fraud had been committed in the State, and by a portion of the people he had the honor to represent, which he by no means admitted, the atonement, according to the custom of the ancients, had been made to a certain extent. We are told by high authority that without the shedding of blood there is no remission of sins. Blood had not only been shed, but one of Mississippi's most valued citizens had lost his life in consequence of difficulties growing out of that investigation. The lives of others were threatened. The public mind had been highly excited.

He hoped that no additional charges would be preferred, nor new excitements created, in relation to the alleged frauds in Mississippi, until they had an opportunity of reading the documentary evidence in cases which had been investigated. Mr. P. said, that he was no favorite with the locating agents, under the Choctaw treaty, but he was in justice bound to them to repel the idea of their having acted fraudulently or even improperly. Their proceedings had already been reported to Congress, and he invited gentlemen to examine them for themselves. He deemed it unnecessary, however, to enter into a defence of them or any portion of his constituents, because he did not understand that allusion had been made to them by any member who had spoken on the subject. Mr. P. concluded, by expressing a wish that no opposition would be made to referring the subject to the Committee on Indian Affairs. The reference he considered appropriate and one that met his most cordial approbation.

The question was then taken on the commitment of the resolution to the Committee on Indian Affairs, and carried.

On motion of Mr. HUBBARD, the House proceeded to the consideration of the orders of the day.

The following bills, and joint resolutions, from the Senate were read twice and committed:

A bill for the relief of the heirs or legal representatives of Col. Jean Hudrey, deceased.

A bill authorizing the construction of a road from the public grounds near Tallahassee to St. Marks in Florida.

A bill for the relief of the heirs of M. Cam[illegible].

A bill for the relief of William Pettiplace and ——— White, legal representatives of Joseph White, deceased.

A bill to improve the navigation of the Mississippi river, in the vicinity of St. Louis.

A bill authorizing the removal of the land office from Clinton to Jackson, Mississippi.

A bill for the completion of certain improvements in Florida:

A bill for the relief of Elizabeth Magruder, of Mississippi.

A bill to improve the harbor at or near the mouth of the river Raisin.

A bill for the relief of William Tharp.

The following bills and joint resolutions, (which originated in the House,) were read a third time and passed:

A bill authorizing letters patent to be issued to Francis B. Ogden.

A bill for the relief of James Middleton [illegible].

A joint resolution authorizing certain papers having reference to claims for revolutionary services, to be placed in the office of the Secretary of War.

Mr. POLK moved to take up the general appropriation bill.

After some conversation between Messrs. ASHLEY, POLK, VANCE, and WILLIAMS, the motion was negatived.

On motion of Mr. JOHNSON, of Kentucky, the

House went into Committee of the Whole, Mr. PATTON in the Chair, on the bill for the relief of Col. John Eugene Leitenadorfer; which was subsequently reported to the House without amendment.

Mr. WARDWELL inquired of the Chairman on Military Affairs the grounds upon which, in addition to pay, the bill proposed to give lands to the individual named?

Mr. JOHNSON, of Kentucky, replied that this donation of land was in consideration of the extraordinary services and sufferings of Col. Leitenadorfer.

The bill was then read a third time and passed.

On motion of Mr. LETCHER, the House went into Committee of the Whole—Mr. EVANS in the Chair—on a bill for the relief of Col. Thomas Buford, which was subsequently reported to the House without amendment, and ordered to be engrossed for a third reading.

The House then adjourned.

HOUSE OF REPRESENTATIVES,
SATURDAY, January 24, 1835.

Mr. E. EVERETT, from the Joint Committee on the Library, reported the following joint resolution; which was read twice and ordered to be engrossed:

Be it resolved by the Senate and House of Representatives of the United States of America in Congress assembled, That in pursuance of the request of Morgan Neville, the Master of the Mint be and he is hereby authorized and directed to cause to be struck a Gold Medal, in honor of the battle of the Cowpens, which was fought on the 17th day of January, 1781, to replace the original medal presented by the Continental Congress to General Daniel Morgan; the said medal to be struck from the original die, and at the expense of the said Morgan Neville.

Mr. PEYTON, on leave, presented a petition; which was referred.

Mr. J. Q. ADAMS, from the select committee appointed on the subject, reported, without amendment, the bill from the Senate providing for the establishment of the northern boundary lines of the States of Ohio, Indiana, and Illinois. Mr. A. stated that the committee recommended the rejection of the bill. It was committed.

On motion of Mr. CLAY,

Resolved, That the Committee on the Public Buildings and grounds be instructed to inquire into the expediency of enlarging the space at present allotted for the Library of this House, and of adapting the same to a more convenient place and arrangement for the use of the members.

Mr. GILMER offered the following resolution, which, under the rule, lies one day:

Resolved, That the Secretary of the Treasury report to this House, at as early a day as practicable, what States, if any, have paid to their officers in the continental establishment, the commutation or other pay due those officers by the resolutions of the Congress, and if any, whether the United States, in pursuance of the laws and resolutions for the final settlement of the accounts between the United States, and the States, has allowed to said State or States credit for such payments for commutation pay, and that the Secretary specially report whether John Pierce, Commissioner of Army Accounts, did not give to the State of Georgia a certificate in 1785, that that State had paid to its officers the commutation and other pay due them ad that there was due to the State of Georgia from the Confederation therefor, the sum of $123,583 70-100, and so, whether the said certificate has ever allowed to the State of Georgia, in the settlement of accounts between that State and the United States, and whether the same yet remains due to said State. And that the Secretary further report whether the States which have found debt due to the United States in the final settlement of accounts between the United States and the States, have paid the same so found to be due to the United States, and if not, what sums remain unpaid to the United States from the several debtor States.

The resolution heretofore offered by Mr. HAMER, requiring the Committee on the Judiciary to inquire into the expediency of amending the constitution of the United States in relation to judicial officers, and the amendment moved by Mr. VANCE, to inquire into the expediency of further amending the constitution in regard to removals from office by the President of the United States, was taken up.

Mr. ALLEN of Ohio, remarked that his colleague who had introduced the resolution, was not then in his seat. He, no doubt desired to be present, when his proposition was acted on. He therefore moved to postpone the consideration of the resolution, to Monday next, which was agreed to.

The following resolution, heretofore offered by Mr. REYNOLDS, came up in course:

Resolved, That hereafter, in all elections made by the House of Representatives (for officers) the votes shall be given *viva voce*, each member in his place, naming aloud the person for whom he votes.

Mr. CROCKETT moved to lay the resolution on the table.

Mr. REYNOLDS, said that the House being thin, and the resolution being of an important character, he would move a call of the House.

The motion was agreed to, and the roll was called, when it appeared that 178 members were present.

Mr. EVANS moved to suspend further proceedings under the call.

Mr. WHEELEY demanded the yeas and nays upon the motion, which were ordered.

Mr. EVANS then withdrew his motion.

Mr. BRIGGS inquired, whether the 19th rule of the House, setting apart Fridays and Saturdays for the consideration of private bills, did not require imperatively that the House should proceed at one o'clock with such bills, without a question?

The SPEAKER replied in the negative.

The doors were then closed, and the absentees were called, and excuses made for those who were necessarily absent on leave or otherwise.

Mr. JOHNSON of Kentucky, moved to suspend further proceedings under the call.

Mr. CROCKETT asked for the yeas and nays; which were ordered.

Mr. JOHNSON withdrew his motion.

Messengers having been despatched by order of the House for the absent members,

Mr. THOMSON moved that the absentees be again called, which was agreed to, when 197 members were ascertained to be in attendance.

Mr. JOHNSON, of Kentucky, renewed the motion to suspend the call.

Mr. CROCKETT demanded the yeas and nays. Ordered.

Mr. JOHNSON withdrew the call.

Mr. TURRILL moved an adjournment.

Mr. CROCKETT demanded the yeas and nays. Ordered.

Mr. TURRILL withdrew the motion.

Mr. HARPER moved to suspend further proceedings under the call.

Mr. CROCKETT demanded the yeas and nays; which were ordered, and were—yeas 95, nays 109. The absentees were again called.

Mr. ANTHONY then moved to suspend all further proceedings under the call; which was agreed to.

Mr. A. H. SHEPPERD moved to proceed to the consideration of the orders of the day.

Mr. CROCKETT demanded the yeas and nays; which were ordered, and were—yeas 64, nays 146.

The question recurred upon the motion to lay the resolution on the table.

Mr. CROCKETT demanded the yeas and nays; which were ordered, and were as follows:

YEAS—Messrs. John Q. Adams, Heman Allen, Chilton Allan, Ashley, Banks, Barber, Barnitz, Barringer, Bates, Baylies, Beaty, Bell, Binney, Briggs, Bull, Bunch, Burges, Cage, Campbell, Carmichael, Chambers, Chilton, William Clark, Clayton, Clowney, Corwin, Crane, Crockett, Amos Davis, Deberry, Denny, Dickson, Dickinson, Evans, Ewing, Felder, Fillmore, Forester, Foster, Fulton, Gamble, Gholson, Gillmer, Gorham, Graham, Grayson, Grennell, Griffin, Hiland Hall, Hard, Hardin, James Harper, Hazeltine, Hiester, Inge, William Jackson, Ebenezer Jackson, Jones, William C. Johnson, Henry Johnson, Seaborn Jones, King, Lea, Letcher, Lewis, Lincoln, Love, Martindale, Marshall, McCarty, McKennan, Mercer, Milligan, Miner, Moore, Peyton, Phillips, Pickens, Pinckney, Potts, Reed, Reacher, William B. Shepard, Augustine H. Shepperd, Slade, Sloane, Spangler, Steele, William P. Taylor, Philemon Thomas, Tompkins, Trumbull, Tweedy, Vance, Vinton, Watmough, Frederick Whittlesey, Wilde, Williams, Wilson, Young—101.

NAYS—Messrs. John Adams, John J. Allen, William Allen, Anthony, Archer, Beale, Bean, Beardsley, Beaumont, Blair, Bockee, Boon, Bouldin, Brown, Burns, Bynum, Cambreleng, Carr, Casey, Chaney, Chinn, Claiborne, Samuel Clark, Clay, Coffee, Coulter, Cramer, Day, Dickerson, Dunlap, Ferris, William K. Fuller, Galbraith, Gillet, Gordon, Joseph Hall, Thomas H. Hall, Halsey, Hamer, Joseph M. Harper, Harrison, Hathaway, Hawkins, Heath, Henderson, Howell, Hubbard, Huntington, Jarvis, Richard M. Johnson, Noadiah Johnson, Benjamin Jones, Kavanagh, Kilgure, Kinnard, Lane, Lansing, Laporte, Lee, Loyall, Lucas, Lyon, Lytle, Abijah Mann, Joel K. Mann, Manning, Mardis, John Y. Mason, Moses Mason, May, McComas, McIntire, McKay, McKim, McKinley, McLene, McVean, Miller, Robert Mitchell, Morgan, Murphy, Osgood, Parks, Parker, Patton, Patterson, Pearce, Pierce, Pierson, Polk, Pope, Ramsay, Reynolds, Robertson, Schenck, Schley, Shinn, Smith, Speight, Standifer, Sutherland, Francis Thomas, Thomson, Turner, Turrill, Vanderpoel, Van Houten, Wagener, Ward, Wardwell, Webster, Whallon—112.

So the House refused to lay the resolution on the table.

Mr. FILMORE, after having called for the reading of the resolution, (which was read by the Clerk,) said it seemed to him to involve principles of some importance, and he would frankly confess that, in determining how he should vote, he had been met by many difficulties. His own opinion with reference to the appointing power of this Government, and of all governments similar to our own, was, that where the legislative power or body exercised the appointing power, peculiarly and especially for itself, i. e. for its own internal rule and regulation, and not for the nation at large, then that power might, with great propriety, be exercised by ballot; and he believed that to be the practice in most legislative bodies in reference to the appointment of those officers, who might be considered special officers of the body, but not of the nation. This was the practice in Mr. F's. own State, (New York) and he really could see no objection to it in principle or practice any where else. It appeared to him to be correct to give the people at large, when they exercised the right of suffrage, the power to exercise that right in secret, by the ballot; and it was equally so to extend the same privilege, the same right, and the same authority to their representatives, when acting for themselves in the election of those officers peculiarly belonging to the body to which they were elected.

The next question that presented itself, would be, what officers had that House the power of appointing or electing? A reference to the constitution of the United States proved that we had the power of appointing all the officers of the House. It says: "The House of Representatives shall choose their Speaker and other officers; and shall have the sole power of impeachment." This, then, was the extent of the appointing power in that House to "choose their Speaker and other officers," alluding, doubtless, to the clerk, sergeant-at-arms, messengers, door-keepers, &c. That they had no appointing power generally, would be seen by referring to another clause of the same instrument, which says, the President of the United States "shall nominate, and by with the advice and consent of the Senate, appoint ambassadors, other public ministers consuls, judges of the Supreme Court, whose other officers of the United States, whose appointments are not herein otherwise provided and which shall be established by law: but Congress may by law vest the appointment of inferior officers, as they think proper, in the president alone; in the courts of law, or in the—

of departments." Here, then, the whole appointing power was vested in the President of United States and the Senate, with certain exceptions—those therein otherwise provided for, and which shall be established by law, &c. This, then, was was all the control that the legislature, or rather this branch of it, had over the appointing power, to "choose their own officers," and to "vest the appointment of such inferior officers as they think proper, in the President alone, in the courts of law, or in the heads of departments." They might create such offices as they should deem necessary or think proper, but the moment the office itself was created, the power of nominating to, or filling up that office, became vested in the President of the United States, by and with the advice and consent of the Senate, unless they shall see fit to vest them in the other way laid down in the clause; but they had no power, no authority to vest the appointment in themselves. Mr. F. said, he furthermore thought, that the distinction taken in the constitution between officers of the body and officers of the nation, was fairly, clearly, and distinctly marked out. They had, under the constitution, the power of appointing officers for that specific body, but none others whatsoever.

Mr. F. supposed the fact would not be disguised, that the object of the present resolution was to reach what was said to be an officer of the House—not the Speaker, Sergeant at Arms, or Messengers; but the Printer. We may as well, sir, said Mr. F., come to it at once, and discuss the matter fairly and openly, and candidly. Now, the first question that arose on this subject would be, (if the object of the resolution be to effect this appointment in any way,) to inquire whether the printer of that House was or was not, in the true acceptation and meaning of the term, an officer of that House. This was a very important inquiry. The question was agitated, he believed, during the last session of Congress, and if his recollection served him aright, there was a strong party who thought he was not an officer, and another who thought he was. From the best investigation he had been able to give, and he had spared neither diligence nor reflection, he confessed his own impression was, that the printer of the House of Representatives was not an officer either of the Government or of that body. It might be somewhat difficult to define what was necessary to constitute an officer, and to draw a distinction, or give such a definition, as should in all cases determine what was an officer; but he would endeavor to give, as briefly as possible, the reasons why he could not regard the individual charged with the Congress printing as an officer. In the first place, Mr. F. did not find that he took any oath of office, which was the practice with all other officers of the Government appointed in the usual manner. There was nothing in the law authorizing the House to employ a public printer which required an oath of office to be administered to that individual when employed. On the contrary, he did find, that after they had designated a person to the employment, if he should fail in the performance of the work, they might employ any other person, who might enter into a contract, and be paid for such work as should be executed by him. Again; the word "employ" was made use of in the law, and not "appoint," as if thereby to regard the printer in a light different from the officers of the House.

But perhaps the best distinction drawn between the contractor and the officer of the Government or of the House, and which showed that the distinction was designed by the framers of the law, was this: that there was not a solitary case in any department of the Government wherein an officer had not the power of resignation; whereas a contractor was bound to the performance of his contract, as was the case with the printer of the House. He had to give security for the due and faithful performance of his contract, but could not himself fix the term of his services by resignation. If they employed a person to build a capi[illegible] any other work, it was immaterial how he [illegible] designated, he was ipso facto, a contractor [illegible] nothing else. The mode of his resignation [illegible] not of itself constitute him an officer of the [illegible]. Because the House had the power to designate the person with whom it would contract for certain services, surely no one would contend that that was sufficient to constitute an officer. An appointment to an office, as he said before, never deprived an individual of the right of tendering his resignation, but would any one pretend to say that were that House to enter into a contract with a person to print, that that person could resign the contract? Mr. F. thought not. The individual in question would stand in the relation and capacity of a contractor to that body, without having had conferred upon him the particular character that created him an officer. We have contracted with him to perform certain services, and we hold him to their performance by certain stipulated obligations which may be enforced in the ordinary courts of law.

But suppose, said Mr. F., that he was mistaken, and that the printer to the House of Representatives be in reality an officer of the government or of that body, could we appoint him for the next Congress? Most clearly not. If we adopt the rule, they will act upon it, and as they have the power to do, will elect their own officers, and make their own regulations. We cannot do it for them, and should be transcending our powers in attempting it. On the contrary, the constitution had taken it out of our power, for it says, "the House of Representatives shall choose their Speaker and other officers," and if this House had the power to choose their printer, regarding him in the light of an officer, so would the next, for we have no power to control the appointment of their officers. This conclusion seems irresistible. The constitution had vested in each House the power of appointing its own officers, and if its printer be an officer, it is out of our power to adopt any rule, the effect of which would be to take the appointment or election out of the hands of the next. It might be well, however, to advert to the power by which we contracted with a person to execute the public printing, and it would be found that it was provided for by a joint resolution, of 1819, which received the sanction of both Houses of Congress, and the approval of the President of the United States. Now, if we intended to alter the mode therein laid down, it would be necessary first to revoke or to repeal that resolution, and enact a new one, in the usual form and manner; for nothing less than the whole legislative power of the nation, could effect the change. What were the provisions of that instrument? First, it provided for the manner in which the printing should be executed. 2d. for the prices; 3d. for the manner of performing the press-work, and 4th. the manner in which the person to be employed should be elected. The last part of the resolution was to the following purport—that as soon as it should receive the approval of the President of the United States, each House should proceed to ballot for a printer, to execute the work during the next Congress; and the person having the greatest number of votes, shall be considered elected, &c. Now then if the person thus to be employed, be an officer of that House, by virtue of that resolution, then it was to Mr. F. incontrovertible, that they could not appoint him for the next Congress. If, however, he be regarded as an officer of the nation, then had the constitution vested the power in the President of the United States, by and with the advice and consent of the Senate. Take either horn of the dilemma, and the difficulty was insurmountable. The only authority by and under which one Congress could appoint for the ensuing one was to regard the printer as a contractor for the performance of certain services, and by legislative authority to enter into a contract with him, and enforce its observance in a court of justice, should he fail therein.

With this view of the subject, said Mr. F. in conclusion, and conceiving it a matter in which we have a right to exercise our own judgment and discretion, so far as the election of our own officers is concerned; and believing that the practice of almost all legislative bodies are at variance with the proposed mode, and that there is no reason for changing the rule, I shall feel myself compelled to vote against the adoption of the resolution.

Mr. REYNOLDS said, the resolution which he had offered to the House some time since, was as follows:

"*Resolved*, That hereafter, in all elections made by the House of Representatives for officers, the votes shall be given *viva voce*, each member in his place naming aloud the person for whom he votes."

Mr. R. observed, that he had not the least intention of producing any excitement, when he had the honor to offer this proposition for the consideration of this House, and he sincerely hoped that none should be now created by it. He was not himself considered at home a violent party man, and he condemned excessive party excitement either at home or abroad.

The gentleman (Mr. Fillmore) from New York, urged in this discussion Mr. R's *motives* in presenting this resolution. He stated them to be to operate on the election of public printer. In this allegation, Mr. Reynolds observed, that his friend (Mr. F.) from New York, was entirely mistaken. He did not now entertain any great feeling or interest about the election of a public printer, and at the time he introduced the resolution, he did not even know there was one to be elected at this session of Congress. He had nothing to do with the election of a public printer, and did not care on whom, or on what printers, the resolution would operate.

He observed, that he moved it because it was the rule of action of the representatives in the State of Illinois, in which he lived, and had the honor to represent in part, and it was adopted when he had the honor to be in the Legislature of that State, and that it was the republican rule in every representative body. This was the reason he offered it, and on these principles he hoped it would be sustained by the House; consequently, the burthen of the song of the gentleman from New York, the election of a public printer, was out of the question. It could not in fact be discussed on the proposition which is now before the House—"Sufficient unto the day is the evil thereof." Let the abstract principle be established; let the republican rule be adopted, and then let it operate on preachers, speakers, printers, and all officers of the House, on which it ought to operate. Do right in all cases, and let the consequences provide for themselves.

Mr. Reynolds remarked, that as his motion and the election of public printer were disposed of, he would bring to the consideration of the House part of the 5th section of the 1st article of the constitution of the United States, which he read as follows:

"Each House shall keep a journal of its proceedings, and from time to time publish the same, excepting such parts as may in their judgment require secrecy; and the yeas and nays of the members of either House on any question shall, at the desire of one-fifth of those present, be entered on the journal."

This is the rule of action in all cases where it is applicable. It is the supreme law of the land.

The object of this part of the constitution was to preserve a record of the proceedings of Congress, and to give them publicity to the People. This is expressly required on all questions in the proceedings of Congress, where one fifth of the members desire it. No member of this House will contend that an election is no question. It is the most important question, if equally, to members of Congress, of any that could be agitated.

M. R. said he recollected well, last summer, it was an important question to your humble servant. He appeared often on the "stump" before his constituents; and each party, candidate and constituent, took it for granted that it was a *question*. Is not the election of a public printer a *question* also? There is too much discussion about it in this House for it to be no question. Some may say that the rule of action under the provisions of the constitution, has been for a long time different, and ought not *now* to be changed [illegible] this mode of balloting.

He considered the principle to be just, and whenever we found an error to exist in our proceedings, if those proceedings were as old as Jerusalem, we should change them.

It may be that this provision of the constitution

was never discussed in relation to this subject, and consequently never acted on. If neither an examination nor discussion has been had on this part of the constitution, the prevailing practice of balloting should not receive much consideration from its antiquity—"an ancient error cannot make a modern right."

The object and meaning of the constitution was to give publicity to the proceedings in Congress; and as all elections were questions in which the people were interested, the conclusion is irresistible, under the provisions of the constitution, that the proceedings in all elections should be *viva voce*, and published to the world in the journals.

It cannot be seriously contended that under the constitution the yeas and nays ought to be used literally in an election; but even this could be done. The candidate proposed for office could be voted for in this language. The voter could say yea or nay to him. And one fifth of the members present may require it.

But independent of the express provision of the constitution, and independent of the spirit and meaning of that instrument, Mr. R. observed, that this proposition was of such a character, arising from our republican institutions, that it is almost as susceptible of demonstration as any mathematical problem.

In this republic, the supreme power rests with the people, under such rules and regulations as are prescribed in our constitutions and laws. The people are sovereign, and of right must be, while our Government continues to exist as a republic. No tyrant or irresponsible lord or representative can rule over us. The people are responsible for their acts to no earthly power, while they remain within the pale of the constitution and the law of the land.

This principle needs no demonstration to an American. It is self-evident to every republican; and I hope I address such.

Arising out of this principle, the system of representation must of necessity be adopted.

It would be folly to suppose that all the people of this widely-extended Republic could assemble together to provide for their various wants, and to transact their public business. If they were present, they could not do any business, as the body would be so unwieldy. Hence resulted the representative form and principle in our Government. It is the great improvement in Governments which gives the modern the great superiority over the ancient Republics. This is the principle, above all others in our Government, which should be preserved *pure* and *sacred*. Any intervening circumstance, although trivial in itself, that tends to injure the *purity* of elections, or the *purity* of the representative principle, should be condemned as dangerous to our liberties.

Judging from the experience of a few years past, Mr. R. said, he had arrived at the conclusion, that the People of the United States are determined, at all hazards, to preserve the purity of elections. This is the greatest evidence of the vigor, strength, and long life, of our Government.

Next in the order of events is the responsibility of the Representative to his constituents. This is as important, and, in fact, as necessary to be cherished and preserved in its purity, as the elective franchise. It is a yoke fellow; one will not exist in vigor when the other is in decay and rottenness. They will both rise or fall together, as they both stand on the same political ground.

A moment's reflection will satisfy all of the necessity of the *responsibility* of the representative to his constituents. The very name will show, that he is not acting for himself in his official capacity. He acts for others, and to them he is responsible for his official conduct. He should be the mirror, to exhibit the sentiments of his people, and, in fact, the miniature picture of the people.

Although I am at a great distance from my constituents, and perhaps not one of them will witness any of my official conduct, yet I consider myself bound, by the nature of my office, and by my own feelings also, to represent in this House the will and sentiments of the people of the First Congressional District in the State of Illinois.—Should I disregard their republican sentiments on the subject now before the House, and vote to hide my vote from their examination, I would be taught a lesson, through the medium of the ballot-box at home, which would be a warning to me on all future occasions. This, I think, would be my lot. I judge not for others.

This principle being established, that the representative is bound to represent the sentiments of his constituents, *truly* and *honestly*, and that he is responsible for the same, the question then arises, how is this fact to be ascertained?

The proposition now before the House, is nothing more or less than to require the best evidence to ascertain the responsibility of the representative of which the nature of the case is susceptible. This is the common sense, and, I may add, the common law rule of evidence in our courts of justice. And should it not be extended also to transactions in the most high and august tribunal in the nation? The record evidence of each individual's vote on the journal is the mode the best calculated to exhibit to the people the acts of their representatives.

This is the mode pointed out by the constitution, and it is found by experience to be the best manner to preserve the history of any transaction in courts of justice, or in legislative bodies. It is much the best for the member himself. There can be no perversion of his vote, if it be recorded, as it falls from his mouth. His constituents and the world, if they please, will know how he acts. Mr. R. said he was satisfied that there was no person in this House, who would want to hide his vote on any *public* transaction.

The people, as they are sovereign and not responsible to the representatives or to any body, have the right to vote as they please, by ballot or otherwise. The ballot system is the best for the people, and the *viva voce* for their public servants.

It is idle to contend that the constitution requires the record of the proceedings and votes of members on *measures*, to be recorded, and not on *men*, in elections. On measures, one-fifth of the members can require the votes to be recorded, and on elections for men to office, the same rule and principle should be applied. They are both within the meaning and letter of the constitution.

Mr. McKINLEY did not consider it a matter of the least consequence, so far as this resolution was concerned, whether the printer to this House be regarded as an officer of the House, or one bound by contract to perform a particular duty. The joint resolution of 1819 could have no influence upon the mere question of election or appointment of printer, because that part of it which directed that the printer to each House should be elected by ballot, was temporary, and expired with the first election under it. The residue of the resolution, which regulates the duties of the printers, is still in force. The joint resolution of 1829, is the law regulating the election of printers; by it there is no mode of election prescribed; consequently there is no law of Congress requiring that the election of public printer shall be by ballot.

But, sir, if there was such a law, it could have no weight in a case like this. The constitution confers the power on each House, to determine the rules of its own proceedings. That part of the resolution of 1819, which directs that the printers shall be elected by ballot, does nothing more than prescribe the rule of proceeding in the election, therefore, is not obligatory on either House longer than either chooses to conform to it. There is nothing, therefore, in the resolution of 1819, if it were in force, which could, or ought to, restrain this House from adopting the resolution under consideration. Sir, I deem it unnecessary to follow the argument of the gentleman from New York, (Mr. Fillmore,) further upon this part of the subject. The resolution under consideration, is one of great importance, in principle; it proposes that the vote of each member of this House shall be entered upon the journal in ever election, and thereby promotes the great and leading principle of the government—the responsibility of the representative to his constituents. In doing this, it conforms to the spirit and intention of the constitution. Why should any gentleman desire to conceal his vote, or to shield himself from just accountability, upon this, more than any other subject. Upon all other *questions*, it is admitted that one fifth of the members present can compel each member to vote *viva voce*, and have his vote recorded in the journal. Are elections exempted, in any way, from the influence of this rule? Is there any reason why they should be? The constitutional rule is broad enough to cover every case that can come before either House. It is in these words, "each House shall keep a journal of its proceedings, and from time to time publish the same, excepting such parts as may, in their judgment require secrecy, and the yeas and nays of the members of either House on any question, shall, at the desire of one fifth of those present, be entered on the journal."

Sir, is not an election a *proceeding* which is, and ought to be, *entered on the journal?* If so, *any question* arising in the course of that proceeding may be so *entered*, or there is no virtue in the rule. There is no provision of the constitution more practised under by this House—none so well calculated to keep the people informed of the proceedings of Congress, and the motives of its members; why then should they not have the full benefit of it in elections as in other cases? It does appear to me, to be utterly impossible to escape from the obligatory form of this provision in this or any other case. The proposition, here, is that a majority of this House, by passing the resolution under discussion, may compel all the members voting upon a *question* of election to have their votes entered on the journal. The constitutional rule is, that one fifth of those present may do so, and yet gentlemen say this resolution ought not to pass.

Why was this provision inserted in the constitution? Was it not to enable the people to see who sustained and who opposed any particular measure? This, sir, is the living principle of this Government; without it the liberties of the country could not be preserved. We see efforts making daily, on the part of the representative, to shake off all responsibility; and to put at defiance the popular will. Let it now be established by the vote of this House, that we are not bound to record our votes, in the election of officers, or on any other *question*, and the boldest step towards irresponsible power ever yet taken in this Government, will have been, so far, established. Is there any exception to the rule laid down in the constitution? If elections of officers, the election, or appointment of printers, or any other act, or thing to be done by this House, is excepted, let the exception be shown. There is just as much danger from the exercise of irresponsible power in the election of officers of the two Houses of Congress, as in innumerable other cases, occurring daily, in which the yeas and nays are required. Your Clerk disburses annually more than one hundred and fifty thousand dollars—has the custody of the papers and journals of the House. The Speaker presides over the deliberations of this House—appoints the committees—examines and corrects the journal—preserves order and decorum—decides questions of order; and in virtue of his office, may be President of the United States; and have the people no interest in the appointment of these officers? It is strange if they have not. Should a worthless individual be appointed to either of these offices, and any signal failure of duty occur, we should hear the inquiry—who voted for him? By which party was he elected? But under the existing rules of this House, these would be unavailing questions—secrets, which the people could not know, and which gentlemen say, they ought not to know.

The framers of the constitution did not put it in the power of a bare majority of either Hou[illegible] suppress, or exclude from the journals, th[illegible] upon any question whatever; but to effect th[illegible] ject, they required that more than four-fifths [illegible] those present should concur. This shows [illegible] jealous apprehensions entertained by those patriots. It shows that they foresaw that the representatives would be disposed to conceal their proceedings and to avoid responsibility; and fearing the combinations of interested members, and the failure of public virtue, they put in the power of one-fifth of those present to coerce the remaining four-fifths and compel them to record their [illegible] the information of the people. And is th[illegible]

tial provision of the constitution to be entirely disregarded—nay violated—because it has been neglected heretofore?

It may be, sir, that I am mistaken on this subject; I am willing, however, to abide the consequences of that mistake, and record my vote in favor of this proposition.

Mr. HARDIN (owing to a considerable stir, Mr. H's. remarks were occasionally inaudible at our reporter's desk,) was believed to say, that without pretending to understand what members of that House proposed by the resolution; but believing that gentlemen did intend it should bear upon all the elections of that House, he was satisfied, so far as the elections of Speaker, Sergeant-at-Arms, Door-keeper, Assistant Door-keeper, Messengers, &c. were concerned, that the resolution should be adopted; nor if his honorable friend from Illinois (Mr. Reynolds,) desired to place the record of his own vote upon the journals would he have any objection; but there were certain officers of the House, if they were officers, in the election of whom certain conditions were stipulated for, and which must be complied with, or the contract made with them would not be worth a cent. Mr. H. then put the case of Sheriffs being elected in a State Legislature in the manner proposed by the resolution, *viva voce*, and the law in force declared he should be appointed in a different way, would the bond required of him be binding? Certainly not. And so in the present case, if they were to direct the election of their printer in any other mode than that provided for by the law in force, the stipulations under the contract made with him would be invalid. He understood there had been a variety of modes of electing the printers of that House and of the Senate, and great complaints made at former periods, on account of their extravagant charges, and the manner in which their accounts were audited by the House. In 1819, a committee was raised for the purpose of investigating the whole subject, who made a report, and presented a resolution, which received the sanction of Congress. Mr. H. here read from the resolution a lengthy extract, showing the manner in which the work was to be executed, the prices to be paid, &c. Now, said Mr. H., here was a certain law, fixing the pay for printing, and prescribing that the printer should give bond for the faithful performance of his contract. It moreover prescribed, that in the event of the printer failing to do so, the Clerk of the House was empowered to employ some one else, the contracting printer to pay for any loss that might accrue in consequence thereof. Mr. H. was proceeding on this point, when

Mr. VANDERPOEL rose to a question of order. He would respectfully inquire of the Chair, if it was in order to argue the question of electing a public printer, when no such proposition was before the House?

The CHAIR deemed the argument of the gentlemen from Kentucky perfectly in order. The resolution under discussion provided for the election of all officers of the House, and as it was made a question whether the printer was an officer or not, the remarks of the gentleman came within the rules of debate.

Mr. HARDIN proceeded by reading a proviso he intended to offer, and asked the honorable mover of the resolution if he were willing to accept it? It was read as follows:

Provided, That elections ordered by joint resolutions of the Senate and House of Representatives, approved and signed by the President, shall be conducted in manner and form as are directed by said resolutions.

Mr. REYNOLDS dissented.

Mr. HARDIN was willing to believe the resolution had no particular case in view; but if his proviso were adopted, every difficulty would be obviated. Suppose we were to disregard the proviso, and, under the resolution, proceed to the election of a printer. Mr. H. would ask, if the printer would be bound by the contract? Not at all. If he fail in furnishing the work, and the clerk should employ any one else, could we deduct the [illegible] from the stipulation? No; we could not. [illegible] solution he had before referred to, prescri[illegible] form, and they must proceed according to it. The gentleman from Alabama (Mr. McKinley) has discovered that the regulation of 1819 has been repealed. We shall see whether it is or not. [Mr. H. here read the resolution.] Now, the resolution repealed only just as much as it altered; and it altered only that part which provided that the election should take place within thirty days of the end of the session. That was the only alteration. Did it alter the price of the work? No. Did it alter the mode of appointing the printer? No. It only prescribed the time of election; but left the price of the work, and the manner of electing, just as the resolution of 1819 did.

We were informed that the constitution of the United States required all these elections to be *viva voce*; that it should be known and spread upon the journals how each member voted. Mr. H. believed this had never been done since the formation of this Government in 1789. The wise men who framed our system came from every quarter of the United States—from the East, where the scripture says they shall come from; but now, said Mr. H. jocosely, things are reversed, and the wise men are to come from the West, (he was glad of this, for he was a western man himself,) and discover errors to which we had been blind for forty years. Now it was discovered to be fraught with danger to elect our own Speaker, Sergeant-at-Arms, Door-keepers, Messengers, &c. Why, so little interest did he take in the election of these officers, that about three times out of four, he took no part in them at all. Now, however, it was ascertained to be a high responsibility the representative owed to his constituents to record his vote upon the journals, and written, he supposed, in sun-shine on the face of the heavens. What did the people of Illinois care about who any of those officers were? He believed they rarely knew their names. Mr. H. would not go so far as to assert that the resolution pointed to the election of Public Printer, but he must say, that if the House agreed to the resolution, it was bound to adopt the proviso. Then he thought—he did not know—but he thought the resolution would be something like a royal birth in England—still-born. Mr. H. concluded by moving the adoption of the proviso.

Mr. GILMER said, it was remarkable to see the attention and excitement of members on this question; and he deemed it important the people should understand the reason of all this intense excitement. Was it a desire to create a reform in the administration of the offices of the House? Not at all—that was not pretended. It could be traced to principles which struck at the very foundations of this Government, and which, if not checked, must render it the most corrupt Government in the world. He asked what was the difference between voting by ballot and *viva voce*. It was this: When an individual voted from his own unbiased judgment, he voted by ballot. But if you would have him operated on by the dictation or influence of others, then let his vote be *viva voce*. This was a question relating to the officers of the House, interesting only to its members, and not to the people at large. He would be glad to know what the people of Illinois knew or cared about the election of those officers. Mr. G. said he he did not believe there were ten men in Illinois who knew who those officers were. How should they know whether the Clerk or the Speaker of that House faithfully and promptly discharged their respective duties? It was not in the nature of things. It was intended that by voting *viva voce*, the voter should become dependant, and not independent, as some of his friends seemed to suppose. It was a fundamental principle in our government, that the vote by ballot rendered the voter independent, while the vote *viva voce* rendered him subservient. It could not be denied that there would be less opportunity for the free and unbiased exercise of the judgment of the members in selecting their own officers when they were brought up to face those who wielded the power, the influence, and the offices of the government, in giving in their suffrages. He asked if it was worthy of that House to thus give an opportunity of rendering its members liable to such undue influence. The practice long pursued of electing the officers of the House, and of re-electing them so long as they discharged their duties with fidelity, had been found safe and satisfactory; and the operation of the proposed change could only tend to render the officers so elected, the mere creature, the tool, the servile instrument of the majority on whom he was dependant for his station. He trusted there was not a member of that House, who wished to see their officers servilely dependant on any individual member or any portion of members. The design was not so much to make members responsible to the *People*, as to a self-constituted power surrounding them. Here was the very evil of our government, which, if not corrected, and sedulously guarded against, must eventually sap its foundations. Sir, said Mr. G. I will vote against any man who will dare to avow himself dependant alone on the majority who are to elect him. He would not, and he trusted the House would not, permit itself to sanction this dangerous principle. Every thing in this country was looking towards this great evil, and should it continue to be countenanced, this Government could not stand.

Mr. MILLER said, that long before he had the honor of a seat in this House, his attention had been turned to the present rule, under which the members vote by *ballot* for the *officers* of the House. He had always thought it wrong. He well recollected when at home among the people, in examining the proceedings of Congress in the papers, the general result of the election could only be seen. But the people could not ascertain from a list of yeas and nays, how their own immediate representative, nor how any other member had voted. He also recollected that one of his predecessors (the late Mr. Ramsey) had, during his term, brought this subject before the House, by moving a resolution very similar to the one now under consideration, and having precisely the same object in view. He then felt astonished that it had not met with a more favorable reception, as he had always thought the proposed change so reasonable in itself, that it was only necessary to bring it to the notice of the House to ensure its adoption. He thought there was a peculiar fitness and propriety in the alteration of the rule as proposed. It was due to the members themselves, and it was also due to their constituents, that the change should be made. The present mode of voting is not only an undeserved reflection upon the independence of members, but it subjects them, in some instances, to unjust imputations. Their political opponents may represent them as having voted for this man or for that man for Speaker or Public Printer, so as to injure them in the estimation of their constituents, and there is no journal, or published list of yeas and nays, to put the question to rest.

The Speaker of this House is one of the most important and dignified officers in the government. He occupies a distinguished and very elevated position in the eyes of the people of this nation. The people, therefore, have a right to know how their representatives vote in his election, as well as that of public printer, and the other officers of the House.

In the State which he had the honor to represent in part, the *people* vote by ballot themselves. This he thought right; their votes are their own and no one has a *right* to inquire how they dispose of them. But it is not so with regard to their representatives. So tenacious and careful had the people of Pennsylvania been on this subject, that they had made it a provision in their constitution, that *all* votes given in a representative capacity, should be *viva voce*. The representative gives the vote of his constituents, and not his own, and consequently they have a *right* to know how he does give it. This, as a general rule, cannot be successfully controverted in a representative government. And surely the case under consideration, forms no exception.

He was no little astonished at the opposition to the resolution by the gentleman from Kentucky. (Mr. Hardin.) He represents a State where the people themselves vote at the polls *viva voce*—an intelligent and independent people, who proclaim aloud for whom they vote; and why should he, as their representative, wish to put in a secret ballot, for any officer of this House, in preference to

naming aloud the individual for whom he votes? Certainly gentlemen who represent those States where the people themselves vote *viva voce*, will be the last to resist the adoption of the resolution under consideration.

Mr. MILLER said he would not enter into a discussion of the abstruce legal question, as to whether the public Printer of this House is an officer or a mere contractor. In his opinion it had nothing to do with the question under consideration. With regard to the objection that is made, that the adoption of this resolution will interfere with the joint resolution of the two Houses relative to electing a printer, he would observe that it is true the first resolution on that subject provides that the choice shall be made by *ballot*. But the last resolution on the subject, passed at the session of 1828–29, provides that the members of each House shall *vote* for a printer, omitting the word by *ballot*. He had always understood that the last or subsequent law repeals the former, when there is any inconsistency or incongruity between them. He therefore thought that the members were in this case at perfect liberty to vote in any manner they may choose to adopt, so far as the joint resolution is concerned.

The resolution now under consideration, is one on which much might be said by travelling into irrelevant and extraneous matters; but it is one that requires but little argument to show the propriety of its adoption.

The question presented, is nothing more nor less than simply this: Shall we change the rule of this House in relation to the election of officers, so that our constituents and all others may know for whom we do vote; or shall we continue the present rule, so that neither they nor any one else shall know for whom *their* votes are given by their representatives?

Mr. BRIGGS said, that a few points had been raised in this discussion in reference to the power of that House in the election of its officers, which seemed to him ought not to be suffered to pass without especial notice. The gentleman from Alabama (Mr. M'Kinley) seemed to admit that the House had the power to prescribe the mode of its own action; and while he also admitted that the law of 1819 had prescribed that mode to be by ballot, he contended that by the subsequent law of 1829, that mode was changed. How was this? The law of 1819 prescribed that the mode should be by ballot, and that the choice should fall on the individual who had a plurality of all the votes, instead of a bare majority. In 1829, the House again took up the subject, and he would call upon the gentleman from Alabama, as a lawyer, to look into the resolution then adopted, and ask himself what the legislature of 1829 intended to do. What were the evils the second law proposed to remedy, and wherein and how far had the previous law been changed? The only principle changed had been that of a majority to a plurality of votes being necessary, and the clause providing that the election should take place within thirty days of the expiration of Congress.

Now, the gentleman from Pennsylvania, (Mr. Miller) who laid down the principle very clearly, told us that the resolution of 1829 did change the mode of election; and how did he prove it? Why, forsooth, because it merely said the House shall proceed to vote for a printer, without, as in the former resolution, specifying the mode and manner in which it should be done. According to the gentleman's rule of construction, the omission of prescribing the mode in the law of 1829, necessarily involved the repeal of the clause in that of 1819, which set forth that the election should be by ballot. If Mr. B. was not entirely mistaken, the provisions of the resolution of 1829 did not touch the mode of election at all.

[Mr McKINLEY here read the joint resolution of that year.]

Mr. BRIGGS. But that resolution distinctly provided that no more of the resolution of 1819 should be repealed than was contrary to the provisions thereof. The gentleman says that the omission is a virtual repeal—we say that the law of 1819 having prescribed the mode of election, and no mention being made of its repeal in the subsequent law, but on the other hand a clause providing that nothing should be repealed contrary to its provisions, that the old mode is still in force.

Another question. It seemed that the great principle of liberty was involved in the mode of electing our officers. The great principle of our constitution—the great principle of representative accountability, now for the first time discovered, after forty years practice and experience. This was extraordinary. The gentleman from Pennsylvania, in his own peculiarly appropriate and chaste manner, has asked if any member upon that floor wished to "sneak" in his vote by the ballot? Mr. B. would ask, if the People of Pennsylvania were wont to "sneak" in their ballots in the election of their State officers? Would the gentleman aver that he was sent to that House by the ballots of the "sneaking" citizens of Pennsylvania? Did the gentleman, in voting, "sneak" in his own ballot? Let those who are sneaks, say so; he did not believe the gentleman to be one. Mr. B. would allude to the People of Massachusetts, and those of New England generally, who had been peculiarly watchful of the right of suffrage, and guarded it with the utmost vigilance. No officer dared to look into the ballot-box of a freeman, and they were still satisfied with their experience of the past, and relied on it as one of the main pillars of their future welfare. He knew that our brethren in other parts of the Union entertained a different idea, and sustained it by arguments of great weight; but, in his opinion, they did not counterbalance the reasons for the mode by ballot. The gentleman from Illinois has told us that by adopting this mode of electing *viva voce*, we should return to the great principles of the constitution. Now, sir, said Mr. B., I will pause to give the gentleman an opportunity of pointing out a single clause of that sacred instrument embracing any provision, or saying one word about voting *viva voce*. The gentleman makes no reply. Mr. B. apprehended it had escaped the gentleman's recollection that the only provision therein that prescribed the manner in which the representatives of the people should vote, related to a subject more interesting to the people of this country than any other—he had almost said, of all others, and that was the choice of a Chief Magistrate; where it was laid down expressly that they should vote by ballot.

The constitution provided first, that "the electors shall meet in their respective States and vote *by ballot*;" and if there be no choice, or two persons have a majority, "then the House of Representatives shall immediately choose, *by ballot*, one of them for President; and if no person have a majority, then from the five highest on the list the said House shall, *in like manner*, choose the President." And again, in the election of Vice President, "if there remain two or more who have equal votes, the Senate shall choose from them *by ballot*, the Vice President." Thus then, we see that the wise framers of that sacred instrument have provided for the election, by ballot, and that too, by the servants of the people upon the floor of Congress. These provisions of the constitution were full, (however gentlemen might talk about the sacred principles of liberty,) and the fact was deduced from them that the legitimate principle of voting in this House must be by ballot. We were told that when the representative went home to his constituents he might, by means of the ballot, shield himself from accountability to them; but Mr. B. said, this brought him to the converse of that conclusion; and under these views his duty would lead him to vote against the adoption of the resolution.

Several members rose to address the House.

The floor was obtained by Mr. PEYTON, who gave way to

Mr. LOVE, who moved an adjournment.

Mr. MANN, of New York, asked for the yeas and nays, but the House refused to order them.

The motion to adjourn was then put and carried without a division.

IN SENATE.

MONDAY, Jan. 26, 1835.

Petitions and memorials were presented by Messrs. TIPTON, TOMLINSON, TYLER, BLACK, and CLAYTON.

Mr. TIPTON, from the Committee of Claims, made an unfavorable report upon the petition of Roger Bond.

Mr. TIPTON, from the same Committee, made an unfavorable report upon the petition of the Marshal of the district of Missouri, for certain allowances.

Mr. WHITE, from the Committee on Indian Affairs, to which was referred the bill from the House of Representatives to authorize the Superintendent of Indian affairs at St. Louis to employ a clerk, reported the same with an amendment, limiting the employment to one year, and the salary to $700.

Mr. MOORE presented certain joint resolutions from the Legislature of Alabama, on the subject of reducing the minimum price of the public lands; which was laid on the table.

Mr. CLAYTON, from the Judiciary Committee, made an unfavorable report upon the petition of Ludwig Ludwigson, for leave to introduce certain slaves into New Orleans; and the Committee was discharged from the further consideration of the same.

Mr. CLAYTON, from the same Committee, also made an unfavorable report upon the petition of Noah Brown and others.

Mr. LEIGH, from the Committee on Revolutionary Claims, made an unfavorable report upon the petitions of Robert Ferroll, Uriah Forest, and Zackguell Morgan.

Mr. LEIGH, from the same Committee, reported a bill for the relief of John Spitfathom; which was read, and ordered to a second reading.

Mr. ROBBINS, pursuant to notice, given on Friday last, submitted the following resolution:

Resolved That the Secretary of the Senate be, and hereby is authorized to furnish the Senators who have been elected since the last distribution of the Register of Debates, published by Gales & Seaton, and who have taken, or shall take their seats in the Senate during the present session, each with a copy of said work.

Mr. PRESTON, from the Committee on Pensions, made on unfavorable report upon the petition of Captain Richard H. Bell.

Mr. BELL, from the Judiciary Committee, reported a bill authorizing the issuing of a patent to John Howard Harris, for his discovery of a method for preserving vegetable substances from decay

Mr. KING, of Alabama, from the Committee on Military Affairs, to whom was referred the bill making appropriations for the repair of certain fortifications in the State of Maryland, reported a bill authorizing the purchase of a lot of land adjoining Fort McHenry, near Baltimore.

The last named bills were read the first time, and ordered to a second reading.

The joint resolution from the House of Representatives authorizing the Secretary of State to deliver to the Secretary of War such of the papers of General Washington, purchased by the Government, as may be necessary in the investigation of pension claims;

The bill from the House of Representatives to authorize the relief of James Middleton Tuttle, of Arkansas, and

The bill authorizing letters patent to be issued to Francis B. Ogden—were each read the first time, and ordered to a second reading.

The following resolutions were submitted:

By Mr. MOORE:

Resolved, That the Committee on the Judiciary be instructed to inquire into the propriety of making a suitable appropriation, to aid in the erection of a court-house, now in progress in Madison county, Alabama, in order to provide for the accommodation of the District Court of the United States, holden at that place.

By Mr. TIPTON:

Resolved, That the Committee on the Post Of and Post Roads be instructed to inquire into the expediency of establishing a post route from Ma- rion to Huntington; thence to Goshen, India a post route from Greensville, by Recovery, to Huntington, Indiana; a post route from Y river Post Office to Laport; a post route Kirk's Cross Road by Frankfort and Delhi to ticello; and a post route from Log .nsport by

key Creek Prairie and Goshen to White Pigeon, in the Michigan Territory.

Mr. EWING, from the Committee on the Post Office and Post Roads made a report.

Mr. E. observed, that as the report was long, he would move to dispense with the reading of it, unless some gentlemen desired to have it read.

A desire having been expressed to hear the report, Mr. EWING commenced reading it, and three hours and a half having been consumed in that process, before it was concluded,

Mr. CLAY, at 4 o'clock, rose and said, that he intended moving the Senate to go into the consideration of Executive business to-day, but this report having intervened, had prevented him. As he understood that there was a counter report to be read, he would now move an adjournment. The motion was agreed to, and

The Senate adjourned.

HOUSE OF REPRESENTATIVES,
Monday, Jan. 26, 1835.

Mr. PLUMMER asked that a correction might be made of the Journal. On the motion to lay the resolution respecting a vote was not for officers of the House, he had voted in the negative, but his name had not been recorded.

Mr. PINCKNEY inquired whether the gentleman from Mississippi was present and voted.

Mr. CAMBRELENG stated, that the gentleman sat near him, at the time, and voted on the question.

The correction was then ordered to be made.

Petitions and memorials were presented by—

Messrs. EVANS and JARVIS, of Maine;

Messrs. HUBBARD and BEAN, of New Hampshire;

Messrs. LINCOLN, PHILLIPS, and JACKSON, of Massachusetts;

Messrs. BARBER and TRUMBULL, of Connecticut;

Mr. JANES, of Vermont;

Messrs. HARD, HUNTINGTON, FILLMORE, P. C. FULLER, DICKSON, WARD, HAZELTINE, and FERRIS, of New York.

[Mr. WARD, of New York, presented a memorial of the York Town Presbyterian Church, New York, and the petition and additional documents in the case of the legal representatives of E. Lockwood; both of which were referred to the Committee on Revolutionary Claims. Also, the petition of Israel Reynolds; referred to the Committee on Revolutionary Pensions.]

Mr. LEE, of New Jersey;

Messrs. WAGENER, SUTHERLAND, WATMOUGH, and STEWART, of Pennsylvania;

Mr. MILLIGAN, of Delaware;

Messrs. TAYLOR and CHINN, of Virginia;

Mr. SPEIGHT, of North Carolina;

Mr. PINCKNEY, of South Carolina;

Messrs. JOHNSON and ALLAN, of Kentucky;

Mr. STANDIFER, of Tennessee;

Messrs. CRANE, MITCHELL, LYTLE, VINTON, and CORWIN, of Ohio;

Messrs. LANE and EWING, of Indiana;

Mr. PLUMMER, of Mississippi;

[Mr. PLUMMER presented the petitions of John H. McKennie; Baylis Nation; William Blanton; Wm. B. Edwards; Robert Belshar; William Ormon; Nathan Edwards; Josiah Edwards; Wm. Sullivan; Calvin Cushman; Woodard Boone; A. McCaslin; Stephen Smith; John H. Byers; Wm. W. Byers; representing that they have been deprived of the benefits of the pre-emption act of March 2, 1833, in consequence of a decision of the land officers against them, and praying for relief: referred to the Committee on Public Lands]

[Mr. CASEY presented the petition of sundry citizens of the southeastern counties of Illinois, bordering on the Ohio and Wabash rivers, praying the erection of a hospital at Shawneetown, in said State.

Upon introducing the petition, Mr. C. made —— appropriate remarks, particularly showing ——reat necessity of such a hospital upon the ——, and especially at that point, which in the ——landing place, not only for a large portion ——interior of Illinois, but for a very great por—— ——f the immense trade of the Big Wabash.]

[Mr. REYNOLDS presented the petition of Capt. Halstead, praying to be paid for his military services in the campaign of 1832 against the hostile Indians in the State of Illinois.

Also, the memorial of the inhabitants of the village of Cahokia, in the State of Illinois.

Mr. R. stated, that this was one of the ancient villages on the Mississippi. The French Government, under which this village was settled, granted to the citizens a tract of land as a common to said village. An act of Congress passed in the year 1791, granting to said inhabitants the use of said land as a common. Now the inhabitants pray the confirmation of said land, and that the fee simple fully be granted to them Said memorial was referred to the Committee on Public Lands.]

Messrs. CLAY and MARDIS, of Alabama;

[Mr. CLAY presented the petition of Richard Cottrell, asking remuneration for provisions, forage, &c. furnished to the army under Gen. Jackson, in the Creek war; which was referred to the Committee on Claims

Mr. C. also presented the petition of numerous citizens of Benton county, Alabama, asking the establishment of certain post routes therein described.]

Messrs. BULL and ASHLEY, of Missouri;

Mr. LYON, of Michigan.

Which petitions and memorials were appropriately referred

On motion of Mr. HAZELTINE,

Resolved, That the Committee on Ways and Means be instructed to inquire into the expediency of making an appropriation for running and continuing the works at Dunkirk Harbor, New York.

On motion of Mr. JOHNSON, of Louisiana,

Resolved, That the Committee on Foreign Affairs be instructed to inquire into the expediency of providing for the complete execution of the 8th article of the Florida treaty, so far as it relates to the claims of lands between the Mississippi and Perdido rivers, and that the report of the late Secretary of State, Edward Livingston, Esq. and the resolution of the Legislature of Louisiana, in relation to that subject, be referred to said committee, with the documents in relation thereto, presented at this session by order of the Senate.

On motion of Mr. MUHLENBERG,

Resolved, That the Committee on the Public Buildings be instructed to inquire into the expediency of procuring such additional Statues as may be necessary to complete the original design of the Capitol, and of employing Luigi Persico to execute the same.

Mr. DENNY offered the following resolution, which, under the rule, lies one day:

Resolved, That the Secretary of War be, and he is hereby requested to communicate to this House, a statement of the amount paid annually, and the price per pound during the last five years for the transportation of arms and other military and public stores from Harper's Ferry, Baltimore, Washington Arsenal, and any other posts or places in Virginia, Maryland, and District of Columbia, to Pittsburg and other posts in the western country.

On motion of Mr. GILMER,

Resolved, That the Clerk of this House lay before it, as soon as practicable, any information in his office upon the subject of a certificate given by John Pierce, Commissioner of Army Accounts, to the State of Georgia, for the sum of $123,283 70 cents in 1785, for payment made by the State of Georgia to its officers for commutation and other pay due them, together with the original certificate, if it be in his office.

On motion of Mr. STANDIFER,

Resolved, That the Committee of Claims be instructed to inquire into the expediency of allowing to Samuel Eskridge the amount of his claim for moneys advanced the agent of the United States, and that the papers and evidence in support of said claim be referred to said committee.

On motion of Mr. MITCHELL,

Resolved, That the Committee on the Post Office and Post Roads be instructed to inquire into the expediency of establishing a post route from New Lancaster, through Baltimore, Lura, Gran-

ville, Predonia, Homer, to Mount Vernon, in the State of Ohio.

On motion of Mr. KILGORE,

Resolved, That the Committee on the Post Office and Post Roads be instructed to inquire into the expediency of establishing a mail route from Washington, Washington county, Pennsylvania, via Wellsburgh, Virginia, Smithfield, Cadiz, Bethesda, Philadelphia, and Worster, to Norwalk, Huron county, Ohio.

On motion of Mr. MAY,

Resolved, That the Committee on Claims be instructed to inquire into the expediency of allowing the claims of Albion T. Crew against the Government for property lost during the late Indian war.

On motion of Mr. MURPHY,

Resolved, That the Committee on Public Lands be instructed to inquire into the expediency of amending the act of Congress passed on the 24 May, 1826, entitled "An act for the relief of purchasers of the public lands that have reverted for the non-payment of the purchase money," and to act on the same subject passed in June, 1832, so as to enable the heirs or legal representatives of deceased persons to draw scrip on all such public land stock remaining in the name of such deceased persons, upon the heirs or legal representatives of such deceased persons giving a refunding bond to be approved of by the Register of the Land Office, in double the amount of the scrip issued, and under such other restrictions as may be thought proper and necessary in all cases where the original certificates given to such deceased persons have been lost or destroyed.

Mr. LYON, by leave, offered the following resolution, which was agreed to:

Resolved, That the Secretary of War be requested to furnish this House, as far as practicable from the information in his office, with an estimate of the expense necessary to complete the opening of the military road from Green Bay to Prairie du Chien, in the Territory of Michigan, so as to allow the transportation of troops and military stores thereon when necessary. Also an estimate of the expense required to open a road from Saginaw to Macinac, in said Territory; for similar purposes.

Mr. LYON offered the following resolution, which was rejected:

Resolved, That this House will, on Thursday, the 5th day of February next, consider and dispose of bills relating to Territories.

Mr. PATTON asked the consent of the House to offer the following resolution:

Resolved, That the Committee on Foreign Affairs, to which was referred that part of the Message of the President which concerns our relations with France, be instructed to report the following resolutions to the House:

1st. Resolved, That the claims of our citizens for reparation from France, provided for in the treaty of the 4th July, 1831, rest upon the strongest ground of right and justice—and that validity and extent have been rendered "incontrovertible" as between the two governments by that convention."

2d. Resolved, That the idea of acquiescing in the refusal of France to execute the treaty ought not to be entertained by any branch of the government, and that we ought to insist, and have a right to expect that France will not persist in her failure to comply with her engagements under that treaty.

3d. Resolved, That as the King of the French has, in some of the most recent communications which have passed between the Minister and relations of our governments, given repeated and reiterated assurances of his sincere desire to have the treaty carried into effect—h-s declared his intention to present the bill for that purpose, as soon as the Chambers can be assembled, and his determination to use every exertion in his power to obtain the appropriation as the bill was heretofore rejected in the Chamber of Deputies by a very small majority, and as that bo ly is now in session at this ——her period than was anticipated when Congress met, we ought, at present, to confide in the sincerity of the professions of the French Executive, and relying still upon the honor and ——

france, notwithstanding the unjustifiable delays which have taken place, not now abandon the hope that the obligations of good faith and a due care of the justice of our claims will not be finally disregarded and overlooked by the French Government in any of its Departments.

Resolved, That it is not expedient, at this time, and under existing circumstances, to adopt any legislative measure in relation to our affairs with France.

Objection being made, Mr. PATTON moved to suspend the rule of the House, in order that he might be enabled to offer the resolution. He did not desire to press it at this time, but merely to lay the resolution on the table.

After some conversation between the SPEAKER and Messrs. CAMBRELENG, CLAY, and PATTON, as to the effect of the motion, the question was taken by yeas and nays, and decided in the negative—yeas 103, nays 109.

Mr. CARR, from the Committee on Private Land Claims, reported a bill from the Senate for the relief of Andrew Know, without amendment, which was read and referred to a Committee of the Whole House on the state of the Union.

Mr. CARR, from the same Committee, reported a bill for the relief of George Douglass and others, therein named; which was read twice and committed to a Committee of the Whole House, and made the order of the day for to-morrow.

Mr. CARR, from the same Committee, asked to be discharged from the further consideration of a petition of James Babbott; and, on motion, it was ordered to be laid upon the table.

Mr. CARR, from the same Committee, reported a bill for the relief of Wm. Bowman, of Morgan county, Indiana; which was read twice and postponed until Friday next.

Mr. MARSHALL, from the Committee on Revolutionary Claims, reported a bill for the relief of heirs of William Northrup; which was read twice and committed.

Mr. CHILTON, from the Committee on Invalid Pensions, reported the following resolution:

Resolved, That Friday, the 6th of February, be apart and specially devoted to the consideration bills for the benefit of such individuals as are asking pensions, as invalid soldiers, and to whose reports have been made from the Committee on Invalid Pensions.

The resolution was agreed to.

Mr. BEALE, from the Committee on Invalid Pensions, reported a bill for the relief of William Aler; which was read twice and committed.

Unfavorable reports upon various petitions, &c. were made by Messrs. MARSHALL, MITCHELL, BANKS, BARBER, and JANES, from their respective committees.

ELECTIONS OF OFFICERS OF THE H. R.

The following resolution, heretofore offered by Mr. REYNOLDS, came up in course:

Resolved, That hereafter, in all elections made by the House of Representatives (for officers) the vote shall be given _viva voce_, each member in his turn, naming aloud the person for whom he votes.

With the following proviso, offered on Saturday by Mr. HARDIN:

Provided, That all elections ordered by joint resolutions of the Senate and House of Representatives, approved and signed by the President, shall be conducted in manner and form as are directed by said resolutions.

Mr. PEYTON rose and addressed the House as follows:

Mr. Speaker I am partial to viva voce voting, and especially to viva voce acting. This partiality and my great anxiety to avoid encroaching upon the Constitutional powers of the next Congress, induced me to vote in favor of laying the resolution offered by the Hon. gentleman from Illinois on the table, that I might offer what I am now about to submit as an amendment, without any encumbrance whatever. What I am about to propose, will secure a viva voce vote in _all elections_, and assert the right of each Congress to elect its own officers. I have never seen the time or place when I was the least embarrassed in declaring for whom I intended to vote, and I hope I never shall be so craven in spirit, so lost to that independence which is native in the bosoms of my constituents,

as to crouch, and hide—_do one thing and say another._ And sir, I must be permitted to defend the citizens of my native State from those imputations which have been cast upon all who vote by ballot in their elections. Tennessee has voted in that manner in the election of all her officers for nearly forty years; and she has not lost her liberty, her gallantry, or independence. And if gentlemen think so, they are much mistaken. No sir, such things depend upon the tone of sentiment amongst men, more than the mere mode of expressing that sentiment. The man who would represent the character and feelings of her people, must be frank, candid, and independent, must be a plain case—no hiding, nor dodging. If you ever see a gentleman at this—who cant be found—you may feel, but cannot see him—who leaves no sign—cant tell which end of the road he has gone—if you catch him out in a snow, get on his track and are confident you have him; but when you come to find out, he has turned the heels of his shoes before and you are on the back track.—Such a man is no Tennessean.

But while I vindicate the character of Tennessee from those suspicions which have been thrown upon her on account of the mode of electing public officers, ingrafted upon that constitution which Andrew Jackson aided in forming, and retained by her recent Convention after 38 years experience, I am willing that all elections by Congress shall be viva voce. I like to hear gentlemen speak out boldly on this floor, as well as elsewhere, for of all things, I have the least taste for hypocrisy or double dealing. But sir, I am equally anxious to secure another object, which must be dear to my honorable colleagues who agree in political sentiment with me, and my friends from Alabama, New York, and elsewhere, and that is the right of each Congress to elect his own officer. I know we all agreed in our Constitutional views on this subject last winter. It was a question which produced much excitement in my district, and in the State generally. I give my views, as I am now about to express them unpledged myself to my constituents, if no one else did, to offer a resolution embracing substantially what I now offer on the subject of printer, and to move to go into the election at the commencement of the last session. I did not do so, and this requires an explanation to my constituents. My apology is to be found in the fact that after I had my resolutions prepared, and was on the eve of presenting them, I was requested to permit an abler and much abler member of this body, my friend from Alabama, (Mr. McKinley,) who addressed the House on Saturday, to offer the resolutions; to this I assented with great pleasure, but he was thwarted by the introduction of Mr. McDuffie's resolution on the despotic question, which was debated the greater part of the session. I am proud of an opportunity of redeeming my pledge to my constituents, and at the same time enabling my honorable friends to act out their principles, and aid me in reclaiming for each Congress, the exercise of its inherent and constitutional rights. I have adopted the only mode by which this can be effected, and at the same time secure a viva voce vote. I have no petty party purpose to subserve. We were for it at the last session upon principle, and cannot be against it at this. Our party is overwhelming in strength, it is committed on this question, we have said that the constitution has been violated by an expiring session of Congress, electing a printer for a new Congress; and let us not bring upon ourselves the reproach of inconsistency, but nobly step forward to the rescue of the constitution. Able unanswerable arguments have been made on this question in the other end of the Capitol, by a great statesman and true democrat, which, I am sure will have due weight with all, and with none more than my friends from New York.

I allude sir, to the powerful argument made by the honorable Thomas H. Benton, in the Senate, on the 19th, and published in the Globe of the 23d February, 1833, on the subject to go into the election of public printer. He had, on the 15th of the same month, introduced a resolution, the substance of which I have embraced in my amendment—It was a _Joint Resolution_ of both Houses—

so is mine. It changed the time of the election of printer, from the end of the expiring Congress, to the first week of the new Congress, so does mine. Here Mr. Benton's Resolution stopped, mine goes further, and declares, that the election of printer, and all other elections shall be viva voce. And this is the only material difference between them. I confess, that I should have been somewhat at a loss, as to the powers of this House, in repealing, or in any measure changing a joint resolution of both Houses, which has received the sanction of the President, but for the light which that able, and indefatigable Senator, has shed upon this subject. I had looked upon the Resolution of 1819, as unconstitutional, and void, so did he, and he appears to have been prepared to sustain that proposition, whenever it should be presented. But when the question arose, whether the Senate could recognise its validity as a Joint Resolution, that it could not. This sir, was with me an unanswerable objection to voting for the resolution of the gentleman from Illinois.

It is a single resolution, which will change the mode of electing a printer from a vote by ballot to viva voce, under a joint resolution, and change it in nothing else—thus recognising its validity in every word and syllable, exc pt as to the mode of making the election. It cannot be done. We have a precedent, directly in point: I quote from Mr. Benton's speech, before alluded to: Mr. B. said:

"His present object was to prevent an election at this session; and for this he had a good precedent, originating in the Senate itself, precisely in point, in every particular. He referred to the election of a public printer towards the close of Mr. Adams's administration, when Mr. Green was elected over Gales and Seaton. This election came on; several ballotings took place; Mr. Green had a plurality of the votes, not a majority of the whole. The joint resolution under which the Senate balloted (the resolution of 1819) expressly declared, that a plurality should be sufficient; but the majority, on the eve of proceeding to the ballot, had passed a single resolution, to control the joint resolution, declaring that a majority of the whole should be necessary to a choice. The supporters of Mr. Green claimed the election; but the majority adhered to their single resolution, against the terms of the joint resolution, and refused to permit the election of Mr. Green to be declared. He, Mr. B., then moved that the balloting should be discontinued. They were discontinued accordingly. No election of printer was declared. The session terminated without any further proceedings on the subject. At the commencement of the next session, a resolution was brought in, declaring that Mr. Green had been duly elected at the preceding session. He, Mr. B., voted for the resolution."

Can there be a stronger, clearer case in point? Here the Senate went into the election under the joint resolution of 1819, but passed a single resolution, altering it so far only as the number of votes necessary to constitute an election was concerned. That single resolution was declared to be a nullity by the Senate at its next session, on the ground that a joint resolution could not be altered or changed by a single resolution. And the Senate and House of Representatives, in 1829, did, by a joint resolution of both Houses, make the alteration which had been attempted to be made the preceding session by the Senate alone, and declared that a majority of the whole number of votes given should be necessary to constitute the election of printer, but leaving the resolution of 1819 unchanged in every other particular. Now, sir, have not the Senate and House of Representatives each acted on this question of altering the resolution of 1829, by a single resolution, and decided that it cannot be done? I think so most clearly. I would have no hesitation in saying that the whole resolution could be set aside by any new Congress which might choose to elect its own printer, but I deny that an expiring Congress, which has made all its elections, can by a single resolution alter a joint resolution in part, the validity of which resolution is recog-

nised as constitutional. I ask gentlemen to deal candidly, and say whether their object is not to go into the election of printer at this session? If not, what other election is coming on at this session. And, sir, I should like to know whether the next Congress will not be as well qualified to judge for *itself* of the *mode* of electing *its* officers, as this Congress is. What right have we to say to our successors you are a "*slippery, sneaking*" set of fellows? We have a high regard for your constituents, but no confidence in you, and have therefore said that *you* shall vote viva voce, in the election of your officers. It is true that we elected all our officers by ballot—there is no complaint—the House is satisfied—the country is well pleased—not a word of discontent, save an occasional groan of disappointment, coming, not from the House or country. Sir, it appears to me to be stepping over the line of our duty, to undertake to dictate to the next Congress with regard to the *mode*, or the *election* of printer.

The constitution secures to *each* House the power to determine the rules of *its* proceedings; but not to prescribe rules to govern the proceedings of the next Congress.

But, sir, as it will stand in the light of a mere recommendation to the next Congress, I am willing to accommodate gentlemen in their fondness for viva voce voting, with a hope of conciliating their support on the main question—that of securing to each Congress the right to elect its own printer. And, sir, I am the more inclined to this, as it is said that it will *certainly* secure *perfect independance* in voting; whereas, now it is complained that the oldest *drill-sergeants* may take out a raw recruit, and drill him for hours, and when he comes to vote, he will not feel those noble, lofty sentiments of *independence* which will prompt him to give the *sergeant's* vote, but will *sneakingly* give his *own*. This is monstrous, and ought to be corrected. For, if it is not, the noble science of drilling will be stripped of half its charms, and wild, rude militia-men will be constantly consulting *their judgments* and their *consciences*, in great national questions, involving the liberty, happiness, and constitutional safety of the country. All of which, it is thought, may be corrected by a combination of the two operations of the sergeant on drill to learn him what is right with the nippers, to pinch the word from him at the right time afterwards. This is so perfect a system of *independence*, that all men must be delighted at the dawn of that bold and glorious republican sun which is about to shed a flood of light upon our hitherto dark and benighted hall of legislation.

But, sir, to the main question—that of postponing the election of printer until the next session of Congress. I beg leave again to refer the House to the able and lucid argument of Mr. Benton on this subject. He said, "His object was, to vindicate the right of the new Congress to choose its own officers. That right belonged to it. It belonged to it, both inherently and by the constitution. It would have required a constitutional provision to take it away, not to secure it; yet, in two places, the constitution guaranties this right. Once, in speaking of the House of Representatives, which is to elect its own Speaker, and other officers; and again, where the Senate is secured in the right of electing its President pro tem. and other officers. Mr. B. then alluded to the early practice of Congress, which had been conformable to the constitution, and proceeded to state, that "in 1819, a joint resolution of the two Houses was adopted, creating the *office* of *Public Printer*, and providing for the election of that officer." He said, "for the first thirty years of the action of this Government, there was no Public Printer, while Congress sat at places where it could supply itself, each new Congress was its own purveyor. When it came to a place where supplies could not be obtained, except upon time and notice, the expiring Congress kindly and providentially took upon itself the business of procuring supplies. This assumption on the part of the expiring Congress, was gratuitous and unauthorized. The new Congress, not yet born, could not have created an agent to do this business. The fact of vital importance, whether the new Congress was to have a friend or an enemy for its printer might depend upon the time when he was elected, and thus it became necessary for the new Congress to stand upon its inherent and constitutional right to reclaim the election for itself, and if not successful in the reclamation, to exercise its indisputable power of rejecting the printer that was *imposed* upon it. Mr. B. remarked *that* was what he had done, and was doing—he complained that his resolution had been referred to a committee which had not reported upon it—said that he could have shown that all the reasons which induced the expiring Congress to provide a printer for the new Congress, had ceased; that the district now abounded with printing materials; that a printer chosen the first week of the session would be ready as soon as necessary to do the work, that would be required of him; that the printer was *an officer*, and *an important* officer of the two Houses; that he was a *confidential officer*, having their secret proceedings in his hand, and almost their masters, from the power which the public printer, in his character of editor, had over the publication of the proceedings of Congress, in suppressing, mutilating, and disfiguring the speeches, and occasional remarks of some members, while bringing out all that is said by others to the best possible advantage."

These views are sound. They were hailed by myself, and many gentlemen who I see around me, as containing the true doctrine of our party, which had watched with so much jealousy all encroachments upon the constitution. It has been our pride and boast, that the venerable and patriotic man now filling the Executive chair of the nation, was the shield of the constitution. And shall we forget all this? Shall we say that right reason, and sound constitutional doctrine is one thing in the Senate, and another in the House of Representatives? that our constitutional opinions change with the seasons? No sir. Let us not bring reproach upon our party and its head, but rather elevate both in the world's estimation, by rescuing the constitution, instead of inflicting upon it another blow. Mr. Benton is correct. This House has the inherent as well as the constitutional right to elect its printer. The constitution says, "each House shall keep a journal of its proceedings." To do this, it must have the power to elect a clerk. "And from time to time *publish* the same." How publish? Does not this important duty imply the power of providing the means to perform it? How can the laws and proceedings of this House be published without a printer? The power to elect the printer is conferred in the obligation to publish. Again, the constitution confers upon *each* House the power to determine the rules of its *own* proceedings—secures to the House of Representatives the right to choose its Speaker and other officers, and to the Senate, the right to choose all its officers. Now, sir, I care not whether you consider your printer an officer of the House, or put him upon the footing of stationary, or fuel, or any other supply, the principle is the same. These are my reasons for the vote which I gave, and mean to give, on this question. I have carefully avoided all remarks which might give offence; my object has been to conciliate support for a measure in which my District and my State take a deep interest. If the election of printer is forced on at this session, I have discharged my obligations to my constituents—I have redeemed a pledge too long, but unavoidably, delayed. And, sir, if I am compelled to vote for that officer at this session, I will vote for that *uniform, firm*, and *consistent* Jackson man who I think best qualified, if there should be more than one of our party running—though it would be a pity for two to run, as it would look like splitting the party. But which of them would be obnoxious to this charge, could not be determined until after the election, and then it would justly fall on the meddling fellow who was beaten, and he should be forthwith handed over to a Sergeant and drilled into submission, and directed to turn his attention to history—*biographical history*.

Mr. Speaker, is it in order to move a commitment of the resolution and amendment to a committee with instructions to report. I move sir, that the resolution and amendment be committed to the Committee on the Judiciary with instructions to report the following resolution:

Resolved by the Senate and House of Representatives of the United States of America in Congress assembled, That the election of Printer to each House of Congress, shall hereafter take place within the first week of the first session of each Congress; and that all elections by the two Houses shall hereafter be decided by a viva voce vote.

Mr. POPE said, inasmuch as this proposition had been placed before the House, he intended to vote for it, and he would detain the House but a short time in submitting his reasons for his vote, and for opposing the motion of the gentleman from Tennessee, (Mr. Peyton.) He could not believe, as had been contended, that any great and fundamental principles were involved in this question, but he did believe that the fidelity of the Representatives to their constituents would be [illegible]cused by its adoption. What was the leading argument of the honorable members from Kentucky, (Mr. Hardin,) and from Georgia, (Mr. Gilmer,) [illegible] both of whom, Mr. P. said he had great confidence. It was, that wise men and patriots had established the present mode of electing by ballot, and had sanctioned it by sitting in that Hall under its operation without attempting any alteration. Mr. P. said he paid as much regard to the wisdom of our ancestors and the [illegible]monitions of antiquity as others; but he did deemed it essential for the proper government of his conduct, to have some opinions [illegible] his own. The opinions of antiquity were not [illegible] was infallible. Many patriots of the revolutionary period of '76, sincerely doubted the practicability of the scheme of republican government. [illegible] other of the doctrines of that day were now [illegible] experince repudiated; and he should feel bound to go according to the best lights afforded to him. [illegible] P. said, he would not stop to inquire whether [illegible] resolution was applicable to a printer of the [illegible] or whether that printer was an officer of [illegible] House. It was enough for him to know [illegible] there were officers to whom it would apply, [illegible] that the principle of voting viva voce was a [illegible]ed one in the State which he had the [illegible] part of representing; and although it [illegible] ridicule of the gentleman from Georgia, ([illegible]mer,) he still believed in its efficacy, and [illegible] continue to cherish and revere it. He referred [illegible] the election of a Speaker. Was it not a most [illegible]ponsible station? And did not the people feel [illegible] deep interest in the selection of the individual [illegible]trusted with the important duty of appointing the committees of that House? They certainly [illegible] And should they not know how their servants [illegible] that floor disposed of the vote intrusted to [illegible] He did not care whether this resolution applied [illegible] the election of a public printer or not. When [illegible] question of such an election came up, it [illegible] then be time enough to indulge in that [illegible]

But it had been alleged that members here [illegible] surrounded with a polluted atmosphere; that [illegible] could not vote openly without subjecting themselves to a corrupting influence. He suggested how easy it was for the balloting representative after casting his vote, to go to the Executive mansion, or elsewhere, if you please, [illegible] there represent that he had carried out [illegible] will he had professed to serve. Now, if the [illegible] were given viva voce, it would place the [illegible] his constituents upon him, and the people [illegible] and would see whether he came there to [illegible] represent them, or play the pander to others. [illegible] had been said, that if the vote by ballot were abolished, the representative would stand too much in terror of his constituents, to suffer him to [illegible] his own unbiased judgment. He would [illegible] who he could with more propriety stand in [illegible] than his own immediate constituents? [illegible] voted in error, he voted in accordance with their wishes—and those wishes he was bound to respect.

Mr. P. had said all that he meant to say on the subject. He believing the resolution ought to pass, whether it applied to the election of a public printer or not, would make no difference in his vote, nor alter the purport of these remarks.

Mr. VANDERPOEL said, it seemed to him that no good reason could be urged against the

involved a question of great importance, viz. ether the representative could in justice, with- t special constitutional leave, be permitted to ecute his agency in such a manner as to exempt from responsibility to his principals, *the peo-*

Mr. V. said he held to the broad principle that representatives, we should do no act here, the owledge of which might be concealed from the ople; that the principle of giving a secret vote s anti-republican, and wholly incompatible with possibility to the *source of all power,* which lies the foundation of all our institutions. The cre- r should always know or have the certain ans of knowing the acts of the creature, espe- ly when the latter was commissioned only to ecute the will of the former.

He asked, upon what principle the practice of giving a secret ballot vote could be justified? had been said by his honorable colleague, (Mr. more,) who opened the first battery upon this lution, that the People themselves, in many, most of the States, voted by ballot, and, refore, the practice was sanctioned by the hest authority. Another honorable gentleman, Georgia, (Mr. Gilmer,) who spoke so sel- in this House, but always spoke so well, had us that the voting by ballot here was calculat- to secure the most upright and independent ecution of this appointing power, with which are invested. Let us examine, for a moment, the soundness of these positions. He (Mr. contended, that the circumstance that the ple sometimes vote by ballot in the exercise of sovereign power, was not a precedent to jus- the practice *here,* acting, as we here do, in a esentative capacity. The gentleman from ressee, (Mr. Peyton,) who had just delivered ble argument in favor of the amendment he introduced, seemed to imagine, that the reso- n involved an imputation upon the people of e States where they voted by ballot, and felt self called upon to shield the people from such ation and reproach. In his (Mr. V.'s) hum- opinion, the People required no such vindica- for the exercise of their undoubted right, be- *their* right to vote by ballot was unques- able. The People, the sovereigns, are re- sible to no one but themselves. When vote, they do it in execution of their own ness. Whereas, when *we* vote, we do it ecution of the business of our constitu- Because a man, sir, has a right to uct his own operations secretly, it by no ns follows that he has a right to conduct those nother in such manner as that his principal, the party interested, cannot learn the manner which his affairs are managed. Let not then right to vote secretly, by ballot, be inferred the practice of the people themselves. To mpt to derive such a right from such a source, founding all distinction between master and ant, between principal and agent. Gentle- who seek to deduce the right to vote by bal- here from the practice of the people, seem to get, that although we are "dressed up in a brief authority," we are nevertheless respon- agents, bound to execute the will of those have clothed us with that authority, and that the right of those who have delegated to us high trusts which we are here called upon to ute, to know the manner in which we execute It struck him (he spoke with all pos- respect for those who urged it) that the con- doctrine was founded in a disregard for, or getfulness of the relation in which we stood *sovereign creating power.*

word now, sir, as to the benefits claimed by gentleman from Georgia, (Mr, Gilmer,) from secret mode of ballot voting. He told us, in tance, that this practice was calculated to en- the most independent exercise of the right ty on our part. I suppose he means by this if we vote *viva voce,* delicacy might some- s restrain or embarrass us. This struck him V.) as the feeblest of all reasons, that could given in favor of the practice of voting by bal- The fear of offending candidates or parties rested!! What an ignoble feeling, sir, to con- the Representative! Why, sir, we should, if this be a valid reason, or a sound argument, extend the principle—we should at once make the effort to amend the constitution, so as to abolish the yeas and nays, because in the ordinary course of legislation we have questions here every day, eminently calculated to exercise and try our delicacy. We are not unfrequently called upon here, to vote for claims preferred by our friends, and to vote against them too sir, and then we are exposed to the reproaches, if not the implacable enmity of those friends. Now, sir, permit me to propose a remedy for all this inconvenience to which we are thus exposed. Let us alter the constitution, abolish the yeas and nays, and tell the world, that we "love darkness rather than light," because our day-light deeds have exposed us to the querulous moanings of our friends.

Why, sir, upon what ground of principle should there be a difference between the operations in this Hall and those at the other end of the building, when we appoint to office? The Senate sits with closed doors; but the journals of that body are always published; and the people of the United States have the means of knowing how the representatives of the States vote upon Executive nominations. And the brief existence of this Government has already taught us, that the people do not always regard the votes of honorable Senators upon Executive nominations with indifference or unconcern. No, *sir,* we can adduce memorable instances to show, that the sensibility and indignation of the people have been awakened against the representatives of the States, for what they deemed an exceptionable exercise of this power. There were not wanting instances in which the people had reversed the sentence of *unworthiness,* which the Senate had seen fit to pronounce. He would ask, if the votes and proceedings of the Senate, when acting on Executive nominations, should always be concealed from the people, if they not only sat with closed doors; but if their journals were always kept secret, how long would the people submit to a practice so repugnant to popular sentiment? That august body would then soon, very soon, sir, in the estimation of the people, acquire all the odious features of a Spanish Inquisition.

But a new discovery had been made by his honorable colleague, (Mr. Fillmore,) whose extraordinary perspicacity and microscopic vision sometimes enable him to see distinctions that were not visible to ordinary optics. My honorable colleague has started the idea, that there is a fair distinction between voting for *officers of this House* and *officers of the nation,* and that as the officers embraced in the resolution under discussion, are merely officers of this House, we have an indubitable right to elect them by ballot, and in such a manner, as that the people may not be able to know how we vote. Sir, with all due deference to my honorable colleague, (who, from his *professed repugnance* to all secret operations, and secret societies, is the *last* man on this floor, whom I could suppose would be the first to come out in favor of secret voting,) I must be permitted to contend that there is no soundness in this distinction, so far as it concerns the principle we are now discussing. How arrogant the idea that the officers, which we here choose, are *our* officers? What are we, sir, (I speak of our official capacity,) but the property of the people? When we speak of the officers of this House, do we mean to speak of instruments, that belong exclusively to ourselves, and in which the people have no property or interest? With whose moneys are they paid? The People's. Whose business are they appointed to execute? Not our own individual business, but that of the people, and may not the people then fairly feel some little interest in their election? Have they not a clear right to know what servants they, through their representatives, have chosen, especially, *when their own money is to pay the hire of the laborer?*

The honorable gentleman from Georgia, (Mr. Gilmer,) in the zealous and animated speech which he made on Saturday, told us, that the people generally neither know or care who are the officers of this House. This, said Mr. V., gentleman,) was presuming entirely too much upon the ignorance and indifference of the people. It was not his (Mr. V.'s) good or ill luck to be blessed with constituents so ignorant or so indifferent to the doings of their representives. They believe and know that the sentiments of those who represent them may be as emphatically indicated and expressed by the election of the officers of this House as by any other means, that an election for these officers may indeed involve much of principle. Take, if you please, the case of Speaker of this House. consider his power and patronage, the power of appointing all the committees, which have very properly been called the eyes and organs of the House, the power of controlling in a great measure the order of the business of this House, and of giving an impulse to, or thwarting and impeding great measures that may call for the action of this House. Is it in truth, a matter of moonshine to the people, who is elevated to this high and responsible station? Let the gentleman ask the free trade elector of the South, when the cry of "*give—give us more protection,*" is raised by the manufacturer of the North and East, whether *he* feels any interest in the election of the Speaker of this House; ask the Northern manufacturer at such a crisis, if it is or is not his interest or desire to know whether his representative has voted for a *free trade* or an *ultra-tariff Speaker,* and you cannot be at a loss to conjecture what the answer would be. Woe! to that representative, who should, at such a conjuncture, dare to violate the will of his constituents. He would not be able to plead in bar to the denunciations of an indignant people the plea of the gentleman from Georgia, that the Speaker of this House is the officer of this House, and that he supposed the people generally did not know or care who were the officers of this House. Those gentlemen, who, on such an occasion, should calculate so fatally upon the ignorance and indifference of the people, would soon enjoy a privilege which is oft-times vouchsafed to the best of gentlemen—I mean, *the privilege of staying at home.*

Or take, if you please, the case of printer to this House. It requires no very vivid imagination to fancy a choice of printer, that would do violence to popular feeling. Suppose this office to be conferred upon a man whose whole life had been devoted to the dissemination of principles to which our constituents are mortally opposed—to doctrines subversive of equal rights and equal privileges—yea, of *the liberty of the People.* Think you, sir, that the People would be supine and indifferent, if we lavished the most lucrative patronage of this House upon such a man? Would they be apt to say, "you have done well by rendering more potent the incendiary's capacity for mischief?" Let us make the experiment, and we will soon hear a response from the ranks of an outraged and a sharp-sighted people; a response, too, that will not be distinguished for stoical indifference or extraordinary ignorance.

An honorable gentleman from Massachusetts (Mr. Briggs) who a few days ago betrayed more warmth on this subject than usually belongs to that Spitzbergen region to which he and I belong, pleaded most eloquently for the practice which the resolution upon your table proposes to abolish, because it was a *very old practice*—our wise fathers had originated it—it had now obtained for forty years, and therefore our sacrilegious hands should not now touch it.

Sir, said Mr. V., I am no believer in the doctrine, that an error is less an error because it is an old one. Sin itself, is not less to be lamented and deprecated, because it dates back to the garden of Eden. You are constantly changing your laws, involving great principles; your States have, many of them, changed and vastly improved their constitutions; and is this to be regarded, sir, as a reflection upon the wisdom of our fathers? No, sir. It only proves that we are not such bigoted admirers of *all that is old,* as to reject the improvements that may be suggested by time and experience. Let the apologists, the advocates of monarchs and despots, plead for the wisdom and sanctity of their despotic institutions, because they are covered with the dust and the cob-web of ages,

it is *our* principle, yes, our *duty*, while making the grand and triumphant experiment of free Government, to repudiate error and embrace improvement, though the genius of antiquity may scowl and shake her hoary locks. We live, sir, in an age of improvement, and that is indeed a false and short-sighted philosophy, a philosophy which has no deeper foundation than *poetry*, which inculcates the wisdom of always "*bearing the ills we have*," lest we incur the risk of encountering "*others, that we know not of*." One of the beauties of our republican system of Government is, that it can accommodate itself to changes which time and circumstances may demand. Its charm is not the inflexibility of a despotism—no, sir, it is not unbending to the spirit of reform and improvement. In its veneration for the *past*, it is not blind to the treasures which lie in the *future*.

The resolution under consideration, sir, seeks to establish a great abstract principle, resulting from the relation in which we stand to the people, and yet gentlemen who have opposed its passage, have seen fit to discuss the resolution on the assumption, that it was introduced solely in reference to the printer of this House, and a most labored attempt has been made to show that a printer is not an *officer*, but a *contractor*. Sir I consider such topics wholly irrelevant.—To talk about a printer to this house, is indeed belittling the subject under discussion. A resolution is introduced to establish a great principle of popular right, and gentlemen take it upon themselves to narrow down the discussion to the query, whether it will change the mode heretofore pursued of electing the printer of this House. I have endeavored, sir, to take a more elevated view of the principle which the resolution contains, as having higher objects and higher game than the mere printer of this House. First establish a rule, a principle sir, and when we are called upon to go into elections, it will be time enough to inquire what officer comes within the rule. It is however, wrong, sir, to contend, as some gentlemen have contended, that the resolution for this session and that Congress must necessarily be perfectly nugatory, as to every officer except the printer to this House. You, Mr. Speaker, are not immortal. The Clerk, the Sergeant-at-Arms, and all the officers of this House, may be called upon to pay the great debt of nature before the termination of this session. I sincerely hope, sir, that we may not be called upon to fill any vacancies; but that the occasion for doing so, is beyond the range of possibility, is contending entirely too much.

It is somewhat strange, sir, (if, to follow the bad example of other gentlemen, I may be permitted to say a word about public printer,) it is "passing strange," that while honorable gentlemen contend, that your public printer is so amply fortified by certain joint resolutions passed in 1819 and 1829, one of the most vigilant and talented gentlemen on this floor (he meant the gentleman from Kentucky, Mr. Hardin,) should have found it necessary to offer a proviso, in order to save your public printer from the operation of the resolution now under consideration. A long discussion has already been had upon the question, whether the joint resolution of the 5th February, 1829, repeals the resolution of the 3d March, 1819, as it regards the manner in which we are to vote for printer. The last section of the resolution of 1819 provides, "that this House shall proceed *to ballot* for a printer," and the resolution of 1829, which is amendatory of the former resolution, provides "that within 30 days before the adjournment of every Congress, each House shall proceed to vote for a printer to execute its work for and during the succeeding Congress, and that the former resolution, so far as it is altered by the latter resolution, be repealed. Permit me here, sir, to urge an idea that does not yet seem to have suggested itself to gentlemen. I contend that the last section of the resolution of 1819, which provides that the two Houses shall "*ballot*" for a printer, expired with the Congress that passed it, and by its own limitation. It provides, "that as soon as this resolution shall have been approved by the President, each House shall proceed to ballot for a printer, to execute its work during the next Congress." It does not provide that each and every Congress thereafter should elect a printer for its successor, but simply that *that Congress* (of 1819) should elect a printer for the then next Congress. It is said, however, that the act of 1829, by repealing so much of the *first* resolution as was altered by the *last*, shows that the whole of the first resolution was intended to be permanent. To this I answer, that the resolution of 1819 contains various sections and provisions besides that which prescribes the manner of electing a printer. But again; if it be true that the last section of the resolution of 1819 had performed its office, after the printers for the two Houses in 1819 were appointed, I am not aware that the repealing words contained in the resolution of 1829 can revive that which was already defunct. He was not aware that the repeal of a certain portion of a dead statute revived the residue. He had always supposed that dead things were void things, and that void things were as no things.

He could not forbear here to remind the House, that the constitution provides that the yeas and nays may be called at the request of one-fifth of the members present. Why do gentlemen daily call for the yeas and nays, but to present the members of this House to their constituents, and to awaken that sense of responsibility which our position here naturally implies? What an incongruity this, sir. You have a right to call the yeas and nays upon a proposition to appropriate the paltry sum of ten dollars, and yet, when the officers of this House, possessing so much power and patronage, are to be chosen, it is said to be best, and most conducive to our own independence, and to the interest of the people, to give a secret vote. Was it necessary further to comment upon the unsoundness of such an argument?

He would here, also, before he sat down, take occasion to premise, that the mode of voting *viva voce* for the officers of this House would very much tend to the saving of time, because it is much the most convenient mode; we should by that means avoid the fuss and parade that now distinguished our elections: the trouble and detention of first collecting the ballots, and then appointing tellers to go through the tedious ceremony, not once, but sometimes eight or ten times of canvassing the votes, would be obviated. Had gentlemen forgotten the time that was consumed here a few months ago, in the election of a Chaplain. He meant nothing derogatory to that respectable office, when he said, that all this parade, and ceremony, and consumption of time, were beneath the dignity of the House; but he freely confessed that the point of *convenience* was a minor one, and was swallowed up in the question of *principle*. The relation in which we stood to our constituents required an open and manly discharge of all our duties here. Delicacy, the fear of offending our friends, these motives weigh but a feather against the right of the People to know what we do in execution of the high trusts confided to us. We should always remember, as a general rule, that honesty requires no concealment, that justice holds no communion with secrecy and darkness.

Mr. PEARCE, of R. I., said he would be willing to adopt the views of the gentleman from Illinois, (Mr. Reynolds,) who proposed this resolution, so far as to say that hereafter, the officers of the House should be elected *viva voce* whenever a majority of that House, by express declaration, should require it. Thus far he would be willing to go, but no farther. This was not a new question in the House. He well remembered, that about six years ago, an honorable member from Kentucky made a similar proposition. Mr. P. said he then thought it unfortunate for the proposal, as it was now, that it was offered for consideration, after the long session of Congress was passed, and we had come nearly to the close of the short session, and was just about going into the election of the public printer. It had been contended, that some great and fundamental principles were involved in this question. If so, why was it now agitated by those gentlemen for the first time. Where had they been all this time, that this subject, of such vital interest, had been suffered to rest *in statu quo*? Why have they been thus long forgetful of those great principles? Mr. P. said it was useless to disguise the matter. We had better speak of things as they are. It was designed to apply, and did apply to the election of printer, and to nothing else. On that question Mr. P. was willing to give his vote *viva voce*. He was willing to, and would now declare for whom he should vote to fill that station. It would be for the candidate who had consistently and faithfully adhered to and supported the administration. It would be for him to whom he believed it of right belonged. In short, he should vote for Mr. Blair, if that gentleman was a candidate before the House. But he could not consent to alter or abolish what he believed to be a most salutary rule as applied to all the other officers of the House—the Speaker, Clerk, Chaplain, the Door-keeper and his assistants, even the very boys in waiting—if the House thought proper, might be chosen by ballot.

Mr. P. said he understood that the Legislature of Illinois, the State from which the honorable member (Mr. Reynolds) who introduced the resolution came, elected their officers *viva voce*. It might be so in some other instances; but more than two-thirds of the States conducted their elections by ballot; and he apprehended if the question were taken by States on that floor, there would be found a large majority opposed to a change of the rule. In his own State, the vote by ballot prevailed in all excepting one vote, which might be considered a *quasi* ballot. He could not, therefore, directly or indirectly, sanction by his vote a course which he deemed improper, nor did he wish to see a future Congress influenced by any act of the present. If the gentleman from New York (Mr. Vanderpoel) was so much attached to the democratical principles of the vote *viva voce*, why did not he, while a member of the legislature of that State, endeavor to secure its blessings to his constituents? Why not have the elections in New York, *viva voce*, like those of Virginia and Kentucky? What, he asked, would have become of the late election in the city of New York had it been conducted *viva voce*? How would the democratic party have stood against the wealth and power of the whigs? The very voters of the democratic party would have lost their employment and their bread. They were compelled to wear secret badges on their coats and hats by which to distinguish each other. Gentlemen may say this state of things ought not to exist. But, as they do exist, we must meet the exigency. It was right sometimes to do goodly stealth, covertly and secretly. The state of things fully authorized it. Mr. P. said, if the vote *viva voce* was to be adopted here, a very different complexion of affairs would soon be exhibited. He was undisguisedly opposed to this system of special legislation. He was indeed opposed to the adoption of any rule for the government of those over whom we could have no control. For his own part, he had never given a vote there that he was unwilling to avow. But, it had been said the People had a right to know the votes of their Representatives. Now, he had never discovered that the People had ever evinced any great curiosity on this subject.

The present system had prevailed for long years, and the People had manifested no special anxiety for its change. When they did so, it would be time enough to act in the matter. The gentleman from New York went on the ground that the course hitherto pursued had been erroneous. If such were the fact, he had only to repeat the inquiry which he had before made—why had they thus long slept upon their oars? Why did they not earlier seek a correction of the evil?

Mr. P. here alluded to the circumstances attending the first election of Gen. Green as printer to the House, and said perhaps he ought to apologise for the frank manner in which he had avowed his intention of supporting a particular candidate at the next election on party grounds. In the city of New York this principle had been carried to its utmost extent; embracing its street commissioners, and he believed, its chimney sweeps. Nay, the leading daily papers openly called upon their adherents to support none but *Whig butchers*, *Whig*

ders, and *Whig every thing*. If this principle was so universally recognised elsewhere, why should it not be here? The Globe was the accredited organ of the Government and of the democratic party, and as such should be sustained by it. In the city of Philadelphia the principle was extended to the watchmen; and in his own town of Providence, to the constables and the town crier—none were allowed to cry but a Whig! He was therefore for Mr. Blair, against any Judge White-man, any John McLean-man, or any Daniel Webster-man.

Mr. P. repeated that he was opposed to this special legislation. If the rule should be adopted, what would be its effect on the election for Speaker in the next Congress? It was not always the most prominent candidate on the first ballot who was finally elected. Such was the case with the honorable gentleman now in the Chair, and when the honorable P. P. Barbour was elected, he received but fourteen votes on the first ballot. It is true, he did not believe that any man who voted for the present Speaker, was unwilling to avow it; but it was the evils which we hazard by the change which he contemplated. Mr. P. said his constituents had not instructed them on this subject, nor did he believe they called for any action upon it. The constitution provided that "the yeas and nays of the members of either House, on any question, shall, at the desire of one-fifth of those present, be entered on the journal." This, he thought, was quite sufficient to secure ample publicity on all votes specially interesting to the people. It was all they desired; and as far as he was willing to go. He would support the proposition if so amended as to say that, on the call of a majority, the vote should be taken *viva voce*. But he did not deem it necessary to compel members to hold up their hands on all occasions, to prevent them from looking one way and rowing another; nor would he presume fraud in them until there was some evidence of its existence.

Mr. GILLET said, he should not have claimed any portion of the time of the House upon the present occasion, but for the fact, that he represented, in part, a State, which held the ballot box system in high estimation, and for the further reason that his colleague (Mr. Fillmore) had presented, in a forcible manner, the reasons which could be urged against the resolution, which seemed to him to render it necessary that he should succinctly state the reasons for the vote he intended to give. Many gentlemen had expressed in strong terms their disapprobation of the introduction of this resolution. Mr. G. said, he had no agency in its introduction, and was not responsible for the act, though he attributed its origin to noble and generous sentiments entertained by its author, and those whom he represented. Whether its presentation at this time was politic or not, or whether it would be operative or not, was not the question. The real question is, whether the principle asserted, is a correct one or not. This is the true question, and he must give a vote for or against it.

It had become necessary to inquire whether the constitution controlled our decision on the question. This was a question of some doubt. He could not agree with the gentleman from Mass. (Mr. Briggs,) that because the constitution had declared, that certain elections should be by ballot, that it followed that the election of officers for this House must be conducted in the same way. If there was any inference to be drawn from thence, it must be the reverse. The constitution gives this House power to "choose their Speaker and other officers," and to "determine the rules of its proceedings," and under these powers we must act. The constitution itself affords but little light to aid in determining the question, except the fifth section of the first article, which declares, "each House shall keep a journal of its proceedings, and from time to time publish the same, except such parts thereof as may, in their opinion, require secrecy, and the yeas and nays of the members of either House, on any question shall, at the desire of one-fifth of those present, be entered upon the journal."

Mr. G. said he presumed no one would contend here that our election of officers would come within the meaning of this clause, so far as relates to secrecy; but that the intention of the constitution was to conceal such discussions as those that preceded the late war, which it was believed to be for the interest of the nation to be concealed for a limited period. Until gentlemen opposed to this resolution can prove that the election of officers of this House, is not *any question*, the clause of the constitution just cited, will be considered by many as having an important bearing, if it is not decisive of the question. If it is not decisive of the point, then the House is left free to decide it upon the ground of expediency and propriety, and in such manner as shall best accord with the genius and spirit of our republican institutions.

Here, however, we are met with what is called precedent, which is so powerful as to sanctify the errors of the past, and to perpetuate them for the future. This is the doctrine which sanctions the Divine right of Kings, gives the old world its accidental Lords and other similar favors, which give wealth, titles, and power, to the few, and dependence and poverty to the many. Thanks to our fathers, these political heresies were repelled from America by the thunders of Bunker Hill, and our title deed to better principles is not only enrolled on that parchment called the constitution, but it is registered in the heart of every American freeman. But how stands precedent on this subject? My colleague (Mr. Fillmore) the other day, speaking on this subject, said:

"His own opinion with reference to the appointing power of this Government, and of all Governments similar to our own, was, that where the legislative power or body exercised the appointing power, peculiarly and especially for itself, i. e. for its own internal rule and regulation, and not for the nation at large, then that power might, with great propriety, be exercised by ballot; and he believed that to be the practice in most legislative bodies in reference to the appointment of those officers, who might be considered special officers of the body, but not of the nation. This was the practice in Mr. F.'s own State, (New York,) and he really could see no objection to it in principle or practice any where else. It appeared to him to be correct to give the people at large, when they exercised the right of suffrage, the power to exercise that right in secret, by the ballot; and it was equally so to extend the same privilege, the same right, and the same authority to their representatives, when acting for themselves in the election of those officers peculiarly belonging to the body to which they were elected."

Now, how was the fact? Mr. G. said, he desired it to be distinctly understood, that he did not himself allude to his native State, (New York,) for the purpose of invoking the aid of her precedents to guide or justify us for acts done here under another constitution, but merely to put his colleague right on the subject of the doings of that State, as a precedent. It would be borne in mind that his colleague, (Mr. F.) had taken the ground that officers of Legislative bodies were the servants of the body, and not agents of the people, and in enumerating them, he said:

"The House of Representatives shall choose their Speaker and other officers; and shall have the sole power of impeachment" This, then, was the extent of the appointing power in that House to "choose their Speaker and other officers," alluding, doubtless, to the clerk, sergeant-at-arms, messengers, door-keepers," &c.

Here the officers he would include are enumerated. Now for the facts. The journals of the Assembly, in New York, he had examined as far back as to 1820. In that year, the sergeant-at-arms, door-keeper, and his assistant, were appointed by motion or resolution.

In 1822, the same officers were appointed in the same way, and in 1823, the clerk was in like manner appointed. In 1825, the sergeant at-arms, door-keeper, and his assistant, and in 1826, the two latter officers were appointed by resolution, and in 1827, all these officers, including the clerk, were appointed in the same way. So in 1828, of all but the clerk. In 1829, 1830, and 1831, my colleague, creditably to bimself, occupied a seat in the Assembly, and in those years, as well as in 1832, 1833, 1834, in this very year, the clerk, sergeant-at-arms, door-keeper, and assistant door-keeper, (he believed all,) were elected on motion or by resolution. Mr. G. said he had not now access to the journals prior to 1820, but he had been informed by one, who could not be mistaken, that anterior to 1820, a Speaker had been elected by resolution.

His colleague must pardon him for saying, that although he entertained the highest respect both for his talents and integrity, and esteemed him as a friend, he must say little in favor of his memory, when he had forgotten to inform the House that in 1830, while he was in the Assembly at Albany, a Speaker *pro tem.* (Mr. Savage) had actually been appointed by resolution or motion; and his colleague, Mr. F., and four others of his colleagues, had voted on that occasion. He believed it was conceded that all officers elected by the Legislature, except officers of the House, were voted for *viva voce*; and after this review of the precedents, he was of opinion that little could be drawn from that quarter, in form of precedents, against the resolution.

But we were referred to this House for precedents. He had not found a precedent for electing a Speaker by resolution or motion, but a large majority of all the officers for this House back as far as the last war, (and he had not been able to examine further back,) had been elected by resolution or on motion. From 1813 to 1829, he believed the Sergeant-at-Arms had regularly been appointed by this House either on motion or resolution. And from that period to this, with but two exceptions, its Door-keeper, with but one of its Assistant-Door-keeper, had been appointed in the same way. In 1819 and 1821, Thomas Dougherty was chosen Clerk in the same manner. In 1823, 1825, 1827, 1829, and 1831, Matthew St. Clair Clarke had been chosen Clerk of this House in this same way. Will gentlemen after this refer to this House for precedents to establish the propriety of choosing "Clerks, Sergeant-at-Arms, Messengers, Door-keepers," &c. by ballot?

He would submit it to the House to say, whether these precedents not only did not prove the point contended for by his colleague, but the reverse. He was confident after this exhibition of precedents, it would not be pretended that they had *settled* the question, but that it at least left the the question with the constitution, where we found it.

But, said M. G., we are told by the gentleman from Georgia, (Mr. Gilmer,) that the members of this House may fall under Executive displeasure, if they vote independently and against his will, and in that manner the just independence of this House will be endangered. It here may be asked how the faithful representative in this House could, if he acted rightly, in accordance with the views of his constituents, be in danger of this dreaded influence? The representative depends upon his constituents, and not upon the Executive for his employment. To his mind, there was more danger that he would here vote in a concealed manner, and unknown to his constituents, to please the Executive, who would, more readily than his constituents, ascertain how he voted, than to vote openly in a manner to displease those whose suffrages had sent him here. The danger of a secret vote was, that those at a distance, the electors, would be the persons whose wishes would be disregarded—vote openly, and experience proves that the representative usually looks to the source of the power which rules his future agency here. There are those, however, who have not acted on these subjects, as was desired by their constituents, and their fate is written in the history of the times. His own State had furnished a prominent instance of the will of the people being violated, and of their inflicting summary punishment.

The gentleman from Georgia (Mr. Gilmer sired so know whether the people knew or about the election of these officers. He d believe there were "ten men in Illinois knew these officers were." He could not the good people of that State knew o he could only draw conclusions from displayed in selecting their representat believed the gentleman was much mista certainly would have been, had his remar

applied to those whom he (Mr. G.) represented They understood these things thoroughly. What, do not the people know who the Speaker is, and is he so small a light? Is that man, who has more power in shaping and controlling legislation than any other in the nation, one of such small consequence as not to be known to the people? But the gentleman from Georgia, and my colleague, say that the officers of the House are our agents, and the people are not interested in their selection. Is this so? Is it of no consequence to the people whether the officer who brings money to pay us, is honest, or runs away with it, as has actually happened? Such losses, it is known, fall upon the people.

The Clerk of this House disburses a contingent fund of several thousand dollars a year, and has charge of much of the people's property, and has a large patronage in the appointment of officers. Is it to be supposed that the people neither know or care who holds this office? Our door-keeper has the appointment of almost as many officers as some small States. The Speaker, also, appoints many persons about the House, and has charge of the furniture of the Hall. In the faithful disbursement of money, in the preservation of property, and in the faithful discharge of the duties of all the officers of the House, the people have a deep interest, and we have but little. If the people were as ignorant and careless about who and what the officers of the House were, he would ask how it happened that the acts of a late Speaker of this House, in the appointment of committees, were made a prominent ground for his rejection as minister to England? It is a little extraordinary, if that grave body had fastened upon the acts of an officer of this House to justify his rejection, when in a whole State, not "ten men" knew who the officer was, and when they did not know or care any thing about his election. This was presuming largely upon the ignorance and carelessness of the people. He, Mr. G. must abide by the conclusion that the people did know and care about these things.

He knew nothing of the facts upon which rumor had predicated her news, but certain it was that her tales had led the people to inquire much after our ballot box transactions here. Whether there was any thing wrong or worthy of censure, was not for him to say. He had, however, been asked to know why, on a recent election for clerk of this House, there had been more ballots than legal qualified voters, and why a recent candidate for printer of this House had not been declared elected, when he had been able to prove he had had a majority of all the votes? Inquiries about the election of other officers had been made, and he had been unable to answer because he did not know; and this had been his reply. The response was, "Vote openly and let us know how these things are done and by whom" Such were the sentiments of all who had spoken to him on this subject, and he doubted not that such would be found to be the views of all, in relation to the doings of their agents here.

Mr. G. thought this the true ground, that when we vote as citizens, in the exercise of free, full, and untrammelled sovereign power—when we were accountable only to ourselves and our Maker for our acts—when no one had a right to question our motives or call us to an account for our doings, we should vote by ballot, and when we voted in our representative capacity, we should vote *viva voce*, or by yeas and nays. In the chivalrous west, from the glowing accounts of their independence, and exemption from reliance upon others for support, it would seem that the ballot box was of less moment than in other parts of the world. But there might be places, such as large cities and manufacturing towns, where things were differently situated. There might be men who had others, even hundreds of them, in their employ, and entirely dependent upon them for the means of supporting their families, and it might so happen that these men would be *required* to [illegible] in a particular manner or be thrown out of [illegible]ployment. He would ask, did not these things [illegible]ly occur in the *distressed* year of 1834? [illegible]n let the People continue the use of the ballot [illegible] in the exercise of the sovereign power of appointing their agents. On the other hand, let us as agents, act openly, manfully, and in such a manner as to enable our principals to judge of our actions, and to protect ourselves from the suspicion of having done what they would not approve. Is there a man here who desires to conceal his vote, or avoid the strictest scrutiny? He hoped not. In the South and West nearly all vote *viva voce*. Those who were appointed agents by a *viva voce* vote, certainly would not claim to be more independent than their constituents, and desire to conceal their vote. He would further remark, if there were those here or elsewhere, who had a horror of secret societies, and secret influences, and who claimed much of the hands of the People from their desire that every thing should be submitted to the scrutiny of open day, he certainly should expect their hearty support and approval of this resolution.

He doubted not that the People would be well pleased, to borrow the figure of my friend from Kentucky (Mr Hardin,) if all the acts of their agents here, were written in sunshine in the firmament of Heaven, that they might read, and approve, or disapprove them. But it is said this resolution will not bind the next Congress, and will have no effect upon the present. If so, it can do no harm. It is before us, and we must vote for or against it, whether it avails us much or little, and whether it embraces officers we have to elect this session or not. Perhaps it would, like many resolutions, result in little but the assertion of principles. He cared not what might be hereafter construed to be within its provisions, or the extent it might be considered binding. He should vote for the resolution, because he believed it right in principle, and ought to receive the sanction of this House, and be the rule of action in "choosing" *all* the officers of the House, as it has been for twenty years, in choosing three-fourths of them. The principle contended for, was not only right in itself, but was sustained by a strong indication of the intention of the makers of the constitution, and has the sanction of the People. He should therefore vote for it.

Mr. CLAYTON said, the proposition before the House strongly reminded him of a celebrated Spanish epitaph, which, when he repeated it, would sufficiently explain itself. The words engraven on the tomb-stone were, "I was well; I wished to be better; I took physic; and here I lie." Now, the House had practised its present mode of election for the last forty years, without finding occasion for alterations or new devices. The gentleman last up but one, had given some specimens of prophecy. Had he confined himself to his prophecies, rather than his pledges, it would perhaps have been more agreeable. He proposed to make a prophecy himself, and he would particularly invoke towards it the attention and recollection of the House. It was, that as soon as the object of that resolution was accomplished, it would be repealed. It was fashionable, too, occasionally to deal a little in poetry. He remembered a couplet not entirely inapplicable to the subject:

"Princes and kings may flourish, or may fade,
A breath can make them, as a breath has made."

Much debate had been elicited to determine whether this resolution was designed to apply to the printer of the House. Mr. C. said he had consulted no witnesses when he declared that such was the fact. What other officer could it apply to, when no other was to be elected? Why else was this resolution deemed so peculiarly important at this late stage of the last session? If they had passed the resolution at the commencement of the preceding session, there would be more plausibility in its aspect. But its passage at the present time would be viewed as an attempt to interfere and tamper with the rights and privileges of the next Congress. One of the first acts of that Congress would doubtless be to repeal the dictatorial resolution. Mr. C. called the attention of the House to the primary organization of legislative bodies. Their first step was doubtless to appoint a Head, and afterwards to elect the subordinate officers and assistants. If one was elected viva voce, the others would come under the same rule. It was more a matter of convenience to themselves than one affecting the liberties of the people. But if the rule applied to the higher officers, it did equally so to the minor ones; for when you stop with these, and denominate the less offices as unimportant matters, you make the viva voce system depend on the importance of the office, and not on the general principle contended for.

Mr. C. said frequent allusions had been made to the interest which the people felt in this question. Now, he would venture to make an assertion, in the truth of which he would call on that House to bear him out, that in eighteen States out of the twenty-four, the elections were conducted by ballot. So that if we go to the people—the great source of all power—for a rule of action, their voice would be found in favor of the balloting system. To himself, personally, it was quite unimportant. The vote *viva voce* would be as acceptable as any other. He cared not if members chose to approach the desk with their votes posted on their foreheads. But he could not justify the perversion of principles which had stood the test of forty years on light and trivial ground.

The gentleman from New York had offered a quotation from the scriptures. This, perhaps would be improper on trifling occasions; but if it was designed to enforce a serious argument, he could have no objection to it. The people, he conceived, were the legitimate masters of their representatives. The effect of the resolution would be to create for them new masters, who "loved darkness rather than light." "We cannot serve two masters;" and where the "treasure is, there will be the heart also."

It was well known that within a short period, some forty or fifty members of Congress had "received the reward of their labors, and were now at rest." Another argument had been advanced in favor of the resolution, that it would be a saving of time. This he deemed of little consequence. The more time the House spent in doing nothing, the better for their constituents. Again, it is urged in support of the resolution by the gentleman from New York (Mr. Vanderpoel) in its application to the other officers of the House, that you, sir, have not a lease of your life—that you are not immortal! He hoped the gentlemen would not admit that the support of their measure would involve the killing of the Speaker. The proper way to test the strength of an argument was to take away all others, and see how it would stand on that alone. Do so in the present case, and how many members would vote for the proposition on that contingency? It had also been gravely alleged that an officer of the House, elected by ballot, forsooth, had formerly decamped with a portion of its funds! Could it be seriously contended that an election viva voce would remedy or prevent such an evil? He could not approve of that species of logic which leads us to jump to conclusions from false or inapplicable premises.

Mr. C. said he had probably occupied the attention of the House already too long in submitting what he had to say. Believing this resolution designed to alter a practice of forty years standing, for the purpose of effecting a single object, and calculated to leave them foundering on the unknown coast of experiment, or subject to an immediate repeal on the accomplishment of its special purpose, he should give his vote against it.

Mr. SEABORN JONES said it seemed to him that if the resolution under consideration were to be adopted by the present Congress, no action would ensue upon it hereafter, because, as each House had, under the constitution, the power "to choose their Speaker and other officers," the next House would not be bound by it. Furthermore, not only was the election, but also the mode of choosing, left entirely with each, and therefore, if the resolution was designed to embrace the officers of the House, it did not belong to the existing body to pass it, since the mode of electing no more belonged to it, than did the election itself, of the officers of the next Congress. We have been told by an honorable colleague of Mr. Jones, and by other gentlemen, that the resolution was offered for a certain specified object, and that

[CONTINUED IN NEXT NUMBER.]

CONGRESSIONAL GLOBE.

| BY BLAIR & RIVES. | ——WEEKLY—— | PRICE $1 A SESSION. |

| 2d Sess......23d Cong. | MONDAY, FEBRUARY 9, 1835. | Volume 2........No. 11. |

TWENTY-THIRD CONGRESS.
SECOND SESSION.

HOUSE OF REPRESENTATIVES.
Monday, January 26, 1835.

[Continued from last number.]
vus, to bear upon the election of printer. If this were so, and if the printer were an officer of the House, then have we, said Mr. J. no right to elect him, for if we did, it would be taking the power from the next Congress to do so, contrary to the above provision of the constitution. Supposing the resolution should pass, in the phraseology in which it is drawn, to wit, that all elections of officers of the House, shall be by viva voce vote of the members, what would be the result? Would the rule be operative in the election of Speaker of the next Congress? He trusted not. What was the regular mode of proceeding at the first assembly? The Clerk of the House took the Chair, and was the presiding officer for the time being, and the House proceeded to elect their Speaker by ballot, or in any other way the assemblage of members thought proper. If, suppose, when the Clerk has called the roll, a member should get up and in defiance of this resolution, propose to proceed to elect a Speaker by ballot, would any man deny their right to do so, because a resolution of the last Congress ordered it otherwise? Certainly not. It was the election of Speaker that organized the House; and it was not fairly organized before the Speaker was placed in possession of the duty—but the resolution would not be obligatory on the next Congress at all, unless they pleased to abide by it. It would be inoperative, and therefore he thought it needless to adopt it. One gentleman had said that the passage of the resolution would be an expression of our opinion as to what ought to be the mode of procedure in matters of description, but that would be as useless as it could be to apprize the House who should be the next Speaker. Suppose, at the close of the present session, a resolution was brought forward expressive of the thanks of the House to the Speaker and asking the next Congress to reinstate him, would any member expect such a resolution would be entertained? Mr. J. presumed not. And yet had we not as much right to advise them thus to elect, as to direct the mode by which they should elect?

It was not necessary at that time to enter at large into the question whether the mode of electing by ballot or viva voce was best calculated to preserve the dignity and character of that House, but he would content himself with recurring to one fact, and see what practical effect the practice had. Now it was well known that for many years past, the whole energies and exertions of the opposition party in England have been directed to obtain the very thing we are proposing to abolish in that House—the vote by ballot, which their opponents have, up to the present time, prevented. We were told by a noble historian that what the crown had lost in prerogative, it had gained in influence, and the minister known he can only ensure and perpetuate that influence by the command he has over the offices. He holds on for viva voce voting, and why? Not, in the ballot, men may not always follow a "single man," when giving their votes. In the then of all that had been said to the contrary, he was induced to believe that election by ballot was the best, if not the only mode calculated to preserve the character of that House. But, by some, our Government has not become so corrupt, and our members are not so deficient in independence as to wish to vote secretly. Here by intimation on one side or the other, not at all visible. He is so independent, and so far removed above corrupting influence, that he may be tempted to give his vote openly; or on the other hand, he cannot be trusted to vote agreeable to the wishes of his constituents, unless he be closely watched at every step? The argument involved a compliment on one side, and a direct censure on the other.

Mr. J. did not believe that our constituents felt that interest in the election of officers of the House which some gentlemen seemed to think they did. He never could bring himself to believe that they desired to know how their members voted in the election of Clerk, Sergeant-at-arms, Deputy Clerks, Door keepers, &c. but he did believe that in the organization of parties, it sometimes became necessary to know how those offices were disposed of, and whether any undue influence had been exercised. Now it was for the purpose of preventing that very thing that he should vote against the adoption of the present resolution. He could not reconcile it to himself to lay down a rule for the guidance of others, which had been no rule for his own conduct. If the resolution be intended to operate upon only a single election, and the only one that may reasonably be expected to come before us, that of printer, and if he be considered an officer of the House, then Mr. J. conceived that the present House could not go into the election at all, for the reasons before assigned. If it be intended not to operate upon him alone, but only in the contingency of a vacancy in the place of Speaker, Clerk, Sergeant-at-Arms, &c. by death or otherwise, then he would say "sufficient unto the day be the evil thereof;" and when it become necessary to elect any of those officers, then it will be time enough to prescribe to ourselves the mode of election. To prescribe it to another House, would lay them under no obligation to follow it. For these reasons he deemed the resolution unnecessary, and should vote against it.

Mr. HAWES said, it must be evident to every member, that this discussion was interrupting all the regular business of the House, and the elaborate debate that had already taken place, had elicited the opinions of both parties, he thought sufficiently; he therefore moved the previous question.

The House refused to sustain the call; ayes 76, noes, 99.

The House then adjourned.

SENATE.
Tuesday, January 27, 1835.

After the Journal of yesterday had been read, Mr. EWING moved that the Senate take up the bill and report of the Post Office Committee.

The motion was agreed to, and the reading of the report was concluded.

Mr. GRUNDY then rose and said, that the report which had just been read embraced the opinions of three members of the committee. The gentleman from Illinois, (Mr. Robinson,) and himself, being the remaining members of the committee, had prepared a paper containing their own views on most of the subjects upon which the majority had given their opinion, and without reference to their report. When it was found that they could not agree upon the report, it was thought the better course for each branch of the committee to present its own views upon the subject of their investigations.

He moved for leave to present the paper he held in his hand, as containing the views of the minority of the committee.

Leave having been granted, Mr. GRUNDY presented the paper which was read, after which, Mr. GRUNDY said, that at the last session there was a great diversity of opinion as to what number of copies of the report should be printed. The committee on this occasion wished to avoid any such difficulty, and by the unanimous consent of the committee, he was directed to move that 2,500 copies of the reports, together with the documents, and 5,000 extra copies of the reports, without the documents, be printed for the use of the Senate.

The CHAIR here remarked that such motion was out of order, until after the bill reported by the committee should be read.

Mr. GRUNDY then yielded the floor, and the bill was read the first time, and ordered to a second reading.

Mr. GRUNDY expressed a wish that the bill might be read the second time by its title, for the purpose of reference to the Committee. He stated that all the members of the Committee had not had an opportunity of examining it. If it was perfect in all its provisions so far as it went, still some additional provisions might be ingrafted upon it, which would be likely to meet the unanimous approbation of the Committee.

Mr. EWING said that owing to the great pressure of other business upon the members of the Committee, they were unable to spend as much time upon the bill as was desirable. He was willing, therefore, that the motion should prevail, that the bill should be read the second time and re-committed, under the assurance that it should be reported without delay.

The bill was then read the second time by its title, to wit: "A bill changing the organization of the General Post Office."

Mr. GRUNDY then moved to re-commit the bill.

Mr. CLAY thought it would be better to order the bill to be printed, and then the Committee could have it, as well as other members of the Senate, and they could prepare any amendments or improvements they might think proper. It was a novel proceeding to report a bill and then re-commit it before it was printed.

Mr. GRUNDY said that if it was re-committed it would be printed to-night. But he was not particular with regard to it, if the Committee would feel it as much their duty to examine it as if it was formally referred.

Mr. CLAY replied, that if the bill was to be printed, he had no objection to the reference.

Mr. CLAYTON said he had attended to the provisions of the bill as they had been read, and he thought many of them of the utmost importance, particularly that submitting the money operations of the department to the government of Congress. He always considered, and still believed, that the distribution of the public treasure without the intervention of Congress, was in direct violation of the constitution. This bill proposed to bring this department back and place it under the supervision and control of Congress. He saw no reason for recommitting the bill, unless the provisions in it were to be altered, and if they were, gentlemen could suggest such amendments as they proposed when the bill came up. He did not meet and recommend the adoption of any other provisions which they might agree upon.

Mr. GRUNDY said he would not persist in his motion. But he hoped the gentleman from Ohio, (Mr. Ewing,) would name a day, where the bill might be taken up.

Mr. PORTER said he agreed with the gentleman from Delaware, (Mr. Clayton,) upon the importance of the provisions of the bill. But, he thought if the Committee could improve it in its details, it ought to be recommitted, and there would be no difficulty in getting it printed. And with regard to printing the reports, he was apprehensive some error might be fallen into, and perhaps he might afterwards be said to have given his assent to all the provisions of the report, a matter which had been imputed to him, on a similar occasion. He rose at this time more particularly to ask a question of the honorable Chairman of the Committee, (Mr. Grundy.) It was whether at the last session of Congress, application had been made for an appropriation for the relief of the Post Office Department.

Mr. GRUNDY replied, that he did not know. Something was said by the Committee on that subject. But he had no recollection that a bill for that purpose was before them.

Mr. PORTER resumed. The explanation of

the hon. gentleman was as he expected. No such thing was before the committee. He desired to make the request he did, on this floor, from the circumstance, that in an address published in the newspapers bearing the signature of a high officer —the President of the United States—his honorable colleague (Mr Waggaman) and himself were charged with having voted against such an appropriation for the purpose of embarrassing that department, and preventing it from granting mail facilities to the citizens of the State they had the honor to represent. This was the reason for his asking the question. He did not accuse that high officer with intentional misrepresentation. But the accusation had gone out from the President of the United States, and was made on the eve of an important election in Louisiana. He (Mr. P.) might have assented to the report of the majority of the committee, but he did so as he assented to all other documents, the general tenor of which he approved.

The CHAIR here observed that such observation were not in order.

After some further remarks from Mr. PORTER, Mr. EWING moved that the bill be made the special order of the day for Monday next.

Mr. CALHOUN said if the committee could be unanimous upon the provisions of the bill, which he looked upon as of great importance, it was very desirable that it should be re-committed.

Mr. GRUNDY said he never saw the bill until yesterday morning, when he was not able to give it a very attentive examination. Since then he had been very much engaged. Some of its provisions he should fully concur in, perhaps all of them—he did not know. But he was satisfied that the bill was susceptible of further important improvements that were not in it, and in which all the members of the committee, he thought, would concur.

Mr. CALHOUN then moved to re-commit, but withdrew the motion, on the suggestion of the the Chair that there was a motion pending.

Mr. PRESTON said, he had no wish to interfere in the disposition which was proposed to be made of the bill, but he was anxious to be further informed on the subject; and first, he would put a question to the honorable Chairman of the committee. We had heard a most voluminous report with regard to the Post Office, together with the views of the minority, and a bill for the reorganization of the Department. He would ask whether it was the conclusion of the committee that the proposed reorganization of the Department was a cure for the evils prevailing there, or in other words, whether all the evils set forth in the report were the result of an improper organization of the Department? Now, could any gentleman say that all the enormous evils set forth in the report were the result of such an improper organization? It would be recollected that this was not the first occasion on which developments of an extraordinary character had been made, and that on the other occasion, there was a unanimous vote of the Senate, strongly censuring the Post Office Department. The gentleman from Louisiana had alluded to the declaration of a high personage in allusion to himself, and he (Mr. P.) would call to mind another declaration of the Chief Magistrate, that he was responsible for, and was the universal organ of the Executive Departments. And while the declaration was fresh on the lips of the President, that he was responsible for the whole Executive power of the Government, was he to be told that these abuses resulted from an improper organization of that Department? He was very loath to form an opinion from hearing the report read, but did any man doubt the turpitude of the Post Office? When, hardly of the age of man, it was found steeped in corruption the most foul, the most melancholy. Why propose the mere reorganization of it, if those who had been fattening on it were still to be kept in? If the President was responsible, and the officers had acted improperly, was this the House to submit the subject to? And should we stand by without saying or doing any thing in regard to the present state of things in that Department? But this was not the proper time to go into it, yet he was anxious for an occasion of exposing the culprit, whoever

he might be, that he might lay his hands upon him, and hold him up to the public gaze. He hoped an opportunity would be afforded him for doing so; when he should think it his duty to brand him as a culprit before the people of this country. Now, were we to be put off with only a prospective reorganization of the Department for the purpose of correcting the evils which had been exposed.

Mr. EWING replied: As to the inquiry of the gentleman from South Carolina, the Committee did not think that all the mystery, and evils which had been exposed, arose from the organization of the Department—they believed that corruption existed in the Department—foul corruption among some of the individuals there, and the report expressed it. But the remedy proposed was the only one which Congress could adopt. As regarded the corrupt individuals, the Committee thought that the President ought long since to have removed them. Perhaps the other branch of Congress ought to have brought them before this body. Nothing, however, could be done here, but legislation—prospective legislation. The Committee did not shrink from a resolution, which should elicit the opinion of the Committee, but that would come as well from any other member of the Senate, as from the Committee. The labors of the Committee were before the Senate, and therefore, they did not report any resolution for the action of the Senate—they had reported their views, and left them to the Senate to dispose of.

Mr. CALHOUN hoped some Senator would present a resolution giving some character to these developements. He listened to the report with sorrow and the deepest mortification. He had been twenty-two years connected with this government, and in all that time, the charges of corruption against all the departments of the government, that he had ever heard, were not equal to the disclosures here made. The exhibition would disgrace the rottenest ages of the Roman Republic. He hoped every Senator would be called on in his place to say whether he sanctioned it. The guilt of the Department was unquestionable, and it remained to be seen whether any Senator would rise here to defend it, and identify himself with it. If he could, and the public sentiment could bear it, and the President could bear it, and the people would submit to it, there was an end forever to freedom. He hoped some gentleman would look into the subject, and propose some resolution suitable to the occasion.

Mr. CUTHBERT said, he was far from agreeing with the Senators from South Carolina. The committee had manifested much more wisdom in the course they had pursued than would have been done by adopting their recommendation. They had recommended Legislative measures for the purpose of remedying evils which we could remedy. Did we want the voice of party again to resound through these Halls? If it was to be made a party cause, let it be made at a proper time, and not mingle it with the proceedings of this committee. Was this country so corrupt that the people were incapable of seeing and correcting any errors which might creep into the government? or was the government so corrupt that an attempt should be made to weaken the attachment of the people to it, and the institutions of this country?

Mr. BENTON said, that the honorable gentleman from South Carolina, (Mr. Calhoun,) if he understood him correctly, was in favor of instituting judicially a criminal proceeding against the Post Office Department, for the purpose of trying Senators here. All he had to say now, was, that he was ready at any time to proceed in any manner which was constitutional, and leave his conduct to say whether he was governed by the trammels of party.

Mr. CALHOUN replied, that he was surprised that honorable gentleman should make this a party question. The minority themselves did not do so. Who ever dreamed of making it a party question? If any party without to identify themselves with these corruptions, let them step forth. Here were volumes of documents which not one-hundredth part of the people would read, and they must receive an impression with regard to them from

what we did here. What he said was, that the people should know the opinions of Senators here on this subject, and how were they to know them but by the incorporation of their sentiments in resolution for the action of this body? Did he from gentleman from Georgia (Mr. Cuthbert) wish to identify himself with the Post Office and its management? He could not believe he did. On hearing the report read; he (Mr. C.) felt a deep and profound melancholy, that so much rottenness should have found its way into a department in so short a time. And the expression of opinion he suggested, was the only way it could meet the people of this Union. It was very ty of opinion existed, it was due to the state that it should be done; and if no one suggested a resolution he would move it. But not to be deterred from it by any fear of consequences whatever. His object was that the people should know what impression this report made here.

Mr. CUTHBERT said that Senators were invited to pursue any course which this party real demanded. What he said was, that it was not good policy to mingle the feelings of party with the efficient proceedings of the Committee.

Mr. PRESTON said, he asked of the committee, whether it was intended by them to offer a resolution expressive of their opinion on the subject. He knew he was a party man, and his party feelings, and therefore he might well have some slight party feelings as having actuated others. Now, the committee had a right to prepare a bill for otherwise, and the bill certainly did not press the feelings of this House. In regard to the subject, last year the committee reported resolutions expressive of their feelings with regard to it. Was there party in that? So far he was in spirit had subsided on that occasion, and ensued, and the Hon. Chairman of the committee who was always a zealous defender of party, which was defensible, concerned with an occasion for the resolutions, in relation to the Post Office; had no other feelings but those of duty engaged at the palpable frauds which had been detected. For no purpose of party would he have introduced the exhibition of frauds go forth. He stated plainly only to the Department—he did not feel any what individuals they existed. He only felt that such an instrument existed against the administration. But he hoped the committee would report a resolution which should express in some sort the views of the Senate, and that it ought to be upon those who wielded the destinies of the country. The honorable gentleman from Georgia alluded to party. Why stir up party feelings now? We were beaten. He felt, and there was no use in exciting party spirit, no good could result from it. But here, sad as we are in a minority, and it was his honest conviction which was flowing through the land ling every thing in the land. He wanted nothing to blot out, so far as it could be done, the plague spot from this young country. Suppose man doubted the malfeasance of the Post Office, and that it was not conducted as it ought to be, to the honor of this nation—that it would be a pass on to the orders of the day with meanness and indifference as if nothing of the kind had occurred.

Mr. CUTHBERT said, if he had felt the essence of the same spirit upon his feelings when he first rose, which now operated upon him, would not have risen. He was pleased with the beautiful tropes of the honorable gentleman, with the delightful melody of his voice; but when he spoke of the defeats of his party, they did not happen to be attributed in a great degree to the monstrous exaggerations of the minority, who magnified mere error into the most heinous crimes. There was no way to——

Mr. EWING, who moved an adjournment, which prevailed.

The Senate adjourned.

HOUSE OF REPRESENTATIVES.

TUESDAY, Jan. 27, 1835.

Mr. SPEIGHT, from the Committee on Military Affairs, reported with an amendment, the joint resolution from the Senate, authorizing a gold medal to be presented to Col. Croghan, and a sword to each of the officers under his command, for their gallant defence of Fort Stephenson, during the late war.

After some conversation between Messrs. PARKER, SPEIGHT, and MERCER, the amendment was concurred in, and the resolution agreed to.

INDIAN RESERVATIONS.

Mr. LOVE, from the Committee on Indian Affairs, to whom the resolution heretofore offered by Mr. McCARTY was committed, reported the same, with an amendment, as follows:

Strike out after the word correspondence, in the fourth line, the words "of all Indian agents, sub-agents, and other persons connected with the Indian Department," and insert after the words "General Land Office, in the eighth line, the words of "all Indian agents, sub-agents, and other persons" and insert after the words reserves of land, in the tenth line, the words "east of the Mississippi river."

Mr. CLAY was understood to ask that the consideration of the resolution might be deferred for the present.

Mr. LOVE said the resolution as reported was changed, except as respected the printing.

Mr. CLAY wished the amendment read again, as he had not perceived its full extent. The resolution having been read,

Mr. LOVE said, he would make a brief explanation. The resolution as amended by the Committee on Indian Affairs was confined in its operations to those States east of the Mississippi river. The committee would have been gratified if it had been in their power to have circumscribed the inquiries asked for within narrower limits; but to have done so, would have been invidious. For instance, if they had recommended an inquiry in relation to the transactions within the State of Alabama alone, the gentlemen from that State might well complain of an invidious distinction, and say, why were not Indiana, Illinois, and Michigan included? The committee have also been anxious to avoid unnecessary expense in the preparation of this correspondence; but their duty to the House and to the country, and the importance of the subject involved, forbade them to limit it to any particular State or Territory.

A few words on the principle of these reservations. It was something like this: in the treaties which gave rise to them, there were two stipulations in relation to these reservations. The first was, that the President of the United States was required to approve of the transfer and sale of the reservation before it should be vested in the purchaser; the second was, that the Indian Agent should testify that the reservation had been sold a valuable consideration, and that no fraud had in practiced on the Indians in the purchase. The object of these stipulations was to protect both the Indians and the Government from fraud. It was impossible, therefore, that the President of the United States or, the Secretary of War, should have been, or could have been, conscious of frauds, if frauds had been committed. The frauds are said to be of this character, that agents had been intrusted with speculators in the purchase of Indian reservations, and had certified that which was not true, viz. that a valuable consideration had been given, thereby defrauding both the Indians and the Government of the United States. Again: many of these reservations belonged to persons, and the commission of these frauds had deprived them of subsistence. The resolution was intended to affect any particular individuals, the Executive, nor any officer of the Government, but its object was to bring to light the compacts and transactions of all those officers on the subject of Indian reservations, so that the country might learn if frauds had been committed—who had been guilty of them—and who had been defrauded—at contracts made were valid, and what not, to enable those who had rights which had been violated, to set aside the contracts, or to institute proceedings in relation thereto. No action was proposed by the committee; but they asked only that the correspondence and necessary documents be furnished to the House, which may then be referred to one of its standing committees for such action as might be deemed requisite.

The committee were well aware, and had duly considered, that those documents could not be got at without labor, and some expense. They were well apprized of it before their recommendation of the resolution; but it was due to the nation, due to the Indians, and due to the Executive himself, that if frauds existed, the fact should be known and investigated; and as he remarked the other day, he did not believe that a single gentleman in that House, if he was satisfied that frauds had been committed in an important branch of the public service, would be deterred from voting for the adoption of the resolution by the consideration of its expense. Besides, Mr. L. was induced to believe that the amount had been very much amplified, and that the labor would not be half as much as had been described. One gentleman said it would take a few days, while another averred it as his opinion it would take months; and these conflicting statements showed it was a mere matter of opinion, without being based on facts. The maps were already prepared; and nothing was required but to copy them, and transcribe the letters and documents necessary.

Mr. CLAY said the gentleman from Kentucky must have misapprehended what he had said, and he presumed many gentlemen who had objected to the adoption of this resolution had done so merely on the score of the expense. Mr. C. had other, and more material objections than the mere item of cost. His first objection was, that he believed the call to be unnecessary. It would be recollected by the House that the resolution called for the services of those engaged in the land office to transcribe all the correspondence and documents in relation to all the Indian reservations. Was the House unaware of the continual and annual complaints in this branch of the Treasury Department, of its inability to perform its duties? Had we not been notified at the commencement of the present session that in spite of all the extra clerk hire already employed, the patents in the land office were upwards of one hundred thousand in arrears? Then the first objection that presented itself to his mind, was that the call was unnecessary for such a mass of documents, not one tenth of which would prove useful to the country or to an individual member of the House. It was true, that in connexion with this objection, we might take into consideration the great expense that would, and necessarily must, be incurred. And again, why call for a mass of documents without any assurance that the public interest required them to be made out at a great expense of labor and of money; without taking into consideration the cost of printing a volume of some seven or eight hundred pages, all at the public expense, and as far as any one knew, not calculated to benefit any one portion or section of the country. This was an objection, but, nevertheless, Mr. C. did not pretend to put it into the scale with the detection of the perpetration of fraud, if such existed. But why have not gentlemen made a specification, and then called for proof, instead of involving the country in an immense expense upon vague rumor? And this brought him to a still more important objection. The House was then discussing a mere ex parte inquiry, and instituting an inquisition into the conduct of every agent of the Government, without any specific charge having been brought against any one of them, or without giving them notice of the trial, or investigation, they were about to undergo. Would not such a course be unjust towards those individuals who had been intrusted with a great public duty to bring their conduct before a committee for investigation, without designating any specific charge, or without giving those individuals any notice thereof? He did not expect a single member of that House to rise in his place and say that he had a well-founded suspicion against either the office or any individual employed in it. As far as regarded the State of which Mr. C. had the honor to be a representative, not even rumor had whispered that any fraudulent transactions had taken place there, and why should the persons engaged there be brought up on an ex parte inquisition? Irreparable and irretrievable injury might be done to individuals in this branch of the service by the proposed measure. If the committee, or any gentleman of the House, were in possession of a well-grounded charge of fraud, designate the party, and if they did, Mr. C. would be the last to vote against having a copy of every record of every description, whether it respected the President or any other functionary of the Government, that could bear upon the case, but do not draw upon one branch of the Treasury Department for labor which it is impracticable to perform, unless its more important duties are neglected—duties which it is already incompetent to fulfil—for the purpose of bringing on a trial without previous notice. It seemed to him that these few objections were unanswerable; he might urge more, but he did not wish to take up the time of the House in a lengthened discussion, the less so as he hoped the House would not adopt it without some modification, or taking some time to examine its details.

Mr. PLUMMER said, having first made war on the resolution, as originally introduced by the gentleman from Indiana, (Mr. McCarty,) for reasons which he then stated to the House, and the original resolution having been amended to meet his views, he withdrew all opposition, and would vote for its adoption in its modified form. It was true that he thought it an unnecessary consumption of time to require the Clerks in the General Land Office, who had not aid enough to keep up the current business of the office, to make out plats of the lands on which the Indian reservations were located. He could not conceive of any benefit the maps would be to the House or the country. That objection, however, was too unimportant to induce him to vote against the whole of the resolution, or jeopardize its adoption by submitting an amendment. He was in favor of the call; it was due to the country, and the officers of the Government, that all of the documents in relation to lands held under the Indian treaties, should be published to the world. There were reservations under the treaty of Doak's Stand, made in 1820, held by purchasers under regulations of the War Department, the titles to which were not definitely understood by those who had a right to know by what tenure and nature of titles all lands within the limits of Mississippi are held. The State has the right to tax those lands, as well as lands the titles to which were acquired directly by purchase from the Government, after the expiration of five years from the time they became private property. In some cases of reservations, it was unknown whether the lands reserved from sale for individuals of the Choctaw tribe, were private property, or whether they had reverted to the General Government. If these reservations were private property, the State had a right to tax them. If they belonged to the general government, they ought to be brought into market and offered for sale as other public lands. There were no records in the State showing these facts. As regards the matter of expense, he said that was of little importance compared with the importance of investigating the frauds charged by the gentleman from Kentucky, (Mr. Love,) who is, on this occasion, the organ of the Committee on Indian Affairs. The objections which he urged, and enlarged upon the other day, in relation to the expense of furnishing and printing the information proposed to be obtained, he repeated, had been obviated by the adoption of the amendment which he then offered, and became incorporated into the body of the resolution. He repelled the idea that the item of expense would induce him on any occasion to screen a public officer, charged with improper conduct, from an investigation, nor deprive the people, or their representatives, of useful information. His only object to a useless and unnecessary expenditure of the people's money, for the publication of new editions of documents and papers which would never be read. He did not understand the gentleman from Kentucky, nor any one who preferred the charge of fraud against the Agents of the government as locating the charge in Mississippi. The gentleman (Mr. Love) says, that he

the hon. gentleman was as he expected. No such thing was before the committee. He desired to make the request he did, on this floor, from the circumstance, that in an address published in the newspapers bearing the signature of a high officer —the President of the United States,—his honorable colleague (Mr Waggaman) and himself were charged with having voted against such an appropriation for the purpose of embarrassing that department, and preventing it from granting mail facilities to the citizens of the State they had the honor to represent. This was the reason for his asking the question. He did not accuse that high officer with intentional misrepresentation. But the accusation had gone out from the President of the United States, and was made on the eve of an important election in Louisiana. He (Mr. P.) might have assented to the report of the majority of the committee, but he did so as he assented to all other documents, the general tenor of which he approved.

The CHAIR here observed that such observation were not in order.

After some further remarks from Mr. PORTER,

Mr. EWING moved that the bill be made the special order of the day for Monday next.

Mr. CALHOUN said if the committee could be unanimous upon the provisions of the bill, which he looked upon as of great importance, it was very desirable that it should be re-committed.

Mr. GRUNDY said he never saw the bill until yesterday morning, when he was not able to give it a very attentive examination. Since then he had been very much engaged. Some of its provisions he should fully concur in, perhaps all of them—he did not know. But he was satisfied that the bill was susceptible of further important improvements that were not in it, and in which all the members of the committee, he thought, would concur.

Mr. CALHOUN then moved to re-commit, but withdrew the motion, on the suggestion of the Chair that there was a motion pending.

Mr. PRESTON said, he had no wish to interfere in the disposition which was proposed to be made of the bill, but he was anxious to be further informed on the subject; and first, he would put a question to the honorable Chairman of the committee. We had heard a most voluminous report with regard to the Post Office, together with the views of the minority, and a bill for the reorganization of the Department. He would ask whether it was the conclusion of the committee that the proposed reorganization of the Department was a cure for the evils prevailing there, or in other words, whether all the evils set forth in the report were the result of an improper organization of the Department? Now, could any gentleman say that all the enormous evils set forth in the report were the result of such an improper organization? It would be recollected that this was not the first occasion on which developments of an extraordinary character had been made, and that on the other occasion, there was a unanimous vote of the Senate, strongly censuring the Post Office Department. The gentleman from Louisiana had alluded to the declaration of a high personage. He alluded to himself, and he (Mr. P.) would ask to mind another declaration of the Chief Magistrate, that he was responsible for, and was the universal organ of the Executive Departments. And while the declaration was fresh on the lips of the President, that he was responsible for the whole Executive power of the Government, was he to be told that these abuses resulted from an improper organization of that Department? He was very loath to form an opinion from hearing the report read, but did any man doubt the turpitude of the Post Office? When, hardly of the age of man, it was found steeped in corruption the most foul, the most melancholy. Why propose the mere reorganization of it, if those who had been fattening on it were still to be kept in? If the President was responsible, and the officers had acted improperly, was this the House to submit the subject? And should we stand by without saying 'doing any thing in regard to the present state things in that Department? But this was not proper time to go into it; yet he was anxious an occasion of exposing the culprit, whoever

he might be, that he might lay his hands upon him, and hold him up to the public gaze. He hoped an opportunity would be afforded him for doing so; when he should think it his duty to brand him as a culprit before the people of this country. Now, were we to be put off with only a prospective reorganization of the Department for the purpose of correcting the evils which had been exposed.

Mr. EWING replied: As to the inquiry of the gentleman from South Carolina, that the Committee did not think that all the mystery, and evils which had been exposed, arose from the organization of the Department—they believed that corruption existed in the Department—foul corruption among some of the individuals there, and the report expressed it. But the remedy proposed was the only one which Congress could adopt. As regarded the corrupt individuals, the Committee thought that the President ought long since to have removed them. Perhaps the other branch of Congress ought to have brought them before this body. Nothing, however, could be done here, but legislation—prospective legislation. The Committee did not shrink from a resolution, which should elicit the opinion of the Committee, but that would come as well from any other member of the Senate, as from the Committee. The labors of the Committee were before the Senate, and therefore, they did not report any resolution for the action of the Senate—they had reported their views, and left them to the Senate to dispose of.

Mr. CALHOUN hoped some Senator would present a resolution giving some character to these developements. He listened to the report with sorrow and the deepest mortification. He had been twenty-two years connected with this government, and in all that time, the charges of corruption against all the departments of the government, that he had ever heard, were not equal to the disclosures here made. The exhibition would disgrace the rottenest ages of the Roman Republic. He hoped every Senator would be called on in his place to say whether he sanctioned it. The guilt of the Department was unquestionable, and it remained to be seen whether any Senator would rise here to defend it, and identify himself with it. If he could, and the public sentiment could bear it, and the President could bear it, and the people would submit to it, there was an end forever to freedom. He hoped some gentleman would look into the subject, and propose some resolution suitable to the occasion.

Mr. CUTHBERT said, he was far from agreeing with the Senators from South Carolina. The committee had manifested much more wisdom in the course they had pursued than would have been done by adopting their recommendation. They had recommended Legislative measures for the purpose of remedying evils which we could remedy. Did we want the voice of party again to resound through these Halls? If it was to be made a party cause, let it be made at a proper time, and not mingle it with the proceedings of this committee. Was this country so corrupt that the people were incapable of seeing and correcting any errors which might creep into the government? or was the government so corrupt that an attempt should be made to weaken the attachment of the people to it, and the institutions of this country?

Mr. BENTON said, that the honorable gentleman from South Carolina, (Mr. Calhoun,) if he understood him correctly, was in favor of instituting judicially a criminal proceeding against the Post Office Department, for the purpose of trying Senators here. All he had to say now, was, that he was ready at any time to proceed in any manner which was constitutional, and leave his conduct to say whether he was governed by the trammels of party.

Mr. CALHOUN replied, that he was surprised that honorable gentlemen should make this a party question. The minority themselves did not do so. Who ever dreamed of making it a party question? If any party wished to identify themselves with these corruptions, let them step forth. Here were volumes of documents which not one-hundredth part of the people woul'l read, and they must receive an impression with regard to them from

what we did here. What he said was, that the people should know the opinions of Senators here on this subject, and how were they to know them, but by the incorporation of their sentiments in a resolution for the action of this body? Did the Hon. gentleman from Georgia (Mr. Cuthbert) wish to identify himself with the Post Office and its management? He could not believe he did. On hearing the report read, he (Mr. C.) felt a deep and profound melancholy, that so much rottenness should have found its way into a department in so short a time. And the expression of opinion he suggested, was the only way in which it could meet the people of this Union. If a vera ty of opinion existed, it was due to the Senate that it should be done; and if no one would present a resolution he would move it. He was not to be deterred from it by any fear of consequences whatever. His object was that the people should know what impression this report made here.

Mr. CUTHBERT said that Hon. gentlemen were invited to pursue any course which this party zeal demanded. What he said was, that it was not good policy to mingle the feelings of party with the efficient proceedings of this Committee.

Mr. PRESTON said, he asked of the committee, whether it was intended by them to offer a resolution expressive of their opinions on this subject. He knew he was a party man, and held its party feelings, and therefore he might well conceal some slight party feelings as having actuated others. Now, the committee had a right to expect a bill or otherwise, and the bill certainly did not press the feelings of this House. In regard to this subject, last year the committee reported resolutions expressive of their feelings with regard to it. Was there party in that? So far from it, party spirit had subsided on that occasion, quite a role ensued, and the Hon. Chairman of the committee who was always a zealous defender of any that which was defensible, concurred with us as I have for the resolutions. In relation to the Post Office he had no other feelings but those of disapprobation at the palpable frauds which had been disclosed. For no purpose of party would he have made exhibition of frauds go forth. He attributed the arrest, so far as was in his power, this burst of corruption which was flowing through all and lingering every thing in the land. He wanted some thing to blot out, so far as it could be done, the plague spot from this young country. Regret man doubted the malfeasance of the Post Office, and that it was not conducted as it ought to be the honor of this nation—that it was disgraceful the United States. And when it was brought before us as it was, he would ask, was it proper pass on to the orders of the day with the same coolness and indifference as if nothing of the sort had occurred.

Mr. CUTHBERT said, if he had felt the influence of the same spirit upon his feelings when he first rose, which now operated upon his own spirit, altered tone of the gentleman's last remark, he would not have risen. He was pleased with the beautiful tropes of the honorable gentleman, as the delightful melody of his voice, but when he spoke of the defeats of his party, they were perhaps to be attributed in a great degree to the strous exaggerations of the period alluded to, which magnified mere error into the most heinous crime.

Mr. SOUTHARD then rose to speak, but gave way to

Mr. EWING, who moved an adjournment, which prevailed.

And

The Senate adjourned.

HOUSE OF REPRESENTATIVES.
TUESDAY, Jan. 27, 1835.

Mr. SPEIGHT, from the Committee on Military Affairs, reported with an amendment, the joint resolution from the Senate, authorizing a gold medal to be presented to Col. Croghan, and a sword to each of the officers under his command, for their gallant defence of Fort Stephenson, during the late war.

After some conversation between Messrs. PARKER, SPEIGHT, and MERCER, the amendment was concurred in, and the resolution agreed to.

INDIAN RESERVATIONS.

Mr. LOVE, from the Committee on Indian Affairs, to whom the resolution heretofore offered by Mr. McCARTY was committed, reported the same, with an amendment, as follows:

Strike out after the word correspondence, in the fourth line, the words "of all Indian agents, sub-agents, and other persons connected with the Indian Department," and insert after the words General Land Office, in the eighth line, the words "of all Indian agents, sub-agents, and other persons," and insert after the words reserves of land, in the tenth line, the words " east of the Mississippi river."

Mr. CLAY was understood to ask that the consideration of the resolution might be deferred for the present.

Mr. LOVE said the resolution as reported was changed, except as respected the printing.

Mr. CLAY wished the amendment read again, he had not perceived its full extent. The resolution having been read,

Mr. LOVE said, he would make a brief explanation. The resolution as amended by the Committee on Indian Affairs was confined in its operation to those States east of the Mississippi river. As committee would have been gratified if it had in its their power to have circumscribed the information asked for within narrower limits; but to be done so, would have been invidious. For instance, if they had recommended an inquiry into the transactions within the State of Alabama alone, the gentlemen from that State might well complain of an invidious distinction, and say, why not Indians, Illinois, and Michigan included? As committee have also been anxious to avoid any unnecessary expense in the preparation of the correspondence; but their duty to the House was to the country, and the importance of the matter involved, forbade them to limit it to any particular State or Territory.

A few words on the principle of these reservations. It was something like this: in the treaties which gave rise to them, there were two stipulations in relation to these reservations. The first was, that the President of the United States was required to approve of the transfer and sale of the reservation before it should be vested in the purchaser; the second was, that the Indian Agent should testify that the reservation had been sold for a valuable consideration, and that no fraud had been practised on the Indians in the purchase. The object of these stipulations was to protect both the Indians and the Government from fraud. It was impossible, therefore, that the President of the United States or, the Secretary of War, should have been, or could have been, conscious of frauds, if frauds had been committed. The frauds were said to be of this character, that agents had combined with speculators in the purchase of Indian reservations, and had certified that which was not true, viz. that a valuable consideration had been given, thereby defrauding both the Indians and the Government of the United States.

Against many of these reservations belonged to orphans; and the commission of those frauds had deprived them of subsistence. The resolution was not intended to affect any particular individuals, or the Executive, nor any officer of the Government; but its object was to bring to light the correspondence of all those officers on the subject of Indian reservations, so that the country might know if frauds had been committed—who had been guilty of them—and who had been defrauded—that contracts made were valid, and what not, and enable those who had rights which had been violated, to set aside the contracts, or to institute proceedings in relation thereto. No action was proposed by the committee; but they asked only that the correspondence and necessary documents be furnished to the House, which may then be referred to one of its standing committees for such action as might be deemed requisite.

The committee were well aware, and had duly considered, that those documents cou'd not be got at without labor, and some expense. They were well apprized of it before their recommendation of the resolution; but it was due to the nation, due to the Indians, and due to the Executive himself, that if frauds existed, the fact should be known and investigated; and as he remarked the other day, he did not believe that a single gentleman in that House, if he was satisfied that frauds had been committed in an important branch of the public service, would be deterred from voting for the adoption of the resolution by the consideration of its expense. Besides, Mr. L. was induced to believe that the amount had been very much amplified, and that the labor would not be half as much as had been described. One gentleman said it would take a few days, while another averred it as his opinion it would take months; and these conflicting statements showed it was a mere matter of opinion, without being based on facts. The maps were already prepared; and nothing was required but to copy them, and transcribe the letters and documents necessary.

Mr. CLAY said the gentlemen from Kentucky must have misapprehended what he had said, and he presumed many gentlemen who had objected to the adoption of this resolution had done so merely on the score of the expense. Mr. C. had other, and more material objections than the mere item of cost. His first objection was, that he believed the call to be unnecessary. It would be recollected by the House that the resolution call'd for the services of those engaged in the head office to transcribe all the correspondence and documents in relation to all the Indian reservations. Was the House unaware of the continual and annual complaints in this branch of the Treasury Department, of its inability to perform its duties? Had we not been notified at the commencement of the present session that in spite of all the extra clerk hire already employed, the patents in the land office were upwards of one hundred thousand in arrear? Then the first objection that presented itself to his mind, was that the call was unnecessary for such a mass of documents, not one tenth of which would prove useful to the country or to an individual member of the House. It was true, that in connexion with this objection, we might take into consideration the great expense that would, and necessarily must, be incurred. And again, why call for a mass of documents without any assurance that the public interest required them to be made out at a great expense of labor and of money; without taking into consideration the cost of print ng a volume of some seven or eight hundred pages, all at the public expense, and as far as any one knew, not calculated to benefit any one portion or section of the country. This was an objection, but, nevertheless, Mr. C. did not pretend to put it into the scale with the detection of the perpetration of fraud, if such existed. But why have not gentlemen made a specification, and then called for proof, instead of involving the country in an immense expense upon vague rumor? And this brought him to a still more important objection. The House was then discussing a mere ex parte inquiry, and instituting an inquisition into the conduct of every agent of the Government, without any specific charge having been brought against any one of them, or without giving them notice of the trial, or investigation, they were about to undergo. Would not such a course be unjust towards those individuals who had been intrusted with a great public duty to bring their conduct before a committee for investigation, without designating any specific charge, or without giving those individuals any notice thereof? He did not expect a single member of that House to rise in his place and say that he had a well-founded suspicion against either the office or any individual employed in it. As far as regarded the State of which Mr. C. had the honor to be a representative, not even rumor had whispered that any fraudulent transactions had taken place there, and why should the persons engaged there be brought up on an ex parte inquisition? Irreparable and irretrievable injury might be done to individuals in this branch of the service by the proposed measure. If the committee, or any gentleman of the House, were in possession of a well-grounded charge of fraud, designate the party, and if they did, Mr. C. would be the last to vote against having a copy of every record of every description, whether it respected the President or any other functionary of the Government, that could bear upon the case, but do not draw upon one branch of the Treasury Department for labor which it is impracticable to perform, unless its more important duties are neglected—duties which it is already incompetent to fulfil—for the purpose of bringing on a trial without previous notice. It seemed to him that these few objections were unanswerable; he might urge more, but he did not wish to take up the time of the House in a lengthened discussion, the less was he hopeful the House would not adopt it without some modification, or taking some time to examine its details.

Mr. PLUMMER said, having first made war on the resolution, as originally introduced by the gentleman from Indiana, (Mr. McCarty,) for reasons which he then stated to the House, and the original resolution having been amended to meet his views, he withdrew all opposition, and would vote for its adoption in its modified form. It was true that he thought it an unnecessary consumption of time to require the Clerks in the General Land Office, who had not aid enough to keep up the current business of the office, to make out plats of the lands on which the Indian reservations were located. He could not conceive of any benefit the maps would be to the House or the country. That objection, however, was too unimportant to induce him to vote against the whole of the resolution, or jeopardize its adoption by subjecting an amendment. He was in favor of the call; it was due to the country, and the officers of the Government, that all of the documents in relation to lands held under the Indian treaties, should be published to the world. There were reservations under the treaty of Doak's Stand, made in 1820, held by purchasers under regulations of the War Department, the titles to which were not distinct; ly understood by those who had a right to know by what tenure and nature of titles all lands within the limits of Missisippi are held. The State has titles to which were acquired directly by purchase from the Government, after the expiration of five years from the time they became private property. In some cases of reservations, it was unknown whether the lands reserved from sale for individuals of the Choctaw tribe, were private property, or whether they had reverted to the General Government. If these reservations were private property, the State had a right to tax them. If they belonged to the general government, they ought to be brought into market and offered for sale as other public lands. There were no records in the State showing these facts. As regards the matter of expense, he said that was of little importance compared with the importance of investigating the frauds charged by the gentleman from Kentucky, (Mr. Love,) who is, on this occasion, the organ of the Committee on Indian Affairs. The objections which he charged, and enlarged upon the other day, in relation to the expense of furnishing and printing the information proposed to be obtained, he repeated, had been obviated by the adoption of the amendment which he then offered, and became incorporated into the body of the resolution. He repelled the idea that the item of expense would induce him on any occasion to screen a public officer, charged with improper conduct, from an investigation, nor deprive the people, or their representatives, of useful information. He only objected to a useless and unnecessary expenditure of the people's money, for the publication of new editions of documents and papers which would never be read. He did not understand the gentleman from Kentucky, nor any one who preferred the charge of fraud against the Agents of the government as locating the charge in Mississippi. The gentleman (Mr. Love) says, that he

tion ' of the revenue from customs, that the salaries of the officers were too high, and that their number had been increased beyond the exigencies of the service, and that they ought to be reduced. He, for one, was not willing to concede that point. He was willing that the subject should undergo the strictest scrutiny of the Committee on Commerce; that the examination should be conducted either at the several Custom-houses or at the bar of this House, and he would venture to predict, that no just ground could be found to sustain any of these allegations; and he would further predict, that the Committee and the House would be constrained to come to the conclusion that the salaries of most of the officers demand an increase rather than a diminution. He, therefore, hoped that this inquiry would be deferred until this examination could be had by the committee to which the subject properly belonged, and to which it had been specially committed.

Mr. GILLET commenced by saying, that it was with reluctance that he had arisen to participate in the present debate. The notice, however, which had been taken of the Committee on Commerce, rendered it proper he should say one word on this subject. He would endeavor to state to the House the real question under consideration, in a few words as possible. Under the acts of Congress, a certain per centage on moneys collected, was paid to the Collectors of the customs as well as certain fees of office; out of which certain officers under them were paid the compensation allowed them by law, and the overplus, if any, was paid into the Treasury, after deducting the salary of the collector. On reducing the duties on imports in 1832, the amount of these commissions and fees became materially diminished, though the labors of these officers continued very much the same. The consequence was, that the fund out of which these officers were paid, became so much lessened, that it did not afford them a reasonable compensation. This led to the adoption of the third section of the act of 1833, which is in these words:

"Sec. 3. And be it further enacted, that the Secretary of the Treasury be, and he is hereby authorized to pay to the collectors, naval officers, surveyors, gaugers, weighers, and measurers, of the several ports of the United States, out of any money in the Treasury, not otherwise appropriated, such sums as will give to the said officers respectively, the same compensation in the year one thousand eight hundred and thirty-three, according to the importations of that year, as they would have been entitled to receive if the act of the 14th July, 1832, had not gone into effect."

Under this law he understood that these officers received the same compensation they did prior to 1832; whether they then received it in the shape of fees or in a salary. On passing the law of 1833 it was expected that the whole subject of paying custom-house officers would be acted upon at the last session; but the destruction of the Treasury building and consequent loss of materials collected by the Secretary to enable him to digest and recommend a plan for that purpose, prevented those expectations from being then realized. And in order to prevent these officers from not being sufficiently compensated, a section was introduced at the last session into the appropriation bill, making the necessary provision for paying them, and it is in the precise words of the law of 1833. It has, however, a proviso, limiting the amount that these officers shall be allowed to receive. Under this law of 1834, it was understood that the officers had been paid their respective compensations. On passing the law of 1834, this House considered that the law of 1833 had expired, at this time the law of 1834 must be equally dead. It could not have the effect to give these officers salaries after 1834, unless 1834 could be made to read 1835, &c. It followed, that there was no provision at this time to pay these men, if the fund alluded to should fail to be sufficient. In this state of the case, the civil appropriation bill comes before us, and the gentleman from Ohio (Mr. Vance) proposed to add to the appropriation bill a section repealing that portion of the act of 1834 which provides for making compensation to the officers referred to, and con-

tinuing a certain other portion of it. This, to his mind, was like firing a park of artillery at a dead lion. It was hardly worthy of grave legislators to be spending days on a question of repealing a dead law. If the bill contained any provision to pay Custom-house officers, there would be some apology for the effort; but it did not provide one cent for them; and the amendment is entirely irrelevant and out of place.

But the gentleman talks much of enormous sums taken from the Treasury to pay certain of these officers. He forgets that much of what many of them receive, and about which he speaks, is fees paid by individuals, and but very little is ever paid them from the Treasury; and he also forgets that many of them disburse much of what they receive, in paying their necessary assistants. It was highly probable that some of these officers were too well, and others too poorly paid. This is not the proper place to examine and act upon that subject. He had profited by experience. He well recollected last session, his venerable friend from Massachusetts, (Mr. Adams,) assumed the ground that appropriation bills ought not to be loaded with extraneous matters. Their office was merely to appropriate money, under existing laws, to compensate public agents, and to execute public works. This was the true rule, and one which he desired to act upon.

But, said Mr. G. we are told that if we do not add this clause now to this bill, we shall not be able to act on the subject this session. He did not deem it important that it should be done, for unless we pass a law to pay these officers, there will be no law to pay them from the Treasury, and the fund referred to cannot give them what they received under the gentleman's amendment of last year. But to his mind it would be less out of place to add the gentleman's present amendment to many of the other bills which were certain to come up this session. He, Mr. G. however, hoped to see this whole subject brought before this House at this session, in a proper form, from the appropriate committee. It was a subject of vast importance, and required much deliberation and care. It was first necessary to establish a proper basis, and then the details would require great consideration and attention. He hoped, if he had any agency in preparing the bill, to aid in infusing into it, so much of liberality and economy as would make it acceptable to all sides of this House. He would diminish the number of these officers to the actual necessities and wants of the Government, and was not for paying them, or any other officers in the Government, a salary larger than was necessary to ensure the services of competent, faithful, and efficient men. More than this would be justly termed extravagance.

On the other hand, that rate of compensation which was so low, as not to ensure the services of such persons as he had described, would be ill timed economy, would result in injury to the public interests. When you pay too low to command the services of men of capacity, and integrity, you are sure of being badly served. Your agent must live, and if you do not give him such compensation as will allow him comfortably to do so, he is sure to cheat you in the time he serves you or in some other way; for a living he must and will have. If he cannot live honestly, he will do so dishonestly. You may obtain capacity to do business at a low price; but integrity is quite as important as talent. The public service requires both. He would, however, avoid, if possible, having any officer, whose compensation should depend upon contingencies. It should not be composed of per centages, or allowances, or any thing of the kind. He preferred paying a distinct annual salary; then the law would inform us how much each public agent received for his services. This would prevent the dishonest from paying or receiving too much, and it would shield the upright from suspicion.

Then, on the last day of the year, the compensation of all officers for the ensuing year could be accurately calculated. All would be paid distinctly under statutes, and Congress would be responsible to the people for the amount paid. Then the executive would be free even from the suspicion of having by his own act increased

the expenses of government. He would be the disbursement of the public money, the executive of the laws of Congress—an agent without discretionary powers. It would relieve him of much of the embarrassment, now necessarily attendant upon his office. The hands of the department, and their accounting officers, would also be relieved from an unpleasant and tedious part of their duty. These suspicions against the integrity of officers would be much less likely to be raised—now he believed most of them suspicious grew out of the fact that many offices were not paid a certain and definite sum as salary.

He had urged these considerations upon the attention of the gentleman from Pennsylvania, (Mr. Watmough,) when considering the Navy pension, and he was happy to learn that they had been so appreciated, and were likely to be ingrafted by common consent. Once adopt a definite salary as the mode of pay, you do away with those difficulties that are said to be so much between those who have accounts and against officers. Should these principles be adopted, the custom-house pay bill, he thought that none of the public service would be relieved from all suspicion. He did not expect, in the making of this bill that could be reported, that we could all agree in opinion, in every instance, as to the mode of compensation of officers. These things were matters of opinion; but in the principles of compensation which he had suggested, he hoped the gentleman from Ohio would acquiesce. He hoped they would be unanimously assented to by the House. After this frank expression of his views and expectations, he hoped the gentleman from Ohio would not further press his notion upon the consideration of the House; he hoped this bill to take the ordinary course through its appropriate committee, untrammelled by the consideration of subjects totally disconnected with those presented to its consideration in the bill.

Mr. McKINLEY called for the previous question, which, however, was not seconded by the House.

On motion of Mr. WISE,
The House then adjourned.

IN SENATE.

WEDNESDAY, JANUARY 28, 1835.
The VICE PRESIDENT laid before the Senate a communication from the Commissioner of the General Land Office, in obedience to a resolution of the 30th ultimo, requiring copies of all orders directed to be administered to all persons required to purchase public lands; which was ordered to be printed, with 500 additional copies.

Petitions were presented by Messrs. MANGUM, PRESTON, PORTER, and MOORE, and referred.

Mr. TYLER, from the Committee on the District of Columbia, reported a bill for the relief of James Young, without amendment.

Also, a bill for the relief of Baily E. Clark, an amendment.

Mr. TIPTON, from the Committee on Claims, reported a bill for the relief of Captain William Morrow.

Mr. ROBINSON, from the Committee on Roads and Canals, to which was referred the bill for the relief of Moses Shepperd, reported the same with an amendment, and a report; which were ordered to be printed.

Mr. LEIGH, from the Judiciary Committee, which was referred the bill from the House for the better organization of the District Courts of Alabama, reported the same, with an amendment.

Mr. POINDEXTER, from the Committee on Public Lands, to which was referred the bill for locating a further issue of scrip for six sections of United States military land warrants, reported the same, without amendment.

Also, the bill authorizing the widening of certain streets in the City of St. Augustine.

The bill for the relief of Richard F. Archer.

The bill for the relief of William O'Neale and Robert Morrison.

Mr. POINDEXTER, from the same committee, made unfavorable reports upon the claims of Peter Morrison and Harvey Perry.

The following resolutions were submitted.

The reference was made accordingly, and the motion to print an extra number of copies, according to the rule of the House, was laid upon the table for one day.

A bill returned from the Senate, entitled an act for the final adjustment of land claims in Louisiana, with an amendment, was then taken up, and on motion of Mr. GARLAND, was postponed till to-morrow.

An act to amend the act providing for the construction of a bridge across the Potomac, was read a third time and passed.

The bill to regulate the United States Circuit Court for the district of West Tennessee, was next taken up.

Mr. PEYTON moved to recommit the bill to the Committee on the Judiciary, with instructions to insert a provision for an increase of the salaries of the judges. He thought this to be due to them, inasmuch as their duties were much extended.

Mr. FOSTER said the bill was founded on a petition which said nothing on the subject of an increase of compensation. He, however, had no objection to the course proposed.

The bill was then recommitted.

The joint resolution, introduced by Mr. E. EVERETT, from the Committee on the Library, directing a gold medal to be struck at the Mint of the United States from the original die, at the expense of Morgan Neville, in honor of the battle of the Cowpens, was read a third time and passed.

GENERAL APPROPRIATION BILL.

The House then resumed the consideration of the bill making appropriations for the civil and diplomatic expenses of the government for the year 1835—being on the amendment offered by Mr. VANCE, relative to the pay of Custom-house officers.

Mr. VANCE supported his amendment at length, and went into a tabular and documentary history of the expense of the collection of the revenue since 1811, and the gradual increase of the same.

He was followed by Mr. CAMBRELENG, who concurred in the general object designed to be effected by this amendment. But he conceived it was improper to incorporate its provisions in the general appropriation bill. It should form the subject of a separate bill. Mr. C. also explained the manner in which the gentleman from Ohio, (Mr. Vance,) had fallen into error in some of his tabular statements.

Mr. SUTHERLAND followed on the same side of the question, and stated the intention of the Commercial Committee soon to bring this matter before the House.

Mr. FILLMORE also spoke at some length on the amendment, and finally offered an amendment to the amendment of the gentleman from Ohio, for acceptance, which was however declined.

The debate was continued by Messrs POPE, PHILLIPS, WARD, WILLIAMS, GILLET, and HARPER.

Mr. WARD said he regretted that the honorable gentleman from Ohio (Mr. Vance) should have taken this occasion to endeavor to correct the abuses which he seems to think exists in the collection of the revenue from customs. The object which the honorable gentleman has in view is to repeal all "that part of the second section of an act entitled an act making appropriations for the civil and diplomatic expenses of Government for the year 1834, which authorizes the Secretary of the Treasury to pay to the collectors, naval officers, surveyors, and their respective clerks, together with the weighers of the several ports of the United States, out of any money in the Treasury not otherwise appropriated, such sums as will give to the said officers respectively the same compensation in the year 1834, according to the importations of that year, as they would have been entitled to receive if the act of the 14th of July had not gone into effect; and that the clerks employed by the respective collectors, naval officers, and surveyors of the several ports, shall be paid for the year 1833, as if they had been specifically provided in the third section of the act of the 2d March, of said year, entitled "an act making appropriations for the civil and diplomatic expenses of government for the year 1834, and to provide that the balance of the said second section of the above recited act of 1834, be continued in force, until otherwise ordered by Congress."

Mr. W. said, the amendment to this amendment, which has been submitted by his colleague, (Mr. Fillmore) did not materially vary the case, and he, for one, was not prepared, at this time, to record his vote in favor of either of the propositions. We had been told by the honorable gentleman who is at the head of the Committee of Commerce, (Mr. Sutherland,) that that committee has the subject of "*the compensation and number of the custom house officers*" under consideration in the committee, and that he has reason to believe that the committee will make a report during the session, and that honorable gentleman had himself opposed this amendment in a forcible and eloquent address to the House.

Now, if the honorable gentleman who had devoted so much of his time particularly to this subject, was of the opinion that the proposed amendment was improper, and if the able and distinguished gentleman at the head of the Committee of Ways and Means, who reported this bill, and who had also given the subject much consideration, entertained the same opinion, he would ask whether gentlemen would sustain it, without allowing themselves time thoroughly to examine the subject, so that they might, at least, act understandingly upon it. He hoped not; and he hoped too that gentlemen were not disposed to delay the passage of this important bill, by a continuance of this discussion, until the extraneous matter now in controversy was investigated and settled. This bill, said Mr. W., now blocks up our way; and he would remind the House that there were but twenty-two days of the session remaining, in which, by the rules of the House, we could transact public business; and yet, as it was well known, we had before us a vast deal of business, of the most important character.

The gentleman from Ohio (Mr. Vance) had entered at large into a statement of the amount of revenue received, for several years past, and of the amount expended in collecting it, and he had alleged that the expense of collection had amounted to from 2½ to 10 per cent. Mr. W. was, he said, induced to believe that the honorable gentleman was mistaken in this statement, so far, at least, as regarded the principal commercial cities; for, it would be found, upon a careful examination, that the expense of collecting the revenue from imports would not, in the aggregate, exceed from 3½ to 4 per cent. The statement of the honorable gentleman showed that, in one instance, the expense of collection had gone up as high as 6 per cent., but that, as he had just remarked, was not true in respect to any of the principal cities. It would be found that in the City of New York, which place seemed to command so much of the gentleman's attention, the cost of collecting the revenue had never exceeded from 3 to 3¼ per cent. on the amount received.

The amount of the revenue collected, and of the expenses of collection, in the year 1833, in *Boston*, *New York*, and *Philadelphia*, was as follows:

Boston	$3,906,356 97	121,978	or a frac'n more than		3	p. c.
N. York	13,081,548 93	429,501	do	do	3 1-4	
Phila.	2,995,663 35	99,877	do	do	3 1-4	

The honorable gentleman did not consider that in making his calculations of the expense, he took the *whole* revenue. Now, there were many ports at which much more was paid than the amount received. If these could be abolished, the expense of collecting would be greatly diminished; and if reduction was necessary, which he was not willing to admit, it should be made in those ports which were a burden on, and not those which support the Government. Nor did the honorable gentleman consider that the amount of duties had been of late greatly reduced by the tariff, which, at the same time, did not allow of a reduction in the number of officer., because the increase of arrivals has been progressive with the diminution of duties. During the last year, more than two thousand vessels from foreign ports entered at the custom-house of N. York; and every one of them must have a custom officer on board, or those which bring articles not dutiable, might avail themselves of the circumstance to smuggle in valuable dutiable articles. And, moreover, there was scarcely a single cargo which did not embrace some dutiable goods. Mr. W. said, he was at a loss to know why the hon. gentleman seemed so desirous of inquiring into the expense of collecting the revenue from customs. Why did he not likewise inquire into the expense of collecting the revenue from the sale of the public lands. If he would compare the expense of collecting the one with the expense of collecting the other, he would find a vast difference in favor of the collection of the revenue from customs. The expense attending the collection of the land revenue varied from 8 to 25 per cent. upon the amount received. Mr. W. said he had no complaint to make with respect to this great and manifest difference. He believed that the officers in charge of the sale of the public lands, and in the receipt of the money therefor, received no more for their services than they were fairly entitled to. The land agents and land receivers were each allowed an annual salary of five hundred dollars, with an addition of one per cent. on the amount of the moneys received; their emoluments being limited to three thousand dollars a year; and he did not hesitate to say, that most, if not all of those officers, receive the maximum amount allowed by law. These offices were places of great responsibility, and require to be filled by men of worth and respectability; and he did not wish to be understood as complaining that they were in the receipt of too great a compensation for their services But if it was not deemed extravagant to allow them three thousand dollars a year for their services, residing, as they did, in the country where living was cheap, it seemed to him that no complaint ought to be made against the small amount received by gaugers, weighers, and other subordinate officers attached to the custom-houses—for their situations were no less responsible, requiring equal talent and respectability, while the expense of living in the principal cities must be acknowledged on all sides to be vastly greater. But we have been told, he said, by his honorable colleague, (Mr. Fillmore,) that some of the weighers receive from four to six thousand dollars a year for their services; one, in particular, in Baltimore, and others either in Philadelphia or Boston; and this was urged as the principal reason why we should vote for the amendment. Did that gentleman suppose that one weigher in each of those cities was competent to perform personally all the duties of his office? Did he not know, that he is compelled, from the nature of the case, to employ deputies? And did not those deputies come in for a portion of these receipts? In fact, on the ground assumed, and on which the honorable gentleman so confidently relied, the compensation, had there been an adequate number of weighers, would have been even less to each than was received in eighteen hundred and thirty-three, by the same class of officers, in New York.

Mr. Ward said, he would inform that gentleman and the House, that the weighers were obliged to pay all the expenses of labor incident to their office, which amounted to about one third of their gross receipts; and although it would seem from the document referred to by the gentlemen who have advocated this amendment, that, by the separate returns of the weighers in the City of New York, one may have received some two or three thousand dollars a year for his services, while another received but four hundred dollars. This inequality would disappear when it was known that the aggrigate amount received for fees was equally divided between the fourteen weighers in that City. The facts were, in the year eighteen hundred and thirty three net amount paid the weighers in the city of York, was eighteen thousand six hundre seventy-five dollars, which being divided bet the fourteen weighers in that city, gave to only the sum of thirteen hundred and thirty- dollars per annum—a sum hardly adequate, the greatest economy, to support themselves and their families. Was there, he asked, a member who heard him, who would say that the amount thus shown to be received by these faithful and vigilant guardians of our revenue, for their in able services, was too great? He trusted n had been said, there existed abuses in the

tion 'of the revenue from customs, that the salaries of the officers were too high, and that their number had been increased beyond the exigencies of the service, and that they ought to be reduced. He, for one, was not willing to concede that point. He was willing that the subject should undergo the strictest scrutiny of the Committee on Commerce; that the examination should be conducted either at the several Custom-houses or at the bar of this House, and he would venture to predict, that no just ground would be found to sustain any of these allegations; and he would further predict, that the Committee and the House would be constrained to come to the conclusion that the salaries of most of the officers demand an increase rather than a diminution. He, therefore, hoped that this inquiry would be deferred until this examination could be had by the committee to which the subject properly belonged, and to which it had been sp. cially committed.

Mr. GILLET commenced by saying, that it was with reluctance that he had arisen to participate in the present debate. The notice, however, which had been taken of the Committee on Commerce, rendered it proper he should say one word on the subject. He would endeavor to state to the House the real question under consideration, in as few words as possible. Under the acts of Congress, a certain per centage on moneys collected, was paid to the Collectors of the customs as well as certain fees of office; out of which certain officers under them were paid the compensation allowed them by law, and the overplus, if any, was paid into the Treasury, after deducting the salary of the collector. On reducing the duties on imports in 1832, the amount of these commissions an l fees became materially diminished, though the labors of these officers continued very much the same. The consequence was, that the fund out of which these officers were paid, became so much lessened, that it did not afford them a reasonable compensation. This led to the adoption of the third section of the act of 1833, which is in these words:

"Sec. 3. And be it further enacted, that the Secretary of the Treasury be, and he is hereby authorized to pay to the collectors, naval officers, surveyors, gaugers, weighers, and measurers, of the several ports of the United States, out of any money in the Treasury, not otherwise appropriated, such sums as will give to the said officers respectively, the same compensation in the year one thousand eight hundred and thirty fifter, according to the importations of that y ar, as they would have been entitled to receive if the act of the 14th July, 1832, had not gone into effect."

Under this law he understood that these officers received the same compensation they did prior to 1832; whether they then received it in the shape of fees or in a s-lary. On passing the law of 1833 it was expected that the whole subject of paying custom-house officers would be acted upon at the last session; but the destruction of the Treasury building and consequent loss of materials collected by the Secretary to enable him to digest and recommend a plan for that purpose, prevented those expectations from being then real sed. And in order to prevent these officers from not being sufficiently compensated, a section was introduced at the last session into the appropriation bill, making the necessary provision for paying them, and it is in the precise words of the law of 1833. It was, however, a proviso, limiting the amount that these officers shall be allowed to receive. Under this law of 1834, it was understood that the officers had been paid their respective compensations. On passing the law of 1834, this House considered that the law of 1833 had expired, at this time the law of 1834 must be equally dead. It could not have the effect to give these officers salaries after 1834, unless 1834 could be made to read 1835, &c. It followed, that there was no provision at this time to pay these men, if the fund alluded to should fail to be sufficient. In this state of the case, the civil appropriation bill comes before us, and the gentleman from Ohio (Mr. Vance) proposed to a lid to appropriation bill a section repealing that portion of the act of 1834 which provides for making provision to the officers referred to, and continuing a certain other portion of it. This, 'to his mind, was like firing a park of artillery at a dead lion. It was hardly worthy of grave legislators to be spending days on a question of repealing a dead law. If the bill contained any provision to pay Custom-house officers, there would be some apology for this effort; but it did not provide one cent for them; and the amendment is entirely irrelevant and out of place.

But the gentleman talks much of enormous sums taken from the Treasury to pay certain of these officers. He forgets that much of what many of them receive, and about which he speaks, is fees paid by individuals, and but very little is ever paid them from the Treasury; and he also forgets that many of them disburse much of what they receive, in paying their necessary assistants. It was highly probable that some of these officers were too well, and others too poorly paid. This is not the proper place to examine and act upon that subject. He had profited by experience. He well recollected last session, his venerable friend from Massachusetts, (Mr. Adams,) assumed the ground that appropriation bills ought not to be loaded with extraneous matters. Their office was merely to appropriate money, under existing laws, to compensate public agents, and to execute public works. This was the true rule, and one which he desired to act upon.

But, said Mr. G. we are told that if we do not add this clause now to this bill, we shall not be able to act on the subject this session. He did not deem it important that it should be done, for unless we pass a law to pay these officers, there will be no law to pay them from the Treasury, and the fund referred to cannot give them what they received under the gentleman's amendment of last year. But to his mind it would be less out of place to add the gentleman's present amendment to many of the other bills which were certain to come up this session. He, Mr. G. however, hoped to see this whole subject brought before this House in a proper form, from the appropriate committee. It was a subject of vast importance, and required much deliberation and care. It was first necessary to establish a proper basis, and then the details would require great consideration and attention. He hoped, if its had any agency in preparing the bill, to aid in infusing into it, so much of liberality and economy as would make it acceptable to all sides of this House. He would diminish the number of these officers to the actual necessities and wants of the Government, and was not for paying them, or any other officers in the Government, a salary larger than was necessary to ensure the services of competent, faithful, and efficient men. More than this would be justly termed extravagance.

On the other hand, that rate of compensation which was so low, as not to ensure the services of such persons as he had described, would be ill timed economy, would result in injury to the public interests. When you pay too low to command the services of men of capacity, and integrity, you are sure of being badly served. Your agent must live, and if you do not give him such compensation as will al ow him comfortably to do so, he is sure to cheat you in the time he serves you or in some other way; for a living he must and will have. If he cannot live honestly, he will do so dishonestly. You may obtain capacity to do business at a low price; but integrity is quite as important as talent. The public service requires both. He would, however, avoid, if possible, having any officer, whose comp nsation should depend upon contingencies. It should not be composed of per centages, or allowances, or any thing of the kind. He preferred paying a distinct annual salary; then the law would inform us how much each publ c agent received for his service. This would prevent the dishonest from paying or receiving too much, and it would shield the upright from suspicion.

Then, on the last day of the year, the compensation of all officers for the ensuing year could be accurately calculated. All would be paid dis tinctly under statutes, and Congress would be responsible to the people for the amount paid. Then the executive would be free even from the suspicion of having by his own act increased

the expenses of government. He would be, in the disbursement of the public moneys, the executive of the laws of Congress—an agent without discretionary powers. It would relieve him of much of the embarrassment, now necessarily attendant upon his office. The heads of the departments, and their accounting officers, would also be rel eved from an unpleasant and vexatious part of their duty. These suspicions against the integrity of officers would be much less likely to be raised—now he believed most of them suspicions grew out of the fact that many officers were not paid a certain and definite sum as salary.

He had urged these considerations upon the attention of the gentleman from Pennsylvania, (Mr. Watmough,) when considering the Navy pay bill, and he was happy to learn that they had been fully appreciated, and were likely to be ingrafted on it by common consent. Once adopt a definite salary as the mode of pay, you do away with all those difficulties that are said to be so common between those who have accounts and accounting officers.. Should these principles be adopted in the custom-house pay bill, he thought that much of the publ c service would be relieved from unjust suspicion. He did not expect, in the details of any bill that could be reported, that we could all agree in opinion, in every instance, as to the number of compensation of officers. These things were not matters of opinion but in the principles of compensation which he had suggested, he hoped the gentleman from Ohio would acquiesce. He even hoped they would be unanimously assented to by the House. After this frank expression of his views and expectations, he hoped the gentleman from Ohio would not further press this matter upon the consideration of the House, but allow this bill to take the ordinary course through it untrammelled by the consideration of subjects not tally disconnected with those presented to our consideration in the bill.

Mr. McKINLEY called for the previous question, which, however, was not seconded by the House.

On motion of Mr. WISE,

The House then adjourned.

IN SENATE.

WEDNESDAY, JANUARY 28, 1835.

The VICE PRESIDENT laid before the Senate a communication from the Commissioner of the General Land Office, in obedience to a resolution of the 30th ultimo, requiring copies of orders directed to be administered to all persons applying to purchase public lands, which was ordered to be printed, with 500 additional copies.

Petitions were presented by Messrs. MANGUM, PRESTON, PORTER, and MOORE, and referred.

Mr. TYLER, from the Committee on the District of Columbia, reported a bill for the relief of James Young, without amendment.

Also, a bill for the relief of Hally E. Clark, with an amendment.

Mr. TIPTON, from the Committee on Claims, reported a bill for the relief of Captain William Morrow.

Mr. ROBINSON, from the Committee on Roads and Canals, to which was referred the bill for the relief of Moses Shepperd, reported the same with an amendment, and a report; which very soon to be printed.

Mr. LEIGH, from the Judiciary Committee, to which was referred the bill from the House for the better organization of the District Courts of Alabama, reported the same, with an amendment.

Mr. POINDEXTER, from the Committee on Public Lands, to which was referred the bill granting a further issuing of scrip for satisfaction of United States military land warrants, reported the same, without amendment.

Also, the bill authorizing the widening of certain streets in the City of St. Augustine.

The bill for the relief of Richard P. Archer, and Robert Morrison.

The bill for the relief of William O'Neile and Mr. POINDEXTER, from the same committee, made unfavorable reports upon the claims of Robert Morrison and Harvey Perry.

The following resolutions were subn

By Mr. BROWN:

Resolved, That the Committee on Revolutionary claims be instructed to inquire into the propriety of allowing commutation pay to the heirs at law of Henry Irwin, late a Lieutenant Colonel of the 5th Regiment of the North Carolina line, on the continental establishment, in the army of the revolution.

Which was considered and adopted.

By Mr. PRENTISS:

Resolved, That the President be requested to communicate to the Senate the correspondence which passed between the Governments of the United States and Spain, through their respective Ministers or Agents, in the negotiation of the late treaty between the two Governments, together with the instructions given to the Ministers of the United States, from time to time, in the course of said negotiation, or so much of said correspondence and instructions as it may not be incompatible with the public interest to communicate.

Mr. TOMLINSON, from the Committee on Pensions, made an unfavorable report upon the petitions of Daniel Maginnis and Francis Patterson.

Mr. MOORE presented certain joint resolutions of the Legislature of Alabama, relative to the 16th sections of the public lands set apart for the use of schools.

Also, joint resolutions, from the same body, for the establishment of a pension agency in Alabama.

Mr. KING, of Alabama, presented a memorial from the same body, for the passage of a law to confirm the titles of persons to lands purchased near the line between Alabama and Georgia, without knowing at the time of purchase in which State the lands lay.

Mr. KING said it also became his duty to present certain joint resolutions from the same Legislature, setting forth their disapprobation of the resolution of the Senate of last session, censuring the Chief Magistrate for certain official acts, and instructing their Senators to use their best efforts to have the same expunged from the journal of the Senate.

Mr. KING moved that the resolutions be laid on the table and printed.

The resolutions having been read,

Mr. CLAY said, before any order should be taken for laying the resolutions on the table, which had been addressed to the Senators from Alabama as instructions, he would be glad to know if it was the purpose of the gentleman who had presented them to submit a proposition to expunge the resolution alluded to from the Journal of the Senate.

Mr. KING, of Alabama, being about to speak, gave way to

Mr. BENTON, who rose and said that the Senate would recollect that when the resolution of censure was adopted, he gave immediate notice to the Senate and to the American people that he would commence a series of motions for the purpose of ...ing the offensive resolution expunged from the journal. He used the word expunge in contradistinction to the words repeal or reverse, because he believed at that time, and experience had confirmed him in the belief, that a repeal of it would not do justice to the case. It required an expurgation of the journal itself, which should operate as a declaration to all future times, that it should not have been there. He gave this notice from a conviction arising from the deepest reflection that the Senate, in adopting that resolution, were trampling under foot the constitution of the U. States, and not only so, but all the forms of administering criminal justice. He gave the notice too, without consultation with any human being, and no being on this earth could say that he asked him whether it was right or wrong. He had not done so, nor never would he consult with any one on such an occasion. No man conferred more with his friends on ordinary occasions than he did but there were some occasions and emergencies in which he consulted with none. And on this ...bject he calculated no consequences—he considered it immaterial if the whole Senate should get up as one man, and vote against it. So strong were his convictions of the propriety of submit[ting] it, that he would present it at the hazard of all consequences.

The presentation of the Alabama resolutions afforded him an opportunity of giving this public notice, which he had often given privately here. He had told hon. members that he should, at a convenient time, move this resolution. On yesterday evening when he saw an attempt made to give to the report of the Committee upon the General Post Office, such a course and destination as was to eventuate in a legislative measure here, and when an attempt was made by the two Senators from South Carolina, to have this measure followed up by something else, which was to be a proceeding upon persons in contradistinction to the subject matter of the report, and in reality was an impeachment in the form of legislation, he then determined to give notice, that at a convenient time, he would offer a resolution to expunge the resolution of censure from the journal. This was an answer to the inquiry.

Mr. KING, of Alabama, said that he thought it was so well understood that the gentleman from Missouri had it in contemplation to offer the resolution he had just spoken of, that he was surprised when the gentleman from Kentucky asked him whether he was disposed to offer it. He could only say, that having voted againt the resolution of censure, he had supposed that his opinions on the subject both then and since were well understood. The Legislature of Alabama had instructed him to do that which would have made it his duty to have brought such a resolution before the Senate, if the gentleman from Missouri had declined doing so. He would in that event have introduced it, embracing as well that subject as the right of instruction. He held that right in its fullest extent. For he held it, not impugning the opinions of others who thought differently. But viewing that right as he did, he should feel himself bound to carry the wishes of his constituents into effect when fairly and fully made known. His course with regard to the resolution complained of, was well known, and therefore, the instructions from the Legislature of Alabama scarcely applied to him. If the movement depended upon him, he should have been disposed to have suffered it to sleep where it was, if the subject had not been urged upon him. But, if it was not brought foward, he should feel himself bound to bring it forward, and when that should be done he would of course vote for it. If there were precedents for it, as he believed there were, he should vote for expunging the objectionable resolution from the journal. He might hesitate as to the mode of doing it, but he would do every thing to effect it, in fact.

Mr. CLAY said that the gentleman from Alabama presented these instructions from the Legislature of Alabama, unaccompanied by any motion to submit a resolution to expunge in accordance with the instructions, and he (Mr. C.) felt quite surprised that the gentleman should not have expected the inquiry which he had made. The inquiry was addressed to that gentleman, and him only. As to the answer which had been given by another Senator, it was known that his relations with him were not of such a character as would enable him to know his purposes. But he hoped these resolutions would be withdrawn for the present; and after the hon. gentleman had made a careful examination of the Constitution of the United States upon the subject of each House keeping a record of its proceedings, if he then thought proper to present them with the resolution proposed, he could do so. For himself, he should think it his duty to his God and his country to oppose such a proposition at the very threshold. He submitted to the gentleman the propriety of withdrawing the resolutions for the present.

Mr. MOORE said, he had not anticipated any discussion would arise upon the presentation of the resolutions from the General Assembly of Alabama, but, as it had so unexpectedly occurred, he would beg leave to say a word or two only.

Sir, said Mr. M., his colleague might have saved himself the trouble of informing the Senate that the resolutions were not intended to influence his conduct on the subject of the expunging resolution; his willingness to vote in conformity with the instructions would not be doubted here or elsewhere. Mr. M. said he was free to admit that he in all probability was entitled to the honor of having given rise to the resolutions, because, he said, he had, in the exercise of his honest convictions of propriety, on some few occasions been compelled to vote differently from his colleague, and possibly on the question referred to by the resolutions; he entertained, however, the same views now that he entertained then.

Mr. M. said, as regarded the right of instruction, he admitted it to the fullest extent ever claimed, as practised upon by the republican party since the establishment of the Government; that right, however, abided with the people as the source of all power. The sovereign people, he said, had the legitimate right, either by themselves or their agents, at their own instance, to instruct their Senators upon matters of policy connected with their interest; these agents, however, as they were only public servants themselves, must also act in pursuance of the will of the sovereign people.

As regarded any matter involving constitutional questions, Mr. M felt himself bound by higher and paramount obligations to his conscience. But upon all questions of policy, he would be found acknowledging the right of instruction by the the people, and the corresponding obligation on the public servant to obey.

Mr. KING expressed his unwillingness to provoke a discussion, or to go further than to move to lay the resolutions on the table: this he would do. He could not accede to the proposition of the gentleman from Kentucky to withdraw them. When he should feel it his duty to call them up, he would introduce such a resolution as he thought proper. And when he thought fit, he would bring the subject forward, and the honorable gentleman would have an opportunity of discharging his duty to his country and his God, by opposing it.

Mr. MOORE said the resolutions did not require either him or his colleague to bring forward a resolution to expunge. They seemed to contemplate that such a resolution would be brought forward. But he submitted to his honorable colleague, whether he would not consider it his duty to introduce a resolution.

Mr. CLAY asked whether it was not better to withdraw the resolutions, and offer them to-morrow.

Mr. PRESTON said that the honorable gentleman from Missouri made reference to the debate of yesterday, and stated that on account of the remarks of the Senators of South Carolina, he felt it to be his duty, earlier than he intended, to submit his resolution. Not having investigated his motives, he was surprised at the connexion which was made by him between the two subjects. Last night he (Mr. P.) stated, that upon the report of the honorable Chairman, (Mr. Grundy,) there could be but one opinion, and therefore that some expression of the Senate should be made upon the subject-matter of it; and the hon gentleman supposed that as he (Mr. P.) was not content with prospective legislation, that he required that some course should be pursued upon the persons implicated in the Department, and that, therefore, the gentleman intended to introduce his resolution. Was it thought that, because he chose to censure the Post Office Department, that a measure should be introduced here to censure the Senate of the United States Admit that the Senate had done wrong, upon what principle would you introduce a censure of the Senate here? Were his lips to be closed, as a Senator of the U. States, in pronouncing censure upon a notoriously corrupt and insolvent Department, because the Senate itself was not free from blame before the people? The gentleman was mistaken, too, in supposing that he intended to censure persons. From the bottom of his heart, he hoped that the head of the Department was free from blame. And, as the honorable Chairman of the committee himself thought that only malfeasance existed there, he would say, neither that gentleman, nor the gentleman from Missouri, had failed to vote at the last session for just such a resolution as he proposed.

[Here Mr. P. read the resolution passed session, declaring the borrowing of money by Post Office Department to be unconstitut

and the ayes and noes upon its passage.]

Mr. P. resumed. The very first name upon the list, he said, was that of the honorable member from Missouri, in the affirmative, in which be had given his authority for the resolution. There could be no stronger argument for censuring the head of a Department than this resolution. We could not differ in regard to these matters. Great blame rested some where, and the affairs of the office demanded reform; and when the Executive claimed to supervise the Executive Departments, and declined to exert his powers to correct such abuses, he thought it necessary that he should reiterate that these were evils which he might correct, or the people should interfere. Whenever he knew there was corruption, he would brand the guilty with it—ay, even to the President of the United States. He thought if there was a unanimous vote upon such a resolution as he suggested, there would be a clearing out at the Department; that the power of the Executive would be interposed to correct the evils which had been exposed. He would not pause here to inquire into the constitutionality of the power of expunging from the records what one party may have done, which was obnoxious to the other party. Nor whether it would be considered less imperative to have it expunged if it applied to a subordinate officer, rather than the Chief Executive He knew that "a saint in crape was twice a saint in lawn." With him there was no difference in rank between the President and a subordinate officer, in making such an inquiry. He said yesterday, that his party had been beaten down. We were not, it was true, in a minority here, but we should shortly be, and should every thing we had done, then be expunged? He hoped and believed that this Government was to live long, but what would it avail to expose and denounce that Post Office? Could such denunciation and exposure affect the great popularity of the President? The man must have a more ardent spirit than he professed to have, who could believe it. No, sir. If it was blackened with a ten fold deeper die than both of the reports together gave it, it would not affect this Administration. When one of the reports stated that one mail contractor had received $100,000 which was not accounted for, and showed that the flood-gates of corruption were opened, the very exposure would tend to strengthen the Administration.

Mr. BENTON said, he could not but regret his extreme poverty of speech, which prevented him from giving his opinions so as to be understood by those who sat nearest to him; and if he was so unfortunate as to be incomprehensible to these, how much more so must he have been to those at a greater distance. In all he said yesterday as to the additional proceedings proposed to be instituted against the Post Office, there was neither retaliation threatened, nor the intention of intimidating any one, even if he were capable of doing so, or the honorable gentleman could be intimidated by any thing he could say. But his design was to keep things of the same sort together. When he saw an attempt made to bring the friends of the administration to act as they did on a former occasion, then he thought proper to bring up the debate upon that expurgation which he had proposed. Although that resolution which the honorable gentleman read from the journal was pressed through at the heel of the session, and was adopted in the dark, yet it was not in darkness to his mental vision. He saw then with the same distinctness of vision, which he saw now, that two hooks were thrown out on which his party were to be hung. If the conduct of Mr. Barry should be condemned, then it should be proclaimed aloud, that it was so indefensible that even his friends could not support him, and we were to be hung on that hook. If we voted against the resolution, we were to hang ourselves on the other hook, as the defenders of this black, rotten, damned administration. He saw the two hooks thrown out then, and when he saw the same process about to be repeated last night, it was that which brought him to his feet. The honorable [illegible] from South Carolina farthest from him, [illegible]un,) said it was his intention to introduce [illegible]solution, in order that it might be seen who would here defend the guilt and blackness of the Post Office. That gentleman had no right to assume that any one here would defend what was wrong. It was unjustifiable in him to assume, that such a state of things as he had described, would find any defenders here. But if such a resolution as had been suggested, against persons, should be brought in, he should protest against it; and he would either be excused from voting in his place, or if that was not permitted him, he would vote against it. If all the resolutions of last session, which were brought in by the Post Office Committee, had been separately put to the question, he would have voted upon each one of them. On some ay, on others no, according to his sense of justice and right. He had looked over that vast mass of documents in one night, in order to prepare himself to give his votes upon them. But it was because he did not mean to be hung on the same hook again, that he gave notice of his design to bring up his resolution—it was not for the purpose of intimidation or retaliation, but for the purpose of raising the preliminary discussion as to the right to bring up this condemnation of persons without a formal impeachment by the House of Representatives. He wished to be distinctly comprehended on another point. He was not to be understood either by implication or by a direct vote to sanction any thing which he did not sanction, neither by implication resulting from a vote of his own or the arguments of any gentleman. Bring up the Post Office in any shape which was constitutional, and he would vote with alacrity upon it according to his sense of right or wrong. But bring it up unconstitutionally, and he would give it his zealous opposition. Whether tried before this tribunal or another, he had but one measure of justice for the Bank of the United States and the Post Office Department.

Mr. PRESTON disclaimed having hung out two hooks to hang any body. He confessed that such was his want of perspicacity that he did not understand the honorable gentleman from Missouri.

Mr. CALHOUN said he rose to move to lay the resolutions on the table, to afford the gentleman from Alabama an opportunity to prepare his resolution to expunge. He had some curiosity to see how the gentleman would reconcile a proposition to expunge, with the constitution of the United States, which said that a journal of the proceedings of this body should be kept. He would like to see a resolution which proposed to rep al a journal—to repeal a fact. He wanted to see the form of the resolution. The principle involved in it was, that we had no right to express our opinions of the conduct of executive officers, or any other officers; and thus affirming the maxim that the King could do no wrong—that his ministers only were responsible for his conduct. And this was the doctrine of the democratic party. He wished to see the extraordinary extremities to which Senators must be reduced in this effort to expunge the journals. The thing could not be done, but the Senate itself might be expunged. And if that should be done by the madness of party, this Government was at an end. He was anxious to see who would attempt to carry out the doctrines of the protest of last year—doctrines as despotic as those which were held by the Autocrat of all the Russias.

Mr. CLAY here said he considered the debate very irregular. He entertained the opinion that these resolutions should not be received at all; and therefore if they were not withdrawn for the present, he proposed to submitted this resolution:

Resolved, That the instructions of the Legislature of Alabama, presented by the Senator from that State, ought not to be acted upon by the Senate, inasmuch as they are not addressed to the Senate, nor contain any request that they be laid before the Senate; and inasmuch, also, as that which those resolutions direct should be done, cannot be done without violating the constitution of the United States.

Mr. CLAYTON said, that so long ago as December, 1830, he had moved an investigation of the Post Office Department—that on that occasion the vials of wrath were poured out on himself and the late Senator from Maine, (Mr. Holmes.) He wished to refer the honorable Senator (Mr. Benton) to that debate. It was then proposed to expunge the proceedings of that day from the journals of the Senate. The Senator from Louisiana, now on a foreign mission, played a part in that farce. It was then this plan of expunging was begun; and had it then been adopted, should we now have succeeded in obtaining these reports—in prosecuting this investigation? He hoped they should learn wisdom from experience. He believed the proposition to expunge perfectly ridiculous. How, said Mr. C., can it be done! I am at a loss to conceive what method would be adopted. The Journals of the Senate have been printed and distributed among the members of this body. If any gentleman wished to expunge an obnoxious article, let him tear it out; but if I, on the contrary, am disposed to retain it, how is it to be expunged from my copy? For I protest no man shall despoil my property. I hope, Mr. President, no such proposition will ever be made.

Mr. BENTON said, if the gentleman from South Carolina, who had just sat down, had not spoken again, it would not have been necessary for him to have risen again. He opposed the inquiry, as being a criminal inquiry made into the conduct of the Postmaster General, upon the ground that the House of Representatives were the Grand Inquest of the Nation, and that we should reserve ourselves until the accusation should be presented in such a shape that we could act upon it as judges. That was the view he took of it. And now, whether he had two measures for the Bank and the Post Office, he would leave to others to judge. For [illegible] years he had been opposed to the Bank of the U. States, and at any period of that time, if he had chosen, he might have had a committee appointed, and according to parliamentary usage, the committee would have been of his political opinions. He had a right to ask it, and that upon strict parliamentary principles. But did he ask it? No; and on the ground that the House of Representatives was the grand inquest of the nation, and because all inquiries into malfeasances ought, properly, to orignate there. But if he ever should do it, it would be because he could perceive no other remedy. With regard to the manner of expunging the journals, which seemed to be so difficult of comprehension by honorable gentlemen, he would say, that in a State contiguous to Georgia, a journal had been burnt. Need he refer to the celebrated case of Wilkes, in which the journal was expunged, not by the childish operation of sending out and having all the copies brought in, and the offensive parts torn out, but by taking up the journal of the House, and having the offensive part read, and then expunging it. Not by marking a St. Andrews cross upon it, but by an entire obliteration of it, line by line. So that the honorable gentleman would see there could be no difficulty either as to the modus operandi, or the constitutionality. One journal had been burnt, and the other had been entirely obliterated. But we had got the Post Office upon us now, and he begged to say that should not divert him from his course. "Sufficient for the day was the evil thereof." Nothing either in or out of the House should throw him off his track. He should move on in that journal with the precision of a steam engine, and nothing should prevail to throw him from his track.

Mr. CALHOUN. The honorable Senator, (Mr. Benton,) said he had the same measure for the Bank and the Post Office. He had succeeded in setting the President against the Bank, but had not yet succeeded in setting him against the Post Office. He wished these resolutions to be laid on the table for the present, to give the gentleman an opportunity to introduce this matter. He renewed the motion to lay on the table, and refused to withdraw it.

bama resolutions

Mr. CALHOUN was opposed the motion.

Mr. KING, of Alabama expressed a wish for an opportunity to make some remarks in rep

honorable member from Kentucky. He (Mr. K) would bring forward such a resolution as the instructions contemplated, and the honorable Senator should be gratified. The gentleman from South Carolina asked whether it was proposed to repeal a fact. The resolution of censure was no fact. When the Senate adopted a resolution which we believed and the people believed was not founded in fact, had we not the power to repeal it? He would say to the gentleman, that the Democracy of this land had spoken and pronounced their condemnation of that proceeding, and the Legislature of Alabama had said to their Senators, if you have the power of expunging it from your journals, do so; if not, so as far as you can, and not suffer a condemnation of the Executive Magistrate to remain there which is in violation of the constitution of the United States. They said, let not a declaration, that the Chief Magistrate had violated the constitution, remain there. He had hoped on a former occasion, when the honorable gentleman declared that he would act for the country, that he would have little more to do with party, but he had since manifested a very different feeling. He had no expectation that the resolutions which he had introduced would have caused this discussion. But an attempt had been made to smother up the Post Office subject with these resolutions. And did it comport with the gravity of the Senate to denounce the Administration of the Government, and rush into the discussion with such unreasonable haste? When time was afforded for examining the documents, he would go as far as any man to punish the guilty. But it had been said that the President held himself responsible for the conduct of his Executive officers. And so was so when the facts came authentically before him. And he would now undertake to say that when they came fairly before him, the President would not hesitate to apply the proper correctives, and do exact justice. He would vouch for his pursuing that course. He would serve the country with that zeal, faithfulness, and devotion, which had always characterized him, by punishing every individual under his control, who was proved to be guilty.

Mr. CALHOUN would not, he said, have risen here, had not a personal allusion been made to him. He was accused of acting under the influence of party spirit. But he utterly disclaimed all such motives. The principles he had voluntarily professed and supported for eight years past were sufficient proof of it. He had voluntarily withdrawn from the side of popular opinion in his action and associated himself with a feeble minority of not more than one in a hundred, not to his own benefit; but as the result had proved, now for the benefit of the honorable Senator himself, (Mr. King, of Alab.) I am not a party man, said Mr. C. I have no purpose to serve; I am no desire to be here. But, as long as it is the will of the People of South Carolina that I should serve them, I shall obey. Sir, continued Mr. C. would not turn upon my heel to be intrusted with the management of the Government. If one has to go into the reformation of these abuses it would not be sustained. The evil is ingrafted upon the very vitals of our political institutions. It cannot be cured by a Presidential election, but by legislative enactments. I am no party man. Sir, I stand here as a citizen of the U. States, or rather as a representative of South Carolina.

The resolutions, and the motion to print, were laid on the table.

Mr. SMITH then moved to lay the motion to print on the table, upon which Mr. HILL demanded the ayes and noes, and they were ordered, and was as follows, to wit.

YEAS—Messrs. Bell, Bibb, Black, Calhoun, Clay, Clayton, Ewing, Frelinghuysen, Goldsborough, Hendricks, Kent, Knight, Leigh, Mangum, Naudain, Poindexter, Porter, Prentiss, Robbins, Silsbee, Smith, Southard, Swift, Tomlinson, Tyler, Waggaman, Webster.—27.

NAYS—Messrs. Benton, Brown, Buchanan, Cuthbert, Grundy, Hill, Kane, King of Ala. King of Georgia, Linn, McKean, Moore, Morris, Preston,

Robinson, Shepley, Tallmadge, Tipton, White, Wright.—20.

So the question was determined in the affirmative, and the whole matter was laid upon the table.

Mr. CLAY then gave notice that when the subject should be moved again, he would move the following resolution:

Resolved, That the instructions of the Legislature of Alabama, presented by the Senator from that State ought not to be acted upon by the Senate, inasmuch as they are not addressed to the Senate, nor contain any request that they be laid before the Senate; and inasmuch, also, as that which those resolutions direct should be done, cannot be done without violating the constitution of the United States.

Mr. SMITH then submitted the following resolution:

Resolved, That the General Post Office is deeply in debt—its affairs in great disorder—its accounts and reports irregular, unsatisfactory, and in many instances untrue—that large sums of public money have been wasted and paid over to favored individuals upon false pretences, and that its conduct and administration are justly the subjects of public complaint, and demand a radical reform.

Mr. GRUNDY then renewed his motion to print the reports of the Committee and documents, which led to a considerable discussion, in which Messrs. GRUNDY, CLAYTON, EWING, LEIGH, WEBSTER, CALHOUN, PORTER, and HILL, participated.

Several motions to print were made, rising from 7500 to 10 and 20,000.

Upon the motion to print 20,000 copies of the reports and documents made by Mr. WEBSTER, Mr. HILL asked the yeas and nays, which were ordered and are as follows:

YEAS—Messrs. Bell, Bibb, Calhoun, Clay, Clayton, Ewing, Frelinghuysen, Goldsborough, Kent, Knight, Mangum, Moore, Naudain, Poindexter, Porter, Prentiss, Robbins, Robinson, Silsbee, Sm th, Southard, Tomlinson, Waggaman, Webster—24.

NAYS—Messrs. Benton, Black, Brown, Buchanan, Cuthbert, Grundy, Hendricks, Hill, Kane, King of Alabama, King of Georgia, Leigh, Linn, McKean, Morris, Preston, Shepley, Tallmadge, Tipton, Tyler, White, Wright.—22.

FRENCH SPOLIATIONS.

Mr. WEBSTER then moved that the Senate take up the bill making compensation for French spoliations prior to 1800, which was agreed to.

The question being upon ordering the bill to be engrossed for a third reading.

Mr. WEBSTER demanded the yeas and nays; which were ordered, and are as follows:

YEAS—Messrs. Bell, Buchanan, Clay, Clayton, Ewing, Frelinghuysen, Goldsborough, Kent, Knight, McKean, Moore, Naudain, Poindexter, Porter, Prentiss, Preston, Robbins, Shepley, Silsbee, Smith, Southard, Swift, Tomlinson, Waggaman, Webster—25.

NAYS—Messrs. Benton, Bibb, Black, Brown, Calhoun, Cuthbert, Grundy, Hendricks, Hill, Kane, King of Alabama, King of Georgia, Leigh, Linn, Mangum, Morris, Robinson, Tallmadge, Tyler, White, Wright—21.

Mr. CLAYTON then gave notice, that at one o'clock to-morrow, he would move the Senate to go into the consideration of Executive business.

On motion of Mr. WEBSTER,

The Senate adjourned.

HOUSE OF REPRESENTATIVES.
WEDNESDAY, JAN. 28, 1835.

Mr. JOHNSON, of Kentucky, from the Committee on Military Affairs, reported, a bill to authorize the Secretary of War to purchase a site for an arsenal at Memphis, Tennessee, and to provide for the erection of an arsenal on the same; which was twice read and committed.

Mr. THOMSON, from the Committee on Military Affairs, reported, without amendment, the

bill from the Senate, for the relief of the heirs of Col. Jean Hudry; which was committed.

Mr. WISE, from the Committee on Naval Affairs, reported the following joint resolution, which was read twice:

be and he is hereby authorized to constitute a Board of Naval Officers, to be composed of the Post Captains, whose duty it shall be, in conjunction with the Secretary of the Navy, to revise the code of Naval Signals.

Mr. WISE, from the Committee on Naval Affairs.

Mr. VINTON, from the Committee on Roads and Canals, reported a bill amendatory of the act for the continuation of the Cumberland road; which was twice read and committed.

Mr. CLAY, from the Committee on the Public Lands, reported, without amendment, a bill from the Senate, to remove the Land Office from Clinton to Jackson, in the State of Mississippi; which was ordered to be read a third time.

Mr. WILLIAMS, from the Committee on the Public Lands, reported a bill to authorize the removal of the Land Office from Wapakhaneta to Lima, in the State of Ohio; which was read twice and ordered to be engrossed.

Mr. FOSTER, from the Committee on the Judiciary, reported a bill to prescribe the punishment of Consuls, Vice Consuls, and Commercial Agents; which was read twice.

Mr. ROBERTSON remarked that there was one feature of the bill, which he considered of great interest and importance, and in which he did not concur with the Committee. He would, therefore, move so to amend the bill, as that the fine and imprisonment provided by it, should be left to the discretion of a jury, instead of the Court.

Mr. FOSTER remarked that the gentleman had moved a similar amendment in the committee. Several members were disposed to favor it; but a majority of the Committee were of opinion that this should not be made an exception to the general rule of proceeding in cases of a similar character.

Mr. ROBERTSON remarked, that the State from which he came held the trial by Jury as a sacred principle, and he was unwilling in this case to yield that principle, and vest the decision in one man. It proposed to give to the Court, a discretion, which he thought dangerous and improper, and which should be left to a jury of the country.

The amendment was disagreed to, and the bill ordered to be engrossed.

Mr. ASHLEY, from the Committee on the Public Lands, reported a bill for the relief of the signees of Peter Albar; which was read twice committed.

Mr. ASHLEY, from the same Committee reported a bill to authorize the sale of certain belonging to a University in Michigan; which read twice and ordered to be engrossed.

Mr. ASHLEY moved the printing of part which he then presented to the House, in relation to the extension of the boundary line of the State of Missouri; which was agreed to.

Mr. ADAMS, of N. Y., from the Committee on Invalid Pensions, reported a bill granting a sion to Justus Cobb; which was read twice, and committed.

Mr. ADAMS, from the same committee, reported a bill for the relief of Lambert L. Vanburg; which was read twice, and committed.

Mr. ALLAN, of Ky., instructed by the committee on Territories, asked the House to se Thursday, the 5th February, for the consideration of bills relating to the Territories.

After some conversation between Mr. POLK, ALLAN, WARDWELL, SEVIER, LAND, and WHITE, in relation to the various measures which remained unacted on, Mr. LAND suggested that the second Mond

February be set apart for the consideration of the bills alluded to.

Mr. ALLAN accepted the amendment as a modification of his motion; when the proposition was agreed to.

Unfavorable reports upon various petitions, &c. were made by Messrs. GILLET, J. Q. ADAMS, THOMSON, McKIM, TOMPKINS, and FUL- from various standing committees

ADAMS, of Massachusetts, offered the fol- resolution, which, under the rule, lies one

olved, That the President of the United be requested to communicate to this House, incompatible with the public interest, any spondence with the Government of France, ny despatches received from the Minister of nited States at Paris, not hitherto communi- to the House, in relation to the failure of rench Government to carry into effect any stipulation of the treaty of the 4th of July, 1831.

Mr. FERRIS offered the following resolution, which, under the rule, lies one day:

Resolved, That the Secretary of the Treasury be requested to furnish this House with the Re- of the Solicitor of the Treasury, together all the documents relative to the compromise claims of the United States against Thomas ith and Son, and their securities.

motion of Mr. THOMAS, of Maryland,

olved, That the Committee on Roads and s be instructed to inquire into the expedien- f aiding, to relieve from embarrassment, the apeake and Ohio Canal Company, by grant- and releasing, for the benefit of the other tholders, the stock now held therein by the ed States.

Petitions and memorials were presented by Messrs J. Q. ADAMS, EWING, ARCHER, and H. EVERETT. Referred.

Mr. POLK called for the orders of the day; agreed to.

When the orders of the day were called,

Mr. POPE reminded the House, that about ten days since, he had given notice that he would, on this day, move the House to resolve itself into Committee of the Whole on the state of the Union, to consider the bill reported by him in relation to the Louisville and Portland canal. As the appropriation bill was still under discussion, he would postpone his motion until that bill was disposed of.

The amendments of the Senate to the bill of the House for the adjustment of land claims in Louisiana, were concurred in.

The bill for the benefit of the city of Alexandria, came up upon the motion to reconsider the vote whereby it was rejected.

On motion of Mr. MERCER, it was postponed until to-morrow.

GENERAL APPROPRIATION BILL.

The House then resumed the consideration of the bill making appropriations for the civil and di- atic expenses of Government for the year

question was on the amendment offered . VANCE, proposing to repeal the second n of the law of 1834 (which gives to cer- ubordinate officers of the customs the same uments as they received prior to the reduc- of duties in 1832) to limit their compensation, oblige them to report annually the amount of pensation by fees, &c. received by them, to- her with an amendment thereto, securing to the same emoluments as they received in , &c

r. WISE said, his object in rising was merely ate some facts, as he was led to believe from emarks he had heard yesterday, that the did not fully understand the manner in our revenue officers were paid. The re- upon the subject was calculated to mislead deceive. The gentleman from North C- (Mr. Williams) had cited the enormous f $6000 as the amount received by a single r or guager. The truth was, no such sum d. Previous to the reduction of the tariff, ghers received 37½ cents per ton, but t reduction their fees were reduced to a adequate compensation. In 1833, Congress law making their fees the same as if the duties had not been reduced, and limiting their income to $2000 per annum. You will find it stated in the report and in the Blue Book that one weigher received upwards of $2000, while another received but $330. The truth was, the one received precisely the same as the other,—averaging $133.80. He put it to the House to say whether this amount was sufficient if they would have respectable and responsible officers. The city of New York was divided into thirteen districts—many of those officers were obliged to go from one to two miles to attend to their duties. In the first place, his house rent should be estimated at least at $450; his fuel at $150; his clothing at $125. This amount might be put to his individual expenses, to which should be added his food, which he is compelled to procure at the eating houses near the scene of his duties, $125. One dollar was surely a moderate estimate of his daily family expenses, making $365 per annum; the clothing of his family might be estimated at $125, and $150 for purposes of education. Thus we have for his yearly expenses the sum of $1490, exclusive of various other items which it would be difficult to enumerate.

Mr. W. said, he would go with the gentleman to restrict the compensation of these officers to the sum of $2000 per annum. They could not receive more under the present law. He believed the poor and pillaging system of paying salaries, which he was sorry to see have so many advocates on that floor this year, was the most unwise and corrupting system in the world. If you set up these offices to the lowest bidder, you would have some very respectable looking men giving in the figure naught; but they would find the ways and means of paying themselves a higher salary than that now allowed. A weigher of sugar, for instance, could make a cask weigh as much when one half of its contents was taken out as it did before. So with wine, returned for a drawback. The cask might be filled with water. A custom house oath was considered by many as the least of all moral obligations. He knew individuals who would smuggle, while he believed them otherwise to be men of honesty and integrity. He hoped that Congress would do justice to these officers, and also do justice to the Government, by securing an honest collection of the revenue, by giving them an adequate compensation.

Mr. JARVIS said he had an amendment to propose, to which he belived the gentleman from Ohio would not object. It was as follows:

"*Provided*, That the whole number of Custom House officers in the United States, on the first of February, 1834, shall not be increased till otherwise allowed by Congress."

Mr. J. said, his object was to empower the Secretary of the Treasury, in conjunction with the Collectors of Customs, to apportion to places where they might be required, Custom-house officers at present in the service. The amendment of the gentleman from Ohio, if adopted, would not permit the Secretary of the Treasury, or the Collectors, however necessary it might be for the public service, to send an inspector to any exposed point, unless there should be an excess in one district. What Mr. J. wanted, was to impower these persons to transfer from one district to another when requisite, which they would be enabled to do under the provision under consideration. If, for instance, there be too many inspectors in the district of New York, and too few in the district of New Haven, he wished to give the Secretary of the Treasury the power of reducing them in the former, and increasing them in the latter. At present, he had the power of decreasing in New York, but he had not the power, provided the amendment of the gentleman from Ohio be adopted, of adding any inspectors in any district, however necessary it might be. Mr. J. presumed the gentleman did not design so to curb and restrain the power of the Secretary of the Treasury.

Mr. VANCE supposed the proviso was a proper one, and he would adopt it.

Mr. JARVIS wished to say a few words in reply to the gentleman from Virginia (Mr. Wise.) The argument used by that gentleman in regard to weighers and gaugers, went farther, perhaps, than he intended; for it applied equally well, and indeed better, to the inspectors. The latter received a *per diem* allowance which, by law, could not exceed three dollars a day, making $1095 per annum. Now, if the weigher and gauger could not live for less than three thousand dollars a year, how were the inspectors to live for a little more than one thousand? They had as many mouths to feed, and as many children to educate, and the responsibility upon them was greater than upon the weighers and gaugers. Mr. J. agreed with the gentleman from Virginia, that it was in the power of the last to defraud the Government by making false returns, and entering a full hogshead of sugar when it was perhaps only half full, or a pipe of wine when its contents might be nothing but water, and procuring the drawback upon the same. But the inspector could, if disposed, go a little further. By law, the inspector was compelled to certify that the goods specified had been actually put on board; but he might certify, without any thing being put on board at all. He might give his certificate, and the exporting merchant would receive the whole amount of duties, when *none* of the goods were on board. This was no imaginary case; for it had fallen under Mr. J.'s own experience. He had known cases where teas were alleged to have been on board, where there was nothing but empty chests, or with stones in them, and wine exported, where not a single pint had gone out of the country.

Mr. J. wished this matter had come up in a better shape, and was sorry that the necessity of having such an amendment introduced in an appropriation should exist; but he was satisfied that unless it was put into an appropriation bill, there was very little chance of any reform ever being made in our custom-house system. It was when officers in the larger ports felt a pressure, that we were to look for action in that House, and not before; and although he was at no time disposed to encumber appropriation bills in this way, yet, as there was never any difficulty of encumbering them with extraneous matter when the object was to draw money out of the Treasury, he could not feel himself adverse to it when the object was to retain money therein.

Mr. HARPER of Penn., stated the process in the port of Philadelphia, which was usually performed by the deputy weighers and laborers, the principal weigher rarely being in attendance, for there was but one for that port. Therefore, all idea about dividing the fees among a number of persons was imaginary, at least as respected the city of Philadelphia. The principal weigher had little discretion compared with the inspectors, who received a compensation of three dollars a day. As soon as a vessel arrived in port, an inspector was put on board, and it was his duty to permit nothing to be taken away without his certificate. The goods for drawback are put on shore, under his control, and placed in custom-house stores or warehouses, and secured under two locks, one key to be kept by him, and the other by the merchant, and the door could not be opened without the presence of both. If the inspector was disposed to connive at fraud, he could do so, but the weigher had no means of doing it. Then, if $1,335 be not enough to keep one honest, how would $1000 be sufficient to keep the other so.

Mr. H. contended further, that the gentleman from Virginia had made a very exaggerated statement in regard to the expense of living in these places. A house amply sufficient for a man of this description could be rented at one-half the sum set down, and the expense of fuel was also too much. But his principal objection was the giving one man a salary of $1000 to perform as much or more labor than another who was to receive $2000. Mr. H. agreed that some legislation on this subject was necessary, and that there might be particular places where the compensation would be found too small, but if officers themselves thought so, we should soon have a multiplicity of applications from them for a remedy.

Mr. McKIM said he had been to the Treasury Department that morning, for the purpose of procuring a return of what the compensation of the Custom-house officers really was. The fees received in Baltimore, Mr. McK. was understood to

say, amounted last year to only $433, making the whole compensation only $1433, and this was the exorbitant salary complained of by several gentlemen. In Baltimore there was but one weigher, and his salary last year was $1917, and out of that he had to pay all the laberers and clerks employed by him Mr. McK. thought the collector of every port should receive a certain fixed salary, and he believed if a plan of that kind was adopted, the country would be a gainer of some thirty or forty thousand dollars, but he thought the general appropriation bill an improper place for it. He therefore trusted that the amendment would not prevail, but that the Committee on Commerce would be permitted to introduce a bill to regulate the whole subject.

Mr. WISE made a brief reply to Messrs. Jarvis and Harper, and said the argument used by the latter did not apply. It did not prove that the compensation of the weighers was too much, but that the inspectors received too little Did any gentleman believe that the inspectors of Philadelphia or New York received no more than three dollars a day? No such thing. Mr. W. defended the accuracy of the statements he had read with regard to the expenses of living, &c. and hoped the House would leave the matter alone in the appropriation bill, and authorize the passage of a special bill on the subject.

Mr. HARPER said a few words in defence of the character of the Custom-house officers of Philadelphia.

Mr. SUTHERLAND said he had one word to say with regard to the allusions which had been made against this class of public officers. He was acquainted with many of them whose characters were unimpeachable. One of them in Philadelphia was an officer of the army during the last war, and he had no hesitation in saying that his reputation stood as high as that of any individual on that floor, or elsewhere. Mr. S. concurred in the opinion of the honorable gentleman from Virginia, (Mr. Wise,) that the salaries of these officers should be established on a more liberal basis. After going into an expose of the inadequacy of the pay of some of the officers employed, Mr. S. said he did not feel it expedient to embark in this argument, as he believed the whole subject was agitated in the wrong place. It did not properly belong to the appropriation bill. The Committee of Commerce had the subject in their custody, and he pledged himself that if the appropriation bill was left unincumbered with the amendment, they would introduce a bill embracing the whole subject.

Mr. BURGES said he had heretofore said nothing on this subject, and it had been his intention to have said nothing, but he could not consent to stand and hear members sneered at, because in their views of liberality and economy, they thought fifteen hundred dollars an adequate compensation. He had been told that these officers in New York could not live on $3 per day. It had been suggested on that floor, a few days ago, that a distinguished officer, if he was not satisfied with his pay, should have resigned. The same rule should apply to these individuals. But no—they still hang on to the Custom House—an army of them—and ten or fifteen thousand recruits could easily be enlisted. He could not subscribe to the argument of the gentleman from Virginia, (Mr. Wise,) that it was necessary to increase the salaries of officers, to keep them honest. He never knew that plan to succeed. Money could not purify the sordid soul. If this doctrine was to prevail, it would be better to give up all our institutions—give up society, and revert back to the savage state.

Mr. B. said he was willing to pay the officers of the United States as other men were paid, and no more; but if gentlemen would look around them, they would see they were paid at least fifty per cent. more. But the House had been told that the Committee on Commerce was about to bring in a bill to provide for this subject. It had long been promised, and there appeared to be no immediate accomplishment of the promise. He would, therefore, vote to place the additional sum in the appropriation bill, to crowd the officers until they should crowd that Committee to its duty.

Mr. MANN, of New York, said that he was not about to debate this question; but he wished, in justice to himself, to assign a reason for the vote he intended to give. He was fully sensible that the subject of the compensation of the collectors of the customs, and their assistants, required attention and regulation. He was the more sensible of this, from having read, with some care, the report of the Secretary of the Treasury on this subject. But he was well informed that the Finance Committee of the Senate are now engaged in a laborious examination of the subject, and that they would probably report to the Senate very soon, and he felt assured that, from the unanimity believed to prevail with the Committee on the subject, their bill, covering the whole ground, would be sent to us in season for our action. He was, moreover, opposed to introducing into appropriation bills provisions so entirely foreign and inconsistent with their objects, and should therefore vote against the amendment.

Mr. HARPER followed with some remarks, in reply to Mr. SUTHERLAND.

Mr. SUTHERLAND rejoined. He concluded by again repeating that the Committee on Commerce had this subject under consideration, and would certainly introduce a bill, providing for the compensation of custom-house officers, if the amendment was rejected, in a very few days.

Mr. VANCE again addressed the House, in favor of his amendment, which he contended could do no harm, even if the projected bill from the Committee of Commerce should be introduced and passed; for in that case, the amendment would be annulled. He hoped the question would now be taken, as he was aware the House was weary of the subject.

The yeas and nays having been ordered on the question of adopting the amendment—

Mr. WILLIAMS moved a call of the House; but the call was not seconded by the House.

Mr. McKAY, (after suggesting a verbal amendment, which was adopted by Mr. Vance,) said, he last year voted against a similar provision to the present, in the appropriation bill, on the promise that a bill would be introduced by the Committee on Commerce, embracing the whole subject. It had not been done, and he should now vote for the amendment.

Mr. HALL, of North Carolina, said, like his colleague, (Mr. McKay,) he last year voted against this proposition. It was on the ground that it introduced strange and foreign matter into the appropriation bill, which was a bill *sui generis*—devoted to particular objects, which he enumerated. He should now vote against it on the same grounds.

Mr. J. Q. ADAMS gave similar reasons for voting against the amendment to those offered by the gentleman who last addressed the Chair, (Mr. Hall,) He also took this occasion to return his sincere thanks to the Committee of Ways and Means, for stripping the appropriation bills of all extraneous matter. It was certainly the wisest course of legislation.

Mr. SCHLEY said he believed some provision was necessary to regulate the pay of those engaged in the public revenue, to give them a sufficient compensation, and to restrict them from obtaining too much. If the amendment under consideration had been of a character consistent with the bill itself, and would have effected the object desired, he would have voted for it; but it was totally unconnected with any part of the bill, its subject, nor embraced or touched upon in a single clause of it; and therefore, Mr. S. could not vote for it. He was in favor of the principle it involved, and should vote against it only because it was introduced in an improper place.

The question on the amendment was then taken by yeas and nays, and resulted as follows: yeas 111, nays 91.

So the amendment was agreed to.

Mr. LINCOLN then moved to strike out the following clause: "For additional clerk hire for the year 1834, $38,355 84;" and entered into an elaborate argument to show that the provision was contrary to law; which had fixed the number of clerks, and that the Postmaster General was not warranted in employing the additional force—quoting the act of Congress, and making sundry references to the Blue Book, and other works.

Mr. WILLIAMS made a motion to adjourn—which was negatived—ayes 54, noes 79.

Mr. POLK said the question was embraced within a very small compass. It was well known to every one that the number of clerks provided by law was inadequate to perform the duties of the Post Office, and applications had been repeatedly made to Congress for additional aid, without success. But although Congress had refused to pass a law to authorize the extra number, it had uniformly sanctioned appropriations for extra clerk hire, from the year 1828 up to the present time, and for years preceding. Had gentlemen forgotten that in the debate of last year, a letter was produced from Judge McLean, the predecessor of the present Postmaster General, averring that the duties of the office could not be performed without the employment of additional force? The fault then lay not with the Post Office in asking for this appropriation, but with Congress, in refusing to authorize a sufficient number of clerks to execute the labors of that Department. If this were not done, what would be the consequence? Why that the work must be left undone. Congress must do one of two things, either provide additional force, or pay for extra clerk hire. If precedents were necessary, Mr. P. could adduce them, of extra clerk hire, granted long before the present time, upon the same principle as the one now called for.

Mr. P. said he was not a little astonished at the gentleman from Massachusetts, (Mr. Lincoln,) whose reputation came there in advance of him, that he should upon so plain a question, and one perfectly intelligible, have misunderstood himself. He takes up the blue book, and says here are seventy-five clerks engaged; while the law only authorizes thirty-eight, and what can be wanted of more? Now, did not the gentleman know that the number set down in the blue book, was the number actually employed last year in the Post Office, and that it was for labor done in 1834, that the appropriation under debate was asked? The labor had been performed, and Congress were told last year when the same item was under consideration, they must grant it, inasmuch as they had failed to provide the necessary force. Congress did grant it, and the work was done. Mr. P. contended that the Postmaster General was not culpable. Bills had been reported from time to time to provide additional and sufficient clerk hire, but they had not been acted on. A resolution was offered a few days ago, adopted by the House, and at that time under consideration in the Committee of Ways and Means, directing that committee to inquire and report what additional number of clerks would be requisite in all the various Departments, to perform the duties of those offices. He invoked the gentleman to come forward with his aid, as soon as the committee should report, which he trusted would be in a few days. They were preparing a bill to reduce the number of clerks where they could be spared, and to provide, by a permanent law, that the business of all the Departments should be substantially done. The committee will make a bold effort and bold appeal to the members of the House, and he called upon those disposed to censure the Departments, to stand up with them. To return to the Post Office; its business had been almost quadrupled since the act of 1828, limiting the number of clerks, and it impossible to do the work with that number. P. said, he hoped the House would not retard the passage of the appropriation bill longer was continually pressed by members of ties, to use his endeavors to get it through expidite the remaining business before the He hoped the House was preparted to vo at once, especially as the question was deci the last session by yeas and nays, and the ple was the same.

Mr. R M. JOHNSON, of Kentucky, would detain the House but a few moment was astonished at the memory of the wor honorable member from Massachusetts coln.) That gentleman's memory app very good in relation to the Post Off

ment, said he could not have forgotten that the same arguments which he had now advanced, were made and rebutted at the last session. Mr. J. said he stood there as the personal friend of the Post-master General, and he could not sit there and hear him denounced as a lawless man without re-pelling the charge.

Mr. LINCOLN explained. He had done certain acts, which he had specified, in violation of law, and was in that respect lawless.

Mr. JOHNSON continued. The gentleman might use such language as he pleased, and he should take the same privilege in reply.

The question was then taken on the motion of Mr. LINCOLN, and decided in the negative without a division.

Mr. BEAUMONT moved to strike out the appropriation of $2,000 for a library for the office of the Attorney General.

The motion was advocated by Messrs. BEAU-MONT and HARDIN, and decided by yeas and nays in the affirmative—ayes 114, noes 48.

Mr. McKAY then submitted an amendment, directing the kind of currency to be received in the collection of the revenue.

Mr. POLK said this was a literal copy of a provision in the former bill, and he had no objection to its adoption.

The amendment was agreed to, and the bill, with the amendments, was then ordered to be engrossed for a third reading to-morrow; whereupon, at half-past 4 o'clock,

The House adjourned.

IN SENATE.

THURSDAY, JAN. 29, 1835.

Petitions were presented by Messrs. GOLDS-BOROUGH, CLAYTON, and TOMLINSON, which were appropriately referred.

Mr. WAGGAMAN submitted the following resolutions:

Resolved, That the Committee on Commerce be instructed to inquire into the expediency of erecting a light-house at the mouth of the Bayou St John, in Louisiana.

Resolved, That a Select Committee on the part of the Senate, be appointed to inquire into the expediency of establishing a Branch of the Mint of the United States, at the city of New Orleans.

Mr. MOORE, from the Committee on Claims, reported a bill for the relief of Isaac Bronson, which was read the first time, and ordered to a second reading.

Mr. WEBSTER said he was instructed by the Committee on Finance, to move to the discharge of from the further consideration of certain petitions which the Committee had under consideration, and to present a resolution which applied to the subject of them. He therefore submitted the following resolution, which, at his request, was considered and adopted:

Resolved, That the Secretary of the Treasury cause to be ascertained the amount of duties assessed and paid on plains, kerseys, and kendall cottons, imported into the United States, which were ordered after the passage of the act of the 14th of July, 1832, and before the passage of the act of the 2d of March, 1833—that he lay an account thereof before the Senate at the next session of Congress.

Mr. BENTON submitted the following resolution, the consideration of which he moved at this time:

Resolved, That the Committee on Military Affairs be instructed to inquire into the expediency of increasing the appropriation for arming the fortifications of the United States.

Mr. POINDEXTER thought the resolution should go to the Committee on Finance.

Mr. WEBSTER said he thought the direction asked for it was the most proper one. The Committee of course were to look after and, but he thought it belonged to the Military committee to judge into the necessity of naming the appropriation. He (Mr. W.) thought most pressing necessity that the appropriation was then adopted.

of Alabama, from the Committee on re, reported a bill for the relief of

Col. Daniel Numan: which was read the first time and ordered to a second reading.

Mr. CLAYTON gave notice, that to-morrow he would ask leave to introduce a bill authorizing the Secretary of the Treasury to settle the claims of the Government on the Allegheny Bank of Pennsylvania.

Mr. BENTON gave notice, that to-morrow he would ask leave to introduce the following joint resolution:

Be it resolved by the Senate and House of Representatives of the United States of America in Congress assembled, That so much of the joint resolution of March 3d, 1819, as prescribes the manner of electing public printers, and so much of the joint resolution of 5th February, 1829, as amends the said resolution in relation to the manner of electing public printers, be and the same hereby is repealed.

On motion of Mr. POINDEXTER, the bill for the relief of the heirs of Nathaniel Tyler was taken up and recommitted to the Committee on the Public Lands.

On motion of Mr. KING, of Alabama, the bill for the relief of Duncan L. Clynch was taken up and recommitted to the Committee on Public Lands.

Mr. HENDRICKS, from the Committee on Roads and Canals, reported a bill making appropriations to improve and complete certain roads in Arkansas; which was read the first time and ordered to a second reading.

The Clerk of the House of Representatives being introduced, announced the death of the Hon. WARREN R. DAVIS, a Representative in Congress from the State of South Carolina, accompanied with the customary resolution relative to his funeral.

Mr. CALHOUN then said, in rising to offer the usual resolution on this melancholy occasion, he felt it to be a duty which he owed to himself and his deceased friend, to make a few remarks commemorative of his many very excellent qualities. He knew him intimately—he was his near neighbor, and personal and political friend, and closely connected with him by the ties of close affinity. And he must say that in forming not a very limited acquaintance in passing through life, he had rarely known an individual more richly endowed. His intellect was of the highest order; clear, rapid, and comprehensive; accompanied with a remarkable facility in expressing and illustrating his thoughts, both in conversation and public discussion. With these high qualities, he combined a rich imagination, and a pure and delicate taste, accompanied by a sportive wit and an uninterrupted flow of good humor, which made him the delight of every circle in which he moved. Nor was he less distinguished for his moral qualities. He was generous, brave, patriotic, and disinterested almost to a fault. For the truth of this picture—that it was not the exaggerated effusions of a warm friendship, he could appeal to many whom he saw around him, who were intimately acquainted with the deceased, and could vouch for its correctness. Such was Warren Ransom Davis. He is now no more. He departed this life at 7 o'clock this morning. He (Mr. C.) witnessed the departing scene. He met his fate with calmness. When his most excellent friend, (Dr. Linn,) the Senator from Missouri, whose kind attentions to the deceased will be long remembered by his surviving friends, announced to him, after the adjournment of the Senate yesterday, his approaching dissolution, though the sad event was unexpected to him, he met it with perfect resignation. He thanked him for his kindness and candor, and said, that he only desired to die in peace and composure. His wish was realized. He fell into a gentle slumber at 1 o'clock in the morning, to awake no more. He departed without a struggle or a groan, but forever to his country and his friends. Mr. C. concluded by moving the following resolutions:

Resolved, That the Senate will attend the funeral of the Hon. WARREN R. DAVIS, late a member of the House of Representatives from the State of South Carolina, at the hour of 12 o'clock to-morrow; and, as a testimony of respect for the

memory of the deceased, they will go into mourning, by wearing crape round the left arm for thirty days.

On motion of Mr. PRESTON,

The Senate adjourned.

HOUSE OF REPRESENTATIVES.

THURSDAY, January 29, 1835.

The House met, pursuant to adjournment, at 12 o'clock.

After the reading of the proceedings of the preceding day, and the receipt of a message from the President of the United States, through his Secretary, Maj. A. J. DONELSON,

Mr. PICKENS, of South Carolina, arose, and addressed the Chair as follows:

Mr. SPEAKER: It becomes my melancholy and painful duty to announce to this House the death of one of my colleagues, WARREN R. DAVIS, of South Carolina. He died this morning, a few moments before 7 o'clock. Sir, it is not my privilege to speak in the language of eulogy, but I trust I may be permitted to say of the deceased, that, whatever were his faults, they were of such a nature as to sink with him into the tomb, and be forgotten; whilst those, who knew him best, will remember only that he had a heart full of human kindness, rich in all those qualities that constitute a gentleman. Under whatever was ever brilliant, and he more that never grew heavy, he covered a shrewd sagacity in relation to men, and a thorough knowledge of human affairs. As a public man, perhaps the ruling feeling of his heart was a deep and burning attachment to his native State. With him it was not as with most men, the ordinary principled patriotism. No! it was a permanent, abiding, passionate affection for her, and all her institutions. In much so, that even in the last days of his lingering illness, at the very mention of South Carolina, you might see the fire of animated, but sinking nature, rekindle in his eye, and burn upon his cheek. It may be gratifying to his relations to know, that in his last suffering hours, even up to the moment of death, he retained the full exercise of all his faculties. And when it was announced to him that he would soon have to meet his God, he received the disclosure with the most perfect calmness and composure, and replied in these remarkable words, that all he "desired was to die easily and gracefully."

It may also be to his relations a source of consolation to know, that, during his protracted sickness up to his death scene, he had around him the kindest and most devoted and personal friends, who ministered to him all that affectionate attention could prompt.

I will conclude by saying, that in his death this House has lost a prominent member, and his State a patriot citizen, who might have been to her an ornament in the brightest days of her proud career.

Mr. P. then offered the following resolutions:

Resolved, That the members of this House will attend the funeral of the late WARREN R. DAVIS, at 12 o'clock, to-morrow.

Resolved, That a Committee be appointed to take order for superintending the funeral of WARREN R. DAVIS, deceased, late a member of this House from the State of South Carolina.

Resolved, That the members of this House will testify their respect for the memory of WARREN R. DAVIS, by wearing crape on the left arm for thirty days.

In pursuance of the foregoing resolutions, which were read and unanimously adopted, the SPEAKER announced the following members to constitute the Committee of Arrangements, to superintend the funeral of the deceased member, viz:

Mr. PICKENS, of South Carolina,
ARCHER, of Virginia,
WILDE, of Georgia,
HARDIN, of Kentucky,
COULTER, of Pennsylvania,
LANSING, of New York,
McINTIRE of Maine,
CLAYS, of Ohio,
LEA, of Tennessee.

On motion of Mr. PINCKNEY, a message was sent to the Senate, announcing the death of the

Hon. WARREN R. DAVIS, a member of this House from South Carolina; when,

On motion of Mr. MANNING,

The House adjourned.

SENATE.

FRIDAY, January 30, 1835.

When the Senate was called to order—

On motion of Mr. WEBSTER, the reading of the Journal was dispensed with.

Some conversation then ensued between Messrs. WEBSTER, POINDEXTER, WRIGHT, and HILSBEE, upon the propriety of adjourning over to Monday, a motion to that effect having been submitted by Mr. MANGUM, when the motion was agreed to.

On motion of Mr. LEIGH, the Senate adjourned, and withdrew to the Hall of the House of Representatives, to attend the Funeral of the Hon. WARREN RANSOM DAVIS.

HOUSE OF REPRESENTATIVES.

FRIDAY, January 30, 1835.

The House met, pursuant to adjournment, for the purpose of attending the funeral obsequies of the Honorable WARREN RANSOM DAVIS, late a Representative in Congress from the State of South Carolina.

The Committee of Arrangements, pall bearers, and mourners, attended at the late residence of the deceased, on Capitol Hill, at eleven o'clock, A. M. at which time the remains were removed, in charge of the Committee of Arrangements, attended by the Sergeant-at-Arms of the House of Representatives, to the Hall of the House, where the funeral service was performed by the Rev. Mr. HAYES.

At 12 o'clock, meridian, the funeral procession moved from the Hall of the House of Representatives to the place of interment, in the following order:

The Chaplains of both Houses.

Physicians and Clergymen who attended the deceased.

Committee of Arrangements:

Mr. Pickens, Mr. Archer, Mr. Wilkie, Mr. Hardin, Mr. Coulter, Mr. Lansing, Mr. McIntire, Mr. Crane, and Mr. Lea, of Tennessee.

Pall Bearers: Pall Bearers:
Mr. Lewis,   Mr. Clayton,
Mr. Williams,   Mr. Gordon,
Mr. Bates,   Mr. McKennan.

The family and friends of the deceased.

The members of the House of Representatives and Senators from South Carolina, as mourners.

The Sergeant-at-Arms of the House of Representatives.

The House of Representatives, preceded by their Speaker and Clerk.

The Sergeant-at-Arms of the Senate.

The Senate of the United States, preceded by the Vice President, and their Secretary.

The President of the United States.

The Heads of Departments.

Judges of the Supreme Court, and its officers.

Foreign Ministers.

Citizens and Strangers.

On the return of the members to the Hall, the House adjourned till to-morrow at 12 o'clock.

HOUSE OF REPRESENTATIVES.

SATURDAY, Jan. 31, 1835.

Mr. CRANE, from the Committee on Revolutionary Claims, reported a bill for the relief of the heirs and legal representatives of Joseph Young, deceased; which was read twice, and committed.

Mr. CHINN, from the Committee on the District of Columbia, reported a bill to extend the charter of the Bank of Potomac, and the Farmer's Bank of Alexandria; which was read twice, and committed.

Mr. ADAMS, of New York, from the Committee on Invalid Pensions, reported a bill granting a pension to Isaac Eckhart; which was read twice, and committed.

Mr. CLAYTON, from the Committee on Public Lands, reported a bill granting a quantity of land in the Territory of Arkansas for public buildings at the seat of government of that Territory. Read twice and committed.

Petitions were presented by—

Messrs. LINCOLN, of Massachusetts,

And DUNLAP, of Tennessee.

Unfavorable Reports were made by—

Messrs. FULTON, CLAY, and CLAYTON.

AMENDMENT OF THE CONSTITUTION—

Mr. GILMER, from the Select Committee to whom was referred that part of the President's Message, relative to the amendment of the Constitution, reported that the committee could come to no decision thereon, and asked leave that they be discharged from its further consideration.

Agreed to.

Mr. G. then asked leave to lay the following resolution upon the table:

Resolved, by the Senate and House of Representatives of the United States of America in Congress assembled, Two-thirds of both Houses concurring:

That the following amendments to the Constitution of the United States be proposed to the Legislatures of the several States, which, when ratified by the Legislatures of three fourths of the States, shall be valid, to all intents and purposes, as part of the Constitution, to wit:

1st. No person who shall have been elected President of the United States, shall be again eligible to that office.

2d. Hereafter, the President and Vice President of the United States shall be chosen by the People of the respective States, in the manner following:

On the 1st Monday and succeeding Tuesday and Wednesday in the month of August, eighteen hundred and thirty-six, and the same days in every fourth year thereafter, an election shall be held for President and Vice President of the United States, at such places and in such manner as elections are held by the laws of each State for members of the most numerous branch of the Legislature thereof. And the citizens of each State who possess the qualifications of electors of the most numerous branch of the State Legislature, shall then and there vote for President and Vice President of the United States, one of whom shall not be an inhabitant of the same State with themselves.' And the superintendents or persons holding elections in each election district shall immediately thereafter make returns thereof to the Governor of the State.

And it shall be the duty of the Governor, together with such other persons as shall be appointed by the authority of each State, to ascertain the result of said returns, and the person receiving the greatest number of votes for President, and the one receiving the greatest number of votes for Vice President, shall be holden to have received the whole number of votes which the State shall be entitled to give for President and Vice President; which fact shall immediately be certified by the Governor, and sent to the seat of Government of the United States, to each of the Senators in Congress from such State, to the President of the Senate, and to the Speaker of the House of Representatives. The places and manner of holding such elections, of canvassing the votes, making returns thereof, and ascertaining their result, shall be prescribed in each State by the Legislature thereof. But Congress may, at any time, make or alter such regulations. 'Congress shall have the power of altering the times of holding the elections; but they shall be held on the same days throughout the United States, and of altering the time hereinafterwards prescribed for the assembling of Congress every fourth year. The Congress of the United States shall be in session on the second Monday in October, in the year one thousand eight hundred and thirty-six, and on the same day in every fourth year thereafter; and the President of the Senate, in the presence of the Senate and House of Representatives, shall, as soon as convenient and practicable, proceed to open all the certificates and returns, and the electoral votes of the States shall be thereupon counted. The person having the greatest number of votes for President shall be President, if such number be a majority of the whole number of votes given. But if no person have such majority, or if the person having the majority of the whole number of votes given shall have died before the counting of the votes, then a second election shall be held on the first Monday and succeeding Tuesday and Wednesday, in the month of December then next ensuing, which shall be confined to the persons having the two highest number of votes at the preceding election. But if two or more persons have the highest and an equal number of votes, then the persons having the highest number of votes: Provided, however, if, in the first election, there were but two persons voted for, and the person receiving the highest number of votes shall have died before the counting of the votes, then, in the second election, the choice shall not be confined to the person previously voted for; but any person may be voted for who may be otherwise qualified by the constitution to be President of the United States; which second election shall be conducted, the returns made, the votes counted, and the result of the election in each State, certified by the Governor in the same manner as in the first; and the final result of the election shall be ascertained in the same manner as the first, and at such time as shall be fixed by law, or resolution of Congress; and the person having the greatest number of votes for President, shall be President; but if the two or more persons shall have received an equal and the highest number of votes at the second election, or if the person who shall have received the majority of the whole number of votes given at the second election, shall have died before the counting of the votes, then the House of Representatives shall choose one of the remaining number of the persons voted for, for President, in the manner prescribed by the constitution. But if there shall have been but two persons voted for in the second election, and the person who shall have received the highest number of votes, shall have died before the counting of the votes, the Vice President then in office, shall be President for the next succeeding term. The person having the greatest number of votes for Vice President, at the first election, shall be Vice President, if such number be a majority of the whole of votes given; And if no person shall have received such majority, or if the person have received the majority of the whole of votes given, shall have died before the taking of the votes, then of the persons having two highest number of votes, the Senate shall choose one for Vice President, but if two or persons have the highest and an equal number of votes, then the persons having the highest of votes; but if there shall have been but two sons voted for, and the person who shall have received the highest number of votes, shall have before the counting of the votes, the remaining person shall be Vice President, or persons voted for shall have died before the counting of the votes, then the Senate shall choose of their own body for Vice President.

4th. No Senator or Representative shall be appointed to any civil office, place, or emolument under the authority of the United States, the time for which he was elected, and months afterward.

Mr. SPEIGHT wished to inquire of the man from Georgia if it was his intention to the consideration of the resolution at the session of Congress. If so, Mr. S. would if it were postponed to a day certain. Mr. he would take that occasion to remark, though the committee could come to no ment generally, they did agree, with o tion, to that part relative to the election dent and Vice President of the United States.

Mr. GILMER said he should be gratified House would consent to refer the subject Committee of the Whole; but he could himself, have ventured to ask it. If it would suffer it to be read a first and second he would ask that permission.

Mr. HUBBARD believed a majority of committee were decidedly opposed to both motions. Whether the gentleman intended tion of Congress upon them during session, Mr. H. knew not; but he was

the course then adopted. He had no objection that they should be merely presented, and laid on the table.

Mr. GILMER would accept either course.

Mr. SPEIGHT believed that he concurred with the gentleman from New Hampshire, as to the amendment. Mr. S. did not desire to press the subject upon the consideration of the House, but only that a subject of so much importance to the rican People should be brought fully before

. ARCHER said he thought it better that the .olution be laid on the table and printed. The motion was then agreed to.

r. J. Q. ADAMS asked the consent of the se to take up and consider the following reso-uuon, offered by him on Wednesday, 28th inst.:

Resolved, That the President of the United States be requested to communicate to this House, if not incompatible with the public interest, any correspondence with the Government of France, and any despatches received from the Minister of 'he United States at Paris, not hitherto communi-ited to the House, in relation to the failure of ', French Government to carry into effect any pulation of the treaty of the 4th of July, 1831. 'he motion was agreed to, and the resolution ed.

. FERRIS asked the consent of the House ke up and consider the following resolution, ;ed by him on Wednesday last.

coolved, That the Secretary of the Treasury ·equested to furnish this House with the Re-t of the Solicitor of the Treasury, together ' all the documents relative to the compro-of the claims of the United States against as H. Smith and Son, and their securities. i ne resolution was agreed to.

Mr. PLUMMER, by consent, offered the fol-lowi g resolution:

Resolved, That the C mmittee on Public Lands tructed to inquire into the expediency of g to the settlers on the public lands within . district of country ceded to the U. States by treaty of Dancing Rabbit creek, in the State of s'ssippi, where improvements have been cov-·d by Indian and Jefferson College claims, and reby d prived of the benefits of the pre-emp-a laws, a pre-empt on right and other lands, in ι thereof, and of granting unto them such other rr··f as they may deem equitable and just.

r. CAGE said he had sometime since prepar-.similar resolution in reference to those lands, in a conversa· on with the Cha rm n of the ·mittee on Public Lands, Mr. C. a certained a bill had been reported by that Co mittee ·racing the same objects, as far as related to States of Alabama and Illinois, and he hon-irman distinctly assured him that wh n that came up for consideration an amendment uld be proposed thereto, to include the State Mississippi, the session being so far advanced ' a separate bill could not be passed.

CLAY said, he did inform the gentleman he would move an amendment embracing the ' of Mississippi, in the bill referred to; not sting that if the House were disposed to pass ·e bill rel·ting to Alabama and Illinois, they would ' object to the proposition for Mississippi. He , however, no objection to the resolution being ted to and referred to the Committee on Pub-l ands.

·. PLUMMER explained, that the resolution aced other objects, relative to settlement ι, than those referred to by his honorable gue.

. CLAY was not at first aware of that, and rfore he trusted the resolution would be adopt-

'he resolution was then agreed to.

. motion of Mr. WATMOUGH, a docu-relating to the bill to regulate the pay of the of the United States, together with certain iments, proposed to meet the views of the ι members, were directed to be printed for ι of the House.

.ARCH called for the consideration of ι made by him on Thursday last, to print ι copies of the Report of Mr. J. N. Rey-

nolds, relative to certain, islands, shoals, &c. in the Pacific Ocean.

Mr. P. said he had. been requested to modify his motion so as to have 2000 extra copies of the report printed. After a few remarks on the im-portance of the work, Mr. P. so modified his mo-tion.

Mr. JARVIS said he would like to hear some good reason advanced for printing any number of extra copies of this work. It was not a report from a Department, Lut was the printed work of an individual, which, it seemed, did not possess in itself sufficient interest to insure its sale, and so it was found desirable to print it at the expense of Congress. He thought it was high time for that body to stay its hand, and no longer be made the instrument for printing worthless books.

Mr. PEARCE said, he believed the gentleman from Maine, (Mr. Jarvis) could not have fully un-derstood the object of the motion. The report in question could not properly be denominated a book. It contained information of great import-ance to the action of committees of the House, as well as individuals engaged in commercial pur-suits. It was an abstract of informa·ion which had been collecting from various authentic sources for the last twenty or thirty years. All who had ever been connected with the important branch of our commerce, the interests of which it involved, would readily admit the high value of the informa-tion contained in the report. He hoped the House would agree to print the extra copies c·lled for.

Mr. JARVIS replied. He said the argument of the gentleman would be an excellent one to in duce the House to publish the "Coast Pilot." That was a work of infinite value to mariners; and if this compilation was of equal value, let the com-piler publish it at his own expense, and there would be no difficulty in effecting a sufficient sale to indemnify him. He repeated, it was high time for that House to stop. They had alre dy done enough of this kind of work for individuals.

Mr. BURGES observed, that he would not have said a word upon this resolution, had it not been for the opposition of the gentleman from Maine, (Mr. Jarvis.) He was astonished that one who would advocate an appropriation of some fifty thousand dollars, for the adornment of the Capi-tol, should oppose the expenditure of a dollar to save the life of the toil-worn and tempest-tost ma-riner of his country. He asked what in·rest was ·more dear to the country ,than that of its com merce? Gentlemen might talk as they pleased of the-predominating influence of agriculture, it re-mained alone for commerce to open a market for the products of agriculture. He should, there-fore, use every means to promote the facilities of navigation. He would rather advocate an aug-mentation of the number of extra copies than its decrease.

Mr. PHILLIPS wished to say one word in favor of this motion. He deemed the information con-tained in the report of essential importance to the House as well as to those directly engaged in na-vigation. The amount of American tonnage en-gaged in the commerce of these seas, was believ-ed to be greater than that of all other nations put together, and yet all the information possessed on the subject, excepting that furnished by individual expense and enterprise, was procured at the ex-pense of other governments. He dwelt on the growing importance of this commerce, and hoped the motion would prevail.

The question was then taken, and the motion agreed to.

On motion of Mr. REYNOLDS,

Resolved, That the Committee on Roads and Canals be instructed to inquire into the expedi-ency of making an examination or survey of the route for the Cumberland Road from Vandalia, in the State of Illinois, to Alton, in said State, and from thence to Jefferson city, in the State of Mis-souri, and make report to the next Congress.

On motion of Mr. WHITE, of Florida,

Resolved, That the Committee on the Post Office and Post Roads be instructed to inquire into the expediency of providing for a post route from Pensacola, by Florida Town, Almirante, Pittman's Ferry, to Campbellton.

On motion of Mr. ASHLEY,

Resolved, That the Committee on Invalid Pen-sions be instructed to inquire into the expediency of reinserting the name of John Davenport, on the roll of invalid pensioners.

On motion of Mr. FILLMORE,

Resolved, That the Committee on Roads and Canals be instructed to inquire into the expedien-cy of causing a survey to be made of the best mode of enlarging and improving the harbor of Buffalo for the reception and security of vessels navigating Lake Erie.

On motion of Mr. SCHLEY,

Resolved, That the Committee on the Post Office and Post Roads be instructed to inquire into the expediency of establishing a post route from Forsyth, in Monroe county, by the w·y of Jeffer-son to Newman, in Courtie county, in the State of Georgia.

On motion of Mr. DUNLAP,

Resolved, That the Committee on Claims be in-structed to inquire into the expediency of paying Robert Marsha l, for a horse lost in the Seminole War.

On motion of Mr. HARDIN,

Resolved, That the Committee on Claims in-quire into the expediency of allowing compensa-tion to Samuel Overton, Bernard Fowler, and James Green, for horses lost during the late war with Great Britain, and that the vouchers to sup-port said claims be als i referred to said Commit-tee.

On motion of Mr. BOON,

Resolved, That the Committee on the Post Offi-ces and Post Roads be instructed to inquire into the expediency of establishing the State Road from Evansville into the State of Indiana to Anthony's Ferry on the Ohio river, and thence to Hender-sonville in Kentucky, as a post road.

On motion of Mr. ROBERTSON,

Resolved, That the Committee of Claims be in-structed to inquire into the propriety of referring to James Herron a sum of money pa d by him into the Treasury, with leave to report by bill or other-wise.

The following resolution was offered by Mr. BLAIR, viz.

Resolved, by the Senate and House of Repre-tatives of the United States in Congress assembled, That the Secretary of War be, and he is hereby directed to cause to be paid to each pensioner of the United States, the amount of pension due from time to time, whether as an invalid or indigent pensioner, at such office or agency as he may se-lect, at which pensions are paid by the United States.

Mr. HUBBARD then called for the orders of the day, wh ch was agree l to.

The SPEAKER laid before the House a letter from the Secretary of War, transmitting a state-ment of the appropriations for the War Depart-ment for the services of the year 1834, showing the amount appropriated under each specific head, the amount expended under each, and the ba-lance remaining unexpended in the Treasury on the 31st December last, prepared in obedience to the act of May 1, 1820, which letter was read and laid on the table.

The SPEAKER laid before the House a letter from the Secretary of War, transmitting a Report from the Chief Engineer and showing the amount of the funds which have been applied to the im-provement of the Cumberland river, and conveying further information in relation to expenditures for the improvement of said river, as called for by the House on the 8th of January instant, which letter and report were referred to the Committee on Roads and Canals.

A message in writing was received from the President of the United States, by Mr. Donelson his Private secretary, which was read, and is as follows:

To the House of Representatives of the U. States.

With reference to the claim of the grand daugh-ters of the Marshall De Rochambeau, and in ad-dition to the papers formerly communicated, re-lating to the same subject, I now transmit to the House of Representatives for their consideration, a memorial to the Congress of the United States, from the Countess d'Ambrugede, and the Mar-quise de la Gorce, together with the

accompanied it.. Translations of these documents are also sent

ANDREW JACKSON.

The message was ordered to be printed and lie on the table.

GENERAL APPROPRIATION BILL.

The bill making appropriations for the Civil and Diplomatic Expenses of the Government for the year 1835, was then taken up, read a third time, and passed.

Mr. POLK gave notice that on Wednesday next he should ask leave of the House to proceed to the consideration of the bill regulating the deposits of the money of the United States in certain local banks.

Mr. HUBBARD also gave notice that on Monday next he should ask leave to move that the House resolve itself into a Committee of the Whole on the State of the Union, on the bill making appropriations for certain harbors.

The House then proceeded to the orders of the day, being private bills.

The question pending being the Whole, of the bill for the relief of the legal representatives of Rich-ard W. Meade.—

Mr. WHITTLESEY, of Ohio, said, he hoped the friends of that bill would consent to its temporary postponement, for he feared if it was taken up, no other business would be acted on that day.

After some conversation between the CHAIR, Messrs. WHITTLESEY, POLK, ARCHER, HUBBARD, MANN, of N. Y., and VINTON.—

The bills for the relief of R. W. Meade, Geo. Gibson, and Mervin P. Mix, were, for the present, laid aside; and the House, on motion of Mr. WHITTLESEY, of Ohio, resolved itself into a Committee of the Whole, Mr. WARD in the Chair, and proceeded to take up and consider the following bills:

A bill for the relief of Samuel Butler.

[Mr. FULTON moved to amend the bill by a further appropriation for the loss of a wagon, horse, &c. Agreed to.]

A bill for the relief of Elizabeth Swain.

A bill to refund David Watkinson & Co. a part of the duties imposed on a quantity of tin and iron imported by them.

A bill for the relief of Richard Putman.

A bill for the relief of the heirs of William Pollard.

A bill for the relief of Sutten Stephens.

A bill for the relief of Thomas Dixon & Co.

A bill for the relief of John Fraser & Co., of Charleston, S. C.

A bill for the relief of Jacob Barton.

A bill for the relief of Noah Chittenden.

[Mr. ALLEN, of Vermont, proposed an amendment to the bill, to pay the pension therein provided for the widow of N. Chittenden, who had died since the bill was reported; which was agreed to.]

A bill for the relief of Job Bass.

[Some conversation ensued on the principle embraced in this bill, between Messrs. CLAY, VINTON GARLAND, and PARKER, who moved a proviso, which was agreed to.]

A bill for the relief of Samuel H. Doxey.

A bill for the relief of John Herrick;

A bill granting a pension to Job Wood;

A bill for the relief of Asa Armington and others;

A bill for the relief of Dominick Lynch;

A bill for the relief of David Kincaid;

A bill for the relief of Stevens Smith and others.

The Committee then rose and reported the several bills to the House.

The bills for the relief of Asa Armington and others, David Watkinson & Co., Job Bass, and Noah Chittenden, were, on motion, postponed till Friday next.

The House agreed to the amendment of the committee to the bill for the relief of Samuel Butler.

All the above bills (except the four postponed) were then ordered to be engrossed for a third reading.

The House again resolved itself into a Committee of the Whole, Mr. HUBBARD in the Chair, and took up and considered the following bills:

A bill for the relief of Robert Abbott and others;

A bill for the relief of Matthew C. Perry;

A bill for the relief of E. R. Shubrick;

A bill for the relief of Biddle, Beckle, and others;

A bill for the relief of John J. Avery;

A bill for the relief of Stephen Gatlin;

A bill for the relief of Theodore Owens;

A bill for the relief of the representatives of Thos. Clemmons;

A bill for the relief of S. Morris Waler and Henry Percival;

A bill for the relief of Shubael Conant;

A bill for the relief of the representatives of Aaron Smith;

A bill for the relief of Thomas Ball;

A bill for the relief of Richard Hargrave Lee;

A bill for the relief of William Haskell and others;

A bill for the relief of Ebenezer Breed;

A bill for the relief of George Davenport;

A bill for the relief of John Carmack;

A bill for the relief of Abijah King.

All of which bills were severally reported to the House without amendment.

The Committee also took up and considered the following, which were severally reported to the House, with amendments:

A bill for the relief of Lieut. Mervin P. Mix;

A bill for the relief of William Lawrence;

A bill for the relief of William Marcus; and

A bill for the relief of Isaac Baker.

The committee then rose and reported the bills to the House.

The amendment to the bill for the relief of Lt. Mervin P. Mix was concurred in.

The further consideration of the bills for the relief of William Lawrence, Isaac Baker, Abijah King, and John Carmack, was postponed till Friday next.

The bill for the relief of William Marcus, as amended, was then taken up

Mr. VINTON made remarks thereon, and

Mr. SEVIER, of Arkansas, rejoined; but before the question was taken, the House, on motion of Mr. MANN, of New York,

Adjourned till Monday 11 o'clock, A. M.

IN SENATE.

MONDAY, February 2, 1835.

The VICE PRESIDENT communicated a letter from the War Department, made in pursuance of the act of May 1, 1820, showing the amount of appropriations for that Department for the year 1834.

He also communicated a memorial from the mayor of the City of Boston, remonstrating against the refusal to make an appropriation for repairing the fortifications of Castle Island, and asking such an appropriation, which was referred to the Committee on Finance.

Mr. HENDRICKS presented a memorial from citizens of Michigan city for the improvement of their harbor and the establishment of a port of entry there; which was referred to the Committee on Commerce.

Also, a memorial and joint resolutions from the legislature of Indiana, praying for the improvement of the Illinois river. Referred to the Committee on Roads and Canals.

Mr. McKEAN presented a memorial from importers, auctioneers, commission merchants, merchants, traders, and dry goods dealers, of Philadelphia, praying Congress to establish a standard of weights and measures throughout the Union, and a uniform mode of applying and conforming to the same. Referred to the Committee on the Judiciary.

Mr. CLAY presented a memorial from inhabitants of Louisville, Kentucky, praying Congress to take stock in the Louisville and Portland canal; which was referred to the Committee on Roads and Canals.

Other petitions of a private nature were presented by Messrs. BENTON, KING of Alabama, KANE, and KENT.

[Mr. BENTON presented a memorial from the expatriated Poles, praying for some alterations in the law passed by Congress last session, giving them land.]

Mr. CALHOUN arose, holding in his hand a copy of the Globe newspaper, and desired that the Secretary of the Senate should be required to read a paragraph which he (Mr. Calhoun) referred to.

The following paragraph from the Globe was then read:

"We were informed by Mr. Wilson, the keeper of the Rotundo, that he had frequently observed th's man about the Capitol—so frequently that he had become an object of curiosity to him—that he had endeavored to draw him into conversation, but found him taciturn and unwilling to talk. Whether Lawrence has caught, in his visits to the Capitol, the mania which has prevailed during the two last sessions in the Senate—whether he has become infatuated with the chimeras which have troubled the brains of the disappointed and ambitious orators who have depicted the President as a Cæsar who ought to have a Brutus—as a Cromwell—a Nero—a Tiberius, we know not. If no secret conspiracy has prompted the perpetration of the horrid deed, we think it not improbable some delusion of intellect has grown out of his visits to the Capitol, and that bearing down every horrible mischief threatened to public, and revolution and all its train of evil imputed as the necessary consequence of the President's measures, it may be that the infatuated fancied he had reason to become his own avenger. If he had heard and believed Mr. Houn's speech the day before yesterday, he have found in it ample justification for his own, who was represented as the cause of the most dreadful calamities to the nation—as charged with the perfect rottenness and corruption to the vitals of the Government—insomuch as was scarcely worth preserving, if it were possible."

Mr. CALHOUN said that he rose to a few remarks on the article which had been read. Not in reference to himself, but on litical bearing and character.

There are some things of themselves so insignificant as to be undeserving of notice, but which, in connection with others, may become important. Such was the present. Whatever may be the character of the paper which contains this—however base and prostitute, it is the authentic, and established organ of the Executive sustained by its power, and pampered hands.

In noticing the article, I pass by the accusation that it contains, and will confine my remarks to the new principles in ethics and which it asserts. What this principle is, who read the article can doubt. It asserts who denounces abuses and corruption, even so great, instigates assassination! A description of denunciation is considered as ing an assassination is not left to doubt. remove all uncertainty on this point the author refers to my remarks the other day. I allude this reference, with a view of defending for I require no defence, but for illustration new code of political morals announce the Executive organ. It asserts, that it has attempted the life of the Chief Magistrate present and heard what I said, he would be justified in doing what he attempted course, if I had made such declarations, as would have justified the attempt, whence would follow that I was the instigator of the crime.

Now, said Mr. C. what was the circumstance of the case? The Post Office report was under consideration. It had made extraordinary exposures of abuses and corruption in that of the administration—abuses and corruption denied, acknowledged—and denied by none but the supporters of the Administration denounced, and at the same time expressed conviction that abuses and corruption were limited to that particular branch, but on the contrary almost every Department of the Administration with which I attributed more to the worthless political machine at this time, than to the direct of those who administer the Government, as great as I believe this misconduct to be this which the Executive organ has authoritatively asserted, would justify assassination.

To what are we coming? In the first place it is intended, that the Senate has no right to express its opinion upon any misconduct of the Executive, because, forsooth, we may become his judges in a trial of impeachment!—acting on this term, a resolution on our journals condemning unconstitutional acts must be expunged. Be what next? It follows as a clear consequence we are not individually to condemn the conduct of the Executive, in debate, for an expression of an opinion individually as much disqualifies vote upon a resolution. Now another step ten still higher! still bolder! We are told to denounce the abuse of the administration, in general terms, without personal reference, instigate the assassination of the Chief Magistrate.

Mr. C. entreated Senators to pause and reflect. they fail in all this to see the near approach of possible despotic power? In looking around, beheld many Senators in the ranks of the Administration, of whose patriotism he could not doubt. He would, in particular, ask them what is to come of all this, and whether it is not time halt? Did they not see that the necessary conse nce is to degrade the Senate to the humble rument of Executive power—to deprive it of usefulness, and ultimately to work an enfe nge in our political institutions?

On my part, said Mr. C. I cannot be mistaken. I in all this an approaching catastrophe. I a repeat what I asserted on another occasion—reform, thorough, radical reform, or revolution is inevitable—there is no other alternative. I comprehend the crisis in which I speak and I have made up my mind as to my duty. I am no candidate for any office—I neither seek nor desire place—nothing shall intimidate—nothing shall prevent me from what I believe is due to my conscience and my country.

Mr. LEIGH, from the Committee on Revolutionary Claims, reported a bill for the relief of the legal representatives of Thornton Taylor.

Also, a bill for the relief of the legal representatives of N. P. Horner, deceased.

Also, a bill for the relief of the legal representatives of James Bell, deceased; which were severally read the first time, and ordered to a second reading.

The following resolutions were submitted:

By Mr. PORTER.

Resolved, That the Committee on the Post Office and Post Roads be instructed to inquire into the expediency of providing by law for the transportation of a daily mail between New Orleans and Mobile.

By Mr. FRELINGHUYSEN.

Resolved, That the Committee on the Judiciary inquire into the expediency of annexing the fourth Circuit to the third Judicial Circuit, and of so arranging the circuit system, as to extend its benefits to all the States, by a even or more circuits.

By Mr. WAGGAMAN.

Resolved, That the Committee on Manufactures be instructed to inquire into the expediency of further providing by law against the evasions of the tariff on refined and other sugars.

By Mr. CLAYTON.

Resolved, That the Committee on the Judiciary instructed to inquire into the expediency of so clearly defining by law the crime of revolt the crews of American ships within the admiral and maritime jurisdiction of the United s, of abolishing the capital punishment now ided by the act of the 30th of April, 1790, that offence; and of substituting a milder punishment for it; which, on motion, was agreed to.

r. CLAYTON, pursuant to notice, and on given, introduced a bill to authorize the etary of the Treasury to compromise the is of the United States on the Alleghany of Pennsylvania; which was read twice, and red.

WHITE, from the Committee on Revolutionary Claims, made an unfavorable report upon dition of John B. White.

WHITE, from the same Committee, made a report on the petition of John Spotswood which were concurred in.

CLAYTON, from the Committee on the Judiciary, reported a bill making provision by law against offences committed on the high seas against the United States; which was read the first time and ordered to a second reading.

Mr. BENTON, agreeably to notice, and on leave given, introduced a joint resolution, repealing a joint resolution of Congress with regard to the election of printer; which was read the first time and ordered to a 2d reading

Mr. PRESTON gave notice that on to-morrow he would ask leave to introduce a joint resolution making an appropriation for the purchase of certain paintings now in this city.

Mr. SOUTHARD, from the Committee on the District of Columbia, reported a bill granting annually for five years, to the City of Washington, $70,000, to the City of Alexandria $17,500, and to Georgetown —— towards extinguishing certain loans made to the Chesapeake and Ohio Canal Company. This bill also provides for the relinquishment of the stock now owned by the said cities in that canal to the United States. The bill was read the first time and ordered to a second reading.

Mr. BENTON offered the following motion in writing:

That the Secretary of the Senate inquire into the state of the printing ordered to be done by the Senate during the last and present session, and report at about what time each piece of printing will be completely; which was agreed to.

The Senate then proceeded to the order of the day, when the following resolutions, heretofore offered, were taken up and agreed to:

By Mr. PRENTISS.

Resolved, That the President be requested to communicate to the Senate the correspondence which passed between the Governments of the United States and Spain, through the respective Ministers or agents, in the negotiation of the late treaty between the two Governments, together with the instructions given to the Ministers of the United States, from time to time, in the course of the negotiation, or so much of said correspondence and instructions as it may not be incompatible with the public interest to communicate.

By Mr. MOORE.

Resolved, That the Committee on the Judiciary be instructed to inquire into the propriety of making a suitable appropriation, to aid in the erection of a court-house, now in progress in Madison county, Alabama, in order to provide for the accommodation of the District Court of the United States, holden at that place.

By Mr. TIPTON.

Resolved, That the Committee on the Post Office and Post Roads be instructed to inquire into the expediency of establishing a post route from Marion to Huntington; thence to Goshen, Indiana; a post route from Greenville, by Recovery, Ohio, to Huntington, Indiana; a post route from Yellow river Post Office to Laport; a post route, from Kirk's Cross Road by Frankfort and Delhi to Monticello; and a post route from Logansport by Turkey Creek Prairie and Goshen to White Pigeon, in the Michigan Territory.

The following resolution being under consideration:

Resolved, That the General Post Office is deeply in debt—its affairs in great disorder—its accounts and reports irregular, unsatisfactory, and in many instances untrue—that large sums of public money have been wasted and paid over to favored individuals upon false pretences. and that its conduct and administration are justly the subjects of public complaint, and demand a radical reform.

Mr. CLAYTON suggested that its discussion might occupy some considerable time, and, as he had given notice on a former day, he now moved that the Senate proceed to the consideration of Executive business; when,

On motion of Mr. POINDEXTER, the resolution was postponed to and made the special order of the day, for to-morrow.

On motion of Mr. GRUNDY, the bill for reorganising the General Post Office was taken up.

Mr. Grundy said, that the bill was framed principally by the majority of the committee; that the minority had some amendments to offer; which,

on his motion, were received and ordered to be printed.

The Senate then proceeded to the consideration of Executive business, after which The Senate adjourned.

HOUSE OF REPRESENTATIVES.

Monday, Feb. 2, 1835.

Several memorials, presented during the last week by Mr. DICKSON, from citizens of New York, praying the abolition of slavery within the District of Columbia, and a petition from citizens on the same subject, came up for consideration.

Mr. DICKSON addressed the House at great length in favor of the prayer of the petition, and the propriety, justice, and expediency of some legislation by Congress thereon. Mr. D. contended that neither the Old and New Testament, the heathen philosophy, nor the Declaration of Independence, recognised a difference of color in the rights of man. He also cited the laws of the District, as derived from the State of Maryland, the cession thereof, and contended that the slave trade, as at present carried on here, was worse than its features and its effects than that of Africa. While the trade was made piracy in almost every country in Europe, even under despotic governments, it was fostered and nourished at the seat of the General Government of the greatest Republic on earth. In all other Republics, slavery had been abolished, and on the whole continent of America, with the exception of the absolute government of the Brazils, it had ceased to exist. Mr. D. disclaimed for himself, and for the petitioners, any intention of interfering, then or thereafter, with the powers of the State Governments, but maintained the full and complete power of Congress over the subject within the District.

His object, in the motion he intended to make, to refer the subject to a select committee, was in consequence of a majority of the committee to whom the District of Columbia being from time to time held, no action had ever been made on the petitions referred to it. Mr. D. then referred to reports, &c. and by former committees, to a petition from upwards of one thousand inhabitants of the District, owning, he said, more than a million of its property, for the abolition of slavery therein, and to a presentation of the grand jury of Alexandria, some years since, declaring the trade to be a nuisance, from all of which he affirmed that to grant the prayer of the petitions he now presented, would conduce to the benefit and prosperity of the District itself.

The question of order, as to whether the honorable member could go into the merits merely of the presentation of a petition, was raised by Mr. CHINN, Mr. CLAY, and Mr. BOON, but, overruled by the CHAIR, on the ground that the question having laid over from a former day, and embracing matters of great importance, touched thereon were in order, so long as the House had not interpose.

Mr. DICKSON moved that the petition be referred to a select committee and printed.

Mr. CHINN said that he did not rise to discuss the course pursued by the present committee, nor by any former Committee of the District of Columbia, upon the subject of this memorial. He hoped that neither the present, nor any committee, required any such defence. He meant to disturb the deep sympathy, or to tender mercies, of the gentleman from New York, still less of the eight hundred fair memorialists who had made the gentleman their champion. He only moved to lay the whole subject on the table, and upon this question he asked the ayes and noes; which were ordered.

Mr. DENNY inquired if they could be called hereafter?

The CHAIR replied, it was in the power of the House to call up the subject whenever it thought proper.

The question was then taken by yeas and nays and resulted as follows: Yeas 117, nays 77.

So the House determined to lay the petition and the motion to refer the same to a select committee on the table.

[Continued in next number.]

CONGRESSIONAL GLOBE.

BY BLAIR & RIVES. ————WEEKLY———— PRICE $1 A SESSION.

2d Sess.....23d Cong. MONDAY, FEBRUARY 16, 1835. Volume 2.......No. 12.

TWENTY-THIRD CONGRESS.
SECOND SESSION.

HOUSE OF REPRESENTATIVES.
Monday, February 2, 1835.
[CONTINUED FROM LAST NUMBER.]

Petitions and memorials were presented by—
Messrs. HALL and SMITH, of Maine;
Messrs. REED, OSGOOD, LINCOLN, and EVERETT, of Massachusetts;
Mr. YOUNG, of Connecticut;
Mr. PEARCE, of Rhode Island;
Messrs. WHITE, CAMBRELENG, PIERSON, TURRILL, HARD, and MARTINDALE, of New York;
Mr. SHINN, of New Jersey;
Messrs. HIESTER, McKENNAN, BINNEY, GALBRAITH, and DENNY, of Pennsylvania;
[Mr. DENNY presented a memorial from a large number of delegates, representing five counties of that town, of Pennsylvania, extending along the Monongahela river from the head of the Ohio to the Virginia State line, asking for an appropriation for the improvement of the Monongahela river from Pittsburg to the National road at Brownsville, according to the plan suggested by Mr. Stewart. Mr. D. moved to refer the memorial and accompanying documents to the Committee on Roads and Canals.

Mr. STEWART suggested to his colleague the propriety of giving the subject a different direction.

This subject, at the last session, had been referred, on his motion, to the Committee on Roads and Canals, and that committee had authorized him to report a bill making an appropriation for the improvement of the Monongahela river, drawing up Brownsville, on the very plan recommended by the memorialists. He hoped this bill would be reached and passed before the close of the session. He therefore suggested the reference of the subject to the Committee of the Whole House, to which this bill had been referred.

Mr. DENNY acquiesced, and the memorial was referred accordingly.]

Mr. MILLIGAN, of Delaware;
Messrs. HEATH and McKIM, of Maryland;
Messrs. CHINN, MERCER, LOYALL, and WISE, of Virginia;
Mr. W. B. SHEPPERD, of North Carolina;
Mr. PICKENS, of South Carolina;
Mr. SCHLEY, of Georgia;
Messrs. POPE, TOMPKINS, BEATY, and JOHNSON, of Kentucky;
Messrs. STANDIFER, DUNLAP, BUNCH, and LEA, of Tennessee;
Messrs. THOMSON and MITCHELL, of Ohio;
Mr. GARLAND, of Louisiana;
Messrs. CARR and HANNEGAN, of Indiana;
[Mr. CARR presented the petition of Gilbert Brown, of the parish of Natchitoches, in the State of Louisiana; which was referred to the Committee on Private Land Claims.

Mr. HANNEGAN presented the petition of sundry citizens of Clinton county, in the State of Indiana, praying the establishment of a post route from that place on the Michigan road, by Frankfort and Delphi, to Monticello, in said State.]

Mr. PLUMMER, of Mississippi;
Mr. CASEY, of Illinois;
[Mr. CASEY presented sundry resolutions of the Legislature of the State of Illinois, in relation to a grant of land to assist in constructing a road from a point on the Wabash river, opposite Vincennes, to Chicago; which, on his motion, was referred to the same Committee of the Whole House to which bill No. 514 on that subject has been referred. The resolutions were ordered to be printed.]

Messrs. CLAY, MARDIS, MURPHY, and LEWIS, of Alabama;
[Mr. CLAY, of Alabama, presented a memorial from the Legislature of Alabama, asking the relinquishment of the 2 per cent. of the net proceeds of sales of public lands in that State, reserved for the purpose of making a road or roads, leading to said State, in order that it may be applied to the construction of a rail road, to connect the waters of Mobile Bay with those of the Tennessee river—and also asking the condemnation of a section of the public land on each side of the contemplated road, for the use thereof—which was referred to the Committee of the Whole on the state of the Union; to which a bill, heretofore reported for the same purpose, had been committed. Mr. Clay also presented a memorial from the same Legislature, asking the extension of the law granting pre-emption rights to settlers on the public lands, to the inhabitants of fractional townships, who are now denied the benefits of that law—which was referred to the Committee on the Public Lands.]

Mr. ASHLEY, of Missouri;
Mr. LYON, of Michigan;
Mr. WHITE, of Florida.

The SPEAKER also presented several memorials and petitions from various States, &c.; which petitions and memorials were appropriately referred.

On motion of Mr. HENDERSON,
Resolved, That the Committee on the Post Office and Post Roads be instructed to inquire into the expediency of establishing a post road from Brown's Mills, Mifflin county, Pennsylvania, by the way of Steudt's Mills and Perrysville, to the Valley Post Office, in said county.

On motion of Mr. STEWART,
Resolved, That the Committee on Revolutionary Claims be instructed to inquire into the expediency of granting commutation and land to the heirs of George Galmes, an officer of the Virginia Continental Line in the revolutionary war.

On motion of Mr. McKIM,
Resolved, That the Committee of Claims inquire into the expediency of paying Hugh McDonald for a horse lost in the service of the United States during the late war with Great Britain.

On motion of Mr. CARMICHAEL,
Resolved, That the Committee on Commerce be instructed to inquire into the expediency of establishing a Port of Entry at Port Deposite, in the State of Maryland.

On motion of Mr. POTTS,
Resolved, That the Committee on the Post Office and Post Roads be instructed to inquire into the expediency of establishing a mail route from Coatesville, by way of Doe Run, Chatham, Westgrove, Rosscommon, and Boyd's Store, to Strickersville, all in the county of Chester, and State of Pennsylvania.

Mr. McKAY offered the following resolutions, which, under the rule, lie one day:
Resolved, That the Secretary of the Treasury be directed to make to this House a statement of all moneys disbursed from the Treasury of the United for expenses and intercourse with the Barbary Powers during the last ten years, therein noting as far as can be ascertained, the sums received by the respective Agents or Consuls, and the purposes to which the same have been applied in each of said years.
Resolved, That all cases during the past ten years wherein any Consul or Agent residing on the Barbary coast, has paid for any purpose or on any pretence, not authorized by law, to any one of said Powers, or to the officers or subjects thereof, a greater sum than three thousand dollars in any one year, with intent to charge the United States with the same, that the Secretary inform this House, whether it is done by the special approbation or writing of the President, first obtained for that purpose.

On motion of Mr. PINCKNEY,
Resolved, That the Secretary of the Navy be, and he is hereby requested to transmit to this House, copies of all such naval reports and other documents in his possession, as relate to the employment of cotton canvass in the American navy, and the propriety of providing cotton clothing for the seamen, and also to accompany his report with an expression of his own views and opinions upon both these subjects.

On motion of Mr. PINCKNEY,
Resolved, That the Committee on Naval Affairs be instructed to ascertain and report to what extent cotton canvass has hitherto been introduced into use in the American navy, and to inquire into the expediency of providing by law for its general employment on board of all vessels of the United States, and also of substituting cotton cloth for the general clothing of the seamen attached to the navy in the place of the linen manufacture now in use.

Mr. HUBBARD, from the Committee on Ways and Means, reported the following resolution; which was agreed to:
Resolved, That the Secretary of War be directed to communicate to this House, as soon as practicable, a map or chart representing the present state of the Breakwater and the adjoining shoals in the river Delaware, with the report of the engineers thereon, or any other information which may be in the possession of the Department, tending to show the policy or impolicy of making further appropriations for the present for the improvement of the said Breakwater.

Mr. MILLER, from the Committee on Invalid Pensions, reported a bill granting a pension to William C. Beard, late a Captain in the Army of the United States; which was read twice and committed.

Mr. ROBERTSON, from the Committee on the Judiciary, reported a bill to extend the provisions of certain laws for the relief of insolvent debtors; which was read twice, and its further consideration postponed for one week.

Mr. TOMPKINS, from the Committee on Revolutionary Pensions, reported a bill to establish a Pension Agency south of Green river, in Kentucky; which was read twice, and ordered to be engrossed.

Unfavorable reports were made by Messrs. MILLER, MARSHALL, TOMPKINS, BANKS, and FULTON, from their respective standing committees.

Mr. WARDWELL (instructed by the Committee on Revolutionary Claims,) moved that the bill to authorize the Secretary of War to appoint agents to examine pensioners, in order to prevent frauds, and for other purposes, be made the special order of the day for to-morrow week.

INDIAN RESERVATIONS.

The following resolution, heretofore offered by Mr. McCARTY—
Resolved, That the President of the U. States be requested to transmit to this House copies of all letters and correspondence of all Indian Agents and sub-agents, and other persons connected with the Indian Department, now in the Executive or War Department, or in the office of the Commissioner of the General Land Office, connected with or relative to the survey, location, sale, and transfer of all Indian reserves of lands since the year 1825, up to this time; and also, all the orders and communications from the Executive of the United States, through the War Department, or General Land Office, or otherwise, in reference to said surveys, locations, sales, and transfers of Indian reserves; together with maps and plots of said surveys, and of the tracts approved and confirmed by the President under said transfers and sale what remains unappropriated, that have be ported and submitted for his approval, to with the evidence of title.

To which Mr. PLUMMER moved an men, to restrict the call for information not already communicated by the Senate, resolutions of that body, adopted at the last session.

And which having been referred to the mittee on Indian Affairs—

Mr. LOVE, from that Committee, reported same, with an amendment, as follows:

rike out after the word correspondence, in the ..h line, the words "of all Indian Agents, sub-nts, and other persons connected with the In-1 Department," and insert after the words General Land Office, in the eighth line, the words "*of all Indian Agents, sub-agents, and other persons,*" and insert after the words reserves of lands, in the tenth line, the words "*east of the Mississippi river*"—

Then came up for consideration.

Mr. McCARTY said: Mr. Speaker: When I closed my remarks upon this subject, more than a week ago, upon the motion of the gentleman from Kentucky (Mr. Love) to refer this subject to the Committee on Indian Affairs, I had no intention of again troubling the House with any further remarks of mine. Nor, sir, important as I consider the subject to the country, should I have done so, but for the reported remarks of one of my colleagues (Mr. Lane) of the debate which took place on that day, and the subsequent debate upon this subject. Mr. Speaker, when I introduced the resolution under consideration, I carefully and studiously avoided locating charges of fraud in any district, or in any particular section of the country, upon any individual officer; nor, in no remark by me on this floor, during the time I occu- the attention of the House upon this subject, I adverted or made any allusion whatever y specific place, or upon any individual, of frauds contemplated to be laid open by this olution. It is not my practice, sir, to stand ..e.e and charge individuals elsewhere, with any act dishonorable to themselves or to the country, where they would be unable to defend themselves. The object of the resolution was, as expressed on its face, simply for the purpose of bringing forward—believing as I do that frauds exist—such evidence as would lead to an investigation into the conduct of public agents which may be thought prejudicial to the public interest, for the purpose of enabling the executive and the the proper departments to correct those fraudulent practices and of exposing the perpetrators. But, notwithstanding my repeated disclaimers against any thing like locating charges in any section of the country, my colleague (Mr. Lane) has been kind enough, in his reported remarks in the Globe, to falsely impute the charge upon myself and an honorable colleague, (Mr. Ewing,) of having located the frauds referred to within the State of Indiana.

Sir, it is needless for me to reiterate this disclaimer here, for every gentleman upon this floor, who participated in that discussion, must well remember it; but it is due to myself that I should expose this misrepresentation, which was intended to operate more *elsewhere* than here. The gentleman (Mr. Lane) after having made his first remarks, in which he goes on to state that he objected to the resolution, because I had not been sufficiently specific, and for that reason he could not vote for it, so fully was he satisfied that I had located charges no where, that he called upon me to put my finger upon the agent who had acted fraudulently. And this was also all the ground objection taken by the gentleman who op-d the resolution: these were the remarks, I ..lieve, of my colleague, in his first speech upon the subject. In his second remarks he changes his ground, and instead of opposing the adoption of the resolution as before, he says, in substance, "that he feels it incumbent upon him to redeem the people of the State of Indiana from the charges imputed to them by *my colleague* and myself," "as they had, if fraud had been commited, located it there." His corrected remarks read thus:—"And that, inasmuch as the resolution originated he gentleman from his own State, and inas- as two of his honorable colleagues (Messrs. ..g and McCarty) had expressed a belief auds had been perpetrated in the transfer of reservations, it might be supposed that ... of those frauds had taken place in Indiana." ..c the gentleman has travelled out of his way, an.. it of the subject under consideration, to seek xcuse to pass a eulogy upon the citizens of ..., entirely gratuitous and uncalled for by ..casion, in reply to charges that not only never made, but upon which nothing had been said. The gentleman has endeavored to show that he had corrected this error, by the publication of a letter in the Globe. But mark! He professes to have written it on Saturday, but instead of appearing in Monday's paper, it did not appear till Tuesday, although the gentleman assured the House that be took the *earliest* occasion to correct the error, but that his letter did not reach the office until late on Sunday night, and after the form of the paper had been made up.

Now, sir, the resolution came from myself, and, in my remarks on its introduction, I distinctly stated that I was personally acquainted with the agent in Indiana, and disavowed any intention of imputing wrong to that individual, whom I believe to be incapable of perpetrating a fraud. Why, then, was the State of Indiana, and the agents there, named by my colleague? Why, he says, "inasmuch as the resolution originated with a gentleman from his own State." Sir, no such inference can be drawn, either from any remarks I made, or from the resolution itself. The resolution was introduced by me for the purpose of getting at the subject *generally*. It was known to the gentleman, that for two years I have been connected with the Committee on Indian Affairs; and that my investigation on this subject was general. How then could he come to the conclusion he states, in the total absence of any thing said or done on my part to warrant such an inference. He could not.

But even admitting that I had been disposed to locate these frauds in the State of Indiana, would it have been considered disreputable to a whole people, because a few dishonest persons may be found among them? Would that have offered a sufficient ground for a gentleman to misrepresent his colleagues, for the purpose of passing a hypocritical eulogy, uncalled for and out of place, and entirely gratuitous on his part? No one thinks higher of my fellow-citizens of Indiana than I do; but would any gentleman believe me if I were to assert it as my opinion, that there was not a man among them capable of committing fraud? Was it an imputation upon the honest portion of any community, to charge some one or two of them with the perpetration of fraud—had I even done so—which is not true? Even the records of the gentleman's own county, which had as honest men as any in the world, would show that things had been done there not *altogether consistent with honesty and fair-dealing*. But where was there a county in this Union, whose records would not show that dishonest and corrupt men had lived there, and yet, is this an imputation upon the inhabitants of the county, does it argue against the integrity and purity of the community generally? Certainly not. My motive, Mr. Speaker, was a general one, in reference to the general interest of the country. Sir, were I disposed, I might instance a circumstance in my own State, not of fraud, sir, but of deep interest to those concerned, as well as the State, which of itself, I think, is of sufficient interest and importance to warrant the call contemplated by this resolution. It is this: a good many reserves were made by the treaty of 1826, in Indiana, to the minor Indian children of a particular school. Those children have mostly gone from the country, and it is believed their lands, or many of them, have been transferred; if so, the titles may be questioned, and innocent purchasers may suffer; and it is important these facts should be known.

I will again, sir, recur to the speech of my colleague, (Mr. Lane,) subsequently made, in reference to his feelings upon this subject. He says, "he would ever be ready to co-operate with 'them [his colleagues] in any thing and every 'thing they may undertake, calculated to promote 'the interests of their constituents, the interest and 'prosperity of our State, and the interest and 'prosperity of the Union."

Now, sir, these sentiments are certainly worthy of a representative and a better heart; but take them in connexion with the following, from another speech, made by the gentleman upon another occasion. I refer to it, sir, to show the insidious design of the gentleman upon that occasion; and that the interest of the State and his district is not so much his object, as to fish for a pretext to fix blame and censure upon others.

"MR. LANE said, be regretted he could not, in 'justice to himself, accept the kind aid of his good 'feeling colleague, (Mr. McCarty,) in the motion 'he had made to reconsider the vote of yesterday, 'rejecting the resolution he had the honor of pre'senting to the House for adoption. That it was 'his intention to present it anew to the House, locating its commencement." Now, he could have no such motive, for its commencement had been designated by the resolution itself.

Now, Mr. Speaker, the resolution was offered by the gentleman himself, referring, as I thought, to a subject already before one of the Standing Committees of the House, and it was for that reason alone I made the suggestion I did upon that occasion. As soon, however, as I discovered the mistake, I myself moved its reconsideration; and the gentleman, although it was his own resolution, his own proposition, objected to its reconsideration, under the pretence that he would "present it anew to the House, locating its commencement." I have quoted this for the purpose of connecting these subjects, and to show that the opposition to the reconsideration of the gentleman's own resolution, and his published remarks on that subject, were intended for political effect at home, and not for the information of the House, because they were made out of this House, and written by the gentleman himself.

Mr. Speaker, I have upon all occasions, carefully avoided any collision with any gentleman upon this floor. It is both unpleasant and disagreeable, and it is especially so with a colleague. But when I see my remarks and my motives misrepresented, and those misrepresentations sent abroad throughout the country, to produce an effect against me at home, I could not, in justice to myself and those I represent, permit them to pass unnoticed. Sir, there are a species of animals in our forests, with whom, notwithstanding their weakness and abject meanness of spirit, the lion himself would shun a controversy. There are, Mr. Speaker, men who owe their impunity from rebuke and chastisement, to their resemblance to these quadrupeds. I hope the House will pardon me for thus trespassing upon its patience, by introducing matter not altogether relevant to the subject under consideration.

I know, sir, the gentleman may suppose that the length of time that has elapsed since his remarks have gone forth, would have enabled them to produce the desired effect; but this being the first occasion that has offered to make the correction, I have thought it due to myself to explain it. I have no objection that gentlemen should take any course they think proper to write out their own speeches, when it is not done at the expense of truth and to the detriment of others.

The gentleman the other day, in reply to my colleague, (Mr. Ewing,) after he had been told in emphatic terms, that his published remarks were not true; that he had written them himself, and that the reporter, therefore, was not chargeable with the misrepresentation, boastingly told the House, that whoever contradicts his assertion, does it at his peril. Why, sir, this reminds me of a very troublesome fellow in my neighborhood, who had offended a very good citizen, and refusing to make the necessary redress, the gentleman took upon himself the responsibility of redressing his own wrong by applying a very unpleasant application to the young man's shoulders. After giving him about thirty, he let him pass. The fellow immediately applied to the clerk for a writ, who asked him why he did not fight him. "Why," said the fellow, "I had determined if he had struck another lick, I would have given him hell!"

Mr. Speaker, when I introduced the subject here, I did it in the character of a representative of the People. I consulted no personal feelings, nor am I responsible to any but my constituents out of this House; but, notwithstanding this, I shall never shrink from any responsibility that may grow out of any thing that I may say here. Nor, sir, have I introduced it for the purpose of hunting out and making charges against the administration. No, sir, I am an older soldier in the support of the administration than that gentleman, and have defended it from the earliest period, and expect to do so, as long as I have th

of a seat here, when I think its measures are correct. But I claim the right of differing in opinion upon all subjects, when my duty to my constituents shall demand it.

There is no intention of bringing any charge upon the Executive by this resolution. On the contrary, its object is to enable the Executive to do justice to the country. I have brought it forward, sir, after due deliberation and reflection, and I trust it will be adopted, so that the country may see where frauds have been perpetrated, and who have been guilty of them, and that those who have been unjustly charged may have it in their power to exculpate themselves. I again repeat, sir, that so far from locating the frauds in Indiana, or intending to locate them there, I located them nowhere, I made no charge against the agent in Indiana, (whom I believe to be as honest and honorable a man as lives,) nor against any other individual whatsoever. I have reason to believe that fraud has been perpetrated somewhere, and I wish it known. In conclusion, sir, let me assure my honorable colleague, that I will never suffer misrepresentations of myself to pass here unheeded, nor, so long as I shall be honored with a seat on this floor, permit them to go without exposing them to public view. I have thus, Mr. Speaker, said all I intended on this subject, and beg to express my acknowledgments to the House for the indulgence afforded me. My main object was to correct this error, and to do justice to myself by placing the whole matter fairly before the public.

Mr. EWING then rose, but

Mr. WATMOUGH called for the order of the day; which motion was not sustained—ayes 55, noes not counted.

Mr. EWING, of Indiana, said, he did not rise to protract the debate upon this resolution, and he would not now add one word after the remarks of his respected colleague, (Mr. McCarty,) who had just taken his seat, were it not that the correction of false and injurious matter made by the member on his right, (Mr. Lane,) was little less offensive than his original publication. In his effort to avert the force of the correction, I felt myself called upon to reply; he seemed to take offence at the language I had used, when it is known to the House that I used no language but what his injurious misrepresentation justly merited. I am in the habit of calling things by their right names, and so are the upright people I represent. I call a spade a spade, when I allude to that implement, and in repelling the charge that I had implicated the people of Indiana, in any participation of fraud, or that the resolution was calculated to do so, or that it justified or required his bald eulogium, I used only such terms as were necessary to expose the falsehood.

The member (Mr. Lane) commenced his remarks by stating that he would not "bandy epithets," but that he would state the truth, and that contradiction would be at "peril." Now, I bandy no "epithets;" I establish the fact that he did not state the truth; and of his "perils," I am here and elsewhere utterly regardless. Indeed, in this case, the "peril" is fudge: what does not appear, does not exist. But if his "perils" are the garbled and untrue reports sent through the medium of the Globe, to injure faithful Representatives at home, I confess I cannot express such indifference. Now, sir, the report of my late remarks in that partisan print were so garbled and shaped as to give covert point to his misrepresentations. I acknowledge, sir, there is art manifested in this course; the same sort of art which he displayed in his uncalled for allusion to the people of Indiana. The people require services, not flattery; and in his case it was dealt out upon the unfounded assumption that the resolution of my colleague (Mr. McCarty) had cast a stigma on them; when in fact the people of Massachusetts, and every other State, were as much implicated as they were, for the resolution is only calculated to bring necessary information to all.

But I suppose the "peril" threatened by the member (Mr. Lane) had reference to the new version of his remarks, and not to those that he prepared for the Globe, which were the original cause of complaint. Now how does the matter stand, the threatened peril notwithstanding? I charged him with having written for the Globe a bald eulogy founded on a false and injurious statement, calculated to do great injustice to myself and my colleague on my right, (Mr. McCarty,) and to deceive our constituents. I further charged him with making such a correction of it as might still gain for him unmerited credit for defending them from the false and injurious statement which originated in his own imagination, and appeared in the Globe. The House has witnessed his pretext, inuendoes, and subterfuge, in reply to these exposures, and heard his declaration that what he then said was "true and not false, and, that the contradicter would himself assert a falsehood." This, too, accompanied by an intimation that I had sought protection under the dome and within the walls and drapery of this House, for the exposure of the impositions. He (Mr. Lane) did not deny that he had written the false statement for the Globe; but he may have wished to convey the idea that I could be intimidated from stating facts. Now, I would have that member to understand, that such an idea is as unfounded as the falsehoods I have already exposed. I claim no protection from the walls, dome, or drapery. It is not these, but my constituents, that I regard; and I have not, nor shall I ever, make any remarks here, which I shall shrink from reiterating elsewhere. The intimation was given as a disclaimer on his part, that he would seek no such protection. He must now know that I hold myself personally responsible, and he may pursue what course he chooses.

As the able exposition of my respected colleague (Mr. McCarty) has placed the matter at issue in its true light, I would say no more, were it not for the degrading perversions of my former remarks, and the declaration of what the member (Mr. Lane) "would never do," which accompanied his perversions. He labored to make the erroneous impression that I took offence at his unnecessary eulogy on my constituents, instead of the false ground on which he based it. He knew I had taken offence only at his attempt to show that his pretended defence of them was required by my course; and he knew, and this House knew, he was attempting to do the very thing he disclaimed. Thank God, sir, I and that member are known to the people of Indiana; and if he does not know me better than his course indicates, I can inform him that I have long known him. This, sir, is no place to play the braggart, and I hope he will hereafter seek some place more suitable. If, as he said, he would indulge in no defamation, why did he not frankly and effectually correct his error in proper time, and why did he labor to avert the force of my correction? I wish only that the constituents of each shall know the facts of this case, as the House knows them; and that each of us may be judged by the tendency of our acts. The resolution I hope will be adopted.

In reply Mr. LANE said, his colleagues, (Mr. McCarty, and Ewing,) were upon a cold trail; that he deemed it a duty to the House and himself to say, he had not in the House on a former occasion, said his colleagues had located the frauds in Indiana—that as soon as he saw the report of his remarks in the Globe, he had detected the error, and sent a note to the office correcting it. That his remarks had, at the request of the reporter, been written out by himself, as is usual in the House. That in setting the type the compositor omitted the following words: "which would seem to locate them;" had this line not been omitted all this difficulty would have been avoided, but as it is the assault on the part of my colleagues was uncalled for, and unprovoked on my part, in as much as the correction was made before the assault.

Mr. Lane said it was extremely unpleasant, repugnant to all his feelings, to be called upon to make even a good natured reply to such language as had been thrown upon the House. It has been said with wisdom, there is a time for all things. A poor thing said in, is better than a good one out of place. The one is the manifestation of a weak mind—the other of a depraved taste.

Sir, we are in the house of mourning. Some for the loss of a personal and esteemed friend—all for the loss of a valuable member. That tongue, lately so eloquent, is silent. Those eyes so bright, are closed in death. Those limbs so active, and face so comely, in the tomb. I could not have found it in my heart to have said ought to have disturbed the repose of the mourner—the solemn feast of feeling—the Sabbath of the mind. Nor would I have forgotten the late tragical attempt in this Capitol; which, had it been acted out as did Othello his part, this Capitol, this nation, would have been shaken as by some mighty earthquake, from its centre to its circumference.

Thus situated, had I never so much cause for revenge—my bow and my arrow in my hand, my eye on the victim, the very thought of these recent events to have flitted across my mind, a look at this badge of mourning on my arm, as a manifestation of regard for departed worth, and my bow and my arrow should have fallen; with my eyes on Heaven. I would have made one effort to rise, in all the pride and glory of man, superior to the brutal passion.

Sir, said Mr. Lane, to the people of Indiana it would be a subject of curiosity how this difficulty should have arisen between himself and colleagues (McCarty and Ewing) in the consideration of a resolution in the adoption of which we agree.

They will see at once it has not grown out of any thing seen or heard in this debate; that the couse lies deeper, not in the virtue, but in the depravity of the human heart.

Man, sir, may dissemble for a while, may deceive, but, sooner or later, like the pent up heated waters, the least enviable qualities will burst forth. The politician who abandons his first love, his principles, and betrays his trust, looks with envy upon the faithful. Sir, there is a manner, a language, a courtesy, a delicacy, and sweetness of expression, in the heat of even angry debate, that characterises the gentleman and the scholar—a language, a look, that distinguishes him from the vulgar ruffian. To look at such a man is to know him a gentleman, elevated in mind, pure in thought, sensitive in feeling, alive to his honor, always respecting the feelings and regarding the honor of others.

Sir, pursue the other through all the walks and shades of life, to his own or his neighbor's fireside, to the gay circle, or to a more elevated station, and he is still no gentleman, but a ruffian, without feeling or honor, regardless of both in others. To see such a man is to know his ruling passions, his weapons of warfare—envy, revenge, detraction, calumny.

Sir, it is to be presumed, neither of my honorable colleagues, (Messrs. McCarty and Ewing,) will claim this picture or desire the garment, not being intended for them. If, however, contrary to my wishes and intentions, a claim should be asserted, I assure the House and my honorable colleagues, (Messrs. McCarty and Ewing,) that nothing shall be charged for the cutting or the making.

Mr. Speaker, I was elected by a highly respectable District, as their immediate representative, to act in harmonious concert with my honorable colleagues, in promoting the best interest of the People of Indiana, to maintain their interests, their honor, the Union, the dignity of this House, and not to tarnish the one or neglect the other, by entering into a private quarrel with them.

Sir, there is a point in the scale of human degradation, to notice or look at no honorable man will descend.

There is a language and men, not, surely, in this House, to notice either, is disgrace—to disregard, a virtue.

Mr. Speaker, I feel myself called upon to say one word in relation to myself. During the last, and so far of the present session, I have been at my post; not a day or an hour absent. I have voted on all occasions; have been the watchful, and, to the extent of my humble abilities, the faithful sentinel over the rights and the honor of the district and State I represent. Unlike my honorable colleague at my right, (Mr. McCarty,) the Clerk of this House has not dashed his pen across my name, as absent, in the taking the ayes and the noes, eighty and two times, and unlike my colleague on the left, (Mr. Ewing,) forty and seven times.

Sir, my sin seems to consist chiefly in the fact, that I took occasion to say of the people of Indiana, that they were as pure, honest, and high-minded as the citizens of any other State. In these general terms of commendation, the constituents of my colleagues (Messrs. McCarty and Ewing) were included. They claim this special privilege themselves. That when they want praise, or their interests require a defender, that their constituents look to them.

Sir, on the eighty-two occasions when my colleague (Mr. McCarty) was absent, a part of which time he was in Baltimore and Philadelphia, and of my other colleague (Mr. Ewing) on forty-seven occasions, what would have been the condition of their constituents, had their honor or their interests required an advocate?

Sir, I shall never shrink from stepping forward as the advocate of any and every portion of Indiana, when, in my judgment, their interests or their honor shall require it at my hands.

Sir, this is a most useless and unpleasant discussion—a wanton waste of the time of the House, and the money of the people, and all this occasioned by my colleages, by this wanton and uncalled for assault. How much better, how much more honorable, if my colleagues had vied with me, in serving our common constituents, to force through this House, by all proper means, the various local, and general bills in which they feel so much interest; to which the people of the State look with so much anxiety.

In this laudable strife I will most cheerfully engage. I have no other object or motive. All my aspirations are for the public good—the interest and honor of my constituents.

I ask pardon of the House for having detained them so long, assuring the House and my colleagues, that on no future occasion I shall consider it a duty to notice them, other than in manly and honorable debate, in promoting the interest of my constituents and the People of the State.

Mr. McCARTY said: This controversy, Mr. Speaker, is unpleasant, but it is not of my seeking. It has been forced upon me, and although uninteresting to this House, I must be permitted to say one word in reply to the gentleman's (Mr. Lane's) remarks, in reference to the non-appearance of my name upon the list of yeas and nays, upon several occasions. Sir, I had been repeatedly informed, during the last, and present session of Congress, by several honorable members of this House, as well as several of its officers, that the gentleman (Mr. Lane) was in the habit of examining the Clerk's books, and taking extracts from them, to show the absence of his colleagues, when their names were called; and I have, Mr. Speaker, known, that he had written on to my district, and published this fact, accompanied with other remarks, regardless of truth, disreputable and unbecoming the station he fills.

But I could not believe it possible that the gentleman would have had the face, hard and unblushing as I know it is, to have got up in this House, before the assembled representatives of the nation, and voluntarily given testimony to his own depravity. Sir, has there ever before been an instance of a member of Congress, no matter by what accident he may have got here, who has had so little regard for himself as to have descended to so low and disgraceful a practice? What! a member of Congress, representing a highminded, intelligent, and patriotic people, in the constant habit of taking, if not filching, from the Clerk's papers, means by which to charge and slander his colleagues at home! Not only so, sir, but that he should openly acknowledge, and avow it here, in a speech to go forth to the country. Sir, when I shall have so far lost sight of all principles of propriety, courtesy, and honorable deportment towards my colleagues and this House, with assumptions of saint-like sanctity, with the pretensions of regard which the gentleman in his speech the other day professed for his colleagues, and, at the same time, make such disclosures of my own conduct, as the gentleman has of himself upon this occasion, I should feel myself no longer worthy the trust confided to me.

have known for a long time the gentleman had lged in this habit, but for the honor of the State, and the feelings of those he represents, I forbore to speak of it. I preferred to risk the injury he intended to inflict upon me, by this course of conduct, rather than it should be generally known that one who could or would descend to such a practice, held a seat in this Hall. But it can be concealed no longer; he has himself made this disclosure. Sir, I will pursue this subject no further. It is painful to speak of it. I will leave the gentleman to enjoy all the *honor* and *glory* he may have fancied himself to have acquired by publishing his own infamy; and I will not, sir, descend to notice anything he may say. One word in reference to myself, upon the subject of my absence from my seat on some occasions, upon the call of the yeas and nays. You know, Mr. Speaker, that members are necessarily and unavoidably many times absent from their seats, in the discharge of their various duties in the committee rooms, and at the public offices, in addition to their absence sometimes from sickness. I know this is not a matter for discussion here—that it is a subject between me and my constituents, and to whose judgment and decision I will most cheerfully submit it; and with no fearful apprehensions of the result, when I return among them and submit the journals of this House, that they may know how often I have been absent from my seat, during the four years they have honored me with their confidence. I have not examined them, nor will I. My constituents have not yet complained of any neglect of attention to their interest; and when they do, permit me to tell the gentleman he is the last man on the floor of this House whom they would call upon, either for aid or information. Sir, many of my constituents know that man; yes sir, they know him, and thank Heaven, many who do not know him personally, know his character, and what estimate to put upon it.

Mr. EWING said, Mr. Speaker: "How use doth breed a habit in a man." The member (Mr. Lane) has strongly exemplified the truth of this remark—contradicting, yet persisting in the truth of all he has said. After disclaiming, on a former occasion, any wish to detract from his colleague's standing, avowing himself unworthy of a seat on this floor when he should be capable of doing so, the House now sees that he still resorts to false and injurious charges, direct and implied, to accomplish the purpose of his original falsehood which my colleague (Mr. McCarty) and myself have distinctly exposed. His disposition and habits are thus clearly manifested in his course, and I disdain to animadvert further. If the charge that I have been absent during the last and present sessions forty times, when the ayes and noes were called, was intended to impress the people of Indiana that I have neglected the business of the State, or my immediate constituents, my reply is, that the charge is false. I may, for aught I know, have been absent as often as he has stated when the ayes and noes were called upon collateral questions; but if he intended to intimate that I have been in Baltimore or Philadelphia while the House was in session—[Here Mr. Lane said he had not asserted any such thing.] Mr. Ewing resumed: Then let that pass. The member (Mr. Lane) omitted to mention the number of times himself and his other colleagues had been absent. For myself, I have so much office business to transact, that the number of missing votes are fewer than I had apprehended. But with one exception—last session, in relation to the Bank of the United States, not conceived to be properly before the House—I have never avoided a vote, nor lost one by neglect.

The melancholy circumstances alluded to by the member, (Mr. Lane,) as a pretext for much he has said, I will not notice; but his implied censure of my course I can only regard with contempt. On this, as on all other occasions, I have done what duty to myself and constituents required; and, holding myself always ready to reciprocate kindness, I am equally prepared to resent imposition, insult, and injury. I will only add that the charge of *envying* the member is too ridiculous to require any other correction than flat denial. I can neither envy nor imitate that member, in his principles, pretensions, disposition, or character. He has said that it is "a wanton waste of time" to correct all his misrepresentations. I now join in that opinion, and abstain from adverting to many, which, I trust, the people at home are sufficiently advised to appreciate as they deserve. Of this number I pass over his preposterous pretension to extraordinary services in this House, and his remark upon politicians who "abandon their *first* love." All such impositions can be detected without notice here, and I think it unnecessary to say more.

Mr. PLUMMER said, he was very anxious for the passage of this resolution; but he had ascertained, and was authorized to state, that if that part relating to the production of a map was retained, the call could not be answered during the present session of Congress. He wished to submit a motion to strike out that part relating to maps.

The CHAIR stated, the question was on the amendment submitted by the Committee on Indian Affairs, and asked the gentleman from Mississippi, (Mr. Plummer,) if he wished to offer an amendment to that?

Being answered in the negative—

Mr. CLOWNEY asked for the yeas and nays on the adoption of the amendment from the Committee on Indian Affairs.

The motion was not sustained by one-fifth, the requisite number of votes.

Mr. CLAY then submitted an amendment, constituting a Select Committee on the subject. He remarked, that neither himself or constituents could have any personal interest in the matter, but he believed the proposition he had just submitted indicated the most suitable course for the House to pursue.

Mr. LOVE opposed this amendment; and on the question of its adoption, demanded the yeas and nays. They were ordered;

And after some conversation between Messrs. BOON, LOVE, and ASHLEY, they were taken, and the amendment was rejected—ayes 22, nays 172.

Mr. PLUMMER then moved to strike out that part of the resolution relating to maps.

Mr. GRENNELL opposed the motion. He thought it would tend to defeat the principal object of the resolution, as the map and surveys were deemed to constitute the most important information sought for. It was not the separate plats that were desired, as seemed to be the impression of some gentlemen, but a single and general map; and he could not think the expense or trouble would be so great as to prevent the call being answered at the present session. However that might be, he deemed the map of sufficient importance to justify the delay. When it was known that this investigation was ordered and progressing, that fact alone would have a tendency to check further frauds, if any now existed.

Mr. PLUMMER, after expressing his readiness to be governed by the opinions of gentlemen around him, in facilitating business, withdrew his motion to an end.

The question was then taken on the passage of the resolution, as reported from the Committee on Indian Affairs, and it was adopted without a division.

On motion of Mr. MANN, of New York.

The House then adjourned.

IN SENATE.

TUESDAY, Feb. 3, 1835.

A message was received from the President of the United States by the hands of A. J. Donelson, Esq., his Private Secretary, giving information that he had approved and signed the bill making an appropriation to repair the military barracks at New Orleans.

The VICE PRESIDENT laid before the Senate a communication from the Treasury Department, transmitting a statement of the revenue which accrued from the duties upon merchandise, for the year 1833.

Also, a communication from the Navy Department, transmitting a statement of the appropriations made for the naval service for the year 1834.

Also, a communication from the War Department, transmitting abstracts of the general returns of the militia of the United States.

Mr. BUCHANAN presented the memorial of a convention of delegates assembled at Brownsville, Pennsylvania, praying an appropriation to improve the Monongahela river, from Brownsville to Pittsburgh; which was referred to the Committee on Commerce.

Mr. SILSBEE, from the Committee on Commerce, to which sundry petitions on the subject were referred, reported a bill fixing the number and pay of the custom-house officers of the United States, which was read twice, and made the special order for Monday next.

Mr. POINDEXTER, from the Committee on Public Lands, to which was referred the bill supplementary to the act granting pre-emption rights to settlers of the public lands, reported the same without amendment, and gave notice that when the bill should be called up, he would move for its indefinite postponement.

Mr. POINDEXTER, from the same Committee, reported a bill for the relief of the heirs of James Latham, deceased.

Mr. POINDEXTER, from the same Committee, to which was recommitted the bill for the relief of Duncan L. Clynch, reported the same with an amendment, which was concurred in, and the bill, as amended, was ordered to be engrossed for a third reading.

Mr. ROBBINS, pursuant to notice, and on leave given, introduced a joint resolution authorizing an equestrian bronze statue of Washington to be executed, which was read twice, and referred to the Library Committee.

Mr. WHITE, from the Committee on Indian Affairs, made an unfavorable report upon the petition of citizens of Michilimackinac, praying a road of a township of land to aid in the instruction of Indian youths at that place, and the committee were discharged from the further consideration of the subject.

Mr. HENDRICKS, from the Committee on Roads and Canals, reported a bill to provide for the transportation of the mail and other property of the United States, on the eastern section of the Chesapeake and Ohio Canal; which was read the second time and ordered to a second reading.

Mr. TOMLINSON, from the Committee on Pensions, made an unfavorable report upon the petition of Timothy M. Bannesu.

The resolution submitted by Mr. CLAY, declaring that the resolutions from Alabama, instructing their Senators to use their exertions to get the resolution of censure, adopted by the late at the last session, expunged from the journals, ought not to be received, was taken up for consideration.

Mr. CLAY said, that when he submitted the resolution, he stated that he did not intend any action on it, until some movement should be made given to those resolutions. Till then, he moved to let it on the table.

The motion was agreed to.

The resolution submitted by Mr. WAGGAMAN, for an inquiry, by a Select Committee, into the expediency of establishing a branch of the United States Mint at New Orleans, was taken up, altered, and agreed to.

Mr. PRESTON, pursuant to notice, and on leave given, introduced a joint resolution authorizing the purchase of certain paintings, now in this city, to be placed in the President's House.

Mr. P. remarked, that the paintings which it in contemplation to purchase, might be appropriately placed in the President's House, and in others, too, where they were needed. He thought the expenditure was within the powers delegated by the constitution, and as vast expenditures had only been made for ornaments of that building, thought this one quite as appropriate—one which should last for ages, and would be honorable to the nation. He moved in this matter, because he could not be suspected of being actuated by any personal feeling. He had not been in that place for twenty years, and thought it probable might not be in it for twenty years to come; he thought the paintings would be appropriate and tasteful to the house, and therefore he had the proposition to purchase them.

The resolution was read the first time, and ordered to a second reading.

The amendments made by the House to the Joint Resolution authorizing a gold medal to be struck and presented to Lieut. Col. Croghan, and swords to the officers who were under his command at Fort Sandusky, were taken up, and concurred in.

The following bills from the House were taken up, read twice, and committed:

The bill making appropriations for the Civil and Diplomatic expenses of the Government for the year 1835.

The bill for the relief of Thomas Buford;

The bill amending the act for constructing a bridge over the Potomac at Washington City, and repealing all other acts relating thereto;

A Joint Resolution, authorizing a gold medal to be struck in honor of the battle of the Cowpens.

The Joint Resolution authorizing the purchase of Gales and Seaton's Register of Debates, to supply the new Senators at the present session, was taken up for consideration, as in Committee of the Whole.

Mr. HILL desired that a day might be assigned for considering the subject, which he thought required some investigation, and suggested Tuesday next.

Mr. KING, of Georgia, moved to lay it on the table, for the purpose of allowing further time to obtain certain information which the Senate had required the Secretary of the Senate to obtain; which was agreed to.

The Joint Resolution repealing a joint resolution prescribing the mode of electing the printer of the Senate, came up on a second reading.

Mr. BENTON said he did not think it necessary that this resolution should go to a committee. A commitment was only necessary to examine details or investigate principles. Such was the case with the three act two years ago, which was not committed, because there was but a single point in it. Neither were the rules of the Senate imperative on this subject, and there was nothing in this proposition which required the supervision of a committee, for the point was a single one. But his objection to sending it to a committee was more substantial. It was because, two years ago, a similar proposition introduced and submitted to a committee, which the Committee did not find leisure to act on until the time had gone by which it was designed to apply to—until after the election of the public printer had taken place which the resolution was intended to prevent. Then it came back without the crossing of a t, or the dotting of an i. He now objected to the commitment for the same reason; he would not move to refer the resolution, but he asked the action of the Senate on it at once.

Mr. MANGUM thought it ought to be referred, and we could have a report in a day or two. The proposition was an important one, going to change the usages of this House, which were of 15 years standing. He moved to refer the resolution to the Committee on the Expenditures of the Senate.

Mr. BENTON said, he resumed his seat for the purpose of giving an opportunity to any member to make a motion to refer if necessary. He was not a member of the Committee indicated by the gentleman who had just sat down. He would barely state, that it was the inherent right of every public body, to provide itself with its own officers; and since the resolution of 1818-19 had been in force and operation, he looked on the public printer as an officer of the House, and a very responsible one. Under the Constitution of the United states, it belongs to each House to choose its own officers. In this view, he considered the existing resolution a dead letter, which might well be disregarded by both Houses. But he did not wish to proceed in this way. As the act was upon the statute book, he proposed to remove it in the ordinary way.

Mr. POINDEXTER said, if we adopted the resolution, we would be nine months without a public printer, and the simple question was whether we should leave no printer in existence, or choose one in advance—the latter, he thought best.

Mr. MANGUM said as there seemed to be an important principle involved in the proposition, he would move to refer it to the Judiciary Committee, instead of the one he had indicated, who could very speedily act upon it.

Mr. BENTON said the whole object of sending it to a committee was to perfect its details. He had no objection to its going to a committee, or preference for any particular one, if it would return again. But he was not willing to let it go to the tomb of the Capulets, never to return. As to having a printer in the recess, it was an abuse which had grown up of late years. Before the passage of the resolution of 1818-19, the Clerk of the House, and the Secretary of the Senate, were directed to make provision for having the public printing executed. When that resolution passed, it changed the mode by which the printing had been done. It was passed on the 3d March 1819, just at the breaking up of Congress, and one of the terms embraced in it, was, that the printer was to give bond for the prompt and faithful execution of the work. Prompt was the word used, and if he failed in having it executed promptly, the Clerk and Secretary were to go on and have it executed as they had formerly done, and if any loss accrued thereby, it was to be at his expense. The vacation printer then, was an abuse which had grown up since that period. And no sooner was he thus created than he went to work immediately, in instanti, to rummage the old documents and files, to find out every possible kind of printing which could be done—obtain authority for doing it, and let it lie over for the vacation. And so successful had the printers been in this work, that members sometimes were the innocent cause of procuring printing to be done to the amount of thousands of dollars, which was not worth as many cents. One job, within his recollection, which it was said would cost $1500, had since cost $46,000, which was not worth one straw; and which not one member would read after it was finished. Another document was in his eye on the table, containing 690 pages, with a great proportion of it table work, for which he declared three prices was paid. This work was ordered to be done on the 9th December, 1834, and it had just been laid on our tables. Mr. B. said, let any gentleman look over it, and see what was contained in it, that was not printed before, and then say what use he could make of it. In a short time we should have another portion of it coming in by instalments.

And thus while we were receiving instalment after instalment, and octavo volume after octavo volume, not one document in it would be read, and if it should be read, it would be of no manner of use afterwards. It was a mere farce, and an abuse which resulted by having an officer in vacation. The Senate were engaged in looking for abuses in the administration of the Government, and none were so great as those which existed in this body. Within seven years the Senate had put on its seven league boots, and had taken strides of twenty-one miles at a time. It became us to look at our own conduct, and arrest the extravagant abuses which this business of printing had engendered. It had degenerated into making fat jobs for the printer, and presents to ourselves, and while another matter was in his recollection, he would take the opportunity to offer a compliment to the honorable gentleman from Georgia, which he well merited, for having arrested at the last session, when it was about to pass almost sub silentio, a project which would have taken thousands more from the Treasury. He would inquire of that honorable gentleman whether he had made a calculation of the probable expense of that projected job, and how much it was?

Mr. KING replied, that he could not answer the inquiry accurately, but from the best information he had obtained, it would have been about $80,000.

Mr. BENTON observed, after that, he would say no more.

Mr. LEIGH—What was the proposition?

Mr. KING—It was for reprinting the old journals, &c. of Congress.

The resolution was then referred to the Judiciary Committee.

The bill making an appropriation of five millions, to satisfy claims for spoliations made on Ame-

rican commerce by France prior to 1800, came up
on its third reading and final passage.

Mr. HILL said it was generally understood, he
believed, in the Senate, and he hoped it would be
also by the American People, that the last section,
added to the bill at the suggestion of the honorable gentleman from Maine, (Mr. Shepley,) would
not, and could not bar the further prosecution of
these claims. Before he concluded, Mr. H. asked
for the yeas and nays on the passage of the bill,
which were ordered, and are as follows:

YEAS—Messrs. Bell, Buchanan, Chy, Clayton,
Ewing, Frelinghuysen, Goldsborough, Kent,
Knight, McKean, Moore, Naudain, Poindexter,
Porter, Prentiss, Preston, Robbins, Shepley, Sil-
bee, Smith, Southard, Swift, Tipton, Tomlinson,
Webster—25.

NAYS—Messrs. Benton, Bibb, Brown, Calhoun,
Cuthbert, Grundy, Hendricks, Hill, Kane, King of
Alabama, King of Georgia, Leigh, Linn, Man-
gum, Morris, Robinson, Tallmadge, Tyler, White,
Wright—20.

So the bill passed.

The bill for the relief of David McCord; a bill
for the relief of Christopher T. Bailey; and a bill
supplementary to an act allowing the people of
Louisiana to settle the back lands—were severally
read a third time and passed.

The bill for allowing interest on certain claims
to the heirs of Lucy Bond and others, being under
consideration.

Mr. WRIGHT said he was constrained to oppose its passage. He believed it a violation of the
rules and principles established by the Senate,
during the last session of Congress. It was then
decided that Government ought not to pay such
demands, unless it was in the wrong, unless it had
failed to satisfy claims which had been fully established. The subject was before the Senate at its
last session. As the bill came from the House, by
some means several names had been stricken
from it, and its passage at this time would go to
establish that a subsequent Congress may rightfully decide on the propriety of the sets of a preceding Congress, in relation to claims rejected by
them. If for once this were established, what
would be the condition of Congress, liable to be
perpetually harassed by every claimant? Mr. W.
here alluded to the bill just passed, (the spoliation
bill,) which had been before Congress since 1802.
Are we to adopt, said Mr. W. the principle, that
every preceding Congress was in the wrong, and
we in the right? He was not willing to allow that
any claim was due until it had been successfully
prosecuted and allowed by Congress.

Mr. SMITH explained the manner in which
the names had been left out through a mistake made
in the Committee, and also why interest had not
been allowed before.

Mr. LEIGH was glad, he said, the Senator from
New York, (Mr. Wright,) had brought the consideration of this subject before the Senate. He
had no need of informing that gentleman, that
he fully agreed with him in the main; but he merely rose to inform him of the rules that had been
adopted on this subject. Here Mr. L. read a report to the Senate made on another subject.

Mr. WRIGHT wished to inquire of the Senator
from Connecticut, (Mr. Smith,) whether the
names stricken from the bill at the last session,
was stricken by order of the Senate or by mistake?

Mr. SMITH was not positive on that point.

Mr. W. resumed: He believed this claim had
been placed on its true grounds—that we are acting on a subject which had already been rejected
one branch of the Government. Mr. W. concluded by asking the yeas and nays, which were ordered.

After some further debate between Messrs.
WRIGHT, LEIGH, SHEPLEY, MILL, PREN-
TISS—during which Mr. HILL read a letter
showing the manner in which claims of this kind
were hunted up by speculators and presented to
Congress—when the question was put and decided
by yeas and nays as follows:

YEAS—Messrs. Bibb, Clay, Cuthbert, Ewing,
(hu)sen, Goldsborough, Hendricks, Kent,
Lien, McKean, Mangum, Moore, Poindex-
arter, Robbins, Shenley, Smith, Southard,
Tomlinson, Tyler, White—23.

NAYS—Messrs. Benton, Brown, Grundy, Hill,
King of Alab., King of Geo., Knight, Morris, Nau-
dain, Prentiss, Robinson, Tallmadge, Tipton,
Wright—14.

So the bill passed.

Mr. POINDEXTER asked to be excused from
from serving longer as a member of the Committee on the Library, which was granted.

The Senate then proceeded by ballot to fill the
vacancy occasioned by the resignation of Mr.
POINDEXTER, and Mr. PRESTON was elected.

A bill for the relief of James Middleton Tuttle
was taken up and read the first time and ordered to
a second reading.

On motion of Mr. WHITE, the bill for the relief of Silas D. Fisher was considered and ordered to be read a third time.

Mr. HENDRICKS gave notice that he will on
to-morrow ask leave to introduce a bill to allow
the inhabitants of Florida to open a canal from
the Apalachicola to ————

And the Senate adjourned.

HOUSE OF REPRESENTATIVES.
Tuesday, Feb. 5, 1833.

After the reading of the Journal—

Mr. GRENNELL moved a call of the House,
in consequence of the thin attendance of members;
which was agreed to.

The roll was then called in part, when Mr.
CLAYTON moved to suspend further proceedings under the call; which was agreed to.

Mr. CLAYTON, from the Committee on the
Public Lands, reported a bill amendatory of the
act of 3d March, 1823, in relation to pre-emptions
to settlers on the public lands; which was read
twice and postponed to Friday week.

Mr. CLAYTON, from the same committee, reported a bill for the relief of Thomas M. Bernard; which was read twice and committed.

Mr. CHAMBERS, from the Committee on Private Land Claims, reported, without amendment,
the bill from the Senate for the relief of M. de
Carrrm; which was committed.

Mr. FARRIS, from the Committee on Naval
Affairs, reported a bill for the relief of Samuel
W. Ruff; which was read twice and committed.

Mr. CASEY, from the Committee on the Public Lands, reported, without amendment, the bill
from the Senate for the relief of Elizabeth Mc-
Gruder, of Mississippi; which was committed.

Mr. SUTHERLAND, from the Committee on
Commerce, reported a bill to allow drawbacks of
duties on merchandise exported from the United
States, via Missouri, to the provinces of New Mexico; which was read twice and committed.

Mr. ADAMS, from the Committee on Invalid
Pensions, reported a bill granting a pension to
Soloman Case; which was read twice and com-
mitted.

Mr. JOHNSON, of Kentucky, from the Committee on Military Affairs, reported a bill, making
an appropriation for the repair of the fortifications
on Castle Island, in Boston harbor; which was
read twice and committed.

Mr. BOCKEE, from the Committee on Agriculture, made a report in relation to the culture and
manufacture of silk in the United States; which
was committed.

Mr. SCHENCK, from the Committee on Invalid Pensions, reported a bill for the relief of Jacob Stewart; which was read twice and committed.

Mr. SCHENCK, from the same committee, reported a bill for the relief of Elijah Blodgett;
which was read twice and committed.

Mr. CLAY, from the Committee on the Public
Lands, reported the following resolution; which
was ordered to lie on the table for one day:

Resolved, That the Secretary of the Treasury
be directed to cause an estimate to be made of the
probable expense of constructing a Levee on the
public lands on the western bank of the Mississippi, and the southern bank of Red river, in the
State of Louisiana; and also an estimate of the
expense of constructing or removing obstructions
from the rivers of Arkansas and Missouri, through
the public lands, where in they may be necessary,
together with the probable advantages or disadvantages of such works respectively; the proba-

---

ble effects upon the health and prosperity of the
country in which any such works may be constructed, and the probable quantity, quality, and
value of land belonging to the United States,
which will be reclaimed by the construction of
any such Levees, and make report thereof to the
next Congress.

Unfavorable reports upon various petitions were
made by Messrs. CHANEY, BARRINGER, MIL-
LER, ANTHONY, CARR, ADAMS of New
York, LOYALL, LEA of Tennessee, T. H.
HALL, and INGE; which were laid on the table.

Mr. CARR, from the Committee on Private
Land Claims, made unfavorable reports upon the
petitions of Joseph W. Hegeman, John E. Goff,
and Wordsop Wren; which were ordered to lie
on the table.

Mr. ASHLEY, by leave, offered the following
resolution:

Resolved, That the Secretary of War be required to furnish this House with annual and detailed statements of the expenses which have oc-
cured on the transportation and disbursement of
money appropriated for the payment of Indian
annuities for the years 1833 and 1834, showing the
amount paid, and such claims, if any, as have been
submitted for payment and rejected by the Department.

Mr. PARKS offered the following resolution,
which, under the rule, lies on the table one day:

Resolved, That the Secretary of War be requested to communicate to this House, the report of Maj. Hartman Bache, of the reconnoisance
for a road through the northern frontier of the
State of Maine, made by him in pursuance of
instructions from the War Department.

On motion of Mr. LYON, of Michigan,
Resolved, That the information called for by a
resolution of this House of the 14th ultimo, requesting the Secretary of the Treasury to furnish
copies of the decisions of the commissioners on
Private Land Claims at Machinac, Green Bay, and
Prairie du Chien, in the Territory of Michigan, be
prepared in season to be submitted at the commencement of the next session of Congress.

On motion of Mr. DUNLAP,
Resolved, That the Committee on the Post
Office and Post Roads be instructed to inquire
into the expediency of establishing a post route
from Bluff Creek Post Office, in Fayette county, Tennessee, to Landspring Post Office, in said
county.

On motion of Mr. MAY,
Resolved, That the Committee on Roads and
Canals be instructed to inquire into the expediency of causing a survey of the Illinois river to
be made, from its junction with the Mississippi to
the town of Ottawa.

On motion of Mr. GILMER,
Resolved, That the Committee on Revolutionary
Claims inquire whether a certificate, issued to
John Pierce, Paymaster General of the United
States, to the State of Georgia, in the year 1792,
for the sum of $23,283 79, for commuted
and other pay, advanced by that State to her officers on the continental establishment, be carried, or, in any manner settled by the United States,
and, if not, that said committee inquire into the
propriety of providing for the payment of the
same to the State of Georgia.

On motion of Mr. GARLAND,
Resolved, That the Committee on the Post Office and Post Roads be instructed to inquire into
the expediency of extending the post route from
the town of Opelousas to the settlements on the
Calcasieu river, to the Sabine river, in the State of
Louisiana.

Mr. FERRIS, by consent, offered the following
resolution:

Resolved, That the Committee of Ways and
Means be instructed to inquire into the expediency of repealing the duty on foreign coal.

Mr. FERRIS said, that in offering this resolution, he requested the indulgence of the House,
while he endeavored to explain the reasons which
induced him to solicit this inquiry, and to obviate some of the objections that he anticipated
would be made to it.

During the short period I have had the honor of
a seat on this floor, I have observed that

itions of this nature have been met with one general objection, deemed by many an insuperable one, which is, that any alteration of the tariff of duties on imports, is considered as an interference with the act of March the 2d, 1833, commonly called the Compromise Bill, and that this bill is regarded by many as a compact which it would be a violation of good faith to alter, amend, modify, or repeal.

I respect as highly as any one the motives in which this bill originated, and duly appreciate the great objects and blessings it was intended to accomplish and secure; and while I would not, on the ground of expediency, disturb its leading principles, or agitate questions that have shaken the country to its foundations, I will not shrink from the responsibility of seeking relief from any particular oppression, occasioned by the present tariff of duties, or refuse my assent to alter or modify such tariff, as the good of the country at large, the welfare of its several parts, its relative position with foreign nations, or its agricultural, manufacturing, and commercial policy may from time to time seem to require.

It cannot be true that this Compromise Bill, or those it proposes to modify, are not subject to the same amendment and repeal as any other bills, or that the Legislature who made this compromise bill had any authority to bind or restrain subsequent Legislatures, who might deem proper to act in relation to it, or that it would be even a violation of good faith to do so; for who, I would ask, could pledge the representatives of the people not to relieve their constituents from the operation of laws proved by reason and experience to be unjust or prejudicial. In the absence of constitutional objections, questions of this kind must be determined with reference to their expediency and the rights and interests of the nation, and of all its parts.

Should our relative position with a foreign nation be changed from a pacific to a belligerent state, all will admit that it would be our duty to modify our tariff of duties so as to meet the new circumstances and relations in which we would be placed, and that our necessities might induce us to encourage the importation of articles which, under other circumstances, it would be our policy to exclude.

All will readily admit that if a foreign nation should change her commercial policy towards the United States, and alter her system of duties so materially to affect our navigation and interests, or should violate the provisions of a treaty by which the commercial intercourse between the two countries had been regulated, that it might become necessary for us to counteract these measures by a corresponding action on our part, in relation to our tariff of duties.

And if from experience, the duty on any article of import shall be found to be extremely partial and oppressive, to a particular section of the country, by reason of its circumscribed operation—to produce but little revenue, but that little collected from a few for the benefit of the many, odious from its increasing the price of the necessaries of life, and from its very nature, bearing hard upon the most needy class of our citizens, is it not equally evident that prudence, justice, and policy, would call for its remission, either immediately, or prospectively as circumstances may render expedient?

Did not the compromise bill itself originate from causes of this kind? and was it not intended to relieve the country from the operation of taxes, alleged to bear unequally and oppressively on particular parts, and if from accident, inadvertence, neglect, or the want of knowledge of the operation of a particular duty, relief was not administered by this compromise bill, shall there be no remedy? Are the doors of legislation forever closed against the oppressed class, because they did not complain of their grievances at the time this bill was under discussion, or add to the troubles of the times when the north was arrayed against the south, and conflicting interests aroused the passions of men in bitter hostility? When our country, torn with dissension and threatened with civil war, filled the patriot with the most gloomy apprehensions for the future, while the enemies of our political system rejoiced in the prospect of its dissolution? If the Representatives of the People shall be convinced that any portion of the community suffers unequal burthens, and consequental oppression, I feel every confidence that their sense of justice will apply the remedy.

The resolution before you proposes this inquiry; and upon examination, it will be found that the duty on foreign coal, a primary necessary of life, is one of the most odious, oppressive, and unequal taxes ever imposed by a free Government on a free people, under similar circumstances. The tax on *light* in England, the result of her necessities, arising from protracted wars, does not reach the laboring classes. Our tax on heat, equivalent to one hundred per cent. on the first cost of the material that produces it, extends to the poorest of the very poor; and is extorted in time of peace and in the midst of abundance, without necessity to excuse, or reason to justify it.

By the act of the 10th of August 1790, a duty of 3 cents per bushel was laid on foreign coal.

By the act of April 1816, this duty was increased to five cents per heaped bushel.

By the act of May 1824, it was further increased to six cents per heaped bushel. The act of July 1832, left it in this situation, and although subject to the general operation of the compromise bill. Coal is not among the articles enumerated in the fifth section of that bill, to be admitted to entry free of duty, after the 30th of June 1842.

By a statement furnished me from the Treasury Department, it appears that the aggregate amount of coal imported into the United States during the year ending the 30th of September, 1834, was 1,626,185 bushels, on which the duties amounted to the sum of $94,425.94, after deducting one tenth of the excess of twenty per cent. authorized by the act of March 2, 1833. The duties on the coal imported into the City of New York alone, the same year, amounted to the sum of $45,119 27.

The income derived from this duty, is paid into the Treasury of the general Government, and applied to the use of the whole American People. The wealthy landholder whose forest supplies him with fuel, is as much benefitted by this tax, as the poor tenant of a garret or cellar in the City, who feels happy if he can gather his hungry and shivering family over a few coals, whilst the winter storm is howling around his comfortless dwelling. But although the benefit of the tax extends to the whole community, it is paid by a part only, and that part but a small fraction when compared to the population of the United States. The whole of this tax, except so far as it may influence the price of manufactures, is paid by the Atlantic cities and the inhabitants of their vicinity, of which the city of New York and its vicinage pay about one half; and upon examination it will be found that the consumers of foreign coal amount to less than two hundred thousand persons who pay this tax, which goes into the common Treasury of upwards of twelve millions of people. Is not this unequal and unjust? But, sir, it is oppressive also—the inhabitants of the interior have their fuel at a moderate price, generally for the mere cost of the labor of procuring it. To the inhabitant of a city, fuel is one of the heaviest burthens he has to shoulder through life; it is one of the largest items in every man's family expenses, and fortunate are those, who, by frugal industry, can obtain it. Many suffer from cold and hunger during our long winters, rejoiced if they can gather a few chips, saw dust, or tanners' bark after being ground and used for tanning purposes, to kindle a smouldering fire over which to warm themselves, their wives and little ones. This is no picture of the fancy, it is literally true, and those who have lived in a large city like New York, and who have been called upon to visit the abodes of poverty and wretchedness, will vouch for the correctness of my statements. And I am persuaded, that if the American people become acquainted with the difficulty and expense of procuring fuel in cities, and the misery many suffer for the want of it—they would approve of the remission of this duty, which makes the poor man's home still more wretched.

Those who are relieved from it, will certainly not complain. And I appeal to the better feelings of our nature, whether the inhabitants of the interior, who obtain fuel from their forests or the extensive coal-beds with which some regions abound, and particularly whether the inhabitants of the South and West in the enjoyment of mild climates and fruitful soils, would wish to extort this revenue from the inhabitants of the cities, and add to the difficulties of those who have to encounter long winters at places where fuel from obvious causes is of a high price, and where it is sold to the poor by the penny worth.

In order to show the operation of this tax in the city of New York, with which I am most familiar, and where it is most severely felt, it will be necessary to make mention of some facts with which many may not be acquainted. By a statement from the Treasury Department it appears that the aggregate amount of foreign coal imported into the United States during the year 1833, was 2,256,143 bushels on which the duties amounted to $135,368 58. That there was imported into the city of New York alone during the same year, 1,237,532 bushels, on which the duties amounted to the sum of $74,251, 92, being more than one-half the entire importation of foreign coal for that year, and this coal was consumed in that city and in its immediate vicinity, and sold at an average price of twenty-five cents per bushel. By a report of the city inspector made in pursuance of the order of the Common Council of the city of New York, it appears that the expense of the fuel consumed in that city during the same year, exclusive of foreign coal amounted to $1,088,658 92, add to this amount the estimated value of the foreign coal, being $309,383, and you have the enormous amount of $1,398,041 92, the cost of the fuel for that single year, exclusive of turf, chips, and other substitutes made use of by the poor for better fuel and without including the cost of domestic fuel in the adjoining city of Brooklyn, which would swell the amount to nearly two millions of dollars, and this enormous consumption of fuel is increasing with the augmentation of the population and extension of manufacturing establishments. Among the articles enumerated in the report of the city inspector, are 53,882½ tons of anthracite coal, varying in price from $8 64½ to $6 29 per ton. From the best information I am able to obtain, the anthracite coal can be brought to the city of New York and sold by retail and yield a fair profit at a price varying from five dollars to six dollars and fifty cents per ton.

When it is considered that the price of fuc all kinds is enhanced to the extent of this nearly so, and that the cost of fuel enters i our domestic and manufacturing calc that the price of board, of bread, of gas, and of every manufactured article, a horse shoe to a steam engine, is more or i fluenced by it, some conception may be f of the extent of oppression occasioned b duty to the city of New York, and the oth lantic cities, in proportion to their consun of foreign and domestic fuel.

Another evil flowing from this source, is tl stacle this duty interposes to the inhabita that city, in selecting the kind of coal best ed to their health, comfort, or convenience. American coal introduced there, is mostly anthracite kind, with the exception of the coal, which is principally used for manufac purposes.

The imported coal is bituminous, and man our citizens, and most of the settlers from Eur prefer it, having been accustomed to it from e life, or believing the use of it more conduciv health than the use of anthracite coal. It also be used to more advantage for steam na tion than the anthracite, as it produces more in its consumption. By the operation of this foreign coal is becoming excluded from our kets, and the quantity imported is gradually min shing. Can any good reason be assigned our citizens should be deprived of using anth or bituminous, foreign or domestic coal, a option, and at a price so reduced, by taking duty, that the humblest individual could the comforts of a fire side, and the growth

prosperity of our cities be promoted by lessening the price of living in them?

If this duty on coal was intended as a source of revenue, it has failed of its object, as the statement from the Treasury Department, shows that it produced during the last fiscal year but $94,425 94, and as the national debt is paid, and we shall have in the treasury an annual surplus, after discharging all necessary expenditures, it is not required for that object; and I submit to the good sense of the House, whether the peace and harmony of the country will not be better promoted by circumscribing our revenue to our wants, as far as may be consistent with the protection of our national industry, than by collecting a surplus by unequal taxation, which will invite to extravagance in expenditures, and engender discord and jealousy under any conceivable plan of distribution; and I trust it will be generally conceded that it is better to retain among the people their own money, to circulate through the channels of commerce and industry, giving activity to business and vigorous impulse to enterprise, than to accumulate it in a national treasury, to become the subject of contention and a source of speculation for the statesman and politician, to devise the least objectionable mode of returning it back from whence it came, unavoidably diminished by the expenses of original collection and ultimate distribution, and subject to contingent losses by defalcation and other causes. If this duty was intended to encourage national industry, it has defeated its object, for while it embarrasses commerce, increases the expense of living, and enhanses the price of the implements of husbandry and of most manufactured articles to the farmer and consumer, it at the same time affords no protection to our manufactures, as heat is generally an agent in their production, and any augmentation in the price of fuel must operate to their disadvantage.

If this duty was intended to enable the coal of our country to compete with foreign coal, it was unnecessary for such a purpose; as, without this duty, domestic coal can be sold cheaper than foreign coal, and yield a fair profit; as can be easily shown by a reference to the calculations made by the various coal and canal companies, in their applications for legislative patronage; and by a fair estimate of the cost of coal at the mines, the cost of transportation, toll, yardage, and other incidental expenses, and the increasing facilities of bringing it to market by rail-roads, canals, and new avenues of communication, will enable it to be sold at still more reduced prices.

Neither do the coal-producing States derive advantages from this duty proportionate to the injury it causes to the districts where its operation is felt; as is evident from the prices at which coal is sold at the collieries. A great portion of the increment of the price of coal arising from this tax, is received by the speculators in coal, mostly consisting of the large incorporated coal companies, principally formed of city capitalists, and non-residents of the coal-producing States, who are the proprietors or lessees of the largest and most valuable collieries, and who retail it to the consumer through their agents, and by monopolizing the market, compel the purchasers to pay what they demand, unrestrained by the competition which foreign coal would oppose to them, if admitted free of duty. In order fairly to estimate the profits of the venders of coal, it may also be proper to observe that anthracite coal is sold in the city of New York by the ton, consisting of the nett weight of two thousand pounds, in conformity with the statute regulation of a ton weight in the State of New York; while coal is purchased at many of the collieries from which the supply is obtained, at the gross weight of two thousand two hundred and forty pounds to the ton.

I would submit to those who may wish to encourage the consumption of domestic coal, whether that object is promoted by unnecessarily increasing its price. I apprehend that the cheaper it is [illegible]d to the consumer, just in that proportion [illegible] force other fuel out of market, and supply [illegible].

[illegible]erpool and other European coals are generally brought as ballast by American and foreign shipping. They could not be brought as a regular cargo, without great loss to the importer. They may serve sometimes to complete a return cargo with advantage; but remit this duty and the Nova Scotia coal mines would pour in a supply which would compel the large coal companies and venders of domestic coal to reduce it to a fair price; and although at such a price, it would compete with foreign coal, yet the foreign coal would operate as a check to any unreasonable increase of price. But waiving for the present the question of policy, would it be a legitimate object of the Government to promote the interest of one section of the country to the prejudice and injury of other sections? Is it in accordance with the principles of our Union, with that spirit of amity and good feeling which should exist between the members of this great confederacy? Is it the meaning of the constitution, or was it ever contemplated by the framers of that instrument, that the citizens of one State should be indirectly taxed for the benefit of a sister State?

What would the farmers of Pennsylvania say, if a duty was put on plaster of Paris, or gypsum—a material which is sent in large quantities from the State of New York to fertilize their lands? and there is as much reason why foreign plaster should be taxed to enrich the owners of plaster beds in the State of New York, as that foreign coal should be taxed to enhance the profits of the proprietors of domestic coal mines.

I will not examine the abstract question, how far our Government may be authorized to raise revenues beyond what may be necessary for the purposes of its organization. But it will be admitted that, as a general rule, it is not in accordance with the principles of sound Government to increase the price of the necessaries of life by unnecessary taxation. Revenue should be raised, as far as practicable, from luxuries, with the double view of discouraging extravagance and of placing the burthen on those who are the best able to bear it, and who voluntarily assume the payment, by the consumption of the articles coming under that denomination. But if the necessities of the Government shall render it proper to impose duties on the necessaries of life, they should be placed on such articles as are of general consumption throughout the nation, and in this point of view, a tax on salt, sugar, tea, or coffee, is far more equitable than the one on coal. Sir, the duty on foreign coal cannot be sustained by the arguments that may be advanced in favor of a duty on most other articles.

A duty on some articles of primary necessity may be defended on the ground of public policy. A duty may be put on sugar with a view to encourage its growth in our country—a duty on wool to encourage the raising of sheep among us; upon any product of the earth, to encourage our agriculture; upon any manufactured articles, to encourage the arts and enterprise of our citizens, to enable them to compete with foreign manufacturers, that our wants may be supplied in time of war, or when our intercourse with foreign nations, from whatever cause, shall be suspended; with a view to create a home market for our agricultural produce by diverting a part of the national labor to manufactures or to meet some extraordinary national expenditure or emergency. But a duty on coal can neither be defended on the ground of necessity or policy. The God of nature, in his divine wisdom, has placed extensive beds of coal in many sections of our country—duty or no duty—they are there—in peace or war, they are there. The price our citizens would pay for domestic coal, without the addition of price occasioned by this duty, will be a sufficient inducement to work the coal mines, and the increased consumption of domestic coal that would be created by the lowering of its price, and the gradual augmentation of the population, with the increasing facilities of transportation from the mines to the market, will at all times place it in fair competition with coal which must be brought over the ocean at much greater expense, with the hazards of the sea or the expense of insurance. But, even admit that foreign coal could be brought to our Atlantic cities cheaper than domestic coal, this circumstance would afford no justification for so unequal a tax as this duty imposes, or for unnecessarily increasing the price of fuel, and no principle of our confederated government established for the benefit and protection of all its members, and guarantying equal rights, immunities, and privileges to all its citizens, can sanction any law or policy which adds a fictitious value to the mineral or other productions of some of the States, by increasing the burthens of the other States, or that enriches one part of the community by impoverishing the other part. If I am answered that this duty on coal is part of the compact formed by the compromise bill, and was the consideration and inducement for the coal-producing States to enter into it, I will reply, that all compromises of this kind ought to be based on the principle of reciprocity, and are intended to secure mutual advantages to the contracting parties—that New York receives no equivalent for submitting to this unequal tax on her citizens, and that in this legislative arrangement, her interests in this respect, have not received that consideration to which they are entitled.

A more suitable time could not be selected to bring forward inquiries of the kind contemplated by the resolution. Our national debt has been paid; one and all of us rejoice at this unprecedented event in the history of modern nations; so animating to the patriot; so cheering to the American people of all parties. Let the joyful tidings, as they roll along the valley of the Mississippi, or reverberate through the hills of Maine and New Hampshire, as they are wafted from the Atlantic to the Lakes, and spread through every part of our country, as they reach the hamlet in the wilderness, the scattered settlements of the prairies, or the dense crowds of the city population, be followed by the equally joyful announcement that the Government is taking measures to lessen the burthens of the people, so far as the same can be done consistent with national faith, and a due regard to our great manufacturing, agricultural, and commercial interests, and while our statesmen are devising the means of disposing of the surplus revenue accumulating in the national treasury, let us not at least refuse the inquiry as to what duties on the necessaries of life may be remitted with benefit to all, and without injury to any.

Feeling unwilling to trespass longer on the time of the House, and grateful for the indulgence I have already experienced, I submit this resolution to your consideration, cherishing the hope that the inquiry will be allowed, and that it will be followed by a remission of the duty on coal, or at least that coal will be admitted to entry free of duty, in the same manner and at the same time, as the articles enumerated in the fifth section of the compromise bill. I repeat, I only solicit an inquiry into the complaints of those who feel themselves aggrieved, and who look to the paternal wisdom of Government for protection. I do not wish to disturb the general provisions of the compromise bill, originating in those fraternal feelings which I cherish and respect; I only seek relief from the oppressive operation of a single duty to which the attention of Congress was not particularly drawn when this compromise bill proclaimed to the nation, that our dissensions had yielded to mutual concession, and that peace, harmony, and sentiments of attachment to our Union prevailed throughout the republic.

The SPEAKER laid before the House the following communications, which were appropriately disposed of:

A message from the President of the United States, transmitting a report from the Secretary of State, in answer to a resolution of the House of the 22d ult. in relation to certain correspondence with the Government of Spain;

A letter from the Secretary of War, transmitting, pursuant to a resolution of 8th April, 1834, a revised system of military discipline;

A letter from the Secretary of War, communicating, pursuant to law, an abstract of the general returns of the militia, arms, &c. of the United States;

A letter from the Secretary of the Treasury, exhibiting the revenue accruing from imports for the year 1833;

A letter from the Clerk of the House in relation to the case of —— Pierce, of Georgia.

CITY OF ALEXANDRIA.

The House proceeded to consider the motion heretofore made by Mr. BOULDIN, to reconsider the vote rejecting the bill for the relief of the City of Alexandria.

Mr. BOULDIN said, he would request the indulgence of the House but for a short time, in stating the reasons that had induced him to move for the reconsideration of this bill. He could not flatter himself that, what he had to say, would change the vote of so large a majority as had been given against it, when last before the House; but inasmuch as he had voted under misapprehension, he desired to explain. He was no advocate for internal improvements at the expense of the General Government, carried on any where; nor was he an advocate for it to an extravagant length within the limit of the District of Columbia; but the case under consideration was a peculiar one. An injury had been done to the town of Alexandria by an act of Congress, and the bill before the House was a proposition for its redress. In 1804, he believed it was, that the main channel of the Potomac was diverted from its course by a causeway placed in its deepest part, so as to throw the channel out of its original course, round by the town of Georgetown, thereby destroying the main channel which had previously ran direct to Alexandria; and thereby destroying the trade of that city, which was the only thing that made it an interesting and prosperous city. The trade came down from the valley of Virginia, passing the old channel that went round the falls of the Potomac, and the boats passed immediately along the deep channel between Mason's Island, by which they were protected. The causeway was constructed on that channel; and it then became necessary for the boats to cross the river, a matter of almost impossibility, or at least of great danger, as he was informed, and verily believed, for small craft—the river being there a mile wide. This was the injury that had been done. Mr. B. referred to the opinions of those who lived at the time in its vicinity, and who took part in the legislation under the authority of which the causeway was constructed, and of the delegation in Congress from Virginia, eleven out of fourteen of whom voted against it. Of the three who voted for it, one lived in Georgetown, which would be benefited by it; another lived above, and therefore cared nothing about it; and the third voted as he pleased. This showed the impression those had of it who might be supposed to have known most about it. Prior to the construction of this causeway, the city of Alexandria was flourishing, since that, it had gone down, and it had a right to complain of injury. When a city grew up, and its commerce prospered, and was increasing, to destroy it at once was little short of an act of violence. The citizens had done all in their power to avert its fall. They had subscribed very largely, to the amount of $—,000, to the Chesapeake and Ohio canal, in the expectation that that would remedy the evil brought upon them by the act of Congress. After subscribing a quarter of a million, and bringing the canal to Georgetown, the very seat of the evil, there it was to stop, and all the money they had laid out gone to build up and strengthen their rival. Mr. B. thought it became Congress to aid them, and with due deference, he thought it not right to refuse. Had Congress, by its act, done them an injury? If so, let it be redressed.

Mr. Bouldin said it created great surprise in his mind, as it no doubt did to many others, when he saw a canal proposed to be constructed on both sides of tide water, and when he first saw it, he had no idea of advocating this appropriation. But when he came to be informed that the old channel of the river had been stopped up by an act of Congress, it altered the case altogether, and he saw at once that injury had been done to that town, and that it became Congress to redress it in the best way it could. His impression was, that the redress could not be easily repaired; but as the injured themselves said they should be satisfied with the plan now proposed, he trusted it would be acceded to. He was for final redress, and he thought they should be put in the situation they were before the injury was done them; but as this could not be done, the best way would be to give them what they asked. We have wronged them, and are bound to remedy the evil we have done; and the easiest mode would be that proposed. If a better could be devised, he would willingly vote for it, and he hoped some gentleman would point it out.

Mr. B. again explained, that in voting for the rejection of this bill, he had done so under the misapprehension that it was an appropriation different from that proposed last spring. He thought the money had been received and expended, and that this was a bill for a new appropriation, and he had no idea that it was the same bill. After some further remarks, Mr. B. concluded by moving to reconsider the vote rejecting the bill.

Mr. CHILTON said, the decisive majority by which the bill had been before rejected, was such that he did not imagine such lights would be thrown upon it by further discussion, as to change that issue; and, moreover, as there were many bills of great importance pressing for action, he would, for the purpose of testing the disposition of the House, move to lay the motion on the table.

Mr. MANN, of New York, called for the yeas and nays, which were ordered.

The question was so taken, and resulted as follows: Yeas 89, nays 104.

So the House refused to lay the motion to reconsider the bill on the table.

Mr. THOMAS, of Louisiana, said he was in favor of a reconsideration of this question; but from very different views from those advanced by the gentleman from Virginia (Mr. Bouldin.) The Congress of the United States stood in the relation of a local Legislature to the ten miles square composing the District of Columbia. This District did not possess the privileges of a State, but looked to the Federal Legislature as a child looked to its parent. He for one felt bound to advocate its interests as much as he would those of the State in which he lived. If the Legislation of a State inflicted injury, it was admitted that the State was bound to make reparation for the evil it had inflicted. Mr. T. felt it his duty to call the attention of the House to this ten miles square. He thought it hard that the whole twenty-four States should be unwilling, or feel themselves unable to take care of so small a territory, deprived of the means of taking care of itself. It was hard that they should shut up their bowels of mercy and compassion against the natural appeals of the child dependent on them, and cut off from all other succor. But gentlemen were in the habit of viewing every appropriation in this District as so much money taken out of the Treasury, and belonging to people at a distance. This position he denied. He asked how the District came to belong to the United States. They asked for its session from two States. The answer of Virginia was that she must first obtain the consent of her citizens. When this was done, some forty years ago, she gave, as it were with her child, a dowry of $120,000; which, if running upon interest, would now amount to about $300,000. Of this fund, the United States had enjoyed the benefit. He denied that the United States was advancing one cent out of the pockets of the People. He believed if we should give this ten miles square a Governor and a little Legislature of their own, they would do this work for themselves; and perhaps it would be much better for them, rather than to depend on the great body so little disposed to do any thing for them. He was in favor of the appropriation as a matter of sheer justice.

Mr. BATES expressed his intention to vote in favor of a re-consideration of this bill. It was to do that which, sooner or later, we should be bound to do. The city of Alexandria had difficulties enough to contend with without the hostile legislation of Congress; or if not its hostile, at least its unwise and prejudicial legislation. In the first place, a dam is placed across their channel of the river, diverting its commerce; and next the termination of the Chesapeake and Ohio Canal in Washington, if left in that condition, was calculated to demolish, to annihilate, the prosperity of Alexandria. Two hundred and fifty thousand dollars of the funds of Alexandria had been appropriated towards the construction of the canal, and one hundred and eighty thousand towards that of their lateral canal. A great portion of the work was completed—two of the abutments and one of the piers of the aqueduct were finished, or in a state of forwardness—the machinery for the further prosecution of the work was all provided; and now it seemed to be the disposition of some gentlemen to abandon it altogether. To this course, Mr. B. said, he could not consent, let the expense be what it might. He could not consent that the ruin of this work should be suffered to stand here under the eyes of Congress a monument of its folly. He contended that the dollars and cents expended on public works gave no criterion of the expediency of their construction. The true standard was the amount of labor which they draw from other employments. The circulation of the money among those requiring employment was its proper appropriation. He concluded by repeating that he could not consent to see this work left only as a monument of the unwise legislation of Congress, and if it required ten times the amount asked for, he would support it rather than see it abandoned.

Mr. SPEIGHT said, he did not suppose his opinion would have a tendency to change the vote of any member on this question, but he felt bound to give the reasons which would impel him to vote against the reconsideration. He held different views from those advanced by the gentleman from Louisiana, (Mr. Thomas,) of the relation in which the District of Columbia stood towards the General Government. He considered this projected appropriation as a mere entering wedge, looking to future expenditures of the money of the People, and of the States, on works of internal improvements. He asked what they were called on to do? To cut a splendid canal alongside of a navigable river, fully equal to all the wants of the people in its vicinity. He could conceive of no project more absurd, and called on gentlemen to go and view the works, and convince themselves. He had always found, when the public purse was opened for such works, individual enterprise was relaxed, and the works thus professedly fostered by the Government were most liable to languish. Mr. S. said he was the friend of internal improvements; but they should be confined to their proper conservators. His doctrine was, that the money requisite for their accomplishment, should remain in the hands of the people, and be by them expended at their own option. Those works which had been prosecuted under the auspices of Government funds, had generally given more evidence of peculation than enterprize. The General Government had been accused of extravagance by interested partisans, and the fault was laid at the door of the President or the present administration, while the extravagant appropriations on that floor, were the source to which all these complaints were attributable. He, therefore, called upon every gentleman on that floor, who professed to sustain the principles of economy avowed by the administration, to put a stop to these extravagant expenditures. Mr. S. said he should vote against the motion for reconsideration, as he believed the work inexpedient, and liable to cost a million of dollars, rather than the hundred thousand applied for.

Mr. VINTON said he should vote for the reconsideration, on the ground that the House had previously appropriated $100,000 for the work—80,000 of which was already expended, and the remainder was under the process of expenditure. When the House decided the question to make the former appropriation, they decided the question of its expediency; and he did not think that question should now be agitated. The question was, whether the sum already expended should be lost, or whether it should be saved by the passage of the bill proposed to be reconsidered. The expediency of the work being decided by the former action of the House, he thought it required the most cogent reasons from gentlemen opposed to the appropriation, for refusing to continue it.

Mr. MILLER said he was in favor of a re

ideration of this question, and of the appropriation, for reasons similar to those given by gentlemen who preceded him. He had, on a former occasion, opposed an appropriation for this work, under the belief that it would require a much larger sum than he was now convinced would be adequate to the completion of the work. He would deprecate the loss of the sums already expended, and he was now willing to vote for the sum required in the bill.

Mr. MINER said: Here was a place located on navigable water, well situated for trade and commerce, and which, by the industry and enterprise of its citizens, was prosperous and flourishing, until by an act of the government, that was perhaps very proper, for of that he knew nothing, an impediment had been placed in the river turning and changing the old natural channel, and thereby substantially destroying the navigation formerly carried on there. This was the case of the city of Alexandria. Now came the question, whether an attempt which had been made to remedy this evil by the formation of a canal, which was called, and certainly was, an internal improvement, for the purpose of placing that city in some degree in the same situation it was before, should be completed. He was in favor of internal improvements generally, but this recommended itself on different grounds from what those usually did. Here was a city possessed of advatages bestowed upon it by the God of nature, a navigable stream to it, and of which it had been deprived by an act of the Government, and surely the application stood upon much higher grounds than those of ordinary cases of internal improvement, for the benefit of those who were not benefitted before, and to whom it was a mere matter of favor, policy, or interest, whether it were done or not. But when the Government has interfered with pre-existing rights, or taken away privileges and advantages given by God himself to them, and when they have laid out almost their whole fortunes in the erection of buildings, warehouses, &c., for the purpose of carrying on their commerce, then he considered it a question resting on an entirely different basis than ordinary cases. It was on that general ground that he was in favor of reconsidering the vote rejecting the bill, and in favor of the grant proposed.

It had been said, and this weighed greatly on his mind, that the people of Alexandria had been led to expect that the canal, or one part of it, should be extended to that city; and that such assurances had been given, or held out to them, as raised expectations in their minds that such would be the case—that the canal would not be carried to Georgetown, or to this city, and there stop, from which they could possibly draw no advantage, but, on the contrary, receive nothing but injury. Under this expectation they subscribed a large sum of money to aid in the completion of the canal, all which money they had lost—worse than lost—provided the canal should stop where it then was, since their trade would be entirely destroyed. Mr. M. apprehended that this consideration alone would lead to the conclusion that the proposed appropriation ought to be made; and he accorded in the idea suggested, that it would be an act of injustice not to do it. He had no fears that it would not meet the views and wishes of their constituents, to extend the work a little further, and not stop in the middle of it. He believed it would redound to the honor, and glory, and wisdom, of the Government, and he hoped the motion to reconsider would prevail, and the application be successful.

Mr. PARKS said, they were told by the gentleman from Ohio, (Mr. Vinton,) that this work having been commenced by the United States, it was incumbent upon those gentlemen who were opposed to the reconsideration of this vote, and opposed, also, to the construction of the work to give good reasons why it should not go on. Mr. P. apprehended it would not be very difficult for any [illegible]eman in justification of his vote on this sub[illegible] to shew that the work, if completed, would [illegible], and that all the money heretofore ex[illegible]pon it, had been entirely, or almost entire[illegible]l. That it was useless a moment's re[illegible] would he thought convince any one. Here was one of the finest rivers upon the face of the earth, flowing between two commercial cities, or rather between two cities once commercial, and one of them asking Congress to dig a canal by the side of that river for the purpose of benefiting commerce. Was it possible for any boat or vessel to be conveyed on that canal that could not float on this majestic river? It was not. But even were it so, that this canal should be made the means of conveying the vast resources of this District, they would not go to Alexandria. The inevitable result was, that commerce would become concentrated at particular spots, in large cities and towns. The commerce of this section of country was once divided among many small rival ports, it was now concentrated in the city of Baltimore. Railroads might be constructed, canals might be dug to this city or to Alexandria, the railroad from the Point of Rocks or to Washington City, from Baltimore, would take every barrel of flour and every species of commodity from the city of Alexandria. Even if it could promote the navigation of the river itself it would be useless, as far as Alexandria was concerned.

Mr. P. had stated that the money already expended had been thrown away; let us see how the fact stood. His recollection was, that the $100,000 voted last session, was for the purpose of building an aqueduct across the river at Georgetown. The gentleman from Massachusetts (Mr. Bates) has said that the abutments were completed. Mr. P. did not know what the gentleman meant by abutments; but he himself had searched on the west side of the river, and could find nothing done that appeared to have any connexion with the aqueduct. On the other side he saw a pile of earth, which any where in the north could have been raised at a trifling expense. That was all he saw; and if the gentleman saw more, he was more fortunate than M. P. had been. The gentleman from Massachusetts further said, inasmuch as the work had been begun, it was the duty of Congress to complete it, whatever might be its cost, and that he, for one, would never consent that this canal should stand as a monument of our folly. Mr. P. would defy that gentleman, on any part of the habitable globe, out of the District of Col. to find such a monument of folly as this canal would be if it were completed. The truth was it was nothing more than voting the public money away for the benefit of the indolent in this District, and Mr. P. was for doing it, if at all, openly, plainly, and avowedly, so that their constituents should understand the purpose for which it was done. He could not bring himself to believe, and he had devoted some attention to the subject, that the canal, if finished, would ever benefit the country, the district, or a single individual except the contractor, and for this reason he should vote against the reconsideration.

Mr. HAWES jocosely remarked that unless he took a hand now and then, he was beginning to fear he should forget how to speak. Moreover, he had another reason. His honorable friend from North Carolina, (Mr. Speight) had sounded the administration trumpet, and called upon all the friends of the administration to come forward and resist this attempt at extravagant expenditure, and as Mr. H. held himself to be as good an administration man as any gentleman upon that floor, he felt bound to obey the summons of the trumpeter. He was, however, somewhat afraid it would turn out like the case of a man in the western country celebrated for raising hogs, who was in the habit every morning of calling them, and when they came up he gave them nothing to eat. At last they refused to come at his call, and the man swore he would change the breed of his hogs, because they refused to obey his summons. (Laughter.) But Mr. H. agreed with his honorable friend, and he would give his reason for it.

The gentleman from Pennsylvania (Mr. Miller) said that he opposed this bill at the last session of Congress, but having at this session a better understanding of the matter, he should support it. And what, let me ask, sir, said Mr. H., is this better understanding of the matter? He says that the people of Alexandria were induced to subscribe for this canal under an agreement, or a compact, or an assurance, or an understanding, that it should terminate at the highest navigable point. Well, and what was the highest navigable point of the river? At Georgetown; and at Georgetown the canal terminated, and there, in his opinion, it ought to terminate. The very compact which induced the people of Alexandria to subscribe to the canal had been carried into effect, and yet, says the gentleman, "upon better understanding of the matter," he is induced to alter his vote from that of last session.

Mr. H. would ask, what would be the consequence if the canal would effect all the people of Alexandria predicted? Why, to build up their city, and, at the same time, destroy Georgetown. There were three cities in this District contending for the trade and commerce from foreign ports, and whichever would be built up, would result in the destruction of the others. For his part, he never would vote for an appropriation of money to build any canal by the side of a navigable river, created by the hand of nature, and better than any canal Congress could construct, if it were to expend the whole resources of the Government in attempting it. A river, in which vessels of almost all sizes could navigate with safety. The argument about compensation amounted to nothing. Suppose the States of New York, Pennsylvania, and Ohio, had been stayed by the principle, that to construct a work in one part of the country might for a time injure another, where would we have been their great works of internal improvement? and their treasures? Remuneration was never thought of by them.

Mr. H. made a few further remarks, and concluded by repeating his intention to vote against the motion to reconsider.

Mr. MERCER entered into a detail of the circumstances and the various proceedings of the corporations of Washington, Alexandria, and Geoegetown, connected with the original location of the Ohio and Chesapeake Canal, and the [illegible] of the contemplated aqueduct. He urged, at length, the importance and utility of the proposed improvements, which he contended could be completed by the appropriation of $135,000 in addition to former appropriations.

Mr. MANN of New York, opposed the resolution at some length.

Mr. ALLEN of Virginia, supported it.

Mr. HARDIN rose to address the House in opposition, and remarked that he was willing now to proceed with his argument; but as it was late in the day, to test the wishes of the House on the subject, he would move an adjournment.

The question on adjournment was taken by tellers, and decided in the affirmative. Ayes [illegible], noes 77.

So the House adjourned till to-morrow at 11 o'clock.

IN SENATE,

Wednesday, February 4, 1835.

The **VICE PRESIDENT** laid before the Senate a certificate of the election of the honorable **JOHN M. ROBINSON**, a senator from the State of Illinois, for six years from the 4th of March next.

The **VICE PRESIDENT** also communicated a further report from the Commissioners of the Sinking Fund, recommending that the commission be discontinued, as the object for which it had been created was accomplished.

He also communicated a report from the Secretary of the Senate, made in obedience to order, relative the state of the printing of the Senate, which on motion of Mr. HILL, was ordered to be printed.

Mr. HENDRICKS, pursuant to notice, and leave given, introduced a bill supplementary to the act to authorize the Florida Territory to open a canal in that Territory; which was twice read and referred.

Petitions of a private nature were presented by Messrs. PORTER, TIPTON, and KANE.

Mr. TIPTON presented a memorial from the Legislature of Indiana, praying Congress to extinguish the Indian title in that State, and to make provision to remove the Indians West of the Mississippi.

Mr. NAUDAIN presented a joint resolution of the Legislature of Delaware, praying an appropriation for the improvement of the harbor at New Castle.

Mr. LEIGH, from the Judiciary Committee, to which was referred the bill for the relief of Theodore Brightwell, reported the same without amendment, but with an expression of opinion on the part of the committee, that the bill ought not to pass.

Mr. TIPTON presented the following resolution, which, on his motion, was considered and adopted:

Resolved, That the Secretary of War be requested to transmit to the Senate a copy of the report, plan, and estimate, of Lieut. Berrien, the officer charged with the survey of the mouth of Trail Creek, at Michigan City, Indiana, with a view to the construction of a harbor at that place.

On motion of Mr. FRELINGHUYSEN, the Senate proceeded to the consideration of the following resolution, submitted by him on Monday last:

Resolved, That the Committee on the Judiciary inquire into the expediency of annexing the fourth circuit to the third Judicial Circuit, and of so arranging the Circuit system, as to extend its benefits to all the States, by seven or more Circuits.

Mr. FRELINGHUYSEN said he desired briefly to explain the motives which had induced him to offer the resolution. It contained two distinct propositions; one to annex the fourth judicial circuit to the third; the other to extend the benefit of the circuit system to all parts of the United States. A very happy occasion had arrived for uniting the third and fourth districts, and dispensing with one of the judges in the Atlantic States, a vacancy, occasioned not by death, not by removal, but by the voluntary and fortunate resignation of the individual holding the office. Mr. F. did not think any disadvantage would arise from the extent of the circuit after the union proposed; it would not exceed the extent of the district composed of the New England States; and he was happy to have it in his power to state that the present judge in the third circuit would willingly take upon himself the additional duties which would arise from such an arrangement. The facilities afforded by steamboat navigation would enable the judge to transport himself to any part of either district in a few hours. With regard to the other part of the resolution, Mr. F. went on to state that by a new arrangement of the western districts, annexing Indiana to the seventh, and Alabama to the sixth, and the creation of a new district embracing the new States in the West, the benefits of this system might be extended to the whole Union.

The resolution was agreed to.

Mr. KENT, pursuant to notice, and on leave given, introduced a bill for the relief of Somerville Pinckney, administrator de bonis non of —— Williams, deceased.

Mr. CLAY said, he held in his hand, and asked leave to present, a memorial, and certain resolutions from a Council held at Running Waters, of a portion of the Cherokee Indians. The Cherokees had a country, (if it could any longer be called their country,) lying in the States of Georgia, Alabama, Mississippi, and Tennessee; containing a population of about 15,000. Of this population, much the greater part was in the State of Georgia. It was well known, that for several years past, it had been the policy of this Government, to transfer the Cherokee Indians west of the Mississippi, and a portion of the tribe had availed themselves of the opportunity, and the facilities afforded them for going there, but a portion of them were disposed to remain. These proceedings came from the minor portion of them, who were desirous of emigrating, who said they found it impossible to live under laws which they could not understand, and which they did not participate in framing. And they said that destruction was hanging over them, if they continued within the United States, that self-government among themselves was destroyed, and they preferred exile with liberty, rather than a residence in their accustomed homes with slavery. They asked this Government to provide means to transport them west of the Mississippi, with guarantees of political rights and self-government, never to be destroyed. These were the objects of the Council of Running Waters. But he took the present occasion to give his own opinions on this entire subject, and to express the general sentiments which he entertained of the relations existing between the Indian tribes, and the People of the United States. The rights of the tribes were to be ascertained by solemn stipulations of numerous treaties. It would be found from the examination, that 14 different treaties had been made with the Cherokee Indians—some one or more of which were concluded under some one of the administrations of this Government, down to the present time, with the exception of the two last administrations. The treaty of Hopewell, made in 1785, was the first, the third artitcle of which, declared that the Indians were placed under the protection of the United States, and no other sovereign whatever. The next treaty was concluded under the auspices of the father of his country, in 1791, and guarantied to the Cherokees, the undisturbed enjoyment of all the lands which were not ceded. The next treaty was in 1794, and that too under the auspicies of Gen. Washington, and containing a solemn guarantee that all parts of the former treaties relating to the Cherokees, were binding on the parties. By another treaty, made in 1798, it was stipulated that the treaties subsisting between the contracting parties, were in full force and operation. The last treaty was concluded in 1817, and it recognised the difference between the two portions of the Cherokee nation, and renewed the provision that the existing relations between the two parties, were to continue in force; and to this treaty was affixed the signature of the present Chief Magistrate, as one of the negotiators on the part of the United States. He also called the attention of the Senate to the treaty of Grenville made forty years ago, recognising the same general principles. "That the tribes should be permitted hunting, or any other pursuit, and when they chose to make sale of their lands, it should be only to the United States." In this treaty too, they acknowledge themselves to be under the protection of the United States, and no other power. Such were the rights which were recognised by treaties, to the Indian tribes in the United States, and in addition, the guarantee that they were to live under their own laws, without any interruption or molestation. He contended too, that these rights had been recognised by the Supreme Court of the United States, on several occasions. In one case it was declared "that the Indians had an unquestioned and unquestionable right to the lands they occupied, until their right was extinguished by voluntary cession to our Government. But these Indian rights were further recognised on one of the most interesting occasions known to this Government. He alluded to the negotiations between Great Britain and the United States, for the termination of the late war. The hinge on which the negotiation turned, he had a distinct recollection, was the claim brought forward by the British negotiators in behalf of the Indians, and which they held as a *sine qua non* to the conclusion of a treaty of peace—that the Indians, her allies, should be included in that treaty—that they should have a permanent boundary assigned them, and that neither party should be at liberty to purchase the lands they set apart. But the American Commissioners would not listen to the proposition so much as to refer it to their Government, informing the British Commissioners that if they did so, they were sure it would meet with a most prompt rejection. They stated that the Indians lived under their own customs, and not the laws of the United States, and that they were placed under the protection of the United States alone, whether they were subjects or otherwise. The correspondence finally terminated in a proposition to which the American Commissioners assented, that the United States should do their best endeavors to restore peace with the Indians with which they were at war, and restore to them all the rights and privileges they enjoyed prior to the commencement of hostilities. And he declared it to be his belief that if the Indian rights had not been thus declared, there would have been a prolongation of the war. If then their rights and treaties were now to be disregarded, were we not justly chargeable with having procured a treaty upon suggestions which were unfounded and erroneous? Thus had the Indian rights been recognised by every branch of this government at home and abroad, and not only this, but the fulfilment of the stipulations of treaties was repeatedly urged by Georgia upon the government in 1802.

Mr. C. said he wished to turn the attention of the Senate to the nature of the wrongs this people had suffered, to the present condition of the Cherokees, whose lands had been guarantied by the United States. He went into the examination with the utmost feelings of sorrow and regret at the miserable state to which these tribes were reduced by the laws of the States. But he would assure the honorable Senators from Georgia he was actuated by no hostile intentions to that State. Georgia was the first that made these encroachments; she originated the plan of invading the Indian rights, and she had carried it far beyond all others. He had not all these various laws before him; it was not necessary to go into details; it was sufficient to notice the results. By the first act Georgia abolished the Government of the Cherokee nation. No nation, said Mr. C. can exist without a Government of some kind. These people had formed and established a Government in imitation of our own. But it was wholly immaterial what the humble form of that Government might be. Georgia had abolished it. She next proceeded to divide their territories into counties and distribute them by lotteries among her citizens; every head of a family being entitled to the land drawn against his number. She did indeed reserve a small pittance of a few acres for those Indians who wished to remain within her limits, but under circumstances that rendered them worthless. She gave them no rights, no franchise, no single privilege; they were denied the power of testifying in courts of justice; no Indian could be a witness in favor of his fellows. Thus had Georgia proceeded by continued aggressions to invade and destroy the rights of the Indians. By a late law they are denied even the privilege of appealing to a foreign tribunal. They did once appeal from the injustice and violence of Georgia to the District Court of the United States; and the Judge, in the performance of his sacred duties, granted them an injunction. But what was the result? Another act of wrong and insult—a law concerning the gold districts. It was the pursuit of gold that led the Spaniards in Mexico and Peru to desolate those beautiful lands and deluge them with blood. Mr. C. here read a section of the law concerning the appointment of agents and granting a military force when any opposition was offered. After, continued Mr. C. having distributed the land by lotteries, grants were made and agents appointed. If an Indian dared to oppose the agent who was driving him from his home, he was seized by a military force, without a trial, and without an investigation, whilst a citizen in such cases would be entitled to the benefits of the law——

Mr. CUTHBERT here interrupted Mr. CLAY: he did not think the remarks consistent with the occasion.

Mr. CLAY explained—and then proceeded. The Courts of Georgia, said Mr. C. are restrained from granting injunctions, unless the Indian, on coming into Court, shall first acknowledge the right of Georgia to pass the laws. Thus he is compelled to renounce his Indian rights, so that he is forever barred from appealing to the Courts of the General Government.

Mr. C. protested he had no feelings hostile to Georgia, and in the remarks he was about to offer, he should carefully abstain from the use of every epithet that might be construed into an unkind feeling towards her.

The whole power of the State, said Mr. C. both civil and military, is brought to bear on the Indians. The law prevents Indian testimony from being brought in their defence—their rights are surrendered to a State where they have no voice whose laws they do not understand, and whose language to them is a foreign tongue. Sir, it impossible to conceive of a community more mi

rable, more wretched. Even the lot of the African slave was preferable, far preferable to the condition of this unhappy nation. The interest of the master prompts him to protect his slave; but what mortal will care for, who will protect the suffering, injured Indian, shut out from the family of man? Such was the case of the Cherokees. He had one more remark before he offered his propositions to the Senate. Was there a remedy, he inquired?

If we had no power, if we had no right to interfere, then we could offer them only our sympathies and consolations; but we were not thus powerless; our hands were not bound. It would be recollected there were two classes, the one, those who wished to emigrate, the other, those who desired to remain. With regard to the first, our rights were ample; the power of the U States over her territory was absolute; there could be no question on that point.

But in regard to those who wished to remain on this side of the river, were we powerless, must we sit still and behold their wrongs? Why, he asked, have we contracted the obligations? Why, by solemn treaties, guarantied to them these rights and privileges and possessions?

These were solemn declarations, made in the face of England, of Europe, of the world. Georgia had shut her doors upon them. Let us now open to them ours. The constitution provides for all cases arising under treaties. The Indians are entitled to come into the courts of the United States in support of their rights; and if we have the power, are we not bound by every sacred obligation to afford them redress? Revelation informs us of a day of retribution; and if we disregard the cries of the oppressed and suffering Indians—if we continue to heap wrong upon wrong, and injury upon injury, how shall we hope to escape the righteous judgments of Heaven?

We are now urging upon France her obligation to regard her solemn stipulations. What force would it give to our arguments, if we could tell her we have always fulfilled all our treaties. How shall we stand before the world, if we suffer these fourteen treaties to be violated? How shall we appear to civilized nations, if we disregard all these obligations to protect this unfortunate people? How appear to Great Britain? How would he, a commissioner who negotiated the treaty with her, be looked upon? For himself, he rejoiced he had been spared and allowed the opportunity to express his feelings in behalf of this unhappy people. If we do our duty, it will be a consolation upon our bed of death, which, to him, could not be very distant.

Mr. C. then submitted the following resolutions:

Resolved, That the Committee on the Judiciary be directed to inquire into the expediency of making further provision by law to enable Indians or tribes, to whose use and occupancy lands are secured by treaties concluded between them and the United States, to defend and maintain their rights to such lands in the courts of the United States.

Resolved, That the Committee on Indian Affairs be directed to inquire into the expediency of making further provisions by law for setting apart a district of country West of the Mississippi river, for such of the Cherokee nation as may be disposed to emigrate and occupy the same, and for securing in perpetuity the peaceful and undisturbed enjoyment thereof to the emigrants and their descendants.

Mr. CUTHBERT said that this subject had been introduced altogether unnecessarily. It was a subject that could not be tried here. Georgia did not plead before this tribunal. He did not plead for her here. To what purpose, then, were the Senator's remarks? (Mr. Clay's) Were they for *show?* We all were willing to acknowledge his merits, his powers, and his eloquence. Was it to display his rhetoric—to charm us with his measured tones—to delight us with a *theatrical exhibition?* We may [illegible] *what part* Roscius *will next enact?* Does he [illegible] the dignity of Georgia, and at the same [illegible]mpare her acts to Peruvian and Mexican [illegible] Does he talk of respect to Georgia, while [illegible] she is actuated by a most detestable [illegible]l, by which she is urged on to the [illegible] of wrongs and injuries upon a defenceless people? Talk of respect? He asked no such respect. Why talk of the day of judgment? Are the injured shades of all the red men, whose bones are scattered over our country from Maine to Mississippi, to be conjured up against her? Must Georgia be loaded with all the injuries and wrongs these people have suffered?

Mr. WHITE said—

Mr. President, I feel it to be my duty to make a few remarks upon this subject before; the present question is disposed of.

When I came to the Senate this morning, I did not know of the intention of the Hon. Senator from Kentucky, to present this memorial, of course I cannot be prepared for the discussion of this subject.

Although I cannot hope any thing I may have it in my power to say will have any influence with the Senate; yet as the subject is one of great importance to the United States, as well as to the Indians, I think the remarks of the Hon. Senator call for some reply.

The object of the memorial is one I heartily approve. The memorialists are a portion of the Cherokees, residing within the limits of the State of Georgia. They wish to emigrate west of the river Mississippi, and there have a country assigned to them, where they can live under a government of their own choice, preserve as far as they may think right their own customs, exercise their privileges in endeavoring to promote the civilization of their own people, and having them instructed in the doctrines of christianity. They wish the United States to furnish them a country to go to, to be at the expense of their removal, and to give them suitable guarantees that they shall never be disturbed in the country to which they may emigrate.

If any additional legislation is found necessary upon this subject, it will give me sincere pleasure to afford my aid in all suitable enactments.

But, in presenting the memorial and resolutions, the Hon. Senator has gone into a discussion of the powers of the States, and the manner in which their powers have been exerted over the Indians.

I do not believe any benefit is likely to result to the people of the United States, or to the Indians, from such discussions; but as the subject has been introduced, it is due to the States that, at least, some of the grounds upon which they have acted, should be brought to the notice of the Senate.

What was the condition of the Indians, *within the limits of the States*, at the close of the revolutionary war?

The people of the United States declared their independence, the revolutionary war in maintenance of that declaration, terminated in a treaty of peace in 1783. The limits and bounds of the States are described in that treaty. Each of the States, within its territorial limits, believed it was free, sovereign, and independent, and that a majority had a right to prescribe whatever rules they pleased for the government of every person, of every age, sex, and color, within their acknowledged boundaries.

Each of these States believe they still possess all these powers, except so far as they have *expressly* granted them to the Federal Government, for the good of the whole.

The articles of confederation gave to the federal government power to regulate trade and intercourse with the Indians, but contain an express proviso that Congress shall not interfere with the territorial rights of the States.

The first treaty with the Cherokees was made in 1785, and although the articles referred to were then in force, the lands allotted to the Indians included a large portion of the *territory* of North Carolina.

That State was not inattentive to her rights. She had an agent present when the treaty was negotiated, and he there entered the solemn protest of his State, more than once, against this exercise of Federal power.

These protests are still on record, and can yet be produced, at any time the Senate may desire.

The next treaty with the Cherokees, was after the present constitution was adopted.

In the mean time, North Carolina had been urged to cede her Western lands to the United States, and one motive for this was, that the United States would be the better enabled to regulate their affairs with the Cherokees, it being then believed, they all, or nearly all, lived on those lands.

In 1789, North Carolina, yielding to these solicitations, made the cession.

The vacant lands, after satisfying all existing claims against North Carolina, were the property of the United States, who also had the sole power of legislation. The United States, thus owning the vacant soil, and having the *entire sovereignty and jurisdiction*, and still believing the Cherokees resident upon this territory, made the treaty of Holston in 1791.

After arguing upon the boundary between the whites and the Indians there is an express guarantee to the Indians of their lands. This, if my memory serves me, is the *first* guarantee to these Indians. This guarantee was inserted, not by the mere motion of our Commissioner, but by the express instructions of President Washington. The reason of this is obvious to me. General Washington believed, at that day, the country guarantied to the Indians was a tract, over which the United States *alone* had the sovereignty and jurisdiction, and that they were the owners of the soil; that neither the sovereign, nor territorial rights of any State were invaded by such a stipulation, and that it would be the means of preventing future encroachments upon the Indians.

We now know by our own Executive journal, kept secret until a few years past, that when the first agreements with Indians were made, after the adoption of the constitution, the President himself doubted whether they ought to go through the forms prescribed for treaties: he sent a message to the Senate; it doubted, but eventually seems to have acted upon the opinion, that the formal sanction of two-thirds of the Senators present, required to ratify treaties, would be a safe rule, as to these compacts or agreements, and the course then adopted has been pursued ever since.

A farther illustration of Gen. Washington's views as to the rights of States, may be given by his conduct in relation to lands within the limits of New York, which were attempted to be secured to Indians, by treaty. He condemned this course on the part of the agent, and made it the subject of a special letter now on record.

The tract of country ceded by the State of North Carolina to the United States in 1789, and which was a territory in 1791, when the Holston treaty was made, continued to be a territory till February 1796, when the people residing upon it formed a constitution, and afterwards were admitted into the Union.

In the treaties with the Cherokees subsequent to that period, (and there were many of them, as has been correctly said by the honorable Senator from Kentucky,) the United States seem to have lost sight of the distinction between their power over a country, of which they had both the right of *soil* and the *jurisdiction*, and one where the *States* had the right of soil and jurisdiction, and to have continued the *guarantee* as inserted in the treaty of 1791.

The States, however, do not acquiesce in this exercise of federal power. The same opinion entertained by North Carolina in 1785 is entertained and acted upon *now*.

They maintain, that they are sovereign and independent communities, within the whole of their chartered limits, upon all points, where they have not transferred their powers to the Federal Government.

They maintain, that these agreements, with a portion of their *own population*, are not treaties within the meaning of the constitution; and they deny that they have ever vested in the federal government the power, by *treaty*, or otherwise, with any portion of the people within their limits, no matter whether the people are French, German, or Indians, to take from the State one acre of its *territory*, and transfer it to any other people whatever.

They maintain, that each State has the right, independently of the federal and all other governments, to enact such laws for the government of their whole population, as in the wisdom of their own legislatures may seem best suited to the [illegible]

est of all; and that in the exercise of this power, now, out of their limits, has the right to interfere.

If the States are right in the operation of these powers, it must clearly follow, that they alone, have the power to judge whether their laws are adapted to the condition and wants of their people.

Whether the States are correct in the assertion and maintenance of these rights and powers or not, they think they are, and many others think with them. They have acted upon them, and will continue to do so, as I firmly believe. Georgia has extended her laws over her whole limits. Tennessee has, to some purposes, done the same thing, and so has North Carolina and Alabama.

How they are these States to be induced to repeal or repeal these laws? Suppose the United States to apply to them for the repeal: they will answer, their laws are approved by their people, they had the power to enact them, and they will not repeal them. What then? Are the United States to apply force to compel the repeal? If they do, and such force is met by an opposing force from the States, we then have presented to our view the most horrid of all spectacles. Armed strife between brothers, and in the midst of it, what becomes of the red men for whose rights this war is waged? They are swept from this state of existence. When the war terminates, there will be no Indians to be protected by the U. States, or by these States individually.

The time has arrived when we must all speak out plainly as we think. These people, if they remain where they are, must submit to the laws of the respective States. They cannot exist in the States as a separate and distinct community, governed by their own customs and laws. Some of them are civilized and enlightened; they will make useful and respectable members of any community. They may still remain where they are, if they choose. But this is not the condition of the class of the Indian population. They are poor, ignorant, and uninformed.

Residing where they now do, certain misery and ruin await them. If they will remove beyond the Mississippi, out of our States and organized Territories, they may be preserved. There they may progress in that civilization which has commenced; they can, as freemen, have a government of their own choice; their interests can be protected and their rights protected by the United States, without collision with any State. Who now doubts that it is their interest to do so? Few men can doubt it, who will take pains to acquire correct information, and then duly consider the subject. I believe the time has nearly arrived, and will certainly soon have arrived, when there will be but one opinion upon this subject throughout our country.

The policy of inducting our Indians to remove west of the Mississippi, did not originate with this administration. As early, at all events, as 1804, it was the policy of Mr. Jefferson. It has been the policy of every succeeding administration; and during the last administration, it had, in the then Secretary of War, one of its ablest advocates. The great distinction between this and prior administrations consists, in the present having succeeded to much greater extent in carrying into effect what it, from the time of Mr. Jefferson, desired to accomplish.

The honorable Senator from Kentucky thinks, the State of Georgia has shut her courts against the people, we ought to open those of the United States to them. And if we can, let me ask, Mr. President, of what practical benefit will such provision be? Useless. Encourage a poor Indian, living surrounded by whites, unfriendly to him, to commence suit in the Federal Circuit court, and then follow it here to the Supreme court, to assert his title to 160 or to 640 acres of land, and by the time the cause is decided, he and his family will have starved to death. Instead of this, let us encourage them, by all means in our power, to remove. Every day by remain the means of the United States to make them comfortable homes, west of the Mississippi, are lessening. Other tribes are going and getting their choice of the country. Let me be encouraged to remove speedily, provide aids for their removal, for their comfortable support for a season. Furnish them a permanent home, guaranty it by all the solemnities which can be deemed necessary, and then faithfully observe this guarantee.

Upon these points, if additional legislation is found to be proper, I am willing to go to any extent which may be deemed necessary, and which is not inconsistent with what is due to the interests of the great body of our community.

Mr. BENTON said, he rose, not to prolong this discussion, but to bring in a voice much more potential than his own. It was the voice of Mr. Jefferson, by which it would be seen that these things which we called treaties, were not so under the constitution of the United States, nor were they treaties upon which the laws of the United States were founded. Such was the ground taken by President Washington. The word treaty in the constitution was to be there understood as it was recognized in the laws of nations, and nothing else but that kind of treaty which was known to the laws of nations. And first, it was to be made with a foreign power, and which an Indian might be received, and suppose that this thing which we called a treaty, was what was understood and contemplated by the constitution of the United States, yet no statesman should take so shallow a view of it. Look at the treaties made with some of these people who had not a blanket round their shoulders, and then say whether they are such things as can put down the laws of a sovereign State. A judge would have widely mistaken his duty who should say that such a proceeding could put down the municipal regulations of a sovereign State. (Mr. B. read an extract from a work of Mr. Jefferson's, to show to what subjects the treaty making power extended.) He said he rose for the more purpose of bringing Mr. Jefferson's voice where it would be heard. He wished the Cherokees well, and comfortably located West of the Mississippi, where they would find a safe home, and he wished them also to be fully informed that these were not treaties which could operate against a sovereign State.

Mr. CLAY rose, he said, to assure the honorable Senator from Georgia (Mr. Cuthbert) he had no intention of making a show, but that the honorable Senator might take the charge to himself, since he (Mr. Cuthbert) had declared he had no object in view, that Georgia did not plead here. With regard to the objections of the honorable Senator from Tennessee (Mr. White) he would say a few words. Mr. C. went on to show the validity of treaties, and the obligation of the United States to fulfil all that these treaties guarantied. The Senator recoiled at the thought of a civil war, where the Indians would be swept from the face of the earth. How was it last session, when the powers of a State were actually arrayed against the General Government? He gave a warm support to the measures then adopted. He himself gave a reluctant vote in its favor. It filled him with the severest feelings of sorrow then; he had reflected upon it with grief ever since. The removal of the Indians was said to have been the policy of former Administrations, but it was not to be done by force of arms; he knew they would all melt away in the midst of civilized society; he wished they would all emigrate to a land where they might be beyond the reach and influence of the white man. He believed that North Carolina had not touched them; Tennessee had interfered only to protect them against the whites. One State only had gone to extremes; Georgia had outstripped all the rest.

Mr. CUTHBERT replied in a few words. The question, said Mr. C., is one due to humanity, and upon that the was willing to go with the gentleman; but to talk of negotiations in regard to the rights of the State, was mockery.

The memorial and resolutions were then referred to the Judiciary Committee.

On motion of Mr. EWING, the Senate proceeded to consider, as in the Committee of the Whole, the bill to change the organization of the Post Office Department.

At the suggestion of Mr. GRUNDY, the reading of the bill was dispensed with, and the amendments prepared by the minority of the committee were considered.

The first amendment, proposing to strike out the provision in the bill for the appointment of an officer to be called the Solicitor of the Post Office, and to impose the duties of that office on the Solicitor of the Treasury, was taken up.

After some explanatory remarks from Mr. GRUNDY,

Mr. EWING accepted the amendment, and it was agreed to.

The next amendment proposed to strike out the provision of the bill, which prohibits the Postmaster General from granting any more extra compensation than shall amount to double the amount of postages received on the route, and to insert in lieu thereof, a provision that the expenditures for the transportation of the mail shall not exceed the revenues of the Department.

After some remarks in support of the amendment by Mr. GRUNDY, it was opposed by Messrs. EWING, BIBB, and SOUTHARD.

Mr. PORTER also objected to the amendment, but as it required some further consideration, and it was now late, he moved an adjournment, which was agreed to, and

The Senate adjourned.

HOUSE OF REPRESENTATIVES,

WEDNESDAY, February 4, 1835.

Petitions and Memorials were presented, on leave, by Messrs. PLUMMER, JACKSON of Connecticut, EWING, SEVIER, and BANKS; which were appropriately referred.

Mr. WHITTLESEY, of Ohio, from the Committee of Claims, made a report in the case of John Smith, concluding with a resolution referring the same to the Secretary of War.

Mr. CAMBRELENG, from the Committee of Foreign Affairs, reported a bill further to extend the time allowed for the execution of the articles of the commission for carrying into effect the treaty with France, which was read twice, and committed.

Mr. CHINN, from the Committee on the District of Columbia, reported a bill to extend the charter of the Bank of Alexandria; which was read twice, and committed.

Mr. LAY, from the Committee on Revolutionary Pensions, reported a bill to authorize the Secretary of War to appoint an additional agent for paying pensioners in the State of Indiana; which was read twice.

Mr. LAY moved, that the bill be ordered to be engrossed.

Mr. LANE suggested that an arrangement was about being made, whereby the State Bank of Indiana, and its ten branches, would act as the agents of the Government in the payment of pensioners. If so, the passage of the bill would be unnecessary. He moved to postpone the bill until to-morrow, in order that the House might act understandingly on the subject.

The postponement was opposed by Messrs. LAY, KINNARD, and EWING, and advocated by Messrs. LANE and WARDWELL. The motion prevailed—yeas 65, nays 63.

Mr. WISE, from the Committee on Naval Affairs, reported a bill to authorize the Secretary of the Navy to cause to be constructed a Steam Plough Ship, which was read twice and committed.

Mr. FOSTER, from the Committee on the Judiciary, reported a bill to change the time of holding the District Courts of the United States for the Western District of Virginia, holden at Clarksburg which was read twice and ordered to be engrossed for a third reading.

Mr. FOSTER, from the same committee, reported, without amendment, the bill from the Senate for the relief of David Thomas; which was committed.

Mr. HARPER, of New Hampshire, from the Committee on Commerce, reported a bill for the relief of Gilbert A. Smith and others; which was read twice and committed.

Mr. LOVE, from the Committee on Indian Affairs, gave notice that the committee would move the House on Tuesday next to take up the bill to establish the Western Territory.

Mr. DICKINSON offered the following resolution, which, under the rule, lies one day:

Resolved, That the Secretary of War be requir-

ed to communicate to this House the amount of money expended in each State of the Union, for fortifications, from the year 1816 up to this time.

Mr. MITCHELL, of Ohio, offered the following resolution, which, under the rule, lies one day:

Resolved, That the Secretary of War be required to report to this House, what has been the amount of contingent expenses for superintending the Cumberland road in the State of Ohio, for each year since its commencement, west of the Ohio river, including clerk hire, office rent, furniture, books, stationary, engineering, travelling expenses of officers, the purchase of horses and carriages, the amount of commission (if any) for paying out the public moneys; what sums of money have been paid for work actually done within each year, distinguishing what was done by contract, from what was done by day labor.

On motion of Mr. LEA,

Resolved, That the Committee on the Post Office and Post Roads be instructed to inquire into the expediency of establishing a mail route from Calhoun, in the county of McMinn, in the State of Tennessee, passing by Richard Taylor's and John Brown's, thence down the Chatooga river and valley, crossing said river near a Camp-ground, thence crossing Coosa river at Nesbett's Ferry, thence crossing Tarrapin creek at Adams's Ford, and thence by Jacksonville, to Talladega Court House, in the State of Alabama.

On motion of Mr. FILLMORE,

Resolved, That the Committee on Revolutionary Pensions be instructed to inquire into the expediency of establishing an Agency for the payment of pensions at Buffalo, in the State of New York.

On motion of Mr. A. H. SHEPPERD,

Resolved, That the Committee on Revolutionary Pensions be instructed to inquire into the expediency of providing by law for the establishment of an Agency for the payment of pensions at Salem, North Carolina.

On motion of Mr. FOSTER,

Resolved, That the Committee on the Post Office and Post Roads be instructed to inquire into the expediency of establishing the following post routes in the State of Georgia:

From Clarksville by Mount Jonah and Loudsville to Blairsville, Union county; from Cumming's, Forsyth county, to the Court-house in Cherokee county; from McDonough by Decatur to Cherokee Court-house; from Camptellton by Marietta, Cherokee Court-house, Aurora, and Dahloblinger to Blairsville; from Villa Ria, Carroll county, by Paulding Court-house, Head of Coosa, and Walker Court-house, to Rossville; from Capsville by Pine Log and Coosa Water to Elligay, Gilmer county; from Murray county to Walker Court-house; from Dublin by Court Hill, Montgomery county, to Jacksonville, Telfair county; and from Sandersville by Dublin to Hopkinsville; and that said Committee further inquire into the expediency of establishing a mail route from Hamilton by way of Greensville to Newnon, to be carried three times a week in two-horse stages.

On motion of Mr. CASEY,

Resolved, That the Committee on the Post Office and Post Roads be instructed to inquire into the expediency of establishing a post route from Mount Carmel to Maysville, in Illinois.

Mr. WHITTLESEY, from the Committee of Claims, reported the following resolution, which lies one day on the table:

Resolved, That the order of the House of the 31st January, 1835, discharging the Committee on Claims from the further consideration of the petition of James Taylor, of Kentucky, and that leave be given to withdraw the same, be rescinded.

On motion of Mr. HARPER, of New Hampshire, the House proceeded to the consideration of the orders of the day and the business upon the Speaker's table.

The SPEAKER laid before the House a Report from the Commissioners of the Sinking Fund; ..ch, on motion of Mr. HUBBARD, was refer.. to the Committee of Ways and Means.

.he following bills from the Senate were read .. and committed:

.. bill supplementary to the act authorizing the ..ens of Louisiana to enter their back lands;

A bill for the relief of David McCord;

A bill for the relief of Christopher T. Baly.

A bill from the Senate to provide satisfaction for the claims of certain American citizens on account of spoliations committed by the French prior to 1800, was read the first time.

Mr. MANN, of New York, remarked, that this was a bill involving considerations of the highest moment to the nation. It proposed an appropriation of $5,000,000 out of the public Treasury, upon grounds of at least a doubtful nature, at a time too, when if all the other demands and appropriations were satisfied, there would not be a single dollar in the Treasury. He had had occasion to make some examination of these claims. He was satisfied that they rested on no just foundation. If the subject should ever hereafter come before the House for discussion, he thought he could demonstrate the impropriety of paying them. Although many of the citizens of his own State were interested in these claims, yet, from the advanced period of the session, he hoped the House would not be troubled with the investigation of the subject at the present. He therefore moved to lay the bill on the table.

Mr. SPEIGHT hoped the gentleman would withdraw the motion, and let the bill take the usual course.

The SPEAKER said that the motion must be to reject the bill. The motion to lay it on the table was not at present in order.

Some conversation took place between the SPEAKER and Mr. POLK, on the point of order, when Mr. MANN varied his motion, in accordance with the foregoing suggestions of the Chair.

Mr. SPEIGHT said his simple purpose in desiring that the motion should be withdrawn was, that the bill might be permitted to go to a committee, as was usual. He did not know whether he should eventually vote for the bill; he wanted light on the subject. He represented a district which was interested to a considerable extent in these claims. If called upon to vote on the question at this time, he should vote against the rejection of the bill. If upon a full investigation, the claims should be found to be just and proper to be paid by the Government, he would favor them, without any reference to what might be the state of the Treasury.

Mr. CAMBRELENG agreed with the gentleman last up, that it was entirely proper that this bill should take the usual course; and he hoped that his colleague would withdraw his motion. The bill involved great and important principles. He did not believe that either a committee or the House would have time to act thoroughly on the subject during the present session; but he was willing to give to it all the investigation which was practicable at present. The Committee might ascertain what documents were necessary to be printed. There were a variety of important points involved in the bill, some of which might be investigated at this time. He therefore hoped that the motion of his colleague, if not withdrawn, would not prevail.

Mr. MANN said he was not much conversant with the rules of proceeding in this House. He thought it possible that the Chair was in error in the decision just made. He had supposed it in order at any time to move to lay a proposition on the table. However, under the solicitation of gentlemen, who seemed desirous that this bill should take the usual course, he would withdraw his motion, and should, at the proper time, move to commit the bill to the Committee of Ways and Means.

The bill was then read a second time.

Mr. MANN moved to refer it to the Committee of Ways and Means.

Mr. CAMBRELENG proposed the Committee on Foreign Relations.

Mr. E. EVERETT suggested that subjects of a similar character were always referred to the Committee on Foreign Relations. The day before yesterday, a claim of a similar nature had been sent to the Committee on Foreign Relations. He hoped the present bill would be committed to that Committee.

Mr. BURGES remarked that it seemed to him hardly a question to which committee the subject should be referred. In his opinion it embraced nothing coming within the high duties of the Committee of Ways and Means, at least not at present. When the subject should be passed upon, if it ever should be, then it might; but in its present condition the question was one relating to treaties, national laws, and foreign intercouse, and its proper reference, therefore, would be to the Committee on Foreign Affairs.

Mr. GILLET remarked that the questions involved in this bill rendered it proper, in his opinion, that it should go to the Committee on the Judiciary. The claims were founded upon documents, and the proper construction of these documents was the appropriate function of a legal committee. He therefore moved to commit the bill to the Committee on the Judiciary.

Mr. FILLMORE said, as this was a claim upon the government, it should go to the Committee on Claims. It was clearly no claim upon a foreign government, and consequently the subject did not belong to the Committee on Foreign Relations; nor was it a judicial question. He read the rule on the subject, and concluded by moving to commit the bill to the Committee of Claims.

Mr. ARCHER thought it a waste of the precious time of the House in a discussion of this sort. Every subject of a similar character had uniformly been committed to the Committee on Foreign Relations. He was apprehensive that the bill could not be acted on at the present session; but he repeated that the subject properly belonged to the Committee on Foreign Relations, and he hoped it would be at once referred to that Committee for investigation.

Mr. McKIM asked to be excused from voting on the question, on account of an indirect interest in the subject; which was agreed to.

Mr. MANN, of New York, said the most material part of the subject related to money. If the bill was to become a law, it should go to the Committee of Ways and Means, in order that the ways and means of raising the necessary funds—might be enquired into. The question was one which did not in the least involve the foreign relations of the country. It was one eminently proper for the consideration of the Committee of Ways and Means. Mr. M. concluded by asking the yeas and nays upon the question of committing the bill to the Committee of Ways and Means.

The House refused to order the yeas and nays.

Mr. VANDERPOEL said, there could be no doubt that the most appropriate Committee to which this bill could be referred, was the Committee on Foreign Affairs. His colleague, (Mr. Mann,) had observed that it was only or mainly a question of money, a matter about dollars; but it was more than this. It involved the question whether the faith of the nation was either expressly or impliedly pledged for the payment of these claims. If pledged, how? Why, sir, by reason of certain results and liabilities springing from our relations with a foreign Government. The question then now to be determined was liability, or no liability; after that was determined, it would be time enough to institute an inquiry into the ways and means of satisfying the obligation, if any should be adjudged to exist. Then the legitimate functions of the Committee of Ways and Means could be invoked, but now it was a question whether, according to the laws of nations, and our past relations with France, this nation was responsible to its citizens.

[Mr. V. here read the 57th rule of the House, to show, that this subject matter did not come within the duties of the Committee of Ways and Means, as there prescribed.]

He said, that when he came to act finally upon this subject, it was more than probable, that he would be found on the side of his colleague, (Mr. Mann,) for he had paid some attention to the subject, and was inclined to the opinion that the United States were not legally or equitably liable to these claimants; but this could not preclude him from voting for *now* giving the bill such a direction as he believed the rules of the House, and the nature of the subject required.

The question was then put upon committing

the bill to the Committee of Ways and Means, and lost—yeas 26, nays 119.

The bill was then committed to the Committee on Foreign Relations

Mr. POLK, pursuant to notice given, some days since, moved to suspend all the previous orders of the day for the purpose of proceeding to the consideration of the bill regulating the deposites of the public moneys in the local Banks, and several other bills in relation to the Bank of the United States, &c.

Mr. McKIM demanded the yeas and nays on the motion, which were ordered, and were, yeas 90, nays 111.

So the House refused to postpone the orders for this purpose.

Mr. POLK regarded the measures to which he had referred as vitally important to the fiscal operations of the Government. He therefore gave notice, that he would, on Tuesday next, make a motion similar to the one which had just failed, and he wished gentlemen to determine at that time whether or not they would be disposed to act on these subjects at the present session.

CITY OF ALEXANDRIA.

The House proceeded to the consideration of the motion to reconsider the vote rejecting the bill for the relief of the city of Alenandria.

Mr. HARDIN said he had given his sentiments on this subject at length when it was last up, but he wished to say a few words in addition. One argument used was, that this was a debt due to the city of Alexandria; if it was, let it be examined by the Committee of Claims, and whether it amounted to one dollar or a million, he was willing it should be paid. He denied, however, that it was a debt. Alexandria had no claim. The cession made by Virginia had never been claimed back by her, and she would consider it an insult to be told so. But again. What had the United States done in Virginia? Expended upwards of half a million of dollars on that part of the Cumberland road which ran through that State. Was that all? No. Congress had given at one time 100,000 dollars to the city of Alexandria, at another $00,000, and at another $12,000; and had moreover purchased out the shares in the long bridge, and made it toll-free—thereby opening three markets to the State of Virginia, instead of one. Here was an outlay of $300,000; and still the Government was in debt! Great God! said Mr. H., he never knew a debt so hard to pay before. It was true that no State in the Union had been more liberal than Virginia; but she had received much in return. She, however, was too high minded to make any claim. It was said we owed a large debt to the District. This was not the fact. How much had the District been benefitted by the location of the seat of Government there? The People complained of taxes; but for what were they laid? To improve their own property, and to provide for the police. And had we not improved it? Yes, at an expense of thousands upon thousands of dollars. Even the very walks had been done at Uncle Sam's expense. The streets of the City of Washington had been paved and improved by Congress at an expense of $130,000. The lots between the famous river Tiber and the City Hall had been first given to the Corporation, and then bought back again. $160,000 had been given for the canal, and $150,000 for the lots, making in all about $500,000; and still we owed them a debt, a heavy debt; and still further applications for money were made. He would ask, would they let us off for six millions? Mr. H. was certain we owed neither the city of Alexandria nor the District one cent.

Mr. H. then referred to the aqueduct, upon which $70,000 had been already expended, and no one seemed to know how much had been done. The gentleman from Massachusetts (Mr. Bates,) said that the abutments had been erected on one side; but Mr. H. was at a loss to know what the gentleman meant. He went and examined the work himself, and a dam or embankment, he was informed, had been made, at an expense of some six or seven thousand dollars; and when he was there, a large part of it had been destroyed. He had had the river measured at Georgetown, and found it fifteen hundred feet wide—the embankment being five hundred feet, left a clear channel of one thousand feet, according to the showing of the gentleman from Virginia, (Mr. Mercer,) who addressed the House on the subject some days ago.

Mr. MERCER explained.

Mr. HARDIN said, he had probably misunderstood the gentleman—besides he knew we were not accountable here for a speech delivered a month ago. We have the right to plead the act of limitation upon it. He contended that the aqueduct would require eleven piers, and if the length of the aqueduct shall prove to be 12 or 1400 feet, it will require more; for he did not believe it practicable to make the span of each 100 feet. Mr. H. said this wooden aqueduct could not last more than six or seven years, subjected as it was to the action of air and water, and in proof of this, appealed to the experience of gentlemen in the construction of mills, &c. He said he was opposed to the expenditure of another dollar on these works. He considered the million already expended on the Chesapeake and Ohio Canal as lost, as likewise the $100,000 already appropriated to the aqueduct. He had opposed, and while he held a seat on that floor, he would continue to oppose, the whole scheme of the Chesapeake and Ohio Canal. He opposed these appropriations on other considerations. He did not believe the government ever received fair return in the labor bestowed. The money was too apt to stick to the fingers of those intrusted with its expenditure. The McAdamizing of Pennsylvania Avenue, cost $100,000, while it should have been done for $20,000. He asked how gentlemen would face their constituents, with the tale that they had voted this $100,000 to construct a canal along side of the finest river in our country? Mr. H. concluded by saying, he had done what he deemed to be his duty. This he would always endeavor to do so while he retained that responsible station; and when he retired from it, and was again placed on one of those western hills, where the eye glances over the vast and fertile regions of the great valley of the Mississippi, he could cast a look to the Eastward and exclaim with the dying christian, "Farewell—farewell! vain world! I'm going home!"

Mr. TURRILL opposed the reconsideration of the bill.

Mr. SUTHERLAND said, notwithstanding what had been said by the gentleman from Kentucky, (Mr. Hardin,) he considered himself a representative of the people of the District of Columbia, and also the representative of the people of the first Congressional District of Pennsylvania, in the vote he intended to give in favor of this bill. When the cession of these ten miles square was made to the General Government, it was upon a full and fair understanding, that the cities therein would have some one to take care of them in Congress. If Alexandria could to-morrow go back to Virginia, how soon would she start from her present condition? Before she was ceded to this government, she had golden prospects before her, but what has been the result? Those prospects ruined, blighted, he had almost said, blasted. But, said the gentleman from Kentucky, when we go back to our constituents, and tell them we have voted away so much of their money, what will they say? This came home. We could say what we pleased in favor of an appropriation in which our constitituents were interested, but these Alexandria people have no one in Virginia to take care of them. If they look to the great State of Virginia, engaged in carrying out national improvements, and make their appeal there, they are told they do not belong to the State; if they come here, they are unrepresented. Where then were they to look? They could not, as the people of Pennsylvania or New York might, look to their State Legislature, for they had none; and when she came to that House, their only resource, they were to be sneered, as it were, from the door. Mr. S. was not afraid of telling his constituents, when he went home, if they should ask him, how he had voted upon this question, and that he regarded the people of these ten miles square, as though they had a right to call upon us to legislate especially for them. The people of Alexandria had no other legislature than that House, and if that House refused to listen to their appeal, they had no other resource left them. Had we not been told, no longer ago than yesterday, that we had so far forgotten these people, that they were still governed by their old musty laws derived from Virginia, though that State had now modelled her own code?

But let him ask, was it fair to talk about what had been done for the District of Columbia on the occasion of an application by the people of Alexandria? It was true that three bridges had been constructed, but were they for them alone? No. They were for the accommodation of the whole Union, to facilitate the transportation of the mail, and were as beneficial to the people generally as to the inhabitants of this District. Mr. S. said, the able and eloquent advocacy of this measure by the delegation of the Old Dominion, reflected honor upon the State, and showed they appreciated the condition of the city of Alexandria. Supposing such an obstruction in the navigation of a river as that which had blocked up the channel of the Potomac, had occurred in one of the States, would the people have been without redress? They would not. But we were told that there was no occasion for this work; and by whom are we told so? By the people of Alexandria? No. By the people of Washington or Georgetown, who might be supposed interested in keeping it down? No. Had any one conversant with the subject told us so? No. On the contrary, all concurred in its expediency. Surely, no one would pretend that the citizens of Alexandria asked for this appropriation merely that the money might be squandered among them; for they have almost embarked all their means in its success, in the expectation that the work would be brought to their town. Would any one think them fools enough to have embarked their money on the scheme, unless they had been led to expect they should reap some benefit from it? They have done all in their power, and they now come to us, as the people of Virginia would go to their Legislature, or those of his own State to Harrisburg, and ask for aid in completing the work. It was their only place of appeal. Mr. S. said he trusted, looking upon that House as the peculiar guardian and representative body of this District, that they would throw aside their prejudices; and as the constitution had placed it under their peculiar care, they would regard it as they would their individual States, and act upon this measure calmly and dispassionately. He hoped the motion to reconsider would prevail.

Mr. CHINN replied at considerable length to Mr. Hardin; and asked if it was fair, in a question of that kind, to array the honest prejudices of the House against the bill, and to quote the expenditures upon the Chessapeake and Ohio canal, this bridge or that bridge, this work or that work, in which the people of Alexandria felt no more interest, nor had any more voice than the gentleman himself. The gentleman also, in the course of his remarks, seemed to advocate what he considered the proper dignity and honor of the State of Virginia, and said that asking for this appropriation was offering an insult to her. Mr. C. hoped he would be the last to do any thing tending to affect either her honor, her dignity, or her character. Mr. Chinn then entered into a general defence of the merits of the proposition, and referred to sundry estimates and surveys, and the opinions of eminent engineers, upon the expediency of the Alexandria canal, together with those of the stockholders of the Chesapeake and Ohio canal, and the Corporations of Washington and Georgetown. Mr. C. also read a table of the expenses already incurred, the works completed, and the probable cost of those in progress; showing that the whole could be completed for the amount now asked.

Mr. CROCKETT said he thought it time that this debate should be arrested. The House was within four weeks of the termination of the session, and many important bills were pressing for consideration, which had been postponed, from time to time, to hear gentlemen make speeches. Look back to last session, and it would be seen that seven months were almost entirely consumed

in long speeches. He should therefore move the
Previous Question.

The call was sustained—ayes 128, noes not
counted.

The main question was then ordered to be put,
without a count, and

Mr. BYNUM called for the yeas and nays; which
were ordered.

The question on the reconsideration of the bill,
was then put and decided as follows: yeas 93,
nays 104.

YEAS.—Messrs. John Quincy Adams, Heman
Allen, J. J. Allen, Anthony, Banks, Barber, Bar-
nitz, Bates, Baylies, Beale, Binney, Bouldin,
Briggs, Burd, Burges, Chambers, Cage, Chinn,
Wm. Clark, Clay, Coulter, Crane, Crockett, Dar-
lington, Davenport, Denny, Evan, E. Everett,
H. Everett, Ewing, Ferris, Fillmore, Garland,
Gholson, Gorham, Grennell, Hiland Hall, Han-
negan, Hard, Heath, Hiester, Huntington, Wm.
Jackson, E. Jackson, Richard M. Johnson, Hen-
ry Johnson, King, Lane, Laporte, Lincoln, Love,
Lucas, Lytle, Martindale, Marshall, Mardis, John
Y. Mason, McComas, McKennan, McKim, Mer-
cer, Miller, Milligan, Miner, Morgan, Murphy,
Patton, Dutee J. Pearce, Pope, Potts, Ramsay,
Reed, Rencher, W. B. Shepard, Slade, Sloane,
Spangler, Stewart, Stoddart, Sutherland, Francis
Thomas, P. Thomas, Turner, Tweedy, Vance,
Vinton, Watmough, F. Whittlesey, E. Whittle-
sey, Wilde, Wilson, Wise, Young—93

NAYS.—Messrs. John Adams, Chilton Allan,
Wm. Allen, Barringer, Bean, Beaumont, Bockee,
Brown, Bunch, Burns, Bynum, Cambreleng,
Carmichael, Carr, Casey, Chaney, Chilton, Clai-
borne, Samuel Clark, Clayton, Clowney, Coffee,
Cramer, Amos Davis, Day, Dickson, Dickinson,
Dunlap, Felder, P. C. Fuller, W. K. Fuller, Fulton,
Galbraith, Gamble, Gillet, Gordon, Graham, Gray-
son, Griffin, Joseph Hall, Thomas H. Hall, Halsey,
Hardin, Joseph M. Harper, J. Harper, Harrison,
Hathaway, Hawkins, Hazeltine, Henderson, How-
all, Hubbard, Inge, Jarvis, W. C. Johnson, Noa-
diah Johnson, Benjamin Jones, Kavanagh, Kil-
gore, Kinnard, Lansing, Lea, Lee, Letcher, Lay-
all, Lyon, Moses Mason, jr., May, McCarty, Mc-
Kay, McLene, McVean, Henry Mitchell, Robert
Mitchell, Moore, Muhlenberg, Osgood, Parks,
Parker, Patterson, Peyt n, F. Pierce, Pierson,
Pinckney, Plummer, Polk, Reynolds, Robertson,
Schenck, A. H. Shepperd, Shinn, Smith, Speight,
Standifer, Steele, Wm. P. Taylor, Thomson,
Tompkins, Turrill, Vanderpool, Van Houten, Wa-
gener, Wardwell, White, Williams—105.

So the House refused to reconsider the bill, and
it is therefore finally rejected by th s Congress.

Mr. WATMOUGH made an ineffectual attempt
to call up the navy bill, but a motion to adjourn
prevailed—ayes 87, noes 70.

And then the House adjourned.

IN SENATE.

THURSDAY, February 5, 1835.

On motion of Mr. WAGGAMAN, the Senate
proceeded to the consideration of the resolution
submitted by h m, for the appointment of a Select
Committee, to inquire into the expediency of establishing a Branch of the United States Mint, at
New Orleans.

On motion of Mr. CALHOUN, the resolution
was amended, so as to add to it, "and also another, some where in the gold region of the South
Atlantic States."

The resolution as amended, was then agreed to,
and on motion of Mr. WAGGAMAN, the Committee was ordered to consist of five members.

The Senate having balloted for the Committee,
it appeared, that Messrs. WAGGAMAN, KING
of Georgia, BENTON, CALHOUN, and MAN-
GUM, were appointed.

Petitions of a private nature, were presented by
Mr. TIPTON and Mr. TYLER.

Mr. McKEAN presented a memorial from merchants, and other citizens of Philadelphia, praying an appropriation to improve the harbor at New
Castle.

Mr. BUCHANAN submitted the following resolution, which, on his motion, was considered and
adopted:

Resolved, That the Committee on Finance be
instructed to inquire into the expediency of appropriating the sum of eight hundred and sixty-two
dollars and eighty one cents, for the payment of
the balance due to Valentine Gea-y, late Superintendent of the Cumberland road, for arrearages of
his salary.

Mr. ROBBINS, from the Library Committee, to
which was referred a resolution on the subject,
reported a joint resolution authorizing the purchase of th re-maining copies of Waterston's Tabular Views of the United States; which was
read the first time, and ordered to a second reading.

The following resolutions, submitted yesterday,
by Mr. CLAY, were taken up, and adopted:

Resolved, That the Committee on the Judiciary
be directed to inquire into the expediency of making further provision by law, to enable Indians or
tribes, to whose use and occupancy lands are secured by treaties concluded between them and
the United States, to defend and maintain their
rights to such lands in the courts of the United
States, in accordance with the laws and constitution
of the United States.

Resolved, That the Committee on Indian Affairs
be directed to inquire into the expediency of making further provisions by law for setting apart a
district of country West of the Mississippi river,
for such of the Cherokee nation as may be disposed
to emigrate and occupy the same, and for securing
in perpetuity the peaceful and undisturbed enjoyment thereof to the emigrants and their descendants.

The resolution submitted by Mr. WAGGAMAN
that the Committee on Manufactures be instructed
to inquire into the expediency of further providing by law against the evasions of the tariff on refined and other sugars, and another submitted by
Mr. PORTER for an inquiry by the Committee
on Commerce into the expediency of establishing
a Light-house at the Bayou St. John, were severally considered and adopted.

On motion of Mr. PRESTON, the Senate proceeded to the consideration of the joint resolut on
authorizing the purchase of certain pictures now
in this city, for the President's House.

Mr. HILL objected to the bill, as involving an
unnecessary expenditure, and moved to lay the
same on the table, which was not agreed to.

The question being on ordering the bill to be
engrossed for a third reading, Mr. HILL aske l
for the yeas and nays, which were ordered.

Mr. CUTHBERT made some remarks in support of the bill, and thought the purchase of those
ornamental pictures were worthy the expenditure,
and would be subjects of just pride to the nation,
and he would be glad to see the hon. member
fr m New Hampshire yield his opposition to the
bill.

Mr POINDEXTER moved to fill the blank left
for the appropriation with " any sum not exceeding $40,000."

Mr. PORTER objecte l to any sum being inserted in the bill at all. He thought if the pictures
were worthy of being purchased, it was much better to leave the price entirely at the discretion of
the President.

Mr. PRESTON observed that the value affixed
to them was about $48,000. He thought the sum
suggested was quite sufficient, and he had no o -
jection to it.

Mr. POINDEXTER said he had examined these
pictures, and $40,000, it was thought, would cov-
er the entire cost; for some of them ought not,
and he believed would not be purchased.

Mr. LEIGH also was opposed to inserting the
sum, he would prefer leaving it to the President's
discretion.—The motion to insert was agreed to.

The question on the engrossment of the bill,
was decided in the negative by a vote of yeas 20,
nays 22, as follows:

YEAS.—Messrs. Bell, Benton, Cuthbert, Ewing,
Goldsborough, King of Alabama, Leigh, Linn, Mc-
Kean, Mangum, Poindexter, Porter, Preston,
Robbins, Robinson, Silsbee, Smith, Tallmadge,
Waggaman, Wright—20.

NAYS.—Messrs. Black, Brown, Buchanan, Calhoun, Clay, Frelinghuysen, Grundy, Hendricks,
Hill, Kane, Kent, King of Georgia, Knight, Morris,

Naudain, Prentiss, Shepley, Swift, Tipton, Tomlinson, Tyler, White.—22.

The bill from the House of Representatives to
grant letters patent to Francis B. Ogden, and

The bill authorizing certain papers in the Department of State to be delivered to the Secretary
of War, to be used in making allowances of pensions, were severally read the second time and
referred.

Mr. PRESTON, from the Committee on the
Judiciary, reported the bill for the relief of the
Judges of Michigan Territory, with an opinion of
the Committee unfavorable to its passage.

Mr. BLACK, from the Committee on Private
Land Claims, reported unfavorably upon the petitions of William Stringer and John B. Treton.

Mr. PRESTON, from the Judiciary Committee,
to which was referred the bill from the House authorizing letters patent to be granted to Jesse
Jones, reported the same without amendment.

Mr. PRESTON, from the Committee on Finance, made an unfavorable report upon the petition of Moses Hawkins.

Mr. WEBSTER, from the Committee on Finance, to which was referred the bill from the
House making appropriations for the naval service
for the year 1835, reported the same without a-
mendment.

Mr. PORTER, from the Committee on Private
Land Claims, reported a bill for the relief of Lemuel Turner, assignee of Pierre Dufresne; which
was read the first time and ordered to a second
reading.

On motion of Mr. EWING, the Senate resumed
the consideration of the bill changing the organization of the General Post Office, as in Committee
of the Whole.

The amendment proposed by Mr. GRUNDY, to
strike out the provision, "that no increase of compensation shall be allowed to more than double
the net amount of postages received on the
route," being still under consideration,

Mr EWING further opposed the amendment,
and said, when it was in order, if the amendment
proposed should be rejected, as he hoped it would,
he intended to follow up the principle contained
in that part of the bill, by offering a further
amendment, that there should be no increase of
compensation on any route which was in excess of
more than ten years.

Mr. GRUNDY declined discussing the proposition, because he saw plainly that it was not to be
adopted. The great evils now complained of
were improvident extra allowances. He then required the Postmaster General to report to Congress, within 30 days from the commencement of
every session, what allowances he had made, the
reasons for them, and the services for which they
had been allowed, which he thought were sufficient guards against the evils complained of if
any others to be apprehended. The bill here to
double the amount of postages on the route was
very uncertain, and in case any thing should happen to obstruct the progress of the mail on any
route, if there was no discretion left to the Postmaster General to send on the mail, it would have
to lie until by the regular recurrence of the mail
it could be carried on. One thing should be observed, that as much security and certainty should
be given to the contractor as possible, and he
would have a greater inducement to make his
low bid. He did not differ from the gentleman
from Ohio upon the principle, but doubted, he
think the machine would operate advantageously
without some discretion being left in the Postmaster General on this subject.

Mr. PORTER was opposed to granting of the
extra allowances whatever, and had proposed last
night, an amendment embracing the principle,
and since yielded to the solicitations of the House,
and would not now press it, but he thought the
inconveniences which the public would feel should
by taking away this unlimited power, would not
be so great as granting extra compensation in any
shape.

Mr. EWING said that the law before was very
imperative and explicit as to the amount of services which was to be performed, as was the present
proposition, and it was disregarded, and should

[CONTINUED IN NEXT NUMBER.]

report of the Committee on Roads and Canals and you will find that some of the steam boats are compelled to pay as much as 180 dollars for a passage through this canal, and must do this whether freighted or empty. Look at the number of boats that pass the canal, and the amount of toll paid by each, and then answer if the evils complained of are not most grievous and unprecedented? Examine the report and you will find that the tolls have increased every year; that notwithstanding the company had to encounter unforeseen difficulties and expense and to repair and guard against unexpected disasters, they yet divided, for the year 1833, 6 per cent. on the original stock subscribed, and also declared a dividend of three and a half per cent. for the first six months of the last year, both on the old and new subscriptions. Sir, the dividends must increase. The company has the uncontrollable power to make them increase. But suppose they do not. Does not the present rate of toll amount to an oppressive impost? Let me invoke honorable gentlemen to view this subject in a proper light. Let me beseech them to examine it with the liberal and expanded understandings of statesmen. I can assure them, that the munificence of Government could not be extended to citizens more attached to their country and its institutions than they are, a more ready to respond to the call of duty. They are enterprising, industrious, patriotic. They ask but for free trade and equal rights—they want no more. That they have been tardy in calling upon you, is no objection to their claim. That the Government has already subscribed for a portion of the stock with the view of aiding the work, is no reason why it should not now purchase the whole stock and make the navigation of the river free to all on the terms suggested by the committee in their report.

Let not the claims of our people be prejudiced by the unfounded suspicion, that this measure is a trick got on foot by designing stockholders for selfish purposes. I assure this body that such is not the fact. They have no such purpose—they have, they can have no motive, no inducement to originate such a scheme. The stock is nearly at par in the market—yields now about 6 per cent. per annum profit on the amount invested, and the company have the chartered right to make it yield eighteen per centum per annum. I do solemnly believe that it is, or will be as most profitable stock in the United States. The stockholders are possessed of the most valuable master in the country, and they know it. No, sir, is the people who are not stockholders that have made this general movement, and have loaded our tables with petitions and memorials for relief. The acts dictates of justice require that Congress should sold to their petitions. Sir, let justice be done though the heavens fall. Deny not their wishes. Now is the accepted time to grant it if you mean ever to grant it. The bill precludes the possibility of imposition upon the Government, because it limits a price to be given at one hundred dollars a share. The purchase of the stock will cause no fiscal inconvenience, no sensible effect upon the treasury, because it will be gradual. By occasional purchase, a Government will obtain a majority of the shares, and can thus control the management of the corporation. Let me not be understood as being willing to perpetrate injustice upon those who have risked their funds in the adventure—I mean no such thing. I scorn to wrong either them or others. But I mean, say, that Congress should assume such a position that they could announce to the stockholders that a work should be a public work—that private interest should yield to the general good—that, remuneration being first made, it is justifiable to appropriate private property to the public use—that, having the power to prevent the imposition of exorbitant tolls, nay, to reduce them as low as they please, a will feel justified in exercising that power, unless the stockholders will part with their stock at a fair a, and permit a great highway of States, to be a highway. Sir, I doubt not that the stockholders or a majority of them, will consent to do so. I that some of them are willing to accede to our proposition. Why then shall it not be done? I have it is stated in casual conversations, that inasmuch

as the canal is already completed, and Congress have aided to complete it, by subscribing $290,000 of the stock, that it is all we should ask. Sir, it is most unfortunate that a private company was ever incorporated for this purpose. The proper way to have accomplished the public wishes, would have been to have applied originally and directly to this body: to have stated that the navigation of the Ohio river was interrupted by a natural obstacle: that a vast portion of the country was vitally interested in overcoming this obstacle: that it could be done with safety and success only by constructing a canal, and *then demand that as it was for a nation's use, it should be accomplished with a nation's purse.* It would then have stood confessedly upon the same footing as applications to improve snags and sand bars in the Ohio and Mississippi rivers, which, we know, have been removed by the sanction of Congress. Would Congress have refused the application, in such a shape? Could they have refused? No, sir, not when the Delaware breakwater, and a thousand other improvements of inferior importance, stand as monuments of the nation's liberality. If Congress would, or ought to have done so in the first instance, is there any legitimate reason why they should not now step forward, and assume upon the nation the expense of the construction of the canal— I think not. Let me state a case which seems to me to be apposite. We all know that light houses are erected and sustained at the common expense. Suppose, under a charter granted by Massachusetts when a colony, a private company had erected a light house, and in the shape of tolls were levying a tax on vessels, to the injury and oppression of the citizens of that and other States, and the parties injured were to apply to Congress to purchase the rights of the Company, and free them from the exactions of the corporation, would Congress hesitate to do so? Could they refuse to place the applicants upon the same footing with the citizens of other States who paid no tax for like benefits? Would Congress tell them you once had a fair claim, but it has been forfeited by the act of Massachusetts.— Sir, every sentiment of justice would forbid it Every impulse of patriotism would prevent it. Let not then, an unwise act of the Legislature of Kentucky forfeit the undoubted rights of the people of the valley of the Mississippi, but extend to them the same measure of justice that you would extend to the people of Massachusetts.

In conclusion Mr. Chairman, let me again invoke the Committee to give to this subject a fair, liberal, and candid consideration. Let them decide upon the bill under the influence of elevated sentiments. Let them bear in mind that the interests of millions is at stake. Let them recollect that the bill proposes to relieve from taxation, (excepting what may be necessary to keep the canal in repair, and pay the requisite charges of superintendence,) the commerce that now flows, and which will flow in all time to come, from the navigable sources of the Allegany and Monongahela rivers, and all the tributaries of the Ohio, and Mississippi, down to New Orleans, and also to relieve from impost, what will be brought from that modern Babel, back to the respective beds of navigation. Let them reflect seriously on this, and then answer in good faith, if the rejection of the bill under. consideration will not be attended with manifold evils, and crying injustice to the people of that country. Sir, let Congress act in the premises, as becomes the legislature of a great nation. At the close of the year 1833, there was paid into the national Treasury, as the portion of the Government's toll, the sum of $14,010. This will annually increase. Let us disdain then to fatten, on the fruits of the energies of our fellow citizens. Let us pass a law authorizing the purchase of the individual stock in the company, and then make an offering of the whole on the altar of the common good. Let this be done with the nation's means, because no State can, will, or ought to do it. Ohio will not do it, Indiana will not do it Kentucky cannot be required to do it. Her interest in the measure is no greater than that of her neighbors, although the Canal is constructed through an elbow, a nook of her territory. No one of the transmontane States will do it with her separate means. It will

never be done with their *united* resources, because the poverty of many, and the disagreeing, disunited, and divided councils of all, will ever prevent it. Let then, I repeat, the common purse be opened to remove, now and forever, the tax imposed on the navigation of a river, whose waters, prolonged as they are, would be freely empurpled with the blood of battle, should the country's voice ever require it to flow in her defence.

Mr. McKIM inquired at what price the stock was in the market.

Mr. POPE replied, he had no precise information on that point.

Mr. BURGES said this was altogether a new project, and he had no recollection that a similar one had ever been presented before. Congress had frequently appropriated money for executing public works, and for the purchase of private property, on which to erect them; but this was a project to purchase of a company of stockholders a work already completed. It was said that it was desirable to relieve the people of the tolls, and that the work would be profitable; but he had no doubt they would always have to pay toll enough to keep it in repair; and he did not believe there would be any profit. But there was another view of the subject. The cost was, in all cases, paid by the consumer, and in the one under consideration, was paid by the people of the East for those productions they required, and by the people of the West Indies for what they consumed. After some further remarks, Mr. B. concluded by declaring his intention to vote against the proposition.

Mr. VANDERPOEL said he had voted to postpone all the orders of the day, for the purpose of giving his friend from Kentucky (Mr. Pope,) the opportunity of bringing this subject, which seemed to be a very favorite one to him, before the House. He had listened to the honorable gentleman with great attention; and he was sorry, so far as his honorable friend was concerned, that he had not succeeded in convincing him (Mr. V.) that he could on principle vote for the bill under consideration. He did not mean to make an elaborate speech on the subject; but he deemed it incumbent upon him, to state that the bill was important, act only in reference to a constitutional principle, but also in regard to the question of expediency. There was a class of gentlemen on this floor, who believed that this Government had no right to appropriate the money of the People for works of internal improvement. There was another class, who believed that such appropriations could not be made by us, unless it were for objects clearly national in their character. He would appeal to those gentlemen, and ask them what the bill under consideration proposed? It proposed to appropriate the formidable sum of six hundred and fifty thousand dollars to purchase the interest of a joint stock company in a short canal in the west. Now, he would ask what was the difference, in a constitutional point of view, between appropriating money to construct a work, and appropriating money to purchase a work of this description, after it was constructed. If the one was unconstitutional, he had not discrimination enough to see why the other was not equally so.

It had, however, been contended by the honorable gentleman from Ky., probably in anticipation of this point, that this was a *national object*. If this was national, could he not present an analogous case, which would certainly not be entertained a moment by this House, if proposed here. Our great New York Erie Canal was certainly more national than the little canal under consideration, both in reference to the vast regions of country which are connected, and the amount of produce and merchandise, which flowed through it. Consider, sir, the immense territory bordering on our western lakes and upon the Ohio, whose rich productions flow through this canal. Suppose the inhabitants of the west, whose exports and imports passed through this canal, were to petition you that it were to tell you that it was very inconvenient for them to pay the tolls and tribute exacted by them from the State of New York, and respectfully prayed you to pay New York the eight or nine million which this canal has cost New York, and make it free, would you not be surprised at the

ported a bill for the relief of Thankful Randall; which was read twice and committed.

Unfavorable reports were made by Messrs. SLADE, MUHLENBERG, TURRILL, and CASEY, on various petitions, &c. referred to their respective committees.

Mr. JOHNSON, of Kentucky, from the Committee on Military Affairs, reported the following resolution:

Resolved, That from 11 to 12 o'clock to-morrow morning be set apart to consider the following bills, viz. A bill for the better organization of the Corps of Engineers; for the gradual increase of the Corps of Engineers; to appoint additional Paymasters; and a bill to continue the Subsistence Department.

After some remarks by Messrs. JOHNSON of Kentucky, ASHLEY, DICKINSON, and WILLIAMS,

Mr. REYNOLDS moved to lay the resolution on the table; which was agreed to—yeas 78, nays 63.

Mr. JARVIS, from the Committee on the Public Buildings, reported a bill to provide for erecting a fire-proof building for the accommodation of the Departments of the Treasury and State; which was read twice and committed.

Mr. POPE moved to proceed to the consideration of the orders of the day; which was agreed to.

Mr. POPE rose to submit a motion, which he said he did with great reluctance. It was a motion in which thirteen States of the Union were deeply interested. He alluded to the bill in relation to the Louisville and Portland Canal. He moved to postpone all the orders of the day previous to this bill, for the purpose of going into Committee of the Whole on the state of the Union, upon it.

A count having been called upon the motion, and the yeas having been announced to be 103,

Mr. WATMOUGH called for the yeas and nays on the motion; which were ordered, and were—yeas 115, nays 76.

So the House determined to go into committee on the bill referred to.

Mr. WARDWELL suggested the propriety of also going into Committee upon the bill from the Senate, for continuing the office of Commissioner of Pensions; which was agreed to.

Mr. WATMOUGH rose to a question of order. He desired to know whether a bare majority could set aside the usual and regular routine of business?

The SPEAKER remarked, that this was the third time that this question had been made. The Chair had again and again decided that a majority was sufficient.

The House then resolved itself into a Committee of the Whole on the state of the Union, Mr. PATTON in the Chair.

The bill to purchase the private stock in the Louisville and Portland Canal, was first considered.

Mr. POPE then moved an amendment, as an additional clause to the bill:

SEC. 2. *And be it further enacted*, That the sum of $654,800 be and the same is hereby appropriated (out of any money in the Treasury not otherwise appropriated) for the purpose aforesaid.

Mr. POPE rose and said—

Mr. CHAIRMAN, I feel profoundly grateful to honorable gentlemen for their kindness in consenting to postpone the orders of the day, to take up the bill under consideration. I will requite their courtesy by being very brief. I should not say a word, sir, but that the bill before the Committee is a highly important one. It involves the interests of the inhabitants of an immense region and is entitled to the grave and respectful consideration of this body. All the citizens of the transmontane States, in greater or less degree, are interested in its fate, and they expect us to legislate upon the subject in a liberal, enlightened, and national spirit. In numerous memorials which have been presented, they invoke the interposition of the National Legislature to disembarrass their ...les of burthens, as injurious as they are ...teous. They tell you that their industry and ...prise are shackled by unwested taxation—that their legitimate gains are subjected to the exactions of a corporation almost wholly irresponsible, and they earnestly and respectfully call upon Congress for relief. Sir, they have a deep stake in this matter. Their rights, their interests, their feelings, are all involved. Blessed with more than plenty, they are yet debarred a free and rightful highway to a ready market. Their surplus productions must either rot on their hands, or in their transit to market be taxed almost at the will of a licensed corporation—a corporation most improvidently clothed with extraordinary powers, and possessed of that pernicious gift, perpetual existence. Let me not be told, sir, that these formidable powers were derived from an act of the Legislature of my own State. This fact does not render them less exceptionable. The motives of those who passed the act of incorporation, were pure and praiseworthy. They intended to do good, although they acted unwisely. In their anxiety to furnish facilities to the navigation of the Ohio river, they went too far. They were apprized of the difficulties and perils which the falls of the Ohio presented to the navigator, and they, therefore, incorporated a company to construct the Louisville and Portland Canal. They were aware, that there was no surplus local capital, and it was to tempt the employment of foreign means in the undertaking, that the act complained of was passed. Be that as it may, the evil is unquestionably inflicted, and it is now the part of wisdom and duty to adopt the best, I may say the only, made of correcting the error.

Mr. Chairman, if it be a part of the settled policy of this country, that objects purely, essentially, and confessedly national, shall receive the favorable consideration of the Government, the one now under discussion is most eminently entitled to it. Recollect, sir, that it is the busy, the enterprising, and increasing thousands of an immense extent of country, who demand relief—of a district of country, which stretches from clime to clime, comprehending within its circuit parts of the States of New York, Pennsylvania, Maryland, Virginia, and the whole of Ohio, Kentucky, Indiana, Illinois, Missouri, Tennessee, Alabama, Mississippi, and Louisiana, and the Territory of Arkansas—of an extent of country which includes within its sweep, the "Great Father of Rivers" himself, and all his beautiful, unrivalled, and magnificent tributaries. Sir, as the "King of Floods" rolls his rushing and turbid waters to the deep, he bears upon his bosom the surplus productions of all these States and many more, much of which find a way through the Louisville and Portland Canal. From its mountain sources to its mouth, the Ohio flows freighted with the exportations of New York, Pennsylvania, Maryland, and Virginia, which States receive in return, by the same communication, the valuable and increasing agricultural and mineral productions of the far South and West. What object then, sir, let me inquire, is more national than the one under consideration? Throughout this wide-spread, far-reaching land, can any one be designated in which so many States and so many people are so deeply interested? Sir, there can be but one answer to these questions.

Mr. Chairman, the value of the annual commerce of the Ohio river, is estimated by the committee that reported this bill at five millions of dollars. Recent information and reflection have satisfied me that this estimate is too low. I have been credibly informed, that during the year 1833, there was freighted from the city of Cincinnati, produce of the value of four millions. If this information be correct, we may safely put down the value of the annual commerce of the Ohio river at this time at ten millions. This immense amount, sir, ought to be sufficient to arrest the attention and enlist the feelings and judgment of Congress in favor of the bill. But if it be not sufficient, let us look into the future, and behold if we can the events which time will reveal—let us look onward to the period when the forests of the west shall disappear before the axe of the emigrant, when its valleys and its hill-tops shall be peopled with laborious millions—when its mighty rivers shall be dotted, and enlivened, and variegated with valuable and beautiful gardens, and farms, and manufacteries, and villages, and towns, and splendid cities—when magnificent steamers never out of view, shall, "rejoicing as they go," bear off the surplus products of its soil, and let us inquire if its population will not have a right *then* to assume a bolder tone, and to demand from the Federal Government a dispensation of benefits and encouragement great as those granted to more favored portions of the country. Sir, do I make a wild, unreal, visionary prediction, when I say that this proud day of prosperity is not distant? I will not pretend to foretell the mighty destinies of the valley of the Mississippi, or to portray the world that is there leaping into existence. But if the lessons afforded by the history of the past give us any right to found calculations upon the future, the lapse of less than fifty years will present the living, moving, and wondrous spectacle which I have depicted. Forty-five years ago, the territory which is now the State of Ohio, was a wilderness. Nature there reposed in primeval and uninvaded grandeur, save only when it was disturbed by the prowlings of the wild beast, and the roaming footsteps of the savage. Now it numbers and sustains more than a million of inhabitants, ranks the third State in the Union, and is still hurrying onward in her bright career.

In 1817, Mr. Chairman, when steam-boats began to obtain general use on the western waters, the commerce between Pittsburgh and New Orleans employed about twenty barges, and one hundred keel boats, generally of small dimensions and capacity. I know not the number now employed in the exclusive trade of those two cities; but I do know, that the whole trade of the Ohio and Mississippi, and their tributaries, gives employment to about three hundred steam-boats, and more than two thousand flat and keel boats. As population increases in the west, its commerce must increase: and no matter how much it may augment, it must endure an oppressive and perpetual tax, unless Congress shall see proper to remove it. Sir, the inhabitants of that region feel and know this. They see that their industry and trade are subjected to a most onerous impost, while that of other portions of the confederacy is entirely freed from it. They see that obstructions to the navigation of eastern and northern rivers, inconsiderable when compared with the Ohio, have been removed entirely at the expense of the General Government, and no *local* tax imposed on those who profited by it. They see that a Delaware Breakwater has been constructed at the common expense, and Philadelphia and the surrounding country paying no *local* charges therefor. They know that large sums are annually appropriated by Congress to construct and improve harbors along the sea-coast and the lakes, to plant buoys, build and support light houses, and no *local* tax paid by those who gain by the expenditure. Sir, they do not cavil about or complain of these things, but they say that the object of this bill is more national than any or all of these. They think that these acts of favor to our northern and eastern brethren, give them a right to claim something from the bounty and liberality of their Government. They tell you, that the Falls of the Ohio constituted an obstruction to the navigation of a river, in the removal of which thirteen States were directly interested, and several others indirectly interested—that the obstruction was only about two miles in length, and should have been removed as in all similar instances, at the expense of the General Government—that it was done (or rather avoided) by a private corporation acting under the authority of a charter most incautiously granted—that the corporation has a right and will in process of time, levy upon their commerce (for who can set bounds to human cupidity?) an annual tax of at least one hundred and fifty thousand dollars—that under most disadvantageous circumstances, the company received in the year 1833, from tolls, the sum of $60,736 92—that this tax is a vampyre which is battening upon their energies—that their trade cannot well sustain it—that it is an unaccustomed and perpetual imposition—and they earnestly call upon Congress for relief. Sir, let me add my feeble voice to theirs in this appeal. Let me invoke this body to give a friendly ear to their complaints. Look, sir, at the list appended to the

report of the Committee on Roads and Canals and you will find that some of the steam boats are compelled to pay as much as 180 dollars for a passage through this canal, and must do this whether freighted or empty. Look at the number of boats that pass the canal, and the amount of toll paid by each, and then answer if the evils complained of are not most grievous and unprecedented? Examine the report and you will find that the tolls have increased every year; that notwithstanding the company had to encounter unforeseen difficulties and expense and to repair and guard against unexpected disasters, they yet divided, for the year 1833, 5 per cent. on the original stock subscribed, and also declared a dividend of three and a half per cent. for the first six months of the last year, both on the old and new subscriptions. Sir, the dividends must increase. The company has the uncontrollable power to make their increase. But suppose they do not. Does not the present rate of toll amount to an oppressive impost? Let me invoke honorable gentlemen to view this subject in a proper light. Let me beseech them to examine it with the liberal and expanded understandings of statesmen. I can assure them, that the munificence of Government could not be extended to citizens more attached to their country and its institutions than they are, or more ready to respond to the call of duty. They are enterprising, industrious, patriotic. They ask but for free trade and equal rights—they want no more. That they have been tardy in calling upon you, is no objection to their claim. That the Government has already subscribed for a portion of the stock with the view of aiding the work, is no reason why it should not now purchase the whole stock and make the navigation of the river free to all on the terms suggested by the committee in their report.

Let not the claims of our people be prejudiced by the unfounded suspicion, that this measure is a trick put on foot by designing stockholders for selfish purposes. I assure this body that such is not the fact. They have no such purpose—they have, they can have no motive, no inducement to originate such a scheme. The stock is nearly at par in the market—yields near about 6 per cent. per annum profit on the amount invested, and the company have the chartered right to make it yield eighteen per centum per annum. I do solemnly believe that it is, or will be the most profitable stock in the United States. The stockholders are possessed of the most valuable charter in the country, and they know it. No, sir, it is the people who are not stockholders that have made this general movement, and have loaded our tables with petitions and memorials for relief. The mere distance of justice require that Congress should yield to their petitions. Sir, let justice be done though the heavens fall. Deny not their wishes. 'Now is the accepted time' to grant it if you mean ever to grant it. The bill precludes the possibility of imposition upon the Government, because it limits the price to be given at one hundred dollars a share. The purchase of the stock will cause no fiscal inconvenience, no sensible effect upon the treasury, because it will be gradual. By occasional purchases, the Government will obtain a majority of the shares, and can thus control the management of the corporation. Let me not be understood as being willing to perpetrate injustice upon those who have risked their funds in the adventure—I mean no such thing. Scorn to wrong either them or others. But I mean to say, that Congress should assume such a position as they could announce to the stockholders that a work should be a public work—that private interests should yield to the general good—that, remuneration being first made, it is justifiable to appropriate private property to the public use—that, having the power to prevent the imposition of exorbitant tolls, nay, to reduce them as low as they please, we will feel justified in subscribing that power, unless the stockholders will part with their stock at a fair price, and permit a great highway of States, to be a free highway. Sir, I doubt not that the stockholders, or a majority of them, will consent to do so. I now that some of them are willing to accede to our proposition. Why then shall it not be done? I have said it stated in casual conversations, that inasmuch

as the canal is already completed, and Congress have aided to complete it, by subscribing $290,000 of the stock, that it is all we should ask. Sir, it is most unfortunate that a private company was ever incorporated for this purpose. The proper way to have accomplished the public wishes, would have been to have applied originally and directly to this body: to have stated that the navigation of the Ohio river was interrupted by a natural obstacle: that a vast portion of the country was vitally interested in overcoming this obstacle: that it could be done with safety and success only by constructing a canal, and then demand that as it was for a nation's use, it should be accomplished with a nation's purse. It would then have stood confessedly upon the same footing as applications to remove snags and sand bars in the Ohio and Mississippi rivers, which, we know, have been removed by the sanction of Congress. Would Congress have refused the application, in such a shape? Could they have refused? No, sir, not when the Delaware breakwater, and a thousand other improvements of inferior importance, stand as monuments of the nation's liberality. If Congress would, or ought to have done so in the first instance, is there any legitimate reason why they should not now step forward, and assume upon the nation the expense of the construction of the canal—I think not. Let me state a case which seems to me to be apposite. We all know that light houses are erected and sustained at the common expense. Suppose, under a charter granted by Massachusetts when a colony, a private company had erected a light house, and in the shape of tolls were levying a tax on vessels, to the injury and oppression of the citizens of that and other States; and the parties injured were to apply to Congress to purchase the rights of the Company, and free them from the exactions of the corporation, would Congress hesitate to do so? Could they refuse to place the applicants upon the same footing with the citizens of other States who paid no tax for like benefits? Would Congress tell them you once had a fair claim, but it has been forfeited by the act of Massachusetts. Sir, every sentiment of justice would forbid it. Every impulse of patriotism would prevent it. Let not then, an unwise act of the Legislature of Kentucky forfeit the undoubted rights of the people of the valley of the Mississippi, but extend to them the same measure of justice that you would extend to the people of Massachusetts.

In conclusion Mr. Chairman, let me again invoke the Committee to give to this subject a fair, liberal, and candid consideration. Let them decide upon the bill under the influence of elevated sentiments. Let them bear in mind that the interests of millions is at stake. Let them recollect that the bill proposes to relieve from taxation, (excepting what may be necessary to keep the canal in repair, and pay the requisite charges of superintendence,) the commerce that now flows, and which will flow in all time to come, from the navigable sources of the Allegany and Monongahela rivers, and all the tributaries of the Ohio, and Mississippi, down to New Orleans, and also to relieve from injustice in relation to the respective rights of navigation. Let them reflect seriously on this, and then answer in good faith, if the rejection of the bill under consideration will not be attended with manifold evils, and crying injustice to the people of that country. Sir, let Congress act in the premises, as becomes the legislature of a great nation. At the close of the year 1833, there was paid into the national Treasury, as the portion of the Government's toll, the sum of $14,010. This will annually increase. Let us disdain then to fatten, on the fruits of the energies of our fellow citizens. Let us pass a law authorizing the purchase of the individual stock in the company; and then make an offering of the whole on the altar of the common good. Let this be done with the nation's means, because no State can, will, or ought to do it. Ohio will not do it, Indiana will not do it. Kentucky cannot be required to do it. Her interest in the measure is no greater than that of her neighbors, although the Canal is constructed through an elbow, a nook of her territory. No one of the transmontane States will do it with her separate means. It will

never be done with their united resources, because the poverty of many, and the disagreeing, disunited, and divided councils of all, will ever prevent it. Let them, I repeat, the common purse be opened to remove, now and forever, the tax imposed on the navigation of a river, whose waters, prolonged as they are, would be freely empurpled with the blood of battle, should the country's voice ever require it to flow in her defence.

Mr. McKIM inquired at what price the stock was in the market.

Mr. POPE replied, he had no precise information on that point.

Mr. BURGES said this was altogether a new project, and he had no recollection that a similar one had ever been presented before. Congress had frequently appropriated money for executing public works, and for the purchase of private property, on which to erect them; but this was a project to purchase of a company of stockholders a work already completed. It was said that it was desirable to relieve the people of the tolls, and that the work would be profitable; but he had no doubt they would always have to pay toll enough to keep it in repair, and he did not believe there would be any profit. But there was another view of the subject. The cost was, in all cases, paid by the consumer, and in the one under consideration, was paid by the people of the East for those productions they required, and by the people of the West Indies for what they consumed. After some further remarks, Mr. B. concluded by declaring his intention to vote against the proposition.

Mr. VANDERPOEL said he had voted to postpone all the orders of the day, for the purpose of giving his friend from Kentucky (Mr. Pope,) the opportunity of bringing this subject, which seemed to be a very favorite one to him, before the House. He had listened to the honorable gentleman with great attention; and he was sorry, so far as his honorable friend was concerned, that he had not succeeded in convincing him (Mr. V.) that he could on principle vote for the bill under consideration. He did not mean to make an elaborate speech on the subject; but he deemed it incumbent upon him, to state that the bill was important, not only in reference to a constitutional principle, but also in regard to the question of expediency. There was a class of gentlemen on this floor, who believed that this Government had no right to appropriate the money of the People for works of internal improvement. There was another class, who believed that such appropriations could not be made by us, unless it were for objects clearly national in their character. He would appeal to these gentlemen, and ask them what the bill under consideration proposed? It proposed to appropriate the formidable sum of six hundred and fifty thousand dollars to purchase the interest of a joint stock company in a short canal in the west. Now, he would ask what was the difference, in a constitutional point of view, between appropriating money to construct a work, and appropriating money to purchase a work of this description, after it was constructed. If the one was unconstitutional, he had not discrimination enough to see why the other was not equally so.

It had, however, been contended by the honorable gentleman from Ky., probably in anticipation of this point, that this was a national object. If this was national, could he not present an analogous case, which would certainly not be entertained a moment by this House, if proposed here. Our great New York Erie Canal was certainly more national than the little one under consideration, both in reference to the vast regions of country which are connected, and the amount of produce and merchandise, which flowed through it. Consider, sir, the immense territory bordering on our western lakes and upon the Ohio, whose rich productions flow through this canal. Suppose the inhabitants of the west, whose exports and imports passed through this canal, were to petition you for relief, were to tell you that it was very inconvenient for them to pay the tolls and tribute exacted by them from the State of New York, and respectfully prayed you to pay New York the eight or nine million which this canal has cost New York, and make it free, would you not be surprised at

assurance which might dictate a request so extravagant? And yet, it could not be denied, that the proposition to buy the Erie canal was full out more defensible on the score of *nationality* than the project contained in this bill. It was also true, that the great West, whose exports and imports passed through this canal, could urge with greater force the argument with which this bill was sought to be supported. Our farmers in the western part of New York did not now find it an object in consequence of the canal tolls to send their coarse grains, their rye and corn, to the New York market. They could not compete as to these articles with those who lived on nature's navigable waters. Let them, if this bill passes, petition Congress to purchase the great western canal and make it a free highway. There will then be a precedent for the enormous appropriation that such a scheme would require.

But there was another objection to the bill. It proposed to take this canal from a company and give it to the Government, which he believed was always most illy calculated to manage a work of this description economically. Pass the bill, and you will create at once a host of agents and superintendents, and new leeches upon your treasury. This Government was already too much connected with canals for its interest. He wished it could be wholly severed from them. For his own part, he would rather retrograde than go further. The interests of our constituents required that we should rather retrace our steps than progress further in this draining and mischievous policy.

Mr. MERCER said, he had heard to-day, most extraordinary doctrines advanced upon that floor. One from a gentleman from New York, in relation to the duty on coal, and now it was contended that artificial navigation was preferable to natural. He said it had been admitted and established by the highest authority that the General Government was bound to remove the obstructions in the Ohio and other great navigable rivers. If it was competent for the government to remove obstructions by cutting out a rock or deepening a channel, it was equally so to improve the navigation, by cutting around a fall. Mr. M. dwelt at considerable length on the great importance of the navigation of this river to the prosperity of the country; and no man, he said, could predict with any degree of certainty, what would be its overwhelming increase of importance in the process of a few years. He deemed the removal of the obstructions at the Indian Shute, a matter of primary interest. Another consideration Mr. M. said would induce him to give a favorable view of this bill. The West, from its natural position, had not shared so liberally in the expenditures of the General Government, in consequence of requiring the erection of no fortifications on her lofty eminences, where no enemy would ever dare to approach. He was anxious, therefore, that a proportionate expenditure should be made in her internal improvements. He was in favor of the bill because it was necessary, before the government could act effectually, to extinguish the title of others to this canal.

Mr. JOHNSON, of Kentucky, said, while he had held a seat on this floor, he had never allowed sectional feelings to control his votes in the appropriation of the public treasure. He had never either felt or shown favoritism for one part of the country more than another. But if gentlemen would cast their eyes over the list of public expenditures, they would see the amount for Kentucky all but a perfect blank, if you except the pension fund. Among the hundreds of millions expended by the Government, how much, he asked, had been appropriated to Kentucky? He repeated, that in all the votes he had ever given on the expenditure of public money for other parts of the country, he had voted with the same feelings that he would have done had it been for the benefit of the county in which he resided. This was a bill for the benefit of nine different States, though the expenditure happened to be in the State of Kentucky; and he did not believe there was a point more interesting to the general prosperity connected with the great waters of the West. Mr. J. said he wished no gentleman to support a measure which he might, by any construction, deem unconstitutional. Here, he contended, was a legitimate object of appropriation, where he supposed no such scruples could exist. He again appealed to the liberality and justice of the Committee, which could only be evinced in the passage of the bill.

Mr. ALLEN, of Virginia, addressed the committee in favor of the bill. He was surprised at the constitutional objection advanced by the gentleman from New York (Mr. Vanderpoel.) He would ask if that gentleman had any constitutional scruples against the improvement of the navigation of the Hudson river, by the removal of the obstructions at the Overslaugh? This work was precisely similar in its nature, and more national in its object. Mr. A. went into a further comparison of this work with other great works of admitted national character. That gentleman had contended that the commerce on the Erie Canal was ten times greater than that on the Ohio. He believed the gentleman could have but a very indistinct idea of the commerce of the West; for he could with greater safety assert that the reverse was the fact—that the Commerce of the Ohio was ten times greater than that of the New York Canal. But what was the prospect ahead! The stock of this company was now at par. In the course of a few years it would doubtless be 3 or 400 per cent. above par. He believed it the duty, therefore, of the Government, as a matter of economy, to seize the earliest opportunity of securing the stock

Mr. BOULDIN said he had voted to take up this bill from courtesy to the mover of it, and with a view to the economy in the time of the House. But he should vote against the passage of the bill in all its stages. He said it was not necessary for him to say any thing to show his conviction that such works of internal improvement could not be constitutionally made by the General Government. He had no idea of voting for the purchase of any such stock as that proposed by this bill to be bought, and should vote against the purchase upon any terms whatever.

Mr. MASON, of Virginia, said it was known that the Government of the United States was a joint stockholder in the Louisville and Portland canal, and that it was also interested in some other improvements in the country. He thought it must be conceded, from common respect to those, who had gone before us, and who had authorized these subscriptions, that they must have been satisfied that the several works in which the government had become interested as a stockholder were calculated to promote the public good, and unquestionably that the investment was not to be thrown away. Now, he thought it became us to reflect that if we adopt the principle involved in the bill under consideration, we could not, in common justice, refuse to act up to it when applications should be made from other companies. The company of whose stock it was proposed the government should become the exclusive proprietor, had not, as yet, so far as he was informed, divided one cent of profit; nor had paid their debt.

Mr. POPE explained. The company had divided six per cent. on the shares in 1833, and the government had received $14,010 on account of its third share of the stock. Moreover, as he had before stated, a dividend of three and a half per cent. had been paid for six months of last year, and there would be a further one of more than two per cent.

Mr. MASON proceeded. He had no other means of information than that afforded by the report, and from which he certainly understood that the debts could not be paid before 1837, and therefore it was a fair inference, that if they had not paid their debts, they could have shared no profits. This was also borne out by the fact, that the stock was still below its par value in the market; and when we took into consideration the immense amount of uninvested capital in the country, in consequence of the liquidation of our national debt and other causes, and that most stocks were now above par, he thought they could not conceal from themselves the fact, that the stock of the Louisville and Portland Canal was not likely to turn out a good investment, or it never would have sunk below par. But setting this aside, he again called the attention of the committee to the fact, that if the Government should become the exclusive proprietor of this stock, we could not, in common justice, refuse to become the exclusive proprietors of the stock of all these companies in which we were interested, whenever the said companies should think fit to make an application to that effect. The same principle which justified the one, would apply with equal force to all other cases. How could they refuse to take the whole stock of the great canal leading from the Potomac to the western waters? How refuse the Dismal Swamp Canal, which, in the opinion of every one conversant with the subject, was one of the most important and valuable works in the country? He had listened with great pleasure and satisfaction yesterday to the able and lucid argument of the gentleman from Kentucky, (Mr. Hardin,) on a subject somewhat similar to the present. That gentleman expressed sentiments which Mr. M. hoped yet to see become the ruling principle of our councils; he meant, that the expenses of the General Government should be confined within its legitimate objects, viz. providing for the army, navy, civil list, &c. as defined by the constitution. He should be rejoiced if he could hear the same gentleman give an exposition of his views on the present subject.

Mr. M. said he should, perhaps, be found in a small minority in the Committee of the Whole upon that question, but he would at once candidly confess that he had a constitutional objection to this measure, and it appeared to him to possess much more force than gentlemen seemed to attribute to it. It was not his intention to go into any argument upon the powers of that House to undertake works of internal improvements. His own opinions were made up, and had long been made up on that question, and although every day's experience in legislation confirmed him in the opinion that the government of the United States could not, under the provisions of the constitution, engage in works of internal improvement in the United States; and although he considered this bill as a violation of that principle, he did not purpose to discuss that question at the present time.

But in what aspect did the bill present itself there? The legislature of Kentucky had chartered a company to undertake and complete a certain work. Individuals had subscribed and paid stock, by which the work had been executed, and which had become their private property. The canal was their real estate. Now it was proposed by this bill that the government of the United States should become the purchaser of this real estate. Where could be found the power to do this? It was not in the constitution of the United States. The only provision in that instrument, relating to this point, was that which authorized Congress to purchase places for the erection of forts, magazines, arsenals, dock-yards, &c. but that purchase must, in all cases, be made "by the consent of the legislature of the State in which the same shall be." This was plainly designated and described, and he could find nothing to justify the exercise of the power claimed in the bill before the Committee. He was fully aware he entertained opinions with regard to the constitution in which he would not be sustained by a majority of the Committee; but this he could not avoid. His own opinion was, that under that instrument, Congress had no right to take this stock.

There was also another view in which this subject should be considered, and it was this: the question was not whether the trade that passed down the river Ohio should cease to be incommoded by the obstruction at the falls—it was not whether the Government should make that improvement, for the improvement was already made; the question was, whether the United States should buy out the shares in the Bank stock from individual stockholders, at a price which must necessarily exceed the present market value of them. He said exceed, because the moment this bill passed, the price of shares would rise to the maximum. It has been urged, as a just ground of complaint, that the trade upon that river was heavily and unnecessarily taxed by the imposition of tolls. He

was astonished to hear such an argument made use of as a subject of complaint. The trade on the Ohio river had been benefited already to a greater extent than any other channel in the United States. Repeated expenditures of public money had been made, for which the people there had never been taxed one cent. The trade which floated on these waters had been promoted by large and repeated expenditures of the public money, for which the Government received nothing in the shape of tolls; and he believed he could safely aver that there was not an internal navigation in the whole Union, not a river or a water course, upon whose bosom the produce of the farmer was carried to market subject to so few charges as upon the Ohio river. Look at the rivers of Virginia, of New York, and of other States; all the improvements had been effected by individual enterprise, and the farmer cheerfully paid his quota of taxation. Look at the young State of Indiana, willing even to exhaust her resources in constructing the great canal to Lake Erie. Besides, the United States had already subscribed one-third of the whole stock to this canal, and the petitioners for the proposition before the Committee had no just cause of complaint.

There was also another point he thought worthy of consideration. There was no provision in the bill, or the amendment, making the navigation free, but it proposed to continue a tariff of tolls. Now he would put it to the committee, who was to regulate that tariff? At whose discretion was it to be? Supposing the tolls were insufficient to keep the canal in repair, who was to fix their rate? If too low, who should raise them, if too high, who was to depress them? This was perhaps comparatively an unimportant question, but still it involved one of no little embarrassment, and one which, with him, if no other consideration presented itself, would induce him to vote against it. If considerations of a public character justified the purchase of the stock of this canal, make it a free high way, do it effectually at once, employ a superintendent, pay him a certain fixed salary, and pay all the needful expenses of keeping the work in repair.

Entertaining, said Mr. M. in conclusion, the opinions he did, that they had no right to become the proprietors of this canal, and consequently no right to make the purchase; believing also that if they did, no good would result, but on the contrary, the very moment that individuals ceased to be interested in it as their own private property, that very moment all security for that vigorous and constant attention which works of this nature required would be lost; furthermore, considering that the projectors were entitled to all the benefits of the enterprise, and in fine that the burdens depicted were not such as the petitioners had a right to complain of, he could not vote for this bill in any possible form in which it might be presented.

Mr. DENNY did not intend to enter into an argument on the merits of the bill; but some remarks which had just fallen from the gentleman from Virginia (Mr. Mason,) seemed to call for a reply. That gentleman contended that the Government had no constitutional right to purchase this stock. If we had become proprietors in part, why could we not be so in full? If the constitutional right, as it had been so often expressed here, by the other branch of the National Legislature and by the Executive, existed to become the owner of a part of the shares of this stock, what should obstruct the right to possess the whole? This principle he conceived to be definitively settled; and it was merely a question of expediency, of policy. Those who opposed the constitutional power of the Government to make appropriations for internal improvements, had ever admitted the improvement of the navigation of the great rivers to be an exception to their general rule. This work, he contended, was truly and emphatically national, involving the vital interest of not only nine States, as had been suggested, but of eleven. Mr. D. alluded to the vast amount of freight paid by the west for the productions of the south and east, and showed by a tabular statement, the tolls of some single boats to be upwards of one hundred dollars. He concluded by urging the importance of the work to the western country, and expressing a hope for the passage of the bill.

Mr. HAWES did not wish to obstruct unnecessarily the passage of the bill; but in justice to himself, he would claim the attention of the House for a few moments, for the purpose of explaining the vote he should give on this subject. The Legislature of his State, had by perhaps a unanimous vote, requested him to vote for this measure. He considered it improper for a member of Congress thus circumstanced, to vote against the wishes of his Legislature, upon light or trivial grounds. When the measure was intended to benefit his own State, he should not oppose it, except upon high considerations. It would probably appear strange, under these circumstances, that he should oppose this bill. He should, nevertheless, do so upon grounds which he had always assumed and maintained, namely, that it was improper for the General Government to appropriate money for improvements within the States. Besides, the Government was incapable of carrying on and superintending this canal so as to produce any practical good or benefit. Pass this bill and pay the private stockholders their money, and, said Mr. H. the canal will be immediately destroyed, and the navigation again impeded. In two years from the passage of such an act as the one proposed, the difficulties in passing the Falls of the Ohio would be equally as great as they were before the canal was made. Such was the history of all of the works made by the National Government. He would do no act calculated to destroy or disturb improperly this important improvement. He could not, conscientiously, vote for this bill, for the reasons which he had assigned.

Mr. PEARCE advocated the bill at considerable length. He combated the idea that it would form a precedent which would lead to the necessity of purchasing of the Dismal Swamp Canal or any other. And as to the New York Canals, gentlemen might be under no apprehensions of their being offered to the Government, while they continued to yield their present profits. In alluding to the importance of improving the navigation of the Ohio, Mr. P. referred to the circumstance of some of his fellow-townsmen, in 1804, having sent hands to Marietta to construct a ship, which would have proved a profitable speculation had it not met with an accident, which rendered it useless, in passing the Falls of the Ohio. Mr. P. after considering some other objections, concluded by saying he could see no impropriety in the passage of the bill, and he should have no objection to giving his vote in its favor.

Mr. McCOMAS said, a large portion of his constituents were interested in this Canal. About two millions bushels of salt annually manufactured at the Kenhawa Saline, passed the Falls of the Ohio, either by way of the Canal or otherwise. Great embarrassments had been experienced, owing to the obstructions in the river at this place. The deleterious effects produced by them, were felt not only in regard to the article to which he had referred, but in relation to every article of produce raised above the Falls, and which was intended for the market below that point. Any gentleman who would turn his attention to the Ohio river, would at once see the peculiarly national character of the improvement, at the Falls of the river. He was in favor of a strict construction of the constitution on subjects of this character, but this was a case which he considered, presented no constitutional difficulty.

His worthy friend and colleague, (Mr. Mason,) seemed alarmed lest we should be asked in some future occasion, to purchase the stock, on various other works—the Dismal Swamp Canal for instance. There was certainly no analogy between those works. The Dismal Swamp Canal was 29 miles in length, and connects itself with the Roanoke river—a stream full of cataracts and obstructions. If the works on the Ohio river were to be put down by comparisons of this sort, we might with equal propriety put down, and destroy your light-houses, &c.

Mr. McC. referred to the great extent of trade carried on through this Canal. It was intimately connected with the best interests of the country. Even the Alantic sea-board was deeply concerned in this improvement. Who were the individuals who passed down the Ohio river? For the most part, the poorer classes who emigrate to the west for the purpose of seeking homes, for themselves and their families. In every aspect in which the subject could be viewed, the propriety of the passage of this bill was rendered obvious He could see no difference in purchasing the Canal, from the individuals who had made it, and an original proposition to clear out the obstructions to the navigation. Besides, the Government was already a stockholder in the Canal. This House possessed the power of judging for itself, of the nationality of this improvement. The objections which might be interposed by the President were obviated by the fact, that a port of entry was established above the Falls of the Ohio, at Pittsburg. This would form no objection with him.

Mr. McC. thought the passage of the bill justly due to the people inhabiting the western country. Very little of the pap of the Treasury had been distributed west of the Alleganies, for public improvements. In times of danger and peril, no portion of the people of this Union, acted with more determined bravery—all they asked was a participation in the benefits which were extended to other sections of the country—that these benefits should not be confined exclusively to those districts where salt water flowed. Upon a full view of the subject, he could see no objection to the passage of the bill, and he hoped that it would receive the favorable consideration of the House.

Mr. FILLMORE rose to put a question relating to some legal points connected with the charter and officers of the company.

Mr. POPE moved as an amendment to add at the end of the bill, "and pay the necessary charges and expenses of superintendence."

The question being taken, it was decided in the negative. The bill was then laid aside; and,

On motion of Mr. WARDWELL,

The committee then proceeded to consider the bill from the Senate for continuing the office of Commissioner of Pensions; which was read and laid aside.

Mr. E. EVERETT moved that the committee proceed to consider the bill providing for the purchase of 200 copies of the *fac simile* accounts of General Washington; which was agreed to. The bill was then read and laid aside.

On motion of Mr. FILLMORE,

The committee then rose and reported the three bills to the House, without amendment.

The SPEAKER having resumed the Chair,

Mr. BARRINGER moved to strike out the enacting clause of the bill relative to the Louisville and Portland Canal; which motion he advocated at some length.

The bill was then, on motion of Mr. LYTLE, postponed till Monday next—ayes 107, noes not counted.

The bill for continuing the office of Commissioner of Pensions was next taken up, and an additional section was offered by Mr. McKIM, as an amendment; which was adopted.

This bill, and that to purchase 200 copies of the *fac simile* of Gen. Washington's accounts were then ordered to be engrossed and read a third time to-morrow.

Several unsuccessful motions were made to go into Committee on various bills; when,

On motion of Mr. BRIGGS,

The House adjourned.

IN SENATE.

FRIDAY, February 6, 1835.

Mr. SHEPLEY presented the credentials of the Hon. JOHN RUGGLES, elected a Senator from the State of Maine, to supply the vacancy occasioned by the resignation of the Hon. PELEG SPRAGUE.

Mr. RUGGLES having presented himself, the oath was administered, and he took his seat in the Senate.

The VICE PRESIDENT laid before the Senate a communication from the Navy Department in compliance with a resolution of the Senate, relative to the claims of the owners of the private armed brig Neptune and Fox.

Mr. PRENTISS, from the Committee on Pensions, reported a bill for the relief of Richard Anderson.

Mr. PRESTON, from the Judiciary Committee, to which was referred the resolution of the Senate directing an inquiry into the expediency of connecting the third and fourth Judicial Districts, and to extend the benefits of the Judiciary system to the Western States, reported a bill reorganizing the Judicial Circuits of the United States, and connecting the two districts formed of the States of New Jersey, Pennsylvania, Delaware, and Maryland, into one district.

Mr. KING, of Alabama, from the Committee on Military Affairs, reported a bill for the relief of John H. Bell.

The said bills were severally read the first time, and ordered to a second reading.

Mr. WEBSTER, from the Committee on Finance, to which was referred the bill to authorize George Witman to import an iron steamboat in detached parts, free of duty, reported the same, with an amendment.

Mr. LEIGH, from the Committee on Revolutionary Claims, made an unfavorable report upon the petition of the heirs of Lieut. Col. John Jamieson, and the committee were discharged from the further consideration of the subject.

On motion of Mr. PORTER, the Senate proceeded to consider, as in Committee of the Whole, the bill appropriating $20,000 to the completion of certain roads in the Territory of Arkansas, and the bill was ordered to be engrossed for a third reading.

On motion of Mr. FRELINGHUYSEN, the Senate resumed the consideratian of the joint resolution providing for the disposition of a Lion and two Horses presented by the Emperor of Morocco to the United States Consul at Tangiers.

The resolution was read the third time, and passed.

Mr. TOMLINSON, from the Committee on Pensions, to which was referred the petition of William W. Hall for arrears of pension, reported unfavorably upon the same, and the committee were discharged from the further consideration of the same.

Mr. TIPTON, from the Committee on Claims, reported unfavorably upon the petitions of Thos. Mullen, and William Mann, from the further consideration of which, the committee were discharged.

POST OFFICE BILL.

The Senate resumed the consideration, as in Committee of the Whole, of the bill to change the organization of the General Post Office.

The question being on the sixteenth section, submitted by Mr. GRUNDY, as an amendment, providing for payment of the debts of the Department, which may be owing on the 31st March, 1835.

Mr. GRUNDY rose, in support of the amendment, as this subject would be properly discussed only by those who have carefully examined it. In answer to the remarks of the honorable Senator from Louisiana (Mr. Porter) made yesterday, he wished to say a few words. That honorable Senator supposed, because he was no favorite of the present administration, injustice had been done to his constituents, in regard to the route leading to New Orleans. This route had been particularly pointed out by the report of the majority of the committee last session, and but one feeble voice raised in its favor, and that not from Louisiana. Mr. G. read from the report of the majority several passages going to condemn this route, and this report was a favorite with the majority of the Senate. He was the only one who supported the conduct of the Postmaster General on that occasion. He wished to do justice to that officer; he wished justice to be rendered where it was due. Last year the head of that Department was condemned for extending facilities; now, he was censured for withdrawing them.

Mr. G. did not think the Department had acted in compliance with either the reports of the majority or of the minority, but to meet the exigencies of the time.

The President of the United States had been censured in the course of this debate. He wished to see if the censure was just. Mr. G. read from the report of the Postmaster General, made to the President; also from the report of the majority of the committee, showing the grounds on which the President had founded his opinions. He thought no injustice had been done to the Senators from Louisiana. If they thought so, let them state to the Senate that they would have voted in favor of the grant. So far from that, he did not believe they would even vote for it now. The Department had been accused of corruptions, said Mr. G. He thought the head of that Department uncorrupt, and incapable of corruption. He feared for him at the commencement of the investigation; not from any suspicions of his integrity, but from perjury and misrepresentation. The order for investigation held out an invitation to all dissatisfied and ill-disposed contractors who had been dismissed or rejected. But to the honor of his countrymen, he was proud to say no one had been found to accuse the Postmaster General of corruption.

Mr. G. said, in accusing the Department of corruption, in general terms, the innocent was involved with the guilty. Distinctions should be made—the dishonest should be pointed out; and then, in the language of the Senator from South Carolina, (Mr. Preston,) the culprit might be held up to the view.

Mr. G. contended that the term *corruption* was improperly applied, where there was no evidence that the individual accused had been profited. He thought mismanagement was severe enough. If there was corruption, he did not believe it attached to the head of the Department.

The Postmaster General, said Mr. G., did not reverse the political maxim, which considers all innocent until they are found guilty; which, perhaps, he ought to have done, and suspected all persons of having improper and selfish designs on the Department. A thousand influences were brought to bear upon; the interest of the contractor, of the inn-keeper, of the stage-driver, of the citizen who provided hay and oats, or chickens and butter, for the support of those employed in this business; and finally, by members of Congress.

The Senator from New Jersey, said Mr. G., had told us the People would not be satisfied with the turning out of a single clerk. That Senator would not be satisfied with the turning out of a single clerk—not with the turning out of the Head of that Department—not with turning out all the clerks in all the Departments—not with the turning out of all the heads of the departments—no, not even of the President of the United States; for then the Vice President would turn himself in.

Mr. G. contended, that if Congress took away the revenues of the Department, they should also pay all just and honest debts. He was not disposed to trust to some future appropriation. It was better to do a thing while they were about it.

Mr. LEIGH said, he understood the report of the minority of the committee at the last session, as a recommendation to pay the debts of the department. But although he did not believe any such debt contracted as these had been, without authority of law, were binding on the United States, yet he thought that perhaps in point of policy, the Government ought to pay the money, because it had received the benefit of it; and he designed to vote for such a proposition, when the department should be placed upon a safe and secure foundation. But he did understand the honorable gentleman then to say, that no proposition was made or intended to be made for such an appropriation. Now as to the payment of these debts, let a schedule be laid before the Senate, and if it should appear that they were *bona fide* debts, he would vote to pay the creditors of the department, but he would not vote it to the Post Office Department. For suppose one of these debts was a contract for extra allowances to Reeside or Robinson for services which were not performed. Would any body say it was right to pay a debt so manifestly unjust, and which any chancellor would order to be refunded? When he saw a schedule, and was satisfied of their honesty, he would vote a liberal appropriation to satisfy them. He would not make charges of corruption, but whether the evils complained of had grown out of want of vigilance, corruption, or any other cause, he must think it was not Obadiah who had tied all these knots.

Mr. EWING denied that there was any thing in the report of last year from which it could be justly inferred that the Committee condemned the carrying of a daily mail between New Orleans and Mobile as a waste of public money. He thought no such thing; he rather thought that the mails, generally, were not carried any too fast. Mr. E. read from the report of the majority of last session, to show that the objection to those contracts was, that the Postmaster General made them by private arrangements, instead of by a public letting, which prevented open bidding. He said there were 150 failures in a year upon the route between Mobile and New Orleans, and yet $40,000 a year were paid for carrying this as a daily mail. And it appeared, too, that Mr. O. B. Brown was interested in that contract. Whether there was corruption in this, he would not argue with the honorable gentleman. But why were these failures? The mail ought to have been carried daily, and ought now to be so carried; but the payment for services which were never performed, was what the Committee condemned. So if other payments which had been made by the Department for services which had not been rendered, had been reserved, and paid usefully for facilitating the mail, the Committee would not have condemned them—the danger of paying which the honorable gentleman feared, was certainly a groundless alarm; for not a single witness had testified against the Department, but his testimony had been confirmed by the documents in the Department itself. It was not the disposition of our people to get up a conspiracy against the head of the Department, or any other person in it. It was with great difficulty that the truth could be got out of the witnesses, and when the officers were examined, the Committee had really to wring the testimony out of them. He thought when a public officer peculated on the public funds, the presumption did arise, that the public suffered to that amount, and it did not require negative proof to show that the public did not suffer. Mr. E. said he was under the impression, from the report of the committee, that the specification of the sum necessary to relieve the Department was to be considered as an application for relief. He cared not how it came, whether from the Postmaster General or the committee, the purport was the same, and it was so believed by the majority of the committee. But as to the report, he admitted it did not produce conviction among the whole community—it was not expected it would do so. It was not till these things were examined that their enormity would be observed. With regard to the appropriation asked, he would state, that there was a very large sum due to small contractors prior to January 1st, 1834, many of whom were now nearly ruined, and now suppose this appropriation of $300,000 should be made, the large contractors, who had performed no service, would come in and sweep it away, while the honest small contractors would get nothing. The gross amount due to contractors, the Postmaster General said was about $400,000, but the accountants employed by the committee, and they were as skilful as any in the District, had made the actual sum only about $199,000. How then could we make a sweeping appropriation to pay them? But there were accepted drafts too in circulation not paid, amounting to $160,000, but payable at a future day, and in the aggregate they amounted on the 1st April last to $160,000, as he had stated. We could not then make an appropriation. He hoped the amendment would be rejected, and then, when sufficient data could be obtained, he would introduce a bill to appropriate annually such sum as would be required for payment of the just and legal debts of the Department.

Mr. BUCHANAN said, he did not rise to extend this discussion; on the contrary, if so young a member of the Senate as himself might be at liberty to express such an opinion, it had already been too much extended. The bill before us, was for the purpose of changing the organization of the Post Office Department. Its most important provisions had received the unanimous approbation of the Committee. It was not denied that the enactment of this bill was indispensable to the useful and successful operations of the Department.

It corrected the strange anomoly now existing, that the same hands which received the public money were those which disbursed it: when it must be admitted that there could be no effectual security against abuses, but by imposing the duty of receiving the money upon one class of officers, and that of paying it out upon annother. The main object was to adopt some measure to correct this evil. The session was rapidly drawing to a close, and unless we should pass this bill and send it to the House of Representatives very soon, it could not become a law at the present session. He was ready to press on an examination of the principles involved in the bill, but not to a discussion of alleged abuses in the administration of the Department, which he deemed out of place at this time. There was a resolution on the table offered by the Senator from Connecticut, (Mr. Smith) on whic, when it should come up, war might be waged on the one side as well as the other. But he would not engage in such discussion now, for another reason. When the reports of the majority and the minority of the Committee were presented and read, the Senate presented the appearance of a "Sleepy Hollow." With very few exceptions, not a Senator then present, paid that attention to them which their importance required. He plead guilty himself: the reports gave details which he did not and could not thoroughly understand from hearing them read. He had, therefore, determined to wait until he could see them in print, and until then, he should be unprepared to express an opinion on the subject. So soon as he could get the printed reports, he would lay aside all other business, and examine them carefully, and when he had done so, he would come to his own conclusions, which, on any proper occasion, he should express fearlessly. But there was another reason why we should have the reports before us. As to most of the facts, it was said both the reports agreed. But from the same facts, the majority and minority of the Committee had drawn very different inferences. To ascertain which was correct in their conclusions, would require a much more minute and attentive examination of all the circumstances attending each transaction, than would have otherwise been necessary. Without saying any thing further, he hoped we would go on to discuss the bill, and leave the other subjects for another occasion. He would merely suggest to the Senator from Ohio, (Mr. Ewing, whether the debts due to the small contractors prior to the year 1834, which were admitted to be honest, might not be provided for by this bill, even if he would consent to do nothing more. Their payment should no longer be delayed. Certainly the gentleman could not be afraid to trust the Commissioner to be appointed under this act, and the Secretary of the Treasury, with the settlement of these claims.

Mr. KANE said, he could not vote for the amendment: by doing so, he might be voting to pay a debt, the consideration for which had entirely failed—it might be to pay for the transportation of the mail when it had never taken place. Was it right, he inquired, to leave the ascertainment of the debts to Congress, hereafter. Such a thing he deemed hopeless, unless Congress were perpetually in session: He believed the ascertainment of the amount of the debts could be effected better by the Treasury Department than through the medium of a committee. He therefore offered the following amendment to the amendment:

"That all the debts now due and owing by the Post Office Department for the actual transportation of the mail, or for money borrowed and actually applied on account of such transportation, when ascertained, adjusted and audited, according to the provisions of existing laws, shall be paid by the treasury of the United States."

Mr. GRUNDY accepted the offer as part of his amendment.

Mr. BIBB rose to offer an amendment to the amendment. He had come to the conclusion never to vote one cent from the Treasury to support the Post Office Department. But as these debts would come in as claims against the government for services performed, under proper regulations, he would consent to the appropriation.

Mr. B. then went on to pay a tribute of respect to the private character of the Postmaster General. He thought the good disposition and kindness of that officer had been laid hold of by interested and selfish persons, to further their own private interests; thus abusing the goodness of the Postmaster General's private feeling by the grossest impositions.

Mr. B. concluded, by moving an amendment providing for the payment of the debts of the Department out of the accruing postages.

Mr. SOUTHARD said, that the amendment did not obviate his difficulty. He stated, yesterday, that the difficulty in his mind was in inserting an appropriation in a bill organizing the Department. He was in favor of organizing the Department first, and then he would think of making an appropriation when he saw where and how the money was to be paid.

Mr. WEBSTER said, a rule of practical wisdom in legislation was, to act for a single object by a single measure. The gentleman from Tennessee, he thought, would have done well to have made this proposition the subject of a distinct bill. The Post Office Department required a substantial reorganization, and if mismanagement, or whatever else it might be called, existed there, and he believed it was not denied, we should make provision, first, for the reconstruction of the Department, and when that was done, introduce a bill making an appropriation for its relief. That seemed to him the proper course, and if so, why introduce into this bill a proposition of this extraneous character. What should hinder us from considering this simple question of reorganization? The gentleman from Pennsylvania, (Mr. Buchanan,) argued, and with great propriety, that the amount of the debts was not pertinent to the question of the mode of reorganization. And he thought so too, but he carried the principle farther—he thought that the means of paying those debts were not so either, they were entirely distinct. The appropriation was a matter to be founded on estimates. The gentlemen on the other side of the House desired to provide for those honest men who were creditors of the department, and he felt every disposition to join them in this matter. But was there any thing more easy than to get a report from the department, with statements of the amount of its debts? He hoped the honorable gentleman (Mr. Grundy) would not thus obstruct the progress of the bill, which he knew the gentleman desired should pass, by the introduction of this debateable matter. Because, if we were called on to pay the debts in this way, it opened the whole question; and must we not inquire what they were, how they were contracted, and the true character of them? So far as they could be discriminated, and shown to be just and honest, he would cheerfully vote a sum sufficient to pay them.

Mr. GRUNDY said, that he had but one object in view, in all that he had advanced on this subject, and that was, that the Department should be paid. He was very anxious that this bill should pass, if proper amendments were incorporated in it, and he therefore withdrew the amendment.

The 17th section (another of Mr. Grundy's amendments) was then taken up. It provides, that the books of the Treasury, so far as relates to the accounts of the General Post Office, shall be kept separate and distinct from all other accounts; and every warrant for the payment of money for demands against the General Post Office, shall express upon its face that the same was issued on account of the General Post Office.

After some explanation from Mr. Grundy, this section was amended so as to require such warrants to be "signed by the Postmaster General and the Commissioner of the General Post Office;" after which it was agreed to.

The 18th section, in the following words, was then considered: "That the Commissioner to be appointed under the provisions of this act, shall have power to transfer debts due from Postmasters by drafts in favor of contractors, in discharge of debts due to such contractors, for services which may have been rendered prior to the time of drawing such drafts."

After the word "Postmaster," the words "who do not make deposites in Bank" were inserted, at the suggestion of Mr. KNIGHT, and the section as amended, was then adopted.

The 19th section was next considered. It provides that the Postmaster General shall report to Congress within the first ten days of each annual session, and specifies at length, the various subjects upon which he shall report. The section is divided into four clauses The fourth clause requires the Commissioner to report to the Postmaster General the condition of the finances of the department.

After being so amended, at the suggestion of Mr. WEBSTER, as to require the report of the Commissioner to be made to Congress, the section was adopted.

The 20th section was next considered, in the following words: "It shall be the duty of the Postmaster General to furnish to the Deputy Postmaster at the termination of each route, a schedule specifying the times of arrival and departure at his office, of each mail; and also furnish a notice, in like manner, of any change or alteration in the arrivals and departures which may be ordered by him."

Mr. EWING moved to insert, after the word "mail," the words "a copy of which, the Postmaster shall set up in some conspicuous place in his office;" which, Mr. GRUNDY not objecting, was agreed to, and the section, as amended, was then adopted.

The 21st and last section was then considered. It requires the Postmaster at the end of a mail route, or at any other place where the time shall be designated at which the mail shall arrive, to subscribe an oath "that he will truly and faithfully report to the General Post Office, all failures to deliver the mail at his office at the times prescribed." It also directs the Postmaster General to report to Congress, annually, each failure to deliver the mail where the same may be conveyed in steamboats, coaches, or stages, and the names of the contractors on whose routes the failures have occurred.

After some immaterial amendments of form, this section was also adopted.

[Mr. CLAY here, on leave, submitted a motion to reconsider the vote by which the joint resolution, authorizing the purchase of certain pictures for the President's House, was negatived. The motion being received, it was laid on the table.]

The amendments having been gone through with—

Mr. CALHOUN made some objection to the first section of the bill, which provides for the appointment of the Commissioner. He also thought the salary ought to be reduced from four thousand to three thousand five hundred dollars per annum. Mr. C. submitted an amendment to be inserted in lieu of the first section:

"That the duties now performed by the Fifth Auditor of the Treasury Department, be, and the same are hereby assigned to the Second Auditor of the Treasury; and those now assigned to the Second, to the Third Auditor; and that the Fifth Auditor shall hereafter be known as the Commissioner of the General Post Office, and shall perform the duties hereby assigned, or which may hereafter be assigned, to said Commissioner.

After some conversation between Mr. CALHOUN and Mr. BUCHANAN on the subject, and before any action was had on the proposition,

Mr. GRUNDY interposed a motion to adjourn, which prevailed, and

The Senate adjourned.

HOUSE OF REPRESENTATIVES.

FRIDAY, February 6, 1835.

Mr. BAYLIES, from the Committee on Revolutionary Claims, reported a bill for the relief of the legal representatives of Tristam Coffin; which was read twice and committed.

Mr. GALBRAITH, from the Committee on Private Land Claims, reported a bill supplementary to the act entitled "An act enabling the claimants to lands within the limits of the State of Missouri, and Territory of Arkansas, to institute proceedings to try the validity of their claims," approved twenty-sixth May eighteen hundred and twenty-four; which was read twice and committed.

Unfavorable reports were made by Messrs. BANKS and FULTON, from the Committee on Claims, upon petitions referred to said committee.

Petitions and memorials were presented, on leave, by Messrs. MITCHELL of Ohio, McVEAN, McCARTY, and REYNOLDS, and appropriately referred.

On motion of Mr. WISE,

Resolved, That the Committee on the Post Office and Post Roads be instructed to inquire into the expediency of establishing a post route from Princess Anne, via Newtown, in Maryland, to Bloxom's tavern, in Virginia; and from Horn Town, in Virginia, to Bloxom's tavern, and from Bloxom's tavern, via Riley's store, Caleb Broadwater's store, Jenkin's bridge, Mesongo bridge, Guilford and Bagwell's mill, to Drummondtown, Accomack county, Virginia.

On motion of Mr. RENCHER,

Resolved, That the Committee on Indian Affairs be instructed to inquire into the expediency of providing by law, for the relief of certain Choctaw Indians, who claim to be entitled to reservations of land under the 14th article of the treaty of Dancing Rabbit Creek.

On motion of Mr. LYON, of Kentucky,

Resolved, That the Committee on the Post Office and Post Roads be instructed to inquire into the expediency of establishing a post route from Wadesboro, Calloway Court House, Kentucky, via Humility, to the mouth of Sandy river, Tennessee.

On motion of Mr. MITCHELL, of Ohio,

Resolved, That so much of the petition of the citizens of Zanesville, in the State of Ohio, as relates to the establishment of a Port of Entry, be referred to the Committee on Commerce, and that so much as relates to the improvement of the navigation of the Muskingum river, be referred to the Committee on Roads and Canals.

On motion of Mr. CHINN,

Resolved, That the Commissioner of Public Buildings be directed to prepare and furnish to this House an estimate of the cost of the Treasury building, recommended by a select committee of this House, if freestone be substituted for granite.

On motion of Mr. KINNARD,

Resolved, That the Committee on the Post Office and Post Roads be instructed to inquire into the expediency of establishing a post route from Noblesville, in the county of Hamilton, to Montezuma, Indiana, via Westfield, Northfield, Lebanon, Jamestown, and Rupeville.

Mr. DICKINSON offered the following resolution; which, under the rule, lies one day:

Resolved, That the Secretary of War be required to communicate to this House the number of Cadets that have been educated at the Military Academy at West Point—the number that joined the Army, and are now in its service—the sums of money that have been appropriated for its support, each year, since 1802, up to this time. Also, the number of Professors now employed at the institution.

The following resolution, offered by Mr. PARKS, on the 3d inst., was considered, and agreed to:

Resolved, That the Secretary of War be requested to communicate to this House, the report of Major Hartman Bache, of the reconnoisance for a road through the northern frontier of the State of Maine, made by him in pursuance of instructions from the War Department.

The following resolution, offered by Mr. DENNY, on the 26th of January, was read, considered, and agreed to:

Resolved, That the Secretary of War be, and he is hereby requested to communicate to this House, a statement of the amount paid annually, and the price per year, during the last five years, for the transportation of arms, and all other military and public stores, from Harper's Ferry, Baltimore, Washington Arsenal, and any other posts or places in Virginia, Maryland, and District of Columbia, to Pittsburg, and other posts in the western country.

Mr. McVEAN, on leave, submitted the following resolution:

Resolved, That the Committee on the District of Columbia be directed to report to this House the amount expended by said committee under the resolution of the sixth of January last, purporting to authorize and instruct them to ascertain the amount of fuel that might be necessary for the relief of the suffering poor of the City of Washington, and to place the same at the disposal of the Corporation for that purpose; and also that said committee be instructed to desist from further expenditure under the color of authority derived from said resolution, ***and that said resolution be expung'd from the journal of this House.***

Mr. EVANS moved the question of consideration.

Mr. HAMER asked for the yeas and nays; which were ordered.

Mr. McVEAN moved a call of the House. Negatived.

Mr. McVEAN made an appeal to Mr. EVANS to withdraw his motion, in order that he might explain his reasons for offering the resolution.

Mr. EVANS thought the gentleman had better withdraw the resolution, or at least modify it by withdrawing the latter clause. If it was so modified, he might withdraw his motion.

Mr. McVEAN said, that at the suggestion of several gentlemen he had no objection to modify his resolution, by striking out the latter clause.

After some remarks between Mr. SPEIGHT and the CHAIR, on a point of order, Mr. McVEAN modified his resolution by striking from it the latter clause, printed in italics.

Mr. EVANS withdrew his motion, asking the question of consideration.

Mr. WILDE renewed the question of consideration

Mr. HAMER demanded the yeas and nays; which were ordered.

The question, "Will the House consider the resolution?" was then put and decided in the affirmative—yeas 124, nays 54.

So the House determined to consider the resolution.

Mr. EVANS said, his objection to the resolution was not founded on any opposition which he might have to the general views of the mover (Mr. McVean,) for he was opposed to the practice which had obtained in the House, of passing resolutions of that nature. But the emergency which called forth the original resolution, had gone by. The money had been expended according to its provisions; and to pass this resolution now, would be a reflection on the proceedings of the House, which he deemed unnecessary and uncalled for. If, however, the honorable mover (Mr. McVean) would adopt the amendment which he was about to propose, he would not object to its passage. The amendment was to strike out the words "purporting to," and let it read, "authorizing and instructing;" and also strike out the words "under color of." These words, Mr. E. considered objectionable, as they seemed to convey a reflection—a censure on the House.

Mr. McVEAN said, that he could not accept of the amendments offered by the honorable member from Maine, because he would thereby defeat the principal object he had in view in offering his resolution. He believed the resolution to which the one he had the honor to offer, referred, was passed by the House without constitutional authority, and he frankly confessed, that the main object he had in view, was to elicit a declaration to that effect from the House, that it might not hereafter be cited as a precedent. He disclaimed any intention to cast any reflection upon the House, upon the mover of the resolution, or on the Committee who acted under it. He believed that all were governed by motives of charity, and that under the influence of such motives, it was unadvisedly passed.

Sir, said Mr. McV., I consider the resolution of the 10th of January, a manifest and palpable violation of the constitution. The constitution provides "that no money shall be drawn from the treasury but in consequence of appropriations made by law." The resolution to which I refer, is not a legislative act, not having received the sanction of those bodies which constitute the legislature, and which is indispensable to give it the character and the efficacy of a law. It was the mere declaration of this House, on a subject entirely beyond the reach of its separate authority, and as wholly inoperative and void, in my opinion, as if it were the dictum of any individual member of this House, assuming to act in his official character as a representative.

I understand that the amount expended under that resolution is to be paid out of a fund which this House has now in its possession, or which it is hereafter to get possession of, to defray its contingent expenses. In other words, this House having got possession of funds for certain specific purposes, it will, or can, by the application of physical force, divert them to other objects not originally contemplated—and thus attempt to evade the provision of the constitution to which I have referred.

It is perhaps proper, although the history of this House will show that it was liable to great abuse—that each House of Congress should have a fund set apart to defray its contingent expenses. We want every thing that will facilitate us in the business in which we are engaged in maturing laws—but, what member of this House will assert that furnishing fuel to the poor of this city is an expense contingent to the legislation of this House? The proposition is too absurd to find an advocate any where. And yet, upon this absurdity rests the authority for the passage of that resolution. Sir, if this House have the power by resolution to appropriate money to furnish the poor of this city with fuel, it has also the power to feed and clothe them, and to educate them, which also includes the power of establishing hospitals, asylums, and schools. Sir, there is no such thing as disguising the fact that this House has assumed on itself the exercise of power which constitutes one of the highest attributes of the legislature and that the resolution which it passed is wholly null and void.

I am aware that it may be said that this is a laudable affair; and that the deed of which I complain as a breach of the constitution, does of itself constitute a deed of charity to the poor of this city, and that therefore, the matter ought not to be disturbed. Had I consulted my inclinations only, I might have yielded to such suggestions, but a sense of duty had prompted me, however ungracious it may appear, to offer the resolution which I have had the honor to submit. I have yet to learn that this House will consider it a small affair that the constitution has been violated, or that Charity's ample folds will cover or cure its breach. The House owed it to itself to declare its opinion on this matter, even although it might be implicated thereby: and if we are to indulge in charity, let it be that charity which is according to law.

Mr. CHINN said, it was due to himself, and to the committee, to make a brief statement to the House. For himself, he would say, that he voted against the original resolution of the House, because, however much his feelings might have been enlisted, he did not consider himself authorized to vote for it. For the Committee on the District of Columbia, he would say, that when the original resolution of this House was taken up by the committee, and considered, they found that the direction to them was *positive*, that they had no discretion, except as to the amount: that they had no *right* to disregard the *positive command* of the House. They therefore made the proper inquiry of the city authority, and upon receiving an answer shewing an appalling degree and extent of distress, and that one hundred and fifty cords of wood were wanted, the committee directed them to draw upon the Clerk of this House for fifty cords upon two occasions, amounting in all to one hundred cords. This was during the recent season of intense cold. Since that the committee had done nothing, nor did he believe that they intended to do more under that resolution, which was for "immediate relief."

Mr. McKENNAN remarked that it seemed to him that the gentleman from New York was too late to effect any good purpose by his proposition. It would have been, perhaps, in good time, when the resolution was first before the House, and before any action was had upon it. But after it had been adopted by the House, and the committee had acted upon it, and the suffering poor had been relieved, it seemed to him to be an idle proposition to entertain the House upon a subject of this kind. They had heard what had been said by the chairman of the Committee on the District (Mr. Chinn,) the committee had distributed [illegible]

mbred cords of wood in the whole, the proportion of which was only sixteen cords to each ward in the city. The accounts of distress which had reached the committee had been heart-rending, and he apprehended if the gentleman from New York had heard them also, his difficulties and scruples would have been dissipated. He would state an instance of a single family that came under the notice of the committee.

This family consisted of five children, besides the two parents. The old gentleman was lying on his bed of sickness—no, not on his bed of sickness, because he had not the means of procuring any thing but a bag of straw, and in order to keep himself from freezing, the bed was cut open, and he was thrust in it up to the neck; that family, in all probability, by the relief extended by that House, under the resolution in question, were kept from being frozen to death. He would not detain the House by any argument on the subject. The gentleman from New York did not urge his constitutional scruples at that time, while his proposition to expunge the resolution now was before it, and it was a waste of time to discuss it. Besides, the committee, so far as Mr. McK. understood, did not intend to proceed further, and were then ready to report what they had done to the House. Believing then, that this discussion was altogether a waste of time, he moved to lay the resolution upon the table.

Before the question was put from the Chair, Mr. BROWN moved for the orders of the day; but being agreed to, the motion to lay the resolution of Mr. McVEAN on the table lies over.

The SPEAKER laid before the House the following communications:

A letter from the Secretary of War, in response to a resolution of the House, relative to certain lands in the Territory of Michigan. Laid on the table and ordered to be printed.

A letter from the Secretary of the Treasury, in answer to a resolution of the 31st ult. relative to a compromise of the claim of Thomas H. Smith &c. Referred to the Committee on the Judiciary and ordered to be printed.

A report from the Secretary of the Treasury, in conformity with a resolution of the House of the 3d March, 1797, exhibiting the amount of duties accruing, and drawback payable, on the several articles imported into the United States, and reported therefrom, during the years ending the 30th December, 1831, 1832, and 1833; which was laid on the table and ordered to be printed.

The following bills were read a third time and passed.

A bill for the removal of the Land Office, from Zanesville, to Lima, in the State of Ohio;
A bill to authorize the sale of certain lands, belonging to the University of Michigan;
A bill prescribing the punishment of Consuls, commercial Agents, and others, in certain cases;
A bill for the relief of Lieutenant Mervin P. Ware;
A bill for the relief of Samuel Butler;
A bill for the relief of Elizabeth Swain;
A bill for the relief of the heirs of William Sharp;
A bill for the relief of Sutton Stevens;
A bill for the relief of Thomas Dixon & Co., New York;
A bill for the relief of Job Barton;
A bill for the relief of Samuel H. Doxey;
A bill for the relief of John Herrick;
A bill for the relief of Job Wool;
A bill for the relief of David Kincaid;
A bill for the relief of Stephen Smith, and heirs,
A bill for the relief of Robert Abbott, and the other heirs of James Abbott, dec'd;
A bill for the relief of Matthew C Perry;
A bill for the relief of E. R. Shubrick, of the U. Navy;
A bill for the relief of Riddle, Bechtel and others;
A bill for the relief of John J. Avery;
A bill for the relief of Stephen Gatlin;
A bill for the relief of Theodore Owens;
A bill for the relief of the representatives of Thomas Clements, dec'd;

A bill for the relief of S. M. Wall and H. Percival;
A bill for the relief of Shubael Conant;
A bill for the relief of the legal representatives of Aaron Smith;
A bill for the relief of Thomas Bally;
A bill for the relief of Richard H. Lee;
A bill for the relief of William Haskell and others.
A bill for the relief of Ebenezer Breed;
A bill for the relief of George Davenport;
A bill for the relief of Richard Butman;
A bill for the relief of the children of Dominick Lynch;
And a bill for the relief of John Fraser & Co.

The House, on motion of Mr. BROWN, went into Committee of the Whole, Mr. GORDON in the Chair, upon the following bills reported by the Committee on Invalid Pensions:

A bill for the benefit of John Cullins;
A bill granting a pension to Amasa A. Tifft;
A bill for the relief of Harry Reynolds and John Casey;
A bill for the relief of Josiah Westlake;
A bill granting a pension to Isaac Janvier;
A bill for the relief of Josiah H. Brown and John Conkin;
A bill to restore to certain invalid pensioners the amount of pension by them relinquished;
A bill for the relief of Enoch Blaisdell;
A bill granting pensions to certain persons therein named;
A bill granting a pension to John F. Wiley, and increasing the pension of George Fields;
A bill granting a pension to William Slocum;
A bill granting a pension to William Wilgus;
A bill for the relief of Samuel M. Asbury
A bill granting a pension to Francis F. St. Coir;
A bill for the relief of the invalid pensioners therein mentioned;
A bill granting a pension to Joseph Meade;
A bill granting a pension to Luke Voorhies;
A bill granting a pension to Col. Gideon Morgan;
A bill granting a pension to Benjamin Leslie;
A bill granting pensions to William Boden and James Harrington;
A bill for the relief of John Ashton;
A bill for the relief of Ephraim F. Gilbert;
A bill granting a pension to Isaac Carter;
A bill granting a pension to John Gerotelle;
A bill for the relief of Samuel Shelmerdine;
A bill for the relief of Thomas Morton;
A bill to increase the pension of Origen Eaton;
A bill granting a pension to John W. Cox;
A bill for the relief of Joseph Swartwood;
A bill granting an arrearage of pension to Edward Nicholson;
A bill for the relief of Abraham E. Boutwell and David Pearson;
A bill granting a pension to Robert Lucas;
A bill for the relief of George McFadden;
A bill for the relief of John Moore;
A bill granting a pension to Simeon S. Morrill;
A bill for the relief of George C. Seaton;
A bill granting a pension to Larned Swallow;
A bill granting a pension to John Bryant;
A bill granting a pension to Noah Miller;
A bill placing Capt. Cole, a Seneca Chief, on the pension roll;
A bill for the relief of Benjamin Holland;
A bill for the relief of William Kelley;
A bill granting a pension to Justus Cobb;
A bill granting a pension to Lambert L. Van Valkenburg;
A bill granting a pension to Isaac Eckright;
A bill for the relief of William C. Beard;
A bill for the relief of Elijah Tate;
A bill for the relief of Jacob Stewart;
A bill for the relief of Elijah Blodgett;
A bill for the relief of Thomas Simpson;
And a bill for the relief of Thankful Randall.

The committee rose, reported the bills to the House, when the amendments to a portion of them were agreed to, and they were ordered to be engrossed and read a third time to-morrow.

The House again went into Committee, Mr. MERCER in the Chair, on the following bills:
A bill for the relief of Col. Daniel Newman;
A bill for the relief of Peter Triplett;

A bill for the relief of Peter Doxtator and Jacob Weaver;
A bill for the relief of John Dal, of Maine;
A bill for the relief of Simeon Meachum;
A bill for the relief of Joseph Gilbert;
A bill for the relief of the widow and heirs of Samuel Southerland;
A bill for the relief of Timothy Jordan;
A bill for the relief of David Page;
A bill for the relief of Walter Phillips;
And a bill for the relief of Elizabeth May.

The committee rose, reported the bills to the House, and they were ordered to be engrossed and read a third time to-morrow.

On motion of Mr. MITCHELL, of Ohio, the Committee of the Whole were discharged from the further consideration of the bill to authorize the survey of certain lands adjacent to the canal reservoir on Licking Summit, in the State of Ohio.

Mr. MITCHELL asked the unanimous consent of the House to order the bill to be engrossed at this time. It was objected to.

The amendments heretofore reported from the Committee of the Whole to the bill for the relief of Stephen Chittenden, were concurred in, and the bill ordered to be engrossed.

The amendment heretofore reported from the Committee of the Whole, to the bill for the relief of Col. William Lawrence, was considered, and, after some remarks by Messrs. THOMAS of Louisiana, MILLER, PARKER, EVANS, HUBBARD, BURGES, MASON of Virginia, and HEATH, disagreed to.

Mr. HUBBARD moved a further amendment, providing that the pension to Col. Lawrence should take effect and commence from July, 1831.

Mr. CAMBRELENG demanded the yeas and nays on this amendment; which were ordered, and were—ayes 90, nays 60.

The bill was then ordered to be engrossed and read a third time, as amended.

On motion of Mr. McKIM,
The House then adjourned.

IN SENATE.

SATURDAY, Feb 7, 1835.

Mr. HENDRICKS, from the Committee on Roads and Canals, reported a bill supplementary to an act authorizing the Territory of Florida to construct certain canals there in named.

Mr. HENDRICKS, from the same committee, reported a bill authorizing certain rail road companies to construct roads through the lands of the U. States; which was read and ordered to a second reading.

Mr. KING, of Alabama, on leave, introduced a bill providing for the erection of a light house at Mobile Point, and for placing buoys near the same.

Mr. BENTON, from the Committee on Military Affairs, in pursuance of a resolution of the Senate directing an inquiry to be made into the propriety of making further appropriations for arming the fortifications of the United States, reported a bill for the purpose; which was read, and ordered to a second reading.

Mr. ROBBINS, from the Committee on the Library, reported the joint resolution, directing certain medals to be struck in honor of the officers engaged in the defence of Fort St. Stephens, with an amendment.

Mr. McKEAN, and Mr. WAGGAMAN, presented petitions of a private nature; which were appropriately referred.

The bill for the relief of Silas D. Fisher;

The bill for the relief of Duncan L. Clynch, and

The bill making an appropriation to complete certain roads in the Territory of Arkansas, were severally read the third time and passed.

The bill, in addition to the act for the relief of the heirs of Geo. Hurlburt, deceased, was read the second time as in Committee of the Whole; when, after some remarks between Messrs. SMITH, LEIGH, WHITE, HILL, and KING, the bill was ordered to be engrossed for a third reading.

Mr. POINDEXTER, from the Committee on Public Lands, to which was referred the petition of H. H. Hall, relative to the location of Virginia military land warrants, reported unfavorable upon

the same, and the committee were discharged from the further consideration of the subject.

Mr. POINDEXTER, from the same Committee, to which was referred the bill from the House for the relief of James M. Tuttle, reported the same without amendment.

Mr. POINDEXTER, from the same Committee to which was referred the memorial from the legislature of Illinois, praying a relinquishment of the 16th section and the entry of other lands in lieu thereof for the use of schools, reported unfavorably upon the same, and the Committee were discharged from the further consideration of the subject.

Mr. LEIGH, from the Committee on Revolutionary Claims, reported a bill for the relief of Sally Springer and others, legal representatives of Col. Wm. Crawford, deceased; which was read the first time and ordered to a second reading.

POST OFFICE BILL.

On motion of Mr. EWING, the Senate resumed the consideration of the bill changing the organization of the General Post Office, when Mr. CALHOUN withdrew the amendment he submitted yesterday.

Mr. EWING moved to amend the bill by striking out $4000, the compensation given to the Commissioners, and inserting $3,500.

Mr. WRIGHT moved to amend the amendment by reducing the salary to $3000 per annum.

Mr. WRIGHT said he was desirous of putting this officer on the same grade, as regarded the salary, with the Auditors of the Treasury; and he saw no reason for the distinction between them. The salary was quite sufficient, and it must be perceived by Senators that the time was very near when all the Auditors would be put on the same footing.

Mr. WRIGHT'S proposition was agreed to.

Several unimportant amendments were then made to the second, third, fourth and fifth sections, when

Mr. EWING moved an amendment, requiring the books in the General Post Office, appropriately belonging to the Commissioners' office, to be delivered up to that officer on the 10th of March next, and requiring the Postmaster General to "deliver to the Solicitor all books and papers in the Post Office, or copies or extracts therefrom relative to suits brought, and a statement of all matters in suit and all judgments remaining unsatisfied;" which were agreed to.

The 12th section prohibits any additional compensation from being made to any mail contractor for additional services in carrying the mail upon any mail route, so as to increase the compensation to more than double the net amount of postages received on the route, &c.

Mr. EWING moved to amend this section by inserting after the word "route," in italics, these words—"which shall have been established for 10 years before the execution of his contract."

This amendment was also agreed to.

The 12th section further provides that "when any extra service shall be ordered, the amount of the allowance therefor, in dollars and cents, shall be signified in the order for such service, and be forthwith entered upon the books of the General Post Office."

Mr. EWING moved to add to this, "and no additional compensation shall be paid for any extra services ordered before the issuing of such order and the making of such entry;" which was agreed to.

Several unimportant amendments were made in other sections of the bill, on motion of Mr. EWING, when

Mr. PORTER moved an amendment as an additional section to the bill, "That it shall be the duty of the Postmaster General to enter into a contract for carrying a daily mail between New Orleans and Mobile."

Upon this proposition a discursive debate ensued.

Mr. SOUTHARD opposed it, not because he was unfavorable to a daily mail between Mobile and New Orleans, for he thought there ought to be one transported there. But his difficulty was in selecting any particular route where there

should be a daily mail carried, and introducing it into this bill. He thought it ought to be incorporated in a particular bill, and unless this was a very grievous case, he would be opposed to it.

Mr. PORTER admitted there was some incongruity in incorporating a provision like this in a general law, but he hoped the Senate would consent to introducing it when his reasons were heard. If the subject had been left to the Postmaster General, to do as he had done for nine months past, they had nothing else to look for but continued interruption; for, by the bill, no change could be made in any contract upon a route which was of ten years standing, and therefore this route would be cut off. Incongruities should yield to general utility and public necessity. The mail was now carried only three times a week, and he believed this interruption was done for the purpose of inducing Louisians to send Senators here who would support the Postmaster General. No other part of the whole country, it appeared, could be selected for making retrenchments upon, but this one. Mr. P. then recurred, at some length, to the President's letter to the people of New Orleans, and the allusions made therein to himself and his colleague. When Mr. P. concluded,

Mr. LINN said, if the amendment should pass, and he was not in favor of it, he would then propose another to carry the mail daily from Louisville to St. Louis—he did not wish to embarrass the bill, but, if this passed he would feel it his duty to offer the one he suggested.

Mr. WAGGAMAN said, the honorable gentleman had not taken a just view of this amendment. New Orleans was the only commercial place which had been made the victim of the curtailment of the expenses of the Post Office Department. The important commercial relations of that city, made it indispensable that a regular daily mail should be kept up. The exports from that city alone, in 1835, would be fifty millions of dollars, and in 10 years it would be doubled. This fact would present to the Senate the necessity of an unrestrained daily intercourse between that city and the north. This was the object of his colleague's amendment, and it occurred to him that New Orleans should be made an exception. He was willing that St. Louis should have equal privileges, if it had as imperative claims. The necessity of a daily mail from Mobile to New Orleans, was self-evident. The amount of postages which were taken in the latter city, was about $46,000, while $40,000 only, was estimated to be sufficient for the transportation of the mail. Why not grant it then? They asked nothing unreasonable, but only that what they paid into the Treasury might be appropriated for their use.

Mr. BIBB said he should vote for the proposition, notwithstanding the objection of the honorable gentleman from New Jersey (Mr. Southard.) Mail routes were established by Congress, and the question now was, whether, if it was manifestly proper that the mail should be transported a certain number of times on a particular route, it was the duty of Congress so to direct. He thought it was. Could there be any more doubt that a daily mail was as necessary between Mobile and New Orleans as between the seat of Government and New Orleans, and between Washington and New York or Philadelphia? If it was self-evident that it was important to have a daily communication between New York and New Orleans, and the Postmaster General would not establish it, ought it not to be done? It was said he would not establish it, but that it was only tri-weekly. Then, he thought a proposition for the purpose ought to be introduced into this bill, and he would go for any other similar proposition where the propriety of it was as manifest as at this was.

Mr. GRUNDY remarked, that having given his opinions very fully yesterday, he would not say any thing to-day on the general topics connected with this bill. But if there had been any person more consistent then another in favor of this mail being carried daily, he was that man. He always was in favor of it, and reported favorably upon it last year. He thought there should be a regular daily mail between New Orleans and the eastern States. But such a case as this never had occur-

red in our legislation before. Congress had never yet said when, and how, the mail should be conveyed from place to place. He believed there was one instance in which Congress had authorized the employment of a steamboat for that purpose. He was very unwilling to see this special kind of legislation. The object was certainly a desirable one; but if this proposition was agreed to, the honorable gentleman from Missouri would also make out his case, and perhaps a very strong one, and how could you refuse it? And another and another would then be presented, and how could you refuse the accommodation? Let this be established as a precedent, and other applications would be irresistible. It would also be trenching upon one of the great principles of this bill, which required the Postmaster General to restrain the expenditures of the Department beyond its revenues. And when, by legislating, you encroached upon this principle, you destroyed his responsibility. He agreed that this daily mail was proper, and ought to be established; but he hoped it would be done in the ordinary way.

Mr. SOUTHARD thought it important that this should be a daily mail route; and if it could not be done otherwise, Congress ought to direct it. But we might command the Postmaster General, and still it would not be done. But his difficulty was, that this was not the proper place to introduce it; it should be inserted in a bill establishing post routes. Such a bill, he had no doubt, would be passed at this session—there were petitions for it both here and in the other House, and it would be easy to say in that bill, that there should be a daily mail between Mobile and New Orleans. He assured the gentlemen from Louisiana, that, in some form or other, he would give them his utmost exertions to carry such a proposition through.

Mr. EWING said he agreed with the honorable Senators from Louisiana; that a daily mail between New Orleans and Mobile, was highly necessary. And he also agreed with the other Senators, (Messrs. Grundy and Southard,) that this bill should not be encumbered with unnecessary provisions. There was another objection—this bill must yet pass through the other House where, if it was most loaded with incumbrances, it would be impossible to get through this session—and it was of the utmost importance that it should be passed.

The question being upon the amendment, Mr. WAGGAMAN asked the yeas and nays, which were ordered.

Mr. PRESTON explained his reasons for voting against the amendment. An important proposition, said Mr. P., had been but yesterday with drawn to prevent every thing unnecessary from being incorporated in the bill; and he was opposed to this amendment on the same ground.

The question was then put and decided in the negative—yeas 8, nays 33, as follows:

YEAS—Messrs. Bibb, Black, Mangum, Moore, Poindexter, Porter, Robbins, Waggaman—8.

NAYS—Messrs. Bell, Brown Buchanan, Calbert, Ewing, Frelinghuysen, Goldsborough, Grundy, Hendricks, Hill, Kane, Kent, King of Alabama, King of Georgia, Knight, Leigh, Linn, McKean, Morris, Naudain, Prentiss, Preston, Robinson, Ruggles, Shepley, Smith, Southard, Swift, Tallmadge, Tipton, Tomlinson, White, Wright—33.

Several other unimportant amendments were then made, so as to conform to others inserted in the examination of the bill, and it was thus reported to the Senate as amended.

The question being then put on all the amendments collectively, they were agreed to.

Mr. KING, of Georgia, then moved further to amend the bill in that part which prescribes the mode of letting contracts. His proposition was that proposals should be handled in sealed, which should then be regularly numbered, and when opened, it should be done in presence of the bidders; also, that all combination or concealment bids should not be received.

After some remarks between Mr. EWING and Mr. KING, the amendment was rejected, on a division—yeas 18, nays 19.

Mr. EWING then adopted a portion of Mr.

ING'S proposition, and moved it as an amendment, as follows: "each route to be bid for, separately, and separate contracts executed for each accepted bids, and every proposal shall be handed sealed."

Mr. WRIGHT inquired whether it had occurred to gentlemen that this amendment would very much increase the price of mail transportation? He had made an inquiry of the former Postmaster general, when he was in office, with a view to this object, and he was then informed that such would be the effect of so strict a measure.

Mr. EWING could not say that it would not be the effect of increasing the cost of transportation. But if there were fairness in consolidation it, it would not have that effect. And he thought it would not in fact increase the expense. Such was the confusion and uncertainty which existed in existing contracts of this kind, that it a better there should be an increase of expense, a this evil should be continued.

Mr. GRUNDY said that this was a subject on which he had found more difficulty in his own mind than on any other. It was an evil; but the body was to save the Department, and at the same time obviate the inconvenience. He thought it would have the effect of increasing the expense carrying the mail, but that was better than the use of complaint.

Some further remarks were made by Messrs. LESTER, King of Georgia, BIBB, PRESTON, SHEPLEY, in favor of the amendment, and Mr. WRIGHT against it.

Mr. WAGGAMAN asked the yeas and nays on its adoption; which were ordered; and the question was determined in the affirmative—yeas 2, as follows:

NAYS—Messrs. Bell, Benton, Bibb, Black, Brown, Buchanan, Calhoun, Cuthbert, Ewing, Frelinghuysen, Goldsborough, Grundy, Hendricks, Kent, King of Alabama, King of Georgia, Leigh, Linn, McKean, Mangum, Moore, Nudain, Poindexter, Prentiss, Preston, Robbins, Simon, Ruggles, Shepley, Silsbee, Smith, Southard, Swift, Tipton, Tomlinson, Tyler, Waggaman, Webster, White—41.

NAYS—Messrs. Tallmadge and Wright—2.

Mr. EWING then moved a further amendment a bill, that "immediately after the lettings the bill containing the register of the bids shall be laid for inspection;" which was agreed to.

Mr. SHEPLEY then offered a further amendment, "that if any person bid for different routes, remotely, which are connected with each other, shall not obtain the principal route, he may have the subordinate route, and it shall be let again."

Mr. BUCHANAN thought there was no ground of apprehension on this subject. The great mail contractors would drive all the small contractors off the public roads of the United States. And though it would not be known to the Department, their bids would be known to each other. It would be combinations as well for the little a great routes, and then they would transfer it to each other. This would be the result in practice. It would be so if it was now, with this difference, that it would not be known at the Department.

The amendment was disagreed to.

Mr. POINDEXTER then offered a further amendment providing that if any Deputy Postmaster shall at any time refuse to deliver, or shall detain letter, newspaper, periodical, or other paper conveyed through the mail, with intent to prevent the same from duly reaching the person to whom it is directed, he shall forfeit a penalty not exceeding $500, and undergo an imprisonment not exceeding six months, be dismissed from office, and ever afterwards incapable of holding the office of Deputy Postmaster.

After some conversation between Messrs. ROBBINS, POINDEXTER, BIBB, and PRESTON, the proposed amendment, it was agreed to.

Mr. KING, of Georgia, then offered a further amendment as an additional section to the bill, it was to prohibit mail contractors from punishes for the conveyance of passengers upon their routes, in opposition to the coaches of regular mail contractor on such route.

After some explanation from Mr. KING of the object of the amendment,

Mr. WRIGHT asked the yeas and nays upon its adoption; which were ordered, and are as follows:

YEAS.—Messrs. Bibb, Calhoun, Cuthbert, King of Alab., King of Georgia, Leigh, Linn, Mangum, Moore, Poindexter.—10.

NAYS.—Messrs. Bell, Benton, Brown, Buchanan, Ewing, Frelinghuysen, Goldsborough, Grundy, Hendricks, Hill, Kent, Knight, McKean, Naudain, Porter, Prentiss, Preston, Robbins, Robinson, Ruggles, Shepley, Silsbee, Smith, Southard, Swift, Tallmadge, Tipton, Tyler, Waggaman, Webster, White, Wright.—33.

So the amendment was disagreed to.

The question being on the engrossment of the bill for a third reading.

Mr. EWING asked for the yeas and nays, which were ordered, and are as follows:

YEAS.—Messrs. Bell, Benton, Bibb, Brown, Buchanan, Calhoun, Cuthbert, Ewing, Frelinghuysen, Goldsborough, Grundy, Hendricks, Hill, Kent, King of Alab., King of Georgia, Knight, Leigh, Linn, McKean, Mangum, Moore, Morris, Naudain, Poindexter, Porter, Prentiss, Preston, Robbins, Robinson, Ruggles, Shepley, Silsbee, Smith, Southard, Swift, Tallmadge, Tipton, Tomlinson, Tyler, Waggaman, Webster, White, Wright.—44.

NAYS.—None.

So the question was unanimously determined in the affirmative.

Mr. WAGGAMAN then gave notice, that on Monday next he would ask leave to introduce a bill directing a daily mail to be run from Mobile to New Orleans.

And then, the Senate adjourned.

HOUSE OF REPRESENTATIVES.

SATURDAY, February 7, 1835.

Mr. MERCER, from the Committee on Roads and Canals, reported a bill to provide for the opening of certain roads in the Territory of Arkansas, and for other purposes; which was read twice and committed.

Mr. MERCER, from the same committee, reported a bill to provide for the improvement of the harbor of Clinton river, in Michigan Territory, and for other purposes; which was read twice and committed.

Mr. CHANEY, from the Committee on Invalid Pensions, reported a bill granting a pension to James Calvert; which was read twice and committed.

Mr. PEARCE, of Rhode Island, from the Committee on Commerce, made a report, accompanied by a bill to provide for an expedition to the Pacific Ocean and South Sea; which was read twice and commited; and, together with the report, ordered to be printed.

Mr. SCHLEY, by consent, submitted the following resolution:

Resolved, That the Committee on the Post Office and Post Roads be instructed to inquire into the expediency of abolishing the office of Draftsman in the House of Representatives, and discontinuing the annual expenditure of fifteen hundred dollars now paid to that officer.

Mr. McKENNAN said he would like to know the reasons which had induced the gentleman from Georgia to offer this resolution. Several years ago the office of draftsman had been, after much discussion, abolished. It had subsequently, however, been found necessary to restore the former order of things and to re-instate this officer of the House.

Mr. SCHLEY said it was true that this office, upon consideration, had heretofore been abolished, and subsequently re-established, for what reasons, he knew not. The individual who occupied this office was daily engaged in reporting the proceedings of this House for a morning paper of this city, while a gentleman by the name of Burr was employed in preparing those maps for the Committee on the Post Office and Post Roads, which it was the peculiar duty of the draftsman of the House to perform. What would be the extra expense thus incurred, he knew not, but presumed it would exceed $1,500. He saw no ne-

cessity for continuing this office if it was necessary to employ another individual to perform its duties, while the incumbent was employed as a Reporter for a newspaper. His attention had been drawn to the subject by the fact, that Mr. Burr had been employed to execute the necessary maps required by the Committee on the Post Office and Post Roads. He could not remain silent, and see such a wasteful and prodigal expenditure of the public money, without interposing an objection. He was aware of the facility with which the hangers on of this House manage to put their hands into the public Treasury. He considered himself, and every member of this House in the capacity of a guardian of the public treasure, and he felt the same obligation to take care of it, that he would to take care of the estate of minors for whom he had been legally appointed the guardian. The maps required by the committees of the House, he was satisfied, could be procured at less expense than the sum now paid. In conclusion, he could see no good reason why another person should be employed to do this work while the regular officer of the House, instead of attending to his duties, was engaged as a reporter of its proceedings.

Mr. McKENNAN admired the spirit of economy which seemed to actuate the gentleman from Georgia, (Mr. Schley.) He was bound to suppose that the resolution was solely dictated by considerations of economy. It was probable, however, that the object was to procure these maps to be made by some other person; that it was intended to make room for some favorite. He had understood that greater facilities had been afforded at the Post Office Department to another individual than were extended to the draftsman of this House. The duties of this officer were not confined to the Post Office Department. He was also assiduously engaged in the performance of duties required by the Committee on Roads and Canals, and other committees. He was unwilling that this office should be abolished, merely for the purpose of transferring its duties to some favorite.

Mr. PEARCE said, if the officer of the House did not execute the duties required of him, it might be a proper subject of inquiry. He could not, however, see the propriety of transferring the duti s from the present officer to another—nothing could be gained by it.

The duties of the draftsman were not confined to the Committee on the Post Office. The Committees on Public and Private Land Claims, and on Roads and Canals, required the constant services of this officer. Several of the members of his family were also engaged in aiding him in the performance of his duties. If an inquiry was necessary, it was a matter of doubt to what committee it should go. About once in two years, when the Committee on the Post Office reported a bill creating new post routes, the services of the draftsman were necessary. The other committees to which he had referred, required his services almost daily. In conclusion, he could see no reason for a change. It was the duty of the Clerk of the House to see that this officer did his duty, and if Mr. Burr had been employed by the Clerk, it was his duty to explain why this had been done.

Mr. LOVE said, as a general rule, he was in favor of resolutions of inquiry. He was satisfied his friend from Georgia, (Mr. Schley,) had no other motive in offering the resolution, than a high regard to duty and the public interest—that he was actuated by no sinister views. He knew that several of the sons of the draftsman of the House, who were every way competent, were engaged in aiding him in the performance of his duties. It should, therefore, not be an objection to him that he spent three hours each day in preparing the speeches of members, (in a manner, too, better than any other reporter.) It would be recollected, that after much debate at a former session, on the subject of reform, the only result was an action of the office of draftsman. It had been subsequently found necessary to reinstate this offi.... If the gentleman would modify his resolution so as to inquire into all the abuses in the public departments, with a view to reform, he should have his hearty assent. He would go with him most

heartily in all attempts to correct abuses. He had been informed that after the office of draftsman was abolished, it had cost ten times more to procure the necessary work to be done by the job, than was paid to this officer. Why had not the regular draftsman of the House been called upon to execute the work which had been done by another? If he had been so called upon, and refused, then it would be a proper subject of inquiry. In conclusion, he repeated that if the gentleman would so shape his resolution as to inquire into any and all abuses which might exist in the departments, he should have his cordial co-operation.

Mr. STEWART said this was rather a small matter, although it seemed likely to lead to a long debate. There was but three weeks remaining of the present session, and much important business to be acted upon. He would, therefore, move to lay the resolution on the table.

Mr. SCHLEY asked for the yeas and nays on the motion; which were ordered.

Mr. LOVE could not vote to lay the resolution on the table, although he was opposed to the adoption of the resolution in its present shape.

Mr. STEWART withdrew his motion to lay the resolution on the table.

Mr. SCHLEY said, it was impossible for him to know the motives which actuated the course of the gentleman from Pennsylvania, (Mr. McKennan.) He had thought fit to attribute improper motives to him, (Mr. S.) It would perhaps be better for the gentleman to look to his own motives, without reflecting upon those of others. He was not in the habit of imputing unworthy motives to others, and he had no evidence that would authorize him to impute such to the gentleman from Pennsylvania, (Mr. McKennan.) But if the old maxim be true, "that we judge others by ourselves," then it would follow that the gentleman made propositions from unworthy motives. He, Mr. S., however, did not believe the gentleman capable of such a course.

In offering the resolution, he had no favorite in view, nor was his motion the result of any management or pre-concert. He had no acquaintance with any person qualified to discharge the duties of draftsman. No applications had been made to him. No persons solicited him for favors here. He had not seen any such persons. His associations did not lead him to such discoveries. He had offered the resolution without consulting any person. He had daily seen the draftsman of the House engaged in reporting speeches here, while another individual was employed at the public expense to discharge his duties. He had inquired why this was the case, and had obtained no satisfactory reply. If Mr. Stansberry was incompetent or unable to perform these duties, another should be appointed in his place. If large sums were to be paid to another for these services, it was proper that this almost useless officer of the House should be dispensed with. He barely knew the present incumbent when he saw him. He had no objections to him personally. He was actuated in offering the resolution by considerations of public duty alone. It had been said that this officer, particularly in relation to the duties required by the land committees, performed his duties faithfully. If, upon inquiry, it should be found that all the services required of this officer were performed properly and with fidelity, there would be an end of the matter, and he, for one, would vote against the abolition of the office. If, on the contrary, this office, under present circumstances, should, upon inquiry, be found to be unnecessary, he presumed no gentleman would vote for its continuance. He was surprised that gentletlemen should be opposed to this inquiry. Do they fear it?

In relation to the suggestion of his friend from Kentucky (Mr. Love) as to the propriety of extending the inquiry to other supposed abuses in the Departments of the Government, he should not object to such a proceeding, if it was brought forward in a separate proposition. It was best to do one thing at a time. If he was aware of any other abuses, he would not hesitate to bring them to the consideration of the House. If the gentleman from Kentucky would propose a resolution of the character indicated by him, he would go for it. He would be perfectly willing that a Select Committee should be raised on any such resolution, with the gentleman from Kentucky at its head, and he would be willing to stand at the foot of such committee, for the purpose of ferreting out any abuses which might be supposed to exist.

Mr. H. EVERETT desired to know, if maps had been made by order of the House, whether the draftsman of the House had been first required to do the service, previous to the employment of another. Mr. Burr, he understood, was the peculiar officer of the Post Office Department. He wished to know, also, whether the maps alluded to had been ordered by the Post Office Committee?

Mr. SCHLEY replied, that he understood Mr. Burr had been employed under a resolution of the House; whether at the instance of the Committee on the Post Office he knew not.

Mr. BRIGGS said, that during the 1st session of Congress, the Committe on the Post Office required various maps connected with their duties. The draftsman of the House had been required to execute them, which he failed to do, owing as he alleged that the proper facilities were withheld from him at the Department. The draftsman had applied at the Department for a map necessary to the performance of the duty required, but he was informed that it could not be taken from the Department, and could only be used in the office. He knew not whether this apology of the draftsman was considered sufficient. The maps were necessary, and the Clerk of the House was required by resolution to procure their execution. The Clerk did not apply to the draftsman of the House, under the circumstances; as he understood, from terms of the resolution, that he was required to employ another individual to perform the service. He considered this officer essentially necessary. The resolution to which he had referred, showed the propriety of continuing this office. The draftsman employed under the resolution had been constantly employed in the discharge of the duty assigned to him, and it would take months to complete the work. If the gentleman was anxious to know whether this officer performed his duties faithfully, he had better direct his enquiry to that point. He was not prepared to say whether this officer had or had not discharged the duties assigned him, with fidelity. He had no objection to the enquiry. If the office was abolished, nothing would be gained by it, as the services would have to be performed by the job or otherwise, at an expense equal, if not greater than that at present allowed.

The resolution was then agreed to.

Mr. ROBERTSON, by leave, offered the following resolutions:

Resolved, That the office or appointment of Printer to the Senate and House of Representatives, respectively, ought to be abolished or dispensed with.

Resolved, That in future all printing on public account, should be done under contracts with such persons, and subject to such regulations, as may be authorized and prescribed by law, and that to this end, the Secretary of the Senate, the Clerk of the House of Representatives, the Postmaster General, and the Secretary of the Treasury, be authorized and required to advertise, respectively, for sealed proposals to execute: first, all printing by order, or on account of the Senate; secondly, all printing on account of the House of Representatives; thirdly, all printing within the District of Columbia for the Post Office Department; and, fourthly, all other printing within the said District, on public account; the said proposals to be returned to and lodged in the office of the Attorney General, and to be opened on some day to be prescribed by law, and mentioned in the advertisements, in the presence of the said Attorney General, and all the officers abovenamed, and the contracts to be then and there entered into by and between the said officers respectively, acting on behalf of the United States, and such persons as may be willing to undertake the said printing on the most advantageous terms to the public, and to give adequate security for the faithful execution of the work. *Provided*, That no person nor company employed by any one of the officers authorized to enter into contracts for the same, shall be employed or concerned in any other printing on public account, authorized to be contracted for by the other officers respectively; and in case of equality in two or more bids, the preference shall be given to the person whose proposals were first lodged in the Attorney General's Office. *Provided also*, that no person, holding any office or appointment under the Government, shall be employed to do any part of the public printing, or to have an interest or concern therein.

Mr. EVANS said, the resolution was one of considerable importance, and as the hour devoted to reports and resolutions had nearly expired, he would prefer that the resolution should be printed and postponed to Monday, and that the House should proceed to the consideration of the orders of the day.

Mr. ROBERTSON would not object to a postponement of his resolution to Monday, provided it should be made the special order for that day. He did not propose to discuss it at the present time. The period had however arrived when, under a joint rule of the two Houses, it became necessary to choose a printer. If, therefore, the resolution offered by him was acted upon, it should be speedily done. He would move that the resolution be postponed to Monday, and made the special order for that day.

The CHAIR reminded the gentleman that the resolution would come up as a matter of course on Monday, as the unfinished business of the morning hour of this day.

Mr. HANNEGAN offered the following resolution, which, under the rule, lies one day:

Resolved, That the Secretary of War be requested to communicate to this House, if in the possession of the War Department, a copy of the survey, plan, and estimate, for the construction of a harbor at the mouth of Trail creek, on lake Michigan, in the State of Indiana, or any information he may possess in relation thereto.

Mr. BEATY offered the following resolution, which, under the rule, lies one day:

Resolved, That the Secretary of War be requested to report to this House the survey and report of the engineers sent during the last year to survey the Cumberland river, from the falls of said river down to meet the survey heretofore made thereon.

The House then, on motion of Mr. Mc[illegible], proceeded to the consideration of the orders of the day.

Mr. BINNEY, (by consent) from the Committee of Ways and Means, reported a bill for the relief of John F. Lewis; which was read twice and committed.

Mr. PHILLIPS, on leave, moved to print extra copies of the report of the Committee of Commerce, in relation to fitting out a South Sea expedition; which, by the rules, lie on the table one day.

The SPEAKER laid before the House the following Message from the President of the United States:

To the House of Representatives of the United States:

I transmit to the House of Representatives a report of the Secretary of State, accompanied by extracts from certain despatches received from the Minister of the United States at Paris, which are communicated in compliance with a resolution of the House of the 31st ultimo. Being of opinion that the residue of the despatches of that Minister cannot, at present, be laid before the House, consistently with the public interest, I decline transmitting them. In doing so, however, I deem it proper to state, that whenever any communication shall be received exhibiting any change in the condition of the business referred to in the resolution, the information will be promptly transmitted to Congress.

ANDREW JACKSON.

Washington, 6th February, 1835.

To the President of the United States:

DEPARTMENT OF STATE,
Washington, 5th Feb. 18[illegible]

The Secretary of State, to whom has been referred the resolution of the House of Representatives of the 31st ult. requesting the President to communicate to that House, if not incompatible with the public interest, any correspondence of

Government of France, and any despatches mixed from the Minister of the United States at ris, not hitherto communicated to the House in ition to the failure of the French Government carry into effect any stipulation of the treaty of fourth day of July, 1831"—has the honor to scr't to the Pr sident that, as far as is known to Department, no correspondence has taken ce with the Government of France, since that municated to the House on the 27th December last. The Secretary is not aware that the despatches received from the Minister of the United tes at Paris, present any material fact which f not appear in the correspondence already ummitted. He nevertheless enclose's so much hose despatches, written subsequently to the amencement of the present session of the nch Chambers, as may serve to show the state the business to which they relate since that e; and also that portion of an early despatch ch contains the substance of the assurances le to him by his Majesty the King of the nch, at a formal audience granted to him for purpose of presenting his credentials, and he may, for the President's consideration, whethhe residue can, consistently with the public rest, be now laid before the House.
JOHN FORSYTH.

Livingston to the Secretary of State of the United States. (Extracts.)

Paris, 4th October, 1833.

ti: On Monday I presented my letter of cre' ce to the King, on which occasion I made the ss to him, a copy of which is enclosed.

s answer was long and earnest. I cannot pre-
tu give you the words of it; but in substance,
us a warm expression of his good feeling to-
is the United States, for the hospitality he had
ived there, &c.

o the convention, he said, assure your Govern-
I that unavoidable circumstances alone pre-
rd its immediate execution, but it will be
fully performed; assure your Government of
he repeated, the necessary laws will be passed
e next meeting of the Chambers. I tell you
not only as King, but as an individual whose
ise will be fulfilled.

r. Livingston to the Secretary of State.
(Extracts.)

Paris, 23d November, 1834.

et hope for any decision on our affairs before
dle of January. One motive for delay is,
pectation that the message of the President
were before the discussion, and that it may
in something to shew a strong national feel-
in the subject. *This is not mere conjecture,
but the fact;* and I repeat now, from a full
rledge of the case, what I have more than
stated in my former despatches as my firm
ssion—that the moderate tone taken by our
mment when the rejection was first known,
attributed by some to indifference, or to a
iction on the part of the President, that he
mnot be supported in any strong measure by
e ople; and by others, to a consciousness that
ervention had given us more than we were
led to ask.

w last night an influential member of the
bear who told me that   *   *
that the King had spoken of our affairs, and
ared extremely anxious to secure the passage
e law. I mention this as one of the many
instances which, independent of official as-
ces, convince me that the King is sincere,
e I have no doubt of the sincerity of his
net. From all th s. you may imagine the
y I'shall feel for the arrival of the Presi-
's message. On its tone will depend very
h, not only the payment of our claims, but
national reputation for energy. I have no
t it will be such as to attain both of these im-
ant objects.

Mr. Livingston to Mr. Forsyth.
(Extract.)
Legation of the United States,
Paris, December 6th, 1834.

The Chambers were convened on the 1st inst, under very exciting circumstances.

The Ministers individually, and the papers supposed to speak their language, having previously announced a design to enter into a full explanation of their conduct to answer all the interrogations and place their continuance in office on the question of approval by the Chambers of their measures.

This, as you will see by the papers, they have finally and explicitly done, and after a warm debate of two days which has just closed, they have gained a decided victory. This gives them confidence, permanence, and I hope influence enough to carry the treaty. I shall now urge the presentation of the law at as early a day as possible, and although I do not yet feel very certain of success, my hopes of it are naturally much increased by the vote of this evening. The conversations I have had with the King and with all the Ministers, convince me that now they are perfectly in earnest, and united on the question, and that it will be urged with zeal and ability.

Many of the Deputies, too, with whom I have entered into explanations on the subject, seem now convinced that the interest as well as the honor of the nation requires the fulfilment of their engagements. This gives me hopes that the endeavors I shall continue to make, without ceasing until the question is decided, may be successful. The intimation I have conceived myself authorized to make of the serious consequences that may be expected from another rejection of the law and of the firm determination of our Government to admit of no reduction or change in the treaty, I think have had an effect. On the whole, I repeat, that without being at all confident, I now entertain better hopes than I have for sometime past done.

Mr. Livingston to the Secretary of State.
(Extracts.)
Paris, 22d Dec. 1834.

Sir: Our Diplomatic Relations with this Government are on the most extraordinary footing. With the Executive branch, I have little to discuss; for they agree with me in every material point on the subject of the Treaty. With the Legislature, where the great difficulty arises, I can have no official communication. Yet, deeply impressed with the importance to my fellow-citizens of securing the indemnity to which they are entitled, and to the country of enforcing the execution of engagements solemnly made to it, as well as of preventing a rupture, which must infallibly follow the final refusal to execute the Convention, I have felt it a duty to use every proper endeavor to avoid this evil. This has been, and continues to be, a subject of much embarrassment.

My last despatch (6th December) was written immediately after the vote of the Chamber of Deputies had, as it was thought, secured a majority to the administration—thought it naturally excited hopes which that supposition was calculated to inspire. I soon found, however, both from the tone of the administration press, and from the language of the King and all the Ministers with whom I conferred on the subject, that they were not willing to put their popularity to the test on our question. It will not be made one, on the determination of which the Ministers are willing to risk their port folios. The very next day after the debate, the ministerial gazette (Les Debats,) declared that, satisfied with the approbation the Chamber had given to their system, it was at perfect liberty to exercise its discretion as to particular measures which do not form an *essential part of that system;* and the communication I subsequently had with the King and the Ministers, confirmed me in the opinion that the law for executing our convention, was to be considered as one of those free questions. I combated this opinion, and asked whether the faithful observance of treaties was not an essential part of their system,

and if so, whether it did not come within their rule. Without answering this argument, I was told of the endeavors they were making to secure the passage of the law, by preparing the statement* mentioned in my former despatch. This, it is said, is nearly finished; and from what I know of its tenor, it will produce all the effect that truth and justice can be expected to have on prejudice and party spirit.

The decision, not to make it a cabinet question, will not be without its favorable operation; * * * * * some of the leaders of the opposition, who may not be willing to take the responsibility of a rupture between the two nations by breaking the treaty, when they are convinced that instead of forcing the Ministers to resign, they will themselves only incur the odium of having caused the national breach. In this view of the subject, I shall be much aided, if, by the tenor of the President's Message, it is seen that we shall resent the breach of faith they contemplated. It is on all hands conceded that it would be imprudent to press the decision before the next month, when the exposition will be printed and laid before the Chambers.

On the whole, I am far from being sanguine of success in the endeavors which I shall not cease to make for the accomplishment of this important object of my mission; and I expect with some solicitude the instructions for my conduct, in the probable case of a rejection of the law.

I have the honor to be, &c.
(Signed)   EDW. LIVINGSTON.
Hon. John Forsyth,
Secretary of State.

*Note.—The paper here referred to by Mr. Livingston, is a memoir to be laid before the commission which may be appointed to examine the law intended to contain all the arguments and facts by which it is to be supported.

Mr. ADAMS, of Massachusetts, moved to refer the Message and documents to the Committee on Foreign Relations, with instructions to report forthwith on the subject.

Mr. McKIM said, as the papers accompanying the message were of an important character, he moved that they be read; which was done.

Mr. CAMBRELENG hoped that the gentleman from Massachusetts, after having heard the correspondence read, would withdraw that part of his motion which proposed to instruct the Committee to report forthwith. He trusted the House would allow the Committee till the last moment to decide upon measures requiring unanimity, and involving such important considerations. On such a question, he would appeal to no particular portion of the House; for he felt assured that whenever we were called upon to decide on a proper measure of redress, there could be but one sentiment where the national character and honor were involved. He trusted that whenever we should be called upon to act decisively, whatever might be proposed by the Committee, would receive the unanimous vote of the House. He rose merely for the purpose of soliciting the gentleman from Massachusetts to withdraw that part of his motion which proposed to instruct the Committee to report forthwith; for, at the present moment, it would be almost impossible to report any measure which would meet the approbation of the Committee or of the House.

Mr. J. Q. ADAMS said, in introducing this resolution, his purpose was that the Committee on Foreign Relations should be instructed to report *forthwith*—he used the word *forthwith* in order to ascertain whether that House thought it inconsistent with their duty, and the interests and honor of the nation, to leave this great subject any longer without action upon it. And as the action of the House must depend upon the report to be made by that committee, there was no other mode of arriving at that result than by instructing the committee to report *forthwith*. He had no objection to any amendment which the honorable Chairman of the Committee on Foreign Relations, (Mr. Cambreleng,) or any other member, might propose, who thought it necessary to allow that committee further time to consider the subject; but he deemed it important that, as we were then

within a short month of the termination of the session, and as from the correspondence just read, as well as from the reports in general circulation throughout the country, he thought it exceedingly doubtful whether any thing more definitive would be received with respect to the action of the French Government upon that treaty. The letter from Mr. Livingston of the 6th of December, the day after the new French ministry had obtained what that gentleman called a victory, speaks in very sanguine terms of the probability of the Chamber of Deputies passing the bill of appropriations. But what did his subsequent letter, dated fifteen days afterwards, say? He tells us that the new ministry were far from willing to hazard their popularity upon proposing the bill. Well, then, Mr. Livingston concluded with saying that he was by no means sanguine; and other reports, from Paris, and from almost every other source, concurred in stating that there was no prospect whatever, that the French Chamber would make any appropriation, to provide for the payment of this debt. That was also the general tenor of all

ber of Deputies had made the appropriation, it would do no harm; but it would show that that House felt what was due to the dignity, the honor, and the interests of the nation. Whatever might be said of the message of the President, Mr. A. for one would say, as was once said in the case of General La Fayette, that whoever censured its imprudence, must yet admire its spirit. It would go forth to all mankind as the sustainer of the rights, the honor, and the interests of this country, and he hoped the House would not suffer itself to appear in a contrasted character with the President of the United States, by shrinking from responsibility, in order not to commit themselves to the nation. At least, let them have the

ernment in a wrong attitude, and would be tantamount to a declaration of war. He also objected to the principle of specially instructing a committee on matters of such deep importance; and reluctant as he would be, he should be compelled to vote against the proposition.

Mr. CLAYTON alluded to what took place on this subject at the commencement of the session, and said he considered that at that time there were two courses for that body to take; one was to act up to the spirit of the President's Message; the other was for the representative branch of the nation to show to the French Government we did not coincide in that recommendation, and by that means avert, if possible, all the consequences that might ensue; but at the same time place the Chamber of Deputies in the same situation they would have been placed in, if that message had not been sent to this House. In the latter course, one branch of the Government had sustained the motion he made on this subject at the commencement of the present session. The Senate had unanimously resolved that it was inexpedient, at the present time, to adopt any legislative measure in regard to the state of affairs between the United States and France. That resolution had accomplished all he wished upon this subject, and if it failed to answer the purpose, he had nothing else in view. If we were now to discuss this subject, short of that proposition, whether we should institute acts of hostility against France, it might involve a collision between the two bodies. The unanimous vote of the Senate upon the first question presented by him, answered his purpose better than a vote against it by that House. Now, then, if all had been done that could be done to effect what he had in view, the next inquiry was, if it failed, should we proceed until we forced conviction that it was necessary to proceed upon the alternative laid down by the President of the United States? Was there testimony before us of a character to justify our doing it? Should we act upon the testimony presented to us, and proceed at once to measures of hostility? or would it not be better for the Committee on Foreign Affairs not to make a report until they could do it upon information that would satisfy that House? He put the question, were gentlemen prepared to proceed to what would be considered acts of hostility? for certainly any legislation growing out of the testimony before them would result in that consequence. He thought they would not, and they ought not so to act. Taking this view of the subject, then, that it was proper for the legislative branch, or rather the popular branch, of the Government, to signify to France that they did not agree with the President in his recommendation, and believing that the alternative had not arrived, he should vote against the motion to instruct the committee forthwith,—reluctantly, because it came from a very high source; but he did not deem immediate action either expedient or called for.

Mr. McKINLEY said he was pleased to see the gentleman from Massachusetts (Mr. Adams) evince so becoming a spirit on the occasion; and if he would delay his motion till a reasonable time was given to hear further from France, he (Mr. M.) would go with him for instructions to the Committee on Foreign Affairs, provided they would not make a proper report without. Mr. M. said that he was prepared to act decisively upon this subject before the adjournment of Congress. The gentleman from Virginia (Mr. Archer) urges forbearance towards our ancient friend and ally. He believes the King of the French sincerely desires that the treaty of the 4th of July, 1831, should be carried into effect; and that we ought not therefore to carry out the recommendation of the President, because it may lead to war; we ought not, he thinks, to involve the country in war for the sum in controversy.

Sir, how long is this forbearance to be urged upon us? There have been four sessions of the French Chambers since the exchange of ratifications of the treaty. At the first, the subject was not noticed; at the second, which lasted about four months, it was laid before the Chamber of Deputies nineteen days only before the adjournment; the bill was referred to a committee, and there

tice.

oes it occur to gentlemen here, that it will France just as much to go to war for these millions, as it will cost us. If war should be result of the course which we may be com- d. to take, is the fault ours? Had France plied with the stipulat ons of the treaty, that dship, which is so highly and so justly appre- d, might, and would, have been preserved— she been as tender of our feelings, and regard- f our rights, as we have been of hers, no dif- y could ever have occurred between us. forgetting that sacred friendship—that ancient ce—which weighs so heavily with us—she elayed to acknowledge a just debt for more twenty years; and, after acknowledging and ising, in the most solemn manner, to pay it, as finally refused, and still continues to enjoy ommercial benefits of the treaty, which were as part consideration for the five millions romised to pay.

would to be sure, be better, in a pecuniary of view, that we should pay our citizens the millions of dollars than to hazard a war with e, if that were the only interest involved. an we thus compromise the honor of the na- Is the national honor to be estimated by s and cents? To submit to this indignity, l be an abandonment of all national charac- nd invite aggression and insult from every quarter. The idea is not to be tolerated for sent. I am willing to wait as long as we can propriety, for further advices from France; ot so long as to prevent decisive action on estion at the present session. We have grounds to justify the proceeding recom- d by the President; and to justify a much er proceeding, if we choose to adopt it; for one, am prepared to act upon it be- re separate. It is true, that those I repre- and the South generally, would be great- red by a war, if war should be the re- which I cannot believe will be the case. have no doubt they would submit to any al privation, rather than submit to national or.

LYTLE said: Mr. Speaker, since I have e honor of a seat upon this floor, it has nev- s my good fortune to listen to speeches in ouse, or elsewhere, or at any time, or up- occasion, in which I felt the same sensa- which have been produced upon me by the ition and appeal made by the venerable r from Massachusetts this morning. Sir, was in it, to my mind, however it may af- e minds of others, I say there was in it to d, a degree of moral grandeur and sublimi- ch, as an American citizen, I was most and happy to see and hear. The ex-repre- e of the Executive Department of this Gov- t now aiding to the extent of his abilities, resentative upon this floor, in the councils ountry, and sustaining with the candor and isoed patriotism of an American freeman rit and proposition of his successful rival, mbent of the Executive chair at this time, on what? Upon a proposition that the of this country should vindicate their na- ride and their national honor. What was racter of the proposition of the honorable an from Massachusetts? Does it amount laration of war if adopted by this House?

It merely proposes to call upon the com- on Foreign Affairs to make a report to vin- his House from the imputation, which I in- him, will rest upon it, of pusillanimously to the juggling and caprices of a foreign e, who is unwilling to render that justice, l over again proposed by himself, and ad- o be due to this country, and after four of the session, for it is now the fourth nce the special call of the French Cham- eputies was made, with reference to the ent of this very claim; here we are, with elligence from France? Why, that your was first seduced into the belief, ed into the belief, by the flourishes of Philippe and his cabinet, that they real- ded to enter, heart and soul, into this , and instantly carry the treaty into hat they meant to pledge the whole weight of the Government, and to throw them- selves into the scale, and make it a national propo- sition. This was the purport of Mr. Livingston's first despatch. But what was the amount of his subsequent correspondence? Why, he grows less and less sanguine up to the date of his last communication, and finally tells us he is now not at all sanguine! That the French King and his cabinet, instead of making it a ministerial measure, and throwing the whole weight and popularity of the Government into the scale, have shuffled out of the controversy, and left it as an open matter, in the decision of which they have no special interest. Now let me ask the members of this House what pledge they will wait for after this shuffling course, before the close of this session? Can they, after this, expect to receive intelligence of a more grateful character? Or may they not reasonably calculate upon hearing, by the first vessel that may arrive from Europe, that this nation, which has thus long procrastinated the payment of a just claim, has determined not to pay it at all? And having come to that conclusion, and knowing that war is inevitable, may we not expect her to take the first step, and as a matter of safety to herself, detain our ships now in the Mediterranean, and blockade the ports there? Well, what are we asked to do by the proposition of the honorable member from Massachusetts? Nothing more than that, in the event of their refusing before the adjournment of this House, to ratify this treaty, the House will pledge itself to answer the call of the President of the United States, by giving him power, or resorting to some other means, in the event of this contingency, to save the nation, and protect it's honor and the just claims of its citizens from the aggressions of this insolent and juggling power. Sir, when I hear the appeal from such a quarter, echoing back the same spirit, so highly and properly lauded on the part of the Executive, by one grown grey in diplomacy, and familiar with the tricks of courts; by one who has a just, a high, and an honorable sense of his own character, and the character of the American People, I say, sir, there is no room left for me to doubt of its propriety at this time. I say, sir, now is the time, and if I, for one, were certain that a messenger would arrive this very night, with intelligence that the French Chamber had acted upon this subject, I would still urge the adoption of the resolution of the gentleman from Massachusetts. It goes the whole to show abroad the sense of the American People in reference to this matter. It goes the whole to show that if it is the intention of France to suffer this Congress to pass over before any intelligence of a satisfactory character should be received, that the Representatives of the American People are not slumbering at their posts, but are aroused at the prospect of injury or insult, and, by an expression of some sort of the character referred to by the gentleman from Massachusetts, that they are prepared to vindicate the character and honor of the country, and let the world know that that power which attempts to cavil with, to special plead with, to juggle with the United States of America, have made a serious, and, for them, an unfortunate mistake. That we are prepared to go the whole for the spirit, if not the measure, of the proposition in the Executive message; and that we will stand by and sustain the President therein—that we will make it a common cause. *That* will be done, and I hope now, upon the proposition of the gentleman from Massachusetts; and I trust the matter will be referred by the unanimous vote of this House — What valid objection can be urged against it? It does not contain a proposition for immediate action; it only anticipates that which I believe will come; and in the event of its coming, we should then have the vantage ground, and be able to show that even before it arrives, we were in a state of preparation to meet it. It is a delicate, but a well-timed and judicious proposition, and one that I hail as an American freeman and a representative of this body, from the bottom of my soul, especially coming from the quarter it does. I again reiterate the hope, that the resolution, as worded, will be unanimously adopted.

Mr. SUTHERLAND expressed his approbation of the exalted and patriotic sentiment expressed by the gentleman from Massachusetts, (Mr. Adams) but he confessed, in the present instance, he could not go with him, to the extent which his remarks seemed to indicate. Give me, (said Mr. S.) the vantage ground, and all the advantage which long suffering and forbearance can give in such a contest as this. But, he asked, shall we gain this ground by precipitation? Shall we not rather injure a just and honest cause? Let us hear once more from France; for she is, after all, our ancient friend and ally. He still cherished the hope, that on the receipt of the President's message, she would be inclined to render us justice. Ten or fifteen days at the uttermost would bring us intelligence from that country; and he fervently hoped with it a message worthy of France. If these sanguine anticipations should not be realized, he would then be prepared to go with the gentleman from Massachusetts, (Mr. Adams) and from Ohio, (Mr. Lytle) to maintain the honor and glory of our country, as far as they could go. We "asked nothing but what is right, and would submit to nothing wrong." He would give France the opportunity, at least, of sending us better tidings. It would be painful to wage a war with France; but she, like other nations, must render us justice—strict, equal, and exact justice. He would give her a last chance of settling her affairs with us on amicable terms. His feelings were such, that he was willing to go back to ancient times, and remember with glowing gratitude the former relations between that government and our own. If we now say we will not go to war with her in consequence of our recollections of these ancient services, will it not excite a corresponding spirit on her part. He was disposed to look on that country as one which had rendered us essential service in the hour of our greatest want of such service. He believed that a week before the closing of the session, would be time enough for the House to take any decisive measures; for it was evident we were prepared, at a moment's warning, if France should refuse to grant us justice, to go with the gentleman from Massachusetts; to go with the President in asserting and vindicating our rights.

After some further remarks, Mr. S. alluded to our ability to maintain a conflict with foreign powers. We had passed through one war with her who had so long been proudly denominated the mistress of the ocean, in which our heroes had won for themselves and their country immortal renown. The stars and stripes of America waved over every sea, a protection to our rights, a terror to our foes.

Mr. S. said, he would not send these documents to the committee on Foreign Relations, with the peremptory instructions suggested by the gentleman from Massachusetts, (Mr. Adams,) but in the language of the gentleman from Alabama, (Mr. McKinley,) he would wait a few days. He would secure to our country in her just and holy cause all the advantage of long suffering and patience. No vessel had yet arrived from France which sailed for this country after the transmission of the President's message to Congress. What new lights had we at the present moment to guide us? Surely none. He was for waiting the effect of that message on the French people. If it is disposed then to retrace their steps and do us justice, it was well—if not, it was even then quite soon enough for the dread alternative.

Mr. HAMER said he did not rise to make a speech, because every gentleman upon the floor understood the subject as well as he did; and because he apprehended every gentleman was prepared to act whenever the proper time should arrive. Although, as to that time, a difference of opinion existed, he trusted however when it should come, all would be prepared to sustain the national honor and dignity. On that subject he had no fears, either with regard to the members of that House, or with regard to the great mass of the people of the country. It was always a matter of regret to him to differ with his honorable friend on the left (Mr. Lytle) upon any question, but especially upon those of great importance; but he rose to say that the reading of the papers on the Clerk's table had produced upon his mind precise-

ly the opposite impression produced upon that of his honorable friend, and upon the minds of some other gentlemen upon that floor.

It was obvious to Mr. H. that two things should take place before requiring the Committee on Foreign Relations to report. The memoir of the French Ministers, spoken of by Mr. Livingston, should be presented to the French Chamber of Deputies, whose action thereon should be known here; and the message of the President should have been received in France, considered, and the effect thereof known here, before we proceed to act definitely upon the subject. Now, it might happen that both these things may occur in the course of a few days; and we might reasonably expect to hear the effect of the message upon the Deputies and the French people in a short time; and till we did, he thought it would be unwise to ask the Committee on Foreign Relations to report on so grave and important a matter. He therefore moved to amend the motion of the gentleman from Massachusetts, by striking out that part of it requiring the Committee to report *forthwith*.

Mr. R. M. JOHNSON, of Kentucky, said he had looked into this difficulty between France and the United States with intense interest—and he would add with great anxiety and anguish of mind. That feeling had not, in the least, been softened, or mitigated by the message and documents now presented to us. He said he had read the correspondence between our minister and government, and the King's ministers here and in Europe—and the subject seemed to be perfectly understood by the government of France. It was clear that the king and his ministers had in vain exerted their influence upon the popular branch of the French Government, to carry the treaty into effect, by making the appropriation which it stipulated to pay our citizens five millions of dollars, for burning their ships and cargoes on the high seas, and for plundering and confiscating their property, without the authority of the law of nations. He said he found the difficulty to exist in the Chamber of Deputies. He had supposed that the Chambers must have been under some strange delusion as to the principles and facts in the negotiation—for they could not seek to violate an obligation so sacred—so imperative upon nations to perform—particularly the gallant and intelligent people of France towards the United States, their ancient friend and ally. But what was his surprise—his astonishment, on reading the debates of the Deputies to discover on their part a perfect knowledge of the whole transaction—of all the facts in the case—and yet these Deputies—these Representatives of the People of France, refused to pay the money due to our citizens—accruing from the invasion of our rights—the plunder of our commerce under the unholy sanction of their illegal decrees!

Mr. J. said, he would gladly avoid this question if he could do so with due regard to the rights and character of his country. We might attempt to avoid this question—our feelings may prompt us to do so, because its tendency is to involve such important—such vital consequence; but we should remember that the price of liberty was blood! It was impossible to maintain our freedom, our character, our independence, and at the same time submit to violation of faith, so pointed, so gross, and so flagrant, if persisted in. It was the people of France, or rather the Chamber of Deputies, representing that people, who had, with their eyes open, refused to do us justice; and not the King and his ministers.

Mr. J. said, it was doubtful whether those who held back and refused to take strong measures, in cases of insult and injury did not do more to plunge nations into war, than those who acted promptly to resent and redress violations of faith, by acting upon the principle of the President, to demand nothing but what was just, and to sumbit to nothing evidently wrong. Mr. J. expressed his utter astonishment at the conduct of France. Here, he said, seemed not only to be wrong and injustice, but *wilful* and *premeditated* wrong—and the question was, could we tamely submit to it? For one, he could, he would not. He would sustain the President in his course. He was not or precipitation—he was willing to wait for the final action of the Chamber of Deputies; but he now believed forbearance had ceased to be a virtue. It would amount to nothing, unless it was known and believed that this nation could not and would not submit to such injustice. And when it was thus believed, that war was inevitable, then, as our cause was so obviously just—as the United States were so palpably in the right—it was possible, perhaps probable, that France might retrace her steps, for the sake of her own honor, and execute the treaty, by paying the indemnity stipulated for the wrongs she had inflicted on our commerce. At all events, this was our only hope. We had made a full experiment of forbearance. It had failed. We must resort to another alternative.

But, Mr. J. said, as he believed the people of the United States were only divided as to the time for resenting and redressing this violation of national faith on the part of France, he, for one, would still yield to that nation a further time, so that no voice could be raised against the course which our country should ultimately be compelled to pursue. The temper of the House manifested great unanimity in relation to the main point—the justice of our complaint, and the utter impossibility of submitting to it. Mr. J. said, he hoped, therefore, it would be distinctly understood, that he feared not the consequences of expressing himself strongly on this subject; and whenever the occasion should arrive, he should vote for strong measures, corresponding with his expressions. War, said Mr. J., is a great calamity—there is none greater, except that of tamely submitting to insult and injury. And here was an instance of wrong so flagrant, and a violation of national faith so palpable, that it had few, if any, parallels in the annals of nations; and in this sentiment he believed he should have the concurrent testimony of the civilized world. France knew as well as ourselves, that we could not submit to it without degradation and disgrace.

With regard to the immediate question before the House, he thought the message and accompanying documents should be referred to the Committee on Foreign Affairs, without instructions.

In conclusion, Mr. J. said he should do injustice to his own *feelings* if he took his seat without admitting that his heart palpitated with joy on hearing the patriotic sentiments of the honorable member from Massachusetts, (Mr. Adams.) Those sentiments were truly American; and, like the gentleman from Ohio, (Mr. Lytle,) he honored them for the source from which they came.

Mr. STEWART rose, he said, mainly to suggest an amendment to the proposition, which he trusted would be calculated to produce a greater degree of unanimity in the vote to be given upon that interesting and important occasion. It would doubtless be conceded by all, that unanimity was of the very utmost consequence abroad, and they should present to France and to the world a united front, since divided councils could lead to no profitable result. He had no serious objections to the proposition of the honorable member from Massachusetts, (Mr. Adams,) in whose patriotic sentiments Mr. S. would take that opportunity of expressing his entire concurrence, except to that part of it which required the Committee on Foreign Affairs to report *forthwith*. In his opinion, it would be premature. In a few days hence another packet might arrive, bringing important advices from France, and which might put a new aspect upon the affair. He would therefore respectfully suggest to the distinguished mover of the proposition, the propriety of modifying it, so as to strike out the word *forthwith*, and allow it to read, that the committee be required to report on or before the 15th or 20th of the present month. This would also, he thought, meet the object of the gentleman from Ohio, (Mr. Hamer,) and, as it seemed to Mr. S., would obviate his objections to the motion of the gentleman from Massachusetts. If this amendment were adopted, it would also, he believed, be calculated to produce a greater degree of unanimity in the vote that would be given upon the subject, and he regarded unanimity as of the utmost importance, and should be glad to see that House act with the same unanimity as did the other branch of the national legislature. If his suggestion were not acceded to, he would move it as an amendment.

The CHAIR said there was a motion to amend already before the House, which must be first disposed of.

Mr. HAMER remarked, that he could not agree to the suggestion, because it did not embrace what he objected to in the motion. He had moved to strike out *all* that part instructing the committee.

Mr. EVANS said, he hardly knew in what position he should now consider the motion of the honorable gentleman from Massachusetts, (Mr. Adams.) It was originally to give instructions to the Committee on Foreign Relations to report upon the subject forthwith. If this was its present shape, he should support it; and as that gentleman had given to the House the reasons which induced his motion, he should also give those which would influence him in voting for it. If he had understood the views of that gentleman, as expressed, Mr. E. said his own object would be to procure a report widely different from that which he seemed to anticipate—one of an entirely opposite character.

Mr. ADAMS explained. He had proposed that the committee be instructed to report *forthwith*, because he thought it a duty they owed to the House and to the world to give that House an opportunity of acting in the matter. He had not declared what position he should take in that [illegible], but he deemed it all important that the subject should be deliberated on by the representatives of the people. It was with this particular view that he had submitted his motion, that time might be had for the discussion, before the adjournment, and he believed from present indications, that the time of the present session would be required for a deliberate comparison of the views of different members. Mr. A. said, from the motion he had made and the position he had taken, it did not follow that he deemed a war necessary—nor did it follow that reprisals should be made—or that any other particular course should be pursued or recommended by the House. It would be competent to the House to pursue the same course that the other Legislative Branch of the Government had done. That branch had come to its conclusion—and what was that conclusion? It would dodge the question. This House could, if it chose, also dodge the question.

The CHAIR interposed. It was not in order to allude to the proceedings of the other branch of the Legislature.

Mr. ADAMS said he merely wished to be understood as to to the motives which prompted him to make his motion. He wished that House to have ample time to deliberate on the momentous question involved in the communications before them.

Mr. EVANS continued. He did not know that he had materially misunderstood the gentleman from Massachusetts. It was true he had not distinctly avowed the opinion he entertained as to the course which should ultimately be pursued; but Mr. E. said he did infer from the spirit of his remarks, that he was for sustaining the recommendations of the Executive in their fullest extent. It was certain that others had drawn the same inferences, else whence the remarks of the gentleman from Virginia (Mr. Archer,) and why the [illegible] encomiums of the gentleman from Ohio (Mr. Lytle) for his generous and disinterested support of "the views and measures of a successful rival?" Mr. E. said, he, like others, only drew his inferences from the general spirit of the gentleman's remarks. He did not see that it would be "dodging the question" if the House should declare that there was at present no occasion for legislative interference in this matter. The character of our country was essentially pacific. It was our policy to exhaust all language—all forms of negotiation, before we appealed to the last dread resort of war.

[CONTINUED IN NEXT NUMBER.]

CONGRESSIONAL GLOBE.

BY BLAIR & RIVES.	———WEEKLY———	PRICE $1 A SESSION.
2d Sess.......23d Cong.	WEDNESDAY, FEBRUARY 18, 1835.	Volume 2.......No. 14.

TWENTY-THIRD CONGRESS.
SECOND SESSION.

HOUSE OF REPRESENTATIVES.
SATURDAY, Feb. 7, 1835.

[CONTINUED FROM LAST NUMBER.]

The gentleman had spoken of what had been termed the imprudence of the message of the President. There were many who viewed it in that light. Mr. E. contended that the House should have more information before it acted, especially when it was known that such information existed; for that fact was avowed in the message now before the House. Would the gentleman contend that either House of Congress should say, although the annual message might be imprudent in some of the sentiments it advanced, yet that, being advanced, we were bound to support them?

Mr. ADAMS said, "No."

Mr. EVANS said he begged the gentleman's pardon. He knew he did not use that language. But such was the general inference. It was hardly necessary for us at once to say that all hopes of a pacific course were at an end. He wished, in common with others from France—to learn the effect which the message had upon her people and their representatives. He wished to hope for the best, until all plausibility of hope was gone. He had but a single word to add. He could not consent to sanction any incipient measure of hostility, on the part of this Government, until the whole facts and correspondence was laid before them. It was a point in our political relations where we must use great consideration and forbearance. The term "juggling" had been used in relation to the French Ministry. He had thought the good faith of the King of the French had never been doubted, and he could not sanction any measure of incipient act of hostility, until every pacific measure in our power had been tried. It was with these views, and a desire to receive a corresponding report from the Committee of Foreign Relations, that he should vote in favor of the motion of the gentleman from Massachusetts.

Mr. CAMBRELENG said that the gentleman from Maine seemed to be apprehensive that the President's Message would produce injurious effects upon our relations with France; and yet the gentleman's argument had convinced him that if the appropriation was not made by the French Chamber, it could not be ascribed to the tone of the President's Message. The gentleman said—as he had lost all hope—the correspondence which he had just heard read, had, for the first time, induced him to believe that serious consequences might result; and yet, when this intelligence, which had extinguished hope, left France, the Meas ge had not arrived. He did not rise, however, to excite debate, or to produce division, but to congratulate the country that but one sentiment was heard from all sides of the House—that however gentlemen might differ as to the time for action, whenever the time arrived they would present an undivided front. He responded entirely to the patriotic sentiments so admirably expressed by the gentleman from Massachusetts, (Mr. Adams.) He thought with him that a more prompt and decided course would have been preferable. Had the two Houses, at the commencement of the session, assumed a bolder attitude, he thought it would have been more consistent with national patriotism, national honor, and sound national policy. Unfortunately, another course was pursued, and a measure adopted which he found would not produce the result anticipated. A more decided policy would have shown to France and to the world, that we were resolved to assert our rights, and that after five and twenty years of wrong and insult, we could no longer consider forbearance a national virtue. But while he concurred with the gentleman from Massachusetts, in desiring to vindicate our character and our rights, and while he would have gone with him at an earlier, or at any period of the session, for the measure recommended by the President, or for any other that the gentleman himself might have proposed which would have accomplished the object, he differed with him as to the propriety of precipitating our action at the expense of our unanimity. It is necessary to secure unanimity not only here, but in the other branch of the Legislature, and that cannot be expected while the attitude of the question remains unchanged.—It is for that reason, and that alone, that he desired that the House might not now be called upon to act definitively upon the question. He felt as sensitive as the gentleman from Massachusetts, at every hour's delay; he felt that they were every moment approaching the period in the history of these relations with France, when forbearance would become pusillanimity. But to give effect to measures, whatever they might be, union was necessary, and however prepared the gentleman from Massachusetts and himself might be for definitive or preparatory action, others in this House, independent of the other body, would prefer postponing the decision of the question to a later period of the session. The gentleman from Pennsylvania (Mr. Stewart) had suggested postponement to the 20th, or some such date; but though he should not object to that, he should prefer that the House would leave the question of time to the discretion of the Committee. He trusted we should not be precipitated into any half way measures, and that whatever might be proposed would meet the approbation of the House. If the gentleman from Massachusetts would not modify or withdraw his proposition to instruct, he hoped that part of the motion would not prevail.

Mr. PATTON. (Mr. P.'s remarks were frequently indistinctly audible at our reporter's desk.) Mr. P. was understood to say, he had not, in the slightest degree, changed his opinion with regard to the propriety of a prompt and immediate report from the Committee on Foreign Affairs, upon the matter under consideration; but entertained the opinion, with unabated conviction, that it was their duty to the House, to the country, and eminently so to the President of the United States, whose opinions and recommendations upon this great subject had been committed to them for deliberation, that the Committee, which constituted a merely incipient organ of the House for digesting materials for its action, should not delay one moment, after their own opinion and judgment had been formed upon the materials committed to them, in reporting their resolutions and deliberations for the concurrence or for the disapprobation of the House. Entertaining that view, and entertaining, moreover, the belief, a belief deeply impressed upon his mind by the information communicated that morning, the material parts of which were before within the knowledge of the Committee on Foreign Affairs, that it was utterly hopeless to expect any decisive information from France, as to the action which would take place in the French Chamber of Deputies upon the bill making appropriations for carrying the treaty into effect, until after the close of the present session of Congress, he did then conceive, and he now conceived, that this subject ought to have been before the House for its deliberation upon the principles involved in the President's message, as well as upon the expediency and propriety of the particular measure of redress he proposed, and the expediency or propriety, at that time, of resorting to any measure of redress whatever. However his own opinions might differ from those of any other, or all the members of the Committee on Foreign Relations, upon that subject, it was, he humbly conceived, a matter that belonged not to the Committee to decide, or to conclude. It was not, he conceived, for them to forestal, but it belonged peculiarly to that House, unaffected and uninfluenced by the action of any other branch of the legislature of the Government. It belonged to the popular body, to the immediate representatives of the People of this country. It belonged to them in a peculiar manner—that as soon as they had maturely deliberated upon the materials presented for their judgment, that they should say to France and to the country what their opinions, what their feelings, what their course, were to be upon this matter. As it was then presented, how did the facts stand? Mr. Livingston's despatch of the 23d of November, showed that, according to the information obtained by him in Paris, the bill which the French King (Mr. P. had no sort of doubt with the utmost sincerity, for he did not take the King's declaration in the literal sense of the terms in which it was couched,) had declared his determination to present to the Chamber of Deputies, as soon as it could be reasonably and judiciously presented, would not be presented to the Chamber for its consideration until the middle of January. All the information we have subsequently received, either from Mr. Livingston or from any private sources, went to satisfy us that this impression was correct, and that in all human probability, instead of being presented earlier, it would not be till a later period. This was a question which, knowing as we did the feelings and opinions, and the conflict of opinion existing in France, and in the Chamber of Deputies, on this subject, would not be, could not be promptly and immediately disposed of. And every one knew that if this subject was not presented to the Chamber before the middle of January, it could not possibly receive the definite action of that body early enough for us to obtain any information of their definite action until the close, or near the close, of the present session of Congress. Mr. P. could not therefore perceive the propriety for further delay, nor did he the other day, when he offered to that House, and asked permission to present for its adoption, certain resolutions containing the principles and opinions upon which he was prepared to show to the House that it was time the subject should come under its deliberation. More than two thirds of the session had elapsed, and only three weeks of it remaining, and there was just time enough that this subject, which was calculated to produce much conflict of opinion, and a great variety of propositions, as to what ought to be the course adopted, should be brought before this body, whose deliberations we all knew, could not be promptly brought to a conclusion; they should have it in their power fully to deliberate upon the principles it involved, and as soon as they had come to an opinion, to express it in the form of resolutions or in the form of action. If there were any who upon deliberation should be of opinion that at that time it was prudent, proper, and necessary, to have action, it might be taken.

It was due, said Mr. Mr. P. to himself, and he felt it certainly due to the honorable and distinguished gentleman from Massachusetts that he should say that he felt much satisfaction in the spirit of his remarks. He understood those remarks precisely as that gentleman had since explained them, viz. For not committing himself to the propriety of any particular measure at that time, but it was his opinion that this House owed it not only to the executive head of the country, whose constitutional duty has made it necessary to present this subject and his opinions to their consideration, but also to the anxious feeling of the country, and to the great interests involved in this high, important, and critical question, that they should say whether they concurred in the views of the President that this treaty was a valid and binding treaty. Whether they concurred in the opinion expressed by the President that this country would not, and could not acquiesce in the final refusal of France to perform the engagements entered into by her; or whether we should, in a manner perfectly respectful to France, and with a proper spirit of forbearance towards her, wait the further action of the French Chamber be-

fore we came to any final and definite conclusion on this subject.

These were the views, Mr. P. said, that prompted him throughout the whole affair. He still entertained a most thorough and undoubting conviction in the correctness of these opinions, but he was bound to regard also, the decision of the House on a proposition submitted to them by himself. It may have been influenced by other considerations than his own, but he was bound to regard that vote as it stood, as the opinion of the majority of the House, that they would not now compel the committee to report as they would not then, for he did not suppose any thing had occurred since to change their judgment, and however contrary it might be to his own convictions of what ought to be done, he yielded as it became him to do, with proper deference to what seemed to be the judgment of the House. Many gentlemen still thought that further delay ought to be allowed, and having every disposition to do all in his power to produce the most happy result, and being, with the gentleman from New York, (Mr. Cambreleng,) desirous to elicit a unanimous vote on this subject, he would, before he sat down, move that the resolution be so referred to the committee that they should report on or before Monday week next. This proposition he thought would answer the views of all of those who thought further delay necessary, and he did not think the House should postpone it beyond that time; and if not presented to the House by that day, there would not be time to deliberate, but that day would still leave time for a patient, temperate, and judicious judgment upon it. Whether it should be necessary for the committee to recommend any legislative action or not, or what should be the particular tone of the report or the resolutions, depended on the committee; for the proposition of the gentleman from Massachusetts left the subject perfectly open to the committee. Having indicated his own opinions, Mr. P. had not the slightest disposition to interfere in any way whatever with the judgment of the committee. All he asked was, that they should report, and he thought the day he had mentioned was the latest period they should be allowed. Mr. P. concluded by moving to modify the motion of Mr. Adams so as to make it read, that the committee should report on Monday week.

Mr. J. Q. ADAMS accepted the modification.

Mr. EDWARD EVERETT observed, that this did not appear to him to be a question of so much importance, as seemed to have been given it in the present discussion. Whether the Committee should be instructed to report on Monday week or Monday fortnight, or forthwith, could not, he conceived, be a matter of great moment. There are but a little more than three weeks remaining of the session. What has fallen from the Chairman of the Committee will, of course, be regarded by the House as an assurance that the Committee will report before the close of the session. Such is my own understanding (said Mr. E.) of the purpose of the Committee. That report cannot well be delayed many days beyond the time now fixed in the resolution as modified; and whether the report came a few days earlier or later, cannot be, I should think, of great consequence. While, therefore, I am willing to concur in the passage of the resolution of my distinguished colleague, I should also have voted for it as first moved by him. I should have been willing that the Committee should be instructed to report *forthwith*. I have been in favor of the Committee's reporting forthwith, from the beginning of the session. I thought it very important—highly desirable, to do so. So much time has since elapsed, and the difference between reporting forthwith and reporting at as late period as it can well be done, is so inconsiderable, that I attach less consequence to it than I did. At the commencement of the session, I thought an immediate report from the Committee would have done great good. I differ, on this point, from the gentleman from New York, (Mr. Cambreleng,) at the head of the Committee on Foreign Affairs. I think it would have been much better if we had reported long ago; if we had taken a ground like that assumed unanimously by the Senate of the United States, and which I understand the gentleman from New York to censure—

Mr. CAMBRELENG explained. He said it would have been proper to have had prompt and bold action at the commencement of the session.

Mr. EVERETT continued: I was for acting as promptly and boldly as the gentleman. It was precisely a prompt and bold course which I desired. I was not for war, nor for reprisals, in the state of affairs then existing, and we are now told that neither of these measures was contemplated by any member of the House. What, then, could we have done promptly and boldly? We could have done this: We could have taken up the subject as one of imminent importance, admitting no delay in the consideration of the House. We could have shown the justice of the American side of the question in the strongest terms. We could have uttered the feelings and views of this House, in the strongest and most emphatic language. Having shown the justice of our claims, we could have expressed our resolute determination to stand upon our rights under the treaty—our firm purpose not to relax one tittle, nor recede one inch, and we could have adduced the reasons—and such reasons there were—which might be urged in support of the opinion, that France would yet do us justice. I would have had a report of this character, bold, firm, and pacific, and would have hoped for it the unanimous concurrence of the House. And here, sir, I should have been inclined to stop. I would have had the rights of the country maintained, and our purpose never to recede from them asserted. But what Congress would do in the contingency—somewhat distant of necessity—never perhaps to arrive, I think I should not then have said. I would reserve my action on the contingency till it ceased to be one, and when that should be the case, then I would act promptly and vigorously, under the state of circumstances which should present itself. But I should have been indisposed to anticipate that event, and would not, therefore, undertake to say what measures I would adopt, should it happen. But I would have asserted our rights so broadly and distinctly, as to leave me at full liberty to adopt any measure of redress, which circumstances unfortunately might render necessary. The same course I would pursue now; though, from the lapse of time, I do not think all the good would result from it, which might have been hoped, from the earlier action of the Committee. I agree with the Chairman of the Committee as to the character which the report must take. He says the Committee are not prepared o recommend any measnre. I so understand it. In the present state of our information, nothing of the kind alluded to, under the name of a *measure*, can be recommended. And for this reason, I would still refrain from recommending any thing hypothetically, to be done upon the happening of a contingency, because the varieties of circumstances, the shades of human action, public as well as private, are infinitely too numerous to be foreseen.

I own, sir, my anticipations are not so cheerful as they were. I entertained a strong hope, at the commencement of the session, of the speedy adjustment of this painful controversy. In the interval, little, I must own, has occurred to strengthen, and more than I could wish to discourage, that hope. I begin to contemplate, as a possible event, that things will go to extremes. But I am not ready, and I think the House, though it may share this apprehension, cannot be ready to act on this anticipation. Even if the French Chamber should refuse again to make an appropriation to execute the treaty, we cannot be sure that it may not be in form, and with qualifications that will justify us in further delay. We cannot know this: as we cannot know that the very reverse may not, by some deplorable fatality, happen. If, for instance, the suggestion of the gentleman from Ohio (Mr. Lytle) should be realized—if the French Government should accompany the refusal by acts of affront and violence—by a hostile attempt on the squadron of the United States in the Mediterranean; an attempt which, every one knows, would be resisted to the last drop of blood of officers and men—then, sir, there would be no delay; there would be no need of instructing the committee to report forthwith; there would be no long debates in this House or the other House; but the two Houses, and the country, rising as one man, would take their position and sustain it. But I would not anticipate any such event as this. I would not take any step whatever, on the presumption that France, to the long denial of justice—to the signal injustice, of which she has given us cause already to complain, could add a procedure of such outrageous madness. I will not say such a thing is beyond the range of possibility: nothing is impossible; but no gentleman, I think, on reflection, can consider it in any degree probable.

I have said already sir, that my anticipations of the satisfactory adjustment of the business are less sanguine than they were. There are, however, some reasons for hope that the French Chambers will reach the appropriation this winter. One of the chief reasons is, that the Chamber of Deputies of last year contained some members, by no means entitled to the compliment paid to them by the gentleman from Kentucky, (Mr. Johnson,) of having understood the question thoroughly, and not having rejected the appropriation through ignorance. On the contrary, sir, there was exhibited, in my opinion, an entire ignorance of some of the most important facts of the case, and in reference to the most important of them all, a gross, not to say a discreditable ignorance, which I believe proved fatal to the passage of the appropriation bill, and which, should the two countries most unhappily be brought into collision, will throw a tremendous responsibility on those members. You are aware, sir, that, on all sides, it was admitted that something was due to the citizens of the United States, and that it was merely on a question of *how much*, that the great issue of annulling or executing a treaty, was made to depend. In this state of the controversy, and just as the question was about to be taken, members arose in the French Chambers, and stated that of the five millions of indemnity, provided by the treaty under discussion, two millions, covering the St. Sebastian's case, had already been paid under the Florida Treaty between the United States and Spain! The assertion was immediately contradicted by the Minister of Foreign affairs, whose exposition of the whole question was one of the most masterly parliamentary efforts I have ever seen. His contradiction was direct and positive, as to its purport; but if one may judge from the report of the debates, (very likely imperfect,) it was less decided and authoritative in manner, than could have been desired. At all events, I have been told by an intelligent American gentleman, who was present on the occasion, that these statements were evidently fatal to the bill. The question was taken immediately after. It was lost by only eight votes. We know, sir, that deliberative bodies may be taken by surprise, by plausible statements. Were we ourselves about to appropriate five millions of dollars, in payment of an acknowledged debt, and should member after member rise, with a treaty in their hands, maintaining that two of the five millions had been already paid, and read us passages of the document to prove it, and if any thing short of the most positive contradiction, accompanied with the most satisfactory explanation, were given, it would very likely prove fatal to the bill; certainly so, if the House were almost equally divided before. For these reasons, as I said, I rely something on the fact, that the bill was rejected last winter, not in a full understanding of the facts, as the gentleman from Kentucky seemed to think, but in an entire ignorance of the most important of them all. And when the *memoir*, which has been mentioned in Mr. Livingston's despatches to-day, shall have proved to the French Chamber, (as I presume it will do, from the character of some of the documents, which, during the recess of Congress, have been furnished to the French Government at its request, by ours,) that the statements I have alluded to were utterly destitute of foundation, that the St. Sebastian's cases were all rejected by the Commissioners under the Florida treaty, as not included in its provisions, and that they have been all admitted by the Commis-

sioners now sitting under the present treaty, as notoriously provided for by that treaty, I trust it will not be without its effect.

But I do not build with entire confidence on this, or any other ground of encouragement. I see something ominous in the character and composition of the opposition to the King and his ministry on this question. What did the King tell Mr. Livingston? That he might rely upon his honor as a King, and his promise as a man, that the treaty should be executed. For myself, I place the most unqualified dependence on this assurance. I believe that, as far as his influence extends, it will be strenuously exerted; that his constitutional powers will be strained to the utmost, to procure the execution of the treaty. But what, sir, is the melancholy truth, as to the condition of the King's Government? I would not in wantonness, say any thing disparagingly of the internal condition of affairs in a country, between which and our own the relations of amity still subsist; but when our own rights and claims are made the sport of the state of parties in a foreign country, it is a fair subject of comment. The King will do his utmost to effect the fulfilment of the treaty; and not merely because it is a just treaty, but because (as he told Mr. Livingston) his faith as a sovereign, and his honor as a man, are pledged. But what is the position of the King himself? Does not all the world know, that he does not fill the throne on the principles of what is called legitimacy? That there are two powerful parties in France, agreeing in nothing else, but united in opposition to the present establishment of the Government; I mean, of course, the party of the late dispossessed family, on one side, and the extreme liberals on the other. It is, as far as we can judge at this distance, mainly a combination of these two parties, taking along with it, of course, the natural opposition to all heavy money bills, which has hitherto defeated the execution of the treaty.

With these two parties, instead of our gaining strength from the circumstance that the King's regal word and personal honor are pledged to fulfil the treaty, it is precisely for this reason that they oppose it. And they oppose it, not with a zeal measured by the simple merits and consequence of the treaty, but with an intensity of purpose, and depth of feeling, inspired by their hostility to the Government. Seeing the opposition to the treaty thus conducted by parties, who would move heaven and earth to shake the King from his throne, I own, sir, I look to see this question linked in with the very elements of the permanence of the present order of things in France. Could it be reduced simply and solely to this issue, all might be well; but with this powerful, deep seated, far-reaching opposition, we must fear, as I have said, that what may be called the natural opposition to all such measures, will unite itself. The King will do every thing to carry the treaty into effect. I am sure, if it were necessary, he would shed his blood to fulfil it. I should hear, with deep regret, a single word that would cast a shade of doubt on his sincerity. But whether he will even be able to sustain himself, who shall vouch? I trust he will. I believe it highly desirable for the peace of France, and the harmony of Europe, that he should. I have little doubt, should his government be overturned, it would be followed by disastrous consequences, not unworthy the high breach of faith toward the United States, with which the war against it seems to have commenced.

Sir, I reciprocate the sentiment of the Chairman of the Committee; I hope the House will act with unanimity on this subject. I trust we shall not allow ourselves to split on any subordinate questions. That of the present reference surely ought not to divide us. On a question of such great magnitude—if things are to go to extremes—it cannot be expected nor asked, that, on every point involved, all should think alike. Independent men, on such points, must differ. Those who think for themselves, that is, who think at all, must differ to some extent, on such subjects. But if the worst come to the worst—if France shall make up her mind to withhold justice from us deliberately and conclusively, and in such a manner that true policy and honor will no longer admit of delay and forbearance, then, sir, I believe, whatever difference of opinion there may be as to any point of secondary consequence, that Congress and the country will move unanimously in the direction which its rights and honor shall point out.

But I think we should do nothing by way of anticipating that contingency. It may never arrive. Every man, I will not say of common humanity, but of common sense, in the U. States and France, must hope it never will arrive. When it does, there will be no division of feeling. I am satisfied from the expression of opinion here, and of public sentiment throughout the country, that we shall come to this result; and however this matter of the reference may be disposed of, (which at this late stage of the session, I regard as of diminished importance,) I believe that in a firm resolution to stand on our rights, under the treaty, we shall be unanimous.

Mr. GILMER said he felt himself called on to say a word in reply to the gentleman from Massachusetts, (Mr. Adams.) There were one or two reasons why he could not vote for the proposition of that gentleman; which seemed to be predicated on the belief that there was an immediate necessity for action on the part of the House. Now, he believed this to be the first proper point of inquiry—whether such a necessity existed; and if it did exist—what was to be the nature of the action. The House must be in possession of facts on which to ground their proceeding, before it could proceed with propriety. Had France refused ultimately the indemnity stipulated in the treaty? We should act definitely on no other ground; otherwise, our action became premature, untimely, and calculated to do wrong rather than obtain right. The question of peace and war involved the individual interests of mankind. Our country and her institutions were so constituted, that forbearance and pacific measures were their most prominent characteristics. Every opposite sentiment prematurely thrown out here, therefore, had a tendency to injure the character of the nation. Much had been said of national honor: he asked what were the law of national honor? That subject would do for the vaporing of crowned heads; but when this matter was brought to its point, and the country involved in war, it would be found it was not then to be sustained by flourishes of rhetoric. He would again repeal his impression that this House could not act on this subject without a full knowledge how far our national rights were involved. He asked gentlemen if they were aware that this very treaty did not sustain our national honor? The spoliations on our commerce were incident to the Berlin and Milan decrees. Did this treaty—did the indemnity heal the wounds inflicted on our national honor? Having waited the length of time we had already done, Mr. G. asked how the Committee on Foreign Affairs could express to this House the course it ought to pursue, without itself having before it any new facts on which to act. We could do nothing until we knew something further of the proceedings of France—either for the honor of the House, or of the nation.

Mr. STEWART suggested the propriety of giving the committee a longer period than the 16th, but allow them to report sooner if they could; he would say till the 20th of February. While up, he would take occasion to say, in reply to the gentleman from Georgia, that the House was not prepared to act until it had learned what was the decision of the French Chamber, that it might act provisionally if not definitively, for war was not the only alternative to coerce France. We might not only declare war and issue letters of marque and reprisal, but we may pass a non-intercourse law with her; we may impose prohibitory duties; indeed, there were various modes in which we might coerce France without resorting to an open declaration of war. Supposing either of these last were adopted before the adjournment of Congress, in case France did not fulfil the stipulations of the treaty, we should throw upon her the whole responsibility. Besides, how much would she suffer? Our imports from her amounted to between fifteen and twenty millions of dollars, and was it likely for the petty sum of five millions that she would risk the loss of such a trade by our passage of a non-intercourse act? By acting provisionally we should throw the responsibility upon her, and he recommended that course. At least, he trusted that Congress would not suffer the session to pass by without some declaration of its will.

Mr. HAMER moved the House adjourn.

On a division, there appeared for the motion 73, against it 108. So the House refused to adjourn.

Mr. HAMER then renewed his motion to strike out all that part of the motion of Mr. Adams which went to instruct the Committee.

Mr. ADAMS remarked that the instructions were all that the motion aimed at, and he should consider the adoption of the amendment as a virtual rejection of the motion.

Mr. CAMBRELENG moved that the time be extended to the 20th instant, for the Committee to report. He said, in order to meet the views of all, he was induced to make the motion.

Mr. ARCHER said he could not consent to vote to give any positive instructions to the Committee; and he put it to the gentlemen from Massachusetts and Virginia (Messrs. Adams and Patton) to say whether we ought not, under all the circumstances, to hold ourselves untrammelled, to act as emergencies might direct a fortnight hence? Suppose the contingency alluded to by the gentleman from Massachusetts (Mr. Everett) that we should have the most untoward accounts from France that could possibly be anticipated;—must the House then wait until the 20th instant, before acting? Such could not be their wish. He repeated, they could gain nothing, and might lose much of their object by persisting in their instructions to the Committee.

Mr. CLAY asked for a division of the question, viz. that that part going to instruct the Committee be taken separately.

Mr. J. Q. ADAMS asked for the yeas and nays, but they were not ordered.

Mr. PATTON, in reply to the suggestion of his colleague, (Mr. Archer,) said that he apprehended his colleague must labor under some misunderstanding of the character and effect of the proposition of the gentleman from Massachusetts. That proposition did not propose, and its adoption could not commit, or trammel, or fetter the action of the House in the slightest; it did not even interfere with the judgment of the committee, as to what should constitute the tenor and character of their report; all that was done was to require them to report by Monday week. He thought, therefore, that full justice was not done to the motion of the gentleman from Massachusetts, when it was said that the adoption of his motion would be equivalent to a declaration of war. I, said Mr. P., am as little inclined as the gentlemen from Georgia (Mr. Gilmer) and Virginia (Mr. Archer) are now, and under the present state of the subject, and of our information, to adopt the measure of reprisal, or any other measure of self redress. But I think we ought to take the subject into consideration, and decide whether we will await the definite action of the French Chambers. Inauspicious as the present aspect of affairs certainly is, Mr. P. said he would still refrain from taking any measure of hostility against France; he would show the utmost possible forbearance, and every just dependence upon her justice. In the hope, with the possibility that France would not persevere, he would still await the issue, "prepared for either fortune," with a proper reliance upon the honor and integrity of France to do us right, and a firm and steady conviction that we need not—cannot—must not submit to wrong, flagrant, grievous, persevered in, and unredressed.

Mr. CAMBRELENG said his only object in proposing the modification of the motion of the gentleman from Massachusetts (Mr. Adams) was to prevent further debate. Failing in that object, and finding many of his friends disposed to send the communications to the Committee without instructions, he would withdraw his proposition.

The question was then taken on Mr. HAMER'S motion to strike out that part of Mr. Adams's proposition going to instruct the Committee on Foreign Affairs to report, &c., and agreed to without a division.

The motion to refer the message of the President, and the accompanying despatches, to the said Committee, was then agreed to, and they were ordered to be printed.

On motion of Mr. VANDERPOEL,

The House then adjourned.

IN SENATE.

MONDAY, FEB. 9, 1835.

Mr. SOUTHARD submitted the following resolutions, which, on his motion, were considered and agreed to:

Resolved, That the Postmaster General be directed to lay before the Senate, estimates of the amount of money necessary for the service of the General Post Office for one year from the 1st day of January, 1835.

Resolved, That the Postmaster General be directed to lay before the Senate a statement of the debts owing by the General Post Office on the 1st day of January, 1835, exhibiting the name and residence of each creditor—the amount due to each creditor—the time or times when the said debt was contracted in each case—and the cause, service, or consideration for which each debt was contracted—and whether the same was contracted for service rendered upon a bid and contract made in conformity with the public advertisements, or upon a bid and contract not in conformity with the public advertisements, or for extra allowances upon the contracts which were executed.

Mr. HILL submitted the following resolutions:

Resolved, That all the responsibilities and debts incurred by the Postmaster General in executing that part of his duty, prescribed by a law of Congress, which requires that he shall "provide for the carriage of the mail on all post roads that are or may be established by law," and "that he shall pay all expenses which may arise in conducting the Post Office, and in the conveyance of the mail, and all other necessary expenses arising on the collection of the revenues and management of the Gerneral Post Office," are good and valid and binding on the Department of the General Post Office; that the faith of the said Department is lawfully pledged to the discharge of all such debts to the full amount of its receipts; and that any law of Congress, which shall divert those receipts to any other purpose than the discharge of such debts, while any shall remain unpaid, will be unjust and improper.

Resolved, That the law of the United States (with the exception of unproductive routes, as particularly specified,) leaves it entirely in the discretion of the Postmaster General how often, and in what manner, whether in carriages, by single horses, or otherwise, the mail of the United States shall be carried over post roads established by law.

Resolved, That the Secretary of the Senate be instructed to report the aggregate of the expense that has been incurred by the Committee on the Post Office and Post Roads, over and above the ordinary pay during each session of the members of said Committee, as Senators—distinguishing the amount expended during the session of the Senate from the amount expended during the recess—the daily pay, and pay for travel, allowed to their Secretary, Clerks, or accountants, and all other persons by them employed, or called on as witnesses—designating the per diem, travel, and amount paid to each individual by name.

Mr. KING, of Alabama, pursuant to notice, and on leave given, introduced a bill making an appropriation for the erection of a light-house on Mobile Point, and placing buoys in Mobile Bay; which, on his motion, was read twice, considered as in Committee of the Whole, and ordered to be engrossed for a third reading.

Mr. NAUDAIN, from the Committee on Claims, made unfavorable reports upon the memorials of John C. Fitzpatrick and James Nicholson, and the Committee were discharged from the further consideration of those subjects.

Mr. MOORE, from the Committee on the Public Lands, to which was referred a memorial from the Legislature of Alabama, on the subject, reported a bill authorizing the citizens of townships where the 16th section has been disposed of, to enter other lands in lieu thereof; which was read the first time, and ordered to a second reading.

Mr. BENTON, from the Committee on Military Affairs, reported a bill for the relief of Catharine E. Clitherel, widow of Dr. George Clitherel; which was read the first time and ordered to a second reading.

Mr. CALHOUN, from the Select Committee to which was referred the resolution directing an inquiry into the extent of Executive patronage, and the expediency and practicability of reducing the same, &c., made a report in part, accompanied by a bill to regulate the deposites of the public money in the State banks. Also, a joint resolution recommending an alteration of the constitution, so as to allow the distribution of the surplus revenue accruing for the coming seven years, among the several States. The Committee also reported the following resolution:

Resolved, That the Secretary of the Treasury be directed to report to the Senate, at the commencement of the next session of Congress, what duties under twenty per cent. ad valorem, as provided by the sixth section of the act of the 2d of March, 1833, entitled "an act to modiy the act of the 14th of July, 1832, and all other acts imposing duties on imports," can be reduced or repealed consistently with a due regard to the manufacturing interest; and an estimate of the probable amount of the reduction.

Mr. CALHOUN moved that the joint resolution have a second reading at this time, for the purpose of reference.

Mr. BENTON objected, when the bill to regulate the deposites was read twice, and on motion of Mr. CALHOUN, made the special order of the day for Thurday next.

Mr. CALHOUN then moved that the report just read, be printed, together with the report of the Select Committee of 1826, on the the same subject, for the use of the Senate.

Mr. POINDEXTER rose, he said, for the purpose of making an additional motion for printing *thirty thousand extra* copies of the report now made, and the same number of the report made in 1826 on the same subject. He was, he said, deeply impressed with the view of the subject taken by the committee. For one, he begged leave to return his thanks to them for their labors. The question now submitted to the nation was, whether power is to be perpetuated in the hands of him who now wields it, and the one he may select as his successor. A misplaced confidence prevailed throughout this country; the people were slow to believe that the man in whom they confided with the utmost confidence, should be capable of such unheard-of encroachments upon the liberties of the country, whose destinies were now unhappily lodged in his hands. This view of Executive patronage, arising from its own constructions of power, was most alarming and dangerous. The doctrines of the Protest, so called, claimed for the Executive, the entire control of the public treasures, of the public property, and the performance of all the public duties, and by virtue of powers pre-existing before the Constitution of the United States.

The President claimed the exercise of these powers under that part of the constitution, which declares, that all executive power shall be vested in the President. But the knowing ones fearing these doctrines might not be as palatable to the People as was expected, contrived to send forth a kind of supplementary message. Congress may legislate concerning the public property, but the President reserved by his veto, an absolute control over the whole, as the individual representative of the government, although 40,000 aids have been given him, to whom he claims, they alone are responsible. The constitution gives him no authority over the public treasure other than to draw his quarter salary and to spend it as he pleases. How did he then get hold of them? Why by removal and appointment. By this means the President put his fingers into the public treasures and distributed them to whom he pleased. If the King of England, said Mr. P. should mete out the public treasures in this manner, giving a favor now to Manchester, now to London, now to one, and now to another—if he should take such a course his head would pay the forfeit. But we in this country had suffered the President to take possession of the Treasury without the least resistance. And why was it? Because the mass of the country was purchased up to support every thing, right or wrong. By means of his power of removal, the President had not only all the other departments of government under his control, but also, even the Judicial Department. He had only to remove those who dared to disobey, and appoint those who would yield to his will. Mr. P. concluded by expressing his thanks to the committee for the investigation they had made.

Mr. KING, of Georgia said, that if he declined following the Senator from Mississippi through the range he had taken on the wrongful exercise of Executive power, he hoped he would find a sufficient apology in the fact, that in no part of the report was the President's construction of the Constitution doubted. He hoped also, he might be pardoned for the suggestion, that the Committee did not expect a discussion of such a character, on the presentation of the report. Not knowing—or rather having forgotten, that the report would probably be presented this morning, he had neglected to furnish himself with some information which would be necessary to sustain him in a few comments which he intended to make upon some branches of the report, and which he should make on a future occasion. But the motion which had been made, seemed to call attention now to one feature of the report. Sir, said Mr. K., I wish it expressly understood that I am in favor of a reduction of the expenses of this Government. And whenever a reasonable proposition was made, from the north or south; from any part or any party, the object of which was to effect this desirable end, he was prepared to concur in it; and that, said Mr. K. is the very reason I am opposed to this motion which was to print 20,000—(some one near mentioned 30,000.) 30,000 declared Mr. K. was more than he had understood it. He had the same objection to 30,000, that he had to the printing of 30 millions. That objection was, that it was an abominable waste of the public treasure. What was the subject of our deliberation? It was the wasteful expenditure of the public money, as well as executive patronage, which in fact only grew out of it.

If, then, said Mr. K., the expenses of the government have lately increased to an enormous extent?—If they have greatly increased between 1825 and 1833, as stated in the report, which he believed to be true—his intention was, when the report came up again, to show where the increase originated, and was determined that the responsibility should rest where it ought to rest, and was not to be attributed to the Executive. What a spectacle did this exhibit from day to day? The Senate had been a week making war on the *extras* of the Post Office Department. They were now warring against the extravagance of the Executive, and whilst brandishing the sword in one hand in defence of the public treasure, against the ravages of the Executive, we were with the other slipping it into our own pockets, or scattering it in profuse and wasteful extravagance.' Mr. K., after enumerating a few features in the report which he intended hereafter briefly to comment upon, principally in the language and reasoning, said it was not his purpose further to trouble the Senate at that time upon the merits of the report, in the conclusions of which he mainly agreed. He concluded by a hope that the extraordinary number of extra copies proposed by the Senator from Mississippi, would not be agreed to, as every copy over 5,000 for distribution would be useless waste, as the report was short, and before even 5,000 extras could be printed, it would be in all respectable journals in the United States. He said he had another objection to the printing of so large a number. It would counteract a principal object of the committee who wished to avoid giving a party character to the report. These orders for printing so large a number of extras, he said were looked upon generally as efforts to give a party importance to the document, and nine times out of ten, it was the object of such orders. He hoped the Senator himself, on reflection, would consent to 5,000 ex-

tion, which he thought as many as would answer any useful purpose.

Mr. BENTON spoke for nearly two hours on the subject of the report. [We hope to be able to give a full report of his speech at some future day.]

Mr. LEIGH rose and said that the credit or discredit of originating the proposition to divide the surplus revenue among the States, did not belong to this Committee, but to the President of the United States. Mr. L. said his attention was turned to the Message, in consequence of the speech of the honorable gentleman from Missouri. [Mr. L. here read extracts from the President's Message of 1830-'31.]

Mr. CALHOUN rose: He had but little to say; he intended only to allude to that part of the subject which seemed especially pointed at himself. He had been blamed, he said, for not going into the cause of the evil and showing the manner in which these abuses had sprung up. He did not wish to quote opinions, nor plunge into the history of the past, it was unnecessary,—the abuses did exist, and the honorable Senator (Mr. Benton) had acknowledged it. That honorable Senator had raised his voice against it in its infancy; and why was he now silent on the increase of that power to such enormous magnitude? It was matter of astonishment that the honorable Senator did not step forth and stem the overwhelming current.

Mr. C. went on to show that a large surplus would be left in the Treasury, after defraying the expenses of the Government. He said there would be $8,000,000 remaining; and contended that the report of the Secretary of the Treasury was fallacious—that it was intended to retain large sums in the treasury.

Mr. C. then explained the manner in which he had made his calculations for retrenchments; that he had made the year 1823 the basis of his estimate. He disclaimed any intention to excite party feelings; he was anxious to be silent as to party; he only looked to the future; if he had unconsciously stepped on party grounds, he only took facts as he found them. He denied ever having joined in prophesying national bankruptcy—on the contrary he had, during the last session, calculated the revenues arising from duties to exceed 16 millions.

Before he set down, Mr. C. said, he would acknowledge the compliment, paid to the report by the motion to print so large a number. For himself he was not anxious as to the number; he would leave it to his friends to decide.

The motion to print was then reduced to the number usually presented, the report of 1826, and 10,000 extra copies of that just presented.

Upon this question, Mr. HILL demanded the yeas and nays; which were ordered, and are as follow:

YEAS—Messrs. Benton, Bibb, Black, Brown, Buchanan, Calhoun, Cuthbert, Ewing, Goldsborough, Grundy, Hendricks, Kane, King of Alabama, Leigh, Linn, McKean, Mangum, Naudain, Poindexter, Porter, Robbins, Robinson, Silsbee, Smith, Southard, Tipton, Tomlinson, Tyler, White—29.

NAYS—Messrs. Hill, King of Georgia, Morris, Shepley, Tallmadge, Wright—6.

The Senate then adjourned.

HOUSE OF REPRESENTATIVES.

MONDAY, Feb. 9, 1835.

On motion of Mr. SEVIER, a bill from the Senate for the completion of certain roads in the Territory of Arkansas, was read twice, and committed to the Committee of Ways and Means.

Petitions and memorials were presented by—
Mr. PARKS, of Maine;
Mr. HUBBARD, of New Hampshire;
Messrs. EVERETT, GORHAM, and REED, of Massachusetts;
Messrs. PEARCE and BURGES, of Rhode Island;
Messrs. BARBER, JACKSON, and YOUNG, of Connecticut;
Messrs. PEARSON, CAMBRELENG, CRAMER, TURRILL, HARD, HUNTINGTON, CLAY, HAZELTINE, and MANN, of New York;
[Mr. MANN, of New York, presented the me-

morial of H. Sternberg, of the State of New York, praying for the passage of a law to reward him for certain discoveries which he represents he has made in Medical Philosophy. Referred to the Committee on the Judiciary.]

Messrs. HIESTER, MUHLENBERG, BANKS, GALBRAITH, McKENNAN, BINNEY, WATMOUGH, SUTHERLAND, HARPER, and BEAUMONT, of Pennsylvania;
Messrs. HEATH, THOMAS, and McKIM, of Maryland;
Messrs. CHINN, WISE, and ARCHER, of Virginia;
Messrs. SPEIGHT and W. B. SHEPARD, of North Carolina;
Messrs. MARSHALL, POPE, LYON, and JOHNSON, of Kentucky;
[Mr. LYON, of Kentucky, presented the petition of Alexander McDaniel, Leonard Jones, and others, who profess to have attained the power of endless existence on this earth, and praying for a grant of public land on the Mississippi, whereupon to erect a city of refuge; the grant to extend only during the natural life of McDaniel, who is now 64 years of age, and in case of his death to revert to the government, with all the improvements thereon. The petition was referred to the Committee on Public Lands, and ordered to be printed.]

Messrs. DICKINSON and DUNLAP, of Tennessee;
[Mr. DUNLAP, after stating the substance of the petition, informed the House this was the third petition he had presented to the House on the same subject—that the letter accompanying the petition informed him that of all the persons at the date of the letter in the hospital at Memphis, there was not one of them a citizen of Tennessee. He moved the reference of the petition to a Committee of the Whole House on the state of the Union, who had charge of the bill providing for the establishment of a marine hospital at Baltimore, Memphis, and other places; which reference was accordingly made.]

Messrs. MITCHELL, THOMSON, PATTERSON, VINTON, BELL, WEBSTER, and CRANE, of Ohio;
[Mr. MITCHELL presented additional testimony in relation to the claim of Adam Smith, for work and labor done on the Cumberland road, west of Louisiana, in the State of Ohio. He also presented the memorial of Seth Adams, of Zanesville, praying indemnity for French spoliations prior to the year 1800; which were referred to appropriate committees.]

[Mr. PATTERSON presented a petition for a mail route from Tiffin to Sandusky City, in the State of Ohio. Also, the claims of Henry St. John, of the State of Ohio, asking indemnity for the loss of a horse during the last war.]

[On motion of Mr. THOMSON, of Ohio, a statement of Mr. Gill, engineer, giving a description of the merits of the summit of the Bandy and Beaver canal, compared with the licking summit of the Ohio canal, was referred to the Committee on Roads and Canals, and ordered to be printed.]

Mr. JOHNSON, of Louisiana;
Messrs. CARR, KINNARD, and HANNEGAN, of Indiana;
[Mr. CARR presented a memorial and joint resolution of the Legislature of the State of Indiana, soliciting measures to be taken to extinguish the Indian title to lands in said State, and to remove the Indians from her border; which was referred to the Committee on Indian Affairs.]

[Mr. KINNARD presented a joint resolution of the General Assembly of Indiana, recommending the establishment of an agency at Indianapolis, for the payment of pensioners.

Also, additional documents in support of the petition of James Calvin.

Also, the petition of citizens of Indiana, for the establishment of a post route therein mentioned.]

[Mr. HANNEGAN presented the petition of Mrs. Mary Becket, for arrears of pension due her late husband, Humphrey Becket, deceased; which was referred to the Committee on Revolutionary Claims.]

Messrs. CAGE and PLUMMER, of Mississippi;

Messrs. CASEY, REYNOLDS, and MAY, of Illinois;
[Mr. CASEY introduced the memorial of the Legislature of Illinois, praying the establishment of a Surveyor General's office for the State; which, on his motion, was referred to the same committee of the whole House on the state of the Union, to which was referred the "bill to establish a Surveyor General's office for the State of Illinois."

Mr. CASEY also presented a memorial of the Legislature of Illinois, praying the privilege of relinquishing sections numbered 16, where they are found to be unfit for cultivation, and locating other lands in lieu thereof; which was referred to the Committee on the Public Lands.]

[Mr. REYNOLDS presented a memorial from the General Assembly of the State of Illinois, praying the Congress of the United States to establish a public road from Shawneetown in Illinois, to St. Louis, in Missouri. The memorial states, that lands over which this road is to pass, have been in market for many years, and remain unsold—that a road in this section of the State would be the means of bringing those lands into market, and thereby be of service to the General Government—that the U. S. mail is now conveyed on this road from Shawneetown to St. Louis, and that it is a great burden on the people to keep said road in repair for stages—that on this consideration the General Government would be induced to assist in the repair of said road.]

[Mr. MAY presented a joint resolution of the Legislature of the State of Illinois, asking a further donation of land, to aid the State in effecting a communication between Lake Michigan and the Illinois river.

Also, a joint resolution from the same body, praying that the provisions of the pre-emption law of 1834 be extended to all persons now settled upon the public lands; which resolutions, on his motion, were referred to the Committee on Public Lands.]

Mr. MARDIS, of Alabama.
Which petitions and memorials were appropriately referred.

On motion of Mr. CHILTON,
Resolved, That the Committee on the Post Office and Post Roads be instructed to inquire into the expediency of establishing a post route from Monroe Post Office, in Hart County, Kentucky, to Lafayette, in Barren county, and thence to Gretna Green, in Green county, of the same State.

On motion of Mr. MARSHALL,
Resolved, That the Committee on Claims be instructed to inquire into the propriety of allowing payment to William Jones, for a horse lost in the service of the United States during the late war, and that the evidences relating thereto, which were referred to said Committee at the last session of Congress, together with those now presented, be referred to said Committee.

On motion of Mr. VINTON,
Resolved, That the Committee on Public Buildings be instructed to inquire into the expediency of extending the public square on which the Capitol is situated, westwardly to the foot of the slope descending towards the canal.

On motion of Mr. WEBSTER,
Resolved, That the Committee on the Post Office and Post Roads be instructed to inquire into the expediency of establishing a mail route from Dayton, Ohio, by Liberty, Farmersville, Winchester, and Newcome, to Oxford, in the same State.

On motion of Mr. JOHNSON, of Louisiana,
Resolved, That the Committee on the Post Office and Post Roads be instructed to inquire into the expediency of providing by law for the transportation of a daily mail between New Orleans and Mobile.

Resolved, That the Committee on Roads and Canals be instructed to inquire into the expediency of making an appropriation to survey the route designated for a rail road, from Point Coupee to Opelousas Court-house, in this State of Louisiana.

On motion of Mr. REYNOLDS,
Resolved, That the Committee on Revolutionary Pensions be instructed to inquire into the expediency of creating, in the State of Illinois, one other

Pension Agency, so that there will be two Agencies in that State.

Mr. HEATH offered the following resolution, which, under the rule, lies one day:

Resolved, That the Secretary of State be requested to communicate to this House such information as his Department may possess, and copies of any correspondence that may have taken place between this Government, or any of its agents, with the European Governments, on the subjects of their quarantine regulations.

On motion of Mr. McCARTY,

Resolved, That the Committee on Claims be instructed to inquire into the expediency of granting indemnity to Samuel C. Duncan, for losses by him sustained, on a contract for excavations and fillings on the east and west banks of the east branch of White water on the Cumberland Road, in Indiana, and that the papers on the files of the House, presented at the last session of Congress, upon this subject, be again referred to said committee.

Mr. LUCAS offered the following resolutions, which, under the rule, lies one day:

Resolved, That the Secretary of War be requested to report to this House, what officers, if any, have been taken from the line of the army and commissioned in the general staff, with rank therein since the re-organization of the army, under the act entitled "An act to reduce and fix the Military Peace Establishment, approved March 2, 1821, and in such form as to show the rank and date of appointments in the staff, the regimental rank and date of commissions, when taken from the line, and if promoted in their regiments whilst holding rank in the staff, the same to be specified.

Resolved, also, That the Secretary of War inform this House what regimental officers now hold appointments in the general staff of the army, if any, which do not confer rank in such manner as to show the denominations and date of such staff appointments, as well as the rank and dates of commissions in their respective regiments.

Mr. McKINLEY, on leave, submitted the following resolution:

Resolved, That this House will, on Thursday next, proceed to the election of printer to the House of Representatives of the next Congress.

Mr. ROBERTSON said he hoped the resolution would not be adopted. A few days ago, he had himself offered a resolution providing for the abolition of the office of printer, both to the House of Representatives and the Senate of the United States, and he hoped it would be the pleasure of the House to consider this resolution before proceeding to adopt that of the gentleman from Alabama, binding the House to proceed to the election of this officer on a given day. If it were the pleasure of the House, Mr. R. would regard it incumbent upon him, at that time, to submit to the House, briefly and concisely, the views which had lead him to the conclusion that the office in question ought to be abolished, and which would recommend his own resolution to the favorable attention of the House.

The CHAIR remarked that it would not be in order, the subject under consideration being the resolution of the gentleman from Alabama.

Mr. ROBERTSON asked leave of the House to proceed.

The CHAIR said the gentleman might proceed to offer any remarks applicable to the resolution just presented.

Mr. ROBERTSON was not aware of the precise mode by which he could attain his object, but he had supposed it would be in order, in discussing the propriety of the resolution offered by the gentleman from Alabama, to show what was the purpose of one, relating to the same subject, offered by himself on Saturday. The more so, as the latter proposed to abolish the office itself, for the appointment of which the other had set apart a given time. He should not occupy much time in urging the reasons which had induced him to propose that resolution to the House.

There were a few considerations that at once presented themselves in connexion with this question. It had been said, that there was, in point of fact, no such office as that of printer to the House, or printer to the Senate; that it was nothing more than a mere contract; and that the mode of appointment, by which he was elected annually or biennially, was nothing more than the designation of the individual with whom the contract was made. To his mind, however, it appeared to possess all the features that constituted an officer, in its most comprehensive sense; like other officers, he was regularly nominated, brought into competition with other candidates, and was elected by regular ballot—in this point of view he was an officer, and the question then presented itself which was amply discussed on a former day, whether he was properly an officer belonging to the Government of the United States, or a peculiar officer of the respective Houses to which they were elected. If he be an officer of the Government, he can only be so from being designated as such in the constitution of the United States, or because he had been, under the constitution, created by law. Now, the printer to either House of Congress was not a constitutional officer of the United States, because he was no where designated in that instrument; nor, so far as Mr. R. was able to find, was there any law by which he had been made such. There was certainly a joint resolution of the two Houses, providing for the time and manner of his election, but a resolution was no law, and ought not to be regarded as of the same force. The constitutional provision authorizing the creation of offices by law, could not be set aside or obviated by a mere resolution.

The next question was, whether the printer to the House was a peculiar officer of the House itself?

The constitution authorized each House to elect its own officers, but that provision never could have contemplated the right in each House to create as many officers as they choose. It could only have referred to such officers as were necessary and essential to the organization of the body, and over which they must necessarily have control; such were the speaker, the clerk, sergeant-at-arms, &c. Was the public printer an officer of this description? Could we pretend that he was? We could not. For the first thirty years of our government the House had been regularly organized without any such officer—but what was the argument on the other side? Why that the public printing must be provided for by law, and that Congress must necessarily have its printing executed. He freely acknowledged that there was a necessity that Congress should have its printing executed, but it was equally necessary that Congress should have a room, and that that room should be furnished with seats, stationary, &c. for their use; but it did not, therefore, follow that they must elect officers under the designations of architect, stationer, and upholsterer, to each House. But even were it so, that the printer was regarded as the peculiar officer of the House, there arose this objection, which he had never yet heard answered, although often urged in that House. What right had one Congress to elect an officer who was a peculiar officer of the House, to hold his office at the ensuing Congress? They would have as much right to elect the speaker, clerk, sergeant-at-arms, or chaplain, as the printer, if he be considered an officer of the House.

But there were even more important objections to the adoption of the resolution of the gentleman from Alabama than those founded on the constitutional right of that House to create or fill such an office as that of public printer, and which would be removed by the adoption of that offered by Mr. R. on Saturday. It would remove from that House, what he thought very essential should long ago have been removed from it, the ground of the strong party excitement that always took place, and produced such angry discussion for the mastery of the public press, by one or the other of the contending parties. Mr. S. conceived the public printing ought to be provided for in such a manner, that he who looked to it should look to it only as concerned the public good, and the only thing to be looked to by that House should be the conduct of the printer, not for the benefit of any political party, but for the benefit of the community. His plan would do this; and if adopted, would avoid what invariably took place, an excited debate and an angry discussion, calculated to do no good, but productive of the reverse. He was for placing the office in the hands of him who would execute the duty best. Why was it that they did not find it necessary, in regard to other contracts, or essential for the good government of the country, to elect other officers upon party principles? Mr. R. would have the press as the constitution of his country intended it should be, free and unshackled—not merely free from the force and influence of the Government, but free from that more dangerous influence to be exerted by means of the public money. He would have the press untrammelled, unshackled, the palladium of our liberty and of our rights, and no longer the vehicle of dirty abuse and disgusting slander. The press should be protected from the effects of this influence, as well as from that patronage exerted by different branches of the Government. What could be expected from a printer to the House, to the Senate, and to the Executive or the Administration, but that every abuse committed by every one of these departments would be overlooked or vindicated by the printer to each? There was no doubt that the public press of this country would be at all times sufficiently under the control of party; but he trusted in God that parties would be allowed to fight their own battles by themselves, and not have the influence and patronage of the Government thrown in their way.

Upon these grounds, and solely upon these grounds, said Mr. R., he had submitted his proposition on Saturday last; and in doing so, he looked to the support of no printer of any party. It proposed to distribute the printing among those who would faithfully execute the work, and he hoped the resolution offered that morning would not be received; and he would also beg leave to state, that a motion was then pending in the other branch to dispense with the joint resolution under which the printer to that body was elected.

The CHAIR said it was not in order to allude to the proceedings of the other House.

Mr. R. said he had merely adverted to the fact; and having said all he intended, he again reiterated the hope that the House would not adopt the resolution of the gentleman from Alabama.

Mr. SUTHERLAND moved to amend the resolution by inserting the words "*viva voce*."

Mr. McKINLEY accepted the amendment.

Mr. McKINLEY then proceeded. He did not know that it was necessary at that time to enter into a discussion upon the question whether the printer to the House of Representatives was an officer or not; or to inquire whether a joint resolution had the force and validity of a law.

Mr. C. ALLAN called for the orders of the day, but the House did not second the motion, the hour devoted to morning business not having expired.

Mr. McKINLEY resumed. It was a little singular, that whenever this question came up, there was always a disposition by those who had not the power to elect, to interrupt its course by raising the question that it was not proper for one Congress to elect a printer for the ensuing one. He would admit that this House had not the right to impose a printer upon the next House of Representatives against its will; and he would freely admit that it belonged exclusively to the House of Representatives to elect their own officers, and that had always been his opinion, and he would go further and say he believed that the next House would have the right to accept or reject the printer elected for them as they might think fit. But as the present practice had existed for some fifteen or sixteen years, during six or seven Congresses, why should they now all at once stop in proceeding to this election merely because a portion of an opposition think otherwise? Mr. McK. then alluded to what he had understood had fallen from Mr. Robertson, with reference to the impropriety of electing editors of newspapers, and said he considered it a question altogether for those who elected the printer, and saw no reason why they should be proscribed, whether he was the editor of a paper or not.

Mr. ROBERTSON explained, and said he must have been misapprehended, for neither in his remarks nor in the resolution, had he contem-

plated any proscription. He asked leave that the resolutions be read, and

Mr. McKINLEY giving way, they were read accordingly.

Mr. M'KINLEY continued. He may have misapprehended a part of the language of the resolution, but he believed himself correct, that the gentleman in his remarks complained that public patronage ought not to be extended to editors of newspapers. It seemed, however, that if the printer were not a friend of the administration, there was no danger of his being bribed. Indeed, experience had proved that the gentleman was mistaken, for he thought the present printers to this House could not be charged with undue partiality to the present administration. He still believed the House of Representatives to be the proper body to designate their own printer, according to the resolutions of 1819 and 27. The duties of the officer might be prescribed by Congress, but the House has the right to choose the printer, and any printer in the United States had the right of being a candidate for the office, whether he was the editor of a newspaper or not.

Mr. McK., after some further remarks, said he felt disposed to go into the election of a public printer; and he hoped that one friendly to the sound Administration would be appointed. He he maintained the principle of electing that officer also now.

The discussion of the resolution was here arrested by a motion, by Mr. C. ALLAN, to proceed to the consideration of the Orders of the Day; which carried.

Mr. McKINLEY, from the Committee of Ways and Means, reported, without amendment, the bill on the Senate to provide for completing certain roads in the Territory of Arkansas.

The SPEAKER laid before the House the following message from the President of the United States; which was referred to the Committee on a Public Lands:

WASHINGTON, February 6, 1835.

To the House of Representatives:

I submit to Congress a Report from the Secretary of War, containing the evidence of certain claims, reservations under the 14th Article of the treaty of 1830, with the Choctaws, which the locating Agent has reserved from sale, in conformity with instructions from the President, who did not consider himself authorized to direct this location.

Should Congress consider the claims just, it will be proper to pass a law authorizing their location, or satisfying them in some other way.

ANDREW JACKSON.

Mr. PLUMMER said, that at the last session of Congress, the Committee of Public Lands on the part of the Senate, were instructed to investigate the conduct of the Land Offices in Mississippi, and the Chairman of that Committee was authorized to conduct the investigation during the recess. The result of that investigation has been reported to the Senate, and is contained in Senate document No 22. Among other matters inquired into during the investigation, was the conduct of Col. George W. Martin, the Agent who made the location referred to, in the message just read. His character, where his conduct is not known, has suffered under the charge. Mr. P. had read the testimony, and so far as he was capable of judging; from a thorough examination of the subject, considered, that the Agent stood honorably acquitted, from anything like fraudulent or improper conduct in the discharge of his duties. To prevent the charge of fraud against the Agent from being raised, to the prejudice of the claimants, and at the conduct of the Agent may be fully before a Committee in its aggravated form, he moved it so much of the testimony as related to the local conduct of Col. Martin, be referred to the a Committee to which the message of the President had been referred.

The motion was agreed to.

Mr. DICKINSON suggested that the reference it made, more properly belonged to the Committee on Indian Affairs, particularly, as subjects connected with it, were already before that Committee. He would move that the papers be referred to the Committee on Indian Affairs, instead of the Committee on Public Lands.

The CHAIR said, this could only be done by unanimous consent, or by a reconsideration of the vote referring the subject to the Committee on the Public Lands.

Mr. PLUMMER objected to the motion.

Mr. CAGE moved a reconsideration of the vote.

Mr. PLUMMER thought the Committee on Public Lands the most appropriate reference, and should therefore vote against a reconsideration, but had no particular objections to the subject going to the Committee on Indian Affairs, if that should be the desire of the House.

The motion to reconsider prevailed, and the documents were referred to the Committee on Indian Affairs.

On motion of Mr. PLUMMER, the vote taken on referring the testimony taken before the Committee of the Senate, was reconsidered, and the same referred to the Committee on Indian Affairs.

The following bills from the Senate were read twice, and committed:

A bill in addition to an act for the relief of: the legal representatives of Lucy Bond and Hannah Douglass; and

A bill for the relief of Duncan L. Clinch.

The amendments proposed by the Senate to the resolution from the House to provide for the sale of the lion and two horses presented to the American Consul at Tangiers by the Emperor of Morocco, were concurred in.

The following bills were read the third time, and passed:

A bill from the Senate to continue the office of Commissioner of Pensions;

A bill amendatory of the act for the continuation of the Cumberland Road;

A bill to change the time of holding the District Courts of the United States for the Western District of Virginia, holden at Clarksburg;

A bill to establish a pension agency south of Green river, in the State of Kentucky;

A bill making an appropriation for the purchase of 200 copies of the _fac simile_ accounts of Gen. Washington;

A bill for the benefit of John Cullins;

A bill granting a pension to Amasa A. Tifft;

A bill for the relief of Harvey Reynolds and John Casey;

A bill for the relief of Josiah Westlake;

A bill granting a pension to Isaac Janvier;

A bill for the relief of Josiah H. Brown and John Conkin;

And a bill to restore to certain invalid pensioners the amount of pensions by them relinquished.

On motion of Mr. HUBBARD, the bill for the relief of Thomas Simpson was recommitted to the Committee on Invalid Pensions.

TERRITORIES.

This day being specially set apart for the consideration of bills relating to the Territories, Mr. ALLAN, of Kentucky, moved to commit to a Committee of the Whole on the state of the Union, the several bills in relation to the Territories, which had been referred to a Committee of the Whole House; which was agreed to.

The House then, on motion of Mr. ALLAN, of Kentucky, resolved itself into a Committee of the Whole on the State of the Union, Mr. POPE in the Chair, on the following bills:

A bill making appropriations to improve the navigation of certain rivers in the Territory of Florida;

A bill to provide for the improvement of the harbor on Clinton river, in the Territory of Michigan;

A bill from the Senate to provide for certain roads in the Territory of Arkansas;

A bill from the Senate to improve the harbor at the mouth of the river Raisin, in the Territory of Michigan;

A bill to authorize the construction of a railroad through the public lands between Tallahassee, and St. Marks, in Florida. [This bill was amended on motion of Mr. LYON, by authorizing a railroad to be constructed through the public lands in Michigan, &c.]

A bill to provide for the opening of certain roads in the Territory of Arkansas, and for other purposes.

A bill establishing the territorial government of Wisconsin.

Mr. LYON moved an amendment to the latter bill, which was agreed to.

Mr. HAMER submitted another amendment relative to, and fixing the boundary lines of the States of Ohio, Illinois, and Indiana.

On the subject of this amendment, a question of order arose, which was debated at great length, in which various members participated.

The CHAIR decided that the question was not in order, inasmuch as it involved a question already before the House, after the committee should rise.

From this decision, Mr. VINTON appealed, when the subject of order was again resumed and discussed by Messrs. VINTON, MASON, ADAMS, of Mass., CLAY, WHITE of Florida, LANE, HAMER, LYON of Michigan, EWING, ALLEN of Ohio, and others.

The subject was finally withdrawn from the consideration of the committee, in order to be renewed in the House, after the committee should rise.

Mr. REYNOLDS then offered an amendment fixing the boundary line between the Territory of Wisconsin and the State of Illinois, at 42 degrees and 30 minutes of north latitude.

This amendment was decided by the Chair to be in order; and was debated until the hour of adjournment.

Mr. LYON, of Michigan, conceived this amendment to be equally objectionable with the one just withdrawn. He could not accept it.

The amendment was advocated by Messrs. REYNOLDS, HARDIN, EWING, MAY, CRANE, HAMER, BINNEY, and ALLEN of Ohio, and opposed by Messrs. GAMBLE, BOON, J. Q. ADAMS, and MASON of Va.

On motion of Mr. MAY, the Committee rose and reported the bills to the House, with the exception of the bill establishing the Territory of Wisconsin.

The House then adjourned.

IN SENATE.

TUESDAY, Jan. 10, 1835.

The CHAIR communicated a letter from the Secretary of War, in obedience to a resolution of the Senate, accompanied by a report of the Engineer who made a survey and estimate relative to the improvement of the harbor at Trail Creek, in Indiana, which on motion of Mr. TIPTON, was ordered to be printed.

Petitions and memorials were presented by Messrs. HENDRICKS, CALHOUN, M'KEAN, ROBINSON, LEIGH, PRESTON, TOMLINSON, ROBBINS, and TIPTON.

Mr. WAGGAMAN, from the Select Committee to which a resolution on the subject was referred, reported a bill to establish branches of the United States Mint at New Orleans, at Mechlenburg Co. North Carolina, and another at Illengo, in Georgia; which was read the first time and ordered to a second reading.

Mr. SOUTHARD, from the Committee on the District of Columbia, reported a bill for the relief of the Alexandria Canal Company.

Mr. TYLER from the same Committee, reported a bill renewing the charters of certain Banks in the District of Columbia, for a limited period; which bills were severally read the first time and ordered to a second reading.

Mr. HILL offered the following resolution:

Resolved, That the Secretary of the Treasury be requested to inform the Senate whether there is evidence in the Department of the payments made to the officers of the army of the revolution for the commutation to which they are entitled in lieu of half-pay for life, or other emoluments, under the several resolutions of Congress, in all cases in which such payments have, in part, been made, or whether the evidence of payment has in any, and in what class or classes of cases, been lost or destroyed;

Whether classes of these officers, entitled to commutation, were paid by their respective States, and the payment so made by the States was subsequently assumed and paid by the General Government, and if so, whether any record of the names of the individual officers so paid by the States was furnished to and has been preserved in the Department;

Whether, to his knowledge, acts of Congress have passed directing commutation pay to be made in cases where payment had been previously made, or in cases where the officer was not entitled to the commutation under the resolutions of Congress before referred to;

And whether other acts of Congress have been passed allowing commutation to officers, or to the heirs and legal representatives of officers, in cases where there is every reason to believe that payment of the same claim had been previously made.

Mr. LEIGH, from the Committee on Revolutionary Claims, made unfavorable reports upon the following cases: The petition of the legal representatives of Richard Dorsey, deceased; the petition of the administrator of Capt. William Sandford, deceased; and the petition of the heirs of Capt. Jacob Hall, deceased.

On motion of Mr. CALHOUN, the Senate proceeded to the third reading of the bill changing the organization of the General Post Office.

Mr. GRUNDY rose and said that, by the instructions of the committee, he moved to fill up a blank in the bill, which was left for the purpose of inserting the number of clerks necessary to be employed in the General Post Office, under the new organization. He therefore submitted an amendment, which he hoped would be agreed to, by unanimous consent, fixing the number of clerks in the General Post Office at twenty-six, and reducing the salary of the Messenger to be employed in the office of the Commissioner of the Post Office to $700, instead of $800, by which, Mr. Grundy said, he would be put upon a footing of equality, in this respect, with other messengers in the Executive Departments.

The amendment was adopted, and the bill was then read the third time and passed.

Mr. TYLER, from the Committee on the District of Columbia, to which the bill from the House relative to the construction of the bridge over the Potomac at the City of Washington, and repealing all other acts in relation thereto, was referred, reported the same without amendment.

The bill for the relief of the legal representatives of George Hurlbut, and

The bill making an appropriation to erect a light-house at Mobile Point, and to establish buoys in Mobile bay, were severally read the third time and passed.

On motion of Mr. WEBSTER, the Senate considered, as in Committee of the Whole, the bill making appropriations for the naval service for the year 1835, and no objection having been made, it was read the third time and passed.

On motion of Mr. CALHOUN, the Senate considered, as in Committee of the Whole, the joint resolution reported yesterday by the joint Committee proposing an amendment of the constitution relative to the distribution of the surplus revenue of the United States; when, on his motion, the resolution was postponed to and made the special order for Thursday next.

On motion of Mr. SILSBEE, the Senate postponed the previous orders, and proceeded to consider, as in Committee of the Whole, the bill fixing the number and salaries of the custom-house officers of the United States.

Mr. SILSBEE briefly explained the object of the bill, which was, to fix the number and compensation of the custom-house officers in the U. States, and to prevent an inequality which existed in the compensation of the subordinate officers of the same grade, in different parts of the country.

Mr. SILSBEE then moved severally the following amendments to the bill:

The appointment of a surveyor at Jersey City, in the district of New York, at a salary of $800 per annum.

A surveyor at Lynn, in the district of Marblehead, at $300 per annum.

A surveyor at Ocracock, in the Newbern District, at $700 per annum.

A surveyor at Camden, N. Jersey, at $250 per annum.

A survey at St. Mary's, in the Annapolis District, at $200 per annum.

These amendments were agreed to.

Mr. SILSBEE then moved a further amendment, "that all fees now payable by law to all collectors, naval officers, and surveyors, or their deputies, or those authorized to receive them, shall be regularly accounted for quarterly and paid into the Treasury by the officers receiving the same," which was agreed to.

Mr. SWIFT offered an amendment requiring temporary officers who received a per diem compensation, to make a report of the duties performed by them, with a statement under oath that their duties were necessary to the public good.

After some conversation between Mr. SHEPLEY, Mr. SILSBEE, and Mr. SWIFT, the proposed amendment was withdrawn by Mr. SWIFT, on the suggestion that the substance of it was already contained in the bill.

Mr. TYLER said he found by this bill that out of the fourteen naval officers now established, only six were to be retained. That the port of Norfolk was to be deprived of this officer. He contended that these officers were necessary as checks over the collectors; he therefore proposed so to amend the bill as to give a naval officer with a salary of $1000 to the port of Norfolk. Mr. T. then read a letter from the Comptroller of the Treasury stating as his opinion, that a naval officer ought not to be dispensed with at the port of Norfolk.

Mr. SILSBEE said he was willing, so far as respected himself, to have dispensed with all the naval officers, but in accordance with the opinion of the committee, they had retained six for the six principal ports of the country.

Mr. WRIGHT thought these officers were necessary at the large ports, and a majority of the committee thought they could be dispensed with at six or seven ports. Where the receipts were very heavy, he operated as a check on the collector, by reviewing and correcting his accounts. The amendment went to extend this officer to another class of ports not in the contemplation of the committee.

Mr. SILSBEE was opposed to the amendment, because, if it prevailed, this officer must be extended to other ports, where there was really no necessity for it.

Mr. TOMLINSON said he thought, in the committee, that it was necessary to abolish all these naval officers. They were merely checks on the collector, and he was already checked by his clerks and the surveyor of the port, and he was also checked at the Treasury, by the accounting officers. The committee thought it expedient, by way of experiment, to reduce the number of naval officers in the small ports first, and if it succeeded there, it was thought that it would afterwards be very easy to extend it, and abolish the office in the other ports. He saw no strong reason, therefore, for establishing one at Norfolk.

Mr. TYLER said he went for checks and balances. If the appointment of a naval officer was necessary as a check upon the collector at six or seven ports, it was so in all. If we could dispense with sentinels over the collector where not more than $10,000 were received, we could where ten millions were collected. He saw no force in the remark, that the clerks were a check upon the collector, under whose control they were, and removable at his pleasure, nor could he understand how the officers of the Treasury were a check upon the collector. He was unable to conceive what check there was upon that officer, except what was afforded by the naval officer. With respect to the collector at Norfolk, he knew him to be a most honest, trust-worthy man, and believed him to be as much so as any other in the Government, but he would trust no man to go into the Treasury and take money out of it without, having a sentinel to watch over him.

Mr. SILSBEE and Mr. TOMLINSON made

some further remarks, when the amendment was disagreed to.

Mr. BIBB then moved a further amendment to increase the salary of the Collector at Sandusky from $400 to $600 per annum.

Mr. B. knew this officer to be a most honest and excellent one. He had been many years in the service of the Government, but his salary was entirely too low to enable him to live. There was a maxim, "make money—honestly, if you can—but at all events make money." This maxim applied with increased force to persons thus situated—they must live; honestly, if they could, but the means of living must be had at every hazard. He thought that $600 was a very moderate salary, and hoped the proposition would be agreed to.

Mr. BUCHANAN said he would vote for the amendment. But while he was up, he would make one or two general observations with regard to this bill. It must be admitted that there was no Government on the globe that had collected its revenue with more punctuality or more faithfully than the Government of the United States. To collect it successfully, required the exercise of great care, and the possession of great practical knowledge ourselves, or the advantage of it in others. The objection to the bill was not that the higher officers intrusted with the duty of collecting the revenue, were not sufficiently provided for; but when we went from the ports on the sea-board to those in the interior, he entertained doubts on the subject. We all knew what corruption existed among the European Governments among the collectors of their revenues and the reason was, that they did not receive a sufficient compensation for their services to live on. They must live, and in order to live, they became corrupt. Although he was as anxious for an economical administration of the Government, and economical expenditures, as any gentleman of the Senate, yet he would be sorry to introduce the spirit of economy to such an extreme as would induce the collectors of the revenue to become dishonest. As the honorable gentleman from Kentucky, (Mr. Bibb,) well remarked, they must live, and if they could not live honestly, they must derive the means of living from some source. He did not know that there were any persons in this bill, which would have the effect of making all officers dishonest. But he felt certain that at the port of Sandusky, a competent officer could not be obtained for $400, or if he could be obtained, he could not live on that salary. At some other time, it was probable he might move to postpone this bill for the present session—he believed it was not to take effect till next January, and if the next session we should all come better prepared to legislate upon a measure which would have so important a bearing upon the collection of the revenue of the country. Mr. B. said so and valued the practical knowledge of the honorable gentleman from Massachusetts, (Mr. Silsbee,) appreciated it more highly than he did, he had hoped the bill would be postponed, although he would not make a motion to that effect, unless he thought it would receive the sanction of a considerable portion of this body.

Mr. SILSBEE said, the Secretary of the Treasury had given him his opinion as to what these collectors ought to have, and he supposed he had founded his estimates upon what he believed to be just and reasonable. Mr. S. said he would be the last man to give less compensation than these officers ought to have, or what was necessary to support them. If the man had lived hereinbefore at $400, he did not know why he might not continue to do so.

Mr. BUCHANAN would only say that he would take the opinion of the honorable gentleman from Massachusetts respecting the sufficiency of the salary of this collector, with as little hesitation as that of the Secretary of the Treasury. But if this honest man, as he had been represented to be, had lived for so many years upon a salary of $400, he thought it was now time to give him six hundred.

Mr. BIBB observed that this gentleman held this situation under the expectation of a higher salary. He (Mr. B.) was not in favor of high salaries, but $400 would not procure the services of

competent man at a place which was so convenient for smuggling as Sandusky. Unless there was a man there who was competent to his duties, the revenue would suffer. And $400 was not such a compensation as the Government ought to offer such a person.

Mr. WRIGHT conceded the general proposition of the gentleman from Pennsylvania, that it was the interest of the Government, fully to compensate its officers. This was the wish and design of the Committee, in framing the bill; but they might have failed in it, and if they had, he was willing and indeed desired, that the Senate of the House should correct it, in acting on the bill. But with regard to the compensation of collectors, he believed as a general principle, it was used upon the amount of revenue which was received at a particular port. [Mr. W. here referred to the Secretary's report, to show, that in 433, the revenue received at Sandusky was 1102.] The amount paid for doing this business was $409. He was acquainted with this district, as he believed that the facility for smuggling here was very much diminished, owing to the location being upon the lake, with perhaps an expanse of 50 miles of water to be crossed, before smuggled goods could be introduced. If this duty should be raised, he thought all the other duties of the same grade ought also to be raised.

Some further remarks were made by Messrs. ROBB, WRIGHT, and SILSBEE, when Mr. EWING interposed a motion to adjourn, which prevailed, and
The Senate adjourned.

HOUSE OF REPRESENTATIVES.

TUESDAY, February 10, 1835.

Mr. CARR, from the Committee on Private Land Claims, reported the following bills; which were read twice and committed:

A bill concerning land claimants;

A bill for the relief of Silvia C. Vick, widow of Hartwell Vick, deceased, and the heirs of the decedent;

And a bill for the relief of John S. Congor.

Mr. PARKER, from the Committee on Naval Affairs, reported a bill for the relief of James Fisbank; which was read twice and committed.

Mr. POLK, from the Committee of Ways and Means, reported a bill to regulate the disbursement of the public money, and to prohibit allowances not made by law; which was read twice and committed.

Mr. ASHLEY, from the Committee on the Public Lands, reported a bill for the relief of Henry Duchesquette, William Hibert, and J. B. Duvoi, and Charles Sanguinette; which was read twice and committed.

Mr. E. EVERETT, from the Committee on Foreign Affairs, reported a bill for the relief of Commodore John Downs; which was read twice and committed.

Unfavorable reports upon various petitions, &c. were made by Messrs. GALBRAITH, PARKER, F. K. FULLER, FOSTER, FULTON, LAY, and THOMSON, from their respective standing committees.

On motion of Mr. GILMER, leave was given to a Committee on Indian Affairs, to prosecute the duties during the sessions of the House.

Petitions were presented, on leave, by—

Messrs. DUNLAP, WHITE, PINCKNEY, BILLIPS, and KAVANAGH; which were appropriately referred.

[Mr. DUNLAP asked leave of the House to present a petition he had this morning received from sundry citizens of Fayette county, Tennessee, for the establishment of a post route from Bluff Creek post office to Sandy Spring, in said county. Leave being granted, said petition was referred to the Committee on the Post Office and Roads.]

The following resolutions, heretofore offered, were considered and agreed to:

By Mr. HANNEGAN:

Resolved, That the Secretary of War be requested to communicate to this House, if in possession of the War Department, a copy of the survey, plan, and estimate, for the construction of a harbor, at the mouth of Trail creek, on lake Michigan, in the State of Indiana, or any information he may possess in relation thereto.

By Mr. BEATY:

Resolved, That the Secretary of War be requested to report to this House the survey and report of the engineers sent during the last year to survey the Cumberland river, from the falls on said river down to meet the survey heretofore made thereon.

On motion of Mr. HARD:

Resolved, That the Committee on Invalid Pensions be instructed to inquire into the expediency of allowing to Ezekiah Jewit, an invalid pensioner, arrearages of pensions from June, 1815, when his disability occurred, to the present time.

ELECTION OF PRINTER TO THE HOUSE OF REPRESENTATIVES.

The following resolution, offered yesterday, by Mr. McKINLEY, as amended by Mr. SUTHERLAND, then came up as the unfinished morning business:

Resolved, That the House will, on Thursday next, proceed to the election of printer to the House of Representatives of the next Congress, by viva voce.

Mr. EVANS moved the following amendment: Strike out viva voce, and insert "under the authority of the joint resolution, approved March 3, 1819."

The amendment having been read,

Mr. EVANS said: It seemed obvious to him, that if the resolution proposed by the gentleman from Alabama, ought to pass at all, it should pass in the shape Mr. E. proposed. If not, he would inquire of the honorable mover, by and under what authority the House could undertake to go into the election of printer at all for the next Congress? There was none except that derived from the resolution of 1819, as amended by the joint resolution of the 5th February, 1829. Now the very introduction of the resolution, by the honorable member from Alabama, recognized the force of those resolutions. It was by virtue of those two joint resolutions alone, that one Congress had the right to appoint a printer for the succeeding one, and the phraseology proposed by Mr. E. was the only phraseology that could consistently be used. He begged leave also to remind the House that such was the phraseology adopt d ever since the former joint resolution was adopted. The motion had always been made and agreed to, that on such a day the House would proceed to the election of a printer, under the authority of the joint resolution of the 3d March, 1819, and to entitle the House to do so, on the present occasion, the same phraseology must be made use of.

Gentlemen had said on a former occasion when this subject came up incidentally for consideration, that the resolution of 1819 was temporary in its nature, and limited to two years. As an answer to that, he could only say, that it was never considered so, neither by the then nor by the succeeding Congresses, each of whom regarded it as binding upon themselves and upon the succeeding Congress. Even so lately as 1829 the journals of the House show this; wherein it was stated that the House proceeded to the election of printer in obedience to the joint resolution of 1819, and this was the phraseology for several years after the adoption of that resolution. Then if that resolution be in force, and had not been repealed, we derived the only authority we had to choose a printer for the next session from these two resolutions.

Then, as to the mode of election, what was the language of the resolution? That the appointment of printer should be made by ballot. Now, the gentleman's resolution proposed to dispense with that provision, but Mr. E. thought one portion of the resolution was as obligatory as another, and that as the authority under which the appointment was made was derived from the resolution alone, the mode must be in the manner therein laid down, and could not be set aside. It had been alleged that the resolution of 1819 was virtually repealed or rescinded by that of 1829, but how could that be? The latter repealed only so much of the former as was inconsistent with it, and what was that? Why, it limited the time to within thirty days of the termination of the session, and required a majority instead of a plurality of votes. These were the only alterations, and in all other particulars the resolution of 1819 stood unrepealed. The nature of the contract, the prices to be paid, and the mode of appointment, were unaffected.

The next question that came up for consideration was, whether the printer was an officer of the House or not. Mr. E. would not go into this at any length, but it was enough for the justification of his own vote to say, that he did not consider the printer an officer, within the meaning of that clause in the constitution giving each House the right to appoint its officers, no more than the person who supplied the House with a stationary, or fuel, or furniture. In Mr. E.'s judgment, it stood upon the same principle. Still, he thought with the gentleman from Virginia (Mr. Robertson) that there was much propriety in leaving to each House to select its own printer, if it was practicable. But this could not be done. Hut we had the lesson of experience to show its impracticability. In the report made to the House on the 3d March, 1819, the inconvenience of that mode was closely and ably examined, and it was shown, by the experience of former years, that the work was badly executed, and often delayed so long beyond the proper time, as to be useless when completed. Mr. E. read an extract from the report in question, and showed that it would be impossible to be furnished with the requisite material, types, presses, &c., unless he was enabled to provide for them beforehand, by having been elected the printer to the ensuing Congress. He also adduced one fact to show the inconvenience of the mode proposed by Mr. Robertson, that a document, providing for the organization of the War Department, had been delayed upwards of a year in the printing office, till the army itself became almost in a state of disorganization. He would have had no objection that the subject should have been committed to a Select Committee, as proposed some time since by a gentleman from Tennessee, (Mr. Peyton,) and if any better mode than the present or the former one could be devised, Mr. E. would cheerfully support it. But let it be examined by competent persons, conversant with printing and public business. He thought they would be incurring great hazard by repealing the joint resolution, or altering the present mode in any way, at this late hour. At present, he believed the existing mode the best; at all events, he was not assured that a better could be devised. There were no complaints made. The prices were sufficiently low, and the work was promptly executed. At the second session of the 19th Congress, a printer, who had formerly had the contract, sent a memorial to the House, offering to do the work for 15 per cent. under the existing tariff of prices, but Congress was satisfied, and refused to disturb the resolution fixing them. These, then, were the reasons why he thought the resolution should be amended as he had proposed.

In relation to the question of viva voce voting, Mr. E. was decidedly opposed to it in this case, because he thought they had no right to adopt it, and because he was opposed to it in every election for officers of that House, and on most other occasions. He knew it was a contested question, and he had intended to have submitted some remarks on the subject when the resolution of the gentleman from Illinois [Mr. Reynolds] was under consideration. He should now make but a few remarks on the subject. It had been advocated there on the ground of the responsibility of members to their constituents, who, it was contended, ought to know the opinions and sentiments of their representatives, but he would ask, how was a man's opinions and sentiments to be known by his vote for officers of that House? Had not the people opportunities enough, and better opportunities, of knowing the sentiments of their representatives? In his judgment, they were to be best judged by the public policy they advocated and pursued, and not by such votes as those. Of what possible consequence could it be to the people of this country to know how their representatives voted for A, B, or C, as an officer of the House? Be—

. was opposed to it as breaking down lence of private judgment, and the inion in individual members of the making them, or tending to make ervient elsewhere. He was much a remark made by a gentleman who io said he thought the ballot very pro- people, because they were accounta- e. Mr. E. would undertake to say, ciple of the ballot was never estab- at ground. It always stood on the ersonal independence; and such a rea- asigned by the gentleman, he ventured r entered into the head of any legisla- r reason, . every argument, went to was established to secure the right of ment and independence As to re- to constituents, Mr. E. admitted as r one, and respected their wishes opinion as much as any one; was a very great difference as onstituted public opinion. It should intelligent, deliberate judgment; a got up and forced into circula- intrigues of designing persons. A from New York used a great many it the duties of the representative; that thing more than the minion of the I talked about the creature and the principal and the agent, why none ases ——

CKETT here called for the orders of

INLEY asked for the yeas and nays; re not ordered. for the orders of the day prevailed;

E, pursuant to notice heretofore giv- o postpone all the previous orders of h a view to the consideration of the iing the Northwestern Territory. K inquired if the bill regulating the the public moneys in the local Banks, other bills in relation to the Bank of the es, did not occupy a position on the lvance of the bill which the gentle- Kentucky had proposed to take up? recollected that he had given notice d move to take up the bills referred to

E said, that the bill which he proposed ras, he conceived, of more importance i mentioned by the gentleman from (Mr. Polk.) It had been already so i that it was highly expedient, If it i to act upon it at the present session, d be now done.

LAP said, he hoped the House would i the motion of the gentleman from Much of the time of this House had n similar motions to change the order The Tennessee land bill, in which nts were immediately interested, was ecial order of the day for the 17th of ast; and it would be strange to his con- w it had happened the bill had not yet on by this House—it had been owing iotions prevailing, and the order of bu- changed. He was very desirous to t on of the House on the bill in which nts were i terested. If the House e to entertain such motions, it would aving of time, and much more business he time spent in changing the order of uld be devoted to the necessary busi- House.

K referred to the importance of the which he had alluded; some of which itely necessary to be acted on at the ion. on made up by Mr. LOVE was rejected. K then moved to postpone all the or- day, for the purpose of considering the i to which he had referred. IM demanded the yeas and nays on this ieh were ordered, and were, yeas 107,

Iouse determined to postpone the or- day, including the business upon the able.

DEPOSITE BANKS.

The House then, on motion of Mr. POLK, pro- ceeded to the consideration of the bill regulating the deposites of the public moneys in certain local banks. The bill was read.

Mr. POLK said, the bill just read was, in its main principles, precisely similar to that passed by the House at the last session of Congress, and upon a careful review of its provisions, the com- mittee had found but few points, in their judg- ment, requiring revision or change. Mr. P. said the whole country was then aware that the pre- sent method of carrying on the financial concerns of the Government was no longer to be continu- ed, and he went on to show that the mode adopted, through the agency of State Banks, had been done promptly, safely, and without charge, not only without the aid of the National Bank, but against the combined weight and influence of that insti- tution, and in defiance of its attempts to cripple their operations, to the advantage of the commu- nity, and without embarrassment to the Treasury. Mr. P. also referred to, and quoted, many state- ments to prove that the losses sustained by the country had been double, or nearly double, from the Bank of the United States, to what had occur- red from the local banks prior to the year 1816, and also to prove that they would be safer deposi- tories for the public money. Not only so, but they conducted the exchanges at a less cost than the United States Bank had ever done.

[We hope to be enabled to give the remarks of the honorable member in full, on an early day, but the short time allowed would not permit our reporter to give even a fair synopsis of a speech, mainly consisting of close reasoning, sustained by matters of fact and arithmetic data.]

Mr. GORDON submitted the following amend- ment:

Be it enacted by the Senate and House of Repre- sentatives of the United States of America in Congress assembled, That, from and after the   day of   in the year   the collectors of the public revenue at places where the sums collected shall not exceed the sum of   dollars per annum, shall be the agents of the Treasurer to keep and disburse the same, and be subject to such rules and regulations, and give such bond and security, as he shall prescribe, for the faithful execution of their office, and shall receive, in addition to the compensation now allowed by law,   per centum on the sums disbursed, so that it does not exceed the sum of   dollars per annum.

SEC. 2. *And be it further enacted,* That, at places where the amount of public revenue collected shall exceed the sum of   dollars per annum, there shall be appointed by the Presi- dent, by and with the advice and consent of the Senate, receivers of the public revenue, to be agents of the Treasurer, who shall give such bond and security to keep and disburse the public reve- nue, and be subject to such rules and regulations, as the Treasurer shall prescribe, and shall receive for their services   per centum per annum on the sums disbursed, provided it does not exceed the sum of   dollars per annum.

SEC. 3. *And be it further enacted,* That, from and after the   day of   the whole revenue of the United States derived from cus- toms, lands, or other sources, shall be paid in the current coins of the United States.

Mr. GORDON said, the blanks were left to be filled by the judgment of the House. He had submitted a similar proposition on a former occa- sion. He did so, under the belief that the Go- vernment of the United States possessed no con- stitutional power to make a Bank of the United States. He also maintained that it was not in ac- cordance with the spirit of our institutions to in- vest one man with the power of controlling the disposal, or keeping of the public revenue. Such a power he would place in the hands of no single created being. It certainly added too much to the responsibilities of the Executive, which he be- lieved to be already too great. This remark was not intended to apply specially to the individual now in the Executive chair, to whose elevation he had contributed the weight of his earnest exer- tions. Mr. G. alluded to the great inequalities in

the distribution of the deposites of the public treasure—thirteen millions being placed in the State of New York alone, while the Ancient Do- minion had but about $100,000 placed in her cus- tody. This reminded him of the fable of Æsop, from which we learn what the Lion's share is. He wished to separate this Government from all con- nection with banks and like institutions. Mr. G. continued to advocate the amendment at consi- derable length. He concluded by appealing to his contemporaries to act the glorious example of re- ther divesting themselves of power, and placing it back in the hands of its legitimate conservators, the people, than seeking to swell its tide by cling- ing to that which, at best, could only be conce... nated constructive.

Mr. MOORE moved to amend the amendment by striking out all after the word 'that' to the end of the second line of the first section of the bill, and insert—

"The public money shall hereafter be deposit- ed in the following banks, to wit:

"The Merchants' Bank of Salem; the Bank of New London, &c." (Here insert the names of all the banks employed as Deposite Banks.)

"*Provided,* That the said banks shall be willing to undertake to do and perform the several duties and services, and conform to the conditions pre- scribed by this act."

Mr. MOORE, under the belief that the Bank of the United States would not be re-chartered, and no new Bank created, was willing to aid in perfecting the bill before the House. He was op- posed to leaving any thing to the discretion of the Secretary of the Treasury, and with this view, he thought it best to insert the names of the Banks in which the public money should be deposited. This would prevent any undue influence, in im- portant elections, which might be exercised if the selection of these Banks was left to the Executive authority.

Mr. EWING had a substitute, which at the pro- per time, he would offer. He was opposed to this amendment of the gentleman from Virginia. He proceeded to reply to the remarks of the gentle- man from Tennessee, (Mr. Polk.) He would be opposed to any amendment which might be offer- ed to the bill, except the substitute which he should himself propose.

Mr. MOORE said, that upon the suggestion of several members, he would withdraw his amend- ment for the present, and would hereafter offer it as an amendment to the original bill.

Mr. EWING then offered his substitute in lieu of the amendment proposed by Mr. Gordon. It contained twenty-eight sections, and provided for the appointment of Commissioners in the seve- ral States, to be styled " Boards of Currency," with authority to issue bills or notes, &c.

The SPEAKER decided that the amendment out of order, inasmuch as the 10th section made an ap- propriation of $30,000 for the purpose of procur- ing engravings, printing of notes, &c. which would render it necessary that the bill should be com- mitted.

Mr. EWING struck out the 10th section, when the substitute was declared to be in order.

Mr. EWING addressed the House in favor of his proposition, and concluded his remarks by moving to refer the bill and amendments to a Se- lect Committee of one member from each State.

The motion was negatived, by a large majority.

Mr. EWING again addressed the House in favor of his substitute.

Mr. ROBERTSON next obtained the floor, and after speaking some time on the various questions presented by the bill, and in opposition to the pro- visions and the views of the Secretary of the Trea- sury, on the subject of the disposition of the pub- lic moneys, he gave way (without concluding his remarks) to a motion by Mr. WISE, for an ad- journment, which carried.

The House then adjourned.

IN SENATE.

WEDNESDAY, February 11, 1835. Petitions and memorials were presented by Messrs. EWING, SHEPLEY, WRIGHT, Mc- KEAN, TOMLINSON, and BUCHANAN.

Mr. TOMLINSON, from the Committee on

tendтом, to which was referred the resolutions of the Legislature of Alabama, praying the establishment of another pension agency in that State, reported unfavorably upon the same, and moved that the Committee be discharged from the further consideration of the same.

Mr. KING, of Ala., made some opposition to recharging the Committee; and, at his suggestion, the motion was laid on the table for the present.

Mr. WHITE, from the Committee on Revolutionary Claims, to which was referred the petition of the representatives of James Parkinson, deceased, reported unfavorably upon the same.

Mr. HENDRICKS gave notice that tomorrow he would ask leave to introduce a bill making an appropriation to repair certain roads in the Territory of Michigan.

Mr. WAGGAMAN, pursuant to notice, and on leave given, introduced a bill to establish a daily mail between Macon, Geo., and New Orleans; which was read twice and referred to the Post Office Committee.

Mr. SOUTHARD, from the Committee on Naval Affairs, reported a bill for the relief of Augustus A. Nicholson; which was read the first time and ordered to a second reading.

Mr. SOUTHARD, from the same Committee, to which was referred the bill from the House for the relief of Com. Isaac Hull, reported the same, with an amendment.

The bill to continue the office of Commissioner of Pensions, which was returned amended by the House of Representatives, was taken up, and the House amendment were referred to the Committee on Pensions.

Mr. PRESTON, from the Judiciary Committee, reported unfavorably upon the memorial of Wil-ham Clark.

Mr. PRESTON, from the same Committee, to which was referred the joint resolution to repeal the joint resolution prescribing the mode of electing the public printers to Congress, reported unfavorably upon the same, and the Committee was discharged from the further consideration of both the subjects.

The following resolution, offered by Mr. SHEPLEY, was read twice by unanimous consent, and agreed to:

Resolved, That the Secretary of War be directed to cause the surveys and maps made in the State of Maine under the direction of Col. J. S. Abert, to be communicated to the Senate; and that cause the maps to be reduced, if necessary, and prepare them for publication.

The following bills from the House, were read and appropriately referred:

a bill for the removal of the Land Office from Poughkeepsie to Lima, in the State of Ohio; a bill to authorize the sale of certain lands belonging to the university of Michigan;

a bill prescribing the punishment of Consuls, commercial Agents, and others in certain cases; a bill for the relief of Lieutenant Mervin P. I.,

a bill for the relief of Samuel Butler; a bill for the relief of Elizabeth Swain; a bill for the relief of the heirs of William Pol-

a bill for the relief of Sutton Stevens; a bill for the relief of Thomas Dixon and Co. of New York;

a bill for the relief of Job Burton; a bill for the relief of Samuel H. Dozey; a bill for the relief of John Herrick; a bill for the relief of Job Wood; a bill for the relief of David Kincaid; a bill for the relief of Stephen Smith and others,

a bill for the relief of Robert Abbott and the heirs of James Abbott, deceased; a bill for the relief of Matthew C. Perry; a bill for the relief of E. R. Shubrick, of the United States Navy;

a bill for the relief of Riddle, Becktel, and others,

a bill for the relief of John J. Avery; a bill for the relief of Stephen Gatlin; a bill for the relief of Theodore Owens; a bill for the relief of the representatives of uas Clements, deceased;

a bill 'or the relief of S. M. Wall and H. Percival;

a bill for the relief of Shubael Conant; a bill for the relief of the legal representative of Aaron Smith;

a bill for the relief of Thomas Ball; a bill for the relief of Richard H. Lee; a bill for the relief of Ebenezer Breed; a bill for the relief of George Davenport; a bill for the relief of Richard Butman; a bill for the relief of John Frazer & Co. a bill for the benefit of John Cullins; a bill for the relief of Harry Reynolds and John Casey;

a bill for the relief of Josiah Westlake; a bill granting a pension to Isaac Janvier; a bill for the relief of Josiah H. Brown and John Conklin;

a bill to restore to certain invalid pensioners, the amount of pension by them relinquished;

A bill amendatory of the act for the repair of the Cumberland road;

A bill making provision for the purchase of the fac similes of Gen. Washington's accounts.

On motion of Mr. HENDRICKS, the Senate postponed the previous orders, and took up the bill making an appropriation for the continuation and repair of the Cumberland road.

Mr. HENDRICKS then moved an amendment to the bill, allowing a percentage to the officer who shall disburse the appropriation; the amount to be settled by the rules and regulations of the War Department.

After some remarks from Mr. HENDRICKS, explanatory thereof, and also of the bill,

Mr. CLAY opposed the amendment; and

Mr. HENDRICKS afterwards withdrew it.

Mr. BUCHANAN said, that the Cumberland road had been a constant subject before Congress, ever since he had first taken his seat in the House of Representatives, in the session of 1821–2. A bill had passed, at that session, to keep it in repair, by establishing toll gates upon it, under the authority of Congress, on which Mr. Monroe, then the President of the United States, had placed his veto, because, in his opinion, Congress had not the power, under the Constitution, to enact such a law. He (Mr. B.) had then carefully examined the message of Mr. Monroe returning this bill, and had been convinced that we had no power to pass any such act. From that momen he had steadily and uniformly, in every shape and form, opposed the erection of toll gates upon this road under the authority of the General Government. If Congress possess the power to enter the territory of a State; to interfere in their domestic concerns; to errect toll gates upon their roads; to establish a police over them and inflict penalties for its violations, and of consequence to create tribunals in which such offences can be tried; then every barrier between Federal and State authority, is at once prostrated. Indeed this principle would lead to perfect consolidation, so far as an entire jurisdiction over the post roads of the country, for the purpose of levying tolls to keep them in repair, could extend.

In this state of things, there was one party in Congress, which, although favorable to the preservation of the road, felt themselves bound to vote against all appropriations for its repair, on the principle of compelling its friends to consent that tolls for this purpose should be levied under the authority of the States through which it passes. Another party wished that it might be forever kept in repair by appropriations from the national treasury, without the collection of tolls, either under the State or National authority. And a third class of politicians were determined to push the doctrine of internal improvements to the dangerous extent of abolishing the principle that Congress not only possessed the power to appropriate money for the construction of roads and canals, but that they were also bound to assume a jurisdiction over them, by erecting gates upon them, and collecting toll.

In regard to myself, I have been more misrepresented upon this question than I ever have been on any other. I have been constantly denounced as an enemy to the road, although I have never entertained a hostile feeling towards it. Jealousy

towards this great national work, because it might injure the Pennsylvania turnpike, has always been imputed to me; when, if I know myself, I am incapable of such a feeling towards such an improvement—so beneficial to the citizens of the country generally.

For several years I voted for appropriations to repair this road; and I did not cease to do so, until I discovered that if this course were continued, the peculiar friends of the road never would consent to the erection of toll gates under State authority.

In this conflict of opinions, the necessary appropriations could not be obtained for the repairs of the road. It got into a ruinous state, and became so dilapidated, that its entire destruction was threatened. At length its friends consented that it should be placed under the protection of the States. Accordingly, Pennsylvania, in April, 1831, and Maryland, in January, 1832, passed acts authorising the erection of toll gates upon it, and agreed to take it under their care, provided it "should be put in a good and complete state of repair" by appropriations made by Congress. Virginia some time afterwards passed a similar act. On the 3d July, 1832, Congress approved of these acts, and appropriated $150,000 towards the repairs of this road.

Here, then, was a contract expressly and solemnly entered into first, that the road should be placed in good and complete repair by Congress, and then, that it should pass under the care of the States, for the purpose of its preservation.

In pursuance of this arrangement, the Engineer Department adopted a plan for its complete repair. The road was to be Ma Adamised. There were to be three strata of stone placed upon it, each of three inches in depth. The repairs proceeded upon this principle. On the 2d March, 1833, $125,000 more was appropriated to continue these repairs. At the last session, an estimate was presented by the Engineer Department, stating that the sum of $652,100 would be required to finish the road; but Congress refused to appropriate more than $300,000 for this purpose, less than half the necessary sum. The act granting this money also declared that it was given "for the entire completion of the repairs of the Cumberland road east of the Ohio."

What have been the consequences? Just such as might have been anticipated by every reflecting man. The Engineer Department had adopted a fixed plan for repairing the road. This plan they had steadily pursued for two years. It was known, or might have been known, to Congress. They were progressing gradually upon this plan, when all at once, without any previous notice, Congress change this plan by granting less than half the money necessary to complete its execution. What was then to be done? It became necessary for the contractor to abandon his system and spread this appropriation over the whole road. He has done so, and the result is, that on about 63 miles of the road—nearly half its whole length —instead of three strata of three inches in depth each, there is now but one. Is there any Senator who does not know not only that this is insufficient for a permanent road, but that the moment the spring opens, it will be cut to pieces by the heavy wagons and carriages? The metal, as it is technically called, will be all in the mud; and by the fatality which has always attended this road, the last appropriation, of $300,000, will be rendered a most entirely useless.

But, sir, the States through which it passes have only agreed to take this road off your hands on the condition that you shall first put it in good and complete repair; and you have assented to these terms. Does any gentleman imagine for a single moment that the State of Pennsylvania will accept this road in its present condition? Is it in good and complete repair, according to the terms of the contract? Your own Engineers answer No, and inform you that it will require the sum of $346,186 58 to complete the repairs agreeably to the system which they have adopted and which they deem indispensable. This sum, you will have to appropriate for the purpose; or you will be compelled to keep the road in repair by annual appropriations, a course which I presume no

Senator intends to adopt as a permanent system. There is no other alternative, unless you devote the road itself to destruction. This idea no gentleman can one moment entertain. The erection of toll gates under the authority of Congress is now out of the question.

But it is said that the sum of $300,000 was appropriated at the last session, for the entire completion of the repairs of this road, and that more ought not now to be demanded. Is there any force in this argument? In settling an account with individuals, where the claimant is an opposing party, it is very proper for Congress to say that the sum appropriated shall be in full of all demands. Unless in very extraordinary cases, I should never vote to re-open such an account, and grant a new appropriation. But what is the state of facts upon the present occasion? Does not this road belong to the United States? Are we not bound by high principles of public duty to keep it in repair? Here is no opposite party with whom we can drive a bargain. It is our own road; and if we have not appropriated a sufficient sum for its repair, shall we suffer it to go to ruin, because we made a mistake in regard to the amount necessary? If the simple declaration of Congress that $300,000 was sufficient could have rendered it so, then there might be some justice in this reasoning. Otherwise, it is a mere fallacy. If, after having granted a certain sum, which was found by experience to be wholly insufficient to complete one of our fortifications, what should we say to a gentleman who would gravely contend, that as we had declared this sum should accomplish the object, we would rather permit it to go to ruin than appropriate another dollar. The cases are precisely parallel. But this is not all. Congress have contracted an obligation to the States through which the road passes, to put it in good and complete repair. How can they acquit themselves from this obligation, by urging that they had appropriated a sum which they declared to be sufficient for this purpose; and they could not, and would not appropriate any more. The States through which the road passes would have a right to say this is not the bargain. Your mistakes cannot justify the violation of your contract. You have agreed to accomplish a specific object; and cost what it may, this object must be accomplished, or we shall not accept the surrender of the road.

The commissioners appointed under the act of the Legislature of Pennsylvania have pledged themselves in the most solemn manner to accept the road and erect toll gates upon it, as soon as Congress shall appropriate the sum deemed necessary by the Engineer Department to put it in repair. That sum is granted by this bill. Pass it, and I will undertake to say for Pennsylvania, that this perplexing question, which has so often and for so many years agitated Congress, will be put forever at rest. You will never more hear of this road, unless it be that it has been preserved and protected with that fostering care which Pennsylvania exercises over all interests in which either the citizens of the State or of the Union are deeply concerned.

Mr. PRESTON said he was tired of making these repeated appropriations, again and again, for an object which he believed to be originally unconstitutional. He was disposed to vote something to get rid of this incubus upon the Treasury, if it was possible to effect it; but he was by no means satisfied that this appropriation would enable us to get it off our hands. He did not know or understand by what new lights gentlemen were governed heretofore upon this matter; but he would now ask the honorable Chairman whether he would rise in his place and say that the appropriation asked for would be sufficient to put the road in repair? For himself, he did not think it would, but that applications would yet be made for the same purpose, year after year. We could not get rid of the road in any way, neither by selling it, giving it away, or losing it. These States would not take the road, or maintain it, because it was left to their own judgments to say whether it was in repair or not.

Mr. EWING contended, that the reservation o the two per cent. fund to the new States, of which Ohio was one, was by a compact made in 1802, and was expressly for the purpose of making roads. This road was made by these funds, and yet the gentleman from South Carolina said that expenditures had been made to the road again and again. Could the road, he asked, be maintained but by appropriations? If it passed through a rich country, it might be repaired by the population; but it passed, in great part, over mountains and through wildernesses, and must necessarily get out of order. The gentleman said that neither of the States would maintain it, but the States had agreed to take it when it was put into complete repair. This never had been done, and they could not be expected to take it and maintain it when it was worn out. Ohio had already expended large sums in repairing it, and if this sum should be expended, he had information that no further appropriation would hereafter be asked for from Congress for the purpose.

Mr. BUCHANAN rose to say but one or two words. He did not know to whom the hon. Senator from South Carolina alluded, by the new lights which he said had influenced gentlemen. Certainly, he could not have meant him, for no new light had burst on his vision since 1822. Whether that gentleman had seen any himself since that period, he would not pretend to say; but from the session of 1822-3, he (Mr. B.) had been uniform, zealous, and consistent in his opposition to all the attempts which had been made to establish toll gates on this road, by Congress. He had at length, much against his inclination, voted in opposition to appropriations for its repair, in order to compel its friends to apply to the States to erect toll gates upon it. He thought, from the tenor of the hon. gentleman's remarks, he had not read the documents in this case with much care. He would inquire of the gentleman, candidly, would South Carolina, under similar circumstances, take this road under her charge, and agree to keep it in repair, when it was in such a condition that it must go to ruin, unless $340,000 should be expended upon it? Could he expect Pennsylvania to take the road, when the officers of this Government declared that it was not in repair? $652,000 was the sum asked for at the last session, $300,000 of which only had been granted. It was the mere balance of the former sum which was now asked, and, if it was appropriated, he for one was willing to pledge himself he would never vote for a single dollar more for the purpose. With respect to the special terms in which the appropriation of last session was made, he would ask the gentleman, suppose he were building a house, and he should give a specific sum of money to his agent for its completion, and declare this was sufficient, and it should afterwards appear that it was entirely insufficient for the purpose, would he allow it to remain useless, and go to decay, or would he advance an additional sum to finish it? Either we must abandon this road to ruin, or we shall be obliged to make a much greater appropriation at the next session, if this be now refused.

Mr. PRESTON contended that it was for a Pennsylvania road we were making this appropriation—it was not for our house, it was not our road, and if there was this great amount of travelling on it which gentlemen said, it proved its value, and that the States in which it laid might derive an income from it. He supposed the honorable gentleman from Pennsylvania never entertained but one opinion upon these matters, but the gentlemen with whom he usually acted entertained different opinions as to the power of Congress to establish toll gates on the road. He made no opposition, however, to the appropriation West of the Ohio. He therefore moved to amend the bill by striking out the second and third sections, upon which motion he asked the yeas and nays; which were ordered.

[The second section appropriates $346,000 to the repairs of the road East of the Ohio.

The third section provides that when the road shall be completed, it shall be surrendered to the States in which it lies.]

Mr. WEBSTER said, if he had the same constitutional scruples with regard to the power of the United States to construct roads, as the Senator from South Carolina, (Mr. Preston,) he should reason in the same manner and come to the same results. But he had no doubt on that subject. And moreover, the Cumberland Road was of more general interest, and less local in its nature, than most subjects that had been objected to as unconstitutional.

There were, said Mr. W., two objects embraced in the bill. One to carry forward the road beyond the Ohio river and extend it to the new States in the west—the other, to appropriate $350,000 for repairs on this side of that river, in order to put it in a condition to induce the States to accept it and keep it in repair. After the enormous expense the government had incurred in constructing the road, Mr. W. contended it should be preserved. He agreed for the most part with the honorable Senator from Pennsylvania, (Mr. Buchanan.) He understood, by the provisions of the bill, that the States to which it would be surrendered, were bound to apply the revenues of the tolls solely to the repairs of the road. He was in favor at the last session of appropriating 600,000 dollars for these repairs, but the other House thought otherwise. Consequently the bill was amended by changing the sum from $600,000 to 300,000. He was in favor of appropriating the full sum at that time, and then have the road finished.

Mr. CLAY said he should vote for the bill. He felt an imperative duty to preserve what was already done on the road, and prevent the whole from being lost. He did not, however, agree with the honorable Senator from Ohio, (Mr. Ewing,) that the Government was pledged to continue the repairs of the road, because a share in the incomes of public lands had been granted in lieu thereof. He contended that the power to construct a road implied a power to preserve it; and the best way to preserve it was to erect toll-gates, and apply the income to that object. He therefore saw no objection to setting up toll-gates, under the authority of the United States. He had not stood alone in that opinion; a large majority of the Senate concurred with him at that time. His opinions were still the same, and he still believed the power existed in the constitution; but the expediency of resorting to it was guarded by popular opinion. He considered that road a great national object; a great national thoroughfare for all the States. He contended against the propriety of surrendering the road to the States. It was giving the privileges of the nation away to communities whose interest was distinct, who had no sympathies, no common feelings, with the rest. We might as well surrender the care of the Mint or any public works, to individual States, as that road. He felt compelled to vote for the bill. Times had changed! He had seen the Bank, Internal Improvements, and other great national objects compelled, of late, to march to the right or left according to the will of those high in authority.

Mr. WRIGHT did not rise, he said, to defeat the bill. He only wished for some modification; as the bill was, he saw no prospect of getting rid of the road, there was no surety that the same demand would not be made again next year.

Mr. HILL said, he had the bill before him as it came from the House last year. He did not believe another dollar should be expended. The bill was passed at the last session with the understanding that it was the last expenditure that would be asked for. But there it was again, and no security against still further demands. It was contended that the sum was not sufficient,—when would it be sufficient? Millions had already been expended upon this expensive undertaking and he saw no end to the prodigality and waste of the public treasures. He for one could not vote for any appropriation under such circumstances.

Mr. BUCHANAN said, he did not rise to say another word on the merits of this appropriation, but merely to make a brief reply to the Senator from Kentucky. He found himself between two fires from opposite sides of the Senate. While the gentleman from South Carolina (Mr. Preston) thinks I go too far in favor of internal improvements, the gentleman from Kentucky blames me for not going far enough. On this subject they are the opposite extremes. For his own part, between the two, he should adopt the maxim

medio tutissimus ibis." He should certainly follow this advice for the regulation of his own conduct. The safest course, in his opinion, lay between the extremes.

He did not intent to argue the question; but he would say to the gentleman from Kentucky, that he, Mr. B., could see a vast difference between the simple power of appropriating money for the construction of roads, and that of exercising jurisdiction over them after they had been completed. As incidental power cannot transcend its principal, the stream cannot rise higher than its fountain—and it does not, by any means, follow that the mere power of appropriation for internal improvements, involves that of entering the territories of the States, erecting toll gates upon the roads, and levying tolls from passengers. The existence of the one power cannot be inferred from that of the other. To give money is one thing; but to exercise jurisdiction is another, and a very different affair. There is no necessary connexion between the two.

In relation to the remark of the gentleman, that whole communities had changed their opinions upon an important subject within the last few years, he had only to say, that if they had done so, sufficient reasons might be adduced to justify his change. He was not among the number himself who had thus changed; but if he had been, he could readily conceive why any gentleman might have been of one opinion at the period alluded to of the gentleman, and of a very different opinion for the disclosures which had since been made. Mr. B. said he entertained now, as he ever had, feelings of the greatest respect for the gentleman from Kentucky, and none of his (Mr. B.'s) marks were made in any unkind spirit.

Some further remarks were made by Messrs. BAY, WRIGHT, and KING of Alabama, when Mr. K. submitted an amendment, which, if adopted, he said, would remove his objection to the third section. If not, he should feel it his duty to be for striking out.

The amendment was, "that before any portion of the appropriation shall be expended upon the road, the same shall be surrendered to the States through which it passes."

Mr. HENDRICKS having made no objection to the amendment, it was agreed to.

The question being on Mr. PRESTON'S motion to strike out, it was determined in the negative—yeas 14, nays 32, as follows:

NEAS—Messrs. Black, Brown, Calhoun, Cuthbert, Hill, King of Georgia, Leigh, Mangum, Moore, Naudain, Ruggles, Shepley, Tyler, White.—14.

NAYS—Messrs. Benton, Bibb, Buchanan, Clay, Ewing, Frelinghuysen, Goldsborough, Grundy, Hendricks, Kane, Kent, King of Alabama, Knight, Linn, McKean, Morris, Naudain, Poindexter, Porter, Prentiss, Robbins, Robinson, Silsbee, Smith, Southard, Swift, Tallmadge, Tipton, Tomlinson, Wagaman, Webster, Wright—32.

Mr. HILL then moved to reduce the appropriation to the road in Ohio from $200,000 to $100,000, which was disagreed to.

The bill was then reported to the Senate, the amendments concurred in, and the bill was ordered to be engrossed for a third reading.

On motion of Mr. KANE, the Senate proceeded to the consideration of Executive business, and on the doors were opened,

The Senate adjourned.

HOUSE OF REPRESENTATIVES,

WEDNESDAY, February 11, 1835.

Mr. MARDIS, on leave, presented a petition; which was referred.

Mr. CHINN, from the Committee on the District of Columbia, reported a bill in relation to the union of the lateral branch of the Baltimore Ohio Rail Road through the District to the city of Washington; which was read twice.

Mr. CHINN moved that the bill be ordered to be engrossed.

Mr. PARKER said that this appeared to be a bill in relation to a contract, and if an error should be committed, it might be difficult to correct it afterwards. However important the passage of the bill. However important measure might be, still, as it was intended that road should pass through the public lands, he

was unwilling that the bill should be engrossed until time was given to examine into the subject.

Mr. McKIM was surprised at the objection raised by the gentleman from New Jersey (Mr. Parker.) He was not himself personally interested in this work; he did not own a share of its stock, nor did he desire any, because he did not believe that it would be profitable. 'The public were, however, deeply interested in the completion of this work. He was authorized by the President of the Rail Road Company to say, that if no difficulty was thrown in the way by Congress, the road would be completed to this City by the 4th of July next. If this bill was not passed, the road must stop at the line of this District. This would subject the public to considerable additional expense, in travelling and transportation between this City and the point at which the Rail Road would terminate. The Directors of the Rail Road Company had visited this place, and had come to a perfect understanding with the Mayor and City Authorities on the subject. It had been arranged that the road should pass along the valley of the Tiber. This and over which it would pass was worth but little, and the company were pledged to pay any damage which might be assessed by a jury, in consequence of the proposed location of the rail road. There was no trick intended. He repeated that great advantages would result to the public by the completion of this improvement. It would enable travellers to pass between the cities of Baltimore and Washington in two hours; and as no injury would result to any one, he trusted that all objection would be withdrawn, and the bill be permitted to progress.

Mr. PARKER could not see why the gentleman from Maryland should be surprised that he (Mr. P.) was not prepared to vote on a bill which he did not understand. He did not believe that any trick was intended by the bill. He thought it improper that a bill of such importance should be hurried through the House, with so little consideration. If it was supposed that the measure must fail if the bill was not ordered to be engrossed to-day, he would ask what would become of the various important bills which were not yet acted on? The same argument would equally apply to other measures. He saw no reason for such haste upon this particular bill. He thought it had better be postponed for a few days, in order to afford time to look into its provisions.

Mr. CHINN remarked that the public interest was not involved, or compromited, by the provisions of the bill.

Mr. PARKER moved to postpone the further consideration of the bill until Monday next, and that it be printed; which was agreed to.

Mr. ASHLEY, from the Committee on the Public Lands, reported, without amendment, the bill from the Senate, extending the time for entering back lands in the State of Louisiana.

On motion of Mr. ASHLEY, the bill was read a third time and passed.

Mr. LEA, of Tennessee, from the Committee on Revolutionary Pensions, reported a bill to provide for paying certain pensioners at Jackson, in the State of Tennessee; which was read twice and ordered to be engrossed.

Unfavorable reports were made by Mr. GRENNELL, from the Committee on Indian Affairs, and Mr. FOSTER, from the Committee on the Judiciary.

Mr. GAMBLE moved to take up and consider a resolution heretofore offered by him, calling on the Secretary of the Treasury for a plan for the keeping and disbursement of the public moneys, without the agency of a Bank or Banks.

The motion being objected to, Mr GAMBLE moved to suspend the rule of the House, in order that he might attain his object; which was negatived.

Mr. FOSTER, from the Committee on the Judiciary, reported a bill further to define and punish the forging and counterfeiting of Consular and other certificates; which was read twice, and after a few remarks by Messrs FOSTER and FILLMORE,

Mr. McKINLEY said, as the bill seemed likely to lead to a discussion, which would interfere with the usual morning business, he would move to

postpone its further consideration to Monday next; which was agreed to—yeas 82, nays 46.

Mr. FOSTER, from the Committee on the Judiciary, reported the following resolution:

Resolved, That the Committee on the Judiciary be discharged from the further consideration of that part of the President's Message which relates to the extension of the judiciary system of the United States, and of the bill from the House of Representatives, to amend the Judiciary system of the United States, it being manifest that the time to elapse before the Constitutional termination of the present Congress, is insufficient to mature and pass any law on the subject, to which the message and bill refer.

Mr. FOSTER said that the resolution had been reported at the instance of a majority of the Committee. Entertaining different views himself, he would move to amend the resolution by substituting the following:

Strike out all after the word _Resolved_, and insert,—'' That the Committee on the Judiciary, to whom was referred that part of the President's message which relates to an extension of the Judicial system of the United States, be instructed to report a bill, by which the benefits of said system, may be equally extended to all the States of the Union."

Mr. FOSTER remarked, that the reason assigned in the resolution of the majority, that there was not sufficient time to mature a bill on the subject referred to, he considered insufficient. A bill had been prepared by the committee, which he believed could be matured and acted on by the House during the present session. It was not calculated to elicit debate. The time had arrived when every one must see, if we are to have a judicial system at all, it should be general. If there was a necessity for Circuit Courts in the Atlantic States, they were equally necessary in the new States. This was the only question to be decided. He considered it improper, after the committee had proposed a bill, they should ask to be discharged from the further consideration of the subject, merely because they were apprehensive that the House would not have time to act upon it.

Mr. HARDIN had the honor to belong to the Committee on the Judiciary. At the last session, a bill was reported for the extension of the Judiciary system, which propose d to increase the number of the Justices of the Supreme Court from seven to nine. Another bill had been reported by the committee at the present session, which did not increase the number of the Judges, but divided the several States into Circuits, to which the present Judges were assigned, and they were required to hold but one term in each year. For his own part, he was not entirely satisfied with either measure. The bills were recommitted to the Committee on the Judiciary. Owing to some embarrassments on the subject, the committee had come to the determination to report the resolution now under consideration. There was not sufficient time to discuss and mature this measure at this late period of the session. Only seventeen parliamentary days remained for the transaction of business, and there were four or five hundred bills on the docket unacted on, and some of them of an important character. He considered it impossible that the subject of the judiciary system could be taken up and examined in all its bearings during the present session. It was the practice for committees, near the close of a session, to ask to be discharged from the consideration of subjects, when, in their opinion, there was not sufficient time to act on them. He concluded by moving to lay the resolution and amendments on the table.

Mr. THOMAS, of Maryland, hoped the gentleman would withdraw the motion. He would move the previous question, if this should be done, in order that a direct vote might be had on the resolution. A vote to lay on the table would be an equivocal one.

Mr. HARDIN said he would withdraw his motion, provided any gentleman desired to make a speech, but not otherwise.

Mr. FOSTER inquired of the Chair, whether

If the resolution to discharge the committee from the further consideration of the subject, was laid on the table, it would not be incumbent on the committee to continue their investigations of the subject?

The SPEAKER replied, that if the motion to lay the subject on the table prevailed, it would be equivalent to a discharge of the committee from the further consideration of the subject.

Mr. GARLAND hoped that the gentleman from Kentucky (Mr. Hardin) would withdraw his motion, and permit the members from the new States, who were more particularly interested in the subject, to give their views.

Mr. HARDIN reminded the gentleman that he had stated that if any gentleman desired to make a speech, he would withdraw the motion. Mr. H. then withdrew his motion to lay the resolutions on the table.

Mr. GARLAND hoped that the amendment proposed by the Chairman of the Judiciary Committee (Mr. Foster) would be adopted. The President of the United States, in several successive messages, had urged this subject upon the attention of Congress. It was well known that several of the new States did not enjoy the same privileges, as regarded the judicial system, which had been extended to the other States. He asked whether the House would, when a bill had been prepared on the subject, permit the committee to withhold it, because it might suppose that there was not time to act upon it? Was it not proper that an attempt, at least, should be made to pass some bill on this subject at the present session? It was certainly due to the importance of the question, and to the new States, that the subject should be acted upon at the earliest practicable period. He could not believe that this House would be disposed to withhold those rights and privileges from the new, which were enjoyed by the old States. He desired that a direct vote should be taken on the resolution, and agreed with the gentleman from Maryland, (Mr. Thomas,) that a vote to lay the subject on the table, would be an equivocal one.

Mr. McKINLEY felt as much solicitude as any other member, that some bill on this subject should receive the sanction of Congress. The subject had, however, from time to time been brought up, without any apparent disposition to do any thing with it. Was it expected, under such circumstances, that any thing would be gained by discussing the subject at this late period of the session. He was desirous that the judicial system should be extended to the new States. This should be done upon due deliberation. He was not satisfied with the bill which had been proposed. He was, moreover, opposed to wasting unnecessarily the time of the House, when it was impossible that the subject could be matured and disposed of at the present session.

Mr. THOMAS, of Maryland, next rose to address the House, but immediately after he had commenced his remarks

Mr. WATMOUGH moved that the House proceed to the consideration of the orders of the day; which was agreed to. Yeas 122, nays not counted.

DEPOSITE BANKS.

The House resumed the consideration of the bill regulating the deposits of the public moneys in certain local banks.

Mr. ROBERTSON continued the argument commenced by him yesterday, in opposition to the bill introduced by the Committee of Ways and Means. His object, he said, was to show that the experiment, as it had been termed, had proved unsuccessful, not having answered the purpose contemplated in taking charge of and disbursing the public revenue—that a hundred thousand dollars per annum were sunk and lost to the Government by the employment of State banks for the public deposites. Such being the case, in a state of profound peace, he asked what might be expected in the emergency of war, which we might perhaps look to as probable at no very distant day? The local banks he considered as peculiarly liable to be affected by the casualties and circumstances of the times. Under the present system, too, they would spring up with every custom-house and land office. Hostilities would be engendered between the favored banks of the Government and the others, which would require the aid of the latter to sustain, with the force of its power and patronage, the banks selected as its fiscal agents. They would thus become the creatures of the government, dependent on it for their very existence. Jealousies would also arise between the favored institutions themselves—one believing another to have too large a share of executive or governmental favor. To regulate all these conflicting interests the office of the Secretary of the Treasury would be totally changed in its character—and that officer be required to possess more than the financial talents of a Rothschild or a Baring. Instead of filling the office with four different individuals in one year, it would be essential that he should have spent a life in the acquirement of the knowledge—that he should be trained up to all the arts of financiering. He alluded to the amount of deposites in the State of New York. He rejoiced, he said, in the growing prosperity of that great State. He did not believe it her wish to retain an undue share of the public treasure. Her natural advantages were quite sufficient without the addition of such extraneous ones.—The State from which he came did not look with jealousy on the prosperity of any portion of our great and happy country. She beheld with pleasure the rapid advances of the western States; and it was gratifying to behold on that floor the representatives of a great, growing, free and intelligent people, and he should not represent the people of Virginia, if he did not express that sentiment. After some further observations on the commercial importance and power of New York, Mr. R. alluded to the system of retrenchment which had been so long called for by the people of the country. That this system was not more closely adhered to, he was aware, was not so essentially the fault of the Executive branch of government as that of the Legislature. On Congress rested the responsibility of ensuring retrenchment. He was anxious to see the Government brought back to its original purity, and he had the right to call on the friends of the administration to go with him on this great question. He concluded, by expressing a hope, that the bill would be re-committed to the Committee, with instructions to report a project dispensing with the use of Banks as fiscal agents of the Government.

Mr. CAMBRELENG replied at first to the remarks of Mr. Gordon, who spoke yesterday, and defended the course of the Executive from the charges made by that gentleman against him. A gentleman said that under the new system, New York enjoyed a larger portion of the public revenue than any other city; that she enjoyed the lion's share. It was true, the did—but she bore the lion's share of the burthen. New York was a loser by the new system; because, prior to it great use was made of the public money by the merchants of New York. Much had been said of the inability of the local banks to collect, disburse, and distribute the public revenue, but he was at a loss to see how they were unable to disburse twenty millions, when a single bank had distributed and disbursed its thousands of millions. He hoped, however, the time would come when the country would be enabled to dispense with the agency of any and every bank whatsoever. At present, it could not be done. Mr. C. deeply regretted that in a question of this matter, things altogether foreign to it had been introduced. The Executive, in directing the removal of the deposites, was said to have usurped the purse and the sword; had gentlemen forgotten the act of 31st March, 1809? He had hoped, the long contest of last year, in which the very ties of society were involved, and our friendships and affections broken, would not have been renewed. He had hoped that after the general battle of last year, strife would have been at an end, but it seemed we were to have a guerilla war; he trusted it would be conducted with less violence than heretofore.

Much had been said about Executive patronage, and that the majority of the House of Representatives were seen on the side of power. He would appeal to the candor of the gentleman from Virginia, (Mr. Gordon,) an old member of that House, to say at what period in the history of the last twenty years, he had ever seen the majority of the House of Representatives like the present, standing by the constitution, or more faithful to their constituents. Mr. C. had been a member of the House for fourteen years, and he had never seen a republican majority standing by the constitution as did the present, and with what justice could the charge be brought against them of being the advocates of power? When the present incumbent of the presidential chair came into office, the federal banner floated triumphantly over the country, and federal usurpation was making, and had long been making, large and rapid strides. What was the situation of the President? On the one hand he might have made himself the leader of power, on the other was that of his country. He made his choice, and selected that imperishable ground, indignantly rejecting all the proffers of the advocates of power. [Still after] bill was presented to him, by which he might have ensured power; he rejected them, and he was the first President of these United States bold enough to recommend a measure to bring the revenue down to the needful expenses of the country. Again, when the bill to recharter the Bank of the United States passed both houses, and was sent to the President for his approval, when he would have obtained the support of every President, director, officer, stockholder, and customer of that institution throughout the Union, did he, by vetoing that bill, show himself the advocate of power? Again and again, when other bills were presented to him, for roads and canals, for almost every State and every congressional district in these States, did he then show himself the advocate of power? When he returned every measure to those two Houses, was the proof of his advocacy of Executive power? A present Chief Magistrate had presented an ordinary spectacle, and one which might probably never be seen again, for it was the inherent tendency of Executive power not only to retain power given it, and take all that was possible, but to absorb all that it could grasp. We have seen the President of the United States limits to and bridging his own power.

Mr. C. then referred to, and congratulated the House that the great question of reform was to be brought before the American people; he hoped that it would go to the fountain of the abuses and not confine themselves to attack upon one subordinate branch. The root of the evil lay deep, and had been unfortunately in the spirits, Hamilton and Jefferson, of opposing sentiments. The evils of the Post Office dated their rise from that time. After some further remarks, Mr. C. again recurred to the state of banks.

These institutions, he said, might be tried by old countries, but whatever nation should betray they never could meet the case, and would be continually bringing the paper standard into conflict with the metallic currency. The argument that the precious metals are diminishing, and that our currency was indispensable, Mr. C. repelled. But we had gone so far in this banking system that agents had been employed in various tries to ascertain how much specie existed. He have told us that there were seven or ten the millions employed in bullion, and from these five millions in current coin.

He hoped the day would come when all speculations about paper currency would be banished from the halls of legislation. If not, he feared the day would come when their hobbies would be filled with speculative capital, and dissension would be sown every where as he had witnessed many revolutions there. A resolution introduced by himself only six years ago, for the reciprocity of trade, was indignantly rejected on second reading, and many voted against it, and had since become the ardent advocates of the system. Who would now be daring enough to introduce a bill to recharter the Bank of the United States? Yet, not long since it passed both Houses. Mr. C. quoted Smith's Wealth of Nations, to show the

of his description of the then state of England with the present condition of the United States, and referred also to the course of William Pitt, Prime Minister of England, and the speeches of Edmund Burke, in support of free trade. He also gave a review of France, Spain, and Portugal, to show that the spirit of reform was marching rapidly onward, and that the time was approaching when the councils of those countries would be governed by principles other than they were at present.

Mr. CLAYTON said he had two objects in wishing to address the House on this subject. One was in justification of himself from certain charges brought against him there and elsewhere; the other, to give reasons why he should vote for the amendment to the bill proposed by the gentleman from Virginia. Mr. C. particularly referred to certain charges that, he said, had been brought against him, chiefly at home, of having received accommodations from the Bank, and of his course having been influenced thereby. Mr. C. entered into an explanation of the grounds of the affair, in substance the same, we believe, as have appeared in some of the Georgia papers. Mr. C. then referred to the passage of the resolutions of the Legislature of his own State, instructing their Senators to vote for expunging Mr. Clay's resolutions of last year from the journals of the Senate of the United States, and read an application from some members of a former Legislature thereof to the Bank of the United States for a branch, &c.

In support of the amendment for which he intended to vote, Mr. C. quoted Mr. McDuffie's report, as to the power of Congress to charter corporations. He then examined into the reasons assigned by the Secretary of the Treasury for removing the deposites, and contended that there was more danger to be apprehended from the numerous local Banks than from one Bank.

Mr. MANN, of New York, rose and said that he had not designed to trouble the House with any remarks upon this subject; and he should not have done so but for some observations which had fallen in the course of the debate, from the two honorable gentlemen from Virginia (Messrs. Gordon and Robertson,) who addressed the House yesterday and to-day, which Mr. M. said he felt himself constrained, as a Representative from New York, to notice. He must, therefore, ask a few moments' indulgence. If, sir, I have not mistaken the scope of their remarks, the honorable gentlemen object to the passage of this bill, because about thirteen millions of the revenues of this Government are collected in the State of New York, to be deposited in her State Banks, and used in the promotion of her already overgrown commerce; thus operating like a pecuniary tariff in her favor. The gentlemen then go on to speak of that State, which, by courtesy, they denominate the Empire, with an army of forty representatives on this floor, possessing population, facilities, resources, and political power; presenting to the vision of gentlemen ideal dangers to the prosperity and welfare of the other States in this Union; and therefore it is argued that great circumspection should be used here in respect to our National Legislation, so as not to increase those advantages and facilities which New York is always so ready to embrace and improve. The inference which it appears to me necessarily follows from the scope of the remarks of the gentlemen, taken altogether, and I take it as an inference, is, that the power of New York is not only too great in the Union, but that she will use it for political and improper purposes of self-aggrandizement.

[Here Mr. M. yielded the floor to the gentlemen from Virginia, (Messrs. Gordon and Robertson,) who explained, and said that they had not intended to utter a word disrespectful to the State of New York—that they admired that State and her rapid progress and improvement, and Mr. Gordon protested against any inferences being drawn by the gentleman from New York, (Mr. M.) which his language did not warrant.]

Mr. M. resumed, and said that he had not understood the gentlemen as using disrespectful or uncomplimentary or uncourteous language towards his State, or her representatives, and he had not misunderstood the scope of their remarks, from which he had drawn the inference which he had stated, as necessarily following from their propositions and premises. This inference, said Mr. M., seems constantly to disturb the imagination of gentlemen in both wings of the the Capitol, presenting a vision continually before their eyes, insomuch that, judging by the observations which a seat on this floor for a single session has enabled me to make, I conclude that no question of general or national importance can be considered and discussed here, without involving considerations and allusions appertaing to the State of New York and her career as a member of the confederacy. Her advantages, her institutions, her legislative and political policy are arrayed and reviewed, censured, and sometimes freely condemned on this floor. Her public men, charged with the administration of her local and State affairs, have sometimes been attacked with epithets as senseless as they are unjust. Her banking systems seem to have the misfortune with gentlemen, to meet with no favor, except distrust and disapproval.

Sir, if gentlemen who discourse so largely about New York, her laws and institutions, her wealth and commerce, would take the trouble to examine them more closely, and learn more of their nature, extent, and utility, I trust they would find more to merit their commendation, and less to denounce and condemn. I do not know that it is proper to arraign the legislative or local policy of any State of the Union upon this floor; yet I have, perhaps too often, been a silent witness of the exhibition here, and in the other branch of the National Legislature, in respect to the State which, in a very humble part, I have the honor to represent. I have supposed that the States keeping within the boundaries established by the Constitution of the United States, had the power to manage their own affairs, in their own way. But if honorable gentlemen are disposed to look into New York for good or for evil, I will join them in aid of the most scrutinizing examination into her political history, her public policy, laws, and institutions. I would ask their particular attention to her systems and provisions for public education; to her social and moral condition; to her jurisprudence and legislation; to her system of internal improvements; to her proud financial condition; to her banking and monetary system; to her internal resources; to her intelligent, industrious, and enterprising population; in which, at last, they will find the secret of the power, the wealth, and expansive greatness of New York, apparently so much dreaded. Let me ask gentlemen, in what State or country will they find the affairs of a local government better conducted, to secure the ends of a good government, the happiness, rights, and liberties of the people, than are those of N. York? Are her finances and resources wasted or perverted to improper objects? I will not here make invidious comparisons but invite gentlemen in their own States, to imitate rather than to indulge unreasonable or unfounded jealousies of the legislation and power of New York.

But, Mr. Speaker, when has New York used her commercial or political power in the Union, for selfish or improper purposes? When has she endangered the Union of these States, or swerved from the political faith and principles which she derived from Virginia through those apostles of political liberty, Washington, Jefferson, Madison, and Monroe. For thirty two years since the adoption of the Constitution, the vaunted "ancient dominion" has held the control of the executive and legislative policy of this Government, during all which time, New York has stood firmly by her side, advocating her faith and practice under the Constitution, without having dreamed of *"the alternative"* which might permit her to change her course or her principles. Let the history of her action during the late war, pouring out her best blood and treasures upon the altar of the country, while another portion of the Union occupied a position at Hartford more than equivocal, while the very Capitol in which we are assembled, was a heap of smoking ruins under the eyes of the *"ancient dominion,"* hild the State of New York from any inferences of a purpose or intention to use her dreaded political power in the confederacy for selfish or improper purposes. Sir, what has been the recent position of New York in the trials to which the strength of our institutions have been subjected? Has she stopped to consider *"any alternatives,"* or has she stood by the Constitution and the principles which she derived from the fathers of the "ancient Dominion," even though the gallant sons of those fathers may have doubted and hesitated as to whether the path of their sires led on to the fountains of patriotism? She has maintained the firm and even tenor of her ways through all the vicissitudes and changes which have been going on around her, and she will continue to adhere to the ancient republican faith promulged from Virginia, even though the talented public men of the latter, may in some instances indulge their fears that such adherence will lead her to a position in the Union which will not permit those who "discourse of Rome, to say that her wide walls contain but one man."

Sir, what is the position of N. York at present on this floor? Is it equivocal or alternative? Is it in opposition to the constitutional doctrines so long cherished in favor of strict construction? Is it opposed to the rights of the States? When have her representatives arraigned at this bar the admitted constitutional legislation, the policy or measures of one of the State Governments of this Union? And when, sir, after having done so, have they then maintained that the State Governments have the power to review and nullify the constitutional measures of the National Government? Sir, the State of New York may present to the views of some honorable gentlemen the political enigma, about which they discourse, but cannot understand; yet, sir, she has never been found to be a political meteor, traversing the abstruse regions and metaphysical mazes of the political firmanent. But, Mr. Speaker, the sin of New York is her physical and numerical greatness—her overgrown external commerce and her internal trade, resources, and advantages. Sir, I know not how to reply to the position that my native State is physically too strong already, and that greater dangers are to be apprehended from its increasing strength and multiplying facilities and resources. I cannot regret it—that would be a "treason most foul." I cannot profess its weakness—the facts would not sustain me. I do most sincerely desire its increasing prosperity, and I must be permitted to enjoy this natural desire. N. York, sir, has never been the recipient of your bounty. She has never asked at your hands more than strict justice, in the distribution of your favors, and has not received even that. Her commercial advantages depend upon the laws of nature, and of these she cannot be deprived by legislation. Transfer your public revenues from the natural aids they afford to her commerce, as the honorable gentleman from Virginia proposes, and you will not materially affect the progress of New York in her commercial career, since she does not rely upon adventitious advantages. She has, however, a right to demand at your hands equal and impartial justice. She asks nothing more. While New York is the medium and instrument by which so large a portion of the public revenues are collected, can you, in common and equal justice, deprive her of the advantages which her situation confers? You cannot, and ought not. For many years past those revenues have been under the selfish and odious control of the U. S. Bank, with interests opposed to those of New York, and has this circumstance arrested the commerce and prosperity of that State? We have sir, I confess, sometimes inconveniently felt the power of an unseen hand striking at our welfare, but not sufficiently to retard permanently our progress.

Mr. Speaker, allow me to express the hope that we may hereafter be able to discuss and consider the various questions presented here, without drawing into review the local affairs and legislative policy of any of the States of the confederacy, unless it shall be to derive useful lessons, to guide us in the path of duty by their example or experience; and let me add the hope that the various amendments proposed to the bill under consideration may be rejected, and the bill passed into a law.

Mr. WILSON, of Virginia, addressed the

House in opposition to the motion to commit the bill as made by his colleague, (Mr. Robertson.) He was also opposed to the amendment of Mr. Gordon. Believing that the Bank of the United States would not be rechartered; he was satisfied that it would be necessary to employ the State Banks as the fiscal agents of the Government. He was, therefore, in favor of perfecting the present bill; and although he had some doubts on the subject, still he should probably vote for the amendment which had been suggested by another colleague (Mr. Moore,) to insert the names of the State Banks in the bill, so as to leave as little discretion as possible to the Secretary of the Treasury.

Mr. VANCE asked what was now the question before the House?

The CHAIR stated it to be on the motion to recommit the bill, with instructions.

Mr. VANCE said he had an amendment to the bill, which he was anxious should be placed before the House, or before the committee, if the bill should be recommitted. He also wished to have it printed. In all legislation, he deemed it important to look at practical results. There were several States in the Union which did not contain a collection district, and his amendment looked to a more equal distribution of the public revenue. Without it, these States would experience pecuniary embarrassments, which no man could now properly appreciate. The amendment was read. Mr. V. said its object was apparent on the face of it; but, after a suggestion from the CHAIR on a point of order, he withdrew it for the present.

Mr. HANNEGAN rose, and alluded to the variety and importance of the business on the table, which must be acted on in the nine business days left of the session. He alluded particularly to the graduation bill—to the Post Office investigation—the public lands—the harbor bill—and various others, involving interests of the highest importance, which he hoped were duly appreciated by the members of the House. He had a dislike, which nearly amounted to aversion, to be either the principal or the agent in any act tending to curtail the freedom of debate; but under the present circumstances, the necessity was urged upon him by the most imperious considerations. He therefore he assured the House it was with great reluctance that he felt compelled to demand the previous question.

Mr. McKINLEY moved a call of the House.

A question of order was raised as to whether that motion could be made before the call for the previous question was seconded; and after some conversation thereon between the CHAIR, Messrs. McKINLEY, WILLIAMS, MASON, MERCER, SUTHERLAND, and BRIGGS,

Mr. McKINLEY withdrew the motion.

The motion for the previous question was then taken by tellers, and decided as follows: Yeas 96, nays 100.

So the House refused to second the previous question.

Mr. BURGES expressed a wish to address the House, but as the hour was late, he moved to adjourn.

Mr. POLK asked for the yeas and nays, which having been ordered,

Mr. BURGES withdrew the motion.

Mr. FILLMORE then asked for a division of the question to recommit with instructions.

The question was then taken by yeas and nays, which had been previously ordered, on the motion to recommit the bill, and decided in the negative. Yeas 91, nays 115.

The question then recurring on the amendment offered by Mr. EWING, that gentleman asked for the yeas and nays, which were ordered.

Mr. SLADE moved to adjourn. Negatived. Yeas 93, nays 102.

The question on Mr. EWING'S amendment was then decided by the following vote:

YEA.—Mr. Ewing—1.

NAYS.—Messrs. John Q. Adams, John Adams, Heman Allen, J. J. Allen, Chilton Allan, William Allen, Archer, Ashley, Banks, Barber, Barringer, Bates, Baylies, Beale, Bean, Beaty, Beaumont, Bell, Binney, Bockee, Boon, Bouldin,

Briggs, Brown, Bull, Bunch, Burns, Bynum, Cage, Cambreleng, Campbell, Carmichael, Carr, Casey, Chambers, Chaney, Chilton, Chinn, Claiborn, Sam'l Clark, Wm. Clark, Clay, Clayton, Coffee, Cramer, Crane, Crockett, Darlington, Amos Davis, Day, Deberry, Denny, Dickerson, Dickinson, Dunlap, Evans, E. Everett, Felder, Ferris, Fillmore, Forester, Foster, Fowler, Wm K. Fuller, Fulton, Gamble, Garland, Gholson, Gillet, Gilmer, Gordon, Gorham, Graham, Grennell, Griffin, Joseph Hall, Hiland Hall, Thomas H. Hall, Halsey, Hamer, Hannegan, Hardin, James Harper, Hathaway, Hawkins, Heath, Henderson, Hiester, Howell, Hubbard, Huntington, Inge, Wm. Jackson, E. Jackson, Jones, Jarvis, Richard M. Johnson, Noadiah Johnson, Cave Johnson, B. Jones, Kavanagh, Kilgore, King, Kinnard, Lane, Lansing, Laporte, Lea, Lee, Letcher, Lewis, Lincoln, Love, Lyon, Lytle, Abijah Mann, jr. Martindale, Marshall, Mardis, John Y. Mason, Moses Mason, jr. May, McCarty, McComas, McIntire, McKay, McKennan, McKim, McKinley, McLene, McVean, Miller, Milligan, Miner, Henry Mitchell, Robert Mitchell, Moore, Morgan, Muhlenberg, Murphy, Osgood, Page, Parks, Parker, Patton, Patterson, Dutee J. Pearce, Philips, Pickens, Franklin Pierce, Pierson, Pinckney, Plummer, Polk, Pope, Potts, Ramsay, Reed, Reynolds, Robertson, Schenck, Schley, A. H. Shepperd, Shinn, Slade, Smith, Spangler, Speight, Standifer, Steele, Wm. Taylor, Wm. P. Taylor, Francis Thomas, Thomson, Tompkins, Trumbull, Tweedy, Vance, Van Houten, Vinton, Wagener, Ward, Wardwell, Watmough, Webster, Whallon, White, Williams, Wise.—189.

So the amendment was rejected.

The question then recurring on the amendment of Mr. GORDON,

Mr. WILLIAMS asked for the yeas and nays; which were ordered.

Mr. VANCE moved an adjournment—negatived, ayes 71. Noes not counted.

The question was then taken, by yeas and nays, on the amendment offered by Mr. GORDON, as follows:

YEAS—Messrs. John Q. Adams, Heman Allen, John J. Allen, Chilton Allan, Archer, Barber, Beale, Beaty, Campbell, Claiborne, William Clark, Clayton, Amos Davis, Davenport, Deberry, Foster, Gamble, Gholson, Gordon, Griffin, Heath, Letcher, Lewis, Martindale, McComas, Pearce, Robertson, Spangler, Steele, William P Taylor, Wilde, Williams, Wise—33.

NAYS.—Messrs. John Adams, William Allen, Ashley, Banks, Barringer, Baylies, Bean, Beaumont, Bell, Binney, Bockee, Boon, Bouldin, Briggs, Brown, Bunch, Burns, Bynum, Cage, Cambreleng, Carmichael, Carr, Casey, Chaney, Chil ton, Chinn, Samuel Clark, Clay, Coffee, Cramer, Crane, Darlington, Day, Denny, Dickerson, Dickinson, Dunlap, Evans, Edward Everett, Ewing, Ferris, Fillmore, Forester, Fowler, William K. Fuller, Fulton, Galbraith, Garland, Gillet, Gilmer, Gorham, Graham, Grayson, Grennell, Joseph Hall, Hiland Hall, Thomas H. Hall, Halsey, Hamer, Hannegan, Hard, Hardin, James Harper, Harrison, Hathaway, Hawkins, Henderson, Hiester, Howell, Hubbard, Huntington, Inge, William Jackson, Ebenezer Jackson, Janes, Jarvis, Richard M. Johnson, Noadiah Johnson, Benjamin Jones, Kavanagh, Kilgore, King, Kinnard, Lane, Lansing, Laporte, Luke Lea, Thomas Lee, Lincoln, Love, Loyall, Lucas, Lyon, Lytle, Abijah Mann, Joel K. Mann, Marshall, Mardis, John Y. Mason, Moses Mason May, McCarty, McIntire, McKay, McKennan, McKim, McKinley, McLene, McVean, Miller, Milligan, Miner, Henry Mitchell, Robert Mitchell, Moore, Morgan, Muhlenberg, Murphy, Osgood, Page, Parks, Parker, Patton Patterson, Dutee J. Pearce, Phillips, Pierce, Pierson, Pinckney, Plummer, Polk, Pope, Potts, Ramsay, Reed, Reynolds, Schenck, Schley, William B. Shepard, Augustine H. Shepperd, Shinn, Slade, Smith, Speight, Standifer, William Taylor, Francis Thomas, Thomson, Trumbull, Turrill, Tweedy, Vance, Van Houten, Wagener, Ward, Wardwell, Watmough, Webster, Whallon, White, Wilson—161.

So the amendment was negatived.

Mr. BOON moved the previous question.

Mr. FOSTER and Mr. MARDIS appealed to

the Hon. member to withdraw the motion, but Mr. Boon not consenting,

Mr. BURGES moved an adjournment. Carried.—Ayes 95, nays 86.

So the House adjourned.

THURSDAY, February 13, 1834.

Petitions and memorials were presented by Messrs. SILSBEE, KING of Ala., EARL, and GOLDSBOROUGH.

The VICE PRESIDENT communicated a letter from the War Department, conveying a statement of the contracts made by the Department in the year 1834.

The VICE PRESIDENT also laid before the Senate, a memorial from the Legislature Council of Michigan Territory, praying for the removal of the light-boat near Waugoshavee Point, to the mouth of the Detroit river, and for the erection of a light-house on said Point; which was referred to the Committee on Commerce.

Mr. POINDEXTER, from the Committee on Public Lands, to which the following bills for the House of Representatives were referred, reported the same:

A bill authorizing the sale of certain lands belonging to the university in Michigan, with amendment;

A bill authorizing the removal of the Land Office at Wapaghkonetta, in Ohio, to Lima, in the State, without amendment;

A bill for the relief of George Davenport, without amendment;

A bill for the relief of Robert Abbott and others, with an amendment.

Mr. SOUTHARD, from the Naval Committee, to which were referred the bills from the House of Representatives, for the relief of Mervin Perry, M. C. Perry, and E. R. Shubrick, reported severally, without amendment.

Mr. SOUTHARD, from the same Committee, made an unfavorable report upon the petition of the children of Benjamin W. Booth, late a lieutenant commandant in the U. S. Navy.

Mr. FRELINGHUYSEN, from the Committee on Revolutionary Claims, made an unfavorable report upon the petition of Richard Anders.

Mr. BELL, from the Judiciary Committee, an unfavorable report upon the petition of L. Wynn.

Mr. BELL, from the same Committee, unfavorable reports upon the petitions of James H. Burr, and John Howe.

He also reported the bill from the House of Representatives for the relief of Frank Boyden, without amendment.

Also, a bill authorizing the Secretary of the Treasury to compromise the claims allowed by the Two Sicilies, concluded in 1832; which read the first time and ordered to a second reading.

Mr. FRELINGHUYSEN, from the Committee on Manufactures, to which was referred the resolution relative to duties upon refined sugar, reported a bill allowing an additional duty on sugar refined in the United States; and they therefore, which was read the first time and ordered to a second reading.

Mr. WRIGHT, from the Committee on Finance, reported a joint resolution requiring a series of experiments to be made to ascertain how it is practicable to subtract from the value of the sugar by chemical process, or by drilling; which read the first time and ordered to a second reading.

Mr. BLACK, from the Committee on Private Affairs, made unfavorable reports upon the petitions of John A. Webster and Samuel Sloan.

Mr. BLACK, from the Committee on Private Land Claims, made an unfavorable report upon the petition of the heirs of Andrew McClish.

Mr. SILSBEE, pursuant to notice, asked and given, introduced a bill for the relief of John Putnam and Nathan Pratt.

Mr. HENDRICKS, pursuant to notice, leave to present certain certain roads in the Territory of Michigan; which bills were read twice and referred.

[CONTINUED IN NEXT NUMBER.]

TWENTY-THIRD CONGRESS.
SECOND SESSION.

IN SENATE.
Thursday, February 12, 1835.

[CONTINUED FROM LAST NUMBER.]

The following resolution was submitted by Mr. BENTON, which was read and ordered to be printed:

Resolved, That the President be requested to cause information to be laid before the Senate, at the commencement of the next session of Congress, on the following points:

1. The amount of revenue which may be reduced on dutiable articles without affecting the protection intended to be continued by the act of March 2d, 1833, to domestic manufactures.

2. The amount of net revenue which will probably be received from customs from 1836 to 1842, inclusively.

3. The amount of revenue which will probably be received from public lands for the same period, if no change takes place in the price of the lands.

4. The amount of revenue from the same source, if the price of the refuse lands should be reduced, and the lands should be so disposed of as to promote the settlement of the country, and should cease to be a source of revenue, except to defray the expenses of their management, and of extinguishing the Indian titles.

5. The times and proportions in which the amount of stock held in the Bank of the United States will probably be returned to the Treasury, if no act is passed by Congress for the sale of said stock.

6. The probable amount of the expenditures of the Government annually to the end of the year 1842.

7. The state of the fortifications; so as to show the number of forts of the first, second, and third class, now constructed in the United States; the number heretofore proposed and recommended by the War Department, but not yet constructed; and the number which would probably be necessary to the complete and adequate defence of the whole, maritime, an l gulf frontier of the United States, and such points of the land frontier as may be believed to require permanent fortifications.

8. The amount expended since 1816, in constructing forts, and the amount that would probably be necessary to complete the construction of the entire system of permanent fortifications for the United States.

9. The amount which has been expended since 1816 in providing for the armament of the fortifications, and the amount which would probably be necessary to complete the armament of all the fortresses required for the defence of the United States.

10. The amount which would probably be necessary to construct an adequate number of armories and arsenals in the United States, and to supply the States, with field artillery (especially brass ones) for their militia, and with side arms and pistols for their cavalry.

11. The amount expended since 1816 on the gradual increase of the navy, on navy yards, and in yards; and the amount necessary to be expended on each of these objects, to place the naval force of the United States upon the footing of strength and respectability which is due to the dignity and to the welfare of the Union.

12. And that the President be requested to cause to be communicated to the Senate, at the same time, any other information connected with the revenue and expenditure of the Government, and with the defence of the Union, which shall fall within the scope of the foregoing inquiries, or which, in his judgment, shall be necessary to be communicated.

The following resolution, submitted on Monday by Mr. CALHOUN, was taken up and agreed to:

Resolved, That the Secretary of the Treasury be directed to report to the Senate, at the commencement of the next session of Congress, what duties under twenty per cent. ad valorem, as provided by the sixth section of the act of the 2d of March, 1833, entitled "an act to modify the act of the 14th of July, 1832, and all other acts imposing duties on imports," can be reduced or repealed consistently with a due regard to the manufacturing interest; and an estimate of the probable amount of the reduction.

Mr. HILL'S resolutions relative to the validity and binding nature of the debts of the Post Office Department, were, on his motion, postponed to and made the special order for Tuesday next.

The resolution submitted some days since by Mr. SMITH, relative to the affairs of the Post office, was also taken up, and on his motion it was made the special order for the same day.

The resolution submitted on Tuesday, by Mr. HILL, calling upon the Secretary of the Treasury for information, whether the evidence of payments of commutation have been lost, and whether there is reason to believe the officers who received their commutation were not entitled to it, &c., was taken up and agreed to.

The bill making appropriations for the continuation and repair of the Cumberland road, was read the third time and passed.

The Senate proceeded to consider, as in Committee of the Whole, the bill authorizing a remission of duties on all rail road cars and cartirons, which were ordered prior to the 1st January last.

Mr. HILL asked that some good reason might be given by the Committee why the bill should pass.

Mr. TYLER said he thought the bill explained itself.

Mr. HILL said his objection was, that he did not know why these large companies should be exempt from the payment of duties rather than individuals.

Mr. TYLER said this was a subject in which the public had a direct interest. It was not simply for the benefit of the large companies.

Mr. FRELINGHUYSEN said, he saw no reason for the remission of the duties upon these articles, or that they should be refunded, if they had been paid. Our iron establishments were quite sufficient to supply all the demand for those articles, as he had been informed by a manufacturer, and at a reasonable price. Why then should we prefer the foreign manufacture to our domestic establishments? He moved that the bill be laid on the table.

The motion was agreed to.

The Senate then proceeded to the consideration of the joint resolution reported by the Library Committee, authorizing the purchase of 500 copies of Carey & Lea's History of Congress.

Mr. HILL asked the committee to give some reason why this bill should pass.

Mr. KING, of Georgia, expressed a wish that the bill might be permitted to lie on the table, until the information called for from the Secretary of the Senate, relative to the amount of printing authorized by Congress, could be had. It was essential, to enable us to act understandingly on this subject, that the information called for, should be obtained; it was indispensable. With regard to the value of this work, Mr. K. said, it might be a good and useful work, and it might be, like many others we had purchased, totally useless and worthless.

Mr. POINDEXTER enlarged upon the merits of the work; he said it could not progress without the patronage of the Government. It was of great utility to every statesman, because it contained the whole history and proceedings of Congress and the Government in a condensed form, and gentlemen could not afford to purchase it for their private libraries.

Mr. BENTON said, that about seven years ago, the Senate purchased one of those works called a

Political Register, and he took occasion to look into it to examine it closely, and found it to be a complete exemplification of the *suggestio falsi* and *suppressio veri*. Many thing were omitted which members said, and manys things were put into their mouths which they never did say. So far as he himself was concerned, Mr. B. said it contained a general libel on him. He looked over the Register of the last session, and he believed that in the matter that there appeared under his name, there was not one paragraph which was not more or less a downright falsification of what he said, and there was hardly a sentiment in it, or a fact stated in it, which he actually said. There were two papers in this city, the Telegraph and National Intelligencer, both of which, three or four years ago, were very very obliging to him. They both uniformly published his speeches, and whenever he desired alterations to be made in them, they did it very obligingly; and whenever he wanted to improve them, (and he did not hesitate to say that he did improve them,) they cheerfully consented to it. But within the last three years, both those papers had entirely changed their conduct towards him. And one of them, the National Intelligencer, refused, out and out, to publish one of his speeches against the Bank of the U. States. Yes, sir, Mr. B. said, they refused to publish his main speech, on the ground that it was too long, and when he afterwards offered to abridge it, they totally refused to publish it, while they published every thing that was said on the other side. The Telegraph did the same thing, and the gentlemen on the other side not only saw the notes, but the proofs too. With respect to the proposition now before the Senate, to buy these books, he perceived there the name of one of the *employees* of the Bank of the United States, and he had received information from Philadelphia that these persons were busily engaged last winter in keeping and fomenting the panic which was in a course of preparation and performance. He was opposed to this proposition, because, among other reasons, this history of the Congress of the United States by Carey & Lea, was a history of Congress by the Bank of the United States. This was all he had to say on this subject at this time. But with regard to this business of printing in the Senate, it exceeded all the other abuses of the government, including the Post Office, put together. In 1819 the expense for printing amounted to $15,000—while last year, he believed, it amounted to $150,000! And propositions for single jobs passed here, almost without opposition, incurring an expenditure equal to the whole sum paid in 1819. He took the opportunity now to give notice that as often as propositions were introduced here for extra jobs, he would be brought to his feet, and on the subject of this great and crying abuse, he would shew them to the country in all their enormity. And also, show, that while we were seeking to remove the mote from the eye of others, we would not perceive the beam in our own.

Mr. KING, of Georgia, said that where propositions had been made to purchase works, in this way, he always purchased them with his own money. But the value and usefulness of them would vanish like a sprite, if a proposition should be introduced to make the expenditure for them out of our own pockets. He did not know the value of this work, as he before remarked. But he did know that it would be very expensive. Honorable gentlemen agreed that such works were necessary to us in the discharge of our legislative duties. If they were so, he would be willing to vote money enough to purchase a sufficient number for our purpose. He would go as high as 50 copies to be placed in the library. And surely this was a liberal number. If the resolution was thus modified, he would support it. He was not in favor of purchasing these for the members to be taken home and used for their individual purposes. We had already engaged in a work for

which we were to pay $420,000, at least, and which, had it not been for the commendable zeal and care of the Committee last year, would have cost the Government, at least, three millions.

Mr. HILL said he had made some calculation of the cost of books and maps and printing ordered at a single session of Congress, leaving out several items of former purchases, which have been supplied to present members.

I am told the printing alone ordered to be executed by the printer of the Senate at the last session of Congress, amounts by computation to the enormous sum of $120,000.

This is more than ten times the amount of the printing ordinarily directed by this body in other times (when the Senate was not at war with the Executive, and when the printer was friendly to the administration and the voice of the People.) It amounts to an average of $2500 to each of the 48 members of the Senate.

Besides this, there were ordered and paid for, according to the statement of the Clerk, printed and laid upon our tables at the commencement of the session, the following articles:

For newspapers,	$832 18
Geo Watterston's Statistical Tables,	20 00
Jonathan Elliot, for Directories,	38 62
William Cranch, Index to District Report,	500 00
Thompson and Homans, Pennsylvania Register,	13 25
J. Elliot, Debates on the Constitution,	175 00
do Diplomatic Code,	99 00
Gales & Seaton, Register of Debates,	1940 00
Paid for selecting and arranging papers for Land Documents and State papers,	1250 00
D. A. Hall's History of Bank United States,	150 00
To Ames & Son, paper for Map of Narragansett Bay,	$376 00
William J. Stone, for printing do	320 00
E. Gilman, joining do	100 00
	—796 20
J. Kennedy, District Laws,	3 05
G. Templeman, 4 copies Laws,	112 00
Gales & Seaton, for 13 copies 8 vols. State Papers, $11 25 each,	1,172 00
	$7,092 25

This will add $145 75 for each member of the Senate.

Still further, $50,000 annually for Gales & Seaton's State Papers, and $50,000 expenditure on Clarke & Force's Documentary History, would average to the 291 Senators, Representatives, and Delegates, for the year, $340 each, and would make in the whole, £2985 75 to each member of the Senate, as the expense of books and printing for a single year.

Of the items I have called over, one or two are deserving comment. One of the Departments had procured as a matter of favor to that part of Rhode Island and Providence plantations, and at a great expense, the survey, engraving, and furnishing, a map of Narragansett Bay, a sufficient quantity to answer all ordinary purposes. This was not enough. Senators living in distant States, who had as little to do with Narragansett Bay as they had with Winnipisaeogee lake and bay, or any other distant water, must be furnished with additional copies of an unwieldy map; and eight hundred dollars more are expended in printing and furnishing an extra number of these for the forty-eight Senators.

The thirteen copies or sets, eight volumes each, of Gales & Seaton's State Papers, also call for comment. I was surprised at the last session, when I was informed that the whole seven hundred and fifty copies of Gales & Seaton's State Papers, furnished for Congress, had already been disposed of, and that a purchase must be made of additional numbers to supply new members. The eight volumes purchased cost only about the sum of ninety dollars for each set; and when the ninety volumes come to be completed, if the publishers shall not see fit to raise the price, which will depend on circumstances, the added expense for each new member, for this one article, will be two hundred and twenty-five dollars.

This work of Gales & Seaton, it should be recollected, originated in this manner: They at first

published in their newspaper proposals for printing a Compilation of Congressional Documents. After several ineffectual attempts, at last a resolution passes, per fas et nefas, both Houses of Congress, authorizing a subscription of seven hundred and fifty copies, embracing a period of time down to 1815. This subscription of Congress obtained, it is believed not a single additional subscriber was sought for or procured.

Afterwards an additional resolution is passed, extending the time, and limiting the extension to eight additional volumes. The price paid in each instance is fixed to the price paid to the printers of Congress for the ordinary printing of the two Houses. This price is from twenty-five to fifty per cent higher than the same work would cost in Philadelphia, in New York, in Boston, and in several other places. And the money thrown away in price over-paid on this work of Gales & Seaton, and that of Clarke and Force, will amount to between two and three hundred thousand dollars!

I will state the items of three contracts on which from two to three hundred thousand dollars are absolutely thrown away, made by resolutions which have, in some way—these interested can tell how—been carried through Congress, when perhaps one member in ten did not understand either their tendency or extent. They are as follows:

Gales and Seaton's American State Papers, 20 volums, 750 copies, probable cost $10,000 each volume,	$200,000
Clarke and Force's Documentary History, 30 to 40 volumes, calculated to be confined to the cost of	$400,000
Duff Green for printing Land Laws, independent of other printing ordered exclusively by the Senate, 16 volumes,	$60,000
	$660,000

Two, if not three, of the last named volumes, I am informed, will be a reprint of the very volumes to be executed by Gales and Seaton!

The art of working through Congress, resolutions or acts, favorable to those whom they are intended to benefit, could not be better exemplified than in those directing the publication of books by the pet printers and publishers for both Houses of Congress. Gales and Seaton, it is understood, printed for Congress 750 copies, and received of Congress entire pay for preparation and composition and distribution of the types, using the same types and composition to print for themselves 750 other copies. The resolution requires that the members of the 21st and 22d Congress shall be supplied with the books; the consequence is, before this work is half way through the press, the seven hundred and fifty copies are all taken up, the $200,000 appropriation is all run through; and at each successive session of Congress, to supply new members, the Secretary of the Senate or Clerk of the House is obliged to go to the publishers and pay them just what price they ask for additional numbers. Thirteen sets of these additional numbers were bought for the Senate last session, and I am told from 125 to 150 additional sets of the same work were required for the House of Representatives.

The resolutions require that the members of the 21st and 22d Congress shall be supplied; with just as much propriety might the resolution provide that members of the first Congress, or members of forty years ago, should be supplied with Gales and Seaton's State Papers, as that members of the twenty first Congress, who were here four years ago, should be supplied. And I would not be at all surprised hereafter, to find members of each and every Congress, or the "heirs and legal representatives" of members of Congress, coming in here and claiming for each, copies of these State Papers, or the value of such State papers, "with interest" for the whole time of delay.

It will be seen that the resolution despatches at once, the seven hundred and fifty copies; and the new Congresses of two terms more, will nearly or quite consume the addition 1750 copies, for which Gales and Seaton get pay, as if printed at their own expense, while the greatest half of the expense of printing has been paid by Congress.

It was admitted on all hands, at the last session, that Congress had been taken in by the bargain which had been made with Clark and Force for the Documentary History; and it was thought to be a momentous affair to procure the assent of those gentlemen to such terms as would limit the whole expense of this printing to four hundred thousand dollars! But the gist of the matter did not then appear. The act of Congress which authorizes the contract with Clarke and Force directs the distribution of those volumes to the members of the twenty-first and twenty-second Congress, in the same manner as the State papers are distributed; and this too when not even the first volume of the Documentary History has yet been printed. So that Clarke and Force's first seven hundred and fifty copies have all been disposed of to old members and others, before the existence of the twenty-third or present Congress, and if this Congress or its successors obtain any, it must be by purchase of the extra copies; and Clarke and Force, long before their work shall be completed, will have sold, sale, at their own price, of double that number which the act of Congress had provided for. The members of Congress who were not here when the act passed, who are no longer members, and who have no stronger claim to them than any real every man, woman, and child, "from every place to every," in the country, are to be supplied with their twenty, thirty, or forty volumes of Documentary History of the Revolution. The restriction to $400,000 for the seven hundred and fifty copies virtually amounts to nothing, if we do not put a stop to furnishing members of Congress with the books that have been furnished their predecessors. If that practice continues, there can be no limit either as to numbers or amount of expense. Gales and Seaton and Clarke and Force may just as well print 2,000 or 3,000, as 750 copies; both are quite as safe in estimating the sum they will finally take from the Treasury, in one instance at a half, and in the other at a whole million of dollars, as at two hundred and four hundred thousand dollars each.

Mr. President, the gift and distribution of books to members of Congress, even of such books as pertain to our duties as legislators, are of little vantage to the public interests. I have heard members of Congress offering their books for sale in this city, and disposing of them at one tenth one-twentieth their cost. I am told there are books now on sale at one or more places in the city, furnished by members of Congress for that purpose. If the friends of this mode of distribution doubt the fact, they have it in their power to disprove it by appointing a committee to investigate the matter. But, sir, in the main, the books are carried to the homes of the respective members, and never to be turned here. Having occasion recently to look into the volumes of State Papers on the subject of Foreign Relations, and containing the several treaties and negotiations with France, it was more than a week before I was able to procure one of the two volumes on those subjects. If books are procured at all for the use of members, they ought to be retained in the Library, to be used by the successors, as well as by the present members. If in such an event, a small number would answer all our purposes; and we should not have occasion to expend the millions which have been, and are to be lavished on pet printers, whose best recommendation to the favor of Congress seems to have been their violence as partisans and editors of newspapers opposed to the great body of freemen of the United States, and to that Administration which that body of freemen have elected.

Sir, the money thrown away in extra patronage to printers and publishers within the District who are opposed to the administration—the money paid them over and above what would have been the actual cost of printing in other places—would be sufficient to relieve the Post Office Department from all its embarrassments, and to enable it to pay all its contractors promptly. And such is the flourishing condition of this Department, under all the embarrassments which have been thrown upon it, that it would be able to repay any loan that might be made in a very few months. If I were to point to any instance of appro-

...ery in this government that most deserved reprehension, I would turn the public attention to some acts of the two Houses of Congress which are thrown or will throw away more than a million or scarcely on printers and publishers within the District distinguished for no other merit than that of having virulently opposed the repeated voice and voice of the People of the United States.

I hope this resolution will be arrested by a decided majority of the Senate, and that no other resolution of a similar tenor will be permitted to be.

There was another resolution laid on the table the other day, for furnishing Gales and Seaton's chates to the new members.

On inquiry of the Secretary of the Senate, I find the quantity of Registers of Debates already published is twelve volumes, and that the cost of the twelve volumes is fifty-six dollars. There is, I believe, four new members of the Senate to be supplied, and the whole amount of cost under this resolution will be two hundred and twenty-four dollars.

The argument heretofore urged in favor of similar resolutions has been, that the old members, having themselves been supplied, would discover themselves to be both selfish and ungenerous now vote against supplying the new members. As applied to myself, I acknowledge no validity or propriety in that argument. I have invariably tried, whenever I had opportunity, against any and every proposition for supplying myself with books, and the acceptance of those books has in this instance been with me a voluntary act.

Now, Mr. President, whether the proposition to furnish a member with books costing one hundred or one hundred thousand dollars, I contend that it here, and at all other times, so far as it will be prudent to contend. I contend against a practice of voting books for our own individual use—books which are regularly carried away at the end of each session of Congress, and which is never, or rarely ever used here, for any public purpose whatever.

I need not advert, Mr. President, to the comparative worthlessness of the volumes which the resolution proposes to procure. They are like so much old lumber—much less valuable then the mass of old newspapers that make any pretensions at to a fair and impartial detail of even's. The senator from Missouri (Mr. Benton) has showed a great injustice which has been done to the proceedings and speeches in the Senate in these volumes. I scarcely need inform the Senate, that volumes proposed to be purchased embrace a part of the three last sessions of Congress. We might be some little pretence of their usefulness, if they embraced late proceedings and debates. But they do not reach within about three of the last proceedings of Congress. To purchase them now, must accommodate only the few, who are paid their own price. They are fully worth one-tenth of the price paid for them. I would sell at auction scarcely above that price. It is proper, in any place, and on any account, to resist the purchase, for the private use of members of Congress, of books, or other articles which may be convenient to them, by taking and appropriating therefor the money in the public treasury, it is proper, in this place, and on this occasion, to contend against it. There will be the to reason, at the next session of Congress, and all succeeding sessions, to purchase these books, there is now; and it will be no less invidious for members then to oppose it, than now.

I would consider it an act of magnanimity if new members would step forward and declare themselves willing to exercise a first act of self-denial in this respect.

When Mr. HILL had concluded, the hour for special orders having arrived, on motion of Mr. CALHOUN, the resolution was laid on the table. The Senate then resumed, as in Committee of a Whole, the consideration of the bill fixing the labor and salaries of the custom-house officers in the United States.

Mr. BIBB offered an amendment increasing the salary of the collector for the District of Sandusky, from $400 to 600.

Mr. SILSBEE opposed the amendment, on the ground, that if this alteration was made, others of a similar class must also be made. The committee, he said, had regulated these salaries as well they could be at present.

Mr. CALHOUN hoped the bill would be suffered to progress, without being overloaded with amendments.

Mr. KING, of Georgia, thought if this amendment prevailed, it would destroy the whole bill. He thought the sum sufficient, where the duty required was so little. But a small part of the time was necessarily occupied.

After some further remarks by Mr. SILSBEE, the question was put, and the amendment rejected.

Mr. ROBBINS then proposed to raise the salary of the collector at Newport, Rhode Island, from $1500 to 1800.

Mr. SILSBEE objected; and after some little discussion between Mr. ROBBINS and Mr. SILSBEE, the question was put on the proposed amendment, and decided in the negative.

So the amendment was rejected.

Mr. GOLDSBOROUGH rose, he said, to propose an amendment. His honorable colleague and himself had received complaints and memorials in regard to the proposed changes at the port of Baltimore. He moved to strike out ten and insert fourteen, as the number of permanent inspectors and that two be inserted instead of six, for temporary inspectors. He believed there was no port in the world where the vigilance of inspectors was more needed than at Baltimore, as the peculiar situation of the place afforded opportunities for evading the laws.

Mr. SILSBEE said, he thought no district in the whole was better provided for than Baltimore. He then went on to show that other places, equally exposed with Baltimore, were placed on the same footing, even where the revenues were greater.

The debate was continued at some length by Mr. GOLDSBOROUGH and Mr. SILSBEE; after which, the amendment was rejected.

Mr. WRIGHT then offered an amendment as an additional section to the bill, authorizing naval officers each to depute a clerk, who might sign papers in the absence of the officer.

No objection being made, the amendment was agreed to.

Mr. KENT then proposed so to amend the bill so as to allow the collector at Georgetown 900 dollars instead of 800.

Mr. SILSBEE objected.

The question being put, the amendment was not agreed to.

Mr. PORTER proposed to allow the collector of the district of Teche $700 instead of $500, but the Senate rejected the proposition.

Mr. KING, of Georgia, said, he perceived by the bill the six districts of Georgia were reduced to three. He proposed adding a fourth at St. Mary's. He felt jealous of the sister State, South Carolina, which had been suffered to retain all her districts, her nullification notwithstanding.

The amendment was rejected.

On motion of Mr. PORTER, the bill was amended by inserting the word Teche after Mobile, in the fourth section, in order allow office rent to the collector at Teche.

Mr. KNIGHT proposed to equalise the salaries of the collectors at Newport and Bristol, giving $1,650 to each, but some objections being made, he withdrew his motion.

Mr. SHEPLEY then offered several amendments with regard to salaries of collectors, &c. in the State of Maine.

Mr. S. said he was not in favor of high salaries, but when he considered the extensive sea coast, and the frontiers, bounded for more than six hundred miles by the British possessions, he felt as though justice was not done to the State. The shipping of Maine was confined in a great measure to the coasting trade, but the committee in their estimate had confined themselves mostly to the revenues of the ports. Besides the coasting trade, a large number of fishing vessels were constantly passing and repassing between our ports and those of the British provinces, and it was highly neces-

sary that all those vessels should be inspected. In order to have this done, the Government must pay the officers enough to enable them to devote their time to the business. These northern ports, of all others, were the most favorable for smuggling, and should be strictly guarded.

The debate was continued at some length between Mr. SILSBEE, Mr. TOMLINSON, and Mr. SHEPLEY.

The question was then put, and the amendments rejected.

Mr. NAUDAIN offered some slight amendments, which was rejected.

The bill was then reported to the Senate, and ordered to be engrossed and read a third time.

On motion of Mr. CALHOUN, all the orders previous to the bills reported by the Select Committee on Executive patronage were postponed, and he then gave notice that to-morrow, at one o'clock, he would move to take up the bill to repeal the four years law.

Mr. KENT moved, that for the balance of the session, the standing hour of meeting of the Senate, shall be 11 o'clock, which was disagreed to.

The Senate then adjourned.

HOUSE OF REPRESENTATIVES.

Thursday, February 12, 1835.

Mr. BANKS, from the Committee of Claims, reported a joint resolution, authorizing the Secretary of the Treasury to settle the claim of O. H. Dibble; which was read twice, and ordered to be engrossed.

Mr. McKINLEY, from the Committee of Ways and Means, reported a bill to establish branches of the Mint of the United States; which was read twice and committed.

Mr. CLAY, from the Committee on the Public Lands, reported a bill granting a bounty in lands to the organized militia men, mounted militia men, and rangers, who defended the frontier during the late war with Great Britain; which was read the first time.

Mr. WILLIAMS moved that the bill be rejected.

Mr. Williams wished to assign, in a few words, the reasons why he was opposed to the passage of this bill. It would create hopes and expectations which the true interests and policy of the Government would never permit to be realised. It proposed to grant a bounty, in lands, to a class of troops regularly employed by the Government, in a contingent service, and who, in consequence of the peculiar duties required of them, were allowed a per diem allowance of one dollar each. If the principles of the bill were adopted, there would be at least one hundred thousand applications to this House for similar donations of land. He did not see why the troops for which this bill provided should be entitled to more pay than the other militia who were engaged in the public service. He believed that the militia on the Atlantic border, during the late war, performed more arduous duties than any other troops in the service. If, therefore, this bounty was to be extended, the militia generally would be as much entitled to it, as those who were embraced in the bill. He repeated, that if the principles of the bill were recognised, it would have a tendency to induce at least 100,000 applications for a similar bounty in lands. It was for the purpose of cutting off the delusive hopes which might be thus created, that he had been induced to make the motion that the bill be rejected.

Mr. CASEY said he would not trespass upon the time of the House by entering into an examination of the claims of those persons who were intended to be benefited by the bill. The subject had been some time before the Committee on the Public Lands, fully matured, and a lengthy report on the subject accompanied the bill now under consideration. He hoped the bill would be permitted to take its usual course—that it would be read a second time and committed, and, together with the report, printed. It would not be difficult to show the difference between the class of troops referred to by the gentleman from North Carolina (Mr. Williams) and those who were em-

braced in the provisions of the bill. But he would not pursue the subject at present, in the hope that the bill would be suffered to take the usual course, and, that at the proper time, it would come up for discussion.

Mr. CLAY said, the gentleman from North Carolina, (Mr. Williams,) seemed disposed to treat this measure most unceremoniously. The provisions of the bill were certainly not so shocking as to require its instantaneous rejection. The gentleman was wholly mistaken in supposing that this bill would encourage the numerous applications from other portions of the militia to which he had referred, for a similar bounty in lands. There was a most essential difference between the ordinary militiamen and that class of troops embraced in the bill. The former generally served but three months, and perhaps in a single instance, six months, while the latter were bound to serve twelve months, and did serve for that period. They served as long as a portion of the regulars, who received a bounty, as well as he recollected. He contended that the mounted rangers had an advantage over the infantry. They were bound, as he understood, to furnish their own horses, arms, and provisions. Nor had the former any advantage over the regular troops.

Mr. C. said, the House was not now called upon to determine the merits of the bill. The only question was, whether the proposition was so palpably absurd and monstrous, as to cause the House to refuse to entertain it at the threshold. He was not prepared to say how he should eventually vote upon this measure. Let it be examined and matured, and if it should be deemed proper, let us (said Mr. C.) not withhold from the meritorious citizen soldier, that which they may be justly entitled to. He hoped, therefore, that the bill would be read a second time and committed.

Mr. CHILTON expressed a hope that a bill, so meritorious in its character, would not be so cavalierly disposed of by rejecting it on its first reading. While he would be opposed to extending the provisions of the bill to all those who were engaged in the service during the late war, he would be extremely gratified if those in indigent circumstances, who had fought the battles of the late war, could receive a bounty in land, for the purpose of securing to themselves, and their families, a home, which they were unable to purchase. The bill was not as explicit in its character as he could desire. When, however, it should come up ultimately for consideration, the House could fashion it to suit its fancy, and at the same time do justice to those who were concerned. Mr. C. concluded by a warm eulogium upon those who were engaged in sustaining the honor and glory of the nation in the late war.

Mr. VINTON was glad that the motion had been made to reject the bill. It was time for the House to take care of the public lands as well as the other public property. This bill, if he understood it, proposed to give a bounty in lands to almost every person who was engaged in the public service during the late war. Even those who had remained in the service fifteen days, and who were regularly discharged, would be entitled to the proposed bounty. Not only the rangers, but the militia, were to be provided for. He would ask whether these rangers were promised any thing more than what they had received? Were they not acquainted with the character of the service in which they were engaged? Were they required to do any other service than that agreed upon, and were they not paid according to contract? Upon what ground then could any one come here and ask, in addition to the sum paid these troops, that they should be allowed each a bounty of 160 acres of land. A bounty of 100 acres of land was given to the soldiers of the revolution. This, too, was to be located in a savage wilderness. The land which this bill proposed to give, would be located in the very heart of a rich and civilized country. One hundred acres of land thus located, was worth five times as much as that which had been given to the soldiers of the revolution. Was this just or proper? He hoped the bill would be immediately rejected, for the reasons assigned by the gentleman from North Carolina (Mr Williams.) Let this bill be entertained and laid over to the next session, and we should most assuredly have thousands of petitions from the militia engaged in the service during the last war, for the benefit of its provisions. He referred to the sickness which prevailed among the troops at Norfolk during the war. He considered the dangers encountered at that station, from sickness alone, as infinitely greater than those experienced by the mounted rangers, who were engaged in a service calculated to invigorate and strengthen the system. For the reasons which he had assigned, he trusted the House would promptly reject the bill.

Mr. SPEIGHT viewed the motion of his colleague (Mr. Williams) as an unfortunate one. The bill had been reported by one of the committees of the House, and we were called upon to reject it, when many of us did not know what were its details. The motion also operated to exclude all other necessary morning business. He thought the bill ought to be committed. While he was the decided advocate of the old States, in regard to their rights and interests connected with the public domain, still there was no person more ready to do entire justice to those brave men who had served the country in the wild West. He would go one step further, and make provision for the troops stationed at Norfolk at the period alluded to by the gentleman from Ohio. He doubted whether a portion of the public domain could be better disposed of than by distributing it among those destitute and meritorious individuals, who had, during the late war, shouldered their muskets and defended the country.

Mr. REYNOLDS remarked, that there seemed to him to be a view of this subject, which had not been yet presented to the House. The General Assembly of the State of Illinois addressed a memorial, praying for a bounty, in land, to be granted to the United States' Rangers. This memorial was addressed to the Congress of the United States, and was referred to the Committee on Public Lands. They have reported the present bill. He considered that a memorial, coming from one of the free and republican States of this confederacy, to this honorable body, should receive a different treatment. Common respect to a State would, in his humble opinion, guaranty a course entirely different. If the Old Boy himself were depicted in the bill, it should not be treated in this manner, and be rejected thus unceremoniously; but as the bill, and the subject-matter of which it treats, are just and right, it ought, like other propositions emanating from a respectable source, go to the proper committee, or take the ordinary course.

Is it right that the claims and petitions of citizen soldiers, who sustained in the war with Great Britain the honor and character of their country, be rejected without investigation? Citizens that left their homes and families and entered the service of their country to fight its battles against the enemy, should their claims for a bounty in land be thus treated in the Congress of the United States? Citizens who, in sustaining the liberty, honor, and prosperity of the country, had fought and bled under the stripes, such as we see presented before us, are their claims to be rejected in the Congress of the United States without a hearing?

[Mr. R. referred to the United States flag, suspended in the Hall of Representatives.]

Mr. WILLIAMS, from North Carolina, (who made the motion to reject the bill on the first reading,) begged to explain, that he made the motion under a rule of the House, which was recognised, and did not consider it "disrespectful" to the House, or to the claims, to make the motion.

Mr. REYNOLDS observed, that he had not thought, or treated, the honorable member from North Carolina, or his motion, with "disrespect." Nor did he consider him treating the soldier's claim with disrespect. He had been informed of his character, and he had no such notion of him; but he did sincerely believe that the motion was wrong.

He said he would repeat, that should the claims of the soldier, who defended the honor and character of the country, and who advanced its prosperity, be rejected without examination, we will not see the brave soldiers so ready to volunteer their services. If their claims be rejected in this manner, we may again hear of burnings and the destruction of property by the enemy. This Capitol may be visited again with the fire of the enemy, should the claims of the soldiers be rejected thus hastily.

If this treatment be visited on the soldier, who will defend the country? If such course be pursued, he feared he would hear, in another war, of the destruction of the capitol again—a thing, he hoped, which never would again take place. The honorable member, (Mr. Vinton,) from Ohio, remarked, that the militia and other troops received the compensation which the Government agreed to give them. Mr. R. said, this may be the notions of the gentleman, who has been raised under the rigid system of contracts, where there was no liberality observed. This was not the course which was pursued by this House. A liberal and generous policy was observed on all occasions.

Mr. R. would refer the House to various cases brought before it, wherein more was asked than a rigid performance of a contract. Justice and equity should be administered to all, whether their claims were founded on a contract or not, or even if the claim exceeded a contract, if it were just and equitable. Look at the claim of Kilgore, from Canada, who claimed pay for more than a contract. He claimed pay for services he exceeding a contract, and which contract it seemed to Mr. R. was founded in treason. Claims even of this character were soberly and candidly investigated in this House; and should not the present bill before the House receive the same consideration?

Should the bill be of the character represented by the gentleman (Mr. Chilton) from Kentucky, it still ought not to be rejected in this manner. The bill was intelligible and easily understood. It would not fall within the definition of metaphysics, such as the gentleman, (Mr. Chilton) described it, that neither the speaker nor his audience understood the subject which they were discussing.

The bill, if it was not right in form or substance, could be altered, and changed to suit the views of the majority of the House. Almost all bills experience changes and alterations in their passage. This could be so changed as to make it right.

The object of the bill was to grant a bounty in land in proportion to the bounty which the soldiers of the regular army received. This bounty was to be given to the U. S. rangers, in proportion to their services, and in relation to the bounties given other troops.

This is so reasonable, and at the same time so just, that he could not believe the House would reject it at all; but he hoped the House would so retain the bill; change it if necessary, and finally pass it, so as to embrace all troops that served in the late war; and give them a bounty in land in proportion to their services, and in proportion to the bounty given other troops.

Mr. C. ALLAN said, let the merits of this bill be what they might, the course proposed by his honorable friend from North Carolina was a very unusual one. The bill was brought into the House in the usual way, through the ordinary organ, one of its standing committees. It was evident that they were not then prepared to act so definitively as proposed; for no two members who had addressed the House, understood the bill the same way, and every one had given it a different interpretration. For himself, he was not disposed to reject this bill without any consideration, though he was not prepared to say how he should finally vote upon it. The subject was an important one, connected with a large class of meritorious citizens of the country; and did not the House from day to day, and hour by hour, patiently consider bills involving the interest of single individuals, and would it reject a proposition for so large a class as that embraced in the present bill, on its first presentation? He hoped his worthy friend would not press his motion, but allow the bill to take the usual course, by referring it to a committee of the whole House, where its principles and provisions wou'd undergo the most mature deliberation. He again repeated, that he could

him say how he should finally vote on the measure.

Mr. STEWART said, that with a view of putting an end to what, in its present situation, was an unprofitable discussion, if the motion were in order, he would move to lay the whole subject on the table.

The CHAIR pronounced the motion out of order.

Mr. ASHLEY wished to say a few words in reply to the gentleman from Ohio, (Mr. Vinton.) Mr. A. believed that no troops during the late war had been engaged in severer duties or performed harder service than the rangers engaged to twelve months in protecting our frontier. It was true they were paid a dollar per day for their services but as stated by the gentleman from Alabama, (Mr. Clay,) they had to furnish their own horses and their own clothes, and any person at all conversant with the services they performed, would at once come to the conclusion that that amount was not more than was paid to the regular troops or infantry of the United States. The former had to furnish their own horses and were in good condition, and in case of one of them becoming disabled, or being lost, they had either to procure another at their own expense, to hire one, or to go on foot. Mr. A. had the honor of commanding some of those men at that time, and from his own experience, he could aver that their expenses amounted to as much, and generally to more, than their pay. He believed there were three times as many rangers proportionate to their numbers, lost on the frontier, where were of any other class of troops in the service of the United States in that quarter. Now, inasmuch as these men did perform services as arduous and as dangerous as if they formed a part of the regular troops in the army of the United States, and inasmuch as the regular infantry received each a quarter section of land for their services, he was of opinion that the men embraced in this bill were fairly entitled to the same bounty, though it was not in their contract.

Mr. A. said, though he was opposed to the immediate rejection of this bill, and in favor of the principles of it, there were several of its provisions to which he did not assent, and at the proper time he intended to submit some amendments to it for the consideration of the House, but he thought it due to the subject, that the bill should be printed and properly considered and disposed of.

Mr. EWING said a few words, which were not distinctly heard by the Reporter. He was understood to be opposed to the motion to reject the bill.

Mr. LINCOLN desired to say a few words in explanation of the vote which he should give on the motion of the gentleman from North Carolina, (Mr. Williams.) He did not propose to discuss the merits of the bill. He referred to its provisions, and contended that it would afford a precedent which would authorize every soldier of the late war to expect similar gratuity. Indeed the bill was broad enough to include the whole. A single ranger who had served three days, would be as much entitled to this bounty as those who had served one year. Such a bill should never pass this House. If it should, it would be a warrant to every militiaman who was in the service in the late war, to come forward and demand one hundred and sixty acres of land, although all had had been promised was previously paid. He did not believe that the public domain would be sufficient to satisfy the demands which would be created by the passage of this bill. Lest it might be construed into a precedent, and encourage applications and hopes which must eventually prove futile, he submitted whether it was not proper that the bill should be rejected at its present

The remarks of Mr. L. were here arrested by a motion of Mr. WATMOUGH, to proceed to the consideration of the orders of the day, which was carried.

Mr. WATMOUGH asked the consent of the House to take up the bill to regulate the pay of the navy. He was desirous that the substitute which had been prepared for the original bill and

amendments, should be adopted, and the bill ordered to be engrossed.

The motion was objected to.

DEPOSITE BANKS.

The order of the day was the bill to regulate the deposite of the public moneys in certain local banks; and the question pending thereon was the previous question, moved yesterday by Mr. BOON.

Mr. PATTON moved a call of the House.

The CHAIR again decided the motion not to be in order, upon the same grounds as on yesterday.

[The same question of order arose in the House yesterday. The CHAIR decided the motion for a call of the House before it was ascertained whether there was a second to the previous question which had been demanded, to be out of order. In making this decision, the SPEAKER declared that he considered the motion in order, but he felt bound to conform to the decision of the House upon the same point at its last session. It was for the House, if it thought proper, to reverse its own decision.]

Mr. PATTON thereupon appealed from the decision of the Chair.

Mr. BRIGGS asked for the yeas and nays; which were ordered.

A long discussion on the point of order ensued. Messrs. PATTON, MILLER, FOSTER, CAGE, SUTHERLAND, MERCER, H. EVERETT, S. JONES, HEATH, and H. EVERETT, were for reversing the decision of the Char, and Messrs. SPEIGHT, MASON of Virginia, and HALL of North Carolina, were in its favor.

The question was taken by yeas and nays, and the result was—yeas 91, nays 113.

YEAS—Messrs. W. Allen, Bayliss, Beaumont, Blair, Bockee, Boon, Brown, Burns, Bynum, Carmichael, Carr, Casey, Chaney, Samuel Clark, Clay, Coffee, Cramer, Day, Dickerson, Dickinson, Dunlap, Ferris, Forester, William K. Fuller, Galbraith, Gillet, Joseph Hall, Thomas H. Hall, Halsey, Hannegan, Joseph M. Harper, Harrison, Hathaway, Hawkins, Heath, Henderson, Howell, Hubbard, Huntingdon, Inge, Richard M. Johnson, Noadiah Johnson, Cave Johnson, Benjamin Jones, Kilgore, Lane, Lansing, Lucas, Lyon, Lytle, Joel K. Mann, Mardis, John T. Mason, Moses Mason, jr. May, McIntire, McKim, McLene, McVean, H. Mitchell, Robert Mitchell, Morgan, Muhlenberg, Murphy, Osgood, Page, Parker, Patterson, Franklin Pierce, Pierson, Polk, Pope, Ramsay, Reynolds, Schenck, A. H. Shepperd, Shinn, Smith, Speight, Standifer, William Taylor, Thomson, Turrill, Vanderpoel, Van Houten, Wagener, Ward, Wardwell, Webster, Whallon, White—91.

NAYS—Messrs. J. Q. Adams, Heman Allen, J. Allen, Anthony, Ashley, Banks, Barber, Barnitz, Barringer, Beaty, Bell, Binney, Briggs, Burd, Burges, Cambreleng, Chambers, Chilton, Claiborne, William Clark, Clayton, Clowney, Corwin, Crane, Crockett, Darlington, Amos Davis, Davenport, Deberry, Denny, Dickson, Evans, E. Everett, Horace Everett, Ewing, Fillmore, Forester, Fowler, Ph lo C. Fuller, Fulton, Gamble, Garland, Gholson, Gilmer, Gordon, Gorham, Graham, Grayson, Grennell, Griffin, Hiland Hall, Hamer, Hard, Hardin, James Harper, Hazeltine, Hiester, William Jackson, Ebenezer Jackson, Janes, Jarvis, Henry Johnson, Seaborn Jones, Kinnard, Laporte, Ley, Lee, Lee, Letcher, Lincoln, Loyall, Abijah Mann, jr., Martindale, Marshall, McCarty, McComas, McKay, McKennan, McKinley, Mercer, Miller, Milligan, Miner, Moore, Patton, Dutee J. Pearce, Phillips, Pickens, Pinckney, Potts, Reed, Rencher, Robertson, William B. Shepard, Slade, Spangler, Steele, Stewart, William P. Taylor, Philemon Thomas, Tompkins, Trumbull, Tweedy, Vance, Vinton, Watmough, Frederick Whittlesey, Elisha Whittlesey, Wilde, Williams, Wilson, Wise, Young—113.

So the House determined that the motion for a call of the House was in order.

The motion for a call of the House was then put, and negatived, without a division.

The question then recurring on the motion for the previous question—

Mr. GRAHAM appealed to the honorable mem-

ber from Indiana to withdraw his motion for the previous question.

Mr. BOON said, though he did not wish to be obstinate, he could not withdraw the motion. The discussion on this bill was arresting all the other business of the country, and he thought had already extended to a sufficient length.

The question was then taken by tellers, and there were ayes 97, noes 105.

So the House refused to second the call for the previous question.

The question being then on the engrossment of the bill,

Mr. BINNEY said he was desirous of proposing certain amendments, which, however, did not conflict with the general principles of the bill, but, as he believed, tended rather to improve, and render it more acceptable to many who were in favor of its passage. He was aware that the House was very desirous of passing to the consideration of other important business; and he coincided in the wish that the question should be taken this day. He should therefore endeavor to economise the time of the House, so far as he could, with a due regard to perspicuity. He had said that the amendment he was about to propose did not conflict with the principles of the bill. Those principles, he wished to be understood, were such as he could never bring his mind to adopt. This consideration, however, did not debar him from making a reasonable effort to render them more consistent with his own views of right, and of the true interests of the country.

The objections which he entertained to the bill, in its present shape, were its insecurity—its partiality, and its tendency to political influence. In relation to the first of these points, its insecurity, he contended that he had the warrant of experience. The system of using the State banks for the depositories of the public treasure, ha l been tried, and failed—egregiously failed, and that, under circumstances remarkably similar to the present. The honorable Chairman of the Committee of Ways an I Means had sa'd that this was "no longer an experiment." In regard to its first trial, h granted, it was not an experiment; but in relation to the present, he d ffered materially from that gentleman. It was, he conceived, as much an experiment now as it was when it was first so denominated. It had been tried but one short year, and we were now told it had succeeded, and must continue to succeed. The experiment, on its former trial, not only for one, for two, or for three years—but for three years and a half, had the same apparent success. At the end of that period, in less than six weeks, it was exploded, and the currency of the country was left, for more than a year, in the most deplorable condition. To contend that this experiment was tested in the short time in which it had been in operation, with the recent trial of a like experiment, and its failure in three and a half years, staring in our faces, was to him preposterous. Not only did he contend that the experiment had not be n fully tried—but it had not been fairly begun. Its result was only postponed. The causes conducing to this postponement were, first, the refusal on the part of the Bank of the United States, to obey the mandate from the Treasury Department to call in its circulation—her refusal to proceed with the work in which she had begun. It was this spirit of opposition—factious opposition if you choose—to the virtual command of the Department to call in her circulation—which formed one principle cause of the postponement, of the effect of the experiment. The other cause to which he referred was, the celebrated and salutary panic of 1833—which induced a curtailment of one-fourth of our imports—and the subst tution of returns in specie. Mr.B. next called the attention of the House to the similarity of the circum tances existing in 1813 and in 1833. There was, he believed, at the former period, as much specie in the country, as at the latter. After pursuing this subject at some length, he referred to the loss s said to have been sustained by the government, by its places of deposites. He content ed that it had, properly speaking, lost nothing by the Bank of the United States. Mr. B. then went into an examination of his second proposition, that the operation of

the present system, was partial towards various portions of the country. He also dwelt, at considerable length, on the possibilities o the fiscal agents of the gov rnment being used for pol tical effect; and concluded by enumerating the advantages to be secured by the provisions of his amendment.

Mr. PATTON said he was in favor of the princ'ples of this bill, and was desirous that it should be adopted; and he was determined, so far as his own action was concerned, that every member of the House should be enabled to present such amendments as he should think necessary, in order to make it as perfect as possible, and in some he might himself concur. Mr. P. said he should not enter at large into the question. He agreed with the gentleman f om Pennsylvania, (Mr. Binney,) that the question of the Bank of the United States was finally settled. The question now was, what were we to do? There were other great questions brought into this discussion. The most important was that of Executive encroachment in relation to the removal of the deposites, again alleged by those who had before fought the battle and lost it. Mr. P. was ready to enter the contest again with any one, and to maintain, as he had maintained before, that the conduct of the Executive, upon that occasion, was neither an encroachment upon the powers of that House, nor an invasion of the constitution, but were in exact conformity with the principles of the Government, as established in 1789. But the question was, whether the Bank of the United States' being about to expire as the fiscal agent of the Government, there was any necessity of making regulations for the d sposition of the public deposites; an what those regulations should be? Much had been said about the experiment that had been m de. Mr. P. denied that it was an experiment, for it had existed and had been going on from the foundation of the Government to the present time. State Banks had been so employed from 1789, not only down to 1816, but down to the present moment.

In 1811 when the Bank of the United States had been in operation for twenty years, and when judgment of death was about to be pronounced against it by Congress, a report was made to that House showing that one-third of the money of the country was in State Banks. That of twenty-one Deposite Banks, eleven of them were chartered State Banks. In many of the States, Massachusetts, Connecticut, a d Rhode Island, there was no Branch of the United States Bank. He referred to the authority of Mr. Gallatin to prove that all the money of the country was deposited in State Banks, except at Norfolk. He also, referred to the speeches of many g ntlemen on both sides of the question at that time, showing that in the event of the Bank go ng down, the use of State Banks for places of the public deposite, was contemplated. If then this system was an experiment, it was an experiment m de in 1789, and continued to be used down to 1816. Mr. P. entered into a review of the circumstances attending the re-charter of the present Bank of the United States, and quoted the opinion of Mr. Webster, Mr. Clay, and other gentlemen then in Congress, and read an extract from the report of Mr. Gallatin to the Senate of the Unite! S ates, in 1811, in favor of the re-charter of the United States Bank, to show that he believed State banks m ght be safely use l by the Treasury. Whether we regarded this as a political or a mere financial question, it mus still be a question between the establishment of the Bank of the U. S. and the State banks. He thought the development of the last three or four years, and the last year especially, had proved the dangerous influence of the form r institution. He once thought the charges brought against it overrated, but he thought so no longer. From the State banks nothing was to be feared; their profits were distributed and dispersed over the whole country; they were under the control of the State governments, and their being in a continual state of rivalry towards each other would all tend to keep them within proper limits. Much had been s id about the influence the State of New Y k

would derive by the passage of this bill. Mr. P. said it was to the city and not to the State, this application should be made. That city ha l g eat influence, and would always possess it, from her immense commercial advantages, and nothing could stop her course. With regard to g ving the Secretary of the Treasury the control over the deposite banks, he did not believe it ever was, or ever would be used as an engine of political power, or that it could to any great extent. Besides, the power of Congress could at any time interpose to prevent his exercise of any undue influence. At the proper opportunity, it was his intention to offer an amendment to the clause prohibiting the employment of any bank as a place of deposite for the public moneys that issued notes, in 1838, of a less denomination than ten dollars, for he thought it better to leave the matter to be acted upon when the time should arrive, according to the circumstances that might then exist. He thought it wrong thus to bind their successors, and the evils the country had endured from the question of the Bank of the United States had grown out of what some called a contract made by the Congress of 1816 with that institution. There was no necessity for passing this clause to restrict the State Banks, and they were not required to do it. It was trammelling, and unnecessarily trammelling, the bill. Mr. P. concluded by again declaring his intention to vote for the bill.

Mr. E. EVERETT said he wished to offer an amendment to the bill when the proper time should arrive. He expressed his approbation of the several amendments of the gentleman from Pennsylvanla (Mr. Binney.) He last year voted against the bill, for he regarded it as part of an illegal system in violation of the existing law chartering the Bank of the United States. He said, if the amendments of the gentleman from Pennsylvania (Mr. Binney) were adopted, he should vote in favor of the bill. He was opposed to placing so much power as that of selecting the deposite Banks in the will and discretion of the Secretary of the Treasury. He was aware of the difficu ty of the case, but his plan,he thought, would obviate it, and that was to place the money in those Banks that would pay most for its use, and all other things being equal, and taking care that it be perfectly secure. Such a provision was equitable, and he hoped would be adopted, and he should offer it hereafter to the consideration of the House.

Mr. WILDE rose to appeal to all parties, the friends of the amendments in particular, to bring the question to a close. There were only sixteen days of the session remaining and the present discussion was arresting all the business of the country. Every speech made in favor of the amendment was virtually in favor of the previous question. The House had shown a disposition to permit the question to be taken directly on the several amendments, and he hoped the discussion would terminate.

Mr. GRAHAM offered an amendment providing that four per cent. per annum should be paid for the use of the public moneys by the Banks in which they were deposited, and that the Secretary of the Treasury keep a proper book of accounts, &c. Mr. G. advocated his amendment in a few words.

Mr. McKINLEY expressed a hope that the question would be taken on the amendment at once.

Mr. POLK asked for a division of the question on the amendments proposed by Mr. Binn y, and replied to the argument used in favor of requiring interest from the deposite Banks. To select those Banks which woul give most for the use of the public moneys, would in almost all cases be selecting the worst Bank. Mr. P. reiterated his remarks made the oth r day, showing the impracticability of enforcing interest upon an fluctuating a capital as that would be, which might be placed in a bank to-day, and called for to-morrow. The only plan he thought that could be devised would be by a sinking fund, regulated at each session of Congress. At present there was only about half a million in the Treasury, and by the end of the session, there would remain very little. As soon as the contingency existed," of a positive unex-

pended balance in the Treasury, it would be l. g enough to provide for it.

Mr. FILLMORE stated that the unexpended balances belonging to the State of New York, l the banks there, did produce an interest of f m four to five per cent.

Mr. GRAHAM again urged the propriety of hi amendment, and asked for the yeas and nays, which were not or dered.

The amendment of the gentleman was then put and negatived, without a division.

The first clause of Mr. BINNEY'S amendment to the third section of the bill, distinguishing private from public funds, was then agreed to, without a division.

The second clause of the amendment being been read—

Mr. McKINLEY made a few remarks thereon.

Mr. JONES moved to strike out one-fourth, and insert one-fifth of the amount of specie, &c. to be kept in the vaults of the Banks.

Mr. BINNEY accepted the modification.

Mr. POLK explained why the provision had been made in the bill by the committee; and thought it should not be changed. At the time when the Bank of the Unit d States was considered the safest institution in the country, it had only six millions to meet forty-two millions—the most of its liabilities only one-seventh.

Mr. PARKER and Mr. McKIM made a few remarks on the amendment.

Mr. CAMBRELENG said if this amendment were adopted, it would virtually defeat the whole bill.

Mr. BINNEY asked for the yeas and nays which were ordered.

Mr. CRAMER moved an adjournment. Negatived.

The question was then taken on the second branch of the amendment; which was agreed to. Yeas 109, nays 99.

Mr. POLK asked leave to introduce a resolution, proposing to make the bill under consideration and another bill in relation to the transfer of certain books &c. from the Bank of the United States, the special orders for 12 o'clock each day except Saturdays, until the same should be disposed of, and provid ng that petitions should be received as usual on Mondays.

Objection being made,

Mr. POLK moved a suspension of the rules, to enable him to offer the resolution. He was desirous that those bills should be disposed of to-morrow.

Mr. BEATY moved that the House adjourned. Carried —Ayes 90, nors 86.

So the House adjourned at a ½ to 6 o'clock.

IN SENATE.

FRIDAY, February 13, 1835.

Petitions and memorials were presented by Messrs. BENTON, TOMLINSON, and LINN.

Mr. FRELINGHUYSEN presented a memorial of the Cherokee delegation complaining of the decision of the War Department in their case and praying the interposition of Congress for their relief which was referred to the Committee on Indian Affairs.

Mr. POINDEXTER, from the Committee on Public Lands, to which was referred the bills from the House for the relief of Sutton Stephens, reported for the relief of Sutton Stephens, reported the same, the first without, and the last with an amendment.

Mr. POINDEXTER, from the same Committee to which was referred the petition of the settlers on the public lands near Michigan City, praying for certain pre-emption rights, reported unfavorably upon the s me, and the Committee were discharged from the further consideration thereof.

Mr. NAUDAIN, f om the Committee on Claims to which was referred the bills from the House for the r lief of Thomas Beaufort and Shobael Conant, reported the same, severally, without amendment.

Mr. HENDRICKS, from the Committee on Roads and Canals to which was referred the bill making an appropriation to construct certain roads in Michigan Territory, reported the same without amendment.

Mr. HENDRICKS from the same Committee, to which was referred the bill in addition to the act for the continuation and repair of the Cumberland road, reported the same without amendment.

Mr. SILSBEE, from the Committee on Commerce to which was referred the bills from the House for the relief of Stephen Smith and others, reported the same severally without amendment.

Mr. SOUTHARD, from the Naval Committee, reported a bill to regulate the pay of the Navy of the United States; which was read the first time and ordered to a second reading.

Mr. PRESTON, from the Judiciary Committee, to which was referred the bill from the House to prescribe the punishment of Consuls, Commercial Agents and others, reported the same without amendment.

Mr. PRESTON, from the same Committee, to which was referred the bill changing the time of holding the District Courts of the United States in Western Virginia, held at Clarksburg, reported the same without amendment.

Mr. WAGGAMAN submitted the following resolution:

Resolved, That the Secretary of War be requested to communicate to the Senate the Report received from the person charged with the Mineralogical and Geological investigation, authorized by an act of Congress, at the last session.

The joint resolution authorizing the purchase of fifty copies of the American Diplomatic Code, for the use of the Senate, was taken up for consideration; and on motion of Mr. HILL, was laid on the table.

The bill to settle the accounts of Colonel Gad Humphreys was taken up, considered as in Committee of the Whole, and on motion of Mr. FELTE, was laid on the table.

The bill fixing the number and compensation of the custom-house officers of the United States, and to alter certain collection districts, came up as a third reading.

Mr. SILSBEE moved to fill a blank in the bill, prescribing the 31st December next as the period when the bill is to take effect, which was agreed to.

The bill was then read the third time and passed.

The bill supplementary to the act for the relief of the representatives of Col. John Lawrence, was considered as in Committee of the Whole, when it was opposed by Mr. HILL, who asked the ayes and nays upon its passage, which were ordered.

After some remarks from Mr. FRELINGHUYSEN, the bill was ordered to be engrossed for a third reading, by the following vote:

YEAS—Messrs. Bell, Bibb, Black, Clay, Ewing, Frelinghuysen, Goldsborough, Hendricks, Kane, Kent, King of Alabama, Knight, Leigh, Linn, McKean, Moore, Naudain, Poindexter, Preston, Robbins, Robinson, Silsbee, Smith, Southard, Swift, Tipton, Tomlinson, Tyler, Waggaman, Webster, White.—32.

NAYS—Messrs. Benton, Brown, Calhoun, Cuthbert, Grundy, Hill, King of Georgia, Mangum, Morris, Ruggles, Shepley, Tallmadge, Wright.—3.

The bill for the relief of Charles J. Catlett was considered as in Committee of the Whole, and after some remarks from Messrs. TYLER, NAUDAIN, WEBSTER, and KING of Alabama, (the hour of one having arrived,)

Mr. CALHOUN moved to lay the bill upon the table, with a view to proceed to the orders of the day; which was agreed to.

The Senate then proceeded to consider, as in Committee of the Whole, the bill to limit the terms of certain officers, commonly called the four years' law.

Mr. CALHOUN rose to make a few remarks. He had not anticipated any particular objections to the bill before the Senate. Eight years ago it would be remembered a bill passed through that body (the Senate) for restricting executive patronage; it was termed the four years' bill; it was an act which imposed the most solemn obligation on the present administration. He would revert to the strong feelings which overthrew that administration and put the present one in power. The principles then professed and held up as the basis of our free institutions he feared had been too soon forgotten. That administration was accused of extravagance; of building up the power and increasing the influence of the Federal Government. One of the first acts that marked the commencement of the administration was the Panama question. Then there was some slight indications that the four years' law would be perverted by the removal of printers and the like. So very sensitive were the party now in power, at that time, that they were instantly aroused to action. The subject of executive patronage was then committed by the Senate to an able committee, who reported thereon. This committee was composed of the honorable Senator from Missouri, (Mr. Benton,) Mr. Macon, of North Carolina. The distinguished individual who presided over that body (Mr. Van Buren,) Mr. White, Mr. Finley, Mr. Dickinson, Mr. Holmes, Mr. Hayne, and Mr. Johnson. Mr. C. then requested his colleague, (Mr. Preston,) to read some extracts from the report of that committee. After the reading, Mr. C. resumed: such were, said he, the principles that had been held up to the People; such were the hopes that had been excited, that if those then in power were expelled and their opposers put in their places these principles should prevail. On the faithful fulfilment of such pledges much depended. If they were neglected the public would loose all confidence in its servants; the People would cease to be interested in public affairs. He would repeat, how had these pledges been redeemed? The Senator (Mr. Benton) had complained that of the fourteen years he had been on that floor, during the first seven he could obtain nothing as a favor from the government. But the last seven, he had wished to employ in retaliation. That spirit had spread through every Department of the Government. Wave after wave had spread over the land. And if that course was pursued, he would ask what would be the result? He would tell the Senator, that although he might be acquitted before those who were interested; although he might be acquitted by the present generation; yet he must be tried before another tribunal, before posterity, where he would be condemned, unless he retraced his footsteps.

[The debate was further continued by Messrs. BENTON, SOUTHARD, CALHOUN, POINDEXTER, KING, of Alabama, WEBSTER, LINN, CUTHBERT, LEIGH, BIBB, GOLDSBOROUGH, HENDRICKS, and FRELINGHUYSEN. Towards the close of the day, the discussion was exceedingly animated and interesting, and became personal between Messrs. BENTON and CALHOUN, to a degree which terminated in repeated calls to order. We abstain from any remarks upon the course which the debate took; but as it has produced great excitement, and as much interest has been felt with regard to it, a report, as accurately as it can be prepared, will be given in a few days.]

'At half past 5 o'clock,
The Senate adjourned.

HOUSE OF REPRESENTATIVES.
FRIDAY, Feb. 13, 1835.

The motion heretofore submitted by Mr. PHILLIPS, to print 3,000 extra copies of the report of the Committee on Commerce, relative to the proposed South Sea expedition, was considered and agreed to.

Mr. PLUMMER moved to reconsider the vote of yesterday, upon the adoption of the amendment offered by Mr. BINNEY, to the bill in relation to the public deposites. [The amendment was in regard to the amount of specie which the deposite banks were required to keep on hand.]

The SPEAKER said the motion would be received, and would regularly come up for consideration when the bill should be taken up.

Mr. GALBRAITH, from the Committee on Public Lands, reported a bill for the relief of Robert Allison, a lieutenant in the Revolutionary war; which was read twice and committed.

Mr. CARR, from the Committee on Private Land Claims, reported a bill for the relief of John Bartlett; which was read twice and committed.

Mr. CHINN, from the Committee on the District of Columbia, reported a bill authorizing the Circuit Court for the District of Columbia to hold an extra term for the trial of criminal causes; which was read twice and committed.

Mr. FULTON, from the Committee on Claims, reported a bill for the relief of John Cowper; which was read twice and committed.

Mr. FULTON, from the same committee, reported a bill for the relief of Thomas Beauchamp; which was read twice and committed.

Unfavorable reports upon various petitions, &c. were made by Messrs. KAVANAGH, BRIGGS, GALBRAITH, CHAMBERS, FULTON, HOWELL, and CLAY, from the respective committees.

Mr. E. WHITTLESEY moved that the National Temperance Society be permitted to have the use of the Hall of Representatives on Monday evening next.

It was objected to.

Mr. W. then moved to suspend the rule of the House, in order that he might be enabled to submit the motion; which was agreed to—yeas 117, nays 37.

The motion was then submitted, and agreed to—yeas 103, nays 41.

Mr. COLE, from the Committee of Ways and Means, reported the following resolution; and the question being taken, it was disagreed to, two-thirds not voting in the affirmative:

Resolved, That the Bill, No. 563, entitled a bill regulating the deposites of the money of the United States in certain local Banks, and the bill No. 564, entitled a bill to repeal so much of the act entitled an act transferring the duties of Commissioners of Loans to the Bank of the United States, as requires the Bank of the United States to perform the duties of Commissioner of Loans for the several States, be the standing order of the day, for this day at 1 o'clock, and in each succeed ng day at 12 o'clock, Saturday excepted, until disposed of, and that until the hour of 12 o'clock on each day, the business of the House shall proceed in the order prescribed by the rules of the House; but it shall be in order to present petitions and memorials on Monday.

Mr. CONNOR, from the Select Committee appointed at the last session to examine into and report the situation of the Post Office Department, made a detailed report.

Mr. C. moved that the report be laid upon the table and printed.

Mr. C. remarked, that the documents accompanying the report were voluminous, and that two of the members of the Committee had undertaken to collate them, and dispense with such as were unimportant. The remainder he moved to print, together with the report.

Mr. GARLAND asked for the reading of the report.

Mr. CONNOR had no objection; but the report was lengthy, and would probably be followed by a counter one of equal length.

Mr. GARLAND withdrew his motion.

The report and documents were then ordered to be printed.

Mr. E. WHITTLESEY, from the minority of the Committee, presented the views of the minority in a separate report; which was laid on the table and ordered to be printed.

Mr. BRIGGS moved to print 25,000 extra copies of each report, together with the documents.

Mr. SPEIGHT suggested 10,000 copies.

The motion, under the rule, lies over for a day.

Mr. GILMER moved to take up certain joint resolutions, heretofore submitted by him, proposing an amendment to the Constitution of the United States, in relation to the election of President and Vice President, and for other purposes. He did not wish to discuss them at present; but desired that they should be read a second time, and postponed to a particular day.

The motion was objected to.

Mr. GILMER moved to suspend the rule.

Mr. DICKINSON demanded the yeas and nays; which were ordered, and were, yeas 153, nays 56.

The resolutions were then taken up, read a second time, and, on motion of Mr. GILMER, their

further consideration was postponed to Thursday next, and made the special order for that day.

Mr. HANNEGAN, by consent, laid on the table an amendment to the foregoing resolutions, providing that Senators in Congress shall be elected directly by the people, by general ticket, in each State.

Petitions and memorials were presented, on leave, by Messrs. HUBBARD, J.T. MASON, ARCHER, and ASHLEY, and appropriately referred.

Mr. YOUNG, from the Committee on Revolutionary Claims, reported, without amendment, the bill from the Senate for the relief of Lucy Bond and Hannah Douglass.

Mr. WILLIAMS, (with the consent of Mr. Lincoln, who was entitled to the floor,) withdrew his motion to reject the bill reported by Mr. Casey, from the Committee on the Public Lands, entitled "a bill granting a bounty in lands to the organized militia men, mounted militia men, and rangers, who defended the frontier during the late war with Grt at Britain."

The bill was then read a second time.

Mr CASEY moved that it be committed to a Committee of the Whole House, made the order of the day for to-morrow, and, together with the report, be printed.

Mr. WILLIAMS was satisfied that the bill could not be acted on at the present session; and he therefore moved to lay the bill on the table.

Mr. CARR demanded the yeas and nays on the motion; which were ordered, and were, yeas 131, nays 86.

So the bill was ordered to lie on the table.

Mr. REYNOLDS moved to proceed to the consideration of the resolution offered by him on the 24th December last, providing that in elections of officers for the House, the vote should be taken *viva voce*. He thought the subject should be disposed of.

The motion was objected to.

On motion of Mr. EVANS, the House proceeded to the consideration of the orders of the day.

The SPEAKER laid before the House the following communications, which were appropriately disposed of:

From the Secretary of War, containing information in relation to the Delaware breakwater;

From the Secretary of War in relation to a road on the northern frontier of the State of Maine;

From the Secretary of War enclosing a re-survey, plan, and estimate, for building a light-house on Brandywine shoal, in the Delaware Bay;

From the Secretary of War covering a report of all the contracts made by the War Department, for the year 1834, made pursuant to law;

A memorial from the Legislative Council of Michigan, in relation to a light-house, light-vessel, and the improvement of the harbor of Mackinaw.

The following bills from the Senate were read twice and committed:

A bill making an appropriation for building a light-house at Mobile Point, and placing a buoy in Mobi'e bay;

A bill in addition to an act for the relief of the legal representatives of Geo. Hubbert, deceased;

A bill to change the organization of the General Post Office,

A bill for the continuation and repair of the Cumberland Road, in the States of Ohio, Illinois, and Indiana;

And a bill to fix the number and compensation of the officers of the customs, and to alter certa'n collection districts.

The following bills were read a third time and passed.

A bill for the relief of Enoch Blaisdell;

A bill granting pensions to certain persons therein named;

A bill granting a pension to John F. Wiley, and increasing the pension of George Fields;

A bill granting a pension to Wm. Slocum;

A bill granting a pension to Wm. Wilgys;

A bill for the relief of Samuel M. Asbury;

A bill granting a pension to Francis F. St. Cuir.

A bill for the relief of the invalid pensioners therein mentioned;

A bill g. anting a pension to Joseph Mead;

A bill granting a pension to Luke Voorhies;

A bill granting a pension to Colonel Gideon Morgan;

A bill granting a pension Benjamin Leslie;

A bill granting pensions to William Baden and James Harrington;

A bill for the relief of John Aston;

A bill for the relief of Ephraim F. Gilbert;

A bill granting a pension to Isaac Carter;

A bill granting a pension to John Gerodelle;

A bill for the relief of Samuel Shelmerline;

A bill for the relief of Thomas Morton;

A bill to increase the pension of Origen Eaton;

A bill granting a pension to John W. Cox;

A bill for the relief of Joseph Swartwood;

A bill granting an arrearage of pension to Edward Nicholson;

A bill for the relief of Abraham E. Boutwell and David Pearson;

A bill granting a pension to Robert Lucas;

A bill for the relief of George McFadden;

A bill for the relief of Simeon S. Morrill and Theophilus Beekman;

A bill for the relief of George C. Seaton;

A bill granting a pension to Larned Swallow;

A bill granting a pension to John Bryant;

A bill granting a pension to Noah Miller;

A bill placing Capt. Cole, a Seneca Chief, on the pension roll;

A bill for the relief of Benjamin Holland;

A bill for the relief of William Keller;

A bill granting a pension to Justus Cobb;

A bill granting a pension to Labert L. Van Velkenburg;

A bill granting a pension to Isaac Eckright;

A bill for the relief of William C. Beard;

A bill for the relief of Jacob Stewart;

A bill for the relief of Elijah Blodgett;

A bill for the relief of Thomas Simpson;

A bill for the relief Thankful Randall;

A bill for the relief of Col. Daniel Newnan;

A bill for the relief of Peter Triplett;

A bill for the relief of Peter Doxtator and Jacob Weaver;

A bill for the relief of John Dal, of Maine;

A bill for the relief of Simeon Meachum;

A bill for the relief of Joseph Gilbert;

A bill for the relief of the widow and heirs of Samuel Southerland;

A bill for the relief of Timothy Jordan;

A bill for the relief of Daniel Page;

A bi l for the relief of Walter Philips;

A bill for the relief of Elizabeth May.

A bill for the relief of Jared Buckingham;

A bill for the relief of Soloman Case;

A bill for the relief of the widow of Noah Chittenden;

A bill for the relief of Col. William Lawrence;

A bill to provide for paying certain pensioners at Jackson, in the State of Tennessee.

And a bill from the Senate to provide for further compensation to the Marshal for the District of Delaware.

The bill to provide additional compensation to the Marshall of the District of South Carolina, was ordered to be engrossed, and read a third time.

The bill for the relief of citizens of Arkansas who lost their improvements in consequence of a treaty with the Choctaw Indians, was taken up.

An amendment reported from the Committee to this bill, and also one offered by Mr. HARDIN, were adopted.

Mr. VINTON opposed the passage of the bill. He considered it tantamount to giving a reward for the violation of the laws.

Mr. SEVIER, (the Delegate from Arkansas,) defended the justice of the provisions of the bill, with great animation. He contended that those who remained upon their lands in defiance of the orders of the government, had been paid, while to those who obeyed, and went off, the just remuneration was denied. The government had taken these improvements and transferred them for a valuable consideration. Its refusal to pay the claims of those citizens, he could look upon as but little better than highway robbery. If ever there was a claim, which appealed most strikingly to the justice of the House, he conceived this to be the one. He dwelt on the merits of those individuals who act as the pioneers in the settlement of our frontiers, denominated *squatters*. They were many of them his particular friends. The bill was his; it would be passed.

Mr. BURGES said he knew the sportive feelings of the gentleman from Arkansas, or he should regret to hear any action of the government compared to highway robbery, but that gentleman defended the system of "*squatting*,"—(a by-word, by the way, which had obtained currency here, but which he did not remember to have ever used before)—as meritorious, and as having been rewarded by the grant of lands from the early day of the government. It was very true, when the savages hung upon our frontiers like a cloud—when the war whoop resounded, and the tomahawk and scalping knife were drinking the blood of their victims, we did give the public lands to all those who put their lives in their hands and acted as pioneers in opening the wilderness to our citizens. But now, in profound peace, when the danger from the savages was gone by—and the settler had nothing to do but to take up the public property at the public expense, the case was widely different. He understood that some of these settlers had made large improvements—large cotton plantations, &c. because there was no obstruction to their settlement. Would the gentleman pretend to compare these men with the hardy pioneers of the West, who planted and defended their habitations in peril? He considered the bill altogether the most singular that had ever been presented. He denied the justice of the claims which it countenanced.

Messrs. EWING and ASHLEY addressed the House in favor of the bill.

Mr. HARDIN proposed another amendment, by adding to one of the provisions of the bill, the words, "which is, by law, subject to entry."

Mr. MASON stated the views which influenced the committee to report the bill, and advocated, at some length, its passage.

Mr. VINTON again rose, and stated the objections he entertained to the bill. The persons here proposed to be indemnified, had gone on the public lands without the sanction or color of law, but in direct violation of law. The land in question had never been authorized to be sold or settled. If the principle sanctioned in the bill was to obtain, the Government had better give up the public domain entirely, as it was no longer safe in its custody.

Mr. BURGES said he agreed with the gentleman from Ohio, (Mr. Vinton,) that if the principles of this bill were to be sanctioned, we had better abandon the public lands altogether. We had subdued the nations who were its true and original owners. They had been driven across the great rivers of the West. They had gone towards the setting sun, and would reach the happy isles of the crest of their fathers before we could render them justice. It was high time, he thought, for this Government to compel some respect for the rules of moral honesty—that the public lands might be held by other property, and depredations committed on it punished in like manner. One of the gentlemen had told us that he represented these people. he let him. He supposed it was "like master—like man." But he would beg of that gentleman not to cast reflections on his constituents. He doubted whether he could name a man among the settlers on the public lands from the State of Rhode Island. If there were any settlers from that State, he had doubtless purchased of some body. He had purchased from a land thief, he had purchased without knowing that it was stol n. Another gentleman (Mr. Mason) had said it was the policy of the old States to prevent their poor from acquiring the lands of the West.

Mr. MASON sa'd such was not his sentiment. He had alluded to it as the language of the West.

Mr. BURGES said he was very glad; he was delighted to hear that this was not the language of the gentleman from Virginia. It might be the West, where such stumps were found, but he should regret to hear it from one coming from the vicinity of the Potomac. Mr. B. said it was the people of the East, by giving employment to their poor, in manufactures, did discourage the

igration of such as were too poor to purchase ands, as it was known they could not get and without plundering it; and he agreed with dam Smith, that of all luggage, the transportation of human beings was the most expensive. We of the East, said Mr. B. know we ave many established in the west who are ow our friends, and who were once our eighbors. We rejoice in their prosperity, nowing, as we do, that they form a chain with which binds the Union together. But it was igh time for the People of this country to set ome value on the public lands. If it continued to e culled out and the best of it sacrificed to speculators, it would be frittered away to a shadow. If e could save enough of it to educate our children, one great object would be gained, and this as the only object which could justify us in laying our hands upon it.

Mr. PARKER said a few words in opposition to he bill. If these individuals had well-grounded laims on the Government, let them be presented ere for payment in money. We had a key to the Treasury here, but none to the Land Treasury. He was opposed to this system of voting 160 acres or every claim of one cent or one dollar.

Mr. CROCKETT said he would go as far as he President in his message proposed to go. He would give every citizen a portion of the public ands who would settle upon it. No act of the President's life pleased him so much as the avowal f this sentiment. He was in favor of the bill; at speaking had become so fashionable on that loor, in this pressing stage of the business of the ession, that he began to believe in the doctrine hat silence was a virtue.

Mr. HANNEGAN said, he did not rise so much or the purpose of debating the merits of the bill nder consideration, as of replying to and repelling the unwarrantable and insidious aspersions so njustly cast upon the western country by the entleman from Rhode Island, (Mr. Burgess;) aspersions for which no cause could be assigned, no eason found in what was then pending before he House, or had been previously uttered in debate; charges the most extraordinary that he had ver heard uttered on that floor, and without the hade of provocation. To them, however, and to he gentleman from Rhode Island, he would not eply in the spirit that had dictated that gentleman's wanton reproaches upon a race of people bout whom he knew nothing, and to whose abits he would, in all likelihood, forever continue stranger. Mr. H. said his surprise had been increased, when he reflected from what quarter this ttack came; from one whose sectional attachments, if we are to judge by what has often escaped him, are as strong as man's can be. One hose tongue was never silent when New England was assailed; whose eloquence had so often tirred his auditory, not only on that floor, but lsewhere, in repelling the thrusts made at the and of "the pilgrim fathers."

For the love borne by the honorable gentleman his native land, for his defence of her, for his evotion to her interests, he (Mr. H.) honored im. But, sir, is it not strange to hear from such source a wantion violaton of those very feelings others, which he professes to hold so sacred in imself? Can we credit the sincerity of his professions of attachment to his own home, when, with old, unfeeling levity, he openly mocks at the attachment of others? Can such a man be sincere? re not his professions false and hollow?

The invidious remark of the gentleman, in replying to the honorable member from Virginia, Mr. Mason,) "that he would not have expected much of the demagogue from one so near the aters of the Potomac; that it was better suited to west, where stumps were plenty," however ight answer the views of the honorable gentleman from Rhode Island, in making his *court* to irginia, was by no means calculated to heighten im *individually* in the estimation of the House, r to elevate his character before the country for andor and justice. For the purpose of exposing he injustice of the remark, so obvious to all, it ill be unnecessary to institute any comparisons, esort to any appeal, make any reference to times ast or present. What the west was, all the world knew; what her sons were, had been tried in the hour of difficulty, of danger, and of death. Promptly responsive to their country's call in the moment of her necessity, when girt around by enemies, they had not, they would not, no, God forbid that they ever should, stop to inquire whether her cause was right or wrong, after the sword had once been drawn, the standard unfurled, and the shrill bugle sounded the rally for her defence. To the call of their whole country they had promptly responded, as a body—in defence of their own loved "West" as individuals, they would be equally prompt, whenever occasion required a sacrifice or a hazard at their hands, for the maintenance of her honor or her interests.

Who would have recognized to-day in the scornful contemner of the habits and the customs of a large portion of the western people, the same individual who, on some former occasion, has so feelingly and beautifully pictured out of his own New England, her smiling fields, her admirable institutions, her evidences of devotion to the common cause of liberty in other times! And true it is she has them, her Bunker's Hill, her Bennington; and not these alone, but with equal pride cannot the west turn to her evidences of devotion to the same holy cause, has she not her New Orleans, her Tippecanoe, her Thames, her Raisin, where the blood of her best, her noblest sons flowed freely out, an offering before the high altar of the whole, the common country? The hour will never come when her sons shall look with coldness or indifference on these fields, or regard with feelings other than those of holy pride, the oft repeated instances of her attachment to the cause of liberty, and the Union. What, said Mr. H., is it a reproach to have sprung from the "West," that "West" whom her sons love so well, whose very name stirs up their hearts, quickens their pulses, as the name of a fond mother in whose lap they have been nurtured? To her they ever turn with fond affection, thankful to God that their eyes had opened first in her unsullied retreats; that first they had seen the sun shine down on her free and green hill tops above, and the waters roll on their way through her rich and beautiful valleys below. And this pride—and this love—every true son she has will carry with him, through life—the dearest of all cherished affections—the deepest imbedded in his heart—he will carry it to every country—to every climate—where destiny may cast him. It will cease—it will be lost—and lost only when the grave closes over the last throbbings of earthly attachment.

The remark of the gentleman intended so sarcastically to be felt in this House, at the expense of my colleague, (Mr. Ewing,) when he treats him as the specimen of the people he represents, and with indecent levity, aims to excite a transitory mirth by the infliction of a deadly wound, not upon his (Mr. Ewing's) feelings, but the character of those from amongst whom he comes, is what I had not expected from the gentleman—it would almost seem to be consistent only with the workings of a heart whose malevolence seeks for its gratification the miseries of others. I would offer no rebuke to the gentleman from Rhode Island, his years are many, his hairs are white, and thinned by time—mine are the reverse—the contrast checks in me that expression of feeling which swells almost too high for control. But that intended sarcasm carried with it a compliment the highest that I would ask at the hands of mortal man—I would ask no more than to be regarded as the personified delineation of the courage, the generosity, the honor, and the chivalry of that people in the midst of whom I first drew breath, and surrounded by whom I have grown to manhood.

A few remarks concerning the people whom the Hon. gentleman is pleased to designate as "land robbers," "thieves," "depredators," whose offences, morally, fall nothing short of the crime of larceny. It requires no little stretch of imagination, to recognise, under these epithets, that industrious portion of our community in the West, numbers of whom have emigrated from New England, and who, being without the means of purchasing, have become, with their families, the actual occupants of small portions of the soil, for which they ask no other favor than a pre emption right, at the minimum price of the Government. Far different are the feelings by which they have been led to make for themselves a home, their families a shelter and a subsistence. It is their aversion to the very crimes of which the gentleman speaks, that has induced them to leave the older and the compactly settled portions of the country, where even industry is pinched too often by want, and to brave the exposures, the severities, and the hardships, incident to the life of him who goes into the bosom of the forest, depending upon his axe for the roof that must shelter, and upon his rifle for the food that must furnish, not him alone, but these to whom nature has given the dearest and holiest claims upon his exertions and his existence. They have gone to avoid the miserable condition of the thousands who are now lingering about the purlieus of the large cities, pressed by want, struggling with famine and cold, the honesty of whose hearts has been crushed, the firmness of whose integrity has finally bowed before the fierce influence of hunger and necessity, and who have been forced to sustain existence by continued depredations upon the persons and property around them, and living alone by plunder and pillage, have sunk into all the excesses of crime. These same miserable outlaws, had their lot been cast amongst the class so bitterly contemned by the honorable gentleman from Rhode Island, would have presented a far different picture of humanity—one more grateful to the heart that looks with benevolence upon the race of human kind.

With all the attachment borne by the gentleman from Rhode Island for his own State, and the high opinion he has of the condition of her working population, I think the contrast between their condition and that of the backwoodsmen—*the squatter*, to use that word which sounds, as the gentleman says, so horrid to his ears—will present, even to his view, a picture more favorable to the latter. Take the class who labor for subsistence in the large manufacturing institutions, and what does that labor produce to them, at the end of each week, more than will barely answer the pressing demands for food and raiment? Successive years of labor will find them still the same—no increase of stores—no addition of comforts; far less of wealth or substance. The scanty pittance is expended, week by week, as it is earned. Wearied with his endless drudgery, and its miserable recompense, the laborer of years at last turns his eyes to the far-off West—that land of promise, whose harvests, fame tells him, are golden—whose lands yield almost spontaneously to the wants of man. He seeks in her bosom the truth of the tale that has lured him; the reality of the vision that has flitted so often over his doubting senses. Is that vision confirmed? Is that tale the tale of truth? Has the land of promise been reached, and its harvests found ripening in the head? Wait the lapse of a few, a very few short years, and then seek the answer of the pilgrim himself. He will give it you beneath his own roof—he who sought the land of the stranger on foot, with scarcely the means of a dinner in his pocket, will furnish forth the comforts of his habitation. Humble it may be to the dweller in cities, but with comfort it abounds, and within is peace, and health, and plenty, and without, the eye is greeted by the bountiful and waving crop, and the grazing herds may be traced through the distant glade. It is his own, all his own, the fruit, the labor of his hands, and with cheerful delight, he gazes over his farm and feels, with honest pride, the independence of a freeholder. However kind may be the recollections with which memory visits the parent land, that memory is unclouded with regret, for he has exchanged toil for rest, penury for plenty, servitude for freedom. If Rhode Island, as often happens, has been his early home, the change is even greater, the cause of his rejoicing still more increased, for *the high instrument*, the paramount law which secures and guaranties his rights as a man; his privileges and his protection as a citizen, is no longer *a Royal Charter, a grant carrying with it the degrading evidence of a Monarch's rule, the humiliating admission that his kingly condescension* had more wisely provided for freedom, than freemen themselves could. No, he has exchanged the government of *this charter* for a com-

stitution, formed, perfected, adopted in all its parts, by the people themselves, created at their will, based upon their confidence, and sustained by their affection, an honored and living commentary upon the great principle of human equality.

It is such men as I have described, that have this day fallen under the denunciations of the honorable gentleman from Rhode Island, and whom he thinks it would be discreditable to represent on this floor. For my own part, I am proud to acknowledge that such are many of my constituents, and I apprehend they would lose but little by any comparison that might be instituted between their moral condition, and that of the people of Rhode Island, or elsewhere. The very industry which they practise in acquiring for themselves a home, is a sufficient compensation to the Government, for her land, as it increases their attachment to her, by extending their interest in the soil. What constitutes the wealth, the reliance, the boast of any nation, but its population? What is the great and paramount object of all government, if it is not the promotion of happiness and security among its people? Of all governments that have existed, ours professes in the highest degree, and is beyond doubt, in the outline, best calculated to promote the end desired. Yet with all its advantages, much of the machinery may be, and is practically misapplied.

We are doing what no good government besides has ever done, and what it is to be hoped will soon be eradicated from our system—we are making the public domain of the country a matter of speculation and profit upon our own citizens, for the purpose of increasing the Treasury spoils, that are annually divided out on this floor. Instead of this course, were we to portion in limited parcels the whole domain as it might become settled by the class of people against whom the anathema of the honorable gentleman has been directed; were we to divide it amongst all the industrious poor of the whole country willing to become its tenants, and reap its harvests, how much would not the sum of human happiness be raised? How immeasurably would the true wealth of the nation be increased?

But to this the hon. gentleman from Rhode Island, and those who act with him on the main question involving the public lands, have an objection so deep,—to the selfish politician so strong,—that notwithstanding the covert under which they would fain hide the true cause, no occasion passes without its exhibition. And this cause, and this alone, I do from the bottom of my heart, believe has prompted the open and violent assault of the hon. gentleman to day, upon a whole race of people.

It is the fact, that political power and strength is gliding too rapidly from the East to the West. The population of the latter, growing in number, anddirecting all their energies to the developement of the many resources kindly provided by nature, presents a scene of advancing power, that has kindled up the jealousy of some in the Eastern section, who can view only the dark side of the picture,—their own downfall in the prosperity of others. Sir, it will be all in vain, no checks can now restrain the growing prospects of the great valley of the West. Her march is steady, sure, and onward.

Against the very kind suggestions of the gentleman, that the proceeds from the sales of the public lands should be taken and distributed amongst the different States, for the purpose of educating all the children of the country, I would beg leave to protest on many accounts. One reason, however, will be sufficient at this time. I do not wish to see Rhode Island raising the means for the education of her children, out of the soil of Indiana. Let her raise those means at home; let her educate her own children with her own means, and we will educate our children in the same way. We will teach them the proper duties of the citizen; instil into them a pure love of the free institutions of their country; a readiness to defend them when assailed by outward foes, *ay! or by intestine traitors; a just regard too for the feelings of all mankind:* in a word, we will teach teach them all that man should be; just so much and no more; and it will be well *for the fame* of Rhode Island, should the same course [illegible] in *times to come.*

Mr. Speaker I have done. The rhetorical flourish of the gentleman in behalf of the poor Indian requires no answer; its use for sympathy, or ornament, in setting off a speech, however it might suit, were the Indians concerned in the matter before the House, is now of little avail either way, being entirely out of place.

To the merits of that class, for a portion of whom the benefits of the bill under consideration are intended, I have borne and can bear every testimony that honest industry deserves. The bill itself has my hearty wishes for its success, and shall most cordially have my vote.

Mr. HUBBARD said, from some remarks which fell from the gentleman from Virginia (Mr. Mason) he was induced to believe he had not fully understood the subject. If the views taken by the gentleman from Ohio (Mr. Vinton) were correct, the bill should certainly be rejected. In order to give gentlemen a further opportunity for investigation, he moved the House adjourn.

The motion was agreed to, and

The House adjourned.

IN SENATE.

SATURDAY, February 14, 1835.

Petitions and memorials were presented by—

Messrs. EWING, KANE, and LINN.

A message was received from the President of the United States, by the hands of Mr. DONELSON, his Private Secretary, calling the attention of Congress to a bill for the relief of Benedict Alfred and Robert Brush, which obtained the form of law without having actually passed the Senate; which on motion of Mr. TOMLINSON, was referred to the Judiciary Committee.

The VICE PRESIDENT laid before the Senate a communication from the Treasury Department, transmitting the information called for by a resolution of the Senate, relative to the claim of the owners of the brig Despatch.

Mr. BROWN, from the Committee on Claims, to which were referred the bills from the House for the relief of Theodore Owners, and for the relief of the legal representatives of Aaron Smith, deceased, reported them severally, without amendment.

Mr. ROBBINS, from the Library Committee, to which was referred the bill from the House, making provision for the purchase of a *fac simile* of Gen Washington's accounts, reported the same without amendment.

Mr BROWN, from the Committee of Claims, to which was referred the petition of George Kyles, reported unfavorably upon the same; and the Committee were discharged from the further consideration of the same.

The following resolution, submitted yesterday by Mr. WAGGAMAN, was considered, and agreed to:

Resolved, That the Secretary of War be requested to communicate to the Senate the report received from the person charged with the Mineralogical and Geological investigation, authorized by an act of Congress at the last session.

Mr. TOMLINSON submitted the following resolution:

Resolved, That the Committee on Commerce be instructed to inquire into the expediency of making an appropriation for the preservation of Black Rock harbor on the northerly side of Long Island Sound.

The bill in addition to the act for the relief of the personal representatives of Col. John Lawrence, deceased, was read the third time, and passed.

On motion of Mr POINDEXTER, the Senate took up for consideration, as in Committee of the Whole, the bill supplementary to the act of last session, granting a township of land to certain exiles from Poland, and after some remarks from Mr. P., on motion of Mr. KING, the bill was laid on the table.

On motion of Mr. FRELINGHUYSEN, the Senate took up for consideration the bill to consolidate the third and fourth Judicial Districts of the United States; when, on his motion, the bill was postponed to, and made the special order for Wednesday next.

The Senate considered, as in Committee of the Whole, the bill for the relief of the legal representatives of Lieut. Robert Jewett, late of the Virginia Continental Line.

After some remarks from Mr. LEIGH, in support, and by Mr. HILL, against the bill, it was ordered to be engrossed for a third reading.

On motion of Mr. TYLER, the Senate took up the bill for the benefit of the Corporations of Washington, Georgetown, and Alexandria; when, on his motion, it was postponed to, and made the special order for Thursday next.

SPECIAL ORDER.

The Senate then resumed the consideration, as in Committee of the Whole, of the bill to repeal that part of the act of 1820, limiting the terms of certain offices, commonly called the four years' law.

Mr. EWING rose and said, the question before the Senate was one of the utmost importance; and one that was deserving a most serious consideration. He should not feel himself bound to sustain the bill from the importance of the first and second sections, but the third involved principles of the most momentous consequences. He had not heard any thing said against that part of the bill, that calls in question the constitutional powers of the Executive. The third section treated upon those powers of the executive which had been claimed as derived directly from the constitution. If the President did hold these powers from the constitution, then the bill came in contact with the constitution itself. He did not believe, however, that the constitution gave the power of removal from office to the executive. He did not deny that the power might be conferred by law; but only contended that it was not a constitutional privilege. The subject was not a new one, nor for the first time set forth. It had been long ago fully discussed by both Houses of Congress, and very recently in the Senate, though without coming to a decision. The section under consideration would test the opinion of the Senate on that point. The constitution vested all executive power in the President; but the term *executive power* was ambiguous, undefined, and loose in its construction. It had long been a question for debate among statesmen, men of the greatest talents, and profoundest sagacity. What was executive power, he would ask? How far did it extend? If it was intended to vest all power in the hands of the executive, then it should have been more clearly defined and not been left uncertain and doubtful. Among the monarchies of Europe, the executive power of the kings was unlimited; but the framers of our constitution did not look to Europe for patterns and models by which to build up the institutions of a free people. By the phrase *executive power*, they did not intend to confer on the President the power of appointment and removal. Neither was it so understood and expressed by writers and books on executive power.

Mr. E. referred to the opinions of Necker and the patriots of the French revolution. The same branch of Government, said Mr. E. ought not to have the power of willing and acting; that the Executive ought not to judge, but fulfil the decisions of others. The President did not even possess all the powers, said Mr. E. necessary for executing the laws, but often needed the assistance of Congress. If he did, he could raise money to support the administration of the laws. But, for this, no one would contend. So the constitution declares that all legislative power shall be vested in Congress. This expression was equally strong with that which declares all Executive power should be vested in the President. But that all legislative power was not vested in Congress was evident from the fact, that the constitution required the sanction of the President upon all laws; and also gave him the veto privilege. Hence it was probable that no powers were conferred, unless particularly specified. That the authors of the constitution first stated the general proposition, where the Executive power should be placed, and then went on to specify wherein it should consist, not, like children, to load it with useless repetitions, but to define and limit the extent of Executive power. Those who claim these powers for the Executive, went upon the supposition that all powers, not

defined by the constitution, belonged to the President. Whereas the very reverse of that was true. The Executive possessed only those particularly specified by that instrument. He contended that the different departments of Government ought not to be entirely separate and independent of each other. He would make an exception of the Judicial branch; it was not necessary to connect that with the others; but the Executive and Judicial Departments ought not to be separate and independent of each other.

He would next proceed to the power of removing from office. It was claimed as correlative to appointing to office. The power of repealing laws did not belong to Congress without the sanction of the President. The concurrence of all the parties who made the law, was necessary to repeal it; the President could not appoint to office without the consent of the Senate; and by the same reasoning as before, the removal could not be made without the concurrence of the Senate. If the nomination of a new candidate was rejected by the Senate, the incumbent should still continue to hold his office and exercise its duties. In 1789, it was fully discussed whether the President had the power of removal or not, derived from the constitution; many gentlemen who had assisted in framing the constitution, participated in that discussion; they were about equally divided between the two opinions. But during the heat and excitement of debate, the popularity of General Washington drew over a majority to the side of Executive power.

Mr. KANE said, he did not mean to enter into this discussion at length. Soon after the formation of this Government, those who had the power—the first Congress—decided that the President had the power of removal from office, as a necessary incident to the Executive power. This decision, he said, had been practically acceded to for near half a century, and he should not take up time to discuss it, and more especially as the question was not presented by the bill before the Senate. The first section only repealed the law of May, 1820, limiting the term of certain officers. Where did this repeal leave the question of removal? Precisely where it was before, and placed the tenure of these offices where the practice of all past time had placed it; dependent upon Executive pleasure. The second section provides that disbursing offices shall be vacated upon the defalcation of the officer. Here is removal by law, but no limitation is imposed thereby upon the pre-existing power of removal in the Executive. The third and last section admits in general terms the right of the President, without consulting the Senate, to remove. And yet it requires the President to lay his reasons therefor before the Senate. This, if no other reason existed, he thought was sufficient to induce him to vote against the bill. Admitting to its fullest extent the power of the President which he can exercise under the constitution, without any responsibility except to the people through the ballot boxes, or to the impeaching power, yet the bill requires the President to give his reasons for exercising his constitutional powers to the Senate, to which, in this respect, he is not *confessedly* responsible. What shall we do with these reasons when we get them? Shall we take the course which was taken with the Secretary of the Treasury, when he laid his reasons for removing the deposites before Congress? Shall we resolve that the Executive has violated the constitution? That we cannot do; because we admit, by this bill, he has the right to do the act, and that he can do it regardless of the Senate. If he had no other reason for the vote he was about to give, this palpable inconsistency would be sufficient.

Mr. BIBB said, he agreed that the Executive power resided, and should reside, in the President; but, at the same time, he believed that Congress had power to regulate it. He thought the President possessed no other executive powers than those particularly specified in the constitution. If more were granted, he would have an unlimited, boundless power, capable of absorbing all the other branches of the Government. Mr. B. alluded to party distinctions and political strife; which he contended were necessary for the healthy administration of public affairs, as much so as the winds, the waves, and tempests were to purify the ocean. No great reforms could be effected without the influence of party to carry it on. Mr. B. went on at some length in his remarks, and finally concluded by disclaiming all ambitious motives and desires of sharing in any further political projects.

Mr. SHEPLEY opposed the bil at some length.

Mr. CLAY said that at the last session he presented resolutions respecting the power of removal by the executive. He still deemed the subject of momentous importance, opening a wide field for discussion, but he did not propose to debate it now. But he would present his views in the shape of an amendment to the section of the bill which relates to the power of appointment by the President; although he did not formally offer it as an amendment, he desired that it might lie on the table. It is as follows: "That in all instances of appointment to office, by and with the advice and consent of the Senate, the power of removal shall be exercised only in concurrence with the Senate; and when the Senate is not in session, the President may suspend any such officer, communicating to the Senate his reasons for the suspension, during the first month of its succeeding session, and if the Senate concur with him, the officer shall be removed; but if it do not concur with him, the officer shall be restored to office." He hoped at another time to be able to show that the President had not this power of removal given him in the constitution—he had searched that instrument with his utmost care, without being able to find it. And he was in hopes that some gentleman of the administration party would have undertaken to show that it did exist. One gentleman over the way (Mr. Kane) had only peeped out at it, and the other, (Mr. Shepley) would not touch it at all. Why not? Why not take up the constitution and discuss it? Why thus diffident in coming out and giving their reasons for the existence of a power, the practical operation of which was to give the executive an influence over an army of men which was not equalled in ancient Rome? If this power exist, let gentlemen show it. And when we come here on Monday, he hoped some of the leaders of the administration party, some of the honorable gentlemen then in his eye, would come prepared to show that the power existed and was rightfully exercised.

Mr. BUCHANAN said he was sorry to see that the honorable gentleman from Kentucky appeared disposed so frequently to pay his compliments to him—

Mr. CLAY interposed, and remarked that he did not mean the honorable member from Pennsylvania; but if he chose to come out upon the question, his respect for that gentleman would induce him to listen to him with great pleasure. He might have turned his eye toward the honorable gentleman, but in truth he meant the Hon. member from New York, who sat in the same range.

Mr. BUCHANAN resumed: He had nothing further to say, except that when the honorable gentleman from Kentucky should come out and show that a practice which was co-existent with the Government itself, and which had been exercised by Mr. Madison, was unconstitutional, he would undertake to show, in his humble manner, that it was constitutional, and that it was a practice under which this country had flourished to an extent unexampled in the world.

Mr. SHEPLEY said that the gentleman from Kentucky did not understand him correctly. He said that he would not *now* discuss a question which opened so wide a field, because there was not time for it. He did not and would not shun an inquiry into the correctness and constitutionality of a practice which was exercised under every administration of the Government, from its organization down to the present time.

The Senate then adjourned.

HOUSE OF REPRESENTATIVES.

SATURDAY, February 14, 1835.

Mr. J. Q. ADAMS, on leave, presented several petitions for the abolition of slavery in the District of Columbia.

Mr. J. Q. ADAMS then said, while he had possession of the floor, he hoped the House would indulge him for a few moments in making a brief explanation in reference to a matter personal to himself, and of considerable interest also to the House.

It would be recollected that, on that day last week, he offered a resolution to the House on the reference of certain documents to the Committee on Foreign Relations, with instructions to report forthwith on the part of the President's message relating to the state of our affairs with France. In the course of the remarks he made at that time, the expression escaped him, that the other branch of the legislature, after deliberating fully and thoroughly upon the subject matter of these relations, had ultimately come to the determination unanimously to "*dodge*" the question. The House would recollect that the moment he used the word, the Speaker arrested his remarks, under the rule of the House forbidding any member thereof to refer to any thing that had taken place, or might be taking place in the other branch of the legislature. By doing so, the Speaker, Mr A. had no doubt without any intention, had deprived him of the means of giving an explanation at the time. He was therefore silenced, and took his seat. But it struck him then, as a very hard case, to be arrested upon a mere simple rule of the House which was violated every day by almost every member, viz., a single reference to the proceedings of the other branch of the legislature, and he thought himself called upon to ask the Speaker privately why it was that he was so arrested under that rule, when other members were allowed the indulgence every day in almost every debate that took place. The Speaker then informed Mr. A. that it was not the simple reference to the proceedings in the other branch which had induced him to stop Mr. A., but that he thought the use of the term "*dodge*," with reference to their proceedings, was disrespectful, and that it was on that account alone he had done so. It was the manner of the allusion, and not the allusion itself upon which the Speaker thought proper to arrest Mr. A.'s remarks. Thus he was precluded from making, as he wished, an explanation at the moment, and for which he now rose to make.

Mr A. then said, he disclaimed all intention whatever, in the most positive and explicit terms of being disrespectful. He not only intended nothing disrespectful, but it was his intention to have recommended the House to do the same thing. His object was that the House should have deliberated upon the subject, and he should then have recommended it to "dodge" the question as the Senate had done, at least for the present. He wished to make this explanation, for he had been given to understand that several individual members of the other branch of the legislature had felt themselves hurt at the expression used by him. He reiterated, therefore, in the most positive and explicit manner, that he was far, very far, from intending any thing disrespectful to the House or to the Senate, by the use of the term "dodge." He thought then, and he still thought, that the Senate had acted in perfect conformity to their duty, and the unanimity with which that body had acted was precisely the unanimity in which he wished the House to have acted. He then informed the House of the object of the motion then made, viz. of calling upon the Committee on Foreign Relations to do what he thought the duty of every committee to do, report as soon as possible, upon any matter referred to them. He wished the House to show the country that they were not sleeping upon a matter involving the rights, the interests, and the honor of the country. That was his intention, and this explanation he desired to make.

There was another matter of much more importance, to which he would also briefly advert. In that great commercial emporium, the City of New York, he had been informed that great excitement had arisen, not from the action of, but in consequence of the debate that took place in the House, on this day week; and mainly from the remarks he was understood to have made—or, as it was ex-

pressed, upon the stand he was supposed to have taken. He had seen, from the newspapers, that the holders of French goods and wares in the cities of New York and Philadelphia, had advanced their prices upon those goods, in consequence of what he had said. He regretted that any such an effect should have been produced, and he should hardly have believed it possible; for he supposed that the merchants of New York, Philadelphia, and all the other commercial cities in the country, would draw their inferences, with respect to the proceedings of this government, not from what was *said* by any one individual member—much less from what was said by Mr. A.—but from the *action* of the House. Whatever, upon that day, might have been his partial propensity, or whatever might have been most erroneously represented to have been his views and wishes, he should have supposed that the merchants of those large cities would have looked to what the House did upon his motion, and not upon what he had said. He would remark, that it appeared he was not supported by any party in the House; for, so far from agreeing with him, they actually rejected his motion by a very large majority, without even giving him the opportunity of taking the yeas and nays. That fact was as widely diffused abroad as his remarks of that day, and he was, therefore, at a loss to conceive how it was possible for such an effect to have taken place, either from what he said or from what the House did.

In conclusion, said Mr. A. I wish to give this notice, if such notice must be given, to all the merchants throughout the Union, that there is not the least danger, not the slightest danger, of any thing that can lead to a war, from this House, or from the other branch of the legislature. I say this, sir, upon my own responsibility to the nation, and I tell them that in the present state of affairs there is no danger of any sort, that any thing will be done by this or the other branch of the Legislature, which can by any possibility have a tendency to create a rupture with France. I say this, that they may quiet and tranquilize themseles upon this supposed danger. And I say it, that they may immediately set about reducing their prices upon the lute strings and silk ribbons, and all those elegant ornaments, so needful to adorn the fair visiters of fancy balls; for God forbid, that I should do or say any thing that should be the means of taxing the ladies for ornamenting their persons.

Mr. A. here concluded, and the petitions were referred to the Committee on the District of Columbia.

Mr. C. JOHNSON offered the following resolution; the consideration of which was postponed until Monday 16th February.

Resolved, That the Report of the Recorder and Commissioners for the adjustment of land titles in the State of Missouri, under the acts of the 9th July 1832, and the 3d March 1833, be referred to the Secretary of the Treasury, and that he report to the next session of Congress; first as to the correctness of the principles adopted and acted upon by the Recorder and Commissioners as set forth in said report.

2d. That he report also, to the House the names of the several claimants in said Report, whose claims are entitled to confirmation under the Spanish regulations, and the several acts of Congress upon that subject.

Mr. PLUMMER, offered the following resolution, which, under the rule, lies one day:

Resolved, That the President of the United States be requested to cause to be communicated to this House, the construction which the proper Department or Departments of the Executive branch of the General Governments placed upon the 12th section of the act of March 3d, 1803, regulating the grants and providing for the sale of lands of the United States, south of Tennessee; the act of March 1st 1817, enabling the people of the Western part of Mississippi Territory to form a Constitution and State Government, and the treaties of Pontatock and Washington, made with the Chicasaw Tribe of Indians, so far as relates to the rights of the inhabitants of each township to the 16th section for the use of schools, and the rights of the Government of Mississippi to five per cent. of the proceeds of the sale of the lands for purposes of Internal Improvement within that District of country ceded to the United States by the aforesaid tribe of Indians, at the treaty of Pontatock creek, made on the 2d day of October 1832, and whether in the opinion of the Executive this treaty making power of the United States, has or has not placed a specific performance of the compact made with the people of Mississippi, beyond the contract of the General Government, and whether any legislation of Congress is deemed necessary to enable the Government to carry into effect, in good faith, either the provisions of the act of 1803, relating to the 18th section, and the act of 1817, relating to the five per cent.on the stipulations contained in the aforesaid treaties with the Chickasaws.

On motion of Mr. HANNEGAN,

Resolved, That the Committee on Commerce be instructed to inquire into the expediency of making Michigan city, on Lake Michigan, in the State of Indiana, a port of entry.

On motion of Mr. POPE,

Resolved, That the Committee on the Post Office and Post Roads be instructed to inquire into the expediency of establishing a post route from Jefferson Town, Jefferson County, Kentucky, to Shelbyville, Shelby County, Indiana.

Mr. SEVIER, by consent, offered the following resolution, which was agreed to:

Resolved, That the Secretary of War be instructed to report to this House the report of Mr. Featherstonhaugh, the Geologist, employed in virtue of the act of June 28th, 1834, appropriating the sum of five thousand dollars to be applied to Geological and Mineralogical surveys and researches.

Mr. C. ALLAN, from the Committee on the Territories, reported the following resolution:

Resolved, That this House will, on Friday, the 20th instant, take up and consider bills relating to the Territories.

Mr. POLK moved to amend the resolution by substituting Tuesday for Friday, which was agreed to.

Mr. VANCE moved to amend the resolution by including as one of the bills to be considered on that day, the bill fixing the northern boundary lines of the States of Ohio, Indiana, and Illinois.

The amendment was discussed by Messrs. VANCE, C. ALLAN, ASHLEY, ALLEN of Ohio, WHITE, LYON of Michigan, and VINTON.

The debate was arrested, by a motion made by Mr. McKIM, to proceed to the orders of the day.

Mr. WILDE moved to reconsider the vote adopting the resolution offered this day by Mr. C. JOHNSON.

After a few remarks by Messrs. C. JOHNSON, ASHLEY, and CLAY, the motion to reconsider was agreed to.

On motion of Mr. ASHLEY, the further consideration of the resolution was postponed to Monday next.

Mr. CLAIBORNE, from the Committee on Elections, reported the following resolution:

Resolved, That Robert P. Letcher having been duly returned as the rightful member of the House of Representatives of the United States from the Fifth Congressional District of Kentucky, is entitled to compensation as a member of the last and present session, and that Thomas P. Moore having attended the last session of Congress by order of the House, be allowed like compensation for the last session of Congress.

Mr. HARDIN said, the House would recollect, that at the last session he entertained the opinion which he now did, that Mr. Letcher was entitled to his seat in this body. The House had, however, came to the conclusion that owing to the difficulties which the question presented, it could not decide which of the gentlemen was the choice of the people. The question was submitted to the voters of the District, not to examine the record, because that would have been absurd, but that it should be decided by a new election. As both of the gentlemen were detained here by the order of the House, it was his opinion that both should be paid. He was in favor of paying both or neither. He therefore moved to amend the resolution so as to compensate Messrs. Letcher and Moore, for their attendance, under the order of the House at the last session.

Mr. JOHNSON, of Kentucky, concurred entirely in the views of his colleague, (Mr. Hardin.) He thought both the gentlemen ought to be paid, as proposed.

Mr. WILDE demanded the yeas and nays on the amendment; which were ordered.

Mr. CLAY was of opinion that both gentlemen should be paid. He thought, however, that the claims should be considered separately. As the committee had reported this resolution, he was opposed to throwing any embarrassment in the way of its passage; and if a similar resolution should be proposed in favor of Mr. Moore, he would also vote for such a proposition.

Mr. McKIM renewed the motion to proceed to the consideration of the orders of the day; which was agreed to. Yeas 87, nays 64.

POST OFFICE DEPARTMENT.

Mr. BRIGGS asked the unanimous consent of the House, to consider the motion submitted by him yesterday, to print 25,000 extra copies of the two Reports of the Post Office Committee, together with the documents accompanying the same.

Objection having been made, Mr. BRIGGS moved to suspend the rule; which carried—yeas 114, nays 28.

The motion was then taken up, the question being on an amendment offered by Mr. SPEIGHT, to substitute 10,000 for 25,000 copies.

Mr. SPEIGHT said that when he yesterday suggested that 10,000 copies of the reports and documents should be printed, he was not aware that they were so voluminous. The printing of the number he had proposed, could not be accomplished in any reasonable time. The reports and documents could not be embraced in a single volume; and as every newspaper in the country would publish such portions of the reports as would suit their purposes, he would modify his amendment by substituting 5,000 for 10,000 copies.

Mr. BRIGGS said, if he was called upon to vary his motion, he should be disposed to increase rather than lessen the number of copies. He would do this for the very reason assigned by the gentleman from North Carolina (Mr. Speight) for reducing the number which that gentleman had originally proposed, namely, that the newspapers would publish such portions of these reports as *would answer their purposes*. By a course of this kind, the entire matter contained in the reports would never reach the People of the United States. Mr. B. referred to the universal concern which was felt on this subject. The People looked with intense interest for the report of the Committee of this House. It had been charged that the affairs of this Department had been heretofore mismanaged. At the instance of the Chairman of the Committee on the Post Office, (Mr. Connor) who was a friend of the Administration, the House, at the last session, appointed a Select Committee to sit in the recess, for the purpose of investigating the affairs of this Department. This committee met in September and had been laboriously engaged in the discharge of its duties up to yesterday. The results of their labors had been reported to the House, and the question now was, how could the country be best made acquainted with these results? He knew of no other way, than the one which he had proposed. It was not a sufficient reason, that because this investigation was voluminous it should not be extensively circulated in the country. In relation to the contents of the reports, he knew but little. He had merely seen the result to which the majority of the committee, who were friendly to the administration, had arrived—a result which the majority declare has given them pain and filled them with astonishment. The people would look with anxiety for this report. He had more calls for it from his constituents than for any other document which had been presented to the House. He repeated, in conclusion, that if he should vary his motion, it would be to print a still larger number of these papers than what he had originally proposed.

Mr. E. WHITTLESEY did not think that the documents would be found to be as voluminous as

ad been supposed by the gentleman from North arolina, (Mr. Speight.) A sub-committee had ndertaken to examine and select such parts of hese documents as might be necessary to be rinted. This duty was not as yet performed; ut he felt warranted in saying that a large mass f the documents would be found unnecessary, nd would be thrown out by the sub-committee. The principal facts were conceded in both reports. This would supersede the necessity of printing all he documents. As to the number of the reports hich should be printed, that was a matter for the ouse to decide. He had no suggestions to make pon that point. In conclusion, Mr. W. said he usted the House would not prematurely enter pon a discussion of the reports.

Mr. BYNUM said, he should consider himself a egraded wretch, were he to attempt to withhold formation from the people. But the fact must e apparent to all, that a species of extravangance ad obtained in this House in relation to the printng of documents which was wholly unauthorized nd improper. He had, on divers occasions, opposed the printing of an extra number of docuents, not one half of which were ever sent from he Capitol. If the number of the reports in quesn, which had been proposed by the gentleman om Massachusetts, (Mr. Briggs,) should be orered, not more than two thirds or one half of hem would ever be send out to the people. An spection of the folding-rooms of the House ould convince any gentleman that he was not istaken in this particular.

If gentlemen were anxious to put a stop to a odigal expenditure of the public money, this ouse was the place which should form the startg point. The Executive Department had been arged in this House with a wasteful expendiure of money, when it was an incontrovertible ct, that this body was more justly liable to such charge. Those who were the most clamorous gainst the Executive, in this particular, were hemselves the peculiar advocates of extravagant nd uncalled for appropriations on this floor. We e the trustees, said he, of the people. They ill not look to us for the information contained in ese reports. They would look to the public rints. Besides, if the proposed number of the ports should be printed, a few may obtain them. would hardly be a drop in the bucket, compared with the circulation which would be given to em in the newspapers. We could not print a fficient number to enlighten the public. If we d so, we must incur an expense which would be ndemned by all.

Mr. B. repeated, in conclusion, that if gentlen were disposed to attempt reformation, this ouse was the place to commence. There appeared to be a greater disposition for extravagance re than elsewhere. He could not vote for the oposition of the gentleman from Massachusetts, Mr. Briggs.) Much the larger proportion of the cuments laid upon the tables of members, were ver sent from the Capitol. They fell to the lot the little pages of the House. The only reason hich could be assigned for publishing so large a mber of these reports, was that it would give a od job to the printers of the House.

Mr. CONNOR regretted that the concluding marks of the Report of the Committee had en lugged into this discussion. He doubted ry much the propriety of the publication which d been given to them in a morning paper. Bere any inferences were drawn from the extracts hich had been published, it was peculiarly oper that the House should be in possession of e whole facts. He alluded to the probable ount of matter contained in the reports. It was e that many of the documents would be cast off unnecessary to be published. The great mass them, however, must necessarily accompany e report. The Committee were desirous that ery ground upon which they had formed their nclusions, should be distinctly understood. The mmittee had performed their duties honestly d faithfully, although the results had not been in cordance with their wishes.

Mr. BRIGGS modified his motion by proposing print 5,000 copies of the report, together with the documents, and 20,000 copies of the report without the documents.

Mr. BEARDSLEY said, if the proposition of the gentleman from Massachusetts (Mr. Briggs) referred simply to the printing of the reports, he should say nothing on the subject. The motion to print the documents was, however, distinct; and if it was viewed in reference to an expenditure of money, was one of importance. While we were looking elsewhere to see if the public money had not been improvidently squandered, it would perhaps be proper that we should reserve to ourselves, to some extent, a portion of the counsels which we were disposed to impart to others. It was at all events just that the House should be informed of the magnitude of the documents which accompanied this report. The sub-committee, to which reference had been made, would exclude but a small portion of them. Those necessary to be published would form, in his belief, certainly two, and perhaps three, volumes of the ordinary size of congressional documents. The number which had been proposed to be printed, would cost a considerable sum of money. If it was intended to send these documents home to every reader, so that the whole people may derive from them the facts which are ordinarily to be found in the newspapers, if that is the object, as is argued by the honorable member from Massachusetts, (Mr. Briggs,) it would be necessary to print 500,000 copies instead of 5,000 copies. If this was the object, the number proposed by the gentleman from Massachusetts, as had been remarked, would be but a drop in the bucket. He was not opposed to printing a reasonable number of these documents for distribution. He believed the object of printing an extra number of copies would be as essentially attained by publishing 2,000 as any other number. If the House thought it a judicious expenditure of the public money to order a large quantity, they could do so.

Mr. BURGES referred to the importance of the reports. The People, he contended, should be made acquainted with their contents. How were they to procure this information? Were they to look for it in the newspapers, or should they not rather look to the types of this House to furnish them with it? The papers would never publish the whole of the reports and documents. They would, as has been said, publish only so much as would suit their particular views. The truth elicited by the Reports could only be furnished to the People by publishing the volumes. He thought the gentleman from New York, (Mr. Beardsley,) had over-estimated the length of the documents. This was, however, immaterial. He did not think, that the House should withhold from the People desirable information from the paltry consideration that by so doing, it would be a saving of their own money. He could not accord in the statement that a large portion of our documents never left the city. It was true that there were some trifling reports and bills, which were never looked at, and, as a matter of course, not sent away. He was opposed to all attempts to save money, where they were intended to stifle information, or withhold it from the People. In conclusion, he proposed to print 5,000 copies of the Reports and documents, and 30,000 copies of the Reports without the documents. He thought no member who desired to inform the People on the subject, could object to the number which he had proposed.

Mr. LANE said, that believing as he did, that the report was interesting and important—the result of a laborious investigation by a committee of this House—a result to which the people looked with solicitude—he felt bound to vote for printing the largest number named by the gentleman from Massachusetts, (Mr. Briggs.)

It had been said by several honorable gentlemen, that the newspapers would publish all that the people were interested in knowing, and therefore any extra number of copies would be a useless expense of public money.

It was well known, that the newspapers would publish *such* extracts as would suit their own views and the result would be to confuse, not to inform the public. Justice to the people and to the Department, requires that the entire report should be exhibited.

He wished that it was possible to place it in the hands of every individual, that each might examine and decide for himself.

It had been said that the people *would not read* the report if placed before them. The people are not so indifferent about the administration of any Department of the Government—much less so as to the administration of the General Post Office—which addresses itself more immediately and more universally than any other to their feelings and interests.

They will read it with care, and they can best judge of its course, who see its operations and feel its benefits.

Shall the important conclusions of this committee go forth in the newspapers, unaccompanied by the facts which indicate the origin, the progress, and the extent of the evils, that are mentioned? Shall the responsibility of these evils be thus unjustly cast upon the persons administering the Department, instead of the true cause—the defects in the organization originally prescribed by law? The same errors have existed from the origin of the Department. The immense increase of mail routes, called for by the rapid improvement of our country, and incessantly urged by members of this House—have developed their injurious practical operation. The distinguished individual who directs that Department, has merely followed in the footsteps of his predecessors in office. Anxious to administer the Department so as to extend its benefits to every part of our country—the defective legal organization has prevented him from keeping the immense business of the Department under his own eyes.

It should be clearly understood and carefully remembered that these errors have been confined mainly to a subdivision—to the fiscal branch of the Department. Whenever errors have been made obvious, I understand that they have been remedied, as far as was possible, under the present laws.

During the last two years, most of the errors admitting correction have ceased to exist; and to those acquainted with the business of the Department, in two of its most important divisions, it is well known that an energetic and accurate system has been applied, that under proper legal provisions will enable the Postmaster General to place the Department on that high ground suited to its importance.

Enable the people to make these discriminations. The friends of the Postmaster General, the supporters of the administration, are those most interested in the wide circulation of this report.

Shall it be said that a democratic majority, whose leading principles are the correction of abuses, the simplification of public business, and its full exhibition to the people, object to the publication of this report? He trusted not.

The inquiry had been made by direction of a democratic majority of this House; the report had been made by the democratic majority of that Committee; it exhibited abuses which had existed under every administration. On that report it was our duty to act. Let the report go to our constituents, that they may judge whether our conduct in reference to these abuses keeps pace with the professions by which we are pledged to reform them.

Mr. CROCKETT said, I belong to the Committee on the Accounts of the House. We yesterday examined the accounts of this committee, and ascertained that it cost more than $25,000 to get this report. What use would it be then if it was not sent out? I want to see it in every neighborhood. I made charges four years ago against this Post Office Department. I was hissed, sir, for doing so. In the report of the committee, my charges are fully and more than realized. A report on this subject, in another quarter, had been called factious. The people wished to have information from this House. I repeat, that the report made yesterday, more than realizes all my charges against the Department. I move to print 50,000 copies without the documents. They are unnecessary. I don't want to leave the publication of the reports to the hireling newspapers,

which just pick out enough to suit their purposes.

Mr. H. EVERETT said the gentleman from Tennessee (Mr. Crockett) was mistaken. The whole expense of the investigation did not amount to more than $2,500. It had been made with the strictest regard to economy.

Mr. STODDERT did not rise to say any thing in relation to the number of the reports which should be printed. He would never be in favor of excluding light from the people. The history of Congress, he believed, did not present a case like the present, where a committee, constituted as this was, in an extensive investigation, had been enabled to concur, so generally, as regarded facts and results. The reports contained an authentic view of the facts—the very evidence which the people would desire to see. The committee had extracted the kernel and thrown away the husk. He therefore thought it wholly unnecessary to print more than the usual number of the documents accompanying the reports. If the gentleman from Rhode Island was desirous of extending information on the subject to as many as possible, his object would be better answered by applying the amount which it would cost to print the 5,000 extra copies of the documents, to the publication of an additional number of the reports.

Mr. BARRINGER thought a sufficient number of the reports and documents should be printed to supply the clerks' offices and the publishers of newspapers in the country. This could not be effected by a less number than 5,000 copies.

Mr. EVERETT, of Vermont, said he had understood that the expense of printing 3,000 copies of the reports and accompanying documents would amount to about 10,000 dollars.

Mr. HAMER said: If there was any business which ought to be done by human beings in the dark, it was not the business of legislation. Those who undertake to prescribe rules for the action of themselves and others, ought at least to have some light upon the subjects with regard to which they propose to legislate.

It had become a very common thing, to traduce the Post Office Department. It was fashionable to condemn it. There seemed to be a general inclination to bear it down. For one, he was not disposed to join in the general "hue and cry" against the Department. He concurred entirely with his honorable friend from Kentucky (Mr. Johnson) in the observations he let fall the other day. He had known the Postmaster General long, and known him well. He had the most implicit confidence in his honor and integrity, both as a public man and private citizen. Entertaining this opinion of him, he would not condemn him, until he had the most unquestionable evidence of the impropriety of his conduct.

He said he did not know, and therefore would not say, but there might have been subordinate officers in the Department, who were not honest. He would not say, for he did not know but these subordinates might have presented statements to the Postmaster General which had deceived him, and upon which he might have made orders that were detrimental to the public interests. But it is time enough to condemn him, when we have heard the proof. It was time enough for him to condemn him, when he had heard the evidence and heard the defence, and the commentary upon that evidence. When the whole subject shall be presented; the reports printed and laid on our tables; when we have had time to read and deliberate upon them, and have heard the Department in reply, then we should be prepared to act. Whatsoever is wrong, said he, I shall be among the first to condemn. If any thing is wrong, but has circumstances connected with it which ought to be received as palliations, I shall insist upon those circumstances having due weight. But whatever is right, although alleged to be wrong, whether the charge be made by political enemies; or those who were political friends *upon the surface*, he would be prepared to defend to the last.

What are we about to do here? We are asked to vote for the printing of 50,000 of these reports, without knowing one word of their contents. They have not been read. All we know of them is, that *they are against the Department*. Sir, I go against this system. I will not thus legislate in the dark upon any question.

What have we seen in another part of this Capitol? I speak of what I learn from the newspapers; every body knows they are good authority. A report was made there, by a majority and a minority of a committee. Before they could be printed and laid upon their, or our tables, a bill is passed which has come down to this House, to reorganize the whole Post Office Department. Thus passing sentence of condemnation upon it without an examination of the reports of their committee, or hearing one word in defence. Thus declaring that the whole department is so rotten and corrupt that reformation is impossible; and it must, therefore, be thrown into the mill and ground over anew. The passage of the bill is claimed by the party press of this city, and understood by the country, to be such a condemnation. Are we to follow this example? Is this the system to be established in this country? Sir, said he, I have the most perfect respect for the members of the Committee who made these reports; but I will not legislate upon the report of any committee without hearing the other side. Have they not examined witnesses against the Department, without the persons implicated having an opportunity to cross-examine? May not many things, seemingly wrong, be satisfactorily explained by cross examination, or by further testimony? Let us *hear before we strike*. Whoever heard of a great department of the Government being reorganized, without consulting the head of that department? If there be defects in its organization, who so competent to point them out, and suggest improvements, as the man whose experience has brought them repeatedly before him?

Does any one believe, that if we order 50,000 copies of these reports to be printed, we shall receive them during the present session? Every man here knows we shall not. Do we not know that the reports ordered to be printed by the Senate, at the last session, were travelling through the country during the whole summer? They had to be sent first to the members, and then taken up, franked, and sent off by mail again to different portions of the country; thus aiding to burden and break down the very Department which they assailed. It will be an immense expense incurred, for no real substantial benefit to the country.

We are all aware that abstracts of these reports will be circulated in the newspapers every where, for the information of the people. Now, there ought to be a sufficient number of the reports through the several districts of country, to enable any one to correct errors or misrepresentations, that may creep into the abstracts. That is enough: all beyond that is unnecessary. I shall, therefore, vote for the smallest number proposed.

Mr. REED was in favor of printing the largest number. He expressed his surprise at some of the remarks of the gentleman who preceded him, (Mr. Hamer) who had appealed to "hear before we strike." He would ask what course the gentleman would have the House pursue. A committee had been appointed by the House to examine the condition of the Post Office Department, and the result of its investigation should now be published to the country.

Mr. SMITH said: Mr. Speaker, I think it was well remarked that it became this House to look well to its own extravagant expenditures at the moment when they are about to impute to other Departments of the government extravagances of an extraordinary character. Sir, I ask the gentlemen who propose to print the extra number of these documents proposed, whether they have counted the cost? Has any gentleman who has addressed the House in favor of so large a number made an estimate, satisfactory to his mind, of the amount of cost which he proposes to impose upon the country. I have made an estimate, which to my mind, is satisfactory against the printing of either number of documents proposed; I lay aside the number suggested by the gentleman from Tennessee (Mr. Crockett) as being wholly beyond the inclination probably, of every other member of the House. I take the proposition of the gentleman from Massachusetts, and invite the House to consider for a moment, whether it be not of an extravagant character.

I understood the proposition to be to print five thousand extra copies of each report, and the several documents appended thereto. The House has already been informed by one of the honorable members of the Post Office Committee (Mr. Beardsley) that these Reports and accompanying documents will certainly make two full sized octavo volumes, consequently this will make ten thousand volumes. Other gentlemen, however, have said that they will amount to three volumes; but I take the lowest estimate. Now, these ten thousand volumes will cost no less, upon an average, according to the best information I have been able to obtain, than three dollars per volume; for a smaller number, say six or seven hundred, which is the ordinary number, the cost per volume will be nearer five dollars. Take the number proposed, in all probability the price cannot be reduced to less than three dollars per volume, and here it is at once a cost of $30,000. The gentleman further proposes to print twenty thousand extra copies of the two Reports alone, without the documents. It has been said that even these will make a volume of from 150 to 200 pages, and if we estimate the cost at only a dollar a volume, you will have an additional charge of $20,000, at the the least, making an aggregate of $50,000 for the publication of one single report!

Sir, let me ask, are gentlemen prepared for this? Is the country prepared for this? Suppose even you go to the extent proposed, what good will be produced? Five thousand copies of the entire work, divided among the members of this House, will not net to them, after reserving the necessary copies for the Capitol, more than ten sets to each member; and of the twenty thousand reports, the net amount of each member for his district will be short of forty copies. Now then, after you have expended your $50,000 in the publication of the report, and you get forty copies of the report, without the documents, and ten copies with them, for each district, put the question home to the constituents of any gentleman, and ask them whether they approve of such an expenditure under the pretence of furnishing such limited means of information to their district? Whatever the motive may be, they will denounce it as an extravagant expenditure.

But, say gentlemen, the information cannot be given through the newspaper organs. Why not? Does any gentleman doubt that all the material information in each of these reports will be furnished to the people through the newspapers? What is the objection? Why, forsooth, that they will garble, to use the language of the gentleman from Massachusetts, that they will garble the reports, and present only such extracts as will suit their own individual feelings or purposes. But the same gentleman has also told us that the report is of such an extraordinary character that it comes with the concurrence of both branches—the majority and the minority of the committee. Why, Mr. Speaker, if the report be the result of so much unanimity, where can be the danger or apprehension that garbled statements will be made, and the people misled? The very character of the report, as represented by those in favor of the larger number, precludes the possibility of the danger suggested as an argument in favor of printing that large number.

But, again, sir, the report being in itself the result almost of unanimity in the committee, and it being agreed on all sides, that all that is now necessary is legislation, where can be the great utility of multiplying copies of this report at such an extraordinary expense to the treasury? Let me submit this proposition to those gentlemen who are for printing so large a number, since it is acknowledged on all sides that legislation only is now necessary, whether it would not be better for this House to legislate and perform its own duty, and then distribute among the people the results of our own labors, rather than distribute among the people information as to the mode in which we have performed those duties? Let the gentlemen do this, and I will go with heart and hand in multiplying copies to any extent. But no; notwithstanding gentlmen are prepared to admit that

ber. It was a document that ought to be distributed throughout every part of the United States, in every congressional district, and in every county; and published in every village newspaper in the country.

Mr. BOON said that he wished to say a very few words for Bunkum. He said that gentlemen on this floor had stated in their places that the subject under consideration was one of great interest—that it had created much excitement among the people of the country. Grant it, Mr. Speaker, said Mr. B., and I put it to honorable gentlemen to say, whether the mere printing of the report made by the Post Office Committee, will remedy the evils which are complained of. Sir, I represent on this floor an intelligent people, who will look to Congress for a correction of those abuses which are so much complained of, should they be found to exist, rather than the mere printing of a report having reference to the past. The gentleman from Massachusetts (Mr. Briggs) has told this House how vastly important it is that the People should have correct information on this subject. Mr. Speaker, I am myself emphatically a "*People's*" man, willing at all times that they should have all necessary information on all subjects in which they may have an interest. But, sir, I am not in the habit of reiterating the fact, either here or elsewhere, least I might subject myself to the charge of being a political *demagogue* If gentlemen are sincere in their professions on the subject of giving information to the people generally, let them authorize the printing of a sufficient number of the report and accompanying documents to have a copy put into the hands of each and every freeman in the United States Any thing short of this would be partial in its operation. I am willing, Mr. Speaker, that a reasonable number of the report and documents together should be printed, and sent among the people of the country. But I am not willing to vote for the printing of so great a number as has been proposed; nor, sir, am I willing to vote for the printing of a greater number of the report than that of the accompanying documents While I am free to declare that I have the most unlimited confidence in the members who compose the Post Office Committee, without any regard to political distinction, I cannot consent to vote for the printing and sending abroad a greater number of the report than of the *proof* upon which it is predicated; believing, as I do, that it would be an act of injustice, on my part, towards the much-abused head of the Post Office Department.

Mr. JACKSON, of Connecticut, considered that if there was any one department more than another upon which the People wished to be illuminated, it was that of the Post Office Department. Admitting, for the sake of argument, that much extravagant expenditure had been manifested in printing documents by that House, the objection could not, he conceived, apply to the case under consideration, because its object was to apply a remedy to almost universally admitted existing abuses, and it was a question on which the People felt peculiar interest. It was highly necessary that the People should understand what were the grounds of the complaints against the Department. If founded upon mal-administration or corruption, to remove the officers; if, on the contrary, the abuses arise from the peculiar organization of the Department, it was important that the fact should be brought to light. In every point of view, therefore, he conceived, the House could not stand justified in refusing the proposition of the honorable gentleman from Massachusetts, and deeming it reasonable, he should, therefore, give it his cordial support.

Mr. VANDERPOEL said he opposed the printing of an extraordinary number of these documents as a waste of the public funds. He would be the last to oppose the promulgation of important information to the People—but, if 30 or 40,000 thousand of these books—these large volumes were printed, how many would reach the great mass of the People by such means? He was for curtailing the enormous expenses of the government, and he called on the friends of the administration, economy, and of retrenchment, to go with him in that curtailment.

Mr. SLADE expressed his surprise at the opposition which has been manifested ro printing the report of a committee, organized and appointed by the friends of the administration.

Mr. CONNOR said, the committee had been appointed by the House, and not by a party. He believed they had also discharged their duty, without reference to party or political feeling.

Mr. SLADE still believed the majority of the committee were the friends of the present administration, and of the Department whose conduct they were appointed to investigate. He spoke, also, of the expense of the publication of the documents, which he conceived to be a minor consideration when compared with their importance.

Mr. PEARCE also advocated the printing of a large number of copies of the reports and documents. He deprecated the allusions which had been made to the profits which it might be supposed the public printer would acquire by the publication. He spoke at some length on the importance of the dissemination of these reports among the people, who certainly demanded it.

Mr. SMITH, of Maine, again addressed the House in explanation of his former remarks, and in reply to those of Messrs. MERCER, BRIGGS, and BURGES.

Mr. BEARDSLEY felt called upon, as a member of the committee, and especially after what had fallen from the gentleman from Ohio, (Mr. Whittlesey,) to say a few words. That gentleman and himself, he thought, could not differ essentially on the fact referred to; and he presumed there was some little misapprehension on the part of the honorable member from Maine, (Mr. Smith) so far as related to an increased expense on the part of the Post Office Department, in consequence of an increased weight of the mails by public documents. It appeared before the committee, that an extra allowance of $10,000 had been made on the route from Philadelphia to Pittsburg, which allowance was made on the representation of the carrier alone; at least there was no other evidence whatever furnished to the Committee, that the Postmaster General had acted on any evidence but a letter from the mail contractor. That letter did not, nor did the evidence before the Committee, discriminate between an increase in weight by newspapers, letters, or packages.

There was another case in which extra allowance was made, but not from the weight of the mail alone. It was the mail between Baltimore and Wheeling: that allowance was made, also, upon the representation of the contractor, sustained by petitions and letters from others. One ground assumed by the contractor, in that application, was an increase of the weight of the mail on that route; but Mr. B. could not call to mind, at that moment, whether the increased weight was alleged to have been owing to the publication of documents by Congress or not. The evidence before the committee showed that there was an increase, and the Postmaster General, unquestionably, relied upon the representations he had received to establish that fact, and accordingly made the extra allowance. Mr. B. did not remember that, in relation to either route, there was any direct evidence to the fact of an increase in the weight in consequence of the publication of documents, or of any publications whatever emanating from this city. But there was some evidence—he would not say satisfactory—yet there was some evidence given before the committee to establish the fact, that the weight of the mails had been greatly increased on both routes. But the fact, whether there was such an increase or not, the committee regarded as quite immaterial; (he alluded to the report of the majority, for of the opinions of the minority he knew nothing;) the Postmaster General being, in their judgment, unauthorized under the act of Congress regulating the Post Office Department, to make an extra allowance of one single cent on any such ground. Entertaining that opinion, he paid very little attention himself to the evidence which went to prove or to disprove the fact of increased weight. If it were proved to weigh five tons, as the law stood, the Postmaster General possessed no authority to make any extra allowance whatever.

While up, Mr. B. would make a remark or two in consequence of what fell from the gentleman from Louisiana, (Mr. Johnson.) That gentleman ascribed all the abuses and embarrassments of the Post Office Department solely and exclusively to its present administration. Not to the President of the United States, nor to any other department; but Mr. B. understood the gentleman to say that the abuses and enormities were all chargeable to the present Postmaster General. Now, it was but justice to that individual, to the public, and to the committee, to say, that to whatever conclusion the committee may have come, the suggestion made by the gentleman from Louisiana, should not be allowed to go abroad without explanation. Mr. B. then took upon himself to say that the papers produced before the committee, the communications they had received, and the evidence adduced, all showed most clearly and satisfactorily, that many and indeed most of the irregularities now prevailing in that Department, prevailed also under the administration of that Department which preceded the present one. He would not go so far as to say that they existed to the same extent, and the same degree, that they existed now; but the irregular course then marked out and adopted, had been followed by the present incumbent: an irregular course, clearly and decidedly so; and which, in Mr. B.'s estimation, had led to a very considerable, if not to the largest portion of the wasteful expenditure of the public money of which the public had a just right to complain.

He particularly referred to the culpable practice of amalgamated bids, extra allowances upon contracts founded on such bids, and other excesses of that nature: each and all of which prevailed to a greater or less extent under the former as well as the present Postmaster General. Mr. B. did not intend to cast the slightest reflection upon the purity of purpose of the present or the preceding incumbent of that office. All he intended to say was that the abuses existed before and had descended to the present time, though not to the same extent, for they were certainly aggravated in later years.

Mr. LYTLE said, that he objected to the course that the debate had taken. If he understood the question properly, it had reference merely to the number of copies which should be printed of this report—and yet it had taken a wide, and in his judgment, an unwarrantable range. Gentlemen had been discussing the merits of the report, before that report was fairly before them. He should like to see it on the tables, and have time to read it, before he passed judgment on its contents, or expressed an opinion on the subject matter to which it had reference.

Upon the question then of printing an [illegible] number of extra copies, Mr. L said he considered any debate unnecessary, if the declarations of the honorable gentleman from Louisiana were to be taken for granted—who, without any report before him, had undertaken to pass sentence of death on the department and its head—if they were realy already convict, he thought the time of the House would be misspent in deliberating on the question now before them, viz. the printing of the testimony by which the guilt or innocence of the accused should be decided. Gentlemen assure us that the people are to be enlightened on this subject, and through the medium of this report, and yet they tell us in the same breath, that the people understand the whole matter, and that Major Barry must be dismissed, and the department re-organized. That the "whole country believe in his guilt," and the mismanagement of his department. Why, sir, what stuff is this. The people already enlightened! The culprit already condemned!—and yet the House called on to pay the enormous expense of printing fifty thousand extra copies, to show, I presume, that it was fairly done. Why, sir, for one, I enter my solemn protest against the whole procedure. This is indeed a new and most unrighteous mode of action in such cases—passing sentence of death upon a man and his whole department by your speeches, and then printing fifty thousand extra copies of a report, by which, it is hoped, something may be gleaned out of which these charitable decrees or predictions may be justified.

Why sir, said Mr. L. the ordinary mode is this,

CONTINUED IN NEXT NUMBER.

CONGRESSIONAL GLOBE.

BY BLAIR & RIVES. ———WEEKLY——— PRICE $1 A SESSION.

2d Sess........23d Cong. MONDAY, MARCH 2, 1835. Volume 2........No. 16.

TWENTY-THIRD CONGRESS.
SECOND SESSION.

HOUSE OF REPRESENTATIVES.
Saturday, Feb. 14, 1835.

[Continued from last number.]

and in every Christian country, is to *try first*, and convict afterwards—if the testimony exacts or warrant it—but the rule is now to be reversed, for the first time in this country. Sir, I undertake to say you are now called on to criminate, by speeches and the circulation of reports, in unusual and extraordinary numbers, an individual, before the very testimony is examined by his *triers*, who are, by this motion, to be made the organs of its publication and distribution. Why, Mr. Speaker, the humblest culprit arraigned at the bar of our country, for crimes the most foul and atrocious, is indulged with the time and opportunity for a fair hearing and a full and complete defence, an ample examination of all the testimony against him, before the sentence of condemnation is passed upon him. And is a high officer of this Government to be debarred the privilege allowed to the common malefactor? Say what you will, sir, the present proceed ings against this Department have the tendency necessarily to produce the results I have named. Whether by accident it design, he is to be the victim Friend and foe are ready for the sacrifice, and he gets it from them all, right and left. Why, sir, not wait for the printing and examination of the two reports of the Senate, which, before they were printed or read, (I mean by the Senators,) produced a bill that body; a bill which has been sent down in us for the reorganization of that Department? I stand here as a sworn juror between the country and the accused; an I for one, I will not act, by the God that made me, except on ample proof. Let us have it. Not o ly this report, but the two reports from the Senate. Why, sir, should we prejudge this case? Why act before the proof is before us? Why attempt to forestal or prejudice the public mind? Why anticipate a decision which may never be made by this body when they have the time and means to investigate for themselves?

These reports may be antagonist to each other, and yet, sir, you are called on to anticipate your own judgment, deliberately formed, by testimony you have not heard, and a system of conduct which may lead to the most unjust and vindictive condemnation of those who may be (as I believe them) completely innocent. Tell me not that the head of this Department is not to be directly and immediately affected by this precipitate and ill-advised action of the House. I know better. You cannot alienate his personal and political identity in this determination. The object is his removal, his political demolition. It shall not appen sir, with my consent, without a full and fair trial. No, sir, I want all the documents—I want all the proofs—show me official derelictions and I will vote for its radical removal. Show me corruption, peculation, defalcation, or negligence, and with all my heart I will join in the effort to remove it—but I must first see and know it, before I attempt a remedy. There is one thing I must here add—that for the first time the Postmaster General has been *personally* the subject of accusation. During the whole of the last session (elsewhere, as in this body) he has escaped unscathed. His character has been held sacred. I avow openly, and with pride, my warm attachment to the head of this Department. I have known him long, and lo e and esteem, and prize his many estimable and exalted properties, and it was a matter of no ordinary compliment, that through all the bitterness of party feeling during the last session of Congress, as well as the result, when the half storms of party malevolence and persecution beat about his Department and himself as its representative—that his person was held sacred, that no harm approached

him—that the full tribute to his individual merits was exacted by a knowledge of his worth, from the bitterest of his opponents; and I now dare and defy any man on or off this floor to impeach the personal or political integrity of William T. Barry.

Notwithstanding (continued Mr. L.,) the long services, unquestioned ability and worth of my honorable colleague, (Mr. Whittlesey,) than to whom no one more readily than myself, is willing to accord the merit of usefulness, and indefatigable zeal, honesty and energy of action as a representative of my state upon this floor, one who has justly earned its confidence and high regard, and mad: me ready, always ready, to acknowledge his ability and claim him with pride and pleasure as a colleague, however widely we may differ in some thing—to-day he has surprised me, by attempting to disprove the statements of the gentleman from Maine, (Mr. Smith,) by shewing in his way that there was *no proof of the fact*, before the House that the burdens of the Department were increased, by the increase of extra printing during the last session of Congress; and therefore, that the statements fallacious! Why sir, it requires on proof, said Mr. L., it is a matter that at least it itself at once to the common sense and understanding of every man upon this floor. Can there be an ar mous increase of documents without the indispensable increase of cost for their circulation by the mail? It is a matter about which there can be no dispute. Add to the tonnage; and you must pay for the increased carriage. Multiply documents, and you must provide means for their transportation. And thus it has been, sir, among other means that the Department has reached the point difficulty complained of.

The trouble exists mainly in my opinion, in the increased burdens imposed on the Department by the legislation of Congress, one way or another, and its willingness and anxiety to meet the demands thus made on it. Sir, I appeal in a spirit of frankness to this body, If they have not by their system of legislation, contributed mainly to produce the state of things of which they now complain against the Post Office Department. By the application of what class of people have new mail routes been established—post offices created, contracts made—and extra allowances granted? My answer is, by members of Congress. (Am I trust the ca alogue will be forthcoming before long, exhibiting a list of all who have thus kindly aided to the distress of the Department, they are now so ready to condemn and execrate.

Sir, by the proposition now before you, we are called on to aggravate the evil which th: document complains of, that we send abroad. You start a diseased herald to report the malady of which the very messenger is the subject—one of a family of fifty thousand!

I am opposed to any new panic, therefore I shall vote against the printing now, and hereafter, of a single *extra* sheet of any thing; especially where the design is to anticipate the action of the House and forestall public judgment. Such printing as is indispensable to the purposes of legislation I am prepared to vote for, but no more. I have ever been opposed to this extravagant propensity of the House. Yet say gentleman on this floor turn to the mass of well bound printed trash of the last session, and say if the load of such matter under which his shelves now groan, of panic speeches, memorials, reports, resolutions, and even names, will not compel him honestly to admit, that there is to be found the true secret of at least one difficulty under which the Department has had to labor; but there are others, which in due time sha'll be noticed. Let the House, I say, however, pause first itself, before it arraigns any other Department of the government. Sir, the extra printing of this House would cover all the extra allowances (occasioned chiefly by the action of Congress) of the Post Office Department for the last two years, I hazard the opinion.—

Look at the abuses too of the franking privilege' One main object avowed in defence of this proposition is to supply the districts of certain gentlemen—yes, sir, to make Uncle Sam pay for the privilege of getting ourselves re-elected by franking home any quantity of documents. My day is over, sir, in that way, but I assure gentlemen, that I never knew much good to come of it—you can't frank to every elector in the Union—one is as much entitled as another—and so far as my experience goes, you make more enemies than friends by franking at all, for I never sent one document to a constituent, that I did not receive, on an average, at least one letter from another, complaining that he had been neglected; so that but little good is done in that way.

But, sir, in conclusion, I desire nothing but what is fair and just in the decision of the House upon this matter. Let us have an opportunity before we condemn pure and upright and hitherto honorable men—let us compare with any precedent of this Department, under the present head, the expenses, the defalcations, the practices, the uses and abuses of those who preceded him. I wish, sir, and hope, that all these matters have come within the observance of the committee, and that as they are greatly regulated by precedent and contrast, we may expect to find no guilt than has been anticipated or hoped for, and an equal amount of integrity, fidelity, and official usefulness, as will compare with any precedent administration of the Department. I have occupied the House longer than I wished or expected, and conclude by hoping that they will at least reduce the number proposed of extra copies.

Messrs. ELISHA WHITTLESEY, and CRAMER, afterwards, addressed the House, and Mr. HUBBARD moved the Previous Question, which was seconded by a majority of the House, and taken—being on the motion, as modified and divided, to print 3,000 extra copies of the reports and documents. The question was taken by yeas and nays, and decided in the affirmative. Yeas 161, nays 47.

The question was then also taken by yeas and nays, on printing 20,000 extra copies of reports without the documents, and passed in the affirmative. Yeas 101, nays 93.

The House then adjourned.

IN SENATE.
Monday, Feb. 16, 1835.

Petitions were presented by Messrs. TOMLINSON and TYLER.

Mr. WAGGAMAN presented a resolution from the Legislature of Louisiana, together with a joint resolution, praying a grant of land from Congress to that Stat; for purposes of public education; which was referred to the Committee on Public Lands.

Mr. MANGUM, from the Committee on Finance, to which the following bills from the House of Re. presentatives were referred, reported the same as follows:

A bill for the relief of John Frazer & Co., without amendment;

A bill for the relief of Richard Butman, without amendment;

A bill for the relief of Riddle, Becktel, and others, without amendment.

On motion of Mr. MANGUM, the Committee on Finance were discharged from the further consideration of the petition of James Robinson.

Mr. WEBSTER, from the same committee, to which was referred the bill from the House of Re. p esentatives making appropriations for the fortification of the United States for the year 1835, reported the same with an amendment.

Mr. McKEAN, from the Committee on Pensions, to which the bill for the relief of Job Barion was committed, reported the same without amendment.

Mr. TOMLINSON, from the same committee, to which was referred the bills for the relief of

John Herrick and Job Wood, reported them, severally, without amendment.

Mr. BELL, from the Committee on Claims, to which was referred the bill from the House of Representatives for the relief of Samuel Bulier, reported the same without amendment.

Mr. SHEPLEY, from the same committee, to which the bill from the House for the relief of Thomas Clements was referred, reported the same without amendment.

Mr. LEIGH, from the Committee on Revolutionary Claims, reported a bill for the relief of the legal representatives of William Ramsey, deceased.

Mr. WHITE, from the Committee on Indian Affairs, reported a bill for the relief of John Dougherty.

Both the last mentioned bills were read the first time, and ordered to a second reading.

Mr. LEIGH, from the Committee on Revolutionary Claims, made an unfavorable report upon the petition of the representatives of Leonard Cooper, deceased; and the committee were discharged from the further consideration of the same.

Mr. MOORE, from the same committee, made unfavorable reports upon the petitions of Margaret Riker, the representatives of Elizabeth Goodwin and Margaret Leitch, of M. St. C. Clarke, agent of the State of Georgia; of the heirs of Samuel Clagett, and George Richards; of Joseph Boggy, heir of Joseph Placy; of the heirs of James Davis; of the heirs of Thomas Wert; of the heirs of Francis Cazeau, and the heirs of Henry Irwin.

On motion of Mr. POINDEXTER, the Senate took up for consideration the bill authorizing the issuing of scrip to holders of unlocated military land warrants; when, on his motion, it was postponed to, and made the special order for Friday next.

Mr. PRESTON submitted the following resolution:

That on Thursday next the Senate will proceed to the election of a printer.

The bill for the relief of the personal representatives of the late Lieut. Robert Jewett, was read the third time, and passed.

On motion of Mr. SHEPLEY, the Senate considered, as in Committee of the Whole, the bill for the relief of the owners of the brig Despatch; and the same was ordered to be engrossed for a third reading.

The following bills from the House were severally read the first and second time, and referred to the Committee on Pensions:

A bill for the relief of Enoch Blaisiell;

A bill granting pensions to certain persons therein named;

A bill granting a pension to John W. Willey, and for increasing the pension of George Fields;

A bill granting a pension to William Sloacum;

A bill granting a pension to William Wilges;

A bill for the relief of Samuel M. Asbury;

A bill granting a pension to Francis F. St. Cuir;

A bill for the relief of certain invalid pensioners therein named;

A bill granting a pension to Joseph Mead;

A bill for the relief of John Dal, of Maine;

A bill for the relief of Simeon Meachum;

A bill granting a pension to Luke Voorhies;

A bill granting a pension to Col. Gideon Mergau;

A bill granting a pension to Benjamin Leslie;

A bill granting a pension to William Baden and James Harrington;

A bill for the relief of John Aston;

A bill for the relief of Ephraim F. Gilbert;

A bill granting a pension to Isaac Carter;

A bill granting a pension to John Gerodelle;

A bill for the relief of Samuel Shelmerdine;

A bill for the relief of Thomas Morton;

A bill to increase the pension of Origen Eat.n;

A bill granting a pension to John W. Cox;

A bill for the relief of Joseph Swartwood;

A bill granting an arrearage of pension to Edward Nicholson;

A bill for the relief of Abram E. Boutwell and David Pearson;

A bill granting a pension to Robert Lucas;

A bill for the relief of George McFadden;

A bill for the relief of Simeon S. Morrill and Theophilus Beekman;

A bill for the relief of George C. Sexton;

A bill granting a pension to Larned Swallow;

A bill granting a pension to John Bryant;

A bill granting a pension to Noah Miller;

A bill placing Capt. Cole, a Seneca Chief, on the pension roll;

A bill for the relief of Benjamin Holland;

A bill for the relief of William Keller;

A bill granting a pension to Justus Cobb;

A bill granting a pension to L. I. Van Velkenburg;

A bill granting a pension to Isaac Eckingle;

A bill for the relief of Wm C. Beard;

A bill for the relief of Jacob Stewart;

A bill for the relief of Elijah Blodget;

A bill for the relief of Thomas Simpson;

A bill for the relief of Thankful Randall;

A bill for the relief of Col. Daniel Newman;

A bill for the relief of Peter Triplett;

A bill for the relief of Peter Doxtator and J. Weaver;

A bill for the relief of Joseph Gilbert;

A bill for the relief of the widow and heirs of Samuel Southerland;

A bill for the relief of Timothy Jordan;

A bill for the relief of Daniel Page;

A bill for the relief of Walter Phillips;

A bill for the relief of Elizabeth May;

A bill for the relief of Jared Buckingham;

A bill for the relief of Solomon Case;

A bill for the relief of the widow of Noah Chittenden;

A bill for the relief of Col. Wm. Lawrence;

A bill to provide for paying certain pensioners at Jackson, Tenn.

The resolution submitted some days since by Mr. BENTON, calling on the President for certain information to be furnished at the next session of Congress, was taken up for consideration.

Mr. POINDEXTER said, that the resolution was of a very extraordinary character. He had no objection to a call on one of the Departments or the President himself for facts. But this call was much more comprehensive than any other he had ever seen. It called for speculative opinions. He would propose, if it was to pass, to add to the end of it, that the President be requested to furnish a treatise on banking, and a history of his administration. It would be quite as applicable, as the subject matter of the resolution. Mr. P. said he objected to the resolution, that it had a tendency to remind the President of his constitutional duties, when he was bound to communicate annually to Congress, information on all these subjects. To call for his opinions as to the administration of the government, came within the line of his constitutional duties. Mr. P. said he never had seen such a resolution as this was, either here or elsewhere. At the organization of the government, there was an opinion seriously held by the democratic side of the House, that we could not properly call on the President for his opinion on any measure involving the great interests of the country, and these were General Hamilton's views on this subject.

Mr. P. said he objected to this resolution on the ground of its being a proceeding sui generis. At present he moved to lay the subject on the table.

Mr. BENTON rose merely to ask the yeas and nays upon this disposition of the resolution.

Mr. POINDEXTER intimated his willingness to call it up on Wednesday next, and Mr. BENTON then withdrew his call, and the resolution was laid on the table.

The following resolution, submitted by Mr. TOMLINSON, on Saturday last, was taken up, considered, and adopted:

Resolved, That the Committee on Commerce be instructed to inquire into the expediency of making an appropriation for the preservation of Black Rock harbor, on the northerly side of Long Island Sound.

The bill for the relief of James L. Stokes was considered as in Committee of the Whole, and on motion of Mr. POINDEXTER, was laid on the table.

The bill for the relief of Paul Poissot was con-

sidered as in Committee of the Whole, and on motion of Mr. PORTER, was laid on the table.

The bill to provide a system of laws for the District of Columbia, was taken up, and considered as in Committee of the Whole.

Mr. TYLER said the bill proposed to enact the system of laws reported by the District Committee two years ago. He said it was almost inconceivable in what a state of confusion the laws of the District were placed. It would require too much prolixity to enter fully into an examination of them. The cession of the District—there is some of the laws now in operation here, very century in existence, some of which would put a christian man to blush. Some of them, it is true, are dormant, but they can be awakened whenever an occasion presents. He objected, to the District of Columbia being made a great slave mart. It is now a depot for the purchase of slaves for the surrounding country—the States of Virginia and Maryland. The code of laws which is proposed to be enacted by this bill attempts the abolition of this practice of making the District a depot for the purchase and sale of slaves. The punishment of the black population here, is under the existence of laws which are any thing but justifiable, and i require great amelioration. As to the penal system, it cannot be in a worse situation than that in which the committee found it. But that which is enough to break down the energies of any system, is the system of administering the law by the magistrates—which would be a case of any country. A host of justices of the peace are living here, with signs over their doors, which seem like proclaiming, "justice bought and sold here." He did not say that this state of things actually existed. But the state of the laws holds out inducements to justices to make fees by making business. There are also an army of constables here, who are affiliated with the justices; and each favor the other. The system makes the justice dependent upon his fees, and whenever your system makes the judicial officer dependent upon his fees, you make him, instead of being an officer of the peace, a disturber of the peace. He spoke now of no particular individual. But the bill proposed to remove this evil, which will save to the District in fees about some thirty or forty thousand dollars. At present nothing is found more profitable to these justices than to get up assaults and batteries—the witnesses that are brought up, the more he obtained. Mr. T. said he had heard something of this sort, though no case had fallen under his own observation. He thought the committee proposed a judicial scheme which would save from 30 to 40,000 dollars in official fees. The business of the courts, when examined, it would be found every species of criminal business; and the court was at the same time invested with the extensive civil jurisdiction. He did not profess to enter fully into this question, but he thought thus much was necessary and due to the District. He would have preferred that bills should be reported, passed one by one, until a code of good laws could be made; but he would be very well satisfied if the Senate would pass the bill and enact the code now. It was impossible that the code could be understood by an examination of it alone.

Mr. T. having concluded,

Mr. CALHOUN moved to lay the bill on the table, for the purpose of proceeding to the special order; which was agreed to.

The Senate then resumed the consideration of the bill to repeal the act of 1820, commonly called the four years law.

Mr. WEBSTER rose, and said he had proposed to give his views on the subject before the Senate, and if no other gentleman wished to occupy the floor, he would embrace that opportunity.

No other Senator rising, Mr. W. proceeded.

The question, he said, involved subjects of most serious consequence to the People of the United States and of great constitutional importance. It had for its object to diminish the increasing power of the Executive Department. He did not consider the powers which the bill

culated to restrain, as belonging to the class of
institutional powers. He fully concurred with
one who thought that it was important, as well
the present, as the future, that some check
could be imposed on Executive power. Opinion should be left free; the right of suffrage
could be exercised on principle, not to promote
private interests and party purposes.

He thought that Executive power, acting on
one who depended on its patronage for offices
d honors, exerted a powerful influence on popular elections. But how was that power of the
resident exerted? Before the act of 1820, the
ticer was continued, unless removed. But now
term of office expired every four years, and
other might be nominated in his stead.

He would admit, that in the case of accounting
officers, frequent changes might be beneficial;
but, on the whole, the results of the four years
he assumed more evil than good. That law gave
a power and influence to the President. Before that time the President could remove from
office, but seldom exerted that power. But since
the law required a renewal once in four years,
as that time approached, those in office were
in a state of continual fear, lest they should
lose their places; while those out of office
were contriving methods of getting it.—
The office-holder would endeavor to hold
it by subserviency to the appointing power;
he, out of office, by greater zeal and devotion,
would hope to secure themselves an appointment,
and thus destroy all that manly independence
which should characterize freemen. In that way
they were plunging deeper and deeper into the
goal at every election. And thus things would
tend to the destruction of all our republican institutions. The theory of government was very
plain and simple. The great difficulty was to
curb back those attractions that act upon the
hopes and fears of the People. To make office,
as a place of honor and profit, but of trust and
confidence; to repress and suppress every thing
that tended to individual aggrandizement. It was
essential that every officer should feel that he was
an officer for the country, not for himself. The
army, the Post Office, and all other departments,
were instituted only for the welfare of the country, not appendages of executive power. The
misuse of that power should be an important
object to all who wished to see the Government
brought back to its original simplicity. Some
gentlemen pretend to see no danger in so small a
number of men as those within the reach of excessive influence. But it must be remembered
that they are men of intelligence, and act in concert. He was willing to admit, with the honorable Senator from Maine, (Mr. Shepley,) that many
advantages would result from frequent changes,
he believed it was opening the door for still greater evils.

But there was another part of the subject of
far greater magnitude, in his opinion. It was
the constitutionality of the law. It was the principal object of his rising to examine that point.
The power of removal had been supposed to be
in the President since the discussion of 1789.
It was then fully and ably discussed by the great
men that formed the constitution, and decided in
favor of the Executive, by the casting vote of the
presiding officer. But Mr. W. believed the majority to have been in the right on that occasion.
He considered the decision as wrong in principle
the question was, had the President the power to
remove from office, except where it was especially
granted by the constitution? He would not trust
that decision; but go to the constitution, the
source whence that controverted power flowed.

Mr. W. went on to argue that, as the power of
removal was not expressly delegated by the constitution, it could only be exercised by construction,
implication, or as incident to the power of appointment. And since the President could not
act without the consent of the Senate, so he
could not to remove without the concurrence of
Senate. He contended that a mere nomination of a new candidate did not vacate the office;
if the Senate rejected the nomination, the incumbent officer should continue in his place. If
constitution had given to the President the

power of appointment without the aid of the Senate, then he might also exercise the power of removal. The argument in favor of such executive
powers rested on their convenience for getting rid
of an unfaithful officer. But granting the inconvenience of not having the removing power, still
inconveniences alone could not confer power. Such
were mere arguments of convenience and constitution.

There had been another proposition thrown out
in the course of the debate, that was, whether
executive power was subject to constraint or not
by law? He believed it might be. For if it was
absolute or beyond the control of law, then nothing could be done respecting it, but all knew
that offices could be created or abolished by Congress, at its pleasure. Even the time of the continuation of an office might be fixed. The power
exercised by Congress in passing the four years
law, was a proof of it. That law not only limited
the term of holding office, but actually took
away commissions which had been signed by the
President and sanctioned by the Senate. If Congress had power to make that law, they had power to repeal it, and place still further restraints.
But he considered the proposition before the Senate, rather as a bill to regulate the tenure of office,
than to restrain the power of the executive.

When Mr Webster concluded,

Mr. WRIGHT rose and spoke at length in opposition to the bill, and was followed by Mr.
WHITE in support of it..

The amendment submitted by Mr. CLAY on
Saturday was then agreed to.

The question being on the engrossment of the
bill,

Mr WEBSTER demanded the yeas and nays,
which were ordered, and are as follows:

YEAS—Messrs. Bibb, Black, Calhoun, Clay,
Ewing, Goldsborough, Kent, King of Georgia,
Leigh, Linn, McKean, Mangum, Moore, Naudain,
Poindexter, Prentiss, Preston, Silsbee, Smith,
Southard, Swift, Tomlinson, Tyler, Waggaman,
Webster, White—26.

NAYS.—Messrs. Brown, Buchanan, Grundy,
Hendricks, Hill, Kane, King, of Alabama, Knight,
Morris, Robinson, Ruggles, Shepley, Tallmadge,
Tipton, Wright—15.

So the bill was ordered to be engrossed and
read a third time, and then
The Senate adjourned.

HOUSE OF REPRESENTATIVES.

MONDAY, February 16, 1835.

Petitions and memorials were presented by—
Messrs. EVANS, KAVANAGH, and SMITH,
of Maine;

[Mr. SMITH presented a copy of the proceedings
of a public meeting, holden in the city of Portland, on the 10th inst., for the purpose of taking
into consideration the expediency of one or more
breakwaters in the harbor of that city. Mr. S. remarked, that the meeting is represented as having
declare the necessity of an expenditure for the protection of their harbor and property. I perceive,
said he, that the Mayor of the city, who is a distinguished and experienced merchant, presided at
the meeting. The subject, sir, is one of vital importance to the prosperity of Portland, and in fact,
to the commercial interests of the State of Maine:
The work has been strongly recommended as of
great utility, after a careful survey, by an Engineer of the Government. An appropriation for it
has also been reported by a committee of this
House, during the present session of Congress.
Under this state of the matter, it will be unnecessary to refer the proceedings now presented to a
committee, but I ask that they may be printed
for the information of the House. The printing
was ordered accordingly.]

Mr. PIERCE, of New Hampshire;
Mr. PHILLIPS, of Massachusetts;

[Mr. PHILLIPS presented the memorial of 3,600
ladies residing in Massachusetts, in favor of the
abolition of slavery in the District of Columbia;
which was laid on the table.]

Messrs. BURGES and PEARCE, of Rhode
Island;

Messrs. DAY, CAMBRELENG, HARD, and
DICKSON, of New York;

Mr. DICKSON presented the memorial of sundry citizens of Rochester, in the State of New
York, praying Congress to take the proper measures for abolishing slavery within the District of
Columbia; which he moved be laid on the table
and printed, together with the names attached to
the same.

Mr. BOON asked for a division of motion.

The question was first put on printing the memorial without the signatures, and agreed to.

After the decision was pronounced by the
Chair, some doubt was expressed by Mr. WISE
whether a majority had voted in the affirmative,
and it was suggested that the question was not understood by the House.

The SPEAKER rose again to propound the
question.

Mr. McKENNAN objected, on the ground that
the decision had already been announced.

Mr. WISE said he did not vote on the question,
and he desired to be informed by the Chair,
whether it was competent for him to move a reconsideration of the vote upon printing the memorial?

The SPEAKER said it was.

Mr. WISE then moved a reconsideration of the
vote.

Mr. HIESTER asked that the memorial be read;
which was done.

Mr. DICKSON said he would not enter into the
merits of the question, but as a motion to reconsider had been made, he would only remark, that
the memorial was signed by the Mayor and many
of the most respectable citizens of Rochester, belonging to both of the two great parties which now
agitated the country.

Mr. CHINN said, that he hoped the motion to
reconsider would prevail. He saw nothing which
distinguished this memorial from any other upon
the subject. Although it was signed, as the gentleman from from New York had stated to the
House, by the Mayor of Rochester and other distinguished persons, he could not perceive that this
fact entitled it to a consideration different from
that which was given to others. It presents no
new argument; it states no fact but what was contained in others; and the grievances which it
recites are common to all which have been offered
here. It was unnecessary for him to assert that
these grievances were in the main unfounded. If
this memorial were printed, why not print all which
had been offered? There was no difference between
them; if there were, it was not such as to entitle
this to unusual consideration. He did not wish to
discuss this question; he did not know that he ever
would discuss it. The whole mischief, perhaps,
consisted in discussion. This had been, and
still was, his opinion; and he had always acted in
conformity with it. He hoped the motion would
prevail, and that the same disposition would be
made of this as of the many others which had been
presented.

Mr. BOULDIN said, that he had not supposed
he would vote for the printing of this memorial until he heard it read. But after having heard
it read, he should vote for printing it; not because
he approved of the presenting of it, or of the object
of it; nor that he dissented from the general propositions about liberty and slavery in it; but because he wished his constituents to know what
feelings were entertained by their northern brethren, (some of them,) of slavery and slaveholders,
and the means of abolishing slavery.

He said he was unwilling to draw any comparisons between the country that had the honor
in part to represent, and any other portion of the
Union; but every remark about slavery, and
slaveholders, and slave-markets, made in that memorial, in relation to this District, applied equally
to the habits, customs, and legal rights of the people of all the South. He wished them to see what
those opinions and feelings were; and therefore,
and for that only, he should vote for printing the
memorial.

Mr. JOHNSON, of Louisiana, hoped that the
motion to reconsider would prevail, and that the
memorial would be laid on the table. He repudiated the interference of the Northern with the

rights and property of the people of the Southern States. Whenever the North should succeed in procuring legislation by Congress in regard to these rights and this species of property, that moment the Union would be dissolved.

Mr. BOON said, as he had asked for a division of the question, and belonged to a non-slaveholding State, it was perhaps proper that he should say a word or two. There was no person more opposed to slavery than himself; but while he was opposed to the principle, he was also opposed to interfering with those rights to property, which were guarantied to the citizens of particular States and Districts by the constitution of the United States. It would be recollected that this question, when the subject of the admission of Missouri into the Union, was before the House, had come very near dividing the Union. He thought the same course which had been adopted by the gentleman from Massachusetts, (Mr. Phillips,) in presenting a similar memorial this morning, which was, to move that it be laid on the table, was the proper one, and that this memorial should be disposed of in a similar manner.

Mr. FILLMORE said, as it was understood that the Committee on the District of Columbia would not act upon this subject at the present session, it was certainly due to the petitioners that the motion which had been made by his colleague (Mr. Dickson) should prevail. It was not unreasonable that the memorial should be printed and preserved among the documents of the House. He disavowed, most unequivocally, now and forever, any desire on his part to interfere with the rights, or what was termed the property, of the citizens of other States. While he did this, he conceived that as a citizen of the State of New York, and a member of this House, he was interested in the claim to property in man, within the District of Columbia. He referred to the effect which was produced in the North by the advertisements in the papers of this city, connected with the purchase and transportation of slaves. The people of that section of the country believed slavery to be improper, and that it should not be tolerated. This was a great national question. There was nothing in the memorial which should prevent its being printed and placed on the files of the House for future reference. Whenever petitions should be presented here from the slave-holding States, of a different tenor, and which might advocate the establishment or cantinuance of slave markets in this District and City, if they could satisfy the people of other sections that this was proper, he would treat their petitions with respect. He was willing that each party should be fully heard, and that each should have the privilege of spreading their views before the people generally.

Mr. McKINLEY regretted that this discussion had sprung up. He thought it manifested more zeal than prudence. He inquired if the printing was intended to enlighten the House or the country? It was admitted on all hands that no action was to take place upon this subject at this session. That being the case, what object would be attained by printing this memorial? He considered it one of the most imprudent memorials which had ever been read in this House. It was a fire-brand from one of the Northern States, which had been thrown into this House, and he was, for one, opposed to giving it any publicity. He denied that this House had the right to lay their hands upon his property, let him live where he might. There was no disrespect intended to the memorialists by refusing to print their memorial. It had been received by the House, and that, he contended, was sufficient. Nothing more ought to be expected. He cared not whether it had come from a Mayor of a City or the President of the United States. He should oppose the motion to print.

Mr. PARKER was at a loss, he said, to perceive how the mere reading and printing of the memorial could produce unpleasant feelings in that House or in the nation at large; nor was it in his opinion calculated to throw a fire brand into the slave holding States. It appeared to him to be more like a respectful address to the House, calling upon them to exercise the undoubted privileges conferred upon it by the constitution, of legislating for the District of Columbia, in removing what the petitioners considered a great and existing grievance, and if it was intended or wished to prevent any debate it could be easily obviated by withdrawing the question of reconsideration. What was the state of the subject, what had been done heretofore, and how did the matter then stand? A portion of the people of this country, considering the evil a national one—as one that ought not to be tolerated by a free people, respectfully ask that House to take measures to redress the evils. Petitions of this nature have been referred to the committee intrusted with the management of the affairs of the District, not only the present session; but the last and several preceding sessions. Now the prayer of the petition was either right or wrong, and their reasons either forcible and conclusive, or otherwise. Let then the committee on the District of Columbia make a report, and tell us what they think ought to be done, and give us their reasons, so that the House might judge of the question. Mr. P. was not prejudiced one way or the other, but he thought an answer to the prayer of the petition should be given, for it was neither unlawful or unrighteous.

The argument of his honorable friend from Alabama (Mr McKinley) that Congress had no right to interfere, Mr. P. could not assent to so readily. Let that gentleman, who was fully competent to give his reasons, give his reasons on this subject. For himself, in accordance with the wishes and opinions of his constituents and the persons presenting this memorial, he should feel it his bounden duty to vote to put their petition upon the files of the House, and he should continue to urge it with all the zeal of which he was capable, at the same time with all due consideration to the feelings, prejudices, interests, and rights of others, and which they were entitled to require at his hands. This he should do until the Committee on the District of Columbia or some other Select Committee of the House, answered the question, and told us, at the same time giving their reasons, whether Congress had a right to legislate on this subject or not, and until the House had concurred in that decision.

Mr. DICKSON then withdrew that part of the motion proposing to print the names of the subscribers to the memorial.

Mr. CLAY said: He was even more opposed to the printing of the memorial itself, than he was to printing the names appended to it, which he regarded as a matter of little consequence compared with the other. He was decidedly opposed to the publication of such a document. In spite of all the fair professions heard there upon the subject as to any non-interference with the rights, interests, and property of the Southern States, or any other property of this kind, gentlemen must be forgetful of the domestic policy and every thing else concerning the peace and tranquillity of those States, when they ask for the printing and publication of a document like the one under consideration. Are these gentlemen ignorant that the printing and publishing of documents of this kind in almost all the southern States are prohibited under high and heavy penalties? and would they compel, or at least sanction the publication of documents by Congress, for doing which, if a southern tribunal could lay their hands upon a printer doing the same on his individual responsibility, he would be treated and punished as a culprit? Do they call this non-interference with the rights of property, where slavery prevailed? Gentlemen might disclaim any intention of interfering with this subject; but when be heard such disclaimers as those made by the gentleman from New York, covered by so thin a veil, as he had employed, Mr. C. could not yield his assent to them. The gentleman told us that this was a subject he had no intention of interfering with, while at the same time he called it a great national question, and consequently one that ought to be agitated in that House. Was it not a subject against which southern people should decidedly protest? And was it not one calculated to excite the most direful calamities in that portion of the Union, whence Mr. C. and many of his friends came?

Mr. C. had no hesitation in giving an unqualified contradiction to the supposition that it was the wish of the intelligent and enlightened citizens of the Northern and Middle States to agitate this question. It was confined to a few fanatics urged and guided the Garrisons, the Tappans, and others, their wire-workers, who had recently attracted public attention, and whose object was well known. He did not, he could not bring himself to believe that it was the wish of the great mass of the population of the New England or Middle States, to bring on this matter. Were we to be told, because a handful of fanatics, who were ready to light the torch of disaffection and civil discord through the country, were moving on this subject, that it was matter connected with the national prosperity, or that it was a matter of right to that description of individuals, to discuss and agitate the subject in that House. The gentleman from New Jersey, (Mr. Parker) called upon the Committee for the District of Columbia to report on the subject, in order that it might be discussed and investigated. Why that was the very course of proceeding calculated to produce the evils contemplated; evils of such a character as no good citizen in any part of this wide-spread and extensive Union ought for a moment to desire. Mr. C. would inquire, how came it that this was a matter of such concern to those individuals? Did it interfere with their domestic policy, their domestic rights, their liberty, their property, or their security, in any point of view? He was at a loss to perceive how it could. Why was it, then, that those persons sought to interfere with the domestic policy of others? It could not be denied that this was a matter of domestic right and policy, and on what grounds, then, could they find themselves warranted or justified in interfering to give direction to that policy? It was a matter that concerned not them, either individually, or as a community. Until the Committee for the District of Columbia, or some other Committee, should report, the gentleman from New Jersey tells us he should hold himself ready and willing to receive and print all memorials on the subject. But had the people of the District called upon Congress to legislate on the subject? They had not, and why should Congress be called upon by others to give a new direction to the domestic policy of others, without consent first obtained? That doctrine was contrary to any expressed wish of theirs. These petitioners might, with equal propriety, memorialize the Legislature of Virginia, or the legislature of any other State, and call upon them, in the name of national honor, to reverse their policy and abolish the laws authorizing the holding of property of this kind.

Mr. C. in conclusion said, for his own part, after the admission, which seemed to have been made on all hands, that this was a matter belonging to the People holding this peculiar species of property, and after the disclaimer that had been made of non-interference, and in the absence of any petition from the inhabitants of the District of Columbia, and without any call on the part of any of the States where property of this kind existed, he did think that these gentlemen ought not to press this subject, in any form whatever, upon the consideration of the House.

Mr. C. P. WHITE moved to lay the motion to reconsider, and the memorial itself, on the table.

On a question from Mr. WISE, some conversation arose on the point whether if the motion to lay on the table prevailed, the motion to print, which had been announced by the Chair as adopted, would be considered and recorded as adopted? Mr. WISE, Mr. J. Q. ADAMS, and Mr. BRIGGS, participated therein.

The CHAIR said, it was a matter not exclusively belonging to him, but as the question had been put to him, he should say, that the Clerk of the House could not order the memorial to be printed, inasmuch as there would be, if the motion to lie on the table prevailed, a motion pending to reconsider the vote to print the memorial. The motion to lie on the table prevailing would not finally dispose of the matter, because the House might call it up, on doing which the question would recur on the motion to reconsider.

Mr. DICKSON asked for the yeas and nays, which were ordered.

Mr. GHOLSON appealed to the gentleman from New York (Mr. White,) to withdraw his motion; for the people of the South were very anxious to know the feeling of the House upon the subject, and he hoped to see it expressed by a direct vote.

Mr. C. E. WHITE said, though he was at all times very glad to accommodate the gentleman, et, in this particular, he must be excused.

The conversation on the point of order, and the Speaker's decision was resumed, and after a few minutes spent thereon—

Mr. C. P. WHITE said, to meet the views of the gentleman from Virginia, he withdrew the motion to lay the subject on the table, and moved the previous question.

The second to the previous question and the main question were both agreed to without a division.

The question then occurred on reconsidering the motion to print the memorial, on which the yeas and nays had been ordered, and it was decided as follows—yeas 125, nays 81.

So the House determined to re-consider their vote.

Mr. WISE said: Although I have my feelings, my prejudices, my passions, and my fixed principles and determination, as a southern man, on this subject, yet I hope I can discuss it without excitement. I rise not, sir, to throw, as some others are thrown, a fire-brand amongst us. I rise simply to state to my constituents and the country at large, the true state of feeling, and of the case as exists here, in the north, and in the south.

I trust I am well assured, that the Representatives on this floor from the North, do not wish or design to interfere with our rights. That they truly feel bound in their representative duty to resist these memorials, so dangerous in their tendency, and incendiary in their character, from respect to a few, a very few only, of their constituents comparatively, and that they do not act from their own impulses.

Sir, on this delicate and vitally important subject, the moderate, considerate, and patriotic men of the South, as well as of the North, have enemies to contend with. In the North we have the misguided fanatics, whose zeal prompts them to rush blindly into the most absurd excesses; and in the South, I am sorry to say it, we are not wanting those who seize upon any pretext to inflame the public mind on the subject of slavery. In this delicate situation what will be the course of the friends of the country and our institutions? Why, sir, the friends of order, of the constitution, and of the existence of this republic, in this House, or out of it, the North, or in the South, must use their influence to moderate and quench these spirits of the extremes of fanaticism and of disorganization.

When memorials of the character of this asked to be printed, are presented, it is restful enough, I should think, to the memorialists, to receive them; if printed, they will be circulated throughout the country, to fan the flames of zealots on one side, and to serve as food for disorganizers on the other. We, who would safe and secure in the blessings we now enjoy, I, therefore, smother these memorials on their presentation. I am willing, sir, to treat all memorials, no matter how extravagant or preposterous, or of what character, with respect, provided they are from a respectable body of citizens, and not dangerous in their tendencies. I, sir, I cannot tolerate, much less give countenance and éclat to memorials and petitions which tax at the very foundations of the social compact, and our civil institutions. I will not hear them; I desire not to see them; and would reject them at once. With what sort of respect, I ask it of the gentleman from the western part of New York, (Mr. Fillmore,) could he treat an incendiary, who should respectfully ask him to permit him to apply a torch to his dwelling? and he regard him as a sober-minded neighbor, or madman, as a fiend or friend? Sir, I was sorry to hear some of the remarks from the gentleman of New York. He says that the people of the North are continually shocked advertisements of slave dealers in the papers of this District. I am sorry, sir, that their nerves are so delicate, when their fathers did more than any other people of the colonies to establish slavery amongst us. And I appeal to Southern gentlemen for the truth of the remarkable fact that the emigrants from the North to the South, some from the gentleman's own district, perhaps, are as ready to become masters as any who are hereditary masters. To strengthen their nerves and change their whole principles and opinions on the subject, they have but to change their climes, their havens. And if they choose to remain at home, they may cease to take these odious papers. If slavery was abolished in the District I know not what would restrain the press still from publishing advertisements. And if the papers here cease to publish for runaways and purchasers of slaves, still the gentleman would have to cease taking the papers of the South, or to silence them too. Sir, slavery is interwoven with our very political existence, is guaranteed by our constitution, and its consequences must be borne with by our Northern brethren, as resulting from our system of Government; and they cannot attack the institution of slavery without attacking the institutions of the country, our safety and welfare. The gentleman says he will ever respect the property of the States, but he claims to legislate away the property of this District. Sir, a slave is as much property here as in Virginia; property by the law and the constitution. And, in addition to the remark of the gentleman from Alabama, (Mr. McKinley,) that you will not surely take private property without just compensation—and that you cannot compensate without taking in part of the taxes of the South to pay the slaves, I will repeat the idea, that, although you have exclusive jurisdiction over this "ten miles square," yet it is common ground, for the good of the whole, and for the use of the whole people of every State in the Union. And I would ask of the gentleman, if he can come upon this ground with his carriage and horses, why cannot I come with my slaves to remain here, to live here as long as I please? Sir, I say it is not in passion, but calmly and dispassionately, that Congress has no right to abolish slavery even here, against the consent of the slaveholders, who are not represented; and I warn gentlemen, that the South—I speak for all as strongly as one man can speak for many, for millions—that the South will fight to the hilt against the abolition of slavery in this District, unless the inhabitants owning slaves themselves petition for it, as they would against any interference with the right of slave property in Virginia.

The gentleman calls this a great "national question." I protest, sir, against its being so considered. The nation has nothing to do with slave property. It is simply a delicate question of private, individual right, wholly and solely under the control of the States where slavery exists. It is a reserved State right, with which the General Government has no right of interference even, and from intermeddling with which the free States and their inhabitants should scrupulously abstain. The pseudo-philanthropists of the North do but defeat their own objects, when they rudely attempt to touch or handle a subject which does not immediately concern them; and true christians and philanthropists will always find their principles, and the cause of humanity, best subserved, by being the friends of slaveholders, instead of being the friends of slaves, and by co-operating with intelligent, humane, enlightened and patriotic slave-owners of the South, by ways and means which the lights of the age have already shown. If violence or intrusion upon our rights be persisted in and pursued, gentlemen will find Union men and nullifiers of the South all united on the subject—ready ripe for revolution, if the worst must come to the worst!

I hope, sir, that this House will not shock the South more by the printing of this memorial, than the constituents of the gentleman from New York, were ever shocked by slave advertisements, and that it and all others like it, will now and for all time to come, be smothered and suppressed.

Mr. BOULDIN said he should not have risen again but for a remark made by his friend and colleague (Mr Wise.) His colleague had

said that he was not for sending a firebrand in the south; but for this part of his colleagues remarks, he would not have risen to say another word. Mr. B. said, far be it from him to cast, or be the means of casting a firebrand in the south, or the north; or any where. But he had said he would vote to print, merely that the south might know what was going on. He would put it to his colleague, if presenting such memorials as this, was not, as his colleague had said, like putting a torch to a man's house, and if a proposition not to print was not like putting a torch to his colleague's house privately, and on detection, asking him to keep it a secret.

Mr. WISE explained, and said he had no allusion to him, and that he was among the last men he would charge with throwing a firebrand.

Mr. BOULDIN said he was sure of that; but did not know that every one would be equally so.

Mr. ARCHER then rose and asked leave to make a suggestion to lay the whole subject on the table.

Mr. BOULDIN said he would answer to that suggestion of his colleague immediately. He wished only to say a word or two.

Mr B. said, far be it from him, and very far had it been from him, to throw any fire-brands, or make any offensive comparisons between his and any other part of the Union. But the memorial did. It alluded to habits and customs, and legal rights common to this district, and of the States of the South in the most disparaging terms. Mr. B. had refused, and did then refuse, to make any comparison of the principles, habits, or laws of the South and North and East.

He said the South had their infirmities, their weaknesses, and their misfortunes, and perhaps the one alluded to, was the greatest misfortune to which the people of the South were liable to. But had gentlemen no misfortunes, no infirmities, in the body politic among them. Suppose he were to go into their country, and inquire into every thing, and see what they had and could not well get rid off. But he would not. He had no idea of being reduced to the necessity of answering and defending every infirmity and misfortune incident to our nature, or cover under the charge. Let them that were without fault, cast the first stone.

He would, before sitting down, say one thing. He had seen, in the testimony taken before the House of Commons in England, proof that a man and his wife had literally starved, for want of the work to which they were brought up, in making negro cotton. He knew that many negroes had died from exposure to weather, for the want of that negro cotton. Clad in a flimsy fabrick, that will turn neither wind nor water, substituted by northern and eastern people, who present these memorials, or from whose region they are presented, which substitute sold, under protecting duties, for the profit of perhaps four pences half-penny in the yard. So the poor Englishman is starved, and the poor slave perishes in the cold for this profit. It appears, then, that after all this piteous ditties, sung and said, their philanthropy does not amount to 6½ cents a yard be thought by any one that he wished to throw a firebrand any where, he would, at the suggestion of his friend and colleague, (Mr. Archer,) with a view to get clear of the whole matter, and lay it on the table, yield to him the floor to make that motion.

Mr. ARCHER said he considered it almost an indiscreet in gentlemen from the south or slave holding States to discuss this question, as it was for the representatives from the north to introduce it. He would add nothing to this remark, but moved to lay the whole subject on the table.

The question was then taken on laying the motion on the table by yeas and nays, and decided on the affirmation—ayes 139, noes 63.

Petitions and memorials were further presented by—

BINNEY, STEWART, and DENNY of Pennsylvania;

[Mr. DENNY presented the memorial from the delegates to a convention assembled at Pittsburg on the 3d of February, 1835, in favor of the Chesapeake and Ohio Canal, and praying Congress to make an appropriation for completing the western section of the canal; which was referred to the Committee on Roads and Canals, and ordered to be printed.

Mr. D. also presented two memorials, one from the ladies of Allegheny and vicinity, the other from inhabitants of Pittsburg and vicinity, relative to the abolition of slavery in the District of Columbia, and the Territories under the control of Congress. Laid on the table.]

Messrs. STODDERT and CARMICHAEL, of Maryland;

Messrs. ALLEN, WISE, and CHINN, of Virginia;

Mr. CLAYTON, of Georgia;

Messrs. POPE, MARSHALL, and LYON, of Kentucky;

[Mr. POPE presented resolutions adopted by the Legislature of Kentucky, asking Congress to purchase the private stock in the Louisville and Portland Canal, in order that it should be made a free highway.

Mr. MARSHALL presented resolutions of the Kentucky Legislature, asking Congress to establish a national armory in said State.

Mr. LYON presented resolutions of the Legislature of Kentucky, asking Congress to establish a military school in said State.

The foregoing resolutions were severally laid on the table, and ordered to be printed.]

Messrs. BLAIR and INGE, of Tennessee;

[Mr. INGE presented the petition of Fanny Blackmore, praying compensation for services performed by her during the Indian war.]

Messrs. WHITTLESEY, VINTON, VANCE, CRANE, and HAMER, of Ohio.

[Mr. HAMER presented petitions from citizens of Adams, Brown, and Highland counties, Ohio, praying for an alteration of the mail route from Bainbridge to Maysville.]

Mr. GARLAND, of Louisiana;

Messrs. LANE, McCARTY, and CARR, of Indiana;

[Mr. LANE presented the memorial of Capt. John Crandon, of Dearborn County, Indiana, praying to be placed upon the roll as an invalid pensioner.]

[Mr. CARR presented the petition of Joshua Kennedy, of the city of Mobile, Alabama, praying the confirmation of a land claim.

Also, the petition of Thomas G. Newbold, of Mobile, Alabama, solicitor in fact for the heirs of Lewis Durette, deceased, praying the confirmation of land claims.

Also, the petition of Elienes (Stephen) La Lande, of the county of Mobile, Alabama, praying the confirmation of a land claim, which, on his motion, were referred to the Committee on private Land Claims.

Mr. CARR presented the petition of John Carney, of Indiana, a soldier of the revolution; which, on his motion, was referred to the Committee on Revolutionary Pensions.]

Mr. PLUMMER, of Mississippi;

Messrs. MAY and REYNOLDS, of Illinois;

[Mr. MAY presented the petition of Samuel Cozard, praying that a pension be allowed him in consequence of sufferings and injuries received whilst in captivity among the Shawnee tribe of Indians; which, on his motion, was referred to the Committee on Revolutionary Pensions.]

[Mr. REYNOLDS presented the memorial of the General Assembly of the State of Illinois, praying, for certain reasons therein contained, an extension of the National Road westward, to cross the Mississippi at Alton, and not at St. Louis.

The memorial states, that to cross the Mississippi at Alton, would be in accordance with the ultimate destination of said road to the Capitol of the State of Missouri. This route would be more advantageous to the commercial and agricultural interest of Illinois, than any other, and would also afford to Illinois and her sister States a more direct and convenient chain of intercommunication than any

other route. That for the National Road to cross the river at St. Louis, in Missouri, "would not only be highly detrimental to the prosperity of this State, (Illinois,) but in violation of her just pretensions, and of her rights of sovereignty, contrary to the avowed policy of the General Government, and in open defiance of those principles of even-handed justice and impartiality which have characterized her dealings with other States in relation to this subject."

On this statement of facts, and the reasoning thereon, the memorial gives to the United States the "consent" of the State to extend the road through the territory of the State, so as to cross the river at Alton.

Mr. R. added one other fact to what is stated in the memorial; that Alton, by the late act of the Legislature of the State, and the vote thereon, is to be the seat of Government, after the constitutional period expires, which requires the seat of Government to be at Vandalia.]

Mr. CLAY, of Alabama;

[Mr. CLAY presented the memorial of the Legislature of that State, asking further relief for that class of the purchasers of public lands who paid for their lands without the benefit of the reduction of price allowed by the acts of 1830 and 1831. Referred to the Committee on the Public Lands.

Mr. C. also presented the petition of Abraham Woodall, asking to be relieved from a mistake made in the entry of a tract of land. Referred to the same committee.

Mr. C. also presented the petition of Upayoho-lo, asking to be allowed his claim to a reservation under the late treaty with the Creek nation. Referred to the same committee.]

Mr. LYON, of Michigan;

Mr. WHITE, of Florida;

Mr. H. EVERETT, of Vermont;

Mr. SEVIER, of Arkansas.

Which petitions and memorials were appropriately disposed of.

On motion of Mr. CRANE,

Resolved, That the Committee on Commerce be instructed to inquire into the expediency of establishing buoys in the mouth of the Maumee river, and in Maumee bay.

On motion of Mr. GARLAND,

Resolved, That the Committee on Indian Affairs be instructed to inquire into the expediency of making an appropriation for the purpose of holding a treaty or convention with the Caddo Indians, for the extinguishment of a title set up by them, to a certain extent of territory in the north-western part of the State of Louisiana, and the south-western part of Arkansas.

On motion of Mr. KINNARD,

Resolved, That the Committee of Claims be instructed to inquire into the expediency of allowing to William Harmon, of Marion, county Indians, compensation for a horse lost by him in the military service of the United States during the late war with Great Britain.

On motion of Mr. FELDER,

Resolved, That the Committee on the Post Office and Post Roads be instructed to inquire into the expediency of so changing the post route from Columbia to Barnwell Court House, as to run from Gordon's Mills, by Dencey Corbitt's, on Goodland Swamp, and by Davis's Mills to Barnwell Court House.

Mr. CHINN, from the Committee on the District of Columbia, reported the following resolution, which was rejected:

Resolved, That Saturday the 21st inst. from and after the hour of twelve be set apart for the consideration of bills reported by the Committee on the District of Columbia.

On motion of Mr. BURD,

Resolved, That the Committee on Private Land Claims inquire into the expediency of granting a patent to Mrs. Margaret Kingsbury, of Bedford, Pennsylvania, widow and relict of Oliver H. Kingsbury, a soldier of the late war, who fell in battle on the northern frontier, such quantity of land as said Oliver was entitled to under his enlistment.

On motion of Mr. HATHAWAY,

Resolved, That the Committee on the Post Office and Post Roads be instructed to inquire into the

expediency of establishing a post route from Cortlandt village, in the county of Cortlandt, State of New York, to the town of Marathon, in said county.

On motion of Mr. WILSON,

Resolved, That the Committee on Roads and Canals be instructed to inquire into the expediency of authorizing the Secretary of the Treasury to transfer the stock of the United States in the Chesapeake and Ohio Canal Company to such States, corporations, or individuals, as shall secure to the board of directors by subscription of stock or otherwise a sum sufficient to complete the canal to the coal mines near Cumberland.

Mr. HAWES asked the consent of the House to submit a resolution making the reports made by the Committee appointed to examine the Post Office Department, the special order for Monday, the 23d inst.

It was objected to.

Mr. PARKER asked the consent of the House to submit certain amendments which he intended to offer to the bill in relation to the Lateral branch of the Baltimore and Ohio Rail-road to the City of Washington, which he desired to have printed.

The motion was objected to.

Mr. ANTHONY from the Committee on Military Affairs, reported a bill for the relief of Sylvester Day; which was read twice and committed.

Mr. CONNOR, from the Committee on the Post Office and Post Roads, reported an amendment to the bill to establish certain post routes, and to alter and discontinue others; which was ordered to be printed. Mr. C. gave notice, that he should on Wednesday next, move the House to proceed to the consideration of the foregoing bills.

Mr. MUHLENBERG, from the Committee on Revolutionary Claims, reported a bill for the relief of Nancy Haggert, which was read twice and committed.

Mr. McKENNAN, from the Committee on the District of Columbia, reported a bill to extend the charters of the Bank of Washington, the Patriotic Bank of Washington, and the Farmers' and Mechanics' Bank of Georgetown; which was read twice and committed.

Mr. JARVIS, from the Committee on the Public Buildings, reported a bill making appropriations for the public buildings and grounds; which was read twice and committed.

Unfavorable reports upon various petitions, &c., were made by Messrs. McINTIRE, JOHNSON, of Ky. CRANE, and GRENNELL, from their respective committees.

Mr. WISE, from a Select Committee, reported a joint resolution, proposing to purchase 1,000 copies of the writings of General Washington, edited by Jared Sparks; which was read twice.

Mr. SMITH, of Maine, hoped the House would now dispose of this resolution. The present Congress, at its last session, had already voted for the expenditure of about $140,000 for books designed for the use of members alone. For one of these works he had himself voted in a preliminary stage; and if there was a vote upon the records of the House of his, which he would wish to blot out, it was that. The work was doubtless one of merit, and he would be glad to see it placed in the hands of every individual in the country. But he could no longer agree to sanction the practice of filling the shelves of their own libraries by the appropriation of the public funds. He moved to lay the resolution on the table; but withdrew the motion at the request of Mr. WISE, who promised to renew it.

Mr. WISE hoped the House would not so summarily dispose of the resolution. He explained its object and the reasons of the committee in introducing it. In conclusion, he said, in fulfillment of the engagement he was under with the gentleman from Maine, he would renew his motion to lay the resolution on the table, but hoped the House would not agree to it.

Mr. VANDERPOEL demanded the yeas and nays on this question; and while he was up, he would ask if this was not the same work for which the House had already subscribed a large sum?

Mr. WISE replied briefly, and

Mr. J. Q. ADAMS rose, but the question not being debatable, it was taken by yeas and nays and decided in the affirmative. Yeas 141, nays 58

Mr. JARVIS, from the Committee on the Public Buildings, reported a resolution directing the equestrian statue of Jefferson to be removed from the rotundo of the Capitol until some disposition should be made of the same by Congress.

Mr. MERCER moved to strike out all after the word "Rotundo," in the resolution.

The question on this motion was taken, when there appeared—yeas 74, nays 36. There being a quorum voting, a discussion ensued, in which Messrs. JARVIS, MERCER, and Adams of Massachusetts took part. Before the question was finally taken,

Mr. POLK called for the orders of the day, and the motion prevailed.—Ayes 79, noes 47.

The SPEAKER laid before the House the following communications, which were appropriately disposed of.

A letter from the Secretary of War, in answer to a resolution of the House, in relation to the transportation of arms from Harpers ferry, Pittsburg, &c. to different points.

A communication from the Secretary of the Navy, in response to a resolution of the House, in regard to the use of Cotton Canvass in the Navy of the United States.

A bill granting additional compensation to the District Attorney for the District of South Carolina was read a third time and passed.

On motion of Mr. CHINN, the regular orders of the day were postponed, in order to take up the bill reported from the Committee on the District of Columbia relating to the Baltimore and Washington rail road.

Mr. PARKER opposed the passage of this bill in its present shape at some length, as partaking of the character of partial legislation. Congress had undoubted authority to legislate for the District, the whole District, but not to pass an act which would be partial in its operation. He concluded by moving a substitute for the bill.

Mr. CHINN replied, and opposed the amendment.

Mr. McKIM called for the previous question. For this motion there appeared ayes 74, noes 28, no quorum voting.

Mr. PARKER moved to adjourn. The motion was lost without a division.

The question was then taken on seconding the motion for the previous question, and decided in the affirmative—ayes 91, noes 32.]

The main question was then put, on the engrossment of the bill, and it was ordered to be engrossed and read a third time.

On motion of Mr. WHITE, of Florida, the House next took up the "bill for the completion of certain improvements in the Territory of Florida;" but before any question on this bill was taken, it was, on motion of Mr. W., postponed till to-morrow.

Mr. W. then moved to take up another bill relating to the Territory of Florida.

Mr. McVEAN moved that the House do now adjourn; which was agreed to.

The House then adjourned.

IN SENATE.

Tuesday, Feb. 17, 1835.

Petitions and memorials were presented by Messrs. TYLER, RUGGLES, BLACK, and BENTON, and referred.

Mr. TIPTON, from the Committee on Claims, to which was referred the bill from the House of Representatives, for the relief of John J. Avery, reported the same without amendment.

Mr. POINDEXTER, from the Committee on Public Claims, to which was recommitted the bill for the relief of the heirs of Nathaniel Tyler, deceased, reported the same without amendment.

Mr. POINDEXTER, from the same Committee, made unfavorable reports on the following subjects, which were submitted to it.

The memorial and resolution of the Legislature of Louisiana, praying a donation of land for education purposes.

The resolutions of the Legislature of Illinois, praying for a grant of 160 acres of land to the village of Cahokia;

A memorial from the Legislature of Alabama,

lands.

Mr. POINDEXTER, from the same Committee, to which was referred the memorial from Michigan, praying an extension of certain pre-emption privileges, reported a bill for the purpose; which was read the first time and ordered to a second reading.

Mr. PORTER, from the Committee on Private Land Claims, made an unfavorable report upon the petitions of Nicholas Girod, and of the heirs of Jacques Millon, deceased; the petitions of A. Foucher, M. V. Robertson, and A. C. Valois.

Mr. TOMLINSON, from the Committee on Pensions, to which was referred the bills from the House of Representatives, granting pensions to John Cullins, Amasa A. Tift, Harvey Reynolds, and John Casey; reported the same, severally, without amendment.

He also reported the bill from the House, granting a pension to Josiah Westlake, but with an expression of opinion by the committee against its passage, and his intention, when the bill shall be called up, to move its indefinite postponement.

Mr. MOORE, from the Committee on Public Lands, reported a bill concerning pre-emptions, which was read the first time, and ordered to a second reading.

Mr. GRUNDY, from the Committee on the Post Office and Post Roads, to which was referred the bill to establish a daily mail between Macon, Geo., and New Orleans, reported the same without amendment.

The following resolutions were severally submitted, considered, and adopted:

By Mr. PRENTISS:

Resolved, That the resolution passed on the second of February inst. requesting the President to communicate to the Senate the correspondence between the Government of the United States and Spain, in the negotiation of the late treaty between the two governments, and the instructions connected therewith, was intended to be restricted, and is hereby restricted to the correspondence and instructions during the official term of the present minister of the United States to Spain.

By Mr. TIPTON:

Resolved, That the Secretary of War be requested to communicate to the Senate, as early as practicable, a copy of the survey, plan, and estimate of Lieut. Berrien, for the improvement of the harbor at the mouth of St. Joseph's river, in Michigan Territory.

By Mr. PORTER:

Resolved, That the Committee on Indian Affairs be instructed to inquire into the expediency of making an appropriation for the purpose of holding a treaty or convention with the Caddo Indians, for the extinguishment of a claim set up by them to a tract of country in the northwestern part of the State of Louisiana, and the southwestern part of the Territory of Arkansas.

This resolution lies one day for consideration.

The resolution submitted yesterday by Mr. PRESTON, fixing Thursday next for the election of a printer, came up for consideration.

Mr. BENTON said, he had heretofore shown that the joint resolution of 1819 was the result of the report of a committee in that year, and that its adoption at that time was designed for a temporary purpose—for one election only. But he said we had gone on ever since, electing our printer under it. The committee then fixed a tariff of prices, which was to last for two years only, as was clear from the terms of the resolution. About four or five years ago, a joint resolution was passed, requiring a majority of the whole number of votes to be necessary for a choice, instead of a plurality, as before. So that we have been holding elections for printer every two years, when we had no right to do so, for the purpose of binding our successors. The committee in their report suggested three modes of having the public printing executed; one of which was, by a national printing office, for the purpose of executing the work of Congress when in session, and of all the other departments of the Government in the recess. The aggregate amount of the printing, binding, and stationary, amounted to the whole to only $65,000 per annum. This was the

This plan of a national printing office, it was then thought, would be the most economical plan. [Here Mr. B. read passages from the report.] Mr. B. said he only read these passages for the purpose of reminding Senators what the committee then reported, and out of which the illegal and extraordinary practice of electing a printer every two years had grown.

Mr. PRESTON said, he would have no objection, where abuses were suggested, to go into an investigation of the facts and produce a reformation. He thought some good to the people might grow out of the present state of things, while one part of this House were engaged in the examination of executive extravagance, and the other of Senatorial extravagance. He wished to see a thorough investigation and reformation of abuses. But that duty would be very imperfectly performed by limiting it to an investigation of the House or of either of the two Houses. He ventured to say, that although the printing of the two Houses had increased to the extent stated by the gentleman from Missouri, yet the executive printing had increased much more. The expense here, only keeps pace with usual prodigality elsewhere. The general ratio of increase to that of printing. In looking into the resolution of 1819 relative to the printing, the highest proof of its being the best mode of having it executed is to be found in the fact that it has been acquiesced in for fourteen years. In 1829 the question arose of electing a printer by a plurality instead of a majority of the votes, and that resolution passed for the purpose of requiring a majority to elect. Whatever, therefore, was the practice anterior to that time, the clear terms of this resolution superseded it. The evil of the system, if it be an evil, can be remedied in no other way but by a repeal of this joint resolution. Mr. P. said he did not consider the printer an officer of the House. He is an agent employed by the House, under a law of the land, directing how he is to be employed. He hoped the resolution would be agreed to; it is about the period of the session when the printer is usually chosen.

Mr. CLAY said he could not concur exactly with the honorable member from South Carolina in his objections to the printing expenses of Congress. There is some increase, it is true, but the honorable member should have accompanied his remarks with some explanation of the cause of the increase of our printing. The true causes are the abuses of this administration. He was not surprised at the friends of the administration objecting to an examination of the printing. Look at the Post Office Department; the abuses there made it necessary to incur the expense of printing the 30,000 copies of the reports on that subject last year, and 20 and perhaps 30,000 this year. This is the great cause. And the misfortune is that the increase of printing can't keep pace with the increase of abuses. If the Post Office Committee could have penetrated the secret recesses of that Department, instead of merely breaking the crust, there would have been a much greater increase of printing. If the Postmaster General had not kept the key and prevented admission, the expense would have been much greater. Look too, at the public lands. This is the cause of the great increase of printing expense, and much more should have been printed. Mr. C. said he got up to remonstrate against fixing the day for the election of a printer, and moved to lay the resolution on the table.

Mr. PRESTON inquired when the gentleman from Kentucky proposed to call it up.

Mr. CLAY said, to be frank with the honorable member, he was not disposed to act on it at all till the House had chosen their printer. We are a small body here, and can ballot at any time.

Mr. PRESTON then gave notice that he would call it up on Tuesday next.

Mr. BENTON then gave notice that before that period, he would call up his joint resolution to repeal the other joint resolutions on the subject of printing.

Mr. PRESTON'S resolution was laid on the table.

On motion of Mr. BENTON, the report of the committee of 1818–19 upon this subject, was ordered to be reprinted for the use of the Senate.

The bill for the relief of the owners of the brig Despatch, was read the third time and passed.

The bill to repeal the two first sections of the act of 1820, commonly called the four years law, came up on its final passage, when

Mr. BUCHANAN rose and spoke at length against the principles of the bill.

After Mr. B. concluded,

Mr. CLAYTON said he proposed to say a few words on the bill before the Senate. He concurred with the honorable Senator from Pennsylvania, (Mr. Buchanan,) that it was an important constitutional question. But he would not at that time enter into a discussion whether it was constitutional or unconstitutional, but whether Congress had the power to regulate executive power or not. He wished to see nothing of party feeling in the discussion. He entered upon the debate entirely destitute of party politics. If it had been his design to serve party purposes, he should not, when his friends were out of office, and his opponents in power, advocate a bill which was to continue in office those who now held places of trust to the seclusion of his own friends.

He wished to go back to the origin of the principles set forth in the bill. In 1826 a special committee of the Senate, consisting of nine highly intelligent gentlemen, eight of whom concurred in the report, and were of the same political faith as the present administration. He believed they were sincere in the principles they advocated, and was willing to give them credit for the correctness of their views. But now there seemed to be an attempt to give a party character to the bill. He did not think it just for his former friends to cast it in the teeth of those who now advocated it. He had been well said, by the Senator from Pennsylvania, that it was discussed in 1789 by those fresh from the hall where the constitution was framed. The most enlightened of those great men discussed it on the ground that the right of removal was contained in that clause of the constitution which says the President shall see all the laws executed; and on that point they rested their opinions. But the great mass, who voted in favor of the construction then given, he believed, grounded their opinions on the expediency and necessity of such powers being vested in the Executive, for the removal of negligent and unfaithful officers. And that was the only use they expected would be made of it. If the power of the Executive was extended only to remove such officers, there would be no abuse; but if it was exercised to remove for party purposes, it was an abuse never apprehended by those who gave such a construction to the constitution. Mr. C. contended that the Executive power was circumscribed and limited to particular clauses of the constitution—that there was no power delegated further than we specially specified. He thought that Congress had the power to legislate on the subject, as the constitution gave them power to pass laws to carry into effect its provisions. The only reason he could assign why the power of removal had remained so long in the hands of the President, was, that Congress had neglected to legislate on the subject.

He thought the Senator from Pennsylvania was mistaken in his apprehension of the bill. It was not intended to take away the removing power from the President; but merely to require his reasons for the act. The Senate ought to know the grounds on which the removal was made. If the President should tell the Senate it was on account of political principles, he, in his place as a Senator, would vote to reject every nomination made to fill the place ad infinitum. He would ask whether they were acting for party effect or as Senators of the country? He regretted that there should be any attempt to introduce the bill as a party question, and gentlemen be denounced as party men. He could find nothing in the present bill impairing the decision of 1789.

Mr. PRESTON said, he had intended to have taken some part in the debate; at least to examine some of its most important points. But he then rose to enter his protest against certain principles that had been advanced by the Senators from New York and Pennsylvania, (Mr. Wright and Mr. Buchanan.) In what he had to say, he should rather offer his opinions than bring forward arguments. He did not intend to go into the report at that time, but would refer to the remarks of the gentleman from New York. He agreed that the source and origin of executive patronage was to be found in the acts of Congress. But when executive power became dangerous, it should find a restraint in the legislation of Congress. The nature of power, said Mr. P., was to augment itself. The tendency of the Government of the United States was to encroach on subjects which did not properly belong to it, to tread on the rights of the States. In these encroachments of Congress, he believed the executive power was increased more than the legislative.

He was willing to go to the source and origin, to Congress. He believed that when examined into it would be found, the vast extent of Executive power had necessarily grown up from the extravagant legislation of Congress; and that if they purified its source, in the acts of Congress, Executive power would be diminished. Could any one deny that there was danger to be apprehended? Yet the Senator from New York propounded the questions one by one analysing each item that went to make up that mighty sum of Executive power. The gentleman asked what was to be feared from the pensioners? Why they increased the number of those who depended on the legislation of Congress; and they came within the influence of Executive power. The very fulfilling of the laws gave power and influence to the Executive. Our institutions were not in danger from the pensioners, nor from the navy, nor army; but all these increased the power and influence of the Executive. The report of 1826 was made, when the Senate was opposed to that administration, and what has been the result? The patronage of the Executive had increased, and was increasing. Was it, then, considered a party question? Not by the Committee. He had it from the honorable gentleman who composed that Committee. They regarded its increase as dangerous to the future prosperity of our country. He was glad to see those who were then in favor of the measures now proposed, come up again to their support. He would retort upon the Senator from New York his own questions: Was the Navy, the Army, the Post Office, dangerous at that time? If they were dangerous then, what were they now? He did not make these remarks as applying particularly to this Administration; but as the results of past legislation. The same reasons would apply in 1835 as in 1826. He would put the question to the opposers of the bill, Why did they not concur with the recorded opinions of the party with which they acted? For himself, he would adhere to the great principles which he professed, let who would be in power.

Mr. P. said, it was with dismay he had heard the Senators from the great State savor doctrines which he considered as infinitely dangerous.— What were their definitions of executive power? We were not to look to Russia, to the Sublime Porte, to Austria, France, nor Spain, for a definition of executive power. We were not to select models from the mouldering monarchies and despotisms of Europe and Asia, by which to fashion and build up our free institutions. Neither were we to look over the catalogues of British royalty to find patterns for a President in this country. The advocates of independent executive power seemed to claim it as the "prerogative" of the President. But let them remember, that "prerogative" is a term of foreign application; we have no such word on this side of the Atlantic. Since his first entrance on public life, he had looked with dismay on the claims of Congress to pass all laws they thought fit. But all claims would be swallowed up in executive power. He did not refer to the present executive; but to that branch of Government as a distinct corporation.

Mr. P. then went on to state that he did not consider any power as belonging to Congress or the President, unless specified in the constitution. Otherwise their enumeration was mere verbiage, and useless repetition. Though he respected highly the framers and expounders of the constitution, he felt at liberty to judge for himself on this great question. He thought if we take the principal report as a specimen of that debate, it must have fallen far short of the intelligence of the present day.

Mr. P. then showed that Congress had by former enactments regulated, in some measure, the power of removal, and consequently the right now contended for, was no innovation of the usage of this Government.

Mr. CUTHBERT here was understood to suggest an objection to the bill, that its terms were so general as to apply to all officers.

At Mr. CALHOUN'S request, who observed that it applied only to disbursing officers, the bill was again read.

Mr. CUTHBERT repeated his opinion that it applied to all officers.

Mr. WRIGHT then occupied a short time in replying to Mr. PRESTON, and after some explanatory remarks from Mr. EWING, who thought Mr. BUCHANAN had misconceived his argument upon the bill,

The Senate adjourned.

HOUSE OF REPRESENTATIVES.
TUESDAY, Feb. 17, 1835.

Petitions and memorials were presented and leave, by Messrs. GORHAM, ASHLEY, and HEATH, and appropriately referred.

Mr. CHINN, from the Committee on the District of Columbia, reported a bill to extend the charter of the Union Bank of Georgetown; which was read twice and committed.

Mr. CHINN, from the Committee on the District of Columbia, reported a resolution setting apart Saturday next, from twelve o'clock, for the consideration of bills reported from the Committee on the District of Columbia.

The CHAIR decided the resolution to be out of order, in as much as a proposition of a similar tenor was rejected by the House yesterday.

Mr. CORWIN, from the Committee of Ways and Means, reported, without amendment, the bill from the Senate making an appropriation for the repair of the Cumberland road; the bill was committed.

Mr. BARRINGER, from the Committee on Revolutionary Pensions, reported a bill for the relief of Jesse Sykes; which was read twice and committed.

Mr. McKINLEY inquired of the Chair whether it would be in order to move to take up the resolution fixing a day for the election of Printer to the House?

The SPEAKER replied that it would require two-thirds to take up the resolution.

Mr. McKINLEY said, that being the case, it would be useless to submit the motion.

Mr. HARPER, of New York, from the Committee on Commerce, reported a bill for the relief of William Stanard, and others; which was read twice and committed.

Unfavorable reports upon various petitions, &c. were made by Messrs. WARDWELL, THOMSON, FOWLER, WISE, BARRINGER, ASHLEY, and WATMOUGH, from their respective committees; they were laid on the table.

The resolution reported by Mr. JARVIS, for the removal of the bronze statue of Jefferson, from the rotunda, come up as the unfinished business of the morning hour of yesterday.

Mr. McKINLEY moved to postpone the resolution until to-morrow, with a view of taking up the resolution fixing a day for the election of Printer to the House, and demanded the yeas and nays on his motion.

The SPEAKER said, it was not competent for the gentleman to include the latter proposition in his motion.

Mr. McKINLEY said, he did not so intend. He merely wished to notify the House, that if the motion which he had made prevailed, he would then propose to consider the resolution to which he had referred.

The House refused to order the yeas and nays on the motion to postpone.

The question was then taken, and the resolution was postponed: yeas 78, nays 63.

Mr. ALLAN, of Ky. moved to take up a resolution, reported by the Committee on Territories, setting apart a day for the consideration of bills reported from said Committee.

It was objected to.

Mr. McKINLEY again moved to take up the resolution fixing a day for the election of printer. He thought it should be disposed of. If the House was opposed to the resolution, or to the election of a printer, their determination should be made known.

The SPEAKER said, the motion was not in order, the resolution reported by the Committee on Elections, proposing to pay Mr. Letcher his per diem and mileage during the last session, having precedence.

Mr. McKINLEY moved to postpone this resolution until to-morrow, which was disagreed to: yeas , nays 81.

The resolution was then taken up.

The question being on the amendment offered yesterday by Mr. HARDIN, to pay Mr. Moore the same amount which was proposed to be paid to Mr. Letcher.

Mr. VANDERPOEL said, as he was a member of the Committee of Elections last year, and was still connected with that Committee, he would take the opportunity of saying a word about the resolution and amendment under consideration. It would be recollected that the Committee had reported that Mr. Moore was duly elected, but had also reported that both gentlemen ought to be paid. The House decided that the question as to who was the elected member, was a matter of so much doubt that it could not satisfactorily decide it and accordingly referred it to the people. This tribunal had decided in favor of Mr. Letcher, and the Committee could not, therefore, reasonably, at least so far as it regarded Mr. Letcher, recede from the ground it had taken last session. If the House was then under obligation to pay either party, that obligation was not discharged by anything that had since transpired. To be sure, Mr. Letcher had said, at the conclusion of the speech which he had made at the bar of the House, that without his seat he would not receive his pay, but this did not absolve the House from its liability, if it ever existed.

Mr. V. said he would vote for the amendment offered by the gentleman from Kentucky, (Mr. Hardin,) which proposed to pay Mr. Moore; but should that be rejected, he would still vote to pay Mr. Letcher. The Committee had proposed to pay both, because they conceived Mr. Moore to be the certificated member, and because both the gentlemen had been detained here under the order of the House. The claim of Mr. Letcher certainly was not weakened by a decision in his favor by the tribunal (the people) to which the case was referred. Still, he would, for the reasons before stated, and in accordance with what the Committee had recommended last year, vote to pay both. It was a very peculiar case, and would not probably very soon occur again. He would prefer having the cases or claims of each gentleman brought before the House in the shape of distinct propositions, that one might not embarrass the other; but as the amendment was proposed, he should vote for it, and repeated that if rejected, he would vote for the original resolution.

Mr. LETCHER said he did not rise by any means to argue the question before the House. That he did not intend to do, but his object was to place himself *rectus in curia*. He had, at the last session disclaimed taking the proffered compensation, *without the seat*, but he had never said, that he would take no pay, if he got the seat, and having obtained it, through trials and tribulations, the question was a very different one, from what it was at the last session.

Mr. MASON of Virginia, said, that he could not vote for the amendment proposed by the gentleman from Kentucky. Its effect was to give to the two gentlemen pay as members of this House during the first session of the present Congress, when neither was permitted to take a seat. He understood the usage of the House to be that a gentleman contesting the right of a sitting member to it, was paid mileage to meet the expense of travelling to the seat of Government to assert an important constitutional right. This rule was founded in a desire to protect the right of suffrage, and to enable one otherwise without adequate means, to assert his rights. It was stated by the committee at the last session that Mr. Letcher was entitled to the certificate of election from the sheriffs. If he had received it, the case would have been but that which always before occurred, of one sitting and another contesting his right to the seat, and Mr. Letcher's right to his pay, would have been undoubted. The House did not permit him to take his seat, but resolved that, "it being impracticable to determine with any certainty, who is the rightful member, there should be a new election" that election has been held, and Mr Letcher is elected.

He would pay Mr. Moore mileage, but he could not give him more.

Mr. BEARDSLEY was in favor of paying each of the gentlemen their mileage, for the reasons which had been assigned by the gentleman from Virginia, (Mr. Mason.) Beyond this he would not go. As to Mr. Moore, as neither the House nor the people had decided that he was entitled to the seat, it was improper to pay him his per diem. In relation to the other gentlemen, (Mr. Letcher,) the House having declared that it could not decide who was entitled to the seat, had ordered a new election, and the question was referred back to the people, not as was supposed by the gentleman from Virginia, (Mr. Mason,) by way of appeal, or to decide the question which was before the House, but that they might choose a representative, without reference to the former election, or the contest which had grown out of it. Mr. Letcher had been chosen. It had been said that this was the first instance in which it was proposed to give full pay to both the individuals claiming a seat in the House. If this principle was established, there might be three or four competitors, and instead of paying the usual sum of $8 per day, we should have to pay 16, 24, or $32 per day. He repeated, in conclusion, that he should not object to paying each of the gentlemen their mileage, but no more.

Mr. JONES of Georgia, said this was a peculiar case. Ordinarily, in contested elections, one of the parties was admitted to the seat in the first instance, and if he was displaced, he was entitled to full pay up to the time of the decision. The successful claimant, in such case, was also paid from the commencement of the session. In the present case, as neither individual was permitted to take his seat, and the attendance of both was required here, by the course adopted by the House, he thought that each should be paid the usual per diem, and mileage. He entered into a history of the proceeeing of the last session, in relation to this contested election, and in conclusion declared his intention to vote for the amendment, and the resolution.

Mr. LANE said, a contested election was the voluntary act of the party or parties, and not the act of the House. In this case, the House was nearly balanced on the question which had been brought before it. They arrived at no satisfactory conclusion, and the question was referred back to the people of the District. They had decided in favor of Mr. Letcher. He belived it was not proper for the House to give full pay to both gentlemen. Under the circumstances, he could not vote to pay Mr. Moore his per diem. He would vote to pay him mileage; but this he would do with reluctance.

Mr. EVANS entered into a history of the proceedings, at the last session, connected with the contested election, and contended that it would be a bad precedent to give full pay to the unsuccessful claimant to a seat in the House.

Mr. CLAYTON, after adverting to the action of the House at the last session, contended that it was not proper for the House to pocket the money or retain it in the treasury, which of right belonged to a member from Kentucky. The House had determined at the last session, to submit the question of fact as to which of the gentlemen were entitled to a seat, to a jury of the people. The question had been very properly stated by the gentleman from Virginia, (Mr. Mason.) The People had decided the matter referred to them. In conclusion, he hoped the resolution would be adopted. He should also be in favor of paying Mr. Moore his mileage. He thought he was justly entitled to it, and it had been the usual practice heretofore to allow mileage to unsuccessful claimants to seats upon this floor.

Mr. BURGES said, the committee who investigated this subject at the last session, decided in favor of Mr. Moore, and the House determined that they could not decide either way, and sent the gentlemen back to the people. He contended that these contested elections should be investigated at the expense of the Government. It was proper to encourage the purification of elections. No person should be admitted to his seat, where there was any doubt as to his right. He would pay a man who came here to contest an election. If this was not done, great advantage would be given to a rich individual, who might come in conflict with a poor man, who was unable to undergo the expense of asserting what he might conceive to be his rights. It was upon this principle that he voted to pay Mr. Letcher, and upon the same principle he would vote to pay Mr. Moore.

Mr. JOHNSON, of Kentucky, said, that as both of the gentlemen were brought and kept here by the operation of law, he could not for his life see any difference between the two. He felt it to be his duty to vote for the original proposition, and he should also vote for the amendment, as he could not make a distinction between the parties.

Mr. CLAY said, it would be recollected that there was much unprofitable discussion at the last session in relation to this contested election. It seems that the same thing was again likely to take place. His purpose was to submit a motion, which would bring the debate to a close, previous to which he would make a remark or two. He agreed with the gentleman from Virginia (Mr. Mason) that the question as to which of the gentlemen was entitled to his seat, was in effect referred to the people. They had determined that question. Could we with propriety, cavil at their decision? As he remarked on a former occasion, he was in favor of paying Mr. Moore as much as the practice of the House would sanction. What that should be he knew not. He thought that the subject should be referred to a committee, that the precedents might be examined, who could report a resolution, allowing Mr. Moore what might be found to be right and proper. He was in favor of doing ample justice to Mr. Moore. The present resolution ought to be adopted. There could be no question of its propriety. While, therefore, he should on a proper occasion, be willing to examine the claim of Mr. Moore in a spirit of liberality, he felt constrained to move the Previous Question.

The motion was not seconded.

Mr. POLK called for the orders of the day. Yeas 93, nays 64.

The SPEAKER laid before the House the following message from the President of the United States; which was referred to the Committee on Revolutionary Claims:

To the House of Representatives of the U. States:

I transmit to the House of Representatives, for their consideration, a petition to the Congress of the United States, from Adelaide Grasse de Grochamps, one of the surviving daughters of the Count de Grasse, together with the letters which accompanied it. Translations of these are also sent.

ANDREW JACKSON.

Washington, 16th Feb., 1835.

Mr. WATMOUGH moved to postpone all the previous orders of the day, for the purpose of taking up the bill to regulate the pay of the navy.

Mr. POLK demanded the yeas and nays; which were ordered, and were, yeas 110, nays 103.

So the motion prevailed.

NAVY PAY BILL.

The House then took up the bill to regulate the pay of the Navy of the United States.

The question pending, was on the following amendment, offered by Mr. POPE:

"That the bill, with its amendments be submitted to the Committee of the Whole on the state of Union, with instructions to amend the same by

striking out from the thirty-second to the thirty-ninth line, inclusive, and inserting in lieu thereof—

"When commanding a squadron on foreign service, three thousand five hundred dollars.

"When commanding a single ship, or in any other service, three thousand dollars.

"When on leave, or waiting orders, two thousand dollars; and by striking out the remainder of the bill from the commencement of the one hundred and ninety-fifth line, beginning with the word 'including.'"

Mr. POPE expressed a hope that the House would at once act upon the bill, without further discussion.

Mr. WATMOUGH said he had hoped that the bill, as modified, and since presented by him to the House, in which the various amendments had been in part embodied, would have met with general concurrence; and he also hoped the House would come to a decision at once.

Mr. POPE said he could not accept the modifications proposed, but must insist on his amendment.

Mr. WISE was opposed to that part of the amendment to recommit, with instructions, and would rather vote against the whole bill.

Mr. HARDIN was of the same opinion.

Mr. WATMOUGH wished to know if it was necessary that the bill should go again into Committee of the Whole.

The CHAIR replied in the affirmative.

Mr. GRENNELL remarked, that inasmuch as the bill was now stripped of all its objectionable features, and would produce a great saving to the country, a'most $100,000 a year, he had hoped no objections would have been urged.

Mr. FILLMORE asked for a division of the question.

Mr. BEAUMONT moved to lay the motion to recommit, &c. on the table

Mr. GRENNELL asked for the yeas and nays; which were ordered.

The question was then taken and decided in the negative—yeas 75, nays 132.

The question then recurring on recommitting the bill—

Mr. POPE proposed to modify his instructions to the committee, so as to except, in the proposition to strike out, that part allowing ten cents per mile when under travelling orders, and proposing also to raise the pay of Captains on foreign service to $4,000

Mr. GILLET said the new bill, subsequently printed, would conflict with the above amendments. If the bill went into committee with the instructions proposed, their hands would be so tied up, that they would be unable to make the bill as perfect as was desired. He hoped the bill would be recommitted with instructions.

Mr. HARDIN also expressed the same wish.

Mr. GILLET then offered the following amendment to the bill:

"Strike out from line 191 to the end of the bill, and insert the following: That no allowance shall hereafter be made to any officer, or person employed in the naval service of the United States, for drawing bills, for receiving or disbursing money, or transacting any business for the Government of the United States, nor shall he be allowed servants, or pay for servants, or clothing or rations for them, or pay for the same, nor shall any allowance be made to him for rent of quarters, or to pay rent for furniture, or for lights or fuel, or for travelling expenses or transporting baggage, nor shall any such officer or person be allowed to transport, or aid in transporting, for pay, any specie or property for any person. It is hereby expressly declared that the yearly allowance provided in this act is all the pay, compensation, and allowance that shall be received under any circumstances whatever, by any such officer or person."

Mr. POPE agreed to accept it as a modification to his instructions.

Some conversation ensued on the subject of this amendment, conflicting with the other, between the CHAIR, Messrs. JONES, GILLET, and WATMOUGH; and Mr. POPE expressed a wish to withdraw his acceptance

The question was then taken on re committing the bill, and agreed to.

The question was then taken on re-committing the bill with instructions; negatived.

The House then, on motion of Mr. WATMOUGH, resolved itself into a Committee of the Whole on the state of the Union, Mr. BRIGGS in the Chair.

Mr. POPE then proposed his amendment as modified.

Mr. WISE proposed to amend the same by fixing the pay of captains in foreign service at $4000; when on other duty $3,500; when off duty 2,500.

Mr. WISE made a few remarks in favor of his amendment, contending that by the amendment offered by Mr. Pope, there was no increase whatever in the pay of the naval officers. Mr. W. hoped his own would be adopted, as the smallest possible increase that could reasonably be adopted.

Mr. JONES said a few words in reply.

Mr. FOSTER said, if much time was consumed in committee, the bill would be lost in the House.

Mr. BATES opposed the original amendment.

Mr. GRENNELL said that nine hundred and fifty, out of every thousand officers, were satisfied with the amendment as offered by the gentleman from Kentucky.

Mr. WATMOUGH hoped the whole ground was not to be gone over again.

Mr. MASON, of Virginia, hoped the amendment of his colleague would be adopted in lieu of the gentleman's from Kentucky, because by the latter, an officer who had been thirty-five years in the service, would receive only five hundred dollars more than one who had only served five years.

After a few further remarks from Mr. C. P. WHITE and Mr. JONES, the question on the amendment was taken, Ayes 68, noes 24. No quorum voting.

Mr. HARPER made a few observations in favor of the increased pay.

Mr. MANN said if the amendment of the gentleman from Virginia should be rejected, he would, as an act of justice to that meritorious class of persons embraced in the bill, renew the proposition heretofore offered by the gentleman from Maine, (Mr. Jarvis.)

The question was again taken on Mr. WISE'S amendment, when there appeared, ayes 72, noes 40. Still no quorum voting, tellers were demanded, and on the division, there were ayes 79, noes 46. So the amendment was agreed to The question then recurred on the amendment as amended, which was agreed to without a division.

Mr. POPE moved to insert an amendment in relation to the mileage of officers when travelling under orders.

Mr. GILLET here moved his amendment, as printed above.

Mr. G. explained that his object was to confine officers in all respects to their salaries: An idea had been advanced on a former occasion by a gentleman from Rhode Island (Mr. Pearce) that officers ought to receive an extra allowance for the transportation of specie, which Mr. G. thought very objectionable.

The CHAIR decided this amendment not to be in order at that time.

The question was then taken on Mr. POPE'S amendment, and there appeared, Ayes 85, noes 16. No quorum voting, it was taken again by tellers, and there were ayes 83, noes 35. So the amendment was adopted.

Mr. JARVIS then called the attention of the committee to the following provision for surgeons of the navy, "and when appointed to perform the duties of surgeon general, his pay shall be increased three-fourths."

Mr. J. moved to strike out this provision, because there was in fact no such officer as that of surgeon general known in the service, and an appropriation bill was not the place for creating such an office.

Mr. WATMOUGH explained: The service had suffered greatly for the want of a surgeon general, and he hoped the provision would not be stricken out.

The question was taken, and there appeared yeas 60, nays 55.

Mr. JARVIS withdrew his motion, whereupon—

Mr. MANN, of New York, renewed it, and the amendment was agreed to. Yeas 95, nays not counted.

Mr. WISE moved that the Committee rise and report the bill to the House.

Mr. GILLET then renewed his amendment. Negatived. Yeas 61, nays 69.

Mr. JACKSON, of Massachusetts, then moved to amend the clause for the provision for officers on furlough entitling them to receive two-thirds of the pay to which they would have been entitled if on leave of absence, by striking out "two-thirds," and inserting one-half. Agreed to.

Mr. GILLET moved to strike out the following clause: "Officers temporarily performing duties belonging to those of a higher grade, shall receive the compensation allowed to such higher grade, while actually so employed."

Mr. C. P. WHITE opposed the motion.

Mr MANN, of New York, was in favor of the motion. The officers in our s rvice should receive a pay corresponding to their rank, and to more.

Mr. BURGES opposed the amendment.

Mr. JONES remarked, that the provision, as it stood, would go to pay two officers for performing the same duty, and he hoped the amendment would be adopted.

Mr. CLAY said, to him it mattered not what might be the grade of an officer, if he performed the duty of a higher grade than his own, he ought to be paid accordingly. If a Lieutenant performed the duty of a Commander, he was equitably entitled to a Commander's pay, for the time he was so employed.

The question was then taken on the amendment—ayes 34, nays 82; no quorum. It was again taken by tellers, when there appeared, ayes 44, nays 96. Still no quorum voting.

The CHAIR ascertained that there was a quorum in the House, and the amendment was then negatived, without a division.

Mr. JARVIS then moved to amend the following provision of the bill: "Lieutenants Commanding, $1,800, on other duty, $1,500, waiting orders, $1,200;" and insert in lieu thereof the following: "Lieutenants Commanding on duty over ten years' service, $1,500; under ten years' service and on duty, $1,200; waiting orders, $1,000." Negatived, without a division.

Mr. JARVIS then moved to amend the following clause: "passed Midshipmen on duty $750; waiting orders $600" by inserting in lieu of those sums respectively, $600 for the former, and $500 for the latter. Negatived without a division.

On motion of Mr. WARD, the Committee then rose and reported the bill with the amendments to the House.

Mr. JONES then moved to amend the two clauses relating to the pay of captains, and asked for the yeas and nays; not ordered—ayes 38, nays 129.

The amendment was then negatived without a division.

The other amendments agreed to in Committee were then concurred in by the House.

Mr GILLET then proposed the amendment to the House which he had submitted in Committee of the Whole, in relation to allowances. Mr G. urged its adoption on the principle that it was best to allow officers a fixed salary than subject them to the contingencies of indirect and extra allowance, and asked for the yeas and nays, which were ordered.

Mr. McKIM opposed the amendment, and asked how could the merchants call upon and expect the captains of ships of war to br ng home specie from South America, unless they were paid for it, and in case of war, how could its safety be insured by any other conveyance.

Mr. GILLET said his amendment was not confined to the allowance incident to the transportation of specie alone.

Mr. McKIM still thought the amendment objectionable, as that was one of the most important articles of transportation. It was allowed in the British navy, and he believed in other countries also.

Mr. BURGES also opposed the amendment.

Mr. HARDIN made some observations on the nature of the services expected of our naval officers

ers connected with commercial transactions, and limited to allowances which had been made by secretaries of the Navy under former administrations.

Mr. ADAMS, of Massachusetts, made some explanatory remarks on the practices which had obtained in the Government, on this subject; and referred also to the practices of the British Government. It was almost indispensable that specie should at times be conveyed in armed vessels.

Mr. MANN moved to amend the amendment of Mr. Gillet, by prohibiting the captains of the navy from carrying specie and other property. He said, he thought the present system productive of gross abuses. Mr. M. also made sundry references to the system of allowing extra rations, and allowances in the army, and he hoped the House would take the present opportunity of cutting loose off from the navy.

Mr. GILLET was understood to except the motion of his colleague.

Mr. VINTON said, as the amendment prohibited officers from having any servants, he wished to know if the clause was intended to prohibit them from employing servants at their own expense?

Mr. WATMOUGH moved a substitute to the amendment by inserting in lieu thereof a proviso, that no allowance should hereafter be made or drawing bills or receiving or disbursing moneys belonging to the Government of the United States, nor for clothing nor rations, &c. Which was negatived.

Mr. PARKER asked for a division of the question on the original amendment, but it was decided not to be in order.

Mr. JONES moved an amendment to the amendment, and said he wished to make the officers of the navy accountable to the department for what they received; otherwise they might charge what they pleased.

Mr. McKIM briefly opposed the amendment. It had long been the practice of the navy to carry money, and if they were to receive nothing for it, how could they be expected to undertake so troublesome and responsible a duty?

Mr. JONES said it was a disgrace to our naval service that the officers should be allowed to receive pay for such labor. Mr. J. then asked for the yeas and nays, which were not ordered, and the amendment was negatived without a division.

Mr. FILLMORE proposed to amend the amendment by leaving in the bill one ration per day for officers on service. Agreed to—ayes 93, noes 43.

Mr. C. P. WHITE moved further to amend the same by striking out the words, person employed.

Mr. LOYAL moved to amend the amendment by a clause prohibiting any officer or other person employed in the naval service, from taking his wife or any female member of his family on board a ship at sea, and asked for the yeas and nays, but they were not ordered.

Mr. L. said that the only occasion on which our navy had been insulted with impunity arose from a lady having been on board.

Mr. STEELE explained that the facts of the case referred to, were not understood. There had been no court of inquiry on the subject, the captain, a very brave and meritorious officer, having died of yellow fever on his return to Savannah.

Mr. J. Q. ADAMS opposed the amendment; and he had no apprehensions on the subject. In time of war there was little probability of a case occurring, and even if it did, he did not believe that a commander would refuse to resent an insult, because his wife was on board. The case mentioned by the gentleman from Virginia might have happened, but one swallow did not make a summer.

Mr. WISE remarked, that the provision might be proper enough, but it had better be left to another bill.

Mr. FOSTER asked, if the amendment was in order?

The CHAIR said, in his opinion, it was not perhaps entirely in order, but as the House had chosen to entertain it, the Chair had not interfered.

Mr. LOYALL explained, that he had no intention of casting any reflection upon a high and gallant officer, in alluding to the case he had, but had merely adverted to it, as going to show the necessity of such a provision as that he had proposed. He was convinced the practice was a bad one.

Mr. BURD made a few remarks in favor of the amendment.

Mr. TURRILL moved that the House adjourn. Negatived.

The question was then taken on Mr. LOYALL'S amendment, and it was negatived. Ayes 60, noes 106.

The question was then taken on Mr. GILLET'S amendment, and carried without a division.

Mr. JARVIS then moved the amendments proposed by him in Committee of the Whole, which were rejected.

The question then recurring, on ordering the bill to be engrossed,

Mr. MARDIS asked for the yeas and nays; which were ordered.

Mr. PARKS moved an adjournment. Negatived. Ayes 74, noes 103.

The question was then taken and decided as follows: Yeas 102, nays 82.

So the bill was ordered to be engrossed for a third reading.

On motion of Mr. WISE,

The House adjourned.

IN SENATE.

Wednesday, Feb. 18, 1835.

The CHAIR communicated a letter from the Post Office Department, made in obedience to a resolution of the Senate, requiring a statement of the debts of the Department; which, on motion of Mr. GRUNDY, was referred to the Post Office Committee, and ordered to be printed.

The CHAIR also laid before the Senate a letter from the War Department, with a communication relative to the disbursements of money, goods, or effects, in the trade and intercourse with the Indians; which, on motion of Mr. WHITE, was referred to the Committee on Indian Affairs, and ordered to be printed.

On motion of Mr. CLAYTON, the Judiciary Committee were discharged from the further consideration of the petition of Samuel H. Thompson, and the petition of James M. Elford, and of the sureties of Archibald H. Sneed.

On motion of Mr. EWING, the Committee on Finance was discharged from the further consideration of the petition of John Sachett.

The CHAIR also laid before the Senate a letter from the War Department, with a communication relative to the disbursements of money, goods, or effects, in the trade and intercourse with the Indians; which, on motion of Mr. WHITE, was referred to the Committee on Indian Affairs, and ordered to be printed.

Mr. TOMLINSON, from the Committee on Pensions, to which was referred the bills from the House of Representatives granting pensions to Isaac Janvier and John Dal, reported the same, severally, without amendment.

On motion of Mr. SHEPLEY, the Committee on Claims was discharged from the further consideration of the petitions of Sylvester Day, Abraham Morrill, Noah Brown, and others.

Mr. BENTON, by the instructions of the Military Committee, made the following report:

That it is expedient to increase the appropriations heretofore made for the national defence; and that in addition to the sums now contained in the bill for fortifications, and in addition to the two sums of $100,000 each, heretofore recommended by this committee to be inserted in the said bill for fortifications and the armament thereof, the further sum of $500,000 be recommended to be inserted therein, for the repair, completion, and construction of fortifications, and to provide the necessary armament thereof. And the committee have directed their Chairman to move an amendment accordingly, at the proper time, to the Fortification Appropriation Bill.

Mr. PRESTON, from the Committee on Pensions, to which was referred the bill from the House of Representatives granting a pension to William Slocum, reported the same without amendment; but with an expression of opinion by the Committee, against its passage.

The following resolutions were submitted:

By Mr. HENDRICKS:

Resolved, That the Secretary of War be directed to cause a survey to be made of a road from the Maumee bay through the northern counties of Indiana, to, or near the rapids of Illinois river, and thence to the Mississippi river, to some point between Rock Island and Quincy.

By Mr. KENT:

Resolved, That the Secretary of the Treasury be directed to transmit to the Senate any information he may possess in relation to the obstructions in the navigation of the Potomac between Washington and Georgetown, in this District.

By Mr. HENDRICKS:

Resolved, That the Committee on Indian Affairs be instructed to inquire into the expediency of allowing to Mr. Marshall, Indian Agent, the amount of certain abstracts herewith submitted, for expenditures in the Indian service. Agreed to.

Mr. BENTON submitted the following resolution:

Resolved, That the resolution adopted by the Senate, on the 28th day of March, in the year 1834, in the following words: "*Resolved, That the President, in the late Executive proceedings, in relation to the public revenue, has assumed upon himself authority and power not conferred by the constitution and laws, but in derogation of both,*" be, and the same is hereby ordered to be expunged from the journals of the Senate: because the said resolution is illegal and unjust, of evil example, indefinite and vague, expressing a criminal charge, without specification, and was irregularly and unconstitutionally adopted by the Senate in subversion of the rights of defence, which belong to an accused and impeachable officers; and at a time, and under circumstances to involve peculiar injury to the political rights and pecuniary interests of the People of the United States.

The resolution having been read,

Mr. POINDEXTER rose and said he doubted, whether it was in order to offer such a proposition, and therefore, he objected to the reception of the motion of the honorable Senator. The constitution of the United States, said Mr. P., makes it the duty of each House of Congress to keep a journal of its proceedings. Each House may incorporate with its journals an unconstitutional act, or Congress may pass an unconstitutional law; but it does not follow that the matter which is a part of the history of the session, should not be on the journals. To omit to place it on the journals would be a violation of its constitutional duty. The journal is only a history of the proceedings of this body—there is no principle involved in it. How are we to fulfil our constitutional obligations, if, after we repeat of having done an act, we allow a proceeding to expunge it? The amendment of a journal must be made on the day when it is read. Is it in order to expunge any part of the journal of the Senate during the administration of John Adams or Thomas Jefferson? If it be, Mr. P. said he could find enough there that he would be willing to expunge. The motion to amend, then, must be made on the day the journal is read, or it is out of order to move it afterwards; and he insisted it should not be received. If the honorable gentleman from Missouri thinks the resolution complained of is wrong in principle, let him introduce a countervailing resolution, and then the Senate can take it into consideration; and if there be an error in it, they can correct it. Mr. P. said he objected to the act that which the constitution forbids—to do that, which, if we had not done it, would have been a violation of the constitution of the United States. Without offering an opinion about the resolution, or whether it is such as the constitution justifies or not, Mr. P. said he considered a record of it, whether it be creditable to the body or not, to be a constitutional duty.

Mr. BROWN said it appeared to him, with great deference to the honorable gentleman from Mississippi, that the remarks he had just made, and the course he had indicated as the most appropriate one to be pursued in this case, were not extremely regular. If the proposition, said he, contains matter derogatory to the dignity of this body, and indecorous in itself, then it may

with propriety be arrested in its incipient state. But it is not said that this resolution is indecorous or derogatory to the Senate. The honorable gentleman says it is unconstitutional to alter a journal. But is it not most manifest that the gentleman anticipates the decision of the case, which would be much more proper at another time? The exact question to be decided is, whether the resolution is constitutional or not. But there is another question intimately connected with this matter, which may well address itself to the consideration of the Senate. Several of the State Legislatures have passed resolutions expressive of their opinions upon the very point to which this proposition distinctly applies, and will the Senate, representing the sovereignties of the several States, refuse to listen to this proposition expressed by the regular constitutional organ of the States? If it be so, however honorable gentlemen may profess to reverence State rights, certain it is that such a course is much better calculated to bring contempt upon the rights of the States, than any other course that could be pursued. Yes, sir, the case is presented of the Senate's refusing to entertain a proposition upon which the States themselves have expressed a solemn and deliberate opinion. If this doctrine be true, the legitimate consequence is that all investigation must be stifled. Whenever an important question is presented which involves a question of constitutionality, and there are many which are supposed to do so at the threshold, the honorable gentleman might rise in his place and move that it be not considered. The practice is calculated to suppress inquiry, and ought not to be admitted. Suppose an arbitrary majority of the Senate should refuse to entertain a proposition which was upon its face manifestly proper, but which did not exactly quadrate with their own notions. Would the Senate suppress or deny inquiry by refusing to receive it? It was so clearly inadmissible that he could not assent to the honorable gentleman's motion.

Mr. LEIGH expressed a wish that the gentleman from Mississippi would withdraw his motion not to receive the proposition. For it must be evident to every gentleman that the debate must come up upon his motion, if it was not withdrawn.

Mr. POINDEXTER here interposed. He begged to put a question to the honorable gentleman from Virginia. Suppose, after a bill had passed the Senate, and had been sent to the other House, a proposition were made to consider it, would the consideration of the motion be proper?

Mr. LEIGH replied, that he was not well acquainted with the rules of the Senate. He could not answer the gentleman's question. But he wanted the debate to come up, for he saw it must come up. He wanted to give full time to the gentlemen on the other side to come out and discuss this question. For himself, he was satisfied that this was a proposition, the effect of which would be, not only to expunge from the journal of this House, but to expunge this body from the constitution. He wanted to meet the resolution—and he was desirous of giving the gentleman from Missouri a full and fair opportunity of discussing the question—he wished to see him come fully prepared, for he knew he was not so now. He wished to hear that gentleman's reasons, and therefore he hoped his friend from Mississippi would withdraw his opposition to the reception of the resolution.

Mr. POINDEXTER said, as he believed the motion involved the merits of the proposition, he would therefore withdraw it.

The resolution having been received,

Mr. BENTON said, as it contained the heads of the topics which he meant to discuss, he moved that it be printed; which was agreed to.

Mr. WAGGAMAN gave notice, that to-morrow he would move to take up, the bill to establish a daily mail between Macon, in Georgia, and New Orleans.

The bill for the relief of David Beard was taken up, considered as in Committee of the Whole, and ordered to be engrossed for a third reading.

On motion of Mr. POINDEXTER, the Senate resumed, as in Committee of the Whole, the bill supplementary to the act granting a township of land to certain exiles from Poland.

After adopting an amendment submitted by Mr. ROBINSON, confining the Poles to such lands as have not been settled, and which have been surveyed,

Mr. KANE asked the yeas and nays upon the engrossment of the bill, which were ordered, and are as follows:

YEAS—Messrs. Benton, Black, Buchanan, Calhoun, Clay, Clayton, Ewing, Frelinghuysen, Goldsborough, Kent, King of Alabama, King of Georgia, Knight, Leigh, Linn, McKean, Moore, Naudain, Poindexter, Porter, Prentiss, Preston, Robbins, Silsbee, Smith, Tallmadge, Tomlinson—27.

NAYS—Messrs. Bell, Brown, Grundy, Hill, Kane, Mangum, Morris, Robinson, Shepley, Swift, Tyler, Waggaman, White, Wright—14.

So the bill was ordered to be engrossed for a third reading.

On motion of Mr. LINN, it was ordered that the standing hour of meeting for the remainder of the session, shall be 11 o'clock.

Mr. CLAYTON, from the Judiciary Committee, reported a bill relative to the boundary line between the States of Alabama and Georgia; which was read the first time, and ordered to a second reading.

The following resolution, submitted yesterday by Mr. PORTER, was taken up, considered, and agreed to:

Resolved, That the Committee on Indian Affairs be instructed to inquire into the expediency of making an appropriation for the purpose of holding a treaty or convention with the Caddo Indians, for the extinguishment of a claim set up by them to a tract of country in the northwestern part of the State of Louisiana, and the southwestern part of the Territory of Arkansas.

The Senate then resumed the consideration of the bill to repeal the act limiting the term of certain officers, commonly called the four years law, approved in May, 1820.

Mr. CLAY said, the subject under consideration was one, on which he had felt extremely anxious; and one involving the same principles as those on which he had the honor at the last session to offer a resolution to the Senate. These principles were the results of long and mature reflection; and from their being incorporated in the bill, he felt called upon to defend it. He would say, that he differed with the gentleman from New York, (Mr. Wright) in his comparison of the dangers last winter and this. He knew that the scenes alluded to, arose from one of the most extraordinary measures ever witnessed in a free government. He saw no congruity between those measures and the present report. That was no less than the assumption of all power by one person, as was shown by the removal of the deposites, by the protest, and by the report of the Secretary of the Treasury. But he regretted that any reference had been made to the Bank. Nothing more could be hoped for in favor of that institution. It was gone, and no one could ever expect its recharter, especially if he looked to the disposition of the other House, and to different sections of the country. He believed its affairs had been justly and properly administered. But he was not disposed to look too much on the bright side of the question. The Bank was gone and the currency of the country deranged; on its ruins a multitude of local Banks would spring up in every part of these twenty four sovereign States. Money would be plenty; property would increase in nominal value, and the country be flooded with spurious bills. It was the misfortune of this country that the great principles of reform should be connected with an unpopular institution. He had warned his friends not to connect the subject of preventing the increase of Executive power with the fortunes of the Bank. He considered the bill before the Senate totally divested of any connexion with the Bank, and separated from all the political questions that distracted the country.

There were duties, said Mr. C., transcendent duties, far paramount to party purposes—duties we owe our country. It had been well said, that in the perpetual flow of the political wheel, those who are up to-day may be down to-morrow; but if we adhered to principles, to manly, independent principles, it was no matter whether we were up or down.

Mr. C. said, in regard to the question under consideration that the paticipation of the Senate in the power of appointment was merely nominal, if it acted without the reasons of the President. For if they sanctioned an appointment, the President could eject the officer from his place the next day, if he pleased. If the office was once vacant, it was beyond the control of the Senate. Should they reject one nomination, the President might nominate another and another of his creatures, until the Senate would be forced to yield, or leave the office vacant.

The power of removal, as now exercised, was entirely despotic in its application. In the recesses of the executive mansion, the question was decided, while the officer remained unseen and unheard. The President was sole judge, jurors, and executioner. And further, it was an irresponsible power, as, without his reasons were given, no one could call him to an account for his actions. He was beyond the power of impeachment, if such a thing was capable of being practically carried out in such a government as ours. Responsibility was as essential an ingredient of a free government, as the vital air which surrounds us, was necessary for animal life. Every officer was responsible to the people; all were public servants; and if one servant removed another, he ought to render an account, to give his reasons to the nation. There would be a day of reckoning to all; and he would appeal to the Senate, if there had not been abuse? Mr. C. then referred to the removal of a marshal in Maryland, and to a friend of his in Kentucky, who had been dismissed from office.

The gentleman from New York, (Mr. Wright,) had ingeniously analized the mass over which Executive power had its influence, and upon each division asked the question, Was there any danger in that? He (Mr. C.) perfectly understood the nature of such appeals; they were better suited for the *stump* than the Senate of the United States. We had not yet felt the weight of executive influence; the power of removal was still in its infancy; scarly six years old. It had not yet been applied to the army and navy, and it could not be brought to bear on the pensioners.

Suppose, said Mr. C., it should be applied to the army; if an officer stood in the way of the President's designs, and he refused to yield, the President would remove him, and put another in his place. In this way, the army and navy might soon be filled with the supple tools of executive power. Whoever would take a just view of these principles, let him look to the nature of man— The very tendency of these things was, to produce servility. There were several stages in the descent: First, silence. If an officer happened to differ with the President on some political points, he would be reserved; his friends and relations would advise him to be prudent, and say nothing. But the place admits of no neutrality; hungry expectants are crowding around, and the officer must become warm and active, or he is dismissed. What a multitude of officers, so situated, did the Post Office Department, the Custom-houses, and the Land Offices, furnish. They were a well-regulated body, a *corps d' armee*, a rallying point for political action, forming committees of correspondence all over the country. It was a revival of the institutions of feudal times, filling the land with barons and feudatories. The Senator from New York had used the term "inherent power." This was a new source of power. He was ignorant of what the Senator meant by inherent power. He had only known implied and expressed power.

[Mr. WRIGHT here rose to explain. He meant no other power than what was derived from the Constitution.]

Mr. C. then proceeded. The Senator from Pennsylvania had spoken of "sovereign power." This was also a new idea in this country. Did the Senator bring back with him his definition of executive power from Russia, where he had seen the wretched serf toiling three days in the week for his lordly master?

Mr. C. went on to show, that the power of removal was not an executive power, but rather a judicial one, as it implied a condemnation. He

believed the constitution pointed out no other way of removal than by impeachment. But if the necessity of the case required a way less tedious, he thought it should be classed as a legislative power, since the legislature had the right to create office, or abolish it.

Mr. C. then went back to examine the decision in 1789. On looking over that debate, Mr. C. said he had found his opinions changed, with regard to some of the great men who acted conspicuous parts then.

Mr. C. concluded by saying, that he had stated, in the beginning, that the power of dismissal or suspension was necessary. He only contended, that it ought to be regulated by law.

When Mr. CLAY concluded,

Mr. GRUNDY rose, and spoke in opposition to the bill.

After some time, Mr. G. yielded the floor to Mr. MANGUM, on whose motion,

The Senate adjourned.

HOUSE OF REPRESENTATIVES.

WEDNESDAY, February 18, 1835.

Mr. DICKERSON, on leave, presented certain amendments to the bill to prevent evasion of the revenue laws; which were ordered to be printed.

Unfavorable reports on various petitions were made by Messrs. E. WHITTLESEY, BANKS, and TURRILL, from their respective committees.

On motion of Mr. CAVE JOHNSON, the bill supplementary to an act passed 4th July, 1832, for the final adjustment of land claims in the Southeastern District of Louisiana, was recommitted to the Committee on Private Land Claims.

On motion of Mr. BINNEY, by leave:

Resolved, That the Committee of Ways and Means be instructed to inquire into the expediency of making an appropriation for the repair of Fort Mifflin and the adjacent pier, on the river Delaware, for the purposes of temporary defence.

Mr. EWING presented certain resolutions of the Legislature of the State of Indiana; which were laid on the table, and ordered to be printed.

Mr. H. EVERETT presented a report and resolutions of the Legislature of Vermont, in favor of the distribution of the proceeds of the sale of the public lands among the several States—in favor of a national Bank—declaring the course of the Executive in removing the deposites from the Bank of the United States, not warranted by the constitution—in opposition to the Protest of the President, &c. &c. Mr. E. moved to lay the report and resolutions on the table, and that they be printed.

On motion, the report and resolutions were read.

The question on printing being propounded from the Chair, there appeared 69 in the affirmative.

Before those in the negative were counted, Mr. SLADE demanded the yeas and nays, which were ordered.

Mr. SLADE said the resolutions emanated from one of the sovereign States of this confederacy, and he thought should be treated at least with so much respect as to order their printing. He referred to the importance of some of the topics embraced in the resolutions, particularly as regarded the public lands, upon which the House might shortly be called on to act, as a reason why the resolutions should be printed.

Mr. CAGE said no man repudiated more than he did some of the principles contained in the resolutions. But he submitted whether it was not going too far to refuse to print this document, coming, as it did, from the Legislature of one of the States of the Union; he hoped that those who agreed with him, in relation to the contents of the resolutions, would withdraw all objection to the printing. It could do no injustice, and he would vote for the printing out of respect to the Legislature of Vermont.

Mr. TURRILL said he was disposed to pay all due respect to the Legislature of Vermont. At the same time he felt greater respect for this body. At the last session he had opposed the printing of the panic memorials which had been sent here. He had done this on account of the expense, and because he believed that by printing and sending those memorials out, an excitement would be created, credit destroyed, and many individuals of large fortunes would, (as the result proved,) be sacrificed and ruined. He was opposed to the present motion to print, not merely because of the expense, but on the ground that the resolutions reflected upon the action of this House. It would be recollected that after a protracted debate of some months, this House, at the last session, sustained the Executive in the course taken in relation to the removal of the deposites from the Bank of the United States.—Months after this decision of the House, and after the adjournment of Congress, the Legislature of Vermont passed these resolutions under consideration, one of which contains an unjustifiable attack, not only upon the Executive, but upon this House.

Mr. H. EVERETT believed this would be the first instance in which any objection had ever been made to the printing of any thing coming from the Legislature of a State to this House; and he could not but express his great surprise at the grounds of exception taken by the gentleman from New York, (Mr. Turrill.) Mr. E. would respectfully ask that gentleman if he was prepared to say that the Legislature of one of the States of the Union might not express their opinion on the acts and proceedings of that House? He begged to hear the gentleman's reasons for the ground he had assumed, before he called upon the House to adopt it, in refusing what was merely a mark of respect, paid to every memorial from every State Legislature, whatever might be its character. He hoped the gentleman would either do this, or withdraw his objection to the motion.

Mr. CLAY asked for the reading of the resolutions; which being done,

Mr. C. said he hoped all opposition to the printing would be withdrawn. It was true they were not addressed to this House, but to the members from Vermont. It had been the uniform practice of the House to print every such communication, when presented. The result was expressed the sentiments of the Legislature of Vermont on particular subjects. He dissented from the position which was assumed in them; but he hoped that, coming as they did from a State Legislature, the opposition to the printing would be withdrawn.

Mr. BYNUM was sorry that any opposition should be made to printing the resolutions. There was no man more opposed than himself to the doctrines which they contained. If he was ten times more opposed to these doctrines than he was, he would not deny to the Legislature of Vermont, or to her members upon this floor, the privilege of printing this document.

It was true, he believed, that in another quarter, a similar application for printing resolutions adopted by an independent State, had been refused. God forbid, said Mr. B. that this House should ever exhibit so factious a spirit, as to follow a factious example. He hoped that opposition to the printing would be withdrawn, and that the House would not countenance the course which had been adopted by another body on a similar case.

Mr. SLADE contended that a refusal to print the resolutions would be disrespectful to the State of Vermont. The State Legislatures had as much right to be heard here, in some form, as individuals. This was the only form in which the Legislatures could be heard. The Legislature of Vermont met in October last. That was the first opportunity which had been presented of expressing their views upon the great questions referred to in their resolutions.

Mr. BEARDSLEY said, it was because the resolutions were disrespectful, and for that cause only, that he objected to printing them. The gentleman from Vermont (Mr. Slade) contended that it would be disrespectful to the Legislature of Vermont, if the House refused to print their resolutions. In reply, he would remark, that he presumed no person would have opposed the motion. If the resolutions had been drawn up in a decent manner, and were respectful to the House. But he contended that they contained a direct denunciation of what had been done by this House. He denied the right of the Legislature

of Vermont to pronounce judgment on this House, and then call upon it to record their condemnation. He read a passage from one of the resolutions, which charged the President with having acted in derogation of the constitution and laws, in the removal of the deposites from the Bank of the United States. The resolution was adopted in November last. This House had previously decided, that the Executive, in the measure referred to, had not transcended his constitutional privilege—that he had not acted "in derogation of the constitution and laws." He repeated in conclusion, that whatever others might do, for one he would not vote to record the judgment of condemnation which had been pronounced against this House by the Legislature of Vermont.

Mr. FOSTER denied that the House had come to any direct decision on the subject of the removal of the deposites. It had been in vain attempted to procure a vote of the House, as to the propriety of the removal of the public moneys. The Committee of Ways and Means had made a labored report on the subject, and had come to the conclusion, that the deposites should not be restored. This was the only point decided. The committee knew to a well the temper and disposition of the House to propose a direct vote as to the propriety of the Executive measure. He was astonished that the gentleman from New York (Mr. Beardsley) should now get up and contend that the House had decided this question. Suppose the Legislature of Vermont had expressed different opinions from those entertained by a majority of this House, was that any reason why the printing of the resolutions should be refused? We were almost every day called upon by individuals to reverse the action of this House, and every year we were asked by the State Legislatures to do the same thing. Was such a course disrespectful? Certainly not.

Mr. SUTHERLAND wished to know whether the Legislature of Vermont had requested that the resolutions should be presented to the House. He asked that they be read.

The resolutions were again read.

They were not addressed to the House.

Mr. PATTON was in favor of the motion to print. There was, he believed, but one precedent, and that was a recent one, where a proposition of this character had failed. He was not at liberty to refer particularly to this precedent; but it was one which the House ought to condemn. He appealed to the House to say, whether an instance of the kind could be found, at least from 1798 to the present time, where either branch of Congress had refused to receive or treat with respect any communication coming from the Legislature of an independent State, regarding the public policy and liberty? He should regard a different decision as portentous. He dissented from each and all of the views contained in the resolutions of the Legislature of Vermont. It was, however, a matter of no sort of importance what were the particular views of this Legislature. They had a right to present them here, and they were entitled to respect. He trusted, as this was the first effort which had been made here out of hundreds and thousands of cases, to adopt a course which he deemed highly improper, that it would be promptly and decidedly condemned by the House.

Mr. P. referred to the history of the proceedings at the last session, on the subject of the removal of the deposites. He did not know what was then the judgment of the House in regard to the propriety of the removal. There was no such proposition presented for the decision of the House. That was a matter of no consequence. It was admitted by all, that the question was one of vital importance, and the Legislature of Vermont, as well as that of every other State, had the right to express their views upon the subject.

Mr. BURGES never expected to hear what he had heard this day. He did not suppose that any member on this floor would attempt to silence the voice of a whole State——

Mr. WATMOUGH here interrupted Mr. Burges, and called for the orders of the day.

Carried.

The SPEAKER laid before the House a letter

from the Secretary of War, enclosing a geological report of Mr. Featherstonhaugh; which was laid on the table, and ordered to be printed.

Mr. BEATY moved to print 1200 extra copies of said report. The motion lies over one day.

A bill from the Senate for the relief of the representative of Robert Jewett, deceased, was read twice, and committed.

The bill supplementary to the act for the construction of a lateral branch of the Baltimore and Ohio Rail Road to the City of Washington, was read the third time.

Mr. PARKER entered at length into his objections against the passage of this bill, quoting the acts passed by Congress and the Legislature of Maryland, chiefly on the ground that it gave the company privileges too great and extensive.

Mr. CHINN said, the objections of the gentleman were extraordinary, for he understood him, the other day, to object to the bill because the Committee on the District of Columbia had refused to grant the company sufficient privileges; and he now opposed it because the privileges were too large.

Mr. PARKER explained: He wished the benefits of the bill to be extended to every part of the District.

Mr. JACKSON, of Massachusetts, was in favor of the bill.

The bill was then read a third time and passed.

NAVY PAY BILL.

The bill to regulate the pay of the officers of the Navy of the United States was then taken up.

The bill was read a third time, and the question recurring on its final passage—

Several members rose, but—

Mr. CROCKETT obtained the floor, and said: Mr. Speaker, as this bill has consumed no less than three weeks in discussion, and as I had a bill made the order of the day, the day after this bill, viz. the 16th of December, and as I see a disposition to speak more on the subject, as speaking has become so fashionable here, I am therefore bound, to move the previous question.

Mr. HARDIN hoped his friend from Tennessee would withdraw the motion.

Mr. CROCKETT. I can't do it, sir.

Mr. JARVIS moved a call of the House.

Ordered. Yeas 125.

The call was proceeded with, and 210 members being found present—

Mr. BOCKEE moved to suspend all further proceedings on the call. Agreed to.

The motion for the previous question was not seconded. Ayes 82, noes 90.

Mr. HARDIN then obtained the floor, and said he wished to submit a few remarks to the House on the bill under consideration, which was one of greater magnitude than was generally supposed. In February 1834, a standing Committee of the House had reported a bill to equalise the pay of officers of the Army and Navy; the bill was referred back to a select Committee, who in May, 1834, reported a substitute in lieu of it, and both the original and substitute were referred to a Committee of the whole House. A variety of amendments were made, in Committee, on the original bill; and yesterday the question was taken upon engrossing the substitute, before it was adopted, in lieu of the original bill, and he called upon the Clerk to say if he was not correct in this statement.

The SPEAKER said, that was not material, and was not then a question of order

Mr. HARDIN did not desire to be understood as making it a question of order, because, although he had had the honor of a seat in parliamentary bodies for nearly twenty-four years, he never once had the honor of presiding over any deliberative body, either as Speaker, or as deputy Speaker, or as Speaker's Chairman, for he was never accustomed to wait round the Speaker's chair, and of course he was ignorant of all the forms of order. He had only referred to the proceeding on the bill for the purpose of showing the anxiety of the House to get the question, by having ordered an amendment to be engrossed instead of the original bill. He regretted that the subject had been so earnestly pressed upon the consideration of the House.

One argument had been urged in favor of legislating upon this subject, which, in his opinion, was altogether unsustainable. It was remarked, that we were out of debt; at peace with all the world; that our finances were in a flourishing condition; and that now was the time to increase the pay of officers of the navy. In answer to this, he would only remark, that we had to legislate for the future; that however we might increase the pay, that increase would remain hereafter for ages to come. In regulating the pay of the army, the navy, and the civil list, we should bear in mind, that we ought to regulate it with a view to its permanent continuance, not for the sun-shine of peace and prosperity; but also with a view to the fiscal embarrassments incident to war; for no nation could expect to go on for more than twenty years, without experiencing the vicissitudes of war. He was opposed, generally, to all propositions for the increase of pay for any officers of the Government, and invariably voted against them; because when a man once got into office, there was a kind of understanding between the officers and the Government, that the salary should not be diminished, and he was therefore opposed to an increase of them. He would ask, why was this bill, then, pressed with such earnestness?

Where was the necessity for it? We were told by gentlemen upon the floor of the House, and we heard it in our private rooms, over and over again from officers of the navy, that those officers could not live upon their present pay. If that were true Mr. H. was ready to admit an increase should be made, but if it could be proved to be enough, it ought to stand as it was. We should bear in mind that our navy was yet in infancy, and it might be necessary and probably would become twice as large as at present, and that therefore we ought to limit our present expenditure of the army and navy both, within what might be considered our capacity and means.

What was the present pay of the navy? The aggregate amount, as certified by the naval department, was $770,000, using round numbers. The officers of the navy were but few in number, perhaps not more than from seven hundred to a thousand, including the whole provided in this bill. How many of them were, now in a time of profound peace, when the necessity for the increase of pay had all at once sprung up, employed? He had made some calculation from the report of the Secretary of Navy, and with an honorable member from Ohio, had compared the number in commission with those out of commission or on the stocks, and he had ascertained that there were not more than one sixth part employed from year to year, one with another With the exception of those employed at the navy yards, who, God knows were well enough provided for, better than any other officers of the government, there were not more than one-fifth employed on the ocean. Where were the residue? Generally at their houses, or taking their pleasure. Now, he would ask, when only about one-fourth or one-fifth of these officers were employed on the ocean, and the balance at home, where was the imperious necessity for the increase of their pay at this particular time? They now received, as he had said, about $770,000, not including the appropriations under the ordinary bill. Now, what was the increase proposed by this bill? As the bill was reported last February twelvemonth it increased the pay of the navy $116,000, and the pay of the officers of the army $70,000, in round numbers, for he would not detain the House with fractions. On referring the bill back again to a Select Committee, they knocked the army off altogether, and reported a substitute for the original bill, increasing the pay of the navy $84,500, making a total increase of $200,500. The bill was then referred to a Committee of the Whole House, where it underwent a variety of modifications, and before it came to the amendment passed yesterday, Mr. H. sent the bill to the Navy Department, and by that means ascertained that the increase amounted to the sum he had stated, $200,500. After that calculation had been made, one of his colleagues (Mr. Pope) moved an amendment proposing to increase the pay of past midshipmen. A gentleman from Maine made a calculation as to how much that amendment would add to the bill, and he made it appear to be $32,000. Mr. H's. calculation, founded upon the returns of the Navy Department, brought it to $31,000, and if these were correct the whole increase would be $266,000.

The modifications of the gentleman from Virginia (Mr. Wise) adopted yesterday, in relation to the pay of captains of the navy, diminished that sum about $15,000. There were thirty-seven captains, about two-thirds of them had their pay lessened about $500 each, and about one-third of them $250 each, making, according to Mr. H's. estimate, about $15,000, leaving the actual increase by the bill, as passed the committee yesterday $251,000—and all this in a time of profound peace, and if ever our navy should be filled up he had no doubt the increase would amount to no less than $500,000 a year. He was perfectly confident that he was not inaccurate to the amount of fifty dollars, in any one calculation. If the estimates of the Navy Department were correct, then by the first bill there would be an increase of $116,000, and by the second bill of $84,500 additional.

If the calculations of the Navy Department were not inaccurate, Mr. H. was satisfied that the whole increase would be $251,000. Gentlemen might say this bill was in lieu of all commutation, and that the $770,000 included every thing except the item of mileage, which could not be calculated with any probable certainty. As this bill was an actual increase upon the present pay of the navy, taking it altogether, of about $257,000, better than one-fourth, and not quite a fifth, the whole would hereafter amount to about $1,026,000 a year; and when the mileage of ten cents a mile was added, they might fairly estimate that our naval officers in times of profound peace, would cost the Government $1,100,000 annually. He had made inquiries as to what the whole civil Government, including the legislative, executive, and judicial departments of the several States of Virginia, Pennsylvania, Ohio, Indiana, Illinois, Missouri, Kentucky, Tennessee, Alabama, North and South Carolina, making eleven States, the whole machinery of the Government of those States put together fell short, by at least $100,000 of what was proposed, in a time of profound peace, for the officers of the navy of the United States. Surely there was something in this. How much was it on the old Jeffersonian plan? That a mere handful of men, in times of profound peace, when not more than one-fifth of them were engaged, should cost the Government of the United States 100,000 dollars more than the whole civil governments together of eleven States of the Union! Surely, surely, we must have fallen on fine days of retrenchment and reform indeed! In the year 1828, it was promulgated to the world what wondrous things would be done upon the subject of retrenchment and reform! How have these promises been fulfilled? Office after office had been created; emolument after emolument, had been added and increased, and now, to sum up all, an increase of pay of officers of the navy to more than a fourth, and little less than a third, was to be made. He called upon those gentlemen associated with him, who were attached to the political party that governed the nation, and who would be held responsible to the country, to look at the reports issued from the House—to look at the circular letters, the speeches published, and those also made on the stump, and they would find themselves held responsibl for all this. For twenty years Mr. H. had been contending to bring the Government back to its original expenditure, and he should continue to do so as long as he had the honor of a seat upon that floor. He had not confined his denunciations of these extravagant expenditures to the stump; he had made them in that House, and he should do it again, and upon every opportunity, when the occasion presented itself. The country would hold the party attach-

ed to the present administration responsible for their profligacy of the public money.

But we have been told that we have been ungrateful to the navy, in the language of one gentleman, "the right arm of the nation." Let us make a comparison of their pay with that of the army. A Lieutenant commanding in the navy got above $1100 a year, a Lieutenant in the army, taking every thing into calculation, got $820, and a Second Lieutenant $762, &c. Mr. H. here went into a statement of the salaries paid to the officers of different grades in both branches, in order to sustain his proposition that the naval received more in proportion to the number of men he commanded than the military officer. A Lieutenant in the navy, he maintained, got as much as a major in the army, and a captain in the navy got higher pay than a Brigadier General, besides the former got ten cents a mile for his travelling expenses. If the latter got more than he had stated, he made it up by left handed charges, by transportation of baggage, quarters, &c, but this would show that abuses had crept in, and if so, Mr. H. for one, was prepared to go into the correction of them.

Mr. WISE explained that a Lieutenant in the Navy acted as a Colonel in the Army, and a Captain as a General, for they were liable to be called upon to command more ships than one.

Mr. HARDIN resumed. In general, a full compliment of a first rate ship did not exceed 733 men men. In the English ships about 750. The French had taken up a foolish idea—he ought not to say foolish, but they had adopted the policy that the more men the better, and their large ships now usually took up a thousand men. But if you took all vessels in the U. States naval service, of different sizes, from a seventy-four down to the smallest, they would not average more, at the outside, than five hundred men each; nay, in general, they would not reach four hundred. When a captain went out with his ship of a complement of four hundred men, he usually took with him a lieutenant to about every seventy men. That was the average Com. Porter took in his expedition to the Pacific; that was the average of the old Constitution in the last war. Mr. H. entered further into this statement to show that a lieutenant and midshipman did not command more men, upon an average, than a first and second lieutenant in the army. Upon the subject of gratitude, also, he would call one fact to the recollection of gentlemen, that if a man died an officer in the naval service, his widow was pensioned from five years to five years. He knew widows of meritorious officers in the army who were starving. One in his own neighborhood, whose husband, an officer in the army, fought at Raisin, Niagara, and at New Orleans, was now without a cent in the world, and he had brought on a letter from her to General Jackson, stating that she was reduced to want and beggary, and the General promised to do all he could for her. He knew a similar instance of a major in the army, who died at New Orleans, whose widow and children were also reduced to want and beggary. Hence it was that he said the navy got more than the army. He wished to God there was a law providing for the widows of all those who lost their lives in the service of their country. But he would again call the attention of the House to the contrast between the pay of the two services. Mr. H. then read an estimate of the different sums paid to the officers and crews of various ships engaged during the late war.

Mr. H. then referred to the addresses of Commodore Porter, Lord Nelson, &c., to show that prize-money was the greatest incentive for sailors to fight well, relating an ancient anecdote to that effect, of a soldier, who, having lost his budget, as he called his wealth, on an assault, was the first to mount the breach, and recovered by the plunder of the town, more than he had lost; on another occasion, being called on by his commander to do the same, he requested some other man to take his place, who had lost his budget, for he possessed one. A gentleman referred to a captain yesterday, who had been 29 years in the service; but who was not worth 700 dollars—Mr. H. said there were some men whom you could not make rich. But he would refer to the numerous captains in this city, living in the finest palaces—no, he must not say palaces—in the most splendid mansions, built by the public money they had obtained. Ask a commander how much he made, and he would reply, why in the last war probably about $100,000. It was said their

"March is on the mountain wave,
Their home is on the deep."

Their march here was too often from the tavern to the Capitol, and their home was ——, several gentlemen around him said, in the gallery's of this House. Mr. H. referred to the officers of the army, who were then toiling in the West, and were not represented there by committees, &c. and complained of the proposal for the army having been rejected by the select committee, and the navy alone taken up and acted on, (Mr. Watmough explained,) contrary to the just expections of all.

In regard to a lavish expenditure of the public money, the history of the last three hundred years furnished us with one fact, that it was the natural tendency of all governments to increase their expenses from year to year. Such was the case with the governments of Europe, and he was afraid the Government of the United States would exhibit the same melancholy picture, that its expenses will be so increased that at last it will become too oppressive and too onerous for the people to bear, and, according to the language of the other House, reform or revolution must be the end of it. It was the lavish waste of the public money that brought Charles I. of England and Louis 16th of France to the block, and it is one of the main causes of all the revolutions of empires that have ever happened. Gentlemen say that the navy was a popular branch of the public service. He agreed. But ought that House to legislate for fashionable attachment? He knew there was a continual struggle to get expenditures on the sea board. He had no wish to impeach the integrity of gentlemen who were so zealous on the subject of fortifications and other works on the sea board; but they could not help being acted on by their feelings. In the language of Sir Robert Walpole, prime minister of England, he said they came up year after year to be shorn like sheep. We, said Mr. H., come from the interior every year to be shorn, for your fortifications on the sea-board, but I for one am not exactly like the sheep, for although I might be willing to be shorn, I will make a noise about it. Mr. H. concluded by saying that he had a great many more observations which he wished to have offered on the present occasion, but he was unwilling to intrude too far upon the indulgence afforded to him by the House, for which he offered his acknowledgments, and he should probably take some other opportunity of giving his sentiments at more length to the public.

Mr. WISE said, he was fully aware that it would be improper for him to detain the House long on the subject of this bill, as he had perhaps spoken too much upon it already. He felt it incumbent on him, however, to make a brief reply to what he considered, without intending the least disrespect towards that honorable member, to be the *ad captundem* remarks of the gentleman from Kentucky, (Mr. Hardin) who had just taken his seat. Were it not for the already well earned reputation of the gentleman as a debater, he might be led to the supposition that he was fighting for fame. He had certainly taken strong ground in opposition to bills involving public expenditure. When the bill to compensate Commodore Hull was before the House, there stood the gentleman from Kentucky to oppose it. When the Alexandria Canal bill was up, there stood the gentleman from Kentucky. When Meade's claim was presented, there stood the gentleman from Kentucky. And now on the question of the passage of the bill to regulate the pay of the Navy, there still stands the gentleman from Kentucky. From this indiscriminate opposition to *all money bills*, we might be led to suppose that the gentleman acts more from habit than from calculation, but always from principles of sound economy. When the Louisville and Portland canal bill came up, *there* was *not* to be found the gentleman from Kentucky. And at the moment the gentleman was so earnestly contending for economy in *navy*-pay, he eloquently—I never heard the gentleman more eloquent than to-day, though he always delightfully entertains me—justified the *pay* of the *army*, when I have on a former occasion, and could now demonstrate the pay of the army to be nearly double that of the navy. But, with the gentleman from Kentucky, it seemed, the Army was like the Louisville and Portland Canal—the army clears the way of the West on the frontiers! Yes, sir, the gentleman from Kentucky is like all the rest of us, when a little wool is to be sheared off we are apt to bleat, but if any is to be stuck on our skins, we are dumb as lambs. But, sir, the West is as much interested in the navy as the seaboard, and no more sheared than we are, in increasing its pay and emoluments.

Mr. W. said, such was the impression which the course of that gentleman had made upon him, and he had watched that course with some attention, though not, he assured him, with a little or invidious spirit. There was probably another cause for the habit of opposition, which the gentleman from Kentucky seemed to have acquired. He was a long-experienced lawyer, and appeared sometimes to conceive himself addressing a jury of unpractised men. Such must have been his impression when he appealed to the friends of the present administration, with a view to arouse their party predilections in opposition to this bill as calculated to render that administration odious. It was true, the administration was sometimes held responsible for expenditures for which it should not be held accountable; but did the gentleman from Kentucky suppose he could frighten the friends of this bill favorable to the Administration from its support by threatening to accuse them of improvidence, if this increase of pay be improvident, in which every party in this House has its full share? In no sense can this bill be viewed as a party measure.

Mr. HARDIN here interposed an explanation relative to a remark of the gentleman from Virginia, (Mr Wise) relative to his course in relation to the bill for the benefit of the Louisville and Portland canal. He had already explained to that gentleman that his own sentiments were in opposition to that bill, but that he had acted under instructions from the Legislature of his State.

Mr. WISE said it was true a conversation had occurred, in which he understood the gentleman to be opposed to that bill; and he now learnt that he acted, in some measure, from instructions of his constituents. He had only alluded to it to show that all have their "budget" to fight for, and that the gentleman from Kentucky could fight for his, as well as others.

Mr. W. hoped the House would not, in its action upon this bill, take such views into consideration. It was merely a question of dollars and cents, and should not be connected with any party or extraneous ideas. He would conclude by adverting to a single remark relative to the fortunes of the officers of our Navy. He believed there was not one who received more than sufficient for subsistence. Not one now in the service, who now possesses more than he derived from inheritance or from marriage. It was not in the Naval service that fortunes were acquired. On the contrary, it was impossible at the present pay, to live as become a gentleman belonging to the American Navy. The Navy Pension fund, too, had often been alluded to. Not one cent of this came out of the pockets of the people. So with prize money. It did not come from the pockets of the people, but was wrested from their foes. As was well said by an intelligent Lieutenant, whose letter he had on a former occasion introduced to the attention of the House—it was hardly fought for and dearly won. It was taken from the enemies of your country, and not from the People's Treasury. What benefit, he asked, accrued to the young officers of the navy from the prize money so often alluded to as having been distributed to the commanders during and prior to the last war? He hoped the House would not suffer itself to be governed by such considerations. He would detain them no longer, as the subject had certainly been sufficiently argued and discussed.

Mr. LYTLE said, Mr. Speaker: Before this

bill goes to a vote on its final passage, I feel constrained to say that I must differ with some of my colleagues with whom I have generally acted, and perhaps with a majority of the delegation from the west. The objections just made to it by the honorable gentleman from Kentucky, (Mr. Hardin,) furnish an additional inducement for me, briefly to make some explanations of my views at this time upon the bill before you.

I know well, sir, that whenever that gentleman chooses to devote the powerful, active energies of his mind, to the investigation of any subject, that he can always present that subject in a clear and plausible, if not a conclusive manner, before this body. The only objection I have to his style and manner of effecting his object, is that his long and successful practice at the bar, has had a tendency to make him forget that he is not here in full practice before a jury—and that having taken sides, he makes his argument, in correspondence with his professional habits, altogether a *one-sided* one. He has omitted nothing in the presentment of his views, from the organization of the Navy to the present time, which was calculated to prejudice the passage of the bill. But, I did hope, sir, that when he undertook to enlighten the House by a comparison between the naval and army expenditures, that his sense of justice would have kept pace with his zealous spirit of inquiry, and that he would have made the contrast perfect. But, alas, sir, it was followed out on the one side by facts in opposition to the navy, and on the other by *assertions* in relation to the pay, the duties, and expenses of the army; in reference to which my honorable friend from Virginia (Mr. Wise) who, by the way, has given to the subject, with a view to this very matter, great attention, entertains a wide and total difference of opinion, both as to facts and conclusions.

But, sir, said Mr. L. I object to such comparisons—they are altogether erroneous. They are calculated to create invidious feelings between the members of those two branches of the service—to awaken jealousies, and produce embarrassments which should never exist amongst members of the same family. Sir, the cause is a common cause. Both are contending for the same great interests, and both should be well paid. If the army is indifferently provided for, let us know it, and apply there also the needful remedy—but as we are now regulating merely the pay of the naval officers; why start objections which may result in envy and the generation of bad blood between the members of these two classes of our public service. It is a just tribute to the officers of the army, to say, that in reference to this bill, I have heard but one expression in relation to it—all have hoped for, and encouraged its passage with a spirit of magnanimity and chivalry, they have always to'd me it was right, and wished it success. Sir, they are sworn brethren in arms, fighting under the same banner, and governed by the same interests and feelings. Let not discord come among them then, by any act of ours, calculated to awaken causeless jealousies, where all is now harmonious and friendly. The matter, Mr. Speaker, is reduced to this point, it is too late in the session, essentially to change the features of this bill, immediate action is required, and we must either take this as we find it or leave the navy in a weak and deplorable condition. I am free to say, sir, if you are not disposed to make it respectable and sound, abolish it at once—burn down your fleets, and block up your harbors, destroy your fortifications, act on the defensive altogether, at the expense of not only the trade and commerce of the country, but so much of its liberty as may be considered dependent on a naval armament—on the marine power of the Government. If, however, it is the desire of the House to place our navy on a rank and power that shall correspond with any and all others that she may come in contact with—that our "stars and stripes" may float proudly and triumphantly wherever a breeze may waft, or a wave may bear it—that the products of our rich and happy country may be safely carried into every port, where any other ship may ride—that the seamen in our service may be enabled by their pay to exhibit, in their intercourse with those they meet, the aspiring, generous, and proud character of the Government they represent. Pass this bill, and furnish the means by which it shall be done. Already, upon the most slender means and diminished resources, have they sustained the national honor, and the national character, at the expense of personal comfort and independence. If you are to have a navy at all, then, let it be such a one as you will not be ashamed of. By your pay bill, show that you do not mean that men shall fight your battles, protect your exiled citizens, cultivate by reciprocal hospitalities with foreign powers, that most desirable feeling of amity and respect, which it is so eminently our duty and policy as a nation to maintain, without the indispensable patronage of the Government they belong to Sir, this is nothing more than naked justice, and so far myself from being horror-stricken at the provisions of this bill, I would be glad to have it improved by the amendments proposed by the gentleman from Georgia, (Mr. Jones,) some time back, in reference to the additional grades in the service, thereby perfecting the navy of our Union, and making it, in all respects, equal with all others. Sir, these opinions may surprise some of my friends with whom I have acted, but they are the same that I have always cherished, and hold myself ready to defend—but not on the grounds assumed by my honorable friend from Kentucky, (Mr. Hardin.) He christens it a *party measure*, and holds, after an eloquent description of the reform and retrenchment measures promised by this administration, that he will hold as responsible for this most extravagant proposition, the *Administration* and its friends! Sir, how is this? when, in the same breath, he tells us that one-third of the administration party is opposed to the bill, and that the two-thirds is made up by the opposition members of the House? The two averments are admirably reconciled to each other. Sir, so far as I have seen or heard any thing in this discussion, it is totally exempt from all spirit of party. I go for the improvement of this great arm of the National Government, upon principles of national policy and right. Party feeling and party interest never entered into my brain. When reflecting or acting on it, party feeling is dead, as it should be, in reference to it, except so far as it may concern the common interest of our common country.

The gentleman from Kentucky did not seem to expect support from the *western country* for this bill. Sir, I admit with him that an opposition might justly and fairly have been anticipated from our quarter. The close, and partial, and exclusive policy of those on the sea board to our western interests, was well calculated to make us return the compliment on this, and on all other such occasions. But I have ever regarded the navy of our country as a subject of the deepest and most thrilling national interest. I have sunk, and have always been willing to sink, my feelings of local or sectional interest, in a question that involved the common welfare, glory, and perpetuity of the country. Born and nurtured in the back-woods; a buckeye in feeling and thought, in education, habits, and action, I trust, as a Representative on this floor, I shall never forget the obligations thus imposed upon me by that station of common, *national, indivisible* interest. Thus, sir, I regard the bill which proposes to protect and sustain the navy of our Union. I have never seen the ocean, never inhaled a breeze from the salt water. I have never but once trod the deck of a man-of-war, and have yet to see a *ship* of the first class under sail. But I hope and belive, sir, if I know myself, that there is that within me, which, if I were on the extremest boundary of our western frontiers, would never, never make me forget that I was an *American citizen*—would never subdue the feelings of proud exultation which I still remember of having felt in early boyhood, when hearing of the result of the well-fought battles of our gallant tars upon the high seas—nor make me pause upon a proposition to amend the unjust policy of the Government towards them; for the gallantry they have displayed, the privations they are still enduring, and the demands which they now have, and are entitled to make, on the justice of their country. Again, sir, we are told of the pensions already received by the widows of deceased naval officers; and my friend before me has instanced one in his own neighborhood. I am glad it is so, and that she is comfortable; and I wish to God that I could say as much of the widows of the *living* officers of our navy. I know one, sir, whose residence is not out of sight of the Capitol, who may now indeed be within the sound of my voice, whose gallant husband is on a two or three cruise in the Pacific, and whose salary amounts to the miserable pittance of eleven hundred dollars; the *one-half* of which he has divided with a lovely and growing family, consisting of his wife and some five or six children; and out of this sum he must interchange civilities as commandant of the station—with the officers of all other governments he may happen to find there.

Sir, if you mean to have a navy that will answer the just purposes and expectations of the Government, you must expect to pay for it; but yet we are furnished with a history of the enormous sums paid to different crews, or received by them in the shape of prize money. Well, sir, it is earned only in time of war, and well earned then, Mr. Speaker—earned as much for the country as for the sailor who enjoys it; for it is a reciprocal benefit to the country, and whoever the country may employ to take it. By crippling the resources of the enemy, you add to the country's strength, no matter into whose pockets the plunder goes, or if one farthing should never reach the coffers of your Treasury. But my worthy friend has had his sensibilities excited, also, by the appearance of navy officers in the city, and has told you, that instead of their "*march*" being "on the mountain wave, and their home upon the deep," their 'march is now from the tavern to the capitol, and their home in our gallery.' He seems offended at the appointment of a committee to come on here to explain to the members of this House, as a committee, matters which could never have been furnished elsewhere. Why, sir, is there any thing unjust or presumptuous in this; their every thing is at stake; the rules and principles by which they they are to be governed, perhaps for the balance of their lives; their whole future destiny dependent on the decision of the House this day, sir, upon the fate of this bill, and they debarred the common privileges of American freemen, of expressing their opinions, or giving their advice, when it is really indispensable to correct action, and denied a seat in the gallery, to ascertain the result!

I am unable to perceive or appreciate the enormity of this offence. The officers of the army do, also, come here, and they have the right to come; and I think the honorable gentleman will find two army to one naval officer at this time in the city; and so great was this grievance, as complained of by the Secretary of War, from the too frequent visitations of his troops here last winter, that he had to issue a proclamation to keep them off, during the session of Congress, as every gentleman here must remember. The order was revoked, and with at least as much propriety as it was made but we all know the fact.

Th officers of the navy then, have done no more than other people—they have looked a little after their own interests—they found them in jeopardy, and came, for the last time, to their rescue. Sir, I deny that the navy is the "spoiled child of the government." She is the abused, neglected, cast off member of the family. It is time her injuries should be redressed, her services rewarded—no better time could have happened than the present—even the vote upon the present bill, sir, may be regarded as b g with the fate of the dearest interests of the country. Sir, it may, it will have an important bearing, as it should, upon our foreign relations—it will show that the People are awakened to a sense of the difficulties that are approaching, and to a correct appreciation of the same. No man can look at the papers from the east this morning, and not be satisfied that a war-cloud is now lowering upon us; it is plainly visible sir, at least in the horizon; if I mistake not, it will soon be upon us, and if I had, or could have my way, so far from being staggered by the provisions of this bill, I would add the

CONTINUED IN NEXT NUMBER.

CONGRESSIONAL GLOBE.

BY BLAIR & RIVES. ——WEEKLY—— PRICE $1 A SESSION.

2d Sess.......23d Cong. TUESDAY, MARCH 3, 1835. Volume 2.......No. 17.

TWENTY-THIRD CONGRESS.

SECOND SESSION.

HOUSE OF REPRESENTATIVES.

WEDNESDAY, February 18, 1835.

[CONTINUED FROM LAST NUMBER.]

full amount claimed by this government from the French as an extra appropriation for repairing the navy—and completing the fortifications of the country, and by hard knocks, make the French pay the whole expense for the trouble of collecting our just debts on that way.

It will come to that at last, and when we send off our gallant seamen to undertake the work, let those who are now anxiously watching the results of our deliberations, start with light hearts and fuller pockets, leaving a better prospect of comforts and happiness behind them, and entering with increased ardour and renewed spirit into the service of a country, liberal enough to reward and honor them; at least sir, the bill shall have my hearty and most ardent support.

Mr. CHILTON here moved the Previous Question.

Mr. WARD moved a call of the House.

On this question Mr. HARDIN called for the yeas and nays, which were ordered, and taken; when there appeared, ayes 101, noes 103.

So the House refused to second the call.

The question was then taken on seconding the Previous Question; which was decided, by tellers, in the affirmative, ayes 116, noes 94.

The main question, "Shall the bill pass," was then put and taken by yeas and nays, as follows, Ayes 117, noes 102.

YEAS—Messrs. J. Q. Adams, John Adams, Heman Allen, Anthony, Archer, Ashley, Banks, Barber, Barnitz, Bates, B glies, Beale, Bell, Binney, Bodle, Boon, Briggs, Brown, Bull, Bur't, Burges, Cage, Cambreleng, Campbell, Carmichael, Chambers, Wm. Clark, Clay, Clayton, Coffee, Cramer, Crane, Crockett, D rlington, H Everett, Denny, Dickson, Evans, E. Everett, H. Everett, Ewing, Ferris, Filmore, Foster Fulton, Gamble, Garland, Gholson, Gorham, Grennell Hannegan, Hazeltine, H dit, Henderson, Howell, Huntington, Wm. Jackson, E. Jackson, Wm C. Johnson, Richard M Johnson, Henry Johnson, Seaborn Jones, Kavanagh, King, Lane, Lay, Lincoln, Love, Lovall, Lucas, Lytle, Manning, Martindale, Marshall, John Y. Mason, McComas, McKim, McKinley, Mercer, Milligan, Miner, Moore, Morgan, Murphy, Parker, Patton, Dutee J. Pearce, Phillips, Pierson, Pinckney, Pope, Potts, Reed, Reencher, Wm. B. Shepard, Slade, Sloane, Spangler, Steele, Stoddert, Wm. P. Taylor, P. Thomas, Trumbull, Turner, Tweedy, Vance, Vanderpoel, Van Houten, Vinton, Ward, Watmough, White, Frec'k Whittlesey, Elisha Whittlesey, Wilde, Wilson, Wise, Young—118.

NAYS—Messrs. J. J. Allen, Chilton Allan, Wm. Allen, Barringer, Bean, Beardsley, Beaty, Beaumont, Bocker, Bunch, Burns, Bynum, Carr, Casey, Chaney, Connor, Coult r, Day, Dickerson, Dunlap, Forester, Fowler, Philo C. Fuller, Wm. K. Fuller, Galbraith, Gillet, Gilmer, Gordon, Graham, Grayson, Griffin, Joseph Hall, Thomas H. Hall, Halsey, Hamer, Hard, Hardin, Harper, Harrison, Hathaway, Hawkins, Hawes, Heister, Hubbard, Inge, James, Jarvis, Noadiah Johnson, Cave Johnson, B. Jones, Kilgore, Kinnard, Lansing, Laporte, Lea, Lee, Lewis, Lyon, Abijah Mann, Joel K. Mann, Mardis, Moses Mason, May, McIntire, McKay, McLene, McVean, Miller, Henry Mitchell, Robert Mitchell, Muhlenberg, Osgood, Page, Parks, Patterson, Franklin Pierce, Pierson, Plummer, Polk, Ramsay, Reynolds, Robertson, Schenck, A. H. Shepperd, Smith, Standifer, Sutherland, Wm. Taylor, Francis Thomas, Thomson, Turrill, Wagener, Wardwell, Webster, Whallon, Williams—102.

So the bill passed.

The joint resolution relative to the settlement of the accounts of O. H. Dibble, was next taken up, and on motion of Mr. WHITTLESEY, of Ohio, postponed till Friday next.

PUBLIC DEPOSITES.

The House next took up the motion submitted some days since by Mr. PLUMMER, to reconsider the vote on the amendment offered by Mr. BINNEY, to the bill regulating the deposite of the public moneys of the United States in certain local banks.

Mr POLK addressed the House, and propounded some inquiries to Mr. Binney, in relation to the nature and intention of his amendment.

Mr. BINNEY replied. He added that he had no special objection to the reconsideration; for he believed he could convince the House of the propriety of his amendment.

Mr. POLK resumed his remarks, but finally gave way to a motion for adjournment.

On motion of Mr. MANN, of New York,

The House then adjourned.

IN SENATE.

THURSDAY, February 19, 1835.

The VICE PRESIDENT communicated a letter from the Treasury Department, transmitting a statement of the contracts authorized, and payments made by that Department, for the year 1834.

Mr. PRENTISS, from the Committee on Pensions, reported the House bill granting a pension to Simeon Meacham, without amendment.

Mr. McKEAN, from the Committee on Pensions, reported the House bills granting pensions to Peter Dostator and Jacob Weaver, without amendment, and intimated that when the bills should be called up, he would move for their indefinite postponement.

Mr. TOMLINSON, from the same Committee, reported the House bills granting pensions to Samuel M. Asberry and Francis St. Cyr, without amendment, and with the expression of an opinion by the Committee against the passage of the last named bill.

Mr. BUCHANAN, on leave given, (previous notice having been dispensed with,) introduced a bill further to suspend the operation of certain provisions of "an act to alter an I amend the several acts imposing duties on imports, approved 14th July, 1834:" which was read twice by unanimous consent, and referred, to the Committee on Finance.

On motion of Mr. TOMLINSON, the Senate considered, as in Committee of the Whole, the bill for the relief of Walter Loomis and Abel Gay; when it was ordered to be engrossed and read a third time.

The following resolutions lying on the table, were considered and adopted:

By Mr. HENDRICKS:

Resolved, That the Secretary of War be directed to cause a survey to be made of a road from the Maumee bay through the northern counties of Indiana, to, or near the rapids of Illinois river, and thence to the Mississippi river, to some point between Rock Island and Quincy.

By Mr. KENT:

Resolved, That the Secretary of the Treasury be directed to transmit to the Senate any information he may possess in relation to the obstructions in the navigation of the Potomac between Washington and Georgetown, in this District.

The following bills from the House of Representatives, were read twice and referred:

The bill to increase the pay of the navy of the United States;

A supplement to the act authorizing an extension of the lateral branch of the Baltimore and Ohio rail road within the District of Columbia;

A bill to allow additional compensation to the District Attorney of the United States, for the district of South Carolina.

On motion of Mr. CLAYTON, the Senate considered, as in Committee of the Whole, the bill amendatory of the act for the punishment of offences against the United States.

Mr. CLAYTON rose briefly to explain the provisions of the bill. He said the object of the Judiciary Committee in report ng it, was to define and punish the revolt of crews of American ships. The act of 1820 makes revolt a crime punishable with death, but does not define the offence. This courts have given it a construction about which, it is true, there is now no doubt; but it was thought better by the Committee to give it a definition by statute. There is another feature of the bill—it changes the punishment. In practice, criminals of this description often escape punishment altogether, owing to the excessive severity now imposed upon the offence. It was therefore thought best by the Committee to define it and attach such severe punishment to it as would effectually suppress it.

Mr. CLAYTON then moved to amend the bill by striking out three years' confinement at hard labor, at the discretion of the court, as the maximum sum of punishment for revolt, and inserting ten years in lieu thereof; which was agreed to.

On motion of Mr. CLAYTON, the bill was further amended by striking out one year and inserting five years' imprisonment as the extremity of punishment for inciting to revolt.

On his motion the bill was further amended by increasing the maximum of punishment from one to five years' imprisonment, against captains, mates, &c., for cruel beating of seamen.

After some further explanation of the legal provisions of the bill, it was reported to the Senate, and the amendments were concurred in.

Mr. SHEPLEY then moved to strike out the words in the bill which authorized punishment to be extended to *neglect of duty.*

Mr. CLAYTON opposed the motion, on the ground that it was only designed to apply to conspiracies by the crew to neglect their duties, so as to endanger the safety of the ship and crew.

The motion was disagreed to, and the bill was then ordered to be engrossed for a third reading.

On motion of Mr. NAUDAIN, the Senate proceeded to consider, as in Committee of the Whole, the bill for the relief of Charles J. Catlett.

[This bill provides payment for a large quantity of tobacco, together with a building in which a portion of it was stored, at Magruder's Ferry warehouse, Nottingham warehouse, and Cedar point warehouse, on the Chesapeake bay, which was destroyed by the British troops, during the last war.]

The merits of the bill were discussed at some length, by Messrs. NAUDAIN, BELL, and SHEPLEY, who contended that the case did not come within the principle which had here ofore governed Congress in making compensation for private property destroyed by the enemy in time of war.

The opposite ground was taken by Messrs. TYLER, POINDEXTER, KING of Alabama, and FRELINGHUYSEN.

The question being on the engrossment of the bill, Mr SHEPLEY asked for the yeas and nays, which were ordered, and are as follows:

YEAS—Messrs Bibb, Clay, Cuthbert, Ewing, Goldsborough, Grundy, Kane, Kent, King of Ala., Linn, McKean, Mangum, Moore, Poindexter, Porter, Robbins, Sm th, Southard, Tyler, Waggaman, Webster, White—22.

NAYS—Messrs. Bell, Benton, Black, Brown, Buchanan. Calhoun, Clayton, Frelinghuysen, Hendricks, Hill, King of Ga., Knight, Moore, Naudain, Prentiss, Preston, Ruggles, Shepley, Swift, Tallmadge, Tipton. Tomlinson, Wright—23.

So the Senate refused to order the bill to be engrossed.

The Senate then proceeded to the special order, being the bill to repeal the act limiting the term of certain officers, commonly called the four years law.

Mr. GRUNDY resumed and concluded his remarks in opposition to the bill, when

Mr. BIBB rose and said, he did not intend to enter into a debate of this question, but to bring forward certain facts, which the honorable Senator from Tennessee (Mr. Grundy) had found convenient to pass over. The Senate were aware that by extracting certain passages and paragraphs, facts might be made to appear far different from what they really were. That honorable Senator had, by reading sentences from the bill, and referring to former votes on the subject, ingeniously attempted to place gentlemen there in the predicament of having changed their opinions on this subject.

Mr. B. then went on to show, by reading from documents, and to explain how the former bill on that subject had been disposed of, and in such a way as he thought would exculpate Senators from the charge brought against them.

Mr. CLAYTON rose, he said, to correct the statement made by the Senator from Tennessee, (Mr. Grundy,) with regard to the resolution calling upon the President for his reasons for making a removal in a certain instance. The honorable Senator had mentioned that as the only instance of the kind; but he believed there were many more.

Mr. C. t en mentioned several other instances where the Senate had called on the President for his reasons. Among others he referred to the proceedings with respect to the "Panama Mission," and the case of the dismissal of certain military officers, whose the nominees had been rejected, not on account of any objection to them, but because the Senate thought that others ought to have the places.

Mr. C. said that he had no doubt of the propriety of calling upon the President for information, with regard to dismissal. But the question before the Senate was, not whether the President had the power of removal or not, but whether Congress had a right to regulate that power by law or not. He was aware that the honorable Senator from Ohio, (Mr. Ewing,) had placed the question on the ground of the constitutionality of that power; and it might, perhaps, be so nearly allied to this bill as to come within the scope of discussion; but still that was not the question to be decided by the Senate.

Mr. C. said he did not deny the right of removal; he stood on the same ground as the decision of 1798. In this, he differed with most of his political friends. He also differed with the opp seers of the bill, inasmuch as he thought that the power flowed, not from the general grant, that all Executive power should be vested in the President, but in that part where it says the President shall see the laws executed, and hence it might be regulated by law Impeachment seemed to be the only restraint on Executive power, contemplated by the constitution. And where that power was exercised by the President for self aggrandizement and political purposes, all would agree that he ought to be impeached. But how was he to be impeached? That was a difficult question.

Mr. C. said the only control the Senate had over the power of removal, was the right of rejection. And if a meritorious officer, who had discharged his duty with fidelity and good faith, should be removed, the only remedy was to reject the partisan who might be nominated by the President to fill his place; and this he would do; rejecting the first, the second, third, and so on, ad infinitum. Such was the maxim he had laid down as the rule of his conduct, and without information he should not know how to act.

He thought the Senator from Tennessee (Mr. Grundy) had artfully attempted to give the question a political cast. He deprecated such a course and hoped the question would not be decided by a party vote.

He was anxious that the reasons of the President should be brought to light and spread before the people. It was a favor that every citizen and officer had a right to demand The charge had been made, and would be filed away in the process of the Post Office or some other office. The accused would be debarred from ever seeing or knowing what they were, and some 50 years afterwards, these charges, made against him by a political enemy, and lodged on the records of some Department, might be brought forward against his posterity. For such reasons he should vote for the bill.

Mr. CUTHBERT said he had the greatest respect for the intelligence, learning, and moral qualities of the honorable Senator from Delaware (Mr. Clayton.) He would appeal to him, what would be the effect, if the doctrines he had advocated should be carried out—that of strenuously rejecting all appointments, if not made to suit his own notions He would ask the Senator, if in thus acting, he was himself entirely free from party motives. And if the Senate acted from party motives, would it not be impeachable as well as the President? What would be the character then, of the Senate? It would be perpetually occupied in examining reasons and rejecting nominations He would repeat, what would be the character of the Senate?

Mr. CLAYTON replied briefly. The Senate was not impeachable; but there is another remedy provided to correct abuses in that body. But the President was impeachable.

Mr. CUTHBERT replied in a few words—

When Mr. POINDEXTER rising, expressed an intention, if the debate was to be continued, of offering his views on the subject under consideration.

The question was called for from different parts of the House, then, but, Mr. CALHOUN moved to adjourn, which was agreed to.

When the Senate adjourned.

HOUSE OF REPRESENTATIVES.
Thursday, Feb. 19, 1835.

Mr. A. H. SHEPPERD rose, and stated that his name had been inadvertently omitted in the yeas and nays on the engrossment of the navy pay bill. He had voted in the negative on that question and he moved that his vote be recorded; which was agreed to.

Mr. DICKINSON, from the Committee on Indian Affairs, reported a bill for the relief of certain Choctaw Indians; which was read twice and committed.

Mr. CHINN, on leave, presented resolutions of the General Assembly of Virginia, on the subject of certain revolutionary claims; which were laid on the table, and directed to be printed.

Mr. CHINN, from the Committee on the District of Columbia, reported a bill concerning the Orphans' Court, of the county of Washington, in the District of Columbia; which was read twice, and committed.

Mr. CHINN, from the Committee on the District of Columbia, reported the following resolution, which was rejected:—

Resolved, That this House will, on Monday next, from and after the hour of twelve, proceed to consider bills reported by the Committee on the District of Columbia.

Mr. GILMER, from the Committee on Indian Affairs, reported a bill to secure in perpetuity to the Cherokee Indians, residing east of the Mississippi, a country west of that river, to extinguish their rights of ownership in Georgia, to provide for the removal of such as are desirous of emigrating, and for other purposes; which was read twice and committed.

Mr GILMER, from the same committee, reported a bill making appropriations for holding Indian treaties; which was read twice, and referred to the Committee of Ways and Means

Mr. VANDERPOEL, from the Committee for the District of Columbia, reported a bill to incorporate the Alexandria Savings Society; which was read twice and committed.

Mr. KING, from the Committee for the District of Columbia, reported a bill for the suppression of lotteries, and the sale of lottery tickets, in the District of Columbia; which was read twice and committed.

Mr. PINCKNEY, from a Special Committee, reported a bill for the relief of the legal representative of Thomas W Bacot, late of Charleston, South Carolina, deceased; which was read twice and committed.

Mr. C. ALLAN, from the Committee on Territories, reported, with an amendment, a bill from the Senate, granting to the corporation of the borough of Mackinaw a lot of ground, for public purposes. The amendment was adopted, and the bill ordered to be read a third time.

Mr. YOUNG, from the Committee on Revolutionary Claims, reported, without amendment, the bill from the Senate, for the relief of George Burl. but; which was committed.

Mr. SUTHERLAND, from the Committee on Commerce, reported a bill to fix the manner and compensation of the officers of the customs, and to alter certain collection districts; which was read twice, committed to a Committee of the Whole on the State of the Union, and made the special order of the day for Thursday next.

On motion of Mr. SUTHERLAND, 2,000 extra copies of the foregoing bill were ordered to be printed.

Mr. SUTHERLAND, from the same Committee, reported, without amendment, the bill from the Senate, making an appropriation for certain improvements at Mobile Point, and in Mobile Bay; which was committed.

Mr. MUHLENBERG, from the Committee on Revolutionary Claims, reported a bill for the relief of the legal representative of Capt. John Wilce, deceased; which was read twice and committed.

Mr. MAY, from the Committee on Private Land Claims, made an unfavorable report upon a petition which had been referred to said Committee.

Mr KINNARD, from the Committee on Revolutionary Claims, made an unfavorable report on the petition of John M. S. McNight, administrator of Dr. Charles McNight.

Mr. KINNARD, from the same Committee, made an unfavorable report on the petition of Marcus Brown. Which reports were ordered to be printed.

Mr. SEVIER made an appeal to the House, to take up and order to a third reading, several bills which had some days previous passed through committee, relating to the Territories, and which were of great importance to those concerned. But, however, varied his motion, to allow Mr. Hawes an opportunity of making a report from a committee.

Mr. HAWES, from the Select Committee raised on the subject, made a report, accompanied by a bill to modify the system of military instruction in the West Point Academy; which was read twice.

Mr. HAWES moved that the bill be committed to a Committee of the Whole on the state of the Union, and that the bill, together with the report, be printed.

Mr. DICKERSON called for the reading of the bill, which being done, Mr. B. rose and said—

Mr. Speaker, I regret that I am called upon to attempt to arrest the progress of the committee, and particularly at this stage of their proceedings. But I consider it my duty, now, here to object, not only to the printing of this report, but to its reception in this House as the report of the committee.

As to the duties and privileges of committees of this House, I contend, in the first place, that it is necessary that every member should be present, or have an opportunity of being present at the meetings of the committee, and if they have not that opportunity, no report can be made which can with propriety be considered the report of that committee

[The Chairman of the Committee (Mr Hawes) here inquire I whether the gentleman from New Jersey intended to assert or insinuate that the Committee had not been properly summoned.]

Mr D. proceeded. I have no such intention but state the general proposition, and will let the House understand the use I intend to make of it before I sit down; and from the feelings of friendship which I have for the Chairman and indeed for all of the majority of that Committee, I have an assurance that any remarks which I may make upon this subject, will not be considered personal or of an unfriendly character.

I contend further, that it is not only the privilege of every member of a Committee, but the duty, to consult together and discuss the matters submitted to their investigation. This is the essential privilege of such members, and the duty of all. If then a majority of a Committee should

deprive the minority of this privilege, I insist that any report which should be made under the circumstances could not be considered as the report of the Committee. In this respect the report of a Committee may justly be compared with the report of arbitrators or referees, their report may be valid and effectual, if signed by a majority; but it is essential to its validity, that it be the result of the consultation of the whole; although by the terms of the submission, it be agreed that the report of the majority shall be final and conclusive.

In order to show the application of the principles which I have submitted to the House, I will now proceed to state the facts connected with the case, and I take this course, not from any personal considerations, but because I believe that if the report be received and adopted as the report of a committee composed of a member from each State, it would have an effect prejudicial to the institution, and believing as I do, that the institution is one which ought not to be destroyed, I cannot consent to any measure which in my opinion will have that tendency.

It will be recollected by the House, that this committee was organized in the early part of the session. Soon afterwards they had a meeting. A majority of the committee appeared, and I have no doubt but that all were regularly summoned. Upon that occasion a sub-committee of five was appointed to investigate certain points which were designated, and to make report thereon to the main committee. I do not at this moment recollect the exact words of the resolution appointing that sub committee, but my impression was, and still is, that the duty assigned to that sub-committee was to report the facts which were designated in the resolution, and not to report arguments or conclusions. The investigation of the facts necessary to enable the committee at large to draw their conclusions, was a duty which could not have been performed by the whole committee, and therefore that duty was assigned to a sub-committee, by whom it could more conveniently be executed. Another circumstance which satisfies me, that I am correct in my impressions as to the duty of the sub-committee is, that the original resolution which was introduced before the committee for the appointment of this sub-committees authorized them in very terms to report their "opinion" upon the different points of investigation. This feature in the resolution became the subject of discussion before the committee, and upon my motion the word "opinion" was stricken out of the resolution, and, as I understood it, upon the express ground that the sub-committee were to report the facts only. I would never have consented to delegate the whole power of the committee to the sub-committee, but was willing that they should report the facts, in order that the committee might discuss those facts, and make such conclusions, and report thereon, as the case might require. About ten days ago, the committee were again summoned to meet in the evening, upon which occasion nineteen of the committee appeared. I attended that meeting, expecting to hear a report of the facts called for by the resolution appointing the sub-committee, and to proceed to execute the duty assigned to us by this House, by discussing the matters referred to us, and reporting the result of our deliberations. But instead of this, a report is made by the sub-committee, occupying more than two hours in reading, and containing facts, opinions, arguments, and conclusions, accompanied by the bill which has just been read. The reading of this report occupied the house until a late hour at night, when it was adopted. Yes sir, this report of the sub-committee, which had occupied them most of the session to make, and taken more than two hours to read, and embracing a great variety of facts and of statistical tables, was adopted by the committee by a vote of 10 to 9, according to my recollection; and this vote taken in opposition to the wishes of the minority, who claimed the right before voting to examine the report. In this respect, I consider it injustice has been done, and that the minority that committees have been deprived of their rights. No opportunity was given for the examination or discussion of the important measure under consideration; and it places the report upon the same ground that it would have stood, if the minority of the committee had never been summoned to attend the meeting. It is a mere mockery to summon a member of a committee to attend, if he cannot have the opportunity, when assembled, of executing, in a free, deliberate, and proper manner, the duties which are assigned to him by his appointment. Mr. D. concluded by moving that the report and bill be recommitted to the same committee.

Mr. HAWES (the Chairman of the Select Committee) said, this was a most singular proceeding. He thought the House would be of the same opinion when the facts should be stated. He would ask if such was the sanctity of this institution, that a committee of twenty four members, selected from each State in the Union, were not at liberty to make a report in relation to it? It was a part of the Government, and was under the control of Congress. What do we are here? An objection has been made at the very outset to a report, which he was bold to say, would blow the institution to atoms.

In a few days after the committee were appointed, he had called a meeting of the same. He had sent a summons to every member of the committee, and if they did not receive them, it was at least, was innocent. A majority attended the meeting. In consequence of the largeness of the committee, it was deemed expedient to appoint a sub-committee of five to collect facts and report to the committee. Could the gentleman from New Jersey, (Mr. Dickinson,) expect that the sub-committee would report the facts without explaining them—that they would give figures without explaining them? If he did, he was a wiser man than he supposed him to be—and he would admit that he was very wise.

The sub committee, after a laborious investigation, announced to him that they were prepared to report. He again called a meeting of the committee. The meeting took place. The House met at 11 o'clock; and for want of time, the committee adjourned to meet at his room, at Brown's, on the same evening. Each member was notified to attend. A majority of the committee accordingly met. The sub-committee made a report, which was read. The bill was not read, because it was substantially set forth in the conclusion of the report. A proposition was made by the gentleman from Alabama, (Mr. Lewis,) that the report of the sub-committee be adopted as the report of the whole committee. This proposition was discussed fully and freely. He recollected that the gentleman from Missouri (Mr. Ashley) made two speeches, the gentleman from Ohio, (Mr. Allen,) and the gentleman from Indiana, (Mr. Hannegan,) also made speeches. Indeed, he believed that all the members present, except the Chairman, took part in the debate. The vote was finally taken, and the report and bill of the sub-committee were adopted—yeas 10, nays 8, (one member having left the room.) It was the privilege of every member of a committee to be present at its meetings, if they chose. The Chairman had no authority to force their attendance. In this instance all were summoned, and nineteen out of the twenty-four atten ied.

The minority of the committee asked that the report should not be made forthwith. The majority yielded to this request, and they were allowed one more day than they required. Under the instructions of the committee, he should have submitting the report to the minority, to which he replied that, under the circumstances of the case, he would take the responsibility of withholding it. These were the facts which preceded the report which he had just made, and he would leave it to the House to say, whether or not the course pursued by the gentleman from New Jersey (Mr. Dickerson) was not most extraordinary and uncalled for.

When Mr. HAWES concluded his remarks, several gentlemen rose to address the House, but further proceedings on the subject were arrested by a motion submitted by

Mr. POLK, to proceed to the consideration of the orders of the day, which was agreed to.

The SPEAKER laid before the House the following message from the President of the United States, which was committed to a committee of the whole on the state of the Union, and directed to be printed:

WASHINGTON, February 18th, 1835.
To the House of Representatives:

Since my message a few days ago relating to Choctaw reservations, other documents on the same subject have been received from the locating agent which are mentioned in the accompanying report of the Secretary of War, and which I also transmit herewith for the information and consideration of Congress.

ANDREW JACKSON.

The SPEAKER laid before the House a letter from the Secretary of the Treasury, inclosing a statement of the contracts entered into by the Department in the year 1834, pursuant to the several acts of Congress, which was laid on the table and ordered to be printed.

DEPOSITE BANKS.

The bill to regulate the deposite of the public moneys of the United States in certain local banks, was then taken.

The question pending, was on the motion of Mr. PLUMMER, to reconsider the vote of the House adopting the following amendment of Mr. BINNEY to the bill:

"Strike out the second article of the section, and in lieu thereof, insert the following:

"To keep in its vaults, an amount of specie, which, together with the balance of all its accounts, with specie paying banks, shall be equal to one-fifth of the amount of its notes and bills in circulation, and its public and private deposites.

"At the end of the fourth article of the second section, insert two additional articles, as follows:

" Fifthly. To do and perform the duties of Pension Agent without any allowance or compensation, except for the actual cost of books and stationery.

" Sixthly. To pay interest, quarterly into the Treasury, at the rate of ten per cent. per annum, on the average balance of the public moneys on deposite, over and above a sum which shall be equal to five per centum of its capital actually paid in; provided, that no interest be payable, when the said average quarterly balance does not exceed fifty thousand dollars."

Mr. POLK, who was entitled to the floor, proceeded to say, that under existing circumstances, he should confine what he had to say, within as brief a space as possible; and proceed to show the inexpediency of adopting the amendment in question. He remarked that he had the other day demonstrated, to some extent, that if the construction of the gentleman from Pennsylvania, (Mr. Binney,) were to be placed upon the amendment, it would utterly destroy and break up the whole system of employing local Banks as fiscal agents of the Government in every part of the country, except in the larger cities. In the cities, the Banks were enabled to make daily settlements, and strike daily balances; but the country Banks had no such opportunity. He would put a strong case. The Choctaw lands were in market, and the deposite Bank at Natchez had necessarily, at occasional times, a large amount of the public money, and the receivers being compelled to receive, not specie, but notes of the Bank of the United States, how would the deposite Bank be able to answer the call required by the above amendment? In September last year, the amount of public deposites in that Bank was half a million or more; and in January of the present year, it was nearly 900,000 dollars. Some of this was in notes payable in Philadelphia, some in Boston, New York, and other cities, and of all the branches, perhaps, in the Union, for it was required to

receive them; and what did the amendment propose? Why, that they should not count any thing as specie that was not metallic. It would be compelled instantly to transmit to Boston, Savannah, New York, and other places, the notes payable there; and receive their balances back to Natchez. This would take months in transmitting, besides running a great risk in the double transportation. Nor was this all; during the time the deposit bank was lying out of all this money, she must procure specie, at whatever cost, so as to keep up the requisite proportion, although the deposites were made in notes of the Bank of the United States. In other words, you would be requiring the deposite bank to receive the paper of the Bank of the U. States, and not specie; while, at the same time, you would require that bank to answer for the same notes in specie, losing the interest upon and use of the money, by the time consumed in procuring the balances and returns from the Bank of the United States. He affirmed, that at no period since the Bank of the United States came into operation, could the bank, or any one of its branches, have stood up under such a restriction as that proposed by the gentleman from Pennsylvania; nor was it a provision of such a character ever required before.

He had procured the several official returns of the branches of the Bank of the United States, which all showed that they could not have existed under such a restriction. Take one, the branch at Mobile. On the 1st of April, 1833, before the public deposites were removed from the Bank of the United States, it had of public and private deposites, notes in circulation, &c. over and above what was owing to the bank, $2,651,000. Now, according to the amendment proposed, this branch bank should have had $526,200, being one-fifth; so far from it, that it had only $136,000 in specie and specie paying banks. The branch bank at Natchez, at the same period, had, of public and private deposites, and notes in circulation, $1,531,000; while of specie, and notes of specie paying banks, it had only $75,000 to meet these liabilities; about a twentieth, instead of a fifth. This would be the result of carrying out the principle of the gentleman from Pennsylvania, that it would be destructive of the whole system of local depositories. Mr. P. would call upon all those gentlemen who desired this system to be carried out, to examine this point thoroughly, and they would see that if this amendment was adopted, it would be impracticable, and would tend to drive them out of the public service, and throw the public treasury into the hands of receivers, or to compel the re-establishment of a national bank; a contingency which would inevitably follow. The provision was altogether a novel one, and had never been imposed upon the Bank of the United States or its branches. It added no greater security for the public money; it was no additional guarantee, and the provisions of the bill offered sufficient security. Mr. P. here referred to several of them, such as the limited powers with which the Secretary of the Treasury was clothed, &c.

There was another view of the matter. The Bank of the United States was not compelled to take the notes of every other Bank unless she chose to do so, while the deposite Bank was compelled to take hers, and to keep a proportionate amount of specie for it also. By the amendment, they would be compelled to increase their specie, as money might be paid in, and to hold it from circulation, however necessary it might be.

Mr. P. said, without intending any disrespect to the honorable member from Pennsylvania, (Mr. Binney,) and without supposing any such intention could have been entertained by that gentleman, yet the conviction forced itself upon Mr. P.'s mind that the source of the amendment had been prepared by that portion of the intelligent men in this country who were most desirous, to bring from improper motives, for the establishment of a National Bank. The effect of all the amendments, if finally adopted by the House, would be to embarrass those new fiscal agents of the Government, and to bring them at least, into disrepute. No plan could have been devised more effectually than these amendments. Why should these depo-

site banks be required to do what had never been done by the Bank of the United States or by any other bank? He alluded now particularly to the requisition that a monthly publication of the affairs of each deposite bank throughout the country, should be made in three newspapers in the city of Washington, so that their condition might be exposed to the bank of the United States and to other banks, whilst the condition of the bank of the United States and all the other banks would be concealed. By doing this the bank of the United States would be enabled to select their victim, and by means of its extensive changes and in other ways, concentrate its immense power to crush one of those fiscal agents, and thus by producing a temporary interruption to business, embarrass the whole country. We were at no loss to know what would be the effect of public clamor. The experience of the past year, especially from the temporary suspension of two or three banks in this District, proved what might be done. Mr. P. had no doubt that there were those who would have rejoiced to have seen every institution of the kind in the country stop specie payments, reckless of the ruin that might be brought about thereby. You would first require a certain proportion of specie to be kept in each bank upon the amount of its deposites, at the same time paying in those deposites not in specie, but in paper or other banks. Not content with this, they must publish in the newspapers a monthly expose of all their affairs! Where was the necessity for this? Under the bill returns were to be made to the Treasury, and every guarantee had been thrown around that was considered forcible and practicable at the same time.

What was the next provision? The first was that of requiring a certain amount of specie in proportion to the liabilities. The second was that throwing open the condition of each bank. And the third was, that the deposite banks should pay interest on the public money in their hands. Mr. P. would ask, had interest ever been required of any depository from the foundation of this Government up to the present time? It was scarcely necessary to go into this branch of the argument. The subject was also amply discussed at the last session of Congress. What duties had these fiscal agents to perform? They would have to perform the duties of pension agent, without any allowance or compensation, except for the actual cost of books and stationary. They had to furnish the Government with facilities in collecting, receiving, and disbursing the public money, and in this way alone, he would venture to affirm, there would not be a great saving to the Government. Besides, how could interest be charged for the use of money, the amount of which was liable to such fluctuation as the public deposites. Mr. P. felt no hesitation, then, in saying, that if you imposed such hard terms upon these banks, you would be driven to select those of a second rate character, instead of the best, the most solvent, and the most efficient. He hoped and trusted that the plan for the employment of these banks would not be so crippled with regulations as to make it altogether impracticable.

The gentleman from Pennsylvania thought the system must fail. Permit him, (Mr. P.) to say that if the bill should have thrown around it the provisions proposed by that gentleman in his judgment those institutions would be so trammelled and fettered as to render it very difficult, perhaps wholly impracticable, for many of them to succeed. They would then have to resort either to the scheme of the gentleman from Virginia or the gentleman from Pennsylvania, or be thrown back again upon a national Bank. The gentleman from Pennsylvania distinctly averred that the system could not succeed, unless it should be converted into a national Bank; he also avowed his hostility to this bill in any and every form or shape, in which it could be presented, and he informed the Senate at the outset that he intended to vote against it. The gentleman, also, further told the House, that if it passed the bill, the responsibility would be upon them, if they rejected it, the responsibility would be elsewhere. The gentleman had predicted that the whole system must fail, and that the scheme was altogether

impracticable. Now, Mr. P. submitted to the gentleman whether it was fair to that part of the House who differed in opinion with himself, and who thought it a practicable scheme to enhance that scheme with these amendments, and then to render it wholly inoperative. To put the proposed provisions into this bill would, indeed, have this effect.

The gentleman from Pennsylvania further said that the success of the State banks as fiscal agents of the Government, for the last six months, was mainly to be attributed to the forbearance exercised by the Bank of the United States during the spring of 1834, and the effect of the pass. For bearance of the United States! Mr. P. then knew not what for forbearance was; he did know that during the whole of last session, nothing was heard or seen but one general outcry of invective from the party sustaining the bank, that that institution could not extend its accommodations, because, on account of the removal of the deposites, they were compelled to make provision to pay off their own liabilities. So far from forbearing, we were again and again assured that the bank had been pushed to extremities, and could not relieve the country; but as soon as Congress adjourned, we saw a correspondence between the Bank, and Committee of merchants of New York, in which the Bank said, that as Congress had adjourned, without doing its duty, it would then generously extend its loans. Was the panic got up by the friends of the State Banks, or by their opponents? By the friends or enemies of the Bank? The whole country would give but one response to this question.

Mr. P. wished to set the gentleman from Pennsylvania right as to another fact. The gentleman had said that the effect of the panic had been to diminish the importation of foreign articles of commerce, but he must have overlooked its returns from the Treasury Department. If he would turn to them, he will see that, so far from an importation trade having decreased, it had increased to an amount of fourteen millions over any one year.

Mr. BINNEY explained. He had referred to the increase of importations in specie, and a diminution of other articles.

Mr. POLK said, still the treasury returns showed a great increase. The argument of the gentleman from Pennsylvania, that the panic had produced an influx of specie into the country, was fallacious. It was true that more specie was imported during the year 1834; but then the amount of imports of goods, or general fabrics, had not diminished, and this fact was borne out by official statements. The country, then, has been prosperous; but she is indebted for that prosperity neither to the Bank nor to the panic; but to the new impulses springing out of the employment of State banks as fiscal agents of the Government, to which the Bank and its friends had been the most inveterate enemies, and did all in their power to sweep them from the face of the earth. They have stood up against the power of that institution, and the effects of the panic also—and have been, so far, successful. The gentleman said that the parallel case of those banks, as formerly existing, as between 1789 and 1816, during which they met constantly employed as fiscal agents, and they hold good, because, said he, there was then a much specie in the country as now; and averred that the calamity of their inability came at a time. But the gentleman's argument did not hold good, for the country was then only just liberated from an expensive war. The cause of their losses ought to be ascribed to their having made their issues too large, many of them, he believed, from patriotic motives, and were not able to meet the sudden call upon them. We had, however, no guarantee now, which did not exist then, and was in the regulation of the standard of our metallic currency, by which it would be kept from exportation. Mr. P. said he would now conclude, with hoping that the House would not adopt the runs and trammel the bill as, in the judgment of those in favor of it, and of those who would be called upon to execute it, to render it impracticable.

ble, and thereby give the vantage ground to the Bank of the United States. He was anxious that the public should be secured in every possible way, but he could see no additional safeguards in the propositions of the gentleman from Pennsylvania.

One word in regard to these amendments. He did not know whether it was improper to allude to what had occurred elsewhere, but this he might say, that the proposition now moved by the gentleman from Pennsylvania, was not heard of when the original bill was discussed in the Committee of Ways and Means. The provision, relative to specie payments was inserted in the present bill, though Mr. P. had deemed it unnecessary last session, still he thought it could do no harm. Mr. P. concluded, by trusting the House would alter its decision by reconsidering its vote and rejecting the amendment.

Mr. BINNEY spoke at considerable length, in reply to the arguments of Mr. Polk, and going to show that the amendment introduced by him, and proposed to be reconsidered, was salutary in its tendency, and necessary in its operation on the general influence of the bill. It was not unreasonable to require of each of the deposite banks to retain within their vaults, at least one fifth of the amount in specie of its circulation and deposites. He pursued his argument and reply, for upwards of an hour; contending that the amendment proposed nothing but which the local banks were fully able to meet. The converse of this opinion must arise from a want of information as to their real s tuation, highly injurious to them.

M. CAMBRELING followed. He expressed his satisfaction at hearing the opinions from the gentleman from Pennsylvania, (Mr. Binney,) that the State banks were in such high reputation. He believed it was the first time such an admission had come from that quarter of the House. Mr. C. then proceeded to show his reasons for advocating a reconsideration of the amendment of the gentleman from Pennsylvania, among which was the fact that the Bank had no effectual control over the public moneys deposited in their vaults, which were liable to be drawn and transferred by the Government, at any moment. On the subject of a hard money system, he believed he would go as far as that gentleman. He concluded, by repeating his conviction that the reconsideration should prevail and the amendment be expunged.

Mr. McKINLEY then addressed the House at length, in favor of a reconsideration of the amendment. He appealed to the House to decide now, whether they were prepared to sanction, in this bill, a system, which would most inevitably have broken down the old one—or to put upon these institutions such restrictions as none could bear.

Mr. SEABORN JONES, of Georgia, next obtained the floor. He was opposed to many of the amendments that had been made to the bill, in its progress through the House, but not to this one. Mr. J. alluded to an amendment proposed to the bill by himself, relative to the deposites from the had offices, which he still deemed highly essential. He proceeded, at length, to explain the reasons which would impel him to oppose the motion for reconsideration.

Mr. HUBBARD, after a few explanatory remarks, moved the previous question.

Mr. VANDERPOEL demanded a call of the House, and on that question asked for the yeas and nays, which were ordered, and taken as follows: Yeas 144, nays 59.

So the call was ordered, and proceeded in, until all the members were found to be in attendance (or excused for cause) excepting nine.

On motion of Mr. BEARDSLEY, the call was suspended.

The question, "Shall the main question be now put?" was then decided by tellers, in the affirmative, 126 members voting for it—the noes were not counted.

The question on reconsidering the amendment was then taken by yeas and nays, and decided in the affirmative, as follows—ayes 119, nays 109.

So the House agreed to the amendment.

Mr. S. JONES, of Georgia, then proposed his amendment above alluded to, as an amendment to the one preceding.

It was rejected without a division.

Mr. MILLER here moved the Previous Question, which would be on the engrossment of the bill.

The motion was not seconded by the House, there appearing 97 in the affirmative and 116 in the negative, being counted by tellers.

Mr. CLAY then moved an adjournment, which prevailed; ayes 105, noes 48.

And the House adjourned.

IN SENATE.

FRIDAY, February 20, 1835.

The VICE PRESIDENT laid before the Senate a communication from the State Department, transmitting an abstract of the number of seamen registered in each port of the United States, in the year 1834, made in pursuance of the act of May, 1796, which, on motion of Mr. SILSBEE, was ordered to be printed.

Petitions and memorials were presented by Messrs. KANE and TIPTON.

Mr. WEBSTER, from the Committee on Finance, to which was referred the bill further to suspend the operation of certain provisions of the act to alter and amend the several acts imposing duties on imports, approved July, '32, reported the same without amendment.

Mr. WEBSTER said, that the act of 1832, in the 10th and 12th sections provided that the collection of the duties on hardware, being impracticable in some of its provisions, should be suspended for a year, and in the mean time the Secretary of the Treasury was to make examination into the practicability of carrying it into effect. Mr. W. read a passage from the late report of the Secretary, to show that it was now expedient to continue to suspend the operation of these provisions until the end of next session of Congress, which this bill provided. He hoped, as it was necessary the bill should pass, that the Senate would take it up and let it have its several readings at this time.

The bill was then considered as in Committee of the Whole; and ordered to be engrossed for a third reading.

Mr. WEBSTER, from the Committee on Finance, reported the bill from the House for the relief of Dominick Lynch, with an amendment.

Mr. SILSBEE, from the Committee on Commerce, reported a bill to allow a drawback of duties on imported hemp when manufactured into cordage; which was read the first time and ordered to a second reading.

Mr. McKEAN, from the Committee on Pensions, reported the bill from the House granting a pension to Jared Buckingham, without amendment, but intimated that the Committee were of opinion that the bill ought not to pass.

Mr. PRENTISS, from the same Committee, reported without amendment the bills from the House granting pensions to Daniel Page and Larnard Swallow.

Mr. TOMLINSON, from the same Committee, reported the bills from the House granting pensions to Stephen Gatlin and Peter Triplett.

The following resolutions were submitted:

By Mr. ROBINSON:

Resolved, That the Secretary of War be directed to cause a survey to be made of the route from Vandalia, the seat of Government of Illinois, to Lower Alton, on the Mississippi river, for the purpose of ascertaining the eligibility of that route for the permanent location of the National Road.

By Mr. TIPTON:

Resolved, That the Secretary of the Navy be requested to report to the Senate the aggregate number of midshipmen in the Navy of the United States, with the dates of warrants, appointments, and a tabular statement showing the number appointed from each state and Territory, and from the District of Columbia; and stating the number that each State and Territory is entitled to under existing laws of Congress and the regulations of the Navy Department.

Mr. PRENTISS moved to re-consider the vote of yesterday, by which the bill for the relief of

Charles J. Catlett was negatived, on the question of engrossment.

On motion of Mr. SHEPLEY, the motion to re-consider was laid on the table.

Mr. FRELINGHUYSEN gave notice that to-morrow he would move to take up the bill to extend the Circuit Court system.

On motion of Mr. KENT, the Senate took up for consideration, as in Committee of the Whole, the joint resolution introduced by him, to amend the constitution relative to the Veto power.

Mr. KENT said he desired to occupy but a few moments of the time of the Senate on this subject. He was at all times opposed to any hasty alterations of the constitution. No man respected that instrument more than himself, nor was any one more inclined to cherish it; but while he entertained these feelings, he regarded the liberties of the country still more. There was always ground to fear, in disturbing the movements of the Government, lest we rush from one evil to another and a greater. The framers of the constitution were far from believing that that an experience would not disclose latent defects in it—they therefore left it to future times to amend such defects. Look only to the prerogative and claims of the Executive at this day, and you will see that the amendment proposed is the only remedy for this evil.

The veto power as exercised tends to unite the Legislative and Executive powers, than which nothing is more dangerous, and the concentration of them in one hand is despotism, and leads to oppression. This has been boldly held forth by our patriotic ancestors, when they asserted that the people alone could enact laws by which the people could be bound. This provision was designed only to prevent legislative encroachment upon the Executive authority—they never designed it to operate upon matters involving no constitutional objections. These doctrines we find throughout the instrument, particularly by that which says the whole Legislative power shall be vested in Congress. It is a principle, that the law-making power, should be vested in the representatives of the people, who are responsible for the proper performance of their duties. If this power ever pass from the people, it is easy to perceive the first step is to perpetuate this power, and every succeeding act would be one of encroachment, and oppression. All legislative power being thus vested in the two Houses, they, and they only, can make laws. It is manifest, therefore, that no President is justified in interfering with this power further than to protect himself. It was intended not to be active but defensive, and to guard against inadvertent legislation. The first practical exposition of this power will be found in a communication of of Thomas Jefferson. The closing sentence of this opinion of Mr. Jefferson, is, that where the President's opinion is equally balanced, a just respect for the legislature, would incline him to lean to their opinion, and he acted upon this principle, never having vetoed a bill during his eight years' term. [Mr. Kent here read from Mr. Madison's writings upon the definition of a despotism—and also, from Blackstone's Commentaries relative to the English veto power—also from Mr. Hamilton's Federalist, to shew that the veto should always be exercised with great caution.] There are many reasons why a King of England should have the power which will not apply to a President of the United States. The King is a hereditary monarch, bound to see his subjects' rights preserved unmolested. He convenes and prorogues the Parliament, and notwithstanding the power of an absolute negative, he has abstained from its exercise since 1667, while in this country the President, regardless of public sentiment, has exercised it till it has become an occurrence of almost every day. The President is only a servant of the people, like us. Has no inviolability of person, no prerogatives, or privileges, distinct from any other citizen, but is liable to impeachment like any other officer. Here is a marked distinction between the two Executives of England, and the United States. One advantage only the veto power possesses, and which the proposed amendment does not disturb. It anticipates a re-examination of a measure which has been vetoed for the purpose of arresting anything which may be prejudicial to

the public good. But when the legislative power shall pass a bill a third time after it has been rejected by the Executive, Mr. K. said he could not consent that the will of one man shall frustrate the repeatedly expressed will of the people. Mr. K. said, he heard an experienced member of the other House say that he believed the President had more power than the King of England, and he believed there was much more to be feared from encroachments by the Executive upon the Legislative, than by the Legislative upon the Executive power. The short periods for which the members of the Legislature are elected, literaly prevents any combinations against the Executive. But the real character of the Executive is unknown to the people, and his will remains in his single breast. Here is the weak point of Republican Governments. Who in the history of the world, have atempted to usurp power? Has it ever been the Legislative power? All history shows that it has always been the chief Executive, who has acted against the liberties of the people. Was it Cæsar or the Senate who attempted the liberties of Rome? It is undeniable that there is a constant tendency in the Executive power to contemn the law, and undermine the provisions of law. This principle is to be found in the writings of all the patriots who wrote prior to the adoption of the present Constitution. But how has the veto power been exercised heretofore? In the commencement of the Government, it was used to correct the effects of hasty and precipitate legislation, and of those acts which are supposed to violate the Constitution. As time progresses, we find it no longer confined to such cases, but it assumes the power to act upon finance, commerce, and in fact every thing which affects the interest of the people. Twice only was it exerted during the first 20 years of the Government.—Seven times within the first five years of this Administration, embracing various interests and deeply interesting to the people. We find the Executive will opposed to the Legislative will, anticipating and controlling the action of Congress, and entering upon the initiating powers of Congress, proposing a law which they may register and he approve. When these examples are before us, what may not be apprehended in succeeding ages? The danger consists, not in the possession of power, but in the illegal and improper exercise of it.

Mr. CLAY said that the gentleman from Maryland had presented a most interesting proposition, and he owed him his thanks for it, as well as for the clear manner in which he had elucidated and sustained it. The subject, he said, was undoubtedly entitled to mature consideration—he was inclined to support it, not only from a conviction of the necessity of curtailing the enormity of executive power, but because from the practical exercise of its effects, it had long since been felt in his State. But he regretted that it was so late in the session that it could not receive a deliberate consideration. He thought a period might arrive when we could do so. But at present he would move to lay the subject on the table, promising to call it up if an occasion should offer, during the residue of the session. The motion tion was agreed to.

On motion of Mr. WAGGAMAN, the Senate proceeded to consider, as in Committee of the Whole, the bill to establish branches of the United States Mint.

Mr. WAGGAMAN, in explanation of the objects of the bill, said that when the Mint was first established, branches of the institution were contemplated. The importations of gold and silver bullion into New Orleans, is now three times as great as it is in any other port of the United States, and it is daily accumulating. In the Globe of today, there is a statement, that on the 26th January last, there was, in two vessels, an importation of upwards of half a million into the port of New Orleans, from which it is obviously necessary to establish a branch of the Mint there, to do away the expense and risk of transportation of the bullion to the Mint at Philadelphia, which amounted to no less than two and a half per cent. But a more impressive argument, he said, was, that it would have the effect of adding to the circulating medium of the country some two and a half or three millions of dollars. The effects of this would be felt throughout the whole West. We, in the Southwest, labor under very great difficulties for want of a specie currency. The great sales of the public lands have caused a constant flow of specie to the Atlantic States—and we have now, in every State of the Union, batches of Banks which are deluging the country with a currency which is utterly useless to us, and which, by its continuance, will be productive of the most ruinous effects in the rise of property, which it will produce. As regards the branches in the Southern country, the necessity of them must be obvious to every gentleman. In a very few years, the mines in that region will yield at least two millions, and the risk of transporting such an immense amount of bullion to Philadelphia, will present almost an insurmountable barrier to sending it there for coinage. Mr. W. declined saying any thing more, until he heard some objections to the bill, which he would undertake to answer, if there should be any offered.

Mr. TALLMADGE then offered an amendmend to the first section, providing for the establishment of a branch at New York.

Mr. T. said, that if the system of branches was to be adopted, the large amount of specie imported into New York, which was the great radiating point for the internal commerce of the country, made it proper that there should be a branch there.

Mr. WAGGAMAN could not accept the amendment, because he did not think a branch of the the mint necessary at New York. It was within six hours of facile transportation to Philadelphia, and certainly it was not immediately necessary.

Mr. CALHOUN hoped the gentleman from New York would not press his amendment. At present, a branch at New York was not necessary. Hereafter, he proposed to extend the system by establishing branches at New York, Boston, Baltimore, and Charleston, the great importing points of the country. But at present he hoped the gentleman would not encumber this bill.

Mr. BENTON rose to say a single word. He belonged to the committee which reported this bill. He had looked over it with an anxious eye, and found that it entered into his views of restoring a metallic currency to the country. He was in favor of establishing branches of the mint wherever they were necessary, and he was also ready to appropriate money out of the Treasury to give a hard-money currency to the people of the United States. In France, which embraces a territory greatly less than that of the United States, there are ten branches of the mint, and in Mexico there exist seven. In the United States, from the peculiar configuration of the country, it might not be necessary to have more than six or seven; but it is of importance to the West that there should be one at New Orleans. On the Atlantic, there may be necessity for more. He was therefore ready to vote as much money as was necessary for this purpose. At a future day, he would be willing to vote for a branch at New York, but at present the amendment proposed was only loading down the bill. In No. 44 of the Federalist, Mr. Madison enters into an exposition of the coining power, and states, that as many local Mints as may be necessary to the wants of the country may be established. Before the confederation, each State had the power of coining at its own Mint; but the power has been surrendered, and as there is not the facility in the Atlantic States to diffuse coin through the West, it becomes the more necessary; a single Mint in Philadelphia partakes, in a great measure, of the character of a local institution. When Mr. Hillhouse was a member of the Senate, many years ago, he actually introduced a resolution for the purpose of abolishing the Mint at Philadelphia, viewing it as a local institution. But happily the resolution did not pass. Mr. B. said he apprehended it was a right of the People of the South and West to have branches of the Mint, and he deemed it necessary in order to prevent the notes of the local Banks from becoming the currency of the Federal Government. In '89 Congress passed a revenue law, in which they expresly required that the revenue should be received and paid out in gold and silver only, and he hoped to see the time when the Government would be restored to as good a condition as it was at that time. He would certainly vote for branches wherever they were necessary.

Mr. TALLMADGE remarked, that as honorable gentlemen had intimated their intention to carry out the system of branches at another time, he would withdraw the amendment.

The Senate then proceeded, on motion of Mr. WAGGAMAN, to fill up the blanks left in the bill, as follows:

For the annual salary of the superintendent of the mint at New Orleans,	$5,000
To the treasurer,	2,000
To the chief coiner,	2,000
To the assayer and refiner, each,	2,000
To two clerks, each,	1,700

Twenty subordinate workmen were also authorized to be employed at that branch.

Other blanks were filled as follows:

For the branches in North Carolina and Georgia, the superintendents, each,	$2,000
The chief coiners, each,	1,500
The assayers, melters, and refiners, each,	1,500
Two clerks, each,	1,000

Five subordinate workmen and servants to be allowed at each branch.

Mr. KING, of Alabama, offered an amendment requiring the appointment of the officers to be made as soon as the necessary building shall be erected.

Mr. CLAY said this bill was a measure of considerable importance, and he had not information sufficient on the subject to enable him to form an opinion upon the propriety of its passage. He did not know whether the mint was or was not sufficient to do the coinage of the country. But he thought, while we were discussing the danger and extent of executive patronage, we ought to be cautious how we passed laws to increase it. But he wanted to examine the subject—he knew nothing at all about it—it was new, and he had not reflected upon it, nor did he know any thing about the expense which would attend it. He therefore, moved to lay the bill on the table, and have it and the amendments printed. Mr. C. however, withdrew the motion at the request of some gentlemen.

Mr. CALHOUN thought the bill would be extending the expense, but he put it to the gentleman from Kentucky, whether all our citizens ought not to be placed on a footing—they were now incurring a loss of more than the whole expense of these branches. Are not the people of the south entitled to have the benefits and advantages of this government, equally with other citizens?

Mr. PORTER opposed the motion—the effect of laying the bill on the table would be that it would not be acted on in the House this session, and the object would therefore be defeated—it was of importance to the whole Union and particularly the western country.

Mr. CLAY said, if we must go on and discuss the bill, let us go at it. The annual expense of these establishments must be near half a million of dollars, and the same in perpetuity, for it was folly to suppose if once established, that they would ever be discontinued. He wanted to look into this question, and see what the probable importations of specie may reasonably be expected to be. The late importations are known to be very extraordinary, and to have arisen from uncommon causes. But he begged he might not be driven into this question—he was not informed on the subject, and could not consent to let it go on. He therefore renewed the motion to lay the bill on the table.

Mr. WAGGAMAN requested that the motion might be withdrawn for a moment.

Mr. CLAY. I withdraw the motion. Let the debate go on.

Mr. W. continued. The expense of these establishments would not cost more than from $30,000 to $32,000 a year at New Orleans, and $15,000 at each of the other two places in the south. The Mint, he said, had paid nearly all its expenses out of the half per cent. retained upon

coinage. He hoped the honorable member would not make any objection to the bill.

On motion of Mr. CALHOUN, the bill was laid on the table, and the amendments were ordered to be printed.

SPECIAL ORDER.

The Senate resumed the bill to repeal the law limiting the terms of certain officers, it being on its final passage.

Mr. POINDEXTER said, that since this subject had been under the consideration of the Senate, he had felt anxious to express his opinions upon its principles. It opened before us the whole theory of our Government. But from respect to the Senate, and a belief that it had been amply discussed to enable the People to understand it, he would not take up the time of the Senate, by entering far into the discussion. He had wished in particular to examine the doctrine of implied powers. He denied the whole theory altogether. The executive powers of the President were derived from legislative enactments. There was no such thing as implied powers in any branch of the Government. Where power was given, it was expressly declared and specified in the constitution. There was another point he wished to have discussed. That was the power of impeachment. But he would forbear.

Mr. CALHOUN said the third section of the bill, involving the question whether the power of removal resided in the President by the constitution or not, was one of no ordinary character. Upon its decision, momentous consequences depended; he believed the future destinies of this Government rested on that decision. But that subject had been ably discussed by gentlemen qualified for the task, and he would not occupy the time of the Senate by repeating their arguments. He intended to confine himself to a single point.

Mr. C. said the power of removal existed either as a power necessary and proper for carrying into effect the provisions of the constitution, or as an express grant of that constitution. If it was necessary for carrying into effect the constitution, it was more properly a legislative than an executive power.

He had relied on the decision of 1789 as the true and proper exposition of the constitution, until last winter, when his attention was particularly called o the subject. He then took up the subject and looked over the debate of that time. He thought the arguments of the minority exhibited a just view of the question and were unanswerable.

Mr. C. said some Senators had grounded their ugyments on the supposition that this power was ontained in that general sweep, where all executive ower is granted to the President. Others main- ain that it was an inherent power; but he disagreed rith both opinions. Mr. C. wished to turn to the ractical operations and see how these powers ould work. Among so many constructions there ould be no government. Every officer, from the 'resident down to the constable, must show some rant of power, either from the constitution or law.

Congress was the great central point where all ower must receive its sanction and direction, instead of being directed according to the views of eparate and conflicting departments. If the different departments of the Government should be laced in hostile array against each other, it was asy to see which would prevail. The President xecuted the laws, and was clothed with their auhority; he put all the machinery of Government i motion, and without him the laws were powerless; the Judicial Department might decide upon e propriety and application of the laws, but the resident must enforce their decisions. Hence it as easy to see which department would prevail i the conflict.

Mr. C. said, he had been unjustly dealt with. e had been represented as saying that all the ofcers of Government were the supple tools of exutive power. That was far from his meaning; believed there were many upright and conscitious officers. But his fears were for the fuure; he had seen within a few years persons of e noblest spirit and purest intentions, quail bere that magic influence, which has power over l, and before which the loftiest bow down. Bere it, Roman firmness had been broken; and every manly virtue blasted beneath its withering influence. And whoever contended for that power upheld a mighty influence which would swallow up our free institutions.

There was, said Mr. C., an immense amount of discretionary power, which must be vested somewhere, and he thought it should be intrusted with Congress, as the immediate Representatives of the People. The President was sufficiently protected by his negative over the laws of Congress. And here, Mr. C. said, he differed with his honorable friend from Maryland (Mr. Kent) in regard to the veto power of the Executive. He believed that power was granted, not only as a protection against the encroachments of Congress, but also to prevent all laws which might embarrass him in the performance of his duties. The Judicial Department was fortified by its permanence and tenure of office.

Mr. C. said that if they wished to have the public business transacted faithfully, the officer should be made safe, as sure of his place as if it were a freehold. Such should be the policy of the Government, unless they meant that offices should be the spoils of victory, and be divided like conquered lands in former times. Every President ought to rejoice in the opportunity of giving his reasons and explaining his conduct to the People.

Mr. C. went on to state, that the doctrines contained in the bill were precisely the same as those which had been advocated by the friends of this administration, and upon which it came into power. He held the grounds of canvass sacred—pledges should be redeemed, and assurances given to the People, be scrupulously fulfilled.

Mr. C. said the Senator from New York (Mr. Wright) had attempted to show there was no danger from the multitude over which executive power was exercised. He then went on to show that there was danger—an irresistible influence exerted through each division and sub-division of that great mass. He referred to rotation in office; he thought where the offices were filled by the people, rotation might be practised; but where they were filled by the will of a single man, it tended to make slaves and supple tools of men.

The debate was further continued by Mr. KANE and Mr. TALLMADGE, in opposition to the bill.

Mr. HILL said: Mr. President, it will be perceived that the principles of the bill which has passed the Senate, relating to appointments of postmasters, comes in direct conflict with the bill under consideration. The Post Office bill assumes for the Senate the power of deciding on the appointment of all postmasters in those post offices the net proceeds of which amount to one thousand dollars annually; and to make the power of the Senate felt in those appointments, it makes provision that the postmaster shall continue in office only four years! This bill, changing the tenure by which every considerable postmaster in the country shall hold his office, is recommended by gentlemen who are the strong friends of repealing that law which limits all other officers to a term of four years. So is appears, when the Senate is grasping at more power for itself, it adopts a principle directly in the face of that which it repudiates when it would deprive the President of his constitutional power.

Some persons, for a few years past, have seemed to manifest a longing desire that the Senate should have a hand in the management of the Executive Departments beyond the power the Senate possesses as a co-ordinate branch of the legislature. The new mode of appointment will enable them to punish those postmasters who shall have the independence to express their opinions on any matter which may be adverse to the opinions of a majority of the members of the Senate—to proscribe, "for opinion's sake," every man as a partisan who shall have the hardihood to act with the mass of the people, in any public meeting adopting resolutions that shall speak the language of freemen in relation to the acts of every public man, and every body of public men.

Did the Senate intend, by making every valuable post office dependent on their will, to create a new corps of "supple and subservient tools," such as the Senator from Kentucky (Mr. Clay) described on Wednesday, as being first put to "silence," and afterwards compelled to become "neutrals" in politics? The Senator complained of the postmasters in Ohio, who had the hardihood to attend a political convention in that State. Doubtless the Senator would like to lay his hands on these offenders who have had the presumption to act with others of their fellow citizens, and express their opinions in relation to public men; and the bill of the Senate will give warning to all postmasters not again to offend in like manner.

There seems to be a sort of hydrophobia-dread of removals from office whenever a certain party is at the bottom of the wheel. The Senator from Kentucky says the principle of dismissing men from office is a new principle—that it commenced about six years ago, when Gen. Jackson first came into office. So great has been the burden on the mind of the Senator since that time, that he may be readily excused for not recollecting what took place during the administration immediately preceding that of Gen. Jackson. Does he remember that the editors of two principal democratic newspapers in Maine and New Hampshire, which had "done the State some service," while contending in a fearful minority during the war with Great Britain, were proscribed because they would not put on and wear the then Executive collar? Does he recollect the declaration then made by a Secretary of State (Mr. Clay) relative to one of those newspapers when the Representatives of the State requested his reasons for proscribing its editor, that he would "have no neutrals?" Does he remember that this Secretary proceeded to make these removals, as was stated at the time, even against the wishes, or without consulting the Representatives of the People of those States?

The Senator has complimented the veteran *Gerry* for his opposition to the doctrine of Executive removals in the Congress of 1789. If he had been conversant with Gerry's administration, while at the head of the Executive of Massachusetts, in 1810 and 1811, he would have seen that he carried the doctrine of removals, in just retaliation of the universal proscription by the opposite party, much farther than it ever has been carried by President Jackson. The name of the revolutionary patriot was made a by-word with the aristocracy of Massachusetts, because he had the independence to prefer his own political friends to his political enemies, in his appointments to office. He was even arrested for debt on the day of the annual election, by his political enemies, to show their spite for his fidelity to the democratic party.

The Senator says, the people of the west cannot and will not submit to the turning out of officers; and he seems to take it for granted that the present administration alone is guilty of the enormous offence of preferring its friends to its enemies. What has the Senator himself been doing for the last six years? Have not his nightly cogitations, and his daily speeches, been directed to the business of turning out the "hungry" and "haggard" crew, who have obtained offices under Gen. Jackson? Can any man believe the Senator would have consented to the confirmation of any officer differing in opinion with him, if he could, by withholding that consent, have forced the appointment of one of his political friends?

It would be difficult for any friend to the administration in the Senate soon to forget the "armor and the attitude" of the honorable Senator from Kentucky, during the session one year ago. The "Long and Hungry"* exultation at the old Hanover election in Virginia, in which our friends were turned out, and the Senator's friends were in the full tide of success, had such an impression on my mind, that I have been scarcely able to think of any thing else than "Long and Hungry" for office every time I have cast my eye at the seat of the honorable Senator. It was most manifest, Mr. President, that the principal pleasure then anticipated by the Senator and his friends, was that of turning every Jackson man out of office that could be reached, either by the Executive, Legislative, or elective power. The whole business of the honorable Senator for years seems to have been, either directly or indirectly, to bring about that

*The name of a place in Virginia.

state of things which should leave the coast clear, to the turning out of every political enemy, that the Senator himself, and his friends, might step into their places.

Speaking of the labors of the Post Office Committee at the last session, and in anticipation of what they were to do in the recess, a Senator from Massachusetts (Mr. Webster) then said: "They have had a laborious winter, and are likely to have a laborious summer. Let them go on fearlessly, and the country will appreciate their services. Let them explore all the sources of corrupt patronage; let them bring all abuses into the broad light of day; let them inquire into the *number of removals of postmasters, with the alleged cause of such removals;* let them inquire at whose bidding honest and faithful men have been removed to make way for partisans," &c.

Well, the Senate's Committee, sitting during the recess, went into the Department agreeably to instructions, to make inquiry of the abuses of the removal of postmasters. The Postmaster General did not acknowledge their authority to catechise him as to the cause of removals. And it is my belief that the Senate alone has not the power to go into any Executive Department in the recess, to call the Executive to account for the reasons why it removes or appoints its subordinate agents.

Removals from office, after all, have been the great and crying sin of the Post Office Department since General Jackson came into office. From the opinions which have been advanced in the Senate Chamber, we might suppose that after a man is once seated in office, he has a right to it for life: it is very inconvenient for him to give it up, since he depends upon it for a living: he has made his arrangements to keep it, and it will but deprive his children of bread to take from him his office.

I care not whence comes such a doctrine, whether from the North or the South, the East or the West. I say no man is entitled to an office one moment longer than he is useful in that office, nor has he the right to complain if the power which gave it, at any time shall see fit to take it away. When a man accepts an office, he either considers it a matter of favor to himself or favor to the public; if it be a favor to himself, how are his rights invaded by discontinuing that favor? If he accepts the office at a personal sacrifice, he ought to be thankful to be relieved of the duty.

The doctrine that once in an office of emoluments gives a man a claim to be always in office, will not stand alone. If we would see this government becoming one of the most corrupt on earth, we should favor the appointment of men to office for life. And this would hardly go far enough; for the poor children who would suffer if their father was deprived of office during his life, would certainly have stronger claims to the same office after the father was dead, when they were still more helpless.

In the elder Adams's time the federalists very well understood the advantage of the influence and emoluments of office. In the State of New Hampshire, from 1797 to 1804, no man who did not subscribe to the doctrines of the alien and sedition laws could even be appointed a justice of the peace. In 1798 a democratic clergyman was turned out of the office of chaplain, after a formal trial before the Legislature, because he happened to omit naming the President of the United States in his morning prayer. All the offices from high to low were filled by friends to the administration. The venerable WHIPPLE and GARDNER, the one collector of Portsmouth, and the other commissioner of loans for the State, who had been appointed by Washington, were both dismissed from office by Adams, because their names were not found upon an adulatory address to the President which had been circulated at Portsmouth.

Mr. Jefferson came into the President's office in 1801, and what did he do? Without assigning his [illegible] to the Senate, he reinstated his own political [illegible], and he dismissed others who were his [illegible] opponents. Whipple and Gardner were [illegible] in New Hampshire. Did Mr. Jefferson place other than a political friend in any considerable office? Did he not remove officers in repeated instances, for no other reason than that they were opposed to the principles which elevated the republican party and raised him to the Presidency?

During his administration and the greater part of that of James Madison, Gideon Granger of Connecticut was the Postmaster General. The post offices in 1800 were not more than one for every ten at this time. Yet during those two administrations in almost every considerable office a change of postmaster was made for no other reason than that the incumbent was not friendly to the administration.

In the two only towns where I ever lived in New Hampshire, changes were made of the postmaster. When but a boy of fifteen years of age, in the year 1803, I well recollect the last mail bag that was opened by Doct. Samuel Curtis, the postmaster at Amherst. The old gentleman parted with his office with great reluctance; he had fought hard against Mr. Jefferson, and he could not but consider it fair play, that inasmuch as Mr. Jefferson had succeeded, it was right that one of his friends should fill the office of postmaster. In the other town, (Concord,) George Hough, a veteran printer of a partisan newspaper that had called Mr. Jefferson as many hard names as have been applied to President Jackson, was the postmaster; he was removed early in 1801, and a democrat and friend to the administration, appointed in his place. For more than twenty years this undeviating old federalist was afterwards my neighbor, always inveterate in his political hostility, but accommodating and kind in the way of business. During the war I an scarcely doubt he would willingly have had me tried and hung, for rejoicing at American victories and urging the sons of New Hampshire to enter the army. Yet the old gentleman in the way of business readily united with me in the publication of a periodical work containing the debates in Congress on both sides and public documents, which were then highly interesting to the people, two large volumes of which we printed without asking Congress to subscribe for them. To the day of his death, on all political questions, he adhered to the doctrines of the aristocracy—he probably never in his life gave his vote or his influence to promote any democrat to office. Although a professing christian of the prevailing sect, he once declared to me that it was sufficient for him if a man was a federalist, to have his support, even though he was Algerine or Turk in his religion.

These two cases are only specimens of the general turning out of federal postmasters in New England, by Gideon Granger. It was not then as it is now: there were no charges exhibited against the incumbent waiting for answers and explanations. If the democrats in any town were dissatisfied with their postmaster, they wrote to the Postmaster General, generally through JOHN LANGDON, the well-known patriot of the Granite State, and the removal was as sure to take place as the day is to succeed the night.

The removals under the Administration of James Madison, were even more decisive in their character than under Thomas Jefferson. All the more lucrative post offices that Mr. Jefferson had left in the hands of the federalists, were by Mr. Madison, changed to other hands. In Boston, in Portsmouth, Newburyport, Hartford, Baltimore, and all other places where a change was desired, changes for political reasons alone, were made; the most of them under Mr. Madison. And it is well known that for refusing to remove the Postmaster at Philadelphia for political reasons only, at the instance and direction of the President, Gideon Granger himself was turned out of the office of Postmaster General. Looking back to the administration of Mr. Madison, it must be recollected, that he had even less affection for his political opponents than almost any other President.

It will thus be seen that the doctrine of change and rotation in office is not new. The old federalists at first insisted that no democrat was fit for any office, and never suffered any to be appointed while they had the power. The democrats, as was natural, when they obtained the ascendency, as a matter of necessity, made removals of their adversaries, because, as Mr. Jefferson then said, "few died, and none resigned." From that day to this, much the largest share of permanent offices, depending on executive appointment, has been held by the party in this country adverse to popular rights. That party has not scrupled, in all instances where they had the power, to turn out their adversaries. Nor has it ceased to claim their right to remain in office, when the tables have been turned upon them. On the one hand, they never cease to cry out "proscription for opinion's sake," while, on the other, their very creed is based on that spirit of persecution which will tolerate in office, or even in prosperous business, no man who thinks differently from themselves.

It is to old Virginia, to JEFFERSON and MADISON, that we are indebted for the republican example of doing justice to our own political friends when we are in the ascendency. They were not quite as magnanimous as Virginians have on some occasions since been. They did not think it of so little consequence what a man's political opinions were, as to elect men as members of the Legislature, who were decided political opponents, and thus give a character to one branch of her representation in Congress hostile to the principles which she has ever professed

After the examples of Jefferson and Madison, sanctioned as they were by the strong public sentiment of the country, should it be imputed to the present administration as a crime, that it prefers its friends to its enemies? It was abundantly evident, during the panic of last winter, that a large majority of the army of office-holders in this District belonged to the opposition. Men who had been neutral before, viewing the triumph of the Bank, in its great contest for power, as certain, did not hesitate to come out. Indeed, at this moment, the enemies of the administration stand a much better chance for favor than its friends, in every thing that depends on Congress. All officers who want increased salaries, increased expenditures, great appropriations, and great patronage; all who want to press doubtful claims to a favorable result; know very well on what side to look for favors.

As to removals of Postmasters, I am of opinion that the present Postmaster General has been in fault, and that fault is, that he has not, in some places, made changes where he ought to have made them. There are counties in New England with thirty, forty, fifty, and sixty Post Offices, and scarcely a democratic Postmaster among them all. Perhaps not one in five of the Post Offices in some of the New England States, is in the hands of a friend of the administration. It is well known that the opposition party in New England not only do not suffer friends of the administration to be appointed to any office, but that they turn every man out, whenever they find a chance. When were they ever known to elect a man to Congress, or to any considerable office, opposed to their views? It is their general practice to exclude all from the highest to the lowest grade of office. Now it might be supposed that a party possessing all their pride and manly bearing would scarcely deign to be whining continually, because when they are beaten in fair fight, they are obliged to give place in the principal offices of trust to those whom the people have declared better deserving of the public favor, than themselves.

In New Hampshire, Mr. President, we repudiate the doctrine that men have life estates in the public offices. With the republicans of that State generally, it has become a practice to send a man to neither branch of the legislature, more than two years in succession; to elect a man Governor not more than three or four times; to choose a man representative in Congress, not more than twice or thrice at most, if he be distinguished; and I hope to see the time arrive, when it shall be considered a rule not to be deviated from, that no man shall be re-elected a Senator in Congress who has served for the term of six years, until a term of years shall have intervened.

The extravagant expenditures and abuses in this government will never be fully remedied until the right of the people to instruct their Senators and Representatives shall be acknowledged in practice as it is admitted in theory—until a swift responsibility, on the part of public servants to their employers, shall be confessed—until *rotation in office* shall be considered a cardinal point in the re-

abl can creed. Scarcely any man can come here
per or six years without being committed on
some one of those precedents which are taken as the
round of unnecessary expenditure: he has some
send who wants a claim allowed, or he comes
on a section of the country where a handsome
appropriation for the improvement of some river;
he bull ing of some canal or road; the erection of
some breakwater or light-house; the fortification of
some harbor—will do immense good to his friends
al neighbors. He goes for that claim or that appropriation; and when he has gone for it, he is
bound in all good conscience to go for almost any
thing that shall be proposed by any other member
to has been so disinterested as to vote for his proposition. I am quite certain that it would be for the
interest of every member of Congress to come
here with the expectation that he shall not, in any
event, continue in the House of Representatives
for four years, and in the Senate beyond six
years, and that he shall retire at any moment the
it shall be ascertained he is misrepresenting the
ideas of a majority of his constituents. Sure I am
that the public interest will be better subserved
under the adoption of such a rule, than by continuing a man once chosen for life, under the repeal at
price of a repudiated politician, than the action
of the representative ought not to be palsied by
the will of his constituents. I, however, am willing that each State should regulate its own practice in relation to rotation in office. The party
with whom I act in the State of New Hampshire,
adopting a rule which, while it makes office accessible to every man who will deserve it, preserves
the purity and economy and simplicity of its administration.

It would be more for the interest of the public
surge at the seat of government if a salutary
system of rotation in office should be adopted
throughout. Many of the evils which now exist here would be remedied by a change of
floors. The idea of dependance on the emoluments of office, is degrading to a republican
country and it has degraded many who have
spent their whole lives as clerks in the Departments, and died, having destitute families. I would have no man expect that he is
to remain in office doing servile duty, or no duty,
for life. If a law should pass providing that a
man should not continue in any one public employment over twelve years—if one third of all the
incumbents in bureaus of this city should be compelled to go out every four years, leaving their
places to be filled by persons who, within the limits of the States, have inhaled the air of freemen,
and know how to procure a livelihood without being paid an office salary—we should find a difference of things in the public offices; we should
visit a population at the seat of Government
using some affinity to that indomitable spirit of
our countrymen which best provides for itself on
its own resources. Weakness and pusillanimity
is always to be expected in that child which is
taught to believe that its parent will furnish its
aliment.

I do not doubt the time will speedily arrive
when offices of profit, depending as well on Executive appointment as on elections by the People, will be changed from one to another, till it
will become a matter of course that each individual shall strive to qualify himself to discharge the
duties of any office to which he may be called.
I could even be willing to see the Postmasters
changed where an incumbent has enjoyed a lucrative place for years, and his more needy neighbor, who was equally capable and worthy, was in
a situation to discharge the duties of the office as
well, or better, than he had done. I would be
glad to witness such a change, even when all were
the party friendly to the Administration. As I
now there never could be a change against us in
the election of a President where a general turn-out
of our friends in office would not take place,
could I not count much on the value of that advice from any preferred political friend who tells
me that we ought, when we succeed in an election ourselves, to let our enemies remain in quiet
possession of all the offices in our Government depending on the Executive will.

Believing the tendency of the bill will be to give

---

the incumbents in office a life-estate in their respective offices—that it will create a corps of men
having interests and feelings adverse to the spirit
of our republican institutions, and to the interests
and feelings of the great body of the People—I
will record my vote against it.

Nevertheless, as the bill seems likely to pass this
body, with my negative, I am anxious it should
pass with at least one feature which I can approve.
I therefore move that the bill be recommitted, with instructions that the committee report
the following additional section:

" Section 4. And be it further enacted, That
the proceedings of the Senate in relation to all
nominations of public officers by the President
shall be with open doors, and that each member
may rise up his place and assign his reasons for or
against the confirmation of the person nominated."

The reason for the Senate acting in public on
nominations is of much greater force than in favor
of the President assigning his reasons for the removal of officers. The President cannot lose his
individual character in that of his office. His reasons, which are written, must all be made public
sooner or later. The indignation of the individual
reported against and that of his friends, will break
on his head alone, inducing even personal attacks,
as we have seen in the case of a late dismissed officer of the navy. Not so the proceedings of the
Senate—the individual there is lost in the corporate or collective character of the body. Hence,
if there be any propriety in requiring the President to communicate his reasons for the removal
of an officer, there is a much stronger reason why
the action of the Senate, on all nominations made
by the President, should be in full view of the people.

Mr. H. concluded by asking the yeas and nays
upon his motion, which were ordered.

Mr. BENTON then moved that the Senate adjourn, which was not agreed to.

Mr. BENTON then spoke for some time, to
show that this bill, and that reported by the committee in 1826, were not identical, and was desirous
of recommitting it to have alterations made, so as
to make it conform to that bill in all particulars.

Mr. HILL then withdrew his motion, in order
to enable Mr. BENTON to move its recommitment,
with the instructions indicated by him.

Mr. CALHOUN compared the two bills, for
the purpose of showing that they were now identically the same, with the exception of one or two
words, indicated by Mr. BENTON.

Mr. WEBSTER expressed his willingness to
see the bill altered, so as to make it exactly like
the bill of 1826.

Mr. LEIGH made some remarks upon the recommitment.

Mr. CUTHBERT desired the commitment, as
the bill was now presented under a new aspect.
He strongly resisted hurrying so important a bill
through at the close of a session where there was
no exigency requiring it.

Mr. WHITE took the same view of this bill as
of the one of 1826.

The recommitment was agreed to, and the
committee having obtained leave to sit during the
sitting of the Senate, withdrew, and after a few
minutes, returned, when

Mr. CALHOUN reported the bill, amended in
conformity with the instructions.

The bill was then considered, as in Committee
of the Whole, and the amendments were concurred in; when it was reported to the Senate.

Mr. HILL then renewed his motion to amend
the bill as before mentioned, and asked the yeas
upon it, which were ordered.

Mr. POINDEXTER opposed the motion as going to change a rule of the Senate; to do this the
proposition must be on the table one day.

Mr. BUCHANAN expressed the hope that the
gentleman from New Hampshire would withdraw
his proposition. It was one which required consideration, and it was now too late to give it that
attention which it required. He could not vote
for it on this account.

Mr. CALHOUN said the proposition goes to establish rules for the Senate by law, when the constitution provides that each House shall make its
own rules for its own government.

The amendment was disagreed to by a vote of
yeas and nays. Yeas 3, nays 40, as follows:

YEAS.—Messrs. Hill, Kane, Linn.—3.

NAYS.—Messrs. Bell, Bibb, Benton, Black,
Brown, Buchanan, Calhoun, Clay, Clayton, Cuthbert, Ewing, Goldsborough, Hendricks, Kent,
King of Alabama, King of Georgia, Leigh, McKean, Mangum, Moore, Naudain, Poindexter,
Porter, Prentiss, Preston, Robbins, Robinson,
Ruggles, Shepley, Silsbee. Smith, Southard, Swift,
Tallmadge, Tipton, Tomlinson, Tyler, Webster,
White, Wright.—40.

The bill was then ordered to be engrossed for a
third reading, and then, at 6 o'clock,
The Senate adjourned.

HOUSE OF REPRESENTATIVES.

FRIDAY, February 20, 1835.

Petitions and memorials were presented, on
leave, by Messrs. BEATY, LOYALL, VINTON,
POTTS, and HANNEGAN.

On motion of Mr. BEATY, the petition of Col.
Henry W. Francis, claiming pay for horses stolen
from his father in his lifetime, by the Cherokee Indians, be referred to the Committee on Indian Affairs, and printed.

On motion of Mr. BEATY, the letter of the
Governor of Kentucky, and resolution of the Legislature of that State, in relation to the establishment of a military school in said State, and a resolution from the Legislature of said State in relation to the establishment of a national armory
therein, were referred to the Committee on Military
Affairs, and printed.

Mr. HANNEGAN presented sundry petitions
for the establishment of a post route from Michigan City to Plymouth, in the State of Indiana;
which were referred to the Committee on the Post
Office and Post Roads.

Mr. CAVE JOHNSON, from the Committee on
Private Land Claims, reported with amendments,
the bill for the relief of the heirs and legal representatives of James Latham, deceased; which were
concurred in, and the bill ordered to be read a
third time.

Mr. C. JOHNSON, from the same Committee,
reported, with amendments, the bill to confirm
certain land claims in the southeastern District of
Louisiana; which were concurred in, and the bill
ordered to be engrossed.

Mr. HUBBARD, from the Committee of Ways
and Means, reported a bill authorizing the employment of additional Clerks in some of the Departments of the Government; which was read twice
and committed.

Mr. FOSTER, from the Committee on the Judiciary, reported a bill authorizing the issuing of
letter-patent to John Howard Kyan, on certain
conditions; which was read twice, and postponed
to Friday next.

Unfavorable reports, upon various petitions,
were made by Messrs. FOSTER and TOMPKINS,
from their respective Committees.

Mr. C. ALLAN, from the Committee on Territories, reported the following resolution; which
was rejected:

Resolved, That this House will, on Saturday, the
21st instant, from and after the hour of 1 o'clock,
P. M., take up and consider bills relating to the
Territories.

Mr. E. WHITTLESEY, from the Committee on
Claims, submitted the following resolution; which
was agreed to:

Resolved, That it is expedient that the Solicitor
of the Treasury stay all further proceedings in the
suits now pending, and judgments obtained in the
Circuit Court of the United States, for the Northern District of New York, against so many of the
persons referred to in bill No. 369, reported on the
18th of March, 1834, as may apply to him for that
purpose, by themselves or attorney, until the close
of the next session of Congress: Provided, That
the endorsers, or securities, in those instances
where they exist, shall assent to the staying of
further proceedings in the cases in which they are
concerned, by a writing, to be lodged with the
said Solicitor.

Mr. SEVIER asked the House to consider certain bills relative to the Territories, which had
been reported by a Committee of the Whole.

Objection being made, Mr. SEVIER moved a suspension of the rule; which was agreed to; yeas 113, nays 27.

The following bills were then read a second time, and ordered to a third reading:

A bill making appropriations for certain improvements in the Territory of Michigan;

A bill to provide for opening certain roads in the Territory of Arkansas, and for other purposes;

A bill from the Senate making an appropriation for completing certain roads in the Territory of Arkansas;

And a bill from the Senate to improve the harbor of the river Raisin.

The bill from the Senate authorizing the construction of a Rail-road upon the public land, from Tallahassee to St. Marks, in Florida, was taken up

Several amendments having been disposed of, the question recurred upon the amendment adopted in Committee authorizing the construction of a Rail-road upon the public lands in the Territory of Michigan.

Mr. WHITE said that he understood the rail-road in Michigan, provided for in the amendment, was connected with the disputed boundary question. he therefore hoped the Delegate from that Territory, would withdraw the amendment, and attach it to one of his own bills, as it would be calculated to embarrass the bill in which his (Mr. White's) constituents were particularly interested.

Mr. MERCER remarked, that the adoption of the amendment would make the bill incongruous, as it was not competent for the House to change the title of a bill from the Senate.

Mr. LYON said he could see no force in the objection of the Delegate from Florida. The boundary question had nothing to do with it. He understood that the members from Ohio intended to resist the amendment because one end of the proposed road touched upon a tract of country claimed by the state of Ohio. He thought an objection of that character, an illiberal one. In order however, to avoid a long debate, and according to a promise which he had made to the Delegate from Florida, not to throw any embarrassment in the way of the passage of the bill, he would withdraw the amendment.

The bill was then ordered to be read a third time.

Mr. CONNOR moved to suspend all the previous orders of the day, for the purpose of taking up the bill reported from the Committee on the Post Office and Post Roads, establishing certain post routes and altering and discontinuing others. It was important that this bill should be acted on.

Mr. VINTON hoped the gentleman would ask for an evening session, for the purpose of considering this bill.

Mr. CONNOR objected to the suggestion, there being usually so much confusion during an evening session.

After some further conversation between several members, Mr. CONNOR yielded his objections, and the afternoon of Tuesday next, from 6 o'clock, was set apart for the purpose of considering the foregoing bill.

Mr. DUNLAP moved to suspend the rules of the House, for the purpose of going into *Committee of the Whole House*, on the Tennessee Land Bill. Mr. D. said, he asked the indulgence of the House to state the situation of the persons provided for in said bill. The citizens of eighteen counties, and the fractions of five others, were directly interested in the passage of this bill: they live on scraps of vacant land. They had been for twelve years asking Congress to provide some means for them to obtain a title to their homes; it had hitherto denied them. The members whose constituents were directly interested in the passage of this bill, had, during the last and present session, contented themselves to give silent votes. They had not occupied the attention of this House with long speeches. Their great anxiety to get this bill passed had prevented them from occupying a portion of the time of the House in debate. Their constituents had a right to a portion of the time of the House, for the consideration of their business: none had been given them during the last or present session. We have been assisting other gentlemen to get the business of their constituents attended to; now we ask them to assist us. The provisions of the bill are such as will give general satisfaction. He did not believe there could be any opposition to the same, and that it would occupy but a short time of the House. He asked it as a matter of favor of the House to take up this bill.

Mr. CROCKETT wished to make a few explanations on the subject of this bill.

Objection being made, Mr. C. resumed his seat.

The question was then taken on Mr. DUNLAP'S motion to suspend the rules; which was negatived.—yeas 77, nays 52—two-thirds being required.

Mr. GILMER moved to suspend all the previous orders of the day, for the purpose of taking up the bill establishing the Western Territory. Mr. G. in submitting this motion, urged the importance and necessity of speedy action upon this measure.

After a few remarks by Messrs. ASHLEY, LOVE, and H. EVERETT, the latter gentleman asked the yeas and nays, on the motion to suspend the rules; which were ordered, and were, yeas 145, nays 50.

So the House determined to consider the bill.

WESTERN TERRITORY.

The House accordingly took up the bill to provide for the establishment of the Western Territory, and for the security and protection of emigrants, and other Indian tribes therein.

The bill had passed through the Committee of the Whole, who had reported sundry amendments thereto, and the question was on agreeing to the same.

On motion of Mr. J. Q. ADAMS, the bill was read at length by the Clerk.

Several verbal amendments were agreed to without discussion.

Mr. HORACE EVERETT entered into a lengthened defence of the provisions of the bill. He examined the relations in which the Government of the United States had placed itself by the several treaties made from time to time with the Indian tribes, and the relations in which it stood towards the Indian tribes, by the claims they had upon the Government of the United States, on account of those treaties. Various engagements had been entered into with those tribes, providing for their removal west of the Mississippi. For the fulfilment of these engagements the faith of the nation was pledged. Among those engagements, was one guarantying to the Indians the possession of their lands against all hostilities whatever, whether arising from other tribes or between themselves. These were the two most important engagements, and it became necessary to take measures for the purpose of fulfilling those obligations.

One great object of the bill was to enable the Indians themselves to make such regulations among themselves as should, in a great measure, relieve us from the burthen, so far as we could induce them to take upon themselves the obligations we have assumed; to defend themselves from foreign hostilities, and maintain peace among themselves. This could only be done by employing such a military force as that provided for under the bill. One word as to the relations between the Government of the United States and the State of Georgia: we had bound ourselves to extinguish the Indian titles to all the lands within the limits of that State; and that would be done if this bill passed, and that embarrassing question forever settled. Mr. E. then referred to the Indian titles in Alabama, Tennessee, Mississippi, &c., which belonged to the United States, and which we should then acquire. The first great object of the bill was to fulfil our obligations towards the Indians; the next to redeem the faith we had pledged towards the State of Georgia; the third to acquire a territory for ourselves in those States wherein the Indian titles belonged exclusively to the Government of the United States.

The great question was, if the bill would effect these objects. First, with regard to the Cherokees in Georgia, it was a belief, well founded, that as soon as the bill was passed, that tribe would emigrate, and one great end would be answered, that of disposing of those intricate and embarrassing questions, which had so long been agitated, not only in the State of Georgia, but also in other sections of the country. Mr. E. then entered into a review of the various sections of the bill seriatim. With regard to the alleged indisposition of the Indians to emigrate, Mr. E. said the committee had satisfactory evidence before them that the tribes were willing to do so, if their territorial government could be ensured. The committee had procured a translation of the bill, and submitted it to a delegation in Washington, who expressed themselves satisfied with it. The object was not to force it upon the Indians, but to organize a plan, and to provide an officer on the spot, who might aid and assist in carrying it into effect. Much error had arisen from the name given to the officer, from his being called Governor, instead of Superintendent; and it was thence imagined that it was the object of the bill to form an Indian Government; but this was not so. The plan of the council was for the purpose of their forming a confederation of the different tribes. It was indispensable that the presiding power should be somewhere; it was in the President of the United States, who, as Commander-in-chief of the army, was required to see the bill carried into effect, which could only be ensured by a military force, and the commander of that force would be appointed in the usual manner. Sufficient powers had been reserved to the United States, in the provisions of the bill, between the different tribes.

With regard to a delegate, it was absolutely necessary that the Indians should have one in the House. What objections might be urged against it he knew not, but if they were to examine the subject minutely, they would find it exceedingly difficult to discover by what authority a delegate from either of the territories come there. The end of the committee had been to provide for every thing which could civilize the Indian tribes, and no provision was thought more conducive to that end than the provision authorizing a delegate to be sent to Congress. It would also be productive of a great saving to the United States, and would eventually do away with much of the expenses of of the Indian Department.

Mr. J. Q. ADAMS regretted to see that there was an evident disposition on the part of the House to pass this bill. It was a bill interfering with the laws of nations, and proposing the establishment of a despotism. It was a bill to alter the Constitution of the United States, and was contrary to the second section of that instrument. He asked the gentleman who reported the bill, (Mr. Everett,) to show him any article of the Constitution authorizing the establishment of an Indian Territory. This land was guarantied to the Indians, and what right had we to take upon ourselves, to form the Indians into an integral part of the United States? Such an instance was never known under the Constitution. If you did this, what could prevent you from having a negro territory in the United States, and authorizing it to send a delegate to Congress? Were gentlemen prepared for this? He believed not, but it might come.

It was also a bill to change the laws of nations. The relations in which the United States existed towards the Indians, were relations under the common compact of the laws of nations. The Indians had retained the power of self-government. We had made treaties with them, and if we proposed any such control over them as that intended by the present bill, it could only be done by treaty. We were assuming more than we had a right to, in doing it by legislation, though he was not aware that an Indian treaty was a mockery.

It was a bill for the establishment of a despotism. It was in contravention of the laws of nations, and was therefore despotic. Under the Constitution, every State must be republican, and the people were so punctillious, that although they reserved certain sovereign rights to the States, they made it a fundamental principle with them all, that no Government in this Union should be established, other than republican. If they did so, the other States were bound to put it down by force. This bill was not republican at all; it established a military despotism. To prove this,

r A. read the second and third sections of the ll and said it was the very essence of despotism. le intended to move to strike out those two secons. The bill had undergone a close and rigid xamination last session, and was proved to be of he character he had designated. Mr. A. concluded by moving to strike out the second section of e bill.

Mr. BURGES was always in favor of every ing that could be done to those wrecks of so any mighty nations, but to see the representatives f a great republic, sitting there to make laws for eople who were unrepresented, was one of the reatest anamolies he could have conceived. It ould be inefficacious. If those people had asked r it, and had requested the wise men of this naon to make a code of laws for them, that would different, but they could not be coerced by ws made without their own consent. He ould shrink from doing so with horror. Mr. B. opposed, particularly, the provision of e bill providing for a reversion of the Indian nds to the United States, and said he could not pport the bill. We were placing these men der the power of our legislation, and then proding for taking back their lands again. In a few ars, he said, by dragoons and bayonets, christian mahawks and scalping knives, not one of these or fellows would exist on his land.

Mr. GILMER said, if they intended to act upon this bill, it was impossible to go into the old estion with the Indians. The clause referred by the gentleman from Rhode Island, (Mr. rges,) was an exact transcript from the agreeent made with the Indians themselves. The dians were in a state of pupilage, regarded as fit to govern themselves. It was said that the ployment of a military force made this a despom. Was not the United States a Republican vernment, and would the gentleman from Maschusetts refuse to employ a military force to rry the laws into execution? And why should the Indian Council do the same? The gentlen himself had once carried it out to a greater tent. Mr. G. contended that the bill was the ly measure that could be devised to secure the dian rights, and yet the bill was objected to by gentleman from Rhode Island on that very ound.

Mr. BURGES explained. He wished their hts to be secured by treaty

Mr. GILMER resumed. With regard to the tion to strike out the second section, he would serve, that the word Territory was used, not in sense of a Government, but as a territory or ct of country. Mr. G. would have no objecn to strike out all that part relating to territoand insert some other words, and also insert a vision to reserve to the Indians the same right the lands they had now. The word territory s introduced by the committee in compliance h the wish of the Indians themselves. Mr. G. ved to insert "lands within," so as to read, nds within said territory," and gave notice of ther amendment, connected with the provision a Delegate to Congress.

Mr. ARCHER regretted the apathy and indifence with which this subject was regarded. contended that the bill under consideration for the establishment of a foreign confederathat might become as great as our own. We as much right to go abroad and incorporate a ernment in a foreign land. We had territonow, but of what are they composed? Of cins of the United States. It had been said y were in a state of pupilage. Who governed m? Who appointed the meetings of their ncils? Did not every one know that the agent the United States could govern these Indians the influence of whisky and presents? When se presents had not proved sufficient, what had ved so? Force! Is this securing to the poor ian a government of his own? The remedy posed grew out of those very acts of oppres. Mr. A. contended that the proposed government would be a despotism—a military government in its worst form. He had a feeling ich he would never surrender, which would ays impel him to discountenance any government in this country composed of people of any other color than his own. There was even now a proposition existing to form a government of blacks on our borders. There was one already established in Canada, formed of the negroes from our own territy, and occupying one of the most fertile sections of the country. He asked, what would be the relation of this government to ourselves? It would be a *province*. Were we dead to the warnings of history? What finally subjugated Rome? Her Provinces. The Territory in contemplation, (though it did not deserve the name of Territory, and he would not call it such,) would make a parallel with fallen Rome. Our Governor or Superintendent would resemble her Proconsuls. He hoped the members of that House would pause before they recognised the principles sanctioned in the bill, and he expressed himself opposed to it in every form.

Mr. HARDIN began by an examination of the claims of Georgia on the United States Government in reference to the Indian titles, to lands in the Cherokee country, &c., and maintained that we were bound to fulfil the engagements we had made with Georgia for extinguishing those claims.

It was the policy of the United States to give them such a form of Government as should induce treaties with all the Indian tribes, and make all those tribes the true friends of the United States. Such was the object of the bill. Notwithstanding the profound respect which he entertained for the opinions of the gentlemen from Massachusetts and Virginia (Messrs. Adams and Archer) on constitutional law, he could not see the subject in the same light in which they appeared to view it. Mr. H. then referred to the act admitting the Territory of Louisiana into the Government as a Territory, for which the gentleman from Massachusetts voted, and which was similar in many of its provisions to the present one. The officers of that Territory were appointed by the President, and where was then the cry of despotism? And he would ask them where was the constitutional objection to this bill? Military force was authorized in the incorporation of Louisiana into the Government. Why then object to it here, where the Indians themselves were allowed a commanding voice in its exercise? He could see no despotism in the matter. The opposition to the bill reminded him of the trick of lawyers so often resorted to to sustain a bad cause.

Mr. H. said he would be happy to see a Delegate from that abused race upon this floor, and he doubted not that nine times out of ten he would go with him. Give these tribes a government—and a standing among nations. What more degraded the otherwise fair character of our country, than the fate of this almost extinct race. The remnant of them left on this side of the setting sun, was a reproach to Spain and to Europe. What could more contribute to our glory, than to be the instruments of making a reparation, so long due to an injured—a pesecuted race? Mr. H. alluded to the indirect and inefficient attempts that had been made to civilize the Indians, by sending missionaries among them, &c. but he would say, give them a government, give them property, give them laws and literature, and every thing would follow. They would then become christians like ourselves. We owed it to Georgia to do it. We owed it to ourselves, and to our God, and he never, in his life, voted more cheerfully for any bill than he should for the present. He had no such fears as those dreaded by the two gentlemen who had addressed the House that morning. Wait till the time come and then meet the contingency. He hoped the bill would pass.

Mr. VINTON said this discussion was unexpected to him. It was a solemn subject, and he feared the character of the bill was not properly understood by the House. If the country was charged with any violation of public faith, which bore with particular force upon its national character, it was this of its obligations to, and contract with, the aborginees. The Territory included in the bill, extended over an immense portion of our continent—bounded on one side by the 29th degree of north latitude, and extending over 13 degrees of longitude. He concurred with the gentleman from Massachusetts, (Mr. Adams,) that the government proposed for this territory was a despotism—a military government in embryo.

How was this Territory to be governed? By a Governor, and a Council consisting of twenty four Chiefs, who were "to be elected or *selected*."—What selected meant, he knew not. Then, it was confined to Chiefs; no other Indian than a Chief. Then the Governor had many despotic powers. Mr. V. recited the various provisions of the bill setting forth the same.

Mr. CLAYTON rose and requested the Chair to call the House to order, as the stir was so great that, though sitting near the gentleman, he was himself unable to hear him distinctly.

Mr. HUBBARD said, as there was a great excitement prevailing, in consequence of the important news that had arrived, he moved that the House adjourn. Negatived.

Mr. VINTON resumed. He was opposed to the bill, because, in the first place, it was unconstitutional, and secondly, it was anti-republican. If it was intended to form a civil government, he was for the employment of civil officers only. If, however, the bill should be adopted, he should move to restrict the limits of the territory within a smaller compass, so that it should not be larger than one, or two, at the utmost, of the Western States.

Mr. CLAYTON reviewed the objections to the bill. Those of the gentleman from Massachusetts (Mr. Adams) were three; first, that it violated the constitution; second, that it violated national law; third, that it would establish a despotism. The objection of the gentleman from Virginia (Mr. Archer) was that we were about to create a dangerous confederacy; and those of the gentleman from Ohio (Mr. Vance) that the territory would be too large. Mr. C. maintained that these objections were more imaginary than real. He took them up and answered them seriatim. He thought that the general government had the same power over its own territories that a state government had over the territory within its own limits. They both had the right to impose what conditions they thought necessary for the regulations of the people residing within the territory. Nor could you stop after having once assumed the right. The United States government had done it in various ways, and they had the same power to extend their regulations as far as it deemed expedient. Mr. C. then gave an historical outline of the incidents and events that had occurred between the state of Georgia and the Cherokee Indians in that state, and advocated the bill at considerable length.

He concluded by insisting that it was not the object of the bill to establish a new territory or a new government. It was to secure a home to the Indian tribes of the country. Such was the wish and feeling of the State of Georgia, and, he trusted such would prove to be the feeling of this House and of this country. Where, he asked, was the evidence of all that benevolence so often manifested in this House? Now was the time to exert it. Now it could be plainly evinced by the passage of this bill.

Mr. ADAMS rose to correct some statements of the gentleman from Kentucky (Mr. Hardin) in relation to the vote he gave on the admission of the Territory of Louisiana into this government. He quoted from the journals of the House from 1804 to 1806 (which he held in his hand,) to prove that the course he pursued on that occasion was directly the reverse of that attributed to him. He made a wide distinction between that case, however, and the present. This was for the admission into our Union of another race of beings—and not the admission of white men belonging to a foreign government.

Mr. FILLMORE proposed an amendment to the bill, which was decided then to be out of order, but at the solicitation of Mr. F. the amendment was read. Mr. F. was induced to offer his amendment, he said, to apply particularly to those tribes of Indians residing in New York.

This amendment not being considered in order,

Mr. GILMER obtained leave to make some explanatory remarks applicable to the subject to which the amendment of Mr. F. alluded.

On motion of Mr. JONES, of Georgia,

The House then adjourned.

IN SENATE.

SATURDAY, February 21, 1835.

The VICE PRESIDENT laid before the Senate a communication from the Treasury Department, made in obedience to a resolution of the Senate, transmitting the information called for relative to obstructions in the Potomac river, between Washington and Georgetown.

Also, a communication from the War Department, transmitting the information called for by a resolution of the Senate, relative to a survey at the mouth of the St. Joseph's river.

Mr. SILSBEE presented the memorial of a number of citizens of Beverly, Massachusetts, praying the passage of a non-intercourse law with France.

After some remarks from Messrs. SILSBEE, CALHOUN, KING of Alabama, BROWN, GOLDSBOROUGH, POINDEXTER, LEIGH, BENTON, WEBSTER, and BUCHANAN, the memorial was laid on the table, and ordered to be printed.

The bill to repeal the two first sections of the act limiting the term of certain officers, commonly called the four year law, came up on its final passage, when Mr. EWING demanded the yeas and nays, which were ordered; and the bill was passed —yeas 31, nays 16, as follows:

YEAS—Messrs. Bell, Benton, Bibb, Black, Calhoun, Clay, Clayton, Ewing, Frelinghuysen, Goldsborough, Kent, King of Georgia, Leigh, McKean, Mangum, Moore, Naudain, Poindexter, Porter, Prentiss, Preston, Robbins, Silsbee, Smith, Southard, Swift, Tomlinson, Tyler, Waggaman, Webster, White—31.

NAYS—Messrs. Brown, Buchanan, Cuthbert, Hendricks, Hill, Kane, King of Alabama, Knight, Linn, Morris, Robinson, Ruggles, Shepley, Tallmadge, Tipton, Wright—16.

The following bills were also read a third time and passed;

The bill further to suspend the operation of certain provisoes of "the act to alter and amend the several acts imposing duties on imports," passed in July, 1832;

The bill for the relief of David Beard;

The supplement to the act granting a township of land to certain exiles from Poland;

The bill for the relief of Walter Loomis and Abel Gay;

The bill for the definition and punishment of offences against the United States.

Mr. WEBSTER, from the Committee on Finance, made an unfavorable report on the petition of Mathias Brumen.

Mr. SOUTHARD, from the Committee on Naval Affairs, reported the bill from the House regulating the pay of the officers in the Navy of the United States.

Mr. TOMLINSON, from the Committee on Pensions, reported the bill from the House granting a pension to Joseph Gilbert.

Also, the bill granting a pension to John Gerodelle.

Also, the bill granting a pension to Luke Vicolise, with an intimation that he should, when it came up before the Senate, move for its indefinite postponement.

Also, a bill granting a pension to Col. Gideon Morgan, with an amendment.

Also, a bill to increase the pension of Origen Eaton, with an amendment.

Mr. PRENTISS, from the same committee, reported a bill for the relief of John Ashton. Also, a bill for the relief of Thomas Morton.

Mr. ROBBINS, from the Committee on the Library, reported a resolution requiring the Secretary of State to cause to be compiled and printed a list of the officers of Government.

On motion of Mr. WAGGAMAN, the Senate resumed, as in Committee of the Whole, the bill to establish branches of the Mint of the United States.

After some remarks from Mr. BROWN,

Mr. CLAY moved for the indefinite postponement of the bill. He reiterated his opposition to the bill, and contended that the Mint at Philadelphia was fully competent to do all the coinage which the country required. He denied the correctness of the argument that the Mint at

New Orleans was necessary to prevent the transportation of the bullion to Philadelphia. It would find its way to the great commercial marts of the country at all events, whether coined or not—he considered it therefore, unwise and injudicious to establish these branches. He supposed it would gratify the pride of the States of North Carolina and Georgia, to have them there where they might conveniently go and get out the precious metals, but when the objection as to the measure was so strong, he could not consent to yield his opposition to it. He moved the indefinite postponement, and asked the yeas and nays upon the motion, which were ordered.

Mr. MANGUM regretted that the gentleman had not all the information which was necessary to enable him to understand this subject; if he had, Mr. M. thought he would not oppose the bill. He thought the necessity to multiply the number of American coins was manifest, and the actual loss of transporting the bullion and foreign coins to Philadelphia for coinage was about three and three-quarters per cent.; a loss which must retard the increase of the coinage. With respect to the gratifying the pride of the Southern States, he would tell the gentleman, they had none to gratify. The actual loss in the gold region of Georgia and North Carolina far exceeds the expense of all the necessary buildings for these establishments. He saw no evil in the multiplication of these mints. It was well said by the gentleman from Missouri, when the bill was up before, that, in the commentaries upon the constitution, it was understood that branches of the mint might be multiplied. He was willing to establish branches wherever the natural advantages of the country required it.

Mr. FRELINGHUYSEN thought the object of having a mint was mistaken, when he heard gentlemen say that there were great quantities of gold in the southern quarter of the Union, and asked the Government to establish mints there for for their accommodation. The mint was established for the accommodation of the Government, and he thought the present one suffice at. Why put an additional burthen on the Government, because the people in that section have been so fortunate as to find gold in abundance? The plain answer is, if you have found gold, you ought to be the last to ask the aid of the Government in transporting it to Philadelphia. The manufacturer asks no aid in transporting his productions to market, and how is the case of the gold digger any stronger? He wished gentlemen to answer this objection.

Mr. BROWN said, the gentleman from New Jersey asked why we apply to Congress to relieve us from the burthen of transporting our bullion to be coined, when the manufacturers of the North did not ask to be paid for transporting their material. Mr. B. said it was true they have not applied for this assistance, but they have applied for that which is much more substantial—protection. The people of the South ask no protection—they rely on their own exertions—they ask but a simple act of justice, which is extended to other parts of the Union—they ask for their rights, under the regulation of Congress—the right to coin money. But the gentleman from Kentucky says that there is no expense imposed upon the South by way of transporting their bullion; that the burthen would be the same as if it was coined there. The remark of the gentleman is founded in mistake. What are the facts? Can the bullion of North Carolina be circulated as a circulating medium? We all know it cannot be done, and its value, therefore, must be necessarily curtailed, and it must be transported at great risk, trouble, and expense. The annual loss sustained by the citizens of North Carolina from these causes amounts to a sum which is very serious to them. But they suffer a much greater loss than the returns of the mint disclose. Much of their gold is sent to South Carolina and Georgia, and from thence it is sent to the mint as Georgia and South Carolina gold, when in fact it is North Carolina gold. Another reason for the passage of the law, and one which he hoped would not be less regarded by the gentlemen on the other side of the house, was that the measure would be auxiliary to the restoration of the metalic

currency of the United States, and contribute to bring the Government back to that currency which was contemplated by the constitution.

A protracted and discursive debate then ensued, in which Messrs. FRELINGHUYSEN, MANGUM, CALHOUN, BENTON, PORTER, WEBSTER, GOLDSBOROUGH, CLAY, and EWING participated, when the principles of the bill of last session were fully gone into.

The question to postpone was determined in the negative by the following vote:

YEAS—Messrs. Bell, Buchanan, Clay, Ewing, Frelinghuysen, Goldsborough, Hill, Knight, McKean, Naudain, Prentiss, Robbins, Smith, Southard, Swift, Tipton—16.

NAYS—Messrs. Benton, Bibb, Black, Brown, Calhoun, Cuthbert, Hendricks, Kane, King of Alabama, King of Georgia, Leigh, Linn, Mangum, Moore, Morris, Poindexter, Porter, Preston, Robinson, Shepley, Silsbee, Tallmadge, Tyler, Waggaman, White, Wright—27.

Mr. CLAY made some further remarks in opposition to the bill, and, with a view to test the opinion of the Senate, he moved its recommitment to the Committee on Finance, with instructions to amend the bill so as to authorize the establishment of one branch only, upon which motion he asked the yeas and nays; which were ordered.

After some further remarks from Messrs. POINDEXTER, WAGGAMAN, CLAY, and CALHOUN, the question was determined in the negative by the following vote:

YEAS—Messrs. Bell, Black, Buchanan, Clay, Ewing, Frelinghuysen, Goldsborough, Hill, Knight, McKean, Naudain, Prentiss, Robbins, Smith, Southard, Swift, Tipton, Tomlinson—18.

NAYS—Messrs. Benton, Bibb, Brown, Calhoun, Cuthbert, Hendricks, Kane, King of Alabama, King of Georgia, Leigh, Linn, Mangum, Moore, Poindexter, Porter, Preston, Robinson, Ruggles, Shepley, Tallmadge, Tyler, Waggaman, White, Wright—24.

Mr. CLAY then moved to postpone the bill till Monday next, and on that motion he asked the yeas and nays; which were ordered, and the question was determined in the negative; yeas 26, nays 22, as follows:

YEAS—Messrs. Bell, Buchanan, Clay, Ewing, Frelinghuysen, Goldsborough, Hill, Knight, McKean, Moore, Naudain, Poindexter, Prentiss, Robbins, Shepley, Smith, Southard, Swift, Tipton, Tomlinson—26.

NAYS—Messrs. Benton, Bibb, Black, Brown, Calhoun, Cuthbert, Hendricks, Kane, King of Alabama, King of Georgia, Leigh, Linn, Mangum, Porter, Preston, Robinson, Ruggles, Tallmadge, Tyler, Waggaman, White, Wright—22.

Mr. CLAY then moved another section, as an amendment to the bill, authorizing the establishment of a branch of the Mint at Louisville, Kentucky.

Mr. C. made some remarks in support of the amendment, and Mr. MANGUM, Mr. BIBB, and Mr. WAGGAMAN, opposed it.

The motion was disagreed to, without a division.

The bill was then reported to the Senate, and the question being on concurring in the amendments made, as in Committee of the Whole, Mr. CLAY moved further to amend the bill by reducing the salary of the superintendent of the branch at New Orleans, from $3,000 to $2,500 per annum, and upon that motion demanded the yeas and nays; which were ordered, and are as follows:

YEAS—Messrs. Buchanan, Clay, Ewing, Goldsborough, Hendricks, Hill, McKean, Moore, Morris, Naudain, Prentiss, Robbins, Shepley, Smith, Southard, Swift, Tipton, Tomlinson, Webster—19.

NAYS—Messrs. Benton, Bibb, Black, Brown, Calhoun, Cuthbert, Kane, King of Alabama, King of Georgia, Leigh, Linn, Mangum, Poindexter, Porter, Preston, Robbins, Ruggles, Tallmadge, Tyler, Waggaman, White, Wright—22.

So the amendment was disagreed to.

Mr. CLAY then moved a further amendment to reduce the salary to $2,500 per annum, and upon that motion demanded the yeas and nays, which were ordered and are as follows:

YEAS—Messrs. Buchanan, Clay, Ewing, Goldsborough, Hendricks, Hill, Linn, McKean, Moore

rris, Naudain, Prentiss, Robbins, Ruggles, Shep-
ly, Sibbee, Smith, Southard, Swift, Tipton,
mlinson, Webster—22.

NAYS.—Messrs. Benton, Bibb, B'ack, Brown,
lhoun, Cuthbert, Kane, King of Alabama, King
of Georgia, Leigh, Mangum, Poindexter, Porter,
Preston, Robinson, Tallmadge, Tyler, Wagga-
an, White, Wright.—20.

So the Senate agreed so to amend the bill.

Mr. EWING then moved to amend by reducing
salary of the Treasurer at New Orleans, from
2,000 to $1,500.

Mr. CLAY moved that the Senate adjourn,
which was lost, yeas 15, nays not counted.

The question recurring on the amendment, it
was determined in the negative, on a division—
yeas 20, nays 21.

Mr. EWING then moved, further to amend by
reducing the salary of the chief coiner, from $2,000
to $1,500 per annum, and demanded the yeas and
nays on the motion, which were ordered, and it
was determined in the negative by the following
vote:

YEAS.—Messrs. Buchanan, Clay, Ewing,
Goldsborough, Hill, Knight, McKean, Moore,
Morris, Naudain, Prentiss, Robbins, Shepley,
Smith, Southard, Swift, Tipton, Tomlinson.—18.

NAYS.—Messrs. Benton, Bibb, Black, Brown,
Calhoun, Cuthbert, Hendricks, Kane, King of Ala-
bama, King of Georgia, Leigh, Mangum, Poin-
dexter, Porter, Preston, Robinson, Ruggles,
Sibbee, Tallmadge, Tyler, Waggaman, Webster,
White, Wright.—25.

Mr. CLAY then moved to reduce the salaries
of the assayer, melter, and refiner from $2,000
each, to $1,500, which was disagreed to.

On motion of Mr. CLAY, the salaries of the
six clerks were reduced from $17,000 to $1,200
each.

Mr. CLAY then moved to reduce the salaries
of the two superintendents of the branches in
North Carolina and Georgia, from $2,000 to
1,500 each, and on that motion demanded the
yeas and nays, which were ordered, and are as
follows:

YEAS.—Messrs. Bell, Buchanan, Clay, Ewing,
Goldsborough, Hill, Knight, McKean, Morris,
Naudain, Prentiss, Robbins, Shepley, Smith,
Southard, Swift, Tipton, Tomlinson.—18.

NAYS.—Messrs. Benton, Bibb, Black, Brown,
Calhoun, Cuthbert, Hendricks, Kane, King of Alabama, King of Georgia, Leigh, Mangum, Poindexter, Porter, Robinson, Ruggles, Sibbee, Tallmadge, Tyler, Waggaman, Webster, White,
Wright.—24.

So the motion was disagreed to.

The bill was then ordered to be engrossed for a
third reading.

The CHAIR laid before the Senate a communication from the honorable George Poindexter,
calling the attention of the Senate to an anonymous letter, stating that affidavits were in the possession of the President of the United States,
proving that interviews had taken place between
POINDEXTER and RICHARD LAWRENCE, a few
days previous to the attempt on the life of
President, and asking the appointment of a
select Committee to investigate the facts and report them to the Senate.

The communication was read; and also a document signed by D. J. PEARCE, a member of the
House, testifying (as the Reporter understood it)
that he saw such depositions in the hands of the
President.

Mr. CLAY rose and said, that the communication and document which had just been read, induced him with nothing but the deepest mortification and regret; and when he saw the anonymous letter to which the communication referred,
he did not believe there was the slightest foundation for it. It was impossible for him to credit the
statement, that affidavits should have been procured at the instance of the Chief Magistrate, for
the purpose of implicating a Senator of the United States in so foul a transaction. That such a
course of injuring a fellow citizen should be adopted, affidavits of such a tenor procured, and not
only for the purpose of producing them under
circumstances as should prevent the charges
being met, he should not credit, but upon

the production of much higher evidence than
had yet been adduced.

But, said Mr. C. the communication calls on us
for the exercise of a most unpleasant duty, and at a
most unpropitious season—at a time when the Senate is within 7 or 8 days of the close of its session,
and when the official existence of the Senator,
himself, for a time at least, is near its close. But
although the time is short, that should not become
a question when the duty of this body requires it
to act. It was the duty of the Senate to examine
into the case, as requested by the Senator, and if
it should turn out to be true that he had the slightest agency in that most nefarious attempt involving
the life of a fellow citizen, and that citizen the
Chief Magistrate of the country, he had no doubt,
painful as the alternative might be, that we would
be called on to exercise the high functions conferred on the Senate by the Constitution, of expelling so unworthy a member. But if it should turn
out that there was not the slightest foundation for
the charge, and that there had been no agency on
the part of the Chief Magistrate in procuring such
affidavits, it was due to the country that he should
be vindicated from the aspersion. Taking this
view of the case, he thought there could not be
the slightest objection to creating the Committee
of Investigation, as asked for.

Mr. C. concluded by moving that a committee
of five be appointed for this purpose, clothed with
power to send for persons and papers.

The motion was agreed to.

On balloting for the Committee, it appeared
that Messrs. TYLER, SMITH, MANGUM, KING,
of Georgia, and WRIGHT, were appointed.

Mr. WEBSTER then gave notice that on Monday next, he would move to take up the bill making appropriations for the support of the fortifications of the United States.

Mr. BUCHANAN, by unanimous consent, offered a resolution, that the Military Committee be
instructed to inquire into the expediency of making an appropriation to repair Fort Mifflin, and to
construct piers or batteries in the river Delaware;
which was ordered and adopted.

The Senate then adjourned.

HOUSE OF REPRESENTATIVES.

SATURDAY, February 21, 1835.

Mr. CAMBRELENG from the Committee on
Foreign Affairs, reported the bill of the Senate to
create a Commission for the adjustment of claims
on account of French spoliations prior to 1800
He said the Committee had instructed him to state
that there was not sufficient time for its members
to investigate a question of such magnitude, and
requiring the examination of so many documents.
The Committee had therefore instructed him to
move that it be discharged from the further consideration of the bill, and that it be laid upon the
table—with the assent of the Committee, he also
moved that two statements, the one prepared by
the gentleman from Massachusetts, (Mr. Everett)
in favor of the claims; the other by himself,
against them, embodying much information on
both sides of the question, should be printed for
the use of the House; which was ordered accordingly.

Mr. FULTON, from the Committee on Claims,
reported a bill for the relief of Abner Stelson;
which was read twice and committed.

Mr. CONNOR, from the Committee on the Post
Office and Post Roads, reported, with an
amendment, the bill from the Senate to provide
for the organization of the Post Office Department. The bill was made the special order, of the
day for Tuesday next, and the amendment was
ordered to be printed.

Mr. WATMOUGH, from the Committee on
Naval Affairs, reported a resolution setting apart
this day, from 12 o'clock, M., for the consideration of the motion to reconsider the vote rejecting the bill for the relief of Mrs. Susan Decatur and others

Mr. W. said, that the committee had been induced to offer the resolution in consequence of
the necessitous condition of one of the parties.

The SPEAKER decided the resolution to be
out of order.

Petitions were presented, on leave, by Messrs.
LOVE and POLK, and referred.

Petitions were presented, on leave, by Messrs.
LOVE and POLK, and referred.

Mr. ASHLEY presented resolutions of the Legislature of Missouri, relative to the boundary line
of that State; which were ordered to be printed.

Mr. CHINN, from the Committee on the District of Columbia, reported a bill making an appropriation for the support of the Penitentiary in
the District of Columbia, for the year 1835; which
was read twice and committed.

Mr. FOSTER, from the Committee on the Judiciary, reported the following bills, which were
read twice and ordered to be read a third time:
A bill for the relief of the heirs of James Wilson, deceased, and a bill for the relief of Sarah H. B. Stith.

Mr. BEATY, by leave, submitted the following joint resolution, which was read twice, and its
further consideration postponed to Monday next,
and it was ordered to be printed.

*Resolved by the Senate and House of Represen-
tatives of the Congress of the United States,* That the
Secretary of War be instructed to expend ten
thousand dollars of the thirty thousand dollars appropriated at the last session of Congress for the
improvement of the navigation of the Cumberland
river, between the mouth of Laurel river, and the
Big South Fork of Cumberland river, in the
neighborhood of the Stone Coal Mine, during the
next summer.

Mr. HAMER, from the Committee on the Judiciary, to which a resolution adopted by the
House on motion of Mr. BURGES, had been referred, directing said committee to inquire into the
expediency of providing that all printing hereafter required for every branch of the public service, should be executed in the District of Columbia, and also into the propriety of excluding all
newspaper editors and publishers of the same,
from a participation in the execution of said printing,—made a lengthy report. Mr. H. moved that
the committee be discharged from the further
consideration of the subject.

Mr. FOSTER asked for the reading of the report.

The reading of the report was commenced,
but before it was concluded—

Mr. WATMOUGH called for the orders of the
day. Yeas 98, nays 48.

The SPEAKER laid before the House a letter
from the Secretary of State, communicating, pursuant to law, the number of American seamen
registered in each port of entry in the United
States, for the year 1834, &c., which was laid on
the table and ordered to be printed.

The following bills were read a third time and
passed:

A bill for relief of the heirs of James Latham,
deceased;

A bill supplementary to the act of 1802, for the
settlement and confirmation of certain land claims
in the Southeastern District of Louisiana;

A bill to provide for the improvement of the
harbor of Clinton river in the Territory of Michigan;

A bill from the Senate making appropriations to
complete certain roads in the Territory of Arkansas;

A bill from the Senate providing for the improvement of the harbor at the mouth of the river
Raisin, in the Territory of Michigan;

A bill from the Senate authorising the construction of a rail-road upon the public lands between
St. Marks and Tallahasse in Florida;

And a bill to provide for opening certain roads
in the Territory of Arkansas, and for other purposes.

The motion heretofore made by Mr. MERCER,
to reconsider the vote on the passage of a joint
resolution, authorising the Secretary of the Treasury to examine and adjust the claim of O. H.
Dibble, for materials, &c., furnished for the erection of a bridge across the Potomac, and report
the state of the same to Congress at its next session, was taken up.

After a few remarks from Messrs. MERCER
and BANKS, the motion to reconsider was agreed
to.

Mr. BANKS, instructed by the Committee on
Claims, and by unanimous consent, submitted a

amendment to the resolution; which was agreed to.

The question recurring on the passage of the joint resolution, as amended, a desultory debate of considerable length ensued, in which Messrs. MERCER, BANKS, ANTHONY, FILLMORE, and MINER participated.

Mr. ANTHONY moved to recommit the resolution to the Committee on Claims.

Mr. HILAND HALL moved the previous question; which was seconded—yeas 80, nays 40.

The House then determined that the main question should be put.

The main question being, "Shall the joint resolution pass?" it was decided in the affirmative—yeas 98, nays 75.

A bill from the Senate, granting to the borough of Mackinaw, certain grounds for public purposes, was read the third time and passed.

The following bills from the Senate, were read twice and committed;

A bill for the relief of the owners of the brig Despatch, and cargo;

A bill for the relief of Walter Loomis and Abel Gay;

A bill for the relief of David Beard;

A bill supplementary to the act granting lands to certain exiles from Poland;

And a bill amendatory of the act for the punishment of certain offences against the United States.

A bill from the Senate to repeal the first and second sections of the "act to limit the term of office of certain officers therein named, and for other purposes," approved, May 1st, 1820, was read twice.

Mr. ARCHER moved that the bill be committed to a Select Committee.

Mr. FOSTER moved that it be postponed to Wednesday next, and made the special order for that day.

Mr. HUBBARD moved to commit the bill to a Committee of the Whole on the state of the Union, and that it be reprinted.

Mr. FOSTER said, if the latter motion prevailed, it would be equivalent to sending the bill to the tomb of the Capulets. He demanded the yeas and nays on the motion; which were ordered.

Mr. HUBBARD referred to the number of appropriation and other important bills which were necessary to be acted on. He did not object to the postponement of the bill as proposed, but he was opposed to making it a special order.

Mr. ARCHER withdrew his motion to commit to a select committee.

The SPEAKER informed the House that there were various special orders upon the calendar, which would have precedence, and that the present bill could not be reached if made the special order for a particular day, unless the House by a vote of two thirds, postponed all the previous special orders.

Mr. E. EVERETT inquired of the Chair, if the bill was of a character which required its commitment?

The SPEAKER replied that as the bill made no appropriation of money, its commitment was not required by the rules of the House.

Mr. HUBBARD withdrew his motion to commit.

The motion of FOSTER was then agreed to.

A bill from the Senate to suspend the operation of portions of the tenth and twelfth clauses of the 7th section of the act supplementary to the acts imposing duties on imports, of July, 1832, was read twice and committed.

The SPEAKER laid before the House a letter from the Secretary of the Treasury communicating a list of balances on the books of the Treasury, against collectors, &c., which was laid on the table and ordered to be printed.

WESTERN TERRITORY.

The House then resumed the consideration of the bill to provide for the establishment of the Western Territory, and for the security and protection of emigrant and other Indians therein.

The question pending was the motion of Mr. GILMER to amend the second section of the

bill, by inserting the words "lands within," so as to read "lands within said Territory."

Mr. SEABORN JONES, who was entitled to the floor, said the provisions of the bill had been sufficiently explained by the gentlemen from Vermont and Georgia, (Mr. H. Everett and Mr. Gilmer.) Mr. J. wished, however, to make a few remarks in reply to the gentleman from Massachusetts (Mr. J. Q. Adams.) That gentleman had objected to this bill because it provided for the employment of a military force; he (Mr. J.) could not avoid expressing his surprise at the objection from that quarter, when all must recollect, but too well, the employment of military force in Georgia, to deprive a State of her just rights. Mr. J. entered into a full defence of the course that had been adopted and pursued by the State of Georgia, arising out of the engagement entered into by the Government of the United States to extinguish the titles to the Indian lands within her limits. Why had not the U. States effected this sooner when they had done it in other parts of the country? Because, by extinguishing the titles to Indian lands within the territorial limits of other States the lands became the property of the United State; but the United States desiring no benefit from the lands in Georgia, had delayed carrying the compact into effect. He maintained that the whole blame rested on the United States for not putting an end to this question in Georgia, as she was bound to do, by fulfilling the obligations to which they were pledged under the treaty of 1802. Every application made by Georgia, every memorial, every remonstrance, received but the monosyllabic answer—No. When Georgia found the Cherokees about to erect themselves into an independent government, she then extended her jurisdiction over those Indians. Was Georgia, said Mr. J. to permit an imperium in imperio within her own limits? Could she permit this with peace and tranquility to herself? Ought a sovereign State to permit it? She could not. What did she do? She remonstrated with the general government, who paid no attention to her complaints, and Georgia was consequently driven to the expedient of surveying the Cherokee country, and enforcing obedience to her laws. This bill was the measure that would effect what was desired in that respect; and if gentlemen were sincere in their professions of philanthropy, he called upon them to sustain it by their votes. Mr. J. concluded by announcing his intent to offer sundry amendments to the bill as soon as the House had passed upon the others under consideration.

Mr. ASHLEY was opposed to the general principles of the bill, and said, at the proper time he should also propose some amendments. His principal objection was that it was contrary to the spirit of the laws made by the Indians themselves. There was scarce an instance in which laws were made for them by us with which they were not dissatisfied. The only way, in his opinion, to civilize the Indian, was to surround them with civilization. He was in favor of giving a certain portion of land to each, binding them to a certain territory, and leaving them to make their own laws and regulations. He was quite sure that the governor would become a despot, at least in the opinion of the Indians themselves. He put the case of murder. If an Indian were to be executed by the order of the Governor, under our laws, it would excite general dissatisfaction among them; but if left to themselves they would do justice with alacrity.

One great object of the bill was to relieve the State of Georgia of the Cherokees, but that very act would burden the territory of Arkansas, and the borders of other States to the same extent.

The amendment was agreed to without a division.

Mr. GILMER then moved to strike out the following from the second section of the bill, " and that the right of such Indians or tribes shall be impaired by their being at any time formed into a territory."

Mr. FILLMORE then submitted the amendment which he had attempted to introduce yesterday, applicable to the Indian tribes in the State of New

York. It was to insert after the word tribe " and Indians "

Mr. EVERETT, of Vermont, thought the amendment unnecessary. It was, however, agreed to.

Mr. BATES then moved to strike out part of the same section, pledging the faith of the United States. Agreed to —ayes 81.

The question then recurred on Mr. J. Q. ADAMS'S amendment, to strike out the second section of the bill. Negatived.

Mr J. Q. ADAMS then waived for the present his intended motion to strike out the third section.

Mr. GILMER proposed a modification of the same, relating to the appointment of the governor by the President of the United States, one of the Cherokee, Choctaw, and Creek tribes of Indians.

Mr. VINTON said, it was a very important and exceedingly imperfect bill, in some of its details; he would suggest that a further time be given for perfecting it before a motion should be made for the previous question, which he understood to be the intention of the gentleman from Georgia, (Mr. Jones,) as soon as the amendments of the Committee on Indian Affairs should be acted on.

Mr. JONES disclaimed such an intention.

Mr. VINTON said he had some important amendments to offer, which he hoped would be permitted to be heard and incorporated in the bill.

The amendment of Mr. GILMER was then adopted.

Several other amendments, of a verbal character, were then agreed to.

Mr. VINTON then proposed to introduce an amendment, extending the right of electing a council to all the individuals in the community. He objected, too, that there was no provision in the bill setting forth whether their proceedings should be by a quorum, or that the votes should be by a majority or a minority; nor was there any provision for framing a code of laws; nor was there any compelled to keep a journal of its proceedings. These points required to be corrected, and he should submit several amendments touching these subjects.

Mr. V. then moved his first amendment, providing that the existing chiefs or other Indians holding or cultivating the soil, or engaged in the occupations of civilized life, should be eligible for members of the council for two years.

Mr. H. EVERETT moved to strike out the part of the amendment, " engaged in the occupations of civilized life."

Mr. ASHLEY said he was opposed to the amendment, as inapplicable to the condition of the Indians. He would leave the whole subject to the Indians themselves, who always schooled their most intelligent men.

Mr. H. EVERETT thought the word Chief had better be omitted.

Mr. VINTON said if the object of the bill was not to civilize the Indian, then the amendment and his amendment ought to prevail; and not otherwise. If gentlemen would say such was not their object, he would better understand them.

Mr. EVERETT of Vermont explained.

Mr. SEVIER gave an explanation of the manner of the Indians with regard to the cultivation of the soil. It was almost invariably in common, and not confined to a few. He hoped the amendment would be adopted.

Mr. GILMER was in favor of the motion as it stood, and any additions thought necessary might be made to it.

After some further conversation between Messrs. VINTON, H. EVERETT, GILMER, and SEVIER, the amendment of Mr. EVERETT was agreed to—ayes 86, noes not counted.

The question recurring on the amendment of Mr. VINTON,

Mr. GARLAND was opposed to the resolutions it would involve.

Mr. VINTON and Mr. S. JONES spoke in favor of it.

After some further conversation, the amendment was agreed to.

Mr. POPE moved an adjournment of the House. Negatived—ayes 56, noes 67.

Mr. VINTON then moved an amendment, providing that the Council should keep a journal of its proceedings, that electors should be 25 years of age, &c.

Mr. GARLAND moved an amendment to this amendment.

Mr. LOVE said he would leave the whole internal regulations of these tribes to themselves.

After some remarks from Mr. EVERETT, of Vermont, the question was then taken on the amendment of Mr. GARLAND, and rejected. The amendment of Mr. VINTON was also rejected.

Mr. GILMER moved to strike out the provision giving the Governor the power, at all times, to adjourn the Council. Agreed to.

Mr. GILMER also proposed sundry verbal amendments, which were agreed to.

Mr. GILMER also proposed an amendment giving the Governor the pardon ing power in cases where the punishment should be death. Agreed to.

Mr. DICKINSON moved to reconsider this vote; which was agreed to. The amendment was then withdrawn.

Mr. ASHLEY offered a proviso, securing the rights of citizens of the United States, travelling in Missouri and on the Western frontier, pursuant and in conformity with treaties with the Osages, which he briefly advocated.

Mr. HUBBARD considered this subject sufficiently provided for in in the first section of the bill, which he read.

Mr. ASHLEY then withdrew the amendment.

Mr. S. JONES then offered an amendment respecting the pardoning powers vested in the Governor, &c.

Mr. ALLEN of Ohio said he should vote against the bill however it might be amended—for he was opposed to the whole principle of it. It would require the most profound attention an l deliberation before it could be perfected. He warned the House that they were about organizing a new system of government in this country. The bill proposed not one single feature known to the constitution. It could not vote for the bill unless by consideration, but his respect for the committee who reported it would induce him at a proper time to give his objections more at length.

After a few remarks from Mr. H. EVERETT, Mr. S. JONES withdrew the amendment.

Mr. DICKINSON proposed an amendment to strike out the word "delegate" and insert "agent." On motion of Mr. MINER, The House adjourned.

sions to Justin Cobb and George C. Seaton, without amendment.

On motion of Mr. PORTER, the Senate considered as in Committee of the Whole, the bill for the relief of Lemuel Porter, and it was ordered to be engrossed for a third reading.

On motion of Mr. LEIGH, the Senate considered the report of the Judiciary Committee upon the case of Silence Elliot, and the resolution referring the same to the Solicitor of the Treasury to be inquired into and to make report to Congress, was adopted.

On motion of Mr. FRELINGHUYSEN, the Senate proceeded to the consideration, as in Committee of the Whole, of the bill supplementary to the act to amend the Judicial system of the United States.

[This bill provides for consolidating the circuits composed of New Jersey and Pennsylvania, with that composed of Delaware and Maryland, and requiring Judge Baldwin to hold the circuit courts in the Delaware and Maryland circuit, so as to obviate the necessity o' appointing a judge of the Supreme Court in that circuit, and thereby to extend the circuit system to the western States.]

The blanks in the bill having been filled up, for the times of sitting of the several courts, &c. as suggested by Mr. FRELINGHUYSEN,

Mr. BENTON rose and said, he could not permit this b ll to go through the Senate without making every resistance to it which it was in his power to put forth, for as it regarded his district it was a perfect monstrosity. It gave them a judicial circuit which extended from the gulf of Mexico to lake Michigan—from the torid to the frigid zone, and proposed to give them one term in a year. The gentleman had better have made it like those planets whose circles are one in twenty years. Mr. B. said that on this bill, so directly affecting their interest neither he nor his colleague had b-en consulted.

Mr. FRELINGHUYSEN. Does the honorable gentleman's colleague say he was not consulted?

Mr. LINN replied that he had been spoken to by the gentleman with respect to one of the amendment's which had just been made to the bill, which was suggested at his instance.

Mr. FRELINGHUYSEN observed that he heard some of the western gentlemen were consulted, not with respect to filling the blanks it was true.

Mr. BENTON continued. He believed the gentleman near him from Alabama, (Mr. King,) was not consulted. The two gentlemen from Illinois were not consulted; so that there were six Senators with whom there had not been the slightest consultation upon the structure of this bill. It is the first time in the history of the American Senate of a bill having been framed, making provision for three entire States, without consultation with the six Senators of those States; and therefore, when this bill was reported, he determined it should not pass without unpractical opposition from him, before the Senate and the whole American People. The important bill is brought up here during a short session, and at the eleventh hour, for re arranging the whole judicial system of the United States. As regards filling these blanks, Mr. B. said, that so far as Missouri was concerned, as to time, he had as lief it was filled with doomsday, and as to distance, with the antipodes. He continued would not be I amboozled with such a bill. A circuit of such extent was mockery, mockery, mockery to the people of Missouri. Under the name of a circuit court, there is a total impossibility in the way of carrying it into execution. No man, who is fit to be a judge, will suffer himself to be appointed for it. Look at the circuit. Louisiana is at one end of it, and then you are to take a huge leap over Tennessee and Kentucky, the Cumberland and Ohio rivers, and then alight on the borders of lake Michigan. The middle of this distance is cut off by another circuit. Can such a circuit be thought possible by practical purposes? The only result can be to answer a temporary purpose, and an object which is not visible on its face. What is the object of this bill? Certainly nothing for the good of the People. Mr. B. said he had, seen in

some of the papers, that Mr. Benton moved to go into executive session, for the purpose of despatching the executive business on hand. He never made any such motion, nor any movement in favor of such a nomination as that alluded to. But it was made 40 days ago. Do we suppose here, that the People are blind, and that every body don't know that we have slept? and now, at the end of 40 days, we are to be bamboozled, and the western Senators are to suffer such a bill to pass without opposing it? There is an old maxim, that "there are many ways to kill a dog," and "there are two ways to drown a man." One is to throw him overboard, and another is, to "scuttle the ship and let him go to the bottom." He might speak in enigmas, but they would be perfectly intelligible, to Senators at least. Mr. B. said no man would consent to receive the salary and perform such duties. Mr. B. then alluded to the number of circuits and terms in the eastern States, and contended that there was no impartiality in extending the proposed circuit over such an immense district, giving to it only one term a year. It is said to be, only deluding the people with expectations which they will never realize. What is the complaint with respect to the present organization? It is that there is now no judge on the Supreme Court bench having a knowledge of the practice of the civil law. And if a judge from the north should be sent to New Orleans the same difficulty would exist—he would have no knowledge of the civil law. There ought therefore, to be a judge upon the Supreme Court bench from Louisiana. He said he had not seen the bill, and therefore did not know how this judge was to be shot from one end of this circuit to the other; how you are to transport him. By steam! There is no steam to effect it. And to get over land from New Orleans to lake Michigan, must depend on a series of connecting conveyances. He thought we ought to wait for organizing this circuit till we have arrived at a greater art in aerial navigation. Or perhaps the judge might in his journeys south, be transported by one of those flights of wild geese, which periodically emigrate from the north, the could manage to have his car attached to them. Sir, said Mr. B. it will require something more than mere appearances to induce the people to suppose that this bill is introduced for the purpose of extending judicial circuits to the west. We say that this circuit should be given to Louisiana, and although we desire its benefits also, yet we are willing to give it to Louisiana, and wait till justice can be done us under the census of 1840. We come in to the aid of Louisiana, and therefore we are willing that the bill should be amended so as to give to her two courts a year, and a judge of the Supreme Court. The amendment proposes that there should be a chief justice and eight associate judges of that court The 8th circuit to be formed of Louisiana, Alabama and Miss as ppi, and the judge to be appointed in that circuit and to reside there. There is also a section in the amendment, providing for transferring the business of the district court into the circuit court, which he believed was wanting in the bill. Mr. Benton concluded by presenting an amendment conforming to his views, which he moved to have printed to be offered as a substitute for the bill, that the bill be laid on the table and that the Senate proceed to the consideration of executive business.

Mr. BENTON withdrew the motion to lay the bill on the table, at the request of

Mr. FRELINGHUYSEN, who observed, that he did not expect that this bill would have met with such an exception from the gentleman from Missouri When the gentleman said the bill was a monstrosity, and that his constituents were bamboozled by it, it was done at the suggestion of the President of the United States. When we look at the map and see the situation of the Mississippi, Louisiana, and Missouri, and see that the judge can travel the whole distance by steam, Mr. F. believed that many gentlemen would be

Monday, Feb 23, 1835.

Mr. HILL presented the credentials of the Hon. HENRY HUBBARD, a Senator elect from the State of New Hampshire, for six years from and for the third of March next.

Mr. BENTON, from the Committee on Military Affairs, reported a bill to increase the Corps of Engineers which was read the first time, and ordered to a second reading.

Mr. BENTON, from the same committee, to which the resolution of Saturday last was referred, made a report, recommending appropriations be inserted in the fortification bill for the repair of Fort Mifflin and the Pea Patch, in the river Delaware.

Mr. McKEAN, from the Committee on Pensions, to which was referred the claim of the house granting pensions to Benjamin Holland and Isaac Eckwright, reported them, severally, without amendment; also, a bill from the House for the relief of Josiah H. Brown and John Noakis, with the expression of opinion, by the committee, against its passage.

Mr. CLAYTON, from the Judiciary Committee, reported the bill from the House granting additional compensation to the District Attorney for the district of South Carolina, without amendment.

Mr. TOMLINSON, from the Committee on Pensions, reported the bills from the House for the relief of Captain Cole, since a Indian Chief, also for the relief of Solomon Case.

Mr. PRINCE, from the same committee, reported the bills from the House granting pensions

found, who would accept the appointment. Suppose he does ship from the torrid to the frozen zone, and he can administer justice by it, why should we not do it? He could well conceive how gentlemen with western aspirations should desire to see ten judges on the bench instead of seven. [Mr. F. here read a passage from the President's late message.] Here is the very enlargement of the Circuit Court system, the very hamboozling which is recommended by the President. A vacancy has happened in the Maryland District, and by giving that district to the judge who presides in Pennsylvania and New Jersey, that extension which the President recommends, can be given to the west. And the circuit spoken of, will be one of the pleasantest in the United States, and the courts in it will be held in the pleasantest months of the year, April, May, and June. The question then is, is the Senate prepared to avail itself of the chasm, which enables us to effect this great object. If we let the opportunity pass, it may be long before one so favorable may be presented again.

Mr. PORTER said he was singularly situated in this matter. He was between his friends on both sides; but he hoped to be able to say what would reconcile both of them. It was of no importance what were the motives of the originators of the bill or the amendment; for as to dodging any question connected with this or any other subject, he dodged nothing. He thanked the gentleman from Missouri for foregoing the benefits of the proposed system, and giving it to the southwest, for, said Mr. P., the present system is so grievous that we cannot bear it much longer. He thought the honorable gentleman's amendment was the best possible plan that could be suggested. To avoid the inconvenience of an increase of the judges, he thought it the best plan that could be hit on. In Louisiana, the whole of our jurisprudence is based upon the civil law; but what is her situation? When her cases are tried and brought to the Supreme Court, there is not a judge on the bench who has any knowledge of it. The requisite knowledge cannot be acquired from books, but only by applying its principles to the affairs of men. There is no man on the bench who is acquainted with its principles, and it cannot be endured much longer. He begged gentlemen to arrange it in such way, now that it is in their power, as to give us the benefits of the system. He hoped the amendment would prevail; but if it did not, he asked the honorable gentleman from Missouri whether it was not better to take half a loaf than no bread. For fourteen years we have been struggling in the West to get the benefits of the Circuit Court system. The justice of Congress has been applied to without avail. He deprecated waiting longer, and he now gave notice, that, if he could not get the amendment, he was willing to go for the original bill. He asked honorable Senators, why they would not take the gentleman from the fourth Circuit, and give him to Illinois, Indiana, and Missouri, and let us have, for the eighth Circuit, Louisiana, Alabama, and Mississippi? But the inconvenience the gentleman from Missouri spoke of, was not so great. A man could travel easier from New Orleans to Missouri, than Judge McLean could go from Ohio to Tennessee and Kentucky. He put it to the honorable gentleman from New Jersey, whether the amendment did not fully meet this view?

Mr. EWING said, he did not see much force in the Senator's (Mr. Benton's) objection on the ground that the Senators whose States were interested in the bill, had not been consulted. The resolution directing the investigation of the subject was presented some weeks since. The subject had been before the Senate since that time. He would ask why did not the Senators go to the committee with their suggestions, if the desirous of making any to them. But the floor of the Senate was the proper place for suggestions. The honorable Senator objected to the extent of the districts, representing the sessions of the court to be like the long periodic returns of an eccentric comet. But what were the purposes of these courts? They were not to decide cases at common law between man and man, but tribunals where the foreigner and citizen might plead. It was not considered so great a favor in his (Mr E's) State, to be dragged into the Courts of the United States. The citizens generally preferred their own Courts, as the expense was much more in the District Court than in the State Courts. The great ends of justice would be as well answered by one court a year as two. The Senator called the bill a mockery! But surely it would answer all the wants of those States. Why should they complain? Because they cannot be sued in the United States Court instead of their own county courts. He also told you of the extent of the proposed district, as if it was impossible for a judge to travel through it. Mr. E. said, that five or six weeks would be sufficient for Louisiana, and a week or two for each of the other States. The honorable gentleman said not be serious in his objections in regard to the judge's transporting himself from place to place. The great natural advantages afforded for steam boat navigation furnished a safe and expeditious communication between all parts of the district, excepting about 100 miles between the Mississippi river and Vandalia. Yet he has told you about flying, and being drawn by wild geese.

Mr. KING, of Alabama, said he recollected well that they had been deprived of the benefits of the circuit system on account of gentlemen's being unable to make up their minds as to the mode of bestowing it. If the system was good, the new States should have the benefit of it; if not, the old States should give it up. He was willing the districts should be formed on geographical principles, and so constructed, as to be permanent, and extend to all the States alike. The additional expense ought not to prevent gentlemen from giving these benefits to the South and West. He regretted that the subject had not been brought forward at an earlier part of the session. He thought it would be better to send back the bill to the Committee, with instructions to report the bill giving an additional judge to Louisiana, Alabama and Mississippi.

Mr. BIBB said, there was one circumstance the advocates of the bill seemed not to have regarded. Those six States had, for more than fourteen years been denied the benefits of the circuit system. There, life and death depend upon the opinion of a single judge. In a civil case also, his opinion was decisive. Congress had gone on, forgetting that justice was the most sacred privilege. It was strange that in a new country, where so many difficulties arose, the rights of the citizens should depend on a single voice. In those six States where many criminal cases, especially in Louisiana, where crimes committed on the high seas were brought, all of which were decided by a single individual, who was a judge of an inferior grade, and limited abilities.

His opinion was, that the Supreme Court and the District Courts ought to be separated. Mr. B. said party feeling had too much to do with the subject. The question often became what President was to appoint the judge? In the dissensions about politics, the claims of justice were too often forgotten. It was a burning shame! He was willing to make seven judges do all the business, but still should prefer an additional circuit, as the wants of the new States, about to be admitted into the Union, must be provided for.

Mr. BLACK said the system should be abolished altogether, or be extended to all alike. The great objection to extending the system was enlarging the number of judges. The only way then was to enlarge the circuits. He was in favor of abolishing the fourth altogether, or to provide some other way of giving two judges to the South and West. He would, however, accept of one if he could get no more. But he had come to the determination, that if the old States withheld the extension of the judicial system, he had given the last vote he ever intended to give for appointing a judge.

Mr. HENDRICKS said he preferred the original bill to the amendment. It had struck him as a favorable opportunity for giving a judge to the new States.

Mr. BUCHANAN said, he should not have risen to make any remarks upon the subject; but he believed the propitious moment had at length arrived when justice might be done to the west. The people of the western States had a right to complain, and to complain loudly, that the Circuit Court system had never been extended to them. It must be admitted, however, that their Representatives, in this and the other House, had, to a great degree, been the cause of this injustice. Whilst he had been a member of the House of Representatives, he had exerted all his feeble powers, first under the lead of the gentleman from Massachusetts, (Mr. Webster,) and afterwards as Chairman of the Judiciary Committee, to direct its attention in this particular to the western States. Every effort had hitherto been in vain, chiefly for want of a cordial and united effort of the western gentlemen themselves.

Although no practical benefit has yet resulted from the repeated discussions of this subject, yet a great and important principle has been settled. At first, many gentlemen whose opinions were entitled to great consideration, thought it best to detach the judges of the Supreme Court from Circuit duties, and convert them into a mere Court of Appeals. He believed that very few, if any, now entertained such an opinion. The truth was, that no man can be a useful judge of the Supreme Court, who has not an opportunity of acquiring a practical knowledge on the circuit of the conflicting and ever varying laws of the different States. It is thus, and thus only, the laws being with him to Washington and contribute to proportion of that sort of local State law which can never be acquired in any other manner. The judges of a mere appellate tribunal never could and never would acquire by study alone, a sufficient knowledge of twenty-four distinct and different systems of the State laws and customs.

It has then been established, that our present judicial system shall not be abandoned. This being the case, no man can doubt but that it must be extended to the six western States. Nature herself has clearly divided these States into two circuits. The three Southwestern States, Alabama, Mississippi, and Louisiana, ought to form one circuit, and the three Northwestern States, Indiana, Illinois, and Missouri, the other. Before he sat down, he should make a motion to recommit the bill to the Judiciary Committee, with instructions to create two circuits.

Mr. B. believed that the circuit as proposed by the bill under consideration was far too extensive. It was possible indeed that the judge might be able to travel over it, though the places of holding the courts were very remote from each other, but was there nothing more necessary? The Judge must acquire an accurate knowledge of the laws of each of the States within his circuit. The work of time and of labor. Every State in the Union had its own system of laws; and these were constantly changing, according to the will of their four distinct Legislatures. If a Judge was to be kept constantly on the road, he could never acquire the knowledge necessary to make him useful to the country. The proposed circuit was greatly too large. He would again repeat, that no State had already formed the two circuits in the West, which he should propose to establish. Alabama, Mississippi, and Louisiana, were so nearly connected by their position, that they might be in feeling and in interest. The same might be said of Indiana, Illinois, and Missouri. He conceived the time had now arrived when these circuits might be formed. In order to try the sense of the nation upon the subject, he now moved,

"That the bill be recommitted to the Committee on the Judiciary, with instructions to amend the bill, to create two new circuits, the one to consist of the States of Louisiana, Alabama, and Mississippi, and the other of the States of Indiana, Illinois, and Missouri.

Mr. CLAY wished to make a few remarks to vindicate the General Government against the eternal cry of injustice from the new States. He did not deny that all the State ought to be on the same footing. He cared but little what system was adopted; he had no objection to enlarging the number of judges; he would even go so far as twelve. The Supreme Court of the United States was no ordinary court. It was a high tribunal,

CONTINUED IN NEXT NUMBER.

CONGRESSIONAL GLOBE.

BY BLAIR & RIVES. ———WEEKLY——— PRICE $1 A SESSION.

2d Sess.......23d Cong. WEDNESDAY, MARCH 4, 1835. Volume 2.......No. 18.

TWENTY-THIRD CONGRESS.
SECOND SESSION.

IN SENATE.
Monday, Feb. 23, 1835.
[CONTINUED FROM LAST NUMBER.]

tribunal to interpret the constitution as well as the civil law. There was a trust committed to it too high for any earthly tribunal. He would not trust it there, if there was any where else to put it. It exercises a power over the constitution transcendent to all the other departments of the Government; a jurisdiction higher than any court in England—either the Court of Cassation or the House of Lords. If its functions were confined to civil cases, a small number would facilitate the business. But, in this view of expounding the constitution, he had no objections to a larger number.

Mr. KING, of Alabama, hoped the bill would be recommitted without instructions, leaving it to the committee to arrange the circuits, otherwise it might lead to a discussion, when the time of the Senate was so precious.

After some further conversation between Messrs. CLAY, BIBB, BENTON, CLAYTON, LEIGH, and BUCHANAN,

On motion by Mr. FRELINGHUYSEN,
To amend said motion by adding thereto the following words:—*And so to arrange the third and fourth circuits, as to form in the whole eight circuits.*

It was determined in the affirmative—yeas 34, nays 10.

On motion of Mr. CLAYTON,
The yeas and nays being desired by one-fifth of the Senators present, those who voted in the affirmative are—

YEAS.—Messrs. Bell, Benton, Bibb, Black, Brown, Calhoun, Clay, Ewing, Frelinghuysen, Goldsborough, Grundy, Hendricks, King of Alabama, King of Georgia, Knight, Linn, McKean, Mangum, Morris, Naudain, Porter, Prentiss, Preston, Robbins, Robinson, Silsbee, Smith, Southard, Swift, Tipton, Tomlinson, Waggaman, Webster, White,—34.

NAYS.—Messrs. Buchanan, Clayton, Cuthbert, Hill, Kane, Kent, Leigh, Huggins, Shepley, Tallmadge.—10.

The motion of Mr. BUCHANAN, as amended, was then agreed to, and the bill recommitted accordingly.

On motion of Mr. SMITH, the committee appointed on the application of the Honorable GEORGE POINDEXTER, had leave to sit during the sittings of the Senate.

FORTIFICATION BILL.

On motion of Mr. WEBSTER, the Senate took up for consideration, in Committee of the Whole, the bill from the House making appropriations for the fortifications of the United States, for the year 1835.

The amendments of the Committee on Finance were taken up successively, as follows, and agreed to.

An appropriation of 75,000 dollars for the repair of Castle Island in the harbor of Boston.

100,000 dollars for the defences within the State of Maryland;

A section authorizing the Secretary of War to purchase 6 acres of land adjoining Fort McHenry, near Baltimore.

The bill was then reported to the Senate, and these amendments were concurred in.

Mr. BENTON then offered an amendment appropriating 75,000 dollars for the repair of Fort Mifflin and the adjacent pier batteries in the river Delaware.

Mr. KING, of Georgia, inquired what repairs there were to be done, which made so large an appropriation necessary.

Mr. BUCHANAN replied that by the destruction of Fort Delaware, Philadelphia was left entirely without protection, and the important question with the War Department was, where that

city could be most readily and cheaply defended. The result of the inquiry was, that it could be better done at Fort Mifflin. He hoped it would not be necessary, but if it should, undoubtedly, the repairs ought to be made.

Mr. BENTON read an extract from the report of the Secretary of War on this subject, when the amendment was agreed to.

Mr. BENTON then moved, by the instructions of the Military Committee, to increase the appropriation for the repair of Fort Delaware (the Pea Patch,) to 150,000 dollars.

Mr. PRESTON made some general observations upon the system of fortifications, and expressed the opinion that if these expenditures were increased unreasonably, or beyond the amounts contemplated in the system, the Treasury would not be competent to sustain it.

After some remarks from Mr. CALHOUN and Mr. CLAYTON, in defence of the system and the necessity of the increased sum, the amendment was agreed to.

Mr. BENTON moved a further amendment of $100,000 to the armament of the several fortifications, which was agreed to.

The amendments were then all concurred in, and the bill ordered to be engrossed for a third reading.

On motion of Mr. HENDRICKS, the Senate proceeded to the consideration of executive business, and after some time spent therein,
The Senate adjourned.

HOUSE OF REPRESENTATIVES.
Monday, February 23, 1835.

The House resumed the consideration of the motion to print the preamble and resolutions of the Legislature of the State of Vermont, in relation to the Public Lands; the Bank of the United States; and the removal of the Deposites.

Mr. SLADE said. it had been contended by the gentlemen from New York (Messrs. Turrill and Beardsley) that the resolutions were disrespectful to the House. He wished the gentlemen to point out in what particular, either in form or substance, these proceedings were disrespectful. He made the request the more earnestly, because if the printing was refused, it would go forth to the world, that resolutions presented by a member of the House, which had passed the Legislature of Vermont, were considered unfit to be entered on the journal of this House.

Mr. BOON moved to lay the motion to print on the table.

On this motion Mr. H. EVERETT demanded the yeas and nays which were ordered, and were, yeas 32, nays 139.

So the House refused to lay the motion to print on the table.

Mr. SLADE reiterated his former remarks, which he said had not had the effect of producing the specifications which he had required of the gentlemen from New York. He was no great stickler for State rights, but he began to think that the advocates of State rights had more reason than heretofore for maintaining their ground. From a source which he need not designate, great danger to the just rights of the States had arisen, and in the present posture of affairs he was disposed to stand upon the ground of State sovereignty, although he could not go so far as some of its advocates. He contended in conclusion that the preamble and resolutions were respectful, and that the Legislature of Vermont had a right to be heard and their proceedings spread upon the journals of the House.

Mr. H. EVERETT said the members from Vermont were requested to use their influence in furthering the objects of the resolutions. This was a sufficient reason for their presentation.

Mr. BOON meant no disrespect to the Legislature or the members from Vermont. He had moved to lay the motion to print on the table, to avoid a long and useless debate, for which there

was no time. He did not object to receiving the views of a sovereign State. The resolutions had been received by the House, and by referring them to a committee, nothing more, he conceived, was necessary to be done.

The question was then taken, and the motion to print carried. Yeas 139, nays 32.

Petitions and memorials were presented by

Mr. JARVIS, of Maine.

Mr. HUBBARD, of New Hampshire.

Messrs. JACKSON and PHILLIPS, of Massachusetts.

Mr. BURGES, of Rhode Island.

Messrs. HALL, SLADE, JAMES, and ALLEN, of Vermont.

Messrs. WHITE, BEARDSLEY, DICKSON, and HAZELTINE, of New York.

Mr. PARKER, of New Jersey.

[Mr. PARKER presented the petition of the citizens of New Jersey, on the subject of the Bank of the United States, the removal of the public deposites, &c.]

Messrs. BANKS, KING, STEWART, CLARK, COULTER, BURD, SUTHERLAND, of Pennsylvania.

Messrs. KNIGHT, and A. H. SHEPPERD, of North Carolina.

Messrs. JOHNSON and DAVIS, of Kentucky.

[Mr. R. M. JOHNSON presented resolutions of the Legislature of Kentucky, in favor of the establishment of a National Armory, in said State.]

Messrs. PATTERSON, VANCE, WHITTLESEY, and HAMER, of Ohio.

[Mr. PATTERSON presented the petition of the citizens of Huron Co. Ohio, praying that a survey and estimate be made of the expense of making a ship navigation round the falls of Niagara.]

[Mr. HAMER, presented petitions from sundry citizens of Ohio, praying an alteration of the post route from Bainbridge to Maysville. Also, petitions from Brown County, Ohio, praying the establishment of a new post route from Decatur to Maysville.]

Mr. GARLAND, of Louisiana.

Messrs. HANNEGAN, KINNARD, and McCARTY, of Indiana.

[Mr. KINNARD presented an additional document in favor of allowing the Leavenworth and Bloomington Rail Road Company, in the State of Indiana, to take materials from the public lands, &c. for the construction of said road, which was referred to the Committee on the Public Lands.]

Mr. PLUMMER, of Mississippi.

Mr. REYNOLDS, of Illinois.

Mr. MARDIS, of Alabama.

[Mr. MARDIS presented the petition of Henrietta Binns,of Sumpter County,Alabama, praying Congress to pass a law granting to her a pre emption to a tract of land described in her petition.]

Mr. ASHLEY, of Missouri.

Mr. WHITE, of Florida.

Mr. Speaker BELL.

Which petitions and memorials were appropriately disposed of.

On motion of Mr. BURGES,
Resolved, That the Committee on Commerce be instructed to report to this House, on the memorial of the Marine Society in Providence,in the State of Rhode Island, in relation to a Marine Hospital to be established in the vicinity of that city; if there be not time for that committee to report on the expediency of that measure,that they be further instructed to report forthwith to this House all the papers and documents which have been referred to them thereby.

Mr. BOCKEE submitted the following resolution, which lies one day:

Resolved, That the Secretary of War be directed to communicate to this House the reason of his omission or refusal to place the names of Ben diet Alvord and Robert Brush on the Revolutionary Pension roll, pursuant to the provisions of an act passed 30th June, 1834, entitled an act for the relief of Benedict Alvord and Robert Brush.

On motion of Mr. THOMAS, of Maryland,

Resolved, That the Committee on Revolutionary Pensions be instructed to inquire into the expediency of providing by law for the payment of the claim of Henry Hoffman for military services in the war of the Revolution.

Mr. GAMBLE submitted the following resolution by consent, which was agreed to:

Resolved, That the Secretary of War be directed to communicate to this House, a copy of the report made to him by the engineer employed the last summer in the examination of certain routes for rail roads from the Atlantic to the Mississippi and its waters.

On motion of Mr. ALLAN, of Kentucky,

Resolved, That the Committee on Revolutionary Pension be instructed to inquire into the propriety of directing payment to be made to the heirs of Levi Todd, of the amount of half pay claimed by them to be due on account of the services of said Levi Todd, as a Lieutenant in the Virginia regiment commanded by Col. George Rogers Clark, in the revolutionary war.

On motion of Mr. WEBSTER,

Resolved, That the Committee on Public Lands be instructed to inquire into the expediency of removing the Land Office from Cincinnati to Greenville, Ohio.

On motion of Mr. JOHNSON, of Louisiana,

Resolved, That the Committee on Military Affairs be instructed to inquire into the expediency of making an appropriation for the erection of Barracks at Donaldsonville, in the State of Louisiana, for the accommodation of the troops of the United States to be stationed at that place.

On motion of Mr. THOMAS, of Louisiana,

Resolved, That the Committee on Commerce be instructed to inquire into the expediency of making an appropriation to remove the obstructions to the navigation of vessels in the rivers Amite, Teche, Chipahaw, and West Pearl, in the State of Louisiana.

On motion of Mr. WHITE, of Florida,

Resolved, That the Secretary of the Treasury be directed to report to this House at his next session, the number of Spanish claims to land in Florida now depending in the Courts of that Territory, under the act of Congress of 1828, the amount of land claimed, the nature of the claims, and by whom granted—with a schedule of those made by the same officers, and for the same objects, of those confirmed by the Supreme Court of the United States, and whether the lands covered by the titles are reserved from survey, or sufficiently designated to be laid down on the township plats.

Mr. MANN, of New York, by consent, offered the following resolution, which was agreed to:

Resolved, That the Secretary of War be requested to report to the next Congress, at the commencement of their first session, a statement showing the state and condition of the Ordnance and Ordnance Stores, under the control of the Ordnance Department; the number and kind of arms and accoutrements and heavy ordnance on hand, specifying the number and kinds fit for service; the amount of money expended in each year at the respective armories and arsenals, and the general objects of such expenditure since their establishment; the average cost of each kind of ordnance and small arms and accoutrements in each year, showing the aggregate expense of buildings, implements, and machinery, devoted to the manufacture of arms at each armory; the number of officers and workmen employed at the respective armories and arsenals in each year, and the number and kinds of arms produced; the aggregate cost of the whole, and the average cost of each description manufactured, and showing separately the expenditure for each year of buildings, machinery, implements, workmen, and their number in each year devoted to the manufacture of Hall's patent rifles, the number annually produced, and the place where manufactured; the average cost of each, including buildings, machinery, and all charges, and the number now belonging to the United States.

Mr. HANNEGAN, on leave, presented the following resolution:

Resolved, That the bill from the Senate, No. 54,

being an act to improve the navigation of the river Wabash, be made the special order of the day for Thursday next, the 26th instant.

Mr. HANNEGAN remarked, on introducing this resolution, that his object in asking the House to make this bill the special order of the day for a day certain, was the perfection of the bill itself so as to ensure its success, should the House feel inclined, as he hoped it did, to pass the bill. As the matter now stood, it was imperfect, and he wished, before the measure was finally acted on, to propose an amendment, by inserting a provision for a port of entry; a provision necessary to the final success of the object contemplated by the bill. He did not wish to excite debate at this time, but when the bill came up, he would so move to amend it, and an opportunity would then be given for any discussion that might be considered necessary. Should the House adopt the resolution, he would, on Thursday morning, move a suspension of all the previous special orders, for the purpose of considering this bill.

Mr. McCARTY was in favor of the resolution. The bill was one of the utmost importance to a large portion of the citizens of Indiana.

Mr. MERCER suggested that the resolution be modified by adding after the word "Wabash," "and such other bills as relate to roads and canals and surveys thereon."

Mr. HANNEGAN accepted the modification, when, after a short explanatory conversation between Messrs. HANNEGAN, MERCER, EVANS, McKENNAN, and SUTHERLAND, the resolution was rejected.

Mr. POLK, from the Committee of Ways and Means, reported, without amendment, a bill making an appropriation for holding a treaty with the Camanche tribe of Indians; which was committed.

Mr. HUBBARD moved to suspend the rules for the purpose of going into committee upon several appropriation bills which he named.

Various other bills were named by different individuals, which they desired to include in the motion.

Mr. HUBBARD varied his motion so as to suspend the rule generally, for the purpose of going into committee, without designating any particular bill or bills; which was agreed to. Yeas 120, nays 38.

The House then, on motion of Mr. HUBBARD, resolved itself into a Committee of the Whole on the state of the Union, Mr. McKENNAN in the chair.

On motion of Mr. HUBBARD, the committee took up the bill No. 648; a bill making additional appropriations for the Delaware breakwater, for certain harbors, and removing obstructions in and at the mouths of certain rivers, for the year 1835.

The bill was read through by the Clerk.

Mr. HUBBARD proposed an additional appropriation for the, pier or break water in Dunkirk harbor, New York, $9,579 16; and also a further appropriation for filling up 380 yards with stone of the outer pier on the said breakwater. Agreed to. Mr. H. also proposed a proviso to the bill, giving the direction of these expenditures to the War Department, &c. Agreed to.

Mr. VINTON then proposed an appropriation of $50,000 for the improvement of the Ohio river between Pittsburg and the Falls, to be expended under the direction of the War Department, and explained the necessity that called for the appropriation,—for the removal of certain bars on the river which obstructed its navigation.

Mr. HAWES opposed the amendment, as altogether unnecessary. He was convinced that as soon as one bar was removed, the same causes which had made it, would make it in some other part of the river, and in this way they might go on and expend the whole treasury of the country, and then effect no good.

Mr. HUBBARD said, the Committee had had the matter under consideration, and had not deemed it necessary to report in its favor.

Mr. LANE was in favor of the amendment, and denied that if one bar was removed, another would take place; at least it would not generally be the case. He hoped the Committee of the Whole House would not reject the appropriation

because the Committee of Ways and Means had not entertained it.

Mr. CHAMBERS said this was an appropriation in which the whole West was concerned, and ought to be deemed a national work, and to be treated as such by that House. It extended over hundreds of miles, and accommodated the interest of millions. It facilitated the great chain of communication between the East and the West, which would be imperfect without the improvement of the stream from Pittsburg to the Falls of the Ohio.

Mr. LYTLE argued in favor of the appropriation with considerable energy, in reply to Mr. Hawes. It was recommended by the appropriate Committee, the Committee on Roads and Canals, and it was grounded upon the report of a gentleman (Capt. Shreeve) in whom the whole county had confidence.

Mr. HARDIN gave an explanation relative to the effect produced by removing the bars, which, he contended, was generally productive of more harm than good. If he thought otherwise, he should cheerfully vote for the item; but his present convictions would lead him to oppose it.

Mr. DICKINSON, of Tennessee, complained of the system by which these appropriations were made, and said, till a better plan was devised, he hoped the bill would be rejected altogether. He believed the work contemplated in the bill would never be completed, and he called upon the members of the South to interpose and put a stop to a expenditure which now, under this bill, amounted to above $300,000 for the present year. It would be inconvenient to resist appropriations for improvements on the sea board, and to vote for one of the same character in the west.

Mr. POPE made a few remarks in favor of the bill.

Mr. LANE was well acquainted with the Ohio river, but he had no constitutional scruples on the subject, for he would not give a fig for the constitution if the Treasury of the nation could not be expended in promoting such works as the present. He explained what was necessary to be done in removing the bars, and denied that they would come up again. The Ohio river was, of all others in the country, the most truly national, and it was the duty of the Government to improve it.

Mr. BOON said that he had lived near the Ohio river upwards of twenty-three years, and within twelve or fifteen miles of three bars, which has presented the greatest obstruction to the passage of flat boats down the river, below the falls, as well as to the passage of steam-boats both up and down the river. The circumstance mentioned by the gentleman from Kentucky, (Mr. Hardin,) of a bottom boat or two having been injured, perhaps lost, I am not disposed to controvert. This has happened, however, when the river was more two or three feet above low water mark. The improvement of those bars by wing dams, is intended to improve the navigation of the river in time of low water. This, sir, I know has been done at the Scuffletown bar, as also the French Island bar, and at the bar above the mouth of Green river, the improvement of it is in a state of progress, which bids fair to result in a successful improvement of the navigation of the river at those places.

My residence near the bars which I have mentioned, has given me an opportunity of knowing something of the effect which has been produced by the improvement of the navigation of the river at those points, by wing dams. Before the improvement which has been made, I have known from twelve to fifteen steam boats at one time to be obstructed in their passage over those bars, to say nothing of the great number of flat boats that were obstructed in their passage down the river before the erection of wing dams at those bars. But now that those improvements have been made, and their utility tested, I am enabled to state that steam boats of middle class can, and do pass over the Scuffletown bar at the lowest stage of water, thereby attending active facilities to the commerce carried on upon that river. I have thought it my duty to say thus much in relation to what has come under my own observation.

Mr. EWING maintained that it was not the West alone that was interested in this improvement, but the South was equally so, and they

section of the Union was more or less so. It was, in his opinion, a perversion of the constitution to oppose the appropriation of the people's money for the people's good. Mr. E. proposed to amend the am ndment, by inserting at th · end of it, " for improv ng the river Wabash $25,000."

Mr. HUBBARD submitted whether the amendment was in order, a bill having been reported providing for the same object.

Mr. EWING said, the bill was not the same as his amendment, for it provided for a different amount, $20,000.

The CHAIR decided the amendment out of order, on the grounds set forth by Mr. Hubbard.

Mr. STEWART, of Pennsylvania, produced a letter from Captain Shrieve, covering a statement of the expenses of the proposed improvement, with his opinion of its propriety and expediency, &c. which was read by the clerk, and Mr. . supported the amendment at some length.

Mr. CHILTON hoped the discussion would be brought to an end, for this question had been argued so frequently, from session to session, that all must be well versed in it.

Mr. BURD hoped the House would not draw a invidious distinction, by rejecting so small an appropriation for this part of the Ohio river, while ny many hundreds of thousands were expended elsewhere. He believed the object within the intent and meaning of the Constitution, for the means of the country could be devoted to no object more national than that of improving its rivers, which are the veins and arteries of the country.

Mr. HAWES gave an explanation with reference to his votes on last session. He added that as communication of the Engineer confirmed him in his opinion that the appropriation was unnecessary, and if made would be endless. If $20,000 were expended, it would necessarily involve an xpenditure of $40,000, and as soon as $40,000 were expended, $80,000 more would be required, and so it would go on. He believed more harm than good would ensue, and he would never give a vote for destroying the navigation of this beautiful river.

Mr. LYTLE again addressed the committee in ror of the amendment, and maintained that its character was peculiarly national, and was scarcely equalled in point of importance. If, however, n issue was to be made of opposing all appropriations for improvements in the West, Mr. L. would oppose equally those in other sections of country, which we e not more national than one now under consideration.

Mr. WHITTLESEY, of Ohio, said a few words n the same subject.

Mr. HARDIN w s as solicitous as any gentleman could be for the improvement of the Ohio river, provided it was productive of benefit, but was still convinced that the removal of the r would do, as it had done heretofore, harm. Then one bar was removed, generally a worse e was formed instead of it. Mr. H. contended at the West had no right to complain. By the npact three per cent. of the proceeds of the ublic lands in Indiana, Ohio, and Illinois, were be expended in Internal Improvements, but if 3 whole of the land within the triangle formed those three States were sold at the full price a dollar and a quarter an acre, it would barely make one third of the amount already expended there upon the Cumberland road. Mr. H. ented into an explanation with reference to his ne on the Portland and Louisville canal. He voted to take up the subject, but he explained the difficulties he was under, whether he should d for it or not, to one of his colleagues, and the been present when the vote was taken, intended to have asked leave to be excused voting.

Mr. JOHNSON, of Louisiana, referred to a ey made for the improvement of the mouth the Mississippi, and thought the amount contemplated in the amendment might with more riety be devoted to this subject.

Mr. VINTON desired the Clerk to read the cluding part of Captain Shrieve's letter, to by the importance of the improvement.

Mr. HUBBARD little thought the bill would re brought up such a discussion. He would

appeal to the gentleman from Tennessee himself (Mr. Dick nson) to say if there was any thing constitutionally objectionable in it. Of the three hundred thousand dollars appropriated in the bill, sixty thousand were for western harbors; and the amount for new entries did not exceed twenty thousand. It moreover contained already $50,000 for the Ohio, Mississippi, and Missouri. It had been argued in favor of the amendment that the Committee on Roads and Canals were for it: why then had they not reported a bill for the purpose? The Committee of Ways and Means could not be expected to do it. He denied that the bill was exclusively for the benefit of the seaboard, for it only appropriated $17,000 for New England. He hoped the bill would be reported as it stood.

Mr. DICKINSON, of Ten. again reiterated his objections to the bill.

Mr. SUTHERLAND rose to urge the friends of the bill not to debate it, but to act, if they did not wish to kill it. He referred to several bills which he was desirous of bringing before the committee involving no constitutional difficulties.

The question was then taken, and the amendment was agreed to.' Yeas 72, nays 54.

Mr. BARBER moved an amendment appropriating $33,000 for removing obstructions in the Thames river, Connecticut. Negatived.

Mr. PARKER proposed an amendment appropriating for the protection and securing Flat Beach, alias Tucker's Island, Little Egg Harbor, New Jersey, $3695 40, and sent to the Clerk's table a report of the Engineer thereon.

Mr. SUTHERLAND objected to the amendment, on the principle that it was for a new work, and was now before the Committee on Commerce, to whom it had been referred by a resolution introduced by the gentleman from New Jersey himself.

The amendment was rejected.

Mr. BEATY moved an item of $25,000 for improving the navigation of the Cumberland river.

Mr. B. made a brief explanation in favor of the proposed appropriation, and said that he had been informed at the War Department, that the report of the Engineer on the subject, would be sent to the House to-morrow. The vicinity of the river contained bituminous coal, iron, coppers, and other ore, sufficient to supply the whole continent, all of which were now lying useless for want of improving the navigation of the Cumberland river.

The amendment was rejected—ayes 49, noes not counted.

Mr. WATMOUGH proposed an item of $7,000 to remove the bar at the mouth of the Schuylkill.

Mr. POPE asked if there had been any survey?

Mr. WATMOUGH replied in the negative.

Mr. SUTHERLAND said, some four or five years ago he had attempted to get a survey made for this very object; and the committee to which Mr. S. belonged, intended to report a bill for that purpose.

Mr. WATMOUGH asked, if the gentleman was opposed to the amendment; as Mr. W. wished that fact should be known elsewhere as well as in that House.

Mr. SUTHERLAND again explained. The subject was under consideration by the committee of which Mr. S. was a member, and he would be reported upon in the present session.

The amendment was rejected without a division.

Mr. MERCER moved an item for defraying the expense of surveys, pursuant to the act of 30th April, 1834, $50,000. Negatived. Ayes 65, noes 71.

Mr. HAWES proposed an amendment for the improvement of Green river, Ky.—$25,000.

Mr. TRUMBULL moved an item of $25,000, for improvements at the mouth of the Connecticut river.

Mr. SUTHERLAND said the subject was embraced in a bill reported from the Committee on Commerce.

The amendment was rejected.

Mr. LYON offered an amendment for the improvement of the harbor at the mouth of St. Joseph's river, in the Territory of Michigan—$10,000.

Mr. HAWES asked if the place was in Canada or in the United States.

Mr. LYON said the whole section of country in its vicinity was in the United States.

The bill was then laid aside, and the Committee, on motion of Mr. MAY, took up the bill No. 587, for providing for the establishment of a Surveyor General's Office in the State of Illinois.

Mr. KINNARD moved to amend the bill by inserting a provision for the appointment of a Surveyor General for Indiana, to reside at Indianapolis.

Mr. K. remarked, that the Committee on the Public Lands, at their last session, were in favor of this proposition. He did not believe that the House would be disposed to give any advantage to one State over another, in this particular. He urged the propriety of his amendment as peculiarly proper in reference to certain constitutional provisions of that State, prohibiting the reduction of the size of any county below a given number of square miles.

The amendment was disagreed to.

The bill was then laid aside, and the committee, on motion of Mr. POLK, took up the bill making appropriations for Indian annuities, and other similar objects for 1835.

Several amendments, some merely of a verbal character, were agreed to.

On motion, the committee then rose, and the chairman (Mr. McKENNAN,) reported the foregoing bills, with their amendments, to the House.

On motion of Mr. HARDIN,

The House then adjourned.

IN SENATE.

TUESDAY, February 24, 1835.

Petitions and memorials were presented by—Messrs. BUCHANAN, HENDRICKS, and LINN.

Mr. FRELINGHUYSEN, from the Committee on Indian Affairs, to which was referred the memorial of John Ross, a Cherokee Indian, reported the following resolution:

Resolved, That the said memorial be referred to the President of the United States, and that the President be requested to ascertain the facts on which said memorial is founded, and the amount of reservations of which the Cherokees have been deprived as stated; and cause a report of the whole case to be laid before the Senate at the opening of the next session of Congress.

Mr. SILSBEE, from the Committee on Commerce, reported a bill from the House for the relief of William McLean, and the owners of the fishing schooner Milo, which, on his motion, was taken up for consideration and postponed indefinitely.

Mr. PRENTISS, from the Committee on Pensions, reported the bills from the House of Representatives, granting pensions to Benjamin Leslie, William Baden, and James Harrington.

Mr. TOMLINSON, from the same Committee, reported the bills from the House granting pensions to Ephraim F. Gilbert and William Wilge, and also, that the bill from the House granting a pension to George McFadden, ought not to pass.

Mr. TOMLINSON, from the same Committee, reported the bill from the House to establish a pension agency at Russelville, in Kentucky.

Also, the bill to provide for paying certain pensioners at Jackson, in the State of Tennessee; both which bills were severally considered as in Committee of the Whole, and ordered to be engrossed for a third reading.

Mr. WEBSTER rose and said it was his intention at an earlier period of the session, to have drawn the attention of the Senate to a matter which he considered a great and growing difficulty in Congress. Those of us who have been here longest, have felt that the accumulation of private business has been so great, and is increasing, that it threatens to overwhelm us. He was desirous that some measure should be introduced for the purpose of reducing the number of applications to Congress upon private business. He

would offer a joint resolution, which he held in his hand, not for consideration now, but to let it lie on the table, that it might meet the attention of Congress and of the People, in the hope, that at the next session, which is the long session, some action may be had upon it.

Mr. W. then submitted the following joint resolution:

Resolved, by the Senate and House of Representatives of the United States of America in Congress assembled, That a joint committee of the two Houses, to consist of —— members of each House, be appointed, for the following purposes, viz.

1. To examine the general nature of the private acts which have passed Congress within the last five years, to ascertain their numbers, and to classify them according to their subjects.

2. To consider the practicability of diminishing the number of private applications to Congress, either by vesting the authority of deciding on such claims, or some of them, in some public board, or in the several Departments, or by other proper provision; and to report thereon.

Agreeably to notice given, Mr. CLAY asked and obtained leave to bring in a joint resolution, directing the appropriation heretofore made for improving the Cumberland river, to be applied as well above as below Nashville; which was read twice by unanimous consent, as in Committee of the Whole, and ordered to be engrossed and read a third time.

The bill making appropriations for the fortifications of the United States, for the year 1835, was read the third time and passed.

The amendments by the House to the bill granting a lot of land to the borough of Mackinaw, for public purposes, were concurred in.

The following bills from the House were read twice and referred:

The bill to confirm certain claims to land in Louisiana;

A bill for the relief of the heirs and legal representatives of James Latham, deceased;

A bill to provide for opening certain roads in the Territory of Arkansas, and for other purposes;

A bill to authorize the Secretary of the Treasury to settle the claim of Orange H. Dibble, for losses upon materials, work, and labor done on his contract for building a bridge over the Potomac, at Washington;

A bill for the improvement of the harbor at lake Michigan.

The amendments of the House to the bill to authorize the construction of a rail-road from Tallahassee to St. Marks, in Florida, were taken up for consideration; and the bill and amendments were referred to the Committee on Roads and Canals.

The bill for the relief of Lemuel Tanner, assignee, &c., was read the third time and passed.

The bill for establishing branches of the mint of the United States in North Carolina, Georgia, and New Orleans, being under consideration on its third reading,

Mr. HILL said, that having voted steadily against the bill for creating three additional mints, which must be conducted exclusively at the expense of the people of the United States, and against some of those Senators with whom he had the happiness generally to agree, he felt a necessity for explaining the grounds on which he gave his votes.

He had been struck very forcibly, when the blanks were filled up, with the fact that the salaries for the several officers of the mint at New Orleans were placed from twenty-five to thirty-three per cent higher than would be expected at any other point of the Union. In addition to this, it was to be observed, that during the sickly season of from three to six months in the year, the operations of the mint at that place must be suspended. The additional expense of coining at New Orleans, must be far greater than the expense of transportation would be from New Orleans back and forward to the mint at Philadelphia.

He considered that Louisville, in Kentucky, would be a far preferable point for a mint: it would be more central for the western country; and the difference of the expense of coinage at the two places in favor of Louisville, would much more than pay all the expenses of transportation back and forward of the bullion or material for coinage.

Mr. H. said, if he could believe for a moment that the establishment of these three new mints would be the means of introducing a specie circulation—would change the circulation of paper for that of the precious metals—he would consent to incur some expense to the treasury to effect such an object. He believed that the introduction of the new mints would not make hard money more plenty. A large portion of the gold which would be coined at New Orleans would not be from bullion or native gold; but from gold already coined. The recent law had made all foreign gold coin a tender—so that the coinage of gold in any vicinity could not and would not make gold more plenty. That circulation must depend on other circumstances—on the prohibition, by the State and local Legislatures, of paper bills of certain denominations.

It had been said that the gold finding business required protection: the bill of the last session of Congress had raised the value of gold six per cent.

Mr. H. referred to the last report of the Director of the Mint at Philadelphia, by which it appeared that the gold coinage at the mint during the last year, (half eagles $3,660,845, and quarter eagles $293,425,) has "exceeded the aggregate coinage of gold during the nine preceding years;" and that the amount of silver coinage in the same time exceeds by about one quarter of a million of dollars the coinage of any previous year. He also showed from that report, that of the gold received during last year, 898,000 dollars was received from the gold regions of the United States; 225,000 dollars from Mexico, South America, and the West Indies; 2,180,000 dollars from Europe; 12,000 dollars from Africa; and 9,000 dollars from sources not ascertained; and that of the whole amount received from Europe, about four fifths were in foreign coins.

This statement from the Mint at Philadelphia showed most conclusively that this institution was ample for all the wants of the country. The gold coinage of the last single half year had exceeded the whole gold coinage of the last nine *years*—while the silver coinage had exceeded that of any previous year. The importation of gold, resulting from its increased value, had been greater during the last year than could be calculated on hereafter, and it was found that the Mint at Philadelphia, even with its present force, was ample for the coinage of all that could be required for the supply of the whole United States. If, in a time like the present, the National Mint is sufficient for all the wants of the nation, of what service can three additional Mints be to the country, when the importation of gold and silver shall be discontinued? In time of war, the operations of the Mint will be stopped; but the salaries of the officers and men will go on; and this bill will establish and create from twenty to thirty officers, with larger salaries than the highest and most responsible officers in many States of the Union.

I object to the bill, (said Mr. H.) because, after incurring an expense in the outlay of half a million of dollars, it will fix a permanent annual expenditure of one hundred thousand dollars; and all this, when the gold, silver, and copper, are coined, not for the benefit of the whole people, but for the benefit of individuals. Even if there should be no coinage, the expenses of the several mint establishments must go on.

Mr. H. said the statement made in the Senate on Saturday, relative to the thirteen Mints in France, had induced him to make inquiry in relation to the fact. He said there were thirteen mints in France; but only three of them were authorized to coin gold. The mints of France had this important difference from the Mint of the United States—they were in the nature of private institutions. The Mint of the U. States was a public institution, coining gratuitously for individuals all of the precious metals that may be committed to its charge. He quoted from Goldsmith's Statistics of France, by which it was shown that the charges for coinage at the Royal Mints in that country, were 29 centimes for every 100 francs in gold; that is, 20 centimes for loss, and 9 centimes for coining; and, on silver, one franc and 50 centimes for every 100 francs; that is, one franc for coining, and 50 centimes for loss. He showed from this book, that in the year 1827, the profits from the Mints, after paying all expenses of recoining and salaries to the Government, amounted to 120,000 francs, or about $23,000. If (said Mr. H.) the Mints in this country were founded on the same principle as they are in France, he would have no objection to adding three to the present number, or any additional number.

In England there is but a single Mint, as there is in this country; and it is a government institution, nearly similar to that of the United States. From Rees' Cyclopedia he found the account, that in former times there was a Mint in nearly every county of England; that at this time there is only one single Mint for the whole of England, Scotland, and Ireland. That Mint is in London; and the single institution produces coin with so great facility, that the whole wants of the country are by it supplied. As one Mint in that country is sufficient for the whole United Kingdom, so one mint will be ample for the coinage of all that the wants of this country may require.

The Senator from Missouri, (Mr. Benton,) has declared the system of Mints to be a part of the hard money system. I will not yield to any gentleman that he is more the friend of a hard money currency than I am myself. He supposes hard money cannot be diffused through the West and the South, if these Mints shall not be established. He should recollect that Banks are the natural enemies of a hard money circulation; especially will bank notes of a small denomination drive out of circulation hard money. Hard money, gold sovereigns, and Spanish milled dollars, and French crowns, was more plenty within the British province of Canada, until local banks were there established, than I have ever known it to be in the United States. Specie was constantly brought from that province in quantities. Yet the Mint at which this hard money was produced, was thousands of miles distant. So at New Orleans, until banks were there established, specie, gold doubloons, and silver dollars, were there always to be had in abundance. Drive small bank notes out of circulation, and no additional Mint can be wanted to give the people all the gold and silver they may desire.

We have had, very recently, (said Mr. H.) a severe lecture on executive patronage, in the report of a committee on that subject. Is it not matter of surprise, that gentlemen who should take a conspicuous part in that committee should, in a few days thereafter, advocate the passage of a law which will invest the Executive with an additional annual patronage of at least one hundred thousand dollars?

The report of the committee he considered a valuable document for some purposes. Mr. H. said he had a large number of extra copies of the report sent to him. He thought the report did not represent facts in their true light; and on that account he did not feel disposed to distribute with alacrity such a document. But he considered it valuable for another purpose. He desired to have it always before members of Congress, when they had under consideration such projects for expending the people's money as that of the Mints which was now before us. Mr. H. read several paragraphs from Mr. Calhoun's report; among which was the following:

"Experience has shown, that it is next to impossible to reduce the public expenditure with an overflowing treasury; and not much less difficult to reduce patronage without a reduction of expenditure; or, in other words, that the most simple and effectual mode of retrenching the superfluous expenditure of the Government, to introduce a spirit of frugality and economy in the administration of public affairs; to correct the corruption and abuses of the Government; and, finally, to arrest the progress of power, is, *to leave the money in the pockets of those who made it,* where all laws, human and divine, place it, and from which it cannot be removed by Government but except for its necessary and indispensable wants, without violation of its highest trust, and the most sacred principles of justice."

He agreed cordially with the opinion here expressed, and hoped that parts of this report would r refer d to as a text book for present and future legislators.

In conclusion, he said he saw no possible advantage in the erection of three new m nts the expenditure was unnecessary; it could not be accomplished by corresponding benefits He must, therefore, continue to oppose the bill, as he had heretofore done.

Mr. BLACK said he found himself in an unpleasant situation, with respect to the bill before the Senate. He stood alone among the southern delegation on this subject. He thought one much enough for the South. There were objections to so many different branches on account of the diversity of dies, and the difference in the alloy that might be used at each place. He would move a recommitment of the bill with instructions, to amend it as to strike out all the branches except one, and that one to be located in either of the States of North Carolina, Georgia, or Louisiana.

Mr. FRELINGHUYSEN said that he found, by the Report of the Director of the Mint, that a never intended more than one branch in the old region, and one at New Orleans. According to the estimates of the director, Mr. F. said, would be cheaper for the United States to pay transporting the gold to Philadelphia, than to establish these branches.

Mr. CLAY said he would acknowledge the efficient support which the Senator from New Hampshire (Mr. Hill) had brought to the opposers of the bill. Politics, said Mr. C. made strange bedfellows sometimes of contending opponents. If a honorable Senator would always stand on such a ground, he would hog him still closer to himself. The occasion gave rise to strange reflections. For who would have thought a few days since, after hearing the eloquent appeal of the Senator from South Carolina (Mr. Calhoun) against the exercise of Executive patronage, that the Senator would so soon be advocating its influence, and the Senator from New Hampshire opposing it?

Mr. C. said he would refer to the practical comments of the honorable gentleman from New Hampshire. Here Mr. C. went into a calculation the expense of transportation, &c. compared to that of establishing these branches.

Mr. WAGGAMAN said, at that late period of session, to recommit the bill was to destroy it, as was well known to the mover.

Mr. W. said the Senator from Kentucky (Mr. y) had argued very disingenuously. He had erected the high ground on which his eloquence placed him, and resorted to ridicule, in order to defeat the bill.

Mr. W. h d made a calculation of the expenses transportation, and differed almost $100,000 in the statements of the Senator from Kentucky. Mr. W. said New Orleans was the greatest exporting city in the Union, and her prospects were daily increasing. It was the outlet of rivers capable more than 30,000 miles, and irrigating a country capable of supporting a population of more than 150,000,000 of inhabitants.

Mr. CLAY said a few words in reply.

Mr. BROWN said, he regretted that the two states (Mr. Hill and Mr. Clay) who seldom act together, had taken that opportunity to use their united efforts to defeat a bill, in which his it was so deeply interested. He had thought arguments exhaust d on Saturday, and if the matter from Kentucky (Mr. Clay) had labored any delusion as to the votes at that time, he said the v.te about to be taken would undoc ire. He could assure the honorable Senator, they did not come as mendicants to ask the city of Government, but they came as citizens to claim their rights.

Mr. CALHOUN said, they were not to be f r neglected. There was a fundamental principle which should be considered, that this Government was not a single community; but composed of separate and independent States. The individual rights of one part were not to be sacrificed to the ideal welfare of the whole. The United States had taken it into their own hands to regulate the coinage, and they were bound to supply the wants of each section. It must be borne in mind that we were a community of States, United for the benefit of the States. He had been accused of advocating an increase of Executive patronage. He was opposed to every measure tending to its increase, where the public wants did not absolutely require it. But we might as well refuse the usual appropriations for fortifications, of which the Senator from Kentucky is a strenuous advocate.

Mr. BLACK replied, that he was not opposed to establishing a branch at New Orleans, but thought the other two altogether unnecessary.

Mr. CALHOUN said the two branches in the gold regions would be five or six hundred miles apart, and the transportation must be carried on wholly by land; therefore two was as necessary as one.

Mr. CLAY said the Senator from South Carolina had retorted upon him the accusation of favoring Executive patronage, because he had voted in favor of fortifications. To be sure, he was in favor of some fortifications, but not to the extent marked out by the aspiring desires of that honorable Senator. The gentleman told us of the necessary extensions of patronage of the Government. All Executive patronage, said Mr. C. was founded on public necessities. All the extras of that wretched Department which had made all sick at the heart—all Obadiah B. Brown's extras, were for public necessities.

The location of one of the branches in a country (the Cherokee country) yet held sacred by the legislation of Congress, was an insuperable objection. While the rightful owners of the lands were in this city beseeching the protection of the Government, should they be turned away, insulted by the establishment of a Mint in their territories?

Mr. CALHOUN explained his views of the system of fortifications. He did not think the Indians had any claim on that portion of country where the location was proposed to be made. He did not believe there was an Indian within 30 miles of the place.

Mr. CUTHBERT said, having heard the name of his State mentioned so often, he felt himself called upon to rise. He would follow the course which the Senate would wish him to follow; he would use no expression which would provoke an angry discussion; he would rest, where Georgia rested, firm and at ease. Georgia did not wish to agitate the Indian question there; she would firmly persevere in her own course.

Mr. FRELINGHUYSEN said he did not wish to bring forward a discussion on the course that Georgia had taken. She might pursue her course as an independent State, but her actions should not be sanctioned there. The American People were bound by the most solemn treaties to protect that injured nation, now hunted down like a privilege on the mountains. Georgia did not plead here, as the Senator has said, but we should plead here. He hoped the Senate would pause before it tarnished the sacred honor of the nation.

Mr. KING, of Georgia, said he had been actively engaged in his duties as a committee, which he could not abandon without a gross dereliction of duty. He had not, therefore, heard the arguments on this subject, except what h d just fallen from the Senator from New Jersey. He understood the objection of that Senator to the establishment of a branch of the mint in Georgia, to be that the territory on which the establishment was to be made, was a subject of negotiation between the United States and Georgia, the subject of which was to restore the country to the Cherokees. He said the validity of such an objection would rest somewhat on the probability of success in any such project. Who believed that the country would ever be receded by Georgia? Did any seriously propose such nonsense? Why should we be influenced in a practical measure of legislation by connecting it with a measure impracticable?

He said this was a practical question, of what is—and not a moral inquiry of what ought to be? Whatever might have been the past history of the Indian country, it could not alter the present condition of the country. Georgia, right or wrong, could not now recede. Georgia ought not to recede. Georgia would not now r. cede. The country was regularly organized—represented in the Legislature—and as fully incorporated with the State Government as any other portion of her territory. Why then speculate upon this measure? It was said by the Senator who had just taken his seat, that the honor of the Union was concerned in obtaining back the Cherokee lands to comply with solemn treaties. If we wished to restore our national honor, we would have to do something more than get back this country. Where were the countless thousands of the aborigines who once reigned in wild in dependence from Maine to Louisiana? Their bones now enriched the soil of which they had been robbed. And although a necessary State policy required that Georgia should have the jurisdiction of this country, the Cherokees were offered more for it than it would sell for if exposed lot by lot at public auction, with fair competition.

He would not go into the Cherokee question at present, further than to add that it could constitute no reasonable objection to the measure proposed.

An argument much dwelt upon, and which seemed to be considered most important, had just been repeated. It was stated that government might as well be called on to transport to market all the products of the country, as to pay the loss on the uncoined metal exported by the mines. Mr. K. did not think the argument at all applicable. There was no restriction upon the States or their citizens in the manufacture of other products, but such products could be manufactured, sold, or appropriated in any way that local policy might dictate as most profitable or advantageous. But a restriction on the right of coinage was surrended to the Union for the common benefit. And, therefore, th loss should be borne as a general charge.

Mr. K. then went into the subject of the present gold coinage, and said that gentlemen were mistaken in fact, when they stated that gold had been raised so high as to depreciate it below a par value with silver on the contrary, at the South, the new coin was generally sold at a premium. After some further remarks, explanatory of the amount of loss to the mines for the want of a mint, and the manner in which it was increased, and the advantages which will accrue to the country by the measure proposed, Mr. K. concluded, with the hope that the bill would pass as a measure due to those parts of the country interested in the measure.

Mr. BENTON said he felt extremely solicitous about the fate of the bill, as at that time of the session the vote on the recommitment would be decisive of a passage. He considered the bill but the commitment of a series of measures to restore a sound and metallic currency to the country; and opposition to the bill was a measure in favor of paper instead of gold. He would continue to combat a paper currency in every form, whether in the Bank of the United States, deposite banks, or local banks.

Mr. BLACK thought the question had nothing to do with the currency. He was in favor of a gold currency.

Mr. CLAY rose to vindicate his State against the insinuation of the Senator from Georgia. He denied that Kentucky had ever taken an acre of land from the Indians without paying for it.

The hour of three o'clock having arrived, the Senate, agreeably to a vote of yesterday, had a recess until five.

EVENING SESSION.

At five o'clock, when the Senate was called to order,

Mr. CLAY objected to putting the question, until the seats of the Senators were filled, and on his motion the Sergeant-at-Arms was directed to bring in the absent members.

After some further discussion by Messrs. KNIGHT, WAGGAMAN, BENTON, EWING, CALHOUN, PORTER, and CLAY, the question on recommitting, with instructions, was put, and decided, by ayes and nays as follows:

YEAS—Messrs. Bell, Black, Buchanan, Clay,

Clayton, Ewing, Frelinghuysen, Goldsborough, Hill, Knight, McKean, Morris, Naudain, Robbins, Silsbee, Smith, Southard, Swift, Tipton, Tomlinson, Webster.—31.

NAYS—Messrs. Benton, Bibb, Brown, Calhoun, Cuthbert, Hendricks, Kane, King of Alabama, King of Georgia, Leigh, Linn, Mangum, Porter, Preston, Robinson, Ruggles, Shepley, Tallmadge, Tyler, Waggaman, White, Wright.—22.

So the motion to recommit was rejected.

On the final passage of the bill, the ayes and noes being desired were ordered; and were as follows:

YEAS—Messrs. Benton, Bibb, Brown, Calhoun, Cuthbert, Hendricks, Kane, King of Alabama, King of Georgia, Leigh, Linn, Mangum, Morris, Porter, Preston, Robinson, Ruggles, Shepley, Tallmadge, Tyler, Waggaman, Webster, White, Wright.—24.

NAYS—Messrs. Bell, Black, Buchanan, Clay, Clayton, Ewing, Frelinghuysen, Goldsborough, Hill, Knight, McKean, Naudain, Robbins, Silsbee, Smith, Southard, Swift, Tipton, Tomlinson.—19.

So the bill passed.

Mr. CLAYTON, from the Judiciary Committee, to which the same was recommitted, reported the bill supplementary to the act to establish the judicial system of the United States, amended, in accordance with the instructions of the Senate.

Mr. CLAYTON briefly explained the nature of the bill as amended. It attaches Maryland to the 5th District, and Delaware to the 3d District, thereby abolishing the 4th District altogether. It also provides for erecting a new District, to be composed of the States of Louisiana, Alabama, and Mississippi, and another of Missouri, Illinois, and Indiana, and provides also for the appointment of another judge of the Supreme Court.

The amendment was concurred in, and the bill was ordered to be engrossed and read a third time.

By unanimous consent, the bill was put upon its third reading, where

Mr. PRELINGHUYSEN asked the yeas and nays, which were ordered, and are as follows, to wit:

YEAS—Messrs. Bell, Benton, Bibb, Black, Brown, Buchanan, Calhoun, Clay, Ewing, Frelinghuysen, Goldsborough, Hendricks, Kane, King of Alabama, King of Georgia, Knight, Leigh, Lane, McKane, Naudain, Porter, Preston, Robbins, Robinson, Silsbee, Southard, Swift, Tipton, Tomlinson, Webster, White.—31.

NAYS—Messrs. Clayton, Cuthbert, Hill, Shepley, Tallmadge.—5.

So the bill was passed.

On motion of Mr. SOUTHARD, the Senate took up for consideration, as in Committee of the Whole, the bill for the relief of the cities of Washington, Georgetown, and Alexandria.

Mr. TYLER said that last year, when this same subject was before Congress, it met with considerable opposition. At this session, the District committees of the two Houses met in joint session, and it was with considerable difficulty that the committees could agree upon a measure of relief. The city of Washington has contracted a large foreign debt, which it cannot discharge without the interposition of this Government. By the arrangements which have been made with regard to their debts, the citizens of this city are rendered liable to have their property sold. Last year, under the same pressing necessity, the sum of $70,000 was voted for their relief; and now the reasons for relief have come before Congress with accumulated force; and the probability is, that for the coming year, there will not be $14,000 of available funds in their Treasury; and their property is subject to the influence of the act of the Government. The agents of the foreign creditors are here, ready to purchase the property of these citizens of Washington under the hammer, so that there is danger emphatically, that this city may be "sold to the Dutch." Two remedies present themselves to our consideration for this case, either to pay off the debt, or grant present relief. To the first, some gentlemen thought a question of principle stood in the way; and he, (Mr. T.,) who was among the straight-laced in regard to the constitutional powers of Congress, confessed that the principle was an obstacle in his mind; for he thought Congress could just as well, and with as much justice, pay off the debts of private individuals. He therefore thought that this was by far the best remedy of granting relief. It is placed in some sort on the footing of a loan, and looks to the Chesapeake and Ohio Canal stock for indemnity, on the ground that they will surrender all their interests in this canal to the Government. He held, that as a fund had arisen from the sale of public lots in Washington, amounting to some $600,000, Congress had a right to apply that sum to any purposes they might think proper, within the District; and the reason for extending them relief was enhanced, when it was recollected that Congress itself held out inducements to subscribe to this stock, and thus to incur the debt.

Mr. BIBB said, he was last year opposed to the bill giving relief to this city, but since then he had examined the question, and deliberately came to the conclusion that we ought to grant relief. On reading the act under which this burthensome loan had been made, he thought Congress were under a pledge to pay the debt. Undoubtedly it it is an act which on its face bears the impression of the encouragement of Congress to go into these expenses and to borrow money on their own responsibility. He believed that the people here had to pay a higher tax than was paid by any other people in the United States—he believed the average of taxes usually was 6 and 10 cents upon the assessment of every $100—here the assessment was $1 25 upon that assessment. And as Congress has been the means by which this state of things has been introduced and imposed upon this city, and as we are their local Legislature, they ought to be freed from so very oppressive a burthen. It is only appropriating those funds which have been donated to the Government of the United States.

Mr. BLACK said he was opposed to this proposition last year, when it was reduced to an appropriation of $70,000 for one year, and then adopted upon the express understanding that it was not to be presented again. The gentleman from Massachusetts (Mr. Webster) then declared in his place, that when the application was made to Congress for permission to incur this debt, the people of Washington used persuasions and supplications for the purpose, and he warned them against incurring it, on the ground, that they never would be able to pay it. The law, he confessed, was a singular one, and it was only to be accounted for, on the ground that it was formed upon their own solicitation. He would rather vote for the bill as a gift than as a loan, for if it is loaned, it is gone forever, just as if it is given, and we have the same authority to give as to loan. But it is brought forward now in a new dress, and in a more imposing form, and appealing to our feelings. He was opposed to the bill on constitutional grounds, and asked the yeas and nays upon the bill, which were ordered.

Some further remarks were made by Mr. SOUTHARD and Mr. LEIGH in favor of the bill, and by Mr. BLACK against it, when, without taking the question,

On motion of Mr. PRELINGHUYSEN,

The Senate adjourned.

HOUSE OF REPRESENTATIVES.

TUESDAY, Feb. 24, 1835.

Petitions were presented on leave, by Messrs. CAGE and BURGES.

Mr. PIERCE, of N. H. from the Committee on the Judiciary, reported a bill to extend the patent of Robert Eastman for seven years, which was read twice and ordered to be engrossed.

Mr. JOHNSON, from the Committee on Military Affairs, reported the following resolution, which was agreed to:

Resolved, That on Wednesday morning, after reading the journals and receiving reports from committees, this House will appropriate one hour to the consideration of the following bills:

A bill to render permanent the present mode of supplying the army of the United States;

A bill respecting the appointment of three addition paymasters;

A bill respecting the Topographical Corps;

A bill respecting the Corps of Engineers.

Mr. CHINN, from the Committee on the District of Columbia, reported the following resolution, which was agreed to:

Resolved, That this House will, on Thursday next, from and after the hour of 1 o'clock, proceed to consider bills reported by the Committee on the District of Columbia.

Mr. R. M. JOHNSON, from the Committee on Military Affairs, reported the following joint resolution, which was read twice and ordered to be engrossed for a third reading:

Resolved by the Senate and House of Representatives of the United States of America in Congress assembled, That the system of Discipline and Tactics prepared by Major General Scott, under the direction of the War Department, and in conformity with a resolution of the House of Representatives of April 8th, 1834, shall be, and the same is hereby established for the government of the army of the United States and of the militia.

Mr. CONNOR, from the Committee on the Post Office and Post Roads, reported the following resolution, which was agreed to:

Resolved, That the Clerk of the House continue the services of the individual employed by him, under a resolution of the last session, to make certain maps for the use of the Committee on the Post Office and Post Roads.

Mr. C. JOHNSON, from the Committee on Private Land Claims, reported the following resolution:

Resolved, That a translator of the French and Spanish language be employed by the clerk of this House for two years, whose duty it shall be to translate for the use of the House as well as the Land Office, all such documents and papers as may be necessary for the action of the House, and its committees, as well as the Land Office, and that the said translator be allowed the sum of eight hundred dollars for each year.

Mr. C. JOHNSON explained the object and necessity of the resolution.

After a few remarks from Messrs. PILLMORE, ASHLEY, E. WHITTLESEY, and WHITE of Florida, the resolution was agreed to.

Mr. BEARDSLEY, from the Committee on the Judiciary, reported, without amendment, the bill from the Senate, amendatory of the acts for the punishment of crimes against the United States.

Mr. B. briefly explained the provisions of the bill, when, after some conversation between Messrs. PHILLIPS, BEARDSLEY, FOSTER, VINTON, and BINNEY, it was ordered to be read a third time to-morrow.

Mr. MASON, of Virginia, moved that the bill "granting an additional quantity of land for the satisfaction of revolutionary bounty land warrants," be included among the bills relating to the District of Columbia, to be considered on Thursday next.

The motion was objected to.

Mr. MASON moved a suspension of the rules which was agreed to; and the proposition to include was adopted.

Mr. CLAY, from the Committee on the Public Lands, reported, with an amendment, the bill from the Senate supplementary to the act granting a quantity of land to certain exiles from Poland which was postponed to Monday next.

Mr. CARR, from the Committee on Private Land Claims, reported a bill for the relief of the heirs of Jacob Smith, of Michigan Territory, deceased; which was read twice and ordered to be engrossed and read a third time.

Mr. CARR, from the same Committee, made an unfavorable report on the memorial of Justin Beirbien; which was ordered to lie on the table.

Mr. DANKS, from the Committee of Claims, reported a bill for the relief of Jacob a different which was read twice and committed.

Unfavorable reports, on various petitions, &c. were made by Messrs. KINNARD, MITCHELL of Ohio, MILLER, SCHENCK, LINCOLN, McINTIRE, CHANEY, PARKS, LEA of Tennessee, ADAMS of New York, and BEALE, from their respective Committees; wh ch were ordered to lie on the table.

[Mr. KINNARD, from the Committee on Revolutionary Claims, made a report on the memorial of Col. Francis Vigo, of Vincennes, Indiana, which

m his motion, was laid on the table and ordered to be printed.]

Mr. FOSTER, from the Committee on the Judiciary, reported, with an amendment, a bill from the Senate for the relief of David Beard; which was committed.

Mr. CAMBRELENG, by consent, moved to print 3,000 extra copies of the document prepared by Mr. E. Everett and himself, the one in favor, and the other adverse to the bill from the Senate, asking an appropriation to satisfy the claims of certain American citizens, on account of spoliations committed by the French, prior to 1800.

Mr. CAMBRELENG moved to suspend the rule requiring the motion to lie over one day, which carried.—Yeas 110, nays 38.

The motion to print, was then agreed to.

Mr. CONNOR remarked that the House had heretofore determined to hold a session this evening at six o'clock. It was proper that there should be a recess, and he therefore moved that the House should adjourn at 4, to meet again at 6 o'clock, P. M.

Mr. C. P. WHITE moved to amend the motion by proposing a recess from 4 to 6 o'clock, P. M. each day, for the remainder of the session; which was disagreed to—yeas 61, nays not counted.

Mr. MARSHALL proposed a recess from 3 to 5 o'clock. Lost, 69 to 72.

Mr. CONNOR'S motion was then agreed to.

Mr. C. P. WHITE called for the orders of the day. Agreed to.

Mr. C. P. WHITE then moved to suspend the rule, for the purpose of going into committee, with the view of considering such bills as might be determined on by the committee; which was agreed to—yeas 154, nays 99.

The House then, on motion of Mr. C. P. WHITE, resolved itself into a Committee of the Whole on the state of the Union—Mr. WARDWELL in the chair.

On motion of Mr. SUTHERLAND, the committee took up the bill (No. 660) making appropriations for building light-boats, beacons, and monuments, and placing buoys, for the year 1835.

The bill was taken up by sections.

Mr. SUTHERLAND moved to strike out the sum of $400 for the erection of a fog bell on Cape Elizabeth, Maine. Agreed to.

Mr. SUTHERLAND also moved to insert $1000 instead of $700, for placing buoys near Lynn, Hunter's rock, Western rocks, Sawyer's river, &c. Massachusetts. Agreed to.

Mr. SUTHERLAND also moved an item of $400 for buoys in New Jersey. Agreed to.

Mr. SUTHERLAND also moved an additional item for placing six buoys on the Potomac river, $250, and a spindle at Potomac Creek, $500. Agreed to.

Mr. PINCKNEY moved an amendment of $5,000 for five beacon lights at Charleston harbor, in lieu of the clause appropriating $750 for three buoys in the north channel of said harbor. Agreed to.

Mr. SUTHERLAND moved an additional item of $3,000 for improvements at the mouth of Portland harbor. Agreed to.

Sundry other amendments were also agreed to.

The bill, with amendments, was then ordered to be reported to the House, and the committee, on motion of Mr. C. P. WHITE, took up and considered the bill authorizing the construction of a dry Dock for the naval service; which was ordered to be reported to the House without amendment.

The committee then, on motion of Mr. C. P. WHITE, took up and considered the bill to carry into effect the Convention with Spain; which was ordered to be reported to the House, without amendment.

On motion of Mr. HUBBARD, the committee took up the bill making appropriations for certain roads, and for examinations and surveys, for the year 1835.

Mr. CORWIN moved to strike out the clause appropriating $546,086 for the repair of the Cumberland road. Agreed to.

Mr. CORWIN also moved an additional item of

$320 for one of the superintendents on the Cumberland road. Agreed to.

Mr. LYON moved an additional clause of $10,000 for certain surveys and improvements in the military road from Mackinaw to Green Bay, &c.

Mr. MERCER opposed the appropriation.

The amendment was rejected. The bill was then laid aside, and

On motion of Mr. PEARCE, the committee took up the bill making appropriations for the erection of Marine Hospitals in the city of Baltimore and other places.

Mr. McKIM moved to strike out that part leaving the designation to the Mayor and City Council, and to give it to the Secretary of the Treasury. Agreed to.

Mr. PEARCE moved to insert an additional item of $3,000 for the purchase of a site, and the erection thereon of a Marine Hospital, at White river, in the Territory of Arkansas.

Mr. SEVIER advocated the amendment. It was, he said, at the mouth of the Arkansas river, where the hospital was proposed to be built, the best site that could be selected. Last year, when the cholera raged at New Orleans, hundreds were landed on that Territory, and would have perished in utter destitution but for the benevolence of the citizens of Arkansas. It was one of the most important channels of trade in the country, and for six hundred each way there was no place of accommodation for persons attacked with disease on any part of the line. The proposition would in no way benefit the citizens of the Territory he represented, but the boatmen, sailors, and other persons engaged in navigating the waters in that section of country.

Mr. POPE would not deny that Marine Hospitals were perhaps required at Pittsburg, New Orleans, and at the mouth of the White river. But he did deny that one was needed in the State of Illinois, at or near the mouth of the Ohio river. There is now a hospital at Smithland, sixty miles above the mouth of the Ohio, and he could not see the necessity of establishing another only fifty or sixty miles off. There is also a Marine Hospital at Louisville Kentucky, which, as well as the one at Smithland, was built at the expense of Kentucky. He was as willing as any man, to provide for the comfort of sick sailors, but he would try to do so in a mode different from that suggested by the bill. It would be better to provide for the support of those already established, than to erect new ones that are not required. When the proper time arrived, he intended to submit a motion to strike out the appropriation for the erection of a Hospital at the mouth of the Ohio, and to insert, in lieu thereof, a clause appropriating five thousand dollars to aid in the support of the one at Louisville, and twenty-five hundred to aid in support of that at Smithland.

A long discussion ensued, upon the general merits of the bill, and the propriety of erecting Marine Hospitals, in which Messrs. MERCER, HARDIN, POPE, DENNY, MASON of Virginia, D. J. PEARCE, BURGES, LYTLE, REYNOLDS, JOHNSON of Louisiana, FILLMORE, REED, WISE, HAWES, SUTHERLAND, and VINTON, took part.

Mr. BURGES moved to strike out the enacting clause of the bill, but subsequently withdrew it.

Before the question was taken on the amendment,

Mr. VINTON said it was evident that the whole day would be consumed on the bill under discussion, and he therefore, for the purpose of expediting other business, moved that the committee rise, and report the other bills to the House—ayes 75, noes 40.

The committee thereupon rose, and reported the bills acted on to the House.

The bill to carry into effect the convention with Spain;

The bill to authorize the construction of a dry dock for the use of the navy, reported without amendment, were both ordered to be engrossed for a third reading.

The amendments to the bill making appropriations for certain roads—

To the bill making appropriations for building light-houses, beacon-lights, and making surveys

for the year 1835; were then concurred in by the House, and the bills ordered to be engrossed for a third reading.

The bill making additional appropriations for the Delaware Break-water, for certain harbors, and removing obstructions in and at the mouths of certain rivers, for the year 1835, reported from the Committee of the Whole, with sundry amendments, was then taken up.

On the question to concur with the Committee of the Whole on the amendment appropriating the sum of $50,000 for the improvement of the Ohio river between Pittsburg and Louisville, at the Falls of the Ohio—

Mr. HAWES asked for the yeas and nays; which were ordered.

Mr. POLK objected to so large an additional appropriation as $50,000 for the Ohio alone, which was already provided for under the bill to an amount of $50,000.

Mr. LANE warmly advocated the appropriation, and said it was trifling compared with the immense extent of trade, and the great interest involved.

Mr. VINTON remarked that the sum of $50,000, appropriated under the bill, was to be divided between the severe Ohio, Missouri, and Mississippi, and it was doubtful whether a cent of it would be expended on the Ohio. One agent could easily disburse the whole of it. When $50,000 was appropriated for the Red river, $40,000 for the Arkansas, $20,000 for the Cape Fear, he deemed it barely just to resist the proposed amendment for the Ohio.

Mr. HUBBARD explained, that the other items were recommended upon reports made by Engineers, and upon positive estimates, whereas, such was not the case with the amendment. He expressed a hope that the House would act upon the question at once, without further discussion.

Mr. MERCER was in favor of the amendment.

Mr. DENNY remarked that it should be borne in mind that the amendment was recommended by one of the standing committees of the House, after mature deliberation, and it was entitled to full as much consideration as if it had come sanctioned by the Committee of Ways and Means.

Mr. VANDERPOEL inquired if the Committee on Internal Improvement had reported a bill embracing this appropriation.

Mr. VINTON explained. The subject had been referred to that committee under a resolution of the House. In consequence of the difficulty of getting a special bill through, Mr. V. was instructed by the committee to move this amendment to one of the appropriation bills.

Mr. POLK said he understood that the whole amount recommended by the War Department, was $350,000, under a report by Captain Shrieve; and the Committee on Roads and Canals, not deeming the estimate large enough, asked for this additional item.

Mr. VINTON explained: The report of Captain Shrieve was predicated on the river below the Falls, and never contemplated any improvement at all above that point.

Mr. POLK was still correct, that all the information upon which any estimates could be made was before the Committee of Ways and Means. If the engineer had not reported, nor any documents furnished from the War Department, to the House, upon what just ground could they venture to vote away so large an amount as that contemplated in the amendment? The importance of the Ohio river as a channel of commerce, the nature of the obstructions, whether sand bars or gravel bars, had nothing to do with the question. The question was, whether the appropriation was founded on proper information?

Mr. LYTLE said, notwithstanding his profound respect for the Committee of Ways and Means, there were other committees which he entertained as high respect as he did for that. From whatever committee a proposition should come, he was prepared to act upon it as he thought best conduced to the interest of the country. The commerce between Pittsburg and Louisville was of immense importance to that section of the country, and the appropriation he believed should be made. He denied the position

that a recommendation from one committee should clothe any measure with more sanctity than that of another.

Mr. BURGES cared not from what quarter a recommendation came, so that it was supported by facts, such as would establish its expediency and benefit, and he would be ever ready to sustain it.

Mr. HUBBARD defended the course pursued by the Committee of Ways and Means. They had confined themselves in this bill, to works already commenced, as its title expressed, for the purpose of carrying on works already begun and in progress. If the Committee on Roads and Canals thought the appropriation now asked for so inadequate, why had not that Committee introduced a bill for the purpose, and not endeavor to thrust this amendment forward? It was altogether out of place in this bill, since it was to commence a new work.

Mr. STEWART said the gentleman from New Hampshire (Mr. Hubbard) labored under a misapprehension in supposing this to be a new work, since an act was passed for it in May, 1824, eleven years ago.

Mr. DICKINSON, of Tennessee, moved to strike out the enacting clause of the bill, but withdrew it on the understanding that the question on the amendment should be taken at once, declaring his intention to renew it hereafter.

The question was then taken by yeas and nays, and decided as follows:—Yeas 109, nays 86

So the House concurred in the amendment.

Mr. DICKINSON, of Tennessee, said, although he believed the amendment just adopted to be one of the best provisions in the bill, still he voted against it, from a dislike to its general principles, and he therefore renewed his motion to strike out the enacting clause of the bill.

Mr. HUBBARD asked for the yeas and nays, which were ordered.

Mr. HANNEGAN moved that the House adjourn. Negatived.

The question was then taken, and decided in the negative—Yeas 56, nays 128.

The House then, at ½ past 4, took a recess till 6 o'clock P. M.

EVENING SESSION.

The House, according to order, re-assembled at 6 o'clock, P. M.

The Speaker laid before the House a communication from the Secretary of War, transmitting a copy of a report and survey of Cumberland river, which was laid on the table and ordered to be printed.

Mr. BEATY, on leave, moved to print 500 extra copies of the foregoing communication and document, which motion, by the rule, lies over one day.

On motion of Mr. CONNOR, the House then went into Committee of the Whole on the state of the Union, Mr. VANCE in the Chair, upon the bill to establish certain post routes, and to alter and discontinue others, and for other purposes.

The bill was read by sections; various amendments were offered and adopted, and others rejected, when—

Mr. JOHNSON, of Louisiana, moved an amendment directing the Postmaster General to cause the mail between New Orleans and Mobile to be carried daily instead of tri-weekly, as at present.

This motion was resisted by Mr. CONNOR, because it was an innovation upon the principles of the bill. He believed the Postmaster General, whenever the finances of the Department would permit, would establish a daily mail between the two points.

The amendment was advocated by Messrs. JOHNSON of La., E. EVERETT, and SEABORN JONES, and opposed by Messrs. CONNOR and BEARDSLEY.

Mr. JOHNSON, of Md., moved to strike out the enacting clause of the bill.

Upon this motion, a desultory and exciting debate ensued, in reference to the management of the Post Office Department, in which Messrs. JOHNSON of Md., WISE, CONNOR, PEYTON, BEARDSLEY, LANE, HAWES, STODDERT, GARLAND, and LYTLE participated.

Without taking the question on the motion to

strike out the enacting clause, the committee, on motion of Mr. POLK, rose, and asked leave to sit again.

On motion of Mr. POLK, the House then, at half past ten o'clock, P. M.

Adjourned.

IN SENATE.

The VICE PRESIDENT communicated a letter from the Treasury Department, transmitting reports from the First and Third Auditors, and Register of the Treasury, in relation to commutation to officers of the revolution; which, on motion of Mr. HILL, was ordered to be printed.

The VICE PRESIDENT also communicated a letter from the Treasury Department, transmitting abstracts of the official emoluments of the officers of the customs, and the fees received for certificates to accompany distilled spirits, wines, and teas, and commissions on disbursements as superintendents of light houses, and as agents for the marine hospitals.

Petitions and memorials were presented by Messrs. KENT, TIPTON, and PORTER.

Mr. KANE presented a joint resolution of the Legislature of Illinois, for rescinding so much of the compact between that State and the United States, as prohibits said State from taxing land sold by the United States for five years after such sale.

Mr. TIPTON presented a joint resolution of the Legislature of Indiana, relative to limiting the enrolment of the militia to able-bodied free male citizens of the United States, between the ages of 21 and 40 years, and providing for better arming and disciplining the militia of the United States.

Mr. McKEAN, from the Committee on Pensions, reported the bills from the House, granting pensions to John Bryan, John Moore, Timothy Jordan, David Pearson, Samuel Shelmerdine, and Abraham E. Boutwell.

He also reported that the bills from the House, granting pensions to Robert Lucas, Isaac Carter, and the widow and heirs of Samuel Southerland, ought not to pass.

Mr. TOMLINSON, from the same committee, reported that the bills from the House, granting pensions to John W. Cox, Edward Nicholas, and Labert L. Van Veltenburg, ought not to pass; and that the bill granting a pension to Joseph Swartwood, ought to pass.

On motion of Mr. KING, of Alabama, the bill for the relief of Rio and H. Bell was considered as in Committee of the Whole, ordered to be engrossed for a third reading, and then read a third time and passed.

On motion of Mr. BENTON, the bill authorising an increase of the corps of Engineers, was taken up, considered as in Committee of the Whole, ordered to be engrossed for a third reading, and finally passed.

On motion of Mr. BELL, the Senate took up for consideration, the bill to continue the patent of Joseph Grant, was considered as in committee of the whole; ordered to be engrossed for a third reading, and then read a third time and passed.

On motion of Mr. WHITE, the Senate took up for consideration, as in committee of the whole, the bill for the relief of John Dougherty, an Indian agent; when it was ordered to be engrossed for a third reading, and then read a third time and passed.

Mr. SHEPLEY submitted the following resolution:

Resolved, That the Secretary of War be directed to furnish the information called for by a resolution of the ——— in regard to the surveys made in the State of Maine, to the Secretary of the Senate during the vacation; and that the surveys be printed under his direction.

On motion of Mr. BLACK, the Senate took up for consideration, as in committee of the whole, the bill authorizing the Secretary of the Treasury to invest the two per cent fund reserved for roads leading to the state of Mississippi when it was ordered to be engrossed and read a third time. Afterwards the bill was read the third time and passed.

On motion of Mr. KING, of Alabama, the Senate took up for consideration, as in committee of

the whole, the bill to authorise the application of the two per cent fund of Alabama, set apart for public purposes, to the construction of a rail road from Mobile Bay to the Tennessee river.

After some remarks by Mr. CLAY in opposition to the bill, and by

Mr. KING in support of it,

Mr. CLAY moved to lay it on the table, which was negatived. Yeas, 12—Nays, 14.

Mr. CLAY then moved the indefinite postponement of the bill, and asked the yeas and nays upon the question, which were ordered.

Some further debate ensued upon the bill, Mr. CLAY renewed the motion to lay it on the table; which was agreed to.

The Senate then resumed the bill granting relief to the cities of Washington, Alexandria, and Georgetown.

Mr. BENTON regretted that he should be compelled to vote against the bill, unless its friends were willing to take the relief it proposed for this year, and leave the rest to future legislation by Congress. The people of this city, he said, labored under peculiar grievances—great expenses had been thrown upon them which entitled them to all the indulgence which we can extend to them. This Government exacted hard terms in getting the ground on which this city is located, for their own use. Many lots in this city have been sold at great amounts, and those which yet remain are estimated at between two and three millions of dollars. He thought the next step we could do would be to set apart the building lots, the proceeds of which should be applied as a sinking fund to pay this debt. One great objection with him was, that to extend this aid in five years was an encroachment for four years upon our successors. His opposition to it was one year, was quiet, easy, and almost imperceptible mode of granting effectual relief, by passing this bill in its present shape, it was unequally imposing upon the treasury of this country, a burthen of near two millions of dollars. Mr. B. said, he would be extremely sorry, if by voting against the bill, it should be lost, for a residence of fourteen years in Washington had convinced him that its citizens should be favored. He wished to be generous to them, but he wished also to prevent the treasury from being saddled with a debt of two millions.

Mr. SOUTHARD said that the bill was the result of the joint consultation of the two Committees on the District, and to alter it as suggested, would be the means of defeat. He was much gratified by the expression of feeling and opinion of the hon. gentleman from Missouri, and as far as he could, he would yield to his views. He said the appropriation was not for payment of the whole debts of the city, but for that which was contracted for the purposes of the canal. We cannot at the present session, form and mature such a bill as the gentleman's views would require, or as he would seem to suggest. A difficulty was presented from the situation of the public grounds. It would require time to investigate how many lots could be spared from the uses or probable cash of the Government.

Mr. BENTON said, he was aware that his suggestion would defeat the bill, and his object in making it was to gain time to make the necessary investigation. He therefore moved the necessary amendment to the bill, so as to make the appropriation to each of the cities for one year only.

After some conversation between Messrs. TILLER, BENTON, and SOUTHARD, the amendment was agreed to.

The question being on the engrossment of the bill,

Mr. CLAY said, he should vote for it in its present shape, for the purpose of relieving the pressing necessities of this city, but he had at once seen that the Committee on the District would introduce a bill to take the stock of the canal, and assume the whole foreign debt. That, he believed to be the only essential relief we could extend to them.

Mr. PRESTON expressed his intention to vote for the bill, but he did so only from dire necessity. He would vote for it only to prevent the city of Washington from being "sold to the Dutch."

Mr. CALHOUN sincerely felt for the situation which the city was placed, but he could understand this bill as nothing more or less than a provision to make a donation of so much of the people's money to them. He really commiserated the unfortunate situation, but he thought we had a right to give the property of the people away as proposed. This bill was setting a bad precedent. These people must suffer, and to relieve them now, would only be an inducement to them incur greater debts, in the belief that Congress would always assist them. He recommended them a friend to depend upon their own resources of industry, which alone could give them lasting relief.

Mr. BUCHANAN said, when this bill first came he thought he had determined to vote against and he certainly should have done so, if it had been for the change which had been made in upon the motion of the honorable gentleman in Missouri. But now, he felt that he was in the measure, under duress with regard to it, and could not vote against it. He differed, however, the gentleman from Virginia, (Mr. Leigh,) the law which authorized this debt to be incurred, could be construed into a guarantee on part of the Government to pay the debt; he disliked entering into that question now. But President of the United States was made the cutor of the law, and if this bill did not pass, it was the President's duty to sell this city. He would vote for the bill for once, but with these clauses from South Carolina, (Mr. Calhoun,) would advise the people of this city to depend on their own energy and industry for substantial relief, and cease their applications to Congress.

Mr. TYLER said he was very sorry the gentleman from Pennsylvania could not vote for further if than by giving his support to this bill. To be candid on the subject, if the relief is to be continued, the appropriation will be of manner of use whatever. The truth is, the gies of these people are entirely crippled, and means and strength prostrated in the dust. Hoped at the next session, the honorable gentleman would open his heart and be willing to permanent relief.

Mr. KING, of Georgia, said that he too wished we in his experience on the subject of this bill. When the conflict between inclination and duty had been a most painful one. And like some, he had made up his mind to vote for the bill with the greatest reluctance. He had been raised by a reference to the act authorizing the loan to find that, as between the government the contractors of the loan, Congress had virtually guaranteed the debt. The honor of the nation was pledged for the payment of the debt. And on a hasty inquiry into the affairs of these cities, he did not believe it in their power, at present, to discharge the debt. And like others, he no idea of seeing the capital of the Union in hands of the Dutch.

Some gentlemen, he said, had constitutional ideas on the subject. It was thought we had power to make a gratuity to the people of the city. He did not feel these scruples, though he not given a studied examination to the act. He was, he thought, generally as much for of a strict construction of the constitution as any other Senator; but as at present indeed, he thought that whatever restrictions placed upon us when legislating for the city, there was no restriction upon our sovereign power, and the propriety of its exercise were different questions. We might as the power we refuse to exercise it, on the of justice and expediency; and here, he felt, was the difficulty in the measure before enacted. For if there was any theory in which I agreed, it was that republican government ought to be, an association upon principles that claims then, said Mr. K., have people of this city, as a part of the great American family, to a gratuity from this Government than Charleston, or any other city in union? They had a claim to our legislation the usual purposes of government, to direct concentrate the energies of the people to the

greatest advantage; but they had no exclusive claims to our bounty, at the expense of the rest of the Union.

With these views, it would be seen with what reluctance he voted for the bill, and he should it further understood that he did not stand pledged to go further at the next session, if, in the meantime, he could ascertain that it was possible for the cities of the District to pay their own debt.

Mr. KING, of Alabama, protested against this law being interpreted as any guarantee on the part of Congress, either to pay this debt or its interest. The question then was, simply whether we shall relieve the people of Washington. He should vote for the bill as it was now, but he would have voted for it as it was originally, because he thought the Congress of the United States ought not quietly to act by and see the Capital of the country sold under the hammer.

After some further observations from Mr. LEIGH, Mr. KING of Alabama, and Mr. WAGAMAN, the question of engrossment was taken, and decided in the affirmative—ayes 27, noes 14, as follows:

YEAS—Messrs. Benton, Bibb, Buchanan, Clay, Cuthbert, Ewing, Frelinghuysen, Gollsborough, Kane, Kent, King of Alabama, King of Georgia, Knight, Leigh, Linn, McKean, Naudain, Porter, Preston, Robbins, Silsbee, Southard, Swift, Tomlinson, Tyler, Waggaman, Webster—27.

NAYS—Messrs. Black, Brown, Calhoun, Grundy, Hendricks, Hill, Mangum, Morris, Prentiss, Robinson, Ruggles, Shepley, Tipton, Wright—14.

The bill was then read a third time and passed.

The hour of 3 having arrived, Mr. BENTON moved to rescind the resolution for the recess, which was disagreed to, 13 to 15.

The Senate then took a recess till 5 o'clock.

EVENING SESSION.

The bill to provide for paying certain pensioners at Jackson, in Tennessee, and

The bill to establish a pension agency at Russelville, in Kentucky, were each read a third time and passed.

The resolution requiring the appropriations to the Cumberland river be applied as well above as below Nashville, came up on the third reading, and, on motion of Mr. WHITE, was laid on the table.

The bill from the House making permanent the supplies of the army, and fixing the salaries of certain clerks in the Commissary General's Office, was read twice and referred.

The resolution relative to the condition of the Post Office, submitted by Mr. HILL and Mr. SMITH, came up in order, when Mr. HILL moved the following, as an amendment to his resolutions:

Resolved, That no evidence appears in the report of any committee of the Senate, which it goes to impeach the private and official integrity of Wm. T. Barry, Postmaster General; that the extra allowance asunder his direction made to mail contractors, and the method of receiving combined mails on advertised proposals for carrying the mails, are a continuation of the former practice of the Post Office Department; and that the defects and irregularities of the Department have been a natural consequence of a want of a due organization of the Department by Congress.

On motion of Mr. HILL, both the resolutions and amendment were laid upon the table.

The bill for distributing the proceeds of the public lands among the several States;

The bill to graduate the price of the public lands which have been longest in market;

The bill to grant to the State of Missouri a portion of the public domain for purposes of internal improvement; and

The bill granting a township of land for the benefit of a University at St. Louis, Missouri;

Were severally taken up, and then laid upon the table.

The Senate proceeded to consider, as in Committee of the Whole, the bill to regulate the deposites of the public money in the State banks.

After an immaterial amendment,

Mr. CALHOUN moved to fill a blank in the bill with the sum of two and a half per cent, the sum to be paid by the deposite banks, for the use of the public money.

After some remarks by Messrs. CALHOUN, KING of Alabama, KING of Georgia, PRESTON, KNIGHT, SILSBEE, SHEPLEY, and EWING,

Mr. BUCHANAN, in order to try the sense of the Senate, moved to strike out the half per cent, which Mr. CALHOUN, after some remarks, acceded to.

Mr. PRESTON then offered an amendment that when the average amount of deposites shall not exceed $100,000 quarterly, in any one Bank, the Secretary of the Treasury shall be at liberty to contract for terms on which such Bank shall have the use of the public money deposited in it.

Mr. EWING moved to reduce the quarterly minimum to $50,000, when a desultory debate ensued, in which Messrs. CALHOUN, PRESTON, KING of Georgia, KING of Alabama, KNIGHT, TALLMADGE, BUCHANAN, SHEPLEY, SILSBEE, WEBSTER, and EWING, participated; when

On motion of Mr. CALHOUN, the bill was laid on the table.

Mr. NAUDAIN then submitted a resolution to rescind the resolution for the recess.

Mr. SOUTHARD, from the Committee on the District of Columbia, reported the bill from the House supplementary to the act extending a branch of the Baltimore and Ohio Railroad into the District of Columbia, without amendment.

After which the Senate adjourned.

HOUSE OF REPRESENTATIVES.
WEDNESDAY, Feb. 25, 1835.

Mr. H. EVERETT, on leave, presented certain amendments to the bill from the Senate, to provide for the organization of the Post Office Department; which were ordered to be printed.

Mr. FORESTER, from the Committee on Claims, reported a bill for the relief of Charles M. Frazier; which was read twice and committed.

Mr. STODDERT asked the consent of the House to print certain amendments, which he contemplated offering to the bill from the Senate to provide for the organization of the Post Office Department.

Mr. CONNOR said, he intended making an effort to-day, to take up this Post Office bill. He should have done so yesterday if he could have obtained the floor. If his motion should succeed, he suggested that there would not be time to print the amendments, as proposed.

The motion to print was agreed to:

Mr. ANTHONY, from the Committee on Military Affairs, reported the following resolution, which was agreed to.

Resolved, That the Secretary of War be directed to settle and adjust the claims of Frederick Bernard, for services as an extra clerk between September, 1823, and March, 1827, according to the principles of equity and justice.

Mr. PINCKNEY (instructed by the Committee on Commerce) moved the printing of a document from the State Department, in relation to the trade between the United States and the Islands of Cuba and Porto Rico; which was agreed to.

Mr. P. referred to the importance of the document in question, particularly as regarded the interests of his co-constituents, and moved to print 2,000 extra copies of the same; which was agreed to.

On motion of Mr. EWING, a report from the Treasury Department in relation to the Vincennes Land District; was ordered to be printed.

The motion submitted yesterday by Mr. BEATTY, to print 500 extra copies of a report and survey of the Cumberland river, was considered and agreed to.

Mr. ASHLEY, from the Committee on Public Lands, reported the following bills; which were read twice and committed.

A bill for the relief of John Howell;

And a bill for the relief of James Baldridge.

On motion of Mr. ASHLEY, three decisions of the Supreme Court, applicable to Land Claims in Missouri, (now pending before the House,) were ordered to be printed.

On motion of Mr. CONNOR, the Committee on the Post Office and Post Roads were dis-

charged from the further consideration of all subjects referred to said committee.

Mr. JANES, from the Committee on Invalid Pensions, reported a bill granting an invalid pension to Daniel Stoddert; which was read twice and committed.

Mr. CRANE, from the Committee on Revolutionary Claims, reported a bill for the relief of the children of William Crawford, deceased; which was read twice and committed.

Mr. BURGES, from a Select Committee, reported a bill for the relief of the officers and soldiers who served in the Rhode Island brigade in the revolutionary war, their heirs and representatives; which was read twice and committed.

Unfavorable reports upon various petitions, &c. were made by Messrs. GRAYSON, KINNARD, JANES, GRAHAM, HUBBARD, and DAY; which were ordered to lie on the table.

[Mr. KINNARD, from the Committee on Revolutionary Claims, moved to discharge said committee from the further consideration of the petition of Dempsey Hicks; which, on his motion, was laid on the table.

Mr. K., from the same committee, moved to be discharged from the consideration of the petition of John Scott, and that he have leave to withdraw his papers; which was agreed to.]

Petitions were presented by Messrs. FULTON and MAY, and referred.

Mr. McKINLEY said he felt it to be his duty once more to ask the House to take up the resolution offered by him fixing a day for the election of Printer. He wished the House to decide this question one way or the other, and so far as he was concerned, without debate.

The SPEAKER decided the motion out of order.

The House then, on motion of Mr. R. M. JOHNSON, went into Committee of the Whole on the state of the Union, Mr. WHITE, of New York, in the Chair, on the bill to render permanent the present mode of supplying the army of the United States.

The committee accordingly took up the bill as amended; which having been read and agreed to, the committee rose, and reported the bill to the House.

The bill was then ordered to be engrossed.

On motion of Mr. R. M. JOHNSON, the House again resolved itself into a Committee of the Whole on the state of the Union—Mr. LYTLE in the Chair—and took up and considered the following bills:

A bill respecting the appointment of three additional Paymasters of the Army;

A bill to provide for the increase of the Corps of Engineers.

Mr. R. M. JOHNSON moved a substitute to the first section of this bill, proposing to increase the corps.

Mr. SPEIGHT was opposed to the bill.

Mr. DUNLAP was opposed to any further increase of the army, and trusted the amendment would be rejected.

Mr. R. M. JOHNSON appealed to gentlemen to permit the bill to come into the House, when he would give every necessary explanation that might be deemed requisite.

Mr. LANE said he trusted the motion to amend would not be sustained by the committee. Every State in the Union are interested in the increase of the corps of Topographical Engineers. They are educated for the purpose, at the public expense. Their services are devoted to the public interest. They are experienced; and their services are called for daily and hourly at the Department, to superintend the surveys of our harbors, our roads, and our canals. The States required their services to superintend their surveys of internal improvements, authorized by the respective States, and carried on with their own resources. Also, by private incorporated companies in every portion of the country, who are engaged in constructing works of great public and local interest.

That he had at the request of a rail-road company in Indiana, made application to the Department for an Engineer without success, because they were all on duty. That the State of Indiana had authorized several surveys of a public and national character, with a view to a general system of internal improvement within the State, to be carried on with their own resources. They have an agent now in this city, for the purpose of obtaining an experienced engineer from the Department.

That the increase of this corps was, in his opinion, called for, by every consideration of national, State, and local interest.

Mr. R. M. JOHNSON withdrew the amendment.

Mr. DUNLAP offered an amendment providing for the repeal of all laws authorizing the appointment of Topographical Engineers.

Mr. D. expressed his great surprise at the gentleman from Indiana, (Mr. Lane,) supporting the bill, but it was not uncommon to see gentlemen elected as friends of the present executive, and when they came to that House they voted in favor of every measure of internal improvement by the general government. Mr. D. wanted these appointments and surveys confined to the States. He called upon gentlemen to redeem their pledges, and sustain the principles of the administration, which was assailed from every quarter of the country, while that House would be really to blame. He did hope that a House, with a Jackson majority, would not be found sustaining every proposition opposed to the principles of the present Executive.

Mr. LANE said, in reply to the gentleman from Tennessee, (Mr. Dunlap,) that the House had received a lesson of party discipline. That a large portion of it seemed to have been intended for himself. That it would have been wisdom in the honorable gentleman if he had applied the discipline to himself, before he should have instructed the House.

He says he is surprised that the gentleman from Indiana, and others who were elected as Jackson men, and sent here to support the principles of the Administration, should vote for these extravagant appropriations for surveys and for works of internal improvement. That to increase the corps of engineers, was to authorize unconstitutional improvements.

Mr. L. said, it was true he had been elected as a friend of the distinguished Chief Magistrate, not to serve the Chief Magistrate, but to serve his constituents, the State, and the Union.

That he wore no collar—no man's yoke. In his votes, and the course he had and would pursue, while honored with a seat in this House, he had and should follow the dictates of his own conscience and judgment, uninfluenced by any other consideration, than the interest and prosperity of his constituents, the State, and the Union. The honorable gentleman from Tennessee, (Mr. Dunlap,) may have been elected because he was a Jackson man, to sustain the administration right or wrong. If so, Mr. L. said, he was proud to say, his selection was a different one. That he had been elected in a district where General Jackson himself had been beaten a few months before.

That he was willing to sustain with the gentleman from Tennessee, (Mr. Dunlap) and let the House and the American People determine who had accorded to the Chief Magistrate the most efficient support. That in the present instance, he was sustaining the Chief Magistrate, while the gentleman from Tennessee (Mr. Dunlap,) was opposing him and his measures. The President recommended it in his message, the Secretary of War requires it; it is emphatically an administration measure. A distinguished officer of one of the bureaus is now in this hall urging the passage of this bill.

That he was in favor of the General Government improving the condition of the country, for the benefit of the People, with the money of the People. That he believed it not only constitutional, but the duty of the General Government to aid the States, and even private companies in the surveys and prosecution of all works calculated to facilitate the commerce and interest of the Union.

That he had no constitutional scruples, nor did he subscribe to the doctrine that a stream, because the water was salt, had the preference over a large and commercial channel of fresh water. If the gentleman means to be understood that to be a Jackson man is to oppose all appropriations for the improvements of our rivers and channels of commerce, and all aid by the General Government for improvements in the several States, he could only say no such Jackson men could be found in Indiana.

That he not only believed the General Government possessed the power, but that it was their duty to improve all the channels of commerce, in every part of the Union. That this principle had been acted upon, so far as they participated in the character of national works. That he understood these to be the principles of the Chief Magistrate. That he desires the passage of this bill increasing the corps of Topographical Engineers, for the purpose of aiding the nation, the States, and companies, in the prosecution of works of internal improvement.

Mr. BOON said he was aware that the remarks which had just been made by his friend from Tennessee, (Mr. Dunlap) were not directed to him individually, but as he (Mr. Boon) should vote for the amendment offered by the gentleman from Kentucky and for the bill itself, he was not, therefore, to be considered as being inconsistent in his course toward the administration. Mr. B. said that no one, perhaps, had been more uncompromising in their support of the present chief Magistrate in three several elections, than himself, and that few, if any, had given a more hearty and uniform support of the general policy of the present Administration than he had done during the time he had been honored with a seat in Congress—and that while he had given his support to the leading measures of the Administration, he had also taken the liberty, on some occasions to go a scruple further in relation to some matters to evolve a mere difference of opinion.

Mr. DUNLAP then withdrew his amendment.

On motion of Mr. R. M. JOHNSON, the committee rose, and reported the bill to the House.

The bill to provide additional paymasters, then came up on its engrossment.

Mr. JOHNSON gave a brief explanation of the merits of the bill.

Mr. SPEIGHT opposed the bill.

Mr. BURGES moved a proviso to the bill, giving the President the power of pointing the additional paymasters, by and with the advice and consent of the Senate.

Some conversation ensued between Messrs. POLK, MERCER, GRENNELL, and R. M. JOHNSON, on some of the provisions of the bill.

Mr. CHILTON opposed the bill with much earnestness, and called upon the friends of retrenchment and economy to vote against a proposition for the creation of a new source of expense.

Mr. WISE maintained that the bill was a direct violation of the principles of the constitution, since it vested the appointing power in an officer not recognised in that instrument. He therefore moved to strike out the third section of the bill, providing for the employment of citizens when soldiers could not be engaged. Agreed to.

Mr. LYTLE said it had been contended that this bill went to create a new office. It had been urgently recommended by the Department, and was believed to be highly essential to the welfare of the service.

Before any question was taken, the House, on motion of Mr. HUBBARD, passed to the order of the day.

An act to render permanent the present mode of supplying the army of the United States, and fixing the salaries of certain clerks therein named, was then read a third time, and passed.

Mr. McKINLEY moved to suspend all the orders of the day, for the purpose of taking up the resolution on the subject of the election of printer.

A question of order arose as to the operation of the rule, whether the motion required more than a bare majority, or a majority of two thirds.

The CHAIR, referring to his decision the other day, that a bare majority was sufficient to postpone the orders of the day, said the question as presented itself in a different shape, inasmuch as it was a resolution, and the first question was set apart for the consideration of members, and, in his opinion, the motion of the gentleman from Alabama would require a vote of two thirds.

r. McKINLEY appealed from the decision of the Chair. He was determined to obtain a decision upon the resolution, if there remained any use of arriving at a decision. He had tried various plans, in order to effect this object; but they invariably been met by the Chair, with the assertion that they were out of order.

he question was discussed by the CHAIR, srs. FOSTER, MERCER, BRIGGS, CLAY, IGES, PATTON, McKINLEY, EVANS, and NOR.

r. McKINLEY then withdrew the appeal, and ed to suspend the rules of the House.

r. CLAY asked for the yeas and nays; which s ordered.

he question was then taken, and decided as was:

EAS—Messrs. John Adams, William Allen, sony, Beale, Bean, Beardsley, Beaumont, ter, Boon, Bouldin, Brown, Burd, Burns, By-, Cambreleng, Carr, Casey, Chaney, Samuel k, Clay, Connor, Coulter, Cramer, Day, Dick-, Dunlap, Fowler, William K. Fuller, Gal-h, Gillet, Joseph Hall, Thomas H. Hall, Hal-Hagner, Hannegan, Hardin, Joseph M. Hur-Hathaway, Hawkins, Hawes, Henderson, ter, Howell, Hubbard, Huntington, Jarvis, ard M. Johnson, Noadiah Johnson, Cave John-Benjamin Jones, Kavanagh, Kilgore, Kin-Lane, Lansing, Laporte, Lee, Lucas, Lyon, s Abijah Mann, Mardis, John Y. Mason, Ma-son, May, McKay, McKinley, McLene, Mc-, Miller, Henry, Mitchell, Robert Mitchell, pan, Muhlenberg, Murphy, Osgood, Page, s Parker, Patterson, Peirce, Pierson, Plum-Polk, Pope, Reynolds, Schenck, Shinn, b, Speight, Sutherland, William Taylor, sis Thomas, Thomson, Turner, Turrill, Van-sel, Van Houten, Wagener, Ward, Ward-Whael on, White—103.

AYS—Messrs. J. Q. Adams, H. Allen, J. J. s C. Allan, Ashley, Banks, Barber, Barnitz, ager, Bates, Baylies, Beaty, Bell, Binney, s Briggs, Bull, Bunch, Burges, Cage, Camp-Carmichael, Chambers, Chilton, Chinn, Clai-s, W. Clark, Clowney, Corwin, Crane, kett, Darlington, A. Davis, Davenport, Jo-s Denny, Evans, E. Everett, H. Everett, s Felder, Fillmore, Forester, Foster, Ful-le, Garland, Gholson, Gilmer, Gordon, Graham, Grayson, Grennell, jr. Griffin, Hard, James Harper, Hazeltine, Inge, son, Janes, H. Johnson, King, Lay, L. Lea, s Lewis, Lincoln, Love, Manning, Martin-arshall, McCarty, McComas, McKennan, Milligan, Miner, Moore, Patton, Peyton, Pickens, Pinckney, Potts, jr. Ramsay, Roberson, W. B. Shepard, A. H. Shep-tandifer, Steele, Stewart, Stoddert, W. P. F. Thomas, Tompkins, Trumbull, Twee-ce, Vinton, Watmough, F. Whittlesey, ttlesey, Wilde, Williams, Wilson, Wise, —110.

e House refused to suspend the rules.

ION OF PRESIDENT AND VICE SIDENT OF THE UNITED STATES.

WILDE moved to suspend the rules for se of taking up the joint resolution re-the election of President and Vice Presi-the United States.

GILMER said all that would be necessary motion to postpone the orders of the day: resolution had been twice read, and he his colleague so to modify his motion.

WILDE assented.

HUBBARD suggested that it be committed the Committee of the Whole on the state Union.

WILDE asked for the yeas and nays; which ordered.

motion prevailed, yeas 112, nays 92.

consent, sundry bills from the Senate were up for reference, and several were refer-

JUDICIAL CIRCUITS.

bill from the Senate relative to the estab-of a Judicial Circuit in the United States, sented by the Chair—

bill provides for consolidating the cir-mposed of New Jersey and Pennsylvania,

with that composed of Delaware and Maryland, and requiring Judge Baldwin to hold the Circuit Courts in the Delaware and Maryland Circuit, so as to obviate the necessity of appointing a Judge of the Supreme Court in that circuit, and there-by to extend the circuit system to the Western States.]

Mr. FOSTER suggested to the House the con-sideration of the question, whether it was worth the while of the House to refer this bill to the Committee on the Judiciary, inasmuch as that committee had already reported that it would be impossible for the House to act upon it during the present session. He moved to commit it to a Committee of the Whole on the state of the Un-ion.

Mr. BEARDSLEY thought the bill too impor-tant to be acted on by the House without its first going through the investigation of a Standing Committee of the House.

Some conversation ensued between Messrs. FOSTER, MERCER, WILDE, THOMAS, of Maryland, and CLAY.

At the suggestion of Mr. CLAY, Mr. FOSTER modified his motion so as to include the pring-in of the bill.

Mr. WILDE demanded the previous question, which motion was not, however, seconded by the House—ayes 68, noes 74.

Mr. COULTER could see no reason why there should be any departure, in this case, from the ordinary course. The bill was a most important one, involving the lives and properties of thou-sands, and he hoped the House would not divest it of those protective proceedings which the rule had thrown around every such measure. He was in favor of extending every privilege enjoyed by the old to the new States, but not at the ex-pense of the former. New Jersey, Delaware, and Maryland had increased in population, and ought not to be deprived of any of their rights and privileges, and he entered his protest against it. The bill proposed a manifest act of injustice and he trusted would undergo the strictest scru-tiny in the standing committee of the House.

Mr. CARMICHAEL addressed the House as follows:

Mr. Speaker: I concur with my honorable friend from Pennsylvania, (Mr. Coulter,) in the opinion he has expressed in regard to the impor-tance of this subject. It is entitled to the most deliberate action of this House. This bill, from the Senate, is designed to operate in a peculiar manner upon the rights and interests of the State in which I reside, and of which I am one of the Representatives upon this floor. I feel myself, therefore, called upon to protest against the adop-tion of the motion of the honorable member from Georgia, (Mr. Foster.) Its effect is to dispense with the usual routine of business, which secures to every measure, before it is submitted to the consideration of the House, a previous examina-tion by one of its constituted organs—by one of its Standing Committees. Sir, why this haste? Why hurry this bill into the Committee of the Whole upon the state of the Union? Where is the mo-tive for all this precipitation? Deeply interested as are the People of Maryland in the result of this proposed alteration of the Judicial Districts of the United States, I must claim for the subject the most mature consideration.

Sir, I have another reason for resisting this unu-sual and unnecessary proceeding. This measure proposes to accomplish one object; it reaches an-other by indirection. Its apparent purpose is to arrange the existing Judicial Districts, and to es-tablish two additional Circuits. It merges the District of Maryland and Delaware, and gives a Circuit to the Northwest and the Southwest.

But whilst it professes—and you know, sir, as it originated in the Senate, I cannot speak of the motives upon which it is based—it would be dis-courtesy to do so—whilst it professes to make a District, its effect is to despatch a Judge. Its effect is to relieve the Senate of a responsibility imposed upon them by the constitution.

Sir, I understand the ready willingness of the honorable member from Alabama (Mr. Clay,) to embrace this measure at once, to disregard the usual and established order of legislation here. It

extends advantages to the people of the southwest. It is enough for him to know there is a benefit he'd out to his constituents. He overlooks the consideration that it works a rank injustice to his friends elsewhere.

I have no objection to extend the contempla-ted advantages to the west; but I cannot do it at the expense of my constituents. It was only by holding out this benefit, never before contempla-ted for the west, that it was hoped to effect this unjust purpose to Maryland.

If this bill is to be adopted, I hope it may be re-quired to pass through the usual routine. I hope it will be referred to the Committee on the Judici-ary. But I must earnestly resist any proceeding, however presented, the manifest tendency of which is to impose upon the House a share of the responsibility devolved by the constitution upon the Senate of the United States; which will re-quire of this House to dispose of executive nomi-nations. And more especially, when the obvious effect of it is to affect injuriously the interests of Maryland, and to crush one of her most valued citi-zens.

I hope the gentleman from Georgia will with-draw his motion to commit this bill to the Com-mittee of the Whole House on the state of the Union.

Mr. CLAY disavowed any personal feel-ing on the subject. When, on the one hand, however, he was disposed to render strict justice to other parts of the Union, he stood then as the representative of Alabama, and gentlemen must not expect him to abandon her interests.

Mr. GARLAND was convinced that the commit-ment of the bill to the Judiciary Committee would only tend to defeat or delay it. His only object was to secure the action of the House, on this all-important subject.

Mr. CAGE adverted to the long withheld jus-tice which this House owed to the new States. He moved the previous question, but withdrew it at the request of

Mr. FOSTER, who made some explanatory re-marks. He was surprised at the opposition which had been elicited by the simple motion which he had made. He avowed his intention of proposing certain amendments when the bill should come before the House. He then renewed, according to usage, the motion for the previous question.

[Here a discussion ensued on the nature of the previous question as applicable to the present case. Mr. SPEIGHT thought the previous question would be the passage, but the Chair decided otherwise.]

Mr. CAGE then withdrew the motion for the previous question.

Mr. THOMAS again addressed the House. He viewed the bill in the light of an attempt to destroy one of the worthy citizens of Maryland. Justice had been denied to that State by the pro-ceedings in this matter, and he demanded, as one of her Representatives, that it should be rendered to her. Mr. T. had protested at the early part of the session and subsequently, against acting up-on this subject, because the facts were not fully in possession of the House, and he would appeal to the Chairman of the Judiciary Committee to say, if he was acquainted with all the circumstances in-volved, or had given the subject such an investi-gation as had put him in possession of the princi-ples of the bill.

Mr. BARRINGER said, were it earlier in the session he would have no objection to gratifying the gentleman from Maryland, by committing this bill; but he was convinced it would be impractica-ble to obtain the action of the House by this course. New Jersey, Delaware, and North Carolina had very little business, and Virginia not a great deal, and he was quite sure that the Judges could per-form the additional duties imposed under this bill. He was quite sure that neither the Chief Justice nor Judge Baldwin would feel themselves unable to discharge the burdens under this bill. Mr. B. referred to what fell from one of the gentlemen from Maryland, that the advocates of the bill de-signed by it to destroy a distinguished citizen of Maryland, and Mr. B. disclaimed it for himself, and hoped such a suggestion would have no in-fluence there or elsewhere. He supported the

bill because he believed the measure it embraced, was required by the wants of the new States. He was convinced there w a no necessity for sending the bill to the Judiciary committee, which would only postpone it till too late for action. Mr. B. asked for the yeas and nays; which were ordered.

Mr. REYNOLDS said, he would not at this late hour address the House, did it not seem to him that Maryland was about to be placed in a similar situation to that in which the Western States had found themselves for many years. He was for acting on the bill without referring it to the Judiciary, as he believed it could not then be acted on at the present session. He demanded too, that the new States might be put on a footing of equality with the old ones, in their judicial system.

Mr. ROBERTSON said a few words on the character and qualifications of the present Chief Justice.

Mr. THOMAS again opposed the motion, and referred to a statement of the business in Baltimore, and also the opinions of the bar.

Mr. MERCER said a few words in reply.

The question was then taken by yeas and nays, as follows—Yeas 119, nays 82.

So the bill was committed to a Committee of the Whole on the state of the Union, and ordered to be printed.

Mr. MANN moved that the House adjourn. Negatived—Ayes 76, noes 84.

The qu stion on engrossing the joint resolutions on the subject of the election of President and Vice President of the United States then came up.

Mr. GILMER said, he had no wish that the resolution should be discuss ed, at that time, and he had risen only to ask that the question on the resolutions and the amendment should be taken separately, and thereon he asked for the yeas and nays, which were ordered.

Mr. SPEIGHT said, like the gentleman from Georgia, (Mr. Gilmer,) it was not his intention to discuss these resolutions. He wished to suggest a single amendment, which was to strike out the word "four," and insert six as the extent of the Presidential and Vice Presidential term. He believed four years too short a period where the duration of the office was restricted to a single term.

Mr. PINCKNEY asked for the reading of the resolutions, which were read.

Mr. BARRINGER regretted that his colleague (Mr. Speight) had thought it necessary to offer the amendment he had. Mr. B. had no intention of provoking a discussion on these resolutions, but he rose to express his entire dissent from the amendment. He was convinced that four years was sufficiently long for a good President, whose place might be supplied by other good men conveniently, and four years was abundantly ample, and rather too ample, for a bad President.

Mr. SPEIGHT asked for the yeas and nays on his amendment, which were ordered.

Mr. PATTON said, he could not vote for the amendment of the gentleman from North Carolina (Mr. Speight,) nor was he in favor of the amendment of the gentleman from Georgia, (Mr. Gilmer.) He believed it to be a cardinal point in our institutions, that no worthy citizen should be disfranchised. That they should at all times be eligible to office, and to being returned to that office at the pleasure of the people. He accorded with the sen im nt of the gentleman from North Carolina (Mr. Barringer) that four years was too long for a bad man to serve us as President—but he would add to that sentiment as amendatory to its force and truth, that eight years was none too long to secure the services of a good man to his country.

The question on the amendment of Mr. SPEIGHT, was decided in the negative—ayes 41, nays 162.

The question then recurred on the first resolution, and the subject was further debated till quarter past 5 o'clock, by Messrs. POLK, PEYTON, GILMER, PEARCE of R I, BURGES, and GHOLSON. Before the question was taken, the House adjourned.

A full sketch of the debate will appear in tomorrow's Globe.

The question then recurring on the first resolution,

Mr. POLK said, he believed he had discovered a very important omission in the resolutions.—They no where stated the number of votes to which each State was entitled, although they laid down the mode and manner in which the elections should be held. Mr. P. said that his views in many points resembled those of the gentleman from Georgia, but in making important fundamental changes in our constitution, it became the House to pause and to deliberate. Mr. P. was for a single term; against an election by that House, and would, in all cases, confine the election to the people; but he did not think that they should pass upon so weighty a subject in half an hour's deliberation. He again avowed himself in favor of the principles of the resolutions, and referred to his former course in support of them.

Mr. GILMER said he would prepare an amendment to meet the defect pointed out by the gentleman.

After some remarks from Mr. PEYTON and Mr. POLK—

Mr. BURGES said he wished to see this subject divided, for in its present shape it was incompatible with his views. On the subject of the first proposition, to render the Chief Magistrate eligible for only one term, he should be in the affirmative; but on the second proposition, he was, and should ever remain in the negative. It swept away all the reserved rights of the less States, which, he contended, in the spirit of our institutions and our original compact, should forever remain inviolable. Mr. B. pursued his argument at some length.

Mr. GILMER then proposed to supply the omission by inserting the following: "according to the rule now fixed by the constitution"

Mr. POLK proposed so to am nd it as that each State should be entitled to the same number of electors as members of Congress.

Mr. GILMER withdrew his own amendment, and accepted Mr. POLK'S.

Mr. WISE remarked that even if it were an omission it did not repeal the existing law, which was sufficiently explicit.

Mr. POLK replied that it might hereafter give rise to great disputes.

The amendment was agreed to.

Mr. GHOLSON then moved an amendment to allow the People an unrestricted choice of a successor in case of the death of a President.

Before the question was taken,

On motion of Mr. HUBBARD,

The House then adjourned.

SENATE.

Thursday, February 26, 1835.

A Message was received from the President of the United States, by the hands of Mr. Donelson, his private Secretary, transmitting the most recent correspondence called for by a resolution of the House, between Mr. LIVINGSTON and the Secretary of State, in relation to our affairs with France.

A motion having been made to print the letter and accompanying documents,

Mr. PRESTON expressed a wish that they might be read, as it would be some days before they would be printed, and some immediate action on the part of Congress might be necessary.

The documents were accordingly read and referred to the Committee on Foreign Relations, and ordered to be printed.

The Message and documents are as follows;

To the House of Representatives of the U. States:

I transmit to Congress a report of the Secretary of State, with copies of all the letters received from Mr. Livingston, since the message to the House of Representatives of the 6th instant, of all the instructions given to that minister, and of all the late correspondence with the French Government in Paris, on the subject of our affairs with France, except a note of M Serrurier, which, or the reasons stated in the report, is not now communicated.

It will be seen that I have deemed it my duty to instruct Mr. Livingston to quit France, with his legation, and return to the United States, if an appropriation for the fulfilment of the convention shall be refused by the Chambers.

The subject being now, in all its present aspects, before Congress, whose right it is to decide

what measures are to be pursued in that event, I d em it unnecessary to make furth r recommendation, being confident that on their part everything will be done to maintain the rights and honor of the country, which the occasion requires.

A. JACKSON.

Washington, Feb. 25, 1835.

To the President of the United States.

DEPARTMENT OF STATE,
Washington, 25th February, 1835.

The Secretary of State has the honor to remit to the President copies of all the letters received from Mr. Livingston, since the message to the House of Representatives of the 6th instant, of the instruction s given to that Minister, and of all the late correspondence with the French Government in Paris, or in Washington, except the last note of M. Serrurier, which it has been considered necessary to submit to the Government of France to be in it made public or answered, that it ma be ascertained whether some exceptionable expressions are to be taken as the resu t of a settled purpose in that Government, or as the mere ebullition of the Minister's indisc tion.

JOHN FORSYTH.

Mr. Livingston to Mr. Forsyth.

LEGATION OF THE UNITED STATES,
Paris, 11th January, 1835.

HON JOHN FORSYTH:

SIR—Believing that it would be important for me to receive the despatches you might think I necessary to send with the President's Message, I ventured on incurring the expense of a courier to bring it to me as soon as it should arrive at Havre. Mr. Bearsley, accordingly, on the arrival of the Sully, despatched a messenger with my letters received by that vessel, and a N w York newspaper containing the m ss ge, but without any communication from the Department; so that our Sa di , is still the last which I have to acknowledge. The courier a rived at 2 o'clock on th morning of the 8th. Other copies were the same morning received by the St.sfette; and the contents being now known, caused the greatest sensati n, which, as yet, is, I think, unfavorable, the few members of the opposition who would have voted for the execution of the treaty, now declaring that they cannot do it und r the threat of reprisals, and the great bo y of that party making use of the offence it has on national pride to gain proselyt s from the Ministerial side of the Chamber, in which, I am no doubt, they have in a great degree, for the time, succeeded.

The Ministers are aware of this, and I will not, I think, imme. lately urge the consideration of the treaty, as I have no doubt they were prepared to do when the mess ge arrived. Should Congress propose commercial restrict ns, or det rmine to make to the end of the session before they s t, this will be considered as a vote agai st reprisals, and that the law will be proposed, and I think carried. But I ought not to conceal from you that the excitement is at present very great; that their pride is deeply wounded by what they call an attempt to coerce them by threats, to the payment of a sum which they persist (in oppositi n to the plain s proof) in declaring not to be du . This feeling is fostered by the language of our oppo-it on papers, particularly by the *Intelligencer* and *New-York Courier*, extracts from which have been sent on by American, declaring them to be the sentiments of a majority of the people. Th se, as you will see, are translated and republished here, with such comments as they might have been expected, and all falsities should take place between the two contending parties, those persons may fl tter themselves with have the credit of a great share in producing them. The only letter I have received from home is one from my family. This, to my great satisfaction, contains, and the President will be supported by all parties, and I am told that this is the language of most of the opposition papers; but as they are not now up to the leg tion, I cannot tell in what degree they support can be depended upon. Wh the the energetic language of the message will be made the pretext with some, or be the cause with t among the Deputies for rejecting the law,

of course, be yet conjectured with any great degree of probability; but I think it will have a good effect. It has certainly raised us in the estimation of other Powers, if I may judge from the demeanor of their representatives here; and my own opinion is, that as soon as the first excitement subsides, it will operate favorably on the Councils of France. Already some of the Journals begin to change their tone; and I am much mistaken if the opposition here, finding that we are in earnest, will incur the responsibility of a rupture between the two nations, which they see must take place if the treaty be rejected. The funds experienced a considerable fall as soon as the message was known, and insurance rose: in short, it has made them feel the commercial, as well as political importance, of our country.

The Count de Rigny had requested me to communicate the message to him as soon as it should be received. This I promised to do, and accordingly, on the morning of the 8th, to avoid any mistake as to the mode of making the communication, I carried the paper to him myself, telling him that I had received a *gazette* containing a paper, said to be the message of the President, which I delivered to him in compliance with my promise, but I requested him to observe, that it was not an authentic paper, nor was it delivered in pursuance of instructions, nor in my official character. I thought it, for obvious reasons, necessary to be very explicit on this point, and he probably understood me, as he had not yet read the message. Little more passed at the interview, and I thought of it, but not immediately, to seek another: I shall probably, however, see him to-night, and shall then appoint some time for a further conference, of which I will, by this same packet, give you the result.

Mr. Middleton had just arrived from Madrid, with the inscriptions for the Spanish indemnity, and a draft for the first payment of interest. His instructions are, he says, to leave them with me, but, as I have heard nothing from the Department, I shall advise the depositing them with Rothschild, to wait the directions of the President.

The importance of obtaining the earliest intelligence at this crisis of our affairs with France, has induced me to direct, that my letters should be sent by the Estafette from Havre, and that, if any important advices should be received, at such an hour in the day as would give a courier an advance of some hours over the Estafette, that a special messenger should be despatched with it.

I have the honor to be, very respectfully, sir, your most obedient servant

EDW. LIVINGSTON.

Mr. Livingston to Mr. Forsyth.

LEGATION OF THE UNITED STATES,
Paris, Jan. 14, 1835.

Hon. JOHN FORSYTH:

Sir: The intended conference with the Minister of Foreign Affairs, of which I spoke to you in my letter, No 70, took place yesterday morning. I began it by expressing my regret that a communication from the President to Congress had been so much misrepresented in that part which related to France, as to be construed into a measure of hostilities. It was, I said, part of a consultation between different members of our Government, as to the proper course to be pursued, if the legislative body of France should persevere in refusing to provide the means of complying with a treaty formally made. That the President, as was his duty, stated the facts truly, and in moderate language, without any irritating comment. That in further pursuance of his official duty he considered the different modes of redress which the law of nations permitted, in order to avoid hostilities; expressing as he ought to do, his reasons for preferring one of them. That in all this there was nothing addressed to the French nation; and I likened it to a proceeding, well known to the French law, (a family council in which the concerns and interests are discussed,) but of which in our case the debates were necessarily made public. That a further elucidation of the nature of the document might be drawn from the circumstance, that no instructions had been given to communicate it to the French Government, and that, if a gazette containing it had been delivered, it was at the request of his Excellency, and expressly declared a private communication, not an official one. I further stated that I made this communication without instructions, merely to counteract misapprehensions, and from an earnest desire to rectify errors which might have serious consequences. I added that it was very unfortunate that an earlier call of the Chambers had not been made in consequence of Mr. Serrurier's promise, the non-compliance with which, was of a nature to cause serious disquietude with the Government of the United States. I found immediately, that this was the part of the message that had most seriously affected the King, for Count de Rigny immediately took up the argument, endeavoring to show that the Government had acted in good faith, relying principally on the danger of a second rejection, had the Chambers been called, at an early day, expressly for this object. I replied, repeating that the declaration made by M. Serrurier was a positive and formal one, and that it had produced a forbearance on the part of the President to lay the state of the case before Congress. In this conference, which was a long one, we both regretted that any misunderstanding should interrupt the good intelligence of two nations having so many reasons to preserve it, and so few of conflicting interests. He told me (what I knew before,) that the exposition was prepared, and that the law would have been presented the day after that on which the message was received. He showed me the document, read part of it to me, and expressed regret that the language of the message prevented it being sent in. I said that I hoped the excitement would soon subside, and give place to better feelings, in which I thought he joined with much sincerity. It is, perhaps, necessary to add, that an allusion was made by me to the change of ministry in November, and the reinstatement of present ministers, which I told him I had considered as a most favorable occurrence, and that I had so expressed myself in my communications to you; but that this circumstance was unknown at Washington when the message was delivered; and I added, that the hopes of success held out in the communication to which I referred, and the assurances it contained that the ministers would zealously urge the adoption of the law, might probably have imparted the same hopes to the President, and have induced some change in the measure he had recommended. But that the formation of the Dupin ministry, if known, must have had a very bad effect on the President's mind, as many of that ministry were known to be hostile to the treaty.

When I took leave, the minister requested me to reflect on the propriety of presenting a note of our conversation; which, he said, should be formal or otherwise, as I should desire. I told him I would do so, and inform him on the next morning by 11 o'clock.

We parted, as I thought, on friendly terms, and in the evening, meeting him at the Austrian Ambassador's, I told him that on reflection I had determined to wait the arrival of the packet of the 16th before I gave the note, to which he made no objection. After all this, you may judge of my surprise, when last night, about ten o'clock, I received the letter, a copy of which is enclosed, and which necessarily closes my mission. In my reply, I shall take care to throw the responsibility of breaking up the diplomatic intercourse between the countries where it ought to rest, and will not fail to expose the misstatements which you will observe are contained in the Minister's note; both as respects my Government and myself—but the late hour at which I received the Cte. de Rigny's note, and the almost immediate departure of the packet, may prevent my sending you a copy of my communication to him, which I shall use the utmost diligence in preparing.

The law, it is said, will be presented to-day, and I have very little doubt it will pass. The ministerial phalanx, reinforced by those of the opposition (and they are not a few) who will not take the responsibility of involving the country in the difficulties which they now see must ensue, will be sufficient to carry the vote. The recal of Serrurier, and the notice to me, are measures which are resorted to to save the pride of the Government and the nation.

I have the honor to be, very respectfully, sir, your most obedient servant,

EDW. LIVINGSTON.

From Count De Rigny to Mr. Livingston.

[TRANSLATION.]

DEPARTMENT OF FOREIGN AFFAIRS,
Paris, January 13*th*, 1835.

SIR: You have well comprehended the nature of the impressions, produced upon the King's Government, by the message which his excellency, President Jackson, addressed on the 1st of December, to the Congress of the United States. Nothing certainly could have prepared us for it. Even though the complaints expressed in it, had been as just, as they are in reality unjust, we should still have had a right to be astonished, on receiving the first communication of them in such a form.

In the explanations which I am now about to make, I cannot enter upon the consideration of any facts, other than those occurring subsequently to the vote, by which the last Chamber of Deputies refused the appropriation, necessary for the payment stipulated in the treaty of July 4th. However this vote may have been regarded by the Government of the United States, it is evident, that by accepting (*accueillant*) the promise of the King's Government, to bring on a second deliberation, before the new Legislature, it had in fact postponed all discussion, and all recrimination on the subject of this first refusal, until another decision should have either repealed or confirmed it. This postponement therefore sets aside, for the time, all difficulties arising either justly or injustly, from the rejection of the treaty, or from the delay by which it had ben preceded; and although the message begins by enumerating them, I think proper, in order to confine myself to the matter in question, only to reply to the imputations made on account of subsequent occurrences.

The reproaches which President Jackson considers himself authorized to address to France, may be summed up in a few words. The King's Government promised to present the treaty of July 4th again to the Chambers, as soon as they could be assembled. They were assembled on the 31st of July, and the treaty has not yet been presented to them. Such is exactly the whole substance of the President's argumentation, and nothing can be easier than to refute it.

I may first observe, that the assembling of the Chambers on the 31st July, in obedience to a legal prescription, that they should be called together within a stated period after a dissolution of the Chamber of Deputies, was nothing more than a piece of formality; and if President Jackson had attended to the internal mechanism of our administrative system, he would have been convinced that the session of 1835 could not have really commenced at that season of 1834. Every one knew beforehand that, after a fortnight spent in the forms of installation, it would be adjourned.

The President of the United States considers that the bill relative to the American claims should have been presented to the Chamber within that fortnight. I cannot understand the propriety of this reproach. The bill was explicitly announced in the speech from the throne; on the very day in which the Chambers met. This was all that was required to make known the opinion and design of the Government, and to prevent that species of moral proscription to which absolute silence would have given authority. With regard to the mere act of presentation, so long before discussion could possibly take place, this proceeding would have been so unusual and extraordinary, that it might have increased the unfavorable prepossessions of the public, already too numerous, without producing any real advantage in return. Above all, the result which the President had in view, of being able to announce the new vote of the Chamber of Deputies in his message would not have been attained.

President Jackson expresses his regret that your solicitations (*instances*) had not determined the King's Government to call the Chambers together at an earlier day. How soon soever they may

have been called, the simplest calculation will serve to show that the discussions in our Chambers could not have been known in the United States at the opening of Congress, and the President's regret is therefore unfounded. Moreover, the same obstacles and the same administrative reasons which rendered a real session impossible during the months of July and August, were almost equally opposed to its taking place before the last weeks of the year. The head of a Government, like that of the United States, should be able to comprehend more clearly than any one else, those moral impossibilities which arise from the fixed character of the principles of a constitutional *regime*, and to see that in such a system the administration is subject to constant and regular forms, from which no special interest, however important, can authorize a deviation.

It is, then, evident, that, far from meriting the reproach of failing to comply with its engagements, far from having deferred, either voluntarily or from negligence, the accomplishment of its promises, the King's Government, ever occupied in the design of fulfilling them, was only arrested for a moment, by insurmountable obstacles. This appears from the explanations now given; and, I must add, that the greater part of them have already been presented by M. Serrurier to the Government of the United States, which, by its silence, seemed to acknowledge their full value.

It is worthy of remark, that, on the first of December, the day on which President Jackson signed the Message to Congress, and remarked with severity that nearly a month was to elapse before the assembling of the Chambers, they were in reality assembled, in virtue of a royal ordinance, calling them together at a period earlier than that first proposed. Their assemblage was not indeed immediately followed by the presentment of the bill relative to the American claims; but, you, sir, know better than any other person, the causes of this new delay. You yourself requested us not to endanger the success of this important affair, by mingling its discussion with debates of a different nature, as their mere coincidence might have the effect of bringing other influences into play, than those by which it should naturally be governed. By this request, you clearly showed that you had, with your judicious spirit, correctly appreciated the situation of things, and the means of advancing the cause which you were called to defend. And permit me to add, that the course which you have thought proper to adopt on this point is the best justification of that which we ourselves have for some months been pursuing, in obedience to the necessities inherent in our political organization, and in order to ensure, as far as lies in our power, the success of the new attempt which we were preparing to make in the Chamber.

However this may be, the King's Government, freed from the internal difficulties, the force of which you have yourself so formally admitted, was preparing to present the bill for giving sanction to the treaty of July 4th, when the strange message of December 1st came, and obliged it again to deliberate on the course which] it should pursue.

The King's Government, though deeply wounded by imputations to which I will not give a name, having demonstrated their purely gratuitous character, still does not wish to retreat absolutely from a determination, already taken, in a spirit of good faith and justice. How great soever may be the difficulties, caused by the provocation which President Jackson has given, and by the irritation which it has produced in the public mind, it will ask the Chambers for an appropriation of twenty-five millions, in order to meet the engagements of July 4th. But, at the same time, his Majesty has considered it due to his own dignity, no longer to leave his Minister exposed to hear language so offensive to France. M. Serrurier will receive orders to return to France.

Such, sir, are the determinations of which I am charged immediately to inform you, in order that you may make them known to the Government of the United States; and that you may yourself take those measures which may seem to you to be the natural consequences of this communication. The passports which you may desire, are, therefore, at your disposition.

Accept, sir, the assurance of my high consideration. DE RIGNY.

To the Hon. EDW. LIVINGSTON.

Mr. Livingston to Mr. Forsyth.

LEGATION OF THE UNITED STATES,
PARIS, January 15th, 1835.

SIR: Having determined to send Mr. Brown, one of the gentlemen attached to the legation, to Havre, with my despatches, I have just time to add to them the copy of the note which I have sent to the Count de Rigny. The course indicated by it was adopted after the best reflections I could give to the subject; and I hope will meet the approbation of the President. My first impressions were, that I ought to follow my inclinations, demand my passports, and leave the Kingdom. This would at once have freed me from a situation extremely painful and embarrassing; but a closer attention convinced me that, by so doing, I should give to the French Government the advantages they expect to derive from the equivocal terms of their note; which, as occasions might serve, they might represent as a suggestion only, leaving upon me the responsibility of breaking up the diplomatic intercourse between the two countries if I demanded my passports; or if I did not, and they found the course convenient, they might call it an order to depart, which I had not complied with. Baron Rothschild also called on me yesterday, saying that he had conversed with the Count de Rigny, who assured him that the note was not intended as a notice to depart, and that he would be glad to see me on the subject. I answered that I could have no verbal explanations on the subject, to which he replied that he had suggested the writing a note on the subject, but that the Minister had declined any written communication. Rothschild added, that he had made an appointment with the Count de Rigny for six o'clock, and would see me again at night: and he called to say that there had been a misunderstanding as to the time of appointment, and that he had not seen M. de Rigny, but would see him this morning; but in the mean time I determined on sending my note, not only for the reasons contained in it, which appear to me conclusive, but because I found that the course was the correct one in diplomacy, and that to ask for a passport merely because the Government near which the Minister was accredited had suggested it would be considered as committing the dignity of his own: that the universal practice in such cases was to wait the order to depart, and not, by a voluntary demand of passports, exonerate the foreign Government from the odium and responsibility of so violent a measure.

My note will force them to take their ground. If the answer is that they intended only a suggestion, which I may follow or not as I choose, I will remain, but keep aloof until I receive your directions. If, on the other hand, I am told to depart, I will retire to Holland or England, and there wait the President's orders. In either case, the arrangement will be extremely expensive, and my situation very disagreeable. The law was not presented yesterday, but will be to-day, and I have been informed that it is to be introduced by an *Expose*, throwing all the blame of the present state of things on M. Serrurier and me, for not truly representing the opinions of our respective Governments. They may treat their own Minister as they please, but they shall not, without exposure, presume to judge of my conduct, and make me the scape-goat for their sins. The truth is, they are sadly embarrassed. If the law should be rejected, I should not be surprised if they anticipated our reprisals by the seizure of our vessels in port, or the attack of our ships in the Mediterranean with a superior force. I shall, without delay, inform Commodore Patterson of the state of things, that he may be on his guard, having already sent him a copy of the message. I have the honor to be, sir, your most obedient servant, EDW. LIVINGSTON.

Mr. Livingston to the Count de Rigny.

LEGATION OF THE UNITED STATES OF AMERICA,
PARIS, January 14, 1835.

The undersigned, Envoy Extraordinary and Minister Plenipotentiary of the United States of America, received late last night the note of His Excellency the Count de Rigny, Minister Secretary of State for Foreign Affairs, dated the 13th inst.

The undersigned sees with great surprise, as well as regret, that a communication made by one branch of the Government of the United States to another, not addressed to that of His Majesty the King of the French, nor even communicated to it, is alleged as the motive for a measure, which not only increases actual subjects of irritation, but which necessarily cuts off all the usual means of restoring harmony to two nations who have the same interest, commercial and political, to unite them, and none but factitious subjects for collision.

The grave matter in the body of His Excellency's note demands, and will receive a full answer; it is to the concluding part that his attention is now requested. The undersigned, after being informed that it is the intention of His Majesty's Government to recall M. Serrurier, is told "that this information is given to the undersigned, in order that he may communicate it to his Government, and in order that he may himself take those measures which may appear to him the natural result of that communication; and that, in consequence thereof, the passports which he might require are at his disposition." This phrase [illegible] be considered as an intimation of the course which in the opinion of His Majesty's Government, the undersigned ought to pursue, as the natural [illegible] of Mr. Serrurier's recall; or it may be constr[illegible] as it seems to have been by the public, into a [illegible]rection by His Majesty's Government to the Minister of the United States to cease his functions [illegible] leave the country.

It is necessary, in a matter involving such [illegible] consequences, that there should be no mis[illegible]standing; the two categories demanding a line [illegible] conduct entirely different the one from the o[illegible]

In the first, he can take no directions, or [illegible] no suggestions but those given by his own Government, which he has been sent here to rep[illegible]sent. The recall of the Minister of France, [illegible] the grounds alleged, could not have been [illegible]pated; of course no instructions have been gi[illegible] to the undersigned on the subject; and he [illegible] not take upon himself the responsibility [illegible] he would incur by a voluntary demand of passports, although made on the suggestion [illegible] Majesty's Government. If this be the se[illegible] the passage in question, the duty of the un[illegible]signed cannot be mistaken. He will transmit [illegible] note of his excellency the Count de Rigny to [illegible] Government, and wait its instructions. W[illegible] different will be his conduct, if he is informed [illegible] the conclusion of the Count de Rigny's note [illegible]tended as a direction that he should quit [illegible] French territory. This he will, without d[illegible] comply with, on being so informed, and on [illegible]ceiving the passports necessary for his prote[illegible] until he shall leave the kingdom.

Leaving the responsibility of this measure [illegible] it ought to rest, the undersigned has the ho[illegible] renew to his excellency the Count de Rig[illegible] assurance, &c., &c.

(Signed) EDW. LIVINGST[illegible]

No. 73.

Mr. Livingston to Mr. Forsyth.

LEGATION OF THE UNITED STATES,
PARIS, January 16, 1[illegible]

SIR: The wind being unfavorable, I h[illegible] this letter may arrive in time for the packet.

By the enclosed semi-official paper, you w[illegible] that a law has been presented for effecti[illegible] payment of 25,000,000 francs capital to the [illegible]ed States, for which the budgets of the six [illegible] next succeeding this are affected, and with a [illegible]tion annexed that our Government shall have [illegible] nothing to affect the interests of Fran[illegible] would seem from this that they mean to [illegible] thing but the capital, and that only in six [illegible] from this time; but, as the law refers to the [illegible] for the execution of which it provides, I [illegible] the intention of the Ministry cannot be [illegible] any change in it, and that the phraseology [illegible] conformity with their usual forms. At [illegible] shall, notwithstanding the situation in w[illegible]

placed, in relation to this Government, endeavor to obtain some explanation on this point.

The packet of the 16th has arrived; but, to my great regret, brought me no despatches, and having received none subsequent to your No. 43, and that not giving me any indication of the conduct that would be expected from me in the event if such measures as might have been expected on he arrival of the President's message, I have been left together to the guidance of my own sense of duty, under circumstances of much difficulty. I have endeavored to shape my course through them a such a way as to maintain the dignity of my Government, and preserve peace, and, if possible, restore the good understanding that existed between the two countries. From the view of the motives of the President's message, contained in the answer of the Globe to the article in the Intelligencer, I am happy in believing that the representations I have made to the Count de Rigny, as detailed in my No. 71, are those entertained by the Government, and that I have not, in this at least, gone further than it would have directed me to do had been favored with your instructions.

I have no answer yet to my note to the Count de Rigny, a copy of which was sent by my last repatch, nor can I form any new conjecture as to its event.

The enclosed paper contains a notice that I had been received by the King. This is unfounded, and shall be contradicted. I shall not, in the present state of things, make my appearance at port, and only in cases where it is indispensable, have any communication with the Ministers.

I have the honor to be, with great respect, your obedient servant,

EDW. LIVINGSTON.

Hon. J. FORSYTH, &c. &c.

Mr. Forsyth to Mr. Livingston.
DEPARTMENT OF STATE,
Washington, Feb. 13, 1835.

SIR: To relieve the anxiety expressed in your communication to the Department of State, as to the course to be pursued in the event of the rejection by the Chamber of Deputies of the law appropriate funds to carry into effect the treaty of 4th July, 1831, I am directed by the President to inform you that if Congress shall adjourn without prescribing some definite course of action, as in as it is known here that the law of appropriation has been again rejected by the French nation, a frigate will be immediately despatched to Havre to bring you back to the United States, with such instructions as the state of the nation may then render necessary and proper.

I am, sir, &c.
JOHN FORSYTH.

EDWARD LIVINGSTON, Esq.

DEPARTMENT OF STATE,
Washington, 24th Feb. 1835.

SIR: Your despatches to No. 73, have been received at the Department.—No. 73 by yesterday's mail. Nos. 70, 71, 72, were delayed until morning, by the mismanagement of the young man to whose care they were committed by the mate of the packet Sully, in New York.

In the very unexpected and unpleasant position in which you have been placed, I am directed by the President, to say to you, that he approves of your conduct, as well becoming the representative of a Government ever slow to manifest resentment, and eager only to fulfil the obligations of justice and good faith, but at the same time to inform you that he should have felt surprise, and certainly would have expressed displeasure, but you yielded to the impulse of personal pride, and at once have quitted France, the whole Legation, on the receipt of the de Rigny's note of the 13th January. Mr. Barton having received his orders, has terminated his Ministerial career by the transmission of a copy of which, and of all the correspondence had with him, is herewith enclosed. Mr. Barton has been presented to me, as charged with affairs of France on the recall of the Minister.

The note of the Count de Rigny having, no according to your intention, received from

you an appropriate reply, it is only necessary for me now to say that the Count is entirely mistaken in supposing that any explanations have been given here by M. Serrurier, of the causes that have led to the disregard, or postponement, of the engagements entered into by France, after the rejection of the appropriation by the last Chamber of Deputies, and of which he was the organ. No written communication whatever has been made on the subject, and none verbally made of sufficient importance to be recorded—a silence with regard to which, could have been justly the foundation of any inference that the President was satisfied that the course of the French administration was either reconcilable to the assurances given him, or necessary to secure a majority of the Chamber of Deputies.

The last note of M. Serrurier will be the subject of separate instructions, which will be immediately prepared and forwarded to you.

In the present posture of our relations with France, the President directs, that, if the appropriation to execute the treaty shall be, or shall have been, rejected by the French legislature, you forthwith quit the territory of France, with all the Legation, and return to the United States, by the ship of war which shall be in readiness at Havre to bring you back to your own country. If the appropriation be made, you may retire to England or Holland, leaving Mr. Barton in charge of affairs; notify the Department of the place selected as your temporary residence, and await further instructions.

I am, sir, your obedient servant,
JOHN FORSYTH.

EDWARD LIVINGSTON, Esq.,
Envoy Extraordinary and Minister Plenipotentiary.

Mr. Forsyth to Mr. Serrurier.
DEPARTMENT OF STATE,
Washington, February 23, 1835.

Official information having been received by the President of the recall of Mr. Serrurier by his Government, and the papers of the morning having announced the arrival of a French sloop of war at New York, for the supposed object of carrying him from the United States, the undersigned Secretary of State of the United States tenders to Mr. Serrurier all possible facilities in the power of this Government to afford, to enable him to comply speedily with the orders he may have received or may receive.

The undersigned avails himself of the occasion to renew to Mr. Serrurier the assurances of his very great consideration, JOHN FORSYTH.

Mr. Serrurier to Mr. Forsyth.—Translation.
WASHINGTON, *February 23, 1835.*

SIR: I have just received orders from my Government, which make it necessary for me to demand of you an immediate audience. I, therefore, request you to name the hour at which it will suit you to receive me at the Department of State.

I have the honor to be, with great consideration, sir, your obedient humble servant,
SERRURIER.

To the Hon. JOHN FORSYTH,
Secretary of State of the United States.

Mr. Forsyth to Mr. Serrurier.
DEPARTMENT OF STATE,
WASHINGTON, Feb. 23, 1835.

The undersigned, Secretary of State of the United States, informs Mr. Serrurier, in reply to his note of this instant, demanding the indication of an hour for an immediate audience, that he is ready to receive, in writing, any communication that the Government of France desires to have made to the Government of the United States.

The undersigned has the honor to offer Mr. Serrurier the assurances of his very great consideration.
JOHN FORSYTH.

Mr. Serrurier to Mr. Forsyth.—Translation.
WASHINGTON, *February 23, 1835.*

SIR: My object in asking you this morning to name the hour at which it would suit you to receive me was in order that I might, in consequence of my recall as Minister of His Majesty near the Unit-

ed States, present and accredit Mr. Pageot, the first Secretary of this Legation, as Chargé d'Affaires of the King; this presentation, which, according to usage, I calculated on making in person, I have the honor, in compliance with the desire expressed to me by you, to make in the form which you appear to prefer.

I thank you, sir, for the facilities which you have been kind enough to afford me, in the note preceding that now answered, also of this morning's date, and which crossed the letter in which I demanded an interview.

I have the honor to renew to you, sir, the assurance of my high consideration.
SERRURIER.

To the Hon. JOHN FORSYTH,
Secretary of State.

Mr. SHEPLEY presented the credentials of the Hon. JOHN RUGGLES, a Senator elected from the State of Maine, for six years from the 4th of March next.

Mr. WEBSTER from the Committee on Finance, reported the bills from the House, for the relief of Richard Hargrave Lee, and Thomas Dixon & Co. of New York, without amendment.

Mr. WEBSTER, from the same Committee, reported the bills from the House for the relief of S. Morris Wain, and H. Percival, and for the relief of Ebenezer Breed, without amendment.

Mr. WEBSTER stated that these persons were owners of goods on which duties had been secured, and which had been burnt while in the custody of the Government, in the Custom House stores. The majority of the committee were of opinion that under such circumstances, where goods were destroyed by fire, the duties ought to be remitted—he believed it was the practice of other Governments to do so.

Mr. WEBSTER also reported unfavorably upon the bill from the House, for the relief of John J. Putnam and Nathan Pratt, and the committee were discharged from the further consideration of the subject.

Mr. HENDRICKS, from the Committee on Roads and Canals, reported the bill from the House for opening certain roads in the Territory of Arkansas, without amendment. Also, the bill from the House for the improvement of the harbor of Clinton river, in Michigan Territory.

Mr. HENDRICKS, from the same Committee, reported the Senate bill to authorize the construction of a rail road upon the public lands from Tallahassee to St. Marks, in Florida, with the amendments made by the House; which, on his motion, were concurred in.

Mr. TOMLINSON, from the Committee on Pensions, to which had been referred the bill from the House granting pensions to Enoch Blaisdel, and reported that it ought not to pass.

Mr. TOMLINSON, from the same Committee, reported the bills granting pensions to John F. Wiley and George Fields, without amendment.

Mr. TOMLINSON also reported, without amendment, the joint resolution from the House, authorizing the delivery of certain papers to the Secretary of War, to be used in deciding upon pension cases, and gave notice that when it came up for consideration, he would move for its indefinite postponement.

Mr. TOMLINSON, from the same Committee, to which had been recommitted the bill to continue the office of Commissioner of Pensions, with the amendment of the House thereto, reported the same with a further amendment which was agreed to, and the amendment was then concurred in.

Mr. PRESTON, from the same Committee, reported the bills from the House granting pensions.

Mr. BENTON, from the Military Committee, reported the bill from the House to render permanent the supplies of the army, and fix the salaries of certain clerks in the Commissary General's Office.

Mr. McKEAN, from the Committee on Pensions, to which had been referred the bills from the House granting pensions to Walter Phillips and Thomas Simpson, reported that that they ought not to pass.

On motion of Mr. PRESTON, the Senate took up the motion to reconsider the vote, by which

was rejected the joint resolution for the purchase of certain paintings for the President's house.

On the question, will the Senate agree to reconsider the vote, it was disagreed to.

Mr. BIBB submitted the following resolution:

Resolved, That the Committee on the Judiciary be instructed to inquire as to the expediency of printing, under the direction of the Secretary of the Senate, a suitable and usual number of copies of the journals of the Senate, up to the 4th of March, 1815; also, of the the Executive Journal complete in separate volume, and also the cost of such printing.

Mr. CLAYTON, submitted the following resolution:

Resolved, That the President of the United States be respectfully requested to consider the expediency of opening negotiations with the Governments of other nations, and particularly with the Government of Central America, and New Grenada, for the purpose of effectually protecting by suitable treaty stipulations with them, such individuals or companies as may undertake to open a comunication between the Atlantic and Pacific Oceans, by the construction of a ship canal across the Isthmus which connects North and South America, and of securing forever, by such stipulations, the free and equal right of navigating such canal, to all such nations, on the payment of such reasonable tolls as may be established to compensate the capitalists who may engage in such undertaking, and complete the work.

Mr. BLACK, from the Committee on Private Land claims, reported the bill to provide for the final adjudication of claims to land in Louisiana.

On motion of Mr. TIPTON, the Senate then proceeded to the consideration of Executive business, and when the doors were opened,

The Senate took up, as in Committee of the Whole, the bill authorizing the Leavenworth and Bloomington Rail Road Companies to construct rail roads through the public lands of the United States, which, after some slight amendments, was reported to the Senate, and ordered to be engrossed and read a third time.

The Senate then resumed the consideration of the bill regulating the deposites in the State Banks.

The *Proviso* offered yesterday by Mr. Calhoun, requiring the payment of 2 per cent. by banks for the use of public deposites on sums under $100,000, to be regulated by the Secretary of the Treasury, being under consideration,

Mr. WEBSTER moved to strike out $100,000, and insert 50,000; which amendment was agreed to.

Mr. WEBSTER moved an additional section, directing that each Bank of deposite should render the same services to the Government as were rendered by the Bank of the United States, in that place.

Mr. CLAYTON said, it was going as far as they could go, but not to the extent of obligation to which the Bank of the United States were subject by the charter.

Mr. KING, of Alabama, said they were asking more of the deposit Banks than of the Bank of the United States. They were 'compelling these Banks to pay two per cent. while the Bank of the United States paid nothing. The notes of that Bank were made a legal tender, while the notes of the State Banks were not.

Mr. K. thought such restrictions would tend to keep the public moneys out of the good banks, and place them in those less secure. He said the Bank of England received pay for all the public services it performed. He believed the bill would produce the same evils which they were endeavoring to prevent, that of endangering the public treasures.

Mr. WEBSTER said the public money was the same as a permanent deposite; for the Bank would soon, by comparing the past and present, be able to calculate upon as a permanent sum which they ought to pay interest for.

Mr. W. said there was a stipulation in the late bill for rechartering the United States Bank, by which it was to pay $200,000 a year into the treasury as a bonus, which would be two per cent.

upon ten millions of dollars. He wished to regulate by law what now was regulated by the Secretary of the Treasury.

Mr. KING, of Alabama, said he was in favor of the additional section. But he wished to turn the attention of the Senate to the other impositions which were laid on the Banks; their tendency would be to prevent the deposites being recieved at any safe and respectable institutions.

Mr. CALHOUN said, the advantages of being a deposite Bank were very great. He thought these would be Banks enough willing to receive them with the imposition of the bill.

Mr. CUTHBERT said, the Bank of the United States, by means of its branches, was enabled to perform transfers and make exchanges, which were in fact advantageous to itself But from the isolated nature of the State Banks, they were in some measure deprived of these advantages.

Mr. WEBSTER said, these same arguments of the honorable Senator had been urged in favor of the Bank of the United States at a former time.

Mr. TIPTON said, he was well satisfied that the Banks of Indiana would not pay one rent.—but that the government would be obliged to carry its moneys out of the State. He should vote against the bill.

Mr. PORTER thought the Senator's, (Mr. Tipton's) remarks, a wretched commentary on what had been said last year, "that the State Banks could perform the services of the government better and cheaper than the Bank of the United States."

The question being on agreeing to the proposed amendment,

Mr. EWING asked the yeas and nays; which were ordered, and the question decided as follows:

YEAY.—Messrs Benton, Bibb, Black, Brown, Buchanan, Calhoun, Clay, Clayton, Ewing, Frelinghuysen, Goldsborough, Grundy, Hendricks, Hill, Kane, Kent, King of Ala, Knight, Leigh, Linn, McKean, Naudain, Porter, Prentiss, Preston, Robbins, Robinson, Ruggles, Shepley, Silsbee, Southard, Swift, Tipton, Tomlinson, Waggaman, Webster, White—37.

YEAS.—None.

So the amendment was adopted.

Mr. WEBSTER then moved further to amend the bill, by inserting a clause requiring the banks to make monthly returns of its condition, and that these returns should be published quarterly.

Mr. KING, of Alabama, thought no bank would become a depository if its private concerns were to be published in to the world every few months. In reply to Mr. Porter, Mr. K. said he would deny that the Secretary of the Treasury ever had said the public business could be done better and cheaper by the State than by the U. States' banks. In support of his assertion, Mr. K. read part of the Secretary's report on that subject.

Mr. CLAYTON thought the returns of the banks ought to be published. It had been required of the United States' Bank, and was also required of the Bank of England. Mr. G. was desirous of getting as much from the State banks as the Bank of the United States paid us in a bonus.

Mr. BENTON said he was in favor of the publication. He wished to do swy all secrecy from banking institutions. The pub lc ought to know how such things were managed. He believed it would be of public use. He would say the community as emed to be recovering their rights against banks. He believed the Bank of the U. States was the greatest opprobrium that had been cast upon the nineteenth century. There were six hundred machines in the Union throwing out paper money—worthless paper. In these institutions were two hundred millions of capital, on which an annual tax was paid of eight per cent. That tax was taken from the people some way or other, either by hook or by crook, for the banks of themselves produced no value.

He wished the People to have money on which they paid no interest. He was in favor of having our real money sifted out from such a mass of paper trash, even if but a speck of gold remained from a bushel of chaff. He was entirely opposed to the paper system. This opportunity struck

him as a favorable opportunity for retributive justice, for making the banks pay for establishing a hard money currency. They should obtain something to defray the expense of the Mints. The while 600 banks were stamping paper money, there might be several mints stamping hard money.

[Mr. CLAYTON, by the unanimous consent of the Senate, made a motion to reverse the order for a recess, which was agreed to.]

Mr KING, of Alabama, called for a division of the question; when that part which directs most ly returns to be made, was agreed to.

On that part requiring the quarterly returns to be published, Mr. CLAYTON asked the yeas and nays; which were ordered, and were as follows:

YEAS—Messrs Benton, Bibb, Calhoun, Clay, Clayton, Ewing, Frelinghuysen, Goldsborough, Hill, Kent, Knight, Leigh, McKean, Naudain, Porter, Prentiss, Preston, Robbins, Robinson, Southard, Swift, Tomlinson, Waggaman, Webster, White—25.

NAYS—Messrs. Black, Brown, Buchanan, Cuthbert, Kane, King of Alabama, Linn, Morris, Ruggles, Shepley, Tallmadge, Tipton—12.

So the amendment was adopted.

Mr. WEBSTER said he had one or two other amendments to offer which he would premise by a few remarks. In the discussion of this measure it seems a necessary consequence that we should be drawn into comparisons between the utility and efficiency of these local Banks to perform the fiscal operations of the Government, and the Bank of the United States. He wished to say now, that he did not go into such comparison with the purpose of reviving the question of a prolongation of the recharter of the Bank of the United States. He considered the recharter of the present Bank or the charter of any other under the authority of the government as settled, at least for some time to come. And he im-gined there was to be no attempt made to revive it. He had determined not only that he would not make any movement towards effecting its recharter, but he would never move for the establishment of another Bank under the authority of this government if this country should be convinced by experience of the utility and the necessity of such a Bank. We live in a government in which the settled opinions of the People must prescribe a certain course of conduct to public men. When the time shall arrive that the People of this country shall be convinced that some national institution of this sort as ill be necessary and useful to the country, he should be as ready as other good men to act upon the subject and bring it before the public. Until then, he should be content passive with respect to it. And the man which he had made upon this bill had no slightest allusion to the revival of the Bank of the United States. The gentleman from Pennsylvania yesterday, and the gentleman from Alabama to-day, spoke of the services of these deposite Banks as if it proved that the system, as a system would be practicable and useful. He would enter into an argument on that subject, but he desired to state it as his conviction that this experiment of receiving and disbursing the revenues and carrying on the exchanges of the country, was an experiment, which, so far from being practical has not yet even been put to the trial, nor can it be tried for some time to come. A vast things will be in existence for two years to come which will predicate such a trial. That same things is, that the Bank of the United States in circulation some twenty millions which is used as the medium of remittance from place to place, which these deposite Banks all use, and which is valuable to every man, every where, to every Bank wishing to make remittances. And that very facility which the Government now enjoys in transacting its business, is by the medium of the bills of the Bank of the United States. Does any member of Congress choose to carry with him the bills of D strict beyond the Alleghany mountains? to make their transmissions by bills of the United States Bank. The trial, therefore, has not come and will not come, till this paper of the Bank is

CONTINUED IN NEXT NUMBER.

CONGRESSIONAL GLOBE.

BY BLAIR & RIVES.   ——WEEKLY——   PRICE 81 A SESSION.

2d Sess........23d Cong.   THURSDAY, MARCH 5, 1835.   Volume 2........No. 19.

TWENTY-THIRD CONGRESS.
SECOND SESSION.

IN SENATE.
Thursday, February 26, 1835.

CONTINUED FROM LAST NUMBER.

the United States is withdrawn from circulation. Then will come the experiment. Some gentlemen think that then will come the golden age; an event which he thought was all ideal and fanciful. If a bank here is called on to make remittances to Pittsburg, a case which he suggested merely for illustration, it does it by procuring the bills of the United States Bank. So that those b lls do form the medium of exchange as much now, as they have done during any period for 20 years past. If this system of the Government is to go on, by the use of the deposite banks, he was far from desiring to put on them any thing onerous. He knew this was difficult to avoid, consistent with that which ought to be done, to wit, to put under the regulation of law. We all know that the seamrity spoken of in the wealth of rich proprietors of the sto k is wholly imaginary and unsubstantial, and therefore something more ought to be required. But there are some circumstances which had met his attention, and which oug t to awaken the country. Within a week past, attempts have been made to pay off warrants of the Treasury, not in specie, but in drafts payable on their face in current bills. Heavy drafts on the Treasury have been presented to one of the deposite banks, payable in this way; and yet this is the specie system to which we are hastening. He made this statement, not with reference to one only, but to several of these banks; and he was saying nothing in conjecture. Now, this he wished to prevent. He wished all drafts to be payable in cash, and that the holders should not be turned off and paid in current bills.

Mr. W. then submitted an amendment, requiring all drafts or warrants to be paid in gold or silver, if wished by the holder; and that they shall not be expressed to be receivable in current bills.

Mr. BENTON said that the fact stated by the gentleman from Massachusetts, he apprehended w be as he had represented it; and he took the occasion to express his highest indignation at it; and he was willing to go as far, or farther than any other gentleman to prevent it. When Mr. Gallatin, in 1811, made arrangements for payment of all Treasury warrants, the expressly required them to be paid in go'd or silver. Th s arrangement was what he expected at this time; and he would not only concur in the amendment, but he would go farther, and concur in an inquiry why here had been any relaxation from what he thought just year would have been the system adopted.

Mr. LEIGH said, that no one who knew the views and opinions of the honorable gentleman from Missouri on this subject, would feel surprised at the expression of his indignation and regret, at such a departure from the principles he has advocated. All believe, that the gentleman wishes to restore a hard-money currency, but he b..l had not been as sanguine, as to the practicability of restoring it so suddenly, as the Hon. gentleman thought it could be done. He begged leave to ask the g ntleman, whether he thought it practicable to r store a hard-money currency by the action of this Government, if the States persisted in their present banking system, and when there was such an increase in banking capital in so many of the States. In order to restore such a currency, he thought it indispensable that the State banks, by a system should be diminished. In Virginia there there is so much hostility to the Bank of the United States, and where the banking system generally is as unpopular as it is in any State of the Union, an effort has recently been made to supply the void, to be occasioned by the withdrawal of the United States Bank bills, though he was glad o may it had not been adopted. He believed there

was no power on earth which could prevent this paper system, if the State banking system continued to prevail. He vot d last year for the bill reducing the standard of gold, but not in reference to its preventing excessive issues of paper, for if you have a $20 bill, you would have a right to claim gold for it to the amount of the nominal value of the gold, whether the standard had been 1 in 16, or 1 in 32. The truth was that paper being the cheaper currency, would always expel the dearer currency, do what you will.

Mr. BENTON said, that with regard to the enquiry which had been made of him by the honorable gentleman from Virginia, it addressed itself to a subject upon which he could not be supposed to have been indifferent. For some years, he had turned his attention to the subject of currency, and he had looked at the difficulty suggested, as the gentleman did. He looked to the co-operation of the State Governments, as highly necessary to the attainment of the great object, but not as the only means. He looked to the action of the State Government's, as the most ready means of checking this most inordinate paper system. But if a man would cast his eye over the United States, and look at the great advances which had been made in public sentiment, in this particular, he would see that there was hardly a State, in which movements had not been made against the paper system, and Mr. B. said, in his State there was not now a single bank—the Legislature of the State had lately refused to charter one, and the Governor said, if one were chartered, he would use his veto power upon it. So wholesome a state of things in the public mind, would tend to get rid of the paper system. But this was not the only mode of getting a metallic currency for common purposes. There was one measure to restore a specie currency for the origin of which, he would have to go back to the Congress of '89, when the revenues of the government were required to be collected, in gold and silver—he placed great reliance on the action of the States, and upon returning to the system of '89. But there was another remedy in the hands of Congress, which could and would be effectual. As to the cheap currency, it was cheap to those who issued it, but dear to those who used it.

Mr. LEIGH said he used the expression in that sense. He took it to be an axiom in political economy, that the two currencies could not exist together, because the one was cheap and the other dear, and therefore the one would necessarily expel the other. The gentleman from Missouri depends upon the action and wisdom of the States, to correct the evil, but he does not depend upon the action of any one State to effect it. If there were no banks in M ssouri now, Mr. L. ventured to say that if her neighbors, Illinois, Indiana, and Kentucky, did not restrain and regulate their paper system, she would be driven to establish her own banks in self defence. He wished to impress it on those who heard him, and if possible, on the whole nation, that there must be a combined effort of all the State Governments to produce a restoration to a hard money system.

Mr. TALLMADGE remarked, with respect to the amendment, that if the holder of a warrant requires his money in gold or silver, he has a right to it, and therefore there is no necessity for making a formal enactment of what is now the law.

The amendment was agreed to.

Mr. WEBSTER said that it was necessary for the safety of the public funds that the deposite banks should have a sufficient specie basis in their operations. He therefore offered an amendment requiring that the deposite banks shall always have on hand an aggregate amount of specie, and of specie paying bank notes, equal to —— of their liabilities.

Mr. W. suggested to fill the blank with one fifth.

Mr. BENTON preferred a fourth, which Mr WEBSTER accepted.

Mr. SHEPLEY opposed the amendment, as being one which would entirely defeat the objects of the bill, because he believed no bank would be willing to put itself under such an obligation.

After some further remarks from Mr. EWING and Mr. SHEPLEY,

Mr. CLAYTON rose and stated that a committee had just come in who had been investigating a very int resting subject, and they desired to report.

At the suggestion of Mr. CALHOUN, the proceedings upon the bill were suspended, when

Mr. SMITH from the Select Committee appointed upon the letter of the Hon. GEORGE POINDEXTER, rose and stated that he was instructed to say that the committee had closed its examinations—that the testimony taken was voluminous, and the committee had not had time to prepare a detailed report; but they had come to the conclusion, unanimously, that there was not a shade of suspicion upon the character of Mr. POINDEXTER of his having any participation in the matter to which their investigations had been directed.

The Senate then resumed the bill, when Messrs. WEBSTER, CALHOUN, BUCHANAN, CLAYTON, SHEPLEY, KNIGHT, and PRESTON, made some remarks upon the amendment; when

Mr. BUCHANAN asked the yeas and nays upon its adoption; which were ordered, and ar as follow:

YEAS—Messrs. Benton, Bibb, Brown, Calhoun, Clayton, Ewing, Goldsborough, Hendricks, McKean, Poindexter, Porter, Robbins, Smith, Southard, Tipton, Tomlinson, White—17.

NAYS—Messrs. Black, Buchanan, Cuthbert, Frelinghuysen, Hill, Kane, Kent, King of Alabama, Knight, Leigh, Linn, Prentiss, Preston, Robinson, Ruggles, Shepley, Talmadge, Waggaman, Webster—19.

So the amendment was disagreed to.

A motion to insert one-fifth was then agreed to.

Mr. WEBSTER having remarked that it was the design of the bill to require the specie and specie paying notes of other banks to be in the vaults of the deposite banks, at the time of making the quarterly returns,

Mr. TALLMADGE offered an amendment, to express such requisition upon the face of the bill.

The amendment was not agreed to.

Mr. TALLMADGE offered an amendment authorising the Secretary of the Treasury to choose additional deposite banks at places where there are already banks so employed, when, in his opinion, it may be necessary.

The amendment was not agreed to.

The bill was then reported to the Senate, and all t e amendments were concurred in except that requiring each bank to have a basis of one fifth specie and notes of specie paying banks to meet its liabilities.

Upon this question Mr. SHEPLEY demanded the yeas and nays, which were ordered, and the amendment was agreed to by the following vote:

YEAS—Messrs. Benton, Bibb, Black, Buchanan, Calhoun, Clayton, Cuthbert, Ewing, Goldsborough, Hendricks, King of Ala., Knight, Leigh, Linn, McKean, Mangum, Poindexter, Porter, Prentiss, Preston, Robbins, Robinson, Southard, Tomlinson, Waggaman, Webster, White—27.

NAYS—Messrs. Hill, Ruggles, Shepley, Tallmadge, Tipton, Wright—6.

The question then being on the engrossment of the bill, Mr. CALHOUN asked the yeas and nays; which were ordered.

Mr. BUCHANAN said he intended to vote against the engrossment of this bill and that there might be no misconstruction of his reasons for this determination, he would state distinctly the sole cause why he could not give it his support.

The bill, in his opinion, had been greatly improved by the amendments which had been adopted. He was opposed to investing the Treasury

Department with any discretion in regard to the deposite banks which was not absolutely necessary. Their duties should be as far as possible distinctly defined by law. This we owed not only to the Department itself, but to the country. The amendments had, in several important particulars, accomplished this purpose—they had, in a great degree, supplied the defects in the original bill.

Why then, it might be asked, should he vote against it? His answer was simply, because it required these banks to pay two per cent. interest on the deposites. Now it might be, and probably was true, that the banks in the middle and eastern States would be able to bear this burthen. But what was the case in the Southwestern States? In that portion of the Union, the Government received large sums of money which must be deposited in their local banks. There was a constant drain upon these banks to supply the funds necessary to be expended by the Government in the middle and eastern cities. This caused the rate of exchange to be always against New Orleans, and that portion of the Union. Under this bill it was made the duty of the Deposite Banks to transfer the funds of the Government to any point, where it became necessary to expend them. This duty they ought to perform. Mr. B. felt confident, however, both from the nature of the business and the information he had received from gentlemen of the South and the West, that their banks would not be able to bear the charge of transferring these funds, and also pay interest upon the deposites at the rate of two per cent. The inevitable consequence would be, that the Government would not, in that portion of the Union, get sound and solvent banks to accept the deposites upon the terms prescribed by this bill. The Treasury Department would thus be embarrassed in its operations, and heavy eventual losses might be sustained by the United States. Surely, said Mr. B. if two per cent. interest on the deposites be enough to demand from the banks at New York or Boston, it is too much to exact from those at New Orleans. There is no equality, there is no justice in subjecting them to the same charge. Whilst the one class of banks must be constantly transmitting funds, the other are constantly receiving them. For this reason and this alone, he should be compelled to vote against the bill.

Mr. PRESTON said, he would vote for the bill, but he did so with great reluctance, because it was in some sort, a justification of the measures of the Executive, in placing the public money where it now was, when he believed that act to be wholly illegal and unconstitutional. He voted for it therefore under a kind of duress.

Mr. TALLMADGE said, he would vote against the bill, not because he was under duress, for he believed the acts of the Executive alluded to by the honorable gentleman, were perfectly legal and constitutional. But he voted against it, because there were provisions in the bill of so extraordinary a character, without consuming time by going into detail, that he could not vote for it.

A discursive debate of some length, then ensued between Messrs. CUTHBERT, PRESTON, and CALHOUN, when the question was taken, and the bill ordered to be engrossed by the following vote:

AYES—Messrs. Benton, Black, Calhoun, Cuthbert, Ewing, Goldsborough, King, of Georgia, Knight, Leigh, Linn, Mangum, Poindexter, Porter, Prentiss, Preston, Robinson, Southard, Tomlinson, Webster, White—30.

NAYS—Messrs Bibb, Brown, Buchanan, Hendricks, Hill, Kane, King of Alabama, Morris, Ruggles, Shepley, Tallmadge, Tipton—12.

On motion of Mr. PORTER, the Senate adjourned.

HOUSE OF REPRESENTATIVES.

Thursday, Feb. 26, 1835.

On motion of Mr. BEARDSLEY, the bill from the Senate in amendment of the acts for the punishment of offences against the United States, was read the third time and passed.

Mr. POPE moved to take up the bill in relation to the Louisville and Portland canal; which was disagreed to.

A bill making appropriations for the Delaware breakwater, for certain harbors, and removing obstructions in and at the mouths of certain rivers, for the year 1835, was taken up.

Mr. McKAY moved to amend the bill so as to prevent any extra allowance or compensation to any officer of the army on account of services performed under the provisions of the bill; which was agreed to.

Mr. BARBER moved to amend the bill by inserting an appropriation of $25,000 for the improvement of the navigation of the river Thames, in the State of Connecticut, and demanded the yeas and nays on his motion; which were ordered, and were—yeas 63, nays 115.

So the amendment was rejected.

Mr. HAWES moved to amend the bill by inserting $20,000, for the improvement of the navigation of Green river, in the State of Kentucky; which was negatived.

Mr. TRUMBULL moved to insert in the bill the sum of $25,000, for the purpose of deepening the channel at the mouth of Connecticut river.

This amendment was supported by Messrs. TRUMBULL, JACKSON of Conn., MERCER, and BURGES, and opposed by Messrs. PIERCE of Rhode Island and SPEIGHT, when

Mr. MILLER moved the previous question; which was seconded—yeas 91, nays 69.

Mr. H. EVERETT demanded the yeas and nays on the previous question; which were ordered.

Mr. EVANS moved to lay the bill on the table, and demanded the yeas and nays on his motion; which were ordered, and were, yeas 81, nays 135.

So the House refused to lay the bill on the table.

The question, "Shall the main question be now put?" was then taken, and decided in the affirmative—yeas 109, nays 104.

Mr. CHINN called for the special order of the day, being the bills reported by the Committee on the District of Columbia.

Mr. CAMBRELENG suggested the propriety of first taking up a message from the President of the United States.

After some conversation between various members, by general consent, the special order was postponed for one hour.

The SPEAKER then laid before the House the following message from the President of the United States:

[The Message and accompanying documents will be found in this day's Senate proceedings.]

As soon as the Message and accompanying despatches had been read—

Mr. CAMBRELENG said, in pursuance of the pledge he before gave, he would merely move that the communication from the President of the United States, together with the accompanying despatches, and the resolutions he intended to submit, should be printed, and the consideration of the whole postponed till to-morrow. Mr. C. would only observe, that he was authorized by a majority of the Committee on Foreign Affairs to submit the resolutions. They were then read as follows:

Resolved, That it would be incompatible with the rights and honor of the United States further to negotiate in relation to the treaty entered into by France on the 4th of July, 1831, and that this House will insist upon its execution as ratified by both Governments.

Resolved, That the Committee on Foreign Affairs be discharged from the further consideration of so much of the President's Message as relates to commercial restrictions, or reprisals on the commerce of France.

Resolved, That preparation ought to be made to meet any emergency growing out of our relations with France.

Mr. E. EVERETT wished to amend the motion by moving to refer the message and documents to the Committee on Foreign Affairs. He understood the gentleman from New York to say that the resolutions moved by him were sanctioned by a majority of the committee. Mr. E. would remark that they had not been considered in committee.

Mr. CAMBRELENG hoped the gentleman would withdraw his motion, and permit the subject to lie over for to-morrow.

Mr. E. EVERETT said, he had an object in making his motion, which he would state when it became necessary.

Mr. J. Q. ADAMS hoped the message would be disposed of, as he wished to offer an amendment to the resolutions of the gentleman from New York, which he then sent to the Chair, and they were read by the Clerk.

1. Resolved, That the rights of the citizens of the United States to the indemnity from the French Government, stipulated by the treaty of the 4th of July, 1831, ought in no event to be sacrificed, abandoned, or impaired by any content or acquiescence of the Government of the United States.

2. That if the President of the United States should, during the interval before the next session of Congress, deem it not incompatible with the honor and interest of the United States to renew the negotiations with the French Government, he be requested so to do.

4. That no legislative measure of a character or tendency hostile towards the French nation, is necessary or expedient at this time.

Mr. CAMBRELENG then moved to postpone the whole subject till to-morrow.

The CHAIR observed that the question must first be taken on the motion to dispose and print the message.

Mr. E. EVERETT had no desire to delay the motion of the gentleman from New York, but as that gentleman had submitted three resolutions, as a concurrence, as he stated, with the opinion of the majority, though the gentleman would admit they had not been acted on in Committee, Mr. E. only asked permission for himself and two other members of the Committee, composing the minority, to have printed (he would not take up so much time as to ask the reading,) their views on the subject.

This motion requiring unanimous consent, and objection being made,

Mr. CAMBRELENG expressed a hope that the motion to print would prevail.

Mr. ARCHER remarked, that it appeared to him the present mode of proceeding was extremely irregular. Certain members of the Committee on Foreign Affairs had presented resolutions, which they would have that House act upon, while in the next breath, they tell us that the committee have not had the subject under investigation.

Mr. CAMBRELENG explained. The gentleman from Vermont was laboring under a misapprehension. The resolutions had been under consideration in the committee for a week past.

Mr. ARCHER resumed. The course was altogether irregular. He would suggest to both the honorable members that it would be better to move the reference of the President's Message to the Committee on Foreign Affairs, and to-morrow morning the committee might report these resolutions, probably with some modifications, when the House would be prepared to act upon the matter. Surely a subject of this dignity and importance demanded that the most ordinary forms of the House should not be dispensed with. No delay could possibly arise from the mode suggested by Mr. A. The committee would doubtless meet in the morning, and, aided by the communication just read, they might mature a report, which the House could consider at once. That was the correct and proper mode, while the other would together unusual.

Mr. CAMBRELENG said he made the motion he did, inasmuch as there were only a few days of the session remaining, and little time left for discussion. In justice to the Committee on Foreign Affairs, he must say that they had the subject under consideration ever since the beginning of the session, and it was not until that day they had come to a conclusion to report, having waited till the latest moment for information from the Foreign Department. He hoped the House would print both the resolutions of himself and the gentleman from Massachusetts, (Mr. Adams.)

Mr. J. Q. ADAMS consented to the suggestion of the gentleman from Virginia, (Mr. A.)

ther) and asked leave of the House to refer his own resolutions also, with the other papers, to the Committee on Foreign Affairs.

Mr COULTER agreed that the course recommended by the gentleman from Virginia, was the ordinary and parliamentary one, and was the best mode of disposing of the subject. He saw neither the necessity nor the propriety of printing the resolution of the Chairman of the Committee, (Mr. Cambreleng,) because the subject must be sent to the committee for deliberation, who must return a report to the House, and it was impossible to say what their report would be. That is, impossible according to the usual course of parliamentary proceedings, for it was not unlikely that the same resolutions would be agreed upon.

He thought it somewhat anomalous and contrary to print resolutions, and then refer the subject upon which the resolutions should be predicated to the committee, for it might be, that they would report differently. He thought therefore, that all the papers should be sent to the committee, and there was no question they would refer it to-morrow morning at farthest.

One word in relation to the course these matters had already taken in that Committee. There was a disposition in any of the members of that Committee to find fault, and they had hitherto personed in harmony together; but it became necessary to explain, that the course taken by the gentleman from Massachusetts, (Mr. Everett,) was in fact, the only course left, or permitted to him. It was true, that three days ago, a majority of the committee had agreed upon certain resolutions, and had instructed their Chairman to report them. The minority, who entertained somewhat different views, had also agreed upon a report, and although there was no substantial difference between them, yet it was decided by the minority to present their views in a different form, and somewhat different aspect. There had been no recent meeting of the Committee but the Chairman, had collected the opinions of the majority, by calling upon them individually. This left the minority no other way of getting their opinions before the country, than that adopted by the gentleman from Massachusetts, (Mr. Everett.)

Mr. PATTON rose, he said, for the purpose of making an inquiry, which had been substantially answered by the gentleman from Pennsylvania, (Mr. Coulter.) Mr P. was not present in the committee when the resolutions were agreed upon, and he wished to know if they were similar to those then offered by the gentleman from New York. He understood from the gentleman who had addressed the House that they were. After that had transpired Mr. P. deemed it proper to be for himself that the resolutions presented by the gentleman from New York, and which he (Mr. P.) had supposed were intended to be presented by him individually as a member of the committee, although they had received the concurrence of the majority, were very politely shown by the gentleman to him, for his consideration, that he might be prepared when the subject came on.

Mr. P. said he had never seen the resolutions or report of the gentleman from Massachusetts, (Mr. Everett,) and he was therefore in the predicament of not having given his sanction to the resolutions either of the majority or of the minority. He was, however, prepared to consider these resolutions and all others, whenever they should come up in a proper form, for the judgment of the House.

Mr. LETCHER suggested to Mr. Cambreleng to withdraw the resolutions, and to move to refer the message and accompanying documents, to the committee on Foreign Affairs, and to-morrow the gentleman might offer his resolutions.

Mr. ARCHER thought that the best course.

Mr. CAMBRELENG would accept the suggestion with pleasure. It was due to himself to state that he submitted these resolutions yesterday to every member of the Committee, though the decision was substantially made by the Committee long ago. He believed also that every member of the Committee was aware of his intention to submit them to day.

It was also due to himself, Mr, C. said, to state

that he had never seen or heard of any report from the minority of that minority, till the gentleman offered them just now.

Mr. C. then withdrew the proposition to print the resolutions, and moved to refer the President's Message and accompanying papers to the Committee on Foreign Affairs, and that they be printed.

Mr. E. EVERETT would interpose no objection to the last motion, but would ask that if the gentleman's resolutions were received as the report of the majority, that he (Mr. E.) might then be permitted to submit a report on behalf of the minority. In regard to the remark of the gentleman that he had never heard of any such thing, Mr. E. said, if the gentleman would charge his recollection more strictly, he would find that he had been made aware of the existence of these papers, for the gentleman himself suggested to Mr. E. to defer their presentation so as to submit them in conjunction with his own report.

Mr. CAMBRELENG said it was so long ago that he had forgotten the circumstance.

Mr. ARCHER raised a question of order. No report had been made, and it could not be debated without the special leave of the House.

Mr. McKINLEY hoped the question of printing would be withdrawn, since he was assured that the publication of these documents would be productive of much mischief, and he hoped they would be referred without being ordered to be printed. He moved a division of the question.

Mr. J. Q. ADAMS then withdrew his resolutions.

Mr. SUTHERLAND thought, perhaps, it would be as well for the House to postpone printing the correspondence till the report from the Committee on Foreign Affairs had been made, which would be to-morrow, so that the correspondence and the report of the committee might go out together.

Mr. CAMBRELENG observing that the motion to print could be made to-morrow morning, and as a disposition had been manifested that the motion should be withdrawn, he would accordingly withdraw it.

Mr. WATMOUGH thereupon renewed the motion.

Mr. WILDE informed the House that the same papers had been ordered to be printed by the other House.

Mr. S. JONES, and

Mr. J. Q. ADAMS hoped the gentleman from Alabama would withdraw his objection to print.

Mr LYTLE said he believed all the mischief had already been done that possibly could be done by publication, by the very reading of those documents with open doors, in the hearing of the reporters, and of the immense concourse then assembled in the galleries of the House.

Mr. McKINLEY said, inasmuch as the papers had been ordered to be printed by the other House, he would withdraw his motion to divide the question.

Mr. BURGES said a few words in favor of the motion to print.

The motion to print and refer the papers to the Committee on Foreign Affairs was then agreed to without a division.

DISTRICT OF COLUMBIA.

The House then, at a quarter before 3 o'clock, proceeded to the special orders of the day.

The bill to organize the several fire companies in the District of Columbia, was first taken up; various verbal amendments were concurred in, and the bill was ordered to be engrossed for a third reading.

The bill to extend the charter of the Fire Insurance company of Alexandria, was next taken up, and disposed of in a similar manner.

The bill regulating the toll on the Eastern Branch bridge.

The bill to extend the charter of the Potomac Fire Insurance Company;

The bill to incorporate the Georgetown Savings Company; and

The bill for the benefit of Georgetown and Alexandria, were severally laid on the table.

The House then went into committee of the

whole on the state of the Union—Mr. MANN, of N. Y. in the chair,—on the bill relating to the Orphans' Court in the District of Columbia, which was considered, and reported to the House without amendment.

The committee then rose, and the bill was ordered to be engrossed for a third reading.

Mr. CHINN, then moved that the House go into committee of the whole on the other bills relating to the District of Columbia.

Mr. THOMAS said, the charters of the banks which it is proposed to extend, would not expire until March, 1836. He did not, therefore, see the necessity of acting on these bills at this session. Three months of the next session of Congress would expire before the expiration of the charters, and the House could then take up, consider, and dispose of the grave questions involved on the recharter of the banks of this District. The Stockholders of all these Banks enjoyed unreasonable privileges: he wished to curtail them; but this is not the time to enter into this consideration, when we are on the eve of an adjournment. To all the bank bills he was, therefore, opposed at this time, and had moved to strike them from the motion of the gentleman from Virginia. To the recharter of some of the banks he had a particular dislike. They had failed during the last session of Congress, under circumstances well calculated to add to the terrible excitement which was then created. Before we can consider the propriety of re-chartering this last class of banks, surely the House owes it to the country to inquire into the causes of these failures. If they failed with good cause they are still embarrassed, and we should not cheat the public by doing any act calculated to give credit to these institutions. If they failed without good cause, they were solvent at the time of failure—then they acted shamefully to increase that disgraceful panic which had so seriously afflicted the whole country. Before we re-charter, let us examine; let the next Congress appoint a committee to make a searching inquiry into the conduct and condition of these institutions, and if found to be worthy, then, and not till then, let a charter be granted on such terms and conditions as the public interest will justify.

On this question a short discussion ensued between Messrs. THOMAS, CHINN, VANDERPOEL, BEARDSLEY, and McKENNAN.

The question was finally taken by yeas and nays, and decided in the affirmative—ayes 102, noes 66.

The House then went into Committee of the Whole, Mr PIERCE, of New Hampshire, in the Chair, on the remaining bills.

The bill to extend the jurisdiction of certain courts in the county of Washington, was considered, and after some verbal amendments, it was laid aside; and

The bill to incorporate the Alexandria Savings Company was taken up.

Mr. GILLET moved to strike out the enacting clause.

The reading of the bill being called for, it was read by the Clerk.

Mr. VANDERPOEL explained the nature of the proposed institution.

Mr. GILLET thought that it would possess all the objectionable features of a Bank—a monopoly. It was decidedly such an institution as the people of this country have, with a loud voice, condemned, and it was the duty of Congress to carry out the views of the people.

Mr. CHINN denied that this institution partook in any degree, of the character of a Bank, and defended the bill.

Mr. MANN, of New York, was apprehensive that if his colleague, (Mr. Vanderpoel,) would more closely examine this bill, he would discover that it was essentially a Savings Bank; but he was unwilling to deprive the city of Alexandria of the benefits of our legislation; he hoped his other colleague (Mr. Gillet) would withdraw his opposition, and suffer the bill to pass, after some slight amendment.

Mr. VANDERPOEL replied. He said if the motion to strike out the enacting clause should not prevail, it was his intention to offer an amendment to the bill, to meet the scruples of his colleague (Mr. Mann.)

Mr. HUBBARD expressed his utter surprise at the evidence of the slightest opposition to this bill. Such institut ons had been of immense benefit to the country, in enabling the poor to lay up th.ir scanty earnings. This he had witnessed in his own neighborhood, and he hoped the motion would not prevail.

Mr. FELDER referred to instances in which the managers of such establishments had been guilty of the grossest abuses. He expressed himself opposed to the whole class of these institutions. They were too often bottomed in fraud and swindling.

Mr. FILLMORE proposed an amendment to the third section, providing that no notes should be made payable to the directors. He then proceeded to defend the nature of the proposed incorporation. He deemed it emphatically the poor man's bank, in opposition to the rich man's monopoly.

Mr. POLK spoke against the passage of the bill. He saw nothing in its nature to prevent the investment of the funds of capitalists for purposes of speculation. Neither did he see any injury that could result to the community by its postponement to another session.

Mr. PARKER went into an examination of those institutes. He was opposed to the bill, and thought the amendment of the gentleman from New York (Mr. Fillmore,) would not remedy it.

The amendment of Mr. FILLMORE was then agreed to; and Mr. P then submitted another, relating to the amount of loans and deposites to be made by the company to, and by a single individual, limiting the same to five hundred dollars.

Mr. HARPER spoke in general terms in favor of g ving institutions, but he feared, sufficient to secure this one from abuse.

Mr. MANN, of New York, said a few words in explanation of the features of the bill.

Mr. GILLET again addressed the House in opposition to the bill, and in favor of his motion to strike out the enacting clause.

Mr. FILLMORE then withdrew his amendment, in order to avoid further discussion.

Mr. PLUMMER said, he never had voted for a Bank charter; but if he ever should do so, it would not be for one in disguise, as he deemed this to be. It was clothed with banking powers, and was, in every point of view, a monopoly.

Mr. CHINN owed it to the applicants to defend their reputation. They were unimpeachable, and he believed their intention to be unexceptionable.

Mr. HARPER expressed his conviction that the bill contained many defects.

The motion to strike out the enacting clause was agreed to.

The bill making appropriations for the Penitentiary in the District of Columbia was read and laid aside.

The bill granting an additional quantity of land for the satisfaction of revolutionary bounty land warrants, was next considered.

On this a discussion ensued, in which Messrs. PARKER, MASON, VINTON, HUBBARD, CLAY, and EVANS, took part.

Mr. PARKER moved the Committee rise.

Mr. EVANS rose to a point of order, whether the motion before the Committee was to rise, and report the bills already acted on, with the exception of the last.

This elicited further consideration, until

Mr. PARKER explained the nature of his motion, which, to save discussion, he withdrew. Mr. P. then continued his remarks in opposition to the bill. He gave way, however, to

Mr. FILLMORE, who renewed the motion that the Committee rise. After a short debate, the question was t ken by tellers, when there appeared ayes 73, noes 45.

There being no quorum, the Committee rose, and the Chairman reported that fact to the House.

A motion was then made to adjourn, on which question Mr. McKENNAN demanded the yeas an l nays. They were not ordered.

The quest on on adjournment, was then taken

by tellers, when there were declared to be, ayes 52, noes 89.

So the House refused to adjourn.

The Committee of the Whole being again in session, the question recurred on rising, when there appeared ayes 80, noes 51.

The committee then rose and reported the bills, with the exception of the last named.

The amendment adopted by the committee to strike out the enacting clause of the bill to incorporate the Alexandria Savings Institution, was concurred in, and the bill consequently rejected.

The amendments to the other bills relating to the District of Columbia, were concurred in, and they were ordered to be engrossed for a third reading.

The House then adjourned.

IN SENATE.
Friday, February 27, 1835.

Mr. PRENTISS, from the Committee on Pensions, reported, without amendment, the bills from the House granting pensions to Theophilus Beekman and Elijah Blodget.

Mr. TOMLINSON, from the same Committee, to which the bill granting pens ons to the widow of Noah Chittenden and to Thankfull Randall, were referred, reported that they ought not to pass.

Mr. EWING presented a joint resolution of the Legislature of Ohio, rescinding the joint resolution of the same body, passed last year, instructing their Senators, &c., to sustain the removal of the deposites, to oppose the re-charter of the United States Bank, and to oppose the said bill, which, on his motion, was laid on the table, and ordered to be printed.

Mr. PORTER submitted the following resolutions:

Resolved, That a committee of three be appointed to examine and report into the expediency of so arranging the seats in the Senate Chamber as will promote the convenience of members and facilitate the despatch of public business.

The resolution was adopted, and, by consent, the Chair appointed Messrs. PORTER, TALLMADGE, and CUTHBERT.

The resolution submitted by Mr. BENTON, to expunge from the journal the resolution passed last session, declaring "that the Executive in the late proceedings with reference to the revenue, has exercised authority and power not authorized by the constitution and laws, and dangerous to the liberties of the people," came up in order for consideration; when

Mr. BENTON spoke at length in support of it. When Mr. B. concluded, the discussion was suspended for the purpose of taking up the following bills, which were read a third time and passed;

The bill authorizing the Leavenworth, Bloomingville, and other railroad companies, to locate railroads through the public lands;

The bill to regulate the public deposites in the State Banks.

Messrs. POINDEXTER, TYLER, BIBB, BROWN, EWING, and CALHOUN, made some remarks upon this bill; when

Mr. BLACK asked the yeas and nays upon its passage; which were ordered, and the bill was passed by the following vote:

YEAS—Messrs. Benton, Black, Calhoun, Clayton, Cuthbert, Ewing, Frelinghuysen, Goldsborough, Kent, Knight, Leigh, Linn, McKean, Mangum, Moore, Porter, Prentiss, Preston, Robbins, Robinson, Smith, Southard, Swift, Tomlinson, Tyler, Waggaman, Webster, White—28.

NAYS—Messrs. Bibb, Brown, Buchanan, Hendricks, Hill, Kane, King of Alabama, Morris, Poindexter, Ruggles, Shepley, Tallmadge—12.

Mr. CLAY, on leave given, and pursuant to notice, introduced a bill to continue the commission for carrying into eff ct the convention with France.

By unanimous consent, the bill was read twice, and ordered to be engrossed.

The bill was afterwards read the third time and passed.

The bill authorizing the Secretary of the Treasury to compromise the claims allowed by the commission against the King of the Two Sicilies, was, on motion of Mr. SILSBEE, considered as

in Committee of the Whole, and ordered to be engrossed for a third reading.

The bill was afterwards read the third time and passed.

The Senate then resumed Mr. BENTON'S resolution, when

Mr. SOUTHARD took the floor, and spoke at length in opposition to the resolution, and entered into an examination and condemnation of the right of instruction.

When he concluded, on motion of Mr. PRESTON, the subject was laid on the table.

The Senate then considered, as in Committee of the Whole, the bill granting an additional quantity of land in satisfaction of unlocated Virginia military bounty land warrants.

Mr. CLAY opposed the bill, on the ground that the number of acres appropriated would not be sufficient for the purpose of satisfying all these claims; we did not know when we should ever stop. The gentleman from Virginia (Mr. Tyler) informed him formerly, that the last appropriation would be sufficient, and yet we appeared to be no nearer the end of this business than we were then.

Mr. EWING said he would much rather appropriate the sum of $687,500 instead of 550,000 acres, and then we should know what we were about. He was opposed to the bill.

Mr. LEIGH made some remarks in favor of the bill. He said its appropriation could not be considered as made to Virginia, any more than to Ohio, Kentucky or Tennessee, for not one twentieth of these claimants resided in that State.

Mr. TYLER said, if the original appropriation of 550,000 acres was just and correct, a further appropriation ought to be made to cover all the claims, even if it should amount to five millions of acres. The report made on the subject showed that the great mass of these claims were already satisfied, and he did not think we would be much troubled on the subject hereafter.

Mr. CLAY said, that the main cause of this great increase was in consequence of the bills passed giving pension and bounty lands, &c. Since the passage of the act of 1830, they have found in the acts story of the capital a large mass of revolutionary papers, out of which the greater part of these claims have sprung. There seems to be no end of these claims; he was willing to vote for the 550,000 acres, provided it was to be the last.

Mr. POINDEXTER offered an amendment requiring all claimants hereafter to file their claims in the office of the Commissioner of the Land Office within two years, or their claims shall be barred.

After some remarks by Mr. TYLER and Mr. CLAY, the amendment was rejected.

On motion of Mr. LEIGH, the blank was filled with 680,000 acres.

On the question, Shall the bill be engrossed and read a third time?

Mr HILL asked the ayes and nays; which being ordered, were as follows:

YEAS—Messrs. Benton, Bibb, Black, Calhoun, Clay, Cuthber, Ewing, Goldsborough, Hendricks, Kane, Kent, King of Alabama, Leigh, Linn, Mangum, Moore, Poindexter, Porter, Robbins, Robinson, Silsbee, Southar l, Tomlinson, Tyler, Waggaman, White—26.

NAYS—Messrs Hill, King of Georgia, Ruggles, Shepley, Swift, Tallmadge, Tipton, Wright—8.

So the bill was ordered to be engrossed and read a third time.

The following bills from the House, were read the first and second time and severally re'erred:

A bill relating to the Orphans' Court in the District of Columbia;

A bill to extend the charter of the Fire Insurance Company in Alexandria;

An act to organize Fire Companies in the District of Columbia;

An act making appropriation for certain roads and surveys;

A bill for the relief of Sarah H. R. Stith;

A bill for the relief of Elizabeth J. Wilson and others;

A bill amen latory of an act establishing the Chesapeake Canal Company;

An act for carrying into effect the convention between the United States and Spain;

An act making an appropriation for the support of the Penitentiary in the District of Columbia;

An act authorizing the Circuit Court of Washington County, District of Columbia, to hold special sessions;

A bill making additional appropriation for the Delaware breakwater, and other purposes;

A bill making appropriations for Indian annuities and other similar objects for 1835;

A bill authorizing the construction of a Dry Dock for the use of the Navy;

A bill extending the patent of Robert Eastman;

A bill for the relief of the heirs of Jacob Smith, deceased;

A bill making provisions for survey, and plats, and establishing a Surveyor General's office in Illinois and Indiana.

The following bills were taken up in Committee of the Whole, considered, and ordered to be engrossed and read a third time:

A bill for the relief of Mary O'Sullivan;

A bill to confirm certain land claims in Missouri;

A bill for making a road from Lime Creek to Chatahoochee.

Mr. PRESTON gave notice that he would to-morrow call up the resolution for electing a printer for the Senate.

Mr. BIBB offered the following resolution:

Resolved, That the joint rules of the two Houses, which declares that no bill that shall have passed one House, shall be sent for concurrence to the other, on either of the last three days of the session, be suspended, so far as to allow bills which shall have passed either House before 12 o'clock P. M. of Saturday, 28th instant, to be sent to the other for concurrence.

The bill for establishing a pension agency south of Green river, returned from the House with an amendment, was laid on the table.

When the Senate adjourned.

HOUSE OF REPRESENTATIVES.

FEBRUARY, Feb. 27, 1835.

Mr. POLK, from the Committee of Ways and Means, to which had been referred the amendments proposed by the Senate to the bill which originated in the House, making appropriations for certain fortifications for the year 1835, made a report recommending a concurrence in a portion of the amendments, and a non-concurrence in the residue. The bill and amendments were committed.

Mr. McKINLEY, from the Committee of Ways and Means, reported without amendment, the bill from the Senate for the establishment of branches of the Mint; which was considered.

Mr. BINNEY, from a Select Committee, made a report on the subject of weights and measures; which was laid on the table, and ordered to be printed.

Mr. WATMOUGH moved to print 3,000 extra copies of the foregoing report; which motion, under the rule, lies over one day.

Mr. MERCER, from the Committee on Roads and Canals, reported two amendments to the harbor bill; which were ordered to be printed.

Mr. ASHLEY, from the Committee on the Public Lands, reported a bill to authorize John Whicott, to enter a certain tract of land; which was read twice and committed.

On motion of Mr. DICKINSON, the Committee of the Whole was discharged from the further consideration of the bill for the relief of certain Choctaw Indians.

Unfavorable reports upon various petitions were made by Messrs. CHAMBERS, F. THOMAS, and McINTIRE, from Standing Committees; which were ordered to lie on the table.

Mr. HAWES moved to suspend the rules of the House for the purpose of considering the report of the Committee on the West Point Academy. His only object was to have the report printed.

Mr. Hawes demanded the yeas and nays on his motion, which were ordered, and were—yeas 70, nays 100.

So the House refused to suspend the rules.

RELATIONS WITH FRANCE.

Mr. CAMBRELENG, from the Committee on Foreign Affairs, made the following report:

The Committee on Foreign Affairs, to which was referred so much of the President's Message as concerns our political relations with France, and the correspondence between the Ministers of the two Governments, submits the following report:

At an early period of the session, the Committee took into consideration the question of authorizing reprisals, and continued from time to time to discuss various motions and resolutions submitted by its different members; they could, however, concur in no proposition, and in that condition, a majority deemed it expedient to postpone their decision till further intelligence should be received from France. The committee had, within the week past, twice instructed its chairman to report resolutions, but the arrival of additional intelligence caused a suspension of these reports until an official communication should be received from the Executive. That communication places the relations between the two countries in a novel and interesting position. While there is satisfactory evidence that the French Government earnestly desires that the appropriation for indemnity should be made in pursuance of the stipulations of the treaty, and while there is reason to hope that the Chamber of Deputies will adopt that measure and faithfully discharge the obligations of France to the United States, it is, on the other hand to be feared that the conduct of that government has placed us in a position at least embarrassing, even should it not produce at entire suspension of diplomatic intercourse between the two nations. In this new position of our relations, it is deemed expedient to dispense with further discussion on the subject of non-intercourse and reprisals on the commerce of France, to which the attention of the committee had been directed, and to leave the question of our political relations with that Government, to the next Congress, whose action will no doubt be governed by the course which France may deem it expedient to pursue. We are not yet informed what may have been the decision of the King of the French as to the dismissal of our Minister, nor can we conjecture what may be the fate of the appropriation in the Chamber of Deputies. While the committee is unwilling to anticipate any but an amicable and favorable result in both cases, it must be recollected that the King and the Chambers may decide adversely to the interests and harmony of the two nations. Such a decision on the part of France, however it may be regretted by the people of both countries, who have great and growing interests, commercial and political, to cherish, may lead to a result upon which the committee, while in doubt and while a hope remains, will not enlarge. The Committee is therefore of opinion, that at such a crisis, when events may occur which cannot be anticipated, and which may lead to important consequences in our external relations, it would not discharge its duty to the country, if it did not express a firm resolution to insist on the full execution of the treaty of 1831, and if it did not recommend to the House a contingent preparation for any emergency which may grow out of our relations with France, previous to the next meeting of Congress. It is a gratifying circumstance that our means are adequate to meet any exigency, without recourse to loans or taxes. The bill now before the House authorizing the sale of our stock in the Bank of the United States, would, if adopted, afford all the revenue necessary. The Committee is of opinion, that the whole or a part of the fund to be derived from that source, should be appropriated for the purpose of arming our fortifications, and for making other military and naval preparations for the defence of the country, in case such expenditures should become necessary before the next meeting of Congress.

The committee therefore submits the following resolutions for the consideration of the House:

Resolved, That it would be incompatible with the rights and honor of the U. States, further to negotiate in relation to the treaty entered into by

France, on the 4th July, 1831, and that this House will insist upon its execution as ratified by both governments.

Resolved, That the Committee on Foreign Affairs be discharged from the further consideration of so much of the President's message as relates to commercial restrictions or reprisals on the commerce of France.

Resolved, That contingent preparations ought to be made to meet any emergency growing out of our relations with France.

Mr. E. EVERETT, on behalf of himself and two of his colleagues of the Committee on Foreign Affairs, asked permission of the House to submit their views on the subject. He would only observe, that the document was somewhat too long to ask for its reading at that time; and therefore he should only move that the same disposition be made of it as of the report of the majority. The minority of the committee did not materially differ in their views from the majority, except in one or two points; but they thought it due to the subject to take a more full and argumentative view of it.

Mr. CAMBRELENG said it was proper that he should remark, in addition to what he had stated yesterday in relation to the report of the gentleman from Massachusetts, that he (Mr. C.) had not at that time the remotest idea that this document was the same as the one prepared by that gentleman a long time ago; and before Mr. C. had been appointed Chairman of the committee, when the two countries stood in a very different attitude towards each other. Before the last communication was made, Mr. C. had even proposed that a motion should be made for printing the document; but the suggestion was not adopted by the committee. In the new relations which had subsequently ensued, it became necessary, Mr. C. thought, to present new views; and supposing the minority of the committee would do so, he stated, what he conceived to be a fair inference, that he had never seen or heard of that document. He thought proper to make this explanation, in consequence of what had occurred yesterday and to reiterate that the document then submitted by the gentleman from Massachusetts had never been read by one of the six members constituting the majority of the committee.

Mr. J. Q. ADAMS then asked leave to submit his resolutions; but before doing so he desired to know whether the paper presented by his honorable colleague concluded with any resolutions.

Mr. E. EVERETT replied, that it did not. He merely wished, as he stated before, to give it the same disposition that the House intended to give to the report of the majority.

Mr. J. Q. ADAMS said, as the report of the minority did not conclude with any resolution or resolutions, he moved that the resolutions which he had presented yesterday should be received as an amendment, or a substitute, to those of the gentleman from New York.

[The resolutions were then read, as they appeared in the Globe of yesterday.]

Mr. A. requested that the word "measures" as printed in the National Intelligencer should be altered to "measure." He also wished to account to the House and to the nation for the verbal variations that existed between the copies printed in the Intelligencer and the Globe of that morning. The reason was this: His resolutions, in his own manuscript, were taken by the editors of the National Intelligencer to be printed in that paper. Shortly afterwards an application was made to Mr. A. on the part of the Globe for a copy of them; he stated the fact, that they were in the possession of the editors of the Intelligencer, but the gentleman who applied to him from the Globe, having expressed a strong desire to have a copy of them to publish in that morning's paper, Mr. A. wrote a transcript from memory, intending it, if he could, to be verbatim et literatim, but he found on reading it over that there were verbal alterations, though making no alteration whatever in the sense. He thought it proper to give this brief explanation, because persons at a distance might be unable to conjecture why such variations should have occurred.

Mr. A. concluded by moving that the resolu-

tions be adopted as an amendment, or substitute, for those of Mr. Cambreleng.

The SPEAKER remarked, that the question would be on the amendment offered by the other gentleman from Massachusetts, (Mr. Everett.)

Mr. ARCHER rose, he said, to move that the report and resolutions of the majority of the committee, together with the report of the minority, be committed to a Committee of the Whole on the state of the Union, and be made the order of the day for that day.

Mr. CAMBRELENG requested the gentleman to amend his motion so as to include the printing of the reports and resolutions.

Mr. ARCHER assented, and further amended the motion so as to make it the order of the day for to-morrow.

The CHAIR remarked, that if the subject was committed to a Committee of the Whole on the state of the Union, it must take the ordinary place on the calendar, and could not be brought up but by a vote of two-thirds of the House for a suspension of the rules.

Mr. ARCHER then said he would confine his motion to make it the order of the day "for to-day."

Mr. POLK begged to inquire of the Chair if it was made the order of the day for "to-day," whether it would then have the precedence?

The CHAIR replied in the negative.

Mr. POLK hoped then it would not be committed.

Mr. WILDE asked what would be its situation if the motion to commit to a Committee of the Whole on the state of the Union prevailed?

The CHAIR replied: They would be placed on the calendar, and could be taken up by postponing all the orders of the day, or by laying each subject on the table as it came up till the House reached this.

This point was further discussed briefly by Mr. SPEIGHT, Mr. MERCER, and Mr. ARCHER.

Mr. SUTHERLAND rose, he said, to put a question to the Chair, the reply to which would govern his vote. He desired to know if the Chair considered this the last day on which bills emanating in that House could be sent to the other branch, and he would request the Clerk to examine the journals to see if Sunday was a *dies non*, or was considered one of the parliamentary days.

The CHAIR replied that he had been informed that a decision of a former Congress had been made on this subject, and that that would be the last day, according to that decision, on which the House could send bills to the other branch.

Mr MILLER said, he expected that answer, and he would suggest whether it would not be better to act on such bills as were indispensable to-day, and to allow the subject then before the House to lie over till to-morrow.

Mr. CAMBRELENG suggested to the gentleman from Virginia, (Mr. Archer) to withdraw his motion to commit to a Committee of the Whole on the state of the Union, because if the motion prevailed, it would defeat all action upon the resolutions during the present session. There was a bill connected with the subject, which if not taken up to-day could not be acted upon without a vote of two thirds of both Houses; he therefore hoped the gentleman would not press his motion.

Mr. ARCHER said he was as anxious as the gentleman from New York to avoid a lengthy discussion on this subject; but it seemed to him that it would be both irregular and derogatory to the subject to discuss it any where else than in Committee of the Whole on the state of the Union. The House might, if it pleased, resolve itsel *instanter* into a Committee of the Whole generally, and take up any business before it.

Mr. BURGES thought every gentleman would at once perceive the importance of the question, and recollect that it was one of as deep an interest to the Union and to the nation as had ever been discussed in a Committee on the state of the Union. Look back to the whole history of the country, and the same course had always been taken, and a deviation from that long established course had never taken place on far less important subjects than this.

With regard to the objections of the gentleman from New York, they had been answered by the gentleman from Virginia. When in Committee of the Whole on the state of the Union, they could take up whatever bills might be referred to it, and these resolutions likewise. Really he must say, that it seemed to him altogether out of the ordinary course not to refer this matter. It was in order every day, and at any time, for the House to go into that committee. He hoped the bills before the House would be taken up and gone through to-day, and they might fully discuss the matter under consideration to-morrow, and he hoped the motion would be so modified.

Mr. POLK rose, he said, to correct an error into which many had fallen, in regard to the particular position in which the bill to regulate the deposite of the public money then was. That bill was not in Committee of the Whole on the state of the Union. It had been made the special order for a certain day, and by a vote of the House some fortnight ago, all the orders of the day had been postponed for the purpose of taking up the several bills relating to the Bank of the United States.

[Mr. P. here enumerated the several bills.]

Since then, by various votes of the House, other measures have obtained precedence by postponing these bills. Now, he understood the state of the business to be this. If the recommendation of the Committee on Foreign Affairs should receive the sanction of the House, the bill involved in it must also be acted upon at the same time, or if not, it would require a majority of two-thirds of both Houses.

He would suggest to the gentleman from Virginia, (Mr. Archer,) what would perhaps economise their time, viz: that they should proceed forthwith to decide upon these resolutions, for to commit them to a Committee of the Whole on the State of the Union, would be to bury them. It was very certain that the House would never hear of them again. If decision was required, the only way to get at it, would be to consider the subject at once.

Mr. J. Q. ADAMS said it appeared to him that the course recommended by the gentleman from Virginia was the only constitutional course; and as the object of the last resolution of the Chairman of the Committee on Foreign Relations was to effect an appropriation for the defence of the country, at least the recommendation contained in it involved an appropriation of money, the resolution itself must, pursuant to the rules of the House, be considered in Committee of the Whole House. It was a proposition to employ money; to expend money; the money of the nation; and a large sum of it too; and was therefore an appropriation. He would remark that it was introduced by an indirect resolution, although it could not be carried into effect but by a bill. The House could not bind itself to pass it, unless it went through committee. By the rules of the House, no motion or proposition for a tax or charge upon the People shall be discussed on the same day it is introduced. and moreover, it was provided that every such proposition should receive its first discussion in a Committee of the whole House. Was this not a proposition for a tax, or a charge upon the People? It was, for it would take the People's' money and appropriate it for purposes which, it was not yet certain that the consent of Congress could be obtained. The object was apparent enough. It was done for the purpose of forcing down in Committee of the Whole on the state of the Union, a bil which ought to be specially discussed in that Committee. It was an ingenious device, now for the first time disclosed, to connect the war with the Bank of the United States. We were to have two wars together He thought one would be as much as we could wage for the good of the country.

Another rule of the House provided that no tax or duty should be increased, without being also discussed in Committee of the Whole on the state of the Union. And the next was, that *all* proceedings touching appropriations of money, should be first discussed in Committee of the whole House. Was this not a proceeding touching the appropriation of money? We were told that it was a proceeding to deliver the United States from the burden of $7,000,000; but Mr. A. thanked God there had as yet been no expression of opinion on the part of the House on the subject

There were two things which in the course of the deep anxiety he had felt on this subject since the commencement of the session, he had observed with deep concern. The first was, that the principle had been assumed—and it was with unfeigned grief he said it—by the majority of that House, that this dispute with France was to be managed upon party grounds: that the supporters of the administration were the only persons to be heard upon this subject; that what they proposed must be carried in spite of all objections; and that the minority were to have no privileges whatever left to them, but to say ay or no, to any proposition presented by the friends of the administration. That was the principle assumed, and one which he deeply deplored.

The second thing was that now for the first time disclosed, and that was, that the two wars were to be blended together. That there was to be a war with France and a war with the Bank of the United States, carried on at the same time, in such a manner as that one of them would break down the other. He repeated, that this principle had been assumed, a principle the reverse of that assumed by the Senate—he hoped he was not out of order in alluding to the other body—but it was the reverse of the principle there assumed, and of the only principle upon which, in his opinion, the country could ever go through a war against a foreign nation, with honor or with advantage to the country. I say, said Mr. A., it was assumed by an act of the minority of the Committee on Foreign Relations, which act that House did not reprobate as I thought it should have done, by displacing, contrary to long established usage, the chairman of that committee, and placing in his stead another chairman chosen, to say the least of it, by his own vote.

The SPEAKER intimated that the gentleman must perceive that these remarks were not in order. They were irrelevant to the subject under consideration.

Mr. J. Q. ADAMS said he had referred to that appointment only by way of illustration of the principle assumed in the management of those affairs, and which he thought extremely pernicious; but he would say no more on that subject.

By the rules of the House then, it was clearly and emphatically laid down, that these resolutions could not constitutionally be passed by the House, unless in the first instance they were considered in Committee of the Whole on the State of the Union. The consequence of not doing so, would be to suppress debate, and whenever the friends of the administration, or the acting Chairman of the Committee on Foreign Affairs thought that discussion had gone far enough, then the screws of the previous question would be applied. And then, we were told that this was the last day in which bills could be sent from this to the other House, and that we must pass this bill to-day, whether we could or not, or it could not pass at all, and the bugle horn of party will be sounded, and we shall be told that we must pass this resolution. When the previous question shall have been applied, and seconded, and when the question shall be taken, then we shall be at liberty to go into Committee of the Whole on the State of the Union After some further remarks, Mr. A. concluded, by again contending that it would be contrary to the constitution to act upon the subject, without going into Committee.

Mr. CAMBRELENG believed the House would readily pardon him if he did not follow in the same tone and temper of the gentleman from Massachusetts. He had too much respect both for himself and for that gentleman, as well as for the House. Mr C regretted that on a subject and an occasion which should of itself command unanimity, the gentleman should have travelled out of his way to cast imputations of the character the House had just heard; and forgetful also of the high dignity which that occasion demand-

ed, suddenly descended from the lofty eminence he had so lately reached. Mr. C. would permit himself to go no further than to disclaim every imputation which the gentleman had thrown out of a desire on his (Mr. C.'s) part to connect the war with France with the Bank of the United States. He was no longer an enemy to the bank, in the sense in which the gentleman seemed to refer to it. As it regarded another question which the gentleman thought proper to allude to, viz. Mr. C.'s election as Chairman of the Committee on Foreign Affairs, the language used by the gentleman was not authorized by the fact. The gentleman stated that Mr. C. was made chairman by his own vote; surely he could not have meant that Mr. C. voted for himself, because he must have been aware of the contrary, and was made aware of it at the time when he first made the statement.

With regard to party Mr. C. could assure the gentleman from Massachusetts, and every other member of the House, that he had not the slightest desire to make this a party question, and he trusted it never would be so made. He would also further assure the House, that whether they should adopt one or all the resolutions, or proposed any modification, which he deemed compatible with the dignity, the honor, an l the interests of the country, he would most willingly and cheerfully join with them. He hoped to see the sentiment pervade all parties, a desire to do the best for the country. He believed that sentiment lid pervade all parties. He saw it there, he saw t in the papers from the North and from the South; or was it confined to administration presses, but he papers of all parties seemed inspired with one sentiment. Again Mr. C. disclaimed the insinuation that had been thrown out that he was actuated by considerations of party.

Mr. COULTER said that this debate seemed likely to be wandering somewhat unpropitiously from that kind of deliberation which ought to precede a discussion upon so momentous a question as that now submitted for consideration. He was sure that every member of that House must appreciate the delicate situation in which the Legislative branches of this country were placed, whose movements might prejudice the peace and prosperity of fourteen millions of human beings. They were, unfortunately, so situated, that every step they took might, by exasperating pride and stirring up the human passions, be raising up obstacles between friends, where no obstacles ought to exist. Every step they took might have a prejudicial and most unfortunate bearing upon the aspect of two countries of immense population, and upon the happiness of a great portion of the human race. It was therefore proper that every thing should be done dispassionately, with due deliberation, and in order. He hoped the House would adopt the usual and ordinary proceedings. They must perceive that too little time remained for the House to adopt any measure upon this subject in the tone of temper and deliberation that was requisite, and it would perhaps be best to leave every thing to the calm deliberation of the people, and to the representatives who would come fresh from them at the next session of Congress; or they might be convened sooner, if he Executive thought the contingency arising from new circumstances demanded it. At all events, he hoped nothing would be done irregularly, and he coincided with the gentleman from Massachusetts, that this, of all other questions, ought to be debated in Committee of the Whole on the state of the Union. The constitution required it, and the rule of the House required it. Mr. C. inquired if it would be in order to move hat to-morrow morning at 11 o'clock, the House should resolve itself into a Committee of the Whole on the state of the Union, for the purpose of considering this question.

The CHAIR said it would be varying the rules of the House, and would require a vote of two-thirds.

Mr. COULTER said, they would approach the subject with more calmness in the morning, and he made the motion he intimated above.

The subject was further discussed by Messrs. MERCER, BURGES, BRIGGS, BEARDSLEY, PINCKNEY, HUBBARD, MARSHALL, McLENNAN, STEWART, J. Q. ADAMS, GREN-

NEL, COULTER, WHITTLESEY, and ARCHER.

Mr. BEARDSLEY moved to strike out that part of the motion to commit—negatived, yeas 110—nays, 111.

Mr. LYTLE moved to reconsider the vote; lost, yeas 111—nays 113.

The question of Mr. COULTER'S motion was further discussed by Messrs. CLAY, E. EVERETT, REED, and SPEIGHT, and it was adopted—yeas 116, Nays 107.

The House then proceeded to the orders of the day, and acted upon a variety of bills, a full report of which will appear in our next, and was still in session when our paper went to press.

The question was then taken on the amendment offered by Mr. BEARDSLEY and, decided in the negative. Yeas 110, nays 111.

[This vote was first announced to be, yeas 112, nays 110. But the vote of one member having been erroneously recorded and an error of another vote having been discovered, the decision was corrected and declared as above.]

Mr. LYTLE moved to reconsider the vote last taken.

Mr. EVANS moved to lay this motion on the table.

Mr. MERCER inquired of the Speaker whether the proposition to lay the motion to reconsider on the table, would not necessarily include the resolution with it.

The CHAIR replied in the affirmative.

Mr. EVANS withdrew his motion.

Mr. BEARDSLEY demanded the yeas and nays on the motion to reconsider, which were ordered, and were yeas 111, nays 113.

So the House refused to reconsider the vote.

Mr. CLAY was not prepared to adopt the resolution offered by the gentleman from Pennsylvania, (Mr. Coulter.) It would be productive of no good at this period of the session. It would be opening the door for a debate which would occupy the whole time of the House for the remainder of the session, and result in nothing. Let the resolutions of the committee be acted on in the House, and adopted or rejected. As the report and resolutions would come up in the morning, as the first unfinished business (as he was informed by the Chair, in answer to an inquiry) he would move to lay the resolution upon the table.

Mr. E. EVERETT rose to a question of order. He inquired whether, if the resolution be laid on the table, it would not require a vote of the House to take up the report and resolutions?

After some suggestions by Mr. MERCER, the CHAIR made an affirmative response to the inquiry propounded by Mr. EVERETT.

Mr. CLAY rose to withdraw his motion. He was not aware of its effect upon the report of the committee. He hoped other resolutions offered by the gentleman from Pennsylvania (Mr. Coulter) would not be adopted. Every member who had the experience of one or two years in this House, must be aware if this subject was sent to a Committee of the Whole, and was thus placed beyond the control of the House, it would lead to a full investigation of the question, but he could not consent, at this late period to send it to a Committee on the State of the Union.

Mr. REED appealed to the experience of members, if a single instance could be found where a question of so much importance was not sent to a Committee of the Whole. This was a question of vast importance, and he was surprised that gentlemen, in order to get time to act on a little private business, should be willing to dispense with the investigation of a subject of such grave import, and which may or may not result in war. A bill involving the trifling sum of $100, could not be passed, under the rules, without first going to a Committee of the Whole. Why, then, should a motion so important as the present, be resisted? It was a question which, it had been correctly said, should be examined and re-examined.

Mr. SPEIGHT desired to refresh the memory of the gentleman from Massachusetts, (Mr. Reed,) who he believed to be a very honest man. When on a former occasion, a motion had been made to commit the force bill, that gentleman could best

tell whether he voted for it. Upon another occasion, when he (Mr. S.) moved to commit the bill rechartering the Bank of the United States, the gentleman could, if he chose, inform the House whether or not he favored the motion.

Mr. REED said, that as to the votes referred to by the gentleman, they were upon minor subjects compared with the one before the House.

Mr. BEARDSLEY moved, a call of the House. Negatived.

The question was then taken on the adoption of the resolution offered by Mr. COULTER, and decided in the affirmative—yeas 116, nays 107.

So the resolution was adopted.

Mr. CLAIBORNE moved to take up and consider the resolution reported by the Committee on Elections, relative to the contested election in Kentucky.

Mr. HUBBARD called for the orders of the day. Agreed to.

On motion of Mr. HUBBARD, the rule setting apart this day for the consideration of private bills, was suspended—yeas 122, nays 37.

Mr. GILMER moved to suspend all the orders of the day for the purpose of proceeding to the consideration of the joint resolutions in relation to an amendment of the constitution upon the subject of electing a President and Vice President of the United States.

The motion was negatived—yeas 99, nays 104.

The SPEAKER laid before the House the following communications:

A letter from the Postmaster General, covering a statement of the net amount of postage received in each State and Territory for the year 1834, which, on motion of Mr. CONNOR, was laid on the table, and 5,000 extra copies ordered to be printed;

A letter from the Postmaster General, transmitting a statement of the contracts entered into by the Department for the past year; which was laid on the table, and ordered to be printed;

A letter from the Secretary of War, transmitting a report and surveys for rail roads, made, in part, between the Mississippi and the Atlantic, which was laid on the table, and ordered to be printed;

Mr. GILMER moved to print 2000 extra copies of the report; which motion lies over one day.

And a letter from the Secretary of the Treasury, enclosing abstracts of the amount of official emoluments of the collectors of the customs; which was laid on the table, and ordered to be printed.

The following bills from the Senate were read and committed:

An act for the benefit of the corporations of Washington, Alexandria, and Georgetown, in the District of Columbia;

An act for the relief of Richard H. Bell;

An act providing for an increase of the corps of Engineers, and for other purposes;

An act authorizing the Secretary of the Treasury to invest the amount of the two per cent. funds for the road leading to the State of Mississippi;

An act to renew the patent of Joseph Grant;

An act for the relief of John Dowedy, an Indian agent;

An act to regulate the deposite of the public money;

An act to authorize the Leavenworth improving company to locate a certain road through the public lands.

A bill from this House, establishing a pension agency south of Green river, in the State of Kentucky, was returned from the Senate with an amendment, striking out a proviso relative to the location of the said agency; which was first concurred in by the House; but subsequently, on the motion of Mr. Hawes, the House reconsidered the vote, and refused to concur in the amendment.

The following bills were read the third time and passed:

A bill making appropriations for certain roads, and for examinations and surveys for the year 1835;

A bill for the relief of the heirs of James Wilson, deceased;

A bill for the relief of Sarah H. B. Smith;

A bill to extend a patent to Robert Eastman for seven years;

A bill for the relief of the heirs of Jacob Smith;

A bill to provide for carrying into effect the convention with Spain;

A bill to provide for the construction of a dry dock for the naval service;

A bill making appropriations for buoys, light-boats, beacons, and monuments, for the year 1835;

A bill to organize the several fire companies in the District of Columbia;

A bill to extend the charter of the Fire Insurance Company of Alexandria;

A bill further to amend an act incorporating the Chesapeake and Ohio Canal Company;

A bill concerning the Orphans' Court of the county of Washington, in the District of Columbia;

A bill making an appropriation for the support of the Penitentiary in the District of Columbia for the year 1835;

And a bill to provide for the holding of extra terms of the Circuit Court for the District of Columbia for the trial of criminal causes.

The bill making additional appropriations for the Delaware Breakwater, for certain harbors, and removing obstructions in, and at the mouth of certain rivers, for the year 1835; was read the third time, and the question being on its passage,

Mr. H. EVERETT demanded the yeas and nays; which were ordered.

Mr. GARLAND moved a call of the House. Negatived.

The bill was then passed: Yeas 109, nays 65.

The bill making appropriation for Indian annuities and other similar objects for the year 1835, was taken up, the amendments reported by the Committee of the Whole concurred in; when the bill was read a third time and passed.

Mr. LYTLE made an ineffectual attempt to take up the joint resolution authorizing Hiram Powers to execute marble busts of the several Presidents of the United States.

The bill to establish the office of Surveyor General within and for the State of Illinois, was taken up.

Mr. KINNARD moved the amendment offered by him in Committee of the Whole, to establish a similar office within and for the State of Indiana.

The amendment was agreed to without a count; and the bill was engrossed, read a third time, and passed as amended.

A bill to provide for the survey of the public lands, was read a third time and passed.

Mr. INGE moved to postpone the orders of the day for the purpose of taking up the bill to amend the act authorizing the State of Tennessee to issue grants and perfect titles to certain lands therein described, and to settle the claims to the vacant and unappropriated lands within the same, passed April 18th 1806, which was negatived without a count.

A bill to authorize writs of error to the Supreme Court of the United States, in cases involving patent rights, was read a third time.

Messrs. FOSTER and BRIGGS briefly explained the provisions, and advocated the passage of the bill.

Mr. BATES, in a few words, assigned his objections to the measure.

Mr. THOMAS, of Maryland, said he was respectedly called on to consider this bill, but he esteemed the principle involved in it, too important to avoid its discussion, solely because of want of preparation.

The bill proposed to grant an appeal to an individual who felt aggrieved by the decision of one of the Circuit Courts on a contested patent right. If it was passed, this House would have disregarded the provisions of the Judiciary law of 1789, without good cause. In the law of '89, an attempt had been made to fix a boundary between the jurisdictions of the several Courts established by the United States. In some cases, the decision of the Circuit Court was final; in others, an appeal was granted to the Supreme Court. In all cases where the constitutionality of a law was question, or the Supreme Court had jurisdiction by appeal, because he supposed the framers of our judiciary system thought questions of that character were of sufficient dignity to need all the knowledge and wisdom of the seven judges in the Supreme Court

Bench to revise and decide them finally. When the two branches of the national Legislature, with the sanction of the Executive Department, had passed a law, there appeared to be no propriety in permitting any Court, inferior either in numbers or attainment to those who presided in the Supreme Court to adjudge it to be null and void. In other cases, by the sum in controversy, suitors were empowered to ascertain when and where the right of appeal was withheld or granted. If the amount in controversy is any case pending upon the Circuit Court, exceeded two thousand dollars, then either of the parties had a right to appeal to the highest judicial tribunal. This bill attempted to suspend the law of 1789, by which the boundaries of the jurisdiction of these several Courts, were thus established. The constitutionality of the patent of law in this case, has not been controverted, neither is it pretended that the amount in controversy exceeds two thousand dollars. Why then should Congress interfere? The House cannot fail to see that this bill must be a precursor of numerous bills of the same character. If we refuse to permit the decision of our Circuit Court to be final in the construction of the patent law, then we must relieve against the decision of the same tribunals, where the true construction of the tariff laws was the matter in issue. In fact the Committee on the Judiciary had before them a petition from Mr. Birchel, of Philadelphia—a person well known for his efficient, persevering opposition to the tariff of 1828, asking from Congress a special law to enable him to appeal to the Supreme Court against the decision of the Circuit Court of Pennsylvania, by which he was compelled to pay duties to the United States on articles which he thought were not liable to pay duties to the Government. How could the Committee, or the House, with propriety grant an appeal in this case and withhold it from Birchel? In his case the amount in controversy did not exceed ten thousand dollars; yet the decision thereon was a rule of conduct for all other persons importing articles of a character such as he had introduced into the country, and thereby thousands of persons and tens of thousands of property, might and possibly would be effected. He had been opposed to a special law for the old patriotic blacksmith, and he was, for these reasons, opposed to interfering in those cases where the numbers of parties alone gave consequence to this petition. The member from Massachusetts (Mr. Briggs) might be forced from the straight line by the clamors of an amenable constituents, but he would not, and he hoped the House would not be driven from safe moorings by any such impulses. He was for a general rule applicable to all, and if the House thought proper to revise the judiciary law of '89, he was willing to inquire into the expediency of providing that appeals should be granted from the decisions of the Circuit Court in cases where the amount in controversy was less than 2,000 dollars. But, until the general law was changed, he was disposed to enforce it against all parties until some very grievous inconvenience had been shown to exist. In this case he saw no great hardship. The party petitioning had enjoyed the benefit of a trial by a jury of his own neighbors, and the privilege of a hearing before too talented and enlightened judges of his vicinage, in a contest with a stranger to both tribunals, and he did not think there was much cause to complain.

Mr. WISE moved to lay the bill on the table, which was decided in the affirmative—yeas 65, nays 61.

AMENDMENTS TO THE CONSTITUTION.

The House next proceeded to consider the resolutions submitted by Mr. GILMER, relative to amendments to the constitution of the United States.

Mr. GHOLSON remarked, that to avoid discussion at this late hour of the session, he was induced to withdraw the amendment heretofore offered by him.

The question then recurring on the passage of the first resolution, Mr. GILMER asked for the yeas and nay. They were ordered.

Mr. GORHAM, after some remarks in opposition to the proposed amendments, and on the in-

adequacy of the time remaining of the session to give them that deliberation which their great importance demanded, moved to lay the whole subject on the table; and, on this question, he asked the yeas and nays, which were ordered.

Mr. PATTON moved a call of the House, but before the question was taken,

Mr. LEWIS moved that the House adjourn, and asked for the yeas and nays, which were ordered; and the question was decided in the negative—ayes 38, noes 136.

Mr. PATTON then withdrew the motion for a call of the House. It was renewed by Mr. GILLET, but not sustained by the House.

The question was then taken on laying the resolutions on the table, by yeas and nays, and decided in the negative as follows: Ayes 40, noes 137.

Mr. MANN, of New York, remarked that, as it was understood the Senate had adjourned, but little good could be attained by continuing the House in session at this late hour, it being now 7 o'clock. He moved the House adjourn.

The question was then taken by tellers, and decided in the negative—ayes 62, noes 89.

So the House again refused to adjourn.

Mr. EVERETT, of Vermont, after some remarks, moved the previous question. The motion was not sustained by the House.

Mr. VANDERPOEL moved an amendment, and called for the yeas and nays; which were ordered and taken, when there appeared, ayes 38, nays 112.

Mr. PLUMMER said, upon a proposition of so much magnitude as that of changing the organic law of the land, he considered the origin, progress, and history of governments a legitimate subject of inquiry; and in order to a correct understanding of the foundation upon which any complex system of Government was predicated, he considered it necessary, as on all questions of government and rights, occasionally to recur to first principles. It was by tracing things to their source that they learned to understand them.

"In the beginning God created the heaven and the earth.

"And God said let the waters under the heaven be gathered together unto one place, and let the dry land appear: and it was so."

Mr. P. was here called to order by several voices.

The CHAIR remarked, that he had not yet discovered what application the gentleman intended to make of the quotations he had commenced with, and could not, therefore, determine whether they were applicable to the subject before the House.

Mr. PLUMMER proceeded. He regretted that his remarks should be deemed to be out of order. He considered the subject of the greatest importance, affecting that organic law, placed in our hands by the fathers of the country, who pledged in its support their lives, their fortunes and their sacred honor. If this was too serious a subject on which to make Scripture quotations, he would like to know where they should be applied. He had believed it to strike at the foundations of Government, and therefore found it necessary to appeal to first principles. In that belief, he would proceed. "And God said let us make man."

Mr. WISE rose to a question of order. It was part of a systematic attempt in the House to kill these resolutions; to speak them to death. This sort of order which he made was grounded on the irreverance and profanity of the words uttered.

Mr. EVANS said, he had called the gentleman to order on the ground that his remarks did not apply to the subject under consideration.

Mr. PLUMMER took his seat, and the SPEAKER decided that he was not in order—according to the rules he could not be permitted to proceed in his speech without leave of the House.

Mr. PLUMMER asked leave to explain. The SPEAKER refused to permit him. He claimed the privilege to explain as a matter of right under the rules of the House. The SPEAKER denied the right, without leave of the House.

After some conversation, the CHAIR put the question, "Shall the gentleman from Mississippi be permitted to proceed with his remarks." It

ken by yeas and nays, and decided in affirmative. yes 135, noes 35.

Mr. PLUMMER then rose and said, anticipating hat the question to amend the constitution of the Inited States would come up for consideration nd discussion, before the adjournment of the House, he had prepared himself according to the est of his skill and abilities on the subject. He ad followed an example set him by more experienced debators than himself, and prepared his peech beforehand, which then lay before him, n his desk. It might not contain as many classical allusions and poetical quotations as the gentleman from Virginia, (Mr. Wise,) was in the habit f weaving into his speeches, but he thought that would be equally intelligible to the people. Although it did not become him to speak in its raise, he flattered himself that it would be worth ublishing in pamphlet form, and in circulating mong his constituents, and in fact, that it would e, when in print, what might be called a pretty ood speech. He referred to the origin of man, nd the first formation of government as registered n that Book where the first written laws for the overnment of mankind are to be found on record, for the purpose of demonstrating to the House the principles he was about to assume in elation to the question under consideration. The harge of the gentleman from Va., (Mr. Wise,) that e was speaking against time was not true. The stimation of the gentleman from Virginia (Mr. Wise,) that he was acting under the influence of party, or any individual on that floor save himself, was unfounded and untrue. He was incapable of being actuated by any such motives, and he ad yet to learn that a quotation from that greatest and best of Books, in debate, was out of order, r could by possibility be construed into profanity. f there was any grave question, upon the discussion of which a quotation might with propriety e made from the Bible, he thought it was that which proposed to amend that sacred instrument, the constitution of the United States, handed down o us by the patriots of the revolution, and for the establishment of which our fathers expended heir money, perilled their lives, and shed their lood. He was highly gratified at the overwhelming vote by which he had been sustained by the House in opposition to the decision of the Chair, nd the prompt and indignant manner that the members had frowned on the attempt to stifle debate on a question of great national importance, involving the rights and liberties of the American people. His remarks were not irrelevant; they were not impertinent; they were not profane, as the House had correctly decided; nor was it his ntention to violate the rules of order or decorum. He intended, in the course of his remarks, to have dverted to the leading principles advocated by hat party, (the working men,) whose cause he spoused, which he could have done, and made an ppropriate application to the question of amending the constitution, and it was true that he was anxious to be heard; but he could get the substance of his intended remarks before the public n the form of a circular, which would answer his urpose. He proposed, therefore, as a return or the high compliment paid him by the House, o yield the floor to the learned and distinguished entleman from Virginia, (Mr. Wise,) who was apable of making a much greater display and flourish on that floor than himself, or to any other entleman who chose to occupy it. [There was as a general call throughout the House for Mr. P. to proceed, but he yielded the floor.]

Mr. EVANS then addressed the House. He ad felt a strong repugnance to claim their attention, notwithstanding the importance of the subject, in consequence of the short time remaining f the session. He was averse to changes in the onstitution, and the resolutions he deemed objectionable. There was but one which he could feel disposed to countenance; and that was the proposition to restrict the Presidential term to six years. There was a generally pervading sentiment among the people of this country, in favor of that project, and he might be induced to yield o it his assent, though he did not esteem it of essential importance. He was utterly opposed to ll the remainder. First, they recognised the plurality system of elections, while various States adhered to the majority mode, and held the other most unsafe and impolitic. It would be deemed extremely unjust in the latter to ask or compel the former to abandon their views and adopt the majority system. Again, they abolished the District system, which would destroy the influence and power of the smaller States. A majority of one vote, in the largest State, might control all of her forty electors, and cause them to be thrown for an individual. Had the last election been conducted on the District system, it would have been seen to have been a much more closely contested one than it had been supposed to be. Mr. E. said, if this resolution was so modified as to give prevalence to the District system of electing, he did not know but he might be induced to go for it. The third resolution he considered decidedly the best of the three, though even for this he could see no urgent necessity. He had been anxious to have these resolutions camly deliberated upon by the House, and had thrown no obstacles in the way of their discussion. If he could not vote for them himself, he would not bar the opinions of others. It would require two-thirds of the House to sanction them, and in their custody he believed they could safely be reposed.

Mr. BOULDIN said, that considering the immense amount of business before the House, and the short time for calm reflection on such an important topic, he should feel impelled to vote against all three of the resolutions. But in doing so, he wished to be distinctly understood, that he expressed no opinion on their merits or expediency.

Mr. HANNEGAN moved that the House adjourn. The question was taken by yeas and nays, and carried—ayes 96, noes 71.

So, at half past eight o'clock, the House adjourned.

IN SENATE.

Saturday, February 28, 1835.

A message was received from the President of the United States, transmitting a communication from the General Post Office in regard to the number of clerks there employed.

Mr. WEBSTER said, as the Committee on Finance were about to report to the Senate the general appropriation bill for defraying the civil and diplomatic expenses of the Government for the year 1835; and as in the army appropriation bill the usual sum for the support of the Military Academy at West Point had been omitted, under the expectation that a special act would come up from the other House on that subject; and as nothing of that kind had yet appeared, he was instructed by the committee to ask the instructions of the Senate to insert the usual sum in the general appropriation bill; which was agreed to.

The VICE PRESIDENT laid before the Senate the credentials of the Hon. Bedford Brown, a Senator elect from the State of North Carolina for six years from and after the third of March next.

Mr. EWING said: Shortly after the report of the Committee on the Post Office and Post Roads was presented to the Senate, an address of O. B. Brown appeared in the Globe, and has since been copied into most of the other papers in the city, containing some charges of grave import against the committee. As to his statements which do not touch the general course pursued by the committee, I shall not notice them. His testimony, and that of the witnesses who speak of his conduct as a public officer, are published with the report, and all who desire it, can satisfy themselves on those subjects. There are, however, two of his statements as to the course adopted by the committee in the examination, which I think it proper here to notice.

He says, that he was "denied by the committee the privilege of being heard in his own defence, or even of being informed of an accusation against him, before he learned it from the report."

Now, sir, on this subject, I can only say, that it was the opinion of the committee, that all persons implicated by the evidence which they took, should have information of all that was alleged against them, and that they should be *heard* and allowed to produce evidence in their own justification. The mode of communicating this information was a subject of frequent discussion between some of the members of the committee, and it was at last settled that the Chairman should exercise his own sound judgment and discretion in giving this information. This was not by any formal order, but precisely in the way in which the Chairman thought he ought to be authorized to communicate to any and each of the officers, and each individual implicated, all the information that might be necessary to give them a full opportunity for explanation. I never inquired of him what information he saw fit to give any one under this authority; but Mr. Brown was called and permitted to testify in exculpation of his own conduct, and of the course of the Department, on every subject on which the Chairman thought proper to call him. The volume of his testimony which accompanies the report, will shew this fully, especially when it is known that he never was called, except by the request of the Chairman, to explain some transaction in which he or the Department seemed to be implicated.

The second allegation which I have thought necessary to notice, is as follows: "When under oath before the committee, I was not advised of any points on which I was to be examined, nor the object of any inquiry made; and after answering all the questions which any member of the committee thought proper to propound, I was not permitted to hear the testimony read over to know whether it was taken down correctly, or to correct any erroneous impression which it might be calculated to make."

The latter clause of this statement is wholly contrary to the fact. The Chairman conducted this part of the business of the committee, and I observed that he frequently, though not always, asked the witnesses to read, or hear read, their testimony before it was signed. He generally did so, if the statement was long or complicated. The question was, I believe, always written down and read to the witness, before he answered, and the answer was always read over to the witness after it was written, before it was passed by; and I know there was no case in which a witness was refused permission to read, or to hear read, his deposition before he signed it.

I wish the Chairman to say what he understands to have been the course pursued by the committee on these subjects.

Mr. GRUNDY remarked, that he would state all he recollected upon the two points referred to by the Senator from Ohio, (Mr. Ewing,) and I can make myself better understood by noticing in the first place the point last named.

As Chairman of the Committee, the form of proceedings seemed to devolve on me. I, of course, when a difficulty presented itself, consulted the other members.

The practice, in relation to the examination of a witness, was this: When he presented himself, he was sworn. A question was then put to him by a member of the committee. I immediately stated to the witness that he was not then to answer, but might consider what his answer should be, until the Clerk wrote down the question and read it to him. After the question was written and read by the Clerk, the witness gave his answer, which was written down, and read to the witness and the committee. After the testimony of a witness was gone through, I stated to the witness, that if he was satisfied with his evidence as read to him, he could then sign his deposition; and if he did not feel satisfied, he could have it read to him by the Clerk, or read it himself. In some few instances, where I was not sure that the answers of the witness, as written, conveyed his true meaning, I named to the witness that he had better take the deposition and read it over himself before he signed it; and this was sometimes done.

This practice, as I have stated it, was generally pursued; and I have no recollection of a departure from it, in the case of Mr. Brown. Of one thing I am confident. No witness was ever refused an opportunity of reading his testimony, if he requested it.

2d. As to the opportunity afforded to persons implicated or affected by testimony taken by the

committee, this was, to my mind, a very delicate subject. To prevent the proceedings of the committee from assuming the character of a trial, rather than an inquiry, and at the same time to procure the introduction of testimony which might place transactions upon their true ground, was a subject of frequent conversations among the members. At last it seemed to be understood that I might act upon that subject according to my own discretion, taking care that no improper use should be made of any communication I might make for the purpose of obtaining the objects in view. Under the authority conferred on me, I did not feel willing to disclose what any particular witness had sworn; but stated, for instance, to Mr. Reeside, that the order of the Postmaster General was to carry a daily mail from Bedford to Washington, (in Pennsylvania;) that the Department had so paid for it; that the proofs taken did not show a performance on his part; and if he would name any witnesses who could establish his performance, they should be summoned. And in this way witnesses were brought forward and examined upon several cases investigated by the committee.

As to Mr. Brown's transactions with Mr. Porter, he did intimate a wish to know what had been sworn by Mr. Porter. I stated I did not feel at liberty to tell him; but stated that I intended to call on him as a witness, and he could tell all about it. My reasons for not stating to Mr. Brown what Mr. Porter had sworn, were, 1st, that it would be disclosing the testimony of a particular witness; and 2d, Mr. Porter and Mr. Brown were the only persons who had a knowledge of the transactions; and I thought the surest way to arrive at the truth, was to let each give his own account, without knowing what the other had said.

I will further add, that I was present at the examination of every witness, whose testimony was taken by the Committee, during the whole investigation.

Mr. SOUTHARD remarked, that he had a perfect recollection that the witness referred to, (Mr. Brown,) did, on more than one occasion, read over the testimony which he had given, as it was taken down by the clerk of the Committee, and that he also did, on one or more occasions, decline reading it, because it had been taken down as he wished it, and had been read to him. If he did not read every part of it, it was his own fault. He was on no occasion, in my presence, refused permission to read it.

This witness was never taken by surprise, so as to be obliged, on any point, to give an answer hastily. When he had any hesitation, or desired to look at books or papers, or refer to the officers of the Department, he was permitted to do so, and frequently had such permission, and availed himself of it; sometimes delaying an answer for one or two days. And it also sometimes happened that he was directed by the Committee to make examination of papers and books, when he had not expressed any desire to do so.

Mr. ROBINSON said as a member of the Committee on the Post Office and Post Roads, indisposition had prevented him from being present during the whole of the investigation. But upon no occasion so far as came within his knowledg, was any witness denied the priviledge of reading over his testimony after it was taken down by the clerk, before the witness signed it; and well recollects of many witnesses so doing.

Mr. CLAYTON said he had warned the members of the committee not to suffer the opportunities which the session offered them to pass, without their unanimous contradiction, on the floor of the Senate, of all such aspersions upon them, and misrepresentations of their conduct while engaged in this investigation, as they had just exposed. He had heretofore had some experience of the injustice done to those who engage in such investigations. As a member of this committee during the last session, he had concurred in the report of the majority made near the close of that session, and after the adjournment of Congress, he had been astonished at the number and enormity of the misrepresentations of the party press sustaining the Department, arraigning the conduct of the committee. But, sir, said he, at the last session a committee had been appointed by the *other House*, to re examine the matter we had inquired of while the Senate's committee was also directed to proceed with their investigation; and, though grossly traduced and calumniated as the committee was pending the last elections, by the party newspaper press, for what had been done, yet I was content to bear this abuse at the time, believing that justice would eventually be done to us by an honest public, when the result of the examinations of all parties should be fairly communicated to that public. Our report has been re-examined, and the result has been, that the different committees have now carried their condemnation of the conduct and management of this department, far beyond the point at which we had arrived last year, by that investigation, for which we were so grossly calumniated by a portion of the newspaper press. What has been the consequence to those who made the last reports? Sir, even the majority of the committee in the other House, composed as it was of the political friends of the Executive, had no sooner presented their report, condemning the outrageous misconduct of the Post Office Department, than an attempt was made to denounce that majority, and the conclusions to which the honorable gentlemen who thus reported, had arrived, were also declared to be the results of party discipline and party spirit. Yes, sir, the very men, who, it was confidently declared last year, would expose our errors, have confirmed our judgment; and though reluctantly driven to this result, a portion of the press has denounced them also as acting merely from party motives! What justice then have my friends on this committee, appointed by a persecuted Senate, to expect from such sources? Sir, I warn them again that the bloodhounds of the political kennel, which is maintained on the spoils of victory, will be let loose on their trail, the moment they shall leave this city, and forego for six months longer an opportunity of exposing every falsehood against them which is now hatched or undergoing the process of incubation. Let them stand on the alert, and resort to their associates on the committee, as well as every other source within their reach, for a justification of their course, while they have an opportunity to do so. The moment the session closes, leaves them powerless and defenceless, while they present a shining mark for the envenomed shafts of the most rancorous and dangerous of all party spirit—that party spirit, sir, which contends for pay.

Mr. HENDRICKS, from the Committee on Roads and Canals, reported a bill making appropriations for certain roads, and examinations, and surveys, for the year 1835.

The VICE PRESIDENT communicated a letter from the War Department, transmitting a list of the persons employed in the Indian Department under the act of 30th June last, for the year 1834. Also, a report of Mr. Featherstonhaugh, who was charged with making a mineralogical and geological survey of the Southwestern territory.

Mr. POINDEXTER, from the Committee on Public Lands, reported, without amendment, the bill to establish a Surveyor General's Office in Illinois and Indiana.

Mr. SOUTHARD, from the Committee on Naval Affairs, reported a bill from the House for the erection of a dry dock for the naval service.

Mr. TOMLINSON, from the Committee on Pensions, reported the bills from the House granting pensions to Joseph Mead and William Lawrence, and reported that the bill granting a pension to Elizabeth Swain, and to restore to certain invalid pensioners the amount of pensions by them relinquished, ought not to pass.

Mr. TYLER, from the Committee on the District of Columbia, reported a bill making an appropriation for the support of the Penitentiary of the District.

Also, the bill to extend the charter of the Fire Insurance Company of Alexandria;

Also, a bill for the relief of Elizabeth Wilson, Ann C. Wilson, and Malinda A. Campbell;

Also, a bill to organize the several Fire Companies in the District;

Also, a bill concerning the Orphans' Court of the county of Washington.

Mr. BLACK, from the Committee on Private Land Claims, reported unfavorably upon the bill for the relief of the heirs of Jacob Smith.

He also reported a bill for the relief of the heirs of William Pollard.

Mr. LEIGH, from the Judiciary Committee, reported a bill to extend the patent of Robert Eastman.

Mr. SHEPLEY, from the Committee on Claims, reported the bill from the House for the relief of Sarah H. B. Stith.

Mr. SOUTHARD, from the Naval Committee, reported the bill from the House for the relief of Elizabeth Mays, without amendment.

Mr. WEBSTER, from the Committee on Finance, reported the bill from the House making appropriations for the civil and diplomatic expenses of the Government for the year 1835, with sundry amendments.

Mr. WEBSTER moved to take up the bill and agree to those amendments, to which he supposed there could be no objection, and leave others proposed by the committee, which were to strike out certain diplomatic appropriations, which might give rise to discussion, until progress had been made in its engrossment.

The bill was then considered as in Committee of the Whole, and the amendments reported by the committee, were severally agreed to.

Mr. CLAY, by instruction of the Committee on Foreign Relations, offered an amendment appropriating $1,300 to pay John Randolph Clay, U. States charge to Russia, the amount found to be due him upon a re-investigation of his accounts. Also, $5,015 62 cents to Nathaniel Niles, late charge to France, being an amount found to be due him on the settlement of his accounts. The amendment was agreed to, and the bill was then laid on the table.

Mr. PRESTON moved that the Senate proceed to the election of a printer, on the part of the Senate, for the next Congress.

Mr. CLAY said he had made some opposition to this motion on a former occasion, in the expectation that the House would, by this time, have chosen their printer. As they had not done so, he now waived any further objection to the proceeding.

Mr. BENTON said he intended to move cotemporaneously, for the consideration of his joint resolution, to repeal the joint resolution of 1819.

Mr. POINDEXTER hoped the Senate would not go to the consideration of the joint resolution; he was fearful of three hours' speeches.

Mr. PRESTON expressed his disposition to accommodate the gentleman from Missouri, but the resolution for electing a printer was offered two weeks ago, and if the law was to be complied with, there was no fitter occasion for it than the present. He, therefore, persisted in his motion, upon which

Mr. WRIGHT demanded the yeas and nays which were ordered.

Mr. BENTON said he had been quite unfortunate for two sessions past in his endeavors to get up his joint resolution. Last session he failed in getting it up, and he was no more successful at this. For when he introduced it, and it was referred to a committee, they reported it back again, saying there was no occasion to act upon it. Mr. B. said, being in the minority as he was here, and having twice exerted himself to get a decision from the majority on the question of repealing the joint resolution of 1819, he now gave notice that we had no right to go into this election—that all proceedings under that statute are as a dead letter, and that whatever we do with regard to the choice of a printer for the next Senate, he considered as null and void, and that it would be the duty of the next Senate, unless they were disposed to acquiesce in the choice, to disregard the election, and have their printing done as they shall think proper. He thought the course which was pursued in 1819 for the purpose of having the printing done, was not the most advantageous for the country. We have had lamentable proofs since, of what it has cost us—perhaps not less than $130,000 at the last session, and the ingenuity of printers has been put to its utmost stretch to find out old objects for employment upon, the effect of which is to sustain party presses during a long

ucation. In this, and in this only, the election of a printer answers a good purpose. Gentlemen are made, and are daily making, complaints of abuses in other branches of the Government, when we have no occasion to go out of our own body to search for them. They exceed here all the other branches of the Government put together, including the Post Office. When large objects come forward, with propositions to print, and inquiries are made as to their utility and expense, some gentlemen are always furnished with an answer, that it is to be done in so many days, and at such a price, and when it is paid for, it sometimes amounts to one, two, three, and four times as much. He wished the Secretary would say what was the amount of the new appropriation for the printing of the Senate in the bill which had just been up, and whether for specific or general objects.

Mr. HILL observed that there was more than one item.

The Secretary read the amendment in the bill—$20,000.

Mr. BENTON resumed: He believed we contended here, the other day, most manfully, from the morning till the stars appeared in the evening, making head against an appropriation of some $15,000 for the establishment of branch mints. We fought manfully against an appropriation which is intimately connected with the currency of the country, in which the People have a direct interest. But here appropriations, of 30 or 40,000 are made for printing with scarcely an inquiry into the amount. And where are those books for which these enormous expenditures are made? Piled up in your ante room against the wall. Too numerous to remove, and, like the Vicar of Wakefield's picture, too large to be got up—there they lie piled up against the wall. If we must go on in this way, it will be necessary after a while to build an additional wing to the Capitol to hold them. These great abuses have their root and their origin in the appointment of these public printers, who are indefatigable in their exertions to find out fat jobs for themselves in the vacation, and there can be no sort of doubt that if this could have been foreseen by those who passed the joint resolution in 1819, the proposition would not have received the slightest countenance. The committee of '19 thought the expenditure then, was large, and introduced that joint resolution as an experiment only, in the hope of correcting it. What would be the astonishment of the survivors of that committee, to see an expenditure of 140 or $150,000 a year founded on their act. Their astonishment would be excessive that we had not got rid of an experiment which had worked so contrary to their views and the perpetuity which has attended it. The House has thus far declined acting on their resolution, and if that body has decided that to elect a printer now, would be an encroachment upon the rights of the next House, ought this branch to act in contradiction to them? Ought we not to postpone that, which is in itself an evil, when so good an example has been given us? The next Senate is competent to provide its own printer, and we can leave the Secretary of the Senate, in the mean time, to have the printing done by jobs. Mr. B. considered the election now, as null and void, and he wished his voice to go forth against it—that the next Senate were no more bound to receive a printer imposed upon them by us than they were to receive the ink, stationary, or wood, that we might provide them, and although they might acquiesce in receiving it, yet, if they did not like it, they might reject the whole of it. So with regard to a printer. If we should elect a man who might be disagreeable to them, they might say they would have no printer, or they would have their printing done on contract of the Secretary, by job. Although the Senate is a permanent body, yet the persons employed by it are not so. Mr. B. said he, for one, would not submit to the imposition; and if a disagreeable man should be imposed upon him by men who were just leaving their seats, every effort should be made to rout him from his place. Ay, to route him from his place; and if that did not succeed, he would try to prevent his obtaining enormous jobs; and he now gave notice of that intention, so that no blame or censure could attach to that body.

Mr. PRESTON said, that when the joint resolution of the honorable gentleman was referred to the Judiciary Committee, his attention was turned to the history of the printing of Congress; and he found that in 1819 a joint resolution was passed, regulating permanently the mode of getting the printing of the two Houses executed, so far as the prices were the subject of regulation; and the practice has been to elect by ballot ever since. Whatever doubt there may be as to the interpretation of the resolution of 1819, there can be none as to that of 1829, because it re-enacted that of '19, and required the printing to be done by a printer who was to be elected by ballot. The practice, then, was of 14 years standing; and it was sustained by a joint resolution of the two Houses. The gentleman from Missouri says that this Senate has no right to impose a printer on the next Senate; but in '29 the honorable gentleman sustained the principle of imposing a printer on the next session; and now, for the first time, is this practice pronounced illegal, and discourteous to that body. The honorable gentleman says, too, that great abuses exist here, which are not exceeded even in the Post Office. Great abuses no doubt exist in every department of the Government. But if the whole sum for printing here were wasted and thrown away, it could not be compared to the abuses in the Post Office. But the increase in the whole expenditure of the Government is in the same ratio as the increase here. In 1819 it was from 15 to $20,000. Now strike out the printing of these land office documents, and it is not double that of 1829. In other branches, the printing has increased in the same ratio. But the Senate is in opposition to the President and the House of Representatives; and it is necessary to appeal to our common masters; and are we, then, to retrench here, and give up the whole field of public opinion to them to operate in. The President and the House of Representatives each incur greater expenses for printing than we do. We are bound to send information of our doings to those who sent us here; it is extremely necessary. The press is used for the purpose of sending abroad *ex parte* information, and we are bound to counteract such proceedings. He was disposed to correct abuses here as much as any gentleman, and would be glad to see the public printing done independently of the public press of the country, and would gladly go for a public printing press, if it was practicable. The honorable gentleman's objection to electing a printer have a two fold effect. First, that the printer solicits useless jobs: And second, that the Senate grants them, and that these abuses are the necessary consequences of electing a printer. If this be so he was willing to reform the evil. He would not vote for any measure, but upon a conscientious conviction that the public welfare required it. He was willing to reform at home first, and to begin upon his own friends too. But if gentlemen are willing to reform here, let them go to reform the executive printing; let them begin at the white house, and he would be very glad to see the honorable gentleman's talents in saving the money of the country employed in that quarter. It is proper therefore, to proceed to this election now—the present printer has a large and expensive establishment—he has a large capital employed, and if he is not to be the printer, he ought to know it. But whether he is elected or not the successful person ought to make his arrangements—he did not know what the result might be, he hoped an individual of his politics might be chosen—he trusted he would, but he wished it might be terminated in some way.

Mr. BENTON said, the plan he would propose for having the public printing done hereafter, was the one he should read. [Mr. B. then read a passage from the report of the committee of 1819, in favor of the establishment of a national printing office.] This, he said, is the way the British Parliament does its printing, and it is the best in the world. He said, when up before, that the abuses of printing in the Senate exceeded that of all the other departments of the Government, the Post Office included; and this is to be dated from the point at which we started. In 1819, the total for the Senate was $8,000, and for the House $15,000. What is it now? He did not know, nor did he believe any body else knew. For here, in the general appropriation bill are some $20,000 for arrearages. What is the increase of $120,000 beyond $8,000? It is not quite 20 to 1, but it is 16 or 17 to 1. Now, in what department of the Government will you find an increase of 16 or 17 fold? Mr. B. said the honorable gentleman from South Carolina wanted him to try to reform at the White House, or some of the other departments. But how should he succeed there, when all his efforts here, although aided by the influence of the gentleman, are so unsuccessful? If, with the assistance of those who preach retrenchment here, he could effect nothing, how could he do it there? Mr. B. said he had taken his stand upon the inherent right of each House to provide its printing, fuel, and stationary. Here we have ordered a document to be printed of some 4,000 pages, 3,500 of which have been delivered. Now what use can be made of it? He had not looked into it, and he had neither seen nor heard any reference made to it. No extra numbers of it have been struck off. Only a single copy for distribution among the members. And as regarded the documents, those of the last year, he believed, had never been distributed yet; he never saw his quota, though perhaps they may have been sent to him to St. Louis. And how many of these documents (the Post Office reports) will each member send away? After sending some 50 or 100, the rest are an encumbrance on their hands. The gentleman from South Carolina very candidly admitted that he had another object in view in this movement—that he wished to keep up a partisan newspaper. Mr. B. said, if he misunderstood the gentleman, he would yield the floor to be corrected.

Mr. PRESTON said, if printing was used elsewhere to sustain party presses, he would consider it but fair to elect a printer on the same ground. He would vote for a printer who corresponded in politics with himself, while others disavowed the intention of making jobs.

M. BENTON resumed: Good! The honorable gentleman would do something here countervailing what was done elsewhere. He Mr. B., would wash foul linen for no party in the world. If corruption exists among partisan printers, and the gentleman denounces it, and they are sustained by corrupt jobs, we will not countenance it. He, Mr. B. came here in 1820, and the printing went on then as it did previously, and therefore, he did not inquire into it. As regards the argument derived from the great expenses of the person whom the gentleman proposed to elect, what is it but an argument in favor of perpetuity of office? If he has made his calculations upon the perpetuation of his party, is that our concern? He was elected for two years and he has kept it, and it is not our affair? If his large establishment shall be paraded before us again next year, Mr. B. said he should pay no attention whatever to it. And if gentlemen will put an officer upon the next Senate, not acceptable to them, it will be the duty of the next Senate to vindicate itself. It is time for gentlemen to take warning now.

Mr. PRESTON said, he could not permit the honorable gentleman from Missouri to put him in a position to defend either here or elsewhere what he did not defend—he new nothing at all about this land document. And if jobs have been improperly given, the gentleman would not be more prompt than he was to correct it. Nor did he say that corruption would bear him out in corruption. Mr. P. said, wherever it existed, he was its enemy. But if the political complexion of the Senate be changed, who will gentlemen elect as their printer? A man opposed to the Executive? No. The gentleman says, each House has the right to appoint its own officers, under the constitution. Certainly it has. But it is competent for both Houses to fix certain principles by which such appointments shall be regulated, and that has been done for this case. He was in favor of a national printing office. But it was useless to think of it now—there was not time to mature and effect such a thing at the present session.

The question being on proceeding to the elec-

tion, it was decided in the affirmative by the following vote:

YEAS—Messrs. Bell, Bibb, Black, Calhoun, Clay, Clayton, Ewing, Frelinghuysen, Goldsborough, Hendricks, Kent, Knight, Leigh, Mangum, Moore, Naudain, Poindexter, Prentiss, Preston, Robbins, Silsbee, Smith, Southard, Swift, Tomlinson, Tyler, Webster—27.

NAYS—Messrs. Benton, Brown, Buchanan, Cuthbert, Grundy, Hill, Kane, King of Geo. Linn, McKean, Morris, Robinson, Ruggles, Shepley, Tallmadge, Tipton, White, Wright—18.

The Senate then proceeded to ballot for printer, when the following was the result:

Gales & Seaton	12
Blair	2
Duff Green	15
Blair & Rives	17
Greer	2

No person having received a majority of the whole number of votes,

Mr. BENTON moved to postpone the subject to the first day of next session, and on that question demanded the yeas and nays; which were ordered, and the question was determined in the negative by a vote of yeas 18, nays 28, as follows:

YEAS—Messrs. Ben on, Brown, Buchanan, Cuthbert, Grundy, Hill, Kane, King of Geo. Linn, McKean, Morris, Robinson, Ruggles, Shepley, Tallmadge, Tipton, White, Wright—18.

NAYS—Messrs. Bell, Bibb, Black, Calhoun, Clay, Clayton, Ewing, Frelinghuysen, Goldsborough, Hendricks, Kent, Knight, Leigh, Mangum, Moore, Naudain, Poindexter, Porter, Prentiss, Preston, Robbins, Silsbee, Southard, Swift, Tomlinson, Tyler, Waggaman, Webster—28.

The Senate then balloted eight times successively without effecting a choice. The ballots were as follows:

	2d.	3d.	4th.	5th.	6th.	7th.	8th.	9th.
Gales & Seaton	13	16	16	17	18	19	20	18
Blair & Rives	16	13	17	12	16	14	13	16
Duff Green	15	15	13	11	10	11	9	10
Blanks	1	1	0	0	0	0	0	0
Mrs. Royall	0	1	1	2	1	4	1	

Mr. POINDEXTER then suggested that it mus't be seen by every Senator that we could not elect a printer now. He would not make a motion, but he thought we had better postpone the matter till Monday next.

The Senate then balloted five times successively, without making a choice. The ballots were as follows:

	10th.	11th.	12th.	13th.	14th.
Gales & Seaton	24	23	20	22	22
Blair & Rives	17	15	9	16	13
Duff Green	9	6	17	7	8
Blanks	0	0	0	0	1
Mrs. Royall	0	1	0	0	0
William R. Rind	0	2	1	2	

Mr. WRIGHT then moved that the subject be indefinitely postponed, and on the question, demanded the yeas and nays; which were ordered, and are as follows:

YEAS—Messrs. Benton, Brown, Buchanan, Grundy, Hill, Kane, King of Alabama, King of Georgia, Linn, McKean, Morris, Robinson, Ruggles, Shepley, Tallmadge, Tipton, White, Wright—18.

NAYS—Messrs. Bell, Bibb, Black, Clay, Clayton, Cuthbert, Ewing, Frelinghuysen, Goldsborough, Hendricks, Kent, Knight, Leigh, Mangum, Moore, Naudain, Poindexter, Porter, Prentiss, Preston, Robbins, Silsbee, Smith, Southard, Swift, Tomlinson, Tyler, Waggaman, Webster—29.

So the question of postponement was disagreed to.

The Senate then balloted three times more, when it appeared that Gales & Seaton received a majority of the whole number of votes, and they were accordingly declared duly elected. The ballotings were as follows:

	15th.	16th.	17th.
Gales & Seaton	22	23	27
Blair & Rives	14	16	14
Duff Green	7	6	3
Wm. A. Rind	3	2	2
Blank	1	0	0

Mr. BIBB then moved to rescind the joint rule

which prohibits the transmission of bills from one House to the other, on the same day.

After some opposition from Mr. EWING and Mr. WEBSTER, the motion was laid on the table, upon a division—ayes 21, noes 13.

On motion of Mr. KING, of Alabama, the Senate at 4 o'clock took a recess till half past 5.

EVENING SESSION.

The following bills from the House, were read twice, and ordered to be engrossed, and read a third time:

A bill to continue in force for one year, an act providing for certain invalid soldiers of the revolutionary war;

A bill for the relief of John Stith;

A bill for the relief of Henry Oxford;

A bill authorizing the Superintendent of the Indian Affairs at St. Louis, to employ a clerk;

A bill for the relief of the heirs and legal representatives of Baily C. Clark;

A bill for the relief of Richard D. Archer;

A bill authorizing the City Council of St. Augustine, in Florida, to widen a street;

A bill authorizing the Secretary of State to issue letters patent to James Jones;

A resolution directing a gold medal in commemoration of the battle of the Cowpens, to be struck at the Mint of the United States;

A bill amending an act for the construction of a bridge across the Potomac;

A bill authorizing the Governor of, Michigan to sell certain lands belonging to the University of that Territory;

A bill for the removal of the Land Office from Wapaghkanetta, to Lima, in the State of Ohio;

A bill for the relief of George Duff;

A bill for the relief of Robert Abbott, and the heirs of James Abbott deceased;

A bill for the relief of Mervin P. Mix;

A bill for the relief of E. R. Shubrick of the United States Navy;

A bill for the relief of Matthew C. Perry;

A bill authorizing the issuing of letters patent to Francis B. Odgen;

A bill for the relief of Sutton Stevens;

A bill for the relief of Shubael Conant;

A bill for the relief of Thomas Hubert;

A bill for the relief of William Haskell, and others;

A bill prescribing the punishment of Consuls and Commercial Agents;

A bill for the relief of Stephen Smith, and others.

A bill for the relief of John Cullins;

A bill for the relief of Amasa A. Tifft;

A bill for the relief of Harvey Reynolds;

A bill for the relief of Isaac Janvier;

A bill for the relief of Simeon Meachum;

A bill to change the time of holding the District Court in the Western District of Virginia;

A bill for the relief of David Kincaid;

A bill for the relief of Theodore Owens;

A bill for the relief of the legal representatives of Aaron Smith;

A bill for the relief of Job Barton;

A bill for the relief of Riddle, Becktel, and others;

A bill to refund certain duties to Richard Butman of the schooner Bandywine;

A bill for the relief of the legal representatives of Thomas Clement;

A bill for the relief of John J. Avery;

A bill for the relief of Nathaniel Tyler;

A bill for the relief of Samuel Butler;

Mr. CLAYTON, from the Committee on the Judiciary, reported a bill from the House authorizing the District Court for the District of Columbia, to hold special sessions for the trial of criminals;

A bill for the removal of the District Court from Natchez, to Jackson, in the State of Mississippi, was read the second and third time, and passed;

The above bills were afterwards read a third time, and passed.

The following bills were read, and laid on the table:

A bill for the relief of Charles Caldwell;

A bill for the relief of Samuel Hunt;

A bill for reviving an act in favor of the officers

and soldiers of the Virginia line, in the revolutionary war;

A bill for the relief of James Tuttle;

A bill for the relief of Comodore Isaac Hull;

A bill for the relief of Samuel H. Doxey.

The following bills were indefinitely postponed.

A bill for the relief of Josiah Westlake;

A bill for the relief of John Dahl;

A bill for the relief of William Slocum.

A bill for the relief of David Weaver;

A bill for the relief of John Herrick;

A bill for the relief of Job Wood;

A bill for the relief of James Young;

And a bill for the relief of William O'Neil, and Robert Morris, were each read three times and passed.

The bill making provision for printing the fac simile accounts of General Washington, was laid on the table, 15 to 13.

The Committee on Naval Affairs were discharged from the further consideration of the papers of Andrew Armstrong.

The following resolutions were offered:

By Mr BENTON:

Resolved, That the Secretary of State be directed to report a plan with an estimate of the expense, at the commencement of the next Congress, for establishing a Printing Office and Book Bindery at the seat of Government, to do all the printing for the two Houses of Congress, and for all the departments of the government, Post Office included.

By Mr. SMITH:

Resolved, That the Secretary of the Senate be and is hereby authorized to employ Samuel S. Osgood, of Boston, Massachusetts, to paint a portrait of Lafayette from the full length, in the House of Representatives, corresponding to the one of George Washington, by Peale; provided that the cost of the same does not exceed the sum of ——dollars to be paid out of the contingent of the Senate.

By Mr. WEBSTER:

Resolved, That the Secretary of the Senate prepare a comparative statement showing the names and number of officers, agents, contractors, and other persons within the employment of the Government, with the compensation and emoluments of each as published in the Register of the year 1823, and 1833, and that there be——number of copies printed for the use of the Senate.

By Mr. KING, of Georgia:

Resolved, That the Secretary of War be directed to communicate to the Senate Col. Long's Report of his late reconnoissance of a route for a Rail-road from Memphis, Tennessee, to Augusta, Georgia. And if it be not sent to the department during the present session, that it be sent to the Secretary of the Senate during the recess, and that it be then printed under his directions for the use of the Senate with the accompanying maps, if any.

Mr. BIBB gave notice that he would offer the following resolution:

Resolved, That there be re-printed for the use of the Senate the usual number of the journals of the Senate up to the 4th of March, 1815, and also so much of the Executive Journal as is made public, in separate volumes.

The Senate then, at 9 o'clock, adjourned.

HOUSE OF REPRESENTATIVES.

SATURDAY, Feb. 28, 1835.

The Speaker laid before the House a letter from the Postmaster General, transmitting a list of the Clerks employed in his Department for the year 1834, which

On motion of Mr. CONNOR, was laid on the table and ordered to be printed.

A bill from the Senate to provide for the settlement of the claim of Mary O'Sullivan, was read twice and committed.

The following bills from the Senate were read the third time and passed:

A bill to authorize the Treasury to compromise the claims allowed by the Commissioners under the treaty with the King of the Two Sicilies, concluded on the 14th October, 1832.

And a bill further to extend the time allowed

for the execution of the duties of the Commissioners to carry into effect the treaty with France.

Mr. HAWES, from the select committee on the West Point Academy, asked the consent of the House to submit a resolution for the printing of 5,000 copies of the Report of said committee.

Objection being made,

Mr. HAWES moved to suspend the rule, which was negatived—yeas 72—nays 98.

Mr. CAVE JOHNSON, from the Committee on Private Land Claims, reported, without amendment, a bill from the Senate, for the relief of Lemuel Tanner, assignee of Pierre Dufresne; which was read a third time and passed.

Mr. BOON, from the Committee on the Public Lands, reported with an amendment, the bill from the Senate, authorizing the construction of the Leavenworth and other rail roads through the public lands. The amendment was agreed to, ordered to be engrossed, and the bill ordered to be read a third time.

Mr. GILMER, from the Committee on Indian Affairs, reported the bill from the Senate for the relief of John Dougherty, without amendment. The bill was then read the third time and passed.

The motion, made yesterday, to print 3,000 extra copies of the report made by Mr. BINNEY, from the Select Committee on Weights and Measures, was considered and agreed to.

The motion made yesterday, to print 2,000 extra copies of the report from the War Department, relative to the surveys of rail-roads, made in part, between the Mississippi and the Atlantic, was taken up.

Mr. GAMBLE moved to amend the motion, by substituting 5,000 for 2,000 copies; which was agreed to; when the proposition was adopted.

Mr. HEATH, on leave, presented the memorial of the members of the Baltimore Bar, remonstrating against the passage of the bill which originated in the Senate, remodeling the judicial limits of the United States, which was committed to a Committee of the Whole on the state of the Union, and ordered to be printed.

RELATIONS WITH FRANCE.

Mr. CAMBRELENG moved to postpone the orders of the day, for the purpose of executing the special order, which was agreed to.

On motion of Mr. CAMBRELENG, the House then resolved itself into a Committee of the Whole on the state of the Union, Mr. MASON of Virginia in the chair.

Mr. CAMBRELENG said, that it was his object to avoid debate on this question—if we were to have peace with them, which he sincerely hoped and expected, the less that was said the better—if war, the next Congress would have enough to say upon that great question. As to the first resolution he cared not for the form, provided the substance could be preserved, and the rights and honor of the country maintained. He would concur in any modification which the House might deem expedient. He should also, to secure unanimity, disembarrass the question of our relations with France, by relieving gentlemen from the miserable question concerning the Bank of the United States. His sole motive in introducing that subject was to show not only to this country, but to France, that if driven into a war, we had the means of carrying it on without recourse to taxes or loans. He proposed that the third resolution declaring that preparation ought to be made should be laid upon the table, as he designed to take a more effective course. He should offer an amendment to the fortification bill, when returned from the Senate, appropriating one million for the army and two millions for the navy, in case it should become necessary before the next meeting of Congress. This he understood would be all that was required by the executive branch of the government. With these modifications, he hoped the resolutions would meet the approbation of the House.

Mr. SPEIGHT called for the reading of the resolutions presented by the Commitee on Foreign Affairs, together with those submitted by the gentleman from Massachusetts, (Mr. Adams.)

The resolutions offered by Mr. CAMBRELENG, from the Committee on Foreign Affairs, were then read as follows:

Resolved, That it would be incompatible with the rights and honor of the United States further to negotiate in relation to the treaty entered into by France on the 4th of July, 1831, and that this House will insist upon its execution as ratified by both Governments.

Resolved, That the Committee on Foreign Affairs be discharged from the further consideration of so much of the President's Message as relates to commercial restrictions, or to reprisals on the commerce of France.

Resolved, That preparation ought to be made to meet any emergency growing out of our relations with France.

The substitute proposed by Mr. J. Q. ADAMS was then also read as follows:

"*Resolved*, That the rights of the citizens of the United States to the indemnity from the French Government, stipulated by the treaty of the 4th of July, 1831, ought in no event to be sacrificed, abandoned, or impaired by any consent or acquiescence of the Government of the United States.

2. That if the President of the United States should, during the interval before the next session of Congress deem it not incompatible with the honor and interest of the United States to resume the negotiations with the French Government, he be requested so to do.

3. That no legislative measure of a character or tendency hostile towards the French nation, is necessary or expedient at this time.

Mr. ADAMS said, he wished the resolutions to be taken up and considered seriatim.

The CHAIR (Mr. Mason) suggested that the latter mode would be for the gentleman to withdraw all but the first resolution for the present.

Mr. J. Q. ADAMS said, it was a matter of indifference to him what was the mode, so that action was had upon each of his resolutions. He did not wish to bring this Committee to a determination to vote *en masse* upon the resolutions of the Chairman of the Committee on Foreign Relations, or upon his own, and therefore, pursuant to the suggestion from the Chair, he would move his first resolution as a substitute for the first resolution of the gentleman from New York.

The CHAIR therefore informed the House, the question would be put in that form.

Mr. J. Q. ADAMS wished to state as briefly as he could, the reasons which urged him to present his own resolutions for adoption in preference to those reported from the majority of the Committee on Foreign Relations.

He objected to the first resolution, because he did not think the state of the country, and the relations existing between the United States and France were such as to make a declaration proper that no further negotiation should take place. Negotiation was the instrument of peace between nations, and it was unanimously acknowledged that the instant nations said they would no longer negotiate, the only alternative, compatible with the honor of nations, was war. He did not think; therefore, that negotiation ought to be foreclosed; much less did he think it proper for that House to declare that there should be no further negotiation on the subject. Why, negotiations implied no concession on the part of either House, and for that reason his resolution was drawn in such a manner as to declare in the most positive manner on the part of the House that no concession should be made upon this subject. (Mr. A. here quoted his first resolution.) Here then the ground was taken. Here was a declaration of peace to the world, that in reference to that treaty the United States would take nothing less than an absolute and complete fulfilment, as far as was possible in the nature of things to obtain it. To that determination he for one was willing to acquiesce, and he hoped that House was willing to acquiesce. And if such a determination should not be sufficient to effect a conciliation, and to preserve peace with France, he was willing also to take the hazard of war. He regarded the interest and the honor of the country at stake upon this question, and he would call upon gentlemen to reflect that the question was very different from what it was before the treaty was made. It was not a question whether your citizens were entitled to this indemnity, or whether they should receive it or not; it was a question whether this country would hold France to the sanctity and obligation of the treaty that had been made with her. It was also a totally different question from any that had ever existed upon this subject before the conclusion of the treaty. Before the conclusion of the treaty, these claims were unsettled and uncertain. The French Government had never admitted or recognised them. The amount was also uncertain. The treaty in fact was a compromise, and a most liberal compromise, although the President himself has told us that that indemnity or compensation was not adequate to the amount of the losses. Now when the indemnity was expressly stipulated by that department of the French Government, authorized by its constitution to make treaties, and to pledge the faith of the nation to all foreigners, the question for us was not whether we should get this amount of money in behalf of our fellow citizens, but whether we should suffer the nation that had made this treaty with us to violate it. This she would do if we did not take the right ground and assert what was just. There was now no question as to the justice of the claims, because the Government of France had admitted them. There was no question as to the amount, because that was admitted also. The only question was, whether you would hold a foreign nation to its engagements, whether those engagements were beneficial to you or not.

What would be the consequences if you gave it up? If you compromised to the value of a cent? Why, that every foreign nation would consider herself at liberty to sport with all treaties she might make with you. You would never have any security, and the most solemn pledges would be set at naught. Whatever engagements any foreign power might enter into, if it suited her interest she would feel herself authorized at any moment to set them at defiance.

This subject, as it was presented to Congress at the commencement of the session by the President of the United States, was also in an entirely different position from that in which it now stood. The President presented the subject to us, and recommended that in the event of the French legislative Chamber refusing, at their next session, to make the appropriation necessary to carry the treaty into effect, letters of reprisal should be issued. Mr. A. had before said in that House that whatever might be said of the imprudence of that recommendation, the opinion of mankind would ever be that it was high spirited and lofty, and such as became the individual from whom it emanated. He said it now, and he repeated, that it was the attitude which that Chief Magistrate would bear before the world, and before mankind, and before all posterity.

It has been supposed, that because Mr. A. had said that, that he was in favor of the measure recommended by the President; but he had explained at the time, most explicitly and distinctly, that he was not, and that he considered it as imprudent. Had he been one of the President's constitutional advisers, he should have recommended a different course, and yet, at this day, he did not know but that the counsel by which the President had been advised, would not be preferred. Mr. A. did not know but that he might ultimately be called upon, by circumstances, to recall even that opinion, that the measure was an imprudent one, for who could tell what the next despatch might contain? Some suppose that the President's Message would have the effect of preventing the appropriation of money from being made by the French Chamber. Others, however, supposed that it would ultimately effect it. Mr. A. was no prophet, and could not pretend to say what the effect of it would be, but he did say, that that which at first view appeared imprudent, was sometimes nothing more than becoming firmness and boldness. At that time he perceived there was a great strife between the two parties of this country, to whom, if the appropriation should be made by the French Chamber, the credit would be due. He found in a paper, well known to be friendly to the Administration, the Globe of that city, the following comment upon some recent news from France:

"A friend in New York writes us a letter of

congratulation on the prospects which the late news has opened on the country; and in conclusion, says: "'*The opposition seem confounded this morning; and even the most desperate in their ranks say the President has had the good fortune to take the right course in this matter. Chance has had no hand in it, my friend; it is parcel of his great, fair, and clear course.*'"

What says another paper of a different description, the National Intelligencer? "The complexion of the news from France is more and more favorable to the preservation of peaceful relations between that country and this; which, as we believe it to be now sincerely the desire of the discreet men of all parties in this country, will, we are persuaded, be universally acceptable to our readers. The latest date of papers which had reached France from America at the last accounts, was the 25th of December. The report of the Foreign Relations Committee of our Senate was made on the 6th January; and it was definitively acted upon on the 14th of the same month. "*We scarcely entertain a doubt that, on the arrival in Paris of authentic accounts of those proceedings, the bill of indemnity will be promptly acted upon, and the treaty carried into full effect.*"

Well, which of the parties was to have the "glory" of this appropriation, if it should be made? He, for one, was in the position of independence, "where Whigs were called Tory, and Tory called Whig." He could not help expressing his regret to the House, for which he had the strongest and profoundest feelings of respect and affection, that which ever of those two parties should attain that glory, of obtaining the appropriation of the money and the fulfilment of the treaty, we, (said Mr. A.) alas, must go without any share of it! We must content ourselves with clapping our hands, and shouting hosannas to the President of the United States for his bold and intrepid spirit, or to the Senate! He, Mr. A. had been for five or six weeks entreating that House to call upon their Committee on Foreign Relations to make a report; to take the subject up, and to deliberate upon it; and he could not help believing that if they had so taken up the subject, if it had so pleased them at an earlier period of the session to deliberate upon it, they too might have shared a little of the glory of obtaining that same appropriation; if, at all events, it should be obtained. But there they were, on the last days of the session, obliged to deliberate upon this subject with a crowd of other important business before them pressing for action, and upon which they must act. Permit him to say, this was to him a painful and melancholy circumstance, and was one of the reasons why he objected to another part of the resolutions of the chairman of the Committee on Foreign Relations, viz. "that this House will insist upon the execution of the treaty as ratified by both governments." Upon what could *that* House insist? In four days from that time, *that* House would be numbered with the dead, and that hall would be the property of their successors. And what could the present House do in the way of insisting upon the execution of the treaty, the fulfilment of which depended upon the action of a foreign government four thousand miles off? What could *that* House do? They would be followed by successors there, and many of the States would meet with heavy losses, in members of as pure hearts and as bright intellects—by which he did not mean to say that he always agreed with them—but, he would say, they were men of as pure hearts and as bright intellects as any that existed in this nation. How did they know what their successors would do? How did they know what their successors would insist upon? or what they would be disposed to concede? That part of the resolution of the gentleman from New York appeared to Mr. A., therefore, to be inconsistent, or to mean nothing. *That* House could insist upon nothing after its own term of service should expire. But the same idea which the gentleman had thus expressed was intended to be expressed by Mr. A. in that resolution which says "that the rights of the citizens of the United States to the indemnity, &c. ought, in no event, to be sacrificed, abandoned, or impaired, by any consent, or acquiescense of the Government of the United States."

It was, therefore, upon these two grounds that he objected to the first resolution of the gentleman from New York. The first was, that it foreclosed all negotiation. The second, because it asserted something that seemed to him to imply that *that* House would have a power to act on the subject; it went to pledge that House, when every one knew that *that* House was entirely inadequate to act upon it.

A word more upon the propriety of negotiation, for although he had offered the first resolution only as a substitute for the one proposed by the gentleman from New York, the second resolution of Mr. A. not only did not countenance the idea of excluding all negociation; but it proposed to recommend to the President of the United States, always in the event of his not deeming it incompatible with the honor and interests of the country, to resume negotiation. Mr. A. would adhere and cling to the idea of negociation, because, as he remarked before, negotiation was the only way by which peace could be preserved and maintained. Let him say, that his second resolution was drawn with that official respect which was due to the Chief Magistrate of the country. And with that sentiment at the bottom of his heart, and which he had expressed with respect to the President's recommendation of reprisals, let him say that one idea of proposing his second resolution, was because he thought the President himself had expressed himself rather too unfavorably of the continuance of negotiation. Mr. A. thought the Chief Magistrate of this country ought never to say, he would not negotiate with a foreign nation. But events had occurred since that message, which, in Mr. A.'s opinion, rendered it further necessary that the House should express its opinion upon this subject; he alluded particularly to the correspondence presented a few days ago. It was natural enough that a great excitement should ensue upon the reception of the President's threat of reprisals in France. The King of the French did not, however, appear to be dissatisfied with it at all. He was only dissatisfied with the language used towards his Minister; because in the message it was strongly intimated that the Minister had not done that which he had promised to do, viz: to bring the subject before the Chamber of Deputies at their first meeting, and in time for the result of their deliberations to be known before the assembling of Congress. It was alleged he had promised this, and had not done it; and it was upon this reproach, personal to himself, the King of the French took fire. Mr A. here made sundry references to the despatches of Mr. Livingston and the conferences held by him with Admiral de Rigny, the Minister for Foreign Affairs, and said, the affair seemed something of the character of a petty pique between the President of the United States and the King of the French.

Mr. A. said he was somewhat alarmed when he saw it stated in the public papers that Mr. Livingston had quitted France, because if we should come to blows, France would say that we were the first to strike. A Minister must always remain till he received an order for his departure, either from his own Government, or from that to which he is sent. To go to war now would be like two boys standing before each other with clenched fists, and each daring the other to strike. If we did go to war with France upon this subject, his word for it, it would all end in an expenditure of millions upon millions of treasure, and oceans of blood, and we should then be asking each other who struck the first blow. Mr. A. further remarked on the impolicy of sending a frigate for Mr. Livingston, which, he maintained, would be considered in the light of a declaration of hostilities by France. He said he should not be at all surprised if the French Government detained her. Mr. A. concluded by remarking that he had not said one tenth part of what the subject would suggest to him, but at this late period of the session he would not trespass upon the House at greater length.

Mr. ARCHER was opposed to both the resolutions, concerning the effect of each would be the same as that of breaking off all further negotiation. The resolutions of the Chairman of the Committee on Foreign Relations, Mr. A. regarded in the light of a menace as much as the message of the President of the United States at the commencement of the session, threatening France with reprisals. Still he thought these resolutions more consistent than those of the gentleman from Massachusetts, because they were more open. Was the country prepared for so determined a measure? Would the circumstance justify it? What would be the effects? These were questions that every man should put to himself. Mr. A. referred to the naval power of France. She had 301 vessels of war, including 44 ships of the line, 40 frigates, and a very large number of steam war vessels. Contrast this with the condition of the American navy. He had conversed with many naval officers, who had assured him that a war on the ocean with France would be far more hazardous than with England, monarch of the sea as she called herself. She had besides, an army of four hundred thousand men, in the finest state of discipline, and kept ready for action at almost a moment's warning. But what could we promise ourselves by going to war? Could we subdue France? He would not conceive a war with France, though the gentleman from Massachusetts seemed to say that the President's instructions to Mr. Livingston amounted to a declaration of war.

Mr. J. Q. ADAMS explained.

Mr. ARCHER resumed, by showing the great sacrifice to trade and commerce by non-intercourse. The exports and imports to France, each averaged about fourteen millions of dollars annually, all of which would be destroyed, besides jeoparding all our other foreign trade. A declaration of war, he would admit, would not destroy this trade, but it would throw it into the hands of two countries, possessing a large commercial marine, England and Holland. In ports where whole forests of American masts were now seen there would be scarcely a single ship owned by native Americans.

If we declared that we would have no further negotiation, coupled with the recal of our minister, it would be tantamount to a declaration of war. And for what? For what was considered almost a desperate debt of five millions, most of which had been long ago transferred from the original creditor at some two or three shillings in the pound. Were two ancient allies to bring upon themselves all the dreadful and horrible consequences of a war, a war that for consequences and dire calamities would be unequaled in the page of history, upon so paltry a ground. The case was disproportionate with the effects, and had no prototype in the whole annals of the civilized world. It would be quixotic, and even romance scarcely presented a precedent, unless that of Sir Lucius O'Trigger. We were going to plunge into a war, not only with the greatest power in the world, but with one also, with which we were united by long bonds of friendship, to sustain the national glory and honor? No; for the payment of a paltry sum of money, two-thirds of which the opposite party were willing at once to pay. It was ironically said that "discretion was the better part of valor," but it did not thence follow that rashness was the best proof of it. If a giant struck him, was he to rush upon him in return, when he was certain to be crushed to atoms? He denied that national honor was yet involved in the question, and if it was, could it be best maintained by bravado, violence, and intemperance?

Mr. A. then maintained that the treaty was incomplete, because all the forms required under the French charter had not been complied with. The constitution of the United States vested the treaty making power in the Executive, but if he made a treaty involving an appropriation, it would be invalid till passed in the House of Representatives of Congress. All appropriations must emanate from the popular branch of the Government, and the same was the case in France. The Representatives of the People held the purse strings. Suppose the President of the United States made a treaty, and that treaty involved an appropriation, and that House refused to pass the bill for the purpose, would there be any breach of national faith? None. But he would say, he had

rather that not only five millions, but five hundred millions should be sacrificed, rather than plunge the country into the calamities that must inevitably ensue from the course he reprobated

Mr. A. said he had just been informed that advices had arrived to-day, from France, which gave strength to the hope heretofore entertained that our affairs in the French Chambers had resulted favorably. He would ask the gentleman from New York, if, under such circumstances, he would deem his resolution either expedient or politic? The gentleman from Massachusetts said something about fear.

Mr. J. Q. ADAMS remarked, that the whole of the gentleman's argument was fear.

Mr. ARCHER admitted it. He feared the dire calamities that would fall upon us, by adopting the course recommended in both series of the resolutions presented that morning.

Mr. CAMBRELENG said, as the gentleman had referred to some recent advices, he should be glad to be informed of their purport.

Mr. ARCHER understood the project of a law presented by the Minister of Finance to the French Chambers had been referred to the Bureau, or Standing Committee of the Chamber.

Mr. A. then alluded to the reference often made by nations to neutral powers, when questions of territory &c. were involved, in proof that this subject might also, without infringing on national honor, be in a like manner disposed of. What had we to fear from negotiation or to arbitry? Nothing. He believed we should lose no portion of the money, but on the contrary, he should expect a great deal more would be asked and obtained. He wanted France and the world to see that nothing had been left undone on our part to prevent a resort to arms; and that if we were forced to it, we should go into it with clean hands. He applauded the spirit of the gentleman from Massachusetts; and if that gentleman thought the national honor insulted, Mr. A. admired that spirit; but he denied that the occasion called for it. We were not to drench the country with oceans of blood, because the autocrat of our country had a spirit which might become him. Mr. A. came there not to exalt the honor of that individual, but to protect the interests of his constituents and of the country at large. Mr. A. concluded by offering the following amendment to the amendment of Mr. Adams:

Resolved, That in the just expectation that the Government of France will have made provision, or will make provision for carrying into effect the stipulations of the treaty of indemnity with that Government of the 4th of July, 1831, this House will forbear at the present time to adopt any measure in relation to that subject

Mr. PICKENS opposed both the resolutions with considerable animation.

Mr. PATTON addressed the House at considerable length in reply to Messrs. ARCHER and PICKENS, and gave the views which had governed him in relation to this subject, both in the Committee on Foreign Affairs, (of which he was a member,) and in the House. He did not fully concur in all points with either of the series of resolutions. Mr. P. read a resolution which he had prepared on the subject, with a view of offering it to the House. It would be seen that it was declarative of the validity of our claim, and preserved the principles advocated by the gentleman from Massachusetts. It was also, he thought, touched in as strong terms as that gentleman should require.

[The great length of Mr. PATTON's remarks precludes even a synopsis; but we hope to give them at length as soon as they can be prepared.]

Mr. BOULDIN said he had a few remarks to make on the subject He said it was not his intention nor had it been his habit to trespass long on the time of the House. He wished to hear what were the views of every member, and supposed that every member wished to understand the opinion and feelings of every one on the floor upon a subject of such magnitude. He would not at any time trespass on the patience of the House, much less would he at this time, looking to the magnitude of this question, and the great press of other business that must be done in the short time left of this session. He thought there was but one question before this House and this nation in relation to this subject, that was to be determined at this time. The question whether the debt secured by this treaty to be paid would be abandoned or insisted on; other questions had been suggested in France and in this country, but no other questions had been made here. The President had advised means under certain contingences. But no other question had been raised by the constituted authorities of this country but this, Shall the debt be abandoned or not? He said this was a very material question to be decided The debates in the French Chamber of Deputies showed that much reliance was placed on the belief that this country would not insist in the last event upon the payment of this money. It was, in his opinion, a very natural inquiry and was the anxious inquiry of this Country and France. He said it was fit that we should answer to it. If we abandoned the claim, there was an end to it. If we did not, the mode and time of asserting our rights was with ourselves. He said he had listened with much pleasure and interest to his colleague, (Mr. Archer,) and had been at a loss to determine what was the conclusion of which he several times spoke, that he would come to. He said he understood him at last to come to the conclusion that the treaty was not obligatory. For this he gives two reasons First, that until the vote of the Chambers was had, making appropriations for the payment, the treaty was not final. Upon this point he would say nothing. His colleague, (Mr. Patton,) had answered to that fully—perfectly. Indeed the gentlemen's argument on that point, if it proved any thing, would prove that, there was no obligation on the part of the Government to pay any officer for services already rendered, until this House shall vote an appropriation. Secondly: My colleague thought we had been precipitate, too hasty. What did he think was hasty? Rather, what did he think reasonable time to negotiate? A quarter of a century he thought not long enough—would he say how long would be long enough—would one hundred and twenty-five years be long enough? Mr. B. said he was willing, if we had acted hasty, to withdraw—negotiate again. But before he entered again into a settlement, he wished to know how we would do. It was not a claim of the Government (which he said he wished might live forever.) It was the claim of individuals, most of whom, he said, were dead and gone, and most of their descendants likewise. If we wait much longer, we shall also be dead and gone; then he supposed there would be an end of the matter so far as we are concerned at least. Mr. B's. colleague said, if we had waited longer we could have done much better—get much more. Mr. B. said he wished to be serious, and was so, but his colleague reminded him of a case (he would not give the names) he knew of. An old gentleman had a daughter who remained single till she was forty five, when she then thought proper to marry, and did so—her father objecting to the match, said, if Peggy had not been in such a hurry she might have done very well. The gentleman asks if we really would go to war for five millions of dollars. Many a suit is brought when the cost is more than the demand—will a man fight if you spit in his face? Suppose the case of my colleague—but the case is not supposable. Yet if it were supposable—and should a man spit in the face of my colleague, would he wash his face and say it was not worth resenting? In such a case it would generally be cheapest with most; if they would wash it off, and be cleaner than they were before. In almost every case it would be best, but for one thing—the next neighbor standing by and seeing we had submitted to that would do another and a much greater indignity to us when it served his turn to do so. We were reminded in the French Chambers that we had taken the like from others, why not from them? He said that he agreed with the gentleman from Massachusetts (Mr. Adams) that his colleague's argument was made up of fear. Did his colleague read the debates in the French Chambers, and did he not see that the most talented men in the opposition then relied mainly that we were a money-loving, money-getting People, and would never spend one hundred millions to obtain five? He knew it was all a fetch, (he asked his colleague's pardon.) He knew there was no fear in him.

The French and his colleague, he thought, were both mistaken. He said he heard with pleasure and pride for his country and his colleague, when he spoke of our commerce, covering with unnumbered millions every sea. He asked if we obtained that commerce or the protection of it, by fear? By arguments, such as his colleague had advanced? We had a name in the world, as a nation, of which every American was proud. We had a respect in the eye of all nations, which had not failed to be acknowledged by them. Did we acquire this by arguments and practices bottomed on considerations of fear? When we were acquiring this, did we show to the world that we regarded more our personal security than our rights and our honor? Did we then consider whether our ducks or our barns were in danger? Far from it. Did the gentleman himself—and he says he thinks the nation's honor is his own honor, and would defend and maintain them both by the same means—when he was acquiring that respect and esteem which he so securely maintains in the bosoms of his friends and his colleagues, act from feelings and arguments, such as those he now advances?

When we receive an injury and resist it—if we get a bloody nose, our adversary is likely to get one also It is well for both to value this. Did the gentleman read the debates in the French Chambers? Are not the very same arguments put into our mouths there? If we refuse to defend our rights and bring the whole to a calculation of dollars and cents, will not all nations deal with us accordingly? We have exacted from other nations payment and received it for similar injuries. We persuaded them we would enforce our claims to justice, and they believed it. If now, after all that, when it comes to the trial, and we have liquidated the claim and taken the bond, and payment is refused, we do not cause our rights to be respected, what may we expect? Clearly that those who have been compelled to pay will say, you bullied us out of it, but when it came to the point with the French, you gave it up; therefore, to be equal, you must pay us back with interest; if you do not, we will go on the high seas—we will shoot your ducks, we will burn your barns, and do worse with you than the French would have done. He said he would repeat the question, shall we give up the money, or insist on the payment of it? This is no uncommon case, after dealing of twenty years standing, upon settlement and bond taken, if any thing is said about suit for the money, that the statute of limitation, usury, and gambling, extortion, or some other plea or bill of injunction is threatened. But the creditor has only to decide whether he will give up the debt or not. A man talks and shuffles with you for 25 years, and at last gives his bond—waits four or five years, and when you call on him for the money, proposes to settle again—draws some nice distinction, admitting the obligation of treaties and bonds, and the authorities of agents to make settlements, but denying the obligation to pay the money. Sir, is not this trifling with a man? Sir, said Mr. B., no more negotiation about this debt. I had rather give it up—the debt—than negotiate again. Sir, when that same France was ground into the dust (justly or unjustly) for peace sake—for love's sake—for gratitude—for past kindness, if not friendship—we forebore, and said to her, "We will not press you now; others we will compel to pay, (we said, by our actions,) but *you*, we will not urge just now; we will settle with you in your own time." And she had settled in her own time—taken her own time of payment. Much was said in those debates in the French Chamber of Deputies about friendship and gratitude, &c They seem to think that the fable of the husbandman and viper would apply to us. He had found a viper frozen, and took him to his bosom, and warmed him into life; the ungrateful viper then bit his benefactor. They spoke of us as foundlings—as some child that has been cast away by its mother—or, being lost, they had found it! Sir, they sit in their Chamber, and we

sit here. I wish to have no words of abuse with them. I, like my colleague, (Mr. Archer,) do not like to hear abuse, or to give it. I wish you distinctly, Mr. Chairman, to understand that I do not deal in abuse towards any individual, or any nation. I want to hear no abuse; and I have heard full as much praise of foreign nations as I want to hear. As much has been said about love, and affection, and gratitude, and obligations, too, between us and the French, as there is any truth in. I want to hear no more about love, and friendship, and gratitude. All I want to hear, and, I am persuaded, all the nation wishes to hear at this time, is, whether we mean to hold on upon the treaty, or give it up. If, then, we give it up, all is done. If we do not give it up, what follows? I do not know. That is the point before us. It is not what the French wish to know, or have the right to require us to tell them. With the greatest possible respect for the feelings and opinions of others, I think it is pusilanimous to be always settling, settling, and resettling.

I do not think it would be dishonorable to give up the debt. I never heard that it was humiliating to give up a debt. The creditor has the right, and no one has the right to complain but the debtor; and I never heard of his taking exceptions. But it is childish to be always settling and unsettling and threatening. I would rather give up the whole, if it be as the gentleman supposes, ten times as much, than be always disputing and quarrelling about it. Perhaps the most dignified position we could assume would be to give it up, and pay the private claims to that amount. It is certainly the cheapest. If the nation is willing I should be willing, I believe my constituents would be. I believe they know the wisdom and necessity of attending to their interest as well as their honor. But I believe they would be willing if all were willing, to give up the claim rather than break the peace between the two countries. Perhaps if we were to return them their bond, and say we have been settling for twenty-five years, and you now refuse to pay after settling even one tenth of what you really owed us; we will hereafter have just as much to do with you as suits our inclinations, and no more than we can well avoid. This might be thought the most independent course by all the world. I know but one objection to this. The claim did not originate in contract, but in violence, and for peace, love, gratitude, and friendship, we have agreed to take money as a satisfaction. I have no idea that such will be the course, and do not mean to advise it, nor do I much fear that war will be the consequence of insisting on a compliance with the treaty. I think the only material question we have to respond to, is the question before stated. Will we give up the money or not? I think any of the resolutions answer sufficiently except those of my colleague, (Mr. Archer) who seems to think we could make something by a new settlement. I cannot agree to that. If they will not comply with this settlement they would not certainly, if we brought them more in debt.

I like rather the resolutions of the highly esteemed and very distinguished gentleman from Massachusetts, (Mr. Adams.) I have no objection even to his second resolution—to give the President discretion to negotiate further with France, if he should think the honor of the nation would not be, in any manner, compromited or sacrificed. If we do not think the President has acted with entire prudence, (and I am not unwilling to admit that I think he has not,) and if some of us do not love him as well as we might, and have not all the confidence that others have, still he is the only organ through which we can constitutionally treat with any nation, in peace or war. It seems admitted by all, unless it might be the Chairman of the Committee on Foreign Affairs, that we ought to have some means in peace to preserve peace, and in war to make peace. This second resolution, therefore, seems distinctly to say to all the world, that however we may differ in degree of personal regard for, or confidence in, the President, still he is our President, and we mean to sustain our own honor and our own institutions, through him, the only constitutional organ for that purpose. Let France see she has no ground to hope to profit by our party provisions.

In saying this, and agreeing to this resolution, I cannot feel what my colleague (Mr. Archer) says we must feel—crouching, yielding, bending the knee, to the President—or to the French Chambers, which seems to me to be more plausible. Simply to say, we will expect the money to be paid, and that we will take our own time and means to obtain it, seems to me to be neither yielding, nor submitting, nor crouching, to France, or the President, or any body in the world. Whether the advice given by the President will be taken, is for after consideration. We have no time to deliberate or act on it now. Whether his message has been prudent or imprudent, wise or unwise, will be determined, like most other things, by the event. Obstinacy, if the thing turn out well, would be firmness; if it turned out ill, it would still be called obstinacy. That which would be rashness, if it turned out ill, would be boldness, nay, wisdom itself, if the event be fortunate. No, sir, said Mr. B., I feel not crouching or humiliation for myself or my country, in this course. I have no severe strictures to make, nor do I think it necessary to add any thing to what the gentleman from Massachusetts (Mr. Adams) has said in relation to the Chief Magistrate. Mr. Chairman, I have said at least four times as much as I at first intended, and will ask pardon of the committee for having detained them so long, and say no more.

Mr. CAMBRELENG said that at the commencement of the debate he had, to avoid discussion, stated, that if we were to remain at peace with France, he thought the less we said upon the subject the better. He sincerely hoped and expected, that the relations between the two countries would not be disturbed; but gentlemen had discussed the question as if we were now on the eve of war. Before he sat down, he should propose some modifications of the resolutions which he hoped would meet the concurrence of the House on all sides. He would cheerfully submit them without further debate, but for the extraordinary arguments of the gentleman from Virginia, (Mr. Archer,) who has addressed the House at length, and which rendered a reply indispensably necessary.

Before he proceeded to reply to the gentleman from Virginia, he would explain as to the resolution proposed by the Committee. That part of it relating to negotiation, he had not proposed—on the other hand, he had himself doubts of the propriety of interferring with the duties of the Executive. But there were members who would not vote for the resolution without that portion relating to further negotiation, and as the minority of the Committee would not vote with him for a modification, he was compelled to report that or none. He hoped, however, that in the House we should have better success.

The gentleman from Virginia, (Mr. Archer,) and he believed the gentleman from South Carolina, (Mr. Pickens,) had both alluded to the right of the Chamber to refuse the appropriation. It had been stated that Mr. Rives was perfectly aware, when making the treaty, that the question must be submitted to the Chamber, and that, therefore, it could not be complete till it had received its sanction.

On this point, very great injustice had been done that distinguished gentleman, (Mr. Rives,) not only here but elsewhere. In a document laid upon our tables—a document to which he was not permitted otherwise to refer—he meant the Report of the Committee on Foreign Relations of the Senate—manifest injustice had been done to our late minister to France. In that report, it is stated that Mr. Rives was aware that the treaty must be submitted to the Chamber, and to sustain that position, the report gives from Mr. R.'s letter to the Secretary of State, detailing a conversation with the French minister, that portion of it relating to what the letter said upon this subject. But by an extraordinary oversight, the committee had suppressed the next paragraph in the same letter—a suppression which had been most successfully exposed by an opposition editor.

In that suppressed paragraph, Mr. Rives says to the Secretary of State, that in reply to the French Minister, he repelled the idea that the Chamber had any thing to do with the treaty-making power; that that power, by the French constitution, was in the King exclusively, and that the French Minister assented to the propriety of his suggestions. It is, said Mr. C., extraordinary, sir, that so pregnant a paragraph should have escaped the attention of the committee of the Senate, following as it did the passage quoted in their report. Mr. Rives never disputed the power of the Chamber to reject an appropriation, but the right of the Chamber is another question. If it be a right, sir, it is one never to be exercised but in the case of a gross and palpable usurpation on the part of the King. It is one never to be exercised on a paltry question of a few millions of francs, but only in great emergencies, involving the question of peace or war. If it be in any sense a right, I trust it is one which will never be enforced in this House; for it is at best but a right to violate the public faith, and to abrogate the solemn obligations of a treaty; a right to disgrace your country.

The gentleman from Virginia thought it extraordinary that we should go to war upon a question of claims. In all the history of war he had never known one for a cause like this. I had not expected such a declaration from a gentleman of his intelligence. [Mr. A. did not mean to be so understood.] What, sir, was our war, which we made, though not declared, against France in 1798—was it not for her depredations on our commerce? What was the war against England in 1812, but for her captures under her orders in council? If we make war for spoliations on our commerce, are we not authorized to do so, when, after five and twenty years negotiation, a treaty founded upon such wrongs, is violated? Wrongs too, which would have compelled us to meet the decrees of France with a declaration of war, had we not been, in 1812, forced to decide whether we should declare war against France or England, for both had violated our national rights, and the law of nations. France had not only violated public law, but the obligations of the treaty of 1800.

The gentleman from Virginia (Mr. Archer) has given us a fallacious argument to alarm our fears of the consequences to result from encountering so formidable a naval power as France is at this time. Such opinions from so respectable a source, are calculated to make an erroneous impression both at home and abroad. The gentleman has furnished us with a statistical table of the number of ships of war of each class belonging to the French navy. The naval power of a nation is not, sir, to be measured by the number of its vessels of war—it is a fallacious standard. It must be measured by the foundation on which naval power rests, the extent and character of its commercial marine. No nation possesses so powerful and effective a commercial marine as the United States, animated and invigorated, as it is, by the spirit of freedom.

The gentleman from Virginia may deceive himself, but France knows our naval strength, and England too; and if our national rights are maintained here, as they ought to be, in a spirit corresponding with the extent of our naval resources, neither France nor England will ever be willing to engage in a war with us. But according to the argument of the gentleman, we are to be overwhelmed with some thirty or forty ships of the line. Sir, the ten thousand mariners whom we have now engaged in the whale trade—that "dreadful trade"—are alone sufficient to sweep from the ocean the whole naval power of France. Our mariners employed in the fisheries on our coast and on the banks, are able of themselves to contend successfully with any naval power existing. The naval resources of France may be great in ships and in her gallant officers—whose daring bravery no nation will dispute—but ships and officers are powerless without a well disciplined and extensive commercial marine; and nations the most commercial must ever be the most powerful on the ocean. In a war with us, France can derive no aid from her army though it were equal to that formidable force which crossed the Niemen in 1812. The war, if there be one, will be on the ocean. We have the materials ready for

CONTINUED IN NEXT NUMBER.

CONGRESSIONAL GLOBE.

BY BLAIR & RIVES. ————WEEKLY———— PRICE $1 A SESSION.

2d Sess.......23d Cong. FRIDAY, MARCH 6, 1835. Volume 2.......No. 20.

HOUSE OF REPRESENTATIVES.
Saturday, February 28, 1835.
Continued from last number.

a immense navy—we have a commercial marine, always ready to avenge our wrongs, and we could not afloat in twelve months a naval force with which no nation could successfully contend. I do not say this, sir, because I anticipate war with France—heaven forbid that the peace between the two nations should ever be disturbed—both nations have every motive to cherish it; and I am sure it never will be sacrificed for five and twenty millions of francs. But, sir, the extraordinary movements of the gentleman from Virginia has compelled me to dissipate the unfounded apprehensions they were calculated to excite and which ought to do us an injury abroad. We have nothing to fear from any nation, come the contest when it may.

The gentleman has referred to the opinions expressed by our officers as to the great superiority and discipline of the French navy at the present time. Modesty, sir, is the characteristic of a brave man—our officers will never underrate those who are, or those who may be, their antagonists. But the opinions of our officers can never sweep away our commercial marine, and while we have that, we shall never concede superiority to any naval power. France, has too another powerful motive for not willingly engaging in a war with us. If she should attempt to interrupt the commerce between this country and Great Britain, or to interfere with British vessels trading between the United States and any part of the world—if she should venture to trespass on our neutrality, England would soon be a party in the war.

We mean, sir, to have no war with France—we mean to avoid it—to do so effectually, we must meet the crisis fearlessly, and maintain our national rights with dignity—adopt that as your rule of conduct in your relations with foreign nations, and you will command the respect of the world, and together with our isolated position avoid war for a century to come. France, sir, will, herself, respect us the more for maintaining our rights with spirit and firmness. Gentlemen who entertained a different opinion must pardon him for really dissenting from the policy adopted by the Senate. A persuasive tone is not the one which will ever obtain indemnity from any nation. The tone of the Message justly responded by the gentleman from Massachusetts, (Mr. Adams) is that which has commanded the respect of France as it ought to have done, and the applause of nations. France respects us because we respect ourselves. For the first time the French Chamber is awakened to the true character of the question. Hitherto it has been trifled away, trifled with, and lost sight of, amidst the struggles for power among the various parties in that body—they never looked abroad. Now, it has become a great national question, in which the honor and welfare of the nation is involved, and the measure will no longer be sacrificed to gratify the spirit of party. If it be denied, it will be because both Houses did not, at an early period of the session, respond to the tone of the message, not by adopting measures of resentment at once, but by doing what we are now about to do, exhibiting a firm determination to sustain the rights and honor of the nation, should the obligations of the treaty be not fulfilled. But, sir, I believe the appropriation will have been, it will be made. The composition of the Chamber differs from this body and the House of Commons. The privilege of voting in France is limited to 160,000 voters, and the Deputies represent more fully the commercial and manufacturing interests of France, having a deep interest in the question—it is essentially a body representing the cities and towns of France. Such representatives will surely not sacrifice the great interests of their constituents, to gratify party

revenge, and in a case where France is clearly in the wrong. But whatever France may do, let us do our duty, and without desiring or anticipating the worst, let us be prepared for it.

I regret sir, that I have been compelled to engage in this debate, contrary to my wish or design; for I anticipate, and sincerely desire nothing but peace between the two great nations. I will now, sir, adopt, in the form of a resolution, a sentiment which I found this morning in the report of the minority of the Committee on Foreign Affairs. Had such a resolution been proposed in the Committee by either of the gentlemen who signed that document, it would have been, with perhaps one exception, unanimously supported. We were always ready to declare that "the treaty of the 4th of July, 1831, should be maintained, and its execution insisted on at all hazards." I unite with them most cordially in the sentiment; and I hope the gentleman from Massachusetts will accept it, as a substitute for his. The first and third resolution will then be abandoned—and I trust that this resolution, with the second, will be adopted with unanimity.

The resolution was then read, and placed in the order of proceedings, in lieu of the amendment originally offered by Mr. Adams. It is as follows:

Resolved, That in the opinion of this House the treaty of the 4th of July 1831, should be maintained and its execution insisted on, at all hazards.

Mr. ARCHER then said, he would withdraw his resolution and adopt that of his colleague, (Mr. Patton,) if the gentleman from Massachusetts (Mr. Adams) would also adopt it.

Mr. ADAMS replied: That he could not take the course indicated in the suggestion of the gentleman from Virginia. He was perfectly willing to accept that of the Chairman of the Committee on Foreign Affairs as a substitute for his own. He had the other day, asked his colleague (Mr. Everett) if his report concluded with resolutions; and, if he had received an affirmative answer to this inquiry, it was not his intention to have offered that which was now on the table. He considered the resolution now proposed for his adoption, by the Chairman of the Committee on Foreign Affairs, (Mr. Cambreleng,) as expressing all that was expressed by his own, and a little more. The difference consisted in this, that his resolution declared that the indemnity secured by the treaty of 1831, should *in no case* be abandoned. The one he now adopted, declared that it should be secured *at all hazards!* He was perfectly willing to adopt that language.

Mr. BURGES contended that the Househshould do nothing which was calculated to throw embarrassment in the way of an amicable adjustment of the question. This House was on the eve of a political dissolution. It could do nothing efficient. It might pass resolutions; but if war was necessary, it did not possess the power, or could not at this late period carry out such a measure Under the circumstances, he thought the members of this House should not throw any embarrassment in the way of their successors. He was pleased with the last resolution of the gentleman from New York, (Mr. Cambreleng,) in some respects. It contained no threat, and every individual in the land would insist upon having the treaty carried into effect as it was,—no person would submit to a reduction of the sum, and it might with propriety, be insisted that it should be increased.

Mr. B. was sorry that the question of war had been discussed upon this occasion. He referred to the maritime force and power of the two nations, and the detriment, to the commerce of the United States which would result from such a war. He thought the House should be extremely cautious in its action upon a question which might result in war. He adverted to the ground of dispute with France. It involved a question of money only, and no case could be cited where a christian nation had went to war merely for plun-

der. He insisted that there was much more cause for war on account of the bad faith and treatment which had originated the controversy with France, than in a refusal to pay the sum of money which was stipulated to be paid us. He thought, that after the United States passed over the insults of France, we should be deeply and ingloriously disgraced by going to war, merely because France would not pay us a sum of money for accumulated wrongs.

Mr. B. entered, at some length, into a history of the difficulties with France, and contended that there existed no just cause of war. The present aspect of the controversy seemed to him to be a mere question of etiquette between the President, and the French King, and the Foreign Minister of this Government, and the Minister of State of France.

In conclusion, Mr. B. said, the House might pass any resolution it choosed. He should not object, unless it was implied that if France did not pay the money, we would go to war. The resolution before the House declared that the treaty should be maintained *at all hazards.* There were but few things which should be maintained *at all hazards.* What were they? Was a mere question of money one? Certainly not. He viewed such a declaration on our part tantamount to saying that we would demand this sum, if refused, through war. France would be cowardly indeed if she should pay the money under such circumstances.

Mr. COULTER felt much gratified that the gentleman from New York, (Mr. Cambreleng,) had offered a modification of the first and had consented to waive the third resolution. This step was calculated to conciliate and ensure unanimity of action, which was so desirable on this occasion. He was opposed to the third resolution because it supposed a rupture with France, and amounted to nothing If the supposition was correct, the resolution should go farther, and some efficient measure should be adopted for putting the country in a state of defence. As, however, this resolution was abandoned, he was willing to vote for the modified resolution of the Chairman of the Committee on Foreign Affairs, (Mr. Cambreleng,) and he would do this with cheerfulness, because the concluding sentence of the resolution was the same language used in the closing paragraph of the report of the minority of the Committee on Foreign Affairs.

Mr. C. felt no apprehension from the phantoms of the member from Rhode Island, (Mr. Burges.) The amount stipulated to be paid by France to American citizens was justly due. Could the American Government, in good faith to her citizens, ever negotiate again with France on this subject? Would France or the Chamber of Deputies ever agree to pay a larger sum? It had been contended in the French Chambers, that this sum should be reduced and cut down. This could not be done. We must insist upon the execution of the treaty as it is. How was this to be done? We must proclaim and insist upon it, from the good faith of France; and if this consideration would not answer the execution of the treaty, we must resort to commercial restrictions. It was useless to open a new negotiation, after the failure to execute an engagement solemnly entered into under the great seal of France. How could the Government approach and ask of the King a renewal of this negotiation, when by his own admission and acknowledgement, the sum stipulated in a former treaty, was justly due to the citizens of this Government? We should certainly encounter no great hazard by insisting on the payment of a sum of money admitted to be justly due us. France would hardly, upon such a pretence seize upon our commercial marine or mulct our fleet in the Mediterranean. She would scarcely go to war upon any such frivolous consideration.

Mr. C. said there two ways in which our just claims might be prejudiced, The first was by

pursuing a vehement and rash line of conduct, and the other by adopting a tame passive and quiescent course, and submitting to every thing. We must either come up to the circumstance of the case or lag behind them. We had carried our part of this treaty into effect. France had not. Why then should we refrain from an expression of a decided opinion on the subject? Should this House evade, should it lag behind the question? Since the power of France had been urged as persuasions against our acting, he, for one, was disposed, with more alacrity than before to meet the question, and to act firmly and decisively. He was the last man who would be disposed causelessly to jeopard the peace of the country. He was still in favor of a middle course. He wished to come up to the crisis—to meet it fully; but he was not in favor of either going a-head, or of remaining behind the crisis.

Various questions had been mooted in the course of the debate, which were not necessarily involved in the subject before the House. The question was not, whether or not we should go to war. It was certainly not just cause of censure, that we should insist upon the payment of a claim which was admitted by the high functionaries of France. After adverting to the position in which France would place herself in the eyes of civilized Europe by a refusal to comply with the stipulations of the treaty, and the stain which she would thereby inflict upon her national power, &c. Mr. C. concluded, by expressing a hope, that the resolution proposed by the gentleman from New York would prevail.

Mr. CHILTON said, that if the three last words of the modified resolution, to wit, "at all hazards," were stricken out, he, and many of those around him, would support the resolution. He hoped that the resolution would be thus modified.

Mr. J. Q. ADAMS said, he could not accept the amendment proposed by the gentleman last up. It was for the sake of harmony and unanimity that he had consented to accept the modification of the gentleman from New York (Mr. Cambreleng.) He now rose to say, that if the resolution as modified was not acceptable to a majority, he would move that the question be taken on his resolution as originally proposed. He stated the difference between the two propositions. The resolution of the gentleman from New York perfectly accorded with his feelings. His own proposition was, however, less harsh in its terms.

Mr. E. EVERETT said, he understood that an express had just arrived in the city, which probably brought additional intelligence from France. He thought the House had better take a recess until seven o'clock, (it being then after 6 o'clock, P. M.) He moved that the Committee rise for this purpose; which was agreed to—yeas 87, nays 82.

The Committee then rose.

[The foregoing embraces only an outline of the debate, which occupied the House from 11 o'clock A. M. to half past 6 P. M.]

Mr. E EVERETT moved that the House take recess until seven o'clock.

A motion was then made to adjourn, but withdrawn at the request of the SPEAKER, who laid before the House the following letter from Mr. EWING of Indiana:

WASHINGTON CITY, }
February 28th, 1835. }

To the Speaker of the House of Representatives:

SIR: My situation compels me to apologize to the House, and through you, to my constituents, for my absence from my seat. While on my way to my boarding house, after the adjournment on the evening of the 26th last. I was way-laid, and assaulted in the most outrageous and dastardly manner, by John F. Lane, a Lieutenant in the army and son of the Hon. A. Lane, of Indiana, for no other known cause than for words spoken in debate some weeks since, in reply to his father on the floor of the House of Representatives.

I had but a casual acquaintance with the person who committed this outrage, and no intercourse whatever with him to lead to this assault. A blow from an iron cane, with a leaden head, &c. companied the first notice of his intention to attack me, and was repeated by several others, with

a violence which I regret to say, at this important and pressing period of the session, has entirely disabled me from taking my seat.

I have the honor to be, sir, your obedient servant,

(Signed)   JNO. EWING.

Mr. HIESTER moved to lay the communication on the table.

Mr. MAY said he understood that the President of the United States had ordered an inquiry into this subject.

Mr. HIESTER, at the request of several members, withdrew his motion.

Mr. BOULDIN doubted the propriety of instituting an inquiry on the part of the House, if one was already progressing in another quarter—

Mr. KINNARD rose to a question of order. The gentleman from Virginia, (Mr. Bouldin,) was speaking of an inquiry, when none was demanded by his colleague. He had, in his letter, done what he had a perfect right to do—apologized to the House and his constituents for his absence at this interesting period of the session. He had assigned the cause which prevented his attendance. But he asked no inquiry; nor did he ask or desire the protection of the House. Mr. K. would say for his colleague, that he was prepared and willing, on fair terms, with any equal and honorable antagonist, to protect and defend himself. Mr. K. would leave to other members of more experience than himself, to propose such measures as might insure to the constituents of a member his services on this floor, if, in the estimation of the House, there had been a breach of its privileges, and of the rights of one of its members.

Mr. HANNEGAN offered a resolution for the appointment of a select committee of seven members, to investigate the facts of the alleged assault, and that the same be reported to the House.

Mr. BRIGGS demanded the yeas and nays upon the adoption of the resolution; which were ordered.

Mr. CLAYTON moved an adjournment.

On this motion Mr. MERCER asked for the yeas and nays—ordered.

Mr. C. P. WHITE renewed it.

Mr. WISE demanded the yeas and nays; which were ordered, and were—yeas 42, nays 156.

So the House refused to adjourn.

Mr. HIESTER renewed the motion to lay the resolution and communication on the table—negatived, yeas 67, noes 128.

A debate of some length, and much animation, ensued on the adoption of the resolution. It was opposed by Mr. POLK, and advocated by Messrs. HARDIN, HANNEGAN, and EVANS, when

Mr. STEWART moved the previous question, which was seconded, and agreed to.

The question being on the adoption of the resolution,

Mr. REED demanded the yeas and nays, which were ordered, and were—yeas 197, nays 63.

So the resolution was agreed to.

Mr. CAMBRELENG moved that the House again go into Committee, on the report of the Committee of Foreign affairs.

Mr. RENCHER moved an adjournment, which carried—yeas 114, noes not counted.

The House adjourned.

IN SENATE.

MONDAY, March 2, 1835.

Mr. RUGGLES presented a joint resolution of the Legislature of Maine, approbatory of the course of the President of the United States, in relation to the Bank of the United States, and in-structing the Senators from that State to use their exertions to have the resolution of last session, condemnatory of the President, expunged from the journal of the Senate.

A message was received from the President of the United States, by the hand of Mr. Donelson, his private Secretary, communicating the correspondence and instructions given to the present minister to Spain, in pursuance of the resolutions of the Senate of the 2d and 17th ultimo.

Mr. WEBSTER, from the Committee on Finance, reported the bill from the House making

appropriations for payment of Indian annuities for the year 1835, with sundry amendments.

On motion of Mr. WEBSTER, the bill was considered as in Committee of the Whole, and the several amendments were agreed to.

Mr. TIPTON offered an amendment appropriating $642 to defray the expenses of Captain Jewett, commandant of Fort Armstrong, on the Mississippi, the amount due him on account of two suits prosecuted against him for seizing a quantity of ardent spirits smuggled into the Indian country in violation of the act of 1802, to regulate trade and intercourse with the Indian tribes. The amendment was agreed to, and the bill was reported to the Senate as-amended. The bill was then ordered to be engrossed, and was afterwards read a third time and passed.

On motion of Mr. SILSBEE, the Committee on Commerce had leave to sit during the sitting of the Senate.

Mr. TOMLINSON, from the Committee on Pensions, reported the bills from the House, granting pensions to Thomas Ball and Col. Daniel Nevan, without amendment, and that the bill granting a pension to William C. Beard ought not to pass.

On motion of Mr. PORTER, the Committee on Private Land Claims were discharged from the further consideration of the petition of the heirs of J. B. Macarty.

Mr. POINDEXTER offered a resolution authorizing the Secretary of the Senate to supply the members of the Senate with the volumes of Gales & Seaton's Register of Debates which have been published since the last distribution, and asked the consideration of the resolution at this time.

As the motion required unanimous consent—

Mr. HILL objected.

Mr. FRELINGHUYSEN suggested that the gentleman could obtain his object by moving the consideration of a resolution lying on the table.

On motion of Mr. POINDEXTER, the Senate took up for consideration the resolution reported by the Library Committee, directing the Secretary to furnish those members of the Senate who have taken their seats during the present session, with Gales and Seaton's Register of Debates.

Mr. BENTON opposed the motion, and demanded the yeas and nays upon it, which were ordered, and are as follows:

YEAS—Messrs. Bibb, Buchanan, Clayton, Ewing, Frelinghuysen, Goldsborough, Knight, Leigh, McKean, Mangum, Naudain, Poindexter, Porter, Prentiss, Robbins, Smith, Southard, Swift, Tipton, Webster—20.

NAYS—Messrs. Benton, Black, Cuthbert, Hill, Kane, King of Georgia, Linn, Morris, Robinson, Shepley, Tallmadge, White, Wright—13.

So the motion to consider was agreed to.

The resolution having been taken up—

Mr. POINDEXTER moved an amendment to furnish each Senator with the volumes published since the last distribution.

Mr. BENTON opposed the amendment, and asked the yeas and nays upon its adoption, which were ordered, and it was agreed to by the following vote:

YEAS—Messrs. Bell, Buchanan, Ewing, Frelinghuysen, Kent, Knight, Leigh, Naudain, Poindexter, Prentiss, Robbins, Southard, Swift, Tipton, Webster—15.

NAYS—Messrs. Benton, Black, Cuthbert, Hill, Kane, King of Georgia, Linn, McKean, Morris, Porter, Robinson, Shepley, Tallmadge, White—14.

The question being on the adoption of the resolution as amended, after some remarks from Messrs. LEIGH, POINDEXTER, BUCHANAN, BENTON, KING of Alabama, and KING of Georgia,

Mr. BENTON moved its indefinite postponement, which he afterwards modified, at the suggestion of Mr. BUCHANAN, to a postponement to the first day of next session, and asked the yeas and nays upon the motion, which were ordered, and are as follows:

YEAS—Messrs. Benton, Black, Brown, Buchanan, Cuthbert, Goldsborough, Grundy, Hill, Kane, King of Alabama, King of Georgia, Linn, McKean, Morris, Robinson, Shepley, Tallmadge, White—18.

NAYS—Messrs. Bell, Bibb, Clay, Clayton,

Ewing, Frelinghuysen, Kent, Knight, Leigh, Mangum, Nauda n, Poindexter, Porter, Prentiss, Robbins, Southard, Swift, Tipton, Webster.—19.

So the motion was disagreed to.

After some further remarks from Messrs. FRE-LINGHUYSEN, BENTON, and POINDEXTER, Mr. BUCHANAN moved to lay the subject on the table; which was agreed to, on a division—yeas 17, nays 17; the Chair voting in the affirmative.

The Senate then resumed the civil and diplomatic appropriation bill.

All the other amendments reported by the Committee on Finance, having been agreed to, that proposing to strike out the salary and outfit of a Minister to Great Britain, was next considered; when a debate of considerable length and much interest ensued, in which Messrs. WEBSTER, WRIGHT, CLAY, CLAYTON, BUCHANAN, BIBB, and TYLER, participated.

Mr. WEBSTER then moved to amend the section before striking out, by inserting a proviso, "that the salary and outfit shall not be paid, unless said Minister shall be appointed at the present sess on of Congress, or in the recess, by and with the advice and consent of the Senate, first had and obtained."

Upon this proposition, Mr. CLAY asked the yeas and nays; which were ordered.

After some further remarks from Messrs. WEBSTER, TYLER, SHEPLEY, CALHOUN, KING of Alabama, and BLACK, the proviso was agreed to by the following vote:

YEAS—Messrs. Bell, Bibb, Black, Clay, Calhoun, Clayton, Ewing, Frelinghuysen, Goldsborough, Hendricks, Kent, Knight, Leigh, Mangum, Moore, Naudain, Poindexter, Porter, Prentiss, Preston, Robbins, Silsbee, Smith, Southard, Swift, Tomlinson, Waggaman, Webster—28.

NAYS—Messrs. Benton, Brown, Buchanan, Cuthbert, Grundy, Hill, Kane, King of Alabama, King of Georgia, Linn, McKean, Morris, Robinson, Ruggles, Shepley, Tallmadge, Tipton, Tyler, White, Wright—20.

M:. EWING proposed to strike out the item for an outfit for a Minister to Spain, and asked the yeas and nays; which were ordered.

Mr. CLAYTON was also in favor of striking out, on the ground of there being no vacancy to require an outfit.

Mr. CLAY said, as a proviso was introduced already into the bill which would shew the President the opinion of the Senate in regard to the right of appointment during the recess of Congress, he was in favor of retaining the sum.

Mr. CLAYTON then read a letter from the Secretary of State, which had just been handed him, stating that the present Minister to Spain had asked and obtained leave to return. Mr. C. said it was sufficient.

Mr. EWING then withdrew his motion.

Mr. WRIGHT offered an amendment to the section of the bill, making a provision in favor of certain custom-house officers, and placing them on the same footing as before 1832, being a provision similar to those made heretofore for that object.

[By unanimous consent the bill was suspended for the introduction of the following.]

Mr. CLAY, from the Committee on Foreign Affairs, by unanimous consent, reported a bill from the House to carry into effect the Convention between the United States and Spain, with an amendment.

The amendment provides, that the distribution of the fund shall be made by the Attorney General, instead of a special commission. The amendment was agreed to, and ordered to be engrossed. The bill was then read the third time and passed.

On motion of Mr. PORTER the 17th joint rule, which prevents bills being sent to the President on the last day of the session, was suspended.

The Senate then took a recess until 5 o'clock.

Mr. SMITH, from the Select Committee appointed upon the letter of the Hon. Gzo. Poindexter, made a report at length, concluding with a resolution that not a shade of suspicion exists that Mr. Poindexter was in any way concerned, directly or indirectly, in the late attempted assassination of the President.

The report was read, and the question being on its adoption,

Mr. WEBSTER asked the yeas and nays; which were ordered, and are as follows:

YEAS—Messrs. Bell, Bibb, Black, Buchanan, Calhoun, Clay, Clayton, Cuthbert, Ewing, Frelinghuysen, Goldsborough, Grundy, Hendricks, Hill, Kane, Kent, King of Alabama, King of Ga., Knight, Leigh, Linn, Mangum, Moore, Morris, Naudain, Porter, Preston, Robbins, Robinson, Ruggles, Shepley, Silsbee, Smith, Southard, Swift, Tallmadge, Tipton, Tomlinson, Tyler, Webster, White, Wright.—42.

NAYS.—None.

On motion of Mr. SMITH, the report and accompanying documents were ordered to be printed.

The Senate then resumed the consideration of the General Appropriation Bill.

The amendment offered by Mr. WRIGHT was still further discussed by Messrs. WRIGHT, BUCHANAN, SILSBEE, KING of Alabama, and CLAY.

Mr. WRIGHT asked the yeas and nays on the adoption of the amendment; which were ordered, and are as follows:

YEAS—Messrs. Benton, Black, Brown, Buchanan, Cuthbert, Frelinghuysen, Grundy, Hill, Kane, Kent, King of Alabama, King of Georgia, Linn, McKean, Morris, Poindexter, Preston, Robinson, Ruggles, Shepley, Tallmadge, White, Wright.—23.

NAYS—Messrs. Bell, Bibb, Calhoun, Clay, Clayton, Ewing, Goldsborough, Hendricks, Knight, Leigh, Mangum, Moore, Naudain, Porter, Robbins, Silsbee, Smith, Southard, Swift, Tipton, Tomlinson, Webster.—22.

So the amendment was agreed to.

The bill was then reported to the Senate.

Mr. CLAY asked the ayes and nays on receiving the amendment offered by Mr. Wright and adopted in Committee of the Whole, which were ordered, and are as follows:

YEAS—Messrs. Benton, Black, Brown, Buchanan, Cuthbert, Frelinghuysen, Grundy, Hill, Kane, Kent, King of Alabama, King of Georgia, Linn, McKean, Poindexter, Preston, Robinson, Ruggles, Shepley, Silsbee, Tallmadge, White, Wright.—23.

NAYS—Messrs. Bell, Bibb, Calhoun, Clay, Clayton, Ewing, Goldsborough, Hendricks, Knight, Leigh, Mangum, Moore, Porter, Prentiss, Robbins, Smith, Southard, Swift, Tipton, Tomlinson, Tyler, Webster.—22.

So the amendment was adopted. The bill was then,

On motion of Mr. WEBSTER, still further amended by incorporating into the provisions of a bill affording relief to certain officers and soldiers of the Virginia line; and of a bill to construct a road from Lyme creek to Chatahoochee and of a bill to confirm certain land titles in Missouri. Which bills had passed the Senate Saturday evening too late to be sent to the House.

The bill was then ordered to be engrossed; and was then read a third time and passed.

Mr. PRESTON moved to take up the resolution offered by Mr. Benton for expunging from the journal of the Senate the resolution condemning the President; on which question the yeas and nays were ordered, and are as follows:

AYES—Messrs. Benton, Brown, Buchanan, Calhoun, Clay, Clayton, Cuthbert, Hill, Kane, King of Alabama, King of Georgia, McKean, Mangum, Moore, Preston, Robinson, Ruggles, Shepley, Tallmadge, White, Wright—21.

NAYS—Messrs. Bibb, Black, Ewing, Goldsborough, Grundy, Hendricks, Kent, Knight, Leigh, Linn, Naudain, Poindexter, Porter, Prentiss, Robbins, Smith, Southard, Swift, Tipton, Tomlinson, Waggaman, Webster—22.

So the motion was lost.

The following resolutions were offered:

By M:. RUGGLES:

Resolved, That the Secretary of War be directed to cause a survey to be taken of the harbor of East Thomaston, Maine, so far as it may be necessary to determine the practicability and propriety of constructing a break-water for the protection of shipping, while lying within the harbor; also an estimate of the probable expense of such construction; that he make report thereof to the Senate at the next session of Congress.

By Mr. POINDEXTER:

Resolved, That the reports of the commissioners for adjusting land titles, made to Congress since the adjournment of the last session of Congress be printed with the documents in relation to the public lands, ordered to be printed at the last session of Congress.

By Mr. BIBB:

Resolved, That the usual number of copies of the journals of the Senate be reprinted for the use of the Senate, arranging the legislative and executive journals in separate volumes; and that the Secretary cause to be prepared and printed therewith a copious index to each volume, and also an analytical index in a separate volume.

This resolution was laid on the table.

By Mr. PRESTON:

Resolved, That a list of the pensioners on the rolls in the Treasury Office be printed and distributed as heretofore ordered in regard to those in the War Office, with the addition of the names of the agents.

The following bills from the House were considered in Committee of the Whole, ordered to be engrossed and read the third time, and passed.

The bill for the relief of Francis F. St. Cyr, and the bill for the relief of Jared Buchanan, were read, and indefinitely postponed.

The following bills were read the first and second time, ordered to be engrossed, and read a third time:

A bill for the relief of Samuel L. Asbury.

A bill for the relief of the children of Dominick Lynch.

A bill for the relief of Daniel Page.

A bill for the relief of Peter Triplett.

A bill for the relief of Stephen Gatlin.

A bill for the relief of Larned Swallow.

A bill to regulate the pay of the officers of the Navy.

While the latter bill was under consideration,

Mr. HILL said, if the bill for raising the salaries of the officers of the navy should pass, he would consider it to be one of the most severe blows ever inflicted on the American navy. As the sincere friend of that navy, he hoped the Senate would pause before they inflicted this blow. There is a point beyond which they would not go; they are willing simply to remunerate every man in their employ to the full amount or his services; but they never will consent that deception shall be palmed upon them.

I have, said Mr. H , before me tables of the pay of the officers of the French and the British navy, and I will present them in contrast with the pay of the officers of the American navy as it stands before the passage of this law.

PAY IN THE FRENCH NAVY.

	Francs.	Dolls.
Maritime Prefects, per annum (commanders at seaports,)	21,600	4,050 00
Vice Admiral,	18,000	5,375 00
Rear Admiral,	12,000	2,250 00
Post Captain, 1st class,	6,000	1,125 00
Captain, 2d class,	5,400	1,012 50
Commander, (capitaine de frigate,)	4,200	787 50
First Lieutenant,	2,400	450 00
Second Lieutenant,	1,800	337 50
Mate, first class,	960	180 00
Midshipman, 2d class, and volunteers, no pay, except when in service, and then	480	52 50
Master gunners and helmsmen, first class, per month, 90_f._	1,080	202 50
Master gunners and helmsmen, 2d class, per month 81_f._	972	182 25
Capitaines d'armes, 1st class, per month 81_f._	972	182 25
Capitaines d'armes, 2d class, per month 72_f._	864	162 00
Master carpenters, caulkers, and sailmakers, 1st class, per month, 81_f._	972	182 25
Master carpenters, caulkers,		

and sailmakers, 2d class, per
month, 72f.	864	162 00
Master Armorers, 1st class, per		
month, 60f.	720	135 00
Master Armorers, 2d class, per		
month, 54f.	648	121 50

One-fifth of the above to be deducted when the
officers are on shore.

When at sea, the officers receive a daily mess
allowance in addition, varying according to the
service or station on which they are to be employed.

The midshipmen (*clerks*) of the 2d class, receive no pay except when in service.

---

*Pay of the British Navy as established by an Order
in Council, June 23, 1824, computing the £ at
$4 44.*

Admiral of the fleet per annum,	$9,723 50
Admiral, - - - -	8,103 00
Vice Admiral, - - -	6,482 40
Rear Admiral or Commodore, 1st class.	4,861 80
Captain of the fleet, - -	4,861 80

In addition to the above, every commander-in-
chief receives a further sum of $13 32 per day,
while his flag is flying within the limits of his station.

Mode of rating Ships in the British Navy.

First rate.—All ships with three decks.
Second rate.—Two deckers of 80 guns and up-
wards.
Third rate.—Ships of 70, and less than 80 guns.
Fourth rate.—Ships of 50, and less than 70 guns.
Fifth rate.—Ships of 36, and less than 50 guns.
Sixth rate.—Ships of 24, and less than 36 guns.
The other vessels in the following table, rank
in the seventh rank:

PAY IN THE BRITISH SERVICE PER ANNUM.

In all rates the same.

RANK.	1st Rate.	2d Rate.	3d Rate.	4th Rate.	5th Rate.	6th Rate.	Sloops, &c.
Captain, pay per month,	$3,542 08	$3,099 95	$2,709 04	$2,213 56	$1,771 04	$1,549 79	$1,549 79
First Lt. Tyger's ditto	3,542 08	3,099 95	2,709 04	2,213 56	1,549 79	1,549 79	1,338 52
All other lieutenants,	663 73	663 73	663 73	673 78	531 02	531 02	531 02
Master,	752 32	531 02	531 02	531 02	531 02	486 77	442 52
Chaplain,	708 03	708 03	708 03	663 78	708 03	708 03	708 03
Surgeon,	708 03	708 03	708 03	619 52	708 03	708 03	708 03
Purser,	531 02	531 02	531 02	531 02	531 02	531 02	404 04
Assistant Surgeon,	531 02	404 04	404 04	404 04	404 04	404 04	404 04
Gunner,	531 02	531 02	531 02	531 02	531 02	531 02	531 02
Boatswain,	531 02	531 02	404 04	404 04	404 04	404 04	404 04
Carpenter,	531 02	531 02	404 04	451 *			
Mate,	404 04						
Midshipmen,	227 03						
Sailmaker,	138 52	249 15	249 15	315 63	303 41	271 28	271 03
Clerk,	271 28	249 15	249 15	227 03	204 90	304 90	

PAY IN THE AMERICAN OR UNITED STATES SERVICE, &c.

RANK.	Pay and rations per annum.	Cabin furniture.	For House rent.	Fuel.	Candles.	Servants & rations.	Total am't.
Captain of a squadron,	$3,660	350					$5,090
Captain of a 74 gun ship,	1,630	300					2,330
Captain of a 32, & upwards,	1,630	340	600	180	63	561 75	2,570
Captain under 32,	1,580						4,066 75
Lieutenant in command,	1,176 25						1,396 25
Master Commandant,	1,176 25						1,356 25
Lieutenant attached to a ship,	965	120					965
Surgeon of a fleet over 20 years	663 50	180					663 60
Handling,	2,430						2,430
Boatswain,	663 50						662 50
Surgeon's mate,	319 25						319 25
Philadelphia,	482 50						482 50
Purser,	492 50						422 50
Gunner,							

INCIDENTAL ALLOWANCES.

$2 per week to officers attached to navy yards
where there are no quarters. Stationery is furnished and all postages upon public letters are
repaid to them. The cabins of the ships are supplied with the permanent furniture, deemed fixtures, as carpets, tables, chairs, sophas, sideboards, dish covers, mirrors, &c. The allowance
in lieu of cabin furniture is for other small articles.

15 cents per mile is allowed to cover the expenses of travelling under orders, to captains and
masters commandants by land, 12 cents to all
others; by water 10 cents, and 8 cents.

Where officers are detained on duty at places
without their regular stations, they are allowed to
captains and masters commandants, 3 dollars
per day. Surgeons, lieutenants, and other officers, 2 dollars per day, during which, their regular pay and emoluments continue.

Officers stationed at the several navy yards, are
allowed a much higher compensation generally,
than when at sea; a capital defect in making an
efficient navy.

Officers returning to the United States from
abroad, have their passage money paid to them.

Prizes.—If of equal or superior force, the whole
value is distributed among the officers and crews.
If of inferior force, one half to the United States
and one-half to the captors. *Note.*—Individuals
fit out privateers for the prizes at their own expense.

Pensions.—Officers wounded are pensioned,
and if killed, their widows are pensioned.

From these several statements (said Mr. H.) it
will be seen that the pay of the officers of the
Navy of the United States, under the law as it
now stands, is better, much better, than the pay
either in the British or French Navy.

Thus it will be seen that the commander of a
frigate in the French Navy receives (besides a
mess allowance of about one-fourth) $787 50; the
same commander in the British Navy receives, in
full of all pay and emoluments, $2,213 56; while
an American commander, of the same grade, receives $2,170, besides other emoluments. Here
an officer of this grade has at least equal pay to an
officer of the same grade in the British Navy, and
nearly double the pay of the same grade of officers in the French Navy. Yet the bill raises the
compensation of this officer from $3,500 as a mini-
mum to $4,890 per annum as a maximum allow-
ance.

But the pay of Lieutenants is raised in still
higher proportion. A first Lieutenant in the
French navy, exclusive of daily mess allowance,
receives while on sea duty $450; a British Lieu-
tenant, as his highest and exclusive allowance, receives $663 78; while an American Lieutenant, of
the highest grade, receives $1,296 25, and of the
lowest grade $965 per annum, under the law as
it now stands. The new bill raises this pay of
Lieutenants of the highest grade to $1820, and
even the lowest to $1500 while on board
ship. This is more than treble the pay of French
officers of the same grade, and, nearly treble that
of the British service.

Take, also, the pay of the most numerous class
of officers. Midshipmen in the French navy receive no pay except when in actual service, and
when in service, besides the daily mess allowance,
they receive as pay only $52 50 per annum. Mid-
shipmen in the British navy receive, as their full
emoluments, $138 52. American midshipmen,
under the law as it stands, receive, as their lowest
allowance, $219 25. The bill under considera-
tion gives the same officer of the lowest grade,
when attached to a ship, $400 per annum, and
even while at home, doing no service, the sum of
$300 per annum. The pay of midshipmen of the
higher grade is carried in the American service to
the amount of $750 per annum.

Other officers, it will be seen by the table I
have presented, present a still greater discrepancy. Thus the commander of a yard is raised from
$4,066 75 to $4,500; masters commandant from
$1,356 25 to $2,500; chaplains from $662 50 to
$1,200; gunners, boatswains, sailmakers, and
carpenters, from $422 50 to $7 50, &c.

Compared with the salaries of the highest civil
officers in most of the States of the Union—with
the salaries of the highest judicial officers requiring expensive education and preparation—the
pay of the officers of the American Navy will be
enormous, if the bill passes: it is out of proportion
to all other compensation in this country, public
or private. If the greatest enemy of the Navy
had meditated the greatest injury to the service,
he could not have devised a more effectual method of doing it than the passage of such a bill as
this.

The People cannot, they will not, stand such
a stride in advancing public salaries, as is sanctioned by the Navy bill. What was the condition
of the officers of the Navy during the late war
with Great Britain? At that time, while they
were fighting and covering themselves with glory
—while they could not get from the impoverished
treasury of the nation the smaller pay that was
their due—they did not ask to have their pay raised, even when the currency was depreciated. But
now a new race seems to have arisen in the
Navy, that knows not Joseph—an influence
which comes from the higher grade, not from
the laboring classes of society. The rush for
midshipmen's births in the navy, for many years,
has been great, even with the low compensation
that the present law affords. The sons of rich
men, or of genteel poor men, not the bone and
muscle of the country, are the most numerous seekers of places as midshipmen in the navy; hundreds
of names are still on the list as seekers for the
places. The number has been increased until probably not one fifth are in active employ. And it is
the time to raise the pay of the boys in the navy?
The midshipmen in the French and British navy
have scarcely sufficient pay to purchase clothing;
their youth go into the service with the sole prospect of reliance on their own exertion. The

American youth who enter the service receive pay both while out of and while in the service sufficient to superinduce habits of dissipation. Can there be a doubt, in which service will ultimately terminate superiority in elevation of character?

The whole increase of pay of officers of the navy by the bill, I am informed, will be to the amount of three hundred thousand dollars per annum. The addition to the pay of the corps of Lieutenants alone, it is said, will exceed one hundred thousand dollars. And this too, when it is said scarcely one-fifth of the officers of the navy are in actual service. Could there be a more unfortunate time to introduce such a bill as this?

The bill has been carried in one branch by an almost exclusive party vote on one side, with just enough of the other side to overbalance the question. This has been done, as I believe, when many of those who voted in favor of the bill did not understand the extent of the increase of pay. There has been a revulsion in that branch since the bill passed, that induces the Senator from New Jersey (Mr. Southard,) now to say the bill will be lost, if it shall be amended so as to include the officers of the marines, and make them equal to those of the navy. The Senate will not suffer this bill to go back to the House. It might have been there passed under entreaties and personal applications of those interested. It is my belief the bill would not again pass that body. Its great friend here will not again trust the bill out of the Senate. I shall regret hereafter, if it shall be seen that the effect of raising the salaries of the officers of the navy, at a time when there is a general press on the Secretary of the Navy to get places in that service, will lower the estimation in which that branch of the public service is held by the People of the United States.

The following House bills were taken up, considered as in the Committee of the Whole, ordered to be engrossed, and afterwards read a third time, and passed.

A bill for the relief of Joseph Gilbert.

A bill for the relief of John Gorodelle.

A bill granting a pension to Col. Gideon Morgan, of Tennessee.

A bill to render permanent the mode of supplying the army, and fixing the salaries of Clerks in the Commissary General's Office.

A bill making appropriations for certain beacons, light-houses, and buoys, for the year 1835.

A bill supplementary to the act to extend a lateral branch of the Baltimore and Ohio rail road into the city of Washington;

A bill granting a pension to Justus Cobb.

Several bills severally granting pensions as follows: to Thomas Swartwood, Benjamin Holland, William Wileges, Isaac Eckwright, Ephraim F. Gilbert, Captain Cole, an Indian chief, Solomon Case, George C. Seaton, Justus Cobb, Benjamin Leslie, Wm. Baden, and James Harrington, Samuel Shelmerdine, Abraham E. Boutwell, and David Pearson, John Moore, John Bryant, John F. Wiley, William Lawrence, Thomas Ball, Joseph Mead, Noah Miller.

[A bill granting a pension to Luke Vorchise, was indefinitely postponed.

Mr. POINDEXTER moved to take up the bill extending the time for issuing scrip for United States military bounty land warrants, which was disagreed to.]

Mr. SILSBEE, from the Committee on Commerce, reported the bill from the House making appropriations for the Delaware breakwater, and for certain harbors, for the year 1835.

On Mr. SILSBEE'S motion, the Senate proceeded to consider the bill, as in committee of the whole, and the amendments having been gone through with,

Mr. TIPTON offered an amendment, appropriating $10,000, to be applied under the direction of the Secretary of War, to the construction of a harbor at Michigan city, mouth of Frail creek, on Lake Michigan.

Mr. T. said he felt it his duty to propose this amendment to the bill. He made a similar proposition last session; but it failed, as he understood, in consequence of no survey having been made of the proposed harbor. A survey, however, was made last fall, by an officer of the engineer corps,

whose report was referred some weeks ago to the Committee on Commerce; and Mr. T. said he was informed by the honorable Chairman, (Mr. Silsbee,) that the committee would not consent to amend this bill, as it provided only for the prosecution of works already commenced. That there were similar propositions before them then, that the committee determined to attach to a bill that was expected from the House, providing for new works. He deemed it unfortunate that he had to encounter the unanimous opposition of the committee; it might defeat his proposition, but would not prevent him from doing his duty. He was told last year this harbor was not surveyed; and now, to wait till a bill came from the other House. Did not honorable gentlemen know, that at this late hour, no other bill need be expected from the other House? Mr. T. said he heard calls from all sides to withdraw the amendment; and he would do so if he could, consistent with duty; but he could not, and would not surrender the rights of those he had the honor in part to represent here. He begged honorable Senators to recollect that Indiana had no other harbors to improve but this. Few States were thus situated. Turn to your statute book, and you will find that no session of Congress passes, without appropriating money for every other State. What has been done for Indiana? We ask nothing as a boon, but claim this appropriation as a matter of right.

Harbors have been constructed at every creek and inlet on the Eastern seaboard, on lake Erie, and almost all other Lakes. This town Michigan City, although new, is a place of immense business. Many of its citizens are business-men, possessing large capitals, and have embarked in commercial enterprises with great spirit. Between 60 and 100 lake vessels arrived at this port last summer. This number will no doubt be doubled the next season. The goods consumed in the north part of Indiana, and a part of Illinois and Michigan, will be landed at this point as soon as the harbor is in a condition to protect the commerce of the place. Appropriations are made each year to construct a harbor at Chicago, 50 miles west of Trail creek, and another is also expected for the St. Joseph's river, forty five miles northwest of our harbor. Mr. T. said he voted with pleasure for the construction of harbors, and would not now complain, could he obtain what is just for his own State. Every dollar laid out to improve harbors on Lake Michigan, turns the business to those which are most secure; thus, by improving that at Chicago, you subtract from the business and the value of our property at Michigan City. He wished to be liberal to his neighbors, but could not consent to vote for others, to the neglect of his own constituents. Having presented the amendment and his views, he asked the yeas and nays, in order that by recording his vote, his constituents might see that he had done his duty. If voted down, he would yield to the decision of the Senate as gravely as any Senator could, who felt that a portion of his constituents were operated upon unjustly. The yeas and nays were ordered, and the amendment was disagreed to, by the following vote:

YEAS.—Messrs. Benton, Black, Goldsborough, Hendricks, Kane, Kent, Linn, Robinson, Tipton, Tomlinson, Webster, White.—12.

NAYS.—Messrs. Bibb, Buchanan, Clayton, Ewing, Hill, King of Geo. Leigh, Mangum, Naudain, Poindexter, Prentiss, Ruggles, Shepley, Silsbee, Southard, Swift, Tallmadge, Tyler.—18.

After the consideration of Executive business, the Senate, at 11 o'clock,
Adjourned.

HOUSE OF REPRESENTATIVES.

Monday, March 2, 1835.

Petitions and memorials were presented by—
Mr. HUBBARD, of New Hampshire;
Messrs. BAYLIES and PHILLIPS, of Massachusetts.
Messrs. DICKSON and HARD, of New York;
Mr. BANKS, of Pennsylvania;

[Mr. Banks presented a memorial signed by citizens of West Greenville, Mercer County, Pennsylvania, praying that a law may be passed abolishing slavery and the slave trade in the District of Columbia and the Territories.]

Messrs. CHINN and MASON, of Virginia;
Messrs. INGE and DUNLAP, of Tennessee;
Mr. REYNOLDS, of Illinois;
Mr. LYON, of Michigan;
Mr. VINTON, of Ohio.
Which petitions and memorials were appropriately disposed of.

On motion of Mr. PLUMMER, several petitions heretofore presented by him in relation to the public lands, were ordered to be printed.

The following resolution offered by Mr. CLAY from the Committee on Public Lands, on the 3d February was taken up, read, considered, and agreed to, viz:

Resolved, That the Secretary of the Treasury be directed to cause an estimate to be made of the probable expense of constructing a levee, on the public land, on the western bank of the Mississippi, and the southern bank of Red river, in the State of Louisiana; also, an estimate of the expense of constructing levees on, or removing obstructions from the rivers of Arkansas and Missouri through the public lands, wherever they may be necessary; together with the probable advantages of disadvantages of such works, respectively; the probable effects upon the health and prosperity of the country in which any of such works may be constructed, and the probable quantity, quality, and value of land, belonging to the United States which will be reclaimed by the construction of any such levees, and make report thereof to the next Congress.

On motion of Mr. BEATY,
Resolved, That the Committee on Revolutionary Claims be instructed to inquire into the propriety of directing payment to be made to the heirs of Capt. Reuben Waggoner, of the amount due him for services as an officer and private in the Virginia State line, or continental establishment; and which said Committee inquire into and ascertain the amount, if any, in money and land there be due to the said heirs for the revolutionary services of Captain Waggoner, either as an officer or private soldier, and report to this House the result of said inquiry.

On motion of Mr. C. P. WHITE,
Resolved, That 10,000 copies be printed of the letter of the Secretary of the Treasury respecting the commerce and navigation of the United States for the year ending September 30, 1834, when the same shall be received.

Mr. POLK, from the Committee of Ways and Means, reported, with amendments, the bill from the Senate in relation to the public depositories, which was committed and the amendments ordered to be printed.

Mr. MUHLENBERG, from the Committee on Revolutionary Claims, reported a bill for the relief of the legal representatives of Doctor Absalon Beard, deceased; which was read twice and committed.

On motion of Mr. CAMBRELENG, the Committee of the Whole on the state of the Union were discharged from the further consideration of the bill from the Senate to suspend the operation of certain provinces of the act to alter and amend the several acts imposing duties on imports.

The amendment reported by the Committee of Ways and Means was then negatived, and the bill was read the third time and passed.

Mr. BANKS, from the Committee on Claims, reported a bill for the relief of the sureties of Nicholas Carter; which was read twice and committed.

Upon the motions of Messrs. CLAY, MUHLENBERG, BROWN, POLK, McINTIRE, and SCHENCK, the Standing Committees to which they belonged, were discharged from the further consideration of various petitions and subjects which had been referred to them.

The report made by Mr. HAMER, from the Judiciary Committee, on the subject of the public printing, came up for consideration.

The reading of the report was concluded.

Mr. WILDE moved to lay the report and motion to print it on the table.

Mr. HUBBARD demanded the yeas and nays.
Ordered.

Mr. WILDE withdrew his motion, when the re

port was laid on the table, and ordered to be printed.

The report of the Select Committee on the West Point Academy, was taken up:—the question being on a motion to recommit the report.

After some suggestions by several members, in regard to the disposition of the report,

Mr. H. HALL (who was entitled to the floor when the subject was last before the House) rose in support of the motion to recommit. After speaking a short time, and without concluding, he gave way to

Mr. CAMBRELENG, who moved that the House proceed to the consideration of the orders of the day; which carried—yeas 118, nays not counted.

Mr. McKENNAN moved to suspend the rules of the House so as to proceed to the consideration of the bill from the Senate for the continuation and repairs of the Cumberland road; but the House refused.

The SPEAKER laid before the House a letter from the Secretary of War, transmitting a report, in pursuant to law, of the persons employed in the Indian Department; which was laid on the table, and ordered to be printed.

The SPEAKER laid before the House a letter from the Postmaster General, transmitting a list of unproductive mail routes; which was laid on the table, and ordered to be printed.

RELATIONS WITH FRANCE.

Mr. CAMBRELENG moved to discharge the Committee of the Whole on the state of the Union, from the further consideration of the report and resolutions of the Committee on Foreign Affairs, on the subject of the relations with France.

On this motion Mr. WILDE asked for the ayes and nays; which were ordered, and were, ayes 104, nays 52.

So the motion prevailed.

The report and resolutions being before the House,

Mr. J. Q. ADAMS said, he had, on Saturday, accepted the amendment of the gentleman from Virginia, (Mr. Archer,) as a modification of his first resolution; but he begged to state, that he wished a direct vote upon his resolution, if the amendment of Mr. Archer should be rejected.

Some conversation ensued upon the question before the House; and after an explanation from Mr. MASON, of Virginia, who was in the Chair in the Committee of the Whole on the state of the Union on Saturday,

The SPEAKER informed the House that the question would be on the amendment of Mr. ARCHER first, which is as follows:

Resolved, That in the just expectation that the Government of France will have made provision, or will make provision for carrying into effect the stipulations of the treaty of indemnity with that Government of the 4th of July, 1831, this House will forbear at the present time to adopt any measure in relation to that subject.

[The resolutions reported by Mr. CAMBRELENG, from the Committee on Foreign Affairs, together with the substitute proposed by Mr J. Q. ADAMS, will be found in the Globe of yesterday.]

Mr. E. EVERETT, who was entitled to the floor, then addressed the House. He said it was not his intention originally to have said a word on this subject, notwithstanding the situation he occupied as a member of the Committee on Foreign Affairs. He had had an opportunity of submitting his views to the House in a report, which it had ordered to be printed; and moreover the state of his health would not permit him to encounter the fatigue necessary to make his voice heard in that Hall. In addition to this, there was another reason operating with greater force upon his mind, and that was, that it was almost impossible to discuss this subject, whatever might be the views of gentlemen on one side or the other, without saying that which perhaps had better not be said, for the public interest at home or abroad. He should be very brief, for he felt how precious the time of the House was.

When this question came before the Committee on Foreign Affairs at the beginning of the session, it was on the recommendation of the President of the United States of an act of Congress ordering reprisals to issue upon the commerce of France. Mr. E. deemed that recommendation inexpedient to be adopted. If the measure were expedient of itself, what could be more inexpedient than to give the adverse party timely notice of it, so as to enable him to anticipate it? It was evident that a majority of the Committee thought with Mr. E. on that point, and he considered it desirable that a report should be made thereon, in order that the effect of that recommendation might be counteracted abroad. The last despatches of Mr. Livingston showed the propriety and justice of such a course. The majority of the committee, however, did not coincide, but thought it expedient not to report. Thus the matter stood till about a week ago, when a resolution, substantially the same as that now reported from the committee, was proposed in committee. He understood the Chairman thereof (Mr. Cambreleng,) to state the other day, that he had found it difficult to collect the sense of the minority of the committee on that resolution. Mr. E. had himself stated, over and over again, that so far as the resolution went to insist upon the obligation of the treaty, he fully concurred in it; but he was distinctly opposed to that part of it which went to shut the door against all negotiation. In truth, he did not think it desirable that any resolution at all should be adopted by the House; for he thought it exceedingly difficult, if not impossible, to frame any resolution which the House would pass with unanimity, and which it would be desirable it should pass. On one occasion, when the pen was put into his hand for the purpose of drafting such a resolution as he would be willing to have adopted, he declined doing so, on the ground that he felt himself incapable of drafting such a resolution as he deemed expedient, and that the House would adopt. The one presented to the House, he never gave his assent to; nor had he concealed his opinions on the subject in the committee. There was then no other course left to the minority but that which they had adopted. They set forth that the recommendation of reprisals was not concurred in by the committee. The same was the opinion of Mr. Livingston, who gave it as his opinion that the French Chamber of Deputies would pass the bill of appropriation, if Congress should *not* pass any act of reprisals. This was the first point to which the attention of the minority had been turned. The next thing to be done was to show that in standing upon the treaty, we were not standing upon a mere piece of parchment, but upon a basis of truth and justice, and that upon that ground we would insist upon the stipulations of the treaty.

The third was the proposition embraced in the President's last message, viz a recall of our Minister from France; and it was upon this that the majority and minority of the committee mainly differed. These views were fully set forth in the report of the minority, which had been directed to be printed by the House.

The fourth point was, that at the present session of Congress it was inexpedient to do any thing further in legislation—leaving it to the consideration and deliberation of the next Congress. This was his sentiment, his feeling, and judgment, but it was not his resolution, nor did he submit it as such. Mr. E. objected to the resolutions under consideration for many reasons. The words, "at all hazards," he thought were superfluous. It was always sufficient to use the word "insist," till the opposite party refused. He thought the former expression rash, and uncalled for by the dignity of the subject. The resolution of the gentleman from Virginia (Mr. Archer) embraced the sentiment of the minority. It was the sense of the House, and of the nation at large, that the treaty should be insisted upon.

The next question was as to the policy to be pursued, and this was the most delicate question of all. He was for insisting upon the treaty at all hazards, but he was not for enforcing the treaty at all hazards He was for avoiding every thing of an irritating character. It was said, we could not negotiate further, and that further negotiation would not ensure our insisting upon the treaty. He was at a loss to see the force of this objection. In 1781 we negotiated, and in the negotiation insisted upon our independence, and secured and maintained it. Supposing negotiation failed? Why then he would not go to war till every other expedient had been tried. Commercial restrictions in favor of France might be removed. If this failed, we might go a step further. We might rid ourselves of the convention of 1822, and then we might pass a non-intercourse act. And if all failed what should we then do? Still insist upon the execution of the treaty. How, after every peaceful remedy had failed? There he would stop. He would not look into the future. The fortunes of nations were subject to vicissitudes which no man could foresee. He would leave that contingency to a future Congress. That was the last day but one that his voice would, perhaps, be ever heard in that hall, and as a farewell sentiment, he would tell them, for Heaven's sake, to preserve peace. He was in the minority, but he appealed to the majority, as they prized the esteem of their fellow-citizens, to preserve peace. This he would say to the President of the United States, if a voice which had never flattered nor vilified could reach his ears. He respectfully abjured the President, whose power was greater than that of any Emperor or King in Christendom, to preserve peace. He admired, as did his respected colleague, the spirit of the President; but moderation, prudence, and discretion, were qualities required in such a crisis as this. A prudent and temperate, as well as a firm and decided course, was what would best carry the country through, with honor and glory, in a crisis like the present.

Mr. ALLEN, of Ohio, followed in an argument of much spirit and energy, and at great length, in support of the resolutions appended to the report of the Committee on Foreign Affairs. He was in favor of the strongest expression of opinion proposed. He contended as a point which had not been dwelt upon by any of those who had preceded him, that there was no propriety in waiting for the French Chamber of Deputies to reject the appropriation for indemnity under the treaty, as that body had already once rejected it. Should we wait for a repetition of the wrong before we sought redress? He urged that the French Government had throughout treated the subject with insincerity and injustice.

[Mr. A.'s remarks will be published in full hereafter.]

Mr. LOVE was understood to be opposed to the adoption of any resolutions; for before the result of the deliberations of that House could be known at Paris, the French Chamber of Deputies will have finally acted upon the subject. He saw no utility in passing either the resolutions or the amendment, because he believed there was but one sentiment prevailing the whole country upon this subject, and that sentiment was that they would abide by the treaty. However we might differ as to our opinions, and the manner in which our views should be carried out, he was well assured that the opinion was general that we should abide by the Chief Magistrate, in asserting what was due to the honor and dignity of the nation. The best time to express our opinions would be when the appropriation should be asked for, and he should then express himself in a much stronger manner than now. All proceedings now were incipient. He should be willing to vote for any sum that the organ of the Executive and that House should deem necessary to appropriate for the purpose of enforcing justice. The resolutions before the House were idle, and a mere consumption of time. He was for taking a ground that should at once show the world what we intended to do.

Mr. L. took that occasion also to say that he dissented totally from the opinion of the gentleman from Massachusetts, (Mr. Adams,) that the course of our Minister to Paris had merited entire approbation, by remaining in that metropolis after he had been notified that his passports were ready for him. Mr. L. thought, on the contrary, that his conduct on that occasion was rather of the character which he regretted to designate as dastardly and cowardly, and such as the country ought not to submit to. He thought our Minister should have acted very differently, and he was borne out in this opinion by the President himself, who i-

forms him, "that he should have felt no surprise, and certainly would have expressed no displeasure, had you yielded to the impulse of national pride, and at once have quitted France, with the whole Legation, on the receipt of the Count de Rigny's note of the 13th January."

Mr L. said, he considered the notification sent to Mr. Livingston as a direct insult, and that that Minister would have better considered the honor and dignity of the country by instant departure out of the country. A strange reason was assigned for his not having done so, that he ought not to leave Paris on account of the expense of breaking up the delegation! What an extraordinary reason for the Minister of this great country! He himself invites a war message, and when he receives it, he is governed by the construction put upon it by the newspapers! So when a gentleman is ordered out of a house, he is to reply, "I will not take the hint!" Was there an American in the world who would thus have acted? Mr. L. further condemned the conduct of Mr. Livingston, and said he was not for war, if it could be avoided, particularly with our ancient friend and ally. He had a veneration for her people, although he could not say much about her present King, but he remembered with gratitude and veneration that King who aided us in effecting our independence. He would never fight France for money, it would be mercenary, and such a one as he hoped would never be heard urging on our seamen to victory.

Mr. McDOWELL MOORE said it was true that one Chamber of Deputies could not bind another; and even if they had paid nine out of ten instalments, they might withhold the tenth; but then they must take the consequences. He must hold the French nation as responsible for the acts of the Executive of France. He held that the moment the treaty was made by the treaty-making power, the nation was bound by it. If the Executive had transcended its powers, or had made a treaty founded in gross injustice, the Chamber might then justly refuse to ratify it, but the one under consideration was of a different character. He was not for plunging the country into a war heedlessly and precipitately; but if it was ascertained that France had resolved not to pay the debt, he would stop short of nothing that became the honor and dignity of the country. He cared not about the power of France; if the honor demanded the contingency, let it be met; the greater the disparity the greater the glory. He was for insisting for a full and prompt execution of the treaty. Mr. M. concluded by reading a resolution he intended to propose to that effect.

Mr. EVANS addressed the House at some length in reply to the gentleman from Ohio, (Mr. Allen,) and upon the general question. He was opposed to any hostile measures, and was in favor of the resolution proposed by the gentleman from Virginia, (Mr. Archer.) He considered this resolution as the most pacific and proper to be adopted on the occasion. He entered into a history of the treaty with France. He hoped that the House would avoid any declarations predicated upon a contingency which might never happen. He contended that the present difficulty was attributable principally to the menaces held by the President in his last annual message. This message, he conceived, presented the chief obstacle to an amicable adjustment of this question. He contended that there was no consideration which called for any action on the part of Congress, until the decision of the French Chambers should be ascertained.

Mr. SUTHERLAND said, he agreed with the gentleman from Ohio, (Mr. Lytle,) that the French Government had no right to take umbrage at the Message of the President. She was the aggressor, and the President had done no more than his duty, in presenting the subject to Congress, in the light in which he viewed it. Mr. S. said, he highly respected the honorable gentleman from Massachusetts, (Mr. Everett,) who addressed the House this morning. He was about to retire from his legislative duties, and would leave it with the esteem of all parties, and not least for his mild, moral, and liberal views which he entertained upon the question under consideration; yet he regretted the feeling in which that gentleman had reflected on the course of the President. He was the head of our government, discharging its functions in the spirit of duty, and as such commanded our respect and support.

France had entered into an engagement with us, and had failed to fulfil her sacred pledges. It became the duty of the President to present the facts to us, with his own views of them. He had done so with candor, dignity, and firmness. It had been urged that the President acted under the undue influence of our Minister to France (Mr. Livingston.) Such an influence had never existed. The Chief Magistrate was bound to lay all the facts before the country. It was required that the treaty on our part should be sanctiod by by our Senate. This was done, and when France was advised of that fact, why did she not confirm it on her part? Mr. S. said emphatically that France *must* pay this stipulated indemnity; and when he said she must, he indicated the relative position in which the two nations stood. It was a contract which must be fulfilled, and few in this country would be found recreant in support of that position. He deemed it totally unnecessary to say "at all hazards;" he cared not for the words; when he said she *must*, he said all. The present period was distinguished for it's pacific policy. By this expression of our opinion, we summon France before the civilized world, and public opinion would stamp its veto on the whole course of her flagrant injustice towards us. She had taken, with avidity, all the advantages secured to her by the treaty, in the introduction of her wines and silks; but when you come to the indemnity, *that* is the pecuniary part of the treaty, and cannot be carried into effect by her Deputies! The French derive about half a million of dollars in her commerce, ($200,000 on her wines, and about $300,000 on her silks,) on the strength of the treaty, and then refuse to fulfil their part of the contract. How could France look us or the world in the face, with gross injustice branded upon her fame? We had been told that we had nothing to do with national honor! It was the first time he had ever heard that strange doctrine promulgated He would tell the gentleman from Georgia, (Mr. Gilmer,) that there was in this country a strong and unconquerable spirit of national pride; not indeed, the spirit that created strife between crowned heads, but that elevated policy which would induce us properly and promptly to meet every emergency in which the honor of a country or of an individual could be involved. The people of this country would insist on the fulfilment to the treaty to the uttermost letter. It was right that they should do so; for if it were infracted with impunity, every puny government in Christendom would turn up its nose with scorn and contempt, at our system of passive obedience and non-resistance. He did not believe there was a man in this country who would go to war for the paltry sum of five millions in contest. No; it was the honor and dignity of our national character that prompted the patriotic feeling which pervaded the community. Much had been said of the blood that was to be shed in this contest. He did not believe that any blood was to be shed, but if it was, it would be better to meet the crisis like men, than to crouch like slaves.

Mr. CLAYTON said the House were acting upon a report of the Committee on Foreign Affairs, founded upon information furnished by the President of the United States. Now if they were to act upon reports of newspapers, or to travel out of the record, they would be acting in a manner unbecoming the dignity of the subject. He observed, also, that it was not those who spoke the loudest who were the most brave, and it generally happened that the war party in peace were the peace party in war. They should also remember that they themselves would never be called upon to face a gun, and they were in the situation of waging war for others. Mr. C. contended that there was no necessity for it. What was the present situation of affairs with France? What said the French Government? Hear the language of the Foreign Minister of France:

"The King's Government, though deeply wounded by imputations to which I will not give a name, having demonstrated their purely gratuitous character, still does not wish to retreat absolutely from a determination, already taken, in a spirit of good faith and justice. How great soever may be the difficulties, caused by the provocation which President Jackson has given, and by the irritation which it has produced in the public mind, it will ask the Chambers for an appropriation of twenty-five millions, in order to meet the engagements of July 4th."

Here, then, we have a distinct assurance from the French Minister that the bill would be presented. Mr. C. also read further extracts from the despatches. The Minister had given an assurance that if Congress failed to act on the recommendation of reprisals, the bill would be submitted, and no doubt passed. Mr. C. also maintained that the French Ministry had acted up to the pledges of the King to Mr. Livingston. How could Congress consistently act upon this subject when every thing had been done that could be done? We now stood as high as we could. We had forfeited nothing, and should we descend from that lofty elevation we had reached? He, for one, had no disposition to commit the nation. The man of true courage never committed himself, but waited silently, patiently, and with confidence, with a perfect determination to meet the crisis when it came. He would move to lay the whole subject on the table, were it not that many gentlemen wished to address the House. He was opposed to any resolutions being adopted, but if any were to be passed upon by the House, that of the gentleman from Virginia (Mr. Archer) was the only one which he could bring himself to vote for.

Mr. GILMER would ask what was intended by the introduction of the resolutions? What was promised or expected to result from them? These questions came home to every one, to the interest of the whole country. Besides, what power had that House to do so? That House had only legislative authority, and to pass these resolutions he contended would be transcending their constitutional limits of power. Mr. G. referred to the consequences and effects of war upon the interests of the country and the stability of its institutions. He contended that nothing had as yet been done by the French Government to justify such a course on our part. So far as the treaty making power of that country was concerned, every thing had been done that could be done. Of whom did we complain? Of the popular branch of the French Government. We should bear in mind that that branch was new to Franch, and every one must perceive, who had read the debates of the French Chamber, that there was a prevailing ignorance on the subject of these claims. They were apprehensive that the monarchy had gone too far, and there was a jealousy which existed between them. But should we, the most popular Government on earth, be the first and foremost to prevent the exercise of the popular branch of a nation just emerging from the shackles of despotism. He was convinced that if we went to war on account of this treaty, as the subject stood at present, public opinion would be against it. He had no doubt whatever, that the force of public opinion alone in Europe would compel France to pay this indemnity. War, it should be borne in mind, would put an end to it. Go to war, and the indemnity would be at an end. He said that neither national honor nor national character was concerned in this dispute.

Mr. LYTLE followed with great energy and at considerable length in support of the resolutions reported by Mr. Cambreleng, and in reply to Mr. Gilmer and Mr. Archer.

Mr. CAMBRELENG said, he rose not to prolong the debate, but to make an attempt to put an end to the only war which he believed would ever grow out of this question. We had on most great questions—particularly on one which divided the House and the country—adjusted it by compromise. He now rose to propose a compromise which he hoped would unite both sides of the House. It was due to the gentleman from Massachusetts, (Mr. Adams,) to explain to him that he could not accept his first resolution as he had promised to do, because, on examining its provisions, he found it referred rather to the rights

of the claimants than of the nation. He thought the House would not adopt a resolution of that character. He, however, proposed to offer the resolution he had presented yesterday, without the words, "at all hazards," for he was compelled to concur in the opinion expressed by the gentleman himself, (Mr. Everett,) that they were unparliamentary.

Mr. E. EVERETT explained. He considered them not unparliamentary in a report, but in the form of a resolution.

Mr. C. continued: That gentleman must pardon me, sir, if I cannot perceive the propriety of the distinction between a report and a resolution, which he makes. Both are alike reported for adoption or rejection by the House. The language was, he thought, not only unparliamentary —but the gentleman must pardon him for saying that it was undignified and even gasconading. He, therefore, most willingly relinquished them as incompatible with the dignity of the House. He should offer the resolution without these words, as soon as the present motion was decided, and he hoped in that form it would meet the approbation of the House.

Mr. ROBERTSON, of Virginia, after some remarks read, two resolutions which he had prepared, and intended to offer, in the event of that offered by his colleague (Mr. Archer,) being rejected. The first one declared that the United States regard the treaty of 1831 as fairly and finally settling the differences between the two Governments; and that there was satisfactory evidence that the French Government was desirous of the fulfilment of the treaty, and reason to hope that the Chamber will carry it into effect. The second resolution, he said, he had extracted from the words of the report of the Committee on Foreign Relations. Mr. R. advocated the position indicated in his resolution at some length.

Mr. BINNEY then obtained the floor but gave way, to enable the Speaker to sign various bills.

Mr. BINNEY then proceeded to address the House in an argument of considerable length on the general principles involved in the dispute between the French Government and our own. He contended that we had nothing to do with the part the Chambers of France possessed in this matter. It was an affair among themselves—between the King and country. We were bound to look to the former, whom, only, we were to know in the transaction. He deprecated the evils of war, but the sacrifice of national honor, he considered a still greater calamity. This House, he said, could never insist on the fulfilment of the treaty of 1831, unless by negotiation. We had agreed in that very treaty to receive this indemnity by instalments, which must be received through the agency of negotiation. He called on gentlemen to pause before they used language which would take away all grace and half the force of their rights. Leave France no pretext, and if she does not enter into the door thus left open for her, it is not for us to answer the consequences. He could not vote for these resolutions submitted by the Committee on Foreign Relations, nor could he support those of the gentleman from Massachusetts, (Mr. Adams,) for the reasons which he had already submitted. He asked if this country was willing to strengthen the hands of the constitutional monarchy of France? That would be the unkindest cut of all, for us to strengthen a monarchy against its republican opponents. Would it oppose the interests of its friends—those who made common cause with us in advocating the execution of this treaty? One of these results was inevitable in the present state of French affairs at home, on the passage of either of these resolutions. Nor would he heed the idle babble of Legislative gossip so often quoted on this floor from the Chamber of Deputies, relating to the patience with which our country is habituated to bear the insult of others. Of all the resolutions proposed, he would prefer that of the gentleman from Virginia (Mr. Archer) for it expressed that which he really felt, a full reliance on the sense of justice on the part of the French nation, which would induce a full requital of the debt.

Mr. SCHLEY said he did not rise to make what might be dignified with the title of "a speech." He was restrained from doing so by two considerations: first, because he labored under a physical disability to do so, in consequence of ill health during the greater part of the session; and secondly, because in his opinion the subject under consideration did not require or admit of much speaking.

The course, said Mr. Schley, which gentlemen have taken in this debate, forcibly reminded him of a Reverend friend of his in Georgia, who is fond of speaking, and who, though he took a text, always sedulously avoided touching it in his discourse, and directed his attention to matters and things in general. Sir, said Mr. S. what is the question before the House? Is it a question of *war*? Is there any thing in the resolution offered, which looks to such a state of things? I humbly apprehend not. Why, then, do gentlemen portray in such vivid colors the horrors and calamities of war? Is it to drive us from the support of this resolution? to drive us from any action in regard to our present relations with France? If this be their object, they will find themselves in error.

Sir, I will not undertake to attribute the motive of such a course. Perhaps gentlemen would not be willing to admit as just, the opinion I have formed; but certainly no adequate motive can be found in the nature and tendency of the resolution itself; and no gentleman who has advocated it on this floor, has intimated a desire for war, nor any thing which could lead to such an idea.

I was somewhat astonished to hear my Hon. colleague, (Mr. Gilmer,) and the Hon. gentleman from Virginia, (Mr. Archer,) assert the doctrine that there was no violation of the treaty on the part of France by the refusal of the Chamber of Deputies to make the appropriation necessary to carry it into effect on their part. On what ground is this opinion held? On this, that the French Chambers is a separate and independent branch of that government, in the same manner that this House is under our constitution. Admit this fact, and what follows: why these honorable gentlemen say, *that the treaty is not complete and binding on the nation until all the departments of the Government have ratified it and provided for its final consummation; and therefore we have no cause of complaint against France.* Is this true, in regard either to the French Government or our own? I presume not. What would be the consequence of such a doctrine? The Executive branch of the Government, to which is intrusted the treaty making power, would enter into a solemn treaty with a foreign nation, but the Chamber of Deputies in France, or this House here, as the case may be, would refuse to make the appropriation necessary to carry it into effect, and consequently the treaty would prove in fact to be *no* treaty. The parties would stand precisely where they stood before the negotiations were commenced, and in this way a nation might forever avoid the payment of money due for any cause to another nation. Sir, this cannot be true. The proposition involves in itself a manifest contradiction. If the Executive branch of the Government has the power to make a treaty, it follows as a necessary consequence that such treaty must be binding and obligatory on the nation: and therefore if another branch of the same government, holding by the constitution the purse strings, shall refuse to pay the money stipulated by the treaty to be paid, such refusal is a violation of the faith of the nation, and *a breach of the treaty*. I admit the right of the Chambers and of this House to refuse the appropriation necessary to carry the treaty into effect; but *they do it at their peril*, and the nation injured or insulted by the refusal, will have the perfect right to demand and take satisfaction.

But his principal object in rising to address the House, was to present to them a view of the subject which had not been taken by any gentleman that had spoken. He would therefore proceed at once to what, in his opinion, was the main and the only question which ought to be considered, and he would detain the House but a few minutes. His honorable colleague (Mr. Gilmer) and the hon. gentleman from Virginia who last addressed the House (Mr. Robertson) had both emphatically asked the question, "what is the object of this resolution, if it be not to excite angry feelings, and lead to a state of hostilities? Sir, said Mr. S., I will tell the honorable gentleman what the object is. Every member on this floor, who has read the debates in the French Chamber, at the time when the law to appropriate money to carry the treaty into full effect, was rejected, knows that the ground upon which the rejection was placed, was that the promised indemnity was too great, and that some twelve or thirteen millions of francs is all that the French people ought in justice to pay. A pamphlet containing these debates, and this reasoning, was furnished by the Executive to every member at the opening of the present Congress. We have been in session three months, with a full knowledge of all these facts; and now, if we adjourn without opening our mouths on the subject, or declaring our view of the matter, will not the conclusion from such conduct be irresistable that we know we have obtained by the treaty more than we are entitled to? Will not the French Chamber and people have a right to say that we know that the ground taken by them is true in point of fact, and that, therefore, we have not denied it? Is not this the fair and legitimate conclusion from these premises? And are gentlemen prepared to do an act which shall lead to such consequences? Will they be silent, by refusing to pass this resolution, and by such silence convey to the French nation and the world, the idea, that we claim more than in justice and equity we are entitled to?

Sir, if there be any gentleman on this floor who really believes that the treaty gives up more than we are entitled to, let him say so, and let him vote against this resolution. But no man in this House, or in this nation, holds this opinion. On the contrary, every member who has addressed the Chair on either side of this question, has declared his firm conviction, that the indemnity offered by the treaty is much too small; that instead of twenty-five millions of francs, it ought to be some sixty or seventy millions. Those gentlemen who oppose this resolution, have declared, in the minority report, and in their speeches, that our claim under the treaty must not be abandoned. Why, then, are they unwilling to say so, by adopting the resolution on your table? No reason has been assigned, except that the resolution contains a menace or a threat. Not so, sir; there is nothing of that character in the resolution—nothing that could insult an individual, or a magnanimous people. No such thing is intended, and the French people cannot so understand it.

We desire not war. We have done nothing to lead to such a result. This resolution has no such bearing, and if the French Government shall choose to make war on us in consequence of its passage, let them do so, and take the odium and the consequences. The civilized world will not sanction, but decidedly condemn such a course.

This is the first opportunity which this House has had to express its opinion upon the conduct of the French Chambers in rejecting the appropriation, and upon the justice of our claims. There is, in fact, no difference of opinion here in regard to either. Let us then say to the French nation, that we know our cause to be just—that the indemnity provided by the treaty, instead of being too large, is, in fact, too small, and that we will insist upon its execution.

Mr. MANN, of New York, demanded the yeas and nays on the amendment offered by Mr. Archer; which were ordered.

Mr. GORHAM was in favor of the amendment offered by the gentleman from Virginia, (Mr. Archer.) He thought it a very proper resolution for the occasion; but he rose simply to enter his decided protest against the views contained in the speech which the gentleman had delivered in favor of his amendment. He was utterly opposed to the speech; but would vote for the resolution.

Mr. MASON, of Virginia, desired to state a single reason why he should vote against the amendment of his colleague, (Mr. Archer.) That gentleman had contended that the treaty with France was not a binding compact. If the amendment of his colleague should be concurred in, and should go out to the country coupled with the foregoing

declaration, it might have a tendency to induce a belief that this House had adopted the resolution in consequence of the reasons expressed by his colleague. For one, he was of opinion that the treaty with France was a solemn and binding compact, which could not be disregarded or set aside by the French Chambers. He repeated, in conclusion, that for the reason which he had assigned, he could not vote for the amendment.

Mr. WATMOUGH said, that the true and only course which he thought should be pursued, had been advocated by the gentleman from Georgia, and his colleague from Pennsylvania, (Mr. Binney and Mr. Clayton.) This course he would indicate in a motion before he sat down. It was not to avoid the terrors of war, that he should make the motion which he intended. War was admitted on all hands to be the most disastrous calamity which could befall the country; and in this case, in his humble opinion, there was no sufficient cause for war. To answer the purpose which accorded with his own judgment, he would move to lay the whole subject upon the table, and, upon this motion, he demanded the yeas and nays, which were ordered.

A call of the House was made and negatived.

Mr. CAMBRELENG called for the reading of the resolution which he had offered, in its modified form. He desired that the House should know what it was, that the gentleman from Pennsylvania, (Mr. Watmough,) had moved to lay on the table.

The resolution was read as follows:

Resolved, That in the opinion of this House, the treaty of the 4th July, 1831, should be maintained, and its execution insisted on.

The question was then taken on Mr. WATMOUGH'S motion to lay the whole subject on the table, by yeas and nays, as follows:

YEAS—Messrs. Chilton Allan, Ashley, Barber, Bates, Beaty, Bell, Binney, Campbell, Clayton, Downey, Corwin, Crane, Crockett, Deberry, Dickson, Horace Everett, Garland, Gilmer, Gorham, Grayson, Grennell, Griffin, Hardin, James Harper, Hazeltine, Ebenezer Jackson, Henry Johnson, King, Letcher, Love, McComas, Mercer, Milligan, Phillips, Pinckney, Potts, Shepard, Steele, Thomas, Tompkins, Trumbull, Tweedy, Vance, Vinton, Watmough, Wilde, Williams, Wise—48.

NAYS—Messrs. J. Q. Adams, John Adams, John J. Allen, William Allen, Anthony, Archer, Banks, Barnitz, Baylies, Beale, Bean, Beardsley, Beaumont, Blair, Bockee, Boon, Bouldin, Briggs, Brown, Bull, Bunch, Burd, Burns, Cage, Cambreleng, Carmichael, Carr, Casey, Chambers, Chaney, Chilton, Chinn, Claiborne, Samuel Clark, William Clark, Clay, Connor, Coulter, Cramer, Darlington, Davis, Davenport, Day, Denny, Dickinson, Dickinson, Evans, Edward Everett, Felder, Ferris, Fillmore, Forester, Foster, Philo C. Fuller, William K. Fuller, Fulton, Galbraith, Gamble, Gholson, Gillet, Gordon, Graham, Joseph Hall, Thomas H. Hall, Halsey, Hamer, Hannegan, Hard, Joseph M. Harper, Harrison, Hathaway, Hawkins, Hawes, Heath, Henderson, Hiester, Howell, Hubbard, Huntington, Inge, William Jackson, Janes, Jarvis, William C. Johnson, Richard M. Johnson, Cadiah Johnson, Seaborn Jones, Benjamin Jones, Kilgore, Kinnard, Lane, Lansing, Laporte, Lay, Lea, Lee, Lewis, Lincoln, Lucas, Lyon, Lytle, Mann, Manning, Martindale, Marshall, Mardis, J. Mason, May, McCarty, McIntire, McKay, McKennan, McKim, McKinley, McLene, McVean, Miller, Miner, Henry Mitchell, Robert Mitchell, R.D. Moore, Morgan, Muhlenberg, Murphy, Osgood, Parks, Parker, Patton, Pearce, Peyton, Pickens, Pierce, Pierson, Plummer, Polk, Ramsey, Reed, Rencher, Reynolds, Robertson, Schenck, Shinn, A. H. Shepperd, Shinn, Slade, Smith, Spangler, Speight, Standefer, Stewart, Sutherland, William Taylor, William P. Taylor, Thomas, Turner, Turrill, Vanderpoel, Van Houten, Wagener, Ward, Wardwell, Whallon, White, Frederick Whittlesey, Elisha Whittlesey, Wilson, Young—166.

So this motion was negatived.

Mr. BEARDSLEY remarked, that the amendment of the gentleman from Virginia (Mr. Archer) on the particular subject now under consideration. It contained two propositions—one declaratory of the views of this House, that no legislative measure was at this time required or proper; the other, a statement of the cause or foundation of the opinion at which the House had arrived. That foundation, as declared in the resolution, was a *"just expectation"* that France would make provision for carrying the treaty of 1831 into effect.

Mr. B. would ask upon what that "expectation" was founded? What ground had we for assuming it as the basis of our action on this most important subject? All might, as all did, desire that result. It was the hope of every one; but, for himself, he saw no sufficient reason for expressing the "just," the confident "expectation," that the government of France had already made, or would make, the required provision.

[Mr. ARCHER explained. He meant by the words "just expectation," as applied in the resolution, not to refer to the conduct of France, or what might be expected from her, but the character of our claims upon her, which he regarded as just.]

Mr. BEARDSLEY said, the explanation would help the matter but little, unless the phraseology of the resolution was changed. That would be understood, at home and abroad, according to the ordinary meaning of the terms used, and not as construed or explained by the honorable mover: and he insisted that the only fair interpretation that could be placed upon the language of the resolution, was that which he had given. At least, that was its natural and common-sense meaning: France would so understand it, if adopted by the House, and she would act accordingly. Then he would ask, again, upon what was that "expectation founded? Upon, as he supposed, the speculative conjecture of our Minister at Paris, and upon that alone. After the omission of France, from 1832 to this time, to perform her treaty—a positive, long-continued neglect and violation of its provisions—and still more, a positive refusal by the Chamber of Deputies to abide by its provisions —after the recall of the French Minister and the dismissal of ours from France, we are called upon, in the face of this mass of evidence, to express a confident, a "just expectation" that France will abide by and perform her treaty, which has hitherto been most unceremoniously neglected and violated. He could see no reasonable ground for that opinion: and he would not, out of mere complaisance to France, express an expectation which, in his opinion, was in no respect warranted by her conduct. This was one, and, with him, a decisive objection to the amendment under consideration. There were others, which might be stated, growing out of the posture of our present relations with France; and which, in his judgment, called for a decided expression of opinion on the part of this House.

Mr. B. said he could not vote for the amendment of the honorable and very distinguished gentleman from Massachusetts, (Mr. Adams,) which proposed to advise the President that further negotiation with France would meet the approbation of this House, if, in the opinion of the President, that course would be compatible with the honor and interest of the United States.

The treaty-making power was not vested in this House, but in the President and Senate. The President was the organ of that power, and of the Union at large—with all Foreign governments. He would leave those, upon whom the Constitution had devolved that responsibility, to exercise it, without obtruding upon them advice, which is not asked for, and for which he could see no necessity. Even if the advice were of itself proper, he would not, at this time, expose to France any strong anxiety for further negotiation. With whom would we negotiate? With the King of the French? He had signed the treaty—he admitted its obligatory force, and was unquestionably desirous to see it fulfilled. It was not his fault that it had not been punctually performed. Why then negotiate further with the King?—or, was it intended to invite a negotiation with the Chamber of Deputies?

Mr. B. said he did not, in all respects, approve of the original resolutions, reported by the chairman of the Committee on Foreign Affairs, although he would vote for them rather than not express any opinion upon the subject. The amendment, however, which had been proposed by the honorable chairman, and which he understood had been accepted by the gentleman from Massachusetts, (Mr. Adams,) as a substitute for his first resolution, met with his entire approbation, and he should give it his vote. If adopted it would express the opinion of this House, that it was the duty of the Government of the United States to insist upon the performance, by France, of the treaty of 1831. The circumstances in which we were placed, demanded an explicit opinion on our part, either that we would or would not insist upon its performance. If we were not prepared to insist upon it, let us say so, and abandon it altogether.

Gentlemen had said such an expression would be equivalent to a declaration of war against France. If so, then the minority of the Committee on Foreign Affairs was for war, for this was their sentiment, expressed in their own language, leaving off those words which were supposed to give it an unbecoming severity, if not indeed some small degree of ferocity. The obnoxious words "at all hazards," had been stricken out, and the only sentiment which the resolution would now contain, was the fixed opinion of this House, that the treaty ought not to be abandoned but that its performance should be insisted on.

And is, have we not a right to express that opinion and to indicate that purpose? Is not such the general sentiment of our constituents? Are we prepared, any one of us, to abandon the treaty, or to say to France that we will not insist on its performance?

Sir, will France have a right to regard this resolution as a menace? Surely not. She has made the question for us and we are bound to decide it. To decide it as the national honor and the national interest requires; as our constituents demand that it should be decided. Sir, is there any reasdoubt of what is the true sentiment of this country? Consult the public press: with the exception of the most degraded and corrupt of its organs, we shall find it united in maintaining the sanctity of the treaty, and insisting that the rights secured by it, shall in no event be sacrificed or abandoned. Sir, let us take counsel from the patriotic feelings of the country, and proclaim to France and to the world, that as the obligation of this treaty is perfect, so on our part we have performed all its stipulations with fidelity, so we will exact and insist upon a similar observance on theirs.

Mr. BRIGGS expressed a disposition to vote for the amendment of the gentleman from Virginia, (Mr. Archer,) because it gave an expression of the opinion of the House, which he deemed necessary. It appeared by the discussion in the French Chambers, that an idea prevailed there that we were divided on the subject of the justice and intention of recovering this claim. This, he apprehended, was not the fact. He believed this House—he believed this people to be united on this subject. The very newspaper (the National Intelligencer) which had been loudest denounced, as opposing the views of the President, had very emphatically declared in favor of the validity of the treaty, and the necessity of its being fulfilled. An expression of the opinion of the House, on this point, and the confidence we entertain in the final adjustment of the claim, seemed to be called for. He, for one, would contribute to that result of the discussion.

Mr. WISE begged to say a word or two only. Instead of spending so much time in idle debate, he thought they would be best doing their duty by putting their country into a state of defence. If this war should come within the next twelve-months, he feared he should be called one of those members of Congress who neglected to take measures to put the country in a state of defence; and when the French fleet should arrive, and seize upon our fortifications it will be asked what was the House of Representatives about, during the last two days of the session; and the only reply will be, that they were spent in debate. Mr. W. wished the subject had been laid on the table, and that they had taken up the subject of appropriation to provide for the means of defence. To the House, and every individual member of it, he would say, in mercy say no more about it.

Mr. CAMBRELENG expressed a hope that the

gentleman from Massachusetts (Mr. Adams) would consent to adopt the resolution which he had proposed, for the purpose of facilitating the business of the House. If that gentleman did not deem it expedient to do so, Mr. C. said he should feel it incumbent on him to move it as an amendment, after the question had been taken on the amendment of the gentleman from Va. He urged the House to come to some action upon the subject. Let us, said Mr. C., do our duty, without reference to the course of the French Chamber of Deputies, and leave them to do theirs.

Mr. ADAMS, of Mass. said he would offer a few reasons why he could not vote for the resolution offered as an amendment, by the gentleman from Virginia, (Mr. Archer,) That resolution expressed a "just *expectation*" that France would have made provision for carrying into effect the treaty, &c. Mr. A. said he was not disposed to bandy words on this subject, but he could not say that he had a *just* expectation—or an expectation at all—that France would willingly render us justice; and he would lie to his own conscience if he said so. He could not, in conscience, vote this, for he did not believe it. Sir, said Mr. A., if, as has been said, there can be no justifiable occasion for a war of words with the French nation, this is neither a place or time for complimenting them. Whence came the compliments to the French? Were they elicited by her virtues? Was it because she had refused the payment of the annual instalments due to us? Was it because she had violated her plighted faith? Did gentlemen find, in all this, cause of compliment?—Was it from the style of the dignified debates in their Chamber of Deputies, where we were characterised as a nation of mercenaries—where the basest and meanest of motives were attributed to the American people—those of sordid avarice, speculation, and gain! Where it was said of us—They wont go to war! No. If you owe them ten millions, they will take up with *three*. Such, Mr. A. said, was the language and style of the French towards us. He asked if on this was founded the "*just expectations*" of the gentleman from Virginia. Mr. A. said he did not believe in the truth of the declaration contained in the gentleman's resolution; and that was one substantial reason why he could not vote for it. Another reason was comprised in what he had heretofore said—and what the gentleman himself, in the honesty and sincerity of his heart, had promptly admitted, that the whole foundation, both of his speech and his resolution, was *fear*. Not that the gentleman was capable of entertaining such a feeling in relation to himself. No: on this point he fully concurred with the gentleman's colleague (Mr. Bouldin,) who, by the way had, in a masterly manner, exposed and dissipated many of his arguments. No man, said Mr. A., is presumed to be more tenacious of his individual reputation—his personal honor. But while he was speaking, an observer could easily detect the conflict in his bosom, between his sense of individual and national honor—that he felt that he could not himself submit to humiliation, while he was pursuading this House to act as cowards—saying to them, you must not do this, for fear of the power of France! Sir, said Mr. A., the gentleman's speech was perfectly consistent with the resolution with which he concluded it. His honorable colleague (Mr. Gorham) had expressed a determination to vote for that resolution, at the same time taking occasion to protest against the gentleman's speech. I protest against both the speech and the resolution: for if it is true that the French are not bound by the treaty, and do not owe the debt, then we have no right to pass the resolution. So he might say to the gentleman from Pennsylvania, (Mr. Binney,) whose speech was also perfectly consistent with the resolution. He admitted that the House should first settle the question, whether that treaty was truly binding. [Mr. A. here read from the French constitution the portion relating to the functions of the King, showing that the treaty-making power reposed in him.] Not a word, said Mr. A., is here said about the Chamber of Deputies. Before God and man that treaty was binding. Another article of the constitution declares that "the public debt is guarantied—every debt entered into by the constituted authorities *shall be inviolable*." So the Chamber of Deputies could not reject this indemnity without violating national faith—without violating their own constitution, which they are sworn to support. He had heard a motion to lay this subject on the floor—no, the table. He had heard much of our obligation to the French, and it incontinently reminded him of one who spoke in

> "Words clothed in reason's garb,
> Courting ignoble ease—not peace."

He would tell gentlemen what his object was from the commencement of this question. The President of the United States had laid before Congress the state of the nation—its relations with the rest of the world, and particularly with that great, that mighty nation, France. He told the tale in unvarnished guise. Such was the condition between the two powers It was not entirely new. Many of the facts were known through unofficial channels to members at the last session. The President, and through him, our nation, had assumed an attitude before the world. I ask not whether he was right or wrong It was enough that the nation was committed. And what was this House about to do. He would not say it was about to "dodge" the question. No—but it *refused to act!* In another place, that body appointed a committee on the subject, in deference to the recommendations of the President. That committee did its duty faithfully. It sustained in its report, the Chief Magistrate, in all the facts—but closed by a resolution, declaring it inexpedient to take any legislative measures on the subject. Now, he asked, if we stop here, how did this matter appear? Why, it would appear that one branch of the legislature recommends that nothing be done, while the other refuses to express any opinion on the subject. The anticipation of such a result had been the source of all the anxiety which he had felt upon this subject. He did believe a declaration of the views of that House due to ourselves, to the world, to the sacred nature of treaties. It was, therefore, with reference to the effect on France, on Europe, on the world, that he had felt it most essentially incumbent on the House to express its feelings, its sentiments. We had heard much on that floor against war, and its horrors. These views were as ancient as the war of Troy—in proof of which, Mr. A. quoted from the Enead. It was said too, that we should go to war and deluge the country with blood for a paltry sum of money. Such too, was the cry in 1775 and '6. When we possessed but a tithe of our present resources—when we had not only a foreign, but a civil and an Indian war! and all for—as was said by the tories of that day—two pence on a pound of tea! It was said it was cheaper to pay the tax than go to war! Even last war, some gentlemen considered the cause a small matter; and asked *how many* American citizens were impressed by Great Britain—declaring their belief, that it was very few! This he then thought a most singular argument, and the present argument was parallel to it. No man, Mr. A. said, could entertain a greater *abhorrence* for war and its calamities than he had. He would do any thing but sacrifice honor and independence to avoid it. But when he heard it advanced on that floor that there was no such thing as national honor—that it was merely ideal—he must take leave to say that he did not subscribe to such doctrine. After some further remarks, Mr. A. said such were the reasons which induced his resolutions. The first was declarative of the rights of our citizens to the indemnity claimed, and the other was declarative of a determination not to omit any possible means of honorable pacification. Mr. A. then referred to the situation of the two countries in 1794, when a non-intercouse was declared between the two countries, and quoted documents on that subject, and concluded by expressing a hope that the amendment of the gentleman from Virginia (Mr. Archer,) would be rejected.

[The above is a mere outline of Mr. A.'s remarks, and has no pretension to literal accuracy.]

Mr. HARDIN had hoped, he said, that the committee on Foreign Affairs would have reported in sufficient time to have allowed every gentleman an opportunity of delivering his sentiments upon this subject. Late as it was, Mr. H. should not have said a word on the subject, but for the last war-speech of the gentleman from New York, (Mr. Cambreleng.)

Mr. H. entered into an examination of the foundation of these claims under the treaty. They had arisen from spoliations made by Napoleon Bonaparte, who had always refused to make any indemnity. Both Louis XVIII and Charles the Xth had also refused to enter into it, and it was only till the elevation of Louis Philippe to the throne of France, that these twenty-five millions had been acknowledged. To this King we owed the treaty, and he had omitted nothing in his power to secure its passage. Mr. H. also contended that the French Chamber, as the popular branch, had the same right to reject a treaty involving an appropriation, as the House of Representatives in Congress had. Besides, the French had the power of making their own laws and their own constitution, and they had the right of putting their interpretation upon them. With these views, he thought it cowardly, he thought it dastardly, for this nation to threaten war. He could see no treachery, no backsliding, in the King or his Ministers. That King was surrounded with difficulties, and had made himself responsible for injuries done twenty-five years ago. What should we go to war for? A paltry sum of five millions. A war would cost us in one year not less than ten or fifteen millions of dollars, and would sweep from the ocean at least fifty millions of our commerce. And upon whom would the expense fall? Upon the hard-working, industrious farmer, almost exclusively. Besides, Mr. H. had no feeling for a French war. He remembered when we had only two millions and a half of people, when we were overwhelmed with debt, and our little band of hardy patriots without arms or clothing, that France shed her blood and expended her treasure for us. Should we forget this? She stood by us when all the nations of the earth stood aloof from us.

Mr. GORHAM rose to reply to some remarks of Mr. Adams. He said the whole bent of that gentleman's resolutions and his speech began and ended in the position that war was inevitable with France. He denied that such was the feeling or the policy of Massachusetts. Mr. G. then proceeded to examine the grounds on which the treaty stood, how it was obtained, &c. He also went into a detail of the difference of sentiments entertained by him from those of other gentlemen who had addressed the House, particularly Mr. Archer and Mr. Adams.

Mr. CHILTON next obtained the floor. He also replied most particularly to the remarks of Mr. Adams. The position which that gentleman first took upon this floor, upon this question, excited the surprise of all, and particularly his friends. He had then accused another branch of the Legislature of *dodging* the question. He had subsequently, in an explanation, declared that he also wished this House to do the same thing. On the last occasion he had assured the country that there was no prospect of a war with France—that there was not a member on that floor who would vote for such a proposition. How were we to reconcile those various and conflicting opinions and sentiments of the gentleman with his present course? Mr. C. said the resolutions of Mr. A. were infinitely weaker than he could approve, though he denounced his *war speech*. He disavowed any personal disrespect to that gentleman, in thus alluding to the inconsistencies of his course. To use a musical phrase, he had looked upon the gentleman heretofore as a sort of political pitch-pipe here. A trumpet of an uncertain sound might lead to disastrous consequences in the field of battle. Hereafter he should follow a trumpeter with an instrument of a less uncertain sound.

Mr. ARCHER also thought the gentleman from Massachusetts, (Mr. Adams,) should be the last to give lectures on consistency. Allusions had been made to his *fears* and to his courage. If he had courage, he was sure he would not show it only, as he would not say whose was shown, in bravado and menace. He had said that he had full confidence in the justice of France. He still retained that opinion. Mr. A. continued further to defend

is amendment.

Mr. HAWES told a story of a bird whose only cry was "fair play." Such was his cry on the present occasion, as he could not abide to see so any birds plucking one. He was well aware, owever, that the gentleman from Massachusetts, (Mr. Adams,) needed no champion to enter the ris in his defence, for, as the roused lion shakes e dew drops from his mane, so could he shake if his antagonists at will. He marvelled what ad brought down the ire of his two colleagues, Messrs. Hardin and Chilton,) and the gentleman om Virginia, (Mr. Archer,) in their united rength upon the distinguished gentleman from Massachusetts! Was it because an American sat high in his bosom? Was it because he oldly stepped forward to sustain the honor of his ountry? Mr. H. said, no man had been accustomd more highly to respect the French nation than imself. He, too, like his honorable colleague, Mr. Hardin,) remembered when with us the lily as accounted the fairest flower of the field. He, xo, had paused with high-wrought feelings before te painting in the rotundo, where the warors of veteran France and infant America were rouped together in the enjoyment of recent vicory—the reward of their mutual prowess. But lould the recollection of those things make us regretful of right? Should they teach us to, see or country trampled upon? His other colleague Mr. Chilton,) had represented the gentleman om Massachusetts as ready at one time to be received with open arms by a party on that floor. ly what party? He asked if there was already French party and an American in that House? No, it was high time the people of Kentucky new it; and he should feel it his duty to go home nd acquaint his constituents of the fact. They are accustomed only to rally under the flag of teir country. Mr. H. said, he rose only to say hat he had said. He did not like to see the tetleman from Massachusetts, whose long career ad been crowned with that brightest of all rowns—the suffrages of a free people for their ighest station, exposed to a rifle here, a musket ore, and a pop-gun there.

The question was then taken by yeas and nays a Mr. Archer's amendment; and was rejected, as ollows, ayes 71; nays 143:

YEAS.—Messrs Heman Allen, Chilton Allan, rcher, Ashley, Barber, Barringer, Bates, Bayes, Bell, Binney, Campbell, Chambers, Chilton, laiborne, William Clarke, Clayton, Clowney, orwin, Crockett, Davis, Davenport, Deberry, ickson, Evans, Horace Everett, Felder, Gamle, Gilmer, Gordon, Gorham, Grayson, Grennell, Griffin, Hiland Hall, Hardin, Hazeltine, Wm. ckson, Ebenezer Jackson, Jones, King, Letcher, ewis, Lincoln, Martindale, Marshall, McComas, treer, Mill gan, Miner, Murphy, Phillips, Pickw, Pinckney, Potts, jr., Ramsay, Reed, Rencher, oberteon, William B. Shepard, Slade, Steele, tompkins. Trumbull, Tweedy, Vinton, Watugh, Elisha Whittlesey, Wilde, Williams, Wise, oung.—71.

NAYS.—Messrs. John Q. Adams, John Adams, ohn J. Allen, Wm. Allen, Anthony, Banks, Barma, Beale, Bean, Beardsley, Blair, Bockee, Boon, oulden, Briggs, Brown, Bull, Bunch, Burch, urns, Cage, Cambreleng, Carmichael, Carr, Cay, Chaney, Chinn, Samuel Clark, Connor, Coulr, Cramer, Day, Denny, Dickerson, Dickinson, unlap, Edward Everett, Ferris, Fillmore, Forese, Foster, Philo C. Fuller, William K. Fuller, alton, Garland, Gholson, Gillet, Graham, Thomas Hall, Halsey, Hamer, Hannegan, Hard, Jos. Harper, James Harper, Harrison, Hathaway, awkins, Hawes, Heath, Henderson, Hiester, owell, Hubbard, Huntington, Inge, Jarvis, R. Johnson, Noadiah Johnson, Henry Johnson, eaborn Jones, Kavanagh, Kilgore, Kinnard, xes, Lansing, Laporte, Lay, Lea, Lee, Love, xes, Lyon, Lytle, Abijah Mann, Joel K. Mann, ansing, Martin, John Y. Mason, Moses Mason, sy, McCarty, McIntire, McKay, McKennan, Mcim, McKinley, McVean, Miller, Henry chell, Robert Mitchell, Moore, Morgan, Muhlenberg, Osgood, Parks, Parker, Patton, Patterk, Pearce, Peyton, Pierce, Pierson, Plummer, xlk, Reynolds, Schenck, Schley, A. H. Shep-

perd, Shinn, Smith, Spangler, Spright, Standefer, Stewart, Sutherland, William Taylor, Wm. P. Taylor, Francis Thomas, Thomson, Turner, Turrill, Vanderpoel, Van Houten, Wagener, Ward, Wardwell, Webster, Whallon, White, Frederick Whittlesey, Wilson.—143.

Mr. CAMBRELENG then moved the following resolution (according to an intimation which he had before made) as an amendment to the first of those introduced by Mr. Adams:

Resolved, That in the opinion of this House, the treaty of the 4th of July, 1831, should be maintained and its execution insisted on.

Mr. ADAMS said he was willing to adopt it. While he was up, he had a word to say on the remarks of his colleague, (Mr. Gorham) who had denounced his course as not being in accordance with the sentiments of Massachusetts. If such was the fact, he could but regret it. He had only to say it was in accordance with the dictates of his own heart.

Mr. GORHAM said there was no man in the United States for whom he had more sincere respect than for his honorable colleague. He had not made his remarks in a spirit of dictation. He was well aware that that gentleman possessed the right to maintain his own opinion—but he (Mr G) must be permitted also to retain the opinion he had already expressed.

Mr. S. JONES, of Georgia, then submitted the following, as an amendment to the above:

Resolved, That, with a solemn treaty, acknowledging the rights of our citizens, entered into under the usual formalities, and with a nation professing to be governed by that code which prescribes the obligation of such instruments, we have every right to expect that the same will be observed in good faith; and that as this House is officially informed the law for executing said treaty is now under consideration in the French Legislature, it is inexpedient, for the present, to legislate on the subject.

Mr. S. JONES briefly advocated the amendment, and called for the yeas and nays, but they were not ordered.

The question was then taken, and the resolution rejected without a division.

Mr. ROBERTSON then offered the following as an amendment,

Strike out from first revolution, words "resolved that," and insert:

"There is satisfactory evidence that the French Government desires that the appropriation for indemnity should be made in pursuance of the stipulations of the treaty of July 4, 1831, and reason to hope that the Chamber of Deputies will adopt that measure, and faithfully discharge the obligations of France to the United States."

Mr. GORHAM asked for the yeas and nays, which were not ordered. The amendment was then rejected.

The question then recurring on the substitute adopted by Mr J. Q. ADAMS, as given above,

Mr. MANN, of New York, called for the yeas and nays.

They were ordered and taken, when the resolution was adopted UNANIMOUSLY, as follows:

YEAS.—Messrs John Q. Adams, John Adams, Heman Allen, John J. Allen, William Allen, Anthony, Archer, Ashley, Banks, Barber, Barnitz, Barringer, Bates, Beale, Bean, Beardsley, Beaumont, Bell, Blair, Bockee, Boon, Boulton, Biggs, Brown, Bull, Bunch, Burd, Burns, Cage, Cambreleng, Campbell, Carmichael, Carr, Casey, Chambers, Chaney, Chilton, Chinn, Claiborne, Samuel Clark, William Clark, Clayton, Clowney, Connor, Corwin, Coulter, Cramer, Crockett, Darlington, Amos Davis, Davenport, Day, Deberry, Denny, Dickson, Dickerson, Dickinson, Dunlap, Evans, Edward Everett, Felder, Ferris, Fillmore, Forester, Foster, Philo C. Fuller, William K. Fuller, Fulton, Galbraith, Gamble, Garland, Gholson, Gillet, Gilmer, Gordon, Gorham, Graham, Grayson, Grennell, Griffin, Hiland Hall, Thomas H. Hall, Halsey, Hamer, Hannegan, Hard, Hardin, Joseph M. Harper, James Harper, Harrison, Hathaway, Hawkins, Hawes, Hazeltine, Heath, Henderson, Hiester, Howell, Hubbard, Huntington, Inge, William Jackson, Ebenezer Jackson, Janes, Jarvis, Richard M. Johnson, Noadiah John-

son, Henry Johnson, Seaborn Jones, Benjamin Jones, Kavanagh, Kilgore, King, Kinnard, Lane, Lansing, Laporte, Lay, Lea, Lee, Letcher, Lewis, Lincoln, Lucas, Lyon, Lytle, Abijah Mann, Joel K. Mann, Manning, Martindale, Marshall, Mardis, John Y. Mason, Moses Mason, May, McCarty, McComas, McIntire, McKay, McKennan, McKim, McKinley, McLene, McVean, Mercer, Miller, Milligan, Miner, Henry Mitchell, Robert Mitchell, Moore, Morgan, Muhlenberg, Murphy, Osgood, Parks, Park r, Patton, Patterson, Pearce, Peyton, Phillips, Pickens, Pierce, Pierson, Pinckney, Plummer, Polk, Potts, Ramsay, Reed, Rencher, Reynolds, Robertson, Schenck, Schley, Augustine H. Shepperd, Shinn, Slade, Smith, Spangler, Spright, Standefer, Steele, Stewart, Sutherland, William Taylor, William P. Taylor, Francis Thomas, Thomson, Tompkins, Trumbull, Turner, Turrill. Tweedy, Vanderpoel, Van Houten, Vinton, Wagener, Ward, Wardwell, Watmough, Webster, Whallon, White, Frederick Whittlesey, Elisha Whittlesey, Williams, Wilson, Wise, Young—312.

NAYS—NONE.

Mr. ADAMS then withdrew his other resolution, and Mr. CAMBRELENG also withdrew the first resolution reported from the Committee on Foreign Affairs, its place being superseded by the one first adopted.

The following resolutions were then also UNANIMOUSLY adopted

Resolved, That the Committee on Foreign Affairs be discharged from the further consideration of so much of the President's Message as relates to commercial restrictions, or to reprisals on the commerce of France.

Resolved, That preparation ought to be made to meet any emergency growing out of our relations with France.

The joint resolution (from the Senate, rescinding the joint rule which prohibits the transmission of bills to the President on the last day of the session, was then adopted, after an ineffectual attempt on the part of Mr. MASON to amend it, so as to rescind that which prohibits the transmission of bills from one House to the other on the same day.

On motion of Mr. POLK, several appropriation bills returned from the Senate with amendments, were referred to the Committee of Ways and Means—when, at 12 o'clock,

The House adjourned.

IN SENATE.

Tuesday, March 3, 1835.

The VICE PRESIDENT laid before the Senate the credentials of the Honorable Bedford Brown, a Senator elect to represent the State of North Carolina for six years from and after the 3d March, 1835.

Mr. WEBSTER, from the Committee on Finance, made a report in regard to the documentary history of the country, as furnished by the Secretary of State, in obedience to a resolution of the Senate of last session.

The report was laid on the table.

Mr. W. moved that the committee be discharged from the further consideration of the circular of the Treasury, in regard to the land offices; which was agreed to.

Mr. W. said the committee had been directed at the last session to inquire into the condition of the United States Bank, the deposite banks, and the currency of the country. He said the two first subjects had already been before the Senate. That in regard to the currency, they had a mass of information, which had been collected, but that it was not in a condition to be laid before the Senate.

Mr. W. said, by a resolution of the Senate, the Committee on Finance had been directed to lay before it information concerning the amount of bullion in the Bank of the United States, and other subjects connected therewith; but that the committee had received no information on that subject.

Mr. W. said he had observed in the official paper of the administration, an allusion to certain statements made by himself in regard to the mode of payment of Treasury drafts by a deposite bank. He did not feel himself bound to make any explanation to an irresponsible editor; but if any honorable Senator in favor of the administration would

call for the name and dates, he was prepared to give them. He did not war with private individuals.

Mr. CLAY, from the Committee on Foreign Relations, to whom was referred the President's Message, transmitting the correspondence between the Governments of the United States and France, asked to be discharged from the further consideration of the subject and from all other subjects before them; which was agreed to.

Mr. WRIGHT, from the Committee on Finance, asked to be discharged from the further consideration of the petition of John F. Lewis; which was agreed to.

Mr. HENDRICKS, from the Committee on Roads and Canals, reported a bill in addition to an act incorporating the Chesapeake and Ohio Canal Company with an amendment.

Mr. NAUDAIN, from the Committee on Claims, asked to be discharged from the further consideration of subjects referred to it; which was agreed to.

Mr. SILSBEE, from the Committee on Commerce;

Mr. BLACK, from the Committee on Private Land Claims;

Mr. TYLER, from the Committee on the District of Columbia;

Mr. TOMLINSON, from the Committee on Pensions;

Mr. ROBBINS, from the Committee on the Library;

Mr. BELL, from the Committee on Claims, and Mr. HENDRICKS, from the Committee on Roads and Canals—each asked to be discharged from the several subjects committed to them; which was agreed to.

Mr. CLAYTON, from the Committee on the Judiciary, made an unfavorable report on the claim of Orange H. Dibble.

Mr. LINN presented a petition; which was laid on the table.

Mr. MANGUM presented certain resolutions of the Legislature of North Carolina, instructing him to vote for expunging from the journals of the Senate the resolution of last March, declaring that the President had violated the law and constitution of the country. Mr. M. desired the instructions might be laid on the table, although he could not obey them. He said he was commanded to do an act that would violate that constitution which he was bound to support. He did not, however, consider the Senate the proper place to give his reasons for disobeying the instructions of the Legislature. That was a point he was to settle with his constituents.

Mr. FRELINGHUYSEN said, he stood in the same predicament as his friend from North Carolina, (Mr. Mangum.) He had constitutional objections to complying. He believed the Senate had no power over the journal. It was a record of the acts of the Senate, guarantied by the constitution, for the benefit of the minority. He would warn the majority who should be in those seats next session, to leave to him untouched the sacred privilege, provided by the constitution, for showing his successors how he had acted.

Mr. CALHOUN expressed his regret that the subject had been deferred to so late a period of the session. He believed it the most important subject that had been brought before Congress; and a subject on which he had wished to be heard. He thought they had the same right to express their disapprobation of as to flatter the Executive. When they had arrived to such a period as either they must flatter or be silent, they should equal the most degenerate days of the Roman Republic, when the horse of the emperor was declared consul.

Mr. KING, of Alabama, said, he was surprised at the language of the Senator from South Carolina, (Mr. Calhoun.) The gentleman spoke of an opportunity of discussing the subject. Did he not remember the presentation of the instructions from Alabama? It was great injustice to insinuate the discussion had been put off by the friends of the administration, when he, (Mr. C.) had occupied the Senate most of the time with his report and bills, since the resolution was introduced. The honorable Senator had spoken of flattering the Executive. Had not that Senator heaped upon

the President, with the utmost license, his censures and invectives, and been listened to with far more attention than he had listened to those who spoke in his defence, believing he had acted honestly and with good intentions? Yet the Senator compared them to the degenerate times of the Roman Senate!

Mr. K. said, he for one was not disposed to be branded as the supple tool of Executive power. If the Senator makes such charges, he must except him from the number. Mr. K. said he would not endure it. There were certain disappointed aspirants to power who always viewed things through a gloomy medium, who were ever croaking over the imaginary ruins of our free institutions.

After some further remarks by Messrs. CALHOUN, MANGUM, and LEIGH,

Mr. CLAYTON said he would say nothing of the instructions. He had himself received instructions, but of a very different nature from those before the Senate. His own State (Delaware) had instructed him to resist any attempt to deface the journals of the Senate, and he had risen to make a motion that would give him an opportunity of obeying. He would first move to lay the instructions on the table, which was agreed to.

Mr. CLAYTON then moved to take up the resolution offered by Mr. Benton, for expunging from the journal's the condemnatory resolution.

Mr. PORTER objected, as the time of the Senate was required for the necessary business before it.

Mr. BLACK demanded the yeas and nays. The motion was supported by Messrs. CLAY, CLAYTON, LEIGH, and FRELINGHUYSEN, and opposed by Messrs. PRESTON, and KING of Georgia.

Mr. BROWN said he wished to reiterate the same sentiments he had expressed there a year ago. He thought the act, for which the President had been censured, was one of the brightest actions of the present administration. It would redound to the honor of President Jackson to the latest period of our republic.

The question was then taken by yeas and nays, and decided in the affirmative.

YEAS—Messrs. Bell, Benton, Brown, Buchanan, Calhoun, Clay, Clayton, Ewing, Frelinghuysen, Goldsborough, Grundy, Hill, Kane, King of Alabama, Knight, Leigh, Linn, M'Kean, Mangum, Morris, Moore, Naudain, Prentiss, Robbins, Robinson, Ruggles, Shepley, Smith, Swift, Tallmadge, Tomlinson, White, Wright—33.

NAYS—Messrs. Bibb, Black, Cuthbert, Hendricks, Kent, King of Georgia, Porter, Preston, Tipton, Tyler, Waggaman, Webster—12.

So the Senate took up the resolution.

Mr. WHITE then moved to amend the resolution by striking out the word "expunge," and inserting "rescind, revere, and to make null and void."

Mr. W. said he could not vote to obliterate and deface the journal of the Senate. He believed it was the right of every Senator to have the votes stand, that the People might know how they had voted. He wished the resolution so framed as to express his feelings on the subject.

Mr. W. desired the yeas and nays on the adoption of his amendment; which were ordered.

Mr. WEBSTER said he should vote against the amendment. He wished to bring the Senate to vote on the original resolution.

Mr. BENTON said, he believed the word "expunge" was strictly parliamentary. He did not wish to obliterate the journal, but to make use of a phraseology which would strongly express that the resolution ought never to have been put into that journal. The word "rescind" was not strong enough; it admitted the lawfulness of the act at the time it was done. It was a convenient term when they merely wished to alter any thing that had been found inexpedient. It was a mere harmless word, expressing no marked disapprobation of the propriety of the resolution at the time it was adopted. Every Senator, said Mr. B. might vote to "rescind" the resolution, without altering his opinion in the least. They might say that President Jackson was the first Executive that had ever been condemned in this manner;

therefore they would rescind the resolution. Such, and no more, was the force of the term "rescind."

Mr. WHITE said, in his opinion, the term "expunge" referred to obliterating the journal, which he could never consent to have done. He wished the proceedings to stand as they transpired, and go down unblemished to posterity. He thought the proposed amendment, which declared the resolution null and void, as much as said it now ought to have been inserted in the journal.

After some further remarks from Mr. WHITE and Mr. WEBSTER, Mr. NAUDAIN moved to amend the amendment by inserting such words as would re-affirm the condemnatory resolution, but afterwards withdrew the motion.

After some remarks from Messrs. BENTON, WHITE, GOLDSBOROUGH, and CLAYTON,

Mr. WRIGHT said, he did not rise to debate this question, but merely to ask the indulgence of the Senate to lay on the table the instructions given him and his colleague by the Legislature of New York.

Mr. CLAYTON objected.

Mr. McKEAN, after some introductory remarks, suggested to Mr. WHITE to modify his amendment so as to adopt the words used by the board of the Pennsylvania Legislature in their resolution of instruction upon this subject, which would make the amendment more acceptable to him—the effective words were to repeal and renew.

Mr. WHITE adopted the words as a modification; when

A discussion of considerable length and much excitement ensued, in which Messrs. BENTON, McKEAN, KING, of Georgia, BUCHANAN, MANGUM, CALHOUN, CUTHBERT, FRELINGHUYSEN, KING of Alabama, CLAY, and WEBSTER, participated.

Mr. MOORE said he did not rise to discuss the question at this moment. The very feeble state of his health would not permit it, even if he was disposed. Yet, the peculiar situation he occupied in connexion with the subject matter, he thought, would be accepted as his apology for the few moments he proposed to detain the Senate.

He said it was true, as had been intimated by the Hon. Senator from South Carolina, (Mr. Calhoun,) that the General Assembly of Alabama had sent him two sets of instructions: the first was instructed to resign his seat here; and in the second, he was instructed to vote in favor of expunging the resolution adopted by the Senate, censuring the course of the Executive in relation to the public treasure of the country.

As these resolutions are contradictory in character, and at variance with each other, he found no little difficulty in complying with them, although an advocate for the right of instruction. If he had complied with the first set of instructions, viz. have forthwith resigned his seat, he, of course could not have complied with the second set of instructions, viz. he could not have voted in favor of the expunging resolution, as instructed in the second. He, therefore, after mature deliberation, had come to the conclusion, that he regarded the first, requiring his resignation, as he could not admit the right of the General Assembly to alter or change the constitutional tenure of office, and he had made an appeal to the same People of the State, to whom the members of the General Assembly and himself were alike responsible.

He said, again, as the subsequent resolution in law is viewed as repealing the former, where that exists inconsistency, he did not know but the General Assembly had thought better of the matter, and, after passing the resolution requiring resignation, therefore adopted the second, in order to repeal the former, in adopting which they had no legitimate power.

Now, said Mr. M., as regards the instruction, vote in favor of expunging the resolution censuring the course of the President, if the General Assembly mean, by "expunging," a repeal, reversal, or a rescinding of the obnoxious resolution, he could have no difficulty in yielding a ready obedience to their instructions; because I am against this resolution; true, sir, under a different

inence from that which operated upon his colleague.

He said he had expressly stated that in his own rate convictions of this matter, in the act of the xecutive in the removal of the public treasure as the place where it had been deposited by , was involved an abuse of Executive power, say the least. Notwithstanding this was his own w, believing as he did at the time, that a majo r of those whom he had the honor to represent artained different views, he had, in obedience the supposed will and wishes of his constituents, corded his vote in opposition to this obnoxious olution, and he was now prepared to re-affirm t vote.

But, said Mr. M., it may be that the General sembly or the leaders in these resolutions of tructions were ignorant of the precise vote that had given; for, said he, he could not believe last General Assembly could have intended to wess the least doubt of the *orthodox political* k of his colleague, nor his willingness to vote favor of the expunging resolution; but he said was glad to find, upon this occasion, that General Assembly and he himself had been taken;—far, said Mr. M., when these resolu s from the Gener.l Assembly of Alabama n first received and presented by his colleague, though his colleague had then given an earnest his views in favor of them altogether; but he now informed by his colleague that he be'iev it would be unconstitutional to expunge, de , or falsify the journals. Sir, said Mr. M., he much gratified to find that his colleague and a.lf thought alike upon this subject—he was I to find they would vote together upon th:s e.

Ir. KING, of Alabama, then moved to amend t part of the resolution proposed to be stricken by first striking out the words "ordered to be anged from the journals."

Ir. MOORE demanded the yeas and nays upon question; which were ordered, and are as follows:

EAS—Messrs. Bell, Benton, Bibb, Black, banan, Clay, Clayton, Cuthbert, Ewing, Fre huy sen, Goldsborough, Grundy, Hendricks, s, Kent, King of Alabama, King of Georgia, ght, Leigh, Linn, McKean, Mangum, Moore, dis, Naudain, Prentiss, Preston, Robbins, inson, S ilabee, Smith, Southard, Swift, Tip. Tomlinson, .Tyler, Waggaman, Webster, te—39.

AYS—Messrs. Brown, Hill, Porter, Ruggles, ley, Tallmadge, Wright—7. the motion to strike out prevailed.

r. WEBSTER then moved to lay the whole ct on the table, refusing to withdraw the mo and demanded the yeas and nays thereon; h were ordered, and the question was deter d in the affirmative by the following vote:

IAS.—Messrs. Bell, Bibb, Black, Calhoun, Clayton, Ewing, Frelinghuysen, Goldsbo h, Kent, Knight, Mangum, Naudain, Poin r, Porter, Prentiss, Preston, Robbins, Sils Smith, Southard, Swift, Tipton, Tomlinson, r, Waggaman, Webster—27.

IYS.—Messrs. Benton, Brown, Buchanan, bert, Grundy, Hill, Kane, King of Alabama, of Georgia, Leigh, Linn, McKean, Moore, s, Robinson, Ruggles, Shepley, Tallmadge, e, Wright—20.

e Senate then took a recess till 5 o'clock.

EVENING SESSION.

. POINDEXTER, from the Committee on ublic Lands, made a report of the investiga of the committee into the subject of frauds in les of the public lands, accompanied by the ony taken under the authority of the Com , in relation thereto.

POINDEXTER then moved that the report ocuments be printed, and referred to the le nt of the United States; which was agreed to.

POINDEXTER then moved that 5,000 ad l copi s of the report and evidence be d for the u c e of the Senate.

t motion was oppos. d by Messrs. HILL, IHT, and BENTON, w.en Mr. WRIGHT

asked the yeas and nays upon the question; which were ordered, and are as follows:

YEAS—Messrs. Bell, Bibb, Calhoun, Clay, Clayton, Ewing, Goldsborough, Hendricks, Kent, Leigh, McKean, Mangum, Moore, Naudain, Poindexter, Porter, Prentiss, Preston, Silsbee, Smith, Southard, Tomlinson, Tyler—23.

NAYS—Messrs. Benton, Brown, Buchanan, Cuthbert, Grundy, Hill, Kane, King of Alabama, King of Georgia, Linn, Morris, Ruggles, Shepley, Tallmadge, Tipton, White, Wright—17.

So the motion was agreed to.

Mr. BENTON then submitted the following resolution, which he desired to stand for the second week of the next session:

Resolved, That the resolution adopted by the Senate on the 28th day of March, in the year 1834, in the following words: "*Resolved, That the President, in the late Executive proceedings in relation to the public revenue, has assumed upon himself authority and power not conferred by the constitution and laws, but in derogation of both*," be, and the same hereby is, ordered to be rescinded and reversed; because the said resolution is illegal and unjust, of evil example, indefinite and vague, expressing a criminal charge without specification; and was irregularly and unconstitutionally adopted by the Senate, in subversion of the rights of defence which belong to an accused and impeachable officer; and at a time, and under circumstances, to endanger the political rights, and to injure the pecuniary interests of the people of the United States.

On motion of Mr. CLAY, the Senate then took up the bill making appropriations for opening certain roads in the Territories, when it was ordered to be engrossed, and it was afterwas read a third time and passed.

On motion of Mr. PORTER, the bill supplementary to the act to provide for the final adjustment of claims to land in Louisiana, was taken up, considered as in Committee of the Whole, ordered to be engrossed, and then read a third time and passed.

On motion of Mr. SOUTHARD, the bill authorising the construction of a dry dock for the naval service, was taken up, considered as in Committee of the Whole, ordered to be engrossed, and then read a third time and passed.

On motion of Mr. RUGGLES, the resolution providing for a survey of the harbor at East Thomastown, in the State of Maine, was taken up, considered and adopted.

The bill entitled an act in addition to the act for the continuation and repair of the Cumberland road, and

The bill to extend the patent of Robert Eastman, were severally read the third time and passed.

At six o'clock the VICE PRESIDENT left the Chair and the Senate proceeded, by ballot, to elect a President pro tempore for the remainder of the session.

On the first ballot, the whole number of votes were 46, necessary for a choice 23. Mr. Poindexter 1, Clay 1, Webster 1, Mangum 2, Silsbee 1, Southard 5, Tyler 15, King of Georgia 18.

The second ballot resulted as follows: Mangum 1, King of Georgia 1, Webster 1, Preston 1, Southard 3, Tyler 15, King of Alabama 20.

Third ballot, Mangum 1, Webster 1, Preston 1, Southard 1, Tyler 20, King of Alabama 21.

Fourth ballot, whole number 45; necessary for a choice 23. Southard 1, Mangum 1, Webster 19, Tyl=r 25.

Mr. TYLER, having received a majority of the whole number of votes, was declared duly elect ed, and having been conducted to the Chair by Mr. KING, of Alabama, he addressed the Senate as follows:

SENATORS: In calling upon me unexpectedly to preside over your deliberations, you have conferred upon me a testimonial of your respect and confidence upon which I place the highest value. I accept it with gratitude, and shall fondly cherish its recollection. You are the representatives of sovereign States, deputed by them to uphold and maintain their rights and interests. Unlike the Roman Senate, so much vaunted of in ancient story, you owe your elevation to the high seats

which you occupy, to no adventitious circumstance of birth or fortune, but to the ennobling traits of intellect and virtue. And what citizen of any one of these States can fail to be proud of you? Who can reflect without high satisfaction on the daily display of intellectual vigor constantly manifested in the debates which here occur. Party contests may divide and sever—those contests constitute the organic principle of free States—you may severally, in your turn, have become the objects of attack and denunciation before the public; but there is not, and cannot be an American who does not turn his eye to the Senate of the United States, as to the great conservative body of our federal system, and to this Chamber as the ark in which the covenant is deposited. To have received, therefore, at your hands, this station, furnishes to me abundant cause for self-gratulation. This feeling is not diminished by the fact that but few hours now remain to this session, and that I shall be probably called upon to render but little active service in this place. Upon this circumstance, I congratulate both you and myself—for although I have, for the greater portion of twenty years, been connected with legislative bodies, this is the first time I have ever been called upon to preside over the deliberations of any; and I have only sought so far to make myself acquainted with the rules of parliamentary proceeding, as to avoid any flagrant violation of them in my personal conduct. For the short period which will now elapse prior to your adjournment, I claim, and shall, doubtless, receive at your hands, for the defects which I may exhibit, and the errors into which I may fall, a liberal indulgence.

On motion of Mr. KING, of Alabama, the Secretary of the Senate was directed to inform the President of the United States, and the House of Representatives, that the Senate had elected the Hon. JOHN TYLER President pro tempore of the Senate.

The bill making a further appropriation in aid of the Chesapeake and Ohio Canal was taken up for consideration. The amendment to insert $300,000 being under consideration, was supported by Mr. KENT and Mr. CLAY, and opposed by Mr. BLACK and Mr. WRIGHT, who asked the yeas and nays upon the question; which were ordered, and are as follows:

YEAS—Messrs. Clay, Clayton, Ewing, Frelinghuysen, Goldsborough, Hendricks, Kent, Linn, McKean, Moore, Naudain, Poindexter, Porter, Robbins, Southard, Tomlinson—16.

NAYS—Messrs. Bell, Benton, Bibb, Black, Brown, Buchanan, Calhoun, Cuthbert, Grundy, Hill, King of Alabama, King of Georgia, Knight, Leigh, Mangum, Morris, Prentiss, Preston, Robinson, Ruggles, Shepley, Smith, Swift, Tallmadge, Tomlinson, Tyler, White, Wright—29.

So the amendment was disagreed to.

Mr. GOLDSBOROUGH then moved to insert an appropriation of $200,000, upon which Mr. BLACK asked the yeas and nays; which were ordered.

Mr. SHEPLEY spoke in opposition to the bill, and Mr. CLAY and Mr. LINN in support of it; when Mr. ROBINSON moved to lay the bill on the table; which was disgreed to, on a division. Yeas 19, nays 20.

After some further opposition from Mr. SHEPLEY—

Mr. WEBSTER renewed the motion to lay the bill on the table; which was agreed to.

The Senate then took up the civil and diplomatic appropriation bill, which was returned from the House, and proceeded to consider the vote of that body disagreeing to the amendment of the Senate, providing that "the salary and outfit of the Minister to Great Britain shall not be paid, unless such Minister shall be appointed by and with the advice and consent of the Senate."

Mr. WEBSTER moved that the Senate insist on their amendment; which was agreed to, and the House directed to be informed thereof; and a Committee of Conference, consisting of Mr. CLAY, Mr. WRIGHT, and Mr. EWING, were appointed on the part of the Senate.

The other amendments of the House to the amendments of the Senate were severally considered, and being immaterial, were gone through

with, some being agreed to and others dissented from.

The Senate then took up the fortification bill, and proceeded to the several amendments made by the House to the amendments of the Senate.

The minor amendments having been gone through, the one placing at the disposal of the President three millions of dollars, to be used, under his directions, in augmenting the army and navy, and repairing the fortifications o the United States, so as to put the country in a posture of defence, i\n case there shall be necessity for it before the next meeting of Congress, was taken up; when

Messrs. WEBSTER, CALHOUN, LEIGH, SOUTHARD, CLAY, and PRESTON opposed the amendment, and Messrs. WRIGHT, LINN, BUCHANAN, and CUTHBERT, supported it.

The question being on disagreeing to the amendment,

Mr. WRIGHT demanded the yeas and nays; which were ordered, and are as follows:

YEAS.—Messrs. Bell, Bibb, Calhoun, Clayton, Ewing, Frelinghuysen, Goldsborough, Hendricks, Kent, Knight, Leigh, Mangum, Moore, Naudain, Poindexter, Porter, Prentiss, Preston, Robbins, Silsbee, Smith, Southard, Swift, Tomlinson, Tyler, Waggaman, Webster, White.—29.

NAYS.—Messrs. Benton, Black, Brown, Buchanan, Cuthbert, Grundy, Hill, Kane, King of Alabama, King of Georgia, Linn, McKean, Morris, Robinson, Ruggles, Shepley, Tallmadge, Tipton, Wright.—19.

So the Senate disagreed to the amendment.

Another amendment of the Senate was, to increase the appropriation of $70,000 to $150,000, for repairing Fort Mifflin.

This was disagreed to by the House, and Mr. CLAYTON moved that the Senate insist on their amendment; which was agreed to, and the House informed thereof accordingly.

A message was then received from the President, returning the bill authorizing the Secretary of the Treasury to compromise the claims upon the indemnity to be paid by the King of the Two Sicilies, with his objections. The message was read, and on motion of Mr. CLAY, laid on the table.

On motion of Mr. CLAYTON, the Senate proceeded to the consideration of Executive Business; and when the doors were opened,

The Senate took up the fortification bill, which was returned by the House, and the amendment of the House placing three millions at the disposal of the President, as stated above.

Mr. WEBSTER moved that the Senate adhere to their disagreeing vote, and asked the ayes and nays upon the question, which were ordered, and are as follows:

YEAS.—Messrs. Bell Bibb, Calhoun, Clay, Clayton, Ewing, Frelinghuysen, Goldsborough, Hendricks, Kent, Knight, Leigh, Mangum, Moore, Naudain, Poindexter, Porter, Prentiss, Preston, Robbins, Silsbee, Smith, Southard, Swift, Tomlinson, Tyler, Waggaman, Webster, White.—29.

NAYS.—Messrs. Benton, Brown, Buchanan, Cuthbert, Grundy, Hill, Kane, King of Ala, King of Georgia, Linn, McKean, Robinson, Ruggles, Shepley, Tallmadge, Tipton, Wright.—17.

So the Senate adhered to their disagreement, and a Committee of Conference, consisting of Messrs. WEBSTER, FRELINGHUYSEN, and WRIGHT, was appointed on the part of the Senate.

On motion of Mr. CLAYTON, the Senate then proceeded to the consideration of Executive Business; and when the doors were opened,

The Senate took up the resolution requiring the publication of a tabular list of revolutionary pensioners now paid by the Treasury Department, similar to that compiled from the books of the War Department.

Mr. BENTON moved to rescind the resolution; which was disagreed to, and the resolution was then adopted.

Mr. POINDEXTER moved to take up the resolution for printing the reports of the Commissioners appointed to settle land titles, when Mr. BENTON moved to rescind the resolution; and,

On motion of Mr. KING, of Georgia, it was laid on the table.

Mr. WEBSTER moved that a message in writing be sent to the House reminding them that the fortification bill was still undisposed of, and that the Senate waited the further action of the House thereon; which was agreed to.

Mr. KING, of Alabama, then moved the usual resolution informing the House that the Senate is ready to adjourn; but withdrew it for a few minutes, at the suggestion of

Mr. WEBSTER, who remarked that a message was every moment expected from the House, with respect to a bill which was before them.

The PRESIDENT, pro tem. laid before the Senate a communication from the War Department, transmitting a statement of the number and kind of arms manufactured at the national armories for the year 1835.

Mr. KING then renewed his resolution; which was adopted.

The Senate then adjourned.

HOUSE OF REPRESENTATIVES.

TUESDAY, March 3, 1835.

By the unanimous consent of the House, Messrs. CLAY, MOSES MASON, and WILDE, were permitted to record their votes in favor of Mr. Cambreleng, on the subject of the French treaty.

On motion of Mr. POLK, the House resolved itself into a Committee of the Whole on the state of the Union, Mr. HUBBARD in the Chair, for the purpose of considering the amendments of the Senate to the several appropriation bills.

The Committee first proceeded to consider the amendments made by the Senate to the bill making appropriations for the support of the Government for the year 1835.

The amendments increasing the appropriations for the contingent expenses of the two Houses of Congress, and increasing the appropriation to the Superintendent and Watchmen of the northeast Executive building, were concurred in.

The amendment providing that the salary and outfit for a Minister to England should not be paid unless a Minister should be appointed at the present session of Congress, or in the recess, by and with the advice and consent of the Senate, was read.

Mr. POLK said he did not rise to make a speech. His purpose was to move that the Committee disagree to this amendment. The amendment was altogether unusual, and he believed wholly unnecessary. We should not presume that the President would not discharge his constitutional duty, and it was not necessary to pre-admonish him in regard to it.

Mr. ADAMS, of Massachusetts, said, he called the attention of the House to this subject when the bill was before it. He had, however, submitted no motion in regard to it. It had now become a matter of more importance that a Minister should be sent to England. If our Minister should be recalled from France, and our negotiations suspended, it was proper that we should have a Minister in the neighborhood. This amendment ought not to be sanctioned. In the first place, it was an attempt at dictation to the President, which was inconsistent with the constitution. In the second place, it made the appointment of a Minister dependent upon a special call of the Senate. He did not agree that the President had not the power, under the constitution, to appoint a Minister in the recess.

The amendment was disagreed to—Yeas 51, nays 74.

The amendment making an appropriation in favor of John Randolph, Clay, and N. Niles, was amended, by inserting the sum of $1080, to be paid to Capt. John Downes for presents to the natives of the Sandwich and Society Islands, was concurred in.

The amendments in favor of Samuel Slater, and for the purchase of iron chests for the safekeeping of the records of the United States Courts, in the City of New York, were non-concurred in.

The amendment appropriating $77,381 98 for the completion of the Warehouse at Baltimore, was amended on the motion of Mr. POLK, by inser-

ting $60,000 instead of the first sum; which was agreed to.

The amendment allowing to Valentine Gill, $802 87, was amended by substituting $865 and agreed to.

An amendment making an appropriation for certain improvements, being read—

Mr. JARVIS moved to amend the amendment by making an appropriation for the erection of a Treasury building, to be constructed of granite.

Mr. CHINN suggested an amendment providing that the building should be constructed of freestone.

The two latter amendments were negatived, and the Senate's amendment concurred in.

Mr. WILDE moved to strike out the same of Persico, and insert that of Mr. Thorwald, an American artist, to be employed in decorating the Capitol.

Mr. WARD said, if there were any works the Capitol more than others, they were those of Mr. Persico. Besides, there were provisions made already in this bill for American artists.

Mr. POLK appealed to the House not to engage in discussions about the merits of artists, at the last day of the session, with so much business before them that must be acted on. He hoped the amendment would at once be rejected.

After a few words from Mr. MERCER, the amendment was negatived.

Mr. WILDE moved to strike out the name of Mr. Persico, and insert that of Mr. Greenough.

Mr. J. Q. ADAMS said, Mr. Greenough was already engaged in a great work.

The amendment was negatived.

Mr. HAMER then moved to strike out the whole paragraph; which was agreed to.

Mr. JARVIS'S amendment was negatived, and the amendment of the Senate was concurred in without a division.

Mr. POLK moved that the House non-concur in the amendment of the Senate providing for recording the opinions of the Judges of the Supreme Court. The clerk already received sufficient.

Mr. HARDIN briefly supported it, and it was agreed to.

Mr. MASON, of Va., proposed an item $7,400 for the System of Military Tactics for the army of the U. States.

Mr. MANN, of N. Y., understood this was for paying General Scott for translating and compiling this work, which he had done without the sanction of any resolution of Congress.

Mr. WARD was understood to say that a resolution on the subject had been adopted.

Mr. MANN had no idea of paying officers twice over. Gen. Scott now received six thousand eight hundred and some odd dollars annually, and the country was entitled to his whole services. It was a case similar to that of Commodore which the House had rejected.

Mr. MASON, of Va., explained the facts of the case. A resolution had been adopted authorizing the Secretary of War to employ a person to compile a system of military tactics for the army of the United States. He had done so; the work had been approved of and adopted by the military Committee of that House; a bookseller had offered Gen. ral Scott more than was now asked. He denied that the case of Commodore was analogous to this, because the services far exceeded that officer claimed extra compensation for within the line of his duty.

Messrs. PATTON, MERCER, ARCHER, and VANCE, further supported the amendment, and Mr. MANN, of N. Y., and Mr. FERRIS opposed it.

Mr. BEALE proposed to insert $2,500 instead of 7,400.

Mr. GRENNELL said it was to him a clear question of contract between the Government and General Scott, and the question was, whether the work was worth the money.

Mr. BEALE'S amendment was negatived without a division.

The amendment of Mr. MASON was also agreed to. Ayes 57, nays 76.

The amendment appropriating $1,380 for the

purchase, (for the use of the public Land Offices,) of copies of Gales and Seaton's documents in relation to the public lands, was taken up.

Mr. LYTLE moved to amend the amendment by appropriating $2,000 for the construction of one or more fountains in the public grounds adjacent to the capitol; which was negatived.

The amendment of the Senate was non-concurred in.

The amendment of the Senate appropriating $40,000 for Gales and Seaton's State Papers for the year 1835, was read.

Mr. POLK referred to the large appropriations hitherto made for this work. A majority of the Committee of Ways and Means were opposed to the amendment.

Mr. PLUMMER opposed the amendment. Every year an appropriation was made to this object. It was considered authority for continuing the work up to the period at which the appropriation was made. He was disposed to limit these appropriations, and stop the future publication of the work, so far as the House was concerned.

Mr. MANNING said, that if a contract had been entered into in this case, it ought to be complied with. He asked the Chair whether there existed a contract in relation to this publication?

Mr. HARDIN said, if the books were published, he would be willing to pay for them. If not, he for one was disposed to put a stop to this useless waste of the public money. He had received at last and present year a number of the copies of this work. They probably cost the government three or four dollars per volume, and they are not worth twelve and a half cents per volume; they would not pay their carriage to Wheeling. It was only intended to give a job to the printers of this city, and it was high time that a stop should be put to it.

The law authorizing the publication of these documents was then read.

Mr. HARDIN said this appropriation was for a present year. He repeated that the work is worthless. The small volumes were not worth more than 6½ cents, and the larger size not 6 cents per volume.

Mr. BARRINGER explained the manner in which the work was compiled and executed. He was surprised that any gentleman should oppose the amendment under the circumstances of the case.

Mr. HAMER said he did not understand this subject. It seemed that 750 copies were to be published, but as to the number or size of the volumes, no provision was made. There had been a ready eight or nine volumes published, and there was no telling where it would end. It might be continued for a hundred years. He was prepared to pay for what had been printed, but would not go further.

The amendment was then concurred in—yeas 69.

The amendment making a further appropriation of $10,800 for completing the printing of the documents ordered by the Senate, was read.

The amendment was supported by Messrs. POLK, PLUMMER, VINTON, and supported by Messrs. GARLAND, and E. WHITTLESEY.

Mr. E. EVERETT moved to amend the amendment, by directing the manner in which the going work should be distributed; which was agreed to.

The amendment of the Senate, as amended, was negatived—yeas 59, nays 61.

Mr. R. M. JOHNSON moved to amend the bill appropriating $2,600 for the publication of the system of discipline and tactics for the use of the army of the United States.

Mr. LETCHER moved to amend the amendment by appropriating to Gen. Winfield Scott $100 for compiling and superintending the location of the foregoing work.

Mr. WILLIAMS proposed $5,030; which was agreed to—yeas 76, nays 63.

Mr. HAWES moved a proviso, that the sum to be paid to Gen. Scott, should be in full of all claims on this account; which was negatived.

The amendment offered by Mr. JOHNSON, of Kentucky, was then agreed to, as amended.

Mr. SMITH moved to strike out the several items of the Senate's amendment regarding appropriations for the West Point Academy.

Mr. SMITH said he did not rise to detain the progress of the bill more than a few minutes. He could not, however, forbear to remark, that the manner and circumstances in which this proposition has been brought before this committee, clearly indicate something new in the history and condition of the institution at West Point. It has been usual, Mr. Chairman, and I believe invariably the practice, for the items now to be passed upon to originate in this House, instead of in the Senate. In no instance, said Mr. S. it is believed, have they ever been brought before this House, until now, in the shape of amendments tacked upon the general appropriation bill of the House by the Senate.

[Mr. WATMOUGH said he would explain the reason of this course if Mr. S. would permit.]

Mr. SMITH said he well understood the reasons for this novel procedure. And the committee well understand the why and wherefore the Senate has thus brought these proposed appropriations before the House, but he would not now go into their reasons. He would, however, observe, that it cannot but appear extraordinary, that appropriations of this magnitude, amounting, as he believed, to more than $120,000, should be asked for the support of the Academy at West Point, while there is lying upon the table of the Speaker, a report of a committee of the House, wholly adverse to the institution. That report, sir, has come from a committee of twenty-four members, and is the result of laborious investigation. And the inability and unprofitableness of the institution is so fully demonstrated by that report, that the friends of the Academy my open this floor, have not dared to have it printed and the contents of it brought home to the knowledge of the members of this House, and of the public. Repeated efforts have been made to have that report printed but the friends of the institution have as frequently defeated it. The report, sir, upon the Speaker's table demonstrates, that only about two in five of those who enter the institution, remain in it to graduate—and that only about two in five of those who graduate, or about one in twelve of those who enter the institution, actually enter the public service, at whose expense they are educated. The report also demonstrates, that such are the influences prevailing at the institution, that more dismissals from it take place annually, than at all the other institutions of a similar high grade in the country. The discipline of the institution has proved insufficient to counteract these influences. A portion of the cadets have been within three or four years past publicly censured by the Head of the War Department, and to succeed in the government of the institution, a tavern stand in the vicinity of it was necessarily bought up a few years since, at an expense of $10,000 to the People. But, said Mr. S. the time of the committee will not admit of my going more into the detail of the developments contained in the report of the Select Committee, which has been thus far suppressed. I will, however, make a motion, and leave every gentleman to take upon himself the responsibility of voting it down, if he chooses; and I presume it may be voted down. I will submit a motion, said Mr. S., that the committee non-concur with each of the amendments of the Senate, making appropriations for the academy.

Mr. HAWES moved to amend the amendments proposed by the Senate, by adding an appropriation for printing 5,000 copies of the report of the Select Committee on the Military Academy, to which Mr. Smith had alluded; which motion was agreed to without opposition.

Whereupon Mr. SMITH withdrew his motion to non-concur in the amendments of the Senate.

The amendment of the Senate, appropriating 650,000 acres of land for the satisfaction of military bounty land warrants, was read.

It was advocated by Messrs. McKINLEY, CHINN, HARDIN, JOHN Y. MASON, and ALLEN of Virginia, and opposed by Messrs. PARKER, MILLER, VINTON, and BURD, when the amendment was agreed to—yeas 83, nays 46.

The amendment making an appropriation of

lands to satisfy certain confirmed land claims in the State of Missouri, was read. It was opposed by Messrs. CAVE JOHNSON and WILLIAMS, and advocated by Messrs. ASHLEY, and WHITE of Florida, when it was disagreed to.

The amendment in relation to the compensation of officers of the customs, was read.

Mr. VANCE opposed the amendment, and it was supported by Messrs. SUTHERLAND, PHILLIPS, and PINCKNEY; when it was concurred in.

Mr. McKINLEY moved an amendment making an additional appropriation for the pay of the naval officers, in pursuance of the late act of Congress; which was agreed to.

Various amendments were concurred in without opposition.

The bill was then laid aside.

The Committee next took up the amendments of the Senate to the bill making appropriations for Indian annuities, and other similar objects, for the year 1835.

The amendment in relation to patents for lands reserved, was non-concurred in.

Mr. POLK objected to the amendment for the appropriation of $1,032,000 provided for under the treaty of Chicago, with various Indian tribes, in 1827. The Committee of Ways and Means had given the subject a most rigid examination.

Mr. LOVE said he had given this subject a most rigid examination also; and he was well convinced that if the House was in possession of all the facts, they would never adopt it. He was well convinced that frauds existed, not on the part of persons in Washington, which should induce its rejection. The Indians had, to say the least of it, made a good bargain, and they might wait another year. He would not vote for so large an appropriation as a million and thirty odd thousand dollars, brought forward for the first time on the last day of the session. Mr. L. then moved to non concur with so much of the Senate's amendment as provided for the removal of the Indians beyond the Mississippi.

Mr. POLK again explained, by making a reference to the various treaties. The Committee of Ways and Means had taken up each item seriatim, and compared it with the provisions of the treaties. He was himself indisposed to recommend so a large a sum, but after a most careful examination, he was convinced the sum was proper.

The amendment was then agreed to.

Mr. McKINLEY moved an additional item of $810 for a Mrs. Mitchel, for teaching Indians.—Agreed to.

The bill was then laid aside.

The Committee next took up the bill making appropriations for certain fortifications for the year 1835.

Sundry amendments of the Senate were concurred in.

The amendment increasing the appropriation for Fort Delaware from $70,000 to $100,000, was, on motion of Mr. POLK, concurred in.

Mr WHITE, of Florida, again renewed his amendment, providing $10,000 for the repair of the sea walls at St. Augustine. Agreed to—yeas 71, nays not counted.

The other amendments of the Senate were then concurred in, and the bill was laid aside.

The Committee then took up the bill making appropriations for light-houses, light-boats, buoys, &c. for the year 1835.

Mr. SUTHERLAND moved to concur in all the amendments of the Senate. Agreed to.

Mr. ASHLEY moved an amendment for the improvement of the harbor of St. Louis, $20,000, but subsequently withdrew it, in consequence of a bill containing the same provision being before the Senate.

On motion of Mr. POLK, the Committee then rose, and the bills and amendments were severally reported to the House.

The general appropriation bill was then taken up.

Mr. POLK moved to concur with the Committee of the Whole in the amendments.

Objection being made, the amendments were taken up seriatim.

The amendment of the Senate, in relation to

the appropriation for the salary of a Minister to Great Britain, was read.

Mr. WILDE asked for the yeas and nays on this amendment, which were ordered.

Mr. EVANS moved to amend the amendment of the Senate, so as to provide that the appropriation should not be applied unless a minister should be first appointed by and with the advice and consent of the Senate; which was disagreed to.

Mr. J. Q. ADAMS said, this amendment proposed to introduce a new principle. The President had hitherto uniformly appointed foreign ministers of all grades, when he deemed such appointments necessary. This was a most important and necessary power reserved to him under the Constitution. The amendment was an assumption on the part of the Senate, that a minister should not be appointed without the consent of that body. This, if adopted, would be one of the most pernicious alterations which the Constitution could endure. It was one among other instances of an attempt to alter the Constitution in an appropriation bill. If this principle should be adopted, we should have other amendments of the Constitution introduced in a similar way, and the President might be compelled in consequence, to veto the general appropriation bill. It was incumbent upon the House to prevent any encroachments of the Executive upon the prerogatives of the Senate. In like manner, the House was bound to resist the encroachments of the Senate upon the Constitutional powers of the Executive. It was also the province of the Senate to check and control the action of this House, which was quite as likely as the other branch, he would not say now, but in other times, to infringe upon the just rights of the Executive. The Constitution provided three powers, who were to co-operate together in the management of the public affairs. They formed checks upon each other, and were so constituted that when one of the three attempted to transcend its constitutional sphere, the other two would interfere to prevent it.

In conclusion Mr. A. said, that the amendment of the Senate proposed to introduce a principle which was contrary to the practice of the government from its commencement. Every President, from Washington down, had pursued a different practice from that proposed in the amendment. It was true, the Senate did not assume directly to declare that a minister should not be appointed by the President, unless previously confirmed by that body; but the means of such appointment were withheld, and the Senate had determined not to pay a minister unless appointed according to the terms of their proviso. He hoped the House would disagree to the amendment of the Senate.

Mr. BARRINGER said, he was opposed to the amendment of the Senate, and should vote against it. He believed the President had the power of appointment during a recess, where a vacancy occurred in that recess, and he held that it made little difference whether he were a Charge or a Minister. The President might equally take upon himself to increase the pay, or to appoint a Minister Plenipotentiary instead of a Charge, or vice versa, during the recess. Mr. B. did not concur with the gentleman from Massachusetts, (Mr. Adams,) in his reasoning, although he said he should concur with him in the vote he intended to give. He, (Mr. B.,) denied the right of the President of the United States, upon former practice or precedent, to appoint a minister during the recess, when the vacancy originated, or created during the session of the Senate, and the President might have nominated. He was aware that it was a contested question, as long ago as under the first administration of this government. But one practice had been generally recognised, that of consulting with the Senate whether they would agree to institute diplomatic relations with any country. It was so during the administrations of Washington and the elder Adams, even down to the time of Mr. Jefferson. The President never presumed until after the administration of the last, to open diplomatic relations with a country without first advising with the Senate. Mr. B. said, he should vote for the appropriation. The question was then taken by yeas and nays, and resulted as follows—yeas 114, nays 46.

So the House concurred with the amendment of the Committee of the Whole, and disagreed to the Senate's amendment.

Mr. JARVIS renewed his amendments offered in Committee, embracing appropriations for the Capitol, the President's House, and the Departments. Agreed to.

On the Senate's amendment, appropriating $40,000 for preparing, printing, and binding public documents, under the act of 1832, a motion was made to disagree, and Mr. HAWES demanded tellers, and the amendment was disagreed to—ayes 58, noes 81.

Some conversation arose on the Senate's amendment, appropriating the sum of $10,800 for printing and binding the documents relating to the public lands, and the accompanying maps, by the printer to the Senate.

Mr. PLUMMER, Mr. EVANS, and Mr. PINCKNEY, spoke briefly in support of it, and Mr. PARKS in opposition.

The amendment was agreed to, without a division.

Mr. PARKER asked for the yeas and nays on the Senate's amendment, granting 650,000 acres of land for the satisfaction of Military Bounty Land Warrants; but they were not ordered, yeas 23, nays 115—not one-fifth.

The question on the adoption of the amendment was taken by tellers, and decided in the affirmative; ayes 97, no s 36.

The amendment relative to the Missouri land claims having been read—

Mr. R. M. JOHNSON renewed the amendment he offered in Committee of the Whole.

Mr. CAVE JOHNSON hoped the House would not agree to the original amendment, but that the claims should be referred to the Secretary of the Treasury.

Mr. ASHLEY advocated the justice of these claims. He believed there were not more than three or four that would not obtain a favorable decision in the Supreme Court. They had been before the Secretary of the Treasury ever since last June, and he had refused to adjudicate upon them. He denied that those claims were founded on fraud.

Mr. MANN, of New York, was disposed to place confidence in the Chairman of the Committee on Private Land Claims, (Mr. Cave Johnson,) and in the absence of more direct information on the subject, he should vote against the amendment.

Mr. PLUMMER hoped the House would not give the amendment the go-by, for it was a proposition founded on justice, and ought to be adopted.

Mr. HAMER thought these claims should be confirmed.

Mr. CAVE JOHNSON again spoke in opposition to the amendment. The claims required more investigation than it was possible for the Secretary of the Treasury to give them. He knew the grossest frauds and perjury would be found to exist in relation to a number of these claims.

Mr. WILLIAMS said, it was impossible to go into a legal adjudication of claims at that late hour, and the better way would be to let the subject lie over to another Congress.

Mr. ASHLEY again advocated the claims, and defended the character of the claimants.

Mr. WILLIAMS again expressed a hope that the subject should be left to a future session.

Mr. POLE demanded the previous question, and explained that he did so from a wish to save the bill, if possible.

The previous question was seconded, and the main question ordered to be put.

The question was then put, and the amendment of the Senate was disagreed to, without a division.

The amendment in relation to the pay of custom-house officers was concurred in—yeas 8 nays 46.

The amendment appropriating $175 for printing 5,000 copies of the report of the Select Committee on the West Point Academy, was agreed to.

The House next proceeded to consider the amendments reported by the committee to the bill making appropriations for Indian annuities, &c., for 1835.

The amendments made in committee to the Senate's amendments, were concurred in.

A portion of the amendments of the Senate were concurred in, and others were disagreed to.

The amendment of the Senate appropriating $1,032,000, for carrying into effect certain Indian treaties, made at Chicago in September 1832, was read.

This item was opposed by Messrs. LOVE, VINTON, and H. EVERETT, and supported by Messrs. POLK, BEARDSLEY, and GILMER.

Mr. STEWART moved the previous question which was seconded and agreed to.

The amendment of the Senate was then concurred in—yeas 93, nays not counted.

The bill making appropriations for certain fortifications already commenced, was taken up.

A portion of the amendments adopted in the Committee to the Senate's amendments, were concurred in.

The amendment of the Senate appropriating $73,000 for the repair of the fortifications in Boston harbor, was read.

The question being on the amendment to this item, adopted in Committee, appropriating $1,000,000 to be expended by the President, in the recess of Congress, if he should deem it expedient, for the military and naval service, including fortifications, ordnance, &c.

Mr. HIESTER demanded the yeas and nays which were ordered, and were as follows

YEAS—Messrs. John Quincy Adams, John Adams, J. J. Allen, William Allen, Beale, Bean, Beardsley, Beaumont, Bockee, Bodle, Bean, Brown, Bull, Bunch, Bynum, Cage, Cambreleng, Carmichael, Casey, Chaney, Samuel Clark, Connor, Coulter, Cramer, Day, Denny, Dickson, Dickinson, Dunlap, Horace Everett, Fowler, William K. Fuller, Fulton, Galbraith, Gillet, Graham, Joseph Hall, Thomas H. Hall, Halsey, Hamer, Hannegan, James Harper, Harrison, Hawkins, Hawes, Heath, Howell, Hubbard, Huntington, Inge, Jarvis, Richard M. Johnson, Noadiah Johnson, Cave Johnson, Kavanagh, Kilgore, Kinnard, Lane, Lansing, Lea, Lee, Leavitt, Lucas, Lyon, Lytle, Abijah Mann, Mason, Job Y. Mason, May, McIntire, McKay, McKim, McKinley, McLene, McVean, Miller, Milligan, Henry Mitchell, Robert Mitchell, Moore, Muhlenberg, Murphy, Osgood, Parks, Parker, Patterson, Peyton, Pierce, Pierson, Plummer, Polk, Reynolds, Schenck, Schley, Shinn, Speight, Steele, Stewart, Sutherland, William Taylor, F. Thomas, Thomas Turner, Turrill, Vanderpoel, Van Houten, Wagener, Ward, White, Wise.—110.

NAYS—Messrs. H. Allen, C. Allan, Ashley, Barringer, Bates, Beaty, Bell, Bouldin, Briggs, Campbell, Chambers, Chinn, Claiborne, W. Clark, Choney, Corwin, Crane, Darlington, A. Davis, Davenport, Deberry, Dickson, Evans, E. Everett, Ewing, Felder, Fillmore, Foster, F. C. Fuller, Gamble, Garland, Gholson, Gilmer, Gordon, Gorham, Grennell, Griffin, H. Hall, Hard, Hardin, Hazeltine, Hiester, W. Jackson, W. C. Johnson, King, Lewis, Lincoln, Martindale, Marshall, Mason, Keenan, Mercer, Miner, Pattoe, Phillips, Pinckney, Potts, Ramsay, Reed, Rencher, Robertson, W. B. Shepard, A. H. Shepperd, Slade, Spangler, W. P. Taylor, P. Thomas, Trumbull, Tweedy, Vance, Vinton, Wardwell, E. Whittlesey, Williams, Wilson, Young.—77.

So the amendment to the amendment was agreed to.

The amendment of the Senate, as amended, was then concurred in.

The bill making appropriations for light-houses, buoys, beacons, &c., was taken up.

The amendments of the Senate, (which had been agreed to in Committee,) were concurred to.

Mr. E. WHITTLESEY submitted the following resolution; which was unanimously agreed to:

Resolved, That the thanks of this House be presented to the Hon. JOHN BELL, for the able, impartial, and dignified manner in which he has presided over its deliberations, and performed the arduous and important duties of the Chair.

The House then resolved itself into a Committee...

CONGRESSIONAL GLOBE.

BY BLAIR & RIVES. ———WEEKLY——— PRICE $1 A SESSION.

2d Sess.........23d Cong. SATURDAY, MARCH 7, 1835. Volume 2........No. 21.

TWENTY-THIRD CONGRESS.
SECOND SESSION.

HOUSE OF REPRESENTATIVES.
Tuesday, March 3, 1835.
CONTINUED FROM LAST NUMBER.

tee of the Whole on the state of the Union, Mr. SPEIGHT in the Chair, on various bills from the Senate, &c.

The first bill considered, was "an act to establish branches of the Mint of the U. States."

Mr. C. P. WHITE moved an amendment establishing a branch at the city of New York.

Mr. McKINLEY said he was favorably disposed towards the amendment, but it was evident it could not be sanctioned by the Senate at this late hour.

Mr. CAMBRELENG advocated the amendment.

The amendment was lost, and the bill was laid aside.

The committee next took up and considered the bill for the continuation of the Cumberland road in Ohio, Indiana, and Illinois, which was laid aside.

The committee then took up the bill entitled an act supplementary to the act entitled an act to amend the Judicial system of the United States.

The provisions of this bill, as before stated in the Globe, are these:

It provides for consolidating the circuits composed of New Jersey and Pennsylvania, with that composed of Delaware and Maryland, and requiring Judge Baldwin to hold the Circuit Courts in the Delaware and Maryland Circuit, so as to obviate the necessity of appointing a Judge of the Supreme Court in that circuit, and thereby to extend the circuit system to the Western States.

Mr. HARDIN proposed an amendment to the bill, the substance of which he stated. Instead of eight Circuit Judges, he proposed nine. If the House would take a review of the United States, it would be evident to every one that eight Judges were too few. The Supreme Court required six days, besides what the States of the new proposed circuit would require. The bill before the House would require about forty weeks of the individual attention of the Judge of the new circuit—more labor than any man could well perform. Besides, there was a great propriety in taking the number of Judges to be an odd number, similar to committees of the House, because if they were equally divided, no adjudication could be made. Mr. H. farther explained the provisions of his amendment as to the regulation of the new circuits.

Mr. ROBERTSON opposed the amendment. A similar proposition was made to that House some time ago, which was debated for three weeks, and defeated, as he feared the present bill would be.

Mr. GARLAND said if the amendment were adopted, the bill would be defeated, as a similar one had been six or seven years ago. This bill passed the Senate, and when it came into the House was defeated by a similar amendment to the present. He urged upon the gentleman from Kentucky, (Mr. Hardin,) if he was favorable to the bill, to withdraw his amendment at once.

Mr. JOHNSON, of Louisiana, also opposed the amendment on the same ground, and called upon the committee to take the question upon it at once.

Mr. THOMAS, of Maryland, expressed his approbation of the amendment offered by the gentleman from Kentucky. It has been offered as an instance by the Committee on the Judiciary, and had one good ingredient at least—it was calculated to accommodate the States without depriving one of the old thirteen of a right enjoyed since the organization of the government. With this fact full before him, he could not feel at the two gentlemen from Louisiana, displayed

their accustomed liberality in urging, as they did, the passage of the bill without amendment. New Orleans, doubtless needed a circuit court. From the character of the causes cognizable by the federal judiciary, that large commercial city ought to have the boon this bill proposed to grant. This was conceded, and the seal of the gentleman from Louisiana commended while it was displayed in behalf of that feature of this bill which secured to their constituents that which they had a right to demand, and could not but feel they were unjust towards the citizens of Maryland. If New Orleans had strong claims to the full benefit of all the courts organised to enforce the laws of the Union, surely Baltimore, one of the first commercial cities of the United States, will be cruelly outraged by the passage of this bill without amendment.

The bill as it came from the Senate, was an act of monstrous injustice to Maryland; and that any representative of that State could stand silently by and witness this sacrifice of the rights of his constituents, was cause to him of great surprise. With what propriety could the fourth circuit be abolished? It appeared from statements furnished to the Judiciary Committee by the clerks of the several circuit courts, that in the year 1833 the circuit court was in session in Maryland eighty-four days, in Delaware six days. From the same statement, we learn that similar courts sit on an average in the Virginia Circuit forty-two days, and in the Georgia circuit, thirty-two days annually. There is then more business to transact in the 4th circuit than there is in the 5th and 6th circuits united; if either of the Atlantic circuits were therefore to be abolished, it would be much more reasonable to blend that of South Carolina and Georgia with Virginia and North Carolina, than to make the unnatural combination which this bill proposes. If the venerable and venerated Chief Justice was required to hold the courts of Maryland, Virginia, and North Carolina, he would be on the circuit bench 132 days, while Judge Wayne would be on the bench only 32 days in the year. The mere statement of these facts must carry conviction to the mind of every man, that the true object of this bill did not appear on its face. In fact, if members would engage seriously and solely in the good work of extending the benefits of the Judiciary to the whole Union, and not in the unholy work of destroying by indirect means an estimable citizen, they would conclude as he had done, that Maryland needed more a separate Circuit Court than any State South or West of Pennsylvania except the State of Louisiana. The States in the interior cannot furnish many causes for the employment of the Federal Judiciary. The cases now pending before State Courts, in the western States, will be found to have originated chiefly from the fact that this Government is a large landholder. Trespasses committed on the national domain, and suits instituted to enforce contracts growing out of the sale of the public lands, will constitute, doubtless, four-fifths of the cases which the Judges will be called on to decide in the Circuit Courts the bill proposes to establish in Illinois, Indiana, and Missouri. The time is rapidly approaching, when such cases can no longer arise, and then the judgeships new about to be created for the benefit of these States, will become mere 'sinecures. How different must be the condition of things in Maryland. Baltimore is a port of entry, at which is collected more revenue than at all the ports of the four southern Atlantic States. To collect this revenue, the Federal Courts are needed, and as its amount will increase with the rapidly augment ing business of that city, the labors of these Judges will also accumulate. The maritime jurisdiction of the Circuit Courts too will afford laborious employment to judges in Baltimore, and (through which city the citizens residing in Virginia, west of the Blue Ridge, and in Pennsylvania, on many of the tributary streams of the Susquehanna, carry

commerce with all the world) while in the interior States, need, few causes, if any could arise under this branch of the jurisdiction of the federal courts.

Mr. Thomas said it was 'too obvious to require illustration, that the object of this bill did not appear on its face and had not been avowed by those with whom it originated. This he would shew more, fully than he had attempted, when it came up for consideration in the House, when he proposed to make a few brief comments on the facts' and statements with which he had now troubled the Committee.

[A message was here received from the Senate, announcing that that body insisted upon their amendments to the General Appropriation Bill, and had appointed a Committee of Conference.]

Mr. POLK moved that the House insist, and that a Committee of Conference be appointed on the part of that House to meet the Committee of the Senate, and that the number be three. Agreed to.

The committee appointed were Mr. POLK, Mr. E. EVERETT, and Mr. BEARDSLEY.

The SPEAKER then left the Chair, and the House resumed its proceedings in Committee of the Whole on the state of the Union, on the Judiciary Bill.

Mr. MILLIGAN, in order to avoid misconstruction, both here and at home, asked the indulgence of the House to say a few words on the subject of this bill. Suits in the State of Delaware were like angels visits, few and far between. He felt perfectly satisfied that his constituents would approve of the bill upon the table. He should support it, believing he had their sanction for so doing. He concluded by eulogizing the character of Judge Marshall.

Mr. CARMICHAEL said, if the amendment of the gentleman from Kentucky (Mr. Hardin) was agreed to, he would vote for this bill, however he should feel it his duty to enter into a detailed discussion of the merits of the bill. After some further remarks, he yielded the floor to

Mr. MILLER, of Pennsylvania, who suggested that it would facilitate the business of the House, if the Committee should rise and report their proceedings to the House.

Mr. FILLMORE expressed a similar wish.

[Mr. CARMICHAEL here yielded the floor, in order that the Report of the Joint Committee of Conference on the disagreement of the two Houses, in relation to amendments to the general appropriation bill, might be made.]

The SPEAKER having resumed the Chair, Mr. POLK, from the Joint Committee of Conference, reported that the Committee had unanimously agreed to recommend to the House to recede from its disagreement to the amendment of the Senate, making appropriations for the salary of a Minister to Great Britain, and Secretary of Legation, and that the salary of a Minister to Great Britain be stricken out. This branch of the Report was concurred in by the House, as also the recommendation that the House recede from its disagreement to the amendments of the Senate, making an appropriation to Samuel Slater, to Gales and Seaton, for printing Congressional documents, and making an appropriation for printing 5,000 copies of the Report of the Committee on the West Point Academy.

The Joint Committee of Conference further recommended that the Senate recede from their amendments in relation to land claims in Missouri, and an appropriation for a road in Alabama.

The House then insisted upon the two latter amendments.

The House being again in Committee of the Whole, Mr. HARDIN proposed to amend the bill by striking out seven and inserting eight as applied to the number of Judges of the Circuit, with several other amendments relative to its location and boundaries.

The amendments were agreed to.

Mr. THOMAS, of Maryland, said his colleague,

(Mr. Carmichael) had given way on the understanding, that when the bill came into the House, he should not be prevented from delivering his views on it by the motion for the previous question.

Mr. BEARDSLEY rose, he said, to propose an amendment to this bill.

A message was here received from the Senate, and the Speaker having resumed the chair, the House took up the amendment to the Fortification bill, appropriating the $3,000,000, and the resolution of the Senate that it would insist on its disagreement.

Mr. GHOLSON expressed a fervent hope that the House would recede from its amendment. He was conscious that no man, woman, or child, in the United States, who had any intelligence of the matter, seriously believed that France would declare war against this country. The appropriation was therefore unnecessary, and the House might with propriety abandon the amendment. He moved that the House do recede.

Mr. CAMBRELENG said, he trusted the House would not recede. If no measures were to be taken for the defence of the country, let the Senate take the responsibility.

Mr. GORDON was in favor of receding. The amendment was extremely objectionable. It was unparalleled in the Legislative history of our country. It placed the purse and the sword, both in the hands of the Executive, and made the Legislative subservient to the Executive power. It was but yesterday that we were told emphatically, that there was to be no war with France. To-night, at the moment of adjournment, we were called upon to place the whole public treasure in the hands of the Executive to provide for the contingencies of war.

Mr. BYNUM said he trusted in God this House would not recede from this amendment. This was an opposition evidently not to the measure, but to the Executive. This question between an Americanized France was about to be tortured into an administration and an anti-administration question. Mr. B. said he was sorry to see the opposition to it come from the quarter it did; there were certain parts of this country and certain men in it, he was aware, who would not intrust to the President the expenditure of ten dollars—but the American People had shown that they would intrust in his hands ten millions.

Mr. GHOLSON here explained. It was far from his intention to make this either an administration or an anti-administration question; the opposition which he made to this measure he would extend to the Father of his Country, were he to rise and propose it.

Mr. BYNUM continued. He could not be deceived—this was evidently a measure of opposition to the administration, and there were men who would willingly see the banner of France waving over your Capitol, rather than lose the opportunity of making a thrust at the administration. He could see through it. Another branch of this Government, not satisfied with endeavoring to thwart the patriotic views of the Executive, must now attempt to legislate for us. Let them triumph, and he asked where is your independence? where your constitutional power; where your Republican Government? Gone, sunk in oblivion, and you have a rank aristocracy for your Government.

Mr. WISE said he agreed with his colleague, (Mr. Gholson,) that this was no pitiful administration or anti-administration question. It was a national question, and in that view, he, for one, had voted for it. But Mr. W. said he rose more especially to notice a remark of another colleague, (Mr. Gordon,) who had said this amendment vested legislative powers in the Executive; that it unites the purse with the sword. This position he denied. He asked how we were situated at the commencement of the last war with Great Britain? Was not the same cry then heard? And how did we then find ourselves prepared for the emergency? He defied the gentleman, as a lawyer—a constitutional lawyer, to show in what respect the legislative power was placed in the hands of the Executive. Mr. W. said he was as much opposed as his honorable colleague could be to the overweening and all grasping tendency of Executive power. He did not distinctly recollect

whether his colleague, (Mr. Gordon,) voted for the "peace resolution" of his other colleague (Mr. Archer.) Mr. W. said for himself he could say he did vote for it. But he believed in the propriety of in peace preparing for war. He did believe there absolutely existed a danger—a prospect of war; and in the event of its occurrence, every fortification on your coast was liable to fall into the hands of a strong maritime power. He wished to give his constituents information—and he regretted that he was compelled to use the time of that House to tell them that such was the danger in which their interests stood. He believed the appropriation to be politic and necessary; and he would adhere to it.

Mr. McKENNAN here moved the previous question, which was seconded.

The main question was then put on the motion of Mr. GHOLSON, to recede from the amendment of the House, appropriating $3,000,000 for the support of fortifications, and taken by yeas and nays, as follows:

YEAS—Messrs. John Q. Adams, Heman Allen, Chilton Allan, Archer, Ashley Barber, Barnitz, Barringer, Beaty, Bouldin, Campbell, Chambers, Chinn, Claiborne, William Clark, Clowney, Corwin, Crane, Crockett, Darlington, Davis, Davenport, Deberry, Dickson, Evans, Edward Everett, Horace Everett, Ewing, Felder, Fillmore, Foster, Philo C. Fuller, Gamble, Garland, Gholson, Gilmer, Gordon, Graham, Grennell, Gr.Bm, Hiland Hall, Hard, Hardin, James Harper, Hazeltine, Hiester, William Jackson, William C. Johnson, Henry Johnson, Seaborn Jones, King, Lay, Letcher, Lewis, Lincoln, Martindale, Marshall, McKay, McKennan, Mercer, Milligan, Miner, Patton, Phillips, Pickens, Pinckney, Potts, Ramsay, Reed, Rencher, Robertson, William B. Shepard, Spangler, Steele, Stewart, William P. Taylor, Philemon Thomas, Trumbull, Tweedy, Vance, Vinton, Watmough, Elisha Whittlesey, Wilde, Williams, Wilson, Young—89.

NAYS—Messrs. J. Adams, J. J. Allen, William Allen, Anthony, Beale, Bean, Beardsley, Beaumont, Blair, Bockee, Boon, Bull, Burns, Bynum, Cage, Cambreleng, Carmichael, Carr, Casey, Samuel Clark, Clay, Connor, Coulter, Cramer, Day, Denny, Dunlap, Forester, William K. Fuller, Fulton, Galbraith, Gillet, Joseph Hall, Thomas H. Hall, Halsey, Hamer, Hannegan, Joseph M. Harper, Harrison, Hathaway, Hawkins, Hawes, Heath, Henderson, Howell, Hubbard, Huntington, Inge, Jarvis, Richard M. Johnson, Nesdiah Johnson, Kavanagh, Kilgore, Kinnard, Lane, Lansing, Lea, Lee, Love, Luce, Lyon, Lytle, Abijah Mann, Joel K. Mann, Manning, Mardis, John Y. Mason, Moses Mason, May, McCarty, McIntire, McKim, McKinley, McLene, McVean, Miller, Henry Mitchell, Robert Mitchell, Moore, Muhlenberg, Murphy, Osgood, Parks, Parker, Patterson, Pearce, Peyton, Pierce, Pierson, Plummer, Polk, Reynolds, Schenck, Schley, Augustine H. Shepperd, Shinn, Smith, Speight, Standifer, Sutherland, William Taylor, Francis Thomas, Turner, Turrill, Vanderpoel, Van Houten, Wagener, Wardwell, Webster, White, Wise—110.

So the House refused to recede from its amendment.

The House went again into Committee on the Judiciary bill.

Mr. BEARDSLEY sent his amendment to the Chair on the Judiciary bill, being an additional section to the bill, providing for certain alterations in the Circuit of New York, and making it the second circuit. Also, that the places of holding the same should be at Albany and Utica

Mr. B. gave a brief explanation of the reasons which had induced him to prepare this amendment. The northern district of New York had now nothing more than one district court, and an extension was greatly desired. It might be inquired what were the population and business that the proposed circuit embraced. It contained twelve or fourteen hundred thousand inhabitants, who employed as much capital as any other region of the same size in the country. The bill provided for the erection of two new circuit courts in the western country, a reason for which Mr. B. was decidedly in favor. The first of these two circuits comprised the States of Missouri, Indiana, and

Illinois. These three states were represented by twelve members in that House, less than one half of the delegation to Congress from the northern district of New York. The second circuit was intended to embrace Louisiana, Alabama and Mississippi, who were there represented by nine members, and all of which were considerably less a population than one half the size of the northern district of New York. In all these States, and throughout the whole region of country, they already enjoyed all the benefits of the judicial system. Mr. B. appealed to his western friends, that while they were anxious, and justly so, to obtain so desirable a matter for themselves, they would not be unmindful of the claims of so large a section of country as that for which he was now advocating.

Mr. FILLMORE begged leave to suggest to his honorable colleague to make one of the places of holding the court farther west. Utica was nearly four hundred miles from the western part of the State of New York, and Albany was still further objectionable from the same ground. Mr. F. would suggest Rochester or Buffalo. He moved to strike out Albany and insert Buffalo.

Mr. BEARDSLEY explained, that he had inserted Albany because it was the capital of the State; and Utica already had one term a year, and it would be better to continue it there. Personally, he would say, he had no objection to the amendment, but the was convinced the public benefit would be better consulted by fixing it as he had done, and he hoped the amendment would not be adopted.

Mr. FOSTER wished to remind gentlemen that there was only one hour and three quarters remaining of the session, and he hoped further discussion would be dropped.

Mr. FILLMORE said, the bill proposed to establish two circuits within one hundred miles of each other, and leave other, and not less important parts of the State, at a distance of four hundred miles.

Mr. FILLMORE'S amendment was adopted without a division.

Mr. BEARDSLEY'S amendment as amended was also adopted—eyes 80, nays 46.

The bill, as amended, was then laid aside, and the Committee took up and considered the following bills:

A bill to increase the engineer corps.

A bill for the relief of David Beard. The amendment to this bill agreed to.

A bill relative to accounts of our Consul at London.

A bill to continue the Subsistence Department.

A bill for the relief of the corporations of Washington, Alexandria, and Georgetown.

All which bills were severally agreed to, and laid aside to be reported to the House.

The Committee then took up the bill to carry into effect the convention with Spain.

The question was on concurring with the Senate in their amendment to this bill.

Mr. CAMBRELENG explained, that the character of the bill had been materially changed by the amendment.

The amendment was concurred in.

The Committee then rose, and the Chairman, (Mr. Speight,) reported the foregoing bills to the House.

The bill to establish branches of the Mint of the United States was then read a third time.

On the passage of the bill, Mr. C. P. WHITE demanded the yeas and nays; which were ordered and taken, when there appeared—yeas 114, nays 59. So the bill was passed.

A message was received from the Senate announcing that that body still adhered to their disagreement to the amendment of the House to the bill making appropriation for certain fortifications.

Mr. CAMBRELENG moved that the House do still adhere to its amendment.

Mr. WILDE said, he believed, if the House should still adhere—there would be the end of the matter. There could be then no further conference with the Senate, and the bill would be lost.

Mr. MERCER moved that the House recede from its amendment.

Mr. LYTLE objected to any conciliatory measures on the part of the House. 'It had already gone as far as prudence or patience could dictate. It had conceded every thing to night, that it could with honor concede, and it was time to tire of concession. Let it, said Mr. L. now remain with the Peers to answer for the consequences. He wished to fasten—to nail the responsibility there. He would not have the House to abandon the elevated ground which it now occupied. Without an appropriation, the country would be left open as a defenceless. That appropriation the House had tendered, and this country would put its seal of reprobation on the pusillanimous act which thus arrested the measure.

Mr. HAWES called for the previous question, which being seconded, the question was taken on the motion of Mr. MERCER to recede. It was decided in the negative by ayes and noes, as follows:—ayes 88, noes 114.

YEAS.—Messrs. John Q. Adams, Heman Allen, Chilton Allan, Archer, Ashley, Barber, Barnitz, Barringer, Beaty, Bouldin, Briggs, Bull, Campbell, Chambers, Chinn, William Clark, Clowney, Corwin, Crane, Crockett, Darlington, Amos Davis, Davenport, Deberry, Dickson, Evans, Edward Everett, Horace Everett, Ewing, Felder, Fillmore, Foster, Phil o C. Fuller, Gamble, Garland, Gholson, Gilmer, Gordon, Grennell, Griffin, Bland Hall, Hard, Hardin, James Harper, Hazeltine, Hiester, William Jackson, William C. Johnson, Henry Johnson, Seaborn Jones, King, Letcher, Lewis, Lincoln, Marshall, McCarty, McKay, McKennan, Mercer, Milligan, Miner, Parker, Patton, Phillips, Pickens, Rjncksey, Potts, Ramsay, Reed, Rencher, Robertson, Slade, Spangler, Steele, Stewart, William P. Taylor, Philemon Thomas, Trumbull, Tweedy, Vance, Vinton, Watmough, Frederick Whittlesey, Elisha Whittlesey, Wilde, Williams, Wilson, Young—88.

NAYS.—Messrs. John Adams, John J. Allen, William Allen, Anthony, Bates, Baylies, Be le,' Bean, Beardsley, Beaumont, Bell, Binney, Blair, Booker, Boon, Brown, Bunch, Cage, Cambreleng, Carmichael, Carr, Casey, Chaney, Samuel Clark, Clay, Coffee, Connor, Coulter, Cramer, Day, Dickerson, Dickinson, Dunlap, Ferris, Forester, William K. Fuller, Fulton, Galbraith, Gillet, Thomas H. Hall, Halsey, Hamer, Hannegan, Joseph M. Harper, Harrison, Hathaway, Hawkins, Hawes, Henderson, Howell, Hubbard, Huntington, Inge, Jarvis, Richard M. Johnson, Noadiah Johnson, Benjamin Jones, Kavanagh, Kilgore, Kinnard, Lane, Lansing, Luke Lea, Thomas Lee, Love, Lucas, Lyon, Lytle, Abijah Mann, Joel K. Mann, Manning, Mardis, John Y. Mason, Moses Mason, May, McIntire, McKim, McKinley, McLene, McVean, Miller, Henry Mitchell, Robert Mitchell, Moore, Muhlenberg, Murphy, Osgood, Parks, Patterson, Pearce, Peyton, Pierce, Pierson, Polk, Reynolds, Schenck, Schley, Shinn, Smith, Speight, Standifer, William Taylor, Francis Thomas, Turner, Turrill, Vanderpoel, Van Houten, Wagener, Ward, Wardwell, Webster, Whallon, White, Wise—114.

Mr. HUBBARD then moved that the House insist upon their amendment, and ask a joint Committee of Conference. Mr. H. asked to be excused from serving on the Committee.

The motion to insist was agreed to, and Messrs. CAMBRELENG and LEWIS appointed on the part of the House.

Mr. ASHLEY moved to take up the bill for improving the harbor of St. Louis, as next in order, which was refused; it being alleged that the 3d March had expired, and that the House had no right to do any further business.

The bill for the continuation and repair of the Cumberland Road in the States of Ohio, Indiana, and Illinois, was on motion of Mr. THOMAS, of Maryland, read the third time and passed—Yeas 93, nays 81.

Mr. JARVIS rose to a question of order. He desired to know whether the functions of the House had not ceased, it being 12 o'clock at night.

The CHAIR intimated a disinclination to entertain the question.

Mr. JONES, of Georgia, moved that the House adjourn.

The SPEAKER said, that the parliamentary course would be to adopt a resolution regularly adjourning the House.

After a few remarks by Messrs. EVANS and J. Q. ADAMS—

The SPEAKER said, it was in order for the House to adjourn, if it thought proper.

Mr. MASON of Va., appealed to the gentleman from Georgia, (Mr. Jones,) to withdraw the motion to adjourn.

Mr. ADAMS said, if it was true that the functions of this House had ceased, the gentleman from Georgia had no right to make the motion, and it would be unnecessary.

Mr. JONES withdrew his motion at the request of

Mr. SMITH, who offered the usual resolution for the appointment of a committee to wait on the President, and inform him that the House was ready to adjourn, and that a similar message be sent to the Senate, &c.

Mr. GARLAND objected to the reception of the resolution.

The SPEAKER decided that it was in order.

Mr. MASON, of Va., asked the gentlemen to withdraw the resolution, for the purpose of taking up the report of the Committee on Elections, to pay the Hon. R. P. Letcher the usual allowance of a member of the House, for the last session of Congress.

The resolution was withdrawn, when the resolution of the Committee on Elections was taken up, the preamble stricken out, and the question being on the amendment proposed by Mr. Hardin, to make a similar provision for Mr. Thomas P. Moore,

Mr. WILDE moved the previous question, which was seconded—yeas 69, nays 65.

The previous question was then agreed to.

The question being on the adoption of the resolution reported by the Committee,

Mr. PARKER demanded the yeas and nays; which were ordered, and were—yeas 113, nays 3—no quorum voting.

Mr. JARVIS moved that the House adjourn.

Mr. WILDE demanded the yeas and nays, which were ordered.

The Clerk proceeded with the call of the roll, but before he had gone through with the same,

Mr. GARLAND rose to a question of order. He inquired whether members who were in their seats were not bound to vote on the question unless excused by the House?

The CHAIR replied in the affirmative.

Mr. GARLAND then stated that a gentleman from New York, (Mr. Beardsley,) had not voted.

Mr. BEARDSLEY said, that making all allowances for difference of time-pieces, it would be admitted by all that the hour of 12 had arrived. Being persuaded of that fact, he considered his constitutional functions as a member of the House, as having ceased, and were at an end. He was, therefore, not called on to vote upon any question which might be propounded.

A motion was then made to excuse Mr. Beardsley from voting; but a majority appearing in the negative,

Mr. GARLAND withdrew his objections, and the roll was called through.

The vote on the motion to adjourn was announced to be—yeas 15, nays 102—no quorum voting.

[Mr. GILMER also declined voting, on the ground that his functions as a member of the House, had ceased at 12 o'clock.]

The SPEAKER by consent, laid before the House, the following communications:

A letter from the Secretary of War, in relation to the expenditures for arms manufactured at the several armories of the United States, which was laid on the table and ordered to be printed.

A communication from the same in relation to the transportation and disbursement of Indian annuities, which was laid on the table and ordered to be printed.

And a communication from the Postmaster General.

Mr. CONNOR moved that it be laid on the table and printed.

Mr. EVANS said the latter communication appeared to be an appeal to the public through this body. It asked no legislative action, and from a glance at its commencement, he discovered that Mr. Barry had styled the report of the committee as aspersion upon his character. He submitted whether it was proper that the House should order the printing of this paper.

Mr. CONNOR said he had read no part of this communication. He understood from one of his colleagues of the committee (Mr. Beardsley,) who had hastily glanced over the communication, that it was respectful to the committee and the House. It was a review of the reports. For one, he would say, that if the committee were mistaken, and if they had fallen into errors, he should be happy to have them corrected. He was in favor of printing the communication.

Mr. MILLER said the House had ordered both of the reports to be printed, without hearing either of them read, and he was in favor of printing this communication in order that it might accompany the documents to which he had referred The Postmaster General had alleged that his character had been implicated, and he had made an explanation. It was nothing but fair that it should be printed. That officer had not an opportunity of being present at the investigations of the committee, which he should have had. It was but an act of common justice to permit his defence; to go along with the reports of the committee.

Mr. E. WHITTLESEY was proceeding to address the House, but gave way to a message from the Senate, by Mr. Lowrie, as follows:

Resolved, That a message be sent to the honorable House of Representatives, respectfully to remind the House of the report of the Committee of Conference appointed on the disagreeing votes of the two Houses, on the amendment of the House to the amendment of the Senate to the bill respecting the fortifications of the United States.

Mr. CAMBRELENG said that the Committee of Conference of the two Houses had not concurred in an amendment which was very unsatisfactory to him. It proposed an unconditional appropriation of 300,000 dollars for arming the fortifications, and 500,000 dollars for repairs of and equipping our vessels of war—an amount to tally inadequate, if it should be required, and more than was necessary if it should not be. When he came into the House from the conference, they were calling the ayes and noes on the resolution to pay the compensation due the gentleman from Kentucky, (Mr. Letcher;) he voted on that resolution, but there was no quorum voting. On subsequent proposition to adjourn, the ayes and noes were called, and again there was no quorum voting. Under such circumstances, and at two o'clock in the morning, he did not feel authorized to present to the House an appropriation of eight hundred thousand dollars. He regretted the loss not only of the appropriation for the defence of the country, but of the whole fortification bill; but let the responsibility fall where it ought—on the Senate of the United States. The House had discharged its duty to the country. It had sent the fortification bill to the Senate with an additional appropriation, entirely for the defence of the country. The Senate had rejected that appropriation without even deigning to propose any amendment whatever, either in form or amount. The House sent it a second time, and a second time an amendment was proposed, but the reverse; the Senate adhered without condescending to ask even a conference. Had that body asked a conference in the first instance, some provision would have been made for the defence, and the fortification bill would have been saved before the hour arrived which terminated the existence of the present House of Representatives. As it was, the committees did not concur till this House had ceased to exist—the ayes and noes had been twice taken without a quorum—the bill was evidently lost, and the Senate must take the responsibility of leaving the country defenceless. He could not feel authorized to report the bill to the House, situated as it was, and at this hour in the morning; but any other member of the Committee of Conference proposed to do it, he should make no objection, though he believed such a proposition utterly

ly ineffectual at this hour—for no member could, at this hour in the morning, be compelled to vote.

Mr. LEWIS asked if there was a quorum in the House?

A count being had, it appeared that only 114 members were in attendance, which was not a quorum.

Mr. FILLMORE moved an adjournment; but withdrew the motion at the request of

Mr. LOVE, who moved a call of the House.

Mr. CARMICHAEL renewed the motion to adjourn.

Mr. WILDE demanded the yeas and nays, which were ordered, and were—Yeas 35, nays 76. No quorum.

Mr. SMITH moved that a message be sent to the Senate, informing that body that the House having completed the business before it was ready to adjourn.

A message was received from the Senate, by Mr. LOWAY, their Secretary, announcing that the Senate having completed its business, were ready to adjourn.

Mr. MERCER contended that under the Constitution and practice of the House, it was not bound to adjourn at 12 o'clock at night on the third of March.

Mr. HARDIN contended that under the Constitution, the House could not continue in session after 12 o'clock at night on the third of March. He insisted that the House had continued in session more than two hours beyond the time which they had a right to sit.

Mr. PARKER said the first Congress assembled at 10 or 11 o'clock on the 4th of March, and the functions of this body would not cease until that time of day on the 4th.

Mr. BRIGGS said, as there was no quorum, he could not see the propriety of sending a message

o the Senate. His honorable colleague (Mr. Adams) had said the other day, that this House would be numbered with the dead on the 3d of March. That day had passed, and he would only say that if we were numbered among the dead, we were the most noisy dead that be had ever seen.

On motion of Mr. WILDE, the resolution paying Mr. LETCHER for his attendance on the House at the last session, was again taken up.

Mr. MANN, of New York, demanded the yeas and nays on the adoption of the resolution.

Mr. BARRINGER said the gentleman from New York had no right to make a motion, inasmuch as he did not believe that the body was in existence.

Mr. MANN replied that he was as much a member of the House as any other gentleman.

The yeas and nays were refused; but a count being called for, there appeared for the resolution 72, against it 3—no quorum.

Mr. SMITH's resolution in relation to the adjournment was then read.

Mr. PARKER wished to ask gentlemen whether they could vote that the business was finished. He referred to the situation of the bill making appropriations for fortifications. The House had appointed a committee of conference. That committee had not reported; and the important measure remained unacted on.

Mr. PHILLIPS inquired whether the report of the Committee of Conference had been submitted.

The CHAIR was understood to say that it had not.

Mr. C. LYON moved to amend Mr. SMITH's resolution, by informing the Senate that the House, having no quorum to do business, was ready to adjourn.

Mr. REED said that we could have a quorum, when one was wanted. That House had not done its duty—

[Here Mr. REED was called to order by several members. He, however, continued his remarks for some moments, amid calls to order, and much confusion.]

Mr. CAMBRELENG regretted as much as the gentleman from Massachusetts (Mr Reed) the loss of the Fortification bill; but he protested against the right of this body at half past two in the morning of the 4th of March, to call gentlemen here, who a longer members of this body. The bill was lost, and the Senate must be held responsible to the country; for no member could now be compelled to answer to the call.

Mr. BARRINGER said that the bill had been lost by intrigue here.

Mr. LEWIS moved a call of the House, which was negatived.

Mr. J. Y. MASON said that he understood that the Senate had adjourned. It was therefore unnecessary to pass a resolution on the subject. He moved that the House adjourn.

Mr. MERCER said he understood that the Senate had not adjourned.

Mr. MASON said he understood his information from a member of the House.

Mr. SPANGLER asked for the yeas and nays on the adjournment; which were ordered.

The Clerk was proceeding with the call of the roll, when Mr. BARRINGER said that the Senate had undoubtedly adjourned. He moved to suspend the call of the yeas and nays, which was agreed to.

The motion to adjourn was agreed to.

Mr. SPEAKER BELL then rose, and after delivering an appropriate valedictory address, adjourned the House, (at 3 o'clock, A. M.) without day.

APPENDIX.

REPORT ON THE PUBLIC PRINTING.

Mr. HAMER, from the Committee on the Judiciary, to whom(on motion of Mr. Burges,) was referred a resolution in these words: "*Resolved*, "That the Committee on the Judiciary be directed to inquire into the expediency and economy "of so altering and amending the laws of the "United States, that thereafter all printing "whatever required to be done for the United "States in any part of the public service, shall "be done and performed within the District of "Columbia, and that no such printing shall be "done by any person or persons who may be "concerned in any way of emolument with any "public journal or newspaper"—presented a Report as follows:

The Committee on the Judiciary have had the foregoing resolution under consideration, and now submit the following report, in reference to the propositions therein contained.

After a mature examination of this subject, with the aid of all the lights of which they have been able to avail themselves, they are of the opinion, that the changes suggested, with regard to the public printing, are inexpedient, and ought not to be adopted.

The resolution contains two propositions; *First*, that all the public printing should be done in the District of Columbia; and *Second*, that the editors or conductors of newspapers shall be excluded from employment, either by the Executive Departments of the Government, or by the two Houses of Congress.

The first is wholly impracticable. The laws of Congress should be widely promulgated, that they may be known to the people, upon whom they are to operate; they should therefore be published in newspapers scattered through the different States of the Union. Proposals for carrying the mail, for furnishing the Army and Navy with provisions, and for the execution of various public works, should be published in the different sections of the country, where the materials and labor are wanted, so as to excite fair and honorable competition. To require all the public printing to be done within this District, is at once to lose sight of important public interests, which are now subserved, in the mode at present followed by the several Departments of the Government.

The second proposition is one of a much more serious character, and deserves a degree of attention and consideration which is not demanded by a former. It proposes to establish a new principle in our Government, which is no less than the proscription by law of a particular profession or occupation from a particular kind of public employment. This principle so startling, and so contrary to the genius of free government, deserves our examination. Monopolies, proscriptions, exclusive privileges, and peculiar castes, are so abhorrent to every system founded upon the doctrines of liberty and equality, that nothing which bears their resemblance should be admitted without the most unanswerable reasoning can be urged in its support. Such is not the case, in the opinion of your committee, with the present proposition.

Upon looking into the constitution of the United States, we will perceive that there are very few disqualifications for offices and appointments under the General Government. To hold the office of President, Vice President, Senator, Representative, it is only necessary to be of a certain age, and to be a citizen as therein described, having resided in the country or State a given number of years. There is no difference made regard to professions, or classes of men. All men are open to all classes, without distinction. Those who are thus eligible can only be constitutionally deprived of their rights by impeachment for high crimes and misdemeanors. Such are the wise and liberal provisions of that great charter, the admirable work of patriots and sages, who achieved and secured our liberties as a confederated people. It may be safely assumed, that Congress have no power to prescribe a disqualification for office, which is unknown to the Constitution. All attempts to require qualifications for office, in the Executive or Legislative branches of the Government, other than those named in the Constitution, would be utterly nugatory. They cannot impose limits upon the elective power, which may rightfully range in its choice, over the whole field left to it by the framers of our liberal and enlightened system. Neither can they restrict the Executive in his appointments. Every American citizen, having the qualifications specified in the Constitution, is eligible to all the appointments in the gift of the President. Congress can neither deprive him of these rights by legislative enactment, nor limit the authority of the Chief Magistrate, by requiring him to select his officers from a particular class, occupation, or profession.

A like principle applies to all legislative appointments. The House of Representatives have power to choose their Speaker and other officers; but they have no power, either in conjunction with the Senate and President, or by a separate resolution, to make any man or class of men ineligible to those appointments. Every gentleman, constitutionally elected a member of the House, is eligible to the office of Speaker; and a law or resolution declaring that farmers, mechanics, merchants, or lawyers should not be eligible, would be unconstitutional and void. So, every citizen of the United States is eligible to the office of clerk, sergeant-at-arms, doorkeeper, or any other, which the House may find it necessary and expedient to establish. All laws, resolutions, rules or orders, proscribing any one class, or attempting to do so, from the enjoyment of these offices, would be equally void. On these subjects the whole House has no right to prescribe rules to its individual members. Each one may judge for himself, whether any particular individual is fit or unfit for the station to which he aspires; and he is accountable to no one for the vote he gives, but to his own constituents. It is not in the power of his co-representatives to compel him to vote for or against any man, on account of the occupation, or profession to which he belongs. If they attempt to do so they attempt a usurpation.

The foregoing observations are equally applicable to all professions in society. On what ground can we draw a distinction, against editors or conductors of newspapers? They are eligible by the constitution to the highest office in the gift of the People. They are frequently elected to the Senate and House of Representatives. All the offices in the State Governments are thrown open to them. Our Speaker and Clerk may both be editors; so may the Sergeant-at-Arms and Doorkeeper. By what authority shall we undertake, without a trial, to reduce them to a level with criminals, who have been adjudged guilty, and disqualified from holding any office of honor, trust, or profit, under the United States? Whilst every other office and agency in the House may be filled by an editor, the place of printer to the House is to be closed against him forever. Suppose a law or resolution to exist, authorising the election of a printer to the House, by a majority of votes, and excluding editors, does any one believe that if an editor were elected, he could not hold the office? If we can exclude them on this ground, we can exclude any other profession from other stations; we can disfranchise all who reside in a certain district of country; who are of a certain age; or who hold particular religious or political doctrines. The truth is, that in all these questions, *the will of the voter* exercised within the constitutional rule, *is the law to himself;* and no one, and no number of his co-representatives, have the right or the power to direct or to bind him. If he believes the occupation of an editor or manager of a newspaper disqualifies a man for any given office or appointment, he may rightfully vote for a person of some other class or occupation, and is responsible for his acts and his reasons to those who clothed him with authority. But there can be no sound reason urged, as your committee believe, for selecting the editorial *corps*, from all other professions, and reducing them to a degraded *caste* in the community.

The exclusion of editors from offices or employments would be not only contrary to the spirit, if not to the letter of the constitution; but, it would also be unjust and impolitic. To demonstrate this, we may inquire who are these men, whom it is proposed to degrade by this disqualification?

That the art of Printing has done more to enlighten and exalt the human mind, than all the other arts together, will perhaps be denied by no one, who has taken the trouble to investigate the history of his race. Its discovery forms an era in human annals. Beyond it all is dreary and obscure, except here and there a bright spot, to relieve the eye from the painful contemplation of a darkness so universal. Art and science, it is true, had made considerable progress in some favored communities; but a knowledge of the discoveries and improvements upon which we delight to dwell, was confined to a fortunate few, who, however they might have been inclined to disseminate what they knew, had it not in their power to effect an object so full of patriotism and benevolence. The living mass that makes up all, of what is denominated either savage or barbarous nations, and constituted a vast majority of the most highly cultivated nations of antiquity, were doomed to perpetual ignorance and degradation in the moral world. No mode of escape could be devised for them. Books were scarce; the process of multiplying them by copies, the work of clerks, and the enormous prices consequent upon this mode of multiplication, must forever have shut out a large majority of such nations from the principal source of mental improvement.

Printing at a single blow demolished these barriers. It threw open all the doors of the temple, and permitted the poor and the ignorant to walk in unmolested, to gaze upon the resplendent beauties that adorned its walls, and to bear off the invaluable treasures that filled its courts—treasures that were the accumulation of ages, and which, till that moment, had been totally concealed from the eye of the multitude. A great moral revolution was effected, as in the twinkling of an eye. Before that period, kings, nobles, and governors, were every thing, and the people nothing. From that period the people became every thing, and kings, nobles, and governors, nothing. The literal existence of this contrast, of this astonishing transformation, it is true, has not been yet realised; but the work has been going on. The rays of light are falling upon the most benighted regions; the force of truth is breaking through all opposition; and the period is not far distant, when man will stand forth in the freedom, the dignity, and majesty of his nature, liberated from the shackles that have so long degraded body and soul; when the people will be completely sovereign; and an enlightened public opinion shall be the

only rule of action to all in authority, from the highest to the lowest station. This time will come, and this will be the work of the *Press*.

Ought this great moral engine to be free? Whatever difference of opinion may have existed elsewhere upon this subject, there seems to have been none among our ancestors. A censorship of the press has been established under most, if not all the, tyrannical governments of Europe. The Court of Rome set the example, in the latter part of the 15th century; other despotic governments adopted the principle, and made the press propagate such opinions and sentiments only, as suited the views of those who controlled its movements. No works, of any kind, could see the light, but such as had been licensed by the government. The people, so far from being blessed by the art, which seemed to have been invented for their use alone, were not only deprived of its benefits; but had its immense power turned against themselves, and their country flooded with doctrines and opinions calculated to rivet their chains more firmly, and to doom them to a perpetual servitude.

To the honor of our ancestors, be it known, that this censorship of the press was first abolished in England. This great event took place in the year 1694. Since that time the English press has been free. A censorship is unknown in this country. The lofty spirit of American liberty would trample upon an effort to limit the freedom of discussion. Truth courts investigation, and he who fears it, is generally. conscious that the truth is against him.

Freedom of speech and of the press are one and the same thing. In a small community, all may assemble for deliberation, and each hear what the other has to advance for the general good. This was the case in some of the ancient Republics. But in a large country this cannot be; and resort must be had to the press, for the circulation of facts and opinions that are connected with the public interest.

The freedom of speech, enjoyed by members of this House, would be of little avail, if they were not allowed to print and circulate their sentiments among their constituents, and in the country at large.

Errors, indiscretions, corruptions, and usurpations, might exist to an alarming extent, yet reform would be utterly hopeless. Before a reform can take place in the Legislation or Administration of a free Government, we must first reform public opinion. How is this to be done, unless the people can be approached through the aid of the Press, and induced to read and consider the productions of those who are laboring for the public welfare?

The history of the world, for the last century, scarcely furnishes an instance of a revolution in government, that has not been produced, in a good degree, by the genial influence of the Press. In some cases, the books and pamphlets, and in others the newspapers, have wrought a change in public opinion, that has been followed up by civil commotions, tending to enlarge the privileges of the people. Uniformly, the newspaper presses have led off, in favor of liberal principles. Witness the recent revolution in France and Belgium. Whenever any portion of the Press lags behind, it is in the pay and under the control of individuals whose interests are adverse to those of the majority. Left free, it goes with the people, as certainly as water seeks to find its level.

A great deal has been said of the licentiousness of the Press; but not a charge can be made against it, that does not apply in principle to the printers and publishers of books, and to the freedom of speech. Do the public journals abuse their liberty? So do those who print pernicious books and circulate scandalous reports. Do the newspapers defame great and good men? So do the others; and often in a more permanent and dangerous form. Have they condemned sound doctrines in ethics and politics, and maintained principles that must overthrow all government, and resolve society into its original elements? Books and orators do the same thing, in a more seductive and effectual manner. It is impossible to separate them. To condemn one, is to pass sentence against the others.

If the press has a great influence in the formation and communication of opinions, is it not all important, that we should elevate and purify it, by all the means in our power? This can never be done by proscription. All experience proves, that men of talents and virtue, who have a desire for distinction, will select that path which is most likely to lead them to their object. Do we desire to see men of high character and splendid talents engaged in conducting the periodicals of our country? Render the profession honorable. To degrade it, is to drive them from it, and to abandon your public press to the superintendence of incompetent and unprincipled individuals, wholly unworthy of so high a trust. There is a great deal of the odium of the profession attaches to each member of it, honest and pure as he may be; and perhaps there is no position in society, where it is so difficult for a man to retain a pure character, as at the editorial desk. If this be true, does it not follow that there is no one, in which a character so preserved, more richly deserves the public approbation? A man who becomes an editor, makes himself a target for the arrows of detraction, and an object of blackening abuse; and if it be difficult in this situation, to maintain perfect purity of character, it is still more difficult to make it appear so. The resolute advocate of free principles in all ages, whether acting as orators, statesmen, or editors, have been objects of brutal attack by the minions of power and corruption. When an individual, in either character, has endured the fiery ordeal for a series of years, and has come out of the contest unscathed by the bolts of his enemies, is it just to tell him, that his very toils and sacrifices in the cause of liberty, have disqualified him to enjoy its honors, and that he must be content to take his station among those who have been convicted of moral treason, or branded as public malefactors?

The existence of bad men among editors wil not justify their proscription as a class; for the same thing may be justly alleged of all other classes. Kings knew how to conciliate the orators of ancient Greece, and to mislead the people, by the instrumentality of those to whom they looked for instruction. In modern times, ambitious men and rich corporations have discovered the means of making editors and presses subservient to their designs. But the poison secretly infused into the fountains, whence a confiding people had been accustomed to drink information, has found its antidote in the pure streams that flow from other sources. It is thus that the health and vigor of the body politic have been preserved, verifying the remarks of a distinguished patriot, "that error may be tolerated when reason is left free to combat it."

If it would be unjust to exclude editors and owners of newspapers from office generally, it would be peculiarly so, to cut them off from employments naturally connected with their business. A large portion of the editors in the United States, own either in whole or in part, the establishments which are under their control. Subscriptions constitute but a part of the means by which they are supported. The rest is made up of advertisements and job printing for individuals, corporations, the State governments, and the United States. If deprived of these latter sources of emolument, a great number, perhaps one-half of the editors in the United States, who are owners of presses, would be obliged to stop them, and the rest would be essentially crippled in their means. It is not just to them, since they have entered upon business with an open field, now to exclude them from a fair competition for this work. It would operate upon them, as the grant of a monopoly does upon the rest of the community, it would cut off one branch of their legitimate business and force them to carry on the remainder under disadvantages which did not exist when they commenced.

A more impolitic measure could not be adopted with regard to the purity of the press, than the one now proposed. The pecuniary independence of editors is one of the surest guarantees of their political independence. It requires no labored argument to prove, that if editors become dependent upon rich men, and powerful corporations, for support, they will naturally incline to promote the objects of those from whom they receive gratuities and loans. Relying upon individuals who sustain it bp their pecuniary means, the press submits to their censorship, speaks their sentiments, obeys their commands, and ministers to their vengeance. Those who seek to maintain the independence of the press, should rather increase its honest emoluments than diminish them; because, in the same proportion as editors are made poor, and rendered dependent upon the rich and designing, in the same proportion will they become the instruments of a sinister ambition. To prevent this, which must be considered one of the greatest disasters that could befall a free people, we must encourage virtue and intellect in the profession, by holding out the same inducements to them, which are presented to all other classes. The controlling patronage of individual and corporate wealth should be counterpoised by the patronage of public honor, public offices, and public esteem.

Editors who advocate liberal principles, under kingly Governments, are kept poor by fines, and intimidated by prosecutions and imprisonment. What is the difference in effect, if we attempt to keep them poor by depriving them of their legitimate business, and treating them as criminals, by a proscription from honorable and profitable employments? If arbitrary power be successful in Europe, editors *there* will become the mere creatures of Kings and nobles; if we drive them from honorable and profitable employments in this country, editors *here* will become the supple tools of rich, aspiring men, and designing combinations. If we thus degrade the profession, talents, virtue, and patriotic ambition will seek rewards through other channels. The press, abandoned by those who ought to cherish and ennoble it, utterly degraded and corrupt, will only speak to the people to mislead them; or, at the best, will become so insignificant and powerless as to oppose no barrier to the approaches of despotism.

The existence of a few bad men in the craft, as before remarked, does not justify the exclusion of all. This House, and the people themselves, are fully able to discriminate, in each individual case, between the corrupt instrument and the independent patriot. If an editor, who has sold his principles, and degraded his noble profession; or one who is steeped in debauchery and reeking with vice; or whose daily sheet is a libel upon all that is virtuous, liberal, and patriotic, should present himself for preferment, it is presumed there will always be virtue enough left among us to treat him with that scorn and contempt which his crimes against society and the republic so richly merit. But if one should appear before us, who, through all the storms of party strife has maintained a private character pure and unsullied; who, whilst showers of libels have been poured upon him, has spoken the truth without fear; whose only fault is the frankness with which he exposes the errors of his friends; who regards no denunciations, cowers at no threats and shrinks from no violence, ever devoted to the cause of liberty, the principles of the constitution, and the welfare of his country; if such a one presents himself for a place of honor, trust, or profit, is it either just or politic to inform him that he belongs to a degraded class, whom it is the will of the Representatives of the People to disfranchise, and proscribe? If the Representatives of the People were so unjust and so cruel to a public benefactor, as to thus reject him, ought not the People to espouse the cause of a faithful sentinel, and to liberally reward him, for the fearless manner in which he has guarded their rights and advocated their interests? That they would do so, no one can doubt who knows and appreciates the justice and generosity of the American character.

Much has been said recently of the corrupt state of the party press of this country. It has become a common topic of remark, and the truth of the charge is admitted by an almost universal acquiescence; very few will admit, however, that the press of their party is corrupt. It is the antagonist press, of which they all complain. A like observation is applicable to public men.

they are accustomed to pour out their denunciations against the press, in the most unlimited profusion. But it is usually the press that abuses them, or their friends. No public man abuses a press that bestows generous and constant praises upon him, and as constantly denounces his rivals and enemies. But, in truth, a great deal of what is called slander, in party times, consists merely in the difference of opinion expressed by editors of different presses; a difference that must always prevail in a free country. Two great parties exist in the community; each one has its statesmen, orators, and presses. They each maintain their doctrines and opinions, and denounce the systems and theories of their antagonists. Each side warns the People to guard themselves against a party that entertains such pernicious doctrines, and against public men who are blind to the public interest and willing to sacrifice the eternal good to promote their own personal aggrandizement. The people hear all, weigh all, and decide upon all. But, in the mean time, the orators and organs pronounce their opponents to be a set of worthless calumniators. It may well be said, therefore, that if the press abuses politicians, they, in turn, abuse the press in the most bitter and vehement terms, and, upon the whole, the account is nearly balanced. In the contest which is thus carried on, abuses are revealed, facts are disclosed, theories are exploded, criminals and speculators are dragged to light, and important reforms are effected in the administration of public affairs. However unpleasant the controversy may be to the persons directly concerned, the people are generally the gainers by these searching, though disagreeable investigations.

But what is a party press? It is, in all other respects, a common newspaper, except, that upon particular questions which divide political parties in the country, it takes sides, one way or the other. Its columns are necessarily filled with other matter, to a very great extent. In general politics, it agrees with all other papers, advocating a right of mankind to personal and political freedom, and the superiority of Republican, to all other forms of Government. The various interests of society, agricultural, commercial, and manufacturing, receive their due share of attention. Modern discoveries in science, and the intelligence of our own and foreign countries, are grouped together and presented daily, or weekly, to us, in the shape of news. Is all this to be discouraged and discountenanced? For what? The sewer is, because the editor or owner exercises a privilege claimed by every other individual in the community, of sustaining one side of the great party questions which agitate the Republic. Such an outrage upon the freedom of discussion should not be tolerated in this country for a moment. Its parallel can be found only in the celebrated SEDITION LAW, to which it bears a strong affinity. That law aroused the indignation of a whole People, and powerfully contributed to the overthrow of the political party that advocated its principles, and enforced its odious provisions. If this proscription of classes is to be introduced, where is it to end? May it not be alleged, that farmers and mechanics are not fit for public life? May not the same principle apply to lawyers? They live by litigation, and it may be said at they have an interest in making laws obscure and equivocal, and ought, therefore, to be excluded from all legislative bodies; upon the same principles that it is proposed to exclude editors from a employment of public printing, lawyers might be excluded from judicial appointments, for which their studies and business have peculiarly qualified them. Such a sentence of condemnation would be considered an act of singular injustice, towards that large and respectable body of citizens. Let each class apply the principle to themselves, and they will at once perceive, how just and impolitic is the proposed exclusion and disfranchisement, of the owners and conductors of public journals.

The only plausible ground on which the present opposition is attempted to be maintained is, that a public patronage ought to be given to practical printers.

This argument is more plausible than sound.

When practical printers become owners and managers of the press and able advocates of the cause of liberty, they, like all others, deserve to be honored in proportion to their merits. The man who raises himself by the force of his own genius and untiring industry, from a mechanical occupation to a place among statesmen and philosophers, and devotes his increased influence to the cause of freedom, deserves to be doubly honored by mankind, and in selecting public servants the People will never forget him or overlook his claims. Our own Franklin is an illustrious example. But when practical printers, the owners and managers of large establishments, undertake jobs for private citizens, or for the State or General Government, they necessarily perform the work by the hands of others.

The contract is not executed by the manual labor of the owner or manager. His capital, his journeymen, and apprentices, perform the agreement, and entitle him to the proceeds, according to the stipulations of his employers.

Whether the undertaker be a practical printer or not, whether he be the owner or editor of a newspaper or not, is a matter of no importance to the craft. In either case, he is but the channel through which they who perform the labor, receive their compensation. In either case, the contract is mainly for the benefit of the practical printers; for the proceeds of the work, after making due allowance for the editor's capital and responsibility, are chiefly paid over to them. They derive employment from the contract, and if the price paid for its fulfilment be but a just remuneration, their profits, in proportion to their investment, are as great as those of the contractor. The practical printer, therefore, has now the same public patronage given to other classes of men. He desires no more; and if he did, he ought not to receive it. It may sometimes happen, that a practical printer should receive the preference over a mere editor; but that is a matter for individual consideration, when the case occurs. It forms no argument for the exclusion of the whole class to which the latter belongs. The constitution, as well as justice and sound policy, demands, that all appointments shall be open to every class, and to every citizen; that equality may be preserved and merit rewarded, whether found at the plough or the plane—the hod or the anvil—the desk or the mortar—the bar or the press. The only distinction acknowledged in our political system, should be, the honors and rewards, which are voluntarily bestowed upon eminent talents, patriotic zeal, and public and private virtue.

All attempts to degrade the press in this country, whilst it is persecuted or silenced under the arbitrary governments of the old world, are calculated to excite alarm. If the time shall ever come when its owners and conductors are proscribed from places of honor, trust, and profit; and denied even the privilege of taking contracts upon the same terms as other men, there will soon be neither honesty nor honor in its management. It will become a false guide to the people; the instrument of the rich and unscrupulous to destroy the poor and honest; the hired advocate of those who are able to pay its price; until destroyed in the public esteem, by its want of character, truth, and independence, it will sink into general contempt—leaving the people without those means of information which now enable them to detect falsehood, baffle corruption, and maintain their rights and liberties against every attempted encroachment. Your Committee are of opinion that the better mode of procuring the public printing to be done, is to employ, either by election or contract, persons of known fidelity and punctuality in the performance of their agreements, and to regulate and supervise the prices and execution of the work, so as to prevent all possible imposition. When these preliminary measures have been adopted, we shall be perfectly safe, not only to admit, but to invite competition from all classes of men in the community. No fears need be entertained for the stability of our institutions, or the purity of the press, from the employment of owners and editors of public journals. Indeed there would seem to be some propriety, in extending the patronage of the people,

through Congress, to such editors, as have distinguished themselves by the advocacy of liberal principles and popular rights. There are cogent reasons why, other circumstances being equal, or nearly so, such men should receive preferment. The aristocracy of a free country founds all its pretensions upon superior wealth. No other distinction can be obtained for them; and seizing upon this, they look down upon their poorer neighbors with an arrogance and contumely, proportioned to the extent of their possessions. These men can always establish and support journals of their own—they have the pecuniary means to do so, but the poorer classes of society have not. An editor who boldly and ably resists the influence, which is unceasingly at war, either openly or secretly, with the great body of the people, deserves the rewards and the emoluments that should always crown the labors of a public benefactor. In private life, he who does not regard and promote the interest and happiness of his friend, when it is in his power, does not deserve to have a friend. How can the people expect, that editors will endure persecution, poverty, and calumny, in their cause, if the friendship thus manifested is repaid with indifference and neglect? What is true among individuals, is true as to the whole body politic. A permanent policy, so cruel and ungrateful, would in all probability be followed by the prostration and bankruptcy of many able and eloquent defenders of civil liberty. Not to serve the cause of our country, is to reward its defenders; and to promote the interest of the people, is to sustain and patronise the men who ardently and ably maintain those interests.

No sound reason has been suggested for changing our laws or rules with regard to public printing, at this particular period. No such proposition was submitted two years ago, when the present printers to the House were elected. No fact has occurred within the last few years that would justify the proposed alteration. It is not probable that contracts of a more extravagant character are made with editors and owners of newspapers than with other men. There has been no agreement made by the House with any editor for printing, that can be compared, for enormity and extravagance, to the one made by Congress with Clark and Force, for collecting and printing a Documentary History of the United States. It is believed that if the work under this contract is not suspended by Congress, it will result in an expenditure of four or five hundred thousand dollars! If those contractors had obtained such a hold upon the Treasury as editors, there might indeed be some plausibility in proposing to guard against that class for the future. Such is not the fact. The only safeguard against these things is to be found in the wisdom and discretion of the members of the House, and in the responsibility they owe to their constituents.

Finally, believing as your Committee do, that the proposed exclusion would be unjust and impolitic; that it would be contrary to the spirit, if not to the letter of the constitution; that it would introduce a new principle into our Government, the tendency of which would be to build up one set of men and depress another; to establish privileged orders and degraded castes in society—they recommend the adoption of the following resolution:

Resolved, That the Committee be discharged from the further consideration of the subject.